LIFE APPLICATION™ BIBLE

NEW REVISED STANDARD VERSION

Published by
WORLD BIBLE PUBLISHERS, INC.
Iowa Falls, Iowa

Also distributed by
TYNDALE HOUSE PUBLISHERS, INC.
Wheaton, Illinois

The publisher gratefully acknowledges the role of Youth for Christ/USA in preparing the Life Application Notes and Bible Helps

The Bible text used in this edition of the *Life Application Bible* is the New Revised Standard Version Bible

WORLD BIBLE PUBLISHERS, INC.
ISBN 0-529-06905-9 Hardcover
ISBN 0-529-06906-7 Hardcover, indexed
ISBN 0-529-06907-5 Burgundy bonded leather
ISBN 0-529-06908-3 Burgundy bonded leather, indexed
ISBN 0-529-06909-1 Blue bonded leather
ISBN 0-529-06910-5 Blue bonded leather, indexed
ISBN 0-529-06911-3 Rose bonded leather
ISBN 0-529-06912-1 Rose bonded leather, indexed
ISBN 0-529-06914-8 Gray bonded leather
ISBN 0-529-06915-6 Gray bonded leather, indexed

Also distributed by TYNDALE HOUSE PUBLISHERS, INC.
ISBN 0-8423-2790-8 Hardcover
ISBN 0-8423-2789-4 Hardcover, indexed
ISBN 0-8423-2791-6 Burgundy bonded leather
ISBN 0-8423-2792-4 Blue bonded leather
ISBN 0-8423-2796-7 Rose bonded leather
ISBN 0-8423-2795-9 Gray bonded leather

Library of Congress Catalog Card Number 90-61239

Printed in the United States of America

97 96 95 94 93 92 91
8 7 6 5 4 3 2

CONTENTS

LIST OF THE BOOKS OF THE BIBLE

TO THE READER

This preface is addressed to you by the Committee of translators, who wish to explain, as briefly as possible, the origin and character of our work. The publication of our revision is yet another step in the long, continual process of making the Bible available in the form of the English language that is most widely current in our day. To summarize in a single sentence: the New Revised Standard Version of the Bible is an authorized revision of the Revised Standard Version, published in 1952, which was a revision of the American Standard Version, published in 1901, which, in turn, embodied earlier revisions of the King James Version, published in 1611.

In the course of time, the King James Version came to be regarded as "the Authorized Version." With good reason it has been termed "the noblest monument of English prose," and it has entered, as no other book has, into the making of the personal character and the public institutions of the English-speaking peoples. We owe to it an incalculable debt.

Yet the King James Version has serious defects. By the middle of the nineteenth century, the development of biblical studies and the discovery of many biblical manuscripts more ancient than those on which the King James Version was based made it apparent that these defects were so many as to call for revision. The task was begun, by authority of the Church of England, in 1870. The (British) Revised Version of the Bible was published in 1881-1885; and the American Standard Version, its variant embodying the preferences of the American scholars associated with the work, was published, as was mentioned above, in 1901. In 1928 the copyright of the latter was acquired by the International Council of Religious Education and thus passed into the ownership of the churches of the United States and Canada that were associated in this Council through their boards of education and publication.

The Council appointed a committee of scholars to have charge of the text of the American Standard Version and to undertake inquiry concerning the need for further revision. After studying the questions whether or not revision should be undertaken, and if so, what its nature and extent should be, in 1937 the Council authorized a revision. The scholars who served as members of the Committee worked in two sections, one dealing with the Old Testament and one with the New Testament. In 1946 the Revised Standard Version of the New Testament was published. The publication of the Revised Standard Version of the Bible, containing the Old and New Testaments, took place on September 30, 1952. A translation of the Apocryphal/Deuterocanonical Books of the Old Testament followed in 1957. In 1977 this collection was issued in an expanded edition, containing three additional texts received by Eastern Orthodox communions (3 and 4 Maccabees and Psalm 151). Thereafter the Revised Standard Version gained the distinction of being officially authorized for use by all major Christian churches: Protestant, Anglican, Roman Catholic, and Eastern Orthodox.

The Revised Standard Version Bible Committee is a continuing body, comprising about thirty members, both men and women. Ecumenical in representation, it includes scholars affiliated with various Protestant denominations, as well as several Roman Catholic members, an Eastern Orthodox member, and a Jewish member who serves in the Old Testament section. For a period of time the Committee included several members from Canada and from England.

Because no translation of the Bible is perfect or is acceptable to all groups of readers, and because discoveries of older manuscripts and further investigation of linguistic features of the text continue to become available, renderings of the Bible have proliferated. During the years following the publication of the Revised Standard Version, twenty-six other English translations and revisions of the Bible were produced by committees and by individual scholars—not to mention twenty-five other translations and revisions of the New Testament alone. One of the latter was the second edition of the RSV New Testament, issued in 1971, twenty-five years after its initial publication.

Following the publication of the RSV Old Testament in 1952, significant advances were made in the discovery and interpretation of documents in Semitic languages related to Hebrew. In addition to the information that had become available in the late 1940s from the Dead Sea texts of Isaiah and Habakkuk, subsequent acquisitions from the same area brought to light many other early copies of all the books of the Hebrew Scriptures (except Esther), though most of these copies are fragmentary. During the same period early Greek manuscript copies of books of the New Testament also became available.

In order to take these discoveries into account, along with recent studies of documents in Semitic languages related to Hebrew, in 1974 the Policies Committee of the Revised Standard Version, which is a standing committee of the National Council of the Churches of Christ in the U.S.A., authorized the preparation of a revision of the entire RSV Bible.

For the Old Testament the Committee has made use of the *Biblia Hebraica Stuttgartensia* (1977; ed. sec. emendata, 1983). This is an edition of the Hebrew and Aramaic text as current early in the Christian era and fixed by Jewish scholars (the "Masoretes") of the sixth to the ninth centuries. The vowel signs, which were added by the Masoretes, are accepted in the main, but where a more probable and convincing reading can be obtained by assuming different vowels, this has been done. No notes are given in such cases, because the vowel points are less ancient and reliable than the consonants. When an alternative reading given by the Masoretes is translated in a footnote, this is identified by the words "Another reading is."

Departures from the consonantal text of the best manuscripts have been made only where it seems clear that errors in copying had been made before the text was standardized. Most of the corrections adopted are based on the ancient versions (translations into Greek, Aramaic, Syriac, and Latin), which were made prior to the time of the work of the Masoretes and which therefore may reflect earlier forms of the Hebrew text. In such instances a footnote specifies the version or versions from which the correction has been derived and also gives a translation of the Masoretic Text. Where it was deemed appropriate to do so, information is supplied in footnotes from subsidiary Jewish traditions concerning other textual readings (the *Tiqqune Sopherim*, "emendations of the scribes"). These are identified in the footnotes as "Ancient Heb tradition."

Occasionally it is evident that the text has suffered in transmission and that none of the versions provides a satisfactory restoration. Here we can only follow the best judgment of competent scholars as to the most probable reconstruction of the original text. Such reconstructions are indicated in footnotes by the abbreviation Cn ("Correction"), and a translation of the Masoretic Text is added.

For the New Testament the Committee has based its work on the most recent edition of *The Greek New Testament*, prepared by an interconfessional and international committee and published by the United Bible Societies (1966; 3rd ed. corrected, 1983; information concerning changes to be introduced into the critical apparatus of the forthcoming 4th edition was available to the Committee). As in that edition, double brackets are used to enclose a few passages that are generally regarded to be later additions to the text, but which we have retained because of their evident antiquity and their importance in the textual tradition. Only in very rare instances have we replaced the text or the punctuation of the Bible Societies' edition by an alternative that seemed to us to be superior. Here and there in the footnotes the phrase, "Other ancient authorities read," identifies alternative readings preserved by Greek manuscripts and early versions. In both Testaments, alternative renderings of the text are indicated by the word "Or."

As for the style of English adopted for the present revision, among the mandates given to the Committee in 1980 by the Division of Education and Ministry of the National Council of Churches of Christ (which now holds the copyright of the RSV Bible) was the directive to continue in the tradition of the King James Bible, but to introduce such changes as are warranted on the basis of accuracy, clarity, euphony, and current English usage. Within the constraints set by the original texts and by the mandates of the Division, the Committee has followed the maxim, "As literal as possible, as free as necessary." As a consequence, the New Revised Standard Version (NRSV) remains essentially a literal translation. Paraphrastic renderings have been adopted only sparingly, and then chiefly to compensate for a deficiency in the English language—the lack of a common gender third person singular pronoun.

During the almost half a century since the publication of the RSV, many in the churches have become sensitive to the danger of linguistic sexism arising from the inherent bias of the English language towards the masculine gender, a bias that in the case of the Bible has often restricted or obscured the meaning of the original text. The mandates from the Division specified that, in references to men and women, masculine-oriented language should be eliminated as far as this can be done without altering passages that reflect the historical situation of ancient patriarchal culture. As can be appreciated, more than once the Committee found that the several mandates stood in tension and even in conflict. The various concerns had to be balanced case by case in order to provide a faithful and acceptable rendering without using contrived English. Only very occasionally has the pronoun "he" or "him" been retained in passages where the reference may have been to a woman as well as to a man; for example, in several legal texts in Leviticus and Deuteronomy. In such instances of formal, legal language, the options of either putting the passage in the plural or of introducing additional nouns to avoid masculine pronouns in English seemed to the Committee to obscure the historic structure and literary character of the original. In the vast majority of cases, however, inclusiveness has been attained by simple rephrasing or by introducing plural forms when this does not distort the meaning of the passage. Of course, in narrative and in parable no attempt was made to generalize the sex of individual persons.

Another aspect of style will be detected by readers who compare the more stately English rendering of the Old Testament with the less formal rendering adopted for the New Testament. For example, the traditional distinction between *shall* and *will* in English has been retained in the Old Testament as appropriate in rendering a document that embodies what may be termed the classic form of Hebrew, while in the New Testament the abandonment of such distinctions in the usage of the future tense in English reflects the more colloquial nature of the koine Greek used by most New Testament authors except when they are quoting the Old Testament.

Careful readers will notice that here and there in the Old Testament the word LORD (or in certain cases GOD) is printed in capital letters. This represents the traditional manner in English versions of rendering the Divine Name, the "Tetragrammaton" (see the notes on Exodus 3.14, 15), following the precedent of the ancient Greek and Latin translators and the long established practice in the reading of the Hebrew Scriptures in the synagogue. While it is almost if not quite certain that the Name was originally pronounced "Yahweh," this pronunciation was not indicated when the Masoretes added vowel sounds to the consonantal Hebrew text. To the four consonants YHWH of the Name, which had come to be regarded as too sacred to be pronounced, they attached vowel signs indicating that in its place should be read the Hebrew word *Adonai* meaning "Lord" (or *Elohim* meaning "God"). Ancient Greek translators employed the word *Kyrios* ("Lord") for the Name. The Vulgate likewise used the Latin word *Dominus* ("Lord"). The form "Jehovah" is of late medieval origin; it is a combination of the consonants of the Divine Name and the vowels attached to it by the Masoretes but belonging to an entirely different word. Although the American Standard Version (1901) had used "Jehovah" to render the Tetragrammaton (the sound of Y being represented by J and the sound of W by V, as in Latin), for two reasons the Committees that produced the RSV and the NRSV returned to the more familiar usage of the King James Version. (1) The word "Jehovah" does not accurately represent any form of the Name ever used in Hebrew. (2) The use of any proper name for the one and only God, as though there were other gods from whom the true God had to be distinguished, began to be discontinued in Judaism before the Christian era and is inappropriate for the universal faith of the Christian Church.

It will be seen that in the Psalms and in other prayers addressed to God the archaic second person singular pronouns (*thee*, *thou*, *thine*) and verb forms (*art*, *hast*, *hadst*) are no longer used. Although some readers may regret this change, it should be pointed out that in the original languages neither the Old Testament nor the New makes any linguistic distinction between addressing a human being and addressing the Deity. Furthermore, in the tradition of the King James Version one will not expect to find the use of capital letters for pronouns that refer to the Deity — such capitalization is an unnecessary innovation that has only recently been introduced into a few English translations of the Bible. Finally, we have left to the discretion of the licensed publishers such matters as section headings, cross-references, and clues to the pronunciation of proper names.

This new version seeks to preserve all that is best in the English Bible as it has been known and used through the years. It is intended for use in public reading and congregational worship, as well as in private study, instruction, and meditation. We have resisted the temptation to introduce terms and phrases that merely reflect current moods, and have tried to put the message of the Scriptures in simple, enduring words and expressions that are worthy to stand in the great tradition of the King James Bible and its predecessors.

In traditional Judaism and Christianity, the Bible has been more than a historical document to be preserved or a classic of literature to be cherished and admired; it is recognized as the unique record of God's dealings with people over the ages. The Old Testament sets forth the call of a special people to enter into covenant relation with the God of justice and steadfast love and to bring God's law to the nations. The New Testament records the life and work of Jesus Christ, the one in whom "the Word became flesh," as well as describes the rise and spread of the early Christian Church. The Bible carries its full message, not to those who regard it simply as a noble literary heritage of the past or who wish to use it to enhance political purposes and advance otherwise desirable goals, but to all persons and communities who read it so that they may discern and understand what God is saying to them. That message must not be disguised in phrases that are no longer clear, or hidden under words that have changed or lost their meaning; it must be presented in language that is direct and plain and meaningful to people today. It is the hope and prayer of the translators that this version of the Bible may continue to hold a large place in congregational life and to speak to all readers, young and old alike, helping them to understand and believe and respond to its message.

For the Committee,
BRUCE M. METZGER

CONTRIBUTORS

Senior Editorial Team
Dr. Bruce B. Barton
Ronald A. Beers
Dr. James C. Galvin
LaVonne Neff
Linda Chaffee Taylor
David R. Veerman

General Editor
Ronald A. Beers

Book Introductions
David R. Veerman

Book Outlines, Blueprints, Harmony
Dr. James C. Galvin

Megathemes
Dr. Bruce B. Barton

Map Development & Computer Operation
Linda Chaffee Taylor

Charts & Diagrams
Neil S. Wilson
Ronald A. Beers
David R. Veerman
Pamela York

Personality Profiles
Neil S. Wilson

Design & Development Team
Dr. Bruce B. Barton
Ronald A. Beers
Dr. James C. Galvin
David R. Veerman

Tyndale House Senior Bible Editor
Philip W. Comfort

Tyndale House Bible Editors
Virginia Muir
Robert Brown
Del Lankford
Mark Norton

Tyndale House Production
Marlene Muller
Joan Major
Edythe Draper

Tyndale House Graphic Design
Timothy R. Botts

A Chronology of Bible Events and World Events
Dr. David Maas

Theological Reviewers

Dr. Kenneth S. Kantzer
General Theological Reviewer
Dean Emeritus and
Distinguished Professor of Bible and Systematic Theology
Trinity Evangelical Divinity School

Dr. V. Gilbert Beers
Senior Editor
Christianity Today, Inc.

Dr. Barry Beitzel
Associate Academic Dean and Professor of Old Testament and Semitic Languages
Trinity Evangelical Divinity School

Dr. Edwin A. Blum
Associate Professor of Historical Theology
Dallas Theological Seminary

Dr. Geoffrey W. Bromiley
Professor
Fuller Theological Seminary

Dr. George K. Brushaber
President
Bethel College & Seminary

Dr. L. Russ Bush
Associate Professor,
Philosophy & Religion
Southwestern Baptist Theological Seminary

C. Donald Cole
Pastor, Moody Radio Network

Mrs. Naomi E. Cole
Speaker & Seminar Leader

Dr. Walter A. Elwell
Dean,
Wheaton College Graduate School

Dr. Gerald F. Hawthorne
Professor of Greek
Wheaton College

Dr. Howard G. Hendricks
Professor-at-Large
Chairman,
Center for Christian Leadership
Dallas Theological Seminary

Dr. Grant R. Osborne
Professor of New Testament
Trinity Evangelical Divinity School

A special thanks to the nationwide staff of Youth for Christ/USA for their suggestions and field-testing, and to the following additional contributing writers: V. Gilbert Beers, Neil Wilson, John Crosby, Joan Young, Jack Crabtree, Philip Craven, Bob Black, Bur Schilling, Arthur Deyo, Annie Lafrentz, Danny Sartin, William Hanawalt, William Bonikowsky, Brian Rathbun, Pamela Barden, Thomas Stobie, Robert Arnold, Greg Monaco, Larry Dunn, Lynn Ziegenfuss, Mitzie Barton, Marijean Hamilton, Larry Kreider, Gary Dausey, William Roland, Kathy Howell, Philip Steffeck, James Coleman, Marty Grasley, O'Ann Steere, Julia Amstutz.

A special thanks also to the following people whose personal counsel, encouragement, and determination helped make this product a reality:

Dr. Kenneth N. Taylor
Translator of *The Living Bible*
Chairman of the Board
Tyndale House Publishers

Mark D. Taylor
President
Tyndale House Publishers

Dr. Wendell C. Hawley
Editor-In-Chief
Tyndale House Publishers

Virginia Muir
Assistant Editor-In-Chief
Tyndale House Publishers

Richard R. Wynn
President, Youth for Christ/USA

Dr. Jay L. Kesler
President, Taylor University

A CHRONOLOGY OF BIBLE EVENTS AND WORLD EVENTS

Creation
undated

Noah builds the ark
undated

Abraham born
2166

Abra
enter
Cana
209

2500 B.C.
Egyptians discover papyrus and ink for writing and build the first libraries; iron objects manufactured in the ancient Near East

2400
Egyptians import gold from Africa

2331
Semitic chieftain, Sargon, conquers Sumer to become first "world conqueror"

2300
Horses domesticated in Egypt; chickens domesticated in Babylon; bows & arrows used in wars

2100
Glass mad
by the
Mesopotan
Ziggurats
(like the to
of Babel)
built in
Mesopotan
Earliest
discovered
Ethyl alcoh
used to
alleviate pa

WHY THE LIFE APPLICATION BIBLE IS UNIQUE

Have you ever opened your Bible and asked the following:

- What does this passage really mean?
- How does it apply to my life?
- Why does some of the Bible seem irrelevant?
- What do these ancient cultures have to do with today?
- I love God; why can't I understand what he is saying to me through his Word?
- What's going on in the lives of these Bible people?

Many Christians do not read the Bible regularly. Why? Because in the pressures of daily living they cannot find a connection between the timeless principles of Scripture and the ever-present problems of day-by-day living.

God urges us to apply his Word (Isaiah 42:23, 1 Corinthians 10:11; 2 Thessalonians 3:4), but too often we stop at accumulating Bible knowledge. This is why the *Life Application Bible* was developed—to show how to put into practice what we have learned.

Applying God's Word is a vital part of one's relationship with God; it is the evidence that we are obeying him. The difficulty in applying the Bible is not with

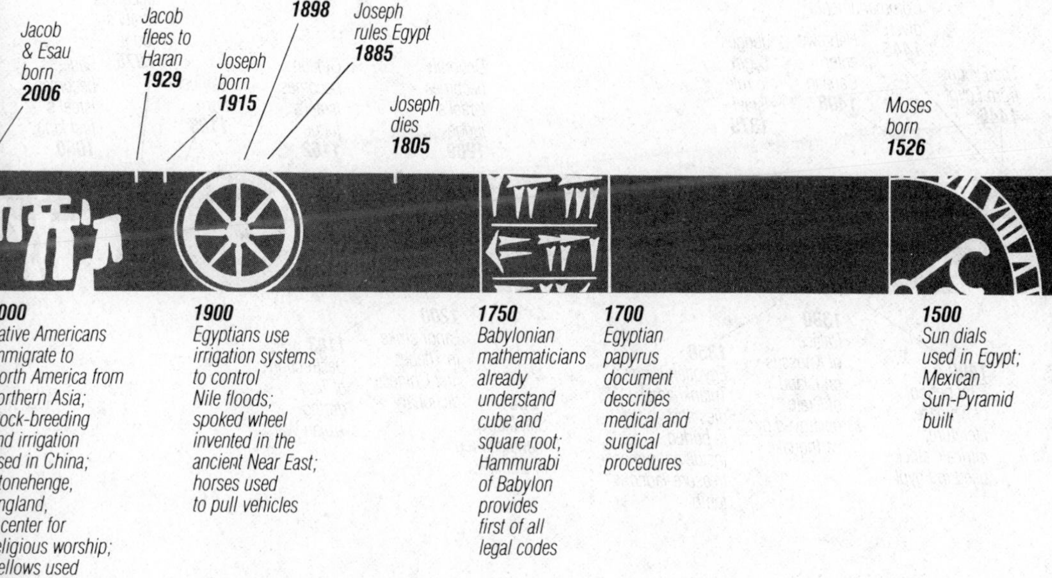

Jacob & Esau born 2006
Jacob flees to Haran 1929
Joseph born 1915
Joseph sold into slavery 1898
Joseph rules Egypt 1885
Joseph dies 1805
Moses born 1526
'000 Native Americans immigrate to North America from northern Asia; stock-breeding and irrigation used in China; Stonehenge, England, a center for religious worship; bellows used in India allowing for higher furnace temperatures
1900 Egyptians use irrigation systems to control Nile floods; spoked wheel invented in the ancient Near East; horses used to pull vehicles
1750 Babylonian mathematicians already understand cube and square root; Hammurabi of Babylon provides first of all legal codes
1700 Egyptian papyrus document describes medical and surgical procedures
1500 Sun dials used in Egypt; Mexican Sun-Pyramid built

the Bible itself, but with the reader's inability to bridge the gap between the past and present, the conceptual and practical. When we don't or can't do this, spiritual dryness, shallowness, and indifference are the results.

The words of Scripture itself cry out to us, "But be doers of the word and not merely hearers who deceive themselves" (James 1.22). The *Life Application Bible* does just that. Developed by an interdenominational team of pastors, scholars, family counselors, and a national organization dedicated to promoting God's Word and spreading the Gospel, the *Life Application Bible* took many years to complete, and all the work was reviewed by several renowned theologians under the directorship of Dr. Kenneth Kantzer.

The *Life Application Bible* does what a good resource Bible should—it helps you understand the context of a passage, gives important background and historical information, explains difficult words and phrases, and helps you see the interrelationships within Scripture. But it does much more. The *Life Application Bible* goes deeper into God's Word, helping you discover the timeless truth being communicated, see the relevance for your life, and make a personal application. While some study Bibles attempt application, over 75% of this Bible is application-oriented. The notes answer the questions, "So what?" and "What does this passage mean to me, my family, my friends, my job, my neighborhood, my church, my country?"

Imagine reading a familiar passage of Scripture and gaining fresh insight, as if it were the first time you had ever read it. How much richer your life would be if you left each Bible reading with a new perspective and a small change for the better. A small change every day adds up to a changed life—and that is the very purpose of Scripture.

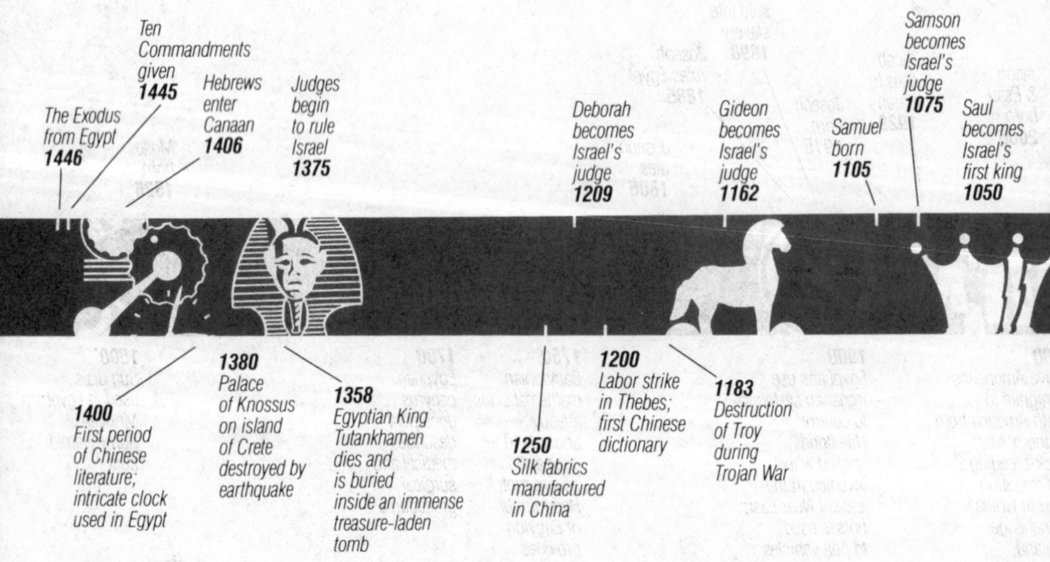
The Exodus from Egypt 1446
Ten Commandments given 1445
Hebrews enter Canaan 1406
Judges begin to rule Israel 1375
Deborah becomes Israel's judge 1209
Gideon becomes Israel's judge 1162
Samuel born 1105
Samson becomes Israel's judge 1075
Saul becomes Israel's first king 1050
1400 First period of Chinese literature; intricate clock used in Egypt
1380 Palace of Knossus on island of Crete destroyed by earthquake
1358 Egyptian King Tutankhamen dies and is buried inside an immense treasure-laden tomb
1250 Silk fabrics manufactured in China
1200 Labor strike in Thebes; first Chinese dictionary
1183 Destruction of Troy during Trojan War

The best way to define application is to first determine what it is *not*. Application is *not* just accumulating knowledge. This helps us discover and understand facts and concepts, but it stops there. History is filled with philosophers who knew what the Bible said, but failed to apply it to their lives, keeping them from believing and changing. Many think that understanding is the end goal of Bible study, but it is really only the beginning.

Application is *not* just illustration. Illustration only tells us how someone else handled a similar situation. While we may empathize with that person, we still have little direction for our personal situation.

Application is *not* just making a passage "relevant." Making the Bible relevant only helps us to see that the same lessons that were true in Bible times are true today; it does not show us how to apply them to the problems and pressures of our individual lives.

What, then, is application? Application begins by knowing and understanding God's Word and its timeless truths. *But you cannot stop there.* If you do, God's Word may not change your life, and it may become dull, difficult, tedious, and tiring. A good application focuses the truth of God's Word, shows the reader what to do about what is being read, and motivates the reader to respond to what God is teaching. All three are essential to application.

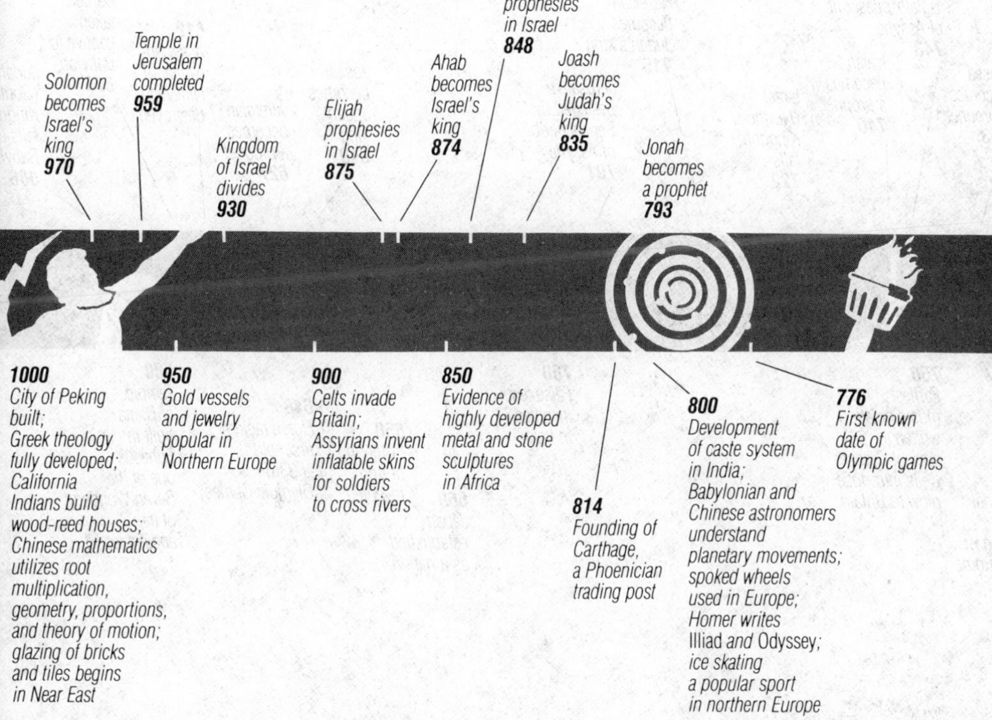
Solomon becomes Israel's king **970**
Temple in Jerusalem completed **959**
Kingdom of Israel divides **930**
Elijah prophesies in Israel **875**
Ahab becomes Israel's king **874**
Elisha prophesies in Israel **848**
Joash becomes Judah's king **835**
Jonah becomes a prophet **793**
1000 City of Peking built; Greek theology fully developed; California Indians build wood-reed houses; Chinese mathematics utilizes root multiplication, geometry, proportions, and theory of motion; glazing of bricks and tiles begins in Near East
950 Gold vessels and jewelry popular in Northern Europe
900 Celts invade Britain; Assyrians invent inflatable skins for soldiers to cross rivers
850 Evidence of highly developed metal and stone sculptures in Africa
814 Founding of Carthage, a Phoenician trading post
800 Development of caste system in India; Babylonian and Chinese astronomers understand planetary movements; spoked wheels used in Europe; Homer writes Illiad and Odyssey; ice skating a popular sport in northern Europe
776 First known date of Olympic games

Application is putting into practice what we already know (see Mark 4.24 and Hebrews 5.14) and answering the question, "So what?" by confronting us with the right questions and motivating us to take action (see 1 John 2.5,6 and James 2.6). Application is deeply personal—unique for each individual. It is making a relevant truth a personal truth, and involves developing a strategy and action plan to live your life in harmony with the Bible. It is the biblical "how to" of life.

You may ask, "How can your application notes be relevant to my life?" Each application note has three parts: (1) an *explanation* that ties the note directly to the Scripture passage and sets up the truth that is being taught, (2) the *bridge* which explains the timeless truth and makes it relevant for today, (3) the *application* which shows you how to take the timeless truth and apply it to your personal situation. No note, by itself, can apply Scripture directly to your life. It can only teach, direct, lead, guide, inspire, recommend, and urge. It can give you the resources and direction you need to apply the Bible; but only you can take these resources and put them into practice.

A good note, therefore, should not only give you knowledge and understanding, but point you to application. Before you buy any kind of resource Bible, you should evaluate the notes and ask the following questions: (1) Does the note contain enough information to help me understand the point of the Scripture passage? (2) Does the note assume I know too much? (3) Does the note avoid denominational bias? (4) Do the notes touch most of life's experiences? (5) Does the note help me *apply* God's Word?

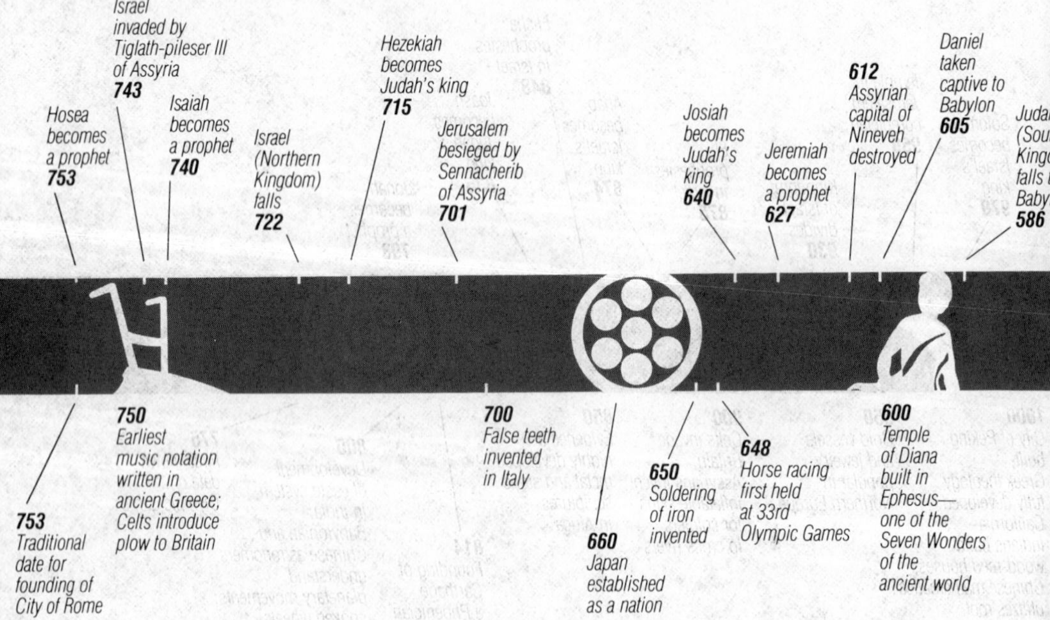

NOTES
In addition to providing the reader with many application notes, the *Life Application Bible* offers several explanatory notes, which are notes that help the reader understand culture, history, context, difficult-to-understand passages, background, places, theological concepts, and the relationship of various passages in Scripture to other passages. Maps, charts, and diagrams are also found on the same page as the passages to which they relate. For an example of an application note, see Mark 15:47. For an example of an explanatory note, see Mark 11:1, 2.

BOOK INTRODUCTIONS
The Book Introductions are divided into several easy-to-find parts:

Timeline. This puts the Bible book into its historical setting. It lists the key events of each book and the date when they occurred.

Vital Statistics. This is a list of straight facts about the book—those pieces of information you need to know at a glance.

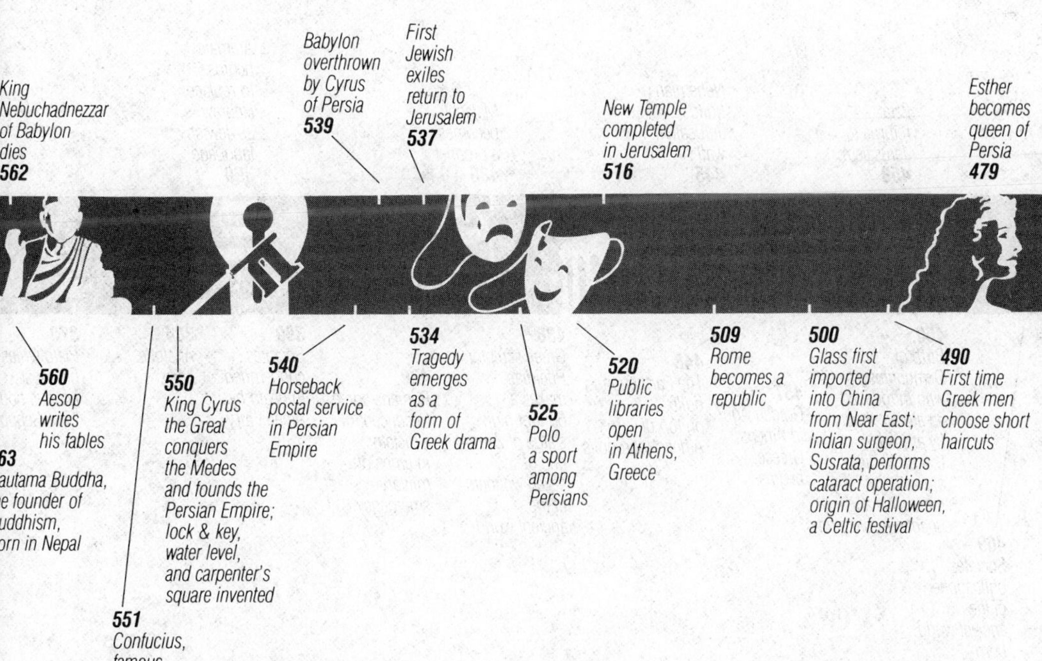

King Nebuchadnezzar of Babylon dies 562
Babylon overthrown by Cyrus of Persia 539
First Jewish exiles return to Jerusalem 537
New Temple completed in Jerusalem 516
Esther becomes queen of Persia 479
560 Aesop writes his fables
563 Gautama Buddha, the founder of Buddhism, born in Nepal
550 King Cyrus the Great conquers the Medes and founds the Persian Empire; lock & key, water level, and carpenter's square invented
551 Confucius, famous Chinese scholar, born
540 Horseback postal service in Persian Empire
534 Tragedy emerges as a form of Greek drama
525 Polo a sport among Persians
520 Public libraries open in Athens, Greece
509 Rome becomes a republic
500 Glass first imported into China from Near East; Indian surgeon, Susrata, performs cataract operation; origin of Halloween, a Celtic festival
490 First time Greek men choose short haircuts

Overview. This is a summary of the book with general lessons and applications that can be learned from the book as a whole.

Blueprint. This is the outline of the book. It is printed in easy-to-understand language and is designed for easy memorization. To the right of each main heading is a key lesson that is taught in that particular section.

Megathemes. This section gives the main themes of the Bible book, explains their significance, and then tells why they are still important for us today.

Map. This shows the key places found in that book and retells the story of the book from a geographical point of view.

OUTLINE

The *Life Application Bible* has a new, custom-made outline that was designed specifically from an application point of view. Several unique features should be noted:

1. To avoid confusion and to aid memory work, each book outline has only three levels for headings. Main outline heads are marked with a capital letter. Subheads are marked by a number. Minor, explanatory heads have no letter or number.
2. Each main outline head marked by a letter also has a brief paragraph below it summarizing the Bible text and offering a general application.
3. Parallel passages are listed where they apply in the Gospels.

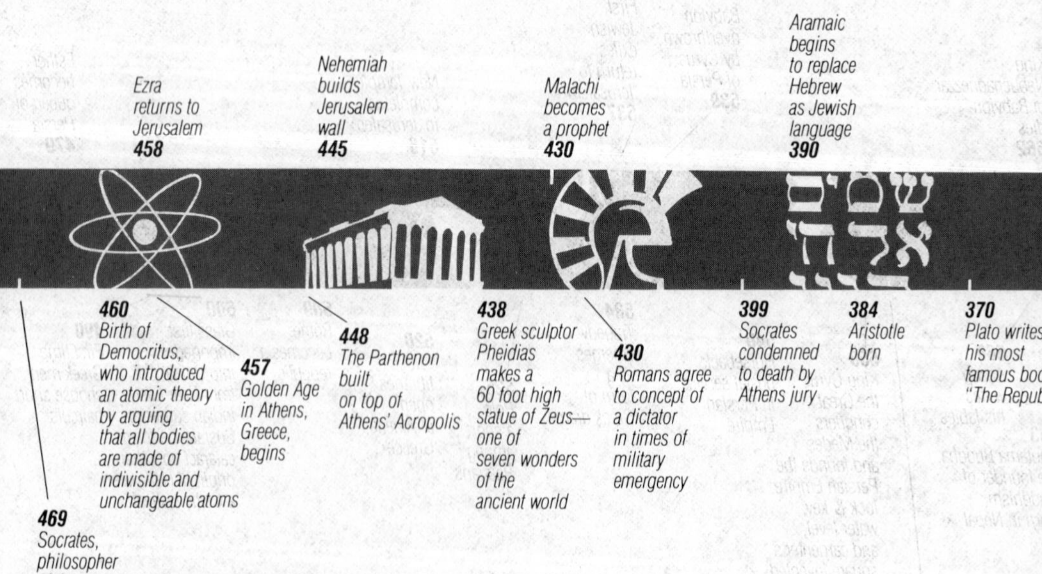

Ezra returns to Jerusalem 458
Nehemiah builds Jerusalem wall 445
Malachi becomes a prophet 430
Aramaic begins to replace Hebrew as Jewish language 390
460 Birth of Democritus, who introduced an atomic theory by arguing that all bodies are made of indivisible and unchangeable atoms
457 Golden Age in Athens, Greece, begins
448 The Parthenon built on top of Athens' Acropolis
438 Greek sculptor Pheidias makes a 60 foot high statue of Zeus—one of seven wonders of the ancient world
430 Romans agree to concept of a dictator in times of military emergency
399 Socrates condemned to death by Athens jury
384 Aristotle born
370 Plato writes his most famous book "The Republ
469 Socrates, philosopher of the ancient world, born

HARMONY OF THE GOSPELS

A harmony of the Gospels was developed specifically for this Bible. It is the first harmony that has ever been incorporated into the Bible text. Through a unique and simple numbering system, you can read any Gospel account and see just where you are in relation to the entire life of Christ. The harmony is located after the Gospel of John and explained in detail there.

PROFILE NOTES

Another unique feature of this Bible is the profiles of many Bible people, including their strengths and weaknesses, greatest accomplishments and mistakes, and key lessons from their lives. The profiles of these people are found in the Bible books where their stories occur.

MAPS

The *Life Application Bible* has more maps than any other Bible. A thorough and comprehensive Bible atlas is built right into each Bible book. There are two kinds of maps: (1) A book introduction map, telling the story of that Bible book. (2) Thumbnail maps in the notes, plotting most geographic movements in the Bible.

CHARTS AND DIAGRAMS

Hundreds of charts and diagrams are included to help the reader better visualize difficult concepts or relationships. Most charts not only present the needed information, but show the significance of the information as well.

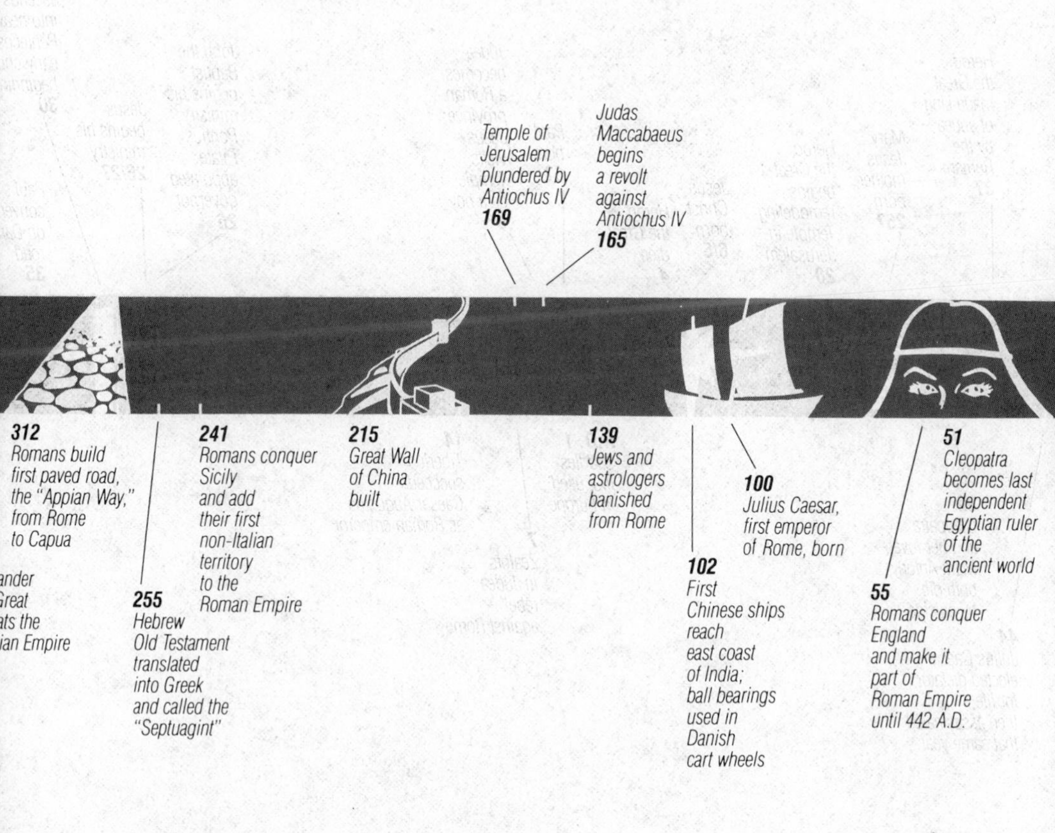
Temple of Jerusalem plundered by Antiochus IV 169
Judas Maccabaeus begins a revolt against Antiochus IV 165
312 Romans build first paved road, the "Appian Way," from Rome to Capua
xander Great ats the sian Empire
255 Hebrew Old Testament translated into Greek and called the "Septuagint"
241 Romans conquer Sicily and add their first non-Italian territory to the Roman Empire
215 Great Wall of China built
139 Jews and astrologers banished from Rome
102 First Chinese ships reach east coast of India; ball bearings used in Danish cart wheels
100 Julius Caesar, first emperor of Rome, born
55 Romans conquer England and make it part of Roman Empire until 442 A.D.
51 Cleopatra becomes last independent Egyptian ruler of the ancient world

CROSS REFERENCES

An updated, exhaustive cross reference system in the margins of the Bible text helps the reader find related passages quickly.

TEXTUAL NOTES

Directly related to *The Living Bible* text, the textual notes provide explanations on certain wording in the translation, alternate translations, and information about readings in the ancient manuscripts.

INDEX

This book contains a complete index to all the notes, charts, maps, and personality profiles. With its emphasis on application it is helpful for group Bible study, sermon preparation, teaching, or personal study.

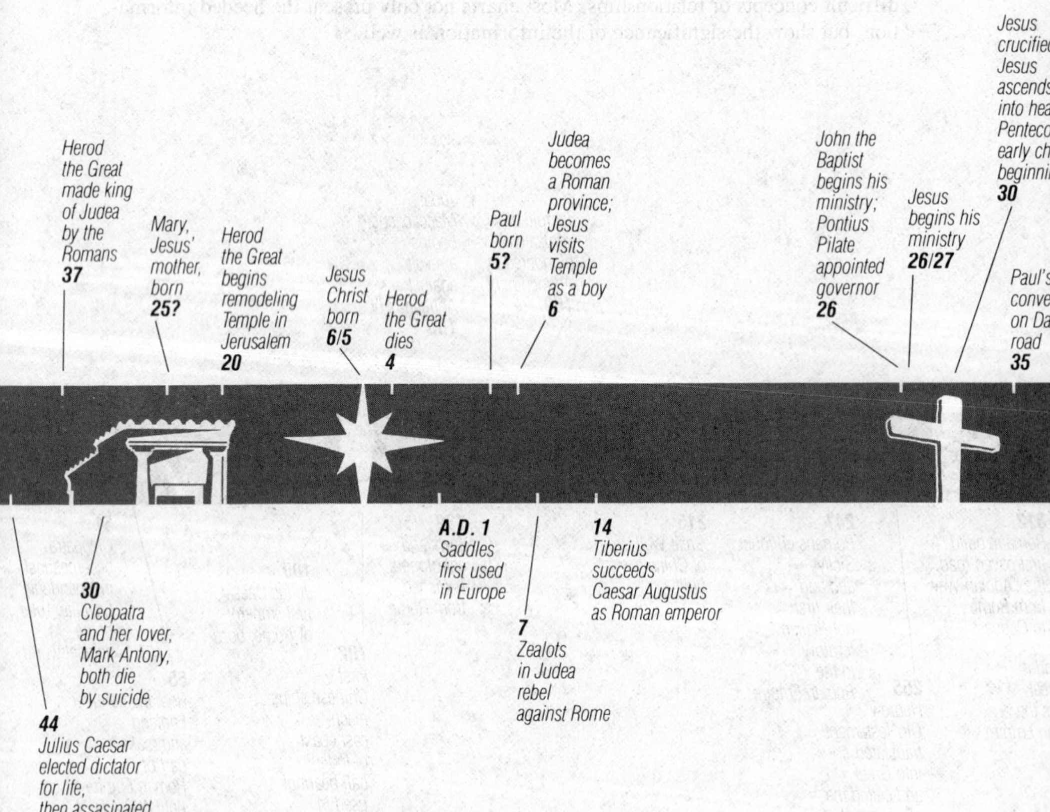

Herod the Great made king of Judea by the Romans 37
Mary, Jesus' mother, born 25?
Herod the Great begins remodeling Temple in Jerusalem 20
Jesus Christ born 6/5
Herod the Great dies 4
Paul born 5?
Judea becomes a Roman province; Jesus visits Temple as a boy 6
John the Baptist begins his ministry; Pontius Pilate appointed governor 26
Jesus begins his ministry 26/27
Jesus crucified; Jesus ascends into heave
Pentecos
early chur
beginning 30
Paul's convers
on Dam
road 35
44 Julius Caesar elected dictator for life, then assasinated that same year
30 Cleopatra and her lover, Mark Antony, both die by suicide
A.D. 1 Saddles first used in Europe
7 Zealots in Judea rebel against Rome
14 Tiberius succeeds Caesar Augustus as Roman emperor

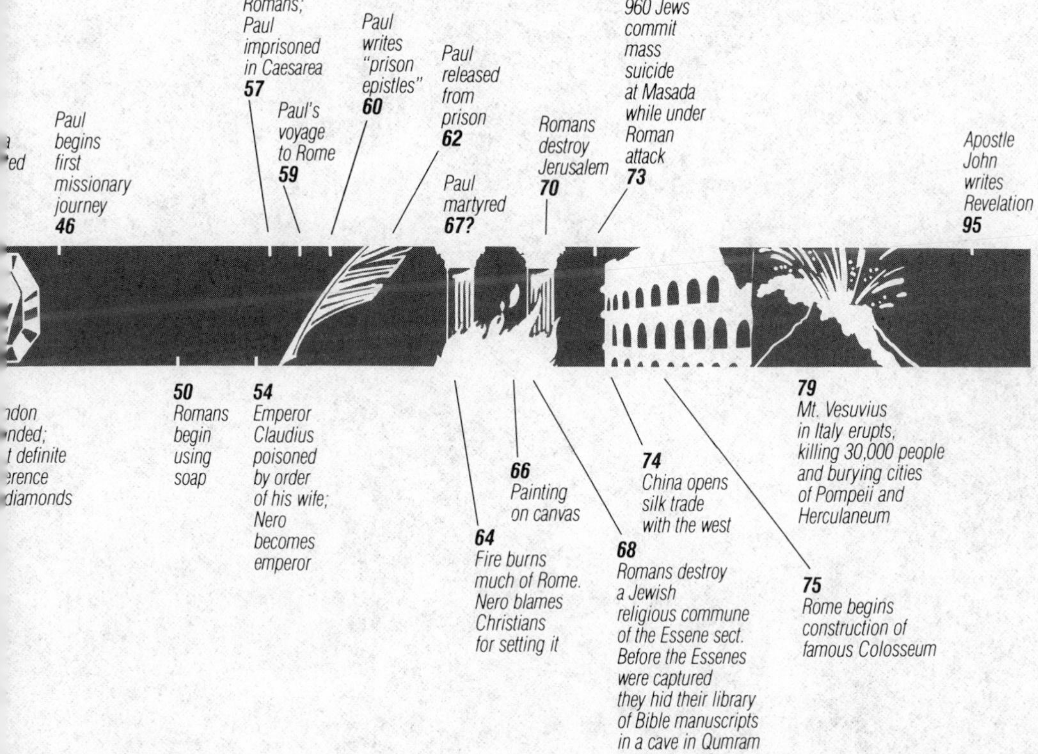
Paul begins first missionary journey 46
Paul writes Romans; Paul imprisoned in Caesarea 57
Paul's voyage to Rome 59
Paul writes "prison epistles" 60
Paul released from prison 62
Paul martyred 67?
Romans destroy Jerusalem 70
960 Jews commit mass suicide at Masada while under Roman attack 73
Apostle John writes Revelation 95
50 Romans begin using soap
54 Emperor Claudius poisoned by order of his wife; Nero becomes emperor
64 Fire burns much of Rome. Nero blames Christians for setting it
66 Painting on canvas
68 Romans destroy a Jewish religious commune of the Essene sect. Before the Essenes were captured they hid their library of Bible manuscripts in a cave in Qumram by the Dead Sea (discovered in 1948).
74 China opens silk trade with the west
75 Rome begins construction of famous Colosseum
79 Mt. Vesuvius in Italy erupts, killing 30,000 people and burying cities of Pompeii and Herculaneum

ABBREVIATIONS

The following abbreviations are used for the books of the Bible:

Old Testament

Gen	Genesis	2 Chron	2 Chronicles	Dan	Daniel
Ex	Exodus	Ezra	Ezra	Hos	Hosea
Lev	Leviticus	Neh	Nehemiah	Joel	Joel
Num	Numbers	Esth	Esther	Am	Amos
Deut	Deuteronomy	Job	Job	Ob	Obadiah
Josh	Joshua	Ps	Psalms	Jon	Jonah
Judg	Judges	Prov	Proverbs	Mic	Micah
Ruth	Ruth	Eccl	Ecclesiastes	Nah	Nahum
1 Sam	1 Samuel	Song	Song of Solomon	Hab	Habakkuk
2 Sam	2 Samuel	Isa	Isaiah	Zeph	Zephaniah
1 Kings	1 Kings	Jer	Jeremiah	Hag	Haggai
2 Kings	2 Kings	Lam	Lamentations	Zech	Zechariah
1 Chron	1 Chronicles	Ezek	Ezekiel	Mal	Malachi

New Testament

Mt	Matthew	Eph	Ephesians	Heb	Hebrews
Mk	Mark	Phil	Philippians	Jas	James
Lk	Luke	Col	Colossians	1 Pet	1 Peter
Jn	John	1 Thess	1 Thessalonians	2 Pet	2 Peter
Acts	Acts of the Apostles	2 Thess	2 Thessalonians	1 Jn	1 John
Rom	Romans	1 Tim	1 Timothy	2 Jn	2 John
1 Cor	1 Corinthians	2 Tim	2 Timothy	3 Jn	3 John
2 Cor	2 Corinthians	Titus	Titus	Jude	Jude
Gal	Galatians	Philem	Philemon	Rev	Revelations

In the notes to the books of the Old Testament the following abbreviations are used:

Ant.	Josephus, *Antiquities of the Jews*
Aram	Aramaic
Ch, chs	Chapter, chapters
Cn	Correction; made where the text has suffered in transmission and the versions provide no satisfactory restoration but where the Standard Bible Committee agrees with the judgment of competent scholars as to the most probable reconstruction of the original text.
Gk	Septuagint, Greek version of the Old Testament
Heb	Hebrew of the consonantal Masoretic Text of the Old Testament
Josephus	Flavius Josephus (Jewish historian, about A.D. 37 to about 95)
Macc.	The book(s) of the Maccabees
Ms(s)	Manuscript(s)
MT	The Hebrew of the pointed Masoretic Text of the Old Testament
OL	Old Latin
Q Ms(s)	Manuscript(s) found at Qumran by the Dead Sea
Sam	Samaritan Hebrew text of the Old Testament
Syr	Syriac Version of the Old Testament
Syr H	Syriac Version of Origen's Hexapla
Tg	Targum
Vg	Vulgate, Latin Version of the Old Testament

THE HEBREW SCRIPTURES

commonly called

THE OLD TESTAMENT

GENESIS

Creation | *Noah undated* | *Abram born 2166 B.C. (2000 B.C.)* | *Abram enters Canaan 2091 (1925)* | *Isaac born 2066 (1900)*

VITAL STATISTICS

PURPOSE:
To record God's creation of the world and his desire to have a people set apart to worship him

AUTHOR:
Moses

TO WHOM WRITTEN:
The people of Israel

DATE WRITTEN:
1450–1410 B.C.

SETTING:
The region presently known as the Middle East

KEY VERSES:
"So God created humankind in his image, in the image of God he created them; male and female he created them" (1.27). "I will make of you a great nation, and I will bless you, and make your name great, so that you will be a blessing. I will bless those who bless you, and the one who curses you I will curse; and in you all the families of the earth shall be blessed" (12.2, 3).

KEY PEOPLE:
Adam, Eve, Noah, Abraham, Sarah, Isaac, Rebekah, Jacob, Joseph

BEGIN . . . start . . . commence . . . open. . . . There's something refreshing and optimistic about these words, whether they refer to the dawn of a new day, the birth of a child, the prelude of a symphony, or the first miles of a family vacation. Free of problems and full of promise, beginnings stir hope and imaginative visions of the future. Genesis means "beginnings" or "origin," and it unfolds the record of the beginning of the world, of human history, of family, of civilization, of salvation. It is the story of God's purpose and plan for his creation. As the book of beginnings, Genesis sets the stage for the entire Bible. It reveals the person and nature of God (Creator, Sustainer, Judge, Redeemer); the value and dignity of human beings (made in God's image, saved by grace, used by God in the world); the tragedy and consequences of sin (the fall, separation from God, judgment); and the promise and assurance of salvation (covenant, forgiveness, promised Messiah).

God. That's where Genesis begins. All at once we see him creating the world in a majestic display of power and purpose, culminating with a man and woman made like himself (1.26, 27). But before long sin entered the world and Satan was unmasked. Bathed in innocence, creation was shattered by the fall (the willful disobedience of Adam and Eve). Fellowship with God was broken, and evil began weaving its destructive web. In rapid succession, we read how Adam and Eve were expelled from the beautiful garden, their first son turned murderer, and evil bred evil until God finally destroyed everyone on earth except a small family led by Noah, the only godly person left.

As we come to Abraham on the plains of Canaan, we discover the beginning of God's covenant people and the broad strokes of his salvation plan: salvation comes by faith, Abraham's descendants will be God's people, and the Savior of the world will come through this chosen nation. The stories of Isaac, Jacob, and Joseph which follow are more than interesting biographies. They emphasize the promises of God and the proof that he is faithful. The people we meet in Genesis are simple, ordinary people, yet through them, God did great things. These are vivid pictures of how God can and does use all kinds of people to accomplish his good purposes . . . even people like you and me.

Read Genesis and be encouraged. There is hope! No matter how dark the world situation seems, God has a plan. No matter how insignificant or useless you feel, God loves you and wants to use you in his plan. No matter how sinful and separated from God you are, his salvation is available. Read Genesis . . . and hope!

Jacob & Esau born 2006 (1840)	Jacob flees to Haran 1929 (1764)	Joseph born 1915 (1750)	Joseph sold into slavery 1898 (1733)	Joseph rules Egypt 1885 (1720)	Joseph dies 1805 (1640)

THE BLUEPRINT

A. THE STORY OF CREATION (1.1—2.3)

Because God created people, we have dignity and worth.

B. THE STORY OF ADAM (2.4—5.32)
1. Adam and Eve
2. Cain and Abel
3. Adam's descendants

Through Adam and Eve we learn about the destructive power of sin and its bitter consequences.

C. THE STORY OF NOAH (6.1—11.32)
1. The great flood
2. Repopulating the earth
3. The tower of Babel

Just as God protected Noah and his family, he protects those who are faithful to him today.

Pride is making ourselves more important than God.

D. THE STORY OF ABRAHAM (12.1—25.18)
1. God promises a nation to Abram
2. Abram and Lot
3. God promises a son to Abram
4. Sodom and Gomorrah
5. Birth and near sacrifice of Isaac
6. Isaac marries Rebekah
7. Abraham dies

Through sharp testing, Abraham remained faithful to God. Abraham's example teaches us how to live a life of faith.

We are to trust God completely, even when it hurts.

E. THE STORY OF ISAAC (25.19—28.9)
1. Jacob and Esau, Isaac's twin sons
2. Isaac and King Abimelech
3. Isaac blesses Jacob instead of Esau

Isaac did not resist when he was about to be sacrificed, and he gladly accepted a wife chosen for him by others. We must put God's will ahead of our own as Isaac did.

F. THE STORY OF JACOB (28.10—36.43)
1. Jacob starts a family
2. Jacob returns home

Although Jacob made many mistakes, his hard work teaches us about living a life of service for our Lord.

God is in the business of changing lives, despite our inadequacies.

G. THE STORY OF JOSEPH (37.1—50.26)
1. Joseph is sold into slavery
2. Judah and Tamar
3. Joseph is thrown into jail
4. Joseph is placed in charge of Egypt
5. Joseph and his brothers meet in Egypt
6. Jacob's family moves to Egypt
7. Jacob and Joseph die in Egypt

Through Joseph, we learn that suffering, no matter how unfair, can develop in us a strong character.

God can turn even our greatest defeats into victory.

MEGATHEMES

THEME	EXPLANATION	IMPORTANCE
Beginnings	Genesis explains the beginning of many important realities: the universe, earth, people, sin, and God's plan of salvation.	Genesis teaches us that the earth is well made and good. Mankind is special to God and unique. God creates and sustains all life.
Disobedience	People are always facing great choices. Disobedience occurs when people choose not to follow God's plan of living.	Genesis explains why men are evil: they choose to do wrong. Even great Bible heroes failed God and disobeyed.
Sin	Sin ruins people's lives. It happens when we disobey God.	Living God's way makes life productive and fulfilling.
Promises	God makes promises to help and protect mankind. This kind of promise is called a "covenant."	God kept his promises then, and he keeps them now. He promises to love us, accept us, forgive us.
Obedience	The opposite of sin is obedience. Obeying God restores our relationship to him.	The only way to enjoy the benefits of God's promises is to obey him.

Prosperity	Prosperity is deeper than mere material wealth. True prosperity and fulfillment come as a result of obeying God.	When people obey God, they find peace with him, with others, and with themselves.
Israel	God started the nation of Israel in order to have a dedicated people who would (1) keep his ways alive in the world, (2) proclaim to the world what he is really like, and (3) prepare the world for the birth of Christ.	God is looking for people today to follow him. We are to proclaim God's truth and love to all nations, not just our own. We must be faithful to carry out the mission God has given us.

KEY PLACES IN GENESIS

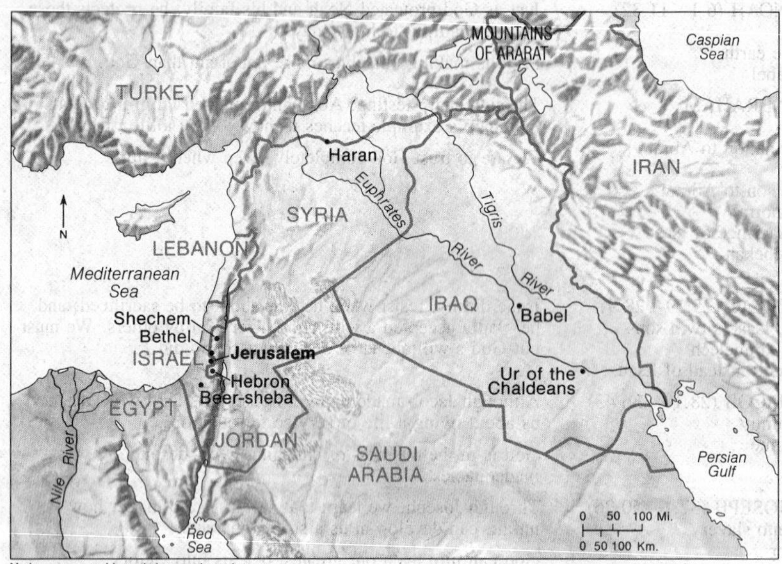

Modern names and boundaries are shown in gray.

God created the universe and the earth. Then he made man and woman, giving them a home in a beautiful garden. Unfortunately, Adam and Eve disobeyed God and were expelled from the garden (3.24).

1 Mountains of Ararat Adam and Eve's sin brought sin into the human race. Years later, sin had run rampant and God decided to destroy the earth with a great flood. But Noah, his family, and two of each animal were safe in the ark. When the floods receded, the ark rested on the mountains of Ararat (8.4).

2 Babel People never learn. Again sin abounded and the pride of the people led them to build a huge tower as a monument to their own greatness—obviously they had no thought of God. As punishment, God scattered the people by giving them different languages (11.8, 9).

3 Ur of the Chaldeans Abram, a descendant of Shem and father of the Hebrew nation, was born in this great city (11.27).

4 Haran Terah, Lot, Abram, and Sarai left Ur and, following the fertile crescent of the Euphrates River, headed toward the land of Canaan. Along the way, they settled in the city of Haran for a while (11.31).

5 Shechem God urged Abram to leave Haran and go to a place where he would become the father of a great nation (12.1, 2). So Abram, Lot, and Sarai traveled to the land of Canaan and settled near a city called Shechem (12.6).

6 Hebron Abraham moved on to Hebron where he put down his deepest roots (13.18). Abraham, Isaac, and Jacob all lived and were buried here.

7 Beer-sheba A well was dug here as a sign of an oath between Abraham and the army of King Abimelech (21.31). Years later, as Isaac was moving from place to place, God appeared to him here and passed on to him the covenant he had made with his father, Abraham (26.23–25).

8 Bethel After deceiving his brother, Jacob left Beer-sheba and fled to Haran. Along the way, God revealed himself to Jacob in a dream and passed on the covenant he had made with Abraham and Isaac (28.10–22). Jacob lived in Haran, worked for Laban, and married Leah and Rachel (29.15–28). After a tense meeting with his brother Esau, Jacob returned to Bethel (35.1).

9 Egypt Jacob had 12 sons, including Joseph, Jacob's favorite. Joseph's ten older brothers grew jealous, until one day the brothers sold him to Ishmaelite traders going to Egypt. Eventually, Joseph rose from Egyptian slave to Pharaoh's "right-hand man," saving Egypt from famine. His entire family moved from Canaan to Egypt and settled there (46.3, 4).

A. THE STORY OF CREATION (1.1—2.3)

We sometimes wonder how our world came to be. But here we find the answer. God created the earth and everything in it, and made man like himself. Although we may not understand the complexity of just how he did it, it is clear that God did create all life. This shows not only God's authority over humanity, but his deep love for all people.

The first six days

1.1 Ps 33.6; 89.11 **1** In the beginning when God created[a] the heavens and the earth, 2 the earth was
a formless void and darkness covered the face of the deep, while a wind from
1.3 Ps 33.9; 104.2 God[b] swept over the face of the waters. 3 Then God said, "Let there be light"; and
there was light. 4 And God saw that the light was good; and God separated the light

[a] Or *when God began to create* or *In the beginning God created* [b] Or *while the spirit of God* or *while a mighty wind*

BEGINNINGS The Bible does not discuss the subject of evolution. Rather, its worldview assumes God created the world. The biblical view of creation is not in conflict with science or with various evolutionary theories; it is in conflict with any worldview that starts with no creator.

Equally committed and sincere Christians have struggled with the subject of beginnings and come to differing conclusions. This, of course, is to be expected since the evidence is very old and, due to the ravages of the ages, quite fragmented. Students of the Bible and of science should avoid polarizations and black/white thinking. Students of the Bible must be careful not to make the Bible say what it doesn't say, and students of science must not make science say what it doesn't say.

The most important aspect of the continuing discussion is not the *process* of creation, but the *origin* of creation. The world is not a product of blind chance and probability; God created it.

The Bible not only tells us that the world was created by God; more important, it tells us who this God is. It reveals God's personality, his character, and his plan for his creation. It also reveals God's deepest desire: to relate to and fellowship with the people he created. God took the ultimate step toward fellowship with us through his historic visit to this planet in the person of his Son, Jesus Christ. We can know this God who created the universe in a very personal way.

The heavens and the earth are here. We are here. God created all that we see and experience. The book of Genesis begins, "God created the heavens and the earth."

Here we begin the most exciting and fulfilling journey imaginable.

1.1 The simple statement that God created the heavens and the earth is one of the most challenging concepts confronting the modern mind. The vast galaxy we live in is spinning at the incredible speed of 490,000 miles an hour. But even at this tremendous speed, our galaxy still needs 200 million years to make one rotation. And there are over one billion other galaxies in the universe.

It has been said that the number of stars in creation is equal to all the grains of all the sands on all the beaches of the world. Yet this complex sea of spinning stars functions with remarkable order and efficiency. To say that the universe "just happened" requires more faith than to believe that God is behind these amazing statistics. God truly did create a wonderful universe.

God did not *need* to create the universe; he *chose* to create it. Why? God is love, and love is best expressed toward something or someone else—so God created the world and people as an expression of his love. Don't reduce God's creation to merely scientific terms. Remember that God created the universe because he loves each of us.

1.1ff The creation story teaches us much about God and ourselves. First, we learn about God: (1) he is creative; (2) as the Creator he is distinct from his creation; (3) he is eternal and in control of the world. Second, we learn about ourselves: (1) since God chose to create us, we are valuable to him; (2) we are more important than the animals. (See 1.28 for more on our role in the created order.)

1.1ff Did God create the world? If so, just how did he do it? This is still a subject of great debate. Some say the universe appeared after a sudden explosion. Others say God started the process, and the universe evolved over billions of years. Almost every ancient religion has its own story to explain how the world came to be; almost every scientist has an opinion on the origin of the universe. But only the Bible shows one supreme God creating the earth out of his great love and giving all people a special place in it. We will never know all the answers to how God created the world, but the Bible tells us that God did create it. That fact alone gives worth and dignity to all people.

1.2 Who created God? To ask that question, we have to assume there was another creator before God. At some time, however, we are forced to stop asking that question and realize that there had to be something which has always existed. God is that infinite Being who has always been and who was created by no one. This is difficult to understand because finite minds cannot comprehend the infinite. For example, what is the highest number? Likewise, we must not limit the infinite God by our finite understanding of him.

1.2 The statement "the earth was a formless void" provides the setting for the creation narrative that follows. During the second and third days of creation, God gave *form* to the universe; during the next three days, God *filled* the earth with living beings. The "darkness covered the face of the deep" was dispelled on the first day, when God created light.

1.3—2.7 How long did it take God to create the world? There are two basic views about the days of creation: (1) each day was a literal 24-hour period; (2) each day represents an indefinite period of time (even millions of years).

The Bible does not say which theory is true. The real question, however, is not how long God took, but how he did it. God created the world in an orderly fashion (he did not make plants before light), and he created men and women as unique beings capable of communication with him. No other part of creation can claim that remarkable privilege. It is important not how long it took God to create the world, but that he created it just the way he wanted it.

from the darkness. 5 God called the light Day, and the darkness he called Night.
And there was evening and there was morning, the first day.
6 And God said, "Let there be a dome in the midst of the waters, and let it
separate the waters from the waters." 7 So God made the dome and separated the
waters that were under the dome from the waters that were above the dome. And it
was so. 8 God called the dome Sky. And there was evening and there was morning,
the second day.
9 And God said, "Let the waters under the sky be gathered together into one
place, and let the dry land appear." And it was so. 10 God called the dry land Earth,
and the waters that were gathered together he called Seas. And God saw that it was
good. 11 Then God said, "Let the earth put forth vegetation: plants yielding seed,
and fruit trees of every kind on earth that bear fruit with the seed in it." And it was
so. 12 The earth brought forth vegetation: plants yielding seed of every kind, and
trees of every kind bearing fruit with the seed in it. And God saw that it was good.
13 And there was evening and there was morning, the third day.
14 And God said, "Let there be lights in the dome of the sky to separate the day
from the night; and let them be for signs and for seasons and for days and years,
15 and let them be lights in the dome of the sky to give light upon the earth." And
it was so. 16 God made the two great lights — the greater light to rule the day and the
lesser light to rule the night — and the stars. 17 God set them in the dome of the sky
to give light upon the earth, 18 to rule over the day and over the night, and to separate the light from the darkness. And God saw that it was good. 19 And there was
evening and there was morning, the fourth day.
20 And God said, "Let the waters bring forth swarms of living creatures, and let
birds fly above the earth across the dome of the sky." 21 So God created the great sea
monsters and every living creature that moves, of every kind, with which the waters swarm, and every winged bird of every kind. And God saw that it was good.
22 God blessed them, saying, "Be fruitful and multiply and fill the waters in the
seas, and let birds multiply on the earth." 23 And there was evening and there was
morning, the fifth day.
24 And God said, "Let the earth bring forth living creatures of every kind: cattle
and creeping things and wild animals of the earth of every kind." And it was so.
25 God made the wild animals of the earth of every kind, and the cattle of every
kind, and everything that creeps upon the ground of every kind. And God saw that
it was good.
26 Then God said, "Let us make humankind[c] in our image, according to our
likeness; and let them have dominion over the fish of the sea, and over the birds of
the air, and over the cattle, and over all the wild animals of the earth,[d] and over
every creeping thing that creeps upon the earth."
27 So God created humankind[c] in his image,

1.4,5 Ps 74.16
1.6 Job 26.10; Ps 136.5,6
1.7,8 Job 38.3; Ps 148.4; Ps 150.1; Prov 8.28
1.9 Job 26.7; Ps 24.1-2; 95.5; Prov 8.9; Jer 5.22; 2 Pet 3.5
1.11,12 Gen 2.9; Ps 104; 14-17; Mt 6.30
1.14,15 Deut 4.19; Ps 74.16; 104.19
1.16 Ps 8.3; 19.1-6; Ps 136.7-9; 1 Cor 15.41; Rev 21.23
1.18 Jer 31.35
1.20 Gen 8.17; Ps 104.24,25; Ps 148.7
1.21,22 Gen 6.20
1.25 Job 12.7-9
1.26 Gen 5.1; 9.6; Ps 8.6-8; Col 3.10
1.27 Mt 19.4; 1 Cor 11.8,9

c Heb *adam* d Syr: Heb *and over all the earth*

1.6 The "dome" was a separation — an expanse of space between the sea and the mists of the skies.

1.25 God saw that his work was good, and he was pleased. People sometimes feel guilty for having a good time or for feeling good about an accomplishment. This need not be so. Just as God was pleased with his work, we can be pleased with ours. However, we cannot be pleased with our work if God is not pleased with it. What are you doing that pleases both you and God?

1.26 Why does God use the plural form: "Let *us* make humankind in *our* image"? One view says this is a reference to the Trinity — God the Father, God the Son, and God the Holy Spirit. Another view is that the plural wording is used to denote majesty. Kings traditionally use the plural form in speaking of themselves. We do know that God's Spirit was present in the creation from Job 33.4 and Psalm 104.30. From Colossians 1.16 we know that Christ, God's Son, was at work in the creation.

1.26 In what ways are we made in God's image? God obviously did not create us exactly like himself, especially in a physical sense. Instead, we are reflections of God's glory. God is sinless, eternal, and unlimited. Although we are given the potential to be sinless and eternal, we are also given the choice to fall short. We will never be totally like God because he is our supreme Creator. Our best hope is to reflect his character in our love, patience, forgiveness, kindness, and faithfulness.

Knowing that we are made in God's image and thus share many of his characteristics provides a solid basis for self-worth. Human worth is not defined by possessions, achievements, physical attractiveness, or public acclaim. Instead, it comes from being made in God's image. Because we are like God we can feel positive about ourselves. Knowing that you are a person of infinite worth gives you the freedom to love God, know him personally, and make a valuable contribution to those around you.

1.27 God made both man and woman in his image. Neither man nor woman is made more in the image of God than the other. From

in the image of God he created them;[e]
male and female he created them.
28God blessed them, and God said to them, "Be fruitful and multiply, and fill the
earth and subdue it; and have dominion over the fish of the sea and over the birds
1.29 Gen 9.3 Ps 115.16 Ps 136.25 145.15 of the air and over every living thing that moves upon the earth." 29God said, "See,
I have given you every plant yielding seed that is upon the face of all the earth, and
every tree with seed in its fruit; you shall have them for food. 30And to every beast
1.30 Ps 104.14 of the earth, and to every bird of the air, and to everything that creeps on the earth,
everything that has the breath of life, I have given every green plant for food." And
1.31 Ps 19.1; 104.24 it was so. 31God saw everything that he had made, and indeed, it was very good.
And there was evening and there was morning, the sixth day.

The seventh day

2.1 Ps 136.5-9 **2** Thus the heavens and the earth were finished, and all their multitude. 2And on
2.2 Ex 31.17 Heb 4.4 the seventh day God finished the work that he had done, and he rested on the
seventh day from all the work that he had done. 3So God blessed the seventh day
2.3 Isa 56.2 and hallowed it, because on it God rested from all the work that he had done in
creation.

B. THE STORY OF ADAM (2.4–5.32)

Learning about our ancestors often helps us understand ourselves. Adam and Eve, our first ancestors, were the highlight of God's creation—the very reason God made the world. But they didn't always live the way God intended. Through their mistakes, we can learn important lessons on how to live rightly. Adam and Eve teach us much about the nature of sin and its consequences.

1. Adam and Eve

The garden of Eden

2.4 Gen 1.3-31; 5.1 6.9 Gen 10.1 4 These are the generations of the heavens and the earth when they were
created.
2.5 Gen 1.12; 3.23 In the day that the LORD God made the earth and the heavens, 5when no plant of
the field was yet in the earth and no herb of the field had yet sprung up—for the
LORD God had not caused it to rain upon the earth, and there was no one to till the
ground; 6but a stream would rise from the earth, and water the whole face of

[e] Heb *him*

DAYS OF CREATION

First Day	Light (so there was light and darkness)
Second Day	Sky and water (vapors separated)
Third Day	Sea and earth (waters gathered); vegetation
Fourth Day	Sun, moon, and stars (to preside over day and night, to bring about the seasons, and to mark days and years)
Fifth Day	Fish and birds (to fill the waters and the sky)
Sixth Day	Animals (to fill the earth) Man and woman (to care for the earth and to commune with God)
Seventh Day	God rested and was pleased

the beginning the Bible places both man and woman at the pinnacle of creation. Neither sex is exalted, and neither is depreciated.

1.28 To have *dominion* over something is to have absolute authority and control over it. God has ultimate dominion over the earth, and he exercises his authority with loving care. When God delegated some of his authority to the human race, he expected us to take responsibility for the environment and the other creatures that inhabit our planet. We must not be careless as we fulfill this charge. Like the Creator, we should care for the earth and its plants and creatures responsibly and lovingly.

1.31 God was pleased with all he created, for he saw that it was very good. You are part of God's creation, and he is pleased with how he made you. If at times you feel worthless, remember that God made you for a good reason. You are valuable to him.

2.2, 3 We live in an action-oriented world! There always seems to be something to do and no time to rest. Yet God demonstrated that rest is appropriate and right. If God himself rested from his work, then it should not amaze us that we also need rest. Jesus demonstrated this principle when he and his disciples left in a boat to get away from the crowds (see Mark 6.31, 32). Our times of rest refresh us for times of service.

2.3 That God "hallowed" the seventh day means that he set it apart for holy use. This act is picked up in the ten commandments where God commanded the observance of the sabbath.

2.4 "Generations" simply means how they came into being.

the ground— 7 then the LORD God formed man from the dust of the ground,[f] and
breathed into his nostrils the breath of life; and the man became a living being.
8 And the LORD God planted a garden in Eden, in the east; and there he put the man
whom he had formed. 9 Out of the ground the LORD God made to grow every tree
that is pleasant to the sight and good for food, the tree of life also in the midst of the
garden, and the tree of the knowledge of good and evil.
10 A river flows out of Eden to water the garden, and from there it divides and
becomes four branches. 11 The name of the first is Pishon; it is the one that flows
around the whole land of Havilah, where there is gold; 12 and the gold of that land
is good; bdellium and onyx stone are there. 13 The name of the second river is Gihon; it is the one that flows around the whole land of Cush. 14 The name of the third
river is Tigris, which flows east of Assyria. And the fourth river is the Euphrates.
15 The LORD God took the man and put him in the garden of Eden to till it and
keep it. 16 And the LORD God commanded the man, "You may freely eat of every
tree of the garden; 17 but of the tree of the knowledge of good and evil you shall not
eat, for in the day that you eat of it you shall die."

Eve is created

18 Then the LORD God said, "It is not good that the man should be alone; I will
make him a helper as his partner." 19 So out of the ground the LORD God formed
every animal of the field and every bird of the air, and brought them to the man to
see what he would call them; and whatever the man called every living creature,
that was its name. 20 The man gave names to all cattle, and to the birds of the air,
and to every animal of the field; but for the man[g] there was not found a helper as
his partner. 21 So the LORD God caused a deep sleep to fall upon the man, and he
slept; then he took one of his ribs and closed up its place with flesh. 22 And the rib
that the LORD God had taken from the man he made into a woman and brought her
to the man. 23 Then the man said,

"This at last is bone of my bones
and flesh of my flesh;
this one shall be called Woman,[h]
for out of Man[i] this one was taken."

2.7 Gen 3.19,23 Job 33.4 Ezek 37.5 Jn 20.22
2.8 Isa 51.3 Ezek 28.13
2.9 Ezek 47.12 Rev 2.7 22.2,14
2.11 1 Sam 15.7
2.14 Dan 10.4
2.16 Gen 2.9 3.1,2
2.17 Rom 5.2; 6.23
2.18 Gen 3.12 Prov 18.22
2.19 Gen 1.20-25 6.20
2.22 1 Cor 11.8 1 Tim 2.13
2.23 Gen 29.14 Eph 5.28-30

[f] Or *formed a man* (Heb *adam*) *of dust from the ground* (Heb *adamah*) [g] Or *for Adam* [h] Heb *ishshah* [i] Heb *ish*

2.7 "From the dust of the ground" implies that there is nothing fancy about the chemical elements from which we are made. The body is a lifeless shell until God brings it alive with his "breath of life." When God removes his life-giving breath, our bodies once again return to dust. Therefore our life and worth come from God's spirit. Many boast of their achievements, only to fail soon after. Others have no achievements to boast about. But in reality, our worth comes not from our achievements but from the God of the universe, who chooses to give us the mysterious and miraculous gift of life. Value life, as he does.

2.9 The name of the tree of the knowledge of good and evil implies that evil had already occurred, if not in the garden, then at the time of Satan's fall.

2.9, 16, 17 Were the tree of life and the tree of knowledge of good and evil real trees? Two views are often expressed:

(1) *The trees were real, but symbolic.* Eternal life with God was symbolized by eating from the tree of life.

(2) *The trees were real, possessing special properties.* By eating the fruit from the tree of life, Adam and Eve could have had eternal life, enjoying a permanent relationship as God's children.

In either case, Adam and Eve's sin separated them from the tree of life and thus kept them from obtaining eternal life. Interestingly, the tree of life again appears in a description in Revelation 22 of people enjoying eternal life with God.

2.15–17 God gave Adam responsibility for the garden and told him not to eat from the tree of the knowledge of good and evil. Rather than physically preventing him from eating, God gave Adam a choice, and thus the possibility of choosing wrongly. God still gives us choices, and we, too, often choose wrongly. These wrong choices may cause us pain, but they can help us learn and grow and make better choices in the future. Living with the consequences of our choices teaches us to become more responsible.

2.16, 17 Why would God place a tree in the garden and then forbid Adam to eat from it? God wanted Adam to obey, but God gave Adam the freedom to choose. Without choice, Adam would have been like a prisoner and his obedience would have been hollow. The two trees provided an exercise in choice, with rewards for choosing to obey and sad consequences for choosing to disobey. When you are faced with the choice, always choose to obey God.

2.18–24 God's creative work was not complete until he made woman. He could have made her from the dust of the ground, as he made man. God chose, however, to make her from the man's flesh and bone. In so doing, he illustrated for us that in marriage man and woman symbolically become one flesh. This is a mystical union of the couple's hearts and lives. Throughout the Bible, God treats this special partnership seriously. If you are married or planning to be married, are you willing to keep the commitment that makes the two of you one? The goal in marriage should be more than friendship; it should be oneness.

2.21–23 God forms and equips men and women for various tasks, but all these tasks lead to the same goal—honoring God. Man gives life to woman; woman gives life to the world. Each role carries exclusive privileges; there is no room for thinking that one sex is superior to the other.

2.24 Mt 19.15 1 Cor 6.16 Eph 5.31

24 Therefore a man leaves his father and his mother and clings to his wife, and they
become one flesh. 25 And the man and his wife were both naked, and were not
ashamed.

Adam and Eve sin

3.1 Ezek 28.12-17 Rev 12.9; 20.2

3.3 Gen 2.16

3.4 2 Cor 2.11 11.3

3 Now the serpent was more crafty than any other wild animal that the LORD God
had made. He said to the woman, "Did God say, 'You shall not eat from any
tree in the garden'?" 2 The woman said to the serpent, "We may eat of the fruit of
the trees in the garden; 3 but God said, 'You shall not eat of the fruit of the tree that
is in the middle of the garden, nor shall you touch it, or you shall die.' " 4 But the
serpent said to the woman, "You will not die; 5 for God knows that when you eat of

WHAT THE BIBLE SAYS ABOUT MARRIAGE

Genesis 2.18–24	Marriage is God's idea
Genesis 24.58–60	Commitment is essential to a successful marriage
Genesis 29.10, 11	Romance is important
Jeremiah 7.34	Marriage holds times of great joy
Malachi 2.14, 15	Marriage creates the best environment for raising children
Matthew 5.32	Unfaithfulness breaks the bond of trust, the foundation of all relationships
Matthew 19.6	Marriage is permanent
Romans 7.2, 3	Ideally, only death should dissolve marriage
Ephesians 5.21–33	Marriage is based on the principled practice of love, not on feelings
Ephesians 5.23, 32	Marriage is a living symbol of Christ and the church
Hebrews 13.4	Marriage is good and honorable

2.24 God gave marriage as a gift to Adam and Eve. Marriage was not just for convenience, nor was it brought about by any culture. It was instituted by God and has three basic aspects: (1) the man leaves his parents and, in a public act, promises himself to his wife; (2) the man and woman are joined together by taking responsibility for each other's welfare and by loving the mate above all others; (3) the two become one flesh in the intimacy and commitment of sexual union, which is reserved for marriage. Strong marriages today include all three of these aspects.

2.25 Have you ever noticed how a little child can run naked through a room full of strangers without embarrassment? He is not aware of his nakedness, just as Adam and Eve were not embarrassed in their innocence. But after Adam and Eve sinned, embarrassment, shame, and awkwardness followed, creating barriers between themselves and God. We often experience these same barriers in marriage. Ideally, a husband and wife have no barriers, feeling no shame in exposing themselves to each other or to God. Like Adam and Eve (3.7), we put on fig leaves (barriers) because we have areas we don't want our spouse, or God, to know about. Then we hide, just as Adam and Eve hid from God. In marriage, lack of spiritual, emotional, and intellectual intimacy usually precedes a breakdown of physical intimacy. In the same way, when we fail to expose our secret thoughts to God, we break our lines of communication with him.

3.1 Disguised as a crafty serpent, Satan came to tempt Eve. Satan at one time was an angelic being who rebelled against God and was thrown out of heaven. As a created being, Satan has definite limitations. Although he is trying to tempt everyone away from God, he will not be the final victor. In 3.14, 15, God promises that Satan will be crushed.

3.1–6 Temptation is Satan's invitation to give in to his kind of life and give up on God's kind of life. Satan tempted Eve and succeeded in getting her to sin. He's been busy getting people to sin ever since. He even tempted Jesus (Matthew 4.11), but Jesus did not sin.

How could Eve have resisted temptation? By following the same guidelines we can follow. First, we must realize that *being tempted* is not a sin. We have not sinned until we *give in* to the temptation. Then, to resist temptation, we must (1) pray for strength to resist, (2) run, sometimes literally, and (3) say no when confronted with what we know is wrong. James 1.12 tells of the blessings and rewards for those who don't give in when tempted.

3.1–6 The serpent, Satan, tempted Eve by getting her to doubt God's goodness. He implied that God was strict, stingy, and selfish for not wanting Eve to share his knowledge of good and evil. Satan made Eve forget all that God had given her and focus on the one thing she couldn't have. We fall into trouble, too, when we focus on the few things we don't have rather than on the countless things God has given us. The next time you are feeling sorry for yourself, consider all you do have and thank God. Don't let your doubts lead you into sin.

3.5 Adam and Eve got what they wanted: an intimate knowledge of both good and evil. But they got it by doing evil, and the results were disastrous. We sometimes have the illusion that freedom is doing anything we want. God says true freedom comes from obedience and knowing what *not* to do. The restrictions he gives us are for our good, helping us avoid evil. We have the freedom to walk in front of a speeding car, but we don't need to be hit to realize it would be foolish to do so. Don't listen to Satan's temptations. Don't think you have to experience evil to learn more about life.

3.5 It wasn't wrong of Eve to want to "be like God." To become more like God is humanity's highest goal. But Satan misled Eve concerning the right way to accomplish this goal. He told her that she could become more like God by defying God's authority, by taking God's place and deciding for herself what was best for her life. In effect, he told her to become her own god.

But to become like God is not the same as trying to become God. Rather, it is to reflect his characteristics and recognize his authority over your life. Like Eve, we often have a worthy goal but try to achieve it in the wrong way. We act like a political candidate who pays off an election judge to be voted into office. When he does this, serving the people is no longer his highest goal.

Self-exaltation leads to rebellion against God. As soon as we begin to leave God out of our plans, we are placing ourselves above him. This is exactly what Satan wants us to do.

it your eyes will be opened, and you will be like God,[j] knowing good and evil."
6 So when the woman saw that the tree was good for food, and that it was a delight
to the eyes, and that the tree was to be desired to make one wise, she took of its fruit
and ate; and she also gave some to her husband, who was with her, and he ate.
7 Then the eyes of both were opened, and they knew that they were naked; and they
sewed fig leaves together and made loincloths for themselves.
8 They heard the sound of the LORD God walking in the garden at the time of the
evening breeze, and the man and his wife hid themselves from the presence of the
LORD God among the trees of the garden. 9 But the LORD God called to the man, and
said to him, "Where are you?" 10 He said, "I heard the sound of you in the garden,
and I was afraid, because I was naked; and I hid myself." 11 He said, "Who told you
that you were naked? Have you eaten from the tree of which I commanded you not
to eat?" 12 The man said, "The woman whom you gave to be with me, she gave me
fruit from the tree, and I ate." 13 Then the LORD God said to the woman, "What is
this that you have done?" The woman said, "The serpent tricked me, and I ate."
14 The LORD God said to the serpent,

"Because you have done this,
cursed are you among all animals
and among all wild creatures;
upon your belly you shall go,
and dust you shall eat

3.5 Gen 2.17 3.22 Ezek 28.2,9 Mt 6.23 Acts 26.18
3.6 2 Cor 11.3 1 Tim 2.14 Jas 1.14 1 Jn 2.16
3.10 Job 23.15 1 Jn 3.20
3.12 Ex 32.21-24 Prov 28.13 Jas 1.13
3.13 2 Cor 11.3 1 Tim 2.14
3.14 Deut 28.15 Isa 65.25

j Or *gods*

3.6 Satan tried to make Eve think that sin is good, pleasant, and desirable. A knowledge of both good and evil seemed harmless to her. People usually choose wrong things because they have become convinced that those things are good, at least for themselves. Our sins do not always appear ugly to us, and the pleasant sins are the hardest to avoid. So prepare yourself for the attractive temptations that may come your way. We cannot always prevent temptation, but there is always a way of escape (1 Corinthians 10.13). Use God's word and God's people to help you stand against it.

3.6, 7 Notice what Eve did: she looked, she took, she ate, and she gave. The battle is often engaged at the first look. Temptation may begin by simply seeing something we want. Are you struggling with temptation because you have not learned that looking is the first step toward sin? We would win over temptation more often if we followed Paul's advice to run from those things that produce evil thoughts (2 Timothy 2.22).

3.6, 7 One of the realities of sin is that its effects spread. After Eve sinned, she involved Adam in her wrongdoing. When we do something wrong, often we try to relieve our guilt by involving someone else. Like toxic waste spilled in a river, sin swiftly spreads. Recognize and confess your sin to God before you are tempted to pollute those around you.

3.7, 8 After sinning, Adam and Eve felt guilt and embarrassment over their nakedness. Their guilty feelings made them run from God and try to hide. A guilty conscience is a warning signal God placed inside you that goes off when you've done wrong. The worst step you could take is to eliminate the guilty feelings without eliminating the cause. That would be like using a pain killer but not treating the disease. Be glad those guilty feelings are there. They make you aware of your sin so you can ask God's forgiveness and then correct your wrongdoing.

3.8 The thought of two humans covered with fig leaves trying to hide from the all-seeing, all-knowing God is humorous. How could they be so silly as to think they could actually hide? Yet we do the same, acting as though God doesn't know what we are doing. Have the courage to share all you do and think with him, and don't try to hide. It can't be done. Honesty will strengthen your relationship with him.

3.8, 9 These verses show God's desire to have fellowship with us. They also show why we are afraid to have fellowship with him. Adam and Eve hid from God when they heard him approaching. God wanted to be with them, but because of their sin, they were afraid to show themselves. Sin had broken their close relationship with God, just as it has broken ours. But Jesus Christ, God's Son, opens the way for us to renew our fellowship with him. God longs to be with us. He actively offers us his unconditional love. Our natural response is fear, because we feel we can't live up to his standards. But understanding that he loves us, regardless of our faults, can help remove that dread.

3.11–13 Adam and Eve failed to heed God's warning recorded in 2.16, 17. They did not understand the reasons for his command, so they chose to act in another way that looked better to them. All of God's commands are for our own good, but we may not always understand the reasons behind them. A person who trusts God will obey because God asks him to, whether or not he understands why God commands it.

3.11–13 When God asked Adam about his sin, Adam blamed Eve. Then Eve blamed the serpent. How easy it is to excuse our sins by blaming someone else or circumstances. But God knows the truth, and he holds each of us responsible for what we do (see 3.14–19). Admit your wrong attitudes and actions and apologize to God. Don't try to get away with sin by blaming someone else.

3.14ff Adam and Eve chose their course of action (disobedience), and then God chose his. As a holy God, he could respond only in a way consistent with his perfect moral nature. He could not allow sin to go unchecked; he had to punish it. If the consequences of Adam and Eve's sin seem extreme, remember that their sin set in motion the world's constant tendency toward disobeying God. That is why we sin today: every human being ever born, with the exception of Jesus, has inherited the sinful nature of Adam and Eve (Romans 5.12–21). Adam and Eve's punishment reflects how seriously God views sin of any kind.

3.14–19 Adam and Eve learned by painful experience that because God is holy and hates sin, he must punish sinners. The rest of the book of Genesis recounts painful stories of lives ruined as a result of sin. Disobedience is sin, and it breaks our fellowship with God. But fortunately, when we disobey, God is willing to forgive us and to restore our relationship with him.

all the days of your life.

3.15 Jn 8.44 Acts 13.10 Rom 16.20 Gal 4.4 1 Jn 3.8-10 Rev 12.7

15 I will put enmity between you and the woman,
and between your offspring and hers;
he will strike your head,
and you will strike his heel."
16 To the woman he said,

ADAM

We can hardly imagine what it must have been like to be the first and only person on earth. It's one thing for us to be lonely; it was another for Adam, who had never known another human being. He missed much that makes us who we are—he had no childhood, no parents, no family or friends. He had to learn to be human on his own. God didn't let him struggle too long before presenting him with an ideal companion and mate, Eve. Theirs was a complete, innocent, and open oneness, without shame.

One of Adam's first conversations with his delightful new companion must have been about the rules of the garden. Before God made Eve he had already given Adam complete freedom in the garden, with the responsibility to tend and care for it. But one tree was off limits, the tree of knowledge of good and evil. Adam would have told Eve all about this. She knew, when Satan approached her, that the tree's fruit was not to be eaten. However, she decided to eat the forbidden fruit. Then she offered some to Adam. At that moment, the fate of creation was on the line. Sadly, Adam didn't pause to consider the consequences. He went ahead and ate.

In that moment of small rebellion something large, beautiful, and free was shattered . . . God's perfect creation. Man was separated from God by his desire to act on his own. The effect on a plate glass window is the same whether a pebble or a boulder is hurled at it—the thousands of fragments can never be regathered.

In the case of man's sin, however, God already had a plan in motion to overcome the effects of the rebellion. The entire Bible is the story of how that plan unfolds, ultimately leading to God's own visit to earth through his Son, Jesus. His sinless life and death made it possible for God to offer forgiveness to all who want it. Our small and large acts of rebellion prove that we are descendants of Adam. Only by asking forgiveness of Jesus Christ can we become children of God.

Strengths and accomplishments:
- The first zoologist—namer of animals
- The first landscape architect, placed in the garden to care for it
- Father of the human race
- The first person made in the image of God, and the first human to share an intimate personal relationship with God

Weaknesses and mistakes:
- Avoided responsibility and blamed others; chose to hide rather than to confront; made excuses rather than admitting the truth
- Greatest mistake: teamed up with Eve to bring sin into the world

Lessons from his life:
- As Adam's descendants, we all reflect to some degree the image of God
- God wants people who, though free to do wrong, choose instead to love him
- We should not blame others for our faults
- We cannot hide from God

Vital statistics:
- Where: Garden of Eden
- Occupation: Caretaker, gardener, farmer
- Relatives: Wife: Eve. Sons: Cain, Abel, Seth. Numerous other children. The only man who never had an earthly mother or father

Key verses:
"The man said, 'The woman whom you gave to be with me, she gave me fruit from the tree, and I ate'" (Genesis 3.12).
"For as all die in Adam, so all will be made alive in Christ" (1 Corinthians 15.22).

Adam's story is told in Genesis 1.26—5.5. He is also mentioned in 1 Chronicles 1.1; Job 31.33; Luke 3.38; Romans 5.14; 1 Corinthians 15.22, 45; 1 Timothy 2.13, 14.

3.15 Satan will do anything he can to get us to follow his evil, deadly path. The phrase "you will strike his heel" refers to Satan's repeated attempts to defeat Christ during his life on earth. "He will strike your head" foreshadows Satan's defeat when Christ rose from the dead. A strike on the heel is not deadly, but a strike on the head is. Already God was revealing his plan to defeat Satan and offer salvation to the world through his Son, Jesus Christ.

3.16–19 Adam and Eve's disobedience affected all creation, including the environment. Years ago people thought nothing of polluting streams with chemical wastes and garbage. This seemed so insignificant, so small. Now we know that just two or three parts per million of certain chemicals can damage human health. Sin in our lives is similar to pollution in streams. Even small amounts are deadly.

"I will greatly increase your pangs in childbearing;
in pain you shall bring forth children,
yet your desire shall be for your husband,
and he shall rule over you."
17 And to the man[k] he said,
"Because you have listened to the voice of your wife,
and have eaten of the tree
about which I commanded you,
'You shall not eat of it,'
cursed is the ground because of you;
in toil you shall eat of it all the days of your life;
18 thorns and thistles it shall bring forth for you;
and you shall eat the plants of the field.
19 By the sweat of your face
you shall eat bread
until you return to the ground,
for out of it you were taken;
you are dust,
and to dust you shall return."

3.16 Gen 35.16; 1 Cor 7.4; 11.3; Eph 5.22; Tit 2.5
3.17 Job 5.6,7; Eccles 1.3; Isa 24.5; Rom 8.20-22
3.18 Prov 22.5; Heb 6.8
3.19 Gen 2.7; Ps 90.3; 104.29; Eccles 12.7; Rom 5.12; 1 Cor 15.21,22

20 The man named his wife Eve,[l] because she was the mother of all living.
21 And the LORD God made garments of skins for the man[m] and for his wife, and
clothed them.
22 Then the LORD God said, "See, the man has become like one of us, knowing
good and evil; and now, he might reach out his hand and take also from the tree of
life, and eat, and live forever"— 23 therefore the LORD God sent him forth from the
garden of Eden, to till the ground from which he was taken. 24 He drove out the
man; and at the east of the garden of Eden he placed the cherubim, and a sword
flaming and turning to guard the way to the tree of life.

3.20 1 Tim 2.13
3.21 2 Cor 5.2,3
3.22 Jn 6.48
3.24 Rev 2.7; 22.2,14

2. Cain and Abel

Cain kills Abel

4 Now the man knew his wife Eve, and she conceived and bore Cain, saying, "I
have produced[n] a man with the help of the LORD." 2 Next she bore his brother
Abel. Now Abel was a keeper of sheep, and Cain a tiller of the ground. 3 In the

4.2 Lk 11.50,51
4.3 Lev 2.1

[k] *Or to Adam* [l] In Heb *Eve* resembles the word for *living* [m] *Or for Adam* [n] The verb in Heb resembles the word for *Cain*

SATAN'S PLAN

Doubt	Makes you question God's Word and his goodness
Discouragement	Makes you look at your problems rather than at God
Diversion	Makes the wrong things seem attractive so that you will want them more than the right things
Defeat	Makes you feel like a failure so that you don't even try
Delay	Makes you put off doing something so that it never gets done

3.22–24 Life in the garden of Eden was like living in heaven. Everything was perfect, and if Adam and Eve had obeyed God, they could have lived there forever. But after disobeying, Adam and Eve no longer deserved paradise, and God told them to leave. If they had continued to live in the garden and eat from the tree of life, they would have lived forever. But eternal life in a state of sin would mean forever trying to hide from God. Like Adam and Eve, all of us have sinned and are separated from fellowship with God. We do not have to stay separated, however. God is preparing a new earth as an eternal paradise for his people (see Revelation 22).

3.24 The cherubim were mighty angels of the Lord.

3.24 This is how Adam and Eve broke their relationship with God: (1) they became convinced their way was better than God's; (2) they became self-conscious and hid; (3) they tried to excuse and defend themselves. To build a relationship with God we must reverse those steps: (1) we must drop our excuses and self-defenses; (2) we must stop trying to hide from God; (3) we must become convinced that God's way is better than our way.

4.1 The word *knew* means "had sexual intercourse with" and is the perfect description of what sexual union means—oneness and total knowledge of the other person. Sexual intercourse is the most intimate of acts, sealing a social, physical, and spiritual relationship. That is why God has reserved it for marriage alone.

4.2 No longer was everything provided for Adam and Eve as it was in the garden of Eden, where their daily tasks were refreshing and delightful. Now they had to struggle against the elements in order to provide food, clothing, and shelter for themselves and their family. Cain became a farmer, while Abel was a shepherd. In parts of the Middle East today, these ancient occupations are still practiced much as they were in Cain and Abel's time.

4.4 Ex 13.12 Lev 3.15,16 Heb 11.4 course of time Cain brought to the LORD an offering of the fruit of the ground, [4]and
Abel for his part brought of the firstlings of his flock, their fat portions. And the
LORD had regard for Abel and his offering, [5]but for Cain and his offering he had no
4.5 Mt 20.15 regard. So Cain was very angry, and his countenance fell. [6]The LORD said to Cain,
4.7 Lk 11.35 Rom 6.12 Jas 1.15 "Why are you angry, and why has your countenance fallen? [7]If you do well, will
you not be accepted? And if you do not do well, sin is lurking at the door; its desire
is for you, but you must master it."

We know very little about Eve, the first woman in the world, yet she is the mother of us all. She was the final piece in the intricate and amazing puzzle of God's creation. Adam now had another human being with whom to fellowship—someone with an equal share in God's image. Here was someone alike enough for companionship, yet different enough for relationship. Together they were greater than either could have been alone.

Eve was approached by Satan in the garden of Eden, where she and Adam lived. He questioned her contentment. How could she be happy when she was not allowed to eat from one of the fruit trees? Satan helped Eve shift her focus from all that God had done and given to the one thing he had withheld. And Eve was willing to accept Satan's viewpoint without checking with God.

Sound familiar? How often is our attention drawn from the much which is ours to the little that isn't? We get that "I've got to have it" feeling. Eve was typical of us all, and we consistently show we are her descendants by repeating her mistakes. Our desires, like Eve's, can be quite easily manipulated. They are not the best basis for actions. We need to keep God in our decision-making process always. His word, the Bible, is our guidebook in decision making.

Strengths and accomplishments:
- First wife and mother
- First female. As such she shared a special relationship with God, had co-responsibility with Adam over creation, and displayed certain characteristics of God

Weaknesses and mistakes:
- Allowed her contentment to be undermined by Satan
- Acted impulsively without talking either to God or to her mate
- Not only sinned, but shared her sin with Adam
- When confronted, blamed others

Lessons from her life:
- The female shares in the image of God
- The necessary ingredients for a strong marriage are commitment to each other, companionship with each other, complete oneness, absence of shame (2.24, 25)
- The basic human tendency to sin goes back to the beginning of the human race

Vital statistics:
- Where: Garden of Eden
- Occupation: Wife, helper, companion, co-manager of Eden
- Relatives: Husband: Adam. Sons: Cain, Abel, Seth. Numerous other children

Key verse:
"Then the Lord God said, 'It is not good that the man should be alone; I will make him a helper as his partner'" (Genesis 2.18).

Eve's story is told in Genesis 2.19—4.26. Her death is not mentioned in scripture.

4.3–5 The Bible does not say why God rejected Cain's offering. Perhaps Cain's attitude was improper, or perhaps his offering was not up to God's standards. God evaluates both our motives and the quality of what we offer him. When we give to God and others, we should have a joyful heart because of what we are able to give. We should not worry about how much we are giving up, for all things are God's in the first place. Instead, we should joyfully give to God our best in time, money, possessions, and talents.

4.6, 7 How do you react when someone suggests you have done something wrong? Do you move to correct the mistake or deny that you need to correct it? After Cain's offering was rejected, God gave him the chance to right his wrong and try again. God even encouraged him to do this! But Cain refused, and the rest of his life is a startling example of what happens to those who refuse to admit their mistakes. The next time someone suggests you are wrong, take an honest look at yourself and choose God's way instead of Cain's.

4.7 Sin still lurks in the world today. Like Cain, we will be victims of sin if we do not master it. We cannot master sin in our own strength. Instead, we must turn to God to receive faith. Through this faith, the power of the Holy Spirit, and the faith and strength of other believers, we will have the strength to master sin. But this will be a lifelong battle. Our struggle with sin will not be over until we are face to face with Christ.

8 Cain said to his brother Abel, "Let us go out to the field."[o] And when they 4.8
were in the field, Cain rose up against his brother Abel, and killed him. 9 Then the Heb 12.24; 1 Jn 3.12
LORD said to Cain, "Where is your brother Abel?" He said, "I do not know; am I my 4.9
brother's keeper?" 10 And the LORD said, "What have you done? Listen; your Ps 9.12; 10.13,14
brother's blood is crying out to me from the ground! 11 And now you are cursed 4.10
from the ground, which has opened its mouth to receive your brother's blood from Deut 21.1; Heb 12.24
your hand. 12 When you till the ground, it will no longer yield to you its strength; 4.11
you will be a fugitive and a wanderer on the earth." 13 Cain said to the LORD, "My Isa 26.21; Gal 3.10
punishment is greater than I can bear! 14 Today you have driven me away from the 4.12
soil, and I shall be hidden from your face; I shall be a fugitive and a wanderer on Deut 28.15-24
the earth, and anyone who meets me may kill me." 15 Then the LORD said to him, 4.14 Gen 9.6
"Not so![p] Whoever kills Cain will suffer a sevenfold vengeance." And the LORD 4.15
put a mark on Cain, so that no one who came upon him would kill him. 16 Then Rev 14.9
Cain went away from the presence of the LORD, and settled in the land of Nod,[q] 4.16 2 Kgs 13.23
east of Eden. Jer 23.39; 52.3

Cain's descendants

17 Cain knew his wife, and she conceived and bore Enoch; and he built a city, 4.17 Ps 49.11
and named it Enoch after his son Enoch. 18 To Enoch was born Irad; and Irad was
the father of Mehujael, and Mehujael the father of Methushael, and Methushael the
father of Lamech. 19 Lamech took two wives; the name of the one was Adah, and
the name of the other Zillah. 20 Adah bore Jabal; he was the ancestor of those who
live in tents and have livestock. 21 His brother's name was Jubal; he was the ancestor of all those who play the lyre and pipe. 22 Zillah bore Tubal-cain, who made all
kinds of bronze and iron tools. The sister of Tubal-cain was Naamah.

23 Lamech said to his wives: 4.23
"Adah and Zillah, hear my voice; Lev 19.18; Deut 32.35
you wives of Lamech, listen to what I say:
I have killed a man for wounding me,
a young man for striking me.
24 If Cain is avenged sevenfold,
truly Lamech seventy-sevenfold."

3. Adam's descendants

25 Adam knew his wife again, and she bore a son and named him Seth, for she 4.25 Gen 4.8; 5.3
said, "God has appointed[r] for me another child instead of Abel, because Cain Lk 3.38

[o] Sam Gk Syr Compare Vg: MT lacks *Let us go out to the field* [p] Gk Syr Vg: Heb *Therefore* [q] That is *Wandering*
[r] The verb in Heb resembles the word for *Seth*

4.8–10 This is the first murder – taking a life by shedding human blood. Blood represents life (Leviticus 17.10–14). If blood is removed from a living creature, it will die. Because God created life, only God should take life away.

4.8–10 Adam and Eve's disobedience brought sin into the human race. They may have thought their sin – eating a "harmless" piece of fruit – wasn't very bad, but notice how quickly their sinful nature developed in their children. Simple disobedience suddenly degenerated into outright murder. Adam and Eve acted only against God, but Cain acted against both God and man. A small sin has a way of growing out of control. Let God help you with your "little" sins before they turn into tragedies.

4.12–15 Cain was severely punished for this murder. God judges all sins and punishes appropriately, but not simply out of anger or vengeance. Rather, God's punishment is meant to correct us and restore our fellowship with him. When you're corrected, don't resent it. Instead, renew your fellowship with God.

4.14 We have heard about only four people so far – Adam, Eve, Cain, and Abel. Two questions arise: why was Cain worried about being killed by others, and where did he get his wife (see 4.17)?

Adam and Eve had numerous children; they had been told to "fill the earth" (1.28). Cain's guilt and fear over killing his brother were heavy, and he probably feared repercussions from his family. If he was capable of killing, so were they. The wife Cain chose may have been one of his sisters or a niece. The human race was still genetically pure, and there was no fear of side effects from marrying relatives.

4.15 The expression "sevenfold vengeance" means that the person's punishment would be complete and thorough and much worse than that received by Cain for his sin.

4.19–26 Unfortunately, when left to themselves, people tend to get worse instead of better. This short summary of Lamech's family shows us the variety of talent and ability God gives humans. It also presents the continuous development of sin as time passes. Another murder has occurred, presumably in self-defense. Violence is on the rise. Two distinct groups are now appearing: (1) those who show indifference to sin and evil, and (2) those who call upon ("invoke") the name of the Lord (the descendants of Seth, 4.26). Seth would take Abel's place as leader of a line of God's faithful people.

4.26 Gen 12.8; 1 Kgs 18.24
5.1 Gen 1.26; 6.9
5.2 Gen 1.27
5.3 Gen 4.25
5.4 1 Chron 1.1
5.5 Gen 3.19; Heb 9.27
5.6 1 Chron 1.1; Lk 3.38
5.9 1 Chron 1.1; Lk 3.37
5.12 1 Chron 1.1; Lk 3.37

killed him." 26 To Seth also a son was born, and he named him Enosh. At that time
people began to invoke the name of the LORD.

5 This is the list of the descendants of Adam. When God created humankind,[s]
he made them[t] in the likeness of God. 2 Male and female he created them, and
he blessed them and named them "Humankind"[s] when they were created.
3 When Adam had lived one hundred thirty years, he became the father of a son
in his likeness, according to his image, and named him Seth. 4 The days of Adam
after he became the father of Seth were eight hundred years; and he had other sons
and daughters. 5 Thus all the days that Adam lived were nine hundred thirty years;
and he died.
6 When Seth had lived one hundred five years, he became the father of Enosh.
7 Seth lived after the birth of Enosh eight hundred seven years, and had other sons
and daughters. 8 Thus all the days of Seth were nine hundred twelve years; and he
died.
9 When Enosh had lived ninety years, he became the father of Kenan. 10 Enosh
lived after the birth of Kenan eight hundred fifteen years, and had other sons and
daughters. 11 Thus all the days of Enosh were nine hundred five years; and he died.
12 When Kenan had lived seventy years, he became the father of Mahalalel.

[s] Heb *adam* [t] Heb *him*

ABEL

Abel was the second child born into the world, but the first one to obey God. All we know about this man is that his parents were Adam and Eve, he was a shepherd, he presented pleasing offerings to God, and his short life was ended at the hands of his jealous older brother, Cain.

The Bible doesn't tell us why God liked Abel's gift and disliked Cain's, but both Cain and Abel knew what God expected. Only Abel obeyed. Throughout history, Abel is remembered for his obedience and faith (Hebrews 11.4), and he is called "righteous" (Matthew 23.35).

The Bible is filled with God's general guidelines and expectations for our lives. It is also filled with more specific directions. Like Abel, we must obey regardless of the cost, and trust God to make things right.

Strengths and accomplishments:
- First member of the Hall of Faith in Hebrews 11
- First shepherd
- First martyr for truth (Matthew 23.35)

Lessons from his life:
- God hears those who come to him
- God recognizes the innocent person, and sooner or later punishes the guilty

Vital statistics:
- Where: Just outside of Eden
- Occupation: Shepherd
- Relatives: Parents: Adam and Eve. Brother: Cain

Key verse:
"By faith Abel offered to God a more acceptable sacrifice than Cain's. Through this he received approval as righteous, God himself giving approval to his gifts; he died, but through his faith he still speaks" (Hebrews 11.4).

Abel's story is told in Genesis 4.1–8. He is also mentioned in Matthew 23.35; Luke 11.51; Hebrews 11.4 and 12.24.

5.1ff The Bible contains several lists of ancestors, called *genealogies.* There are two basic views concerning these lists: (1) they are complete, recording the entire history of a family, tribe, or nation; or (2) they are not intended to be exhaustive and may include only famous people or the heads of families. ("Became the father of" could also mean "was the descendant of.")

Why are genealogies included in the Bible? The Hebrews passed on their beliefs through oral tradition. For many years in many places, writing was primitive or nonexistent. Stories were told to children who passed them on to their children. Genealogies gave a skeletal outline that helped people remember the stories. For centuries these genealogies were added to and passed down from family to family. Even more important than preserving family tradition, genealogies were included to confirm the Bible's promise that the coming Messiah, Jesus Christ, would be born into the line of Abraham.

Genealogies point out an interesting characteristic of God. People are important to him as individuals, not just as races or nations. Therefore God refers to people by name, mentioning their lifespan and descendants. The next time you feel overwhelmed in a vast crowd, remember that the focus of God's attention and love is on the individual – and on you!

5.3–5 All human beings are related, going back to Adam and Eve. Mankind is a family that shares one flesh and blood. Remember this when prejudice enters your mind or hatred invades your feelings. Each person is a valuable and unique creation of God.

13 Kenan lived after the birth of Mahalalel eight hundred and forty years, and had
other sons and daughters. 14 Thus all the days of Kenan were nine hundred and ten
years; and he died.
15 When Mahalalel had lived sixty-five years, he became the father of Jared.
16 Mahalalel lived after the birth of Jared eight hundred thirty years, and had other
sons and daughters. 17 Thus all the days of Mahalalel were eight hundred ninety-
five years; and he died.
18 When Jared had lived one hundred sixty-two years he became the father of **5.18**
Enoch. 19 Jared lived after the birth of Enoch eight hundred years, and had other 1 Chron 1.1 Lk 3.37
sons and daughters. 20 Thus all the days of Jared were nine hundred sixty-two years; Jude 14
and he died.
21 When Enoch had lived sixty-five years, he became the father of Methuselah.
22 Enoch walked with God after the birth of Methuselah three hundred years, and **5.22**
had other sons and daughters. 23 Thus all the days of Enoch were three hundred Gen 6.9; 24.20 48.15
sixty-five years. 24 Enoch walked with God; then he was no more, because God Heb 11.5 Jude 14
took him. **5.24**
25 When Methuselah had lived one hundred eighty-seven years, he became the 2 Kgs 2.11 Ps 49.5; 73.24
father of Lamech. 26 Methuselah lived after the birth of Lamech seven hundred
eighty-two years, and had other sons and daughters. 27 Thus all the days of Methuselah were nine hundred sixty-nine years; and he died.
28 When Lamech had lived one hundred eighty-two years, he became the father
of a son; 29 he named him Noah, saying, "Out of the ground that the LORD has **5.29**
cursed this one shall bring us relief from our work and from the toil of our hands." Gen 3.17; 8.21 Rom 8.20
30 Lamech lived after the birth of Noah five hundred ninety-five years, and had
other sons and daughters. 31 Thus all the days of Lamech were seven hundred
seventy-seven years; and he died.
32 After Noah was five hundred years old, Noah became the father of Shem, **5.32**
Ham, and Japheth. Gen 7.6; 9.18

C. THE STORY OF NOAH (6.1 – 11.32)

Earth was no longer the perfect paradise that God had intended. It is frightening to see how quickly all of humanity forgot about God. Incredibly, in all the world, only one man and his family still worshiped God. That man was Noah. Because of his faithfulness and obedience, God saved him and his family from a vast flood that destroyed every other human being on earth. This section shows us how God hates sin and judges those who enjoy it.

1. The great flood

God promises to save Noah

6 When people began to multiply on the face of the ground, and daughters were
born to them, 2 the sons of God saw that they were fair; and they took wives for **6.3**
themselves of all that they chose. 3 Then the LORD said, "My spirit shall not abide[u] Num 11.17 Ps 78.39
in mortals forever, for they are flesh; their days shall be one hundred twenty years." Isa 63.10 1 Pet 3.20

[u] Meaning of Heb uncertain

5.24 At first glance it looks as if Enoch fared worse than the other patriarchs: he lived on earth only 365 years! Hebrews 11.5 explains what this verse means. Enoch was translated directly to heaven without seeing death. Enoch, then, lived longer than any of the other patriarchs, because he never died at all.

5.25–27 How did these people live so long? Some believe that the ages listed here were lengths of family dynasties rather than ages of individual men. Those who think these were actual ages offer three explanations: (1) the human race was genetically purer in this early time period, so there was less disease to shorten the lifespan; (2) the "waters that were above the dome" (1.7) kept out harmful cosmic rays and shielded people from environmental factors that hasten aging; (3) God gave people longer lives so they would have time to "fill the earth" (1.28) and make a significant impact for him.

6.1–4 Some people have thought that the "sons of God" were fallen angels. But the "sons of God" were probably not angels, because angels do not marry or reproduce (Matthew 22.30; Mark 12.25). Some experts believe this phrase refers to the descendants of Seth who intermarried with Cain's evil descendants ("the daughters of humans"). This would have weakened the good influence of the faithful and increased moral depravity in the world. The result was an explosion of evil. "Nephilim" refers to a powerful race of giants.

6.3 "Their days shall be one hundred twenty years" means that God was allowing the people of Noah's day 120 years to change their sinful ways. God shows his great patience with us as well. He is giving us time to quit living our way and begin living his way, the way he shows us in his word. While 120 years seems like a long time, eventually the time ran out and the flood waters swept across the earth. Your time also may be running out. Turn to God to forgive your sins.

6.4 Num 13.33
6.5 Ps 14.2,3
6.6 Ex 32.14 Num 23.19 1 Sam 15.29 2 Sam 24.16
6.7 Deut 29.19,20
6.9 Job 1.1 Ezek 14.14

4 The Nephilim were on the earth in those days—and also afterward—when the
sons of God went in to the daughters of humans, who bore children to them. These
were the heroes that were of old, warriors of renown.
5 The LORD saw that the wickedness of humankind was great in the earth, and
that every inclination of the thoughts of their hearts was only evil continually. 6 And
the LORD was sorry that he had made humankind on the earth, and it grieved him
to his heart. 7 So the LORD said, "I will blot out from the earth the human beings I
have created—people together with animals and creeping things and birds of the
air, for I am sorry that I have made them." 8 But Noah found favor in the sight of
the LORD.
9 These are the descendants of Noah. Noah was a righteous man, blameless in

CAIN

In spite of parents' efforts and worries, conflicts between children in a family seem inevitable. Sibling relationships allow both competition and cooperation. In most cases, the mixture of loving and fighting eventually creates a strong bond between brothers and sisters. It isn't unusual, though, to hear parents say, "They fight so much I hope they don't kill each other before they grow up." In Cain's case, the troubling potential became a tragedy. And while we don't know many details of this first child's life, his story can still teach us.

Cain got angry. Furious. Both he and his brother Abel had made offerings to God, and his had been rejected. Cain's reaction gives us a clue that his attitude was probably wrong from the start. Cain had a choice to make. He could correct his attitude about his sacrifice to God, or he could take out his anger on his brother. His decision is a clear reminder of how often we are aware of opposite choices, yet choose the wrong just as Cain did. We may not be choosing to murder, but we are still intentionally choosing what we shouldn't.

The feelings motivating our behavior can't always be changed by thought-power. But here we can begin to experience God's willingness to help. Asking for his help to do what is right can prevent us from setting into motion actions that we will later regret.

Strengths and accomplishments:
- First human child
- First to follow in father's profession, farming

Weaknesses and mistakes:
- When disappointed, reacted in anger
- Took the negative option even when a positive possibility was offered
- Was the first murderer

Lessons from his life:
- Anger is not necessarily a sin, but actions motivated by anger can be sinful. Anger should be the energy behind good action, not evil action
- What we offer to God must be from the heart—the best we are and have
- The consequences of sin may last a lifetime

Vital statistics:
- Where: Near Eden, which was probably located in present-day Iraq or Iran
- Occupation: Farmer, then nomad
- Relatives: Parents: Adam and Eve. Brothers: Abel, Seth, and others not mentioned by name

Key verse:
"If you do well, will you not be accepted? And if you do not do well, sin is lurking at the door" (Genesis 4.7).

Cain's story is told in Genesis 4.1–17. He is also mentioned in Hebrews 11.4; 1 John 3.12; Jude 1.11.

6.4 The giants ("Nephilim") mentioned here probably were nine or ten feet tall. These may have been the same people mentioned in Numbers 13.33. Goliath, who was nine feet tall, appears in 1 Samuel 17. The Nephilim used their physical advantage to oppress the people around them.

6.6, 7 Does this mean God regretted creating humanity? Was he admitting he made a mistake? No, God does not change his mind (1 Samuel 15.29). Instead, he was expressing sorrow for what the people had done to themselves, as a parent might express sorrow over a rebellious child. God was sorry that the people chose sin and death instead of a relationship with him.

6.6–8 The people's sin grieved God's heart. Our sins break God's heart as much as sin did in Noah's day. Noah, however, pleased God. Although he was far from perfect, we can follow Noah's example and find "favor in the sight of the Lord" in spite of the sin that surrounds us.

6.9 To say that Noah was "blameless in his generation" does not mean that he never sinned (the Bible records one of his sins in 9.20ff). Rather, it means that he wholeheartedly loved and obeyed God. For a lifetime he walked step by step in faith as a living example to his generation. Like Noah, we live in a world filled with evil. Are we influencing others or being influenced by them?

his generation; Noah walked with God. 10 And Noah had three sons, Shem, Ham,
and Japheth.
11 Now the earth was corrupt in God's sight, and the earth was filled with vio- 6.11
lence. 12 And God saw that the earth was corrupt; for all flesh had corrupted its Deut 31.29 Judg 2.19
ways upon the earth. 13 And God said to Noah, "I have determined to make an end Ezek 8.17
of all flesh, for the earth is filled with violence because of them; now I am going to 6.12 Ps 14.1-3
destroy them along with the earth. 14 Make yourself an ark of cypress[v] wood; make 53.2,3 Rom 3.23
rooms in the ark, and cover it inside and out with pitch. 15 This is how you are to 6.13
make it: the length of the ark three hundred cubits, its width fifty cubits, and its Isa 34.1-4 Ezek 7.2,3
height thirty cubits. 16 Make a roof[w] for the ark, and finish it to a cubit above; and 6.14
put the door of the ark in its side; make it with lower, second, and third decks. 17 For Ex 2.3
my part, I am going to bring a flood of waters on the earth, to destroy from under 6.17
heaven all flesh in which is the breath of life; everything that is on the earth shall Lev 26.28 Ps 29.10
die. 18 But I will establish my covenant with you; and you shall come into the ark, Isa 54.9 2 Pet 2.5
you, your sons, your wife, and your sons' wives with you. 19 And of every living
thing, of all flesh, you shall bring two of every kind into the ark, to keep them alive
with you; they shall be male and female. 20 Of the birds according to their kinds,
and of the animals according to their kinds, of every creeping thing of the ground
according to its kind, two of every kind shall come in to you, to keep them alive. 6.21
21 Also take with you every kind of food that is eaten, and store it up; and it shall Gen 1.29
serve as food for you and for them." 22 Noah did this; he did all that God com- 6.22 Gen 7.5
manded him. Ex 40.16

The flood waters cover the earth

7 Then the LORD said to Noah, "Go into the ark, you and all your household, for 7.1 Gen 6.18
I have seen that you alone are righteous before me in this generation. 2 Take Job 5.19 Prov 11.8
with you seven pairs of all clean animals, the male and its mate; and a pair of the Isa 26.20
animals that are not clean, the male and its mate; 3 and seven pairs of the birds of the Mt 24.38 Lk 17.26
air also, male and female, to keep their kind alive on the face of all the earth. 4 For Heb 11.17 1 Pet 3.20
in seven days I will send rain on the earth for forty days and forty nights; and every
living thing that I have made I will blot out from the face of the ground." 5 And 7.2 Lev 11.2-47
Noah did all that the LORD had commanded him. Deut 14.3-20 Ezek 44.23
6 Noah was six hundred years old when the flood of waters came on the earth. 7.4
7 And Noah with his sons and his wife and his sons' wives went into the ark to Gen 6.7,13 7.10,12,17
escape the waters of the flood. 8 Of clean animals, and of animals that are not clean, 7.11
and of birds, and of everything that creeps on the ground, 9 two and two, male and Ps 78.23 Ezek 26.19
female, went into the ark with Noah, as God had commanded Noah. 10 And after Mal 3.10
seven days the waters of the flood came on the earth. 7.12 Ex 24.18
11 In the six hundredth year of Noah's life, in the second month, on the seven- Deut 9.9
teenth day of the month, on that day all the fountains of the great deep burst forth, 1 Kgs 19.8 Mt 4.2
and the windows of the heavens were opened. 12 The rain fell on the earth forty days 7.13
and forty nights. 13 On the very same day Noah with his sons, Shem and Ham and Heb 11.7 1 Pet 3.20
Japheth, and Noah's wife and the three wives of his sons entered the ark, 14 they and 2 Pet 2.5

[v] Meaning of Heb uncertain [w] Or *window*

6.14 Pitch was a tarlike substance used to make the ark watertight.

6.15 A cubit was about 18 inches long. The boat Noah built was no canoe! Picture yourself building a boat the length of one and a half football fields and as high as a four-story building. The ark was exactly six times longer than it was wide—the same ratio used by modern shipbuilders. This huge boat was probably built miles from any body of water by only a few faithful men who believed God's promises and obeyed his commands.

6.18 *Covenant* means "promise." This is a familiar theme in Scripture—God making covenants with his people. For more on the covenant, see Genesis 9.8–13; 12.1–3; 15.17.

6.22 Noah got right to work when God told him to build the ark. The other people must have been warned about the coming disaster (1 Peter 3.20), but apparently they did not expect it to happen. Today things haven't changed much. Each day thousands of people are warned of God's inevitable judgment, yet most of them don't really believe it will happen. Don't expect people to welcome or accept your message of God's coming judgment on sin. Those who don't believe in God will deny his judgment and try to get you to deny God as well. But remember God's promise to Noah to keep him safe. This can inspire you to trust God for deliverance in the judgment that is sure to come.

7.1ff Pairs of every animal joined Noah in the ark; seven pairs were taken of those animals used for sacrifice. Scholars have estimated that almost 45,000 animals could have fit into the ark.

every wild animal of every kind, and all domestic animals of every kind, and every
creeping thing that creeps on the earth, and every bird of every kind—every bird,
7.15 Gen 6.19; 7.8 every winged creature. 15 They went into the ark with Noah, two and two of all
flesh in which there was the breath of life. 16 And those that entered, male and
female of all flesh, went in as God had commanded him; and the LORD shut him in.
17 The flood continued forty days on the earth; and the waters increased, and
7.18 Ex 14.28 bore up the ark, and it rose high above the earth. 18 The waters swelled and in-
Ps 69.14,15 creased greatly on the earth; and the ark floated on the face of the waters. 19 The
7.19 Ps 46.2,3 waters swelled so mightily on the earth that all the high mountains under the whole
2 Pet 3.6 heaven were covered; 20 the waters swelled above the mountains, covering them
7.20 Ps 104.6 fifteen cubits deep. 21 And all flesh died that moved on the earth, birds, domestic
animals, wild animals, all swarming creatures that swarm on the earth, and all
human beings; 22 everything on dry land in whose nostrils was the breath of life
7.23 Mt 24.37-39 died. 23 He blotted out every living thing that was on the face of the ground, human
1 Pet 3.20 beings and animals and creeping things and birds of the air; they were blotted out
2 Pet 2.5 from the earth. Only Noah was left, and those that were with him in the ark. 24 And
7.24 Gen 7.11; 8.4 the waters swelled on the earth for one hundred fifty days.

NOAH

The story of Noah's life involves not one, but two great and tragic floods. The world in Noah's day was flooded with evil. The number of those who remembered the God of creation, perfection, and love had dwindled to one. Of God's people, only Noah was left. God's response to the severe situation was a 120–year-long last chance, during which he had Noah build a graphic illustration of the message of his life. Nothing like a huge boat on dry land to make a point! For Noah, obedience meant a long-term commitment to a project.

Many of us have trouble sticking to any project, whether or not it is directed by God. It is interesting that the length of Noah's obedience was greater than the lifespan of people today. Our only comparable long-term project is our very lives. But perhaps this is one great challenge Noah's life gives us—to live, in acceptance of God's grace, an entire lifetime of obedience and gratitude.

Strengths and accomplishments:
- Only follower of God left in his generation
- Second father of the human race
- Man of patience, consistency, and obedience
- First major shipbuilder

Weakness and mistake:
- Got drunk and embarrassed himself in front of his sons

Lessons from his life:
- God is faithful to those who obey him
- God does not always protect us from trouble, but cares for us in spite of trouble
- Obedience is a long-term commitment
- A man may be faithful, but his sinful nature always travels with him

Vital statistics:
- Where: We're not told how far from the garden of Eden people had settled
- Occupation: Farmer, shipbuilder, preacher
- Relatives: Grandfather: Methuselah. Father: Lamech. Sons: Ham, Shem, and Japheth

Key verse:
"Noah did this; he did all that God commanded him" (Genesis 6.22).

Noah's story is told in Genesis 5.29—10.32. He is also mentioned in 1 Chronicles 1.4; Isaiah 54.9; Ezekiel 14.14, 20; Matthew 24.37, 38; Luke 3.36; 17.26, 27; Hebrews 11.7; 1 Peter 3.20; 2 Peter 2.5.

7.16 Many have wondered how this animal kingdom roundup happened. Did Noah and his sons spend years collecting them? In reality the creation, along with Noah, was doing just as God had commanded. There seemed to be no problem gathering the animals – God took care of the details of that job while Noah was doing his part by building the ark. Often we do just the opposite of Noah. We worry about details over which we have no control, while neglecting specific areas (such as attitudes, relationships, responsibilities) that *are* under our control. Like Noah, concentrate on what God has given you to do, and leave the rest to him.

7.17–24 Was the flood a local event, or did it cover the entire earth? A universal flood was certainly possible. There is enough water on the earth to cover all dry land (the earth began that way; see 1.9, 10). Afterward, God promised never again to destroy the earth with a flood. Thus this flood must have either covered the entire earth or destroyed all the inhabitants of the earth. Remember, God's reason for sending the flood was to destroy all the earth's wickedness. It would have taken a major flood to accomplish this.

The flood waters recede

8 But God remembered Noah and all the wild animals and all the domestic animals that were with him in the ark. And God made a wind blow over the earth,
and the waters subsided; 2 the fountains of the deep and the windows of the heavens
were closed, the rain from the heavens was restrained, 3 and the waters gradually
receded from the earth. At the end of one hundred fifty days the waters had abated;
4 and in the seventh month, on the seventeenth day of the month, the ark came to
rest on the mountains of Ararat. 5 The waters continued to abate until the tenth
month; in the tenth month, on the first day of the month, the tops of the mountains
appeared.
6 At the end of forty days Noah opened the window of the ark that he had made
7 and sent out the raven; and it went to and fro until the waters were dried up from
the earth. 8 Then he sent out the dove from him, to see if the waters had subsided
from the face of the ground; 9 but the dove found no place to set its foot, and it
returned to him to the ark, for the waters were still on the face of the whole earth.
So he put out his hand and took it and brought it into the ark with him. 10 He waited
another seven days, and again he sent out the dove from the ark; 11 and the dove
came back to him in the evening, and there in its beak was a freshly plucked olive
leaf; so Noah knew that the waters had subsided from the earth. 12 Then he waited
another seven days, and sent out the dove; and it did not return to him any more.
13 In the six hundred first year, in the first month, the first day of the month, the
waters were dried up from the earth; and Noah removed the covering of the ark, and
looked, and saw that the face of the ground was drying. 14 In the second month, on
the twenty-seventh day of the month, the earth was dry. 15 Then God said to Noah,
16 "Go out of the ark, you and your wife, and your sons and your sons' wives with
you. 17 Bring out with you every living thing that is with you of all flesh—birds and
animals and every creeping thing that creeps on the earth—so that they may
abound on the earth, and be fruitful and multiply on the earth." 18 So Noah went out
with his sons and his wife and his sons' wives. 19 And every animal, every creeping
thing, and every bird, everything that moves on the earth, went out of the ark by
families.
20 Then Noah built an altar to the LORD, and took of every clean animal and of
every clean bird, and offered burnt offerings on the altar. 21 And when the LORD
smelled the pleasing odor, the LORD said in his heart, "I will never again curse the
ground because of humankind, for the inclination of the human heart is evil from
youth; nor will I ever again destroy every living creature as I have done.
22 As long as the earth endures,
seedtime and harvest, cold and heat,
summer and winter, day and night,
shall not cease."

8.1 a)Gen 19.29 30.22 Ex 2.24 Job 12.15 Isa 44.27 Jer 2.2 2 Pet 2.5 b)Ex 14.21 Ps 104.7
8.4 Isa 37.38
8.7 Lev 11.15 Deut 14.14 1 Kgs 17.4 Lk 12.24
8.8 Isa 60.8 Hos 11.11 Mt 10.16
8.13 Gen 7.11
8.15 Gen 6.13; 7.1
8.17 Gen 7.8,14
8.19 Gen 7.2,3,8,9
8.20 Gen 4.4; 12.7 13.18; 22.2
8.21 Gen 3.17; 5.29 Lev 1.9 Isa 54.9
8.22 Gen 45.6 Ps 74.16,17

8.6–16 Noah occasionally sent a bird out to test the earth and see if it was dry, but he didn't get out of the ark until God told him to. He was waiting for God's timing. God knew that even though the water was gone, the earth was not dry enough for Noah and his family to venture out. What patience Noah showed, especially after spending an entire year inside his boat! We, like Noah, must trust God to give us patience during those difficult times when we must wait.

8.21, 22 Countless times throughout the Bible we see God showing his love and patience toward men and women in order to save them. Realizing that their hearts are evil, he continues to try to reach them. When we sin or fall away from God, we surely deserve to be destroyed by his judgment. But God has promised never again to destroy everything on earth until the judgment day when Christ returns to destroy evil forever. Now every change of season is a reminder of his promise.

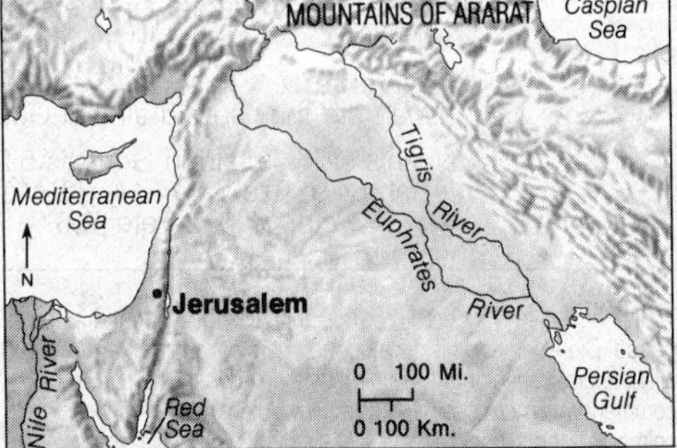

MOUNTAINS OF ARARAT The boat touched land in the mountains of Ararat, located in present-day Turkey near the USSR border. There it rested for almost eight months before Noah, his family, and the animals stepped onto dry land.

2. Repopulating the earth

Be fruitful and multiply

9 God blessed Noah and his sons, and said to them, "Be fruitful and multiply,
9.2 Gen 1.26 Ps 8.6-8 and fill the earth. 2 The fear and dread of you shall rest on every animal of the
earth, and on every bird of the air, on everything that creeps on the ground, and on
9.3 Deut 12.15 Ps 104.14 all the fish of the sea; into your hand they are delivered. 3 Every moving thing that
lives shall be food for you; and just as I gave you the green plants, I give you
9.4 Lev 3.17 7.26,27; 17.10 Deut 12.16 Acts 15.29 everything. 4 Only, you shall not eat flesh with its life, that is, its blood. 5 For your
own lifeblood I will surely require a reckoning: from every animal I will require it
and from human beings, each one for the blood of another, I will require a reckoning for human life.
9.5 Ex 21.12,28,29 Lev 19.17 6 Whoever sheds the blood of a human,
by a human shall that person's blood be shed;
9.6 Ex 20.13 Num 35.33 for in his own image
God made humankind.
7 And you, be fruitful and multiply, abound on the earth and multiply in it."

The rainbow

8 Then God said to Noah and to his sons with him, 9 "As for me, I am establishing my covenant with you and your descendants after you, 10 and with every living
creature that is with you, the birds, the domestic animals, and every animal of the
9.11 Isa 54.9 2 Pet 3.6 earth with you, as many as came out of the ark.[x] 11 I establish my covenant with
you, that never again shall all flesh be cut off by the waters of a flood, and never
9.12 Gen 17.11 Mt 26.26-28 again shall there be a flood to destroy the earth." 12 God said, "This is the sign of the
covenant that I make between me and you and every living creature that is with
9.13 Ezek 1.28 you, for all future generations: 13 I have set my bow in the clouds, and it shall be a
sign of the covenant between me and the earth. 14 When I bring clouds over the
9.15 Gen 6.18 Deut 7.9 earth and the bow is seen in the clouds, 15 I will remember my covenant that is
between me and you and every living creature of all flesh; and the waters shall
never again become a flood to destroy all flesh. 16 When the bow is in the clouds,
I will see it and remember the everlasting covenant between God and every living
creature of all flesh that is on the earth." 17 God said to Noah, "This is the sign of
the covenant that I have established between me and all flesh that is on the earth."

Noah's descendants

9.20 Gen 5.29 18 The sons of Noah who went out of the ark were Shem, Ham, and Japheth.
Ham was the father of Canaan. 19 These three were the sons of Noah; and from
9.21 Gen 19.32 Prov 20.1 these the whole earth was peopled.
20 Noah, a man of the soil, was the first to plant a vineyard. 21 He drank some

[x] Gk: Heb adds *every animal of the earth*

BIBLE NATIONS DESCENDED FROM NOAH'S SONS

Shem	*Ham*	*Japheth*	
Hebrews	Canaanites	Greeks	Shem's descendants were called Semites. Abraham, David, and Jesus descended from Shem. Ham's descendants settled in Canaan, Egypt, and the rest of Africa. Japheth's descendants settled for the most part in Europe and Asia minor.
Chaldeans	Egyptians	Thracians	
Assyrians	Philistines	Scythians	
Persians	Hittites		
Syrians	Amorites		

9.5 To "require a reckoning" means to "account for your actions." We cannot harm or kill another human being with impunity. A penalty must be paid. Justice will be served.

9.5, 6 Here God explains why murder is so wrong: to kill a person is to kill one made in God's image. Because human beings are made in God's image, all people possess the qualities that distinguish us from animals: morality, reason, creativity, and self-worth. When we interact with others, we are interacting with beings made by God, beings to whom God offers eternal life.

9.8–13 Noah stepped out of the ark onto an earth devoid of human life. But God gave him a reassuring promise. This promise, or covenant, had three parts: (1) never again will a flood do such destruction; (2) as long as the earth remains, the seasons will always come as expected; (3) a rainbow will be visible when it rains as a sign to all that God will keep his promises. The earth's order and seasons are still preserved, and rainbows still remind us of God's faithfulness to his word.

9.20–27 Noah, the great hero of faith, got drunk – a poor example of godliness to his sons. Perhaps this story is included to show us that even godly people can sin and that their bad influence affects their families. The possibility of evil still existed in the hearts of Noah and his family.

of the wine and became drunk, and he lay uncovered in his tent. 22 And Ham, the
father of Canaan, saw the nakedness of his father, and told his two brothers outside.
23 Then Shem and Japheth took a garment, laid it on both their shoulders, and
walked backward and covered the nakedness of their father; their faces were turned
away, and they did not see their father's nakedness. 24 When Noah awoke from his
wine and knew what his youngest son had done to him, 25 he said,

"Cursed be Canaan;
lowest of slaves shall he be to his brothers."

26 He also said,
"Blessed by the LORD my God be Shem;
and let Canaan be his slave.

27 May God make space for[y] Japheth,
and let him live in the tents of Shem;
and let Canaan be his slave."

28 After the flood Noah lived three hundred fifty years. 29 All the days of Noah
were nine hundred fifty years; and he died.

10 These are the descendants of Noah's sons, Shem, Ham, and Japheth; children were born to them after the flood.

2 The descendants of Japheth: Gomer, Magog, Madai, Javan, Tubal, Meshech,
and Tiras. 3 The descendants of Gomer: Ashkenaz, Riphath, and Togarmah. 4 The
descendants of Javan: Elishah, Tarshish, Kittim, and Rodanim.[z] 5 From these the
coastland peoples spread. These are the descendants of Japheth[a] in their lands,
with their own language, by their families, in their nations.

6 The descendants of Ham: Cush, Egypt, Put, and Canaan. 7 The descendants
of Cush: Seba, Havilah, Sabtah, Raamah, and Sabteca. The descendants of Raamah: Sheba and Dedan. 8 Cush became the father of Nimrod; he was the first on
earth to become a mighty warrior. 9 He was a mighty hunter before the LORD; therefore it is said, "Like Nimrod a mighty hunter before the LORD." 10 The beginning of
his kingdom was Babel, Erech, and Accad, all of them in the land of Shinar.
11 From that land he went into Assyria, and built Nineveh, Rehoboth-ir, Calah, and
12 Resen between Nineveh and Calah; that is the great city. 13 Egypt became the
father of Ludim, Anamim, Lehabim, Naphtuhim, 14 Pathrusim, Casluhim, and
Caphtorim, from which the Philistines come.[b]

15 Canaan became the father of Sidon his firstborn, and Heth, 16 and the Jebusites, the Amorites, the Girgashites, 17 the Hivites, the Arkites, the Sinites, 18 the
Arvadites, the Zemarites, and the Hamathites. Afterward the families of the Canaanites spread abroad. 19 And the territory of the Canaanites extended from Sidon,
in the direction of Gerar, as far as Gaza, and in the direction of Sodom, Gomorrah,
Admah, and Zeboiim, as far as Lasha. 20 These are the descendants of Ham, by
their families, their languages, their lands, and their nations.

21 To Shem also, the father of all the children of Eber, the elder brother of
Japheth, children were born. 22 The descendants of Shem: Elam, Asshur, Arpachshad, Lud, and Aram. 23 The descendants of Aram: Uz, Hul, Gether, and Mash.
24 Arpachshad became the father of Shelah; and Shelah became the father of Eber.
25 To Eber were born two sons: the name of the one was Peleg,[c] for in his days the
earth was divided, and his brother's name was Joktan. 26 Joktan became the father
of Almodad, Sheleph, Hazarmaveth, Jerah, 27 Hadoram, Uzal, Diklah, 28 Obal,
Abimael, Sheba, 29 Ophir, Havilah, and Jobab; all these were the descendants of
Joktan. 30 The territory in which they lived extended from Mesha in the direction of

9.22 Prov 30.17
9.23 Ex 20.12
9.24 Deut 27.16
9.25 Judg 1.28
9.26 Gen 14.20; 27.40
9.27 Gen 10.2-5 Isa 66.19
9.29 Gen 5.32; 7.11
10.1 Gen 6.9; 9.18 1 Chron 1.4
10.2 1 Chron 1.5-7 Isa 66.19 Ezek 27.13 38.2,3,6
10.3 Jer 51.27 Ezek 27.14
10.4 1 Chron 1.6,7
10.6 1 Chron 1.8,9
10.7 Isa 43.3 Ezek 27.15,20, 22
10.10 Gen 11.9
10.11 a)Mic 5.6 b)Num 4.22,24 Ezra 4.2
10.13 1 Chron 1.11,12 Jer 46.9
10.15 Gen 15.19-21 23.3 1 Chron 1.13 Jer 47.4
10.16 Gen 15.19-21
10.19 Gen 14.2,3
10.22 Gen 11.10-26 2 Kgs 15.29 1 Chron 1.17-23 Isa 66.19
10.23 Job 1.1 Jer 25.30
10.24 Lk 3.35

[y] Heb *yapht,* a play on *Japheth* [z] Heb Mss Sam Gk See 1 Chr 1.7: MT *Dodanim* [a] Compare verses 20, 31. Heb lacks *These are the descendants of Japheth* [b] Cn: Heb *Casluhim, from which the Philistines come, and Caphtorim* [c] That is *Division*

9.25 This verse has been wrongfully used to support racial prejudice and even slavery. Noah's curse, however, wasn't directed toward any particular race, but rather at the Canaanite nation – a nation God knew would become wicked. The curse was fulfilled when the Israelites entered the promised land and drove the Canaanites out (see the book of Joshua).

10.8–10 Not much is known about Nimrod except that he was a mighty hunter. But people with great gifts can become proud, and that is probably what happened to Nimrod. Some consider him the founder of the great, godless Babylonian Empire.

Sephar, the hill country of the east. 31 These are the descendants of Shem, by their
families, their languages, their lands, and their nations.
10.32 Gen 9.19; 10.1 32 These are the families of Noah's sons, according to their genealogies, in
their nations; and from these the nations spread abroad on the earth after the flood.

3. The tower of Babel

God scatters the people

11.2 Gen 10.10; 14.1 Isa 11.11 Dan 1.2 Zech 5.11 **11** Now the whole earth had one language and the same words. 2 And as they
migrated from the east,[d] they came upon a plain in the land of Shinar and
settled there. 3 And they said to one another, "Come, let us make bricks, and burn
11.4 2 Sam 8.13 Ps 49.11-13 them thoroughly." And they had brick for stone, and bitumen for mortar. 4 Then
they said, "Come, let us build ourselves a city, and a tower with its top in the
11.5 Gen 18.21 Ex 19.11 heavens, and let us make a name for ourselves; otherwise we shall be scattered
abroad upon the face of the whole earth." 5 The LORD came down to see the city and
11.6 Gen 9.19; 11.1 the tower, which mortals had built. 6 And the LORD said, "Look, they are one people, and they have all one language; and this is only the beginning of what they will
11.7 Gen 1.26; 3.22 10.5 do; nothing that they propose to do will now be impossible for them. 7 Come, let us
go down, and confuse their language there, so that they will not understand one
11.8 Gen 10.25,32 another's speech." 8 So the LORD scattered them abroad from there over the face of
all the earth, and they left off building the city. 9 Therefore it was called Babel,
11.9 Gen 10.10 1 Cor 14.23 because there the LORD confused[e] the language of all the earth; and from there the
LORD scattered them abroad over the face of all the earth.

Shem's descendants

11.10 Gen 10.22-25 10 These are the descendants of Shem. When Shem was one hundred years old,
he became the father of Arpachshad two years after the flood; 11 and Shem lived
after the birth of Arpachshad five hundred years, and had other sons and daughters.
12 When Arpachshad had lived thirty-five years, he became the father of She-
11.13 1 Chron 1.17 lah; 13 and Arpachshad lived after the birth of Shelah four hundred three years, and
had other sons and daughters.
14 When Shelah had lived thirty years, he became the father of Eber; 15 and
Shelah lived after the birth of Eber four hundred three years, and had other sons and
daughters.
16 When Eber had lived thirty-four years, he became the father of Peleg; 17 and
Eber lived after the birth of Peleg four hundred thirty years, and had other sons and
daughters.

[d] Or *migrated eastward* [e] Heb *balal*, meaning *to confuse*

11.3 The brick used to build this tower was a man-made substance, not as hard as stone. Bitumen was a sticky, tarlike substance.

11.3, 4 The tower of Babel was most likely a ziggurat, a common structure in the area at this time. Most often built as temples, ziggurats looked like pyramids with steps or ramps leading up the sides. Ziggurats stood as high as 300 feet and were often just as wide; thus they were the focal point of the city. The people in this story built their tower as a monument to their own greatness.

11.4 The tower of Babel was a great human achievement, a wonder of the world. But it was a monument to the people themselves rather than to God. We often build monuments to ourselves (expensive clothes, big house, fancy car, important job) to call attention to our achievements. These may not be wrong in themselves, but when we use them to give us identity and self-worth, they take God's place in our lives. We are free to develop in many areas, but we are not free to think we have replaced God. What "towers" are in your life?

11.10–27 In 9.24–27 we read Noah's curse on Canaan, Ham's son (10.6) and ancestor of the evil Canaanites. Here and in 10.22–31 we have a list of Shem's descendants, who were blessed (9.26). From Shem's line came Abram and the entire Jewish nation, which would eventually conquer the land of Canaan in the days of Joshua.

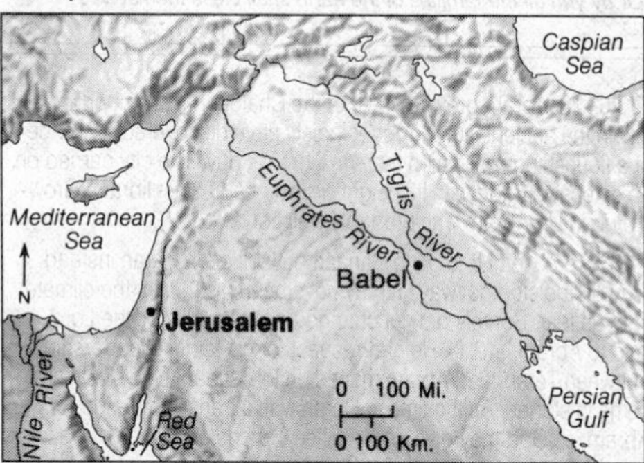

THE TOWER OF BABEL The plain between the Tigris and Euphrates Rivers offered a perfect location for the city and tower, "with its top in the heavens."

18 When Peleg had lived thirty years, he became the father of Reu; 19 and Peleg
lived after the birth of Reu two hundred nine years, and had other sons and daughters.
20 When Reu had lived thirty-two years, he became the father of Serug; 21 and
Reu lived after the birth of Serug two hundred seven years, and had other sons and
daughters.
22 When Serug had lived thirty years, he became the father of Nahor; 23 and
Serug lived after the birth of Nahor two hundred years, and had other sons and
daughters.
24 When Nahor had lived twenty-nine years, he became the father of Terah; **11.24**
25 and Nahor lived after the birth of Terah one hundred nineteen years, and had Josh 24.2
other sons and daughters.
26 When Terah had lived seventy years, he became the father of Abram, Na- **11.26**
hor, and Haran. Gen 22.20 1 Chron 1.26,27
27 Now these are the descendants of Terah. Terah was the father of Abram,
Nahor, and Haran; and Haran was the father of Lot. 28 Haran died before his father
Terah in the land of his birth, in Ur of the Chaldeans. 29 Abram and Nahor took **11.29** Gen 17.15
wives; the name of Abram's wife was Sarai, and the name of Nahor's wife was 20.12; 22.20 31.53
Milcah. She was the daughter of Haran the father of Milcah and Iscah. 30 Now Sarai **11.30**
was barren; she had no child. Gen 15.2; 16.1 18.11; 25.21
31 Terah took his son Abram and his grandson Lot son of Haran, and his 1 Sam 1.5
daughter-in-law Sarai, his son Abram's wife, and they went out together from Ur Luke 1.7
of the Chaldeans to go into the land of Canaan; but when they came to Haran, they **11.31** Gen 27.43
settled there. 32 The days of Terah were two hundred five years; and Terah died in Josh 24.2 Heb 11.8
Haran. Acts 7.2

D. THE STORY OF ABRAHAM (12.1—25.18)

Despite God's swift judgment of sin, most people ignored him and continued to sin. But a handful of people really tried to follow him. One of these was Abraham. God appeared to Abraham one day and promised to make his descendants into a great nation. Abraham's part of the agreement was to obey God. Through sharp testing and an incident that almost destroyed his family, Abraham remained faithful to God. Throughout this section we discover how to live a life of faith.

1. God promises a nation to Abram

12 Now the LORD said to Abram, "Go from your country and your kindred and **12.1** Gen 15.7
your father's house to the land that I will show you. 2 I will make of you a **12.2**
great nation, and I will bless you, and make your name great, so that you will be a Gen 13.16
blessing. 3 I will bless those who bless you, and the one who curses you I will curse; 15.5; 17.5 **12.3**
and in you all the families of the earth shall be blessed."[f] Gen 22.18
4 So Abram went, as the LORD had told him; and Lot went with him. Abram Ex 23.22 **12.4**
was seventy-five years old when he departed from Haran. 5 Abram took his wife Gen 11.26,31

[f] *Or by you all the families of the earth shall bless themselves*

11.26–28 Abram grew up in Ur of the Chaldeans, an important city in the ancient world. Archeologists have discovered evidence of a flourishing civilization there in Abram's day. The city carried on an extensive trade with its neighbors and had a vast library. Growing up in Ur, Abram was probably well educated.

11.31 Terah left Ur to go to Canaan but settled in Haran instead. Why did he stop halfway? It may have been his health, the climate, or even fear. But this did not change Abram's calling ("the Lord said to Abram," 12.1). He had respect for his father's leadership, but when Terah died Abram moved on to Canaan. God's will may come in stages. As the time in Haran was a transition period for Abram, so God may give us transition periods and times of waiting to help us depend on him and trust his timing. If we patiently do his will during the transition times, we will be better prepared to serve him as we should when he calls us.

12.1–3 Abram moved out in faith from Ur to Haran and finally to Canaan. God then established a covenant with him, telling him that he would found a great nation. Not only would this nation be blessed, God said, but the other nations of the earth would be blessed through Abram's descendants. Israel, the nation that would come from Abram, was to follow God and influence those with whom it came in contact. Through Abram's family tree, Jesus Christ was born to save humanity. Through Christ, people can have a personal relationship with God and be blessed beyond measure.

12.2 God promised to bless Abram and make him great, but there was one condition. Abram had to do what God wanted him to do. This meant leaving his home and friends and traveling to a new land where God promised to build a great nation from Abram's family. Abram obeyed, walking away from his home for God's promise of even greater blessings in the future. God may be trying to lead you to a place of greater service and usefulness for him. Don't let the comfort and security of your present position make you miss God's plan for you.

Sarai and his brother's son Lot, and all the possessions that they had gathered, and
the persons whom they had acquired in Haran; and they set forth to go to the land
12.6 Gen 33.18; 35.4 of Canaan. When they had come to the land of Canaan, [6] Abram passed through the
Deut 11.30 land to the place at Shechem, to the oak[g] of Moreh. At that time the Canaanites
12.7 were in the land. [7] Then the LORD appeared to Abram, and said, "To your off-
Gen 13.15 17.1; 18.1 spring[h] I will give this land." So he built there an altar to the LORD, who had
Gal 3.16 appeared to him. [8] From there he moved on to the hill country on the east of Bethel,
12.8 Gen 4.26; 8.20 and pitched his tent, with Bethel on the west and Ai on the east; and there he built
22.9 an altar to the LORD and invoked the name of the LORD. [9] And Abram journeyed on
12.9 Gen 13.1; 20.1 by stages toward the Negeb.
12.10 10 Now there was a famine in the land. So Abram went down to Egypt to reside
Gen 26.1; 42.5 there as an alien, for the famine was severe in the land. [11] When he was about to
12.11 Gen 26.7; 29.17 enter Egypt, he said to his wife Sarai, "I know well that you are a woman beautiful
12.12 in appearance; [12] and when the Egyptians see you, they will say, 'This is his wife';
Gen 20.11 then they will kill me, but they will let you live. [13] Say you are my sister, so that it
may go well with me because of you, and that my life may be spared on your
account." [14] When Abram entered Egypt the Egyptians saw that the woman was
very beautiful. [15] When the officials of Pharaoh saw her, they praised her to

[g] Or *terebinth* [h] Heb *seed*

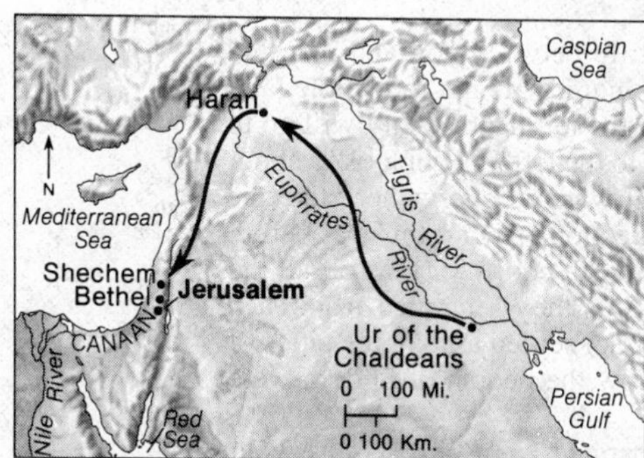

ABRAM'S JOURNEY TO CANAAN Abram, Sarai, and Lot traveled from Ur of the Chaldeans to Canaan by way of Haran. Though indirect, this route followed the rivers rather than attempting to cross the vast desert.

12.5 God planned to develop a nation of people he would call his own. He called Abram from the godless, self-centered city of Ur to a fertile region called Canaan, where a God-centered, moral nation could be established. Though small in dimension, the land of Canaan was the focal point for most of the history of Israel as well as for the rise of Christianity. This small land given to one man, Abram, has had a tremendous impact on world history.

12.7 Altars were used in many religions, but for God's people, altars were more than places of sacrifice. Altars symbolized communion with God and commemorated notable encounters with him. Built of rough stones and earth, they often remained in place for years as continual reminders of God's protection and promises.

Abram regularly built altars to God for two reasons: (1) for prayer and worship, and (2) as reminders of God's promise to bless him. He couldn't survive spiritually without regularly renewing his love and loyalty to God. Building altars helped Abram remember that God was at the center of his life. Regular worship helps us remember what God desires and motivates us to obey him.

12.8 To "invoke the name of the Lord" means to call on God or to pray to him.

12.10 When famine struck, Abram went to Egypt where there was food. Why would there be a famine in the land where God had just called Abram? This was a test of Abram's faith. Abram didn't question God's leading when he faced this difficulty. Many believers find that when they determine to follow God, they immediately encounter great obstacles. The next time you face such a test, don't try to second-guess what God is doing. Use the intelligence God gave you, as Abram did when he temporarily moved to Egypt, and wait for new opportunities.

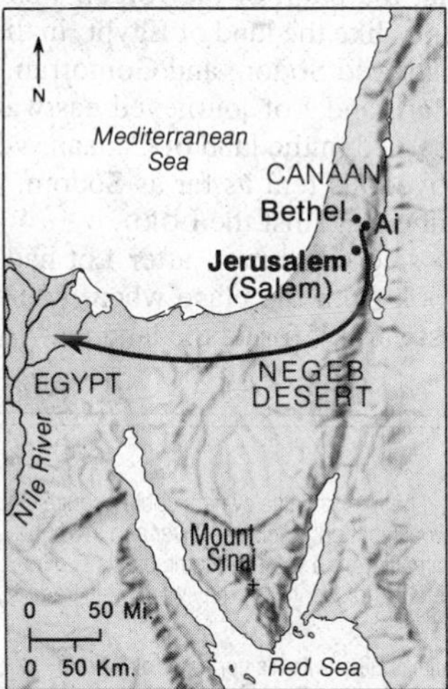

ABRAM'S JOURNEY TO EGYPT A famine could cause the loss of a shepherd's wealth. So Abram traveled through the Negeb Desert to Egypt, where there was plenty of food and good land for his flocks.

12.11–13 Abram, acting out of fear, asked Sarai to tell a half-truth by saying she was his sister. She *was* his half sister, but she was also his wife.

Abram's intent was to deceive the Egyptians. He feared that if they knew the truth, they would kill him to get Sarai. She would have been a desirable addition to Pharaoh's harem because of her wealth, beauty, and potential for political alliance. As Sarai's brother, Abram would have been given a place of honor. As her husband, however, his life would be in danger, because Sarai could not enter Pharaoh's harem unless Abram was dead. So Abram lost faith in God's protection, even after all God had promised him, and told a half-truth. This shows how lying compounds the effects of sin. When he lied, Abram's problems multiplied.

Pharaoh. And the woman was taken into Pharaoh's house. 16 And for her sake he
dealt well with Abram; and he had sheep, oxen, male donkeys, male and female
slaves, female donkeys, and camels.
17 But the LORD afflicted Pharaoh and his house with great plagues because of
Sarai, Abram's wife. 18 So Pharaoh called Abram, and said, "What is this you have
done to me? Why did you not tell me that she was your wife? 19 Why did you say,
'She is my sister,' so that I took her for my wife? Now then, here is your wife, take
her, and be gone." 20 And Pharaoh gave his men orders concerning him; and they
set him on the way, with his wife and all that he had.

12.16 Gen 13.2 20.14; 24.35
12.17 1 Chron 16.21 Ps 105.14
12.18 Gen 3.13; 4.10 20.9

2. Abram and Lot

Abram and Lot separate

13 So Abram went up from Egypt, he and his wife, and all that he had, and Lot
with him, into the Negeb.
2 Now Abram was very rich in livestock, in silver, and in gold. 3 He journeyed
on by stages from the Negeb as far as Bethel, to the place where his tent had been
at the beginning, between Bethel and Ai, 4 to the place where he had made an altar
at the first; and there Abram called on the name of the LORD. 5 Now Lot, who went
with Abram, also had flocks and herds and tents, 6 so that the land could not support
both of them living together; for their possessions were so great that they could not
live together, 7 and there was strife between the herders of Abram's livestock and
the herders of Lot's livestock. At that time the Canaanites and the Perizzites lived
in the land.
8 Then Abram said to Lot, "Let there be no strife between you and me, and
between your herders and my herders; for we are kindred. 9 Is not the whole land
before you? Separate yourself from me. If you take the left hand, then I will go to
the right; or if you take the right hand, then I will go to the left." 10 Lot looked about
him, and saw that the plain of the Jordan was well watered everywhere like the
garden of the LORD, like the land of Egypt, in the direction of Zoar; this was before
the LORD had destroyed Sodom and Gomorrah. 11 So Lot chose for himself all the
plain of the Jordan, and Lot journeyed eastward; thus they separated from each
other. 12 Abram settled in the land of Canaan, while Lot settled among the cities of
the Plain and moved his tent as far as Sodom. 13 Now the people of Sodom were
wicked, great sinners against the LORD.
14 The LORD said to Abram, after Lot had separated from him, "Raise your
eyes now, and look from the place where you are, northward and southward and
eastward and westward; 15 for all the land that you see I will give to you and to your

13.1 Gen 12.9; 20.1
13.2 Gen 12.16 20.14; 24.35
13.3 Gen 12.8; 28.19
13.5 Gen 12.4,5
13.6 Gen 36.6,7
13.7 a)Gen 21.25 26.20 b)Gen 12.6 15.19-21
13.8 Mt 5.9 Heb 12.14
13.9 Gen 20.15
13.10 Gen 2.8
13.13 Gen 18.20 Isa 1.9; 3.9 Rom 9.29 2 Pet 2.7
13.14 Gen 28.14 Deut 3.27 34.1-4
13.15 Gen 12.2,7 15.18; 17.7,8

13.1, 2 In Abram's day, sheep and cattle owners could acquire great wealth. Abram's wealth not only included silver and gold but also livestock. These animals were a valuable commodity used for food, clothing, tent material, and sacrifices. They were often traded for other goods and services.

13.5–9 Facing a potential conflict with his nephew Lot, Abram took the initiative in settling the dispute. He gave Lot first choice, even though Abram, being older, had the right to choose first. Abram also showed a willingness to risk being cheated. Abram's example shows us how to respond to difficult family situations: (1) take the initiative in resolving conflicts; (2) let others have first choice, even if that means not getting what we want; (3) put family peace above personal desires.

13.7, 8 Surrounded by hostile neighbors, the herdsmen of Abram and Lot should have pulled together. Instead, they let petty jealousy tear them apart. Similar situations exist today. Christians often bicker while Satan is at work all around them.

Rivalries, arguments, and disagreements among believers can be destructive in three ways. (1) They damage good will, trust, and peace—the foundations of good human relations. (2) They hamper progress toward important goals. (3) They make us self-centered rather than love-centered. Jesus understood how destructive arguments among brothers could be. In his final prayer before being betrayed and arrested, Jesus asked God that his followers be "one" (John 17.21).

13.10, 11 Lot's character is revealed by his choices. He took the best share of the land even though it meant living near Sodom, a city known for its sin. He was greedy, wanting the best for himself without thinking about his uncle Abram's needs or what was fair.

Life is a series of choices. We too can choose the best while ignoring the needs and feelings of others. But this kind of choice, as Lot's life shows, leads to problems. When we stop making choices in God's direction, all that is left is to make choices in the wrong direction.

13.12 Good pasture and available water seemed like a wise choice to Lot at first. But he failed to recognize that wicked Sodom could provide temptations strong enough to destroy his family. Have you chosen to live or work in a "Sodom"? Even though you may be strong enough to resist the temptations, other members of your family may not. While God commands us to reach people in the "Sodom" near us, we must be careful not to become like the very people we are trying to reach.

13.16 Gen 15.5; 28.14 Num 23.10 offspring[i] forever. 16 I will make your offspring like the dust of the earth; so that
if one can count the dust of the earth, your offspring also can be counted. 17 Rise up,
13.17 Num 13.17-24 walk through the length and the breadth of the land, for I will give it to you." 18 So
13.18 Gen 8.20; 12.7 Abram moved his tent, and came and settled by the oaks[j] of Mamre, which are at
Hebron; and there he built an altar to the LORD.

Abram rescues Lot

14.1 Gen 10.10 11.2; 14.9 **14** In the days of King Amraphel of Shinar, King Arioch of Ellasar, King Chedorlaomer of Elam, and King Tidal of Goiim, 2 these kings made war with
14.3 Num 34.12 Deut 3.17 Josh 3.16 King Bera of Sodom, King Birsha of Gomorrah, King Shinab of Admah, King
Shemeber of Zeboiim, and the king of Bela (that is, Zoar). 3 All these joined forces
in the Valley of Siddim (that is, the Dead Sea).[k] 4 Twelve years they had served

[i] Heb *seed* [j] Or *terebinths* [k] Heb *Salt Sea*

LOT

Some people simply drift through life. Their choices, when they can muster the will to choose, tend to follow the course of least resistance. Lot, Abram's nephew, was such a person.

While still young, Lot lost his father. Although this must have been hard on him, he was not left without strong role models in his grandfather Terah and his uncle Abram, who raised him. Still, Lot did not develop their sense of purpose. Throughout his life he was so caught up in the present moment that he seemed incapable of seeing the consequences of his actions. It is hard to imagine what his life would have been like without Abram's careful attention and God's intervention.

By the time Lot drifted out of the picture, his life had taken an ugly turn. He had so blended into the sinful culture of his day that he did not want to leave it. Then his daughters committed incest with him. His drifting finally took him in a very specific direction—destruction.

Lot, however, is called "righteous" in the New Testament (2 Peter 2.7, 8). Ruth, a descendant of Moab, was an ancestor of Jesus, even though Moab was born as a result of Lot's incestuous relationship with one of his daughters. Lot's story gives hope to us that God forgives and often brings about positive circumstances from evil.

What is the direction of your life? Are you headed toward God or away from him? If you're a drifter, the choice for God may seem difficult, but it is the one choice that puts all other choices in a different light.

Strengths and accomplishments:
- He was a successful businessman
- Peter calls him a righteous man (2 Peter 2.7, 8)

Weaknesses and mistakes:
- When faced with decisions, he tended to put off deciding, then chose the easiest course of action
- When given a choice, his first reaction was to think of himself

Lesson from his life:
- God wants us to do more than drift through life; he wants us to be an influence for him

Vital statistics:
- Where: Lived first in Ur of the Chaldeans, then moved to Canaan with Abram. Eventually he moved to the wicked city of Sodom
- Occupation: Wealthy sheep and cattle rancher; also a city official
- Relatives: Father: Haran. Adopted by Abram when his father died. The name of his wife, who turned into a pillar of salt, is not mentioned

Key verse:
"But he lingered; so the men seized him and his wife and his two daughters by the hand, the Lord being merciful to him, and they brought him out and left him outside the city" (Genesis 19.16).

Lot's story is told in Genesis 11—14; 19. He is also mentioned in Deuteronomy 2.9; Luke 17.28–32; 2 Peter 2.7.

14.4–16 Who was Chedorlaomer, and why was he important? In Abram's time, most cities had their own kings. Wars and rivalries among kings were common. A conquered city paid tribute to the victorious king. Nothing is known about Chedorlaomer except what we read in the Bible, but apparently he was quite powerful. Five cities including Sodom had paid tribute to him for 12 years. The five cities formed an alliance and rebelled by withholding tribute. Chedorlaomer reacted swiftly and reconquered them all. When he defeated Sodom, he captured Lot, his family, and his possessions. Abram, with only 318 men, chased Chedorlaomer's army and attacked him near Damascus. With God's help, he defeated them and recovered Lot, his family, and their possessions.

Chedorlaomer, but in the thirteenth year they rebelled. 5 In the fourteenth year
Chedorlaomer and the kings who were with him came and subdued the Rephaim in
Ashteroth-karnaim, the Zuzim in Ham, the Emim in Shaveh-kiriathaim, 6 and the
Horites in the hill country of Seir as far as El-paran on the edge of the wilderness;
7 then they turned back and came to En-mishpat (that is, Kadesh), and subdued all
the country of the Amalekites, and also the Amorites who lived in Hazazon-tamar.
8 Then the king of Sodom, the king of Gomorrah, the king of Admah, the king of
Zeboiim, and the king of Bela (that is, Zoar) went out, and they joined battle in the
Valley of Siddim 9 with King Chedorlaomer of Elam, King Tidal of Goiim, King
Amraphel of Shinar, and King Arioch of Ellasar, four kings against five. 10 Now
the Valley of Siddim was full of bitumen pits; and as the kings of Sodom and Gomorrah fled, some fell into them, and the rest fled to the hill country. 11 So the
enemy took all the goods of Sodom and Gomorrah, and all their provisions, and
went their way; 12 they also took Lot, the son of Abram's brother, who lived in
Sodom, and his goods, and departed.

13 Then one who had escaped came and told Abram the Hebrew, who was
living by the oaks[l] of Mamre the Amorite, brother of Eshcol and of Aner; these
were allies of Abram. 14 When Abram heard that his nephew had been taken captive, he led forth his trained men, born in his house, three hundred eighteen of
them, and went in pursuit as far as Dan. 15 He divided his forces against them by
night, he and his servants, and routed them and pursued them to Hobah, north of
Damascus. 16 Then he brought back all the goods, and also brought back his
nephew Lot with his goods, and the women and the people.

17 After his return from the defeat of Chedorlaomer and the kings who were
with him, the king of Sodom went out to meet him at the Valley of Shaveh (that is,
the King's Valley). 18 And King Melchizedek of Salem brought out bread and wine;
he was priest of God Most High.[m] 19 He blessed him and said,

"Blessed be Abram by God Most High,[m]
maker of heaven and earth;
20 and blessed be God Most High,[m]

[l] Or *terebinths* [m] Heb *El Elyon*

14.5 Gen 15.20 Deut 1.4 2.10,20; 3.11 Josh 13.19
14.7 Gen 16.14; 20.1 Num 13.26 Deut 1.19 2 Chron 20.2
14.12 Gen 11.27 13.6,12
14.13 Gen 10.16 13.18; 39.14
14.14 Gen 12.5 Deut 34.1
14.15 Gen 15.2 1 Kgs 15.8 Acts 9.2
14.16 Gen 14.12,14
14.17 Gen 14.5 2 Sam 18.18
14.18 Ps 7.17; 50.14 76.2; 110.4 Heb 5.6,10; 7.1
14.19 Gen 27.25; 48.9 Mk 10.16
14.20 Gen 9.26; 24.27 Ps 44.3 72.17-19 Heb 7.4,6

14.12 Lot's greedy desire for the best of everything led him into sinful surroundings. His burning desire for possessions and success cost him his freedom and enjoyment. As a captive to Chedorlaomer, he faced torture, slavery, or death. In much the same way, we can be enticed into doing things or going places we shouldn't. The prosperity we long for is captivating; it can both entice us and enslave us if our motives are not in line with God's desires.

14.14–16 These incidents portray two of Abram's characteristics: (1) He had courage that came from God. Facing a powerful foe, he attacked. (2) He was prepared. He had taken time to train his men for a potential conflict. We never know when we will be called upon to complete difficult tasks. Like Abram, we should prepare for those times and take courage from God when they come.

14.14–16 When Abram learned that Lot was a prisoner, he immediately tried to help his nephew. It is easier and safer not to become involved. But with Lot in serious trouble, Abram acted at once. Sometimes we must get involved in a messy or painful situation in order to help others. We should be willing to act immediately when others need our help.

14.18 Who was Melchizedek? He was obviously a God-fearing man, for his name means "king of righteousness" and "king of peace" (Hebrews 7.2). He was a "priest of God Most High." He recognized God as Creator of heaven and earth. What else is known about him? Four main theories have been suggested. (1) Melchizedek was a respected king of that region. Abram was simply showing him the respect he deserved. (2) The name Melchizedek may have been a standing title for all the kings of Salem. (3) Melchizedek was a "type" of Christ (Hebrews 7.3). A type is an Old Testament event or teaching that is so closely related to what Christ did that it illustrates a lesson about Christ. (4) Melchizedek was the appearance on earth of the preincarnate Christ in a temporary bodily form.

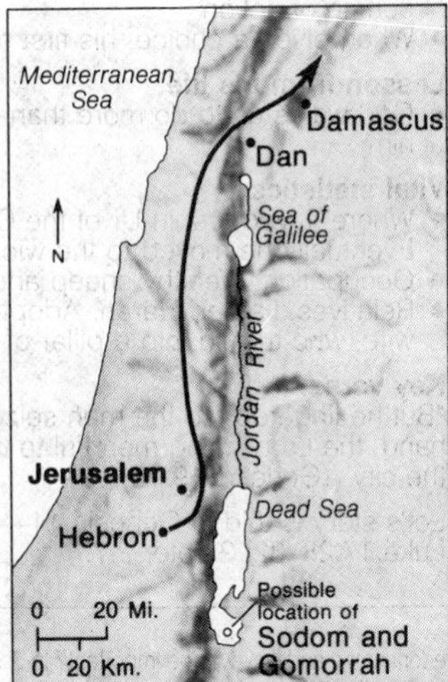

LOT'S RESCUE Having conquered Sodom, Chedorlaomer left for his home country, taking many captives with him. Abram learned what had happened and chased Chedorlaomer past Dan and beyond Damascus. There he defeated the king and rescued the captives, among them Lot.

14.20 Abram gave one-tenth of the booty to Melchizedek. Even in some pagan religions, it was traditional to give a tenth of one's earnings to the gods. Abram followed accepted tradition; however, he refused to take any booty from the king of Sodom. Even though

who has delivered your enemies into your hand!"
And Abram gave him one tenth of everything. 21 Then the king of Sodom said to
14.22 Gen 1.1 Abram, "Give me the persons, but take the goods for yourself." 22 But Abram said
to the king of Sodom, "I have sworn to the LORD, God Most High,[n] maker of
14.23 2 Kgs 5.16 heaven and earth, 23 that I would not take a thread or a sandal-thong or anything that
14.24 Gen 14.13 is yours, so that you might not say, 'I have made Abram rich.' 24 I will take nothing
but what the young men have eaten, and the share of the men who went with
me—Aner, Eshcol, and Mamre. Let them take their share."

3. God promises a son to Abram

Abram believes the Lord

15.1 Gen 21.17 26.24; 46.2 Ps 3.3 **15** After these things the word of the LORD came to Abram in a vision, "Do not
be afraid, Abram, I am your shield; your reward shall be very great." 2 But
Abram said, "O Lord GOD, what will you give me, for I continue childless, and the
15.4 Gen 17.16 Gal 4.28 heir of my house is Eliezer of Damascus?"[o] 3 And Abram said, "You have given
me no offspring, and so a slave born in my house is to be my heir." 4 But the word
15.5 Gen 12.2 22.17; 32.12 Rom 4.18 of the LORD came to him, "This man shall not be your heir; no one but your very
own issue shall be your heir." 5 He brought him outside and said, "Look toward
heaven and count the stars, if you are able to count them." Then he said to him, "So
15.6 Ps 106.31 Rom 4.3 shall your descendants be." 6 And he believed the LORD; and the LORD[p] reckoned
it to him as righteousness.
15.7 Gen 12.1; 13.15 Acts 7.2-4 7 Then he said to him, "I am the LORD who brought you from Ur of the Chaldeans, to give you this land to possess." 8 But he said, "O Lord GOD, how am I to
15.8 Lk 1.18 know that I shall possess it?" 9 He said to him, "Bring me a heifer three years old,
15.9 Lev 1.2 a female goat three years old, a ram three years old, a turtledove, and a young
pigeon." 10 He brought him all these and cut them in two, laying each half over
15.10 Lev 1.17 against the other; but he did not cut the birds in two. 11 And when birds of prey came
15.12 Gen 2.21; 28.11 down on the carcasses, Abram drove them away.
12 As the sun was going down, a deep sleep fell upon Abram, and a deep and
15.13 Ex 12.40 Acts 7.6 Gal 3.17 terrifying darkness descended upon him. 13 Then the LORD[p] said to Abram, "Know
this for certain, that your offspring shall be aliens in a land that is not theirs, and
15.14 Ex 6.5 shall be slaves there, and they shall be oppressed for four hundred years; 14 but I
will bring judgment on the nation that they serve, and afterward they shall come out

[n] Heb *El Elyon* [o] Meaning of Heb uncertain [p] Heb *he*

---

this huge amount would significantly increase what he could have given to God, he chose to reject it for more important reasons—he didn't want the ungodly king of Sodom to say, "I have made Abram rich." Instead, Abram wanted them to say, "God has made Abram rich." In this case, accepting the gifts would have focused everyone's attention on Abram or the king of Sodom rather than on God, the giver of victory. When people look at us, they need to see what God has accomplished in our lives.

15.1 Why would Abram be afraid? Perhaps he feared revenge from the kings he had just defeated (14.15). God gave him two good reasons for courage: (1) he promised to defend Abram ("I am your shield"), and (2) he promised Abram a great reward. When you fear what lies ahead, remember that God will stay with you through difficult times and that he has promised you great blessings.

15.2, 3 Eliezer was Abram's most trusted servant, acting as household administrator (see also Genesis 24). According to custom, if Abram were to die without a son, his eldest servant would become his heir. Although Abram loved his servant, he wanted a son to carry on the family line.

15.5 "Your very own issue" means that Abram's heir would come from his own body, his own flesh and blood.

15.5 Abram wasn't promised wealth or fame; he already had that. Instead God promised descendants like the stars or the grains of sand on the seashore (22.17), too numerous to count. To appreciate the vast number of stars scattered through the sky, you need to be, like Abram, away from any distractions. Or pick up a handful of sand and try to count the grains—it can't be done! Just when Abram was despairing of ever having an heir, God promised descendants too numerous to imagine. God's blessings are beyond our imaginations!

15.6 Although Abram had been demonstrating his faith through his actions, it was believing in the Lord, not actions, that made Abram right with God (Romans 4.1–5). God "reckoned" or credited righteousness to Abram because of his faith. We too can have a right relationship with God by trusting him with our lives. Our outward actions—church attendance, prayer, good deeds—will not by themselves make us right with God. A right relationship is based on faith—the heartfelt inner confidence that God is who he says he is and does what he says he will do. Right actions follow naturally as by-products.

15.6 We have read of Abram's mistakes, and we know he was only human. How could God call him righteous? Although human and sinful, Abram believed God. It was faith, not perfection, that made him right in God's eyes. This principle holds for us: when we believe in God, he declares us righteous.

15.8 Abram was looking for confirmation and assurance that he was doing God's will. We also want assurance when we ask for guidance. But we can know for sure that what we are doing is right if we do what the Bible says. Abram didn't have the Bible—we do.

15.13, 14 The book of Exodus tells the story of the enslavement and miraculous deliverance of Abram's descendants.

with great possessions. 15 As for yourself, you shall go to your ancestors in peace;
you shall be buried in a good old age. 16 And they shall come back here in the fourth
generation; for the iniquity of the Amorites is not yet complete."
17 When the sun had gone down and it was dark, a smoking fire pot and a
flaming torch passed between these pieces. 18 On that day the LORD made a covenant with Abram, saying, "To your descendants I give this land, from the river of
Egypt to the great river, the river Euphrates, 19 the land of the Kenites, the Keniz-
zites, the Kadmonites, 20 the Hittites, the Perizzites, the Rephaim, 21 the Amorites,
the Canaanites, the Girgashites, and the Jebusites."

15.15 Gen 25.7,8
15.16 Ex 33.2
15.17 Jer 34.18,19
15.18 Num 34.1-15; Deut 1.7,8
15.21 Gen 10.15; Ex 23.23,28

Abram's second wife

16 Now Sarai, Abram's wife, bore him no children. She had an Egyptian slave-
girl whose name was Hagar, 2 and Sarai said to Abram, "You see that the
LORD has prevented me from bearing children; go in to my slave-girl; it may be that
I shall obtain children by her." And Abram listened to the voice of Sarai. 3 So, after
Abram had lived ten years in the land of Canaan, Sarai, Abram's wife, took Hagar
the Egyptian, her slave-girl, and gave her to her husband Abram as a wife. 4 He
went in to Hagar, and she conceived; and when she saw that she had conceived, she
looked with contempt on her mistress. 5 Then Sarai said to Abram, "May the wrong
done to me be on you! I gave my slave-girl to your embrace, and when she saw that
she had conceived, she looked on me with contempt. May the LORD judge between
you and me!" 6 But Abram said to Sarai, "Your slave-girl is in your power; do to her
as you please." Then Sarai dealt harshly with her, and she ran away from her.
7 The angel of the LORD found her by a spring of water in the wilderness, the
spring on the way to Shur. 8 And he said, "Hagar, slave-girl of Sarai, where have
you come from and where are you going?" She said, "I am running away from my
mistress Sarai." 9 The angel of the LORD said to her, "Return to your mistress, and
submit to her." 10 The angel of the LORD also said to her, "I will so greatly multiply
your offspring that they cannot be counted for multitude." 11 And the angel of the
LORD said to her,

"Now you have conceived and shall bear a son;
you shall call him Ishmael,[q]

16.1 Gen 11.30; 15.2; 21.9; Gal 4.24,25
16.2 Gen 30.3; Ex 21.4
16.3 Gen 13.1
16.4 Gen 16.15
16.5 Gen 31.53
16.8 Gen 3.9; 4.9
16.9 Gen 21.12; Eccles 10.4; Eph 6.5; Tit 2.9
16.10 Gen 17.20
16.11 Gen 16.15; Ex 3.7,8

[q] That is *God hears*

15.16 The Amorites were one of the nations living in Canaan, the land God promised Abram. God knew the people would grow more wicked and would someday need to be punished. Part of that punishment would involve taking away their land and giving it to Abram's descendants. God in his mercy was giving the Amorites plenty of time to repent, but he already knew they would not. At the right time, they would have to be punished. Everything God does is true to his character. He is merciful, knows all, and acts justly—and his timing is perfect.

15.17 Why did God send this strange vision to Abram? God's covenant with Abram was serious business. It represented an incredible promise from God and a huge responsibility for Abram. To confirm his promise, God gave Abram a sign—the smoking fire pot and flaming torch. God took the initiative, gave the confirmation, and followed through on his promises. The sign to Abram was a visible assurance to him that the covenant God had made was real.

16.1–3 Sarai gave Hagar to Abram as a substitute wife, a common practice of that time. A married woman who could not have children was shamed by her peers and was often required to give a female servant to her husband in order to produce heirs. The children born to the servant woman were considered the children of the wife. Abram was acting in line with the custom of the day, but his action showed a lack of faith that God would fulfill his promise.

16.3 Sarai took matters into her own hands by giving Hagar to Abram. Like Abram she had trouble believing God's promise, which was apparently directed specifically toward Abram and Sarai. Out of this lack of faith came a series of problems. This invariably happens when we take over for God, trying to make his promise come true through efforts that are not in line with his specific directions. In this case, time was the greatest test of Abram and Sarai's willingness to let God work in their lives. Sometimes we too must simply wait. When we ask God for something and have to wait, it is a temptation to take matters into our own hands and interfere with God's plans.

16.5 Although Sarai arranged for Hagar to have a child by Abram, she later blamed Abram for the results. It is often easier to strike out in frustration and accuse someone else than to admit an error and ask forgiveness. (Adam and Eve did the same thing in 3.12, 13.)

16.6 Sarai took out her anger against Abram and herself on Hagar, and her treatment was harsh enough to cause Hagar to run away. Anger, especially when it arises from our own shortcomings, can be dangerous.

16.8 Hagar was running away from her mistress and her problem. The angel of the Lord gave her this advice: (1) to return and face Sarai, the cause of her problem, and (2) to act as she should. Hagar needed to work on her attitude toward Sarai, no matter how justified it may have been. Running away from our problems rarely solves them. It is wise to return to our problems, face them squarely, accept God's promise of help, correct our attitudes, and act as we should.

for the LORD has given heed to your affliction.
12 He shall be a wild ass of a man,
with his hand against everyone,
and everyone's hand against him;
and he shall live at odds with all his kin."
13So she named the LORD who spoke to her, "You are El-roi";[r] for she said, "Have
I really seen God and remained alive after seeing him?"[s] 14Therefore the well was
called Beer-lahai-roi;[t] it lies between Kadesh and Bered.
15 Hagar bore Abram a son; and Abram named his son, whom Hagar bore,
Ishmael. 16Abram was eighty-six years old when Hagar bore him[u] Ishmael.

16.12 Gen 21.20 Job 39.5-8
16.13 Gen 12.8; 32.30
16.14 Gen 14.7
16.15 Gen 21.9; 25.12
16.16 Gen 12.4; 16.3

[r] Perhaps *God of seeing* or *God who sees* [s] Meaning of Heb uncertain [t] That is *the Well of the Living One who sees me* [u] Heb *Abram*

MELCHIZEDEK

Do you like a good mystery? History is full of them! They usually involve people. One of the most mysterious people in the Bible is the King of Peace, Melchizedek. He appeared one day in the life of Abraham (then Abram) and was never heard from again. What happened that day, however, was to be remembered throughout history and eventually became a subject of a New Testament letter (Hebrews).

This meeting between Abram and Melchizedek was most unusual. Although the two men were strangers and foreigners to each other, they shared a most important characteristic: both worshiped and served the one God who made heaven and earth. This was a great moment of triumph for Abram. He had just defeated an army and regained the freedom of a large group of captives. If there was any doubt in his mind about whose victory it was, Melchizedek set the record straight by reminding Abram, "Blessed be God Most High, who has delivered your enemies into your hand!" (Genesis 14.20). Abram recognized that this man worshiped the same God he did.

Melchizedek was one of a small group of God-honoring people throughout the Old Testament who came in contact with the Jews (Israelites) but were not Jews themselves. This indicates that the requirement to be a follower of God is not genetic, but is based on faithfully obeying his teachings and recognizing his greatness.

Do you let God speak to you through other people? In evaluating others, do you consider God's impact on their lives? Are you aware of the similarities between yourself and others who worship God, even if their form of worship is quite different from yours? Do you know the God of the Bible well enough to know if you truly worship him? Allow Melchizedek, Abraham, David, and Jesus, along with many other persons in the Bible, to show you this great God, creator of heaven and earth. He wants you to know how much he loves you; he wants you to know him personally.

Strengths and accomplishments:
- The first priest/king of Scripture—a leader with a heart tuned to God
- Good at encouraging others to serve God wholeheartedly
- A man whose character reflected his love for God
- A person in the Old Testament who reminds us of Jesus and who some believe really was Jesus

Lesson from his life:
- Live for God and you're likely to be at the right place at the right time. Examine your heart: to whom or what is your greatest loyalty? If you can honestly answer *God,* you are living for him.

Vital statistics:
- Where: Ruled in Salem, site of the future Jerusalem
- Occupation: King of Salem and priest of God Most High

Key verses:
"This 'King Melchizedek of Salem, priest of the Most High God, met Abraham as he was returning from defeating the kings and blessed him'; . . . See how great he is! Even Abraham the patriarch gave him a tenth of the spoils" (Hebrews 7.1, 4).

Melchizedek's story is told in Genesis 14.17–20. He is also mentioned in Psalm 110.4; Hebrews 5—7.

16.13 We have watched three people make serious mistakes: (1) Sarai, who took matters into her own hands and gave her servant girl to Abram; (2) Abram, who went along with the plan but, when circumstances began to go wrong, refused to help solve the problem; and (3) Hagar, who ran away from the problem. In spite of this messy situation, God demonstrated his ability to work all things together for good (Romans 8.28). Sarai and Abram still received the son they so desperately wanted, and God solved Hagar's problem despite Abram's refusal to get involved. No problem is too complicated for God if you are willing to let him help you.

The terms of the promise

17 When Abram was ninety-nine years old, the LORD appeared to Abram, and
said to him, "I am God Almighty;[v] walk before me, and be blameless. 2 And
I will make my covenant between me and you, and will make you exceedingly
numerous." 3 Then Abram fell on his face; and God said to him, 4 "As for me, this
is my covenant with you: You shall be the ancestor of a multitude of nations. 5 No
longer shall your name be Abram,[w] but your name shall be Abraham;[x] for I have
made you the ancestor of a multitude of nations. 6 I will make you exceedingly
fruitful; and I will make nations of you, and kings shall come from you. 7 I will
establish my covenant between me and you, and your offspring after you throughout their generations, for an everlasting covenant, to be God to you and to your
offspring[y] after you. 8 And I will give to you, and to your offspring after you, the
land where you are now an alien, all the land of Canaan, for a perpetual holding;
and I will be their God."

9 God said to Abraham, "As for you, you shall keep my covenant, you and your
offspring after you throughout their generations. 10 This is my covenant, which you
shall keep, between me and you and your offspring after you: Every male among
you shall be circumcised. 11 You shall circumcise the flesh of your foreskins, and
it shall be a sign of the covenant between me and you. 12 Throughout your generations every male among you shall be circumcised when he is eight days old, including the slave born in your house and the one bought with your money from any
foreigner who is not of your offspring. 13 Both the slave born in your house and the
one bought with your money must be circumcised. So shall my covenant be in your
flesh an everlasting covenant. 14 Any uncircumcised male who is not circumcised
in the flesh of his foreskin shall be cut off from his people; he has broken my covenant."

15 God said to Abraham, "As for Sarah your wife, you shall not call her Sarai,
but Sarah shall be her name. 16 I will bless her, and moreover I will give you a son
by her. I will bless her, and she shall give rise to nations; kings of peoples shall
come from her." 17 Then Abraham fell on his face and laughed, and said to himself,
"Can a child be born to a man who is a hundred years old? Can Sarah, who is ninety
years old, bear a child?" 18 And Abraham said to God, "O that Ishmael might live
in your sight!" 19 God said, "No, but your wife Sarah shall bear you a son, and you
shall name him Isaac.[z] I will establish my covenant with him as an everlasting
covenant for his offspring after him. 20 As for Ishmael, I have heard you; I will bless

17.1 a)Gen 12.7 16.16 b)Gen 28.3 35.11; 48.3 c)Gen 6.9 Deut 18.13 Mt 5.48
17.2 Gen 13.16 15.5; 17.2 35.11
17.3 Gen 17.17; 18.2 Ex 3.6
17.5 Neh 9.7 Rom 4.17
17.6 Gen 35.11
17.7 Gen 12.7; 13.15 Lev 11.45; 26.12 Ps 105.8-11
17.9 Ex 19.5; 26.5 Ps 25.10
17.10 Acts 7.8
17.11 Ex 12.48 Deut 10.16 Josh 5.3
17.12 Gen 21.4 Lev 12.3 Lk 1.59; 2.21
17.14 Ex 30.33 Lev 7.20
17.15 Gen 17.5
17.16 Gen 18.10
17.17 Gen 17.3; 18.13
17.19 Gen 21.1,2 26.3-5

v Traditional rendering of Heb *El Shaddai* w That is *exalted ancestor* x Here taken to mean *ancestor of a multitude*
y Heb *seed* z That is *he laughs*

17.1 The Lord told Abram, "I am God Almighty; walk before me." He has the same message for us today. We are to obey because he is God—that is reason enough. If you don't think the benefits of obedience are worth it, consider who God is—the only one with the power and ability to meet your every need.

17.2–8 Why did God repeat his covenant to Abram? Twice before, he had mentioned this agreement (Genesis 12 and 15). Here, however, God was bringing it into focus and preparing to carry it out. He now revealed to Abram several specific parts of his covenant: (1) God would give Abram many descendants; (2) many nations would descend from him; (3) God would maintain his covenant with Abram's descendants; (4) God would give Abram's descendants the land of Canaan.

17.5 God changed Abram's name to Abraham ("the ancestor of a multitude of nations") shortly before the promised son was conceived. From this point on, the Bible calls him Abraham.

17.5–14 God was making a covenant, or contract, between himself and Abraham. The terms were simple: Abraham would obey God and circumcise all the males in his household; God's part was to give Abraham heirs, property, power, and wealth. Most contracts are even trades: we give something and in turn receive something of equal value. But when we become part of God's covenant family, the blessings received outweigh what we give up.

17.9, 10 Why did God require circumcision? (1) As a sign of obedience to him in all matters. (2) As a sign of belonging to his covenant people. Once circumcised, there was no turning back. The man would be identified as a Jew forever. (3) As a symbol of "cutting off" the old life of sin, purifying one's heart and dedicating oneself to God. (4) Possibly as a health measure.

Circumcision more than any other practice separated God's people from their heathen neighbors. In Abraham's day, this was essential to develop the pure worship of the one true God.

17.17–27 How could Abraham doubt God? It seemed incredible that he and Sarah in their advanced years could have a child. Abraham, the man God considered righteous because of his faith, had trouble believing God's promise to him. Despite his doubts, however, he followed God's commands (17.22–27). Even people of great faith may have doubts. When God seems to want the impossible and you begin to doubt his leading, be like Abraham. Focus on God's commitment to fulfill his promises to you, and then continue to obey.

17.20 God did not forget Ishmael. Although he was not to be Abraham's heir, he would also be the father of a great nation. Regardless of your circumstances, God has not forgotten you. Obey him and trust in his plan.

17.20 Gen 21.13 25.16
17.21 Gen 17.7,19
17.22 Gen 18.33 35.13
17.23 Gen 14.14
17.24 Gen 16.16; 17.1 Rom 4.11
17.25 Gen 16.16

him and make him fruitful and exceedingly numerous; he shall be the father of
twelve princes, and I will make him a great nation. 21 But my covenant I will establish with Isaac, whom Sarah shall bear to you at this season next year." 22 And when
he had finished talking with him, God went up from Abraham.
23 Then Abraham took his son Ishmael and all the slaves born in his house or
bought with his money, every male among the men of Abraham's house, and he
circumcised the flesh of their foreskins that very day, as God had said to him.
24 Abraham was ninety-nine years old when he was circumcised in the flesh of his
foreskin. 25 And his son Ishmael was thirteen years old when he was circumcised in
the flesh of his foreskin. 26 That very day Abraham and his son Ishmael were circumcised; 27 and all the men of his house, slaves born in the house and those bought
with money from a foreigner, were circumcised with him.

ISHMAEL

Have you ever wondered if you were born into the wrong family? We don't know much about how Ishmael viewed life, but that question must have haunted him at times. His life, his name, and his position were bound up in a conflict between two jealous women. Sarah, impatient with God's timetable, had taken matters into her own hands, deciding to have a child through another woman. Hagar, servant that she was, submitted to being used this way. But her pregnancy gave birth to strong feelings of superiority toward Sarah. Into this tense atmosphere, Ishmael was born.

For 16 years Abraham thought Ishmael's birth had fulfilled God's promise. He was surprised to hear God say that the promised child would be Abraham and Sarah's very own. Sarah's pregnancy and Isaac's birth must have had a devastating impact on Ishmael. Until then he had been treated as a son and heir, but this late arrival made his future uncertain. During Isaac's weaning celebration, Sarah caught Ishmael teasing his half brother. As a result, Hagar and Ishmael were permanently expelled from Abraham's family.

Much of what happened throughout his life cannot be blamed on Ishmael. He was caught in a process much bigger than himself. However, his own actions showed that he had chosen to become part of the problem and not part of the solution. He chose to live under his circumstances rather than above them.

The choice he made is one we must all make. There are circumstances over which we have no control (heredity, for instance), but there are others that we can control (decisions we make). At the heart of the matter is the sin-oriented nature we have all inherited. It can be partly controlled, although not overcome, by human effort. In the context of history, Ishmael's life represents the mess we make when we don't try to change the things we could change. The God of the Bible has offered a solution. His answer is not control, but a changed life. To have a changed life, turn to God, trust him to forgive your sinful past, and begin to change your attitude toward him and others.

Strengths and accomplishments:
- One of the first to experience the physical sign of God's covenant, circumcision
- Known for his ability as an archer and hunter
- Fathered 12 sons who became leaders of warrior tribes

Weakness and mistake:
- Failed to recognize the place of his half brother, Isaac, and mocked him

Lesson from his life:
- God's plans incorporate people's mistakes

Vital statistics:
- Where: Canaan and Egypt
- Occupation: Hunter, archer, warrior
- Relatives: Parents: Hagar and Abraham. Half brother: Isaac

Key verses:
"And God heard the voice of the boy; and the angel of God called to Hagar from heaven, and said unto her, 'What troubles you, Hagar? Do not be afraid; for God has heard the voice of the boy where he is. Come, lift up the boy and hold him fast with your hand, for I will make a great nation of him'" (Genesis 21.17, 18).

Ishmael's story is told in Genesis 16—17; 25.12–18; 28.8, 9; 36. He is also mentioned in 1 Chronicles 1.28–31; Romans 9.7–9; Galatians 4.21–31.

4. Sodom and Gomorrah

Three angels visit Abraham

18 The LORD appeared to Abraham[a] by the oaks[b] of Mamre, as he sat at the
entrance of his tent in the heat of the day. 2 He looked up and saw three men
standing near him. When he saw them, he ran from the tent entrance to meet them,
and bowed down to the ground. 3 He said, "My lord, if I find favor with you, do not
pass by your servant. 4 Let a little water be brought, and wash your feet, and rest
yourselves under the tree. 5 Let me bring a little bread, that you may refresh yourselves, and after that you may pass on — since you have come to your servant." So
they said, "Do as you have said." 6 And Abraham hastened into the tent to Sarah,
and said, "Make ready quickly three measures[c] of choice flour, knead it, and make
cakes." 7 Abraham ran to the herd, and took a calf, tender and good, and gave it to
the servant, who hastened to prepare it. 8 Then he took curds and milk and the calf
that he had prepared, and set it before them; and he stood by them under the tree
while they ate.

9 They said to him, "Where is your wife Sarah?" And he said, "There, in the
tent." 10 Then one said, "I will surely return to you in due season, and your wife
Sarah shall have a son." And Sarah was listening at the tent entrance behind him.
11 Now Abraham and Sarah were old, advanced in age; it had ceased to be with
Sarah after the manner of women. 12 So Sarah laughed to herself, saying, "After I
have grown old, and my husband is old, shall I have pleasure?" 13 The LORD said to
Abraham, "Why did Sarah laugh, and say, 'Shall I indeed bear a child, now that I
am old?' 14 Is anything too wonderful for the LORD? At the set time I will return to
you, in due season, and Sarah shall have a son." 15 But Sarah denied, saying, "I did
not laugh"; for she was afraid. He said, "Oh yes, you did laugh."

16 Then the men set out from there, and they looked toward Sodom; and Abraham went with them to set them on their way. 17 The LORD said, "Shall I hide from
Abraham what I am about to do, 18 seeing that Abraham shall become a great and
mighty nation, and all the nations of the earth shall be blessed in him?[d] 19 No, for
I have chosen[e] him, that he may charge his children and his household after him to
keep the way of the LORD by doing righteousness and justice; so that the LORD may
bring about for Abraham what he has promised him." 20 Then the LORD said, "How
great is the outcry against Sodom and Gomorrah and how very grave their sin! 21 I

18.1 Gen 12.7; 13.18 Gen 14.13
18.2 Gen 19.1; 23.7 33.3,6,7 Josh 5.13-15
18.3 Gen 19.2; 24.31
18.5 Judg 6.18; 13.15, 16
18.7 Judg 13.15
18.8 Deut 32.14
18.10 Gen 22.15 Judg 13.3 Rom 9.9
18.11 Gen 17.17
18.12 1 Pet 3.6
18.14 Gen 18.10 Jer 32.17,27 Lk 1.37
18.16 Gen 18.22; 19.1
18.17 Gen 19.24
18.18 Gen 12.2,3 Gal 3.18
18.19 Neh 9.7
18.20 Gen 13.13 19.13
18.21 Gen 11.5 Ex 3.8

[a] Heb *him* [b] Or *terebinths* [c] Heb *seahs* [d] *Or and all the nations of the earth shall bless themselves by him*
[e] Heb *known*

18.2-5 Abraham was eager to show hospitality to these men, as was Lot (19.2). In Abraham's day, a person's reputation was largely connected to his hospitality – the sharing of home and food. Even strangers were to be treated as highly honored guests. Meeting another's need for food or shelter was and still is one of the most immediate and practical ways to obey God. It is also a time-honored relationship builder. Hebrews 13.2 suggests that we, like Abraham, might actually entertain angels. This thought should be on our minds the next time we have the opportunity to meet a stranger's needs.

18.14 "Is anything too wonderful [hard] for the Lord?" The obvious answer is, "Of course not!" This question reveals much about God. Make it a habit to insert your specific needs into the question. "Is this day in my life too hard for the Lord?" "Is this habit I'm trying to break too hard for him?" "Is the communication problem I'm having too hard for him?" Asking the question this way reminds you that God is personally involved in your life and nudges you to ask for his power to help you.

18.15 Sarah lied because she was afraid of being discovered. Fear is the most common motive for lying. We are afraid that our inner thoughts and emotions will be exposed or our wrongdoings discovered. But lying causes greater complications than telling the truth and brings even more problems. If God can't be trusted with our innermost thoughts and fears, we are in greater trouble than we first imagined.

18.20-33 Did Abraham change God's mind? Of course not. The more likely answer is that God changed Abraham's mind. Abraham knew that God is just and that he punishes sin. But he may have wondered about God's mercy. Abraham seemed to be probing God's mind to see how merciful he really was. He left his conversation with God convinced that God was both kind and fair. Our prayers won't change God's mind, but they may change ours just as Abraham's prayer changed his. Prayer is a means to better comprehend the mind of God.

18.20-33 Why did God let Abraham question his justice and intercede for a wicked city? Abraham knew God must punish sin, but he also knew from experience that God is merciful to sinners. God knew there were not ten righteous people in the city, but he was merciful enough to allow Abraham to intercede. He was also merciful enough to help Lot, Abraham's nephew, get out of Sodom before it was destroyed. God does not take pleasure in destroying the wicked, but he must punish sin. He is both just and merciful. We should be thankful that God's mercy extends to us.

18.21 God gave the men of Sodom a fair test. He was not ignorant of the city's wicked practices, but in his patience he gave the people of Sodom one last chance to turn to him. God is still waiting with the hope that all people will turn to him (2 Peter 3.9). Those who are wise will turn to him before his patience wears out.

must go down and see whether they have done altogether according to the outcry
that has come to me; and if not, I will know."

Abraham prays for Sodom

18.22 Gen 18.16; 19.1
18.23 Ex 23.7
18.25 Deut 1.16; 32.4 Ps 58.11
18.26 Isa 65.8 Jer 5.1

22 So the men turned from there, and went toward Sodom, while Abraham
remained standing before the LORD.[f] 23 Then Abraham came near and said, "Will
you indeed sweep away the righteous with the wicked? 24 Suppose there are fifty
righteous within the city; will you then sweep away the place and not forgive it for
the fifty righteous who are in it? 25 Far be it from you to do such a thing, to slay the
righteous with the wicked, so that the righteous fare as the wicked! Far be that from
you! Shall not the Judge of all the earth do what is just?" 26 And the LORD said, "If
I find at Sodom fifty righteous in the city, I will forgive the whole place for their
sake." 27 Abraham answered, "Let me take it upon myself to speak to the Lord, I

[f] Another ancient tradition reads *while the LORD remained standing before Abraham*

ABRAHAM

We all know that there are consequences to any action we take. What we do can set into motion a series of events that may continue long after we're gone. Unfortunately, when we are making a decision most of us think only of the immediate consequences. These are often misleading because they are short-lived.

Abraham had a choice to make. His decision was between setting out with his family and belongings for parts unknown or staying right where he was. He had to decide between the security of what he already had and the uncertainty of traveling under God's direction. All he had to go on was God's promise to guide and bless him. Abraham could hardly have been expected to visualize how much of the future was resting on his decision of whether to go or stay, but his obedience affected the history of the world. His decision to follow God set into motion the development of the nation that God would eventually use as his own when he visited earth himself. When Jesus Christ came to earth, God's promise was fulfilled; through Abraham the entire world was blessed.

You probably don't know the long-term effects of most decisions you make. But shouldn't the fact that there will be long-term results cause you to think carefully and seek God's guidance as you make choices and take action today?

Strengths and accomplishments:
- His faith pleased God
- Became the founder of the Jewish nation
- Was respected by others and courageous in defending his family at any cost
- Was not only a caring father to his own family, but practiced hospitality to others
- Was a successful and wealthy rancher
- Usually avoided conflicts, but when they were unavoidable, he allowed his opponent to set the rules for settling the dispute

Weakness and mistake:
- Under direct pressure, he distorted the truth

Lessons from his life:
- God desires dependence, trust, and faith in him—not faith in our ability to please him
- God's plan from the beginning has been to make himself known to all people

Vital statistics:
- Where: Born in Ur of the Chaldeans; spent most of his life in the land of Canaan
- Occupation: Wealthy livestock owner
- Relatives: Brothers: Nahor and Haran. Father: Terah. Wife: Sarah. Nephew: Lot. Sons: Ishmael and Isaac
- Contemporaries: Abimelech, Melchizedek

Key verse:
"And he believed the Lord; and the Lord reckoned it to him as righteousness" (Genesis 15.6).

Abraham's story is told in Genesis 11—25. He is also mentioned in Exodus 2.24; Acts 7.2–8; Romans 4; Galatians 3; Hebrews 2, 6, 7, 11.

18.25 Was God being unfair to the people of Sodom? Did he really plan to destroy the good with the wicked? On the contrary, God's fairness stood out. (1) He agreed to spare the entire city if only ten righteous people lived there. (2) He showed great mercy toward Lot, apparently the only man in the city who had any kind of relationship with him (and even that was questionable). (3) He showed great patience toward Lot, almost forcing him to leave Sodom before it was destroyed. Remember God's patience when you are tempted to think he is unfair. Even the most godly people deserve his justice. We should be glad God doesn't direct his justice toward us as he did toward Sodom.

who am but dust and ashes. 28 Suppose five of the fifty righteous are lacking? Will 18.27 Ezra 9.6
you destroy the whole city for lack of five?" And he said, "I will not destroy it if I Isa 6.5
find forty-five there." 29 Again he spoke to him, "Suppose forty are found there." Lk 18.1
He answered, "For the sake of forty I will not do it." 30 Then he said, "Oh do not let 18.30
the Lord be angry if I speak. Suppose thirty are found there." He answered, "I will Ex 32.32
not do it, if I find thirty there." 31 He said, "Let me take it upon myself to speak to
the Lord. Suppose twenty are found there." He answered, "For the sake of twenty
I will not destroy it." 32 Then he said, "Oh do not let the Lord be angry if I speak just
once more. Suppose ten are found there." He answered, "For the sake of ten I will
not destroy it." 33 And the LORD went his way, when he had finished speaking to 18.33
Abraham; and Abraham returned to his place. Gen 17.22; 35.13

God rescues Lot

19 The two angels came to Sodom in the evening, and Lot was sitting in the 19.1
gateway of Sodom. When Lot saw them, he rose to meet them, and bowed Gen 18.2
down with his face to the ground. 2 He said, "Please, my lords, turn aside to your 19.2
servant's house and spend the night, and wash your feet; then you can rise early and Gen 18.3 Lk 24.28
go on your way." They said, "No; we will spend the night in the square." 3 But he 19.3
urged them strongly; so they turned aside to him and entered his house; and he Gen 18.6-8
made them a feast, and baked unleavened bread, and they ate. 4 But before they lay 19.4
down, the men of the city, the men of Sodom, both young and old, all the people Gen 13.13; 18.20 Prov 4.16
to the last man, surrounded the house; 5 and they called to Lot, "Where are the men 19.5
who came to you tonight? Bring them out to us, so that we may know them." 6 Lot Lev 18.22; 20.13 Judg 19.22
went out of the door to the men, shut the door after him, 7 and said, "I beg you, my
brothers, do not act so wickedly. 8 Look, I have two daughters who have not known 19.8 Deut 23.17
a man; let me bring them out to you, and do to them as you please; only do nothing 19.9
to these men, for they have come under the shelter of my roof." 9 But they replied, Ex 2.14 Prov 9.7,8
"Stand back!" And they said, "This fellow came here as an alien, and he would play 19.10
the judge! Now we will deal worse with you than with them." Then they pressed Gen 19.1
hard against the man Lot, and came near the door to break it down. 10 But the men 19.11 Deut 28.28
inside reached out their hands and brought Lot into the house with them, and shut 2 Kgs 6.18
the door. 11 And they struck with blindness the men who were at the door of the Acts 9.8
house, both small and great, so that they were unable to find the door. 19.13 Gen 18.20
12 Then the men said to Lot, "Have you anyone else here? Sons-in-law, sons, 1 Chron 21.15 Jude 7
daughters, or anyone you have in the city—bring them out of the place. 13 For we 19.14
are about to destroy this place, because the outcry against its people has become Ex 9.21 Jer 5.11,12
great before the LORD, and the LORD has sent us to destroy it." 14 So Lot went out 43.1-3

18.33 God showed Abraham that asking for anything is allowed, with the understanding that God's answers come from God's perspective. They are not always in harmony with our expectations, for only he knows the whole story. Are you missing God's answer to a prayer because you haven't considered any possible answers other than the one you expect?

19.1 The city gate was the meeting place for city officials and other men to discuss current events and transact business. It was a place of authority and status where one could see and be seen. Evidently Lot held an important position in the government or associated with those who did, for the angels found him at the city gate. Perhaps Lot's status in Sodom was one reason he was so reluctant to leave (19.16, 18–22).

19.5 The phrase "that we may know them" means the men wanted to have sexual relations with Lot's guests. The sins of the Sodomites included homosexuality, which was forbidden by the law in Leviticus 18.22 and 20.13. The New Testament expressly forbids it. See Romans 1.26–27; 1 Corinthians 6.9; and 1 Timothy 1.10.

19.8 How could any father give his daughters to be ravished by a mob of perverts, just to protect two strangers? Possibly Lot was scheming to save both the girls and the visitors, hoping the girls' fiancés would rescue them or that the homosexual men would be uninterested in the girls and simply go away. Although it was the custom of the day to protect guests at any cost, this terrible suggestion reveals how deeply sin had been absorbed into Lot's life. He had become hardened to evil acts in an evil city. Whatever Lot's motives were, we see here an illustration of Sodom's terrible wickedness—a wickedness so great that God had to destroy the entire city.

19.13 God promised to spare Sodom if only ten righteous people lived there (18.32). Obviously not even ten could be found, for the angels arrived to destroy the city. Archaeological evidence points to an advanced civilization in this area during Abraham's day. Most researchers also confirm some kind of sudden and devastating destruction. It is now widely thought that the buried city lies beneath the waters of the southern end of the Dead Sea. The story of Sodom reveals that the people of Lot's day had to deal with the same kinds of repulsive sins the world faces today. We should follow Abraham's example of trusting God. His selfless faith stands in sharp contrast to the self-gratifying people of Sodom.

19.14 Lot had lived so long, and was so content among ungodly people that he was no longer a believable witness for God. He had allowed his environment to shape him, rather than he shaping his environment. Do those who know you see you as a witness for

and said to his sons-in-law, who were to marry his daughters, "Up, get out of this place; for the LORD is about to destroy the city." But he seemed to his sons-in-law to be jesting.

15 When morning dawned, the angels urged Lot, saying, "Get up, take your wife and your two daughters who are here, or else you will be consumed in the
19.16 Ps 119.60 punishment of the city." 16 But he lingered; so the men seized him and his wife and
his two daughters by the hand, the LORD being merciful to him, and they brought

SARAH

There probably isn't anything harder to do than wait, whether we are expecting something good, something bad, or an unknown.

One way we often cope with a long wait (or even a short one) is to begin helping God get his plan into action. Sarah tried this approach. She was too old to expect to have a child of her own, so she thought God must have something else in mind. From Sarah's limited point of view this could only be to give Abraham a son through another woman—a common practice in her day. The plan seemed harmless enough. Abraham would sleep with Sarah's servant girl, who would then give birth to a child. Sarah would take the child as her own. The plan worked beautifully—at first. But as you read about the events that followed, you will be struck by how often Sarah must have regretted the day she decided to push God's timetable ahead.

Another way we cope with a long wait is to gradually conclude that what we're waiting for is never going to happen. Sarah waited 90 years for a baby! When God told her she would finally have one of her own, she laughed, not so much from a lack of faith in what God could do, but from doubt about what he could do *through her.* When confronted about her laughter, she lied—as she had seen her husband do from time to time. She probably didn't want her true feelings to be known.

What parts of your life seem to be "on hold" right now? Do you understand that this may be part of God's plan for you? The Bible has more than enough clear direction to keep us busy while we're waiting for some particular part of life to move ahead.

Strengths and accomplishments:
- Was intensely loyal to her own child
- Became the mother of a nation and an ancestor of Jesus
- Was a woman of faith, the first woman listed in the Hall of Faith in Hebrews 11

Weaknesses and mistakes:
- Had trouble believing God's promises to her
- Attempted to work problems out on her own, without consulting God
- Tried to cover her faults by blaming others

Lessons from her life:
- God responds to faith even in the midst of failure
- God is not bound by what usually happens; he can stretch the limits and cause unheard-of events to occur

Vital statistics:
- Where: Married Abram in Ur of the Chaldeans, then moved with him to Canaan
- Occupation: Wife, mother, household manager
- Relatives: Father: Terah. Husband: Abraham. Brothers: Nahor and Haran. Nephew: Lot. Son: Isaac

Key verses:
"God said to Abraham, 'As for Sarah your wife, you shall not call her Sarai, but Sarah shall be her name. I will bless her, and moreover I will give you a son by her. I will bless her, and she shall give rise to nations; kings of peoples shall come from her'" (Genesis 17.15, 16).

Sarah's story is told in Genesis 11—25. She is also mentioned in Isaiah 51.2; Romans 4.19; 9.9; Hebrews 11.11; 1 Peter 3.6.

God, or are you just one of the crowd, blending in unnoticed? Lot had compromised to the point that he was almost useless to God. When he finally made a stand, nobody listened. Have you too become useless to God because you are too much like your environment? To make a difference, you must first decide to be different in your faith and your conduct.

19.16 Lot hesitated, and the angel seized his hand and rushed him to safety. He did not want to abandon the wealth, position, and comfort he enjoyed in Sodom. It is easy to criticize Lot for being hypnotized by Sodom when the choice seems so clear to us. To be wiser than Lot, we must see that our hesitation to obey stems from the false attractions of our culture's pleasures.

19.16, 29 Notice how God's mercy toward Abraham extended to Lot and his family. Because Abraham pleaded for Lot, God was merciful and saved Lot from the fiery death that engulfed Sodom. A righteous person can often affect others for good. James says that the prayers of a righteous person are powerful (see James 5.16). All Christians should follow Abraham's example and pray for others to be saved.

him out and left him outside the city. 17 When they had brought them outside, they[g]
said, "Flee for your life; do not look back or stop anywhere in the Plain; flee to the
hills, or else you will be consumed." 18 And Lot said to them, "Oh, no, my lords;
19 your servant has found favor with you, and you have shown me great kindness in
saving my life; but I cannot flee to the hills, for fear the disaster will overtake me
and I die. 20 Look, that city is near enough to flee to, and it is a little one. Let me
escape there — is it not a little one? — and my life will be saved!" 21 He said to him,
"Very well, I grant you this favor too, and will not overthrow the city of which you
have spoken. 22 Hurry, escape there, for I can do nothing until you arrive there."
Therefore the city was called Zoar.[h] 23 The sun had risen on the earth when Lot
came to Zoar.

24 Then the LORD rained on Sodom and Gomorrah sulfur and fire from the
LORD out of heaven; 25 and he overthrew those cities, and all the Plain, and all the
inhabitants of the cities, and what grew on the ground. 26 But Lot's wife, behind
him, looked back, and she became a pillar of salt.

27 Abraham went early in the morning to the place where he had stood before
the LORD; 28 and he looked down toward Sodom and Gomorrah and toward all the
land of the Plain and saw the smoke of the land going up like the smoke of a furnace.

29 So it was that, when God destroyed the cities of the Plain, God remembered
Abraham, and sent Lot out of the midst of the overthrow, when he overthrew the
cities in which Lot had settled.

19.17 Gen 13.10 19.26 1 Sam 19.11 Jer 48.6
19.21 Ps 102.17 145.19
19.22 Gen 13.10 19.30 Isa 15.5
19.24 Lk 17.29 2 Pet 2.6 Jude 7
19.25 Deut 29.23 Isa 3.9; 13.19 Lam 4.6 2 Pet 2.6
19.26 Gen 19.17 Lk 17.32
19.27 Gen 18.22,32
19.28 Rev 9.2
19.29 Gen 8.1 Deut 7.8; 9.5 2 Pet 2.7,8

The sin of Lot's daughters

30 Now Lot went up out of Zoar and settled in the hills with his two daughters,
for he was afraid to stay in Zoar; so he lived in a cave with his two daughters. 31 And
the firstborn said to the younger, "Our father is old, and there is not a man on earth
to come in to us after the manner of all the world. 32 Come, let us make our father
drink wine, and we will lie with him, so that we may preserve offspring through our
father." 33 So they made their father drink wine that night; and the firstborn went in,
and lay with her father; he did not know when she lay down or when she rose. 34 On
the next day, the firstborn said to the younger, "Look, I lay last night with my
father; let us make him drink wine tonight also; then you go in and lie with him, so
that we may preserve offspring through our father." 35 So they made their father
drink wine that night also; and the younger rose, and lay with him; and he did not
know when she lay down or when she rose. 36 Thus both the daughters of Lot became pregnant by their father. 37 The firstborn bore a son, and named him Moab; he
is the ancestor of the Moabites to this day. 38 The younger also bore a son and
named him Ben-ammi; he is the ancestor of the Ammonites to this day.

19.30 Gen 13.10 1 Sam 22.1 1 Kgs 18.4
19.31 Gen 19.14 38.8,9,18
19.32 Prov 23.31-33 Hab 2.15
19.33 Gen 9.21 Lev 18.6 Prov 20.1
19.37 Gen 36.35 Ex 15.15 Deut 2.9 Ruth 1.1
19.38 Num 21.24 Deut 2.19

[g] Gk Syr Vg: Heb *he* [h] That is *Little*

19.24 In the story of Sodom and Gomorrah, we see two facets of God's character: his great patience (agreeing to spare a wicked city for ten good people) and his fierce anger (destroying both cities). As we grow spiritually, we should find ourselves developing a deeper respect for God because of his anger toward sin, and also a deeper love for God because of his patience when we sin.

19.26 Lot's wife turned back to look at the smoldering city of Sodom. Clinging to the past, she was unwilling to turn completely away from sin. Are you looking back longingly at sin while trying to move forward with God? You can't make progress with God as long as you are holding on to pieces of your old life. Jesus said it this way in Matthew 6.24: "No one can be the slave of two masters."

19.30–38 In this pitiful sequel to the story of the destruction of Sodom, we see two women compelled to preserve their family line. They were driven not by lust, but by desperation — they feared they would never marry. Lot's tendency to compromise and refusal to act reached its peak. He should have found right partners for his daughters long before this; Abraham's family wasn't far away. Now the two daughters stooped to incest, showing their acceptance of the morals of Sodom. When we are desperate for what we feel we must have, we are most likely to sin.

19.30–38 Why doesn't the Bible openly condemn these sisters for what they did? In many cases, the Bible does not judge people for their actions. It simply reports the events. However, incest is clearly condemned in other parts of scripture (Leviticus 18.6–18; 20.11, 12, 17, 19–21; Deuteronomy 22.30; 27.20–23; Ezekiel 22.11; 1 Corinthians 5.1). Perhaps the consequence of their action — Moab and Ammon became enemies of Israel — was God's way of judging their sin.

19.37, 38 Moab and Ben-ammi were the products of incest. They became the fathers of two of Israel's greatest enemies, the Moabites and the Ammonites. These nations settled east of the Jordan River, and Israel never conquered them. Because of the family connection, Moses was forbidden to attack them (Deuteronomy 2.9). Ruth, great-grandmother of David and an ancestor of Jesus, was from Moab.

Abraham deceives the king

20.1 Gen 13.1; 14.7 26.1 **20** From there Abraham journeyed toward the region of the Negeb, and settled
between Kadesh and Shur. While residing in Gerar as an alien, 2 Abraham
said of his wife Sarah, "She is my sister." And King Abimelech of Gerar sent and
20.3 Gen 28.12 31.24,37.5 took Sarah. 3 But God came to Abimelech in a dream by night, and said to him,
"You are about to die because of the woman whom you have taken; for she is a
20.4 Gen 18.23-25 married woman." 4 Now Abimelech had not approached her; so he said, "Lord, will
you destroy an innocent people? 5 Did he not himself say to me, 'She is my sister'?
20.5 Gen 12.17 1 Kgs 9.4 Ps 7.8; 26.6 And she herself said, 'He is my brother.' I did this in the integrity of my heart and
the innocence of my hands." 6 Then God said to him in the dream, "Yes, I know
20.6 Gen 15.1; 31.7 Ps 84.11 that you did this in the integrity of your heart; furthermore it was I who kept you
from sinning against me. Therefore I did not let you touch her. 7 Now then, return
20.7 Ex 7.1 1 Sam 7.5 Job 42.8 the man's wife; for he is a prophet, and he will pray for you and you shall live. But
if you do not restore her, know that you shall surely die, you and all that are yours."
8 So Abimelech rose early in the morning, and called all his servants and told
20.9 Gen 12.18 them all these things; and the men were very much afraid. 9 Then Abimelech called
Abraham, and said to him, "What have you done to us? How have I sinned against
you, that you have brought such great guilt on me and my kingdom? You have done
things to me that ought not to be done." 10 And Abimelech said to Abraham, "What
20.11 Gen 12.12 22.12; 42.18 were you thinking of, that you did this thing?" 11 Abraham said, "I did it because I
thought, There is no fear of God at all in this place, and they will kill me because
of my wife. 12 Besides, she is indeed my sister, the daughter of my father but not the
20.13 Gen 11.31; 12.1 daughter of my mother; and she became my wife. 13 And when God caused me to
wander from my father's house, I said to her, 'This is the kindness you must do me:
20.14 Gen 12.16 at every place to which we come, say of me, He is my brother.' " 14 Then Abimelech took sheep and oxen, and male and female slaves, and gave them to Abraham,
20.15 Gen 47.6 and restored his wife Sarah to him. 15 Abimelech said, "My land is before you;
20.16 Gen 23.15 settle where it pleases you." 16 To Sarah he said, "Look, I have given your brother
a thousand pieces of silver; it is your exoneration before all who are with you; you
20.17 Num 12.13; 21.7 are completely vindicated." 17 Then Abraham prayed to God; and God healed
Abimelech, and also healed his wife and female slaves so that they bore children.
20.18 Gen 12.17 18 For the LORD had closed fast all the wombs of the house of Abimelech because
of Sarah, Abraham's wife.

5. Birth and near sacrifice of Isaac

Isaac is born

21.2 Gen 18.10 Gal 4.22,28 **21** The LORD dealt with Sarah as he had said, and the LORD did for Sarah as he
had promised. 2 Sarah conceived and bore Abraham a son in his old age, at
the time of which God had spoken to him. 3 Abraham gave the name Isaac to his son

---

20.2 Abraham had used this same trick before to protect himself (12.11–13). Although Abraham is one of our heroes of faith, he did not learn his lesson well enough the first time. In fact, by giving in to the temptation again, he risked turning a sinful act into a sinful pattern of lying whenever he suspected his life was in danger.

However much we love God, certain temptations are especially difficult to resist. These are the vulnerable spots in our spiritual armor. As we struggle with these weaknesses, we can be encouraged to know that God is watching out for us just as he did for Abraham.

20.6 Abimelech had unknowingly taken a married woman to be his wife and was about to commit adultery. But God somehow prevented him from touching Sarah and held him back from sinning. What mercy on God's part! How many times has God done the same for us, holding us back from sin in ways we can't even detect? We have no way of knowing – we just know from this story that he can. God works just as often in ways we can't see as in ways we can.

20.11, 12 Because Abraham mistakenly assumed that Abimelech was a wicked man, he made a quick decision to tell a half-truth. Abraham thought it would be more effective to deceive Abimelech than to trust God to work in the king's life. Don't assume that God will not work in a situation that has potential problems. You may not completely understand the situation, and God may intervene when you least expect it.

20.17, 18 Why did God punish Abimelech when he had no idea Sarah was married? (1) Even though Abimelech's intentions were good, as long as Sarah was living in his harem he was in danger of sinning. A person who eats a poisonous toadstool, thinking it's a harmless mushroom, no doubt has perfectly good intentions – but will still suffer. Sin is a poison that damages us and those around us, whatever our intentions. (2) The punishment, closing up "all the wombs of the house of Abimelech," lasted only as long as Abimelech was in danger of sleeping with Sarah. It was meant to change the situation, not to harm Abimelech. (3) The punishment clearly showed that Abraham was in league with Almighty God.

21.1–7 Who could believe Abraham would have a son at 100 years of age – and live to raise him to adulthood? But doing the impossible is everyday business for God. Our big problems may not seem so impossible if we let God handle them.

whom Sarah bore him. 4 And Abraham circumcised his son Isaac when he was
eight days old, as God had commanded him. 5 Abraham was a hundred years old
when his son Isaac was born to him. 6 Now Sarah said, "God has brought laughter
for me; everyone who hears will laugh with me." 7 And she said, "Who would ever
have said to Abraham that Sarah would nurse children? Yet I have borne him a son
in his old age."

Hagar and Ishmael sent away

8 The child grew, and was weaned; and Abraham made a great feast on the day
that Isaac was weaned. 9 But Sarah saw the son of Hagar the Egyptian, whom she
had borne to Abraham, playing with her son Isaac.[i] 10 So she said to Abraham,
"Cast out this slave woman with her son; for the son of this slave woman shall not
inherit along with my son Isaac." 11 The matter was very distressing to Abraham on
account of his son. 12 But God said to Abraham, "Do not be distressed because of
the boy and because of your slave woman; whatever Sarah says to you, do as she
tells you, for it is through Isaac that offspring shall be named for you. 13 As for the
son of the slave woman, I will make a nation of him also, because he is your offspring." 14 So Abraham rose early in the morning, and took bread and a skin of
water, and gave it to Hagar, putting it on her shoulder, along with the child, and
sent her away. And she departed, and wandered about in the wilderness of Beer-
sheba.

15 When the water in the skin was gone, she cast the child under one of the
bushes. 16 Then she went and sat down opposite him a good way off, about the
distance of a bowshot; for she said, "Do not let me look on the death of the child."
And as she sat opposite him, she lifted up her voice and wept. 17 And God heard the
voice of the boy; and the angel of God called to Hagar from heaven, and said to her,
"What troubles you, Hagar? Do not be afraid; for God has heard the voice of the
boy where he is. 18 Come, lift up the boy and hold him fast with your hand, for I will
make a great nation of him." 19 Then God opened her eyes and she saw a well of
water. She went, and filled the skin with water, and gave the boy a drink.

20 God was with the boy, and he grew up; he lived in the wilderness, and became an expert with the bow. 21 He lived in the wilderness of Paran; and his mother
got a wife for him from the land of Egypt.

A treaty by a well

22 At that time Abimelech, with Phicol the commander of his army, said to
Abraham, "God is with you in all that you do; 23 now therefore swear to me here by
God that you will not deal falsely with me or with my offspring or with my posterity, but as I have dealt loyally with you, you will deal with me and with the land
where you have resided as an alien." 24 And Abraham said, "I swear it."

25 When Abraham complained to Abimelech about a well of water that Abimelech's servants had seized, 26 Abimelech said, "I do not know who has done this;
you did not tell me, and I have not heard of it until today." 27 So Abraham took
sheep and oxen and gave them to Abimelech, and the two men made a covenant.
28 Abraham set apart seven ewe lambs of the flock. 29 And Abimelech said to Abraham, "What is the meaning of these seven ewe lambs that you have set apart?" 30 He
said, "These seven ewe lambs you shall accept from my hand, in order that you
may be a witness for me that I dug this well." 31 Therefore that place was called

21.5 Rom 4.19
21.6 Gen 18.12 Isa 54.1
21.7 Gen 18.14 Lk 1.37
21.8 1 Sam 1.22
21.9 Gal 4.29
21.10 Gen 16.4,5 Gal 4.30
21.12 Rom 9.7 Heb 11.18
21.13 Gen 16.10; 21.18 25.12-18
21.14 Gen 16.7
21.16 Jer 6.26
21.17 Ex 3.7 Deut 26.7 Ps 6.8
21.18 Gen 16.1-12 25.12
21.19 Isa 48.15
21.20 Gen 28.15
21.21 Gen 14.6; 25.18
21.22 Gen 26.26
21.23 Gen 24.2
21.24 Gen 14.22
21.25 Gen 13.7; 26.15
21.27 Gen 26.31 Prov 18.16 21.14
21.30 Gen 31.44
21.31 Gen 21.14 26.33 Josh 15.28

[i] Gk Vg: Heb lacks *with her son Isaac*

21.7 After repeated promises, a visit by two angels, and the appearance of the Lord himself, Sarah finally cried out with surprise and joy at the birth of her son. Because of her doubt, worry, and fear, she had forfeited the peace she could have felt in God's wonderful promise to her. The way to bring peace to a troubled heart is to focus on God's promises. Trust him to do what he says.

21.18 What happened to Ishmael, and who are his descendants? Ishmael became ruler of a large tribe or nation. The Ishmaelites were nomads living in the wilderness of Sinai and Paran, south of Israel. One of Ishmael's daughters married Esau, Ishmael's nephew (28.9). The Bible pictures the Ishmaelites as hostile to Israel and to God (Psalm 83.6).

21.31 Beer-sheba, the southernmost city of Israel, lay on the edge of a vast wilderness that stretched as far as Egypt to the southwest and Mount Sinai to the south. The phrase "from Dan to Beer-sheba" was often used to describe the traditional boundaries of the

Beer-sheba;[j] because there both of them swore an oath. 32 When they had made a
covenant at Beer-sheba, Abimelech, with Phicol the commander of his army, left
21.33 1 Sam 22.6; 31.13; Ps 90.2; Isa 9.6; 40.28
and returned to the land of the Philistines. 33 Abraham[k] planted a tamarisk tree in
Beer-sheba, and called there on the name of the LORD, the Everlasting God.[l]
34 And Abraham resided as an alien many days in the land of the Philistines.

God tests Abraham's obedience

22.1 Ex 15.25; 16.4; Deut 8.2; Prov 17.3
22 After these things God tested Abraham. He said to him, "Abraham!" And he
said, "Here I am." 2 He said, "Take your son, your only son Isaac, whom
22.2 2 Kgs 3.27; 2 Chron 3.1; Jn 3.16
you love, and go to the land of Moriah, and offer him there as a burnt offering on
one of the mountains that I shall show you." 3 So Abraham rose early in the morning, saddled his donkey, and took two of his young men with him, and his son
22.3 Mt 10.37
Isaac; he cut the wood for the burnt offering, and set out and went to the place in the
distance that God had shown him. 4 On the third day Abraham looked up and saw
the place far away. 5 Then Abraham said to his young men, "Stay here with the
22.7 Gen 8.20; Ex 29.38; Jn 1.29; Rev 13.7
donkey; the boy and I will go over there; we will worship, and then we will come
back to you." 6 Abraham took the wood of the burnt offering and laid it on his son
Isaac, and he himself carried the fire and the knife. So the two of them walked on
22.8 Gen 18.14; Mt 19.26; 1 Pet 1.19; Rev 5.6
together. 7 Isaac said to his father Abraham, "Father!" And he said, "Here I am, my
son." He said, "The fire and the wood are here, but where is the lamb for a burnt
offering?" 8 Abraham said, "God himself will provide the lamb for a burnt offering,
22.9 Gen 12.7; Heb 11.17; Jas 2.21
my son." So the two of them walked on together.
9 When they came to the place that God had shown him, Abraham built an altar
there and laid the wood in order. He bound his son Isaac, and laid him on the altar,
22.11 Gen 16.7; 21.17; Ex 3.2
on top of the wood. 10 Then Abraham reached out his hand and took the knife to
kill[m] his son. 11 But the angel of the LORD called to him from heaven, and said,
22.12 Heb 11.17
"Abraham, Abraham!" And he said, "Here I am." 12 He said, "Do not lay your hand
22.13 Gen 8.20
on the boy or do anything to him; for now I know that you fear God, since you have
not withheld your son, your only son, from me." 13 And Abraham looked up and

[j] That is *Well of seven* or *Well of the oath* [k] Heb *He* [l] Or *the* LORD, *El Olam* [m] Or *to slaughter*

---

promised land (2 Samuel 17.11). Beer-sheba's southern location and the presence of several wells in the area may explain why Abraham settled there. Beer-sheba was also the home of Isaac, Abraham's son.

22.1 God gave Abraham a test, not to trip him and watch him fall, but to deepen his capacity to obey God and thus to develop his character. Just as fire refines ore to extract precious metals, God refines us through difficult circumstances. When we are tested we can complain, or we can try to see how God is stretching us to develop our character.

22.3 That morning Abraham began one of the greatest acts of obedience in recorded history. Over the years he had learned many tough lessons about the importance of obeying God. This time his obedience was prompt and complete. Obeying God is often a struggle because it may mean giving up something we truly want. We should not expect our obedience to God to be easy or to come naturally.

22.6 We don't know how Abraham carried the fire. Perhaps he carried a live coal or a flint to start a fire.

22.7, 8 Why did God ask Abraham to perform human sacrifice? Heathen nations practiced human sacrifice, but God condemned this as a terrible sin (Leviticus 20.1–5). God did not want Isaac to die, but he wanted Abraham to sacrifice Isaac in his heart so it would be clear that Abraham loved God more than he loved his promised and long-awaited son. God was testing Abraham, and the purpose of testing is to strengthen our character and deepen our commitment to God and his perfect timing. Through this difficult experience, Abraham strengthened his commitment to obey God. He also learned about God's ability to provide.

22.13 Notice the parallel between the ram offered on the altar as a substitute for Isaac and Christ offered on the cross as a substitute for us. Whereas God stopped Abraham from sacrificing his son, God did not spare his own Son, Jesus, from dying on the cross. If Jesus had lived, the rest of humankind would have died. God sent his only Son to die for us so that we can be spared from the eternal death we deserve and instead receive eternal life (John 3.16).

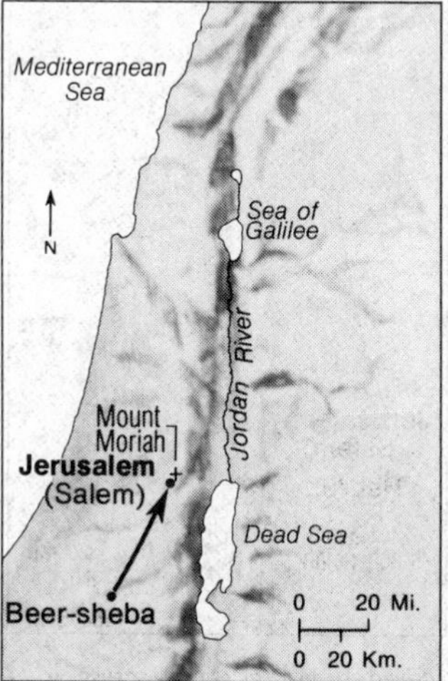

ABRAHAM'S TRIP TO MOUNT MORIAH
Abraham and Isaac traveled the 50 or 60 miles from Beer-sheba to Mount Moriah in about three days. This was a very difficult time for Abraham, who was on his way to sacrifice his beloved son, Isaac.

saw a ram, caught in a thicket by its horns. Abraham went and took the ram and
offered it up as a burnt offering instead of his son. 14 So Abraham called that place
"The LORD will provide";[n] as it is said to this day, "On the mount of the LORD it
shall be provided."[o]
15 The angel of the LORD called to Abraham a second time from heaven, 16 and
said, "By myself I have sworn, says the LORD: Because you have done this, and
have not withheld your son, your only son, 17 I will indeed bless you, and I will
make your offspring as numerous as the stars of heaven and as the sand that is on
the seashore. And your offspring shall possess the gate of their enemies, 18 and by
your offspring shall all the nations of the earth gain blessing for themselves, because you have obeyed my voice." 19 So Abraham returned to his young men, and
they arose and went together to Beer-sheba; and Abraham lived at Beer-sheba.
20 Now after these things it was told Abraham, "Milcah also has borne children, to your brother Nahor: 21 Uz the firstborn, Buz his brother, Kemuel the father
of Aram, 22 Chesed, Hazo, Pildash, Jidlaph, and Bethuel." 23 Bethuel became the
father of Rebekah. These eight Milcah bore to Nahor, Abraham's brother. 24 Moreover, his concubine, whose name was Reumah, bore Tebah, Gaham, Tahash, and
Maacah.

Abraham buries Sarah

23 Sarah lived one hundred twenty-seven years; this was the length of Sarah's
life. 2 And Sarah died at Kiriath-arba (that is, Hebron) in the land of Canaan;
and Abraham went in to mourn for Sarah and to weep for her. 3 Abraham rose up
from beside his dead, and said to the Hittites, 4 "I am a stranger and an alien residing among you; give me property among you for a burying place, so that I may bury
my dead out of my sight." 5 The Hittites answered Abraham, 6 "Hear us, my lord;
you are a mighty prince among us. Bury your dead in the choicest of our burial
places; none of us will withhold from you any burial ground for burying your
dead." 7 Abraham rose and bowed to the Hittites, the people of the land. 8 He said
to them, "If you are willing that I should bury my dead out of my sight, hear me,
and entreat for me Ephron son of Zohar, 9 so that he may give me the cave of Machpelah, which he owns; it is at the end of his field. For the full price let him give it
to me in your presence as a possession for a burying place." 10 Now Ephron was

22.15 Gen 22.11
22.16 Heb 6.13 Lk 1.73,74
22.17 Gen 12.12 13.16; 15.15 17.5
22.18 Gen 18.18 Acts 3.25 Gal 3.8,16
22.19 Gen 21.31
22.20 Gen 11.29 31.53
22.23 Gen 24.15
23.2 Josh 14.15
23.3 Gen 10.15
23.4 Lev 25.23 1 Chron 29.15 Ps 39.12 Heb 11.9
23.6 Gen 13.2; 21.22
23.7 Gen 18.2; 19.1
23.9 Gen 25.9
23.10 Ruth 4.11

[n] Or *will see*; Heb traditionally transliterated *Jehovah Jireh* [o] Or *he shall be seen*

CAVE OF MACHPELAH
Sarah died in Hebron. Abraham bought the Cave of Machpelah, near Hebron, as her burial place. Abraham was also buried there, as were his son and grandson, Isaac and Jacob.

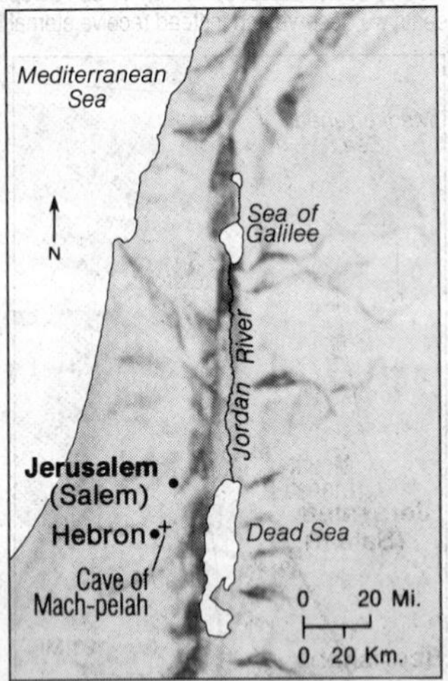

22.17, 18 Abraham received abundant blessings because he obeyed God. First, God gave Abraham's descendants the ability to conquer their enemies. Second, God promised Abraham children and grandchildren who would in turn bless the whole earth. People's lives would be changed as a result of knowing of the faith of Abraham and his descendants. Most often we think of blessings as gifts to be enjoyed. But when God blesses us, his blessings are intended to overflow to others.

23.1–4 In Abraham's day, death and burial were steeped in ritual and traditions. Failing to honor a dead person demonstrated the greatest possible lack of respect. An improper burial was the equivalent of a curse. Mourning was an essential part of the death ritual. Friends and relatives let out loud cries for the whole neighborhood to hear. Because there were no funeral homes or undertakers, these same friends and relatives helped prepare the body for burial, which usually took place on the same day because of the warm climate.

23.4–6 Abraham was in a foreign land looking for a place to bury his wife. Strangers offered to help him because he was "a mighty prince" and they respected him. Although Abraham had not established roots in the area, his reputation was above reproach. Those who invest their time and money in serving God often earn a pleasant return on their investment—a good reputation and the respect of others.

23.10–15 The polite interchange between Abraham and Ephron was typical of bargaining at that time. Ephron graciously offered to give his land to Abraham at no charge; Abraham insisted on paying for it; Ephron politely mentioned the price but said, in effect,

sitting among the Hittites; and Ephron the Hittite answered Abraham in the hearing
of the Hittites, of all who went in at the gate of his city, 11 "No, my lord, hear me;
I give you the field, and I give you the cave that is in it; in the presence of my people
I give it to you; bury your dead." 12 Then Abraham bowed down before the people
23.13 of the land. 13 He said to Ephron in the hearing of the people of the land, "If you
Gen 14.23 2 Sam 24.24 only will listen to me! I will give the price of the field; accept it from me, so that I
23.15 may bury my dead there." 14 Ephron answered Abraham, 15 "My lord, listen to me;
Ex 30.13 a piece of land worth four hundred shekels of silver—what is that between you and

ISAAC

A name carries great authority. It sets you apart. It triggers memories. The sound of it calls you to attention anywhere.

Many Bible names accomplished even more. They were often descriptions of important facts about one's past and hopes for the future. The choice of the name *Isaac,* "laughter," for Abraham and Sarah's son must have created a variety of feelings in them each time it was spoken. At times it must have recalled their shocked laughter at God's announcement that they would be parents in their old age. At other times, it must have brought back the joyful feelings of receiving their long-awaited answer to prayer for a child. Most important, it was a testimony to God's power in making his promise a reality.

In a family of forceful initiators, Isaac was the quiet, "mind-my-own-business" type unless he was specifically called on to take action. He was the protected only child from the time Sarah got rid of Ishmael until Abraham arranged his marriage to Rebekah.

In his own family, Isaac had the patriarchal position, but Rebekah had the power. Rather than stand his ground, Isaac found it easier to compromise or lie to avoid confrontations.

In spite of these shortcomings, Isaac was part of God's plan. The model his father gave him included a great gift of faith in the one true God. God's promise to create a great nation through which he would bless the world was passed on by Isaac to his twin sons.

It is usually not hard to identify with Isaac in his weaknesses. But consider for a moment that God works through people in spite of their shortcomings and, often, through them. As you pray, put into words your desire to be available to God. You will discover that his willingness to use you is even greater than your desire to be used.

Strengths and accomplishments:
- He was the miracle child born to Sarah and Abraham when she was 90 years old and he was 100
- He was the first descendant in fulfillment of God's promise to Abraham
- He seems to have been a caring and consistent husband, at least until his sons were born
- He demonstrated great patience

Weaknesses and mistakes:
- Under pressure he tended to lie
- In conflict he sought to avoid confrontation
- He played favorites between his sons and alienated his wife

Lessons from his life:
- Patience often brings rewards
- Both God's plans and his promises are larger than people
- God keeps his promises! He remains faithful though we are often faithless
- Playing favorites is sure to bring family conflict

Vital statistics:
- Where: The area called the Negeb, in the southern part of Palestine, between Kadesh and Shur (Genesis 20.1)
- Occupation: Wealthy livestock owner
- Relatives: Parents: Abraham and Sarah. Half brother: Ishmael. Wife: Rebekah. Sons: Jacob and Esau

Key verse:
"God said, 'No, but your wife Sarah shall bear you a son, and you shall name him Isaac. I will establish my covenant with him as an everlasting covenant for his offspring after him'" (Genesis 17.19).

Isaac's story is told in Genesis 17.15—35.29. He is also mentioned in Romans 9.7, 8; Hebrews 11.17–20; James 2.21–24.

that it wasn't important; Abraham paid the 400 shekels of silver. Both men knew what was going on as they went through the bargaining process. If Abraham had accepted the land as a gift when it was offered, he would have insulted Ephron, who then would have rescinded his offer. Many Middle Eastern shopkeepers still follow this ritual with their customers.

me? Bury your dead." 16 Abraham agreed with Ephron; and Abraham weighed out 23.16
for Ephron the silver that he had named in the hearing of the Hittites, four hundred Ezra 8.25 Jer 32.9
shekels of silver, according to the weights current among the merchants.
17 So the field of Ephron in Machpelah, which was to the east of Mamre, the 23.17,18
field with the cave that was in it and all the trees that were in the field, throughout Gen 25.9 49.29; 50.13
its whole area, passed 18 to Abraham as a possession in the presence of the Hittites,
in the presence of all who went in at the gate of his city. 19 After this, Abraham
buried Sarah his wife in the cave of the field of Machpelah facing Mamre (that is,
Hebron) in the land of Canaan. 20 The field and the cave that is in it passed from the
Hittites into Abraham's possession as a burying place.

6. Isaac marries Rebekah

24 Now Abraham was old, well advanced in years; and the LORD had blessed 24.1
Abraham in all things. 2 Abraham said to his servant, the oldest of his house, Gen 12.2 18.11; 24.35
who had charge of all that he had, "Put your hand under my thigh 3 and I will make 24.3
you swear by the LORD, the God of heaven and earth, that you will not get a wife Gen 21.23 26.34; 28.1
for my son from the daughters of the Canaanites, among whom I live, 4 but will go 24.4
to my country and to my kindred and get a wife for my son Isaac." 5 The servant Gen 12.1
said to him, "Perhaps the woman may not be willing to follow me to this land; must 24.5
I then take your son back to the land from which you came?" 6 Abraham said to Gen 24.58
him, "See to it that you do not take my son back there. 7 The LORD, the God of 24.7
heaven, who took me from my father's house and from the land of my birth, and Gen 12.7; 15.18 16.17; 22.11
who spoke to me and swore to me, 'To your offspring I will give this land,' he will Ex 23.20,23
send his angel before you, and you shall take a wife for my son from there. 8 But if
the woman is not willing to follow you, then you will be free from this oath of mine;
only you must not take my son back there." 9 So the servant put his hand under the 24.10
thigh of Abraham his master and swore to him concerning this matter. Gen 11.22 22.20
10 Then the servant took ten of his master's camels and departed, taking all Deut 23.4
kinds of choice gifts from his master; and he set out and went to Aram-naharaim, 24.11
to the city of Nahor. 11 He made the camels kneel down outside the city by the well Gen 24.43
of water; it was toward evening, the time when women go out to draw water. 12 And 24.12 Gen 24.27,48
he said, "O LORD, God of my master Abraham, please grant me success today and 24.14
show steadfast love to my master Abraham. 13 I am standing here by the spring of a)Judg 6.17 1 Sam 14.9,10
water, and the daughters of the townspeople are coming out to draw water. 14 Let Prov 19.14 b)Gen 15.8
the girl to whom I shall say, 'Please offer your jar that I may drink,' and who shall Ex 4.1-9

23.16 Four hundred shekels of silver was a high price for the piece of property Abraham bought. The Hittites weren't thrilled about foreigners buying up lots of property, so Abraham had little bargaining leverage.

Ephron asked an outrageous price. The custom of the day was to ask double the fair market value of the land, fully expecting the buyer to offer half the stated price. Abraham, however, did not bargain. He simply paid the initial price. He was not trying to take anything he didn't deserve. Even though God had promised the land to Abraham, he did not just take it away from Ephron.

24.3, 9 In Abraham's culture, putting a hand under the thigh was how an agreement was sealed or a covenant ratified. To accomplish the same purpose, we shake hands, swear oaths, or sign documents in the presence of a notary public.

24.4 Abraham wanted Isaac to marry within the family, a common and acceptable practice at this time that had the added advantage of avoiding intermarriage with heathen neighbors. A son's wife was usually chosen by the parents. It was common for a woman to be married in her early teens, although Rebekah was probably older.

24.6 Abraham wanted Isaac to stay in Canaan but not marry one of the local girls. This contrasts to the way Hagar selected a wife for Ishmael in 21.21. To have Isaac stay and marry someone locally or to send him back to live in their homeland and marry a relative would have been easier. But Abraham wanted to obey God in the "who" as well as in the "where." Make your obedience full and complete.

24.11 The well, the chief source of water for an entire village, was usually located outside town along the main road. Many people had to walk a mile or more for their water. They could use only what they could carry home. Farmers and shepherds would come from nearby fields to draw water for their animals. The well was a good place to meet new friends or chat with old ones. Rebekah would have visited the well twice daily to draw water for her family.

24.12 Abraham's servant asked God for guidance in this very important task. Obviously Eliezer had learned much about faith and about God from his master. What are your family members, friends, and associates learning about God from watching you? Be like Abraham, setting an example of dependent faith. And be like Eliezer, asking God for guidance before any venture.

24.14 Was it right for Abraham's servant to ask God for such a specific sign? The sign he requested was only slightly out of the ordinary. The hospitality of the day required women at the well to offer water to weary travelers, but not to their animals. Eliezer was simply asking God to show him a woman with an attitude of service—someone who would go beyond the expected. Eliezer did not ask for a woman with looks or wealth. He knew the importance of having the right heart, and he asked God to help him with his task.

say, 'Drink, and I will water your camels'—let her be the one whom you have
appointed for your servant Isaac. By this I shall know that you have shown steadfast love to my master."
24.15 Gen 22.20-24 15 Before he had finished speaking, there was Rebekah, who was born to Be-
25.20 thuel son of Milcah, the wife of Nahor, Abraham's brother, coming out with her
24.16 Gen 12.11 water jar on her shoulder. 16 The girl was very fair to look upon, a virgin, whom no
26.7; 29.17 man had known. She went down to the spring, filled her jar, and came up. 17 Then
24.17 1 Kgs 17.10 the servant ran to meet her and said, "Please let me sip a little water from your jar."
Jn 4.7 18 "Drink, my lord," she said, and quickly lowered her jar upon her hand and gave
24.19 Gen 24.14,45, him a drink. 19 When she had finished giving him a drink, she said, "I will draw for
46 your camels also, until they have finished drinking." 20 So she quickly emptied her
jar into the trough and ran again to the well to draw, and she drew for all his camels.
24.21 2 Sam 7.18-20 21 The man gazed at her in silence to learn whether or not the LORD had made his
journey successful.

HAGAR

Escape of some kind is usually the most tempting solution to our problems. In fact, it can become a habit. Hagar was a person who used that approach. When the going got tough, she usually got going—in the other direction.

However, it is worthwhile to note that the biggest challenges Hagar faced were brought on by *other* people's choices. Sarah chose her to be a substitute child-bearer, and Hagar probably had little to say in the matter.

It isn't hard to understand how Hagar's pregnancy caused her to look down on Sarah. But that brought on hard feelings, and Sarah consequently punished Hagar. This motivated her first escape. When she returned to the family and gave birth to Ishmael, Sarah's continued barrenness must have contributed to bitterness on both sides.

When Isaac was finally born, Sarah looked for any excuse to have Hagar and Ishmael sent away. She found it when she caught Ishmael teasing Isaac. In the desert, out of water and facing the death of her son, Hagar once again tried to escape. She walked away so she wouldn't have to watch her son die. Once again, God graciously intervened.

Have you noticed how patiently God operates to make our escape attempts fail? Have you begun to learn that escape is only a temporary solution? God's continual desire is for us to face our problems with his help. We experience his help most clearly in and through conflicts and difficulties, not away from them. Are there problems in your life for which you've been using the "Hagar solution"? Choose one of those problems, ask for God's help, and begin to face it today.

Strength and accomplishment:
- Mother of Abraham's first child, Ishmael, who became founder of the Arab nations

Weaknesses and mistakes:
- When faced with problems, she tended to run away
- Her pregnancy brought out strong feelings of pride and arrogance

Lessons from her life:
- God is faithful to his plan and promises, even when humans complicate the process
- God shows himself as one who knows us and wants to be known by us
- The New Testament uses Hagar as a symbol of those who would pursue favor with God by their own efforts, rather than by trusting in his mercy and forgiveness

Vital statistics:
- Where: Canaan and Egypt
- Occupation: Servant, mother
- Relatives: Son: Ishmael

Key verse:
"The angel of the Lord said to her, 'Return to your mistress, and submit to her'" (Genesis 16.9).

Hagar's story is told in Genesis 16—21. She is also mentioned in Galatians 4.24, 25.

24.15, 16 Rebekah had physical beauty, but the servant was looking for a sign of inner beauty. Appearance is important to us, and we spend time and money improving it. But how do we develop our inner beauty? Patience, kindness, and joy are the beauty treatments that help us become truly lovely—on the inside.

24.18–20 Rebekah's servant spirit was clearly demonstrated as she willingly and quickly drew water for Eliezer and his camels. The pots used for carrying water were large and heavy. It took a lot of water to satisfy a thirsty camel—up to 25 gallons per camel after a week's travel. Seeing Rebekah go to work, Eliezer knew this was a woman with a heart for doing far more than the bare minimum. Do you have a "servant spirit"? When asked to help or when you see a need, go beyond the minimum.

22 When the camels had finished drinking, the man took a gold nose-ring
weighing a half shekel, and two bracelets for her arms weighing ten gold shekels,
23 and said, "Tell me whose daughter you are. Is there room in your father's house
for us to spend the night?" 24 She said to him, "I am the daughter of Bethuel son of
Milcah, whom she bore to Nahor." 25 She added, "We have plenty of straw and
fodder and a place to spend the night." 26 The man bowed his head and worshiped
the LORD 27 and said, "Blessed be the LORD, the God of my master Abraham, who
has not forsaken his steadfast love and his faithfulness toward my master. As for
me, the LORD has led me on the way to the house of my master's kin."

28 Then the girl ran and told her mother's household about these things. 29 Rebekah had a brother whose name was Laban; and Laban ran out to the man, to the
spring. 30 As soon as he had seen the nose-ring, and the bracelets on his sister's
arms, and when he heard the words of his sister Rebekah, "Thus the man spoke to
me," he went to the man; and there he was, standing by the camels at the spring.
31 He said, "Come in, O blessed of the LORD. Why do you stand outside when I
have prepared the house and a place for the camels?" 32 So the man came into the
house; and Laban unloaded the camels, and gave him straw and fodder for the
camels, and water to wash his feet and the feet of the men who were with him.
33 Then food was set before him to eat; but he said, "I will not eat until I have told
my errand." He said, "Speak on."

34 So he said, "I am Abraham's servant. 35 The LORD has greatly blessed my
master, and he has become wealthy; he has given him flocks and herds, silver and
gold, male and female slaves, camels and donkeys. 36 And Sarah my master's wife
bore a son to my master when she was old; and he has given him all that he has.
37 My master made me swear, saying, 'You shall not take a wife for my son from
the daughters of the Canaanites, in whose land I live; 38 but you shall go to my
father's house, to my kindred, and get a wife for my son.' 39 I said to my master,
'Perhaps the woman will not follow me.' 40 But he said to me, 'The LORD, before
whom I walk, will send his angel with you and make your way successful. You
shall get a wife for my son from my kindred, from my father's house. 41 Then you
will be free from my oath, when you come to my kindred; even if they will not give
her to you, you will be free from my oath.'

42 "I came today to the spring, and said, 'O LORD, the God of my master Abraham, if now you will only make successful the way I am going! 43 I am standing
here by the spring of water; let the young woman who comes out to draw, to whom
I shall say, "Please give me a little water from your jar to drink," 44 and who will
say to me, "Drink, and I will draw for your camels also"—let her be the woman
whom the LORD has appointed for my master's son.'

45 "Before I had finished speaking in my heart, there was Rebekah coming out
with her water jar on her shoulder; and she went down to the spring, and drew. I
said to her, 'Please let me drink.' 46 She quickly let down her jar from her shoulder,
and said, 'Drink, and I will also water your camels.' So I drank, and she also watered the camels. 47 Then I asked her, 'Whose daughter are you?' She said, 'The
daughter of Bethuel, Nahor's son, whom Milcah bore to him.' So I put the ring on
her nose, and the bracelets on her arms. 48 Then I bowed my head and worshiped
the LORD, and blessed the LORD, the God of my master Abraham, who had led me
by the right way to obtain the daughter of my master's kinsman for his son. 49 Now
then, if you will deal loyally and truly with my master, tell me; and if not, tell me,
so that I may turn either to the right hand or to the left."

50 Then Laban and Bethuel answered, "The thing comes from the LORD; we
cannot speak to you anything bad or good. 51 Look, Rebekah is before you, take her

24.22 Gen 24.47
24.24 Gen 24.15
24.26 Ex 4.31
24.27 Gen 14.20 24.12,48
24.28 Gen 29.12
24.29 Gen 24.50 25.20; 29.5
24.30 Gen 24.22,47
24.31 Gen 18.3-5 19.2
24.34 Gen 24.2
24.35 Gen 12.2; 13.2
24.36 Gen 21.1-7 25.5
24.37 Gen 24.3; 28.1
24.40 Gen 24.7
24.45 1 Sam 1.13
24.47 Gen 24.23,24
24.49 Gen 32.10 47.29
24.50 Ps 118.23 Mt 21.42
24.51 Gen 20.15

24.26, 27 As soon as Abraham's servant knew that God had answered his prayer, he thanked God for his goodness and guidance. God will also use and lead us if we are available like Eliezer. And our first response should be praise and thanksgiving that God would choose to work in and through us.

24.42, 48 When Eliezer told his story to Laban, he spoke openly of God and his goodness. Often we do the opposite, afraid that we will be misunderstood or rejected or seen as too religious. Instead, we should share openly what God is doing for us.

and go, and let her be the wife of your master's son, as the LORD has spoken."
24.52 Gen 24.26 52 When Abraham's servant heard their words, he bowed himself to the ground
before the LORD. 53 And the servant brought out jewelry of silver and of gold, and
garments, and gave them to Rebekah; he also gave to her brother and to her mother
24.54 Gen 28.6; 30.25 costly ornaments. 54 Then he and the men who were with him ate and drank, and
they spent the night there. When they rose in the morning, he said, "Send me back
24.55 Judg 19.4 to my master." 55 Her brother and her mother said, "Let the girl remain with us a
while, at least ten days; after that she may go." 56 But he said to them, "Do not delay
me, since the LORD has made my journey successful; let me go that I may go to my
24.58 Ps 45.10 master." 57 They said, "We will call the girl, and ask her." 58 And they called Re-
24.59 bekah, and said to her, "Will you go with this man?" She said, "I will." 59 So they
Gen 35.8 sent away their sister Rebekah and her nurse along with Abraham's servant and his
24.60 Gen 17.16 men. 60 And they blessed Rebekah and said to her,
22.17 "May you, our sister, become
Dan 7.10 thousands of myriads;
may your offspring gain possession
of the gates of their foes."

REBEKAH

Some people are initiators. They help get the ball rolling. Rebekah would easily stand out in this group. Her life was characterized by initiative. When she saw a need she took action, even though the action was not always right.

It was Rebekah's initiative that first caught the attention of Eliezer, the servant Abraham sent to find a wife for Isaac. It was common courtesy to give a drink to a stranger, but it took added character to also fetch water for ten thirsty camels. Later, after hearing the details of Eliezer's mission, Rebekah was immediately willing to be Isaac's bride.

Several later events help us see how initiative can be misdirected. Rebekah was aware that God's plan would be channeled through Jacob, not Esau (Genesis 25.23). So not only did Jacob become her favorite; she actually planned ways to ensure that he would overshadow his older twin. Meanwhile, Isaac preferred Esau. This created a conflict between the couple. She felt justified in deceiving her husband when the time came to bless the sons, and her ingenious plan was carried out to perfection.

Most of the time we try to justify the things we choose to do. Often we attempt to add God's approval to our actions. While it is true that our actions will not spoil God's plan, it is also true that we are responsible for what we do and must always be cautious about our motives. When thinking about a course of action, are you simply seeking God's stamp of approval on something you've already decided to do? Or are you willing to set the plan aside if the principles and commands of God's word are against the action? Initiative and action are admirable and right when they are controlled by God's wisdom.

Strengths and accomplishments:
- When confronted with a need, she took immediate action
- She was accomplishment oriented

Weaknesses and mistakes:
- Her initiative was not always balanced by wisdom
- She favored one of her sons
- She deceived her husband

Lessons from her life:
- Our actions must be guided by God's word
- God makes use even of our mistakes in his plan
- Parental favoritism hurts a family

Vital statistics:
- Where: Haran, Canaan
- Occupation: Wife, mother, household manager
- Relatives: Grandparents: Nahor and Milcah. Father: Bethuel. Husband: Isaac. Brother: Laban. Twin sons: Esau and Jacob

Key verses:
"Then Isaac brought her into his mother Sarah's tent. He took Rebekah, and she became his wife; and he loved her. So Isaac was comforted after his mother's death" (Genesis 24.67).
"Isaac loved Esau, because he was fond of game; but Rebekah loved Jacob" (Genesis 25.28).

Rebekah's story is told in Genesis 24—49. She is also mentioned in Romans 9.10.

61 Then Rebekah and her maids rose up, mounted the camels, and followed the
man; thus the servant took Rebekah, and went his way.
62 Now Isaac had come from[p] Beer-lahai-roi, and was settled in the Negeb. **24.62**
63 Isaac went out in the evening to walk[q] in the field; and looking up, he saw camels Gen 16.14 25.11
coming. 64 And Rebekah looked up, and when she saw Isaac, she slipped quickly **24.63**
from the camel, 65 and said to the servant, "Who is the man over there, walking in Ps 119.15,27, 47,48
the field to meet us?" The servant said, "It is my master." So she took her veil and **24.66**
covered herself. 66 And the servant told Isaac all the things that he had done. 67 Then Mk 6.30
Isaac brought her into his mother Sarah's tent. He took Rebekah, and she became **24.67** Gen 23.2
his wife; and he loved her. So Isaac was comforted after his mother's death. 25.20; 29.18

7. Abraham dies

25 Abraham took another wife, whose name was Keturah. 2 She bore him Zim- **25.1**
ran, Jokshan, Medan, Midian, Ishbak, and Shuah. 3 Jokshan was the father 1 Chron 1.32
of Sheba and Dedan. The sons of Dedan were Asshurim, Letushim, and Leum-
mim. 4 The sons of Midian were Ephah, Epher, Hanoch, Abida, and Eldaah. All
these were the children of Keturah. 5 Abraham gave all he had to Isaac. 6 But to the **25.5**
sons of his concubines Abraham gave gifts, while he was still living, and he sent Gen 24.36
them away from his son Isaac, eastward to the east country.
7 This is the length of Abraham's life, one hundred seventy-five years. 8 Abra- **25.7**
ham breathed his last and died in a good old age, an old man and full of years, and Gen 12.4 **25.8**
was gathered to his people. 9 His sons Isaac and Ishmael buried him in the cave of Gen 25.17
Machpelah, in the field of Ephron son of Zohar the Hittite, east of Mamre, 10 the 35.29; 49.29,33
field that Abraham purchased from the Hittites. There Abraham was buried, with **25.9,10** Gen 23.17
his wife Sarah. 11 After the death of Abraham God blessed his son Isaac. And Isaac 49.29; 50.13
settled at Beer-lahai-roi. **25.11** Gen 24.62; 26.3
12 These are the descendants of Ishmael, Abraham's son, whom Hagar the **25.12**
Egyptian, Sarah's slave-girl, bore to Abraham. 13 These are the names of the sons Gen 16.15 1 Chron 1.28-31
of Ishmael, named in the order of their birth: Nebaioth, the firstborn of Ishmael; **25.13**
and Kedar, Adbeel, Mibsam, 14 Mishma, Dumah, Massa, 15 Hadad, Tema, Jetur, Gen 17.20
Naphish, and Kedemah. 16 These are the sons of Ishmael and these are their names,
by their villages and by their encampments, twelve princes according to their
tribes. 17 (This is the length of the life of Ishmael, one hundred thirty-seven years; **25.17**
he breathed his last and died, and was gathered to his people.) 18 They settled from Gen 25.8 **25.18**
Havilah to Shur, which is opposite Egypt in the direction of Assyria; he settled a)Gen 20.1
down[r] alongside of[s] all his people. b)Gen 16.12

E. THE STORY OF ISAAC (25.19—28.9)

Isaac inherited everything from his father, including God's promise to make his descendants into a great nation. As a boy, Isaac did not resist as his father prepared to sacrifice him, and as a man, he gladly accepted the wife that others chose for him. Through Isaac, we learn how to let God guide our life and place his will ahead of our own.

1. Jacob and Esau, Isaac's twin sons

Jacob and Esau are born

19 These are the descendants of Isaac, Abraham's son: Abraham was the father **25.19** Gen 21.3
of Isaac, 20 and Isaac was forty years old when he married Rebekah, daughter of 1 Chron 1.34

[p] Syr Tg: Heb *from coming to* [q] Meaning of Heb word is uncertain [r] Heb *he fell* [s] Or *down in opposition to*

24.65 When Rebekah learned that the man coming to greet them was Isaac, her husband-to-be, she followed two oriental customs. She dismounted from her camel to show respect, and she placed a veil over her face as a bride.

25.1–6 Abraham took another wife, Keturah, after Sarah died. Although the sons and grandsons of Abraham and Keturah received many gifts from Abraham, all his property and authority went to Isaac, his principle heir.

25.21 As Isaac pleaded with God for children, so the Bible encourages us to ask and even plead for our most personal and important requests. God wants to grant our requests, but he wants us to ask him. Even then, as Isaac learned, God may decide to withhold his answer for a while in order to (1) deepen our insight into what we really need, (2) broaden our appreciation for his answers,

25.21 Gen 21.2 Bethuel the Aramean of Paddan-aram, sister of Laban the Aramean. 21 Isaac prayed
to the LORD for his wife, because she was barren; and the LORD granted his prayer,
and his wife Rebekah conceived. 22 The children struggled together within her; and
25.23 Gen 17.2-4 she said, "If it is to be this way, why do I live?"[t] So she went to inquire of the
27.29; 48.19 LORD. 23 And the LORD said to her,
Num 20.14 "Two nations are in your womb,
Deut 2.4,8 Rom 9.12 and two peoples born of you shall be divided;
the one shall be stronger than the other,
25.25 Gen 27.11 the elder shall serve the younger."
24 When her time to give birth was at hand, there were twins in her womb. 25 The
25.26 Hos 12.3 first came out red, all his body like a hairy mantle; so they named him Esau. 26 Afterward his brother came out, with his hand gripping Esau's heel; so he was named
Jacob.[u] Isaac was sixty years old when she bore them.

Esau sells his birthright

27 When the boys grew up, Esau was a skillful hunter, a man of the field, while
Jacob was a quiet man, living in tents. 28 Isaac loved Esau, because he was fond of
game; but Rebekah loved Jacob.
29 Once when Jacob was cooking a stew, Esau came in from the field, and he
25.30 Gen 36.1,9 was famished. 30 Esau said to Jacob, "Let me eat some of that red stuff, for I am
Ex 15.15 famished!" (Therefore he was called Edom.[v]) 31 Jacob said, "First sell me your
25.31 Deut 21.15-17 birthright." 32 Esau said, "I am about to die; of what use is a birthright to me?"
33 Jacob said, "Swear to me first."[w] So he swore to him, and sold his birthright to
25.33 Gen 27.36 Jacob. 34 Then Jacob gave Esau bread and lentil stew, and he ate and drank, and
Heb 12.16 rose and went his way. Thus Esau despised his birthright.

[t] Syr: Meaning of Heb uncertain [u] That is *He takes by the heel* or *He supplants* [v] That is *Red* [w] Heb *today*

ELIEZER: PROFILE OF A TRUE SERVANT

Have you ever approached a responsibility with this kind of singlemindedness and careful planning, while ultimately depending on God?

Reference	Action
24.3, 9	Accepted the challenge
24.5	Examined alternatives
24.9	Promised to follow instructions
24.12–14	Made a plan
24.12–14	Submitted the plan to God
24.12–14	Prayed for guidance
24.12–14	Devised a strategy with room for God to operate
24.21	Waited
24.21	Watched carefully
24.26	Accepted the answer thankfully
24.34–49	Explained the situation to concerned parties
24.56	Refused unnecessary delay
24.66	Followed through with entire plan

or (3) allow us to mature so we can use his gifts more wisely.

25.25 *Esau* sounds like the Hebrew word for "hair." A *mantle* is a cloak.

25.31 A birthright was a special honor given to the firstborn son. It included a double portion of the family inheritance along with the honor of one day becoming the family's leader. The oldest son could sell his birthright or give it away if he chose, but in so doing, he would lose both material goods and his leadership position. By trading his birthright, Esau showed complete disregard for the spiritual blessings that would have come his way if he had kept it. In effect, Esau "despised" his birthright (v. 34).

25.32, 33 Esau traded the lasting benefits of his birthright for the immediate pleasure of food. He acted on impulse, satisfying his immediate desires without pausing to consider the long-range consequences of what he was about to do. We can fall into the same trap. When we see something we want, our first impulse is to get it. At first we feel intensely satisfied and sometimes even powerful because we have obtained what we set out to get. But immediate pleasure often loses sight of the future. We can avoid making Esau's mistake by comparing the short-term satisfaction with its long-range consequences before we act.

Esau exaggerated his hunger. "I am famished," he said. This thought made his choice much easier, because if he was starving, what good was an inheritance anyway? The pressure of the moment distorted his perspective and made his decision seem urgent. We often experience similar pressures. For example, when we feel sexual pressure, a marriage vow may seem unimportant. We might feel such great pressure in one area that nothing else seems to matter, and we lose our perspective. Getting through that short, pressure-filled moment is often the most difficult part of overcoming a temptation.

2. Isaac and King Abimelech

Isaac moves to Gerar

26 Now there was a famine in the land, besides the former famine that had **26.1**
occurred in the days of Abraham. And Isaac went to Gerar, to King Abime- Gen 12.10 20.1,2; 41.54
lech of the Philistines. 2 The LORD appeared to Isaac[x] and said, "Do not go down **26.2**
to Egypt; settle in the land that I shall show you. 3 Reside in this land as an alien, Gen 12.1,7
and I will be with you, and will bless you; for to you and to your descendants I will **26.3**
give all these lands, and I will fulfill the oath that I swore to your father Abraham. Gen 12.7; 15.8
4 I will make your offspring as numerous as the stars of heaven, and will give to **26.4**
your offspring all these lands; and all the nations of the earth shall gain blessing for Gen 15.15 22.17
themselves through your offspring, 5 because Abraham obeyed my voice and kept Ex 32.13
my charge, my commandments, my statutes, and my laws." Gal 3.8

Isaac deceives the king

6 So Isaac settled in Gerar. 7 When the men of the place asked him about his **26.7**
wife, he said, "She is my sister"; for he was afraid to say, "My wife," thinking, "or Gen 12.11,12 20.12
else the men of the place might kill me for the sake of Rebekah, because she is
attractive in appearance." 8 When Isaac had been there a long time, King Abime- **26.8**
lech of the Philistines looked out of a window and saw him fondling his wife Re- Prov 5.18,19 Eccles 9.9
bekah. 9 So Abimelech called for Isaac, and said, "So she is your wife! Why then
did you say, 'She is my sister'?" Isaac said to him, "Because I thought I might die
because of her." 10 Abimelech said, "What is this you have done to us? One of the **26.10**
people might easily have lain with your wife, and you would have brought guilt Gen 20.7-10
upon us." 11 So Abimelech warned all the people, saying, "Whoever touches this **26.11**
man or his wife shall be put to death." Prov 6.29

Isaac refuses to fight

12 Isaac sowed seed in that land, and in the same year reaped a hundredfold. **26.12**
The LORD blessed him, 13 and the man became rich; he prospered more and more Gen 26.3 **26.13**
until he became very wealthy. 14 He had possessions of flocks and herds, and a Gen 24.35; 25.5
great household, so that the Philistines envied him. 15 (Now the Philistines had **26.15**
stopped up and filled with earth all the wells that his father's servants had dug in the Gen 21.15

[x] Heb *him*

26.1 The Philistine tribe would become one of Israel's fiercest enemies. *Philistine* means "sea people," because they originally were sailors from the Mediterranean Sea. These people, living along the southwest coast, were few but ferocious in battle. Although friendly to Isaac, this small group was the forerunner of the nation that would plague Israel during the time of Joshua, the judges, and David.

26.1 This king Abimelech was not the same Abimelech that Abraham encountered (chapter 22). "Abimelech" may have been a dynastic name of the Philistine rulers.

26.7–11 Isaac was afraid that the men in Gerar would kill him to get his beautiful wife, Rebekah. So he lied, claiming that Rebekah was his sister. Where did he learn that trick? Evidently he knew about the actions of his father, Abraham (see 12.10–14 and 20.1–4). Parents help shape the world's future by the way they shape their children's values. The first step toward helping children live rightly is for the parents to live rightly. Your actions are often copied by those closest to you. What kind of example are you setting for your children?

26.12–16 God kept his promise to bless Isaac. The neighboring Philistines grew jealous because everything Isaac did seemed to go right. So they plugged his wells and tried to get rid of him. Jealousy is a dividing force strong enough to tear apart the mightiest of nations or the closest of friends. It forces you to separate yourself from what you were longing for in the first place. When you find yourself becoming jealous of others, try thanking God for their good fortune. Before striking out in anger, consider what you could lose (a friend, a job, a spouse?).

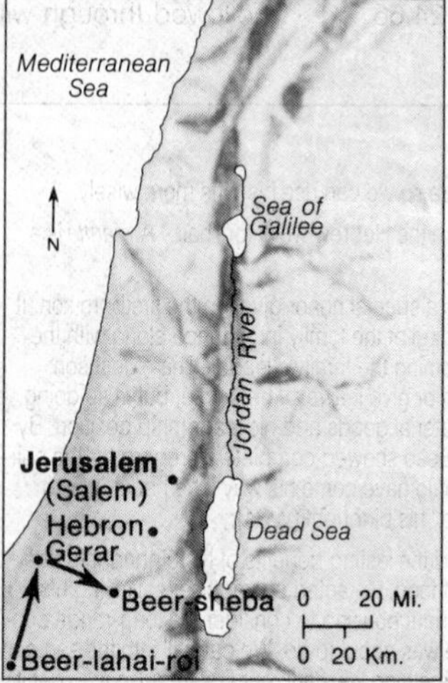

ISAAC'S MOVE TO GERAR
Isaac had settled near Beer-lahai-roi ("the well Lahairoi"), where his sons, Jacob and Esau, were born. A famine drove him to Gerar. But when he became wealthy, his jealous neighbors asked him to leave. From Gerar he moved to Beer-sheba.

26.16 Ex 1.9 days of his father Abraham.) 16 And Abimelech said to Isaac, "Go away from us;
you have become too powerful for us."
17 So Isaac departed from there and camped in the valley of Gerar and settled
there. 18 Isaac dug again the wells of water that had been dug in the days of his
father Abraham; for the Philistines had stopped them up after the death of Abra-
26.19 Jn 4.10,11 ham; and he gave them the names that his father had given them. 19 But when
Isaac's servants dug in the valley and found there a well of spring water, 20 the
herders of Gerar quarreled with Isaac's herders, saying, "The water is ours." So he

---

ESAU

Common sense isn't all that common. In fact, the common thread in many decisions is that they don't make sense. Esau's life was filled with choices he must have regretted bitterly. He appears to have been a person who found it hard to consider consequences, reacting to the need of the moment without realizing what he was giving up to meet that need. Trading his birthright for a bowl of stew was the clearest example of this weakness. He also chose wives in direct opposition to his parents' wishes. He learned the hard way.

What are you willing to trade for the things you want? Do you find yourself, at times, willing to negotiate *anything* for what you feel you need *now?* Do your family, spouse, integrity, body, or soul get included in these deals? Do you sometimes feel that the important parts of life escaped while you were grabbing for something else?

If so, your initial response, like Esau's, may be deep anger. In itself that isn't wrong, as long as you direct the energy of that anger toward a solution and not toward yourself or others as the cause of the problem. Your greatest need is to find a focal point other than "what I need now." The only worthy focal point is God. A relationship with him will not only give an ultimate purpose to your life; it will also be a daily guideline for living. Meet him in the pages of the Bible.

Strengths and accomplishments:
- Ancestor of the Edomites
- Known for his archery skill
- Able to forgive after explosive anger

Weaknesses and mistakes:
- When faced with important decisions, tended to choose according to the immediate need rather than the long-range effect
- Angered his parents by poor marriage choices

Lessons from his life:
- God allows certain events in our lives to accomplish his overall purposes, but we are still responsible for our actions
- Consequences are important to consider
- It is possible to have great anger and yet not sin

Vital statistics:
- Where: Canaan
- Occupation: Skillful hunter
- Relatives: Parents: Isaac and Rebekah. Brother: Jacob. Wives: Judith, Basemath, and Mahalath

Key verses:
"Pursue peace with everyone, and the holiness without which no one will see the Lord. See to it that no one fails to obtain the grace of God; that no root of bitterness springs up and causes trouble, and through it many become defiled. See to it that no one becomes like Esau, an immoral and godless person, who sold his birthright for a single meal. You know that later, when he wanted to inherit the blessing, he was rejected, for he found no chance to repent, even though he sought the blessing with tears" (Hebrews 12.14–17).

Esau's story is told in Genesis 25—36. He is also mentioned in Malachi 1.2; Romans 9.13; Hebrews 12.16, 17.

26.17–22 Three times Isaac and his men dug new wells. When the first two disputes arose, Isaac moved on. Finally there was enough room for everyone. Rather than start a huge conflict, Isaac compromised for the sake of peace. Would you be willing to forsake an important position or valuable possession to keep peace? Ask God for the wisdom to know when to withdraw and when to stand and fight.

26.18 The desolate Gerar area was located on the edge of a wilderness. Water was as precious as gold. If someone dug a well, he was staking a claim to the land. Some wells had locks to keep thieves from stealing the water. To "stop" or plug up someone's well was an act of war; it was one of the most serious crimes in the land. Isaac had every right to fight back when the Philistines ruined his wells, and yet he chose to keep the peace. In the end, the Philistines respected him for his patience.

26.20–22 The names of these wells had specific meanings. *Esek* means "The Well of Argument;" *Sitnah* means "The Well of Anger;" *Rehoboth* means "The Well of Room Enough for Us at Last."

called the well Esek,[y] because they contended with him. 21 Then they dug another
well, and they quarreled over that one also; so he called it Sitnah.[z] 22 He moved
from there and dug another well, and they did not quarrel over it; so he called it
Rehoboth,[a] saying, "Now the LORD has made room for us, and we shall be fruitful
in the land."
23 From there he went up to Beer-sheba. 24 And that very night the LORD appeared to him and said, "I am the God of your father Abraham; do not be afraid, for
I am with you and will bless you and make your offspring numerous for my servant
Abraham's sake." 25 So he built an altar there, called on the name of the LORD, and
pitched his tent there. And there Isaac's servants dug a well.
26 Then Abimelech went to him from Gerar, with Ahuzzath his adviser and
Phicol the commander of his army. 27 Isaac said to them, "Why have you come to
me, seeing that you hate me and have sent me away from you?" 28 They said, "We
see plainly that the LORD has been with you; so we say, let there be an oath between
you and us, and let us make a covenant with you 29 so that you will do us no harm,
just as we have not touched you and have done to you nothing but good and have
sent you away in peace. You are now the blessed of the LORD." 30 So he made them
a feast, and they ate and drank. 31 In the morning they rose early and exchanged
oaths; and Isaac set them on their way, and they departed from him in peace. 32 That
same day Isaac's servants came and told him about the well that they had dug, and
said to him, "We have found water!" 33 He called it Shibah;[b] therefore the name of
the city is Beer-sheba[c] to this day.

3. Isaac blesses Jacob instead of Esau

34 When Esau was forty years old, he married Judith daughter of Beeri the
Hittite, and Basemath daughter of Elon the Hittite; 35 and they made life bitter for
Isaac and Rebekah.

27 When Isaac was old and his eyes were dim so that he could not see, he called
his elder son Esau and said to him, "My son"; and he answered, "Here I
am." 2 He said, "See, I am old; I do not know the day of my death. 3 Now then, take
your weapons, your quiver and your bow, and go out to the field, and hunt game for
me. 4 Then prepare for me savory food, such as I like, and bring it to me to eat, so
that I may bless you before I die."
5 Now Rebekah was listening when Isaac spoke to his son Esau. So when Esau
went to the field to hunt for game and bring it, 6 Rebekah said to her son Jacob, "I
heard your father say to your brother Esau, 7 'Bring me game, and prepare for me
savory food to eat, that I may bless you before the LORD before I die.' 8 Now therefore, my son, obey my word as I command you. 9 Go to the flock, and get me two
choice kids, so that I may prepare from them savory food for your father, such as
he likes; 10 and you shall take it to your father to eat, so that he may bless you before
he dies." 11 But Jacob said to his mother Rebekah, "Look, my brother Esau is a

26.22 Ps 4.1; 18.19; 118.5; Isa 54.2
26.23 Gen 21.31; 46.1
26.24 Gen 12.1,2; 17.1-7; Ex 3.6
26.25 Gen 12.7; 13.3,4
26.26 Gen 21.22,23
26.27 Gen 26.14,16
26.28 Gen 26.3,12-16
26.29 Ps 115.15
26.30 Gen 21.8; 31.54
26.31 Gen 14.22; 21.31; 31.55
26.33 Gen 21.31
26.34 Gen 28.6-8
26.35 Gen 27.46
27.1 Gen 25.25; 48.10
27.2 Gen 47.29
27.3 Gen 25.28
27.4 Gen 24.60; 27.19; 48.9
27.6 Gen 25.28
27.8 Gen 27.13,43
27.9 Judg 13.15
27.11 Gen 25.25

[y] That is *Contention* [z] That is *Enmity* [a] That is *Broad places* or *Room* [b] A word resembling the word for *oath*
[c] That is *Well of the oath* or *Well of seven*

26.26–31 With his enemies wanting to make peace, Isaac was quick to respond, turning the occasion into a celebration. We should be just as receptive to those who want to make peace with us. When God's influence in our lives begins to attract people—even enemies—we must take the opportunity to reach out to them with God's love.

26.34, 35 Esau married heathen women, and this upset his parents greatly. Most parents can be a storehouse of good advice because they have a lifetime of insight into their children's character. You may not agree with everything your parents say, but at least talk with them and listen carefully. This will help avoid the hard feelings Esau experienced.

27.5–10 When Rebekah learned that Isaac was preparing to bless Esau, she quickly devised a plan to trick him into blessing Jacob instead. Although God had already told her that Jacob would become the family leader (25.23–26), Rebekah took matters into her own hands. She resorted to doing something wrong to try to bring about what God had already said would happen. For Rebekah, the end justified the means. No matter how good we think our goals are, we should not attempt to achieve them unjustly. Would God approve of the methods you are using to accomplish your goals?

27.11, 12 How we react to a moral dilemma often exposes our real motives. Frequently we are more worried about getting caught than about doing what is right. Jacob did not seem concerned about the deceitfulness of his mother's plan; instead he was afraid of getting in trouble while carrying it out. If you are worried about getting caught, you are probably in a position that is less than honest. Let your fear of getting caught be a warning to do right. Jacob paid a huge price for carrying out this dishonest plan.

27.11–13 Jacob hesitated when he heard Rebekah's deceitful plan. Although he questioned it for the wrong reason (fear of getting caught), he protested and thus gave her one last chance to

27.12 Gen 9.25 27.21,22

hairy man, and I am a man of smooth skin. [12]Perhaps my father will feel me, and I shall seem to be mocking him, and bring a curse on myself and not a blessing." [13]His mother said to him, "Let your curse be on me, my son; only obey my word,

JACOB

Abraham, Isaac, and Jacob are among the most significant people in the Old Testament. It is important to realize that this significance is not based upon their personal characters, but upon the character of God. They were all men who earned the grudging respect and even fear of their peers; they were wealthy and powerful, and yet each was capable of lying, deceit, and selfishness. They were not the perfect heroes we might have expected; instead, they were just like us, trying to please God, but often falling short.

Jacob was the third link in God's plan to start a nation from Abraham. The success of that plan was more often in spite of than because of Jacob's life. Before Jacob was born, God promised that his plan would be worked out through Jacob and not his twin brother, Esau. Although Jacob's methods were not always respectable, his skill, determination, and patience have to be admired. As we follow him from birth to death, we are able to see God's work.

Jacob's life had four stages, each marked by a personal encounter with God. In the first stage, Jacob lived up to his name, which means "one who supplants, undermines, or grabs." He grabbed Esau's heel at birth, and by the time he fled from home, he had also grabbed his brother's birthright and blessing. During his flight, God first appeared to him. Not only did God confirm to Jacob his blessing, but he awakened in Jacob a personal knowledge of himself. In the second stage, Jacob experienced life from the other side, being manipulated and deceived by Laban. But there is a curious change: the Jacob of stage one would simply have left Laban, whereas the Jacob of stage two, after deciding to leave, waited six years for God's permission. In the third stage, Jacob was in a new role as grabber. This time, by the Jordan River, he grabbed on to God and wouldn't let go. He realized his dependence on the God who had continued to bless him. His relationship to God became essential to his life, and his name was changed to Israel, "a prince who prevails with God." Jacob's last stage of life was to *be* grabbed—God achieved a firm hold on him. In responding to Joseph's invitation to come to Egypt, Jacob was clearly unwilling to make a move without God's approval.

Can you think of times when God has made himself known to you? Do you allow yourself to meet him as you study his Word? What difference have these experiences made in your life? Are you more like the young Jacob, forcing God to track you down in the wilderness of your own plans and mistakes? Or are you more like the Jacob who placed his desires and plans before God for his approval before taking any action?

Strengths and accomplishments:
- Father of the 12 tribes of Israel
- Third in the Abrahamic line of God's plan
- Determined, willing to work long and hard for what he wanted
- Good businessman

Weaknesses and mistakes:
- When faced with conflict, relied on his own resources rather than going to God for help
- Tended to accumulate wealth for its own sake

Lessons from his life:
- Security does not lie in the accumulation of goods
- All human intentions and actions—for good or evil—are woven by God into his ongoing plan

Vital statistics:
- Where: Canaan
- Occupation: Shepherd, livestock owner
- Relatives: Parents: Isaac and Rebekah. Brother: Esau. Father-in-law: Laban. Wives: Rachel and Leah. Twelve sons and one daughter are mentioned in the Bible

Key verse:
"Know that I am with you and will keep you wherever you go, and will bring you back to this land; for I will not leave you until I have done what I have promised you" (Genesis 28.15).

Jacob's story is told in Genesis 25—50. He is also mentioned in Hosea 12.2–5; Matthew 1.2; 22.32; Acts 3.13; 7.46; Romans 9.11–13; 11.26; Hebrews 11.9, 20, 21.

reconsider. But Rebekah had become so wrapped up in her plan that she no longer saw clearly what she was doing. Sin had trapped her and was degrading her character. Correcting yourself in the middle of doing wrong can bring hurt and disappointment, but it also brings freedom from sin's control.

and go, get them for me." 14 So he went and got them and brought them to his
mother; and his mother prepared savory food, such as his father loved. 15 Then
Rebekah took the best garments of her elder son Esau, which were with her in the
house, and put them on her younger son Jacob; 16 and she put the skins of the kids
on his hands and on the smooth part of his neck. 17 Then she handed the savory
food, and the bread that she had prepared, to her son Jacob.
18 So he went in to his father, and said, "My father"; and he said, "Here I am;
who are you, my son?" 19 Jacob said to his father, "I am Esau your firstborn. I have
done as you told me; now sit up and eat of my game, so that you may bless me."
20 But Isaac said to his son, "How is it that you have found it so quickly, my son?"
He answered, "Because the LORD your God granted me success." 21 Then Isaac said
to Jacob, "Come near, that I may feel you, my son, to know whether you are really
my son Esau or not." 22 So Jacob went up to his father Isaac, who felt him and said,
"The voice is Jacob's voice, but the hands are the hands of Esau." 23 He did not
recognize him, because his hands were hairy like his brother Esau's hands; so he
blessed him. 24 He said, "Are you really my son Esau?" He answered, "I am."
25 Then he said, "Bring it to me, that I may eat of my son's game and bless you."
So he brought it to him, and he ate; and he brought him wine, and he drank. 26 Then
his father Isaac said to him, "Come near and kiss me, my son." 27 So he came near
and kissed him; and he smelled the smell of his garments, and blessed him, and
said,

"Ah, the smell of my son
is like the smell of a field that the LORD has blessed.
28 May God give you of the dew of heaven,
and of the fatness of the earth,
and plenty of grain and wine.
29 Let peoples serve you,
and nations bow down to you.
Be lord over your brothers,
and may your mother's sons bow down to you.
Cursed be everyone who curses you,
and blessed be everyone who blesses you!"

30 As soon as Isaac had finished blessing Jacob, when Jacob had scarcely gone
out from the presence of his father Isaac, his brother Esau came in from his hunting.
31 He also prepared savory food, and brought it to his father. And he said to his
father, "Let my father sit up and eat of his son's game, so that you may bless me."
32 His father Isaac said to him, "Who are you?" He answered, "I am your firstborn
son, Esau." 33 Then Isaac trembled violently, and said, "Who was it then that
hunted game and brought it to me, and I ate it all[d] before you came, and I have
blessed him?—yes, and blessed he shall be!" 34 When Esau heard his father's
words, he cried out with an exceedingly great and bitter cry, and said to his father,
"Bless me, me also, father!" 35 But he said, "Your brother came deceitfully, and he
has taken away your blessing." 36 Esau said, "Is he not rightly named Jacob?[e] For
he has supplanted me these two times. He took away my birthright; and look, now
he has taken away my blessing." Then he said, "Have you not reserved a blessing
for me?" 37 Isaac answered Esau, "I have already made him your lord, and I have

27.13 Gen 27.8,43
27.15 Gen 27.27
27.19 Gen 27.21,24, 31
27.21 Gen 27.12
27.23 Gen 27.4,16
27.24 Prov 12.19,22
27.25 Gen 27.4
27.27 Ps 65.9,10 Heb 11.20
27.28 Gen 27.39 45.18 Deut 7.13; 33.13, 28 Zech 8.12
27.29 Gen 9.25; 12.3 22.17; 49.8 Num 24.9 Isa 45.14
27.31 Gen 27.4,19
27.32 Gen 27.18
27.33 Gen 27.35 Ps 55.5
27.34 Heb 12.17
27.35 Gen 27.12, 19-23
27.36 Gen 25.26 32.28
27.37 Gen 27.27-29 2 Sam 8.14

d Cn: Heb *of all* e That is *He supplants* or *He takes by the heel*

27.14 Although Jacob got the blessing he wanted, deceiving his father cost him dearly. These are some of the consequences of that deceit: (1) he never saw his mother again; (2) his brother wanted to kill him; (3) he was deceived by his uncle, Laban; (4) his family became torn by strife; (5) Esau became the founder of an enemy nation; (6) he was exiled from his family for years. Ironically, Jacob would have received the birthright and blessing anyway (25.23). Imagine how different his life would have been had he and his mother waited for God to work his way, in his time!

27.33 In ancient times, a person's word was binding (much like a written contract today), especially when it was a formal oath. This is why Isaac's blessing was irrevocable.

27.36 *Supplant* means to take someone's place by force or treachery.

27.33–37 Before the father died, he performed a ceremony of blessing, in which he officially handed over the birthright to the rightful heir. Although the firstborn son was entitled to the birthright, it was not actually his until the blessing was pronounced. Before the blessing was given, the father could take the birthright away from the oldest son and give it to a more deserving son. But after

given him all his brothers as servants, and with grain and wine I have sustained
27.38 Gen 27.34 Heb 12.17 him. What then can I do for you, my son?" 38 Esau said to his father, "Have you
only one blessing, father? Bless me, me also, father!" And Esau lifted up his voice
and wept.
27.39 Heb 11.20 39 Then his father Isaac answered him:
"See, away from[f] the fatness of the earth shall your home be,
and away from[g] the dew of heaven on high.
27.40 2 Kgs 8.20 2 Chron 21.8 40 By your sword you shall live,
and you shall serve your brother;
but when you break loose,[h]
you shall break his yoke from your neck."
27.41 Gen 32.6 35.29; 37.4 Deut 34.8 41 Now Esau hated Jacob because of the blessing with which his father had
blessed him, and Esau said to himself, "The days of mourning for my father are
approaching; then I will kill my brother Jacob." 42 But the words of her elder son
Esau were told to Rebekah; so she sent and called her younger son Jacob and said
27.43 Gen 11.31 12.4; 27.8,13 28.10 to him, "Your brother Esau is consoling himself by planning to kill you. 43 Now
therefore, my son, obey my voice; flee at once to my brother Laban in Haran, 44 and
stay with him a while, until your brother's fury turns away— 45 until your brother's
27.44 Gen 31.41 anger against you turns away, and he forgets what you have done to him; then I will
27.45 Prov 20.21 send, and bring you back from there. Why should I lose both of you in one day?"
46 Then Rebekah said to Isaac, "I am weary of my life because of the Hittite
27.46 Gen 26.34,35 women. If Jacob marries one of the Hittite women such as these, one of the women
of the land, what good will my life be to me?"
28.1 Gen 24.3,4 **28** Then Isaac called Jacob and blessed him, and charged him, "You shall not
28.3 Gen 17.1-4 27.4,7 35.11 marry one of the Canaanite women. 2 Go at once to Paddan-aram to the
house of Bethuel, your mother's father; and take as wife from there one of the
daughters of Laban, your mother's brother. 3 May God Almighty[i] bless you and

[f] Or *See, of* [g] Or *and of* [h] Meaning of Heb uncertain [i] Traditional rendering of Heb *El Shaddai*

JACOB'S FAMILY TREE
Marrying within the extended family was common and acceptable in this day. Had Jacob married outside his family, he would have married someone who didn't believe in God. So Jacob married his cousins, Rachel and Leah.

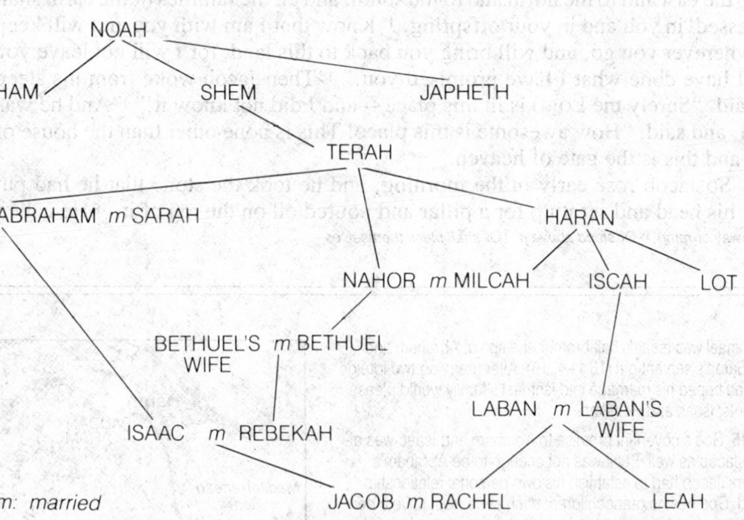

the blessing was given, the birthright could no longer be taken away. This is why fathers usually waited until late in life to pronounce the blessing. Although Jacob had been given the birthright by his older brother years before, he still needed his father's blessing to make it binding.

27.41 Esau was so angry at Jacob that he failed to see his own wrong in giving away the birthright in the first place. Jealous anger blinds us from seeing the benefits we have and makes us dwell on what we don't have.

27.41 When Esau lost the valuable family blessing, his future suddenly changed. Reacting in anger, he decided to kill Jacob. When you lose something of great value, or if others conspire against you and succeed, anger is the first and most natural reaction. But you can control your feelings by (1) recognizing your reaction for what it is, (2) praying for strength, and (3) asking God for help to see the opportunities that even your bad situation may provide.

make you fruitful and numerous, that you may become a company of peoples.
4 May he give to you the blessing of Abraham, to you and to your offspring with 28.4
you, so that you may take possession of the land where you now live as an Gen 12.1-3 15.7; 35.11
alien — land that God gave to Abraham." 5 Thus Isaac sent Jacob away; and he went 48.3
to Paddan-aram, to Laban son of Bethuel the Aramean, the brother of Rebekah,
Jacob's and Esau's mother.
6 Now Esau saw that Isaac had blessed Jacob and sent him away to Paddan-
aram to take a wife from there, and that as he blessed him he charged him, "You
shall not marry one of the Canaanite women," 7 and that Jacob had obeyed his fa- 28.7
ther and his mother and gone to Paddan-aram. 8 So when Esau saw that the Canaan- Gen 27.8 28.8
ite women did not please his father Isaac, 9 Esau went to Ishmael and took Mahalath Gen 26.34
daughter of Abraham's son Ishmael, and sister of Nebaioth, to be his wife in addi- 28.9
tion to the wives he had. Gen 36.3

F. THE STORY OF JACOB (28.10–36.43)

Jacob did everything, both right and wrong, with great zeal. He deceived his own brother Esau and his father Isaac. He wrestled with an angel and worked fourteen years to marry the woman he loved. Through Jacob we learn how a strong leader can also be a servant. We also see how wrong actions will always come back to haunt us.

1. Jacob starts a family

Jacob's dream

10 Jacob left Beer-sheba and went toward Haran. 11 He came to a certain place 28.10 Gen 12.4,5
and stayed there for the night, because the sun had set. Taking one of the stones of 26.23; 46.1
the place, he put it under his head and lay down in that place. 12 And he dreamed 28.12
that there was a ladder[j] set up on the earth, the top of it reaching to heaven; and the Gen 20.3 32.1,2; 37.5
angels of God were ascending and descending on it. 13 And the LORD stood beside Num 12.6 Jn 1.51
him[k] and said, "I am the LORD, the God of Abraham your father and the God of 28.13
Isaac; the land on which you lie I will give to you and to your offspring; 14 and your Gen 15.18
offspring shall be like the dust of the earth, and you shall spread abroad to the west 28.14 Gen 12.2
and to the east and to the north and to the south; and all the families of the earth shall 13.14,16; 22.18
be blessed[l] in you and in your offspring. 15 Know that I am with you and will keep 28.15 Gen 26.3; 48.21
you wherever you go, and will bring you back to this land; for I will not leave you Deut 7.9; 31.6,8
until I have done what I have promised you." 16 Then Jacob woke from his sleep 28.16 Ex 3.5
and said, "Surely the LORD is in this place — and I did not know it!" 17 And he was 28.17
afraid, and said, "How awesome is this place! This is none other than the house of 2 Chron 5.14
God, and this is the gate of heaven." 28.18
18 So Jacob rose early in the morning, and he took the stone that he had put Gen 35.14 28.19
under his head and set it up for a pillar and poured oil on the top of it. 19 He called Gen 12.8; 35.6

[j] Or *stairway* or *ramp* [k] Or *stood above it* [l] Or *shall bless themselves*

28.9 Ishmael was Isaac's half brother, the son of Abraham and Hagar, Sarah's servant girl (16.1–4, 15). After marrying two foreign girls, Esau hoped his marriage into Ishmael's family would please his parents, Isaac and Rebekah.

28.10–15 God's covenant promise to Abraham and Isaac was offered to Jacob as well. But it was not enough to be Abraham's grandson; Jacob had to establish his own personal relationship with God. God has no grandchildren; each of us must have a personal relationship with him. It is not enough to hear wonderful stories about Christians in your family. You need to become part of the story yourself (see Galatians 3.6, 7).

28.19 Bethel was about ten miles north of Jerusalem and 60 miles north of Beer-sheba, where Jacob left his family. This was where Abraham made one of his first sacrifices to God when he entered the land. Later Bethel became a center of idol worship, and the prophet Hosea condemned its evil practices.

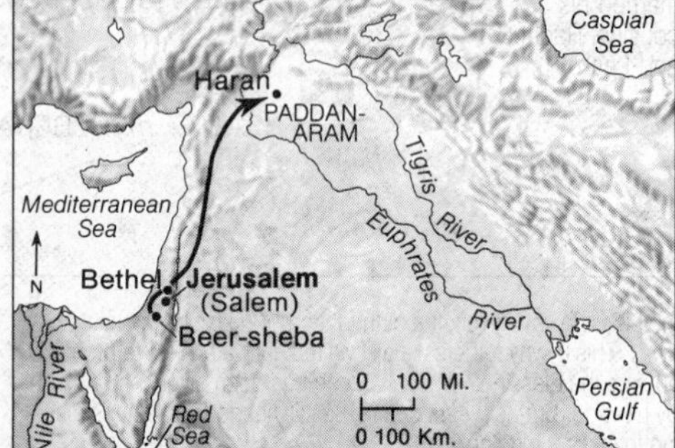

JACOB'S TRIP TO HARAN After deceiving Esau, Jacob ran for his life, traveling more than 400 miles to Haran where an uncle, Laban, lived. In Haran, Jacob married and started a family.

that place Bethel;[m] but the name of the city was Luz at the first. 20 Then Jacob made
a vow, saying, "If God will be with me, and will keep me in this way that I go, and
28.21 Gen 35.3 will give me bread to eat and clothing to wear, 21 so that I come again to my father's
Ex 15.2 house in peace, then the LORD shall be my God, 22 and this stone, which I have set
28.22 Gen 14.20; 35.7 up for a pillar, shall be God's house; and of all that you give me I will surely give
Deut 14.22 one tenth to you."

Jacob meets Rachel

29.1 Judg 6.3,33 **29** Then Jacob went on his journey, and came to the land of the people of the
east. 2 As he looked, he saw a well in the field and three flocks of sheep lying
29.2 Gen 24.11 there beside it; for out of that well the flocks were watered. The stone on the well's
mouth was large, 3 and when all the flocks were gathered there, the shepherds
would roll the stone from the mouth of the well, and water the sheep, and put the
stone back in its place on the mouth of the well.

29.4 Gen 11.31 4 Jacob said to them, "My brothers, where do you come from?" They said, "We
28.10 are from Haran." 5 He said to them, "Do you know Laban son of Nahor?" They
29.5 said, "We do." 6 He said to them, "Is it well with him?" "Yes," they replied, "and
Gen 24.29 here is his daughter Rachel, coming with the sheep." 7 He said, "Look, it is still
29.6 Gen 37.14 broad daylight; it is not time for the animals to be gathered together. Water the
43.27 sheep, and go, pasture them." 8 But they said, "We cannot until all the flocks are
gathered together, and the stone is rolled from the mouth of the well; then we water
the sheep."

9 While he was still speaking with them, Rachel came with her father's sheep;
29.10 Ex 2.16 for she kept them. 10 Now when Jacob saw Rachel, the daughter of his mother's
brother Laban, and the sheep of his mother's brother Laban, Jacob went up and
rolled the stone from the well's mouth, and watered the flock of his mother's
29.11 Gen 27.26; 33.4 brother Laban. 11 Then Jacob kissed Rachel, and wept aloud. 12 And Jacob told
29.12 Rachel that he was her father's kinsman, and that he was Rebekah's son; and she
Gen 28.5 ran and told her father.

13 When Laban heard the news about his sister's son Jacob, he ran to meet him;
he embraced him and kissed him, and brought him to his house. Jacob[n] told Laban
29.14 all these things, 14 and Laban said to him, "Surely you are my bone and my flesh!"
Judg 9.2 2 Sam 5.1 And he stayed with him a month.

Jacob marries two sisters

29.15 15 Then Laban said to Jacob, "Because you are my kinsman, should you there-
Gen 30.28 31.7,41 fore serve me for nothing? Tell me, what shall your wages be?" 16 Now Laban had
29.16 two daughters; the name of the elder was Leah, and the name of the younger was
Gen 29.25,26 Rachel. 17 Leah's eyes were lovely,[o] and Rachel was graceful and beautiful. 18 Ja-
29.17 Gen 12.11; 26.7 cob loved Rachel; so he said, "I will serve you seven years for your younger daugh-
1 Sam 25.3 ter Rachel." 19 Laban said, "It is better that I give her to you than that I should give
29.18 Gen 24.67 her to any other man; stay with me." 20 So Jacob served seven years for Rachel, and
Hos 12.12 they seemed to him but a few days because of the love he had for her.

21 Then Jacob said to Laban, "Give me my wife that I may go in to her, for my

[m] That is *House of God* [n] Heb *He* [o] Meaning of Heb uncertain

28.20–22 Was Jacob trying to bargain with God? It is possible that he, in his ignorance of how to worship and serve God, treated God like a servant who would perform a service for a tip? Or perhaps Jacob was not bargaining, but pledging his future to God. He may have been saying, in effect, "Because you have blessed me, I will follow you." Whether Jacob was bargaining or pledging, God blessed him. But God also had some difficult lessons for Jacob to learn.

29.18–27 It was the custom of the day for a man to present a dowry, or substantial gift, to the family of his future wife. This was to compensate the family for the loss of the girl. Jacob's dowry was not a material possession, for he had none to offer. Instead he agreed to work seven years for Laban. But there was another custom of the land that Laban did not tell Jacob. The older daughter had to be married first. By giving Jacob Leah and not Rachel, Laban tricked him into promising another seven years of hard work.

29.20–28 People often wonder if waiting a long time for something they desire is worth it. Jacob waited seven years to marry Rachel. After being tricked, he agreed to work seven more years for her! The most important goals and desires are worth working and waiting for. Movies and television have created the illusion that people have to wait only about an hour to solve their problems or get what they want. Don't be trapped into thinking the same is true in real life. Patience is hardest when we need it the most, but it is the key to achieving our goals.

time is completed." 22 So Laban gathered together all the people of the place, and
made a feast. 23 But in the evening he took his daughter Leah and brought her to
Jacob; and he went in to her. 24 (Laban gave his maid Zilpah to his daughter Leah
to be her maid.) 25 When morning came, it was Leah! And Jacob said to Laban,
"What is this you have done to me? Did I not serve with you for Rachel? Why then
have you deceived me?" 26 Laban said, "This is not done in our country—giving
the younger before the firstborn. 27 Complete the week of this one, and we will give
you the other also in return for serving me another seven years." 28 Jacob did so,
and completed her week; then Laban gave him his daughter Rachel as a wife.
29 (Laban gave his maid Bilhah to his daughter Rachel to be her maid.) 30 So Jacob
went in to Rachel also, and he loved Rachel more than Leah. He served Laban[p] for
another seven years.

Jacob's many sons

31 When the LORD saw that Leah was unloved, he opened her womb; but Rachel was barren. 32 Leah conceived and bore a son, and she named him Reuben;[q]
for she said, "Because the LORD has looked on my affliction; surely now my husband will love me." 33 She conceived again and bore a son, and said, "Because the
LORD has heard[r] that I am hated, he has given me this son also"; and she named
him Simeon. 34 Again she conceived and bore a son, and said, "Now this time my
husband will be joined[s] to me, because I have borne him three sons"; therefore he
was named Levi. 35 She conceived again and bore a son, and said, "This time I will
praise[t] the LORD"; therefore she named him Judah; then she ceased bearing.

30 When Rachel saw that she bore Jacob no children, she envied her sister; and
she said to Jacob, "Give me children, or I shall die!" 2 Jacob became very
angry with Rachel and said, "Am I in the place of God, who has withheld from you
the fruit of the womb?" 3 Then she said, "Here is my maid Bilhah; go in to her, that
she may bear upon my knees and that I too may have children through her." 4 So she
gave him her maid Bilhah as a wife; and Jacob went in to her. 5 And Bilhah conceived and bore Jacob a son. 6 Then Rachel said, "God has judged me, and has also
heard my voice and given me a son"; therefore she named him Dan.[u] 7 Rachel's
maid Bilhah conceived again and bore Jacob a second son. 8 Then Rachel said,
"With mighty wrestlings I have wrestled[v] with my sister, and have prevailed"; so
she named him Naphtali.

9 When Leah saw that she had ceased bearing children, she took her maid Zilpah and gave her to Jacob as a wife. 10 Then Leah's maid Zilpah bore Jacob a son.
11 And Leah said, "Good fortune!" so she named him Gad.[w] 12 Leah's maid Zilpah

29.22 Judg 14.10
29.23 Gen 24.65
29.24 Gen 30.9
29.25 Gen 12.18 27.35
29.27 Lev 18.18 Judg 14.10,12
29.29 Gen 30.3-8
29.30 Gen 29.17
29.31 Gen 20.18 Deut 21.15 Mal 1.2,3
29.32 Gen 35.23 37.21; 42.22 46.8,9
29.33 Gen 30.6
29.34 Gen 49.5
29.35 Gen 49.8
30.1 1 Sam 1.4-7
30.2 Gen 25.21
30.3 Gen 16.2
30.4 Gen 22.24 35.22
30.6 Gen 29.32
30.8 Gen 32.24 Mt 4.13
30.11 Gen 35.26 46.16; 49.19

[p] Heb *him* [q] That is *See, a son* [r] Heb *shama* [s] Heb *lawah* [t] Heb *hodah* [u] That is *He judged* [v] Heb *niphtal*
[w] That is *Fortune*

29.23–25 Jacob flew into a rage when he learned that Laban had tricked him. The deceiver of Esau was now deceived himself. How natural it is for us to become enraged at an injustice done to us while closing our eyes to the injustices we do to others. Sin has a way of coming back to haunt us.

29.28–30 Although Jacob was tricked by Laban, he kept his part of the bargain. There was more at stake than just Jacob's hurt. There was Rachel to think about, as well as God's plan for his life. When we are tricked by others, keeping our part of the bargain may still be wise. Nursing our wounds or plotting revenge makes us unable to see from God's perspective.

29.32 Today parents usually give their children names that sound good or have sentimental appeal. But the Old Testament portrays a more dynamic use of names. Parents hoped their children would fulfill the meaning of the names given them. Later the parents could look back and see if their grown children had lived up to their names. Sometimes a person's name was changed because his or her character and name did not match. This happened to Jacob ("one who supplants"), whose name was changed to Israel ("a prince who prevails with God"). Jacob's character had changed to the point that he was no longer seen as a deceiver, but as a God-honoring man.

30.3 "Bear upon my knees" means to "have a child in my place." Each of the three great patriarchs (Abraham, Isaac, and Jacob) had wives who had difficulty conceiving children. It is interesting to note how each man reacted to his wife's predicament. Abraham had relations with Sarah's servant girl in order to have his own child, thus introducing bitterness and jealousy into his family. Isaac, by contrast, prayed to God when his wife was barren. God eventually answered his prayers, and Rebekah had twin sons. Jacob, however, followed his grandfather's example and had children by his wives' servant girls, leading to sad and sometimes bitter consequences.

30.4–12 Rachel and Leah were locked in a cruel contest. In their race to have more children, they both gave their servant girls to Jacob as concubines. Jacob would have been wise to refuse, even though this was an accepted custom of the day. The fact that a custom is socially acceptable does not mean it is wise or right. You will be spared much heartbreak if you look at the potential consequences, to you or others, of your actions. Are you doing anything now that might cause future problems?

bore Jacob a second son. 13 And Leah said, "Happy am I! For the women will call
me happy"; so she named him Asher.[x]
30.14 Song 7.13 14 In the days of wheat harvest Reuben went and found mandrakes in the field,
and brought them to his mother Leah. Then Rachel said to Leah, "Please give me
some of your son's mandrakes." 15 But she said to her, "Is it a small matter that you
have taken away my husband? Would you take away my son's mandrakes also?"
Rachel said, "Then he may lie with you tonight for your son's mandrakes." 16 When
Jacob came from the field in the evening, Leah went out to meet him, and said,
"You must come in to me; for I have hired you with my son's mandrakes." So he
30.17 Gen 29.31; 30.6 Ex 3.7 lay with her that night. 17 And God heeded Leah, and she conceived and bore Jacob
a fifth son. 18 Leah said, "God has given me my hire[y] because I gave my maid to
30.18 Gen 35.23 49.14,15 my husband"; so she named him Issachar. 19 And Leah conceived again, and she
bore Jacob a sixth son. 20 Then Leah said, "God has endowed me with a good
30.20 Mt 4.13 dowry; now my husband will honor[z] me, because I have borne him six sons"; so
she named him Zebulun. 21 Afterwards she bore a daughter, and named her Dinah.

[x] That is *Happy* [y] Heb *sakar* [z] Heb *zabal*

RACHEL

History seems to repeat itself here. Twice a town well at Haran was the site of significant events in one family's story. It was here that Rebekah met Eliezer, Abraham's servant, who had come to find a wife for Isaac. Some 40 years later, Rebekah's son Jacob returned the favor by serving his cousin Rachel and her sheep from the same well. The relationship that developed between them not only reminds us that romance is not a modern invention, but also teaches us a few lessons about patience and love.

Jacob's love for Rachel was both patient and practical. Jacob had the patience to wait seven years for her, but he kept busy in the meantime. His commitment to Rachel kindled a strong loyalty within her. In fact, her loyalty to Jacob got out of hand and became self-destructive. She was frustrated by her barrenness and desperate to compete with her sister for Jacob's affection. She was trying to gain from Jacob what he had already given: devoted love.

Rachel's attempts to earn the unearnable are a picture of a much greater error we can make. Like her, we find ourselves trying somehow to earn love—God's love. But apart from his Word, we end up with one of two false ideas. Either we think we've been good enough to deserve his love or we recognize we aren't able to earn his love and assume that it cannot be ours. If the Bible makes no other point, it shouts this one: God loves us! His love had no beginning and is incredibly patient. All we need to do is respond, not try to earn what is freely offered. God has said in many ways, "I love you. I have demonstrated that love to you by all I've done for you. I have even sacrificed my Son, Jesus, to pay the price for what is unacceptable about you—your sin. Now, live because of my love. Respond to me; love me with your whole being; give yourself to me in thanksgiving, not as payment." Live life fully, in the freedom of knowing you are loved.

Strengths and accomplishments:
- She showed great loyalty to her family
- She mothered Joseph and Benjamin after being barren for many years

Weaknesses and mistakes:
- Her envy and competitiveness marred her relationship with her sister, Leah
- She was capable of dishonesty when she took her loyalty too far
- She failed to recognize that Jacob's devotion was not dependent on her ability to have children

Lessons from her life:
- Loyalty must be controlled by what is true and right
- Love is accepted, not earned

Vital statistics:
- Where: Haran
- Occupation: Shepherdess, housewife
- Relatives: Father: Laban. Aunt: Rebekah. Sister: Leah. Husband: Jacob. Sons: Joseph and Benjamin

Key verse:
"So Jacob served seven years for Rachel, and they seemed to him but a few days because of the love he had for her" (Genesis 29.20).

Rachel's story is told in Genesis 29—35.20. She is also mentioned in Ruth 4.11.

22 Then God remembered Rachel, and God heeded her and opened her womb. **30.22**
23 She conceived and bore a son, and said, "God has taken away my reproach"; 1 Sam 1.19
24 and she named him Joseph,[a] saying, "May the LORD add to me another son!" **30.24** Gen 35.17

Jacob becomes wealthy

25 When Rachel had borne Joseph, Jacob said to Laban, "Send me away, that
I may go to my own home and country. 26 Give me my wives and my children for **30.26**
whom I have served you, and let me go; for you know very well the service I have Gen 29.18,27 Hos 12.12
given you." 27 But Laban said to him, "If you will allow me to say so, I have learned **30.27**
by divination that the LORD has blessed me because of you; 28 name your wages, Gen 18.3 39.2-5
and I will give it." 29 Jacob said to him, "You yourself know how I have served you, **30.28**
and how your cattle have fared with me. 30 For you had little before I came, and it Gen 29.15; 31.7
has increased abundantly; and the LORD has blessed you wherever I turned. But **30.30** Gen 30.43
now when shall I provide for my own household also?" 31 He said, "What shall I
give you?" Jacob said, "You shall not give me anything; if you will do this for me,
I will again feed your flock and keep it: 32 let me pass through all your flock today, **30.32**
removing from it every speckled and spotted sheep and every black lamb, and the Gen 31.8,10,12
spotted and speckled among the goats; and such shall be my wages. 33 So my honesty will answer for me later, when you come to look into my wages with you.
Every one that is not speckled and spotted among the goats and black among the
lambs, if found with me, shall be counted stolen." 34 Laban said, "Good! Let it be
as you have said." 35 But that day Laban removed the male goats that were striped
and spotted, and all the female goats that were speckled and spotted, every one that
had white on it, and every lamb that was black, and put them in charge of his sons;
36 and he set a distance of three days' journey between himself and Jacob, while
Jacob was pasturing the rest of Laban's flock.

37 Then Jacob took fresh rods of poplar and almond and plane, and peeled **30.37**
white streaks in them, exposing the white of the rods. 38 He set the rods that he had Gen 31.9-13
peeled in front of the flocks in the troughs, that is, the watering places, where the
flocks came to drink. And since they bred when they came to drink, 39 the flocks
bred in front of the rods, and so the flocks produced young that were striped, speckled, and spotted. 40 Jacob separated the lambs, and set the faces of the flocks toward
the striped and the completely black animals in the flock of Laban; and he put his
own droves apart, and did not put them with Laban's flock. 41 Whenever the stronger
of the flock were breeding, Jacob laid the rods in the troughs before the eyes of
the flock, that they might breed among the rods, 42 but for the feebler of the flock
he did not lay them there; so the feebler were Laban's, and the stronger Jacob's. **30.43**
43 Thus the man grew exceedingly rich, and had large flocks, and male and female Gen 13.2 24.35; 26.13
slaves, and camels and donkeys. 33.11

2. Jacob returns home

Jacob flees Laban

31 Now Jacob heard that the sons of Laban were saying, "Jacob has taken all **31.1**
that was our father's; he has gained all this wealth from what belonged to Prov 27.4
our father." 2 And Jacob saw that Laban did not regard him as favorably as he did **31.2**
before. 3 Then the LORD said to Jacob, "Return to the land of your ancestors and to Gen 31.36 1 Sam 18.9

[a] That is *He adds*

30.22–24 Eventually God answered Rachel's prayers and gave her a child of her own. In the meantime, however, she had given her servant girl to Jacob. Trusting God when nothing seems to happen is difficult. But it is harder still to live with the consequences of taking matters into our own hands. Resist the temptation to think God has forgotten you. Have patience and courage to wait for God to act.

30.27 Laban claimed to have learned by "divination" that God had blessed him because of Jacob. In other words, he thought his idols had given him this insight.

31.1–3 Jacob's wealth made Laban's sons jealous. It is sometimes difficult to be happy when others are doing better than we are. To compare our success with that of others is a dangerous way to judge the quality of our lives. By comparing ourselves to others, we may be giving jealousy a foothold. We can avoid jealousy by rejoicing in others' successes (see Romans 12.15).

31.3 Gen 28.15; 32.9
31.5 Gen 31.42,53
31.6 Gen 30.29
31.7 Gen 29.15; 30.28; 31.41
31.8 Gen 30.32
31.9 Gen 31.1,16
31.10 Gen 31.24
31.11 Gen 16.7-13; 18.1; 22.1,11
31.12 Gen 30.37-43; Ex 3.7; Lev 19.13; Deut 24.14,15
31.13 Gen 28.13-19; 35.7
31.15 Gen 29.20,27; 30.26-28

your kindred, and I will be with you." 4 So Jacob sent and called Rachel and Leah
into the field where his flock was, 5 and said to them, "I see that your father does not
regard me as favorably as he did before. But the God of my father has been with
me. 6 You know that I have served your father with all my strength; 7 yet your father
has cheated me and changed my wages ten times, but God did not permit him to
harm me. 8 If he said, 'The speckled shall be your wages,' then all the flock bore
speckled; and if he said, 'The striped shall be your wages,' then all the flock bore
striped. 9 Thus God has taken away the livestock of your father, and given them to
me.

10 During the mating of the flock I once had a dream in which I looked up and
saw that the male goats that leaped upon the flock were striped, speckled, and mottled. 11 Then the angel of God said to me in the dream, 'Jacob,' and I said, 'Here I
am!' 12 And he said, 'Look up and see that all the goats that leap on the flock are
striped, speckled, and mottled; for I have seen all that Laban is doing to you. 13 I am
the God of Bethel,[b] where you anointed a pillar and made a vow to me. Now leave
this land at once and return to the land of your birth.' " 14 Then Rachel and Leah
answered him, "Is there any portion or inheritance left to us in our father's house?
15 Are we not regarded by him as foreigners? For he has sold us, and he has been
using up the money given for us. 16 All the property that God has taken away from
our father belongs to us and to our children; now then, do whatever God has said to
you."

17 So Jacob arose, and set his children and his wives on camels; 18 and he drove

[b] Cn: Meaning of Heb uncertain

JACOB'S CHILDREN
This chart shows from left to right Jacob's children in the order in which they were born.

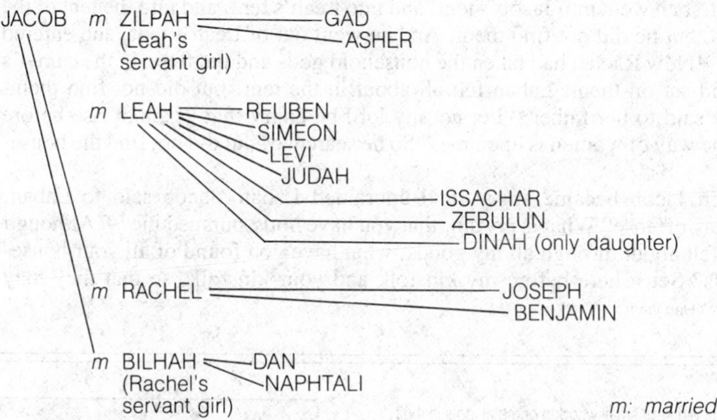

Jacob's many wives (two wives and two "substitute" wives) led to sad and bitter consequences among the children. Anger, resentment, and jealousy were common among Jacob's sons. It is interesting to note that the worst fighting and rivalry occurred between Leah's children and Rachel's children, and among the tribes that descended from them.

31.4–13 Although Laban treated Jacob unfairly, God still increased Jacob's prosperity. God's power is not limited by lack of fair play. He has the ability to meet our needs and make us thrive even though others mistreat us. To give in and respond unfairly in return is to be no different from your enemies.

31.14, 15 Leaving home was not difficult for Rachel and Leah because their father had treated them as poorly as he had Jacob. According to custom, they were supposed to receive the benefits of the dowry Jacob paid for them, which was 14 years of hard work. When Laban did not give them what was rightfully theirs, they knew they would never inherit anything from their father. Thus they wholeheartedly approved of Jacob's plan to take the wealth he had gained and leave.

away all his livestock, all the property that he had gained, the livestock in his possession that he had acquired in Paddan-aram, to go to his father Isaac in the land of
Canaan.
19 Now Laban had gone to shear his sheep, and Rachel stole her father's household gods. 20 And Jacob deceived Laban the Aramean, in that he did not tell him
that he intended to flee. 21 So he fled with all that he had; starting out he crossed the
Euphrates,[c] and set his face toward the hill country of Gilead.

Laban pursues Jacob

22 On the third day Laban was told that Jacob had fled. 23 So he took his kinsfolk with him and pursued him for seven days until he caught up with him in the hill
country of Gilead. 24 But God came to Laban the Aramean in a dream by night, and
said to him, "Take heed that you say not a word to Jacob, either good or bad."
25 Laban overtook Jacob. Now Jacob had pitched his tent in the hill country,
and Laban with his kinsfolk camped in the hill country of Gilead. 26 Laban said to
Jacob, "What have you done? You have deceived me, and carried away my daughters like captives of the sword. 27 Why did you flee secretly and deceive me and not
tell me? I would have sent you away with mirth and songs, with tambourine and
lyre. 28 And why did you not permit me to kiss my sons and my daughters farewell?
What you have done is foolish. 29 It is in my power to do you harm; but the God of
your father spoke to me last night, saying, 'Take heed that you speak to Jacob
neither good nor bad.' 30 Even though you had to go because you longed greatly for
your father's house, why did you steal my gods?" 31 Jacob answered Laban, "Because I was afraid, for I thought that you would take your daughters from me by
force. 32 But anyone with whom you find your gods shall not live. In the presence
of our kinsfolk, point out what I have that is yours, and take it." Now Jacob did not
know that Rachel had stolen the gods.[d]
33 So Laban went into Jacob's tent, and into Leah's tent, and into the tent of the
two maids, but he did not find them. And he went out of Leah's tent, and entered
Rachel's. 34 Now Rachel had taken the household gods and put them in the camel's
saddle, and sat on them. Laban felt all about in the tent, but did not find them.
35 And she said to her father, "Let not my lord be angry that I cannot rise before
you, for the way of women is upon me." So he searched, but did not find the household gods.
36 Then Jacob became angry, and upbraided Laban. Jacob said to Laban,
"What is my offense? What is my sin, that you have hotly pursued me? 37 Although
you have felt about through all my goods, what have you found of all your household goods? Set it here before my kinsfolk and your kinsfolk, so that they may

31.18 Gen 24.29 25.20
31.20 Gen 31.27
31.21 Gen 15.18 Num 32.1 Deut 3.12 Judg 17.4,5
31.22 Gen 30.36
31.24 Gen 25.20 31.10
31.25 Gen 33.18
31.28 Gen 29.13 31.55 Ex 4.27
31.29 Gen 31.24,42
31.30 Gen 31.21
31.31 Gen 20.11
31.32 Gen 44.9 1 Sam 12.3
31.35 Gen 18.11
31.36 Gen 30.2 Num 16.15
31.37 Gen 31.32 Josh 7.23

[c] Heb *the river* [d] Heb *them*

31.19 Many people kept small wooden or metal idols in their homes. These idols were called *teraphim,* and they were thought to protect the home and offer advice in times of need. They had legal significance as well, for when they were passed on to an heir, the person who received them could rightfully claim the greatest part of the family inheritance. No wonder Laban was concerned when he realized his idols were missing (31.30). Most likely Rachel stole her father's idols because she was afraid Laban would consult them and learn where she and Jacob had gone, or perhaps she wanted to claim the family inheritance.

31.32 Can you remember feeling absolutely sure about something? Jacob was so sure that no one had stolen Laban's idols that he vowed to kill the offender. Since Rachel took them, this statement put her safety in serious jeopardy. Even when you are absolutely sure about a matter, it is safer to avoid rash statements. Someone may hold you to them.

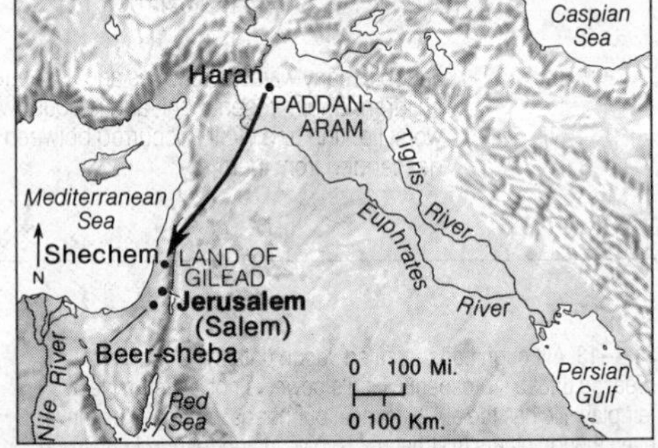

JACOB'S RETURN TO CANAAN God told Jacob to leave Haran and return to his homeland. Jacob took his family, crossed the Euphrates River, and headed first for the land of Gilead. Laban caught up with him there.

31.38 Gen 31.41
31.39 Ex 22.10-13
31.41 Gen 29.27 30.27-32
31.42 Gen 28.13-15, 20; 31.29
31.44 Gen 21.27 26.28-31
31.45 Gen 28.18 Josh 24.26,27

decide between us two. 38 These twenty years I have been with you; your ewes and
your female goats have not miscarried, and I have not eaten the rams of your flocks.
39 That which was torn by wild beasts I did not bring to you; I bore the loss of it
myself; of my hand you required it, whether stolen by day or stolen by night. 40 It
was like this with me: by day the heat consumed me, and the cold by night, and my
sleep fled from my eyes. 41 These twenty years I have been in your house; I served
you fourteen years for your two daughters, and six years for your flock, and you
have changed my wages ten times. 42 If the God of my father, the God of Abraham
and the Fear[e] of Isaac, had not been on my side, surely now you would have sent
me away empty-handed. God saw my affliction and the labor of my hands, and
rebuked you last night."

43 Then Laban answered and said to Jacob, "The daughters are my daughters,
the children are my children, the flocks are my flocks, and all that you see is mine.
But what can I do today about these daughters of mine, or about their children
whom they have borne? 44 Come now, let us make a covenant, you and I; and let it
be a witness between you and me." 45 So Jacob took a stone, and set it up as a pillar.

[e] Meaning of Heb uncertain

LABAN

We're all selfish, but some of us have a real corner on the weakness. Laban's whole life was stamped by self-centeredness. His chief goal was to look out for himself. The way he treated others was controlled by that goal. He made profitable arrangements for his sister Rebekah's marriage to Isaac and used his daughters' lives as bargaining chips. Jacob eventually outmaneuvered Laban, but the older man was unwilling to admit defeat. His hold on Jacob was broken, but he still tried to maintain some kind of control by getting Jacob to promise to be gone for good. He realized that Jacob and Jacob's God were more than he could handle.

On the surface, we may find it difficult to identify with Laban. But his selfishness is one point we have in common. Like him, we often have a strong tendency to control people and events to our benefit. Our "good" reasons for treating others the way we do may simply be a thin cover on our self-centered motives. We may not even recognize our own selfishness. One way to discover it is to examine our willingness to admit we're wrong. Laban could not bring himself to do this. If you ever amaze yourself by what you say and do to avoid facing up to wrong actions, you are getting a glimpse of your selfishness in action. Recognizing selfishness is painful, but it is the first step on the road back to God.

Strengths and accomplishments:
- Controlled two generations of marriages in the Abrahamic family (Rebekah, Rachel, Leah)
- Quick-witted

Weaknesses and mistakes:
- Manipulated others for his own benefit
- Unwilling to admit wrongdoing
- Benefited financially by using Jacob, but never fully benefited spiritually by knowing and worshiping Jacob's God

Lessons from his life:
- Those who set out to use people will eventually find themselves used
- God's plan cannot be blocked

Vital statistics:
- Where: Haran
- Occupation: Wealthy sheep breeder
- Relatives: Father: Bethuel. Sister: Rebekah. Brother-in-law: Isaac. Daughters: Rachel and Leah. Son-in-law: Jacob

Key verse:
"If the God of my father, the God of Abraham and the Fear of Isaac, had not been on my side, surely now you would have sent me away empty-handed. God saw my affliction and the labor of my hands and rebuked you last night" (Genesis 31.42).

Laban's story is told in Genesis 24.1—31.55.

31.38–42 Jacob made it a habit to do more than was expected of him. When his flocks were attacked, he took the losses rather than splitting them with Laban. He worked hard even after several pay cuts. His diligence eventually paid off; his flocks began to multiply. Making a habit of doing more than expected can pay off. It (1) pleases God, (2) earns recognition and advancement, (3) enhances your reputation, (4) builds others' confidence in you, (5) gives you more experience and knowledge, and (6) develops your spiritual maturity.

46 And Jacob said to his kinsfolk, "Gather stones," and they took stones, and made
a heap; and they ate there by the heap. 47 Laban called it Jegar-sahadutha:[f] but
Jacob called it Galeed.[g] 48 Laban said, "This heap is a witness between you and me
today." Therefore he called it Galeed, 49 and the pillar[h] Mizpah,[i] for he said, "The
LORD watch between you and me, when we are absent one from the other. 50 If you
ill-treat my daughters, or if you take wives in addition to my daughters, though no
one else is with us, remember that God is witness between you and me."
51 Then Laban said to Jacob, "See this heap and see the pillar, which I have set
between you and me. 52 This heap is a witness, and the pillar is a witness, that I will
not pass beyond this heap to you, and you will not pass beyond this heap and this
pillar to me, for harm. 53 May the God of Abraham and the God of Nahor"—the
God of their father—"judge between us." So Jacob swore by the Fear[j] of his father
Isaac, 54 and Jacob offered a sacrifice on the height and called his kinsfolk to eat
bread; and they ate bread and tarried all night in the hill country.
55[k] Early in the morning Laban rose up, and kissed his grandchildren and his
daughters and blessed them; then he departed and returned home.

Jacob takes gifts to Esau

32 Jacob went on his way and the angels of God met him; 2 and when Jacob saw
them he said, "This is God's camp!" So he called that place Mahanaim.[l]
3 Jacob sent messengers before him to his brother Esau in the land of Seir, the
country of Edom, 4 instructing them, "Thus you shall say to my lord Esau: Thus
says your servant Jacob, 'I have lived with Laban as an alien, and stayed until now;
5 and I have oxen, donkeys, flocks, male and female slaves; and I have sent to tell
my lord, in order that I may find favor in your sight.' "
6 The messengers returned to Jacob, saying, "We came to your brother Esau,
and he is coming to meet you, and four hundred men are with him." 7 Then Jacob
was greatly afraid and distressed; and he divided the people that were with him, and
the flocks and herds and camels, into two companies, 8 thinking, "If Esau comes to
the one company and destroys it, then the company that is left will escape."
9 And Jacob said, "O God of my father Abraham and God of my father Isaac,
O LORD who said to me, 'Return to your country and to your kindred, and I will do
you good,' 10 I am not worthy of the least of all the steadfast love and all the faithfulness that you have shown to your servant, for with only my staff I crossed this
Jordan; and now I have become two companies. 11 Deliver me, please, from the
hand of my brother, from the hand of Esau, for I am afraid of him; he may come and
kill us all, the mothers with the children. 12 Yet you have said, 'I will surely do you
good, and make your offspring as the sand of the sea, which cannot be counted
because of their number.' "
13 So he spent that night there, and from what he had with him he took a present
for his brother Esau, 14 two hundred female goats and twenty male goats, two hundred ewes and twenty rams, 15 thirty milch camels and their colts, forty cows and
ten bulls, twenty female donkeys and ten male donkeys. 16 These he delivered into
the hand of his servants, every drove by itself, and said to his servants, "Pass on
ahead of me, and put a space between drove and drove." 17 He instructed the fore-

31.46 Gen 35.14 Josh 4.5
31.48 Gen 21.30 Deut 4.26
31.49 Judg 10.17 11.11,29
31.50 Judg 11.10 1 Sam 12.5 Jer 29.23; 42.5
31.52 Gen 31.29,42
31.53 Gen 28.13
31.54 Gen 26.30 Ex 18.12
31.55 Gen 31.28; 33.4
32.1 Gen 16.7 18.1,2; 19.1 22.11; 31.11 2 Kgs 6.16,17 Ps 34.7
32.2 Josh 13.26 21.38 2 Sam 2.8
32.3 Gen 14.5,6 25.30; 27.41 Mal 3.1
32.4 Gen 31.17,18
32.8 Gen 33.1-3
32.9 Gen 28.13-15 31.13
32.10 Gen 24.27
32.11 Gen 27.41; 33.4
32.12 Gen 28.14,15

[f] In Aramaic *The heap of witness* [g] In Hebrew *The heap of witness* [h] Compare Sam: MT lacks *the pillar* [i] That is *Watchpost* [j] Meaning of Heb uncertain [k] Ch 32.1 in Heb [l] Here taken to mean *Two camps*

31.49 To be binding, an agreement had to be witnessed by a third party. In this case, Jacob and Laban used God as their witness that they would keep their word.

32.1 Why did angels of God meet Jacob? In the Bible, angels often intervened in human situations. Although angels often came in human form, these angels must have looked different, for Jacob recognized them at once. The reason these angels met Jacob is unclear; but because of their visit, Jacob knew God was with him.

32.3 The last time Jacob had seen Esau, his brother was ready to kill him for stealing the family blessing (25.29–27.42). Esau was so angry he had vowed to kill Jacob as soon as their father, Isaac, died (27.41). Fearing their reunion, Jacob sent a messenger ahead with gifts. He hoped to buy Esau's favor.

32.9–12 How would you feel knowing you were about to meet the person you had cheated out of his most precious possession? Jacob had taken Esau's birthright (25.33) and his blessings (27.27–40). Now he was about to meet this brother for the first time in 20 years, and he was frantic with fear. He collected his thoughts, however, and decided to pray. When we face a difficult conflict, we can run about frantically or we can pause to pray. Which approach will be more effective?

32.18 Gen 32.4,5
32.20 Gen 43.11,12; 1 Sam 25.18; Prov 21.14

most, "When Esau my brother meets you, and asks you, 'To whom do you belong?
Where are you going? And whose are these ahead of you?' 18 then you shall say,
'They belong to your servant Jacob; they are a present sent to my lord Esau; and
moreover he is behind us.' " 19 He likewise instructed the second and the third and
all who followed the droves, "You shall say the same thing to Esau when you meet
him, 20 and you shall say, 'Moreover your servant Jacob is behind us.' " For he
thought, "I may appease him with the present that goes ahead of me, and afterwards
I shall see his face; perhaps he will accept me." 21 So the present passed on ahead
of him; and he himself spent that night in the camp.

Jacob wrestles with an angel

32.22 Deut 3.16; Josh 12.2
32.24 Gen 18.3; Hos 12.3,4
32.26 Ex 32.10; 1 Chron 4.10; Ps 67.1,6,7
32.28 Gen 35.10; 1 Kgs 18.31
32.29 Ex 3.13; Judg 13.17
32.30 Gen 16.13; Ex 24.10; 33.20; Deut 5.24; 34.10; Judg 6.22
32.31 Judg 8.8,9,17

22 The same night he got up and took his two wives, his two maids, and his
eleven children, and crossed the ford of the Jabbok. 23 He took them and sent them
across the stream, and likewise everything that he had. 24 Jacob was left alone; and
a man wrestled with him until daybreak. 25 When the man saw that he did not prevail against Jacob, he struck him on the hip socket; and Jacob's hip was put out of
joint as he wrestled with him. 26 Then he said, "Let me go, for the day is breaking."
But Jacob said, "I will not let you go, unless you bless me." 27 So he said to him,
"What is your name?" And he said, "Jacob." 28 Then the man[m] said, "You shall no
longer be called Jacob, but Israel,[n] for you have striven with God and with humans,[o] and have prevailed." 29 Then Jacob asked him, "Please tell me your name."
But he said, "Why is it that you ask my name?" And there he blessed him. 30 So
Jacob called the place Peniel,[p] saying, "For I have seen God face to face, and yet
my life is preserved." 31 The sun rose upon him as he passed Penuel, limping because of his hip. 32 Therefore to this day the Israelites do not eat the thigh muscle
that is on the hip socket, because he struck Jacob on the hip socket at the thigh
muscle.

The brothers make peace

33.1 Gen 32.6,16
33.3 Gen 18.2; 42.6; Prov 6.3
33.4 Gen 45.14; 46.29
33.5 Gen 48.8,9

33 Now Jacob looked up and saw Esau coming, and four hundred men with
him. So he divided the children among Leah and Rachel and the two maids.
2 He put the maids with their children in front, then Leah with her children, and
Rachel and Joseph last of all. 3 He himself went on ahead of them, bowing himself
to the ground seven times, until he came near his brother.
4 But Esau ran to meet him, and embraced him, and fell on his neck and kissed
him, and they wept. 5 When Esau looked up and saw the women and children, he
said, "Who are these with you?" Jacob said, "The children whom God has graciously given your servant." 6 Then the maids drew near, they and their children,
and bowed down; 7 Leah likewise and her children drew near and bowed down; and

[m] Heb *he* [n] That is *The one who strives with God* or *God strives* [o] Or *with divine and human beings* [p] That is *The face of God*

32.26 Jacob continued this wrestling match all night just to be blessed. He was persistent. God encourages persistence in all areas of our lives, including the spiritual. Where in your spiritual life do you need more persistence? Strong character develops as you struggle through tough conditions.

32.27–29 God gave many Bible people new names (Abraham, Sarah, Peter). Their new names were symbols of how God had changed their lives. Here we see how Jacob's character had changed. Jacob, the ambitious deceiver, had now become Israel, the prince who struggles with God and prevails.

33.1–11 It is refreshing to see Esau's change of heart when the two brothers meet again. The bitterness over losing his birthright and blessing (25.29–34) seems gone. Instead Esau is content with what he has. Jacob even exclaims how great it is to see his brother obviously pleased with him (33.10).

Life can bring us some bad situations. We can feel cheated, as Esau did, but we don't have to remain bitter. We can remove bitterness from our lives by honestly expressing our feelings to God, forgiving those who have wronged us, and being content with what we have.

33.3 Bowing low seven times was the sign of respect given to a king. Jacob was taking every precaution as he met Esau, hoping to dispel any thoughts of revenge.

33.4 Esau greeted his brother, Jacob, with a great hug. Imagine how difficult this must have been for a man who once had actually plotted his brother's death (27.41). But time away from each other allowed the bitter wounds to heal. With the passing of time, each brother was able to see that their relationship was more important than their real estate.

finally Joseph and Rachel drew near, and they bowed down. 8 Esau said, "What do 33.8
you mean by all this company that I met?" Jacob answered, "To find favor with my Gen 32.5,13-16
lord." 9 But Esau said, "I have enough, my brother; keep what you have for your- 33.9 Gen 27.39
self." 10 Jacob said, "No, please; if I find favor with you, then accept my present 33.10
from my hand; for truly to see your face is like seeing the face of God—since you Gen 19.19 47.29; 50.4
have received me with such favor. 11 Please accept my gift that is brought to you, 33.11
because God has dealt graciously with me, and because I have everything I want." Gen 32.13-15
So he urged him, and he took it.
12 Then Esau said, "Let us journey on our way, and I will go alongside you."
13 But Jacob said to him, "My lord knows that the children are frail and that the
flocks and herds, which are nursing, are a care to me; and if they are overdriven for
one day, all the flocks will die. 14 Let my lord pass on ahead of his servant, and I 33.14
will lead on slowly, according to the pace of the cattle that are before me and ac- Gen 32.3 Deut 2.1
cording to the pace of the children, until I come to my lord in Seir."
15 So Esau said, "Let me leave with you some of the people who are with me."
But he said, "Why should my lord be so kind to me?" 16 So Esau returned that day 33.17 Josh 13.27
on his way to Seir. 17 But Jacob journeyed to Succoth,[q] and built himself a house, Judg 8.5 Ps 60.6
and made booths for his cattle; therefore the place is called Succoth.
18 Jacob came safely to the city of Shechem, which is in the land of Canaan, on 33.18 Gen 12.6
his way from Paddan-aram; and he camped before the city. 19 And from the sons of 25.20; 28.6,7
Hamor, Shechem's father, he bought for one hundred pieces of money[r] the plot of 33.19 Gen 23.17
land on which he had pitched his tent. 20 There he erected an altar and called it 33.20
El-Elohe-Israel.[s] Josh 24.32 Jn 4.5

Jacob's sons take revenge

34 Now Dinah the daughter of Leah, whom she had borne to Jacob, went out 34.1
to visit the women of the region. 2 When Shechem son of Hamor the Hivite, Gen 30.21
prince of the region, saw her, he seized her and lay with her by force. 3 And his soul 34.2 Deut 21.14
was drawn to Dinah daughter of Jacob; he loved the girl, and spoke tenderly to her. 22.29 2 Sam 11.2
4 So Shechem spoke to his father Hamor, saying, "Get me this girl to be my wife." 34.4
5 Now Jacob heard that Shechem[t] had defiled his daughter Dinah; but his sons Judg 14.2,6
were with his cattle in the field, so Jacob held his peace until they came. 6 And
Hamor the father of Shechem went out to Jacob to speak with him, 7 just as the sons 34.7 2 Sam 13.12

[q] That is *Booths* [r] Heb *one hundred qesitah* [s] That is *God, the God of Israel* [t] Heb *he*

JACOB'S JOURNEY TO SHECHEM
After a joyful reunion with his brother Esau (who journeyed from Edom), Jacob set up camp in Succoth. Later he moved on to Shechem where his daughter, Dinah, was raped and two of his sons took revenge on the city.

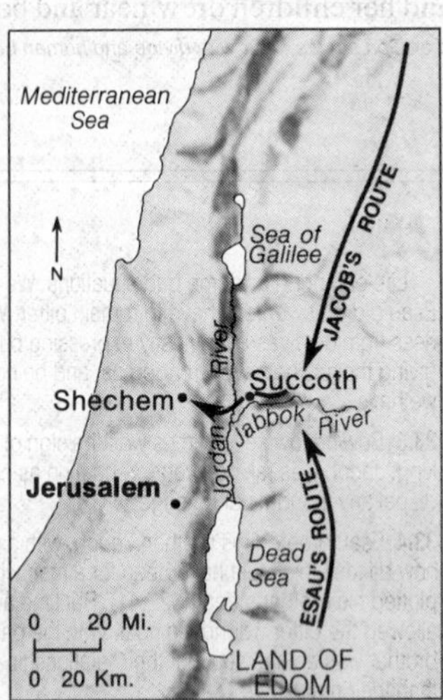

33.11 Why did Jacob send gifts ahead for Esau? In Bible times, gifts were given for several reasons. (1) This may have been a bribe. Gifts are still given to win someone over or buy his or her support. Esau may first have refused Jacob's gifts (33.9) because he didn't want or need a bribe. He had already forgiven Jacob, and he had ample wealth of his own. (2) This may have been an expression of affection. (3) It may have been the customary way of greeting someone before an important meeting. Such gifts were often related to a person's occupation. This explains why Jacob sent Esau, who was a herdsman, sheep, goats, and cattle.

33.14–17 Why did Jacob imply that he was going to Seir but then stay on at Succoth? We don't know the answer, but perhaps Jacob decided to stay at Seir as they journeyed. Succoth is a beautiful site on the eastern side of the Jordan and west of the Jabbok. Whatever the reason, Jacob and Esau parted in peace. They lived fairly close to each other until after their father's death (36.6–8).

34.1–4 Shechem may have been a victim of "love at first sight," but his actions were impulsive and evil. Not only did he sin against Dinah; he sinned against the entire family (34.6, 7). The consequences of his deed were severe both for his family and for Jacob's (34.25–31). Even Shechem's declared love for Dinah could not excuse the evil he did by raping her. Don't allow sexual passion to boil over into evil actions. Passion must be controlled.

of Jacob came in from the field. When they heard of it, the men were indignant and
very angry, because he had committed an outrage in Israel by lying with Jacob's
daughter, for such a thing ought not to be done.
8 But Hamor spoke with them, saying, "The heart of my son Shechem longs for
34.9 Gen 24.3; 28.1
your daughter; please give her to him in marriage. 9 Make marriages with us; give
your daughters to us, and take our daughters for yourselves. 10 You shall live with
us; and the land shall be open to you; live and trade in it, and get property in it."
34.11 Gen 33.10
11 Shechem also said to her father and to her brothers, "Let me find favor with you,
34.12 Gen 24.53 29.18; 31.41 Ex 22.16
and whatever you say to me I will give. 12 Put the marriage present and gift as high
as you like, and I will give whatever you ask me; only give me the girl to be my
wife."
34.13 Gen 27.35 31.7; 34.31
13 The sons of Jacob answered Shechem and his father Hamor deceitfully, because he had defiled their sister Dinah. 14 They said to them, "We cannot do this
34.14 Gen 17.13,14 Josh 5.2
thing, to give our sister to one who is uncircumcised, for that would be a disgrace
to us. 15 Only on this condition will we consent to you: that you will become as we
are and every male among you be circumcised. 16 Then we will give our daughters
to you, and we will take your daughters for ourselves, and we will live among you
and become one people. 17 But if you will not listen to us and be circumcised, then
we will take our daughter and be gone."
34.19 Gen 29.20
18 Their words pleased Hamor and Hamor's son Shechem. 19 And the young
man did not delay to do the thing, because he was delighted with Jacob's daughter.
34.20 Gen 23.10 Deut 17.5
Now he was the most honored of all his family. 20 So Hamor and his son Shechem
came to the gate of their city and spoke to the men of their city, saying, 21 "These
people are friendly with us; let them live in the land and trade in it, for the land is
large enough for them; let us take their daughters in marriage, and let us give them
34.22 Gen 34.15
our daughters. 22 Only on this condition will they agree to live among us, to become
one people: that every male among us be circumcised as they are circumcised.
23 Will not their livestock, their property, and all their animals be ours? Only let us
34.24 Gen 17.23 Josh 5.2
agree with them, and they will live among us." 24 And all who went out of the city
gate heeded Hamor and his son Shechem; and every male was circumcised, all who
went out of the gate of his city.
34.25 Gen 49.5,6 Josh 5.8
25 On the third day, when they were still in pain, two of the sons of Jacob,
Simeon and Levi, Dinah's brothers, took their swords and came against the city
unawares, and killed all the males. 26 They killed Hamor and his son Shechem with
the sword, and took Dinah out of Shechem's house, and went away. 27 And the
other sons of Jacob came upon the slain, and plundered the city, because their sister
34.28 Josh 7.21
had been defiled. 28 They took their flocks and their herds, their donkeys, and whatever was in the city and in the field. 29 All their wealth, all their little ones and their
34.30 Gen 13.7 49.5-7 Ex 5.21 1 Chron 16.19
wives, all that was in the houses, they captured and made their prey. 30 Then Jacob
said to Simeon and Levi, "You have brought trouble on me by making me odious
to the inhabitants of the land, the Canaanites and the Perizzites; my numbers are
few, and if they gather themselves against me and attack me, I shall be destroyed,
both I and my household." 31 But they said, "Should our sister be treated like a
whore?"

34.25–31 Why did Simeon and Levi take such harsh action against the city of Shechem? Jacob's family saw themselves as set apart from others. God wanted them to remain separate from their heathen neighbors. But the brothers wrongly thought that being set apart also meant being better. This arrogant attitude led to the terrible slaughter of innocent people.

34.27–29 When Shechem raped Dinah, the consequences were far greater than he could have imagined. Dinah's brothers were outraged and took revenge. Pain, deceit, and murder followed. Sexual sin is devastating because its consequences are so far reaching.

34.30 *Odius* means stench or smell.

34.30, 31 In seeking revenge against Shechem, Simeon and Levi lied, stole, and murdered. Their desire for justice was right, but their ways of achieving it were wrong. Because of their sin, their father cursed them with his dying breath (49.5–7). Generations later, their descendants lost the part of the promised land allotted to them. When tempted to return evil for evil, leave revenge to God and spare yourself the dreadful consequences of sin.

Rachel and Isaac die

35 God said to Jacob, "Arise, go up to Bethel, and settle there. Make an altar 35.1 Gen 12.1; 22.1
there to the God who appeared to you when you fled from your brother 28.19; 31.3
Esau." 2 So Jacob said to his household and to all who were with him, "Put away the 35.2
foreign gods that are among you, and purify yourselves, and change your clothes; Gen 31.19 35.3
3 then come, let us go up to Bethel, that I may make an altar there to the God who Gen 28.15-22
answered me in the day of my distress and has been with me wherever I have 35.4 Josh 24.23-26
gone." 4 So they gave to Jacob all the foreign gods that they had, and the rings that Judg 8.24
were in their ears; and Jacob hid them under the oak that was near Shechem. 35.5 Gen 34.30
5 As they journeyed, a terror from God fell upon the cities all around them, so Ex 15.16
that no one pursued them. 6 Jacob came to Luz (that is, Bethel), which is in the land 35.6 Gen 12.8
of Canaan, he and all the people who were with him, 7 and there he built an altar and 35.7
called the place El-bethel,[u] because it was there that God had revealed himself to Gen 28.19
him when he fled from his brother. 8 And Deborah, Rebekah's nurse, died, and she 35.8 Gen 24.59
was buried under an oak below Bethel. So it was called Allon-bacuth.[v] 35.9
9 God appeared to Jacob again when he came from Paddan-aram, and he Gen 26.2
blessed him. 10 God said to him, "Your name is Jacob; no longer shall you be called 35.10 Gen 17.5,15
Jacob, but Israel shall be your name." So he was called Israel. 11 God said to him, 35.11
"I am God Almighty:[w] be fruitful and multiply; a nation and a company of nations Gen 12.1
shall come from you, and kings shall spring from you. 12 The land that I gave to 35.12 Gen 13.15
Abraham and Isaac I will give to you, and I will give the land to your offspring after 28.13
you." 13 Then God went up from him at the place where he had spoken with him. 35.13 Judg 6.21; 13.20
14 Jacob set up a pillar in the place where he had spoken with him, a pillar of stone; 35.14
and he poured out a drink offering on it, and poured oil on it. 15 So Jacob called the Gen 28.18,19
place where God had spoken with him Bethel. 35.16 Ruth 4.11
16 Then they journeyed from Bethel; and when they were still some distance 35.17
from Ephrath, Rachel was in childbirth, and she had hard labor. 17 When she was Gen 30.23,24 1 Sam 4.19,20
in her hard labor, the midwife said to her, "Do not be afraid; for now you will have 35.18
another son." 18 As her soul was departing (for she died), she named him Ben-oni;[x] Gen 46.19 49.27
but his father called him Benjamin.[y] 19 So Rachel died, and she was buried on the 35.19
way to Ephrath (that is, Bethlehem), 20 and Jacob set up a pillar at her grave; it is the Gen 48.7

[u] That is *God of Bethel* [v] That is *Oak of weeping* [w] Traditional rendering of Heb *El Shaddai* [x] That is *Son of my sorrow* [y] That is *Son of the right hand* or *Son of the South*

JACOB'S JOURNEY BACK TO HEBRON
After Jacob's sons Simeon and Levi destroyed Shechem, God told Jacob to move to Bethel, where God reminded him that his name had been changed to *Israel.* He then traveled to Hebron, but along the way, his dear wife Rachel died in Ephrath (Bethlehem).

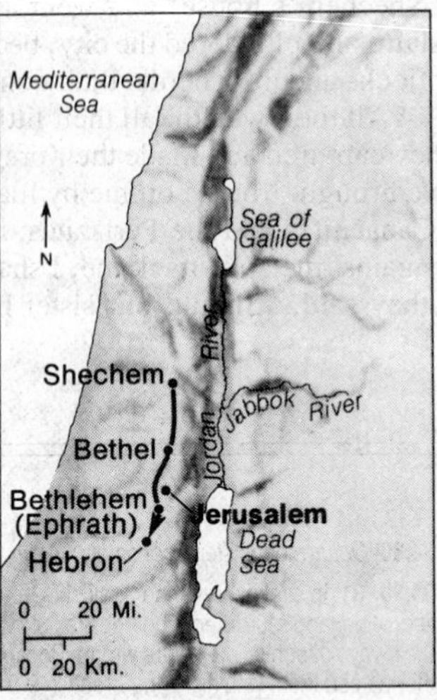

35.2 Why did the people have these idols? Idols were sometimes seen more as good-luck charms than as gods. Some Israelites, even though they worshiped God, had idols in their homes, just as some Christians today own good-luck trinkets. Jacob believed that idols should have no place in his household. He wanted nothing to divert his family's spiritual focus.

Jacob ordered his household to destroy all their idols. Unless we remove idols from our lives, they can ruin our faith. What idols do we have? An idol is anything we put before God. Idols don't have to be physical objects; they can be thoughts or desires. Like Jacob, we should get rid of anything that could stand between us and God.

35.4 Why did the people give Jacob their earrings? Jewelry in itself was not evil, but in Jacob's day earrings were often worn as good-luck charms to ward off evil. The people in his family had to cleanse themselves of all heathen influences, including reminders of foreign gods.

35.10 God reminded Jacob of his new name, Israel, which meant "a prince who prevails with God." Although Jacob's life was littered with difficulties and trials, his new name was a tribute to his desire to stay close to God despite life's disappointments.

Many people believe that Christianity should offer a problem-free life. Consequently, as life gets tough, they draw back disappointed. Instead, they should determine to prevail with God through life's storm. Problems and difficulties are painful but inevitable; you might as well see them as opportunities for growth. You can't prevail with God unless you have troubles to prevail over.

35.13, 14 This oil was olive oil of the finest grade of purity. It was expensive, so using it showed the high value placed on the anointed object. Jacob was showing the greatest respect for the place where he met with God.

35.22 Gen 49.4; Lev 18.8; 1 Chron 5.1
35.23 Gen 29.32-35; 46.8-14
35.24 Gen 30.22-24
35.25 Gen 30.4-8; 46.23-25
35.26 Gen 30.9-13; 46.16-18
35.27 Gen 13.18; 23.2; 37.14

pillar of Rachel's tomb, which is there to this day. 21 Israel journeyed on, and pitched his tent beyond the tower of Eder.

22 While Israel lived in that land, Reuben went and lay with Bilhah his father's concubine; and Israel heard of it.

Now the sons of Jacob were twelve. 23 The sons of Leah: Reuben (Jacob's firstborn), Simeon, Levi, Judah, Issachar, and Zebulun. 24 The sons of Rachel: Joseph and Benjamin. 25 The sons of Bilhah, Rachel's maid: Dan and Naphtali. 26 The sons of Zilpah, Leah's maid: Gad and Asher. These were the sons of Jacob who were born to him in Paddan-aram.

27 Jacob came to his father Isaac at Mamre, or Kiriath-arba (that is, Hebron), where Abraham and Isaac had resided as aliens. 28 Now the days of Isaac were one hundred eighty years. 29 And Isaac breathed his last; he died and was gathered to his people, old and full of days; and his sons Esau and Jacob buried him.

36.1 Gen 25.25-34; 32.3-7; 1 Chron 1.35
36.2 Gen 26.34; 36.10,14
36.4 Gen 36.10,11, 13
36.5 Gen 36.18
36.7 Gen 13.6
36.8 Gen 14.6; 25.30; 32.3
36.9 Gen 36.43; 1 Kgs 11.1
36.10 1 Chron 1.35
36.11 1 Chron 1.36

Esau's descendants

36 These are the descendants of Esau (that is, Edom). 2 Esau took his wives from the Canaanites: Adah daughter of Elon the Hittite, Oholibamah daughter of Anah son[z] of Zibeon the Hivite, 3 and Basemath, Ishmael's daughter, sister of Nebaioth. 4 Adah bore Eliphaz to Esau; Basemath bore Reuel; 5 and Oholibamah bore Jeush, Jalam, and Korah. These are the sons of Esau who were born to him in the land of Canaan.

6 Then Esau took his wives, his sons, his daughters, and all the members of his household, his cattle, all his livestock, and all the property he had acquired in the land of Canaan; and he moved to a land some distance from his brother Jacob. 7 For their possessions were too great for them to live together; the land where they were staying could not support them because of their livestock. 8 So Esau settled in the hill country of Seir; Esau is Edom.

9 These are the descendants of Esau, ancestor of the Edomites, in the hill country of Seir. 10 These are the names of Esau's sons: Eliphaz son of Adah the wife of Esau; Reuel, the son of Esau's wife Basemath. 11 The sons of Eliphaz were Teman, Omar, Zepho, Gatam, and Kenaz. 12 (Timna was a concubine of Eliphaz, Esau's son; she bore Amalek to Eliphaz.) These were the sons of Adah, Esau's wife. 13 These were the sons of Reuel: Nahath, Zerah, Shammah, and Mizzah. These were the sons of Esau's wife, Basemath. 14 These were the sons of Esau's wife Oholibamah, daughter of Anah son[a] of Zibeon: she bore to Esau Jeush, Jalam, and Korah.

36.18 1 Chron 1.35
36.19 Gen 36.1,9
36.20 Gen 14.6; Deut 2.12,22; 1 Chron 1.38-42

15 These are the clans[b] of the sons of Esau. The sons of Eliphaz the firstborn of Esau: the clans[b] Teman, Omar, Zepho, Kenaz, 16 Korah, Gatam, and Amalek; these are the clans[b] of Eliphaz in the land of Edom; they are the sons of Adah. 17 These are the sons of Esau's son Reuel: the clans[b] Nahath, Zerah, Shammah, and Mizzah; these are the clans[b] of Reuel in the land of Edom; they are the sons of Esau's wife Basemath. 18 These are the sons of Esau's wife Oholibamah: the clans[b] Jeush, Jalam, and Korah; these are the clans[b] born of Esau's wife Oholibamah, the daughter of Anah. 19 These are the sons of Esau (that is, Edom), and these are their clans.[b]

20 These are the sons of Seir the Horite, the inhabitants of the land: Lotan,

[z] Sam Gk Syr: Heb *daughter* [a] Gk Syr: Heb *daughter* [b] Or *chiefs*

35.22 Reuben's sin was costly, although not right away. As the oldest son, he stood to receive a double portion of the family inheritance and a place of leadership among his people. Reuben may have thought he got away with his sin. No more is mentioned of it until Jacob, on his deathbed, assembled his family for the final blessing. Suddenly Jacob took away Reuben's double portion and gave it to someone else. The reason? "You went up onto your father's bed; then you defiled it" (49.4).

Sin's consequences can plague us long after the sin is committed. When we do something wrong we may think we can escape unnoticed, only to discover later that the sin has been quietly breeding serious consequences.

36.9 The Edomites were descendants of Esau who lived south and east of the Dead Sea. The country featured rugged mountains and desolate wilderness. Several major roads led through Edom, because it was rich in natural resources. During the exodus, God told Israel to leave the Edomites alone (Deuteronomy 2.4, 5) because they were "kindred." But Edom refused to let them enter the land, and later they became bitter enemies of King David. The nations of Edom and Israel shared the same ancestor, Isaac, and the same border. Israel looked down on the Edomites because they intermarried with the Canaanites.

Shobal, Zibeon, Anah, 21 Dishon, Ezer, and Dishan; these are the clans[c] of the
Horites, the sons of Seir in the land of Edom. 22 The sons of Lotan were Hori and **36.22** 1 Chron 1.39
Heman; and Lotan's sister was Timna. 23 These are the sons of Shobal: Alvan, **36.23** 1 Chron 1.40
Manahath, Ebal, Shepho, and Onam. 24 These are the sons of Zibeon: Aiah and
Anah; he is the Anah who found the springs[d] in the wilderness, as he pastured the
donkeys of his father Zibeon. 25 These are the children of Anah: Dishon and Oholi- **36.25** Gen 36.2,5,14,18; 1 Chron 1.41
bamah daughter of Anah. 26 These are the sons of Dishon: Hemdan, Eshban, Ith-
ran, and Cheran. 27 These are the sons of Ezer: Bilhan, Zaavan, and Akan. 28 These
are the sons of Dishan: Uz and Aran. 29 These are the clans[c] of the Horites: the **36.27** 1 Chron 1.38,42
clans[c] Lotan, Shobal, Zibeon, Anah, 30 Dishon, Ezer, and Dishan; these are the **36.29,30** Gen 36.20
clans[c] of the Horites, clan by clan[e] in the land of Seir.

31 These are the kings who reigned in the land of Edom, before any king **36.31** Gen 17.6,16; 20.14; 1 Chron 1.43
reigned over the Israelites. 32 Bela son of Beor reigned in Edom, the name of his
city being Dinhabah. 33 Bela died, and Jobab son of Zerah of Bozrah succeeded him
as king. 34 Jobab died, and Husham of the land of the Temanites succeeded him as
king. 35 Husham died, and Hadad son of Bedad, who defeated Midian in the coun- **36.35** 1 Chron 1.46
try of Moab, succeeded him as king, the name of his city being Avith. 36 Hadad
died, and Samlah of Masrekah succeeded him as king. 37 Samlah died, and Shaul of **36.37** 1 Chron 1.48
Rehoboth on the Euphrates succeeded him as king. 38 Shaul died, and Baal-hanan
son of Achbor succeeded him as king. 39 Baal-hanan son of Achbor died, and Hadar
succeeded him as king, the name of his city being Pau; his wife's name was Mehetabel, the daughter of Matred, daughter of Me-zahab.

40 These are the names of the clans[c] of Esau, according to their families and **36.40** 1 Chron 1.51
their localities by their names: the clans[c] Timna, Alvah, Jetheth, 41 Oholibamah,
Elah, Pinon, 42 Kenaz, Teman, Mibzar, 43 Magdiel, and Iram; these are the clans[c]
of Edom (that is, Esau, the father of Edom), according to their settlements in the
land that they held.

G. THE STORY OF JOSEPH (37.1 – 50.26)

Joseph, one of Jacob's twelve sons, was obviously the favorite. Hated by his brothers for this, Joseph was sold to slave traders only to emerge as ruler of all Egypt. Through Joseph, we learn how suffering, no matter how unfair, develops strong character and deep wisdom.

1. Joseph is sold into slavery

37 Jacob settled in the land where his father had lived as an alien, the land of **37.1** Gen 17.8; 28.4
Canaan. 2 This is the story of the family of Jacob.

Joseph, being seventeen years old, was shepherding the flock with his brothers; **37.2** Gen 6.9; 35.22-26; 41.46
he was a helper to the sons of Bilhah and Zilpah, his father's wives; and Joseph
brought a bad report of them to their father. 3 Now Israel loved Joseph more than **37.3** Gen 37.23,32; 44.20
any other of his children, because he was the son of his old age; and he had made
him a long robe with sleeves.[f] 4 But when his brothers saw that their father loved **37.4** Gen 27.41
him more than all his brothers, they hated him, and could not speak peaceably to
him.

5 Once Joseph had a dream, and when he told it to his brothers, they hated him **37.5** Gen 28.12; Num 12.6; Dan 2.1
even more. 6 He said to them, "Listen to this dream that I dreamed. 7 There we

[c] Or *chiefs* [d] Meaning of Heb uncertain [e] Or *chief by chief* [f] Traditional rendering (compare Gk): *a coat of many colors*; Meaning of Heb uncertain

37.3 In Joseph's day, everyone had a "robe," or cloak. Cloaks were used to warm oneself, to bundle up belongings for a trip, to wrap babies, to sit on, or even to serve as security for a loan. Most cloaks were knee length, short sleeved, and plain. In contrast, Joseph's coat was probably of the kind worn by royalty – long sleeved, ankle length, and colorful. The coat became a symbol of Jacob's favoritism toward Joseph, and it aggravated the already strained relations between Joseph and his brothers. Favoritism in families may be unavoidable, but its divisive effects should be minimized. Parents may not be able to change their feelings toward a favorite child, but they can change their actions toward the others.

37.6-11 Joseph's brothers were already angry over the possibility of being ruled by their little brother. Joseph then fueled the fire with his immature attitude and boastful manner. No one enjoys a braggart. Joseph learned his lesson the hard way. His angry brothers sold him into slavery to get rid of him. After several years of hardship, Joseph learned an important lesson: because our talents and knowledge come from God, it is more appropriate to thank him for them than to brag about them. Later, Joseph gives God the credit (41.16).

were, binding sheaves in the field. Suddenly my sheaf rose and stood upright; then
your sheaves gathered around it, and bowed down to my sheaf." 8 His brothers said
to him, "Are you indeed to reign over us? Are you indeed to have dominion over
us?" So they hated him even more because of his dreams and his words.
9 He had another dream, and told it to his brothers, saying, "Look, I have had
another dream: the sun, the moon, and eleven stars were bowing down to me."
10 But when he told it to his father and to his brothers, his father rebuked him, and
said to him, "What kind of dream is this that you have had? Shall we indeed come,
I and your mother and your brothers, and bow to the ground before you?" 11 So his
brothers were jealous of him, but his father kept the matter in mind.
12 Now his brothers went to pasture their father's flock near Shechem. 13 And
Israel said to Joseph, "Are not your brothers pasturing the flock at Shechem?
Come, I will send you to them." He answered, "Here I am." 14 So he said to him,
"Go now, see if it is well with your brothers and with the flock; and bring word
back to me." So he sent him from the valley of Hebron.
He came to Shechem, 15 and a man found him wandering in the fields; the man
asked him, "What are you seeking?" 16 "I am seeking my brothers," he said; "tell

37.7 Gen 42.6,9 43.26
37.8 Ex 2.14 Deut 33.16
37.9 Gen 41.25,32
37.10 Gen 27.29 Isa 60.14 Phil 2.10
37.11 Ps 106.16 Isa 11.13 Mt 27.18 Acts 7.9
37.12 Gen 33.18; 37.1
37.14 Gen 29.6; 35.27

JOSEPH

As a youngster, Joseph was overconfident. His natural self-assurance, increased by being Jacob's favorite son and by knowing of God's designs on his life, was unbearable to his ten older brothers, who eventually conspired against him. But this self-assurance, molded by pain and combined with a personal knowledge of God, allowed him to survive and prosper where most would have failed. He added quiet wisdom to his confidence and won the hearts of everyone he met—Potiphar, the jailer, other prisoners, the king, and after many years, even those ten brothers.

Perhaps you can identify with one or more of these hardships Joseph experienced: he was betrayed and deserted by his family, exposed to sexual temptation, and punished for doing the right thing; he endured a long imprisonment and was forgotten by those he helped. As you read his story, note what Joseph did in each case. His positive response transformed each setback into a step forward. He didn't spend much time asking "Why?" His approach was "What shall I do now?" Those who met Joseph were aware that wherever he went and whatever he did, God was with him. When you're facing a setback, the beginning of a Joseph-like attitude is to acknowledge that God is with you. There is nothing like his presence to shed new light on a dark situation.

Strengths and accomplishments:
- Rose in power from slave to ruler of Egypt
- Was known for his personal integrity
- Was a man of spiritual sensitivity
- Prepared a nation to survive a famine

Weakness and mistake:
- His youthful pride caused friction with his brothers

Lessons from his life:
- What matters is not so much the events or circumstances of life, but your response to them
- With God's help, any situation can be used for good, even when others intend it for evil

Vital statistics:
- Where: Canaan, Egypt
- Occupation: Shepherd, slave, convict, ruler
- Relatives: Parents: Jacob and Rachel. Eleven brothers and one sister named in the Bible. Wife: Asenath. Sons: Manasseh and Ephraim

Key verse:
"Pharaoh said to his servants, 'Can we find anyone else like this—one in whom is the spirit of God?'" (Genesis 41.38).

Joseph's story is told in Genesis 30—50. He is also mentioned in Hebrews 11.22.

me, please, where they are pasturing the flock." 17 The man said, "They have gone
away, for I heard them say, 'Let us go to Dothan.' " So Joseph went after his brothers, and found them at Dothan. 18 They saw him from a distance, and before he
came near to them, they conspired to kill him. 19 They said to one another, "Here
comes this dreamer. 20 Come now, let us kill him and throw him into one of the pits;
then we shall say that a wild animal has devoured him, and we shall see what will
become of his dreams." 21 But when Reuben heard it, he delivered him out of their
hands, saying, "Let us not take his life." 22 Reuben said to them, "Shed no blood;
throw him into this pit here in the wilderness, but lay no hand on him"—that he
might rescue him out of their hand and restore him to his father. 23 So when Joseph
came to his brothers, they stripped him of his robe, the long robe with sleeves[g] that
he wore; 24 and they took him and threw him into a pit. The pit was empty; there
was no water in it.
25 Then they sat down to eat; and looking up they saw a caravan of Ishmaelites
coming from Gilead, with their camels carrying gum, balm, and resin, on their way
to carry it down to Egypt. 26 Then Judah said to his brothers, "What profit is it if we
kill our brother and conceal his blood? 27 Come, let us sell him to the Ishmaelites,
and not lay our hands on him, for he is our brother, our own flesh." And his brothers agreed. 28 When some Midianite traders passed by, they drew Joseph up, lifting
him out of the pit, and sold him to the Ishmaelites for twenty pieces of silver. And
they took Joseph to Egypt.
29 When Reuben returned to the pit and saw that Joseph was not in the pit, he
tore his clothes. 30 He returned to his brothers, and said, "The boy is gone; and I,
where can I turn?" 31 Then they took Joseph's robe, slaughtered a goat, and dipped
the robe in the blood. 32 They had the long robe with sleeves[g] taken to their father,
and they said, "This we have found; see now whether it is your son's robe or not."
33 He recognized it, and said, "It is my son's robe! A wild animal has devoured him;
Joseph is without doubt torn to pieces." 34 Then Jacob tore his garments, and put

37.17 2 Kgs 6.13
37.20 Gen 37.33 Prov 1.11
37.21 Gen 42.22
37.22 Gen 37.29
37.23 Gen 37.3
37.24 Jer 38.6
37.25 Gen 25.16-18 31.23; 37.28 Jer 8.22; 46.11
37.27 Ex 21.16 Neh 5.8
37.28 Gen 39.1; 45.4 Judg 8.22-24 Acts 7.9
37.29 Gen 37.34 44.13 Num 14.6
37.30 Gen 5.24 42.13,32,36
37.32 Lk 15.30
37.33 Gen 37.20 44.28
37.34 Gen 37.29 44.13

[g] See note on 37.3

JOSEPH GOES TO MEET HIS BROTHERS Jacob asked Joseph to go find his brothers, who were grazing their flocks near Shechem. When Joseph arrived, he learned that his brothers had gone on to Dothan, which lay along a major trade route to Egypt. There the jealous brothers sold Joseph as a slave to a group of Ishmaelite traders on their way to Egypt.

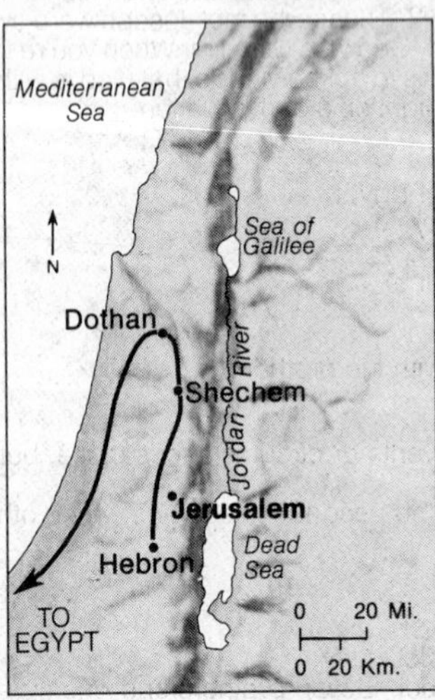

37.19, 20 Could jealousy ever make you feel like killing someone? Before saying, "Of course not," look at what happened in this story. Ten men were willing to kill their younger brother over a coat and a few reported dreams. Their deep jealousy had grown into ugly rage, blinding them completely to what was right. Jealousy can be hard to recognize, because our reasons for it seem to make sense. But left unchecked, jealousy grows quickly and leads to serious sins. The longer you cultivate jealous feelings, the harder it is to uproot them. The time to deal with jealousy is when you notice yourself keeping score of what others have.

37.26, 27 The brothers were worried about bearing the guilt of Joseph's death. Judah suggested an option that was not right, but would leave them guiltless of murder. Sometimes we jump at a solution because it is the lesser of two evils, but it still is not the right action to take. When someone proposes a seemingly workable solution, first ask, "Is it right?"

37.28 Although Joseph's brothers didn't kill him outright, they probably didn't expect him to survive for long as a slave. They were quite willing to let cruel slave traders do their dirty work for them. Joseph faced a 30-day journey through the desert, probably chained and on foot. He would be treated like baggage, and once in Egypt, would be sold as a piece of merchandise. His brothers thought they would never see him again.

37.30 Reuben returned to the pit to find Joseph, but his little brother was gone. His first response, in effect, was "What is going to happen to me?" ("Where can I turn?") rather than "What is going to happen to Joseph?" In a tough situation, are you usually concerned first about yourself? Consider the person most affected by the problem, and you will be more likely to find a solution for it.

37.31–34 To cover their evil action, Jacob's sons deceived their father into thinking Joseph was dead. Jacob himself had deceived others many times (including his own father; 27.35). Now, though blessed by God, he still had to face the consequences of his sins. God may not have punished Jacob immediately for his sins of deceit, but the consequences came nevertheless and stayed with him for the rest of his life.

37.34 Tearing one's clothes and wearing sackcloth was a sign of mourning, much like wearing black today.

37.35 Gen 31.43 44.29 2 Sam 12.17 Ps 77.2
37.36 Gen 39.1; 40.4

sackcloth on his loins, and mourned for his son many days. 35 All his sons and all
his daughters sought to comfort him; but he refused to be comforted, and said, "No,
I shall go down to Sheol to my son, mourning." Thus his father bewailed him.
36 Meanwhile the Midianites had sold him in Egypt to Potiphar, one of Pharaoh's
officials, the captain of the guard.

2. Judah and Tamar

38.1 Josh 12.15 15.35 1 Sam 22.1
38.2 Gen 24.3; 34.2
38.3 Gen 46.12
38.6 Mt 1.3

38 It happened at that time that Judah went down from his brothers and settled
near a certain Adullamite whose name was Hirah. 2 There Judah saw the
daughter of a certain Canaanite whose name was Shua; he married her and went in
to her. 3 She conceived and bore a son; and he named him Er. 4 Again she conceived
and bore a son whom she named Onan. 5 Yet again she bore a son, and she named
him Shelah. She[h] was in Chezib when she bore him. 6 Judah took a wife for Er his
firstborn; her name was Tamar. 7 But Er, Judah's firstborn, was wicked in the sight

[h] Gk: Heb *He*

REUBEN

Parents are usually the best judges of their children's character. Jacob summarized the personality of his son Reuben by comparing him to water. Except when frozen, water has no stable shape of its own. It always shapes itself to its container or environment. Reuben usually had good intentions, but he seemed unable to stand against a crowd. His instability made him hard to trust. He had both private and public values, but these contradicted each other. He went along with his brothers in their action against Joseph while hoping to counteract the evil in private. The plan failed. Compromise has a way of destroying convictions. Without convictions, lack of direction will destroy life. Reuben's sleeping with his father's concubine showed how little he had left of the integrity he had displayed earlier in life.

How consistent are your public and private lives? We may want to think they are separate, but we can't deny that they affect each other. What convictions are present in your life at all times? How closely does Jacob's description of his son—"unstable as water"—describe your life?

Strengths and accomplishments:
- Saved Joseph's life by talking the other brothers out of murder
- Showed intense love for his father by offering his own sons as a guarantee that Benjamin's life would be safe

Weaknesses and mistakes:
- Gave in quickly to group pressure
- Did not directly protect Joseph from his brothers, although as eldest son he had the authority to do so
- Slept with his father's concubine

Lessons from his life:
- Public and private integrity must be the same, or one will destroy the other
- Punishment for sin may not be immediate, but it is certain

Vital statistics:
- Where: Canaan, Egypt
- Occupation: Shepherd
- Relatives: Parents: Jacob and Leah. Eleven brothers, one sister

Key verses:
"Reuben, you are my firstborn, my might and the first fruits of my vigor, excelling in rank and excelling in power. Unstable as water, you shall no longer excell because you went up onto your father's bed; then you defiled it—you went up onto my couch!" (Genesis 49.3, 4).

Reuben's story is told in Genesis 29—50.

37.36 Imagine the culture shock Joseph experienced upon arriving in Egypt. Joseph had lived as a nomad, traveling the countryside with his family, caring for sheep. Suddenly he was thrust into the world's most advanced civilization with great pyramids, beautiful homes, sophisticated people, and a new language. While Joseph saw Egypt's skill and intelligence at their best, he also saw the Egyptians' spiritual blindness. They worshiped countless gods related to every aspect of life.

38.1ff This chapter vividly portrays the immoral character of Judah in contrast to the moral character of Joseph. Judah's lack of integrity resulted in family strife and deception. In the following chapter, we see Joseph's godliness. His integrity and wise choices reflected his godly character. His faithfulness was rewarded with blessings greater than he could imagine, both for himself and for his family.

of the LORD, and the LORD put him to death. 8 Then Judah said to Onan, "Go in to
your brother's wife and perform the duty of a brother-in-law to her; raise up offspring for your brother." 9 But since Onan knew that the offspring would not be his,
he spilled his semen on the ground whenever he went in to his brother's wife, so
that he would not give offspring to his brother. 10 What he did was displeasing in the
sight of the LORD, and he put him to death also. 11 Then Judah said to his daughter-
in-law Tamar, "Remain a widow in your father's house until my son Shelah grows
up"—for he feared that he too would die, like his brothers. So Tamar went to live
in her father's house.

12 In course of time the wife of Judah, Shua's daughter, died; when Judah's
time of mourning was over,[i] he went up to Timnah to his sheepshearers, he and his
friend Hirah the Adullamite. 13 When Tamar was told, "Your father-in-law is going
up to Timnah to shear his sheep," 14 she put off her widow's garments, put on a veil,
wrapped herself up, and sat down at the entrance to Enaim, which is on the road to
Timnah. She saw that Shelah was grown up, yet she had not been given to him in
marriage. 15 When Judah saw her, he thought her to be a prostitute, for she had
covered her face. 16 He went over to her at the road side, and said, "Come, let me
come in to you," for he did not know that she was his daughter-in-law. She said,
"What will you give me, that you may come in to me?" 17 He answered, "I will send
you a kid from the flock." And she said, "Only if you give me a pledge, until you
send it." 18 He said, "What pledge shall I give you?" She replied, "Your signet and
your cord, and the staff that is in your hand." So he gave them to her, and went in
to her, and she conceived by him. 19 Then she got up and went away, and taking off
her veil she put on the garments of her widowhood.

20 When Judah sent the kid by his friend the Adullamite, to recover the pledge
from the woman, he could not find her. 21 He asked the townspeople, "Where is the
temple prostitute who was at Enaim by the wayside?" But they said, "No prostitute
has been here." 22 So he returned to Judah, and said, "I have not found her; moreover the townspeople said, 'No prostitute has been here.' " 23 Judah replied, "Let
her keep the things as her own, otherwise we will be laughed at; you see, I sent this
kid, and you could not find her."

24 About three months later Judah was told, "Your daughter-in-law Tamar has

38.7 Gen 6.5,13.13 19.13; 38.10 2 Chron 33.6
38.8 Lev 18.16 Num 36.8 Deut 25.5-10 Mt 22.24
38.10 2 Sam 11.27 1 Chron 21.7
38.11 Ruth 1.13
38.12 Gen 31.19 Josh 13.23-27 1 Sam 25.4 2 Sam 13.23-27
38.14 Gen 23.10 Josh 15.34
38.15 Gen 24.65
38.16 2 Sam 13.11 Deut 23.18 Ezek 16.33
38.17 Gen 38.20,25
38.18 Gen 41.42 Hos 4.11
38.23 Prov 6.32,33
38.24 Gen 34.31 Lev 20.10; 21.9 Eccles 7.26

[i] Heb *when Judah was comforted*

38.8–10 This law about marrying a widow in the family is explained in Deuteronomy 25.5–10. Its purpose was to ensure that a childless widow would have a son who would receive her late husband's inheritance and who, in turn, would care for her. Because Judah's son (Tamar's husband) had no children, there was no family line through which the inheritance and the blessing of the covenant could continue. God killed Onan because he refused to fulfill his obligation to his brother and to Tamar.

38.15–23 Prostitutes were common in heathen cultures such as Canaan. Public prostitutes served heathen goddesses and were common elements of the religious cults. They were more highly respected than private prostitutes who were sometimes punished when caught. Tamar was driven to seduce Judah because of her intense desire to have children; Judah was driven by his lust. Neither case was justified.

38.15–24 Why was Judah so open about his relations with a prostitute, yet ready to execute his daughter-in-law for being one? To understand this apparent contradiction, we must understand the place of women in Canaan. A woman's most important function was bearing children who would perpetuate the family line. To ensure that children belonged to the husband, the bride was expected to be a virgin and the wife was expected to have relations only with him. If a wife committed adultery, she could be executed. Some women, however, did not belong to families. They might be temple prostitutes supported by offerings or common harlots supported by the men who used their services. Their children were nobody's heirs, and men who hired them adulterated nobody's bloodlines.

Judah saw no harm in hiring a prostitute for a night; after all, he was more than willing to pay. He was ready to execute Tamar, however, because if she was pregnant "as a result of whoredom," his grandchild would not be part of his family line. Apparently the question of sexual morality never entered Judah's mind; his concern was for keeping his inheritance in the family. Ironically, it was Tamar, not Judah, who acted to provide him with legal heirs. By seducing him, she acted more in the spirit of the law than he did when he refused to send his third son to her.

This story in no way implies that God winks at prostitution. Throughout Scripture, prostitution is condemned as a serious sin. If the story has a moral, it is that faithfulness to family obligations is important. Incidentally, Judah and Tamar are direct ancestors of Jesus Christ.

38.18 A signet was a form of identification used to authenticate legal documents. Usually a unique design carved in stone and worn on a ring or necklace inseparable from its owner, it was used by the wealthy and powerful to mark clay or wax. Since Tamar had Judah's seal, she could prove beyond a doubt that he had been with her.

38.24–26 When Tamar revealed she was pregnant, Judah, who unknowingly had gotten her pregnant, moved to have her killed. Judah had concealed his own sin, yet he came down harshly on Tamar. Often the sins we try to cover up are the ones that anger us most when we see them in others. If you become indignant at the sins of others, you may have a similar tendency to sin that you don't wish to face. When we admit our sins and ask God to forgive us, forgiving others becomes easier.

played the whore; moreover she is pregnant as a result of whoredom." And Judah
38.25 Gen 37.32 said, "Bring her out, and let her be burned." 25 As she was being brought out, she
sent word to her father-in-law, "It was the owner of these who made me pregnant."
And she said, "Take note, please, whose these are, the signet and the cord and the
38.26 1 Sam 24.17 Ezek 16.52 staff." 26 Then Judah acknowledged them and said, "She is more in the right than I,
since I did not give her to my son Shelah." And he did not lie with her again.
38.27 Gen 25.24 27 When the time of her delivery came, there were twins in her womb. 28 While
she was in labor, one put out a hand; and the midwife took and bound on his hand
38.29 Gen 46.12 Num 26.20 Ruth 4.12 1 Chron 2.4 Mt 1.3 Lk 3.33 a crimson thread, saying, "This one came out first." 29 But just then he drew back
his hand, and out came his brother; and she said, "What a breach you have made for
yourself!" Therefore he was named Perez.[j] 30 Afterward his brother came out with
the crimson thread on his hand; and he was named Zerah.[k]

3. Joseph is thrown into jail

Joseph in Potiphar's house

39.1 Acts 7.9 **39** Now Joseph was taken down to Egypt, and Potiphar, an officer of Pharaoh,
the captain of the guard, an Egyptian, bought him from the Ishmaelites who
39.2 Gen 21.22 26.24,28; 28.15 had brought him down there. 2 The LORD was with Joseph, and he became a successful man; he was in the house of his Egyptian master. 3 His master saw that the
39.4 Gen 32.5; 41.40 LORD was with him, and that the LORD caused all that he did to prosper in his hands.
39.5 Deut 28.3-6 4 So Joseph found favor in his sight and attended him; he made him overseer of his
39.6 Gen 29.17 1 Sam 16.12,18 house and put him in charge of all that he had. 5 From the time that he made him
overseer in his house and over all that he had, the LORD blessed the Egyptian's
39.7 Ps 119.37 Ezek 23.5 house for Joseph's sake; the blessing of the LORD was on all that he had, in house
and field. 6 So he left all that he had in Joseph's charge; and, with him there, he had
39.8 Gen 39.5 Prov 1.10 6.23,24 no concern for anything but the food that he ate.
Now Joseph was handsome and good-looking. 7 And after a time his master's
wife cast her eyes on Joseph and said, "Lie with me." 8 But he refused and said to
39.9 2 Sam 12.13 Ps 51.4 his master's wife, "Look, with me here, my master has no concern about anything
in the house, and he has put everything that he has in my hand. 9 He is not greater
39.10 1 Cor 6.18 15.33 1 Thess 5.22 2 Tim 2.22 in this house than I am, nor has he kept back anything from me except yourself,
because you are his wife. How then could I do this great wickedness, and sin
against God?" 10 And although she spoke to Joseph day after day, he would not
consent to lie beside her or to be with her. 11 One day, however, when he went into

[j] That is *A breach* [k] That is *Brightness*; perhaps alluding to the crimson thread

WOMEN IN JESUS' FAMILY TREE

Name	Origin	Reference
Tamar	Canaanite	Genesis 38.1–30
Rahab	Canaanite	Joshua 6.22–25
Ruth	Moabite	Ruth 4.13–22
Bathsheba	Israelite	2 Samuel 12.24, 25

39.1 The date of Joseph's arrival in Egypt is debatable. Many believe he arrived during the period of the Hyksos rulers, foreigners who came from the region of Canaan. They invaded Egypt and controlled the land for almost 150 years. If Joseph arrived during their rule, it is easy to see why he was rapidly promoted up the royal ladder. Because the Hyksos were foreigners themselves, they would not hold this brilliant young foreigner's ancestry against him.

39.1 *Pharaoh* was the general name for all the kings of Egypt. It was a title like "King" or "President" used to address the country's leader. The Pharaohs in Genesis and Exodus were not the same man.

39.1 Ancient Egypt was a land of great contrasts. People were either rich beyond measure or poverty stricken. There wasn't much middle ground. Joseph found himself serving Potiphar, an extremely rich officer in Pharaoh's service. Rich families like Potiphar's had elaborate homes two or three stories tall with beautiful gardens and balconies. They enjoyed live entertainment at home as they chose delicious fruit from expensive bowls. They surrounded themselves with alabaster vases, paintings, beautiful rugs, and hand-carved chairs. Dinner was served on golden tableware, and the rooms were lighted with gold candlesticks. Servants, like Joseph, worked on the first floor, while the family occupied the upper stories.

39.9 Potiphar's wife failed to seduce Joseph, who resisted this temptation by saying it would be a sin against God. Joseph didn't say, "I'd be hurting you," or "I'd be sinning against Potiphar," or "I'd be sinning against myself." Under pressure, such excuses are easily rationalized away. Remember that sexual sin is not just between two consenting adults. It is an act of disobedience to God.

39.10–15 Joseph avoided Potiphar's wife as much as possible. He refused her advances and finally *ran* from her. Sometimes merely trying to avoid temptation is not enough. We must turn and run, especially when the temptations seem very strong, as is often the case in sexual temptations.

the house to do his work, and while no one else was in the house, 12 she caught hold
of his garment, saying, "Lie with me!" But he left his garment in her hand, and fled
and ran outside. 13 When she saw that he had left his garment in her hand and had
fled outside, 14 she called out to the members of her household and said to them,
"See, my husband[l] has brought among us a Hebrew to insult us! He came in to me
to lie with me, and I cried out with a loud voice; 15 and when he heard me raise my
voice and cry out, he left his garment beside me, and fled outside." 16 Then she kept
his garment by her until his master came home, 17 and she told him the same story,
saying, "The Hebrew servant, whom you have brought among us, came in to me to
insult me; 18 but as soon as I raised my voice and cried out, he left his garment
beside me, and fled outside."

19 When his master heard the words that his wife spoke to him, saying, "This
is the way your servant treated me," he became enraged. 20 And Joseph's master
took him and put him into the prison, the place where the king's prisoners were
confined; he remained there in prison. 21 But the LORD was with Joseph and showed
him steadfast love; he gave him favor in the sight of the chief jailer. 22 The chief
jailer committed to Joseph's care all the prisoners who were in the prison, and
whatever was done there, he was the one who did it. 23 The chief jailer paid no heed
to anything that was in Joseph's care, because the LORD was with him; and whatever he did, the LORD made it prosper.

Joseph interprets two dreams

40 Some time after this, the cupbearer of the king of Egypt and his baker offended their lord the king of Egypt. 2 Pharaoh was angry with his two officers, the chief cupbearer and the chief baker, 3 and he put them in custody in the
house of the captain of the guard, in the prison where Joseph was confined. 4 The
captain of the guard charged Joseph with them, and he waited on them; and they
continued for some time in custody. 5 One night they both dreamed — the cupbearer
and the baker of the king of Egypt, who were confined in the prison — each his own
dream, and each dream with its own meaning. 6 When Joseph came to them in the
morning, he saw that they were troubled. 7 So he asked Pharaoh's officers, who
were with him in custody in his master's house, "Why are your faces downcast
today?" 8 They said to him, "We have had dreams, and there is no one to interpret
them." And Joseph said to them, "Do not interpretations belong to God? Please tell
them to me."

9 So the chief cupbearer told his dream to Joseph, and said to him, "In my
dream there was a vine before me, 10 and on the vine there were three branches. As
soon as it budded, its blossoms came out and the clusters ripened into grapes.
11 Pharaoh's cup was in my hand; and I took the grapes and pressed them into Pharaoh's cup, and placed the cup in Pharaoh's hand." 12 Then Joseph said to him,
"This is its interpretation: the three branches are three days; 13 within three days
Pharaoh will lift up your head and restore you to your office; and you shall place

39.12 Prov 7.13 Eccles 7.26 Ezek 16.30
39.14 Isa 54.17
39.17 Ex 20.16; 23.1 Ps 37.14; 55.3
39.19 Prov 6.34; 18.17
39.20 Gen 40.1-3,15 41.12,14 Ps 105.18
39.21 Gen 39.2,3 49.25 Acts 7.9
39.22 Gen 39.4; 41.40
39.23 Gen 39.3 Ps 1.3
40.1 Neh 1.11
40.4 Gen 37.36; 39.1
40.5 Gen 20.3 37.5-10; 40.8 41.1-7,11
40.8 Gen 41.15,16 Job 33.15,16 Dan 2.28
40.9 Gen 37.5 Judg 7.13
40.12 Gen 41.12 Judg 7.14 Dan 2.36
40.13 Gen 40.19,20

[l] Heb *he*

39.20 Prisons were grim places with vile conditions. They were used to house forced laborers or, like Joseph, the accused who were awaiting trial. In ancient days, prisoners were guilty until proven innocent, and there was no right to a speedy trial. Many prisoners never made it to court, because trials were held at the whim of the ruler. Joseph was in prison two years until he appeared before Pharaoh, and then he was called out to interpret a dream, not to stand trial.

39.21–23 As a prisoner and slave, Joseph could have seen his situation as hopeless. Instead, he did his best with each small task given him. His diligence and positive attitude were soon noticed by the jail warden, who promoted him to prison administrator. Are you facing a seemingly hopeless predicament? At work, at home, or at school, follow Joseph's example by taking each small task and doing your best. Remember how God turned Joseph's situation around. He will see your efforts and can reverse even overwhelming odds.

40.1–3 The cupbearer and the baker were two of the most trusted men in Pharaoh's kingdom. The baker was in charge of making the king's food, and the cupbearer tasted all the king's food and drink before giving it to him, in case any of it was contaminated or poisoned. These trusted men must have been suspected of a serious wrong, perhaps of conspiring against Pharaoh. Later the cupbearer was released and the baker executed.

40.8 When the subject of dreams came up, Joseph focused everyone's attention on God. Rather than using the situation to make himself look good, he turned it into a powerful witness for the Lord. One secret of effective witnessing is to recognize opportunities to relate God to the other person's experience. When the opportunity arises, we must have the courage to speak, as Joseph did.

Pharaoh's cup in his hand, just as you used to do when you were his cupbeares.
14 But remember me when it is well with you; please do me the kindness to make
mention of me to Pharaoh, and so get me out of this place. 15 For in fact I was stolen
out of the land of the Hebrews; and here also I have done nothing that they should
have put me into the dungeon."
16 When the chief baker saw that the interpretation was favorable, he said to
Joseph, "I also had a dream: there were three cake baskets on my head, 17 and in the
uppermost basket there were all sorts of baked food for Pharaoh, but the birds were
eating it out of the basket on my head." 18 And Joseph answered, "This is its interpretation: the three baskets are three days; 19 within three days Pharaoh will lift up
your head—from you!—and hang you on a pole; and the birds will eat the flesh
from you."
20 On the third day, which was Pharaoh's birthday, he made a feast for all his
servants, and lifted up the head of the chief cupbearer and the head of the chief
baker among his servants. 21 He restored the chief cupbearer to his cupbearing, and
he placed the cup in Pharaoh's hand; 22 but the chief baker he hanged, just as Joseph
had interpreted to them. 23 Yet the chief cupbearer did not remember Joseph, but
forgot him.

40.14 Josh 2.12; 1 Sam 20.13,14
40.15 Gen 37.28; 39.1,20
40.16 Gen 40.1,2
40.18 Gen 40.12; 41.13
40.19 Gen 40.22; 41.13; Deut 21.22
40.20 Gen 40.13,18; 2 Kgs 25.27-30; Jer 52.31-34
40.22 Gen 40.19
40.23 Gen 40.14; 41.9

4. Joseph is placed in charge of Egypt

Pharaoh's strange dream

41 After two whole years, Pharaoh dreamed that he was standing by the Nile,
2 and there came up out of the Nile seven sleek and fat cows, and they grazed
in the reed grass. 3 Then seven other cows, ugly and thin, came up out of the Nile
after them, and stood by the other cows on the bank of the Nile. 4 The ugly and thin
cows ate up the seven sleek and fat cows. And Pharaoh awoke. 5 Then he fell asleep
and dreamed a second time; seven ears of grain, plump and good, were growing on
one stalk. 6 Then seven ears, thin and blighted by the east wind, sprouted after
them. 7 The thin ears swallowed up the seven plump and full ears. Pharaoh awoke,
and it was a dream. 8 In the morning his spirit was troubled; so he sent and called

41.2 Job 8.11; Isa 19.7
41.3 Gen 41.20,21
41.4 1 Kgs 3.15
41.6 Ezek 17.10; 19.12

PARALLELS BETWEEN JOSEPH AND JESUS
Genesis 37—50

Joseph	Parallels	Jesus
37.3	His father loved him dearly	Matthew 3.17
37.2	A shepherd of his father's sheep	John 10.11, 27
37.13, 14	Sent by father to brothers	Hebrews 2.11
37.4	Hated by brothers	John 7.5
37.20	Others plotted to harm them	John 11.53
39.7	Tempted	Matthew 4.1
37.25	Taken to Egypt	Matthew 2.14, 15
37.23	Robes taken from them	John 19.23
37.28	Sold for the price of a slave	Matthew 26.15
39.20	Bound in chains	Matthew 27.2
39.16–18	Falsely accused	Matthew 26.59, 60
40.2, 3	Placed with two other prisoners, one who was saved and the other lost	Luke 23.32
41.46	Both 30 years old at the beginning of public recognition	Luke 3.23
41.41	Exalted after suffering	Philippians 2.9–11
45.1–15	Forgave those who wronged them	Luke 23.34
45.7	Saved their nation	Matthew 1.21
50.20	What men did to hurt them God turned to good	1 Corinthians 2.7, 8

40.23 When Pharaoh's cupbearer was freed from prison, he forgot about Joseph. It was two full years before Joseph had another opportunity to be freed (41.1). Yet Joseph's faith was deep, and he would be ready when the next chance came. When you feel passed by, over looked, or forgotten, trust God as Joseph did. More opportunities may be waiting.

41.8 Magicians and wise men were common in the palaces of ancient rulers. Their job description included studying sacred arts and sciences, reading the stars, interpreting dreams, predicting the future, and performing magic. These men had power (see Exodus 7.11, 12), but their power was satanic. They were unable to interpret Pharaoh's dream, but God had revealed it to Joseph.

for all the magicians of Egypt and all its wise men. Pharaoh told them his dreams,
but there was no one who could interpret them to Pharaoh.
9 Then the chief cupbearer said to Pharaoh, "I remember my faults today.
10 Once Pharaoh was angry with his servants, and put me and the chief baker in
custody in the house of the captain of the guard. 11 We dreamed on the same night,
he and I, each having a dream with its own meaning. 12 A young Hebrew was there
with us, a servant of the captain of the guard. When we told him, he interpreted our
dreams to us, giving an interpretation to each according to his dream. 13 As he interpreted to us, so it turned out; I was restored to my office, and the baker was
hanged."
14 Then Pharaoh sent for Joseph, and he was hurriedly brought out of the dungeon. When he had shaved himself and changed his clothes, he came in before
Pharaoh. 15 And Pharaoh said to Joseph, "I have had a dream, and there is no one
who can interpret it. I have heard it said of you that when you hear a dream you can
interpret it." 16 Joseph answered Pharaoh, "It is not I; God will give Pharaoh a favorable answer." 17 Then Pharaoh said to Joseph, "In my dream I was standing on
the banks of the Nile; 18 and seven cows, fat and sleek, came up out of the Nile and
fed in the reed grass. 19 Then seven other cows came up after them, poor, very ugly,
and thin. Never had I seen such ugly ones in all the land of Egypt. 20 The thin and
ugly cows ate up the first seven fat cows, 21 but when they had eaten them no one
would have known that they had done so, for they were still as ugly as before. Then
I awoke. 22 I fell asleep a second time[m] and I saw in my dream seven ears of grain,
full and good, growing on one stalk, 23 and seven ears, withered, thin, and blighted
by the east wind, sprouting after them; 24 and the thin ears swallowed up the seven
good ears. But when I told it to the magicians, there was no one who could explain
it to me."
25 Then Joseph said to Pharaoh, "Pharaoh's dreams are one and the same; God
has revealed to Pharaoh what he is about to do. 26 The seven good cows are seven
years, and the seven good ears are seven years; the dreams are one. 27 The seven
lean and ugly cows that came up after them are seven years, as are the seven empty
ears blighted by the east wind. They are seven years of famine. 28 It is as I told
Pharaoh; God has shown to Pharaoh what he is about to do. 29 There will come
seven years of great plenty throughout all the land of Egypt. 30 After them there will
arise seven years of famine, and all the plenty will be forgotten in the land of Egypt;
the famine will consume the land. 31 The plenty will no longer be known in the land
because of the famine that will follow, for it will be very grievous. 32 And the dou-
bling of Pharaoh's dream means that the thing is fixed by God, and God will shortly
bring it about. 33 Now therefore let Pharaoh select a man who is discerning and
wise, and set him over the land of Egypt. 34 Let Pharaoh proceed to appoint overseers over the land, and take one-fifth of the produce of the land of Egypt during the
seven plenteous years. 35 Let them gather all the food of these good years that are
coming, and lay up grain under the authority of Pharaoh for food in the cities, and
let them keep it. 36 That food shall be a reserve for the land against the seven years
of famine that are to befall the land of Egypt, so that the land may not perish
through the famine."

[m] Gk Syr Vg: Heb lacks *I fell asleep a second time*

41.8 Ex 7.11; Dan 2.1-3; 4.5; Mt 2.1
41.9 Gen 40.14,23
41.10 Gen 40.2
41.11 Gen 40.5-8
41.12 Gen 40.12-19
41.13 Gen 40.22
41.14 Ex 10.16; Ps 105.16-22
41.15 Gen 41.8; Dan 2.25
41.16 Gen 40.8; Num 12.6; Dan 2.28-30; Acts 3.12
41.17 Gen 41.1-7, 26,27
41.18 Gen 41.28,32
41.26 Gen 40.12,18
41.27 Gen 41.30,54; 2 Sam 24.13; 2 Kgs 8.1
41.29 Gen 41.47
41.30 Gen 47.13
41.32 Gen 37.9; Job 33.14; Isa 14.24; 46.10
41.33 Gen 41.39; Dan 4.27
41.34 Ex 18.19; Deut 1.13; 2 Chron 34.12
41.36 Gen 47.13

41.14 Our most important opportunities may come when we least expect them. Joseph was brought hastily from the dungeon and pushed before Pharaoh. Did he have time to prepare? Yes and no. He had no warning that he would be suddenly pulled from prison and questioned by the king. Yet Joseph was ready for almost anything because of his right relationship with God. It was not Joseph's knowledge of dreams that helped him interpret their meaning. It was his knowledge of God. Be ready for opportunities by getting to know more about God. Then you will be ready to call on him when opportunities come your way.

41.16 Joseph made sure that he gave the credit to God. We should be careful to do the same. To take the honor for ourselves is a form of stealing God's honor. Don't be silent when you know you should be giving glory and credit to God.

41.28–36 After interpreting Pharaoh's dream, Joseph gave the king a survival plan for the next 14 years. The only way to prevent starvation was through careful planning; without a "famine plan" Egypt would have turned from prosperity to ruin. Many find detailed planning boring and unnecessary. But planning is a responsibility, not an option. Joseph was able to save a nation by translating God's plan for Egypt into practical actions. We must take time to translate God's plan for us into practical actions too.

Joseph becomes a ruler

37 The proposal pleased Pharaoh and all his servants. 38 Pharaoh said to his
servants, "Can we find anyone else like this—one in whom is the spirit of God?"
39 So Pharaoh said to Joseph, "Since God has shown you all this, there is no one so
discerning and wise as you. 40 You shall be over my house, and all my people shall
order themselves as you command; only with regard to the throne will I be greater
than you." 41 And Pharaoh said to Joseph, "See, I have set you over all the land of
Egypt." 42 Removing his signet ring from his hand, Pharaoh put it on Joseph's
hand; he arrayed him in garments of fine linen, and put a gold chain around his
neck. 43 He had him ride in the chariot of his second-in-command; and they cried
out in front of him, "Bow the knee!"[n] Thus he set him over all the land of Egypt.
44 Moreover Pharaoh said to Joseph, "I am Pharaoh, and without your consent no
one shall lift up hand or foot in all the land of Egypt." 45 Pharaoh gave Joseph the
name Zaphenath-paneah; and he gave him Asenath daughter of Potiphera, priest of
On, as his wife. Thus Joseph gained authority over the land of Egypt.

46 Joseph was thirty years old when he entered the service of Pharaoh king of
Egypt. And Joseph went out from the presence of Pharaoh, and went through all the
land of Egypt. 47 During the seven plenteous years the earth produced abundantly.
48 He gathered up all the food of the seven years when there was plenty[o] in the land
of Egypt, and stored up food in the cities; he stored up in every city the food from
the fields around it. 49 So Joseph stored up grain in such abundance—like the sand
of the sea—that he stopped measuring it; it was beyond measure.

50 Before the years of famine came, Joseph had two sons, whom Asenath
daughter of Potiphera, priest of On, bore to him. 51 Joseph named the firstborn
Manasseh,[p] "For," he said, "God has made me forget all my hardship and all my
father's house." 52 The second he named Ephraim,[q] "For God has made me fruitful
in the land of my misfortunes."

53 The seven years of plenty that prevailed in the land of Egypt came to an end;
54 and the seven years of famine began to come, just as Joseph had said. There was
famine in every country, but throughout the land of Egypt there was bread. 55 When
all the land of Egypt was famished, the people cried to Pharaoh for bread. Pharaoh
said to all the Egyptians, "Go to Joseph; what he says to you, do." 56 And since the
famine had spread over all the land, Joseph opened all the storehouses,[r] and sold
to the Egyptians, for the famine was severe in the land of Egypt. 57 Moreover, all
the world came to Joseph in Egypt to buy grain, because the famine became severe
throughout the world.

[n] *Abrek*, apparently an Egyptian word similar in sound to the Hebrew word meaning *to kneel* [o] Sam Gk: MT *the seven years that were* [p] That is *Making to forget* [q] From a Hebrew word meaning *to be fruitful* [r] Gk Vg Compare Syr: Heb *opened all that was in* (or, *among*) *them*

41.37 Prov 25.11 Acts 7.10
41.38 Job 32.8 Dan 4.8,18 5.11,14
41.39 Gen 41.28,33
41.40 Gen 39.4,22 42.6; 45.8 Ps 105.21 Prov 22.29 Acts 7.10
41.41 Esth 10.3 Prov 17.2 Dan 6.3
41.42 Esth 3.10,6.8
41.44 Gen 45.8 Ps 105.21,22
41.45 Ezek 30.17
41.46 Gen 37.2; 50.22
41.47 Gen 26.12
41.48 Gen 47.21
41.49 Judg 6.5; 7.12 1 Sam 13.5
41.50 Gen 46.20
41.51 Gen 48.5
41.54 Gen 41.27 45.11 Acts 7.11
41.55 Gen 41.40,41, 49 Jer 14.1
41.57 Gen 42.5; 50.20 Ps 105.16

41.38 Pharaoh recognized that Joseph was a man "in whom is the spirit of God." You probably won't get to interpret dreams for a king, but those who know you should be able to see God in you, through your kind words, merciful acts, and wise advice. Do your relatives, neighbors, and co-workers see you as a person in whom the spirit of God lives?

41.38–40 Joseph rose quickly to the top, from prison walls to Pharaoh's palace. His training for this important position involved being first a slave and then a prisoner. In each situation he learned the importance of serving God and others. Whatever your situation, no matter how undesirable, consider it part of your training program for serving God.

41.45 Pharaoh may have been trying to make Joseph more acceptable by giving him an Egyptian name and wife. He probably wanted to (1) play down the fact that Joseph was a nomadic shepherd, an occupation disliked by the Egyptians, (2) make Joseph's name easier for Egyptians to pronounce and remember, and (3) show how highly he was honored by giving him the daughter of a prominent Egyptian official.

41.46 Joseph was 30 years old when he became governor of Egypt. He was 17 when he was sold into slavery by his brothers, thus he must have spent 11 years as an Egyptian slave and 2 years in prison.

41.54 Famine was a catastrophe in ancient times, just as it still is in many parts of the world today. Almost perfect conditions were needed to produce good crops, because there were no chemical fertilizers or pesticides. Any variances in rainfall or insect activity could cause crop failure and great hunger because the people relied almost exclusively on their own crops for food. Lack of storage, refrigeration, or transportation turned a moderate famine into a desperate situation. The famine Joseph prepared for was described as "severe." Without God's intervention, the Egyptian nation would have crumbled.

5. Joseph and his brothers meet in Egypt

Joseph's brothers go to buy grain

42 When Jacob learned that there was grain in Egypt, he said to his sons, "Why
do you keep looking at one another? 2 I have heard," he said, "that there is
grain in Egypt; go down and buy grain for us there, that we may live and not die."
3 So ten of Joseph's brothers went down to buy grain in Egypt. 4 But Jacob did not
send Joseph's brother Benjamin with his brothers, for he feared that harm might
come to him. 5 Thus the sons of Israel were among the other people who came to
buy grain, for the famine had reached the land of Canaan.
6 Now Joseph was governor over the land; it was he who sold to all the people
of the land. And Joseph's brothers came and bowed themselves before him with
their faces to the ground. 7 When Joseph saw his brothers, he recognized them, but
he treated them like strangers and spoke harshly to them. "Where do you come
from?" he said. They said, "From the land of Canaan, to buy food." 8 Although
Joseph had recognized his brothers, they did not recognize him. 9 Joseph also remembered the dreams that he had dreamed about them. He said to them, "You are
spies; you have come to see the nakedness of the land!" 10 They said to him, "No,
my lord; your servants have come to buy food. 11 We are all sons of one man; we
are honest men; your servants have never been spies." 12 But he said to them, "No,
you have come to see the nakedness of the land!" 13 They said, "We, your servants,
are twelve brothers, the sons of a certain man in the land of Canaan; the youngest,
however, is now with our father, and one is no more." 14 But Joseph said to them,
"It is just as I have said to you; you are spies! 15 Here is how you shall be tested: as
Pharaoh lives, you shall not leave this place unless your youngest brother comes
here! 16 Let one of you go and bring your brother, while the rest of you remain in
prison, in order that your words may be tested, whether there is truth in you; or
else, as Pharaoh lives, surely you are spies." 17 And he put them all together in
prison for three days.
18 On the third day Joseph said to them, "Do this and you will live, for I fear
God: 19 if you are honest men, let one of your brothers stay here where you are
imprisoned. The rest of you shall go and carry grain for the famine of your households, 20 and bring your youngest brother to me. Thus your words will be verified,
and you shall not die." And they agreed to do so. 21 They said to one another, "Alas,
we are paying the penalty for what we did to our brother; we saw his anguish when
he pleaded with us, but we would not listen. That is why this anguish has come
upon us." 22 Then Reuben answered them, "Did I not tell you not to wrong the boy?
But you would not listen. So now there comes a reckoning for his blood." 23 They
did not know that Joseph understood them, since he spoke with them through an
interpreter. 24 He turned away from them and wept; then he returned and spoke to
them. And he picked out Simeon and had him bound before their eyes. 25 Joseph
then gave orders to fill their bags with grain, to return every man's money to his
sack, and to give them provisions for their journey. This was done for them.
26 They loaded their donkeys with their grain, and departed. 27 When one of
them opened his sack to give his donkey fodder at the lodging place, he saw his

42.1 Acts 7.12
42.2 Gen 43.2; 45.9
42.3 Gen 42.13
42.4 Gen 43.8
42.5 Gen 41.57 Acts 7.11
42.6 Ps 105.16-21
42.7 Gen 42.14-17
42.8 Gen 37.2,6-9
42.9 Gen 42.16, 30-34
42.10 Gen 27.29 37.8; 42.2
42.11 Gen 42.19, 31-34
42.13 Gen 37.30 42.4; 43.7 44.20; 46.8-26
42.14 Gen 42.9
42.15 Gen 42.34
42.17 Gen 40.4
42.18 Gen 20.11 Lev 25.43
42.20 Gen 42.34 43.15
42.21 Gen 37.23-28 41.9 Num 32.23
42.22 Gen 9.6 37.21,22 Lk 23.41
42.24 Gen 43.14,23, 30; 45.14
42.25 Gen 44.1
42.27 Gen 43.21 Ex 4.24

42.1, 2 Why was grain so valuable in those days? As a food source it was universal and used in nearly everything eaten. It could be dried and stored much longer than any vegetables, milk products, or meat. It was so important that it was even used as money.

42.4 Jacob was especially fond of Benjamin because he was Joseph's only full brother and—as far as Jacob knew—the only surviving son of his beloved wife, Rachel. Benjamin was Jacob's youngest son and a child of his old age.

42.7 Joseph could have revealed his identity to his brothers at once. But Joseph's last memory of them was of staring in horror at their faces as slave traders carried him away. Were his brothers still evil and treacherous, or had they changed over the years? Joseph decided to put them through a few tests to find out.

42.8, 9 Joseph remembered his dreams about his brothers bowing down to him (37.6–9). Those dreams were coming true! As a young boy, Joseph was boastful about his dreams. As a man, he no longer flaunted his superior status. He did not feel the need to say "I told you so." It was not yet time to reveal his identity, so he kept quiet. Sometimes it is best for us to remain quiet, even when we would like to have the last word.

42.15 Joseph was testing his brothers to make sure they had not been as cruel to Benjamin as they had been to him. Benjamin was his only full brother, and he wanted to see him face to face.

42.22 Reuben couldn't resist saying, "I told you so." "Reckoning for his blood" means that they thought they were being punished by God for what they had done to Joseph.

money at the top of the sack. 28He said to his brothers, "My money has been put
back; here it is in my sack!" At this they lost heart and turned trembling to one
another, saying, "What is this that God has done to us?"
29 When they came to their father Jacob in the land of Canaan, they told him all
that had happened to them, saying, 30"The man, the lord of the land, spoke harshly
to us, and charged us with spying on the land. 31But we said to him, 'We are honest
men, we are not spies. 32We are twelve brothers, sons of our father; one is no more,
and the youngest is now with our father in the land of Canaan.' 33Then the man, the
lord of the land, said to us, 'By this I shall know that you are honest men: leave one
of your brothers with me, take grain for the famine of your households, and go your
way. 34Bring your youngest brother to me, and I shall know that you are not spies
but honest men. Then I will release your brother to you, and you may trade in the
land.' "
35 As they were emptying their sacks, there in each one's sack was his bag of
money. When they and their father saw their bundles of money, they were dismayed. 36And their father Jacob said to them, "I am the one you have bereaved of
children: Joseph is no more, and Simeon is no more, and now you would take
Benjamin. All this has happened to me!" 37Then Reuben said to his father, "You
may kill my two sons if I do not bring him back to you. Put him in my hands, and
I will bring him back to you." 38But he said, "My son shall not go down with you,
for his brother is dead, and he alone is left. If harm should come to him on the
journey that you are to make, you would bring down my gray hairs with sorrow to
Sheol."

Jacob lets Benjamin go

43 Now the famine was severe in the land. 2And when they had eaten up the
grain that they had brought from Egypt, their father said to them, "Go again,
buy us a little more food." 3But Judah said to him, "The man solemnly warned us,
saying, 'You shall not see my face unless your brother is with you.' 4If you will
send our brother with us, we will go down and buy you food; 5but if you will not
send him, we will not go down, for the man said to us, 'You shall not see my face,
unless your brother is with you.' " 6Israel said, "Why did you treat me so badly as
to tell the man that you had another brother?" 7They replied, "The man questioned
us carefully about ourselves and our kindred, saying, 'Is your father still alive?
Have you another brother?' What we told him was in answer to these questions.
Could we in any way know that he would say, 'Bring your brother down'?" 8Then
Judah said to his father Israel, "Send the boy with me, and let us be on our way, so
that we may live and not die—you and we and also our little ones. 9I myself will
be surety for him; you can hold me accountable for him. If I do not bring him back
to you and set him before you, then let me bear the blame forever. 10If we had not
delayed, we would now have returned twice."
11 Then their father Israel said to them, "If it must be so, then do this: take some
of the choice fruits of the land in your bags, and carry them down as a present to the
man—a little balm and a little honey, gum, resin, pistachio nuts, and almonds.
12Take double the money with you. Carry back with you the money that was

42.28 Gen 27.33; Isa 45.7; Lam 3.37
42.30 Gen 42.7
42.31 Gen 42.11
42.32 Gen 42.13
42.33 Gen 42.19
42.34 Gen 42.20
42.35 Gen 42.27; 43.12,21
42.36 Gen 43.14; 44.20-22
42.37 Gen 43.9; 44.32
42.38 Gen 37.35; 44.20-22,29; 1 Kgs 2.6
43.1 Gen 41.5,6,7; 42.5
43.2 Gen 43.15
43.3 Gen 42.15; 44.23
43.7 Gen 42.13; 43.27
43.8 Gen 42.2; 44.26; 45.18,19
43.9 Gen 42.37; 44.32; Heb 7.22
43.11 Gen 32.13; 37.25; 43.25
43.12 Gen 42.35

43.1 Jacob and his sons had no relief from the famine. They could not see God's overall plan of sending them to Egypt to be reunited with Joseph and fed from Egypt's storehouses. If you are praying for relief from suffering or pressure and God is not bringing it as quickly as you would like, remember that God may be leading you to special treasures.

43.9 A "security" is a guarantee or pledge for the fulfillment of a promise. Judah accepted full responsibility for Benjamin's safety. He did not know what that might mean for him, but he was determined to do his duty. It was Judah's stirring words that caused Joseph to reveal himself to his brothers (44.18–34). Accepting responsibilities is difficult, but it builds character and confidence, earns others' respect, and motivates us to complete our work.

43.11 These gifts of balm, honey, gum, resin, pistachio nuts, and almonds were highly valuable specialty items not common in Egypt. Because of the famine, they were even more rare.

43.12 Joseph's brothers arrived home from Egypt only to find in their grain sacks the money they had used to pay for the grain (42.35). Some months later, when it was time to return to Egypt for more food, Jacob instructed them to take extra money so they could pay for the previous purchase as well as for additional grain. He was a man of integrity who paid for what he bought, whether he had to or not. We should follow his example and guard our integrity. A reputation for honesty is worth far more than the money we might save by compromising it.

returned in the top of your sacks; perhaps it was an oversight. 13 Take your brother
also, and be on your way again to the man; 14 may God Almighty[s] grant you mercy
before the man, so that he may send back your other brother and Benjamin. As for
me, if I am bereaved of my children, I am bereaved." 15 So the men took the
present, and they took double the money with them, as well as Benjamin. Then
they went on their way down to Egypt, and stood before Joseph.

16 When Joseph saw Benjamin with them, he said to the steward of his house,
"Bring the men into the house, and slaughter an animal and make ready, for the
men are to dine with me at noon." 17 The man did as Joseph said, and brought the
men to Joseph's house. 18 Now the men were afraid because they were brought to
Joseph's house, and they said, "It is because of the money, replaced in our sacks
the first time, that we have been brought in, so that he may have an opportunity to
fall upon us, to make slaves of us and take our donkeys." 19 So they went up to the
steward of Joseph's house and spoke with him at the entrance to the house. 20 They
said, "Oh, my lord, we came down the first time to buy food; 21 and when we came
to the lodging place we opened our sacks, and there was each one's money in the
top of his sack, our money in full weight. So we have brought it back with us.
22 Moreover we have brought down with us additional money to buy food. We do
not know who put our money in our sacks." 23 He replied, "Rest assured, do not be
afraid; your God and the God of your father must have put treasure in your sacks for
you; I received your money." Then he brought Simeon out to them. 24 When the
steward[t] had brought the men into Joseph's house, and given them water, and they
had washed their feet, and when he had given their donkeys fodder, 25 they made
the present ready for Joseph's coming at noon, for they had heard that they would
dine there.

26 When Joseph came home, they brought him the present that they had carried
into the house, and bowed to the ground before him. 27 He inquired about their
welfare, and said, "Is your father well, the old man of whom you spoke? Is he still
alive?" 28 They said, "Your servant our father is well; he is still alive." And they
bowed their heads and did obeisance. 29 Then he looked up and saw his brother
Benjamin, his mother's son, and said, "Is this your youngest brother, of whom you
spoke to me? God be gracious to you, my son!" 30 With that, Joseph hurried out,
because he was overcome with affection for his brother, and he was about to weep.
So he went into a private room and wept there. 31 Then he washed his face and came
out; and controlling himself he said, "Serve the meal." 32 They served him by himself, and them by themselves, and the Egyptians who ate with him by themselves,
because the Egyptians could not eat with the Hebrews, for that is an abomination to
the Egyptians. 33 When they were seated before him, the firstborn according to his
birthright and the youngest according to his youth, the men looked at one another
in amazement. 34 Portions were taken to them from Joseph's table, but Benjamin's
portion was five times as much as any of theirs. So they drank and were merry with
him.

44 Then he commanded the steward of his house, "Fill the men's sacks with
food, as much as they can carry, and put each man's money in the top of his
sack. 2 Put my cup, the silver cup, in the top of the sack of the youngest, with his
money for the grain." And he did as Joseph told him. 3 As soon as the morning was

[s] Traditional rendering of Heb *El Shaddai* [t] Heb *the man*

43.13 Gen 42.38; 43.4
43.14 Gen 39.21; 42.36; Ps 106.46
43.16 Gen 31.54; 44.1
43.18 Gen 42.28,35
43.21 Gen 42.27,35; 43.12
43.22 Gen 42.25
43.23 Gen 42.24
43.24 Gen 18.4; 24.32; Lk 7.44
43.26 Gen 42.6
43.27 Gen 43.7; 45.3; Ex 18.7
43.28 Ex 18.7
43.29 Num 6.25; Ps 67.1
43.30 Gen 42.24; 45.2,14,15; 46.29
43.31 Gen 43.25; 45.1; Isa 42.14
43.32 Gen 46.34; Ex 8.26
43.33 Gen 44.12
44.1 Gen 42.25; 43.16

43.23 How did the money get into the sacks? Most likely, Joseph instructed his steward to replace the money and then explain it with this response. Note that the steward credited their God, not some Egyptian deity.

43.28 To do *obeisance* means to show respect and give honor by kneeling and placing one's face on the ground.

43.32 Why did Joseph eat by himself? He was following the laws of the Egyptians' caste system. Egyptians considered themselves highly intelligent and sophisticated. They looked upon shepherds and nomads as uncultured and even vulgar. As a Hebrew, Joseph could not eat with Egyptians even though he outranked them. As foreigners and shepherds, his brothers were lower in rank than any Egyptian citizens, so they had to eat separately too.

44.2 Joseph's silver cup was a symbol of his authority. It was thought to have supernatural powers, and to steal it was a serious crime. Such goblets were used for predicting the future. A person poured water into the cup and interpreted the reflections, ripples, and bubbles. Joseph wouldn't have needed his cup, since God told him everything he needed to know about the future.

light, the men were sent away with their donkeys. 4 When they had gone only a
short distance from the city, Joseph said to his steward, "Go, follow after the men;
and when you overtake them, say to them, 'Why have you returned evil for good?
Why have you stolen my silver cup?[u] 5 Is it not from this that my lord drinks? Does
he not indeed use it for divination? You have done wrong in doing this.' "
6 When he overtook them, he repeated these words to them. 7 They said to him,
"Why does my lord speak such words as these? Far be it from your servants that
they should do such a thing! 8 Look, the money that we found at the top of our
sacks, we brought back to you from the land of Canaan; why then would we steal
silver or gold from your lord's house? 9 Should it be found with any one of your
servants, let him die; moreover the rest of us will become my lord's slaves." 10 He
said, "Even so; in accordance with your words, let it be: he with whom it is found
shall become my slave, but the rest of you shall go free." 11 Then each one quickly
lowered his sack to the ground, and each opened his sack. 12 He searched, beginning with the eldest and ending with the youngest; and the cup was found in Benjamin's sack. 13 At this they tore their clothes. Then each one loaded his donkey, and
they returned to the city.
14 Judah and his brothers came to Joseph's house while he was still there; and
they fell to the ground before him. 15 Joseph said to them, "What deed is this that
you have done? Do you not know that one such as I can practice divination?" 16 And
Judah said, "What can we say to my lord? What can we speak? How can we clear
ourselves? God has found out the guilt of your servants; here we are then, my lord's
slaves, both we and also the one in whose possession the cup has been found."
17 But he said, "Far be it from me that I should do so! Only the one in whose possession the cup was found shall be my slave; but as for you, go up in peace to your
father."
18 Then Judah stepped up to him and said, "O my lord, let your servant please
speak a word in my lord's ears, and do not be angry with your servant; for you are
like Pharaoh himself. 19 My lord asked his servants, saying, 'Have you a father or
a brother?' 20 And we said to my lord, 'We have a father, an old man, and a young
brother, the child of his old age. His brother is dead; he alone is left of his mother's
children, and his father loves him.' 21 Then you said to your servants, 'Bring him
down to me, so that I may set my eyes on him.' 22 We said to my lord, 'The boy
cannot leave his father, for if he should leave his father, his father would die.'
23 Then you said to your servants, 'Unless your youngest brother comes down with
you, you shall see my face no more.' 24 When we went back to your servant my
father we told him the words of my lord. 25 And when our father said, 'Go again,
buy us a little food,' 26 we said, 'We cannot go down. Only if our youngest brother
goes with us, will we go down; for we cannot see the man's face unless our youngest brother is with us.' 27 Then your servant my father said to us, 'You know that
my wife bore me two sons; 28 one left me, and I said, Surely he has been torn to
pieces; and I have never seen him since. 29 If you take this one also from me, and
harm comes to him, you will bring down my gray hairs in sorrow to Sheol.' 30 Now
therefore, when I come to your servant my father and the boy is not with us, then,

[u] Gk Compare Vg: Heb lacks *Why have you stolen my silver cup?*

44.4 Prov 17.13
44.5 Gen 30.27 Lev 19.26 Deut 18.10-14
44.8 Gen 43.21 Ex 20.15
44.9 Gen 31.32 44.16 Ps 7.3-5
44.12 Gen 44.2
44.13 Gen 37.29,34 Num 14.6
44.14 Gen 43.26
44.15 Gen 41.38; 44.5
44.16 Gen 42.21 43.8,9 Num 32.23 Ezra 9.10
44.18 Gen 37.7,8 41.40
44.19 Gen 42.13-16 43.7
44.21 Gen 42.20,34 43.7
44.22 Gen 42.38
44.23 Gen 42.20
44.24 Gen 42.29-34
44.25 Gen 43.2
44.26 Gen 43.4,5
44.27 Gen 46.19
44.28 Gen 37.33
44.29 Gen 42.38
44.30 1 Sam 18.1

44.13 Tearing clothes was an expression of deep sorrow, a customary manner of showing grief. The brothers were terrified that Benjamin might be harmed.

44.15 Did Joseph really practice divination? Probably not—he had no desire or need to because of his relationship with God. This statement was probably part of the test to emphasize how important the cup was.

44.16–34 When Judah was younger, he showed no regard for his brother Joseph or his father, Jacob. First he convinced his brothers to sell Joseph as a slave (37.27); then he joined his brothers in lying to his father about Joseph's fate (37.32). But what a change had taken place in Judah! The man who sold one favored little brother into slavery now offered to become a slave himself to save another favored little brother. He was so concerned for his father and younger brother that he was willing to die for them. When you are ready to give up hope on yourself or others, remember that God can change even the most selfish personality.

44.18–34 Judah finally can take no more and steps forward to plead their case. Joseph could have had him killed, but Judah courageously defends himself and his brothers and pleads for mercy, offering to put himself in Benjamin's place. There are times when we should be silent; but there are also times when we should speak up, even if there could be serious repercussions. When faced with a situation that needs a strong voice and courageous action, remember Judah and speak up.

as his life is bound up in the boy's life, 31 when he sees that the boy is not with us,
he will die; and your servants will bring down the gray hairs of your servant our
father with sorrow to Sheol. 32 For your servant became surety for the boy to my **44.32**
father, saying, 'If I do not bring him back to you, then I will bear the blame in the Gen 43.9
sight of my father all my life.' 33 Now therefore, please let your servant remain as
a slave to my lord in place of the boy; and let the boy go back with his brothers.
34 For how can I go back to my father if the boy is not with me? I fear to see the
suffering that would come upon my father."

Joseph sends for Jacob

45 Then Joseph could no longer control himself before all those who stood by **45.1**
him, and he cried out, "Send everyone away from me." So no one stayed Gen 42.24 43.30
with him when Joseph made himself known to his brothers. 2 And he wept so loudly
that the Egyptians heard it, and the household of Pharaoh heard it. 3 Joseph said to **45.3**
his brothers, "I am Joseph. Is my father still alive?" But his brothers could not Gen 50.17-19 Mt 14.27
answer him, so dismayed were they at his presence. Acts 7.13
4 Then Joseph said to his brothers, "Come closer to me." And they came closer. **45.4**
He said, "I am your brother, Joseph, whom you sold into Egypt. 5 And now do not Gen 37.28
be distressed, or angry with yourselves, because you sold me here; for God sent me **45.5** Gen 50.20
before you to preserve life. 6 For the famine has been in the land these two years; **45.6**
and there are five more years in which there will be neither plowing nor harvest. Gen 41.29,30 47.18,23
7 God sent me before you to preserve for you a remnant on earth, and to keep alive
for you many survivors. 8 So it was not you who sent me here, but God; he has made **45.8**
me a father to Pharaoh, and lord of all his house and ruler over all the land of Egypt. Gen 41.39 Judg 17.10
9 Hurry and go up to my father and say to him, 'Thus says your son Joseph, God has Ps 105.21
made me lord of all Egypt; come down to me, do not delay. 10 You shall settle in the Jn 15.16; 19.11
land of Goshen, and you shall be near me, you and your children and your chil- **45.9** Acts 7.14
dren's children, as well as your flocks, your herds, and all that you have. 11 I will **45.10** Gen 46.28,34
provide for you there — since there are five more years of famine to come — so that 47.6
you and your household, and all that you have, will not come to poverty.' 12 And Ex 8.22
now your eyes and the eyes of my brother Benjamin see that it is my own mouth **45.11** Gen 45.8; 47.12
that speaks to you. 13 You must tell my father how greatly I am honored in Egypt, **45.13**
and all that you have seen. Hurry and bring my father down here." 14 Then he fell Acts 7.14
upon his brother Benjamin's neck and wept, while Benjamin wept upon his neck. **45.14** Gen 43.30
15 And he kissed all his brothers and wept upon them; and after that his brothers 46.29
talked with him.
16 When the report was heard in Pharaoh's house, "Joseph's brothers have **45.16**
come," Pharaoh and his servants were pleased. 17 Pharaoh said to Joseph, "Say to Acts 7.13
your brothers, 'Do this: load your animals and go back to the land of Canaan. **45.17** Gen 42.25; 44.1
18 Take your father and your households and come to me, so that I may give you the **45.18**
best of the land of Egypt, and you may enjoy the fat of the land.' 19 You are further Gen 27.28; 47.6
charged to say, 'Do this: take wagons from the land of Egypt for your little ones and **45.19** Gen 45.27; 46.5
for your wives, and bring your father, and come. 20 Give no thought to your posses- **45.20**
sions, for the best of all the land of Egypt is yours.' " Gen 20.15

44.32, 33 Judah had promised Jacob that he would guarantee young Benjamin's safety (43.9). Now Judah had a chance to keep that promise. Becoming a slave was a terrible fate, but Judah was determined to keep his word to his father. He showed great courage in carrying out his promise. Accepting a responsibility means carrying it out with determination and courage, regardless of the personal sacrifice.

44.33 Joseph wanted to see if his brothers' attitudes had changed for the better, so he tested the way they treated each other. Judah, the brother who had stepped forward with the plan to sell Joseph (37.27), now stepped forward to take Benjamin's punishment so that Benjamin could return to their father. This courageous act convinced Joseph that his brothers had dramatically changed for the better.

45.4–8 Although Joseph's brothers had wanted to get rid of him, God used even their evil actions to fulfill his ultimate plan. He sent Joseph ahead to preserve their lives, save Egypt, and prepare the way for the beginning of the nation of Israel. God is sovereign. His plans are not dictated by human actions. When others intend evil toward you, remember that they are only God's tools. As Joseph said to his brothers, "Even though you intended to do harm to me, God intended it for good" (50.20).

45.17–20 Joseph was rejected, kidnaped, enslaved, and imprisoned. Although his brothers had been unfaithful to him, he graciously forgave them and shared his prosperity. Joseph demonstrated how God forgives us and showers us with goodness even though we have sinned against him. The same forgiveness and blessings are ours if we ask for them.

45.22 Gen 43.34 Judg 14.12 2 Kgs 5.5
45.23 Gen 43.11
45.24 Gen 37.22 42.21 Ps 133.1-3
45.26 Gen 37.31-35
45.27 Gen 45.19,21 Judg 15.19 1 Sam 30.12
45.28 Gen 46.30 Lk 2.28-30

21 The sons of Israel did so. Joseph gave them wagons according to the instruction of Pharaoh, and he gave them provisions for the journey. 22 To each one of
them he gave a set of garments; but to Benjamin he gave three hundred pieces of
silver and five sets of garments. 23 To his father he sent the following: ten donkeys
loaded with the good things of Egypt, and ten female donkeys loaded with grain,
bread, and provision for his father on the journey. 24 Then he sent his brothers on
their way, and as they were leaving he said to them, "Do not quarrel[v] along the
way."

25 So they went up out of Egypt and came to their father Jacob in the land of
Canaan. 26 And they told him, "Joseph is still alive! He is even ruler over all the
land of Egypt." He was stunned; he could not believe them. 27 But when they told
him all the words of Joseph that he had said to them, and when he saw the wagons
that Joseph had sent to carry him, the spirit of their father Jacob revived. 28 Israel
said, "Enough! My son Joseph is still alive. I must go and see him before I die."

[v] Or *be agitated*

JUDAH

People who are leaders stand out. They don't necessarily look or act a certain way until the need for their action is apparent. Among their skills are outspokenness, decisiveness, action, and control. These skills can be used for great good or great evil. Jacob's fourth son, Judah, was a natural leader. The events of his life provided many opportunities to exercise those skills. Unfortunately Judah's decisions were often shaped more by the pressures of the moment than by a conscious desire to cooperate with God's plan. But when he did recognize his mistakes, he was willing to admit them. His experience with Tamar and the final confrontation with Joseph are both examples of Judah's willingness to bear the blame when confronted. It was one of the qualities he passed on to his descendant David.

Whether or not we have Judah's natural leadership qualities, we share with him a tendency to be blind toward our own sin. Too often, however, we don't share his willingness to admit mistakes. From Judah we can learn that it is not wise to wait until our errors force us to admit to wrongdoing. It is far better to admit our mistakes openly, to shoulder the blame, and to seek forgiveness.

Strengths and accomplishments:
- Was a natural leader—outspoken and decisive
- Thought clearly and took action in high-pressure situations
- Was willing to stand by his word and put himself on the line when necessary
- Was the fourth son of 12, through whom God would eventually bring David and Jesus, the Messiah

Weaknesses and mistakes:
- Suggested to his brothers they sell Joseph into slavery
- Failed to keep his promise to his daughter-in-law, Tamar

Lessons from his life:
- God is in control, far beyond the immediate situation
- Procrastination often makes matters worse
- Judah's offer to substitute his life for Benjamin's is a picture of what his descendant Jesus would do for all people

Vital statistics:
- Where: Canaan and Egypt
- Occupation: Shepherd
- Relatives: Parents: Jacob and Leah. Wife: Bathshua. Daughter-in-law: Tamar. Eleven brothers, at least one sister, and at least five sons

Key verses:
"Judah, your brothers shall praise you; your hand shall be on the neck of your enemies; your father's sons shall bow down before you. Judah is a lion's whelp; from the prey, my son, you have gone up. He crouches down, he stretches out like a lion, like a lioness—who dares rouse him up? The scepter shall not depart from Judah, nor the ruler's staff from between his feet, until tribute comes to him; and the obedience of the peoples is his" (Genesis 49.8–10).

Judah's story is told in Genesis 29.35—50.26. He is also mentioned in 1 Chronicles 2—4.

45.26, 27 Jacob needed some evidence before he could believe the incredible news that Joseph was alive. Similarly, Thomas refused to believe that Jesus had risen from the dead until he could see and touch him (John 20.25). It is hard to change what you believe without all the facts – or sometimes even with the facts. Don't ever give up hope that God has a wonderful future in store for you.

6. Jacob's family moves to Egypt

46 When Israel set out on his journey with all that he had and came to Beer-
sheba, he offered sacrifices to the God of his father Isaac. 2 God spoke to
Israel in visions of the night, and said, "Jacob, Jacob." And he said, "Here I am."
3 Then he said, "I am God,[w] the God of your father; do not be afraid to go down to
Egypt, for I will make of you a great nation there. 4 I myself will go down with you
to Egypt, and I will also bring you up again; and Joseph's own hand shall close your
eyes."

5 Then Jacob set out from Beer-sheba; and the sons of Israel carried their father
Jacob, their little ones, and their wives, in the wagons that Pharaoh had sent to
carry him. 6 They also took their livestock and the goods that they had acquired in
the land of Canaan, and they came into Egypt, Jacob and all his offspring with him,
7 his sons, and his sons' sons with him, his daughters, and his sons' daughters; all
his offspring he brought with him into Egypt.

8 Now these are the names of the Israelites, Jacob and his offspring, who came
to Egypt. Reuben, Jacob's firstborn, 9 and the children of Reuben: Hanoch, Pallu,
Hezron, and Carmi. 10 The children of Simeon: Jemuel, Jamin, Ohad, Jachin, Zohar, and Shaul,[x] the son of a Canaanite woman. 11 The children of Levi: Gershon,
Kohath, and Merari. 12 The children of Judah: Er, Onan, Shelah, Perez, and Zerah
(but Er and Onan died in the land of Canaan); and the children of Perez were Hezron and Hamul. 13 The children of Issachar: Tola, Puvah, Jashub,[y] and Shimron.
14 The children of Zebulun: Sered, Elon, and Jahleel 15 (these are the sons of Leah,
whom she bore to Jacob in Paddan-aram, together with his daughter Dinah; in all
his sons and his daughters numbered thirty-three). 16 The children of Gad: Ziphion,
Haggi, Shuni, Ezbon, Eri, Arodi, and Areli. 17 The children of Asher: Imnah, Ishvah, Ishvi, Beriah, and their sister Serah. The children of Beriah: Heber and Malchiel 18 (these are the children of Zilpah, whom Laban gave to his daughter Leah;
and these she bore to Jacob — sixteen persons). 19 The children of Jacob's wife Rachel: Joseph and Benjamin. 20 To Joseph in the land of Egypt were born Manasseh
and Ephraim, whom Asenath daughter of Potiphera, priest of On, bore to him.
21 The children of Benjamin: Bela, Becher, Ashbel, Gera, Naaman, Ehi, Rosh,
Muppim, Huppim, and Ard 22 (these are the children of Rachel, who were born to
Jacob — fourteen persons in all). 23 The children of Dan: Hashum.[z] 24 The children
of Naphtali: Jahzeel, Guni, Jezer, and Shillem 25 (these are the children of Bilhah,

46.1 Gen 21.14 26.22 28.10,13 31.42; 33.20 35.7
46.2 Gen 22.11 31.11
46.3 Gen 15.1; 17.1
46.4 Gen 28.15 48.21; 50.5 Ex 3.8
46.6 Acts 7.14,15
46.8 Gen 29.32 35.23; 49.3
46.9 1 Chron 5.3
46.10 1 Chron 4.24
46.11 1 Chron 6.1
46.12 1 Chron 2.3
46.16 Num 26.15 1 Chron 5.11
46.19 Gen 30.24 35.18
46.20 Gen 41.45, 50-52
46.21 Num 26.38 1 Chron 7.6
46.23 Gen 30.6 35.25; 49.16 Num 26.42

[w] Heb *the God* [x] Or *Saul* [y] Compare Sam Gk Num 26.24 1 Chr 7.1: MT *Iob* [z] Gk; Heb *Hushim*

46.3, 4 The Israelites did become a great nation, and Jacob's descendants eventually returned to Canaan. The book of Exodus recounts the story of Israel's slavery in Egypt for 400 years (fulfilling God's words to Abram in 15.13–16), and the book of Joshua gives an exciting account of the Israelites entering and conquering Canaan, the promised land.

46.3, 4 God told Jacob to leave his home and travel to a strange and faraway land. But God reassured him by promising to go with him and take care of him. When new situations or surroundings frighten you, recognize that experiencing fear is normal. To be paralyzed by fear, however, is an indication that you question God's ability to take care of you.

46.4 Jacob never returned to Canaan. This was a promise to his descendants that they would return. "Joseph's own hand shall close your eyes" refers to attending to him as he faced death. It was God's promise to Jacob that he would never know the bitterness of being lonely again.

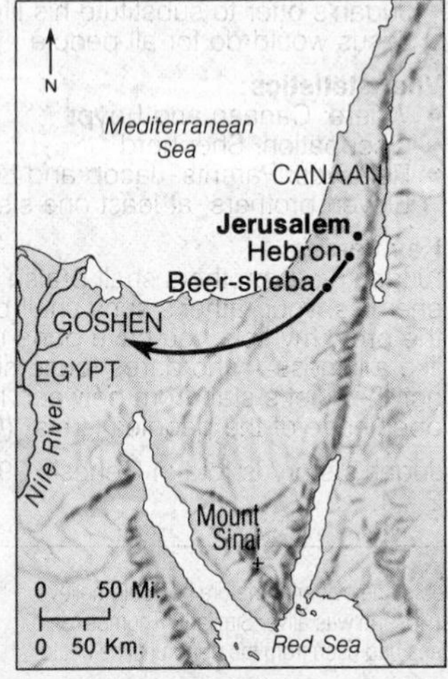

JACOB MOVES TO EGYPT
After hearing the joyful news that Joseph was alive, Jacob packed up and moved his family to Egypt. Stopping first in Beer-sheba, Jacob offered sacrifices and received assurance from God that Egypt was where he should go. Jacob and his family settled in the land of Goshen, in the northeastern part of Egypt.

46.25 Gen 35.25
46.27 Ex 1.5; 24.1 Deut 10.22 Acts 7.14
46.28 Gen 43.8 45.10; 47.1
46.29 Gen 33.4 45.10,14 Lk 15.20
46.30 Gen 45.28 Lk 2.29
46.31 Gen 45.16; 47.1
46.32 Gen 37.2,14 47.3
46.33 Gen 47.2
46.34 Gen 13.7 43.32; 47.4
47.1 Gen 46.31
47.2 Acts 7.13
47.3 Gen 46.33 Amos 7.14
47.4 Gen 15.13 43.1; 46.34 Deut 26.5
47.6 Gen 45.18 46.34; 47.11 Ex 18.21
47.7 Gen 47.10 Ex 12.32 Num 6.23
47.9 Gen 35.28 1 Chron 29.15
47.10 Gen 14.19
47.11 Ex 1.11; 12.37
47.12 Gen 45.11 47.24
47.13 Gen 41.30 Jer 14.1-6 Acts 7.11
47.14 Gen 41.56 1 Cor 4.2
47.15 Gen 47.18, 19,24

whom Laban gave to his daughter Rachel, and these she bore to Jacob—seven
persons in all). 26 All the persons belonging to Jacob who came into Egypt, who
were his own offspring, not including the wives of his sons, were sixty-six persons
in all. 27 The children of Joseph, who were born to him in Egypt, were two; all the
persons of the house of Jacob who came into Egypt were seventy.

28 Israel[a] sent Judah ahead to Joseph to lead the way before him into Goshen.
When they came to the land of Goshen, 29 Joseph made ready his chariot and went
up to meet his father Israel in Goshen. He presented himself to him, fell on his
neck, and wept on his neck a good while. 30 Israel said to Joseph, "I can die now,
having seen for myself that you are still alive." 31 Joseph said to his brothers and to
his father's household, "I will go up and tell Pharaoh, and will say to him, 'My
brothers and my father's household, who were in the land of Canaan, have come to
me. 32 The men are shepherds, for they have been keepers of livestock; and they
have brought their flocks, and their herds, and all that they have.' 33 When Pharaoh
calls you, and says, 'What is your occupation?' 34 you shall say, 'Your servants
have been keepers of livestock from our youth even until now, both we and our
ancestors'—in order that you may settle in the land of Goshen, because all shepherds are abhorrent to the Egyptians."

47 So Joseph went and told Pharaoh, "My father and my brothers, with their
flocks and herds and all that they possess, have come from the land of Canaan; they are now in the land of Goshen." 2 From among his brothers he took five
men and presented them to Pharaoh. 3 Pharaoh said to his brothers, "What is your
occupation?" And they said to Pharaoh, "Your servants are shepherds, as our ancestors were." 4 They said to Pharaoh, "We have come to reside as aliens in the
land; for there is no pasture for your servants' flocks because the famine is severe
in the land of Canaan. Now, we ask you, let your servants settle in the land of
Goshen." 5 Then Pharaoh said to Joseph, "Your father and your brothers have come
to you. 6 The land of Egypt is before you; settle your father and your brothers in the
best part of the land; let them live in the land of Goshen; and if you know that there
are capable men among them, put them in charge of my livestock."

7 Then Joseph brought in his father Jacob, and presented him before Pharaoh,
and Jacob blessed Pharaoh. 8 Pharaoh said to Jacob, "How many are the years of
your life?" 9 Jacob said to Pharaoh, "The years of my earthly sojourn are one hundred thirty; few and hard have been the years of my life. They do not compare with
the years of the life of my ancestors during their long sojourn." 10 Then Jacob
blessed Pharaoh, and went out from the presence of Pharaoh. 11 Joseph settled his
father and his brothers, and granted them a holding in the land of Egypt, in the best
part of the land, in the land of Rameses, as Pharaoh had instructed. 12 And Joseph
provided his father, his brothers, and all his father's household with food, according to the number of their dependents.

13 Now there was no food in all the land, for the famine was very severe. The
land of Egypt and the land of Canaan languished because of the famine. 14 Joseph
collected all the money to be found in the land of Egypt and in the land of Canaan,
in exchange for the grain that they bought; and Joseph brought the money into
Pharaoh's house. 15 When the money from the land of Egypt and from the land of
Canaan was spent, all the Egyptians came to Joseph, and said, "Give us food! Why
should we die before your eyes? For our money is gone." 16 And Joseph answered,
"Give me your livestock, and I will give you food in exchange for your livestock,

[a] Heb *He*

46.31–34 Jacob moved his whole family to Egypt, but they wanted to live apart from the Egyptians. To ensure this, Joseph told them to let Pharaoh know they were shepherds. Although Pharaoh may have been sympathetic to shepherds (for he was probably descended from the nomadic Hyksos line), the Egyptian culture would not willingly accept shepherds in their midst. The strategy worked, and Jacob's family was able to benefit from Pharaoh's generosity as well as from the Egyptians' prejudice.

47.1–6 The faithfulness of Joseph affected his entire family. When he was in the pit and in prison, Joseph must have wondered about his future. Instead of despairing, he faithfully obeyed God and did what was right. Here we see one of the exciting results. We may not always see the effects of our faith, but we can be sure that God will honor faithfulness.

if your money is gone." 17 So they brought their livestock to Joseph; and Joseph 47.17
gave them food in exchange for the horses, the flocks, the herds, and the donkeys. Ex 9.3 1 Kgs 10.28
That year he supplied them with food in exchange for all their livestock. 18 When
that year was ended, they came to him the following year, and said to him, "We can
not hide from my lord that our money is all spent; and the herds of cattle are my
lord's. There is nothing left in the sight of my lord but our bodies and our lands.
19 Shall we die before your eyes, both we and our land? Buy us and our land in 47.19
exchange for food. We with our land will become slaves to Pharaoh; just give us Neh 5.2 Job 2.4
seed, so that we may live and not die, and that the land may not become desolate." Lam 1.11 Mt 16.26

20 So Joseph bought all the land of Egypt for Pharaoh. All the Egyptians sold
their fields, because the famine was severe upon them; and the land became Pharaoh's. 21 As for the people, he made slaves of them[b] from one end of Egypt to the
other. 22 Only the land of the priests he did not buy; for the priests had a fixed 47.22 Gen 41.45
allowance from Pharaoh, and lived on the allowance that Pharaoh gave them; there- Deut 12.19
fore they did not sell their land. 23 Then Joseph said to the people, "Now that I have 47.23 Gen 45.6
this day bought you and your land for Pharaoh, here is seed for you; sow the land. Prov 11.26
24 And at the harvests you shall give one-fifth to Pharaoh, and four-fifths shall be 47.24 Gen 41.34
your own, as seed for the field and as food for yourselves and your households, and Lev 27.32
as food for your little ones." 25 They said, "You have saved our lives; may it please 47.25 Gen 33.15
my lord, we will be slaves to Pharaoh." 26 So Joseph made it a statute concerning 45.7; 50.20
the land of Egypt, and it stands to this day, that Pharaoh should have the fifth. The Ruth 2.13
land of the priests alone did not become Pharaoh's. 47.26 Gen 47.22

7. Jacob and Joseph die in Egypt

Jacob blesses Joseph

27 Thus Israel settled in the land of Egypt, in the region of Goshen; and they 47.27
gained possessions in it, and were fruitful and multiplied exceedingly. 28 Jacob Gen 13.16; 46.3 Ex 1.7
lived in the land of Egypt seventeen years; so the days of Jacob, the years of his life,
were one hundred forty-seven years.

29 When the time of Israel's death drew near, he called his son Joseph and said 47.29
to him, "If I have found favor with you, put your hand under my thigh and promise Gen 24.2,49 50.24,25
to deal loyally and truly with me. Do not bury me in Egypt. 30 When I lie down with Acts 7.15,16 Heb 11.21
my ancestors, carry me out of Egypt and bury me in their burial place." He an- 47.30
swered, "I will do as you have said." 31 And he said, "Swear to me"; and he swore Gen 15.15 23.19; 25.9
to him. Then Israel bowed himself on the head of his bed. 49.29

48 After this Joseph was told, "Your father is ill." So he took with him his two 48.1
sons, Manasseh and Ephraim. 2 When Jacob was told, "Your son Joseph has Gen 41.50-52 Heb 11.21
come to you," he[c] summoned his strength and sat up in bed. 3 And Jacob said to 48.3
Joseph, "God Almighty[d] appeared to me at Luz in the land of Canaan, and he Gen 28.3, 12-19; 35.9-15
blessed me, 4 and said to me, 'I am going to make you fruitful and increase your
numbers; I will make of you a company of peoples, and will give this land to your
offspring after you for a perpetual holding.' 5 Therefore your two sons, who were 48.5
born to you in the land of Egypt before I came to you in Egypt, are now mine; Gen 46.20,27
Ephraim and Manasseh shall be mine, just as Reuben and Simeon are. 6 As for the 48.6
offspring born to you after them, they shall be yours. They shall be recorded under Josh 14.4
the names of their brothers with regard to their inheritance. 7 For when I came from 48.7
Paddan, Rachel, alas, died in the land of Canaan on the way, while there was still Gen 35.19 1 Sam 10.2
some distance to go to Ephrath; and I buried her there on the way to Ephrath" (that Mt 2.18
is, Bethlehem). 48.9

8 When Israel saw Joseph's sons, he said, "Who are these?" 9 Joseph said to his Gen 27.4; 33.5 49.28

[b] Sam Gk Compare Vg: MT *He removed them to the cities* [c] Heb *Israel* [d] Traditional rendering of Heb *El Shaddai*

47.29–31 Putting a hand under the thigh was a sign of making a promise, much like shaking hands today. Jacob had Joseph promise to bury him in his homeland. Few things were written in this culture, so a person's word then carried as much force as a written contract today. People today seem to find it easy to say, "I didn't mean that." God's people, however, are to speak the truth and live the truth. Let your words be as binding as a written contract.

48.8–20 Jacob gave Ephraim, instead of his older brother Manasseh, the greater blessing. When Joseph objected, Jacob refused to listen, for God had told him that Ephraim would become greater. God often works in unexpected ways. When he chooses people to fulfill his plans, he always goes deeper than appearance, tradition,

father, "They are my sons, whom God has given me here." And he said, "Bring
them to me, please, that I may bless them." 10 Now the eyes of Israel were dim with
age, and he could not see well. So Joseph brought them near him; and he kissed
them and embraced them. 11 Israel said to Joseph, "I did not expect to see your face;
and here God has let me see your children also." 12 Then Joseph removed them
from his father's knees,[e] and he bowed himself with his face to the earth. 13 Joseph
took them both, Ephraim in his right hand toward Israel's left, and Manasseh in his
left hand toward Israel's right, and brought them near him. 14 But Israel stretched
out his right hand and laid it on the head of Ephraim, who was the younger, and his
left hand on the head of Manasseh, crossing his hands, for Manasseh was the firstborn. 15 He blessed Joseph, and said,

"The God before whom my ancestors Abraham and Isaac walked,
the God who has been my shepherd all my life to this day,
16 the angel who has redeemed me from all harm, bless the boys;
and in them let my name be perpetuated, and the name of my ancestors
Abraham and Isaac;
and let them grow into a multitude on the earth."

17 When Joseph saw that his father laid his right hand on the head of Ephraim,
it displeased him; so he took his father's hand, to remove it from Ephraim's head
to Manasseh's head. 18 Joseph said to his father, "Not so, my father! Since this one
is the firstborn, put your right hand on his head." 19 But his father refused, and said,
"I know, my son, I know; he also shall become a people, and he also shall be great.
Nevertheless his younger brother shall be greater than he, and his offspring shall
become a multitude of nations." 20 So he blessed them that day, saying,

"By you[f] Israel will invoke blessings, saying,
'God make you[f] like Ephraim and like Manasseh.'"

So he put Ephraim ahead of Manasseh. 21 Then Israel said to Joseph, "I am about
to die, but God will be with you and will bring you again to the land of your ancestors. 22 I now give to you one portion[g] more than to your brothers, the portion[g] that
I took from the hand of the Amorites with my sword and with my bow."

Jacob's prophecies

49 Then Jacob called his sons, and said: "Gather around, that I may tell you
what will happen to you in days to come.

2 Assemble and hear, O sons of Jacob;
listen to Israel your father.

3 Reuben, you are my firstborn,
my might and the first fruits of my vigor,
excelling in rank and excelling in power.

48.10 Gen 27.1
48.11 Gen 37.33,34 42.36
48.12 Gen 33.3; 42.6
48.14 Gen 41.51,52 Ex 15.6 Ps 110.1
48.15 Gen 17.1; 27.4 28.20,21 49.24,28
48.16 Gen 22.11 28.13; 31.11 32.28 Deut 28.11
48.19 Gen 28.14; 46.3 Deut 1.10
48.20 Gen 28.3 Ruth 4.11
48.21 Gen 28.15 46.4; 50.24
48.22 Gen 15.16 Josh 17.17,18 24.32; Jn 4.5
49.3 Num 26.5 Deut 21.17 1 Chron 2.1; 5.1

[e] Heb *from his knees* [f] *you* here is singular in Heb [g] Or *mountain slope* (Heb *shekem*, a play on the name of the town and district of Shechem)

---

or position. He sometimes surprises us by choosing the less obvious person. God can use you to carry out his plans, even if you don't think you have all the qualifications.

48.11 When Joseph became a slave, Jacob thought he was dead and wept in despair (37.30). But eventually God's plan allowed Jacob to regain not only his son, but his grandchildren as well. Circumstances are never so bad that they are beyond God's help. Jacob regained his son. Job got a new family (Job 42.10–17). Mary regained her brother Lazarus (John 11.1–44). We need never despair, because we belong to a loving God. We never know what good he will bring out of a seemingly hopeless situation.

48.15 Jacob spoke of God as one who was his shepherd throughout his life. In his old age, he could clearly see his dependence upon God. This marks a total attitude change from that of his scheming and dishonest youth. To develop an attitude like Jacob's, trust in God's provision and care. When you realize that every good thing comes from God, you can quit trying to grab them for yourself.

48.20–22 Jacob was giving these young boys land occupied by the Philistines and Canaanites. His gift became reality when the tribes of Ephraim and Manasseh occupied the east and west sides of the Jordan River (Joshua 16).

49.3–28 Jacob blessed each of his sons and then made a prediction about each son's future. The way the men had lived played an important part in Jacob's blessing and prophecy. Our past also affects our present and future. By sunrise tomorrow, our actions of today will have become part of the past. Yet they will already have begun to shape the future. What actions can you choose or avoid that will positively shape your future?

4 Unstable as water, you shall no longer excel
because you went up onto your father's bed;
then you defiled it—you[h] went up onto my couch!

49.4 Gen 35.22 Deut 27.20

5 Simeon and Levi are brothers;
weapons of violence are their swords.
6 May I never come into their council;
may I not be joined to their company—
for in their anger they killed men,
and at their whim they hamstrung oxen.
7 Cursed be their anger, for it is fierce,
and their wrath, for it is cruel!
I will divide them in Jacob,
and scatter them in Israel.

49.5 Gen 29.33,34 34.25
49.6 Gen 34.30
49.7 Josh 1.9 21.1-42

8 Judah, your brothers shall praise you;
your hand shall be on the neck of your enemies;
your father's sons shall bow down before you.
9 Judah is a lion's whelp;
from the prey, my son, you have gone up.
He crouches down, he stretches out like a lion,
like a lioness—who dares rouse him up?
10 The scepter shall not depart from Judah,
nor the ruler's staff from between his feet,
until tribute comes to him;[i]
and the obedience of the peoples is his.
11 Binding his foal to the vine
and his donkey's colt to the choice vine,
he washes his garments in wine
and his robe in the blood of grapes;
12 his eyes are darker than wine,
and his teeth whiter than milk.

49.8 Deut 33.7 Judg 1.1,2 20.18; Heb 7.14
49.9 Num 24.9 Mic 5.8
49.10 Num 24.17 Ps 2.6-9; 60.7

13 Zebulun shall settle at the shore of the sea;
he shall be a haven for ships,
and his border shall be at Sidon.

49.13 Deut 33.19 Josh 19.10

14 Issachar is a strong donkey,
lying down between the sheepfolds;
15 he saw that a resting place was good,
and that the land was pleasant;
so he bowed his shoulder to the burden,
and became a slave at forced labor.

49.14 Josh 19.17 Judg 5.16

16 Dan shall judge his people
as one of the tribes of Israel.
17 Dan shall be a snake by the roadside,
a viper along the path,

49.16 Deut 33.22 Judg 13.2; 15.20 Judg 18.26

[h] Gk Syr Tg: Heb *he* [i] Or *until Shiloh comes* or *until he comes to Shiloh* or (with Syr) *until he comes to whom it belongs*

49.4 The oldest son was supposed to receive a double inheritance, but Reuben lost his special honor. Unstable and untrustworthy, especially in his younger days, he had gone so far as to sleep with one of his father's concubines. Jacob could not give the birthright blessing to such a dishonorable son.

49.8–12 Why was Judah—known for selling Joseph into slavery and trying to defraud his daughter-in-law—so greatly blessed? God had chosen Judah to be the ancestor of Israel's line of kings (that is the meaning of "the scepter shall not depart from Judah"). This may have been due to Judah's dramatic change of character (44.33, 34). Judah's line would produce the promised Messiah, Jesus.

49.9 A whelp is a young offspring of a carnivorous animal.

that bites the horse's heels
so that its rider falls backward.

18 I wait for your salvation, O LORD.

49.19 Deut 33.20

19 Gad shall be raided by raiders,
but he shall raid at their heels.

49.20 Deut 33.24

20 Asher's[j] food shall be rich,
and he shall provide royal delicacies.

49.21 Deut 33.23

21 Naphtali is a doe let loose
that bears lovely fawns.[k]

49.22 Deut 33.13-17

22 Joseph is a fruitful bough,
a fruitful bough by a spring;
his branches run over the wall.[l]

49.23 Gen 37.4,18

23 The archers fiercely attacked him;
they shot at him and pressed him hard.

49.24 Isa 28.16; 49.26

24 Yet his bow remained taut,
and his arms[m] were made agile
by the hands of the Mighty One of Jacob,
by the name of the Shepherd, the Rock of Israel,
25 by the God of your father, who will help you,
by the Almighty[n] who will bless you
with blessings of heaven above,
blessings of the deep that lies beneath,
blessings of the breasts and of the womb.

49.26 Num 6.2 Deut 33.15,16

26 The blessings of your father
are stronger than the blessings of the eternal mountains,
the bounties[o] of the everlasting hills;
may they be on the head of Joseph,
on the brow of him who was set apart from his brothers.

49.27 Deut 33.12 Judg 3.15

27 Benjamin is a ravenous wolf,
in the morning devouring the prey,
and at evening dividing the spoil."

28 All these are the twelve tribes of Israel, and this is what their father said to
them when he blessed them, blessing each one of them with a suitable blessing.

49.29 Gen 23.16 25.8,9; 35.29 47.29; 50.5

29 Then he charged them, saying to them, "I am about to be gathered to my
people. Bury me with my ancestors—in the cave in the field of Ephron the Hittite,
30 in the cave in the field at Machpelah, near Mamre, in the land of Canaan, in the
field that Abraham bought from Ephron the Hittite as a burial site. 31 There Abraham and his wife Sarah were buried; there Isaac and his wife Rebekah were buried;
and there I buried Leah— 32 the field and the cave that is in it were purchased from

49.31 Gen 23.19 25.9; 35.29

[j] Gk Vg Syr: Heb *From Asher* [k] Or *that gives beautiful words* [l] Meaning of Heb uncertain [m] Heb *the arms of his hands* [n] Traditional rendering of Heb *Shaddai* [o] Cn Compare Gk: Heb *of my progenitors to the boundaries*

49.18 In the middle of his prophecy to Dan, Jacob exclaimed, "I wait for your salvation, O Lord." He was emphasizing to Dan that he would be a strong leader only if his trust was in God, not in his natural strength or ability. Those who are strong, attractive, or talented often find it easier to trust in themselves than in God, who gave them their gifts. Remember to thank God for what you are and have so your trust does not become misplaced.

49.22 Joseph was indeed fruitful, with some heroic descendants. Among them were Joshua, who would lead the Israelites into the promised land (Joshua 1.10, 11); Deborah, Gideon, and Jephthah, judges of Israel (Judges 4.4; 6.11, 12; 11.11); and Samuel, a great prophet (1 Samuel 3.19).

49.23, 24 These verses celebrate the times God rescued Joseph when his enemies attacked him. So often we struggle by ourselves, forgetting that God is able to help us fight our battles, whether they are against men with weapons or against spiritual forces. Joseph was able to draw closer to God as adversity mounted. To trust God to rescue you shows great faith. Can you trust him when injury or persecution is directed at you? Such spiritual battles require teamwork between courageous, faithful people and a mighty God.

the Hittites." 33 When Jacob ended his charge to his sons, he drew up his feet into
the bed, breathed his last, and was gathered to his people.

49.33 Gen 25.8,17 35.29

Jacob is buried in Canaan

50 Then Joseph threw himself on his father's face and wept over him and kissed
him. 2 Joseph commanded the physicians in his service to embalm his father. So the physicians embalmed Israel; 3 they spent forty days in doing this, for
that is the time required for embalming. And the Egyptians wept for him seventy
days.
4 When the days of weeping for him were past, Joseph addressed the household
of Pharaoh, "If now I have found favor with you, please speak to Pharaoh as follows: 5 My father made me swear an oath; he said, 'I am about to die. In the tomb
that I hewed out for myself in the land of Canaan, there you shall bury me.' Now
therefore let me go up, so that I may bury my father; then I will return." 6 Pharaoh
answered, "Go up, and bury your father, as he made you swear to do."
7 So Joseph went up to bury his father. With him went up all the servants of
Pharaoh, the elders of his household, and all the elders of the land of Egypt, 8 as
well as all the household of Joseph, his brothers, and his father's household. Only
their children, their flocks, and their herds were left in the land of Goshen. 9 Both
chariots and charioteers went up with him. It was a very great company. 10 When
they came to the threshing floor of Atad, which is beyond the Jordan, they held
there a very great and sorrowful lamentation; and he observed a time of mourning
for his father seven days. 11 When the Canaanite inhabitants of the land saw the
mourning on the threshing floor of Atad, they said, "This is a grievous mourning on
the part of the Egyptians." Therefore the place was named Abel-mizraim;[p] it is
beyond the Jordan. 12 Thus his sons did for him as he had instructed them. 13 They
carried him to the land of Canaan and buried him in the cave of the field at Machpelah, the field near Mamre, which Abraham bought as a burial site from Ephron the
Hittite. 14 After he had buried his father, Joseph returned to Egypt with his brothers
and all who had gone up with him to bury his father.

50.1 Gen 23.2 46.4,29
50.2 Gen 50.26
50.3 Num 20.29 Deut 34.8
50.5 Gen 47.29 48.21
50.8 Ex 10.9 Num 32.24
50.9 Gen 41.43 46.29 Ex 14.7
50.12 Ex 20.12 Acts 7.16
50.13 Gen 23.16-18

Joseph treats his brothers kindly

15 Realizing that their father was dead, Joseph's brothers said, "What if Joseph
still bears a grudge against us and pays us back in full for all the wrong that we did
to him?" 16 So they approached[q] Joseph, saying, "Your father gave this instruction
before he died, 17 'Say to Joseph: I beg you, forgive the crime of your brothers and
the wrong they did in harming you.' Now therefore please forgive the crime of the
servants of the God of your father." Joseph wept when they spoke to him. 18 Then
his brothers also wept,[r] fell down before him, and said, "We are here as your
slaves." 19 But Joseph said to them, "Do not be afraid! Am I in the place of God?
20 Even though you intended to do harm to me, God intended it for good, in order

50.17 Gen 45.5 Deut 32.35 Mt 6.12 Lk 6.27 Rom 12.19
50.18 Gen 37.7-11 42.6; 44.14
50.19 Gen 30.2
50.20 Gen 37.26

[p] That is *mourning* (or *meadow*) *of Egypt* [q] Gk Syr: Heb *they commanded* [r] Cn: Heb *also came*

50.1–11 When Jacob died at the age of 147, Joseph wept and mourned for months. When someone close to us dies, we need a long period of time to work through our grief. Crying and sharing our feelings with others helps us recover and go on with life. Allow yourself and others the freedom to grieve over the loss of a loved one, and give yourself time enough to complete your grieving process.

50.2, 3 Embalming was typical for Egyptians but unusual for nomadic shepherds. Believing that the dead went to the next world in their physical bodies, the Egyptians embalmed bodies to preserve them so they could function in the world to come. Jacob's family allowed him to be embalmed as a sign of courtesy and respect to the Egyptians.

50.5 Joseph had proven himself trustworthy as Pharaoh's adviser. Because of his good record, Pharaoh was sure that he would return to Egypt as promised after burying his father in Canaan. Privileges and freedom often result when we have demonstrated our trustworthiness. Since trust must be built gradually over time, take every opportunity to prove your reliability even in minor matters.

50.12, 13 Abraham had purchased the cave of Machpelah as a burial place for his wife, Sarah (23.1–9). It was to be a burial place for his entire family. Jacob was Abraham's grandson, and Jacob's sons returned to Canaan to bury him in this cave along with Abraham and Isaac. Their desire to be buried in this cave expressed their faith in God's promise to give their descendants the land of Canaan.

50.15–21 Now that Jacob (or Israel) was dead, the brothers feared revenge from Joseph. Could he really have forgiven them for selling him into slavery? But to their surprise, Joseph not only forgave them but offered to care for them and their families. Joseph's forgiveness was complete. He demonstrated how God graciously accepts us even though we don't deserve it. Because God forgives us even when we have ignored or rejected him, we should graciously forgive others.

50.21 Gen 45.11	to preserve a numerous people, as he is doing today. [21] So have no fear; I myself will provide for you and your little ones." In this way he reassured them, speaking kindly to them.

Joseph dies

22 So Joseph remained in Egypt, he and his father's household; and Joseph
lived one hundred ten years. [23] Joseph saw Ephraim's children of the third generation; the children of Machir son of Manasseh were also born on Joseph's knees.
24 Then Joseph said to his brothers, "I am about to die; but God will surely
come to you, and bring you up out of this land to the land that he swore to Abraham,
to Isaac, and to Jacob." [25] So Joseph made the Israelites swear, saying, "When God
comes to you, you shall carry up my bones from here." [26] And Joseph died, being
one hundred ten years old; he was embalmed and placed in a coffin in Egypt.

50.23 Gen 16.3; 30.3
50.24 Gen 13.15; 28.13; 35.12; 48.21; 49.29
50.25 Gen 47.29; Ex 13.19; Josh 24.32; Heb 11.22

JACOB'S SONS AND THEIR NOTABLE DESCENDANTS

Jacob's 12 sons were the ancestors of the 12 tribes of Israel. The entire nation of Israel came from these men.

REUBEN	none
SIMEON	none
LEVI	Aaron, Moses, Eli, John the Baptist
JUDAH	David, Jesus
DAN	Samson
NAPHTALI	Barak, Elijah (?)
GAD	Jephthah (?)
ASHER	none
ISSACHAR	none
ZEBULUN	none
JOSEPH	Joshua, Gideon, Samuel
BENJAMIN	Saul, Esther, Paul

50.20 God brought good from the brothers' evil deed, Potiphar's wife's false accusation, the cupbearer's neglect, and seven years of famine. The experiences in Joseph's life taught him that God brings good from evil for those who trust him. Do you trust God enough to wait patiently for him to bring good out of bad situations? You can trust him because, as Joseph learned, God can overrule people's evil intentions to bring about his intended results.

50.23 The expression "born on Joseph's knees" means that these children were like his own.

50.24 Joseph was ready to die. He had no doubts that God would keep his promise and one day bring the Israelites back to their homeland. What a tremendous example! The secret of that kind of faith is a lifetime of trusting God. Your faith is like a muscle—it grows with exercise, gaining strength over time. After a lifetime of exercising trust, your faith can be as strong as Joseph's. Then at your death, you can be confident that God will fulfill all his promises to you and to all those faithful to him who may live after you.

50.24 This verse sets the stage for what would begin to happen in Exodus and come to completion in Joshua. God was going to make Jacob's family into a great nation, lead them out of Egypt, and bring them into the land he had promised them. The nation would rely heavily on this promise, and Joseph emphasized his belief that God would do what he had promised.

50.26 The book of Genesis gives us rich descriptions of the lives of many great men and women who walked with God. They sometimes succeeded and often failed. Yet we learn much by reading the biographies of these people. Where did they get their motivation and courage? They got it by realizing God was with them despite their inadequacies. Knowing this should encourage us to be faithful to God, to rely on him for guidance and utilize the potential he has given us.

Joseph dies 1805 B.C. (1640 B.C.)

VITAL STATISTICS

PURPOSE:
To record the events of Israel's deliverance from Egypt and development as a nation

AUTHOR:
Moses

DATE WRITTEN:
1450–1410 B.C., approximately the same as Genesis

WHERE WRITTEN:
In the wilderness during Israel's wanderings, somewhere in the Sinai peninsula

SETTING:
Egypt. God's people, once highly favored in the land, are now slaves. God is about to set them free.

KEY VERSES:
"Then the Lord said, 'I have observed the misery of my people who are in Egypt; I have heard their cry on account of their taskmasters. . . . So come, I will send you to Pharaoh to bring my people, the Israelites, out of Egypt' " (3.7, 10).

KEY PEOPLE:
Moses, Miriam, Pharaoh, Pharaoh's daughter, Jethro, Aaron, Joshua, Bezalel

KEY PLACES:
Egypt, Goshen, Nile River, Land of Midian, Red Sea, Sinai peninsula, Mount Sinai

SPECIAL FEATURES:
Exodus relates more miracles than any other Old Testament book and is noted for containing the ten commandments

GET UP . . . leave . . . take off—these words are good ones for those trapped or enslaved. Some resist their marching orders, however, preferring present surroundings to a new, unknown environment. It's not easy to trade the comfortable security of the known for an uncertain future. But what if God gives the order to move? Will we follow his lead? Exodus describes a series of God's calls and the responses of his people.

Four hundred years had passed since Joseph moved his family to Egypt. These descendants of Abraham had now grown to over two million strong. To Egypt's new Pharaoh, these Hebrews were foreigners, and their numbers were frightening. Pharaoh decided to make them slaves so they wouldn't upset his balance of power. As it turned out, that was his biggest mistake, for God then came to the rescue of his people. Through a series of strange events, a Hebrew boy named Moses became a prince in Pharaoh's palace and then an outcast in a desert land.

God visited Moses in the mysterious flames of a burning bush, and, after some discussion, Moses agreed to return to Egypt to lead God's people out of slavery. Pharaoh was confronted, and through a cycle of plagues and promises made and broken, Israel was torn from his grasp. It was no easy task to mobilize this mass of humanity, but they marched out of Egypt, through the Red Sea, and into the wilderness behind Moses and the pillars of fire and cloud. Despite continual evidence of God's love and power, the people complained and began to yearn for their days in Egypt. God provided for their physical and spiritual needs with food and a place to worship, but he also judged their disobedience and unbelief. Then in the dramatic Sinai meeting with Moses, God gave his laws for right living.

God called Moses and the nation of Israel, and he wants to lead us as well. Is he preparing you, like Moses, for a specific task? He will be with you; obey and follow. Is he delivering you from an enemy or a temptation? Trust him, and do what he says. Have you heard his clear moral directions? Read, study, and obey his Word. Is he calling you to true worship? Discover God's presence in your life, in your home, and in the body of assembled believers. Exodus is the exciting story of God's guidance. Read with the determination to follow God wherever he leads.

Moses born 1526 (1350)	Exodus from Egypt 1446 (1280)	Ten commandments given 1445 (1279)	Israel enters Canaan 1406 (1240)	Judges begin to rule 1375 (1220)

THE BLUEPRINT

A. ISRAEL IN EGYPT (1.1—12.36) 1. Slavery in Egypt 2. God chooses Moses 3. God sends Moses to Pharaoh 4. Plagues strike Egypt 5. The passover	God heard the cries of his people in Egypt; he hears our cries and answers us too. Just as God prepared Moses for his work, God is still preparing leaders today.
B. ISRAEL IN THE WILDERNESS (12.37—18.27) 1. Escape from Egypt 2. Rescue through the Red Sea 3. Complaining in the wilderness	God's rescuing the Israelites from Egypt teaches us much about how he delivers Christians from sin and death. The events here parallel the Christian's life after salvation. Christians still have struggles. Complaining and dissatisfaction come easy for us.
C. ISRAEL AT SINAI (19.1—40.38) 1. Giving the law 2. Tabernacle instructions 3. Breaking the law 4. Tabernacle construction	Israel's experiences at Sinai show us the beginning of a relationship between God and man. Through God's law, we have a way to expose and identify sin and the standard for righteous living.

MEGATHEMES

THEME	EXPLANATION	IMPORTANCE
Slavery	The Israelites were slaves for 400 years. Pharaoh, the king of Egypt, oppressed them cruelly. They prayed to God for deliverance from this system.	Like the Israelites, we need both human and divine leadership to escape from the slavery of sin. After their escape, the memory of slavery helped Israel learn to treat others generously. We need to stand against those who oppress others.
Rescue/ Redemption	God rescued Israel through the leader Moses and through mighty miracles. The passover celebration was an annual reminder of their escape from slavery.	God delivers us from the slavery of sin. Jesus Christ celebrated the passover with his disciples at the last supper and then went on to rescue us from sin by dying in our place.
Guidance	God guided Israel out of Egypt by using the plagues, Moses' heroic courage, the miracle of the Red Sea, and the ten commandments. God is a trustworthy guide.	Although God is all-powerful and can do miracles, he normally leads us by wise leadership and team effort. His words give us the wisdom to make daily decisions and govern our lives.
Ten Commandments	God's law system had three parts. The ten commandments were the first part, containing the absolutes of spiritual and moral life. The civil law was the second part, giving the people rules to manage their lives. The ceremonial law was the third part, showing them patterns for building the tabernacle and regular worship.	God was teaching Israel the importance of choice and responsibility. When they obeyed the conditions of the law, he blessed them; if they forgot or disobeyed, he punished them or allowed calamities to come. Many great countries of the world base their laws on the moral system set up in the book of Exodus. God's moral law is valid today.
The Nation	God founded the nation of Israel to be the source of truth and salvation to all the world. His relationship to his people was loving yet firm. The Israelites had no army, schools, governors, mayors, or police when they left Egypt. God had to instruct them in their constitutional laws and daily practices. He showed them how to worship and how to have national holidays.	Israel's newly formed nation had all the behavioral characteristics of Christians today. We are often disorganized, sometimes rebellious, and sometimes victorious. God's Person and Word are still our only guide. If our churches reflect his leadership, they will be effective in serving him.

KEY PLACES IN EXODUS

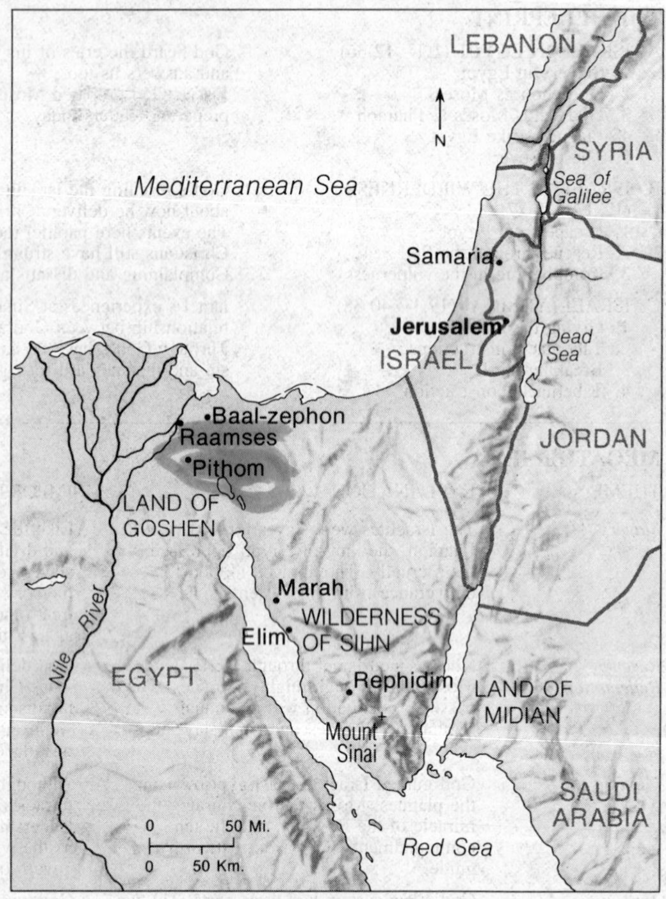

1 Land of Goshen This area was given to Jacob and his family when they moved to Egypt (Genesis 47.5, 6). It became the Hebrews' homeland for 400 years, and remained separate from the main Egyptian centers, for Egyptian culture looked down upon shepherds and nomads. As the years passed, Jacob's family grew into a large nation (1.7).

2, 3 Pithom and Raamses After 400 years, a Pharaoh came to the throne who had no respect for these descendants of Joseph and feared their large numbers. He forced them into slavery in order to oppress and subdue them. Out of their slave labor, the supply cities of Pithom and Raamses were built (1.11).

4 Land of Midian Moses, an Egyptian prince who was born a Hebrew, killed an Egyptian taskmaster and fled for his life to the land of Midian. Here he became a shepherd and married a woman named Zipporah. It was while he was here that God commissioned him for the job of leading the Hebrew people out of Egypt (2.15—4.31).

5 Baal-zephon Slavery was not to last because God planned to deliver his people. After choosing Moses and Aaron to be his spokesmen to Pharaoh, God worked a series of dramatic miracles in the land of Egypt to convince Pharaoh to let the Hebrews go (5.1—12.33). When finally freed, the entire nation set out with the riches of Egypt (12.34–36). One of their first stops was at Baal-zephon (14.1), where Pharaoh, who had changed his mind, chased the Hebrews and trapped them against the Red Sea. But God parted the waters and led the people through the sea on dry land. When Pharaoh's army tried to pursue, the waters collapsed around them, and they were drowned (14.5–31).

6 Marah Moses now led the people southward. The long trek across the desert brought hot tempers and parched throats for this mass of people. At Marah, the water they found was bitter, but God sweetened it (15.22–25).

7 Elim As they continued their journey, the Hebrews (now called Israelites) came to Elim, an oasis with twelve springs (15.27).

8 Wilderness of Sihn (Sin) Leaving Elim, the people headed into the wilderness of Sihn (Sin). Here the people became hungry, so God provided them with manna that came from heaven and covered the ground each morning (16.1, 13–15). The people ate this manna until they entered the promised land.

9 Rephidim Moses led the people to Rephidim where they found no water. But God miraculously provided water from a rock (17.1, 5, 6). Here the Israelites encountered their first test in battle: the Amalekites attacked and were defeated (17.9–13). Moses' father-in-law, Jethro, then arrived on the scene with some sound advice on delegating responsibilities (18).

10 Mount Sinai God had previously appeared to Moses on this mountain and commissioned him to lead Israel (3.1, 2). Now Moses returned with the people God had asked him to lead. For almost a year the people camped at the foot of Mount Sinai. During this time God gave them his ten commandments as well as other laws for right living. He also provided the blueprint for building the tabernacle (19–40).

God was forging a holy nation, prepared to live for and serve him alone.

A. ISRAEL IN EGYPT (1.1–12.36)

Joseph brought his family to Egypt and protected them there. But after Joseph's death, as they multiplied into a nation, they were forced into slavery. God then prepared Moses to free his people from slavery and lead them out of Egypt. To help Moses, God unleashed ten plagues upon the land. After the tenth plague, Pharaoh let the people go. On the night before the great exodus, God's new nation celebrated the passover. Just as God delivered Israel from Egypt, he delivers us from sin, death, and evil.

1. Slavery in Egypt

1.1 Gen 46.8-26 49.3-27 1 Chron 2.1,2 Rev 7.4-8
1.2 Ex 6.14-16
1.5 Gen 46.27
1.6 Gen 50.26 Acts 7.15,16
1.7 Gen 1.27; 12.2 35.11; 46.3 47.27; 48.4 Ex 12.37 Acts 7.17
1.8 Acts 7.18
1.9 Ps 105.24
1.10 Ps 105.25 Acts 7.19
1.11 Ex 2.11; 3.7
1.14 Ex 2.23
1.16 Acts 7.19

1 These are the names of the sons of Israel who came to Egypt with Jacob, each
with his household: 2 Reuben, Simeon, Levi, and Judah, 3 Issachar, Zebulun,
and Benjamin, 4 Dan and Naphtali, Gad and Asher. 5 The total number of people
born to Jacob was seventy. Joseph was already in Egypt. 6 Then Joseph died, and
all his brothers, and that whole generation. 7 But the Israelites were fruitful and
prolific; they multiplied and grew exceedingly strong, so that the land was filled
with them.
8 Now a new king arose over Egypt, who did not know Joseph. 9 He said to his
people, "Look, the Israelite people are more numerous and more powerful than we.
10 Come, let us deal shrewdly with them, or they will increase and, in the event of
war, join our enemies and fight against us and escape from the land." 11 Therefore
they set taskmasters over them to oppress them with forced labor. They built supply
cities, Pithom and Rameses, for Pharaoh. 12 But the more they were oppressed, the
more they multiplied and spread, so that the Egyptians came to dread the Israelites.
13 The Egyptians became ruthless in imposing tasks on the Israelites, 14 and made
their lives bitter with hard service in mortar and brick and in every kind of field
labor. They were ruthless in all the tasks that they imposed on them.
15 The king of Egypt said to the Hebrew midwives, one of whom was named
Shiphrah and the other Puah, 16 "When you act as midwives to the Hebrew women,
and see them on the birthstool, if it is a boy, kill him; but if it is a girl, she shall
live." 17 But the midwives feared God; they did not do as the king of Egypt commanded them, but they let the boys live. 18 So the king of Egypt summoned the

---

1.1 The sons of Israel, or Israelites, were the descendants of Jacob, whose name was changed to Israel after he wrestled with the angel (see Genesis 32.24–30). Jacob's family had moved to Egypt at the invitation of Joseph, one of Jacob's sons, who had become a great ruler under Pharaoh. Jacob's family grew into a large nation. But, as foreigners and newcomers, their lives were quite different from the lives of the Egyptians. The Hebrews worshiped one God; the Egyptians worshiped many gods. The Hebrews were wanderers; the Egyptians had a deeply rooted culture. The Hebrews were shepherds; the Egyptians were builders. The Hebrews were also physically separated from the rest of the Egyptians: they lived in Goshen, north of the great Egyptian cultural centers.

1.9, 10 Pharaoh was afraid the Israelites were becoming so numerous that they would organize and threaten his kingdom. So he made them slaves to kill their spirit and stop their growth. Slavery was an ancient practice used by almost all nations to "employ" conquered people and other captives. The great pyramids of Egypt were most likely built with slave labor. Although Israel was not a conquered nation, the people were foreigners and thus lacked the rights of native Egyptians.

1.11 There were levels of slavery in Egypt. Some slaves worked long hours in mud pits while others were skilled carpenters, jewelers, and craftsmen. Regardless of their skill or level, all slaves were watched closely by ruthless taskmasters, supervisors whose assignment was to keep the slaves working as fast as possible.

1.11 Ancient records indicate that these cities were built in 1290 B.C., which is why some scholars believe the exodus occurred early in the 13th century. Looking at other evidence, however, other scholars believe the Hebrews left Egypt in 1446 B.C. How could they build two cities 150 years after they left? These scholars suggest that Raamses II, the Pharaoh in 1290 B.C., did not build the cities of Pithom and Raamses. Instead, he renamed two cities which actually had been built 150 years previously. It was a common practice for an Egyptian ruler to make improvements on a city and then take credit for building it, thus wiping out all records of previous founders. Also see the note on 14.27, 28.

1.12 The Egyptians tried to wear down the Hebrew people by forcing them into slavery and mistreating them. Instead, the Hebrews multiplied and grew stronger. When we are burdened or mistreated, we may feel defeated. But our burdens can make us stronger and develop qualities in us that will prepare us for the future. Be true to God in the hard times, because even the worst situations can make us better people.

1.15–17 Hebrew midwives helped women give birth and cared for the baby until the mother was stronger. When Pharaoh ordered the midwives to kill the Hebrew baby boys, he was asking the wrong people. Most midwives were friends, neighbors, or relatives of the mothers. These women showed great courage and love for God by risking their lives to disobey Pharaoh's command. Note: the birth stool was the stool upon which the Hebrew women crouched when delivering their babies.

1.17–21 Against Pharaoh's orders, the midwives spared the lives of the Hebrew babies. Their faith in God gave them the courage to take a stand for what they knew was right. In this situation, disobeying the authority was proper. God does not expect us to obey those in authority when they ask us to disobey him or his word. The Bible is filled with examples of those who were willing to sacrifice their very lives in order to obey God or save others. Esther and Mordecai (Esther 3.2; 4.13–16) and Shadrach, Meshach, and Abednego (Daniel 3.16–18) took a bold stand for what was right. Whole nations can be caught up in immorality (racial hatred, slavery, prison cruelty); thus following the majority or the authority is not always right. Whenever we are ordered to disobey God, we must "obey God rather than any human authority" (Acts 5.29).

midwives and said to them, "Why have you done this, and allowed the boys to
live?" 19 The midwives said to Pharaoh, "Because the Hebrew women are not like 1.19
the Egyptian women; for they are vigorous and give birth before the midwife comes Josh 2.4 2 Sam 17.20
to them." 20 So God dealt well with the midwives; and the people multiplied and 1.20
became very strong. 21 And because the midwives feared God, he gave them fami- Ex 1.12
lies. 22 Then Pharaoh commanded all his people, "Every boy that is born to the 1.22
Hebrews[a] you shall throw into the Nile, but you shall let every girl live." Mt 2.16

2. God chooses Moses

Moses is born

2 Now a man from the house of Levi went and married a Levite woman. 2 The 2.1
woman conceived and bore a son; and when she saw that he was a fine baby, Ex 6.16,20 Num 26.59
she hid him three months. 3 When she could hide him no longer she got a papyrus 2.2
basket for him, and plastered it with bitumen and pitch; she put the child in it and Acts 7.20 Heb 11.23
placed it among the reeds on the bank of the river. 4 His sister stood at a distance, 2.3
to see what would happen to him. Gen 6.14 Ex 1.22
5 The daughter of Pharaoh came down to bathe at the river, while her attendants 2.4
walked beside the river. She saw the basket among the reeds and sent her maid to Ex 15.20 Num 26.59
bring it. 6 When she opened it, she saw the child. He was crying, and she took pity 2.5
on him, "This must be one of the Hebrews' children," she said. 7 Then his sister Ex 8.20 Acts 7.21
said to Pharaoh's daughter, "Shall I go and get you a nurse from the Hebrew 2.6
women to nurse the child for you?" 8 Pharaoh's daughter said to her, "Yes." So the Ps 106.46
girl went and called the child's mother. 9 Pharaoh's daughter said to her, "Take this
child and nurse it for me, and I will give you your wages." So the woman took the
child and nursed it. 10 When the child grew up, she brought him to Pharaoh's 2.10
daughter, and she took him as her son. She named him Moses,[b] "because," she 1 Sam 1.20 2 Sam 22.17
said, "I drew him out[c] of the water."

Moses runs away

11 One day, after Moses had grown up, he went out to his people and saw their 2.11
forced labor. He saw an Egyptian beating a Hebrew, one of his kinsfolk. 12 He Acts 7.23,24 Heb 11.24

[a] Sam Gk Tg: Heb lacks *to the Hebrews* [b] Heb *Mosheh* [c] Heb *mashah*

1.19–21 Did God bless the Hebrew midwives for lying to Pharaoh? God blessed them not because they lied, but because they saved the lives of innocent children. This doesn't mean that a lie was necessarily the best way to answer Pharaoh. The midwives were blessed, however, for not violating the higher law of God which forbids the senseless slaughter of innocent lives.

2.1, 2 Although a name is not mentioned yet, the baby in this story was Moses. Moses' mother and father were named Jochebed and Amram. His brother was Aaron and his sister, Miriam.

2.3 This tiny boat made of papyrus reeds was fashioned by a woman who knew what she was doing. Egyptian river boats were made with these same reeds and waterproofed with bitumen and pitch. The reeds, which grew as tall as 16 feet, could be gathered in swampy areas along the Nile. Thus a tiny basket hidden among the reeds would be well insulated from the weather and difficult to see.

2.3ff Moses' mother knew how wrong it would be to destroy her child. But there was little she could do to change Pharaoh's new law. Her only alternative was to hide the child and later place him in a tiny reed basket on the river. God used her courageous act to place her son, the Hebrew of his choice, in the house of Pharaoh. Do you sometimes feel surrounded by evil and frustrated by how little you can do about it? When faced with evil, look for ways to act against it. Then trust God to use your effort, however small it seems, in his war against evil.

2.5 Who was Pharaoh's daughter? There are two popular explanations. (1) Some think that Hatshepsut was the woman who pulled Moses from the river. Her husband was the Pharaoh Thutmose II. (This would match the earlier exodus date.) Apparently Hatshepsut could not have children, so Thutmose had a son by another woman who became heir to the throne. Hatshepsut would have considered Moses a gift from the gods, because now she had her own son who would be the legal heir to the throne. (2) Some think the princess who rescued baby Moses was the daughter of Raamses II, an especially cruel Pharaoh who would have made life miserable for the Hebrew slaves. (This would match the later exodus date.)

2.7, 8 Miriam, the baby's sister, saw that Pharaoh's daughter had discovered Moses. Quickly she took the initiative to suggest a nurse (her mother) who might care for the baby. The Bible doesn't say if Miriam was afraid to approach the Egyptian princess, or if the princess was suspicious of the Hebrew girl. But Miriam did approach her, and the princess bought the services of Miriam and her mother. Their family was reunited. Special opportunities may come our way unexpectedly. Don't let the fear of what might happen cause you to miss an opportunity. Be alert for the opportunities God gives you, and take full advantage of them.

2.9 Moses' mother was reunited with her baby! God used her courageous act of saving and hiding her baby to begin his plan to rescue his people from Egypt. God doesn't need much from us to accomplish his plan for our lives. Focusing on our human predicament may paralyze us because the situation may appear humanly impossible. But concentrating on God and his power helps us see the way out. Right now you may be unable to see beyond your troubles. Focus instead on God, and trust him for the way out. That is all he needs to begin his work in you.

2.14 Gen 19.9; 37.8 Acts 7.28,33
2.15 Gen 24.11; 29.2 1 Kgs 19.1-3 Acts 7.29
2.16 Gen 14.18 Ex 3.1; 18.7,12
2.17 Gen 29.10
2.18 Num 10.29
2.20 Gen 18.5; 24.31 Job 31.32
2.21 Ex 4.25; 18.2 Acts 7.29
2.22 Gen 23.4 Ex 4.20; 18.3
2.23 Ex 6.5,9 Deut 26.7
2.24 Gen 22.16-18 26.2,3; 28.13 46.3,4
3.2 Acts 7.30

looked this way and that, and seeing no one he killed the Egyptian and hid him in
the sand. 13 When he went out the next day, he saw two Hebrews fighting; and he
said to the one who was in the wrong, "Why do you strike your fellow Hebrew?"
14 He answered, "Who made you a ruler and judge over us? Do you mean to kill me
as you killed the Egyptian?" Then Moses was afraid and thought, "Surely the thing
is known." 15 When Pharaoh heard of it, he sought to kill Moses.
But Moses fled from Pharaoh. He settled in the land of Midian, and sat down by
a well. 16 The priest of Midian had seven daughters. They came to draw water, and
filled the troughs to water their father's flock. 17 But some shepherds came and
drove them away. Moses got up and came to their defense and watered their flock.
18 When they returned to their father Reuel, he said, "How is it that you have come
back so soon today?" 19 They said, "An Egyptian helped us against the shepherds;
he even drew water for us and watered the flock." 20 He said to his daughters,
"Where is he? Why did you leave the man? Invite him to break bread." 21 Moses
agreed to stay with the man, and he gave Moses his daughter Zipporah in marriage.
22 She bore a son, and he named him Gershom; for he said, "I have been an alien[d]
residing in a foreign land."
23 After a long time the king of Egypt died. The Israelites groaned under their
slavery, and cried out. Out of the slavery their cry for help rose up to God. 24 God
heard their groaning, and God remembered his covenant with Abraham, Isaac, and
Jacob. 25 God looked upon the Israelites, and God took notice of them.

The burning bush

3 Moses was keeping the flock of his father-in-law Jethro, the priest of Midian;
he led his flock beyond the wilderness, and came to Horeb, the mountain of
God. 2 There the angel of the LORD appeared to him in a flame of fire out of a bush;

[d] Heb *ger*

2.12–14 Moses tried to make sure no one was watching before he killed the Egyptian. But as it turned out, someone did see, and Moses had to flee the country. Sometimes we mistakenly think we can get away with doing wrong if no one sees or catches us. Sooner or later, however, doing wrong will catch up with us as it did with Moses. Even if we are not caught in this life, we will still have to face God's evaluation of our actions.

2.17 How did Moses handle these shepherds so easily? As an Egyptian prince, Moses would have been well trained in the Egyptian military, the most advanced army in the world. Even a large group of shepherds would have been no match for the sophisticated fighting techniques of this trained warrior.

2.20 "Break bread" means to eat together.

2.22 To escape punishment for killing the Egyptian, Moses ran away to the land of Midian. He became a stranger in a strange land, separated from his home and family. It took many years after this incident for Moses to be ready to serve God. But he trusted God instead of fearing the king (Hebrews 11.27). We may feel abandoned or isolated because of something we have done. But though we feel afraid and separated, we should not give up. Moses didn't. He trusted God to deliver him, no matter how dark his past or bleak his future.

2.23–25 God's rescue doesn't always come the moment we want it. God had promised to bring the Hebrew slaves out of Egypt (Genesis 15.16; 46.3, 4). The people had waited a long time for that promise to be kept, but God rescued them when he knew the right time had come. God knows the best time to act. When you feel that God has forgotten you in your troubles, remember that God has a time schedule we can't see.

3.1 What a contrast between Moses' life as an Egyptian prince and his life as a Midianite shepherd! As a prince he had everything done for him. As a shepherd he had to do everything for himself; he was holding the very job he had been taught to despise (Genesis 43.32; 46.32–34), and he lived as an unknown foreigner. What a humbling experience this must have been! But God was preparing Moses for leadership. Living the life of a shepherd and nomad, Moses learned about the ways of the people he would be leading and also about life in the wilderness. God was getting him ready to free Israel from Pharaoh's grasp.

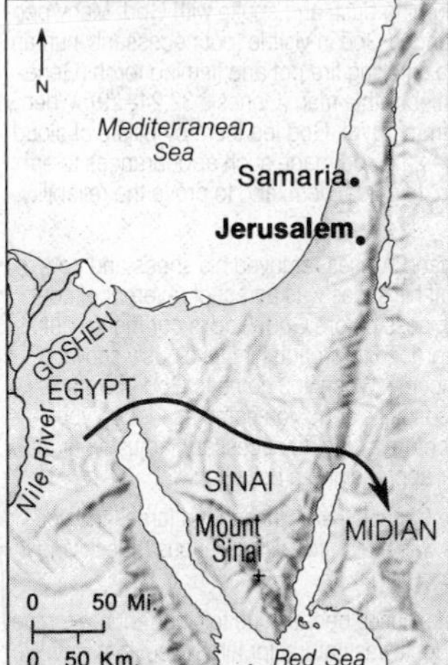

MOSES FLEES TO MIDIAN
After murdering an Egyptian, Moses escaped into the land of Midian. There he married Zipporah and became a shepherd.

3.2 God spoke to Moses from an unexpected source: a burning bush. When Moses saw it, he went to investigate. God may use unexpected sources when communicating to us too, whether people, thoughts, or experiences. Be willing to investigate, and be open to God's surprises.

he looked, and the bush was blazing, yet it was not consumed. 3Then Moses said,
"I must turn aside and look at this great sight, and see why the bush is not burned
up." 4When the LORD saw that he had turned aside to see, God called to him out of
the bush, "Moses, Moses!" And he said, "Here I am." 5Then he said, "Come no
closer! Remove the sandals from your feet, for the place on which you are standing
is holy ground." 6He said further, "I am the God of your father, the God of Abraham, the God of Isaac, and the God of Jacob." And Moses hid his face, for he was
afraid to look at God.
7 Then the LORD said, "I have observed the misery of my people who are in
Egypt; I have heard their cry on account of their taskmasters. Indeed, I know their
sufferings, 8and I have come down to deliver them from the Egyptians, and to bring
them up out of that land to a good and broad land, a land flowing with milk and
honey, to the country of the Canaanites, the Hittites, the Amorites, the Perizzites,
the Hivites, and the Jebusites. 9The cry of the Israelites has now come to me; I have
also seen how the Egyptians oppress them. 10So come, I will send you to Pharaoh
to bring my people, the Israelites, out of Egypt." 11But Moses said to God, "Who
am I that I should go to Pharaoh, and bring the Israelites out of Egypt?" 12He said,
"I will be with you; and this shall be the sign for you that it is I who sent you: when
you have brought the people out of Egypt, you shall worship God on this mountain."
13 But Moses said to God, "If I come to the Israelites and say to them, 'The
God of your ancestors has sent me to you,' and they ask me, 'What is his name?'
what shall I say to them?" 14God said to Moses, "I AM WHO I AM."[e] He said further, "Thus you shall say to the Israelites, 'I AM has sent me to you.' " 15God also
said to Moses, "Thus you shall say to the Israelites, 'The LORD,[f] the God of your
ancestors, the God of Abraham, the God of Isaac, and the God of Jacob, has sent
me to you':

This is my name forever,
and this my title for all generations.

16Go and assemble the elders of Israel, and say to them, 'The LORD, the God of
your ancestors, the God of Abraham, of Isaac, and of Jacob, has appeared to me,
saying: I have given heed to you and to what has been done to you in Egypt. 17I

3.3 Acts 7.31
3.5 Gen 28.16,17; Ex 19.12; Josh 5.15; Acts 7.33
3.6 Gen 31.42; 32.9; Mt 22.32; Mk 12.26; Lk 20.37; Acts 7.32
3.7 Acts 7.34
3.8 a)Gen 15.16; 46.4; 50.24; b)Gen 15.19; Ex 3.17; Deut 6.3; 8.7-9; 11.9; 26.9
3.10 Acts 7.34; 12.6
3.11 Ex 4.10; 6.12
3.12 Ex 4.12; 19.2; Acts 7.7
3.13 Ex 15.3
3.14 Ex 6.3; Jn 8.58; Rev 1.8; 4.8
3.15 Ps 72.17; 102.12; 135.13; 145.1; Acts 7.32
3.16 Ex 4.29; 18.12

[e] Or *I AM WHAT I AM* or *I WILL BE WHAT I WILL BE* [f] The word "LORD" when spelled with capital letters stands for the divine name, *YHWH,* which is here connected with the verb *hayah,* "to be"

3.3, 4 Moses saw a burning bush and spoke with God. Many people in the Bible experienced God in visible (not necessarily human) form. Abraham saw the smoking fire pot and flaming torch (Genesis 15.17); Jacob wrestled with a man (Genesis 32.24–29). When the slaves were freed from Egypt, God led them by pillars of cloud and fire (Exodus 13.17–22). God made such appearances to encourage his new nation, to guide them, and to prove the reliability of his verbal message.

3.5, 6 At God's command, Moses removed his shoes and covered his face. Taking off his shoes was an act of reverence, conveying his own unworthiness before God. God is our friend, but he is also our sovereign Lord. To approach him frivolously shows a lack of respect and sincerity. When you come to God in worship, do you approach him casually, or do you come as though you were an invited guest before a king? If necessary, adjust your attitude so it is suitable for approaching a holy God.

3.8 "The country of the Canaanites" is the land of Israel and Jordan today. *Canaanites* was a term for all the various tribes living in that land.

3.10–12 Moses made excuses because he felt inadequate for the job God asked him to do. It was natural for him to feel that way. He *was* inadequate all by himself. But God wasn't asking Moses to work alone. He offered other resources to help (God himself, Aaron, and the ability to do miracles). God often calls us to tasks that seem too difficult, but he doesn't ask us to do them alone. God offers us his resources, just as he did to Moses. We should not hide behind our inadequacies, as Moses did, but look beyond ourselves to the great resources available. Then we can allow God to use our unique contributions.

3.13–15 The Egyptians had many gods by many different names. Moses wanted to know God's name so the Hebrew people would know exactly who had sent him to them. God called himself *I Am,* an appellation describing his eternal power and unchangeable character. In a world where values, morals, and laws change constantly, we can find stability and security in our unchanging God. The God who appeared to Moses is the same God who can live in us today. Hebrews 13.8 says God is the same "yesterday and today and forever." Because God's nature is stable and trustworthy, we are free to enjoy and follow him rather than spend our time trying to figure him out.

3.14, 15 *Jehovah* or *Yahweh* means "I Am." God reminded Moses of his covenant promises to Abraham (Genesis 12.1–3; 15; 17), Isaac (Genesis 26.2–5), and Jacob (Genesis 28.13–15), and used the name *I Am* to show his unchanging nature. What God promised to the great patriarchs hundreds of years earlier he would fulfill through Moses.

3.16–18 God told Moses to tell the people what he saw and heard at the burning bush. Our God is a God who acts and speaks. One of the most convincing ways to tell others about him is to describe what he has done and how he has spoken to his people. If you are trying to explain God to others, talk about what he has done for you, for people you know, or for people whose stories are told in the Bible.

3.17 Ex 3.8; Josh 24.11
3.18 Ex 4.31; 5.1,3; Num 23.4,16
3.19 Ex 5.2; 6.1; 7.4; Deut 6.22
3.20 Ex 11.1; 12.31; 15.11; Neh 9.10; Acts 7.36
3.21 Ex 11.3; 12.36
3.22 Ex 11.2; 12.35

declare that I will bring you up out of the misery of Egypt, to the land of the Canaanites, the Hittites, the Amorites, the Perizzites, the Hivites, and the Jebusites,
a land flowing with milk and honey.' 18 They will listen to your voice; and you and
the elders of Israel shall go to the king of Egypt and say to him, 'The LORD, the God
of the Hebrews, has met with us; let us now go a three days' journey into the wilderness, so that we may sacrifice to the LORD our God.' 19 I know, however, that the
king of Egypt will not let you go unless compelled by a mighty hand.[g] 20 So I will
stretch out my hand and strike Egypt with all my wonders that I will perform in it;
after that he will let you go. 21 I will bring this people into such favor with the
Egyptians that, when you go, you will not go empty-handed; 22 each woman shall
ask her neighbor and any woman living in the neighbor's house for jewelry of silver
and of gold, and clothing, and you shall put them on your sons and on your daughters; and so you shall plunder the Egyptians."

Moses asks for help

4.1 Ex 3.11,13-16
4.2 Ex 4.17,20
4.3 Ex 7.10-12
4.5 Ex 4.30,31; 19.9
4.6 Ex 12.10; Num 12.10
4.7 Num 12.13,14; Deut 32.39; 2 Kgs 5.14; Mt 8.3; Lk 17.12-14
4.9 Ex 7.19
4.10 Jer 1.6; Acts 7.22
4.11 Ps 94.9; Isa 35.6; Mt 11.5

4 Then Moses answered, "But suppose they do not believe me or listen to me,
but say, 'The LORD did not appear to you.' " 2 The LORD said to him, "What is
that in your hand?" He said, "A staff." 3 And he said, "Throw it on the ground." So
he threw the staff on the ground, and it became a snake; and Moses drew back from
it. 4 Then the LORD said to Moses, "Reach out your hand, and seize it by the
tail" — so he reached out his hand and grasped it, and it became a staff in his hand —
5 "so that they may believe that the LORD, the God of their ancestors, the God of
Abraham, the God of Isaac, and the God of Jacob, has appeared to you."
6 Again, the LORD said to him, "Put your hand inside your cloak." He put his
hand into his cloak; and when he took it out, his hand was leprous,[h] as white as
snow. 7 Then God said, "Put your hand back into your cloak" — so he put his hand
back into his cloak, and when he took it out, it was restored like the rest of his
body — 8 "If they will not believe you or heed the first sign, they may believe the
second sign. 9 If they will not believe even these two signs or heed you, you shall
take some water from the Nile and pour it on the dry ground; and the water that you
shall take from the Nile will become blood on the dry ground."
10 But Moses said to the LORD, "O my Lord, I have never been eloquent, neither in the past nor even now that you have spoken to your servant; but I am slow
of speech and slow of tongue." 11 Then the LORD said to him, "Who gives speech

[g] Gk Vg: Heb *no, not by a mighty hand* [h] A term for several skin diseases; precise meaning uncertain

---

3.17 "A land flowing with milk and honey" is a poetic word picture expressing the beauty and productivity of the promised land.

3.18–20 The leaders of Israel would accept God's message, and the leaders of Egypt would reject it. God knew what both reactions would be before they happened. This is more than good psychology—God knows the future. Any believer can trust his or her future to God, because God already knows what is going to happen.

3.22 The jewelry and clothing were not merely borrowed, but they were asked for and easily received. The Egyptians were so glad to see the Israelites go that they sent them out with gifts. These items were used later in building the tabernacle (35.5, 22). The promise of being able to plunder their captors seemed impossible to Moses at this time.

4.1 Moses' fear was caused by worrying about how the people might respond to him. We often panic over what might go wrong. God does not ask us to go where he has not provided the means to help. Trust him to supply courage and resources at the right moment.

4.2–4 A shepherd's staff was commonly a three- to six-foot wooden rod with a curved hook at the top. The shepherd used it for walking, guiding his sheep, killing snakes, and many other tasks. Still, it was just a stick. But God used the simple shepherd's rod Moses carried to teach him an important lesson. God sometimes takes joy in using ordinary things for extraordinary purposes. What are the ordinary things in your life—your voice, a pen, a hammer, a broom, a musical instrument? While it is easy to assume God can use only special skills, you must not hinder his use of the everyday contributions you can make. Little did Moses imagine the power his simple staff would wield when it became the rod of God.

4.6, 7 Leprosy was one of the most feared diseases of this time. There was no cure, and a great deal of suffering preceded eventual death. Through this experience, Moses learned that God could cause or cure any kind of problem. He saw that God indeed had all power and was commissioning him to exercise that power to lead the Hebrews out of Egypt.

4.10–12 Moses pleaded with God to let him out of his mission. After all, he was not a good speaker and would probably embarrass both himself and God. But God looked at Moses' problem quite differently. All Moses needed was some help, and who better than God could help him say and do the right things. God made his mouth and would give him the words to say. It is easy for us to focus on our weaknesses, but if God asks us to do something, then he will help us get the job done by providing weak areas, then we can trust that he will provide words, strength, courage, and ability where needed.

to mortals? Who makes them mute or deaf, seeing or blind? Is it not I, the LORD?
12 Now go, and I will be with your mouth and teach you what you are to speak."
13 But he said, "O my Lord, please send someone else." 14 Then the anger of the
LORD was kindled against Moses and he said, "What of your brother Aaron, the
Levite? I know that he can speak fluently; even now he is coming out to meet you,
and when he sees you his heart will be glad. 15 You shall speak to him and put the
words in his mouth; and I will be with your mouth and with his mouth, and will
teach you what you shall do. 16 He indeed shall speak for you to the people; he shall
serve as a mouth for you, and you shall serve as God for him. 17 Take in your hand
this staff, with which you shall perform the signs."

Moses and Aaron go to Egypt

18 Moses went back to his father-in-law Jethro and said to him, "Please let me
go back to my kindred in Egypt and see whether they are still living." And Jethro
said to Moses, "Go in peace." 19 The LORD said to Moses in Midian, "Go back to
Egypt; for all those who were seeking your life are dead." 20 So Moses took his wife
and his sons, put them on a donkey and went back to the land of Egypt; and Moses
carried the staff of God in his hand.

21 And the LORD said to Moses, "When you go back to Egypt, see that you
perform before Pharaoh all the wonders that I have put in your power; but I will
harden his heart, so that he will not let the people go. 22 Then you shall say to
Pharaoh, 'Thus says the LORD: Israel is my firstborn son. 23 I said to you, "Let my
son go that he may worship me." But you refused to let him go; now I will kill your
firstborn son.' "

24 On the way, at a place where they spent the night, the LORD met him and
tried to kill him. 25 But Zipporah took a flint and cut off her son's foreskin, and
touched Moses'[i] feet with it, and said, "Truly you are a bridegroom of blood to
me!" 26 So he let him alone. It was then she said, "A bridegroom of blood by circumcision."

27 The LORD said to Aaron, "Go into the wilderness to meet Moses." So he
went; and he met him at the mountain of God and kissed him. 28 Moses told Aaron
all the words of the LORD with which he had sent him, and all the signs with which
he had charged him. 29 Then Moses and Aaron went and assembled all the elders of
the Israelites. 30 Aaron spoke all the words that the LORD had spoken to Moses, and
performed the signs in the sight of the people. 31 The people believed; and when
they heard that the LORD had given heed to the Israelites and that he had seen their
misery, they bowed down and worshiped.

i Heb *his*

4.14 Ex 4.27; 6.7
4.15 Num 22.38 Jer 1.9
4.16 Ex 7.1; 18.19
4.17 Ex 14.16; 17.9
4.18 Ex 3.1; 18.5
4.19 Ex 2.15,23
4.20 Ex 4.17; 18.3 Mt 2.20
4.21 Ex 7.3,13; 9.12 Deut 2.30 Jn 12.40
4.22 Isa 63.17; 64.8 Jer 31.9 Hos 11.1 Rom 9.4
4.23 Ex 5.1; 6.11 7.16; 12.29
4.24 Num 22.22 1 Chron 21.16
4.25,26 Gen 17.14 Josh 5.2
4.27 Ex 4.14
4.28 Ex 4.15,16
4.29 Ex 3.16
4.30 Ex 4.16,17
4.31 Ex 3.18; 12.27

4.14 God finally agreed to let Aaron speak for Moses. Moses' feelings of inadequacy were so strong that he could not trust even God's ability to help him. Moses had to deal with his deep sense of inadequacy many times. When we face difficult or frightening situations, we must be willing to let God help us.

4.16 The phrase "you shall serve as God for him" means that Moses would tell Aaron what to say as God was telling Moses.

4.17–20 Moses clung tightly to the shepherd's staff as he left for Egypt to face the greatest challenge of his life. The staff was his assurance of God's presence and power. When feeling uncertain, some people need something to stabilize and reassure them. For assurance when facing great trials, God has given promises from his word and examples from great heroes of faith. Any Christian may cling tightly to these.

4.24–26 God intended to kill Moses because Moses had not circumcised his son. Why hadn't Moses done this? Remember that Moses had spent half his life in Pharaoh's palace and half his life in the Midianite desert. He might not have been too familiar with God's laws, especially since all the requirements of God's covenant with Israel (Genesis 17) had not been actively carried out for over 400 years. In addition, Moses' wife, due to her Midianite background, may have opposed circumcision. But Moses could not effectively serve as deliverer of God's people until he had fulfilled the conditions of God's covenant, and one of those conditions was circumcision. Before they could go any farther, Moses and his family had to follow God's commands completely. Under Old Testament law, failing to circumcise your son was to remove yourself and your family from God's blessings. Moses learned that disobeying God was even more dangerous than tangling with an Egyptian Pharaoh.

4.25, 26 Why did Zipporah perform the circumcision? It may have been Zipporah who, as a Midianite unfamiliar with the circumcision requirement, had persuaded Moses not to circumcise their son. If she prevented the action, now she would have to perform it. It is also possible that Moses fell ill as a result of permitting disobedience and that Zipporah had to perform the circumcision herself to save both her husband and son. This would not have made her happy—hence, her unflattering comment to Moses.

3. God sends Moses to Pharaoh

Bricks without straw

5.1 Ex 3.18; 4.21 10.9
5.2 Ex 3.19 2 Kgs 18.35 Job 21.15
5.3 Ex 3.18 Deut 28.21
5.4,5 Ex 1.11; 2.11 Jer 38.4 Amos 7.10
5.6 Ex 3.7; 5.10,14
5.7 Gen 11.13
5.14 Ex 5.6 Isa 10.24

5 Afterward Moses and Aaron went to Pharaoh and said, "Thus says the LORD, the God of Israel, 'Let my people go, so that they may celebrate a festival to me in the wilderness.' " 2 But Pharaoh said, "Who is the LORD, that I should heed him and let Israel go? I do not know the LORD, and I will not let Israel go." 3 Then they said, "The God of the Hebrews has revealed himself to us; let us go a three days' journey into the wilderness to sacrifice to the LORD our God, or he will fall upon us with pestilence or sword." 4 But the king of Egypt said to them, "Moses and Aaron, why are you taking the people away from their work? Get to your labors!" 5 Pharaoh continued, "Now they are more numerous than the people of the land[j] and yet you want them to stop working!" 6 That same day Pharaoh commanded the taskmasters of the people, as well as their supervisors, 7 "You shall no longer give the people straw to make bricks, as before; let them go and gather straw for themselves. 8 But you shall require of them the same quantity of bricks as they have made previously; do not diminish it, for they are lazy; that is why they cry, 'Let us go and offer sacrifice to our God.' 9 Let heavier work be laid on them; then they will labor at it and pay no attention to deceptive words."

10 So the taskmasters and the supervisors of the people went out and said to the people, "Thus says Pharaoh, 'I will not give you straw. 11 Go and get straw yourselves, wherever you can find it; but your work will not be lessened in the least.' " 12 So the people scattered throughout the land of Egypt, to gather stubble for straw. 13 The taskmasters were urgent, saying, "Complete your work, the same daily assignment as when you were given straw." 14 And the supervisors of the Israelites, whom Pharaoh's taskmasters had set over them, were beaten, and were asked, "Why did you not finish the required quantity of bricks yesterday and today, as you did before?"

15 Then the Israelite supervisors came to Pharaoh and cried, "Why do you treat your servants like this? 16 No straw is given to your servants, yet they say to us, 'Make bricks!' Look how your servants are beaten! You are unjust to your own

j Sam: Heb *The people of the land are now many*

MOSES RETURNS TO EGYPT
God appeared to Moses in a mysterious burning bush on Mount Sinai (also called Mount Horeb). Later Aaron met Moses at the mountain and together they returned to Egypt, a 200-mile trip.

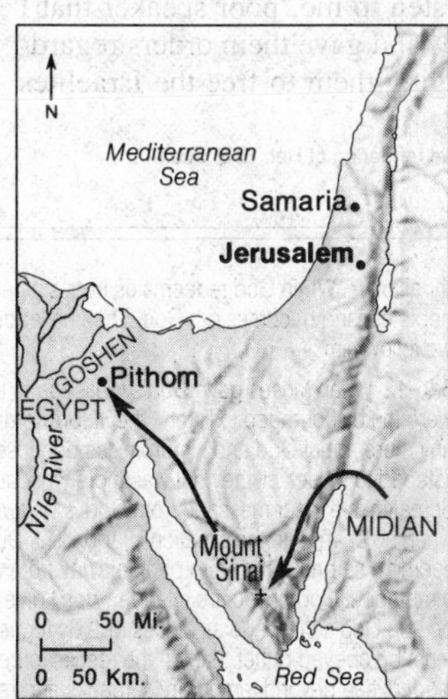

5.1, 2 Pharaoh was familiar with many gods (Egypt was filled with them), but he had never heard of the God of Israel. Pharaoh assumed the God of the Hebrew slaves couldn't be too powerful. At first Pharaoh was not at all worried about Moses' message, for he had not yet seen any evidence of the Lord's power.

5.3 Pharaoh would not listen to Moses and Aaron because he did not know or respect God. People who do not know God may not listen to his word or his messengers. Like Moses and Aaron, we need to persist. When others reject you or your faith, don't be surprised or discouraged. Continue to tell them about God, trusting him to open minds and soften stubborn hearts.

5.4–9 Moses and Aaron took their message to Pharaoh just as God directed. The unhappy result was harder work and more oppression for the Hebrews. Sometimes hardship comes as a result of obeying God. Are you following God, but still suffering—or suffering even worse than before? If your life is miserable, don't assume you have fallen out of God's favor. You may be suffering for doing good in an evil world.

5.7, 8 Mixing straw with mud made bricks stronger and more durable. Pharaoh had supplied the slaves with straw, but now he made them find their own straw and increase their production of bricks as well.

5.15 "Brought us into bad odor" means he made them a stench or repulsive to Pharaoh and his officials.

5.15–21 The supervisors were caught in the middle. First they tried to get the people to produce the same amount, then they complained to Pharaoh, finally they turned on Moses. Perhaps you have felt caught in the middle at work or in relationships in your family or church. Complaining or turning on the leadership does not solve the problem. In the case of these supervisors, God had a larger purpose in mind, just as he might in your situation. So rather than turning on the leadership when you feel pressured by both sides, turn to God to see what else he might be doing in this situation.

people."[k] 17 He said, "You are lazy, lazy; that is why you say, 'Let us go and
sacrifice to the LORD.' 18 Go now, and work; for no straw shall be given you, but
you shall still deliver the same number of bricks." 19 The Israelite supervisors saw
that they were in trouble when they were told, "You shall not lessen your daily
number of bricks." 20 As they left Pharaoh, they came upon Moses and Aaron who
were waiting to meet them. 21 They said to them, "The LORD look upon you and
judge! You have brought us into bad odor with Pharaoh and his officials, and have
put a sword in their hand to kill us."
22 Then Moses turned again to the LORD and said, "O LORD, why have you
mistreated this people? Why did you ever send me? 23 Since I first came to Pharaoh
to speak in your name, he has mistreated this people, and you have done nothing at
all to deliver your people."

The Hebrews refuse to listen to Moses

6 Then the LORD said to Moses, "Now you shall see what I will do to Pharaoh:
Indeed, by a mighty hand he will let them go; by a mighty hand he will drive
them out of his land."
2 God also spoke to Moses and said to him: "I am the LORD. 3 I appeared to
Abraham, Isaac, and Jacob as God Almighty,[l] but by my name 'The LORD'[m] I did
not make myself known to them. 4 I also established my covenant with them, to
give them the land of Canaan, the land in which they resided as aliens. 5 I have also
heard the groaning of the Israelites whom the Egyptians are holding as slaves, and
I have remembered my covenant. 6 Say therefore to the Israelites, 'I am the LORD,
and I will free you from the burdens of the Egyptians and deliver you from slavery
to them. I will redeem you with an outstretched arm and with mighty acts of judgment. 7 I will take you as my people, and I will be your God. You shall know that
I am the LORD your God, who has freed you from the burdens of the Egyptians. 8 I
will bring you into the land that I swore to give to Abraham, Isaac, and Jacob; I will
give it to you for a possession. I am the LORD.' " 9 Moses told this to the Israelites;
but they would not listen to Moses, because of their broken spirit and their cruel
slavery.
10 Then the LORD spoke to Moses, 11 "Go and tell Pharaoh king of Egypt to let
the Israelites go out of his land." 12 But Moses spoke to the LORD, "The Israelites
have not listened to me; how then shall Pharaoh listen to me, poor speaker that I
am?"[n] 13 Thus the LORD spoke to Moses and Aaron, and gave them orders regarding the Israelites and Pharaoh king of Egypt, charging them to free the Israelites
from the land of Egypt.

5.17 Ex 5.8
5.21 Gen 16.5; 34.30 Ex 14.11; 15.24
5.22 Num 11.11 Jer 4.10; 20.7
5.23 Ex 3.8,19
6.1 Ex 3.19,20 11.1; 12.31
6.2,3 Gen 15.7 Ex 3.14; 14.18 Ps 83.18 Isa 42.8; 52.6 Ezek 37.6,13 Jn 8.58
6.4 Gen 15.18
6.5 Ex 2.24 Deut 6.12 Ps 105.8
6.6 Ex 3.17; 7.4 Deut 26.8
6.7 Ex 16.12 Deut 4.20 Isa 60.16
6.8 Num 14.30 Josh 24.13
6.11 Ex 5.1; 7.2
6.12 Ex 4.10; 6.30

[k] Gk Compare Syr Vg: Heb *beaten, and the sin of your people* [l] Traditional rendering of Heb *El Shaddai*
[m] Heb *YHWH*; see note at 3.15 [n] Heb *me? I am uncircumcised of lips*

5.22, 23 Pharaoh had just increased the Hebrews' workload, and Moses protested that God was mistreating his people by not delivering them. He expected faster results and fewer problems. When God is at work, however, suffering, setbacks, and hardship may still occur. In James 1.2–4, we are encouraged to be happy when difficulties come our way. Problems exercise our patience and develop our character by teaching us to (1) trust God to do what is best for us, (2) look for ways to honor God in our present situation, (3) remember that God will not abandon us, and (4) watch for God's plan for us.

6.6 Small problems need only small answers. But when we face great problems, God has an opportunity to exercise his great power. As the Hebrews' troubles grew steadily worse, God planned to intervene with his mighty power and perform great miracles to deliver them. How big are your problems? Big problems put you in a perfect position to watch God give big answers.

6.6–8 God's promises in these verses were fulfilled to the letter when the Hebrews left Egypt. He delivered them from slavery, became their God, and accepted them as his people. Then he led them toward the land he had promised them. When the Hebrews were rescued from slavery, they portrayed the drama of salvation for all of us. When God redeems us from sin he delivers us, accepts us, and becomes our God. Then he leads us to a new life as we follow him.

6.9–12 When Moses gave God's message to the people, they were too discouraged to listen. The Hebrews didn't want to hear any more about God and his promises because the last time they listened to Moses all they got was more work and greater suffering. Sometimes a clear message from God is followed by a period when no change in the situation is apparent. During that time, seeming setbacks may turn people away from wanting to hear more about God. If you are a leader, don't give up. Keep bringing people God's message as Moses did. By focusing on God who must be obeyed rather than on the results to be achieved, good leaders see beyond temporary setbacks and reversals.

6.10–12 Think how hard it must have been for Moses to bring God's message to Pharaoh when his own people had trouble believing it. He must have felt very alone. Moses obeyed God, however, and what a difference it made! When the chances for success appear slim, remember that anyone can obey God when the task is easy and everyone is behind it. Only those with persistent faith can obey when the task seems impossible.

The genealogy of Moses and Aaron

14 The following are the heads of their ancestral houses: the sons of Reuben,
the firstborn of Israel: Hanoch, Pallu, Hezron, and Carmi; these are the families of
Reuben. 15 The sons of Simeon: Jemuel, Jamin, Ohad, Jachin, Zohar, and Shaul,[o]
the son of a Canaanite woman; these are the families of Simeon. 16 The following
are the names of the sons of Levi according to their genealogies: Gershon,[p] Kohath, and Merari, and the length of Levi's life was one hundred thirty-seven years.
17 The sons of Gershon:[p] Libni and Shimei, by their families. 18 The sons of Kohath: Amram, Izhar, Hebron, and Uzziel, and the length of Kohath's life was one
hundred thirty-three years. 19 The sons of Merari: Mahli and Mushi. These are the
families of the Levites according to their genealogies. 20 Amram married Jochebed
his father's sister and she bore him Aaron and Moses, and the length of Amram's
life was one hundred thirty-seven years. 21 The sons of Izhar: Korah, Nepheg, and
Zichri. 22 The sons of Uzziel: Mishael, Elzaphan, and Sithri. 23 Aaron married
Elisheba, daughter of Amminadab and sister of Nahshon, and she bore him Nadab,
Abihu, Eleazar, and Ithamar. 24 The sons of Korah: Assir, Elkanah, and Abiasaph;
these are the families of the Korahites. 25 Aaron's son Eleazar married one of the
daughters of Putiel, and she bore him Phinehas. These are the heads of the ancestral
houses of the Levites by their families.

26 It was this same Aaron and Moses to whom the LORD said, "Bring the Israel-
ites out of the land of Egypt, company by company." 27 It was they who spoke to
Pharaoh king of Egypt to bring the Israelites out of Egypt, the same Moses and
Aaron.

Aaron's rod becomes a snake

28 On the day when the LORD spoke to Moses in the land of Egypt, 29 he said to
him, "I am the LORD; tell Pharaoh king of Egypt all that I am speaking to you."
30 But Moses said in the LORD's presence, "Since I am a poor speaker,[q] why would
Pharaoh listen to me?"

7 The LORD said to Moses, "See, I have made you like God to Pharaoh, and your
brother Aaron shall be your prophet. 2 You shall speak all that I command you,
and your brother Aaron shall tell Pharaoh to let the Israelites go out of his land.
3 But I will harden Pharaoh's heart, and I will multiply my signs and wonders in the
land of Egypt. 4 When Pharaoh does not listen to you, I will lay my hand upon
Egypt and bring my people the Israelites, company by company, out of the land of
Egypt by great acts of judgment. 5 The Egyptians shall know that I am the LORD,
when I stretch out my hand against Egypt and bring the Israelites out from among
them." 6 Moses and Aaron did so; they did just as the LORD commanded them.
7 Moses was eighty years old and Aaron eighty-three when they spoke to Pharaoh.

8 The LORD said to Moses and Aaron, 9 "When Pharaoh says to you, 'Perform
a wonder,' then you shall say to Aaron, 'Take your staff and throw it down before
Pharaoh, and it will become a snake.' " 10 So Moses and Aaron went to Pharaoh and
did as the LORD had commanded; Aaron threw down his staff before Pharaoh and his
officials, and it became a snake. 11 Then Pharaoh summoned the wise men and the
sorcerers; and they also, the magicians of Egypt, did the same by their secret
arts. 12 Each one threw down his staff, and they became snakes; but Aaron's staff

6.14 Gen 46.9 Num 26.5
6.15 Gen 46.10 Num 26.12
6.16 Gen 46.11 Num 3.18 1 Chron 6.1,16
6.23 Ex 24.1 Ruth 4.19,20 Lk 1.5
6.24 Ex 6.21 Num 16.1
6.25 Num 25.7,11 Josh 22.13
6.26 Ex 6.13 Josh 24.5
6.28,29 Ex 6.2; 7.16
6.30 Ex 4.10; 6.12
7.1 Ex 4.16; 18.19
7.3 Ex 4.21; 8.19 9.16,34
7.4 Ex 11.9; 12.51
7.5 Ex 8.10,19
7.7 Deut 31.2; 34.7 Acts 7.23,30
7.9 Ex 4.3 Isa 7.11
7.11 Gen 41.8 Ex 8.7,18 Dan 2.4 2 Tim 3.8,9
7.12 Ex 8.19

[o] Or *Saul* [p] Also spelled *Gershom*; see 2.22 [q] Heb *am uncircumcised of lips*; see 6.12

6.14–25 This genealogy or family tree was placed here to identify more firmly Moses and Aaron. Genealogies were used to establish credentials and authority as well as outlining the history of a family.

7.1 God made Moses "like God to Pharaoh"—in other words, a powerful person who deserved to be listened to. Pharaoh himself was considered a god, so he recognized Moses as one of his peers.

7.11 How were these wise men and sorcerers able to duplicate Moses' miracles? Some of their feats involved trickery or illusion, and some may have used satanic power, since worshiping gods of the underworld was part of their religion. Ironically, whenever the sorcerers duplicated one of Moses' plagues, it only made matters worse. If the magicians had been as powerful as God, they would have reversed the plagues, not added to them.

7.12 God performed a miracle by turning Aaron's staff into a snake, and Pharaoh's magicians duplicated it through trickery or sorcery. Although miracles can help us believe, it is dangerous to rely on them alone. Satan can imitate some parts of God's work and lead people astray. Pharaoh focused on the miracle rather than the message. We can avoid this error by letting the word of God be the basis of our faith. No miracle from God would endorse any message that is contrary to the teachings of his word.

swallowed up theirs. 13 Still Pharaoh's heart was hardened, and he would not listen **7.13** Ex 4.21
to them, as the LORD had said. Deut 2.30

4. Plagues strike Egypt

The first plague: water to blood

14 Then the LORD said to Moses, "Pharaoh's heart is hardened; he refuses to let **7.14** Ex 7.4; 8.15
the people go. 15 Go to Pharaoh in the morning, as he is going out to the water; stand **7.15**
by at the river bank to meet him, and take in your hand the staff that was turned into Ex 2.5; 8.20
a snake. 16 Say to him, 'The LORD, the God of the Hebrews, sent me to you to say, **7.16** Ex 4.23; 8.1
"Let my people go, so that they may worship me in the wilderness." But until now
you have not listened.' 17 Thus says the LORD, "By this you shall know that I am the **7.17** Ex 7.20
LORD." See, with the staff that is in my hand I will strike the water that is in the Rev 11.6; 16.4-6
Nile, and it shall be turned to blood. 18 The fish in the river shall die, the river itself
shall stink, and the Egyptians shall be unable to drink water from the Nile.' " 19 The **7.19** Ex 8.5,16; 9.22
LORD said to Moses, "Say to Aaron, 'Take your staff and stretch out your hand over
the waters of Egypt—over its rivers, its canals, and its ponds, and all its pools of
water—so that they may become blood; and there shall be blood throughout the
whole land of Egypt, even in vessels of wood and in vessels of stone.' "

20 Moses and Aaron did just as the LORD commanded. In the sight of Pharaoh **7.20** Ps 78.44; 105.28,
and of his officials he lifted up the staff and struck the water in the river, and all the 29
water in the river was turned into blood, 21 and the fish in the river died. The river
stank so that the Egyptians could not drink its water, and there was blood throughout the whole land of Egypt. 22 But the magicians of Egypt did the same by their **7.22** Ex 8.7
secret arts; so Pharaoh's heart remained hardened, and he would not listen to them;
as the LORD had said. 23 Pharaoh turned and went into his house, and he did not take **7.23** Ex 9.21
even this to heart. 24 And all the Egyptians had to dig along the Nile for water to
drink, for they could not drink the water of the river.

25 Seven days passed after the LORD had struck the Nile.

The second plague: hordes of frogs

8 [r] Then the LORD said to Moses, "Go to Pharaoh and say to him, 'Thus says the **8.1** Ex 5.1
LORD: Let my people go, so that they may worship me. 2 If you refuse to let
them go, I will plague your whole country with frogs. 3 The river shall swarm with **8.3** Ps 105.30
frogs; they shall come up into your palace, into your bedchamber and your bed, and
into the houses of your officials and of your people,[s] and into your ovens and your
kneading bowls. 4 The frogs shall come up on you and on your people and on all
your officials.' " 5[t] And the LORD said to Moses, "Say to Aaron, 'Stretch out your **8.5** Ex 7.19; 8.16
hand with your staff over the rivers, the canals, and the pools, and make frogs come
up on the land of Egypt.' " 6 So Aaron stretched out his hand over the waters of **8.6** Ps 78.45
Egypt; and the frogs came up and covered the land of Egypt. 7 But the magicians 105.30
did the same by their secret arts, and brought frogs up on the land of Egypt. **8.7** Ex 7.11; 8.18

8 Then Pharaoh called Moses and Aaron, and said, "Pray to the LORD to take **8.8**
away the frogs from me and my people, and I will let the people go to sacrifice to Ex 5.2; 9.28
the LORD." 9 Moses said to Pharaoh, "Kindly tell me when I am to pray for you and 10.10,17

[r] Ch 7.26 in Heb [s] Gk: Heb *upon your people* [t] Ch 8.1 in Heb

---

7.17 God dramatically turned the waters of the Nile into blood to show Pharaoh who he was. Do you sometimes wish for miraculous signs so you can be sure about God? God has given you the miracle of eternal life through your faith in him, something Pharaoh never obtained. This is a quiet miracle and, though less evident right now, just as extraordinary as water turned to blood. The desire for spectacular signs may cause us to ignore the more subtle miracles God is working every day.

7.20 Egypt was a large country, but most of the population lived along the banks of the Nile River. This 3,000-mile waterway was truly a river of life for the Egyptians. It made life possible in a land that was mostly desert by providing water for drinking, farming, bathing, and fishing. Egyptian society was a ribbon of civilization lining the banks of this life source, rarely reaching very far into the surrounding desert. Without the Nile's water, Egypt could not have existed. Imagine Pharaoh's dismay when Moses turned this sacred river to blood!

8.3ff Moses predicted that every house in Egypt would be infested with frogs. The poor of Egypt lived in small, mud-brick houses of one or two rooms with palm-trunk roofs. The homes of the rich, however, were often two or three stories high, surrounded by landscaped gardens and enclosed by a high wall. Servants lived and worked on the first floor while the family occupied the upper floors. Thus if the frogs got into the royal bedrooms, they had infiltrated even the upper floors. No place in Egypt would be safe from them.

for your officials and for your people, that the frogs may be removed from you and
8.10 Ex 9.14,29 15.11 Deut 4.35 Ps 83.18 Isa 46.9 your houses and be left only in the Nile." 10 And he said, "Tomorrow." Moses said,
"As you say! So that you may know that there is no one like the LORD our God,
11 the frogs shall leave you and your houses and your officials and your people; they
shall be left only in the Nile." 12 Then Moses and Aaron went out from Pharaoh; and
8.12 Ex 8.30; 9.33 10.18 Moses cried out to the LORD concerning the frogs that he had brought upon Pharaoh.[u] 13 And the LORD did as Moses requested: the frogs died in the houses, the
8.15 Ex 7.22; 9.34 14.5 Eccles 8.11 courtyards, and the fields. 14 And they gathered them together in heaps, and the
land stank. 15 But when Pharaoh saw that there was a respite, he hardened his heart,
and would not listen to them, just as the LORD had said.

The third plague: dust to gnats

8.16 Ex 8.5; 9.22 16 Then the LORD said to Moses, "Say to Aaron, 'Stretch out your staff and
strike the dust of the earth, so that it may become gnats throughout the whole land
8.17 Ps 105.31 of Egypt.' " 17 And they did so; Aaron stretched out his hand with his staff and
struck the dust of the earth, and gnats came on humans and animals alike; all the
8.18 Ex 7.11; 9.11 dust of the earth turned into gnats throughout the whole land of Egypt. 18 The magicians tried to produce gnats by their secret arts, but they could not. There were
8.19 Ex 7.5; 8.15 1 Sam 6.9 gnats on both humans and animals. 19 And the magicians said to Pharaoh, "This is
the finger of God!" But Pharaoh's heart was hardened, and he would not listen to
them, just as the LORD had said.

The fourth plague: swarms of flies

8.20 Ex 7.15 20 Then the LORD said to Moses, "Rise early in the morning and present yourself before Pharaoh, as he goes out to the water, and say to him, 'Thus says the
LORD: Let my people go, so that they may worship me. 21 For if you will not let my
people go, I will send swarms of flies on you, your officials, and your people, and
into your houses; and the houses of the Egyptians shall be filled with swarms of
8.22 Ex 8.10; 9.4 10.23 flies; so also the land where they live. 22 But on that day I will set apart the land of
Goshen, where my people live, so that no swarms of flies shall be there, that you
may know that I the LORD am in this land. 23 Thus I will make a distinction[v] be-
8.24 Ps 78.45 105.31 tween my people and your people. This sign shall appear tomorrow.' " 24 The LORD
did so, and great swarms of flies came into the house of Pharaoh and into his officials' houses; in all of Egypt the land was ruined because of the flies.
8.25 Gen 46.34 Ex 8.8; 10.8 25 Then Pharaoh summoned Moses and Aaron, and said, "Go, sacrifice to your
God within the land." 26 But Moses said, "It would not be right to do so; for the
8.26 Ex 3.18; 9.3 sacrifices that we offer to the LORD our God are offensive to the Egyptians. If we
offer in the sight of the Egyptians sacrifices that are offensive to them, will they not
8.27 Ex 10.26 stone us? 27 We must go a three days' journey into the wilderness and sacrifice to
8.28 Ex 8.8; 9.28 1 Kgs 13.6 the LORD our God as he commands us." 28 So Pharaoh said, "I will let you go to
sacrifice to the LORD your God in the wilderness, provided you do not go very far
away. Pray for me." 29 Then Moses said, "As soon as I leave you, I will pray to the
LORD that the swarms of flies may depart tomorrow from Pharaoh, from his

[u] Or *frogs, as he had agreed with Pharaoh* [v] Gk Vg: Heb *will set redemption*

8.15 After repeated warnings, Pharaoh still refused to obey God. He hardened his heart every time there was a break in the plagues. His stubborn disobedience brought suffering upon himself and his entire country. While persistence is good, stubbornness is usually self-centered. Stubbornness toward God is always disobedience. Avoid disobedience, because the consequences may spill onto others.

8.19 Some people think, "If only I could see a miracle, I could believe in God." God gave Pharaoh just such an opportunity. When gnats infested Egypt, even the magicians agreed that this was God's work ("the finger of God")—but still Pharaoh refused to believe. He was stubborn, and stubbornness can blind a person to the truth. When you rid yourself of stubbornness, you may be surprised by abundant evidence of God's hand in your life.

8.25–29 Pharaoh wanted a compromise. He would allow the Hebrews to sacrifice, but only if they would do it nearby. God's requirement, however, was firm: the Hebrews had to leave Egypt. Sometimes people urge believers to compromise and give only partial obedience to God's commands. But commitment and obedience to God cannot be negotiated. When it comes to obeying God, half measures won't do.

8.26 The Hebrews' sacrifices would be offensive to the Egyptians because they sacrificed animals that the Egyptians regarded as sacred. Moses was concerned about a violent reaction to sacrificing these animals near the Egyptians.

officials, and from his people; only do not let Pharaoh again deal falsely by not
letting the people go to sacrifice to the LORD."
30 So Moses went out from Pharaoh and prayed to the LORD. 31 And the LORD 8.30
did as Moses asked: he removed the swarms of flies from Pharaoh, from his offi- Ex 8.12
cials, and from his people; not one remained. 32 But Pharaoh hardened his heart this 8.31,32 Ex 7.13; 9.12
time also, and would not let the people go.

The fifth plague: livestock destroyed

9 Then the LORD said to Moses, "Go to Pharaoh, and say to him, 'Thus says the 9.1
LORD, the God of the Hebrews: Let my people go, so that they may worship Ex 8.1; 10.3
me. 2 For if you refuse to let them go and still hold them, 3 the hand of the LORD will 9.3
strike with a deadly pestilence your livestock in the field: the horses, the donkeys, Ex 7.4; 9.18
the camels, the herds, and the flocks. 4 But the LORD will make a distinction be- 9.4
tween the livestock of Israel and the livestock of Egypt, so that nothing shall die of Ex 8.22; 9.26
all that belongs to the Israelites.' " 5 The LORD set a time, saying, "Tomorrow the 9.5
LORD will do this thing in the land." 6 And on the next day the LORD did so; all the Ex 8.23; 10.4
livestock of the Egyptians died, but of the livestock of the Israelites not one died.
7 Pharaoh inquired and found that not one of the livestock of the Israelites was dead. 9.7 Ex 7.14; 8.32
But the heart of Pharaoh was hardened, and he would not let the people go. 9.35

The sixth plague: ashes cause boils

8 Then the LORD said to Moses and Aaron, "Take handfuls of soot from the 9.8
kiln, and let Moses throw it in the air in the sight of Pharaoh. 9 It shall become fine Ex 8.16
dust all over the land of Egypt, and shall cause festering boils on humans and ani- 9.9 Lev 13.18
mals throughout the whole land of Egypt." 10 So they took soot from the kiln, and Rev 16.2
stood before Pharaoh, and Moses threw it in the air, and it caused festering boils on
humans and animals. 11 The magicians could not stand before Moses because of the 9.11
boils, for the boils afflicted the magicians as well as all the Egyptians. 12 But the Ex 8.18
LORD hardened the heart of Pharaoh, and he would not listen to them, just as 9.12 Ex 7.13; 10.1
the LORD had spoken to Moses.

The seventh plague: thunder and hail

13 Then the LORD said to Moses, "Rise up early in the morning and present your- 9.13
self before Pharaoh, and say to him, 'Thus says the LORD, the God of the Hebrews: Ex 8.20
Let my people go, so that they may worship me. 14 For this time I will send all my 9.14
plagues upon you yourself, and upon your officials, and upon your people, so that Ex 8.10; 5.11
you may know that there is no one like me in all the earth. 15 For by now I could 9.15
have stretched out my hand and struck you and your people with pestilence, and Ex 11.6; 14.28
you would have been cut off from the earth. 16 But this is why I have let you live: 9.16
to show you my power, and to make my name resound through all the earth. 17 You Ex 14.4,17 18.11
are still exalting yourself against my people, and will not let them go. 18 Tomorrow Rom 9.17
at this time I will cause the heaviest hail to fall that has ever fallen in Egypt from the 9.17
day it was founded until now. 19 Send, therefore, and have your livestock and ev- Job 9.4; 15.25 Isa 37.23
erything that you have in the open field brought to a secure place; every human or 9.18
animal that is in the open field and is not brought under shelter will die when the Ex 9.5; 10.4
hail comes down upon them.' " 20 Those officials of Pharaoh who feared the word 9.20
of the LORD hurried their slaves and livestock off to a secure place. 21 Those who Prov 13.13 Heb 11.7

9.1 This was the fifth time God sent Moses back to Pharaoh with the demand, "Let my people go!" Moses may have been tired and discouraged by this time, but he continued to obey. Is there a difficult conflict you must face again and again? Don't give up when you know what is right to do. As Moses discovered, persistence is rewarded.

9.12 God gave Pharaoh many opportunities to heed Moses' warnings. But finally God seemed to say, "All right, Pharaoh, have it your way," and Pharaoh's heart became permanently hardened. Did God intentionally harden Pharaoh's heart and overrule his free will? No, he simply confirmed that Pharaoh freely chose a life of resisting God. Similarly, after a lifetime of resisting God, you may find it impossible to turn to him. Don't wait until "just the right time" before turning to God. Do it now while you still have the chance. If you continually ignore God's voice, eventually you will be unable to hear it at all.

9.20–21 If all the Egyptians' livestock were killed in the earlier plague (9.6), how could the servants of Pharaoh put their cattle inside? The answer is probably that the earlier plague killed all the animals in the fields (v.3) but not those in the shelters. (Animals are also mentioned in verse 10.)

did not regard the word of the LORD left their slaves and livestock in the open field.
9.22 Ex 8.5 22 The LORD said to Moses, "Stretch out your hand toward heaven so that hail
may fall on the whole land of Egypt, on humans and animals and all the plants of
9.23 Ex 19.16 Josh 10.11 Ps 18.13; 78.47 105.32 Rev 8.3; 16.21 the field in the land of Egypt." 23 Then Moses stretched out his staff toward heaven,
and the LORD sent thunder and hail, and fire came down on the earth. And the LORD
rained hail on the land of Egypt; 24 there was hail with fire flashing continually in
the midst of it, such heavy hail as had never fallen in all the land of Egypt since it
became a nation. 25 The hail struck down everything that was in the open field
throughout all the land of Egypt, both human and animal; the hail also struck down
9.26 Ex 8.22; 10.23 all the plants of the field, and shattered every tree in the field. 26 Only in the land of
Goshen, where the Israelites were, there was no hail.
9.27 2 Chron 12.6 Ps 129.4 27 Then Pharaoh summoned Moses and Aaron, and said to them, "This time I
have sinned; the LORD is in the right, and I and my people are in the wrong. 28 Pray

THE PLAGUES

Reference	Plague	What Happened	Result
7.14–24	Blood	Fish die, the river smells, the people are without water	Pharaoh's magicians duplicate the miracle by "secret arts" so Pharaoh is unmoved
8.1–15	Frogs	Frogs come up from the water and completely cover the land	Again Pharaoh's magicians duplicate the miracle by sorcery and Pharaoh is unmoved.
8.16–19	Lice	All the dust of Egypt becomes a massive swarm of gnats	Magicians are unable to duplicate this and say it is the "finger of God," but Pharaoh's heart remains hard
8.20–32	Flies	Swarms of flies cover the land	Pharaoh promises to let the Hebrews go, but then hardens his heart and refuses
9.1–7	Livestock	All the Egyptian livestock dies—but none of Israel's is even sick	Pharaoh still refuses to let the people go
9.8–12	Boils	Horrible boils break out on everyone in Egypt	Magicians cannot respond as they are struck down with boils as well—Pharaoh refuses to listen
9.13–35	Hail	Hailstorms kill all the slaves and animals left out or unprotected and strip or destroy almost every plant	Pharaoh admits his sin, but then changes his mind and refuses to let Israel go
10.1–20	Locusts	Locusts cover Egypt and eat everything left by the hail	Everyone advises Pharaoh to let the Hebrews go, but God hardens Pharaoh's heart and he refuses
10.21–29	Darkness	Total darkness covers Egypt for three days so no one can even move—except the Hebrews, who have light as usual	Pharaoh again promises to let Israel go, but again changes his mind
11.1—12.33	Death of Firstborn	The firstborn of all the people and cattle of Egypt die—but Israel is spared	Pharaoh and the Egyptians urge Israel to leave quickly; but after they are gone, Pharaoh again changes his mind and chases after them

9.27–34 After promising to let the Hebrews go, Pharaoh immediately broke his promise and brought even more trouble upon the land. His actions revealed that his repentance was not real. We do damage to ourselves and to others if we pretend to change but don't mean it.

to the LORD! Enough of God's thunder and hail! I will let you go; you need stay no 9.28 Ex 8.8; 10.17
longer." 29 Moses said to him, "As soon as I have gone out of the city, I will stretch 9.29
out my hands to the LORD; the thunder will cease, and there will be no more hail, Deut 10.14
so that you may know that the earth is the LORD's. 30 But as for you and your offi- Ps 24.1 1 Cor 10.26,28
cials, I know that you do not yet fear the LORD God." 31 (Now the flax and the 9.30
barley were ruined, for the barley was in the ear and the flax was in bud. 32 But the Ex 8.29; 11.9
wheat and the spelt were not ruined, for they are late in coming up.) 33 So Moses left
Pharaoh, went out of the city, and stretched out his hands to the LORD; then the
thunder and the hail ceased, and the rain no longer poured down on the earth. 34 But 9.34
when Pharaoh saw that the rain and the hail and the thunder had ceased, he sinned Ex 8.15; 11.9
once more and hardened his heart, he and his officials. 35 So the heart of Pharaoh
was hardened, and he would not let the Israelites go, just as the LORD had spoken
through Moses.

The eighth plague: devouring locusts

10 Then the LORD said to Moses, "Go to Pharaoh; for I have hardened his heart 10.1 Ex 4.21; 7.13
and the heart of his officials, in order that I may show these signs of mine 14.17
among them, 2 and that you may tell your children and grandchildren how I have 10.2
made fools of the Egyptians and what signs I have done among them — so that you Ex 13.8 Deut 4.9
may know that I am the LORD." Ps 44.1
3 So Moses and Aaron went to Pharaoh, and said to him, "Thus says the LORD, 10.3
the God of the Hebrews, 'How long will you refuse to humble yourself before me? Ex 4.23; 16.28
Let my people go, so that they may worship me. 4 For if you refuse to let my people 10.4,5
go, tomorrow I will bring locusts into your country. 5 They shall cover the surface Ex 9.18; 11.4,5 Joel 1.4; 2.25
of the land, so that no one will be able to see the land. They shall devour the last
remnant left you after the hail, and they shall devour every tree of yours that grows
in the field. 6 They shall fill your houses, and the houses of all your officials and of
all the Egyptians — something that neither your parents nor your grandparents have
seen, from the day they came on earth to this day.' " Then he turned and went out
from Pharaoh.
7 Pharaoh's officials said to him, "How long shall this fellow be a snare to us? 10.7 Ex 5.1; 12.33
Let the people go, so that they may worship the LORD their God; do you not yet
understand that Egypt is ruined?" 8 So Moses and Aaron were brought back to Phar- 10.8
aoh, and he said to them, "Go, worship the LORD your God! But which ones are to Ex 5.1; 8.25
go?" 9 Moses said, "We will go with our young and our old; we will go with our 10.9
sons and daughters and with our flocks and herds, because we have the LORD's Ex 12.37
festival to celebrate." 10 He said to them, "The LORD indeed will be with you, if 10.10 Gen 50.8
ever I let your little ones go with you! Plainly, you have some evil purpose in mind. Ex 12.31
11 No, never! Your men may go and worship the LORD, for that is what you are 10.11 Ex 10.28; 11.8
asking." And they were driven out from Pharaoh's presence.
12 Then the LORD said to Moses, "Stretch out your hand over the land of Egypt, 10.12 Ex 7.19; 9.22
so that the locusts may come upon it and eat every plant in the land, all that the hail 10.13 Ps 78.46
has left." 13 So Moses stretched out his staff over the land of Egypt, and the LORD 105.34
brought an east wind upon the land all that day and all that night; when morning 10.14 Joel 1.4,7
came, the east wind had brought the locusts. 14 The locusts came upon all the land 2.1,11
of Egypt and settled on the whole country of Egypt, such a dense swarm of locusts 10.15 Ex 10.5
as had never been before, nor ever shall be again. 15 They covered the surface of the Ps 78.46
whole land, so that the land was black; and they ate all the plants in the land and all 105.35
the fruit of the trees that the hail had left; nothing green was left, no tree, no plant 10.16 Ex 8.8; 9.27
in the field, in all the land of Egypt. 16 Pharaoh hurriedly summoned Moses and 10.17
Aaron and said, "I have sinned against the LORD your God, and against you. 17 Do Ex 8.28 Num 21.7
forgive my sin just this once, and pray to the LORD your God that at the least he 1 Sam 15.25

10.2 God told Moses that his miraculous experiences with Pharaoh should be retold to his descendants. What stories Moses had to tell! Living out one of the greatest dramas in biblical history, he witnessed events few people would ever see. It is important to tell our children about God's work in our past and to help them see what he is doing right now. What are the turning points in your life where God intervened? What is God doing for you now? Your stories will lay the foundations of your children's belief in God.

10.18 Ex 8.30 remove this deadly thing from me." 18 So he went out from Pharaoh and prayed to
the LORD. 19 The LORD changed the wind into a very strong west wind, which lifted
the locusts and drove them into the Red Sea;[w] not a single locust was left in all the
10.20 Ex 4.21; 9.12 11.10 country of Egypt. 20 But the LORD hardened Pharaoh's heart, and he would not let
the Israelites go.

The ninth plague: three days of darkness

10.21 Ex 9.22 Deut 28.29 21 Then the LORD said to Moses, "Stretch out your hand toward heaven so that
there may be darkness over the land of Egypt, a darkness that can be felt." 22 So
10.22 Ex 20.21 Ps 105.28 Joel 2.2 Moses stretched out his hand toward heaven, and there was dense darkness in all
the land of Egypt for three days. 23 People could not see one another, and for three
days they could not move from where they were; but all the Israelites had light
10.23 Ex 8.22; 9.4 14.20 where they lived. 24 Then Pharaoh summoned Moses, and said, "Go, worship the
LORD. Only your flocks and your herds shall remain behind. Even your children
10.24 Ex 8.28; 10.8 may go with you." 25 But Moses said, "You must also let us have sacrifices and
10.26 Ex 10.9; 12.32 burnt offerings to sacrifice to the LORD our God. 26 Our livestock also must go with
us; not a hoof shall be left behind, for we must choose some of them for the worship
of the LORD our God, and we will not know what to use to worship the LORD until
10.27 Ex 4.21; 9.12 11.10; 14.4 we arrive there." 27 But the LORD hardened Pharaoh's heart, and he was unwilling
to let them go. 28 Then Pharaoh said to him, "Get away from me! Take care that you
10.29 Heb 11.27 do not see my face again, for on the day you see my face you shall die." 29 Moses
said, "Just as you say! I will never see your face again."

Moses warns of the final plague

11.1 Ex 3.20,21 12.31 **11** The LORD said to Moses, "I will bring one more plague upon Pharaoh and
upon Egypt; afterwards he will let you go from here; indeed, when he lets
11.2 Ex 12.35 you go, he will drive you away. 2 Tell the people that every man is to ask his neigh-
11.3 Deut 34.10-12 bor and every woman is to ask her neighbor for objects of silver and gold." 3 The
LORD gave the people favor in the sight of the Egyptians. Moreover, Moses himself
was a man of great importance in the land of Egypt, in the sight of Pharaoh's officials and in the sight of the people.
11.4 Ex 12.29 Amos 4.10 4 Moses said, "Thus says the LORD: About midnight I will go out through
Egypt. 5 Every firstborn in the land of Egypt shall die, from the firstborn of Pharaoh
11.5 Ex 4.23; 12.12 13.15 who sits on his throne to the firstborn of the female slave who is behind the hand-
mill, and all the firstborn of the livestock. 6 Then there will be a loud cry throughout
11.6 Ex 12.30 Amos 5.17 the whole land of Egypt, such as has never been or will ever be again. 7 But not a
dog shall growl at any of the Israelites — not at people, not at animals — so that you
11.7 Ex 8.22; 10.23 may know that the LORD makes a distinction between Egypt and Israel. 8 Then all
these officials of yours shall come down to me, and bow low to me, saying, 'Leave
11.8 Ex 12.31 Heb 11.27 us, you and all the people who follow you.' After that I will leave." And in hot
anger he left Pharaoh.

[w] Or *Sea of Reeds*

10.22 As each gloomy plague descended upon the land, the Egyptian people realized how powerless their own gods were to stop it. Hapi, the "powerful" god of the Nile River, could not prevent the waters from turning to blood (7.20). Hathor, the crafty cow-goddess, was helpless as Egyptian cattle died in droves (9.6). Amon-Ra, the sun god and chief of the Egyptian gods, could not stop an eerie darkness from covering the land for three full days (10.21, 22). The Egyptian gods were (1) nonpersonal, centering around images like the sun or the river; (2) numerous; (3) nonexclusive. By contrast, the God of the Hebrews was (1) a living personal Being, (2) the only true God, and (3) the only God who should be worshiped. God was proving to both the Hebrews and the Egyptians that he alone is the living and all-powerful God.

10.27, 28 Why was Pharaoh so reluctant to let the people go? The Hebrews were Egypt's free labor – the builders of their great cities. As Egypt's leader, Pharaoh would not easily let such a great resource go.

11.7 Moses told Pharaoh that God made a distinction between the Hebrews and the Egyptians. At this time the distinction was very clear in God's mind: he knew the Hebrews would become his chosen people. The distinction was taking shape in Moses' mind also. But the Hebrews still saw the distinction only in terms of slave and free. Later, when they were in the desert, God would teach them the laws, principles, and values that would make them distinct as his people. Remember that God sees us in terms of what we will become and not just what we are right now.

9 The LORD said to Moses, "Pharaoh will not listen to you, in order that my
wonders may be multiplied in the land of Egypt." 10 Moses and Aaron performed all
these wonders before Pharaoh; but the LORD hardened Pharaoh's heart, and he did
not let the people of Israel go out of his land.

11.9 Ex 7.4; 10.1
11.10 Ex 4.21 Rom 2.2; 9.17

5. The passover

The first passover is instituted

12 The LORD said to Moses and Aaron in the land of Egypt: 2 This month shall
mark for you the beginning of months; it shall be the first month of the year
for you. 3 Tell the whole congregation of Israel that on the tenth of this month they
are to take a lamb for each family, a lamb for each household. 4 If a household is too
small for a whole lamb, it shall join its closest neighbor in obtaining one; the lamb
shall be divided in proportion to the number of people who eat of it. 5 Your lamb
shall be without blemish, a year-old male; you may take it from the sheep or from
the goats. 6 You shall keep it until the fourteenth day of this month; then the whole
assembled congregation of Israel shall slaughter it at twilight. 7 They shall take
some of the blood and put it on the two doorposts and the lintel of the houses in
which they eat it. 8 They shall eat the lamb that same night; they shall eat it roasted
over the fire with unleavened bread and bitter herbs. 9 Do not eat any of it raw or
boiled in water, but roasted over the fire, with its head, legs, and inner organs.
10 You shall let none of it remain until the morning; anything that remains until the
morning you shall burn. 11 This is how you shall eat it: your loins girded, your
sandals on your feet, and your staff in your hand; and you shall eat it hurriedly. It
is the passover of the LORD. 12 For I will pass through the land of Egypt that night,
and I will strike down every firstborn in the land of Egypt, both human beings and
animals; on all the gods of Egypt I will execute judgments: I am the LORD. 13 The
blood shall be a sign for you on the houses where you live: when I see the blood,
I will pass over you, and no plague shall destroy you when I strike the land of
Egypt.
14 This day shall be a day of remembrance for you. You shall celebrate it as a

12.2 Ex 12.14; 13.4 23.15; 34.18
12.3,4 Lev 1.5 Jn 12.1 1 Cor 5.7
12.5 Lev 22.18-20 Heb 9.14
12.6 Lev 23.5 Num 9.3; 28.16 Deut 16.1 Mk 14.12
12.7 Ex 12.22 Heb 9.13,14
12.8 Ex 13.3; 34.25 Num 9.11 Deut 16.7
12.10 Ex 23.18; 29.34 Lev 7.15
12.11 Num 28.16
12.12 Ex 11.4,5 Num 33.4
12.13 Heb 11.28

11.9, 10 You may wonder how Pharaoh could be so foolish as to see God's miraculous power and still not listen to Moses. But Pharaoh had his mind made up long before the plagues began. He couldn't believe that someone was greater than he. His stubborn unbelief led to a heart so hard that even a major catastrophe couldn't soften him. Finally, it took the greatest of all calamities, the loss of his son, to force him to recognize God's authority. But even then he wanted God to leave, not to rule his country. We must not wait for great calamities to drive us to God, but must open our hearts and minds to his direction now.

11.10 Did God really harden Pharaoh's heart and force him to do wrong? Before the ten plagues began, Moses and Aaron announced what God would do if Pharaoh didn't let the people go. But their message only made Pharaoh stubborn—he was hardening his own heart. In so doing, he defied both God and his messengers. Through the first six plagues, Pharaoh's heart grew even more stubborn. After the sixth plague, God passed judgment. Sooner or later, evil people will be punished for their sins. When it became evident he wouldn't change, God confirmed Pharaoh's prideful decision and set the painful consequences of his actions in motion. God didn't force Pharaoh to reject him; rather, he gave him every opportunity to change his mind. In Ezekiel 33.11, God says, "I have no pleasure in the death of the wicked."

12.1–3 Certain holidays were instituted by God himself. Passover was a holiday designed to celebrate Israel's deliverance from Egypt and to remind the people of what God had done. Holidays can be important today, too, as annual reminders of what God has done for us. Develop traditions in your family to highlight the religious significance of certain holidays. These serve as reminders to the older people and learning experiences for the younger ones.

12.3ff For the Israelites to be spared from the plague of death, a lamb with no defects had to be killed and its blood placed on the doorposts of each home. What was the significance of the lamb? In killing the lamb, the Israelites shed innocent blood. The lamb was a sacrifice, a substitute for the person who would have died in the plague. From this point on, the Hebrew people would clearly understand that for them to be spared from death, an innocent life had to be sacrificed in their place.

12.6–11 The feast of the passover was to be an annual holiday in honor of the night when the Lord "passed over" the homes of the Israelites. The Hebrews followed God's instructions by placing the blood of a lamb on the doorposts of their homes. That night the firstborn son of every family who did not have blood on the doorposts was killed. The lamb had to be killed in order to get the blood that would protect them. (This foreshadowed the blood of Christ, the Lamb of God, who gave his blood for the sins of all people.) Inside their homes, the Israelites ate a meal of roast lamb, unleavened bread, and bitter herbs. Unleavened bread could be made quickly because the dough did not have to rise. They were dressed ("loins girded") and ready to go. Thus they could leave at any time. Bitter herbs signified the bitterness of slavery.

12.11 Eating the passover feast while wearing traveling clothes was a sign of the Hebrews' faith. Although they were not yet free, they were to prepare themselves, for God had said he would lead them out of Egypt. Their preparation was an act of faith. Preparing ourselves for the fulfillment of God's scriptural promises, however unlikely they may seem, demonstrates our faith.

12.13 Unleavened bread was bread made without yeast (leaven). It was not leavened because they could not wait for it to rise (12.39). They had to leave quickly and take their bread with them.

12.15
Ex 13.6; 34.18
Lev 23.5-8
Deut 16.3
12.16
Ex 20.10
Num 28.18
12.17
Ex 13.3
Num 9.4; 28.16
Josh 5.10
2 Kgs 23.21
Mk 14.12-16
12.19
Ex 12.15
12.21
Ex 3.16; 17.5
Heb 11.28
12.22
Lev 14.6
Num 19.18
Ps 51.7
Heb 9.13,14
11.28
12.23
Ex 12.12
2 Sam 24.16
Isa 37.36

festival to the LORD; throughout your generations you shall observe it as a perpetual
ordinance. 15 Seven days you shall eat unleavened bread; on the first day you shall
remove leaven from your houses, for whoever eats leavened bread from the first
day until the seventh day shall be cut off from Israel. 16 On the first day you shall
hold a solemn assembly, and on the seventh day a solemn assembly; no work shall
be done on those days; only what everyone must eat, that alone may be prepared by
you. 17 You shall observe the festival of unleavened bread, for on this very day I
brought your companies out of the land of Egypt: you shall observe this day
throughout your generations as a perpetual ordinance. 18 In the first month, from
the evening of the fourteenth day until the evening of the twenty-first day, you shall
eat unleavened bread. 19 For seven days no leaven shall be found in your houses; for
whoever eats what is leavened shall be cut off from the congregation of Israel,
whether an alien or a native of the land. 20 You shall eat nothing leavened; in all
your settlements you shall eat unleavened bread.
21 Then Moses called all the elders of Israel and said to them, "Go, select lambs
for your families, and slaughter the passover lamb. 22 Take a bunch of hyssop, dip
it in the blood that is in the basin, and touch the lintel and the two doorposts with
the blood in the basin. None of you shall go outside the door of your house until
morning. 23 For the LORD will pass through to strike down the Egyptians; when he

THE HEBREW CALENDAR
A Hebrew month began in the middle of a month on our calendar today. Crops are planted in November and December and harvested in March and April.

	Month	*Today's Calendar*	*Bible Reference*	*Israel's Holidays*
1	Nisan (Abib)	March–April	Exodus 13.4; 23.15; 34.18; Deuteronomy 16.1	Passover (Leviticus 23.5) Unleavened Bread (Leviticus 23.6) Firstfruits (Leviticus 23.10)
2	Iyyar (Zif)	April–May	1 Kings 6.1, 37	
3	Sivan	May–June	Esther 8.9	Pentecost (Leviticus 23.16)
4	Tammuz	June–July		
5	Ab	July–August		
6	Elul	August–September	Nehemiah 6.15	
7	Tishri (Ethanim)	September–October	1 Kings 8.2	Trumpets (Numbers 29.1; Leviticus 23.24) Day of Atonement (Leviticus 23.27) Tabernacles (Leviticus 23.34)
8	Marchesvan (Bul)	October–November	1 Kings 6.38	
9	Chisleu	November–December	Nehemiah 1.1	Dedication (John 10.22)
10	Tebeth	December–January	Esther 2.16	
11	Shebat (Sebat)	January–February	Zechariah 1.7	
12	Adar	February–March	Esther 3.7	

12.17, 23 Passover became an annual remembrance of how God delivered the Hebrews from Egypt. Each year the people would pause to remember the day when God's angel of death passed over their homes. They gave thanks to God for saving them from death and bringing them out of a land of slavery and sin. Believers today have experienced a day of deliverance as well – the day we were delivered from spiritual death and slavery to sin. The Lord's Supper is our "passover remembrance" of our new life and freedom from sin. The next time struggles and trials come, remember how God has delivered you in the past and focus on his promise of new life with him.

sees the blood on the lintel and on the two doorposts, the LORD will pass over that
door and will not allow the destroyer to enter your houses to strike you down.
24 You shall observe this rite as a perpetual ordinance for you and your children.
25 When you come to the land that the LORD will give you, as he has promised, you
shall keep this observance. 26 And when your children ask you, 'What do you mean
by this observance?' 27 you shall say, 'It is the passover sacrifice to the LORD, for
he passed over the houses of the Israelites in Egypt, when he struck down the Egyptians but spared our houses.' " And the people bowed down and worshiped.
28 The Israelites went and did just as the LORD had commanded Moses and
Aaron.

12.24 Gen 17.8
12.25 Gen 50.24 Ex 3.8 Deut 4.5; 12.9
12.26 Ex 13.8 Deut 6.7 Josh 4.6 Ps 78.5
12.27 a)Deut 16.2 1 Cor 5.7 b)Ex 4.31

The tenth plague: firstborn die

29 At midnight the LORD struck down all the firstborn in the land of Egypt,
from the firstborn of Pharaoh who sat on his throne to the firstborn of the prisoner
who was in the dungeon, and all the firstborn of the livestock. 30 Pharaoh arose in
the night, he and all his officials and all the Egyptians; and there was a loud cry in
Egypt, for there was not a house without someone dead. 31 Then he summoned
Moses and Aaron in the night, and said, "Rise up, go away from my people, both
you and the Israelites! Go, worship the LORD, as you said. 32 Take your flocks and
your herds, as you said, and be gone. And bring a blessing on me too!"
33 The Egyptians urged the people to hasten their departure from the land, for
they said, "We shall all be dead." 34 So the people took their dough before it was
leavened, with their kneading bowls wrapped up in their cloaks on their shoulders.
35 The Israelites had done as Moses told them; they had asked the Egyptians for
jewelry of silver and gold, and for clothing, 36 and the LORD had given the people
favor in the sight of the Egyptians, so that they let them have what they asked. And
so they plundered the Egyptians.

12.29 Ex 4.23 Ps 78.51 105.36
12.30 Ex 11.6
12.31 Ex 3.19 10.9,29; 11.8 Ps 105.38
12.33 Gen 20.3 Ex 11.1 Num 17.12
12.35 Ex 3.22
12.36 Gen 39.21 Ex 11.3 Ps 105.37

B. ISRAEL IN THE WILDERNESS (12.37—18.27)

As Egypt buried its dead, the Hebrew slaves left the country, a free people at last. Pharaoh made one last attempt to bring them back, but the people escaped when God miraculously parted the waters of the Red Sea. But on the other side, the people soon became dissatisfied and complained bitterly to Moses and Aaron about their trek through the wilderness. Through these experiences of the Hebrews, we learn that the Christian life is not always trouble-free. We still have struggles and often complain bitterly to God about conditions in our lives.

1. Escape from Egypt

The Israelites leave Egypt

37 The Israelites journeyed from Rameses to Succoth, about six hundred thousand men on foot, besides children. 38 A mixed crowd also went up with them, and
livestock in great numbers, both flocks and herds. 39 They baked unleavened cakes
of the dough that they had brought out of Egypt; it was not leavened, because they

12.37 Ex 1.11; 38.26 Num 1.46
12.38 Num 11.4 Deut 3.19

12.29, 30 Every firstborn child of the Egyptians died, but the Israelite children were spared because the blood of the lamb had been placed on their doorposts. So begins the story of redemption, the central theme of the Bible.

Redemption means "to buy back" or "to save from captivity by paying a ransom." One way to buy back a slave was to offer an equivalent or superior slave in exchange. That is the way God chose to buy us back—he offered his Son in exchange for us.

In Old Testament times, God accepted symbolic offerings. Jesus had not yet been sacrificed, so God accepted the life of an animal in place of the life of the sinner. When Jesus came, he substituted his perfect life for our sinful lives, taking the penalty for sin that we deserve. Thus he redeemed us from the power of sin and restored us to God. Jesus' sacrifice made animal sacrifice no longer necessary.

We must recognize that if we want to be freed from the deadly consequences of our sins, a tremendous price must be paid. But we don't have to pay it. Jesus Christ, our substitute, has already redeemed us by his death on the cross. Our part is to trust him and accept his gift of eternal life. Our sins have been paid for, and the way has been cleared for us to begin a relationship with God (Titus 2.14; Hebrews 9.13–15, 23–26).

12.32 Pharaoh's statement of "bring a blessing on me too" was probably a sarcastic way of saying, "Good riddance!"

12.34 A kneading bowl was large, made of wood, bronze, or pottery, and used for kneading dough. Bread was made by mixing water and flour in the bowl with a small piece of leavened dough saved from the previous day's batch. Bread was the primary food in the Hebrews' diet, and thus it was vital to bring the bowl along. It could be easily carried on the shoulder.

12.37, 38 The total number of people leaving Egypt is estimated to have been about two million. The "mixed crowd" may have been Egyptians and others who were drawn to the Hebrews by God's mighty works and who decided to leave Egypt with them.

were driven out of Egypt and could not wait, nor had they prepared any provisions
for themselves.
40 The time that the Israelites had lived in Egypt was four hundred thirty years.
41 At the end of four hundred thirty years, on that very day, all the companies of the
LORD went out from the land of Egypt. 42 That was for the LORD a night of vigil, to
bring them out of the land of Egypt. That same night is a vigil to be kept for the
LORD by all the Israelites throughout their generations.

Passover instructions

43 The LORD said to Moses and Aaron: This is the ordinance for the passover:
no foreigner shall eat of it, 44 but any slave who has been purchased may eat of it
after he has been circumcised; 45 no bound or hired servant may eat of it. 46 It shall
be eaten in one house; you shall not take any of the animal outside the house, and
you shall not break any of its bones. 47 The whole congregation of Israel shall celebrate it. 48 If an alien who resides with you wants to celebrate the passover to the
LORD, all his males shall be circumcised; then he may draw near to celebrate it; he
shall be regarded as a native of the land. But no uncircumcised person shall eat of
it; 49 there shall be one law for the native and for the alien who resides among you.
50 All the Israelites did just as the LORD had commanded Moses and Aaron.
51 That very day the LORD brought the Israelites out of the land of Egypt, company
by company.

The firstborn are dedicated to God

13 The LORD said to Moses: 2 Consecrate to me all the firstborn; whatever is the
first to open the womb among the Israelites, of human beings and animals,
is mine.
3 Moses said to the people, "Remember this day on which you came out of
Egypt, out of the house of slavery, because the LORD brought you out from there by
strength of hand; no leavened bread shall be eaten. 4 Today, in the month of Abib,
you are going out. 5 When the LORD brings you into the land of the Canaanites, the
Hittites, the Amorites, the Hivites, and the Jebusites, which he swore to your ancestors to give you, a land flowing with milk and honey, you shall keep this observance in this month. 6 Seven days you shall eat unleavened bread, and on the
seventh day there shall be a festival to the LORD. 7 Unleavened bread shall be eaten
for seven days; no leavened bread shall be seen in your possession, and no leaven
shall be seen among you in all your territory. 8 You shall tell your child on that day,
'It is because of what the LORD did for me when I came out of Egypt.' 9 It shall
serve for you as a sign on your hand and as a reminder on your forehead, so that the
teaching of the LORD may be on your lips; for with a strong hand the LORD brought
you out of Egypt. 10 You shall keep this ordinance at its proper time from year to
year.
11 "When the LORD has brought you into the land of the Canaanites, as he
swore to you and your ancestors, and has given it to you, 12 you shall set apart to the
LORD all that first opens the womb. All the firstborn of your livestock that are males
shall be the LORD's. 13 But every firstborn donkey you shall redeem with a sheep;
if you do not redeem it, you must break its neck. Every firstborn male among your

12.39 Ex 6.1; 11.1
12.40,41 Gen 15.13,16 Acts 7.6 Gal 3.16,17
12.42 Ex 13.3 Deut 16.1
12.43 Num 9.14
12.44 Gen 17.12,13 Lev 22.11
12.46 a)1 Cor 12.12 Eph 2.19 b)Num 9.12 Jn 19.33,36
12.48 Gen 17.12 Num 9.14; 15.15 Gal 3.28
12.49 Lev 24.22
13.1,2 Ex 13.11; 22.29 34.19 Lev 27.26 Num 3.13 Deut 15.19 Lk 2.23
13.3 Ex 12.42; 23.15 Deut 5.15
13.4,5 Gen 17.7,8 Ex 3.8,17 34.11 Deut 7.1
13.6 Ex 12.15,19
13.9 Ex 12.14 Num 15.39 Deut 6.8
13.10 Ex 12.14; 23.15 Lev 23.6-8 Deut 16.3,4
13.12 Ex 13.2; 22.29 Num 8.17 Deut 15.19
13.13 Ex 34.20 Num 18.15 Rev 14.4

13.4 "In the month of Abib" corresponds to late March on our calendar.

13.9 The festival of unleavened bread marked the Hebrews as a unique people—as though they were branded on their hands and foreheads. What do you do that marks you as a follower of God? The way you raise your children, demonstrate love for others, show concern for the poor, and live in devotion to God—these actions will leave visible marks for all to see. While national groups are marked by customs and traditions, Christians are marked by loving one another (John 13.34, 35).

13.12–14 What did it mean to redeem all the firstborn? During the night the Israelites escaped from Egypt, God spared the oldest son of every house marked with blood on the doorposts. Because God saved the lives of the firstborn, he had a rightful claim to them. But God commanded the Israelites to buy their sons back from him. This ritual served three main purposes: (1) it was a reminder to the people of how God had spared their sons from death and freed them all from slavery; (2) it showed God's high respect for human life in contrast to the heathen gods who, their worshipers believed, demanded human sacrifice; (3) it looked forward to the day when Jesus Christ would buy us back by paying the price of sin once and for all.

children you shall redeem. 14 When in the future your child asks you, 'What does 13.14 Ex 12.26; 13.8
this mean?' you shall answer, 'By strength of hand the LORD brought us out of Deut 6.20
Egypt, from the house of slavery. 15 When Pharaoh stubbornly refused to let us go, 13.15
the LORD killed all the firstborn in the land of Egypt, from human firstborn to the Ex 12.29; 13.12
firstborn of animals. Therefore I sacrifice to the LORD every male that first opens
the womb, but every firstborn of my sons I redeem.' 16 It shall serve as a sign on 13.16
your hand and as an emblem[x] on your forehead that by strength of hand the LORD Ex 12.13; 13.9 Deut 6.7-9
brought us out of Egypt." 11.18

Pillar of cloud, pillar of fire

17 When Pharaoh let the people go, God did not lead them by way of the land 13.17,18
of the Philistines, although that was nearer; for God thought, "If the people face Ex 14.11; 16.12 Num 14.1-4
war, they may change their minds and return to Egypt." 18 So God led the people by Deut 17.16
the roundabout way of the wilderness toward the Red Sea.[y] The Israelites went up Josh 1.14; 4.12, 13
out of the land of Egypt prepared for battle. 19 And Moses took with him the bones 13.19
of Joseph who had required a solemn oath of the Israelites, saying, "God will surely Gen 50.24,25 Josh 24.32
take notice of you, and then you must carry my bones with you from here." 20 They Acts 7.15,16
set out from Succoth, and camped at Etham, on the edge of the wilderness. 21 The 13.20 Ex 12.37
LORD went in front of them in a pillar of cloud by day, to lead them along the way, Num 33.5,6
and in a pillar of fire by night, to give them light, so that they might travel by day 13.21 Ex 14.19,20
and by night. 22 Neither the pillar of cloud by day nor the pillar of fire by night left 33.9,10 Ps 105.39
its place in front of the people. 1 Cor 10.1

14 Then the LORD said to Moses: 2 Tell the Israelites to turn back and camp in 14.2 Ex 13.17
front of Pi-hahiroth, between Migdol and the sea, in front of Baal-zephon; Num 33.3,7
you shall camp opposite it, by the sea. 3 Pharaoh will say of the Israelites, 'They are Jer 44.1
wandering aimlessly in the land; the wilderness has closed in on them.' 4 I will 14.4
harden Pharaoh's heart, and he will pursue them, so that I will gain glory for myself Ex 4.21; 7.3 14.17
over Pharaoh and all his army; and the Egyptians shall know that I am the LORD. Rom 9.17,22
And they did so.

[x] Or *as a frontlet*; Meaning of Heb uncertain [y] Or *Sea of Reeds*

13.17, 18 God doesn't always work in the way that seems best to us. Instead of guiding the Israelites along the direct route from Egypt to the promised land, he took them by a longer route to avoid fighting with the Philistines. If God does not lead you along the shortest path to your goal, don't complain or resist. Follow him willingly and trust him to lead you safely around unseen obstacles. He can see the end of your journey from the beginning, and he knows the safest and best route.

13.17, 18 When did the Hebrews leave Egypt? There are two theories. The "early" theory says the exodus occurred around 1446–1445 B.C. The "late" theory suggests the exodus happened between 1300 and 1200 B.C. Those who hold to the earlier date point to 1 Kings 6.1, where the Bible clearly states that Solomon began building the temple 480 years after the Hebrews left Egypt. Since almost all scholars agree that Solomon began building the temple in 966, this puts the exodus in the year 1446. But those who hold to the later date suggest that the 480 years cannot be taken literally. They point to Exodus 1.11, which says that the Hebrews built the store-cities of Pithom and Raamses, named after the Pharaoh Raamses, who reigned around 1290 B.C. Regardless of which date is correct, the fact is that God led the Hebrews out of Egypt, just as he had promised. This showed his great power and his great love for his people.

13.21, 22 God gave the Hebrews a pillar of cloud and a pillar of fire so they would know day and night that God was with them on their journey to the promised land. What has he given us so that we can have the same assurance? The Bible – something the Israelites did not have. Look to God's Word for reassurance of his presence. As the Hebrews looked to the pillars of cloud and fire, we can look to God's Word day and night to know he is with us, helping us on our journey.

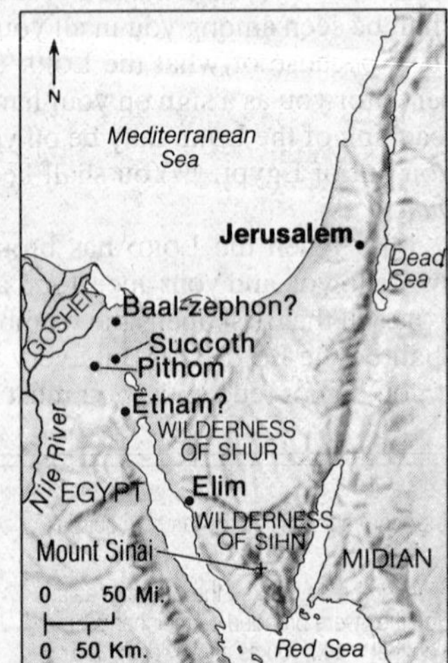

THE EXODUS
The Israelites left Succoth and camped first at Etham before going toward Baal-zephon to camp "by the sea" (14.2). God miraculously brought them across the sea, into the wilderness of Shur (15.22). After stopping at the oasis of Elim, the people moved into the wilderness of Sihn (Sin) (16.1).

13.21, 22 The pillars of fire and cloud were examples of *theophany* – God appearing in a physical form. In this form, God lighted Israel's path, protected them from their enemies, provided reassurance, controlled their movements, and inspired the burning zeal that Israel should have for their God.

The Egyptian army pursues the people of Israel

5 When the king of Egypt was told that the people had fled, the minds of Pharaoh and his officials were changed toward the people, and they said, "What have
we done, letting Israel leave our service?" 6 So he had his chariot made ready, and
took his army with him; 7 he took six hundred picked chariots and all the other
chariots of Egypt with officers over all of them. 8 The LORD hardened the heart of
Pharaoh king of Egypt and he pursued the Israelites, who were going out boldly.
9 The Egyptians pursued them, all Pharaoh's horses and chariots, his chariot drivers
and his army; they overtook them camped by the sea, by Pi-hahiroth, in front of
Baal-zephon.
10 As Pharaoh drew near, the Israelites looked back, and there were the Egyptians advancing on them. In great fear the Israelites cried out to the LORD. 11 They
said to Moses, "Was it because there were no graves in Egypt that you have taken
us away to die in the wilderness? What have you done to us, bringing us out of
Egypt? 12 Is this not the very thing we told you in Egypt, 'Let us alone and let us
serve the Egyptians'? For it would have been better for us to serve the Egyptians
than to die in the wilderness." 13 But Moses said to the people, "Do not be afraid,
stand firm, and see the deliverance that the LORD will accomplish for you today; for
the Egyptians whom you see today you shall never see again. 14 The LORD will fight
for you, and you have only to keep still."

2. Rescue through the Red Sea

The Israelites cross on dry ground

15 Then the LORD said to Moses, "Why do you cry out to me? Tell the Israelites
to go forward. 16 But you lift up your staff, and stretch out your hand over the sea
and divide it, that the Israelites may go into the sea on dry ground. 17 Then I will
harden the hearts of the Egyptians so that they will go in after them; and so I will
gain glory for myself over Pharaoh and all his army, his chariots, and his chariot
drivers. 18 And the Egyptians shall know that I am the LORD, when I have gained
glory for myself over Pharaoh, his chariots, and his chariot drivers."
19 The angel of God who was going before the Israelite army moved and went
behind them; and the pillar of cloud moved from in front of them and took its place
behind them. 20 It came between the army of Egypt and the army of Israel. And so
the cloud was there with the darkness, and it lit up the night; one did not come near
the other all night.
21 Then Moses stretched out his hand over the sea. The LORD drove the sea

14.5 Ex 12.33; Ps 105.25; Jer 34.10
14.7 Ex 14.23; 15.4
14.8 Ex 15.9
14.9 Ex 14.2; Josh 24.6
14.10 Josh 24.7; Neh 9.9
14.11 Ex 5.21; 15.24; Ps 106.6,7; Acts 7.39
14.13 Gen 15.1; Ex 14.30; 20.20
14.14 Ex 15.3; Deut 1.30; 3.22; Isa 30.15; 31.4,5
14.15 Josh 7.10
14.16 Ex 4.2; 7.9; Num 20.8
14.18 Ex 7.5; 14.25
14.19 Gen 24.7; Ex 13.21,22; 23.20
14.20 Ps 18.11
14.21 Ex 7.19; Ps 106.9; 114.3,5; 136.13; Isa 63.12,13

14.6–9 Six hundred Egyptian war chariots were bearing down on the helpless Israelites, who were trapped between the mountains and the sea. The war chariots each carried two people – one to drive and one to fight. They were made of a wood or leather cab placed over two wheels and pulled by horses. These were the armored tanks of Bible times. But even their power was no match for God, who destroyed both the chariots and their soldiers.

14.10, 11 Trapped against the sea, the Israelites faced the Egyptian army sweeping in for the kill. The Israelites thought they were doomed. After watching God's powerful hand deliver them from Egypt, their only response was fear, whining, and despair. Where was their trust in God? Israel had to learn from repeated experience that God was able to provide for them. God has preserved these examples in the Bible so that we can learn to trust him the first time. By focusing on God's faithfulness in the past we can face crises with confidence rather than with fear and complaining.

14.11 This is the first instance of grumbling and complaining by the Israelites. Their lack of faith in God is startling. Yet how often do we find ourselves doing the same thing – complaining over inconveniences or discomforts? The Israelites were about to learn some tough lessons. Had they trusted God, they would have been spared much grief.

14.13 The people were hostile and despairing, but Moses encouraged them to watch the wonderful way God would rescue them. Moses had a positive attitude! When it looked as if they were trapped, Moses called upon God to intervene. We may not be chased by an army, but we may still feel trapped. Instead of giving in to despair, we should adopt Moses' attitude to "stand firm, and see the deliverance that the Lord will accomplish."

14.15 The Lord told Moses to stop praying and get moving! Prayer must have a vital place in our lives, but there is also a place for action. Sometimes we know what to do, but we pray for more guidance as an excuse to postpone doing it. If we know what we should do, then it is time to get moving.

14.21 There was no apparent way of escape, but the Lord opened up a dry path through the sea. Sometimes we find ourselves caught in a problem and see no way out. Don't panic; God can open up a way.

14.21, 22 Some scholars believe the Israelites did not cross the main body of the Red Sea but one of the shallow lakes or marshes north of it that dry up at certain times of the year, or perhaps a smaller branch of the Red Sea where the water would have been shallow enough to wade across. But the Bible clearly states that the Lord "drove the sea back by a strong east wind all night" (14.21; see also Joshua 3.15, 16; and 2 Kings 2.13, 14). The God who created the earth and water performed a mighty miracle at exactly the right time to demonstrate his great power and love for his people.

back by a strong east wind all night, and turned the sea into dry land; and the waters
were divided. 22 The Israelites went into the sea on dry ground, the waters forming
a wall for them on their right and on their left. 23 The Egyptians pursued, and went
into the sea after them, all of Pharaoh's horses, chariots, and chariot drivers. 24 At
the morning watch the LORD in the pillar of fire and cloud looked down upon the
Egyptian army, and threw the Egyptian army into panic. 25 He clogged[z] their chariot wheels so that they turned with difficulty. The Egyptians said, "Let us flee from
the Israelites, for the LORD is fighting for them against Egypt."

14.22 Num 33.8; Ps 66.6; 78.13; Isa 11.15; Heb 11.29

The Egyptians are drowned

26 Then the LORD said to Moses, "Stretch out your hand over the sea, so that
the water may come back upon the Egyptians, upon their chariots and chariot drivers." 27 So Moses stretched out his hand over the sea, and at dawn the sea returned
to its normal depth. As the Egyptians fled before it, the LORD tossed the Egyptians
into the sea. 28 The waters returned and covered the chariots and the chariot drivers,
the entire army of Pharaoh that had followed them into the sea; not one of them
remained. 29 But the Israelites walked on dry ground through the sea, the waters
forming a wall for them on their right and on their left.
30 Thus the LORD saved Israel that day from the Egyptians; and Israel saw the
Egyptians dead on the seashore. 31 Israel saw the great work that the LORD did
against the Egyptians. So the people feared the LORD and believed in the LORD and
in his servant Moses.

14.26 Ex 7.19; 14.21
14.27 Ex 15.1,7; Deut 11.4; Josh 4.18
14.28 Ex 15.10; Neh 9.11
14.29 Isa 11.15
14.30 Ps 58.10; Isa 63.11
14.31 Ex 4.31; 19.9; 2 Chron 20.20

Songs to the Lord

15 Then Moses and the Israelites sang this song to the LORD:
"I will sing to the LORD, for he has triumphed gloriously;
horse and rider he has thrown into the sea.
2 The LORD is my strength and my might,[a]
and he has become my salvation;
this is my God, and I will praise him,
my father's God, and I will exalt him.
3 The LORD is a warrior;
the LORD is his name.

4 "Pharaoh's chariots and his army he cast into the sea;
his picked officers were sunk in the Red Sea.[b]
5 The floods covered them;
they went down into the depths like a stone.
6 Your right hand, O LORD, glorious in power—
your right hand, O LORD, shattered the enemy.
7 In the greatness of your majesty you overthrew your adversaries;
you sent out your fury, it consumed them like stubble.
8 At the blast of your nostrils the waters piled up,
the floods stood up in a heap;
the deeps congealed in the heart of the sea.
9 The enemy said, 'I will pursue, I will overtake,

15.1 Ps 106.12; Isa 12.5; Rev 15.3
15.2 Ex 3.15,16; 2 Sam 22.47,51; Ps 18.1,2; 140.7
15.3 Ex 6.2; 14.14; Ps 24.8
15.4 Ex 14.6,7,27,28
15.5 Neh 9.11
15.6 Ex 3.20; Ps 17.7; 118.15
15.7 Ex 9.16; 14.24; Ps 78.49,50
15.8 Ex 14.22,29; 2 Sam 22.16; Ps 78.13; 114.5
15.9 Ex 14.5,8,9

[z] Sam Gk Syr: MT *removed* [a] Or *song* [b] Or *Sea of Reeds*

14.27, 28 No evidence of this great exodus has been discovered in Egyptian historical records because it was a common practice for Egyptian Pharaohs not to record their defeats. They even went so far as to take existing records and delete the names of traitors and political adversaries. Pharaoh would have been especially anxious not to record that his great army was destroyed chasing a band of runaway slaves. Since either the Egyptians failed to record the exodus or the record has not yet been found, it is impossible to place a precise date on the event.

15.1ff Music played an important part in Israel's worship and celebration. Singing was an expression of love and thanks, and it was a creative way to pass down oral traditions. Some say this song of Moses' is the oldest recorded song in the world. It was a festive epic poem celebrating God's victory, lifting the hearts and voices of the people outward and upward. After having been delivered from great danger, they sang with joy! Psalms and hymns can be great ways to express relief, praise, and thanks when you have been through trouble.

15.8 The phrase "The deeps congealed in the heart of the sea" means that the waters became like hard walls for them to walk between.

I will divide the spoil, my desire shall have its fill of them.
I will draw my sword, my hand shall destroy them.'
15.10 Ex 14.27
10 You blew with your wind, the sea covered them;
they sank like lead in the mighty waters.

15.11 Ex 8.10 Deut 3.24 Isa 6.3; 57.15 Rev 4.8
11 "Who is like you, O LORD, among the gods?
Who is like you, majestic in holiness,
awesome in splendor, doing wonders?
15.12 Ex 15.6
12 You stretched out your right hand,
the earth swallowed them.

MOSES

Some people can't stay out of trouble. When conflict breaks out, they always manage to be nearby. Reaction is their favorite action. This was Moses. He seemed drawn to what needed to be righted. Throughout his life, he was at his finest and his worst responding to the conflicts around him. Even the burning bush experience was an illustration of his character. Having spotted the fire and seen that the bush did not burn, he had to investigate. Whether jumping into a fight to defend a Hebrew slave or trying to referee a struggle between two kinsmen, when Moses saw conflict, he reacted.

Over the years, however, an amazing thing happened to Moses' character. He didn't stop reacting, but rather learned to react correctly. The kaleidoscopic action of each day of leading two million people in the wilderness was more than enough challenge for Moses' reacting ability. Much of the time he served as a buffer between God and the people. At one moment he had to respond to God's anger at the people's stubbornness and forgetfulness. At another moment he had to react to the people's bickering and complaining. At still another moment he had to react to their unjustified attacks on his character.

Leadership often involves reaction. If we want to react with instincts consistent with God's will, we must develop habits of obedience to God. Consistent obedience to God is best developed in times of less stress. Then when stress comes, our natural reaction will be to obey God.

In our age of lowering moral standards, we find it almost impossible to believe that God would punish Moses for the one time he disobeyed outright. What we fail to see, however, is that God did not reject Moses; Moses simply disqualified himself to enter the promised land. Personal greatness does not make a person immune to error or its consequences.

In Moses we see an outstanding personality shaped by God. But we must not misunderstand what God did. He did not change who or what Moses was; he did not give Moses new abilities and strengths. Instead, he took Moses' characteristics and molded them until they were suited to his purposes. Does knowing this make a difference in your understanding of God's purpose in your life? He is trying to take what he created in the first place and use it for its intended purposes. The next time you talk with God, don't ask, "What should I change into?" but "How should I use my own abilities and strengths to do your will?"

Strengths and accomplishments:
- Egyptian education; desert training
- Greatest Jewish leader; set the exodus in motion
- Prophet and lawgiver; recorder of the ten commandments
- Author of the Pentateuch

Weaknesses and mistakes:
- Failed to enter the promised land because of disobedience to God
- Did not always recognize and use the talents of others

Lessons from his life:
- God prepares, then uses. His timetable is life-sized
- God does his greatest work through frail people

Vital statistics:
- Where: Egypt, Midian, Sinai desert
- Occupation: Prince, shepherd, leader of the Israelites
- Relatives: Sister: Miriam. Brother: Aaron. Wife: Zipporah. Son: Gershom

Key verses:
"By faith Moses, when he was grown up, refused to be called a son of Pharaoh's daughter, choosing rather to share ill-treatment with the people of God than to enjoy the fleeting pleasures of sin" (Hebrews 11.24, 25).

Moses' story is told in the books of Exodus through Deuteronomy. He is also mentioned in Acts 7.22–37; Hebrews 11.23–29.

13 "In your steadfast love you led the people whom you redeemed;
you guided them by your strength to your holy abode.
14 The peoples heard, they trembled;
pangs seized the inhabitants of Philistia.
15 Then the chiefs of Edom were dismayed;
trembling seized the leaders of Moab;
all the inhabitants of Canaan melted away.
16 Terror and dread fell upon them;
by the might of your arm, they became still as a stone
until your people, O LORD, passed by,
until the people whom you acquired passed by.
17 You brought them in and planted them on the mountain of your own possession,
the place, O LORD, that you made your abode,
the sanctuary, O LORD, that your hands have established.
18 The LORD will reign forever and ever."

19 When the horses of Pharaoh with his chariots and his chariot drivers went
into the sea, the LORD brought back the waters of the sea upon them; but the Israelites walked through the sea on dry ground.

20 Then the prophet Miriam, Aaron's sister, took a tambourine in her hand; and
all the women went out after her with tambourines and with dancing. 21 And Miriam sang to them:
"Sing to the LORD, for he has triumphed gloriously;
horse and rider he has thrown into the sea."

15.13 Neh 9.12 Ps 77.14,15,20
15.14 Num 14.14 Deut 2.25
15.15 Num 22.3 Deut 2.4
15.17 Ex 23.20; 32.34 Ps 2.6 78.54,68 Isa 5.1,2
15.18 Rev 11.15
15.19 Ex 14.22,23,29 Heb 11.29
15.20 Ex 2.4 Num 26.59 1 Sam 18.6

3. Complaining in the wilderness

The people complain about bitter water

22 Then Moses ordered Israel to set out from the Red Sea,[c] and they went into
the wilderness of Shur. They went three days in the wilderness and found no water.
23 When they came to Marah, they could not drink the water of Marah because it
was bitter. That is why it was called Marah.[d] 24 And the people complained against
Moses, saying, "What shall we drink?" 25 He cried out to the LORD; and the LORD
showed him a piece of wood;[e] he threw it into the water, and the water became
sweet.

There the LORD[f] made for them a statute and an ordinance and there he put them
to the test. 26 He said, "If you will listen carefully to the voice of the LORD your
God, and do what is right in his sight, and give heed to his commandments and
keep all his statutes, I will not bring upon you any of the diseases that I brought
upon the Egyptians; for I am the LORD who heals you."

27 Then they came to Elim, where there were twelve springs of water and seventy palm trees; and they camped there by the water.

15.22 Gen 16.7; 25.18 Ex 3.18
15.23 Num 33.8 Ruth 1.20
15.24 Ex 14.11; 16.2 Ps 106.13
15.25 Ex 14.10; 16.4
15.26 Ex 19.5; 20.2-17 Deut 7.15; 12.28 Ps 103.3
15.27 Num 33.9

God provides meat and bread

16 The whole congregation of the Israelites set out from Elim; and Israel came
to the wilderness of Sin, which is between Elim and Sinai, on the fifteenth
day of the second month after they had departed from the land of Egypt. 2 The

16.1 Ex 17.1; 19.1 Num 33.10

[c] Or *Sea of Reeds* [d] That is *Bitterness* [e] Or *a tree* [f] Heb *he*

15.20 Miriam was called a prophet not only because she received revelations from God (Numbers 12.1, 2; Micah 6.4) but also for her musical skill. Prophecy and music were often closely related in the Bible (1 Samuel 10.5; 1 Chronicles 25.1).

15.26 God promised that if the people obeyed him they would be free from the diseases that plagued the Egyptians. Little did they know that many of the moral laws he later gave them were designed to keep them free from sickness. For example, following God's law against prostitution would keep them free of venereal disease. God's laws for us are often designed to keep us from harm. Men and women are complex beings. Our physical, emotional, and spiritual lives are intertwined. Modern medicine is now acknowledging what these laws assumed. If we want God to care for us, we need to submit to his directions for living.

16.1 The wilderness of Sin was a vast and hostile environment of sand and stone. Its barren surroundings provided the perfect place for God to test and shape the character of his people.

16.2 It happened again. As the Israelites encountered danger, shortages, and inconvenience, they complained bitterly and longed to be back in Egypt. But as always, God provided for their

16.2 Ex 14.11 Acts 7.39 1 Cor 10.10
16.4 Ex 15.25 Deut 8.2,16 Ps 78.24 105.40 Jn 6.31 1 Cor 10.3
16.5 Ex 16.22; 35.2
16.6 Ex 12.51; 16.28
16.7-9 Ex 16.12 Num 14.27 17.5; 21.7 1 Sam 8.7 Mt 9.4
16.10 Ex 13.21; 40.34 Num 14.10
16.11,12 Ex 4.5; 16.6

whole congregation of the Israelites complained against Moses and Aaron in the
wilderness. 3 The Israelites said to them, "If only we had died by the hand of the
LORD in the land of Egypt, when we sat by the fleshpots and ate our fill of bread;
for you have brought us out into this wilderness to kill this whole assembly with
hunger."
4 Then the LORD said to Moses, "I am going to rain bread from heaven for you,
and each day the people shall go out and gather enough for that day. In that way I
will test them, whether they will follow my instruction or not. 5 On the sixth day,
when they prepare what they bring in, it will be twice as much as they gather on
other days." 6 So Moses and Aaron said to all the Israelites, "In the evening you
shall know that it was the LORD who brought you out of the land of Egypt, 7 and in
the morning you shall see the glory of the LORD, because he has heard your complaining against the LORD. For what are we, that you complain against us?" 8 And
Moses said, "When the LORD gives you meat to eat in the evening and your fill of
bread in the morning, because the LORD has heard the complaining that you utter
against him—what are we? Your complaining is not against us but against the
LORD."
9 Then Moses said to Aaron, "Say to the whole congregation of the Israelites,
'Draw near to the LORD, for he has heard your complaining.' " 10 And as Aaron
spoke to the whole congregation of the Israelites, they looked toward the wilderness, and the glory of the LORD appeared in the cloud. 11 The LORD spoke to Moses
and said, 12 "I have heard the complaining of the Israelites; say to them, 'At twilight

FAMOUS SONGS IN THE BIBLE

Where	*Purpose of Song*
Exodus 15.1–21	Moses' song of victory and praise after God led Israel out of Egypt and saved them by parting the Red Sea; Miriam joined in the singing too
Numbers 21.17	Israel's song of praise to God for giving them water in the wilderness
Deuteronomy 32.1–43	Moses' song of Israel's history with thanksgiving and praise as the Hebrews were about to enter the promised land
Judges 5.2–31	Deborah and Barak's song of praise thanking God for Israel's victory over King Jabin's army at Mount Tabor
2 Samuel 22.2–51	David's song of thanks and praise to God for rescuing him from Saul and his other enemies
Song of Solomon	Solomon's song of love celebrating the union of husband and wife
Isaiah 26.1	Isaiah's prophetic song about how the redeemed will sing in the New Jerusalem
Ezra 3.11	Israel's song of praise at the completion of the temple's foundation
Luke 1.46–55	Mary's song of praise to God for the conception of Jesus
Luke 1.68–79	Zechariah's song of praise for the promise of a son
Acts 16.25	Paul and Silas sang hymns in prison
Revelation 5.9, 10	The "new song" of the 24 elders acclaiming Christ as worthy to break the seven seals of God's scroll
Revelation 14.3	The song of the 144,000 redeemed from the earth
Revelation 15.3, 4	The song of all the redeemed in praise of the Lamb who redeemed them

needs. Difficult circumstances often lead to stress, and complaining is a natural response. The Israelites didn't really want to be back in Egypt; they just wanted life to get a little easier. In the pressure of the moment, they could not focus on the cause of their stress (in this case, lack of trust in God); they could only think about the quickest way of escape. When pressure comes your way, resist the temptation to make a quick escape. Instead, focus on God's power and wisdom to help you deal with the cause of your stress.

16.3 Fleshpots were pots filled with meat. The Israelites were saying that they had plenty of food in Egypt, but here they were starving.

16.4, 5 God promised to meet the Hebrews' need for food in the wilderness, but he decided to test their obedience. God wanted to see if they would obey his detailed instructions. We can learn to trust him as our Lord only by following. We can learn to obey by taking small steps of obedience.

you shall eat meat, and in the morning you shall have your fill of bread; then you
shall know that I am the LORD your God.' "
13 In the evening quails came up and covered the camp; and in the morning
there was a layer of dew around the camp. 14 When the layer of dew lifted, there on
the surface of the wilderness was a fine flaky substance, as fine as frost on the
ground. 15 When the Israelites saw it, they said to one another, "What is it?"[g] For
they did not know what it was. Moses said to them, "It is the bread that the LORD
has given you to eat. 16 This is what the LORD has commanded: 'Gather as much of
it as each of you needs, an omer to a person according to the number of persons, all
providing for those in their own tents.' " 17 The Israelites did so, some gathering
more, some less. 18 But when they measured it with an omer, those who gathered
much had nothing over, and those who gathered little had no shortage; they gathered as much as each of them needed. 19 And Moses said to them, "Let no one leave
any of it over until morning." 20 But they did not listen to Moses; some left part of
it until morning, and it bred worms and became foul. And Moses was angry with
them. 21 Morning by morning they gathered it, as much as each needed; but when
the sun grew hot, it melted.
22 On the sixth day they gathered twice as much food, two omers apiece. When
all the leaders of the congregation came and told Moses, 23 he said to them, "This
is what the LORD has commanded: 'Tomorrow is a day of solemn rest, a holy sabbath to the LORD; bake what you want to bake and boil what you want to boil, and
all that is left over put aside to be kept until morning.' " 24 So they put it aside until
morning, as Moses commanded them; and it did not become foul, and there were
no worms in it. 25 Moses said, "Eat it today, for today is a sabbath to the LORD;
today you will not find it in the field. 26 Six days you shall gather it; but on the
seventh day, which is a sabbath, there will be none."
27 On the seventh day some of the people went out to gather, and they found
none. 28 The LORD said to Moses, "How long will you refuse to keep my commandments and instructions? 29 See! The LORD has given you the sabbath, therefore on
the sixth day he gives you food for two days; each of you stay where you are; do not
leave your place on the seventh day." 30 So the people rested on the seventh day.
31 The house of Israel called it manna; it was like coriander seed, white, and the
taste of it was like wafers made with honey. 32 Moses said, "This is what the LORD
has commanded: 'Let an omer of it be kept throughout your generations, in order
that they may see the food with which I fed you in the wilderness, when I brought
you out of the land of Egypt.' " 33 And Moses said to Aaron, "Take a jar, and put
an omer of manna in it, and place it before the LORD, to be kept throughout your
generations." 34 As the LORD commanded Moses, so Aaron placed it before the
covenant,[h] for safekeeping. 35 The Israelites ate manna forty years, until they came
to a habitable land; they ate manna, until they came to the border of the land of
Canaan. 36 An omer is a tenth of an ephah.

[g] Or *"It is manna"* (Heb *man hu*, see verse 31) [h] Or *treaty* or *testimony*; Heb *eduth*

16.13 Ex 16.31-33 Ps 78.27-29 105.40
16.14 Num 11.7-9 Deut 8.3
16.15 Ex 16.31 Josh 5.12 Neh 9.5 Jn 6.31
16.16 Ex 16.18,33,36
16.18 2 Cor 8.15
16.19 Ex 12.10; 23.18 Mt 6.34
16.20 Num 16.15
16.22 Ex 16.5; 34.31 Lev 25.11,12,22
16.23 Gen 2.2 Ex 20.8; 23.12 31.14,15 Neh 9.14 Mk 2.27
16.24 Ex 16.20,33
16.26 Deut 5.13
16.28,29 Num 14.11 Ps 78.10,18-24
16.30 Lev 23.3 Deut 5.12
16.31 Ex 16.15 Num 11.6 Deut 8.3,16
16.32 Ps 111.4,5
16.33 Heb 9.4 Rev 2.17
16.34 Ex 25.16; 30.6 Num 1.50
16.35 Josh 5.12 Neh 9.15,20,21 Ps 78.24

16.14–16 Manna appeared on the ground each day as fresh white grains the size of pearls. The people gathered it, ground it like grain, and made it into honey-tasting pancakes. For the Israelites the manna was a gift—it came every day and was just what they needed. It satisfied their temporary physical need. In John 6.48–51 Jesus compares himself to manna. Christ is our daily bread who satisfies our eternal, spiritual need.

16.23 The Israelites were not to work on the sabbath—not even to cook food. Why? God knew that the busy routine of daily living could distract people from worshiping him. It is so easy to let work, family responsibilities, and recreation crowd our schedules so tightly that we don't take time for God. Carefully guard your time with God.

16.32 The Hebrews put some manna in a special jar as a reminder of the way God provided for them in the wilderness. Symbols have always been an important part of Christian worship also. We use special objects as symbols to remind us of God's work in our lives. Such symbols can be valuable aids to our worship as long as we are careful to keep them from becoming objects of worship.

16.36 An "Omer . . . a tenth of an ephah" is about two quarts or a tenth of a bushel.

17.1
Ex 16.1; 19.2
Num 33.14
17.2
Ex 5.21; 14.11
Num 14.22; 20.2
Deut 6.16
17.3
Ex 16.3
Num 11.4,5
17.4
Ex 15.25
Num 11.11
14.10; 16.19
17.5,6
Ex 3.1,16; 7.20
Num 20.8-10
Neh 9.15
1 Cor 10.4
17.7
Deut 6.16; 9.22
Heb 3.8
17.8
Gen 36.12,16
Num 24.20
Deut 25.17
1 Sam 15.2
17.9
Ex 24.13
Num 11.28
17.10
Ex 24.14; 31.2
1 Chron 2.18,19
17.11,12
Heb 12.12
17.14
Ex 24.4; 34.27
Num 33.2
Deut 25.19
17.15,16
Gen 22.14
Ps 60.4

The people complain about lack of water

17 From the wilderness of Sin the whole congregation of the Israelites journeyed by stages, as the LORD commanded. They camped at Rephidim, but
there was no water for the people to drink. 2 The people quarreled with Moses, and
said, "Give us water to drink." Moses said to them, "Why do you quarrel with me?
Why do you test the LORD?" 3 But the people thirsted there for water; and the people
complained against Moses and said, "Why did you bring us out of Egypt, to kill us
and our children and livestock with thirst?" 4 So Moses cried out to the LORD,
"What shall I do with this people? They are almost ready to stone me." 5 The LORD
said to Moses, "Go on ahead of the people, and take some of the elders of Israel
with you; take in your hand the staff with which you struck the Nile, and go. 6 I will
be standing there in front of you on the rock at Horeb. Strike the rock, and water
will come out of it, so that the people may drink." Moses did so, in the sight of the
elders of Israel. 7 He called the place Massah[i] and Meribah,[j] because the Israelites
quarreled and tested the LORD, saying, "Is the LORD among us or not?"
8 Then Amalek came and fought with Israel at Rephidim. 9 Moses said to
Joshua, "Choose some men for us and go out, fight with Amalek. Tomorrow I will
stand on the top of the hill with the staff of God in my hand." 10 So Joshua did as
Moses told him, and fought with Amalek, while Moses, Aaron, and Hur went up
to the top of the hill. 11 Whenever Moses held up his hand, Israel prevailed; and
whenever he lowered his hand, Amalek prevailed. 12 But Moses' hands grew
weary; so they took a stone and put it under him, and he sat on it. Aaron and Hur
held up his hands, one on one side, and the other on the other side; so his hands
were steady until the sun set. 13 And Joshua defeated Amalek and his people with
the sword.
14 Then the LORD said to Moses, "Write this as a reminder in a book and recite
it in the hearing of Joshua: I will utterly blot out the remembrance of Amalek from
under heaven." 15 And Moses built an altar and called it, The LORD is my banner.
16 He said, "A hand upon the banner of the LORD![k] The LORD will have war with
Amalek from generation to generation."

[i] That is *Test* [j] That is *Quarrel* [k] Cn: Meaning of Heb uncertain

---

JOURNEY TO MOUNT SINAI
God miraculously supplied food and water in the wilderness for the Israelites. In the Sihn (Sin) wilderness, he provided manna (16). At Rephidim, he provided water from a rock (17.1–7). Finally God brought them to the foot of Mount Sinai, where he gave them his holy laws.

17.2 Again the people complained about their problem instead of praying. Some problems can be solved by careful thought or by rearranging our priorities. Some can be solved by discussion and good counsel. But some problems can be solved only by prayer. We should make a determined effort to pray when we feel like complaining because complaining only raises our level of stress. Prayer quiets our thoughts and emotions and prepares us to listen.

17.8 The Amalekites were descendants of Amalek, a grandson of Esau. They were a fierce nomadic tribe who lived in the desert region of the Dead Sea. They made part of their livelihood by conducting frequent raids on other settlements and carrying off booty. They killed for pleasure. One of the greatest insults in Israelite culture was to call someone "a friend of Amalek." When the Israelites entered the region, the Amalekites saw this as a perfect opportunity for both pleasure and profit. But this hostile tribe was moving in on the wrong group—a people led by God. For the Israelite slaves to defeat such a warlike nation was more than enough proof that God was with them as he had promised to be.

17.9 Here we meet Joshua for the first time. Later he would become the great leader who brought God's people into the promised land. As a general of the Israelite army, he was gaining valuable experience for the greater battles to come.

17.10–13 Aaron and Hur stood by Moses' side and held up his arms to insure victory against Amalek. We need to "lift up the hands" of our spiritual leaders as well. Shouldering some responsibility, lending a word of encouragement, or offering a prayer are ways of refreshing spiritual leaders in their work.

17.16 "A hand upon the banner of the Lord" means to raise up the banner of the Lord.

Jethro visits Moses

18 Jethro, the priest of Midian, Moses' father-in-law, heard of all that God
had done for Moses and for his people Israel, how the LORD had brought
Israel out of Egypt. 2 After Moses had sent away his wife Zipporah, his father-
in-law Jethro took her back, 3 along with her two sons. The name of the one was
Gershom (for he said, "I have been an alien[l] in a foreign land"), 4 and the name of
the other, Eliezer[m] (for he said, "The God of my father was my help, and delivered
me from the sword of Pharaoh"). 5 Jethro, Moses' father-in-law, came into the
wilderness where Moses was encamped at the mountain of God, bringing Moses'
sons and wife to him. 6 He sent word to Moses, "I, your father-in-law Jethro,
am coming to you, with your wife and her two sons." 7 Moses went out to meet his
father-in-law; he bowed down and kissed him; each asked after the other's welfare,
and they went into the tent. 8 Then Moses told his father-in-law all that the
LORD had done to Pharaoh and to the Egyptians for Israel's sake, all the hardship
that had beset them on the way, and how the LORD had delivered them. 9 Jethro
rejoiced for all the good that the LORD had done to Israel, in delivering them from
the Egyptians.
10 Jethro said, "Blessed be the LORD, who has delivered you from the Egyptians and from Pharaoh. 11 Now I know that the LORD is greater than all gods, because he delivered the people from the Egyptians,[n] when they dealt arrogantly
with them." 12 And Jethro, Moses' father-in-law, brought a burnt offering and sacrifices to God; and Aaron came with all the elders of Israel to eat bread with Moses'
father-in-law in the presence of God.

Jethro's wise advice

13 The next day Moses sat as judge for the people, while the people stood
around him from morning until evening. 14 When Moses' father-in-law saw all that
he was doing for the people, he said, "What is this that you are doing for the people? Why do you sit alone, while all the people stand around you from morning
until evening?" 15 Moses said to his father-in-law, "Because the people come to me
to inquire of God. 16 When they have a dispute, they come to me and I decide between one person and another, and I make known to them the statutes and instructions of God." 17 Moses' father-in-law said to him, "What you are doing is not
good. 18 You will surely wear yourself out, both you and these people with you. For
the task is too heavy for you; you cannot do it alone. 19 Now listen to me. I will give
you counsel, and God be with you! You should represent the people before God,

18.1 Ex 2.16,18; 3.1
18.2 Ex 2.21; 4.25
18.3 Ex 2.22; 4.20 Acts 7.29 Heb 11.13
18.4 Gen 28.13 49.25 Isa 50.7
18.5,6 Ex 3.1; 4.27
18.7 Gen 43.26
18.8 Ex 15.4,8,22 Num 20.14 Neh 9.9-15
18.9 Isa 44.23; 63.7
18.10 1 Kgs 8.56
18.11 Ex 10.2; 15.11
18.12 Gen 31.54 Ex 24.5
18.15,16 Lev 24.12-14 Num 9.6-8 15.34 Deut 17.8-13 2 Sam 15.3
18.18 Num 11.14 Deut 1.9 Acts 6.1-4
18.19,20 Deut 1.17; 4.1

[l] Heb *ger* [m] Heb *Eli*, my God; *ezer*, help [n] The clause *because . . . Egyptians* has been transposed from verse 10

18.7 Jethro entered Moses' tent where the two talked. Tents were the homes of shepherds. In shape and design, they resembled the tents of today, but they were very large and made of a thick cloth woven from goat or camel hair. This fabric breathed in warm weather and contracted in stormy weather to offer protection from the winter winds and rains. The floor was often covered with animal-skin rugs, while curtains divided the inside space into rooms.

18.8–11 Moses told his father-in-law all that God had done, convincing him that the Lord was greater than any other god. Our relatives are often the hardest people to tell about God. Yet we should look for opportunities to tell them what God is doing in our lives, because we can have an important influence on them.

18.12 The Israelites frequently shared a sacrificial meal among themselves. A burnt offering was sacrificed to God, and then the meal taken from the sacrifice was dedicated to God and eaten ceremonially as a fellowship dinner.

18.13–26 Moses was spending so much time and energy hearing the Hebrews' complaints that he could not get to other important work. Jethro suggested that Moses delegate most of this work to others and focus his efforts on jobs only he could do. People in positions of responsibility sometimes feel they are the only ones who can do necessary tasks; but others are capable of handling part of the load. Delegation relieved Moses' stress and improved the quality of the government of the people. It helped prepare them for the system of government set up in Canaan. Proper delegation can multiply your effectiveness while giving others a chance to grow.

18.16 Moses not only decided these cases, he also taught the people God's laws. Whenever we help others settle disputes or resolve conflicts, we should also look for opportunities to learn and teach about God: "What is he teaching us in this situation?"

and you should bring their cases before God; 20 teach them the statutes and instructions and make known to them the way they are to go and the things they are to do.
18.21 Deut 1.12-15; 16.18; 1 Kgs 3.9; Ps 15.1-5 — 21 You should also look for able men among all the people, men who fear God, are
trustworthy, and hate dishonest gain; set such men over them as officers over thou-
sands, hundreds, fifties and tens. 22 Let them sit as judges for the people at all times;
18.22 Num 15.33; 27.2; 36.1; Deut 17.8 — let them bring every important case to you, but decide every minor case themselves. So it will be easier for you, and they will bear the burden with you. 23 If you
do this, and God so commands you, then you will be able to endure, and all these
people will go to their home in peace."

18.25 Deut 1.15; 16.18 — 24 So Moses listened to his father-in-law and did all that he had said. 25 Moses
chose able men from all Israel and appointed them as heads over the people, as
18.26 Deut 17.8 — officers over thousands, hundreds, fifties, and tens. 26 And they judged the people
at all times; hard cases they brought to Moses, but any minor case they decided
18.27 Num 10.29,30 — themselves. 27 Then Moses let his father-in-law depart, and he went off to his own
country.

JETHRO

People such as Jethro and Melchizedek—not Hebrews, but nevertheless worshipers of the true God—play an important role in the Old Testament. They remind us of God's commitment to the world. God chose one nation through whom to work, but his love and concern are for all nations!

Jethro's religious background prepared him for, rather than prevented him from, responding in faith to God. When he saw and heard what God had done for the Israelites, he worshiped God wholeheartedly. We can guess that for 40 years as Moses' father-in-law, Jethro had been watching God at work, molding a leader. Moses' and Jethro's relationship must have been close, for Moses readily accepted his father-in-law's advice. Each benefited from knowing the other. Jethro met God through Moses, and Moses received hospitality, his wife, and wisdom from Jethro.

The greatest gift one person can give another is an introduction to God. But that gift is hindered if the believer's attitude is, "I have the greatest gift to pass on to you, while you have nothing to give me in return." Real friends give to and receive from each other. The importance of introducing a friend to God does not make the friend's gifts to us insignificant. Rather, the believer is doubly blessed—first by receiving the gifts the friend wishes to give; then by growing in knowledge of the Lord. For we discover that in introducing another person to God, we increase our own awareness of God. As we give God away, he gives himself even more to us.

Is all you know about God a miscellaneous collection of trivia, or do you have a living relationship with him? Only with a vital relationship can you pass on to others the excitement of allowing God to guide your life. Have you reached the point of saying, with Jethro, "Now I know that the Lord is greater than all gods" (Exodus 18.11)?

Strengths and accomplishments:
- As father-in-law to Moses, he came to recognize the one true God
- He was a practical troubleshooter and organizer

Lessons from his life:
- Supervision and administration are team efforts
- God's plan includes all nations

Vital statistics:
- Where: The land of Midian and the Sinai desert
- Occupation: Shepherd, priest
- Relatives: Daughter: Zipporah. Son-in-law: Moses. Son: Hobab

Key verse:
"Jethro rejoiced for all the good that the Lord had done to Israel, in delivering them from the Egyptians" (Exodus 18.9).

Jethro's story is told in Exodus 2.15—3.1; 18.1–27. He is also mentioned in Judges 1.16; 4.11.

C. ISRAEL AT SINAI (19.1—40.38)

After escaping through the Red Sea, the Hebrews traveled through the wilderness and arrived at Sinai, God's holy mountain. There they received the ten commandments, as well as instructions for building a tabernacle as a center of worship. Through Israel's experiences at Mount Sinai, we learn about the importance of obedience in our relationship with God. His laws help expose sin, and they give standards for righteous living.

1. Giving the law

Moses climbs Mount Sinai

19 On the third new moon after the Israelites had gone out of the land of Egypt,
on that very day, they came into the wilderness of Sinai. 2 They had journeyed from Rephidim, entered the wilderness of Sinai, and camped in the wilderness; Israel camped there in front of the mountain. 3 Then Moses went up to God;
the LORD called to him from the mountain, saying, "Thus you shall say to the house
of Jacob, and tell the Israelites: 4 You have seen what I did to the Egyptians, and
how I bore you on eagles' wings and brought you to myself. 5 Now therefore, if you
obey my voice and keep my covenant, you shall be my treasured possession out of
all the peoples. Indeed, the whole earth is mine, 6 but you shall be for me a priestly
kingdom and a holy nation. These are the words that you shall speak to the Israelites."
7 So Moses came, summoned the elders of the people, and set before them all
these words that the LORD had commanded him. 8 The people all answered as one:
"Everything that the LORD has spoken we will do." Moses reported the words of the
people to the LORD. 9 Then the LORD said to Moses, "I am going to come to you in
a dense cloud, in order that the people may hear when I speak with you and so trust
you ever after."
When Moses had told the words of the people to the LORD, 10 the LORD said to
Moses: "Go to the people and consecrate them today and tomorrow. Have them
wash their clothes 11 and prepare for the third day, because on the third day the
LORD will come down upon Mount Sinai in the sight of all the people. 12 You shall
set limits for the people all around, saying, 'Be careful not to go up the mountain
or to touch the edge of it. Any who touch the mountain shall be put to death. 13 No
hand shall touch them, but they shall be stoned or shot with arrows;[o] whether animal or human being, they shall not live.' When the trumpet sounds a long blast,
they may go up on the mountain." 14 So Moses went down from the mountain to the

19.1 Ex 12.51; 16.1
19.4 Deut 4.9; 32.11; Isa 40.31; 63.9; Rev 12.14
19.5 Ex 15.26; 23.22; 24.7; Deut 4.20; 14.2; Isa 41.8
19.6 Lev 11.44,45; Deut 33.2-4; Isa 61.6; 1 Pet 2.5,9; Rev 1.6; 5.10
19.7 Ex 4.29,30; 24.9
19.8 Ex 4.31; 24.3,7; Deut 5.27; 26.17
19.9 Ex 14.31; 19.16; Deut 4.11; Ps 99.7; 1 Kgs 8.12
19.10 Gen 35.2; Josh 3.5; Heb 10.22; Rev 7.14; 22.14
19.11 Ex 19.16; 34.5
19.13 Heb 12.20

[o] Heb lacks *with arrows*

19.2, 3 Mount Sinai is one of the most sacred locations in Israel's history. Located in the south-central Sinai peninsula, this mountain is where Moses met God in a burning bush, God made his covenant with Israel, and Elijah heard God in the still small voice. Here God gave his people the laws and guidelines for right living. They learned the potential blessings of obedience (34.4–28) and the tragic consequences of disobedience (v. 32).

19.4–6 God had a reason for rescuing the Israelites from slavery. Now he was ready to tell them what it was: Israel was to become a holy nation, a kingdom of priests where anyone could approach God freely. It didn't take long, however, for the people to corrupt God's plan. God then established Aaron's descendants from the tribe of Levi as priests, representing what the entire nation should have been (Leviticus 8, 9). But with the coming of Jesus Christ, God has once again extended his plan to all believers. We are to become holy, a "royal priesthood" (1 Peter 2.9). The death and resurrection of Christ has allowed each of us to approach God freely.

19.5 Why did God choose Israel as his nation? God knew that no nation on earth was good enough to deserve to be called his people. He chose Israel, not because of anything they had done, but in his love and mercy he chose Israel in spite of the wrong the nation had done and would do. Why did he want to have a special nation on earth? To represent his way of life, to teach his word, and to be an agent of salvation to the world. "All the nations of the earth" would be blessed through Abraham's descendants (Genesis 18.18). Gentiles and kings would come to the Lord through Israel, predicted Isaiah (Isaiah 60.3). Through the nation of Israel the Messiah, God's chosen son, would be born. God chose one nation and put it through a rigorous training program, so that one day it could be a channel for his blessings to the whole world.

19.5–8 In Genesis 15 and 17, God made a covenant with Abraham, promising to make his descendants into a great nation. Now that promise was being realized as God restated his agreement with the Israelite nation, the descendants of Abraham. God promised to bless and care for them. The people promised to obey him. The covenant was thus sealed. But the good intentions of the people quickly wore off. Have you made a commitment to God? How are you holding up your end of the bargain?

19.9, 10 Moses was told to "consecrate" the people. This meant getting them physically and spiritually ready to meet God. The people were to set themselves apart from sin and even ordinary daily routine in order to dedicate themselves to God. The act of washing and preparing served to get their minds and hearts ready. When we meet God for worship, we should set aside the cares and preoccupations of everyday life. Use your time of physical preparation to get your mind ready to meet God.

19.15 1 Sam 21.4 Mt 3.2 1 Cor 7.5
19.16 Ex 9.23; 20.18 Heb 12.18,19
19.17 Deut 4.10; 5.5
19.18 Ex 24.17 Deut 5.4 Ps 68.7,8 104.32
19.19 Ps 81.7
19.20 Ex 24.12 Neh 9.13
19.21 Ex 3.5; 33.20
19.22 Lev 10.2,3 21.5-8
19.24 Ex 24.1,9,12

people. He consecrated the people, and they washed their clothes. 15 And he said to
the people, "Prepare for the third day; do not go near a woman."
16 On the morning of the third day there was thunder and lightning, as well as
a thick cloud on the mountain, and a blast of a trumpet so loud that all the people
who were in the camp trembled. 17 Moses brought the people out of the camp to
meet God. They took their stand at the foot of the mountain. 18 Now Mount Sinai
was wrapped in smoke, because the LORD had descended upon it in fire; the smoke
went up like the smoke of a kiln, while the whole mountain shook violently. 19 As
the blast of the trumpet grew louder and louder, Moses would speak and God would
answer him in thunder. 20 When the LORD descended upon Mount Sinai, to the top
of the mountain, the LORD summoned Moses to the top of the mountain, and Moses
went up. 21 Then the LORD said to Moses, "Go down and warn the people not to
break through to the LORD to look; otherwise many of them will perish. 22 Even the
priests who approach the LORD must consecrate themselves or the LORD will break
out against them." 23 Moses said to the LORD, "The people are not permitted to
come up to Mount Sinai; for you yourself warned us, saying, 'Set limits around the
mountain and keep it holy.'" 24 The LORD said to him, "Go down, and come up
bringing Aaron with you; but do not let either the priests or the people break
through to come up to the LORD; otherwise he will break out against them." 25 So
Moses went down to the people and told them.

The ten commandments

20.3 Ex 15.11; 20.23 Deut 5.7; 6.14
20.4 Deut 4.15-20
20.5 Ex 23.24; 34.14 Deut 4.24; 5.9
20.6 Ex 34.6,7 Deut 7.9
20.7 Deut 5.11; 6.13
20.8 Gen 2.3 Ex 16.23 Deut 5.12

20 Then God spoke all these words:
2 I am the LORD your God, who brought you out of the land of Egypt, out
of the house of slavery; 3 you shall have no other gods before[p] me.
4 You shall not make for yourself an idol, whether in the form of anything that
is in heaven above, or that is on the earth beneath, or that is in the water under the
earth. 5 You shall not bow down to them or worship them; for I the LORD your God
am a jealous God, punishing children for the iniquity of parents, to the third and the
fourth generation of those who reject me, 6 but showing steadfast love to the thousandth generation[q] of those who love me and keep my commandments.
7 You shall not make wrongful use of the name of the LORD your God, for the
LORD will not acquit anyone who misuses his name.
8 Remember the sabbath day, and keep it holy. 9 Six days you shall labor and do

[p] Or *besides* [q] Or *to thousands*

19.22 By stating that he "would break out against them," God was saying that he would destroy anyone who was not ready to meet him fully consecrated.

20.1ff Why was the law necessary for God's new nation? At the foot of Mount Sinai, God showed his people the true function and beauty of the law. The law was designed to lead Israel to a life of practical holiness. In it people could see the nature of God and his plan for how they should live. Its commands and guidelines were intended to direct the community to meet the needs of each individual in a loving and responsible manner. By Jesus' time, however, most people looked at the law the wrong way. They saw it as a means to prosperity in both this world and the next. To obey every law was the way to earn God's protection from foreign invasion and natural disaster, they thought. Lawkeeping became an end in itself, not the means to fulfill God's ultimate law of love.

20.1–5 The Israelites had just come from Egypt, a land of many idols and many gods. Since each god represented a different aspect of life, it was common to worship many gods in order to get the maximum number of blessings. When God told his people to worship and believe in him, that wasn't so hard for them—he was just one more god to add to the list. But when he said, "You shall have no other gods before me," that was hard for the people to accept. However, if they didn't learn that the God who led them out of Egypt was the only true God, they could not be his people—no matter how faithfully they kept the other nine commandments. Thus, God made this his first commandment and emphasized it more than the others. Today we can allow many things to become gods to us. Money, fame, work, or pleasure can become gods when we concentrate too much on them for personal identity, meaning, and security. No one sets out with the intention of worshiping these things. But with the amount of time we devote to them, they can grow into gods that ultimately control our thoughts and energies. Letting God hold the central place in our lives keeps these things from turning into gods.

20.7 God's name is special because it carries his personal identity. Using it frivolously or in a curse is so common today that we may fail to realize how serious it is. The way we use God's name conveys how we really feel about him. We should respect his name and use it appropriately, speaking it in praise or worship rather than in curse or jest. We should not take lightly the abuse of or dishonoring of his name.

20.8–11 The sabbath was a day set aside for rest and worship. God commanded a sabbath because human beings need to spend unhurried time in worship and rest each week. A God who is concerned enough to provide a day each week for us to rest is indeed wonderful. To observe a regular time of rest and worship in our fast-paced world demonstrates how important God is to us, and it gives us the extra benefit of refreshing our spirits. Don't neglect God's provision.

all your work. 10 But the seventh day is a sabbath to the LORD your God; you shall
not do any work—you, your son or your daughter, your male or female slave, your
livestock, or the alien resident in your towns. 11 For in six days the LORD made
heaven and earth, the sea, and all that is in them, but rested the seventh day; therefore the LORD blessed the sabbath day and consecrated it.

12 Honor your father and your mother, so that your days may be long in the
land that the LORD your God is giving you.

13 You shall not murder.[r]

14 You shall not commit adultery.

15 You shall not steal.

16 You shall not bear false witness against your neighbor.

17 You shall not covet your neighbor's house; you shall not covet your neighbor's wife, or male or female slave, or ox, or donkey, or anything that belongs to
your neighbor.

18 When all the people witnessed the thunder and lightning, the sound of the
trumpet, and the mountain smoking, they were afraid[s] and trembled and stood at
a distance, 19 and said to Moses, "You speak to us, and we will listen; but do not let
God speak to us, or we will die." 20 Moses said to the people, "Do not be afraid; for
God has come only to test you and to put the fear of him upon you so that you do
not sin." 21 Then the people stood at a distance, while Moses drew near to the thick
darkness where God was.

22 The LORD said to Moses: Thus you shall say to the Israelites: "You have seen
for yourselves that I spoke with you from heaven. 23 You shall not make gods of
silver alongside me, nor shall you make for yourselves gods of gold. 24 You need
make for me only an altar of earth and sacrifice on it your burnt offerings and your
offerings of well-being, your sheep and your oxen; in every place where I cause my
name to be remembered I will come to you and bless you. 25 But if you make for me
an altar of stone, do not build it of hewn stones; for if you use a chisel upon it you
profane it. 26 You shall not go up by steps to my altar, so that your nakedness may
not be exposed on it."

r Or *kill* s Sam Gk Syr Vg: MT *they saw*

20.9 Ex 23.12; 34.21 Deut 5.13
20.11 Gen 2.2,3 Mk 2.27
20.12 Lev 19.1-3 Deut 5.16,33 Mt 15.4; Eph 6.2
20.13 Deut 5.17 Mt 5.21,22
20.14 Lev 20.10 Mt 5.27,28
20.15 Lev 6.1-7 Mt 15.19; 19.18
20.16 Deut 5.20
20.18 Heb 12.18
20.19 Gen 32.30 Ex 33.20
20.21 Deut 5.22 Ps 97.2
20.23 Ex 20.4; 32.4 Deut 29.17
20.24 Ex 10.25; 18.12 24.5; 27.1-8 Deut 12.4,5
20.25 Deut 27.5 Josh 8.31
20.26 Ex 28.42

20.12 This is the first commandment with a promise attached. To live in peace for generations in the promised land, the Israelites would need to respect authority and build strong families. But what does it mean to "honor" parents? Partly, it means speaking well of them and politely to them. It also means acting in a way that shows them courtesy and respect (but not to obey them if this means disobedience to God). It means following their teaching and example of putting God first. Parents have a special place in God's sight. Even those who find it difficult to get along with their parents are still commanded to honor them.

20.16 Bearing false witness means giving false evidence in court. God knew that Israel could not survive unless its system of justice was incorruptible. We should be honest in our private dealings as well as in our public statements. In either situation, we "bear false witness" by leaving something out of a story, telling a half-truth, twisting the facts, or inventing a falsehood. God warns us against deception. Even though deception is a way of life for many people, God's people must not give in to it!

20.17 To covet is to wish to have the possessions of others. It goes beyond simply admiring someone else's possessions or thinking, "I'd like to have one of those." Coveting includes envy—resenting the fact that others have what you don't. God knows, however, that possessions never make anyone happy for long. Since only God can supply all our needs, true contentment is found only in him. When you begin to covet, try to determine if a more basic need is leading you to envy. For example, you may covet someone's success, not because you want to take it away from him, but because you would like to feel as appreciated by others as he is. If this is the case, pray that God will help you deal with your resentment and meet your basic needs.

20.18 Sometimes God speaks to his people with a majestic display of power; at other times he speaks quietly. Why the difference? God speaks in the way that best accomplishes his purposes. At Sinai, the awesome display of light and sound was necessary to show Israel God's great power and authority. Only then would they listen to Moses and Aaron.

20.20 Throughout the Bible we find this phrase, "Do not be afraid!" God wasn't trying to scare the people. He was showing his mighty power so the Israelites would know he was the true God and would therefore obey him. If they would do this, he would make his power available to them. God wants us to follow him out of love rather than fear. To overcome fear, we must think more about his love. First John 4.18 says, "Perfect love casts out fear."

20.24–26 Why were specific directions given for building altars? God's people had no Bible and few religious traditions to learn from. God had to start from scratch and teach them how to worship him. God gave specific instructions about building altars because he wanted to control the way sacrifices were offered. To prevent idolatry from creeping into worship, God did not allow the altar stones to be cut or shaped into any form. Nor did God let the people build an altar just anywhere. This was designed to prevent them from starting their own religions or making changes in the way God wanted things done. God is not against creativity, but he is against us creating our own religion.

Laws concerning people

21.1 Lev 18.4,5,26 Deut 5.1,31
21.2 Lev 25.39-43 Deut 15.12 Neh 5.1,2 Jer 34.9-11
21.5 Deut 15.16
21.6 Ex 18.21
21.7 Neh 5.5
21.8 Deut 21.11-14
21.10 1 Cor 7.2-6
21.11 Ex 20.2,3
21.12 Gen 9.5 Ex 20.13 Lev 24.21
21.13 Num 35.9-29,32 Deut 19.1-10

21 These are the ordinances that you shall set before them:
2 When you buy a male Hebrew slave, he shall serve six years, but in the
seventh he shall go out a free person, without debt. 3 If he comes in single, he shall
go out single; if he comes in married, then his wife shall go out with him. 4 If his
master gives him a wife and she bears him sons or daughters, the wife and her
children shall be her master's and he shall go out alone. 5 But if the slave declares,
"I love my master, my wife, and my children; I will not go out a free person," 6 then
his master shall bring him before God.[t] He shall be brought to the door or the
doorpost; and his master shall pierce his ear with an awl; and he shall serve him for
life.
7 When a man sells his daughter as a slave, she shall not go out as the male
slaves do. 8 If she does not please her master, who designated her for himself, then
he shall let her be redeemed; he shall have no right to sell her to a foreign people,
since he has dealt unfairly with her. 9 If he designates her for his son, he shall deal
with her as with a daughter. 10 If he takes another wife to himself, he shall not
diminish the food, clothing, or marital rights of the first wife.[u] 11 And if he does not
do these three things for her, she shall go out without debt, without payment of
money.
12 Whoever strikes a person mortally shall be put to death. 13 If it was not premeditated, but came about by an act of God, then I will appoint for you a place to

[t] Or *to the judges* [u] Heb *of her*

JESUS AND THE TEN COMMANDMENTS

The ten commandments said . . .	*Jesus said . . .*
Exodus 20.3 "Have no other gods before me"	Matthew 4.10 "Worship the Lord your God, and serve only him"
Exodus 20.4 "You shall not make for yourself an idol"	Luke 16.13 "No one can be the slave of two masters"
Exodus 20.7 "You shall not make wrongful use of the name of the Lord your God"	Matthew 5.23 "Do not swear at all, either by heaven, for it is the throne of God"
Exodus 20.8 "Remember the sabbath day, and keep it holy"	Mark 2.27, 28 "God made the sabbath for you, and not you for the sabbath; so the Son of Man is lord even of the sabbath"
Exodus 20.12 "Honor your father and your mother"	Matthew 10.37 "Whoever loves father or mother more than me is not worthy of me"
Exodus 20.13 "You shall not murder"	Matthew 5.22 "If you are angry with brother or sister, you will be liable to judgment"
Exodus 20.14 "You shall not commit adultery"	Matthew 5.28 "Everyone who looks at a woman with lust has already committed adultery with her in his heart"
Exodus 20.15 "You shall not steal"	Matthew 5.40 "If anyone wants to sue you and take your coat, give your cloak as well"
Exodus 20.16 "You shall not bear false witness"	Matthew 12.36 "On the day of judgment you will have to give an account for every careless word you utter"
Exodus 20.17 "You shall not covet"	Luke 12.15 "Be on your guard against all kinds of greed"

21.1ff These laws were given because everything we do has consequences. It is vital to think before acting, to consider the effects of our choices. Think of your plans for today and consider what their long-range results will be. As we deal with others, we should keep the principles of these laws in mind. We should act responsibly and justly with all people – friends and enemies alike.

21.2 The Hebrews, though freed from slavery, had slaves themselves. A person could become a slave because of poverty, debt, or even crime. But Hebrew slaves were treated as humans, not property, and were allowed to work their way to freedom. The Bible acknowledges the existence of slavery but never encourages it.

which the killer may flee. 14 But if someone willfully attacks and kills another by
treachery, you shall take the killer from my altar for execution.
15 Whoever strikes father or mother shall be put to death.
16 Whoever kidnaps a person, whether that person has been sold or is still held
in possession, shall be put to death.
17 Whoever curses father or mother shall be put to death.
18 When individuals quarrel and one strikes the other with a stone or fist so that
the injured party, though not dead, is confined to bed, 19 but recovers and walks
around outside with the help of a staff, then the assailant shall be free of liability,
except to pay for the loss of time, and to arrange for full recovery.
20 When a slaveowner strikes a male or female slave with a rod and the slave
dies immediately, the owner shall be punished. 21 But if the slave survives a day or
two, there is no punishment; for the slave is the owner's property.
22 When people who are fighting injure a pregnant woman so that there is a
miscarriage, and yet no further harm follows, the one responsible shall be fined
what the woman's husband demands, paying as much as the judges determine. 23 If
any harm follows, then you shall give life for life, 24 eye for eye, tooth for tooth,
hand for hand, foot for foot, 25 burn for burn, wound for wound, stripe for stripe.
26 When a slaveowner strikes the eye of a male or female slave, destroying it,
the owner shall let the slave go, a free person, to compensate for the eye. 27 If the
owner knocks out a tooth of a male or female slave, the slave shall be let go, a free
person, to compensate for the tooth.
28 When an ox gores a man or a woman to death, the ox shall be stoned, and its
flesh shall not be eaten; but the owner of the ox shall not be liable. 29 If the ox has
been accustomed to gore in the past, and its owner has been warned but has not
restrained it, and it kills a man or a woman, the ox shall be stoned, and its owner
also shall be put to death. 30 If a ransom is imposed on the owner, then the owner
shall pay whatever is imposed for the redemption of the victim's life. 31 If it gores
a boy or a girl, the owner shall be dealt with according to this same rule. 32 If the ox
gores a male or female slave, the owner shall pay to the slaveowner thirty shekels
of silver, and the ox shall be stoned.

Laws about property

33 If someone leaves a pit open, or digs a pit and does not cover it, and an ox
or a donkey falls into it, 34 the owner of the pit shall make restitution, giving money
to its owner, but keeping the dead animal.
35 If someone's ox hurts the ox of another, so that it dies, then they shall sell the
live ox and divide the price of it; and the dead animal they shall also divide. 36 But
if it was known that the ox was accustomed to gore in the past, and its owner has
not restrained it, the owner shall restore ox for ox, but keep the dead animal.
22 [v] When someone steals an ox or a sheep, and slaughters it or sells it, the thief
shall pay five oxen for an ox, and four sheep for a sheep.[w] The thief shall
make restitution, but if unable to do so, shall be sold for the theft. 4 When the animal, whether ox or donkey or sheep, is found alive in the thief's possession, the
thief shall pay double.

[v] Ch 21.37 in Heb [w] Verses 2, 3, and 4 rearranged thus: 3b, 4, 2, 3a

21.14 Ex 20.13 Num 35.30,31 Deut 19.11-13 1 Kgs 2.28-34
21.15 Ex 20.12 Deut 21.18 Prov 30.11,17
21.16 Deut 24.7 1 Tim 1.10
21.17 Lev 20.9 Deut 27.16 Mt 15.4 Mk 7.10
21.18 Num 35.16,17
21.21 Lev 25.44-46
21.23 Ex 20.13; 21.12
21.24,25 Lev 24.20-22 Deut 19.21 Mt 5.38
21.26 Job 31.13
21.28 Gen 9.5
21.30 Num 30.11,12 35.31
21.32 Gen 37.28 Zech 11.12 Mt 26.15; 27.3,9
21.34 Ex 22.5
22.1 Lev 6.1-7 2 Sam 12.6 Prov 6.31 Lk 19.8
22.4 Prov 6.30 Jer 2.26 Jn 12.6

21.24, 25 The "eye for eye" rule was instituted as a guide for judges, not as a rule for personal relationships or to justify revenge. This rule made the punishment fit the crime, thereby preventing the cruel and barbaric punishments that characterized many ancient countries. Jesus used this principle in Matthew 5.38–48 to teach us not to retaliate. Judges, parents, teachers, and others who work with people must make wise decisions in order for discipline to be effective. A punishment too harsh is unfair, and one too lenient is powerless to teach. Ask God for wisdom before you judge.

22.1ff These are not a collection of picky laws but are case studies of God's principles in action. God was taking potential situations and showing how his laws would work in the Israelites' everyday lives. These case studies had several objectives: (1) to protect the nation, (2) to organize the nation, and (3) to focus the nation's attention on God. The laws listed here do not cover every possible situation, but they give practical examples that make it easier to decide what God wants.

22.3ff Throughout chapter 22 we find examples of the principle of restitution—making wrongs right. For example, if a man stole an animal, he had to repay double the beast's market value. If you have done someone wrong, perhaps you should go beyond what is expected to make things right. This will (1) help ease any pain you've caused, (2) help the other person be more forgiving, and (3) make you more likely to think before you do it again.

22.2 Num 35.26,27
22.3 Ex 20.13; 21.2,14
22.5 Ex 21.34
22.7 Lev 6.1-7; Prov 6.30,31
22.8 Ex 21.6; Deut 1.17
22.9 Num 5.7; Deut 25.1; 2 Chron 19.10
22.12 Lev 6.2
22.13 Gen 37.33
22.14 Deut 23.19; Neh 5.4; Ps 37.21
22.16 Deut 22.28,29
22.17 Deut 7.3
22.18 Lev 19.26; 20.27; Deut 18.10
22.19 Lev 18.23; 20.15
22.20 Ex 32.8; 34.15
22.21 Lev 19.33,34
22.22 Deut 24.17
22.25 Lev 25.36; Deut 23.19
22.26 Deut 24.6,10-13

2[x] If a thief is found breaking in, and is beaten to death, no bloodguilt is incurred; 3 but if it happens after sunrise, bloodguilt is incurred.
5 When someone causes a field or vineyard to be grazed over, or lets livestock
loose to graze in someone else's field, restitution shall be made from the best in the
owner's field or vineyard.
6 When fire breaks out and catches in thorns so that the stacked grain or the
standing grain or the field is consumed, the one who started the fire shall make full
restitution.
7 When someone delivers to a neighbor money or goods for safekeeping, and
they are stolen from the neighbor's house, then the thief, if caught, shall pay double. 8 If the thief is not caught, the owner of the house shall be brought before
God,[y] to determine whether or not the owner had laid hands on the neighbor's
goods.
9 In any case of disputed ownership involving ox, donkey, sheep, clothing, or
any other loss, of which one party says, "This is mine," the case of both parties
shall come before God;[y] the one whom God condemns[z] shall pay double to the
other.
10 When someone delivers to another a donkey, ox, sheep, or any other animal
for safekeeping, and it dies or is injured or is carried off, without anyone seeing it,
11 an oath before the LORD shall decide between the two of them that the one has not
laid hands on the property of the other; the owner shall accept the oath, and no
restitution shall be made. 12 But if it was stolen, restitution shall be made to its
owner. 13 If it was mangled by beasts, let it be brought as evidence; restitution shall
not be made for the mangled remains.
14 When someone borrows an animal from another and it is injured or dies, the
owner not being present, full restitution shall be made. 15 If the owner was present,
there shall be no restitution; if it was hired, only the hiring fee is due.

General laws

16 When a man seduces a virgin who is not engaged to be married, and lies with
her, he shall give the bride-price for her and make her his wife. 17 But if her father
refuses to give her to him, he shall pay an amount equal to the bride-price for virgins.
18 You shall not permit a female sorcerer to live.
19 Whoever lies with an animal shall be put to death.
20 Whoever sacrifices to any god, other than the LORD alone, shall be devoted
to destruction.
21 You shall not wrong or oppress a resident alien, for you were aliens in the
land of Egypt. 22 You shall not abuse any widow or orphan. 23 If you do abuse them,
when they cry out to me, I will surely heed their cry; 24 my wrath will burn, and I
will kill you with the sword, and your wives shall become widows and your children orphans.
25 If you lend money to my people, to the poor among you, you shall not deal
with them as a creditor; you shall not exact interest from them. 26 If you take your
neighbor's cloak in pawn, you shall restore it before the sun goes down; 27 for it

[x] Ch 22.1 in Heb [y] Or *before the judges* [z] Or *the judges condemn*

22.18 Why did God's laws speak so strongly against sorcery (Leviticus 19.31; 20.6, 27; Deuteronomy 18.10–12)? Sorcery was punishable by death because it was a crime against God himself. To invoke evil powers violated the first commandment to "have no other gods." Sorcery was rebellion against God and his authority. In essence, it was teaming up with Satan instead of with God.

22.21 God warned the Israelites not to treat strangers unfairly, for they themselves were once strangers in Egypt. It is not easy coming to a new environment where you feel alone and out of place. Are there strangers in your corner of the world? New arrivals at school? Immigrants from another country? Be sensitive to their struggles, and express God's love by your kindness and generosity.

22.22–27 The Hebrew law is noted for fairness toward the poor. God insisted that the poor and powerless be well treated and given the chance to restore their fortunes. We should reflect God's concern for the poor by helping those less fortunate than ourselves.

22.26 Why did the law insist on returning a person's cloak by evening? A cloak was one of an Israelite's most valuable possessions. Making clothing was difficult and time-consuming. As a result, cloaks were expensive, and most people owned only one. The cloak was used as a blanket, a sack to carry things in, a place to sit, a pledge for a debt, and as clothing.

may be your neighbor's only clothing to use as cover; in what else shall that person
sleep? And if your neighbor cries out to me, I will listen, for I am compassionate.
28 You shall not revile God, or curse a leader of your people.
29 You shall not delay to make offerings from the fullness of your harvest and
from the outflow of your presses.[a]
The firstborn of your sons you shall give to me. 30 You shall do the same with
your oxen and with your sheep: seven days it shall remain with its mother; on the
eighth day you shall give it to me.
31 You shall be people consecrated to me; therefore you shall not eat any meat
that is mangled by beasts in the field; you shall throw it to the dogs.
23 You shall not spread a false report. You shall not join hands with the wicked
to act as a malicious witness. 2 You shall not follow a majority in wrongdoing; when you bear witness in a lawsuit, you shall not side with the majority so as
to pervert justice; 3 nor shall you be partial to the poor in a lawsuit.
4 When you come upon your enemy's ox or donkey going astray, you shall
bring it back.
5 When you see the donkey of one who hates you lying under its burden and you
would hold back from setting it free, you must help to set it free.[a]
6 You shall not pervert the justice due to your poor in their lawsuits. 7 Keep far
from a false charge, and do not kill the innocent and those in the right, for I will not
acquit the guilty. 8 You shall take no bribe, for a bribe blinds the officials, and
subverts the cause of those who are in the right.
9 You shall not oppress a resident alien; you know the heart of an alien, for you
were aliens in the land of Egypt.
10 For six years you shall sow your land and gather in its yield; 11 but the seventh year you shall let it rest and lie fallow, so that the poor of your people may eat;
and what they leave the wild animals may eat. You shall do the same with your
vineyard, and with your olive orchard.
12 Six days you shall do your work, but on the seventh day you shall rest, so
that your ox and your donkey may have relief, and your homeborn slave and the
resident alien may be refreshed. 13 Be attentive to all that I have said to you. Do not
invoke the names of other gods; do not let them be heard on your lips.
14 Three times in the year you shall hold a festival for me. 15 You shall observe
the festival of unleavened bread; as I commanded you, you shall eat unleavened
bread for seven days at the appointed time in the month of Abib, for in it you came
out of Egypt.
No one shall appear before me empty-handed.
16 You shall observe the festival of harvest, of the first fruits of your labor, of
what you sow in the field. You shall observe the festival of ingathering at the end
of the year, when you gather in from the field the fruit of your labor. 17 Three times
in the year all your males shall appear before the Lord GOD.
18 You shall not offer the blood of my sacrifice with anything leavened, or let
the fat of my festival remain until the morning.

[a] Meaning of Heb uncertain

22.27 Ex 2.23 Isa 19.20
22.28 Lev 24.15
22.29 Ex 13.2 23.16,19 34.19,20 Deut 26.2
22.30 Gen 17.12 Lev 12.3; 22.27
22.31 Ex 19.6 Lev 7.24; 17.15 22.8
23.1 Deut 5.20; 19.16
23.2,3 Deut 1.17; 16.19
23.4 Deut 22.1-4
23.6 Ex 22.21-24 Deut 27.19
23.7 Ex 20.13,16 Deut 27.15
23.8 Deut 16.19 1 Sam 8.3; 12.3
23.9 Ex 22.21 Lev 19.33,34
23.10 Lev 25.1
23.11 Lev 26.34,35
23.12 Ex 20.8-11 Deut 5.13
23.13 Deut 4.9,23
23.14 Ex 34.22 Lev 23.4 Deut 16.16
23.15 Ex 12.2; 13.4 Lev 23.5 Num 9.2
23.16 Ex 34.22 Lev 23.9,34 Deut 16.9,13
23.17 Deut 12.5; 16.16
23.18 Ex 12.10; 34.25 Lev 2.11; 7.15

22.29 The Israelites were to be prompt in giving God their offerings. The first of the harvest was to be dedicated to him. Since God doesn't send payment overdue notices, it is easy to take care of other financial responsibilities while letting our gifts to him slide. Giving to God first out of what he has allowed you to have demonstrates that he has first priority in your life.

23.1 Making up or passing along untrue reports was strictly forbidden by God. Gossip, slander, and false witnessing undermined families, strained neighborhood cooperation, and made chaos of the justice system. Destructive gossip still causes problems. Even if you do not initiate a lie, you become responsible if you pass it along. Don't circulate rumors; squelch them.

23.2, 3 Justice is often perverted in favor of the rich. Here the people are warned against twisting justice in favor of the poor. Justice should be impartial, treating rich and poor alike. Giving special privileges to either rich or poor only makes justice for everyone more unlikely. Withstand the pressure of the crowd to sway your decision about a person. Let God's fairness guide your judgment.

23.4, 5 The thought of being kind to enemies was new and startling in a world where revenge was the common form of justice. God not only introduced this idea to the Israelites, he made it law! If a man found a lost animal owned by his enemy, he was to return it at once, even if his enemy would use it to harm him. Jesus clearly taught in Luke 10.30–37 to reach out to all people in need, even our enemies. Following the laws of right living is hard enough with friends. When we apply God's laws of fairness and kindness to our enemies, we show how different we are from the world.

23.19 Ex 22.29; 34.26 Lev 23.10

19 The choicest of the first fruits of your ground you shall bring into the house
of the LORD your God.
You shall not boil a kid in its mother's milk.

Instructions regarding enemies

23.20 Ex 3.2; 14.19
23.21 Ex 3.14; 34.5 Num 14.10,11

20 I am going to send an angel in front of you, to guard you on the way and to
bring you to the place that I have prepared. 21 Be attentive to him and listen to his
voice; do not rebel against him, for he will not pardon your transgression; for my
name is in him.

23.22 Num 24.9 Deut 30.7

22 But if you listen attentively to his voice and do all that I say, then I will be
an enemy to your enemies and a foe to your foes.

23.23 Deut 7.1 Josh 24.11
23.24 Ex 20.5; 34.13
23.25 Ex 15.26 Lev 26.3 Deut 7.15
23.27 Gen 35.5 Ex 15.16 Deut 2.25
23.28 Deut 7.20
23.30 Deut 7.22 Josh 15.63 16.10; 17.12
23.31 Gen 15.18 Josh 21.44 24.12,18
23.32 Deut 7.2
23.33 Deut 7.16; 12.30

23 When my angel goes in front of you, and brings you to the Amorites, the
Hittites, the Perizzites, the Canaanites, the Hivites, and the Jebusites, and I blot
them out, 24 you shall not bow down to their gods, or worship them, or follow their
practices, but you shall utterly demolish them and break their pillars in pieces.
25 You shall worship the LORD your God, and I[b] will bless your bread and your
water; and I will take sickness away from among you. 26 No one shall miscarry or
be barren in your land; I will fulfill the number of your days. 27 I will send my terror
in front of you, and will throw into confusion all the people against whom you shall
come, and I will make all your enemies turn their backs to you. 28 And I will send
the pestilence[c] in front of you, which shall drive out the Hivites, the Canaanites,
and the Hittites from before you. 29 I will not drive them out from before you in one
year, or the land would become desolate and the wild animals would multiply
against you. 30 Little by little I will drive them out from before you, until you have
increased and possess the land. 31 I will set your borders from the Red Sea[d] to the
sea of the Philistines, and from the wilderness to the Euphrates; for I will hand over
to you the inhabitants of the land, and you shall drive them out before you. 32 You
shall make no covenant with them and their gods. 33 They shall not live in your
land, or they will make you sin against me; for if you worship their gods, it will
surely be a snare to you.

The people promise to obey

24.1 Ex 6.23; 19.24
24.2 Ex 20.21

24 Then he said to Moses, "Come up to the LORD, you and Aaron, Nadab, and
Abihu, and seventy of the elders of Israel, and worship at a distance. 2 Moses alone shall come near the LORD; but the others shall not come near, and the
people shall not come up with him."

24.3 Ex 19.8; 24.7 Deut 5.27; 11.1
24.4 Deut 31.9
24.5 Ex 18.12 Lev 1.2; 7.11

3 Moses came and told the people all the words of the LORD and all the ordinances; and all the people answered with one voice, and said, "All the words that
the LORD has spoken we will do." 4 And Moses wrote down all the words of the
LORD. He rose early in the morning, and built an altar at the foot of the mountain,
and set up twelve pillars, corresponding to the twelve tribes of Israel. 5 He sent
young men of the people of Israel, who offered burnt offerings and sacrificed oxen

[b] Gk Vg: Heb *he* [c] Or *hornets*: Meaning of Heb uncertain [d] Or *Sea of Reeds*

23.20, 21 Who was this angel that went with the Israelites? Most likely the angel was a manifestation of God. God was in the angel in the same way he was present in the pillars of cloud and fire (13.21, 22). "My name is in him" means the essential nature and power of God were made known in this angel.

23.24, 25 If you're in the furnace, it's easy to catch fire. God warned the Israelites about their neighbors, whose beliefs and actions could turn them away from him. We also live with neighbors whose values may be completely different from ours. We are called to maintain a life-style that shows our faith. This can be a struggle, especially if our Christian life-style differs from the norm. Our lives should show that we put obeying God before doing what is praised and accepted by society.

23.32, 33 God continually warned the people to avoid false religions and false gods. In Egypt they had been surrounded by idols and sorcerers, but leaving that land did not mean they were free from heathen religious influences. The land of Canaan was just as infested with idol worship. God knew his people needed extra strength, so he continually emphasized guarding against the influence of heathen religions.

as offerings of well-being to the LORD. 6 Moses took half of the blood and put it in
basins, and half of the blood he dashed against the altar. 7 Then he took the book of
the covenant, and read it in the hearing of the people; and they said, "All that the
LORD has spoken we will do, and we will be obedient." 8 Moses took the blood and
dashed it on the people, and said, "See the blood of the covenant that the LORD has
made with you in accordance with all these words."
9 Then Moses and Aaron, Nadab, and Abihu, and seventy of the elders of Israel
went up, 10 and they saw the God of Israel. Under his feet there was something like
a pavement of sapphire stone, like the very heaven for clearness. 11 God[e] did not
lay his hand on the chief men of the people of Israel; also they beheld God, and they
ate and drank.
12 The LORD said to Moses, "Come up to me on the mountain, and wait there;
and I will give you the tablets of stone, with the law and the commandment, which
I have written for their instruction." 13 So Moses set out with his assistant Joshua,
and Moses went up into the mountain of God. 14 To the elders he had said, "Wait
here for us, until we come to you again; for Aaron and Hur are with you; whoever
has a dispute may go to them."
15 Then Moses went up on the mountain, and the cloud covered the mountain.
16 The glory of the LORD settled on Mount Sinai, and the cloud covered it for six
days; on the seventh day he called to Moses out of the cloud. 17 Now the appearance
of the glory of the LORD was like a devouring fire on the top of the mountain in the
sight of the people of Israel. 18 Moses entered the cloud, and went up on the mountain. Moses was on the mountain for forty days and forty nights.

24.6 Ex 12.7; 29.16
24.7 Ex 19.8; 24.3; Deut 5.27
24.8 Lev 8.30; Zech 9.11; Mt 26.28
24.10 Ex 33.20; Num 12.8; Isa 6.5; Ezek 1.26
24.12 Ex 31.18; Jer 31.33
24.13 Ex 17.9; 32.17; 33.11
24.15 Ex 19.9; 2 Chron 6.1
24.16 Lev 9.23; Num 14.10
24.17 Ex 3.2; 16.10; Deut 4.24,36; Ezek 1.27
24.18 Ex 19.20,34.28; Deut 9.9; 10.10

2. Tabernacle instructions

Offerings for the tabernacle

25 The LORD said to Moses: 2 Tell the Israelites to take for me an offering; from
all whose hearts prompt them to give you shall receive the offering for me.
3 This is the offering that you shall receive from them: gold, silver, and bronze,
4 blue, purple, and crimson yarns and fine linen, goats' hair, 5 tanned rams' skins,
fine leather,[f] acacia wood, 6 oil for the lamps, spices for the anointing oil and for
the fragrant incense, 7 onyx stones and gems to be set in the ephod and for the
breastpiece. 8 And have them make me a sanctuary, so that I may dwell among
them. 9 In accordance with all that I show you concerning the pattern of the tabernacle and of all its furniture, so you shall make it.

25.1 Ex 35.5-9; 1 Chron 29.2-5
25.8 Ex 29.45; 36.1; Deut 12.11; Rev 21.3
25.9 Acts 7.44; Heb 8.5

The Ark

10 They shall make an ark of acacia wood; it shall be two and a half cubits long,
a cubit and a half wide, and a cubit and a half high. 11 You shall overlay it with pure
gold, inside and outside you shall overlay it, and you shall make a molding of gold

25.10 Ex 37.1-5

[e] Heb *He* [f] Meaning of Heb uncertain

24.6–8 To understand this unusual covenant ratification ceremony, we need to understand the Bible's view of sin and forgiveness. God is the sovereign judge of the universe. He is also absolutely holy. As the holy judge of all, he condemns sin and judges it worthy of death. In the Old Testament God accepted the death of an animal as a substitute for the sinner. The animal's shed blood was proof that one life had been given for another. So on the one hand blood symbolized the death of the animal, but on the other hand it symbolized the life that was spared as a result. Of course the death of the animal that brought forgiveness in the Old Testament was only a temporary provision, looking forward to the death of Jesus Christ (Hebrews 9.9 – 10.24).

In this ceremony described here, Moses sprinkled half the blood from the sacrificed animals on the altar to show that the sinner could once again approach God because something had died in his place. The other half of the blood he sprinkled on the people to show that the penalty for their sin had been paid and they could be reunited with God. Through this symbolic act God's promises to Israel were reaffirmed and lessons are taught to us about the future sacrificial death (or atonement) of Jesus Christ.

25.1ff Chapters 25 through 31 record God's directions for building the tabernacle. Chapters 35 through 39 tell how these instructions were carried out. But what can all these ancient, complicated construction details show us today? First, the high quality of the precious materials making up the tabernacle shows God's greatness and transcendence. Second, the veil surrounding the most holy place shows God's moral perfection as symbolized by his separation from the common and unclean. Third, the portable nature of the tabernacle shows God's desire to be with his people as they traveled.

25.10 Much of the tabernacle and its furniture was made of acacia wood. Acacia trees flourished in barren regions and were fairly common in Old Testament times. The wood was brownish-orange and very hard, making it an excellent material for furniture. Acacia wood is still used in furniture-making today.

upon it all around. 12 You shall cast four rings of gold for it and put them on its four
feet, two rings on the one side of it, and two rings on the other side. 13 You shall
make poles of acacia wood, and overlay them with gold. 14 And you shall put the
poles into the rings on the sides of the ark, by which to carry the ark. 15 The poles
shall remain in the rings of the ark; they shall not be taken from it. 16 You shall put
into the ark the covenant[g] that I shall give you.

17 Then you shall make a mercy seat[h] of pure gold; two cubits and a half shall
be its length, and a cubit and a half its width. 18 You shall make two cherubim of
gold; you shall make them of hammered work, at the two ends of the mercy seat.[i]
19 Make one cherub at the one end, and one cherub at the other; of one piece with
the mercy seat[i] you shall make the cherubim at its two ends. 20 The cherubim shall
spread out their wings above, overshadowing the mercy seat[i] with their wings.
They shall face one to another; the faces of the cherubim shall be turned toward the
mercy seat.[i] 21 You shall put the mercy seat[i] on the top of the ark; and in the ark
you shall put the covenant[g] that I shall give you. 22 There I will meet with you, and
from above the mercy seat,[i] from between the two cherubim that are on the ark of
the covenant,[g] I will deliver to you all my commands for the Israelites.

The table

23 You shall make a table of acacia wood, two cubits long, one cubit wide, and
a cubit and a half high. 24 You shall overlay it with pure gold, and make a molding
of gold around it. 25 You shall make around it a rim a handbreadth wide, and a
molding of gold around the rim. 26 You shall make for it four rings of gold, and
fasten the rings to the four corners at its four legs. 27 The rings that hold the poles
used for carrying the table shall be close to the rim. 28 You shall make the poles of
acacia wood, and overlay them with gold, and the table shall be carried with these.
29 You shall make its plates and dishes for incense, and its flagons and bowls with
which to pour drink offerings; you shall make them of pure gold. 30 And you shall
set the bread of the Presence on the table before me always.

The lampstand

31 You shall make a lampstand of pure gold. The base and the shaft of the
lampstand shall be made of hammered work; its cups, its calyxes, and its petals
shall be of one piece with it; 32 and there shall be six branches going out of its sides,
three branches of the lampstand out of one side of it and three branches of the
lampstand out of the other side of it; 33 three cups shaped like almond blossoms,

[g] Or *treaty,* or *testimony;* Heb *eduth* [h] Or *a cover* [i] Or *the cover*

25.12 Ex 26.29; 27.7 37.5; 38.7
25.13 Ex 30.5; 37.4 40.20
25.15 1 Kgs 8.8
25.16 Ex 16.34; 30.6 Heb 9.4
25.17 Ex 37.6; 40.20 Lev 16.13 Rom 3.25 Heb 9.5
25.18 Ex 37.7
25.20 1 Kgs 8.7 Heb 9.5
25.22 Ex 30.6,36 Lev 1.1
25.23 Ex 37.10; 40.22
25.29 Ex 37.16 Num 4.7
25.30 Ex 35.13; 39.36 40.23 Lev 24.5 Num 4.7 2 Chron 13.11
25.31 Ex 37.17; 40.24 1 Kgs 7.49 Heb 9.2

THEOPHANIES IN THE SCRIPTURE

At the foot of Mount Sinai, God appeared to the people of Israel in a physical form. This is called a *theophany.* Here are some of the other times God appeared to Bible people.

Verse	*Theophany*
Genesis 16.7	The Angel of the Lord appeared to Sarah's maid, Hagar, announcing the birth of Abraham's son, Ishmael
Genesis 18.1–11	The Lord appeared to Abraham, foretelling Isaac's birth
Genesis 22.11, 12	The Angel of the Lord stopped Abraham from sacrificing Isaac
Exodus 3.2	The Angel of the Lord appeared to Moses as a flame in a bush
Exodus 14.19	God appeared to Israel in pillars of cloud and fire to guide them through the wilderness
Exodus 33.11	The Lord spoke to Moses face to face
Daniel 3.25	God appeared as the fourth man with Shadrach, Meshach, and Abednego in the fiery furnace

("Angel of the Lord" is a reverential way to refer to God in these passages.)

25.17 The cover of the ark of the covenant was called the "mercy seat." This is where, between the two golden cherubim, the real presence of God would dwell in a cloud above their outstretched wings. The mercy seat was where the highest and most perfect act of atonement would be made when the high priest would enter the most holy place on the day of atonement and sacrifice a lamb for the sin of the people (Exodus 30.10).

25.18 Cherubim are mighty angels.

25.33 A calyx is the center spread of leaves at the base of a flower.

each with calyx and petals, on one branch, and three cups shaped like almond
blossoms, each with calyx and petals, on the other branch—so for the six branches
going out of the lampstand. 34 On the lampstand itself there shall be four cups
shaped like almond blossoms, each with its calyxes and petals. 35 There shall be a
calyx of one piece with it under the first pair of branches, a calyx of one piece with
it under the next pair of branches, and a calyx of one piece with it under the last pair
of branches—so for the six branches that go out of the lampstand. 36 Their calyxes
and their branches shall be of one piece with it, the whole of it one hammered piece **25.37** Ex 37.23
of pure gold. 37 You shall make the seven lamps for it; and the lamps shall be set up Zech 4.2 Rev 1.4,12,20
so as to give light on the space in front of it. 38 Its snuffers and trays shall be of pure 4.5
gold. 39 It, and all these utensils, shall be made from a talent of pure gold. 40 And **25.40** Acts 7.44
see that you make them according to the pattern for them, which is being shown Heb 8.5
you on the mountain.

The tabernacle

26 Moreover you shall make the tabernacle with ten curtains of fine twisted **26.1**
linen, and blue, purple, and crimson yarns; you shall make them with cheru- Ex 36.8-19
bim skillfully worked into them. 2 The length of each curtain shall be twenty-eight
cubits, and the width of each curtain four cubits; all the curtains shall be of the same
size. 3 Five curtains shall be joined to one another; and the other five curtains shall
be joined to one another. 4 You shall make loops of blue on the edge of the outermost curtain in the first set; and likewise you shall make loops on the edge of the
outermost curtain in the second set. 5 You shall make fifty loops on the one curtain,
and you shall make fifty loops on the edge of the curtain that is in the second set;
the loops shall be opposite one another. 6 You shall make fifty clasps of gold, and
join the curtains to one another with the clasps, so that the tabernacle may be one
whole.

7 You shall also make curtains of goats' hair for a tent over the tabernacle; you **26.7**
shall make eleven curtains. 8 The length of each curtain shall be thirty cubits, and Ex 35.26; 36.14
the width of each curtain four cubits; the eleven curtains shall be of the same size.
9 You shall join five curtains by themselves, and six curtains by themselves, and the
sixth curtain you shall double over at the front of the tent. 10 You shall make fifty
loops on the edge of the curtain that is outermost in one set, and fifty loops on the
edge of the curtain that is outermost in the second set.

11 You shall make fifty clasps of bronze, and put the clasps into the loops, and
join the tent together, so that it may be one whole. 12 The part that remains of the
curtains of the tent, the half curtain that remains, shall hang over the back of the
tabernacle. 13 The cubit on the one side, and the cubit on the other side, of what
remains in the length of the curtains of the tent, shall hang over the sides of the
tabernacle, on this side and that side, to cover it. 14 You shall make for the tent a **26.14**
covering of tanned rams' skins and an outer covering of fine leather.[j] Ex 36.19

15 You shall make upright frames of acacia wood for the tabernacle. 16 Ten **26.15**
cubits shall be the length of a frame, and a cubit and a half the width of each Ex 36.20 40.18,19
frame. 17 There shall be two pegs in each frame to fit the frames together; you Num 4.31
shall make these for all the frames of the tabernacle. 18 You shall make the frames
for the tabernacle: twenty frames for the south side; 19 and you shall make forty bases
of silver under the twenty frames, two bases under the first frame for its two pegs,
and two bases under the next frame for its two pegs; 20 and for the second side of
the tabernacle, on the north side twenty frames, 21 and their forty bases of silver,
two bases under the first frame, and two bases under the next frame; 22 and for the
rear of the tabernacle westward you shall make six frames. 23 You shall make two
frames for corners of the tabernacle in the rear; 24 they shall be separate beneath,
but joined at the top, at the first ring; it shall be the same with both of them; they
shall form the two corners. 25 And so there shall be eight frames, with their bases
of silver, sixteen bases; two bases under the first frame, and two bases under the
next frame.

[j] Meaning of Heb uncertain

26 You shall make bars of acacia wood, five for the frames of the one side of the
tabernacle, 27 and five bars for the frames of the other side of the tabernacle, and
five bars for the frames of the side of the tabernacle at the rear westward. 28 The
middle bar, halfway up the frames, shall pass through from end to end. 29 You shall
overlay the frames with gold, and shall make their rings of gold to hold the bars;
and you shall overlay the bars with gold. 30 Then you shall erect the tabernacle
according to the plan for it that you were shown on the mountain.

26.30 Ex 25.40; 39.42 Num 8.4 Acts 7.44 Heb 8.5

The curtain

26.31 Ex 36.35; 40.3 Lev 16.2 2 Chron 3.14 Mt 27.51 Heb 9.3; 10.20
26.33 Ex 25.16; 40.21
26.34 Ex 25.17; 37.6

31 You shall make a curtain of blue, purple, and crimson yarns, and of fine
twisted linen; it shall be made with cherubim skillfully worked into it. 32 You shall
hang it on four pillars of acacia overlaid with gold, which have hooks of gold and
rest on four bases of silver. 33 You shall hang the curtain under the clasps, and bring
the ark of the covenant[k] in there, within the curtain; and the curtain shall separate
for you the holy place from the most holy. 34 You shall put the mercy seat[l] on the
ark of the covenant[k] in the most holy place. 35 You shall set the table outside the
curtain, and the lampstand on the south side of the tabernacle opposite the table;
and you shall put the table on the north side.

26.36 Ex 40.28

36 You shall make a screen for the entrance of the tent, of blue, purple, and
crimson yarns, and of fine twisted linen, embroidered with needlework. 37 You
shall make for the screen five pillars of acacia, and overlay them with gold; their
hooks shall be of gold, and you shall cast five bases of bronze for them.

The altar

27.1 Ex 20.24; 38.1 40.10,29 Ezek 43.13 Heb 13.10
27.2 Ex 29.12 Lev 4.7; 16.18 Num 16.38

27 You shall make the altar of acacia wood, five cubits long and five cubits
wide; the altar shall be square, and it shall be three cubits high. 2 You shall
make horns for it on its four corners; its horns shall be of one piece with it, and you
shall overlay it with bronze. 3 You shall make pots for it to receive its ashes, and
shovels and basins and forks and firepans; you shall make all its utensils of bronze.
4 You shall also make for it a grating, a network of bronze; and on the net you shall
make four bronze rings at its four corners. 5 You shall set it under the ledge of the
altar so that the net shall extend halfway down the altar. 6 You shall make poles for
the altar, poles of acacia wood, and overlay them with bronze; 7 the poles shall be
put through the rings, so that the poles shall be on the two sides of the altar when
it is carried. 8 You shall make it hollow, with boards. They shall be made just as you
were shown on the mountain.

27.8 Ex 25.40; 26.30

The court

27.9 Ex 38.9-20; 40.8 1 Kgs 6.36; 8.64

9 You shall make the court of the tabernacle. On the south side the court shall
have hangings of fine twisted linen one hundred cubits long for that side; 10 its
twenty pillars and their twenty bases shall be of bronze, but the hooks of the pillars
and their bands shall be of silver. 11 Likewise for its length on the north side there
shall be hangings one hundred cubits long, their pillars twenty and their bases
twenty, of bronze, but the hooks of the pillars and their bands shall be of silver.
12 For the width of the court on the west side there shall be fifty cubits of hangings,
with ten pillars and ten bases. 13 The width of the court on the front to the east shall

[k] Or *treaty*, or *testimony*; Heb *eduth* [l] Or *the cover*

26.1 Cherubim are mighty angels.

26.31 The curtain separated the two sacred rooms in the tabernacle – the holy place and the most holy place. The priest entered the holy place each day to commune with God and tend to the altar of incense, the lampstand, and the table of the bread of the Presence. The most holy place was where God himself dwelt, his presence resting on the mercy seat, which covered the ark of the covenant. Only the high priest could enter the most holy place. Even he could do so only once a year (on the day of atonement) to make atonement for the sins of the nation as a whole. When Jesus Christ died on the cross, the curtain in the temple (which had replaced the tabernacle) tore from top to bottom (Mark 15.38), symbolizing our free access to God because of Jesus' death. No longer did people have to approach God through priests and sacrifices.

27.1 A cubit is about 1 1/2 feet or .43 meters.

be fifty cubits. 14 There shall be fifteen cubits of hangings on the one side, with
three pillars and three bases. 15 There shall be fifteen cubits of hangings on the other
side, with three pillars and three bases. 16 For the gate of the court there shall be a
screen twenty cubits long, of blue, purple, and crimson yarns, and of fine twisted
linen, embroidered with needlework; it shall have four pillars and with them four
bases. 17 All the pillars around the court shall be banded with silver; their hooks
shall be of silver, and their bases of bronze. 18 The length of the court shall be one
hundred cubits, the width fifty, and the height five cubits, with hangings of fine
twisted linen and bases of bronze. 19 All the utensils of the tabernacle for every use,
and all its pegs and all the pegs of the court, shall be of bronze.

20 You shall further command the Israelites to bring you pure oil of beaten **27.20**
olives for the light, so that a lamp may be set up to burn regularly. 21 In the tent of Ex 35.8 Lev 24.2
meeting, outside the curtain that is before the covenant,[m] Aaron and his sons shall Zech 4.11,12
tend it from evening to morning before the LORD. It shall be a perpetual ordinance **27.21** Lev 24.3
to be observed throughout their generations by the Israelites. Ps 134.1

The garments for the priests

28 Then bring near to you your brother Aaron, and his sons with him, from **28.1**
among the Israelites, to serve me as priests — Aaron and Aaron's sons, Na- Ex 24.1-9 Ps 99.6
dab and Abihu, Eleazar and Ithamar. 2 You shall make sacred vestments for the Heb 5.4
glorious adornment of your brother Aaron. 3 And you shall speak to all who have **28.2** Ex 29.5; 31.10
ability, whom I have endowed with skill, that they make Aaron's vestments to 39.1
consecrate him for my priesthood. 4 These are the vestments that they shall make: Lev 8.7,30 Num 20.26
a breastpiece, an ephod, a robe, a checkered tunic, a turban, and a sash. When they
make these sacred vestments for your brother Aaron and his sons to serve me as
priests, 5 they shall use gold, blue, purple, and crimson yarns, and fine linen. **28.5**

6 They shall make the ephod of gold, of blue, purple, and crimson yarns, and Ex 39.2 Lev 8.7
of fine twisted linen, skillfully worked. 7 It shall have two shoulder-pieces attached
to its two edges, so that it may be joined together. 8 The decorated band on it shall
be of the same workmanship and materials, of gold, of blue, purple, and crimson
yarns, and of fine twisted linen. 9 You shall take two onyx stones, and engrave on
them the names of the sons of Israel, 10 six of their names on the one stone, and the
names of the remaining six on the other stone, in the order of their birth. 11 As a
gem-cutter engraves signets, so you shall engrave the two stones with the names of
the sons of Israel; you shall mount them in settings of gold filigree. 12 You shall set **28.12**
the two stones on the shoulder-pieces of the ephod, as stones of remembrance for Ex 39.7
the sons of Israel; and Aaron shall bear their names before the LORD on his two
shoulders for remembrance. 13 You shall make settings of gold filigree, 14 and two
chains of pure gold, twisted like cords; and you shall attach the corded chains to the
settings.

[m] Or *treaty*, or *testimony*; Heb *eduth*

28.1ff God was teaching his people how to worship him. To do so, he needed ministers to oversee the operations of the tabernacle and help the people maintain their relationship with God. These men were called priests and Levites, and they could be members only of the tribe of Levi. Chapters 28 and 29 give some details about priests. A priest not only was from the tribe of Levi, but also was a descendant of Aaron, Israel's first high priest. Priests had more responsibilities than Levites. As high priest, Aaron was in charge of all the priests and Levites. The priests performed the daily sacrifices, maintained the tabernacle, and counseled the people on how to follow God. They were the people's representatives before God and thus were required to live worthy of their office. Jesus is now our High Priest (Hebrews 8). Daily sacrifices are no longer required, because he sacrificed himself on the cross for our sins. Ministers today no longer sacrifice animals. Instead they lead us in prayer and teach us about both the benefits and the commandments that characterize our new life as Christians.

28.3 The tailors who made Aaron's garments were "endowed with skill" by God in order to do their task. All of us have special skills. God wants to fill us with his spirit so we will use them for his glory. Think about your special talents and abilities and the ways you could use them for God's work in the world. A talent must be used and polished or it will tarnish.

28.15 Ex 39.8 15 You shall make a breastpiece of judgment, in skilled work; you shall make
it in the style of the ephod; of gold, of blue and purple and crimson yarns, and of
fine twisted linen you shall make it. 16 It shall be square and doubled, a span in
28.17 Ex 39.10 length and a span in width. 17 You shall set in it four rows of stones. A row of
carnelian,[n] chrysolite, and emerald shall be the first row; 18 and the second row a
turquoise, a sapphire[o] and a moonstone; 19 and the third row a jacinth, an agate,
and an amethyst; 20 and the fourth row a beryl, an onyx, and a jasper; they shall be
set in gold filigree. 21 There shall be twelve stones with names corresponding to the
names of the sons of Israel; they shall be like signets, each engraved with its name,
for the twelve tribes. 22 You shall make for the breastpiece chains of pure gold,
twisted like cords; 23 and you shall make for the breastpiece two rings of gold, and
put the two rings on the two edges of the breastpiece. 24 You shall put the two cords
of gold in the two rings at the edges of the breastpiece; 25 the two ends of the two
cords you shall attach to the two settings, and so attach it in front to the shoulder-
pieces of the ephod. 26 You shall make two rings of gold, and put them at the two
ends of the breastpiece, on its inside edge next to the ephod. 27 You shall make two
rings of gold, and attach them in front to the lower part of the two shoulder-pieces
of the ephod, at its joining above the decorated band of the ephod. 28 The breastpiece shall be bound by its rings to the rings of the ephod with a blue cord, so that
it may lie on the decorated band of the ephod, and so that the breastpiece shall not
come loose from the ephod. 29 So Aaron shall bear the names of the sons of Israel
in the breastpiece of judgment on his heart when he goes into the holy place, for a
continual remembrance before the LORD. 30 In the breastpiece of judgment you
shall put the Urim and the Thummim, and they shall be on Aaron's heart when he
goes in before the LORD; thus Aaron shall bear the judgment of the Israelites on his
heart before the LORD continually.

28.31 Ex 39.22 31 You shall make the robe of the ephod all of blue. 32 It shall have an opening
for the head in the middle of it, with a woven binding around the opening, like the
opening in a coat of mail,[p] so that it may not be torn. 33 On its lower hem you shall
make pomegranates of blue, purple, and crimson yarns, all around the lower hem,
with bells of gold between them all around— 34 a golden bell and a pomegranate
alternating all around the lower hem of the robe. 35 Aaron shall wear it when he
ministers, and its sound shall be heard when he goes into the holy place before the
LORD, and when he comes out, so that he may not die.

28.36 Ex 39.30 36 You shall make a rosette of pure gold, and engrave on it, like the engraving
28.37,38 Lev 8.9 of a signet, "Holy to the LORD." 37 You shall fasten it on the turban with a blue cord;
Lev 10.17; 22.16 it shall be on the front of the turban. 38 It shall be on Aaron's forehead, and Aaron
Num 18.1 shall take on himself any guilt incurred in the holy offering that the Israelites consecrate as their sacred donations; it shall always be on his forehead, in order that they
may find favor before the LORD.

39 You shall make the checkered tunic of fine linen, and you shall make a turban of fine linen, and you shall make a sash embroidered with needlework.

28.40 Ex 39.27 Lev 8.13 40 For Aaron's sons you shall make tunics and sashes and headdresses; you
shall make them for their glorious adornment. 41 You shall put them on your brother
Aaron, and on his sons with him, and shall anoint them and ordain them and conse-
28.42 Ex 20.26 crate them, so that they may serve me as priests. 42 You shall make for them linen
undergarments to cover their naked flesh; they shall reach from the hips to the
thighs; 43 Aaron and his sons shall wear them when they go into the tent of meeting,
or when they come near the altar to minister in the holy place; or they will bring
guilt on themselves and die. This shall be a perpetual ordinance for him and for his
descendants after him.

[n] The identity of several of these stones is uncertain [o] Or *lapis lazuli* [p] Meaning of Heb uncertain

28.15ff The ephod was a kind of apron, elaborately embroidered, with two pieces, back and front, joined at the shoulders and also at the back near the waist. On each shoulder strap was a stone with the names of the twelve tribes of Israel (six tribes on each stone) so that the priest symbolically carried the burdens of the whole nation on his shoulders as he represented them before God.

The dedication of the priests

29 Now this is what you shall do to them to consecrate them, so that they may 29.1
serve me as priests. Take one young bull and two rams without blemish, Lev 8.1,2; 9.2 16.3
2 and unleavened bread, unleavened cakes mixed with oil, and unleavened wafers 29.2
spread with oil. You shall make them of choice wheat flour. 3 You shall put them Lev 2.4; 6.19
in one basket and bring them in the basket, and bring the bull and the two rams.
4 You shall bring Aaron and his sons to the entrance of the tent of meeting, and
wash them with water. 5 Then you shall take the vestments, and put on Aaron the 29.5
tunic and the robe of the ephod, and the ephod, and the breastpiece, and gird him Ex 28.4,8,15, 31,39
with the decorated band of the ephod; 6 and you shall set the turban on his head, and 29.6
put the holy diadem on the turban. 7 You shall take the anointing oil, and pour it on Ex 28.36
his head and anoint him. 8 Then you shall bring his sons, and put tunics on them, 29.7 Ex 28.41
9 and you shall gird them with sashes[q] and tie headdresses on them; and the priest- Lev 8.10; 10.7 Ps 133.2
hood shall be theirs by a perpetual ordinance. You shall then ordain Aaron and his 29.9
sons. Ex 40.15 Num 3.10; 18.7
10 You shall bring the bull in front of the tent of meeting. Aaron and his sons 25.13
shall lay their hands on the head of the bull, 11 and you shall slaughter the bull Deut 18.5 Heb 5.4
before the LORD, at the entrance of the tent of meeting, 12 and shall take some of the 29.10
blood of the bull and put it on the horns of the altar with your finger, and all the rest Lev 1.4; 3.2 8.14
of the blood you shall pour out at the base of the altar. 13 You shall take all the fat 29.12
that covers the entrails, and the appendage of the liver, and the two kidneys with the Ex 27.2
fat that is on them, and turn them into smoke on the altar. 14 But the flesh of the bull, Lev 8.15,16 29.13
and its skin, and its dung, you shall burn with fire outside the camp; it is a sin Lev 3.3-5
offering. 29.14
15 Then you shall take one of the rams, and Aaron and his sons shall lay their Lev 4.11,12,21 Heb 13.11,12
hands on the head of the ram, 16 and you shall slaughter the ram, and shall take its 29.15
blood and dash it against all sides of the altar. 17 Then you shall cut the ram into its Ex 29.10 Lev 1.4
parts, and wash its entrails and its legs, and put them with its parts and its head,
18 and turn the whole ram into smoke on the altar; it is a burnt offering to the LORD; 29.18
it is a pleasing odor, an offering by fire to the LORD. Gen 8.21 Lev 2.2,9; 6.15
19 You shall take the other ram; and Aaron and his sons shall lay their hands on
the head of the ram, 20 and you shall slaughter the ram, and take some of its blood
and put it on the lobe of Aaron's right ear and on the lobes of the right ears of his
sons, and on the thumbs of their right hands, and on the big toes of their right feet,
and dash the rest of the blood against all sides of the altar. 21 Then you shall take 29.21
some of the blood that is on the altar, and some of the anointing oil, and sprinkle it Ex 30.25,31
on Aaron and his vestments and on his sons and his sons' vestments with him; then
he and his vestments shall be holy, as well as his sons and his sons' vestments.
22 You shall also take the fat of the ram, the fat tail, the fat that covers the
entrails, the appendage of the liver, the two kidneys with the fat that is on them, and
the right thigh (for it is a ram of ordination), 23 and one loaf of bread, one cake of 29.23
bread made with oil, and one wafer, out of the basket of unleavened bread that is Lev 8.26
before the LORD; 24 and you shall place all these on the palms of Aaron and on the 29.24
palms of his sons, and raise them as an elevation offering before the LORD. 25 Then Lev 7.30

q Gk: Heb *sashes, Aaron and his sons*

29.1ff Why did God set up the priesthood? God had originally intended that his chosen people be a nation of priests with both the nation as a whole and each individual dealing directly with God. But the people's sin prevented this from happening, because a sinful person is not worthy to approach a perfect God. God then appointed priests from the tribe of Levi and set up the system of sacrifices to help the people approach him. He promised to forgive the people's sins if they would offer certain sacrifices, which the priests administered on behalf of the people. Through these priests and their work, God wished to prepare all people for the coming of Jesus Christ, who would once again offer a direct relationship with God for anyone who would come to him. But until Christ came, the priests were the people's representatives before God. Through this Old Testament system, we can better understand the significance of what Christ did for us (see Hebrews 10.1–14).

29.6 A diadem is a crown.

29.10–41 Why the detailed rituals in connection with these sacrifices? Partly, it was for "quality control." A centralized, standardized form of worship prevented problems of belief which could arise from individuals creating their own worship. Also, it differentiated the Hebrews from the pagan Canaanites they would meet in the promised land. By closely following God's instructions, the Hebrews could not possibly join the Canaanites in their immoral religious practices. Finally, it showed Israel that God was serious about his relationship with them.

you shall take them from their hands, and turn them into smoke on the altar on top of the burnt offering of pleasing odor before the LORD; it is an offering by fire to the LORD.

29.26 Lev 7.31; 8.29 9.21
29.27 Lev 7.31-33 Num 18.11,18 Deut 18.3

26 You shall take the breast of the ram of Aaron's ordination and raise it as an elevation offering before the LORD; and it shall be your portion. 27 You shall consecrate the breast that was raised as an elevation offering and the thigh that was raised as an elevation offering from the ram of ordination, from that which belonged to Aaron and his sons. 28 These things shall be a perpetual ordinance for Aaron and his sons from the Israelites, for this is an offering; and it shall be an offering by the Israelites from their sacrifice of offerings of well-being, their offering to the LORD.

29.29 Num 20.26,28
29.30 Lev 8.35

29 The sacred vestments of Aaron shall be passed on to his sons after him; they shall be anointed in them and ordained in them. 30 The son who is priest in his place shall wear them seven days, when he comes into the tent of meeting to minister in the holy place.

29.33 Lev 22.10 Num 1.51 3.10,38

31 You shall take the ram of ordination, and boil its flesh in a holy place; 32 and Aaron and his sons shall eat the flesh of the ram and the bread that is in the basket, at the entrance of the tent of meeting. 33 They themselves shall eat the food by which atonement is made, to ordain and consecrate them, but no one else shall eat of them, because they are holy. 34 If any of the flesh for the ordination, or of the bread, remains until the morning, then you shall burn the remainder with fire; it shall not be eaten, because it is holy.

29.37 Mt 23.19

35 Thus you shall do to Aaron and to his sons, just as I have commanded you; through seven days you shall ordain them. 36 Also every day you shall offer a bull as a sin offering for atonement. Also you shall offer a sin offering for the altar, when you make atonement for it, and shall anoint it, to consecrate it. 37 Seven days you shall make atonement for the altar, and consecrate it, and the altar shall be most holy; whatever touches the altar shall become holy.

29.38,39 Num 28.3; 29.6 1 Chron 16.40 Ezra 3.3 Dan 12.11
29.41 1 Kgs 29.36 2 Kgs 16.15 Ezra 9.4 Ps 141.2
29.45 Ex 25.8 Rev 21.3
29.46 Ex 20.2 Jer 31.33

38 Now this is what you shall offer on the altar: two lambs a year old regularly each day. 39 One lamb you shall offer in the morning, and the other lamb you shall offer in the evening; 40 and with the first lamb one-tenth of a measure of choice flour mixed with one-fourth of a hin of beaten oil, and one-fourth of a hin of wine for a drink offering. 41 And the other lamb you shall offer in the evening, and shall offer with it a grain offering and its drink offering, as in the morning, for a pleasing odor, an offering by fire to the LORD. 42 It shall be a regular burnt offering throughout your generations at the entrance of the tent of meeting before the LORD, where I will meet with you, to speak to you there. 43 I will meet with the Israelites there, and it shall be sanctified by my glory; 44 I will consecrate the tent of meeting and the altar; Aaron also and his sons I will consecrate, to serve me as priests. 45 I will dwell among the Israelites, and I will be their God. 46 And they shall know that I am the LORD their God, who brought them out of the land of Egypt that I might dwell among them; I am the LORD their God.

The procedures to prepare for worship

30.1 Ex 27.1; 37.25 Lev 4.7 1 Kgs 6.22 Rev 8.3

30 You shall make an altar on which to offer incense; you shall make it of acacia wood. 2 It shall be one cubit long, and one cubit wide; it shall be square, and shall be two cubits high; its horns shall be of one piece with it. 3 You shall overlay it with pure gold, its top, and its sides all around and its horns; and you shall make for it a molding of gold all around. 4 And you shall make two golden

---

29.40 A measure was probably about two quarts (two liters) and a hin was probably about one quart (one liter).

29.45, 46 God's action in bringing the Israelites out of Egypt showed his great desire to be with them and protect them. Throughout the Bible, God shows that he is not an absentee landlord. He wants to live among us, even in our hearts. Don't exclude God from your life. Allow him to be your God as you obey his word and communicate with him in prayer. Let him be your resident landlord.

29.46 Notice the overwhelming emphasis on the holiness of God. The priests, the clothes, the tabernacle, and the sacrifices all had to be clean and consecrated, prepared to come before God. In contrast, today we tend to take God for granted, rushing into worship and treating him often with casual disregard. But we worship the almighty Creator and Sustainer of the Universe. Remembering that profound truth when you pray and worship will help you come before God with reverence and repentence.

rings for it; under its molding on two opposite sides of it you shall make them, and
they shall hold the poles with which to carry it. 5 You shall make the poles of acacia
wood, and overlay them with gold. 6 You shall place it in front of the curtain that
is above the ark of the covenant,[r] in front of the mercy seat[s] that is over the covenant,[r] where I will meet with you. 7 Aaron shall offer fragrant incense on it; every **30.7**
morning when he dresses the lamps he shall offer it, 8 and when Aaron sets up the Ex 27.20; 30.34; 1 Sam 2.28
lamps in the evening, he shall offer it, a regular incense offering before the LORD Lk 1.9
throughout your generations. 9 You shall not offer unholy incense on it, or a burnt
offering, or a grain offering; and you shall not pour a drink offering on it. 10 Once **30.10**
a year Aaron shall perform the rite of atonement on its horns. Throughout your Lev 16.8
generations he shall perform the atonement for it once a year with the blood of the
atoning sin offering. It is most holy to the LORD.

11 The LORD spoke to Moses: 12 When you take a census of the Israelites to **30.11,12**
register them, at registration all of them shall give a ransom for their lives to the Ex 38.25; Num 1.2; 26.2
LORD, so that no plague may come upon them for being registered. 13 This is what 2 Sam 24.1; Mt 20.28
each one who is registered shall give: half a shekel according to the shekel of the 1 Pet 1.18,19
sanctuary (the shekel is twenty gerahs), half a shekel as an offering to the LORD. **30.13**
14 Each one who is registered, from twenty years old and upward, shall give the Mt 17.24
LORD's offering. 15 The rich shall not give more, and the poor shall not give less, **30.15**
than the half shekel, when you bring this offering to the LORD to make atonement Prov 22.2
for your lives. 16 You shall take the atonement money from the Israelites and shall
designate it for the service of the tent of meeting; before the LORD it will be a
reminder to the Israelites of the ransom given for your lives.

17 The LORD spoke to Moses: 18 You shall make a bronze basin with a bronze **30.17**
stand for washing. You shall put it between the tent of meeting and the altar, and Ex 31.9; 38.8; Lev 8.11
you shall put water in it; 19 with the water[t] Aaron and his sons shall wash their **30.19**
hands and their feet. 20 When they go into the tent of meeting, or when they come Ex 40.31
near the altar to minister, to make an offering by fire to the LORD, they shall wash
with water, so that they may not die. 21 They shall wash their hands and their feet, **30.21**
so that they may not die: it shall be a perpetual ordinance for them, for him and for Ex 28.43
his descendants throughout their generations.

22 The LORD spoke to Moses: 23 Take the finest spices: of liquid myrrh five **30.22**
hundred shekels, and of sweet-smelling cinnamon half as much, that is, two hun- Ps 45.8
dred fifty, and two hundred fifty of aromatic cane, 24 and five hundred of
cassia—measured by the sanctuary shekel—and a hin of olive oil; 25 and you shall **30.25**
make of these a sacred anointing oil blended as by the perfumer; it shall be a holy Ex 37.29; 40.9; Lev 8.10
anointing oil. 26 With it you shall anoint the tent of meeting and the ark of the cove- **30.26**
nant,[r] 27 and the table and all its utensils, and the lampstand and its utensils, and Num 7.1
the altar of incense, 28 and the altar of burnt offering with all its utensils, and the
basin with its stand; 29 you shall consecrate them, so that they may be most holy;
whatever touches them will become holy. 30 You shall anoint Aaron and his sons,
and consecrate them, in order that they may serve me as priests. 31 You shall say to
the Israelites, "This shall be my holy anointing oil throughout your generations.
32 It shall not be used in any ordinary anointing of the body, and you shall make no
other like it in composition; it is holy, and it shall be holy to you. 33 Whoever com- **30.33**
pounds any like it or whoever puts any of it on an unqualified person shall be cut off Gen 17.4; Ex 12.15
from the people." Lev 7.20,21

[r] Or *treaty*, or *testimony*; Heb *eduth* [s] Or *the cover* [t] Heb *it*

30.10 This once-a-year ceremony was called the day of atonement. On this day a sacrifice was made for the sins of the entire Israelite nation. This was the only day the high priest could enter the most holy place, the innermost room of the tabernacle. Here he asked God to forgive the people. The day of atonement served as a reminder that the daily, weekly, and monthly sacrifices could cover sins only temporarily. It pointed toward Jesus Christ, the perfect atonement, who could remove sins forever.

30.11–15 Whenever a census took place, everyone, both rich and poor, was required to pay a ransom. God does not discriminate between people (see Acts 10.34; Galatians 3.28). All of us need mercy and forgiveness because of our sinful thoughts and actions. There is no way the rich person can buy off God, and no way the poor can avoid paying. God's demand is that all of us come humbly before him to be forgiven and restored to his family.

30.13 A shekel was about one-fifth of an ounce (6 grams).

34 The LORD said to Moses: Take sweet spices, stacte, and onycha, and galba-
num, sweet spices with pure frankincense (an equal part of each), 35 and make an
incense blended as by the perfumer, seasoned with salt, pure and holy; 36 and you
shall beat some of it into powder, and put part of it before the covenant[u] in the tent
of meeting where I shall meet with you; it shall be for you most holy. 37 When you
make incense according to this composition, you shall not make it for yourselves;
it shall be regarded by you as holy to the LORD. 38 Whoever makes any like it to use
as perfume shall be cut off from the people.

Craftsmen given special skill

31.1 Ex 35.30,36.1 37.1 1 Chron 2.20
31.3 1 Kgs 7.14
31.6 Ex 35.34; 36.1
31.7 Ex 25.9
31.8 Ex 25.31 Lev 24.4

31 The LORD spoke to Moses: 2 See, I have called by name Bezalel son of Uri
son of Hur, of the tribe of Judah: 3 and I have filled him with divine spirit,[v]
with ability, intelligence, and knowledge in every kind of craft, 4 to devise artistic
designs, to work in gold, silver, and bronze, 5 in cutting stones for setting, and in
carving wood, in every kind of craft. 6 Moreover, I have appointed with him Oholiab son of Ahisamach, of the tribe of Dan; and I have given skill to all the skillful,
so that they may make all that I have commanded you: 7 the tent of meeting, and the
ark of the covenant,[u] and the mercy seat[w] that is on it, and all the furnishings of
the tent, 8 the table and its utensils, and the pure lampstand with all its utensils, and
the altar of incense, 9 and the altar of burnt offering with all its utensils, and the basin
with its stand, 10 and the finely worked vestments, the holy vestments for the priest
Aaron and the vestments of his sons, for their service as priests, 11 and the anointing
oil and the fragrant incense for the holy place. They shall do just as I have commanded you.

Resting on the sabbath

31.12 Ex 20.8,12 Lev 19.30; 26.2 Deut 5.12
31.14 Ex 16.23; 35.2 Jn 7.21
31.16 Ex 20.9 Deut 5.13
31.17 Gen 2.2,3 Ex 20.11 Heb 4.4
31.18 Ex 24.12 34.1,28; 32.15

12 The LORD said to Moses: 13 You yourself are to speak to the Israelites: "You
shall keep my sabbaths, for this is a sign between me and you throughout your
generations, given in order that you may know that I, the LORD, sanctify you.
14 You shall keep the sabbath, because it is holy for you; everyone who profanes it
shall be put to death; whoever does any work on it shall be cut off from among the
people. 15 Six days shall work be done, but the seventh day is a sabbath of solemn
rest, holy to the LORD; whoever does any work on the sabbath day shall be put to
death. 16 Therefore the Israelites shall keep the sabbath, observing the sabbath
throughout their generations, as a perpetual covenant. 17 It is a sign forever between
me and the people of Israel that in six days the LORD made heaven and earth, and
on the seventh day he rested, and was refreshed."

18 When God[x] finished speaking with Moses on Mount Sinai, he gave him the
two tablets of the covenant,[m] tablets of stone, written with the finger of God.

[u] Or *treaty*, or *testimony*; Heb *eduth* [v] Or *with the spirit of God* [w] Or *the cover* [x] Heb *he*

30.34–38 The Israelites often burned incense, but only holy incense could be burned in the tabernacle. Here God gives the recipe for this special incense. The sweet-smelling incense burned in shallow dishes called censers and was used to show honor and reverence to God. It was also a vital part of the sacred ceremony on the day of atonement, when the high priest carried his smoking censer into the most holy place. This incense was so holy that the people were strictly forbidden to copy it for personal use.

31.12–17 The sabbath had two purposes: it was a time to rest and a time to remember what God had done. We need rest. Without time out from the bustle, life loses its meaning. In our day as in Moses' day, taking time out is not easy, but God reminds us that without sabbaths we will forget the purpose for our activity and lose the balance crucial to a faithful life. Make sure your sabbath provides a time of both refreshment and remembrance of God.

31.18 The ten commandments were not the only code of laws in the ancient world. Other law codes had come into existence when cities or nations decided that there must be standards of judgment, ways to correct specific wrongs. But God's laws for Israel were unique in that (1) they alleviated the harsh judgments typical of the day; (2) they were egalitarian – the poor and the powerful received the same punishment; and (3) they did not separate religious and social law. All law rested on God's authority.

3. Breaking the law

The golden calf

32 When the people saw that Moses delayed to come down from the mountain,
the people gathered around Aaron, and said to him, "Come, make gods for
us, who shall go before us; as for this Moses, the man who brought us up out of the
land of Egypt, we do not know what has become of him." 2 Aaron said to them,
"Take off the gold rings that are on the ears of your wives, your sons, and your
daughters, and bring them to me." 3 So all the people took off the gold rings from
their ears, and brought them to Aaron. 4 He took the gold from them, formed it in
a mold,[y] and cast an image of a calf; and they said, "These are your gods, O Israel,
who brought you up out of the land of Egypt!" 5 When Aaron saw this, he built an
altar before it; and Aaron made proclamation and said, "Tomorrow shall be a festival to the LORD." 6 They rose early the next day, and offered burnt offerings and
brought sacrifices of well-being; and the people sat down to eat and drink, and rose
up to revel.

7 The LORD said to Moses, "Go down at once! Your people, whom you brought
up out of the land of Egypt, have acted perversely; 8 they have been quick to turn
aside from the way that I commanded them; they have cast for themselves an image
of a calf, and have worshiped it and sacrificed to it, and said, 'These are your gods,
O Israel, who brought you up out of the land of Egypt!' " 9 The LORD said to Moses, "I have seen this people, how stiff-necked they are. 10 Now let me alone, so
that my wrath may burn hot against them and I may consume them; and of you I
will make a great nation."

11 But Moses implored the LORD his God, and said, "O LORD, why does your
wrath burn hot against your people, whom you brought out of the land of Egypt
with great power and with a mighty hand? 12 Why should the Egyptians say, 'It was
with evil intent that he brought them out to kill them in the mountains, and to consume them from the face of the earth'? Turn from your fierce wrath; change your
mind and do not bring disaster on your people. 13 Remember Abraham, Isaac, and
Israel, your servants, how you swore to them by your own self, saying to them, 'I
will multiply your descendants like the stars of heaven, and all this land that I have
promised I will give to your descendants, and they shall inherit it forever.' " 14 And
the LORD changed his mind about the disaster that he planned to bring on his people.

15 Then Moses turned and went down from the mountain, carrying the two
tablets of the covenant[z] in his hands, tablets that were written on both sides, writ-

32.1 Ex 24.18 Deut 9.10 Acts 7.40
32.2 Ex 12.35; 35.22
32.4 Ex 20.23 Deut 9.16 Ps 106.19 Acts 7.41
32.5 Hos 8.11
32.6 Num 25.2 Acts 7.41 1 Cor 10.7
32.7 Ex 19.24; 33.1 Deut 9.12
32.8 Ex 22.20; 34.15 Deut 32.17
32.9 Ex 33.5 Num 14.11 Acts 7.42,51
32.10 Gen 18.32 Deut 9.13,14
32.11 Num 14.17-19 Deut 9.18,26 Ps 106.23
32.12 Deut 9.28 Josh 7.9
32.13 Gen 15.5 22.16-18 Ex 13.5,11 Lev 26.42
32.14 Gen 6.5,6 1 Sam 15.35 2 Sam 24.16
32.15 Ex 24.18 Deut 9.15

[y] Or *fashioned it with a graving tool*; Meaning of Heb uncertain [z] Or *treaty*, or *testimony*; Heb *eduth*

32.1–10 Idols again! Even though Israel had seen the invisible God in action, they still wanted the familiar gods they could see and shape into whatever image they desired. How much like them we are! Our great temptation is still to shape God to our liking, to make him convenient to obey or ignore. God responds in great anger when his mercy is trampled on. The gods we create blind us to the love the loving God wants to shower on us. God cannot work in us when we elevate anyone or anything above him. Are any false gods in your life preventing the true God from living in you?

32.4, 5 Two popular Egyptian gods, Hapi and Hathor, were thought of as a bull and a heifer. The Canaanites around them worshiped Baal, thought of as a bull. Baal was their sacred symbol of power and fertility and was closely connected to immoral sexual practices. No doubt the Israelites, fresh from Egypt, found it quite natural to make a golden calf to represent the God that had just delivered them from their oppressors. They were weary of a god without a face. But in doing so, they were ignoring the command he had just given them: "You shall not make for yourself an idol" (20.4). They may even have thought they were worshiping God. Their apparent sincerity was no substitute for obedience.

Even if we do not make idols, we are often guilty of trying to make God in our image, molding him to fit our expectations, desires, and circumstances. When we do this, we end up worshiping ourselves rather than the God who created us—and self worship, today as in the Israelites' time, leads to all kinds of immorality. What is your favorite image of God? Is it biblical? Is it adequate? Do you need to destroy it in order to worship the immeasurably powerful God who delivered you from bondage to sin?

32.9–14 God was ready to destroy the whole nation because of their sin. But Moses pleaded for mercy, and God spared them. This is one of the countless examples in the Bible of God's mercy. Although we deserve his anger, he is willing to forgive and restore us to himself. We can receive God's forgiveness from sin by asking him. Like Moses, we can pray that he will forgive others as well, and use us to bring them the message of his mercy.

32.14 How could God change his mind? God did not change his mind in the same way that a parent decides not to discipline a child. Instead, God changed his behavior to remain consistent with his nature. When God first wanted to destroy the people, he was acting consistently with his justice. When Moses interceded for the people, God "changed" in order to act consistently with his mercy. God had often told the people that if they changed their ways he would not condemn them. They changed, and God did as he promised.

32.16 Ex 31.18; 34.1 Deut 9.9 ten on the front and on the back. 16 The tablets were the work of God, and the
writing was the writing of God, engraved upon the tablets. 17 When Joshua heard
the noise of the people as they shouted, he said to Moses, "There is a noise of war
in the camp." 18 But he said,

"It is not the sound made by victors,
or the sound made by losers;
it is the sound of revelers that I hear."

32.19 Ex 32.6 Deut 9.16,17 19 As soon as he came near the camp and saw the calf and the dancing, Moses' anger
burned hot, and he threw the tablets from his hands and broke them at the foot of
32.20 Deut 9.21 the mountain. 20 He took the calf that they had made, burned it with fire, ground it
to powder, scattered it on the water, and made the Israelites drink it.

21 Moses said to Aaron, "What did this people do to you that you have brought
32.22 Deut 9.6,24 31.27 so great a sin upon them?" 22 And Aaron said, "Do not let the anger of my lord burn
hot; you know the people, that they are bent on evil. 23 They said to me, 'Make us
32.23 Ex 32.1 gods, who shall go before us; as for this Moses, the man who brought us up out of
the land of Egypt, we do not know what has become of him.' 24 So I said to them,
'Whoever has gold, take it off'; so they gave it to me, and I threw it into the fire,
and out came this calf!"

32.25 1 Kgs 12.25 25 When Moses saw that the people were running wild (for Aaron had let them

AARON

Effective teamwork happens when each team member uses his or her special skills. Ideally, each member's strengths will contribute something important to the team effort. In this way, members make up for one another's weaknesses. Aaron made a good team with Moses. He provided Moses with one skill he lacked—effective public speaking. But while Aaron was necessary to Moses, he needed Moses as well. Without a guide, Aaron had little direction of his own. There was never any doubt as to who God's chosen and trained leader was. The pliability that made Aaron a good follower made him a weak leader. His major failures were caused by his inability to stand alone. His yielding to public pressure and making an idol was a good example of this weakness.

Most of us have more of the follower than the leader in us. We may even be good followers, following a good leader. But no leader is perfect, and no human deserves our complete allegiance. Only God deserves our complete loyalty and obedience. We need to be effective team members in using the skills and abilities God has given us. But if the team or the leader goes against God's Word, we must be willing to stand alone.

Strengths and accomplishments:
- First high priest of God in Israel
- Effective communicator; Moses' mouthpiece

Weaknesses and mistakes:
- Pliable personality; gave in to people's demands for a golden calf
- Joined with Moses in disobeying God's orders about the water-giving rock
- Joined sister Miriam in complaining against Moses

Lessons from his life:
- God gives individuals special abilities, which he weaves together for his use
- The very skills that make a good team player sometimes also make a poor leader

Vital statistics:
- Where: Egypt, Sinai peninsula
- Occupation: Priest; Moses' second in command
- Relatives: Brother: Moses. Sister: Miriam. Sons: Nadab, Abihu, Eleazar, and Ithamar

Key verses:
"Then the anger of the Lord was kindled against Moses and he said, 'What of your brother Aaron, the Levite? I know that he can speak fluently; even now he is coming out to meet you, and when he sees you his heart will be glad. . . . He indeed shall speak for you to the people' " (Exodus 4.14, 16).

Aaron's story is told in Exodus—Deuteronomy 10.6. He is also mentioned in Hebrews 7.11.

32.19–20 Overwhelmed by the sight of the blatant idolatry and revelry, Moses broke the tablets containing the commandments which had already been broken by the people. But however angry Moses might have been, God was angrier still. He wanted to destroy the people and start over again. There is a place for righteous anger. Anger at sin is a sign of spiritual vitality. Don't squelch this kind of anger. But when you are experiencing this kind of anger be careful not to let it get out of control to where you will do something you might regret later.

run wild, to the derision of their enemies), 26 then Moses stood in the gate of the **32.26**
camp, and said, "Who is on the LORD's side? Come to me!" And all the sons of 2 Sam 20.11
Levi gathered around him. 27 He said to them, "Thus says the LORD, the God of **32.27**
Israel, 'Put your sword on your side, each of you! Go back and forth from gate to Num 25.5
gate throughout the camp, and each of you kill your brother, your friend, and your
neighbor.' " 28 The sons of Levi did as Moses commanded, and about three thou- **32.28**
sand of the people fell on that day. 29 Moses said, "Today you have ordained your- Num 16.32; 25.9
selves[a] for the service of the LORD, each one at the cost of a son or a brother, and **32.29** Deut 13.6; 33.9
so have brought a blessing on yourselves this day."

Moses pleads for the people

30 On the next day Moses said to the people, "You have sinned a great sin. But **32.31**
now I will go up to the LORD; perhaps I can make atonement for your sin." 31 So Ex 20.23
Moses returned to the LORD and said, "Alas, this people has sinned a great sin; they **32.32**
have made for themselves gods of gold. 32 But now, if you will only forgive their Deut 9.14 Isa 4.3
sin—but if not, blot me out of the book that you have written." 33 But the LORD said Dan 12.1 Mal 3.16
to Moses, "Whoever has sinned against me I will blot out of my book. 34 But now Rev 3.5
go, lead the people to the place about which I have spoken to you; see, my angel **32.33** Deut 29.20
shall go in front of you. Nevertheless, when the day comes for punishment, I will Ps 9.5; 69.28 Ezek 18.4
punish them for their sin." **32.34**

35 Then the LORD sent a plague on the people, because they made the calf—the Ex 3.17; 23.20 33.2
one that Aaron made. Num 20.16

The people mourn

33 The LORD said to Moses, "Go, leave this place, you and the people whom **33.1**
you have brought up out of the land of Egypt, and go to the land of which I Gen 12.7; 22.16 Ex 32.13,34
swore to Abraham, Isaac, and Jacob, saying, 'To your descendants I will give it.'
2 I will send an angel before you, and I will drive out the Canaanites, the Amorites, **33.2**
the Hittites, the Perizzites, the Hivites, and the Jebusites. 3 Go up to a land flowing Ex 23.23,27
with milk and honey; but I will not go up among you, or I would consume you on **33.3** Ex 3.8; 13.5
the way, for you are a stiff-necked people." 32.9,10,14

4 When the people heard these harsh words, they mourned, and no one put on **33.4**
ornaments. 5 For the LORD had said to Moses, "Say to the Israelites, 'You are a Num 14.1,3,9
stiff-necked people; if for a single moment I should go up among you, I would **33.5** Num 16.45
consume you. So now take off your ornaments, and I will decide what to do to
you.' " 6 Therefore the Israelites stripped themselves of their ornaments, from
Mount Horeb onward.

The tent of meeting

7 Now Moses used to take the tent and pitch it outside the camp, far off from the **33.7**
camp; he called it the tent of meeting. And everyone who sought the LORD would Ex 18.26; 29.43
go out to the tent of meeting, which was outside the camp. 8 Whenever Moses went **33.8**
out to the tent, all the people would rise and stand, each of them, at the entrance of Num 16.27
their tents and watch Moses until he had gone into the tent. 9 When Moses entered **33.9**
the tent, the pillar of cloud would descend and stand at the entrance of the tent, and Ex 13.21; 19.9 25.22
the LORD would speak with Moses. 10 When all the people saw the pillar of cloud Ps 99.7
standing at the entrance of the tent, all the people would rise and bow down, all of
them, at the entrance of their tent. 11 Thus the LORD used to speak to Moses face to **33.11**
face, as one speaks to a friend. Then he would return to the camp; but his young Gen 32.30 Num 12.8
assistant, Joshua son of Nun, would not leave the tent. Deut 34.10

[a] Gk Vg Compare Tg: Heb *Today ordain yourselves*

33.5, 6 This ban on jewelry was not permanent, but a temporary sign of repentance and mourning. In 35.22 we read that the people still had their jewelry.

33.11 God and Moses talked back and forth with each other, just as friends do. Why did Moses find such favor with God? It certainly was not because he was perfect, gifted, or powerful. Rather, it was because God chose Moses, and Moses in turn relied wholeheartedly on God's wisdom and direction. Friendship with God was a true privilege for Moses, out of reach for the other Hebrews. But it is not out of reach for us today. Jesus called his disciples—and, by extension, all of his followers—his friends (John 15.15). He has called you to be his friend. Will you trust him as Moses did?

Moses asks to see God

33.12 Ex 3.10; 32.34
33.13 Ex 3.10; 5.1 Ps 25.4; 27.11
33.14 Ex 13.21 Josh 22.4 Isa 63.9
33.15 Ps 80.3,7,19
33.16 Ex 8.22 Lev 20.24,26 Num 14.14

12 Moses said to the LORD, "See, you have said to me, 'Bring up this people';
but you have not let me know whom you will send with me. Yet you have said, 'I
know you by name, and you have also found favor in my sight.' 13 Now if I have
found favor in your sight, show me your ways, so that I may know you and find
favor in your sight. Consider too that this nation is your people." 14 He said, "My
presence will go with you, and I will give you rest." 15 And he said to him, "If your
presence will not go, do not carry us up from here. 16 For how shall it be known that
I have found favor in your sight, I and your people, unless you go with us? In this
way, we shall be distinct, I and your people, from every people on the face of the
earth."

33.17 Gen 19.21 Ex 33.12
33.18 2 Cor 3.18
33.20 Ex 24.10 Isa 6.5 Jn 1.18 1 Tim 6.16
33.22 Ps 18.2 Isa 2.21; 49.2 51.16

17 The LORD said to Moses, "I will do the very thing that you have asked; for
you have found favor in my sight, and I know you by name." 18 Moses said, "Show
me your glory, I pray." 19 And he said, "I will make all my goodness pass before
you, and will proclaim before you the name, 'The LORD';[b] and I will be gracious
to whom I will be gracious, and will show mercy on whom I will show mercy.
20 But," he said, "you cannot see my face; for no one shall see me and live." 21 And
the LORD continued, "See, there is a place by me where you shall stand on the rock;
22 and while my glory passes by I will put you in a cleft of the rock, and I will cover
you with my hand until I have passed by; 23 then I will take away my hand, and you
shall see my back; but my face shall not be seen."

The ten commandments written again

34.1 Ex 24.12; 31.18 Deut 10.1
34.3 Ex 19.12 Lev 16.17
34.5,6 Ex 19.9; 33.9 Num 14.17,18 Neh 9.17 Ps 86.15; 103.8

34 The LORD said to Moses, "Cut two tablets of stone like the former ones, and
I will write on the tablets the words that were on the former tablets, which
you broke. 2 Be ready in the morning, and come up in the morning to Mount Sinai
and present yourself there to me, on the top of the mountain. 3 No one shall come
up with you, and do not let anyone be seen throughout all the mountain; and do not
let flocks or herds graze in front of that mountain." 4 So Moses cut two tablets of
stone like the former ones; and he rose early in the morning and went up on Mount
Sinai, as the LORD had commanded him, and took in his hand the two tablets of
stone. 5 The LORD descended in the cloud and stood with him there, and proclaimed
the name, "The LORD."[b] 6 The LORD passed before him, and proclaimed,

"The LORD, the LORD,
a God merciful and gracious,
slow to anger,
and abounding in steadfast love and faithfulness,
7 keeping steadfast love for the thousandth generation,[c]
forgiving iniquity and transgression and sin,
yet by no means clearing the guilty,
but visiting the iniquity of the parents
upon the children
and the children's children,
to the third and the fourth generation."

34.7 Ex 20.5,6; 23.7 Deut 5.10 Neh 1.5
34.9 Num 14.19 Deut 4.20; 32.9 Ps 25.11

8 And Moses quickly bowed his head toward the earth, and worshiped. 9 He said, "If
now I have found favor in your sight, O Lord, I pray, let the Lord go with us,

[b] Heb *YHWH*; see note at 3.15 [c] Or *for thousands*

33.23 Moses' prayer was to see the manifest glory of God. Because we are finite and morally imperfect, we cannot exist and see God as he is. To see God's "back" means we can only see where God has passed by. We can only know him by what he does and how he acts. We cannot comprehend God as he really is apart from Jesus Christ (John 14.9).

34.6, 7 Moses had asked to see God's glory (33.18), and this was God's response. What is God's glory? It is his character, his nature, his way of relating to his creatures. Notice that God did not give Moses a vision of his power and majesty, but rather of his love. God's glory is revealed in his mercy, grace, longsuffering, goodness, truth, forgiveness, justice. God's love and mercy are truly wonderful and we benefit from them.

34.7 Why would sins affect grandchildren and great-grandchildren? This is no arbitrary punishment. Children still suffer for the sins of their parents. Consider child abuse or alcoholism, for example. While these sins are obvious, sins like selfishness and greed can be passed along as well. The dire consequences of sin are not limited to the individual family member. Be careful not to treat sin casually, but repent and turn from it.

Although this is a stiff-necked people, pardon our iniquity and our sin, and take us
for your inheritance."
10 He said: I hereby make a covenant. Before all your people I will perform
marvels, such as have not been performed in all the earth or in any nation; and all
the people among whom you live shall see the work of the LORD; for it is an awesome thing that I will do with you.
11 Observe what I command you today. See, I will drive out before you the
Amorites, the Canaanites, the Hittites, the Perizzites, the Hivites, and the Jebusites. 12 Take care not to make a covenant with the inhabitants of the land to which
you are going, or it will become a snare among you. 13 You shall tear down their
altars, break their pillars, and cut down their sacred poles[d] 14 (for you shall worship
no other god, because the LORD, whose name is Jealous, is a jealous God). 15 You
shall not make a covenant with the inhabitants of the land, for when they prostitute
themselves to their gods and sacrifice to their gods, someone among them will
invite you, and you will eat of the sacrifice. 16 And you will take wives from among
their daughters for your sons, and their daughters who prostitute themselves to their
gods will make your sons also prostitute themselves to their gods.
17 You shall not make cast idols.
18 You shall keep the festival of unleavened bread. Seven days you shall eat
unleavened bread, as I commanded you, at the time appointed in the month of
Abib; for in the month of Abib you came out from Egypt.
19 All that first opens the womb is mine, all your male[e] livestock, the firstborn
of cow and sheep. 20 The firstborn of a donkey you shall redeem with a lamb, or if
you will not redeem it you shall break its neck. All the firstborn of your sons you
shall redeem.
No one shall appear before me empty-handed.
21 Six days you shall work, but on the seventh day you shall rest; even in plowing time and in harvest time you shall rest. 22 You shall observe the festival of
weeks, the first fruits of wheat harvest, and the festival of ingathering at the turn of
the year. 23 Three times in the year all your males shall appear before the LORD
God, the God of Israel. 24 For I will cast out nations before you, and enlarge your
borders; no one shall covet your land when you go up to appear before the LORD
your God three times in the year.
25 You shall not offer the blood of my sacrifice with leaven, and the sacrifice
of the festival of the passover shall not be left until the morning.
26 The best of the first fruits of your ground you shall bring to the house of the
LORD your God.
You shall not boil a kid in its mother's milk.
27 The LORD said to Moses: Write these words; in accordance with these words
I have made a covenant with you and with Israel. 28 He was there with the LORD
forty days and forty nights; he neither ate bread nor drank water. And he wrote on
the tablets the words of the covenant, the ten commandments.[f]
29 Moses came down from Mount Sinai. As he came down from the mountain
with the two tablets of the covenant[g] in his hand, Moses did not know that the skin
of his face shone because he had been talking with God. 30 When Aaron and all
the Israelites saw Moses, the skin of his face was shining, and they were afraid to
come near him. 31 But Moses called to them; and Aaron and all the leaders of the

34.10 Ex 8.10 Deut 4.35 Ps 72.18; 136.4
34.11 Ex 33.2 Deut 4.1,40; 6.3
34.12 Ex 23.32,33 Deut 7.1-4
34.13 Ex 23.24 Deut 7.5; 12.2 16.21 2 Chron 34.4
34.14 Ex 20.3,4 Deut 4.24
34.15 Num 25.1,2 Deut 31.16
34.16 Deut 7.3 Josh 23.12
34.17 Lev 19.3,4 Deut 29.17
34.18 Ex 12.2,15,17 23.15 Deut 16.1
34.19 Ex 13.2 22.29,30
34.20 Ex 13.13 Num 3.45 Lk 2.23
34.21 Ex 20.8; 31.15 35.2
34.22 Ex 23.16 Lev 23.4
34.23 Ex 23.14-17 Deut 16.16
34.24 Ex 23.27; 33.2
34.25 Ex 12.10,20 23.18 Lev 2.11
34.26 Ex 23.19 Deut 26.2
34.27 Ex 17.14; 24.4 Deut 1.5; 31.9
34.28 Ex 24.18 Deut 4.13; 10.4
34.29 Ex 32.15 Mt 17.2 Acts 6.15 2 Cor 3.7

[d] Heb *Asherim* [e] Gk Theodotion Vg Tg: Meaning of Heb uncertain [f] Heb *words* [g] Or *treaty*, or *testimony*; Heb *eduth*

34.12–14 God told the Israelites not to join in religious rites with the sinful people around them, but to give their absolute loyalty and exclusive devotion to him. Heathen worship simply cannot be mixed with the worship of the holy God. As Jesus pointed out, "No one can be the slave of two masters. . . . You cannot be the slave of both God and wealth" (Luke 16.13). The love of money is the god of this age, and many Christians attempt to "make a covenant" with this enslaving god. Are you trying to worship two gods at once? Where is your first allegiance? Do you need to break any "pillars" or cut down any "poles"?

34.28–35 Moses' face actually glowed after he spent time with God. The people could clearly see God's presence in him. How often do you spend time alone with God? Time spent in prayer, reading the Bible, and meditating should have such an effect on your life that people will know you have been with God.

34.31 Ex 4.29; 24.1 congregation returned to him, and Moses spoke with them. 32 Afterward all the Israelites came near, and he gave them in commandment all that the LORD had spoken
34.33 2 Cor 3.13 with him on Mount Sinai. 33 When Moses had finished speaking with them, he put
34.34 2 Cor 3.16 a veil on his face; 34 but whenever Moses went in before the LORD to speak with him,
he would take the veil off, until he came out; and when he came out, and told the
Israelites what he had been commanded, 35 the Israelites would see the face of Moses, that the skin of his face was shining; and Moses would put the veil on his face
again, until he went in to speak with him.

4. Tabernacle construction

Work prohibited on the sabbath

35.1 Ex 25.1; 34.32 **35** Moses assembled all the congregation of the Israelites and said to them:
These are the things that the LORD has commanded you to do:
35.2 Ex 16.23; 20.8; 23.12; 34.21; Num 15.32; Deut 5.13,14 2 Six days shall work be done, but on the seventh day you shall have a holy
sabbath of solemn rest to the LORD; whoever does any work on it shall be put to
death. 3 You shall kindle no fire in all your dwellings on the sabbath day.

Gathering the material

4 Moses said to all the congregation of the Israelites: This is the thing that the
35.5-9 Ex 25.1-7 LORD has commanded: 5 Take from among you an offering to the LORD; let whoever is of a generous heart bring the LORD's offering: gold, silver, and bronze;
6 blue, purple, and crimson yarns, and fine linen; goats' hair, 7 tanned rams' skins,
and fine leather;[h] acacia wood, 8 oil for the light, spices for the anointing oil and for
the fragrant incense, 9 and onyx stones and gems to be set in the ephod and the
breastpiece.
35.10-19 Ex 39.32-41 10 All who are skillful among you shall come and make all that the LORD has
commanded: the tabernacle, 11 its tent and its covering, its clasps and its frames, its
bars, its pillars, and its bases; 12 the ark with its poles, the mercy seat,[i] and the
curtain for the screen; 13 the table with its poles and all its utensils, and the bread of
the Presence; 14 the lampstand also for the light, with its utensils and its lamps, and
the oil for the light; 15 and the altar of incense, with its poles, and the anointing oil
and the fragrant incense, and the screen for the entrance, the entrance of the tabernacle; 16 the altar of burnt offering, with its grating of bronze, its poles, and all its
utensils, the basin with its stand; 17 the hangings of the court, its pillars and its
bases, and the screen for the gate of the court; 18 the pegs of the tabernacle and the
pegs of the court, and their cords; 19 the finely worked vestments for ministering in
the holy place, the holy vestments for the priest Aaron, and the vestments of his
sons, for their service as priests.
20 Then all the congregation of the Israelites withdrew from the presence of
35.21 Ex 25.2; 35.5 Moses. 21 And they came, everyone whose heart was stirred, and everyone whose
spirit was willing, and brought the LORD's offering to be used for the tent of meeting, and for all its service, and for the sacred vestments. 22 So they came, both men
and women; all who were of a willing heart brought brooches and earrings and
signet rings and pendants, all sorts of gold objects, everyone bringing an offering

[h] Meaning of Heb uncertain [i] Or *the cover*

35.5–21 God did not require these special offerings, but he appealed to those with generous hearts. Only those who were willing to give were invited to participate. God loves cheerful givers (2 Corinthians 9.7). Our giving should be from a generous heart, not a guilty conscience.

35.10–19 Moses asked people with various abilities to help with the tabernacle. Every one of God's people has been given special abilities. We are responsible to develop these abilities – even the ones not considered "religious" – and to use them for God's glory. We can become skilled through study, by watching others, and through practice. Work on your skills or abilities that could help your church or community.

35.20–24 Where did the Israelites, who were once Egyptian slaves, get all this gold and jewelry? When the Hebrews left Egypt, they took with them the spoils from the land – all the booty they could carry (12.35, 36). This included gold, silver, jewels, linen, skins, and other valuables.

35.21 Those whose hearts were stirred gave cheerfully to the tabernacle. With great enthusiasm they gave because they knew how important their giving was to the completion of God's house. Airline pilots and computer operators can push test buttons to see if their equipment is functioning properly. God has a quick test button he can push to see the level of our commitment – our pocketbooks. Generous people aren't necessarily faithful to God. But faithful people are always generous.

of gold to the LORD. 23 And everyone who possessed blue or purple or crimson yarn
or fine linen or goats' hair or tanned rams' skins or fine leather,[j] brought them.
24 Everyone who could make an offering of silver or bronze brought it as the LORD's
offering; and everyone who possessed acacia wood of any use in the work, brought
it. 25 All the skillful women spun with their hands, and brought what they had spun
in blue and purple and crimson yarns and fine linen; 26 all the women whose hearts
moved them to use their skill spun the goats' hair. 27 And the leaders brought onyx
stones and gems to be set in the ephod and the breastpiece, 28 and spices and oil for
the light, and for the anointing oil, and for the fragrant incense. 29 All the Israelite
men and women whose hearts made them willing to bring anything for the work
that the LORD had commanded by Moses to be done, brought it as a freewill offering to the LORD.

30 Then Moses said to the Israelites: See, the LORD has called by name Bezalel
son of Uri son of Hur, of the tribe of Judah; 31 he has filled him with divine spirit,[k]
with skill, intelligence, and knowledge in every kind of craft, 32 to devise artistic
designs, to work in gold, silver, and bronze, 33 in cutting stones for setting, and in
carving wood, in every kind of craft. 34 And he has inspired him to teach, both him
and Oholiab son of Ahisamach, of the tribe of Dan. 35 He has filled them with skill
to do every kind of work done by an artisan or by a designer or by an embroiderer
in blue, purple, and crimson yarns, and in fine linen, or by a weaver—by any sort
of artisan or skilled designer.

36 Bezalel and Oholiab and every skillful one to whom the LORD has given skill
and understanding to know how to do any work in the construction of the
sanctuary shall work in accordance with all that the LORD has commanded.

2 Moses then called Bezalel and Oholiab and every skillful one to whom the
LORD had given skill, everyone whose heart was stirred to come to do the work;
3 and they received from Moses all the freewill offerings that the Israelites had
brought for doing the work on the sanctuary. They still kept bringing him freewill
offerings every morning, 4 so that all the artisans who were doing every sort of task
on the sanctuary came, each from the task being performed, 5 and said to Moses,
"The people are bringing much more than enough for doing the work that the LORD
has commanded us to do." 6 So Moses gave command, and word was proclaimed
throughout the camp: "No man or woman is to make anything else as an offering for
the sanctuary." So the people were restrained from bringing; 7 for what they had
already brought was more than enough to do all the work.

Building the tabernacle

8 All those with skill among the workers made the tabernacle with ten curtains;
they were made of fine twisted linen, and blue, purple, and crimson yarns, with
cherubim skillfully worked into them. 9 The length of each curtain was twenty-
eight cubits, and the width of each curtain four cubits; all the curtains were of the
same size.

10 He joined five curtains to one another, and the other five curtains he joined
to one another. 11 He made loops of blue on the edge of the outermost curtain of the
first set; likewise he made them on the edge of the outermost curtain of the second
set; 12 he made fifty loops on the one curtain, and he made fifty loops on the edge
of the curtain that was in the second set; the loops were opposite one another.
13 And he made fifty clasps of gold, and joined the curtains one to the other with
clasps; so the tabernacle was one whole.

[j] Meaning of Heb uncertain [k] Or *the spirit of God*

35.25 Ex 28.3; 31.6; 36.1
35.27 1 Chron 29.6; Ezra 2.68
35.29 1 Chron 29.9
35.30,31 Ex 31.1; 38.22; 1 Chron 2.20; 1 Cor 3.10
35.32 1 Kgs 7.13; 2 Chron 2.14
35.35 Ex 31.3; 1 Kgs 3.12; 7.13; 2 Chron 2.14; Isa 28.26
36.2 1 Chron 29.5
36.5 2 Chron 31.10; 2 Cor 8.2,3
36.7 1 Kgs 8.64
36.8-38 Ex 26.1-37

35.26 Those who sewed and spun cloth made a beautiful contribution to the tabernacle. Good workers take pride in the quality and beauty of their work. God is concerned with the quality and beauty of what you do. Whether you are a corporate executive or a drug store cashier, your work should reflect the creative abilities God has given you.

36.8, 9 Making cloth (spinning and weaving) took a great deal of time in Moses' day. To own more than two or three changes of clothes was a sign of wealth. The effort involved in making enough cloth for the tabernacle was staggering. The tabernacle would never have been built without tremendous community involvement. Churches and neighborhoods today often require this same kind of pulling together. Without it, many essential services wouldn't get done.

36.14 Ex 26.7; 35.26

14 He also made curtains of goats' hair for a tent over the tabernacle; he made
eleven curtains. 15 The length of each curtain was thirty cubits, and the width of
each curtain four cubits; the eleven curtains were of the same size. 16 He joined five
curtains by themselves, and six curtains by themselves. 17 He made fifty loops on
the edge of the outermost curtain of the one set, and fifty loops on the edge of the
other connecting curtain. 18 He made fifty clasps of bronze to join the tent together
so that it might be one whole. 19 And he made for the tent a covering of tanned
rams' skins and an outer covering of fine leather.[l]

36.20-34 Ex 26.15-29 40.18,19 Num 4.31

20 Then he made the upright frames for the tabernacle of acacia wood. 21 Ten
cubits was the length of a frame, and a cubit and a half the width of each frame.
22 Each frame had two pegs for fitting together; he did this for all the frames of the
tabernacle. 23 The frames for the tabernacle he made in this way: twenty frames for
the south side; 24 and he made forty bases of silver under the twenty frames, two
bases under the first frame for its two pegs, and two bases under the next frame for
its two pegs. 25 For the second side of the tabernacle, on the north side, he made
twenty frames 26 and their forty bases of silver, two bases under the first frame and
two bases under the next frame. 27 For the rear of the tabernacle westward he made
six frames. 28 He made two frames for corners of the tabernacle in the rear. 29 They
were separate beneath, but joined at the top, at the first ring; he made two of them

[l] Meaning of Heb uncertain

KEY TABERNACLE PIECES

Name	*Function and Significance*
Ark of the Covenant	• A golden rectangular box that contained the ten commandments • Symbolized God's covenant with Israel's people • Located in the most holy place
Mercy Seat	• The lid to the ark of the covenant • Symbolized the presence of God among his people
Curtain	• The curtain that divided the two sacred rooms of the tabernacle—the holy place and the most holy place • Symbolized how the people were separated from God because of sin
Table of Showbread	• A wooden table located in the holy place of the tabernacle. The bread of the Presence and various utensils were kept on this table
Bread of the Presence	• Twelve loaves of baked bread, one for each tribe of Israel • Symbolized the spiritual nourishment God offers his people
Lampholders and Lamps	• A golden lampstand located in the holy place, which held seven burning oil lamps • The lampstand lighted the holy place for the priests
Incense Altar	• An altar in the holy place in front of the curtain • Used for burning God's special incense and symbolic of acceptable prayer
Anointing Oil	• A special oil used to anoint the priests and all the pieces in the tabernacle • A sign of being set apart for God
Altar for the Burnt Offerings	• The bronze altar outside the tabernacle used for the sacrifices • Symbolized how sacrifice restored one's relationship with God
Basin (Laver) (or Bason)	• A large wash basin outside the tabernacle used by the priests to cleanse themselves before performing their duties • Symbolized the need for spiritual cleansing

in this way, for the two corners. 30 There were eight frames with their bases of silver: sixteen bases, under every frame two bases.

31 He made bars of acacia wood, five for the frames of the one side of the tabernacle, 32 and five bars for the frames of the other side of the tabernacle, and five bars for the frames of the tabernacle at the rear westward. 33 He made the middle bar to pass through from end to end halfway up the frames. 34 And he overlaid the frames with gold, and made rings of gold for them to hold the bars, and overlaid the bars with gold.

36.35-38 Ex 26.31-37 40.3 Lev 16.2

35 He made the curtain of blue, purple, and crimson yarns, and fine twisted linen, with cherubim skillfully worked into it. 36 For it he made four pillars of acacia, and overlaid them with gold; their hooks were of gold, and he cast for them four bases of silver. 37 He also made a screen for the entrance to the tent, of blue, purple, and crimson yarns, and fine twisted linen, embroidered with needlework; 38 and its five pillars with their hooks. He overlaid their capitals and their bases with gold, but their five bases were of bronze.

Building the ark

37.1-9 Ex 25.10-20 26.33 Deut 10.3

37 Bezalel made the ark of acacia wood; it was two and a half cubits long, a cubit and a half wide, and a cubit and a half high. 2 He overlaid it with pure gold inside and outside, and made a molding of gold around it. 3 He cast for it four rings of gold for its four feet, two rings on its one side and two rings on its other side. 4 He made poles of acacia wood, and overlaid them with gold, 5 and put the poles into the rings on the sides of the ark, to carry the ark. 6 He made a mercy seat[m] of pure gold; two cubits and a half was its length, and a cubit and a half its width. 7 He made two cherubim of hammered gold; at the two ends of the mercy seat[n] he made them, 8 one cherub at the one end, and one cherub at the other end; of one piece with the mercy seat[n] he made the cherubim at its two ends. 9 The cherubim spread out their wings above, overshadowing the mercy seat[n] with their wings. They faced one another; the faces of the cherubim were turned toward the mercy seat.[n]

37.10-16 Ex 25.23-29 40.22

10 He also made the table of acacia wood, two cubits long, one cubit wide, and a cubit and a half high. 11 He overlaid it with pure gold, and made a molding of gold around it. 12 He made around it a rim a handbreadth wide, and made a molding of gold around the rim. 13 He cast for it four rings of gold, and fastened the rings to the four corners at its four legs. 14 The rings that held the poles used for carrying the table were close to the rim. 15 He made the poles of acacia wood to carry the table, and overlaid them with gold. 16 And he made the vessels of pure gold that were to be on the table, its plates and dishes for incense, and its bowls and flagons with which to pour drink offerings.

Building the lampstand

37.17-24 Ex 25.31-39 40.24

17 He also made the lampstand of pure gold. The base and the shaft of the lampstand were made of hammered work; its cups, its calyxes, and its petals were of one piece with it. 18 There were six branches going out of its sides, three branches of the lampstand out of one side of it and three branches of the lampstand out of the other side of it; 19 three cups shaped like almond blossoms, each with calyx and petals, on one branch, and three cups shaped like almond blossoms, each with calyx and petals, on the other branch — so for the six branches going out of the lampstand. 20 On the lampstand itself there were four cups shaped like almond blossoms, each with its calyxes and petals. 21 There was a calyx of one piece with it under the first pair of branches, a calyx of one piece with it under the next pair of

[m] Or *a cover* [n] Or *the cover*

37.1 The ark of the covenant was built to hold the ten commandments. It symbolized God's covenant with his people. Two gold angels called cherubim were placed on its top. The ark was Israel's most sacred object and was kept in the most holy place in the tabernacle. Only once each year the high priest entered the most holy place to sprinkle blood on the top of the ark (called the mercy seat) to atone for the sins of the entire nation.

37.1ff The ark of the covenant, the altars, and everything connected with the tabernacle was built according to the detailed instructions given earlier (Exodus 25–30).

branches, and a calyx of one piece with it under the last pair of branches. 22 Their
calyxes and their branches were of one piece with it, the whole of it one hammered
piece of pure gold. 23 He made its seven lamps and its snuffers and its trays of pure
gold. 24 He made it and all its utensils of a talent of pure gold.

Building the altar of incense

37.25-29 Ex 30.1-5 Lev 4.7 1 Kgs 6.22

25 He made the altar of incense of acacia wood, one cubit long, and one cubit
wide; it was square, and was two cubits high; its horns were of one piece with it.
26 He overlaid it with pure gold, its top, and its sides all around, and its horns; and
he made for it a molding of gold all around, 27 and made two golden rings for it
under its molding, on two opposite sides of it, to hold the poles with which to carry
it. 28 And he made the poles of acacia wood, and overlaid them with gold.

37.29 Ex 30.22,23 40.9 Lev 8.10

29 He made the holy anointing oil also, and the pure fragrant incense, blended
as by the perfumer.

Building the altar of burnt offering

38.1-7 Ex 20.24; 27.1-8 40.10,29 Heb 13.10

38 He made the altar of burnt offering also of acacia wood; it was five cubits
long, and five cubits wide; it was square, and three cubits high. 2 He made
horns for it on its four corners; its horns were of one piece with it, and he overlaid
it with bronze. 3 He made all the utensils of the altar, the pots, the shovels, the
basins, the forks, and the firepans: all its utensils he made of bronze. 4 He made for
the altar a grating, a network of bronze, under its ledge, extending halfway down.
5 He cast four rings on the four corners of the bronze grating to hold the poles; 6 he
made the poles of acacia wood, and overlaid them with bronze. 7 And he put the
poles through the rings on the sides of the altar, to carry it with them; he made it
hollow, with boards.

38.8 Ex 30.18; 31.9 Lev 8.11

8 He made the basin of bronze with its stand of bronze, from the mirrors of the
women who served at the entrance to the tent of meeting.

Building the court

38.9-20 Ex 27.9-19; 40.8 1 Kgs 6.36; 8.64

9 He made the court; for the south side the hangings of the court were of fine
twisted linen, one hundred cubits long; 10 its twenty pillars and their twenty bases
were of bronze, but the hooks of the pillars and their bands were of silver. 11 For the
north side there were hangings one hundred cubits long; its twenty pillars and their
twenty bases were of bronze, but the hooks of the pillars and their bands were of
silver. 12 For the west side there were hangings fifty cubits long, with ten pillars and
ten bases; the hooks of the pillars and their bands were of silver. 13 And for the front
to the east, fifty cubits. 14 The hangings for one side of the gate were fifteen cubits,
with three pillars and three bases. 15 And so for the other side; on each side of the
gate of the court were hangings of fifteen cubits, with three pillars and three bases.
16 All the hangings around the court were of fine twisted linen. 17 The bases for the
pillars were of bronze, but the hooks of the pillars and their bands were of silver;
the overlaying of their capitals was also of silver, and all the pillars of the court
were banded with silver. 18 The screen for the entrance to the court was embroidered with needlework in blue, purple, and crimson yarns and fine twisted linen. It
was twenty cubits long and, along the width of it, five cubits high, corresponding
to the hangings of the court. 19 There were four pillars; their four bases were of
bronze, their hooks of silver, and the overlaying of their capitals and their bands of
silver. 20 All the pegs for the tabernacle and for the court all around were of bronze.

The materials used

21 These are the records of the tabernacle, the tabernacle of the covenant,[o]
which were drawn up at the commandment of Moses, the work of the Levites being

[o] Or *treaty*, or *testimony*; Heb *eduth*

38.21 In building the tabernacle, Moses laid out the steps, but Ithamar supervised the project. We all have different talents and abilities. God didn't ask Moses to build the tabernacle but to motivate the experts to do it. Look for the areas where God has gifted you and then seek opportunities to allow God to use your gifts.

under the direction of Ithamar son of the priest Aaron. 22 Bezalel son of Uri son of
Hur, of the tribe of Judah, made all that the LORD commanded Moses; 23 and with
him was Oholiab son of Ahisamach, of the tribe of Dan, engraver, designer, and
embroiderer in blue, purple, and crimson yarns, and in fine linen.

24 All the gold that was used for the work, in all the construction of the sanctuary, the gold from the offering, was twenty-nine talents and seven hundred thirty
shekels, measured by the sanctuary shekel. 25 The silver from those of the congre- **38.25,26**
gation who were counted was one hundred talents and one thousand seven hundred Ex 12.37 30.11-16
seventy-five shekels, measured by the sanctuary shekel; 26 a beka a head (that is, Num 1.2,46 26.2,51
half a shekel, measured by the sanctuary shekel), for everyone who was counted in
the census, from twenty years old and upward, for six hundred three thousand, five
hundred fifty men. 27 The hundred talents of silver were for casting the bases of the
sanctuary, and the bases of the curtain; one hundred bases for the hundred talents,
a talent for a base. 28 Of the thousand seven hundred seventy-five shekels he made
hooks for the pillars, and overlaid their capitals and made bands for them. 29 The
bronze that was contributed was seventy talents, and two thousand four hundred
shekels; 30 with it he made the bases for the entrance of the tent of meeting, the
bronze altar and the bronze grating for it and all the utensils of the altar, 31 the bases
all around the court, and the bases of the gate of the court, all the pegs of the tabernacle, and all the pegs around the court.

Making the garments for the priests

39 Of the blue, purple, and crimson yarns they made finely worked vestments,
for ministering in the holy place; they made the sacred vestments for Aaron;
as the LORD had commanded Moses.

2 He made the ephod of gold, of blue, purple, and crimson yarns, and of fine **39.2**
twisted linen. 3 Gold leaf was hammered out and cut into threads to work into the Ex 28.6 Lev 8.7
blue, purple, and crimson yarns and into the fine twisted linen, in skilled design.
4 They made for the ephod shoulder-pieces, joined to it at its two edges. 5 The decorated band on it was of the same materials and workmanship, of gold, of blue,
purple, and crimson yarns, and of fine twisted linen; as the LORD had commanded
Moses.

6 The onyx stones were prepared, enclosed in settings of gold filigree and engraved like the engravings of a signet, according to the names of the sons of Israel.
7 He set them on the shoulder-pieces of the ephod, to be stones of remembrance for
the sons of Israel; as the LORD had commanded Moses.

8 He made the breastpiece, in skilled work, like the work of the ephod, of gold, **39.8-21**
of blue, purple, and crimson yarns, and of fine twisted linen. 9 It was square; the Ex 28.15-28
breastpiece was made double, a span in length and a span in width when doubled.
10 They set in it four rows of stones. A row of carnelian,[p] chrysolite, and emerald
was the first row; 11 and the second row, a turquoise, a sapphire,[q] and a moonstone;
12 and the third row, a jacinth, an agate, and an amethyst; 13 and the fourth row, a
beryl, an onyx, and a jasper; they were enclosed in settings of gold filigree. 14 There **39.14**
were twelve stones with names corresponding to the names of the sons of Israel; Rev 21.12
they were like signets, each engraved with its name, for the twelve tribes. 15 They
made on the breastpiece chains of pure gold, twisted like cords; 16 and they made
two settings of gold filigree and two gold rings, and put the two rings on the two
edges of the breastpiece; 17 and they put the two cords of gold in the two rings at the
edges of the breastpiece. 18 Two ends of the two cords they had attached to the two

[p] The identification of several of these stones is uncertain [q] Or *lapis lazuli*

39.1–21 The priests wore a uniform to the tabernacle each day. Some of the pieces of their uniform were not only beautiful but also significant. Two parts of the high priest's uniform were the ephod and breastplate. The ephod looked like a vest and was worn over the outer clothing. The breastplate was fitted to the ephod (and sometimes was called the ephod). The breastplate was made of colored linens about nine inches square. On its front were attached 12 precious stones, each inscribed with the name of a tribe of Israel. This symbolized how the high priest represented all the people before God. The breastplate also contained pockets that held two stones or plates called the Urim and Thummim. Somehow the high priest could determine God's will for the nation by consulting the Urim and Thummim.

settings of filigree; in this way they attached it in front to the shoulder-pieces of the
ephod. 19 Then they made two rings of gold, and put them at the two ends of the
breastpiece, on its inside edge next to the ephod. 20 They made two rings of gold,
and attached them in front to the lower part of the two shoulder-pieces of the ephod,
at its joining above the decorated band of the ephod. 21 They bound the breastpiece
by its rings to the rings of the ephod with a blue cord, so that it should lie on the
decorated band of the ephod, and that the breastpiece should not come loose from
the ephod; as the LORD had commanded Moses.

39.22 22 He also made the robe of the ephod woven all of blue yarn; 23 and the open-
Ex 28.31 ing of the robe in the middle of it was like the opening in a coat of mail,[r] with a
binding around the opening, so that it might not be torn. 24 On the lower hem of the
robe they made pomegranates of blue, purple, and crimson yarns, and of fine
twisted linen. 25 They also made bells of pure gold, and put the bells between the
pomegranates on the lower hem of the robe all around, between the pomegranates;
26 a bell and a pomegranate, a bell and a pomegranate all around on the lower hem
of the robe for ministering; as the LORD had commanded Moses.

39.27 27 They also made the tunics, woven of fine linen, for Aaron and his sons,
Ex 28.40 Lev 8.13 28 and the turban of fine linen, and the head-dresses of fine linen, and the linen
undergarments of fine twisted linen, 29 and the sash of fine twisted linen, and of
blue, purple, and crimson yarns, embroidered with needlework; as the LORD had
commanded Moses.

39.30 30 They made the rosette of the holy diadem of pure gold, and wrote on it an
Ex 38.36 Lev 8.9 inscription, like the engraving of a signet, "Holy to the LORD." 31 They tied to it a
blue cord, to fasten it on the turban above; as the LORD had commanded Moses.

Moses inspects the work

32 In this way all the work of the tabernacle of the tent of meeting was finished;
the Israelites had done everything just as the LORD had commanded Moses. 33 Then
they brought the tabernacle to Moses, the tent and all its utensils, its hooks, its
frames, its bars, its pillars, and its bases; 34 the covering of tanned rams' skins and
the covering of fine leather,[r] and the curtain for the screen; 35 the ark of the covenant[s] with its poles and the mercy seat;[t] 36 the table with all its utensils, and the
bread of the Presence; 37 the pure lampstand with its lamps set on it and all its utensils, and the oil for the light; 38 the golden altar, the anointing oil and the fragrant
incense, and the screen for the entrance of the tent; 39 the bronze altar, and its grating of bronze, its poles, and all its utensils; the basin with its stand; 40 the hangings
of the court, its pillars, and its bases, and the screen for the gate of the court, its
cords, and its pegs; and all the utensils for the service of the tabernacle, for the tent
of meeting; 41 the finely worked vestments for ministering in the holy place, the
39.43 sacred vestments for the priest Aaron, and the vestments of his sons to serve as
Lev 9.22,23 Num 6.23 priests. 42 The Israelites had done all of the work just as the LORD had commanded
Josh 22.6 1 Kgs 8.14 Moses. 43 When Moses saw that they had done all the work just as the LORD had
2 Chron 30.27 commanded, he blessed them.

[r] Meaning of Heb uncertain [s] Or *treaty*, or *testimony*; Heb *eduth* [t] Or *the cover*

39.32 The tabernacle was finally complete to the last detail. God was keenly interested in every minute part. The creator of the universe was concerned about even the little things. Matthew 10.30 says that God knows the number of hairs on our heads. This shows that God is greatly interested in you. Don't be afraid to talk with him about any of your concerns – no matter how small or unimportant they might seem.

39.42 Moses had learned his management lesson well. He gave important responsibilities to others and then trusted them to do the job. Great leaders, like Moses, give plans and direction while letting others participate on the team. If you are a leader, trust your assistants with key responsibilities.

39.43 Moses inspected the finished work, saw that it was done the way God wanted, and then blessed the people. A good leader follows up on assigned tasks and gives rewards for good work. In whatever responsible position you find yourself, follow up to make sure tasks are completed as intended, and show your appreciation to the people who have helped.

Putting the tabernacle together

40 The LORD spoke to Moses: 2 On the first day of the first month you shall set **40.2**
up the tabernacle of the tent of meeting. 3 You shall put in it the ark of the Ex 12.1; 19.1 40.17
covenant,[u] and you shall screen the ark with the curtain. 4 You shall bring in the Num 1.1; 7.1
table, and arrange its setting; and you shall bring in the lampstand, and set up its **40.3** Ex 25.9,10
lamps. 5 You shall put the golden altar for incense before the ark of the covenant,[u] Num 4.5
and set up the screen for the entrance of the tabernacle. 6 You shall set the altar of
burnt offering before the entrance of the tabernacle of the tent of meeting, 7 and
place the basin between the tent of meeting and the altar, and put water in it. 8 You
shall set up the court all around, and hang up the screen for the gate of the court.
9 Then you shall take the anointing oil, and anoint the tabernacle and all that is in it,
and consecrate it and all its furniture, so that it shall become holy. 10 You shall also
anoint the altar of burnt offering and all its utensils, and consecrate the altar, so that
the altar shall be most holy. 11 You shall also anoint the basin with its stand, and
consecrate it. 12 Then you shall bring Aaron and his sons to the entrance of the tent **40.12**
of meeting, and shall wash them with water, 13 and put on Aaron the sacred vest- Ex 28.41; 29.1 Lev 8.1-13
ments, and you shall anoint him and consecrate him, so that he may serve me as
priest. 14 You shall bring his sons also and put tunics on them, 15 and anoint them, **40.15**
as you anointed their father, that they may serve me as priests: and their anointing Ex 29.9 Num 3.10
shall admit them to a perpetual priesthood throughout all generations to come. Deut 18.5 Heb 5.4
16 Moses did everything just as the LORD had commanded him. 17 In the first **40.17**
month in the second year, on the first day of the month, the tabernacle was set up. Ex 40.2 Num 7.1
18 Moses set up the tabernacle; he laid its bases, and set up its frames, and put in its
poles, and raised up its pillars; 19 and he spread the tent over the tabernacle, and put
the covering of the tent over it; as the LORD had commanded Moses. 20 He took the **40.20**
covenant[u] and put it into the ark, and put the poles on the ark, and set the mercy Deut 10.5 1 Kgs 8.9
seat[v] above the ark; 21 and he brought the ark into the tabernacle, and set up the Heb 9.4
curtain for screening, and screened the ark of the covenant;[u] as the LORD had commanded Moses. 22 He put the table in the tent of meeting, on the north side of the
tabernacle, outside the curtain, 23 and set the bread in order on it before the LORD; **40.23**
as the LORD had commanded Moses. 24 He put the lampstand in the tent of meeting, Ex 25.30; 35.13 Lev 24.5
opposite the table on the south side of the tabernacle, 25 and set up the lamps before
the LORD; as the LORD had commanded Moses. 26 He put the golden altar in the tent
of meeting before the curtain, 27 and offered fragrant incense on it; as the LORD had
commanded Moses. 28 He also put in place the screen for the entrance of the tabernacle. 29 He set the altar of burnt offering at the entrance of the tabernacle of the tent
of meeting, and offered on it the burnt offering and the grain offering as the LORD
had commanded Moses. 30 He set the basin between the tent of meeting and the
altar, and put water in it for washing, 31 with which Moses and Aaron and his sons **40.31**
washed their hands and their feet. 32 When they went into the tent of meeting, and Ex 30.19
when they approached the altar, they washed; as the LORD had commanded Moses.
33 He set up the court around the tabernacle and the altar, and put up the screen at
the gate of the court. So Moses finished the work.

The glory of the Lord

34 Then the cloud covered the tent of meeting, and the glory of the LORD filled **40.34**
the tabernacle. 35 Moses was not able to enter the tent of meeting because the cloud 1 Kgs 8.10,11 Hag 2.7,9

[u] Or *treaty, or testimony*; Heb *eduth* [v] Or *the cover*

40.1ff Moses was careful to obey God's instructions to the smallest detail. Notice that he didn't make a reasonable facsimile of God's description but an exact copy. We should follow Moses' example and be meticulous about obedience. When obeying a command of God, we must do it, do it right, and do it completely.

40.16 God told Moses how to build the tabernacle, and Moses delegated jobs in order to do it. God allows people to participate with him in carrying out his will. Your task is not just to sit and watch God work, but to give your best effort when work needs to be done.

40.17–33 The physical care of the tabernacle required a long list of tasks, and each was important to the work of God's house. This principle is important to remember today, when God's house is the church. There are many seemingly unimportant tasks that must be done to keep your church building maintained. Washing dishes, painting walls, or shoveling snow may not seem very spiritual, but they are vital to the ministry of the church and have an important role in our worship of God.

40.34 The tabernacle was God's home on earth. He filled it with his glory – the overpowering sense of his presence. Almost 500

40.35 1 Kgs 8.1
40.36 Num 9.17; 10.11
40.37,38 Num 9.15-23

settled upon it, and the glory of the LORD filled the tabernacle. 36 Whenever the
cloud was taken up from the tabernacle, the Israelites would set out on each stage
of their journey; 37 but if the cloud was not taken up, then they did not set out until
the day that it was taken up. 38 For the cloud of the LORD was on the tabernacle by
day, and fire was in the cloud[w] by night, before the eyes of all the house of Israel
at each stage of their journey.

[w] Heb *it*

---

years later, Solomon built the temple, which replaced the tabernacle as the central place of worship. God also filled the temple with his glory (2 Chronicles 5.13, 14). But when Israel turned from God, his glory and presence departed from the temple and it was destroyed by invading armies (2 Kings 25). The temple was rebuilt in 516 B.C., and God's glory returned in even greater splendor nearly five centuries later when Jesus Christ, God's Son, entered it and taught. When Jesus was crucified, God's glory again left the temple. However, God no longer needed a physical building after Jesus rose from the dead. God's temple now is his church, the body of believers.

40.38 The Israelites were once Egyptian slaves making bricks without straw. Now they were following the pillar of cloud and the pillar of fire, carrying the tabernacle they had built for God. Exodus begins in gloom and ends in glory, which parallels our progress through the Christian life. We begin as slaves to sin, are redeemed by God, and end our pilgrimage living with God forever. The lessons the Israelites learned along the way are practical lessons for us, too.

LEVITICUS

Joseph dies 1805 B.C. (1640 B.C.)

S L A V E R Y I N E G Y P T

VITAL STATISTICS

PURPOSE:
A handbook for the priests and Levites outlining their duties in worship, and a guidebook of holy living for the Hebrews

AUTHOR:
Moses

DATE OF EVENTS:
1445–1444 B.C.

SETTING:
At the foot of Mount Sinai. God is teaching the Israelites how to live as holy people.

KEY VERSE:
"You shall be holy, for I the Lord your God am holy" (19.2).

KEY PEOPLE:
Moses, Aaron, Nadab, Abihu, Eleazar, Ithamar

KEY PLACE:
Mount Sinai

SPECIAL FEATURE:
Holiness is mentioned more times (152) than in any other book of the Bible.

"GOD seems so far away . . . if only I could see or hear him." When have you felt this way—struggling with loneliness, burdened by despair, riddled with sin, overwhelmed by problems? Made in God's image, we were created to have a close relationship with him; and when fellowship is broken, we are incomplete and need restoration. Communion with the living God is the essence of worship. It is vital, touching the very core of our lives. Perhaps this is why a whole book of the Bible is dedicated to worship. After Israel's dramatic exit from Egypt, the nation was camped at the foot of Mount Sinai for two years to listen to God (Exodus 19 to Numbers 10). It was a time of resting, teaching, building, and meeting with him face to face. Redemption in Exodus is the foundation for cleansing, worship, and service in Leviticus.

The overwhelming message of Leviticus is the holiness of God—"You shall be holy, for I the Lord your God am holy" (19.2). But how can unholy people approach a holy God? The answer—first sin must be dealt with. Thus the opening chapters of Leviticus give detailed instructions for offering sacrifices, which were the active symbols of repentance and obedience. Whether bulls, grain, goats, or sheep, the sacrificial offerings had to be perfect, with no defects or bruises—pictures of the ultimate sacrifice to come, Jesus, the Lamb of God. Jesus has come and opened the way to God by giving up his life as the final sacrifice in our place. True worship and oneness with God begin as we confess our sin and accept Christ as the only one who can redeem us from sin and help us approach God.

In Leviticus, sacrifices, priests, and the sacred day of atonement opened the way for the Israelites to come to God. God's people were also to worship him with their lives. Thus we read of purity laws (11—15) and rules for daily living concerning family responsibilities, sexual conduct, relationships, worldliness (18—20), and vows (27). These instructions involve one's holy walk with God, and the patterns of spiritual living still apply today. Worship, therefore, has a horizontal aspect—that is, God is honored by our lives as we relate to others.

The final emphasis in Leviticus is celebration. The book gives instructions for the festivals. These were special, regular, and corporate occasions for remembering what God had done, giving thanks to him, and rededicating lives to his service (23). Our Christian traditions and holidays are different, but they are necessary ingredients of worship. We too need special days of worship and celebration with our brothers and sisters to remember God's goodness in our lives. As you read Leviticus, rededicate yourself to holiness, worshiping God in private confession, public service, and group celebration.

Exodus from Egypt 1446 (1280)	Ten commandments given 1445 (1279)	Israel camps at Mt. Sinai 1444 (1278)	Moses dies, Canaan entered 1406 (1240)	Judges begin to rule 1375 (1220)	United kingdom under Saul 1050 (1045)

THE BLUEPRINT

A. WORSHIPING A HOLY GOD (1.1—17.16) 1. Instructions for the offerings 2. Instructions for the priests 3. Instructions for the people 4. Instructions for the altar	God's instructions for worship provide guidelines about our attitude toward worship today. Through the offerings we learn of the seriousness of sin and the importance of bringing our sins to God for forgiveness. The day of atonement foreshadows how Christ became the sacrifice for our sins.
B. LIVING A HOLY LIFE (18.1—27.34) 1. Standards for the people 2. Standards for the priests 3. Seasons and festivals 4. Receiving God's blessing	Seeing how God combated sin in the nation of Israel shows us how God wants to remove sin from our lives. God made a distinction between the Israelites and the heathen nations around them. Christians today are to be separated from sin and dedicated to God. All people, including priests, had to perform a special cleansing ceremony before they could approach God. From this we learn about the purity and holiness of God.

MEGATHEMES

THEME	EXPLANATION	IMPORTANCE
Sacrifice/Offering	There are five kinds of offerings that fulfill two main purposes: one to show praise, thankfulness, and devotion; the other for atonement, the covering and removal of guilt and sin. Animal offerings demonstrated that the person was giving his or her life to God by means of the life of the animal.	The sacrifices (offerings) were for worship and forgiveness of sin. Through them we learn about the cost of sin, for we see that we cannot forgive ourselves. God's system says that a life must be given for a life. In the Old Testament, an animal's life was given to save the life of a person. But this was only a temporary measure until Jesus' death paid the penalty of sin for all people forever.
Worship	Seven festivals were designated religious and national holidays. They were often celebrated in family settings. These events teach us much about worshiping God in both celebration and quiet dedication.	God's rules about worship set up an orderly, regular pattern of fellowship with him. They allowed times for celebration and thanksgiving as well as for reverence and rededication. Our worship should demonstrate our deep devotion.
Health	Civil rules for handling food, disease, and sex were taught. In these physical principles, many spiritual principles were suggested. Israel was to be different from the surrounding nations. God was preserving Israel from disease and community health problems.	We are to be different morally and spiritually from the unbelievers around us. Principles for healthy living are as important today as in Moses' time. A healthy environment and a healthy body make our service to God more effective.
Holiness	Holy means "separated" or "devoted." God removed his people from Egypt; now he was removing Egypt from the people. He was showing them how to exchange Egyptian ways of living and thinking for his ways.	We must devote every area of life to God. God desires absolute obedience in motives as well as practices. Though we do not observe all the worship practices of Israel, we are to have the same spirit of preparation and devotion.
Levites	The Levites and priests instructed the people in their worship. They were the ministers of their day. They also regulated the moral, civil, and ceremonial laws and supervised the health, justice, and welfare of the nation.	The Levites were servants who showed Israel the way to God. They provide the historical backdrop for Christ, who is our High Priest and yet our servant. God's true servants care for all the needs of their people.

A. WORSHIPING A HOLY GOD (1.1 – 17.16)

The Israelites have arrived safely at the foot of Mount Sinai, and the tabernacle has been completed. The people will spend a great deal of time here as God shows them a new way of life with clear instructions on how sinful people can relate to a holy God. These instructions help us avoid taking our relationship with the same holy God too lightly. We learn about the holiness and majesty of the God with whom we are allowed to have a personal relationship.

1. Instructions for the offerings

The burnt offering

1 The LORD summoned Moses and spoke to him from the tent of meeting, say- **1.1** Ex 25.22 Num 7.89
ing: 2 Speak to the people of Israel and say to them: When any of you bring an
offering of livestock to the LORD, you shall bring your offering from the herd or **1.2** Lev 6.9-13 22.19,20-25 Heb 9.14
from the flock.
3 If the offering is a burnt offering from the herd, you shall offer a male without

---

1.1 The book of Leviticus begins where the book of Exodus ends – at the foot of Mount Sinai. The tabernacle has just been completed (Exodus 35 – 40). Now God is ready to teach the people how to worship there.

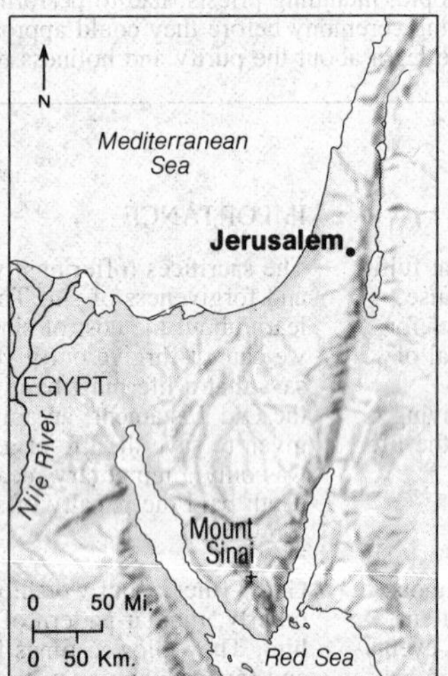

THE ISRAELITES AT MOUNT SINAI Throughout the book of Leviticus, the Israelites were camped at the foot of Mount Sinai. It was time to regroup as a nation and learn the importance of following God as they prepared to march toward the promised land.

1.1 The tent of meeting was the smaller structure inside the larger tabernacle. The tent of meeting contained the holy place and the most holy place. These two parts were separated from the rest of the tabernacle by a curtain. Moses often spoke with God in this tent of meeting. Exodus 33.7 mentions a tent of meeting outside the camp where Moses met with God before the tabernacle was constructed. Many believe that tent of meeting served the same function as the one described here.

1.1ff We may be tempted to dismiss Leviticus as a record of bizarre rituals of a different age. But its practices made sense to the people of the day and offer important insights for us into God's nature and character. Animal sacrifice seems obsolete and repulsive to many people today. Yet animal sacrifices were practiced in many cultures in the Middle East. God used the form of sacrifice to teach his people about faith. Sin needed to be taken seriously. When people saw the sacrificial animals being killed, they were sensitized to the importance of their sin and guilt. Our culture's casual attitude toward sin ignores the cost of sin and need for repentance and restoration. Although many of the rituals of Leviticus were fitted to the culture of the day, their purpose was to reveal a high and holy God who should be loved, obeyed, and worshiped. God's laws and sacrifices were intended to bring out true devotion of the heart. The ceremonies and rituals were the best way for the Israelites to focus their hearts on God.

1.2, 3 Was there any difference between a sacrifice and an offering? In Leviticus the words are interchanged. Usually a specific sacrifice was called an offering (burnt offering, grain offering, thank offering). Offerings in general were called sacrifices. The point is that each person *offered* a gift to God by *sacrificing* it on the altar. In the Old Testament, the sacrifice was the only way to approach God and restore a relationship with him. There was more than one kind of offering or sacrifice. The variety of sacrifices made them more meaningful, because each one related to a specific life situation. Sacrifices were given in praise, worship, and thanksgiving, as well as for forgiveness and fellowship. The first seven chapters of Leviticus describe the variety of offerings and how they were to be used.

1.2, 3 When God taught his people to worship him, he placed great emphasis on sacrifices. Why? Sacrifices were God's Old Testament way for people to ask forgiveness for their sins. Since Creation, God made it clear that sin separated people from him, and that those who sinned deserved to die. Since "all have sinned" (Romans 3.23), God designed sacrifice as a way to seek forgiveness and restore a relationship with him. Because he is a God of love and mercy, God decided from the very first that he would come down into our world and die to pay the penalty for all humans. This he did in his Son who, while still God, took the form and characteristics of a human being. In the meantime, before God made this ultimate sacrifice of his Son, he instructed people to kill animals as sacrifices for sin.

Animal sacrifice accomplished two purposes: (1) the animal symbolically took the sinner's place and paid the penalty for sin, and (2) the animal's death represented one life given so that another life could be saved. This method of sacrifice continued throughout Old Testament times. It was effective in teaching and guiding the people and bringing them back to God. But in New Testament times, Christ's death became the last sacrifice needed. He took our punishment once and for all. Animal sacrifice was no longer required. All people can now be freed from the penalty of sin by simply believing in Jesus and accepting the forgiveness he offers.

1.3, 4 The first offering God described was the burnt offering. A person who had sinned brought an animal with no defects to a priest. The unblemished animal symbolized the moral perfection demanded by a holy God and the perfect nature of the real sacrifice to come – Jesus Christ. The person then placed his hand on the head of the animal while it was killed by the priest. This symbolized the person's complete identification with the animal as his substitute. He symbolically transferred his sins to the animal, and thus his sins were taken away (atonement). Finally the animal (except for the blood and skin) was burned on the altar, signifying the person's complete dedication to God. God required more than a sacrifice, of course. He also asked the sinner to have an attitude of repentance. The outward symbol (the sacrifice) and the inner change (repentance) were to work together. But it is important to remember that neither sacrifice nor repentance actually caused

1.4 Ex 29.10,15,19 Lev 4.13-35 Num 8.10-12 15.25 2 Chron 29.23, 24
1.5 Lev 1.11; 3.7,8 16.15 Heb 12.24
1.6 Lev 7.8 Neh 13.31
1.8 Ex 29.17 Lev 3.3,4,5
1.9 Gen 8.21 Ex 29.17,18 Num 15.8,9 Eph 5.2 Phil 4.18

blemish; you shall bring it to the entrance of the tent of meeting, for acceptance in
your behalf before the LORD. 4 You shall lay your hand on the head of the burnt
offering, and it shall be acceptable in your behalf as atonement for you. 5 The bull
shall be slaughtered before the LORD; and Aaron's sons the priests shall offer the
blood, dashing the blood against all sides of the altar that is at the entrance of the
tent of meeting. 6 The burnt offering shall be flayed and cut up into its parts. 7 The
sons of the priest Aaron shall put fire on the altar and arrange wood on the fire.
8 Aaron's sons the priests shall arrange the parts, with the head and the suet, on the
wood that is on the fire on the altar; 9 but its entrails and its legs shall be washed
with water. Then the priest shall turn the whole into smoke on the altar as a burnt
offering, an offering by fire of pleasing odor to the LORD.
10 If your gift for a burnt offering is from the flock, from the sheep or goats,
your offering shall be a male without blemish. 11 It shall be slaughtered on the north
side of the altar before the LORD, and Aaron's sons the priests shall dash its blood
against all sides of the altar. 12 It shall be cut up into its parts, with its head and its
suet, and the priest shall arrange them on the wood that is on the fire on the altar;
13 but the entrails and the legs shall be washed with water. Then the priest shall offer

THE OFFERINGS
Listed here are the five key offerings the Israelites made to God. The Jews made these offerings in order to have their sins forgiven and to restore their fellowship with God. The death of Jesus Christ made these sacrifices unnecessary. Because of his death our sins were completely forgiven and fellowship with God has been restored.

Offering	*Purpose*	*Significance*	*Christ, the Perfect Offering*
Burnt Offering (Lev. 1—voluntary)	To make payment for sins in general	Showed a person's devotion to God	Christ's death was the perfect offering
Grain Offering (Lev. 2—voluntary)	To show honor and respect to God in worship	Acknowledged that all we have belongs to God	Christ was the perfect man, who gave all of himself to God and others
Offering of Well-Being (Lev. 3—voluntary)	To express gratitude to God	Symbolized peace and fellowship with God	Christ is the only way to fellowship with God
Sin Offering (Lev. 4—required)	To make payment for unintentional sins of uncleanness, neglect, or thoughtlessness	Restored the sinner to fellowship with God; showed seriousness of sin	Christ's death restores our fellowship with God
Guilt Offering (Lev. 5—required)	To make payment for sins against God and others. A sacrifice was made to God and the injured person was repaid or compensated	Provided compensation for injured parties	Christ's death takes away the deadly consequences of sin

the sin to be taken away. God alone forgives sin. Fortunately for us, forgiveness is part of God's loving nature.

1.3ff What did sacrifices teach the people? (1) By requiring perfect animals and holy priests, they taught reverence for a holy God. (2) By demanding exact obedience, they taught total submission to God's laws. (3) By requiring an animal of great value, they showed the high cost of sin and demonstrated the sincerity of their commitment to God.

1.4ff Israel was not the only nation to sacrifice animals. Many other religions did it as well, to try to please their gods. Some cultures even included human sacrifice, which was strictly forbidden by God. However, the meaning of Israel's animal sacrifices was clearly different from that of their heathen neighbors. Israelites sacrificed animals not to appease God, but as a substitute for the punishment they deserved for their sins. A sacrifice showed faith in God and commitment to his laws. Most important, this system foreshadowed the day when the Lamb of God (Jesus Christ) would die and conquer sin once and for all.

1.4–13 Why such detailed regulations for each offering? God had a purpose in giving these commands. Starting from scratch, he was teaching his people a whole new way of life, cleansing them from the many heathen practices they had learned in Egypt, and restoring true worship of himself. The strict details kept Israel from slipping back into their old life-style. In addition, each law paints a graphic picture of the seriousness of sin and of God's great mercy in forgiving sinners.

1.8 "Suet" is the fatty part of the animal.

1.13 The "pleasing odor to the Lord" is a way of saying that God accepted the sacrifice because of the attitude of the people.

the whole and turn it into smoke on the altar; it is a burnt offering, an offering by
fire of pleasing odor to the LORD.
14 If your offering to the LORD is a burnt offering of birds, you shall choose
your offering from turtledoves or pigeons. 15 The priest shall bring it to the altar and
wring off its head, and turn it into smoke on the altar; and its blood shall be drained
out against the side of the altar. 16 He shall remove its crop with its contents[a] and
throw it at the east side of the altar, in the place for ashes. 17 He shall tear it open by
its wings without severing it. Then the priest shall turn it into smoke on the altar,
on the wood that is on the fire; it is a burnt offering, an offering by fire of pleasing
odor to the LORD.

The grain offering

2 When anyone presents a grain offering to the LORD, the offering shall be of
choice flour; the worshiper shall pour oil on it, and put frankincense on it, 2 and
bring it to Aaron's sons the priests. After taking from it a handful of the choice flour
and oil, with all its frankincense, the priest shall turn this token portion into smoke
on the altar, an offering by fire of pleasing odor to the LORD. 3 And what is left of
the grain offering shall be for Aaron and his sons, a most holy part of the offerings
by fire to the LORD.
4 When you present a grain offering baked in the oven, it shall be of choice
flour: unleavened cakes mixed with oil, or unleavened wafers spread with oil. 5 If
your offering is grain prepared on a griddle, it shall be of choice flour mixed with
oil, unleavened; 6 break it in pieces, and pour oil on it; it is a grain offering. 7 If your
offering is grain prepared in a pan, it shall be made of choice flour in oil. 8 You shall
bring to the LORD the grain offering that is prepared in any of these ways; and when
it is presented to the priest, he shall take it to the altar. 9 The priest shall remove
from the grain offering its token portion and turn this into smoke on the altar, an
offering by fire of pleasing odor to the LORD. 10 And what is left of the grain offering shall be for Aaron and his sons; it is a most holy part of the offerings by fire to
the LORD.
11 No grain offering that you bring to the LORD shall be made with leaven, for
you must not turn any leaven or honey into smoke as an offering by fire to the
LORD. 12 You may bring them to the LORD as an offering of choice products, but
they shall not be offered on the altar for a pleasing odor. 13 You shall not omit from
your grain offerings the salt of the covenant with your God; with all your offerings
you shall offer salt.
14 If you bring a grain offering of first fruits to the LORD, you shall bring as the
grain offering of your first fruits coarse new grain from fresh ears, parched with
fire. 15 You shall add oil to it and lay frankincense on it; it is a grain offering. 16 And

a Meaning of Heb uncertain

1.14 Gen 15.9 Lev 12.8
1.15 Lev 5.9
2.1 Ex 29.2 Lev 6.14-18 24.7 Num 15.4-21
2.2 Lev 2.9 5.12,13 6.15-18
2.3 Lev 10.12,13 Num 8.8-11
2.4 Ex 29.2 Lev 7.12
2.9 Gen 8.21 Ex 29.18 Lev 2.2; 6.15
2.10 Lev 2.3
2.11 Lev 6.16,17
2.12 Lev 7.13 23.9-14
2.13 Num 18.19 2 Chron 13.5 Ezek 43.24 Mk 9.49
2.14 Lev 23.9-14 2 Kgs 4.42
2.16 Lev 2.1,2

2.1ff The grain offering accompanied all burnt offerings and was a gift of thanks to God. It reminded the people that their food came from God and that therefore they owed their lives to him. Three kinds of grain offerings are listed: (1) fine flour with oil and frankincense, (2) baked cakes or wafers of fine flour and oil, (3) roasted kernels of grain (corn) with oil and frankincense. Frankincense was a balsamic resin obtained from shrubs. It was symbolic of holiness and devotion. The absence of leaven symbolized the absence of sin, and the oil symbolized God's presence. Part of the grain offering was burned on the altar as a gift to God, and the rest was eaten by the priests. The offerings helped support them in their work.

2.11 Why was no leaven (yeast) allowed in the meat offerings? Yeast is a bacterial fungus or mold, the active ingredient in leaven. Yeast, therefore, is an appropriate symbol for sin. It grows in bread dough just as sin grows in a life. A little yeast will affect the whole loaf, just as a little sin can ruin a whole life. Jesus continued this analogy by warning about the "yeast of the Pharisees and Sadducees" (Matthew 16.6; Mark 8.15).

2.13 The offerings were seasoned with salt as a reminder of the people's covenant (contract) with God. Salt is a good symbol of God's activity in a person's life because it penetrates, preserves, and aids in healing. God wants to be active in your life. Let him become part of you, penetrating every aspect of your life, preserving you from the evil all around, and healing you of your sins and shortcomings.

2.13 In Arab countries, an agreement was sealed with a gift of salt to show the strength and permanence of the contract. In Matthew 5.13 believers are called "the salt of the earth." Let the salt we use each day remind us that we are now God's covenant people who actively help preserve and purify our world.

2.14 Coarse new grain mixed with olive oil and cooked was typical food for the average person. This offering was a token presentation of a person's daily food. In this way people acknowledged God as provider of their food. Even a poor person could fulfill this offering. God was pleased by the motivation and dedication of the person making it.

the priest shall turn a token portion of it into smoke—some of the coarse grain and
oil with all its frankincense; it is an offering by fire to the LORD.

The offering of well-being

3.1 Lev 1.2; 7.11-21
3 If the offering is a sacrifice of well-being, if you offer an animal of the herd,
whether male or female, you shall offer one without blemish before the LORD.
3.2 Ex 29.11 Lev 1.4; 7.14
2 You shall lay your hand on the head of the offering and slaughter it at the entrance
of the tent of meeting; and Aaron's sons the priests shall dash the blood against all
3.3-5 Ex 29.13,22 Lev 3.9-11, 14-16
sides of the altar. 3 You shall offer from the sacrifice of well-being, as an offering
by fire to the LORD, the fat that covers the entrails and all the fat that is around the
entrails; 4 the two kidneys with the fat that is on them at the loins, and the appendage of the liver, which he shall remove with the kidneys. 5 Then Aaron's sons shall
turn these into smoke on the altar, with the burnt offering that is on the wood on the
fire, as an offering by fire of pleasing odor to the LORD.
3.6 Lev 1.2; 3.1
6 If your offering for a sacrifice of well-being to the LORD is from the flock,
male or female, you shall offer one without blemish. 7 If you present a sheep as
your offering, you shall bring it before the LORD 8 and lay your hand on the head of
the offering. It shall be slaughtered before the tent of meeting, and Aaron's sons
shall dash its blood against all sides of the altar. 9 You shall present its fat from the
sacrifice of well-being, as an offering by fire to the LORD: the whole broad tail,
which shall be removed close to the backbone, the fat that covers the entrails, and
all the fat that is around the entrails; 10 the two kidneys with the fat that is on them
at the loins, and the appendage of the liver, which you shall remove with the kidneys. 11 Then the priest shall turn these into smoke on the altar as a food offering by
fire to the LORD.
3.12 Num 15.6,11-16
12 If your offering is a goat, you shall bring it before the LORD 13 and lay your
3.13 Lev 1.2
hand on its head; it shall be slaughtered before the tent of meeting; and the sons of
Aaron shall dash its blood against all sides of the altar. 14 You shall present as your
3.15,16 Lev 4.26 7.23-25 Ezek 44.7
offering from it, as an offering by fire to the LORD, the fat that covers the entrails,
and all the fat that is around the entrails; 15 the two kidneys with the fat that is on
them at the loins, and the appendage of the liver, which you shall remove with the
3.17 Lev 7.26,27 17.10 Deut 12.16 Acts 15.20, 27-29
kidneys. 16 Then the priest shall turn these into smoke on the altar as a food offering
by fire for a pleasing odor.
All fat is the LORD's. 17 It shall be a perpetual statute throughout your generations, in all your settlements: you must not eat any fat or any blood.

The sin offering

4.2 Lev 4.22; 22.14 Num 15.22-29
4 The LORD spoke to Moses, saying, 2 Speak to the people of Israel, saying:
When anyone sins unintentionally in any of the LORD's commandments about
things not to be done, and does any one of them:
4.3 Lev 4.14; 9.2 Ezek 43.19
3 If it is the anointed priest who sins, thus bringing guilt on the people, he shall
offer for the sin that he has committed a bull of the herd without blemish as a sin
offering to the LORD. 4 He shall bring the bull to the entrance of the tent of meeting
before the LORD and lay his hand on the head of the bull; the bull shall be slaugh-
4.5,6 Lev 4.17; 16.14 Num 19.4
tered before the LORD. 5 The anointed priest shall take some of the blood of the bull
and bring it into the tent of meeting. 6 The priest shall dip his finger in the blood and
sprinkle some of the blood seven times before the LORD in front of the curtain of the

---

3.1ff A person gave an offering of well-being (or peace offering) as an expression of gratitude and a means of establishing fellowship between himself and God. It is called well-being because God as healer and restorer made people complete. He made up any lack as the offerer came to him in faith. Because it symbolized peace with God, part of the offering could be eaten by the person presenting it.

4.1ff Have you ever done something wrong without realizing it until later? Although your sin was unintentional, it was still sin. One of the purposes of God's law was to make the Israelites aware of their unintentional sins so they would not repeat them and so they could be forgiven for them. Leviticus 4 and 5 mention some of these unintentional sins and the way the Israelites could be forgiven for them. As you read more of God's laws, keep in mind that they were meant to teach and guide the people. Let them help you become more aware of sin in your life.

4.2 The sin offering was for those who (1) committed a sin without realizing it or (2) committed a sin out of weakness or negligence as opposed to outright rebellion against God. Different animals were sacrificed for the different kinds of sin. The death of Jesus Christ was the final sin offering in the Bible (Hebrews 9.25–28 tells why).

sanctuary. 7 The priest shall put some of the blood on the horns of the altar of fra- 4.7
grant incense that is in the tent of meeting before the LORD; and the rest of the blood Ex 30.10 Lev 8.15
of the bull he shall pour out at the base of the altar of burnt offering, which is at the
entrance of the tent of meeting. 8 He shall remove all the fat from the bull of sin 4.8
offering: the fat that covers the entrails and all the fat that is around the entrails; 9 the Lev 3.3
two kidneys with the fat that is on them at the loins; and the appendage of the liver,
which he shall remove with the kidneys, 10 just as these are removed from the ox of
the sacrifice of well-being. The priest shall turn them into smoke upon the altar of
burnt offering. 11 But the skin of the bull and all its flesh, as well as its head, its 4.11
legs, its entrails, and its dung— 12 all the rest of the bull—he shall carry out to a Ex 29.14 Lev 6.11
clean place outside the camp, to the ash heap, and shall burn it on a wood fire; at Num 19.9
the ash heap it shall be burned. Heb 13.11

13 If the whole congregation of Israel errs unintentionally and the matter es- 4.13
capes the notice of the assembly, and they do any one of the things that by the Num 15.23-26 1 Sam 14.32-34
LORD's commandments ought not to be done and incur guilt; 14 when the sin that 4.14
they have committed becomes known, the assembly shall offer a bull of the herd for Lev 4.3
a sin offering and bring it before the tent of meeting. 15 The elders of the congrega- 4.15
tion shall lay their hands on the head of the bull before the LORD, and the bull shall Lev 8.14 Num 8.10-12
be slaughtered before the LORD. 16 The anointed priest shall bring some of the blood
of the bull into the tent of meeting, 17 and the priest shall dip his finger in the blood 4.17
and sprinkle it seven times before the LORD, in front of the curtain. 18 He shall put Lev 4.6
some of the blood on the horns of the altar that is before the LORD in the tent of
meeting; and the rest of the blood he shall pour out at the base of the altar of burnt
offering that is at the entrance of the tent of meeting. 19 He shall remove all its fat 4.19
and turn it into smoke on the altar. 20 He shall do with the bull just as is done with Lev 4.8
the bull of sin offering; he shall do the same with this. The priest shall make atone- 4.20 Num 15.25
ment for them, and they shall be forgiven. 21 He shall carry the bull outside the 4.21
camp, and burn it as he burned the first bull; it is the sin offering for the assembly. Lev 4.11

22 When a ruler sins, doing unintentionally any one of all the things that by 4.22
commandments of the LORD his God ought not to be done and incurs guilt, 23 once Lev 4.2,13
the sin that he has committed is made known to him, he shall bring as his offering
a male goat without blemish. 24 He shall lay his hand on the head of the goat; it shall 4.24
be slaughtered at the spot where the burnt offering is slaughtered before the LORD; Lev 6.25-30 9.2-11
it is a sin offering. 25 The priest shall take some of the blood of the sin offering with 4.25
his finger and put it on the horns of the altar of burnt offering, and pour out the rest Lev 4.7
of its blood at the base of the altar of burnt offering. 26 All its fat he shall turn into 4.26
smoke on the altar, like the fat of the sacrifice of well-being. Thus the priest shall Lev 4.8-12
make atonement on his behalf for his sin, and he shall be forgiven.

27 If anyone of the ordinary people among you sins unintentionally in doing 4.27
any one of the things that by the LORD's commandments ought not to be done and Lev 4.23
incurs guilt, 28 when the sin that you have committed is made known to you, you 4.28
shall bring a female goat without blemish as your offering, for the sin that you have Lev 1.2-4
committed. 29 You shall lay your hand on the head of the sin offering; and the sin
offering shall be slaughtered at the place of the burnt offering. 30 The priest shall 4.30
take some of its blood with his finger and put it on the horns of the altar of burnt Lev 9.9-11
offering, and he shall pour out the rest of its blood at the base of the altar. 31 He shall 4.31
remove all its fat, as the fat is removed from the offering of well-being, and the Gen 8.21 Ex 29.18
priest shall turn it into smoke on the altar for a pleasing odor to the LORD. Thus the Lev 2.2; 4.8; 6.15
priest shall make atonement on your behalf, and you shall be forgiven.

32 If the offering you bring as a sin offering is a sheep, you shall bring a female 4.32
without blemish. 33 You shall lay your hand on the head of the sin offering; and it Lev 4.28
shall be slaughtered as a sin offering at the spot where the burnt offering is slaughtered. 34 The priest shall take some of the blood of the sin offering with his finger
and put it on the horns of the altar of burnt offering, and pour out the rest of its
blood at the base of the altar. 35 You shall remove all its fat, as the fat of the sheep 4.35
is removed from the sacrifice of well-being, and the priest shall turn it into smoke Lev 3.3
on the altar, with the offerings by fire to the LORD. Thus the priest shall make

atonement on your behalf for the sin that you have committed, and you shall be
forgiven.

5 When any of you sin in that you have heard a public adjuration to testify
and—though able to testify as one who has seen or learned of the
5.2 Lev 11.4-11, 24-39 Num 19.11-16 Deut 14.3-21 matter—does not speak up, you are subject to punishment. 2 Or when any of you
touch any unclean thing—whether the carcass of an unclean beast or the carcass of
unclean livestock or the carcass of an unclean swarming thing—and are unaware of
it, you have become unclean, and are guilty. 3 Or when you touch human
uncleanness—any uncleanness by which one can become unclean—and are un-
5.4 Judg 11.31 1 Sam 14.24,25 Acts 23.12 aware of it, when you come to know it, you shall be guilty. 4 Or when any of you
utter aloud a rash oath for a bad or a good purpose, whatever people utter in an oath,
and are unaware of it, when you come to know it, you shall in any of these be
5.5 Lev 16.21 Num 5.7 Josh 7.19 Ezra 10.11 guilty. 5 When you realize your guilt in any of these, you shall confess the sin that
you have committed. 6 And you shall bring to the LORD, as your penalty for the sin
that you have committed, a female from the flock, a sheep or a goat, as a sin offer-
5.6 Lev 4.28,32 7.1-10 ing; and the priest shall make atonement on your behalf for your sin.
7 But if you cannot afford a sheep, you shall bring to the LORD, as your penalty
5.7 Lk 2.24 for the sin that you have committed, two turtledoves or two pigeons, one for a sin
offering and the other for a burnt offering. 8 You shall bring them to the priest, who
5.8 Lev 1.15-17 shall offer first the one for the sin offering, wringing its head at the nape without
5.9 Lev 4.7; 7.2 severing it. 9 He shall sprinkle some of the blood of the sin offering on the side of
the altar, while the rest of the blood shall be drained out at the base of the altar; it
5.10 Lev 1.14-17 is a sin offering. 10 And the second he shall offer for a burnt offering according to
the regulation. Thus the priest shall make atonement on your behalf for the sin that
you have committed, and you shall be forgiven.
5.11 Lev 14.21 Num 15.3-9 5.15 11 But if you cannot afford two turtledoves or two pigeons, you shall bring as
your offering for the sin that you have committed one-tenth of an ephah of choice
flour for a sin offering; you shall not put oil on it or lay frankincense on it, for it is
5.12 Lev 6.25-30 a sin offering. 12 You shall bring it to the priest, and the priest shall scoop up a
handful of it as its memorial portion, and turn this into smoke on the altar, with the
offerings by fire to the LORD; it is a sin offering. 13 Thus the priest shall make atonement on your behalf for whichever of these sins you have committed, and you shall
be forgiven. Like the grain offering, the rest shall be for the priest.

The guilt offering

5.15 Ex 30.13 Lev 6.6; 7.1-10 22.14-16 27.3,25 14 The LORD spoke to Moses, saying: 15 When any of you commit a trespass
and sins unintentionally in any of the holy things of the LORD, you shall bring, as
your guilt offering to the LORD, a ram without blemish from the flock, convertible
into silver by the sanctuary shekel; it is a guilt offering. 16 And you shall make
restitution for the holy thing in which you were remiss, and shall add one-fifth to it

---

5.1 A public adjuration is literally a "sound of an oath," and meant a public charge to testify, or a public call for reluctant witnesses. Some would be tempted to remain silent out of fear. Even today, people are often afraid to testify about a crime they have witnessed because of fear of retribution.

5.4 Have you ever sworn to do or not do something and then realized what a foolish thing you had done? God's people are called to keep their word, even if they make promises that are tough to keep. Jesus was warning against swearing (in the sense of making vows or oaths) when he said, "Let your word be 'Yes, Yes' or 'No, No'; anything more than this comes from the evil one" (Matthew 5.37). Our word should be enough. If we feel we have to strengthen it with an oath, something is wrong. The only promises we ought not to keep are promises that lead to sin. A wise and self-controlled person avoids making rash vows.

5.5 The entire system of sacrifices could not help a sinner unless he brought his offering with an attitude of repentance and a willingness to confess sin. Today, because of Christ's death on the cross, we do not have to sacrifice animals. But it is still vital to confess sin, because confession shows realization of sin, awareness of God's holiness, humility before God, and willingness to turn from this sin (Psalm 51.16, 17). Even Jesus' death is of little value to us if we do not repent and follow him. It is like a vaccine for a dangerous disease—it is of little value unless it enters the bloodstream.

5.14–19 The guilt offering was a way of taking care of sin committed unknowingly. It was for those who sinned in some way against "holy things"—the tabernacle or the priesthood—as well as for those who unintentionally sinned against someone. In either case, a ram with no defects had to be sacrificed, plus those harmed by the sin had to be compensated for their loss, plus a 20 percent penalty. Even though Christ's death has made trespass offerings unnecessary for us today, we still need to make things right with those we hurt.

and give it to the priest. The priest shall make atonement on your behalf with the
ram of the guilt offering, and you shall be forgiven.
17 If any of you sin without knowing it, doing any of the things that by the
LORD's commandments ought not to be done, you have incurred guilt, and are
subject to punishment. 18 You shall bring to the priest a ram without blemish from
the flock, or the equivalent, as a guilt offering; and the priest shall make atonement
on your behalf for the error that you committed unintentionally, and you shall be
forgiven. 19 It is a guilt offering; you have incurred guilt before the LORD.

6 [b] The LORD spoke to Moses, saying: 2 When any of you sin and commit a trespass against the LORD by deceiving a neighbor in a matter of a deposit or a
pledge, or by robbery, or if you have defrauded a neighbor, 3 or have found something lost and lied about it—if you swear falsely regarding any of the various things
that one may do and sin thereby— 4 when you have sinned and realize your guilt,
and would restore what you took by robbery or by fraud or the deposit that was
committed to you, or the lost thing that you found, 5 or anything else about which
you have sworn falsely, you shall repay the principal amount and shall add one-
fifth to it. You shall pay it to its owner when you realize your guilt. 6 And you shall
bring to the priest, as your guilt offering to the LORD, a ram without blemish from
the flock, or its equivalent, for a guilt offering. 7 The priest shall make atonement
on your behalf before the LORD, and you shall be forgiven for any of the things that
one may do and incur guilt thereby.

Burnt offerings

8 [c] The LORD spoke to Moses, saying: 9 Command Aaron and his sons, saying:
This is the ritual of the burnt offering. The burnt offering itself shall remain on the
hearth upon the altar all night until the morning, while the fire on the altar shall be
kept burning. 10 The priest shall put on his linen vestments after putting on his linen
undergarments next to his body; and he shall take up the ashes to which the fire has
reduced the burnt offering on the altar, and place them beside the altar. 11 Then he
shall take off his vestments and put on other garments, and carry the ashes out to a
clean place outside the camp. 12 The fire on the altar shall be kept burning; it shall
not go out. Every morning the priest shall add wood to it, lay out the burnt offering
on it, and turn into smoke the fat pieces of the offerings of well-being. 13 A perpetual fire shall be kept burning on the altar; it shall not go out.

Grain offerings

14 This is the ritual of the grain offering: The sons of Aaron shall offer it before
the LORD, in front of the altar. 15 They shall take from it a handful of the choice
flour and oil of the grain offering, with all the frankincense that is on the offering,
and they shall turn its memorial portion into smoke on the altar as a pleasing odor
to the LORD. 16 Aaron and his sons shall eat what is left of it; it shall be eaten as
unleavened cakes in a holy place; in the court of the tent of meeting they shall eat
it. 17 It shall not be baked with leaven. I have given it as their portion of my offerings by fire; it is most holy, like the sin offering and the guilt offering. 18 Every
male among the descendants of Aaron shall eat of it, as their perpetual due throughout your generations, from the LORD's offerings by fire; anything that touches them
shall become holy.
19 The LORD spoke to Moses, saying: 20 This is the offering that Aaron and his

5.16 Lev 6.4-6 22.15; 27.13
5.17 Lev 5.17,19
6.2 Ex 22.7-15 Num 5.6 Col 3.9
6.3 Lev 19.12 Deut 22.1-3
6.4 Ex 22.1,4,7,9 Lev 5.16 Prov 6.31 Jer 7.9 Zech 5.4 Lk 19.8
6.9 Ex 29.38-42 Lev 1.2-17 Num 28.1-25
6.10 Ex 28.39-43 Lev 16.4
6.11 Lev 16.23-25
6.12 Lev 3.3; 6.9
6.13 Ex 27.20,21 Lev 6.9,12 24.1-4
6.14 Lev 2.1-16
6.15 Lev 2.1,2,9
6.16 Lev 10.12-15 Num 18.8-11
6.17 Ex 29.33,34,37 Lev 2.11 6.26,29; 10.17
6.18 Lev 6.29 Num 18.10 1 Cor 9.13
6.19 Ex 29.40 Lev 8.12

[b] Ch 5.20 in Heb [c] Ch 6.1 in Heb

6.1–7 Here we discover that stealing involves more than just taking from someone. Finding something and not returning it or refusing to return something borrowed are other forms of stealing. These are sins against God and not just your neighbor, a stranger, or a large business. If you have gotten something deceitfully, then confess your sin to God, apologize to the owner, and return the stolen items—with interest.

6.12, 13 The holy fire on the altar had to keep burning because God had started it. This represented God's eternal presence in the sacrificial system. It showed the people that only by God's gracious favor could their sacrifice be acceptable. God's fire is present in each believer's life today. He lights the fire when the Holy Spirit comes to live in us, and he tends it so that we will grow in grace as we walk with him. When we are aware that God lives in us, we have confidence to come to him for forgiveness and restoration.

sons shall offer to the LORD on the day when he is anointed: one-tenth of an ephah
of choice flour as a regular offering, half of it in the morning and half in the evening. 21 It shall be made with oil on a griddle; you shall bring it well soaked, as a
grain offering of baked[d] pieces, and you shall present it as a pleasing odor to the
LORD. 22 And so the priest, anointed from among Aaron's descendants as a successor, shall prepare it; it is the LORD's — a perpetual due — to be turned entirely into
smoke. 23 Every grain offering of a priest shall be wholly burned; it shall not be
eaten.

Sin offerings

24 The LORD spoke to Moses, saying: 25 Speak to Aaron and his sons, saying:
This is the ritual of the sin offering. The sin offering shall be slaughtered before the
LORD at the spot where the burnt offering is slaughtered; it is most holy. 26 The
priest who offers it as a sin offering shall eat of it; it shall be eaten in a holy place,
in the court of the tent of meeting. 27 Whatever touches its flesh shall become holy;
and when any of its blood is spattered on a garment, you shall wash the bespattered
part in a holy place. 28 An earthen vessel in which it was boiled shall be broken; but
if it is boiled in a bronze vessel, that shall be scoured and rinsed in water. 29 Every
male among the priests shall eat of it; it is most holy. 30 But no sin offering shall be
eaten from which any blood is brought into the tent of meeting for atonement in the
holy place; it shall be burned with fire.

Guilt offerings

7 This is the ritual of the guilt offering. It is most holy; 2 at the spot where the
burnt offering is slaughtered, they shall slaughter the guilt offering, and its
blood shall be dashed against all sides of the altar. 3 All its fat shall be offered: the
broad tail, the fat that covers the entrails, 4 the two kidneys with the fat that is on
them at the loins, and the appendage of the liver, which shall be removed with the
kidneys. 5 The priest shall turn them into smoke on the altar as an offering by fire
to the LORD; it is a guilt offering. 6 Every male among the priests shall eat of it; it
shall be eaten in a holy place; it is most holy.

7 The guilt offering is like the sin offering, there is the same ritual for them; the
priest who makes atonement with it shall have it. 8 So, too, the priest who offers
anyone's burnt offering shall keep the skin of the burnt offering that he has offered.
9 And every grain offering baked in the oven, and all that is prepared in a pan or on
a griddle, shall belong to the priest who offers it. 10 But every other grain offering,
mixed with oil or dry, shall belong to all the sons of Aaron equally.

Offerings of well-being

11 This is the ritual of the sacrifice of the offering of well-being that one may
offer to the LORD. 12 If you offer it for thanksgiving, you shall offer with the thank
offering unleavened cakes mixed with oil, unleavened wafers spread with oil, and
cakes of choice flour well soaked in oil. 13 With your thanksgiving sacrifice of well-
being you shall bring your offering with cakes of leavened bread. 14 From this you
shall offer one cake from each offering, as a gift to the LORD; it shall belong to the
priest who dashes the blood of the offering of well-being. 15 And the flesh of your
thanksgiving sacrifice of well-being shall be eaten on the day it is offered; you shall
not leave any of it until morning. 16 But if the sacrifice you offer is a votive offering
or a freewill offering, it shall be eaten on the day that you offer your sacrifice, and
what is left of it shall be eaten the next day; 17 but what is left of the flesh of the
sacrifice shall be burned up on the third day. 18 If any of the flesh of your sacrifice

6.21 Lev 2.5,8; 7.9
6.22,23 Ex 29.25
6.25 Lev 4.24,29
6.27 Ex 29.37; 30.29,30; Lev 6.18
6.28 Lev 11.33; 15.12
6.29 Lev 6.18; Num 18.10
6.30 Lev 16.27; Heb 9.11; 13.11
7.1 Lev 5.14-19; 6.1-7; Num 6.12
7.2 Lev 4.29
7.3 Lev 3.3,9
7.6 Lev 6.18,29
7.7 Lev 14.13
7.9 Lev 2.5,8; Num 18.9; Ezek 44.29
7.11 Lev 3.1-17; Ezek 45.15
7.12 Lev 2.4; Num 6.15
7.13 Lev 2.12; 23.17
7.14 Ex 29.27
7.15 Lev 22.29,30
7.16 Lev 19.5-8
7.17 Ex 29.14

[d] Meaning of Heb uncertain

6.20 One-tenth of an ephah was about two quarts.

7.11–18 The offering of well-being was divided into three kinds according to purpose: thank offering, votive offering, and freewill offering. A thank offering was appropriate whenever one wished to show thanks to God, as when recovering from a serious illness or surviving a dangerous calamity (Psalm 107). A votive offering was given in fulfillment of a vow (2 Samuel 15.7–8). A freewill offering, however, needed no special occasion or reason.

of well-being is eaten on the third day, it shall not be acceptable, nor shall it be
credited to the one who offers it; it shall be an abomination, and the one who eats
of it shall incur guilt.
19 Flesh that touches any unclean thing shall not be eaten; it shall be burned up.
As for other flesh, all who are clean may eat such flesh. 20 But those who eat flesh
from the LORD's sacrifice of well-being while in a state of uncleanness shall be cut
off from their kin. 21 When any one of you touches any unclean thing—human
uncleanness or an unclean animal or any unclean creature—and then eats flesh
from the LORD's sacrifice of well-being, you shall be cut off from your kin.
22 The LORD spoke to Moses, saying: 23 Speak to the people of Israel, saying:
You shall eat no fat of ox or sheep or goat. 24 The fat of an animal that died or was
torn by wild animals may be put to any use, but you must not eat it. 25 If any one of
you eats the fat from an animal of which an offering by fire may be made to the
LORD, you who eat it shall be cut off from your kin. 26 You must not eat any blood
whatever, either of bird or of animal, in any of your settlements. 27 Any one of you
who eats any blood shall be cut off from your kin.
28 The LORD spoke to Moses, saying: 29 Speak to the people of Israel, saying:
Any one of you who would offer to the LORD your sacrifice of well-being must
yourself bring to the LORD your offering from your sacrifice of well-being. 30 Your
own hands shall bring the LORD's offering by fire; you shall bring the fat with the
breast, so that the breast may be raised as an elevation offering before the LORD.
31 The priest shall turn the fat into smoke on the altar, but the breast shall belong to
Aaron and his sons. 32 And the right thigh from your sacrifices of well-being you
shall give to the priest as an offering; 33 the one among the sons of Aaron who offers
the blood and fat of the offering of well-being shall have the right thigh for a portion. 34 For I have taken the breast of the elevation offering, and the thigh that is
offered, from the people of Israel, from their sacrifices of well-being, and have
given them to Aaron the priest and to his sons, as a perpetual due from the people
of Israel. 35 This is the portion allotted to Aaron and to his sons from the offerings
made by fire to the LORD, once they have been brought forward to serve the LORD
as priests; 36 these the LORD commanded to be given them, when he anointed them,
as a perpetual due from the people of Israel throughout their generations.
37 This is the ritual of the burnt offering, the grain offering, the sin offering, the
guilt offering, the offering of ordination, and the sacrifice of well-being, 38 which
the LORD commanded Moses on Mount Sinai, when he commanded the people of
Israel to bring their offerings to the LORD, in the wilderness of Sinai.

7.19 Lev 11.47
7.20 Gen 17.14 Lev 22.3-7 Num 19.13 1 Cor 11.27,28
7.21 Lev 5.2,3 Deut 14.8
7.23 Lev 3.17
7.24 Ex 22.31 Lev 17.15 Deut 14.21
7.26 Gen 9.4 Lev 3.17 17.10-14 Ezek 33.25 John 6.53 Acts 15.20,29
7.29 Ezek 45.15
7.30 Ex 29.24,27 Lev 8.27; 9.21 Num 6.20
7.31 Lev 7.34 Num 18.18
7.32 Num 18.18
7.34 Ex 29.28 Lev 7.31; 10.14, 15 Deut 18.3
7.36 Ex 29.22-34 40.13-15
7.38 Lev 26.46

2. Instructions for the priests

Moses consecrates the priests

8 The LORD spoke to Moses, saying: 2 Take Aaron and his sons with him, the
vestments, the anointing oil, the bull of sin offering, the two rams, and the
basket of unleavened bread; 3 and assemble the whole congregation at the entrance

8.1 Ex 29.1-4
8.2 Ex 28.1

7.29, 30 God told the people of Israel to bring their sacrifices of well-being personally, with their own hands. They were to take time and effort to express thanks to God. You are the only person who can express your thankfulness to God and to others. Do you leave it to others to express thanks for what people have done? Do you rely on the one leading the prayer to thank God for you? Take time yourself to express thanks both to God and to others who have helped and blessed you.

7.31–36 The "elevation offering" is also called the wave offering because it was lifted up and waved before the altar. The part of the offering the priests waved was theirs to keep. The waving motion toward and away from the altar symbolized the offering of the sacrifice to God and his returning it to the priests. These offerings helped to care for the priests, who cared for God's house. The New Testament teaches that ministers should be paid by the people they serve (1 Corinthians 9.10). We should give generously to those who minister to us.

7.37 The "offering of ordination" refers to the offering given at the ceremony when priests were inducted into office (8.22).

7.38 God gave his people many rituals and instructions to follow. All the rituals in Leviticus were meant to teach the people valuable lessons. But over time, the people became indifferent to the meanings of these rituals and they began to lose touch with God. When your church appears to be conducting dry, meaningless rituals, try rediscovering the original meaning and purpose behind each, and your worship will be revitalized.

8.1ff Why did Aaron and his sons need to be cleansed and set apart? Although all the men from the tribe of Levi were dedicated for service to God, only Aaron's descendants could be priests. They alone had the honor and responsibility of performing the sacrifices. These priests had to cleanse and dedicate themselves before they could help the people do the same.

of the tent of meeting. 4 And Moses did as the LORD commanded him. When the
congregation was assembled at the entrance of the tent of meeting, 5 Moses said to
the congregation, "This is what the LORD has commanded to be done."
6 Then Moses brought Aaron and his sons forward, and washed them with water. 7 He put the tunic on him, fastened the sash around him, clothed him with the
robe, and put the ephod on him. He then put the decorated band of the ephod
around him, tying the ephod to him with it. 8 He placed the breastpiece on him, and
in the breastpiece he put the Urim and the Thummim. 9 And he set the turban on his
head, and on the turban, in front, he set the golden ornament, the holy crown, as the
LORD commanded Moses.
10 Then Moses took the anointing oil and anointed the tabernacle and all that
was in it, and consecrated them. 11 He sprinkled some of it on the altar seven times,
and anointed the altar and all its utensils, and the basin and its base, to consecrate
them. 12 He poured some of the anointing oil on Aaron's head and anointed him, to
consecrate him. 13 And Moses brought forward Aaron's sons, and clothed them
with tunics, and fastened sashes around them, and tied headdresses on them, as the
LORD commanded Moses.
14 He led forward the bull of sin offering; and Aaron and his sons laid their
hands upon the head of the bull of sin offering, 15 and it was slaughtered. Moses
took the blood and with his finger put some on each of the horns of the altar, purifying the altar; then he poured out the blood at the base of the altar. Thus he consecrated it, to make atonement for it. 16 Moses took all the fat that was around the
entrails, and the appendage of the liver, and the two kidneys with their fat, and
turned them into smoke on the altar. 17 But the bull itself, its skin and flesh and its
dung, he burned with fire outside the camp, as the LORD commanded Moses.
18 Then he brought forward the ram of burnt offering. Aaron and his sons laid
their hands on the head of the ram, 19 and it was slaughtered. Moses dashed the
blood against all sides of the altar. 20 The ram was cut into its parts, and Moses
turned into smoke the head and the parts and the suet. 21 And after the entrails and
the legs were washed with water, Moses turned into smoke the whole ram on the
altar; it was a burnt offering for a pleasing odor, an offering by fire to the LORD, as
the LORD commanded Moses.
22 Then he brought forward the second ram, the ram of ordination. Aaron and
his sons laid their hands on the head of the ram, 23 and it was slaughtered. Moses
took some of its blood and put it on the lobe of Aaron's right ear and on the thumb
of his right hand and on the big toe of his right foot. 24 After Aaron's sons were
brought forward, Moses put some of the blood on the lobes of their right ears and

8.6 Ex 29.3,4
8.8 Ex 28.30,31 Ezra 2.62,63
8.9 Ex 28.4,36-38 29.6; 39.27-31 Zech 6.11-14
8.10 Ex 30.26-33 40.9-11
8.11 Ex 29.37 Lev 16.14
8.12 Ex 28.41; 30.30 Lev 21.10-12
8.13 Ex 28.36-38
8.14 Ex 29.10-14 Lev 16.6
8.15 Ex 30.10 Lev 4.7
8.17 Lev 4.11 Num 19.9
8.18 Ex 29.15-19
8.22 Ex 29.31
8.23 Ex 29.19,20

The ceremony described in Leviticus 8 and 9 was their ordination ceremony. Aaron and his sons were washed with water (8.6), clothed with special garments (8.7–9), and anointed with oil (8.12). They placed their hands on a young bull as it was killed (8.14), and on two rams as they were killed (8.18, 19, 22). This showed that holiness came from God alone, not from the priestly role. Similarly, we are not spiritually cleansed because we have a religious position. Spiritual cleansing comes only from God.

8.2, 3 Why were priests needed in Israel? In Exodus 19.6, the Israelites were instructed to be a kingdom of priests; ideally they would all be holy and relate to God. But from the time of Adam's fall, sin has separated man and God, and people have needed mediators to help them find forgiveness. At first, the patriarchs—heads of households like Abraham and Job—were priests of the house or clan and made sacrifices for the family. When the Israelites left Egypt, the descendants of Aaron were chosen to serve as priests for the nation. The priests stood in the gap between God and man. They were the full-time spiritual leaders and overseers of offerings. The priestly system was a concession to people's inability, because of sin, to confront and relate to God individually and corporately. In Christ, this imperfect system was transformed. Jesus Christ himself is our High Priest, so now all believers can approach God through him.

8.8 What were the Urim and Thummim? Little is known about them, but they were probably precious stones or flat objects that God used to give guidance to his people. The priest kept them in a pouch attached to his breastplate. Some scholars think the Urim may have been the "no" answer and the Thummim the "yes" answer. The priest would shake one of the stones out of the pouch, and God would cause the proper one to fall out. Another view is that the Urim and Thummim were small flat objects, each with a "yes" side and a "no" side. The priest spilled both from his pouch. If both landed on their "yes" sides, God's answer was positive. Two "no" sides were negative. A "yes" and a "no" meant no reply. God had a specific purpose for using this method of guidance, as he was teaching a nation the principles of following him. Our situation is not the same, however, so we must not assume God will guide us in ways like this today.

8.12 What was the significance of anointing Aaron as high priest? The high priest had special duties that no other priest had. He alone could enter the most holy place in the tabernacle on the yearly day of atonement to atone for the sins of the nation. Therefore he was in charge of all the other priests. The high priest was a picture of Jesus Christ, who is our High Priest (Hebrews 7.26–28).

on the thumbs of their right hands and on the big toes of their right feet; and Moses
dashed the rest of the blood against all sides of the altar. 25He took the fat—the 8.25
broad tail, all the fat that was around the entrails, the appendage of the liver, and Ex 29.22 Lev 3.9-11
the two kidneys with their fat—and the right thigh. 26From the basket of unleav- 8.26
ened bread that was before the LORD, he took one cake of unleavened bread, one Ex 29.23
cake of bread with oil, and one wafer, and placed them on the fat and on the right
thigh. 27He placed all these on the palms of Aaron and on the palms of his sons, and 8.27
raised them as an elevation offering before the LORD. 28Then Moses took them Ex 29.24 8.28
from their hands and turned them into smoke on the altar with the burnt offering. Ex 29.25
This was an ordination offering for a pleasing odor, an offering by fire to the LORD.
29Moses took the breast and raised it as an elevation offering before the LORD; it 8.29
was Moses' portion of the ram of ordination, as the LORD commanded Moses. Ex 29.26 Lev 8.22
30 Then Moses took some of the anointing oil and some of the blood that was 8.30
on the altar and sprinkled them on Aaron and his vestments, and also on his sons Ex 29.21
and their vestments. Thus he consecrated Aaron and his vestments, and also his
sons and their vestments.
31 And Moses said to Aaron and his sons, "Boil the flesh at the entrance of the 8.31
tent of meeting, and eat it there with the bread that is in the basket of ordination Ex 29.31,32 1 Sam 2.12-17
offerings, as I was commanded, 'Aaron and his sons shall eat it'; 32and what re- 8.32
mains of the flesh and the bread you shall burn with fire. 33You shall not go outside Lev 7.17,18 8.33
the entrance of the tent of meeting for seven days, until the day when your period Ex 29.35
of ordination is completed. For it will take seven days to ordain you; 34as has been
done today, the LORD has commanded to be done to make atonement for you.
35You shall remain at the entrance of the tent of meeting day and night for seven 8.35
days, keeping the LORD's charge so that you do not die; for so I am commanded." Lev 8.33
36Aaron and his sons did all the things that the LORD commanded through Moses.

The priests present the offerings

9 On the eighth day Moses summoned Aaron and his sons and the elders of Israel. 2He said to Aaron, "Take a bull calf for a sin offering and a ram for a 9.2
burnt offering, without blemish, and offer them before the LORD. 3And say to the Ex 29.24 9.3
people of Israel, 'Take a male goat for a sin offering; a calf and a lamb, yearlings Ezra 6.17
without blemish, for a burnt offering; 4and an ox and a ram for an offering of well- 9.4
being to sacrifice before the LORD; and a grain offering mixed with oil. For today Ex 29.43 Lev 2.4
the LORD will appear to you.'" 5They brought what Moses commanded to the front
of the tent of meeting; and the whole congregation drew near and stood before the
LORD. 6And Moses said, "This is the thing that the LORD commanded you to do, so 9.6
that the glory of the LORD may appear to you." 7Then Moses said to Aaron, "Draw Ex 40.34 Lev 9.23
near to the altar and sacrifice your sin offering and your burnt offering, and make 9.7
atonement for yourself and for the people; and sacrifice the offering of the people, Heb 5.1-3; 7.27 9.7
and make atonement for them; as the LORD has commanded."
8 Aaron drew near to the altar, and slaughtered the calf of the sin offering,
which was for himself. 9The sons of Aaron presented the blood to him, and he 9.9
dipped his finger in the blood and put it on the horns of the altar; and the rest of the Lev 4.6,7 Heb 9.22
blood he poured out at the base of the altar. 10But the fat, the kidneys, and the
appendage of the liver from the sin offering he turned into smoke on the altar, as
the LORD commanded Moses; 11and the flesh and the skin he burned with fire outside the camp.
12 Then he slaughtered the burnt offering. Aaron's sons brought him the blood,
and he dashed it against all sides of the altar. 13And they brought him the burnt
offering piece by piece, and the head, which he turned into smoke on the altar.

8.36 Aaron and his sons did "all the things that the Lord commanded." Considering the many detailed lists of Leviticus, that was a remarkable feat. They knew what God wanted, how he wanted it done, and with what attitude it was to be carried out. This can serve as a model for how carefully we ought to obey God. God wants us to be thoroughly holy people, not a rough approximation of the way his followers should be.

14 He washed the entrails and the legs and, with the burnt offering, turned them into
smoke on the altar.
15 Next he presented the people's offering. He took the goat of the sin offering
that was for the people, and slaughtered it, and presented it as a sin offering like the
first one. 16 He presented the burnt offering, and sacrificed it according to regulation. 17 He presented the grain offering, and, taking a handful of it, he turned it into
smoke on the altar, in addition to the burnt offering of the morning.
18 He slaughtered the ox and the ram as a sacrifice of well-being for the people.
Aaron's sons brought him the blood, which he dashed against all sides of the altar,
19 and the fat of the ox and of the ram—the broad tail, the fat that covers the entrails, the two kidneys and the fat on them,[e] and the appendage of the liver. 20 They
first laid the fat on the breasts, and the fat was turned into smoke on the altar; 21 and
the breasts and the right thigh Aaron raised as an elevation offering before the
LORD, as Moses had commanded.
22 Aaron lifted his hands toward the people and blessed them; and he came
down after sacrificing the sin offering, the burnt offering, and the offering of well-
being. 23 Moses and Aaron entered the tent of meeting, and then came out and
blessed the people; and the glory of the LORD appeared to all the people. 24 Fire
came out from the LORD and consumed the burnt offering and the fat on the altar;
and when all the people saw it, they shouted and fell on their faces.

Aaron's sons destroyed by fire

10 Now Aaron's sons, Nadab and Abihu, each took his censer, put fire in it,
and laid incense on it; and they offered unholy fire before the LORD, such as
he had not commanded them. 2 And fire came out from the presence of the LORD
and consumed them, and they died before the LORD. 3 Then Moses said to Aaron,
"This is what the LORD meant when he said,

'Through those who are near me
I will show myself holy,
and before all the people
I will be glorified.' "

And Aaron was silent.
4 Moses summoned Mishael and Elzaphan, sons of Uzziel the uncle of Aaron,
and said to them, "Come forward, and carry your kinsmen away from the front of
the sanctuary to a place outside the camp." 5 They came forward and carried them
by their tunics out of the camp, as Moses had ordered. 6 And Moses said to Aaron
and to his sons Eleazar and Ithamar, "Do not dishevel your hair, and do not tear
your vestments, or you will die and wrath will strike all the congregation; but your
kindred, the whole house of Israel, may mourn the burning that the LORD has sent.

[e] Gk: Heb *the broad tail, and that which covers, and the kidneys*

9.15 Lev 4.27-31; 9.3 Heb 5.1-3; 7.27 9.7
9.16 Lev 1.3-10 8.18-21
9.17 Ex 29.38-42 Lev 2.1-16 6.14-18
9.18 Lev 3.1-11 7.11-18
9.19 Lev 3.3; 9.10
9.21 Lev 7.30,32
9.22 Num 6.24-26
9.23 Num 16.19,42
9.24 Gen 15.17 1 Kgs 18.38
10.1 Ex 6.23 Num 3.2
10.2 Lev 16.1 Num 26.61
10.3 Ex 19.22 30.29,30 Ezek 38.16 Rom 14.11
10.4 Ex 6.18 Num 3.25-30
10.6 Lev 21.1-15 Num 1.53 Deut 33.9 Josh 7.1

9.22, 23 In 9.6 Moses said to the people, "This is the thing that the Lord commanded you to do, so that the glory of the Lord may appear to you." Moses, Aaron, and the people then got to work and completed God's instructions. Soon after, the glory of the Lord appeared. Often we look for God's glorious acts without concern for following his instructions. Do you serve God in the daily routines of life, or do you wait for him to do a mighty act? If you depend on his glorious acts, you may find yourself sidestepping your everyday duty to obey.

9.24 As a display of his mighty power, God sent fire from the sky to consume Aaron's offering. The people fell to the ground in awe. Some people wonder if God really exists because they don't see his activity in the world. But God is at work in today's world as he was in Moses' world. Where a large body of believers is active for him, God tends not to display his power in the form of mighty physical acts. Instead he works to change people's lives through the work of these believers. When you realize that, you will begin to see acts of love and faith in your life that are just as supernatural.

10.1 What was the unholy fire that Nadab and Abihu offered before the Lord? The fire on the altar of burnt offering was never to go out (6.12, 13), implying that it was holy. It is possible that Nadab and Abihu brought coals of fire to the altar from another source, making the sacrifice unholy. It has also been suggested that the two priests gave an offering at an unprescribed time. Whatever explanation is correct, the point is that Nadab and Abihu abused their office as priests in a flagrant act of disrespect to God, who had just reviewed with them precisely how they were to conduct worship. As leaders, they had special responsibility to obey God. In their position, they could easily lead many people astray.

10.2 Aaron's sons were careless about following the laws for sacrifices. In response, God destroyed them with a blast of fire. Performing the sacrifices was an act of obedience. Doing them correctly showed respect for God. It is easy for us to grow careless about obeying God, to live our way instead of God's. But if one way were just as good as another, God would not command us to live his way. He always has good reasons for his commands, and we always place ourselves in danger when we consciously or carelessly disobey them.

7 You shall not go outside the entrance of the tent of meeting, or you will die; for the
anointing oil of the LORD is on you." And they did as Moses had ordered.
8 And the LORD spoke to Aaron: 9 Drink no wine or strong drink, neither you
nor your sons, when you enter the tent of meeting, that you may not die; it is a
statute forever throughout your generations. 10 You are to distinguish between the
holy and the common, and between the unclean and the clean; 11 and you are to
teach the people of Israel all the statutes that the LORD has spoken to them through
Moses.
12 Moses spoke to Aaron and to his remaining sons, Eleazar and Ithamar: Take
the grain offering that is left from the LORD's offerings by fire, and eat it unleavened beside the altar, for it is most holy; 13 you shall eat it in a holy place, because
it is your due and your sons' due, from the offerings by fire to the LORD; for so I am
commanded. 14 But the breast that is elevated and the thigh that is raised, you and
your sons and daughters as well may eat in any clean place; for they have been
assigned to you and your children from the sacrifices of the offerings of well-being
of the people of Israel. 15 The thigh that is raised and the breast that is elevated they
shall bring, together with the offerings by fire of the fat, to raise for an elevation
offering before the LORD; they are to be your due and that of your children forever,
as the LORD has commanded.
16 Then Moses made inquiry about the goat of the sin offering, and—it had
already been burned! He was angry with Eleazar and Ithamar, Aaron's remaining
sons, and said, 17 "Why did you not eat the sin offering in the sacred area? For it is
most holy, and God[f] has given it to you that you may remove the guilt of the
congregation, to make atonement on their behalf before the LORD. 18 Its blood was
not brought into the inner part of the sanctuary. You should certainly have eaten it
in the sanctuary, as I commanded." 19 And Aaron spoke to Moses, "See, today they
offered their sin offering and their burnt offering before the LORD; and yet such
things as these have befallen me! If I had eaten the sin offering today, would it have
been agreeable to the LORD?" 20 And when Moses heard that, he agreed.

3. Instructions for the people

Clean and unclean animals

11 The LORD spoke to Moses and Aaron, saying to them: 2 Speak to the people
of Israel, saying:
From among all the land animals, these are the creatures that you may eat. 3 Any
animal that has divided hoofs and is cleft-footed and chews the cud—such you may
eat. 4 But among those that chew the cud or have divided hoofs, you shall not eat the
following: the camel, for even though it chews the cud, it does not have divided
hoofs; it is unclean for you. 5 The rock badger, for even though it chews the cud, it
does not have divided hoofs; it is unclean for you. 6 The hare, for even though it
chews the cud, it does not have divided hoofs; it is unclean for you. 7 The pig, for
even though it has divided hoofs and is cleft-footed, it does not chew the cud; it is
unclean for you. 8 Of their flesh you shall not eat, and their carcasses you shall not
touch; they are unclean for you.

10.7 Lev 21.12
10.8,9 Ezek 44.21
10.10 Lev 11.47 Ezek 22.26
10.11 Deut 6.4-9 33.10
10.12 Lev 2.1-3; 21.22 Num 3.2
10.13 Lev 16.14-18
10.14 Lev 7.28-36
10.15 Lev 7.30-34
10.16 Lev 6.25-30; 9.3
10.17 Lev 7.6
10.18 Lev 6.29,30
11.2-19 Deut 14.3-21
11.4 Ezek 4.14 Dan 1.8 Mt 15.11 Acts 10.14 Rom 14.2,3 Heb 9.10; 13.9
11.7 Isa 65.4; 66.3,17
11.8 Mk 7.15,18 Acts 10.14,15 1 Cor 8.8 Heb 9.10

[f] Heb *he*

10.8–11 The priests could not drink wine or other alcoholic beverages before going into the tabernacle. If their senses were dulled by alcohol, they might repeat Nadab and Abihu's sin and bring something unholy into the worship ceremony. In addition, drinking would disqualify them to teach the people God's requirements of self-discipline. Drunkenness was also associated with pagan practices and the Jewish priests were to be distinctively different.

10.10, 11 This passage (along with 19.1, 2) shows the focus of Leviticus. The ten commandments recorded in Exodus 20 were God's fundamental laws, and Leviticus explained and supplemented them with many other guidelines and principles that helped the Israelites put them into practice. The purpose of God's laws was to teach people how to distinguish right from wrong, and the holy from the common. The nation that lived by God's laws would obviously be set apart, dedicated to his service.

10.16–20 The priest who offered the sin offering was supposed to eat a portion of the animal and then burn the rest (6.24–30). Moses was angry because Eleazar and Ithamar burned the sin offering, but did not eat any of it. Aaron explained to Moses that his two sons did not feel it appropriate to eat the sacrifice after their two brothers, Nadab and Abihu, had just been killed for sacrificing wrongly. Moses then understood that Eleazar and Ithamar were not trying to disobey God. They were simply afraid and upset over what had just happened to their brothers.

11.8 God had strictly forbidden eating the meat of certain animals; to make sure, he forbade even touching them. He wanted the peo-

9 These you may eat, of all that are in the waters. Everything in the waters that
has fins and scales, whether in the seas or in the streams—such you may eat. 10 But
anything in the seas or the streams that does not have fins and scales, of the swarming creatures in the waters and among all the other living creatures that are in the
waters—they are detestable to you 11 and detestable they shall remain. Of their
flesh you shall not eat, and their carcasses you shall regard as detestable. 12 Everything in the waters that does not have fins and scales is detestable to you.
13 These you shall regard as detestable among the birds. They shall not be
eaten; they are an abomination: the eagle, the vulture, the osprey, 14 the buzzard,
the kite of any kind; 15 every raven of any kind; 16 the ostrich, the nighthawk, the sea
gull, the hawk of any kind; 17 the little owl, the cormorant, the great owl, 18 the
water hen, the desert owl,[g] the carrion vulture, 19 the stork, the heron of any kind,
the hoopoe, and the bat.[h]
20 All winged insects that walk upon all fours are detestable to you. 21 But
among the winged insects that walk on all fours you may eat those that have jointed
11.22 Mt 3.4 Mk 1.6 legs above their feet, with which to leap on the ground. 22 Of them you may eat: the
locust according to its kind, the bald locust according to its kind, the cricket according to its kind, and the grasshopper according to its kind. 23 But all other winged
insects that have four feet are detestable to you.

[g] Or *pelican* [h] Identification of several of the birds in verses 13-19 is uncertain

NADAB/ABIHU

Some brothers, like Cain and Abel or Jacob and Esau, get each other in trouble. Nadab and Abihu got in trouble together.

Although little is known of their early years, the Bible gives us an abundance of information about the environment in which they grew up. Born in Egypt, they were eyewitnesses of God's mighty acts of the exodus. They saw their father, Aaron, their uncle, Moses, and their aunt, Miriam, in action many times. They had first-hand knowledge of God's holiness as few men have ever had, and for a while at least, they followed God wholeheartedly (Leviticus 8.36). But at a crucial moment they chose to treat with indifference the clear instructions from God. The consequence of their sin was fiery, instant, and shocking to all.

We are in danger of making the same mistake as these brothers when we treat lightly the justice and holiness of God. We must draw near to God while realizing that there is a proper fear of God. Don't forget that the opportunity to know God personally is based on his gracious invitation to an always unworthy people, not a gift to be taken for granted. Do your thoughts about God include a humble recognition of his great holiness?

Strengths and accomplishments:
- Oldest sons of Aaron
- Primary candidates to become high priest after their father
- Involved with the original consecration of the tabernacle
- Commended for doing "all the things that the Lord commanded" (8.36)

Weakness and mistake:
- Treated lightly God's direct commands

Lesson from their lives:
- Sin has deadly consequences

Vital statistics:
- Where: The Sinai peninsula
- Occupation: Priests-in-training
- Relatives: Father: Aaron. Uncle and Aunt: Moses and Miriam. Brothers: Eleazar and Ithamar

Key verses:
"Now Aaron's sons, Nadab and Abihu, each took his censer, put fire in it, and laid incense on it; and they offered unholy fire before the Lord, such as he had not commanded them. And fire came out from the presence of the Lord and consumed them, and they died before the Lord" (Leviticus 10.1, 2).

The story of Nadab and Abihu is told in Leviticus 8—10. They are also mentioned in Exodus 24.1, 9; 28.1; Numbers 3.2–4; 26.61.

ple to be totally separated from those things he had forbidden. So often we flirt with temptation, rationalizing that at least we are technically keeping the commandment not to commit the sin. But God wants us to separate ourselves completely from all sin and tempting situations.

24 By these you shall become unclean; whoever touches the carcass of any of
them shall be unclean until the evening, 25 and whoever carries any part of the car- **11.25**
cass of any of them shall wash his clothes and be unclean until the evening. 26 Every Lev 11.28,40 Num 19.11-13
animal that has divided hoofs but is not cleft-footed or does not chew the cud is
unclean for you; everyone who touches one of them shall be unclean. 27 All that
walk on their paws, among the animals that walk on all fours, are unclean for you;
whoever touches the carcass of any of them shall be unclean until the evening,
28 and the one who carries the carcass shall wash his clothes and be unclean until the
evening; they are unclean for you.

29 These are unclean for you among the creatures that swarm upon the earth:
the weasel, the mouse, the great lizard according to its kind, 30 the gecko, the land
crocodile, the lizard, the sand lizard, and the chameleon. 31 These are unclean for
you among all that swarm; whoever touches one of them when they are dead shall
be unclean until the evening. 32 And anything upon which any of them falls when **11.32**
they are dead shall be unclean, whether an article of wood or cloth or skin or sack- Lev 15.12
ing, any article that is used for any purpose; it shall be dipped into water, and it
shall be unclean until the evening, and then it shall be clean. 33 And if any of them **11.33**
falls into any earthen vessel, all that is in it shall be unclean, and you shall break the Lev 6.28 2 Tim 2.20,21
vessel. 34 Any food that could be eaten shall be unclean if water from any such
vessel comes upon it; and any liquid that could be drunk shall be unclean if it was
in any such vessel. 35 Everything on which any part of the carcass falls shall be
unclean; whether an oven or stove, it shall be broken in pieces; they are unclean,
and shall remain unclean for you. 36 But a spring or a cistern holding water shall be
clean, while whatever touches the carcass in it shall be unclean. 37 If any part of
their carcass falls upon any seed set aside for sowing, it is clean; 38 but if water is
put on the seed and any part of their carcass falls on it, it is unclean for you.

39 If an animal of which you may eat dies, anyone who touches its carcass shall
be unclean until the evening. 40 Those who eat of its carcass shall wash their clothes **11.40**
and be unclean until the evening; and those who carry the carcass shall wash their Lev 11.25; 17.15 Deut 14.21
clothes and be unclean until the evening. Ezek 4.14; 44.31

41 All creatures that swarm upon the earth are detestable; they shall not be **11.41**
eaten. 42 Whatever moves on its belly, and whatever moves on all fours, or what- Lev 11.20,23 Deut 14.19,20
ever has many feet, all the creatures that swarm upon the earth, you shall not eat;
for they are detestable. 43 You shall not make yourselves detestable with any crea- **11.44**
ture that swarms; you shall not defile yourselves with them, and so become un- Ex 19.6; 20.2 Lev 19.2
clean. 44 For I am the LORD your God; sanctify yourselves therefore, and be holy, 20.7,26 Isa 6.3,4
for I am holy. You shall not defile yourselves with any swarming creature that Amos 3.3
moves on the earth. 45 For I am the LORD who brought you up from the land of Mt 5.48 1 Thess 4.7
Egypt, to be your God; you shall be holy, for I am holy. 1 Pet 1.16 Rev 4.8; 22.11

46 This is the law pertaining to land animal and bird and every living creature **11.47**
that moves through the waters and every creature that swarms upon the earth, 47 to Lev 10.10

11.25 In order to worship, people need to be prepared. There were some acts of disobedience, some natural acts (such as childbirth, menstruation, or sex), or some accidents (such as touching a dead or diseased body) that would make a person ceremonially defiled and thus forbidden to participate in worship. This chapter describes many of the intentional.or accidental occurrences that would disqualify a person from worship until they were "cleansed" or straightened out. One had to be *prepared* for worship. Similarly, we cannot live any way we want during the week then rush into God's presence on Sunday. Our relationship with him must be one of constant repentance and cleansing so we are prepared for worship.

11.44, 45 There is more to this chapter than eating right. These verses provide a key to understanding all the laws and regulations in Leviticus. God wanted his people to be *holy* (set apart, different, unique), just as he is holy. He knew they had only two options: to be separate and holy, or to compromise with their heathen neighbors and become corrupt. That is why he called them out of idolatrous Egypt and set them apart as a unique nation, dedicated to worshiping him alone and leading moral lives. That is also why he designed laws and restrictions to help them remain separate—both socially and spiritually—from the wicked heathen nations they would encounter in Canaan. Christians also are called to be holy (1 Peter 1.15). Like the Israelites, we are to remain spiritually separate from the world's wickedness, even though, unlike them, we rub shoulders with unbelievers every day. It is no easy task to be holy in an unholy world, but God doesn't ask you to accomplish this on your own. Through the death of his Son, he will "present you holy and blameless and irreproachable before him" (Colossians 1.22).

11.47 The designations *clean* and *unclean* were used to define the kind of animals the Israelites could and could not eat. There were several reasons for this restricted diet: (1) To insure the health of the nation. The forbidden foods were usually scavenging animals that fed on dead animals; thus disease could be transmitted through them. (2) To visibly distinguish Israel from other nations.

make a distinction between the unclean and the clean, and between the living creature that may be eaten and the living creature that may not be eaten.

Purification after childbirth

12.2 Lev 15.19; 18.19

12 The LORD spoke to Moses, saying: 2 Speak to the people of Israel, saying:
If a woman conceives and bears a male child, she shall be ceremonially un-

12.3 Gen 17.12-14 Josh 5.2-7 Lk 1.59; 2.21 Phil 3.5

clean seven days; as at the time of her menstruation, she shall be unclean. 3 On the
eighth day the flesh of his foreskin shall be circumcised. 4 Her time of blood purification shall be thirty-three days; she shall not touch any holy thing, or come into the
sanctuary, until the days of her purification are completed. 5 If she bears a female
child, she shall be unclean two weeks, as in her menstruation; her time of blood
purification shall be sixty-six days.

12.6 Lev 14.21,22 Lk 2.22

6 When the days of her purification are completed, whether for a son or for a
daughter, she shall bring to the priest at the entrance of the tent of meeting a lamb
in its first year for a burnt offering, and a pigeon or a turtledove for a sin offering.
7 He shall offer it before the LORD, and make atonement on her behalf; then she
shall be clean from her flow of blood. This is the law for her who bears a child,

12.8 Lev 5.7 15.29-31 Lk 2.24

male or female. 8 If she cannot afford a sheep, she shall take two turtledoves or two
pigeons, one for a burnt offering and the other for a sin offering; and the priest shall
make atonement on her behalf, and she shall be clean.

Rules about leprosy

13 The LORD spoke to Moses and Aaron, saying:

13.2,3 Lev 13.38; 14.56 Deut 24.8 Lk 17.14

2 When a person has on the skin of his body a swelling or an eruption or a
spot, and it turns into a leprous[i] disease on the skin of his body, he shall be brought
to Aaron the priest or to one of his sons the priests. 3 The priest shall examine the
disease on the skin of his body, and if the hair in the diseased area has turned white
and the disease appears to be deeper than the skin of his body, it is a leprous[i]
disease; after the priest has examined him he shall pronounce him ceremonially
unclean. 4 But if the spot is white in the skin of his body, and appears no deeper than
the skin, and the hair in it has not turned white, the priest shall confine the diseased
person for seven days. 5 The priest shall examine him on the seventh day, and if he
sees that the disease is checked and the disease has not spread in the skin, then the

13.6 Lev 11.25

priest shall confine him seven days more. 6 The priest shall examine him again on
the seventh day, and if the disease has abated and the disease has not spread in the
skin, the priest shall pronounce him clean; it is only an eruption; and he shall wash
his clothes, and be clean. 7 But if the eruption spreads in the skin after he has shown
himself to the priest for his cleansing, he shall appear again before the priest. 8 The
priest shall make an examination, and if the eruption has spread in the skin, the

13.9,10 Num 12.10 2 Kgs 5.27

priest shall pronounce him unclean; it is a leprous[i] disease.
9 When a person contracts a leprous[i] disease, he shall be brought to the priest.

[i] A term for several skin diseases; precise meaning uncertain

---

The pig, for example, was a common sacrifice of heathen religions. (3) To avoid objectionable associations. Animals that 'swarmed upon the earth' (crawled on the ground) for example, were reminiscent of serpents, which often symbolized sin.

12.1–4 Why was a woman considered unclean after the wonderful miracle of birth? It was due to the bodily emissions and secretions occurring during and after childbirth. These were considered unclean and made the woman unprepared to enter the pure surroundings of the tabernacle.

12.1–4 *Unclean* did not mean "sinful" or "dirty." God created us male and female, and he ordered us to be fruitful and multiply (Genesis 1.27, 28). He did not change his mind and say that sex and procreation were now somehow defiled. Instead, he made a distinction between his worship and the popular worship of fertility gods and goddesses. Canaanite religions incorporated prostitution and immoral rites as the people begged their gods to make their crops, herds, and families increase. By contrast, Israel's religion avoided all sexual connotations. By keeping worship and sex entirely separate, God helped the Israelites avoid confusion with heathen rites. The Israelites worshiped God as their loving Creator and Provider, and they thanked him for bountiful crops and safe childbirth.

13.1ff Leprosy, a name applied to several different diseases, was greatly feared in Bible times. Some of these diseases, unlike the disease we call leprosy or Hansen's disease today, were highly contagious. The worst of them slowly ruined the body and, in most cases, were fatal. Lepers were separated from family and friends and confined outside the camp. Since priests were responsible for the health of the camp, it was their duty to expel and readmit lepers. If someone's leprosy appeared to go away, only the priest could decide if he was truly cured. Leprosy is often used in the Bible as an illustration of sin because sin is contagious and destructive and leads to separation.

10 The priest shall make an examination, and if there is a white swelling in the skin
that has turned the hair white, and there is quick raw flesh in the swelling, 11 it is a
chronic leprous[j] disease in the skin of his body. The priest shall pronounce him
unclean; he shall not confine him, for he is unclean. 12 But if the disease breaks out
in the skin, so that it covers all the skin of the diseased person from head to foot, so
far as the priest can see, 13 then the priest shall make an examination, and if the
disease has covered all his body, he shall pronounce him clean of the disease; since
it has all turned white, he is clean. 14 But if raw flesh ever appears on him, he shall
be unclean; 15 the priest shall examine the raw flesh and pronounce him unclean.
Raw flesh is unclean, for it is a leprous[j] disease. 16 But if the raw flesh again turns
white, he shall come to the priest; 17 the priest shall examine him, and if the disease
has turned white, the priest shall pronounce the diseased person clean. He is clean.

18 When there is on the skin of one's body a boil that has healed, 19 and in the **13.18**
place of the boil there appears a white swelling or a reddish-white spot, it shall be Ex 9.9
shown to the priest. 20 The priest shall make an examination, and if it appears
deeper than the skin and its hair has turned white, the priest shall pronounce him
unclean; this is a leprous[j] disease, broken out in the boil. 21 But if the priest examines it and the hair on it is not white, nor is it deeper than the skin but has abated,
the priest shall confine him seven days. 22 If it spreads in the skin, the priest shall
pronounce him unclean; it is diseased. 23 But if the spot remains in one place and
does not spread, it is the scar of the boil; the priest shall pronounce him clean.

24 Or, when the body has a burn on the skin and the raw flesh of the burn
becomes a spot, reddish-white or white, 25 the priest shall examine it. If the hair in
the spot has turned white and it appears deeper than the skin, it is a leprous[j] disease; it has broken out in the burn, and the priest shall pronounce him unclean. This
is a leprous[j] disease. 26 But if the priest examines it and the hair in the spot is not
white, and it is no deeper than the skin but has abated, the priest shall confine him
seven days. 27 The priest shall examine him the seventh day; if it is spreading in the **13.27**
skin, the priest shall pronounce him unclean. This is a leprous[j] disease. 28 But if Deut 24.8
the spot remains in one place and does not spread in the skin but has abated, it is a
swelling from the burn, and the priest shall pronounce him clean; for it is the scar
of the burn.

29 When a man or woman has a disease on the head or in the beard, 30 the priest
shall examine the disease. If it appears deeper than the skin and the hair in it is
yellow and thin, the priest shall pronounce him unclean; it is an itch, a leprous[j]
disease of the head or the beard. 31 If the priest examines the itching disease, and it
appears no deeper than the skin and there is no black hair in it, the priest shall
confine the person with the itching disease for seven days. 32 On the seventh day the
priest shall examine the itch; if the itch has not spread, and there is no yellow hair
in it, and the itch appears to be no deeper than the skin, 33 he shall shave, but the itch **13.33**
he shall not shave. The priest shall confine the person with the itch for seven days Lev 14.9
more. 34 On the seventh day the priest shall examine the itch; if the itch has not **13.34**
spread in the skin and it appears to be no deeper than the skin, the priest shall Lev 14.8
pronounce him clean. He shall wash his clothes and be clean. 35 But if the itch
spreads in the skin after he was pronounced clean, 36 the priest shall examine him.
If the itch has spread in the skin, the priest need not seek for the yellow hair; he is
unclean. 37 But if in his eyes the itch is checked, and black hair has grown in it, the
itch is healed, he is clean; and the priest shall pronounce him clean.

38 When a man or a woman has spots on the skin of the body, white spots, 39 the
priest shall make an examination, and if the spots on the skin of the body are of a
dull white, it is a rash that has broken out on the skin; he is clean.

40 If anyone loses the hair from his head, he is bald but he is clean. 41 If he loses
the hair from his forehead and temples, he has baldness of the forehead but he is
clean. 42 But if there is on the bald head or the bald forehead a reddish-white diseased spot, it is a leprous[j] disease breaking out on his bald head or his bald forehead. 43 The priest shall examine him; if the diseased swelling is reddish-white on
his bald head or on his bald forehead, which resembles a leprous[j] disease in the

[j] A term for several skin diseases; precise meaning uncertain

skin of the body, 44 he is leprous,[k] he is unclean. The priest shall pronounce him
unclean; the disease is on his head.

13.45 Lam 4.15 Ezek 24.17,22 Mic 3.7
13.46 Num 5.1-4 12.14 2 Kgs 7.3; 15.5 2 Chron 26.21 Lk 17.12

45 The person who has the leprous[k] disease shall wear torn clothes and let the
hair of his head be disheveled; and he shall cover his upper lip and cry out, "Unclean, unclean." 46 He shall remain unclean as long as he has the disease; he is
unclean. He shall live alone; his dwelling shall be outside the camp.
47 Concerning clothing: when a leprous[k] disease appears in it, in woolen or
linen cloth, 48 in warp or woof of linen or wool, or in a skin or in anything made of
skin, 49 if the disease shows greenish or reddish in the garment, whether in warp or
woof or in skin or in anything made of skin, it is a leprous[k] disease and shall be
shown to the priest. 50 The priest shall examine the disease, and put the diseased

13.51 Lev 14.44

article aside for seven days. 51 He shall examine the disease on the seventh day. If
the disease has spread in the cloth, in warp or woof, or in the skin, whatever be the
use of the skin, this is a spreading leprous[k] disease; it is unclean. 52 He shall burn
the clothing, whether diseased in warp or woof, woolen or linen, or anything of
skin, for it is a spreading leprous[k] disease; it shall be burned in fire.
53 If the priest makes an examination, and the disease has not spread in the
clothing, in warp or woof or in anything of skin, 54 the priest shall command them
to wash the article in which the disease appears, and he shall put it aside seven days
more. 55 The priest shall examine the diseased article after it has been washed. If the
diseased spot has not changed color, though the disease has not spread, it is unclean; you shall burn it in fire, whether the leprous[k] spot is on the inside or on the
outside.
56 If the priest makes an examination, and the disease has abated after it is
washed, he shall tear the spot out of the cloth, in warp or woof, or out of skin. 57 If
it appears again in the garment, in warp or woof, or in anything of skin, it is spreading; you shall burn with fire that in which the disease appears. 58 But the cloth, warp
or woof, or anything of skin from which the disease disappears when you have
washed it, shall then be washed a second time, and it shall be clean.
59 This is the ritual for a leprous[k] disease in a cloth of wool or linen, either in
warp or woof, or in anything of skin, to decide whether it is clean or unclean.

Purification after leprosy

14.2 Mt 8.4 Mk 1.40-45 Lk 5.12-14 17.12-14
14.3 Lev 13.36
14.4 Lev 14.6,49-53 Num 19.6
14.6 Ps 51.7 Heb 9.19

14 The LORD spoke to Moses, saying: 2 This shall be the ritual for the leprous[k]
person at the time of his cleansing:
He shall be brought to the priest; 3 the priest shall go out of the camp, and the
priest shall make an examination. If the disease is healed in the leprous[k] person,
4 the priest shall command that two living clean birds and cedarwood and crimson
yarn and hyssop be brought for the one who is to be cleansed. 5 The priest shall
command that one of the birds be slaughtered over fresh water in an earthen vessel.
6 He shall take the living bird with the cedarwood and the crimson yarn and the
hyssop, and dip them and the living bird in the blood of the bird that was slaughtered over the fresh water. 7 He shall sprinkle it seven times upon the one who is to
be cleansed of the leprous[k] disease; then he shall pronounce him clean, and he shall

14.8 Lev 14.9 Num 8.7
14.9 Lev 13.33; 14.8 Num 6.9

let the living bird go into the open field. 8 The one who is to be cleansed shall wash
his clothes, and shave off all his hair, and bathe himself in water, and he shall be
clean. After that he shall come into the camp, but shall live outside his tent seven
days. 9 On the seventh day he shall shave all his hair: of head, beard, eyebrows; he
shall shave all his hair. Then he shall wash his clothes, and bathe his body in water,
and he shall be clean.

14.10 Lev 23.12,13 Num 6.14,15

10 On the eighth day he shall take two male lambs without blemish, and one
ewe lamb in its first year without blemish, and a grain offering of three-tenths of an

[k] A term for several skin diseases; precise meaning uncertain

13.45, 46 A person with leprosy had to perform this strange ritual to protect others from coming too near. Since the disease described in Leviticus was often contagious, it was important that people stay away from those who had it.

13.48 Warp and woof are the vertical and horizontal strands in woven fabric.

ephah of choice flour mixed with oil, and one log[l] of oil. 11 The priest who
cleanses shall set the person to be cleansed, along with these things, before the
LORD, at the entrance of the tent of meeting. 12 The priest shall take one of the **14.12**
lambs, and offer it as a guilt offering, along with the log[l] of oil, and raise them as Ex 29.24
an elevation offering before the LORD. 13 He shall slaughter the lamb in the place **14.13**
where the sin offering and the burnt offering are slaughtered in the holy place; for Lev 1.11-13 4.4-12
the guilt offering, like the sin offering, belongs to the priest: it is most holy. 14 The 6.1–7.10
priest shall take some of the blood of the guilt offering and put it on the lobe of the **14.14**
right ear of the one to be cleansed, and on the thumb of the right hand, and on the Ex 29.19-21 Lev 8.23,24
big toe of the right foot. 15 The priest shall take some of the log[l] of oil and pour it
into the palm of his own left hand, 16 and dip his right finger in the oil that is in his
left hand and sprinkle some oil with his finger seven times before the LORD.
17 Some of the oil that remains in his hand the priest shall put on the lobe of the right
ear of the one to be cleansed, and on the thumb of the right hand, and on the big toe
of the right foot, on top of the blood of the guilt offering. 18 The rest of the oil that **14.18**
is in the priest's hand he shall put on the head of the one to be cleansed. Then the Lev 8.30
priest shall make atonement on his behalf before the LORD: 19 the priest shall offer **14.19**
the sin offering, to make atonement for the one to be cleansed from his unclean- Lev 6.24-30
ness. Afterward he shall slaughter the burnt offering; 20 and the priest shall offer the **14.20**
burnt offering and the grain offering on the altar. Thus the priest shall make atone- Lev 23.12,13
ment on his behalf and he shall be clean.

21 But if he is poor and cannot afford so much, he shall take one male lamb for **14.21**
a guilt offering to be elevated, to make atonement on his behalf, and one-tenth of Lev 5.7,11 12.8
an ephah of choice flour mixed with oil for a grain offering and a log[l] of oil; 22 also **14.22**
two turtledoves or two pigeons, such as he can afford, one for a sin offering and the Lev 5.7
other for a burnt offering. 23 On the eighth day he shall bring them for his cleansing **14.23**
to the priest, to the entrance of the tent of meeting, before the LORD; 24 and the priest Lev 14.11
shall take the lamb of the guilt offering and the log[l] of oil, and the priest shall raise
them as an elevation offering before the LORD. 25 The priest shall slaughter the lamb **14.25**
of the guilt offering and shall take some of the blood of the guilt offering, and put Lev 14.14
it on the lobe of the right ear of the one to be cleansed, and on the thumb of the right
hand, and on the big toe of the right foot. 26 The priest shall pour some of the oil into
the palm of his own left hand, 27 and shall sprinkle with his right finger some of the
oil that is in his left hand seven times before the LORD. 28 The priest shall put some
of the oil that is in his hand on the lobe of the right ear of the one to be cleansed, and
on the thumb of the right hand, and the big toe of the right foot, where the blood of
the guilt offering was placed. 29 The rest of the oil that is in the priest's hand he shall
put on the head of the one to be cleansed, to make atonement on his behalf before
the LORD. 30 And he shall offer, of the turtledoves or pigeons such as he can afford,
31 one[m] for a sin offering and the other for a burnt offering, along with a grain
offering; and the priest shall make atonement before the LORD on behalf of the one
being cleansed. 32 This is the ritual for the one who has a leprous[n] disease, who
cannot afford the offerings for his cleansing.

33 The LORD spoke to Moses and Aaron, saying:

34 When you come into the land of Canaan, which I give you for a possession,
and I put a leprous[n] disease in a house in the land of your possession, 35 the owner **14.35**
of the house shall come and tell the priest, saying, "There seems to me to be some Ps 91.10 Zech 5.4
sort of disease in my house." 36 The priest shall command that they empty the house
before the priest goes to examine the disease, or all that is in the house will become
unclean; and afterward the priest shall go in to inspect the house. 37 He shall examine the disease; if the disease is in the walls of the house with greenish or reddish

[l] A liquid measure [m] Gk Syr: Heb *afford, 31 such as he can afford, one* [n] A term for several skin diseases; precise meaning uncertain

14.34, 35 Could leprosy really infect one's clothing or house? The Hebrew word for leprosy included a variety of skin diseases as well as other molds and fungi. The "leprosy" found on clothing or house walls was more like a mold, fungus, or bacteria. Like mildew, this fungus could spread rapidly and promote disease. It was therefore important to check its spread as soon as possible. In extreme cases, if the fungus had done enough damage, the clothing was burned or the house destroyed.

spots, and if it appears to be deeper than the surface, 38 the priest shall go outside to
14.39 the door of the house and shut up the house seven days. 39 The priest shall come
Lev 13.6-8 again on the seventh day and make an inspection; if the disease has spread in the
walls of the house, 40 the priest shall command that the stones in which the disease
appears be taken out and thrown into an unclean place outside the city. 41 He shall
have the inside of the house scraped thoroughly, and the plaster that is scraped off
shall be dumped in an unclean place outside the city. 42 They shall take other stones
and put them in the place of those stones, and take other plaster and plaster the
house.

43 If the disease breaks out again in the house, after he has taken out the stones
and scraped the house and plastered it, 44 the priest shall go and make inspection; if
the disease has spread in the house, it is a spreading leprous[o] disease in the house;
14.45 it is unclean. 45 He shall have the house torn down, its stones and timber and all the
Lev 14.41-45 plaster of the house, and taken outside the city to an unclean place. 46 All who enter
the house while it is shut up shall be unclean until the evening; 47 and all who sleep
in the house shall wash their clothes; and all who eat in the house shall wash their
clothes.

48 If the priest comes and makes an inspection, and the disease has not spread
in the house after the house was plastered, the priest shall pronounce the house
14.49 clean; the disease is healed. 49 For the cleansing of the house he shall take two birds,
Lev 14.4-7 Num 19.6 with cedarwood and crimson yarn and hyssop, 50 and shall slaughter one of the
birds over fresh water in an earthen vessel, 51 and shall take the cedarwood and the
hyssop and the crimson yarn, along with the living bird, and dip them in the blood
of the slaughtered bird and the fresh water, and sprinkle the house seven times.
52 Thus he shall cleanse the house with the blood of the bird, and with the fresh
water, and with the living bird, and with the cedarwood and hyssop and crimson
yarn; 53 and he shall let the living bird go out of the city into the open field; so he
shall make atonement for the house, and it shall be clean.

54 This is the ritual for any leprous[o] disease: for an itch, 55 for leprous[o] dis-
14.57 eases in clothing and houses, 56 and for a swelling or an eruption or a spot, 57 to
Deut 24.8 Ezek 44.23 determine when it is unclean and when it is clean. This is the ritual for leprous[o]
diseases.

Purification after bodily discharges

15.1-3 Lev 22.4 Num 5.2 **15** The LORD spoke to Moses and Aaron, saying: 2 Speak to the people of Israel
and say to them:

When any man has a discharge from his member,[p] his discharge makes him
ceremonially unclean. 3 The uncleanness of his discharge is this: whether his member[p] flows with his discharge, or his member[p] is stopped from discharging, it is
15.4 uncleanness for him. 4 Every bed on which the one with the discharge lies shall be
Lev 15.20-23 unclean; and everything on which he sits shall be unclean. 5 Anyone who touches
his bed shall wash his clothes, and bathe in water, and be unclean until the evening.
6 All who sit on anything on which the one with the discharge has sat shall wash
their clothes, and bathe in water, and be unclean until the evening. 7 All who touch

[o] A term for several skin diseases; precise meaning uncertain [p] Heb *flesh*

14.54–57 God told the Israelites how to diagnose leprosy so they could avoid it or treat it. These laws were given for the people's health and protection. They helped the Israelites avoid diseases that were serious threats in that time and place. Although they wouldn't have understood the medical reasons for some of these laws, their obedience to them made them healthier. Many of God's laws must have seemed strange to the Israelites. His laws, however, helped them avoid not only physical contamination, but moral and spiritual infection as well.

The word of God still provides a pattern for physically, spiritually, and morally healthy living. We may not always understand the wisdom of God's laws, but if we obey them we will thrive. Does this mean we are to follow the Old Testament health and dietary restrictions? In general, the basic principles of health and cleanliness are still healthful practices. But it would be legalistic, if not wrong, to adhere to each specific restriction today. Some of these regulations were intended to mark the Israelites as different from the wicked people around them. Others were given to prevent God's people from becoming involved in pagan religious practices, one of the most serious problems of the day. Still others related to quarantines in a culture where exact medical diagnosis was impossible. Today, for example, physicians can diagnose the different forms of leprosy, and they know which ones are contagious. Treatment methods have greatly improved, and quarantine for leprosy is rarely necessary.

the body of the one with the discharge shall wash their clothes, and bathe in water,
and be unclean until the evening. 8 If the one with the discharge spits on persons
who are clean, then they shall wash their clothes, and bathe in water, and be unclean until the evening. 9 Any saddle on which the one with the discharge rides shall
be unclean. 10 All who touch anything that was under him shall be unclean until the
evening, and all who carry such a thing shall wash their clothes, and bathe in water,
and be unclean until the evening. 11 All those whom the one with the discharge
touches without his having rinsed his hands in water shall wash their clothes, and
bathe in water, and be unclean until the evening. 12 Any earthen vessel that the one
with the discharge touches shall be broken; and every vessel of wood shall be rinsed
in water.

13 When the one with a discharge is cleansed of his discharge, he shall count
seven days for his cleansing; he shall wash his clothes and bathe his body in fresh
water, and he shall be clean. 14 On the eighth day he shall take two turtledoves or
two pigeons and come before the LORD to the entrance of the tent of meeting and
give them to the priest. 15 The priest shall offer them, one for a sin offering and the
other for a burnt offering; and the priest shall make atonement on his behalf before
the LORD for his discharge.

16 If a man has an emission of semen, he shall bathe his whole body in water,
and be unclean until the evening. 17 Everything made of cloth or of skin on which
the semen falls shall be washed with water, and be unclean until the evening. 18 If
a man lies with a woman and has an emission of semen, both of them shall bathe in
water, and be unclean until the evening.

19 When a woman has a discharge of blood that is her regular discharge from
her body, she shall be in her impurity for seven days, and whoever touches her shall
be unclean until the evening. 20 Everything upon which she lies during her impurity
shall be unclean; everything also upon which she sits shall be unclean. 21 Whoever
touches her bed shall wash his clothes, and bathe in water, and be unclean until the
evening. 22 Whoever touches anything upon which she sits shall wash his clothes,
and bathe in water, and be unclean until the evening; 23 whether it is the bed or
anything upon which she sits, when he touches it he shall be unclean until the evening. 24 If any man lies with her, and her impurity falls on him, he shall be unclean
seven days; and every bed on which he lies shall be unclean.

25 If a woman has a discharge of blood for many days, not at the time of her
impurity, or if she has a discharge beyond the time of her impurity, all the days of
the discharge she shall continue in uncleanness; as in the days of her impurity, she
shall be unclean. 26 Every bed on which she lies during all the days of her discharge
shall be treated as the bed of her impurity; and everything on which she sits shall be
unclean, as in the uncleanness of her impurity. 27 Whoever touches these things
shall be unclean, and shall wash his clothes, and bathe in water, and be unclean
until the evening. 28 If she is cleansed of her discharge, she shall count seven days,
and after that she shall be clean. 29 On the eighth day she shall take two turtledoves
or two pigeons and bring them to the priest to the entrance of the tent of meeting.
30 The priest shall offer one for a sin offering and the other for a burnt offering; and
the priest shall make atonement on her behalf before the LORD for her unclean discharge.

31 Thus you shall keep the people of Israel separate from their uncleanness, so
that they do not die in their uncleanness by defiling my tabernacle that is in their
midst.

32 This is the ritual for those who have a discharge: for him who has an emis-

15.12 Lev 6.28; 11.33
15.13 Num 19.11,12
15.15 Lev 14.22
15.16 Lev 15.5; 22.6 Deut 23.10,11
15.18 Ex 19.15 1 Sam 21.4
15.19 Lev 12.2-5
15.20 Lev 15.4,5
15.24 Lev 15.33 18.19; 20.18 Ezek 18.6; 22.10
15.25 Mt 9.20 Mk 5.25 Lk 8.43,44
15.30 Lev 5.7; 14.22 15.15
15.31 Num 5.3; 19.13, 20

15.18 This verse is not implying that sex is dirty or disgusting. God created sex, both for the enjoyment of married couples, as well as for continuing the race and continuing the covenant. Everything must be seen and done with a view toward God's love and control. Sex is not separate from spirituality and God's care. God is concerned about our sexual habits. We tend to separate our physical and spiritual lives, but there is an inseparable intertwining. God must be Lord over our whole selves – including our private lives.

15.32, 33 God is concerned about health, the dignity of the person, the dignity of the body, and the dignity of the sexual experience. His commands call the people to avoid unhealthy practices and promote healthy ones. To wash was the physical health response, to be purified or cleansed was the spiritual dignity response. This shows God's high regard for sex and sexuality. In our

sion of semen, becoming unclean thereby, 33 for her who is in the infirmity of her
period, for anyone, male or female, who has a discharge, and for the man who lies
with a woman who is unclean.

4. Instructions for the altar

The day of atonement for sin

16.1,2 Ex 25.17-22 30.10 Lev 10.1,2 Heb 9.7,25
16.3 Lev 16.6,7 Num 29.7-11
16.4 Ex 28.39-43 39.27-29 Lev 6.10 Ezek 44.17-19
16.6 Lev 9.7 Heb 5.1-3; 7.27, 28; 9.7

16 The LORD spoke to Moses after the death of the two sons of Aaron, when
they drew near before the LORD and died. 2 The LORD said to Moses:
Tell your brother Aaron not to come just at any time into the sanctuary inside the
curtain before the mercy seat[q] that is upon the ark, or he will die; for I appear in the
cloud upon the mercy seat.[q] 3 Thus shall Aaron come into the holy place: with a
young bull for a sin offering and a ram for a burnt offering. 4 He shall put on the
holy linen tunic, and shall have the linen undergarments next to his body, fasten the
linen sash, and wear the linen turban; these are the holy vestments. He shall bathe
his body in water, and then put them on. 5 He shall take from the congregation of
the people of Israel two male goats for a sin offering, and one ram for a burnt
offering.
6 Aaron shall offer the bull as a sin offering for himself, and shall make atonement for himself and for his house. 7 He shall take the two goats and set them before
the LORD at the entrance of the tent of meeting; 8 and Aaron shall cast lots on the two
goats, one lot for the LORD and the other lot for Azazel.[r] 9 Aaron shall present the

[q] Or *the cover* [r] Traditionally rendered *a scapegoat*

OLD/NEW SYSTEMS OF SACRIFICE

Old System of Sacrifice	*New System of Sacrifice*
Was temporary (Hebrews 8.13)	Is permanent (Hebrews 7.21)
Aaron first high priest (Leviticus 16.32)	Jesus only High Priest (Hebrews 4.14)
From tribe of Levi (Hebrews 7.5)	From tribe of Judah (Hebrews 7.14)
Ministered on earth (Hebrews 8.4)	Ministers in heaven (Hebrews 8.1,2)
Used blood of animals (Leviticus 16.15)	Uses blood of Christ (Hebrews 10.5)
Required many sacrifices (Leviticus 22.19)	Requires one sacrifice (Hebrews 9.28)
Needed perfect animals (Leviticus 22.19)	Needs a perfect life (Hebrews 5.9)
Required careful approach to tabernacle (Leviticus 16.2)	Encourages bold approach to Throne (Hebrews 4.16)
Looked forward to new system (Hebrews 10.1)	Cancels old system (Hebrews 10.9)

day, sex has been degraded by publicity; it has become public domain, not private celebration. We are called to have a high regard for sex, both in good health and purity.

16.1ff The day of atonement was the greatest day of the year for Israel. The Hebrew word for *atone* means "to cover." Old Testament sacrifices could not actually remove sins, only cover them. On this day, the people confessed their sins as a nation, and the high priest went into the most holy place to make atonement for them. Sacrifices were made and blood was shed so that the people's sins could be "covered" until Christ's sacrifice on the cross would give people the opportunity to have their sin removed forever.

16.1–25 Aaron had to spend hours preparing himself to meet God. But we can approach God anytime (Hebrews 4.16). What a privilege! We are offered easier access to God than the high priests of Old Testament times! Still, we must never forget that God is holy nor let this privilege cause us to approach God carelessly. The way to God has been opened to us by Christ. But easy access to God does not eliminate our need to prepare our hearts as we draw near in prayer.

16.5–28 This event with the two goats occurred on the day of atonement. The two goats represented the two ways God was dealing with the Israelites' sin: (1) he was forgiving their sin through the first goat, which was sacrificed, and (2) he was removing their guilt through the second goat, the scapegoat, which was sent into the wilderness. The same ritual had to be repeated every year. Jesus Christ's death replaced this system once and for all. We can have our sins forgiven and guilt removed by placing our trust in Christ (Hebrews 10.1–18).

16.8–10 The word "Azazel" has been traditionally understood as "the goat which escapes" or scapegoat. Some have suggested that the word means "the precipice" because of a similar sounding word and because it was a custom on the day of atonement in later times to push the scapegoat off a cliff three or four miles outside Jerusalem. But the word is a proper name that means something like "complete removal of community guilt."

goat on which the lot fell for the LORD, and offer it as a sin offering; 10 but the goat
on which the lot fell for Azazel[s] shall be presented alive before the LORD to make
atonement over it, that it may be sent away into the wilderness to Azazel.[s]
11 Aaron shall present the bull as a sin offering for himself, and shall make
atonement for himself and for his house; he shall slaughter the bull as a sin offering
for himself. 12 He shall take a censer full of coals of fire from the altar before the
LORD, and two handfuls of crushed sweet incense, and he shall bring it inside
the curtain 13 and put the incense on the fire before the LORD, that the cloud of the
incense may cover the mercy seat[t] that is upon the covenant,[u] or he will die. 14 He
shall take some of the blood of the bull, and sprinkle it with his finger on the front
of the mercy seat,[t] and before the mercy seat[t] he shall sprinkle the blood with his
finger seven times.
15 He shall slaughter the goat of the sin offering that is for the people and bring
its blood inside the curtain, and do with its blood as he did with the blood of the
bull, sprinkling it upon the mercy seat[t] and before the mercy seat.[t] 16 Thus he
shall make atonement for the sanctuary, because of the uncleannesses of the people
of Israel, and because of their transgressions, all their sins; and so he shall do for
the tent of meeting, which remains with them in the midst of their uncleannesses.
17 No one shall be in the tent of meeting from the time he enters to make atonement
in the sanctuary until he comes out and has made atonement for himself and for his
house and for all the assembly of Israel. 18 Then he shall go out to the altar that is
before the LORD and make atonement on its behalf, and shall take some of the blood
of the bull and of the blood of the goat, and put it on each of the horns of the altar.
19 He shall sprinkle some of the blood on it with his finger seven times, and cleanse
it and hallow it from the uncleannesses of the people of Israel.
20 When he has finished atoning for the holy place and the tent of meeting and
the altar, he shall present the live goat. 21 Then Aaron shall lay both his hands on the
head of the live goat, and confess over it all the iniquities of the people of Israel,
and all their transgressions, all their sins, putting them on the head of the goat, and
sending it away into the wilderness by means of someone designated for the task.[v]
22 The goat shall bear on itself all their iniquities to a barren region; and the goat
shall be set free in the wilderness.
23 Then Aaron shall enter the tent of meeting, and shall take off the linen vestments that he put on when he went into the holy place, and shall leave them there.
24 He shall bathe his body in water in a holy place, and put on his vestments; then
he shall come out and offer his burnt offering and the burnt offering of the people,
making atonement for himself and for the people. 25 The fat of the sin offering he
shall turn into smoke on the altar. 26 The one who sets the goat free for Azazel[s]
shall wash his clothes and bathe his body in water, and afterward may come into the
camp. 27 The bull of the sin offering and the goat of the sin offering, whose blood
was brought in to make atonement in the holy place, shall be taken outside the
camp; their skin and their flesh and their dung shall be consumed in fire. 28 The one
who burns them shall wash his clothes and bathe his body in water, and afterward
may come into the camp.
29 This shall be a statute to you forever: In the seventh month, on the tenth day
of the month, you shall deny yourselves,[w] and shall do no work, neither the citizen
nor the alien who resides among you. 30 For on this day atonement shall be made for
you, to cleanse you; from all your sins you shall be clean before the LORD. 31 It is
a sabbath of complete rest to you, and you shall deny yourselves;[w] it is a statute
forever. 32 The priest who is anointed and consecrated as priest in his father's place

16.10 Isa 53.4-10
16.11 Lev 9.7; Heb 9.7
16.12 Ex 30.34-38; Num 16.18,46; Isa 6.6,7; Rev 8.3-5
16.13 Ex 25.21; 30.1,7,8; Lev 22.9
16.14 Lev 4.17
16.15 Heb 6.19; 9.3,7,12
16.16 Ex 30.10; Ezek 45.18; Heb 9.22,23
16.17 Lk 1.10
16.18 Lev 4.7,17,25; Ezek 43.20
16.19 Lev 4.6; 16.14
16.21 Lev 5.5; Num 5.7
16.22 Isa 53.4-7
16.23 Ex 28.39-43; Lev 16.4
16.24 Ex 29.3-9
16.26 Num 19.7
16.27 Lev 4.11,12; 8.17
16.28 Lev 16.26
16.29 Lev 23.26-32; Num 27.7; Ps 51.7
16.31 Ex 12.16; 20.10; Lev 23.32; Ezra 8.21
16.32 Ex 28.39-43

[s] Traditionally rendered *a scapegoat* [t] Or *the cover* [u] Or *treaty*, or *testament*; Heb *eduth* [v] Meaning of Heb uncertain [w] Or *shall fast*

16.12 A censer was a dish or shallow bowl that hung by a chain or was carried with tongs. Inside the censer were placed incense (a combination of sweet-smelling spices) and live coals from the altar. On the day of atonement, the high priest entered the most holy place carrying a smoking censer. The smoke shielded him from the ark of the covenant and the presence of God – otherwise he would die. Incense may also have had a very practical purpose. The sweet smell drew the people's attention to the morning and evening sacrifices and helped cover their sometimes foul smell.

shall make atonement, wearing the linen vestments, the holy vestments. 33 He shall
make atonement for the sanctuary, and he shall make atonement for the tent of
meeting and for the altar, and he shall make atonement for the priests and for all the
people of the assembly. 34 This shall be an everlasting statute for you, to make
atonement for the people of Israel once in the year for all their sins. And Moses did
as the LORD had commanded him.

16.34 Ex 30.10; Lev 23.14,21,30,31; Heb 9.7

Warnings against improper sacrifice

17 The LORD spoke to Moses:
2 Speak to Aaron and his sons and to all the people of Israel and say to
them: This is what the LORD has commanded. 3 If anyone of the house of Israel
slaughters an ox or a lamb or a goat in the camp, or slaughters it outside the camp,
4 and does not bring it to the entrance of the tent of meeting, to present it as an
offering to the LORD before the tabernacle of the LORD, he shall be held guilty of
bloodshed; he has shed blood, and he shall be cut off from the people. 5 This is in
order that the people of Israel may bring their sacrifices that they offer in the open
field, that they may bring them to the LORD, to the priest at the entrance of the tent
of meeting, and offer them as sacrifices of well-being to the LORD. 6 The priest shall
dash the blood against the altar of the LORD at the entrance of the tent of meeting,
and turn the fat into smoke as a pleasing odor to the LORD, 7 so that they may no
longer offer their sacrifices for goat-demons, to whom they prostitute themselves.
This shall be a statute forever to them throughout their generations.
8 And say to them further: Anyone of the house of Israel or of the aliens who
reside among them who offers a burnt offering or sacrifice, 9 and does not bring it
to the entrance of the tent of meeting, to sacrifice it to the LORD, shall be cut off
from the people.
10 If anyone of the house of Israel or of the aliens who reside among them eats
any blood, I will set my face against that person who eats blood, and will cut that
person off from the people. 11 For the life of the flesh is in the blood; and I have
given it to you for making atonement for your lives on the altar; for, as life, it is the
blood that makes atonement. 12 Therefore I have said to the people of Israel: No
person among you shall eat blood, nor shall any alien who resides among you eat
blood. 13 And anyone of the people of Israel, or of the aliens who reside among
them, who hunts down an animal or bird that may be eaten shall pour out its blood
and cover it with earth.
14 For the life of every creature — its blood is its life; therefore I have said to the

17.3,4 Lev 1.2,3; Deut 12.5-7
17.5 Deut 12.4-7
17.6 Ex 29.18
17.7 Ex 22.20; 32.8; Deut 32.17; 2 Chron 11.15; 1 Cor 10.20
17.9 Lev 17.3,4; Deut 12.4-7
17.10 Lev 3.17; 19.26; Deut 12.23
17.11 Gen 9.4; Lev 17.14; Matt 26.28; Rom 3.25; Eph 1.7; Col 1.14,20; Heb 9.22; 1 Pet 1.2; 1 Jn 1.7
17.13 Deut 12.16,24,25; 15.23; Ezek 24.7
17.14 Lev 7.26,27; 17.11

17.1ff Chapters 17–26 are sometimes called the "holiness code" because they focus on what it means to live a holy life. The central verse is 19.2, "You shall be holy, for I the Lord your God am holy."

17.3–9 Why were the Israelites prohibited from sacrificing outside the tabernacle area? God had established specific times and places for sacrifices, and each occasion was permeated with symbolism. If people sacrificed on their own, they might easily add to or subtract from God's laws to fit their own life-styles. Many heathen religions allowed every individual priest to set his own rules; God's command helped the Israelites resist the temptation to follow the heathen pattern. When the Israelites slipped into idolatry, it was because "all the people did what was right in their own eyes" (Judges 17.6).

17.7 The goat-demons (also called satyrs) were objects of worship and sacrifice in ancient times. Evidently, the people were already beginning to make this kind of sacrifice in the open fields.

17.11–14 How does blood make atonement for sin? When offered with the right attitude, the sacrifice and the blood shed from it made forgiveness of sin possible. On the one hand, blood represented the sinner's life, infected by his sin and headed for death. On the other hand, the blood represented the innocent life of the animal that was sacrificed in place of the guilty person making the offering. The death of the animal (of which the blood was proof) fulfilled the penalty of death. God therefore granted forgiveness to the sinner. It is God who forgives based on the faith of the one sacrificing.

17.14 Why was eating or drinking blood prohibited? The prohibition against eating blood can be traced all the way back to Noah (Genesis 9.4). God prohibited eating or drinking blood for several reasons. (1) To discourage heathen practices. Israel was to be separate and distinct from the heathen nations around them. Eating blood was a common pagan practice. It was often done in hopes of gaining the characteristics of the slain animal (strength, speed, etc.). God's people were to rely on him, not on ingested blood, for their strength. (2) To preserve the symbolism of the sacrifice. Blood symbolized the life of the animal that was sacrificed in the sinner's place. To drink it would change the symbolism of the sacrificial penalty and destroy the evidence of the sacrifice. (3) To protect the people from infection, since many deadly diseases are transmitted through the blood. The Jews took this prohibition seriously, and that is why Jesus' hearers were so upset when Jesus told them to drink his blood (John 6.53–56). However Jesus, as God himself and the last sacrifice ever needed for sins, was asking believers to identify with him completely. He wants us to take his life into us, and he wants to participate in our lives as well.

people of Israel: You shall not eat the blood of any creature, for the life of every
creature is its blood; whoever eats it shall be cut off. 15 All persons, citizens or 17.15
aliens, who eat what dies of itself or what has been torn by wild animals, shall wash Lev 7.24 11.24,39
their clothes, and bathe themselves in water, and be unclean until the evening; then Num 19.8
they shall be clean. 16 But if they do not wash themselves or bathe their body, they
shall bear their guilt.

B. LIVING A HOLY LIFE (18.1—27.34)

After the sacrificial system for forgiving sins was in place, the people were instructed on how to live as forgiven people. Applying these standards to our lives helps us grow in obedience and live a life pleasing to God.

1. Standards for the people

Sexual perversions forbidden

18 The LORD spoke to Moses, saying: 18.1
2 Speak to the people of Israel and say to them: I am the LORD your God. Ex 20.2
3 You shall not do as they do in the land of Egypt, where you lived, and you shall
not do as they do in the land of Canaan, to which I am bringing you. You shall not
follow their statutes. 4 My ordinances you shall observe and my statutes you shall 18.4
keep, following them: I am the LORD your God. 5 You shall keep my statutes and Lev 19.37; 20.22 Deut 4.1; 6.1
my ordinances; by doing so one shall live: I am the LORD. Ezek 20.11
6 None of you shall approach anyone near of kin to uncover nakedness: I am the
LORD. 7 You shall not uncover the nakedness of your father, which is the nakedness 18.7
of your mother; she is your mother, you shall not uncover her nakedness. 8 You Lev 20.11
shall not uncover the nakedness of your father's wife; it is the nakedness of your 18.8 Gen 35.22
father. 9 You shall not uncover the nakedness of your sister, your father's daughter Lev 20.10 Deut 27.20
or your mother's daughter, whether born at home or born abroad. 10 You shall not 18.9
uncover the nakedness of your son's daughter or of your daughter's daughter, for Lev 20.17
their nakedness is your own nakedness. 11 You shall not uncover the nakedness of
your father's wife's daughter, begotten by your father, since she is your sister. 18.12 Lev 20.19
12 You shall not uncover the nakedness of your father's sister; she is your father's 18.14
flesh. 13 You shall not uncover the nakedness of your mother's sister, for she is your Lev 20.20
mother's flesh. 14 You shall not uncover the nakedness of your father's brother, that 18.15 Lev 20.15
is, you shall not approach his wife; she is your aunt. 15 You shall not uncover the Ezek 22.11
nakedness of your daughter-in-law: she is your son's wife; you shall not uncover 18.16
her nakedness. 16 You shall not uncover the nakedness of your brother's wife; it is Lev 20.21 Deut 25.5
your brother's nakedness. 17 You shall not uncover the nakedness of a woman and Mt 22.24
her daughter, and you shall not take[x] her son's daughter or her daughter's daughter 18.17 Lev 20.14
to uncover her nakedness; they are your[y] flesh; it is depravity. 18 And you shall not 18.19
take[x] a woman as a rival to her sister, uncovering her nakedness while her sister is Lev 15.24; 20.18 Ezek 18.6; 22.10
still alive.
19 You shall not approach a woman to uncover her nakedness while she is in 18.20 Ex 20.14
her menstrual uncleanness. 20 You shall not have sexual relations with your kins- Deut 5.18 22.22-27

[x] Or *marry* [y] Gk: Heb lacks *your*

18.3 The Israelites moved from one idol-infested country to another. As God helped them form a new culture, he warned them to leave all aspects of their heathen background behind. He also warned them how easy it would be to slip into the heathen culture of Canaan, where they were going. Canaan's society and religions appealed to carnal desires, especially sexual immorality and drunkenness. The Israelites were to keep themselves pure and set apart for God. God did not want his people absorbed into the surrounding culture and environment. Society may pressure us to conform to its way of life and thought, but yielding to that pressure will (1) create confusion as to which side we should be on and (2) eliminate our effectiveness in serving God. Follow God, and don't let the culture around you mold your thoughts and actions.

18.6–18 "Uncover the nakedness" means to have sexual relations. Marrying relatives was prohibited by God for physical, social, and moral reasons. Children born to near relatives may experience serious health problems. Without these specific laws, sexual promiscuity would have been more likely, first in families, then outside. Improper sexual relations destroy family life.

18.6–27 Several abominations, or wicked actions, are listed here: (1) having sexual relations with close relatives, (2) committing adultery, (3) offering children as sacrifices, (4) having homosexual relations, (5) having sexual relations with animals. These practices were common in pagan religions, and it is easy to see why God dealt harshly with those who began to follow them. Such practices lead to disease, deformity, and death. They disrupt family life and society and reveal a low regard for the value of oneself and of others. Society today takes some of these practices lightly, even trying to make them acceptable. But they are still sins in God's eyes. If you consider them acceptable, you are not judging by God's standards.

man's wife, and defile yourself with her. 21 You shall not give any of your offspring
to sacrifice them[z] to Molech, and so profane the name of your God: I am the LORD.
22 You shall not lie with a male as with a woman; it is an abomination. 23 You shall
not have sexual relations with any animal and defile yourself with it, nor shall any
woman give herself to an animal to have sexual relations with it: it is perversion.
24 Do not defile yourselves in any of these ways, for by all these practices the
nations I am casting out before you have defiled themselves. 25 Thus the land became defiled; and I punished it for its iniquity, and the land vomited out its inhabitants. 26 But you shall keep my statutes and my ordinances and commit none of
these abominations, either the citizen or the alien who resides among you 27 (for the
inhabitants of the land, who were before you, committed all of these abominations,
and the land became defiled); 28 otherwise the land will vomit you out for defiling
it, as it vomited out the nation that was before you. 29 For whoever commits any of
these abominations shall be cut off from their people. 30 So keep my charge not to
commit any of these abominations that were done before you, and not to defile
yourselves by them: I am the LORD your God.

Commands for daily life

19 The LORD spoke to Moses, saying:
2 Speak to all the congregation of the people of Israel and say to them: You
shall be holy, for I the LORD your God am holy. 3 You shall each revere your mother
and father, and you shall keep my sabbaths: I am the LORD your God. 4 Do not turn
to idols or make cast images for yourselves: I am the LORD your God.
5 When you offer a sacrifice of well-being to the LORD, offer it in such a way
that it is acceptable on your behalf. 6 It shall be eaten on the same day you offer it,
or on the next day; and anything left over until the third day shall be consumed in
fire. 7 If it is eaten at all on the third day, it is an abomination; it will not be acceptable. 8 All who eat it shall be subject to punishment, because they have profaned
what is holy to the LORD; and any such person shall be cut off from the people.
9 When you reap the harvest of your land, you shall not reap to the very edges
of your field, or gather the gleanings of your harvest. 10 You shall not strip your
vineyard bare, or gather the fallen grapes of your vineyard; you shall leave them for
the poor and the alien: I am the LORD your God.
11 You shall not steal; you shall not deal falsely; and you shall not lie to one
another. 12 And you shall not swear falsely by my name, profaning the name of
your God: I am the LORD.
13 You shall not defraud your neighbor; you shall not steal; and you shall not
keep for yourself the wages of a laborer until morning. 14 You shall not revile the
deaf or put a stumbling block before the blind; you shall fear your God: I am the
LORD.
15 You shall not render an unjust judgment; you shall not be partial to the poor
or defer to the great: with justice you shall judge your neighbor. 16 You shall not go
around as a slanderer[a] among your people, and you shall not profit by the blood[b]
of your neighbor: I am the LORD.
17 You shall not hate in your heart anyone of your kin; you shall reprove your
neighbor, or you will incur guilt yourself. 18 You shall not take vengeance or bear

[z] Heb *to pass them over* [a] Meaning of Heb uncertain [b] Heb *stand against the blood*

18.21 Lev 19.12; 20.1-5; 21.6; Deut 12.31; 2 Kgs 23.10; Mal 1.12
18.22 Gen 19.4-8; Lev 20.13; Judg 19.22-24; Rom 1.26,27; 1 Tim 1.10
18.23 Ex 22.19; Lev 20.15,16; Deut 27.21
18.24 Deut 12.31
18.25 Lev 20.22,23; Deut 9.5
19.1 Ex 20.8-11; Lev 11.44,45
19.3 Ex 20.3-5,23; Lev 26.1; Deut 27.15
19.5 Lev 3.1-17; 7.11-21,28-38
19.8 Num 15.31
19.9 Lev 23.22; Deut 24.19-22
19.11 Ex 20.15,16; Deut 5.19,20
19.13 Ex 22.7-15, 21-27; 23.4-9; Deut 24.14,15; Prov 22.22; Mal 3.5
19.14 Deut 27.18
19.15 Ex 23.2,3,6; Deut 1.17; 16.19,20; Prov 24.23; Jas 2.1-7
19.16 Ex 23.1,7; Prov 20.19; Ezek 22.9; Mt 26.60,61; Acts 6.11-14
19.17 Prov 9.7,8; 27.5,6; Mt 17.17,18; 1 Jn 3.15

19.9, 10 This law was a protection for the poor. Laws such as this showed God's generosity and liberality. As people of God, the Israelites were to reflect his nature and characteristics in their attitudes and actions. Ruth and Naomi were two people who benefited from this merciful law (Ruth 2.2).

19.9, 10 God instructed the Hebrews to provide for those in need. He required that the people leave the corners of their fields unharvested, providing food for travelers and the poor. It is easy to ignore the poor or forget about those who have less than we do. But God desires generosity. In what ways can you leave "the corners of your fields" for those in need?

19.16 "You shall not profit by the blood of your neighbor" means that we should not bear false witness against someone who is on trial for his life when we can profit from his death in some way. It may also mean that we should not stand idly by, indifferent to our neighbor's life.

19.18 "You shall not. . . ." Some people think the Bible is nothing but a book of don'ts. But Jesus neatly summarized all these rules when he said to love God with all your heart, and your neighbor as yourself. He called these the greatest commandments (or rules) of all (Matthew 22.34–40). By carrying out Jesus' simple commands, we find ourselves following all of God's other laws as well.

a grudge against any of your people, but you shall love your neighbor as yourself:
I am the LORD.
19 You shall keep my statutes. You shall not let your animals breed with a
different kind; you shall not sow your field with two kinds of seed; nor shall you put
on a garment made of two different materials.
20 If a man has sexual relations with a woman who is a slave, designated for
another man but not ransomed or given her freedom, an inquiry shall be held. They
shall not be put to death, since she has not been freed; 21 but he shall bring a guilt
offering for himself to the LORD, at the entrance of the tent of meeting, a ram as
guilt offering. 22 And the priest shall make atonement for him with the ram of guilt
offering before the LORD for his sin that he committed; and the sin he committed
shall be forgiven him.
23 When you come into the land and plant all kinds of trees for food, then you
shall regard their fruit as forbidden;[c] three years it shall be forbidden[d] to you, it
must not be eaten. 24 In the fourth year all their fruit shall be set apart for rejoicing
in the LORD. 25 But in the fifth year you may eat of their fruit, that their yield may
be increased for you: I am the LORD your God.
26 You shall not eat anything with its blood. You shall not practice augury or
witchcraft. 27 You shall not round off the hair on your temples or mar the edges of
your beard. 28 You shall not make any gashes in your flesh for the dead or tattoo any
marks upon you: I am the LORD.
29 Do not profane your daughter by making her a prostitute, that the land not
become prostituted and full of depravity. 30 You shall keep my sabbaths and reverence my sanctuary: I am the LORD.
31 Do not turn to mediums or wizards; do not seek them out, to be defiled by
them: I am the LORD your God.
32 You shall rise before the aged, and defer to the old; and you shall fear your
God: I am the LORD.
33 When an alien resides with you in your land, you shall not oppress the alien.
34 The alien who resides with you shall be to you as the citizen among you; you shall
love the alien as yourself, for you were aliens in the land of Egypt: I am the LORD
your God.
35 You shall not cheat in measuring length, weight, or quantity. 36 You shall
have honest balances, honest weights, an honest ephah, and an honest hin: I am the
LORD your God, who brought you out of the land of Egypt. 37 You shall keep all my
statutes and all my ordinances, and observe them: I am the LORD.

Punishments for sin

20 The LORD spoke to Moses, saying: 2 Say further to the people of Israel:
Any of the people of Israel, or of the aliens who reside in Israel, who give
any of their offspring to Molech shall be put to death; the people of the land shall
stone them to death. 3 I myself will set my face against them, and will cut them off

19.18 Ex 23.4,5 Deut 32.35 Ps 103.9 Mt 5.43; 19.19 Mk 12.31-33 Lk 10.27-37 Rom 12.17-21 Gal 5.14 Heb 10.30
19.19 Deut 22.9-11
19.20 Ex 21.20,21
19.21 Lev 5.14-19
19.26 Ex 22.18
19.27 Ezek 44.20
19.28 Deut 14.1 Jer 16.6; 48.37
19.29 Lev 21.9 Deut 23.17,18 Hos 4.13
19.30 Ex 20.8-11 Lev 26.2
19.31 Lev 19.26
19.32 1 Tim 5.1,2
19.34 Lev 19.18
19.35 Deut 25.13-16 Prov 11.1 16.11; 20.10 Amos 8.5 Mic 6.11
20.2 Lev 18.21 Deut 13.10
20.3 Num 19.20 Ezek 5.11; 23.38

c Heb *as their uncircumcision* d Heb *uncircumcision*

19.26 "Augury" is fortune telling or divination.

19.32 People often find it easy to dismiss the opinions of the elderly and avoid taking time to visit with them. But the fact that God commanded the Israelites to honor the elderly shows how seriously we should take the responsibility of respecting those older than we. Their wisdom gained from experience can keep us from many pitfalls.

19.33, 34 How do you feel when you encounter foreigners, especially those who don't speak your language? Are you impatient? Do you think or act as if they should go back where they came from? Are you tempted to take advantage of them? God says to treat foreigners as you'd treat a fellow countryman, to love them as you love yourself. In reality, we are all foreigners in this world because it is only our temporary home. View strangers, newcomers, and foreigners as opportunities to demonstrate God's love.

20.1–3 Sacrificing children to the gods was a common practice in ancient religions. The Ammonites, Israel's neighbors, made child sacrifice to Molech (their national god) a vital part of their religion. They saw this as the greatest gift they could offer to ward off evil or appease angry gods. God made it clear that this practice was detestable and strictly forbidden. In Old Testament times as well as New, his character made human sacrifice unthinkable. (1) Unlike the heathen gods, he is a God of love, who does not need to be appeased (Exodus 34.6). (2) He is a God of life, who prohibits murder and encourages practices that lead to health and happiness (Deuteronomy 30.15, 16). (3) He is God of the helpless, who shows special concern for children (Psalm 72.4). (4) He is a God of unselfishness, who instead of demanding blood gives his life for others (Isaiah 53.4, 5).

from the people, because they have given of their offspring to Molech, defiling my
sanctuary and profaning my holy name. [4]And if the people of the land should ever
close their eyes to them, when they give of their offspring to Molech, and do not
put them to death, [5]I myself will set my face against them and against their family,
and will cut them off from among their people, them and all who follow them in
prostituting themselves to Molech.
6 If any turn to mediums and wizards, prostituting themselves to them, I will set
my face against them, and will cut them off from the people. [7]Consecrate yourselves therefore, and be holy; for I am the LORD your God. [8]Keep my statutes, and
observe them; I am the LORD; I sanctify you. [9]All who curse father or mother shall
be put to death; having cursed father or mother, their blood is upon them.
10 If a man commits adultery with the wife of[e] his neighbor, both the adulterer
and the adulteress shall be put to death. [11]The man who lies with his father's wife
has uncovered his father's nakedness; both of them shall be put to death; their blood
is upon them. [12]If a man lies with his daughter-in-law, both of them shall be put to
death; they have committed perversion, their blood is upon them. [13]If a man lies
with a male as with a woman, both of them have committed an abomination; they
shall be put to death; their blood is upon them. [14]If a man takes a wife and her
mother also, it is depravity; they shall be burned to death, both he and they, that
there may be no depravity among you. [15]If a man has sexual relations with an
animal, he shall be put to death; and you shall kill the animal. [16]If a woman approaches any animal and has sexual relations with it, you shall kill the woman and
the animal; they shall be put to death, their blood is upon them.
17 If a man takes his sister, a daughter of his father or a daughter of his mother,
and sees her nakedness, and she sees his nakedness, it is a disgrace, and they shall
be cut off in the sight of their people; he has uncovered his sister's nakedness, he
shall be subject to punishment. [18]If a man lies with a woman having her sickness
and uncovers her nakedness, he has laid bare her flow and she has laid bare her flow
of blood; both of them shall be cut off from their people. [19]You shall not uncover
the nakedness of your mother's sister or of your father's sister, for that is to lay bare
one's own flesh; they shall be subject to punishment. [20]If a man lies with his uncle's wife, he has uncovered his uncle's nakedness; they shall be subject to punishment; they shall die childless. [21]If a man takes his brother's wife, it is impurity; he
has uncovered his brother's nakedness; they shall be childless.
22 You shall keep all my statutes and all my ordinances, and observe them, so
that the land to which I bring you to settle in may not vomit you out. [23]You shall
not follow the practices of the nation that I am driving out before you. Because they
did all these things, I abhorred them. [24]But I have said to you: You shall inherit

20.5 Lev 17.10
20.6 Lev 19.26,31
20.7 Lev 11.44
20.9 Ex 21.17; Deut 27.16; Mt 15.4
20.10 Ex 20.14; Deut 22.22-24
20.11 Lev 18.7,8; Deut 27.20
20.12 Lev 18.15
20.13 Gen 19.5; Lev 18.22; Deut 23.17; Judg 19.22
20.14 Lev 18.17; Deut 27.23
20.15 Lev 18.23; Deut 27.21
20.17 Lev 18.9
20.18 Lev 15.24; 18.19
20.19 Lev 18.12,13
20.20 Lev 18.14
20.21 Lev 18.16
20.22 Lev 18.28
20.23 Lev 18.1-3, 24-30; Deut 9.5
20.24 Gen 15.16; Ex 3.17; 6.8,9; Deut 6.3; 8.7-9; 11.9; 26.9; 27.3; Josh 5.6; 24.11

[e] Heb repeats *if a man commits adultery with the wife of*

20.6 Everyone is interested in what the future holds, and we often look to others for guidance. But God warned about looking to the occult for advice. Mediums and wizards were outlawed because God was not the source of their information. At best, occult practitioners are fakes whose predictions cannot be trusted. At worst, they are in contact with evil spirits and are thus extremely dangerous. We don't need to look to the occult for information about the future. God has given us the Bible so that we may obtain all the information we need—and the Bible's teaching is trustworthy.

20.10–21 This list of commands against sexual sins includes extremely harsh punishments. Why? God had no tolerance for such acts for the following reasons: (1) they shatter the mutual commitment of married partners; (2) they destroy the sanctity of the family; (3) they twist people's mental well-being; and (4) they spread disease. Sexual sin has always been widely available, but the glorification of sex between people who are not married to each other often hides deep tragedy and hurt behind the scenes. When society portrays sexual sins as attractive, it is easy to forget the dark side. God had good reasons for prohibiting sexual sins: he loves us and wants the very best for us.

20.10–21 The detestable acts listed here were very common in the heathen nations of Canaan; their religions were rampant with sex goddesses, temple prostitution, and other gross sins. The Canaanites' immoral religious practices reflected a decadent culture that tended to corrupt whoever came in contact with it. By contrast, God was building a nation to make a positive influence on the world. He did not want the Israelites to adopt the Canaanites' practices and slide into debauchery. So he prepared the people for what they would face in the promised land by commanding them to steer clear of sexual sins.

20.22, 23 God gave many rules to his people—but not without reason. He did not withhold good from them; he only prohibited those acts that would bring them to ruin. All of us understand God's physical laws of nature. For example, jumping off a ten-story building means death because of the law of gravity. But some of us don't understand how God's spiritual laws work. God forbids us to do certain things because he wants to keep us from self-destruction. Next time you are drawn to a forbidden physical or emotional pleasure, remind yourself that its consequences might be suffering and separation from the God who is trying to help you.

their land, and I will give it to you to possess, a land flowing with milk and honey.
I am the LORD your God; I have separated you from the peoples. 25 You shall therefore make a distinction between the clean animal and the unclean, and between the
unclean bird and the clean; you shall not bring abomination on yourselves by animal or by bird or by anything with which the ground teems, which I have set apart
for you to hold unclean. 26 You shall be holy to me; for I the LORD am holy, and I
have separated you from the other peoples to be mine.
27 A man or a woman who is a medium or a wizard shall be put to death; they
shall be stoned to death, their blood is upon them.

2. Standards for the priests

The holiness of priests

21 The LORD said to Moses: Speak to the priests, the sons of Aaron, and say to
them:
No one shall defile himself for a dead person among his relatives, 2 except for his
nearest kin: his mother, his father, his son, his daughter, his brother; 3 likewise, for
a virgin sister, close to him because she has had no husband, he may defile himself
for her. 4 But he shall not defile himself as a husband among his people and so
profane himself. 5 They shall not make bald spots upon their heads, or shave off the
edges of their beards, or make any gashes in their flesh. 6 They shall be holy to their
God, and not profane the name of their God; for they offer the LORD's offerings by
fire, the food of their God; therefore they shall be holy. 7 They shall not marry a
prostitute or a woman who has been defiled; neither shall they marry a woman
divorced from her husband. For they are holy to their God, 8 and you shall treat
them as holy, since they offer the food of your God; they shall be holy to you, for
I the LORD, I who sanctify you, am holy. 9 When the daughter of a priest profanes
herself through prostitution, she profanes her father; she shall be burned to death.
10 The priest who is exalted above his fellows, on whose head the anointing oil
has been poured and who has been consecrated to wear the vestments, shall not
dishevel his hair, nor tear his vestments. 11 He shall not go where there is a dead
body; he shall not defile himself even for his father or mother. 12 He shall not go
outside the sanctuary and thus profane the sanctuary of his God; for the consecration of the anointing oil of his God is upon him: I am the LORD. 13 He shall marry
only a woman who is a virgin. 14 A widow, or a divorced woman, or a woman who
has been defiled, a prostitute, these he shall not marry. He shall marry a virgin of
his own kin, 15 that he may not profane his offspring among his kin; for I am the
LORD; I sanctify him.
16 The LORD spoke to Moses, saying: 17 Speak to Aaron and say: No one of
your offspring throughout their generations who has a blemish may approach to
offer the food of his God. 18 For no one who has a blemish shall draw near, one who
is blind or lame, or one who has a mutilated face or a limb too long, 19 or one who
has a broken foot or a broken hand, 20 or a hunchback, or a dwarf, or a man with a
blemish in his eyes or an itching disease or scabs or crushed testicles. 21 No descendant of Aaron the priest who has a blemish shall come near to offer the LORD's
offerings by fire; since he has a blemish, he shall not come near to offer the food of
his God. 22 He may eat the food of his God, of the most holy as well as of the holy.
23 But he shall not come near the curtain or approach the altar, because he has a
blemish, that he may not profane my sanctuaries; for I am the LORD; I sanctify
them. 24 Thus Moses spoke to Aaron and to his sons and to all the people of Israel.

20.25 Lev 11.1-47 Deut 14.3-5
20.26 Lev 11.44
20.27 Lev 19.26,31 Deut 18.10-12
21.1 Lev 21.11 Num 19.14,16 Ezek 44.25
21.2 Lev 21.11
21.5 Lev 19.27,28 Deut 14.1 Jer 16.6; 48.37
21.6 Ex 29.44 Lev 10.3
21.7 Lev 21.14 Ezek 44.22
21.8 Lev 11.44
21.10 Lev 10.6,7
21.11 Lev 21.1-4 Ezek 44.25
21.12 Ex 29.7 Lev 10.7 Num 19.11-13
21.13 Ezek 44.22
21.14 Lev 21.7,13 Ezra 2.62,63 9.2 Neh 13.29
21.16,17 Deut 23.1,2
21.21 Lev 21.17-21
21.22 Lev 6.16,29 24.9 Num 18.8-11 1 Cor 9.13
21.23 Lev 21.17

21.1–2 Defiling "himself for a dead person" means touching a dead body.

21.16–23 Was God unfairly discriminating against handicapped people when he said they were unqualified to offer sacrifices? Just as God demanded that no imperfect animals be used for sacrifice, he required that no handicapped priests offer sacrifices. This was not meant as an insult; rather, it had to do with the fact that the priest must match as closely as possible the perfect God he served. Of course, such perfection was not fully realized until Jesus Christ came. As Levites, the handicapped priests were protected and supported with food from the sacrifices. They were not abandoned, for they still performed many essential services within the tabernacle.

The holiness of offerings

22.2 Lev 10.1-4 **22** The LORD spoke to Moses, saying: [2]Direct Aaron and his sons to deal carefully with the sacred donations of the people of Israel, which they dedicate
22.3 Lev 7.20,21 Num 19.13 to me, so that they may not profane my holy name; I am the LORD. [3]Say to them:
If anyone among all your offspring throughout your generations comes near the
sacred donations, which the people of Israel dedicate to the LORD, while he is in a
22.4 Lev 11.24,28, 31,39,40 13.45,46 14.1-32 Num 5.1; 19.11 state of uncleanness, that person shall be cut off from my presence: I am the LORD.
[4]No one of Aaron's offspring who has a leprous[f] disease or suffers a discharge
may eat of the sacred donations until he is clean. Whoever touches anything made
unclean by a corpse or a man who has had an emission of semen, [5]and whoever
22.5 Lev 11.24,25, 41-44 touches any swarming thing by which he may be made unclean or any human being
by whom he may be made unclean — whatever his uncleanness may be — [6]the per-
22.6 Num 19.7-10 son who touches any such shall be unclean until evening and shall not eat of the
sacred donations unless he has washed his body in water. [7]When the sun sets he
22.8 Ex 22.31 Lev 17.15 Deut 14.21 Ezek 44.31 shall be clean; and afterward he may eat of the sacred donations, for they are his
food. [8]That which died or was torn by wild animals he shall not eat, becoming
unclean by it: I am the LORD. [9]They shall keep my charge, so that they may not
22.9 Ex 28.43 Lev 22.16 Num 18.1-7 incur guilt and die in the sanctuary[g] for having profaned it: I am the LORD; I sanctify them.

10 No lay person shall eat of the sacred donations. No bound or hired servant of
22.10 Ex 29.31-34 Lev 22.13 the priest shall eat of the sacred donations; [11]but if a priest acquires anyone by
purchase, the person may eat of them; and those that are born in his house may eat
22.11 Num 18.11 of his food. [12]If a priest's daughter marries a layman, she shall not eat of the offering of the sacred donations; [13]but if a priest's daughter is widowed or divorced,
22.13 Lev 22.10 without offspring, and returns to her father's house, as in her youth, she may eat of
22.14 Lev 5.16 Num 15.22-26 her father's food. No lay person shall eat of it. [14]If a man eats of the sacred donation unintentionally, he shall add one-fifth of its value to it, and give the sacred
22.15 Lev 19.8 donation to the priest. [15]No one shall profane the sacred donations of the people of
22.16 Lev 22.9 Israel, which they offer to the LORD, [16]causing them to bear guilt requiring a guilt
offering, by eating their sacred donations: for I am the LORD; I sanctify them.

Acceptable animals for sacrifice

17 The LORD spoke to Moses, saying: [18]Speak to Aaron and his sons and all the
people of Israel and say to them: When anyone of the house of Israel or of the aliens
residing in Israel presents an offering, whether in payment of a vow or as a freewill
22.19 Lev 1.2; 4.3 offering that is offered to the LORD as a burnt offering, [19]to be acceptable in your
behalf it shall be a male without blemish, of the cattle or the sheep or the goats.
22.20 Lev 22.22-25 Deut 15.21 [20]You shall not offer anything that has a blemish, for it will not be acceptable in
your behalf.

21 When anyone offers a sacrifice of well-being to the LORD, in fulfillment of
a vow or as a freewill offering, from the herd or from the flock, to be acceptable it
22.22 Lev 22.20 Mal 1.8 must be perfect; there shall be no blemish in it. [22]Anything blind, or injured, or
maimed, or having a discharge or an itch or scabs — these you shall not offer to the
LORD or put any of them on the altar as offerings by fire to the LORD. [23]An ox or
a lamb that has a limb too long or too short you may present for a freewill offering;
but it will not be accepted for a vow. [24]Any animal that has its testicles bruised or

[f] A term for several skin diseases; precise meaning uncertain [g] Vg: Heb *incur guilt for it and die in it*

22.1–4 Why were there so many specific guidelines for the priests? The Israelites would have been quite familiar with priests from Egypt. Egyptian priests were mainly interested in politics. They viewed religion as a way to gain power. Thus the Israelites would have been suspicious of the establishment of a new priestly order. But God wanted his priests to serve him and the people. Their duties were religious – to help people draw near to God and worship him. They could not use their position to gain power, because they were not allowed to own land or take money from anyone. All these guidelines reassured the people and helped the priests accomplish their purpose.

22.10 Lay people, in this context, means anyone outside of the priest's family. The sacred donations were the priest's portions of the offerings to the Lord.

22.19–25 Animals with defects were not acceptable as sacrifices, because they did not represent God's holy nature. Furthermore, the animal had to be without blemish in order to foreshadow the perfect, sinless life of Jesus Christ. When we give our best time, talent, and treasure to God rather than what is tarnished or common, we show the true meaning of worship and testify to God's supreme worth.

crushed or torn or cut, you shall not offer to the LORD; such you shall not do within
your land, 25 nor shall you accept any such animals from a foreigner to offer as food
to your God; since they are mutilated, with a blemish in them, they shall not be
accepted in your behalf.

22.25 Num 15.15,16 Mal 1.14

26 The LORD spoke to Moses, saying: 27 When an ox or a sheep or a goat is
born, it shall remain seven days with its mother, and from the eighth day on it shall
be acceptable as the LORD's offering by fire. 28 But you shall not slaughter, from the
herd or the flock, an animal with its young on the same day. 29 When you sacrifice
a thanksgiving offering to the LORD, you shall sacrifice it so that it may be acceptable in your behalf. 30 It shall be eaten on the same day; you shall not leave any of
it until morning: I am the LORD.

22.26 Ex 22.30 **22.28** Deut 22.6 **22.29** Ex 16.19 Lev 7.15

31 Thus you shall keep my commandments and observe them: I am the LORD.
32 You shall not profane my holy name, that I may be sanctified among the people
of Israel: I am the LORD; I sanctify you, 33 I who brought you out of the land of
Egypt to be your God: I am the LORD.

22.31 Ex 20.2 Lev 18.4 **22.33** Lev 22.31

3. Seasons and festivals

23 The LORD spoke to Moses, saying: 2 Speak to the people of Israel and say to
them: These are the appointed festivals of the LORD that you shall proclaim
as holy convocations, my appointed festivals.

23.1 Ex 23.17; 34.22 Lev 23.4,37,44 Num 29.39

3 Six days shall work be done; but the seventh day is a sabbath of complete rest,
a holy convocation; you shall do no work: it is a sabbath to the LORD throughout
your settlements.

23.3 Ex 20.8-11 23.12; 31.15 Deut 5.13,14 Lk 13.14

The passover and festival of unleavened bread

4 These are the appointed festivals of the LORD, the holy convocations, which
you shall celebrate at the time appointed for them. 5 In the first month, on the fourteenth day of the month, at twilight,[h] there shall be a passover offering to the
LORD, 6 and on the fifteenth day of the same month is the festival of unleavened
bread to the LORD; seven days you shall eat unleavened bread. 7 On the first day you
shall have a holy convocation; you shall not work at your occupations. 8 For seven
days you shall present the LORD's offerings by fire; on the seventh day there shall
be a holy convocation: you shall not work at your occupations.

23.5 Ex 12.3-20 Mt 26.17 Mk 14.12 **23.6** Mk 14.1-12 Lk 22.1 **23.7** Ex 12.6 Num 28.18

The offering of first fruits

9 The LORD spoke to Moses: 10 Speak to the people of Israel and say to them:
When you enter the land that I am giving you and you reap its harvest, you shall
bring the sheaf of the first fruits of your harvest to the priest. 11 He shall raise the
sheaf before the LORD, that you may find acceptance; on the day after the sabbath
the priest shall raise it. 12 On the day when you raise the sheaf, you shall offer a
lamb a year old, without blemish, as a burnt offering to the LORD. 13 And the grain
offering with it shall be two-tenths of an ephah of choice flour mixed with oil, an
offering by fire of pleasing odor to the LORD; and the drink offering with it shall be
of wine, one-fourth of a hin. 14 You shall eat no bread or parched grain or fresh ears

23.9-11 Ex 23.16,19 34.22 Num 15.17-21 28.26-31 Deut 16.9-12 Rom 11.16 Jas 1.18 Rev 14.4 **23.13** Lev 6.14-23 Num 15.3-10

[h] Heb *between the two evenings*

23.1ff Festivals played a major role in Israel's culture. Israel's festivals were different from those of any other nation because, being ordained by God, they were times of celebrating with him, not times of moral depravity. God wanted to set aside special days for the people to come together for rest, refreshment, and remembering with thanksgiving all he had done for them.

23.1–4 God established several national holidays each year for celebration, fellowship, and worship. Much can be learned about people by observing the holidays they celebrate and the way they celebrate them. Take note of your holiday traditions. What do they say about your values?

23.6 The festival of unleavened bread reminded Israel of their escape from Egypt. For seven days they ate unleavened bread, just as they had eaten it back then (Exodus 12.14, 15). The symbolism of this bread made without yeast was important to the Israelites. First, because the bread was unique, it illustrated Israel's uniqueness as a nation. Second, since yeast was a symbol of sin, the bread represented Israel's moral purity. Third, the bread reminded them to obey quickly. Their ancestors left the yeast out of their dough so they could leave Egypt quickly without waiting for the dough to rise.

23.9–14 The offering of first fruits required that the first crops harvested be offered to God. The Israelites could not eat the food from their harvest until they had made this offering. Today God still expects us to set aside his portion first, not last. Giving leftovers to God is no way to express thanks.

23.14 Lev 3.17

until that very day, until you have brought the offering of your God: it is a statute
forever throughout your generations in all your settlements.

The festival of weeks

23.15,16 Lev 23.9-14 Num 28.26-31 Acts 2.1

15 And from the day after the sabbath, from the day on which you bring the
sheaf of the elevation offering, you shall count off seven weeks; they shall be complete. 16 You shall count until the day after the seventh sabbath, fifty days; then you
shall present an offering of new grain to the LORD. 17 You shall bring from your
settlements two loaves of bread as an elevation offering, each made of two-tenths
of an ephah; they shall be of choice flour, baked with leaven, as first fruits to the
LORD. 18 You shall present with the bread seven lambs a year old without blemish,
one young bull, and two rams; they shall be a burnt offering to the LORD, along
with their grain offering and their drink offerings, an offering by fire of pleasing

23.19 Lev 16.15

23.20 Num 18.12 Deut 18.4

odor to the LORD. 19 You shall also offer one male goat for a sin offering, and two
male lambs a year old as a sacrifice of well-being. 20 The priest shall raise them with
the bread of the first fruits as an elevation offering before the LORD, together with
the two lambs; they shall be holy to the LORD for the priest. 21 On that same day you
shall make proclamation; you shall hold a holy convocation; you shall not work at
your occupations. This is a statute forever in all your settlements throughout your
generations.

23.22 Lev 19.9,10 Deut 24.19-21 Prov 11.24,25

22 When you reap the harvest of your land, you shall not reap to the very edges
of your field, or gather the gleanings of your harvest; you shall leave them for the
poor and for the alien: I am the LORD your God.

The festival of trumpets

23.23,24 Num 10.10 29.1-6

23.25 Lev 23.7

23 The LORD spoke to Moses, saying: 24 Speak to the people of Israel, saying:
In the seventh month, on the first day of the month, you shall observe a day of
complete rest, a holy convocation commemorated with trumpet blasts. 25 You shall
not work at your occupations; and you shall present the LORD's offering by fire.

THE FEASTS
Besides enjoying one sabbath day of rest each week, the Israelites also enjoyed 19 days when national holidays were celebrated.

Feast	*What It Celebrated*	*Its Importance*
Passover One day (Leviticus 23.5)	When God spared the lives of Israel's firstborn children in Egypt and freed the Hebrews from slavery	Reminded the people of God's deliverance
Unleavened Bread Seven days (Leviticus 23.6–8)	The exodus from Egypt	Reminded the people they were leaving the old life behind and entering a new way of living
First Fruits One day (Leviticus 23.9–14)	The first crops of the barley harvest	Reminded the people how God provided for them
Weeks One day (Leviticus 23.15–22)	The end of the barley harvest and beginning of the wheat harvest	Showed joy and thanksgiving over the bountiful harvest
Trumpets One day (Leviticus 23.23–25)	The beginning of the seventh month (civil new year)	Expressed joy and thanksgiving to God
Day of Atonement One day (Leviticus 23.26–32)	The removal of sin from the people and the nation	Restored fellowship with God
Booths Seven days (Leviticus 23.33–43)	God's protection and guidance in the wilderness	Renewed Israel's commitment to God and trust in his guidance and protection

23.23, 24 Most of the trumpets used were rams' horns, although some of the more special trumpets were made of beaten silver. Trumpets were blown to announce the beginning of each month as well as the start of festivals.

The day of atonement

26 The LORD spoke to Moses, saying: 27 Now, the tenth day of this seventh 23.26
month is the day of atonement; it shall be a holy convocation for you: you shall Lev 16.3-34 Num 29.7-11
deny yourselves[i] and present the LORD's offering by fire; 28 and you shall do no 23.28
work during that entire day; for it is a day of atonement, to make atonement on your Lev 23.7
behalf before the LORD your God. 29 For anyone who does not practice self-denial[j] 23.29
during that entire day shall be cut off from the people. 30 And anyone who does any Lev 23.32
work during that entire day, such a one I will destroy from the midst of the people.
31 You shall do no work: it is a statute forever throughout your generations in all
your settlements. 32 It shall be to you a sabbath of complete rest, and you shall deny 23.32
yourselves;[i] on the ninth day of the month at evening, from evening to evening Lev 16.29-31
you shall keep your sabbath.

The festival of booths

33 The LORD spoke to Moses, saying: 34 Speak to the people of Israel, saying: 23.33,34
On the fifteenth day of this seventh month, and lasting seven days, there shall be Ex 23.16 Lev 23.39-43
the festival of booths[k] to the LORD. 35 The first day shall be a holy convocation; you Num 29.12-39
shall not work at your occupations. 36 Seven days you shall present the LORD's Deut 16.13-16 Ezra 3.4
offerings by fire; on the eighth day you shall observe a holy convocation and Neh 8.14 Zech 14.16
present the LORD's offerings by fire; it is a solemn assembly; you shall not work at Jn 7.2
your occupations. 23.35 Lev 23.7
37 These are the appointed festivals of the LORD, which you shall celebrate as 23.36
times of holy convocation, for presenting to the LORD offerings by fire—burnt Lev 23.34
offerings and grain offerings, sacrifices and drink offerings, each on its proper Neh 8.18 Jn 7.39
day— 38 apart from the sabbaths of the LORD, and apart from your gifts, and apart 23.37
from all your votive offerings, and apart from all your freewill offerings, which Ex 34.22 Deut 16.16
you give to the LORD. 23.38
39 Now, the fifteenth day of the seventh month, when you have gathered in the Num 29.39
produce of the land, you shall keep the festival of the LORD, lasting seven days; a
complete rest on the first day, and a complete rest on the eighth day. 40 On the first
day you shall take the fruit of majestic[l] trees, branches of palm trees, boughs of
leafy trees, and willows of the brook; and you shall rejoice before the LORD your
God for seven days. 41 You shall keep it as a festival to the LORD seven days in the
year; you shall keep it in the seventh month as a statute forever throughout your
generations. 42 You shall live in booths for seven days; all that are citizens in Israel 23.42
shall live in booths, 43 so that your generations may know that I made the people of Neh 8.14-18
Israel live in booths when I brought them out of the land of Egypt: I am the LORD 23.43 Ex 13.14-18
your God. Deut 13.31 Ps 78.1-8
44 Thus Moses declared to the people of Israel the appointed festivals of the
LORD. 23.44 Lev 23.37

The memorial offering

24 The LORD spoke to Moses, saying: 2 Command the people of Israel to bring 24.1
you pure oil of beaten olives for the lamp, that a light may be kept burning Ex 27.20,21
regularly. 3 Aaron shall set it up in the tent of meeting, outside the curtain of the 24.3
covenant,[m] to burn from evening to morning before the LORD regularly; it shall be Ex 25.31-39 37.17-24
a statute forever throughout your generations. 4 He shall set up the lamps on the
lampstand of pure gold[n] before the LORD regularly.

[i] Or *shall fast* [j] Or *does not fast* [k] Or *tabernacles*: Heb *succoth* [l] Meaning of Heb uncertain [m] Or *treaty*, or *testament*; Heb *eduth* [n] Heb *pure lampstand*

23.43 The festival of booths was a special celebration involving the whole family (see 23.34; Exodus 23.16; Deuteronomy 16.13). Like passover, this festival taught family members of all ages about God's nature and what he had done for them, and was a time of renewed commitment to God. Our families also need rituals of celebration to renew our faith and to pass it on to our children. In addition to Christmas and Easter, we should select other special days to commemorate God's goodness.

23.44 Worship involves both celebration and confession. But in Israel's national holidays, the balance seems heavily tipped in favor of celebration—five joyous occasions to two solemn occasions. The God of the Bible encourages joy! God does not intend for religion to be only meditation and introspection. He also wants us to celebrate. Serious reflection and immediate confession of sin is essential, of course. But this should be balanced by celebrating who God is and what he has done for his people.

24.5 Ex 25.30 37.10-13; 40.23 Lev 2.9,16 5.12; 6.15 Heb 9.2
24.9 Lev 6.16-18 Mt 12.4

5 You shall take choice flour, and bake twelve loaves of it; two-tenths of an
ephah shall be in each loaf. 6You shall place them in two rows, six in a row, on the
table of pure gold.[o] 7You shall put pure frankincense with each row, to be a token
offering for the bread, as an offering by fire to the LORD. 8Every sabbath day Aaron
shall set them in order before the LORD regularly as a commitment of the people of
Israel, as a covenant forever. 9They shall be for Aaron and his descendants, who
shall eat them in a holy place, for they are most holy portions for him from the
offerings by fire to the LORD, a perpetual due.

The penalty for cursing God

24.11 Ex 22.28 Job 1.5,11,22 Ps 74.18
24.13 Lev 4.15 Deut 13.9; 17.7 21.21
24.15,16 Ex 22.28
24.17 Gen 9.5 Ex 20.13 21.12,14 Num 35.30,31 Deut 19.11-13
24.18 Ex 21.33-36 Lev 24.21
24.20 Ex 21.24,25 Deut 19.21 Mt 5.38
24.21 Lev 24.18
24.22 Ex 12.49 Num 15.15, 16,29

10 A man whose mother was an Israelite and whose father was an Egyptian
came out among the people of Israel; and the Israelite woman's son and a certain
Israelite began fighting in the camp. 11The Israelite woman's son blasphemed the
Name in a curse. And they brought him to Moses—now his mother's name was
Shelomith, daughter of Dibri, of the tribe of Dan— 12and they put him in custody,
until the decision of the LORD should be made clear to them.

13 The LORD said to Moses, saying: 14Take the blasphemer outside the camp;
and let all who were within hearing lay their hands on his head, and let the whole
congregation stone him. 15And speak to the people of Israel, saying: Anyone who
curses God shall bear the sin. 16One who blasphemes the name of the LORD shall
be put to death; the whole congregation shall stone the blasphemer. Aliens as well
as citizens, when they blaspheme the Name, shall be put to death. 17Anyone who
kills a human being shall be put to death. 18Anyone who kills an animal shall make
restitution for it, life for life. 19Anyone who maims another shall suffer the same
injury in return: 20fracture for fracture, eye for eye, tooth for tooth; the injury inflicted is the injury to be suffered. 21One who kills an animal shall make restitution
for it; but one who kills a human being shall be put to death. 22You shall have one
law for the alien and for the citizen: for I am the LORD your God. 23Moses spoke
thus to the people of Israel; and they took the blasphemer outside the camp, and
stoned him to death. The people of Israel did as the LORD had commanded Moses.

Rest every seventh year

25.2 Ex 23.11 Lev 26.33-35,43
25.3 Ex 23.10
25.4 Lev 25.1,20-23
25.5 2 Kgs 19.29
25.6 Lev 25.20-22

25 The LORD spoke to Moses on Mount Sinai, saying: 2Speak to the people of
Israel and say to them: When you enter the land that I am giving you, the
land shall observe a sabbath for the LORD. 3Six years you shall sow your field, and
six years you shall prune your vineyard, and gather in their yield; 4but in the seventh year there shall be a sabbath of complete rest for the land, a sabbath for the
LORD: you shall not sow your field or prune your vineyard. 5You shall not reap the
aftergrowth of your harvest or gather the grapes of your unpruned vine: it shall be
a year of complete rest for the land. 6You may eat what the land yields during its
sabbath—you, your male and female slaves, your hired and your bound laborers
who live with you; 7for your livestock also, and for the wild animals in your land
all its yield shall be for food.

The year of jubilee

25.9 Num 10.10
25.10 Lev 25.8-16, 28-54 Isa 61.1,2 Jer 34.8,15,17 Lk 4.17-20

8 You shall count off seven weeks[p] of years, seven times seven years, so that
the period of seven weeks of years gives forty-nine years. 9Then you shall have the
trumpet sounded loud; on the tenth day of the seventh month—on the day of
atonement—you shall have the trumpet sounded throughout all your land. 10And
you shall hallow the fiftieth year and you shall proclaim liberty throughout the land
to all its inhabitants. It shall be a jubilee for you: you shall return, every one of you,

[o] Heb *pure table* [p] Or *sabbaths*

24.19–20 This was a code for judges, not an endorsement of personal vengeance. In effect it was saying that the punishment should fit the crime.

25.8–16 The year of jubilee was meant to be celebrated every 50 years. It included canceling all debts, freeing all slaves, and returning to its original owners all land that had been sold. There is no indication in the Bible that the year of jubilee was ever carried out. If Israel had followed this practice faithfully, they would have been a society without permanent poverty.

to your property and every one of you to your family. 11 That fiftieth year shall be
a jubilee for you: you shall not sow, or reap the aftergrowth, or harvest the unpruned vines. 12 For it is a jubilee; it shall be holy to you: you shall eat only what the **25.12**
field itself produces. Lev 25.5

13 In this year of jubilee you shall return, every one of you, to your property. **25.13**
14 When you make a sale to your neighbor or buy from your neighbor, you shall not Lev 25.10,24-31 **25.14**
cheat one another. 15 When you buy from your neighbor, you shall pay only for the Lev 25.17,51,52
number of years since the jubilee; the seller shall charge you only for the remaining
crop years. 16 If the years are more, you shall increase the price, and if the years are
fewer, you shall diminish the price; for it is a certain number of harvests that are
being sold to you. 17 You shall not cheat one another, but you shall fear your God; **25.17**
for I am the LORD your God. Lev 25.14-16

18 You shall observe my statutes and faithfully keep my ordinances, so that you
may live on the land securely. 19 The land will yield its fruit, and you will eat your
fill and live on it securely. 20 Should you ask, What shall we eat in the seventh year,
if we may not sow or gather in our crop? 21 I will order my blessing for you in the **25.21**
sixth year, so that it will yield a crop for three years. 22 When you sow in the eighth Lev 25.3,4
year, you will be eating from the old crop; until the ninth year, when its produce
comes in, you shall eat the old. 23 The land shall not be sold in perpetuity, for the **25.23**
land is mine; with me you are but aliens and tenants. 24 Throughout the land that Ex 19.5 2 Chron 7.20
you hold, you shall provide for the redemption of the land. Ezek 48.14

25 If anyone of your kin falls into difficulty and sells a piece of property, then **25.25**
the next of kin shall come and redeem what the relative has sold. 26 If the person has Lev 25.35 Ruth 2.20; 4.4,6
no one to redeem it, but then prospers and finds sufficient means to do so, 27 the Jer 32.6-8
years since its sale shall be computed and the difference shall be refunded to the **25.27**
person to whom it was sold, and the property shall be returned. 28 But if there is not Lev 25.50-53 **25.28**
sufficient means to recover it, what was sold shall remain with the purchaser until Lev 25.10,13
the year of jubilee; in the jubilee it shall be released, and the property shall be
returned.

29 If anyone sells a dwelling house in a walled city, it may be redeemed until
a year has elapsed since its sale; the right of redemption shall be one year. 30 If it is
not redeemed before a full year has elapsed, a house that is in a walled city shall
pass in perpetuity to the purchaser, throughout the generations; it shall not be released in the jubilee. 31 But houses in villages that have no walls around them shall
be classed as open country; they may be redeemed, and they shall be released in the
jubilee. 32 As for the cities of the Levites, the Levites shall forever have the right of
redemption of the houses in the cities belonging to them. 33 Such property as may
be redeemed from the Levites — houses sold in a city belonging to them — shall be **25.34**
released in the jubilee; because the houses in the cities of the Levites are their pos- Num 35.2-5
session among the people of Israel. 34 But the open land around their cities may not **25.35**
be sold; for that is their possession for all time. Lev 25.25 Deut 15.7-11

35 If any of your kin fall into difficulty and become dependent on you,[q] you Prov 14.21 19.17
shall support them; they shall live with you as though resident aliens. 36 Do not take **25.36**
interest in advance or otherwise make a profit from them, but fear your God; let Ex 22.25 Deut 23.19,20
them live with you. 37 You shall not lend them your money at interest taken in Neh 5.10

[q] Meaning of Heb uncertain

25.23 The people would one day possess land in Canaan, but in God's plan, only God's ownership was absolute. He wanted his people to avoid greed and materialism. If you have the attitude that you are taking care of the Lord's property, you will make what you have more available to others. This is difficult to do if you have an attitude of ownership. Think of yourself as a manager of all that is under your care, not as an owner.

25.35–37 God said that neglecting the poor was a sin. Permanent poverty was not allowed in Israel. Financially secure families were responsible to help and house those in need. Many times we do nothing, not because we lack compassion, but because we are overwhelmed by the size of the problem and don't know where to begin. God doesn't expect you to eliminate poverty, nor does he expect you to neglect your family while providing for others. He does expect that when you see an individual in need you will reach out with whatever help you can offer, including hospitality.

25.35ff The Bible places great emphasis on assisting the poor and helpless, especially orphans, widows, and the handicapped. In Israelite society, no paid work was available to women; thus a widow and her children had no livelihood. Neither was work available for the seriously handicapped in this nation of farmers and shepherds. The poor were to be helped without charging any interest. Individual and family responsibility for the poor was crucial since there was no government aid.

25.38 Ex 20.2 Lev 11.45 advance, or provide them food at a profit. 38 I am the LORD your God, who brought
you out of the land of Egypt, to give you the land of Canaan, to be your God.
25.39 Ex 21.2-11 Deut 15.12-18 39 If any who are dependent on you become so impoverished that they sell
themselves to you, you shall not make them serve as slaves. 40 They shall remain
25.40 Lev 25.53 with you as hired or bound laborers. They shall serve with you until the year of the
jubilee. 41 Then they and their children with them shall be free from your authority;
25.42 Rom 6.22 1 Cor 7.23 they shall go back to their own family and return to their ancestral property. 42 For
they are my servants, whom I brought out of the land of Egypt; they shall not be
25.43 Eph 6.9 sold as slaves are sold. 43 You shall not rule over them with harshness, but shall fear
your God. 44 As for the male and female slaves whom you may have, it is from the
nations around you that you may acquire male and female slaves. 45 You may also
acquire them from among the aliens residing with you, and from their families that
are with you, who have been born in your land; and they may be your property.
25.46 Lev 25.40,53 46 You may keep them as a possession for your children after you, for them to inherit as property. These you may treat as slaves, but as for your fellow Israelites,
no one shall rule over the other with harshness.
25.47 Lev 25.39 47 If resident aliens among you prosper, and if any of your kin fall into difficulty with one of them and sell themselves to an alien, or to a branch of the alien's
25.48 Neh 5.5 family, 48 after they have sold themselves they shall have the right of redemption;
one of their brothers may redeem them, 49 or their uncle or their uncle's son may
25.49 Lev 25.26 redeem them, or anyone of their family who is of their own flesh may redeem them;
25.50 Lev 25.27 Job 7.1 or if they prosper they may redeem themselves. 50 They shall compute with the
purchaser the total from the year when they sold themselves to the alien until the
jubilee year; the price of the sale shall be applied to the number of years: the time
they were with the owner shall be rated as the time of a hired laborer. 51 If many
years remain, they shall pay for their redemption in proportion to the purchase
price; 52 and if few years remain until the jubilee year, they shall compute thus:
25.53 Lev 25.40,46 according to the years involved they shall make payment for their redemption. 53 As
a laborer hired by the year they shall be under the alien's authority, who shall not,
25.54 Ex 21.3-6 Lev 25.41 however, rule with harshness over them in your sight. 54 And if they have not been
redeemed in any of these ways, they and their children with them shall go free in
the jubilee year. 55 For to me the people of Israel are servants; they are my servants
whom I brought out from the land of Egypt: I am the LORD your God.

4. Receiving God's blessing

Rewards for obedience

26.1 Ex 20.4; 34.17 **26** You shall make for yourselves no idols and erect no carved images or pillars, and you shall not place figured stones in your land, to worship at them;
26.2 Ex 20.8-11 for I am the LORD your God. 2 You shall keep my sabbaths and reverence my sanctuary: I am the LORD.
3 If you follow my statutes and keep my commandments and observe them
26.4 Lev 25.19-22 Deut 11.14,15 Amos 9.13 faithfully, 4 I will give you your rains in their season, and the land shall yield its
produce, and the trees of the field shall yield their fruit. 5 Your threshing shall over-
take the vintage, and the vintage shall overtake the sowing; you shall eat your bread
to the full, and live securely in your land. 6 And I will grant peace in the land, and
you shall lie down, and no one shall make you afraid; I will remove dangerous
animals from the land, and no sword shall go through your land. 7 You shall give
26.8 Deut 28.7; 32.30 chase to your enemies, and they shall fall before you by the sword. 8 Five of
you shall give chase to a hundred, and a hundred of you shall give chase to ten

25.44 Why did God allow the Israelites to purchase slaves? Under Hebrew laws, slaves were treated differently from slaves in other nations. They were seen as human beings with dignity, and not as animals. Hebrew slaves, for example, took part in the religious festivals and rested on the sabbath. Nowhere does the Bible condone slavery, but it recognizes its existence. God's laws offered many guidelines for treating slaves properly.

26.1 The people of the Old Testament were warned over and over against worshiping idols. We wonder how they could deceive themselves with these objects of wood and stone. Yet God could well give us the same warning, for we are prone to put idols before him. Idolatry is making anything more important than God, and our lives are full of that temptation. Money, looks, success, reputation, security – these are today's idols. As you look at these false gods that promise everything you want but nothing you need, does idolatry seem so far removed from your experience?

thousand; your enemies shall fall before you by the sword. [9]I will look with favor
upon you and make you fruitful and multiply you; and I will maintain my covenant
with you. [10]You shall eat old grain long stored, and you shall have to clear out the
old to make way for the new. [11]I will place my dwelling in your midst, and I shall
not abhor you. [12]And I will walk among you, and will be your God, and you shall
be my people. [13]I am the LORD your God who brought you out of the land of Egypt,
to be their slaves no more; I have broken the bars of your yoke and made you walk
erect.

Results of disobedience

14 But if you will not obey me, and do not observe all these commandments,
[15]if you spurn my statutes, and abhor my ordinances, so that you will not observe
all my commandments, and you break my covenant, [16]I in turn will do this to you:
I will bring terror on you; consumption and fever that waste the eyes and cause life
to pine away. You shall sow your seed in vain, for your enemies shall eat it. [17]I will
set my face against you, and you shall be struck down by your enemies; your foes
shall rule over you, and you shall flee though no one pursues you. [18]And if in spite
of this you will not obey me, I will continue to punish you sevenfold for your sins.
[19]I will break your proud glory, and I will make your sky like iron and your earth
like copper. [20]Your strength shall be spent to no purpose: your land shall not yield
its produce, and the trees of the land shall not yield their fruit.

21 If you continue hostile to me, and will not obey me, I will continue to plague
you sevenfold for your sins. [22]I will let loose wild animals against you, and they
shall bereave you of your children and destroy your livestock; they shall make you
few in number, and your roads shall be deserted.

23 If in spite of these punishments you have not turned back to me, but continue
hostile to me, [24]then I too will continue hostile to you: I myself will strike you
sevenfold for your sins. [25]I will bring the sword against you, executing vengeance
for the covenant; and if you withdraw within your cities, I will send pestilence
among you, and you shall be delivered into enemy hands. [26]When I break your
staff of bread, ten women shall bake your bread in a single oven, and they shall dole
out your bread by weight; and though you eat, you shall not be satisfied.

27 But if, despite this, you disobey me, and continue hostile to me, [28]I will
continue hostile to you in fury; I in turn will punish you myself sevenfold for your
sins. [29]You shall eat the flesh of your sons, and you shall eat the flesh of your
daughters. [30]I will destroy your high places and cut down your incense altars; I will
heap your carcasses on the carcasses of your idols. I will abhor you. [31]I will lay
your cities waste, will make your sanctuaries desolate, and I will not smell your
pleasing odors. [32]I will devastate the land, so that your enemies who come to settle
in it shall be appalled at it. [33]And you I will scatter among the nations, and I will
unsheathe the sword against you; your land shall be a desolation, and your cities a
waste.

34 Then the land shall enjoy[r] its sabbath years as long as it lies desolate, while

[r] Or *make up for*

26.9 Ex 6.4,5
26.10 Lev 26.5
26.11 Ex 29.45,46
26.12 Jer 32.38
26.13 Ex 20.2
26.15 Num 15.30,31
26.16 Deut 28.22,33, 65-67; 32.25 Jer 5.17
26.17 Deut 28.25 Neh 9.27-30 Ps 106.41,42
26.19 Deut 28.23 Isa 25.11; 26.5
26.20 Ps 127.1 Hab 2.13
26.22 Deut 32.24
26.23 Isa 1.18-20
26.25 Deut 28.21,22, 27-29; 32.35
26.26 Isa 3.1; 9.19,20 Ezek 4.16
26.29 Deut 28.53-57 2 Kgs 6.26-30
26.30 1 Kgs 13.2-5 Isa 27.9
26.31 2 Kgs 25.4-10 Isa 24.10-13 Jer 52.13
26.32 Deut 28.37 29.23 Jer 12.11; 18.16 Ezek 33.28 Dan 9.2
26.33 Deut 28.64-68

26.13 Imagine the joy of a slave set free. God took the children of Israel out of bitter slavery and gave them freedom and dignity. We too are set free when we accept Christ's payment that redeems us from sin's slavery. We no longer need to be bogged down in shame over our past sins; we can walk with dignity because God has forgiven us and forgotten them. But just as the Israelites were still in danger of returning to a slave mentality, we need to beware of the temptation to return to our old lives of sin.

26.18 If the Israelites obeyed, there would be peace in the land. If they disobeyed, disaster would follow. God used sin's consequences to draw them to repentance, not to get back at them. Today, sin's consequences are not always so apparent. When calamity strikes us we may not know the reason. It may be (1) the result of our own disobedience, (2) the result of someone else's sin, (3) the result of natural disaster. Since we don't know, we should search our hearts and be sure we are at peace with God. His spirit, like a great searchlight, will reveal those areas we need to deal with. Since calamity is not always the result of wrongdoing, we must guard against assigning or accepting blame for every tragedy we encounter. Misplaced guilt is one of Satan's favorite weapons against believers.

26.33–35 In 2 Kings 17 and 25 the warning pronounced in these verses came true. The people persistently disobeyed, and eventually they were conquered and carried off to the lands of Assyria and Babylon. The nation was held in captivity for seventy years, making up for all of the years that the Israelites did not observe the law of the sabbatical year (2 Chronicles 36.21).

26.34 2 Chron 36.21 Jer 29.10
26.36 Deut 28.65,67 Ezek 21.7
26.38 Deut 4.25-27 Jer 42.17,18
26.39 Ezek 20.43 33.10
26.40 Deut 30.1-3 2 Chron 7.17 Ezek 36.31 Mt 23.12 Lk 14.11 1 Jn 1.9
26.42 Gen 12.1-3 15.1-4,13-16 26.2-5 28.13-15
26.44 Deut 4.29-31 Neh 9.31 Rom 11.2,26
26.45 Ex 2.24; 20.2 Lev 22.32,33 Lk 1.72,73
26.46 Lev 27.34 Deut 6.1; 12.1

you are in the land of your enemies; then the land shall rest, and enjoy[s] its sabbath
years. 35 As long as it lies desolate, it shall have the rest it did not have on your
sabbaths when you were living on it. 36 And as for those of you who survive, I will
send faintness into their hearts in the lands of their enemies; the sound of a driven
leaf shall put them to flight, and they shall flee as one flees from the sword, and
they shall fall though no one pursues. 37 They shall stumble over one another, as if
to escape a sword, though no one pursues; and you shall have no power to stand
against your enemies. 38 You shall perish among the nations, and the land of your
enemies shall devour you. 39 And those of you who survive shall languish in the
land of your enemies because of their iniquities; also they shall languish because of
the iniquities of their ancestors.
40 But if they confess their iniquity and the iniquity of their ancestors, in that
they committed treachery against me and, moreover, that they continued hostile to
me— 41 so that I, in turn, continued hostile to them and brought them into the land
of their enemies; if then their uncircumcised heart is humbled and they make
amends for their iniquity, 42 then will I remember my covenant with Jacob; I will
remember also my covenant with Isaac and also my covenant with Abraham, and
I will remember the land. 43 For the land shall be deserted by them, and enjoy[s] its
sabbath years by lying desolate without them, while they shall make amends for
their iniquity, because they dared to spurn my ordinances, and they abhorred my
statutes. 44 Yet for all that, when they are in the land of their enemies, I will not
spurn them, or abhor them so as to destroy them utterly and break my covenant with
them; for I am the LORD their God; 45 but I will remember in their favor the covenant
with their ancestors whom I brought out of the land of Egypt in the sight of the
nations, to be their God: I am the LORD.
46 These are the statutes and ordinances and laws that the LORD established
between himself and the people of Israel on Mount Sinai through Moses.

Payments to the Lord

27.3 Ex 30.13 Lev 5.15; 27.25
27.6 Num 3.46-48 18.14-16
27.8 Lev 14.21,22

27 The LORD spoke to Moses, saying: 2 Speak to the people of Israel and say to
them: When a person makes an explicit vow to the LORD concerning the
equivalent for a human being, 3 the equivalent for a male shall be: from twenty to
sixty years of age the equivalent shall be fifty shekels of silver by the sanctuary
shekel. 4 If the person is a female, the equivalent is thirty shekels. 5 If the age is
from five to twenty years of age, the equivalent is twenty shekels for a male and ten
shekels for a female. 6 If the age is from one month to five years, the equivalent for
a male is five shekels of silver, and for a female the equivalent is three shekels of
silver. 7 And if the person is sixty years old or over, then the equivalent for a male
is fifteen shekels, and for a female ten shekels. 8 If any cannot afford the equivalent,
they shall be brought before the priest and the priest shall assess them; the priest
shall assess them according to what each one making a vow can afford.
9 If it concerns an animal that may be brought as an offering to the LORD, any

[s] Or *make up for*

26.40–45 These verses show what God meant when he said he is longsuffering (Exodus 34.6). Even if the Israelites chose to disobey and were scattered among the heathen, God would still give them the opportunity to repent and return to him. His purpose was not to destroy them, but to help them grow. Our day-to-day experiences and hardships are sometimes overwhelming; unless we can see that God's purpose is to bring about continual growth in us, we may despair. The hope we need is well expressed in Jeremiah 29.11, 12: "For surely I know the plans I have for you, says the Lord, plans for your welfare and not for harm, to give you a future with hope. Then when you call upon me and come and pray to me, I will hear you." To retain hope while we suffer shows we understand God's merciful ways of relating to his people.

27.1ff The Israelites were required to give or dedicate certain things to the Lord and to his service: the first fruits of their harvests, firstborn animals, their firstborn sons, a tithe of their increase. Many wished to go beyond this and dedicate themselves or another family member, additional animals, a house, or a field to God. In these cases, it was possible to donate money instead of the actual person, animal, or property. Some people made rash or unrealistic vows. To urge people to think first before they made a vow, a 20% penalty was placed on those items purchased back with money after the vow had been made. This chapter explains how valuations were to be made and what to do if a donor later wished to buy back what had been donated to God.

27.9, 10 God taught the Israelites that when they made a vow to him, they must not go back on their promise even if it turned out to cost more than expected. God takes our promises seriously. If you vow to give 10 precent of your income and suddenly some unexpected bills come along, your faithful stewardship will be costly. God, however, expects you to fulfill your vow even if it is difficult to do so.

such that may be given to the LORD shall be holy. 10 Another shall not be exchanged 27.10 Lev 27.14-33
or substituted for it, either good for bad or bad for good; and if one animal is substituted for another, both that one and its substitute shall be holy. 11 If it concerns any
unclean animal that may not be brought as an offering to the LORD, the animal shall
be presented before the priest. 12 The priest shall assess it: whether good or bad,
according to the assessment of the priest, so it shall be. 13 But if it is to be redeemed
one-fifth must be added to the assessment.

14 If a person consecrates a house to the LORD, the priest shall assess it: whether
good or bad, as the priest assesses it, so it shall stand. 15 And if the one who consecrates the house wishes to redeem it, one-fifth shall be added to its assessed value,
and it shall revert to the original owner.

16 If a person consecrates to the LORD any inherited landholding, its assessment
shall be in accordance with its seed requirements: fifty shekels of silver to a homer
of barley seed. 17 If the person consecrates the field as of the year of jubilee, that
assessment shall stand; 18 but if the field is consecrated after the jubilee, the priest 27.18
shall compute the price for it according to the years that remain until the year of Lev 25.14-16
jubilee, and the assessment shall be reduced. 19 And if the one who consecrates the
field wishes to redeem it, then one-fifth shall be added to its assessed value, and it
shall revert to the original owner; 20 but if the field is not redeemed, or if it has been
sold to someone else, it shall no longer be redeemable. 21 But when the field is 27.21
released in the jubilee, it shall be holy to the LORD as a devoted field; it becomes the Lev 25.8-54 Num 18.14
priest's holding. 22 If someone consecrates to the LORD a field that has been pur- Ezek 44.29
chased, which is not a part of the inherited landholding, 23 the priest shall compute
for it the proportionate assessment up to the year of jubilee, and the assessment
shall be paid as of that day, a sacred donation to the LORD. 24 In the year of jubilee 27.24
the field shall return to the one from whom it was bought, whose holding the land Lev 27.21
is. 25 All assessments shall be by the sanctuary shekel: twenty gerahs shall make a 27.25
shekel. Ex 30.13 Lev 5.15

26 A firstling of animals, however, which as a firstling belongs to the LORD, Num 3.47; 18.16 Ezek 45.12
cannot be consecrated by anyone; whether ox or sheep, it is the LORD's. 27 If it is an 27.26
unclean animal, it shall be ransomed at its assessment, with one-fifth added; if it is Ex 13.2,12
not redeemed, it shall be sold at its assessment. 22.30

28 Nothing that a person owns that has been devoted to destruction for the 27.28
LORD, be it human or animal, or inherited landholding, may be sold or redeemed; Lev 27.21 Jos 6.17-19
every devoted thing is most holy to the LORD. 29 No human beings who have been
devoted to destruction can be ransomed; they shall be put to death.

30 All tithes from the land, whether the seed from the ground or the fruit from 27.30
the tree, are the LORD's; they are holy to the LORD. 31 If persons wish to redeem any Gen 28.22 Num 18.21,24
of their tithes, they must add one-fifth to them. 32 All tithes of herd and flock, every 2 Chron 31.5,6
tenth one that passes under the shepherd's staff, shall be holy to the LORD. 33 Let no Neh 3.12 Mal 3.8
one inquire whether it is good or bad, or make substitution for it; if one makes 27.33
substitution for it, then both it and the substitute shall be holy and cannot be re- Lev 27.10
deemed.

34 These are the commandments that the LORD gave to Moses for the people of 27.34
Israel on Mount Sinai. Lev 26.46

27.14–25 Real estate could be given as a voluntary offering similar to the way in which people today will donate property or proceeds from the sale of property to the church or Christian organizations.

27.28 Things "devoted to destruction" applies to personal property placed under God's ban, such as captured booty from idol worshipers, or idols themselves. These were to be destroyed and could not be redeemed.

27.33 Many of the principles regarding sacrifices and tithes were intended to encourage inward attitudes as well as outward actions. If a person gives grudgingly, he shows that he has a stingy heart. God wants us to be cheerful givers (2 Corinthians 9.7) who give with grateful eyes turned on him, the object of our giving.

27.34 The book of Leviticus is filled with the commands God gave his people at the foot of Mount Sinai. From these commands we can learn much about God's nature and character. At first glance, Leviticus seems irrelevant to our high-tech world. But digging a little deeper, we realize that the book still speaks to us today because God has not changed and his principles are for all times. As people and society change, we need constantly to search for ways to apply the principles of God's law to our present circumstances. God was the same in Leviticus as he is today and will be forever (Hebrews 13.8).

EIGHT WORDS FOR LAW

Hebrew law served as the personal and national guide for living under God's authority. It directed the moral, spiritual, and social life. Its purpose was to produce better understanding of God and commitment to him.

Word	*Meaning*	*Examples*	*Significance*
Torah	Direction, Guidance, Instruction	Exodus 24.12; Isaiah 12.23; 30.20	Need for law in general; a command from a higher person to a lower.
Mitsvah	Commandment, Command	Genesis 25.5; Exodus 15.26; 20.2-17; Deuteronomy 5.6-21	God's specific instruction to be obeyed rather than a general law; used of the ten commandments.
Mishpat	Judgment, Ordinance	Genesis 18.19; Deuteronomy 34.2; 16.18; 17.9	This refers to the civil, social, and sanitation laws.
Eduth	Admonition, Testimony	Exodus 25.22	Refers to God's law as he deals with his people.
Huqqim	Statutes, Oracles	Leviticus 18.4; Deuteronomy 4.1	Dealt with the royal pronouncements; mainly connected to worship and festivals.
Piqqudim	Orders, Precepts	Psalms 19.8; 103.8	Used often in the Psalms to describe God's orders and assignments.
Dabar	Word	Exodus 34.28; Deuteronomy 4.13	Used to indicate divine oracles or revelations of God.
Dath	Royal Edict, Public Law	Ezekiel 7.26; Daniel 2.3, 15; 6.8, 12	Refers to the divine law or Jewish religious traditions in general.

NUMBERS

Joseph dies 1805 B.C. (1640 B.C.)	SLAVERY IN EGYPT	Exodus from Egypt 1446 (1280)	Ten command-ments given 1445 (1279)	First census 1444 (1278)	First spy mission 1443 (1277)

VITAL STATISTICS

PURPOSE:
To tell the story of how Israel prepared to enter the promised land, how they sinned and were punished, and how they prepared to try again

AUTHOR:
Moses

TO WHOM WRITTEN:
The people of Israel

DATE WRITTEN:
1450–1410 B.C.

SETTING:
The vast desert of the Sinai region, as well as lands just south and east of Canaan

KEY VERSES:
"None of the people who have seen my glory and the signs that I did in Egypt and in the wilderness, and yet have tested me these ten times and have not obeyed my voice, shall see the land that I swore to give to their ancestors; none of those who despised me shall see it" (14.22, 23).

KEY PEOPLE:
Moses, Aaron, Miriam, Joshua, Caleb, Eleazar, Korah, Balaam

KEY PLACES:
Mount Sinai, promised land (Canaan), Kadesh, Mount Hor, plains of Moab

EVERY parent knows the shrill whine of a young child—a slow, high-pitched complaint that grates on the eardrums and aggravates the soul. The tone of voice is difficult to bear, but the real irritation is the underlying cause—discontentment and disobedience. As the "children" of Israel journeyed from the foot of Mount Sinai to the land of Canaan, they grumbled, whined, and complained at every turn. They focused on their present discomforts. Faith had fled, and they added an extra 40 years to their trip.

Numbers, which records the tragic story of Israel's unbelief, should serve as a dramatic lesson for all of God's people. God loves us and wants the very best for us. He can and should be trusted. Numbers also gives a clear portrayal of God's patience. Again and again he withholds judgment and preserves the nation. But his patience must not be taken for granted. His judgment will come. We must obey.

As Numbers begins, the nation of Israel was camped at the foot of Mount Sinai. The people had received God's laws and were preparing to move. A census was taken to determine the number of men fit for military service. Next, the people were set apart for God. God was making the people, both spiritually and physically, ready to receive their inheritance.

But then the complaining began. First, the people complained over the food. Next, it was over Moses' authority. God punished some people but spared the nation because of Moses' prayers. The nation then arrived at Kadesh, and spies were sent into Canaan to assess its strength. Ten returned with fearful stories of giants. Only Caleb and Joshua encouraged them to "go up at once and occupy" the land! The minority report fell on deaf ears full of the ominous message of the majority. Because of their unbelief, God declared that the present generation would not live to see the promised land. Thus the "wanderings" began. During these wilderness wanderings there is a continuous pattern of grumbling, defiance, discipline, and death. How much better it would have been to have trusted God and entered his land! Now the terrible waiting began—waiting for the old generation to die off and waiting to see if the new generation could faithfully obey God.

Numbers ends as it begins, with preparation. This new generation of Israelites are numbered and sanctified. After defeating numerous armies, they settle the east side of the Jordan River. Now they face their greatest test: they must cross the river and possess the beautiful land God promised them.

The lesson is clear. God's people must trust him, moving ahead by *faith*, if they are to claim his promised land.

WILDERNESS WANDERINGS	Second census, Balaam prophesies 1407 (1241)	Joshua appointed, Canaan entered 1406 (1240)	Judges begin to rule 1375 (1220)	United kingdom under Saul 1050 (1045)

THE BLUEPRINT

A. PREPARING FOR THE JOURNEY (1.1—10.10)
1. The first numbering of the nation
2. The role of the Levites
3. Maintaining purity in the camp
4. Receiving guidance for the journey

God abundantly provided for the Israelites on their journey to the promised land. He supplies all that we need for our journey through life too.
The Lord gave strict guidelines to the Israelites regarding purity in the camp. We, too, need to concern ourselves with purity in the church.

B. FIRST APPROACH TO THE PROMISED LAND (10.11—14.45)
1. The people complain
2. Miriam and Aaron criticize Moses
3. The spies incite rebellion

When the people complained and criticized Moses, they were severely punished. We must guard against complaining and criticizing our leaders.
The Israelites were prevented from entering the promised land because of their unbelief. We must prevent unbelief from gaining a foothold in our lives, for it will keep us from enjoying the blessings which God has promised.

C. WANDERING IN THE WILDERNESS (15.1—21.35)
1. Additional regulations
2. Many leaders rebel against Moses
3. Directions to the priests and Levites
4. The new generation

After years of wandering in the wilderness, Israel developed a stronger relationship with God. The hard times in our lives help make us better and stronger Christians.
Over 14,000 people died in the rebellion against Moses. Dissatisfaction and discontent, if allowed to remain in our lives, can easily lead to disaster.

D. SECOND APPROACH TO THE PROMISED LAND (22.1—36.13)
1. The story of Balaam
2. The second numbering of the nation
3. Instructions concerning offerings
4. The war against Midian
5. Two and a half tribes receive their land
6. Camped on the plains of Moab

Balaam was a man who knew what was right, but he gave in to the temptation of material rewards and sinned. Knowing what is right is not enough. We must also do what is right.
Two and a half tribes chose the land they could see over the land they were promised. We sometimes think we can make better choices than the Lord can, but he can see farther than we can, and he has our spiritual well-being in mind.

MEGATHEMES

THEME	EXPLANATION	IMPORTANCE
Census	Moses counted the Israelites twice. The first census organized the people into marching units to better defend themselves. The second prepared them to conquer the country east of the Jordan River.	People have to be organized, trained, and led to be effective in great movements. It is always wise to count the cost before setting out on some great undertaking. When we are aware of the obstacles before us we can more easily avoid them. In God's work, we must remove barriers in our relationships with others so that our effectiveness is not diminished.
Rebellion	At Kadesh, 12 spies were sent out into the land of Canaan to report on the fortifications of the enemies. When the spies returned, ten said that they should give up and go back to Egypt. As a result, the people refused to enter the land. Faced with a choice, Israel rebelled against God. Rebellion did not start with an uprising, but with griping and murmuring against Moses and God.	Rebellion against God is always a serious matter. It is not something to take lightly, for God's punishment for sin is often very severe. Our rebellion does not usually begin with all-out warfare, but in subtle ways—with griping and criticizing. Make sure your negative comments are not the product of a rebellious spirit.
Wandering	Because they rebelled, the Israelites wandered 40 years in the wilderness. This shows how severely God can punish sin. Forty years was enough time for all those who held on to Egypt's customs and values to die off. It gave time to train up a new generation in the ways of God.	God judges sin harshly because he is holy. The wanderings in the wilderness demonstrate how serious God considers flagrant disobedience of his commands. Purging our lives of sin is vital to God's purpose.

Canaan	Canaan is the promised land. It was the land God had promised to Abraham, Isaac, and Jacob—the land of the covenant. Canaan was to be the dwelling place of God's people, those set apart for true spiritual worship.	Although God's punishment for sin is often severe, he offers reconciliation and hope—his love is truly amazing. Just as God's love and law led Israel to the promised land, God desires to give purpose and destiny to our lives.

KEY PLACES IN NUMBERS

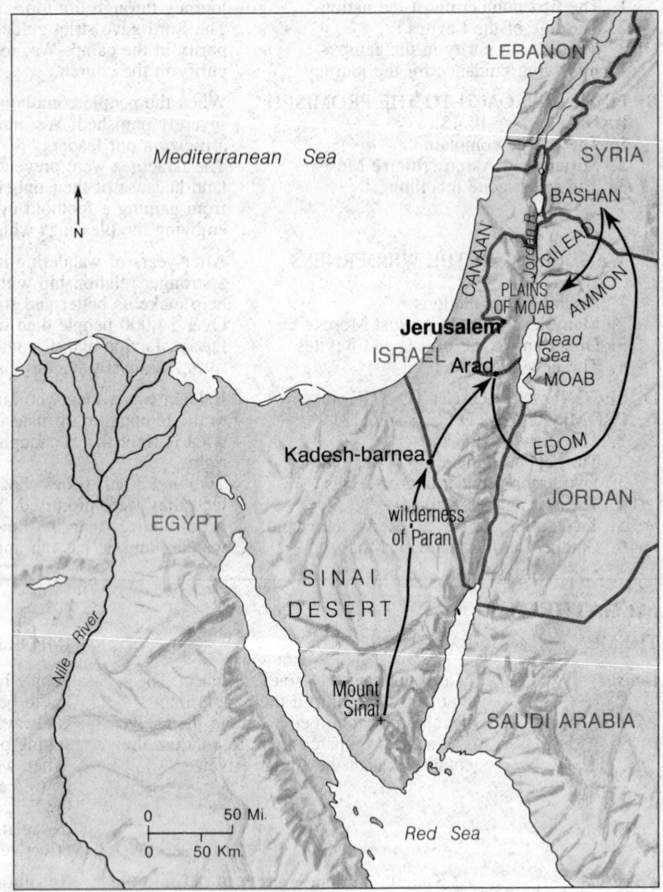

Modern names and boundaries are shown in gray.

1 Mount Sinai Numbers begins at Mount Sinai with Moses taking a census of the men eligible for battle. As the battle preparations began, the people also prepared for the spiritual warfare they would face. The promised land was full of wicked people who would try to entice the Israelites to sin. God, therefore, taught Moses and the Israelites how to live rightly (1.1—12.15).

2 Wilderness of Paran After a full year at Mount Sinai, the Israelites broke camp and began their march toward the promised land by moving into the wilderness of Paran. From there, one leader from each tribe was sent to spy out the new land. After 40 days they returned, and all but Joshua and Caleb were too afraid to enter. Because of their lack of faith, the Israelites were made to wander in the desert for 40 years (12.16—19.22).

3 Kadesh With the years of wandering nearing an end, the Israelites set their sights once again on the promised land. Kadesh was the oasis where they spent most of their wilderness years. Miriam died here. And it was here that Moses angrily struck the rock, which kept him from entering the promised land (20).

4 Arad When the king there heard that Israel was on the move, he attacked, but he was soundly defeated. Moses then led the people southward and eastward around the Dead Sea (21.1–3).

5 Edom The Israelites wanted to travel through Edom, but the king of Edom refused them passage (20.14–22). So they traveled around Edom and became very discouraged. The people complained, and God sent poisonous snakes to punish them. Only by looking at a bronze serpent on a pole could those bitten be healed (21.4–9).

6 Ammon Next, King Sihon of the Amorites refused Israel passage. When he attacked, Israel defeated his army and conquered the territory as far as the border of Ammon (21.21–32).

7 Bashan Moses sent spies to Bashan. King Og attacked, but he was also defeated (21.33–35).

8 Plains of Moab The people camped on the plains of Moab, east of the Jordan River opposite Jericho. They were on the verge of entering the promised land (22.1).

9 Moab King Balak of Moab, terrified of the Israelites, called upon Balaam, a famous sorcerer, to curse Israel from the mountains above where the Israelites camped. But the Lord caused Balaam to bless them instead (22.2—24.25).

10 Gilead The tribes of Reuben and Gad decided to settle in the fertile country of Gilead east of the Jordan River because it was a good land for their sheep. But first they promised to help the other tribes conquer the land west of the Jordan River (32).

A. PREPARING FOR THE JOURNEY (1.1—10.10)

At Mount Sinai, the Israelites received specific directions for their life-style in the new land God would give to them. A census was taken and the second passover was celebrated, marking one year of freedom from slavery in Egypt. The people were now prepared to continue their journey to the promised land. Just as the Lord prepared the Israelites, he prepares us for our journey through life.

1. The first numbering of the nation

The Lord orders a census

1 The LORD spoke to Moses in the wilderness of Sinai, in the tent of meeting, on
the first day of the second month, in the second year after they had come out
of the land of Egypt, saying: 2 Take a census of the whole congregation of Israelites, in their clans, by ancestral houses, according to the number of names, every
male individually; 3 from twenty years old and upward, everyone in Israel able to
go to war. You and Aaron shall enroll them, company by company. 4 A man from
each tribe shall be with you, each man the head of his ancestral house. 5 These are
the names of the men who shall assist you:

1.2 Ex 25.22; 30.11, 12; 38.26 Num 26.2-4, 63-65 2 Sam 24.1-3 1 Chron 21.2

From Reuben, Elizur son of Shedeur.
6 From Simeon, Shelumiel son of Zurishaddai.
7 From Judah, Nahshon son of Amminadab.
8 From Issachar, Nethanel son of Zuar.
9 From Zebulun, Eliab son of Helon.
10 From the sons of Joseph:
from Ephraim, Elishama son of Ammihud;
from Manasseh, Gamaliel son of Pedahzur.
11 From Benjamin, Abidan son of Gideoni.
12 From Dan, Ahiezer son of Ammishaddai.
13 From Asher, Pagiel son of Ochran.
14 From Gad, Eliasaph son of Deuel.
15 From Naphtali, Ahira son of Enan.

16 These were the ones chosen from the congregation, the leaders of their ancestral
tribes, the heads of the divisions of Israel.
17 Moses and Aaron took these men who had been designated by name, 18 and
on the first day of the second month they assembled the whole congregation together. They registered themselves in their clans, by their ancestral houses, according to the number of names from twenty years old and upward, individually, 19 as
the LORD commanded Moses. So he enrolled them in the wilderness of Sinai.
20 The descendants of Reuben, Israel's firstborn, their lineage, in their clans,
by their ancestral houses, according to the number of names, individually, every

1.16 Num 1.2-15 7.2; 26.3-51 1 Chron 27.16-22

1.17 Num 1.2 Ezra 2.59 Neh 7.61

1.20 Num 2.32,33 26.5-51

1.1 As the book of Numbers opens, the Israelites have been camped near Mount Sinai for more than a year. While there, they received all the laws and regulations as recorded in the book of Leviticus. They had been transformed into a new nation and equipped for its task. Now they were ready to move out and receive their land. In preparation, Moses and Aaron were told to number all the fighting men. This book received its name from this census, or numbering, of the people.

1.1 The tent of meeting was the smaller structure inside the larger tabernacle. The tent of meeting contained the sanctuary in one part and the most holy place with the ark in another part. These two parts were separated by a curtain. God revealed himself to Moses in the most holy place. Exodus 33.7 mentions the tent of meeting as the place where Moses met with God before the tabernacle was constructed. Many believe that the tent of meeting in Exodus served the same function as the one described here.

1.2 An "ancestral house" means a family or clan.

1.2–15 Taking a census was long and tedious, but it was an important task. The fighting men had to be counted to determine Israel's military strength before entering the promised land. In addition, the tribes had to be organized to determine the amount of land each would need, as well as to provide genealogical records. Without such a census, the task of conquering and organizing the promised land would have been more difficult. Whenever we are at a crossroads, it is important to take inventory of our resources. We will serve more effectively if, before plunging in, we set aside time to take a "census" of all we have—possessions, relationships, spiritual condition, time, goals.

1.20–46 If there were 603,550 men, not counting the Levites or women and children, there must have been a total population of more than two million Israelites. How could such a large population grow from Jacob's family of 70 who moved down to Egypt? The book of Exodus tells us that the Israelites who descended from Jacob's family "multiplied and grew exceedingly strong" (Exodus 1.7). Because they remained in Egypt more than 400 years, they had more than enough time to grow into a large group of people. After leaving Egypt, they were able to survive in the desert because God miraculously provided the food and water they needed. The leaders of Moab were terrified because of the large number of Israelites (22.3).

male from twenty years old and upward, everyone able to go to war: 21 those enrolled of the tribe of Reuben were forty-six thousand five hundred.

22 The descendants of Simeon, their lineage, in their clans, by their ancestral
houses, those of them that were numbered, according to the number of names,
individually, every male from twenty years old and upward, everyone able to go to
war: 23 those enrolled of the tribe of Simeon were fifty-nine thousand three hundred.

24 The descendants of Gad, their lineage, in their clans, by their ancestral
houses, according to the number of the names, from twenty years old and upward,
everyone able to go to war: 25 those enrolled of the tribe of Gad were forty-five
thousand six hundred fifty.

26 The descendants of Judah, their lineage, in their clans, by their ancestral
houses, according to the number of names, from twenty years old and upward,
everyone able to go to war: 27 those enrolled of the tribe of Judah were seventy-four
thousand six hundred.

28 The descendants of Issachar, their lineage, in their clans, by their ancestral
houses, according to the number of names, from twenty years old and upward,
everyone able to go to war: 29 those enrolled of the tribe of Issachar were fifty-four
thousand four hundred.

30 The descendants of Zebulun, their lineage, in their clans, by their ancestral
houses, according to the number of names, from twenty years old and upward,
everyone able to go to war: 31 those enrolled of the tribe of Zebulun were fifty-seven
thousand four hundred.

32 The descendants of Joseph, namely, the descendants of Ephraim, their lineage, in their clans, by their ancestral houses, according to the number of names,
from twenty years old and upward, everyone able to go to war: 33 those enrolled of
the tribe of Ephraim were forty thousand five hundred.

34 The descendants of Manasseh, their lineage, in their clans, by their ancestral
houses, according to the number of names, from twenty years old and upward,
everyone able to go to war: 35 those enrolled of the tribe of Manasseh were thirty-
two thousand two hundred.

36 The descendants of Benjamin, their lineage, in their clans, by their ancestral
houses, according to the number of names, from twenty years old and upward,
everyone able to go to war: 37 those enrolled of the tribe of Benjamin were thirty-
five thousand four hundred.

38 The descendants of Dan, their lineage, in their clans, by their ancestral
houses, according to the number of names, from twenty years old and upward,
everyone able to go to war: 39 those enrolled of the tribe of Dan were sixty-two
thousand seven hundred.

40 The descendants of Asher, their lineage, in their clans, by their ancestral
houses, according to the number of names, from twenty years old and upward,
everyone able to go to war: 41 those enrolled of the tribe of Asher were forty-one
thousand five hundred.

42 The descendants of Naphtali, their lineage, in their clans, by their ancestral
houses, according to the number of names, from twenty years old and upward,
everyone able to go to war: 43 those enrolled of the tribe of Naphtali were fifty-three
thousand four hundred.

44 These are those who were enrolled, whom Moses and Aaron enrolled with
the help of the leaders of Israel, twelve men, each representing his ancestral house.
45 So the whole number of the Israelites, by their ancestral houses, from twenty
years old and upward, everyone able to go to war in Israel— 46 their whole number
was six hundred three thousand five hundred fifty. 47 The Levites, however, were **1.47-49**
not numbered by their ancestral tribe along with them. Num 2.32,33 26.62

48 The LORD had said to Moses: 49 Only the tribe of Levi you shall not enroll,
and you shall not take a census of them with the other Israelites. 50 Rather you shall **1.50**
appoint the Levites over the tabernacle of the covenant,[a] and over all its equip- Num 3.6-10, 25-37; 4.25-48
ment, and over all that belongs to it; they are to carry the tabernacle and all its

[a] Or *treaty*, or *testimony*; Heb *eduth*

1.51 equipment, and they shall tend it, and shall camp around the tabernacle. 51 When
Num 3.38; 18.22 the tabernacle is to set out, the Levites shall take it down; and when the tabernacle
is to be pitched, the Levites shall set it up. And any outsider who comes near shall
1.52 be put to death. 52 The other Israelites shall camp in their respective regimental
Num 2.1 camps, by companies; 53 but the Levites shall camp around the tabernacle of the
1.53 Num 1.50 covenant,[b] that there may be no wrath on the congregation of the Israelites; and the
1.54 Levites shall perform the guard duty of the tabernacle of the covenant.[b] 54 The
Ex 39.43 Israelites did so; they did just as the LORD commanded Moses.

Where the tribes camped

2.1 Num 1.52 **2** The LORD spoke to Moses and Aaron, saying: 2 The Israelites shall camp each
in their respective regiments, under ensigns by their ancestral houses; they
shall camp facing the tent of meeting on every side. 3 Those to camp on the east side
toward the sunrise shall be of the regimental encampment of Judah by companies.
The leader of the people of Judah shall be Nahshon son of Amminadab, 4 with a
company as enrolled of seventy-four thousand six hundred. 5 Those to camp next to
him shall be the tribe of Issachar. The leader of the Issacharites shall be Nethanel
son of Zuar, 6 with a company as enrolled of fifty-four thousand four hundred.
7 Then the tribe of Zebulun: The leader of the Zebulunites shall be Eliab son of
Helon, 8 with a company as enrolled of fifty-seven thousand four hundred. 9 The
total enrollment of the camp of Judah, by companies, is one hundred eighty-six
thousand four hundred. They shall set out first on the march.

10 On the south side shall be the regimental encampment of Reuben by companies. The leader of the Reubenites shall be Elizur son of Shedeur, 11 with a company as enrolled of forty-six thousand five hundred. 12 And those to camp next to
him shall be the tribe of Simeon. The leader of the Simeonites shall be Shelumiel
son of Zurishaddai, 13 with a company as enrolled of fifty-nine thousand three hundred. 14 Then the tribe of Gad: The leader of the Gadites shall be Eliasaph son of
Reuel, 15 with a company as enrolled of forty-five thousand six hundred fifty. 16 The

[b] Or *treaty*, or *testimony*; Heb *eduth*

SUMMARY OF THE FIRST CENSUS

Tribe	*Total*
Reuben (the oldest son of Jacob)	46,500
Simeon	59,300
Gad	45,650
Judah	74,600
Issachar	54,400
Zebulun	57,400
Ephraim (son of Joseph)	40,500
Manasseh (son of Joseph)	32,200
Benjamin	35,400
Dan	62,700
Asher	41,500
Naphtali	53,400
Grand Total:	603,550

So he enrolled them in the wilderness of Sinai (1.19).

1.51 "Any outsider" was anyone who was not a Levite.

1.52–54 The very organization of the Israelite camp was ordered by God! By obeying God's commands for organization, even when the reason for them was not apparent, the people became more effective. When a group disintegrates into a collection of individuals each going his or her own way, its ability to be used by God is diminished. But if the group unites and looks to God for direction and organization, its effectiveness will be enhanced.

2.2 The nation of Israel was organized according to tribes for several reasons. (1) It was an effective way to manage and govern a large group. (2) It made dividing the promised land easier. (3) It was part of their culture and heritage (people were not known by a last name, but by their family, clan, and tribe). (4) It made it easier to keep detailed genealogies, and genealogies were the only way to prove membership in God's chosen nation. (5) It made travel much more efficient. The people followed the tribe's standard (a kind of flag), and thus stayed together and kept from getting lost.

total enrollment of the camp of Reuben, by companies, is one hundred fifty-one
thousand four hundred fifty. They shall set out second.
17 The tent of meeting, with the camp of the Levites, shall set out in the center
of the camps; they shall set out just as they camp, each in position, by their regiments.
18 On the west side shall be the regimental encampment of Ephraim by companies. The leader of the people of Ephraim shall be Elishama son of Ammihud,
19 with a company as enrolled of forty thousand five hundred. 20 Next to him shall
be the tribe of Manasseh. The leader of the people of Manasseh shall be Gamaliel
son of Pedahzur, 21 with a company as enrolled of thirty-two thousand two hundred. 22 Then the tribe of Benjamin: The leader of the Benjaminites shall be Abidan
son of Gideoni, 23 with a company as enrolled of thirty-five thousand four hundred.
24 The total enrollment of the camp of Ephraim, by companies, is one hundred eight
thousand one hundred. They shall set out third on the march.
25 On the north side shall be the regimental encampment of Dan by companies.
The leader of the Danites shall be Ahiezer son of Ammishaddai, 26 with a company
as enrolled of sixty-two thousand seven hundred. 27 Those to camp next to him shall
be the tribe of Asher. The leader of the Asherites shall be Pagiel son of Ochran,
28 with a company as enrolled of forty-one thousand five hundred. 29 Then the tribe
of Naphtali: The leader of the Naphtalites shall be Ahira son of Enan, 30 with a
company as enrolled of fifty-three thousand four hundred. 31 The total enrollment
of the camp of Dan is one hundred fifty-seven thousand six hundred. They shall set
out last, by companies.[c]
32 This was the enrollment of the Israelites by their ancestral houses; the total **2.32**
enrollment in the camps by their companies was six hundred three thousand five Ex 12.37; 38.26
hundred fifty. 33 Just as the LORD had commanded Moses, the Levites were not Num 1.20
enrolled among the other Israelites. 11.21; 26.51
34 The Israelites did just as the LORD had commanded Moses: They camped by **2.34**
regiments, and they set out the same way, everyone by clans, according to ances- Num 1.54
tral houses.

2. The role of the Levites

The Levites assist Aaron

3 This is the lineage of Aaron and Moses at the time when the LORD spoke with **3.2** Lev 10.1,2,6
Moses on Mount Sinai. 2 These are the names of the sons of Aaron: Nadab the Num 26.60
firstborn, and Abihu, Eleazar, and Ithamar; 3 these are the names of the sons of **3.3**
Aaron, the anointed priests, whom he ordained to minister as priests. 4 Nadab and Ex 29.1-37 **3.4**
Abihu died before the LORD when they offered illicit fire before the LORD in the Lev 10.1,2
wilderness of Sinai, and they had no children. Eleazar and Ithamar served as priests Num 26.61 **3.6**
in the lifetime of their father Aaron. Num 8.6-15, 22-26; 18.2-6
5 Then the LORD spoke to Moses, saying: 6 Bring the tribe of Levi near, and set Deut 33.10
them before Aaron the priest, so that they may assist him. 7 They shall perform **3.7**
duties for him and for the whole congregation in front of the tent of meeting, doing Num 3.11,12, 41; 8.16-18

[c] Compare verses 9, 16, 24: Heb *by their regiments*

2.34 This must have been one of the biggest campsites the world has ever seen! It would have taken about 12 square miles to set up tents for just the 600,000 fighting men – not to mention the women and children. Moses must have had a difficult time managing such a group. In the early stages of the journey and at Mount Sinai, the people were generally obedient to both God and Moses. But when the people left Mount Sinai and traveled across the rugged wilderness, they began to complain, grumble, and disobey. Soon problems erupted, and Moses could no longer effectively manage the Israelites. The books of Exodus, Leviticus, and Numbers present a striking contrast between how much we can accomplish when we obey God and how little we can accomplish when we don't.

3.4 See Leviticus 10.1, 2 for the story of Nadab and Abihu. "Illicit fire" is the same as "unholy fire."

3.6–13 At the time of the first passover (Exodus 13.2), God instructed every Israelite family to dedicate its firstborn son to him. They were set apart to assist Moses and Aaron in ministering to the people. This was only a temporary measure, however. Here God chooses all the men from the tribe of Levi to replace the firstborn sons from every Israelite tribe. These men, called Levites, were required to do "service," or do the work of the tabernacle. They assumed the responsibilities of ministering to the people. Once the tabernacle was built, it was their job to maintain it and assist with the sacrifices. All the priests had to belong to the tribe of Levi, but not all Levites were priests. The Levites were to be 25 years old before entering service. They probably received five years of on-the-job training before being admitted to full service at age 30.

service at the tabernacle; 8 they shall be in charge of all the furnishings of the tent
of meeting, and attend to the duties for the Israelites as they do service at the tabernacle. 9 You shall give the Levites to Aaron and his descendants; they are unreservedly given to him from among the Israelites. 10 But you shall make a register of
Aaron and his descendants; it is they who shall attend to the priesthood, and any
outsider who comes near shall be put to death.
3.11 Num 3.7,41,45 — 11 Then the LORD spoke to Moses, saying: 12 I hereby accept the Levites from
among the Israelites as substitutes for all the firstborn that open the womb among
3.13 Ex 13.2,12,15 Lev 27.26 Num 8.16,17 Lk 2.23 — the Israelites. The Levites shall be mine, 13 for all the firstborn are mine; when I
killed all the firstborn in the land of Egypt, I consecrated for my own all the first-
born in Israel, both human and animal; they shall be mine. I am the LORD.

Census of the Levites

3.14 Num 26.57-62 — 14 Then the LORD spoke to Moses in the wilderness of Sinai, saying: 15 Enroll
the Levites by ancestral houses and by clans. You shall enroll every male from a
3.16 Ex 16.16-22 — month old and upward. 16 So Moses enrolled them according to the word of the
LORD, as he was commanded. 17 The following were the sons of Levi, by their
names: Gershon, Kohath, and Merari. 18 These are the names of the sons of Gershon by their clans: Libni and Shimei. 19 The sons of Kohath by their clans: Amram, Izhar, Hebron, and Uzziel. 20 The sons of Merari by their clans: Mahli and
Mushi. These are the clans of the Levites, by their ancestral houses.
21 To Gershon belonged the clan of the Libnites and the clan of the Shimeites;
these were the clans of the Gershonites. 22 Their enrollment, counting all the males
from a month old and upward, was seven thousand five hundred. 23 The clans of the
Gershonites were to camp behind the tabernacle on the west, 24 with Eliasaph son
3.25 Num 1.50 4.25-28 — of Lael as head of the ancestral house of the Gershonites. 25 The responsibility of
the sons of Gershon in the tent of meeting was to be the tabernacle, the tent with its
covering, the screen for the entrance of the tent of meeting, 26 the hangings of the
court, the screen for the entrance of the court that is around the tabernacle and the
altar, and its cords – all the service pertaining to these.
27 To Kohath belonged the clan of the Amramites, the clan of the Izharites, the
clan of the Hebronites, and the clan of the Uzzielites; these are the clans of the

ARRANGEMENT OF TRIBES AROUND THE TABERNACLE WHILE IN THE WILDERNESS

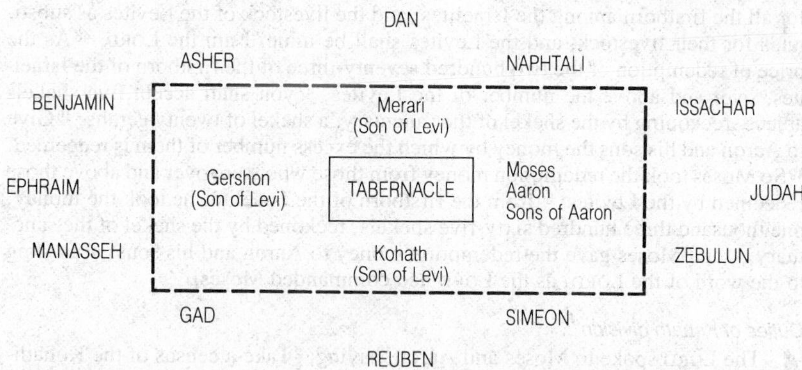

3.10 "Make a register" means "appoint." Aaron and his descendants were appointed to the priesthood. There is a tremendous contrast between the priesthood of Aaron in the Old Testament and the priesthood of Christ in the New Testament. Aaron and his descendants were the only ones who could carry out the duties of the priests and approach God's dwelling place. Now that Christ is our High Priest – our intermediary with God – anyone who follows him is also called a priest (1 Peter 2.5, 9). Now all Christians may come into God's presence without fear, because God's own Son encourages his followers to do so. We can put guilt behind us when we have a special relationship with God based on what Christ has done for us.

3.12 The Levites were "the substitutes for all the firstborn." The idea of "substitutionary atonement" was central to the Israelites ever since Abraham and Isaac (Genesis 22.13). It was reiterated by the passover lamb in their escape from Egypt (Exodus 12), and repeated in their regular sacrifices (Leviticus 4). It was meant by God to prepare them for the firstborn Son, Jesus Christ (Mark 10.45).

Kohathites. 28 Counting all the males, from a month old and upward, there were
eight thousand six hundred, attending to the duties of the sanctuary. 29 The clans of
the Kohathites were to camp on the south side of the tabernacle, 30 with Elizaphan
son of Uzziel as head of the ancestral house of the clans of the Kohathites. 31 Their
responsibility was to be the ark, the table, the lampstand, the altars, the vessels of
the sanctuary with which the priests minister, and the screen—all the service pertaining to these. 32 Eleazar son of Aaron the priest was to be chief over the leaders
of the Levites, and to have oversight of those who had charge of the sanctuary.

33 To Merari belonged the clan of the Mahlites and the clan of the Mushites:
these are the clans of Merari. 34 Their enrollment, counting all the males from a
month old and upward, was six thousand two hundred. 35 The head of the ancestral
house of the clans of Merari was Zuriel son of Abihail; they were to camp on the
north side of the tabernacle. 36 The responsibility assigned to the sons of Merari was
to be the frames of the tabernacle, the bars, the pillars, the bases, and all their
accessories—all the service pertaining to these; 37 also the pillars of the court all
around, with their bases and pegs and cords.

38 Those who were to camp in front of the tabernacle on the east—in front of **3.38**
the tent of meeting toward the east—were Moses and Aaron and Aaron's sons, Num 1.51; 3.10
having charge of the rites within the sanctuary, whatever had to be done for the
Israelites; and any outsider who came near was to be put to death. 39 The total en- **3.39**
rollment of the Levites whom Moses and Aaron enrolled at the commandment of Num 26.62
the LORD, by their clans, all the males from a month old and upward, was twenty-
two thousand.

Census of Israel's firstborn males

40 Then the LORD said to Moses: Enroll all the firstborn males of the Israelites, **3.40**
from a month old and upward, and count their names. 41 But you shall accept the Num 1.2
Levites for me—I am the LORD—as substitutes for all the firstborn among the Isra- **3.41** Num 3.11,13,45
elites, and the livestock of the Levites as substitutes for all the firstborn among the
livestock of the Israelites. 42 So Moses enrolled all the firstborn among the Israelites, as the LORD commanded him. 43 The total enrollment, all the firstborn males **3.43**
from a month old and upward, counting the number of names, was twenty-two Num 3.39
thousand two hundred seventy-three.

44 Then the LORD spoke to Moses, saying: 45 Accept the Levites as substitutes **3.45**
for all the firstborn among the Israelites, and the livestock of the Levites as substi- Num 3.11,13,41
tutes for their livestock; and the Levites shall be mine. I am the LORD. 46 As the **3.46**
price of redemption of the two hundred seventy-three of the firstborn of the Israel- Ex 13.13,15 Num 18.14-16
ites, over and above the number of the Levites, 47 you shall accept five shekels **3.47,48**
apiece, reckoning by the shekel of the sanctuary, a shekel of twenty gerahs. 48 Give Lev 27.1-8 Num 18.16
to Aaron and his sons the money by which the excess number of them is redeemed.
49 So Moses took the redemption money from those who were over and above those
redeemed by the Levites; 50 from the firstborn of the Israelites he took the money, **3.50**
one thousand three hundred sixty-five shekels, reckoned by the shekel of the sanc- Lev 25.25 Ezek 45.12
tuary; 51 and Moses gave the redemption money to Aaron and his sons, according
to the word of the LORD, as the LORD had commanded Moses.

Duties of Kohath division

4 The LORD spoke to Moses and Aaron, saying: 2 Take a census of the Kohath- **4.1**
ites separate from the other Levites, by their clans and their ancestral houses, Num 3.25-30
3 from thirty years old up to fifty years old, all who qualify to do work relating to **4.3**
the tent of meeting. 4 The service of the Kohathites relating to the tent of meeting Num 4.21-23 8.23,24
concerns the most holy things.

4.1ff The Kohathites, Gershonites, and Merarites were families of Levites who were assigned special tasks in Israel's worship. For the duties described in this chapter, a Levite had to be between 30 and 50 years of age. They were expected to carry out their duties as described here in every detail. In fact, failure to do so would mean death (4.20). Worshiping our holy God must not be taken lightly.

4.5 Num 4.15 5 When the camp is to set out, Aaron and his sons shall go in and take down the
4.6 Ex 26.31 Num 4.25 screening curtain, and cover the ark of the covenant[d] with it; 6 then they shall put
on it a covering of fine leather,[e] and spread over that a cloth all of blue, and shall
4.7 Ex 37.10-16 Lev 24.5-8 put its poles in place. 7 Over the table of the bread of the Presence they shall spread
a blue cloth, and put on it the plates, the dishes for incense, the bowls, and the
4.8 Num 4.25 flagons for the drink offering; the regular bread also shall be on it; 8 then they shall
spread over them a crimson cloth, and cover it with a covering of fine leather,[e] and
4.9 Ex 25.37,38 shall put its poles in place. 9 They shall take a blue cloth, and cover the lampstand
for the light, with its lamps, its snuffers, its trays, and all the vessels for oil with
which it is supplied; 10 and they shall put it with all its utensils in a covering of fine
leather,[e] and put it on the carrying frame. 11 Over the golden altar they shall spread
a blue cloth, and cover it with a covering of fine leather,[e] and shall put its poles in
place; 12 and they shall take all the utensils of the service that are used in the sanctuary, and put them in a blue cloth, and cover them with a covering of fine leather,[e]
and put them on the carrying frame. 13 They shall take away the ashes from the
altar, and spread a purple cloth over it; 14 and they shall put on it all the utensils of
the altar, which are used for the service there, the firepans, the forks, the shovels,
and the basins, all the utensils of the altar; and they shall spread on it a covering of
4.15 Num 3.38 4.5,17-19 fine leather,[e] and shall put its poles in place. 15 When Aaron and his sons have
finished covering the sanctuary and all the furnishings of the sanctuary, as the camp
sets out, after that the Kohathites shall come to carry these, but they must not touch
the holy things, or they will die. These are the things of the tent of meeting that the
Kohathites are to carry.

4.16 Ex 25.1-7 30.22-38 16 Eleazar son of Aaron the priest shall have charge of the oil for the light, the
fragrant incense, the regular grain offering, and the anointing oil, the oversight of
all the tabernacle and all that is in it, in the sanctuary and in its utensils.

4.17 Num 4.15 17 Then the LORD spoke to Moses and Aaron, saying: 18 You must not let the
tribe of the clans of the Kohathites be destroyed from among the Levites. 19 This is
how you must deal with them in order that they may live and not die when they
come near to the most holy things: Aaron and his sons shall go in and assign each
to a particular task or burden. 20 But the Kohathites[f] must not go in to look on the
holy things even for a moment; otherwise they will die.

Duties of Gershon division

4.21 Num 3.3, 14-24,35 21 Then the LORD spoke to Moses, saying: 22 Take a census of the Gershonites
also, by their ancestral houses and by their clans; 23 from thirty years old up to fifty
years old you shall enroll them, all who qualify to do work in the tent of meeting.
24 This is the service of the clans of the Gershonites, in serving and bearing burdens:
4.25 Num 3.25-30 25 They shall carry the curtains of the tabernacle, and the tent of meeting with its
covering, and the outer covering of fine leather[e] that is on top of it, and the screen
for the entrance of the tent of meeting, 26 and the hangings of the court, and the
screen for the entrance of the gate of the court that is around the tabernacle and the
altar, and their cords, and all the equipment for their service; and they shall do all

[d] Or *treaty*, or *testimony*; Heb *eduth* [e] Meaning of Heb uncertain [f] Heb *they*

CENSUS OF LEVI'S TRIBES

Levi's son	*Clan names*	*Census*	*Leader*	*Camp Location*
Gershon	Libni Shimei	7,500	Elisaph (son of Lael)	West side of tabernacle
Kohath	Amran Izhar Hebron Uzziel	8,600	Elizaphan (son of Uzziel)	South side of tabernacle
Merari	Mahli Mushi	6,200	Zuriel (son of Abihail)	North side of tabernacle

The total enrollment of the Levites . . . all the males from a month old and upward, was twenty-two thousand (3.39).

that needs to be done with regard to them. [27] All the service of the Gershonites shall
be at the command of Aaron and his sons, in all that they are to carry, and in all that
they have to do; and you shall assign to their charge all that they are to carry. [28] This
is the service of the clans of the Gershonites relating to the tent of meeting, and
their responsibilities are to be under the oversight of Ithamar son of Aaron the
priest.

Duties of Merari division

29 As for the Merarites, you shall enroll them by their clans and their ancestral **4.29** Num 3.31-35
houses; [30] from thirty years old up to fifty years old you shall enroll them, everyone **4.30-32**
who qualifies to do the work of the tent of meeting. [31] This is what they are charged Ex 26.15,16
to carry, as the whole of their service in the tent of meeting: the frames of the Num 4.3
tabernacle, with its bars, pillars, and bases, [32] and the pillars of the court all around
with their bases, pegs, and cords, with all their equipment and all their related
service; and you shall assign by name the objects that they are required to carry.
[33] This is the service of the clans of the Merarites, the whole of their service relating
to the tent of meeting, under the hand of Ithamar son of Aaron the priest.

Census of men eligible for tabernacle service

34 So Moses and Aaron and the leaders of the congregation enrolled the Kohathites, by their clans and their ancestral houses, [35] from thirty years old up to fifty **4.35**
years old, everyone who qualified for work relating to the tent of meeting; [36] and Num 3.3,21,35
their enrollment by clans was two thousand seven hundred fifty. [37] This was the
enrollment of the clans of the Kohathites, all who served at the tent of meeting,
whom Moses and Aaron enrolled according to the commandment of the LORD by
Moses.

38 The enrollment of the Gershonites, by their clans and their ancestral houses,
[39] from thirty years old up to fifty years old, everyone who qualified for work relating to the tent of meeting— [40] their enrollment by their clans and their ancestral
houses was two thousand six hundred thirty. [41] This was the enrollment of the clans
of the Gershonites, all who served at the tent of meeting, whom Moses and Aaron
enrolled according to the commandment of the LORD.

42 The enrollment of the clans of the Merarites, by their clans and their ancestral houses, [43] from thirty years old up to fifty years old, everyone who qualified for
work relating to the tent of meeting— [44] their enrollment by their clans was three
thousand two hundred. [45] This is the enrollment of the clans of the Merarites, whom
Moses and Aaron enrolled according to the commandment of the LORD by Moses.

46 All those who were enrolled of the Levites, whom Moses and Aaron and the **4.46**
leaders of Israel enrolled, by their clans and their ancestral houses, [47] from thirty Num 3.39
years old up to fifty years old, everyone who qualified to do the work of service and
the work of bearing burdens relating to the tent of meeting, [48] their enrollment was
eight thousand five hundred eighty. [49] According to the commandment of the LORD **4.49**
through Moses they were appointed to their several tasks of serving or carrying; Num 1.47-49
thus they were enrolled by him, as the LORD commanded Moses. 3.14,15

3. Maintaining purity in the camp

Removing unclean persons

5 The LORD spoke to Moses, saying: [2] Command the Israelites to put out of the **5.1**
camp everyone who is leprous,[g] or has a discharge, and everyone who is un- Lev 13.45,46
clean through contact with a corpse; [3] you shall put out both male and female, put- Num 19.11
ting them outside the camp; they must not defile their camp, where I dwell among **5.3** 2 Cor 6.16

[g] A term for several skin diseases; precise meaning uncertain

4.27, 28 The Gershonites could receive directions from any of Aaron's sons, but they were directly responsible to Ithamar only. The lines of authority and accountability were clearly communicated to all. As you function with others in service to God, make sure the lines of authority between you and those you work with are clearly understood. Good communication builds good relationships.

them. 4 The Israelites did so, putting them outside the camp; as the LORD had spoken to Moses, so the Israelites did.

Making restitution

5.5 Lev 6.1-3 — 5 The LORD spoke to Moses, saying: 6 Speak to the Israelites: When a man or a
5.7 — woman wrongs another, breaking faith with the LORD, that person incurs guilt 7 and
Lev 5.5,16; 6.4,5; 16.21 — shall confess the sin that has been committed. The person shall make full restitution
for the wrong, adding one fifth to it, and giving it to the one who was wronged. 8 If
the injured party has no next of kin to whom restitution may be made for the wrong,
the restitution for wrong shall go to the LORD for the priest, in addition to the ram
5.9 Ex 29.27,28 Lev 6.17,18 — of atonement with which atonement is made for the guilty party. 9 Among all the
sacred donations of the Israelites, every gift that they bring to the priest shall be his.
10 The sacred donations of all are their own; whatever anyone gives to the priest
shall be his.

A test to uncover adultery

5.11 Ex 20.14 Lev 18.20; 20.10 Num 5.4,29 — 11 The LORD spoke to Moses, saying: 12 Speak to the Israelites and say to them:
If any man's wife goes astray and is unfaithful to him, 13 if a man has had inter-
course with her but it is hidden from her husband, so that she is undetected though
she has defiled herself, and there is no witness against her since she was not caught
in the act; 14 if a spirit of jealousy comes on him, and he is jealous of his wife who
has defiled herself; or if a spirit of jealousy comes on him, and he is jealous of his
5.15 Num 15.1-10 — wife, though she has not defiled herself; 15 then the man shall bring his wife to the
priest. And he shall bring the offering required for her, one-tenth of an ephah of
barley flour. He shall pour no oil on it and put no frankincense on it, for it is a grain
offering of jealousy, a grain offering of remembrance, bringing iniquity to remembrance.

16 Then the priest shall bring her near, and set her before the LORD; 17 the priest
shall take holy water in an earthen vessel, and take some of the dust that is on the
floor of the tabernacle and put it into the water. 18 The priest shall set the woman
before the LORD, dishevel the woman's hair, and place in her hands the grain offering of remembrance, which is the grain offering of jealousy. In his own hand the
priest shall have the water of bitterness that brings the curse. 19 Then the priest shall
make her take an oath, saying, "If no man has lain with you, if you have not turned
aside to uncleanness while under your husband's authority, be immune to this water of bitterness that brings the curse. 20 But if you have gone astray while under
your husband's authority, if you have defiled yourself and some man other than
5.21 2 Chron 21.15 Neh 10.29 Jer 29.22 Isa 65.16 — your husband has had intercourse with you," 21 —let the priest make the woman
take the oath of the curse and say to the woman—"the LORD make you an execra-
tion and an oath among your people, when the LORD makes your uterus drop, your
womb discharge; 22 now may this water that brings the curse enter your bowels and
make your womb discharge, your uterus drop!" And the woman shall say, "Amen.
Amen."

23 Then the priest shall put these curses in writing, and wash them off into the
water of bitterness. 24 He shall make the woman drink the water of bitterness that
brings the curse, and the water that brings the curse shall enter her and cause bitter
pain. 25 The priest shall take the grain offering of jealousy out of the woman's hand,
5.26 Lev 5.12; 6.15 — and shall elevate the grain offering before the LORD and bring it to the altar; 26 and
the priest shall take a handful of the grain offering, as its memorial portion, and turn

---

5.5–8 God included restitution, a unique concept for that day, as part of his law for Israel. When someone was robbed, the guilty person was required to restore to the victim what had been taken and pay an additional interest penalty. When we have wronged others, we should look for ways to set matters right and, if possible, leave the victim even better off than when we harmed him or her. When we have been wronged, we should still seek restoration rather than striking out in revenge.

5.11–31 This test for adultery served to remove a jealous husband's suspicion. Trust between husband and wife had to be completely eroded for a man to bring his wife to the priest for this type of test. Today priests and pastors help restore marriages by counseling couples who have lost faith in each other. Whether justified or not, suspicion must be removed for a marriage to survive and thrive.

it into smoke on the altar, and afterward shall make the woman drink the water.
27 When he has made her drink the water, then, if she has defiled herself and has **5.27**
been unfaithful to her husband, the water that brings the curse shall enter into her Num 5.11,21 Jer 29.18; 42.18
and cause bitter pain, and her womb shall discharge, her uterus drop, and the 44.12
woman shall become an execration among her people. 28 But if the woman has not
defiled herself and is clean, then she shall be immune and be able to conceive children.
29 This is the law in cases of jealousy, when a wife, while under her husband's **5.29** Num 5.11
authority, goes astray and defiles herself, 30 or when a spirit of jealousy comes on
a man and he is jealous of his wife; then he shall set the woman before the LORD, **5.30** Num 5.15,16
and the priest shall apply this entire law to her. 31 The man shall be free from iniquity, but the woman shall bear her iniquity.

Rules for the nazirite vow

6 The LORD spoke to Moses, saying: 2 Speak to the Israelites and say to them: **6.1,2**
When either men or women make a special vow, the vow of a nazirite,[h] to Lev 20.26 Num 6.3-8
separate themselves to the LORD, 3 they shall separate themselves from wine and Judg 13.4,5 16.16,17
strong drink; they shall drink no wine vinegar or other vinegar, and shall not drink Amos 2.11,12
any grape juice or eat grapes, fresh or dried. 4 All their days as nazirites[i] they shall **6.3**
eat nothing that is produced by the grapevine, not even the seeds or the skins. Lev 10.8,9 Jer 35.6-8
5 All the days of their nazirite vow no razor shall come upon the head; until the **6.5**
time is completed for which they separate themselves to the LORD, they shall be Num 1.1 1 Sam 1.11
holy; they shall let the locks of the head grow long.
6 All the days that they separate themselves to the LORD they shall not go near **6.6**
a corpse. 7 Even if their father or mother, brother or sister, should die, they may not Lev 21.1-3 Num 19.11-22
defile themselves; because their consecration to God is upon the head. 8 All their
days as nazirites[i] they are holy to the LORD.
9 If someone dies very suddenly nearby, defiling the consecrated head, then **6.9**
they shall shave the head on the day of their cleansing; on the seventh day they shall Num 6.18 Acts 18.18
shave it. 10 On the eighth day they shall bring two turtledoves or two young pigeons 21.23,24
to the priest at the entrance of the tent of meeting, 11 and the priest shall offer one **6.11**
as a sin offering and the other as a burnt offering, and make atonement for them, Lev 5.7; 12.6-8
because they incurred guilt by reason of the corpse. They shall sanctify the head
that same day, 12 and separate themselves to the LORD for their days as nazirites,[i] **6.12**
and bring a male lamb a year old as a guilt offering. The former time shall be void, Lev 7.1-10 14.24,25
because the consecrated head was defiled.
13 This is the law for the nazirites[i] when the time of their consecration has
been completed: they shall be brought to the entrance of the tent of meeting, 14 and **6.14**
they shall offer their gift to the LORD, one male lamb a year old without blemish as Lev 1.2-17 7.1-10
a burnt offering, one ewe lamb a year old without blemish as a sin offering, one ram
without blemish as an offering of well-being, 15 and a basket of unleavened bread, **6.15**
cakes of choice flour mixed with oil and unleavened wafers spread with oil, with Num 15.1-7
their grain offering and their drink offerings. 16 The priest shall present them before
the LORD and offer their sin offering and burnt offering, 17 and shall offer the ram
as a sacrifice of well-being to the LORD, with the basket of unleavened bread; the
priest also shall make the accompanying grain offering and drink offering. 18 Then **6.18**
the nazirites[i] shall shave the consecrated head at the entrance of the tent of meet- Num 6.9
ing, and shall take the hair from the consecrated head and put it on the fire under the

[h] That is *one separated* or *one consecrated* [i] That is *those separated* or *those consecrated*

5.27 Today we are unsure what the bitter water, womb's discharge, and the dropping uterus were. But the intent of the strange procedure is that in the absence of positive proof, the priest appealed to God to determine the guilt or innocence of the accused person. "Execration" means "curse," or object of scorn.

6.1, 2 The nazirite vow was for people who wanted to devote some time exclusively to serving God. This vow could be taken for as little as 30 days or as long as a lifetime. It was voluntary, with one exception—parents could take the vow for their young children, making them nazirites for life. The vow included three distinct restrictions: (1) the hair could not be cut and the beard could not be shaved; (2) wine and strong drink could never be tasted; and (3) touching a dead body was prohibited. The purpose of the nazirite vow was to raise up a group of leaders devoted completely to God. Samson, Samuel, and John the Baptist were probably nazirites for life.

sacrifice of well-being. 19 The priest shall take the shoulder of the ram, when it is
boiled, and one unleavened cake out of the basket, and one unleavened wafer, and
shall put them in the palms of the nazirites,[j] after they have shaved the consecrated
6.20 Lev 7.28-34 Num 18.18 head. 20 Then the priest shall elevate them as an elevation offering before the LORD;
they are a holy portion for the priest, together with the breast that is elevated and the
thigh that is offered. After that the nazirites[j] may drink wine.

6.21 Num 6.1-5 21 This is the law for the nazirites[j] who take a vow. Their offering to the LORD
must be in accordance with the nazirite[k] vow, apart from what else they can afford.
In accordance with whatever vow they take, so they shall do, following the law for
their consecration.

How to bless the people

6.22 Deut 21.5; 33.1 Josh 8.33 1 Chron 23.13 22 The LORD spoke to Moses, saying: 23 Speak to Aaron and his sons, saying,
Thus you shall bless the Israelites: You shall say to them,

6.24-26 Deut 28.3-6 Ps 4.6; 17.8 29.11; 44.3 80.3,7,19 24 The LORD bless you and keep you;
25 the LORD make his face to shine upon you, and be gracious to you;
26 the LORD lift up his countenance upon you, and give you peace.
27 So they shall put my name on the Israelites, and I will bless them.

Gifts for the dedication of the tabernacle

7.1 Ex 40.9-11 Lev 8.10 **7** On the day when Moses had finished setting up the tabernacle, and had
anointed and consecrated it with all its furnishings, and had anointed and con-
7.2 Num 1.2-16 secrated the altar with all its utensils, 2 the leaders of Israel, heads of their ancestral
houses, the leaders of the tribes, who were over those who were enrolled, made
offerings. 3 They brought their offerings before the LORD, six covered wagons and
twelve oxen, a wagon for every two of the leaders, and for each one an ox; they
presented them before the tabernacle. 4 Then the LORD said to Moses: 5 Accept
these from them, that they may be used in doing the service of the tent of meeting,
and give them to the Levites, to each according to his service. 6 So Moses took the
7.7 Num 4.26 wagons and the oxen, and gave them to the Levites. 7 Two wagons and four oxen
7.8 Num 4.33 he gave to the Gershonites, according to their service; 8 and four wagons and eight
oxen he gave to the Merarites, according to their service, under the direction of
7.9 Num 4.5-15 Ithamar son of Aaron the priest. 9 But to the Kohathites he gave none, because they
were charged with the care of the holy things that had to be carried on the shoulders.

10 The leaders also presented offerings for the dedication of the altar at the time
when it was anointed; the leaders presented their offering before the altar. 11 The
LORD said to Moses: They shall present their offerings, one leader each day, for the
dedication of the altar.

12 The one who presented his offering the first day was Nahshon son of Amminadab, of the tribe of Judah; 13 his offering was one silver plate weighing one
hundred thirty shekels, one silver basin weighing seventy shekels, according to the
shekel of the sanctuary, both of them full of choice flour mixed with oil for a grain
7.15 Lev 6.9-13 offering; 14 one golden dish weighing ten shekels, full of incense; 15 one young bull,
7.16 Lev 6.25-30 one ram, one male lamb a year old, for a burnt offering; 16 one male goat for a sin
offering; 17 and for the sacrifice of well-being, two oxen, five rams, five male
7.17 Lev 7.11-21 goats, and five male lambs a year old. This was the offering of Nahshon son of
Amminadab.

18 On the second day Nethanel son of Zuar, the leader of Issachar, presented an

[j] That is *those separated* or *those consecrated* [k] That is *one separated* or *one consecrated*

6.24–26 A blessing was one way of asking for God's divine favor to rest upon others. The ancient blessing in these verses helps us understand what a blessing was supposed to do. Its five parts conveyed hope that God would (1) favor and protect; (2) be pleased; (3) be gracious (merciful and compassionate); (4) give his approval; (5) give peace. When you ask God to bless others or yourself, you are asking him to do these five things. The blessing you offer will not only help the one receiving it, it will also demonstrate love, encourage others, and provide a model of caring.

7.1ff After the tabernacle was set up, anointed, and sanctified, the leaders of the 12 tribes brought gifts and offerings for its use and maintenance. This way, all of the people participated. It was a tabernacle for everyone.

offering; 19 he presented for his offering one silver plate weighing one hundred
thirty shekels, one silver basin weighing seventy shekels, according to the shekel of
the sanctuary, both of them full of choice flour mixed with oil for a grain offering;
20 one golden dish weighing ten shekels, full of incense; 21 one young bull, one ram,
one male lamb a year old, as a burnt offering; 22 one male goat as a sin offering;
23 and for the sacrifice of well-being, two oxen, five rams, five male goats, and five
male lambs a year old. This was the offering of Nethanel son of Zuar.

24 On the third day Eliab son of Helon, the leader of the Zebulunites: 25 his
offering was one silver plate weighing one hundred thirty shekels, one silver basin
weighing seventy shekels, according to the shekel of the sanctuary, both of them
full of choice flour mixed with oil for a grain offering; 26 one golden dish weighing
ten shekels, full of incense; 27 one young bull, one ram, one male lamb a year old,
for a burnt offering; 28 one male goat for a sin offering; 29 and for the sacrifice of
well-being, two oxen, five rams, five male goats, and five male lambs a year old.
This was the offering of Eliab son of Helon.

30 On the fourth day Elizur son of Shedeur, the leader of the Reubenites: 31 his
offering was one silver plate weighing one hundred thirty shekels, one silver basin
weighing seventy shekels, according to the shekel of the sanctuary, both of them
full of choice flour mixed with oil for a grain offering; 32 one golden dish weighing
ten shekels, full of incense; 33 one young bull, one ram, one male lamb a year old,
for a burnt offering; 34 one male goat for a sin offering; 35 and for the sacrifice of
well-being, two oxen, five rams, five male goats, and five male lambs a year old.
This was the offering of Elizur son of Shedeur.

36 On the fifth day Shelumiel son of Zurishaddai, the leader of the Simeonites:
37 his offering was one silver plate weighing one hundred thirty shekels, one silver
basin weighing seventy shekels, according to the shekel of the sanctuary, both of
them full of choice flour mixed with oil for a grain offering; 38 one golden dish
weighing ten shekels, full of incense; 39 one young bull, one ram, one male lamb a
year old, for a burnt offering; 40 one male goat for a sin offering; 41 and for the
sacrifice of well-being, two oxen, five rams, five male goats, and five male lambs
a year old. This was the offering of Shelumiel son of Zurishaddai.

42 On the sixth day Eliasaph son of Deuel, the leader of the Gadites: 43 his offering was one silver plate weighing one hundred thirty shekels, one silver basin
weighing seventy shekels, according to the shekel of the sanctuary, both of them
full of choice flour mixed with oil for a grain offering; 44 one golden dish weighing
ten shekels, full of incense; 45 one young bull, one ram, one male lamb a year old,
for a burnt offering; 46 one male goat for a sin offering; 47 and for the sacrifice of
well-being, two oxen, five rams, five male goats, and five male lambs a year old.
This was the offering of Eliasaph son of Deuel.

48 On the seventh day Elishama son of Ammihud, the leader of the Ephraimites: 49 his offering was one silver plate weighing one hundred thirty shekels, one
silver basin weighing seventy shekels, according to the shekel of the sanctuary,
both of them full of choice flour mixed with oil for a grain offering; 50 one golden
dish weighing ten shekels, full of incense; 51 one young bull, one ram, one male
lamb a year old, for a burnt offering; 52 one male goat for a sin offering; 53 and for
the sacrifice of well-being, two oxen, five rams, five male goats, and five male
lambs a year old. This was the offering of Elishama son of Ammihud.

54 On the eighth day Gamaliel son of Pedahzur, the leader of the Manassites:
55 his offering was one silver plate weighing one hundred thirty shekels, one silver
basin weighing seventy shekels, according to the shekel of the sanctuary, both of
them full of choice flour mixed with oil for a grain offering; 56 one golden dish
weighing ten shekels, full of incense; 57 one young bull, one ram, one male lamb a
year old, for a burnt offering; 58 one male goat for a sin offering; 59 and for the
sacrifice of well-being, two oxen, five rams, five male goats, and five male lambs
a year old. This was the offering of Gamaliel son of Pedahzur.

60 On the ninth day Abidan son of Gideoni, the leader of the Benjaminites:
61 his offering was one silver plate weighing one hundred thirty shekels, one silver
basin weighing seventy shekels, according to the shekel of the sanctuary, both of

them full of choice flour mixed with oil for a grain offering; [62]one golden dish
weighing ten shekels, full of incense; [63]one young bull, one ram, one male lamb a
year old, for a burnt offering; [64]one male goat for a sin offering; [65]and for the
sacrifice of well-being, two oxen, five rams, five male goats, and five male lambs
a year old. This was the offering of Abidan son of Gideoni.

66 On the tenth day Ahiezer son of Ammishaddai, the leader of the Danites:
[67]his offering was one silver plate weighing one hundred thirty shekels, one silver
basin weighing seventy shekels, according to the shekel of the sanctuary, both of
them full of choice flour mixed with oil for a grain offering; [68]one golden dish
weighing ten shekels, full of incense; [69]one young bull, one ram, one male lamb a
year old, for a burnt offering; [70]one male goat for a sin offering; [71]and for the
sacrifice of well-being, two oxen, five rams, five male goats, and five male lambs
a year old. This was the offering of Ahiezer son of Ammishaddai.

72 On the eleventh day Pagiel son of Ochran, the leader of the Asherites: [73]his
offering was one silver plate weighing one hundred thirty shekels, one silver basin
weighing seventy shekels, according to the shekel of the sanctuary, both of them
full of choice flour mixed with oil for a grain offering; [74]one golden dish weighing
ten shekels, full of incense; [75]one young bull, one ram, one male lamb a year old,
for a burnt offering; [76]one male goat for a sin offering; [77]and for the sacrifice of
well-being, two oxen, five rams, five male goats, and five male lambs a year old.
This was the offering of Pagiel son of Ochran.

78 On the twelfth day Ahira son of Enan, the leader of the Naphtalites: [79]his
offering was one silver plate weighing one hundred thirty shekels, one silver basin
weighing seventy shekels, according to the shekel of the sanctuary, both of them
full of choice flour mixed with oil for a grain offering; [80]one golden dish weighing
ten shekels, full of incense; [81]one young bull, one ram, one male lamb a year old,
for a burnt offering; [82]one male goat for a sin offering; [83]and for the sacrifice of
well-being, two oxen, five rams, five male goats, and five male lambs a year old.
This was the offering of Ahira son of Enan.

7.84 Num 7.10
84 This was the dedication offering for the altar, at the time when it was
anointed, from the leaders of Israel: twelve silver plates, twelve silver basins,
twelve golden dishes, [85]each silver plate weighing one hundred thirty shekels and
each basin seventy, all the silver of the vessels two thousand four hundred shekels
according to the shekel of the sanctuary, [86]the twelve golden dishes, full of incense, weighing ten shekels apiece according to the shekel of the sanctuary, all the
7.87 Lev 1.2-17 6.9-13
gold of the dishes being one hundred twenty shekels; [87]all the livestock for the
burnt offering twelve bulls, twelve rams, twelve male lambs a year old, with their
7.88 Num 7.17
grain offering; and twelve male goats for a sin offering; [88]and all the livestock for
the sacrifice of well-being twenty-four bulls, the rams sixty, the male goats sixty,
the male lambs a year old sixty. This was the dedication offering for the altar, after
it was anointed.

DEDICATION GIFTS FOR THE ALTAR

The leaders of each tribe presented dedication gifts when the altar was anointed. Moses asked each to bring gifts on a different day.

Day	*Leader*	*Tribe*
1	Nahshon	Judah
2	Nethaneel	Issachar
3	Eliab	Zebulun
4	Elizur	Reuben
5	Shelumiel	Simeon
6	Eliasaph	Gad
7	Elishama	Ephraim
8	Gamaliel	Manasseh
9	Abidan	Benjamin
10	Ahiezer	Dan
11	Pagiel	Asher
12	Ahira	Naphtali

89 When Moses went into the tent of meeting to speak with the LORD,[l] he would hear the voice speaking to him from above the mercy seat[m] that was on the ark of the covenant[n] from between the two cherubim; thus it spoke to him.

7.89 Ex 25.22 33.9-11 Lev 1.1 Ps 80.1; 99.1

Setting up the lamps

8 The LORD spoke to Moses, saying: 2 Speak to Aaron and say to him: When you set up the lamps, the seven lamps shall give light in front of the lampstand.
3 Aaron did so; he set up its lamps to give light in front of the lampstand, as the
LORD had commanded Moses. 4 Now this was how the lampstand was made, out of
hammered work of gold. From its base to its flowers, it was hammered work; according to the pattern that the LORD had shown Moses, so he made the lampstand.

8.2 Ex 25.37
8.4 Ex 25.18,31-36, 40; 37.17-22 Heb 8.5

The Levites are dedicated

5 The LORD spoke to Moses, saying: 6 Take the Levites from among the Israelites and cleanse them. 7 Thus you shall do to them, to cleanse them: sprinkle the
water of purification on them, have them shave their whole body with a razor and
wash their clothes, and so cleanse themselves. 8 Then let them take a young bull and
its grain offering of choice flour mixed with oil, and you shall take another young
bull for a sin offering. 9 You shall bring the Levites before the tent of meeting, and
assemble the whole congregation of the Israelites. 10 When you bring the Levites
before the LORD, the Israelites shall lay their hands on the Levites, 11 and Aaron
shall present the Levites before the LORD as an elevation offering from the Israelites, that they may do the service of the LORD. 12 The Levites shall lay their hands
on the heads of the bulls, and he shall offer the one for a sin offering and the other
for a burnt offering to the LORD, to make atonement for the Levites. 13 Then you
shall have the Levites stand before Aaron and his sons, and you shall present them
as an elevation offering to the LORD.

8.7 Ex 19.10 Lev 14.8,9 15.6; 16.28
8.8 Num 15.3-12
8.10 Lev 4.15
8.11 Num 3.5-9
8.12 Ex 29.10-14 Lev 16.20-22 Num 8.10

14 Thus you shall separate the Levites from among the other Israelites, and the
Levites shall be mine. 15 Thereafter the Levites may go in to do service at the tent
of meeting, once you have cleansed them and presented them as an elevation offering. 16 For they are unreservedly given to me from among the Israelites; I have
taken them for myself, in place of all that open the womb, the firstborn of all the
Israelites. 17 For all the firstborn among the Israelites are mine, both human and
animal. On the day that I struck down all the firstborn in the land of Egypt I consecrated them for myself, 18 but I have taken the Levites in place of all the firstborn
among the Israelites. 19 Moreover, I have given the Levites as a gift to Aaron and
his sons from among the Israelites, to do the service for the Israelites at the tent of
meeting, and to make atonement for the Israelites, in order that there may be no
plague among the Israelites for coming too close to the sanctuary.

8.14 Num 8.11
8.16 Num 3.13
8.17 Ex 13.12,13
8.19 Num 1.53

20 Moses and Aaron and the whole congregation of the Israelites did with the
Levites accordingly; the Israelites did with the Levites just as the LORD had commanded Moses concerning them. 21 The Levites purified themselves from sin and
washed their clothes; then Aaron presented them as an elevation offering before the
LORD, and Aaron made atonement for them to cleanse them. 22 Thereafter the Levites went in to do their service in the tent of meeting in attendance on Aaron and
his sons. As the LORD had commanded Moses concerning the Levites, so they did
with them.

23 The LORD spoke to Moses, saying: 24 This applies to the Levites: from
twenty-five years old and upward they shall begin to do duty in the service of the
tent of meeting; 25 and from the age of fifty years they shall retire from the duty of

8.23 Num 4.3

l Heb *him* m Or *the cover* n Or *treaty*, or *testimony*; Heb *eduth*

7.89 Imagine hearing the very voice of God! Moses must have trembled at the sound. Yet we have God's words recorded for us in the Bible, and we should have no less reverence and awe for them. God sometimes spoke directly to his people to tell them the proper way to live. The Bible records these conversations to give us insights into God's character. How tragic when we take these very words of God lightly. (Note: cherubim were mighty angels.)

8.1–4 The lampstand provided light for the priests as they carried out their duties. The light was also an expression of God's presence. Jesus said, "I am the light of the world" (John 8.12). The golden lampstand is still one of the major symbols of the Jewish faith.

the service and serve no more. 26 They may assist their brothers in the tent of meeting in carrying out their duties, but they shall perform no service. Thus you shall do
with the Levites in assigning their duties.

The second passover

9.1 Ex 40.2,17 **9** The LORD spoke to Moses in the wilderness of Sinai, in the first month of the
9.2 Ex 12.1-6 second year after they had come out of the land of Egypt, saying: 2 Let the
Israelites keep the passover at its appointed time. 3 On the fourteenth day of this
month, at twilight,[o] you shall keep it at its appointed time; according to all its
statutes and all its regulations you shall keep it. 4 So Moses told the Israelites that
they should keep the passover. 5 They kept the passover in the first month, on the
fourteenth day of the month, at twilight,[o] in the wilderness of Sinai. Just as the
9.6 Lev 21.1-4 LORD had commanded Moses, so the Israelites did. 6 Now there were certain people
who were unclean through touching a corpse, so that they could not keep the passover on that day. They came before Moses and Aaron on that day, 7 and said to him,
"Although we are unclean through touching a corpse, why must we be kept from
presenting the LORD's offering at its appointed time among the Israelites?" 8 Moses
spoke to them, "Wait, so that I may hear what the LORD will command concerning
you."
9 The LORD spoke to Moses, saying: 10 Speak to the Israelites, saying: Anyone
of you or your descendants who is unclean through touching a corpse, or is away on
a journey, shall still keep the passover to the LORD. 11 In the second month on the
fourteenth day, at twilight,[o] they shall keep it; they shall eat it with unleavened
9.12 Ex 12.1-50 Lev 23.5-14 Num 28.16-25 Jn 19.36 bread and bitter herbs. 12 They shall leave none of it until morning, nor break a bone
of it; according to all the statute for the passover they shall keep it. 13 But anyone
who is clean and is not on a journey, and yet refrains from keeping the passover,
9.13 Ex 12.15 Num 15.30,31 shall be cut off from the people for not presenting the LORD's offering at its appointed time; such a one shall bear the consequences for the sin. 14 Any alien resid-
9.14 Ex 12.48,49 ing among you who wishes to keep the passover to the LORD shall do so according
to the statute of the passover and according to its regulation; you shall have one
statute for both the resident alien and the native.

4. Receiving guidance for the journey

The pillars of cloud and fire

15 On the day the tabernacle was set up, the cloud covered the tabernacle, the

[o] Heb *between the two evenings*

8.25, 26 Why were the Levites supposed to retire at age 50? The reasons were probably more practical than theological. (1) Moving the tabernacle and its furniture through the wilderness required strength. The younger men were more suited for the work of lifting the heavy articles. (2) The Levites over 50 did not stop working altogether. They were allowed to assist with various light duties in the tabernacle. This helped the younger men assume more responsibilities, and it allowed the older men to be in a position to advise and counsel them.

9.6–12 Several men came to Moses because of the predicament they faced: attendance at a funeral prevented them from participating in the passover meal because it had made them unclean. Notice that God did not adjust the requirements of the passover. The standards of holiness were maintained, and the men were not allowed to participate. But God did make an exception and allowed the men to celebrate the passover at a later date. This upheld the sacred requirements while allowing the men to participate in the feast—a duty for all Israelite men. We sometimes face predicaments where the most obvious solution might cause us to compromise God's standards. Like Moses, we should use wisdom and prayer to reach a workable solution.

9.14 Sometimes we are tempted to excuse non-Christians from following God's guidelines for living. Christmas and Easter, for example, often have other meanings for them. We would not expect them to understand Lent. Yet foreigners ("aliens") at this time were expected to follow the same laws and ordinances as the Israelites. God did not have a separate set of standards for unbelievers and he still does not today. The phrase "You shall have one statute" emphasizes that non-Israelites were also subject to God's commands and promises. God singled out Israel for a special purpose—to be an example of how one nation could, and should, follow him. His aim, however, was to have all people obey and worship him.

9.15 The cloud is used in Scripture to describe the majestic, awe-inspiring presence of God. He spoke from it when he gave the 10 commandments at Sinai (Exodus 19.9). Christ was covered with a cloud at his transfiguration (Luke 9.34), and he disappeared into a cloud at the Ascension (Acts 1.9).

9.15–22 A pillar of cloud by day and a pillar of fire by night guided and protected the Israelites as they traveled across the wilderness. Some have said this pillar may have been a burning bowl of pitch whose smoke was visible during the day and whose fire could be seen at night. However, a bowl of pitch would not have lifted itself up and moved ahead of the people, and the Bible is clear that the cloud and fire moved in accordance with the will of God. The cloud and the fire were not merely natural phenomena; they were the vehicle of God's presence and the visible evidence of his moving and directing his people.

tent of the covenant;[p] and from evening until morning it was over the tabernacle,
having the appearance of fire. 16 It was always so: the cloud covered it by day[q] and
the appearance of fire by night. 17 Whenever the cloud lifted from over the tent,
then the Israelites would set out; and in the place where the cloud settled down,
there the Israelites would camp. 18 At the command of the LORD the Israelites would
set out, and at the command of the LORD they would camp. As long as the cloud
rested over the tabernacle, they would remain in camp. 19 Even when the cloud
continued over the tabernacle many days, the Israelites would keep the charge of
the LORD, and would not set out. 20 Sometimes the cloud would remain a few days
over the tabernacle, and according to the command of the LORD they would remain
in camp; then according to the command of the LORD they would set out. 21 Sometimes the cloud would remain from evening until morning; and when the cloud
lifted in the morning, they would set out, or if it continued for a day and a night,
when the cloud lifted they would set out. 22 Whether it was two days, or a month,
or a longer time, that the cloud continued over the tabernacle, resting upon it, the
Israelites would remain in camp and would not set out; but when it lifted they would
set out. 23 At the command of the LORD they would camp, and at the command of
the LORD they would set out. They kept the charge of the LORD, at the command of
the LORD by Moses.

9.15 Ex 14.20,24 40.2,18 Num 14.14 Neh 9.12,19 Ps 78.14
9.17 Ex 40.36-38 Num 10.11,33, 34
9.23 Josh 22.2,3

The silver trumpets

10 The LORD spoke to Moses, saying: 2 Make two silver trumpets; you shall
make them of hammered work; and you shall use them for summoning the
congregation, and for breaking camp. 3 When both are blown, the whole congregation shall assemble before you at the entrance of the tent of meeting. 4 But if only
one is blown, then the leaders, the heads of the tribes of Israel, shall assemble
before you. 5 When you blow an alarm, the camps on the east side shall set out;
6 when you blow a second alarm, the camps on the south side shall set out. An alarm
is to be blown whenever they are to set out. 7 But when the assembly is to be gathered, you shall blow, but you shall not sound an alarm. 8 The sons of Aaron, the
priests, shall blow the trumpets; this shall be a perpetual institution for you
throughout your generations. 9 When you go to war in your land against the adversary who oppresses you, you shall sound an alarm with the trumpets, so that you
may be remembered before the LORD your God and be saved from your enemies.
10 Also on your days of rejoicing, at your appointed festivals, and at the beginnings
of your months, you shall blow the trumpets over your burnt offerings and over
your sacrifices of well-being; they shall serve as a reminder on your behalf before
the LORD your God: I am the LORD your God.

10.2 Lev 25.9 2 Kgs 12.13
10.5,7 Ex 19.13 Judg 3.27 Joel 2.1
10.8 Num 31.6 Josh 6.3-9 2 Chron 5.11,12
10.9 Judg 3.27 Ezek 33.3 Joel 2.1 Zeph 2.5
10.10 Lev 23.33,34 Num 29.1 Ezra 3.10 Ps 81.3-5

B. FIRST APPROACH TO THE PROMISED LAND (10.11—14.45)

As the Israelites approached the promised land, Moses sent leaders to spy out the land and its people. But the spies returned with a discouraging report—"It is a magnificent country, but the people living there are too powerful." Although Joshua and Caleb disagreed, the Israelites had already made up their minds and began to complain. As punishment for their lack of faith, God condemned them to wander in the wilderness for forty years. Our obedience must be complete and timely.

1. The people complain

A good start

11 In the second year, in the second month, on the twentieth day of the month,

[p] Or *treaty,* or *testimony;* Heb *eduth* [q] Gk Syr Vg: Heb lacks *by day*

9.23 The Hebrews traveled and camped as God guided. "They kept the charge of the Lord" means they obeyed the orders. When you follow God's guidance, you know you are where God wants you, whether you're moving or staying in one place. You are physically somewhere right now. Instead of praying, "God, what do you want me to do next?" ask, "God, what do you want me to do while I'm right here?" Direction from God is not just for your next big move. He has a purpose in placing you where you are right now. Begin to understand God's purpose for your life by discovering what he wants you to do now!

10.1–10 The two silver trumpets were used to coordinate the tribes as they moved through the wilderness. Their tight formations required clear communication and control. Their blast also reminded Israel of God's protection over them. They may have had this promise in mind (10.9) as they later marched around the city of Jericho (Joshua 6).

10.12 Gen 21.20,21 the cloud lifted from over the tabernacle of the covenant.[r] 12 Then the Israelites set
Num 12.16 out by stages from the wilderness of Sinai, and the cloud settled down in the wilder-
13.3,26 ness of Paran. 13 They set out for the first time at the command of the LORD by
10.13 Deut 1.6 Moses. 14 The standard of the camp of Judah set out first, company by company,
10.14 Num 2.3-31 and over the whole company was Nahshon son of Amminadab. 15 Over the company of the tribe of Issachar was Nethanel son of Zuar; 16 and over the company of
the tribe of Zebulun was Eliab son of Helon.

10.17 Num 4.21-23 17 Then the tabernacle was taken down, and the Gershonites and the Merarites,
10.18 who carried the tabernacle, set out. 18 Next the standard of the camp of Reuben set
Num 2.3-31 out, company by company; and over the whole company was Elizur son of Shed-
26.5-18 eur. 19 Over the company of the tribe of Simeon was Shelumiel son of Zurishaddai,
20 and over the company of the tribe of Gad was Eliasaph son of Deuel.

10.21 Num 4.1-20 21 Then the Kohathites, who carried the holy things, set out; and the tabernacle
10.22 was set up before their arrival. 22 Next the standard of the Ephraimite camp set out,
Num 2.3-31 company by company, and over the whole company was Elishama son of Ammihud. 23 Over the company of the tribe of Manasseh was Gamaliel son of Pedahzur,
24 and over the company of the tribe of Benjamin was Abidan son of Gideoni.

25 Then the standard of the camp of Dan, acting as the rear guard of all the
camps, set out, company by company, and over the whole company was Ahiezer
son of Ammishaddai. 26 Over the company of the tribe of Asher was Pagiel son of
Ochran, 27 and over the company of the tribe of Naphtali was Ahira son of Enan.
28 This was the order of march of the Israelites, company by company, when they
set out.

10.29 Ex 2.18-21; 3.1 29 Moses said to Hobab son of Reuel the Midianite, Moses' father-in-law, "We
18.1,5-27 are setting out for the place of which the LORD said, 'I will give it to you'; come
Judg 1.16; 4.11 with us, and we will treat you well; for the LORD has promised good to Israel."
30 But he said to him, "I will not go, but I will go back to my own land and to my
10.32 kindred." 31 He said, "Do not leave us, for you know where we should camp in the
Num 10.29 Ps 67.5-7 wilderness, and you will serve as eyes for us. 32 Moreover, if you go with us, what-
10.33 Josh 3.2-6, ever good the LORD does for us, the same we will do for you."
11-17 33 So they set out from the mount of the LORD three days' journey with the ark
10.34 Ex 14.20,24 of the covenant of the LORD going before them three days' journey, to seek out a
Num 9.15-22 resting place for them, 34 the cloud of the LORD being over them by day when they
10.35 set out from the camp.
Ps 68.1,2 132.8 35 Whenever the ark set out, Moses would say,
Isa 51.9 "Arise, O LORD, let your enemies be scattered,

[r] Or *treaty*, or *testimony*; Heb *eduth*

ISRAEL'S DEPARTURE FROM SINAI
It has been two years since Israel left Egypt. Having received God's travel instructions through Moses, Israel set out from Mount Sinai into the wilderness of Paran on their way toward the promised land.

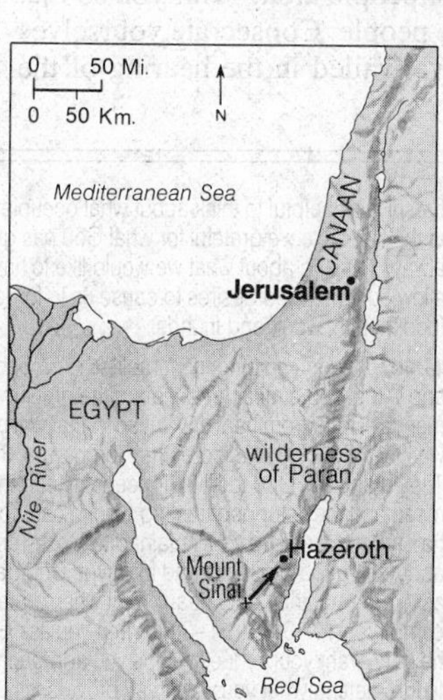

10.21 Those who travel, move, or face new challenges know what it is to be uprooted. Life is full of changes, and few things remain stable. The Israelites were constantly moving through the wilderness. They were able to handle change only because God's presence in the tabernacle was always with them. The portable tabernacle signified God and his people moving together. For us, stability does not mean lack of change, but moving with God in every circumstance.

10.29–32 By complimenting Hobab's wilderness skills, Moses let him know he was needed. People cannot know you appreciate them if you do not tell them they are important to you. Complimenting those who deserve it builds lasting relationships and helps people know they are valued. Think about those who have helped you this month. What can you do to let them know how much you need and appreciate them?

and your foes flee before you.”
36 And whenever it came to rest, he would say, **10.36**
“Return, O LORD of the ten thousand thousands of Israel.”[s] Deut 1.10,11 Ps 90.13-17

God sends fire upon the complaining people

11 Now when the people complained in the hearing of the LORD about their **11.1**
misfortunes, the LORD heard it and his anger was kindled. Then the fire of Ex 16.2-9 17.2,3
the LORD burned against them, and consumed some outlying parts of the camp. Lev 10.1,2 Num 14.2
2 But the people cried out to Moses; and Moses prayed to the LORD, and the fire 16.35; 17.5
abated. 3 So that place was called Taberah,[t] because the fire of the LORD burned 20.2-5 Deut 32.22
against them.

God sends meat to the complaining people

4 The rabble among them had a strong craving; and the Israelites also wept **11.4**
again, and said, “If only we had meat to eat! 5 We remember the fish we used to eat Ps 78.18 1 Cor 10.6
in Egypt for nothing, the cucumbers, the melons, the leeks, the onions, and the
garlic; 6 but now our strength is dried up, and there is nothing at all but this manna **11.6**
to look at.” Num 21.5
7 Now the manna was like coriander seed, and its color was like the color of **11.7**
gum resin. 8 The people went around and gathered it, ground it in mills or beat it in Ex 16.14,31
mortars, then boiled it in pots and made cakes of it; and the taste of it was like the **11.9**
taste of cakes baked with oil. 9 When the dew fell on the camp in the night, the Ex 16.13 Ps 78.23-25
manna would fall with it. **11.10**
10 Moses heard the people weeping throughout their families, all at the en- Num 11.1 14.1,2; 16.27
trances of their tents. Then the LORD became very angry, and Moses was dis- Deut 32.22
pleased. 11 So Moses said to the LORD, “Why have you treated your servant so Isa 5.25
badly? Why have I not found favor in your sight, that you lay the burden of all this **11.11** Ex 17.4
people on me? 12 Did I conceive all this people? Did I give birth to them, that you Num 11.15
should say to me, ‘Carry them in your bosom, as a nurse carries a sucking child,’ **11.12** Gen 13.14-17
to the land that you promised on oath to their ancestors? 13 Where am I to get meat 26.3; 50.24,25 Ex 13.4,5
to give to all this people? For they come weeping to me and say, ‘Give us meat to Isa 49.15
eat!’ 14 I am not able to carry all this people alone, for they are too heavy for me. **11.14**
15 If this is the way you are going to treat me, put me to death at once—if I have Ex 18.18 Deut 1.9-13
found favor in your sight—and do not let me see my misery.” **11.15** Ex 32.32
16 So the LORD said to Moses, “Gather for me seventy of the elders of Israel, **11.16**
whom you know to be the elders of the people and officers over them; bring them Ex 4.29; 24.1,9
to the tent of meeting, and have them take their place there with you. 17 I will come Lk 10.1,17
down and talk with you there; and I will take some of the spirit that is on you and **11.17** Ex 34.5,6
put it on them; and they shall bear the burden of the people along with you so that Num 11.25; 12.5
you will not bear it all by yourself. 18 And say to the people: Consecrate yourselves **11.18** Ex 19.10,14,15
for tomorrow, and you shall eat meat; for you have wailed in the hearing of the Josh 7.13

[s] Meaning of Heb uncertain [t] That is *Burning*

11.1, 11–15 The Israelites complained, and then Moses complained. But God responded positively to Moses and negatively to the rest of the people. Why? The people complained *to one another,* and nothing was accomplished. Moses took his complaint *to God,* who could solve any problem. Many of us are good at complaining to each other. We need to learn to take our problems to the One who can do something about them.

11.4 The "rabble" refers to a mixed crowd of Egyptians and others who had followed Israel out of Egypt (Exodus 12.38).

11.4–6 Dissatisfaction comes when our attention shifts from what we have to what we don't have. The people of Israel didn't seem to notice what God was doing for them—setting them free, making them a nation, giving them a new land—because they were so wrapped up in what God wasn't doing for them. They could think of nothing but the delicious Egyptian melons they had left behind. Somehow they forgot that the brutal whip of Egyptian slavery was the cost of eating those melons. Before we judge the Israelites too harshly, it's helpful to think about what occupies our attention most of the time. Are we grateful for what God has given us, or are we always thinking about what we would like to have? We should not allow our unfulfilled desires to cause us to forget God's gifts of life, food, health, work, and friends.

11.4–10 Every morning the Israelites drew back their tent doors and witnessed a miracle. Covering the ground was white, fluffy manna—food from heaven. But soon that wasn't enough. Feeling it was their right to have more, they forgot what they already had. They didn't ask God to fill their need; instead they demanded meat, and they stopped trusting God to care for them. "If only we had meat to eat!" they complained to Moses as they reminisced about the good food they had in Egypt. God gave them what they asked for, but they paid dearly for it when a plague struck the camp (see 11.18–20, 31–34). When you ask God for something, he may grant your request. But if you approach him with a sinful attitude, getting what you want may prove costly.

LORD, saying, 'If only we had meat to eat! Surely it was better for us in Egypt.'
Therefore the LORD will give you meat, and you shall eat. 19 You shall eat not only
one day, or two days, or five days, or ten days, or twenty days, 20 but for a whole
month—until it comes out of your nostrils and becomes loathsome to
you—because you have rejected the LORD who is among you, and have wailed
11.21 before him, saying, 'Why did we ever leave Egypt?' " 21 But Moses said, "The
Ex 12.37 Num 1.20-46 people I am with number six hundred thousand on foot; and you say, 'I will give
2.32,33 them meat, that they may eat for a whole month'! 22 Are there enough flocks and
herds to slaughter for them? Are there enough fish in the sea to catch for them?"
11.23 23 The LORD said to Moses, "Is the LORD's power limited?[u] Now you shall see
Gen 18.14 whether my word will come true for you or not."

24 So Moses went out and told the people the words of the LORD; and he gath-
11.25 ered seventy elders of the people, and placed them all around the tent. 25 Then the
Num 11.16,17 Isa 50.2 LORD came down in the cloud and spoke to him, and took some of the spirit that
was on him and put it on the seventy elders; and when the spirit rested upon them,
they prophesied. But they did not do so again.

26 Two men remained in the camp, one named Eldad, and the other named

[u] Heb *LORD's hand too short?*

ISRAEL'S COMPLAINING

Reference	Complaint	Sin	Result
11.1	About their misfortunes	Complained about their problems instead of praying to God about them	Thousands of people were destroyed when God sent a plague of fire to punish them
11.4	About the lack of meat	Lusted after things they didn't have	God sent quail; but as the people began to eat, God struck them with a plague that killed many
14.1–4	About being stuck in the wilderness, facing the giants of the promised land, and wishing to return to Egypt	Openly rebelled against God's leaders and failed to trust in his promises	All who complained were not allowed to enter the promised land, being doomed to wander in the wilderness until they died
16.3	About Moses' and Aaron's authority and leadership	Were greedy for more power and authority	The families, friends, and possessions of Korah, Dathan, and Abiram were swallowed up by the earth. Fire then burned up the 250 other men who rebelled
16.41	That Moses and Aaron caused the deaths of Korah and his conspirators	Blamed others for their own troubles	God began to destroy Israel with a plague. Moses and Aaron made atonement for the people, but 14,700 of them were killed
20.2, 3	About the lack of water	Refused to believe that God would provide as he had promised	Moses sinned along with the people. For this he was barred from entering the promised land
21.5	That God and Moses brought them into the wilderness	Failed to recognize that their problems were brought on by their own disobedience	God sent poisonous snakes which killed many people and seriously injured many others

11.21, 22 Moses had witnessed God's power in spectacular miracles, yet at this time he questioned God's ability to feed the wandering Israelites. If Moses doubted God's power, how much easier it is for us to do the same. But completely depending upon God is essential, regardless of our level of spiritual maturity. When we begin to rely on our own understanding, we are in danger of ignoring God's assessment of the situation. By remembering his past works and his present power, we can be sure that we are not cutting off his potential help.

11.23 How strong is God? It is easy to trust God when we see his mighty acts (the Israelites saw many), but after a while, in the routine of daily life, his strength may appear to diminish. God doesn't change, but our view of him often does. The monotony of day-by-day living lulls us into forgetting how powerful God can be. As Moses learned, God's strength is always available.

11.26–29 This incident is similar to a story told in Mark 9.38–41. The disciples wanted Jesus to forbid others to cast out demons because they were not part of the disciples' group. But this type of narrow attitude was condemned by both Moses and Jesus. Beware of putting limits on God because he can work through whomever he chooses.

Medad, and the spirit rested on them; they were among those registered, but they
had not gone out to the tent, and so they prophesied in the camp. 27 And a young
man ran and told Moses, "Eldad and Medad are prophesying in the camp." 28 And **11.28**
Joshua son of Nun, the assistant of Moses, one of his chosen men,[v] said, "My lord Josh 1.1 Mk 9.38-40
Moses, stop them!" 29 But Moses said to him, "Are you jealous for my sake? Would
that all the LORD's people were prophets, and that the LORD would put his spirit on
them!" 30 And Moses and the elders of Israel returned to the camp.
31 Then a wind went out from the LORD, and it brought quails from the sea and **11.31** Ex 16.13
let them fall beside the camp, about a day's journey on this side and a day's journey Ps 78.26-33
on the other side, all around the camp, about two cubits deep on the ground. 32 So 105.40
the people worked all that day and night and all the next day, gathering the quails;
the least anyone gathered was ten homers; and they spread them out for themselves
all around the camp. 33 But while the meat was still between their teeth, before it **11.33** Num 11.10
was consumed, the anger of the LORD was kindled against the people, and the LORD **11.34**
struck the people with a very great plague. 34 So that place was called Kibroth- Num 33.15-37 Deut 9.22
hattaavah,[w] because there they buried the people who had the craving. 35 From **11.35**
Kibroth-hattaavah the people journeyed to Hazeroth. Num 12.16

2. Miriam and Aaron criticize Moses

12 While they were at Hazeroth, Miriam and Aaron spoke against Moses be- **12.1** Ex 2.21; 15.20
cause of the Cushite woman whom he had married (for he had indeed mar-
ried a Cushite woman); 2 and they said, "Has the LORD spoken only through Moses? **12.2**
Has he not spoken through us also?" And the LORD heard it. 3 Now the man Moses Num 16.3 Mic 6.4
was very humble,[x] more so than anyone else on the face of the earth. 4 Suddenly **12.3**
the LORD said to Moses, Aaron, and Miriam, "Come out, you three, to the tent of Num 16.16-21
meeting." So the three of them came out. 5 Then the LORD came down in a pillar of **12.5**
cloud, and stood at the entrance of the tent, and called Aaron and Miriam; and they Num 11.25
both came forward. 6 And he said, "Hear my words: **12.6**

When there are prophets among you, Gen 15.1 31.10; 46.2
 I the LORD make myself known to them in visions; 1 Kgs 3.5 Ezek 1.1
 I speak to them in dreams. Dan 8.2 Mt 1.20
7 Not so with my servant Moses; 2.12,13,19
 he is entrusted with all my house. Acts 22.17,18
8 With him I speak face to face— **12.7,8** Ex 33.11
 clearly, not in riddles; Num 14.14 Deut 18.15-19
 and he beholds the form of the LORD. 34.10

Why then were you not afraid to speak against my servant Moses?" 9 And the anger Acts 3.21-23 Heb 3.2,5
of the LORD was kindled against them, and he departed.
10 When the cloud went away from over the tent, Miriam had become lep- **12.10**
rous,[y] as white as snow. And Aaron turned towards Miriam and saw that she was Deut 24.9

[v] Or *of Moses from his youth* [w] That is *Graves of craving* [x] Or *devout* [y] A term for several skin diseases; precise meaning uncertain

---

11.29 When it comes to serving God, there is plenty of room for everyone. Moses was recognized as Israel's leader, yet when others showed leadership ability, he was overjoyed. Joshua, however, was so faithful to Moses' leadership that he forgot the objective—creating a nation of faithful people. As a result, he tried to restrict God's work in order to keep Moses in the limelight. Focusing on individuals and their abilities may cause us to lose sight of our overall objective. In God's service, shared accomplishments are more important than individual achievements.

11.34 Craving or lust is more than inappropriate sexual desire. It can be an unnatural or greedy desire for anything (sports, knowledge, possessions, influence over others). In this circumstance, God punished the Israelites for craving good food! Their desire was not wrong; the sin was in allowing that desire to turn into greed. They felt it was their right to have fine food, and they could think of nothing else. When you become preoccupied with something until it affects your perspective on everything else, you may have moved from desire to lust.

12.1 People often argue over minor disagreements, leaving the real issue untouched. Such was the case when Miriam and Aaron came to Moses with a complaint. The real issue was their growing jealousy of Moses' position and influence. Since they could not find fault with the way Moses was leading the people, they chose to criticize his wife. Rather than face the problem squarely by dealing with their envy and pride, they chose to create a diversion from the real issue. When you are in a disagreement, stop and ask yourself if you are arguing over the real issue or if you have introduced a smoke screen by attacking someone's character. If you are unjustly criticized, remember that your critics may be afraid to face the real problem. Don't take this type of criticism personally. Ask God to help you identify the real issue and deal with it.

12.1 Moses didn't have a Jewish wife because he lived with the Egyptians the first 40 years of his life, and he was in the desert the next 40 years. A "Cushite" was an Ethiopian.

leprous. 11 Then Aaron said to Moses, "Oh, my lord, do not punish us[z] for a sin
that we have so foolishly committed. 12 Do not let her be like one stillborn, whose
flesh is half consumed when it comes out of its mother's womb." 13 And Moses
cried to the LORD, "O God, please heal her." 14 But the LORD said to Moses, "If her
father had but spit in her face, would she not bear her shame for seven days? Let her
be shut out of the camp for seven days, and after that she may be brought in again."

12.14 Lev 14.8,9; 15.8; Num 5.1-3; Deut 25.9

[z] Heb *do not lay sin upon us*

MIRIAM

Ask older brothers or sisters what their greatest trial in life is and they will often answer, "My younger brother (or sister)!" This is especially true when the younger sibling is more successful than the older. The bonds of family loyalty can be strained to the breaking point.

When we first meet Miriam she is involved in one of history's most unusual baby-sitting jobs. She is watching her infant brother float on the Nile River in a waterproof cradle. Miriam's quick thinking allowed Moses to be raised by his own mother. Her protective superiority, reinforced by that event, must have been hard to give up as she watched her little brother rise to greatness.

Eventually Moses' choice of a wife gave Miriam an opportunity to criticize. It was natural for her insecurity to break out over this issue. With Moses married, Miriam was clearly no longer the most important woman in his life. The real issue, however, was not the kind of woman Moses had married. It was the fact that he was now the most important man in Israel. "Has the Lord spoken only through Moses? Has he not spoken through us also?" No mention is made of Moses' response, but God had a quick answer for Miriam and Aaron. Without denying their role in his plan, God clearly pointed out his special relationship with Moses. Miriam was stricken with leprosy, a deadly disease, as punishment for her insubordination. But Moses, true to his character, intervened for his sister, so that God healed Miriam of her leprosy.

Before criticizing someone else, we need to pause long enough to discover our own motives. Failing to do this can bring disastrous results. What is often labeled "constructive criticism" may actually be destructive jealousy, since the easiest way to raise our own status is to bring someone else down. Are you willing to question your motives before you offer criticism? Does the critical finger you point need to be pointed first toward yourself?

Strengths and accomplishments:
- Quick thinker under pressure
- Able leader
- Song writer
- Prophetess

Weaknesses and mistakes:
- Was jealous of Moses' authority
- Openly criticized Moses' leadership

Lesson from her life:
- The motives behind criticism are often more important to deal with than the criticism itself

Vital statistics:
- Where: Egypt, Sinai peninsula
- Relatives: Brothers: Aaron and Moses

Key verses:
"Then the prophet Miriam, Aaron's sister, took a tambourine in her hand; and all the women went out after her with tambourines and with dancing. And Miriam sang to them: 'Sing to the Lord, for he has triumphed gloriously; horse and rider he has thrown into the sea' " (Exodus 15.20, 21).

Miriam's story is told in Exodus 2 and 15; Numbers 12 and 20. She is also mentioned in Deuteronomy 24.9; 1 Chronicles 6.3; Micah 6.4.

12.11 Aaron cried out, "Do not punish us for a sin that we have so foolishly committed." It is easy to look back at our mistakes and recognize their foolishness. It is much harder to recognize foolish plans while we are carrying them out, because somehow then they seem appropriate. To get rid of foolish ideas before they turn into foolish actions requires eliminating our wrong thoughts and motives. Failing to do this caused Miriam and Aaron much grief.

12.14 Spitting in someone's face was considered the ultimate insult and a sign of shame imposed on wrongdoers. The religious leaders spat in Jesus' face to insult him (Matthew 26.67). God punished Miriam for her smug attitude toward not only Moses' authority, but also God's. He struck her with leprosy, then ordered her out of the camp for a week. This punishment was actually quite lenient. A week was the length of time she would have been excluded if her father had spat in her face. How much more she deserved for wronging God! Once again, God was merciful while retaining an effective discipline.

15 So Miriam was shut out of the camp for seven days; and the people did not set out
on the march until Miriam had been brought in again. 16 After that the people set out **12.16**
from Hazeroth, and camped in the wilderness of Paran. Num 11.35

3. The spies incite rebellion

The spies are sent out

13 The LORD said to Moses, 2 "Send men to spy out the land of Canaan, which **13.2**
I am giving to the Israelites; from each of their ancestral tribes you shall send Ex 18.25 Num 11.16; 32.8
a man, every one a leader among them." 3 So Moses sent them from the wilderness Deut 1.22-25 Josh 2.1
of Paran, according to the command of the LORD, all of them leading men among **13.3**
the Israelites. 4 These were their names: From the tribe of Reuben, Shammua son of Num 1.2-15 12.16; 13.26
Zaccur; 5 from the tribe of Simeon, Shaphat son of Hori; 6 from the tribe of Judah, 34.16-28
Caleb son of Jephunneh; 7 from the tribe of Issachar, Igal son of Joseph; 8 from the
tribe of Ephraim, Hoshea son of Nun; 9 from the tribe of Benjamin, Palti son of
Raphu; 10 from the tribe of Zebulun, Gaddiel son of Sodi; 11 from the tribe of Joseph
(that is, from the tribe of Manasseh), Gaddi son of Susi; 12 from the tribe of Dan,
Ammiel son of Gemalli; 13 from the tribe of Asher, Sethur son of Michael; 14 from
the tribe of Naphtali, Nahbi son of Vophsi; 15 from the tribe of Gad, Geuel son of
Machi. 16 These were the names of the men whom Moses sent to spy out the land. **13.16** Num 13.3-15
And Moses changed the name of Hoshea son of Nun to Joshua. Acts 7.45

The spies explore the land

17 Moses sent them to spy out the land of Canaan, and said to them, "Go up **13.17**
there into the Negeb, and go up into the hill country, 18 and see what the land is like, Gen 12.9; 13.1 Num 13.22
and whether the people who live in it are strong or weak, whether they are few or Josh 15.1
many, 19 and whether the land they live in is good or bad, and whether the towns
that they live in are unwalled or fortified, 20 and whether the land is rich or poor, **13.20**
and whether there are trees in it or not. Be bold, and bring some of the fruit of the Num 13.23,24
land." Now it was the season of the first ripe grapes. **13.21** Num 20.1; 27.14
21 So they went up and spied out the land from the wilderness of Zin to Rehob, Josh 19.28 Judg 1.31,32
near Lebo-hamath. 22 They went up into the Negeb, and came to Hebron; and Ahi- 2 Sam 8.9 Amos 6.2
man, Sheshai, and Talmai, the Anakites, were there. (Hebron was built seven years **13.22**
before Zoan in Egypt.) 23 And they came to the Wadi Eshcol, and cut down from Num 13.33
there a branch with a single cluster of grapes, and they carried it on a pole between Josh 11.21 15.14
two of them. They also brought some pomegranates and figs. 24 That place was Judg 1.10
called the Wadi Eshcol,[a] because of the cluster that the Israelites cut down from **13.23**
there. Num 13.24; 32.9 Deut 1.24,25

The people rebel at the spies' report

25 At the end of forty days they returned from spying out the land. 26 And they **13.26**
came to Moses and Aaron and to all the congregation of the Israelites in the wilder- Num 12.16 13.3; 20.1; 32.8
ness of Paran, at Kadesh; they brought back word to them and to all the congrega- Deut 1.19
tion, and showed them the fruit of the land. 27 And they told him, "We came to the Josh 14.6
land to which you sent us; it flows with milk and honey, and this is its fruit. 28 Yet
the people who live in the land are strong, and the towns are fortified and very
large; and besides, we saw the descendants of Anak there. 29 The Amalekites live **13.29** Gen 15.19-21
in the land of the Negeb; the Hittites, the Jebusites, and the Amorites live in the hill Ex 3.8,17 17.8-16
country; and the Canaanites live by the sea, and along the Jordan." Num 14.43

[a] That is *Cluster*

13.17–20 Moses decided what information was needed before the people could enter the promised land, and he took careful steps to get that information. When you are making decisions or assuming new responsibilities, remember these two important steps. Ask yourself what you need to know about the opportunity, and then obtain that knowledge. Common sense is a valuable aid in accomplishing God's purposes.

13.25–29 God told the Israelites that the promised land was rich and plentiful. Not only that, he promised that this bountiful land would be theirs. When the spies reported back to Moses, they gave plenty of good reasons for entering the land, but they couldn't stop focusing on their fear. Talk of giants and walled cities made it easy to forget about God's promise to help. When facing a tough decision, don't let the negatives cause you to lose sight of the positives. Weigh both sides carefully. Don't let potential difficulties blind you to God's power to help and his promise to guide.

13.30 Num 14.6-9 Josh 14.6-8 Isa 41.10-16
13.31 Num 32.9 Heb 3.19
13.32 Deut 1.28

30 But Caleb quieted the people before Moses, and said, "Let us go up at once
and occupy it, for we are well able to overcome it." 31 Then the men who had gone
up with him said, "We are not able to go up against this people, for they are stronger than we." 32 So they brought to the Israelites an unfavorable report of the land
that they had spied out, saying, "The land that we have gone through as spies is a
land that devours its inhabitants; and all the people that we saw in it are of great

THE SPIES MOSES SENT OUT

Of the 12 spies Moses sent out, only Caleb and Joshua (Oshea, Jehoshua) brought back a positive report and encouraged the people to go up and possess the land.

Tribe	*Name*
Reuben	Shammua, son of Zaccur
Simeon	Shaphat, son of Hori
Judah	Caleb, son of Jephunneh
Issachar	Igal, son of Joseph
Ephraim	Oshea, son of Nun
Benjamin	Palti, son of Raphu
Zebulun	Gaddiel, son of Sodi
Joseph (Manasseh)	Gaddi, son of Susi
Dan	Ammiel, son of Gemalli
Asher	Sethur, son of Michael
Naphtali	Nahbi, son of Vophsi
Gad	Geuel, son of Machi

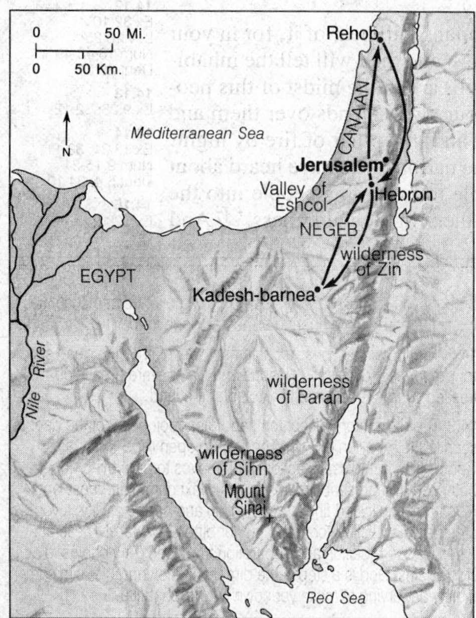

ROUTE OF THE SPIES The spies traveled from Kadesh-barnea (Kadesh) at the northern edge of the wilderness of Paran to Rehob at the northern end of the Jordan Valley and back, a round trip of about 300 miles.

13.26 Although Kadesh was only a desert oasis, it was a crossroads in Israel's history. When the spies returned to Kadesh from scouting the new land, the people had to decide either to enter the land or to retreat. They chose to retreat and were condemned to wander 40 years in the wilderness. It was also at Kadesh that Moses disobeyed God (20.7–12). For this, he too was denied entrance into the promised land. Aaron and Miriam died there, for they could not enter the new land either. Kadesh was near Canaan's southern borders, but because of the Israelites' lack of faith, they needed more than a lifetime to go from Kadesh to the promised land.

13.27 The promised land, also called the land of Canaan, was indeed magnificent, as the 12 spies discovered. The Bible often calls it the "land flowing with milk and honey." Although the land was relatively small – 150 miles long and 60 miles wide – its lush hillsides were covered with fig, date, and nut trees. It was the land God had promised to Abraham, Isaac, and Jacob.

13.28 The "descendants of Anak" were a race of abnormally large people. The family of Goliath may have descended from these people (see 2 Samuel 21.16–22).

13.28, 29 The fortified cities the spies talked about were surrounded by high walls as much as 20 feet thick and 25 feet tall. Guards were often stationed on top, where there was a commanding view of the countryside. Some of the inhabitants, said the spies, were formidable men – from seven to nine feet tall – so that the Israelites felt like grasshoppers next to them. The walled cities and the giants struck fear into the hearts of most of the spies.

13.30 Imagine standing before a crowd and loudly voicing an unpopular opinion! Caleb was willing to take the unpopular stand to do as God had commanded. To be effective when you go against the crowd, you must (1) have the facts (Caleb had seen the land himself); (2) have the right attitude (Caleb trusted God's promise to give Israel the land); and (3) state clearly what you believe (Caleb said, "We are well able to overcome it").

13.31, 32 The Israelites didn't trust God – they believed victory was impossible. In their self-doubt, their decision made sense. But they failed to realize that God doesn't always operate from a human perspective. A promise from God is a sure thing, no matter how unlikely it seems. God's word isn't subject to majority opinion. His truth is set apart from feelings, situations, or opinions. Caleb stood for the truth he knew about God, apart from what he saw. He knew that God's promises could be depended on. God had said very plainly that he would help the people conquer the promised land. But the other spies forgot what they knew about God and made their decision on the basis of what they knew of themselves. Are you willing to stand against the pressure of popular opinion to do what God's word says?

size. 33 There we saw the Nephilim (the Anakites come from the Nephilim); and to
ourselves we seemed like grasshoppers, and so we seemed to them."
14 Then all the congregation raised a loud cry, and the people wept that night.
2 And all the Israelites complained against Moses and Aaron; the whole congregation said to them, "Would that we had died in the land of Egypt! Or would that
we had died in this wilderness! 3 Why is the LORD bringing us into this land to fall
by the sword? Our wives and our little ones will become booty; would it not be
better for us to go back to Egypt?" 4 So they said to one another, "Let us choose a
captain, and go back to Egypt."

Moses prays for the rebellious people

5 Then Moses and Aaron fell on their faces before all the assembly of the congregation of the Israelites. 6 And Joshua son of Nun and Caleb son of Jephunneh,
who were among those who had spied out the land, tore their clothes 7 and said to
all the congregation of the Israelites, "The land that we went through as spies is an
exceedingly good land. 8 If the LORD is pleased with us, he will bring us into this
land and give it to us, a land that flows with milk and honey. 9 Only, do not rebel
against the LORD; and do not fear the people of the land, for they are no more than
bread for us; their protection is removed from them, and the LORD is with us; do not
fear them." 10 But the whole congregation threatened to stone them.
Then the glory of the LORD appeared at the tent of meeting to all the Israelites.
11 And the LORD said to Moses, "How long will this people despise me? And how
long will they refuse to believe in me, in spite of all the signs that I have done
among them? 12 I will strike them with pestilence and disinherit them, and I will
make of you a nation greater and mightier than they."
13 But Moses said to the LORD, "Then the Egyptians will hear of it, for in your
might you brought up this people from among them, 14 and they will tell the inhabitants of this land. They have heard that you, O LORD, are in the midst of this people; for you, O LORD, are seen face to face, and your cloud stands over them and
you go in front of them, in a pillar of cloud by day and in a pillar of fire by night.
15 Now if you kill this people all at one time, then the nations who have heard about
you will say, 16 'It is because the LORD was not able to bring this people into the
land he swore to give them that he has slaughtered them in the wilderness.' 17 And

13.33 1 Sam 17.4-7 2 Sam 21.20-22 1 Chron 11.23
14.2 Ex 15.24; 16.3 Num 11.1,5 16.41; 20.3,4 21.5
14.3 Ex 5.21; 16.3 Num 14.31 Deut 1.39
14.5 Gen 17.3 Num 16.22,45 Josh 5.14
14.7 Deut 1.25 6.10,11; 8.7-9
14.8 Ex 3.8 Num 13.27
14.9 Deut 1.21,29 7.18; 9.7,23,24
14.10 Ex 16.7,10 17.4; 24.16,17 Lev 9.23 Num 20.6 1 Sam 30.6
14.12 Ex 32.10 Lev 26.25 Num 16.46-49 Deut 28.21
14.13 Ex 9.28; 32.12
14.14 Ex 13.21; 33.11 Num 9.15-21 Deut 5.4; 34.10
14.15 Ex 32.12

13.33 The Nephilim were giants who lived on the earth before the flood (Genesis 6.4).

13.33–14.4 The negative opinion of ten men caused a great rebellion among the people. Because it is human nature to accept opinion as fact, we must be especially careful when voicing our negative opinions. What we say may heavily influence the actions of those who trust us to give sound advice.

14.1–4 When the chorus of despair went up, everyone joined in. Their greatest fears were being realized. Losing their perspective, the people were caught up in the emotion of the moment, forgetting what they knew about God's character. What if the people had spent as much energy moving forward as they did moving back? They could have enjoyed their land—instead they never even entered it. When a cry of despair goes up around you, consider the larger perspective before you join in. You probably have more to do with your energy than complain.

14.5–9 With great miracles, God led the Israelites out of slavery, through the desolate wilderness, and up to the very edge of the promised land. He protected them, fed them, and fulfilled every promise. Yet when encouraged to take that last step of faith and enter the land, the people refused. After witnessing so many miracles, why did they stop trusting God? Why did they refuse to enter the promised land when that had been their goal since leaving Egypt? Often we do the same thing. We trust God to handle the smaller issues but doubt his ability to take care of the big problems, the tough decisions, the frightening situations. Don't stop trusting God just as you are ready to reach your goal. If he has brought you this far, he won't let you down now. We can continue trusting God by remembering all he has done for us.

14.6 Tearing clothing was a customary way of showing deep sorrow, mourning, or despair. Joshua and Caleb were greatly distressed by the people's refusal to enter the land.

14.9 The discomfort, discontent, and disappointment of the people soon led to rebellion (16.1ff). The path to open rebellion against God begins with dissatisfaction, then moves to grumbling about both God and present circumstances. Next come bitterness and resentment, followed finally by rebellion and open hostility. If you are often dissatisfied, complaining, or bitter—beware! These attitudes lead to rebellion and separation from God. Any choice to side against God is a step in the direction of letting go of him completely and trying to make your own way through life.

14.10 Two wise men, Joshua and Caleb, encouraged the people to act on God's promise and move ahead into the land. The people rejected their advice and even talked of killing them. Don't be too quick to reject advice you don't like. Evaluate it carefully, comparing it to the teaching in God's word. Those who offer the advice may be giving God's message.

14.13–16 The people didn't deserve it, but Moses pleaded for them because he was concerned about God's reputation among unbelievers. Pharaoh would hear about it and this would be a disgrace to the Lord in the eyes of the nations. Instead, Israel was to be a light for the nations. Think of the reputation you give God by the way you live. What your friends and neighbors think about God is more important than what they think about you.

now, therefore, let the power of the LORD be great in the way that you promised
when you spoke, saying,
18 'The LORD is slow to anger,
and abounding in steadfast love,
forgiving iniquity and transgression,
but by no means clearing the guilty,
visiting the iniquity of the parents
upon the children
to the third and the fourth generation.'
19 Forgive the iniquity of this people according to the greatness of your steadfast
love, just as you have pardoned this people, from Egypt even until now."

God condemns the people to wander for 40 years

20 Then the LORD said, "I do forgive, just as you have asked; 21 nevertheless—as I live, and as all the earth shall be filled with the glory of the LORD—
22 none of the people who have seen my glory and the signs that I did in Egypt and
in the wilderness, and yet have tested me these ten times and have not obeyed my
voice, 23 shall see the land that I swore to give to their ancestors; none of those who
despised me shall see it. 24 But my servant Caleb, because he has a different spirit
and has followed me wholeheartedly, I will bring into the land into which he went,
and his descendants shall possess it. 25 Now, since the Amalekites and the Canaanites live in the valleys, turn tomorrow and set out for the wilderness by the way to
the Red Sea."[b]
26 And the LORD spoke to Moses and to Aaron, saying: 27 How long shall this
wicked congregation complain against me? I have heard the complaints of the Israelites, which they complain against me. 28 Say to them, "As I live," says the LORD,
"I will do to you the very things I heard you say: 29 your dead bodies shall fall in this
very wilderness; and of all your number, included in the census, from twenty years
old and upward, who have complained against me, 30 not one of you shall come into
the land in which I swore to settle you, except Caleb son of Jephunneh and Joshua
son of Nun. 31 But your little ones, who you said would become booty, I will bring
in, and they shall know the land that you have despised. 32 But as for you, your dead
bodies shall fall in this wilderness. 33 And your children shall be shepherds in the
wilderness for forty years, and shall suffer for your faithlessness, until the last of

[b] Or *Sea of Reeds*

14.17 Ex 20.5; 34.6,7 Ps 103.8
14.19 Ex 32.32; 34.9
14.20 Num 14.28 Deut 32.40 Mic 7.18-20
14.23 Num 26.65 32.11 Deut 1.35
14.24 Num 13.30 14.6; 26.65 Josh 14.6-15
14.25 Num 13.29
14.26 Num 11.1
14.28 Num 14.21 Heb 3.17
14.29 Num 1.17-19 26.2
14.30 Num 14.24,38 32.12
14.31 Num 14.3
14.32 Num 14.29 26.64; 32.13 1 Cor 10.5

14.17–19 Moses and Aaron asked God to have mercy on the very people who rebelled against them. They prayed for those with whom they were most angry and frustrated. Do you pray for those who try to hurt you? Or do you seek revenge, asking God to help you to get even? Only men and women who have a deep relationship with God can remain firm under pressure and pray for their attackers. They understand that the God who called them to their task will take the responsibility for settling the score with those who rebel. It is not the child's job to discipline a sibling, but the parents'. In the same way, it is not our job to seek revenge against those who wrong us. God will make certain that, in the end, justice is carried out.

14.17–20 Moses pleaded with God, asking him to forgive his people. His plea reveals several characteristics of God: (1) God is immensely patient; (2) God's love is one promise we can always count on; (3) God forgives again and again; and (4) God is merciful, listening to and answering our requests. God has not changed since Moses' day. Like Moses, we can rely on God's love, patience, forgiveness, and mercy.

14.18 This phrase, "visiting the iniquity of the parents upon the children," points to a truth that many want to ignore—how we act affects others, especially children. We must never forget that our actions as parents will affect our children, and they will suffer from our sins.

14.20–23 The people of Israel had a clearer view of God than any people before them, for they had both his laws and his physical presence. Their refusal to follow God after witnessing his miraculous deeds and listening to his words made the judgment against them more severe. Increased opportunity brings increased responsibility. As Jesus said: "From everyone to whom much has been given, much will be required" (Luke 12.48). How much greater is our responsibility to obey and serve God, for we have the whole Bible and we know God's Son, Jesus Christ.

14.22 God wasn't exaggerating when he said that the Israelites had already failed ten times to trust and obey him. Here is a list of their ten failures: (1) lacking trust at the crossing of the Red Sea (Exodus 14.11, 12); (2) complaining over bitter water at Marah (Exodus 15.24); (3) complaining in the wilderness of Sin (Exodus 16.3); (4) collecting more than the daily quota of manna (Exodus 16.20); (5) collecting manna on the sabbath (Exodus 16.27–29); (6) complaining over lack of water at Rephidim (Exodus 17.2, 3); (7) committing idolatry with a golden calf (Exodus 32.7–10); (8) complaining at Taberah (Numbers 11.1); (9) more complaining over the lack of delicious food (Numbers 11.4); (10) failing to trust God and enter the promised land (Numbers 14.1–4).

14.24 The fulfillment of this verse is recorded in Joshua 14.6–15, when Caleb received his inheritance in the promised land. Caleb followed God with all his heart and was rewarded for his obedience. Are you wholehearted in your commitment to obey God?

your dead bodies lies in the wilderness. [34]According to the number of the days in 14.33 Num 33.38 Deut 2.7; 8.2
which you spied out the land, forty days, for every day a year, you shall bear your
iniquity, forty years, and you shall know my displeasure." [35]I the LORD have spoken; surely I will do thus to all this wicked congregation gathered together against
me: in this wilderness they shall come to a full end, and there they shall die.
36 And the men whom Moses sent to spy out the land, who returned and made 14.36 Num 13.26-29, 31-33; 16.49 25.9
all the congregation complain against him by bringing a bad report about the
land— [37]the men who brought an unfavorable report about the land died by a
plague before the LORD. [38]But Joshua son of Nun and Caleb son of Jephunneh
alone remained alive, of those men who went to spy out the land.
39 When Moses told these words to all the Israelites, the people mourned 14.39 Ex 33.4
greatly.

The people try to enter the promised land on their own

[40]They rose early in the morning and went up to the heights of the hill country, 14.40 Deut 1.41-44
saying, "Here we are. We will go up to the place that the LORD has promised, for
we have sinned." [41]But Moses said, "Why do you continue to transgress the command of the LORD? That will not succeed. [42]Do not go up, for the LORD is not with
you; do not let yourselves be struck down before your enemies. [43]For the Amalekites and the Canaanites will confront you there, and you shall fall by the sword;
because you have turned back from following the LORD, the LORD will not be with
you." [44]But they presumed to go up to the heights of the hill country, even though 14.44 Num 10.33; 31.6
the ark of the covenant of the LORD, and Moses, had not left the camp. [45]Then the 14.45 Num 21.3 Judg 1.17
Amalekites and the Canaanites who lived in that hill country came down and de-
feated them, pursuing them as far as Hormah.

C. WANDERING IN THE WILDERNESS (15.1—21.35)

After their disobedience and unsuccessful attempt to enter the promised land, the Israelites are condemned to wander 40 years in the desert. Even in the midst of this punishment, the people continued to rebel and thus God continued to punish them. But the hearts of the people remained hard and rebellious. Hard hearts toward God may bring similar calamity to us.

1. Additional regulations

For offerings

15 The LORD spoke to Moses, saying: [2]Speak to the Israelites and say to them:
When you come into the land you are to inhabit, which I am giving you,
[3]and you make an offering by fire to the LORD from the herd or from the 15.3 Lev 1.1; 2.1-16 6.9-11 6.14-21; 22.21 23.37,38; 27.2 Deut 12.6,17 16.16
flock—whether a burnt offering or a sacrifice, to fulfill a vow or as a freewill offer-
ing or at your appointed festivals—to make a pleasing odor for the LORD, [4]then
whoever presents such an offering to the LORD shall present also a grain offering,
one-tenth of an ephah of choice flour, mixed with one-fourth of a hin of oil. [5]More-
over, you shall offer one-fourth of a hin of wine as a drink offering with the burnt 15.5 Num 15.5-10 28.7
offering or the sacrifice, for each lamb. [6]For a ram, you shall offer a grain offering,
two-tenths of an ephah of choice flour mixed with one-third of a hin of oil; [7]and as

---

14.34 God's judgment came in the form the people feared most. The people were afraid of dying in the wilderness, so God punished them by making them wander in the wilderness until they died. Now they wished they had the problem of facing the giants and the fortified cities of the promised land. Failing to trust God often brings even greater problems than those we originally faced. When we run from God, we inevitably run into problems.

14.35 Was this judgment—wandering 40 years in the wilderness—too harsh? Not compared to the instant death that God first threatened (14.12). Instead, God allowed the people to live. God had brought his people to the edge of the promised land, just as he said he would. He was ready to give them the rich land, but the people didn't want it (14.1, 2). By this time, God had put up with a lot. At least ten times the people had refused to trust and obey him (14.22). The whole nation (except for Joshua, Caleb, Moses, and Aaron) showed contempt for and distrust of God. But God's punishment was not permanent. In 40 years, a new generation would have a chance to enter Canaan (Joshua 1—3).

14.40–44 When the Israelites realized their foolish mistake, they were suddenly ready to return to God. But God didn't confuse their admission of guilt with true repentance, because he knew their hearts. Sure enough, they soon went their own way again. Sometimes right actions or good intentions come too late. We must not only act rightly, but also do it at the right time. God wants complete and instant obedience.

15.3 "A pleasing odor for the Lord" means that God would be pleased with their sacrifices.

a drink offering you shall offer one-third of a hin of wine, a pleasing odor to the
15.8 Lev 3.1; 7.11-18 LORD. 8 When you offer a bull as a burnt offering or a sacrifice, to fulfill a vow or
as an offering of well-being to the LORD, 9 then you shall present with the bull a
grain offering, three-tenths of an ephah of choice flour, mixed with half a hin of oil,
15.10 Num 15.5 10 and you shall present as a drink offering half a hin of wine, as an offering by fire,
a pleasing odor to the LORD.

11 Thus it shall be done for each ox or ram, or for each of the male lambs or the
kids. 12 According to the number that you offer, so you shall do with each and every
one. 13 Every native Israelite shall do these things in this way, in presenting an
offering by fire, a pleasing odor to the LORD. 14 An alien who lives with you, or who
takes up permanent residence among you, and wishes to offer an offering by fire,
15.15 Ex 12.49 Lev 24.22 Num 9.14; 15.29 a pleasing odor to the LORD, shall do as you do. 15 As for the assembly, there shall
be for both you and the resident alien a single statute, a perpetual statute throughout
your generations; you and the alien shall be alike before the LORD. 16 You and the
alien who resides with you shall have the same law and the same ordinance.

17 The LORD spoke to Moses, saying: 18 Speak to the Israelites and say to them:
15.19 Lev 23.10,17 Num 18.12 After you come into the land to which I am bringing you, 19 whenever you eat of the
bread of the land, you shall present a donation to the LORD. 20 From your first batch
of dough you shall present a loaf as a donation; you shall present it just as you
present a donation from the threshing floor. 21 Throughout your generations you
shall give to the LORD a donation from the first of your batch of dough.

22 But if you unintentionally fail to observe all these commandments that the
15.23 Lev 4.2,22,27 5.15,18 LORD has spoken to Moses— 23 everything that the LORD has commanded you by
Moses, from the day the LORD gave commandment and thereafter, throughout your
generations— 24 then if it was done unintentionally without the knowledge of
the congregation, the whole congregation shall offer one young bull for a burnt

---

CALEB

The voice of the minority is not often given a hearing. Nevertheless, truth cannot be measured by numbers. On the contrary, it often stands against majority opinion. Truth remains unchanged because it is guaranteed by the character of God. God is truth; what he says is the last word. At times, a person must even stand alone on the side of truth.

Caleb was not so much a man of great faith as a man of faith in a great God! His boldness rested on his understanding of God, not on his confidence in Israel's abilities to conquer. He could not agree with the majority, for that would be to disagree with God.

We, on the other hand, often base our decisions on what everyone else is doing. Few of us are first-order cowards like the ten spies. We are more like the people of Israel, getting our cowardice secondhand. Our search for right and wrong usually starts with questions such as "What do the experts say?" or "What do my friends say?" The question we most often avoid is "What does God say?" The principles we learn as we study the Bible provide a dependable road map for life. They draw us into a personal relationship with the God whose word is the Bible. The God who gave Caleb his boldness is the same God who offers us the gift of eternal life through his Son, Jesus. That's truth worth believing!

Strengths and accomplishments:
- One of the spies sent by Moses to survey the land of Canaan
- One of the only two adults who left Egypt and entered the promised land
- Voiced the minority opinion in favor of conquering the land
- Expressed faith in God's promises, in spite of apparent obstacles

Lessons from his life:
- Majority opinion is not an accurate measurement of right and wrong
- Boldness based on God's faithfulness is appropriate
- For courage and faith to be effective, they must combine words and actions

Vital statistics:
- Where: From Egypt to the Sinai peninsula to the promised land, specifically Hebron
- Occupation: Spy, soldier, shepherd

Key verse:
"But my servant Caleb, because he has a different spirit and has followed me wholeheartedly, I will bring into the land into which he went, and his descendants shall possess it" (Numbers 14.24).

Caleb's story is told in Numbers 13; 14 and Joshua 14; 15. He is also mentioned in Judges 1 and 1 Chronicles 4.15.

offering, a pleasing odor to the LORD, together with its grain offering and its drink
offer ing, according to the ordinance, and one male goat for a sin offering. 25 The 15.25
priest shall make atonement for all the congregation of the Israelites, and they shall Lev 4.20
be forgiven; it was unintentional, and they have brought their offering, an offering
by fire to the LORD, and their sin offering before the LORD, for their error. 26 All the
congregation of the Israelites shall be forgiven, as well as the aliens residing among
them, because the whole people was involved in the error.

27 An individual who sins unintentionally shall present a female goat a year old
for a sin offering. 28 And the priest shall make atonement before the LORD for the
one who commits an error, when it is unintentional, to make atonement for the
person, who then shall be forgiven. 29 For both the native among the Israelites and 15.29
the alien residing among them—you shall have the same law for anyone who acts Num 15.15
in error. 30 But whoever acts high-handedly, whether a native or an alien, affronts 15.30
the LORD, and shall be cut off from among the people. 31 Because of having de- Num 14.40-44 Deut 1.43
spised the word of the LORD and broken his commandment, such a person shall be 17.12,13
utterly cut off and bear the guilt.

For breaking the sabbath

32 When the Israelites were in the wilderness, they found a man gathering 15.32
sticks on the sabbath day. 33 Those who found him gathering sticks brought him to Ex 31.14,15 35.2,3
Moses, Aaron, and to the whole congregation. 34 They put him in custody, because
it was not clear what should be done to him. 35 Then the LORD said to Moses, "The 15.35
man shall be put to death; all the congregation shall stone him outside the camp." Lev 24.14,23 Deut 21.21
36 The whole congregation brought him outside the camp and stoned him to death,
just as the LORD had commanded Moses.

For clothing

37 The LORD said to Moses: 38 Speak to the Israelites, and tell them to make 15.37,38
fringes on the corners of their garments throughout their generations and to put a Mt 9.20; 23.5
blue cord on the fringe at each corner. 39 You have the fringe so that, when you see 15.39
it, you will remember all the commandments of the LORD and do them, and not Ex 13.9 Deut 6.12; 8.11
follow the lust of your own heart and your own eyes. 40 So you shall remember and Jude 16
do all my commandments, and you shall be holy to your God. 41 I am the LORD your 15.40
God, who brought you out of the land of Egypt, to be your God: I am the LORD your 1 Pet 1.15,16
God. 15.41 Ex 20.1

2. Many leaders rebel against Moses

Rebellion in the camp

16 Now Korah son of Izhar son of Kohath son of Levi, along with Dathan and 16.1
Abiram sons of Eliab, and On son of Peleth—descendants of Reuben—took Ex 6.21 Num 26.9,10
2 two hundred fifty Israelite men, leaders of the congregation, chosen from the as- Deut 11.6
sembly, well-known men,[c] and they confronted Moses. 3 They assembled against Jude 11
Moses and against Aaron, and said to them, "You have gone too far! All the con- 16.2 Num 1.16
gregation are holy, everyone of them, and the LORD is among them. So why then

[c] Cn: Heb *and they confronted Moses, and two hundred fifty men . . . well-known men*

15.30, 31 God was willing to forgive those who made unintentional errors if they realized their mistakes quickly and corrected them. However, those who deliberately sinned (acted "high-handedly") received a harsher judgment. Intentional sin grows out of an improper attitude toward God. A child who knowingly disobeys his parents challenges their authority and dares them to respond. Both the act and the attitude have to be dealt with.

15.32–35 Executing a man for picking up sticks on the sabbath seems like a severe punishment, and it was. This act was a deliberate sin, defying God's law against working on the sabbath. Picking up the sticks was gathering firewood. Perhaps this man was trying to get ahead of everyone else, in addition to breaking the sabbath.

15.39 The fringe was to remind people not to seek after their own lustful desires, but to seek the Lord. Idol worship is self-centered, focusing on what a person can get. Good luck, prosperity, long life, and success in battle were expected from the gods. So were power and prestige. The worship of God is a striking contrast. Believers are to be selfless rather than self-centered. We serve God for who he is, not for what we get out of him.

16.2, 3 Korah and his associates had seen the advantages of the priesthood in Egypt. Egyptian priests had great wealth and political influence, something Korah desired for himself. Korah might have assumed that the Israelite priesthood would be the same kind of political machine. He did not understand that Moses' main ambition was to serve God rather than control others.

16.3 Ex 19.6 Num 16.7; 35.34
16.4 Num 14.5 16.45; 20.6
16.5 Lev 10.3 21.6-8,12-15 Jn 15.16
16.7 Num 16.3
16.10 Num 3.6-10

do you exalt yourselves above the assembly of the LORD?" 4 When Moses heard it,
he fell on his face. 5 Then he said to Korah and all his company, "In the morning the
LORD will make known who is his, and who is holy, and who will be allowed to
approach him; the one whom he will choose he will allow to approach him. 6 Do
this: take censers, Korah and all your[d] company, 7 and tomorrow put fire in them,
and lay incense on them before the LORD; and the man whom the LORD chooses
shall be the holy one. You Levites have gone too far!" 8 Then Moses said to Korah,
"Hear now, you Levites! 9 Is it too little for you that the God of Israel has separated
you from the congregation of Israel, to allow you to approach him in order to perform the duties of the LORD's tabernacle, and to stand before the congregation and
serve them? 10 He has allowed you to approach him, and all your brother Levites

[d] Heb *his*

KORAH

Some notorious historical figures might have remained anonymous if they hadn't tried to grab onto more than they could hold. But by refusing to be content with what they had, and by trying to get more than they deserved, they ended up with nothing. Korah, one of the Israelite leaders, was such a person.

Korah was a Levite who assisted in the daily functions of the tabernacle. Shortly after Israel's great rebellion against God (Numbers 13, 14), Korah instigated his own mini-rebellion. He recruited a grievance committee and confronted Moses and Aaron. Their list of complaints boils down to three statements: (1) you are no better than anyone else; (2) everyone in Israel has been chosen of the Lord; (3) we don't need to obey you. It is amazing to see how Korah twisted the first two statements—both true—to reach the wrong conclusion.

Moses would have agreed that he was no better than anyone else. He would also have agreed that all Israelites were God's chosen people. But Korah's application of these truths was wrong. Not all Israelites were chosen to lead. Korah's hidden claim was this: "I have as much right to lead as Moses does." His error cost him not only his job—a position of service that he enjoyed—but also his life.

Korah's story gives us numerous warnings: (1) Don't let desire for what someone else has make you discontented with what you already have. (2) Don't try to raise your own self-esteem by attacking someone else's. (3) Don't use part of God's word to support what you want, rather than allowing its entirety to shape your wants. (4) Don't expect to find satisfaction in power and position; God may want to work through you in the position you are now in.

Strengths and accomplishments:
- Popular leader; influential figure during the exodus
- Mentioned among the chief men of Israel (Exodus 6)
- One of the first Levites appointed for special service in the tabernacle

Weaknesses and mistakes:
- Failed to recognize the significant position God had placed him in
- Forgot that his fight was against someone greater than Moses
- Allowed greed to blind his common sense

Lessons from his life:
- There is sometimes a fine line between goals and greed
- If we are discontented with what we have, we may lose it without gaining anything better

Vital statistics:
- Where: Egypt, Sinai peninsula
- Occupation: Levite (tabernacle assistant)

Key verses:
"Then Moses said to Korah, 'Hear now, you Levites! Is it too little for you that the God of Israel has separated you from the congregation of Israel, to allow you to approach him in order to perform the duties of the Lord's tabernacle, and to stand before the congregation and serve them? He has allowed you to approach him, and all your brother Levites with you; yet you seek the priesthood as well' " (Numbers 16.8–10).

Korah's story is told in Numbers 16.1–40. He is also mentioned in Numbers 26.9; Jude 1.11.

16.8–10 Moses saw through their charge to their true motivation—some of the Levites wanted the power of the priesthood. Like Korah, we often desire the special qualities God has given others. Korah had significant, worthwhile abilities and responsibilities of his own. In the end, however, his ambition for more caused him to lose everything. Inappropriate ambition is greed in disguise. Concentrate on finding the special purpose God has for you.

with you; yet you seek the priesthood as well! 11 Therefore you and all your com- **16.11**
pany have gathered together against the LORD. What is Aaron that you rail against Num 16.3 1 Sam 8.7
him?"
12 Moses sent for Dathan and Abiram sons of Eliab; but they said, "We will not
come! 13 Is it too little that you have brought us up out of a land flowing with milk **16.13**
and honey to kill us in the wilderness, that you must also lord it over us? 14 It is clear Ex 16.3,17 Num 11.5
you have not brought us into a land flowing with milk and honey, or given us an 14.2,3; 20.3,4
inheritance of fields and vineyards. Would you put out the eyes of these men? We **16.14** Ex 22.5
will not come!" Num 20.5
15 Moses was very angry and said to the LORD, "Pay no attention to their offer- **16.15**
ing. I have not taken one donkey from them, and I have not harmed any one of Gen 4.4 1 Sam 12.3
them." 16 And Moses said to Korah, "As for you and all your company, be present
tomorrow before the LORD, you and they and Aaron; 17 and let each one of you take
his censer, and put incense on it, and each one of you present his censer before the
LORD, two hundred fifty censers; you also, and Aaron, each his censer." 18 So each
man took his censer, and they put fire in the censers and laid incense on them, and
they stood at the entrance of the tent of meeting with Moses and Aaron. 19 Then **16.19**
Korah assembled the whole congregation against them at the entrance of the tent of Lev 9.6 Num 12.5
meeting. And the glory of the LORD appeared to the whole congregation. 14.10; 16.42 20.6
20 Then the LORD spoke to Moses and to Aaron, saying: 21 Separate yourselves **16.21**
from this congregation, so that I may consume them in a moment. 22 They fell on Ex 32.10
their faces, and said, "O God, the God of the spirits of all flesh, shall one person sin Num 14.12
and you become angry with the whole congregation?" **16.22** Gen 18.23-32

Punishment for the rebellion

23 And the LORD spoke to Moses, saying: 24 Say to the congregation: Get away **16.24**
from the dwellings of Korah, Dathan, and Abiram. 25 So Moses got up and went to Num 16.45
Dathan and Abiram; the elders of Israel followed him. 26 He said to the congrega- **16.26**
tion, "Turn away from the tents of these wicked men, and touch nothing of theirs, Gen 19.12-17 Deut 13.17
or you will be swept away for all their sins." 27 So they got away from the dwellings
of Korah, Dathan, and Abiram; and Dathan and Abiram came out and stood at the
entrance of their tents, together with their wives, their children, and their little
ones. 28 And Moses said, "This is how you shall know that the LORD has sent me to **16.28**
do all these works; it has not been of my own accord: 29 If these people die a natural Ex 3.12; 4.1-9 7.9
death, or if a natural fate comes on them, then the LORD has not sent me. 30 But if Deut 18.22
the LORD creates something new, and the ground opens its mouth and swallows
them up, with all that belongs to them, and they go down alive into Sheol, then you
shall know that these men have despised the LORD."
31 As soon as he finished speaking all these words, the ground under them was
split apart. 32 The earth opened its mouth and swallowed them up, along with their **16.32**
households—everyone who belonged to Korah and all their goods. 33 So they with Num 16.30 26.10
all that belonged to them went down alive into Sheol; the earth closed over them,
and they perished from the midst of the assembly. 34 All Israel around them fled at

---

16.13, 14 One of the easiest ways to fall away from following God is to look at our present problems and inflate their unpleasantness. Dathan and Abiram did just that when they began to long for better food and more pleasant surroundings. Egypt, the place they had longed to leave, was now looking better and better—not because of slavery and taskmasters, of course, but because of its mouth-watering food! These two men and their followers had completely lost their perspective. When we take our eyes off God and start looking at ourselves and our problems, we begin to lose our perspective as well. Overrating problems can hinder our relationship with God. Don't let difficulties make you lose sight of God's direction for your life. (Note: "put out the eyes" means "to fool" or "to pull a fast one.")

16.26 The Israelites were told not even to touch the belongings of the wicked rebels. In this case, doing so would have shown sympathy to their cause and agreement with their principles. Korah, Dathan, and Abiram were directly challenging Moses and God. Moses clearly stated what God intended to do to the rebels (16.28–30). He did this so that everyone would have to choose between following Korah or following Moses, God's chosen leader. When God asks us to make a fundamental choice between siding with wicked people or siding with him, we should not hesitate or waver, but commit ourselves to be 100 percent on the Lord's side.

16.27–35 Although the families of Dathan and Abiram were swallowed up, the sons of Korah were not wiped out (26.11).

16.33 *Sheol* is a term often applied to the grave or the world of the dead. Korah and the other rebels were buried alive when the earth split open. God executed swift and final judgment against those who had rejected him.

their outcry, for they said, "The earth will swallow us too!" 35 And fire came out
from the LORD and consumed the two hundred fifty men offering the incense.
36[e] Then the LORD spoke to Moses, saying: 37 Tell Eleazar son of Aaron the
priest to take the censers out of the blaze; then scatter the fire far and wide. 38 For
the censers of these sinners have become holy at the cost of their lives. Make them
into hammered plates as a covering for the altar, for they presented them before the
LORD and they became holy. Thus they shall be a sign to the Israelites. 39 So Eleazar
the priest took the bronze censers that had been presented by those who were
burned; and they were hammered out as a covering for the altar— 40 a reminder to
the Israelites that no outsider, who is not of the descendants of Aaron, shall approach to offer incense before the LORD, so as not to become like Korah and his
company—just as the LORD had said to him through Moses.
41 On the next day, however, the whole congregation of the Israelites rebelled
against Moses and against Aaron, saying, "You have killed the people of the
LORD." 42 And when the congregation had assembled against them, Moses and
Aaron turned toward the tent of meeting; the cloud had covered it and the glory of
the LORD appeared. 43 Then Moses and Aaron came to the front of the tent of meeting, 44 and the LORD spoke to Moses, saying, 45 "Get away from this congregation,
so that I may consume them in a moment." And they fell on their faces. 46 Moses
said to Aaron, "Take your censer, put fire on it from the altar and lay incense on it,
and carry it quickly to the congregation and make atonement for them. For wrath
has gone out from the LORD; the plague has begun." 47 So Aaron took it as Moses
had ordered, and ran into the middle of the assembly, where the plague had already
begun among the people. He put on the incense, and made atonement for the people. 48 He stood between the dead and the living; and the plague was stopped.
49 Those who died by the plague were fourteen thousand seven hundred, besides
those who died in the affair of Korah. 50 When the plague was stopped, Aaron returned to Moses at the entrance of the tent of meeting.

Aaron's budding staff proves his authority

17[f] The LORD spoke to Moses, saying: 2 Speak to the Israelites, and get twelve
staffs from them, one for each ancestral house, from all the leaders of their
ancestral houses. Write each man's name on his staff, 3 and write Aaron's name on
the staff of Levi. For there shall be one staff for the head of each ancestral house.
4 Place them in the tent of meeting before the covenant,[g] where I meet with you.
5 And the staff of the man whom I choose shall sprout; thus I will put a stop to the
complaints of the Israelites that they continually make against you. 6 Moses spoke
to the Israelites; and all their leaders gave him staffs, one for each leader, according
to their ancestral houses, twelve staffs; and the staff of Aaron was among theirs.
7 So Moses placed the staffs before the LORD in the tent of the covenant.[g]
8 When Moses went into the tent of the covenant[g] on the next day, the staff of
Aaron for the house of Levi had sprouted. It put forth buds, produced blossoms,
and bore ripe almonds. 9 Then Moses brought out all the staffs from before the
LORD to all the Israelites; and they looked, and each man took his staff. 10 And the
LORD said to Moses, "Put back the staff of Aaron before the covenant,[g] to be kept
as a warning to rebels, so that you may make an end of their complaints against me,
or else they will die." 11 Moses did so; just as the LORD commanded him, so he did.
12 The Israelites said to Moses, "We are perishing; we are lost, all of us are

16.35 Lev 10.2 Num 11.1; 16.2 26.10
16.40 Num 1.51 3.10,38
16.41 Num 16.3
16.42 Ex 24.16 40.34,35 Num 14.10 16.19
16.45 Num 16.21,24
16.46 Ex 30.7-10 Lev 10.6 Num 8.19; 18.5 25.13 Deut 9.22
16.47 Num 16.36 25.7,8,13 Deut 33.10
16.49 Num 16.32-35 25.9 1 Chron 21.14
17.4 Ex 25.16-22 Num 17.10
17.5 Num 16.5; 17.8 Heb 9.4
17.7 Num 18.2
17.8 Num 17.5 Heb 9.4
17.10 Num 17.4 Deut 9.7,24
17.12 Num 1.51-53 18.4-7; 26.11 Isa 6.5

[e] Ch 17.1 in Heb [f] Ch 17.16 in Heb [g] Or *treaty*, or *testimony*; Heb *eduth*

17.5, 10 After witnessing spectacular miracles, seeing the Egyptians punished by the plagues, and experiencing the actual presence of God, the Israelites still complained and rebelled. We wonder how they could be so blind and ignorant, and yet we often repeat this same pattern. We have centuries of evidence, the Bible in many translations, and the convincing results of archeological and historical studies. But people today continue to disobey God and go their own way. Like the Israelites, we pay more attention to our physical condition than to our spiritual condition. We can escape this pattern only by paying attention to all the signs of God's presence that we have been given. Has God guided and protected you? Has he answered your prayers? Do you know people who have experienced remarkable blessings and healings? Do you know Bible stories about the way God has led his people? Focus your thoughts on what God has done, and rebellion will become unthinkable. Concentrate on your spiritual condition.

lost! 13 Everyone who approaches the tabernacle of the LORD will die. Are we all to
perish?"

3. Directions to the priests and Levites

Division of duties

18 The LORD said to Aaron: You and your sons and your ancestral house with **18.1**
you shall bear responsibility for offenses connected with the sanctuary, Ex 28.38
while you and your sons alone shall bear responsibility for offenses connected with
the priesthood. 2 So bring with you also your brothers of the tribe of Levi, your **18.2**
ancestral tribe, in order that they may be joined to you, and serve you while you and Num 1.51 3.5-10
your sons with you are in front of the tent of the covenant.[h] 3 They shall perform 4.15-20 8.19,22; 18.7
duties for you and for the whole tent. But they must not approach either the utensils
of the sanctuary or the altar, otherwise both they and you will die. 4 They are attached to you in order to perform the duties of the tent of meeting, for all the service
of the tent; no outsider shall approach you. 5 You yourselves shall perform the du- **18.5**
ties of the sanctuary and the duties of the altar, so that wrath may never again come Num 8.19; 16.46
upon the Israelites. 6 It is I who now take your brother Levites from among the **18.6**
Israelites; they are now yours as a gift, dedicated to the LORD, to perform the ser- Num 3.9 8.16-19
vice of the tent of meeting. 7 But you and your sons with you shall diligently per- **18.7**
form your priestly duties in all that concerns the altar and the area behind the Ex 29.9 Num 1.51; 3.10
curtain. I give your priesthood as a gift;[i] any outsider who approaches shall be put
to death.

Portion of the offerings

8 The LORD spoke to Aaron: I have given you charge of the offerings made to **18.8**
me, all the holy gifts of the Israelites; I have given them to you and your sons as a Lev 7.28-34 Deut 12.6
priestly portion due you in perpetuity. 9 This shall be yours from the most holy **18.9**
things, reserved from the fire: every offering of theirs that they render to me as a Lev 2.2; 4.22 6.25-30
most holy thing, whether grain offering, sin offering, or guilt offering, shall belong 10.12,13
to you and your sons. 10 As a most holy thing you shall eat it; every male may eat
it; it shall be holy to you. 11 This also is yours: I have given to you, together with **18.11**
your sons and daughters, as a perpetual due, whatever is set aside from the gifts of Lev 22.2,3, 11-13
all the elevation offerings of the Israelites; everyone who is clean in your house
may eat them. 12 All the best of the oil and all the best of the wine and of the grain, **18.12**
the choice produce that they give to the LORD, I have given to you. 13 The first fruits Ex 22.29 Num 15.19-21
of all that is in their land, which they bring to the LORD, shall be yours; everyone Deut 18.4
who is clean in your house may eat of it. 14 Every devoted thing in Israel shall be **18.14**
yours. 15 The first issue of the womb of all creatures, human and animal, which is Lev 27.28
offered to the LORD, shall be yours; but the firstborn of human beings you shall
redeem, and the firstborn of unclean animals you shall redeem. 16 Their redemption
price, reckoned from one month of age, you shall fix at five shekels of silver, according to the shekel of the sanctuary (that is, twenty gerahs). 17 But the firstborn
of a cow, or the firstborn of a sheep, or the firstborn of a goat, you shall not redeem;
they are holy. You shall dash their blood on the altar, and shall turn their fat into
smoke as an offering by fire for a pleasing odor to the LORD; 18 but their flesh shall
be yours, just as the breast that is elevated and as the right thigh are yours. 19 All the **18.19**
holy offerings that the Israelites present to the LORD I have given to you, together 2 Chron 13.5
with your sons and daughters, as a perpetual due; it is a covenant of salt forever
before the LORD for you and your descendants as well. 20 Then the LORD said to **18.20**
Aaron: You shall have no allotment in their land, nor shall you have any share Num 18.23 Deut 10.9; 18.2
among them; I am your share and your possession among the Israelites. Josh 13.33 Ezek 44.28

21 To the Levites I have given every tithe in Israel for a possession in return for **18.21**
the service that they perform, the service in the tent of meeting. 22 From now on the Lev 27.30-33
Israelites shall no longer approach the tent of meeting, or else they will incur guilt
and die. 23 But the Levites shall perform the service of the tent of meeting, and they **18.23**
shall bear responsibility for their own offenses; it shall be a perpetual statute Num 18.1,20
throughout your generations. But among the Israelites they shall have no allotment,

[h] Or *treaty*, or *testimony*; Heb *eduth* [i] Heb *as a service of gift*

24 because I have given to the Levites as their portion the tithe of the Israelites,
which they set apart as an offering to the LORD. Therefore I have said of them that
they shall have no allotment among the Israelites.
25 Then the LORD spoke to Moses, saying: 26 You shall speak to the Levites,
saying: When you receive from the Israelites the tithe that I have given you from
them for your portion, you shall set apart an offering from it to the LORD, a tithe of
the tithe. 27 It shall be reckoned to you as your gift, the same as the grain of the
threshing floor and the fullness of the wine press. 28 Thus you also shall set apart an
offering to the LORD from all the tithes that you receive from the Israelites; and
from them you shall give the LORD's offering to the priest Aaron. 29 Out of all the
gifts to you, you shall set apart every offering due to the LORD; the best of all of
them is the part to be consecrated. 30 Say also to them: When you have set apart the
best of it, then the rest shall be reckoned to the Levites as produce of the threshing
floor, and as produce of the wine press. 31 You may eat it in any place, you and your
households; for it is your payment for your service in the tent of meeting. 32 You
shall incur no guilt by reason of it, when you have offered the best of it. But you
shall not profane the holy gifts of the Israelites, on pain of death.

Purification after defilement

19 The LORD spoke to Moses and Aaron, saying: 2 This is a statute of the law
that the LORD has commanded: Tell the Israelites to bring you a red heifer
without defect, in which there is no blemish and on which no yoke has been laid.
3 You shall give it to the priest Eleazar, and it shall be taken outside the camp and
slaughtered in his presence. 4 The priest Eleazar shall take some of its blood with
his finger and sprinkle it seven times towards the front of the tent of meeting. 5 Then
the heifer shall be burned in his sight; its skin, its flesh, and its blood, with its dung,
shall be burned. 6 The priest shall take cedarwood, hyssop, and crimson material,
and throw them into the fire in which the heifer is burning. 7 Then the priest shall
wash his clothes and bathe his body in water, and afterwards he may come into the
camp; but the priest shall remain unclean until evening. 8 The one who burns the
heifer[j] shall wash his clothes in water and bathe his body in water; he shall remain
unclean until evening. 9 Then someone who is clean shall gather up the ashes of the
heifer, and deposit them outside the camp in a clean place; and they shall be kept
for the congregation of the Israelites for the water for cleansing. It is a purification
offering. 10 The one who gathers the ashes of the heifer shall wash his clothes and
be unclean until evening.
This shall be a perpetual statute for the Israelites and for the alien residing among
them. 11 Those who touch the dead body of any human being shall be unclean seven
days. 12 They shall purify themselves with the water on the third day and on the
seventh day, and so be clean; but if they do not purify themselves on the third day
and on the seventh day, they will not become clean. 13 All who touch a corpse, the
body of a human being who has died, and do not purify themselves, defile the

j Heb *it*

18.25,26 Num 18.28 Neh 10.38
18.28 Num 18.25
18.31 Mt 10.10 Lk 10.7 1 Cor 9.13 1 Tim 5.18
18.32 Lev 22.2,15,16
19.2 Lev 10.6 22.20-25 Num 3.4 Deut 21.3
19.4 Lev 4.6,17 16.14
19.6 Lev 14.4,6,49
19.7 Lev 11.25,40 16.26-28
19.9 Num 8.7 19.13,20,21
19.10 Num 19.7,8,19
19.11 Lev 11.27,31 21.1,11
19.12 Num 19.17-19
19.13 Lev 7.20,21 15.31; 20.3 22.3-7

18.25, 26 Even the Levites, who were ministers, had to tithe to support the work of the tabernacle. No one was exempt from returning to God a portion of what was received from him. Though the Levites owned no land and operated no great enterprises, they were to treat their income the same as everyone else did by giving a portion to care for the needs of the other Levites and of the tabernacle. The tithing principle is still relevant today. God expects all his followers to supply the material needs of those who devote themselves to meeting the spiritual needs of the community of faith.

18.32 Gifts dedicated to God were to be treated with respect. Churches today also have the responsibility to manage carefully the money and time people have dedicated to God. To mishandle it is to "profane the holy gifts." If you are involved in raising or handling your church's money, insist that people show respect for gifts made to God by their careful management and responsible stewardship of his resources.

19.9, 10 What is the significance of the red heifer's ashes? When a person touched a dead body, he was considered unclean (i.e., unable to approach God in worship). This ritual purified the unclean person so that once again he could offer sacrifices and worship God. Death was the strongest of defilements because it was the final result of sin. Thus a special sacrifice—a red heifer—was required. It had to be offered by someone who was not unclean. When it had been burned on the altar, its ashes were used as a filter through which water was poured in order to be purified—not so much literally as symbolically. The unclean person then washed himself, and often his clothes and belongings, with this purified water as an act of becoming clean again.

tabernacle of the LORD; such persons shall be cut off from Israel. Since water for
cleansing was not dashed on them, they remain unclean; their uncleanness is still
on them.
14 This is the law when someone dies in a tent: everyone who comes into the
tent, and everyone who is in the tent, shall be unclean seven days. 15 And every
open vessel with no cover fastened on it is unclean. 16 Whoever in the open field
touches one who has been killed by a sword, or who has died naturally,[k] or a
human bone, or a grave, shall be unclean seven days. 17 For the unclean they shall
take some ashes of the burnt purification offering, and running water shall be added
in a vessel; 18 then a clean person shall take hyssop, dip it in the water, and sprinkle
it on the tent, on all the furnishings, on the persons who were there, and on whoever
touched the bone, the slain, the corpse, or the grave. 19 The clean person shall
sprinkle the unclean ones on the third day and on the seventh day, thus purifying
them on the seventh day. Then they shall wash their clothes and bathe themselves
in water, and at evening they shall be clean. 20 Any who are unclean but do not
purify themselves, those persons shall be cut off from the assembly, for they have
defiled the sanctuary of the LORD. Since the water for cleansing has not been
dashed on them, they are unclean.
21 It shall be a perpetual statute for them. The one who sprinkles the water for
cleansing shall wash his clothes, and whoever touches the water for cleansing shall
be unclean until evening. 22 Whatever the unclean person touches shall be unclean,
and anyone who touches it shall be unclean until evening.

19.16 Num 19.11; 31.19
19.17 Num 19.9
19.19 Num 19.9; Ps 51.7; Ezek 36.25-27
19.20 Num 15.30; 19.13
19.21 Lev 11.25,40; 16.26-28; Num 19.7
19.22 Lev 5.2,3; 7.21

4. The new generation

Moses strikes the rock and is judged

20 The Israelites, the whole congregation, came into the wilderness of Zin in
the first month, and the people stayed in Kadesh. Miriam died there, and
was buried there.
2 Now there was no water for the congregation; so they gathered together
against Moses and against Aaron. 3 The people quarreled with Moses and said,
"Would that we had died when our kindred died before the LORD! 4 Why have you
brought the assembly of the LORD into this wilderness for us and our livestock to die
here? 5 Why have you brought us up out of Egypt, to bring us to this wretched
place? It is no place for grain, or figs, or vines, or pomegranates; and there is no
water to drink." 6 Then Moses and Aaron went away from the assembly to the entrance of the tent of meeting; they fell on their faces, and the glory of the LORD
appeared to them. 7 The LORD spoke to Moses, saying: 8 Take the staff, and assemble the congregation, you and your brother Aaron, and command the rock before
their eyes to yield its water. Thus you shall bring water out of the rock for them;
thus you shall provide drink for the congregation and their livestock.
9 So Moses took the staff from before the LORD, as he had commanded him.
10 Moses and Aaron gathered the assembly together before the rock, and he said to
them, "Listen, you rebels, shall we bring water for you out of this rock?" 11 Then
Moses lifted up his hand and struck the rock twice with his staff; water came out
abundantly, and the congregation and their livestock drank. 12 But the LORD said to
Moses and Aaron, "Because you did not trust in me, to show my holiness before the
eyes of the Israelites, therefore you shall not bring this assembly into the land that

20.1 Num 13.21
20.2 Ex 17.1-4
20.3 Ex 17.2; Num 11.1, 33,34; 14.1,2,36,37; 16.31-35
20.5 Num 16.14
20.8 Ex 4.2,17; Num 21.18
20.11 Ex 17.6; Ps 78.16; Isa 48.21; 1 Cor 10.4
20.12 Lev 10.3; Num 20.24; Ezek 36.23

[k] Heb lacks *naturally*

20.1 It had been 37 years since Israel's first spy mission into the promised land (Numbers 13, 14) and 40 years since the exodus from Egypt. The Bible is virtually silent about those 37 years of aimless wandering. The generation of those who had lived in Egypt had almost died off, and the new generation would soon be ready to enter the land. Moses, Aaron, Joshua, and Caleb were among the few who remained from those who had left Egypt. Once again they camped at Kadesh, the site of the first spy mission that had ended in disaster. Now Moses hoped the people were ready for a fresh start.

20.3–5 After 37 years in the wilderness, the Israelites forgot that their wanderings were a result of their parents' and their own sin. They could not accept the fact that they brought their problems upon themselves, so they blamed Moses for their condition. Often our troubles result from our own disobedience or lack of faith. We cannot blame God for our sins. Until we face this reality, there will be little peace and no spiritual growth in our lives.

20.13 Ex 17.7 I have given them." 13 These are the waters of Meribah,[l] where the people of Israel
Deut 32.51 quarreled with the LORD, and by which he showed his holiness.

Edom refuses to let Israel pass through

20.14 Gen 36.31-39 14 Moses sent messengers from Kadesh to the king of Edom, "Thus says your
Josh 2.10 brother Israel: You know all the adversity that has befallen us: 15 how our ancestors
9.9,10 went down to Egypt, and we lived in Egypt a long time; and the Egyptians op-
20.16 Ex 3.2-6; 14.19 pressed us and our ancestors; 16 and when we cried to the LORD, he heard our voice,
23.30 and sent an angel and brought us out of Egypt; and here we are in Kadesh, a town
on the edge of your territory. 17 Now let us pass through your land. We will not pass
through field or vineyard, or drink water from any well; we will go along the King's
Highway, not turning aside to the right hand or to the left until we have passed
through your territory."

18 But Edom said to him, "You shall not pass through, or we will come out
with the sword against you." 19 The Israelites said to him, "We will stay on the
highway; and if we drink of your water, we and our livestock, then we will pay for
it. It is only a small matter; just let us pass through on foot." 20 But he said, "You
20.21 Num 20.1,14 shall not pass through." And Edom came out against them with a large force, heav-
21.4 Deut 2.8,29 ily armed. 21 Thus Edom refused to give Israel passage through their territory; so
Judg 11.17 Israel turned away from them.

Aaron dies

22 They set out from Kadesh, and the Israelites, the whole congregation, came
to Mount Hor. 23 Then the LORD said to Moses and Aaron at Mount Hor, on the
border of the land of Edom, 24 "Let Aaron be gathered to his people. For he shall not
enter the land that I have given to the Israelites, because you rebelled against my
20.25 command at the waters of Meribah. 25 Take Aaron and his son Eleazar, and bring
Num 3.4; 19.3,4 them up Mount Hor; 26 strip Aaron of his vestments, and put them on his son Elea-
20.26 Num 20.24 zar. But Aaron shall be gathered to his people,[m] and shall die there." 27 Moses did
as the LORD had commanded; they went up Mount Hor in the sight of the whole

[l] That is *Quarrel* [m] Heb lacks *to his people*

EVENTS AT KADESH
After wandering in the wilderness for 40 years, Israel arrived at Kadesh-barnea (Kadesh), where Miriam died. There was not enough water and the people complained bitterly. Moses struck a rock, and it gave enough water for everyone. The king of Edom refused Israel passage through his land, forcing them to travel around his country.

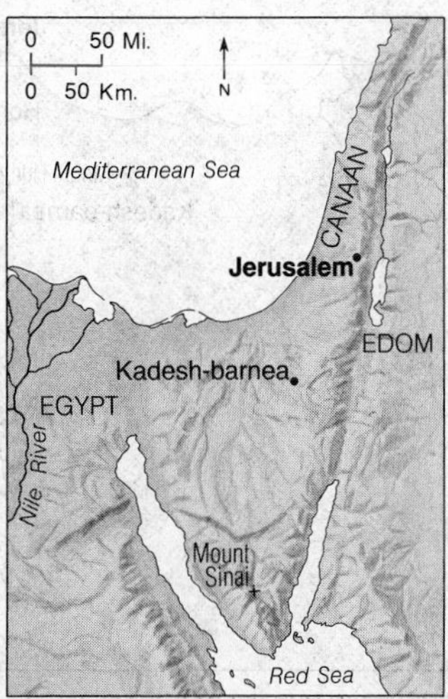

20.12 The Lord had told Moses to speak to the rock; Moses struck it, not once, but twice. For this he was forbidden to enter the promised land. Was God's punishment of Moses too harsh? After all, the people had nagged him, slandered him, and rebelled against both him and God. Now they were at it again (20.5). But Moses was the leader and model for the entire nation. Because of this great responsibility to the people, he could not be let off lightly. By striking the rock, Moses disobeyed God's direct command and dishonored God in the presence of his people.

20.14 Two brothers became the ancestors of two nations. The Edomites descended from Esau; the Israelites from Jacob. Thus the Edomites were "brothers" to the Israelites. Israel sent a brotherly message to Edom requesting passage through their land on the main road, a well-traveled trade route. Israel promised to stay on the road, thus harmlessly bypassing Edom's fields, vineyards, and wells. Edom refused, however, because they did not trust Israel's word. They were afraid that this great horde of people would either attack them or devour their crops (Deuteronomy 2.4, 5). Since brothers should not fight, God told the Israelites to turn back and travel by a different route to the promised land.

20.17 The King's Highway was an old caravan route. Long before this time it was used as a major public road.

20.21 Moses negotiated and reasoned with the Edomite king. When nothing worked, he was left with two choices – force a conflict or avoid it. Moses knew there would be enough barriers in the days and months ahead. There was no point in adding another one unnecessarily. Sometimes conflict is unavoidable. Sometimes, however, it isn't worth the consequences. Open warfare may seem heroic, courageous, and even righteous, but it is not always the best choice. We should consider Moses' example and find another way to solve our problems, even if it is harder for us to do.

congregation. 28 Moses stripped Aaron of his vestments, and put them on his son 20.28
Eleazar; and Aaron died there on the top of the mountain. Moses and Eleazar came Num 33.38
down from the mountain. 29 When all the congregation saw that Aaron had died, all
the house of Israel mourned for Aaron thirty days.

Israel defeats the king of Arad

21 When the Canaanite, the king of Arad, who lived in the Negeb, heard that 21.1
Israel was coming by the way of Atharim, he fought against Israel and took Num 33.40
some of them captive. 2 Then Israel made a vow to the LORD and said, "If you will Josh 12.14
indeed give this people into our hands, then we will utterly destroy their towns." Judg 1.16
3 The LORD listened to the voice of Israel, and handed over the Canaanites; and they 21.3 Num 14.45
utterly destroyed them and their towns; so the place was called Hormah.[n] 1 Sam 30.30

The bronze serpent

4 From Mount Hor they set out by the way to the Red Sea,[o] to go around the 21.4
land of Edom; but the people became impatient on the way. 5 The people spoke Deut 2.8
against God and against Moses, "Why have you brought us up out of Egypt to die 21.5 Ex 16.15
in the wilderness? For there is no food and no water, and we detest this miserable Num 11.1-9
food." 6 Then the LORD sent poisonous[p] serpents among the people, and they bit 14.1-4; 16.13
the people, so that many Israelites died. 7 The people came to Moses and said, "We 21.6 Deut 8.15
have sinned by speaking against the LORD and against you; pray to the LORD to take
away the serpents from us." So Moses prayed for the people. 8 And the LORD said 21.8
to Moses, "Make a poisonous[q] serpent, and set it on a pole; and everyone who is Isa 14.29 Jn 3.14,15
bitten shall look at it and live." 9 So Moses made a serpent of bronze, and put it 21.9
upon a pole; and whenever a serpent bit someone, that person would look at the 2 Kgs 18.4
serpent of bronze and live. Jn 3.14; 12.32

[n] Heb *Destruction* [o] Or *Sea of Reeds* [p] Or *fiery*; Heb *seraphim* [q] Or *fiery*; Heb *seraph*

20.28 Aaron died just before entering the promised land, probably as punishment for his sin of rebellion (Exodus 32; Numbers 12.1–9). This was the first time that a new high priest was appointed. The priestly clothing was removed from Aaron and placed on his son Eleazar, following the commands recorded in the book of Leviticus.

21.5 In Psalm 78, we learn the sources of Israel's complaining: (1) their spirit was not faithful to God; (2) they refused to obey God's law; (3) they forgot the miracles God had done for them. Our complaining often has its roots in one of these thoughtless actions and attitudes. If we can deal with the cause of our complaining, it will not take hold and grow in our lives.

21.6 God used poisonous serpents to punish the people for their unbelief and complaining. The Sinai desert has a variety of snakes. Some hide in the sand and attack without warning. Both the Israelites and the Egyptians had a great fear of snakes. A bite by a poisonous snake often meant a slow death with intense suffering.

21.8, 9 When the bronze snake was hung on the pole, the Israelites didn't know the fuller meaning Jesus Christ would bring to this event (see John 3.14, 15). Jesus explained that just as the Israelites were healed of their sickness by looking at the serpent on the pole, all believers today can be saved from the sickness of sin by looking to Jesus' death on the cross. It was not the snake that healed the people, but their belief that God could heal them. This belief was demonstrated by their obedience to God's instructions. In the same way, we should continue to look to Christ (see Hebrews 12.2).

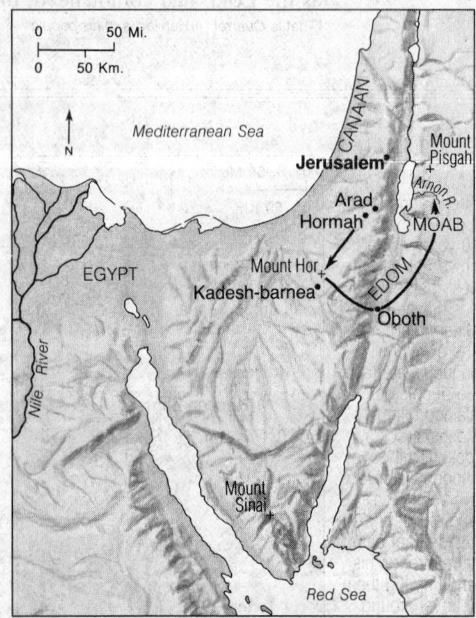

EVENTS IN THE WILDERNESS Israel next met resistance from the king of Arad, but soundly defeated him. The next stop was Mount Hor (where Aaron had died); then they traveled south and east around Edom. After camping at Oboth, they moved toward the Arnon River and onto the plains of Moab near Mount Pisgah.

10 The Israelites set out, and camped in Oboth. 11 They set out from Oboth, and
camped at Iye-abarim, in the wilderness bordering Moab toward the sunrise.
12 From there they set out, and camped in the Wadi Zered. 13 From there they set
out, and camped on the other side of the Arnon, in[r] the wilderness that extends
from the boundary of the Amorites; for the Arnon is the boundary of Moab, between Moab and the Amorites. 14 Wherefore it is said in the Book of the Wars of the
LORD,

"Waheb in Suphah and the wadis.

21.15 Num 21.28 Deut 2.9

The Arnon 15 and the slopes of the wadis
that extend to the seat of Ar,
and lie along the border of Moab."[s]

21.16 Judg 9.21 Jn 4.14

16 From there they continued to Beer;[t] that is the well of which the LORD said
to Moses, "Gather the people together, and I will give them water." 17 Then Israel
sang this song:

"Spring up, O well! — Sing to it! —
18 the well that the leaders sank,
that the nobles of the people dug,
with the scepter, with the staff."

From the wilderness to Mattanah, 19 from Mattanah to Nahaliel, from Nahaliel to
Bamoth, 20 and from Bamoth to the valley lying in the region of Moab by the top of
Pisgah that overlooks the wasteland.[u]

Israel defeats King Sihon

21.21 Deut 2.26-28 Judg 11.19-21

21 Then Israel sent messengers to King Sihon of the Amorites, saying, 22 "Let
me pass through your land; we will not turn aside into field or vineyard; we will not

[r] Gk: Heb *which is in* [s] Meaning of Heb uncertain [t] That is *Well* [u] Or *Jeshimon*

ELEAZAR

An understudy must know the lead role completely and be willing to step into it at a moment's notice. Eleazar was an excellent understudy, well trained for his eventual leading role. However, his moments in the spotlight were painful. On one occasion, he watched his two older brothers burn to death for failing to take God's holiness seriously. Later, as his father was dying, he was made high priest, surely one of the most responsible—and therefore potentially most stressful—positions in Israel.

An understudy benefits from having both the script and a human model of the role. Ever since childhood, Eleazar had been able to observe Moses and Aaron. Now he could learn from watching Joshua. In addition, he had God's laws to guide him as he worked as priest and adviser to Joshua.

Strengths and accomplishments:
- Succeeded his father, Aaron, as high priest
- Completed his father's work by helping lead the people into the promised land
- Teamed up with Joshua
- Acted as God's spokesman to the people

Lessons from his life:
- Concentrating on our present challenges and responsibilities is the best way to prepare for what God has planned for our future
- God's desire is consistent obedience throughout our lives

Vital statistics:
- Where: Sinai wilderness, promised land
- Occupation: Priest and high priest
- Relatives: Father: Aaron. Brothers: Nadab and Abihu. Aunt and uncle: Miriam and Moses. Contemporaries: Joshua, Caleb

Key verses:
"Then the Lord said to Moses and Aaron at Mount Hor, on the border of the land of Edom, 'Let Aaron be gathered to his people. For he shall not enter the land. . . . Take Aaron of his vestments, and put them on his son Eleazar' " (Numbers 20.23–26).

Eleazar is mentioned in Exodus 6.23; Leviticus 10.16–20; Numbers 3.1–4; 4.16; 16.36–40; 20.25–29; 26.1–3, 63; 27.2, 15–23; 32.2; 34.17; Deuteronomy 10.6; Joshua 14.1; 17.4; 24.33.

21.12 A "wadi" is a stream, streambed, or valley. A wadi may or may not have water in it.

21.14 There is no existing record of the Book of the Wars of the Lord. Most likely, it was a collection of victory songs or poems.

drink the water of any well; we will go by the King's Highway until we have passed
through your territory." 23 But Sihon would not allow Israel to pass through his 21.23 Num 20.21 Deut 2.32 Judg 11.20
territory. Sihon gathered all his people together, and went out against Israel to the
wilderness; he came to Jahaz, and fought against Israel. 24 Israel put him to the
sword, and took possession of his land from the Arnon to the Jabbok, as far as to 21.24 Deut 2.19,31-37 Josh 12.1-3 13.8-10
the Ammonites; for the boundary of the Ammonites was strong. 25 Israel took all
these towns, and Israel settled in all the towns of the Amorites, in Heshbon, and in
all its villages. 26 For Heshbon was the city of King Sihon of the Amorites, who had 21.25,26 Neh 9.22 Ps 135.9,10 136.19 Amos 2.9
fought against the former king of Moab and captured all his land as far as the Ar-
non. 27 Therefore the ballad singers say,

"Come to Heshbon, let it be built; 21.27 Num 21.15 Deut 2.9,18 Judg 11.24 1 Kgs 11.33 Jer 48.45,46
let the city of Sihon be established.
28 For fire came out from Heshbon,
flame from the city of Sihon.
It devoured Ar of Moab,
and swallowed up[v] the heights of the Arnon.
29 Woe to you, O Moab!
You are undone, O people of Chemosh!
He has made his sons fugitives,
and his daughters captives,
to an Amorite king, Sihon.
30 So their posterity perished
from Heshbon[w] to Dibon,
and we laid waste until fire spread to Medeba."[x]

31 Thus Israel settled in the land of the Amorites. 32 Moses sent to spy out Jazer; 21.31 Num 32.1,35 Isa 16.8,9 Jer 48.32
and they captured its villages, and dispossessed the Amorites who were there.

Israel defeats King Og

33 Then they turned and went up the road to Bashan; and King Og of Bashan 21.33 Deut 32.14
came out against them, he and all his people, to battle at Edrei. 34 But the LORD said
to Moses, "Do not be afraid of him; for I have given him into your hand, with all
his people, and all his land. You shall do to him as you did to King Sihon of the
Amorites, who ruled in Heshbon." 35 So they killed him, his sons, and all his people, until there was no survivor left; and they took possession of his land.

[v] Gk: Heb *and the lords of* [w] Gk: Heb *we have shot at them; Heshbon has perished* [x] Compare Sam Gk: Meaning of MT uncertain

---

21.23 How could this horde of wilderness wanderers sucessfully fight against Sihon's well-organized army? (1) The Israelites had already engaged in several military encounters (Exodus 17.8; Numbers 21.1); (2) Moses was well trained in warfare from his days as an Egyptian prince; (3) the people were prepared for war (Numbers 1). God had given the promised land to Israel. Any country who got in their way would be destroyed, for God, who is mightier than any army, was with his people. Sihon was outmatched without knowing it.

21.27–30 Chemosh, the national god of Moab and Ammon, was worshiped as a god of war. This false god, however, was no help to these nations when they fought against Israel. Israel's God was stronger than any of Canaan's war gods.

21.34 God assured Moses that Israel's enemy was conquered even before the battle began! God wants to give us victory over our enemies (which are usually problems related to sin rather than armed soldiers). But first we must believe that he can help us. Second, we must trust him to help us. Third, we must take the steps he shows us.

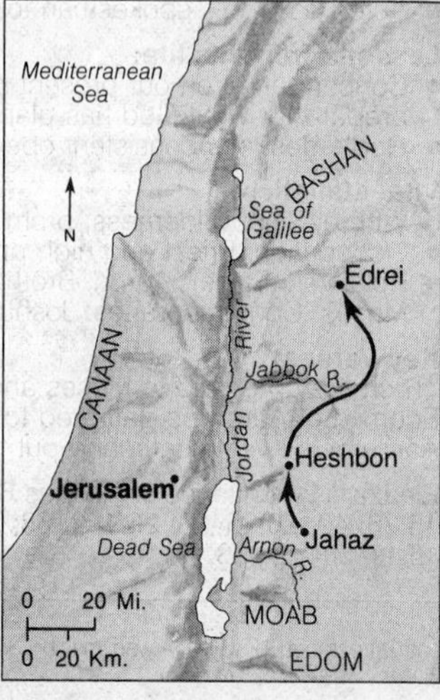

BATTLES WITH SIHON AND OG
King Sihon refused passage to the Israelites through his land, and he attacked Israel at Jahaz. Israel defeated him, occupying the land between the Arnon and Jabbok rivers, including the capital city, Heshbon. As they moved north, they defeated King Og of Bashan at Edrei.

D. SECOND APPROACH TO THE PROMISED LAND (22.1–36.13)

Now the old generation has died and a new generation stands poised at the border, ready to enter the promised land. Neighboring nations, however, cause Israel to begin worshiping other gods. Without Moses' quick action, the nation may never have entered Canaan. We must never let down our guard in resisting sin.

1. The story of Balaam

Balaam asked to curse Israel

22.1 Num 33.48,49 **22** The Israelites set out, and camped in the plains of Moab across the Jordan
from Jericho. 2 Now Balak son of Zippor saw all that Israel had done to the
22.2 Ex 15.15 Deut 2.25 Amorites. 3 Moab was in great dread of the people, because they were so numerous;
Moab was overcome with fear of the people of Israel. 4 And Moab said to the elders
22.4 Num 22.7 25.15-18 of Midian, "This horde will now lick up all that is around us, as an ox licks up the
grass of the field." Now Balak son of Zippor was king of Moab at that time. 5 He
22.5 Num 22.17 23.7,8; 24.9 Deut 23.4 sent messengers to Balaam son of Beor at Pethor, which is on the Euphrates, in the
land of Amaw,[y] to summon him, saying, "A people has come out of Egypt; they
have spread over the face of the earth, and they have settled next to me. 6 Come
now, curse this people for me, since they are stronger than I; perhaps I shall be able
to defeat them and drive them from the land; for I know that whomever you bless
is blessed, and whomever you curse is cursed."
22.7 1 Sam 9.7,8 Isa 56.11 7 So the elders of Moab and the elders of Midian departed with the fees for
divination in their hand; and they came to Balaam, and gave him Balak's message.
8 He said to them, "Stay here tonight, and I will bring back word to you, just as the
LORD speaks to me"; so the officials of Moab stayed with Balaam. 9 God came to
Balaam and said, "Who are these men with you?" 10 Balaam said to God, "King
Balak son of Zippor of Moab, has sent me this message: 11 'A people has come out
of Egypt and has spread over the face of the earth; now come, curse them for me;
22.12 Num 23.13-15 perhaps I shall be able to fight against them and drive them out.' " 12 God said to

[y] *Or land of his kinsfolk*

THE SERPENT IN THE WILDERNESS Compare the texts for yourself: Numbers 21.7–9 and John 3.14, 15.

Israelites	*Christians*
Bitten by snakes	Bitten by sin
Little initial pain, then intense suffering	Little initial pain, then intense suffering
Physical death from snakes' poison	Spiritual death from sin's poison
Bronze snake lifted up in the wilderness	Christ lifted up on the cross
Looking to the snake spared one's life	Looking to Christ saves from eternal death

---

THE STORY OF BALAAM At King Balak's request Balaam traveled nearly 400 miles to curse Israel. Balak took Balaam to Bamoth-baal ("the high places of Baal"), then to Mount Pisgah, and finally to Mount Peor. Each place looked over the plains of Moab where the Israelites were camped. But to the king's dismay, Balaam blessed, not cursed, Israel.

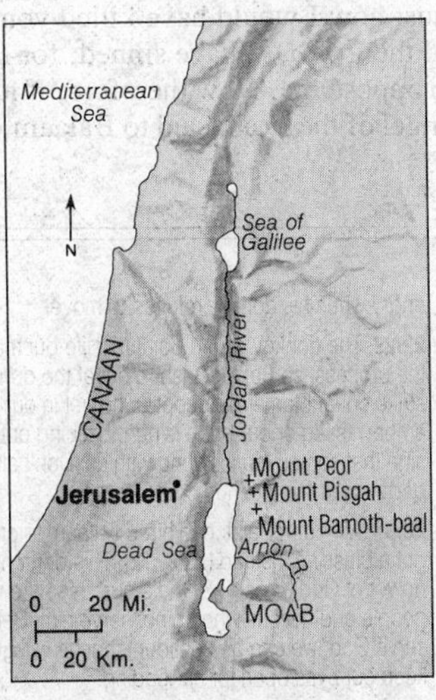

22.4–6 Balaam was a sorcerer, one called upon to place curses on others. Belief in curses and blessings was common in Old Testament times. Sorcerers were thought to have power with the gods. Thus the king of Moab wanted Balaam to use his powers with the God of Israel to place a curse on Israel—hoping that, by magic, God would turn against his people. He thought he could buy a curse with the "fees for divination" (22.7). Neither Balaam nor Balak had any idea whom they were dealing with!

22.9 Why would God speak through a sorcerer like Balaam? God wanted to give a message to the Moabites, and they had already chosen to employ Balaam. So Balaam was available for God to use, much as he used the wicked pharaoh to accomplish his will in Egypt (Exodus 10.1). Balaam entered into his prophetic role seriously, but his heart was mixed. He had some knowledge of God, but not enough to forsake his magic and turn wholeheartedly to God. Although this story leads us to believe he turned completely to God, later passages in the Bible show that Balaam couldn't resist the tempting pull of money and idolatry (31.16; 2 Peter 2.15; Jude 1.11).

Balaam, "You shall not go with them; you shall not curse the people, for they are
blessed." [13]So Balaam rose in the morning, and said to the officials of Balak, "Go
to your own land, for the LORD has refused to let me go with you." [14]So the officials of Moab rose and went to Balak, and said, "Balaam refuses to come with us."
15 Once again Balak sent officials, more numerous and more distinguished
than these. [16]They came to Balaam and said to him, "Thus says Balak son of Zip- **22.16**
por: 'Do not let anything hinder you from coming to me; [17]for I will surely do you Num 22.6
great honor, and whatever you say to me I will do; come, curse this people for
me.'" [18]But Balaam replied to the servants of Balak, "Although Balak were to **22.18**
give me his house full of silver and gold, I could not go beyond the command of the Num 23.26 24.13
LORD my God, to do less or more. [19]You remain here, as the others did, so that I
may learn what more the LORD may say to me." [20]That night God came to Balaam **22.20**
and said to him, "If the men have come to summon you, get up and go with them; Num 22.35 23.12,26
but do only what I tell you to do." [21]So Balaam got up in the morning, saddled his **22.21**
donkey, and went with the officials of Moab. 2 Pet 2.15

Balaam's donkey speaks

22 God's anger was kindled because he was going, and the angel of the LORD
took his stand in the road as his adversary. Now he was riding on the donkey, and
his two servants were with him. [23]The donkey saw the angel of the LORD standing
in the road, with a drawn sword in his hand; so the donkey turned off the road, and
went into the field; and Balaam struck the donkey, to turn it back onto the road.
[24]Then the angel of the LORD stood in a narrow path between the vineyards, with
a wall on either side. [25]When the donkey saw the angel of the LORD, it scraped
against the wall, and scraped Balaam's foot against the wall; so he struck it again.
[26]Then the angel of the LORD went ahead, and stood in a narrow place, where there
was no way to turn either to the right or to the left. [27]When the donkey saw the
angel of the LORD, it lay down under Balaam; and Balaam's anger was kindled, and
he struck the donkey with his staff. [28]Then the LORD opened the mouth of the don- **22.28**
key, and it said to Balaam, "What have I done to you, that you have struck me these 2 Pet 2.16
three times?" [29]Balaam said to the donkey, "Because you have made a fool of me!
I wish I had a sword in my hand! I would kill you right now!" [30]But the donkey said
to Balaam, "Am I not your donkey, which you have ridden all your life to this day?
Have I been in the habit of treating you this way?" And he said, "No."
31 Then the LORD opened the eyes of Balaam, and he saw the angel of the LORD **22.31**
standing in the road, with his drawn sword in his hand; and he bowed down, falling Num 24.4
on his face. [32]The angel of the LORD said to him, "Why have you struck your Josh 5.13-15
donkey these three times? I have come out as an adversary, because your way is
perverse[z] before me. [33]The donkey saw me, and turned away from me these three
times. If it had not turned away from me, surely just now I would have killed you
and let it live." [34]Then Balaam said to the angel of the LORD, "I have sinned, for I **22.34** Ex 9.27
did not know that you were standing in the road to oppose me. Now therefore, if it 1 Sam 15.24
is displeasing to you, I will return home." [35]The angel of the LORD said to Balaam, **22.35** Num 22.20,21

[z] Meaning of Heb uncertain

22.20–23 God let Balaam go with Balak's messengers, but he was angry about Balaam's greedy attitude. Balaam claimed that he would not go against God just for money, but his resolve was beginning to slip. His greed for the wealth offered by the king blinded him so that he could not see how God was trying to stop him. Though we may know what God wants us to do, we can become blinded by the desire for money, possessions, or prestige. We can avoid Balaam's mistake by looking past the allure of fame or fortune to the long-range benefits of following God.

22.27 Donkeys were all-purpose vehicles used for transportation, carrying loads, grinding grain, and plowing fields. They were usually highly dependable, which explains why Balaam became so angry when his donkey refused to move.

22.29 The donkey saved Balaam's life but made him look foolish in the process, so Balaam lashed out at the donkey. We sometimes strike out at blameless people who get in our way because we are embarrassed or our pride is hurt. Lashing out at others can be a sign that something is wrong with us. Don't allow your own hurt pride to lead you to hurt others.

22.31 Although Balak had hired Balaam to curse the Israelites, he got a blessing instead (22.6, 12). This demonstrates the hidden power of God in history. God's purposes are worked out even by people and nations who do not serve him. Because we love and serve God, we can be confident that he will guide our paths. Let us keep our eyes open for his leading.

"Go with the men; but speak only what I tell you to speak." So Balaam went on
with the officials of Balak.

Balaam's first blessing

36 When Balak heard that Balaam had come, he went out to meet him at Ir-
moab, on the boundary formed by the Arnon, at the farthest point of the boundary.
22.37,38 Num 22.18 37 Balak said to Balaam, "Did I not send to summon you? Why did you not come to
me? Am I not able to honor you?" 38 Balaam said to Balak, "I have come to you
now, but do I have power to say just anything? The word God puts in my mouth,
that is what I must say." 39 Then Balaam went with Balak, and they came to Kiriath-
huzoth. 40 Balak sacrificed oxen and sheep, and sent them to Balaam and to the
officials who were with him.
22.41 Num 21.19,20 23.13 41 On the next day Balak took Balaam and brought him up to Bamoth-baal; and
23 from there he could see part of the people of Israel.[a] 1 Then Balaam said to
Balak, "Build me seven altars here, and prepare seven bulls and seven rams
for me." 2 Balak did as Balaam had said; and Balak and Balaam offered a bull and
a ram on each altar. 3 Then Balaam said to Balak, "Stay here beside your burnt

[a] Heb lacks *of Israel*

BALAAM

Balaam was one of those noteworthy Old Testament characters who, though not one of God's chosen people, was willing to acknowledge that Jehovah was indeed a powerful God. But he did not believe in Jehovah as the only true God. His story exposes the deception of maintaining an outward facade of spirituality over a corrupt inward life. Balaam was a man ready to obey God's command as long as he could profit from doing so. This mixture of motives—obedience and profit—eventually led to Balaam's death. Although he realized the awesome power of Israel's God, his heart was occupied with the wealth he could gain in Moab. There he returned to die when the armies of Israel invaded.

Eventually, each of us lives through the same process. Who and what we are will somehow come to the surface, destroying any masks we may have put on to cover up our real selves. Efforts spent on keeping up appearances would be much better spent on finding the answer to sin in our lives. We can avoid Balaam's mistake by facing ourselves and realizing that God is willing to accept us, forgive us, and literally make us over from within. Don't miss this great discovery that eluded Balaam.

Strengths and accomplishments:
- Widely known for his effective curses and blessings
- Obeyed God and blessed Israel, in spite of Balak's bribe

Weaknesses and mistakes:
- Encouraged the Israelites to worship idols (Numbers 31.16)
- Returned to Moab and was killed in war

Lessons from his life:
- Motives are just as important as actions
- Your treasure is where your heart is

Vital statistics:
- Where: Lived near the Euphrates River, traveled to Moab
- Occupation: Prophet
- Relatives: Father: Bosor
- Contemp[illegible]ries: Balak (king of Mo[illegible]b), Moses, Aaron

Key [illegible]

[illegible] one astray, following the road of Balaam
[illegible] ong, but was rebuked for his own
[illegible] a human voice and restrained the

[illegible] lso mentioned in Numbers
[illegible] 13.2; Micah 6.5; 2 Peter

22.40 Balak held a large fe[illegible] e point they could see the entire
practice to have a sacrificia[illegible]
(see 1 Samuel 9.12–14). [illegible] among many of the nations

22.41 Bamoth-baal means the [illegible] eans a place at a higher
and Dibon. It was the first stopp[illegible]

offerings while I go aside. Perhaps the LORD will come to meet me. Whatever he
shows me I will tell you." And he went to a bare height.
4 Then God met Balaam; and Balaam said to him, "I have arranged the seven
altars, and have offered a bull and a ram on each altar." 5 The LORD put a word in
Balaam's mouth, and said, "Return to Balak, and this is what you must say." 6 So
he returned to Balak,[b] who was standing beside his burnt offerings with all the
officials of Moab. 7 Then Balaam[c] uttered his oracle, saying:

"Balak has brought me from Aram,
the king of Moab from the eastern mountains:
'Come, curse Jacob for me;
Come, denounce Israel!'
8 How can I curse whom God has not cursed?
How can I denounce those whom the LORD has not denounced?
9 For from the top of the crags I see him,
from the hills I behold him;
Here is a people living alone,
and not reckoning itself among the nations!
10 Who can count the dust of Jacob,
or number the dust-cloud[d] of Israel?
Let me die the death of the upright,
and let my end be like his!"

23.5 Num 22.20,35 23.16

23.7-10 Gen 10.22 13.16; 22.17 28.14 Ex 19.5,6 33.16 Num 22.5,6,11, 12,17 Deut 33.28 Ps 37.37 Isa 57.1,2

11 Then Balak said to Balaam, "What have you done to me? I brought you to
curse my enemies, but now you have done nothing but bless them." 12 He answered, "Must I not take care to say what the LORD puts into my mouth?"

23.12 Num 22.38 23.20,26

Balaam's second blessing

13 So Balak said to him, "Come with me to another place from which you may
see them; you shall see only part of them, and shall not see them all; then curse
them for me from there." 14 So he took him to the field of Zophim, to the top of
Pisgah. He built seven altars, and offered a bull and a ram on each altar. 15 Balaam
said to Balak, "Stand here beside your burnt offerings, while I meet the LORD over
there. 16 The LORD met Balaam, put a word into his mouth, and said, "Return to
Balak, and this is what you shall say." 17 When he came to him, he was standing
beside his burnt offerings with the officials of Moab. Balak said to him, "What has
the LORD said?" 18 Then Balaam uttered his oracle, saying:

23.16 Num 22.35

"Rise, Balak, and hear;
listen to me, O son of Zippor:
19 God is not a human being, that he should lie,
or a mortal, that he should change his mind.
Has he promised, and will he not do it?
Has he spoken, and will he not fulfill it?
20 See, I received a command to bless;
he has blessed, and I cannot revoke it.
21 He has not beheld misfortune in Jacob;
nor has he seen trouble in Israel.
The LORD their God is with them,
acclaimed as a king among them.
22 God, who brings them out of Egypt,
is like the horns of a wild ox for them.
23 Surely there is no enchantment against Jacob,
no divination against Israel;
now it shall be said of Jacob and Israel,
'See what God has done!'
24 Look, a people rising up like a lioness,
and rousing itself like a lion!
It does not lie down until it has eaten the prey
and drunk the blood of the slain."

23.18-24 Ex 3.12; 20.1,2 Num 22.18,38 Deut 31.23 1 Sam 15.29 Isa 40.8; 43.13 55.11

[b] Heb *him* [c] Heb *he* [d] Or *fourth part*

23.25,26
Num 22.18,38

25 Then Balak said to Balaam, "Do not curse them at all, and do not bless them
at all." 26 But Balaam answered Balak, "Did I not tell you, 'Whatever the LORD
says, that is what I must do'?"

Balaam's third blessing

27 So Balak said to Balaam, "Come now, I will take you to another place; perhaps it will please God that you may curse them for me from there." 28 So Balak
took Balaam to the top of Peor, which overlooks the wasteland.[e] 29 Balaam said to
Balak, "Build me seven altars here, and prepare seven bulls and seven rams for
me." 30 So Balak did as Balaam had said, and offered a bull and a ram on each altar.

23.28
Num 31.16
Josh 22.17,18

24.1
Num 23.3,15

24 Now Balaam saw that it pleased the LORD to bless Israel, so he did not go,
as at other times, to look for omens, but set his face toward the wilderness.
2 Balaam looked up and saw Israel camping tribe by tribe. Then the spirit of God
came upon him, 3 and he uttered his oracle, saying:

24.2
Num 11.25-29
1 Sam 10.10
2 Chron 15.1

24.3-9
Gen 12.3
15.1,2; 27.29
Ex 20.1,2
Num 12.6; 14.9
23.7-10,18-24
24.15-24
Deut 7.1
1 Sam 15.8
Ps 45.8
145.11-13
Dan 8.26,27

"The oracle of Balaam son of Beor,
the oracle of the man whose eye is clear,[f]
4 the oracle of one who hears the words of God,
who sees the vision of the Almighty,[g]
who falls down, but with eyes uncovered:
5 how fair are your tents, O Jacob,
your encampments, O Israel!
6 Like palm-groves that stretch far away,
like gardens beside a river,
like aloes that the LORD has planted,
like cedar trees beside the waters.
7 Water shall flow from his buckets,
and his seed shall have abundant water,
his king shall be higher than Agag,
and his kingdom shall be exalted.
8 God who brings him out of Egypt,
is like the horns of a wild ox for him;
he shall devour the nations that are his foes
and break their bones.
He shall strike with his arrows.[h]
9 He crouched, he lay down like a lion,
and like a lioness; who will rouse him up?
Blessed is everyone who blesses you,
and cursed is everyone who curses you."

10 Then Balak's anger was kindled against Balaam, and he struck his hands
together. Balak said to Balaam, "I summoned you to curse my enemies, but instead
you have blessed them these three times. 11 Now be off with you! Go home! I said,
'I will reward you richly,' but the LORD has denied you any reward." 12 And Balaam said to Balak, "Did I not tell your messengers whom you sent to me, 13 'If
Balak should give me his house full of silver and gold, I would not be able to go
beyond the word of the LORD, to do either good or bad of my own will; what the

24.13
Num 22.18,20

[e] Or *overlooks Jeshimon* [f] Or *closed* or *open* [g] Traditional rendering of Heb *Shaddai* [h] Meaning of Heb uncertain

23.27 Balak took Balaam to several places to try to entice him to curse the Israelites. He thought a change of scenery might help change Balaam's mind. But changing locations won't change God's will. We must learn to face the source of our problems. Moving to escape problems only makes solving them more difficult. Problems rooted in us are not solved by a change of scenery. A change in location or job may only distract us from the need for us to change our hearts.

24.1 Because Balaam was a sorcerer, he would look for omens or signs to help him tell the future. In this situation, however, it was clear that God himself was speaking, and so Balaam needed no other signs, real or imagined.

24.7 Who was Agag? "Agag" was the title for the king of the Amalekites, just as "Pharaoh" was the ruler of Egypt. Saul, the first king of Israel, defeated Agag (1 Samuel 15.8). Balaam prophesied correctly the ruin of Israel's oldest enemy (Exodus 17.14–16).

24.11 Although Balaam's motives were not correct, in blessing Israel he acted with integrity. God's message had so filled him that Balaam spoke the truth. In so doing, he forfeited the promotion that had lured him to speak in the first place. Staying true to God's word may cost us promotions and advantages in the short run, but those who choose God over money will one day acquire heavenly wealth beyond measure (Matthew 6.19–21).

LORD says, that is what I will say'? 14 So now, I am going to my people; let me
advise you what this people will do to your people in days to come."

Balaam's fourth blessing

15 So he uttered his oracle, saying: **24.15** Gen 49.10 Num 21.29 Isa 15.1–16.4 Amos 9.11,12 Mt 2.2 Rev 22.16
"The oracle of Balaam son of Beor,
the oracle of the man whose eye is clear,[i]
16 the oracle of one who hears the words of God,
and knows the knowledge of the Most High,[j]
who sees the vision of the Almighty,[k]
who falls down, but with his eyes uncovered:
17 I see him, but not now;
I behold him, but not near—
a star shall come out of Jacob,
and a scepter shall rise out of Israel;
it shall crush the borderlands[l] of Moab,
and the territory[m] of all the Shethites.
18 Edom will become a possession,
Seir a possession of its enemies,[n]
while Israel does valiantly.
19 One out of Jacob shall rule,
and destroy the survivors of Ir."
20 Then he looked on Amalek, and uttered his oracle, saying: **24.20** Ex 17.14
"First among the nations was Amalek,
but its end is to perish forever."
21 Then he looked on the Kenite, and uttered his oracle, saying: **24.21** Gen 15.19 Judg 1.16 Ezra 4.2
"Enduring is your dwelling place,
and your nest is set in the rock;
22 yet Kain is destined for burning.
How long shall Asshur take you away captive?"
23 Again he uttered his oracle, saying: **24.23** Gen 10.4,21-25 Dan 9.26,27
"Alas, who shall live when God does this?
24 But ships shall come from Kittim
and shall afflict Asshur and Eber;
and he also shall perish forever."
25 Then Balaam got up and went back to his place, and Balak also went his
way.

The Israelites worship Baal

25 While Israel was staying at Shittim, the people began to have sexual rela- **25.1** Josh 2.1
tions with the women of Moab. 2 These invited the people to the sacrifices of **25.2** Ex 34.15,16
their gods, and the people ate and bowed down to their gods. 3 Thus Israel yoked

[i] Or *closed* or *open* [j] Or *of Elyon* [k] Traditional rendering of Heb *Shaddai* [l] Or *forehead* [m] Some Mss read *skull*
[n] Heb *Seir, its enemies, a possession*

24.15–19 The "star . . . out of Jacob" is often thought to refer to the coming Messiah. It was probably this prophecy that convinced the wise men to travel to Israel to search for the baby Jesus (see Matthew 2.1, 2). It seems strange that God would use a sorcerer like Balaam to foretell the coming of the Messiah. But this teaches us that God can use anything or anyone to accomplish his plans. By using a sorcerer, God did not make sorcery acceptable; in fact, the Bible condemns it in several places (Exodus 22.18; 2 Chronicles 33.6; Revelation 18.23). Rather, God showed his ultimate sovereignty over good and evil.

25.1 This verse shows the great challenge Israel had to face. The most dangerous problem for Moses and Joshua was not Jericho's hostile army, but the ever-present temptation to compromise with the heathen Canaanite religions and cultures.

25.1, 2 At first the Israelite men were interested in sex, not idol worship. Soon, however, in addition to visiting Moabite prostitutes they were also participating in heathen feasts. Scripture frequently links adultery and idolatry because one sin so often leads to the other.

25.1–3 This combination of sexual sin and idolatry, it turns out, was Balaam's idea (see 31.16; Revelation 2.14), the same Balaam who had just blessed Israel and who appeared to be on their side. It is easy to see how the Israelites were misled, for Balaam seemed to say and do all the right things—at least for a while (22–24). Not until Balaam had inflicted great damage on them did the Israelites realize that he was greedy, that he used sorcery, and that he was deeply involved in heathen religious practices. We must be careful to weigh both the words and the deeds of those who claim to offer spiritual help.

25.3 Baal was the most popular god in Canaan, the land Israel

25.3 Num 25.5 Deut 4.3,4 itself to the Baal of Peor, and the LORD's anger was kindled against Israel. 4The
LORD said to Moses, "Take all the chiefs of the people, and impale them in the sun
before the LORD, in order that the fierce anger of the LORD may turn away from
Israel." 5And Moses said to the judges of Israel, "Each of you shall kill any of your
people who have yoked themselves to the Baal of Peor."

25.6 Num 22.4 31.2,9-16 6 Just then one of the Israelites came and brought a Midianite woman into his
family, in the sight of Moses and in the sight of the whole congregation of the
25.7 Ex 6.25 Josh 22.30,31 Israelites, while they were weeping at the entrance of the tent of meeting. 7When
Phinehas son of Eleazar, son of Aaron the priest, saw it, he got up and left the
congregation. Taking a spear in his hand, 8he went after the Israelite man into the
tent, and pierced the two of them, the Israelite and the woman, through the belly.
25.9 1 Cor 10.8 So the plague was stopped among the people of Israel. 9Nevertheless those that
died by the plague were twenty-four thousand.

10 The LORD spoke to Moses, saying: 11"Phinehas son of Eleazar, son of Aaron
the priest, has turned back my wrath from the Israelites by manifesting such zeal
among them on my behalf that in my jealousy I did not consume the Israelites.
25.12 Ex 29.9; 32.30 40.15 Num 16.46 Isa 54.10 Ezek 37.26 12Therefore say, 'I hereby grant him my covenant of peace. 13It shall be for him
and for his descendants after him a covenant of perpetual priesthood, because he
was zealous for his God, and made atonement for the Israelites.' "

14 The name of the slain Israelite man, who was killed with the Midianite
woman, was Zimri son of Salu, head of an ancestral house belonging to the Sime-
25.15 Num 25.18; 31.8 Josh 13.21 onites. 15The name of the Midianite woman who was killed was Cozbi daughter of
Zur, who was the head of a clan, an ancestral house in Midian.

25.16 Num 31.2 16 The LORD said to Moses, 17"Harass the Midianites, and defeat them; 18for
25.18 Num 25.15 they have harassed you by the trickery with which they deceived you in the affair
of Peor, and in the affair of Cozbi, the daughter of a leader of Midian, their sister;
she was killed on the day of the plague that resulted from Peor."

2. The second numbering of the nation

A census of the new generation

26.1 Num 25.6-9 **26** After the plague the LORD said to Moses and to Eleazar son of Aaron the
26.2 Num 1.2-15 4.1-4 priest, 2"Take a census of the whole congregation of the Israelites, from
twenty years old and upward, by their ancestral houses, everyone in Israel able to
go to war." 3Moses and Eleazar the priest spoke with them in the plains of Moab
by the Jordan opposite Jericho, saying, 4"Take a census of the people,[o] from
twenty years old and upward," as the LORD commanded Moses.

26.5 Gen 46.8-14 Num 1.20-46 16.1 1 Chron 5.1-5 The Israelites, who came out of the land of Egypt, were:

5 Reuben, the firstborn of Israel. The descendants of Reuben: of Hanoch, the
clan of the Hanochites; of Pallu, the clan of the Palluites; 6of Hezron, the clan of

[o] Heb lacks *take a census of the people*: Compare verse 2

---

was about to enter. Represented by a bull, symbol of strength and fertility, he was the god of the rains and harvest. The Israelites were continually attracted to Baal worship, in which prostitution played a large part, throughout their years in Canaan. Since Baal was so popular, his name was often used as a generic title for all the local gods.

25.6 The phrase, "brought . . . into his family," referred to the person's inner room of his tent, or his bedroom. Clearly the woman was brought into his tent for sex. Zimri so disregarded the law of God that he brought the woman right into the camp.

25.8 Evidently God punished Israel for its adultery and idolatry by sending a terrible plague. The plague was stopped when Phinehas killed the latest offenders.

25.10, 11 It is clear from Phinehas's story that some anger is proper and justified. But how can we know when our anger is appropriate and when it should be restrained? Ask these questions when you become angry: (1) Why am I angry? (2) Whose rights are being violated (mine or another's)? (3) Is the truth (a principle of God) being violated? If only your rights are at stake, it may be wiser to keep angry feelings under control. But if the truth is at stake, anger is often justified, although violence and retaliation are usually the wrong way to express it (Phinehas's case was unique). If we are becoming more and more like God, we should be angered by sin.

25.12, 13 Phinehas's act made atonement for the nation of Israel; in effect, what he did averted God's judgment. Because of this, his descendants would become the high priests of Israel. They continued so throughout the history of the tabernacle and the temple.

26.2 This is the second great census in the book of Numbers. Both were taken to count the number of men able to go to war. The first census (1.1 – 2.33) counted the Hebrews who had left Egypt. When the old generation died in the wilderness, another census was needed to count the Hebrews ready to enter the promised land. The new census revealed that although over 600,000 men (not counting women and children) had died in the wilderness, the male population of Israel now numbered 601,730. The census was one of the first major steps in preparing the people to enter the land they had waited so long to possess.

the Hezronites; of Carmi, the clan of the Carmites. 7 These are the clans of the
Reubenites; the number of those enrolled was forty-three thousand seven hundred
thirty. 8 And the descendants of Pallu: Eliab. 9 The descendants of Eliab: Nemuel,
Dathan, and Abiram. These are the same Dathan and Abiram, chosen from the
congregation, who rebelled against Moses and Aaron in the company of Korah,
when they rebelled against the LORD, 10 and the earth opened its mouth and swallowed them up along with Korah, when that company died, when the fire devoured
two hundred fifty men; and they became a warning. 11 Notwithstanding, the sons of
Korah did not die.

12 The descendants of Simeon by their clans: of Nemuel, the clan of the Nemu- **26.12**
elites; of Jamin, the clan of the Jaminites; of Jachin, the clan of the Jachinites; 13 of 1 Chron 4.24-43
Zerah, the clan of the Zerahites; of Shaul, the clan of the Shaulites.[p] 14 These are
the clans of the Simeonites, twenty-two thousand two hundred.

15 The children of Gad by their clans: of Zephon, the clan of the Zephonites; of
Haggi, the clan of the Haggites; of Shuni, the clan of the Shunites; 16 of Ozni, the
clan of the Oznites; of Eri, the clan of the Erites; 17 of Arod, the clan of the Aro-
dites; of Areli, the clan of the Arelites. 18 These are the clans of the Gadites: the
number of those enrolled was forty thousand five hundred.

19 The sons of Judah: Er and Onan; Er and Onan died in the land of Canaan. **26.19**
20 The descendants of Judah by their clans were: of Shelah, the clan of the Shelan- 1 Chron 4.1-4
ites; of Perez, the clan of the Perezites; of Zerah, the clan of the Zerahites. 21 The
descendants of Perez were: of Hezron, the clan of the Hezronites; of Hamul, the
clan of the Hamulites. 22 These are the clans of Judah: the number of those enrolled
was seventy-six thousand five hundred.

23 The descendants of Issachar by their clans: of Tola, the clan of the Tolaites; **26.23**
of Puvah, the clan of the Punites; 24 of Jashub, the clan of the Jashubites; of Shim- 1 Chron 7.1-5
ron, the clan of the Shimronites. 25 These are the clans of Issachar: sixty-four thousand three hundred enrolled.

26 The descendants of Zebulun by their clans: of Sered, the clan of the Sere-
dites; of Elon, the clan of the Elonites; of Jahleel, the clan of the Jahleelites.
27 These are the clans of the Zebulunites; the number of those enrolled was sixty
thousand five hundred.

28 The sons of Joseph by their clans: Manasseh and Ephraim. 29 The descen- **26.28**
dants of Manasseh: of Machir, the clan of the Machirites; and Machir was the father Gen 46.19-22
of Gilead; of Gilead, the clan of the Gileadites. 30 These are the descendants of 1 Chron 7.14-40
Gilead: of Iezer, the clan of the Iezerites; of Helek, the clan of the Helekites; 31 and
of Asriel, the clan of the Asrielites; and of Shechem, the clan of the Shechemites;
32 and of Shemida, the clan of the Shemidaites; and of Hepher, the clan of the He-
pherites. 33 Now Zelophehad son of Hepher had no sons, but daughters: and the
names of the daughters of Zelophehad were Mahlah, Noah, Hoglah, Milcah, and
Tirzah. 34 These are the clans of Manasseh; the number of those enrolled was fifty-
two thousand seven hundred.

35 These are the descendants of Ephraim according to their clans: of Shuthelah,
the clan of the Shuthelahites; of Becher, the clan of the Becherites; of Tahan, the
clan of the Tahanites. 36 And these are the descendants of Shuthelah: of Eran, the
clan of the Eranites. 37 These are the clans of the Ephraimites: the number of those
enrolled was thirty-two thousand five hundred. These are the descendants of Joseph by their clans.

38 The descendants of Benjamin by their clans: of Bela, the clan of the Belaites; **26.38**
of Ashbel, the clan of the Ashbelites; of Ahiram, the clan of the Ahiramites; 39 of Gen 46.19-22
Shephupham, the clan of the Shuphamites; of Hupham, the clan of the Hupham- 1 Chron 7.6-12
ites. 40 And the sons of Bela were Ard and Naaman: of Ard, the clan of the Ardites; 8.1-40
of Naaman, the clan of the Naamites. 41 These are the descendants of Benjamin by
their clans; the number of those enrolled was forty-five thousand six hundred.

42 These are the descendants of Dan by their clans: of Shuham, the clan of the **26.42**
Shuhamites. These are the clans of Dan by their clans. 43 All the clans of the Shu- Gen 46.23-25
hamites: sixty-four thousand four hundred enrolled.

[p] Or *Saul . . . Saulites*

26.44 Gen 46.16,17 44 The descendants of Asher by their families: of Imnah, the clan of the Im-
nites; of Ishvi, the clan of the Ishvites; of Beriah, the clan of the Beriites. 45 Of the
descendants of Beriah: of Heber, the clan of the Heberites; of Malchiel, the clan of
the Malchielites. 46 And the name of the daughter of Asher was Serah. 47 These are
the clans of the Asherites: the number of those enrolled was fifty-three thousand
four hundred.
26.48 1 Chron 7.13 48 The descendants of Naphtali by their clans: of Jahzeel, the clan of the Jahze-
elites; of Guni, the clan of the Gunites; 49 of Jezer, the clan of the Jezerites; of
Shillem, the clan of the Shillemites. 50 These are the Naphtalites[q] by their clans:
the number of those enrolled was forty-five thousand four hundred.
26.51 Num 2.32,33 26.5 51 This was the number of the Israelites enrolled: six hundred and one thousand
seven hundred thirty.
52 The LORD spoke to Moses, saying: 53 To these the land shall be apportioned
26.54 Num 33.54 for inheritance according to the number of names. 54 To a large tribe you shall give
a large inheritance, and to a small tribe you shall give a small inheritance; every
26.55 Num 33.54 34.13 Josh 14.2; 17.14 tribe shall be given its inheritance according to its enrollment. 55 But the land shall
be apportioned by lot; according to the names of their ancestral tribes they shall
inherit. 56 Their inheritance shall be apportioned according to lot between the larger
and the smaller.
26.57 Num 3.16-38 1 Chron 6.1 57 This is the enrollment of the Levites by their clans: of Gershon, the clan of
the Gershonites; of Kohath, the clan of the Kohathites; of Merari, the clan of the
26.58 Num 3.16-35 Merarites. 58 These are the clans of Levi: the clan of the Libnites, the clan of the
Hebronites, the clan of the Mahlites, the clan of the Mushites, the clan of the Korahites. Now Kohath was the father of Amram. 59 The name of Amram's wife was
Jochebed daughter of Levi, who was born to Levi in Egypt; and she bore to Amram:
26.60 Num 3.2,8 Aaron, Moses, and their sister Miriam. 60 To Aaron were born Nadab, Abihu, Elea-
26.61 Lev 10.1,2 Num 3.4 zar, and Ithamar. 61 But Nadab and Abihu died when they offered illicit fire before
the LORD. 62 The number of those enrolled was twenty-three thousand, every male
26.62 Num 3.39 4.46-48 Deut 10.9 one month old and up; for they were not enrolled among the Israelites because there
was no allotment given to them among the Israelites.
63 These were those enrolled by Moses and Eleazar the priest, who enrolled the
26.64 Num 14.20-43 Deut 2.14,15 Israelites in the plains of Moab by the Jordan opposite Jericho. 64 Among these
there was not one of those enrolled by Moses and Aaron the priest, who had en-
rolled the Israelites in the wilderness of Sinai. 65 For the LORD had said of them,

q Heb *clans of Naphtali*

SUMMARY OF THE SECOND CENSUS
The Lord spoke to Moses, saying: To these the land shall be apportioned for inheritance according to the number of names (26.52, 53).

Tribe	*All men 20 and older*
Reuben	43,730
Simeon	22,200
Gad	40,500
Judah	76,500
Issachar	64,300
Zebulun	60,500
Ephraim	32,500
Manasseh	52,700
Benjamin	45,600
Dan	64,400
Asher	53,400
Naphtali	45,400
Grand Total	601,730

26.61 "Illicit fire" here is called "unholy fire" in Leviticus 10.1.

26.64 A new census for a new generation. Thirty-eight years had elapsed since the first great census recorded in Numbers. During that time, every Israelite man and woman over 20 years of age—except Caleb, Joshua, and Moses—had died, and yet God's laws and the spiritual character of the nation were still intact. Numbers records some dramatic miracles. This is a quiet but powerful miracle often overlooked: a whole nation moved from one land to another, lost its entire adult population, yet managed to maintain its spiritual direction. Sometimes it may feel like God isn't working dramatic miracles in our lives. But God often works in quiet ways to bring about his long-range purposes.

"They shall die in the wilderness." Not one of them was left, except Caleb son of
Jephunneh and Joshua son of Nun.

The inheritance for daughters

27 Then the daughters of Zelophehad came forward. Zelophehad was son of 27.1
Hepher son of Gilead son of Machir son of Manasseh son of Joseph, a mem- Num 26.28-37 36.1-4
ber of the Manassite clans. The names of his daughters were: Mahlah, Noah, Hog- Josh 17.3,4
lah, Milcah, and Tirzah. 2 They stood before Moses, Eleazar the priest, the leaders,
and all the congregation, at the entrance of the tent of meeting, and they said,
3 "Our father died in the wilderness; he was not among the company of those who
gathered themselves together against the LORD in the company of Korah, but died
for his own sin; and he had no sons. 4 Why should the name of our father be taken
away from his clan because he had no son? Give to us a possession among our
father's brothers."

5 Moses brought their case before the LORD. 6 And the LORD spoke to Moses, 27.6,7
saying: 7 The daughters of Zelophehad are right in what they are saying; you shall Num 36.1-4 Josh 17.5,6
indeed let them possess an inheritance among their father's brothers and pass the
inheritance of their father on to them. 8 You shall also say to the Israelites, "If a man
dies, and has no son, then you shall pass his inheritance on to his daughter. 9 If he
has no daughter, then you shall give his inheritance to his brothers. 10 If he has no
brothers, then you shall give his inheritance to his father's brothers. 11 And if his 27.11
father has no brothers, then you shall give his inheritance to the nearest kinsman of Lev 25.25,49
his clan, and he shall possess it. It shall be for the Israelites a statute and ordinance,
as the LORD commanded Moses."

Moses appoints Joshua as his successor

12 The LORD said to Moses, "Go up this mountain of the Abarim range, and see 27.12
the land that I have given to the Israelites. 13 When you have seen it, you also shall Num 33.47 Deut 32.49
be gathered to your people, as your brother Aaron was, 14 because you rebelled 27.13
against my word in the wilderness of Zin when the congregation quarreled with Deut 32.50,51 34.1-6
me.[r] You did not show my holiness before their eyes at the waters." (These are the 27.14
waters of Meribah of Kadesh in the wilderness of Zin.) 15 Moses spoke to the LORD, Num 20.9-13 Deut 32.48-52
saying, 16 "Let the LORD, the God of the spirits of all flesh, appoint someone over 34.1-6
the congregation 17 who shall go out before them and come in before them, who 27.17
shall lead them out and bring them in, so that the congregation of the LORD may not 1 Kgs 22.17 Ezek 34.1-24
be like sheep without a shepherd." 18 So the LORD said to Moses, "Take Joshua son Zech 10.2 Mt 9.36
of Nun, a man in whom is the spirit, and lay your hand upon him; 19 have him stand 27.18
before Eleazar the priest and all the congregation, and commission him in their Deut 3.28 31.7,8; 34.9
sight. 20 You shall give him some of your authority, so that all the congregation of 27.20
the Israelites may obey. 21 But he shall stand before Eleazar the priest, who shall Deut 31.3
inquire for him by the decision of the Urim before the LORD; at his word they shall 27.21 Ex 28.30
go out, and at his word they shall come in, both he and all the Israelites with him, Lev 8.8 Deut 33.8
the whole congregation." 22 So Moses did as the LORD commanded him. He took 1 Sam 28.6

[r] Heb lacks *with me*

27.3 "Died for his own sin" means that he died a natural death. His death fell under the judgment of the entire nation for believing the false spies.

27.3, 4 Up to this point, the Hebrew law gave sons alone the right to inherit. The daughters of Zelophehad, having no brothers, came to Moses to ask for their father's possessions. God told Moses that if a man died without sons, his inheritance would go to his daughters (27.8). But the daughters could keep it only if they married within their own tribe, probably so the territorial lines would remain intact (36.5–12).

27.15–21 Moses did not want to leave his work without making sure a new leader was ready to replace him. First he asked God to help him find a replacement. Then, when Joshua was selected, Moses gave him a variety of tasks to ease the transition into his new position. Moses also clearly told the people that Joshua had the authority and the ability to lead the nation. His display of confidence in Joshua was good for both Joshua and the people. To minimize leadership gaps, anyone in a leadership position should train others to carry on the duties should he or she suddenly or eventually have to leave. While you have the opportunity, follow Moses' pattern: pray, select, develop, and commission.

27.16, 17 Moses asked God to appoint a leader who was capable of directing both external and internal affairs – one who could lead them in battle, but who would also care for their needs. The Lord responded by appointing Joshua. Many people want to be known as leaders. Some are very capable of reaching their goals, while others care deeply for the people in their charge. The best leaders are both goal-oriented and people-oriented.

Joshua and had him stand before Eleazar the priest and the whole congregation;
23 he laid his hands on him and commissioned him—as the LORD had directed
through Moses.

3. Instructions concerning offerings

Daily offerings

28 The LORD spoke to Moses, saying: 2 Command the Israelites, and say to
them: My offering, the food for my offerings by fire, my pleasing odor, you
shall take care to offer to me at its appointed time. 3 And you shall say to them, This
is the offering by fire that you shall offer to the LORD: two male lambs a year old
without blemish, daily, as a regular offering. 4 One lamb you shall offer in the
morning, and the other lamb you shall offer at twilight[s] 5 also one-tenth of an
ephah of choice flour for a grain offering, mixed with one-fourth of a hin of beaten
oil. 6 It is a regular burnt offering, ordained at Mount Sinai for a pleasing odor, an
offering by fire to the LORD. 7 Its drink offering shall be one-fourth of a hin for each
lamb; in the sanctuary you shall pour out a drink offering of strong drink to the
LORD. 8 The other lamb you shall offer at twilight[s] with a grain offering and a drink
offering like the one in the morning; you shall offer it as an offering by fire, a
pleasing odor to the LORD.

Sabbath offerings

9 On the sabbath day: two male lambs a year old without blemish, and two-
tenths of an ephah of choice flour for a grain offering, mixed with oil, and its drink
offering— 10 this is the burnt offering for every sabbath, in addition to the regular
burnt offering and its drink offering.

Monthly offerings

11 At the beginnings of your months you shall offer a burnt offering to the
LORD: two young bulls, one ram, seven male lambs a year old without blemish;
12 also three-tenths of an ephah of choice flour for a grain offering, mixed with oil,
for each bull; and two-tenths of choice flour for a grain offering, mixed with oil, for
the one ram; 13 and one-tenth of choice flour mixed with oil as a grain offering for
every lamb—a burnt offering of pleasing odor, an offering by fire to the LORD.
14 Their drink offerings shall be half a hin of wine for a bull, one-third of a hin for
a ram, and one-fourth of a hin for a lamb. This is the burnt offering of every month
throughout the months of the year. 15 And there shall be one male goat for a sin
offering to the LORD; it shall be offered in addition to the regular burnt offering and
its drink offering.

Offerings for passover

16 On the fourteenth day of the first month there shall be a passover offering to
the LORD. 17 And on the fifteenth day of this month is a festival; seven days shall
unleavened bread be eaten. 18 On the first day there shall be a holy convocation.
You shall not work at your occupations. 19 You shall offer an offering by fire, a
burnt offering to the LORD: two young bulls, one ram, and seven male lambs a year
old; see that they are without blemish. 20 Their grain offering shall be of choice
flour mixed with oil: three-tenths of an ephah shall you offer for a bull, and two-
tenths for a ram; 21 one-tenth shall you offer for each of the seven lambs; 22 also one

s Heb *between the two evenings*

28.3 Ex 29.38-41 Ezek 46.13-15
28.4 Lev 6.19,20
28.5 Num 15.3-12
28.7 Ex 29.41 Lev 23.12-14 Num 28.31
28.11 Num 10.10 28.19 1 Chron 23.31 2 Chron 2.4 Ezra 3.5 Neh 10.33 Isa 1.12,13 Ezek 46.6,7 Col 2.16
28.12 Num 15.4-12
28.15 Lev 6.8-13 Num 28.3
28.16 Ex 23.15 Lev 23.5-14 Num 9.3-5 Deut 16.1-8
28.19 Num 29.11

28.1, 2 Offerings had to be brought regularly and presented according to prescribed rituals under the priests' supervision. Following these rituals took time, and this gave the people the opportunity to prepare their hearts for worship. God is delighted, and we get more from it, when our hearts are prepared to come before him in a spirit of thankfulness.

28.5–7 This was a fine flour, and the oil was from crushed olives. The strong drink was wine. This food offering showed respect for God as the Giver of all gifts, and represented the first of the fruit of the earth.

28.9, 10 Why were extra offerings made on the sabbath? The sabbath was a special day of rest and worship commemorating both creation (Exodus 20.8–11) and the deliverance from Egypt (Deuteronomy 5.12–15). Because of the significance of this special day, it was only natural to offer extra sacrifices on it.

male goat for a sin offering, to make atonement for you. 23 You shall offer these in
addition to the burnt offering of the morning, which belongs to the regular burnt
offering. 24 In the same way you shall offer daily, for seven days, the food of an
offering by fire, a pleasing odor to the LORD; it shall be offered in addition to the
regular burnt offering and its drink offering. 25 And on the seventh day you shall
have a holy convocation; you shall not work at your occupations.

Offerings for pentecost

26 On the day of the first fruits, when you offer a grain offering of new grain to **28.26**
the LORD at your festival of weeks, you shall have a holy convocation; you shall not Ex 23.16
work at your occupations. 27 You shall offer a burnt offering, a pleasing odor to the Lev 23.9-22
LORD: two young bulls, one ram, seven male lambs a year old. 28 Their grain offer- Deut 16.16
ing shall be of choice flour mixed with oil, three-tenths of an ephah for each bull, Acts 2.1
two-tenths for one ram, 29 one-tenth for each of the seven lambs; 30 with one male
goat, to make atonement for you. 31 In addition to the regular burnt offering with its **28.31**
grain offering, you shall offer them and their drink offering. They shall be without Num 28.3
blemish.

Offerings for the festival of trumpets

29 On the first day of the seventh month you shall have a holy convocation; you **29.1**
shall not work at your occupations. It is a day for you to blow the trumpets, Lev 23.23-25
2 and you shall offer a burnt offering, a pleasing odor to the LORD: one young bull, Num 10.10
one ram, seven male lambs a year old without blemish. 3 Their grain offering shall
be of choice flour mixed with oil, three-tenths of one ephah for the bull, two-tenths
for the ram, 4 and one-tenth for each of the seven lambs; 5 with one male goat for a
sin offering, to make atonement for you. 6 These are in addition to the burnt offer- **29.6**
ing of the new moon and its grain offering, and the regular burnt offering and its Num 28.3
grain offering, and their drink offerings, according to the ordinance for them, a
pleasing odor, an offering by fire to the LORD.

Offerings for the day of atonement

7 On the tenth day of this seventh month you shall have a holy convocation, and **29.7**
deny yourselves;[t] you shall do no work. 8 You shall offer a burnt offering to the Lev 16.29-31
LORD, a pleasing odor: one young bull, one ram, seven male lambs a year old. They 23.23-27
shall be without blemish. 9 Their grain offering shall be of choice flour mixed with
oil, three-tenths of an ephah for the bull, two-tenths for the one ram, 10 one-tenth
for each of the seven lambs; 11 with one male goat for a sin offering, in addition to **29.11**
the sin offering of atonement, and the regular burnt offering and its grain offering, Lev 16.1-35
and their drink offerings. 23.26-32

Offerings for the festival of booths

12 On the fifteenth day of the seventh month you shall have a holy convocation; **29.12**
you shall not work at your occupations. You shall celebrate a festival to the LORD Lev 23.33-43
seven days. 13 You shall offer a burnt offering, an offering by fire, a pleasing odor Deut 16.13,14
to the LORD: thirteen young bulls, two rams, fourteen male lambs a year old. They Ezek 45.25
shall be without blemish. 14 Their grain offering shall be of choice flour mixed with
oil, three-tenths of an ephah for each of the thirteen bulls, two-tenths for each of the

[t] *Or and fast*

28.25 A "holy convocation" was a sacred and solemn assembly of all the people.

29.1ff God placed many holidays on Israel's calendar. The festival of trumpets was one of three great holidays celebrated in the seventh month (the festival of booths and day of atonement were the other two). These holidays provided a time to refresh the mind and body and to renew one's commitment to God. If you feel tired or far from God, try taking a "spiritual holiday." Separate yourself from your daily routine and concentrate on renewing your commitment to God.

29.1, 2 The festival of trumpets demonstrated three important principles that we should follow in our worship today: (1) The people gathered together to celebrate and worship. There is an extra benefit to be gained from worshiping with other believers. (2) The normal daily routine was suspended, and no hard work was done. It takes time to worship, and setting aside the time allows us to adjust our attitudes before and reflect afterwards. (3) The people sacrificed animals as burnt offerings to God. We show our commitment to God when we give something of value to him. The best gift, of course, is ourselves.

two rams, 15 and one-tenth for each of the fourteen lambs; 16 also one male goat for
a sin offering, in addition to the regular burnt offering, its grain offering and its
drink offering.
17 On the second day: twelve young bulls, two rams, fourteen male lambs a
year old without blemish, 18 with the grain offering and the drink offerings for the
bulls, for the rams, and for the lambs, as prescribed in accordance with their num-
29.19 Num 28.3,11,31
ber; 19 also one male goat for a sin offering, in addition to the regular burnt offering
and its grain offering, and their drink offerings.
20 On the third day: eleven bulls, two rams, fourteen male lambs a year old
without blemish, 21 with the grain offering and the drink offerings for the bulls, for
the rams, and for the lambs, as prescribed in accordance with their number; 22 also
one male goat for a sin offering, in addition to the regular burnt offering and its
grain offering and its drink offering.
23 On the fourth day: ten bulls, two rams, fourteen male lambs a year old without blemish, 24 with the grain offering and the drink offerings for the bulls, for the
rams, and for the lambs, as prescribed in accordance with their number; 25 also one
male goat for a sin offering, in addition to the regular burnt offering, its grain offering and its drink offering.
26 On the fifth day: nine bulls, two rams, fourteen male lambs a year old without blemish, 27 with the grain offering and the drink offerings for the bulls, for the
rams, and for the lambs, as prescribed in accordance with their number; 28 also one
male goat for a sin offering, in addition to the regular burnt offering and its grain
offering and its drink offering.
29 On the sixth day: eight bulls, two rams, fourteen male lambs a year old without blemish, 30 with the grain offering and the drink offerings for the bulls, for the
rams, and for the lambs, as prescribed in accordance with their number; 31 also one
male goat for a sin offering, in addition to the regular burnt offering, its grain offering, and its drink offerings.
32 On the seventh day: seven bulls, two rams, fourteen male lambs a year old
without blemish, 33 with the grain offering and the drink offerings for the bulls, for
the rams, and for the lambs, as prescribed in accordance with their number; 34 also
one male goat for a sin offering, besides the regular burnt offering, its grain offering, and its drink offering.
29.35 Lev 23.3,7, 21,36
35 On the eighth day you shall have a solemn assembly; you shall not work at
your occupations. 36 You shall offer a burnt offering, an offering by fire, a pleasing
odor to the LORD: one bull, one ram, seven male lambs a year old without blemish,
37 and the grain offering and the drink offerings for the bull, for the ram, and for the
lambs, as prescribed in accordance with their number; 38 also one male goat for a
sin offering, in addition to the regular burnt offering and its grain offering and its
drink offering.
29.39 Lev 22.20,21 2 Chron 31.3 Ezra 3.5 Neh 10.33
39 These you shall offer to the LORD at your appointed festivals, in addition to
your votive offerings and your freewill offerings, as your burnt offerings, your
grain offerings, your drink offerings, and your offerings of well-being.
40[u] So Moses told the Israelites everything just as the LORD had commanded
Moses.

Rules about vows

30.1,2 Lev 5.4; 27.2-13 Deut 23.21-25 Judg 11.30-35 Eccles 5.4
30 Then Moses said to the heads of the tribes of the Israelites: This is what the
LORD has commanded. 2 When a man makes a vow to the LORD, or swears
an oath to bind himself by a pledge, he shall not break his word; he shall do according to all that proceeds out of his mouth.

[u] Ch 30.1 in Heb

29.39 A "votive offering" was an offering given with a solemn vow. Chapter 6 describes one of these vows (the nazirite vow).

30.1, 2 Moses reminded the people that their promises must be kept. In ancient times, a person's word was as binding as a signature. No one was forced by law to make a vow; but once made, vows had to be fulfilled. Breaking a vow meant a broken trust and a broken relationship. Trust is still the basis of our relationships with God and others. Thus a broken promise today is just as harmful as it was in Moses' day.

3 When a woman makes a vow to the LORD, or binds herself by a pledge, while
within her father's house, in her youth, 4 and her father hears of her vow or her
pledge by which she has bound herself, and says nothing to her; then all her vows
shall stand, and any pledge by which she has bound herself shall stand. 5 But if her
father expresses disapproval to her at the time that he hears of it, no vow of hers,
and no pledge by which she has bound herself, shall stand; and the LORD will forgive her, because her father had expressed to her his disapproval.
6 If she marries, while obligated by her vows or any thoughtless utterance of **30.6**
her lips by which she has bound herself, 7 and her husband hears of it and says Judg 11.30,31
nothing to her at the time that he hears, then her vows shall stand, and her pledges
by which she has bound herself shall stand. 8 But if, at the time that her husband
hears of it, he expresses disapproval to her, then he shall nullify the vow by which
she was obligated, or the thoughtless utterance of her lips, by which she bound
herself; and the LORD will forgive her. 9 (But every vow of a widow or of a divorced
woman, by which she has bound herself, shall be binding upon her.) 10 And if she
made a vow in her husband's house, or bound herself by a pledge with an oath,
11 and her husband heard it and said nothing to her, and did not express disapproval
to her, then all her vows shall stand, and any pledge by which she bound herself
shall stand. 12 But if her husband nullifies them at the time that he hears them, then
whatever proceeds out of her lips concerning her vows, or concerning her pledge of
herself, shall not stand. Her husband has nullified them, and the LORD will forgive
her. 13 Any vow or any binding oath to deny herself,[v] her husband may allow to
stand, or her husband may nullify. 14 But if her husband says nothing to her from
day to day,[w] then he validates all her vows, or all her pledges, by which she is
obligated; he has validated them, because he said nothing to her at the time that he
heard of them. 15 But if he nullifies them some time after he has heard of them, then
he shall bear her guilt.
16 These are the statutes that the LORD commanded Moses concerning a hus- **30.16**
band and his wife, and a father and his daughter while she is still young and in her Num 5.29
father's house.

4. The war against Midian

31 The LORD spoke to Moses, saying, 2 "Avenge the Israelites on the Midian- **31.1,2**
ites; afterward you shall be gathered to your people." 3 So Moses said to the Num 25.6-18 Deut 32.35
people, "Arm some of your number for the war, so that they may go against Midian, to execute the LORD's vengeance on Midian. 4 You shall send a thousand from
each of the tribes of Israel to the war." 5 So out of the thousands of Israel, a thousand from each tribe were conscripted, twelve thousand armed for battle. 6 Moses **31.6**
sent them to the war, a thousand from each tribe, along with Phinehas son of Elea- Num 10.10 Josh 6.4-6,
zar the priest,[x] with the vessels of the sanctuary and the trumpets for sounding the 1 Sam 4.4,5,17 2 Chron 13.12-15
alarm in his hand. 7 They did battle against Midian, as the LORD had commanded
Moses, and killed every male. 8 They killed the kings of Midian: Evi, Rekem, Zur, **31.8**
Hur, and Reba, the five kings of Midian, in addition to others who were slain by Josh 13.21,22
them; and they also killed Balaam son of Beor with the sword. 9 The Israelites took
the women of Midian and their little ones captive; and they took all their cattle,
their flocks, and all their goods as booty. 10 All their towns where they had settled,
and all their encampments, they burned, 11 but they took all the spoil and all the

[v] *Or to fast* [w] *Or from that day to the next* [x] Gk: Heb adds *to the war*

30.3–8 Under Israelite law, parents could overrule their children's vows. This helped young people avoid the consequences of making foolish promises or costly commitments. From this law comes an important principle for both parents and children. Young people still living at home should seek their parents' help when they make decisions. A parent's experience could save a child from a serious mistake. Parents, however, should exercise their authority with caution and grace. They should let children learn from their mistakes while protecting them from disaster.

31.1ff The Midianites were a nomadic people who descended from Abraham and his second wife, Keturah. The land of Midian lay far to the south of Canaan, but large bands of Midianites roamed many miles from their homeland, searching for grazing areas for their flocks. Such a group was near the promised land when the Israelites arrived. When Moses fled from Egypt (Exodus 2), he took refuge in the land of Midian. His wife and father-in-law were Midianites. But despite this alliance, the Israelites and Midianites were always bitter enemies.

booty, both people and animals. 12 Then they brought the captives and the booty
and the spoil to Moses, to Eleazar the priest, and to the congregation of the Israelites, at the camp on the plains of Moab by the Jordan at Jericho.
13 Moses, Eleazar the priest, and all the leaders of the congregation went to
meet them outside the camp. 14 Moses became angry with the officers of the army,
the commanders of thousands and the commanders of hundreds, who had come
from service in the war. 15 Moses said to them, "Have you allowed all the women
to live? 16 These women here, on Balaam's advice, made the Israelites act treacherously against the LORD in the affair of Peor, so that the plague came among the
congregation of the LORD. 17 Now therefore, kill every male among the little ones,
and kill every woman who has known a man by sleeping with him. 18 But all the
young girls who have not known a man by sleeping with him, keep alive for yourselves. 19 Camp outside the camp seven days; whoever of you has killed any person
or touched a corpse, purify yourselves and your captives on the third and on the
seventh day. 20 You shall purify every garment, every article of skin, everything
made of goats' hair, and every article of wood."
21 Eleazar the priest said to the troops who had gone to battle: "This is the
statute of the law that the LORD has commanded Moses: 22 gold, silver, bronze,
iron, tin, and lead — 23 everything that can withstand fire, shall be passed through
fire, and it shall be clean. Nevertheless it shall also be purified with the water for
purification; and whatever cannot withstand fire, shall be passed through the water.
24 You must wash your clothes on the seventh day, and you shall be clean; afterward you may come into the camp."
25 The LORD spoke to Moses, saying, 26 "You and Eleazar the priest and the
heads of the ancestral houses of the congregation make an inventory of the booty
captured, both human and animal. 27 Divide the booty into two parts, between the
warriors who went out to battle and all the congregation. 28 From the share of the
warriors who went out to battle, set aside as tribute for the LORD, one item out of
every five hundred, whether persons, oxen, donkeys, sheep, or goats. 29 Take it
from their half and give it to Eleazar the priest as an offering to the LORD. 30 But
from the Israelites' half you shall take one out of every fifty, whether persons,
oxen, donkeys, sheep, or goats — all the animals — and give them to the Levites
who have charge of the tabernacle of the LORD."
31 Then Moses and Eleazar the priest did as the LORD had commanded Moses:
32 The booty remaining from the spoil that the troops had taken totaled six
hundred seventy-five thousand sheep, 33 seventy-two thousand oxen, 34 sixty-one
thousand donkeys, 35 and thirty-two thousand persons in all, women who had not
known a man by sleeping with him.
36 The half-share, the portion of those who had gone out to war, was in number
three hundred thirty-seven thousand five hundred sheep and goats, 37 and the
LORD's tribute of sheep and goats was six hundred seventy-five. 38 The oxen were
thirty-six thousand, of which the LORD's tribute was seventy-two. 39 The donkeys
were thirty thousand five hundred, of which the LORD's tribute was sixty-one.
40 The persons were sixteen thousand, of which the LORD's tribute was thirty-two

31.16 Num 25.1-18 Deut 4.3 Josh 22.17,18 2 Pet 2.15,16
31.17 Judg 21.10-12 Deut 7.2 20.16-18
31.20 Lev 13.52
31.24 Lev 11.25; 14.9 Num 19.19
31.27 Josh 22.8 1 Sam 30.23,24
31.28 2 Sam 8.11,12
31.29 Num 18.25,26

31.14–16 Because Midianites were responsible for enticing Israel into Baal worship, God commanded Israel to destroy them (25.16–18). But Israel took the women as captives, rather than killing them, probably because of the tempting enticements of the Midianites' sinful life-style. When we discover sin in our lives, it is a mistake to deal with it in a halfhearted manner. When the Israelites later entered the promised land, it was their indifferent attitude to sin that eventually ruined them. Moses dealt with the sin promptly and completely. When God points out sin, move quickly to remove it from your life.

31.16 Balaam's story (22.1 – 24.25), taken alone, would lead us to believe that Balaam was an honest and God-fearing man. But here is the first of much biblical evidence that Balaam was not the good man he could easily appear to be. For more on Balaam see the notes on 22.9 and 25.1–3, and Balaam's Profile in chapter 23.

31.22, 23 The Israelites could ceremonially purify certain captured possessions by passing them through a fire. If the material goods passed through without being destroyed, they could be used and enjoyed by God's people. Here we learn that some things, if purified through dedication to God, can be used for his service.

31.25–30 Moses told the Israelites to give a portion of the war spoils to God. Another portion was to go to the people who remained behind. Similarly, the money we earn is not ours alone. Everything we possess comes directly or indirectly from God and ultimately belongs to him. We should return a portion to him (our "tribute") and also share a portion with those in need.

persons. 41 Moses gave the tribute, the offering for the LORD, to Eleazar the priest,
as the LORD had commanded Moses.
42 As for the Israelites' half, which Moses separated from that of the troops,
43 the congregation's half was three hundred thirty-seven thousand five hundred
sheep and goats, 44 thirty-six thousand oxen, 45 thirty thousand five hundred donkeys, 46 and sixteen thousand persons. 47 From the Israelites' half Moses took one of
every fifty, both of persons and of animals, and gave them to the Levites who had
charge of the tabernacle of the LORD; as the LORD had commanded Moses.
48 Then the officers who were over the thousands of the army, the commanders
of thousands and the commanders of hundreds, approached Moses, 49 and said to
Moses, "Your servants have counted the warriors who are under our command, and
not one of us is missing. 50 And we have brought the LORD's offering, what each of
us found, articles of gold, armlets and bracelets, signet rings, earrings, and pendants, to make atonement for ourselves before the LORD." 51 Moses and Eleazar the
priest received the gold from them, all in the form of crafted articles. 52 And all the
gold of the offering that they offered to the LORD, from the commanders of thousands and the commanders of hundreds, was sixteen thousand seven hundred fifty
shekels. 53 (The troops had all taken plunder for themselves.) 54 So Moses and Elea- **31.53**
zar the priest received the gold from the commanders of thousands and of hun- Deut 20.14
dreds, and brought it into the tent of meeting as a memorial for the Israelites before
the LORD.

5. Two and a half tribes receive their land

32 Now the Reubenites and the Gadites owned a very great number of cattle. **32.1**
When they saw that the land of Jazer and the land of Gilead was a good place Num 21.32 Josh 13.25
for cattle, 2 the Gadites and the Reubenites came and spoke to Moses, to Eleazar the 2 Sam 24.5
priest, and to the leaders of the congregation, saying, 3 "Ataroth, Dibon, Jazer, **32.3**
Nimrah, Heshbon, Elealeh, Sebam, Nebo, and Beon— 4 the land that the LORD Num 32.33-42
subdued before the congregation of Israel—is a land for cattle; and your servants Josh 13.17-19
have cattle." 5 They continued, "If we have found favor in your sight, let this land Isa 15.2-6; 16.8
be given to your servants for a possession; do not make us cross the Jordan."
6 But Moses said to the Gadites and to the Reubenites, "Shall your brothers go **32.8**
to war while you sit here? 7 Why will you discourage the hearts of the Israelites Num 13.2-26 14.2
from going over into the land that the LORD has given them? 8 Your fathers did this, Deut 1.19-21
when I sent them from Kadesh-barnea to see the land. 9 When they went up to the **32.9**
Wadi Eshcol and saw the land, they discouraged the hearts of the Israelites from Num 13.23,24, 27-33; 14.1-12

31.48–50 After carefully accounting for all their men, the officers discovered that not one soldier had been lost in battle. At once they thanked God. After going through tough times, we should be quick to thank God for delivering us and protecting us from severe loss. (Note: the "officers who were over the thousands of the army" probably refers to all of the commanders.)

32.1ff Three tribes (Reuben, Gad, and the half-tribe of Manasseh) wanted to live east of the Jordan River on land they had already conquered. Moses immediately assumed they had selfish motives and were trying to avoid helping the others fight for the land across the river. But Moses jumped to the wrong conclusion. In dealing with people, we must find out all the facts before making up our minds. We shouldn't automatically assume that their motives are wrong, even if their plans sound suspicious.

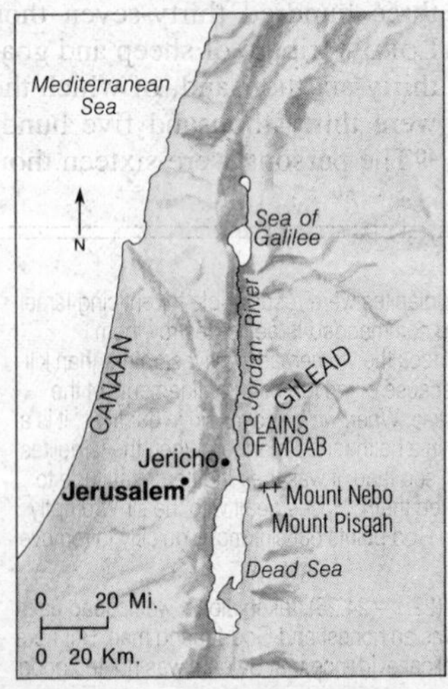

PREPARING TO ENTER THE PROMISED LAND
The Israelites had been camped in the plains of Moab, opposite Jericho. From this position, they were ready to enter the promised land.

32.10,11 Num 14.28-30 Deut 1.34,35

going into the land that the LORD had given them. 10 The LORD's anger was kindled
on that day and he swore, saying, 11 'Surely none of the people who came up out of
Egypt, from twenty years old and upward, shall see the land that I swore to give to
Abraham, to Isaac, and to Jacob, because they have not unreservedly followed

32.12 Num 14.6,24,30 Deut 1.36 Josh 14.8,9

me— 12 none except Caleb son of Jephunneh the Kenizzite and Joshua son of Nun,
for they have unreservedly followed the LORD.' 13 And the LORD's anger was kindled against Israel, and he made them wander in the wilderness for forty years,

32.13 Num 14.31-39 Deut 2.14,15

until all the generation that had done evil in the sight of the LORD had disappeared.
14 And now you, a brood of sinners, have risen in place of your fathers, to increase

32.15 Deut 30.17 Josh 22.16

the LORD's fierce anger against Israel! 15 If you turn away from following him, he
will again abandon them in the wilderness; and you will destroy all this people."

16 Then they came up to him and said, "We will build sheepfolds here for our

32.17 Deut 3.18-20 Josh 4.12,13

flocks, and towns for our little ones, 17 but we will take up arms as a vanguard[y]
before the Israelites, until we have brought them to their place. Meanwhile our
little ones will stay in the fortified towns because of the inhabitants of the land.

32.18,19 Josh 13.8; 22.4

18 We will not return to our homes until all the Israelites have obtained their inheritance. 19 We will not inherit with them on the other side of the Jordan and beyond,
because our inheritance has come to us on this side of the Jordan to the east."

20 So Moses said to them, "If you do this—if you take up arms to go before the

32.21 Deut 3.18 Josh 1.12-18

LORD for the war, 21 and all those of you who bear arms cross the Jordan before the
LORD, until he has driven out his enemies from before him 22 and the land is sub-

32.22 Deut 3.20 Josh 2.4-9

dued before the LORD—then after that you may return and be free of obligation to
the LORD and to Israel, and this land shall be your possession before the LORD.
23 But if you do not do this, you have sinned against the LORD; and be sure your sin

32.24 Num 30.2

will find you out. 24 Build towns for your little ones, and folds for your flocks; but
do what you have promised."

25 Then the Gadites and the Reubenites said to Moses, "Your servants will do
as my lord commands. 26 Our little ones, our wives, our flocks, and all our livestock shall remain there in the towns of Gilead; 27 but your servants will cross over,
everyone armed for war, to do battle for the LORD, just as my lord orders."

28 So Moses gave command concerning them to Eleazar the priest, to Joshua
son of Nun, and to the heads of the ancestral houses of the Israelite tribes. 29 And
Moses said to them, "If the Gadites and the Reubenites, everyone armed for battle
before the LORD, will cross over the Jordan with you and the land shall be subdued
before you, then you shall give them the land of Gilead for a possession; 30 but if
they will not cross over with you armed, they shall have possessions among you in
the land of Canaan." 31 The Gadites and the Reubenites answered, "As the LORD
has spoken to your servants, so we will do. 32 We will cross over armed before the
LORD into the land of Canaan, but the possession of our inheritance shall remain
with us on this side of[z] the Jordan."

32.33 Num 21.23-26 32.22; 34.14,15 Deut 2.32-37 3.8-17 Josh 12.1-6

33 Moses gave to them—to the Gadites and to the Reubenites and to the half-
tribe of Manasseh son of Joseph—the kingdom of King Sihon of the Amorites and
the kingdom of King Og of Bashan, the land and its towns, with the territories of
the surrounding towns. 34 And the Gadites rebuilt Dibon, Ataroth, Aroer, 35 Atroth-
shophan, Jazer, Jogbehah, 36 Beth-nimrah, and Beth-haran, fortified cities, and
folds for sheep. 37 And the Reubenites rebuilt Heshbon, Elealeh, Kiriathaim,

[y] Cn: Heb *hurrying* [z] Heb *beyond*

32.16 A sheepfold was a shelter for enclosing and protecting sheep. A simple sheepfold had four roughly built stone walls, high enough to keep wild animals out. Sometimes the top of the wall was lined with thorns to further discourage predators and thieves. The fold's single entrance made it easier for a shepherd to guard his flock. Often several shepherds used a single fold and took turns guarding the entrance. Mingling the animals was no problem since each flock responded readily to its own shepherd's voice. The three tribes who chose to remain east of the Jordan River wanted to build sheepfolds to protect their flocks, and cities to protect their families, before the men crossed the river to help the rest of the tribes conquer the promised land.

32.16–19 The land on the east side of the Jordan had been conquered. The hard work was done by all of the tribes together. But the tribes of Reuben and Gad and the half-tribe of Manasseh did not stop after their land was cleared. They promised to keep working with the others until everyone's land was conquered. After others have helped you, do you make excuses to escape helping them? Finish the whole job, even those parts that may not benefit you directly.

38 Nebo, and Baal-meon (some names being changed), and Sibmah; and they gave
names to the towns that they rebuilt. 39 The descendants of Machir son of Manasseh
went to Gilead, captured it, and dispossessed the Amorites who were there; 40 so
Moses gave Gilead to Machir son of Manasseh, and he settled there. 41 Jair son of **32.41**
Manasseh went and captured their villages, and renamed them Havvoth-jair.[a] Deut 3.14
42 And Nobah went and captured Kenath and its villages, and renamed it Nobah Josh 13.30 1 Chron 2.22
after himself.

6. Camped on the plains of Moab

Israel's travel route

33 These are the stages by which the Israelites went out of the land of Egypt in
military formation under the leadership of Moses and Aaron. 2 Moses wrote
down their starting points, stage by stage, by command of the LORD; and these are
their stages according to their starting places. 3 They set out from Rameses in the **33.3**
first month, on the fifteenth day of the first month; on the day after the passover the Ex 12.11-51
Israelites went out boldly in the sight of all the Egyptians, 4 while the Egyptians
were burying all their firstborn, whom the LORD had struck down among them. The
LORD executed judgments even against their gods.

5 So the Israelites set out from Rameses, and camped at Succoth. 6 They set out **33.5**
from Succoth, and camped at Etham, which is on the edge of the wilderness. 7 They Ex 13.20
set out from Etham, and turned back to Pi-hahiroth, which faces Baal-zephon; and **33.7** Ex 14.2,9
they camped before Migdol. 8 They set out from Pi-hahiroth, passed through the **33.8**
sea into the wilderness, went a three days' journey in the wilderness of Etham, and Ex 14.21,22
camped at Marah. 9 They set out from Marah and came to Elim; at Elim there were **33.9**
twelve springs of water and seventy palm trees, and they camped there. 10 They set Ex 15.27; 16.1
out from Elim and camped by the Red Sea.[b] 11 They set out from the Red Sea[u] and **33.11**
camped in the wilderness of Sin. 12 They set out from the wilderness of Sin and Ex 16.1; 17.1
camped at Dophkah. 13 They set out from Dophkah and camped at Alush. 14 They **33.14**
set out from Alush and camped at Rephidim, where there was no water for the Ex 17.1-8 19.2,3
people to drink. 15 They set out from Rephidim and camped in the wilderness of **33.15**
Sinai. 16 They set out from the wilderness of Sinai and camped at Kibroth- Num 11.34,35 13.21; 20.1
hattaavah. 17 They set out from Kibroth-hattaavah and camped at Hazeroth. 18 They Deut 2.2-8
set out from Hazeroth and camped at Rithmah. 19 They set out from Rithmah and 10.6,7; 32.51 1 Kgs 9.26
camped at Rimmon-perez. 20 They set out from Rimmon-perez and camped at Lib- 2 Chron 20.36
nah. 21 They set out from Libnah and camped at Rissah. 22 They set out from Rissah
and camped at Kehelathah. 23 They set out from Kehelathah and camped at Mount
Shepher. 24 They set out from Mount Shepher and camped at Haradah. 25 They set
out from Haradah and camped at Makheloth. 26 They set out from Makheloth and
camped at Tahath. 27 They set out from Tahath and camped at Terah. 28 They set out
from Terah and camped at Mithkah. 29 They set out from Mithkah and camped at
Hashmonah. 30 They set out from Hashmonah and camped at Moseroth. 31 They set
out from Moseroth and camped at Bene-jaakan. 32 They set out from Bene-jaakan
and camped at Hor-haggidgad. 33 They set out from Hor-haggidgad and camped at
Jotbathah. 34 They set out from Jotbathah and camped at Abronah. 35 They set out
from Abronah and camped at Ezion-geber. 36 They set out from Ezion-geber and
camped in the wilderness of Zin (that is, Kadesh). 37 They set out from Kadesh and
camped at Mount Hor, on the edge of the land of Edom.

38 Aaron the priest went up Mount Hor at the command of the LORD and died **33.38**
there in the fortieth year after the Israelites had come out of the land of Egypt, on Num 20.28

[a] That is *the villages of Jair* [b] Or *Sea of Reeds*

33.1ff Look at the map in the introduction to this book to see the travels of the Israelites.

33.2 Moses recorded the Israelites' journeys as God instructed him, providing a record of their spiritual as well as geographic progress. Have you made spiritual progress lately? Recording your thoughts about God and lessons you have learned over a period of time can be a valuable aid to spiritual growth. A record of your spiritual pilgrimage will let you check up on your progress and avoid repeating past mistakes.

33.4 God "executed judgments" against Egypt's gods by sending the plagues. See the note on Exodus 9.6 for further explanation.

the first day of the fifth month. 39 Aaron was one hundred twenty-three years old
when he died on Mount Hor.

33.40 Num 21.1
40 The Canaanite, the king of Arad, who lived in the Negeb in the land of Canaan, heard of the coming of the Israelites.

33.42 Num 21.10,11
41 They set out from Mount Hor and camped at Zalmonah. 42 They set out from
Zalmonah and camped at Punon. 43 They set out from Punon and camped at Oboth.
44 They set out from Oboth and camped at Iye-abarim, in the territory of Moab.
45 They set out from Iyim and camped at Dibon-gad. 46 They set out from Dibon-

33.47 Num 27.12
gad and camped at Almon-diblathaim. 47 They set out from Almon-diblathaim and

33.48 Num 22.1
camped in the mountains of Abarim, before Nebo. 48 They set out from the mountains of Abarim and camped in the plains of Moab by the Jordan at Jericho; 49 they

33.49 Num 25.1 Josh 2.1
camped by the Jordan from Beth-jeshimoth as far as Abel-shittim in the plains of
Moab.

How to settle and conquer the new land

50 In the plains of Moab by the Jordan at Jericho, the LORD spoke to Moses,
saying: 51 Speak to the Israelites, and say to them: When you cross over the Jordan

33.52 Ex 23.24 34.12-17 Deut 7.2-5,25, 26 Josh 23.7 Judg 2.2
into the land of Canaan, 52 you shall drive out all the inhabitants of the land from
before you, destroy all their figured stones, destroy all their cast images, and demolish all their high places. 53 You shall take possession of the land and settle in it,
for I have given you the land to possess. 54 You shall apportion the land by lot

33.54 Num 26.53-56
according to your clans; to a large one you shall give a large inheritance, and to a
small one you shall give a small inheritance; the inheritance shall belong to the
person on whom the lot falls; according to your ancestral tribes you shall inherit.

33.55 Ex 23.33 Deut 7.4,16-20 Ps 106.34-36
55 But if you do not drive out the inhabitants of the land from before you, then those
whom you let remain shall be as barbs in your eyes and thorns in your sides; they
shall trouble you in the land where you are settling. 56 And I will do to you as I

33.56 Deut 28.63
thought to do to them.

33.50–53 God told Moses that before the Israelites settled in the promised land, they should drive out the wicked inhabitants and destroy their idols. In Colossians 3, Paul encourages us to live as Christians in the same manner: throwing away our old way of living and moving ahead into our new life of obedience to God and faith in Jesus Christ. Like the Israelites moving into the promised land, we can destroy the wickedness in our lives or we can settle down and live with it. To move in and possess the new life, we must drive out the sinful thoughts and practices to make room for the new.

33.50–56 Why were the Israelites told to destroy the people living in Canaan? God had several compelling reasons for giving this command: (1) God was stamping out the wickedness of an extremely sinful nation. The Canaanites brought on their own punishment. Idol worship expressed their deepest evil desires. It ultimately led to the worship of Satan and the total rejection of God. (2) God was using Moses and Israel to judge Canaan for its sins in fulfillment of the prophecy in Genesis 9.25. (3) God wanted to remove all trace of pagan beliefs and practices from the land. He did not want his people to mix or compromise with idolatry in any way. The Israelites did not fully understand God's reasons, and they did not carry out his command. This eventually led them to compromise and corruption. In all areas of life, we should obey God's word without question because we know he is just, even if we cannot fully understand his overall purposes.

33.55 If you don't do the job right the first time, it often becomes much more difficult to accomplish. God warned that if the Israelites did not drive the wicked inhabitants out of the promised land, later they would become a source of great irritation. That is exactly what happened. Just as the Israelites were hesitant to clear out all the wicked people, we are sometimes hesitant to clear out all the sin in our lives, either because we are afraid of it (as the Israelites feared the giants), or because it seems harmless and attractive (as sexual sin seemed). But Hebrews 12.1, 2 tells us to throw off the sin that "clings so closely." We all have "idols" we don't want to let go of (a bad habit, an unhealthy relationship, a certain life-style). If we allow these idols to dominate us, they will cause serious problems later.

33.55, 56 God never goes back on his word, and this is one warning the Israelites should not have taken lightly. God made it perfectly clear: "If you do not drive out the inhabitants of the land, . . . I will do to you as I thought to do to them." Yet for some reason the people did not obey. The Israelites did not drive all the wicked nations out, and soon they began to assimilate their evil religious beliefs and practices. After a while, an Israelite was no different from a Canaanite. God fulfilled his warning in these verses during the period of the judges, and in a fuller sense during the time of the kings when he sent the Assyrians (2 Kings 17) and the Babylonians (2 Kings 25) to destroy Israel and carry the people away captive. The Israelites learned that God's words should be taken seriously.

The boundaries of the land

34 The LORD spoke to Moses, saying: 2 Command the Israelites, and say to **34.2** Gen 17.8
them: When you enter the land of Canaan (this is the land that shall fall to Deut 1.7,8
you for an inheritance, the land of Canaan, defined by its boundaries), 3 your south Ezek 47.14
sector shall extend from the wilderness of Zin along the side of Edom. Your south- **34.3** Ex 23.31
ern boundary shall begin from the end of the Dead Sea[c] on the east; 4 your bound- Josh 15.1-4
ary shall turn south of the ascent of Akrabbim, and cross to Zin, and its outer limit **34.4** Num 34.4
shall be south of Kadesh-barnea; then it shall go on to Hazar-addar, and cross to
Azmon; 5 the boundary shall turn from Azmon to the Wadi of Egypt, and its termination shall be at the Sea.
6 For the western boundary, you shall have the Great Sea and its[d] coast; this
shall be your western boundary.
7 This shall be your northern boundary: from the Great Sea you shall mark out **34.7**
your line to Mount Hor; 8 from Mount Hor you shall mark it out to Lebo-hamath, Josh 13.5 15.5-11
and the outer limit of the boundary shall be at Zedad; 9 then the boundary shall Ezek 47.15-17
extend to Ziphron, and its end shall be at Hazar-enan; this shall be your northern
boundary.
10 You shall mark out your eastern boundary from Hazar-enan to Shepham; **34.10**
11 and the boundary shall continue down from Shepham to Riblah on the east side Deut 3.17 Josh 15.5,12
of Ain; and the boundary shall go down, and reach the eastern slope of the sea of 2 Kgs 23.33 25.6
Chinnereth; 12 and the boundary shall go down to the Jordan, and its end shall be at Jer 52.9
the Dead Sea.[c] This shall be your land with its boundaries all around. Mt 14.34 Lk 5.1
13 Moses commanded the Israelites, saying: This is the land that you shall in- Jn 6.1
herit by lot, which the LORD has commanded to give to the nine tribes and to the **34.13** Josh 14.1,2
half-tribe; 14 for the tribe of the Reubenites by their ancestral houses and the tribe of **34.14**
the Gadites by their ancestral houses have taken their inheritance, and also the half- Num 32.33
tribe of Manasseh; 15 the two tribes and the half-tribe have taken their inheritance
beyond the Jordan at Jericho eastward, toward the sunrise.
16 The LORD spoke to Moses, saying: 17 These are the names of the men who **34.16**
shall apportion the land to you for inheritance: the priest Eleazar and Joshua son of Num 1.2-15 2.3-21
Nun. 18 You shall take one leader of every tribe to apportion the land for inheritance. 19 These are the names of the men: Of the tribe of Judah, Caleb son of Jephunneh. 20 Of the tribe of the Simeonites, Shemuel son of Ammihud. 21 Of the
tribe of Benjamin, Elidad son of Chislon. 22 Of the tribe of the Danites a leader,
Bukki son of Jogli. 23 Of the Josephites: of the tribe of the Manassites a leader,
Hanniel son of Ephod, 24 and of the tribe of the Ephraimites a leader, Kemuel son

[c] Heb *Salt Sea* [d] Syr: Heb lacks *its*

34.1ff The division of the territory was determined by sacred lot. No tribe was to claim its own land. Everything was an inheritance, a gift from God. The boundaries declared by God are larger than the area actually occupied by the Hebrews. The boundaries correspond more to the land conquered by David and to the ideal territory portrayed by Ezekiel (Ezekiel 47–48). The size of the land portrays God's generosity. He always gives us more than than we could ask or think.

34.16–29 In God's plan for settling the land, he (1) explained what to do, (2) communicated this clearly to Moses, and (3) assigned specific people to oversee the apportionment of the land. No plan is complete until each job is assigned and everyone understands his or her responsibilities. When you have a job to do, determine what must be done, give clear instructions, and put people in charge of each part.

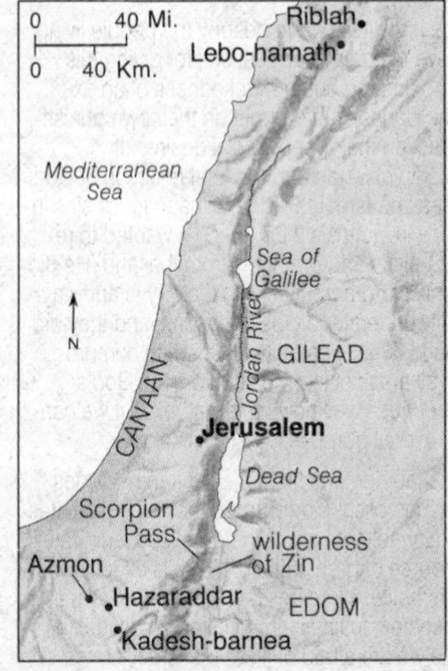

THE BORDERS OF THE PROMISED LAND
The borders of the promised land stretched from the wilderness of Zin and Kadesh-barnea in the south to Lebo-hamath and Riblah in the north, and from the Mediterranean sea coast (the Great Sea) on the west to the Jordan River on the east. The land of Gilead was also included.

of Shiphtan. 25 Of the tribe of the Zebulunites a leader, Eli-zaphan son of Parnach.
26 Of the tribe of the Issacharites a leader, Paltiel son of Azzan. 27 And of the tribe
of the Asherites a leader, Ahihud son of Shelomi. 28 Of the tribe of the Naphtalites
a leader, Pedahel son of Ammihud. 29 These were the ones whom the LORD commanded to apportion the inheritance for the Israelites in the land of Canaan.

The cities for the Levites

35 In the plains of Moab by the Jordan at Jericho, the LORD spoke to Moses,
35.2 Lev 25.32-34 Josh 14.3,4 Ezek 45.1; 48.8 saying: 2 Command the Israelites to give, from the inheritance that they possess, towns for the Levites to live in; you shall also give to the Levites pasture lands
surrounding the towns. 3 The towns shall be theirs to live in, and their pasture lands
shall be for their cattle, for their livestock, and for all their animals. 4 The pasture
lands of the towns, which you shall give to the Levites, shall reach from the wall of
the town outward a thousand cubits all around. 5 You shall measure, outside the
town, for the east side two thousand cubits, for the south side two thousand cubits,
for the west side two thousand cubits, and for the north side two thousand cubits,
with the town in the middle; this shall belong to them as pasture land for their
towns.
35.6 Deut 4.41-43 Josh 20.2-9 21.3,13,21-38 6 The towns that you give to the Levites shall include the six cities of refuge,
where you shall permit a slayer to flee, and in addition to them you shall give
forty-two towns. 7 The towns that you give to the Levites shall total forty-eight,
35.7 Josh 21.3-42 1 Chron 6.54-81 with their pasture lands. 8 And as for the towns that you shall give from the possession of the Israelites, from the larger tribes you shall take many, and from the
35.8 Num 26.54 smaller tribes you shall take few; each, in proportion to the inheritance that it obtains, shall give of its towns to the Levites.

The cities of refuge

9 The LORD spoke to Moses, saying: 10 Speak to the Israelites, and say to them:
35.11 Num 35.6 When you cross the Jordan into the land of Canaan, 11 then you shall select cities to
be cities of refuge for you, so that a slayer who kills a person without intent may
35.12 Num 35.16-29 flee there. 12 The cities shall be for you a refuge from the avenger, so that the slayer
may not die until there is a trial before the congregation.

DIVIDING THE LAND
These are the men appointed by Moses to oversee the division of the promised land among the tribes.

Tribe	*Leader*
Judah	Caleb, son of Jephunneh
Simeon	Shemuel, son of Ammihud
Benjamin	Elidad, son of Chislon
Dan	Bukki, son of Jogli
Manasseh	Hanniel, son of Ephod
Ephraim	Kemuel, son of Shiphtan
Zebulun	Elizaphan, son of Parnach
Issachar	Paltiel, son of Azzan
Asher	Ahihud, son of Shelomi
Naphtali	Pedahel, son of Ammihud

35.2–4 The Levites were ministers. They were supported by the tithes of the people. Likewise, we are responsible to provide for the needs of our ministers and missionaries so they can be free to do their God-ordained work.

35.6 Of the 48 cities given to the Levites, six were cities of refuge. Such cities were needed because the ancient customs of justice called for revenge in the event of the death of a relative or loved one (2 Samuel 14.7). The Levites would hold a preliminary hearing outside the gates; then the accused person was kept in the city until the time of his trial. If the killing was judged accidental, the person stayed in the city until the death of the high priest. At that time, he was allowed to go free. He could start a new life without worrying about avengers. This system of justice shows how God's law and his mercy go hand in hand.

35.11–28 If anyone died because of violence, murder was assumed, but the murder suspect was not automatically assumed guilty. The cities of refuge assured the accused that justice would be served. But if the accused left the city (35.27), then he/she would be assumed guilty and able to be killed by the avenging party. The people were to be intolerant of the sin, yet impartial to the accused so that he or she could have a fair trial. The cities of refuge represented God's concern for justice in a culture that did not always protect the innocent. It is unjust both to overlook wrongdoing and to jump to conclusions about guilt. When someone is accused of wrongdoing, stand up for justice, protect those not yet proven guilty, and listen carefully to all sides of the story.

13 The cities that you designate shall be six cities of refuge for you: 14 you shall
designate three cities beyond the Jordan, and three cities in the land of Canaan, to
be cities of refuge. 15 These six cities shall serve as refuge for the Israelites, for the
resident or transient alien among them, so that anyone who kills a person without
intent may flee there.
16 But anyone who strikes another with an iron object, and death ensues, is a **35.16**
murderer; the murderer shall be put to death. 17 Or anyone who strikes another with Ex 21.12-14 Lev 24.17
a stone in hand that could cause death, and death ensues, is a murderer; the mur- Deut 19.11-13
derer shall be put to death. 18 Or anyone who strikes another with a weapon of wood
in hand that could cause death, and death ensues, is a murderer; the murderer shall
be put to death. 19 The avenger of blood is the one who shall put the murderer to **35.19**
death; when they meet, the avenger of blood shall execute the sentence. 20 Like- Deut 19.6,7,12 Josh 20.3,5
wise, if someone pushes another from hatred, or hurls something at another, lying
in wait, and death ensues, 21 or in enmity strikes another with the hand, and death
ensues, then the one who struck the blow shall be put to death; that person is a
murderer; the avenger of blood shall put the murderer to death, when they meet.
22 But if someone pushes another suddenly without enmity, or hurls any object
without lying in wait, 23 or, while handling any stone that could cause death, unintentionally[e] drops it on another and death ensues, though they were not enemies,
and no harm was intended, 24 then the congregation shall judge between the slayer
and the avenger of blood, in accordance with these ordinances; 25 and the congregation shall rescue the slayer from the avenger of blood. Then the congregation shall
send the slayer back to the original city of refuge. The slayer shall live in it until the
death of the high priest who was anointed with the holy oil. 26 But if the slayer shall
at any time go outside the bounds of the original city of refuge, 27 and is found by
the avenger of blood outside the bounds of the city of refuge, and is killed by the
avenger, no bloodguilt shall be incurred. 28 For the slayer must remain in the city of
refuge until the death of the high priest; but after the death of the high priest the
slayer may return home.

e Heb *without seeing*

PRIESTS IN ISRAEL'S HISTORY

Numbers 35.25–28 mentions the death of a high priest. Each new high priest had to come from the lineage of Aaron. Listed here are the ones whose stories are told elsewhere in the Bible.

Priest	*Importance*	*Reference*
Aaron	Moses' brother and first priest	Exodus 28.1–3
Eleazar	Watched two of his brothers die in a fire from God because they did not follow God's instructions. He obeyed God and became chief administrator of the tabernacle.	Leviticus 10 Numbers 3.32
Phinehas	Executed a young Israeli idol worshiper and his Midianite mistress to end a plague. He was then promised that his priestly line would never end.	Numbers 25.1–15
Ahitub	A priest during King Saul's reign	1 Samuel 14.3
Zadok	A faithful high priest under King David. He and Nathan anointed Solomon as the next king.	2 Samuel 8.17 1 Kings 1.38, 39
Ahimaaz	Carried the message of Absalom's death to King David, but was apparently afraid to tell about it.	2 Samuel 18.19–29
Azariah	High priest under King Solomon	1 Kings 4.2
Azariah	High priest under Uzziah. He rebuked the king for burning incense himself.	2 Chronicles 26.17–21
	When Hezekiah became king he reopened the temple. Azariah again served as high priest.	2 Chronicles 26.17–21
Amariah	King Jehoshaphat appointed him to judge religious disputes.	2 Chronicles 19.11
Hilkiah	Found the book of the law during Josiah's reign	2 Kings 22.3–13 2 Chronicles 34.14–21
Azariah	Probably one of the first to return to Israel from Babylon	1 Chronicles 9.10, 11
Seraiah	The father of Ezra	Ezra 7.1–5

29 These things shall be a statute and ordinance for you throughout your generations wherever you live.

35.30 Deut 17.6,7 19.15 Mt 18.16 2 Cor 13.1 Heb 10.28

30 If anyone kills another, the murderer shall be put to death on the evidence of
witnesses; but no one shall be put to death on the testimony of a single witness.
31 Moreover you shall accept no ransom for the life of a murderer who is subject to
the death penalty; a murderer must be put to death. 32 Nor shall you accept ransom
for one who has fled to a city of refuge, enabling the fugitive to return to live in the
land before the death of the high priest. 33 You shall not pollute the land in which
you live; for blood pollutes the land, and no expiation can be made for the land, for
the blood that is shed in it, except by the blood of the one who shed it. 34 You shall
not defile the land in which you live, in which I also dwell; for I the LORD dwell
among the Israelites.

35.34 Lev 18.25 Deut 21.1-8 2 Kgs 24.4 Ezek 22.24-27

The inheritance of each tribe to remain secure

36.1,2 Num 27.1-11 Josh 17.3,4

36 The heads of the ancestral houses of the clans of the descendants of Gilead
son of Machir son of Manasseh, of the Josephite clans, came forward and
spoke in the presence of Moses and the leaders, the heads of the ancestral houses of
the Israelites; 2 they said, "The LORD commanded my lord to give the land for inheritance
by lot to the Israelites; and my lord was commanded by the LORD to give the
inheritance of our brother Zelophehad to his daughters. 3 But if they are married
into another Israelite tribe, then their inheritance will be taken from the inheritance
of our ancestors and added to the inheritance of the tribe into which they marry; so
it will be taken away from the alloted portion of our inheritance. 4 And when the
jubilee of the Israelites comes, then their inheritance will be added to the inheritance
of the tribe into which they have married; and their inheritance will be taken
from the inheritance of our ancestral tribe."

5 Then Moses commanded the Israelites according to the word of the LORD,
saying, "The descendants of the tribe of Joseph are right in what they are saying.

36.6 Gen 24.3,57,58

6 This is what the LORD commands concerning the daughters of Zelophehad, 'Let
them marry whom they think best; only it must be into a clan of their father's tribe
that they are married, 7 so that no inheritance of the Israelites shall be transferred
from one tribe to another; for all Israelites shall retain the inheritance of their ancestral
tribes. 8 Every daughter who possesses an inheritance in any tribe of the Israelites
shall marry one from the clan of her father's tribe, so that all Israelites may
continue to possess their ancestral inheritance. 9 No inheritance shall be transferred
from one tribe to another; for each of the tribes of the Israelites shall retain its own
inheritance.' "

36.8 1 Chron 23.22

CITIES OF REFUGE

Six of the Levites' cities were designated as cities of refuge. They were spaced throughout the land and protected those who had accidentally committed a crime or who were awaiting trial.

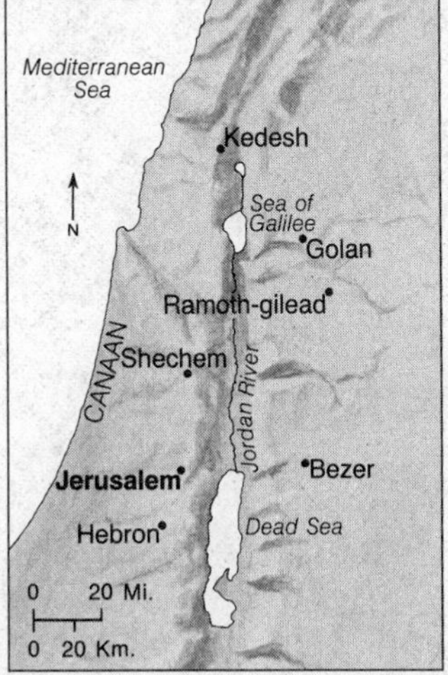

35.33 Murderers were to be executed, for they corrupted the land. But Jesus startles us by saying that even becoming angry at someone for no reason is a sin like murder (Matthew 5.21, 22). Murder and anger stem from the same root, and while one seems a lesser sin, it will often lead to the greater sin. Unchecked bitterness and anger will ultimately destroy us. We need to deal with these unhealthy emotions before they fester and corrupt our lives.

36.1-9 Zelophad had no sons, but he did have five daughters. After he died, his daughters appealed to Moses. If the inheritance would pass on only through the male heirs, then the family line of Zelophad would disappear. God Told Moses that if a man died without sons, then the inheritance would go to his daughters (Numbers 27.8). Now the question of marriage arose. If the duaghter were to marry outside of their tribe, the land would belong to another tribe at the Year of Jubilee. Moses commanded that in such cases the women should marry someone in their own clan and tribe so that each tribe would retain its original inheritance. Later, when the tribes received their land under Joshua, the daughters of Zelophad received their inheritance as God had instructed (Joshua 17.3-6). We don't have to look far to find those who want to be considered "special cases" and "exceptions to the rules." But wise leaders will sort out those who have legitimate complaints and make sure that justice is done in these special situations.

10 The daughters of Zelophehad did as the LORD had commanded Moses.
11 Mahlah, Tirzah, Hoglah, Milcah, and Noah, the daughters of Zelophehad, mar- **36.11** Num 27.1-11 36.1
ried sons of their father's brothers. 12 They were married into the clans of the descendants of Manasseh son of Joseph, and their inheritance remained in the tribe of
their father's clan.
13 These are the commandments and the ordinances that the LORD commanded **36.13** Lev 7.37,38 27.34
through Moses to the Israelites in the plains of Moab by the Jordan at Jericho.

36.13 The book of Numbers covers 39 years and closes with the Israelites poised near the banks of the Jordan River with the promised land in sight. The wanderings in the wilderness have come to an end, and the people are preparing for their next big move—the conquest of the land. The apostle Paul says that the events described in Numbers are examples that warn us and help us avoid the Israelites' mistakes (1 Corinthians 10.1–12). From their experiences we learn that unbelief is disastrous. We also learn not to long for the sinful pleasures of the past, to avoid complaining, and to stay away from all forms of compromise. If we choose to let God lead us, we should not ignore his message in the book of Numbers.

NAMES OF GOD

Name of God	Meaning	Reference	Significance
Elohim	God	Genesis 1.1; Numbers 23.19; Psalms 19.1	Refers to God's power and might. He is the only supreme and true God.
Jehovah (Yahweh)	The Lord	Genesis 2.4; Exodus 6.2, 3	The proper name of the divine person.
El-Elyon	God Most High	Genesis 14.17-20; Numbers 24.16; Psalms 7.19; Isaiah 14.13, 14	He is above all gods; nothing in life is more sacred.
El-Roi	God Who Sees	Genesis 16.12	God oversees all creation and the affairs of people.
El-Shaddai	God Almighty	Genesis 17.1; Psalms 91.1	God is all powerful.
Jehovah-Jireh	The Lord Will Provide	Genesis 22.13, 14	God will provide our real needs.
Jehovah Nissi	The Lord Is My Banner	Exodus 17.15	We should remember God for helping us.
Adonai	Lord	Deuteronomy 6.4	God alone is the head over all.
Yahweh-Elohe Israel	Lord God of Israel	Judges 5.3; Psalms 58.5; Isaiah 17.6; Zephaniah 2.9	He is the God of the nation.
Jehovah-Shalom	The Lord Is Peace	Judges 6.24	God gives us peace so we need not fear.
Kedosh Israel	Holy One of Israel	Isaiah 1.4	God is morally perfect.
Jehovah-Sabbaoth	Lord of Hosts Host refers to armies but also to all the heavenly powers.	1Samuel 1.3; Isaiah 6.1-3	God is our savior and protector.
El-Olam	The Everlasting God	Isaiah 40.28-31	God is eternal. He will never die.
Jehovah-Tsidkenu	The Lord Is Our Righteousness	Jeremiah 23.6; 33.16	God is our standard for right behavior. He alone can make us righteous.
Jehovah-Shammah	The Lord is There	Ezekiel 48.35	God is always present with us.
Attiq Yomin	Ancient of Days	Daniel 7.9; 13.12	God is the ultimate authority. He will one day judge all nations.

DEUTERONOMY

Joseph dies 1805 B.C. (1640 B.C.) — *S L A V E R Y I N E G Y P T* — *Exodus from Egypt 1446 (1280)* — *Ten commandments given 1445 (1279)*

WILDERNESS WANDERIN

VITAL STATISTICS

PURPOSE:
To remind the people of what God has done and encourage them to rededicate their lives to him

AUTHOR:
Moses (except for the final summary which was probably written by Joshua after Moses' death)

TO WHOM WRITTEN:
Israel (the new generation entering the promised land)

DATE WRITTEN:
About 1407/6 B.C.

SETTING:
The east side of the Jordan River, in view of Canaan

KEY VERSE:
"Know therefore that the Lord your God is God, the faithful God who maintains covenant loyalty with those who love him and keep his commandments, to a thousand generations" (7.9).

KEY PEOPLE:
Moses, Joshua

KEY PLACE:
The valley of Arabah in Moab

CLASS reunions, scrapbooks and photo albums, familiar songs, and old neighborhoods—like long-time friends they awaken our memories and stir our emotions. The past is a kaleidoscope of promises, failures, victories, and embarrassments. Sometimes we want to forget memories that are too painful. However, as the years pass, memories of unpleasant events usually fade into our subconscious. But there is a time to remember: mistakes should not be repeated; commitments made must be fulfilled; and the memory of special events can encourage us and move us to action.

Deuteronomy is written in the form of a treaty between a king and his vassal state typical of the second millenium B.C. The book of Deuteronomy calls Israel to remember who God is and what he has done. Lacking faith, the old generation wandered for 40 years and died in the wilderness. They left Egypt behind, but never knew the promised land. Now on the east bank of the Jordan River, Moses prepares the sons and daughters of that faithless generation to possess the land. After a brief history lesson emphasizing God's great acts on behalf of his people, Moses reviews the law. Then he restates the covenant—God's contract with his people.

The lessons are clear. Because of what God has done, Israel should have hope and follow him; because of what he expects, they should listen and obey; because of who he is, they should love him completely. Learning these lessons will prepare them to possess the promised land.

As you hear the message of Deuteronomy, remember how God has expressed his kindness in your life, and then commit yourself anew to trust, love, and obey him.

THE BLUEPRINT

A. WHAT GOD HAS DONE FOR US: MOSES' FIRST ADDRESS (1.1—4.43)

Moses reviewed the mighty acts of God for the nation of Israel. Remembering God's special involvement in our lives gives us hope and encouragement for the future.

B. PRINCIPLES FOR GODLY LIVING: MOSES' SECOND ADDRESS (4.44—29.1)

1. Review of the ten commandments
2. Love God and obey his commandments
3. Laws for proper worship
4. Laws for ruling the nation
5. Laws for human relationships
6. Consequences of obedience and disobedience

Moses reviews God's commands and applies them to specific situations. Knowing what God requires is not enough. We must put God's word into action, making it a part of our lives.

Obeying God's laws brought blessings to the Israelites and disobeying brought misfortune. This was part of the written agreement God made with his people. Although we are not part of this covenant, the principle holds true: obedience and disobedience carry inevitable consequences in this life and the next.

Moses' death; Israelites enter Canaan 1406 (1240)	Judges begin to rule 1375 (1220)	United kingdom under Saul 1050 (1045)

C. A CALL FOR COMMITMENT TO GOD: MOSES' THIRD ADDRESS (29.2—30.20)	Moses called the people to commitment. God still calls us to be committed to love him with all our heart, soul, mind, and strength.
D. THE CHANGE IN LEADERSHIP: MOSES' LAST DAYS (31.1—34.12)	Although Moses made some serious mistakes, he had lived uprightly and carried out God's commands. Moses died with integrity. We too may make some serious mistakes, but that should not stop us from living with integrity and godly commitment.

MEGATHEMES

THEME	EXPLANATION	IMPORTANCE
History	Moses reviewed the mighty acts of God whereby he liberated Israel from slavery in Egypt. He recounted how God had helped them and how the people had disobeyed.	By reviewing God's promises and mighty acts in history, we can learn about his character. We come to know God more intimately through understanding how he has acted in the past. We can also avoid mistakes in our own lives through learning from Israel's past failures.
Laws	God reviewed his laws for the people. The legal contract between God and his people had to be renewed by the new generation about to enter the promised land.	Commitment to God and his truth cannot be taken for granted. Each generation and each person must respond afresh to God's call for obedience.
Love	God's faithful and patient love is portrayed more often than his punishment. God shows his love by being faithful to his people and his promises. In response, God desires love from the heart, not merely legalistically keeping his law.	God's love forms the foundation for our trust in him. We trust him because he loves us. Because God loves us, we should maintain justice and respect.
Choices	God reminded his people that in order to ratify his agreement they must choose the path of obedience. A personal decision to obey would bring benefits to their lives; rebellion would bring severe calamity.	Our choices make a difference. Choosing to follow God benefits us and improves our relationships with others. Choosing to abandon God's ways brings harm to ourselves and others.
Teaching	God commanded the Israelites to teach their children his ways. They were to use ritual, instruction, and memorization to make sure their children understood God's principles and passed them on to the next generation.	Quality teaching for our children must be a priority. It is important to pass on God's truth to future generations in our traditions. But God desires that his truth be in our hearts and minds and not merely in our traditions.

A. WHAT GOD HAS DONE FOR US: MOSES' FIRST ADDRESS (1.1—4.43)

God has led his people out of Egypt and across the great wilderness. Now they stand ready to enter the promised land. But before the Israelites go into the land, Moses has some important advice to give them. He delivers his advice in three parts. In the first part, Moses reviews the history of God's previous care for the people of Israel. Through God's actions in the past, we can learn about the God we serve today.

1 These are the words that Moses spoke to all Israel beyond the Jordan — in the **1.1**
wilderness, on the plain opposite Suph, between Paran and Tophel, Laban, Gen 32.3 Num 21.24,33
Hazeroth, and Di-zahab. 2 (By the way of Mount Seir it takes eleven days to reach Deut 2.8,24
Kadesh-barnea from Horeb.) 3 In the fortieth year, on the first day of the eleventh 3.3; 4.1,44-46
month, Moses spoke to the Israelites just as the LORD had commanded him to speak
to them. 4 This was after he had defeated King Sihon of the Amorites, who reigned
in Heshbon, and King Og of Bashan, who reigned in Ashtaroth and[a] in Edrei.
5 Beyond the Jordan in the land of Moab, Moses undertook to expound this law as
follows:

Leaders chosen from each tribe

6 The LORD our God spoke to us at Horeb, saying, "You have stayed long **1.6**
enough at this mountain. 7 Resume your journey, and go into the hill country of the Ex 19.1 Num 10.11-13
Amorites as well as into the neighboring regions — the Arabah, the hill country, the **1.7**
Shephelah, the Negeb, and the seacoast — the land of the Canaanites and the Leba- Gen 15.18-21
non, as far as the great river, the river Euphrates. 8 See, I have set the land before Deut 4.49 Josh 10.5,40
you; go in and take possession of the land that I[b] swore to your ancestors, to Abra- **1.8**
ham, to Isaac, and to Jacob, to give to them and to their descendants after them." Gen 12.7; 26.3 Ex 33.1
9 At that time I said to you, "I am unable by myself to bear you. 10 The LORD

[a] Gk Syr Vg Compare Josh 12.4: Heb lacks *and* [b] Sam Gk: MT *the LORD*

1.1ff The Israelites spent 40 years on a journey that should have lasted 11 days. It wasn't distance that stood between them and the promised land. It was the condition of their hearts. God's purpose went deeper than simply transporting a huge group of people to a new land. He was preparing them to live in obedience to him once they arrived. What good was the promised land if the Israelites were just as wicked as the nations already living there? The journey was a painful but necessary part of their preparation. Through it God taught the Israelites who he was: the living God, the Leader of their nation. He also taught them who they were: people who were fallen, sinful, prone to rebellion and doubt. He gave his rebellious people the law to help them understand how to relate to their God and to other people. Your spiritual pilgrimage may be lengthy and you may face pain, discouragement, and difficulties. But remember that God isn't just trying to keep you alive. He wants to prepare you to live in service and devotion to him.

1.1–5 The 40 years of desert wandering come to an end in this book. The events of Deuteronomy cover only a week or two of the 11th month of the 40th year (1.3). The 12th and last month was spent in mourning for Moses (34.8). The Israelites then entered the promised land the first month of the 41st year after the exodus (Joshua 4.19).

1.6 Notice that Moses' summary of Israel's 40-year journey begins at Mount Horeb (Sinai), not in Egypt. Why did Moses leave out the first part of the exodus? Moses was not giving an itinerary — he was summarizing the nation's development. In Moses' mind the nation of Israel began at the base of Mount Sinai, not in Egypt, for it was at Mount Sinai that God gave his covenant to the people (Exodus 19, 20). Along with this covenant came knowledge and responsibility. After the people chose to follow God (and it was their choice), they had to know *how* to follow him. Therefore, God gave them a comprehensive set of laws and guidelines that told them how he wanted them to live (these are found in the books of Exodus, Leviticus, and Numbers). The people could no longer say they didn't know the difference between right and wrong. Now that the people had promised to follow God and knew how to follow him, they had a responsibility to do it. Moses probably gave his first speech at Mount Sinai to remind the people of this responsibility as they faced their biggest challenge to date — finally entering the promised land and starting a nation that was to obey God and be a light and example to others.

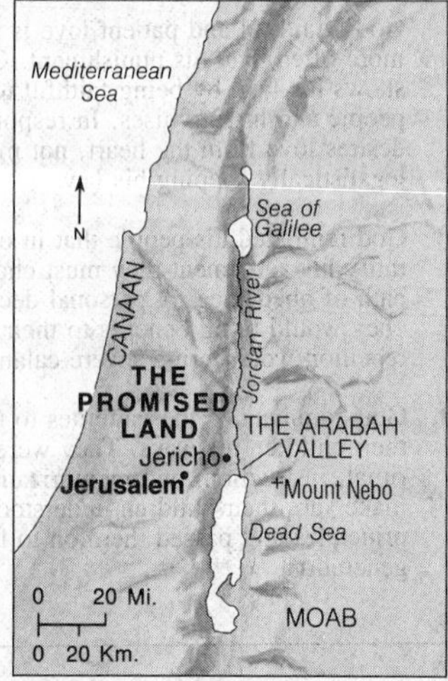

EVENTS IN DEUTERONOMY The book of Deuteronomy opens with Israel camped east of the Jordan River in the Arabah Valley in the land of Moab. Just before the people crossed the river into the promised land, Moses delivered an inspirational speech indicating how they were to live.

1.9–13 It was a tremendous burden for Moses to lead the nation by himself. He could not accomplish the task single-handedly. As churches and families grow, they become more complex. Conflicting needs and quarrels arise. No longer can one leader make all the decisions. Like Moses, you may have a natural tendency to try to do all the work alone. You may be afraid or embarrassed to ask for help. Moses made a wise decision to share the leadership with others. Look for ways of sharing the load so that others may exercise their God-given gifts and abilities.

1.10 Gen 15.5; 22.17 Deut 10.22 26.5; 28.62 Heb 11.12
1.11 Deut 8.1 Ps 115.14
1.12 Ex 18.13,14
1.13 Ex 18.21,22 Num 11.16,17
1.16 Ex 22.21; 23.9 Deut 10.18 24.14
1.17 Ex 18.25,26 Deut 10.17 16.19; 24.17 Prov 24.23 Jas 2.1,9
1.19 Deut 1.2; 8.15 32.10

your God has multiplied you, so that today you are as numerous as the stars of
heaven. 11 May the LORD, the God of your ancestors, increase you a thousand times
more and bless you, as he has promised you! 12 But how can I bear the heavy burden
of your disputes all by myself? 13 Choose for each of your tribes individuals who are
wise, discerning, and reputable to be your leaders." 14 You answered me, "The plan
you have proposed is a good one." 15 So I took the leaders of your tribes, wise and
reputable individuals, and installed them as leaders over you, commanders of thousands, commanders of hundreds, commanders of fifties, commanders of tens, and
officials, throughout your tribes. 16 I charged your judges at that time: "Give the
members of your community a fair hearing, and judge rightly between one person
and another, whether citizen or resident alien. 17 You must not be partial in judging:
hear out the small and the great alike; you shall not be intimidated by anyone, for
the judgment is God's. Any case that is too hard for you, bring to me, and I will
hear it." 18 So I charged you at that time with all the things that you should do.
19 Then, just as the LORD our God had ordered us, we set out from Horeb and
went through all that great and terrible wilderness that you saw, on the way to the
hill country of the Amorites, until we reached Kadesh-barnea. 20 I said to you,
"You have reached the hill country of the Amorites, which the LORD our God is
giving us. 21 See, the LORD your God has given the land to you; go up, take possession, as the LORD, the God of your ancestors, has promised you; do not fear or be
dismayed."

1.22 Num 13.1,2
1.23 Num 13.3-15
1.24 Num 13.21-25

22 All of you came to me and said, "Let us send men ahead of us to explore the
land for us and bring back a report to us regarding the route by which we should go
up and the cities we will come to." 23 The plan seemed good to me, and I selected
twelve of you, one from each tribe. 24 They set out and went up into the hill country,
and when they reached the Valley of Eshcol they spied it out 25 and gathered some
of the land's produce, which they brought down to us. They brought back a report
to us, and said, "It is a good land that the LORD our God is giving us."

Rebellion against God

1.26 Num 14.1-3
1.27 Ex 16.3 Num 14.3 Ps 106.25
1.28 Num 13.28,33 Deut 9.1,2
1.29 Deut 3.22; 7.18 Josh 8.1

26 But you were unwilling to go up. You rebelled against the command of the
LORD your God; 27 you grumbled in your tents and said, "It is because the LORD
hates us that he has brought us out of the land of Egypt, to hand us over to the
Amorites to destroy us. 28 Where are we headed? Our kindred have made our hearts
melt by reporting, 'The people are stronger and taller than we; the cities are large
and fortified up to heaven! We actually saw there the offspring of the Anakim!' "
29 I said to you, "Have no dread or fear of them. 30 The LORD your God, who goes
before you, is the one who will fight for you, just as he did for you in Egypt before

---

1.14–18 Moses identified some of the inner qualities of good leaders: (1) wisdom, (2) fairness, (3) impartiality, and (4) the ability to recognize their limitations. These characteristics differ markedly from the ones that often help elect leaders today: good looks, wealth, popularity, willingness to do anything to get to the top. The qualities Moses identified should be evident in us as we lead, and we should look for them in those we elect to positions of leadership.

1.19–21 God gave the land to his people and told them to take possession of it. By remaining outside the land, the Israelites were disobeying. When God offers a gift, he offers it in good faith. Often, however, when he opens up opportunities, we have doubts and are afraid of failure. Seize your opportunities to grow, to share your faith, and to live in a manner pleasing to God. He will lead the way and give you strength.

1.22 The spies were sent into the land to determine not *whether* they should enter, but *where* they should enter. Upon returning, however, most of the spies concluded that the land was not worth the obstacles. God gave the Israelites the power to conquer the land, but they failed to enter because of the risk and because they did not trust God. God gives us the power to overcome our obstacles, but like the Israelites filled with fear and skepticism, we often let difficulties control our lives. Following God regardless of the difficulties is the way to have courageous, overcoming faith.

1.23–40 Moses retold the story of the spy mission into the promised land (Numbers 13; 14). When the spies returned with reports of giants and walled cities, the people were afraid to move ahead and began to complain about their predicament. But the minority report of Joshua and Caleb pointed out that the land was fertile, the enemy was vulnerable, and God was on their side. We become fearful and immobile when we focus on the negative aspects of a situation. How much better it is to focus on the positive – God's direction and promises. When confronted with an important decision and you know what you should do, move out in faith. Discover and focus on the positives while trusting God to overcome the negatives. Problems don't have to rob you of the victory.

1.28 Canaan was a land with giants and imposing fortresses. The "offspring of the Anakim" may have been seven to nine feet tall. Many of the land's fortified cities had walls as high as 30 feet. The Israelites' fear was understandable, but not justified, for the all-powerful God had already promised them victory.

your very eyes, 31 and in the wilderness, where you saw how the LORD your God
carried you, just as one carries a child, all the way that you traveled until you
reached this place. 32 But in spite of this, you have no trust in the LORD your God,
33 who goes before you on the way to seek out a place for you to camp, in fire by
night, and in the cloud by day, to show you the route you should take."
34 When the LORD heard your words, he was wrathful and swore: 35 "Not one
of these—not one of this evil generation—shall see the good land that I swore to
give to your ancestors, 36 except Caleb son of Jephunneh. He shall see it, and to him
and to his descendants I will give the land on which he set foot, because of his
complete fidelity to the LORD." 37 Even with me the LORD was angry on your account, saying, "You also shall not enter there. 38 Joshua son of Nun, your assistant,
shall enter there; encourage him, for he is the one who will secure Israel's possession of it. 39 And as for your little ones, who you thought would become booty,
your children, who today do not yet know right from wrong, they shall enter there;
to them I will give it, and they shall take possession of it. 40 But as for you, journey
back into the wilderness, in the direction of the Red Sea."[c]
41 You answered me, "We have sinned against the LORD! We are ready to go
up and fight, just as the LORD our God commanded us." So all of you strapped on
your battle gear, and thought it easy to go up into the hill country. 42 The LORD said
to me, "Say to them, 'Do not go up and do not fight, for I am not in the midst of
you; otherwise you will be defeated by your enemies.' " 43 Although I told you, you
would not listen. You rebelled against the command of the LORD and presumptuously went up into the hill country. 44 The Amorites who lived in that hill country
then came out against you and chased you as bees do. They beat you down in Seir
as far as Hormah. 45 When you returned and wept before the LORD, the LORD would
neither heed your voice nor pay you any attention.

Review of the wanderings

2 46 After you had stayed at Kadesh as many days as you did, 1 we journeyed
back into the wilderness, in the direction of the Red Sea,[c] as the LORD had told
me and skirted Mount Seir for many days. 2 Then the LORD said to me: 3 "You have
been skirting this hill country long enough. Head north, 4 and charge the people as
follows: You are about to pass through the territory of your kindred, the descendants of Esau, who live in Seir. They will be afraid of you, so, be very careful 5 not
to engage in battle with them, for I will not give you even so much as a foot's length
of their land, since I have given Mount Seir to Esau as a possession. 6 You shall
purchase food from them for money, so that you may eat; and you shall also buy
water from them for money, so that you may drink. 7 Surely the LORD your God has
blessed you in all your undertakings; he knows your going through this great wilderness. These forty years the LORD your God has been with you; you have lacked
nothing." 8 So we passed by our kin, the descendants of Esau who live in Seir,
leaving behind the route of the Arabah, and leaving behind Elath and Ezion-geber.
When we had headed out along the route of the wilderness of Moab, 9 the LORD
said to me: "Do not harass Moab or engage them in battle, for I will not give you
any of its land as a possession, since I have given Ar as a possession to the descendants of Lot." 10 (The Emim—a large and numerous people, as tall as the
Anakim—had formerly inhabited it. 11 Like the Anakim, they are usually reckoned
as Rephaim, though the Moabites call them Emim. 12 Moreover, the Horim had
formerly inhabited Seir, but the descendants of Esau dispossessed them, destroying

[c] Or *Sea of Reeds*

1.30 Ex 14.14 Deut 20.4
1.31 Deut 32.11 Isa 40.11 Acts 13.18
1.33 Ex 13.21 Num 9.15-23 10.33-36
1.34 Num 14.28-30 32.8-12 Deut 2.14
1.36 Num 14.24 Josh 14.6
1.37 Num 20.12 27.18
1.38 Num 34.16-28 Deut 3.28; 31.7
1.39 Num 14.3,31
1.40 Num 14.25
1.41 Num 14.40
1.42 Num 14.41-43
1.43 Num 14.44
1.44 Num 14.45
2.1 Num 21.4
2.4 Ex 15.15 Num 20.14 Judg 11.17
2.5 Deut 23.7
2.6 Num 20.19
2.7 Deut 8.2; 29.5
2.8 Num 20.20
2.9 Gen 19.37 Deut 1.1-5
2.10 Num 13.28 Josh 14.12
2.11 Deut 2.20 3.11,13 Josh 12.4
2.12 Gen 14.5,6 Num 21.25,35 Deut 2.22

2.4–6 When the Israelites passed through Seir, God advised them to be careful. The Israelites were known as warriors, and the children of Esau—the Edomites—would be understandably nervous as the great crowd passed through their land. God warned the Israelites not to start a fight, to respect the Edomites' territory, and to pay for whatever they used. God wanted the Israelites to deal justly with these neighbors. We must also act justly in dealing with others. Recognize the rights of others, even your opponents. By behaving wisely and justly you may be able to establish or restore a relationship.

2.11 Each nation had removed a tall, Anakim-like people, usually known as the Rephaim, but called Emim by the Moabites, and Zamzummim by the Ammonites (2.20).

them and settling in their place, as Israel has done in the land that the LORD gave
them as a possession.) 13“Now then, proceed to cross over the Wadi Zered.”

2.14,15 Num 14.29-35; 26.64,65; Deut 2.7; Ps 106.26; 1 Cor 10.5; Jude 5

So we crossed over the Wadi Zered. 14And the length of time we had traveled
from Kadesh-barnea until we crossed the Wadi Zered was thirty-eight years, until
the entire generation of warriors had perished from the camp, as the LORD had
sworn concerning them. 15Indeed, the LORD's own hand was against them, to root
them out from the camp, until all had perished.

2.18 Num 21.15; Deut 2.9

2.20 Deut 2.11

16 Just as soon as all the warriors had died off from among the people, 17the
LORD spoke to me, saying, 18“Today you are going to cross the boundary of Moab
at Ar. 19When you approach the frontier of the Ammonites, do not harass them or
engage them in battle, for I will not give the land of the Ammonites to you as a
possession, because I have given it to the descendants of Lot.” 20(It also is usually
reckoned as a land of Rephaim. Rephaim formerly inhabited it, though the Ammonites call them Zamzummim, 21a strong and numerous people, as tall as the
Anakim. But the LORD destroyed them from before the Ammonites so that they
could dispossess them and settle in their place. 22He did the same for the descendants of Esau, who live in Seir, by destroying the Horim before them so that they
could dispossess them and settle in their place even to this day. 23As for the Avvim,
who had lived in settlements in the vicinity of Gaza, the Caphtorim, who came
from Caphtor, destroyed them and settled in their place.) 24“Proceed on your journey and cross the Wadi Arnon. See, I have handed over to you King Sihon the
Amorite of Heshbon, and his land. Begin to take possession by engaging him in
battle. 25This day I will begin to put the dread and fear of you upon the peoples
everywhere under heaven; when they hear report of you, they will tremble and be
in anguish because of you.”

2.23 Gen 10.13,14; 1 Chron 1.11,12; Jer 47.4; Amos 9.7

2.24 Num 21.13; Judg 11.18

2.25 Ex 15.14-16; 23.27; Deut 11.25; Josh 2.9

Review of battles

2.26 Num 21.21; Deut 20.10-13; Judg 11.19

2.29 Deut 2.8,9; 23.3

2.30 Ex 11.10; Num 21.23; Josh 11.20

26 So I sent messengers from the wilderness of Kedemoth to King Sihon of
Heshbon with the following terms of peace: 27“If you let me pass through your
land, I will travel only along the road; I will turn aside neither to the right nor to the
left. 28You shall sell me food for money, so that I may eat, and supply me water for
money, so that I may drink. Only allow me to pass through on foot— 29just as the
descendants of Esau who live in Seir have done for me and likewise the Moabites
who live in Ar—until I cross the Jordan into the land that the LORD our God is
giving us.” 30But King Sihon of Heshbon was not willing to let us pass through, for
the LORD your God had hardened his spirit and made his heart defiant in order to
hand him over to you, as he has now done.

2.33 Num 21.24-30; Deut 3.6; 29.7

2.35,36 Num 31.9-11; Deut 3.7,10; Ps 44.3

2.37 Deut 3.16

31 The LORD said to me, “See, I have begun to give Sihon and his land over to
you. Begin now to take possession of his land.” 32So when Sihon came out against
us, he and all his people for battle at Jahaz, 33the LORD our God gave him over to
us; and we struck him down, along with his offspring and all his people. 34At that
time we captured all his towns, and in each town we utterly destroyed men,
women, and children. We left not a single survivor. 35Only the livestock we kept
as spoil for ourselves, as well as the plunder of the towns that we had captured.
36From Aroer on the edge of the Wadi Arnon (including the town that is in the wadi
itself) as far as Gilead, there was no citadel too high for us. The LORD our God gave
everything to us. 37You did not encroach, however, on the land of the Ammonites,

---

2.13 A “wadi” is a brook, valley, or dry riverbed.

2.14, 15 Israel did not have to spend 40 years on the way to the promised land. God sentenced them to desert wanderings because they rebelled against his love, ignored his commands for right living, and willfully broke their end of the agreement made in Exodus 19.8 and 24.3–8. In short, they disobeyed God. We often make life's journey more difficult than necessary by disobedience. Accept God's love, read and follow his commands in the Bible, and make a promise to stick with God whatever your situation. You will find your life will be less complicated and more rewarding.

2.25 God told Moses he would make the enemy nations afraid of the Israelites. By worldly standards, Israel's army was not intimidating, but Israel had God on its side. Moses no longer had to worry about his enemies, because his enemies were worried about him. The important issue is not whether you are the biggest or strongest, but whether or not you are on God's side.

avoiding the whole upper region of the Wadi Jabbok as well as the towns of the hill
country, just as[d] the LORD our God had charged.

3 When we headed up the road to Bashan, King Og of Bashan came out against
us, he and all his people, for battle at Edrei. 2 The LORD said to me, "Do not
fear him, for I have handed him over to you, along with his people and his land. Do
to him as you did to King Sihon of the Amorites, who reigned in Heshbon." 3 So the
LORD our God also handed over to us King Og of Bashan and all his people. We
struck him down until not a single survivor was left. 4 At that time we captured all
his towns; there was no citadel that we did not take from them—sixty towns, the
whole region of Argob, the kingdom of Og in Bashan. 5 All these were fortress
towns with high walls, double gates, and bars, besides a great many villages. 6 And
we utterly destroyed them, as we had done to King Sihon of Heshbon, in each city
utterly destroying men, women, and children. 7 But all the livestock and the plunder of the towns we kept as spoil for ourselves.

Dividing the land

8 So at that time we took from the two kings of the Amorites the land beyond
the Jordan, from the Wadi Arnon to Mount Hermon 9 (the Sidonians call Hermon
Sirion, while the Amorites call it Senir), 10 all the towns of the tableland, the whole
of Gilead, and all of Bashan, as far as Salecah and Edrei, towns of Og's kingdom
in Bashan. 11 (Now only King Og of Bashan was left of the remnant of the Rephaim. In fact his bed, an iron bed, can still be seen in Rabbah of the Ammonites. By
the common cubit it is nine cubits long and four cubits wide.) 12 As for the land that
we took possession of at that time, I gave to the Reubenites and Gadites the territory
north of Aroer,[e] that is on the edge of the Wadi Arnon, as well as half the hill
country of Gilead with its towns, 13 and I gave to the half-tribe of Manasseh the rest
of Gilead and all of Bashan, Og's kingdom. (The whole region of Argob: all that
portion of Bashan used to be called a land of Rephaim; 14 Jair the Manassite acquired the whole region of Argob as far as the border of the Geshurites and the
Maacathites, and he named them—that is, Bashan—after himself, Havvoth-jair,[f]
as it is to this day.) 15 To Machir I gave Gilead. 16 And to the Reubenites and the
Gadites I gave the territory from Gilead as far as the Wadi Arnon, with the middle
of the wadi as a boundary, and up to the Jabbok, the wadi being boundary of the
Ammonites; 17 the Arabah also, with the Jordan and its banks, from Chinnereth
down to the sea of the Arabah, the Dead Sea,[g] with the lower slopes of Pisgah on
the east.

18 At that time, I charged you as follows: "Although the LORD your God has
given you this land to occupy, all your troops shall cross over armed as the vanguard of your Israelite kin. 19 Only your wives, your children, and your
livestock—I know that you have much livestock—shall stay behind in the towns
that I have given to you. 20 When the LORD gives rest to your kindred, as to you, and
they too have occupied the land that the LORD your God is giving them beyond the
Jordan, then each of you may return to the property that I have given to you."
21 And I charged Joshua as well at that time, saying: "Your own eyes have seen
everything that the LORD your God has done to these two kings; so the LORD will
do to all the kingdoms into which you are about to cross. 22 Do not fear them, for
it is the LORD your God who fights for you."

[d] Gk Tg: Heb *and all* [e] Heb *territory from Aroer* [f] That is *Settlement of Jair* [g] Heb *Salt Sea*

3.1 Num 21.33-35 Deut 1.1-5
3.3 Josh 9.10
3.4 Num 32.33-42 Josh 12.4
3.6 Num 21.2 Deut 2.33,34 20.16 Josh 11.11 Ps 135.10-12
3.7 Josh 8.27
3.8 Num 32.33-42 Josh 12.1-6 13.8-13 Amos 3.9,10
3.9 Deut 4.48 Josh 11.17 Ps 29.5,6
3.12 Num 32.33-42 Deut 2.35,36 Josh 13.8-13
3.13 Num 32.41 Judg 10.4
3.15 Num 32.40
3.17 Josh 13.27
3.18 Num 32.20 Josh 1.12,13 4.12,13
3.19 Num 32.26 Deut 20.5-8 Josh 1.14
3.21 Num 27.18
3.22 Deut 1.30; 20.4 Josh 10.25

3.1–3 The Israelites faced a big problem—the well-trained army of Og, king of Bashan. The Israelites hardly stood a chance. But they won because God fought for them. God can help his people regardless of the problems they face. No matter how insurmountable the obstacles may seem, remember that God is sovereign, and he will keep his promises.

3.11 King Og's bed was about 13 1/2 feet long and 6 feet wide.

3.18 A vanguard was an armed unit that led the rest of the army.

3.21, 22 What encouraging news for Joshua, who was to lead his men against the persistent forces of evil in the promised land! Since God promised to help him win every battle, he had nothing to fear. Our battles may not be against godless armies, but they are just as real as Joshua's. Whether we are resisting temptation or battling fear, God has promised to fight with and for us as we obey him.

Moses' prayer to God

3.23 Jer 15.1
3.26 Num 20.12; 27.14; Deut 1.37; 32.51
3.27 Num 23.14; 27.12; Deut 1.37
3.28 Num 27.18

23 At that time, too, I entreated the LORD, saying: 24 "O Lord GOD, you have
only begun to show your servant your greatness and your might; what god in
heaven or on earth can perform deeds and mighty acts like yours! 25 Let me cross
over to see the good land beyond the Jordan, that good hill country and the Lebanon." 26 But the LORD was angry with me on your account and would not heed me.
The LORD said to me, "Enough from you! Never speak to me of this matter again!
27 Go up to the top of Pisgah and look around you to the west, to the north, to the
south, and to the east. Look well, for you shall not cross over this Jordan. 28 But
charge Joshua, and encourage and strengthen him, because it is he who shall cross
over at the head of this people and who shall secure their possession of the land that
you will see." 29 So we remained in the valley opposite Beth-peor.

Moses urges the people to obey

4.1 Lev 19.37; Deut 5.32,33; 8.1; 16.20; 30.16; Ezek 11.20; 20.11; Rom 10.5
4.2 Mt 5.18
4.3 Num 25.1-9; Deut 3.29
4.5 Lev 26.46; 27.34
4.6 Deut 32.46,47; Ps 19.7,8
4.7 Ps 148.14
4.8 Ps 89.14,15

4 So now, Israel, give heed to the statutes and ordinances that I am teaching you
to observe, so that you may live to enter and occupy the land that the LORD, the
God of your ancestors, is giving you. 2 You must neither add anything to what I
command you nor take away anything from it, but keep the commandments of the
LORD your God with which I am charging you. 3 You have seen for yourselves what
the LORD did with regard to the Baal of Peor—how the LORD your God destroyed
from among you everyone who followed the Baal of Peor, 4 while those of you who
held fast to the LORD your God are all alive today.
5 See, just as the LORD my God has charged me, I now teach you statutes and
ordinances for you to observe in the land that you are about to enter and occupy.
6 You must observe them diligently, for this will show your wisdom and discernment to the peoples, who, when they hear all these statutes, will say, "Surely this
great nation is a wise and discerning people!" 7 For what other great nation has a
god so near to it as the LORD our God is whenever we call to him? 8 And what other
great nation has statutes and ordinances as just as this entire law that I am setting
before you today?
9 But take care and watch yourselves closely, so as neither to forget the things

---

3.28 God had made it clear that Moses would not enter the promised land (Numbers 20.12). So God told Moses to commission Joshua as the new leader and encourage him in this new role. This is a good example to churches and organizations who must eventually replace their leaders. Good leaders prepare their people to function without them by discovering those with leadership potential, providing the training they need, and looking for ways to encourage them.

4.2 What is meant by adding and taking away? These laws were the word of God, and they were complete. How could any human being, with limited wisdom and knowledge, edit God's perfect laws? To add to the laws would make them a burden; to subtract from the laws would make them incomplete. Thus the laws were to remain unchanged. To presume to make changes in God's law is to assume a position of authority over God who gave the laws (Matthew 5.17–19; 15.3–9; Revelation 22.18, 19). The religious leaders at the time of Christ did exactly this; they elevated their own laws to the same level as God's. Jesus rebuked them for this (Matthew 23.1–4).

4.6 Some people work hard to make others think they are smart. The books they carry and the facts they quote are impressive. But Moses said that a reputation for wisdom comes by obeying God's word. This may not be the easiest or most glamorous way to earn a reputation, but it is the most authentic. Do you try to make others think you are intelligent because of what you know or pretend to know? Obeying God's Word will give you a far greater reputation, because it's not just what you know, but what you do that counts.

4.8 Do the laws God gave to the Israelites still apply to Christians today? Their purpose was to point out sin (or potential sin) and show the proper way to deal with that sin. God's laws are just as applicable today as they were 3,000 years ago because they are the perfect expression of (1) who God is and (2) how he wants people to live.

But God gave other laws besides the ten commandments. Are these just as important? God never issued a law that didn't have a purpose. However, many of the laws we read in the Pentateuch were directed specifically to people of that time and culture. Although the specific law may not apply to us, the timeless truth or principle behind the law does.

For example, Christians do not practice animal sacrifice in worship today. However, the principles behind the sacrifices—forgiveness for sin and thankfulness to God—still apply. The sacrifices pointed to the ultimate sacrifice made for us by Jesus Christ. The New Testament says that with the death and resurrection of Jesus Christ the Old Testament laws were fulfilled. This means that while the Old Testament laws help us recognize our sins and correct our wrongdoings, it is Jesus Christ who takes our sins away. Jesus is now our primary example to follow because he alone perfectly obeyed the law and modeled its true intent. Although many of the specific Old Testament laws are no longer necessary, Jesus showed that the spirit of these laws is still applicable today, because the principles they uphold continue to point us to God.

4.9 Moses wanted to make sure that the people did not forget all they had seen God do, so he urged parents to tell their children about God's great miracles. This helped parents remember God's faithfulness, and it provided the means for passing on from one generation to the next the stories recounting God's great acts. It is easy to forget the wonderful ways God has worked in the lives of his people. But you can remember God's great acts of faithfulness by telling your children, friends, or associates what you have seen him do.

that your eyes have seen nor to let them slip from your mind all the days of your life; **4.9**
make them known to your children and your children's children— 10 how you once Ex 13.8 Josh 4.6
stood before the LORD your God at Horeb, when the LORD said to me, "Assemble **4.10**
the people for me, and I will let them hear my words, so that they may learn to fear Ex 19.7-9,16
me as long as they live on the earth, and may teach their children so"; 11 you ap- **4.11**
proached and stood at the foot of the mountain while the mountain was blazing up Ex 19.18 Heb 12.18
to the very heavens, shrouded in dark clouds. 12 Then the LORD spoke to you out of
the fire. You heard the sound of words but saw no form; there was only a voice.
13 He declared to you his covenant, which he charged you to observe, that is, the ten **4.13**
commandments;[h] and he wrote them on two stone tablets. 14 And the LORD charged Ex 31.18 34.1,28
me at that time to teach you statutes and ordinances for you to observe in the land Deut 10.4
that you are about to cross into and occupy.

Moses' warning against idols

15 Since you saw no form when the LORD spoke to you at Horeb out of the fire, **4.15**
take care and watch yourselves closely, 16 so that you do not act corruptly by mak- Ex 19.9,18,21 **4.16**
ing an idol for yourselves, in the form of any figure—the likeness of male or fe- Ex 20.4,5; 32.8
male, 17 the likeness of any animal that is on the earth, the likeness of any winged
bird that flies in the air, 18 the likeness of anything that creeps on the ground, the
likeness of any fish that is in the water under the earth. 19 And when you look up to **4.19**
the heavens and see the sun, the moon, and the stars, all the host of heaven, do not Acts 7.43
be led astray and bow down to them and serve them, things that the LORD your God
has allotted to all the peoples everywhere under heaven. 20 But the LORD has taken **4.20**
you and brought you out of the iron-smelter, out of Egypt, to become a people of 1 Kgs 8.51 Jer 11.4
his very own possession, as you are now.
21 The LORD was angry with me because of you, and he vowed that I should not **4.21**
cross the Jordan and that I should not enter the good land that the LORD your God Num 27.14 Deut 1.37
is giving for your possession. 22 For I am going to die in this land without crossing
over the Jordan, but you are going to cross over to take possession of that good
land. 23 So be careful not to forget the covenant that the LORD your God made with **4.23**
you, and not to make for yourselves an idol in the form of anything that the LORD Josh 23.11
your God has forbidden you. 24 For the LORD your God is a devouring fire, a jealous **4.24**
God. Ex 24.17; 34.14 Heb 12.29
25 When you have had children and children's children, and become compla- **4.25**
cent in the land, if you act corruptly by making an idol in the form of anything, thus Deut 4.16; 31.29
doing what is evil in the sight of the LORD your God, and provoking him to anger,
26 I call heaven and earth to witness against you today that you will soon utterly **4.26**
perish from the land that you are crossing the Jordan to occupy; you will not live Deut 7.4; 8.19 31.29
long on it, but will be utterly destroyed. 27 The LORD will scatter you among the **4.27**
peoples; only a few of you will be left among the nations where the LORD will lead Deut 28.64

h Heb *the ten words*

4.19 God was not excusing the other nations for their idol worship. He was simply saying that while judgment might be delayed for those other nations, it would be swift and complete for Israel because Israel knew God's laws. We must remember that idol worship was not just keeping statues around the house—harmless lumps of clay, wood, or iron. It was the commitment to the evil qualities, beliefs, and practices the idol represented (such as murder, prostitution, cruelty in war, self-centeredness). Because God had so clearly revealed himself in Israel's history, the Israelites had no excuse for worshiping anyone but the true God.

4.24 God is a devouring fire. Because he is morally perfect, he hates sin and cannot accept those who practice it. Moses' sin kept him from entering the promised land, and no sacrifice could remove that judgment. Sin kept us from entering God's presence, but Jesus Christ paid the penalty for our sin and removed God's judgment forever by his death. Trusting in Jesus Christ will save you from God's anger and will allow you to begin a personal relationship with him.

4.24 Jealousy is a demand for someone else's exclusive affection or loyalty. Some jealousy is bad. It is destructive for a man to get upset when his wife talks pleasantly with another man. But other jealousy is good. It is right for a man to demand that his wife treat him, and only him, as her husband. Usually we use the word *jealousy* only for the bad reaction. But God's kind of jealousy is appropriate and good. He is defending his Word and his high honor. He makes a strong, exclusive demand on us: we must treat only Jehovah—and no one else in all the universe—as God.

4.25–28 This warning eventually came true. Again and again, the Israelites turned from God; but God, in his great patience, gave them time to recognize their wrongs and return to him. Finally God's patience was spent, so he allowed the Israelites to be captured and carried off to foreign lands. The warnings in the book of Deuteronomy were clear enough to help the Israelites, but they failed to heed them. A clear warning is not enough to make people obey—they need to take God's warnings to heart.

4.28 Deut 28.36,64 29.17 Ps 115.4-8
4.29 2 Chron 15.4 Neh 1.8,9
4.31 Josh 1.5 Heb 13.5

you. 28 There you will serve other gods made by human hands, objects of wood and
stone that neither see, nor hear, nor eat, nor smell. 29 From there you will seek the
LORD your God, and you will find him if you search after him with all your heart
and soul. 30 In your distress, when all these things have happened to you in time to
come, you will return to the LORD your God and heed him. 31 Because the LORD
your God is a merciful God, he will neither abandon you nor destroy you; he will
not forget the covenant with your ancestors that he swore to them.

There is no other God

4.32 Gen 1.27
4.33 Ex 20.22 Deut 5.24,26
4.34 Ex 14.30 Deut 5.15; 6.21 7.19; 33.29 Ps 136.12
4.35 Ex 8.10; 9.14 Deut 4.39 1 Sam 17.46 Mk 12.29
4.36 Ex 19.9,19 Neh 9.13
4.37 Deut 7.7,8 Ps 105.5-11
4.38 Ex 23.27-30 Num 32.3,4
4.40 Ex 23.26

32 For ask now about former ages, long before your own, ever since the day
that God created human beings on the earth; ask from one end of heaven to the
other: has anything so great as this ever happened or has its like ever been heard of?
33 Has any people ever heard the voice of a god speaking out of a fire, as you have
heard, and lived? 34 Or has any god ever attempted to go and take a nation for himself from the midst of another nation, by trials, by signs and wonders, by war, by
a mighty hand and an outstretched arm, and by terrifying displays of power, as the
LORD your God did for you in Egypt before your very eyes? 35 To you it was shown
so that you would acknowledge that the LORD is God; there is no other besides him.
36 From heaven he made you hear his voice to discipline you. On earth he showed
you his great fire, while you heard his words coming out of the fire. 37 And because
he loved your ancestors, he chose their descendants after them. He brought you out
of Egypt with his own presence, by his great power, 38 driving out before you nations greater and mightier than yourselves, to bring you in, giving you their land for
a possession, as it is still today. 39 So acknowledge today and take to heart that the
LORD is God in heaven above and on the earth beneath; there is no other. 40 Keep his
statutes and his commandments, which I am commanding you today for your own
well-being and that of your descendants after you, so that you may long remain in
the land that the LORD your God is giving you for all time.

Cities of refuge

4.41 Num 35.6 Deut 19.1-13 Josh 20.7

41 Then Moses set apart on the east side of the Jordan three cities 42 to which a
homicide could flee, someone who unintentionally kills another person, the two
not having been at enmity before; the homicide could flee to one of these cities and
live: 43 Bezer in the wilderness on the tableland belonging to the Reubenites, Ramoth in Gilead belonging to the Gadites, and Golan in Bashan belonging to the
Manassites.

B. PRINCIPLES FOR GODLY LIVING: MOSES' SECOND ADDRESS (4.44–29.1)

After reviewing the history of Israel's journey, Moses recounts the ten commandments and the other laws given to the Israelites at Mount Sinai. He urges them to obey the law and reminds them of the consequences of disobeying God's laws. The ten commandments and all of God's laws point out to us where we fall short and show us how we should act as God's people.

44 This is the law that Moses set before the Israelites. 45 These are the decrees
and the statutes and ordinances that Moses spoke to the Israelites when they had
come out of Egypt, 46 beyond the Jordan in the valley opposite Beth-peor, in the
land of King Sihon of the Amorites, who reigned at Heshbon, whom Moses and the

4.29 Do you want to know God? This verse promised the Israelites that they would find God when they searched with all their hearts and souls. God is knowable and wants to be known – but we have to want to know him. Acts of service and worship must be accompanied by sincere devotion of the heart. As Hebrews 11.6 says, "Whoever would approach him must believe that he exists and that he rewards those who seek him." God will reward those who pursue a relationship with him.

4.40 Was Israel guaranteed prosperity for obeying God's laws? Yes – but we have to look carefully at what that means. God's laws were designed to make his chosen nation healthy, just, and merciful. When they followed those laws, they prospered. This does not mean, however, that no sickness, no sadness, and no misunderstandings existed among them. Rather, it means that as a nation they prospered, and that individuals' problems were handled as fairly as possible. Today God's promise of prosperity – his constant presence, comfort, and the resources to live as we should – extends to all believers. We will face trials; Jesus assured us of that. But we will avoid the misery that directly results from intentional sin, and we will know that a great treasure awaits us in heaven.

Israelites defeated when they came out of Egypt. 47 They occupied his land and the
land of King Og of Bashan, the two kings of the Amorites on the eastern side of the
Jordan: 48 from Aroer, which is on the edge of the Wadi Arnon, as far as Mount **4.48**
Sirion[i] (that is, Hermon), 49 together with all the Arabah on the east side of the Deut 2.35,36
Jordan as far as the Sea of the Arabah, under the slopes of Pisgah.

1. Review of the ten commandments

5 Moses convened all Israel, and said to them: **5.1**
Hear, O Israel, the statutes and ordinances that I am addressing to you today; Deut 6.4; 9.1 20.3; 27.9
you shall learn them and observe them diligently. 2 The LORD our God made a cove- **5.2**
nant with us at Horeb. 3 Not with our ancestors did the LORD make this covenant, Ex 19.5 Num 26.64,65
but with us, who are all of us here alive today. 4 The LORD spoke with you face to **5.4**
face at the mountain, out of the fire. 5 (At that time I was standing between the Num 14.14
LORD and you to declare to you the words[j] of the LORD; for you were afraid be- **5.5**
cause of the fire and did not go up the mountain.) And he said: Ex 19.16,25
6 I am the LORD your God, who brought you out of the land of Egypt, out of the **5.6**
house of slavery; 7 you shall have no other gods before[k] me. Ex 20.2-17
8 You shall not make for yourself an idol, whether in the form of anything that **5.7** Ex 20.3
is in heaven above, or that is on the earth beneath, or that is in the water under the Mt 4.10
earth. 9 You shall not bow down to them or worship them; for I the LORD your God **5.8** Ex 20.4
am a jealous God, punishing children for the iniquity of parents, to the third and Lev 26.1
fourth generation of those who reject me, 10 but showing steadfast love to the thou- Deut 4.16,17 **5.9,10**
sandth generation[l] of those who love me and keep my commandments. Ex 20.4-6
11 You shall not make wrongful use of the name of the LORD your God, for the **5.11**
LORD will not acquit anyone who misuses his name. Deut 6.13; 10.20 Mt 5.33
12 Observe the sabbath day and keep it holy, as the LORD your God com- **5.12**
manded you. 13 Six days you shall labor and do all your work. 14 But the seventh day Ex 20.8-11 Lev 26.2
is a sabbath to the LORD your God; you shall not do any work — you, or your son or
your daughter, or your male or female slave, or your ox or your donkey, or any of
your livestock, or the resident alien in your towns, so that your male and female
slave may rest as well as you. 15 Remember that you were a slave in the land of **5.15**
Egypt, and the LORD your God brought you out from there with a mighty hand and Ex 20.11 Deut 15.15
an outstretched arm; therefore the LORD your God commanded you to keep the 16.12
sabbath day. **5.16**
16 Honor your father and your mother, as the LORD your God commanded you, Ex 20.12; 21.17 Eph 6.2,3

[i] Syr: Heb *Sion* [j] Q Mss Sam Gk Syr Vg Tg: MT *word* [k] Or *besides* [l] Or *to thousands*

5.1 The people had entered into a covenant with God, and Moses commanded them to hear, learn, and observe his statutes. Christians also have entered into a covenant with God (through Jesus Christ) and should be responsive to what God expects. Moses' threefold command to the Israelites is excellent advice for all God's followers. *Hearing* is absorbing and accepting information about God. *Learning* is understanding its meaning and implications. *Observing* is putting into action all we have learned and understood. All three parts are essential to a growing relationship with God.

5.7 A "god" is whatever people put first in their lives. Some people literally worship other gods by joining cults or strange religions. In a more subtle way, many of us worship other gods by building our lives around something other than the one true God. If your greatest desire is for popularity, power, or money, you are devoting yourself to something other than God. To put God first, (1) recognize what is taking his place in your life; (2) renounce this substitute god as unworthy of your devotion; (3) ask God for forgiveness; (4) restructure your priorities so that love for God is the motive for everything you do; and (5) examine yourself daily to be sure you are giving God first place.

5.8–10 How would you feel if someone took a picture of you, framed it, stared at it a lot, showed it to others, but completely ignored the real you? God does not want to be treated this way either. He wants a genuine relationship with us, not mere ritual. He wants us to know him. God knows that if we put anything other than him at the center of our lives, we will not reach our potential and become all that he wants us to be.

5.11 We are familiar with the sin to be avoided in this commandment, that we should not use the name of the Lord in an empty or worthless way. But there is also a good work that is commanded: to praise God and ascribe to him glory. This is the opposite of taking his name in vain. While you might be able to keep yourself from swearing, how have you done at finding time to praise God and honor his name?

5.16 Obeying our parents is our main task when we are young, but respect for them should continue even beyond their death. One way to honor parents is to provide for them in times of financial need or when they are ill and unable to care for themselves. Perhaps the best way to honor them is to pass on their godly values to our children. Honoring involves all that sons and daughters do with their lives — the way they work and talk, the values they hold, and the morals they practice. What are you doing to honor your parents? Are you living in a way that brings honor to them?

so that your days may be long and that it may go well with you in the land that the
LORD your God is giving you.
17 You shall not murder.[m]
18 Neither shall you commit adultery.
19 Neither shall you steal.
20 Neither shall you bear false witness against your neighbor.
21 Neither shall you covet your neighbor's wife.
Neither shall you desire your neighbor's house, or field, or male or female slave,
or ox, or donkey, or anything that belongs to your neighbor.
22 These words the LORD spoke with a loud voice to your whole assembly at the
mountain, out of the fire, the cloud, and the thick darkness, and he added no more.
He wrote them on two stone tablets, and gave them to me. 23 When you heard the
voice out of the darkness, while the mountain was burning with fire, you approached me, all the heads of your tribes and your elders; 24 and you said, "Look,
the LORD our God has shown us his glory and greatness, and we have heard his
voice out of the fire. Today we have seen that God may speak to someone and the
person may still live. 25 So now why should we die? For this great fire will consume
us; if we hear the voice of the LORD our God any longer, we shall die. 26 For who
is there of all flesh that has heard the voice of the living God speaking out of fire,
as we have, and remained alive? 27 Go near, you yourself, and hear all that the
LORD our God will say. Then tell us everything that the LORD our God tells you,
and we will listen and do it."
28 The LORD heard your words when you spoke to me, and the LORD said to

5.17 Ex 20.13; Mt 5.21
5.18 Ex 20.14; Lk 18.20; Jas 2.11
5.19 Ex 20.15; Rom 13.9
5.20 Ex 20.16
5.21 Rom 7.7; 13.9
5.22 Ex 19.16-19
5.25 Ex 20.18,19; Deut 18.16; Heb 12.19
5.26 Ex 24.3
5.28 Deut 18.17

[m] Or *kill*

BROKEN COMMANDMENTS

The ten commandments were God's standards for right living. To obey them was to obey God. Yet throughout the Old Testament, we can see how each commandment was broken. As you read the stories, notice the tragic consequences that occurred as a result of violating God's law.

Ten Commandments	*Notable Violations*
"You shall have no other gods before me."	Solomon (1 Kings 11)
"You shall not make for yourself an idol. . . . You shall not bow down to them or worship them."	The golden calf-idol incident (Exodus 32); generations after Joshua (Judges 2.10–14; 2 Kings 21.1–15; Jeremiah 1.16)
"You shall not make wrongful use of the name of the Lord your God."	Zedekiah (Ezekiel 17.15–21)
"Observe the sabbath day and keep it holy."	Judah (2 Chronicles 36.21)
"Honor your father and your mother."	Eli's sons—Hophni and Phinheas (1 Samuel 2.12, 23–25)
"You shall not murder."	Hazael (2 Kings 8.15)
"Neither shall you commit adultery."	David (2 Samuel 11.2–5)
"Neither shall you steal."	Ahab (1 Kings 21.1–19)
"Neither shall you bear false witness against your neighbor."	Saul (1 Samuel 15.13–25)
"Neither shall you covet your neighbor's wife. Neither shall you desire your neighbor's house, or field . . . or any thing that belongs to your neighbor."	Achan (Joshua 7.19–26)

5.17 "But I don't murder people," you may say. Good. That fulfills the letter of the law. But Jesus explained that hateful anger breaks this commandment (Matthew 5.21, 22). Have you ever been so angry with someone who mistreated you that for a moment you wished that person were dead? Have you ever fantasized that you could "do someone in"? Jesus' teaching concerning this law demonstrates that we are capable of murder in our hearts. Even if we are legally innocent, we are all morally guilty of murder and need to ask God's forgiveness. We need to commit ourselves to the opposite of hatred and anger – love and reconciliation.

5.21 We are not to covet anything. Not only can coveting make us miserable, it can also lead us to other sins such as adultery and stealing. Coveting is a useless exercise because God is able to provide everything we really need, even if he does not always give us everything we want. To drive out covetousness, we need to practice being content with what we have. The apostle Paul emphasizes the significance of contentment in Philippians 4.11. It's a matter of perspective. Instead of thinking about what we don't have, we should thank God for what he has given and strive to be content. After all, our most important possession is free and available to everyone – eternal life through Christ.

me: "I have heard the words of this people, which they have spoken to you; they are
right in all that they have spoken. 29 If only they had such a mind as this, to fear me
and to keep all my commandments always, so that it might go well with them and
with their children forever! 30 Go say to them, 'Return to your tents.' 31 But you,
stand here by me, and I will tell you all the commandments, the statutes and the
ordinances, that you shall teach them, so that they may do them in the land that I am
giving them to possess." 32 You must therefore be careful to do as the LORD your
God has commanded you; you shall not turn to the right or to the left. 33 You must
follow exactly the path that the LORD your God has commanded you, so that you
may live, and that it may go well with you, and that you may live long in the land
that you are to possess.

5.29 Ps 81.13 Isa 48.18 Mt 23.37 Lk 19.42
5.31 Ex 24.12 Ezek 20.11
5.32 Deut 17.20 28.14 Josh 1.7; 23.6
5.33 Ex 20.12 Deut 4.1,40 25.13-15

2. Love God and obey his commandments

Teach your children to obey God

6 Now this is the commandment—the statutes and the ordinances—that the
LORD your God charged me to teach you to observe in the land that you are
about to cross into and occupy, 2 so that you and your children and your children's
children, may fear the LORD your God all the days of your life, and keep all his
decrees and his commandments that I am commanding you, so that your days may
be long. 3 Hear therefore, O Israel, and observe them diligently, so that it may go
well with you, and so that you may multiply greatly in a land flowing with milk and
honey, as the LORD, the God of your ancestors, has promised you.
4 Hear, O Israel: The LORD is our God, the LORD alone.[n] 5 You shall love the
LORD your God with all your heart, and with all your soul, and with all your might.
6 Keep these words that I am commanding you today in your heart. 7 Recite them to
your children and talk about them when you are at home and when you are away,
when you lie down and when you rise. 8 Bind them as a sign on your hand, fix them
as an emblem[o] on your forehead, 9 and write them on the doorposts of your house
and on your gates.
10 When the LORD your God has brought you into the land that he swore to your

6.1 Deut 5.1; 12.1
6.2 Deut 4.9; 10.12
6.3 Ex 3.8,17
6.4,5 Mt 22.37 Mk 12.29,30 Lk 10.27 1 Cor 8.4,6
6.6 Deut 10.12 11.13 Josh 1.8
6.7 Ex 12.26 Ps 78.4-6
6.8 Ex 13.9 Deut 11.18
6.9 Deut 11.20

[n] Or *The LORD our God is one LORD,* or *The LORD our God, the LORD is one,* or *The LORD is our God, the LORD is one*
[o] Or *as a frontlet*

5.29 God told Moses that he wanted the people to have a heart for him—to *want* to obey him. There is a difference between doing something because it is required and doing something because we want to. God is not interested in forced religious exercises and rule-keeping. He wants our hearts and lives completely dedicated to him. If we love him, obedience will follow.

5.33 How closely do we need to follow the commands of God? How good is good enough? This verse shows us plainly that God expects what we are unable to give—absolute obedience. He wants us to follow exactly the path that he has laid out for us. And this is where God's grace enters the picture. When we see how far we have strayed off of his path, we can turn to him through faith in Christ for forgiveness of our sins. After he has placed us back on the path, these commandments show us how to live pleasing to him.

6.3 For a nation that had wandered 40 years in a parched desert, a land flowing with milk and honey sounded like paradise. It brought to mind rich crops, rushing streams, gentle rains, and lush fields filled with livestock. The Israelites could have had all that 40 years earlier. Numbers 13 and 14 explain how the people missed their chance. Now Moses was determined to help the people avoid the same mistake by whetting their appetite for the beautiful land and then clearly explaining the conditions for entering the land.

6.4 Monotheism—belief in only one God—was a distinctive feature of Hebrew religion. Many ancient religions believed in many gods. But the God of Abraham, Isaac, and Jacob is the God of the whole earth, the only true God. This was an important insight for the nation of Israel, because they were about to enter a land filled with people who believed in many gods. Both then and today, there are people who prefer to place their trust in many different "gods." But the day is coming when God will be recognized as the only one. He will be the King over all the earth (Zechariah 14.9).

6.4–9 This passage is often said to be the central theme of Deuteronomy. It sets a pattern that helps us relate the word of God to our daily lives. We are to love God, think constantly about his commandments, teach his commandments to our children, and live each day by the guidelines in his Word. God emphasized the importance of parents' teaching the Bible to their children. The church and Christian schools cannot be used to escape from this responsibility. The Bible provides so many opportunities for object lessons and practical teaching that it would be a shame to study it only one day a week. Eternal truths are most effectively learned in the loving environment of a God-fearing home.

6.5 Jesus said that loving God with all your heart, soul, and mind is the first and greatest commandment (Matthew 22.37–39). This command, combined with the command to love your neighbor (Leviticus 19.18), encompasses all the other Old Testament laws.

6.6 To keep God's words in our hearts means to know and believe them so well that they become part of us.

6.7 The Hebrews were extremely successful at making religion an integral part of life. The reason for their success was that religious education was life-oriented, not information-oriented. They used the context of daily life to teach about God. The key to teaching your children to love God is stated simply and clearly in these verses. If you want your children to follow God, you must make God a part of your everyday experience. You must teach your children to see God in all aspects of life, not just those that are church related.

6.10 Deut 8.10; 9.1 Josh 24.13
6.13 Mt 4.10 Lk 4.8
6.15 Deut 4.24 5.9,10 11.16,17
6.16 Ex 17.7 Mt 4.7 Lk 4.12 1 Cor 10.9
6.17 Ex 15.26 Deut 11.22
6.18 Deut 4.40; 8.11 12.24,25
6.20 Ex 13.8,14
6.24 Deut 6.17; 10.12

ancestors, to Abraham, to Isaac, and to Jacob, to give you—a land with fine, large
cities that you did not build, 11 houses filled with all sorts of goods that you did not
fill, hewn cisterns that you did not hew, vineyards and olive groves that you did not
plant—and when you have eaten your fill, 12 take care that you do not forget the
LORD, who brought you out of the land of Egypt, out of the house of slavery. 13 The
LORD your God you shall fear; him you shall serve, and by his name alone you shall
swear. 14 Do not follow other gods, any of the gods of the peoples who are all
around you, 15 because the LORD your God, who is present with you, is a jealous
God. The anger of the LORD your God would be kindled against you and he would
destroy you from the face of the earth.

16 Do not put the LORD your God to the test, as you tested him at Massah.
17 You must diligently keep the commandments of the LORD your God, and his
decrees, and his statutes that he has commanded you. 18 Do what is right and good
in the sight of the LORD, so that it may go well with you, and so that you may go
in and occupy the good land that the LORD swore to your ancestors to give you,
19 thrusting out all your enemies from before you, as the LORD has promised.

20 When your children ask you in time to come, "What is the meaning of the
decrees and the statutes and the ordinances that the LORD our God has commanded
you?" 21 then you shall say to your children, "We were Pharaoh's slaves in Egypt,
but the LORD brought us out of Egypt with a mighty hand. 22 The LORD displayed
before our eyes great and awesome signs and wonders against Egypt, against Pharaoh and all his household. 23 He brought us out from there in order to bring us in,
to give us the land that he promised on oath to our ancestors. 24 Then the LORD
commanded us to observe all these statutes, to fear the LORD our God, for our
lasting good, so as to keep us alive, as is now the case. 25 If we diligently observe

DANGER IN PLENTY

"... When you have eaten your fill, take care that you do not forget the Lord ..." (Deuteronomy 6.11, 12). It is often most difficult to follow God when life is easy—we can fall prey to temptation and fall away from God. Here are some notable examples of this truth.

Person	*Reference*	*Comment*
Adam	Genesis 3	Adam lived in a perfect world and had a perfect relationship with God. His needs were met; he had everything. But he fell to Satan's deception.
Noah	Genesis 9	Noah and his family had survived the flood and the whole world was theirs. They were prosperous, and life was easy. Noah shamed himself by becoming drunk and cursed his son Ham.
The nation of Israel	Judges 2	God had given Israel the promised land—rest at last with no more wandering. But as soon as brave and faithful Joshua died, they fell into the idolatrous practices of the Canaanites.
David	2 Samuel 11	David ruled well, and Israel was a dominant nation, politically, economically, and militarily. In the midst of prosperity and success, he committed adultery with Bathsheba and had her husband Uriah murdered.
Solomon	1 Kings 11	Solomon truly had it all: power, wealth, fame, and wisdom. But his very abundance was the source of his downfall. He loved his pagan, idolatrous wives so much that he allowed himself and Israel to copy their detestable religious rites.

6.10-13 Moses warned the people not to forget God when they entered the promised land and became prosperous. Prosperity, more than poverty, can dull our spiritual vision, because it tends to make us self-sufficient and eager to acquire still more of everything – except God. The same thing can happen in our church. Once we become successful in terms of numbers, programs, and buildings, we can easily become self-sufficient and less sensitive to our need for God. This leads us to concentrate on self-preservation rather than thankfulness and service to God. Note: a "hewn cistern" was a well dug by hand.

6.24 Does "for our lasting good" mean that we can expect only prosperity and no suffering when we obey God? What is promised here is a right relationship with God for all those who love him with all their heart. It speaks of a good relationship with God and the ultimate benefit of knowing him. It is not blanket protection against poverty, adversity, or suffering. We can have this right relationship with him by obeying his command to love him with all that we are.

6.25 "We will be in the right" means that we will be right with God, or "righteous."

this entire commandment before the LORD our God, as he has commanded us, we
will be in the right."

Conquer the enemy nations

7 When the LORD your God brings you into the land that you are about to enter
and occupy, and he clears away many nations before you—the Hittites, the
Girgashites, the Amorites, the Canaanites, the Perizzites, the Hivites, and the Jebusites, seven nations mightier and more numerous than you—2 and when the LORD
your God gives them over to you and you defeat them, then you must utterly destroy them. Make no covenant with them and show them no mercy. 3 Do not intermarry with them, giving your daughters to their sons or taking their daughters for
your sons, 4 for that would turn away your children from following me, to serve
other gods. Then the anger of the LORD would be kindled against you, and he would
destroy you quickly. 5 But this is how you must deal with them: break down their
altars, smash their pillars, hew down their sacred poles,[p] and burn their idols with
fire. 6 For you are a people holy to the LORD your God; the LORD your God has
chosen you out of all the peoples on earth to be his people, his treasured possession.
7 It was not because you were more numerous than any other people that the
LORD set his heart on you and chose you—for you were the fewest of all peoples.
8 It was because the LORD loved you and kept the oath that he swore to your ancestors, that the LORD has brought you out with a mighty hand, and redeemed you
from the house of slavery, from the hand of Pharaoh king of Egypt. 9 Know therefore that the LORD your God is God, the faithful God who maintains covenant loyalty with those who love him and keep his commandments, to a thousand
generations, 10 and who repays in their own person those who reject him. He does
not delay but repays in their own person those who reject him. 11 Therefore, observe diligently the commandment—the statutes, and the ordinances—that I am
commanding you today.
12 If you heed these ordinances, by diligently observing them, the LORD your
God will maintain with you the covenant loyalty that he swore to your ancestors;
13 he will love you, bless you, and multiply you; he will bless the fruit of your
womb and the fruit of your ground, your grain and your wine and your oil, the
increase of your cattle and the issue of your flock, in the land that he swore to your
ancestors to give you. 14 You shall be the most blessed of peoples, with neither
sterility nor barrenness among you or your livestock. 15 The LORD will turn away
from you every illness; all the dread diseases of Egypt that you experienced, he will
not inflict on you, but he will lay them on all who hate you. 16 You shall devour all
the peoples that the LORD your God is giving over to you, showing them no pity;
you shall not serve their gods, for that would be a snare to you.
17 If you say to yourself, "These nations are more numerous than I; how can I
dispossess them?" 18 do not be afraid of them. Just remember what the LORD your
God did to Pharaoh and to all Egypt, 19 the great trials that your eyes saw, the signs
and wonders, the mighty hand and the outstretched arm by which the LORD your
God brought you out. The LORD your God will do the same to all the peoples of
whom you are afraid. 20 Moreover, the LORD your God will send the pestilence[q]
against them, until even the survivors and the fugitives are destroyed. 21 Have no

7.1 Ex 3.8 Deut 20.17 Josh 3.10 Acts 13.19
7.2 Ex 23-32
7.3 Josh 23.12
7.5 Ex 23.24; 34.13
7.6 Ex 19.5,6 Deut 14.2; 26.18 Amos 3.2 1 Pet 2.9
7.7 Deut 4.37 Jn 15.16
7.8 Lk 1.55,72,73
7.9 Ex 20.6; 34.7 Deut 4.39 5.9,10 1 Cor 1.9 2 Cor 1.18 2 Thess 3.3 2 Tim 2.13 Heb 11.11
7.12 Lev 26.3 Deut 28.1
7.13 Lev 26.9 Deut 28.2-6 30.5,6
7.14 Ex 23.26 Deut 33.29 Ps 147.19,20
7.15 Ex 15.26; 23.26
7.16 Ex 23.32 Deut 7.2
7.17 Deut 8.17
7.18 Num 14.9 Deut 1.19,20, 21; 8.2
7.19 Deut 4.34; 8.17 11.3,4 Neh 9.10
7.20 Ex 23.28 Josh 24.12

[p] Heb *Asherim* [q] Or *hornets*: Meaning of Heb uncertain

7.2 God instructed the Israelites to utterly destroy their enemies. How can a God of love and mercy wipe out everyone, even children? Although God is loving and merciful, he is also just. These enemy nations were as much a part of God's creation as Israel was, but God does not allow evil to continue unchecked. God had punished Israel by not allowing those who had disobeyed to enter the promised land. The command to destroy these nations was both a judgment and a safety measure. On one hand, the people living in the land were being judged for their sin, and Israel was God's instrument of judgment—just as God would one day use other nations to judge Israel for its sin (2 Chronicles 36.17; Isaiah 10.12). On the other hand, God's command was designed to protect Israel from being ruined by the idolatry and immorality of its enemies. To think that God is too "nice" to judge sin would be to underestimate him.

7.6 How did Israel deserve to be chosen above all of the other nations at that time? It was not a matter of Israel's merit, but of God keeping his promise to their ancestors. Just as God chose the nation of Israel, he has chosen all believers today to be a part of his treasured possession. Similarly, it is not because of our merit that we have come to faith in Christ, but he chose us out of his goodness and grace.

7.21 Ex 29.45 Lev 26.11 Ps 68.18
7.22 Ex 23.27-30
7.24 Deut 11.25 Josh 1.5; 6.2 10.8; 23.9
7.25 Deut 7.2; 12.3 Josh 7.1,21
7.26 Deut 13.17 Josh 6.18,19

dread of them, for the LORD your God, who is present with you, is a great and
awesome God. 22 The LORD your God will clear away these nations before you little
by little; you will not be able to make a quick end of them, otherwise the wild
animals would become too numerous for you. 23 But the LORD your God will give
them over to you, and throw them into great panic, until they are destroyed. 24 He
will hand their kings over to you and you shall blot out their name from under
heaven; no one will be able to stand against you, until you have destroyed them.
25 The images of their gods you shall burn with fire. Do not covet the silver or the
gold that is on them and take it for yourself, because you could be ensnared by it;
for it is abhorrent to the LORD your God. 26 Do not bring an abhorrent thing into
your house, or you will be set apart for destruction like it. You must utterly detest
and abhor it, for it is set apart for destruction.

8.1 Lev 26.3
8.2 Ex 15.25 Deut 13.3 Job 33.16-18 Ps 81.7
8.3 Ps 78.24
8.4 Deut 29.5 Neh 9.21
8.5 Ps 89.30-32 Prov 3.11,12 Heb 12.6

Do not forget God

8 This entire commandment that I command you today you must diligently observe, so that you may live and increase, and go in and occupy the land that the
LORD promised on oath to your ancestors. 2 Remember the long way that the LORD
your God has led you these forty years in the wilderness, in order to humble you,
testing you to know what was in your heart, whether or not you would keep his
commandments. 3 He humbled you by letting you hunger, then by feeding you with
manna, with which neither you nor your ancestors were acquainted, in order to
make you understand that one does not live by bread alone, but by every word that
comes from the mouth of the LORD.[r] 4 The clothes on your back did not wear out
and your feet did not swell these forty years. 5 Know then in your heart that as a
parent disciplines a child so the LORD your God disciplines you. 6 Therefore keep

[r] Or *by anything that the LORD decrees*

OBEDIENCE Deuteronomy 8.1 tells us to obey God's commandments. We do this by obeying God with . . .

OUR HEART	By loving him more than any relationship, activity, achievement, or possession.
OUR WILL	By committing ourselves completely to him.
OUR MIND	By seeking to know him and his Word, so his principles and values form the foundation of all we think and do.
OUR BODY	By recognizing that our strengths, talents, and sexuality are given to us by God to be used for pleasure and fulfillment according to his rules, not ours.
OUR FINANCES	By deciding that all of the resources we have ultimately come from God, and that we are to be managers of them and not owners.
OUR FUTURE	By deciding to make service to God and man the main purpose of our life's work.

7.21–24 Moses told the Israelites that God would destroy Israel's enemies, but not all at once. God had the power to destroy those nations instantly, but he chose to do it in stages. In the same way and with the same power, God could miraculously and instantaneously change your life. Usually, however, he chooses to help you gradually, teaching you one lesson at a time. Rather than expect instant spiritual maturity and solutions to all your problems, slow down and work one step at a time, trusting God to make up the difference between where you should be and where you are now. You'll soon look back and see that a miraculous transformation has occurred.

7.25, 26 Moses warned Israel against becoming ensnared by the idols of the defeated nations by coveting the silver and gold on them. We may think it's all right to be close to sin as long as we don't participate. "After all," we say, "I didn't do anything wrong!" But being close can hurt as we become attracted and finally give in. The only sure way to stay from sin is to stay away!

8.3 Jesus quoted this verse when the devil tempted him to turn stones into bread (Matthew 4.4). Many people think that life is based on satisfying their appetites. If they can earn enough money to dress, eat, and play in high style, they think they are living "the good life." But such things do not satisfy our deepest longings. In the end they leave us empty and dissatisfied. Real life, according to Moses, comes from total commitment to God, the one who created life itself. It requires discipline, sacrifice, and hard work, and that's why most people never find it. At first it may not seem to be as much fun as the world's way of living, but gradually, as our friendship with God deepens, it leads to strength of character, peace of mind, and deep satisfaction. The long-term rewards of obeying God are greater than anything the world has to offer.

8.4 It's usually easy for us to take God's protection for granted. We seldom take notice or thank God when our car doesn't break down, our clothes don't rip, and our tools don't break. The people of Israel also failed to take notice, it seems. At least they did not appear very thankful. Like us, they expected their clothes to last and work well. And that's all right, but they did not remember to give thanks to God for these blessings. What has been working well for you? What has been giving you good service? What has been lasting for a long time without breaking down or apart? Remember to thank God for those quiet blessings.

the commandments of the LORD your God, by walking in his ways and by fearing
him. 7 For the LORD your God is bringing you into a good land, a land with flowing
streams, with springs and underground waters welling up in valleys and hills, 8 a
land of wheat and barley, of vines and fig trees and pomegranates, a land of olive
trees and honey, 9 a land where you may eat bread without scarcity, where you will
lack nothing, a land whose stones are iron and from whose hills you may mine
copper. 10 You shall eat your fill and bless the LORD your God for the good land that
he has given you.

11 Take care that you do not forget the LORD your God, by failing to keep his
commandments, his ordinances, and his statutes, which I am commanding you
today. 12 When you have eaten your fill and have built fine houses and live in them,
13 and when your herds and flocks have multiplied, and your silver and gold is
multiplied, and all that you have is multiplied, 14 then do not exalt yourself, forgetting the LORD your God, who brought you out of the land of Egypt, out of the house
of slavery, 15 who led you through the great and terrible wilderness, an arid wasteland with poisonous[s] snakes and scorpions. He made water flow for you from flint
rock, 16 and fed you in the wilderness with manna that your ancestors did not know,
to humble you and to test you, and in the end to do you good. 17 Do not say to
yourself, "My power and the might of my own hand have gotten me this wealth."
18 But remember the LORD your God, for it is he who gives you power to get wealth,
so that he may confirm his covenant that he swore to your ancestors, as he is doing
today. 19 If you do forget the LORD your God and follow other gods to serve and
worship them, I solemnly warn you today that you shall surely perish. 20 Like the
nations that the LORD is destroying before you, so shall you perish, because you
would not obey the voice of the LORD your God.

8.7 Deut 10.7; 11.9-15; Jer 2.7
8.8 Deut 32.13
8.10 Ps 103.2
8.11 Deut 4.9,23; 6.10-12
8.12 Prov 3.9; Hos 13.6
8.15 Ex 17.6; Num 20.11; 21.6; Deut 1.19-21; 32.13; Ps 78.15; 114.8
8.16 Ex 16.15; Deut 8.2; Jn 6.30,31
8.18 Prov 10.22; Hos 2.8
8.19 Deut 4.26; 30.18
8.20 Dan 9.11,12

Do not forget God's mercy

9 Hear, O Israel! You are about to cross the Jordan today, to go in and dispossess nations larger and mightier than you, great cities, fortified to the heavens,
2 a strong and tall people, the offspring of the Anakim, whom you know. You have
heard it said of them, "Who can stand up to the Anakim?" 3 Know then today that
the LORD your God is the one who crosses over before you as a devouring fire; he
will defeat them and subdue them before you, so that you may dispossess and destroy them quickly, as the LORD has promised you.

4 When the LORD your God thrusts them out before you, do not say to yourself,
"It is because of my righteousness that the LORD has brought me in to occupy this
land"; it is rather because of the wickedness of these nations that the LORD is dispossessing them before you. 5 It is not because of your righteousness or the upright-

9.1 Num 13.27-30; Deut 2.18; 12.10; Josh 1.10; 11.21
9.3 Ps 78.52,53
9.4 Lev 18.23-30; Deut 7.24; 12.31; 18.9-14; 31.27

[s] Or *fiery*; Heb *seraph*

8.10 The Israelites were to bless the Lord after eating their fill in the promised land. This verse is traditionally cited as the reason we say grace before or after meals. Its purpose, however, was to warn the Israelites not to forget God when their needs and wants were satisfied. Let your table prayers serve as a constant reminder of the Lord's goodness to you and your duty to those less fortunate.

8.11–20 In times of plenty, we often take credit for our prosperity and begin to feel that our own hard work and cleverness have made us rich. It is easy to get so busy collecting and managing our wealth that we push God right out of our lives. But it is God who gives us everything we have, and it is God who asks us to manage it for him. Don't forget God in your abundance, or he will remove his blessing from you. Remember that the most valuable thing in life—your relationship with God—is free.

9.2, 3 The Anakim were enormous people, some almost ten feet tall. Goliath, probably a descendant of this race, was over nine feet tall (1 Samuel 17.4–7). Unfortunately, these great men used their stature as a means of intimidation rather than for noble causes. Their appearance alone frightened the Israelite spies (Numbers 13.28), and their bad reputation may have been the deciding factor that kept the Israelites out of the land 40 years earlier (Numbers 13, 14). Moses used all his persuasive power to convince his people that God could handle these bullies. He used the illustration of God as a devouring fire, for not even a giant could stand up to that.

9.3 God promised to go before the Israelites as a "devouring fire" to help them conquer their enemies. Fire was a symbol of holiness and purification, illustrating God's desire to purify the land of wicked people in order to make Israel a holy nation.

9.5, 6 If the Israelites were so stubborn, why did God make such wonderful promises to them? There are two good reasons: (1) A promise is a promise. God and Israel had made a treaty (Genesis 15, 17; Exodus 19, 20). God promised to be faithful to them and they promised to obey him. The agreement was irrevocable and eternal. Even though the Israelites rarely upheld their end of the agreement, God would always be faithful to his part. (Although he has punished them several times, he has always remained faithful.) (2) God's mercy is unconditional. No matter how many times the people turned from God, he was always there to restore them. It is comforting to know that despite our inconsistencies and sins, God

ness of your heart that you are going in to occupy their land; but because of the
wickedness of these nations the LORD your God is dispossessing them before you,
in order to fulfill the promise that the LORD made on oath to your ancestors, to
Abraham, to Isaac, and to Jacob.
6 Know, then, that the LORD your God is not giving you this good land to occupy because of your righteousness; for you are a stubborn people. 7 Remember
and do not forget how you provoked the LORD your God to wrath in the wilderness;
you have been rebellious against the LORD from the day you came out of the land
of Egypt until you came to this place.
8 Even at Horeb you provoked the LORD to wrath, and the LORD was so angry
with you that he was ready to destroy you. 9 When I went up the mountain to receive
the stone tablets, the tablets of the covenant that the LORD made with you, I remained on the mountain forty days and forty nights; I neither ate bread nor drank
water. 10 And the LORD gave me the two stone tablets written with the finger of
God; on them were all the words that the LORD had spoken to you at the mountain
out of the fire on the day of the assembly. 11 At the end of forty days and forty nights
the LORD gave me the two stone tablets, the tablets of the covenant. 12 Then the
LORD said to me, "Get up, go down quickly from here, for your people whom you
have brought from Egypt have acted corruptly. They have been quick to turn from
the way that I commanded them; they have cast an image for themselves." 13 Furthermore the LORD said to me, "I have seen that this people is indeed a stubborn
people. 14 Let me alone that I may destroy them and blot out their name from under
heaven; and I will make of you a nation mightier and more numerous than they."
15 So I turned and went down from the mountain, while the mountain was
ablaze; the two tablets of the covenant were in my two hands. 16 Then I saw that you
had indeed sinned against the LORD your God, by casting for yourselves an image
of a calf; you had been quick to turn from the way that the LORD had commanded
you. 17 So I took hold of the two tablets and flung them from my two hands, smash-
ing them before your eyes. 18 Then I lay prostrate before the LORD as before, forty
days and forty nights; I neither ate bread nor drank water, because of all the sin you
had committed, provoking the LORD by doing what was evil in his sight. 19 For I
was afraid that the anger that the LORD bore against you was so fierce that he would
destroy you. But the LORD listened to me that time also. 20 The LORD was so angry
with Aaron that he was ready to destroy him, but I interceded also on behalf of
Aaron at that same time. 21 Then I took the sinful thing you had made, the calf, and
burned it with fire and crushed it, grinding it thoroughly, until it was reduced to
dust; and I threw the dust of it into the stream that runs down the mountain.
22 At Taberah also, and at Massah, and at Kibroth-hattaavah, you provoked the
LORD to wrath. 23 And when the LORD sent you from Kadesh-barnea, saying, "Go
up and occupy the land that I have given you," you rebelled against the command
of the LORD your God, neither trusting him nor obeying him. 24 You have been
rebellious against the LORD as long as he has[t] known you.
25 Throughout the forty days and forty nights that I lay prostrate before the
LORD when the LORD intended to destroy you, 26 I prayed to the LORD and said,
"Lord GOD, do not destroy the people who are your very own possession, whom
you redeemed in your greatness, whom you brought out of Egypt with a mighty
hand. 27 Remember your servants, Abraham, Isaac, and Jacob; pay no attention to
the stubbornness of this people, their wickedness and their sin, 28 otherwise the land

9.6 Deut 9.13,14 10.16; 31.27 Ps 78.17,40
9.7 Ex 14.11 Num 11.4,5 14.20-22 Deut 8.2; 31.27 32.5,6
9.8 Ex 32.7 Ps 106.19,20
9.9 Ex 24.18 Deut 9.18
9.12 Ex 32.7,8
9.13 Ex 32.10
9.15 Ex 32.15
9.16 Ex 32.19 Acts 7.40,41
9.17 Ex 32.19
9.18 Ex 34.8,9,28 Deut 9.9; 10.10
9.19 Ex 32.10,11 Heb 12.21
9.20 Ex 32.2,3,21
9.21 Ex 32.20
9.22 Ex 17.7 Num 11.3,34
9.24 Ex 32.9 Deut 9.7; 31.27
9.25 Ex 34.8 Deut 9.18
9.26 Ex 32.11-13 34.9 Num 14.13
9.27 Ex 32.31 Ps 78.7,8

[t] Sam Gk: MT *I have*

loves us unconditionally. Eternal life is not achieved on the merit system, but on the mercy system. God loves us no matter who we are or what we have done.

9.18 In the record of this event in Exodus 32, it seems as though Moses acted immediately, grinding the golden calf and forcing the people to drink water mixed with it. But that should not be taken as a strict chronological order. Apparently Moses spent 40 days and nights interceding for the people.

9.23 Moses was reminding the people of the nation's unbelief 40 years earlier, when they feared to enter Canaan. The Israelites had not believed God would be able to help them – in spite of all he had already done. They refused to follow, because they looked only to their own limited resources instead of to God. Unbelief is the root of many sins and problems. When you feel lost, it may be because you're looking everywhere but to God for your help and guidance. (See Psalms 81.6–12; 95.8; 106.13–20; Hebrews 3.)

from which you have brought us might say, 'Because the LORD was not able to
bring them into the land that he promised them, and because he hated them, he has
brought them out to let them die in the wilderness.' 29 For they are the people of 9.29
your very own possession, whom you brought out by your great power and by your Deut 4.34
outstretched arm."

Do not forget to fear God

10 At that time the LORD said to me, "Carve out two tablets of stone like the 10.1
former ones, and come up to me on the mountain, and make an ark of wood. Ex 25.10; 34.1
2 I will write on the tablets the words that were on the former tablets, which you 10.2
smashed, and you shall put them in the ark." 3 So I made an ark of acacia wood, cut Ex 25.16 Deut 4.13
two tablets of stone like the former ones, and went up the mountain with the two Heb 9.4
tablets in my hand. 4 Then he wrote on the tablets the same words as before, the ten 10.3 Ex 34.4; 37.1
commandments[u] that the LORD had spoken to you on the mountain out of the fire 10.4
on the day of the assembly; and the LORD gave them to me. 5 So I turned and came Ex 34.28
down from the mountain, and put the tablets in the ark that I had made; and there Deut 4.13 10.5
they are, as the LORD commanded me. Ex 40.20
6 (The Israelites journeyed from Beeroth Bene-jaakan[v] to Moserah. There 10.6
Aaron died, and there he was buried; his son Eleazar succeeded him as priest. Num 20.25,26 33.15-38
7 From there they journeyed to Gudgodah, and from Gudgodah to Jotbathah, a land 10.8
with flowing streams. 8 At that time the LORD set apart the tribe of Levi to carry the Num 3.6; 18.1
ark of the covenant of the LORD, to stand before the LORD to minister to him, and Deut 18.5; 21.5 31.9
to bless in his name, to this day. 9 Therefore Levi has no allotment or inheritance 10.9
with his kindred; the LORD is his inheritance, as the LORD your God promised him.) Num 18.20,24 26.62
10 I stayed on the mountain forty days and forty nights, as I had done the first Deut 18.2
time. And once again the LORD listened to me. The LORD was unwilling to destroy Josh 14.3,4 Ezek 44.28
you. 11 The LORD said to me, "Get up, go on your journey at the head of the people, 10.10
that they may go in and occupy the land that I swore to their ancestors to give Deut 9.18 10.11
them." Ex 32.34; 33.1

Do not forget to obey God

12 So now, O Israel, what does the LORD your God require of you? Only to fear 10.12
the LORD your God, to walk in all his ways, to love him, to serve the LORD your Deut 6.5 Jer 7.22,23
God with all your heart and with all your soul, 13 and to keep the commandments of
the LORD your God[w] and his decrees that I am commanding you today, for your 10.14
own well-being. 14 Although heaven and the heaven of heavens belong to the LORD Ps 68.33 115.16
your God, the earth with all that is in it, 15 yet the LORD set his heart in love on your 10.16
ancestors alone and chose you, their descendants after them, out of all the peoples, Lev 26.41,42 Deut 30.6
as it is today. 16 Circumcise, then, the foreskin of your heart, and do not be stubborn Jer 4.4 Rom 2.29
any longer. 17 For the LORD your God is God of gods and Lord of lords, the great 10.17
God, mighty and awesome, who is not partial and takes no bribe, 18 who executes Ps 136.2

[u] Heb *the ten words* [v] Or *the wells of the Bene-jaakan* [w] Q Ms Gk Syr: MT lacks *your God*

10.5 The tables of the law were still in the ark about 500 years later, when Solomon put it in his newly built temple (1 Kings 8.9). The ark last appears in the Israelites' history during the reign of Josiah, about 300 years after Solomon (2 Chronicles 35.3).

10.12, 13 Often we ask, "What does God expect of me?" Here Moses gives a summary that is simple in form and easy to remember. Here are the essentials: (1) Fear God (have reverence for him). (2) Walk in all his ways. (3) Love and serve him with all your heart. How often we complicate faith with man-made rules, regulations, and requirements. Are you frustrated and burned out from trying hard to please God? Concentrate on his real requirements and find peace. Respect, follow, and love.

10.16–19 God required all male Israelites to be circumcised, but he wanted them to go beyond performing the surgery to understanding its meaning. They needed to submit to God inside, in their hearts, as well as outside, in their bodies. Then they could begin to imitate God's love and justice in their relationships with others. If our hearts are right with God, then our relationships with other people can be made right too. When your heart has been cleansed and you have been reconciled to God, you will begin to see a difference in the way you treat others.

10.17 In saying that the Lord is God of gods and Lord of lords, Moses was distinguishing the true God from all the local gods worshiped throughout the land. Then Moses went a step further, calling God "mighty and awesome." God has such awesome power and justice that people cannot stand before him without his mercy. Fortunately, his mercy toward his people is unlimited. When we begin to grasp the extent of God's mercy toward us, we see what true love is and how deeply God loves us. Although our sins deserve severe judgment, God has chosen to show love and mercy to all who seek him.

10.18 Ex 22.22 Deut 27.19 Ps 68.5; 103.6
10.19 Ex 22.21 Lev 19.34
10.21 Ex 15.2
10.22 Gen 46.27
11.1 Lev 18.29,30 Deut 6.5,6 10.12,13 11.8,31; 28.1
11.2 Deut 5.2,3 7.19; 8.3
11.4 Ex 14.28; 15.4 Ps 106.6-11
11.5 Ps 77.19,20
11.6 Num 16.31 26.5-11

justice for the orphan and the widow, and who loves the strangers, providing them
food and clothing. 19 You shall also love the stranger, for you were strangers in the
land of Egypt. 20 You shall fear the LORD your God; him alone you shall worship;
to him you shall hold fast, and by his name you shall swear. 21 He is your praise; he
is your God, who has done for you these great and awesome things that your own
eyes have seen. 22 Your ancestors went down to Egypt seventy persons; and now
the LORD your God has made you as numerous as the stars in heaven.
11 You shall love the LORD your God, therefore, and keep his charge, his decrees, his ordinances, and his commandments always. 2 Remember today
that it was not your children (who have not known or seen the discipline of the
LORD your God), but it is you who must acknowledge his greatness, his mighty
hand and his outstretched arm, 3 his signs and his deeds that he did in Egypt to
Pharaoh, the king of Egypt, and to all his land; 4 what he did to the Egyptian army,
to their horses and chariots, how he made the water of the Red Sea[x] flow over them
as they pursued you, so that the LORD has destroyed them to this day; 5 what he did
to you in the wilderness, until you came to this place; 6 and what he did to Dathan
and Abiram, sons of Eliab son of Reuben, how in the midst of all Israel the earth
opened its mouth and swallowed them up, along with their households, their tents,
and every living being in their company; 7 for it is your own eyes that have seen
every great deed that the LORD did.

Choose between blessings and curses

11.8 Deut 26.17 31.6,7,23 Josh 1.6,7
11.9 Deut 4.40; 5.33 6.2 Ps 34.12 Prov 3.1,2
11.11 Deut 8.7-9 Ps 104.10-13 Jer 2.7
11.13 Deut 4.29; 6.5 8.6
11.14 Lev 26.4,5 Deut 28.12
11.15 Deut 6.10-12 8.10 Joel 2.19
11.16 Deut 8.19; 30.17
11.17 Deut 4.26; 28.24 Josh 23.13
11.18 Ex 13.16 Ps 119.11
11.19 Ps 78.5,6

8 Keep, then, this entire commandment that I am commanding you today, so
that you may have strength to go in and occupy the land that you are crossing over
to occupy, 9 and so that you may live long in the land that the LORD swore to your
ancestors to give them and to their descendants, a land flowing with milk and
honey. 10 For the land that you are about to enter to occupy is not like the land of
Egypt, from which you have come, where you sow your seed and irrigate by foot
like a vegetable garden. 11 But the land that you are crossing over to occupy is a land
of hills and valleys, watered by rain from the sky, 12 a land that the LORD your God
looks after. The eyes of the LORD your God are always on it, from the beginning of
the year to the end of the year.
13 If you will only heed his every commandment[y] that I am commanding you
today—loving the LORD your God, and serving him with all your heart and with all
your soul— 14 then he[z] will give the rain for your land in its season, the early rain
and the later rain, and you will gather in your grain, your wine, and your oil; 15 and
he[z] will give grass in your fields for your livestock, and you will eat your fill.
16 Take care, or you will be seduced into turning away, serving other gods and
worshiping them, 17 for then the anger of the LORD will be kindled against you and
he will shut up the heavens, so that there will be no rain and the land will yield no
fruit; then you will perish quickly off the good land that the LORD is giving you.
18 You shall put these words of mine in your heart and soul, and you shall bind
them as a sign on your hand, and fix them as an emblem[a] on your forehead.
19 Teach them to your children, talking about them when you are at home and
when you are away, when you lie down and when you rise. 20 Write them on the

[x] Or *Sea of Reeds* [y] Compare Gk: Heb *my commandments* [z] Sam Gk Vg: MT *I* [a] Or *as a frontlet*

10.19 Just as the Israelites' ancestors were at one time strangers in a strange land, so they were to be friends to foreigners who were seeking a new life with them. Likewise, we are commanded to love foreigners. By showing genuine love, we may bring those who are not yet Christians to Christ. We must remember that all of us were brought to Christ through someone else's loving concern.

10.20 "By his name you shall swear" means that God alone should have their allegiance.

11.7 Israel had strong reasons to believe in God and obey his commandments. They had witnessed a parade of mighty miracles that demonstrated God's love and care for them. Incredibly, they still had trouble remaining faithful. Since few of us have seen such dramatic miracles, it may seem even more difficult for us to obey God and remain faithful. However, we have the Bible, the written record of God's acts throughout history. Reading God's Word gives us a panoramic view of both the miracles Israel saw and others they didn't see. The lessons from the past, the instructions for the present, and the glimpses into the future give us many opportunities to strengthen our faith in God.

11.13 This statement sums up the entire law of God—to love and serve God completely. Often people think that God has a whole list of rules and requirements. But everything will be fulfilled if we love him and serve him.

doorposts of your house and on your gates, 21 so that your days and the days of
your children may be multiplied in the land that the LORD swore to your ancestors
to give them, as long as the heavens are above the earth.
22 If you will diligently observe this entire commandment that I am command- 11.22
ing you, loving the LORD your God, walking in all his ways, and holding fast to Deut 6.17; 10.20; 11.1
him, 23 then the LORD will drive out all these nations before you, and you will dis- 11.23
possess nations larger and mightier than yourselves. 24 Every place on which you Deut 4.38; 7.1
set foot shall be yours; your territory shall extend from the wilderness to the Leba- 11.24 Gen 15.8
non and from the River, the river Euphrates, to the Western Sea. 25 No one will be Ex 23.31 Deut 1.7,8
able to stand against you; the LORD your God will put the fear and dread of you on Josh 1.3
all the land on which you set foot, as he promised you. 11.25 Ex 23.27
26 See, I am setting before you today a blessing and a curse: 27 the blessing, if Deut 7.24
you obey the commandments of the LORD your God that I am commanding you 11.26
today; 28 and the curse, if you do not obey the commandments of the LORD your Deut 30.1,15-20
God, but turn from the way that I am commanding you today, to follow other gods
that you have not known.
29 When the LORD your God has brought you into the land that you are entering 11.29
to occupy, you shall set the blessing on Mount Gerizim and the curse on Mount Deut 27.12-26 Josh 8.30-35
Ebal. 30 As you know, they are beyond the Jordan, some distance to the west, in the 11.30
land of the Canaanites who live in the Arabah, opposite Gilgal, beside the oak[b] of Gen 12.6 Josh 4.19; 24.26
Moreh.
31 When you cross the Jordan to go in to occupy the land that the LORD your 11.31
God is giving you, and when you occupy it and live in it, 32 you must diligently Josh 1.10,11
observe all the statutes and ordinances that I am setting before you today.

3. Laws for proper worship

12 These are the statutes and ordinances that you must diligently observe in the 12.1
land that the LORD, the God of your ancestors, has given you to occupy all Deut 4.1; 6.1
the days that you live on the earth.

Only one altar for sacrifice

2 You must demolish completely all the places where the nations whom you are 12.2
about to dispossess served their gods, on the mountain heights, on the hills, and Ex 34.13 Lev 26.30
under every leafy tree. 3 Break down their altars, smash their pillars, burn their Num 33.52 Judg 2.2
sacred poles[c] with fire, and hew down the idols of their gods, and thus blot out
their name from their places. 4 You shall not worship the LORD your God in such 12.4,5 Ex 20.24
ways. 5 But you shall seek the place that the LORD your God will choose out of all Josh 9.27; 18.1 2 Kgs 16.4
your tribes as his habitation to put his name there. You shall go there, 6 bringing 17.10,11 Jer 3.6
there your burnt offerings and your sacrifices, your tithes and your donations, your Jn 4.19,20

[b] Gk Syr: Compare Gen 12.6; Heb *oaks* or *terebinths* [c] Heb *Asherim*

11.26 What is God's curse? It is not a magician's spell. To understand it, we must remember the conditions of the treaty between God and Israel. Both parties had agreed to the terms. The blessings would benefit Israel if they kept their part of the treaty: they would receive the land, live there forever, have fruitful crops, and expel their enemies. The curse would fall on Israel only if they broke their agreement; then they would forfeit God's blessing and would be in danger of crop failure, invasion, and expulsion from their land. Joshua later reviewed these blessings and curses with the entire nation (Joshua 8.34).

11.26 It is amazing that God offered the Israelites a choice between blessings and curses. It is even more amazing that most of them, through their disobedience, chose the curses. We have the same fundamental choice today. We can live for ourselves or live in service to God. To choose our own way is to travel on a dead-end road, but to choose God's way is to receive eternal life (John 5.24).

12.2, 3 When taking over a nation, the Israelites were supposed to destroy every heathen altar and idol in the land. God knew it would be easy for them to change their beliefs if they started using those altars, so nothing was to remain that might tempt them to worship idols. We too should ruthlessly find and remove any centers of false worship in our lives. These may be activities, attitudes, possessions, relationships, places, or habits – anything that tempts us to turn our hearts from God and do wrong. We should never flatter ourselves by thinking we're too strong to be tempted. Israel learned that lesson.

12.4, 5 God continued to separate himself and his people from the practices of the heathen. In Canaan, pagan sacrifice could be carried out anywhere and in any way. But the Israelites were to worship one God, one way, at one specified place. This was a type of "quality control" to keep the people from falling into their own ways of worshiping, which could lead to idolatry. Moses was not denouncing individual and spontaneous worship. Instead, he was emphasizing the importance of a body of believers gathering together at a specified place and time to worship God.

12.6 "Votive gifts" were offerings given in fulfillment of a vow.

12.6 Lev 17.3,4 Deut 14.22 26.2,3
12.7 Deut 12.12,18 14.26; 15.20
12.8 Judg 17.6
12.10 Josh 3.17; 11.23
12.12 Deut 10.9 12.7,18,19 26.11
12.13 Deut 12.4,5
12.15 Deut 12.20-23 14.3-5
12.16 Lev 17.10-12 Deut 15.23
12.17 Deut 12.26 14.22; 26.12
12.18 Deut 12.4,5,26
12.20 Lev 11.2,3 Deut 12.16 15.23; 18.3-5
12.24 Deut 4.40
12.26 Lev 3.1 Deut 12.20

votive gifts, your freewill offerings, and the firstlings of your herds and flocks.
7 And you shall eat there in the presence of the LORD your God, you and your households together, rejoicing in all the undertakings in which the LORD your God has
blessed you.

8 You shall not act as we are acting here today, all of us according to our own
desires, 9 for you have not yet come into the rest and the possession that the LORD
your God is giving you. 10 When you cross over the Jordan and live in the land that
the LORD your God is allotting to you, and when he gives you rest from your enemies all around so that you live in safety, 11 then you shall bring everything that I
command you to the place that the LORD your God will choose as a dwelling for his
name: your burnt offerings and your sacrifices, your tithes and your donations, and
all your choice votive gifts that you vow to the LORD. 12 And you shall rejoice before the LORD your God, you together with your sons and your daughters, your
male and female slaves, and the Levites who reside in your towns (since they have
no allotment or inheritance with you).

13 Take care that you do not offer your burnt offerings at any place you happen
to see. 14 But only at the place that the LORD will choose in one of your
tribes—there you shall offer your burnt offerings and there you shall do everything
I command you.

15 Yet whenever you desire you may slaughter and eat meat within any of your
towns, according to the blessing that the LORD your God has given you; the unclean
and the clean may eat of it, as they would of gazelle or deer. 16 The blood, however,
you must not eat; you shall pour it out on the ground like water. 17 Nor may you eat
within your towns the tithe of your grain, your wine, and your oil, the firstlings of
your herds and your flocks, any of your votive gifts that you vow, your freewill
offerings, or your donations; 18 these you shall eat in the presence of the LORD your
God at the place that the LORD your God will choose, you together with your son
and your daughter, your male and female slaves, and the Levites resident in your
towns, rejoicing in the presence of the LORD your God in all your undertakings.
19 Take care that you do not neglect the Levite as long as you live in your land.

20 When the LORD your God enlarges your territory, as he has promised you,
and you say, "I am going to eat some meat," because you wish to eat meat, you may
eat meat whenever you have the desire. 21 If the place where the LORD your God
will choose to put his name is too far from you, and you slaughter as I have commanded you any of your herd or flock that the LORD has given you, then you may
eat within your towns whenever you desire. 22 Indeed, just as gazelle or deer is
eaten, so you may eat it; the unclean and the clean alike may eat it. 23 Only be sure
that you do not eat the blood; for the blood is the life, and you shall not eat the life
with the meat. 24 Do not eat it; you shall pour it out on the ground like water. 25 Do
not eat it, so that all may go well with you and your children after you, because you
do what is right in the sight of the LORD. 26 But the sacred donations that are due
from you, and your votive gifts, you shall bring to the place that the LORD will
choose. 27 You shall present your burnt offerings, both the meat and the blood, on
the altar of the LORD your God; the blood of your other sacrifices shall be poured
out beside[d] the altar of the LORD your God, but the meat you may eat.

[d] *Or on*

12.12, 18 The Hebrews placed great emphasis on family worship. Whether offering a sacrifice or attending a great feast, the family was often together. This gave the children a healthy attitude toward worship, and it put extra meaning into it for the adults. Watching a family member confess his or her sin was just as important as celebrating a great holiday together. Although there are appropriate times to separate people by ages, some of the most meaningful worship can be experienced only when shared by old and young.

12.13, 14 While the pagans offered sacrifices to their gods, they offered them in many places. In contrast, the Israelites were only to offer sacrifices in the prescribed manner and in the prescribed places. This restriction was meant to insure purity of worship for the nation of Israel. Later, they would neglect this injunction and offer sacrifices at the high places where pagan deities were worshiped (see for example, 2 Kings 23 where Josiah destroyed these other altars). While we do not generally have the problem of offering sacrifices at other locations, we should still take steps to safeguard the purity of worship in our congregations.

12.16 Eating blood was forbidden for several reasons: (1) it was an integral part of the pagan practices of the land the Israelites were about to enter; (2) it represented life, which is sacred to God; (3) it was a symbol of the sacrifice that had to be made for sin. (For more on why eating blood was prohibited see the note on Leviticus 17.14.)

28 Be careful to obey all these words that I command you today,[e] so that it may — **12.28**
go well with you and with your children after you forever, because you will be — Deut 4.40
doing what is good and right in the sight of the LORD your God.

Warnings against worshiping other gods

29 When the LORD your God has cut off before you the nations whom you are
about to enter to dispossess them, when you have dispossessed them and live in
their land, 30 take care that you are not snared into imitating them, after they have — **12.30**
been destroyed before you: do not inquire concerning their gods, saying, "How did — Rom 16.19
these nations worship their gods? I also want to do the same." 31 You must not do — **12.31**
the same for the LORD your God, because every abhorrent thing that the LORD hates — Lev 18.21; Deut 9.5; 18.10
they have done for their gods. They would even burn their sons and their daughters — Ps 106.37,38
in the fire to their gods. 32[f] You must diligently observe everything that I com- — **12.32**
mand you; do not add to it or take anything from it. — Deut 4.2

13 [g] If prophets or those who divine by dreams appear among you and promise — **13.1,2**
you omens or portents, 2 and the omens or the portents declared by them take — Num 12.6; Deut 18.20-22
place, and they say, "Let us follow other gods" (whom you have not known) "and
let us serve them," 3 you must not heed the words of those prophets or those who — **13.3**
divine by dreams; for the LORD your God is testing you, to know whether you — Deut 6.5; 8.2,16; Ps 81.7
indeed love the LORD your God with all your heart and soul. 4 The LORD your God — **13.4**
you shall follow, him alone you shall fear, his commandments you shall keep, his — Deut 10.20; Jer 7.23
voice you shall obey, him you shall serve, and to him you shall hold fast. 5 But — **13.5**
those prophets or those who divine by dreams shall be put to death for having spo- — Deut 7.4; 13.9; 17.5; 22.21
ken treason against the LORD your God — who brought you out of the land of Egypt — Jer 14.15
and redeemed you from the house of slavery — to turn you from the way in which — Zech 13.3
the LORD your God commanded you to walk. So you shall purge the evil from your
midst.
6 If anyone secretly entices you — even if it is your brother, your father's son — **13.6,7** Deut 13.2
or[h] your mother's son, or your own son or daughter, or the wife you embrace, or — 17.2-7; 29.18; Mic 7.5
your most intimate friend — saying, "Let us go worship other gods," whom neither — **13.8**
you nor your ancestors have known, 7 any of the gods of the peoples that are around — Deut 7.2; Ezek 9.5
you, whether near you or far away from you, from one end of the earth to the other, — **13.9**
8 you must not yield to or heed any such persons. Show them no pity or compassion — Lev 24.13,14; Deut 13.5; 17.7
and do not shield them. 9 But you shall surely kill them; your own hand shall be first — **13.10**
against them to execute them, and afterwards the hand of all the people. 10 Stone — Lev 24.15; Num 15.35
them to death for trying to turn you away from the LORD your God, who brought — Josh 7.25

[e] Gk Sam Syr: MT lacks *today* [f] Ch 13.1 in Heb [g] Ch 13.2 in Heb [h] Sam Gk Compare Tg: MT lacks *your father's son or*

12.30, 31 God did not want the Israelites even to ask about the heathen religions surrounding them. Idolatry completely permeated the land of Canaan. It was too easy to get drawn into the subtle temptations of seemingly harmless practices. Sometimes curiosity can cause us to stumble. Knowledge of evil is harmful if the evil becomes too tempting to resist. To resist curiosity about harmful practices shows discretion and obedience.

12.32 Taking away from God's commands is looking for an easy way around them. Adding to them sounds religious, but it can crush people with unnecessary requirements. Strangely enough, when we add one command we often wind up subtracting another. For example, the Pharisees in Jesus' day added many restrictions to the sabbath commandment. But by trying to keep Jesus from healing on the sabbath (see John 9), they were breaking God's commandment to "love your neighbor as yourself" (Leviticus 19.18). God gave his laws to point people to himself. Making them simpler or more difficult than they really are gets in the way of God's purpose and makes it harder for people to see him clearly.

13.1–3 Attractive leaders are not always led by God. Moses warned the Israelites against false prophets who encouraged worship of other gods. New ideas from inspiring people may sound good, but we must judge them by whether or not they are consistent with God's Word. When people claim to speak for God today, check them in these areas: Are they telling the truth? Is their focus on God? Are their words consistent with what you already know to be true? Some people speak the truth while directing you toward God, but others speak persuasively while directing you toward themselves. It is even possible to say the right words but still lead people in the wrong direction. God is not against new ideas, but he is for discernment. When you hear a new, attractive idea, examine it carefully before getting too excited. False prophets are still around today. The wise person will carefully test ideas against the truth of God's word.

13.5–11 The Israelites were warned not to listen to false prophets or to anyone else who tried to get them to worship other gods — even if this person was a close friend or family member. The temptation to abandon God's commands often sneaks up on us. It may come not with a loud shout but in a whispering doubt. And whispers can be very persuasive, especially if they come from loved ones. But love for relatives should not take precedence over devotion to God. We can overcome whispered temptations by pouring out our hearts to God in prayer and by diligently studying his Word.

13.11 Deut 17.13 you out of the land of Egypt, out of the house of slavery. 11 Then all Israel shall hear
19.20 and be afraid, and never again do any such wickedness.
13.12 12 If you hear it said about one of the towns that the LORD your God is giving
Deut 13.2 you to live in, 13 that scoundrels from among you have gone out and led the inhabi-
Josh 22.11 tants of the town astray, saying, "Let us go and worship other gods," whom you
have not known, 14 then you shall inquire and make a thorough investigation. If the
charge is established that such an abhorrent thing has been done among you, 15 you
shall put the inhabitants of that town to the sword, utterly destroying it and every-
13.16 Num 21.2 thing in it—even putting its livestock to the sword. 16 All of its spoil you shall
Deut 7.25,26 gather into its public square; then burn the town and all its spoil with fire, as a
Josh 6.24 whole burnt offering to the LORD your God. It shall remain a perpetual ruin, never
13.17 Ex 32.12 to be rebuilt. 17 Do not let anything devoted to destruction stick to your hand, so that
Num 25.4 the LORD may turn from his fierce anger and show you compassion, and in his
Deut 7.13; 30.3 compassion multiply you, as he swore to your ancestors, 18 if you obey the voice of
13.18 Deut 12.28 the LORD your God by keeping all his commandments that I am commanding you
Mt 6.33,34 today, doing what is right in the sight of the LORD your God.

Clean and unclean foods

14.1 Lev 19.27,28 **14** You are children of the LORD your God. You must not lacerate yourselves or
21.5 shave your forelocks for the dead. 2 For you are a people holy to the LORD
Jer 16.6 your God; it is you the LORD has chosen out of all the peoples on earth to be his
14.2 Ex 19.5 people, his treasured possession.
14.3 Lev 11.2-43 3 You shall not eat any abhorrent thing. 4 These are the animals you may eat: the
Ezek 4.14 ox, the sheep, the goat, 5 the deer, the gazelle, the roebuck, the wild goat, the ibex,
Acts 10.12-14 the antelope, and the mountain-sheep. 6 Any animal that divides the hoof and has
the hoof cleft in two, and chews the cud, among the animals, you may eat. 7 Yet of
those that chew the cud or have the hoof cleft you shall not eat these: the camel, the
hare, and the rock badger, because they chew the cud but do not divide the hoof;
they are unclean for you. 8 And the pig, because it divides the hoof but does not
chew the cud, is unclean for you. You shall not eat their meat, and you shall not
touch their carcasses.
9 Of all that live in water you may eat these: whatever has fins and scales you
may eat. 10 And whatever does not have fins and scales you shall not eat; it is unclean for you.
11 You may eat any clean birds. 12 But these are the ones that you shall not eat:
the eagle, the vulture, the osprey, 13 the buzzard, the kite, of any kind; 14 every
raven of any kind; 15 the ostrich, the nighthawk, the sea gull, the hawk, of any kind;
16 the little owl and the great owl, the water hen 17 and the desert owl,[i] the carrion
vulture and the cormorant, 18 the stork, the heron, of any kind; the hoopoe and the
bat.[j] 19 And all winged insects are unclean for you; they shall not be eaten. 20 You
may eat any clean winged creature.

[i] Or *pelican* [j] Identification of several of the birds in verses 12-18 is uncertain

---

13.12–17 A city that completely rejected God was to be destroyed so as not to lead the rest of the nation astray. But Israel was not to take action against a city until the rumor about its rejecting God was proven true. This guideline saved many lives when the leaders of Israel wrongly accused three tribes of falling away from their faith (Joshua 22). If we hear of friends who have wandered from the Lord or of entire congregations that have fallen away, we should check the facts and find the truth before doing or saying anything that could prove harmful. There are times, of course, when God wants us to take action—to rebuke a wayward friend, to discipline a child, to reject false teaching—but first we must be sure we have all the facts straight.

14.1 The actions described here refer to a cult. Many other religions today have some kind of worship of or service to the dead. But Christianity and Judaism are very different because they focus on serving God in this life. Don't let concern or worry over the dead distract you from the tasks that God has for you while you are still alive.

14.3–21 Why was Israel forbidden to eat certain foods? There are several reasons: (1) Predatory animals ate the blood of other animals. Since the people could not eat blood, they could not eat such animals. (2) Some forbidden animals had bad associations in the Israelite culture, as bats, snakes, and spiders do for some people today. Some may have been used in heathen religious practices (Isaiah 66.17). To the Israelites, the unclean animals represented sin or unhealthy habits. (3) Perhaps some restrictions were given to Israel just to remind them continually that they were a different and separate people committed to God. Although we no longer must follow these laws about food (Acts 10.9–16), we can still learn from them the lesson that holiness is to be carried into all parts of life. We can't restrict holiness only to the spiritual side; we must be holy in the everyday practical part of life as well. Health practices, finances, use of leisure—all provide opportunities to put "holy living" into "daily living."

21 You shall not eat anything that dies of itself; you may give it to aliens residing in your towns for them to eat, or you may sell it to a foreigner. For you are a
people holy to the LORD your God.
You shall not boil a kid in its mother's milk.

Tithes

22 Set apart a tithe of all the yield of your seed that is brought in yearly from the
field. 23 In the presence of the LORD your God, in the place that he will choose as
a dwelling for his name, you shall eat the tithe of your grain, your wine, and your
oil, as well as the firstlings of your herd and flock, so that you may learn to fear
the LORD your God always. 24 But if, when the LORD your God has blessed you, the
distance is so great that you are unable to transport it, because the place where the
LORD your God will choose to set his name is too far away from you, 25 then you
may turn it into money. With the money secure in hand, go to the place that the
LORD your God will choose; 26 spend the money for whatever you wish—oxen,
sheep, wine, strong drink, or whatever you desire. And you shall eat there in the
presence of the LORD your God, you and your household rejoicing together. 27 As
for the Levites resident in your towns, do not neglect them, because they have no
allotment or inheritance with you.
28 Every third year you shall bring out the full tithe of your produce for that
year, and store it within your towns; 29 the Levites, because they have no allotment
or inheritance with you, as well as the resident aliens, the orphans, and the widows
in your towns, may come and eat their fill so that the LORD your God may bless you
in all the work that you undertake.

Lending money

15 Every seventh year you shall grant a remission of debts. 2 And this is the
manner of the remission: every creditor shall remit the claim that is held
against a neighbor, not exacting it of a neighbor who is a member of the community, because the LORD's remission has been proclaimed. 3 Of a foreigner you may
exact it, but you must remit your claim on whatever any member of your community owes you. 4 There will, however, be no one in need among you, because the
LORD is sure to bless you in the land that the LORD your God is giving you as a
possession to occupy, 5 if only you will obey the LORD your God by diligently observing this entire commandment that I command you today. 6 When the LORD your
God has blessed you, as he promised you, you will lend to many nations, but you
will not borrow; you will rule over many nations, but they will not rule over you.
7 If there is among you anyone in need, a member of your community in any of
your towns within the land that the LORD your God is giving you, do not be hard-
hearted or tight-fisted toward your needy neighbor. 8 You should rather open your
hand, willingly lending enough to meet the need, whatever it may be. 9 Be careful
that you do not entertain a mean thought, thinking, "The seventh year, the year of
remission, is near," and therefore view your needy neighbor with hostility and give

14.21 Ex 23.19; 34.26 Lev 17.15; 22.8 Deut 14.2 Ezek 4.14
14.22 Deut 12.6,17 26.12
14.23 Deut 4.10; 12.4
14.24 Deut 12.20
14.26 Deut 12.18
14.27 Num 18.20 Deut 10.9; 12.12
14.28 Deut 26.12
14.29 Deut 16.11,14 24.19
15.1 Deut 31.10,11
15.2 Neh 5.7 Amos 8.4-8
15.3 Deut 23.20
15.4 Deut 14.29 28.1-8
15.6 Deut 28.12,13
15.7 Deut 15.11 Prov 19.11
15.9 Ex 22.22,23 Deut 15.1 24.14,15 Job 34.28

14.21 This prohibition against boiling a young goat in its mother's milk may reflect a Canaanite fertility rite. Or it may just mean that the Israelites were not to take what was intended to promote life and use it to kill or destroy life. This commandment is also given in Exodus 23.19.

14.28, 29 The Bible supports an organized system of caring for the poor. God told his people to use their tithe every third year for those who were helpless, hungry, or poor. These regulations were designed to prevent the country from sinking under crushing poverty and oppression. It was everyone's responsibility to care for those less fortunate. Families were to help other family members, and towns were to help members of their community. National laws protected the rights of the poor, but helping the poor was also an active part of religious life. God counts on believers to provide for the needy, and we should use what God has given us to aid those less fortunate. Look beyond your regular giving and think of ways to help the needy. This will help you show your regard for God as Creator of all people, share God's goodness with others, and draw them to him. It is a practical and essential way to make faith work in everyday life.

15.7–11 God told the Israelites to help the poor among them when they arrived in the promised land. This was an important part of possessing the land. Many people conclude that people are poor through some fault of their own. This kind of reasoning makes it easy to close their hearts and hands against them. But we are not to invent reasons for ignoring the care of the poor. We are to respond to their needs no matter who or what was responsible for their condition. Who are the poor in your community? If your church does not have a program to identify the poor and assist in fulfilling their needs, why not help start one? What can you do to help someone in need?

nothing; your neighbor might cry to the LORD against you, and you would incur
15.10 guilt. 10 Give liberally and be ungrudging when you do so, for on this account the
2 Cor 9.7 LORD your God will bless you in all your work and in all that you undertake.
15.11 11 Since there will never cease to be some in need on the earth, I therefore command
Jn 12.8 you, "Open your hand to the poor and needy neighbor in your land."

Hebrew slaves

15.12 12 If a member of your community, whether a Hebrew man or a Hebrew
Ex 21.2 Lev 25.39 woman, is sold[k] to you and works for you six years, in the seventh year you shall
Jer 34.14 set that person free. 13 And when you send a male slave[l] out from you a free person, you shall not send him out empty-handed. 14 Provide liberally out of your
flock, your threshing floor, and your wine press, thus giving to him some of the
15.15 Ex 20.2 bounty with which the LORD your God has blessed you. 15 Remember that you were
Deut 5.15; 16.12 a slave in the land of Egypt, and the LORD your God redeemed you; for this reason
15.16 I lay this command upon you today. 16 But if he says to you, "I will not go out from
Ex 21.5,6 you," because he loves you and your household, since he is well off with you,
15.17 17 then you shall take an awl and thrust it through his earlobe into the door, and he
Lev 25.39 shall be your slave[m] forever.
You shall do the same with regard to your female slave.[n]
18 Do not consider it a hardship when you send them out from you free persons,
because for six years they have given you services worth the wages of hired laborers; and the LORD your God will bless you in all that you do.

Firstborn animals

15.19 19 Every firstling male born of your herd and flock you shall consecrate to the
Ex 13.1; 34.19 LORD your God; you shall not do work with your firstling ox nor shear the firstling
Lev 27.26 Num 3.13 of your flock. 20 You shall eat it, you together with your household, in the presence
15.20 Lev 7.15 of the LORD your God year by year at the place that the LORD will choose. 21 But if
15.21 it has any defect—any serious defect, such as lameness or blindness—you shall
Lev 22.19 not sacrifice it to the LORD your God; 22 within your towns you may eat it, the
Mal 1.7,8 15.22 unclean and the clean alike, as you would a gazelle or deer. 23 Its blood, however,
Deut 12.15 you must not eat; you shall pour it out on the ground like water.

Festivals reviewed

16.1 Ex 12.2 **16** Observe the month[o] of Abib by keeping the passover for the LORD your
Lev 23.5 God, for in the month of Abib the LORD your God brought you out of Egypt
Num 9.2,3 28.16 by night. 2 You shall offer the passover sacrifice for the LORD your God, from the
16.2 flock and the herd, at the place that the LORD will choose as a dwelling for his
Ex 12.5 name. 3 You must not eat with it anything leavened. For seven days you shall eat
16.3 Ex 12.8,15 unleavened bread with it—the bread of affliction—because you came out of the
34.18 land of Egypt in great haste, so that all the days of your life you may remember the
16.4 day of your departure from the land of Egypt. 4 No leaven shall be seen with you in
Ex 13.6,7 34.25 all your territory for seven days; and none of the meat of what you slaughter on the
evening of the first day shall remain until morning. 5 You are not permitted to offer
the passover sacrifice within any of your towns that the LORD your God is giving
16.6 you. 6 But at the place that the LORD your God will choose as a dwelling for his
Deut 12.4,5 2 Kgs 23.21-23 name, only there shall you offer the passover sacrifice, in the evening at sunset, the
Jn 2.13; 11.55 time of day when you departed from Egypt. 7 You shall cook it and eat it at the place
16.7 2 Chron 35.13 that the LORD your God will choose; the next morning you may go back to your
tents. 8 For six days you shall continue to eat unleavened bread, and on the seventh

[k] *Or sells himself or herself* [l] *Heb him* [m] *Or bondman* [n] *Or bondwoman* [o] *Or new moon*

15.12–15 The Israelites were to release their slaves after six years, sending them away with enough food so that they would be amply supplied until their needs could be met by some other means. This humanitarian act recognized that God created each person with dignity and worth. It also reminded the Israelites that they, too, had once been slaves in Egypt, and that their present freedom was a gift from God. We do not have slaves today, but these instructions still apply to us: we must still be sure to treat our employees with respect and economic fairness.

day there shall be a solemn assembly for the LORD your God, when you shall do no
work.
9 You shall count seven weeks; begin to count the seven weeks from the time 16.9
the sickle is first put to the standing grain. 10 Then you shall keep the festival of Ex 23.16; 34.22 Lev 23.15
weeks for the LORD your God, contributing a freewill offering in proportion to the Num 28.26
blessing that you have received from the LORD your God. 11 Rejoice before the 16.10 Lev 5.7; 12.8
LORD your God—you and your sons and your daughters, your male and female 16.11
slaves, the Levites resident in your towns, as well as the strangers, the orphans, and Deut 12.7,12
the widows who are among you—at the place that the LORD your God will choose 14.29; 24.19
as a dwelling for his name. 12 Remember that you were a slave in Egypt, and dili- 16.12
gently observe these statutes. Ex 21.2 Deut 15.15
13 You shall keep the festival of booths[p] for seven days, when you have gath- 16.13
ered in the produce from your threshing floor and your wine press. 14 Rejoice dur- Lev 23.40 Ezek 45.25
ing your festival, you and your sons and your daughters, your male and female
slaves, as well as the Levites, the strangers, the orphans, and the widows resident
in your towns. 15 Seven days you shall keep the festival for the LORD your God at
the place that the LORD will choose; for the LORD your God will bless you in all
your produce and in all your undertakings, and you shall surely celebrate.
16 Three times a year all your males shall appear before the LORD your God at 16.16
the place that he will choose: at the festival of unleavened bread, at the festival of Ex 22.29 23.14; 34.20
weeks, and at the festival of booths.[p] They shall not appear before the LORD 22-24
empty-handed; 17 all shall give as they are able, according to the blessing of the 16.17
LORD your God that he has given you. Deut 16.10

4. Laws for ruling the nation

Justice in the courts

18 You shall appoint judges and officials throughout your tribes, in all your 16.18
towns that the LORD your God is giving you, and they shall render just decisions for Ex 18.25 Deut 1.17
the people. 19 You must not distort justice; you must not show partiality; and you 16.19
must not accept bribes, for a bribe blinds the eyes of the wise and subverts the cause Ex 23.2,3 Lev 19.15
of those who are in the right. 20 Justice, and only justice, you shall pursue, so that 16.20
you may live and occupy the land that the LORD your God is giving you. Deut 25.13-15
21 You shall not plant any tree as a sacred pole[q] beside the altar that you make 16.21
for the LORD your God; 22 nor shall you set up a stone pillar—things that the LORD Ex 34.13
your God hates. 16.22 Lev 26.1

17 You must not sacrifice to the LORD your God an ox or a sheep that has a 17.1
defect, anything seriously wrong; for that is abhorrent to the LORD your Lev 22.20 Deut 15.21
God. 17.2
2 If there is found among you, in one of your towns that the LORD your God is Deut 4.19,23 29.26
giving you, a man or woman who does what is evil in the sight of the LORD your Josh 22.16 2 Kgs 21.3-5
God, and transgresses his covenant 3 by going to serve other gods and worshiping Acts 7.43

p Or *tabernacles*; Heb *succoth* q Heb *Asherah*

16.16, 17 Three times a year every male was to make a journey to the sanctuary in the city that would be designated as Israel's religious capital. At these festivals, each participant was encouraged to give what he could in proportion to what God had given him. God does not expect us to give more than we can, but we are blessed when we are able to give cheerfully. For some of us, 10 percent may be a burden. For most of us, it is far too little. Look around at what you have, and then give in proportion to what you have been given.

16.18–20 These verses anticipated a great problem the Israelites would face when they arrived in the promised land. Although they had Joshua as their national leader, they failed to complete the task and choose other spiritual leaders who would guide the tribes, districts, and cities with justice and God's wisdom. Because they did not appoint wise judges and faithful administrators, rebellion and injustice plagued their communities. It is a serious responsibility to appoint or elect wise and just officials. In your sphere of influence—home, church, school, job—are you ensuring that justice and godliness prevail? Failing to choose leaders who uphold justice can lead to much trouble, as Israel would discover.

17.1 The fact that this command was included probably indicates that some Israelites were sacrificing imperfect or deformed animals to God. Then, as now, it is difficult and expensive to offer God our best (i.e., the first part of what we earn). It is always tempting to shortchange God, because we think we won't get caught. But our giving shows our real priorities. When we give God the leftovers, he is obviously not at the center of our lives. Give God the honor of having first claim on your money, your time, and your talents.

17.2, 3 It was common to worship not only idols of wood and stone, but also the sun, moon, and stars. This was simply another form of idol worship—bowing down to a created thing, rather than the Creator.

them — whether the sun or the moon or any of the host of heaven, which I have
17.4 Deut 13.12-14; 19.18
forbidden — 4 and if it is reported to you or you hear of it, and you make a thorough
inquiry, and the charge is proved true that such an abhorrent thing has occurred in
17.5 Deut 13.10; 21.21
Israel, 5 then you shall bring out to your gates that man or that woman who has
committed this crime and you shall stone the man or woman to death. 6 On the
17.6 Num 35.30; Deut 19.15
evidence of two or three witnesses the death sentence shall be executed; a person
must not be put to death on the evidence of only one witness. 7 The hands of the
17.7 Lev 24.13,14; Deut 13.9
witnesses shall be the first raised against the person to execute the death penalty,
and afterward the hands of all the people. So you shall purge the evil from your
midst.
17.8 Deut 1.17; 19.17
8 If a judicial decision is too difficult for you to make between one kind of
bloodshed and another, one kind of legal right and another, or one kind of assault
and another — any such matters of dispute in your towns — then you shall immediately go up to the place that the LORD your God will choose, 9 where you shall
consult with the levitical priests and the judge who is in office in those days; they
shall announce to you the decision in the case. 10 Carry out exactly the decision that
they announce to you from the place that the LORD will choose, diligently observ-
17.11 Deut 25.1
ing everything they instruct you. 11 You must carry out fully the law that they interpret for you or the ruling that they announce to you; do not turn aside from the
decision that they announce to you, either to the right or to the left. 12 As for anyone
who presumes to disobey the priest appointed to minister there to the LORD your
17.13 Deut 13.11; 19.20
God, or the judge, that person shall die. So you shall purge the evil from Israel.
13 All the people will hear and be afraid, and will not act presumptuously again.

Guidelines for the king

17.14 Deut 11.31; Josh 21.43
14 When you have come into the land that the LORD your God is giving you,
and have taken possession of it and settled in it, and you say, "I will set a king over
me, like all the nations that are around me," 15 you may indeed set over you a king
whom the LORD your God will choose. One of your own community you may set
as king over you; you are not permitted to put a foreigner over you, who is not of
17.16 1 Kgs 4.26
your own community. 16 Even so, he must not acquire many horses for himself, or
return the people to Egypt in order to acquire more horses, since the LORD has said
17.17 2 Sam 5.13; 1 Kgs 11.3,4
to you, "You must never return that way again." 17 And he must not acquire many
wives for himself, or else his heart will turn away; also silver and gold he must not
17.18 Deut 31.9,24; 2 Kgs 11.12; 22.8
acquire in great quantity for himself. 18 When he has taken the throne of his kingdom, he shall have a copy of this law written for him in the presence of the levitical

---

17.6, 7 A person was not put to death on the testimony of only one witness. On the witness of two or three, a person could be condemned and then sentenced to death by stoning. The condemned person was taken outside the city gates, and the witnesses were the first to throw heavy stones down on him or her. Bystanders would then pelt the dying person with stones. This system would "purge the evil" by putting the idolater to death. At the same time, it protected the rights of accused persons two ways. First, by requiring several witnesses, it prevented any angry individual from "bearing false witness." Second, by requiring the accusers to throw the first stones, it made them think twice about accusing unjustly. They were responsible to finish what they had started.

17.8–13 Sometimes a case would come up that was too difficult for the local community to decide. Perhaps there were no witnesses, or the evidence was insufficient, or unusual circumstances made the truth hard to see. When this happened, the case was to be taken to God's sanctuary. There the priest in charge of judging these special cases would make a decision. His word was final. This was the fairest way to settle the matter once and for all. It was vitally important to have a just man who obeyed God in this position.

17.14–20 God was not encouraging Israel to appoint a king to rule their nation. He was actually against the idea because he was their King, and the people were to obey and follow him. But God knew that the people would one day demand a king for selfish reasons — they would want to be like the nations around them (1 Samuel 8). If they insisted on having a king, he wanted to make sure they chose the right person. That is why he included these instructions both for the people's benefit as they chose their king and for the king himself as he sought to lead the nation according to God's laws.

17.16, 17 Israel's kings did not heed this warning, and their behavior led to their downfall. Solomon had everything going for him, but when he became rich, built up a large army, and married many wives, his heart turned from God (1 Kings 11). Out of Solomon's sin came Israel's disobedience, division, and captivity.

17.18–20 The king was to be a man of God's Word. He was to (1) have a copy of the law made for his personal use, (2) keep it with him all the time, (3) read from it every day, and (4) obey it completely. By this process he would learn respect for God, keep himself from feeling more important than others, and avoid neglecting God in times of prosperity. We can't know what God wants except through his Word, and his Word won't affect our lives unless we read and think about it regularly. With the abundant availability of the Bible today, it is not difficult to gain access to the source of the king's wisdom. What is more of a challenge is following its directives.

priests. 19 It shall remain with him and he shall read in it all the days of his life, so
that he may learn to fear the LORD his God, diligently observing all the words of
this law and these statutes, 20 neither exalting himself above other members of the
community nor turning aside from the commandment, either to the right or to the
left, so that he and his descendants may reign long over his kingdom in Israel.

Offerings for the priests and Levites

18 The levitical priests, the whole tribe of Levi, shall have no allotment or inheritance within Israel. They may eat the sacrifices that are the LORD's portion[r] 2 but they shall have no inheritance among the other members of the
community; the LORD is their inheritance, as he promised them.
3 This shall be the priests' due from the people, from those offering a sacrifice,
whether an ox or a sheep: they shall give to the priest the shoulder, the two jowls,
and the stomach. 4 The first fruits of your grain, your wine, and your oil, as well as
the first of the fleece of your sheep, you shall give him. 5 For the LORD your God
has chosen Levi[s] out of all your tribes, to stand and minister in the name of the
LORD, him and his sons for all time.
6 If a Levite leaves any of your towns, from wherever he has been residing in
Israel, and comes to the place that the LORD will choose (and he may come whenever he wishes), 7 then he may minister in the name of the LORD his God, like all his
fellow-Levites who stand to minister there before the LORD. 8 They shall have equal
portions to eat, even though they have income from the sale of family possessions.[r]

Warnings against unholy practices

9 When you come into the land that the LORD your God is giving you, you must
not learn to imitate the abhorrent practices of those nations. 10 No one shall be
found among you who makes a son or daughter pass through fire, or who practices
divination, or is a soothsayer, or an augur, or a sorcerer, 11 or one who casts spells,
or who consults ghosts or spirits, or who seeks oracles from the dead. 12 For whoever does these things is abhorrent to the LORD; it is because of such abhorrent
practices that the LORD your God is driving them out before you. 13 You must remain completely loyal to the LORD your God. 14 Although these nations that you are
about to dispossess do give heed to soothsayers and diviners, as for you, the LORD
your God does not permit you to do so.

[r] Meaning of Heb uncertain [s] Heb *him*

17.19 Deut 6.6; 11.18 Ps 119
18.1 Deut 10.9 1 Cor 9.13
18.2 Deut 12.12 Ps 16.5
18.3 Lev 7.32 Num 18.11
18.4 Ex 22.29; 23.19
18.5 Ex 28.1 Num 3.10 Deut 10.8
18.6 Num 35.2,3
18.8 Lev 27.30 Num 18.21
18.9 Lev 18.26 Deut 9.5 12.29,30
18.10 Ex 22.18 Lev 19.26,31 20.6 Deut 12.31 Jer 27.9,10
18.13 Gen 6.7-10 17.1 Job 1.1 Mt 5.48

18.1–8 The priests and Levites served much the same function as our ministers today. Their duties included (1) teaching the people about God, (2) setting an example of godly living, (3) caring for the sanctuary and its workers, and (4) distributing the offerings. Because priests could not own property or pursue outside business interests, God made special arrangements so the people would not take advantage of them. Often churches take advantage of the men and women God has brought to lead them. For example, pastors may not be paid in accordance with their skills or the time they put in. Or maybe they are expected to attend every evening meeting, even if this continual absence is harmful to their families. As you look at your own church in light of God's Word, what ways do you see to honor the leaders God has given you?

18.9 God warned the Israelites that the promised land wasn't paradise. God did not insulate them from the evils they would face, but he gave them the support they needed to live in the land and conquer the enemy. Earth has no trouble-free environments. There will always be problems as long as the world is filled with sinful people. Not even Christian churches, schools, ministries, or homes are problem free. But you can deal with your problem-filled environment by applying God's Word to your situation. Rather than looking for a safe, secure retreat from corrupting influences, we must look to God for the courage to deal with our problems and the power to conquer them.

18.10 Child sacrifice and occult practices were strictly forbidden by God. These practices were common among heathen religions. Israel's own neighbors actually sacrificed their children to the god Molech ("pass through fire," see also Leviticus 20.2–5). Other neighboring religions used supernatural means, such as contacting the spirit world and interpreting omens ("augur"), to foretell the future and gain guidance. Because of these wicked practices, God would drive out the heathen nations (18.12). The Israelites were to replace their evil practices with the worship of the one true God.

18.10–13 The Israelites were naturally curious about the occult practices of the Canaanite religions. But Satan is behind the occult, and God flatly forbade Israel to have anything to do with it. Today people are still fascinated by horoscopes, fortune-telling, witchcraft, and bizarre cults. Often their interest comes from a desire to know and control the future. But Satan is no less dangerous today than he was in Moses' time. In the Bible, God tells us all we need to know about what is going to happen. The information Satan offers is likely to be distorted or completely false. With the trustworthy guidance of the Holy Spirit through the Bible and the church, we don't need to turn to occult sources for faulty information.

Advice concerning prophets

18.15 Lk 24.19 Jn 1.21,24,25 6.14; 7.52 Acts 3.20-22 7.37 Heb 3.2
18.16 Deut 5.23-27
18.18 Acts 3.21-23
18.19 Deut 17.12 Heb 12.25
18.20 Deut 13.1-4 Jer 28.15,16
18.22 Isa 41.22 Jer 28.9

15 The LORD your God will raise up for you a prophet[t] like me from among
your own people; you shall heed such a prophet.[u] 16 This is what you requested of
the LORD your God at Horeb on the day of the assembly when you said: "If I hear
the voice of the LORD my God any more, or ever again see this great fire, I will
die." 17 Then the LORD replied to me: "They are right in what they have said. 18 I
will raise up for them a prophet[t] like you from among their own people; I will put
my words in the mouth of the prophet,[v] who shall speak to them everything that I
command. 19 Anyone who does not heed the words that the prophet[w] shall speak in
my name, I myself will hold accountable. 20 But any prophet who speaks in the
name of other gods, or who presumes to speak in my name a word that I have not
commanded the prophet to speak — that prophet shall die." 21 You may say to yourself, "How can we recognize a word that the LORD has not spoken?" 22 If a prophet
speaks in the name of the LORD but the thing does not take place or prove true, it is
a word that the LORD has not spoken. The prophet has spoken it presumptuously; do
not be frightened by it.

Cities of refuge

19.1 Deut 6.10-12 17.14
19.2,3 Num 35.6 Deut 4.41,42 Josh 20.7
19.4 Num 35.9-34

19 When the LORD your God has cut off the nations whose land the LORD your
God is giving you, and you have dispossessed them and settled in their towns
and in their houses, 2 you shall set apart three cities in the land that the LORD your
God is giving you to possess. 3 You shall calculate the distances[x] and divide into
three regions the land that the LORD your God gives you as a possession, so that any
homicide can flee to one of them.

4 Now this is the case of a homicide who might flee there and live, that is,
someone who has killed another person unintentionally when the two had not been
at enmity before: 5 Suppose someone goes into the forest with another to cut wood,
and when one of them swings the ax to cut down a tree, the head slips from the
handle and strikes the other person who then dies; the killer may flee to one of these
cities and live. 6 But if the distance is too great, the avenger of blood in hot anger
might pursue and overtake and put the killer to death, although a death sentence
was not deserved, since the two had not been at enmity before. 7 Therefore I command you: You shall set apart three cities.

19.8 Deut 11.24 12.20-24
19.9 Deut 6.15; 11.22
19.10 Num 35.33 Deut 21.1-9
19.11 Deut 27.24
19.12 Num 35.21,24

8 If the LORD your God enlarges your territory, as he swore to your
ancestors — and he will give you all the land that he promised your ancestors to give
you, 9 provided you diligently observe this entire commandment that I command
you today, by loving the LORD your God and walking always in his ways — then
you shall add three more cities to these three, 10 so that the blood of an innocent
person may not be shed in the land that the LORD your God is giving you as an
inheritance, thereby bringing bloodguilt upon you.

11 But if someone at enmity with another lies in wait and attacks and takes the
life of that person, and flees into one of these cities, 12 then the elders of the killer's
city shall send to have the culprit taken from there and handed over to the avenger

[t] Or *prophets* [u] Or *such prophets* [v] Or *mouths of the prophets* [w] Heb *he* [x] Or *prepare roads to them*

18.15 Who is this prophet? Stephen used this verse to support his claim that Jesus Christ is God's Son, the Messiah (Acts 7.37). The coming of Jesus Christ to earth was not an afterthought, but part of God's original plan.

18.21, 22 As in the days of ancient Israel, some people today claim to have messages from God. God still speaks to his people, but we must be cautious before saying that the Lord has spoken through a prophet. How can we tell when people are speaking for the Lord? (1) We can see whether or not their prophecies come true — the ancient test for judging prophets. (2) We can check their words against the Bible. God never contradicts himself, so if someone says something contrary to the Bible, we can know that this is not God's Word. We should give our trust carefully and in accordance with what we already know about God from the church and the Bible.

19.2–7 Every society must deal with the problem of murder. But how should society treat those who have innocently or accidentally killed someone? God had an answer for the Israelites. Since revenge was common and swift in Moses' day, God had the Israelites set apart several "cities of refuge." Anyone who claimed to have accidentally killed someone could flee to one of these cities until he could have a fair trial. If he was found innocent of intentional murder, he could remain in that city and be safe from those seeking revenge. This is a beautiful example of how God blended his justice and mercy toward his people. (For more information on cities of refuge see the note on Numbers 35.6.)

19.12 The "avenger of blood" was the nearest male relative to the person killed. He acted as the family protector (see Numbers 35.19).

of blood to be put to death. 13 Show no pity; you shall purge the guilt of innocent
blood from Israel, so that it may go well with you.
14 You must not move your neighbor's boundary marker, set up by former generations, on the property that will be allotted to you in the land that the LORD your
God is giving you to possess.
15 A single witness shall not suffice to convict a person of any crime or wrongdoing in connection with any offense that may be committed. Only on the evidence
of two or three witnesses shall a charge be sustained. 16 If a malicious witness
comes forward to accuse someone of wrongdoing, 17 then both parties to the dispute
shall appear before the LORD, before the priests and the judges who are in office in
those days, 18 and the judges shall make a thorough inquiry. If the witness is a false
witness, having testified falsely against another, 19 then you shall do to the false
witness just as the false witness had meant to do to the other. So you shall purge the
evil from your midst. 20 The rest shall hear and be afraid, and a crime such as this
shall never again be committed among you. 21 Show no pity: life for life, eye for
eye, tooth for tooth, hand for hand, foot for foot.

19.13 Deut 7.16; 13.8
19.14 Deut 27.17 Prov 23.10,11
19.15 Num 35.30 Deut 17.16 Mt 18.16 2 Cor 13.1
19.16 Ex 23.1 Prov 14.5,25
19.17 Deut 17.9; 21.5
19.19 Deut 13.5; 17.7 Prov 19.5,9
19.21 Ex 21.23 Lev 24.17,20 Mt 5.38

Instructions for soldiers

20 When you go out to war against your enemies, and see horses and chariots,
an army larger than your own, you shall not be afraid of them; for the LORD
your God is with you, who brought you up from the land of Egypt. 2 Before you
engage in battle, the priest shall come forward and speak to the troops, 3 and shall
say to them: "Hear, O Israel! Today you are drawing near to do battle against your
enemies. Do not lose heart, or be afraid, or panic, or be in dread of them; 4 for it is
the LORD your God who goes with you, to fight for you against your enemies, to
give you victory." 5 Then the officials shall address the troops, saying, "Has anyone built a new house but not dedicated it? He should go back to his house, or he
might die in the battle and another dedicate it. 6 Has anyone planted a vineyard but
not yet enjoyed its fruit? He should go back to his house, or he might die in the
battle and another be first to enjoy its fruit. 7 Has anyone become engaged to a
woman but not yet married her? He should go back to his house, or he might die in
the battle and another marry her." 8 The officials shall continue to address the
troops, saying, "Is anyone afraid or disheartened? He should go back to his house,
or he might cause the heart of his comrades to melt like his own." 9 When the officials have finished addressing the troops, then the commanders shall take charge of
them.
10 When you draw near to a town to fight against it, offer it terms of peace. 11 If
it accepts your terms of peace and surrenders to you, then all the people in it shall
serve you at forced labor. 12 If it does not submit to you peacefully, but makes war
against you, then you shall besiege it; 13 and when the LORD your God gives it into
your hand, you shall put all its males to the sword. 14 You may, however, take as
your booty the women, the children, livestock, and everything else in the town, all

20.1 Deut 1.29,30 3.22; 7.18
20.2 Num 10.8; 31.6
20.3 Ps 27.1-3 Isa 35.4; 41.10
20.5 Neh 12.27
20.6 Lev 19.23
20.7 Deut 24.5
20.8 Judg 7.3
20.10 2 Sam 20.17-21
20.13 Num 31.7-11 1 Kgs 11.15
20.14 Josh 8.2 11.14 2 Chron 14.13-15

19.19 This punishment for being a false witness would be well fitted for each instance of the crime. If someone was lying about a small matter, he would receive a small punishment. If he was lying about a life and death issue, his own life was also at stake. According to this law, those who were hired to bring false charges against Jesus (Mark 14.56–58) were in danger of losing their own lives.

19.21 This principle was for the judges to use, not a plan for personal vengeance. This attitude toward punishment may seem primitive, but it was actually a breakthrough for justice and fairness in ancient times when most nations used arbitrary methods to punish criminals. This guideline reflects a concern for evenhandedness and justice—ensuring that those who violated the law were not punished more severely than their particular crime deserved. In the same spirit of justice, a false witness was to receive the same punishment the accused person would have suffered. The principle of making the punishment fit the crime should still be observed today.

20.1 Just like the Israelites, we sometimes face overwhelming opposition. Whether at school, at work, or even at home, we can feel outnumbered and helpless. God bolstered the Israelites' confidence by reminding them that he was always with them and that he had already saved them from the potential danger. We too can feel secure when we consider that God is able to overcome even the most difficult odds.

20.13–18 How could a merciful and just God order the destruction of entire population centers? He did this to protect his people from idol worship, which was certain to bring ruin to Israel (20.18). In fact, because Israel did not completely destroy these evil people as God commanded, Israel was constantly oppressed by them and experienced greater bloodshed and destruction than if they had followed God's instructions in the first place.

its spoil. You may enjoy the spoil of your enemies, which the LORD your God has
given you. 15 Thus you shall treat all the towns that are very far from you, which are
20.16 Ex 23.31; Deut 7.1,2
not towns of the nations here. 16 But as for the towns of these peoples that the LORD
your God is giving you as an inheritance, you must not let anything that breathes
remain alive. 17 You shall annihilate them—the Hittites and the Amorites, the Canaanites and the Perizzites, the Hivites and the Jebusites—just as the LORD your
20.18 Deut 7.4; 9.5; 12.31
God has commanded, 18 so that they may not teach you to do all the abhorrent
things that they do for their gods, and you thus sin against the LORD your God.
20.19,20 2 Chron 26.15
19 If you besiege a town for a long time, making war against it in order to take
it, you must not destroy its trees by wielding an ax against them. Although you may
take food from them, you must not cut them down. Are trees in the field human
beings that they should come under siege from you? 20 You may destroy only the
trees that you know do not produce food; you may cut them down for use in building siegeworks against the town that makes war with you, until it falls.

5. Laws for human relationships

Forgiveness for an unsolved murder

21 If, in the land that the LORD your God is giving you to possess, a body is
found lying in open country, and it is not known who struck the person
down, 2 then your elders and your judges shall come out to measure the distances to
the towns that are near the body. 3 The elders of the town nearest the body shall take
a heifer that has never been worked, one that has not pulled in the yoke; 4 the elders
of that town shall bring the heifer down to a wadi with running water, which is
21.5 Deut 10.8; 17.9; 19.17
neither plowed nor sown, and shall break the heifer's neck there in the wadi. 5 Then
the priests, the sons of Levi, shall come forward, for the LORD your God has chosen
them to minister to him and to pronounce blessings in the name of the LORD, and
21.6,7 Ps 26.6; Mt 27.24
by their decision all cases of dispute and assault shall be settled. 6 All the elders of
that town nearest the body shall wash their hands over the heifer whose neck was
broken in the wadi, 7 and they shall declare: "Our hands did not shed this blood, nor
21.8 Num 35.33,34; Jonah 1.14
were we witnesses to it. 8 Absolve, O LORD, your people Israel, whom you redeemed; do not let the guilt of innocent blood remain in the midst of your people
21.9 Deut 19.13
Israel." Then they will be absolved of bloodguilt. 9 So you shall purge the guilt of
innocent blood from your midst, because you must do what is right in the sight of
the LORD.

Marriage and family

21.10 Deut 20.1
10 When you go out to war against your enemies, and the LORD your God hands
21.11 Deut 20.14
them over to you and you take them captive, 11 suppose you see among the captives
a beautiful woman whom you desire and want to marry, 12 and so you bring her
21.12 Lev 14.8,9; Num 6.9
home to your house: she shall shave her head, pare her nails, 13 discard her captive's garb, and shall remain in your house a full month, mourning for her father
21.13 Ps 45.10
and mother; after that you may go in to her and be her husband, and she shall be
21.14 Ex 21.8,11; Deut 22.19
your wife. 14 But if you are not satisfied with her, you shall let her go free and not
sell her for money. You must not treat her as a slave, since you have dishonored
her.
15 If a man has two wives, one of them loved and the other disliked, and if both
the loved and the disliked have borne him sons, the firstborn being the son of the

---

20.19, 20 To keep from destroying the land, the people were warned against needlessly cutting down valuable fruit trees. Israel remained a fruitful, fertile land until medieval times, when the Crusaders destroyed most of the trees and thus prevented the land from replenishing itself. This is what God was warning against.

20.20 Archaeologists have uncovered the remnants of many well-fortified cities in Canaan. Some had tall walls (up to 30 feet high), ramparts, moats, and towers. Accustomed to fighting on the open plains, the Israelites were going to have to learn new battle strategies to conquer these massive fortresses.

21.1–9 When a crime was committed and the criminal got away, the whole community was held responsible. In much the same way, if a city has a dangerous intersection and someone is killed there, the community may be held responsible for both damages and repairs. God was pointing to the need for the whole community to feel a keen sense of responsibility for what was going on around them and to move to correct any situations that were potentially harmful—physically, socially, or morally.

21.4 A "wadi" was a brook, valley, or dry riverbed.

one who is disliked, 16 then on the day when he wills his possessions to his sons, he
is not permitted to treat the son of the loved as the firstborn in preference to the son
of the disliked, who is the firstborn. 17 He must acknowledge as firstborn the son of 21.17
the one who is disliked, giving him a double portion[y] of all that he has; since he is Gen 49.3
the first issue of his virility, the right of the firstborn is his.
18 If someone has a stubborn and rebellious son who will not obey his father 21.18
and mother, who does not heed them when they discipline him, 19 then his father Deut 27.16 Prov 28.24
and his mother shall take hold of him and bring him out to the elders of his town at 30.11,12
the gate of that place. 20 They shall say to the elders of his town, "This son of ours
is stubborn and rebellious. He will not obey us. He is a glutton and a drunkard." 21.21
21 Then all the men of the town shall stone him to death. So you shall purge the evil Lev 20.2,27 24.13,14
from your midst; and all Israel will hear, and be afraid. Num 15.35

Burying criminals

22 When someone is convicted of a crime punishable by death and is executed, 21.22 2 Sam 21.5,6,9
and you hang him on a tree, 23 his corpse must not remain all night upon the tree; Mt 26.65,66
you shall bury him that same day, for anyone hung on a tree is under God's curse. Mk 14.63,64
You must not defile the land that the LORD your God is giving you for possession. 21.23 Gal 3.13

Helping neighbors

22 You shall not watch your neighbor's ox or sheep straying away and ignore 22.1 Ex 23.4
them; you shall take them back to their owner. 2 If the owner does not reside Lev 20.4
near you or you do not know who the owner is, you shall bring it to your own
house, and it shall remain with you until the owner claims it; then you shall return
it. 3 You shall do the same with a neighbor's donkey; you shall do the same with a
neighbor's garment; and you shall do the same with anything else that your neighbor loses and you find. You may not withhold your help.
4 You shall not see your neighbor's donkey or ox fallen on the road and ignore
it; you shall help to lift it up.

Various rules

5 A woman shall not wear a man's apparel, nor shall a man put on a woman's
garment; for whoever does such things is abhorrent to the LORD your God.
6 If you come on a bird's nest, in any tree or on the ground, with fledglings or 22.6 Lev 22.28
eggs, with the mother sitting on the fledglings or on the eggs, you shall not take the
mother with the young. 7 Let the mother go, taking only the young for yourself, in
order that it may go well with you and you may live long.
8 When you build a new house, you shall make a parapet for your roof; otherwise you might have bloodguilt on your house, if anyone should fall from it.
9 You shall not sow your vineyard with a second kind of seed, or the whole 22.9 Lev 19.19
yield will have to be forfeited, both the crop that you have sown and the yield of the
vineyard itself.
10 You shall not plow with an ox and a donkey yoked together. 22.10 2 Cor 6.14

[y] Heb *two-thirds*

21.18–21 Disobedient and rebellious children were to be brought before the elders of the city and stoned to death. There is no biblical or archeological evidence that this punishment was ever carried out, but the point was that disobedience and rebellion were not to be tolerated in the home or allowed to continue unchecked.

22.1–3 The Hebrews were to care for and return lost animals or possessions to their rightful owners. The way of the world, by contrast, is "Finders keepers, losers weepers." To go beyond the finders-keepers rule by protecting and returning the property of others keeps us from being envious and greedy.

22.5 This verse commands men and women not to reverse their sexual roles. It is not a statement about clothing styles. Today role rejections are common—there are men who want to become women and women who want to become men. It's not the clothing style that offends God, but using the style to act out a different sex role. God had a purpose in making us uniquely male and female.

22.8–11 These are practical laws, helpful for establishing good habits for everyday living. Verse 8: Since people used their flat roofs as porches, a guardrail (parapet) was a wise safety precaution. Verse 9: If you plant two different crops side by side, one of them will not survive, since the stronger, taller one will block the sunlight and take most of the vital nutrients from the soil. Verse 10: A donkey and an ox, due to differences in strength and size, cannot pull a plow evenly. Verse 11: Two different kinds of thread wear unevenly and wash differently. Combining them reduces the life of the garment. Don't think of God's laws as arbitrary restrictions. Look for the reasons behind the laws. They are not made just to teach or restrict, but also to protect.

11 You shall not wear clothes made of wool and linen woven together.
22.12 Num 15.37-39 Mt 23.5 12 You shall make tassels on the four corners of the cloak with which you cover
yourself.

Violations of marriage laws

22.13 Deut 24.1 13 Suppose a man marries a woman, but after going in to her, he dislikes her
14 and makes up charges against her, slandering her by saying, "I married this
woman; but when I lay with her, I did not find evidence of her virginity." 15 The
father of the young woman and her mother shall then submit the evidence of the
young woman's virginity to the elders of the city at the gate. 16 The father of the
young woman shall say to the elders: "I gave my daughter in marriage to this man
but he dislikes her; 17 now he has made up charges against her, saying, 'I did not
find evidence of your daughter's virginity.' But here is the evidence of my daughter's virginity." Then they shall spread out the cloth before the elders of the town.
18 The elders of that town shall take the man and punish him; 19 they shall fine him
one hundred shekels of silver (which they shall give to the young woman's father)
because he has slandered a virgin of Israel. She shall remain his wife; he shall not
be permitted to divorce her as long as he lives.
20 If, however, this charge is true, that evidence of the young woman's virgin-
22.21 Lev 19.29; 21.9 Deut 23.17,18 ity was not found, 21 then they shall bring the young woman out to the entrance of
her father's house and the men of her town shall stone her to death, because she
committed a disgraceful act in Israel by prostituting herself in her father's house.
So you shall purge the evil from your midst.
22.22 Lev 20.10 Ezek 16.38 Jn 8.5 22 If a man is caught lying with the wife of another man, both of them shall die,
the man who lay with the woman as well as the woman. So you shall purge the evil
from Israel.
22.23 Lev 19.20 Deut 20.7 23 If there is a young woman, a virgin already engaged to be married, and a
man meets her in the town and lies with her, 24 you shall bring both of them to the
gate of that town and stone them to death, the young woman because she did not cry
for help in the town and the man because he violated his neighbor's wife. So you
shall purge the evil from your midst.
25 But if the man meets the engaged woman in the open country, and the man
seizes her and lies with her, then only the man who lay with her shall die. 26 You
shall do nothing to the young woman; the young woman has not committed an
offense punishable by death, because this case is like that of someone who attacks
and murders a neighbor. 27 Since he found her in the open country, the engaged
woman may have cried for help, but there was no one to rescue her.
22.28 Ex 22.16 28 If a man meets a virgin who is not engaged, and seizes her and lies with her,
and they are caught in the act, 29 the man who lay with her shall give fifty shekels
of silver to the young woman's father, and she shall become his wife. Because he
violated her he shall not be permitted to divorce her as long as he lives.
22.30 Lev 18.8; 20.11 Deut 27.20 30[z] A man shall not marry his father's wife, thereby violating his father's
rights.[a]

The sanctuary

23.1 Lev 21.20; 22.24 **23** No one whose testicles are crushed or whose penis is cut off shall be admitted to the assembly of the LORD.
2 Those born of an illicit union shall not be admitted to the assembly of the
LORD. Even to the tenth generation, none of their descendants shall be admitted to
the assembly of the LORD.

[z] Ch 23.1 in Heb [a] Heb *uncovering his father's skirt*

22.13–30 Why did God include all these laws about sexual sins? Instructions about sexual behavior would have been vital for three million people on a 40-year camping trip. But they would be equally important when they entered the promised land and settled down as a nation. Paul, in Colossians 3.5–8, recognizes the importance of strong rules about sex for believers, because sexual sins have the power to disrupt and destroy the church. Sins involving sex are not innocent dabblings in forbidden pleasures, as is so often portrayed, but powerful destroyers of relationships. They confuse and tear down the climate of respect, trust, and credibility so essential for solid marriages and secure children.

3 No Ammonite or Moabite shall be admitted to the assembly of the LORD. **23.3**
Even to the tenth generation, none of their descendants shall be admitted to the Deut 7.1
assembly of the LORD, 4 because they did not meet you with food and water on your **23.4**
journey out of Egypt, and because they hired against you Balaam son of Beor, from Num 23.4,7-10 Neh 13.1
Pethor of Mesopotamia, to curse you. 5 (Yet the LORD your God refused to heed 2 Pet 2.15 Jude 11
Balaam; the LORD your God turned the curse into a blessing for you, because the **23.5**
LORD your God loved you.) 6 You shall never promote their welfare or their pros- Num 22.35 24.3-9
perity as long as you live.

7 You shall not abhor any of the Edomites, for they are your kin. You shall not **23.7**
abhor any of the Egyptians, because you were an alien residing in their land. 8 The Lev 19.34 Num 20.14
children of the third generation that are born to them may be admitted to the assem- Deut 10.19
bly of the LORD. **23.8** Num 11.4

The camps

9 When you are encamped against your enemies you shall guard against any
impropriety.

10 If one of you becomes unclean because of a nocturnal emission, then he shall
go outside the camp; he must not come within the camp. 11 When evening comes, **23.11**
he shall wash himself with water, and when the sun has set, he may come back into Lev 15.5,16
the camp.

12 You shall have a designated area outside the camp to which you shall go.
13 With your utensils you shall have a trowel; when you relieve yourself outside,
you shall dig a hole with it and then cover up your excrement. 14 Because the LORD **23.14**
your God travels along with your camp, to save you and to hand over your enemies Lev 26.12
to you, therefore your camp must be holy, so that he may not see anything indecent
among you and turn away from you.

Various rules

15 Slaves who have escaped to you from their owners shall not be given back **23.15**
to them. 16 They shall reside with you, in your midst, in any place they choose in 1 Sam 22.2 25.10
any one of your towns, wherever they please; you shall not oppress them.

17 None of the daughters of Israel shall be a temple prostitute; none of the sons **23.17**
of Israel shall be a temple prostitute. 18 You shall not bring the fee of a prostitute or Lev 18.22; 20.13 Deut 22.21
the wages of a male prostitute[b] into the house of the LORD your God in payment for
any vow, for both of these are abhorrent to the LORD your God.

19 You shall not charge interest on loans to another Israelite, interest on **23.19**
money, interest on provisions, interest on anything that is lent. 20 On loans to a Ex 22.25 Lev 25.36
foreigner you may charge interest, but on loans to another Israelite you may not **23.20**
charge interest, so that the LORD your God may bless you in all your undertakings Deut 28.12
in the land that you are about to enter and possess.

21 If you make a vow to the LORD your God, do not postpone fulfilling it; for **23.21**
the LORD your God will surely require it of you, and you would incur guilt. 22 But Lev 5.4 Num 15.4
if you refrain from vowing, you will not incur guilt. 23 Whatever your lips utter you 30.1,2 Eccles 5.4
must diligently perform, just as you have freely vowed to the LORD your God with Mt 5.33
your own mouth.

24 If you go into your neighbor's vineyard, you may eat your fill of grapes, as
many as you wish, but you shall not put any in a container.

[b] Heb *a dog*

23.17, 18 Prostitution was not overlooked in God's law – it was strictly forbidden. To forbid this practice may seem obvious to us, but it may not have been so obvious to the Israelites. Almost every other religion known to them included prostitution as an integral part of its worship services. Prostitution makes a mockery of God's original idea for sex. It treats sex as an isolated physical act rather than an act of commitment to another. Outside of marriage, sex destroys relationships. Within marriage, if approached with the right attitude, it can be a relationship builder. God frequently had to warn the people against the practice of extramarital sex. Today we still need to hear his warnings; young people need to be reminded about premarital sex, and adults need to be reminded about sexual fidelity.

23.24, 25 This commandment guarded against selfishly holding onto one's possessions. It also insured that no one had to go hungry. It was not, however, an excuse for taking advantage of one's neighbor. The Pharisees did not interpret this appropriately when they accused Jesus and the disciples of harvesting on the sabbath (Matthew 12.1, 2).

23.25 Mt 12.1,2 Mk 2.23 Lk 6.1
24.1 Num 5.12-28 Deut 22.13-21 Jer 3.1 Mal 2.16 Mt 5.31; 19.7 Mk 10.4
24.5 Deut 20.7
24.8 Lev 13.1,59
24.9 Num 12.10
24.10 Deut 15.8
24.12 Ex 22.26
24.14 Lev 19.13 Mt 20.8 1 Tim 5.18 Jas 5.4
24.16 2 Kgs 14.6 2 Chron 25.4 Ezek 18.4,20
24.17 Ex 22.21,22 23.2,3 Deut 1.17; 10.17
24.18 Deut 5.15; 24.22
24.19 Lev 19.9,10 Deut 14.28,29

25 If you go into your neighbor's standing grain, you may pluck the ears with
your hand, but you shall not put a sickle to your neighbor's standing grain.

24 Suppose a man enters into marriage with a woman, but she does not please
him because he finds something objectionable about her, and so he writes
her a certificate of divorce, puts it in her hand, and sends her out of his house; she
then leaves his house 2 and goes off to become another man's wife. 3 Then suppose
the second man dislikes her, writes her a bill of divorce, puts it in her hand, and
sends her out of his house (or the second man who married her dies); 4 her first
husband, who sent her away, is not permitted to take her again to be his wife after
she has been defiled; for that would be abhorrent to the LORD, and you shall not
bring guilt on the land that the LORD your God is giving you as a possession.

5 When a man is newly married, he shall not go out with the army or be charged
with any related duty. He shall be free at home one year, to be happy with the wife
whom he has married.

6 No one shall take a mill or an upper millstone in pledge, for that would be
taking a life in pledge.

7 If someone is caught kidnaping another Israelite, enslaving or selling the Israelite, then that kidnaper shall die. So you shall purge the evil from your midst.

8 Guard against an outbreak of a leprous[c] skin disease by being very careful;
you shall carefully observe whatever the levitical priests instruct you, just as I have
commanded them. 9 Remember what the LORD your God did to Miriam on your
journey out of Egypt.

10 When you make your neighbor a loan of any kind, you shall not go into the
house to take the pledge. 11 You shall wait outside, while the person to whom you
are making the loan brings the pledge out to you. 12 If the person is poor, you shall
not sleep in the garment given you as[d] the pledge. 13 You shall give the pledge back
by sunset, so that your neighbor may sleep in the cloak and bless you; and it will be
to your credit before the LORD your God.

14 You shall not withhold the wages of poor and needy laborers, whether other
Israelites or aliens who reside in your land in one of your towns. 15 You shall pay
them their wages daily before sunset, because they are poor and their livelihood
depends on them; otherwise they might cry to the LORD against you, and you would
incur guilt.

16 Parents shall not be put to death for their children, nor shall children be put
to death for their parents; only for their own crimes may persons be put to death.

17 You shall not deprive a resident alien or an orphan of justice; you shall not
take a widow's garment in pledge. 18 Remember that you were a slave in Egypt and
the LORD your God redeemed you from there; therefore I command you to do this.

19 When you reap your harvest in your field and forget a sheaf in the field, you

[c] A term for several skin diseases; precise meaning uncertain [d] Heb lacks *the garment given you as*

24.1–4 Some think this passage supports divorce, but that is not the case. It simply recognizes a practice that already existed in Israel. All four verses must be read to understand the point of the passage. Divorce was a permanent and final act for the couple. Once divorced and remarried to others, they could never be remarried to each other (24.4). This restriction was to prevent casual remarriage after a frivolous separation. The intention was to make people think twice before divorcing.

24.5 Newly married couples were to remain together their first year. This was to avoid placing an excessive burden upon a new, unproven relationship and to give it a chance to mature and strengthen before confronting it with numerous responsibilities. Let your marriage grow strong by protecting your relationship from too much outside pressure and distraction—especially in the beginning. And don't expect or demand so much from newlyweds that they have inadequate time or energy to establish their marriage.

24.10–13 The Israelites were not to take advantage of others when seeking justice for themselves. Whenever we demand our own legal rights, we must also be concerned about the needs of our opponent. If we seek justice for others, we may find that we too are being treated more fairly.

24.10–22 God told his people to treat the poor with justice. The powerless and poverty-stricken are often looked upon as incompetent or lazy when, in fact, they may be victims of oppression and circumstance. God says we must do all we can to help these needy ones. His justice did not permit the Israelites to insist on profits or quick payment from those who were less fortunate. Instead, his laws gave the poor every opportunity to better their situation, while providing humane options for those who couldn't. God wants us to treat the poor fairly and to see their needs met.

24.19–21 God's people were instructed to leave some of their harvest in the fields so travelers and the poor could "glean" it. Gleaning was a way for them to provide food for themselves. Years later, Ruth obtained food for herself and Naomi by gleaning behind the reapers in Boaz's field, picking up the leftovers (Ruth 2.2). Because this law was being obeyed years after it was written, Ruth, a woman in Christ's lineage, was able to find food.

shall not go back to get it; it shall be left for the alien, the orphan, and the widow,
so that the LORD your God may bless you in all your undertakings. 20When you
beat your olive trees, do not strip what is left; it shall be for the alien, the orphan,
and the widow.
21 When you gather the grapes of your vineyard, do not glean what is left; it
shall be for the alien, the orphan, and the widow. 22Remember that you were a
slave in the land of Egypt; therefore I am commanding you to do this.

25 Suppose two persons have a dispute and enter into litigation, and the judges
decide between them, declaring one to be in the right and the other to be in
the wrong. 2If the one in the wrong deserves to be flogged, the judge shall make
that person lie down and be beaten in his presence with the number of lashes proportionate to the offense. 3Forty lashes may be given but not more; if more lashes
than these are given, your neighbor will be degraded in your sight.
4 You shall not muzzle an ox while it is treading out the grain.
5 When brothers reside together, and one of them dies and has no son, the wife
of the deceased shall not be married outside the family to a stranger. Her husband's
brother shall go in to her, taking her in marriage, and performing the duty of a
husband's brother to her, 6and the firstborn whom she bears shall succeed to the
name of the deceased brother, so that his name may not be blotted out of Israel.
7But if the man has no desire to marry his brother's widow, then his brother's
widow shall go up to the elders at the gate and say, "My husband's brother refuses
to perpetuate his brother's name in Israel; he will not perform the duty of a husband's brother to me." 8Then the elders of his town shall summon him and speak
to him. If he persists, saying, "I have no desire to marry her," 9then his brother's
wife shall go up to him in the presence of the elders, pull his sandal off his foot, spit
in his face, and declare, "This is what is done to the man who does not build up his
brother's house." 10Throughout Israel his family shall be known as "the house of
him whose sandal was pulled off."
11 If men get into a fight with one another, and the wife of one intervenes to
rescue her husband from the grip of his opponent by reaching out and seizing his
genitals, 12you shall cut off her hand; show no pity.
13 You shall not have in your bag two kinds of weights, large and small. 14You
shall not have in your house two kinds of measures, large and small. 15You shall
have only a full and honest weight; you shall have only a full and honest measure,
so that your days may be long in the land that the LORD your God is giving you.
16For all who do such things, all who act dishonestly, are abhorrent to the LORD
your God.
17 Remember what Amalek did to you on your journey out of Egypt, 18how he
attacked you on the way, when you were faint and weary, and struck down all who
lagged behind you; he did not fear God. 19Therefore when the LORD your God has
given you rest from all your enemies on every hand, in the land that the LORD your
God is giving you as an inheritance to possess, you shall blot out the remembrance
of Amalek from under heaven; do not forget.

24.20 Lev 19.10
24.22 Deut 15.15 16.12
25.1-3 Deut 17.11 Acts 16.33 2 Cor 11.24
25.4 1 Cor 9.9 1 Tim 5.18
25.5 Gen 38.8 Ruth 1.11,12 Mt 22.24 Mk 12.19 Lk 20.28
25.6 Ruth 4.5
25.9,10 Ruth 4.7,8
25.12 Deut 7.2
25.13 Lev 19.35 Prov 11.1; 16.11 Ezek 45.10,11
25.16 Deut 18.12; 22.5
25.17 Ex 17.8-16
25.19 Deut 12.9

25.1–3 At first glance these verses appear irrelevant today. But a closer look reveals some important principles about discipline. Are you responsible for the discipline of a child, a student, or an employee? Three important points will help you carry out your responsibility: (1) let the punishment follow quickly after the offense; (2) let the degree of punishment reflect the seriousness of the offense; and (3) don't overdo the punishment. Discipline that is swift, just, and restrained makes its point while preserving the dignity of the offender.

25.4 What is the point of this Old Testament regulation? Oxen were often used to tread out the grain on a threshing floor. The animal was attached by poles to a large millstone. As it walked around the millstone, its hooves trampled the grain, separating the kernels from the chaff. At the same time, the millstone ground the grain into flour. To muzzle the ox would prevent it from eating while it was working. Paul used this illustration in the New Testament to argue that people productive in Christian work should not be denied its benefits—they should receive financial support (2 Corinthians 9.10; 1 Timothy 5.17, 18). The fact that one is in Christian ministry doesn't mean he or she should be unfairly paid. There is also a broader application: don't be stingy with those who work for you.

25.5–10 This law describes a "levirate" marriage, the marriage of a widow to the brother of her dead husband. The purpose of such a marriage was to carry on the dead man's name and inheritance. Family ties were an important aspect of Israelite culture. The best way to be remembered was through your line of descendants. If a widow married someone outside the family, her first husband's line would come to an end. Tamar fought for this right in Genesis 38.

Prayers to God

26.1 Deut 6.1 **26** When you have come into the land that the LORD your God is giving you as
an inheritance to possess, and you possess it, and settle in it, 2 you shall take
26.2 Ex 22.29 23.16,19 some of the first of all the fruit of the ground, which you harvest from the land that
the LORD your God is giving you, and you shall put it in a basket and go to the place
that the LORD your God will choose as a dwelling for his name. 3 You shall go to the
priest who is in office at that time, and say to him, "Today I declare to the LORD
your God that I have come into the land that the LORD swore to our ancestors to give
us." 4 When the priest takes the basket from your hand and sets it down before the
26.5 Gen 43.1; 46.27 Deut 1.10; 10.22 altar of the LORD your God, 5 you shall make this response before the LORD your
God: "A wandering Aramean was my ancestor; he went down into Egypt and lived
there as an alien, few in number, and there he became a great nation, mighty and
26.6 Ex 1.11,12 Deut 4.20 populous. 6 When the Egyptians treated us harshly and afflicted us, by imposing
hard labor on us, 7 we cried to the LORD, the God of our ancestors; the LORD heard
26.8 Deut 4.34 our voice and saw our affliction, our toil, and our oppression. 8 The LORD brought
us out of Egypt with a mighty hand and an outstretched arm, with a terrifying dis-
26.9 Ex 3.8,17 Deut 27.2-4 Josh 5.6 play of power, and with signs and wonders; 9 and he brought us into this place and
gave us this land, a land flowing with milk and honey. 10 So now I bring the first of
the fruit of the ground that you, O LORD, have given me." You shall set it down
26.11 Deut 12.7,12 before the LORD your God and bow down before the LORD your God. 11 Then you,
together with the Levites and the aliens who reside among you, shall celebrate with
all the bounty that the LORD your God has given to you and to your house.
26.12 Deut 14.28,29 Heb 7.5,9,10 12 When you have finished paying all the tithe of your produce in the third year
(which is the year of the tithe), giving it to the Levites, the aliens, the orphans, and
the widows, so that they may eat their fill within your towns, 13 then you shall say
before the LORD your God: "I have removed the sacred portion from the house, and
I have given it to the Levites, the resident aliens, the orphans, and the widows, in
accordance with your entire commandment that you commanded me; I have neither
transgressed nor forgotten any of your commandments: 14 I have not eaten of it
while in mourning; I have not removed any of it while I was unclean; and I have not
offered any of it to the dead. I have obeyed the LORD my God, doing just as you
26.15 1 Kgs 8.30 2 Chron 30.27 Zech 2.13 commanded me. 15 Look down from your holy habitation, from heaven, and bless
your people Israel and the ground that you have given us, as you swore to our
ancestors—a land flowing with milk and honey."

Keeping God's laws

26.16 Deut 6.5,17 16 This very day the LORD your God is commanding you to observe these statutes and ordinances; so observe them diligently with all your heart and with all your
26.17 Ex 24.3 Lev 18.4,5 Deut 5.1 soul. 17 Today you have obtained the LORD's agreement: to be your God; and for
you to walk in his ways, to keep his statutes, his commandments, and his ordi-
nances, and to obey him. 18 Today the LORD has obtained your agreement: to be his
26.18 Deut 7.6 treasured people, as he promised you, and to keep his commandments; 19 for him to
26.19 Deut 28.1,13 set you high above all nations that he has made, in praise and in fame and in honor;
and for you to be a people holy to the LORD your God, as he promised.

26.1ff The festival of first fruits (Leviticus 23.9–14) was a reminder to the people of all God had provided for them. When they arrived in the promised land, the people were to recite a confession of faith that would retell the story of their small beginnings in Egypt, their growth into a mighty nation, and their journey to claim and conquer the land given them by God.

26.5 This wandering Aramean was Jacob. When Abraham's family left Ur, they settled at Haran in Paddan-aram (Genesis 11.28-32). Those who lived there were called Arameans, after the name of the region. Most of the family stayed there. Abraham, however, went on to Canaan. Later, the wives of both Isaac (Genesis 24.1-4) and Jacob (Genesis 27.41–28.5) came from the Aramean branch of the family. Jacob lived for at least fourteen years with the Arameans (Genesis 31.17-18). So the claim of being a descendent of a "wandering Aramean" is fully supported by the family ancestry.

26.5–10 In Israelite tradition, each person was required to recite the history of God's dealings with his people. What is the history of your relationship with God? Can you put into clear and concise words what God has done for you? Find a friend with whom you can share your spiritual journey. Take turns telling your stories. This will help you clearly understand your personal spiritual history, as well as encouraging and inspiring you both. Note: "Wandering" can mean lost or dying. Also, Arameans were the people of northern Syria and among the ancestors of Abraham. This is also used as a reference to Jacob who spent many years in their country (Genesis 29–31) and got his wife there.

6. Consequences of obedience and disobedience

A monument for God's laws

27 Then Moses and the elders of Israel charged all the people as follows: Keep
the entire commandment that I am commanding you today. 2 On the day that
you cross over the Jordan into the land that the LORD your God is giving you, you
shall set up large stones and cover them with plaster. 3 You shall write on them all
the words of this law when you have crossed over, to enter the land that the LORD
your God is giving you, a land flowing with milk and honey, as the LORD, the God
of your ancestors, promised you. 4 So when you have crossed over the Jordan, you
shall set up these stones, about which I am commanding you today, on Mount Ebal,
and you shall cover them with plaster. 5 And you shall build an altar there to the
LORD your God, an altar of stones on which you have not used an iron tool. 6 You
must build the altar of the LORD your God of unhewn[e] stones. Then offer up burnt
offerings on it to the LORD your God, 7 make sacrifices of well-being, and eat them
there, rejoicing before the LORD your God. 8 You shall write on the stones all the
words of this law very clearly.
9 Then Moses and the levitical priests spoke to all Israel, saying: Keep silence
and hear, O Israel! This very day you have become the people of the LORD your
God. 10 Therefore obey the LORD your God, observing his commandments and his
statutes that I am commanding you today.

The Levites shout 12 curses

11 The same day Moses charged the people as follows: 12 When you have
crossed over the Jordan, these shall stand on Mount Gerizim for the blessing of the
people: Simeon, Levi, Judah, Issachar, Joseph, and Benjamin. 13 And these shall
stand on Mount Ebal for the curse: Reuben, Gad, Asher, Zebulun, Dan, and Naphtali. 14 Then the Levites shall declare in a loud voice to all the Israelites:
15 "Cursed be anyone who makes an idol or casts an image, anything abhorrent
to the LORD, the work of an artisan, and sets it up in secret." All the people shall
respond, saying, "Amen!"
16 "Cursed be anyone who dishonors father or mother." All the people shall
say, "Amen!"
17 "Cursed be anyone who moves a neighbor's boundary marker." All the people shall say, "Amen!"
18 "Cursed be anyone who misleads a blind person on the road." All the people
shall say, "Amen!"
19 "Cursed be anyone who deprives the alien, the orphan, and the widow of
justice." All the people shall say, "Amen!"
20 "Cursed be anyone who lies with his father's wife, because he has violated
his father's rights."[f] All the people shall say, "Amen!"

[e] Heb *whole* [f] Heb *uncovered his father's skirt*

27.2 Deut 26.9; Josh 8.30-32
27.7 Lev 7.11; Num 6.14; 7.88
27.9 Deut 26.17
27.12 Deut 11.26; Josh 8.33-35
27.15 Ex 20.4,23; 34.17; Lev 19.3,4; Deut 4.16; 5.8
27.16 Ex 21.15; Lev 20.9; Deut 21.18; Ezek 22.7
27.17 Deut 19.14
27.18 Lev 19.14
27.19 Ex 22.21; Lev 19.33; Deut 10.18; 24.17; Ezek 22.7
27.20 Lev 18.8; 20.11; Deut 22.30

27.5, 6 The Lord had specified an altar made of uncut rocks so that the people would not begin worshiping the altars as idols. To use a chisel on a stone of the altar would be to profane it (Exodus 20.24–26). Also, since the Israelites did not have the capacity to work with iron at this time, using iron tools might mean using the cooperation and expertise of the other nations in the land.

27.9, 10 Moses said that because the Israelites were now God's people, they needed to start obeying God's commands. When we decide to believe in God, we must also decide to follow his ways. What we do shows what we really believe. Are people able to discern that you are a member of God's family?

27.15–26 These curses were a series of oaths, spoken by the priests and affirmed by the people, by which the people promised to stay away from wrong actions. By saying *Amen,* "So be it," the people took responsibility for their actions. Sometimes looking at a list of curses like this gives us the idea that God has a bad temper and is out to crush anyone who steps out of line. But we need to see these restrictions not as threats, but as loving warnings about the plain facts of life. Just as we warn children to stay away from hot stoves and busy streets, God warns us to stay away from dangerous actions. The natural law of his universe makes it clear that wrongdoing toward others or God has tragic consequences. God is merciful enough to tell us this truth plainly. Motivated by love and not anger, his strong words help us avoid the serious consequences that result from neglecting God or wronging others. But God does not leave us with only curses or consequences. Immediately following these curses, we discover the great blessings (positive consequences) that come from living for God (28.1–14). These give us extra incentive to obey God's laws. While all these blessings may not come in our lifetime on earth, those who obey God will experience the fullness of his blessing when he establishes the new heavens and the new earth.

21 "Cursed be anyone who lies with any animal." All the people shall say,
"Amen!"
22 "Cursed be anyone who lies with his sister, whether the daughter of his father or the daughter of his mother." All the people shall say, "Amen!"
23 "Cursed be anyone who lies with his mother-in-law." All the people shall
say, "Amen!"
24 "Cursed be anyone who strikes down a neighbor in secret." All the people
shall say, "Amen!"
25 "Cursed be anyone who takes a bribe to shed innocent blood." All the people
shall say, "Amen!"
26 "Cursed be anyone who does not uphold the words of this law by observing
them." All the people shall say, "Amen!"

Blessings for obedience

28 If you will only obey the LORD your God, by diligently observing all his
commandments that I am commanding you today, the LORD your God will
set you high above all the nations of the earth; 2 all these blessings shall come upon
you and overtake you, if you obey the LORD your God:
3 Blessed shall you be in the city, and blessed shall you be in the field.
4 Blessed shall be the fruit of your womb, the fruit of your ground, and the fruit
of your livestock, both the increase of your cattle and the issue of your flock.
5 Blessed shall be your basket and your kneading bowl.
6 Blessed shall you be when you come in, and blessed shall you be when you go
out.
7 The LORD will cause your enemies who rise against you to be defeated before
you; they shall come out against you one way, and flee before you seven ways.
8 The LORD will command the blessing upon you in your barns, and in all that you
undertake; he will bless you in the land that the LORD your God is giving you. 9 The
LORD will establish you as his holy people, as he has sworn to you, if you keep the
commandments of the LORD your God and walk in his ways. 10 All the peoples of
the earth shall see that you are called by the name of the LORD, and they shall be
afraid of you. 11 The LORD will make you abound in prosperity, in the fruit of your
womb, in the fruit of your livestock, and in the fruit of your ground in the land that
the LORD swore to your ancestors to give you. 12 The LORD will open for you his
rich storehouse, the heavens, to give the rain of your land in its season and to bless
all your undertakings. You will lend to many nations, but you will not borrow.
13 The LORD will make you the head, and not the tail; you shall be only at the top,
and not at the bottom—if you obey the commandments of the LORD your God,
which I am commanding you today, by diligently observing them, 14 and if you do
not turn aside from any of the words that I am commanding you today, either to the
right or to the left, following other gods to serve them.

Curses for disobedience

15 But if you will not obey the LORD your God by diligently observing all his
commandments and decrees, which I am commanding you today, then all these
curses shall come upon you and overtake you:
16 Cursed shall you be in the city, and cursed shall you be in the field.
17 Cursed shall be your basket and your kneading bowl.
18 Cursed shall be the fruit of your womb, the fruit of your ground, the increase
of your cattle and the issue of your flock.
19 Cursed shall you be when you come in, and cursed shall you be when you go
out.
20 The LORD will send upon you disaster, panic, and frustration in everything
you attempt to do, until you are destroyed and perish quickly, on account of the evil
of your deeds, because you have forsaken me. 21 The LORD will make the pestilence
cling to you until it has consumed you off the land that you are entering to possess.
22 The LORD will afflict you with consumption, fever, inflammation, with fiery heat
and drought, and with blight and mildew; they shall pursue you until you perish.

27.21 Ex 22.19 Lev 18.23; 20.15
27.22 Lev 18.9; 20.17
27.23 Lev 18.17; 20.14
27.24 Num 35.30 Deut 19.13
27.25 Ex 23.8 Deut 10.17
27.26 Deut 5.1; 28.15 Gal 3.10
28.1 Ex 15.26; 23.22 Lev 26.3 Deut 7.12; 11.13
28.2 Lev 26.9 Deut 28.8 Ps 107.36-38 Amos 9.13
28.7 Lev 26.7 Deut 32.30 Josh 10.10 Ps 89.23
28.8 Lev 25.21,22 26.4,5
28.9 Ex 19.5 Deut 7.6; 26.18
28.11 Lev 26.9 Deut 28.2-6,8 30.9
28.12 Lev 26.4 Deut 11.14 23.20
28.13 Deut 28.1,44
28.14 Deut 5.32,33 19.9
28.15 Lev 26.14 Deut 27.15 28.1-6 Josh 23.15,16
28.20 Deut 8.11; 28.25
28.21 Lev 26.25 Num 14.12 1 Kgs 8.37 Amos 4.10

23 The sky over your head shall be bronze, and the earth under you iron. 24 The
LORD will change the rain of your land into powder, and only dust shall come down
upon you from the sky until you are destroyed.

25 The LORD will cause you to be defeated before your enemies; you shall go
out against them one way and flee before them seven ways. You shall become an
object of horror to all the kingdoms of the earth. 26 Your corpses shall be food for
every bird of the air and animal of the earth, and there shall be no one to frighten
them away. 27 The LORD will afflict you with the boils of Egypt, with ulcers,
scurvy, and itch, of which you cannot be healed. 28 The LORD will afflict you with
madness, blindness, and confusion of mind; 29 you shall grope about at noon as
blind people grope in darkness, but you shall be unable to find your way; and you
shall be continually abused and robbed, without anyone to help. 30 You shall become engaged to a woman, but another man shall lie with her. You shall build a
house, but not live in it. You shall plant a vineyard, but not enjoy its fruit. 31 Your
ox shall be butchered before your eyes, but you shall not eat of it. Your donkey
shall be stolen in front of you, and shall not be restored to you. Your sheep shall be
given to your enemies, without anyone to help you. 32 Your sons and daughters
shall be given to another people, while you look on; you will strain your eyes looking for them all day but be powerless to do anything. 33 A people whom you do not
know shall eat up the fruit of your ground and of all your labors; you shall be continually abused and crushed, 34 and driven mad by the sight that your eyes shall see.
35 The LORD will strike you on the knees and on the legs with grievous boils of
which you cannot be healed, from the sole of your foot to the crown of your head.
36 The LORD will bring you, and the king whom you set over you, to a nation that
neither you nor your ancestors have known, where you shall serve other gods, of
wood and stone. 37 You shall become an object of horror, a proverb, and a byword
among all the peoples where the LORD will lead you.

38 You shall carry much seed into the field but shall gather little in, for the
locust shall consume it. 39 You shall plant vineyards and dress them, but you shall
neither drink the wine nor gather the grapes, for the worm shall eat them. 40 You
shall have olive trees throughout all your territory, but you shall not anoint yourself
with the oil, for your olives shall drop off. 41 You shall have sons and daughters, but
they shall not remain yours, for they shall go into captivity. 42 All your trees and the
fruit of your ground the cicada shall take over. 43 Aliens residing among you shall
ascend above you higher and higher, while you shall descend lower and lower.
44 They shall lend to you but you shall not lend to them; they shall be the head and
you shall be the tail.

45 All these curses shall come upon you, pursuing and overtaking you until you
are destroyed, because you did not obey the LORD your God, by observing the
commandments and the decrees that he commanded you. 46 They shall be among
you and your descendants as a sign and a portent forever.

47 Because you did not serve the LORD your God joyfully and with gladness of
heart for the abundance of everything, 48 therefore you shall serve your enemies
whom the LORD will send against you, in hunger and thirst, in nakedness and lack
of everything. He will put an iron yoke on your neck until he has destroyed you.
49 The LORD will bring a nation from far away, from the end of the earth, to swoop
down on you like an eagle, a nation whose language you do not understand, 50 a
grim-faced nation showing no respect to the old or favor to the young. 51 It shall

28.23 Lev 26.19
28.24 Deut 11.17; 1 Kgs 17.1; Jer 14.1
28.25 Lev 26.17,36; 2 Chron 29.8; Isa 30.17; Jer 15.4
28.26 Ps 79.2; Jer 7.33; 16.4; 19.7; 34.20
28.27 Ex 9.9; 15.26; Lev 13.1,2; 1 Sam 5.6,9,12
28.28 Isa 19.14
28.29 Ex 10.21; Job 5.14; Ps 69.23; Isa 59.10
28.30 Job 31.10; Isa 65.21; Jer 8.10; Amos 5.11
28.32 2 Chron 29.9; Neh 5.2,5
28.35 Job 2.7; Isa 3.17
28.36 2 Kgs 17.4,6; 24.12,14; 25.7,11
28.37 Deut 29.22
28.38 Lev 26.20; Isa 5.10; Joel 1.4; Mic 6.15
28.39 Amos 5.11; Mic 6.15
28.41 Deut 28.32
28.42 Deut 28.38; Amos 7.11
28.44 Deut 28.12,13
28.45 Lev 26.28; Deut 4.25,26
28.47 Lev 26.13; Jer 28.14; Lam 1.3
28.49 Deut 28.36; Isa 5.26; 7.18; Jer 5.15

28.23, 24 This refers to a drought.

28.34 One of the curses for those who rejected God was that they would go mad from seeing all the tragedy around them. Do you ever feel that you will go crazy if you hear about one more rape, kidnaping, murder, or war? Much of the world's evil is a result of people's failure to acknowledge and serve God. When you hear bad news, don't groan helplessly as do unbelievers who have no hope for the future. Remind yourself that in spite of it all, God has ultimate control and will one day come back to make everything right.

28.36 This happened when Assyria and Babylon took the Israelites captive to their lands (2 Kings 17.23; 25.11).

28.46 A "portent" is a prophetic indication. These curses will be warnings to others.

consume the fruit of your livestock and the fruit of your ground until you are destroyed, leaving you neither grain, wine, and oil, nor the increase of your cattle and
the issue of your flock, until it has made you perish. 52 It shall besiege you in all
your towns until your high and fortified walls, in which you trusted, come down
throughout your land; it shall besiege you in all your towns throughout the land that
the LORD your God has given you. 53 In the desperate straits to which the enemy
siege reduces you, you will eat the fruit of your womb, the flesh of your own sons
and daughters whom the LORD your God has given you. 54 Even the most refined
and gentle of men among you will begrudge food to his own brother, to the wife
whom he embraces, and to the last of his remaining children, 55 giving to none of
them any of the flesh of his children whom he is eating, because nothing else remains to him, in the desperate straits to which the enemy siege will reduce you in
all your towns. 56 She who is the most refined and gentle among you, so gentle and
refined that she does not venture to set the sole of her foot on the ground, will
begrudge food to the husband whom she embraces, to her own son, and to her own
daughter, 57 begrudging even the afterbirth that comes out from between her thighs,
and the children that she bears, because she is eating them in secret for lack of
anything else, in the desperate straits to which the enemy siege will reduce you in
your towns.

58 If you do not diligently observe all the words of this law that are written in
this book, fearing this glorious and awesome name, the LORD your God, 59 then the
LORD will overwhelm both you and your offspring with severe and lasting afflictions and grievous and lasting maladies. 60 He will bring back upon you all the
diseases of Egypt, of which you were in dread, and they shall cling to you. 61 Every
other malady and affliction, even though not recorded in the book of this law, the
LORD will inflict on you until you are destroyed. 62 Although once you were as
numerous as the stars in heaven, you shall be left few in number, because you did
not obey the LORD your God. 63 And just as the LORD took delight in making you
prosperous and numerous, so the LORD will take delight in bringing you to ruin and
destruction; you shall be plucked off the land that you are entering to possess.
64 The LORD will scatter you among all peoples, from one end of the earth to the
other; and there you shall serve other gods, of wood and stone, which neither you
nor your ancestors have known. 65 Among those nations you shall find no ease, no
resting place for the sole of your foot. There the LORD will give you a trembling
heart, failing eyes, and a languishing spirit. 66 Your life shall hang in doubt before
you; night and day you shall be in dread, with no assurance of your life. 67 In the
morning you shall say, "If only it were evening!" and at evening you shall say, "If
only it were morning!"—because of the dread that your heart shall feel and the
sights that your eyes shall see. 68 The LORD will bring you back in ships to Egypt,
by a route that I promised you would never see again; and there you shall offer
yourselves for sale to your enemies as male and female slaves, but there will be no
buyer.

29 [g] These are the words of the covenant that the LORD commanded Moses to
make with the Israelites in the land of Moab, in addition to the covenant that
he had made with them at Horeb.

[g] Ch 28.69 in Heb

28.52 2 Kgs 19.30; 25.1; 2 Chron 32.1; Jer 10.17,18; Zeph 1.14,15
28.53 Lev 26.29
28.58 Lev 26.14; Deut 28.15
28.60 Deut 28.21,27
28.62 Deut 1.10
28.63 Deut 30.9; Jer 45.4
28.64 Lev 26.33; Deut 4.27; 32.17; Neh 1.8; Jer 16.13; Lk 21.24
28.65 Lam 1.3
28.66 Heb 10.27
28.67 Deut 28.34
28.68 Deut 17.16
29.1 Lev 27.34; Deut 1.1-5; 5.1

28.64 This severe warning tragically came true when Israel was defeated and carried away into captivity by Assyria (722 B.C.), and Judah to Babylon (586 B.C.). Later, in A.D. 70, Roman oppression forced many Jews to flee their homeland. Thus the people were dispersed throughout the various nations.

29.1ff At Mount Sinai, 40 years earlier, God and Israel had made a covenant (Exodus 19, 20). Although there were many parts to the covenant (the books of Exodus, Leviticus, and Numbers), its purpose can be summed up in two sentences: God promised to bless the Israelites by making them the nation through whom the rest of the world could know God. In return, the Israelites promised to love and obey God in order to receive physical and spiritual blessings. Here Moses reviews this covenant. God was still keeping his part of the bargain (and he always would), but the Israelites were already neglecting their part. Moses restated the covenant to warn the people that if they did not keep their part of the agreement, they would experience severe discipline.

C. A CALL FOR COMMITMENT TO GOD: MOSES' THIRD ADDRESS (29.2—30.20)

After reviewing God's laws, Moses calls for commitment, urging the people to honor the contract they had previously made with God. Knowing God's Word is not enough, we must obey it.

Moses reviews God's covenant

2[h] Moses summoned all Israel and said to them: You have seen all that the LORD did before your eyes in the land of Egypt, to Pharaoh and to all his servants and to all his land, 3 the great trials that your eyes saw, the signs, and those great wonders. 4 But to this day the LORD has not given you a mind to understand, or eyes to see, or ears to hear. 5 I have led you forty years in the wilderness. The clothes on your back have not worn out, and the sandals on your feet have not worn out; 6 you have not eaten bread, and you have not drunk wine or strong drink— so that you may know that I am the LORD your God. 7 When you came to this place, King Sihon of Heshbon and King Og of Bashan came out against us for battle, but we defeated them. 8 We took their land and gave it as an inheritance to the Reubenites, the Gadites, and the half-tribe of Manasseh. 9 Therefore diligently observe the words of this covenant, in order that you may succeed[i] in everything that you do.

10 You stand assembled today, all of you, before the LORD your God—the leaders of your tribes,[j] your elders, and your officials, all the men of Israel, 11 your children, your women, and the aliens who are in your camp, both those who cut your wood and those who draw your water— 12 to enter into the covenant of the LORD your God, sworn by an oath, which the LORD your God is making with you today; 13 in order that he may establish you today as his people, and that he may be your God, as he promised you and as he swore to your ancestors, to Abraham, to Isaac, and to Jacob. 14 I am making this covenant, sworn by an oath, not only with you who stand here with us today before the LORD our God, 15 but also with those who are not here with us today. 16 You know how we lived in the land of Egypt, and how we came through the midst of the nations through which you passed. 17 You have seen their detestable things, the filthy idols of wood and stone, of silver and gold, that were among them. 18 It may be that there is among you a man or woman, or a family or tribe, whose heart is already turning away from the LORD our God to serve the gods of those nations. It may be that there is among you a root sprouting poisonous and bitter growth. 19 All who hear the words of this oath and bless themselves, thinking in their hearts, "We are safe even though we go our own stubborn ways" (thus bringing disaster on moist and dry alike)[k]— 20 the LORD will be unwilling to pardon them, for the LORD's anger and passion will smoke against them. All the curses written in this book will descend on them, and the LORD will blot out their names from under heaven. 21 The LORD will single them out from all the tribes of Israel for calamity, in accordance with all the curses of the covenant written in this book of the law. 22 The next generation, your children who rise up after you, as well as the foreigner who comes from a distant country, will see the devastation of that land and the afflictions with which the LORD has afflicted it— 23 all its soil burned out by sulfur and salt, nothing planted, nothing sprouting, unable to support any vegetation, like the destruction of Sodom and Gomorrah, Admah and Zeboiim, which the LORD destroyed in his fierce anger— 24 they and indeed all the nations will wonder, "Why has the LORD done thus to this land? What caused this great

29.2 Lev 8.1 Num 1.17-19
29.4 Isa 6.9,10 Acts 28.26 Rom 11.8
29.5 Deut 8.2,4
29.7 Num 21.21 Deut 1.2-5; 2.26
29.8 Num 32.31 Deut 3.12
29.9 Ex 19.5 Deut 4.6 Josh 1.7
29.11 Josh 9.21,23,27
29.12 Deut 5.2
29.13 Gen 17.7 Ex 6.7
29.14 Jer 31.31 Heb 8.7
29.16 Deut 2.4
29.17 Ex 20.23
29.18 Jer 9.15 Hos 10.4 Heb 12.15
29.19 Num 15.30,39 Ps 10.4-6 49.18,19 Prov 29.1 Jer 5.12
29.20 Deut 9.14 2 Kgs 14.27 Ps 74.1; 80.4
29.22 Jer 19.8
29.23 Gen 19.24 Isa 1.7; 34.9 64.11
29.24 1 Kgs 9.8 2 Chron 7.21 Jer 22.8 Lam 2.15

[h] Ch 29.1 in Heb [i] Or *deal wisely* [j] Gk Syr: Heb *your leaders, your tribes* [k] Meaning of Heb uncertain

---

29.5 Just as Israel did not notice God's care for them along their journey, we sometimes do not notice all of the ways that God takes care of us, that all of our daily needs have been supplied and we have been well fed and well clothed. Worse yet, we mistakenly take the credit ourselves for being good providers, instead of recognizing God's hand in the process.

29.9 What is the best way to find success in life? For the Israelites, their first step was to keep their part of the covenant. They were to love God with all their heart, soul, and might (Deuteronomy 6.4, 5). We too are to seek first the kingdom of God and his righteousness (Matthew 6.33); then, true success in life will follow as a blessing from the hand of God.

29.18 Moses cautioned that the day the Hebrews chose to turn from God, a root would be planted that would produce poisonous and bitter growth. When we decide to do what we know is wrong, we plant an evil seed that begins to grow out of control, eventually yielding a crop of sorrow and pain. But we can prevent those seeds of sin from taking root. If you have done something wrong, confess it to God and others immediately. If the seed never finds fertile soil, its bitter fruit will never ripen.

29.25 2 Kgs 17.9; 2 Chron 36.13; Jer 40.2,3; 50.7
29.27 Deut 29.20
29.28 1 Kgs 14.15; Ezek 19.12
29.29 Job 11.6,7; Ps 25.14; 78.2-7

display of anger?" 25 They will conclude, "It is because they abandoned the covenant of the LORD, the God of their ancestors, which he made with them when he
brought them out of the land of Egypt. 26 They turned and served other gods, worshiping them, gods whom they had not known and whom he had not allotted to
them; 27 so the anger of the LORD was kindled against that land, bringing on it every
curse written in this book. 28 The LORD uprooted them from their land in anger,
fury, and great wrath, and cast them into another land, as is now the case." 29 The
secret things belong to the LORD our God, but the revealed things belong to us and
to our children forever, to observe all the words of this law.

Returning to the Lord

30.1 Lev 26.40,41; Deut 4.30; 11.26
30.2 Lev 26.3; Deut 26.16; Neh 1.8,9
30.3 Gen 28.15; 48.21; Ps 106.45-47; Isa 56.8; Mt 23.37; Jn 12.51,52
30.4 Isa 43.5,6; 48.20; 62.11
30.5 Deut 13.17; Jer 29.14; 30.3
30.7 Ex 23.22; Deut 25.19; 28.7; 30.2
30.9 Deut 15.10; 29.9
30.10 Deut 4.29; Ezek 18.21

30 When all these things have happened to you, the blessings and the curses
that I have set before you, if you call them to mind among all the nations
where the LORD your God has driven you, 2 and return to the LORD your God, and
you and your children obey him with all your heart and with all your soul, just as
I am commanding you today, 3 then the LORD your God will restore your fortunes
and have compassion on you, gathering you again from all the peoples among
whom the LORD your God has scattered you. 4 Even if you are exiled to the ends of
the world,[l] from there the LORD your God will gather you, and from there he will
bring you back. 5 The LORD your God will bring you into the land that your ancestors possessed, and you will possess it; he will make you more prosperous and
numerous than your ancestors.

6 Moreover, the LORD your God will circumcise your heart and the heart of
your descendants, so that you will love the LORD your God with all your heart and
with all your soul, in order that you may live. 7 The LORD your God will put all
these curses on your enemies and on the adversaries who took advantage of you.
8 Then you shall again obey the LORD, observing all his commandments that I am
commanding you today, 9 and the LORD your God will make you abundantly prosperous in all your undertakings, in the fruit of your body, in the fruit of your livestock, and in the fruit of your soil. For the LORD will again take delight in
prospering you, just as he delighted in prospering your ancestors, 10 when you obey
the LORD your God by observing his commandments and decrees that are written in
this book of the law, because you turn to the LORD your God with all your heart and
with all your soul.

The choice of life or death

30.11-14 Isa 45.19; Rom 16.25-27

11 Surely, this commandment that I am commanding you today is not too hard
for you, nor is it too far away. 12 It is not in heaven, that you should say, "Who will

[l] Heb *of heaven*

29.29 There are some things God has chosen not to reveal to us, possibly for the following reasons: (1) our finite minds cannot fully understand the infinite aspects of God's nature and the universe (Ecclesiastes 3.11); (2) some things are unnecessary for us to know until we are more mature; and (3) God is infinite and all-knowing, and we do not have the capacity to know everything he does. This verse shows that although God has not told us everything there is to know about obeying him, he has told us enough. Thus disobedience comes from an act of the will, not a lack of knowledge. Through God's Word we know enough about him to be saved by faith and to serve him. We must not use the limitation of our knowledge as an excuse to reject his claim on our lives.

30.1–6 The theme of verses 1–6 is frequently found in the writings of the prophets. Although the Israelites will be punished for their sin, made captives, and exiled to distant lands, God will let them return one day to their homeland. This prediction was fulfilled in part when many Israelites returned from 70 years of captivity in Babylon (Ezra 1, 2). It will be fulfilled completely at the second coming of Jesus Christ. Then all believers, Jews and non-Jews, will be gathered from the ends of the earth to worship Christ in his new kingdom.

30.1–6 Moses told the Hebrews that when they were ready to return to God, he would be ready to receive them. God's mercy is unbelievable. It goes far beyond what we can imagine. Even if the Jews deliberately walked away from him and ruined their lives, God would still take them back. God wants to forgive us and bring us back to himself too. Some people will not learn this until their world has crashed in around them. Then the sorrow and pain seem to open their eyes to what God has been saying all along. Are you separated from God by sin? No matter how far you have wandered, God promises a fresh beginning if only you will turn to him.

30.11–14 God has called us to obey his commandments while reminding us that his laws are not hidden from us or beyond our reach. Have you ever said you would obey God if you knew what he wanted? Have you ever complained that obedience is too difficult for a mere human? These are unacceptable excuses. God's laws are written in the Bible and are clearly evident in the world around us. Obeying them is reasonable, sensible, and beneficial. The most difficult part of obeying God's laws is simply deciding to start now.

go up to heaven for us, and get it for us so that we may hear it and observe it?" 30.12-14 Rom 10.6-8
13 Neither is it beyond the sea, that you should say, "Who will cross to the other side
of the sea for us, and get it for us so that we may hear it and observe it?" 14 No, the
word is very near to you; it is in your mouth and in your heart for you to observe. 30.15 Deut 11.26
15 See, I have set before you today life and prosperity, death and adversity. 16 If Jer 21.8
you obey the commandments of the LORD your God[m] that I am commanding you Mt 7.13,14
today, by loving the LORD your God, walking in his ways, and observing his com- 30.16 Deut 4.1; 6.5
mandments, decrees, and ordinances, then you shall live and become numerous, 30.6
and the LORD your God will bless you in the land that you are entering to possess. 30.17 Deut 28.15,36,
17 But if your heart turns away and you do not hear, but are led astray to bow down 64; 29.18
to other gods and serve them, 18 I declare to you today that you shall perish; you 30.18
shall not live long in the land that you are crossing the Jordan to enter and possess. Deut 25.13-15 31.29
19 I call heaven and earth to witness against you today that I have set before you life 30.19
and death, blessings and curses. Choose life so that you and your descendants may Deut 4.26 31.28; 32.1
live, 20 loving the LORD your God, obeying him, and holding fast to him; for that Isa 1.2
means life to you and length of days, so that you may live in the land that the LORD 30.20 Deut 10.20; 13.4
swore to give to your ancestors, to Abraham, to Isaac, and to Jacob. Josh 22.5

D. THE CHANGE IN LEADERSHIP: MOSES' LAST DAYS (31.1—34.12)

Realizing that he is about to die, Moses commissions Joshua, records the laws in a permanent form, and teaches a special song to the Israelites. Thus Moses prepared the people for his departure. Similarly, we should not allow others to become dependent upon us for their spiritual growth, but help them to become dependent upon God.

Moses commissions Joshua

31 When Moses had finished speaking all[n] these words to all Israel, 2 he said 31.2
to them: "I am now one hundred twenty years old. I am no longer able to get Deut 1.37; 34.7 Acts 7.23,30
about, and the LORD has told me, 'You shall not cross over this Jordan.' 3 The LORD 31.3
your God himself will cross over before you. He will destroy these nations before Num 27.18 Deut 3.28; 34.9
you, and you shall dispossess them. Joshua also will cross over before you, as the Josh 1.2; 3.7
LORD promised. 4 The LORD will do to them as he did to Sihon and Og, the kings
of the Amorites, and to their land, when he destroyed them. 5 The LORD will give
them over to you and you shall deal with them in full accord with the command that
I have given to you. 6 Be strong and bold; have no fear or dread of them, because 31.6 Deut 20.1
it is the LORD your God who goes with you; he will not fail you or forsake you." Heb 13.5
7 Then Moses summoned Joshua and said to him in the sight of all Israel: "Be 31.7
strong and bold, for you are the one who will go with this people into the land that Deut 1.38; 3.28
the LORD has sworn to their ancestors to give them; and you will put them in possession of it. 8 It is the LORD who goes before you. He will be with you; he will not fail
you or forsake you. Do not fear or be dismayed."

Moses records the laws

9 Then Moses wrote down this law, and gave it to the priests, the sons of Levi, 31.9 Num 4.5,6
who carried the ark of the covenant of the LORD, and to all the elders of Israel. Deut 10.8
10 Moses commanded them: "Every seventh year, in the scheduled year of remis- 31.10
sion, during the festival of booths,[o] 11 when all Israel comes to appear before the Deut 12.4,5 15.1
LORD your God at the place that he will choose, you shall read this law before all

[m] Gk: Heb lacks *If you obey the commandments of the LORD your God* [n] Q Ms Gk: MT *Moses went and spoke*
[o] Or *tabernacles*; Heb *succoth*

30.19, 20 Moses challenged Israel to choose to obey God and therefore continue to experience his blessings. God doesn't force his will on anyone. He lets us decide whether to follow him or reject him. This decision, however, is a life-or-death matter. God wants us to realize this, for he would like us all to choose life. Daily, in each new situation, we must affirm and reinforce this commitment.

31.10–13 The laws were to be read to the whole assembly so that everyone, including the children, could hear them. Every seven years the entire nation would gather together and listen as a priest read the law to them. There were no books, Bibles, or newsstands to spread God's Word, so the people had to rely on word of mouth and an accurate memory. Memorization was an important part of worship, for if everyone knew the law, ignorance would be no excuse for breaking it. To fulfill God's purpose and will in our lives, we need the content and substance of his Word in our hearts and minds. For the Hebrews, this process began in childhood. Teaching our children and new believers should be one of our top priorities. Our finest teachers, best resources, and most careful thought should be directed toward showing them how to follow God in all life's situations.

31.12 Deut 4.10; 29.11 Israel in their hearing. 12 Assemble the people—men, women, and children, as
well as the aliens residing in your towns—so that they may hear and learn to fear
the LORD your God and to observe diligently all the words of this law, 13 and so that
their children, who have not known it, may hear and learn to fear the LORD your
God, as long as you live in the land that you are crossing over the Jordan to possess."

Israel's disobedience predicted

31.14 Num 27.13 Deut 34.5 14 The LORD said to Moses, "Your time to die is near; call Joshua and present
yourselves in the tent of meeting, so that I may commission him." So Moses and
31.15 Ex 16.10 Joshua went and presented themselves in the tent of meeting, 15 and the LORD appeared at the tent in a pillar of cloud; the pillar of cloud stood at the entrance to the
tent.
31.16 Deut 4.25; 32.50 Judg 2.11; 10.6 16 The LORD said to Moses, "Soon you will lie down with your ancestors. Then
this people will begin to prostitute themselves to the foreign gods in their midst, the
gods of the land into which they are going; they will forsake me, breaking my
31.17 Judg 2.12-14 covenant that I have made with them. 17 My anger will be kindled against them in
that day. I will forsake them and hide my face from them; they will become easy
prey, and many terrible troubles will come upon them. In that day they will say,
'Have not these troubles come upon us because our God is not in our midst?' 18 On
that day I will surely hide my face on account of all the evil they have done by
turning to other gods. 19 Now therefore write this song, and teach it to the Israelites;
put it in their mouths, in order that this song may be a witness for me against the
31.20 Deut 6.10-12 8.10,19 11.16,17 Israelites. 20 For when I have brought them into the land flowing with milk and
honey, which I promised on oath to their ancestors, and they have eaten their fill
and grown fat, they will turn to other gods and serve them, despising me and break-
31.21 Lev 26.40,41 ing my covenant. 21 And when many terrible troubles come upon them, this song
will confront them as a witness, because it will not be lost from the mouths of their
descendants. For I know what they are inclined to do even now, before I have
brought them into the land that I promised them on oath." 22 That very day Moses
wrote this song and taught it to the Israelites.
23 Then the LORD commissioned Joshua son of Nun and said, "Be strong and
bold, for you shall bring the Israelites into the land that I promised them; I will be
with you."
24 When Moses had finished writing down in a book the words of this law to
31.25 Deut 31.9 the very end, 25 Moses commanded the Levites who carried the ark of the covenant
of the LORD, saying, 26 "Take this book of the law and put it beside the ark of the
31.27 Deut 9.6,7,13, 14 covenant of the LORD your God; let it remain there as a witness against you. 27 For
I know well how rebellious and stubborn you are. If you already have been so
rebellious toward the LORD while I am still alive among you, how much more after
31.28 Deut 30.19; 32.1 my death! 28 Assemble to me all the elders of your tribes and your officials, so that
I may recite these words in their hearing and call heaven and earth to witness
31.29 Deut 32.5 against them. 29 For I know that after my death you will surely act corruptly, turning aside from the way that I have commanded you. In time to come trouble will

---

31.19–21 There is a place for music in Christian education, and for the building up of all believers. Some people memorize classic hymns of the church to help them think of what is true, right, and good. Others find tapes to play when they are in the car or at home. What creative ways can music be used to teach in your church? How could you maximize the benefit of music in your family?

31.23 Joshua had been appointed to take over the leadership of Israel and guide the people into the promised land (Moses could not enter the land due to his disobedience—Numbers 20.12). Joshua, first mentioned in Exodus 17.9, had been Moses' assistant for many years (Joshua 1.1). One of his key qualifications was his faith. As one of the 12 spies to first enter Canaan, only he and Caleb believed that God could help Israel conquer the land (Numbers 13.1–14.30). Moses told Joshua to be strong and courageous twice in this chapter (see 31.7, 23). Indeed, this was a frightening task with three million people to care for, settle disputes for, and lead into battle. Finding courage would be Joshua's greatest test. He was strong and courageous because he knew God was with him, and he had faith that God would do all he had promised Israel.

31.27–29 Moses knew that the Israelites, in spite of all they had seen of God's work, were rebellious at heart. They deserved God's punishment, although they often received his mercy instead. We too are stubborn and rebellious by nature. Throughout our lives we struggle with sin. Repentance once a month or once a week is not enough. We must constantly turn from our sins to God and let his mercy save us.

befall you, because you will do what is evil in the sight of the LORD, provoking him
to anger through the work of your hands."

Moses' song

30 Then Moses recited the words of this song, to the very end, in the hearing of
the whole assembly of Israel:

32 Give ear, O heavens, and I will speak; 32.1 Deut 4.26
let the earth hear the words of my mouth. Isa 1.2
2 May my teaching drop like the rain, 32.2 Ps 72.6
my speech condense like the dew; Isa 55.10
like gentle rain on grass,
like showers on new growth.
3 For I will proclaim the name of the LORD; 32.3 Gen 18.25
ascribe greatness to our God! Ex 34.5,6 Deut 3.23-25
4 The Rock, his work is perfect, 32.4 Gen 49.24
and all his ways are just. Deut 32.18
A faithful God, without deceit, 2 Sam 22.2
just and upright is he;
5 yet his degenerate children have dealt falsely with him,[p] 32.5 Deut 4.25; 31.27
a perverse and crooked generation. Mt 17.17
6 Do you thus repay the LORD, 32.6 Deut 1.31; 32.28
O foolish and senseless people?
Is not he your father, who created you,
who made you and established you?
7 Remember the days of old, 32.7 Deut 7.18; 8.2
consider the years long past;
ask your father, and he will inform you;
your elders, and they will tell you.
8 When the Most High[q] apportioned the nations,
when he divided humankind,
he fixed the boundaries of the peoples
according to the number of the gods;[r]
9 the LORD's own portion was his people, 32.9 1 Kgs 8.51
Jacob his allotted share. Jer 10.16

10 He sustained[s] him in a desert land, 32.10 Ps 17.8
in a howling wilderness waste;
he shielded him, cared for him,
guarded him as the apple of his eye.
11 As an eagle stirs up its nest, 32.11 Ex 19.4
and hovers over its young; Ps 17.8; 91.4
as it spreads its wings, takes them up,
and bears them aloft on its pinions,
12 the LORD alone guided him; 32.12 Deut 4.36
no foreign god was with him. Isa 43.12
13 He set him atop the heights of the land, 32.13 Job 29.6
and fed him with[t] produce of the field; Ps 81.16
he nursed him with honey from the crags,
with oil from flinty rock;

[p] Meaning of Heb uncertain [q] Traditional rendering of Heb *Elyon* [r] Q Ms Compare Gk Tg: MT *the Israelites*
[s] Sam Gk Compare Tg: MT *found* [t] Sam Gk Syr Tg: MT *he ate*

32.1ff Moses was not only a great prophet but a song leader as well. After three sermons, he changed the form of his message to singing. Sometimes reciting something in a different form makes it easier to remember. This song gives a brief history of Israel. It reminds the people of their mistakes, warns them to avoid repetition of those mistakes, and offers the hope that comes only in trusting God.

32.8 The phrase "according to the number of the gods" could mean "Israel" or "sons of God."

32.14 Ps 147.14

14 curds from the herd, and milk from the flock,
with fat of lambs and rams;
Bashan bulls and goats,
together with the choicest wheat—
you drank fine wine from the blood of grapes.

32.15 Judg 10.6

15 Jacob ate his fill;[u]
Jeshurun grew fat, and kicked.
You grew fat, bloated, and gorged!
He abandoned God who made him,
and scoffed at the Rock of his salvation.

32.16 Ps 78.58; 106.29

16 They made him jealous with strange gods,
with abhorrent things they provoked him.

32.17 Lev 17.7; 1 Cor 10.20

17 They sacrificed to demons, not God,
to deities they had never known,
to new ones recently arrived,
whom your ancestors had not feared.

32.18 Ps 106.21; Deut 8.11; 32.4

18 You were unmindful of the Rock that bore you;[v]
you forgot the God who gave you birth.

32.19 Lev 26.30; Ps 106.40

19 The LORD saw it, and was jealous[w]
he spurned[x] his sons and daughters.

32.20 Deut 32.5; Mt 17.17

20 He said: I will hide my face from them,
I will see what their end will be;
for they are a perverse generation,
children in whom there is no faithfulness.

32.21 1 Kgs 16.13,26; Rom 10.19

21 They made me jealous with what is no god,
provoked me with their idols.
So I will make them jealous with what is no people,
provoke them with a foolish nation.

32.22 Lev 26.20; Ps 18.7,8

22 For a fire is kindled by my anger,
and burns to the depths of Sheol;
it devours the earth and its increase,
and sets on fire the foundations of the mountains.

32.23 Lev 26.18; Deut 28.15-19; 2 Sam 22.15; Ps 85.5

23 I will heap disasters upon them,
spend my arrows against them:

32.24 Deut 28.53; Ps 91.6

24 wasting hunger,
burning consumption,
bitter pestilence.
The teeth of beasts I will send against them,
with venom of things crawling in the dust.

32.25 2 Chron 36.17; Lam 1.20; 2.21; Ezek 7.15

25 In the street the sword shall bereave,
and in the chambers terror,
for young man and woman alike,
nursing child and old gray head.

32.26 Deut 4.27; 28.64

26 I thought to scatter them[y]

[u] Q Mss Sam Gk: MT lacks *Jacob ate his fill* [v] Or *that begot you* [w] Q Mss Gk: MT lacks *was jealous* [x] Cn: Heb *he spurned because of provocation* [y] Gk: Meaning of Heb uncertain

---

VARIETY IN WORSHIP

Israel's worship used all of the senses. They reinforced the meaning of the ceremony. Every sense can be used to worship God.

SIGHT	the beauty and symbolism of the tabernacle; every color and hue had a meaning
HEARING	the use of music; there were instructions for the use of a variety of instruments, and the Bible records many songs
TOUCH	the head of the animal to be sacrificed was touched, symbolizing the fact that it was taking their place
SMELL	the sacrifices were burned, emitting a familiar aroma
TASTE	the feasts were celebrations and memorials—much of the food was symbolic

and blot out the memory of them from humankind;
27 but I feared provocation by the enemy,
for their adversaries might misunderstand
and say, "Our hand is triumphant;
it was not the LORD who did all this."

28 They are a nation void of sense;
there is no understanding in them.
29 If they were wise, they would understand this;
they would discern what the end would be.
30 How could one have routed a thousand,
and two put a myriad to flight,
unless their Rock had sold them,
the LORD had given them up?
31 Indeed their rock is not like our Rock;
our enemies are fools. [z]
32 Their vine comes from the vinestock of Sodom,
from the vineyards of Gomorrah;
their grapes are grapes of poison,
their clusters are bitter;
33 their wine is the poison of serpents,
the cruel venom of asps.

34 Is not this laid up in store with me,
sealed up in my treasuries?
35 Vengeance is mine, and recompense,
for the time when their foot shall slip;
because the day of their calamity is at hand,
their doom comes swiftly.

36 Indeed the LORD will vindicate his people,
have compassion on his servants,
when he sees that their power is gone,
neither bond nor free remaining.
37 Then he will say: Where are their gods,
the rock in which they took refuge,
38 who ate the fat of their sacrifices,
and drank the wine of their libations?
Let them rise up and help you,
let them be your protection!

39 See now that I, even I, am he;
there is no god beside me.
I kill and I make alive;
I wound and I heal;
and no one can deliver from my hand.
40 For I lift up my hand to heaven,
and swear: As I live forever,
41 when I whet my flashing sword,
and my hand takes hold on judgment;
I will take vengeance on my adversaries,
and will repay those who hate me.

z Gk: Meaning of Heb uncertain

32.29 Deut 5.29
32.30 Lev 26.7,8 Josh 23.10 Judg 7.22 Deut 32.4,18
32.32 Gen 19.4,5 Deut 29.18
32.35 Jer 23.12 Ezek 7.5 Rom 12.19
32.36 Lev 26.44,45 Deut 30.2,3 Heb 10.30
32.37 Jer 2.28
32.38 Num 25.1,2 Jer 11.12
32.39 1 Sam 2.6 Ps 50.22 Isa 41.4; 43.10
32.40 Num 8.21 Ps 65.5 Isa 1.24; 34.6 Jer 12.12 46.10; 50.28-32

32.38 A "libation" is a drink offering that was poured out over the sacrifical animal after it was killed. For an example of this, see 2 Kings 16.13.

32.42 "Long-haired enemy" could also mean the leaders of the enemies.

42 I will make my arrows drunk with blood,
and my sword shall devour flesh—
with the blood of the slain and the captives,
from the long-haired enemy.

43 Praise, O heavens,[a] his people,
worship him, all you gods![b]
For he will avenge the blood of his children,[c]
and take vengeance on his adversaries;
he will repay those who hate him,[b]
and cleanse the land for his people.[d]

32.46 Deut 4.9; Ezek 40.4; 44.5
32.47 Deut 4.40; 8.3; 30.20

44 Moses came and recited all the words of this song in the hearing of the people, he and Joshua[e] son of Nun. 45 When Moses had finished reciting all these
words to all Israel, 46 he said to them: "Take to heart all the words that I am giving
in witness against you today; give them as a command to your children, so that they
may diligently observe all the words of this law. 47 This is no trifling matter for you,
but rather your very life; through it you may live long in the land that you are
crossing over the Jordan to possess."

Moses is told he is about to die

32.49 Num 27.12; Deut 3.27
32.50 Gen 25.17; Num 27.13,14; Deut 31.16
32.51 Num 20.12
32.52 Deut 1.37; 3.27

48 On that very day the LORD addressed Moses as follows: 49 "Ascend this
mountain of the Abarim, Mount Nebo, which is in the land of Moab, across from
Jericho, and view the land of Canaan, which I am giving to the Israelites for a
possession; 50 you shall die there on the mountain that you ascend and shall be gathered to your kin, as your brother Aaron died on Mount Hor and was gathered to his
kin; 51 because both of you broke faith with me among the Israelites at the waters of
Meribath-kadesh in the wilderness of Zin, by failing to maintain my holiness
among the Israelites. 52 Although you may view the land from a distance, you shall
not enter it—the land that I am giving to the Israelites."

Moses blesses all the tribes

33.1 1 Sam 2.27
33.2 Ex 19.18,20; Judg 5.4; Ps 68.8,17; Dan 7.10

33 This is the blessing with which Moses, the man of God, blessed the Israelites before his death. 2 He said:
The LORD came from Sinai,
and dawned from Seir upon us;[f]
he shone forth from Mount Paran.
With him were myriads of holy ones;[g]
at his right, a host of his own.[h]

33.3 Deut 4.37; 6.1-9; 7.6; 14.2

3 Indeed, O favorite among[i] peoples,
all his holy ones were in your charge;
they marched at your heels,
accepted direction from you.

33.4 Deut 4.2; Ps 119.111
33.5 Num 23.18-24; Ps 10.16; 22.28

4 Moses charged us with the law,
as a possession for the assembly of Jacob.
5 There arose a king in Jeshurun,
when the leaders of the people assembled—
the united tribes of Israel.

[a] Q Ms Gk: MT *nations* [b] Q Ms Gk: MT lacks this line [c] Q Ms Gk: MT *his servants* [d] Q Ms Sam Gk Vg: MT *his land his people* [e] Sam Gk Syr Vg: MT *Hoshea* [f] Gk Syr Vg Compare Tg: Heb *upon them* [g] Cn Compare Gk Sam Syr Vg: MT *He came from Ribeboth-kodesh,* [h] Cn Compare Gk: meaning of Heb uncertain [i] Or *O lover of the*

32.46, 47 Moses urged the people to think about God's Word and teach it to their children. The Bible can sit on your bookshelf and gather dust, or you can make it a vital part of your life by regularly setting aside time to study it. When you discover the wisdom of God's message, you will want to apply it to your life and pass it on to your family and others. The Bible is not merely good reading—it's real help for real life.

32.51 Moses broke faith with God by striking the rock to obtain water for the thirsty Israelites.

33.6-25 Note the difference in blessings God gave each tribe. To one he gave the best land, to another strength, to another safety. Too often we see someone with a particular blessing and think that God must love that person more than others. Think rather that God draws out in all people their unique talents. All these gifts are needed to complete his plan. Don't be envious of the gifts others have. Instead, look for the gifts God has given you, and resolve to do the tasks he has uniquely qualified you to do.

6 May Reuben live, and not die out,
even though his numbers are few.

33.6 Gen 49.3

7And this he said of Judah:
O LORD, give heed to Judah,
and bring him to his people;
strengthen his hands for him,[j]
and be a help against his adversaries.

33.7 Gen 49.8-12

8And of Levi he said:
Give to Levi[k] your Thummim,
and your Urim to your loyal one,
whom you tested at Massah,
with whom you contended at the waters of Meribah;
9 who said of his father and mother,
"I regard them not";
he ignored his kin,
and did not acknowledge his children.
For they observed your word,
and kept your covenant.
10 They teach Jacob your ordinances,
and Israel your law;
they place incense before you,
and whole burnt offerings on your altar.
11 Bless, O LORD, his substance,
and accept the work of his hands;
crush the loins of his adversaries,
of those that hate him, so that they do not rise again.

33.8 Ex 17.7 Lev 8.8 Num 20.13,24
33.9 Ex 32.27 Lev 10.6; 21.11
33.10 Lev 10.11 16.12,13 Deut 17.9; 31.9

12Of Benjamin he said:
The beloved of the LORD rests in safety—
the High God[l] surrounds him all day long—
the beloved[m] rests between his shoulders.

33.12 Gen 49.27 Deut 12.10 32.11

13And of Joseph he said:
Blessed by the LORD be his land,
with the choice gifts of heaven above,
and of the deep that lies beneath;
14 with the choice fruits of the sun,
and the rich yield of the months;
15 with the finest produce of the ancient mountains,
and the abundance of the everlasting hills;
16 with the choice gifts of the earth and its fullness,
and the favor of the one who dwells on Sinai.[n]
Let these come on the head of Joseph,
on the brow of the prince among his brothers.
17 A firstborn[o] bull—majesty is his!
His horns are the horns of a wild ox;
with them he gores the peoples,
driving them to[p] the ends of the earth;
such are the myriads of Ephraim,
such the thousands of Manasseh.

33.13 Gen 27.27-29 49.22
33.14 Deut 28.8
33.16 Ps 24.1; 50.12 89.11
33.17 Num 23.22; 24.8 1 Kgs 22.11

18And of Zebulun he said:
Rejoice, Zebulun, in your going out;
and Issachar, in your tents.

33.18 Gen 49.13

j Cn: Heb *with his hands he contended* k Q Ms Gk: MT lacks *Give to Levi* l Heb *above him* m Heb *he* n Cn: Heb *in the bush* o Q Ms Gk Syr Vg: MT *His firstborn* p Cn: Heb *the peoples, together*

33.19 Deut 32.13 Ps 4.5; 51.19

19 They call peoples to the mountain;
there they offer the right sacrifices;
for they suck the affluence of the seas
and the hidden treasures of the sand.

33.20 Gen 49.19

20 And of Gad he said:
Blessed be the enlargement of Gad!
Gad lives like a lion;
he tears at arm and scalp.

33.21 Num 32.1 34.14,15 Josh 4.12; 22.1

21 He chose the best for himself,
for there a commander's allotment was reserved;
he came at the head of the people,
he executed the justice of the LORD,
and his ordinances for Israel.

33.22 Gen 49.16 Josh 19.47,48 Ezek 19.2

22 And of Dan he said:
Dan is a lion's whelp
that leaps forth from Bashan.

33.23 Gen 49.21 Isa 9.1,2

23 And of Naphtali he said:
O Naphtali, sated with favor,
full of the blessing of the LORD,
possess the west and the south.

33.24 Gen 49.20 Job 29.6

24 And of Asher he said:
Most blessed of sons be Asher;
may he be the favorite of his brothers,
and may he dip his foot in oil.

33.25 Ps 147.13

25 Your bars are iron and bronze;
and as your days, so is your strength.

33.26 Ex 15.11 Deut 4.35 Ps 68.33

26 There is none like God, O Jeshurun,
who rides through the heavens to your help,
majestic through the skies.

33.27 Gen 49.24 Deut 7.2 Josh 24.18 Ps 90.1

27 He subdues the ancient gods,[q]
shatters[r] the forces of old;[s]
he drove out the enemy before you,
and said, "Destroy!"

33.28 Gen 27.27-29, 37 Deut 33.12,13

28 So Israel lives in safety,
untroubled is Jacob's abode[t]
in a land of grain and wine,
where the heavens drop down dew.

33.29 Gen 15.1 Deut 4.32 2 Sam 22.3 Ps 66.3; 115.11

29 Happy are you, O Israel! Who is like you,
a people saved by the LORD,
the shield of your help,
and the sword of your triumph!

[q] Or *The eternal God is a dwelling place* [r] Cn: Heb *from underneath* [s] Or *the everlasting arms* [t] Or *fountain*

33.20, 21 The people of the tribe of Gad received the best of the new land because they obeyed God by punishing Israel's wicked enemies. Punishment is unpleasant for both the giver and the receiver, but it is a necessary part of growth. If you are in a position that sometimes requires you to correct others, don't hold back from fulfilling your task. Understand that realistic discipline is important to character development. Always strive to be both just and merciful, keeping in mind the best interests of the person who must receive the punishment.

33.24 Dipping feet in oil was a sign of prosperity.

33.27 Moses' song declares that God is our refuge, our only true security. How often we entrust our lives to other things – perhaps money, career, a noble cause, or a lifelong dream. But our onl[illegible] true refuge is the eternal God, who always holds out his a[illegible] catch us when the shaky supports we trust in colla[illegible] No storm can destroy us when we take refuge i[illegible] out God, however, must forever be cautious. [illegible] wipe them out. Living for God in this world ma[illegible] ness. But it is the godless who are on shaky g[illegible] is our refuge, we can dare to be bold.

Your enemies shall come fawning to you,
and you shall tread on their backs.

Moses dies

34 Then Moses went up from the plains of Moab to Mount Nebo, to the top of
Pisgah, which is opposite Jericho, and the LORD showed him the whole
land: Gilead as far as Dan, 2all Naphtali, the land of Ephraim and Manasseh, all the
land of Judah as far as the Western Sea, 3the Negeb, and the Plain—that is, the
valley of Jericho, the city of palm trees—as far as Zoar. 4The LORD said to him,
"This is the land of which I swore to Abraham, to Isaac, and to Jacob, saying, 'I
will give it to your descendants'; I have let you see it with your eyes, but you shall
not cross over there." 5Then Moses, the servant of the LORD, died there in the land
of Moab, at the LORD's command. 6He was buried in a valley in the land of Moab,
opposite Beth-peor, but no one knows his burial place to this day. 7Moses was one
hundred twenty years old when he died; his sight was unimpaired and his vigor had
not abated. 8The Israelites wept for Moses in the plains of Moab thirty days; then
the period of mourning for Moses was ended.
9 Joshua son of Nun was full of the spirit of wisdom, because Moses had laid
his hands on him; and the Israelites obeyed him, doing as the LORD had commanded Moses.
10 Never since has there arisen a prophet in Israel like Moses, whom the LORD
knew face to face. 11He was unequaled for all the signs and wonders that the LORD
sent him to perform in the land of Egypt, against Pharaoh and all his servants and
his entire land, 12and for all the mighty deeds and all the terrifying displays of
power that Moses performed in the sight of all Israel.

34.1 Num 21.20; 27.12; Deut 32.49,52
34.2 Ex 23.31; Deut 11.24; Josh 19.32
34.4 Gen 12.7; 26.3; Ps 105.10,11
34.5 Num 12.7,8; Deut 32.50
34.6 Deut 3.29; 4.44-46; Jude 9
34.7 Deut 31.2; Acts 7.23,30
34.9 Ex 31.3; Num 27.18
34.10 Num 12.7,8; Acts 3.22,23
34.11 Deut 4.34; 7.19

34.4, 10 Moses was the only person who ever spoke with God face to face. He was called Israel's greatest prophet. Yet even this great man was not allowed to enter the promised land because he disobeyed God (Numbers 20.12). No matter how good we are, or how much we've done for God, we sometimes disobey him. The result of our disobedience is that we will be disciplined. God disciplined Moses severely, yet still called him his friend. When you experience the sting of God's discipline, respond as Moses did. Don't turn away in anger, embarrassment, or resentment. Instead, turn toward God with love, openness, and a desire to do better.

34.10–12 Moses, the man who did not want to be sent to Egypt because he was "slow of speech" (Exodus 4.10), delivered the three addresses to Israel that make up the book of Deuteronomy. God gave him the power to develop from a stuttering shepherd into a national leader and powerful orator. His courage, humility, and wisdom molded the Hebrew slaves into a nation. But Moses was one person who did not let success go to his head. In the end, God was still Moses' best friend. His love, respect, and awe for God had grown daily throughout his life. Moses knew that it was not any greatness in himself that made him successful; it was the greatness of the all-powerful God in whom he trusted. There were many great and powerful prophets during the time of the kings. But it would be a thousand years before one greater than Moses would appear—Jesus Christ.

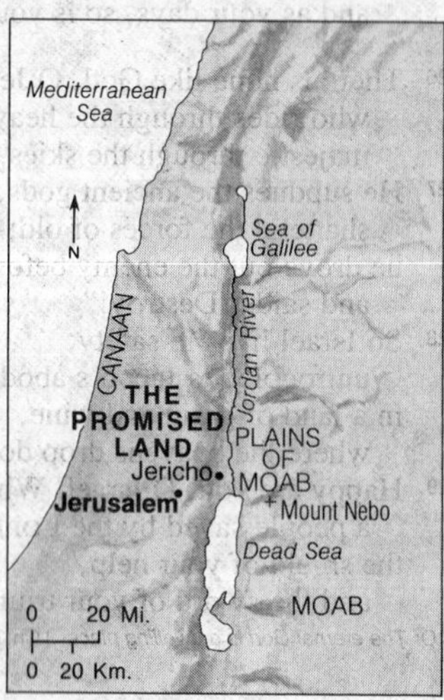

THE DEATH OF MOSES
Just before Moses died, he climbed Mount Nebo. Although he could not enter the promised land, God showed him its beauty from Mount Nebo's peak.

ISRAEL'S OPPRESSORS

THE AMMONITES were descendants of Ben-Ammi. He was born from the incestuous relationship between Lot and his younger daughter (Genesis 19.38). Jephthah delivered Israel from this enemy (Judges 10.6—12.7).

THE AMORITES were descendants of Canaan. They were scattered throughout the hill country on both sides of the Jordan. The people of Ai were Amorites (Joshua 7.7).

descendants of Abraham through Keturah. They were a nomadic people and inhabited the desert area southeast of Moab and Edom. They raided the Israelites during the time of harvest. Gideon delivered Israel from this enemy (Judges 6.1—8.32).

THE MOABITES were descendants of Moab. He was born from the incestuous relationship between Lot and his older daughter (Genesis 19.37).

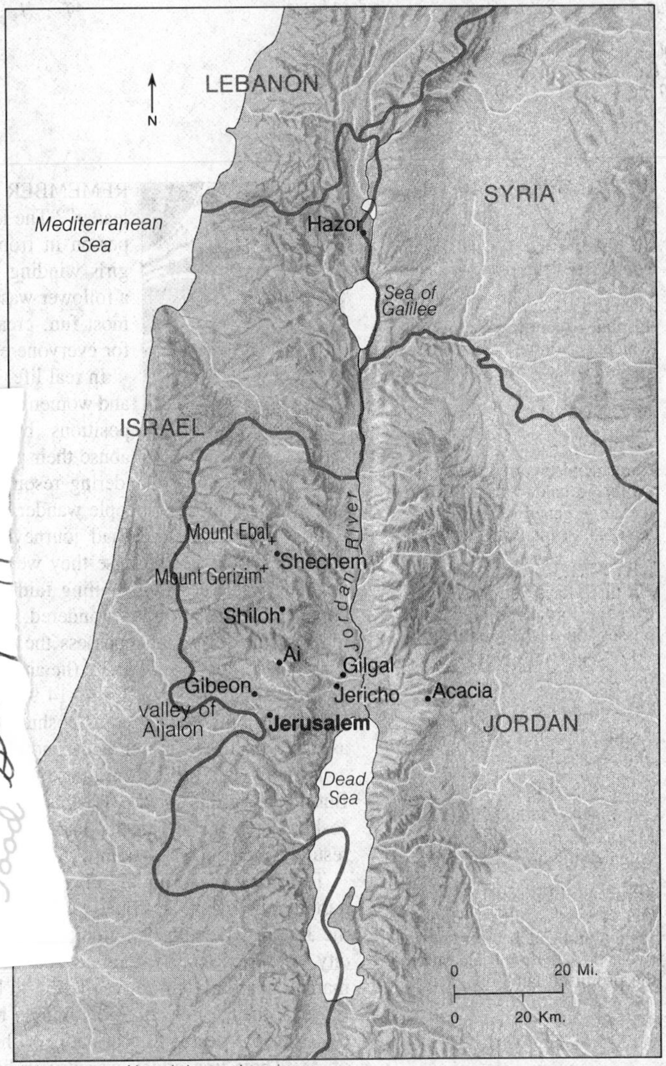

Modern names and boundaries are shown in gray.

THE PERIZZITES were mentioned among the other Canaanite peoples. Joshua defeated them at the waters of Merom (Joshua 11.3).

THE PHILISTINES migrated from somewhere in the Mediterranean world, possibly Crete. They inhabited the lowlands near the Mediterranean Sea and caused continual trouble for the Israelites until the time of David. Shamgar (Judges 3.31) and Samson (Judges 13.1—16.31) were two judges that fought against them.

JOSHUA

Exodus from Egypt 1446 B.C. (1280 B.C.)	Israelites enter Canaan 1406 (1240)	Judges begin to rule 1375 (1220)

CONQUEST OF CANAAN

T H E D A Y S O F

VITAL STATISTICS

PURPOSE:
To give the history of Israel's conquest of the promised land

AUTHOR:
Joshua, except for the ending which may have been written by the high priest Phinehas, an eyewitness to the events recounted there

SETTING:
Canaan, also called the promised land, which occupied the same general geographical territory of modern-day Israel

KEY VERSE:
"In three days you are to cross over the Jordan, to go in to take possession of the land that the Lord your God gives you to possess" (1.11).

KEY PEOPLE:
Joshua, Rahab, Achan, Phinehas, Eleazar

KEY PLACES:
Jericho, Ai, Mount Ebal, Mount Gerizim, Gibeon, Gilgal, Shiloh, Shechem

SPECIAL FEATURE:
Out of over a million people, Joshua and Caleb were the only two who left Egypt and entered the promised land.

REMEMBER the childhood game "follow the leader"? The idea was to mimic the antics of the person in front of you in the line of boys and girls winding through the neighborhood. Being a follower was all right, but being leader was the most fun, creating imaginative routes and tasks for everyone else to copy.

In real life, great leaders are rare. Often, men and women are elected or appointed to leadership positions, but then falter or fail to act. Others abuse their power to satisfy their egos, crushing their subjects and squandering resources. But without faithful, ethical, and effective leaders, people wander.

For 40 years, Israel had journeyed a circuitous route through the wilderness, but *not* because they were following their leader. Quite the opposite was true—with failing faith, they refused to obey God and to conquer Canaan. So they wandered. Now the new generation was ready to cross the Jordan and possess the land. Having distinguished himself as a man of faith and courage (he and Caleb gave the minority spy report recorded in Numbers 13.30—14.9), Joshua was chosen to be Moses' successor. This book records Joshua's leadership of the people of God as they finish their march and conquer the promised land.

Joshua was a brilliant military leader and a strong spiritual influence. But the key to his success was his submission to God. When God spoke, Joshua listened and obeyed. Joshua's obedience served as a model. As a result, Israel remained faithful to God throughout Joshua's lifetime.

The book of Joshua is divided into two main parts. The first part narrates the events surrounding the conquest of Canaan. After crossing the Jordan River on dry ground, the Israelites camped near the mighty city of Jericho. God commanded the people to conquer Jericho by marching around the city 13 times, blowing trumpets, and shouting. Because they followed God's unique battle strategy, they won (chapter 6). After the destruction of Jericho, they set out against the small town of Ai. Their first attack was driven back because one of the Israelites (Achan) had sinned (chapter 7). After the men of Israel stoned Achan and his family—purging the community of its sin—the Israelites succeeded in capturing Ai (chapter 8). In their next battle against the Amorites, God even made the sun stand still to aid them in their victory (chapter 10). Finally, after defeating other assorted Canaanites led by Jabin and his allies (chapter 11), they possessed most of the land.

Part two of the book of Joshua records the assignment and settlement of the captured territory (chapters 13—22). The book concludes with Joshua's farewell address and his death (chapters 23, 24).

Joshua was committed to obeying God, and this book is about obedience. Whether conquering enemies or settling the land, God's people were required to do it God's way. In his final message to the people, Joshua underscored the importance of obeying God. "Be very careful, therefore, to love the Lord your God" (23.11), and "choose this day whom you will serve . . . but as for me and my household, we will serve the Lord" (24.15). Read Joshua and make a fresh commitment to obey God today—wherever he leads and whatever it costs.

T H E   J U D G E S

United kingdom under Saul 1050 (1045)

David becomes king 1010

THE BLUEPRINT

A. ENTERING THE PROMISED LAND (1.1—5.12) 1. Joshua leads the nation 2. The nation crosses the Jordan River	Joshua demonstrated his faith in God as he took up the challenge to lead the nation. The Israelites reaffirmed their commitment to God by obediently setting out across the Jordan River to possess the land. As we live the Christian life, we need to cross over from the old life to the new, put off our selfish desires, and press on to possess all God has planned for us. Like Joshua and Israel, we need courageous faith to live the new life.
B. CONQUERING THE PROMISED LAND (5.13—12.24) 1. Joshua attacks the center of the land 2. Joshua attacks the southern kings 3. Joshua attacks the northern kings 4. Summary of conquests	Joshua and his army moved from city to city, cleansing the land of its wickedness by destroying every trace of idol worship. Conflict with evil is inevitable, and we should be as merciless as Israel in destroying sin in our lives.
C. DIVIDING THE PROMISED LAND (13.1—24.33) 1. The tribes receive their land 2. Special cities are set aside 3. The eastern tribes build an altar 4. Joshua's last message	Joshua urged the Israelites to continue to follow the Lord and worship him alone. The people had seen God deliver them from many enemies and miraculously provide for all their needs, but they were prone to wandering from the Lord. Even though we may have experienced God at work in our lives, we too must continually renew our commitment to obey him above all other authority and to worship him alone.

MEGATHEMES

THEME	EXPLANATION	IMPORTANCE
Success	God gave success to the Israelites when they obeyed his master plan, not when they followed their own desires. Victory came when they trusted in him rather than in their military power, money, muscle, or mental capacity.	God's work done in God's way will bring his success. The standard for success, however, is not to be set by the society around us but by God's word. We must adjust our minds to God's way of thinking in order to see his standard for success.
Faith	The Israelites demonstrated their faith by trusting God daily to save and guide them. By noticing how God fulfilled his promises in the past, they developed strong confidence that he would be faithful in the future.	Our strength to do God's work comes from trusting him. His promises reassure us of his love and that he will be there to guide us in the decisions and struggles we face. Faith begins with believing he can be trusted.
Guidance	God gave instructions to Israel for every aspect of their lives. His law guided their daily living and his specific marching orders gave them victory in battle.	Guidance from God for daily living can be found in his word. By staying in touch with God, we will have the needed wisdom to meet the great challenges of life.
Leadership	Joshua was an example of an excellent leader. He was confident in God's strength, courageous in the face of opposition, and willing to seek God's advice.	To be a strong leader like Joshua we must be ready to listen and to move quickly when God instructs us. Once we have his instructions, we must be diligent in carrying them out. Strong leaders are led by God.
Conquest	God commanded his people to conquer the Canaanites and take all their land. Completing this mission would have fulfilled God's promise to Abraham and brought judgment on the evil people living there. Unfortunately, Israel never finished the job.	Israel was faithful in accomplishing their mission at first, but their commitment faltered. To love God means more than being enthusiastic about him. We must complete all the work he gives us and apply his instructions to every corner of our lives.

KEY PLACES IN JOSHUA

1 Acacia (Shittim) The story of Joshua begins with the Israelites camping at Acacia. The Israelites under Joshua were ready to enter and conquer Canaan. But before the nation moved out, Joshua received instructions from God (1.1—18).

2 Jordan River The entire nation prepared to cross this river, which was swollen from spring rains. After the spies returned from Jericho with a positive report, Joshua prepared the priests and people for a miracle. As the priests carried the ark into the Jordan River, the water stopped flowing and the entire nation crossed on dry ground into the promised land (2.1—4.24).

3 Gilgal After crossing the Jordan River, the Israelites camped at Gilgal where they renewed their commitment to God and celebrated the passover, the feast commemorating their deliverance from Egypt (see Exodus). As Joshua made plans for the attack on Jericho, an angel appeared to him (5.1–15).

4 Jericho The walled city of Jericho seemed a formidable enemy. But when Joshua followed God's plans, the great walls were no obstacle. The city was conquered with only the obedient marching of the people (6.1–27).

5 Ai Victory could not continue without obedience to God. That is why the disobedience of one man, Achan, brought defeat to the entire nation in the first battle against Ai. But once the sin was recognized and punished, God told Joshua to take heart and try Ai once again. This time the city was taken (7.1—8.29).

Modern names and boundaries are shown in gray.

6 The Mountains of Ebal and Gerizim After the defeat of Ai, Joshua built an altar at Mount Ebal. Then the people divided themselves, half at the foot of Mount Ebal, half at the foot of Mount Gerizim. The priests stood between the mountains holding the ark of the covenant as Joshua read God's law to all the people (8.30–35).

7 Gibeon It was just after the Israelites reaffirmed their covenant with God that their leaders made a major mistake in judgment: they were tricked into making a peace treaty with the city of Gibeon. The Gibeonites pretended that they had traveled a long distance and asked the Israelites for a treaty. The leaders made the agreement without consulting God. The trick was soon discovered, but because the treaty had been made Israel could not go back on its word. As a result, the Gibeonites saved their own lives, but they were forced to become Israel's slaves (9.1–27).

8 Valley of Aijalon The king of Jerusalem was very angry at Gibeon for making a peace treaty with the Israelites. He gathered armies from four other cities to attack the city. Gibeon summoned Joshua for help. Joshua took immediate action. Leaving Gilgal, he attacked the coalition by surprise. As the battle waged on and moved into the valley of Aijalon, Joshua prayed for the sun to stand still until the enemy could be destroyed (10.1–43).

9 Hazor Up north in Hazor, King Jabin mobilized the kings of the surrounding cities to unite and crush Israel. But God gave Joshua and Israel victory. (11.1–23).

10 Shiloh After the armies of Canaan were conquered, Israel gathered at Shiloh to set up the tabernacle. This movable building had been the nation's center of worship during their years of wandering. The seven tribes who had not received their land were given their allotments (18.1—19.51).

11 Shechem Before Joshua died he called the entire nation together at Shechem to remind them that it was God who had given them their land and that only with God's help could they keep it. The people vowed to follow God. As long as Joshua was alive, the land was at rest from war and trouble (24.1–33).

A. ENTERING THE PROMISED LAND (1.1 – 5.12)

After wandering for 40 years in the wilderness, a new generation is ready to enter Canaan. But first God prepares both Joshua and the nation by teaching them the importance of courageous and consistent faith. The nation then miraculously crosses the Jordan River to begin the long-awaited conquest of the promised land. Like Joshua, we too need faith to begin and continue living the Christian life.

1. Joshua leads the nation

God's charge to Joshua

1.1 Deut 34.7,8
1.2 Num 12.7,8; 1 Kgs 8.56
1.3 Deut 11.24
1.5 Deut 7.24; 31.6-8; Heb 13.5

1 After the death of Moses the servant of the LORD, the LORD spoke to Joshua
son of Nun, Moses' assistant, saying, 2"My servant Moses is dead. Now proceed to cross the Jordan, you and all this people, into the land that I am giving to
them, to the Israelites. 3Every place that the sole of your foot will tread upon I have
given to you, as I promised to Moses. 4From the wilderness and the Lebanon as far
as the great river, the river Euphrates, all the land of the Hittites, to the Great Sea
in the west shall be your territory. 5No one shall be able to stand against you all the
days of your life. As I was with Moses, so I will be with you; I will not fail you or

TAKE THE LAND
God told Joshua to lead the Israelites into the promised land (also called Canaan) and conquer it. This was not an act of imperialism or aggression, but an act of judgment. Here are some of the earlier passages in the Bible where God promised to give this land to the Israelites and the reasons for doing so.

Genesis 12.1–3	God promised to bless Abraham and make his descendants into a great nation
Genesis 15.16	God would choose the right time for Israel to enter Canaan because the nations living there then would be wicked and ripe for judgment (their iniquity would be full)
Genesis 17.7, 8	God promised to give all the land of Canaan to Abraham's descendants
Exodus 33.1–3	God promised to help the Israelites drive out all the evil nations from Canaan
Deuteronomy 4.5–8	The Israelites were to be an example of right living to the whole world; this would not work if they intermingled with the wicked Canaanites
Deuteronomy 7.1–5	The Israelites were to utterly wipe the Canaanites out because of their wickedness and because of Israel's call to purity
Deuteronomy 12.2	The Israelites were to completely destroy the Canaanite altars so nothing would tempt them away from worshiping God alone

1.1 As the book of Joshua opens, the Israelites are camped along the east bank of the Jordan River at the very edge of the promised land and they are completing the mourning period for Moses, who has just died (Deuteronomy 34.7, 8). Thirty-nine years earlier (after spending a year at Mount Sinai receiving God's law), the Israelites had an opportunity to enter the promised land, but they failed to trust God to give them victory. As a result, God did not allow them to enter the land, but made them wander in the wilderness until the disobedient generation all died.

During their wilderness wanderings, the Israelites obeyed God's laws. They also taught the new generation to obey God's laws so that they might enter the promised land (also called Canaan). As the children grew, they were often reminded that faith and obedience to God brought victory, while unbelief and disobedience brought tragedy. When the last of the older generation had died and the new generation had become adults, the Israelites prepared to make their long-awaited claim on the promised land.

1.1–5 Joshua succeeded Moses as Israel's leader. What qualifications did he have to become the leader of a nation? (1) God appointed him (Numbers 27.18–23). (2) He was one of only two living eyewitnesses to the Egyptian plagues and the exodus from Egypt. (3) He was Moses' personal assistant for 40 years. (4) Of the 12 spies, only he and Caleb showed complete confidence that God would help them conquer the land.

1.2 Because Joshua had assisted Moses for many years, he was well prepared to take over the leadership of the nation. Changes in leadership are common in many organizations. At such times, a smooth transition is essential for the establishment of the new administration. This doesn't happen unless new leaders are trained. If you are currently in a leadership position, begin preparing someone to take your place. Then, when you leave or are promoted, operations can continue to run efficiently. If you desire to be a leader, learn from others so you will be prepared when the opportunity comes.

1.5 Joshua's new job consisted of leading more than two million people into a strange new land and conquering it. What a challenge – even for a man of Joshua's caliber! Every new job is a challenge. Without God it can be frightening. With God it can be a great adventure. Just as God assured Joshua he would be with him, he is with us as we face our new challenges. We may not conquer nations, but every day we face tough situations, difficult people, and temptations. However, God promises that he will never abandon us or fail to help us, regardless of how we feel. By asking God to direct us we can conquer many of life's problems.

forsake you. [6]Be strong and courageous; for you shall put this people in possession
of the land that I swore to their ancestors to give them. [7]Only be strong and very 1.7
courageous, being careful to act in accordance with all the law that my servant Deut 5.29,32 28.14; 29.9
Moses commanded you; do not turn from it to the right hand or to the left, so that
you may be successful wherever you go. [8]This book of the law shall not depart out 1.8
of your mouth; you shall meditate on it day and night, so that you may be careful Deut 6.6,7 11.18; 17.19
to act in accordance with all that is written in it. For then you shall make your way Ps 1.1-3
prosperous, and then you shall be successful. [9]I hereby command you: Be strong 1.9
and courageous; do not be frightened or dismayed, for the LORD your God is with Deut 31.6,8
you wherever you go."

Joshua prepares the people to enter

10 Then Joshua commanded the officers of the people, [11]"Pass through the 1.10
camp, and command the people: 'Prepare your provisions; for in three days you are Deut 3.2-4, 15-17
to cross over the Jordan, to go in to take possession of the land that the LORD your
God gives you to possess.' "
12 To the Reubenites, the Gadites, and the half-tribe of Manasseh Joshua said, 1.12
[13]"Remember the word that Moses the servant of the LORD commanded you, say- Num 32.20
ing, 'The LORD your God is providing you a place of rest, and will give you this Deut 3.18 Josh 22.1
land.' [14]Your wives, your little ones, and your livestock shall remain in the land
that Moses gave you beyond the Jordan. But all the warriors among you shall cross
over armed before your kindred and shall help them, [15]until the LORD gives rest to 1.15
your kindred as well as to you, and they too take possession of the land that the Josh 22.4
LORD your God is giving them. Then you shall return to your own land and take
possession of it, the land that Moses the servant of the LORD gave you beyond the
Jordan to the east."
16 They answered Joshua: "All that you have commanded us we will do, and 1.16
wherever you send us we will go. [17]Just as we obeyed Moses in all things, so we Num 32.25
will obey you. Only may the LORD your God be with you, as he was with Moses! 1.17 Ex 19.8; 24.3
[18]Whoever rebels against your orders and disobeys your words, whatever you Deut 5.27
command, shall be put to death. Only be strong and courageous."

Rahab protects the spies

2 Then Joshua son of Nun sent two men secretly from Shittim as spies, saying, 2.1
"Go, view the land, especially Jericho." So they went, and entered the house Num 13.2 Mt 1.5

1.6–8 Many people think prosperity is based on power, influential personal contacts, and a relentless desire to get ahead. But the strategy for prosperity that God taught Joshua goes against such criteria. He told Joshua that to succeed he must (1) be strong and courageous because the task ahead would not be easy, (2) obey God's law, and (3) constantly read and study God's Word. To be successful, follow God's words to Joshua. You may not succeed by the world's standards, but you will be a success in God's eyes, and his opinion lasts forever.

1.7, 8 How strange to equate success with obedience. For many, success is controlling others; for Joshua it meant being controlled by God. God told Joshua that to succeed he must obey the rules for living found in God's law. Often we can't see what the results or future benefits of following God will be. When we are not certain what to do, obedience to what God has revealed in the Scriptures is the only sure step we can take. Resolve to set aside time each day to read and think about God's Word. Remind yourself of God's words day and night. Act today on what you know God has said, and God will assure your success in carrying out his purposes.

1.12–15 During the previous year, the tribes of Reuben and Gad and the half-tribe of Manasseh had asked Moses if they could settle just east of the promised land. The area was excellent pastureland for their large flocks. Moses agreed to give them the land on one condition—that they help their fellow tribes enter and conquer the land. Only after the land was conquered could they return to their homes. Now it was time for these three tribes to live up to their agreement.

1.13 A place of rest was highly meaningful and desirable to the people of a nation that had been on the move its entire history. This people who had no land would be given a land of their own.

1.16 What would have happened if everyone had tried to conquer the promised land his own way? Chaos would have resulted. In order to complete the enormous task of conquering the land, everyone had to agree to the leader's plan and be willing to support and obey him. If we are going to complete the tasks God has given us, we must fully agree to his plan and pledge ourselves to obey it, and put his principles into action. Agreeing to God's plan means both knowing his plan for us as found in the Bible and carrying it out daily.

1.18 When God commissioned Joshua, he was told three times to be strong and courageous (see 1.6, 7, 9). Now, he was giving the same kind of encouragement to the rest of the people. Apparently, he took God's message to heart and found the strength and courage he needed in his relationship with God. The next time you are afraid to do what you know is right, remember that strength and courage are readily available from God.

of a prostitute whose name was Rahab, and spent the night there. 2The king of
Jericho was told, "Some Israelites have come here tonight to search out the land."
3Then the king of Jericho sent orders to Rahab, "Bring out the men who have come
to you, who entered your house, for they have come only to search out the whole

JOSHUA

One of the greatest challenges facing leaders is to replace themselves, training others to become leaders. Many outstanding accomplishments have been started by someone with great ability whose life or career ended before the vision became reality. The fulfillment of that dream then became the responsibility of that person's successor. Death is the ultimate deadline for leadership. One of the best tests of our leadership is our willingness and ability to train another for our position.

Moses made an excellent decision when he chose Joshua as his assistant. That choice was later confirmed by God himself when he instructed Moses to commission Joshua as his successor (Numbers 27.15–23). Joshua had played a key role in the exodus. Introduced as the field general of Israel's army, he was the only person allowed to accompany Moses partway up the mountain when Moses received the law. Joshua and Caleb were the only two among the 12 spies to bring back an encouraging report after being sent into the promised land the first time. Other references show him to have been Moses' constant shadow. His basic training was living with Moses—experiencing firsthand what it meant to lead God's people. This was modeling at its best!

Who is your Moses? Who is your Joshua? You are part of the chain of God's ongoing work in the world. You are modeling yourself after others, and others are patterning their lives after you. How important is God to those you want to be like? Do those who are watching you see God reflected in every area of your life? Ask God to lead you to a trustworthy Moses. Ask him to make you a good Joshua.

Strengths and accomplishments:
- Moses' assistant and successor
- One of only two adults who experienced Egyptian slavery and lived to enter the promised land
- Led the Israelites into their God-given homeland
- Brilliant military strategist
- Faithful to ask God's direction in the challenges he faced

Lessons from his life:
- Effective leadership is often the product of good preparation and encouragement
- The persons after whom we pattern ourselves will have a definite effect on us
- A person committed to God provides the best model for us

Vital statistics:
- Where: Egypt, the Sinai wilderness, and Canaan (the promised land)
- Occupation: Special assistant to Moses, warrior, leader
- Relatives: Father: Nun
- Contemporaries: Moses, Caleb, Miriam, Aaron

Key verses:
"So Moses did as the Lord commanded him. He took Joshua and had him stand before Eleazar the priest and the whole congregation; he laid his hands on him and commissioned him—as the Lord had directed through Moses" (Numbers 27.22, 23).

Joshua is also mentioned in Exodus 17.9–14; 24.13; 32.17; 33.11; Numbers 11.28; 13; 14; 26.65; 27.18–23; 32.12, 28; 34.17; Deuteronomy 1.38; 3.21, 28; 31.3, 7, 14, 23; 34.9; the book of Joshua; Judges 2.6–10; and 1 Kings 16.34.

2.1 Why would the spies stop at the house of Rahab the prostitute? (1) It was a good place to gather information and have no questions asked in return. (2) Rahab's house was in an ideal location for a quick escape because it was built into the city wall. (3) God directed the spies to Rahab's house because he knew her heart was open to him and that she would be instrumental in the Israelite victory over Jericho. God often uses people with simple faith to accomplish his great purposes, no matter what kind of past they have had or how insignificant they seem to be. Rahab didn't allow her past to keep her from the new role God had for her.

2.1 Why did Joshua send the spies secretly? As far as he knew at this point, he would be attacking a heavily fortified city using conventional means. He needed strategic information about the city for the upcoming battle, but he also knew that this might draw criticism from the other leaders. After all, the last time spies were sent, the report they brought back caused problems (see Numbers 13.1–14.4). While he did not want to move ahead without information, he also did not want to cause the people to stumble and question his wisdom and ability to lead them.

land." 4 But the woman took the two men and hid them. Then she said, "True, the 2.4
men came to me, but I did not know where they came from. 5 And when it was time Ex 1.19
to close the gate at dark, the men went out. Where the men went I do not know. 2 Sam 17.20
Pursue them quickly, for you can overtake them." 6 She had, however, brought 2.6
them up to the roof and hidden them with the stalks of flax that she had laid out on Jas 2.25
the roof. 7 So the men pursued them on the way to the Jordan as far as the fords. As
soon as the pursuers had gone out, the gate was shut.
8 Before they went to sleep, she came up to them on the roof 9 and said to the 2.9
men: "I know that the LORD has given you the land, and that dread of you has fallen Ex 23.27 Deut 2.25
on us, and that all the inhabitants of the land melt in fear before you. 10 For we have Josh 9.24
heard how the LORD dried up the water of the Red Sea[a] before you when you came Heb 11.31 2.10
out of Egypt, and what you did to the two kings of the Amorites that were beyond Ex 14.21-31
the Jordan, to Sihon and Og, whom you utterly destroyed. 11 As soon as we heard Num 21.21 Deut 2.30; 3.1
it, our hearts melted, and there was no courage left in any of us because of you. The 2.11
LORD your God is indeed God in heaven above and on earth below. 12 Now then, Deut 4.39 1 Kgs 8.60
since I have dealt kindly with you, swear to me by the LORD that you in turn will Ps 83.18
deal kindly with my family. Give me a sign of good faith 13 that you will spare my 2.12
father and mother, my brothers and sisters, and all who belong to them, and deliver Josh 6.22,23 9.14,15,18
our lives from death." 14 The men said to her, "Our life for yours! If you do not tell
this business of ours, then we will deal kindly and faithfully with you when the
LORD gives us the land."
15 Then she let them down by a rope through the window, for her house was on 2.15
the outer side of the city wall and she resided within the wall itself. 16 She said to Josh 2.17,18,21
them, "Go toward the hill country, so that the pursuers may not come upon you. 2.16 Jas 2.25
Hide yourselves there three days, until the pursuers have returned; then afterward
you may go your way." 17 The men said to her, "We will be released from this oath
that you have made us swear to you 18 if we invade the land and you do not tie this

[a] Or *Sea of Reeds*

SPY MISSION TO JERICHO
Two spies left the Israelite camp at Acacia (Shittim), crossed the Jordan River, and slipped into Jericho. The city was built around an oasis in the midst of a hot and desolate valley 840 feet below sea level. Jericho was the first major city the Israelites set out to conquer.

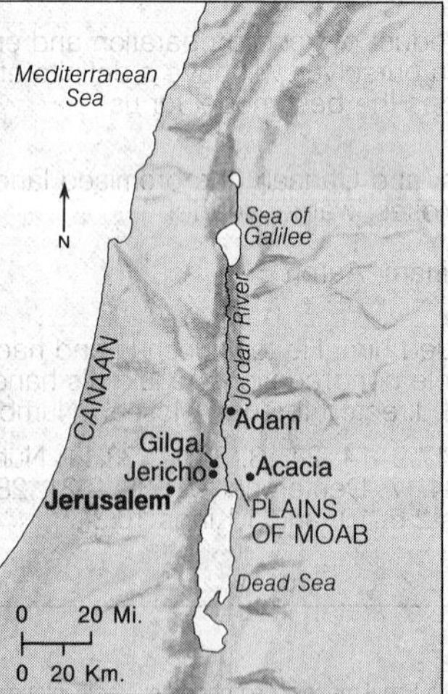

2.4, 5 Was Rahab justified in lying to save the lives of the spies? Although the Bible does not speak negatively about her lie, it is clear that lying is sin. In Hebrews 11.31, however, Rahab is commended for her faith in God. Her lie is not mentioned. Several explanations have been offered: (1) God forgave Rahab's lie because of her faith; (2) Rahab was simply deceiving the enemy, a normal and acceptable practice in wartime; (3) Since Rahab was not a Jew, she could not be held responsible for keeping the moral standards set forth in God's law; (4) Rahab broke a lesser principle—telling the truth—to uphold a higher principle—protecting God's people.

There may have been another way to save the lives of the Israelite spies. But under the pressure of the moment, Rahab had to make a choice. Most of us will face dilemmas at one time or another. We may feel that there is no perfect solution to our problem. Fortunately, God does not demand that our judgment be perfect in all situations. He simply asks us to put our trust in him and to do the best we know how. Rahab did that and was commended for her faith.

2.6 Flax was harvested in the fields and piled high on the rooftops to dry. It was then made into yarn which was used to make linen cloth. Flax grows to a height of three or four feet. Stacked on the roof, it made an excellent hiding place for the spies.

2.9–13 Many would assume that Rahab—a heathen, a Canaanite, and a prostitute—would never be interested in God. Yet Rahab was willing to risk everything she had for a God she barely knew. We must not gauge a person's interest in God by his or her background, life-style, or appearance. We should let nothing get in the way of our telling people about God.

2.11 Rahab recognized something that many of the Israelites did not—the God of heaven is not an ordinary god! He is all-powerful. The people of Jericho were afraid, for they had heard the news of God's extraordinary power in defeating the armies across the Jordan River. Today we can worship this same powerful, miracle-working God. He is powerful enough to destroy mighty, wicked armies, as he did in Jericho. He is also powerful enough to save us from certain death, as he did with Rahab.

2.15 In Joshua's day it was common to build houses on town walls. Many cities had two walls about 12 to 15 feet apart. Houses were built on wooden logs laid across the tops of the two walls. Rahab may have lived in such a house with a window that looked out over the outside wall.

crimson cord in the window through which you let us down, and you do not gather
into your house your father and mother, your brothers, and all your family. [19]If any
of you go out of the doors of your house into the street, they shall be responsible for
their own death, and we shall be innocent; but if a hand is laid upon any who are
with you in the house, we shall bear the responsibility for their death. [20]But if you
tell this business of ours, then we shall be released from this oath that you made us
swear to you." [21]She said, "According to your words, so be it." She sent them
away and they departed. Then she tied the crimson cord in the window.
22 They departed and went into the hill country and stayed there three days,
until the pursuers returned. The pursuers had searched all along the way and found
nothing. [23]Then the two men came down again from the hill country. They crossed
over, came to Joshua son of Nun, and told him all that had happened to them.
2.24 Josh 5.1; 9.24 [24]They said to Joshua, "Truly the LORD has given all the land into our hands; moreover all the inhabitants of the land melt in fear before us."

RAHAB

Rahab was a survivor. She was accustomed to figuring the odds. As a prostitute, she lived on the edge of society, one stop short of rejection. Her inn, built right into the city walls, provided both lodging and favors to travelers. It was a natural place for the Israelite spies to stay. These were undoubtedly not the first men she had hidden from the police. Her lie to the authorities was a calculated risk: she hoped it would guarantee her (and her guests) immediate safety and also set into motion her plan for long-term survival. By protecting the spies, Rahab hoped that her future safety would be secure.

Stories about the Israelites had been circulating for some time, but now it was evident that the Israelites were about to invade. Living on the wall, Rahab felt especially vulnerable. Yet while she shared the general mood of fear with the rest of Jericho's population, she alone looked for a way of survival. Her faith began with the thought, "If we can't beat them, maybe I can join them." Rahab knew her position was dangerous. In harboring the spies, she was in danger of being caught and killed. She knew that siding with the strangers was risky business: they might lose the battle, or they might refuse to guarantee her safety. Against these real dangers, Rahab sensed that the Israelites relied on a God worth trusting.

God works through people—like Rahab—whom we are inclined to reject. We remember her because of her moral failure; God remembers her because of her faith! If at times you feel like a failure, remember that Rahab rose above her situation through her trust in God. You can do the same!

Strengths and accomplishments:
- Relative of Boaz, and thus an ancestor of David and Jesus
- One of only two women listed in the Hall of Faith in Hebrews 11
- Resourceful, willing to help others at great cost to herself

Weakness and mistake:
- She was a prostitute

Lesson from her life:
- She did not let fear affect her faith in God's ability to deliver

Vital statistics:
- Where: Jericho
- Occupation: Prostitute/innkeeper, later became a wife
- Relatives: Ancestor of David and Jesus (Matthew 1.5)
- Contemporaries: Joshua

Key verse:
"By faith the prostitute Rahab did not perish with those who were disobedient, because she had received the spies in peace" (Hebrews 11.31).

Rahab's story is told in Joshua 2 and 6. She is also mentioned in Matthew 1.5; Hebrews 11.31; and James 2.25.

2.23, 24 This was not the first time spies were sent into the promised land. Thirty-nine years earlier, another spy mission had been conducted (Numbers 13, 14). Then, however, most of the spies came back afraid. They doubted God's ability to help them conquer the land. Joshua was one of those spies; only he and Caleb encouraged the people to follow God's plan. This time Joshua sent spies secretly. He did not want the possibility of another negative report to stir up the people to revolt.

2. The nation crosses the Jordan River

The people miraculously cross the Jordan River

3 Early in the morning Joshua rose and set out from Shittim with all the Israel- **3.1**
ites, and they came to the Jordan. They camped there before crossing over. Josh 2.1
2 At the end of three days the officers went through the camp 3 and commanded the **3.2**
people, "When you see the ark of the covenant of the LORD your God being carried Deut 31.9 Josh 1.10,11
by the levitical priests, then you shall set out from your place. Follow it, 4 so that
you may know the way you should go, for you have not passed this way before. Yet
there shall be a space between you and it, a distance of about two thousand cubits;
do not come any nearer to it." 5 Then Joshua said to the people, "Sanctify your- **3.5**
selves; for tomorrow the LORD will do wonders among you." 6 To the priests Joshua Ex 19.10 Josh 7.13
said, "Take up the ark of the covenant, and pass on in front of the people." So they
took up the ark of the covenant and went in front of the people.
7 The LORD said to Joshua, "This day I will begin to exalt you in the sight of all **3.7**
Israel, so that they may know that I will be with you as I was with Moses. 8 You are Josh 4.14 **3.8**
the one who shall command the priests who bear the ark of the covenant, 'When Josh 3.13,14
you come to the edge of the waters of the Jordan, you shall stand still in the Jordan.' " 9 Joshua then said to the Israelites, "Draw near and hear the words of the
LORD your God." 10 Joshua said, "By this you shall know that among you is the **3.10**
living God who without fail will drive out from before you the Canaanites, Hittites, Gen 15.19, 20,21
Hivites, Perizzites, Girgashites, Amorites, and Jebusites: 11 the ark of the covenant Deut 7.1
of the Lord of all the earth is going to pass before you into the Jordan. 12 So now **3.12**
select twelve men from the tribes of Israel, one from each tribe. 13 When the soles Josh 4.2,3 **3.13**
of the feet of the priests who bear the ark of the LORD, the Lord of all the earth, rest Ex 15.8
in the waters of the Jordan, the waters of the Jordan flowing from above shall be cut
off; they shall stand in a single heap."

3.2–4 The ark of the covenant was Israel's most sacred treasure. It was a symbol of God's presence and power. The ark was a golden rectangular box with two cherubim (angels) facing each other on the lid. Inside the ark were the ten commandments Moses received from God, a jar of manna (the bread God miraculously sent from heaven during the wilderness wanderings), and Aaron's rod (the symbol of the high priest's authority). According to God's law, only the Levites could carry the ark. The ark was constructed at the same time as the tabernacle (Exodus 37.1–9) and placed in the sanctuary's most sacred room.

3.4 Two thousand cubits is about half a mile.

3.5 Before entering the promised land, the Israelites were to perform a purification ceremony. This was often done before making a sacrifice or, as in this case, before witnessing a great act of God. God's law stated that a person could become unclean for many reasons – eating certain foods (Leviticus 11), childbirth (Leviticus 12), disease (Leviticus 13, 14), touching a dead person (Numbers 19.11–22). God used these various outward signs of uncleanness to illustrate man's inward uncleanness, which comes as a result of sin. The purification ceremony pictured the importance of approaching God with a pure heart. Like the Israelites, we need God's forgiveness before we approach him.

3.9 Just before crossing over into the promised land, Joshua gathered the people to hear the words of the Lord. Their excitement was high. No doubt they wanted to rush on, but Joshua made them stop and listen. We live in a fast-paced age where everyone rushes just to keep up. It is easy to get caught up in our tasks, becoming too busy for what God says is most important – listening to his words. Before making your schedule, take time to focus on what God wants from all your activities. Knowing what God has said before you rush into your day may help you avoid foolish mistakes.

3.10 Why would God help the Israelites drive out these nations from their native land? God had punished Israel first for its disobedience. He then turned to the rest of the nations. Genesis 15.16 implies that the people of Canaan were wicked and deserved to be punished for their terrible sins. Israel was to be a vehicle for this punishment. More important was the fact that Israel, as a holy nation, could not live among such evil and idolatrous people. To do so would be to invite sin into their lives. The only way to prevent Israel from being infected by evil religions was to drive out those who practiced them. Israel, however, failed to drive everyone out as God had told them to do. It wasn't long before Israel – the nation God chose to be his "holy" people – began following the evil practices of the Canaanites.

3.11 As the Israelites prepared to enter the land and divide up the territory, Joshua reminded them that God is Lord of the whole earth, not just one part of it. Understanding this truth delivers us from thinking of *our* church, *our* nation, *our* family, or *ourselves* as the central figures on God's stage. We are not central; God is. Although we are valuable in God's sight, we must realize that he is weaving a grand design much larger than our personal interests and limited perspectives. God doesn't exist to grant us personal success in all we do. We were created to serve him and fulfill his desires.

3.13, 14 The Israelites were eager to enter the promised land, conquer nations, and live peacefully. But first they had to cross the flood-level waters of the Jordan River. God gave them specific instructions: in order to cross, they had to step into the water. What if they had been afraid to take that first step? Often God provides no solution to our problems until we trust him and move ahead with what we know we should do. What are the rivers, or obstacles, in your life? In obedience to God, take that first step into the water.

3.13–17 God had parted the waters of the Red Sea to let the people out of Egypt (Exodus 14), and now he parts the Jordan River to let them enter Canaan. These miracles showed Israel that God keeps his promises. God's presence among his people and his faithfulness to them made the entire journey from Egypt to the promised land possible. He was with them at the end of their wanderings just as he was with them in the beginning.

14 When the people set out from their tents to cross over the Jordan, the priests
3.15,16 1 Chron 12.15 Ps 66.6; 74.15 114.3,5 bearing the ark of the covenant were in front of the people. 15 Now the Jordan overflows all its banks throughout the time of harvest. So when those who bore the ark
had come to the Jordan, and the feet of the priests bearing the ark were dipped in the
edge of the water, 16 the waters flowing from above stood still, rising up in a single
heap far off at Adam, the city that is beside Zarethan, while those flowing toward
the sea of the Arabah, the Dead Sea,[b] were wholly cut off. Then the people crossed
3.17 Ex 14.21,22,29 Josh 3.6-8 2 Kgs 2.8 over opposite Jericho. 17 While all Israel were crossing over on dry ground, the
priests who bore the ark of the covenant of the LORD stood on dry ground in the
middle of the Jordan, until the entire nation finished crossing over the Jordan.

The people build a monument

4 When the entire nation had finished crossing over the Jordan, the LORD said to
Joshua: 2 "Select twelve men from the people, one from each tribe, 3 and command them, 'Take twelve stones from here out of the middle of the Jordan, from the
place where the priests' feet stood, carry them over with you, and lay them down
in the place where you camp tonight.' " 4 Then Joshua summoned the twelve men
from the Israelites, whom he had appointed, one from each tribe. 5 Joshua said to
them, "Pass on before the ark of the LORD your God into the middle of the Jordan,
and each of you take up a stone on his shoulder, one for each of the tribes of the
4.6 Ex 12.26; 13.14 Deut 6.20 Josh 4.20,21 Israelites, 6 so that this may be a sign among you. When your children ask in time
to come, 'What do those stones mean to you?' 7 then you shall tell them that the
waters of the Jordan were cut off in front of the ark of the covenant of the LORD.
When it crossed over the Jordan, the waters of the Jordan were cut off. So these
stones shall be to the Israelites a memorial forever."
4.8 Josh 1.16 8 The Israelites did as Joshua commanded. They took up twelve stones out of
the middle of the Jordan, according to the number of the tribes of the Israelites, as
the LORD told Joshua, carried them over with them to the place where they camped,
4.9 Josh 5.8,9 and laid them down there. 9 (Joshua set up twelve stones in the middle of the Jordan, in the place where the feet of the priests bearing the ark of the covenant had
stood; and they are there to this day.)
10 The priests who bore the ark remained standing in the middle of the Jordan,
until everything was finished that the LORD commanded Joshua to tell the people,
according to all that Moses had commanded Joshua. The people crossed over in
haste. 11 As soon as all the people had finished crossing over, the ark of the LORD,
4.12 Num 32.1,17,25 Josh 1.12,13 and the priests, crossed over in front of the people. 12 The Reubenites, the Gadites,
and the half-tribe of Manasseh crossed over armed before the Israelites, as Moses
had ordered them. 13 About forty thousand armed for war crossed over before the
LORD to the plains of Jericho for battle.

[b] Heb *Salt Sea*

3.15, 16 The Israelites crossed the Jordan River in the spring, when it was overflowing its banks. God chose the time when the river was at its highest to demonstrate his power—parting the waters so that the entire nation could cross on dry ground. Some say that God used a natural occurrence (such as a landslide) to stop the waters of the Jordan; others say he did it by a direct miracle. In either case, God showed his great power by working a miracle of timing and location to allow his people to cross the river on dry ground. This testimony of God's supernatural power served to build the Israelites' hope in God and to give them a great reputation with their enemies, who greatly outnumbered them.

4.1ff After the people safely crossed the river, what would be next? Conquering the land? Not yet. First, God directed them to build a monument from 12 stones drawn from the river by 12 men, one from each tribe. This may seem like an insignificant step in their mission of conquering the land, but God did not want his people to plunge into their task unprepared. They were to focus on him and remember who was guiding them. As you are busy doing your God-given tasks, set aside quiet moments, times to build your own memorial "altar" to God's power. Too much activity can shift your focus away from God.

4.2–7 Joshua and the nation erected a memorial to the end of their wandering and the beginning of their new life in a new land. While monuments are usually erected to commemorate great events or acknowledge heroic deeds, each of us has memorials, though often less visible—a special event, an answered prayer, a miracle. Think back over what God has done for you. Let your memories serve as monuments, reminders of God's work and of his care for you.

14 On that day the LORD exalted Joshua in the sight of all Israel; and they stood 4.14
in awe of him, as they had stood in awe of Moses, all the days of his life. Josh 24.31 1 Chron 29.25
15 The LORD said to Joshua, 16 "Command the priests who bear the ark of 4.15
the covenant,[c] to come up out of the Jordan." 17 Joshua therefore commanded the Josh 3.8
priests, "Come up out of the Jordan." 18 When the priests bearing the ark of the
covenant of the LORD came up from the middle of the Jordan, and the soles of
the priests' feet touched dry ground, the waters of the Jordan returned to their place
and overflowed all its banks, as before.
19 The people came up out of the Jordan on the tenth day of the first month, and 4.19
they camped in Gilgal on the east border of Jericho. 20 Those twelve stones, which Ex 12.3
they had taken out of the Jordan, Joshua set up in Gilgal, 21 saying to the Israelites,
"When your children ask their parents in time to come, 'What do these stones
mean?' 22 then you shall let your children know, 'Israel crossed over the Jordan 4.22
here on dry ground.' 23 For the LORD your God dried up the waters of the Jordan for Josh 3.17
you until you crossed over, as the LORD your God did to the Red Sea,[d] which he
dried up for us until we crossed over, 24 so that all the peoples of the earth may 4.24
know that the hand of the LORD is mighty, and so that you may fear the LORD your Ex 7.3
God forever."

The nation reaffirms its commitment to God

5 When all the kings of the Amorites beyond the Jordan to the west, and all the 5.1
kings of the Canaanites by the sea, heard that the LORD had dried up the waters Num 13.29 Josh 2.9-11
of the Jordan for the Israelites until they had crossed over, their hearts melted, and
there was no longer any spirit in them, because of the Israelites.
2 At that time the LORD said to Joshua, "Make flint knives and circumcise the 5.2,3
Israelites a second time." 3 So Joshua made flint knives, and circumcised the Israel- Gen 17.9,10,23
ites at Gibeath-haaraloth.[e] 4 This is the reason why Joshua circumcised them: all 5.4
the males of the people who came out of Egypt, all the warriors, had died during the Deut 2.14
journey through the wilderness after they had come out of Egypt. 5 Although all the
people who came out had been circumcised, yet all the people born on the journey
through the wilderness after they had come out of Egypt had not been circumcised.
6 For the Israelites traveled forty years in the wilderness, until all the nation, the 5.6
warriors who came out of Egypt, perished, not having listened to the voice of the Num 14.29-35 26.64,65
LORD. To them the LORD swore that he would not let them see the land that he had Deut 2.7
sworn to their ancestors to give us, a land flowing with milk and honey. 7 So it was 5.7 Deut 1.39

[c] Or *treaty*, or *testimony*; Heb *eduth* [d] Or *Sea of Reeds* [e] That is *the Hill of the Foreskins*

4.14 The Israelites respected Joshua for his role in leading them across the Jordan River. He, like Moses, would receive Israel's praises generation after generation. Although Israel was not a world power at that time, Joshua's reputation for handling his responsibilities God's way brought him greater glory than if he had been a hero in a "super-power" nation. Doing right is more important than doing well.

4.21–24 The monument of 12 stones was to be a constant reminder of the day the Israelites crossed the Jordan River on dry ground. Their children would see the stones, hear the story, and learn about God. Do you have traditions—special dates or special places—to help your children learn about God's work in your life? Do you take time to tell them what God has done for you—forgiving and saving you, answering your prayers, supplying your needs? Retelling your story will help keep memories of God's faithfulness alive in your family.

5.1 The Israelites spent 39 years in the wilderness unnecessarily because they were terrified of the Canaanites. They underestimated God's ability. Their first attempt to enter the promised land had failed (Numbers 13, 14). Now Israel saw that the Canaanites were terrified of their army. They had heard about Israel's great victories through God (2.9–11). Their last hope was that the Jordan River would slow Israel down or discourage them from entering the land. But news that the Israelites had crossed the Jordan on dry land caused any courage the Canaanites still had to melt away.

Don't underestimate God. If we are faithful to God, he will cause great opposition to melt away. He can change the attitudes of those who oppose him.

5.1 The Canaanites and Amorites were the two major groups living in Canaan at the time of Israel's invasion. The Canaanites worshiped a variety of gods, but Baal was their favorite. Their culture was materialistic, their religion, sensual. The Israelites continually turned to Baal after entering Canaan. The Amorite gods also infected Israel's worship and turned people away from worshiping the true God. Worshiping these false gods eventually brought about Israel's downfall.

5.2, 3 The rite of circumcision marked Israel's position as God's covenant people. When God made the original covenant with Abraham, he required that each male be circumcised as a sign of

their children, whom he raised up in their place, that Joshua circumcised; for they
were uncircumcised, because they had not been circumcised on the way.
8 When the circumcising of all the nation was done, they remained in their
places in the camp until they were healed. 9 The LORD said to Joshua, "Today I have
rolled away from you the disgrace of Egypt." And so that place is called Gilgal[f] to
this day.
5.10 10 While the Israelites were camped in Gilgal they kept the passover in the
Ex 12.18 Josh 4.19 evening on the fourteenth day of the month in the plains of Jericho. 11 On the day
5.11 after the passover, on that very day, they ate the produce of the land, unleavened
Ex 16.35 Neh 9.20 cakes and parched grain. 12 The manna ceased on the day they ate the produce of the
land, and the Israelites no longer had manna; they ate the crops of the land of Canaan that year.

B. CONQUERING THE PROMISED LAND (5.13—12.24)

After crossing the Jordan River, the Israelites begin to conquer Canaan. Jericho is the first to fall. Then Israel suffers its first defeat because of one man's disobedience. After the people remove the sin from their community, they strike again—this time with success. Soon great kings attack from the north and south, but they are defeated because God is with Israel. Evil could not be tolerated in the promised land, nor can it be tolerated in our lives. We, like Israel, must ruthlessly remove sin from our lives before it takes control of us.

1. Joshua attacks the center of the land

Joshua meets an angel

5.13 13 Once when Joshua was by Jericho, he looked up and saw a man standing
Gen 18.2 32.22-24 before him with a drawn sword in his hand. Joshua went to him and said to him,
Ex 23.23 Num 22.31 "Are you one of us, or one of our adversaries?" 14 He replied, "Neither; but as
Judg 13.9 commander of the army of the LORD I have now come." And Joshua fell on his face
5.14 to the earth and worshiped, and he said to him, "What do you command your ser-
Ex 3.5 vant, my lord?" 15 The commander of the army of the LORD said to Joshua, "Re-
move the sandals from your feet, for the place where you stand is holy." And
Joshua did so.

[f] Related to Heb *galal* to roll

---

cutting off the old life and beginning a new life with God (Genesis 17.13). Other cultures at that time used circumcision as a sign of entry into adulthood, but only Israel used it as a sign of following God.

5.8, 9 Located about two miles northeast of Jericho, Gilgal was Israel's base camp and their temporary center of government and worship during their invasion of Canaan. Here the people renewed their commitment to God and covenant with him before attempting to conquer the new land. At Gilgal the angelic commander of God's army appeared to Joshua with further instructions for battle and encouragement for the conquest. After the conquest, Gilgal continued to be an important place in Israel. It was here that Israel's first king, Saul, was crowned (1 Samuel 11.14, 15).

5.10 This joyous passover was the first to be celebrated in the promised land and only the third celebrated by Israel since the exodus from Egypt. The last time was at the foot of Mount Sinai, 39 years earlier. This celebration reminded Israel of God's mighty miracles that brought them out of Egypt. There they had to eat in fear and haste; now they ate in celebration of God's blessings and promises. (See Exodus 12 for a description of the night the angel "passed over" Israel.)

5.11, 12 God had miraculously supplied manna to the hungry Israelites during their 40 years in the wilderness (Exodus 16.14–31). In the bountiful promised land they no longer needed this daily food supply because the land was ready for planting and harvesting. God had miraculously provided food for the Israelites while they were in the desert; now he provided food from the land itself. Prayer is not an alternative to preparation, and faith is not a substitute for hard work. God can and does provide miraculously for his people as needed, but he also expects them to use their God-given talents and resources to provide for themselves. If your prayers have gone unanswered, perhaps what you need is within your reach. Pray instead for the wisdom to see it and the energy and motivation to do it.

5.14, 15 This was an angel of superior rank, the commander of the army of the Lord. Some say he was Christ himself as he appeared before his birth on earth. As a sign of respect, Joshua took off his shoes. Although Joshua was Israel's leader, he was still subordinate to God, the absolute leader. Awe and respect are the responses due to our holy God. How can we show respect for God? By our attitudes and actions. We should recognize God's power, authority, and deep love, and our actions must model our attitudes before others. Respect for God is just as important today as it was in Joshua's day, even though removing sandals is no longer our cultural way of showing it.

The walls of Jericho fall

6 Now Jericho was shut up inside and out because of the Israelites; no one came 6.1
out and no one went in. 2The LORD said to Joshua, "See, I have handed Jericho Josh 5.1
over to you, along with its king and soldiers. 3You shall march around the city, all 6.2 Deut 7.24
the warriors circling the city once. Thus you shall do for six days, 4with seven Josh 10.8
priests bearing seven trumpets of rams' horns before the ark. On the seventh day 6.3 Lev 25.9
you shall march around the city seven times, the priests blowing the trumpets.
5When they make a long blast with the ram's horn, as soon as you hear the sound
of the trumpet, then all the people shall shout with a great shout; and the wall of the
city will fall down flat, and all the people shall charge straight ahead." 6So Joshua 6.6
son of Nun summoned the priests and said to them, "Take up the ark of the cove- Josh 1.10; 3.2
nant, and have seven priests carry seven trumpets of rams' horns in front of the ark
of the LORD." 7To the people he said, "Go forward and march around the city; have
the armed men pass on before the ark of the LORD."

8 As Joshua had commanded the people, the seven priests carrying the seven
trumpets of rams' horns before the LORD went forward, blowing the trumpets, with
the ark of the covenant of the LORD following them. 9And the armed men went
before the priests who blew the trumpets; the rear guard came after the ark, while
the trumpets blew continually. 10To the people Joshua gave this command: "You
shall not shout or let your voice be heard, nor shall you utter a word, until the day
I tell you to shout. Then you shall shout." 11So the ark of the LORD went around the
city, circling it once; and they came into the camp, and spent the night in the camp.

12 Then Joshua rose early in the morning, and the priests took up the ark of the 6.12
LORD. 13The seven priests carrying the seven trumpets of rams' horns before the Josh 6.3,4
ark of the LORD passed on, blowing the trumpets continually. The armed men went
before them, and the rear guard came after the ark of the LORD, while the trumpets
blew continually. 14On the second day they marched around the city once and then
returned to the camp. They did this for six days.

15 On the seventh day they rose early, at dawn, and marched around the city in
the same manner seven times. It was only on that day that they marched around the
city seven times. 16And at the seventh time, when the priests had blown the trumpets, Joshua said to the people, "Shout! For the LORD has given you the city. 17The 6.17
city and all that is in it shall be devoted to the LORD for destruction. Only Rahab the Josh 2.15; 6.22
prostitute and all who are with her in her house shall live because she hid the messengers we sent. 18As for you, keep away from the things devoted to destruction, 6.18
so as not to covet[g] and take any of the devoted things and make the camp of Israel Deut 20.17 Josh 7.1

g Gk: Heb *devote to destruction* Compare 7.21

6.1 The city of Jericho, built thousands of years before Joshua was born, was one of the oldest cities in the world. In some places it had fortified walls up to 25 feet high and 20 feet thick. Soldiers standing guard on top of the walls could see for miles. Jericho was a symbol of military power and strength—the Canaanites considered it invincible.

Israel would attack this city first, and its destruction would put the fear of Israel into the heart of every person in Canaan. The Canaanites saw Israel's God as a nature god because he parted the Jordan and as a war god because he defeated Sihon and Og. But the Canaanites did not consider him a fortress god—one who could prevail against a walled city. The defeat of Jericho showed not only that Israel's God was superior to the Canaanite gods, but also that he was invincible.

6.2–5 God told Joshua that Jericho was already given into his hand—the enemy was already defeated! What confidence Joshua must have had as he went into battle! Christians also fight against a defeated enemy. Our enemy, Satan, has been defeated by Christ (Romans 8.37–39; Hebrews 2.14, 15; 1 John 3.8). Although we still fight battles every day and sin runs rampant in the world, we have the assurance that the war has already been won. We do not have to be paralyzed by the power of a defeated enemy; we can overcome him through Christ's power.

6.3–5 Why did the Lord give Joshua all these complicated instructions for the battle? Several answers are possible: (1) God was making it undeniably clear that the battle would depend upon him, and not upon Israel's weapons and expertise. This is why priests carrying the ark, not soldiers, led the Israelites into battle. (2) God's method of taking the city accentuated the terror already felt in Jericho (2.9). (3) This strange military maneuver was a test of the Israelites' faith and their willingness to follow God completely. The blowing of the trumpets had a special significance. Earlier, they had been instructed to blow the same trumpets used in the religious festivals in their battles to remind them that their victory would come from the Lord, not their own military might (Numbers 10.9).

6.14–20 It must have seemed strange to the Israelites that, instead of going to battle, they were going to march around the city for a week! But this was God's plan, and the Israelites had a guaranteed victory if they would follow it (6.2). As strange as the plan sounded, it worked. God's instructions may require you to take steps that don't make sense at first. Even as you follow him, you may wonder how things can possibly work out. Like the Israelites, take one day at a time and follow step by step. You may not see the logic of God's plan until after you have obeyed.

6.19 Num 31.22,23 an object for destruction, bringing trouble upon it. 19 But all silver and gold, and
vessels of bronze and iron, are sacred to the LORD; they shall go into the treasury of
6.20 Heb 11.30 the LORD." 20 So the people shouted, and the trumpets were blown. As soon as the
people heard the sound of the trumpets, they raised a great shout, and the wall fell
6.21 Deut 20.16 down flat; so the people charged straight ahead into the city and captured it. 21 Then
they devoted to destruction by the edge of the sword all in the city, both men and
women, young and old, oxen, sheep, and donkeys.

The spies rescue Rahab's family

6.22 Josh 2.15 Judg 1.25 22 Joshua said to the two men who had spied out the land, "Go into the prostitute's house, and bring the woman out of it and all who belong to her, as you swore
6.23 Heb 11.31 to her." 23 So the young men who had been spies went in and brought Rahab out,
along with her father, her mother, her brothers, and all who belonged to her—they
brought all her kindred out—and set them outside the camp of Israel. 24 They
burned down the city, and everything in it; only the silver and gold, and the vessels
6.25 Josh 2.6 Heb 11.31 of bronze and iron, they put into the treasury of the house of the LORD. 25 But Rahab
the prostitute, with her family and all who belonged to her, Joshua spared. Her
family[h] has lived in Israel ever since. For she hid the messengers whom Joshua
sent to spy out Jericho.
6.26 2 Sam 10.5 1 Kgs 16.34 26 Joshua then pronounced this oath, saying,
"Cursed before the LORD be anyone who tries
to build this city—this Jericho!
At the cost of his firstborn he shall lay its foundation,
and at the cost of his youngest he shall set up its gates!"
6.27 Deut 31.7 27 So the LORD was with Joshua; and his fame was in all the land.

Achan's sin of disobedience

7.1 Josh 6.17-19 1 Chron 2.7 **7** But the Israelites broke faith in regard to the devoted things: Achan son of
Carmi son of Zabdi son of Zerah, of the tribe of Judah, took some of the de-
voted things; and the anger of the LORD burned against the Israelites.
7.2 Gen 28.19 Josh 16.2 2 Joshua sent men from Jericho to Ai, which is near Beth-aven, east of Bethel,
and said to them, "Go up and spy out the land." And the men went up and spied out
Ai. 3 Then they returned to Joshua and said to him, "Not all the people need go up;
about two or three thousand men should go up and attack Ai. Since they are so few,
do not make the whole people toil up there." 4 So about three thousand of the people

[h] Heb *She*

6.21 Why did God demand that the Israelites destroy almost everyone and everything in Jericho? He was carrying out severe judgment against the wickedness of the Canaanites. This judgment, or "ban," usually required that everything be destroyed (Deuteronomy 12.2, 3; 13.12–18). Because of their evil practices and intense idolatry, the Canaanites were a stronghold of rebellion against God. This threat to the the right kind of living that God required had to be removed. If not, it would affect all Israel like a cancerous growth (as it did in the sad story told in the book of Judges). A few people and some items in Jericho were not destroyed, but this was a special case. Rahab and her household were saved because she had faith in God and because she helped the Israelite spies. The silver and gold were kept, not to enrich the people, but to beautify the tabernacle and its services.

God's purpose in all this was to keep the people's faith and religion uncontaminated. He did not want the loot to remind Israel of Canaanite practices.

God desires purity in each of us as well. He wants us to clean up our behavior when we begin a new life with him. We must not let the desire for personal gain distract us from our spiritual purpose. We must also reject any objects that commemorate a life of rebellion to God. (For more information on how Israel handled its booty, see the note on Numbers 31.22, 23.)

6.22 In return for information, Joshua's spies had promised to protect Rahab and her family from the battle (2.14, 15). Rahab kept her part of the promise, and Joshua took time from the battle to tell the spies to keep their part.

6.26 This curse was fulfilled in 1 Kings 16.34 when a man rebuilt Jericho and consequently lost his oldest and youngest sons.

7.1 "The devoted things" refer to all the clothing, cattle, and other loot that God said Israel should destroy when they conquered Jericho (see 6.17–19). This was more than finding a good use for something that was going to be thrown out anyway. This was a serious offense because it was in direct defiance to an explicit command of God.

7.1ff Notice the results of Achan's sin: (1) many men died (7.5); (2) Israel's army was paralyzed with fear (7.5); (3) the leader faltered and was confused (7.7–9); (4) God said he might withdraw his presence from the people (7.12); (5) Achan and his family had to be destroyed (7.24–26).

When Israel eliminated the sin in their community, these were the results: (1) encouragement from God (8.1); (2) God's presence in battle (8.1); (3) God's guidance and promise of victory (8.2); (4) God's permission to keep the loot from the battle for themselves (8.2). Throughout Israel's history, blessings came when the people got rid of their sin. You will also experience victory when you turn from your sin and follow God's plan wholeheartedly.

went up there; and they fled before the men of Ai. 5 The men of Ai killed about 7.5
thirty-six of them, chasing them from outside the gate as far as Shebarim and kill- Josh 8.1
ing them on the slope. The hearts of the people melted and turned to water.
6 Then Joshua tore his clothes, and fell to the ground on his face before the ark 7.6
of the LORD until the evening, he and the elders of Israel; and they put dust on their Job 2.12; 42.6 Lam 2.10
heads. 7 Joshua said, "Ah, Lord GOD! Why have you brought this people across the 7.7
Jordan at all, to hand us over to the Amorites so as to destroy us? Would that we had Ex 14.11; 17.3
been content to settle beyond the Jordan! 8 O Lord, what can I say, now that Israel
has turned their backs to their enemies! 9 The Canaanites and all the inhabitants of 7.9
the land will hear of it, and surround us, and cut off our name from the earth. Then Ex 32.12 Deut 9.28
what will you do for your great name?"
10 The LORD said to Joshua, "Stand up! Why have you fallen upon your face? 7.10
11 Israel has sinned; they have transgressed my covenant that I imposed on them. Ex 14.15 1 Sam 15.22
They have taken some of the devoted things; they have stolen, they have acted 16.1
deceitfully, and they have put them among their own belongings. 12 Therefore the
Israelites are unable to stand before their enemies; they turn their backs to their
enemies, because they have become a thing devoted for destruction themselves. I
will be with you no more, unless you destroy the devoted things from among you.
13 Proceed to sanctify the people, and say, 'Sanctify yourselves for tomorrow; for 7.13
thus says the LORD, the God of Israel, "There are devoted things among you, Ex 19.10 Joel 2.16,17
O Israel; you will be unable to stand before your enemies until you take away the Zeph 2.1-3
devoted things from among you." 14 In the morning therefore you shall come forward tribe by tribe. The tribe that the LORD takes shall come near by clans, the clan
that the LORD takes shall come near by households, and the household that the
LORD takes shall come near one by one. 15 And the one who is taken as having the
devoted things shall be burned with fire, together with all that he has, for having
transgressed the covenant of the LORD, and for having done an outrageous thing in
Israel.' "
16 So Joshua rose early in the morning, and brought Israel near tribe by tribe,
and the tribe of Judah was taken. 17 He brought near the clans of Judah, and the clan
of the Zerahites was taken; and he brought near the clan of the Zerahites, family by

---

7.6 Joshua and the elders tore their clothing and put dust upon their heads as signs of deep mourning before God. They were confused by their defeat at the small city of Ai after the spectacular Jericho victory, so they went before God in deep humility and sorrow to receive his instructions. When our lives fall apart, we also should turn to God for direction and help. Like Joshua and the elders, we should humble ourselves so that we will be able to hear his word.

7.7 When Joshua first went against Ai (7.3), he did not consult God but relied on the strength of his army to defeat the small city. Only after Israel was defeated did they turn to God and ask, "What happened?"

Too often we rely on our own skills and strength, especially when the task before us seems easy. We go to God only when the obstacles seem too great. However, only God knows what lies ahead. Consulting him, even when we are on a winning streak, may save us from grave mistakes or misjudgments. God may want us to learn lessons, remove pride, or consult others before he will work through us.

7.7–9 Imagine praying this way to God. This is not a formal church prayer; it is the prayer of a man who is afraid and confused by what is happening around him. Joshua poured out his real thoughts to God. Hiding your needs from God is ignoring the only one who can really help. God welcomes your honest prayers and wants you to express your true feelings to him. Any believer can become more honest in prayer by remembering that God is all-knowing and all-powerful, and his love is everlasting.

7.10, 11 Once Achan started covering up, he couldn't stop until it was too late. Covering his sin only led to further sinning. First Achan disobeyed God and took the loot from Jericho, then he hid it, then he lied. When you sin, beware of compounding your problems by deceit. Confess your sin and turn away from it before you go beyond the point of no return.

7.10–12 Why did Achan's sin bring judgment on the entire nation? Although it was one man's failure, God saw it as national disobedience to a national law. God needed the entire nation to be committed to the job they had agreed to do – conquer the land. Thus, when one person failed, everyone failed. If Achan's sin went unpunished, unlimited looting could break out. The nation as a whole had to take responsibility for preventing this undisciplined disobedience.

Achan's sin was not merely his keeping some of the booty (God allowed it in some cases), but his disobeying God's explicit command to destroy everything connected with Jericho. His sin was indifference to the evil and idolatry of the city, not just a desire for money and clothes. God would not protect Israel's army again until the sin was removed and the army returned to obeying him without reservation. God is not content with our doing what is right some of the time. He wants us to do what is right all the time. We are under his orders to eliminate any thought, practice, or possession that hinders our devotion to him.

7.13 "Sanctify yourselves" meant that the Israelites were to undergo purification rites like those mentioned in 3.5 when they were preparing to cross the Jordan River. Such rites prepared the people to approach God and constantly reminded them of their sinfulness and his holiness.

family,[i] and Zabdi was taken. 18 And he brought near his household one by one,
and Achan son of Carmi son of Zabdi son of Zerah, of the tribe of Judah, was taken.
19 Then Joshua said to Achan, "My son, give glory to the LORD God of Israel and
make confession to him. Tell me now what you have done; do not hide it from me."
20 And Achan answered Joshua, "It is true; I am the one who sinned against the
LORD God of Israel. This is what I did: 21 when I saw among the spoil a beautiful
mantle from Shinar, and two hundred shekels of silver, and a bar of gold weighing
fifty shekels, then I coveted them and took them. They now lie hidden in the ground
inside my tent, with the silver underneath."
22 So Joshua sent messengers, and they ran to the tent; and there it was, hidden
in his tent with the silver underneath. 23 They took them out of the tent and brought
them to Joshua and all the Israelites; and they spread them out before the LORD.
24 Then Joshua and all Israel with him took Achan son of Zerah, with the silver, the
mantle, and the bar of gold, with his sons and daughters, with his oxen, donkeys,
and sheep, and his tent and all that he had; and they brought them up to the Valley
of Achor. 25 Joshua said, "Why did you bring trouble on us? The LORD is bringing
trouble on you today." And all Israel stoned him to death; they burned them with
fire, cast stones on them, 26 and raised over him a great heap of stones that remains
to this day. Then the LORD turned from his burning anger. Therefore that place to
this day is called the Valley of Achor.[j]

Israel destroys the city of Ai

8 Then the LORD said to Joshua, "Do not fear or be dismayed; take all the fighting men with you, and go up now to Ai. See, I have handed over to you the
king of Ai with his people, his city, and his land. 2 You shall do to Ai and its king
as you did to Jericho and its king; only its spoil and its livestock you may take as
booty for yourselves. Set an ambush against the city, behind it."
3 So Joshua and all the fighting men set out to go up against Ai. Joshua chose
thirty thousand warriors and sent them out by night 4 with the command, "You shall
lie in ambush against the city, behind it; do not go very far from the city, but all of
you stay alert. 5 I and all the people who are with me will approach the city. When
they come out against us, as before, we shall flee from them. 6 They will come out

7.19 Jer 13.16 Jn 9.24
7.20 Ex 10.16
7.24 Josh 15.7
7.25 Deut 13.17 24.16 Josh 6.18
7.26 Gen 31.46, 51,52 Josh 8.28,29 Isa 65.10 Hos 2.15
8.1 Deut 1.19-21 Josh 1.9; 6.2 10.8
8.2 Josh 6.18; 8.27
8.6 Josh 7.5

[i] Mss Syr: MT *man by man* [j] That is *Trouble*

7.21 The "mantle from Shinar" was a beautiful and costly cloak from Babylon.

7.24, 25 Achan underestimated God and didn't take his commands seriously (6.18). It may have seemed a small thing to Achan, but the effects of his sin were felt by the entire nation, especially his family. Like Achan, our actions affect more people than just ourselves. Beware of the temptation to rationalize your sins by saying they are too small or too personal to hurt anyone but you.

7.24–26 Why did Achan's entire family pay for his sin? The biblical record does not tell us if they were accomplices to his crime, but in the ancient world, the family was treated as a whole. Achan, as the head of his family, was like a king. If he prospered, the family prospered with him. If he suffered, so did they. Many Israelites had already died in battle because of Achan's sin. Now he was to be completely cut off from Israel.

His entire family was to be stoned along with him so that no trace of Achan would remain in Israel. In our individualistic culture we have a hard time understanding such a decree, but in ancient cultures it was a common punishment. The punishment fit the crime: Achan had disobeyed God's command to destroy everything in Jericho; thus everything that belonged to Achan would be destroyed. Sin has drastic consequences, so we should take drastic measures to avoid it.

8.1 Now that Israel was cleansed from Achan's sin, Joshua prepared to attack Ai again—this time to win. Joshua had learned some lessons which we can follow in our daily lives: (1) confess your sins when God reveals them to you (7.19–21); (2) when you fail, refocus on God, deal with the problem, and move on (7.22–25; 8.1). God wants the cycle of sin, repentance, and forgiveness to strengthen us, not weaken us. The lessons we learn from our failures should make us better able to handle the same situation the second time around. Since God is eager to give us cleansing, forgiveness, and strength, the only way to lose is to give up. We can tell what kind of people we are by what we do on the second and third attempts.

8.2 Why did God allow the Israelites to keep the loot this time? Israel's laws for handling the spoils of war covered two situations. (1) Cities like Jericho which were under God's *ban* (judgment for idolatry) could not be looted. God's people were to be kept holy and separate from every influence of idolatry. (2) The distribution of loot from cities not under the ban was a normal part of warfare. It provided the army and the nation with the necessary food, flocks, and weapons needed to sustain itself in wartime. Ai was not under the ban. The conquering army needed the food and equipment. Since soldiers were not paid, the loot was part of their incentive and reward for going to war.

8.3 The conquest of Ai was very important to the Israelites. Only 11 miles away from Jericho, Ai was a key stronghold for the Caananites and a buffer fortress for Bethel (8.12). If the Caananite kings got wind of an Israelite defeat at Ai, they could unite in a coordinated attack. They did not know that God had restored his power and protection to Joshua's troops. We must depend on God with absolute obedience to be sure of the victory he has promised.

after us until we have drawn them away from the city; for they will say, 'They are
fleeing from us, as before.' While we flee from them, 7 you shall rise up from the
ambush and seize the city; for the LORD your God will give it into your hand. 8 And 8.8
when you have taken the city, you shall set the city on fire, doing as the LORD has Josh 6.24 8.20,21
ordered; see, I have commanded you." 9 So Joshua sent them out; and they went to
the place of ambush, and lay between Bethel and Ai, to the west of Ai; but Joshua
spent that night in the camp.[k]
10 In the morning Joshua rose early and mustered the people, and went up, with
the elders of Israel, before the people to Ai. 11 All the fighting men who were with
him went up, and drew near before the city, and camped on the north side of Ai,
with a ravine between them and Ai. 12 Taking about five thousand men, he set them
in ambush between Bethel and Ai, to the west of the city. 13 So they stationed the
forces, the main encampment that was north of the city and its rear guard west of
the city. But Joshua spent that night in the valley. 14 When the king of Ai saw this, 8.14
he and all his people, the inhabitants of the city, hurried out early in the morning to Deut 1.1; 4.49 Josh 11.1
the meeting place facing the Arabah to meet Israel in battle; but he did not know
that there was an ambush against him behind the city. 15 And Joshua and all Israel
made a pretense of being beaten before them, and fled in the direction of the wilderness. 16 So all the people who were in the city were called together to pursue them,
and as they pursued Joshua they were drawn away from the city. 17 There was not 8.17
a man left in Ai or Bethel who did not go out after Israel; they left the city open, and Josh 12.8-24
pursued Israel.
18 Then the LORD said to Joshua, "Stretch out the sword that is in your hand 8.18
toward Ai; for I will give it into your hand." And Joshua stretched out the sword Ex 14.16; 17.9 Josh 8.26
that was in his hand toward the city. 19 As soon as he stretched out his hand, the
troops in ambush rose quickly out of their place and rushed forward. They entered
the city, took it, and at once set the city on fire. 20 So when the men of Ai looked
back, the smoke of the city was rising to the sky. They had no power to flee this
way or that, for the people who fled to the wilderness turned back against the pursuers. 21 When Joshua and all Israel saw that the ambush had taken the city and that
the smoke of the city was rising, then they turned back and struck down the men of
Ai. 22 And the others came out from the city against them; so they were surrounded 8.22
by Israelites, some on one side, and some on the other; and Israel struck them down Num 21.35 Deut 3.6
until no one was left who survived or escaped. 23 But the king of Ai was taken alive
and brought to Joshua.
24 When Israel had finished slaughtering all the inhabitants of Ai in the open

[k] Heb *among the people*

8.15 Joshua used a brilliant military maneuver to destroy this fortified city with minimal loss of life among his own soldiers. According to God's instructions (8.2), he set an ambush by dividing his troops into three groups. The first group was sent by night to hide just west of the city. They would rush in and burn it when the soldiers left to join the main battle. The second group camped on the north side of the city in plain view of the men of Ai. They were to be the decoy to draw the soldiers out of Ai. The third group was positioned between Bethel and Ai to cut off the possibility of reinforcements arriving from Bethel or of the enemy soldiers fleeing to Bethel. As the battle began, Joshua pretended that they were being defeated in the same way once again. The king of Ai took the bait as planned.

8.18 The Lord gave Joshua the city. Yesterday's defeat became today's victory. Once sin is dealt with, forgiveness and victory lie ahead. With God's direction we need not stay discouraged or burdened with guilt. No matter how difficult a setback sin may bring, we must renew our efforts to carry out God's will.

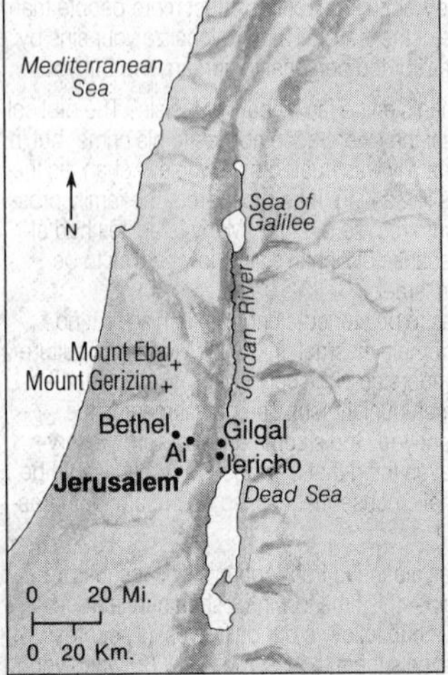

THE BATTLE FOR AI
During the night, Joshua sent one detachment of soldiers to the west of Ai to lie in wait. The next morning he led a second group north of Ai. When the army of Ai attacked, the Israelites to the north pretended to scatter, only to turn on the enemy as the men lying in ambush moved in and burned the city.

wilderness where they pursued them, and when all of them to the very last had
fallen by the edge of the sword, all Israel returned to Ai, and attacked it with the
8.25 Deut 20.16 edge of the sword. 25 The total of those who fell that day, both men and women,
8.26 Ex 17.11 Josh 8.18 was twelve thousand—all the people of Ai. 26 For Joshua did not draw back his
hand, with which he stretched out the sword, until he had utterly destroyed all the
inhabitants of Ai. 27 Only the livestock and the spoil of that city Israel took as their
8.27 Josh 8.2 booty, according to the word of the LORD that he had issued to Joshua. 28 So Joshua
8.28 Josh 7.26 burned Ai, and made it forever a heap of ruins, as it is to this day. 29 And he hanged
the king of Ai on a tree until evening; and at sunset Joshua commanded, and they
8.29 Deut 21.22,23 took his body down from the tree, threw it down at the entrance of the gate of the
city, and raised over it a great heap of stones, which stands there to this day.

Joshua reads the law to the entire nation

8.30 Gen 8.20 12.7,8 Josh 22.10 Judg 6.24 30 Then Joshua built on Mount Ebal an altar to the LORD, the God of Israel,
31 just as Moses the servant of the LORD had commanded the Israelites, as it is writ-
ten in the book of the law of Moses, "an altar of unhewn[l] stones, on which no iron
8.31 Ex 20.25 Deut 27.5,6 tool has been used"; and they offered on it burnt offerings to the LORD, and sacrificed offerings of well-being. 32 And there, in the presence of the Israelites,
Joshua[m] wrote on the stones a copy of the law of Moses, which he had written.
8.33 Deut 27.12,13 33 All Israel, alien as well as citizen, with their elders and officers and their judges,
stood on opposite sides of the ark in front of the levitical priests who carried the ark
of the covenant of the LORD, half of them in front of Mount Gerizim and half of
them in front of Mount Ebal, as Moses the servant of the LORD had commanded at
8.34 Deut 11.26 28.2-6,15-19 the first, that they should bless the people of Israel. 34 And afterward he read all the
words of the law, blessings and curses, according to all that is written in the book
of the law. 35 There was not a word of all that Moses commanded that Joshua did
not read before all the assembly of Israel, and the women, and the little ones, and
the aliens who resided among them.

2. Joshua attacks the southern kings

The people of Gibeon trick Joshua

9.1 Num 13.17,29 Deut 1.7 Josh 3.10 10.40; 11.16 9 Now when all the kings who were beyond the Jordan in the hill country and in
the lowland all along the coast of the Great Sea toward Lebanon—the Hittites,
the Amorites, the Canaanites, the Perizzites, the Hivites, and the Jebusites—heard
of this, 2 they gathered together with one accord to fight Joshua and Israel.
9.3 Josh 10.2,7 11.19 Prov 13.17 3 But when the inhabitants of Gibeon heard what Joshua had done to Jericho
and to Ai, 4 they on their part acted with cunning: they went and prepared provi-
sions,[n] and took worn-out sacks for their donkeys, and wineskins, worn-out and
torn and mended, 5 with worn-out, patched sandals on their feet, and worn-out
clothes; and all their provisions were dry and moldy. 6 They went to Joshua in the
camp at Gilgal, and said to him and to the Israelites, "We have come from a far
9.7 Ex 23.32 Josh 11.19 country; so now make a treaty with us." 7 But the Israelites said to the Hivites,
"Perhaps you live among us; then how can we make a treaty with you?" 8 They said
9.9 Josh 2.9 9.16,17 to Joshua, "We are your servants." And Joshua said to them, "Who are you? And
where do you come from?" 9 They said to him, "Your servants have come from a

[l] Heb *whole* [m] Heb *he* [n] Cn: Meaning of Heb uncertain

---

8.31 The altar was to be built out of natural stones so it would not be profaned (see Exodus 20.25). This would prevent the people from worshiping altars like idols, or worshiping the craftsmanship of the workers rather than the great works of God.

8.32 It was most likely the ten commandments (recorded in Exodus 20) that Joshua carved into the altar. These were the heart of all God's laws, and they are still relevant today.

8.33, 35 After Israel's military victory, Joshua obeyed God's command by gathering the people together and reminding them of God's laws (1.8). God knows how easily we forget. We need to review what God says. We should not read the Bible as we do most other books—once through quickly. We should read it daily as a constant reminder of who God is and what we can become.

9.1–6 As the news about their victory became widespread, the Israelites experienced opposition in two forms: direct (kings in the area began to unite against them); and indirect (the Gibeonites resorted to trickery). We can expect similar opposition as we obey God's commands. To guard against these pressures, we must rely on God and communicate daily with him. He will give us strength to endure the direct pressures and wisdom to see through the indirect trickery.

very far country, because of the name of the LORD your God; for we have heard a
report of him, of all that he did in Egypt, [10]and of all that he did to the two kings
of the Amorites who were beyond the Jordan, King Sihon of Heshbon, and King
Og of Bashan who lived in Ashtaroth. [11]So our elders and all the inhabitants of our
country said to us, 'Take provisions in your hand for the journey; go to meet them,
and say to them, "We are your servants; come now, make a treaty with us."'
[12]Here is our bread; it was still warm when we took it from our houses as our food
for the journey, on the day we set out to come to you, but now, see, it is dry and
moldy; [13]these wineskins were new when we filled them, and see, they are burst;
and these garments and sandals of ours are worn out from the very long journey."
[14]So the leaders[o] partook of their provisions, and did not ask direction from the **9.14**
LORD. [15]And Joshua made peace with them, guaranteeing their lives by a treaty; Ex 23.32
and the leaders of the congregation swore an oath to them. Num 27.21

16 But when three days had passed after they had made a treaty with them, they
heard that they were their neighbors and were living among them. [17]So the Israel-
ites set out and reached their cities on the third day. Now their cities were Gibeon, **9.17** Josh 18.15,25,
Chephirah, Beeroth, and Kiriath-jearim. [18]But the Israelites did not attack them, 26; 15.9,60 1 Sam 7.1,2
because the leaders of the congregation had sworn to them by the LORD, the God of 1 Chron 13.5,6
Israel. Then all the congregation murmured against the leaders. [19]But all the leaders said to all the congregation, "We have sworn to them by the LORD, the God of
Israel, and now we must not touch them. [20]This is what we will do to them: We will **9.20**
let them live, so that wrath may not come upon us, because of the oath that we 2 Sam 21.1
swore to them." [21]The leaders said to them, "Let them live." So they became hew- **9.21**
ers of wood and drawers of water for all the congregation, as the leaders had de- Gen 9.25
cided concerning them.

22 Joshua summoned them, and said to them, "Why did you deceive us, saying, 'We are very far from you,' while in fact you are living among us? [23]Now
therefore you are cursed, and some of you shall always be slaves, hewers of wood
and drawers of water for the house of my God." [24]They answered Joshua, "Be- **9.24**
cause it was told to your servants for a certainty that the LORD your God had com- Deut 7.1 20.16,17
manded his servant Moses to give you all the land, and to destroy all the inhabitants Josh 2.24; 5.1
of the land before you; so we were in great fear for our lives because of you, and did
this thing. [25]And now we are in your hand: do as it seems good and right in your
sight to do to us." [26]This is what he did for them: he saved them from the Israelites;
and they did not kill them. [27]But on that day Joshua made them hewers of wood and **9.27**
drawers of water for the congregation and for the altar of the LORD, to continue to Deut 12.4,5,6
this day, in the place that he should choose.

The sun stands still

10 When King Adoni-zedek of Jerusalem heard how Joshua had taken Ai, and **10.1**
had utterly destroyed it, doing to Ai and its king as he had done to Jericho Josh 8.25 9.14,15
and its king, and how the inhabitants of Gibeon had made peace with Israel and

o Gk: Heb *men*

9.14–17 When the leaders partook of their provisions, they inspected them for themselves. While they saw that the bread was really moldy and the shoes were really worn out, they did not see through the trick. After the promise had been made and the treaty ratified, the facts came out – Israel's leaders had been deceived. God had specifically instructed Israel to make no treaties with the inhabitants of Canaan (Exodus 23.32; 34.12; Numbers 33.55; Deuteronomy 7.2; 20.17, 18). As a strategist, Joshua knew enough to talk to God before leading his troops into battle. But the peace treaty seemed innocent enough, so Joshua and the leaders made this decision on their own. By failing to seek God's guidance and rushing ahead with their own plans, they had to deal with angry people and an awkward alliance.

Successful people may feel they can "go it on their own." Thinking they have all the facts and understand the situation, they may not ask for advice in untried ventures. But seeking God's will before entering into agreements can keep minor matters from becoming major headaches.

9.19, 20 Joshua and his advisers had made a mistake. But because they had vowed to protect the Gibeonites, they would keep their word. The vow was not nullified by the Gibeonites' trickery. God had commanded that vows be kept (Leviticus 5.4; 27.1, 28), and breaking a vow was serious. This encourages us not to take vows and promises lightly.

10.1–9 The Israelites, who were supposed to have destroyed the Gibeonites, were now allied with them. Even though this was a big mistake, God would remain faithful to his promise and help Israel defeat the coalition of nations now on the attack. God forgives sin and helps us move on, but he does not cancel all its conse-

10.2 1 Kgs 3.4,5; 9.2,3; 1 Chron 21.29; 2 Chron 1.2,3
were among them, 2 he[p] became greatly frightened, because Gibeon was a large
city, like one of the royal cities, and was larger than Ai, and all its men were warriors. 3 So King Adoni-zedek of Jerusalem sent a message to King Hoham of Hebron, to King Piram of Jarmuth, to King Japhia of Lachish, and to King Debir of
Eglon, saying, 4 "Come up and help me, and let us attack Gibeon; for it has made
10.5 Num 13.29; Josh 9.1
peace with Joshua and with the Israelites." 5 Then the five kings of the
Amorites—the king of Jerusalem, the king of Hebron, the king of Jarmuth, the
king of Lachish, and the king of Eglon—gathered their forces, and went up with all
their armies and camped against Gibeon, and made war against it.
6 And the Gibeonites sent to Joshua at the camp in Gilgal, saying, "Do not
abandon your servants; come up to us quickly, and save us, and help us; for all the
kings of the Amorites who live in the hill country are gathered against us." 7 So
Joshua went up from Gilgal, he and all the fighting force with him, all the mighty
10.8 Josh 1.5,9; 6.2; 8.1
warriors. 8 The LORD said to Joshua, "Do not fear them, for I have handed them
over to you; not one of them shall stand before you." 9 So Joshua came upon
10.10 Judg 4.15
them suddenly, having marched up all night from Gilgal. 10 And the LORD threw
them into a panic before Israel, who inflicted a great slaughter on them at Gibeon,
chased them by the way of the ascent of Beth-horon, and struck them down as far
as Azekah and Makkedah. 11 As they fled before Israel, while they were going
down the slope of Beth-horon, the LORD threw down huge stones from heaven on
them as far as Azekah, and they died; there were more who died because of the hailstones than the Israelites killed with the sword.
12 On the day when the LORD gave the Amorites over to the Israelites, Joshua
spoke to the LORD; and he said in the sight of Israel,

"Sun, stand still at Gibeon,
and Moon, in the valley of Aijalon."

10.13 Isa 38.8
13 And the sun stood still, and the moon stopped,
until the nation took vengeance on their enemies.

Is this not written in the Book of Jashar? The sun stopped in mid-heaven, and did
10.14 Ex 14.14; Deut 1.30
not hurry to set for about a whole day. 14 There has been no day like it before or
10.15 Josh 10.6,43
since, when the LORD heeded a human voice; for the LORD fought for Israel.
15 Then Joshua returned, and all Israel with him, to the camp at Gilgal.

[p] Heb *they*

---

quences. Even so, God can use our bad situations for his purposes.

10.5–8 This alliance of enemy kings from the south actually helped Joshua and his army. Because the enemies had united to attack Gibeon, Joshua didn't have to spend the time and resources required to wage separate campaigns against each fortified city represented in the coalition. Joshua confidently confronted this coalition of armies and defeated them in a single battle because he trusted God to give Israel the victory.

10.6 Joshua's response shows the integrity of the people. After having been tricked, Joshua and the leaders could have been slow in rescuing these people. How willing would you be to help someone who just took advantage of you in a business deal? We should take our word as seriously as these leaders did.

10.12–14 How did the sun stand still? Of course, in relation to the earth the sun always stands still—it is the earth that travels around the sun. But the terminology used in Joshua should not cause us to doubt the miracle. After all, we are not confused when someone tells us the sun rises or sets. The point is that the day was prolonged, not that God used a particular method to prolong it.

Two explanations have been given for how this event occurred: (1) A slowing of the earth's normal rotation gave Joshua more time, as the original Hebrew language seems to indicate. (2) Some unusual refraction of the sun's rays gave additional hours of light. Regardless of God's chosen method, the Bible is clear that the day was prolonged by a miracle, and that God's intervention turned the tide of battle for his people.

10.13 The book of Jashar (also mentioned in 2 Samuel 1.18) was probably a collection of historical events put to music. Many parts of the Bible contain quotations from previous books, songs, poems, or other spoken and written materials. Because God guided the writer to select this material, his message comes with divine authority.

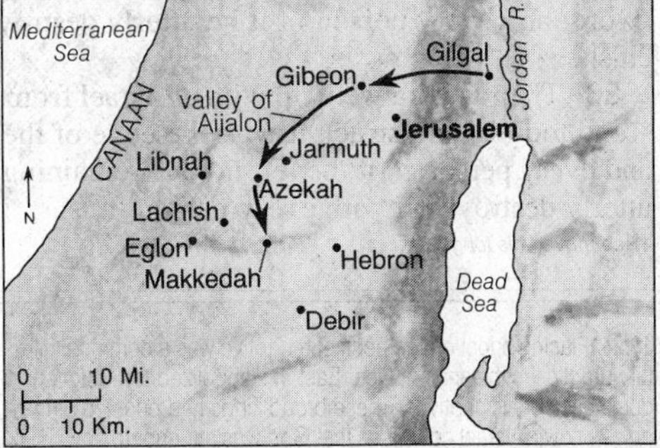

THE BATTLE FOR GIBEON Five Amorite kings conspired to destroy Gibeon. Israel came to the aid of the Gibeonites. The Israelites attacked the enemy armies outside of Gibeon and chased them through the Aijalon Valley as far as Makkedah and Azekah.

The five kings are killed

16 Meanwhile, these five kings fled and hid themselves in the cave at Makke- 10.16
dah. 17 And it was told Joshua, "The five kings have been found, hidden in the cave Josh 10.28
at Makkedah." 18 Joshua said, "Roll large stones against the mouth of the cave, and
set men by it to guard them; 19 but do not stay there yourselves; pursue your enemies, and attack them from the rear. Do not let them enter their towns, for the LORD
your God has given them into your hand." 20 When Joshua and the Israelites had 10.20
finished inflicting a very great slaughter on them, until they were wiped out, and Deut 20.16
when the survivors had entered into the fortified towns, 21 all the people returned 10.21
safe to Joshua in the camp at Makkedah; no one dared to speak[q] against any of the Josh 10.16
Israelites.

22 Then Joshua said, "Open the mouth of the cave, and bring those five kings 10.22
out to me from the cave." 23 They did so, and brought the five kings out to him from Deut 7.24
the cave, the king of Jerusalem, the king of Hebron, the king of Jarmuth, the king 1 Sam 15.32,33
of Lachish, and the king of Eglon. 24 When they brought the kings out to Joshua,
Joshua summoned all the Israelites, and said to the chiefs of the warriors who had
gone with him, "Come near, put your feet on the necks of these kings." Then they
came near and put their feet on their necks. 25 And Joshua said to them, "Do not be 10.25
afraid or dismayed; be strong and courageous; for thus the LORD will do to all the Josh 10.8
enemies against whom you fight." 26 Afterward Joshua struck them down and put 10.26
them to death, and he hung them on five trees. And they hung on the trees until Josh 8.29
evening. 27 At sunset Joshua commanded, and they took them down from the trees 10.27
and threw them into the cave where they had hidden themselves; they set large Deut 21.22,23
stones against the mouth of the cave, which remain to this very day.

Israel destroys cities in the south

28 Joshua took Makkedah on that day, and struck it and its king with the edge
of the sword; he utterly destroyed every person in it; he left no one remaining. And
he did to the king of Makkedah as he had done to the king of Jericho.

29 Then Joshua passed on from Makkedah, and all Israel with him, to Libnah, 10.29
and fought against Libnah. 30 The LORD gave it also and its king into the hand of Num 33.15-37
Israel; and he struck it with the edge of the sword, and every person in it; he left no Josh 12.8-24
one remaining in it; and he did to its king as he had done to the king of Jericho.

31 Next Joshua passed on from Libnah, and all Israel with him, to Lachish, and
laid siege to it, and assaulted it. 32 The LORD gave Lachish into the hand of Israel,
and he took it on the second day, and struck it with the edge of the sword, and every
person in it, as he had done to Libnah.

33 Then King Horam of Gezer came up to help Lachish; and Joshua struck him
and his people, leaving him no survivors.

34 From Lachish Joshua passed on with all Israel to Eglon; and they laid siege
to it, and assaulted it; 35 and they took it that day, and struck it with the edge of the
sword; and every person in it he utterly destroyed that day, as he had done to Lachish.

36 Then Joshua went up with all Israel from Eglon to Hebron; they assaulted it, 10.36
37 and took it, and struck it with the edge of the sword, and its king and its towns, Josh 10.3
and every person in it; he left no one remaining, just as he had done to Eglon, and
utterly destroyed it with every person in it.

[q] Heb *moved his tongue*

10.24 Placing a foot on the neck of a captive was a common military practice in the ancient Near East. It symbolized the victor's domination of his captives. These proud kings had boasted of their power; now all Israel could see that God was superior to any earthly army.

10.25 With God's help, Israel won the battle against five armies. Such a triumph was part of God's daily business as he worked with his people for victory. Joshua told his men never to be afraid because God would give them similar victories over all their enemies. God has often protected us and won victories for us. The same God who empowered Joshua and who has led us in the past will help us with our present and future needs. Reminding ourselves of his help in the past will give us hope for the struggles that lie ahead.

10.32 Notice that in every Israeli victory, the text says, "The Lord gave." All of their victories came from God. When we are successful, the temptation is to take all the credit and glory as though we did it by ourselves, in our own strength. In reality, *God* gives us the victories; and he alone delivers us from our enemies. We should give him the credit and praise him for his goodness.

38 Then Joshua, with all Israel, turned back to Debir and assaulted it, 39 and he
took it with its king and all its towns; they struck them with the edge of the sword,
and utterly destroyed every person in it; he left no one remaining; just as he had
done to Hebron, and, as he had done to Libnah and its king, so he did to Debir and
its king.
10.40 Deut 1.7; 7.24 20.16 — 40 So Joshua defeated the whole land, the hill country and the Negeb and the
lowland and the slopes, and all their kings; he left no one remaining, but utterly
10.41 Josh 11.16 15.48-62 — destroyed all that breathed, as the LORD God of Israel commanded. 41 And Joshua
defeated them from Kadesh-barnea to Gaza, and all the country of Goshen, as far
as Gibeon. 42 Joshua took all these kings and their land at one time, because the
10.43 Josh 10.6 — LORD God of Israel fought for Israel. 43 Then Joshua returned, and all Israel with
him, to the camp at Gilgal.

3. Joshua attacks the northern kings

11.1 Josh 10.3,4 11.10; 12.8-24 19.35-39 Judg 4.2,17 — 11 When King Jabin of Hazor heard of this, he sent to King Jobab of Madon, to
the king of Shimron, to the king of Achshaph, 2 and to the kings who were in
the northern hill country, and in the Arabah south of Chinneroth, and in the lowland, and in Naphoth-dor on the west, 3 to the Canaanites in the east and the west,
the Amorites, the Hittites, the Perizzites, and the Jebusites in the hill country, and
11.4 Josh 11.20 — the Hivites under Hermon in the land of Mizpah. 4 They came out, with all their
troops, a great army, in number like the sand on the seashore, with very many
horses and chariots. 5 All these kings joined their forces, and came and camped
together at the waters of Merom, to fight with Israel.
11.6 Josh 8.1; 10.8 2 Sam 8.4 — 6 And the LORD said to Joshua, "Do not be afraid of them, for tomorrow at this
time I will hand over all of them, slain, to Israel; you shall hamstring their horses,
and burn their chariots with fire." 7 So Joshua came suddenly upon them with all his
fighting force, by the waters of Merom, and fell upon them. 8 And the LORD handed
them over to Israel, who attacked them and chased them as far as Great Sidon and
Misrephoth-maim, and eastward as far as the valley of Mizpeh. They struck them
down, until they had left no one remaining. 9 And Joshua did to them as the LORD
11.10 Judg 4.2,3 1 Sam 12.9 1 Kgs 9.15 2 Kgs 15.29 — commanded him; he hamstrung their horses, and burned their chariots with fire.
10 Joshua turned back at that time, and took Hazor, and struck its king down
with the sword. Before that time Hazor was the head of all those kingdoms. 11 And
11.11 Deut 20.16 Josh 8.8,20,21 10.28,30 — they put to the sword all who were in it, utterly destroying them; there was no one
left who breathed, and he burned Hazor with fire. 12 And all the towns of those
kings, and all their kings, Joshua took, and struck them with the edge of the sword,

---

10.40–43 God had commanded Joshua to take the leadership in ridding the land of sin so God's people could occupy it. Joshua did his part thoroughly—leading the united army to weaken the inhabitants. When God orders us to stop sinning, we must not pause to debate, consider the options, negotiate a compromise, or rationalize. Instead, like Joshua, our response must be swift and complete. We must be ruthless in avoiding relationships and activities that can lead us to sin.

11.1–4 There were two kings of Hazor named Jabin. The other, apparently a weak ruler, is mentioned in Judges 4.2, 3. The Jabin of this story was quite powerful, for he was able to build an alliance with dozens of kings. By all appearances, Jabin had a clear advantage over Joshua and his outnumbered forces. But those who honor God can be victorious regardless of the odds.

11.10–13 Victorious invaders usually kept captured cities intact, moving into them and making them centers of commerce and defense. For example, Moses predicted in Deuteronomy 6.10–12 that Israel would occupy cities they themselves had not built. Hazor, however, was burned. As a former capital of the land, it symbolized the wicked culture Israel had come to destroy. In addition, its capture and destruction broke the backbone of the federation and weakened the rest of the people's will to resist.

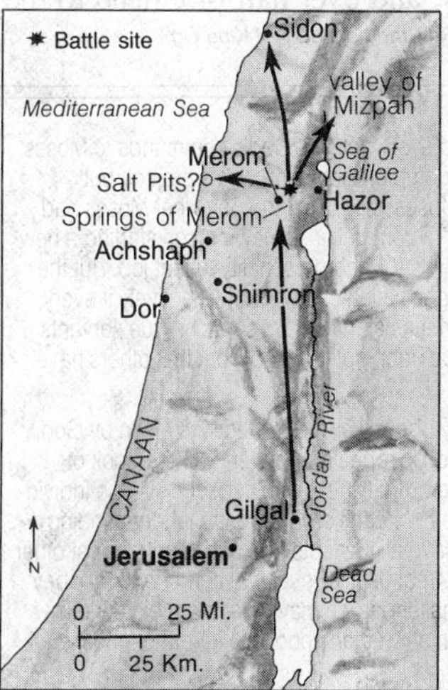

THE BATTLE FOR HAZOR
Kings from the north joined together to battle the Israelites who controlled the southern half of Canaan. They gathered by the Springs ("waters") of Merom, but Joshua attacked them by surprise—the enemies' chariots were useless in the dense forests. Hazor, the largest Canaanite center in Galilee, was destroyed.

utterly destroying them, as Moses the servant of the LORD had commanded. 13 But
Israel burned none of the towns that stood on mounds except Hazor, which Joshua
did burn. 14 All the spoil of these towns, and the livestock, the Israelites took for 11.14
their booty; but all the people they struck down with the edge of the sword, until Josh 8.27
they had destroyed them, and they did not leave any who breathed. 15 As the LORD 11.15
had commanded his servant Moses, so Moses commanded Joshua, and so Joshua Ex 34.11 Deut 31.7
did; he left nothing undone of all that the LORD had commanded Moses.

4. Summary of conquests

The whole land conquered

16 So Joshua took all that land: the hill country and all the Negeb and all the 11.16
land of Goshen and the lowland and the Arabah and the hill country of Israel and its Josh 10.40,41
lowland, 17 from Mount Halak, which rises toward Seir, as far as Baal-gad in the 11.17
valley of Lebanon below Mount Hermon. He took all their kings, struck them Deut 7.24 Josh 12.7
down, and put them to death. 18 Joshua made war a long time with all those kings.
19 There was not a town that made peace with the Israelites, except the Hivites, the 11.19
inhabitants of Gibeon; all were taken in battle. 20 For it was the LORD's doing to Josh 9.3-15
harden their hearts so that they would come against Israel in battle, in order that 11.20 Ex 14.17
they might be utterly destroyed, and might receive no mercy, but be exterminated, Deut 20.16 Josh 11.4
just as the LORD had commanded Moses.

21 At that time Joshua came and wiped out the Anakim from the hill country, 11.21
from Hebron, from Debir, from Anab, and from all the hill country of Judah, and Num 13.33 Deut 9.1,2
from all the hill country of Israel; Joshua utterly destroyed them with their towns. Josh 14.12 15.13
22 None of the Anakim was left in the land of the Israelites; some remained only in
Gaza, in Gath, and in Ashdod. 23 So Joshua took the whole land, according to all 11.23
that the LORD had spoken to Moses; and Joshua gave it for an inheritance to Israel Deut 1.38 12.9,10; 25.19
according to their tribal allotments. And the land had rest from war. Heb 4.8

A list of the conquered kings

12 Now these are the kings of the land, whom the Israelites defeated, whose 12.1
land they occupied beyond the Jordan toward the east, from the Wadi Arnon Num 32.33 Deut 3.8
to Mount Hermon, with all the Arabah eastward: 2 King Sihon of the Amorites who Josh 11.1-3
lived at Heshbon, and ruled from Aroer, which is on the edge of the Wadi Arnon, 12.2 Num 21.23
and from the middle of the valley as far as the river Jabbok, the boundary of the Deut 2.35
Ammonites, that is, half of Gilead, 3 and the Arabah to the Sea of Chinneroth eastward, and in the direction of Beth-jeshimoth, to the sea of the Arabah, the Dead
Sea,[r] southward to the foot of the slopes of Pisgah; 4 and King Og[s] of Bashan, one 12.4
of the last of the Rephaim, who lived at Ashtaroth and at Edrei 5 and ruled over Num 21.33 Josh 13.12
Mount Hermon and Salecah and all Bashan to the boundary of the Geshurites and
the Maacathites, and over half of Gilead to the boundary of King Sihon of Hesh-

[r] Heb *Salt Sea* [s] Gk: Heb *the boundary of King Og*

11.15 Joshua followed every detail of God's commands to Moses. It is usually difficult to complete someone else's project, but Joshua stepped into Moses' job, building upon what Moses had started, and brought it to completion. A new person starting a new job usually brings a new style and personality to that job. But the church or any other organization cannot work effectively if every change of personnel means starting from scratch. True servants will step in and continue or complete good work that others have begun.

11.15 Joshua carefully obeyed all the instructions given by God. This theme of obedience is repeated frequently in the book of Joshua, partly because obedience is one aspect of life the individual believer can control. We can't always control understanding because we may not have all the facts. We can't control what other people do or how they treat us. However, we can *choose* to obey God. Whatever new challenges we may face, the Bible contains relevant instructions which we can choose to ignore or choose to follow.

11.18 The conquest of much of the land of Canaan seems to have happened quickly (we can read about it in one sitting), but it actually took seven years. We often expect quick changes in our lives and quick victories over sin. But our journey with God is a lifelong process, and the changes and victories may take time. It is easy to grow impatient with God and feel like giving up hope because things are moving too slowly. When we are close to a situation, it is difficult to see progress. But when we look back we can see that God never stopped working.

11.21 The Anakim were the tribes of giants the Israelite spies described when they gave their negative report on the promised land (Numbers 13, 14). This time the people did not let their fear of the giants prevent them from engaging in battle and claiming the land God had promised.

12.1ff Chapter 12 is a summary of the first half of Joshua. It lists the kings and nations conquered by Joshua to both the east and the west of the Jordan River. As long as the people trusted and obeyed God, one evil nation after another fell in defeat.

bon. [6]Moses, the servant of the LORD, and the Israelites defeated them; and Moses
the servant of the LORD gave their land for a possession to the Reubenites and the
Gadites and the half-tribe of Manasseh.

12.7 Josh 11.17

7 The following are the kings of the land whom Joshua and the Israelites defeated on the west side of the Jordan, from Baal-gad in the valley of Lebanon to
Mount Halak, that rises toward Seir (and Joshua gave their land to the tribes of
Israel as a possession according to their allotments, [8]in the hill country, in the lowland, in the Arabah, in the slopes, in the wilderness, and in the Negeb, the land of
the Hittites, Amorites, Canaanites, Perizzites, Hivites, and Jebusites):

12.8 Num 21.1-3 Deut 7.24 Josh 11.16

9 the king of Jericho — one
the king of Ai, which is next to Bethel — one
10 the king of Jerusalem — one
the king of Hebron — one
11 the king of Jarmuth — one

THE CONQUERED LAND
Joshua displayed brilliant military strategy in the way he went about conquering the land of Canaan. He first captured the well-fortified Jericho to gain a foothold in Canaan and to demonstrate the awesome might of the God of Israel. Then he gained the hill country around Bethel and Gibeon. From there he subdued towns in the lowlands. Then his army conquered important cities in the north, such as Hazor. In all, Israel conquered land both east (12.1–6) and west (12.7–24) of the Jordan River; from Mount Hermon in the north to beyond the Negeb to Mount Halak in the south. Thirty-one kings and their cities had been defeated. The Israelites had overpowered the Hittites, the Amorites, the Canaanites, the Perizzites, the Hivites, and the Jebusites. Other peoples living in Canaan were yet to be conquered.

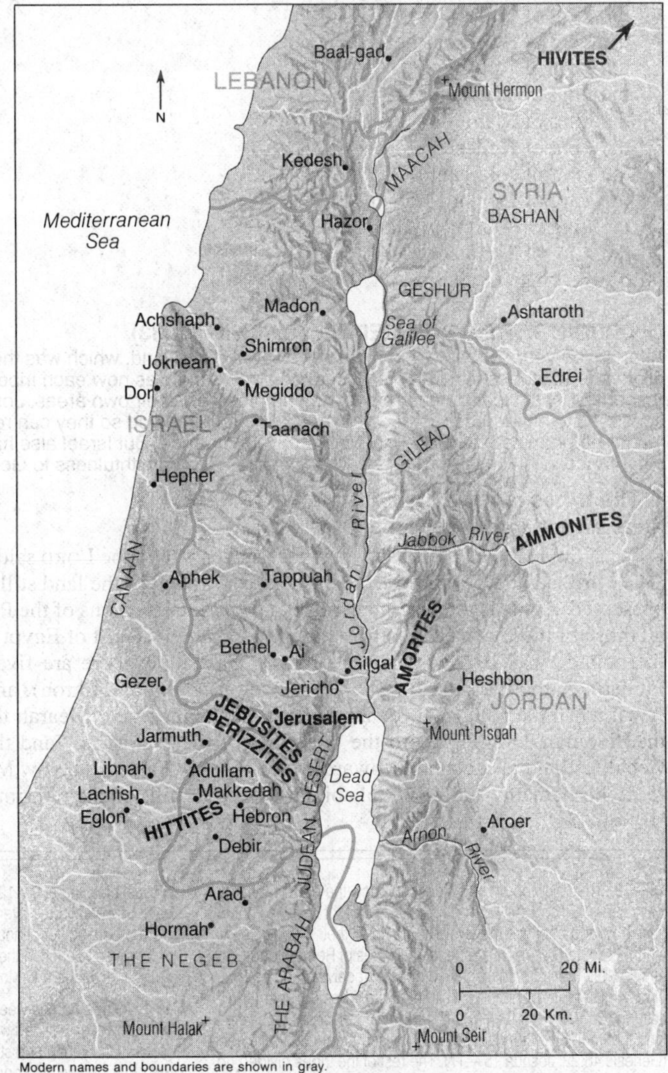

Modern names and boundaries are shown in gray.

	the king of Lachish	one
12	the king of Eglon	one
	the king of Gezer	one
13	the king of Debir	one
	the king of Geder	one
14	the king of Hormah	one
	the king of Arad	one
15	the king of Libnah	one
	the king of Adullam	one
16	the king of Makkedah	one
	the king of Bethel	one
17	the king of Tappuah	one
	the king of Hepher	one
18	the king of Aphek	one
	the king of Lasharon	one
19	the king of Madon	one
	the king of Hazor	one
20	the king of Shimron-meron	one
	the king of Achshaph	one
21	the king of Taanach	one
	the king of Megiddo	one
22	the king of Kedesh	one
	the king of Jokneam in Carmel	one
23	the king of Dor in Naphath-dor	one
	the king of Goiim in Galilee,[t]	one
24	the king of Tirzah	one

thirty-one kings in all.

C. DIVIDING THE PROMISED LAND (13.1—24.33)

After seven years of battle, Israel gained control of the land, which was then divided and allotted to the tribes. Joshua dismisses the army, for it was now each tribe's responsibility to clear out the remaining enemies from their own areas. Joshua continues to encourage the people to remain faithful to God so they can remain in the land. The promised land was Israel's earthly inheritance. But Israel also had a spiritual inheritance in which we can share when we live a life of faithfulness to God.

1. The tribes receive their land

Areas still to be occupied

13 Now Joshua was old and advanced in years; and the LORD said to him, "You
are old and advanced in years, and very much of the land still remains to be
possessed. 2 This is the land that still remains: all the regions of the Philistines, and
all those of the Geshurites 3 (from the Shihor, which is east of Egypt, northward to
the boundary of Ekron, it is reckoned as Canaanite; there are five rulers of the
Philistines, those of Gaza, Ashdod, Ashkelon, Gath, and Ekron), and those of the
Avvim, 4 in the south, all the land of the Canaanites, and Mearah that belongs to
the Sidonians, to Aphek, to the boundary of the Amorites, 5 and the land of the
Gebalites, and all Lebanon, toward the east, from Baal-gad below Mount Hermon
to Lebo-hamath, 6 all the inhabitants of the hill country from Lebanon to

13.1 Josh 14.10

13.2 Josh 12.3; Judg 3.1-3

[t] Gk: Heb *Gilgal*

13–19 The following chapters describe how the promised land was divided among the 12 tribes. First, the tribe of Levi was not to have any land because they were to spend all their energies serving the people (13.14; 21). Second, the tribes of Reuben and Gad and the half-tribe of Manasseh had already received land east of the Jordan River (Numbers 32). Third, the tribes of Judah and Joseph (Ephraim and the other half-tribe of Manasseh) received land that their ancestor Jacob had promised them 450 years earlier (Genesis 48.22; Joshua 15—17). The rest of the tribes divided up the remaining land by casting lots (chapter 18).

Through Jacob's original blessing of his sons (Genesis 49) and Moses' blessing of the 12 tribes (Deuteronomy 33), the type of land each tribe would receive was already known. The two blessings were prophetic, for although Joshua cast lots to determine the land to be given to each of the remaining tribes, the allotments came out just as Jacob and Moses had predicted.

13.1 Joshua was between 85 and 100 years of age at this time. God, however, still had work for him to do. Our culture often glorifies the young and strong and sets aside those who are older. Yet older people are very capable of serving if given the chance and should be encouraged to do so.

Misrephoth-maim, even all the Sidonians. I will myself drive them out from before
the Israelites; only allot the land to Israel for an inheritance, as I have commanded
you. 7 Now therefore divide this land for an inheritance to the nine tribes and the
half-tribe of Manasseh."

Assignment of the land east of the Jordan

13.8 Num 32.33 Deut 3.12 8 With the other half-tribe of Manasseh[u] the Reubenites and the Gadites received their inheritance, which Moses gave them, beyond the Jordan eastward, as
Moses the servant of the LORD gave them: 9 from Aroer, which is on the edge of the
Wadi Arnon, and the town that is in the middle of the valley, and all the tableland
from[v] Medeba as far as Dibon; 10 and all the cities of King Sihon of the Amorites,
who reigned in Heshbon, as far as the boundary of the Ammonites; 11 and Gilead,
and the region of the Geshurites and Maacathites, and all Mount Hermon, and all
13.12 Josh 12.4 Bashan to Salecah; 12 all the kingdom of Og in Bashan, who reigned in Ashtaroth
and in Edrei (he alone was left of the survivors of the Rephaim); these Moses had
13.13 Josh 6.25; 13.13 defeated and driven out. 13 Yet the Israelites did not drive out the Geshurites or the
Maacathites; but Geshur and Maacath live within Israel to this day.
13.14 Deut 18.1 14 To the tribe of Levi alone Moses gave no inheritance; the offerings by fire to
the LORD God of Israel are their inheritance, as he said to them.
13.15 Josh 18.7 15 Moses gave an inheritance to the tribe of the Reubenites according to their

[u] Cn: Heb *With it* [v] Compare Gk: Heb lacks *from*

THE LAND YET TO BE CONQUERED
Canaan was now controlled by the Israelites, although much land and several cities still needed to be conquered. Joshua told the people to include both conquered and unconquered lands in the territorial allotments (13.7). He was certain the people would complete the conquest as God had commanded.

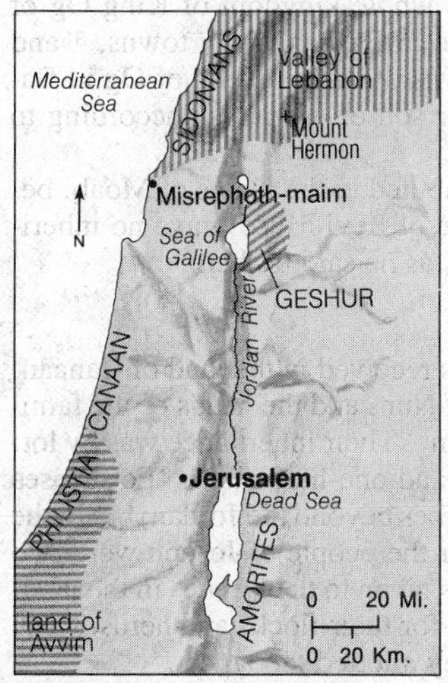

13.7 Much of the land was unconquered at this point, but God's plan was to go ahead and include it in the divisions among the tribes. God's desire was that it would eventually be conquered by the Israelites. God knows the future, and as he leads you he already knows about the victories that lie ahead. But just as the Israelites still had to go to battle and fight, we must still face the trials and fight the battles of our unconquered land.

What are our unconquered lands today? They may be overseas missionary territories, new languages in which to translate the Bible, new missionary areas in our neighborhoods, interest groups or institutions that need redemptive work, unchallenged public problems or ethical issues, unconfessed sin in our lives, or underdeveloped talents and resources. What territory has God given you to conquer? This territory is your "promised land." Our inheritance will be a new heaven and a new earth (Revelation 21.1), if we fulfill the mission God has given us to do.

13.13 One reason the Israelites encountered so many problems as they settled the land was that they failed to conquer *fully* the land and drive out all its inhabitants. The cancer-like presence of the remaining heathen peoples of Canaan caused unending difficulties for the Israelites, as the book of Judges records. Just as they failed to completely remove sin from the land, believers today often fail to completely remove sin from their lives – with equally disastrous results. As a test, reread the ten commandments in Exodus 20.1–17. Ask yourself, "Am I tolerating sinful practices or thoughts? Have I accepted half-measures as good enough? Do I condemn the faults of others, but condone my own?"

THE TRIBES EAST OF THE JORDAN
Joshua assigned territory to the tribes of Reuben, Gad, and the half-tribe of Manasseh on the east side of the Jordan where they had chosen to remain because of the wonderful sheep country (Numbers 32.1–5).

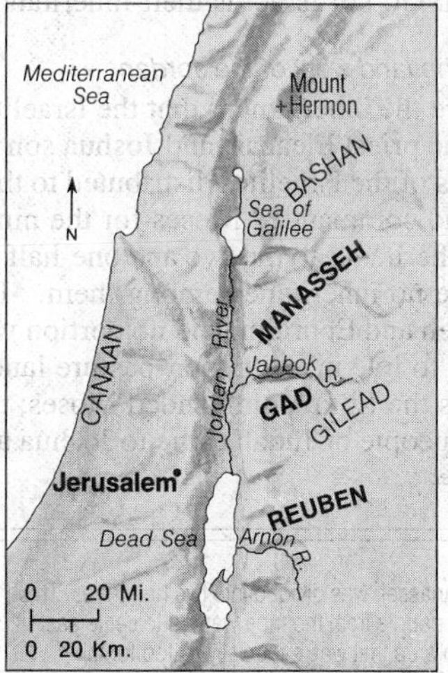

13.15–23 There is often an interesting connection between the land a tribe received and the character of the tribe's founder. For example, because of Joseph's godly character (Genesis 49.22–26), the tribes descended from him – Ephraim and Manasseh – were given the richest, most fertile land in all of Canaan. Judah, who offered himself in exchange for his brother Benjamin's safety (Genesis 44.18–34), received the largest portion of land, which eventually became the Southern Kingdom and the seat of David's dynasty. Reuben, who slept with one of his father's wives (Genesis 49.4), was given desert land, the region described here.

clans. 16 Their territory was from Aroer, which is on the edge of the Wadi Arnon,
and the town that is in the middle of the valley, and all the tableland by Medeba;
17 with Heshbon, and all its towns that are in the tableland; Dibon, and Bamoth-
baal, and Beth-baal-meon, 18 and Jahaz, and Kedemoth, and Mephaath, 19 and Kiriathaim, and Sibmah, and Zereth-shahar on the hill of the valley, 20 and Beth-peor,
and the slopes of Pisgah, and Beth-jeshimoth, 21 that is, all the towns of the table- **13.21**
land, and all the kingdom of King Sihon of the Amorites, who reigned in Heshbon, Num 31.8
whom Moses defeated with the leaders of Midian, Evi and Rekem and Zur and Hur
and Reba, as princes of Sihon, who lived in the land. 22 Along with the rest of those **13.22**
they put to death, the Israelites also put to the sword Balaam son of Beor, who Num 22.5 32.34-36
practiced divination. 23 And the border of the Reubenites was the Jordan and its
banks. This was the inheritance of the Reubenites, according to their families with
their towns and villages.

24 Moses gave an inheritance also to the tribe of the Gadites, according to their
families. 25 Their territory was Jazer, and all the towns of Gilead, and half the land
of the Ammonites, to Aroer, which is east of Rabbah, 26 and from Heshbon to
Ramath-mizpeh and Betonim, and from Mahanaim to the territory of Debir,[w]
27 and in the valley Beth-haram, Beth-nimrah, Succoth, and Zaphon, the rest of the **13.27**
kingdom of King Sihon of Heshbon, the Jordan and its banks, as far as the lower Deut 3.17
end of the Sea of Chinnereth, eastward beyond the Jordan. 28 This is the inheritance
of the Gadites according to their clans, with their towns and villages.

29 Moses gave an inheritance to the half-tribe of Manasseh; it was allotted to
the half-tribe of the Manassites according to their families. 30 Their territory extended from Mahanaim, through all Bashan, the whole kingdom of King Og of
Bashan, and all the settlements of Jair, which are in Bashan, sixty towns, 31 and
half of Gilead, and Ashtaroth, and Edrei, the towns of the kingdom of Og in Bashan; these were allotted to the people of Machir son of Manasseh according to
their clans — for half the Machirites.

32 These are the inheritances that Moses distributed in the plains of Moab, beyond the Jordan east of Jericho. 33 But to the tribe of Levi Moses gave no inheri- **13.33**
tance; the LORD God of Israel is their inheritance, as he said to them. Josh 13.14

Assignment of the land west of the Jordan

14 These are the inheritances that the Israelites received in the land of Canaan, **14.1**
which the priest Eleazar, and Joshua son of Nun, and the heads of the fami- Num 34.10-29 Josh 18.5,6
lies of the tribes of the Israelites distributed to them. 2 Their inheritance was by lot,
as the LORD had commanded Moses for the nine and one-half tribes. 3 For Moses **14.3**
had given an inheritance to the two and one-half tribes beyond the Jordan; but to the Num 32.33 Josh 13.14
Levites he gave no inheritance among them. 4 For the people of Joseph were two
tribes, Manasseh and Ephraim; and no portion was given to the Levites in the land,
but only towns to live in, with their pasture lands for their flocks and herds. 5 The **14.6**
Israelites did as the LORD commanded Moses; they allotted the land. Num 13.30 14.6,24,30
6 Then the people of Judah came to Joshua at Gilgal; and Caleb son of Jephun- Josh 15.13

w Gk Syr Vg: Heb *Lidebir*

13.29 The tribe of Manasseh was divided into two half-tribes. This occurred when many people from the tribe wanted to settle east of the Jordan River in an area that was especially suited for their flocks (Numbers 32.33). The rest of the tribe preferred to settle west of the Jordan River in the land of Canaan.

13.33 The Levites were dedicated to serving God. They needed more time and mobility than a landowner could possibly have. Giving them land would mean saddling them with responsibilities and loyalties that would hinder their service to God. Instead, God arranged for the other tribes to meet the Levites' needs through donations. (See Numbers 35.2–4 for how the Levites were to receive cities within each tribal territory.)

14.5 The land was divided exactly as God had instructed Moses years before. Joshua did not change a word. He followed God's commands precisely. Often we believe that "almost" is close enough, and this idea can carry over into our spiritual life. For example, we may follow God's Word as long as we agree with it, but ignore it when the demands seem harsh. But God is looking for leaders who follow instructions thoroughly.

14.6–12 Caleb was faithful from the start. As one of the original spies sent into the promised land (Numbers 13.30–33), he saw great cities and giants, yet he knew God would help the people conquer the land. Because of his faith, God promised him a personal inheritance of land (Numbers 14.24; Deuteronomy 1.34–36). Now, 45 years later, the land was given to him. His faith was still unwavering. Although his inherited land still had giants, he knew the Lord would help him conquer them. Like Caleb, we must be faithful to God, not only at the start of our walk with him, but

neh the Kenizzite said to him, "You know what the LORD said to Moses the man of
God in Kadesh-barnea concerning you and me. 7 I was forty years old when Moses
the servant of the LORD sent me from Kadesh-barnea to spy out the land; and I
brought him an honest report. 8 But my companions who went up with me made the
14.9 heart of the people melt; yet I wholeheartedly followed the LORD my God. 9 And
Deut 1.36 Moses swore on that day, saying, 'Surely the land on which your foot has trodden
shall be an inheritance for you and your children forever, because you have wholeheartedly followed the LORD my God.' 10 And now, as you see, the LORD has kept
me alive, as he said, these forty-five years since the time that the LORD spoke this
word to Moses, while Israel was journeying through the wilderness; and here I am
today, eighty-five years old. 11 I am still as strong today as I was on the day that
Moses sent me; my strength now is as my strength was then, for war, and for going
14.12 and coming. 12 So now give me this hill country of which the LORD spoke on that
Num 13.33 day; for you heard on that day how the Anakim were there, with great fortified
cities; it may be that the LORD will be with me, and I shall drive them out, as the
LORD said."

13 Then Joshua blessed him, and gave Hebron to Caleb son of Jephunneh for an
inheritance. 14 So Hebron became the inheritance of Caleb son of Jephunneh the
Kenizzite to this day, because he wholeheartedly followed the LORD, the God of
14.15 Israel. 15 Now the name of Hebron formerly was Kiriath-arba;[x] this Arba was[y] the
Gen 35.27 Josh 15.48-62 greatest man among the Anakim. And the land had rest from war.

20.7 Judg 1.10 **15** The lot for the tribe of the people of Judah according to their families
15.1 reached southward to the boundary of Edom, to the wilderness of Zin at the
Num 34.3,4 farthest south. 2 And their south boundary ran from the end of the Dead Sea,[z] from
Deut 32.51 Josh 15.13 the bay that faces southward; 3 it goes out southward of the ascent of Akrabbim,
19.1,36 passes along to Zin, and goes up south of Kadesh-barnea, along by Hezron, up to
Addar, makes a turn to Karka, 4 passes along to Azmon, goes out by the Wadi of
15.5 Egypt, and comes to its end at the sea. This shall be your south boundary. 5 And the
Josh 18.15 east boundary is the Dead Sea,[z] to the mouth of the Jordan. And the boundary on
the north side runs from the bay of the sea at the mouth of the Jordan; 6 and the
boundary goes up to Beth-hoglah, and passes along north of Beth-arabah; and the
boundary goes up to the Stone of Bohan, Reuben's son; 7 and the boundary goes up
to Debir from the Valley of Achor, and so northward, turning toward Gilgal, which
is opposite the ascent of Adummim, which is on the south side of the valley; and the
15.8 boundary passes along to the waters of En-shemesh, and ends at En-rogel; 8 then the
Josh 15.63 boundary goes up by the valley of the son of Hinnom at the southern slope of
the Jebusites (that is, Jerusalem); and the boundary goes up to the top of the mountain that lies over against the valley of Hinnom, on the west, at the northern end of
the valley of Rephaim; 9 then the boundary extends from the top of the mountain to
the spring of the Waters of Nephtoah, and from there to the towns of Mount
Ephron; then the boundary bends around to Baalah (that is, Kiriath-jearim); 10 and
the boundary circles west of Baalah to Mount Seir, passes along to the northern
slope of Mount Jearim (that is, Chesalon), and goes down to Beth-shemesh, and
passes along by Timnah; 11 the boundary goes out to the slope of the hill north of
Ekron, then the boundary bends around to Shikkeron, and passes along to Mount
Baalah, and goes out to Jabneel; then the boundary comes to an end at the sea.

[x] That is *the city of Arba* [y] Heb lacks *this Arba was* [z] Heb *Salt Sea*

---

through our entire lives. We must never allow ourselves to rest on our past accomplishments or reputations.

14.6–12 When Joshua gave Caleb his land, it fulfilled a promise God had made to Caleb 45 years earlier. We expect such integrity and reliability from God, but do we expect the same from his followers? How about you? Is your word this reliable? Would you honor a 45-year-old promise? God would—and does. Even today he is honoring promises he made *thousands* of years ago. In fact, some of his greatest promises are yet to be fulfilled. This gives us much to look forward to. Let your faith grow as you realize how God keeps his word.

14.15 The Anakim were a race of giants who inhabited parts of the land before Israel's conquest.

15.4 Notice that these boundaries and descriptions of the promised land are very specific. God was telling Israel exactly what to do, and he was giving them just what they needed. There was no excuse for disobedience.

12 And the west boundary was the Mediterranean with its coast. This is the boundary surrounding the people of Judah according to their families.

13 According to the commandment of the LORD to Joshua, he gave to Caleb son
of Jephunneh a portion among the people of Judah, Kiriath-arba,[a] that is, Hebron
(Arba was the father of Anak). 14 And Caleb drove out from there the three sons of
Anak: Sheshai, Ahiman, and Talmai, the descendants of Anak. 15 From there he
went up against the inhabitants of Debir; now the name of Debir formerly was
Kiriath-sepher. 16 And Caleb said, "Whoever attacks Kiriath-sepher and takes it, to
him I will give my daughter Achsah as wife." 17 Othniel son of Kenaz, the brother
of Caleb, took it; and he gave him his daughter Achsah as wife. 18 When she came
to him, she urged him to ask her father for a field. As she dismounted from her
donkey, Caleb said to her, "What do you wish?" 19 She said to him, "Give me a
present; since you have set me in the land of the Negeb, give me springs of water
as well." So Caleb gave her the upper springs and the lower springs.

20 This is the inheritance of the tribe of the people of Judah according to
their families. 21 The towns belonging to the tribe of the people of Judah in the
extreme South, toward the boundary of Edom, were Kabzeel, Eder, Jagur, 22 Ki-
nah, Dimonah, Adadah, 23 Kedesh, Hazor, Ithnan, 24 Ziph, Telem, Bealoth,
25 Hazor-hadattah, Kerioth-hezron (that is, Hazor), 26 Amam, Shema, Moladah,
27 Hazar-gaddah, Heshmon, Beth-pelet, 28 Hazar-shual, Beer-sheba, Biziothiah,
29 Baalah, Iim, Ezem, 30 Eltolad, Chesil, Hormah, 31 Ziklag, Madmannah, Sansan-
nah, 32 Lebaoth, Shilhim, Ain, and Rimmon: in all, twenty-nine towns, with their
villages.

33 And in the Lowland, Eshtaol, Zorah, Ashnah, 34 Zanoah, En-gannim, Tappuah, Enam, 35 Jarmuth, Adullam, Socoh, Azekah, 36 Shaaraim, Adithaim, Gederah, Gederothaim: fourteen towns with their villages.

37 Zenan, Hadashah, Migdal-gad, 38 Dilan, Mizpeh, Jokthe-el, 39 Lachish,
Bozkath, Eglon, 40 Cabbon, Lahmam, Chitlish, 41 Gederoth, Beth-dagon, Naamah, and Makkedah: sixteen towns with their villages.

42 Libnah, Ether, Ashan, 43 Iphtah, Ashnah, Nezib, 44 Keilah, Achzib, and
Mareshah: nine towns with their villages.

45 Ekron, with its dependencies and its villages; 46 from Ekron to the sea, all
that were near Ashdod, with their villages.

47 Ashdod, its towns and its villages; Gaza, its towns and its villages; to the
Wadi of Egypt, and the Great Sea with its coast.

48 And in the hill country, Shamir, Jattir, Socoh, 49 Dannah, Kiriath-sannah
(that is, Debir), 50 Anab, Eshtemoh, Anim, 51 Goshen, Holon, and Giloh: eleven
towns with their villages.

52 Arab, Dumah, Eshan, 53 Janim, Beth-tappuah, Aphekah, 54 Humtah,
Kiriath-arba (that is, Hebron), and Zior: nine towns with their villages.

55 Maon, Carmel, Ziph, Juttah, 56 Jezreel, Jokdeam, Zanoah, 57 Kain, Gibeah,
and Timnah: ten towns with their villages.

58 Halhul, Beth-zur, Gedor, 59 Maarath, Beth-anoth, and Eltekon: six towns
with their villages.

60 Kiriath-baal (that is, Kiriath-jearim), and Rabbah: two towns with their villages.

61 In the wilderness, Beth-arabah, Middin, Secacah, 62 Nibshan, the City of
Salt, and En-gedi: six towns with their villages.

63 But the people of Judah could not drive out the Jebusites, the inhabitants of
Jerusalem; so the Jebusites live with the people of Judah in Jerusalem to this day.

[a] That is *the city of Arba*

15.13 Josh 14.13-15 Judg 1.12-15
15.14 Num 13.33 Deut 9.2 Josh 11.21,22
15.17 Judg 1.13; 3.9
15.21 Gen 21.31 35.21 1 Sam 27.6 30.1 2 Kgs 14.19
15.33 Judg 13.25 16.31 1 Sam 22.1
15.37 Josh 10.3 2 Kgs 14.19
15.47 Josh 13.2-7
15.63 Judg 1.21 2 Sam 5.6

15.16–19 Othniel became Israel's first judge after Joshua's death (Judges 1.13; 3.9–11). He played an important role in reforming Israel by chasing away an oppressive enemy army and bringing peace back to the land. Thus Caleb's legacy of faithfulness continued to the next generation.

15.19 Achsah asked Caleb for springs of water because her land was in the south and was very arid. Caleb probably granted her request as a wedding present (see 15.17).

16.1 Josh 8.15; 10.33; 18.13; 1 Kgs 9.17

16 The allotment of the Josephites went from the Jordan by Jericho, east of the
waters of Jericho, into the wilderness, going up from Jericho into the hill
country to Bethel; 2 then going from Bethel to Luz, it passes along to Ataroth, the
territory of the Archites; 3 then it goes down westward to the territory of the Japhle-
tites, as far as the territory of Lower Beth-horon, then to Gezer, and it ends at the
sea.

4 The Josephites — Manasseh and Ephraim — received their inheritance.

16.5 Josh 17.7; 18.13

5 The territory of the Ephraimites by their families was as follows: the boundary
of their inheritance on the east was Ataroth-addar as far as Upper Beth-horon, 6 and
the boundary goes from there to the sea; on the north is Michmethath; then on the
east the boundary makes a turn toward Taanath-shiloh, and passes along beyond it
on the east to Janoah, 7 then it goes down from Janoah to Ataroth and to Naarah,

16.8 Josh 17.8

and touches Jericho, ending at the Jordan. 8 From Tappuah the boundary goes westward to the Wadi Kanah, and ends at the sea. Such is the inheritance of the tribe of
the Ephraimites by their families, 9 together with the towns that were set apart for
the Ephraimites within the inheritance of the Manassites, all those towns with their

16.10 Josh 13.13; 15.63; 17.12,13; Judg 1.29; 1 Kgs 9.16

villages. 10 They did not, however, drive out the Canaanites who lived in Gezer: so
the Canaanites have lived within Ephraim to this day but have been made to do
forced labor.

17.1 Josh 13.8

17 Then allotment was made to the tribe of Manasseh, for he was the firstborn
of Joseph. To Machir the firstborn of Manasseh, the father of Gilead, were
allotted Gilead and Bashan, because he was a warrior. 2 And allotments were made
to the rest of the tribe of Manasseh, by their families, Abiezer, Helek, Asriel, Shechem, Hepher, and Shemida; these were the male descendants of Manasseh son of
Joseph, by their families.

17.3 Num 26.28-37; 27.1-7; 36.1-12

3 Now Zelophehad son of Hepher son of Gilead son of Machir son of Manasseh
had no sons, but only daughters; and these are the names of his daughters: Mahlah,
Noah, Hoglah, Milcah, and Tirzah. 4 They came before the priest Eleazar and
Joshua son of Nun and the leaders, and said, "The LORD commanded Moses to give
us an inheritance along with our male kin." So according to the commandment of

17.5 Josh 13.30

the LORD he gave them an inheritance among the kinsmen of their father. 5 Thus
there fell to Manasseh ten portions, besides the land of Gilead and Bashan, which
is on the other side of the Jordan, 6 because the daughters of Manasseh received an
inheritance along with his sons. The land of Gilead was allotted to the rest of the
Manassites.

7 The territory of Manasseh reached from Asher to Michmethath, which is east
of Shechem; then the boundary goes along southward to the inhabitants of En-
tappuah. 8 The land of Tappuah belonged to Manasseh, but the town of Tappuah on
the boundary of Manasseh belonged to the Ephraimites. 9 Then the boundary went
down to the Wadi Kanah. The towns here, to the south of the wadi, among the
towns of Manasseh, belong to Ephraim. Then the boundary of Manasseh goes
along the north side of the wadi and ends at the sea. 10 The land to the south is
Ephraim's and that to the north is Manasseh's, with the sea forming its boundary;

17.11 1 Chron 7.29

on the north Asher is reached, and on the east Issachar. 11 Within Issachar and
Asher, Manasseh had Beth-shean and its villages, Ibleam and its villages, the inhabitants of Dor and its villages, the inhabitants of En-dor and its villages, the

---

16.1ff Although Joseph was one of Jacob's 12 sons, he did not have a tribe named after him. This was because Joseph, as the oldest son of Jacob's wife Rachel, received a double portion of the inheritance. This double portion was given to Joseph's two sons, Ephraim and Manasseh, whom Jacob considered as his own (Genesis 48.5). The largest territory and the greatest influence in the northern half of Israel belonged to their tribes.

16.10 Occasionally this short phrase appears: "they did not . . . drive out the Canaanites" (see also 15.63; 17.12). This was contrary to God's explicit desire and command (13.1–6). The failure to remove completely the pagan people and their gods from the land would cause many problems for the nation. The book of Judges records many of these struggles.

17.3, 4 Although women did not traditionally inherit property in Israelite society, Moses put justice ahead of tradition and gave these five women the land they deserved (see Numbers 27.1–11). In fact, God told Moses to add a law that would help other women in similar circumstances inherit property. Joshua was now carrying out this law. It is easy to refuse to honor a reasonable request because "things have never been done that way before." But, like Moses and Joshua, it is best to look carefully at the purpose of the law and the merits of each case before deciding.

inhabitants of Taanach and its villages, and the inhabitants of Megiddo and its villages (the third is Naphath).[b] 12 Yet the Manassites could not take possession of 17.12
those towns; but the Canaanites continued to live in that land. 13 But when the Isra- Josh 16.10 Judg 1.27
elites grew strong, they put the Canaanites to forced labor, but did not utterly drive
them out.

14 The tribe of Joseph spoke to Joshua, saying, "Why have you given me but 17.14
one lot and one portion as an inheritance, since we are a numerous people, whom Num 26.28-37
all along the LORD has blessed?" 15 And Joshua said to them, "If you are a numerous
people, go up to the forest, and clear ground there for yourselves in the land of the
Perizzites and the Rephaim, since the hill country of Ephraim is too narrow for
you." 16 The tribe of Joseph said, "The hill country is not enough for us; yet all the 17.16
Canaanites who live in the plain have chariots of iron, both those in Beth-shean and Judg 1.19
its villages and those in the Valley of Jezreel." 17 Then Joshua said to the house of 4.3,13
Joseph, to Ephraim and Manasseh, "You are indeed a numerous people, and have
great power; you shall not have one lot only, 18 but the hill country shall be yours,
for though it is a forest, you shall clear it and possess it to its farthest borders; for
you shall drive out the Canaanites, though they have chariots of iron, and though
they are strong."

The remaining tribes receive their territory

18 Then the whole congregation of the Israelites assembled at Shiloh, and set 18.1
up the tent of meeting there. The land lay subdued before them. Gen 49.10 Deut 12.10,11
2 There remained among the Israelites seven tribes whose inheritance had not Judg 21.19
yet been apportioned. 3 So Joshua said to the Israelites, "How long will you be slack 18.3
about going in and taking possession of the land that the LORD, the God of your Josh 14.1

[b] Meaning of Heb uncertain

17.14, 15 Notice the two contrasting attitudes toward settling the promised land: Caleb took what God gave him and moved ahead to fulfill God's plan for him (14.12). He was confident that God would help him drive out the wicked inhabitants and that he would soon fully occupy his land (15.14, 15). In contrast, the two tribes of Joseph were given rich land and lots of it, but they were afraid to drive out the inhabitants and take full possession of it. Instead they begged for more land. But Joshua asked them to prove their sincerity first by clearing the unclaimed forest areas. They agreed, but they failed to carry through (Judges 1.27).

18.1, 2 With most of the conquest behind them, Israel moved their religious center from Gilgal (see note on 5.8, 9) to Shiloh. This was probably the first place where the tabernacle was set up permanently. The tent of meeting was part of the tabernacle and was where God lived among his people (Exodus 25.8). Its central location in the land made it easier for the people to attend the special worship services and yearly festivals.

The family of Samuel, a great priest and prophet, often traveled to Shiloh, and Samuel was taken there when he was a small boy (1 Samuel 1.3, 22). The tabernacle remained in Shiloh through the period of the judges (about 300 years). Apparently the city was destroyed by the Philistines when the ark of the covenant was captured (1 Samuel 4, 5). Shiloh never lived up to its reputation as Israel's religious center, for later references in the Bible point to the wickedness and idolatry in the city (Psalm 78.56–60; Jeremiah 7.12–15).

18.3ff Seven of the tribes had not yet been assigned their land. They gathered at Shiloh, where Joshua cast lots to determine which areas would be given to them. Using the sacred lottery, God would make the choice, not Joshua or any other human leader.

By this time, the Canaanites were, in most places, so weakened that they were no longer a threat. Instead of fulfilling God's command to destroy the remaining Canaanites, however, these seven tribes would often take the path of least resistance. As nomadic people, they may have been reluctant to settle down, preferring to depend economically on the people they were supposed to eliminate. Others may have feared the high cost of continued warfare. It was easier and more profitable to trade for goods than to destroy the suppliers and have to provide for themselves.

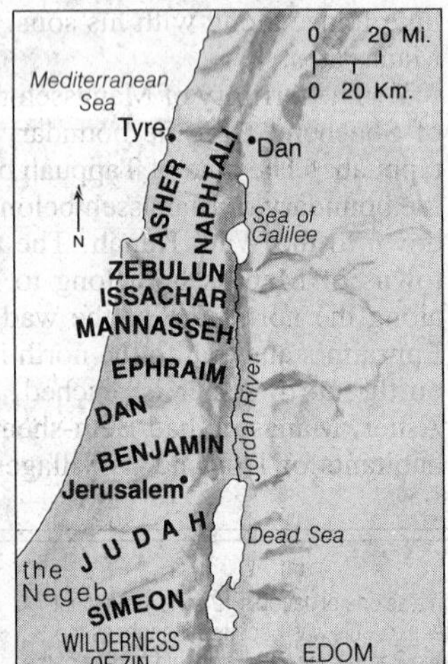

THE TRIBES WEST OF THE JORDAN
Judah, Ephraim, and the other half-tribe of Manasseh were the first tribes to receive land west of the Jordan because of their past acts of faith. The remaining seven tribes—Benjamin, Zebulun, Issachar, Asher, Naphtali, Simeon, and Dan—were slow to conquer and possess the land allotted to them.

18.3–6 Joshua asked why some of the tribes were putting off the job of possessing the land. Often we delay doing jobs that seem large, difficult, boring, or disagreeable. But to continue putting them off shows lack of discipline, poor stewardship of time, and in some cases disobedience to God. Jobs we don't enjoy require concentration, teamwork, twice as much time, lots of encouragement, and accountability. Remember this when you are tempted to procrastinate.

ancestors, has given you? 4 Provide three men from each tribe, and I will send them
out that they may begin to go throughout the land, writing a description of it with
a view to their inheritances. Then come back to me. 5 They shall divide it into seven
portions, Judah continuing in its territory on the south, and the house of Joseph in
their territory on the north. 6 You shall describe the land in seven divisions and
bring the description here to me; and I will cast lots for you here before the LORD
18.7 our God. 7 The Levites have no portion among you, for the priesthood of the LORD
Num 18.7,20 is their heritage; and Gad and Reuben and the half-tribe of Manasseh have received
Josh 13.32,33 their inheritance beyond the Jordan eastward, which Moses the servant of the LORD
gave them."

18.8 8 So the men started on their way; and Joshua charged those who went to write
Judg 1.22 the description of the land, saying, "Go throughout the land and write a description
of it, and come back to me; and I will cast lots for you here before the LORD in
Shiloh." 9 So the men went and traversed the land and set down in a book a descrip-
tion of it by towns in seven divisions; then they came back to Joshua in the camp at
18.10 Shiloh, 10 and Joshua cast lots for them in Shiloh before the LORD; and there Joshua
Num 34.16-29 apportioned the land to the Israelites, to each a portion.
Josh 19.51

11 The lot of the tribe of Benjamin according to its families came up, and the
territory allotted to it fell between the tribe of Judah and the tribe of Joseph. 12 On
the north side their boundary began at the Jordan; then the boundary goes up to the
slope of Jericho on the north, then up through the hill country westward; and it ends
at the wilderness of Beth-aven. 13 From there the boundary passes along southward
in the direction of Luz, to the slope of Luz (that is, Bethel), then the boundary goes
down to Ataroth-addar, on the mountain that lies south of Lower Beth-horon.
18.14 14 Then the boundary goes in another direction, turning on the western side south-
Josh 15.9,48-62 ward from the mountain that lies to the south, opposite Beth-horon, and it ends at
Kiriath-baal (that is, Kiriath-jearim), a town belonging to the tribe of Judah. This
forms the western side. 15 The southern side begins at the outskirts of Kiriath-
jearim; and the boundary goes from there to Ephron,[c] to the spring of the Waters
of Nephtoah; 16 then the boundary goes down to the border of the mountain that
overlooks the valley of the son of Hinnom, which is at the north end of the valley
of Rephaim; and it then goes down the valley of Hinnom, south of the slope of the
Jebusites, and downward to En-rogel; 17 then it bends in a northerly direction going
on to En-shemesh, and from there goes to Geliloth, which is opposite the ascent of
Adummim; then it goes down to the Stone of Bohan, Reuben's son; 18 and passing
on to the north of the slope of Beth-arabah[d] it goes down to the Arabah; 19 then the
boundary passes on to the north of the slope of Beth-hoglah; and the boundary ends
at the northern bay of the Dead Sea,[e] at the south end of the Jordan: this is the
southern border. 20 The Jordan forms its boundary on the eastern side. This is the
inheritance of the tribe of Benjamin, according to its families, boundary by boundary all around.

21 Now the towns of the tribe of Benjamin according to their families were
Jericho, Beth-hoglah, Emek-keziz, 22 Beth-arabah, Zemaraim, Bethel, 23 Avvim,
Parah, Ophrah, 24 Chephar-ammoni, Ophni, and Geba—twelve towns with their
villages: 25 Gibeon, Ramah, Beeroth, 26 Mizpeh, Chephirah, Mozah, 27 Rekem, Ir-
peel, Taralah, 28 Zela, Haeleph, Jebus[f] (that is, Jerusalem), Gibeah[g] and Kiriath-

[c] Cn See 15.9. Heb *westward* [d] Gk: Heb *to the slope over against the Arabah* [e] Heb *Salt Sea* [f] Gk Syr Vg: Heb *the Jebusite* [g] Heb *Gibeath*

18.8 Making decisions by casting lots was a common practice among the Hebrews. Little is known about the actual method used in Joshua's day. Dice may have been used. Another possibility is that two urns were used: one containing tribal names; the other, the divisions of the land. Drawing one name from each urn matched a tribe to a region. The Urim and Thummim (explained in the note on Leviticus 8.8) may also have been used. No matter how it was done, the process removed human choice from the decision-making process and allowed God to match tribes and lands as he saw fit.

18.11 The tribe of Benjamin was given a narrow strip of land that served as a buffer zone between Judah and Ephraim, the two tribes that would later dominate the land.

18.16 "The valley of Hinnom" became associated with the worship of Molech (the Ammonite god) in Jeremiah's time. These terrible rites involved the sacrifice of children. Later the valley was used for burning garbage and the corpses of criminals and animals. Thus the name became a synonym for hell.

jearim[h] — fourteen towns with their villages. This is the inheritance of the tribe of
Benjamin according to its families.

19 The second lot came out for Simeon, for the tribe of Simeon, according to its
families; its inheritance lay within the inheritance of the tribe of Judah. 2 It
had for its inheritance Beer-sheba, Sheba, Moladah, 3 Hazar-shual, Balah, Ezem,
4 Eltolad, Bethul, Hormah, 5 Ziklag, Beth-marcaboth, Hazar-susah, 6 Beth-lebaoth,
and Sharuhen — thirteen towns with their villages; 7 Ain, Rimmon, Ether, and
Ashan — four towns with their villages; 8 together with all the villages all around
these towns as far as Baalath-beer, Ramah of the Negeb. This was the inheritance
of the tribe of Simeon according to its families. 9 The inheritance of the tribe of
Simeon formed part of the territory of Judah; because the portion of the tribe of
Judah was too large for them, the tribe of Simeon obtained an inheritance within
their inheritance.

10 The third lot came up for the tribe of Zebulun, according to its families. The
boundary of its inheritance reached as far as Sarid; 11 then its boundary goes up
westward, and on to Maralah, and touches Dabbesheth, then the wadi that is east of
Jokneam; 12 from Sarid it goes in the other direction eastward toward the sunrise to
the boundary of Chisloth-tabor; from there it goes to Daberath, then up to Japhia;
13 from there it passes along on the east toward the sunrise to Gath-hepher, to Eth-
kazin, and going on to Rimmon it bends toward Neah; 14 then on the north the
boundary makes a turn to Hannathon, and it ends at the valley of Iphtah-el; 15 and
Kattath, Nahalal, Shimron, Idalah, and Bethlehem — twelve towns with their villages. 16 This is the inheritance of the tribe of Zebulun, according to its
families — these towns with their villages.

17 The fourth lot came out for Issachar, for the tribe of Issachar, according to
its families. 18 Its territory included Jezreel, Chesulloth, Shunem, 19 Hapharaim,
Shion, Anaharath, 20 Rabbith, Kishion, Ebez, 21 Remeth, En-gannim, En-haddah,
Beth-pazzez; 22 the boundary also touches Tabor, Shahazumah, and Beth-shemesh,
and its boundary ends at the Jordan — sixteen towns with their villages. 23 This is
the inheritance of the tribe of Issachar, according to its families — the towns with
their villages.

24 The fifth lot came out for the tribe of Asher according to its families. 25 Its
boundary included Helkath, Hali, Beten, Achshaph, 26 Allammelech, Amad, and
Mishal; on the west it touches Carmel and Shihor-libnath, 27 then it turns eastward,
goes to Beth-dagon, and touches Zebulun and the valley of Iphtah-el northward to
Beth-emek and Neiel; then it continues in the north to Cabul, 28 Ebron, Rehob,
Hammon, Kanah, as far as Sidon the Great; 29 then the boundary turns to Ramah,
reaching to the fortified city of Tyre; then the boundary turns to Hosah, and it ends
at the sea; Mahalab,[i] Achzib, 30 Ummah, Aphek, and Rehob — twenty-two towns
with their villages. 31 This is the inheritance of the tribe of Asher according to its
families — these towns with their villages.

32 The sixth lot came out for the tribe of Naphtali, for the tribe of Naphtali,
according to its families. 33 And its boundary ran from Heleph, from the oak in
Zaanannim, and Adami-nekeb, and Jabneel, as far as Lakkum; and it ended at the
Jordan; 34 then the boundary turns westward to Aznoth-tabor, and goes from there
to Hukkok, touching Zebulun at the south, and Asher on the west, and Judah on the
east at the Jordan. 35 The fortified towns are Ziddim, Zer, Hammath, Rakkath,
Chinnereth, 36 Adamah, Ramah, Hazor, 37 Kedesh, Edrei, En-hazor, 38 Iron,
Migdal-el, Horem, Beth-anath, and Beth-shemesh — nineteen towns with their
villages. 39 This is the inheritance of the tribe of Naphtali according to its
families — the towns with their villages.

40 The seventh lot came out for the tribe of Dan, according to its families.
41 The territory of its inheritance included Zorah, Eshtaol, Ir-shemesh, 42 Shaalab-
bin, Aijalon, Ithlah, 43 Elon, Timnah, Ekron, 44 Eltekeh, Gibbethon, Baalath, 45 Je-
hud, Bene-berak, Gath-rimmon, 46 Me-jarkon, and Rakkon at the border opposite
Joppa. 47 When the territory of the Danites was lost to them, the Danites went
up and fought against Leshem, and after capturing it and putting it to the sword,

[h] Gk: Heb *Kiriath* [i] Cn Compare Gk: Heb *Mehebel*

they took possession of it and settled in it, calling Leshem, Dan, after their ancestor
Dan. 48 This is the inheritance of the tribe of Dan, according to their
families — these towns with their villages.

Land is given to Joshua

49 When they had finished distributing the several territories of the land as inheritances, the Israelites gave an inheritance among them to Joshua son of Nun.
19.50 Josh 24.30 Judg 2.7-9 50 By command of the LORD they gave him the town that he asked for, Timnath-
serah in the hill country of Ephraim; he rebuilt the town, and settled in it.
19.51 Josh 14.1; 18.10 51 These are the inheritances that the priest Eleazar and Joshua son of Nun and
the heads of the families of the tribes of the Israelites distributed by lot at Shiloh
before the LORD, at the entrance of the tent of meeting. So they finished dividing
the land.

2. Special cities are set aside

Cities of refuge named

20.2 Num 35.6 Deut 4.41 19.2,3 1 Chron 6.58,59 **20** Then the LORD spoke to Joshua, saying, 2 "Say to the Israelites, 'Appoint the
cities of refuge, of which I spoke to you through Moses, 3 so that anyone
who kills a person without intent or by mistake may flee there; they shall be for you
a refuge from the avenger of blood. 4 The slayer shall flee to one of these cities and
shall stand at the entrance of the gate of the city, and explain the case to the elders
of that city; then the fugitive shall be taken into the city, and given a place, and shall
remain with them. 5 And if the avenger of blood is in pursuit, they shall not give up
the slayer, because the neighbor was killed by mistake, there having been no enmity between them before. 6 The slayer shall remain in that city until there is a trial
before the congregation, until the death of the one who is high priest at the time:
then the slayer may return home, to the town in which the deed was done.' "
20.7 Josh 21.9-16,32 1 Chron 6.76 Lk 1.39 7 So they set apart Kedesh in Galilee in the hill country of Naphtali, and Shechem in the hill country of Ephraim, and Kiriath-arba (that is, Hebron) in the hill
country of Judah. 8 And beyond the Jordan east of Jericho, they appointed Bezer in
the wilderness on the tableland, from the tribe of Reuben, and Ramoth in Gilead,

---

19.47, 48 The tribe of Dan thought that some of their land looked difficult to conquer, so they chose to migrate to Leshem where they knew victory would be easier. Anyone can trust God when the going is easy. It is when everything looks impossible that our faith and courage are put to the test. Have faith that God is great enough to tackle your most difficult situations.

19.49 There were several good reasons for establishing these well-set boundaries instead of turning the promised land into a single undivided nation. (1) The boundaries gave each tribe ownership of an area, promoting loyalty and unity that would strengthen each tribe. (2) The boundaries delineated areas of responsibility and privilege, which would help each tribe develop and mature. (3) The boundaries reduced conflicts that might have broken out if everyone had wanted to live in the choicest areas. (4) The boundaries fulfilled the promised inheritance to each tribe that began to be given as early as the days of Jacob (Genesis 48.21, 22).

19.50 After the land was divided and given to each tribe, Joshua was given his own inheritance, a city of his choosing. This was probably given to him in recognition of his devotion to God and strong leadership. God-fearing and faithful leaders are scarce, and too often we take them for granted. Then, when they are gone, we grieve over the loss. Don't wait until it's too late. Honor and thank your leaders now while you still have them.

20.6 A new nation in a new land needed a new government. Many years earlier God had told Moses how this government should function. One of the tasks God wanted the Israelites to do when they entered the promised land was to designate certain cities as "cities of refuge." These were to be scattered throughout the land. Their purpose was to prevent injustice, especially in cases of revenge. For example, if someone accidentally killed another person, he could flee to a city of refuge where he was safe until he could have a fair trial. The Levites were in charge of these cities. They were to ensure that God's principles of justice and fairness were kept. (For more on cities of refuge, see the notes on Numbers 35.6; 35.11–28.)

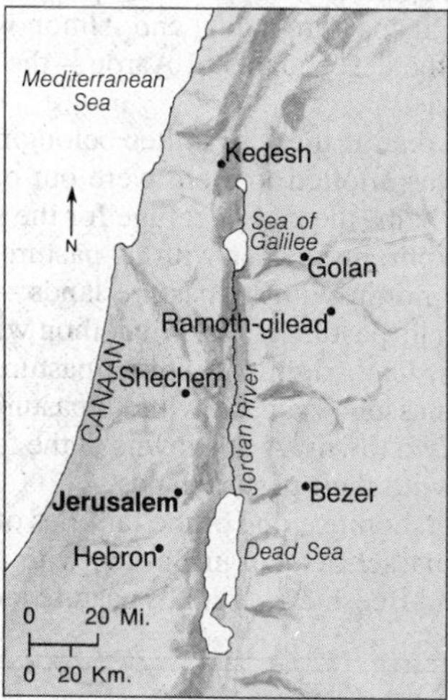

THE CITIES OF REFUGE
A city of refuge was just that—refuge for someone who committed an unintentional murder which would evoke revenge from the victim's friends and relatives. The six cities of refuge were spaced throughout the land so that a person was never too far from one.

from the tribe of Gad, and Golan in Bashan, from the tribe of Manasseh. 9 These
were the cities designated for all the Israelites, and for the aliens residing among
them, that anyone who killed a person without intent could flee there, so as not to
die by the hand of the avenger of blood, until there was a trial before the congregation.

Cities given to the Levites

21 Then the heads of the families of the Levites came to the priest Eleazar and **21.1**
to Joshua son of Nun and to the heads of the families of the tribes of the Josh 14.1; 17.4
Israelites; 2 they said to them at Shiloh in the land of Canaan, "The LORD com- **21.2**
manded through Moses that we be given towns to live in, along with their pasture Num 35.1,2 1 Chron 6.54
lands for our livestock." 3 So by command of the LORD the Israelites gave to the
Levites the following towns and pasture lands out of their inheritance.
4 The lot came out for the families of the Kohathites. So those Levites who
were descendants of Aaron the priest received by lot thirteen towns from the tribes
of Judah, Simeon, and Benjamin.
5 The rest of the Kohathites received by lot ten towns from the families of the
tribe of Ephraim, from the tribe of Dan, and the half-tribe of Manasseh.
6 The Gershonites received by lot thirteen towns from the families of the tribe
of Issachar, from the tribe of Asher, from the tribe of Naphtali, and from the half-
tribe of Manasseh in Bashan.
7 The Merarites according to their families received twelve towns from the tribe
of Reuben, the tribe of Gad, and the tribe of Zebulun.
8 These towns and their pasture lands the Israelites gave by lot to the Levites,
as the LORD had commanded through Moses.
9 Out of the tribe of Judah and the tribe of Simeon they gave the following
towns mentioned by name, 10 which went to the descendants of Aaron, one of the
families of the Kohathites who belonged to the Levites, since the lot fell to them
first. 11 They gave them Kiriath-arba (Arba being the father of Anak), that is Hebron, in the hill country of Judah, along with the pasture lands around it. 12 But the
fields of the town and its villages had been given to Caleb son of Jephunneh as his
holding.
13 To the descendants of Aaron the priest they gave Hebron, the city of refuge
for the slayer, with its pasture lands, Libnah with its pasture lands, 14 Jattir with its
pasture lands, Eshtemoa with its pasture lands, 15 Holon with its pasture lands, Debir with its pasture lands, 16 Ain with its pasture lands, Juttah with its pasture lands,
and Beth-shemesh with its pasture lands—nine towns out of these two tribes. 17 Out
of the tribe of Benjamin: Gibeon with its pasture lands, Geba with its pasture lands,
18 Anathoth with its pasture lands, and Almon with its pasture lands—four towns.
19 The towns of the descendants of Aaron—the priests—were thirteen in all, with
their pasture lands.
20 As to the rest of the Kohathites belonging to the Kohathite families of the
Levites, the towns allotted to them were out of the tribe of Ephraim. 21 To them
were given Shechem, the city of refuge for the slayer, with its pasture lands in the
hill country of Ephraim, Gezer with its pasture lands, 22 Kibzaim with its pasture
lands, and Beth-horon with its pasture lands—four towns. 23 Out of the tribe of
Dan: Elteke with its pasture lands, Gibbethon with its pasture lands, 24 Aijalon with
its pasture lands, Gath-rimmon with its pasture lands—four towns. 25 Out of the
half-tribe of Manasseh: Taanach with its pasture lands, and Gath-rimmon with its
pasture lands—two towns. 26 The towns of the families of the rest of the Kohathites
were ten in all, with their pasture lands.
27 To the Gershonites, one of the families of the Levites, were given out of the
half-tribe of Manasseh, Golan in Bashan with its pasture lands, the city of refuge
for the slayer, and Beeshterah with its pasture lands—two towns. 28 Out of the tribe

---

21.2 The Levites were to minister before God on behalf of all the people, so they were given cities scattered throughout the land. Although Jerusalem was far away from the homes of many Israelites, almost no one lived more than a day's journey from a levitical city.

of Issachar: Kishion with its pasture lands, Daberath with its pasture lands, 29 Jarmuth with its pasture lands, En-gannim with its pasture lands — four towns; 30 Out
of the tribe of Asher: Mishal with its pasture lands, Abdon with its pasture lands,
31 Helkath with its pasture lands, and Rehob with its pasture lands — four towns.
32 Out of the tribe of Naphtali: Kedesh in Galilee with its pasture lands, the city of
refuge for the slayer, Hammoth-dor with its pasture lands, and Kartan with its pasture lands — three towns. 33 The towns of the several families of the Gershonites
were in all thirteen, with their pasture lands.

34 To the rest of the Levites — the Merarite families — were given out of the
tribe of Zebulun: Jokneam with its pasture lands, Kartah with its pasture lands,
35 Dimnah with its pasture lands, Nahalal with its pasture lands — four towns. 36 Out
of the tribe of Reuben: Bezer with its pasture lands, Jahzah with its pasture lands,
37 Kedemoth with its pasture lands, and Mephaath with its pasture lands — four
towns. 38 Out of the tribe of Gad: Ramoth in Gilead with its pasture lands, the city
of refuge for the slayer, Mahanaim with its pasture lands, 39 Heshbon with its pasture lands, Jazer with its pasture lands — four towns in all. 40 As for the towns of the
several Merarite families, that is, the remainder of the families of the Levites, those
allotted to them were twelve in all.

21.41 Num 35.7 41 The towns of the Levites within the holdings of the Israelites were in all
forty-eight towns with their pasture lands. 42 Each of these towns had its pasture
lands around it; so it was with all these towns.

The Lord gives the nation peace

21.43 Num 33.53 Deut 11.31 17.14; 34.4 43 Thus the LORD gave to Israel all the land that he swore to their ancestors that
he would give them; and having taken possession of it, they settled there. 44 And the
LORD gave them rest on every side just as he had sworn to their ancestors; not one
21.44 Ex 23.31 Deut 7.24 of all their enemies had withstood them, for the LORD had given all their enemies
into their hands. 45 Not one of all the good promises that the LORD had made to the
house of Israel had failed; all came to pass.

3. The eastern tribes build an altar

22.1 Num 32.29-41 **22** Then Joshua summoned the Reubenites, the Gadites, and the half-tribe of
22.2 Josh 1.12-18 Manasseh, 2 and said to them, "You have observed all that Moses the servant of the LORD commanded you, and have obeyed me in all that I have commanded you; 3 you have not forsaken your kindred these many days, down to this
22.4 Num 32.18 Deut 3.20 day, but have been careful to keep the charge of the LORD your God. 4 And now the
LORD your God has given rest to your kindred, as he promised them; therefore turn
and go to your tents in the land where your possession lies, which Moses the ser-
22.5 Deut 5.1 vant of the LORD gave you on the other side of the Jordan. 5 Take good care to
observe the commandment and instruction that Moses the servant of the LORD commanded you, to love the LORD your God, to walk in all his ways, to keep his commandments, and to hold fast to him, and to serve him with all your heart and with
all your soul." 6 So Joshua blessed them and sent them away, and they went to their
22.7 Num 32.33 Josh 17.1 tents.

7 Now to the one half of the tribe of Manasseh Moses had given a possession in

---

21.43–45 God proved faithful in fulfilling every promise he had given to Israel. Fulfillment of some promises took several years, but "all came to pass." His promises will be fulfilled according to his timetable, not ours, but we know that his word is sure. The more we learn of those promises God has fulfilled and continues to fulfill, the easier it is to hope for those yet to come. It is easy to become impatient, wanting God to act in a certain way *now.* Instead, we should faithfully do what we know he wants us to do and trust him for the future.

22.2–4 Before the conquest had begun, these tribes were given land on the east side of the Jordan River. But before they could settle down, they had to first promise to help the other tribes conquer the land on the west side (Numbers 32.20–22). They had patiently and diligently carried out their promised duties. Joshua now commended them for doing just that. At last they were permitted to return to their families and build their cities. Follow-through is vital in God's work. Beware of the temptation to quit early and leave God's work undone.

22.5 Here Joshua briefly restated the central message Moses gave the people in Deuteronomy: obedience should be based on love for God. Although the Israelites had completed their military responsibility, Joshua reminded them of their spiritual responsibility. Sometimes we think so much about what we are to do that we neglect thinking about who we are to be. If we know we are God's children, we will love him and joyfully serve him. We must not let daily service take away from our love for God.

Bashan; but to the other half Joshua had given a possession beside their fellow
Israelites in the land west of the Jordan. And when Joshua sent them away to their
tents and blessed them, 8 he said to them, "Go back to your tents with much wealth,
and with very much livestock, with silver, gold, bronze, and iron, and with a great
quantity of clothing; divide the spoil of your enemies with your kindred." 9 So the
Reubenites and the Gadites and the half-tribe of Manasseh returned home, parting
from the Israelites at Shiloh, which is in the land of Canaan, to go to the land of
Gilead, their own land of which they had taken possession by command of the
LORD through Moses.

10 When they came to the region[j] near the Jordan that lies in the land of Ca- **22.10** Deut 12.5
naan, the Reubenites and the Gadites and the half-tribe of Manasseh built there an
altar by the Jordan, an altar of great size. 11 The Israelites heard that the Reubenites **22.11** Deut 13.12-14
and the Gadites and the half-tribe of Manasseh had built an altar at the frontier of
the land of Canaan, in the region[k] near the Jordan, on the side that belongs to the
Israelites. 12 And when the people of Israel heard of it, the whole assembly of the
Israelites gathered at Shiloh, to make war against them.

13 Then the Israelites sent the priest Phinehas son of Eleazar to the Reubenites **22.13** Num 25.7,10,
and the Gadites and the half-tribe of Manasseh, in the land of Gilead, 14 and with 11; 31.6
him ten chiefs, one from each of the tribal families of Israel, every one of them the
head of a family among the clans of Israel. 15 They came to the Reubenites, the
Gadites, and the half-tribe of Manasseh, in the land of Gilead, and they said to
them, 16 "Thus says the whole congregation of the LORD, 'What is this treachery
that you have committed against the God of Israel in turning away today from following the LORD, by building yourselves an altar today in rebellion against the
LORD? 17 Have we not had enough of the sin at Peor from which even yet we have **22.17** Num 25.1-9
not cleansed ourselves, and for which a plague came upon the congregation of the
LORD, 18 that you must turn away today from following the LORD! If you rebel
against the LORD today, he will be angry with the whole congregation of Israel
tomorrow. 19 But now, if your land is unclean, cross over into the LORD's land
where the LORD's tabernacle now stands, and take for yourselves a possession
among us; only do not rebel against the LORD, or rebel against us[l] by building
yourselves an altar other than the altar of the LORD our God. 20 Did not Achan son **22.20** Josh 7.1
of Zerah break faith in the matter of the devoted things, and wrath fell upon all the
congregation of Israel? And he did not perish alone for his iniquity!' "

21 Then the Reubenites, the Gadites, and the half-tribe of Manasseh said in
answer to the heads of the families of Israel, 22 "The LORD, God of gods! The LORD, **22.22** Deut 12.1,2
God of gods! He knows; and let Israel itself know! If it was in rebellion or in breach
of faith toward the LORD, do not spare us today 23 for building an altar to turn away
from following the LORD; or if we did so to offer burnt offerings or grain offerings
or offerings of well-being on it, may the LORD himself take vengeance. 24 No! We
did it from fear that in time to come your children might say to our children, 'What
have you to do with the LORD, the God of Israel? 25 For the LORD has made the
Jordan a boundary between us and you, you Reubenites and Gadites; you have no
portion in the LORD.' So your children might make our children cease to worship

[j] Or *to Geliloth* [k] Or *at Geliloth* [l] Or *make rebels of us*

22.8 Joshua's parting counsel to these tribes was to share their new wealth with the relatives back home. We often neglect this vital part of the Christian life – sharing what we have been given. This does not mean, "When I'm wealthy, I'll share." It means willingly sharing whatever we have right now with those not fortunate enough to enjoy the same blessings.

22.11–34 When the tribes of Reuben and Gad and the half-tribe of Manasseh built an altar at the Jordan River, the rest of Israel feared that these tribes were starting their own religion and rebelling against God. But before beginning an all-out war, Phinehas led a delegation to learn the truth. He was prepared to negotiate rather than fight if a battle was not necessary. When he learned that the altar was for a memorial rather than for heathen sacrifice, war was averted and unity restored.

As nations and as individuals, we would benefit from a similar approach to resolving conflicts. Assuming the worst about the intentions of others only brings trouble. Israel averted the threat of civil war by asking before assaulting. Beware of reacting before you hear the whole story.

22.17 For the story of how Israel turned away from God and began to worship Baal-peor, see Numbers 25.1–18.

22.20 For the story of Achan, a man who allowed greed to get the best of him, see chapter 7.

the LORD. 26 Therefore we said, 'Let us now build an altar, not for burnt offering,
nor for sacrifice, 27 but to be a witness between us and you, and between the generations after us, that we do perform the service of the LORD in his presence with our
burnt offerings and sacrifices and offerings of well-being; so that your children may
never say to our children in time to come, "You have no portion in the LORD." '
28 And we thought, If this should be said to us or to our descendants in time to
come, we could say, 'Look at this copy of the altar of the LORD, which our ancestors made, not for burnt offerings, nor for sacrifice, but to be a witness between us
and you.' 29 Far be it from us that we should rebel against the LORD, and turn away
this day from following the LORD by building an altar for burnt offering, grain
offering, or sacrifice, other than the altar of the LORD our God that stands before his
tabernacle!"

30 When the priest Phinehas and the chiefs of the congregation, the heads of the
families of Israel who were with him, heard the words that the Reubenites and the
Gadites and the Manassites spoke, they were satisfied. 31 The priest Phinehas son of
Eleazar said to the Reubenites and the Gadites and the Manassites, "Today we
know that the LORD is among us, because you have not committed this treachery
against the LORD; now you have saved the Israelites from the hand of the LORD."

32 Then the priest Phinehas son of Eleazar and the chiefs returned from the
Reubenites and the Gadites in the land of Gilead to the land of Canaan, to the
Israelites, and brought back word to them. 33 The report pleased the Israelites; and
the Israelites blessed God and spoke no more of making war against them, to de-
22.34 Gen 31.47-49 stroy the land where the Reubenites and the Gadites were settled. 34 The Reubenites
and the Gadites called the altar Witness;[m] "For," said they, "it is a witness between
us that the LORD is God."

4. Joshua's last message

Joshua addresses the leaders

23.1 Josh 21.44 **23** A long time afterward, when the LORD had given rest to Israel from all their
enemies all around, and Joshua was old and well advanced in years, 2 Joshua
23.2 Deut 31.28 Josh 24.1 summoned all Israel, their elders and heads, their judges and officers, and said to
them, "I am now old and well advanced in years; 3 and you have seen all that the
LORD your God has done to all these nations for your sake, for it is the LORD your
23.4 Ex 23.30 Num 33.53 God who has fought for you. 4 I have allotted to you as an inheritance for your tribes
those nations that remain, along with all the nations that I have already cut off, from
the Jordan to the Great Sea in the west. 5 The LORD your God will push them back
23.6 Deut 5.32 Josh 1.7; 22.5 before you, and drive them out of your sight; and you shall possess their land, as the
LORD your God promised you. 6 Therefore be very steadfast to observe and do all
23.7 Ex 20.5; 23.13 Deut 6.13; 10.20 Ps 16.4 that is written in the book of the law of Moses, turning aside from it neither to the
right nor to the left, 7 so that you may not be mixed with these nations left here
among you, or make mention of the names of their gods, or swear by them, or serve
23.9 Ex 23.23,30 Deut 7.24 them, or bow yourselves down to them, 8 but hold fast to the LORD your God, as
you have done to this day. 9 For the LORD has driven out before you great and strong

m Cn Compare Syr: Heb lacks *Witness*

22.26–28 The tribes were concerned that, without some visible sign of unity between the people on the two sides of the Jordan, future generations might see conflict between them. The altar, patterned after the altar of Jehovah, was to remind these people that they all worshiped the same God. Often we need to be reminded of the faith of our fathers. What actions demonstrate to your children your reliance on God and remind them of what he has done? Take the time to establish family traditions that will help your children remember.

23.6–13 Joshua knew the nation's weak spots. Before dying, he called the people together and gave commands to help them where they were most likely to slip: (1) follow all Moses' instructions without deviating; (2) don't mix with the heathen nations or worship their idols; (3) don't intermarry with the heathen nations. These temptations were right in their backyard. Similar temptations afflict us as well. It's wise to identify our weak spots *before* we break down. Then we can develop strategies to overcome these temptations instead of being overcome by them.

23.8 Joshua was dying and so he called all the leaders of the nation together to give them his final words of encouragement and instruction. His whole message can be summarized in this verse, "Hold fast to the Lord your God." Joshua had been a living example of those words, and he wanted that to be his legacy. For what do you want to be remembered, and what do you want to pass on to your children and associates? You can leave them nothing better than the admonition to hold on to God and the memory of a person who did.

nations; and as for you, no one has been able to withstand you to this day. 10One 23.10
of you puts to flight a thousand, since it is the LORD your God who fights for you, Lev 26.8 Deut 28.7
as he promised you. 11Be very careful, therefore, to love the LORD your God. 12For Judg 15.15
if you turn back, and join the survivors of these nations left here among you, and 23.12 Deut 7.3
intermarry with them, so that you marry their women and they yours, 13know as- Ezra 9.2
suredly that the LORD your God will not continue to drive out these nations before 23.13 Ex 23.33; 34.12
you; but they shall be a snare and a trap for you, a scourge on your sides, and thorns Deut 7.16
in your eyes, until you perish from this good land that the LORD your God has given
you.

14 "And now I am about to go the way of all the earth, and you know in your
hearts and souls, all of you, that not one thing has failed of all the good things that
the LORD your God promised concerning you; all have come to pass for you, not
one of them has failed. 15But just as all the good things that the LORD your God 23.15
promised concerning you have been fulfilled for you, so the LORD will bring upon Lev 26.14 Deut 4.25
you all the bad things, until he has destroyed you from this good land that the LORD 28.15-19; 32.30
your God has given you. 16If you transgress the covenant of the LORD your God,
which he enjoined on you, and go and serve other gods and bow down to them, then
the anger of the LORD will be kindled against you, and you shall perish quickly
from the good land that he has given to you."

Joshua addresses all the people

24 Then Joshua gathered all the tribes of Israel to Shechem, and summoned the 24.1 Josh 23.1
elders, the heads, the judges, and the officers of Israel; and they presented 24.2
themselves before God. 2And Joshua said to all the people, "Thus says the LORD, Gen 11.27-32
the God of Israel: Long ago your ancestors—Terah and his sons Abraham and 24.3 Gen 12.1; 15.5
Nahor—lived beyond the Euphrates and served other gods. 3Then I took your fa- 21.1-3; 24.7
ther Abraham from beyond the River and led him through all the land of Canaan 24.4
and made his offspring many. I gave him Isaac; 4and to Isaac I gave Jacob and Gen 25.25,26 36.9; 46.6
Esau. I gave Esau the hill country of Seir to possess, but Jacob and his children Deut 2.5
went down to Egypt. 5Then I sent Moses and Aaron, and I plagued Egypt with 24.5 Ex 4.14-17
what I did in its midst; and afterwards I brought you out. 6When I brought your Ps 105.26
ancestors out of Egypt, you came to the sea; and the Egyptians pursued your ances- 24.6 Ex 14.2-8
tors with chariots and horsemen to the Red Sea.[n] 7When they cried out to the Neh 9.11
LORD, he put darkness between you and the Egyptians, and made the sea come Ps 77.15
upon them and cover them; and your eyes saw what I did to Egypt. Afterwards you 24.7 Ex 14.19-31
lived in the wilderness a long time. 8Then I brought you to the land of the Amo- Num 14.33

[n] Or *Sea of Reeds*

23.12–14 This chilling prediction about the consequences of intermarriage with the Canaanite nations eventually became a reality. Numerous stories in the book of Judges show what Israel had to suffer because of failure to follow God wholeheartedly. God was supremely loving and patient with Israel, just as he is today. But we must not confuse his patience with us as approval of or indifference to our sin. Beware of demanding your own way, because eventually you may get it—along with all its painful consequences.

24.2–13 Joshua reminded the people of God's goodness and his provision for them by reviewing past times when God blessed them. Reviewing past blessings can encourage us to continue to serve God faithfully. When you need a reminder of God's love, review how God has blessed you in the past. Then turn to the Bible and see how unchanging his love is.

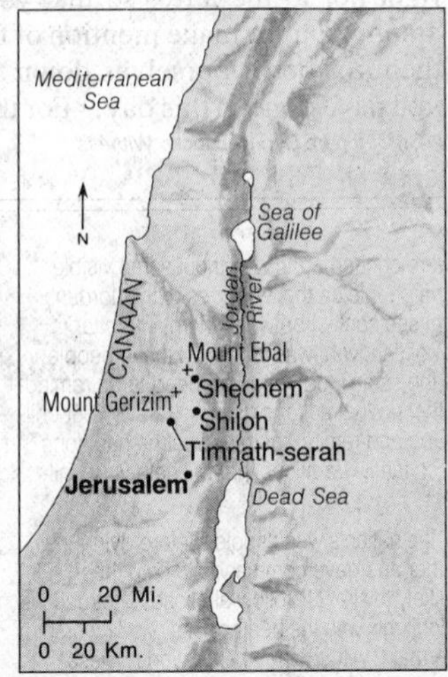

JOSHUA'S FINAL SPEECH
Joshua called all the Israelites to Shechem to hear his final words. He challenged the people to make a conscious choice to always serve God. Soon afterwards, Joshua died and was buried in his hometown of Timnath-serah.

24.8 Num 21.21-35
24.9 Num 22.2-6
24.11 Ex 23.23,31 Deut 7.1 Josh 3.15-17
24.12 Ex 23.28 Deut 7.20 Ps 44.3
24.13 Deut 6.10-12
24.14 Deut 10.12,13 18.13 1 Sam 12.24 Ps 111.10
24.15 Ruth 1.15,16 1 Kgs 18.21

rites, who lived on the other side of the Jordan; they fought with you, and I handed
them over to you, and you took possession of their land, and I destroyed them
before you. 9 Then King Balak son of Zippor of Moab, set out to fight against Israel. He sent and invited Balaam son of Beor to curse you, 10 but I would not listen
to Balaam; therefore he blessed you; so I rescued you out of his hand. 11 When you
went over the Jordan and came to Jericho, the citizens of Jericho fought against
you, and also the Amorites, the Perizzites, the Canaanites, the Hittites, the Girgashites, the Hivites, and the Jebusites; and I handed them over to you. 12 I sent the
hornet[o] ahead of you, which drove out before you the two kings of the Amorites;
it was not by your sword or by your bow. 13 I gave you a land on which you had not
labored, and towns that you had not built, and you live in them; you eat the fruit of
vineyards and oliveyards that you did not plant.
14 "Now therefore revere the LORD, and serve him in sincerity and in faithfulness; put away the gods that your ancestors served beyond the River and in Egypt,
and serve the LORD. 15 Now if you are unwilling to serve the LORD, choose this day
whom you will serve, whether the gods your ancestors served in the region beyond
the River or the gods of the Amorites in whose land you are living; but as for me and
my household, we will serve the LORD."

The nation promises to worship and obey the Lord

24.19 Ex 20.5; 23.21 34.14 Lev 19.1,2 20.7,26
24.20 Deut 4.25 Josh 23.12 Acts 7.42
24.24 Ex 19.8; 24.3,7 Deut 5.26,27
24.25 Ex 24.8

16 Then the people answered, "Far be it from us that we should forsake the
LORD to serve other gods; 17 for it is the LORD our God who brought us and our
ancestors up from the land of Egypt, out of the house of slavery, and who did those
great signs in our sight. He protected us along all the way that we went, and among
all the peoples through whom we passed; 18 and the LORD drove out before us all the
peoples, the Amorites who lived in the land. Therefore we also will serve the
LORD, for he is our God."
19 But Joshua said to the people, "You cannot serve the LORD, for he is a holy
God. He is a jealous God; he will not forgive your transgressions or your sins. 20 If
you forsake the LORD and serve foreign gods, then he will turn and do you harm,
and consume you, after having done you good." 21 And the people said to Joshua,
"No, we will serve the LORD!" 22 Then Joshua said to the people, "You are witnesses against yourselves that you have chosen the LORD, to serve him." And they
said, "We are witnesses." 23 He said, "Then put away the foreign gods that are
among you, and incline your hearts to the LORD, the God of Israel." 24 The people
said to Joshua, "The LORD our God we will serve, and him we will obey." 25 So
Joshua made a covenant with the people that day, and made statutes and ordinances
for them at Shechem. 26 Joshua wrote these words in the book of the law of God;

[o] Meaning of Heb uncertain

24.15 The people had to decide whether they would obey the Lord, who had proven his trustworthiness, or obey the local gods, which were only man-made idols. It's easy to slip into a quiet rebellion—going about life in your own way. But the time comes when you have to choose who or what will control you. The choice is yours. Will it be God, your own limited personality, or another imperfect substitute? Once you have chosen to be controlled by God's spirit, reaffirm your choice every day.

24.15 In taking a definite stand for the Lord, Joshua again displayed his spiritual leadership. Regardless of what others decided, Joshua had made a commitment to God, and he was willing to set the example of living by that decision. The way we live shows others the strength of our commitment to serving God.

24.16–18, 21 All the people boldly claimed that they would never forsake the Lord. But all the people did not keep that promise. Very soon God would charge them with breaking their contract with him (Judges 2.2, 3). Talk is cheap. It is easy to say we will follow God, but it is much more important to live like it. Yet the nation followed God through Joshua's lifetime, a great tribute to Joshua's faith in God and powerful leadership.

24.23 Joshua told the Israelites to put away their foreign gods, or idols. To follow God requires destroying whatever gets in the way of worshiping him. We have our own form of idols—greed, wrong priorities, jealousies, prejudices—that get in the way of worshiping God. God is not satisfied if we merely hide these idols. We must completely remove them from our lives.

24.24–26 The permanent contract between Israel and God was that the people would worship and obey the Lord alone. Their purpose was to become a holy nation that would influence the rest of the world for God. The conquest of Canaan was a means to achieve this purpose, but Israel became preoccupied with the land and lost sight of the Lord God.

The same can happen to us. We can spend so much time on the means that we forget the end—to glorify God. Churches may make this mistake as well. For example, the congregation may pour all of its energies into a new facility, only to become self-satisfied or fearful of letting certain groups use it. If this happens, they have focused on the building and lost sight of its purpose—to bring others to God.

and he took a large stone, and set it up there under the oak in the sanctuary of the
LORD. 27 Joshua said to all the people, "See, this stone shall be a witness against us; **24.27**
for it has heard all the words of the LORD that he spoke to us; therefore it shall be Ex 22.26,27
a witness against you, if you deal falsely with your God." 28 So Joshua sent the
people away to their inheritances.

Leaders are buried in the promised land

29 After these things Joshua son of Nun, the servant of the LORD, died, being **24.29**
one hundred ten years old. 30 They buried him in his own inheritance at Timnath- Judg 2.7-9 **24.30**
serah, which is in the hill country of Ephraim, north of Mount Gaash. Josh 19.50
31 Israel served the LORD all the days of Joshua, and all the days of the elders
who outlived Joshua and had known all the work that the LORD did for Israel.
32 The bones of Joseph, which the Israelites had brought up from Egypt, were **24.32** Gen 50.25
buried at Shechem, in the portion of ground that Jacob had bought from the chil- Ex 13.19
dren of Hamor, the father of Shechem, for one hundred pieces of money;[p] it be- Acts 7.16 Heb 11.22
came an inheritance of the descendants of Joseph.
33 Eleazar son of Aaron died; and they buried him at Gibeah, the town of his **24.33** Judg 19.12,13
son Phinehas, which had been given him in the hill country of Ephraim. 1 Sam 10.26

p Heb *one hundred qesitah*

24.29–31 The book of Joshua opens with a new leader being handed a seemingly impossible task – to take over the land of Canaan. By following God closely, Joshua led the people through military victories and faithful spiritual obedience. In 24.16 we read that the people were sure they would never forsake the Lord. The response of the whole nation during these many years is a tribute both to Joshua's leadership and to the God he faithfully served.

24.33 Joshua and Eleazar had died, but not before laying before the people the fundamentals of what it means to have faith in God. We are to fear and serve the Lord alone (24.14). This is based on a choice: to obey him instead of following other gods (24.15). We are incapable, however, of properly worshiping him because of our rebellion and sin (24.19). By choosing God as Lord we enter into a covenant with him (24.25) whereby he promises not only to forgive and love us, but also to enable us by his spirit to do his work here on earth. This covenant requires us to renounce the principles and practices of the culture around us that are hostile to God's plan (24.23). This is not to be done alone, but by binding ourselves together with others who have faith in God. (See Deuteronomy 30.15–20 for a similar message from Moses.)

THE ANCESTORS OF JESUS
The book of Ruth is not just a nice story, or an inconsequential incident. The events recorded in Ruth were part of God's preparation for the births of David and eventually Jesus, the promised Messiah.
In Matthew, the opening genealogy looks back to Ruth and Boaz as ancestors of Jesus (see Matthew 1.5).

"An account of the genealogy of Jesus the Messiah, the son of David, the son of Abraham.

"Abraham was the father of Isaac, and Isaac the father of Jacob, and Jacob the father of Judah and his brothers, and Judah the father of Perez and Zerah by Tamar, and Perez the father of Hezron, and Hezron the father of Aram, and Aram the father of Aminadab, and Aminadab the father of Nahshon, and Nahshon the father of Salmon, and Salmon the father of **Boaz** by Rahab, and **Boaz** the father of Obed by **Ruth**, and Obed the father of Jesse, and Jesse the father of King David.

"And David was the father of Solomon by the wife of Uriah, and Solomon the father of Rehoboam, and Rehoboam the father of Abijah, and Abijah the father of Asaph, and Asaph the father of Jehoshaphat, and Jehoshaphat the father of Joram, and Joram the father of Uzziah, and Uzziah the father of Jotham, and Jotham the father of Ahaz, and Ahaz the father of Hezekiah, and Hezekiah the father of Manasseh, and Manasseh the father of Amos, and Amos the father of Josiah, and Josiah the father of Jechoniah and his brothers, at the time of the deportation to Babylon.

"And after the deportation to Babylon: Jechoniah was the father of Salathiel, and Salathiel the father of Zerubbabel, and Zerubbabel the father of Abiud, and Abiud the father of Eliakim, and Eliakim the father of Azor, and Azor the father of Zadok, and Zadok the father of Achim, and Achim the father of Eliud, and Eliud the father of Eleazar, and Eleazar the father of Matthan, and Matthan the father of Jacob, and Jacob the father of Joseph the husband of Mary, of whom Jesus was born, who is called the Messiah." (Matthew 1.1-16)

Exodus from Egypt 1446 B.C. (1280 B.C.)	Israelites enter Canaan 1406 (1240)	Period of the Judges begins 1375 (1220)	Othniel 1367–1327 (1202–1162)	Ehud 1309–1229 (1184–1104)	Deborah 1209–1169 (1192–1152)

VITAL STATISTICS

PURPOSE:
To show that God's judgment against sin is certain, and his forgiveness of sin and restoration to relationship is just as certain for those who repent

AUTHOR:
Probably Samuel

SETTING:
The land of Canaan, later called Israel. God had helped the Israelites conquer Canaan, which had been inhabited by a host of wicked nations. But they were in danger of losing this promised land because they compromised their convictions and disobeyed God.

KEY VERSE:
"In those days there was no king in Israel; all the people did what was right in their own eyes" (17.6).

KEY PEOPLE:
Othniel, Ehud, Deborah, Gideon, Abimelech, Jephthah, Samson, Delilah

SPECIAL FEATURE:
Records Israel's first civil war

REAL heroes are hard to find these days. Modern research and the media have made the foibles and weaknesses of our leaders very apparent; we search in vain for men and women to emulate. The music, movie, and sports industries produce a steady stream of "stars" who shoot to the top and then quickly fade from view.

Judges is a book about heroes—12 men and women who delivered Israel from her oppressors. These judges were not perfect; in fact, they included an assassin, a sexually promiscuous man, and a person who broke all the laws of hospitality. But they were submissive to God, and God used them.

Judges is also a book about sin and its consequences. Like a minor cut or abrasion which becomes infected when left untreated, sin grows and soon poisons the whole body. The book of Joshua ends with the nation taking a stand for God, ready to experience all the blessings of the promised land. After settling in Canaan, however, the Israelites lost their spiritual commitment and motivation. When Joshua and the elders died, the nation experienced a leadership vacuum, leaving them without a strong central government. Instead of enjoying freedom and prosperity in the promised land, Israel entered the dark ages of her history.

Simply stated, the reason for this rapid decline was sin—individual and corporate. The first step away from God was incomplete obedience (1.11—2.5); the Israelites refused to eliminate the enemy completely from the land. This led to intermarriage and idolatry (2.6—3.7) and people doing "what was right in their own eyes" (17.6). Before long the Israelites became captives. Out of their desperation they begged God to rescue them. In faithfulness to his promise and out of his lovingkindness, God would raise up a judge to deliver his people and, for a time, there would be peace. Then complacency and disobedience would set in, and the cycle would begin again.

The book of Judges spans a period of over 325 years, recording six successive periods of oppression and deliverance, and the careers of 12 deliverers. Their captors included the Mesopotamians, Moabites, Philistines, Canaanites, Midianites, and Ammonites. A variety of deliverers—from Othniel to Samson—were used by God to lead his people to freedom and true worship. God's deliverance through the judges is a powerful demonstration of his love and mercy toward his people.

As you read the book of Judges, take a good look at these heroes from Jewish history. Take note of their dependence on God and obedience to his commands. Observe Israel's repeated downward spiral into sin, refusing to learn from history and living only for the moment. But most of all, stand in awe of God's mercy as he delivers his people over and over again.

Gideon 1162–1122 (1146–1106)	Samuel born 1105 (1083)	Samson 1075–1055 (1083–1063)	Saul anointed king 1050 (1045)	David becomes king 1010

THE BLUEPRINT

A. THE MILITARY FAILURE OF ISRAEL (1.1—3.6)
1. Incomplete conquest of the land
2. Religious rebellion of the people

The tribes had compromised God's command to drive out the inhabitants of the land. Incomplete removal of evil often means disaster in the end. We must beware of compromising with wickedness.

B. THE RESCUE OF ISRAEL BY THE JUDGES (3.7—16.31)
1. First period: Othniel
2. Second period: Ehud and Shamgar
3. Third period: Deborah and Barak
4. Fourth period: Gideon, Tola, and Jair
5. Fifth period: Jephthah, Ibzan, Elon, and Abdon
6. Sixth period: Samson

Repeatedly we see the nation of Israel sinning against God and God allowing suffering to come upon the land and the people. Sin always has its consequences. Where there is sin we can expect suffering to follow. Rather than living in an endless cycle of abandoning God and then crying out to him for rescue, we should seek to live a consistent life of faithfulness.

C. THE MORAL FAILURE OF ISRAEL (17.1—21.25)
1. Idolatry in the tribe of Dan
2. War against the tribe of Benjamin

Despite the efforts of Israel's judges, the people still would not turn wholeheartedly to God. They all did whatever they thought was best for themselves. The result was the spiritual, moral, and political decline of the nation. Our lives will also fall into decline and decay unless we live by the guidelines God has given us.

MEGATHEMES

THEME	EXPLANATION	IMPORTANCE
Decline/ Compromise	Whenever a judge died, the people faced decline and failure because they compromised their high spiritual purpose in many ways. They abandoned their mission to drive all the people out of the land, and they adopted the customs of the people living around them.	Society has many rewards to offer those who compromise their faith: wealth, acceptance, recognition, power, and influence. When God gives us a mission, it must not be polluted by a desire for approval from society. We must keep our eyes on Christ who is our Judge and Deliverer.
Decay/Apostasy	Israel's moral downfall had its roots in the fierce independence that each tribe cherished. It led to everyone doing whatever seemed good in his own eyes. There was no unity in government or in worship. Law and order broke down. Finally idol worship and man-made religion led to the complete abandoning of faith in God.	We can expect decay when we value anything more highly than God. If we value our own independence more than dedication to God, we have placed an idol in our hearts. Soon our lives become temples to that god. We must constantly regard God's first claim on our lives and all our desires.
Defeat/ Oppression	God used evil oppressors to punish the Israelites for their sin, to bring them to the point of repentance, and to test their allegiance to him.	Rebellion against God leads to disaster. God may use defeat to bring wandering hearts back to him. When all else is stripped away, we recognize the importance of serving only him.
Repentance	Decline, decay, and defeat caused the people to cry out to God for help. They vowed to turn from idolatry and to turn to God for mercy and deliverance. When they repented, God delivered them.	Idolatry gains a foothold in our hearts when we make anything more important than God. We must identify modern idols in our hearts, renounce them, and turn to God for his love and mercy.

Deliverance/ Heroes	Because Israel repented, God raised up heroes to deliver his people from their path of sin and the oppression it brought. He used many kinds of people to accomplish this purpose by filling them with his Holy Spirit.	God's Holy Spirit is available to all people. Anyone who is dedicated to God can be used for his service. Real heroes recognize the futility of human effort without God's guidance and power.

KEY PLACES IN JUDGES

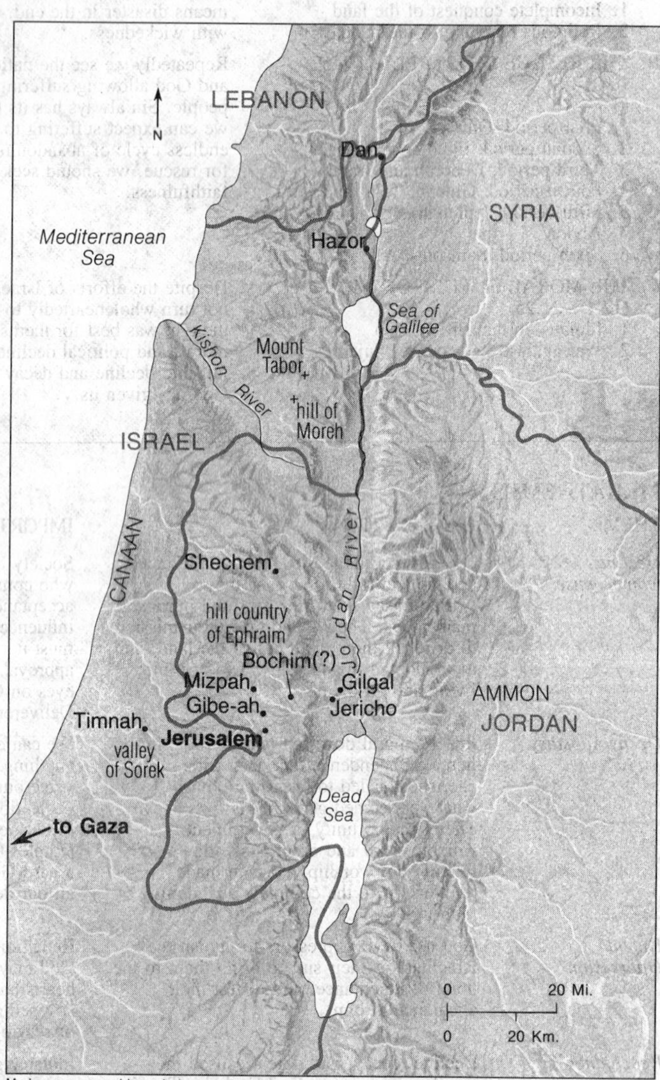

Modern names and boundaries are shown in gray.

1 Bochim The book of Judges opens with the Israelites continuing their conquest of the promised land. Their failure to obey God and destroy all the evil inhabitants soon comes back to haunt them in two ways: (1) the enemies reorganized and counterattacked, and (2) Israel turned away from God, adopting the evil and idolatrous practices of the inhabitants of the land. The angel of the Lord appeared at Bochim to inform the Israelites that their sin and disobedience had broken their agreement with God and would result in punishment through oppression (1.1—3.10).

2 Jericho The nation of Moab was one of the first to oppress Israel. Moab's King Eglon conquered much of Israel—including the city of Jericho ("the city of palms")—and forced the people to pay unreasonable taxes. The messenger chosen to deliver this tax money to King Eglon was named Ehud. But he had more than money to deliver, for he drew his hidden sword and killed the Moabite king. Ehud then escaped, only to return with an army that chased out the Moabites and freed Israel from its oppressors (3.11–31).

3 Hazor After Ehud's death, King Jabin of Hazor conquered Israel and oppressed the people for 20 years. Then Deborah became Israel's leader. She summoned Barak to fight General Sisera, the leader of King Jabin's army. Together Deborah and Barak led their army into battle against Jabin's forces in the land between Mount Tabor and the Kishon River and conquered them (4.1—5.31).

4 Hill of Moreh After 40 years of peace, the Midianites began to harass the Israelites by destroying their flocks and crops. When the Israelites finally cried out to God, he chose Gideon, a poor and humble farmer, to be their deliverer. After struggling with doubt and feelings of inferiority, Gideon took courage and knocked down his town's altar to Baal, causing a great uproar among the citizens. Filled with the Spirit of God, he attacked the vast army of Midian which was camped near the hill of Moreh. With just a handful of men he sent the enemy running away in confusion (6.1—7.25).

5 Shechem Even great leaders make mistakes. Gideon's relations with a concubine in Shechem resulted in the birth of a son named Abimelech. Abimelech turned out to be treacherous and power hungry—stirring up the people to proclaim him king. To carry out his plan, he went so far as to kill 69 of his 70 half brothers. Eventually some men of Shechem rebelled against Abimelech, but he gathered together an army and defeated them. His lust for power led him to ransack two other cities, but he was killed by a woman who dropped a millstone onto his head (8.28—9.57).

6 Land of Ammon Again Israel turned completely from God; so God turned from them. But when the Ammonites mobilized their army to attack, Israel threw away her idols and called upon God once again. Jephthah, a prostitute's son who had been run out of Israel, was asked to return and lead Israel's forces against the enemy. After defeating the Ammonites, Jephthah became involved in a war with the tribe of Ephraim over a misunderstanding (10.1—12.15).

7 Timnah Israel's next judge, Samson, was a miracle child promised by God to a barren couple. He was the one who would begin to free Israel from their next and most powerful oppressor, the Philistines. According to God's command, Samson was to be a nazirite—one who took a vow to be set apart for special service to God. One of the stipulations of the vow was that Samson's hair could never be cut. But when Samson grew up, he did not always take his special responsibility to God seriously. He even fell in love with a Philistine girl in Timnah and asked to marry her. Before the wedding, Samson held a party for some men in the city, using a riddle to place a bet with them. The men, however, forced Samson's fiancée into giving the answer. Furious at being tricked, Samson paid his bet with the lives of 30 Philistines who lived in the nearby city of Ashkelon (13.1—14.20).

8 Valley of Sorek Samson killed thousands of Philistines with his incredible strength. The nation's leaders looked for a way to stop him. They got their chance when another Philistine woman stole Samson's heart. Her name was Delilah, and she lived in the valley of Sorek. In exchange for a great sum of money, Delilah deceived Samson into confiding in her the secret of his strength. One night while he slept, Delilah cut off his hair. As a result, Samson fell helplessly into the hands of the enemy (15.1—16.20).

9 Gaza Samson was blinded and led captive to a prison in Gaza. There his hair began to grow again. After a while, the Philistines held a great festival to celebrate Samson's imprisonment and to humiliate him before the crowds. When he was brought out as the entertainment, he literally brought down the house when he pushed on the main pillars of the banquet hall and killed the thousands trapped inside. The prophecy that he would begin to free Israel from the Philistines had come true (16.21–31).

10 Hill Country of Ephraim In the hill country of Ephraim lived a man named Micah. Micah hired his own priest to perform priestly duties in the shrine which housed his collection of idols. He thought he was pleasing God with all his religiosity! Like many of the Israelites, Micah assumed that his own opinions of what was right would agree with God's (17.1–13).

11 Dan The tribe of Dan migrated north in order to find new territory. They sent spies ahead of them to scout out the land. One night the spies stopped at Micah's home. Looking for some assurance of victory, the spies stole Micah's idols and priest. Rejoining the tribe, they came upon the city of Laish and slaughtered the unarmed and innocent citizens, renaming the conquered city Dan. Micah's idols were then set up in the city and became the focal point of the tribe's worship for many years (18.1–31).

12 Gibeah The extent to which many people had fallen away from God became clear in Gibeah, a village in the territory of Benjamin. A man and his concubine were traveling north toward the hill country of Ephraim. They stopped for the night in Gibeah, thinking they would be safe. But some perverts in the city gathered around the home where they were staying and demanded that the man come out to have sexual relations with them. Instead, the man and his host pushed the concubine out the door. She was raped and abused all night. When the man found her lifeless body the next morning, he cut it into 12 pieces and sent the parts to each tribe of Israel. This tragic event demonstrated that the nation had sunk to its lowest spiritual level (19.1–30).

13 Mizpah The leaders of Israel came to Mizpah to decide how to punish the wicked men from the city of Gibeah. When the city leaders refused to turn the criminals over, the whole nation of Israel took vengeance upon both Gibeah and the tribe of Benjamin where the city was located. When the battle ended, the entire tribe had been destroyed except for a handful of men who took refuge in the hills. Israel had become morally depraved. The stage was now set for the much-needed spiritual renewal that would come under the prophet Samuel (20.1–21.25).

A. THE MILITARY FAILURE OF ISRAEL (1.1 – 3.6)

By faithfully obeying the Lord, Joshua led the Israelites to military victory. After his death, however, the tribes failed to clear the inhabitants from the land, so the Lord withdrew his promise to help drive the people out and bless the Israelites in battle. The new generation abandoned God and worshiped idols. This part of Judges shows what can happen when we neglect to teach our children to follow the Lord.

1. Incomplete conquest of the land

Israel begins clearing out the land

1 After the death of Joshua, the Israelites inquired of the LORD, "Who shall go **1.1**
up first for us against the Canaanites, to fight against them?" 2 The LORD said, Num 27.21
"Judah shall go up. I hereby give the land into his hand." 3 Judah said to his brother **1.2** Gen 49.8
Simeon, "Come up with me into the territory allotted to me, that we may fight **1.3**
against the Canaanites; then I too will go with you into the territory allotted to you." Josh 19.1
So Simeon went with him. 4 Then Judah went up and the LORD gave the Canaanites **1.4**
and the Perizzites into their hand; and they defeated ten thousand of them at Bezek. Gen 13.7; 34.30 1 Sam 11.8
5 They came upon Adoni-bezek at Bezek, and fought against him, and defeated the
Canaanites and the Perizzites. 6 Adoni-bezek fled; but they pursued him, and
caught him, and cut off his thumbs and big toes. 7 Adoni-bezek said, "Seventy
kings with their thumbs and big toes cut off used to pick up scraps under my table;
as I have done, so God has paid me back." They brought him to Jerusalem, and he
died there.
8 Then the people of Judah fought against Jerusalem and took it. They put it to **1.8**
the sword and set the city on fire. 9 Afterward the people of Judah went down to Josh 15.63
fight against the Canaanites who lived in the hill country, in the Negeb, and in the
lowland. 10 Judah went against the Canaanites who lived in Hebron (the name of **1.10**
Hebron was formerly Kiriath-arba); and they defeated Sheshai and Ahiman and Josh 15.14 20.7; 21.9-16
Talmai. **1.11**
11 From there they went against the inhabitants of Debir (the name of Debir Josh 15.15
was formerly Kiriath-sepher). 12 Then Caleb said, "Whoever attacks Kiriath-sepher **1.12**
and takes it, I will give him my daughter Achsah as wife." 13 And Othniel son of Josh 15.16 **1.13**
Kenaz, Caleb's younger brother, took it; and he gave him his daughter Achsah as Judg 3.9

1.1 The people of Israel had finally entered and taken control of the land promised to their ancestors (Genesis 12.7; Exodus 3.16, 17). The book of Judges continues the story of this conquest which began in the book of Joshua. By God's strength, the Israelites had conquered many enemies and overcome many difficulties, but their work was not yet finished. They had effectively met many political and military challenges, but facing spiritual challenges was more difficult. The unholy but attractive life-style of the Canaanites proved more dangerous than their military might. The Israelites gave in to the pressure and compromised their faith. If we attempt to meet life's challenges with human effort alone, we will find the pressures and temptations around us too great to resist.

1.1 Everyone wants guidance in making tough decisions. The Israelites were no different. To ask for this national guidance, the elders probably gathered at the tabernacle in Shiloh as they had done when the land was divided (Joshua 18). There they may have used the Urim and Thummim to seek God's answers. These were two stones or plates made according to God's instructions and used to seek his guidance in making difficult decisions that involved the entire nation. They were used to take away the possibility of human error and allow God to make the choice.

1.1 The Canaanites were all the people who lived in Canaan (the promised land). They lived in city-states where each city had its own government, army, and laws. One reason Canaan was so difficult to conquer was that each city had to be defeated individually. There was no single king who could surrender the entire country into the hands of the Israelites.

However, Canaan's greatest threat to Israel was not its army, but its religion. Canaanite religion idealized evil traits: cruelty in war, sexual immorality, selfish greed, and materialism. It was a "me first, anything goes" society. Obviously, the religions of Israel and Canaan could not coexist.

1.2 The book of Joshua tells of a swift and thorough conquest of enemy armies and cities, while the book of Judges seems to suggest a more lengthy and gradual conquest. When the Israelites first entered the promised land (Joshua 1 – 12), they united as one army to crush the inhabitants until they were too weak to retaliate. Then, after the land was divided among the 12 tribes (Joshua 13 – 24), each tribe was responsible for clearing out the remaining enemy from its own territory. The book of Judges tells of their failure to do this.

Some tribes were more successful than others. Under Joshua, they all began strong, but soon most were sidetracked by fear, weariness, lack of discipline, or pursuit of their own interests. As a result their faith began to fade away, and "all the people did what was right in their own eyes" (17.6). In order for our faith to survive, it must be practiced day by day. It must penetrate every aspect of our lives. Beware of starting out strong and then getting sidetracked from your real purpose – loving God and living for him.

1.6 The Israelites cut off the thumbs and big toes of Adoni-bezek to humiliate him and make him ineffective in battle. But according to God's instructions for conquering the promised land, he should have been killed.

1.8 Although the Israelites conquered Jerusalem, they did not occupy the city until the days of David (2 Samuel 5.6–10).

1.12–15 This same event is recorded in Joshua 15.16–19. Caleb was one of the original spies who scouted out the promised land (Numbers 13; 14) and, with Joshua, encouraged the people to conquer it. For his faithfulness, he was given the land of his choice.

wife. 14 When she came to him, she urged him to ask her father for a field. As she
dismounted from her donkey, Caleb said to her, "What do you wish?" 15 She said
to him, "Give me a present; since you have set me in the land of the Negeb, give me
also Gulloth-mayim."[a] So Caleb gave her Upper Gulloth and Lower Gulloth.

Israel fails to drive out the enemy

1.16 Deut 34.3 — 16 The descendants of Hobab[b] the Kenite, Moses' father-in-law, went up with
Judg 3.13; 4.11 — the people of Judah from the city of palms into the wilderness of Judah, which lies
1.17 — in the Negeb near Arad. Then they went and settled with the Amalekites.[c] 17 Judah
Num 21.3 — went with his brother Simeon, and they defeated the Canaanites who inhabited
Zephath, and devoted it to destruction. So the city was called Hormah. 18 Judah
took Gaza with its territory, Ashkelon with its territory, and Ekron with its terri-
1.19 — tory. 19 The LORD was with Judah, and he took possession of the hill country, but
Josh 17.16 Judg 4.2,3 — could not drive out the inhabitants of the plain, because they had chariots of iron.
1.20 — 20 Hebron was given to Caleb, as Moses had said; and he drove out from it the three
Josh 14.6-9 15.14 — sons of Anak. 21 But the Benjaminites did not drive out the Jebusites who lived in
1.21 — Jerusalem; so the Jebusites have lived in Jerusalem among the Benjaminites to this
Josh 15.63 2 Sam 5.6 — day.
1.22 — 22 The house of Joseph also went up against Bethel; and the LORD was with
Gen 28.19 — them. 23 The house of Joseph sent out spies to Bethel (the name of the city was
Josh 14.3,4 **1.24** — formerly Luz). 24 When the spies saw a man coming out of the city, they said to
Josh 6.22 — him, "Show us the way into the city, and we will deal kindly with you." 25 So he
1.25 — showed them the way into the city; and they put the city to the sword, but they let
Josh 6.25 — the man and all his family go. 26 So the man went to the land of the Hittites and built
a city, and named it Luz; that is its name to this day.
1.27 — 27 Manasseh did not drive out the inhabitants of Beth-shean and its villages, or
Josh 17.11,12 — Taanach and its villages, or the inhabitants of Dor and its villages, or the inhabitants of Ibleam and its villages, or the inhabitants of Megiddo and its villages; but
the Canaanites continued to live in that land. 28 When Israel grew strong, they put
the Canaanites to forced labor, but did not in fact drive them out.

[a] That is *Basins of Water* [b] Gk: Heb lacks *Hobab* [c] See 1 Sam 15.6: Heb *people*

JUDAH FIGHTS FOR ITS LAND
The tribe of Judah wasted no time beginning their conquest of the territory allotted to them. With help from the tribe of Simeon, Jerusalem was conquered, as were the Canaanites in the Negeb and along the coast. Hebron and Debir fell to Judah, and later Gaza, Ashkelon (Askelon), and Ekron.

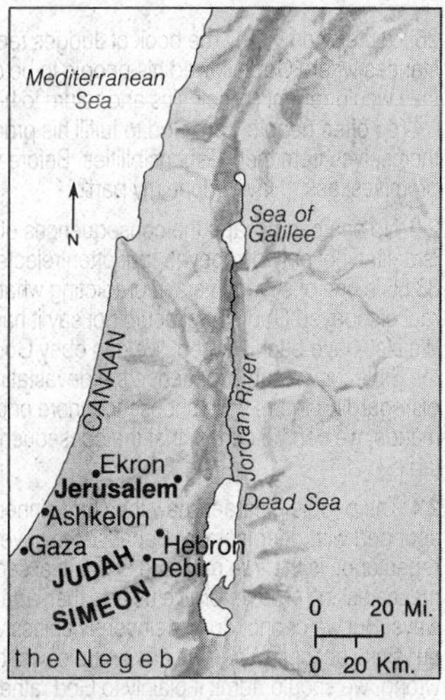

1.19 Why did God order the Israelites to drive the Canaanites off their land? Although the command seems cruel, the Israelites were under God's order to execute judgment on those wicked people. The other nations were to be judged for their sin as God had judged Israel's sin in the 40 years they wandered in the wilderness before they were allowed to enter the promised land. Over 700 years earlier God had told Abraham that when the Israelites entered the promised land, the gross evil of the native people would be ready for judgment (Genesis 15.16). But God wasn't playing favorites with the Israelites, for eventually they too would be severely punished for becoming as evil as the people they were ordered to drive out (2 Kings 17, 25; Jeremiah 6.18, 19; Ezekiel 8). God is not partial; all people are eligible for God's gracious forgiveness as well as his firm justice.

1.19 Canaanite chariots pulled by horses were among the most sophisticated weapons of the day. Israelite foot soldiers were absolutely powerless when a speeding iron chariot bore down upon them. This is why Israel preferred to fight in the hills where chariots couldn't venture.

1.21ff Tribe after tribe failed to drive the evil Canaanites from their land. Why didn't they follow through and completely obey God's commands? (1) They had been fighting for a long time and were tired. Although the goal was in sight, they lacked the discipline and energy to reach it. (2) They were afraid the enemy was too strong – the iron chariots seemed invincible. (3) Spiritual decay had infected them from within. They thought they could handle the temptation and be more prosperous by doing business with the Canaanites.

We, too, often fail to drive sin from our lives. Often we know what to do but just don't follow through. This results in a gradual deterioration of our relationship with God. In our battles, we may grow tired and want rest, but we need more than a break from our work. We need to know that God loves us and has given us a purpose for life. Victory comes from living according to his purpose.

29 And Ephraim did not drive out the Canaanites who lived in Gezer; but the **1.29**
Canaanites lived among them in Gezer. Josh 16.10
30 Zebulun did not drive out the inhabitants of Kitron, or the inhabitants of
Nahalol; but the Canaanites lived among them, and became subject to forced labor.
31 Asher did not drive out the inhabitants of Acco, or the inhabitants of Sidon,
or of Ahlab, or of Achzib, or of Helbah, or of Aphik, or of Rehob; 32 but the Asherites lived among the Canaanites, the inhabitants of the land; for they did not drive
them out.
33 Naphtali did not drive out the inhabitants of Beth-shemesh, or the inhabitants of Beth-anath, but lived among the Canaanites, the inhabitants of the land;
nevertheless the inhabitants of Beth-shemesh and of Beth-anath became subject to
forced labor for them.
34 The Amorites pressed the Danites back into the hill country; they did not **1.34**
allow them to come down to the plain. 35 The Amorites continued to live in Har- Josh 19.47
heres, in Aijalon, and in Shaalbim, but the hand of the house of Joseph rested Judg 18.1
heavily on them, and they became subject to forced labor. 36 The border of the
Amorites ran from the ascent of Akrabbim, from Sela and upward.

An angel announces that the covenant is broken

2 Now the angel of the LORD went up from Gilgal to Bochim, and said, "I **2.1**
brought you up from Egypt, and brought you into the land that I had promised Ex 20.2 Josh 3.10
to your ancestors. I said, 'I will never break my covenant with you. 2 For your part, Judg 6.11
do not make a covenant with the inhabitants of this land; tear down their altars.' But **2.2**
you have not obeyed my command. See what you have done! 3 So now I say, I will Gen 17.7,8 Ex 23.32
not drive them out before you; but they shall become adversaries[d] to you, and their 34.12,13
gods shall be a snare to you." 4 When the angel of the LORD spoke these words to **2.3** Num 33.55,56
all the Israelites, the people lifted up their voices and wept. 5 So they named that Deut 29.25
place Bochim,[e] and there they sacrificed to the LORD. **2.5** Josh 7.26

The death of Joshua

6 When Joshua dismissed the people, the Israelites all went to their own inheri- **2.6**
tances to take possession of the land. 7 The people worshiped the LORD all the days Josh 24.28

[d] OL Vg Compare Gk: Heb *sides* [e] That is *Weepers*

2.1 The angel of the Lord was either (1) a divine messenger sent by God or (2) God appearing in a human form. In either case, the message was so important that God used a special visitation to communicate the seriousness of breaking the agreement with him.

Did this angel speak to all two million Israelites at once? One possible answer is that the angel spoke only to the tribal leaders as representatives of the entire nation. (We say, "The President addressed the nation," even though he doesn't speak to each individual.) Possibly, by miraculous means, every Israelite actually heard the speech. One way or the other, it is certain that God wanted all the people to know the consequences of their sins.

2.1–3 This event marks a significant change in Israel's relationship with God. At Mount Sinai, God made a sacred and binding agreement with the Israelites called a covenant (Exodus 19.5–8). God's part was to make Israel a special nation (see the note on Genesis 12.1–3), to protect them, and to give them unique blessings for following him. Israel's part was to love God and obey his laws. But because they rejected and disobeyed God, the agreement to protect them was no longer in effect. However, God wasn't going to abandon his people. They would receive wonderful blessings if they asked God to forgive them and sincerely followed him once again.

Although God's agreement to help Israel conquer the land was no longer in effect, his promise to make Israel a nation through whom the whole world would be blessed (fulfilled in the Messiah's coming) remained valid. God still wanted the Israelites to be a holy people (just as he wants us to be holy), and he often used oppression to bring them back to him, just as he said he would (Leviticus 26; Deuteronomy 28). The book of Judges records a number of instances where God allowed his people to be oppressed so that they would repent of their sins and return to him.

Too often people want God to fulfill his promises while excusing themselves from their responsibilities. Before you claim God's promises, ask, "Have I done my part?"

2.3 No one can escape the consequences of disobeying God. The Israelites not only disobeyed, but often rejected him. Numbers 33.55 is one of several verses predicting what would happen if Israel disobeyed God. Israel could not say it hadn't been warned. We also have been warned. We can obey God's clear warnings in the Bible, or we can experience the devastating consequences of disregarding them. If we choose to ignore or disobey God's commands, we can be certain that the consequences will be regrettable.

2.4 The people of Israel knew they had sinned, and they responded with deep sorrow. Because we have a tendency to sin, repentance is the true measure of spiritual sensitivity. Repentance means asking God to forgive us and then abandoning our sinful ways. But we cannot do this sincerely unless we are truly sorry for our sinful actions. When we are aware of what we have done wrong, we should admit it plainly to God rather than try to cover it up or hope we can get away with it.

2.7–9 The account of Joshua's death is found here and at the end of the book of Joshua (24.29). Either this account is a summary of what happened earlier, or the account in the book of Joshua omitted the events in the first chapter of Judges. (For more on Joshua see his Profile in Joshua 2.)

2.7 Josh 24.29
of Joshua, and all the days of the elders who outlived Joshua, who had seen all the
great work that the LORD had done for Israel. 8 Joshua son of Nun, the servant of the
LORD, died at the age of one hundred ten years. 9 So they buried him within
the bounds of his inheritance in Timnath-heres, in the hill country of Ephraim,
north of Mount Gaash.

2. Religious rebellion of the people

2.10 Ps 81.11
10 Moreover, that whole generation was gathered to their ancestors, and another
generation grew up after them, who did not know the LORD or the work that he had
done for Israel.

2.11 Judg 4.1; 6.1 8.33; 10.6
11 Then the Israelites did what was evil in the sight of the LORD and worshiped
the Baals; 12 and they abandoned the LORD, the God of their ancestors, who had

THE JUDGES OF ISRAEL

Judge	*Years of Judging*	*Memorable Act(s)*	*Reference*
OTHNIEL	40	He captured a powerful Canaanite city	Judges 3.7–11
EHUD	80	He killed Eglon and defeated the Moabites	Judges 3.12–30
SHAMGAR	unrecorded	He killed 600 Philistines with an oxgoad	Judges 3.31
DEBORAH (w/Barak)	40	She defeated General Sisera and the Canaanites and later sang a victory song with Barak	Judges 4 and 5
GIDEON	40	He destroyed his family idols, used a fleece to determine God's will, raised an army of 10,000, and defeated 135,000 Midianites with 300 soldiers	Judges 6–8
TOLA	23	He judged Israel for 23 years	Judges 10.1, 2
JAIR	22	He had 30 sons	Judges 10.3–5
JEPHTHAH	6	He made a rash vow, defeated the Ammonites, and later battled jealous Ephraim	Judges 10.6—12.7
IBZAN	7	He had 30 sons and 30 daughters	Judges 12.8–10
ELON	10	unrecorded	Judges 12.11, 12
ABDON	8	He had 40 sons and 30 grandsons each of whom had his own donkey	Judges 12.13–15
SAMSON	20	He was a nazirite, killed a lion with his bare hands, burned the Philistine wheat fields, killed 1,000 Philistines with an ass' jawbone, tore off an iron gate, was betrayed by Delilah, and destroyed thousands of Philistines in one last mighty act	Judges 13—16

2.10ff One generation died, and the next did not follow God. Judges 2.10–3.7 is a brief preview of the cycle of sin, judgment, and repentance that Israel experienced again and again. Each generation failed to teach the next generation to love and follow God. Yet this was at the very center of God's law (Deuteronomy 6.4–9). It is tempting to leave the job of teaching the Christian faith to the church or Christian school. Yet God says that the responsibility for this task belongs primarily to the family. Because children learn so much by our example, faith must be a family matter.

2.11ff Soon after Joshua died, Israel began to slip away from God. Although Joshua was a great commander, the people missed his spiritual leadership even more than his military skill, because he had kept the people focused on God and his purposes. Joshua had been the obvious successor to Moses, but there was no obvious successor to Joshua. During this crisis of leadership, Israel needed to learn that no matter how powerful and wise the current leader was, its real leader was God. We often focus our hope and confidence on some influential leader, failing to realize that in reality it is God who is in command. Acknowledge God as your commander in chief, and don't rely on human leaders alone, regardless of their spiritual wisdom.

2.11–14 Baal was the god of the storm and rains, therefore he supposedly controlled vegetation and agriculture. Astarte was the goddess of war and fertility (she was called Ishtar in Babylonia). Lascivious practices and child sacrifice were part of worshiping the Canaanite idols. This generation of Israelites abandoned the faith of their parents and began worshiping the gods of their neighbors. Many things can tempt us to abandon what we know is right. The desire to be accepted by our neighbors can lead us into behavior that is unacceptable to God. Don't be pressured into disobedience.

2.12–14 God often saved his harshest criticism and punishment for those who worshiped idols. Why were idols so bad in God's sight? To worship an idol violated two of the ten commandments (Exodus 20.3–6). The Canaanites had gods for almost every season, activity, or place. To them, Jehovah was just another god to add to their collection of gods. Israel, by contrast, was to worship only Jehovah. They could not possibly believe God is the one true God and at the same time bow to an idol. Adding the worship of idols to the worship of God could not be tolerated.

2.12–14 God was angry with Israel, and he allowed them to be punished by their enemies. Anger, in itself, is not a sin. God's anger was the reaction of his holy nature to sin. One side of God's nature is his anger against sin; the other side is his love and mercy toward sinners. We cannot fully appreciate God's mercy without understanding his fierce wrath.

brought them out of the land of Egypt; they followed other gods, from among the **2.12**
gods of the peoples who were all around them, and bowed down to them; and they Deut 28.25 31.16,17; 32.30
provoked the LORD to anger. 13 They abandoned the LORD, and worshiped Baal and Judg 10.6
the Astartes. 14 So the anger of the LORD was kindled against Israel, and he gave Ps 106.40
them over to plunderers who plundered them, and he sold them into the power of
their enemies all around, so that they could no longer withstand their enemies.
15 Whenever they marched out, the hand of the LORD was against them to bring
misfortune, as the LORD had warned them and sworn to them; and they were in
great distress.

16 Then the LORD raised up judges, who delivered them out of the power of **2.16**
those who plundered them. 17 Yet they did not listen even to their judges; for they Judg 6.6 Ps 106.43-45
lusted after other gods and bowed down to them. They soon turned aside from the **2.17**
way in which their ancestors had walked, who had obeyed the commandments of Ps 81.11,12
the LORD; they did not follow their example. 18 Whenever the LORD raised up
judges for them, the LORD was with the judge, and he delivered them from the hand
of their enemies all the days of the judge; for the LORD would be moved to pity by
their groaning because of those who persecuted and oppressed them. 19 But when- **2.19**
ever the judge died, they would relapse and behave worse than their ancestors, Judg 3.11,12 4.1; 8.33
following other gods, worshiping them and bowing down to them. They would not 2 Chron 24.17, 18
drop any of their practices or their stubborn ways. 20 So the anger of the LORD was Ps 78.8
kindled against Israel; and he said, "Because this people have transgressed my covenant that I commanded their ancestors, and have not obeyed my voice, 21 I will no **2.21**
longer drive out before them any of the nations that Joshua left when he died." 22 In Josh 23.13
order to test Israel, whether or not they would take care to walk in the way of the **2.22** 2 Chron 32.31
LORD as their ancestors did, 23 the LORD had left those nations, not driving them out
at once, and had not handed them over to Joshua.

3 Now these are the nations that the LORD left to test all those in Israel who had **3.1**
no experience of any war in Canaan 2 (it was only that successive generations Ps 78.7 Josh 11.19
of Israelites might know war, to teach those who had no experience of it before):
3 the five lords of the Philistines, and all the Canaanites, and the Sidonians, and the
Hivites who lived on Mount Lebanon, from Mount Baal-hermon as far as Lebo- **3.4**
hamath. 4 They were for the testing of Israel, to know whether Israel would obey Deut 8.2
the commandments of the LORD, which he commanded their ancestors by Moses. Judg 2.22
5 So the Israelites lived among the Canaanites, the Hittites, the Amorites, the Periz- **3.5** Judg 1.29-32

2.15, 16 Despite Israel's disobedience, God showed his great mercy by providing judges to save the people from their oppressors. Mercy has been defined as "not giving a person what he or she deserves." This is exactly what God did for Israel and what he does for us. Our disobedience demands judgment! But God shows mercy toward us by providing an escape from sin's penalty through Jesus Christ, who alone saves us from sin. When we pray for forgiveness, we are asking for what we do not deserve. Yet when we take this step and trust in Christ's saving work on our behalf, we can experience God's forgiveness.

2.17 Why would the people of Israel turn so quickly from their faith in God? Simply put, the Canaanite religion appeared more attractive to their sensual nature and offered more short-range benefits (they believed their idols could increase their fertility in childbearing and in farming). One of its most attractive features was that people could remain selfish and yet fulfill their religious requirements. They could do almost anything they wished and still be obeying at least one of the many Canaanite gods. Male and female prostitution were not only allowed, but encouraged as forms of worship.

Faith in the one true God, however, does not offer short-range benefits that appeal to our sinful human nature. The essence of sin is selfishness; the essence of God's way of life is selflessness. We must seek Christ's help to live God's way.

2.17–19 Throughout this period of history Israel went through seven cycles of (1) rebelling against God, (2) being overrun by enemy nations, (3) being delivered by a God-fearing judge, (4) remaining loyal to God under that judge, and (5) again forgetting God when the judge died. We tend to follow the same cycle—remaining loyal to God as long as we are near those who are devoted to him. But when we are on our own, the pressure to be drawn away from God increases. Determine to be faithful to God despite the difficult situations you may encounter.

3.1–3 We learn from chapter one that these enemy nations were still in the land because the Israelites had failed to obey God and drive them out. Now God would allow the enemies to remain in order to "test" the Israelites; that is, to give them an opportunity to exercise faith and obedience. By now the younger generation that had not fought in the great battles of conquest was coming of age. It was their job to complete the conquest of the land. There were many obstacles yet to be overcome in their new homeland. How they would handle these obstacles would be a test of their faith.

Perhaps God has left obstacles in your life—hostile people, difficult situations, baffling problems—for the purpose of allowing you to develop faith and obedience.

3.5–7 The Israelites discovered that relationships affect faith. The men and women of the surrounding nations were attractive to the Israelites. Soon they intermarried, and the Israelites accepted their pagan gods. This was clearly prohibited by God (Exodus 34.15–17; Deuteronomy 7.1–4). By accepting these gods into their homes, the Israelites gradually began to accept the immoral practices associated with them. Most Israelites didn't start out de-

3.6 Ex 34.15,16 Deut 7.3,4

zites, the Hivites, and the Jebusites; 6 and they took their daughters as wives for
themselves, and their own daughters they gave to their sons; and they worshiped
their gods.

B. THE RESCUE OF ISRAEL BY THE JUDGES (3.7—16.31)

The Israelites began a series of cycles of sinning, worshiping idols, being punished, crying out for help, being rescued by a judge sent from God, obeying God for a while, then falling back into idolatry. They were conquered by Syria, Moab, Canaan, Midian, Ammon, and Philistia. They even faced the threat of civil war. Just as God sent help to the people when they cried out to him, he will deliver us when we call on him.

1. First period: Othniel

3.8 Ex 22.24 Deut 29.20 Judg 2.12-14,20
3.9 Judg 1.13
3.10 Num 11.17 27.18 Judg 6.34; 11.29 1 Sam 10.6
3.11 Judg 5.31; 8.28

7 The Israelites did what was evil in the sight of the LORD, forgetting the LORD
their God, and worshiping the Baals and the Asherahs. 8 Therefore the anger of the
LORD was kindled against Israel, and he sold them into the hand of King Cushan-
rishathaim of Aram-naharaim; and the Israelites served Cushan-rishathaim eight
years. 9 But when the Israelites cried out to the LORD, the LORD raised up a deliverer
for the Israelites, who delivered them, Othniel son of Kenaz, Caleb's younger
brother. 10 The spirit of the LORD came upon him, and he judged Israel; he went out
to war, and the LORD gave King Cushan-rishathaim of Aram into his hand; and his
hand prevailed over Cushan-rishathaim. 11 So the land had rest forty years. Then
Othniel son of Kenaz died.

WHY DID ISRAEL WANT TO WORSHIP IDOLS?

Worshiping God	*Worshiping idols*
long-range benefits	short-range benefits
gratification postponed	self-gratification immediate
morality required	sensuality approved
high ethical standards demanded	low ethical standards tolerated
neighbors' sins disapproved	neighbors' sins approved
unseen God worshiped	visible idols worshiped
unselfishness expected	selfishness condoned
business relations hindered	business relations improved
strict religious practices maintained	religious practices loosely regulated
changed life demanded	changed life not demanded
ethical stand expected	compromise and cooperation practiced
concern for others taught	no concern for others expected

The temptation to follow false gods because of short-term benefits, good feelings, easy "rules," or convenience was always present. *But the benefits were deceptive because the gods were false.* We worship God because he is the one and only true God.

termined to be idolaters, they just added the idols to their worship of God. But before long they found themselves absorbed in pagan worship.

A similar danger faces us. We want to befriend those who don't know God, but through those friendships we can become entangled in unhealthy practices. Friendships with unbelievers are important, but we must accept people without adopting their patterns of behavior. Don't compromise and become entangled in sinful practices.

3.7 Baal was the most worshiped god of the Canaanites. Most often cast in the form of a bull, he symbolized strength and fertility and was considered the god of agriculture. Asherah was Baal's female consort; she was worshiped by means of wooden pillars that substituted for sacred trees. In times of famine, the Canaanites believed Baal was angry with them and was withholding rain as punishment. Archaeologists have uncovered many Baal idols in Israel. It is difficult to imagine the people of Israel trading worship of the Lord for worship of idols of wood, stone, and iron. But we do the same when we forsake worshiping God for other activities or priorities. Our idols are not made of wood or stone, but they are every bit as sinful.

3.9 Othniel was Israel's first judge. In 1.13 we read that he volunteered to lead an attack against a fortified city. Here he was to lead the nation back to God. Othniel had a rich spiritual heritage, for his uncle was Caleb, a man with unwavering faith in God (Numbers 13.30; 14.24). Othniel's leadership brought the people back to God and freed them from the oppression of the king of Mesopotamia. But after Othniel's death, it didn't take the Israelites long to fall back into their neighbors' comfortable but sinful ways.

3.10 This phrase, "The spirit of the Lord came upon him," was also spoken of the judges Gideon, Jephthah, and Samson, among others. It expresses a temporary and spontaneous increase of physical, spiritual, or mental ability. This was an extraordinary and supernatural occurrence to prepare a person for a special task. Even though the Holy Spirit is available to all believers today, he still comes upon believers in an extraordinary way for special tasks. We should ask for the Holy Spirit's help as we face our daily problems as well as the major challenges.

2. Second period: Ehud and Shamgar

The Moabites oppress Israel

12 The Israelites again did what was evil in the sight of the LORD; and the LORD 3.12
strengthened King Eglon of Moab against Israel, because they had done what was Judg 2.19
evil in the sight of the LORD. 13 In alliance with the Ammonites and the Amalekites, Hos 6.4 3.13
he went and defeated Israel; and they took possession of the city of palms. 14 So the Judg 1.16
Israelites served King Eglon of Moab eighteen years.

Ehud

15 But when the Israelites cried out to the LORD, the LORD raised up for them 3.15
a deliverer, Ehud son of Gera, the Benjaminite, a left-handed man. The Israelites Judg 3.9; 20.16 1 Chron 12.2
sent tribute by him to King Eglon of Moab. 16 Ehud made for himself a sword with
two edges, a cubit in length; and he fastened it on his right thigh under his clothes.
17 Then he presented the tribute to King Eglon of Moab. Now Eglon was a very fat
man. 18 When Ehud had finished presenting the tribute, he sent the people who
carried the tribute on their way. 19 But he himself turned back at the sculptured
stones near Gilgal, and said, "I have a secret message for you, O king." So the king
said,[f] "Silence!" and all his attendants went out from his presence. 20 Ehud came
to him, while he was sitting alone in his cool roof chamber, and said, "I have a
message from God for you." So he rose from his seat. 21 Then Ehud reached with
his left hand, took the sword from his right thigh, and thrust it into Eglon's[g] belly;
22 the hilt also went in after the blade, and the fat closed over the blade, for he did
not draw the sword out of his belly; and the dirt came out.[h] 23 Then Ehud went out
into the vestibule,[i] and closed the doors of the roof chamber on him, and locked
them.

24 After he had gone, the servants came. When they saw that the doors of the 3.24
roof chamber were locked, they thought, "He must be relieving himself[j] in the 1 Sam 24.3
cool chamber." 25 So they waited until they were embarrassed. When he still did not
open the doors of the roof chamber, they took the key and opened them. There was
their lord lying dead on the floor.

26 Ehud escaped while they delayed, and passed beyond the sculptured stones,
and escaped to Seirah. 27 When he arrived, he sounded the trumpet in the hill coun-

[f] Heb *he said* [g] Heb *his* [h] With Tg Vg: Meaning of Heb uncertain [i] Meaning of Heb uncertain [j] Heb *covering his feet*

3.12, 13 The Moabites, Ammonites, and Amalekites were nomadic tribes that lived near each other southeast of Canaan. These tribes were notorious raiders, possessing great military skill. The Moabites were descended from Moab, the son of Lot's oldest daughter by an incestuous relationship (Genesis 19.37). When the nation of Israel was at Kadesh, they were refused permission to pass through the land of the Moabites (Judges 11.17). When they were preparing to enter the Promised Land, they were seduced by the Moabite and Midianite women to participate in idolatrous practices (Numbers 25.1-18).

3.13 This was the first time nations outside Canaan attacked the Israelites in their own land. The city of palms is most likely Jericho.

3.15 Ehud is called a "deliverer." In the broadest sense, all the judges can be looked upon as foreshadowing the perfect Deliverer, Jesus Christ. While Ehud delivered Israel from its enemies, Jesus delivers us from sin, our greatest enemy.

3.15–30 This is a strange story, but it teaches us that God can use us just the way he made us. Being left-handed in Ehud's day was considered a handicap. Many Benjaminites were left-handed (see 20.16). But God used Ehud's perceived weakness to give Israel victory. Let God use you the way you are to accomplish his work.

3.16 The sword was about 1 1/2 feet long.

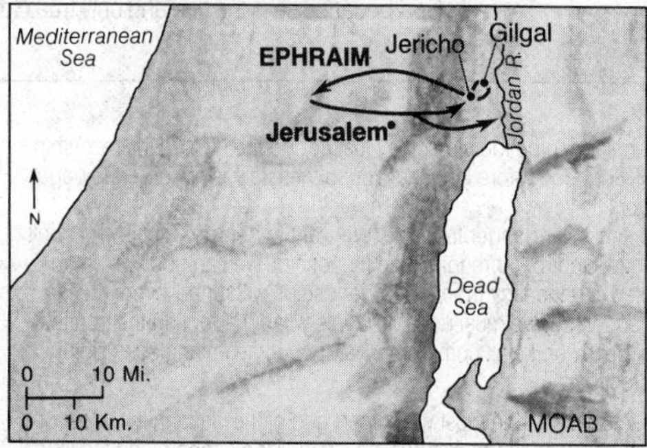

EHUD FREES ISRAEL FROM MOAB When King Eglon of Moab conquered part of Israel, he set up his throne in the city of Jericho. Ehud was chosen to take Israel's tribute there. After delivering Israel's tribute, Ehud killed King Eglon and escaped into the hill country of Ephraim. From there he gathered together an army to cut off any Moabites trying to escape across the Jordan River.

try of Ephraim; and the Israelites went down with him from the hill country, having
3.28 Judg 7.24; 12.5 him at their head. 28 He said to them, "Follow after me; for the LORD has given your
enemies the Moabites into your hand." So they went down after him, and seized the
fords of the Jordan against the Moabites, and allowed no one to cross over. 29 At
that time they killed about ten thousand of the Moabites, all strong, able-bodied
men; no one escaped. 30 So Moab was subdued that day under the hand of Israel.
And the land had rest eighty years.

Shamgar

3.31 Judg 5.6 31 After him came Shamgar son of Anath, who killed six hundred of the Philistines with an oxgoad. He too delivered Israel.

At first glance, Ehud's career as a judge in Israel may not seem relevant to us. He clearly lived in another time. He took radical and violent action to free his people. His murder of Eglon shocks us. His war on Moab was swift and deadly. His life is difficult to relate to. But our commitment to God's word challenges us not to ignore this leader. As we read about his life, some questions come to mind: (1) When was the last time God showed me something wrong in my life and I took immediate and painful action to correct the error? (2) When was the last time I asked God to show me how he could use something unique about me (as he used Ehud's left-handedness)? (3) When was the last time I made a plan to obey God in some specific area of my life and then followed through on that plan? (4) When was the last time my life was an example to others of obedience to God?

The enemies we face are as real as Ehud's, but they are most often within ourselves. The battles we fight are not against other people but against the power of sin. We need God's help in doing battle against sin. We also need to remember that he has already won the war. He has defeated sin at the cross of his Son, Jesus. His help is the cause of each success, and his forgiveness is sufficient for each failure.

Strengths and accomplishments:
- Second judge of Israel
- A man of direct action, a front-line leader
- Used a perceived weakness (left-handedness) to do a great work for God
- Led the revolt against Moabite domination and gave Israel 80 years of peace

Lessons from his life:
- Some conditions call for radical action
- God responds to the cry of repentance
- God is ready to use our unique qualities to accomplish his work

Vital statistics:
- Where: Born during the last years of the wilderness wanderings or during Israel's early years in the promised land
- Occupation: Messenger, judge
- Relatives: Father: Gera
- Contemporary: Eglon of Moab

Key verse:
"But when the Israelites cried out to the Lord, the Lord raised up for them a deliverer, Ehud son of Gera, the Benjaminite, a left-handed man" (Judges 3.15).

His story is told in Judges 3.12–30.

3.22 The phrase, "and the dirt came out," refers to the contents of Eglon's intestines when he was stabbed in the abdomen.

3.28–30 Ehud's courageous faith brought peace to the nation of Israel for 80 years. Genuine faith grows stronger in the face of opposition. By bravely following God, we can present an inspiring example that helps others stand up for him.

3.31 To kill 600 Philistines with an oxgoad was quite a feat. A goad was a long stick with a small flat piece of iron on one side and a sharp point on the other. The sharp side was used to drive the oxen during the times of plowing, and the flat end was used to clean the mud off the plow. Eight-foot-long ancient oxgoads have been found. In times of crisis they could easily have been used as spears, as in Shamgar's case. Oxgoads are still used in the Middle East to drive oxen.

3. Third period: Deborah and Barak

4 The Israelites again did what was evil in the sight of the LORD, after Ehud died. 4.1 Judg 2.19
2 So the LORD sold them into the hand of King Jabin of Canaan, who reigned
in Hazor; the commander of his army was Sisera, who lived in Harosheth-ha- 4.2 Josh 11.1 Ps 83.9
goiim. 3 Then the Israelites cried out to the LORD for help; for he had nine hundred
chariots of iron, and had oppressed the Israelites cruelly twenty years.

Deborah and Barak

4 At that time Deborah, a prophetess, wife of Lappidoth, was judging Israel.
5 She used to sit under the palm of Deborah between Ramah and Bethel in the hill
country of Ephraim; and the Israelites came up to her for judgment. 6 She sent and 4.6
summoned Barak son of Abinoam from Kedesh in Naphtali, and said to him, "The 1 Sam 12.11 Heb 11.32
LORD, the God of Israel, commands you, 'Go, take position at Mount Tabor, bringing ten thousand from the tribe of Naphtali and the tribe of Zebulun. 7 I will draw 4.7
out Sisera, the general of Jabin's army, to meet you by the Wadi Kishon with his Ps 83.9
chariots and his troops; and I will give him into your hand.' " 8 Barak said to her,
"If you will go with me, I will go; but if you will not go with me, I will not go."
9 And she said, "I will surely go with you; nevertheless, the road on which you are
going will not lead to your glory, for the LORD will sell Sisera into the hand of a 4.10
woman." Then Deborah got up and went with Barak to Kedesh. 10 Barak sum- Judg 5.18

4.1 Israel's sin was not only "in the sight of the Lord"; it was also against the Lord. Our sins harm both ourselves and others, but all sin is ultimately against God because it disregards his commands and his authority over us. When confessing his sin David prayed, "Against you, you alone, have I sinned, and done what is evil in your sight" (Psalm 51.4). Recognizing the seriousness of sin is the first step toward removing it from our lives.

4.2, 3 Nothing is known about Jabin. Joshua had defeated a king by that name years earlier and burned the city of Hazor to the ground (Joshua 11.1–11). Either the city was rebuilt by this time, or Jabin was hoping to rebuild it.

This is the only time during the period of the judges when the Israelites' enemies came from within their land. The Israelites had failed to expel all the Canaanites. These Canaanites had regrouped and were attempting to restore their lost power. If the Israelites had obeyed God in the first place and driven the Canaanites from the land, this incident would not have happened.

4.2, 3 Chariots were the tanks of the ancient world. Made of iron or wood, they were pulled by one or two horses and were the most feared and powerful weapons of the day. Some chariots even had razor sharp knives extending from the wheels designed to mutilate helpless foot soldiers. The Canaanite army had 900 iron chariots. Israel was not powerful enough to defeat such an invincible army. Therefore, Jabin and Sisera had no trouble oppressing the people – until a faithful woman named Deborah called upon God.

4.3 After 20 years of unbearable circumstances, the Israelites finally turned to God for help. But God should be the first place we turn when we are facing struggles or dilemmas. The Israelites chose to go their own way and got into a mess. We often do the same. Trying to control our own lives without God's help often leads to struggle and confusion. By contrast, when we stay in daily contact with God, we are less likely to create painful circumstances for ourselves. This is a lesson the Israelites never fully learned. When struggles come our way, God wants us to come to him first, seeking his strength and guidance.

4.4ff The Bible records few women in national leadership positions – Deborah was an exceptional woman. Obviously she was the best person for the job, and God chose her to lead Israel. God can choose anyone to lead his people, young or old, man or woman. Don't let your prejudices get in the way of those God may have chosen to lead you.

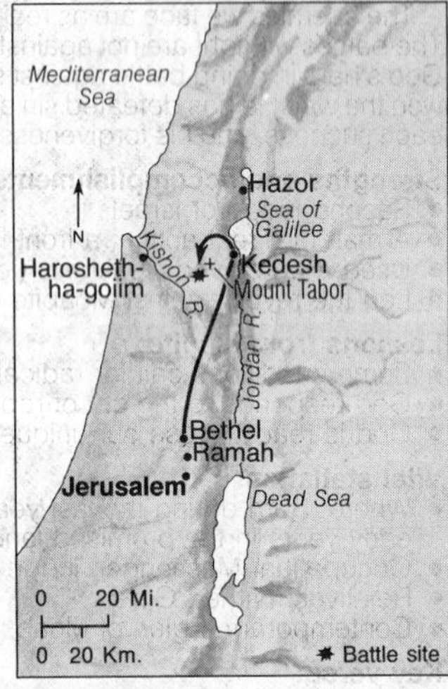

KING JABIN IS DEFEATED
Deborah traveled from her home between Ramah and Bethel to march with Barak and the Israelite army against Hazor. Sisera, commander of Hazor's army, assembled his men at Harosheth. In spite of Sisera's 900 chariots and expertly trained army, Israel was victorious.

4.6–8 Was Barak cowardly or just in need of support? We don't know Barak's character, but we see the character of a great leader in Deborah, who took charge as God directed. Deborah told Barak that God would be with him in battle, but that was not enough for Barak. He wanted Deborah to go with him. Barak's request shows that at heart he trusted human strength more than God's promise. A person of real faith steps out at God's command, even if he or she must do so alone.

4.9 How did Deborah command such respect? She was responsible for leading the people into battle, but more than that, she influenced them to live for God after the battle was over. Her personality drew people together and commanded the respect of even Barak, a military general. She was also a prophetess, whose main role was to encourage the people to obey God. Those who lead must not forget about the spiritual condition of those being led. A true leader is concerned for persons, not just success.

4.9 "Sell" means to give or hand over.

4.11 Josh 19.33 Judg 1.16

moned Zebulun and Naphtali to Kedesh; and ten thousand warriors went up behind
him; and Deborah went up with him.
11 Now Heber the Kenite had separated from the other Kenites,[k] that is, the
descendants of Hobab the father-in-law of Moses, and had encamped as far away
as Elon-bezaanannim, which is near Kedesh.
12 When Sisera was told that Barak son of Abinoam had gone up to Mount
Tabor, 13 Sisera called out all his chariots, nine hundred chariots of iron, and all the
troops who were with him, from Harosheth-ha-goiim to the Wadi Kishon. 14 Then
Deborah said to Barak, "Up! For this is the day on which the LORD has given Sisera
into your hand. The LORD is indeed going out before you." So Barak went down
from Mount Tabor with ten thousand warriors following him. 15 And the LORD
threw Sisera and all his chariots and all his army into a panic[l] before Barak; Sisera
got down from his chariot and fled away on foot, 16 while Barak pursued the chariots and the army to Harosheth-ha-goiim. All the army of Sisera fell by the sword;
no one was left.

4.15 Josh 10.10 Judg 7.21
4.16 Judg 4.2,3 Ps 83.9

17 Now Sisera had fled away on foot to the tent of Jael wife of Heber the Kenite; for there was peace between King Jabin of Hazor and the clan of Heber the
Kenite. 18 Jael came out to meet Sisera, and said to him, "Turn aside, my lord, turn
aside to me; have no fear." So he turned aside to her into the tent, and she covered
him with a rug. 19 Then he said to her, "Please give me a little water to drink; for I
am thirsty." So she opened a skin of milk and gave him a drink and covered him.
20 He said to her, "Stand at the entrance of the tent, and if anybody comes and asks
you, 'Is anyone here?' say, 'No.' " 21 But Jael wife of Heber took a tent peg,
and took a hammer in her hand, and went softly to him and drove the peg into his
temple, until it went down into the ground—he was lying fast asleep from
weariness—and he died. 22 Then, as Barak came in pursuit of Sisera, Jael went out
to meet him, and said to him, "Come, and I will show you the man whom you are
seeking." So he went into her tent; and there was Sisera lying dead, with the tent
peg in his temple.
23 So on that day God subdued King Jabin of Canaan before the Israelites.
24 Then the hand of the Israelites bore harder and harder on King Jabin of Canaan,
until they destroyed King Jabin of Canaan.

4.19 Judg 5.25

[k] Heb *from the Kain* [l] Heb adds *to the sword*; compare verse 16

THE JUDGES' FUNCTIONS
Regardless of an individual judge's leadership style, each one demonstrated that God's judgment follows apostasy, while repentance brings restoration.

Judges of Israel could be:

saviors (deliverers) and redeemers (Gideon)	or mediators and administrators (Tola)
providers of rest and peace (Ehud and Jair)	or rude, petty dictators (Jephthah)
famous and powerful (Samson)	or hardworking yet unsung (Elon and Abdon)
leaders of the nation (Othniel and Deborah)	or local heroes (Shamgar and Ibzan)

4.11 Heber was Jael's husband (4.17). He was from the Kenite tribe, a longtime ally of Israel. But for some reason, Heber decided to side with Jabin, maybe because Jabin's army appeared to have the military advantage. It was probably Heber who told Sisera that the Israelites were camped near Mount Tabor (4.12; see map). Although Heber threw his lot with Jabin and his forces, his wife Jael did not (4.21).

4.18–21 Sisera couldn't have been more pleased when Jael offered him her tent as a hiding place. First, because Jael was the wife of Heber, a man loyal to Sisera's forces (see the note on 4.11), he thought she certainly could be trusted. Second, because men were never allowed to enter a woman's tent, no one would think to look for Sisera there.

Even though her husband, Heber, was loyal to Sisera's forces, Jael certainly was not. Since women of that day were in charge of pitching the tents, Jael had no problem driving the tent peg into Sisera's head while he slept. Deborah's prediction was thus fulfilled: the honor of conquering Sisera went to a brave and resourceful woman (4.9).

The song of Deborah

5 Then Deborah and Barak son of Abinoam sang on that day, saying: **5.1** Ex 15.1,21 Num 21.17,18 1 Sam 2.1
2 "When locks are long in Israel,
when the people offer themselves willingly —
bless[m] the LORD! **5.2** Ps 110.3

3 "Hear, O kings; give ear, O princes;
to the LORD I will sing,
I will make melody to the LORD, the God of Israel.

4 "LORD, when you went out from Seir, **5.4** Deut 33.2 Hab 3.3
when you marched from the region of Edom,
the earth trembled,
and the heavens poured,
the clouds indeed poured water.
5 The mountains quaked before the LORD, the One of Sinai, **5.5** Ex 19.18; 20.18 Ps 97.5; 114.6 Isa 64.3
before the LORD, the God of Israel.

6 "In the days of Shamgar son of Anath, **5.6** Judg 3.31; 4.17
in the days of Jael, caravans ceased
and travelers kept to the byways.
7 The peasantry prospered in Israel,
they grew fat on plunder,
because you arose, Deborah,
arose as a mother in Israel.
8 When new gods were chosen, **5.8** Deut 32.17 1 Sam 13.22
then war was in the gates.
Was shield or spear to be seen
among forty thousand in Israel?
9 My heart goes out to the commanders of Israel
who offered themselves willingly among the people.
Bless the LORD.

10 "Tell of it, you who ride on white donkeys, **5.10** Judg 10.4; 12.14
you who sit on rich carpets[n]
and you who walk by the way.
11 To the sound of musicians[n] at the watering places, **5.11** Gen 24.11 1 Sam 12.7
there they repeat the triumphs of the LORD,
the triumphs of his peasantry in Israel.

"Then down to the gates marched the people of the LORD.

12 "Awake, awake, Deborah!
Awake, awake, utter a song!

[m] Or *You who offer yourselves willingly among the people, bless* [n] Meaning of Heb uncertain

---

5.1ff Music and singing were a cherished part of Israel's culture. Chapter five is a song, possibly composed and sung by Deborah and Barak. It sets to music the story of Israel's great victory recounted in chapter four. This victory song was accompanied by joyous celebration. It proclaimed God's greatness by giving him credit for the victory. It was an excellent way to preserve and retell this wonderful story from generation to generation. (Other songs in the Bible are listed in the chart in Exodus 16.)

5.1ff In victory, Barak and Deborah sang praises to God. Songs of praise focus our attention on God, give us an outlet for spiritual celebration, and remind us of God's faithfulness and character. Whether you are experiencing a great victory or a major dilemma, singing praises to God can have a positive effect on your attitude.

5.2 This expression, "When locks are long," may be a poetic reference to the nazirite vow, with which freedom, strength, and dedication to God were associated. Soldiers left their hair uncut to show they were engaged in a holy war.

5.8 War was the inevitable result when Israel chose to follow false gods. Although God had given clear directions, the people failed to heed his words. Without God at the center of their national life, pressure from the outside soon became greater than power from within, and they were an easy prey for their ene mies. If you are letting a desire for recognition, craving for power, or love of money rule your life, you may find yourself besieged by enemies — stress, anxiety, illness, fatigue. Keep God at the center of your life, and you will have the power you need to fight these destroyers.

Arise, Barak, lead away your captives,
O son of Abinoam.
13 Then down marched the remnant of the noble;
the people of the LORD marched down for him[o] against the mighty.
14 From Ephraim they set out[p] into the valley,[q]
following you, Benjamin, with your kin;
from Machir marched down the commanders,
and from Zebulun those who bear the marshal's staff;
15 the chiefs of Issachar came with Deborah,
and Issachar faithful to Barak;
into the valley they rushed out at his heels.
Among the clans of Reuben
there were great searchings of heart.
5.16 Num 32.24
16 Why did you tarry among the sheepfolds,
to hear the piping for the flocks?
Among the clans of Reuben
there were great searchings of heart.

[o] Gk: Heb *me* [p] Cn: Heb *From Ephraim their root* [q] Gk: Heb *in Amalek*

DEBORAH

Wise leaders are rare. They accomplish great amounts of work without direct involvement because they know how to work through other people. They are able to see the big picture which often escapes those directly involved, so they make good mediators, advisers, and planners. Deborah fit this description perfectly. She had all these leadership skills, and she had a remarkable relationship with God. The insight and confidence God gave this woman placed her in a unique position in the Old Testament. Deborah is among the outstanding women of history.

Her story shows that she was not power hungry. She wanted to serve God. Whenever praise came her way, she gave God the credit. She didn't deny or resist her position in the culture as a woman and wife, but she never allowed herself to be hindered by it either. Her story shows that God can accomplish great things through people who are willing to be led by him.

Deborah's life challenges us in several ways. She reminds us of the need to be available both to God and to others. She encourages us to spend our efforts on what we can do rather than on worrying about what we can't do. Deborah challenges us to be wise leaders. She demonstrates what a person can accomplish when God is in control.

Strengths and accomplishments:
- Fourth and only female judge of Israel
- Special abilities as a mediator, adviser, and counselor
- When called on to lead, was able to plan, direct, and delegate
- Known for her prophetic power
- A writer of songs

Lessons from her life:
- God chooses leaders by his standards, not ours
- Wise leaders choose good helpers

Vital statistics:
- Where: Canaan
- Occupation: Prophetess and judge
- Relatives: Husband: Lapidoth
- Contemporaries: Barak, Jael, Jabin of Hazor, Sisera

Key verse:
"At that time Deborah, a prophetess, wife of Lappidoth, was judging Israel" (Judges 4.4).

Her story is told in Judges 4; 5.

5.13, 14 Despite the odds, God's people could boldly and confidently attack the mighty. If you are struggling with something greater than you can handle, turn to the Bible for God's encouragement. When the odds seem stacked against us, God can swiftly turn them to our favor.

5.15–17 Four tribes – Reuben, Gilead (either Gad or Manasseh), Dan, and Asher – were accused of not lending a helping hand in the battle. No reasons are given for their refusal to help their fellow Israelites, but they may be the same ones that stopped them from driving out the Canaanites in the first place: (1) lack of faith in God to help, (2) lack of effort, (3) fear of the enemy, (4) fear of antagonizing those with whom they did business and thus from whom they prospered. This disobedience showed a lack of enthusiasm for God's plan.

17 Gilead stayed beyond the Jordan;
and Dan, why did he abide with the ships?
Asher sat still at the coast of the sea,
settling down by his landings.
18 Zebulun is a people that scorned death;
Naphtali too, on the heights of the field.

5.17 Josh 13.25; 22.9

19 "The kings came, they fought;
then fought the kings of Canaan,
at Taanach, by the waters of Megiddo;
they got no spoils of silver.
20 The stars fought from heaven,
from their courses they fought against Sisera.
21 The torrent Kishon swept them away,
the onrushing torrent, the torrent Kishon.
March on, my soul, with might!

5.19 Josh 11.1,2 Judg 1.27

5.21 Judg 4.7

22 "Then loud beat the horses' hoofs
with the galloping, galloping of his steeds.

5.22 Job 39.19-25

23 "Curse Meroz, says the angel of the LORD,
curse bitterly its inhabitants,
because they did not come to the help of the LORD,
to the help of the LORD against the mighty.

24 "Most blessed of women be Jael,
the wife of Heber the Kenite,
of tent-dwelling women most blessed.
25 He asked water and she gave him milk,
she brought him curds in a lordly bowl.
26 She put her hand to the tent peg
and her right hand to the workmen's mallet;
she struck Sisera a blow,
she crushed his head,
she shattered and pierced his temple.
27 He sank, he fell,
he lay still at her feet;
at her feet he sank, he fell;
where he sank, there he fell dead.

28 "Out of the window she peered,
the mother of Sisera gazed[r] through the lattice:
'Why is his chariot so long in coming?
Why tarry the hoofbeats of his chariots?'
29 Her wisest ladies make answer,
indeed, she answers the question herself:
30 'Are they not finding and dividing the spoil?—
A girl or two for every man;
spoil of dyed stuffs for Sisera,
spoil of dyed stuffs embroidered,
two pieces of dyed work embroidered for my neck as spoil?'

5.30 Ex 15.9

31 "So perish all your enemies, O LORD!

5.31 Ps 68.1,2 92.8,9

[r] Gk Compare Tg: Heb *exclaimed*

5.23 Meroz was probably a city near the scene of the great battle between the Canaanites and Israelites. It must have been an Israelite city, because it was cursed for not sending help against Sisera's forces.

But may your friends be like the sun as it rises in its might."

And the land had rest forty years.

4. Fourth period: Gideon, Tola, and Jair

The Midianites oppress Israel

6.1 Num 22.4 25.15; 31.1 Judg 2.11-14
6 The Israelites did what was evil in the sight of the LORD, and the LORD gave
them into the hand of Midian seven years. 2 The hand of Midian prevailed over
Israel; and because of Midian the Israelites provided for themselves hiding places
6.3 Isa 21.2
in the mountains, caves and strongholds. 3 For whenever the Israelites put in seed,
the Midianites and the Amalekites and the people of the East would come up
against them. 4 They would encamp against them and destroy the produce of the
land, as far as the neighborhood of Gaza, and leave no sustenance in Israel, and no
6.5 1 Sam 30.17
sheep or ox or donkey. 5 For they and their livestock would come up, and they
would even bring their tents, as thick as locusts; neither they nor their camels could
6.6 Deut 28.43
be counted; so they wasted the land as they came in. 6 Thus Israel was greatly impoverished because of Midian; and the Israelites cried out to the LORD for help.
6.8 Ex 18.9 Judg 2.1,2,18 10.12
7 When the Israelites cried to the LORD on account of the Midianites, 8 the LORD
sent a prophet to the Israelites; and he said to them, "Thus says the LORD, the God
of Israel: I led you up from Egypt, and brought you out of the house of slavery; 9 and
I delivered you from the hand of the Egyptians, and from the hand of all who op-
6.10 Josh 24.15
pressed you, and drove them out before you, and gave you their land; 10 and I said
to you, 'I am the LORD your God; you shall not pay reverence to the gods of the
Amorites, in whose land you live.' But you have not given heed to my voice."

God commissions Gideon

6.11 Judg 13.2,3 Heb 11.32
11 Now the angel of the LORD came and sat under the oak at Ophrah, which
belonged to Joash the Abiezrite, as his son Gideon was beating out wheat in the
wine press, to hide it from the Midianites. 12 The angel of the LORD appeared to him
and said to him, "The LORD is with you, you mighty warrior." 13 Gideon answered

---

6.2 The Midianites were desert people descended from Abraham's second wife, Keturah (Genesis 25.1, 2). From this relationship came a nation that was always in conflict with Israel. Years earlier the Israelites, while still wandering in the wilderness, battled the Midianites and almost totally destroyed them (Numbers 31.1–20). Because of their failure to completely destroy them, however, the tribe repopulated. Here they were once again oppressing Israel.

6.6, 7 Again Israel hit rock bottom before turning back to God. How much suffering they could have avoided if they had trusted him! Turning to God shouldn't be a last resort; we should look to him for help each day. This isn't to say he will always give us an easy life. There will be struggles, but God will give us the strength to live through them. Don't wait until you're desperate. Call on God first in every situation.

6.8 The Bible does not say who this prophet was. Prophets were those who brought God's messages to the people. Their main role was to urge people to turn away from their sins and back to God. This is exactly what this prophet did.

6.11 The Old Testament records several appearances of an angel of the Lord: Genesis 16.7; 22.11; 31.11; Exodus 3.2; 14.19; Judges 2.1; 13.3; Zechariah 3.1–6. It is not known whether the same angel appeared in each case. The angel mentioned here appears to be separate from God in one place (6.12) and yet the same as God in another place (6.14). This has led many to believe that the angel was a special appearance of Jesus Christ prior to his mission on earth as recorded in the New Testament. It is also possible that as a special messenger from God, the angel had authority to speak for God. In either case, God sent a special messenger to deliver an important message to Gideon.

6.11 "Beating out the wheat" was the process of separating the grains of wheat from the useless outer shell called chaff. Also called "threshing," this was normally done in a large area, often on a hill, where the wind could blow away the lighter chaff when the farmer tossed the beaten wheat into the air. If Gideon had done this, however, he would have been an easy target for the bands of raiders who were overrunning the land. Therefore, he was forced to thresh his wheat in a winepress, a pit that was probably hidden from view and that would not be suspected as a place to find a farmer's crops.

6.13 Gideon questioned God about the problems he and his nation faced and about God's apparent lack of help. What he didn't acknowledge was the fact that the people had brought calamity upon themselves when they decided to disobey and neglect God. How easy it is to overlook personal accountability and blame our problems on God and others. Unfortunately this does not solve our problems. It brings us no closer to God, and it escorts us to the very edge of rebellion and backsliding.

When problems come, the first place to look is within. Our first action should be confession to God of sins that may have created our problems.

6.13 Gideon had heard about the great miracles God had done for his people, but he hadn't seen any. It had been almost 250 years since the ten plagues and the parting of the Red Sea (Exodus 7–14), and 200 years had passed since the last great miracle, the parting of the Jordan River (Joshua 3). Because of this lack of miracles, Gideon wrongly assumed that God had given up on his people. But it was the people who had given up on God. They knew what God expected of them. They had his laws, but they chose not to obey them. God's blessings, as Moses and Joshua had foretold, came only when the people were obedient.

him, "But sir, if the LORD is with us, why then has all this happened to us? And 6.13
where are all his wonderful deeds that our ancestors recounted to us, saying, 'Did Deut 31.17 2 Chron 15.2
not the LORD bring us up from Egypt?' But now the LORD has cast us off, and given Ps 44.9
us into the hand of Midian." 14 Then the LORD turned to him and said, "Go in this
might of yours and deliver Israel from the hand of Midian; I hereby commission
you." 15 He responded, "But sir, how can I deliver Israel? My clan is the weakest 6.15
in Manasseh, and I am the least in my family." 16 The LORD said to him, "But I will Ex 3.11
be with you, and you shall strike down the Midianites, every one of them." 17 Then 6.17
he said to him, "If now I have found favor with you, then show me a sign that it is Isa 38.7
you who speak with me. 18 Do not depart from here until I come to you, and bring
out my present, and set it before you." And he said, "I will stay until you return."
19 So Gideon went into his house and prepared a kid, and unleavened cakes 6.19
from an ephah of flour; the meat he put in a basket, and the broth he put in a pot, Gen 18.8
and brought them to him under the oak and presented them. 20 The angel of God
said to him, "Take the meat and the unleavened cakes, and put them on this rock,
and pour out the broth." And he did so. 21 Then the angel of the LORD reached out 6.21
the tip of the staff that was in his hand, and touched the meat and the unleavened Lev 9.24
cakes; and fire sprang up from the rock and consumed the meat and the unleavened
cakes; and the angel of the LORD vanished from his sight. 22 Then Gideon perceived 6.22
that it was the angel of the LORD; and Gideon said, "Help me, Lord GOD! For I have Gen 16.13 32.30
seen the angel of the LORD face to face." 23 But the LORD said to him, "Peace be to Ex 33.20
you; do not fear, you shall not die." 24 Then Gideon built an altar there to the LORD, Judg 13.22
and called it, The LORD is peace. To this day it still stands at Ophrah, which belongs to the Abiezrites.

Gideon destroys idols

25 That night the LORD said to him, "Take your father's bull, the second bull 6.25
seven years old, and pull down the altar of Baal that belongs to your father, and cut Ex 34.13 Deut 7.5
down the sacred pole[s] that is beside it; 26 and build an altar to the LORD your God
on the top of the stronghold here, in proper order; then take the second bull, and
offer it as a burnt offering with the wood of the sacred pole[s] that you shall cut
down." 27 So Gideon took ten of his servants, and did as the LORD had told him; but
because he was too afraid of his family and the townspeople to do it by day, he did
it by night.
28 When the townspeople rose early in the morning, the altar of Baal was broken down, and the sacred pole[s] beside it was cut down, and the second bull was
offered on the altar that had been built. 29 So they said to one another, "Who has
done this?" After searching and inquiring, they were told, "Gideon son of Joash did
it." 30 Then the townspeople said to Joash, "Bring out your son, so that he may die,
for he has pulled down the altar of Baal and cut down the sacred pole[s] beside it."
31 But Joash said to all who were arrayed against him, "Will you contend for Baal?

[s] Heb *Asherah*

6.14–16 "I will be with you," God told Gideon, and God promised to give him the strength he needed to overcome the opposition. In spite of this clear promise for strength, Gideon made excuses. Seeing only his limitations and weaknesses, he failed to see how God could work through him.

Like Gideon, we are called to serve God in specific ways. Although God promises us the tools and strength we need, we often make excuses. But reminding God of our limitations only implies that he does not know all about us or that he has made a mistake in evaluating our character. Don't spend time making excuses. Instead spend it doing what God wants.

6.22 Why was Gideon afraid of seeing an angel? The Israelites believed that no one could see God and live (see God's words to Moses in Exodus 33.20). Evidently Gideon thought this also applied to angels.

6.25–30 After God called Gideon to be Israel's deliverer, he immediately asked him to tear down the altar of the pagan god, Baal—an act that would test Gideon's faith and commitment. Canaanite religion was very political, so an attack on a god was often seen as an attack on the local government supporting that god. If caught, Gideon would face serious social problems and probable physical attack.

Gideon took a great risk by following God's higher law which specifically forbids idol worship (Exodus 20.1–5). After learning what Gideon had done, the townspeople wanted to kill him. Many of those people were fellow Israelites. This shows how immoral God's people had become. God said in Deuteronomy 13.6–11 that idolaters must be stoned to death, but these Israelites wanted to stone Gideon for tearing down an idol and worshiping God! When you begin to accomplish something for God, you may be criticized by the very people who should support you.

Or will you defend his cause? Whoever contends for him shall be put to death by
morning. If he is a god, let him contend for himself, because his altar has been
pulled down." 32 Therefore on that day Gideon[t] was called Jerubbaal, that is to
say, "Let Baal contend against him," because he pulled down his altar.

Gideon puts out the fleece

6.33 Josh 17.16-18 Judg 7.1,12,13
6.34 Judg 3.10
6.35 Judg 7.24; 9.31
6.36 Judg 6.14

33 Then all the Midianites and the Amalekites and the people of the East came
together, and crossing the Jordan they encamped in the Valley of Jezreel. 34 But the
spirit of the LORD took possession of Gideon; and he sounded the trumpet, and the
Abiezrites were called out to follow him. 35 He sent messengers throughout all Manasseh, and they too were called out to follow him. He also sent messengers to
Asher, Zebulun, and Naphtali, and they went up to meet them.

36 Then Gideon said to God, "In order to see whether you will deliver Israel by
my hand, as you have said, 37 I am going to lay a fleece of wool on the threshing
floor; if there is dew on the fleece alone, and it is dry on all the ground, then I shall
know that you will deliver Israel by my hand, as you have said." 38 And it was so.

[t] Heb *he*

GOD USES COMMON PEOPLE

God uses all sorts of people to do his work—like you and me!

Person	*Known as*	*Task*	*Reference*
JACOB	A liar	To "father" the Israelite nation	Genesis 27
JOSEPH	A slave	To save his family	Genesis 39ff
MOSES	Shepherd in exile (and murderer)	To lead Israel out of bondage, to the promised land	Exodus 3
GIDEON	A farmer	To deliver Israel from Midian	Judges 6.11
JEPHTHAH	Son of a prostitute	To deliver Israel from the Ammonites	Judges 11.1
HANNAH	A housewife	To be the mother of Samuel	I Samuel 1
DAVID	A shepherd boy and last-born of the family	To be Israel's greatest king	I Samuel 16
EZRA	A scribe	To lead the return to Judah and to write some of the Bible	Ezra, Nehemiah
ESTHER	A slave girl	To save her people from massacre	Esther
MARY	A peasant girl	To be the mother of Christ	Luke 1.27–38
MATTHEW	A tax-collector	To be an apostle and gospel writer	Matthew 9.9
LUKE	A Greek physician	To be a companion of Paul and a gospel writer	Colossians 4.14
PETER	A fisherman	To be an apostle, a leader of the early church, and a writer of two New Testament epistles	Matthew 4.18–20

6.33 The armies of Midian and Amalek camped in the Valley of Jezreel, the agricultural center for the area. Whoever controlled the valley's rich and fertile land controlled the people who lived in and around it. Because of the valley's vast resources, many major trade routes converged at the pass which led into it. This made it the site of many great battles. Gideon's men attacked the enemy armies from the hills, and the only escape route was through the pass toward the Jordan River. That is why Gideon urged some of his troops to take control of the river's crossing points (7.24).

6.34 The spirit of the Lord took such control of Gideon that it was as though the spirit was clothed with Gideon. Thus empowered, Gideon was ready for the task God gave him to carry out.

6.37 Was Gideon really testing God, or was he simply asking God for more encouragement? In either case, though his motive was right (to obey God and defeat the enemy), his method was less than ideal. Gideon seems to have known that his requests might displease God (6.39), and yet he demanded two miracles (6.37, 39) even after witnessing the miraculous fire from the rock (6.21). It is true that to make good decisions we need facts. Gideon had all the facts, but still he hesitated. He delayed obeying God because he wanted even more proof.

Demanding extra signs was an indication of unbelief. Fear often makes us wait for more confirmation when we should be taking action. Visible signs are unnecessary if they only confirm what we already know is true.

Today the greatest means of God's guidance is his Word. Unlike Gideon, we have God's complete, revealed Word. If you want to have more of God's guidance, don't ask for signs; study God's Word (2 Timothy 3.16, 17).

When he rose early next morning and squeezed the fleece, he wrung enough dew
from the fleece to fill a bowl with water. 39 Then Gideon said to God, "Do not let **6.39**
your anger burn against me, let me speak one more time; let me, please, make trial Gen 18.32
with the fleece just once more; let it be dry only on the fleece, and on all the ground
let there be dew." 40 And God did so that night. It was dry on the fleece only, and
on all the ground there was dew.

Gideon selects an army and defeats Midian

7 Then Jerubbaal (that is, Gideon) and all the troops that were with him rose **7.1**
early and encamped beside the spring of Harod; and the camp of Midian was Gen 12.6 Deut 11.30
north of them, below[u] the hill of Moreh, in the valley. Judg 6.32
2 The LORD said to Gideon, "The troops with you are too many for me to give **7.2**
the Midianites into their hand. Israel would only take the credit away from me, Deut 8.18 Isa 10.13
saying, 'My own hand has delivered me.' 3 Now therefore proclaim this in the hear- Ezek 28.2,17
ing of the troops, 'Whoever is fearful and trembling, let him return home.'" Thus **7.3** Deut 20.8
Gideon sifted them out;[v] twenty-two thousand returned, and ten thousand remained.
4 Then the LORD said to Gideon, "The troops are still too many; take them down **7.4**
to the water and I will sift them out for you there. When I say, 'This one shall go 1 Sam 14.6
with you,' he shall go with you; and when I say, 'This one shall not go with you,'
he shall not go." 5 So he brought the troops down to the water; and the LORD said
to Gideon, "All those who lap the water with their tongues, as a dog laps, you shall
put to one side; all those who kneel down to drink, putting their hands to their
mouths,[w] you shall put to the other side." 6 The number of those that lapped was
three hundred; but all the rest of the troops knelt down to drink water. 7 Then the
LORD said to Gideon, "With the three hundred that lapped I will deliver you, and
give the Midianites into your hand. Let all the others go to their homes." 8 So he **7.8**
took the jars of the troops from their hands,[x] and their trumpets; and he sent all the Josh 2.24; 10.8 11.6
rest of Israel back to their own tents, but retained the three hundred. The camp of Judg 3.28; 4.14
Midian was below him in the valley.
9 That same night the LORD said to him, "Get up, attack the camp; for I have

[u] Heb *from* [v] Cn: Heb *home, and depart from Mount Gilead'"* [w] Heb places the words *putting their hands to their mouths* after the word *lapped* in verse 6 [x] Cn: Heb *So the people took provisions in their hands*

6.39 After seeing the miracle of the wet fleece, why did Gideon ask for another miracle? Perhaps he thought the results of the first test could have happened naturally. A thick fleece could retain moisture long after the sun had dried the surrounding ground. "Putting out fleeces" is a poor decision-making method. Those who do this put limitations on God. They ask him to fit their expectations. The results of such experiments are usually inconclusive and thus fail to make us any more confident about our choices. Don't let a "fleece" become a substitute for God's wisdom that comes through Bible study and prayer.

7.2 Self-sufficiency is an enemy when it causes us to believe we can always do what needs to be done in our own strength. To prevent this attitude among Gideon's soldiers, God reduced their number from 32,000 to 300. With an army this small, there could be no doubt that victory was from God. The men could not take the credit. Like Gideon, we must recognize the danger of fighting in our own strength. We can be confident of victory only if we put our confidence in God and not ourselves.

7.10, 11 Facing overwhelming odds, Gideon was afraid. God understood his fear, but he didn't excuse Gideon from his task. Instead he allowed Gideon to slip into the enemy camp and overhear a conversation that would give him courage (7.12–15). Are you facing a battle? God can give you the strength you need for any situation. And don't be startled by the way he helps you. Like Gideon, you must listen to God and be ready to take the first step. Only after you begin to obey God will you find the courage to move ahead.

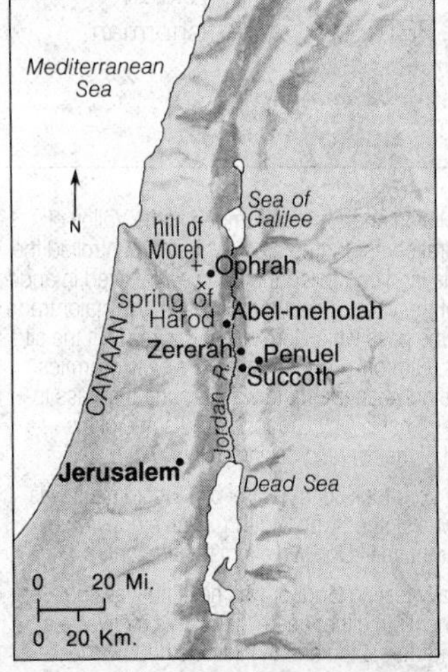

GIDEON'S BATTLE
In spite of Deborah and Barak's victory, the Canaanites still caused trouble in this fertile region. God appeared to Gideon at Ophrah and called him to defeat them. With only 300 fighting men, Gideon routed thousands of Midianites, chasing them to Zererah and Abel-meholah.

given it into your hand. 10 But if you fear to attack, go down to the camp with your
servant Purah; 11 and you shall hear what they say, and afterward your hands shall
be strengthened to attack the camp." Then he went down with his servant Purah to
7.12 Josh 11.4 Judg 6.5; 8.10
the outposts of the armed men that were in the camp. 12 The Midianites and the
Amalekites and all the people of the East lay along the valley as thick as locusts;
and their camels were without number, countless as the sand on the seashore.
13 When Gideon arrived, there was a man telling a dream to his comrade; and he
said, "I had a dream, and in it a cake of barley bread tumbled into the camp of
Midian, and came to the tent, and struck it so that it fell; it turned upside down, and
the tent collapsed." 14 And his comrade answered, "This is no other than the sword
of Gideon son of Joash, a man of Israel; into his hand God has given Midian and all
the army."

15 When Gideon heard the telling of the dream and its interpretation, he worshiped; and he returned to the camp of Israel, and said, "Get up; for the LORD has
given the army of Midian into your hand." 16 After he divided the three hundred
men into three companies, and put trumpets into the hands of all of them, and
empty jars, with torches inside the jars, 17 he said to them, "Look at me, and do the
same; when I come to the outskirts of the camp, do as I do. 18 When I blow the
trumpet, I and all who are with me, then you also blow the trumpets around
the whole camp, and shout, 'For the LORD and for Gideon!' "

19 So Gideon and the hundred who were with him came to the outskirts of the
camp at the beginning of the middle watch, when they had just set the watch; and
they blew the trumpets and smashed the jars that were in their hands. 20 So the three
companies blew the trumpets and broke the jars, holding in their left hands the
torches, and in their right hands the trumpets to blow; and they cried, "A sword for
7.21 Ex 14.25 2 Kgs 7.7
the LORD and for Gideon!" 21 Every man stood in his place all around the camp, and
all the men in camp ran; they cried out and fled. 22 When they blew the three hundred trumpets, the LORD set every man's sword against his fellow and against all
the army; and the army fled as far as Beth-shittah toward Zererah,[y] as far as the
border of Abel-meholah, by Tabbath. 23 And the men of Israel were called out from
Naphtali and from Asher and from all Manasseh, and they pursued after the Midianites.

7.24 Judg 3:28; 12.5
24 Then Gideon sent messengers throughout all the hill country of Ephraim,
saying, "Come down against the Midianites and seize the waters against them, as
far as Beth-barah, and also the Jordan." So all the men of Ephraim were called out,
7.25 Judg 8.2,3 Ps 83.11 Isa 10.26
and they seized the waters as far as Beth-barah, and also the Jordan. 25 They captured the two captains of Midian, Oreb and Zeeb; they killed Oreb at the rock of
Oreb, and Zeeb they killed at the wine press of Zeeb, as they pursued the Midianites. They brought the heads of Oreb and Zeeb to Gideon beyond the Jordan.

[y] Another reading is *Zeredah*

7.12, 13 An enemy soldier dreamed of a loaf of barley bread tumbling into camp. Barley grain was only half the value of wheat, and the bread made from it was considered inferior. In the same way, Israel's tiny band of men was considered inferior to the vast forces of Midian and Amalek. But God would make the underdog Israelites seem invincible.

7.15 Gideon stood just outside the enemy camp and worshiped. Rituals, motions, and loud praise would have announced his presence to the enemy, so Gideon's worship must have been a silent attitude of joy, thanksgiving, and praise to God. Worship is not limited to a particular form or building. We can worship anywhere by changing our focus from life's struggles to the God who cares. True worship begins with a worshipful attitude.

7.19 The night was divided equally into three watches. The beginning of the second watch would have been around 10:00 at night. Many in the camp would have still been awake.

7.21 Gideon's army simply watched as the army of Midian fell into panic, confusion, and disordered retreat. Not one man had to draw a sword to defeat the enemy. Gideon's small army could never have brought about such a victory in their own strength. God wanted to demonstrate to Israel that victory depends not on strength or numbers, but on obedience and commitment to him.

Gideon punishes those who refuse to help

8 Then the Ephraimites said to him, "What have you done to us, not to call us 8.1
when you went to fight against the Midianites?" And they upbraided him vio- Judg 12.1
lently. 2 So he said to them, "What have I done now in comparison with you? Is not
the gleaning of the grapes of Ephraim better than the vintage of Abiezer? 3 God has
given into your hands the captains of Midian, Oreb and Zeeb; what have I been able
to do in comparison with you?" When he said this, their anger against him subsided.
4 Then Gideon came to the Jordan and crossed over, he and the three hundred
who were with him, exhausted and famished.[z] 5 So he said to the people of Suc- 8.5
coth, "Please give some loaves of bread to my followers, for they are exhausted, Gen 33.17 Judg 8.15
and I am pursuing Zebah and Zalmunna, the kings of Midian." 6 But the officials of
Succoth said, "Do you already have in your possession the hands of Zebah and
Zalmunna, that we should give bread to your army?" 7 Gideon replied, "Well then, 8.7
when the LORD has given Zebah and Zalmunna into my hand, I will trample your Judg 4.14; 7.15
flesh on the thorns of the wilderness and on briers." 8 From there he went up to 8.8
Penuel, and made the same request of them; and the people of Penuel answered him Gen 32.30 1 Kgs 12.25
as the people of Succoth had answered. 9 So he said to the people of Penuel, "When
I come back victorious, I will break down this tower."
10 Now Zebah and Zalmunna were in Karkor with their army, about fifteen 8.10
thousand men, all who were left of all the army of the people of the East; for one Ps 83.9 Isa 9.4
hundred twenty thousand men bearing arms had fallen. 11 So Gideon went up by the
caravan route east of Nobah and Jogbehah, and attacked the army; for the army was
off its guard. 12 Zebah and Zalmunna fled; and he pursued them and took the two
kings of Midian, Zebah and Zalmunna, and threw all the army into a panic.
13 When Gideon son of Joash returned from the battle by the ascent of Heres,
14 he caught a young man, one of the people of Succoth, and questioned him; and
he listed for him the officials and elders of Succoth, seventy-seven people. 15 Then 8.15
he came to the people of Succoth, and said, "Here are Zebah and Zalmunna, about Judg 8.7
whom you taunted me, saying, 'Do you already have in your possession the hands
of Zebah and Zalmunna, that we should give bread to your troops who are exhausted?' " 16 So he took the elders of the city and he took thorns of the wilderness
and briers and with them he trampled[a] the people of Succoth. 17 He also broke 8.17
down the tower of Penuel, and killed the men of the city. Judg 8.8
18 Then he said to Zebah and Zalmunna, "What about the men whom you
killed at Tabor?" They answered, "As you are, so were they, every one of them;
they resembled the sons of a king." 19 And he replied, "They were my brothers, the
sons of my mother; as the LORD lives, if you had saved them alive, I would not kill

[z] Gk: Heb *pursuing* [a] With verse 7, Compare Gk: Heb *he taught*

8.1–3 Ephraim's leaders felt left out because Gideon had not called them to join the battle, but had left them in place to "clean up" the escaping Midianites ("gleaning of the grapes"), and so they angrily confronted him ("upbraided him violently"). Gideon assured the leaders of Ephraim that their accomplishment was even greater than his own clan's ("Abi-ezer"). His diplomatic explanation pointed out that this rear guard had managed to capture the enemy's generals, thus cutting off the leaders from their army. Not every necessary job is a highly visible leadership role. Much of the necessary labor of any effective enterprise is considered by many to be dirty work. But such work is vital to getting any big task done. Engineers and millionaires may design and finance an elegant building, but it is the bricklayers who get the work done. Pride causes us to want recognition. Are you content to be God's bricklayer, or do you resent the work God has given you?

8.5–9 The leaders of Succoth and Penuel refused to help Gideon, probably fearing Midian's revenge should he fail. (Gideon's army was 300 men chasing 15,000.) They should have realized that victory was certain because God was with Gideon. But they were so worried about saving themselves that they never thought about God's power to save.

Because of fear for ourselves, we may not recognize God's presence in other people and therefore miss God's victory. Then we must face the often bitter consequences of failing to join forces with those God has chosen to do his work. Since God's work will prevail with or without you, be quick to join others who are engaged in God's work. Lend support with your time, money, talents, or prayer.

8.11 The Midianites were escaping into the desert area, where only the tent-dwelling nomads lived. They didn't expect Gideon to follow them that far.

8.15–17 Gideon carried out the threat he had made in 8.7. It is difficult to determine whether this act of revenge was justified or whether he should have left the punishment up to God. Gideon was God's appointed leader, but the officials of Succoth and Penuel refused to help him in any way because they feared the enemy. They showed neither faith or respect for God nor the man God chose to save them. We should help others because it is right, regardless of whether we will benefit personally.

you." 20 So he said to Jether his firstborn, "Go kill them!" But the boy did not draw
his sword, for he was afraid, because he was still a boy. 21 Then Zebah and Zalmunna said, "You come and kill us; for as the man is, so is his strength." So Gideon

GIDEON

Most of us want to know God's plan for our lives, but we're not always sure how to find it. One common misunderstanding is the idea that God's guidance will come to us out of the blue, that it has nothing to do with what we're doing now. But if we're always looking around for God's next assignment, we run the risk of ruining whatever we're working on right now. Fortunately, the Bible points to a kind of guidance that does not put our current projects in jeopardy. In the Bible's descriptions of how God guided many people, we can see that often God's call came while people were completely immersed in the challenge of the moment. A good example of this kind of guidance is seen in Gideon's life.

Gideon had a limited vision, but he was committed to it. His challenge was to obtain food for his family even though hostile invaders were making the growing, gathering, and preparation of the food almost impossible. Gideon was resourceful. He put a winepress to double duty by turning it into a sunken threshing floor. It lacked ventilation to blow the chaff away, but at least it was hidden from the Midianites. Gideon was working in his threshing floor when God sent him a messenger with a challenge.

Gideon was surprised by what God told him to do. He did not want to jump into a task for which he was ill prepared. The angel had to overcome three objections before Gideon was convinced: (1) Gideon's feelings of responsibility for his family's welfare, (2) his doubts about the call itself, and (3) his feelings of inadequacy for the job. Once Gideon was convinced, however, he obeyed with zest, resourcefulness, and speed. He dedicated those personality traits to God, with whom he was now personally acquainted.

Gideon had his weak moments and failures, but he was still God's servant. If you can easily see yourself in Gideon's weakness, can you also see yourself in being willing to serve? Remember Gideon as a man who obeyed God by giving his attention to the task at hand. Then give your full attention to believing God will prepare you for tomorrow when it comes.

Strengths and accomplishments:
- Israel's fifth judge. A military strategist who was expert at surprise
- A member of the Hall of Faith in Hebrews 11
- Defeated the Midianite army
- Was offered a hereditary kingship by the men of Israel
- Though slow to be convinced, acted on his convictions

Weaknesses and mistakes:
- Feared that his own limitations would prevent God from working
- Collected Midianite gold and made a symbol which became an evil object of worship
- Through a concubine, fathered a son who would bring great grief and tragedy to both Gideon's family and the nation of Israel
- Failed to establish the nation in God's ways; after he died they all went back to idol worship

Lessons from his life:
- God calls in the middle of our present obedience. As we are faithful, he gives us more responsibility
- God expands and uses the abilities he has already built into us
- God uses us in spite of our limitations and failures
- Even those who make great spiritual progress can easily fall into sin if they don't consistently follow God

Vital statistics:
- Where: Ophrah, valley of Jezreel, well of Harod
- Occupation: Farmer, warrior, and judge
- Relatives: Father: Joash. Son: Abimelech
- Contemporaries: Zebah, Zalmunna

Key verses:
"He [Gideon] responded, 'But sir, how can I deliver Israel? My clan is the weakest in Manasseh, and I am the least in my family.' The Lord said to him, 'But I will be with you, and you shall strike down the Midianites, every one of them' " (Judges 6.15, 16).

His story is told in Judges 6—8. He is also mentioned in Hebrews 11.32.

8.20, 21 For a general to be killed by a boy was humiliating because it would look as though he was no match for a boy ("for as the man is, so is his strength"). The two men wanted to avoid that disgrace, as well as the slower and more painful death which an inexperienced swordsman might inflict.

proceeded to kill Zebah and Zalmunna; and he took the crescents that were on the
necks of their camels.

Gideon refuses to become king

22 Then the Israelites said to Gideon, "Rule over us, you and your son and your
grandson also; for you have delivered us out of the hand of Midian." 23 Gideon said
to them, "I will not rule over you, and my son will not rule over you; the LORD will
rule over you." 24 Then Gideon said to them, "Let me make a request of you; each
of you give me an earring he has taken as booty." (For the enemy[b] had golden
earrings, because they were Ishmaelites.) 25 "We will willingly give them," they
answered. So they spread a garment, and each threw into it an earring he had taken
as booty. 26 The weight of the golden earrings that he requested was one thousand
seven hundred shekels of gold (apart from the crescents and the pendants and the
purple garments worn by the kings of Midian, and the collars that were on the necks
of their camels). 27 Gideon made an ephod of it and put it in his town, in Ophrah; **8.27**
and all Israel prostituted themselves to it there, and it became a snare to Gideon and Ex 28.5,6 Judg 17.4,5
to his family. 28 So Midian was subdued before the Israelites, and they lifted up
their heads no more. So the land had rest forty years in the days of Gideon.

Gideon dies

29 Jerubbaal son of Joash went to live in his own house. 30 Now Gideon had **8.30**
seventy sons, his own offspring, for he had many wives. 31 His concubine who was Judg 9.2,5 **8.31**
in Shechem also bore him a son, and he named him Abimelech. 32 Then Gideon son Judg 9.1,2
of Joash died at a good old age, and was buried in the tomb of his father Joash at
Ophrah of the Abiezrites.
33 As soon as Gideon died, the Israelites relapsed and prostituted themselves **8.33**
with the Baals, making Baal-berith their god. 34 The Israelites did not remember the Judg 2.11 **8.34**
LORD their God, who had rescued them from the hand of all their enemies on every Deut 4.9
side; 35 and they did not exhibit loyalty to the house of Jerubbaal (that is, Gideon) Judg 3.7
in return for all the good that he had done to Israel.

Abimelech tries to become king of Israel

9 Now Abimelech son of Jerubbaal went to Shechem to his mother's kinsfolk
and said to them and to the whole clan of his mother's family, 2 "Say in the
hearing of all the lords of Shechem, 'Which is better for you, that all seventy of the
sons of Jerubbaal rule over you, or that one rule over you?' Remember also that I

[b] Heb *they*

8.23 The people wanted to make Gideon their king, but Gideon stressed that God was their true King. Despite his inconsistencies, Gideon never lost sight of the importance, for both a nation and an individual, of putting God first. Is God first in your life? If he is, he must affect every dimension of your life, not just what you do in church.

8.26, 27 Those who were very wealthy put jewelry on their camels as a way of displaying their riches. Women wore vast amounts of jewelry as well, often up to 15 pairs of earrings. Jewelry was also worn for good luck. After Gideon's rise to power, he seems to have become carried away with this accumulation of wealth. Eventually it led the Israelites to idolatry.

8.27 An ephod was a linen garment worn by priests over their chests. It was considered holy (Exodus 28.5–35; 39.2–24; Leviticus 8.7, 8). Gideon probably had good motives for making the ephod (a visible remembrance commemorating the victory). Unfortunately, the people began to worship the ephod as an idol ("unfaithful with it"). Sadly, many decisions that stem from good motives produce negative results. Perhaps no one stops to ask, "What might go wrong?" or "Is there a possibility of negative consequences?" In your plans and decisions, take time to anticipate how a good idea might lead to a potential problem.

8.31 This relationship between Gideon and a concubine produced a son who tore apart Gideon's family and caused tragedy for the nation. Gideon's story illustrates the fact that heroes in battle are not always heroes in daily life. Gideon led the nation but could not lead his family. No matter who you are, moral laxness will cause problems. Just because you have won a single battle with temptation does not mean you will automatically win the next. We need to be constantly watchful against temptation. Sometimes Satan's strongest attacks come after a victory.

9.1–3 With Gideon dead, Abimelech wanted to take his father's place. (Jerubbaal is another name for Gideon; see 6.32.) To set his plan in motion he went to the city of Shechem, his mother's hometown, to drum up support. Here he felt kinship with the residents. These relatives were Canaanites and would be glad to unite against Israel. Shechem was an important city, a crossroads for trade routes, and a natural link between the coastal plain and the Jordan valley. Whoever controlled Shechem would dominate the countryside.

9.2–5 Israel's king was to be the Lord and not a man. But Abimelech wanted to usurp the position reserved for God alone. In his selfish quest, he killed all but one of his 70 half brothers. People with selfish desires often seek to fulfill them in ruthless ways. Examine your ambitions to see if they are self-centered or God-centered. Be sure you fulfill your desires in ways God would approve.

am your bone and your flesh." 3 So his mother's kinsfolk spoke all these words on
his behalf in the hearing of all the lords of Shechem; and their hearts inclined to
follow Abimelech, for they said, "He is our brother." 4 They gave him seventy
pieces of silver out of the temple of Baal-berith with which Abimelech hired worthless and reckless fellows, who followed him. 5 He went to his father's house at
Ophrah, and killed his brothers the sons of Jerubbaal, seventy men, on one stone;
but Jotham, the youngest son of Jerubbaal, survived, for he hid himself. 6 Then all
the lords of Shechem and all Beth-millo came together, and they went and made
Abimelech king, by the oak of the pillar[c] at Shechem.

[c] Cn: Meaning of Heb uncertain

9.4 Judg 8.33; 9.46

9.5 Judg 6.11; 8.32

9.6 Josh 24.26

ABIMELECH

People who desire power always outnumber those who are able to use power wisely once they have it. Perhaps this is because power has a way of taking over and controlling the person using it. This is especially true in cases of inherited but unmerited power. Abimelech's life shows us what happens when hunger for power corrupts judgment.

Abimelech's position in Gideon's family as the son of a concubine must have created great tension between him and Gideon's many other sons. One against 70: such odds can either crush a person or make him ruthless. It is obvious which direction Abimelech chose. Gideon's position as warrior and judge had placed Abimelech in an environment of power; Gideon's death provided an opportunity for this son to seize power. Once the process began, the disastrous results were inevitable. A person's thirst for power is not satisfied when he gets power—it only becomes more intense. Abimelech's life was consumed by that thirst. Eventually, he could not tolerate any threat to his power.

By this time, ownership had changed: Abimelech no longer had power—power had him. One lesson we can learn from his life is that our goals control our actions. The amount of control is related to the importance of the goal. Abimelech's most important goal was to have power. His lust for power led him to wipe out not only his brothers, but also whole cities that refused to submit to him. Nothing but death could stop his bloodthirsty drive to conquer. How ironic that he was fatally injured by a woman! The contrast between Abimelech and the great people of the Bible is great. He wanted to control the nation; they were willing to be controlled by God.

Strengths and accomplishments:
- The first self-declared king of Israel
- Qualified tactical planner and organizer

Weaknesses and mistakes:
- Power hungry and ruthless
- Overconfident
- Took advantage of his father's position without imitating his character
- Had 69 of his 70 half brothers killed

Vital statistics:
- Where: Shechem, Arumah, Thebez
- Occupation: Self-acclaimed king, judge, political troublemaker
- Relatives: Father: Gideon. Only surviving brother: Jotham

Key verses:
"Thus God repaid Abimelech for the crime he committed against his father in killing his seventy brothers; and God also made all the wickedness of the people of Shechem fall back on their heads, and on them came the curse of Jotham son of Jerubbaal" (Judges 9.56, 57).

His story is told in Judges 8.31—9.57. He is also mentioned in 2 Samuel 11.21.

9.4 Politics played a major part in heathen religions such as the worship of Baal-berith. Governments often went so far as to hire temple prostitutes to bring in additional money. In many cases a religious system was set up and supported by the government so the offerings could fund community projects. Religion became a profit-making business. In Israel's religion, this was strictly forbidden. God's system of religion was designed to come from an attitude of the heart, not from calculated plans and business opportunities. It was also designed to serve people and help those in need, not to oppress the needy. Is your faith genuine and sincere or is it based on convenience, comfort, and availability?

9.6 Abimelech was declared ruler of Israel at Shechem, the site of other key Bible events. It was one of Abraham's first stops upon arriving in Canaan (Genesis 12.6, 7). When Jacob lived there, two of his sons killed all the men in Shechem because the prince's son raped their sister (Genesis 34). Joseph's bones were buried in Shechem (Joshua 24.32); Israel renewed its covenant with God there (Joshua 24); and the kingdom of Israel split apart at this same city (1 Kings 12).

7 When it was told to Jotham, he went and stood on the top of Mount Gerizim, 9.7 Deut 11.29 27.12 Jn 4.20
and cried aloud and said to them, "Listen to me, you lords of Shechem, so that God
may listen to you.

8 The trees once went out 9.8 2 Kgs 14.9 Ezek 17.3 Dan 4.10
to anoint a king over themselves.
So they said to the olive tree,
'Reign over us.'
9 The olive tree answered them,
'Shall I stop producing my rich oil
by which gods and mortals are honored,
and go to sway over the trees?'
10 Then the trees said to the fig tree,
'You come and reign over us.'
11 But the fig tree answered them,
'Shall I stop producing my sweetness
and my delicious fruit,
and go to sway over the trees?'
12 Then the trees said to the vine,
'You come and reign over us.'
13 But the vine said to them,
'Shall I stop producing my wine
that cheers gods and mortals,
and go to sway over the trees?'
14 So all the trees said to the bramble,
'You come and reign over us.'
15 And the bramble said to the trees,
'If in good faith you are anointing me king over you,
then come and take refuge in my shade;
but if not, let fire come out of the bramble
and devour the cedars of Lebanon.'

16 "Now therefore, if you acted in good faith and honor when you made Abimelech king, and if you have dealt well with Jerubbaal and his house, and have done
to him as his actions deserved— 17 for my father fought for you, and risked his life,
and rescued you from the hand of Midian; 18 but you have risen up against my fa- 9.18 Judg 9.5
ther's house this day, and have killed his sons, seventy men on one stone, and have
made Abimelech, the son of his slave woman, king over the lords of Shechem,
because he is your kinsman— 19 if, I say, you have acted in good faith and honor

9.7-15 In Jotham's parable the trees represented Gideon's 70 sons, and the bramble represented Abimelech. Jotham's point was this: a productive person would be too busy doing good to want to bother with power politics. A worthless person, on the other hand, would be glad to accept the honor–but he would destroy the people he ruled. Abimelech, like a bramble, could offer Israel no real protection or security. Jotham's parable came true when Abimelech destroyed the city of Shechem (9.45), burned "the Tower of Shechem" (the city of Migdal, 9.46–49), and was finally killed at Thebez (9.53, 54).

9.16 Jotham told the story about the trees in order to help the people set good priorities. He did not want them to appoint a leader of low character. As we serve in leadership positions, we should examine our motives. Do we just want praise, prestige, or power? In the parable, the good trees chose to be productive and to provide benefits to people. Make sure these are your priorities as you aspire to leadership.

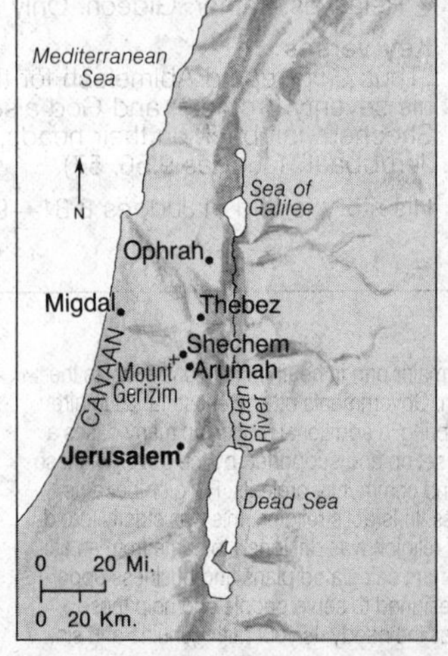

ABIMELECH'S FALL
Gideon's illegitimate son killed 69 of his half brothers in Ophrah and returned to Shechem to be acclaimed king. But three years later, Shechem rebelled. From Arumah, Abimelech attacked Shechem, Migdal ("the tower of Shechem"), and Thebez where he was killed.

with Jerubbaal and with his house this day, then rejoice in Abimelech, and let him
also rejoice in you; 20 but if not, let fire come out from Abimelech, and devour the
lords of Shechem, and Beth-millo; and let fire come out from the lords of Shechem,
and from Beth-millo, and devour Abimelech." 21 Then Jotham ran away and fled,
going to Beer, where he remained for fear of his brother Abimelech.
9.22 1 Sam 16.14 22 Abimelech ruled over Israel three years. 23 But God sent an evil spirit between Abimelech and the lords of Shechem; and the lords of Shechem dealt treach-
9.24 Num 35.33 Deut 27.25 erously with Abimelech. 24 This happened so that the violence done to the seventy
sons of Jerubbaal might be avenged[d] and their blood be laid on their brother Abim-
elech, who killed them, and on the lords of Shechem, who strengthened his hands
to kill his brothers. 25 So, out of hostility to him, the lords of Shechem set ambushes
on the mountain tops. They robbed all who passed by them along that way; and it
was reported to Abimelech.
26 When Gaal son of Ebed moved into Shechem with his kinsfolk, the lords of
9.27 Judg 8.33 Shechem put confidence in him. 27 They went out into the field and gathered the
grapes from their vineyards, trod them, and celebrated. Then they went into the
temple of their god, ate and drank, and ridiculed Abimelech. 28 Gaal son of Ebed
said, "Who is Abimelech, and who are we of Shechem, that we should serve him?
Did not the son of Jerubbaal and Zebul his officer serve the men of Hamor father of
Shechem? Why then should we serve him? 29 If only this people were under my
command! Then I would remove Abimelech; I would say[e] to him, 'Increase your
army, and come out.' "
30 When Zebul the ruler of the city heard the words of Gaal son of Ebed, his
anger was kindled. 31 He sent messengers to Abimelech at Arumah,[f] saying,
"Look, Gaal son of Ebed and his kinsfolk have come to Shechem, and they are
stirring up[g] the city against you. 32 Now therefore, go by night, you and the troops
9.33 1 Sam 10.7 that are with you, and lie in wait in the fields. 33 Then early in the morning, as soon
as the sun rises, get up and rush on the city; and when he and the troops that are with
him come out against you, you may deal with them as best you can."
34 So Abimelech and all the troops with him got up by night and lay in wait
against Shechem in four companies. 35 When Gaal son of Ebed went out and stood
in the entrance of the gate of the city, Abimelech and the troops with him rose from
the ambush. 36 And when Gaal saw them, he said to Zebul, "Look, people are coming down from the mountain tops!" And Zebul said to him, "The shadows on the
mountains look like people to you." 37 Gaal spoke again and said, "Look, people
are coming down from Tabbur-erez, and one company is coming from the direction
of Elon-meonenim."[h] 38 Then Zebul said to him, "Where is your boast[i] now, you
who said, 'Who is Abimelech, that we should serve him?' Are not these the troops
you made light of? Go out now and fight with them." 39 So Gaal went out at the
head of the lords of Shechem, and fought with Abimelech. 40 Abimelech chased
him, and he fled before him. Many fell wounded, up to the entrance of the gate.
41 So Abimelech resided at Arumah; and Zebul drove out Gaal and his kinsfolk, so
that they could not live on at Shechem.
42 On the following day the people went out into the fields. When Abimelech
was told, 43 he took his troops and divided them into three companies, and lay in
wait in the fields. When he looked and saw the people coming out of the city, he

[d] Heb *might come* [e] Gk: Heb *and he said* [f] Cn See 9.41. Heb *Tormah* [g] Cn: Heb *are besieging* [h] That is *Diviners' Oak* [i] Heb *mouth*

9.22–24 Abimelech was the opposite of what God wanted in a judge, but it was three years before God moved against him, fulfilling Jotham's parable. Those three years must have seemed like forever to Jotham. Why wasn't Abimelech punished sooner for his evil ways?

We are not alone when we wonder why evil seems to prevail (Job 10.3; 21.1–18; Jeremiah 12.1; Habakkuk 1.2–4, 12–17). God promises to deal with sin, but in his time, not ours. Actually it is good news that God doesn't punish *us* immediately, for we all have sinned and deserve God's punishment. God, in his mercy, often spares us from immediate punishment and allows us time to turn from our sins and turn to him in repentance. Trusting God for justice means (1) we must first recognize our own sins and repent, and (2) we may face a difficult time of waiting for the wicked to be punished. But in God's time, all evil will be destroyed.

9.23 This evil spirit was not just an "attitude of strife," but a demon. It was not Satan himself but one of the fallen angels under Satan's influence. God used this evil spirit to bring about judgment on Shechem. First Samuel 16.14 records how God judged Saul in a similar way.

rose against them and killed them. 44 Abimelech and the company that was[j] with
him rushed forward and stood at the entrance of the gate of the city, while the two
companies rushed on all who were in the fields and killed them. 45 Abimelech
fought against the city all that day; he took the city, and killed the people that were
in it; and he razed the city and sowed it with salt.
46 When all the lords of the Tower of Shechem heard of it, they entered the **9.46**
stronghold of the temple of El-berith. 47 Abimelech was told that all the lords of the Judg 8.33 **9.47**
Tower of Shechem were gathered together. 48 So Abimelech went up to Mount Zal- Ps 68.14
mon, he and all the troops that were with him. Abimelech took an ax in his hand,
cut down a bundle of brushwood, and took it up and laid it on his shoulder. Then
he said to the troops with him, "What you have seen me do, do quickly, as I have
done." 49 So every one of the troops cut down a bundle and following Abimelech
put it against the stronghold, and they set the stronghold on fire over them, so that
all the people of the Tower of Shechem also died, about a thousand men and
women.
50 Then Abimelech went to Thebez, and encamped against Thebez, and took
it. 51 But there was a strong tower within the city, and all the men and women and
all the lords of the city fled to it and shut themselves in; and they went to the roof
of the tower. 52 Abimelech came to the tower, and fought against it, and came near
to the entrance of the tower to burn it with fire. 53 But a certain woman threw an **9.53**
upper millstone on Abimelech's head, and crushed his skull. 54 Immediately he 2 Sam 11.19-21
called to the young man who carried his armor and said to him, "Draw your sword
and kill me, so people will not say about me, 'A woman killed him.' " So the young
man thrust him through, and he died. 55 When the Israelites saw that Abimelech
was dead, they all went home. 56 Thus God repaid Abimelech for the crime he
committed against his father in killing his seventy brothers; 57 and God also made
all the wickedness of the people of Shechem fall back on their heads, and on them
came the curse of Jotham son of Jerubbaal.

Tola

10 After Abimelech, Tola son of Puah son of Dodo, a man of Issachar, who
lived at Shamir in the hill country of Ephraim, rose to deliver Israel. 2 He
judged Israel twenty-three years. Then he died, and was buried at Shamir.

Jair

3 After him came Jair the Gileadite, who judged Israel twenty-two years. 4 He **10.4**
had thirty sons who rode on thirty donkeys; and they had thirty towns, which are in Num 32.41
the land of Gilead, and are called Havvoth-jair to this day. 5 Jair died, and was
buried in Kamon.

j Vg and some Gk Mss: Heb *companies that were*

9.45 To sow a city with salt was a ritual to symbolize its perpetual desolation. This city would not be rebuilt for 150 years.

9.53 In times of battle, women were sometimes asked to join the men at the city wall to drop heavy objects on the soldiers below. A millstone would have been an ideal object for this purpose. It was a round stone about two feet in diameter with a hole in the center. It weighed several hundred pounds. Millstones were used to grind grain into flour. The grain was placed between two millstones. The top millstone was turned, crushing the grain.

Abimelech's death was especially humiliating: he was killed by a woman, not by fighting; and he was killed by a farm implement instead of a weapon. Abimelech therefore asked his armor bearer to stab him with his sword before he died from the blow of the millstone.

9.56, 57 Gideon, Abimelech's father, succeeded in military battles, but sometimes failed in his personal struggles. Gideon was not condemned for taking a concubine (8.31), but the family problems that resulted from this relationship are clearly stated.

In the end, Abimelech killed 69 of his 70 half brothers, tore apart a nation, and then was killed himself. From Gideon's life we learn that no matter how much good we do for God's kingdom, sin in our lives will still produce powerful, damaging consequences.

9.56, 57 Jotham's curse is found in 9.16–20.

10.1–5 In five verses we read about two men who judged Israel for a total of 45 years, yet all we know about them besides the length of their rules is that one had 30 sons who rode around on 30 donkeys. What are you doing for God that is worth noting? When your life is over, will people remember more than just what was in your bank account or the number of years you lived?

5. Fifth period: Jephthah, Ibzan, Elon, and Abdon

The Ammonites oppress Israel

10.6 Judg 4.1; 6.1 10.16; 13.1 2 Kgs 17.7 2 Chron 7.21,22
10.7 Judg 4.2 1 Sam 12.9

6 The Israelites again did what was evil in the sight of the LORD, worshiping the
Baals and the Astartes, the gods of Aram, the gods of Sidon, the gods of Moab, the
gods of the Ammonites, and the gods of the Philistines. Thus they abandoned
the LORD, and did not worship him. 7 So the anger of the LORD was kindled against
Israel, and he sold them into the hand of the Philistines and into the hand of the
Ammonites, 8 and they crushed and oppressed the Israelites that year. For eighteen
years they oppressed all the Israelites that were beyond the Jordan in the land of the
Amorites, which is in Gilead. 9 The Ammonites also crossed the Jordan to fight
against Judah and against Benjamin and against the house of Ephraim; so that Israel
was greatly distressed.

10.10 Judg 3.9 Ps 106.43
10.11 Judg 2.1-3 1 Kgs 9.9
10.14 Deut 32.37
10.15 2 Sam 12.13
10.16 Deut 32.43 Josh 24.23 2 Chron 7.14 15.8; 33.15 Jer 18.7,8

10 So the Israelites cried to the LORD, saying, "We have sinned against you,
because we have abandoned our God and have worshiped the Baals." 11 And the
LORD said to the Israelites, "Did I not deliver you[k] from the Egyptians and from the
Amorites, from the Ammonites and from the Philistines? 12 The Sidonians also,
and the Amalekites, and the Maonites, oppressed you; and you cried to me, and I
delivered you out of their hand. 13 Yet you have abandoned me and worshiped other
gods; therefore I will deliver you no more. 14 Go and cry to the gods whom you have
chosen; let them deliver you in the time of your distress." 15 And the Israelites said
to the LORD, "We have sinned; do to us whatever seems good to you; but deliver us
this day!" 16 So they put away the foreign gods from among them and worshiped the
LORD; and he could no longer bear to see Israel suffer.

17 Then the Ammonites were called to arms, and they encamped in Gilead; and
the Israelites came together, and they encamped at Mizpah. 18 The commanders of
the people of Gilead said to one another, "Who will begin the fight against the
Ammonites? He shall be head over all the inhabitants of Gilead."

Jephthah defeats the Ammonites

11.1 1 Sam 12.11 20.30 Heb 11.32
11.3 Judg 9.4; 12.4 1 Sam 22.2 30.22 2 Sam 10.6,8

11 Now Jephthah the Gileadite, the son of a prostitute, was a mighty warrior.
Gilead was the father of Jephthah. 2 Gilead's wife also bore him sons; and
when his wife's sons grew up, they drove Jephthah away, saying to him, "You
shall not inherit anything in our father's house; for you are the son of another
woman." 3 Then Jephthah fled from his brothers and lived in the land of Tob. Outlaws collected around Jephthah and went raiding with him.

[k] Heb lacks *Did I not deliver you*

10.7–10 God permitted the heathen nations to oppress the Israelites because of their sin (2.1–3). Because God is just, he will punish sin (Leviticus 26). God allows problems and pressures to come our way in order to draw us lovingly back into relationship with him. When problems arise, before you ask, "Why me?" ask, "Is God trying to say something to me through this?"

10.9, 10 Once again the Israelites suffered for many years before they gave up their sinful ways and called out to God for help (see 4.1–3; 6.1–7). Notice that when the Israelites were at the end of their rope they did not look to their heathen gods for help, but to the only One who was really able to help.

Is God your last resort? So much unnecessary suffering takes place because we don't call on God until we've used up all other resources. Rather than waiting until the situation becomes desperate, turn to God first. He has the necessary resources to meet every kind of problem.

10.11–16 These verses show how difficult it can be to follow God over the long haul. The Israelites always seemed to forget God when all was well. But despite being rejected by his own people, God never failed to rescue them when they called out to him in repentance. God never fails to rescue us either. We act just like the Israelites when we put God outside our daily events instead of at the center of them. Just as a loving parent feels great rejection when a child rebels, so God feels great rejection when we ignore or neglect him (1 Samuel 8.4–9; 10.17–19; John 12.44–50). We should strive to stay close to God rather than see how far we can go before judgment comes.

10.17, 18 The power of the Ammonite nation was at its peak during the period of the judges. The land of Ammon was located just east of the Jordan River across from Jerusalem. South of Ammon lay the land of Moab. Moab and Ammon were usually allies. It was a formidable task to defeat these nations.

11.1, 2 Jephthah, an illegitimate son of Gilead, was chased out of the country by his half brothers. He suffered as a result of another's decision and not for any wrong he had done. Yet in spite of his brothers' rejection, God used him. If you are suffering from unfair rejection, don't blame others and become discouraged. Remember how God used Jephthah despite his unjust circumstances, and realize that he is able to use you even if you feel rejected by some.

11.3 Circumstances beyond his control forced Jephthah away from his people and into life as an outcast. Today, both believers and nonbelievers may drive away those who do not fit the norms dictated by our society, neighborhoods, or churches. Often, as in Jephthah's case, great potential is wasted because of prejudice—a refusal to look beyond ill-conceived stereotypes. Look around you to see if there are potential Jephthahs being kept out due to factors beyond their control. Can you do anything to help these people gain acceptance for their character and abilities?

4 After a time the Ammonites made war against Israel. 5 And when the Ammon- 11.4
ites made war against Israel, the elders of Gilead went to bring Jephthah from the Judg 10.9
land of Tob. 6 They said to Jephthah, "Come and be our commander, so that we
may fight with the Ammonites." 7 But Jephthah said to the elders of Gilead, "Are
you not the very ones who rejected me and drove me out of my father's house? So
why do you come to me now when you are in trouble?" 8 The elders of Gilead said
to Jephthah, "Nevertheless, we have now turned back to you, so that you may go
with us and fight with the Ammonites, and become head over us, over all the inhabitants of Gilead." 9 Jephthah said to the elders of Gilead, "If you bring me home
again to fight with the Ammonites, and the LORD gives them over to me, I will be
your head." 10 And the elders of Gilead said to Jephthah, "The LORD will be witness 11.10
between us; we will surely do as you say." 11 So Jephthah went with the elders of Gen 21.23 31.51-53
Gilead, and the people made him head and commander over them; and Jephthah 11.11
spoke all his words before the LORD at Mizpah. Judg 9.14,15

12 Then Jephthah sent messengers to the king of the Ammonites and said,
"What is there between you and me, that you have come to me to fight against my
land?" 13 The king of the Ammonites answered the messengers of Jephthah, "Be- 11.13
cause Israel, on coming from Egypt, took away my land from the Arnon to the Josh 13.10
Jabbok and to the Jordan; now therefore restore it peaceably." 14 Once again Jephthah sent messengers to the king of the Ammonites 15 and said to him: "Thus says
Jephthah: Israel did not take away the land of Moab or the land of the Ammonites,
16 but when they came up from Egypt, Israel went through the wilderness to the Red 11.16
Sea[l] and came to Kadesh. 17 Israel then sent messengers to the king of Edom, Num 20.1-22
saying, 'Let us pass through your land'; but the king of Edom would not listen. 11.17 Josh 24.9
They also sent to the king of Moab, but he would not consent. So Israel remained
at Kadesh. 18 Then they journeyed through the wilderness, went around the land of 11.18
Edom and the land of Moab, arrived on the east side of the land of Moab, and Num 21.4 Deut 2.8,9,18,
camped on the other side of the Arnon. They did not enter the territory of Moab, for 19
the Arnon was the boundary of Moab. 19 Israel then sent messengers to King Sihon 11.19
of the Amorites, king of Heshbon; and Israel said to him, 'Let us pass through your Num 21.21-32
land to our country.' 20 But Sihon did not trust Israel to pass through his territory;
so Sihon gathered all his people together, and encamped at Jahaz, and fought with
Israel. 21 Then the LORD, the God of Israel, gave Sihon and all his people into the 11.21
hand of Israel, and they defeated them; so Israel occupied all the land of the Amo- Deut 2.19,37 3.3
rites, who inhabited that country. 22 They occupied all the territory of the Amorites
from the Arnon to the Jabbok and from the wilderness to the Jordan. 23 So now the
LORD, the God of Israel, has conquered the Amorites for the benefit of his people
Israel. Do you intend to take their place? 24 Should you not possess what your god 11.24
Chemosh gives you to possess? And should we not be the ones to possess every- Num 21.27-30 1 Kgs 11.7
thing that the LORD our God has conquered for our benefit? 25 Now are you any
better than King Balak son of Zippor of Moab? Did he ever enter into conflict with
Israel, or did he ever go to war with them? 26 While Israel lived in Heshbon and its
villages, and in Aroer and its villages, and in all the towns that are along the Arnon,
three hundred years, why did you not recover them within that time? 27 It is not I
who have sinned against you, but you are the one who does me wrong by making

[l] Or *Sea of Reeds*

11.11 What does it mean that Jephthah spoke all of his words before the Lord? Those making covenants in ancient times often made them at shrines so that they would be witnessed by deities. Often a written copy was also deposited at the shrine as well. This was much like a coronation ceremony for Jephthah.

11.14ff Jephthah sent a dispatch to the king of Ammon wanting to know why the Israelites in the land of Gilead were being attacked (11.12). The king replied that Israel had stolen this land and he wanted it back (11.13).

Jephthah sent another message to the king (11.14–27). In it he gave three arguments against the king's claim: (1) Gilead was never the king's land in the first place because Israel took it from the Amorites, not the Ammonites (11.16–22); (2) Israel should possess land given by Israel's God, and Ammon should possess land given by Ammon's god; (3) no one had contested Israel's ownership of the land since its conquest 300 years earlier (11.25, 26).

To Jephthah's credit, he tried to solve the problem without bloodshed. But the king of Ammon ignored his message and prepared his troops for battle.

11.27 Over the years, Israel had many judges to lead them. But Jephthah recognized God as the people's true Judge, the only One who could really lead them and help them conquer the invading enemies.

war on me. Let the LORD, who is judge, decide today for the Israelites or for the
Ammonites." 28 But the king of the Ammonites did not heed the message that Jephthah sent him.
11.29 Judg 3.10; 6.34 13.25 — 29 Then the spirit of the LORD came upon Jephthah, and he passed through
Gilead and Manasseh. He passed on to Mizpah of Gilead, and from Mizpah of
Gilead he passed on to the Ammonites. 30 And Jephthah made a vow to the LORD,
and said, "If you will give the Ammonites into my hand, 31 then whoever comes out
of the doors of my house to meet me, when I return victorious from the Ammonites,
shall be the LORD's, to be offered up by me as a burnt offering." 32 So Jephthah
crossed over to the Ammonites to fight against them; and the LORD gave them into
his hand. 33 He inflicted a massive defeat on them from Aroer to the neighborhood
of Minnith, twenty towns, and as far as Abel-keramim. So the Ammonites were
subdued before the people of Israel.
11.34 Ex 15.20 1 Sam 18.6 Jer 31.4 — 34 Then Jephthah came to his home at Mizpah; and there was his daughter

RASH VOWS

Ecclesiastes 5.2 says: "Never be rash with your mouth, nor let your heart be quick to utter a word before God. . . ." Scripture records the vows of many men and women. Some of these vows proved to be rash and unwise, and others, though extreme, were kept to the letter by those who made them. Let us learn from the examples in God's word not to make rash vows.

Person	*Vow*	*Result*	*Reference*
JACOB	To "choose" the true God and to give back a tenth to him if he kept him safe	God protected Jacob, who kept his vow to follow God	Genesis 28.20
JEPHTHAH	To offer to the Lord whomever came out to meet him after battle (it turned out to be his daughter)	He lost his daughter	Judges 11.30, 31
HANNAH	To give her son back to God, if God would give her a son	When Samuel was born, she dedicated him to God	1 Samuel 1.9–11
SAUL	To kill anyone who ate before evening (Jonathan, his son, had not heard the command and broke it)	Saul would have killed Jonathan if soldiers had not intervened	1 Samuel 14.24–45
DAVID	To be kind to Jonathan's family	Mephibosheth, Jonathan's son, was treated royally by David	2 Samuel 9.7
ITTAI	To remain loyal to David	He became one of the great men in David's army	2 Samuel 15.21
MICAIAH	To say only what God told him to say	He was put in prison	1 Kings 22.14
JOB	That he was not rebelling against God	His fortunes were restored	Job 27.2
HEROD ANTIPAS	To give Herodias's daughter anything she requested	Herod was forced to order John the Baptist's death	Mark 6.22,23
PAUL	To offer a sacrifice of thanksgiving in Jerusalem	He made the sacrifice despite the danger	Acts 18.18

11.29 The spirit of the Lord came upon Jephthah as he did with many of the Old Testament judges, kings, and prophets. Generally when the spirit came upon a person in the Old Testament, he empowered the person for a specific task or mission. Sometimes this special empowering did not produce an accompanying moral transformation.

11.30, 31 In God's law, a vow was a promise to God that should not be broken (Numbers 30.1, 2; Deuteronomy 23.21–23). It carried as much force as a written contract. Many people made vows in biblical times. Some, like Jephthah's, were very foolish.

11.30, 31 When Jephthah made his vow, did he stop to consider that a person, not a sheep or goat, might come out to meet him? Scholars are divided over the issue. Those who say Jephthah was considering human sacrifice use the following arguments: (1) He was from an area where heathen religion and human sacrifice were common. In his eyes, it may not have seemed like a sin. (2) Jephthah may not have had a background in religious law. Perhaps he was ignorant of God's command against human sacrifice.

Those who say Jephthah could not have been thinking about human sacrifice point to other evidence: (1) As leader of the people, Jephthah must have been familiar with God's law; human sacrifice was clearly forbidden (Leviticus 18.21; 20.1–5). (2) No legitimate priest would have helped Jephthah carry out his vow if a person was to be the sacrifice.

Whatever Jephthah had in mind when he made the vow, did he or did he not sacrifice his daughter? Some think he did, because his vow was to make a burnt offering. Some think he did not, and they offer several reasons: (1) If the girl was to die, she would not have spent her last two months in the mountains. (2) God would not have honored a vow based on a wicked practice. (3) Verse 39 says that she never married, not that she died, implying that she was set apart for service to God, not killed.

11.34, 35 Jephthah's rash vow brought him unspeakable grief. In the heat of emotion or personal turmoil it is easy to make foolish promises to God. These promises may sound very spiritual when we make them, but they may produce only guilt and frustration when we are forced to fulfill them. Making spiritual "deals" only brings disappointment. God does not want promises for the future, but obedience for today.

coming out to meet him with timbrels and with dancing. She was his only child; he
had no son or daughter except her. 35 When he saw her, he tore his clothes, and 11.35
said, "Alas, my daughter! You have brought me very low; you have become the Num 30.1,2
cause of great trouble to me. For I have opened my mouth to the LORD, and I can- Eccles 5.4,5
not take back my vow." 36 She said to him, "My father, if you have opened your
mouth to the LORD, do to me according to what has gone out of your mouth, now
that the LORD has given you vengeance against your enemies, the Ammonites."
37 And she said to her father, "Let this thing be done for me: Grant me two months,
so that I may go and wander[m] on the mountains, and bewail my virginity, my
companions and I." 38 "Go," he said and sent her away for two months. So she departed, she and her companions, and bewailed her virginity on the mountains. 39 At
the end of two months, she returned to her father, who did with her according to
the vow he had made. She had never slept with a man. So there arose an Israelite
custom that 40 for four days every year the daughters of Israel would go out to lament
the daughter of Jephthah the Gileadite.

Jephthah attacks the tribe of Ephraim

12 The men of Ephraim were called to arms, and they crossed to Zaphon and 12.1
said to Jephthah, "Why did you cross over to fight against the Ammonites, Judg 8.1
and did not call us to go with you? We will burn your house down over you!"
2 Jephthah said to them, "My people and I were engaged in conflict with the Ammonites who oppressed us[n] severely. But when I called you, you did not deliver
me from their hand. 3 When I saw that you would not deliver me, I took my life in 12.3
my hand, and crossed over against the Ammonites, and the LORD gave them into 1 Sam 19.5 Job 13.14
my hand. Why then have you come up to me this day, to fight against me?" 4 Then 12.4
Jephthah gathered all the men of Gilead and fought with Ephraim; and the men of Judg 11.3
Gilead defeated Ephraim, because they said, "You are fugitives from Ephraim, you 1 Sam 22.2
Gileadites—in the heart of Ephraim and Manasseh."[o] 5 Then the Gileadites took 12.5-7
the fords of the Jordan against the Ephraimites. Whenever one of the fugitives of Josh 2.7
Ephraim said, "Let me go over," the men of Gilead would say to him, "Are you an Judg 3.28; 7.24
Ephraimite?" When he said, "No," 6 they said to him, "Then say Shibboleth," and
he said, "Sibboleth," for he could not pronounce it right. Then they seized him and
killed him at the fords of the Jordan. Forty-two thousand of the Ephraimites fell at
that time.

[m] Cn: Heb *go down* [n] Gk OL, Syr H: Heb lacks *who oppressed us* [o] Meaning of Heb uncertain: Gk omits *because . . . Manasseh*

12.1ff Israel had just won a great battle, but instead of joy, there was pettiness and quarreling. The tribe of Ephraim was angry and jealous that they were not invited to join in the fighting (although Jephthah said he had invited them). The insults of the Ephraimites enraged Jephthah, who called out his troops and killed 42,000 men from Ephraim.

Jephthah usually talked before he acted, but this time his revenge was swift. It cost Israel dearly, and it might have been avoided. Insulting others and being jealous are not right responses when we feel left out.

But seeking revenge for an insult is just as wrong, and very costly.

12.4–7 The Ephraimites caused Jephthah trouble just as they had Gideon (8.1–3). Jephthah captured the fords of the Jordan, the boundary of Ephraim, and was able to defeat his countrymen as they crossed the river. He used a pronunciation test. *Shibboleth* is the word for stream. The Ephraimites pronounced "sh" as "s," so Jephthah's army could easily identify them.

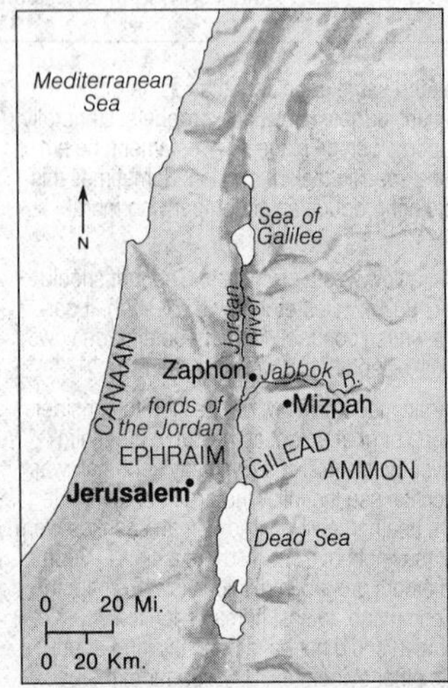

JEPHTHAH'S VICTORY
The Ephraimites mobilized an army because they were angry at not being included in the battle against Ammon. They planned to attack Jephthah at his home in Gilead. Jephthah captured the fords of the Jordan at the Jabbok River and killed the Ephraimites who tried to cross.

7 Jephthah judged Israel six years. Then Jephthah the Gileadite died, and was
buried in his town in Gilead.[p]

Ibzan

8 After him Ibzan of Bethlehem judged Israel. 9 He had thirty sons. He gave his
thirty daughters in marriage outside his clan and brought in thirty young women
from outside for his sons. He judged Israel seven years. 10 Then Ibzan died, and
was buried at Bethlehem.

Elon

11 After him Elon the Zebulunite judged Israel; and he judged Israel ten years.
12 Then Elon the Zebulunite died, and was buried at Aijalon in the land of Zebulun.

Abdon

13 After him Abdon son of Hillel the Pirathonite judged Israel. 14 He had forty
sons and thirty grandsons, who rode on seventy donkeys; he judged Israel eight
years. 15 Then Abdon son of Hillel the Pirathonite died, and was buried at Pirathon
in the land of Ephraim, in the hill country of the Amalekites.

[p] Gk: Heb *in the towns of Gilead*

JEPHTHAH

It's hard not to admire people whose word can be depended on completely and whose actions are consistent with their words. For such people, talking is not avoiding action; it is the beginning of action. People like this can make excellent negotiators. They approach a conflict with the full intention of settling issues verbally, but they do not hesitate to use other means if verbal attempts fail. Jephthah was this kind of person.

In most of his conflicts, Jephthah's first move was to talk. In the war with the Ammonites, his strategy was negotiation. He clarified the issues so that everyone knew the cause of the conflict. His opponent's response determined his next action.

The fate of Jephthah's daughter is difficult to understand. We are not sure what Jephthah meant by his vow recorded in Judges 11.31. In any case, his vow was unnecessary. We do not know what actually happened to his daughter—whether she was burned as an offering or set apart as a virgin, thus denying Jephthah any hope of descendants since she was his only child. What we do know is that Jephthah was a person of his word, even when it was a word spoken in haste, and even when keeping his word cost him great pain.

How do you approach conflicts? There is a big difference between trying to settle a conflict through words and simply counterattacking someone verbally. How dependable are the statements you make? Do your children, friends, and fellow workers know you to be a person of your word? The measure of your trustworthiness is your willingness to take responsibility, even if you must pay a painful price because of something you said.

Strengths and accomplishments:
- Listed in the Hall of Faith in Hebrews 11
- Controlled by God's Spirit
- Brilliant military strategist who negotiated before fighting

Weaknesses and mistakes:
- Was bitter over the treatment he received from his half brothers
- Made a rash and foolish vow that was costly

Lesson from his life:
- A person's background does not prevent God from working powerfully in his or her life

Vital statistics:
- Where: Gilead
- Occupation: Warrior, judge
- Relatives: Father: Gilead

Key verse:
"So Jephthah crossed over to the Ammonites to fight against them; and the Lord gave them into his hand" (Judges 11.32).

His story is told in Judges 11.1—12.7. He is also mentioned in 1 Samuel 12.11 and Hebrews 11.32.

12.8–14 We are unsure whether Izban was from the Bethlehem near Jerusalem or the place with the same name northwest of Narzareth (Joshua 19.15). There is little else known about these three judges or their importance. But the large number of children and cattle are an indication of their wealth and status.

6. Sixth period: Samson

The birth of Samson

13 The Israelites again did what was evil in the sight of the LORD, and the LORD **13.1**
gave them into the hand of the Philistines forty years. Judg 2.11; 3.8 4.2,3; 10.6-8
2 There was a certain man of Zorah, of the tribe of the Danites, whose name **13.2**
was Manoah. His wife was barren, having borne no children. 3 And the angel of the Gen 16.7; 17.17 Judg 2.1
LORD appeared to the woman and said to her, "Although you are barren, having 6.11,12
borne no children, you shall conceive and bear a son. 4 Now be careful not to drink **13.4**
wine or strong drink, or to eat anything unclean, 5 for you shall conceive and bear Num 6.1-4 Judg 13.13,14
a son. No razor is to come on his head, for the boy shall be a nazirite[q] to God from **13.5**
birth. It is he who shall begin to deliver Israel from the hand of the Philistines." Judg 16.16,17
6 Then the woman came and told her husband, "A man of God came to me, and his
appearance was like that of an angel[r] of God, most awe-inspiring; I did not ask him
where he came from, and he did not tell me his name; 7 but he said to me, 'You shall
conceive and bear a son. So then drink no wine or strong drink, and eat nothing
unclean, for the boy shall be a nazirite[q] to God from birth to the day of his death.' "
8 Then Manoah entreated the LORD, and said, "O, LORD, I pray, let the man of
God whom you sent come to us again and teach us what we are to do concerning the
boy who will be born." 9 God listened to Manoah, and the angel of God came again
to the woman as she sat in the field; but her husband Manoah was not with her. 10 So
the woman ran quickly and told her husband, "The man who came to me the other
day has appeared to me." 11 Manoah got up and followed his wife, and came to the
man and said to him, "Are you the man who spoke to this woman?" And he said,
"I am." 12 Then Manoah said, "Now when your words come true, what is to be the
boy's rule of life; what is he to do?" 13 The angel of the LORD said to Manoah, "Let **13.13**
the woman give heed to all that I said to her. 14 She may not eat of anything that Judg 13.4
comes from the vine. She is not to drink wine or strong drink, or eat any unclean
thing. She is to observe everything that I commanded her."
15 Manoah said to the angel of the LORD, "Allow us to detain you, and prepare **13.15**
a kid for you." 16 The angel of the LORD said to Manoah, "If you detain me, I will Gen 18.3,4 Judg 6.18
not eat your food; but if you want to prepare a burnt offering, then offer it to the
LORD." (For Manoah did not know that he was the angel of the LORD.) 17 Then **13.17**
Manoah said to the angel of the LORD, "What is your name, so that we may honor Gen 32.29
you when your words come true?" 18 But the angel of the LORD said to him, "Why
do you ask my name? It is too wonderful."

[q] That is *one separated* or *one consecrated* [r] Or *the angel*

13.1 The Philistines lived on the west side of Canaan, along the Mediterranean seacoast. From Samson's day until the time of David they were the major enemy force in the land and a constant threat to Israel. The Philistines were fierce warriors; they had the advantage over Israel in numbers, tactical expertise, and technology. They knew the secret of making weapons out of iron (1 Samuel 13.19–22). But none of that mattered when God was fighting for Israel.

13.1ff Once again the cycle of sin, judgment, and repentance began (3.8, 9, 14, 15; 4.1–4; 6.1–14; 10.6–11.11). The Israelites would not turn to God unless they had been stunned by suffering, oppression, and death. This suffering was not caused by God, but resulted from the fact that the people ignored God, their Judge and Ruler. What will it take for you to follow God? The warnings in God's Word are clear: if we continue to harden our hearts against God, we can expect the same fate as Israel.

13.2, 3 The angel of the Lord could have been a special divine messenger sent from God or a pre-incarnation appearance of Jesus Christ. The reason for the angel's visit was to give Samson's parents the vital news that Samson would begin to rescue Israel from the Philistines. (For more on the angel see the notes on 2.1 and 6.11.)

13.5 Samson was to be a nazirite—a person who took a vow to be set apart for God's service. Samson's parents made the vow for him. A nazirite vow was sometimes temporary, but in Samson's case, it was for life. As a nazirite, Samson could not cut his hair, touch a dead body, or drink anything containing alcohol.

Although Samson often used poor judgment and sinned terribly, he accomplished much when he determined to be set apart for God. In this way he was like the nation Israel. As long as the Israelites remained set apart for God, the nation thrived. But they fell into terrible sin when they ignored God.

13.5 Manoah's wife was told that her son would *begin* to rescue the Israelites from Philistine oppression. It wasn't until David's day that the Philistine opposition was completely crushed (2 Samuel 8.1). Samson's part in subduing the Philistines was just the beginning, but it was important nonetheless. It was the task God had given Samson to do. Be faithful in following God even if you don't see instant results, because you might be beginning an important job that others will finish.

13.18 Why did the angel keep his name a secret? In those days people believed that if they knew someone's name, they knew his character and how to control him. By keeping his name a secret, the angel was saying he would not allow himself to be controlled by Manoah. He was also saying that his name was a mystery beyond understanding and too wonderful to imagine. Manoah asked the angel for an answer that he wouldn't have understood. Sometimes we ask God questions and then receive no answer. This may

13.19 19 So Manoah took the kid with the grain offering, and offered it on the rock to
Judg 6.19 the LORD, to him who works[s] wonders.[t] 20 When the flame went up toward
heaven from the altar, the angel of the LORD ascended in the flame of the altar while
Manoah and his wife looked on; and they fell on their faces to the ground. 21 The
13.22 angel of the LORD did not appear again to Manoah and his wife. Then Manoah
Gen 32.30 Ex 33.20 realized that it was the angel of the LORD. 22 And Manoah said to his wife, "We
Judg 6.22 shall surely die, for we have seen God." 23 But his wife said to him, "If the LORD

[s] Gk Vg: Heb *and working* [t] Heb *wonders, while Manoah and his wife looked on*

SAMSON

It is sad to be remembered for what one might have been. Samson had tremendous potential. Not many people have started life with credentials like his. Born as a result of God's plan in the lives of Manoah and his wife, Samson was to do a great work for God—to "begin to deliver Israel from the hand of the Philistines." To help him accomplish God's plan, he was given enormous physical strength.

Because Samson wasted his strength on practical jokes and getting out of scrapes, and because he eventually gave it up altogether to satisfy the woman he loved, we tend to see him as a failure. We remember him as the judge in Israel who spent his last days grinding grain in an enemy prison, and we say, "What wasted potential!"

Yes, Samson wasted his life. He could have strengthened his nation. He could have returned his people to the worship of God. He could have wiped out the Philistines. But even though he did none of those things, Samson still accomplished the purpose announced by the angel who visited his parents before his birth. In his final act, Samson began to rescue Israel from the Philistines.

Interestingly, the New Testament does not mention Samson's failures or his heroic feats of strength. In Hebrews, he is simply listed with others "who through faith conquered kingdoms, administered justice, obtained promises," and in other ways were given superhuman aid. In the end, Samson recognized his dependence on God. When he died, God turned his failures and defeats into victory. Samson's story teaches us that it is never too late to start over. However badly we may have failed in the past, today is not too late for us to put our complete trust in God.

Strengths and accomplishments:
- Dedicated to God from birth as a nazirite
- Known for his feats of strength
- Listed in the Hall of Faith in Hebrews 11
- Began to free Israel from Philistine oppression

Weaknesses and mistakes:
- Violated his vow and God's laws on many occasions
- Was controlled by sensuality
- Confided in the wrong people
- Used his gifts and abilities unwisely

Lessons from his life:
- Great strength in one area of life does not make up for great weaknesses in other areas
- God's presence does not overwhelm a person's will
- God can use a person of faith in spite of his or her mistakes

Vital statistics:
- Where: Zorah, Timnah, Ashkelon, Gaza, valley of Sorek
- Occupation: Judge
- Relatives: Father: Manoah
- Contemporaries: Delilah; Samuel, who might have been born while Samson was a judge

Key verse:
"For you shall conceive and bear a son. No razor is to come on his head, for the boy shall be a nazirite to God from birth. It is he who shall begin to deliver Israel from the hand of the Philistines" (Judges 13.5).

His story is told in Judges 13—16. He is also mentioned in Hebrews 11.32.

not be because God is saying no. We may have asked for knowledge beyond our ability to understand or accept.

13.19 Manoah sacrificed a *grain offering* to the Lord. This offering was grain, oil, and flour shaped into a cake and burned on the altar along with the *burnt offering* (the young goat). The grain offering, described in Leviticus 2, was offered to God as a sign of honor, respect, and worship. It was an acknowledgment that because the Israelites' food came from God, they owed their lives to him. With the grain offering, Manoah showed his desire to serve God and demonstrated his respect.

13.22 Manoah thought that he would die because of the Lord's words to Moses recorded in Exodus 33.20. Gideon also had the same experience (6.22).

had meant to kill us, he would not have accepted a burnt offering and a grain offering at our hands, or shown us all these things, or now announced to us such things
as these." **13.24** Heb 11.32
24 The woman bore a son, and named him Samson. The boy grew, and the **13.25**
LORD blessed him. 25 The spirit of the LORD began to stir him in Mahaneh-dan, Judg 3.10; 6.34 14.6
between Zorah and Eshtaol. 1 Sam 10.6,10

Samson asks a riddle

14 Once Samson went down to Timnah, and at Timnah he saw a Philistine
woman. 2 Then he came up, and told his father and mother, "I saw a Philistine woman at Timnah; now get her for me as my wife." 3 But his father and mother **14.3**
said to him, "Is there not a woman among your kin, or among all our[u] people, that Deut 7.3
you must go to take a wife from the uncircumcised Philistines?" But Samson said Josh 23.12
to his father, "Get her for me, because she pleases me." 4 His father and mother did **14.4**
not know that this was from the LORD; for he was seeking a pretext to act against the Josh 11.20
Philistines. At that time the Philistines had dominion over Israel. 1 Kgs 12.15
5 Then Samson went down with his father and mother to Timnah. When he
came to the vineyards of Timnah, suddenly a young lion roared at him. 6 The spirit **14.6**
of the LORD rushed on him, and he tore the lion apart barehanded as one might tear Judg 11.29 13.25; 15.14
apart a kid. But he did not tell his father or his mother what he had done. 7 Then he 1 Sam 17.34-36
went down and talked with the woman, and she pleased Samson. 8 After a while he
returned to marry her, and he turned aside to see the carcass of the lion, and there
was a swarm of bees in the body of the lion, and honey. 9 He scraped it out into his
hands, and went on, eating as he went. When he came to his father and mother, he
gave some to them, and they ate it. But he did not tell them that he had taken the
honey from the carcass of the lion.
10 His father went down to the woman, and Samson made a feast there as the
young men were accustomed to do. 11 When the people saw him, they brought
thirty companions to be with him. 12 Samson said to them, "Let me now put a riddle **14.12**
to you. If you can explain it to me within the seven days of the feast, and find it out, Gen 29.27 Dan 5.12
then I will give you thirty linen garments and thirty festal garments. 13 But if you Ezek 17.2
cannot explain it to me, then you shall give me thirty linen garments and thirty
festal garments." So they said to him, "Ask your riddle; let us hear it." 14 He said
to them,

"Out of the eater came something to eat.

[u] Cn: Heb *my*

13.25 Samson's tribe, Dan, continued to wander in their inherited land (18.1), which was yet unconquered (Joshua 19.47, 48). Samson must have grown up with his warlike tribe's yearnings for a permanent and settled territory. Thus his visits to the tribal army camp stirred his heart, and God's Spirit began preparing him for his role as judge and leader against the Philistines.

Perhaps there are things that stir your heart. These may indicate areas where God wants to use you. God uses a variety of means to develop and prepare us: hereditary traits, environmental influences, and personal experiences. As with Samson, this preparation often begins long before adulthood. Work at being sensitive to the Holy Spirit's leading and the tasks God has prepared for you. Your past may be more useful to you than you imagine.

14.3 Samson's parents objected to his marrying the Philistine woman for several reasons: (1) It was against God's law (Exodus 34.15–17; Deuteronomy 7.1–4). A stark example of what happened when the Israelites married pagans can be found in 3.5–7. (2) The Philistines were Israel's greatest enemies. Marriage to a hated Philistine would be a disgrace to Samson's family. But Samson's father gave in to Samson's demand and allowed the marriage, even though he had the right to refuse his son.

14.6 "The spirit of the Lord rushed on him" refers to the unusual physical strength given Samson by the spirit of the Lord. Samson did not seem to be affected in any way other than increased physical power.

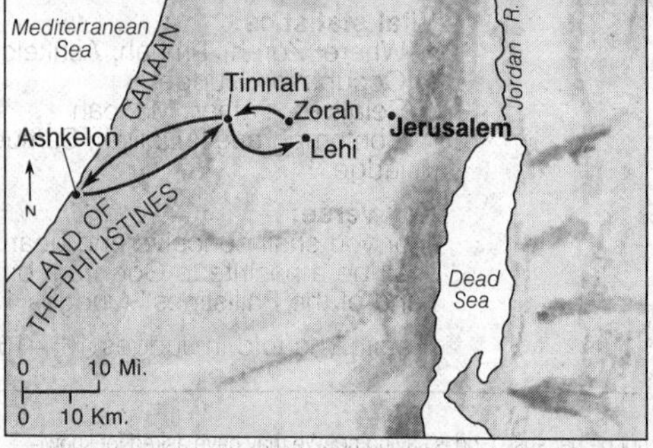

SAMSON'S VENTURES Samson grew up in Zorah and wanted to marry a Philistine girl from Timnah. Tricked at his own wedding feast, he went to Ashkelon and killed some Philistine men and stole their coats to pay off a bet. Samson then let himself be captured and brought to Lehi where he snapped his ropes and killed 1,000 people.

Out of the strong came something sweet."
But for three days they could not explain the riddle.
14.15 Judg 15.6 15 On the fourth[v] day they said to Samson's wife, "Coax your husband to explain the riddle to us, or we will burn you and your father's house with fire. Have
you invited us here to impoverish us?" 16 So Samson's wife wept before him, saying, "You hate me; you do not really love me. You have asked a riddle of my
people, but you have not explained it to me." He said to her, "Look, I have not told
my father or my mother. Why should I tell you?" 17 She wept before him the seven
days that their feast lasted; and because she nagged him, on the seventh day he told
her. Then she explained the riddle to her people. 18 The men of the town said to him
on the seventh day before the sun went down,
"What is sweeter than honey?
What is stronger than a lion?"
And he said to them,
"If you had not plowed with my heifer,
you would not have found out my riddle."
14.19 Judg 14.6; 15.14 19 Then the spirit of the LORD rushed on him, and he went down to Ashkelon. He
killed thirty men of the town, took their spoil, and gave the festal garments to those
who had explained the riddle. In hot anger he went back to his father's house.
14.20 Jn 3.29 20 And Samson's wife was given to his companion, who had been his best man.

Samson kills many enemies

15 After a while, at the time of the wheat harvest, Samson went to visit his wife,
bringing along a kid. He said, "I want to go into my wife's room." But her
father would not allow him to go in. 2 Her father said, "I was sure that you had
rejected her; so I gave her to your companion. Is not her younger sister prettier than
she? Why not take her instead?" 3 Samson said to them, "This time, when I do
mischief to the Philistines, I will be without blame." 4 So Samson went and caught
three hundred foxes, and took some torches; and he turned the foxes[w] tail to tail,
and put a torch between each pair of tails. 5 When he had set fire to the torches, he
let the foxes go into the standing grain of the Philistines, and burned up the shocks
15.6 Judg 14.15 and the standing grain, as well as the vineyards and[x] olive groves. 6 Then the Philistines asked, "Who has done this?" And they said, "Samson, the son-in-law of the
Timnite, because he has taken Samson's wife and given her to his companion." So
the Philistines came up, and burned her and her father. 7 Samson said to them, "If
this is what you do, I swear I will not stop until I have taken revenge on you." 8 He
struck them down hip and thigh with great slaughter; and he went down and stayed
in the cleft of the rock of Etam.
9 Then the Philistines came up and encamped in Judah, and made a raid on
Lehi. 10 The men of Judah said, "Why have you come up against us?" They said,
15.11 Judg 13.1; 15.20 "We have come up to bind Samson, to do to him as he did to us." 11 Then three
thousand men of Judah went down to the cleft of the rock of Etam, and they said to
Samson, "Do you not know that the Philistines are rulers over us? What then have
you done to us?" He replied, "As they did to me, so I have done to them." 12 They
said to him, "We have come down to bind you, so that we may give you into
the hands of the Philistines." Samson answered them, "Swear to me that you

[v] Gk Syr: Heb *seventh* [w] Heb *them* [x] Gk Tg Vg: Heb lacks *and*

14.18 "If you had not plowed with my heifer" means "If you hadn't manipulated my wife." If they hadn't threatened his wife, they wouldn't have learned the answer to his riddle.

14.19 Samson impulsively used the special gift God gave him for selfish purposes. Today, God distributes abilities and skills throughout the church (1 Corinthians 12.1ff). The apostle Paul states that these gifts are to be used "for building up the body of Christ," that is, the church (Ephesians 4.12). To use these abilities for selfish purposes is to rob the church and fellow believers of strength. As you use the gifts God has given you, be sure you are helping others, not just yourself.

15.1ff Samson's reply in 15.11 tells the story of this chapter: "As they did to me, so I have done to them." Revenge is an uncontrollable monster. Each act of retaliation brings another. It is a boomerang which cannot be thrown without cost to the thrower. The revenge cycle can be halted only by forgiveness.

15.7 God had given all the land of the Philistines to Israel (Joshua 13.2), but Israel had failed to drive the Philistines out and were now dominated by them. God used Samson and his short temper to judge these oppressors. God can cause even sinful "human wrath" to bring himself glory (Psalm 76.10). He is not limited by our weaknesses.

yourselves will not attack me." 13 They said to him, "No, we will only bind you and
give you into their hands; we will not kill you." So they bound him with two new
ropes, and brought him up from the rock.
14 When he came to Lehi, the Philistines came shouting to meet him; and the 15.14
spirit of the LORD rushed on him, and the ropes that were on his arms became like Judg 14.6,19
flax that has caught fire, and his bonds melted off his hands. 15 Then he found a
fresh jawbone of a donkey, reached down and took it, and with it he killed a thousand men. 16 And Samson said,

"With the jawbone of a donkey,
heaps upon heaps,
with the jawbone of a donkey
I have slain a thousand men."

17 When he had finished speaking, he threw away the jawbone; and that place was
called Ramath-lehi.[y]
18 By then he was very thirsty, and he called on the LORD, saying, "You have
granted this great victory by the hand of your servant. Am I now to die of thirst, and 15.19
fall into the hands of the uncircumcised?" 19 So God split open the hollow place that Gen 45.27 1 Sam 30.11
is at Lehi, and water came from it. When he drank, his spirit returned, and he 15.20
revived. Therefore it was named En-hakkore,[z] which is at Lehi to this day. 20 And Judg 13.1,5 16.31
he judged Israel in the days of the Philistines twenty years. Heb 11.32

Samson reveals his secret to Delilah

16 Once Samson went to Gaza, where he saw a prostitute and went in to her. 16.1
2 The Gazites were told,[a] "Samson has come here." So they circled around Josh 15.47
and lay in wait for him all night at the city gate. They kept quiet all night, thinking,
"Let us wait until the light of the morning; then we will kill him." 3 But Samson lay
only until midnight. Then at midnight he rose up, took hold of the doors of the city
gate and the two posts, pulled them up, bar and all, put them on his shoulders, and
carried them to the top of the hill that is in front of Hebron.
4 After this he fell in love with a woman in the valley of Sorek, whose name
was Delilah. 5 The lords of the Philistines came to her and said to her, "Coax him,

[y] That is *The Hill of the Jawbone* [z] That is *The Spring of the One who Called* [a] Gk: Heb lacks *were told*

15.14–17 The Lord's strength came upon Samson, but he was proud and boasted only of his own strength. "With the jawbone of a donkey I have slain a thousand men" he said, and later asked God to refresh him because of *his* accomplishments (15.16–18). Pride can cause us to take credit for work we've done only because of God's strength.

15.18 Samson was physically and emotionally exhausted. After a great personal victory, his attitude declined quickly into self-pity—"Am I now to die of thirst?" Emotionally, we are most vulnerable after a great effort or when faced with real physical needs. Severe depression often follows great achievements, so don't be surprised if you feel drained after a personal victory.

During these times of vulnerability, avoid the temptation to think that God owes you for your efforts. It was *his* strength that gave you victory. Concentrate on keeping your attitudes, actions, and words focused on God instead of yourself.

15.19 This miracle of God to revive Samson was water flowing out of a gap in the rock where God caused a fountain to flow. It was God, the Creator and Lord of nature, helping Samson.

15.20 Apparently Samson was appointed Israel's judge after this victory over the Philistines.

16.3 Samson was set apart from birth for special service to God. But for the most part he ignored his vow of devotion and depended more and more on his own strength rather than on God's. This verse marks the first time that the spirit of the Lord is not mentioned as directly affecting one of Samson's great feats of strength (14.6, 19; 15.14).

If we become successful using our God-given gifts, we must not forget (1) who gave us these gifts, skills, and abilities or (2) the moral purpose that directs the use of those gifts. Notice what happened when Samson forgot (16.20, 21). We must always remember that all our gifts and abilities come from God. They must be used with his interests in mind.

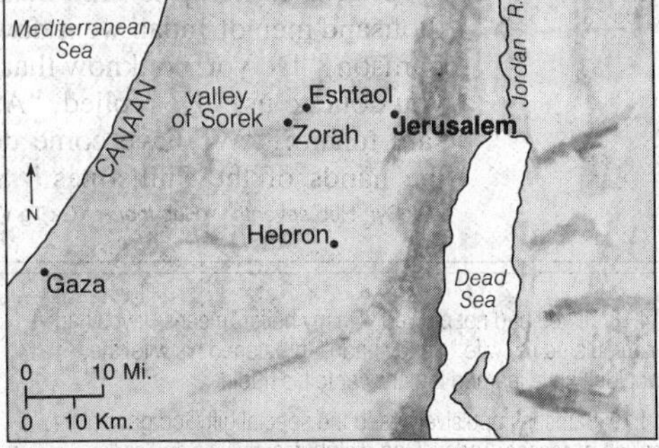

SAMSON AND DELILAH Samson was seduced by a Philistine woman named Delilah who lived in the valley of Sorek. She betrayed the secret of his strength to the Philistines who captured him and led him away in chains to Gaza. There he died. His relatives buried him between Zorah and Eshtaol.

and find out what makes his strength so great, and how we may overpower him, so
that we may bind him in order to subdue him; and we will each give you eleven
hundred pieces of silver." 6 So Delilah said to Samson, "Please tell me what makes
your strength so great, and how you could be bound, so that one could subdue
you." 7 Samson said to her, "If they bind me with seven fresh bowstrings that are
not dried out, then I shall become weak, and be like anyone else." 8 Then the lords
of the Philistines brought her seven fresh bowstrings that had not dried out, and she
bound him with them. 9 While men were lying in wait in an inner chamber, she said
to him, "The Philistines are upon you, Samson!" But he snapped the bowstrings, as
a strand of fiber snaps when it touches the fire. So the secret of his strength was not
known.

10 Then Delilah said to Samson, "You have mocked me and told me lies; please
tell me how you could be bound." 11 He said to her, "If they bind me with new ropes
that have not been used, then I shall become weak, and be like anyone else." 12 So
Delilah took new ropes and bound him with them, and said to him, "The Philistines
are upon you, Samson!" (The men lying in wait were in an inner chamber.) But he
snapped the ropes off his arms like a thread.

13 Then Delilah said to Samson, "Until now you have mocked me and told me
lies; tell me how you could be bound." He said to her, "If you weave the seven
locks of my head with the web and make it tight with the pin, then I shall become
weak, and be like anyone else." 14 So while he slept, Delilah took the seven locks
of his head and wove them into the web,[b] and made them tight with the pin. Then
she said to him, "The Philistines are upon you, Samson!" But he awoke from his
sleep, and pulled away the pin, the loom, and the web.

[b] Compare Gk: in verses 13-14, Heb lacks *and make it tight . . . into the web*

DELILAH

A person's greatest accomplishment may well be helping others accomplish great things. Likewise, a person's greatest failure may be preventing others from achieving greatness. Delilah played a minor role in Samson's life, but her effect was devastating, for she influenced him to betray his special calling from God. Motivated by greed, Delilah used her persistence to wear down Samson. His infatuation with her made Samson a vulnerable target. For all his physical strength, he was no match for her, and he paid a great price for giving in to her. Delilah is never mentioned again in the Bible. Her unfaithfulness to Samson brought ruin to him and to her people.

Are people helped by knowing you? Do they find that knowing you challenges them to be the best they can be? Even more important, does knowing you help their relationship with God? What do your demands for their time and attention tell them about your real care for them? Are you willing to be God's instrument in the lives of others?

Strength and accomplishment:
- Persistent when faced with obstacles

Weaknesses and mistakes:
- Valued money more than relationships
- Betrayed the man who trusted her

Lesson from her life:
- We need to be careful to place our trust only in people who are trustworthy

Vital statistics:
- Where: valley of Sorek
- Contemporary: Samson

Key verses:
"Finally, after she had nagged him with her words day after day, and pestered him, he was tired to death. So he told her his whole secret" (Judges 16.16, 17).

Her story is told in Judges 16.

16.5 The Philistines were ruled by five "lords," or leaders, not just one. Each leader ruled from a different city—Ashdod, Ashkelon, Ekron, Gath, or Gaza. Each of these cities was an important center for trade and commerce. Given Delilah's character, it is little wonder that she betrayed Samson when these rich and powerful men paid her a personal visit.

15 Then she said to him, "How can you say, 'I love you,' when your heart is not **16.15**
with me? You have mocked me three times now and have not told me what makes Judg 14.16
your strength so great." 16 Finally, after she had nagged him with her words day **16.16**
after day, and pestered him, he was tired to death. 17 So he told her his whole secret, Num 6.5 Judg 13.5
and said to her, "A razor has never come upon my head; for I have been a nazirite[c]
to God from my mother's womb. If my head were shaved, then my strength would
leave me; I would become weak, and be like anyone else."
18 When Delilah realized that he had told her his whole secret, she sent and
called the lords of the Philistines, saying, "This time come up, for he has told his
whole secret to me." Then the lords of the Philistines came up to her, and brought
the money in their hands. 19 She let him fall asleep on her lap; and she called a man,
and had him shave off the seven locks of his head. He began to weaken,[d] and his
strength left him. 20 Then she said, "The Philistines are upon you, Samson!" When **16.20**
he awoke from his sleep, he thought, "I will go out as at other times, and shake 1 Sam 16.14 18.11,12
myself free." But he did not know that the LORD had left him. 21 So the Philistines
seized him and gouged out his eyes. They brought him down to Gaza and bound
him with bronze shackles; and he ground at the mill in the prison. 22 But the hair of
his head began to grow again after it had been shaved.

Samson triumphs in death

23 Now the lords of the Philistines gathered to offer a great sacrifice to their god **16.23**
Dagon, and to rejoice; for they said, "Our god has given Samson our enemy into 1 Sam 5.1,2
our hand." 24 When the people saw him, they praised their god; for they said, "Our
god has given our enemy into our hand, the ravager of our country, who has killed
many of us." 25 And when their hearts were merry, they said, "Call Samson, and let
him entertain us." So they called Samson out of the prison, and he performed for

[c] That is *one separated* or *one consecrated* [d] Gk: Heb *She began to torment him*

16.15 Samson was deceived because he wanted to believe Delilah's lies. Although he could strangle a lion, he could not smother his burning lust and see Delilah for who she really was. How can you keep your desire for love and sexual pleasure from deceiving you? (1) You must decide what kind of a person you will love *before* passion takes over. Determine whether a person's character and faith in God are as desirable as his or her physical appearance. (2) Since most of the time you spend with your spouse will *not* involve sex, your companion's personality, temperament, and commitment to solve problems must be as gratifying as his or her kisses. (3) Be patient. Wait for time to reveal what is beneath the pleasant appearance and attentive touch.

16.16, 17 Delilah kept asking Samson for the secret of his strength until he finally grew tired of hearing her nagging and gave in. What a pitiful excuse for disobedience. Don't allow anyone, no matter how attractive or persuasive, to talk you into doing wrong. This was the second time that Samson allowed himself to be worn down by the nagging of a woman (14.17).

16.19 Delilah was a deceitful woman with honey on her lips and poison in her heart. Cold and calculating, she toyed with Samson, pretending to love him while looking for personal gain. How could Samson be so foolish? Four times Delilah took advantage of him. If he didn't realize what was happening after the first or second experience, surely he should have understood the situation by the fourth time! We think Samson is foolish; but how many times do we allow ourselves to be deceived by flattery and give in to temptation and wrong beliefs? Avoid falling prey to deceit by asking God to help you distinguish between deception and truth.

16.20 Samson's relationship with God had deteriorated so much that he didn't even realize God had left him. He took his strength as well as God's presence for granted. God offered Samson all he would ever need, yet Samson chose instead to put himself into Delilah's deceitful hands. As a result he lost his strength. We must be careful not to put our lives into the wrong hands. Our only true security is found in God.

16.21 Samson, the mighty warrior, became a slave. Rather than kill him, the Philistines preferred to humiliate him by gouging out his eyes and making him grind grain. Samson now had plenty of time to wonder if Delilah's charms were worth spending the rest of his life in humiliation.

Although God did not completely abandon Samson (16.28–30), he allowed Samson's decision to stand, and the consequences of his decision followed naturally. We may choose to be close to God or to go our own way, but there are consequences resulting from our choice. Samson didn't choose to be captured, but he chose to be with Delilah, and he could not escape the consequences of his decision.

16.21 Blinded and without strength, Samson was taken to Gaza where he would spend the rest of his short life. Gaza was one of the five capital cities of the Philistines. Known for its many wells, Gaza was a vital stop along a great caravan route that connected Egypt to the south with Syria to the north. The Philistines probably showed off their prize captive Samson to many dignitaries passing through.

Ironically, it was in Gaza that Samson had earlier demonstrated his great strength by uprooting the city gates (16.1–3). Now he was an example of weakness.

16.23, 24 Dagon was the chief god of the Philistines, the god of grain and harvest. Many temples were built to Dagon, and the worship there included human sacrifice. The temples were also the local entertainment centers. Just as people today crowd into theaters, Philistine townspeople crowded into the local temple. They sat on the flat temple roof and looked into the courtyard below. What they often saw was the torture and humiliation of prisoners.

Since the Philistines had control over the Israelites, they thought their god was stronger. But when the ark of God was placed before Dagon in a similar temple, the idol fell over and broke into pieces (1 Samuel 5.1–7). God's strength goes beyond numbers or physical might.

them. They made him stand between the pillars; 26 and Samson said to the attendant
who held him by the hand, "Let me feel the pillars on which the house rests, so that
I may lean against them." 27 Now the house was full of men and women; all the
lords of the Philistines were there, and on the roof there were about three thousand
men and women, who looked on while Samson performed.
16.28 Judg 15.18 28 Then Samson called to the LORD and said, "Lord GOD, remember me and
strengthen me only this once, O God, so that with this one act of revenge I may pay
back the Philistines for my two eyes."[e] 29 And Samson grasped the two middle
pillars on which the house rested, and he leaned his weight against them, his right
hand on the one and his left hand on the other. 30 Then Samson said, "Let me die
with the Philistines." He strained with all his might; and the house fell on the lords
and all the people who were in it. So those he killed at his death were more than
those he had killed during his life. 31 Then his brothers and all his family came
down and took him and brought him up and buried him between Zorah and Eshtaol
in the tomb of his father Manoah. He had judged Israel twenty years.

C. THE MORAL FAILURE OF ISRAEL (17.1 – 21.25)

Please pray for a happy marriage for Eric + Candy. For Eric to excel in the Air Force and for his safety. For Mike to ~~make~~ make good career choices and for him to be able to play water polo overseas, for his safety + happiness. Judy

...to idolatry, moral decline, and petty fighting. Israel,
...ple for spiritual living, had instead become morally
...od, and that was seldom, it was often from selfish
...ot bring us far. Genuine obedience is motivated by a
...

...l country of Ephraim whose name was Micah. 2 He
...eleven hundred pieces of silver that were taken from
...urse, and even spoke it in my hearing, — that silver
...now I will return it to you."[f] And his mother said,
... LORD!" 3 Then he returned the eleven hundred
...d his mother said, "I consecrate the silver to the
..., to make an idol of cast metal." 4 So when he
...r, his mother took two hundred pieces of silver,
...o made it into an idol of cast metal; and it was in
... Micah had a shrine, and he made an ephod and
...sons, who became his priest. 6 In those days there
...ple did what was right in their own eyes.

...s for one of my two eyes [f] The words *but now I will return it to you*

...pentance and use him this final time. One of the effects of sin in our lives is to keep us from feeling like praying. But perfect moral behavior is not a condition for prayer. Don't let guilt feelings over sin keep you from your only means of restoration. No matter how long you have been away from God, he is ready to hear from you and restore you to a right relationship. Every situation can be salvaged if you are willing to turn again to him. If God could still work in Samson's situation, he can certainly make something worthwhile out of yours.

17.2 Micah and his mother seemed to be good and moral and may have sincerely desired to worship God, but they disobeyed God by following their own desires instead of doing what God wanted. The attitude that prevailed in Micah's day was this: "All the people did what was right in their own eyes" (17.6). This is remarkably similar to today's prevailing attitudes. But God has given us standards. He has not left our conduct up to us and our opinions. We can avoid conforming to society's low standards by taking God's commands seriously and applying them to life. Independence and self-reliance are positive traits, but only within the framework of God's standards.

17.4, 5 Micah may have felt religious because of his collection of idols, his confession of wrongdoing, and the appointment of his son as a priest. He obviously wanted to maintain a religious influence in his home, but he went about it the wrong way. His apparently good intentions were not enough; he needed to follow God's laws and not his own ideas of what was right. If Micah truly loved God, he would have desired to know what God had communicated to his people and what he should do about it. Instead, Micah set up his own religious system for his own benefit. Don't think sincerity and good intentions are enough. Everyone, no matter how sincere, needs instruction from God's Word and other believers.

17.6 Today, as in Micah's day, everyone seems to put his or her own interests first. Time has not changed human nature. Most people still reject God's right way of living. The people in Micah's time replaced the true worship of God with a homemade version of worship. As a result, justice was soon replaced by revenge and chaos. Ignoring God's direction led to confusion and destruction. Anyone who has not submitted to God will end up doing whatever seems right at the time. This tendency is present in all of us. To know what is really right and to have the strength to do it, we need to draw closer to God and his Word.

7 Now there was a young man of Bethlehem in Judah, of the clan of Judah. He **17.7**
was a Levite residing there. 8 This man left the town of Bethlehem in Judah, to live Judg 19.1 Ruth 1.1,2
wherever he could find a place. He came to the house of Micah in the hill country Mic 5.2 Mt 2.1
of Ephraim to carry on his work.[g] 9 Micah said to him, "From where do you
come?" He replied, "I am a Levite of Bethlehem in Judah, and I am going to live
wherever I can find a place." 10 Then Micah said to him, "Stay with me, and be to
me a father and a priest, and I will give you ten pieces of silver a year, a set of
clothes, and your living."[h] 11 The Levite agreed to stay with the man; and the
young man became to him like one of his sons. 12 So Micah installed the Levite, and **17.12**
the young man became his priest, and was in the house of Micah. 13 Then Micah Num 16.10 Judg 18.30
said, "Now I know that the LORD will prosper me, because the Levite has become 1 Kgs 12.31
my priest."

The Danites steal Micah's idols

18 In those days there was no king in Israel. And in those days the tribe of the **18.1**
Danites was seeking for itself a territory to live in; for until then no territory Josh 19.40 Judg 17.6; 21.25
among the tribes of Israel had been allotted to them. 2 So the Danites sent five val- **18.2**
iant men from the whole number of their clan, from Zorah and from Eshtaol, to spy Judg 13.2,3,25
out the land and to explore it; and they said to them, "Go, explore the land." When
they came to the hill country of Ephraim, to the house of Micah, they stayed there.
3 While they were at Micah's house, they recognized the voice of the young Levite;
so they went over and asked him, "Who brought you here? What are you doing in
this place? What is your business here?" 4 He said to them, "Micah did such and **18.4**
such for me, and he hired me, and I have become his priest." 5 Then they said to Judg 17.10,11
him, "Inquire of God that we may know whether the mission we are undertaking
will succeed." 6 The priest replied, "Go in peace. The mission you are on is under
the eye of the LORD."
7 The five men went on, and when they came to Laish, they observed the peo- **18.7**
ple who were there living securely, after the manner of the Sidonians, quiet and Josh 19.47,48
unsuspecting, lacking[i] nothing on earth, and possessing wealth.[j] Furthermore,
they were far from the Sidonians and had no dealings with Aram.[k] 8 When they
came to their kinsfolk at Zorah and Eshtaol, they said to them, "What do you re-

[g] Or *Ephraim, continuing his journey* [h] Heb *living, and the Levite went* [i] Cn Compare 18.10: Meaning of Heb uncertain [j] Meaning of Heb uncertain [k] Symmachus: Heb *with anyone*

17.7–12 Apparently the Israelites no longer supported the priests and Levites with their tithes, because so many of the people no longer worshiped God. The young Levite in this story probably left his home in Bethlehem because the money he received from the people there was not enough to live on. But Israel's moral decay affected even the priests and Levites. This man accepted money (17.10, 11), idols (18.20), and position (17.12) in a way that was inconsistent with God's laws. While Micah revealed the religious downfall of individual Israelites, this priest illustrated the religious downfall of priests and Levites.

18.1 The tribe of Dan had been assigned enough land to meet their needs (Joshua 19.40–48). However, because they failed to trust God to help them conquer their territory, the Amorites forced them into the hill country and wouldn't let them settle in the plains (1.34). Rather than fight for their allotted territory, they preferred to look for new land in the north where resistance from the enemy wouldn't be so tough. It was while they were traveling north that some of their men passed Micah's home and stole some of his idols.

18.4–6 Priests and their assistants were all members of the tribe of Levi (Numbers 3.5–13). They were to serve the people, teach them how to worship God, and perform the rituals involved in the worship services both at the tabernacle in Shiloh and in the designated cities throughout the land. But this disobedient priest showed disrespect for God because (1) he performed his duties in a house. Priestly duties were to be performed only in the tabernacle or a designated city. This requirement was intended to prevent God's laws from being changed. (2) He carried idols with him (18.20). (3) He claimed to speak for God when God had not spoken through him (18.6).

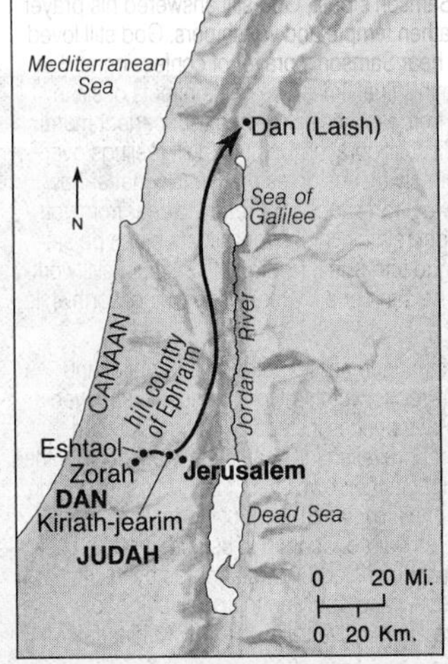

THE TRIBE OF DAN MOVES NORTH
Troops from the tribe of Dan traveled from Zorah and Eshtaol into the hill country of Ephraim where they persuaded Micah's priest to come with them. They continued north to Laish where they ruthlessly butchered its citizens. The city was renamed Dan and the priest's idols became the focus of their worship.

port?" 9 They said, "Come, let us go up against them; for we have seen the land, and
it is very good. Will you do nothing? Do not be slow to go, but enter in and possess
the land. 10 When you go, you will come to an unsuspecting people. The land is
broad—God has indeed given it into your hands—a place where there is no lack of
anything on earth."
11 Six hundred men of the Danite clan, armed with weapons of war, set out
from Zorah and Eshtaol, 12 and went up and encamped at Kiriath-jearim in Judah.
On this account that place is called Mahaneh-dan[l] to this day; it is west of Kiriath-
jearim. 13 From there they passed on to the hill country of Ephraim, and came to the
house of Micah.
18.14 Judg 17.4,5 14 Then the five men who had gone to spy out the land (that is, Laish) said to
their comrades, "Do you know that in these buildings there are an ephod, teraphim,
and an idol of cast metal? Now therefore consider what you will do." 15 So they
turned in that direction and came to the house of the young Levite, at the home of
Micah, and greeted him. 16 While the six hundred men of the Danites, armed with
their weapons of war, stood by the entrance of the gate, 17 the five men who had
gone to spy out the land proceeded to enter and take the idol of cast metal, the
ephod, and the teraphim.[m] The priest was standing by the entrance of the gate with
the six hundred men armed with weapons of war. 18 When the men went into Micah's house and took the idol of cast metal, the ephod, and the teraphim, the priest
18.19 Judg 17.10,11 said to them, "What are you doing?" 19 They said to him, "Keep quiet! Put your
hand over your mouth, and come with us, and be to us a father and a priest. Is it
better for you to be priest to the house of one person, or to be priest to a tribe and
clan in Israel?" 20 Then the priest accepted the offer. He took the ephod, the teraphim, and the idol, and went along with the people.
18.21 Gen 33.2 Ex 12.37 21 So they resumed their journey, putting the little ones, the livestock, and the
goods in front of them. 22 When they were some distance from the home of Micah,
the men who were in the houses near Micah's house were called out, and they
overtook the Danites. 23 They shouted to the Danites, who turned around and said
to Micah, "What is the matter that you come with such a company?" 24 He replied,
"You take my gods that I made, and the priest, and go away, and what have I left?
How then can you ask me, 'What is the matter?' " 25 And the Danites said to him,
"You had better not let your voice be heard among us or else hot-tempered fellows
will attack you, and you will lose your life and the lives of your household." 26 Then
the Danites went their way. When Micah saw that they were too strong for him, he
turned and went back to his home.
27 The Danites, having taken what Micah had made, and the priest who belonged to him, came to Laish, to a people quiet and unsuspecting, put them to the
18.28 2 Sam 10.6 sword, and burned down the city. 28 There was no deliverer, because it was far from
Sidon and they had no dealings with Aram.[n] It was in the valley that belongs to

[l] That is *Camp of Dan* [m] Compare 17.4, 5; 18.14: Heb *teraphim and the cast metal* [n] Cn Compare verse 7: Heb *with anyone*

18.11–26 Through this entire incident, no one desired to worship God; instead, they wanted to use God for selfish gain. Today some people go to church to feel better, be accepted, relieve guilt, and gain business contacts or friends. Beware of following God for selfish gain rather than selfless service.

18.14 An ephod was a ceremonial vest worn by a priest. Teraphim were household gods.

18.24 Micah made idols and hired a priest to run his personal religion. When the men of Dan took his idols and priest, nothing remained. What an empty spiritual condition! An idol is anything that takes God's place in a person's life. Some people invest all their energy in pursuit of money, success, possessions or a career. If these idols are taken away, only an empty shell is left. The only way to protect yourself against such loss is to invest your life in the living God, whom you can never lose.

18.27 Did the tribe of Dan have the right to kill the citizens of Laish? No. God had commanded Israel to clean out and destroy certain cities because of their idolatry and wickedness. But Laish did not fall under that judgment. It was not within the assigned boundaries of Dan, and its people were peaceful in contrast to the warlike Canaanites. But the tribe of Dan had no regard for God's law. God's law said to destroy a city for idolatry (Deuteronomy 13.12–15). The Danites themselves were guilty of this sin. This story shows how far some of the tribes had wandered from God's law.

18.27 Just because the Danites successfully defeated Laish doesn't mean their actions were right. Their idolatry showed that God was not guiding them. Today many justify their wrong actions by outward signs of success. They think that wealth, popularity, or lack of suffering is an indication of God's blessing. But many stories in the Bible indicate that evil and earthly success can go hand in hand (see, for example, 2 Kings 14.23–29). Success doesn't indicate God's approval. Don't allow personal success to become a measuring rod of whether or not you are pleasing God.

Beth-rehob. They rebuilt the city, and lived in it. 29 They named the city Dan, after
their ancestor Dan, who was born to Israel; but the name of the city was formerly
Laish. 30 Then the Danites set up the idol for themselves. Jonathan son of Gershom, **18.30**
son of Moses,[o] and his sons were priests to the tribe of the Danites until the time Ex 2.22; 18.3
the land went into captivity. 31 So they maintained as their own Micah's idol that he
had made, as long as the house of God was at Shiloh.

2. War against the tribe of Benjamin

The runaway concubine

19 In those days, when there was no king in Israel, a certain Levite, residing in **19.1**
the remote parts of the hill country of Ephraim, took to himself a concubine Judg 17.6; 21.25
from Bethlehem in Judah. 2 But his concubine became angry with[p] him, and she
went away from him to her father's house at Bethlehem in Judah, and was there
some four months. 3 Then her husband set out after her, to speak tenderly to her and **19.3**
bring her back. He had with him his servant and a couple of donkeys. When he Gen 34.3
reached[q] her father's house, the girl's father saw him and came with joy to meet
him. 4 His father-in-law, the girl's father, made him stay, and he remained with him
three days; so they ate and drank, and he[r] stayed there. 5 On the fourth day they got **19.5**
up early in the morning, and he prepared to go; but the girl's father said to his Gen 18.5
son-in-law, "Fortify yourself with a bit of food, and after that you may go." 6 So the
two men sat and ate and drank together; and the girl's father said to the man, "Why
not spend the night and enjoy yourself?" 7 When the man got up to go, his father-in-
law kept urging him until he spent the night there again. 8 On the fifth day he got up
early in the morning to leave; and the girl's father said, "Fortify yourself." So they
lingered[s] until the day declined, and the two of them ate and drank.[t] 9 When the
man with his concubine and his servant got up to leave, his father-in-law, the girl's
father, said to him, "Look, the day has worn on until it is almost evening. Spend the
night. See, the day has drawn to a close. Spend the night here and enjoy yourself.
Tomorrow you can get up early in the morning for your journey, and go home."
10 But the man would not spend the night; he got up and departed, and arrived **19.10**
opposite Jebus (that is, Jerusalem). He had with him a couple of saddled donkeys, Josh 15.8; 18.21-28
and his concubine was with him. 11 When they were near Jebus, the day was far 1 Chron 11.4
spent, and the servant said to his master, "Come now, let us turn aside to this city

[o] Another reading is *son of Manasseh* [p] Gk OL: Heb *prostituted herself against* [q] Gk: Heb *she brought him*
[r] Compare verse 7 and Gk: Heb *they* [s] Cn: Heb *Linger* [t] Gk: Heb lacks *and drank*

18.30, 31 The tribe of Dan had stolen Micah's idols, and now they set them up in Laish. Although the Danites were actually denying God by worshiping these images (Exodus 20.1–5), they probably assumed they were worshiping God through them (see the note on Exodus 32.4, 5). Worshiping images of God is *not* worshiping God, even if it resembles true worship in some ways. People repeat the same mistake today when they claim to be Christians without really believing in God's power or changing their conduct to conform to his expectations. Godliness cannot be merely a claim. It must be a reality in our motives and in our actions.

18.31 Shiloh was probably destroyed during the events reported in 1 Samuel 4 and 5, not long after the time described here. Because Shiloh was the religious center for Israel, all adult males were required to travel there for certain religious feasts. The tribe of Dan, however, set up idols and priests in the new territory they conquered. The fact that they were over 80 miles away from Shiloh may have been their excuse for not fulfilling the law's requirements. This act was a further demonstration of their disregard for God.

18.31 The true worship of God should have been maintained through the levitical priests scattered throughout the land and the influence of the tabernacle in Shiloh. This story shows how pagan influences and moral depravity had crept into every corner of Israelite culture. Although 300 years had passed since they entered the promised land, they still had not destroyed the idolatry and evil practices within it.

There may be a tendency in your life to allow "harmless" habits to have their own small corners, but they can become dominating forces. The values, attitudes, and practices you have adopted from the world's system can be exposed by applying the light of God's truth to them. Once you see them for what they are, you can begin to uproot them.

19.1 Having concubines was an accepted part of Israelite society, although this is not what God intended (Genesis 2.24). A concubine had most of the duties but only some of the privileges of a wife. Although she was legally attached to one man, she and her children usually did not have the inheritance rights of the legal wife and legitimate children. Her primary purpose was giving the man sexual pleasure, bearing additional children, and contributing more help to the household or estate. Concubines were often foreign prisoners of war. But they could also be Israelites, as was probably the case in this story.

19.1–21.25 What is the significance of this tragic story? When the Israelites' faith in God disintegrated, their unity as a nation also disintegrated. They could have taken complete possession of the land if they had obeyed God and trusted him to keep his promises. But when they forgot to include him in their lives, they lost their purpose, and soon "all the people did what was right in their own eyes" (21.25). When they stopped letting God lead them, they became no better than the evil people around them. When they made laws for their own benefit, they set standards far below God's. When you leave God out of your life you may be shocked at what you are capable of doing (19.30).

19.12 Josh 24.33 Judg 20.4 of the Jebusites, and spend the night in it." 12 But his master said to him, "We will
not turn aside into a city of foreigners, who do not belong to the people of Israel; but
we will continue on to Gibeah." 13 Then he said to his servant, "Come, let us try to
reach one of these places, and spend the night at Gibeah or at Ramah." 14 So they
passed on and went their way; and the sun went down on them near Gibeah, which
belongs to Benjamin. 15 They turned aside there, to go in and spend the night at
Gibeah. He went in and sat down in the open square of the city, but no one took
them in to spend the night.
16 Then at evening there was an old man coming from his work in the field. The
man was from the hill country of Ephraim, and he was residing in Gibeah. (The
19.17 Esth 4.6 people of the place were Benjaminites.) 17 When the old man looked up and saw the
wayfarer in the open square of the city, he said, "Where are you going and where
do you come from?" 18 He answered him, "We are passing from Bethlehem in Judah to the remote parts of the hill country of Ephraim, from which I come. I went
to Bethlehem in Judah; and I am going to my home.[u] Nobody has offered to take
me in. 19 We your servants have straw and fodder for our donkeys, with bread and
wine for me and the woman and the young man along with us. We need nothing
more." 20 The old man said, "Peace be to you. I will care for all your wants; only
19.21 Gen 18.4; 19.2 24.32 do not spend the night in the square." 21 So he brought him into his house, and fed
the donkeys; they washed their feet, and ate and drank.
19.22 Gen 19.4,5 22 While they were enjoying themselves, the men of the city, a perverse lot,
surrounded the house, and started pounding on the door. They said to the old man,
the master of the house, "Bring out the man who came into your house, so that we
19.23 2 Sam 13.12 may have intercourse with him." 23 And the man, the master of the house, went out
to them and said to them, "No, my brothers, do not act so wickedly. Since this man
19.24 Gen 19.8 is my guest, do not do this vile thing. 24 Here are my virgin daughter and his concubine; let me bring them out now. Ravish them and do whatever you want to them;
but against this man do not do such a vile thing." 25 But the men would not listen to
him. So the man seized his concubine, and put her out to them. They wantonly
raped her, and abused her all through the night until the morning. And as the dawn
began to break, they let her go. 26 As morning appeared, the woman came and fell
down at the door of the man's house where her master was, until it was light.
27 In the morning her master got up, opened the doors of the house, and when
he went out to go on his way, there was his concubine lying at the door of the house,
with her hands on the threshold. 28 "Get up," he said to her, "we are going." But
there was no answer. Then he put her on the donkey; and the man set out for his
home. 29 When he had entered his house, he took a knife, and grasping his concubine he cut her into twelve pieces, limb by limb, and sent her throughout all the
territory of Israel. 30 Then he commanded the men whom he sent, saying, "Thus
shall you say to all the Israelites, 'Has such a thing ever happened[v] since the day

[u] Gk Compare 19.29. Heb *to the house of the* LORD [v] Compare Gk: Heb *30And all who saw it said, "Such a thing has not happened or been seen*

19.15 It was a custom of the times for a stranger to enter the square of the town where all the social and business activity took place. The laws of hospitality required that the stranger be invited for food and lodging.

19.24 Nowhere is the unwritten law of hospitality stronger than in the Middle East. Protecting a guest at any cost ranked at the top of a man's code of honor. But here the hospitality code turned to fanaticism. The rape and abuse of a daughter and companion was preferable to the *possibility* of a conflict between a guest and a neighbor. The two men were selfish (they didn't want to get hurt themselves); they lacked courage (they didn't want to face a conflict even when lives were at stake); and they disobeyed God's law (they allowed deliberate abuse and murder). What drastic consequences can result when social protocol carries more authority than moral convictions!

19.29, 30 Although this was a terrible way to communicate the news, it effectively communicated the horror of the crime and called the people to action. Saul used a similar method in 1 Samuel 11.7. Ironically, the man who alerted Israel to the murder of his concubine was just as guilty for her death as the men who actually killed her.

19.30 The horrible crime described in this chapter wasn't Israel's worst offense. Even worse was the nation's failure to establish a government based upon God's moral principles, where the law of God was the law of the land. As a result, laws were usually unenforced and crime was ignored. Sexual perversion and lawlessness were a by-product of Israel's disobedience to God. The Israelites weren't willing to speak up until events had gone too far.

Whenever we get away from God and his Word, all sorts of evil can follow. Our drifting away from God may be slow and almost imperceptible, with the ultimate results affecting a future generation. We must continually call our nation back to God and work toward the establishment of God's moral and spiritual reign in the heart of every person.

that the Israelites came up from the land of Egypt until this day? Consider it, take
counsel, and speak out.' "

Israel attacks the tribe of Benjamin

20 Then all the Israelites came out, from Dan to Beer-sheba, including the land **20.1**
of Gilead, and the congregation assembled in one body before the LORD at 1 Sam 7.5 2 Sam 19.14
Mizpah. 2 The chiefs of all the people, of all the tribes of Israel, presented themselves in the assembly of the people of God, four hundred thousand foot-soldiers
bearing arms. 3 (Now the Benjaminites heard that the people of Israel had gone up
to Mizpah.) And the Israelites said, "Tell us, how did this criminal act come
about?" 4 The Levite, the husband of the woman who was murdered, answered, "I
came to Gibeah that belongs to Benjamin, I and my concubine, to spend the night.
5 The lords of Gibeah rose up against me, and surrounded the house at night. They
intended to kill me, and they raped my concubine until she died. 6 Then I took my
concubine and cut her into pieces, and sent her throughout the whole extent of
Israel's territory; for they have committed a vile outrage in Israel. 7 So now, you
Israelites, all of you, give your advice and counsel here."

8 All the people got up as one, saying, "We will not any of us go to our tents,
nor will any of us return to our houses. 9 But now this is what we will do to Gibeah:
we will go up[w] against it by lot. 10 We will take ten men of a hundred throughout
all the tribes of Israel, and a hundred of a thousand, and a thousand of ten thousand,
to bring provisions for the troops, who are going to repay[x] Gibeah of Benjamin for
all the disgrace that they have done in Israel." 11 So all the men of Israel gathered
against the city, united as one.

12 The tribes of Israel sent men through all the tribe of Benjamin, saying,
"What crime is this that has been committed among you? 13 Now then, hand over
those scoundrels in Gibeah, so that we may put them to death, and purge the evil
from Israel." But the Benjaminites would not listen to their kinsfolk, the Israelites.
14 The Benjaminites came together out of the towns to Gibeah, to go out to battle **20.14**
against the Israelites. 15 On that day the Benjaminites mustered twenty-six thousand Num 2.23
armed men from their towns, besides the inhabitants of Gibeah. 16 Of all this force, **20.16**
there were seven hundred picked men who were left-handed; every one could sling Judg 3.15
a stone at a hair, and not miss. 17 And the Israelites, apart from Benjamin, mustered
four hundred thousand armed men, all of them warriors.

18 The Israelites proceeded to go up to Bethel, where they inquired of God, **20.18**
"Which of us shall go up first to battle against the Benjaminites?" And the LORD Num 27.21 Judg 1.1
answered, "Judah shall go up first."

19 Then the Israelites got up in the morning, and encamped against Gibeah.
20 The Israelites went out to battle against Benjamin; and the Israelites drew up the
battle line against them at Gibeah. 21 The Benjaminites came out of Gibeah, and
struck down on that day twenty-two thousand of the Israelites. 22[y] The Israelites **20.22**
went up and wept before the LORD until the evening; and they inquired of the LORD, Josh 7.6,7
"Shall we again draw near to battle against our kinsfolk the Benjaminites?" And the
LORD said, "Go up against them." 23 The Israelites took courage, and again formed
the battle line in the same place where they had formed it on the first day.

24 So the Israelites advanced against the Benjaminites the second day. 25 Benja-

[w] Gk: Heb lacks *we will go up* [x] Compare Gk: Meaning of Heb uncertain [y] Verses 22 and 23 are transposed

20.1, 2 Dan was the northernmost city in Israel and Beer-sheba the southernmost. The two were often mentioned together as a reference to the entire nation.

20.13 Perhaps the Benjamite leaders had been given distorted facts about the serious crime in their territory, or perhaps they were too proud to admit that some of their people had stooped so low. In either case, they would not listen to the rest of Israel and hand over the accused criminals. They were more loyal to their own tribe than to God's law.

By covering for their kinsmen, the entire tribe of Benjamin sank to a level of immorality as low as the criminals'. Through this act, we get a glimpse of how thoroughly the nation's moral fabric had unraveled. The time period of the judges ends in a bloody civil war that sets the stage for the spiritual renewal to come under Samuel (see 1 Samuel).

20.13 Israel called for the execution of the perverted men who had committed rape and murder. Since the entire nation was responsible for the acts of its individuals (Deuteronomy 13.12–15; Joshua 7.10–12), the nation stood guilty until justice was served.

min moved out against them from Gibeah the second day, and struck down eigh-
20.26 Judg 21.4 teen thousand of the Israelites, all of them armed men. 26 Then all the Israelites, the
1 Sam 13.9 whole army, went back to Bethel and wept, sitting there before the LORD; they
2 Sam 24.25 fasted that day until evening. Then they offered burnt offerings and sacrifices of
20.27 well-being before the LORD. 27 And the Israelites inquired of the LORD (for the ark
Judg 7.9 of the covenant of God was there in those days, 28 and Phinehas son of Eleazar, son
of Aaron, ministered before it in those days), saying, "Shall we go out once more
to battle against our kinsfolk the Benjaminites, or shall we desist?" The LORD answered, "Go up, for tomorrow I will give them into your hand."
29 So Israel stationed men in ambush around Gibeah. 30 Then the Israelites
went up against the Benjaminites on the third day, and set themselves in array
20.31 against Gibeah, as before. 31 When the Benjaminites went out against the army,
Josh 8.16 they were drawn away from the city. As before they began to inflict casualties on
the troops, along the main roads, one of which goes up to Bethel and the other to
Gibeah, as well as in the open country, killing about thirty men of Israel. 32 The
Benjaminites thought, "They are being routed before us, as previously." But the
Israelites said, "Let us retreat and draw them away from the city toward the roads."
20.33 33 The main body of the Israelites drew back its battle line to Baal-tamar, while
Josh 8.19 those Israelites who were in ambush rushed out of their place west[z] of Geba.
34 There came against Gibeah ten thousand picked men out of all Israel, and the
battle was fierce. But the Benjaminites did not realize that disaster was close upon
them.
35 The LORD defeated Benjamin before Israel; and the Israelites destroyed
twenty-five thousand one hundred men of Benjamin that day, all of them armed.
36 Then the Benjaminites saw that they were defeated.[a]
The Israelites gave ground to Benjamin, because they trusted to the troops in
ambush that they had stationed against Gibeah. 37 The troops in ambush rushed
quickly upon Gibeah. Then they put the whole city to the sword. 38 Now the agreement between the main body of Israel and the men in ambush was that when they
sent up a cloud of smoke out of the city 39 the main body of Israel should turn in
battle. But Benjamin had begun to inflict casualties on the Israelites, killing about
thirty of them; so they thought, "Surely they are defeated before us, as in the first
battle." 40 But when the cloud, a column of smoke, began to rise out of the city, the
Benjaminites looked behind them—and there was the whole city going up in
smoke toward the sky! 41 Then the main body of Israel turned, and the Benjaminites
20.42 were dismayed, for they saw that disaster was close upon them. 42 Therefore they
Josh 8.15,24 turned away from the Israelites in the direction of the wilderness; but the battle
overtook them, and those who came out of the city[b] were slaughtering them in
between.[c] 43 Cutting down[d] the Benjaminites, they pursued them from Nohah[e]
and trod them down as far as a place east of Gibeah. 44 Eighteen thousand Benja-
20.45 minites fell, all of them courageous fighters. 45 When they turned and fled toward
Judg 21.13 the wilderness to the rock of Rimmon, five thousand of them were cut down on the
main roads, and they were pursued as far as Gidom, and two thousand of them were
slain. 46 So all who fell that day of Benjamin were twenty-five thousand arms-
bearing men, all of them courageous fighters. 47 But six hundred turned and fled

[z] Gk Vg: Heb *in the plain* [a] This sentence is continued by verse 45. [b] Compare Vg and some Gk Mss: Heb *cities*
[c] Compare Syr: Meaning of Heb uncertain [d] Gk: Heb *Surrounding* [e] Gk: Heb *pursued them at their resting place*

20.27, 28 This is the only place in Judges where the ark of the covenant is mentioned. This probably indicates how seldom the people consulted God.

Phinehas, the high priest, was also the high priest under Joshua (Joshua 22.13). The reference to Phinehas as high priest and the location of the tabernacle in Bethel instead of Shiloh probably indicate that the events of this story occurred during the early years of the judges.

20.29ff After their first battle against the Benjamites had failed, Israel used the battle plan Joshua had devised against Ai (Joshua 8). However, the ambush would not have defeated the tribe of Benjamin without God's promise of victory (20.28).

20.46–48 The effects of the horrible rape and murder should never have been felt outside the community where the crime happened. The local people should have brought the criminals to justice and corrected the laxness that originally permitted the crime. Instead, first the town and then the entire tribe defended this wickedness, even going to war over it.

To prevent unresolved problems from turning into major conflicts, firm action must be taken quickly, wisely, and forcefully *before* the situation gets out of hand.

toward the wilderness to the rock of Rimmon, and remained at the rock of Rimmon
for four months. 48 Meanwhile, the Israelites turned back against the Benjaminites,
and put them to the sword — the city, the people, the animals, and all that remained.
Also the remaining towns they set on fire.

Wives for the men of Benjamin

21 Now the Israelites had sworn at Mizpah, "No one of us shall give his daugh- **21.1**
ter in marriage to Benjamin." 2 And the people came to Bethel, and sat there Judg 20.1
until evening before God, and they lifted up their voices and wept bitterly. 3 They **21.2** Judg 20.31
said, "O LORD, the God of Israel, why has it come to pass that today there should 21.19
be one tribe lacking in Israel?" 4 On the next day, the people got up early, and built **21.4**
an altar there, and offered burnt offerings and sacrifices of well-being. 5 Then the Deut 12.4,5
Israelites said, "Which of all the tribes of Israel did not come up in the assembly to 2 Sam 24.25
the LORD?" For a solemn oath had been taken concerning whoever did not come up
to the LORD to Mizpah, saying, "That one shall be put to death." 6 But the Israelites
had compassion for Benjamin their kin, and said, "One tribe is cut off from Israel
this day. 7 What shall we do for wives for those who are left, since we have sworn
by the LORD that we will not give them any of our daughters as wives?"

8 Then they said, "Is there anyone from the tribes of Israel who did not come up
to the LORD to Mizpah?" It turned out that no one from Jabesh-gilead had come to
the camp, to the assembly. 9 For when the roll was called among the people, not one
of the inhabitants of Jabesh-gilead was there. 10 So the congregation sent twelve **21.10**
thousand soldiers there and commanded them, "Go, put the inhabitants of Jabesh- Num 31.18
gilead to the sword, including the women and the little ones. 11 This is what you
shall do; every male and every woman that has lain with a male you shall devote to
destruction." 12 And they found among the inhabitants of Jabesh-gilead four hundred young virgins who had never slept with a man and brought them to the camp
at Shiloh, which is in the land of Canaan.

13 Then the whole congregation sent word to the Benjaminites who were at the **21.13**
rock of Rimmon, and proclaimed peace to them. 14 Benjamin returned at that time; Deut 20.10
and they gave them the women whom they had saved alive of the women of Jabesh-
gilead; but they did not suffice for them.

15 The people had compassion on Benjamin because the LORD had made a
breach in the tribes of Israel. 16 So the elders of the congregation said, "What shall
we do for wives for those who are left, since there are no women left in Benjamin?"
17 And they said, "There must be heirs for the survivors of Benjamin, in order that
a tribe may not be blotted out from Israel. 18 Yet we cannot give any of our daughters to them as wives." For the Israelites had sworn, "Cursed be anyone who gives
a wife to Benjamin." 19 So they said, "Look, the yearly festival of the LORD is **21.19**
taking place at Shiloh, which is north of Bethel, on the east of the highway that Josh 18.1 Judg 18.31
goes up from Bethel to Shechem, and south of Lebonah." 20 And they instructed 1 Sam 1.3
the Benjaminites, saying, "Go and lie in wait in the vineyards, 21 and watch; when **21.21**
the young women of Shiloh come out to dance in the dances, then come out of the Ex 15.20 Judg 11.34
vineyards and each of you carry off a wife for himself from the young women of
Shiloh, and go to the land of Benjamin. 22 Then if their fathers or their brothers
come to complain to us, we will say to them, 'Be generous and allow us to have
them; because we did not capture in battle a wife for each man. But neither did you **21.23**
incur guilt by giving your daughters to them.' " 23 The Benjaminites did so; they Judg 20.48

20.48 The tribe of Benjamin eventually recovered from this slaughter. Saul, Israel's first king, was from this tribe (1 Samuel 9.21). So were Queen Esther (Esther 2.5–7) and the apostle Paul (Romans 11.1). However, the tribe was always known for being smaller than the rest (as in Psalm 68.27).

21.8–12 The Israelites moved from one mess to another. Because of a rash vow made in the heat of emotion (21.5), they now destroyed another town. Israel probably justified their action with the following arguments: (1) An oath could not be broken, and Israel had vowed that anyone who did not help them fight the Benjamites would be killed. (2) Since all the women from Benjamin had been killed, the few remaining men needed wives to prevent the tribe from disappearing. To spare the unmarried women from Jabesh-gilead seemed the right solution.

We do not know all the circumstances behind the brutal massacre at Jabesh-gilead, but it seems that the rest of Israel followed Benjamin's pattern. They put tribal loyalties above God's commands, and they justified wrong actions to correct past mistakes.

took wives for each of them from the dancers whom they abducted. Then they went
and returned to their territory, and rebuilt the towns, and lived in them. 24 So the
Israelites departed from there at that time by tribes and families, and they went out
from there to their own territories.
25 In those days there was no king in Israel; all the people did what was right in
their own eyes.

21.25 During the time of the judges, the people of Israel experienced trouble because everyone became his own authority and acted on his own opinions of right and wrong. This produced horrendous results. Our world is similar. Individuals, groups, and societies have made themselves the final authorities without reference to God. When people selfishly satisfy their personal desires at all costs, everyone pays the price.

It is the ultimate heroic act to submit all our plans, desires, and motives to God. Men like Gideon, Jephthah, and Samson are known for their heroism in battle. But their personal lives were far from heroic.

To be truly heroic, we must go into battle each day in our home, job, church, and society to make God's kingdom a reality. Our weapons are the standards, morals, truths, and convictions we receive from God's word. We will lose the battle if we gather the spoils of earthly treasures rather than seeking the treasures of heaven.

VITAL STATISTICS

PURPOSE:
To show how three people remained strong in character and true to God even when the society around them was collapsing

AUTHOR:
Unknown. Some think it was Samuel, but internal evidence suggests that it was written after his death.

DATE WRITTEN:
Sometime after the period of the judges (1375–1050 B.C.)

SETTING:
A dark time in Israel's history when people lived to please themselves, not God (Judges 17.6)

KEY VERSE:
"But Ruth said, 'Do not press me to leave you or to turn back from following you! Where you go, I will go; Where you lodge, I will lodge; your people shall be my people, and your God my God' " (1.16).

KEY PEOPLE:
Ruth, Naomi, Boaz

KEY PLACES:
Moab, Bethlehem

WHEN someone says, "Let me tell you about my mother-in-law," we expect some kind of negative statement or humorous anecdote because the mother-in-law caricature has been a standard centerpiece of ridicule or comedy. The book of Ruth, however, tells a different story. Ruth loved her mother-in-law, Naomi. Recently widowed, she begged to stay with Naomi wherever she went even though it would mean leaving her homeland. In heartfelt words Ruth said, "Your people shall be my people, and your God my God" (1.16). Naomi agreed, and Ruth traveled with her to Bethlehem.

Not much is said about Naomi except that she loved and cared for Ruth. Obviously, Naomi's life was a powerful witness to the reality of God. Ruth was drawn to her—and to the God she worshiped. In the succeeding months and years, God led this young Moabite widow to a man named Boaz, whom she eventually married. As a result, she became the great-grandmother of David and an ancestor in the line of the Messiah. What a profound impact Naomi's life made!

The book of Ruth is also the story of God's grace in the midst of difficult circumstances. Ruth's story occurred during the time of the judges—a period of disobedience, idolatry, and violence. Even in times of crisis and deepest despair, there are those who follow God and through whom God works. No matter how discouraging or antagonistic the world may seem, there are always people who follow God. He will use anyone who is open to him to achieve his purposes. Ruth was a Moabitess and Boaz was a descendant of Rahab, a former prostitute from Jericho. Nevertheless, their offspring continued the family line through which the Messiah came into our world.

Read this book and be encouraged. God is at work in the world, and he wants to use you. God could use you, as he used Naomi, to bring family and friends to him.

THE BLUEPRINT

1. Ruth remains loyal to Naomi (1.1–22)
2. Ruth gleans in Boaz's field (2.1–23)
3. Ruth follows Naomi's plan (3.1–18)
4. Ruth and Boaz are married (4.1–22)

When we first meet Ruth, she is a destitute widow. We follow her as she joins God's people, gleans in the grain fields, and risks her honor at the threshing floor of Boaz. In the end, we see Ruth becoming the wife of Boaz. What a picture of how we come to faith in Christ. We begin with no hope and are rebellious aliens with no part in the kingdom of God. Then as we risk everything by putting our faith in Christ, God saves us, forgives us, rebuilds our lives, and gives us blessings which will last through eternity. Boaz's redeeming of Ruth is a picture of Christ redeeming us.

MEGATHEMES

THEME	EXPLANATION	IMPORTANCE
Faithfulness	Ruth's faithfulness to Naomi as a daughter-in-law and friend is a great example of love and loyalty. Ruth, Naomi, and Boaz are also faithful to God and his laws. Throughout the story we see God's faithfulness to his people.	Ruth's life was guided by faithfulness toward God and showed itself in loyalty toward the people she knew. To be loyal and loving in relationships, we must imitate God's faithfulness in our relationships with others.
Kindness	Ruth showed great kindness to Naomi. In turn, Boaz showed kindness to Ruth—a despised Moabite woman with no money. God showed his kindness to Ruth, Naomi, and Boaz by bringing them together for his purposes.	Just as Boaz showed his kindness by buying back land to guarantee Ruth and Naomi's inheritance, so Christ showed his kindness by dying for us to guarantee our eternal life. God's kindness should motivate us to love and honor him.
Integrity	Ruth showed high moral character by being loyal to Naomi, by her clean break from her former land and customs, and by her hard work in the fields. Boaz showed integrity in his moral standards, his honesty, and by following through on his commitments.	When we have experienced God's faithfulness and kindness, we should respond by showing integrity. Just as the values by which Ruth and Boaz lived were in sharp contrast to those of the culture portrayed in Judges, so our lives should stand out from the world around us.
Protection	We see God's care and protection over the lives of Naomi and Ruth. His supreme control over circumstances brings them safety and security. He guides the minds and activities of people to fulfill his purpose.	No matter how devastating our present situation may be, our hope is in God. His resources are infinite. We must believe that he can work in the life of any person—whether that person is a king or a stranger in a foreign land. Trust his protection.
Prosperity/ Blessing	Ruth and Naomi came to Bethlehem as poor widows, but they soon became prosperous through Ruth's marriage to Boaz. Ruth became the great-grandmother of King David. Yet the greatest blessing was not the money, the marriage, or the child; it was the quality of love and respect between Ruth, Boaz, and Naomi.	We tend to think of blessings in terms of prosperity rather than the high-quality relationships God makes possible for us. No matter what our economic situation, we can love and respect the people God has brought into our lives. In so doing, we give and receive blessings. Love is the greatest blessing.

1. Ruth remains loyal to Naomi
Naomi's husband and sons die

1.1 Judg 2.16-18

1 In the days when the judges ruled, there was a famine in the land, and a certain
man of Bethlehem in Judah went to live in the country of Moab, he and his
wife and two sons. 2 The name of the man was Elimelech and the name of his wife
Naomi, and the names of his two sons were Mahlon and Chilion; they were Ephrathites from Bethlehem in Judah. They went into the country of Moab and remained there. 3 But Elimelech, the husband of Naomi, died, and she was left with

1.1 The story of Ruth takes place sometime during the period of the judges. These were dark days for Israel, when "all the people did what was right in their own eyes" (Judges 17.6; 21.25). But during those dark and evil times, there were still some who followed God. Naomi and Ruth are a beautiful example of loyalty, friendship, and commitment – to God and to each other.

1.1, 2 Moab was the land east of the Dead Sea. It was one of the nations that oppressed Israel during the period of the judges (Judges 3.12ff). The famine must have been quite severe in Israel for Elimelech to move his family here. They were called Ephrathites because Ephrath was an earlier name for Bethlehem. Even if Israel had already defeated Moab, there still would have been tensions between them.

her two sons. 4 These took Moabite wives; the name of the one was Orpah and the
name of the other Ruth. When they had lived there about ten years, 5 both Mahlon
and Chilion also died, so that the woman was left without her two sons and her
husband.

6 Then she started to return with her daughters-in-law from the country of 1.6
Moab, for she had heard in the country of Moab that the LORD had considered his Ex 4.31
people and given them food. 7 So she set out from the place where she had been
living, she and her two daughters-in-law, and they went on their way to go back to
the land of Judah. 8 But Naomi said to her two daughters-in-law, "Go back each of
you to your mother's house. May the LORD deal kindly with you, as you have dealt
with the dead and with me. 9 The LORD grant that you may find security, each of
you in the house of your husband." Then she kissed them, and they wept aloud.
10 They said to her, "No, we will return with you to your people." 11 But Naomi 1.11
said, "Turn back, my daughters, why will you go with me? Do I still have sons in Deut 25.5
my womb that they may become your husbands? 12 Turn back, my daughters, go
your way, for I am too old to have a husband. Even if I thought there was hope for
me, even if I should have a husband tonight and bear sons, 13 would you then wait
until they were grown? Would you then refrain from marrying? No, my daughters,
it has been far more bitter for me than for you, because the hand of the LORD has
turned against me." 14 Then they wept aloud again. Orpah kissed her mother-in-
law, but Ruth clung to her.

Ruth decides to go with Naomi to Bethlehem

15 So she said, "See, your sister-in-law has gone back to her people and to her
gods; return after your sister-in-law." 16 But Ruth said,

SETTING FOR THE STORY Elimelech, Naomi, and their sons traveled from Bethlehem to the land of Moab because of a famine. After her husband and sons died, Naomi returned to Bethlehem with her daughter-in-law Ruth.

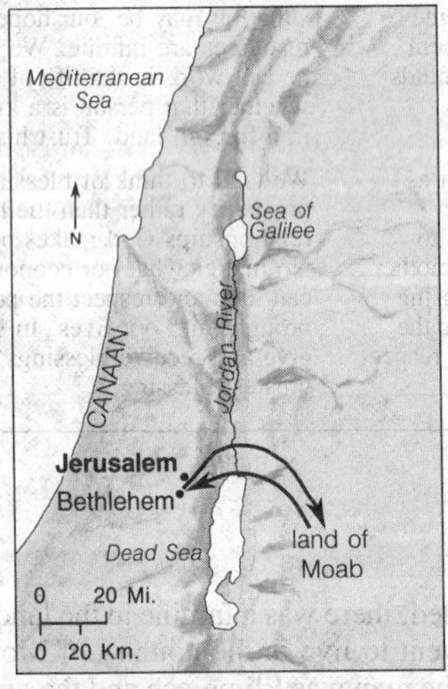

1.4, 5 Friendly relations with the Moabites were discouraged (Deuteronomy 23.6) but probably not forbidden since the Moabites lived outside the promised land. Marrying a Canaanite, however, was against God's law (Deuteronomy 7.1–4). Moabites were not allowed to worship at the tabernacle because they had not let the Israelites pass through their land during the exodus from Egypt (Deuteronomy 23.3, 4).

As God's chosen nation, Israel should have set the standards of high moral living for the other nations. Ironically it was Ruth, a Moabitess, whom God used as an example of genuine spiritual character. This shows just how bleak life had become in Israel during those days.

1.8, 9 There was almost nothing worse than being a widow in the ancient world. Widows were taken advantage of or ignored. They were almost always poverty-stricken. God's law, therefore, provided that the nearest relative of the dead husband should care for the widow; but Naomi had no relatives in Moab, and she did not know if any of her relatives were alive in Israel.

Even in her desperate situation, Naomi had a selfless attitude. Although she had decided to return to Israel, she encouraged Ruth and Orpah to stay in Moab and start their lives over, even though this would mean hardship for herself. Like Naomi, we must consider the needs of others and not just our own. As Naomi discovered, when you act selflessly, others are encouraged to follow your example.

1.11 Naomi's comment here refers to *levirate marriage,* the obligation of a dead man's brother to care for his widow (Deuteronomy 25.5–10). This law kept the widow from poverty and provided a way for the family name of the dead husband to continue.

Naomi, however, had no other sons for Ruth or Orpah to marry, so she encouraged them to remain in their homeland and remarry. Orpah agreed, which was her right. But Ruth was willing to give up the possibility of security and children in order to care for Naomi.

1.16 Ruth was a Moabitess, but that didn't stop her from worshiping the true God, nor did it stop God from accepting her worship and blessing her greatly. The Jews were not the only people God loved. God chose the Jews to be the people through whom the rest of the world would come to know him. This was fulfilled when Jesus Christ was born as a Jew. Through him, the entire world can come to know God. Acts 10.35 says that "in every nation anyone who fears him and does what is right is acceptable to him." God accepts all who worship him; he works through people regardless of their race, sex, or nationality. Ruth is a perfect example of God's impartiality. Although she belonged to a race often despised by Israel, she was blessed because of her faithfulness. She became a great-grandmother of King David and a direct ancestor of Jesus. No one should feel disqualified to serve God because of race, sex, or national background. And God can use every circumstance to build his kingdom.

"Do not press me to leave you
or to turn back from following you!
Where you go, I will go;
Where you lodge, I will lodge;
your people shall be my people,
and your God my God.
17 Where you die, I will die—
there will I be buried.
May the LORD do thus and so to me,
and more as well,
if even death parts me from you!"
18 When Naomi saw that she was determined to go with her, she said no more to her.
19 So the two of them went on until they came to Bethlehem. When they came
to Bethlehem, the whole town was stirred because of them; and the women said, "Is
1.20 Job 6.4 this Naomi?" 20 She said to them,
"Call me no longer Naomi,[a]
call me Mara,[b]

[a] That is *Pleasant* [b] That is *Bitter*

RUTH & NAOMI

The stories of several people in the Bible are woven together so closely that they are almost inseparable. We know more about their relationship than we know about them as individuals. And in an age that worships individualism, their stories become helpful models of good relationships. Naomi and Ruth are beautiful examples of this blending of lives. Their cultures, family backgrounds, and ages were very different. As mother-in-law and daughter-in-law, they probably had as many opportunities for tension as they did for tenderness. And yet they were bound to each other.

They shared deep sorrow, great affection for each other, and an overriding commitment to the God of Israel. And yet as much as they depended on each other, they also gave each other freedom in their commitment to one another. Naomi was willing to let Ruth return to her family. Ruth was willing to leave her homeland to go to Israel. Naomi even helped arrange Ruth's marriage to Boaz, although it would change their relationship.

God was at the center of their intimate communication. Ruth came to know the God of Israel through Naomi. The older woman allowed Ruth to see, hear, and feel all the joy and anguish of her relationship to God. How often do you feel that your thoughts and questions about God should be left out of a close relationship? How often do you share your unedited thoughts about God with your spouse or friends? Sharing openly about our relationship with God can bring depth and intimacy to our relationships with others.

Strengths and accomplishments:
- A relationship where the greatest bond was faith in God
- A relationship of strong mutual commitment
- A relationship in which each person tried to do what was best for the other

Lesson from their lives:
- God's living presence in a relationship overcomes differences that might otherwise create division and disharmony

Vital statistics:
- Where: Moab, Bethlehem
- Occupation: Wives, widows
- Relatives: Elimelech, Mahlon, Chilion, Orpah, Boaz

Key verses:
"But Ruth said, 'Do not press me to leave you or to turn back from following you! Where you go, I will go; Where you lodge, I will lodge; your people shall be my people, and your God my God. Where you die, I will die—there will I be buried. May the Lord do thus and so to me, and more as well, if even death parts me from you!' " (Ruth 1.16, 17).

Their story is told in the book of Ruth. Ruth is also mentioned in Matthew 1.5.

1.20, 21 Naomi had experienced severe hardships. She had left Israel married and secure; she returned widowed and poor. Naomi changed her name to express the bitterness and pain she felt. Naomi was not rejecting God by openly expressing her pain. However, she seems to have lost sight of the tremendous resources she had in her relationship with Ruth and with God. When you face bitter times, God welcomes your honest prayers, but be careful not to overlook the love, strength, and resources that he provides in your present relationships. And don't allow bitterness and disappointment to blind you to your opportunities.

for the Almighty[c] has dealt bitterly with me.
21 I went away full,
but the LORD has brought me back empty;
why call me Naomi
when the LORD has dealt harshly with[d] me,
and the Almighty[c] has brought calamity upon me?"

22 So Naomi returned together with Ruth the Moabite, her daughter-in-law, who came back with her from the country of Moab. They came to Bethlehem at the beginning of the barley harvest.

2. Ruth gleans in Boaz's field

2 Now Naomi had a kinsman on her husband's side, a prominent rich man, of
the family of Elimelech, whose name was Boaz. 2 And Ruth the Moabite said 2.2
to Naomi, "Let me go to the field and glean among the ears of grain, behind some- Lev 19.9,10 23.22
one in whose sight I may find favor." She said to her, "Go, my daughter." 3 So she
went. She came and gleaned in the field behind the reapers. As it happened, she
came to the part of the field belonging to Boaz, who was of the family of Elimelech. 4 Just then Boaz came from Bethlehem. He said to the reapers, "The LORD be
with you." They answered, "The LORD bless you." 5 Then Boaz said to his servant
who was in charge of the reapers, "To whom does this young woman belong?"
6 The servant who was in charge of the reapers answered, "She is the Moabite who
came back with Naomi from the country of Moab. 7 She said, 'Please, let me glean
and gather among the sheaves behind the reapers.' So she came, and she has been
on her feet from early this morning until now, without resting even for a moment."[e]

8 Then Boaz said to Ruth, "Now listen, my daughter, do not go to glean in
another field or leave this one, but keep close to my young women. 9 Keep your
eyes on the field that is being reaped, and follow behind them. I have ordered the

[c] Traditional rendering of Heb *Shaddai* [d] Or *has testified against* [e] Compare Gk Vg: Meaning of Heb uncertain

---

1.22 Bethlehem is about five miles southwest of Jerusalem. The town was surrounded by lush fields and olive groves. Its harvests were abundant.

Ruth and Naomi's return to Bethlehem was certainly part of God's plan, for in this town David would be born (1 Samuel 16.1); and, as predicted by the prophet Micah (Micah 5.2), Jesus Christ would also be born there. This move, then, was more than merely convenient for Ruth and Naomi. It led to the fulfillment of Scripture.

1.22 Because Israel's climate is quite moderate, there are two harvests each year, in the spring and in the fall. The barley harvest took place in the spring, and it was during this time of hope and plenty that Ruth and Naomi returned to Bethlehem. Bethlehem was a farming community, and because it was the time of the harvest, there was plenty of leftover grain in the fields. This grain could be collected, or *gleaned,* and then made into food. (See the note on 2.2 for more information on gleaning.)

2.2 When the wheat and barley were ready to be harvested, reapers were hired to cut down the stalks and tie them into bundles. Israelite law demanded that the corners of the fields not be harvested. In addition, any grain that was dropped was to be left for poor people who picked it up (*gleaned*) and used it for food (Leviticus 19.9; 23.22; Deuteronomy 24.19). The purpose of this law was to feed the poor and prevent the owners from hoarding. This law served as a type of welfare program in Israel. Because she was a widow with no means of providing for herself, Ruth went into the fields to glean the grain.

2.2, 3 Ruth made her home in a foreign land. Instead of depending on Naomi or waiting for good fortune to happen, she took the initiative. She went to work. She was not afraid of admitting her need or working hard to supply it. When Ruth went out to the fields, God provided for her. If you are waiting for God to provide, consider this: he may be waiting for you to take the first step to demonstrate just how important your need is.

2.3 "As it happened," Ruth came to a field belonging to Boaz. As far as she was concerned it seemed a matter of chance. But God was at work behind the scenes setting up the "chance" meeting of these two. God still works behind the scenes in people's lives. What we consider chance, a lucky break, or fate is often the unseen hand of God guiding us in decisions and actions that may seem insignificant to us at the time. The next time that you "happen" to meet someone, consider what God's purposes in the situation might be.

2.4 When Boaz came to the field, his greeting to his men of "The Lord be with you" showed the quality of his character. His faith made a difference in the way he treated his workers. Similarly, our faith should make a difference in our daily work that will be clearly evident to others.

2.7 Ruth's task, though menial, tiring, and perhaps degrading, was done faithfully. What is your attitude when the task you have been given is not up to your true potential? The task at hand may be all you can do, or it may be the work God wants you to do. Or, as in Ruth's case, it may be a test of your character that can open up new doors of opportunity.

2.8, 9 Not only did Ruth take the initiative to work, she worked hard. There are times when hard work with little rest is our only option. Boaz noticed Ruth's hard work. Had she considered herself too proud or embarrassed to glean, she would have missed the opportunity of meeting Boaz, changing her life, and becoming the ancestor of a king and the Messiah.

young men not to bother you. If you get thirsty, go to the vessels and drink from
what the young men have drawn." 10 Then she fell prostrate, with her face to the
ground, and said to him, "Why have I found favor in your sight, that you should
take notice of me, when I am a foreigner?" 11 But Boaz answered her, "All that you
have done for your mother-in-law since the death of your husband has been fully
told me, and how you left your father and mother and your native land and came to
2.12 Ruth 1.16 a people that you did not know before. 12 May the LORD reward you for your deeds,
and may you have a full reward from the LORD, the God of Israel, under whose
wings you have come for refuge!" 13 Then she said, "May I continue to find favor
in your sight, my lord, for you have comforted me and spoken kindly to your servant, even though I am not one of your servants."

14 At mealtime Boaz said to her, "Come here, and eat some of this bread, and
dip your morsel in the sour wine." So she sat beside the reapers, and he heaped up
for her some parched grain. She ate until she was satisfied, and she had some left
over. 15 When she got up to glean, Boaz instructed his young men, "Let her glean
even among the standing sheaves, and do not reproach her. 16 You must also pull
out some handfuls for her from the bundles, and leave them for her to glean, and do
not rebuke her."

17 So she gleaned in the field until evening. Then she beat out what she had
gleaned, and it was about an ephah of barley. 18 She picked it up and came into the
town, and her mother-in-law saw how much she had gleaned. Then she took out
and gave her what was left over after she herself had been satisfied. 19 Her mother-
in-law said to her, "Where did you glean today? And where have you worked?
Blessed be the man who took notice of you." So she told her mother-in-law with
whom she had worked, and said, "The name of the man with whom I worked today
is Boaz." 20 Then Naomi said to her daughter-in-law, "Blessed be he by the LORD,
whose kindness has not forsaken the living or the dead!" Naomi also said to her,
"The man is a relative of ours, one of our nearest kin."[f] 21 Then Ruth the Moabite
said, "He even said to me, 'Stay close by my servants, until they have finished all
my harvest.' " 22 Naomi said to Ruth, her daughter-in-law, "It is better, my daughter, that you go out with his young women, otherwise you might be bothered in
another field." 23 So she stayed close to the young women of Boaz, gleaning until
the end of the barley and wheat harvests; and she lived with her mother-in-law.

[f] Or *one with the right to redeem*

2.10, 11 Foreigners were not always warmly welcomed in Israel, but Boaz gladly welcomed Ruth, because she had gained a reputation for showing kindness and generosity to others. Boaz was so impressed with Ruth that he let her follow directly behind his reapers so she could pick up the choicest grain that was dropped.

Ruth was judged by her past actions. Her good reputation was her most valuable asset. It came as a result of her hard work, her strong moral character, and her sensitivity, kindness, and loyalty to Naomi. A good reputation is built upon God-honoring character and kindness toward others.

2.10–12 Ruth's life exhibited admirable qualities: she was hardworking, loving, kind, faithful, and brave. These qualities gained for her a good reputation, but only because she displayed them *consistently* in all areas of her life. Wherever Ruth went or whatever she did, her character remained the same.

Your reputation is formed by the people who watch you at work, in town, at home, and in church. A good reputation comes by *consistently* living out the qualities you believe in—no matter what group of people or surroundings you are in.

2.14 Sour wine is vinegar. Parched grain is freshly picked grain that is roasted.

2.15, 16 The characters in the book of Ruth are classic examples of good people in action. Boaz went far beyond the intent of the gleaners' law in demonstrating his kindness and generosity. Not only did he let Ruth glean in his field, but he also told his workers to let some of the grain fall on purpose in her path. Out of his abundance, he provided for the needy. How often do you go beyond the accepted patterns of providing for those less fortunate? Do more than the minimum for others.

2.17, 18 When Ruth returned with this much grain (an ephah is half a bushel), plus her lunch leftovers, Naomi knew someone had taken special care of her.

2.19, 20 Naomi had felt bitter (1.20, 21), but her faith in God was still alive, and she praised God for Boaz's kindness to Ruth. In her sorrows, she still trusted God and acknowledged his goodness. We may feel bitter about a situation, but we must never despair. Today is always a new opportunity for experiencing God's care.

2.20 Though Ruth may not have always recognized God's guidance, he had been with her every step of the way. She went to glean and "just happened" to end up in the field owned by Boaz, who "just happened" to be a close relative. This was more than mere coincidence. As you go about your daily tasks, God is working in your life in ways you may not even notice. We must not close the door on what God can do. Events do not occur by luck or coincidence. We should have faith that God is directing our lives for his purpose.

3. Ruth follows Naomi's plan

3 Naomi her mother-in-law said to her, "My daughter, I need to seek some security for you, so that it may be well with you. 2 Now here is our kinsman Boaz, 3.2 Deut 25.5-10
with whose young women you have been working. See, he is winnowing barley
tonight at the threshing floor. 3 Now wash and anoint yourself, and put on your best
clothes and go down to the threshing floor; but do not make yourself known to the
man until he has finished eating and drinking. 4 When he lies down, observe the
place where he lies; then, go and uncover his feet and lie down; and he will tell you
what to do." 5 She said to her, "All that you tell me I will do."

Ruth approaches Boaz at the threshing floor

6 So she went down to the threshing floor and did just as her mother-in-law had
instructed her. 7 When Boaz had eaten and drunk, and he was in a contented mood,
he went to lie down at the end of the heap of grain. Then she came stealthily and
uncovered his feet, and lay down. 8 At midnight the man was startled, and turned
over, and there, lying at his feet, was a woman! 9 He said, "Who are you?" And she
answered, "I am Ruth, your servant; spread your cloak over your servant, for you
are next-of-kin."[g] 10 He said, "May you be blessed by the LORD, my daughter; this
last instance of your loyalty is better than the first; you have not gone after young
men, whether poor or rich. 11 And now, my daughter, do not be afraid, I will do for 3.11 Prov 31.10
you all that you ask, for all the assembly of my people know that you are a worthy
woman. 12 But now, though it is true that I am a near kinsman, there is another
kinsman more closely related than I. 13 Remain this night, and in the morning, if he
will act as next-of-kin[g] for you, good; let him do it. If he is not willing to act as
next-of-kin[g] for you, then, as the LORD lives, I will act as next-of-kin[g] for you. Lie
down until the morning."

[g] *Or one with the right to redeem*

3.1 As widows, Ruth and Naomi could look forward only to difficult times. (See the note on 1.8, 9 for more on a widow's life.) But when Naomi heard the news about Boaz, her hope for the future was renewed (2.20). Typical of her character, she thought first of Ruth, encouraging her to see if Boaz would take the responsibility of being a "kinsman-redeemer" to her.

A kinsman-redeemer was a relative who volunteered to take responsibility for the extended family. When a woman's husband died, the law (Deuteronomy 25.5–10) provided that she could marry a brother of her dead husband. But Naomi had no more sons. In such a case, the nearest relative to the deceased husband could become a kinsman-redeemer and marry the widow. The nearest relative did not have to marry the widow. If he chose not to, the next nearest relative could take his place. If no one chose to help the widow, she would probably live in poverty the rest of her life because in Israelite culture the inheritance was passed on to the son or nearest male relative, not to the wife. To take the sting out of these inheritance rules, there were laws for the provision of gleaning and kinsman-redeemers.

We have a "kinsman-redeemer" in Jesus Christ, who though he was God, came to earth as a man in order to save us. By his death on the cross, he has redeemed us from sin and hopelessness and thereby purchased us to be his own possession (1 Peter 1.18, 19). This guarantees our eternal inheritance.

3.2 The threshing floor was the place where the grain was separated from the harvested wheat. The wheat stalks were crushed, either by hand or by oxen, and the valuable grain (inner kernels) separated from the worthless chaff (the outside shell). The floor was made from rock or soil and located outside the village, usually on an elevated site where the winds would blow away the lighter chaff when the crushed wheat was thrown into the air (or winnowed). Boaz spent the night beside the threshing floor for two reasons: (1) to prevent theft and (2) to wait for his turn to thresh grain. (Threshing was often done at night, because daylight hours were spent harvesting.)

3.3 *Anoint* means to put on some fragrant lotion.

3.4 Naomi's advice seems strange, but she was not suggesting a seductive act. In reality, Naomi was telling Ruth to act in accordance with Israelite custom and law. It was common for a servant to lie at the feet of his master and even share a part of his covering. By observing this custom, Ruth would inform Boaz that he could be her kinsman-redeemer – that he could find someone to marry her or marry her himself. It was family business, nothing romantic. But the story later became beautifully romantic as Ruth and Boaz developed an unselfish love and deep respect for each other.

3.5 As a foreigner, Ruth may have thought that Naomi's advice was odd. But Ruth followed the advice because she knew Naomi was kind, trustworthy, and filled with moral integrity. Each of us knows a parent, older friend, or relative who is always looking out for our best interests. Be willing to listen to the advice of those older and wiser than you are. The experience and knowledge of such a person can be invaluable. Imagine what Ruth's life would have been like had she ignored her mother-in-law.

3.10 Boaz was an unselfish man. He had much to lose by honoring Ruth's request, especially since their first child would be Naomi's heir, not his. But Boaz focused on Ruth's virtuous qualities and was honored that she had come to him. This was remarkable in a culture that looked upon women, especially foreign women, more as property than as human beings.

Boaz had much to lose and very little to gain; but he did what was right, and God honored him. How do you respond when the choice is between doing something for yourself or doing what is right? Do what is right, and let God take care of the results.

3.12 Ruth and Naomi must have assumed that Boaz was their closest relative. Boaz, too, must have already considered marrying Ruth, because his answer to her shows he had been thinking about it. One man in the city was a closer relative than Boaz, and this man had the first right to take Ruth as his wife. If he chose not to, then Boaz could marry Ruth (3.13).

14 So she lay at his feet until morning, but got up before one person could
recognize another; for he said, "It must not be known that the woman came to the
threshing floor." 15 Then he said, "Bring the cloak you are wearing and hold it out."
So she held it, and he measured out six measures of barley, and put it on her back;
then he went into the city. 16 She came to her mother-in-law, who said, "How did
things go with you,[h] my daughter?" Then she told her all that the man had done for
her, 17 saying, "He gave me these six measures of barley, for he said, 'Do not go
back to your mother-in-law empty-handed.' " 18 She replied, "Wait, my daughter,
until you learn how the matter turns out, for the man will not rest, but will settle the
matter today."

4. Ruth and Boaz are married

Boaz speaks to the nearest relative

4 No sooner had Boaz gone up to the gate and sat down there than the next-of-
kin,[i] of whom Boaz had spoken, came passing by. So Boaz said, "Come

[h] Or *"Who are you,* [i] Or *one with the right to redeem*

Heroes are easier to admire than to define. They are seldom conscious of their moments of heroism, and others may not recognize their acts as heroic. Heroes simply do the right thing at the right time, whether or not they realize the impact their action will have. Perhaps the one quality they share is a tendency to think of others before they think of themselves. Boaz was a hero.

In his dealings with other people, he was always sensitive to their needs. His words to his employees, relatives, and others were colored with kindness. He offered help openly, not grudgingly. When he discovered who Ruth was, he took several steps to help her because she had been faithful to his relative Naomi. When Naomi advised Ruth to request his protection, he was ready to marry her if the legal complications could be worked out.

Boaz not only did what was right; he also did it right away. Of course he could not foresee all that his actions would accomplish. He could not have known that the child he would have by Ruth would be an ancestor of both David and Jesus. He only met the challenge of taking the right action in the situation facing him.

We are faced with this challenge in our daily choices. Like Naomi's closer relative, we are often more concerned with making the easy choice than with making the right one. Yet more often than not, the right choice is clear. Ask God to give you a special awareness in your choices today, as well as renewed commitment to make the right ones.

Strengths and accomplishments:
- A man of his word
- Sensitive to those in need, caring for his workers
- A keen sense of responsibility, integrity
- A successful and shrewd businessman

Lessons from his life:
- It can be heroic to do what must be done and to do it right
- God often uses little decisions to carry out his big plan

Vital statistics:
- Where: Bethlehem
- Occupation: Wealthy farmer
- Relatives: Elimelech, Naomi, Ruth

Key verse:
"I have also acquired Ruth the Moabite, the wife of Mahlon, to be my wife, to maintain the dead man's name on his inheritance, in order that the name of the dead may not be cut off from his kindred and from the gate of his native place; today you are witnesses" (Ruth 4.10).

His story is told in the book of Ruth. He is also mentioned in Matthew 1.5.

3.18–4.1 Naomi said Boaz would follow through with his promise at once. He obviously had a reputation for keeping his word. He did not rest until his task was completed. Such reliable people stand out in any age and culture. Do others regard you as one who will do what you say? Keeping your word and following through on assignments should be high on anyone's priority list.

4.1 Boaz knew he could find his relative at the city gate. This was the center of activity. Merchants set up their temporary shops near the gate, which also served as "city hall." Here city officials gathered to transact business. Since there was so much activity, it was a good place to find witnesses (4.2) and an appropriate place for Boaz to make his transaction.

over, friend; sit down here." And he went over and sat down. 2 Then Boaz took ten
men of the elders of the city, and said, "Sit down here"; so they sat down. 3 He then 4.3 Lev 25.25
said to the next-of-kin,[j] "Naomi, who has come back from the country of Moab,
is selling the parcel of land that belonged to our kinsman Elimelech. 4 So I thought
I would tell you of it, and say: Buy it in the presence of those sitting here, and in the
presence of the elders of my people. If you will redeem it, redeem it; but if you will
not, tell me, so that I may know; for there is no one prior to you to redeem it, and
I come after you." So he said, "I will redeem it." 5 Then Boaz said, "The day you
acquire the field from the hand of Naomi, you are also acquiring Ruth[k] the Moabite, the widow of the dead man, to maintain the dead man's name on his inheritance." 6 At this, the next-of-kin[j] said, "I cannot redeem it for myself without 4.6 Lev 25.25
damaging my own inheritance. Take my right of redemption yourself, for I cannot
redeem it."

7 Now this was the custom in former times in Israel concerning redeeming and 4.7 Deut 25.8-10
exchanging: to confirm a transaction, the one took off a sandal and gave it to the
other; this was the manner of attesting in Israel. 8 So when the next-of-kin[j] said to
Boaz, "Acquire it for yourself," he took off his sandal. 9 Then Boaz said to the
elders and all the people, "Today you are witnesses that I have acquired from the
hand of Naomi all that belonged to Elimelech and all that belonged to Chilion and
Mahlon. 10 I have also acquired Ruth the Moabite, the wife of Mahlon, to be my
wife, to maintain the dead man's name on his inheritance, in order that the name of
the dead may not be cut off from his kindred and from the gate of his native place;
today you are witnesses." 11 Then all the people who were at the gate, along with 4.11 Gen 29.25-30
the elders, said, "We are witnesses. May the LORD make the woman who is coming
into your house like Rachel and Leah, who together built up the house of Israel.
May you produce children in Ephrathah and bestow a name in Bethlehem; 12 and, 4.12 Gen 38.29 46.12
through the children that the LORD will give you by this young woman, may your
house be like the house of Perez, whom Tamar bore to Judah."

The descendants of Boaz and Ruth

13 So Boaz took Ruth and she became his wife. When they came together, the
LORD made her conceive, and she bore a son. 14 Then the women said to Naomi,
"Blessed be the LORD, who has not left you this day without next-of-kin;[j] and may
his name be renowned in Israel! 15 He shall be to you a restorer of life and a nour-
isher of your old age; for your daughter-in-law who loves you, who is more to you

[j] Or *one with the right to redeem* [k] OL Vg: Heb *from the hand of Naomi and from Ruth*

4.3 Boaz cleverly presented his case to the relative. First he brought in new information not yet mentioned in the story—Elimelech, Naomi's former husband, still had some property in the area that was now for sale. As the nearest relative, this man had the first right to buy the land, which he agreed to do (Leviticus 25.25). But then Boaz said that, according to the law, if the relative bought the property he also had to marry the widow (probably because Mahlon, Ruth's former husband and Elimelech's son, had inherited the property). At this stipulation, the relative backed down. He did not want to complicate his inheritance. He may have feared that if he had a son through Ruth, some of his estate would transfer away from his family to the family of Elimelech. Whatever his reason, the way was now clear for Boaz to marry Ruth.

4.12 Of all the ancestors (including Abraham) they could have named, why did these men mention Perez? The birth of Perez was an example of the "levirate" practice, whereby the brother or relative of the dead husband married his widow (Genesis 38). Boaz, as kinsman-redeemer, was following this levirate practice since Ruth's former husband had no living brothers. (See the note on 3.1.) The descendants of Perez made Judah a prominent tribe. Boaz, David, and all the Judean kings were descendants of Perez.

4.15 Ruth's love for her mother-in-law was known and recognized throughout the city. From the beginning of the book of Ruth to the end, her kindness toward others remained unchanged.

4.15 God brought great blessings out of Naomi's tragedy, even greater than "seven sons," or an abundance of heirs. Throughout her tough times, Naomi continued to trust God. Even in our sorrow and calamity, God can bring great blessings. Be like Naomi, and don't turn your back on God when tragedy strikes. Instead of asking "How can God allow this to happen to me?" trust him. He will be with you even in the hard times.

than seven sons, has borne him." 16 Then Naomi took the child and laid him in her
bosom, and became his nurse. 17 The women of the neighborhood gave him a
name, saying, "A son has been born to Naomi." They named him Obed; he became
the father of Jesse, the father of David.

4.18-22
Mt 1.3-6

18 Now these are the descendants of Perez: Perez became the father of Hezron,
19 Hezron of Ram, Ram of Amminadab, 20 Amminadab of Nahshon, Nahshon of
Salmon, 21 Salmon of Boaz, Boaz of Obed, 22 Obed of Jesse, and Jesse of David.

4.16, 17 To some, the book of Ruth may be just a nice story about a girl who got lucky. But in reality, the events recorded in Ruth were part of God's preparations for the births of David and of Jesus, the promised Messiah. Just as Ruth was unaware of this larger purpose in her life, we will not know the full purpose and importance of our lives until we are able to look back from the perspective of eternity. We must make our choices with God's eternal values in mind. Taking moral shortcuts and living for short-range pleasures are not good ways to move ahead. Because of Ruth's faithful obedience, her life and legacy were significant even though she couldn't see all the results. Live in faithfulness to God, knowing that the significance of your life will extend beyond your lifetime. The rewards will outweigh any sacrifice you may have made.

1 SAMUEL

Judges begin to rule 1375 B.C. (1220 B.C.)	Samuel born 1105 (1083)	Saul born 1080

VITAL STATISTICS

PURPOSE:
To record the life of Samuel, Israel's last judge; the reign and decline of Saul, the first king; and the choice and preparation of David, Israel's greatest king

AUTHOR:
Probably Samuel, but also includes writings from the prophets Nathan and Gad (1 Chronicles 29.29)

SETTING:
The book begins in the days of the judges and describes Israel's transition from a theocracy (led by God) to a monarchy (led by a king)

KEY VERSES:
"And the Lord said to Samuel, 'Listen to the voice of the people in all that they say to you; for they have not rejected you, but they have rejected me from being king over them. . . . Now then, listen to their voice; only—you shall solemnly warn them, and show them the ways of the king who shall reign over them' " (8.7, 9).

KEY PEOPLE:
Eli, Hannah, Samuel, Saul, Jonathan, David

"RUNNERS take your marks," the starter barks his signal, and the crowd turns quiet attention to the athletes walking toward the line. "Get set" . . . in position now, muscles tense, nervously anticipating the sound of the gun. It resounds! And the race begins. In any contest, the start is important, but the finish is even more crucial. Often a front-runner will lose strength and fade to the middle of the pack. There is the tragedy of the brilliant beginner who sets the pace for a time, but does not even finish. He quits the race burned out, exhausted, or injured.

First Samuel is a book of great beginnings . . . and tragic endings. It begins with Eli as high priest during the time of the judges. As a religious leader, Eli certainly must have begun his life in close communication with God. In his communication with Hannah, and in his training of her son Samuel, he demonstrated a clear understanding of God's purposes and call (chapters 1, 3). But his life ended in ignominy as his sacrilegious sons were judged by God and the sacred ark of the covenant fell into enemy hands (chapter 4). Eli's death marked the decline of the influence of the priesthood and the rise of the prophets in Israel.

Samuel was dedicated to God's service by his mother, Hannah. He became one of Israel's greatest prophets. He was a man of prayer who finished the work of the judges, began the school of the prophets, and anointed Israel's first kings. But even Samuel was not immune to finishing poorly. Like Eli's family, Samuel's sons turned away from God; they took bribes and perverted justice. The people rejected the leadership of the judges and priests and clamored for a king "like other nations" (8.5).

Saul also started fast. A striking figure, this handsome (9.2) and humble (9.21; 10.22) man was God's choice as Israel's first king (10.24). His early reign was marked by leadership (chapter 11) and bravery (14.46–48). But he disobeyed God (chapter 15), became jealous and paranoid (chapters 18, 19), and finally had his kingship taken away from him by God (chapter 16). Saul's life continued steadily downward. Obsessed with killing David (chapters 20—30), he consulted a medium (chapter 28) and finally committed suicide (chapter 31).

Among the events of Saul's life is another great beginner—David. A man who follows God (13.14; 16.7), David ministers to Saul (chapter 16), slays Goliath (chapter 17), and becomes a great warrior. But we'll have to wait until the book of 2 Samuel to see how David finishes.

As you read 1 Samuel, note the transition from theocracy to monarchy, exult in the classic stories of David and Goliath, David and Jonathan, David and Abigail, and watch the rise of the influence of the prophets. But in the midst of reading all the history and adventure, determine to run your race as God's person from start to finish.

Samson becomes judge 1075 (1083)	Saul becomes king 1050 (1045)	David born 1040	David anointed; Goliath slain 1025	David becomes king of Judah 1010	David becomes king of all Israel 1003	Solomon becomes king 970	The kingdom is divided 930

THE BLUEPRINT

A. ELI AND SAMUEL (1.1—7.17)
1. Samuel's birth and childhood
2. War with the Philistines

We see a vivid contrast between young Samuel and Eli's sons. Eli's sons were selfish, but Samuel was helpful. Eli's sons defrauded people, but Samuel grew in wisdom and gave the people messages from God. As an adult, Samuel became a prophet, priest, and judge over Israel. A person's actions reflect his character. This was true of Samuel and Eli's sons. It is also true of us. Strive, like Samuel, to keep your heart pure before God.

B. SAMUEL AND SAUL (8.1—15.35)
1. Saul becomes king of Israel
2. God rejects Saul for disobedience

Saul showed great promise. He was strong, tall, and modest. God's Spirit came upon him, and Samuel was his counselor. But Saul deliberately disobeyed God and became an evil king. We must not base our hopes or future on our potential. Instead, we must consistently obey God in all areas of life. God evaluates obedience, not potential.

C. SAUL AND DAVID (16.1—31.13)
1. Samuel anoints David as king
2. David and Goliath
3. David and Jonathan become friends
4. Saul pursues David
5. Saul's defeat and death

David quickly killed Goliath, but waited patiently for God to deal with Saul. Although David was anointed to be Israel's next king, he had to wait years to realize this promise. The difficult circumstances in life and the times of waiting often refine, teach, and prepare us for the future responsibilities God has for us.

MEGATHEMES

THEME	EXPLANATION	IMPORTANCE
King	Because Israel suffered from corrupt priests and judges, the people wanted a king. They wanted to be organized like the surrounding nations. Though it was against his original purpose, God chose a king for them.	Establishing a monarchy did not solve Israel's problems. What God desires is the genuine devotion of each person's mind and heart to him. No government or set of laws can substitute for the rule of God in your heart and life.
God's Control	Israel prospered as long as the people regarded God as their true king. When the leaders strayed from God's law, God intervened in their personal lives and overruled their actions. In this way, God maintained ultimate control over Israel's history.	God is always at work in this world, even when we can't see what he is doing. No matter what kinds of pressures we must endure or how many changes we must face, God is ultimately in control of our situation. Being confident of God's sovereignty, we can face the difficult situations in our lives with boldness.
Leadership	God guided his people using different forms of leadership: judges, priests, prophets, kings. Those whom he chose for these different offices, such as Eli, Samuel, Saul, and David, portrayed different styles of leadership. Yet the success of each leader depended on his devotion to God, not his position, leadership style, wisdom, age, or strength.	When Eli, Samuel, Saul, and David disobeyed God, they faced tragic consequences. Sin affected what they accomplished for God and how some of them raised their children. Being a real leader means letting God guide all aspects of your activities, values, and goals, including the way you raise your children.
Obedience	For God, "to obey is better than sacrifice" (15.22). God wanted his people to obey, serve, and follow him with a whole heart rather than to maintain a superficial commitment based on tradition or ceremonial systems.	Although we are free from the sacrificial system of the Jewish law, we may still rely on outward observances to substitute for inward commitment. God desires that all our work and worship be motivated by genuine, heartfelt devotion to him.

God's Faithfulness	God faithfully kept the promises he made to Israel. He responded to his people with tender mercy and swift justice. In showing mercy, he faithfully acted in the best interest of his people. In showing justice, he was faithful to his word and perfect moral nature.	Because God is faithful, he can be counted on to be merciful toward us. Yet God is also just, and he will not tolerate rebellion against him. His faithfulness and unselfish love should inspire us to dedicate ourselves to him completely. We must never take his mercy for granted.

KEY PLACES IN 1 SAMUEL

1 Ramah Samuel was born in Ramah. Before his birth, Samuel's mother Hannah made a promise to God that she would dedicate her son to serve God alongside the priests in the tabernacle at Shiloh (1.1—2.11).

2 Shiloh The focal point of Israel's worship was at Shiloh, where the tabernacle and the ark of the covenant resided. Eli was the high priest, but his sons, Hophni and Phinehas, were evil men who took advantage of the people. Samuel, however, served God faithfully, and God blessed him as he grew (2.12—3.21).

3 Kiriath-jearim Israel was constantly at odds with the Philistines, and another battle was brewing. Hophni and Phinehas brought the ark of the covenant from Shiloh to the battlefield, believing that its mere presence would bring the Israelites victory. The Israelites were defeated by the Philistines at Ebenezer, and the ark was captured. However, the Philistines soon found out that the ark was not quite the great battle trophy they expected. For God sent plagues upon every Philistine city into which the ark was brought. Finally, the Philistines sent it back to Kiriath-jearim in Israel (4.1—7.4).

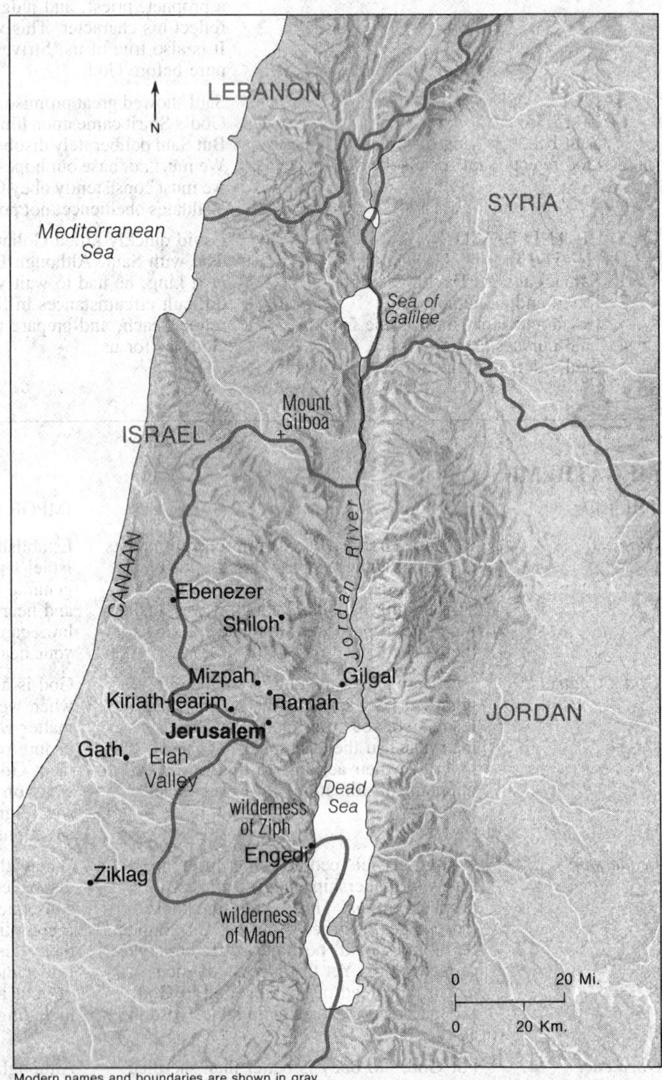

Modern names and boundaries are shown in gray.

4 Mizpah The Israelites' defeat made them realize that God was no longer blessing them. Samuel called the people together at Mizpah and asked them to fast and pray in sorrow for their sins. The convocation at Mizpah was a tempting target for the confident Philistines who advanced for an attack. But God intervened and routed their mighty army. Meanwhile, Samuel was judging cases throughout Israel. But as Samuel grew old, the people came to him at Ramah (his home base) demanding a king in order to be like the other nations. At Mizpah, Saul was chosen by sacred lot to be Israel's first king with the blessing, but not the approval, of God and Samuel (7.5—10.27).

5 Gilgal A battle with the Ammonites proved Saul's leadership abilities to the people of Israel. He protected the people of Jabesh-gilead and scattered the Ammonite army. Samuel and the people crowned Saul as king of Israel at Gilgal (11.1–15).

6 Elah Valley Saul won many other battles, but over time he proved to be arrogant, sinful, and rebellious until God finally rejected him as king. Unknown to Saul, a young shepherd and musician named David was anointed to be Israel's next king. But it would be many years before David sat upon the throne. Ironically, Saul hired David to play the harp in his palace. Saul grew to like David so much that he made him his personal bodyguard. In one particular battle with the Philistines in the Elah Valley, David killed Goliath, the Philistines' mightiest soldier. But this victory was the beginning of the end of Saul's love for David. The Israelites praised David more than Saul, causing Saul to become so jealous that he plotted to kill David (12.1—22.23).

7 The Wilderness Even anointed kings are not exempt from troubles. David literally ran for his life from King Saul, hiding with his band of followers in the wilderness of Ziph (where the men of Ziph constantly betrayed him), the wilderness of Maon, and the caves of Engedi. Though he had opportunities to kill Saul, David refused to do so because Saul was God's anointed king (23.1—26.25).

8 Gath David moved his men and family to Gath, the Philistine city where King Achish lived. Saul then stopped chasing him. The Philistines seemed to welcome this famous fugitive from Israel (27.1–4).

9 Ziklag Desiring privacy in return for his pretended loyalty to King Achish, David asked for a city in which to house his men and family. Achish gave him Ziklag. From there David conducted raids against the cities of the Geshurites, Girzites, and Amalekites, making sure no one escaped to tell the tale (27.5–12). David later conquered the Amalekites after they raided Ziklag (30.1–31).

10 Mount Gilboa War with the Philistines broke out again in the north, near Mount Gilboa. Saul, who no longer relied on God, consulted a witch in a desperate attempt to contact Samuel for help. In the meantime, David was sent back to Ziklag because the Philistine commanders did not trust his loyalty in battle against Israel. The Philistines slaughtered the Israelites on Mount Gilboa, killing King Saul and his three sons, including David's loyal friend Jonathan. Without God, Saul led a bitter and misguided life. The consequences of his sinful actions affected not only him, but hurt his family and the entire nation as well (28.1—31.13).

A. ELI AND SAMUEL (1.1 – 7.17)

Israel has been ruled by judges for over 200 years. Eli and Samuel are the last of those judges. Samuel is born near the end of Eli's life. He grows up in the tabernacle as a priest-in-training under Eli and is well qualified to serve Israel as both a priest and a judge. Although the nation has fallen away from God, it is clear that God is preparing Samuel from the very beginning to lead the nation back to right living. God is always in control; he is able to bring his people back to him.

1. Samuel's birth and childhood

God answers Hannah's prayer for a son

1.1 1 Chron 6.22-28 6.33-38

1.2 Gen 29.30; 30.1 Deut 21.15-17

1 There was a certain man of Ramathaim, a Zuphite[a] from the hill country of
Ephraim, whose name was Elkanah son of Jeroham son of Elihu son of Tohu
son of Zuph, an Ephraimite. 2 He had two wives; the name of the one was Hannah,
and the name of the other Peninnah. Peninnah had children, but Hannah had no
children.
3 Now this man used to go up year by year from his town to worship and to
sacrifice to the LORD of hosts at Shiloh, where the two sons of Eli, Hophni and

[a] Compare Gk and 1 Chr 6.35-36: Heb *Ramathaim-zophim*

1.1 The book of 1 Samuel begins in the days when the judges still ruled Israel, possibly during the closing years of Samson's life. Samuel was Israel's last judge and the first priest and prophet to serve during the time of a king. He was the best example of what a good judge should be, governing the people by God's Word and not by his own impulses. Samuel was the man who anointed Saul as Israel's first king.

1.2 Although many great Old Testament leaders (such as Abraham, Jacob, and David) had more than one wife, this was not God's original intention for marriage. Genesis 2.24 states that in marriage, two people become one flesh. Why then did polygamy exist among God's people? First, it was to produce more offspring to help in the man's work and to assure the continuation of the man's family line. Numerous children were a symbol of status and wealth. Second, in societies where many young men were killed in battle, polygamy became an accepted way of supporting women who otherwise would have remained unmarried and, very likely, destitute. Nevertheless, polygamy often caused serious family problems, as we see in this story of Hannah and Peninnah.

1.3 The tabernacle was located at Shiloh, the religious center of the nation. Three times a year all Israelite men were required to attend a religious feast held at the tabernacle: the passover with the festival of unleavened bread, the festival of weeks, and the festival of booths (Deuteronomy 16.16). Elkanah made this pilgrimage regularly to fulfill God's commands. (See Exodus 23.14–17 for the regulations concerning the pilgrimage, and see the note on Exodus 40.34 for more on the tabernacle.)

Phinehas, were priests of the LORD. 4On the day when Elkanah sacrificed, he 1.3 Ex 34.22,23
would give portions to his wife Peninnah and to all her sons and daughters; 5but to Deut 12.4-7
Hannah he gave a double portion,[b] because he loved her, though the LORD had Josh 18.1,2 1 Sam 2.12
closed her womb. 6Her rival used to provoke her severely, to irritate her, because 4.4,11
the LORD had closed her womb. 7So it went on year by year; as often as she went Lk 2.41,42
up to the house of the LORD, she used to provoke her. Therefore Hannah wept and 1.5 Gen 20.18; 30.2
would not eat. 8Her husband Elkanah said to her, "Hannah, why do you weep? 1.8
Why do you not eat? Why is your heart sad? Am I not more to you than ten sons?" Ruth 4.15

9 After they had eaten and drunk at Shiloh, Hannah rose and presented herself
before the LORD.[c] Now Eli the priest was sitting on the seat beside the doorpost of
the temple of the LORD. 10She was deeply distressed and prayed to the LORD, and
wept bitterly. 11She made this vow: "O LORD of hosts, if only you will look on the 1.11
misery of your servant, and remember me, and not forget your servant, but will Gen 29.32 Num 6.1-6
give to your servant a male child, then I will set him before you as a nazirite[d] until 30.6-11
the day of his death. He shall drink neither wine nor intoxicants,[e] and no razor Judg 13.5 Lk 1.15
shall touch his head."

12 As she continued praying before the LORD, Eli observed her mouth. 13Han-
nah was praying silently; only her lips moved, but her voice was not heard; there- 1.14
fore Eli thought she was drunk. 14So Eli said to her, "How long will you make a Acts 2.13

[b] Syr: Meaning of Heb uncertain [c] Gk: Heb lacks *and presented herself before the LORD* [d] That is *one separated* or *one consecrated* [e] Cn Compare Gk Q Ms 1.22: MT *then I will give him to the LORD all the days of his life*

THE JOURNEY TO SHILOH
Each year Elkanah and his family traveled from their home at Ramah to Shiloh, where they worshiped and sacrificed at God's tabernacle.

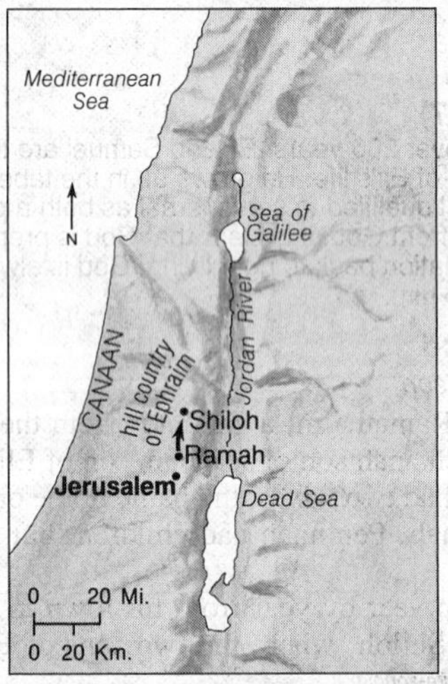

1.6 Hannah had been unable to conceive children, and in Old Testament times, a childless woman was considered a failure. Her barrenness was a social embarrassment for her husband. Children were a very important part of the society's economic structure. They were a source of labor for the family, and it was their duty to care for their parents in their old age. If a wife could not bear children she was often obligated, by ancient Middle Eastern custom, to give one of her servant girls to her husband to bear children for her. Although Elkanah could have left Hannah (a husband was permitted to divorce a barren wife), he remained lovingly devoted to her despite social criticism and his rights under civil law.

1.7 Part of God's plan for Hannah involved postponing her years of childbearing. While Peninnah and Elkanah looked at Hannah's outward circumstances, God was moving ahead with his plan. Can you think of others who are struggling with God's timing in answering their prayers and who need your support? By supporting those who are struggling, you may help them remain steadfast in their faith and confident in his timing to bring fulfillment to their lives.

1.8 Hannah knew her husband loved her, but even his encouragement could not comfort her. She could not keep from listening to Peninnah's jeers and letting her words erode her self-confidence. Although we cannot keep others from unjustly criticizing us, we can choose how we will react to the criticism. Rather than dwelling upon our problems, we can enjoy the loving relationships God has given us. By so doing, we can exchange self-pity for hope.

1.10 Hannah had good reason to feel discouraged. She was unable to bear children; she shared her husband with a woman who ridiculed her (1.7); her loving husband could not solve her problem (1.8); and even the high priest misunderstood her motives (1.14). But instead of retaliating or giving up hope, Hannah prayed. She brought her problem honestly before God.

Each of us may face times of barrenness when nothing "comes to birth" in our work, service, or relationships. It is difficult to pray in faith when we feel so ineffective. But, as Hannah discovered, prayer opens the way for God to work (1.19, 20).

1.11 In return for conceiving a son, Hannah vowed to dedicate this son to God for lifetime service. Hannah may have been making a nazirite vow, which parents could take for their unborn children. The nazirite vow was a promise to be set apart for special service to God. (See the note on Numbers 6.1, 2 and the first note on Judges 13.5.) As long as the vow was in effect, the person's hair could not be cut. Although some vows were temporary, Hannah's vow was for life.

1.11 Be careful what you promise in prayer, because God may take you up on it. Hannah so desperately wanted her prayer to be answered that she was willing to strike a bargain with God. God took her up on her promise, and to Hannah's credit, she did her part, even though it was painful (1.27, 28).

Although we are not in a position to barter with God, he may still choose to answer a prayer which has an attached promise. When you pray, ask yourself, "Will I follow through on any promises I make to God if he grants my request?" It is dishonest and dangerous to ignore a promise, especially to God. God keeps his promises, and he expects you to keep yours.

1.12–14 When you notice something is wrong with another person, what is your first reaction? Eli made a snap judgment before he knew all the facts. It is easy to misunderstand motives and actions. Be sensitive to the fact that, like Hannah, someone may be facing tremendous burdens. Before you make a judgment, find out what a person may be going through (16.7).

1.15 Ps 42.4 142.1,2 Lam 2.19
drunken spectacle of yourself? Put away your wine." 15 But Hannah answered,
"No, my lord, I am a woman deeply troubled; I have drunk neither wine nor strong
drink, but I have been pouring out my soul before the LORD. 16 Do not regard your
servant as a worthless woman, for I have been speaking out of my great anxiety and
1.17 Ps 20.3
vexation all this time." 17 Then Eli answered, "Go in peace; the God of Israel grant
the petition you have made to him." 18 And she said, "Let your servant find favor
in your sight." Then the woman went to her quarters,[f] ate and drank with her
husband,[g] and her countenance was sad no longer.[h]

1.19 Gen 21.1,2 30.22 Ex 2.24 Ps 106.45
19 They rose early in the morning and worshiped before the LORD; then they
went back to their house at Ramah. Elkanah knew his wife Hannah, and the LORD
remembered her. 20 In due time Hannah conceived and bore a son. She named him
Samuel, for she said, "I have asked him of the LORD."

Hannah fulfills her promise to God

1.21 Lk 2.22
21 The man Elkanah and all his household went up to offer to the LORD the
yearly sacrifice, and to pay his vow. 22 But Hannah did not go up, for she said to her
husband, "As soon as the child is weaned, I will bring him, that he may appear in
the presence of the LORD, and remain there forever; I will offer him as a nazirite[i]
for all time."[j] 23 Her husband Elkanah said to her, "Do what seems best to you,
wait until you have weaned him; only—may the LORD establish his word."[k] So the
1.24 Num 15.8,9,10
woman remained and nursed her son, until she weaned him. 24 When she had
weaned him, she took him up with her, along with a three-year-old bull,[l] an ephah
of flour, and a skin of wine. She brought him to the house of the LORD at Shiloh;
and the child was young. 25 Then they slaughtered the bull, and they brought the
child to Eli. 26 And she said, "Oh, my lord! As you live, my lord, I am the woman
who was standing here in your presence, praying to the LORD. 27 For this child I
prayed; and the LORD has granted me the petition that I made to him. 28 Therefore
I have lent him to the LORD; as long as he lives, he is given to the LORD."

She left him there for[m] the LORD.

Hannah's prayer of thanks

2.1 Ex 15.1,2 Deut 32.3,4 Lk 1.47,68
2 Hannah prayed and said,
"My heart exults in the LORD;
my strength is exalted in my God.[n]
My mouth derides my enemies,

[f] Gk: Heb *went her way* [g] Gk: Heb lacks *and drank with her husband* [h] Gk: Meaning of Heb uncertain [i] That is *one separated* or *one consecrated* [j] Cn Compare Q Ms: MT lacks *I will offer him as a nazirite for all time* [k] MT: Q Ms Gk Compare Syr *that which goes out of your mouth* [l] Q Ms Gk Syr: MT *three bulls* [m] Gk (Compare Q Ms) and Gk at 2.11: MT *And he* (that is, Elkanah) *worshiped there before* [n] Gk: Heb *the LORD*

1.18 Earlier Hannah had been discouraged to the point of being physically sick and unable to eat. Here she returns home well and happy. The change in her attitude may be attributed to three factors: (1) she honestly prayed to God (1.11), (2) she received encouragement from Eli (1.17), (3) she resolved to leave the problem with God (1.18). This is the antidote for discouragement: tell God how you really feel and leave your problems with him. Then rely upon the support of good friends and counselors.

1.24, 25 At each of the great annual festivals, several different types of sacrifices were offered to God. Some required animal sacrifices for the forgiveness of sins, some required food or grain offerings for praise and thanksgiving, and some required wine to be poured out at the base of the altar for dedication. Elkanah and Hannah took a three-year-old bull, some flour, and some wine to the annual feast in order to offer several types of sacrifices, including one to dedicate their child Samuel to God. (See Numbers 15.1–10 for more on the different types of offerings.)

1.26–28 To do what she promised (1.11), Hannah gave up what she wanted most—her son—and presented him to Eli to serve God in the tabernacle. In dedicating her only son to God, Hannah was dedicating her entire life and future to God. Since Samuel's life was from God, Hannah was not really giving him up. Rather, she was returning him to God, who had given him to Hannah in the first place. These verses show us the nature of the gifts we are to give to God. Are they gifts which cost us little (Sunday mornings, a comfortable tithe), or are they gifts of sacrifice? Are you presenting God with tokens, or are you presenting him with your entire life?

1.28 Samuel was probably three years old—the customary age for weaning—when his mother left him at the tabernacle. By saying, "I have lent him to the Lord," Hannah meant that she was dedicating Samuel to God for lifetime service. She did not, of course, forget her much-wanted son. She visited him regularly. And each year she brought him a robe just like Eli's (2.19). In later years, Samuel lived in Ramah (7.17), his parents' hometown (1.19, 20).

2.1–10 Hannah praised God for his answer to her prayer for a son. The theme of her poetic prayer was her confidence in God's sovereignty and her thankfulness for everything he had done. Mary, the mother of Jesus, modeled her own praise song, called the Magnificat, after Hannah's prayer (Luke 1.46–55). Like Hannah and Mary, we should be confident of God's ultimate control over the events in our lives, and we should be thankful for the ways he has blessed us. By praising him for all good gifts, we acknowledge his ultimate control over all the affairs of life.

because I rejoice in my[o] victory.

2 "There is no Holy One like the LORD,
no one besides you;
there is no Rock like our God.
3 Talk no more so very proudly,
let not arrogance come from your mouth;
for the LORD is a God of knowledge,
and by him actions are weighed.
4 The bows of the mighty are broken,
but the feeble gird on strength.
5 Those who were full have hired themselves out for bread,
but those who were hungry are fat with spoil.
The barren has borne seven,
but she who has many children is forlorn.
6 The LORD kills and brings to life;
he brings down to Sheol and raises up.
7 The LORD makes poor and makes rich;
he brings low, he also exalts.
8 He raises up the poor from the dust;
he lifts the needy from the ash heap,
to make them sit with princes
and inherit a seat of honor.[p]
For the pillars of the earth are the LORD's,
and on them he has set the world.

9 "He will guard the feet of his faithful ones,
but the wicked shall be cut off in darkness;
for not by might does one prevail.
10 The LORD! His adversaries shall be shattered;
the Most High[q] will thunder in heaven.
The LORD will judge the ends of the earth;
he will give strength to his king,
and exalt the power of his anointed."

11 Then Elkanah went home to Ramah, while the boy remained to minister to
the LORD, in the presence of the priest Eli.

Samuel serves the Lord

12 Now the sons of Eli were scoundrels; they had no regard for the LORD 13 or

2.2 Ex 15.11
2.3 1 Sam 16.7; 1 Kgs 8.39
2.4 Ps 37.15; 46.7-9
2.5 Ruth 4.15; Lk 1.53
2.6 Deut 32.39
2.7 Deut 8.17,18; Job 1.21; 5.10,11; Eccl 2.24-26; Jas 4.10
2.8 Job 36.7; 38.4-7; 42.10; Jas 2.5
2.9 Ps 33.16,17; Jer 9.23,24; Mt 8.12
2.10 Ex 15.6; 19.18; Ps 18.13; 21.1,7; 96.13

[o] Q Ms: MT *your* [p] Gk (Compare Q Ms) adds *He grants the vow of the one who vows, and blesses the years of the just* [q] Cn Heb *against him he*

2.2 Hannah praises God for being a rock—firm, strong, and unchanging. In our fast-paced world, friends come and go and circumstances change. It's difficult to find a solid foundation that will not change. Those who devote their lives to achievements, causes, or possessions have as their security that which is finite and changeable. The possessions that we work so hard to obtain will all pass away. But God is always present. Hope in him. He will never fail.

2.3–5 No doubt as Hannah said these words, she was thinking of Peninnah's arrogance and chiding. Hannah did not have to get even with Peninnah. She knew that God is all-knowing, and that he will judge all sin and pride. Hannah wisely left judgment up to God. Resist the temptation to take justice into your own hands.

2.10 Living in a world where evil abounds and the threat of a nuclear holocaust is always present can cause us to forget that God is in control of our world. Hannah saw God as (1) solid as a rock (2.2); (2) the one who watches what we do (2.3); (3) sovereign over all the affairs of people (2.4–8); and (4) the supreme judge who administers perfect justice (2.10). If we remember God's sovereign control, we will put both world and personal events in perspective.

2.11 As Eli's assistant, Samuel's responsibilities would have included opening the tabernacle doors each morning (3.15), cleaning the furniture, and sweeping the floors. As he grew older, Samuel would have assisted Eli in offering sacrifices. The fact that he was wearing a linen ephod (a garment worn only by priests) shows that he was a priest-in-training (2.18). Because Samuel was Eli's helper, he was God's helper too. When you serve others—even in carrying out ordinary tasks—you are serving God. Because ultimately we serve God, every job has dignity.

2.12ff It was stipulated in the law that the needs of all the Levites were to be met through the people's tithes (Numbers 18.20–24; Joshua 13.14, 33). Because Eli's sons were priests, they were to be taken care of this way. But Eli's sons took advantage of their position to satisfy their lust for power, possessions, and control. Their contempt and arrogance toward both people and worship undermined the integrity of the whole priesthood.

2.13 Lev 7.20,28-36 for the duties of the priests to the people. When anyone offered sacrifice, the
priest's servant would come, while the meat was boiling, with a three-pronged fork
in his hand, 14 and he would thrust it into the pan, or kettle, or caldron, or pot; all
that the fork brought up the priest would take for himself.[r] This is what they did at
2.15 Lev 3.2-5; 7.30 Shiloh to all the Israelites who came there. 15 Moreover, before the fat was burned,
the priest's servant would come and say to the one who was sacrificing, "Give meat
for the priest to roast; for he will not accept boiled meat from you, but only raw."
16 And if the man said to him, "Let them burn the fat first, and then take whatever
you wish," he would say, "No, you must give it now; if not, I will take it by force."
2.17 Mal 2.7-9 17 Thus the sin of the young men was very great in the sight of the LORD; for they
treated the offerings of the LORD with contempt.

[r] Gk Syr Vg: Heb *with it*

HANNAH

Hannah's prayer shows us that all we have and receive is on loan from God. Hannah might have had many excuses for being a possessive mother. But when God answered her prayer, she followed through on her promise to dedicate Samuel to God's service.

She discovered that the greatest joy in having a child is to give that child fully and freely back to God. She entered motherhood prepared to do what all mothers must eventually do—let go of their children.

When children are born, they are completely dependent upon their parents for all their basic necessities. This causes some parents to forget that those same children will grow toward independence within the span of a few short years. Being sensitive to the different stages of that healthy process will greatly strengthen family relationships; resisting or denying that process will cause great pain. We must gradually let go of our children in order to allow them to become mature, interdependent adults.

Strengths and accomplishments:
- Mother of Samuel, Israel's greatest judge
- Fervent in worship; effective in prayer
- Willing to follow through on even a costly commitment

Weakness and mistake:
- Struggled with her sense of self-worth because she was unable to have children

Lessons from her life:
- God hears and answers prayer
- Our children are gifts from God
- God is concerned for the oppressed and afflicted

Vital statistics:
- Where: Ephraim
- Occupation: Homemaker
- Relatives: Husband: Elkanah. Son: Samuel. Later, three other sons and two daughters
- Contemporaries: Eli, the priest

Key verses:
"And she said, 'Oh, my lord! As you live, my lord, I am the woman who was standing here in your presence, praying to the Lord. For this child I prayed; and the Lord has granted me the petition that I made to him. Therefore I have lent him to the Lord; as long as he lives, he is given to the Lord' " (1 Samuel 1.26–28).

Her story is told in 1 Samuel 1; 2.

Eli knew that his sons were evil, but he did little to correct or stop them, even when the integrity of God's sanctuary was threatened. As the high priest, Eli should have responded by executing his sons (Numbers 15.22–31). No wonder Eli chose not to confront the situation. But by ignoring their selfish actions, Eli let his sons ruin their own lives and the lives of many others. There are times when serious problems must be confronted, even if the process and consequences could be painful.

2.13, 14 This fork was a utensil used in the tabernacle for offering sacrifices. Made of bronze (Exodus 27.3), it usually had three prongs to hook the meat that was to be offered on the altar. Eli's sons used the fork to take more meat from the pot than was due them.

2.13–17 What were Eli's sons doing wrong? They were taking parts of the sacrifices *before* they were offered to God on the altar. They were also eating meat before the fat was burned off. This was against God's law (Leviticus 3.3–5). In effect, Eli's sons were treating God's offerings with contempt. Offerings were given to show honor and respect to God while seeking forgiveness for sins, but through their irreverence, Eli's sons were actually sinning while making the offerings. To add to their sins, they were also seducing women who came to the tabernacle (2.22).

Like Eli's sons, some religious leaders look down on the faith of ordinary people and treat their offerings to God casually or even with contempt. God harshly judges those who lead his people astray or scorn what is devoted to him (Numbers 18.32).

18 Samuel was ministering before the LORD, a boy wearing a linen ephod.
19 His mother used to make for him a little robe and take it to him each year, when **2.19**
she went up with her husband to offer the yearly sacrifice. 20 Then Eli would bless 1 Sam 1.3
Elkanah and his wife, and say, "May the LORD repay[s] you with children by this
woman for the gift that she made to[t] the LORD"; and then they would return to their
home.
21 And[u] the LORD took note of Hannah; she conceived and bore three sons and **2.21**
two daughters. And the boy Samuel grew up in the presence of the LORD. Gen 21.1 1 Sam 3.19-21
22 Now Eli was very old. He heard all that his sons were doing to all Israel, and Lk 2.40
how they lay with the women who served at the entrance to the tent of meeting.
23 He said to them, "Why do you do such things? For I hear of your evil dealings **2.23**
from all these people. 24 No, my sons; it is not a good report that I hear the people Num 15.30 Deut 1.17
of the LORD spreading abroad. 25 If one person sins against another, someone can
intercede for the sinner with the LORD;[v] but if someone sins against the LORD, who
can make intercession?" But they would not listen to the voice of their father; for it
was the will of the LORD to kill them.
26 Now the boy Samuel continued to grow both in stature and in favor with the **2.26** Lk 1.80
LORD and with the people. 2.40,52

A prophet speaks to Eli

27 A man of God came to Eli and said to him, "Thus the LORD has said, 'I **2.27**
revealed[w] myself to the family of your ancestor in Egypt when they were slaves[x] Ex 13.16 Deut 6.21
to the house of Pharaoh. 28 I chose him out of all the tribes of Israel to be my priest, Jos 2.10
to go up to my altar, to offer incense, to wear an ephod before me; and I gave to the Judg 6.8
family of your ancestor all my offerings by fire from the people of Israel. 29 Why **2.28** Ex 28.1-4
then look with greedy eye[y] at my sacrifices and my offerings that I commanded, 30.7,8 Deut 10.9
and honor your sons more than me by fattening yourselves on the choicest parts of **2.29**
every offering of my people Israel?' 30 Therefore the LORD the God of Israel de- Mt 10.37
clares: 'I promised that your family and the family of your ancestor should go in **2.30** Num 25.12,13
and out before me forever'; but now the LORD declares: 'Far be it from me; for Ps 50.23 Mal 2.7-9
those who honor me I will honor, and those who despise me shall be treated with
contempt. 31 See, a time is coming when I will cut off your strength and the strength

[s] Q Ms Gk: MT *give* [t] Q Ms Gk: MT *for the petition that she asked of* [u] Q Ms Gk: MT *When* [v] Gk Compare Q Ms: MT *another, God will mediate for him* [w] Gk Tg Syr: Heb *Did I reveal* [x] Q Ms Gk: MT lacks *slaves* [y] Q Ms Gk: MT *then kick*

2.18 Samuel was a young child, and yet he "was ministering before the Lord." Children can often serve God just as effectively as adults. God will use anyone who is willing to learn from him and to serve him. He has no age limits. Don't discount the faith of a child or let your age keep you from serving God. See also the note on 1 Timothy 4.12, 13.

2.18 Samuel wore a linen robe called an *ephod.* Ephods, long sleeveless vests made of plain linen, were worn by all priests. The high priest's ephod carried special significance. It was embroidered with a variety of bright colors. Attached to it was the breastplate, a bib-like garment with gold embroidered shoulder straps. Twelve precious gemstones were attached to the breastplate, each stone representing one of the tribes of Israel. A pouch attached to the ephod held the Urim and Thummim, two small objects used to determine God's will in certain national matters.

2.21 God honored the desires of faithful Hannah. We never hear about Peninnah or her children again, but Samuel was used mightily by God. God also gave Hannah five children in addition to Samuel. God often blesses us in ways we do not expect. Hannah never expected to have a child at her age, much less six children! Don't resent God's timing. His blessings might not be immediate, but they will come if we are faithful to do what he says in his Word.

2.23–25 Eli's sons knew better, but they continued to disobey God deliberately by cheating, seducing, and robbing the people. Therefore, God planned to kill them. Any sin is wrong, but sin carried out deliberately and deceitfully is the worst kind. When we sin out of ignorance, we deserve punishment. But when we sin intentionally, the consequences will be more severe. Don't ignore God's warnings about sin. Abandon it before it becomes a way of life.

2.25 Does a loving God really plan to kill people? Consider the situation in the tabernacle. A person made an offering in order to have his sins forgiven, and Eli's sons stole the offering and made a sham of the person's repentant attitude. God, in his love for Israel, could not permit this situation to continue. He allowed Eli's sons to die as a result of their own boastful presumption. They took the ark into battle, thinking it would protect them. But God withdrew his protection and the wicked sons of Eli were killed (4.10, 11).

2.29 Eli had a difficult time rearing his sons. He apparently did not take any strong disciplinary action with them when he became aware of their wrongdoing. But Eli was not just a father trying to handle his rebellious sons; he was the high priest ignoring the sins of priests under his jurisdiction. As a result, the Lord took the necessary disciplinary action that Eli would not.

Eli was guilty of honoring his sons above God by letting them continue in their sinful ways. Is there a situation in your life, family, or work that you allow to continue even though you know it is wrong? If so, you may become as guilty as those engaged in the wrong act.

2.31–34 God is just, and he will judge all sin. Eli's sons had sinned by despising God, and Eli had sinned by not correcting them. Because they were religious leaders, they may have thought they would get away with it. But God brought judgment.

2.31 1 Sam 4.11 22.17-20
of your ancestor's family, so that no one in your family will live to old age. 32 Then
in distress you will look with greedy eye[z] on all the prosperity that shall be bestowed upon Israel; and no one in your family shall ever live to old age. 33 The only
one of you whom I shall not cut off from my altar shall be spared to weep out his[a]
eyes and grieve his[b] heart; all the members of your household shall die by the
2.34 1 Sam 4.11,17
sword.[c] 34 The fate of your two sons, Hophni and Phinehas, shall be the sign to
you—both of them shall die on the same day. 35 I will raise up for myself a faithful
priest, who shall do according to what is in my heart and in my mind. I will build
him a sure house, and he shall go in and out before my anointed one forever. 36 Everyone who is left in your family shall come to implore him for a piece of silver or
a loaf of bread, and shall say, Please put me in one of the priest's places, that I may
eat a morsel of bread.' "

God calls Samuel to serve him

3.1 1 Sam 3.21 Isa 1.1 Jer 1.1 Ezek 13.17
3 Now the boy Samuel was ministering to the LORD under Eli. The word of the
LORD was rare in those days; visions were not widespread.
2 At that time Eli, whose eyesight had begun to grow dim so that he could not
see, was lying down in his room; 3 the lamp of God had not yet gone out, and
Samuel was lying down in the temple of the LORD, where the ark of God was.
3.4 Isa 6.8
4 Then the LORD called, "Samuel! Samuel!"[d] and he said, "Here I am!" 5 and ran to
Eli, and said, "Here I am, for you called me." But he said, "I did not call; lie down
again." So he went and lay down. 6 The LORD called again, "Samuel!" Samuel got
up and went to Eli, and said, "Here I am, for you called me." But he said, "I did not
call, my son; lie down again." 7 Now Samuel did not yet know the LORD, and the
word of the LORD had not yet been revealed to him. 8 The LORD called Samuel
again, a third time. And he got up and went to Eli, and said, "Here I am, for you
called me." Then Eli perceived that the LORD was calling the boy. 9 Therefore Eli
said to Samuel, "Go, lie down; and if he calls you, you shall say, 'Speak, LORD, for
your servant is listening.' " So Samuel went and lay down in his place.
10 Now the LORD came and stood there, calling as before, "Samuel! Samuel!"
3.11 Deut 31.21 2 Kgs 21.12 Isa 29.14 Jer 19.3
And Samuel said, "Speak, for your servant is listening." 11 Then the LORD said to
Samuel, "See, I am about to do something in Israel that will make both ears of
anyone who hears of it tingle. 12 On that day I will fulfill against Eli all that I have
spoken concerning his house, from beginning to end. 13 For I have told him that I

[z] Q Ms Gk: MT *will kick* [a] Q Ms Gk: MT *your* [b] Q Ms Gk: Heb *your* [c] Q Ms See Gk: MT *die like mortals* [d] Q Ms Gk See 3.10: MT *the LORD called Samuel*

If you are in a position of authority, don't rationalize away God's standards for right living. God expects leaders to lead fairly and to eliminate evil practices. God will not overlook those who justify their own sin.

2.31, 35, 36 For the fulfillment of this prediction see 1 Kings 2.26, 27. This is where Solomon removed Abiathar from his position, thus ending Eli's line. Then God raised up Zadok, a priest under David and then high priest under Solomon. Zadok's line was probably still in place as late as the days of Ezra.

2.35 "My anointed one" refers to the king (see 2.10). God was saying that his faithful priest would serve his king forever.

2.35 God is looking for faithfulness. Eli and his sons were not faithful, so God said he would choose someone else who was. When God has given you a job, do it faithfully — or God may find someone else to do it in your place.

3.1-5 Although God had spoken directly and audibly with Moses and Joshua, his word became rare during the three centuries of rule by judges. By Eli's time, no prophets were speaking God's messages to Israel. Why? Look at the attitude of Eli's sons. They either refused to listen to God or allowed greed to get in the way of any communication with him.

Listening and responding are vital in a relationship with God. Although God does not always use the sound of a human voice, he always speaks clearly through his word. To receive his messages, we must be ready to listen and to act upon what he tells us. Like Samuel, be ready to say "Here I am" when God calls you to action.

3.2, 3 The ark of the covenant was kept in the most holy place, the innermost room of the tabernacle where only the high priest could enter once a year. In front of the most holy place was the holy place, a small room where the sacred furniture of the tabernacle was kept. Just outside the holy place was a court with small rooms where the priests were to stay. Samuel probably slept here with the other priests, only a few yards away from the ark.

3.8, 9 One would naturally expect an audible message from God to be given to the priest Eli and not to the child Samuel. Eli was older and more experienced, and he held the proper position. But God's chain of command is based on faith, not on age or position. In finding faithful followers, God may use unexpected channels. Be prepared for the Lord to work at any place, at any time, and through anyone he chooses.

3.13 Eli had spent his entire life in service to God. He was responsible to oversee all the worship in Israel. But in pursuing this great mission he neglected the responsibilities in his own home. Don't let your desire to do God's work cause you to neglect God in your home. If you do, your mission may degenerate into a quest for personal importance, and your family will suffer the consequences of your neglect.

am about to punish his house forever, for the iniquity that he knew, because his
sons were blaspheming God,[e] and he did not restrain them. 14 Therefore I swear to
the house of Eli that the iniquity of Eli's house shall not be expiated by sacrifice or
offering forever."
15 Samuel lay there until morning; then he opened the doors of the house of the
LORD. Samuel was afraid to tell the vision to Eli. 16 But Eli called Samuel and said,
"Samuel, my son." He said, "Here I am." 17 Eli said, "What was it that he told you?
Do not hide it from me. May God do so to you and more also, if you hide anything
from me of all that he told you." 18 So Samuel told him everything and hid nothing
from him. Then he said, "It is the LORD; let him do what seems good to him."
19 As Samuel grew up, the LORD was with him and let none of his words fall to
the ground. 20 And all Israel from Dan to Beer-sheba knew that Samuel was a trustworthy prophet of the LORD. 21 The LORD continued to appear at Shiloh, for the
4 LORD revealed himself to Samuel at Shiloh by the word of the LORD. 1 And the
word of Samuel came to all Israel.
In those days the Philistines mustered for war against Israel,[f] and Israel went out
to battle against them;[g] they encamped at Ebenezer, and the Philistines encamped
at Aphek. 2 The Philistines drew up in line against Israel, and when the battle was
joined,[h] Israel was defeated by the Philistines, who killed about four thousand men
on the field of battle. 3 When the troops came to the camp, the elders of Israel said,
"Why has the LORD put us to rout today before the Philistines? Let us bring the ark
of the covenant of the LORD here from Shiloh, so that he may come among us and
save us from the power of our enemies." 4 So the people sent to Shiloh, and brought
from there the ark of the covenant of the LORD of hosts, who is enthroned on the
cherubim. The two sons of Eli, Hophni and Phinehas, were there with the ark of the
covenant of God.
5 When the ark of the covenant of the LORD came into the camp, all Israel gave

3.14 Lev 15.31; 1 Sam 2.25; Ps 51.16,17; Isa 22.14; Jer 7.16
3.15 Jer 1.8
3.18 2 Sam 16.10; Job 2.10; Ps 39.9; Isa 39.8
3.19 Gen 21.22; Judg 13.24; Lk 1.80; 2.40,52
3.20 Judg 20.1; 2 Sam 3.9,10; 17.11
4.1 Josh 13.2-7; Judg 13.1; 1 Sam 29.1
4.2 Josh 7.5,12; Ps 44.9,10
4.3 Num 10.35; 31.6; Josh 7.7; 1 Sam 14.18
4.4 1 Sam 1.3; 4.11; 2 Sam 6.2; 2 Kgs 19.15; Ps 80.1
4.5 Josh 6.5

[e] Another reading is *for themselves* [f] Gk: Heb lacks *In those days the Philistines mustered for war against Israel*
[g] Gk: Heb *against the Philistines* [h] Meaning of Heb uncertain

---

3.14 *Expiated* means "atoned for" or "forgiven." God was saying that the sin of Eli's sons could not be covered by sacrifice, and they would be punished.

3.20 The phrase "from Dan to Beer-sheba" was often used to describe the boundaries of the promised land. Dan was one of the northernmost cities in the land, and Beer-sheba one of the cities farthest south. In this context, it was a way of emphasizing that *everyone* in Israel knew that Samuel was called to be a prophet.

4.1 The Philistines, descendants of Noah's son Ham, settled along the southeastern Mediterranean coast between Egypt and Gaza. They were originally called "Sea People" because they migrated to the Middle East in ships from Greece and Crete. By Samuel's time, these warlike people were well established in five of Gaza's cities in southwest Canaan and were constantly pressing inland against the Israelites. Throughout this book, the Philistines are Israel's major enemy.

4.3 The ark of the covenant contained the ten commandments given by God to Moses. The ark was supposed to be kept in the most holy place, a sacred part of the tabernacle that only the high priest could enter once a year. Hophni and Phinehas desecrated the room by unlawfully entering it and removing the ark.

The Israelites rightly recognized the great holiness of the ark, but they thought that the ark itself – the wood and metal box – was their source of power. They began to use it as a good luck charm, expecting it to protect them from their enemies. A symbol of God does not guarantee his presence and power. Their attitude toward the ark came perilously close to idol worship. When the ark was captured by their enemies, they thought that Israel's glory was gone (4.19–22) and that God had deserted them (7.1, 2). God uses his power according to his own wisdom and will. He responds to the faith of those who seek him.

4.4 "The Lord of hosts, who is enthroned on the cherubim" is another way of saying that God's presence rested on the ark of the covenant between the two golden cherubim (or angels) attached to its lid. The people believed that the ark would bring victory when Hophni and Phinehas carried it into battle.

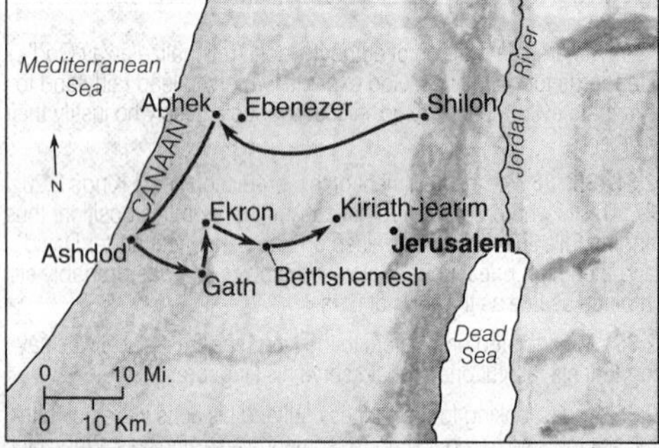

THE ARK'S TRAVELS Eli's sons took the ark from Shiloh to the battlefield on the lower plains at Ebenezer and Aphek. The Philistines captured the ark and took it to Ashdod, Gath, and Ekron. Plagues forced the people to send the ark back to Israel, where it finally was taken by cattle-driven carts to Bethshemesh and on to the home of Eleazar in Kiriath-jearim.

4.5–8 The Philistines were frightened by their recollection of stories about God's intervention for Israel when they left Egypt. But Israel had turned away from God and now clung to only a form of godliness, a symbol of former victories.

People (and churches) often try to live on the memories of

4.7 Ex 14.25; 15.14
4.9 Judg 13.1; 2 Sam 10.12
4.10 Deut 28.15,25; Ps 78.9
4.11 1 Sam 2.34; Ps 78.60,61
4.12 Josh 7.6; 2 Sam 1.1,2; 13.19; Neh 9.1

a mighty shout, so that the earth resounded. 6 When the Philistines heard the noise
of the shouting, they said, "What does this great shouting in the camp of the Hebrews mean?" When they learned that the ark of the LORD had come to the camp,
7 the Philistines were afraid; for they said, "Gods have[i] come into the camp." They
also said, "Woe to us! For nothing like this has happened before. 8 Woe to us! Who
can deliver us from the power of these mighty gods? These are the gods who struck
the Egyptians with every sort of plague in the wilderness. 9 Take courage, and be
men, O Philistines, in order not to become slaves to the Hebrews as they have been
to you; be men and fight."
10 So the Philistines fought; Israel was defeated, and they fled, everyone to his
home. There was a very great slaughter, for there fell of Israel thirty thousand foot
soldiers. 11 The ark of God was captured; and the two sons of Eli, Hophni and Phinehas, died.
12 A man of Benjamin ran from the battle line, and came to Shiloh the same

[i] Or *A god has*

ISRAELITES VS. PHILISTINES
The Israelites and Philistines were archenemies and constantly fighting. Here are some of their confrontations, found in 1 and 2 Samuel. When Israel trusted God for the victory, they always won.

Location of the Battle	*Winner*	*Comments*	*Reference*
Aphek to Ebenezer	Philistines	The ark was captured and Eli's sons killed	1 Samuel 4.1–11
Mizpah	Israelites	After the ark was returned, the Philistines planned to attack again, but God confused them. Israel chased the Philistines back to Beth-car	1 Samuel 7.7–14
Geba	Israelites under Jonathan	One garrison destroyed	1 Samuel 13.3, 4
Gilgal	A standoff	The Israelites lost their nerve and hid	1 Samuel 13.6–17
Michmash	Israelites	Jonathan and his bodyguard said it didn't matter how many enemies there were. If God was with them, they would win. They began the battle, and the army completed it	1 Samuel 13.23—14.23
Elah Valley	Israelites	David and Goliath	1 Samuel 17.1–58
?	Israelites	David killed 200 Philistines to earn a wife	1 Samuel 18.17–30
Keilah	Israelites under David	David protected the threshing floors from Philistine robbers	1 Samuel 23.1–5
Aphek, Jezreel, to Mount Gilboa	Philistines	Saul and Jonathan killed	1 Samuel 29.1; 31.1–13
Baal-perazim	Israelites	The Philistines tried to capture King David	2 Samuel 5.17–25
Gath	Israelites	There was very little trouble with the Philistines after this defeat in their largest city	2 Samuel 8.1
?	Israelites	Abishai saved David from a Philistine giant	2 Samuel 21.15–17
Gob	Israelites	Other giants were killed, including Goliath's brother	2 Samuel 21.18–22

God's blessings. The Israelites wrongly assumed that since God had given them victory in the past, he would do it again, even though they had strayed far from him. Today as in Bible times, spiritual victories come through a continually renewed relationship with God. Don't live off the past. Keep your relationship with God new and fresh.

4.11 This is a fulfillment of the prophecy in 2.34 stating that Eli's sons, Hophni and Phinehas, would die "on the same day."

4.12 At this time, the city of Shiloh was Israel's religious center (Joshua 18.1; 1 Samuel 4.3). The tabernacle was permanently set up there. Because Israel did not have a civil capital – a seat of national government – Shiloh was the natural place for a messenger to deliver the sad news from the battle. Many scholars believe that it was during this battle that Shiloh was destroyed (Jeremiah 7.12; 26.2–6; also see the note on 7.1).

day, with his clothes torn and with earth upon his head. 13 When he arrived, Eli was
sitting upon his seat by the road watching, for his heart trembled for the ark of God.
When the man came into the city and told the news, all the city cried out. 14 When **4.14**
Eli heard the sound of the outcry, he said, "What is this uproar?" Then the man 2 Sam 1.4
came quickly and told Eli. 15 Now Eli was ninety-eight years old and his eyes were **4.15** Gen 27.1
set, so that he could not see. 1 Sam 3.2

2. War with the Philistines

The Philistines capture the ark

16 The man said to Eli, "I have just come from the battle; I fled from the battle
today." He said, "How did it go, my son?" 17 The messenger replied, "Israel has **4.17**
fled before the Philistines, and there has also been a great slaughter among the 1 Sam 2.34 4.11
troops; your two sons also, Hophni and Phinehas, are dead, and the ark of God has
been captured." 18 When he mentioned the ark of God, Eli[j] fell over backward
from his seat by the side of the gate; and his neck was broken and he died, for he
was an old man, and heavy. He had judged Israel forty years.

19 Now his daughter-in-law, the wife of Phinehas, was pregnant, about to give
birth. When she heard the news that the ark of God was captured, and that her
father-in-law and her husband were dead, she bowed and gave birth; for her labor
pains overwhelmed her. 20 As she was about to die, the women attending her said **4.20**
to her, "Do not be afraid, for you have borne a son." But she did not answer or give Gen 35.17,18
heed. 21 She named the child Ichabod, meaning, "The glory has departed from Is- **4.21**
rael," because the ark of God had been captured and because of her father-in-law 1 Sam 14.3 Ps 78.61
and her husband. 22 She said, "The glory has departed from Israel, for the ark of 106.19,20
God has been captured."

God punishes the Philistines

5 When the Philistines captured the ark of God, they brought it from Ebenezer to **5.1**
Ashdod; 2 then the Philistines took the ark of God and brought it into the house 1 Sam 4.11,17
of Dagon and placed it beside Dagon. 3 When the people of Ashdod rose early the **5.3**
next day, there was Dagon, fallen on his face to the ground before the ark of the Isa 19.1 46.1,2,7
LORD. So they took Dagon and put him back in his place. 4 But when they rose early
on the next morning, Dagon had fallen on his face to the ground before the ark of
the LORD, and the head of Dagon and both his hands were lying cut off upon the
threshold; only the trunk of[k] Dagon was left to him. 5 This is why the priests of
Dagon and all who enter the house of Dagon do not step on the threshold of Dagon **5.6**
in Ashdod to this day. Ex 9.3 Deut 28.27

6 The hand of the LORD was heavy upon the people of Ashdod, and he terrified 1 Sam 6.4,5
and struck them with tumors, both in Ashdod and in its territory. 7 And when the **5.7**
inhabitants of Ashdod saw how things were, they said, "The ark of the God of Ex 8.8; 12.33 1 Sam 6.20

[j] Heb *he* [k] Heb lacks *the trunk of*

4.18 Eli was Israel's judge and high priest. His death marked the end of the dark period of the judges when most of the nation ignored God. Although Samuel was also a judge, his career saw the transition from Israel's rule by judges to the nation's monarchy. He began the great revival that Israel would experience for the next century. The Bible does not say who became the next high priest (Samuel was not eligible because he was not a direct descendant of Aaron), but Samuel acted as high priest at this time by offering the important sacrifices throughout Israel.

4.19–22 This incident illustrates the spiritual darkness and decline of Israel. This young boy, Ichabod, was supposed to succeed his father Phinehas in the priesthood, but his father had been killed because he was an evil man who desecrated the tabernacle. The terror of God's leaving his people overshadowed the joy of childbirth. When sin dominates our lives, even God-given joys and pleasures seem empty.

5.1ff Dagon was the chief god of the Philistines, whom they believed sent rain and assured a bountiful harvest. But the Philistines, like most of their heathen neighbors, worshiped many gods. The more gods they could have on their side, the more secure they felt. That was why they wanted the ark. They thought that if it helped the Israelites, it could help them too. But when the people living nearby began to get sick and die, the Philistines realized that the ark was not a good omen. It was a source of greater power than they had ever seen—power they could not control.

5.6, 7 Although the Philistines had just witnessed a great victory by Israel's God over their idol, Dagon, they didn't act upon that insight until they were afflicted with tumors (possibly bubonic plague). Similarly, many people don't respond to biblical truth until they experience pain. Are you willing to listen to God for truth's sake, or do you turn to him only when you are hurting?

5.7 The Philistines thought they had defeated God because they had beaten Israel and captured the ark. They soon learned that no one defeats God. Their sweet victory turned sour as God began to destroy them with a plague.

Israel must not remain with us; for his hand is heavy on us and on our god Dagon."
[8]So they sent and gathered together all the lords of the Philistines, and said, "What
shall we do with the ark of the God of Israel?" The inhabitants of Gath replied, "Let
the ark of God be moved on to us."[l] So they moved the ark of the God of Israel to
5.9 1 Sam 7.13; 12.15 Gath.[m] [9]But after they had brought it to Gath,[n] the hand of the LORD was against
the city, causing a very great panic; he struck the inhabitants of the city, both young
5.10 Josh 15.45; Judg 1.18; 2 Kgs 1.2 and old, so that tumors broke out on them. [10]So they sent the ark of the God of
Israel[o] to Ekron. But when the ark of God came to Ekron, the people of Ekron
cried out, "Why[p] have they brought around to us[q] the ark of the God of Israel to

[l] Gk Compare Q Ms: MT *They answered, "Let the ark of the God of Israel be brought around to Gath."* [m] Gk: Heb lacks *to Gath* [n] Q Ms: MT lacks *to Gath* [o] Q Ms Gk: MT lacks *of Israel* [p] Q Ms Gk: MT lacks *Why* [q] Heb *me*

Eli was one Old Testament person with a very modern problem. The recognition and respect he earned in public did not extend to his handling of his private affairs. He may have been an excellent priest, but he was a poor parent. His sons brought him grief and ruin. He lacked two important qualities needed for effective parental discipline: firm resolve and corrective action.

Eli responded to situations rather than solving them. But even his responses tended to be weak. God pointed out his sons' errors, but Eli did little to correct them. The contrast between God's dealing with Eli and Eli's dealing with his sons is clear—God gave warning, spelled out the consequences of disobedience, and then acted. Eli only warned. Children need to learn that their parents' words and actions go together. Both love and discipline must be spoken as well as acted out.

But Eli had another problem. He was more concerned with the symbols of his religion than with the God they represented. For Eli, the ark of the covenant had become a relic to be protected rather than a reminder of the Protector. His faith shifted from the Creator to the created.

It may be easier to worship things we can see, whether buildings, people, or Scripture itself, but such tangible things have no power in themselves. This book you hold is either merely a respectable religious relic, or it is the sharp and effective word of God. Your attitude toward it is largely shaped by your relationship to the God from whom it comes. A relic or antique has to be carefully stored away; God's Word has to be used and obeyed. Which attitude accurately describes your approach to the word of God?

Strengths and accomplishments:
- Judged Israel for 40 years
- Spoke with Hannah, the mother of Samuel, and assured her of God's blessing
- Reared and trained Samuel, the greatest judge of Israel

Weaknesses and mistakes:
- Failed to discipline his sons or correct them when they sinned
- Tended to react to situations rather than take decisive action
- Saw the ark of the covenant as a relic to be cherished, rather than as a symbol of God's presence with Israel

Lessons from his life:
- Parents need to discipline their children responsibly
- Life is more than simply reacting; it demands action
- Past victories cannot substitute for present trust

Vital statistics:
- Where: Shiloh
- Occupation: High priest and judge of Israel
- Relatives: Sons: Hophni and Phinehas
- Contemporary: Samuel

Key verses:
"Then the Lord said to Samuel, 'See, I am about to do something in Israel that will make both ears of anyone who hears of it tingle. On that day I will fulfill against Eli all that I have spoken concerning his house, from beginning to end. For I have told him that I am about to punish his house forever, for the iniquity that he knew, because his sons were blaspheming God, and he did not restrain them. Therefore I swear to the house of Eli that the iniquity of Eli's house shall not be expiated by sacrifice or offering forever' " (1 Samuel 3.11–14).

His story is told in 1 Samuel 1—4. He is also mentioned in 1 Kings 2.26, 27.

5.8 The Philistines were governed by five rulers, or lords. Each lord lived in a different city – Gath, Ekron, Ashdod, Ashkelon, Gaza. The ark was taken to three of these capital cities, but in each case it brought great trouble and chaos to the citizens.

kill us[r] and our[s] people?" 11 They sent therefore and gathered together all the lords
of the Philistines, and said, "Send away the ark of the God of Israel, and let it return
to its own place, that it may not kill us and our people." For there was a deathly
panic[t] throughout the whole city. The hand of God was very heavy there; 12 those
who did not die were stricken with tumors, and the cry of the city went up to
heaven.

The Philistines return the ark

6 The ark of the LORD was in the country of the Philistines seven months. 2 Then 6.1
the Philistines called for the priests and the diviners and said, "What shall we 1 Sam 5.1
do with the ark of the LORD? Tell us what we should send with it to its place." 6.2 Gen 41.8
3 They said, "If you send away the ark of the God of Israel, do not send it empty, Dan 2.1; 5.7
but by all means return him a guilt offering. Then you will be healed and will be 6.3
ransomed;[u] will not his hand then turn from you?" 4 And they said, "What is the Lev 5.15,16 7.1-7
guilt offering that we shall return to him?" They answered, "Five gold tumors and 1 Sam 6.9
five gold mice, according to the number of the lords of the Philistines; for the same
plague was upon all of you and upon your lords. 5 So you must make images of your
tumors and images of your mice that ravage the land, and give glory to the God of
Israel; perhaps he will lighten his hand on you and your gods and your land. 6 Why 6.6
should you harden your hearts as the Egyptians and Pharaoh hardened their hearts? Ex 8.15,31,32 12.31
After he had made fools of them, did they not let the people go, and they departed?
7 Now then, get ready a new cart and two milch cows that have never borne a yoke, 6.7
and yoke the cows to the cart, but take their calves home, away from them. 8 Take Deut 21.3 2 Sam 6.3
the ark of the LORD and place it on the cart, and put in a box at its side the figures
of gold, which you are returning to him as a guilt offering. Then send it off, and let
it go its way. 9 And watch; if it goes up on the way to its own land, to Beth- 6.9
shemesh, then it is he who has done us this great harm; but if not, then we shall Josh 15.10,11 Judg 1.33
know that it is not his hand that struck us; it happened to us by chance." 1 Sam 6.3
10 The men did so; they took two milch cows and yoked them to the cart, and
shut up their calves at home. 11 They put the ark of the LORD on the cart, and the box 6.11
with the gold mice and the images of their tumors. 12 The cows went straight in the 2 Sam 6.3 1 Chron 13.7
direction of Beth-shemesh along one highway, lowing as they went; they turned
neither to the right nor to the left, and the lords of the Philistines went after them as
far as the border of Beth-shemesh.
13 Now the people of Beth-shemesh were reaping their wheat harvest in the
valley. When they looked up and saw the ark, they went with rejoicing to meet it.[v]
14 The cart came into the field of Joshua of Beth-shemesh, and stopped there. A 6.14
large stone was there; so they split up the wood of the cart and offered the cows as Judg 6.26 1 Kgs 18.30
a burnt offering to the LORD. 15 The Levites took down the ark of the LORD and the 2 Sam 24.22
box that was beside it, in which were the gold objects, and set them upon the large 6.15
stone. Then the people of Beth-shemesh offered burnt offerings and presented sac- Josh 3.2-4

[r] Heb *me* [s] Heb *my* [t] Q Ms reads *a panic from the* LORD [u] Q Ms Gk: MT *and it will be known to you* [v] Gk: Heb *rejoiced to see it*

6.3 What was this guilt offering supposed to accomplish? This was a normal reaction to trouble in the Canaanite religion. The Philistines thought their problems were the result of their gods being angry. They recognized their guilt in taking the ark and now were trying everything they could to placate Israel's God. The diviners (6.2) probably helped choose the gift they thought would placate Jehovah. But the offering consisted of images of tumors and mice, not the kind of guilt offering prescribed in God's laws (Leviticus 5.14–6.7; 7.1–10). How easy it is to design our own methods of acknowledging God rather than serving him in the way he requires.

6.7–12 The Philistine priests and diviners devised a test to see if God was really the one who had caused all their recent troubles. Two cows who had just given birth ("milch cows") were hitched to a cart and sent toward Israel's border carrying the ark of the covenant. For a cow to leave her calf, she would have to go against all her motherly instincts. Only God, who has power over the natural order, could cause this to happen. God sent the cows to Israel, not to pass the Philistines' test, but to show them his mighty power.

6.9 The Philistines acknowledged the existence of the Hebrew God, but only as one of many deities whose favor they sought. Thinking of God in this way made it easy for them to ignore his demand that people worship him alone. Many people "worship" God this way. They see God as just one ingredient in a successful life. But God is far more than an ingredient—he is the source of life itself. Are you a "Philistine," seeing God's favor as only an ingredient of the good life?

6.15 The men of Beth-shemesh sacrificed a burnt offering to God. Wherever there is a burnt offering in Scripture, it represents a renewing of a person's relationship with God. Although some of the people of Beth-shemesh later mishandled the ark (6.19), when they first received it, they rededicated their lives to God. They wanted to start over with him as their leader.

rifices on that day to the LORD. 16 When the five lords of the Philistines saw it, they
returned that day to Ekron.

6.17 1 Sam 6.4,5

17 These are the gold tumors, which the Philistines returned as a guilt offering
to the LORD: one for Ashdod, one for Gaza, one for Ashkelon, one for Gath, one for

6.18 Num 4.1,15,20 Deut 3.5 2 Sam 6.7

Ekron; 18 also the gold mice, according to the number of all the cities of the Philistines belonging to the five lords, both fortified cities and unwalled villages. The
great stone, beside which they set down the ark of the LORD, is a witness to this day
in the field of Joshua of Beth-shemesh.

19 The descendants of Jeconiah did not rejoice with the people of Beth-
shemesh when they greeted[w] the ark of the LORD; and he killed seventy men of
them.[x] The people mourned because the LORD had made a great slaughter among

6.20 Lev 11.44,45 2 Sam 6.9

the people. 20 Then the people of Beth-shemesh said, "Who is able to stand before
the LORD, this holy God? To whom shall he go so that we may be rid of him?" 21 So

6.21 Josh 15.9,60

they sent messengers to the inhabitants of Kiriath-jearim, saying, "The Philistines

7.1 2 Sam 6.3,4

7 have returned the ark of the LORD. Come down and take it up to you." 1 And
the people of Kiriath-jearim came and took up the ark of the LORD, and
brought it to the house of Abinadab on the hill. They consecrated his son, Eleazar,
to have charge of the ark of the LORD.

7.2 Judg 2.3

2 From the day that the ark was lodged at Kiriath-jearim, a long time passed,
some twenty years, and all the house of Israel lamented[y] after the LORD.

Samuel becomes a judge

7.3 Deut 6.13; 13.4 Josh 24.14,23 Judg 2.12-14 2 Chron 19.13 Joel 2.12-14

3 Then Samuel said to all the house of Israel, "If you are returning to the LORD
with all your heart, then put away the foreign gods and the Astartes from among
you. Direct your heart to the LORD, and serve him only, and he will deliver you out
of the hand of the Philistines." 4 So Israel put away the Baals and the Astartes, and

7.5 1 Sam 12.17-19 1 Kgs 18.24

they served the LORD only.
5 Then Samuel said, "Gather all Israel at Mizpah, and I will pray to the LORD

[w] Gk: Heb *And he killed some of the people of Beth-shemesh, because they looked into* [x] Heb *killed seventy men, fifty thousand men* [y] Meaning of Heb uncertain

---

6.19 Why were people killed for looking into the ark? The Israelites had made an idol of the ark. They had tried to harness God's power, to use it for their own purposes (victory in battle). He had warned them not to even look at the sacred sanctuary objects in the most holy place or they would die (Numbers 4.20). Only Levites were allowed to move the ark. Because of their disobedience, God carried out his promised judgment.

God could not allow the people to think they could use his power for their own ends. He could not permit them to disregard his warnings and come into his presence lightly. He did not want the cycle of disrespect, disobedience, and defeat to start all over again. God did not kill the men of Beth-shemesh to be cruel. He killed them because overlooking their presumptuous sin would lead the whole nation of Israel into overlooking God.

7.1 The ark was taken to Kiriath-jearim, a city near the battlefield, for safekeeping, and Eleazar was given the task of caring for it. Why wasn't it taken back to the tabernacle at Shiloh? Shiloh had probably been captured and destroyed by the Philistines in an earlier battle (4.1–18; Jeremiah 26.2–6) because of the evil deeds of its priests (2.12–17). The tabernacle and its furniture were apparently saved, because we read that it was set up in Nob during Saul's reign (21.1–6) and in Gibeon during the reigns of David and Solomon (1 Chronicles 16.39; 21.29, 30; 2 Chronicles 1). Shiloh, however, is never again mentioned in the historical books of the Old Testament. Samuel's new home became Ramah (7.15–17; 8.4), his birthplace (further evidence of Shiloh's destruction).

7.2, 3 Sorrow gripped Israel for 20 years. The ark was put away like an unwanted box in an attic, and it seemed as if the Lord had abandoned his people. Samuel, now a grown man, roused them to action by saying that if they were truly sorry, they should do something about it. How easy it is for us to complain about our problems, even to God, while we refuse to act, change, and do what he requires. We don't even take the advice he has already given us. Do you ever feel as if God has abandoned you? Check to see if there is anything he has already told you to do. You may not be able to receive new guidance until you have acted on his previous directions.

7.3 Samuel told the people they had to return to the Lord and "serve him only." This kind of commitment means setting your mind on a course of action and not backing out. If you have made a decision to follow God, don't allow excuses, distractions, or second thoughts to deter you.

7.3 Samuel urged the Israelites to get rid of their foreign gods—that is, idols. Idols today are much more subtle than gods of wood and stone, but they are just as dangerous. Whatever holds first place in our lives or controls us is our god. Money, success, material goods, pride, or anything else can be an idol if it takes the place of God in our lives. The Lord alone is worthy of our service and worship, and we must let nothing rival him.

7.3, 4 Baal was the son of El, chief deity of the Canaanites. Baal was regarded as the god of thunder and rain, and thus he controlled vegetation and agriculture. Astarte was a goddess of love and war (she was called Ishtar in Babylon and Aphrodite in Greece). She represented fertility. The Canaanites believed that by the sexual union of Baal and Astarte, the earth was magically rejuvenated and made fertile.

7.5 Mizpah held special significance for the Israelite nation. It was there that the Israelites had gathered to mobilize against the tribe of Benjamin (Judges 20.1). Samuel was appointed to be judge there (7.6), and Saul, Israel's first king, was identified and presented to the people there (10.17ff).

for you." 6 So they gathered at Mizpah, and drew water and poured it out before the 7.6
LORD. They fasted that day, and said, "We have sinned against the LORD." And Judg 10.10 Neh 9.1
Samuel judged the people of Israel at Mizpah. Lam 2.19
7 When the Philistines heard that the people of Israel had gathered at Mizpah, 7.7
the lords of the Philistines went up against Israel. And when the people of Israel 1 Sam 13.6
heard of it they were afraid of the Philistines. 8 The people of Israel said to Samuel, 7.8
"Do not cease to cry out to the LORD our God for us, and pray that he may save us 1 Sam 12.19 Isa 37.4
from the hand of the Philistines." 9 So Samuel took a sucking lamb and offered it as 7.9
a whole burnt offering to the LORD; Samuel cried out to the LORD for Israel, and the Lev 22.26,27 Jer 15.1
LORD answered him. 10 As Samuel was offering up the burnt offering, the Philis- 7.10
tines drew near to attack Israel; but the LORD thundered with a mighty voice that 1 Sam 2.10 2 Sam 22.14
day against the Philistines and threw them into confusion; and they were routed Ps 18.14
before Israel. 11 And the men of Israel went out of Mizpah and pursued the Philistines, and struck them down as far as beyond Beth-car. 7.12
12 Then Samuel took a stone and set it up between Mizpah and Jeshanah,[z] and Gen 28.18
named it Ebenezer;[a] for he said, "Thus far the LORD has helped us." 13 So the 35.13-15 Josh 4.9; 24.26
Philistines were subdued and did not again enter the territory of Israel; the hand of 7.13
the LORD was against the Philistines all the days of Samuel. 14 The towns that the 1 Sam 13.5
Philistines had taken from Israel were restored to Israel, from Ekron to Gath; and 7.15 1 Sam 7.6
Israel recovered their territory from the hand of the Philistines. There was peace 12.11
also between Israel and the Amorites. 7.16 Gen 28.19
15 Samuel judged Israel all the days of his life. 16 He went on a circuit year by Josh 5.8; 11.1
year to Bethel, Gilgal, and Mizpah; and he judged Israel in all these places. 17 Then 1 Sam 7.5 7.17
he would come back to Ramah, for his home was there; he administered justice 1 Sam 1.1,19 2.11; 15.34
there to Israel, and built there an altar to the LORD. 16.13

B. SAMUEL AND SAUL (8.1—15.35)

Samuel judges Israel well, saves them from the Philistines, and leads them back to God. But when he retires, the nation does not want another judge. Instead they demand to be given a king in order to be like the nations around them. Although God is unhappy with their request, he tells Samuel to anoint Saul as Israel's first king. Saul is a skillful soldier who successfully leads the nation into many battles against their enemies. But in God's eyes Saul is a failure because he constantly disobeys and does things his own way. God eventually rejected Saul as king. Sometimes we want to go our own way rather than follow the ways of God. This will always end in ruin as it did for Saul.

1. Saul becomes king of Israel

The people demand a king

8 When Samuel became old, he made his sons judges over Israel. 2 The name of 8.1
his firstborn son was Joel, and the name of his second, Abijah; they were Deut 16.18,19
judges in Beer-sheba. 3 Yet his sons did not follow in his ways, but turned aside
after gain; they took bribes and perverted justice.

[z] Gk Syr: Heb *Shen* [a] That is *Stone of Help*

7.6 Pouring water on the ground "before the Lord" was a sign of repentance for sin, turning from idols, and determining to obey God alone.

7.6 Samuel became the last in the long line of Israel's judges, a line that began when Israel first conquered the promised land. For a list of these judges see the chart in Judges 2. A judge was both a political and a religious leader. God was Israel's true leader, while the judge was to be God's spokesman to the people and administrator of justice throughout the land. While some of Israel's judges relied more on their own judgment than on God's, Samuel's obedience and dedication to God made him one of the better judges in Israel's history. (For more on Samuel as a judge, see the note on 4.18.)

7.12 The Israelites had great difficulty with the Philistines, but God rescued them. In response, the people set up a stone as a memorial of God's great deliverance. During tough times, we may need to remember the crucial turning points in our past to help us through the present. Memorials can help us remember God's past victories and gain confidence and strength for the present.

7.14 In Joshua's time, the Amorites were a powerful tribe occupying the east side of the Jordan River opposite the Dead Sea. In the context of this verse, however, *Amorites* is another general name for all the inhabitants of Canaan who were not Israelites.

7.15, 16 Samuel was established as Israel's judge, assuring justice for the people as God's representative. He would travel from town to town administering justice.

8.1–3 By this time, Samuel was an old man. He appointed his sons to be judges over Israel in his place, but they turned out to be corrupt, much like Eli's sons (2.12). We don't know why Samuel's sons were bad, but we do know that Eli was held responsible for his own sons' corruption (2.29–34).

It is impossible to know if Samuel was a bad parent. His children were old enough to be on their own. We need to be careful not to blame ourselves for the sins of our children. On the other

8.4 1 Sam 7.17
8.5 Deut 17.14,15 1 Sam 12.19
8.6 1 Sam 15.11

4 Then all the elders of Israel gathered together and came to Samuel at Ramah,
5 and said to him, "You are old and your sons do not follow in your ways; appoint
for us, then, a king to govern us, like other nations." 6 But the thing displeased
Samuel when they said, "Give us a king to govern us." Samuel prayed to the LORD,
7 and the LORD said to Samuel, "Listen to the voice of the people in all that they say

---

SAMUEL

We often wonder about the childhoods of great people. We have little information about the early years of most of the people mentioned in the Bible. One delightful exception is Samuel; he came as a result of God's answer to Hannah's fervent prayer for a child. (In fact, the name *Samuel* comes from the Hebrew expression, "asked of God.") God shaped Samuel from the start. Like Moses, Samuel was called to fill many different roles: judge, priest, prophet, counselor, and God's man at a turning point in the history of Israel. God worked through Samuel because Samuel was willing to be one thing: God's servant.

Samuel showed that those whom God finds faithful in small things will be trusted with greater things. He grew up assisting the high priest (Eli) in the tabernacle until God directed him to other responsibilities. God was able to use Samuel because he was genuinely dedicated to God.

Samuel moved ahead because he was listening to God's directions. Too often we ask God to control our lives without making us give up the goals for which we strive. We ask God to help us get where *we* want to go. The first step in correcting this tendency is to turn over both the control and the destination of our lives to him. The second step is to do what we *already* know God requires of us. The third step is to listen for further direction from his Word—God's map for life.

Strengths and accomplishments:
- Used by God to assist Israel's transition from a loosely governed tribal people to a monarchy
- Anointed the first two kings of Israel
- Was the last and most effective of Israel's judges
- Is listed in the Hall of Faith in Hebrews 11

Weakness and mistake:
- Was unable to lead his sons into a close relationship with God

Lessons from his life:
- The significance of what people accomplish is directly related to their relationship with God
- The kind of person we are is more important than anything we might do

Vital statistics:
- Where: Ephraim
- Occupation: Judge, prophet, priest
- Relatives: Mother: Hannah. Father: Elkanah. Sons: Joel and Abiah
- Contemporaries: Eli, Saul, David

Key verses:
"As Samuel grew up, the Lord was with him and let none of his words fall to the ground. And all Israel from Dan to Beer-sheba knew that Samuel was a trustworthy prophet of the Lord" (1 Samuel 3.19, 20).

His story is told in 1 Samuel 1—28. He is also mentioned in Psalm 99.6; Jeremiah 15.1; Acts 3.24; 13.20; Hebrews 11.32.

---

hand, parenthood is an awesome responsibility, and nothing is more important than molding and shaping the lives of our children.

If your grown children are not following God, realize that you can't control them any longer. Don't blame yourself for something for which you can no longer be responsible. But if your children are still in your care, know that what you do and teach can have a profound effect upon your children that will last the rest of their lives.

8.4–9 Israel wanted a king for several reasons: (1) Samuel's sons were not fit to lead Israel. (2) The 12 tribes of Israel continually had problems working together because each tribe had its own leader and territory. It was hoped that a king would unite the tribes into one nation and one army. (3) The people wanted to be like the neighboring nations. This is exactly what God didn't want. Having a king would make it easy to forget that God was their real leader. It was not wrong for Israel to want a king; God had mentioned the possibility in Deuteronomy 17.14–20. Yet God was disappointed because the people were rejecting him as their leader. The Israelites wanted laws, an army, and a human monarch in the place of God. They wanted to run the nation through human strength, even though only God's strength could make them flourish in the hostile land of Canaan.

8.5, 6 Israel's 12 tribes were weak and disorganized. The people attributed this problem to the lack of a united army, central capital, and ruling authority. They clamored for a king, thinking that a new system of government would bring about a change in the nation. But since their basic problem was disobedience to God, their other problems would only continue under the new administration. What they needed was a unified faith, not a uniform rule.

Had the Israelites submitted to God's leadership, they would have thrived beyond their expectations (Deuteronomy 28.1). Our obedience is weak if we ask God to lead our family or personal life but continue to live by the world's standards and values. If we think that believing in God pertains only to worship, we may end up rejecting his leadership in practical areas of life.

to you; for they have not rejected you, but they have rejected me from being king
over them. 8 Just as they have done to me,[b] from the day I brought them up out of
Egypt to this day, forsaking me and serving other gods, so also they are doing to
you. 9 Now then, listen to their voice; only—you shall solemnly warn them, and
show them the ways of the king who shall reign over them."

10 So Samuel reported all the words of the LORD to the people who were asking
him for a king. 11 He said, "These will be the ways of the king who will reign over
you: he will take your sons and appoint them to his chariots and to be his horsemen,
and to run before his chariots; 12 and he will appoint for himself commanders of
thousands and commanders of fifties, and some to plow his ground and to reap his
harvest, and to make his implements of war and the equipment of his chariots. 13 He
will take your daughters to be perfumers and cooks and bakers. 14 He will take the
best of your fields and vineyards and olive orchards and give them to his courtiers.
15 He will take one-tenth of your grain and of your vineyards and give it to his
officers and his courtiers. 16 He will take your male and female slaves, and the best
of your cattle[c] and donkeys, and put them to his work. 17 He will take one-tenth of
your flocks, and you shall be his slaves. 18 And in that day you will cry out because
of your king, whom you have chosen for yourselves; but the LORD will not answer
you in that day."

19 But the people refused to listen to the voice of Samuel; they said, "No! but
we are determined to have a king over us, 20 so that we also may be like other
nations, and that our king may govern us and go out before us and fight our battles." 21 When Samuel had heard all the words of the people, he repeated them in
the ears of the LORD. 22 The LORD said to Samuel, "Listen to their voice and set a
king over them." Samuel then said to the people of Israel, "Each of you return
home."

Saul hunts for his father's donkeys

9 There was a man of Benjamin whose name was Kish son of Abiel son of Zeror
son of Becorath son of Aphiah, a Benjaminite, a man of wealth. 2 He had a son
whose name was Saul, a handsome young man. There was not a man among the
people of Israel more handsome than he; he stood head and shoulders above everyone else.

8.7 Ex 16.8
8.8 Ex 14.11; 16.3 Deut 9.24 Judg 2.1,2 1 Sam 10.18,19
8.11 Deut 17.14-20 1 Sam 10.24 14.52 2 Sam 15.1 1 Kgs 1.5
8.12 1 Sam 22.7 1 Kgs 4.7
8.14 1 Sam 22.7 1 Kgs 21.7 Ezek 46.18
8.18 Job 27.9 Prov 1.25-28 Isa 8.21 Mic 3.4
8.19 1 Sam 8.5
9.1 1 Chron 8.33 9.36-39
9.2 2 Sam 14.25

[b] Gk: Heb lacks *to me* [c] Gk: Heb *young men*

8.18 Samuel warned the people that they would regret their decision to have a king. Israel (including the future northern and southern kingdoms) eventually had 41 kings over a period of 450 years. Only 11 kings followed God at all, and seven of those forgot God at the end of their reigns. It was the spiritual rebellion of the kings that paved the way for the later captivities by foreign nations (2 Kings 17; 25). Israel would learn that a human leader was not the complete answer to their problems. Only God, their true leader, and faith in him could bring the reform they sought.

8.19, 20 Samuel carefully explained all the negative consequences of having a king, but the Israelites refused to listen. When you have an important decision to make, weigh the positives and negatives carefully, considering everyone who might be affected by your choice. When you want something badly enough, it is difficult to see the potential problems. But don't discount the negatives. Unless you have a plan to handle each one, they will cause you great difficulty later.

8.19, 20 Israel was called to be a holy nation, separate from and unique among all others (Leviticus 20.26). The Israelites' motive in asking for a king was to be like the nations around them. This was in total opposition to God's original plan. It was not their desire for a king that was wrong, but their reasons for wanting a king.

Often we let others' values and actions dictate our attitudes and behavior. Have you ever made a wrong choice because you wanted to be like everyone else? Be careful that the values of your friends or "heroes" don't pull you away from what God says is right. When God's people want to be like unbelievers, they are heading for spiritual disaster.

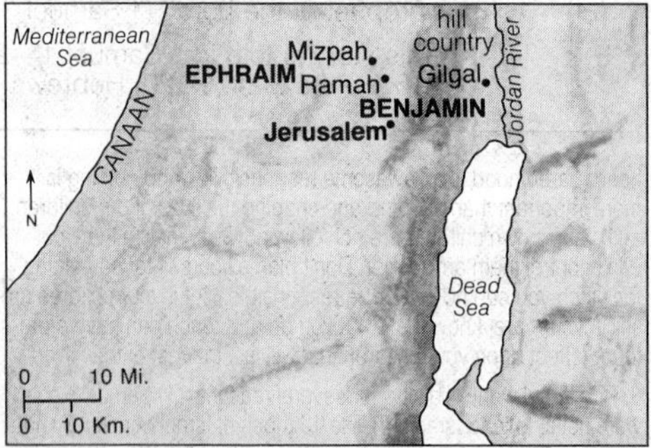

SAUL CHOSEN AS KING Saul and a servant searched for their lost donkeys in the hill country of Ephraim and the territory of Benjamin. They went to Ramah, looking for help from Samuel the prophet. While Saul was there, he found himself unexpectedly anointed by Samuel as Israel's first king. Samuel called Israel together at Mizpah to tell them God's choice for their king.

3 Now the donkeys of Kish, Saul's father, had strayed. So Kish said to his son
Saul, "Take one of the boys with you; go and look for the donkeys." 4 He passed
through the hill country of Ephraim and passed through the land of Shalishah, but
they did not find them. And they passed through the land of Shaalim, but they were
not there. Then he passed through the land of Benjamin, but they did not find them.
5 When they came to the land of Zuph, Saul said to the boy who was with him,
"Let us turn back, or my father will stop worrying about the donkeys and worry
about us." 6 But he said to him, "There is a man of God in this town; he is a man
held in honor. Whatever he says always comes true. Let us go there now; perhaps
he will tell us about the journey on which we have set out." 7 Then Saul replied to
the boy, "But if we go, what can we bring the man? For the bread in our sacks is
gone, and there is no present to bring to the man of God. What have we?" 8 The boy
answered Saul again, "Here, I have with me a quarter shekel of silver; I will give
it to the man of God, to tell us our way." 9 (Formerly in Israel, anyone who went to
inquire of God would say, "Come, let us go to the seer"; for the one who is now
called a prophet was formerly called a seer.) 10 Saul said to the boy, "Good; come,
let us go." So they went to the town where the man of God was.
11 As they went up the hill to the town, they met some girls coming out to draw
water, and said to them, "Is the seer here?" 12 They answered, "Yes, there he is just
ahead of you. Hurry; he has come just now to the town, because the people have a
sacrifice today at the shrine. 13 As soon as you enter the town, you will find him,
before he goes up to the shrine to eat. For the people will not eat until he comes,
since he must bless the sacrifice; afterward those eat who are invited. Now go up,
for you will meet him immediately." 14 So they went up to the town. As they were
entering the town, they saw Samuel coming out toward them on his way up to the
shrine.
15 Now the day before Saul came, the LORD had revealed to Samuel: 16 "Tomorrow about this time I will send to you a man from the land of Benjamin, and you
shall anoint him to be ruler over my people Israel. He shall save my people from the
hand of the Philistines; for I have seen the suffering of[d] my people, because their

9.3 1 Sam 10.2,14
9.5 1 Sam 1.1
9.6 Deut 18.20,21; 1 Sam 3.19,20; 2 Kgs 5.8
9.7 1 Kgs 14.3; 2 Kgs 5.15; 8.8,9; Ezek 13.19
9.9 Ex 2.16; 1 Chron 26.28
9.12 Lk 9.16; Jn 6.11
9.15 1 Sam 15.1; Acts 13.21
9.16 Ex 3.7,9; Ps 106.44

[d] Gk: Heb lacks *the suffering of*

THE PROBLEMS WITH HAVING A KING

Problems (warned by Samuel)	*Reference*	*Fulfillment*
Conscripting young men into the army	8.11, 12	14.52—"When Saul saw any strong or valiant warrior, he took him into his service."
Having the young men "run before his [the king's] chariots"	8.11	2 Samuel 15.1—"Absalom got himself a chariot and horses, and fifty men to run ahead of him."
Making slave laborers	8.12, 17	2 Chronicles 2.17, 18—Solomon conscripted laborers to build the temple.
Taking the best of your fields and vineyards	8.14	1 Kings 21.5–16—Jezebel stole Naboth's vineyard.
Using your property for his personal gain	8.14–16	1 Kings 9.10–15—Solomon gave away 20 cities to Hiram of Tyre.
Demanding a tenth of your harvest and flocks	8.15, 17	1 Kings 12.1–16—Rehoboam was going to demand heavier taxation than Solomon.

9.3 Saul was sent by his father on an important mission – to find their stray donkeys. Donkeys were all-purpose animals, the "pick-up trucks" of Bible times. Used for transportation, hauling, and farming, they were considered necessities. Even the poorest family owned one. To own many donkeys was a sign of wealth, and to lose them was a disaster. Saul's father was wealthy, and his many donkeys were evidence of that wealth.

9.3ff Often we think that events just happen to us, but as we learn from this story about Saul, God may use common occurrences to lead us where he wants. It is important to evaluate all situations as potential "divine appointments" designed to shape our lives. Think of all the good and bad circumstances that have affected you lately. Can you see God's purpose in them? Perhaps he is building a certain quality in you or leading you to serve him in a new area.

9.6 The city where the servant said the prophet lived was probably Ramah, where Samuel moved after the Philistine battle near Shiloh (7.17). Saul's lack of knowledge about Samuel showed his ignorance of spiritual matters. Saul and Samuel even lived in the same territory – Benjamin.

outcry has come to me." 17 When Samuel saw Saul, the LORD told him, "Here is the 9.17
man of whom I spoke to you. He it is who shall rule over my people." 18 Then Saul 1 Sam 10.1 12.13; 16.12
approached Samuel inside the gate, and said, "Tell me, please, where is the house
of the seer?" 19 Samuel answered Saul, "I am the seer; go up before me to the
shrine, for today you shall eat with me, and in the morning I will let you go and will
tell you all that is on your mind. 20 As for your donkeys that were lost three days 9.20
ago, give no further thought to them, for they have been found. And on whom is all 1 Sam 9.6 1 Sam 10.16
Israel's desire fixed, if not on you and on all your ancestral house?" 21 Saul an- 9.21
swered, "I am only a Benjaminite, from the least of the tribes of Israel, and my Judg 20.46-48 1 Sam 15.17
family is the humblest of all the families of the tribe of Benjamin. Why then have
you spoken to me in this way?"

22 Then Samuel took Saul and his servant-boy and brought them into the hall,
and gave them a place at the head of those who had been invited, of whom there
were about thirty. 23 And Samuel said to the cook, "Bring the portion I gave you, 9.23
the one I asked you to put aside." 24 The cook took up the thigh and what went with Gen 43.34
it[e] and set them before Saul. Samuel said, "See, what was kept is set before you.
Eat; for it is set[f] before you at the appointed time, so that you might eat with the
guests."[g]

So Saul ate with Samuel that day. 25 When they came down from the shrine into 9.25
the town, a bed was spread for Saul[h] on the roof, and he lay down to sleep.[i] Deut 22.8 2 Kgs 4.10
26 Then at the break of dawn[j] Samuel called to Saul upon the roof, "Get up, so that Neh 8.16
I may send you on your way." Saul got up, and both he and Samuel went out into Acts 10.9,10
the street.

Samuel anoints Saul to be king

27 As they were going down to the outskirts of the town, Samuel said to Saul,
"Tell the boy to go on before us, and when he has passed on, stop here yourself for
10 a while, that I may make known to you the word of God." 1 Samuel took a 10.1
vial of oil and poured it on his head, and kissed him; he said, "The LORD has Ex 30.22-25 Lev 8.12
anointed you ruler over his people Israel. You shall reign over the people of the 1 Sam 9.16 16.13; 26.9
LORD and you will save them from the hand of their enemies all around. Now this 2 Sam 1.14
shall be the sign to you that the LORD has anointed you ruler[k] over his heritage:
2 When you depart from me today you will meet two men by Rachel's tomb in the 10.2
territory of Benjamin at Zelzah; they will say to you, 'The donkeys that you went Gen 35.19; 48.7
to seek are found, and now your father has stopped worrying about them and is
worrying about you, saying: What shall I do about my son?' 3 Then you shall go on 10.3
from there further and come to the oak of Tabor; three men going up to God at Gen 28.16,22 35.1,3,7
Bethel will meet you there, one carrying three kids, another carrying three loaves
of bread, and another carrying a skin of wine. 4 They will greet you and give you

[e] Meaning of Heb uncertain [f] Q Ms Gk: MT *it was kept* [g] Cn: Heb *it was kept for you, saying, I have invited the people* [h] Gk: Heb *and he spoke with Saul* [i] Gk: Heb lacks *and he lay down to sleep* [j] Gk: Heb *and they arose early and at break of dawn* [k] Gk: Heb lacks *over his people Israel. You shall . . . anointed you ruler*

9.18–21 Saul was unaware of what God was going to do with his life. He was so intent on finding his lost animals that he was slow to grasp God's new role for him and all its opportunities. Our problems and needs can make our attitude negative and pessimistic. Evaluate your situation in light of God's love for you and his resources. Don't let your problems rob you of God's opportunities for you.

9.21 "Why then have you spoken to me in this way?" Saul's outburst reveals a problem he would face repeatedly—inferiority. Like a leaf tossed about by the wind, Saul vacillated between his feelings and his convictions. Everything he said and did was selfish because he was worried about himself. For example, Saul said his family was "the humblest" in the "least" tribe in Israel, but 9.1 says his father was "a man of wealth." (The tribe of Benjamin was the "least" or smallest because they were nearly wiped out as punishment for their immorality—see Judges 19—21.) Saul didn't want to face the responsibility God had given him. In another situation, Saul kept some war booty he shouldn't have and then tried to blame his soldiers (15.21) while claiming that they had really taken it to sacrifice to God (15.15).

Although he had been called by God and had a mission in life, Saul struggled constantly with jealousy, insecurity, arrogance, impulsiveness, and deceit. He did not decide to be wholeheartedly committed to God. Because Saul would not let God's love give rest to his heart, he never became God's man.

10.1 When an Israelite king took office he was not only crowned, he was anointed as well. The coronation was the political act of establishing the king as ruler; the anointing was the religious act of making the king God's representative to the people. A king was always anointed by a priest or a prophet. The special anointing oil was a mixture of olive oil, myrrh, and other expensive spices. It was poured over the king's head to symbolize the presence and power of the Holy Spirit of God in his life. This anointing ceremony was to remind the king of his great responsibility to lead his people by God's wisdom and not his own.

10.5 1 Sam 19.20; 2 Kgs 2.3,5,15; 1 Chron 25.1
10.6 Num 11.25,29; Judg 3.10; 14.6; 1 Sam 16.13; 19.23,24
10.8 1 Sam 7.16; 11.14,15; 13.7; 15.33
10.9 1 Sam 10.6
10.11 1 Sam 19.24; Amos 7.14,15; Mt 13.54-57
10.14 1 Sam 9.3
10.16 1 Sam 9.20

two loaves of bread, which you shall accept from them. 5 After that you shall come
to Gibeath-elohim,[l] at the place where the Philistine garrison is; there, as you
come to the town, you will meet a band of prophets coming down from the shrine
with harp, tambourine, flute, and lyre playing in front of them; they will be in a
prophetic frenzy. 6 Then the spirit of the LORD will possess you, and you will be in
a prophetic frenzy along with them and be turned into a different person. 7 Now
when these signs meet you, do whatever you see fit to do, for God is with you.
8 And you shall go down to Gilgal ahead of me; then I will come down to you to
present burnt offerings and offer sacrifices of well-being. Seven days you shall
wait, until I come to you and show you what you shall do."
9 As he turned away to leave Samuel, God gave him another heart; and all these
signs were fulfilled that day. 10 When they were going from there[m] to Gibeah,[n] a
band of prophets met him; and the spirit of God possessed him, and he fell into a
prophetic frenzy along with them. 11 When all who knew him before saw how he
prophesied with the prophets, the people said to one another, "What has come over
the son of Kish? Is Saul also among the prophets?" 12 A man of the place answered,
"And who is their father?" Therefore it became a proverb, "Is Saul also among the
prophets?" 13 When his prophetic frenzy had ended, he went home.[o]
14 Saul's uncle said to him and to the boy, "Where did you go?" And he replied, "To seek the donkeys; and when we saw they were not to be found, we went
to Samuel." 15 Saul's uncle said, "Tell me what Samuel said to you." 16 Saul said to

[l] Or *the Hill of God* [m] Gk: Heb *they came there* [n] Or *the hill* [o] Cn: Heb *he came to the shrine*

RELIGIOUS AND POLITICAL CENTERS OF ISRAEL

GILGAL	Joshua 4.19; Judges 2.1; Hosea 4.15; Micah 6.5
SHILOH	Joshua 18.1–10; 19.51; Judges 18.31; 1 Samuel 1.3; Jeremiah 7.12–14
SHECHEM	Joshua 24.1
RAMAH	1 Samuel 7.17; 8.4
MIZPAH	Judges 11.11; 20.1; 1 Samuel 10.17
BETHEL	Judges 20.18, 26; 1 Samuel 10.3
GIBEAH (political center only)	1 Samuel 10.26
GIBEON (religious center only)	1 Kings 3.4; 2 Chronicles 1.2, 3
JERUSALEM	1 Kings 8.1ff; Psalm 51.16–19

During the period of the Judges, Israel may have had more than one capital. This may explain why the Scriptures overlap with reference to some cities.

Samuel called the Israelites together at Mizpah, where he would anoint Saul as their first king. Up to this point, the political seat of the nation seems to have been the religious center of the nation as well. Above are the cities which probably served as both the religious and political centers of Israel since the days of Joshua. Saul may have been the first Israelite leader to separate the nation's religious center (probably Mizpah at this time) from its political center (Gibeah—1 Samuel 11.4; 26.1). Politically, the nation grew strong for a while. But when Saul and his officials stopped seeking God's will, internal jealousies and strife soon began to decay the nation from within. When David became king he brought the ark of the covenant back to Jerusalem, his capital. King Solomon then completely united the religious and political centers at Jerusalem.

10.6 How could Saul be so filled with the Spirit and yet later commit such evil acts? Throughout the Old Testament, God's Spirit "came upon" a person temporarily so that God could use him or her for great acts. This happened frequently to Israel's judges when they were called by God to rescue the nation (Judges 3.8–10). This was not always a permanent, abiding influence, but sometimes a temporary manifestation of the Holy Spirit. In many ways it corresponds to the "filling" of the Holy Spirit in the New Testament. Yet, at times in the Old Testament, the Spirit even came upon unbelievers to enable them to do unusual tasks (Numbers 24; 2 Chronicles 36.22, 23). Saul, in his early years as king, had "another heart" (10.1–10) as a result of the Holy Spirit's work in him. But as Saul's power grew, so did his pride. After a while he refused to seek God; the Spirit left him (16.14); and his good attitude melted away. The Holy Spirit temporarily took control of Saul, but he did not take residence in him. The Holy Spirit can use anyone to accomplish his will, but takes residence *only* in those who have put their faith in Jesus Christ, trusting in his sacrifice for their salvation.

10.8 "Sacrifices of well-being" are also called "peace offerings" or "fellowship offerings."

10.10, 11 A prophet is someone who speaks God's words. While God told many prophets to predict certain events, what God wanted most was for them to instruct and inspire people to live in faithfulness to God. When Saul's friends heard inspired words coming from Saul they exclaimed, "Is Saul also among the prophets?" This was an expression of surprise at worldly Saul's becoming religious. It is equivalent to, "What? Has he got religion?"

his uncle, "He told us that the donkeys had been found." But about the matter of the
kingship, of which Samuel had spoken, he did not tell him anything.

The people accept Saul as king

17 Samuel summoned the people to the LORD at Mizpah 18 and said to them,[p] **10.17**
"Thus says the LORD, the God of Israel, 'I brought up Israel out of Egypt, and I Judg 20.1 1 Sam 7.5,6
rescued you from the hand of the Egyptians and from the hand of all the kingdoms **10.18**
that were oppressing you.' 19 But today you have rejected your God, who saves you Josh 24.5 Judg 6.8
from all your calamities and your distresses; and you have said, 'No! but set a king 1 Sam 8.6,7
over us.' Now therefore present yourselves before the LORD by your tribes and by
your clans."
20 Then Samuel brought all the tribes of Israel near, and the tribe of Benjamin **10.20**
was taken by lot. 21 He brought the tribe of Benjamin near by its families, and the Josh 7.16 1 Sam 14.41
family of the Matrites was taken by lot. Finally he brought the family of the Ma- Acts 1.24,25
trites near man by man,[q] and Saul the son of Kish was taken by lot. But when they
sought him, he could not be found. 22 So they inquired again of the LORD, "Did the **10.22**
man come here?"[r] and the LORD said, "See, he has hidden himself among the Num 27.21
baggage." 23 Then they ran and brought him from there. When he took his stand **10.23**
among the people, he was head and shoulders taller than any of them. 24 Samuel 1 Sam 9.2; 16.7
said to all the people, "Do you see the one whom the LORD has chosen? There is no **10.24** 1 Kgs 1.25,
one like him among all the people." And all the people shouted, "Long live the 34,39 2 Kgs 11.12
king!"
25 Samuel told the people the rights and duties of the kingship; and he wrote **10.25**
them in a book and laid it up before the LORD. Then Samuel sent all the people back Deut 17.15 1 Sam 8.11-18
to their homes. 26 Saul also went to his home at Gibeah, and with him went warriors
whose hearts God had touched. 27 But some worthless fellows said, "How can this **10.27**
man save us?" They despised him and brought him no present. But he held his 1 Kgs 10.24 Ps 72.10
peace.

Now Nahash, king of the Ammonites, had been grievously oppressing the Gadites and the Reubenites. He would gouge out the right eye of each of them and

[p] Heb *to the people of Israel* [q] Gk: Heb lacks *Finally . . . man by man* [r] Gk: Heb *Is there yet a man to come here?*

10.19 Israel's true king was God, but the nation demanded another. Imagine wanting a human being instead of God as guide and leader! Men and women have rejected God throughout history, and they continue to do it today. Are you rejecting God by pushing him aside and acknowledging someone or something else as your "king" or top priority? Learn from these stories of Israel's kings, and be careful not to push God aside.

10.20 The Israelites chose their first king by casting lots or by using the Urim and Thummim, two plates or flat stones carried by the high priest. The fact that Saul was chosen may seem like luck, but it was really the opposite. God had instructed the Israelites to make the Urim and Thummim for the specific purpose of consulting him in times such as this (Exodus 28.30; Numbers 27.12–21). By using the Urim and Thummim, the Israelites were taking the decision out of their own hands and turning it over to God.

Only the high priest could use the Urim and Thummim, which were designed to give only yes or no answers.

10.22 When the Israelites assembled to choose a king, Saul already knew he was the one (10.1). Instead of coming forward, however, he hid among the baggage. Often we hide from important responsibilities because we are afraid of failure, afraid of what others will think, or perhaps unsure about how to proceed. Prepare now to step up to your future responsibilities. Count on God's provision rather than your feelings of adequacy.

10.24 Saul, who not long before had been a farmer searching for donkeys, was now king. Although he was tall, handsome, and wealthy, he was a surprising choice to be king because he was not a deeply religious man. But God does not choose people according to our expectations. He may not even choose the one best qualified for the task, but rather the one who will fulfill his larger purpose. Sometimes this means allowing a poor leader to be selected to teach people a valuable lesson. God may want to use you for a great work, or he may choose someone else who seems less fit. In either case, try to look for God's greater purpose.

10.25 The kings of Israel, unlike kings of other nations, had specific duties outlined for them (Deuteronomy 17.14–20). Heathen kings were considered gods; they made their own laws and answered to no one. Israel's king, by contrast, had to answer to a higher authority—the Lord of heaven and earth. The Israelites now had a king like everyone else, just as they wanted. But Samuel, in his charge to both the king and the people, wanted to make sure that the rule of Israel's king would be different from that of his pagan counterparts. (Note: "laid it up before the Lord" means that Samuel put the book, as a witness to the agreement, in a special place at Mizpah.)

10.26 Because Israel had no political capital at this time, Saul returned to Gibeah, his hometown, which eventually became the first capital of the kingdom. Saul's move to Gibeah marked the first time that the political center of Israel was separated from the religious center. During this time, the religious center was in Ramah, Samuel's home.

10.26, 27 Some men became Saul's constant companions, while others despised him. Criticism will always be directed toward those who lead, because they are in a vulnerable position. At this time, Saul took no notice of those who seemed to be against him, although later he would become consumed with jealousy (19.1–3; 26.17–21). As you lead, listen to constructive criticism, but don't spend valuable time and energy worrying about those who may oppose you. Instead, focus your attention on those who are ready and willing to help.

would not grant Israel a deliverer. No one was left of the Israelites across the Jordan
whose right eye Nahash, king of the Ammonites, had not gouged out. But there
were seven thousand men who had escaped from the Ammonites and had entered
Jabesh-gilead.[s]

Saul defeats the Ammonite army

11.1 Judg 11.4-6 21.8 1 Sam 31.11 **11** About a month later,[t] Nahash the Ammonite went up and besieged Jabesh-
gilead; and all the men of Jabesh said to Nahash, "Make a treaty with us, and
we will serve you." 2 But Nahash the Ammonite said to them, "On this condition I
will make a treaty with you, namely that I gouge out everyone's right eye, and thus
put disgrace upon all Israel." 3 The elders of Jabesh said to him, "Give us seven
days' respite that we may send messengers through all the territory of Israel. Then,
11.4 1 Sam 10.26 14.2; 30.4 if there is no one to save us, we will give ourselves up to you." 4 When the messengers came to Gibeah of Saul, they reported the matter in the hearing of the people;
and all the people wept aloud.
11.5 1 Kgs 19.19 5 Now Saul was coming from the field behind the oxen; and Saul said, "What
is the matter with the people, that they are weeping?" So they told him the message
11.6 Judg 3.10; 6.34 1 Sam 10.6; 7,10 from the inhabitants of Jabesh. 6 And the spirit of God came upon Saul in power
when he heard these words, and his anger was greatly kindled. 7 He took a yoke of
11.7 Judg 19.29; 20.1 oxen, and cut them in pieces and sent them throughout all the territory of Israel by
messengers, saying, "Whoever does not come out after Saul and Samuel, so shall
it be done to his oxen!" Then the dread of the LORD fell upon the people, and they
11.8 Judg 1.4-6 came out as one. 8 When he mustered them at Bezek, those from Israel were three
hundred thousand, and those from Judah seventy[u] thousand. 9 They said to the
messengers who had come, "Thus shall you say to the inhabitants of Jabesh-gilead:
'Tomorrow, by the time the sun is hot, you shall have deliverance.'" When the
messengers came and told the inhabitants of Jabesh, they rejoiced. 10 So the inhabitants of Jabesh said, "Tomorrow we will give ourselves up to you, and you may do
11.11 Judg 7.16; 9.43 to us whatever seems good to you." 11 The next day Saul put the people in three
companies. At the morning watch they came into the camp and cut down the Ammonites until the heat of the day; and those who survived were scattered, so that no
11.12 1 Sam 10.27 Lk 19.27 two of them were left together.
12 The people said to Samuel, "Who is it that said, 'Shall Saul reign over us?'

[s] Q Ms Compare Josephus, *Antiquities* VI.v.1 (68-71): MT lacks *Now Nahash . . . entered Jabesh-gilead.* [t] Q Ms Gk: MT lacks *About a month later* [u] Q Ms Gk: MT *thirty*

11.1ff At this time, Israel was very susceptible to invasion by marauding tribes such as these Ammonites from east of the Jordan River. Saul's leadership in battle against this warlike tribe helped unify the nation and proved that he was a worthy military ruler. Saul's kingship was solidified when he saved the nation from disgrace and spared the people who had criticized him.

11.3 Why would Nahash give the city of Jabesh-gilead seven days to find an army to help them? Because Israel was still disorganized, Nahash was betting that no one would come to the city's aid. He was hoping to take the city without a fight and avoid a battle. He also may not have been prepared to attack the city, because a siege against its walls could last weeks or months.

11.6 Anger is a powerful emotion. Often it may drive people to hurt others with words or physical violence. But anger directed at sin and the mistreatment of others is not wrong. Saul was angered by the Ammonites' threat to humiliate and mistreat his fellow Israelites. God used Saul's anger to bring justice and freedom. When injustice or sin makes you angry, ask God how you can channel that anger in constructive ways to help bring about a positive change.

11.8 Judah, one of the 12 tribes of Israel, is often mentioned separately from the other 11. There are several reasons for this. Judah was the largest tribe (Numbers 1.20–46), and it was the tribe from which most of Israel's kings would come (Genesis 49.8–12). Later, Judah would be one of the few tribes to return to God after a century of captivity under a hostile foreign power. Judah would also be the tribe through which the Messiah would come (Micah 5.2).

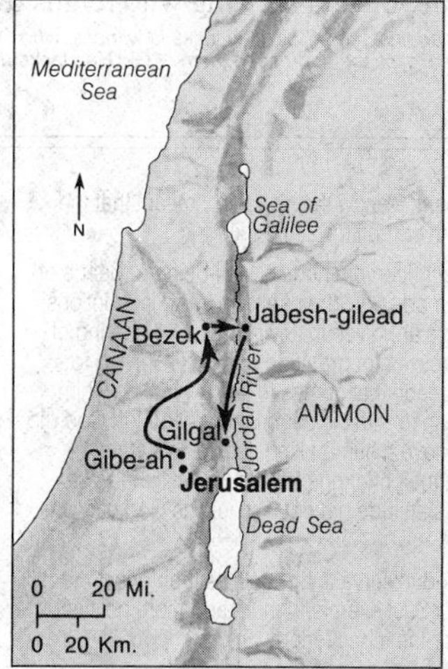

SAUL DEFEATS THE AMMONITES
The Ammonites prepared to attack Jabesh-gilead. The people of Jabesh sent messengers to Saul in Gibeah asking for help. Saul mobilized an army at Bezek and then attacked the Ammonites. After the battle, the Israelites returned to Gilgal to crown Saul as king.

Give them to us so that we may put them to death." 13 But Saul said, "No one shall
be put to death this day, for today the LORD has brought deliverance to Israel."
14 Samuel said to the people, "Come, let us go to Gilgal and there renew the
kingship." 15 So all the people went to Gilgal, and there they made Saul king before
the LORD in Gilgal. There they sacrificed offerings of well-being before the LORD,
and there Saul and all the Israelites rejoiced greatly.

Samuel reminds the people of God's blessing

12 Samuel said to all Israel, "I have listened to you in all that you have said to
me, and have set a king over you. 2 See, it is the king who leads you now; I
am old and gray, but my sons are with you. I have led you from my youth until this
day. 3 Here I am; testify against me before the LORD and before his anointed.
Whose ox have I taken? Or whose donkey have I taken? Or whom have I defrauded? Whom have I oppressed? Or from whose hand have I taken a bribe to
blind my eyes with it? Testify against me[v] and I will restore it to you." 4 They said,
"You have not defrauded us or oppressed us or taken anything from the hand of
anyone." 5 He said to them, "The LORD is witness against you, and his anointed is
witness this day, that you have not found anything in my hand." And they said, "He
is witness."
6 Samuel said to the people, "The LORD is witness, who[w] appointed Moses and
Aaron and brought your ancestors up out of the land of Egypt. 7 Now therefore take
your stand, so that I may enter into judgment with you before the LORD, and I will
declare to you[x] all the saving deeds of the LORD that he performed for you and for
your ancestors. 8 When Jacob went into Egypt and the Egyptians oppressed them,[y]
then your ancestors cried to the LORD and the LORD sent Moses and Aaron, who
brought forth your ancestors out of Egypt, and settled them in this place. 9 But they
forgot the LORD their God; and he sold them into the hand of Sisera, commander of
the army of King Jabin of[z] Hazor, and into the hand of the Philistines, and into the
hand of the king of Moab; and they fought against them. 10 Then they cried to the
LORD, and said, 'We have sinned, because we have forsaken the LORD, and have
served the Baals and the Astartes; but now rescue us out of the hand of our enemies,
and we will serve you.' 11 And the LORD sent Jerubbaal and Barak,[a] and Jephthah,
and Samson,[b] and rescued you out of the hand of your enemies on every side; and
you lived in safety. 12 But when you saw that King Nahash of the Ammonites came
against you, you said to me, 'No, but a king shall reign over us,' though the LORD
your God was your king. 13 See, here is the king whom you have chosen, for whom
you have asked; see, the LORD has set a king over you. 14 If you will fear the LORD
and serve him and heed his voice and not rebel against the commandment of the
LORD, and if both you and the king who reigns over you will follow the LORD your

11.13 Ex 14.13; 1 Sam 14.45; 19.5; 2 Sam 19.22
11.14 1 Sam 10.1,8
12.2 1 Sam 3.10,19, 20; 8.1,5
12.3 Ex 23.8; Num 16.15; Deut 16.19
12.4 1 Sam 8.3
12.5 Ex 22.4; Ps 17.3
12.6 Ex 6.26
12.7 Deut 4.9; Judg 5.11; Ps 78.4; Mic 6.4
12.8 Ex 2.23-25; 3.10; 4.14-16
12.9 Deut 32.18; Judg 3.7; 10.7; 13.1; Ps 106.21
12.10 Judg 3.15; 10.10,15,16
12.11 Judg 4.6; 6.32; 11.1; 1 Sam 1.19,20; Heb 11.32
12.12 Judg 8.23,24
12.13 Hos 13.11
12.14 Josh 24.14,20; Ps 81.12-15; Isa 3.10

[v] Gk: Heb lacks *Testify against me* [w] Gk: Heb lacks *is witness, who* [x] Gk: Heb lacks *and I will declare to you* [y] Gk: Heb lacks *and the Egyptians oppressed them* [z] Gk: Heb lacks *Jabin king of* [a] Gk Syr: Heb *Bedan* [b] Gk: Heb *Samuel*

11.14 Samuel's comment, "renew the kingship," meant that the people should reconfirm or reaffirm Saul as king.

11.15 The Israelites sacrificed offerings of well-being or peace offerings to God as they made Saul their first king. The instructions for giving these offerings are given in Leviticus 3. The offering of well-being was an expression of gratitude and thanksgiving to God, symbolizing the peace that comes to those who know him and who live in accordance with his commands. Although God did not want his people to have a human king, the people were demonstrating through their offerings that he was still their true King. Unfortunately, this attitude did not last, just as God had predicted (8.7–19).

12.1ff Samuel continued to serve the people as their priest, prophet, and judge, but Saul exercised more and more political and military control over the tribes (see 7.15).

12.1–3 By asking the Israelites to point out any wrongs he had committed during his time as Israel's judge, Samuel was reminding them that he could be trusted to tell the truth. He was also reminding them that having a king was their idea, not his. Samuel was setting the stage for the miraculous thunderstorm recorded in 12.16–19, so that the people could not blame him when God punished them for their selfish motives.

12.10 "Baals and Astartes" were pagan gods. See the note on 7.3, 4.

12.11 Jerubbaal was the name given to Gideon when he demolished the altar of Baal (see Judges 6.32).

12.12–15 God granted the nation's request for a king, but his commandments and requirements remained the same. God was to be their true King, and both Saul and the people were to be subject to his law. No person is ever exempt from God's law. No human action is outside his jurisdiction. God is the true King of every area of life. We must recognize his kingship and pattern our relationships, worklife, and homelife according to his principles.

12.15 Deut 28.15 Josh 24.20 Isa 1.2,20
12.17 Ps 99.6 Jer 15.1
12.20 Ex 20.20 Deut 11.16
12.21 Isa 41.29 Hab 2.18 1 Cor 8.4
12.22 Ex 32.12 Num 14.13 1 Pet 2.9
12.23 Prov 4.11 Rom 1.9 Col 1.9 1 Thess 3.10
12.24 Eccles 12.13 Rom 12.1
12.25 Isa 1.20 Hos 10.3

God, it will be well; 15 but if you will not heed the voice of the LORD, but rebel
against the commandment of the LORD, then the hand of the LORD will be against
you and your king.[c] 16 Now therefore take your stand and see this great thing that
the LORD will do before your eyes. 17 Is it not the wheat harvest today? I will call
upon the LORD, that he may send thunder and rain; and you shall know and see that
the wickedness that you have done in the sight of the LORD is great in demanding
a king for yourselves." 18 So Samuel called upon the LORD, and the LORD sent thunder and rain that day; and all the people greatly feared the LORD and Samuel.
19 All the people said to Samuel, "Pray to the LORD your God for your servants,
so that we may not die; for we have added to all our sins the evil of demanding a
king for ourselves." 20 And Samuel said to the people, "Do not be afraid; you have
done all this evil, yet do not turn aside from following the LORD, but serve the LORD
with all your heart; 21 and do not turn aside after useless things that cannot profit or
save, for they are useless. 22 For the LORD will not cast away his people, for his
great name's sake, because it has pleased the LORD to make you a people for himself. 23 Moreover as for me, far be it from me that I should sin against the LORD by
ceasing to pray for you; and I will instruct you in the good and the right way.
24 Only fear the LORD, and serve him faithfully with all your heart; for consider
what great things he has done for you. 25 But if you still do wickedly, you shall be
swept away, both you and your king."

2. God rejects Saul for disobedience

Saul disobeys God by wrongly making a sacrifice

13 Saul was . . .[d] years old when he began to reign; and he reigned . . . and
two[e] years over Israel.

13.2 1 Sam 10.26 13.23 14.2,5,52
13.3 Judg 3.27; 6.34 2 Sam 2.28 20.1

2 Saul chose three thousand out of Israel; two thousand were with Saul in Michmash and the hill country of Bethel, and a thousand were with Jonathan in Gibeah
of Benjamin; the rest of the people he sent home to their tents. 3 Jonathan defeated
the garrison of the Philistines that was at Geba; and the Philistines heard of it. And
Saul blew the trumpet throughout all the land, saying, "Let the Hebrews hear!"

[c] Gk: Heb *and your ancestors* [d] The number is lacking in the Heb text (the verse is lacking in the Septuagint).
[e] *Two* is not the entire number; something has dropped out.

12.17 The wheat harvest came near the end of the dry season during the months of May and June. Since rain rarely fell during this period, a great thunderstorm was considered a miraculous event. It was not a beneficial miracle, however, because rain during the wheat harvest could damage the crops and cause them to rot quickly. This unusual occurrence showed God's displeasure with Israel's demand for a king.

12.22 Why did God make Israel "his people"? God did not choose them because they deserved it (Deuteronomy 7.7, 8), but in order that they might become his channel of blessing to all people through the Messiah (Genesis 12.1–3). Because God chose the people of Israel, he would never abandon them; but because they were his special nation, he would often punish them for their disobedience in order to bring them back to a right relationship with him.

12.23 Is failing to pray for others a sin? Samuel's words seem to indicate that it is. His actions illustrate two of God's people's responsibilities: (1) they should pray consistently for others (Ephesians 6.18), and (2) they should teach others the right way to God (2 Timothy 2.2). Samuel disagreed with the Israelites' demand for a king, but he assured them that he would continue to pray for them and teach them. We may disagree with someone, but we shouldn't stop praying for him or her.

12.23 Samuel also became irritated with Saul because he was always looking for a military answer to his problems instead of a spiritual one. Saul often performed spiritual functions out of duty rather than from his heart. Be sure your serving is based on love of God and his people, and not merely out of duty. Samuel was hoping that God would answer his prayers and change Saul.

12.24 This is the second time in this chapter that Samuel reminded the people to take time to recall all the good things God had done for them (see 12.7). Taking time for reflection allows us to focus our attention upon God's goodness and strengthens our faith. Sometimes we are so progress- and future-oriented that we fail to take time to consider all that God has already done. Remember what God has done for you so that you may move ahead with a heart of gratitude.

12.25 If we "still do wickedly" (continue in sin), we will not enjoy fellowship with God and we will end up destroying ourselves. Persisting in destructive habits, immoral thoughts, harbored resentments, and failing to heed God's Word are examples of continuing in sin.

13.1 According to a few late manuscripts of the Septuagint (an ancient Greek version of the Old Testament), Saul was 30 years old when he began to reign. The missing number in this verse for the length of his reign may be 40, as recorded in Acts 13.21.

13.3, 4 Jonathan attacked and destroyed the Philistine garrison, but Saul took all the credit for it. Although this was normal in that culture, it didn't make his action right. Saul's growing pride started out small—taking credit for a battle which was won by his son. Left unchecked, his pride grew into an ugly obsession, thus it destroyed him, tore his family apart, and threatened the well-being of the nation. Taking credit for the accomplishments of others indicates that pride is controlling your life. When you notice pride taking a foothold, take immediate steps to put it in check by giving credit to those who deserve it.

4 When all Israel heard that Saul had defeated the garrison of the Philistines, and
also that Israel had become odious to the Philistines, the people were called out to
join Saul at Gilgal.
5 The Philistines mustered to fight with Israel, thirty thousand chariots, and six **13.5**
thousand horsemen, and troops like the sand on the seashore in multitude; they Josh 11.4
came up and encamped at Michmash, to the east of Beth-aven. 6 When the Israelites **13.6**
saw that they were in distress (for the troops were hard pressed), the people hid Judg 6.2 1 Sam 14.11
themselves in caves and in holes and in rocks and in tombs and in cisterns. 7 Some 23.19
Hebrews crossed the Jordan to the land of Gad and Gilead. Saul was still at Gilgal,
and all the people followed him trembling.
8 He waited seven days, the time appointed by Samuel; but Samuel did not **13.8**
come to Gilgal, and the people began to slip away from Saul.[f] 9 So Saul said, 1 Sam 10.8
"Bring the burnt offering here to me, and the offerings of well-being." And he **13.9** 2 Sam 24.25
offered the burnt offering. 10 As soon as he had finished offering the burnt offering, 1 Kgs 3.4
Samuel arrived; and Saul went out to meet him and salute him. 11 Samuel said, **13.10** 1 Sam 15.13
"What have you done?" Saul replied, "When I saw that the people were slipping **13.11**
away from me, and that you did not come within the days appointed, and that the 2 Sam 3.23,24
Philistines were mustering at Michmash, 12 I said, 'Now the Philistines will come
down upon me at Gilgal, and I have not entreated the favor of the LORD'; so I forced
myself, and offered the burnt offering." 13 Samuel said to Saul, "You have done **13.13**
foolishly; you have not kept the commandment of the LORD your God, which he 1 Sam 15.22,28 2 Chron 16.9
commanded you. The LORD would have established your kingdom over Israel for-
ever, 14 but now your kingdom will not continue; the LORD has sought out a man **13.14**
after his own heart; and the LORD has appointed him to be ruler over his people, Acts 13.22
because you have not kept what the LORD commanded you." 15 And Samuel left and
went on his way from Gilgal.[g] The rest of the people followed Saul to join the
army; they went up from Gilgal toward Gibeah of Benjamin.[h]

Saul's military hindrances

Saul counted the people who were present with him, about six hundred men. **13.16**
16 Saul, his son Jonathan, and the people who were present with them stayed in 1 Sam 14.2
Geba of Benjamin; but the Philistines encamped at Michmash. 17 And raiders came **13.17** 1 Sam 11.11
out of the camp of the Philistines in three companies; one company turned toward **13.18**
Ophrah, to the land of Shual, 18 another company turned toward Beth-horon, and 1 Kgs 9.17 Neh 11.31-35
another company turned toward the mountain[i] that looks down upon the valley of **13.19**
Zeboim toward the wilderness. Judg 5.8 2 Kgs 24.14
19 Now there was no smith to be found throughout all the land of Israel; for the Jer 24.1

[f] Heb *him* [g] Gk: Heb *went up from Gilgal to Gibeah of Benjamin* [h] Gk: Heb lacks *The rest . . . of Benjamin*
[i] Cn Compare Gk: Heb *toward the border*

13.6 When we forget who is on our side, or see only our own resources, we tend to panic at the sight of the opposition. The Israelites became terrified and hid when they saw the mighty Philistine army. They forgot that God was on their side and that he couldn't be defeated. As you face problems and temptations, focus your attention on God and his resources, trusting him to help you (Romans 8.31–37).

13.9 Rather than wait for a priest, Saul offered the sacrifice himself. This was against the law. Under pressure from the approaching Philistines, he took matters into his own hands and disobeyed God. He was doing a good thing (offering a sacrifice to God before a crucial battle), but he did it in the wrong way. Like Saul, our true spiritual character is revealed under pressure. The methods we use to accomplish our goals are as important as the attainment of those goals.

13.11, 12 It is difficult to trust God when you feel your resources slipping away. When Saul felt that time was running out, he became impatient with God's timing. In thinking that the ritual was all he needed, he substituted the ritual for faith in God.

When faced with a difficult decision, don't allow impatience to drive you to disobey God. When you know what God wants, don't go against that plan regardless of the consequences. God often uses delays to test our obedience and patience.

13.12, 13 "I forced myself" means "I felt compelled." Saul had plenty of excuses for his disobedience. But Samuel zeroed in on the real issue: "You have not kept the commandment of the Lord your God." Like Saul, we often gloss over our mistakes and sins, trying to justify and spiritualize our actions because of our "special" circumstances. Our excuses, however, are nothing more than disobedience. God knows our true motives. He forgives, restores, and blesses only when we are honest about our sins. By trying to hide his sins behind excuses, Saul lost his kingship (13.14).

13.13 Why did Samuel react to Saul's disobedience in such a harsh way? Only priests were permitted to offer sacrifices. By offering the sacrifice himself, Saul directly violated God's law.

Saul was already ignoring the charge Samuel had given him in 12.14, 15. Almost at once he began to work independently of God's law, priests, and prophets. Such actions disqualified him from his real task, which was to be God's representative. God wants servants who will obey. Then he will communicate through them to his people.

Philistines said, "The Hebrews must not make swords or spears for themselves";
20 so all the Israelites went down to the Philistines to sharpen their plowshares, mattocks, axes, or sickles;[j] 21 The charge was two-thirds of a shekel[k] for the plowshares and for the mattocks, and one-third of a shekel for sharpening the axes and for setting the goads.[l] 22 So on the day of the battle neither sword nor spear was to be found in the possession of any of the people with Saul and Jonathan; but Saul and his son Jonathan had them.

Jonathan's brave plan

23 Now a garrison of the Philistines had gone out to the pass of Michmash.

[j] Gk: Heb *plowshare* [k] Heb *was a pim* [l] Cn: Meaning of Heb uncertain

SAUL

First impressions can be deceiving, especially when the image created by a person's appearance is contradicted by his or her qualities and abilities. Saul presented the ideal visual image of a king, but the tendencies of his character often went contrary to God's commands for a king. Saul was God's chosen leader, but this did not mean he was capable of being king on his own.

During his reign, Saul had his greatest successes when he obeyed God. His greatest failures resulted from acting on his own. Saul had the raw materials to be a good leader—appearance, courage, and action. Even his weaknesses could have been used by God if Saul had recognized them and left them in God's hands. His own choices cut him off from God and eventually alienated him from his own people.

From Saul we learn that while our strengths and abilities make us useful, it is our weaknesses that make us usable. Our skills and talents make us tools, but our failures and shortcomings remind us that we need a Craftsman in control of our lives. Whatever we accomplish on our own is only a hint of what God could do through our lives. Does he control your life?

Strengths and accomplishments:
- First God-appointed king of Israel
- Known for his personal courage and generosity
- Stood tall, with a striking appearance

Weaknesses and mistakes:
- His leadership abilities did not match the expectations created by his appearance
- Impulsive by nature, he tended to overstep his bounds
- Jealous of David, he tried to kill him
- He specifically disobeyed God on several occasions

Lessons from his life:
- God wants obedience from the heart, not mere acts of religious ritual
- Obedience always involves sacrifice; but sacrifice is not always obedience
- God wants to make use of our strengths and weaknesses
- Weaknesses should help us remember our need for God's guidance and help

Vital statistics:
- Where: The land of Benjamin
- Occupation: King of Israel
- Relatives: Father: Kish. Sons: Jonathan and Ishbosheth. Wife: Ahinoam. Daughters: Merab and Michal

Key verses:
"And Samuel said, 'Has the Lord as great delight in burnt offerings and sacrifices, as in obeying the voice of the Lord? Surely, to obey is better than sacrifice, and to heed than the fat of rams. For rebellion is no less a sin than divination, and stubbornness is like iniquity and idolatry. Because you have rejected the word of the Lord, he has also rejected you from being king' " (1 Samuel 15.22, 23).

His story is told in 1 Samuel 9—31. He is also mentioned in Acts 13.21.

13.19–22 Israel was in no position to conquer anyone. The army had no iron weapons, and there were no facilities for turning their tools into weapons. In fact, if an Israelite wanted to sharpen his tools, he had to pay a Philistine blacksmith to do it, because the Philistines had a carefully guarded monopoly on iron and blacksmithing. They charged high prices for sharpening their farm implements. Their tight control over the technology, along with their surprise raids, demoralized the Israelites and kept them in subjection.

Against such superiority, the Israelites were at a serious disadvantage. How could they hope to rout their oppressors? Only with God's help. God wanted to give Israel victory without swords so they would realize their true source of strength.

14 1 One day Jonathan son of Saul said to the young man who carried his armor, 14.1 1 Sam 13.2,22
"Come, let us go over to the Philistine garrison on the other side." But he did 14.39-45; 18.1
not tell his father. 2 Saul was staying in the outskirts of Gibeah under the pomegran- 14.2
ate tree that is at Migron; the troops that were with him were about six hundred 1 Sam 13.16
men, 3 along with Ahijah son of Ahitub, Ichabod's brother, son of Phinehas son of 14.3 1 Sam 1.3
Eli, the priest of the LORD in Shiloh, carrying an ephod. Now the people did not 4.21,22
know that Jonathan had gone. 4 In the pass,[m] by which Jonathan tried to go over to 22.11,12
the Philistine garrison, there was a rocky crag on one side and a rocky crag on the
other; the name of the one was Bozez, and the name of the other Seneh. 5 One crag 14.5
rose on the north in front of Michmash, and the other on the south in front of Geba. 1 Sam 13.23
6 Jonathan said to the young man who carried his armor, "Come, let us go over 14.6 Judg 7.4
to the garrison of these uncircumcised; it may be that the LORD will act for us; for 2 Chron 14.11
nothing can hinder the LORD from saving by many or by few." 7 His armor-bearer
said to him, "Do all that your mind inclines to.[n] I am with you; as your mind is, so
is mine."[o] 8 Then Jonathan said, "Now we will cross over to those men and will
show ourselves to them. 9 If they say to us, 'Wait until we come to you,' then we
will stand still in our place, and we will not go up to them. 10 But if they say, 'Come 14.10
up to us,' then we will go up; for the LORD has given them into our hand. That will Gen 24.14 Judg 6.36
be the sign for us." 11 So both of them showed themselves to the garrison of the 14.11
Philistines; and the Philistines said, "Look, Hebrews are coming out of the holes 1 Sam 13.6
where they have hidden themselves." 12 The men of the garrison hailed Jonathan 14.12
and his armor-bearer, saying, "Come up to us, and we will show you something." Judg 5.14; 7.15 2 Sam 5.24
Jonathan said to his armor-bearer, "Come up after me; for the LORD has given them
into the hand of Israel." 13 Then Jonathan climbed up on his hands and feet, with his
armor-bearer following after him. The Philistines[p] fell before Jonathan, and his
armor-bearer, coming after him, killed them. 14 In that first slaughter Jonathan and
his armor-bearer killed about twenty men within an area about half a furrow long in
an acre[q] of land. 15 There was a panic in the camp, in the field, and among all the 14.15
people; the garrison and even the raiders trembled; the earth quaked; and it became Josh 2.9 1 Sam 7.10
a very great panic. 2 Kgs 7.6
16 Saul's lookouts in Gibeah of Benjamin were watching as the multitude was
surging back and forth.[r] 17 Then Saul said to the troops that were with him, "Call
the roll and see who has gone from us." When they had called the roll, Jonathan and
his armor-bearer were not there. 18 Saul said to Ahijah, "Bring the ark[s] of God 14.18 1 Sam 4.3
here." For at that time the ark[r] of God went with the Israelites. 19 While Saul was 23.9; 30.7
talking to the priest, the tumult in the camp of the Philistines increased more and 14.19
more; and Saul said to the priest, "Withdraw your hand." 20 Then Saul and all the Num 27.21
people who were with him rallied and went into the battle; and every sword was 14.20 Judg 7.21
against the other, so that there was very great confusion. 21 Now the Hebrews who 2 Chron 20.23
previously had been with the Philistines and had gone up with them into the camp 14.21 1 Sam 29.4

[m] Heb *Between the passes* [n] Gk: Heb *Do all that is in your mind. Turn* [o] Gk: Heb lacks *so is mine* [p] Heb *They*
[q] Heb *yoke* [r] Gk: Heb *they went and there* [s] Gk *the ephod*

14.1 Why would Jonathan go alone to attack the Philistines? Jonathan may have been weary of the long, hopeless standoff in the battle; he trusted God to give the victory and wanted to act on that trust. He also knew that the number of Philistines was no problem for God. Perhaps he didn't tell his father about his mission because he thought Saul would not let him go.

14.1ff In this chapter we read about the miserable job Saul did as leader: he had no communication with Jonathan (14.1, 17); he made a rash vow (14.24); and he ignored the well-being of his own soldiers (14.31). Saul's poor leadership was not a result of personality traits, but of decaying spiritual character. What we do is often a direct result of our spiritual condition. We cannot ignore the importance of spiritual character in effective leadership.

14.6 Jonathan and his armor-bearer weren't much of a force to attack the huge Philistine army. But while everyone else was afraid, they trusted God, knowing that the size of the enemy army would not restrict God's ability to help them. God honored the faith and brave action of these two men with a tremendous victory.

Have you ever felt surrounded by the "enemy" or faced overwhelming odds? God is never intimidated by the size of the enemy or the complexity of a problem. With him, there are always enough resources to resist the pressures and win the battle. If God has called you to action, then bravely commit what resources you have to God, and rely upon him to lead you to victory.

14.12 Jonathan did not have the authority to lead all the troops into battle, but he could start a small skirmish in one corner of the enemy camp. When he did, panic broke out among the Philistines, the Hebrews who had been drafted into the Philistine army revolted, and the men who were hiding in the hills regained their courage and returned to fight.

When you are facing a difficult situation that is beyond your control, ask yourself, "What steps can I take now to work toward a solution?" A few small steps may be just what are needed to begin the chain of events leading to eventual victory.

14.22 1 Sam 13.6 31.7 turned and joined the Israelites who were with Saul and Jonathan. 22 Likewise,
when all the Israelites who had gone into hiding in the hill country of Ephraim
heard that the Philistines were fleeing, they too followed closely after them in the
14.23 Ex 14.30 2 Chron 32.22 battle. 23 So the LORD gave Israel the victory that day.
The battle passed beyond Beth-aven, and the troops with Saul numbered altogether about ten thousand men. The battle spread out over the hill country of Ephraim.

Saul's foolish order to eat nothing

14.24 Josh 6.26 24 Now Saul committed a very rash act on that day.[t] He had laid an oath on the
troops, saying, "Cursed be anyone who eats food before it is evening and I have
been avenged on my enemies." So none of the troops tasted food. 25 All the troops[u]
came upon a honeycomb; and there was honey on the ground. 26 When the troops
came upon the honeycomb, the honey was dripping out; but they did not put their
hands to their mouths, for they feared the oath. 27 But Jonathan had not heard his
father charge the troops with the oath; so he extended the staff that was in his hand,
and dipped the tip of it in the honeycomb, and put his hand to his mouth; and his
eyes brightened. 28 Then one of the soldiers said, "Your father strictly charged the
troops with an oath, saying, 'Cursed be anyone who eats food this day.' And so the
troops are faint." 29 Then Jonathan said, "My father has troubled the land; see how
my eyes have brightened because I tasted a little of this honey. 30 How much better

[t] Gk: Heb *The Israelites were distressed that day* [u] Heb *land*

GLOOM AND DOOM

Reference	Message
3.11–14	Judgment will come to the house of Eli.
7.1–4	The nation must turn from idol worship.
8.10–22	Your kings will bring you nothing but trouble.
12.25	If you continue in sin, you will be destroyed by God.
13.13, 14	Saul's kingdom will not continue.
15.17–31	Saul, you have sinned before God.

It wasn't easy being a prophet. Most of the messages they had to give were very unpleasant to hear. They preached of repentance, judgment, impending destruction, sin, and in general, how displeased God was over the behavior of his people. Prophets were not the most popular people in town (unless they were *false* prophets and said just what the people wanted to hear). But popularity was not the bottom line for true prophets of God—it was obedience to God and faithfully proclaiming his word. Samuel is a good example of a faithful prophet.

God has words for us to proclaim as well. And although his messages are loaded with "good news," there is also "bad news" to give. May we, like true prophets, faithfully deliver *all* God's words, regardless of their popularity or lack of it.

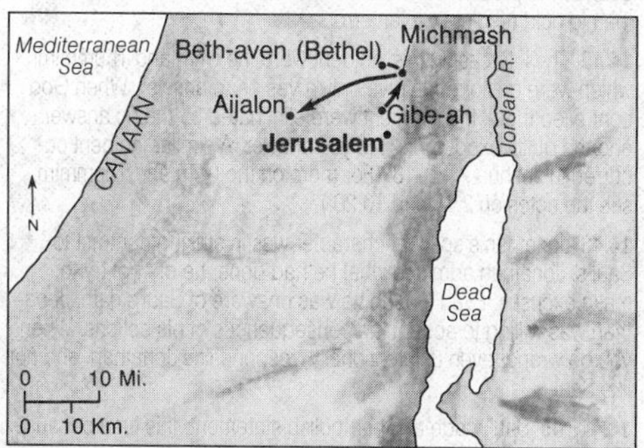

JONATHAN'S BRAVERY Jonathan, Saul's son, left the camp at Gibeah and crept to the Philistine camp at Michmash. With God's help, Jonathan and his bodyguard surprised the Philistines, who panicked and began killing each other! Saul's army heard the commotion and chased the Philistines as far as Beth-aven and Aijalon.

14.19 "Withdraw your hand" refers to the use of the Urim and Thummim. They were withdrawn from the linen ephod (vest) as a way to determine God's will (see the note on 10.20). Saul was rushing the formalities of getting an answer from God so he could hurry and get into battle to take advantage of the confusion of the Philistines.

14.24, 25 Saul made a vow without thinking through the implications. The results: (1) His men were too tired to fight; (2) they were so hungry they ate meat that still contained blood, which was against God's law; (3) Saul almost killed his own son (14.42–44).

Saul's impulsive vow sounded heroic, but it had disastrous side effects. If you are in the middle of a conflict, guard against impulsive statements that you may be forced to honor.

if today the troops had eaten freely of the spoil taken from their enemies; for now
the slaughter among the Philistines has not been great."
31 After they had struck down the Philistines that day from Michmash to Aijalon, the troops were very faint; 32 so the troops flew upon the spoil, and took sheep
and oxen and calves, and slaughtered them on the ground; and the troops ate them
with the blood. 33 Then it was reported to Saul, "Look, the troops are sinning
against the LORD by eating with the blood." And he said, "You have dealt treacherously; roll a large stone before me here."[v] 34 Saul said, "Disperse yourselves
among the troops, and say to them, 'Let all bring their oxen or their sheep, and
slaughter them here, and eat; and do not sin against the LORD by eating with the
blood.' " So all of the troops brought their oxen with them that night, and slaughtered them there. 35 And Saul built an altar to the LORD; it was the first altar that he
built to the LORD.
36 Then Saul said, "Let us go down after the Philistines by night and despoil
them until the morning light; let us not leave one of them." They said, "Do whatever seems good to you." But the priest said, "Let us draw near to God here." 37 So
Saul inquired of God, "Shall I go down after the Philistines? Will you give them
into the hand of Israel?" But he did not answer him that day. 38 Saul said, "Come
here, all you leaders of the people; and let us find out how this sin has arisen today.
39 For as the LORD lives who saves Israel, even if it is in my son Jonathan, he shall
surely die!" But there was no one among all the people who answered him. 40 He
said to all Israel, "You shall be on one side, and I and my son Jonathan will be on
the other side." The people said to Saul, "Do what seems good to you." 41 Then
Saul said, "O LORD God of Israel, why have you not answered your servant today?
If this guilt is in me or in my son Jonathan, O LORD God of Israel, give Urim; but
if this guilt is in your people Israel,[w] give Thummim." And Jonathan and Saul were
indicated by the lot, but the people were cleared. 42 Then Saul said, "Cast the lot
between me and my son Jonathan." And Jonathan was taken.
43 Then Saul said to Jonathan, "Tell me what you have done." Jonathan told
him, "I tasted a little honey with the tip of the staff that was in my hand; here I am,
I will die." 44 Saul said, "God do so to me and more also; you shall surely die,
Jonathan!" 45 Then the people said to Saul, "Shall Jonathan die, who has accom-

14.31 Josh 10.12
14.32 Gen 9.4; Lev 17.10; 1 Sam 15.19; Acts 15.20
14.35 1 Sam 7.12,17
14.36 Josh 10.14
14.37 1 Sam 23.4; 28.5,6; 30.7,8
14.38 Josh 7.10-12
14.39 1 Sam 14.24-44; 19.6
14.41 Prov 16.33; Acts 1.24
14.43 Josh 7.19; 1 Sam 14.27
14.44 Gen 38.24; 1 Sam 3.17; 14.39; 25.22; 2 Sam 12.5
14.45 2 Sam 14.11; Lk 21.18; Acts 27.34

[v] Gk: Heb *me this day* [w] Vg Compare Gk: Heb *41 Saul said to the LORD, the God of Israel*

14.32–34 One of the oldest and strongest Hebrew food laws was the prohibition against eating meat containing the animal's blood (Leviticus 7.26, 27). This law began in Noah's day (Genesis 9.4) and was still observed by the early Christians (Acts 15.27–29). It was wrong to eat blood because blood represented life. (For a further explanation, see Leviticus 17.10–14.)

14.35, 36 After being king for several years, Saul finally built his first altar to God, but only as a last resort. Throughout Saul's reign he consistently approached God only after he had tried everything else. This was in sharp contrast to the priest, who suggested that God be consulted *first* (14.36). How much better if Saul had gone to God first, building an altar as his first official act as king. God is too great to be an afterthought. When we turn to him first, we will never have to turn to him as a last resort.

14.38, 39 Instead of recognizing and admitting his faults, Saul tried to cover them up by blaming everyone but himself. When your life is in a mess, stop and consider how *your* actions and attitudes may be a big part of the problem.

14.39 Saul made the first of his two rash vows (14.24–26) because he was overly anxious to defeat the Philistines and wanted to give his soldiers an incentive to finish the battle quickly. In the Bible, God never asked people to make vows, but if they did, he expected them to keep them (Leviticus 5.4; Numbers 30).

Saul's vow was not something God would have condoned, but still it was a vow. And Jonathan, although he didn't know about Saul's vow, was nevertheless guilty of breaking it. Like Jephthah (Judges 11), Saul made a vow that risked the life of his own child. Fortunately, the people intervened and spared Jonathan's life.

14.39 Saul had issued a ridiculous command and had driven his men to sin, and still he wouldn't back down even if it meant killing his son. When we make ridiculous statements, it is difficult to admit we are wrong. Sticking to the story, just to save face, only compounds the problem. It takes more courage to admit a mistake than to hold resolutely to an error.

14.42 The lots cast in this incident were the Urim and Thummim, which were designed to give only a yes or no answer. When God controlled them, the innocent were eliminated by the no answer and the guilty exposed by the yes answer. A similar incident occurred in Joshua 7.14–18. (For more on the Urim and Thummim see the notes on 2.18 and 10.20.)

14.43 Jonathan's spiritual character was in striking contrast to Saul's. Jonathan admitted what he had done; he did not try to make excuses. Even though he was unaware of Saul's oath, Jonathan was willing to accept the consequences of his actions. When you do wrong, even unintentionally, respond like Jonathan, and not like Saul.

14.44, 45 Saul made another foolish statement, this time because he was more concerned about saving face than being right. To spare Jonathan's life would require him to admit he had acted foolishly, an embarrassment for a king. Saul was really more interested in protecting his image than in enforcing his vow. Fortunately, the people came to Jonathan's rescue. Don't be like Saul. Admit your mistakes, and show that you are more interested in doing what is right than in looking good.

plished this great victory in Israel? Far from it! As the LORD lives, not one hair of his head shall fall to the ground; for he has worked with God today." So the people ransomed Jonathan, and he did not die. 46 Then Saul withdrew from pursuing the Philistines; and the Philistines went to their own place.

Saul's military successes

47 When Saul had taken the kingship over Israel, he fought against all his enemies on every side—against Moab, against the Ammonites, against Edom, against
the kings of Zobah, and against the Philistines; wherever he turned he routed them.
48 He did valiantly, and struck down the Amalekites, and rescued Israel out of the
hands of those who plundered them.
49 Now the sons of Saul were Jonathan, Ishvi, and Malchishua; and the names
of his two daughters were these: the name of the firstborn was Merab, and the name
of the younger, Michal. 50 The name of Saul's wife was Ahinoam daughter of
Ahimaaz. And the name of the commander of his army was Abner son of Ner,
Saul's uncle; 51 Kish was the father of Saul, and Ner the father of Abner was the son
of Abiel.
52 There was hard fighting against the Philistines all the days of Saul; and when
Saul saw any strong or valiant warrior, he took him into his service.

14.48 1 Sam 15.3,7
14.49 1 Sam 18.17,20, 27; 19.11,12 31.2 2 Sam 6.20 1 Chron 10.2
14.50 1 Sam 17.55 2 Sam 2.8
14.52 1 Sam 8.11 1 Kgs 9.22

Saul disobeys God by keeping plunder

15 Samuel said to Saul, "The LORD sent me to anoint you king over his people
Israel; now therefore listen to the words of the LORD. 2 Thus says the LORD
of hosts, 'I will punish the Amalekites for what they did in opposing the Israelites
when they came up out of Egypt. 3 Now go and attack Amalek, and utterly destroy
all that they have; do not spare them, but kill both man and woman, child and
infant, ox and sheep, camel and donkey.'"
4 So Saul summoned the people, and numbered them in Telaim, two hundred
thousand foot soldiers, and ten thousand soldiers of Judah. 5 Saul came to the city
of the Amalekites and lay in wait in the valley. 6 Saul said to the Kenites, "Go!
Leave! Withdraw from among the Amalekites, or I will destroy you with them; for
you showed kindness to all the people of Israel when they came up out of Egypt."
So the Kenites withdrew from the Amalekites. 7 Saul defeated the Amalekites,
from Havilah as far as Shur, which is east of Egypt. 8 He took King Agag of the
Amalekites alive, but utterly destroyed all the people with the edge of the sword.
9 Saul and the people spared Agag, and the best of the sheep and of the cattle and
of the fatlings, and the lambs, and all that was valuable, and would not utterly
destroy them; all that was despised and worthless they utterly destroyed.
10 The word of the LORD came to Samuel: 11 "I regret that I made Saul king, for
he has turned back from following me, and has not carried out my commands."

15.1 1 Sam 9.16 10.1
15.2 Ex 17.8-16 Num 24.20 Deut 25.17
15.3 Deut 20.16-18 Josh 6.17,18
15.6 Num 24.21,22 Judg 1.16; 4.11
15.7 Gen 16.7; 25.18 Ex 15.22 1 Sam 27.8
15.8 Num 24.7
15.9 1 Sam 15.15,21
15.11 Gen 6.6,7 Ex 32.9,11,14 2 Sam 24.16 Luke 6.12

14.47 Why was Saul so successful right after he had disobeyed God and been told that his reign would end (13.13, 14)? God might have given Saul success for the sake of the people, not for Saul. He may have left Saul on the throne for a while to utilize his military talents so that David, Israel's next king, could spend more time focusing on the nation's spiritual battles. Regardless of God's reasons for delaying Saul's demise, his reign ended exactly the way God had foretold. The timing of God's plans and promises are known only to him. Our task is to commit our ways to him and trust him for the outcome.

15.2–5 Why did God command such utter destruction? The Amalekites were a band of guerrilla terrorists. They lived by attacking other nations and carrying off their wealth and their families. They were the first to attack the Israelites as they entered the promised land, and they continued to raid Israelite camps at every opportunity. God knew that the Israelites could never live peacefully in the promised land as long as the Amalekites existed. He also knew that their corrupt, idolatrous religious practices threatened Israel's relationship with him. The only way to protect the Israelites' bodies and souls was to utterly destroy the people of this warlike nation and all their possessions, including their idols.

15.9 Saul and his men did not destroy all the booty from the battle as God commanded (15.3). The law of devoting something—setting it aside—entirely for destruction was well known to the Israelites. Anything under God's ban was to be completely destroyed (Deuteronomy 20.16–18). This was set up in order to prevent idolatry from taking hold in Israel because many of the valuables were idols. To break this law was punishable by death (Joshua 7).

When we gloss over sin in order to protect what we have or for material gain, we aren't being shrewd; we are disobeying God's law. Selective obedience is just another form of disobedience.

15.11 When God said he regretted making Saul king, was he saying he had made a mistake? God's comment was an expression of sorrow, not an admission of error (Genesis 6.5–7). An omniscient God cannot make a mistake; therefore, God did not change his mind. He did, however, change his attitude toward Saul when Saul changed. Saul's heart no longer belonged to God, but to his own interests.

Samuel was angry; and he cried out to the LORD all night. 12 Samuel rose early in the
morning to meet Saul, and Samuel was told, "Saul went to Carmel, where he set up
a monument for himself, and on returning he passed on down to Gilgal." 13 When
Samuel came to Saul, Saul said to him, "May you be blessed by the LORD; I have
carried out the command of the LORD." 14 But Samuel said, "What then is this bleat-
ing of sheep in my ears, and the lowing of cattle that I hear?" 15 Saul said, "They **15.15** Gen 3.12,13
have brought them from the Amalekites; for the people spared the best of the sheep 1 Sam 15.9,21
and the cattle, to sacrifice to the LORD your God; but the rest we have utterly destroyed." 16 Then Samuel said to Saul, "Stop! I will tell you what the LORD said to
me last night." He replied, "Speak."
17 Samuel said, "Though you are little in your own eyes, are you not the head **15.17** Judg 6.15
of the tribes of Israel? The LORD anointed you king over Israel. 18 And the LORD 1 Sam 9.21
sent you on a mission, and said, 'Go, utterly destroy the sinners, the Amalekites, 10.22
and fight against them until they are consumed.' 19 Why then did you not obey the **15.19**
voice of the LORD? Why did you swoop down on the spoil, and do what was evil in 1 Sam 14.32
the sight of the LORD?" 20 Saul said to Samuel, "I have obeyed the voice of the
LORD, I have gone on the mission on which the LORD sent me, I have brought Agag
the king of Amalek, and I have utterly destroyed the Amalekites. 21 But from the **15.21**
spoil the people took sheep and cattle, the best of the things devoted to destruction, 1 Sam 15.9,15
to sacrifice to the LORD your God in Gilgal." 22 And Samuel said, **15.22**

"Has the LORD as great delight in burnt offerings and sacrifices, Ps 40.6-8 51.16-17
as in obeying the voice of the LORD? Isa 1.11 Jer 7.22
Surely, to obey is better than sacrifice, Hos 6.6 Mic 6.7,8
and to heed than the fat of rams. Mk 12.33
23 For rebellion is no less a sin than divination, **15.23** Deut 18.10
and stubbornness is like iniquity and idolatry. 1 Sam 13.14
Because you have rejected the word of the LORD,
he has also rejected you from being king."

Saul pleads for forgiveness

24 Saul said to Samuel, "I have sinned; for I have transgressed the command- **15.24** Num 22.34
ment of the LORD and your words, because I feared the people and obeyed their 2 Sam 12.13
voice. 25 Now therefore, I pray, pardon my sin, and return with me, so that I may Ps 51.4
worship the LORD." 26 Samuel said to Saul, "I will not return with you; for you have **15.25** Ex 10.17
rejected the word of the LORD, and the LORD has rejected you from being king over

---

15.12 Saul built a monument in honor of himself. What a contrast to Moses and Joshua, who gave all the credit to God.

15.13, 14 Saul thought he had won a great victory over the Amalekites, but God saw it as a great failure because Saul had disobeyed him and then lied to Samuel about the results of the battle. Saul may have thought his lie wouldn't be detected, or that what he had done was not wrong. Saul was deceiving himself.

Dishonest people soon begin to believe the lies they construct around themselves. Then they lose the ability to tell the difference between truth and lies. By believing your own lies you deceive yourself, you alienate yourself from God, and you lose credibility in all your relationships. In the long run, honesty wins out.

15.15 Saul was told to destroy everything, but he kept part of the spoils, including the choicest cattle. When Samuel arrived, he could see and hear the evidence of Saul's wrong actions. When confronted, Saul said the spoils taken were to be sacrificed to God. This is like saying, "But I only stole the money so I could put it in the offering plate!" Offerings, worship, and service are meaningless if they flow from a heart that is covering up for sin.

15.22, 23 This is the first of numerous places in the Bible where the theme "to obey is better than sacrifice" is repeated (Psalms 40.6–8; 51.16, 17; Proverbs 21.3; Isaiah 1.11–17; Jeremiah 7.21–23; Hosea 6.6; Micah 6.6–8; Matthew 12.7; Mark 12.33; Hebrews 10.8, 9). Was Samuel saying that sacrifice is unimportant? No, he was urging Saul to look at his reasons for making the sacrifice rather than at the sacrifice itself. A sacrifice was a ritual transaction between man and God that physically demonstrated a relationship between them. But if the person's heart was not truly repentant or if he did not truly love God, the sacrifice was a hollow ritual. Religious ceremonies or rituals are empty unless they are performed with an attitude of love and obedience. "Being religious" (going to church, serving on a committee, giving to charity) is not enough if we do not act out of devotion and obedience to God.

15.23 Rebellion and stubbornness are serious sins. They involve far more than being independent and strong-minded. Scripture equates them with witchcraft and idol worship, sins worthy of death (Exodus 22.18; Leviticus 20.6; Deuteronomy 13.12–15; 18.10; Micah 5.10–14).

Since Saul became both rebellious and stubborn, it is little wonder that God finally rejected him and took away his kingdom. Rebellion against God is perhaps the most serious sin of all, because as long as a person rebels, he or she closes the door to forgiveness and restoration with God.

15.26 Saul's excuses had come to an end. It was the time of reckoning. God wasn't rejecting Saul as a person; the king could still seek forgiveness and restore his relationship with God, but it was too late to get his kingdom back. If you do not act responsibly with what God has entrusted to you, eventually you will run out of excuses. All of us must one day give an account for our actions (Romans 14.12; Revelation 22.12).

15.27 1 Kgs 11.30,31 15.28 1 Sam 28.17,18 15.29 Num 23.19 Ezek 24.14 2 Tim 2.13 15.30 Isa 29.13

Israel." 27 As Samuel turned to go away, Saul caught hold of the hem of his robe,
and it tore. 28 And Samuel said to him, "The LORD has torn the kingdom of Israel
from you this very day, and has given it to a neighbor of yours, who is better than
you. 29 Moreover the Glory of Israel will not recant[x] or change his mind; for he is
not a mortal, that he should change his mind." 30 Then Saul[y] said, "I have sinned;
yet honor me now before the elders of my people and before Israel, and return with
me, so that I may worship the LORD your God." 31 So Samuel turned back after
Saul; and Saul worshiped the LORD.

32 Then Samuel said, "Bring Agag king of the Amalekites here to me." And
Agag came to him haltingly.[z] Agag said, "Surely this is the bitterness of death."[a]
33 But Samuel said,

15.33 Gen 9.5,6 Judg 1.7

"As your sword has made women childless,
so your mother shall be childless among women."

And Samuel hewed Agag in pieces before the LORD in Gilgal.

15.34 1 Sam 7.17 11.4; 15.35 1 Sam 15.11

34 Then Samuel went to Ramah; and Saul went up to his house in Gibeah of
Saul. 35 Samuel did not see Saul again until the day of his death, but Samuel grieved
over Saul. And the LORD was sorry that he had made Saul king over Israel.

C. SAUL AND DAVID (16.1—31.13)

While Saul is still on the throne, Samuel anoints David as Israel's next king. Young David then bravely conquers Goliath, the Philistine champion, and establishes a lifelong friendship with Jonathan, Saul's son. When Saul realizes that David will become king one day, he grows very jealous and tries to kill David on several occasions. David escapes into Philistine territory until Saul is killed in battle. When treated unjustly, we should not take matters into our own hands. God, who is faithful and just, sees all that is happening and will judge all evil.

1. Samuel anoints David as king

Samuel goes to Bethlehem

16.1 Ruth 4.18-22 1 Sam 9.16 13.13; 14 2 Kgs 9.1,2 16.2 1 Sam 20.28,29 16.3 Deut 17.14,15 16.4 1 Sam 16.18 Lk 2.4 16.5 Gen 35.2 Ex 19.10 Josh 3.5

16 The LORD said to Samuel, "How long will you grieve over Saul? I have
rejected him from being king over Israel. Fill your horn with oil and set out;
I will send you to Jesse the Bethlehemite, for I have provided for myself a king
among his sons." 2 Samuel said, "How can I go? If Saul hears of it, he will kill me."
And the LORD said, "Take a heifer with you, and say, 'I have come to sacrifice to
the LORD.' 3 Invite Jesse to the sacrifice, and I will show you what you shall do; and
you shall anoint for me the one whom I name to you." 4 Samuel did what the LORD
commanded, and came to Bethlehem. The elders of the city came to meet him
trembling, and said, "Do you come peaceably?" 5 He said, "Peaceably; I have come
to sacrifice to the LORD; sanctify yourselves and come with me to the sacrifice."
And he sanctified Jesse and his sons and invited them to the sacrifice.

6 When they came, he looked on Eliab and thought, "Surely the LORD's
anointed is now before the LORD."[b] 7 But the LORD said to Samuel, "Do not look
on his appearance or on the height of his stature, because I have rejected him; for

[x] Q Ms Gk: MT *deceive* [y] Heb *he* [z] Cn Compare Gk: Meaning of Heb uncertain [a] Q Ms Gk: MT *Surely the bitterness of death is past* [b] Heb *him*

15.30 Saul was more concerned about what others would think of him than he was about the status of his relationship with God. He begged Samuel to go with him to worship as a public demonstration that Samuel still supported him. If Samuel had refused, the people probably would have lost all confidence in Saul.

15.35 Samuel had to confront Saul with his disobedience and give him the news of God's judgment. He and Saul were not the best of friends. Saul had wronged and hurt both God and Samuel deeply. In spite of this, Samuel mourned for Saul when God promised to take his kingdom away. This is a great example of love. Never give up on people. Even if you'll never see them again, continue to pray for their repentance and eventual right relationship with God.

16.5 Samuel "sanctified" Jesse and his sons to prepare them to come before God to worship and to sacrifice. For more on the purification ceremony, see Genesis 35.2 and the note on Joshua 3.5.

16.7 Saul was tall and handsome; he was an impressive-looking man. Samuel may have been trying to find someone who looked like Saul to be Israel's next king, but God warned him against judging by appearance alone. When people judge by outward appearance, they may overlook individuals who lack the particular physical qualities society currently admires. But appearance doesn't reveal what people are really like or their true value.

Fortunately, God judges by faith and character, not appearances. And because only God can see on the inside, only he can accurately judge people. Most people spend hours each week maintaining their outward appearance; they should do even more to develop their inner character. While everyone can see your face, only you and God know what your heart really looks like. Which is the more attractive part of you?

the LORD does not see as mortals see; they look on the outward appearance, but the
LORD looks on the heart." [8]Then Jesse called Abinadab, and made him pass before
Samuel. He said, "Neither has the LORD chosen this one." [9]Then Jesse made
Shammah pass by. And he said, "Neither has the LORD chosen this one." [10]Jesse
made seven of his sons pass before Samuel, and Samuel said to Jesse, "The LORD
has not chosen any of these." [11]Samuel said to Jesse, "Are all your sons here?" And
he said, "There remains yet the youngest, but he is keeping the sheep." And Samuel said to Jesse, "Send and bring him; for we will not sit down until he comes
here." [12]He sent and brought him in. Now he was ruddy, and had beautiful eyes,
and was handsome. The LORD said, "Rise and anoint him; for this is the one."
[13]Then Samuel took the horn of oil, and anointed him in the presence of his brothers; and the spirit of the LORD came mightily upon David from that day forward.
Samuel then set out and went to Ramah.

16.7 1 Sam 9.2; 1 Kgs 8.39; 1 Chron 28.9; Lk 16.15
16.8 1 Sam 17.13
16.10 2 Sam 7.8; 1 Chron 17.7
16.12 Gen 39.6; Ex 2.1,2; 1 Sam 9.17; Acts 7.20
16.13 1 Sam 10.6, 9,10

David joins Saul's staff

14 Now the spirit of the LORD departed from Saul, and an evil spirit from the
LORD tormented him. [15]And Saul's servants said to him, "See now, an evil spirit
from God is tormenting you. [16]Let our lord now command the servants who attend
you to look for someone who is skillful in playing the lyre; and when the evil spirit
from God is upon you, he will play it, and you will feel better." [17]So Saul said to
his servants, "Provide for me someone who can play well, and bring him to me."
[18]One of the young men answered, "I have seen a son of Jesse the Bethlehemite
who is skillful in playing, a man of valor, a warrior, prudent in speech, and a man
of good presence; and the LORD is with him." [19]So Saul sent messengers to Jesse,
and said, "Send me your son David who is with the sheep." [20]Jesse took a donkey
loaded with bread, a skin of wine, and a kid, and sent them by his son David to
Saul. [21]And David came to Saul, and entered his service. Saul loved him greatly,
and he became his armor-bearer. [22]Saul sent to Jesse, saying, "Let David remain in
my service, for he has found favor in my sight." [23]And whenever the evil spirit
from God came upon Saul, David took the lyre and played it with his hand, and
Saul would be relieved and feel better, and the evil spirit would depart from him.

16.14 1 Sam 11.6; 18.10-12; 19.9; 1 Kgs 22.22
16.15 2 Kgs 3.15
16.18 1 Sam 3.19; 18.11,12
16.21 1 Sam 22.14

2. David and Goliath

Goliath challenges Israel

17 Now the Philistines gathered their armies for battle; they were gathered at
Socoh, which belongs to Judah, and encamped between Socoh and Azekah,
in Ephes-dammim. [2]Saul and the Israelites gathered and encamped in the valley of
Elah, and formed ranks against the Philistines. [3]The Philistines stood on the mountain on the one side, and Israel stood on the mountain on the other side, with a
valley between them. [4]And there came out from the camp of the Philistines a cham-

17.1 1 Sam 13.5; 1 Chron 11.13
17.2 1 Sam 21.9
17.4 Josh 11.21,22; 2 Sam 21.19

16.13 David was anointed king, but it was done in secret; he was not publicly anointed until much later (2 Samuel 2.4; 5.3). Saul was still legally the king, but God was preparing David for his future responsibilities. The anointing oil poured over David's head stood for holiness. It was used to set people or objects apart for God's service. Each king and high priest of Israel was anointed with oil. This commissioned him as God's representative to the nation. Although God rejected Saul's kingship by not allowing any of his descendants to sit on Israel's throne, Saul himself remained in his position until his death.

16.14 What was this evil spirit the Lord sent? Perhaps Saul was simply depressed. Or perhaps the Holy Spirit had left Saul and God allowed an evil spirit (a demon) to torment him as judgment for his disobedience (this would demonstrate God's power over the spirit world – 1 Kings 22.19–23). Either way, Saul was driven to insanity, which led him to attempt to murder David.

16.15, 16 Harps were popular musical instruments in Saul's day, and their music is still known for its soothing qualities. The simplest harps were merely two pieces of wood fastened at right angles to each other. The strings were stretched across the wood to give the harp a triangular shape. Simple strings could be made of twisted grasses, but better strings were made of dried animal intestine. Harps could have up to 40 strings and were louder than the smaller three- or four-stringed instruments called lyres. David, known for his shepherding skills and bravery, was also an accomplished harpist and musician who would eventually write many of the psalms found in the Bible.

16.19–21 When Saul asked David to join his palace staff, he obviously did not know that David had been secretly anointed king (16.12). Saul's invitation presented an excellent opportunity for the young future king to gain firsthand information about leading a nation ("David went back and forth from Saul," 17.15).

Sometimes our plans – even the ones we think God has approved – have to be put on hold indefinitely. Like David, we can use this waiting time profitably. We can choose to learn and grow in our present circumstances, whatever they may be.

pion named Goliath, of Gath, whose height was six[c] cubits and a span. 5 He had a
helmet of bronze on his head, and he was armed with a coat of mail; the weight of
the coat was five thousand shekels of bronze. 6 He had greaves of bronze on his legs
and a javelin of bronze slung between his shoulders. 7 The shaft of his spear was
like a weaver's beam, and his spear's head weighed six hundred shekels of iron;
and his shield-bearer went before him. 8 He stood and shouted to the ranks of Israel,
"Why have you come out to draw up for battle? Am I not a Philistine, and are you
not servants of Saul? Choose a man for yourselves, and let him come down to me.
17.9 2 Sam 2.12-16 9 If he is able to fight with me and kill me, then we will be your servants; but if I
prevail against him and kill him, then you shall be our servants and serve us."
10 And the Philistine said, "Today I defy the ranks of Israel! Give me a man, that we
may fight together." 11 When Saul and all Israel heard these words of the Philistine,
they were dismayed and greatly afraid.
17.12 Gen 35.19 Ruth 4.18-22 1 Chron 2.13 12 Now David was the son of an Ephrathite of Bethlehem in Judah, named
Jesse, who had eight sons. In the days of Saul the man was already old and ad-
vanced in years.[d] 13 The three eldest sons of Jesse had followed Saul to the battle;
the names of his three sons who went to the battle were Eliab the firstborn, and next
to him Abinadab, and the third Shammah. 14 David was the youngest; the three
eldest followed Saul, 15 but David went back and forth from Saul to feed his father's
sheep at Bethlehem. 16 For forty days the Philistine came forward and took his
stand, morning and evening.
17.17 1 Sam 25.18 17 Jesse said to his son David, "Take for your brothers an ephah of this parched
grain and these ten loaves, and carry them quickly to the camp to your brothers;
17.18 Gen 37.13,14 18 also take these ten cheeses to the commander of their thousand. See how your
brothers fare, and bring some token from them."
19 Now Saul, and they, and all the men of Israel, were in the valley of Elah,
17.20 1 Sam 26.5,7 fighting with the Philistines. 20 David rose early in the morning, left the sheep with
a keeper, took the provisions, and went as Jesse had commanded him. He came to
the encampment as the army was going forth to the battle line, shouting the war cry.
21 Israel and the Philistines drew up for battle, army against army. 22 David left the
things in charge of the keeper of the baggage, ran to the ranks, and went and
greeted his brothers. 23 As he talked with them, the champion, the Philistine of
Gath, Goliath by name, came up out of the ranks of the Philistines, and spoke the
same words as before. And David heard him.
24 All the Israelites, when they saw the man, fled from him and were very

[c] MT: Q Ms Gk *four* [d] Gk Syr: Heb *among men*

DAVID AND GOLIATH The armies of Israel and Philistia faced each other across the Elah Valley. David arrived from Bethlehem and offered to fight the giant Goliath. After David defeated Goliath, the Israelite army chased the Philistines to Ekron and Gath (Goliath's hometown).

17.4–7 In the days of the exodus, most of the Israelites had been afraid to enter the promised land because of the giants living there (Numbers 13.32, 33). King Og of Bashan needed a bed over 13 feet long (Deuteronomy 3.11). Now Goliath, nearly ten feet tall ("six cubits and a span"), taunted Israel's soldiers and appeared invincible to them. Saul, the tallest of the Israelites, may have been especially worried because he was obviously the best match for Goliath. In God's eyes, however, Goliath was no different from anyone else.

17.9 An army often avoided the high cost of battle by pitting its strongest warrior against the strongest warrior of the enemy. This avoided great bloodshed because the winner of the fight was considered the winner of the battle. Goliath had the definite advantage over David from a human standpoint. But Goliath didn't realize that in fighting David, he also had to fight God.

17.16 Why would this go on for 40 days without one side attacking the other? They were camped on opposite sides of a valley with steep walls. Whoever would rush down the valley and up the steep cliffs would be at a disadvantage at the beginning of the battle and probably suffer great casualties. Each side was waiting for the other to attack first.

17.18 "Bring some token from them" means that David should bring back proof that he had fulfilled his mission, and perhaps a personal greeting.

much afraid. 25 The Israelites said, "Have you seen this man who has come up?
Surely he has come up to defy Israel. The king will greatly enrich the man who kills
him, and will give him his daughter and make his family free in Israel." 26 David
said to the men who stood by him, "What shall be done for the man who kills this
Philistine, and takes away the reproach from Israel? For who is this uncircumcised
Philistine that he should defy the armies of the living God?" 27 The people answered
him in the same way, "So shall it be done for the man who kills him."
28 His eldest brother Eliab heard him talking to the men; and Eliab's anger was
kindled against David. He said, "Why have you come down? With whom have you
left those few sheep in the wilderness? I know your presumption and the evil of
your heart; for you have come down just to see the battle." 29 David said, "What
have I done now? It was only a question." 30 He turned away from him toward
another and spoke in the same way; and the people answered him again as before.

David kills Goliath

31 When the words that David spoke were heard, they repeated them before
Saul; and he sent for him. 32 David said to Saul, "Let no one's heart fail because of
him; your servant will go and fight with this Philistine." 33 Saul said to David, "You
are not able to go against this Philistine to fight with him; for you are just a boy, and
he has been a warrior from his youth." 34 But David said to Saul, "Your servant
used to keep sheep for his father; and whenever a lion or a bear came, and took a
lamb from the flock, 35 I went after it and struck it down, rescuing the lamb from its
mouth; and if it turned against me, I would catch it by the jaw, strike it down, and
kill it. 36 Your servant has killed both lions and bears; and this uncircumcised Philistine shall be like one of them, since he has defied the armies of the living God."
37 David said, "The LORD, who saved me from the paw of the lion and from the paw
of the bear, will save me from the hand of this Philistine." So Saul said to David,
"Go, and may the LORD be with you!"
38 Saul clothed David with his armor; he put a bronze helmet on his head and
clothed him with a coat of mail. 39 David strapped Saul's sword over the armor, and
he tried in vain to walk, for he was not used to them. Then David said to Saul, "I
cannot walk with these; for I am not used to them." So David removed them.
40 Then he took his staff in his hand, and chose five smooth stones from the wadi,
and put them in his shepherd's bag, in the pouch; his sling was in his hand, and he
drew near to the Philistine.
41 The Philistine came on and drew near to David, with his shield-bearer in
front of him. 42 When the Philistine looked and saw David, he disdained him, for he
was only a youth, ruddy and handsome in appearance. 43 The Philistine said to David, "Am I a dog, that you come to me with sticks?" And the Philistine cursed
David by his gods. 44 The Philistine said to David, "Come to me, and I will give
your flesh to the birds of the air and to the wild animals of the field." 45 But David
said to the Philistine, "You come to me with sword and spear and javelin; but I
come to you in the name of the LORD of hosts, the God of the armies of Israel,
whom you have defied. 46 This very day the LORD will deliver you into my hand,
and I will strike you down and cut off your head; and I will give the dead bodies of
the Philistine army this very day to the birds of the air and to the wild animals of the
earth, so that all the earth may know that there is a God in Israel, 47 and that all this
assembly may know that the LORD does not save by sword and spear; for the battle
is the LORD's and he will give you into our hand."
48 When the Philistine drew nearer to meet David, David ran quickly toward

17.25 Josh 15.16; 1 Sam 18.17
17.26 1 Sam 14.6; 2 Kgs 19.4
17.28 Gen 37.4,8
17.32 Deut 20.1; Ps 27.3
17.35 Amos 3.12
17.36 1 Sam 17.26
17.37 1 Sam 20.13; Ps 18.16,17; 2 Tim 4.17
17.42 1 Sam 16.12
17.43 2 Sam 3.8; 9.8; 16.9; 1 Kgs 20.10
17.45 2 Chron 32.8; Ps 124.8; Prov 18.10; Heb 11.34
17.46 Ex 7.5; Josh 4.24; 2 Kgs 19.19; Isa 37.20; Dan 2.47
17.47 1 Sam 14.6; 2 Chron 14.11; 20.15; Ps 44.6

17.26 What a difference perspective can make. Most of the onlookers saw only a giant. David, however, saw a mortal man defying almighty God. He knew he would not be alone when he faced Goliath; God would fight with him. He looked at his situation from God's point of view. Viewing impossible situations from God's point of view helps us put giant problems into perspective. Once we see clearly we can fight more effectively.

17.28–32 Criticism couldn't stop David. While the rest of the army stood around, he knew the importance of taking action. With God to fight for him, there was no reason to wait. People may try to discourage you with negative comments or mockery, but continue to do what you know is right. By doing what is right, you will be pleasing God, whose opinion matters most.

17.40 A wadi is a dry stream or riverbed.

the battle line to meet the Philistine. 49 David put his hand in his bag, took out a
stone, slung it, and struck the Philistine on his forehead; the stone sank into his
forehead, and he fell face down on the ground.
17.50 1 Sam 21.9 2 Sam 23.21 50 So David prevailed over the Philistine with a sling and a stone, striking
down the Philistine and killing him; there was no sword in David's hand. 51 Then
David ran and stood over the Philistine; he grasped his sword, drew it out of its
sheath, and killed him; then he cut off his head with it.
17.52 Josh 15.10,11, 33-36 When the Philistines saw that their champion was dead, they fled. 52 The troops
of Israel and Judah rose up with a shout and pursued the Philistines as far as Gath[e]
and the gates of Ekron, so that the wounded Philistines fell on the way from

[e] Gk Syr: Heb *Gai*

DAVID

When we think of David, we think: shepherd, poet, giant-killer, king, ancestor of Jesus—in short, one of the greatest men in the Old Testament. But alongside that list stands another: betrayer, liar, adulterer, murderer. The first list gives qualities we all might like to have; the second, qualities that might be true of any one of us. The Bible makes no effort to hide David's failures. Yet he is remembered and respected for his heart for God. Knowing how much more we share in David's failures than in his greatness, we should be curious to find out what made God refer to David as "a man after my heart."

David, more than anything else, had an unchangeable belief in the faithful and forgiving nature of God. He was a man who lived with great zest. He sinned many times, but he was quick to confess his sins. His confessions were from the heart, and his repentance was genuine. David never took God's forgiveness lightly or his blessing for granted. In return, God never held back from David either his forgiveness or the consequences of David's actions. David experienced the joy of forgiveness even when he had to suffer the consequences of his sins.

We tend to get these two reversed. Too often we would rather avoid the consequences than experience forgiveness. Another big difference between us and David is that, while he sinned greatly, he did not sin repeatedly. He learned from his mistakes because he accepted the suffering they brought. Often we don't seem to learn from our mistakes or the consequences that result from those mistakes. What changes would it take for God to find this kind of obedience in you?

Strengths and accomplishments:
- Greatest king of Israel
- Ancestor of Jesus Christ
- Listed in the Hall of Faith in Hebrews 11
- A man described by God himself as a man after his own heart (1 Samuel 13.14)

Weaknesses and mistakes:
- Committed adultery with Bathsheba
- Arranged the murder of Uriah, Bathsheba's husband
- Directly disobeyed God in taking a census of the people
- Did not deal decisively with the sins of his children

Lessons from his life:
- Willingness to honestly admit our mistakes is the first step in dealing with them
- Forgiveness does not remove the consequences of sin
- God greatly desires our complete trust and worship

Vital statistics:
- Where: Bethlehem, Jerusalem
- Occupation: Shepherd, musician, poet, soldier, king
- Relatives: Father, Jesse. Wives included Michal, Ahinoam, Bathsheba, Abigail. Sons included Absalom, Amnon, Solomon, Adonijah. Daughters included Tamar. Seven brothers
- Contemporaries: Saul, Jonathan, Samuel, Nathan

Key verses:
"And now, O Lord God, you are God, and your words are true, and you have promised this good thing to your servant; now therefore may it please you to bless the house of your servant, so that it may continue forever before you; for you, O Lord God, have spoken, and with your blessing shall the house of your servant be blessed forever" (2 Samuel 7.28, 29).

His story is told in 1 Samuel 16—1 Kings 2. He is also mentioned in Amos 6.5; Matthew 1.1; 22.43–45; Luke 1.32; Acts 13.22; Romans 1.3; Hebrews 11.32.

17.51 The Philistines fled when Goliath fell because he was their champion. They did not believe any of Israel's soldiers could defeat him in battle. If a boy like David could defeat the mightiest warrior with God's help, think what the entire army could do!

Shaaraim as far as Gath and Ekron. 53 The Israelites came back from chasing the
Philistines, and they plundered their camp. 54 David took the head of the Philistine
and brought it to Jerusalem; but he put his armor in his tent.
55 When Saul saw David go out against the Philistine, he said to Abner, the **17.55**
commander of the army, "Abner, whose son is this young man?" Abner said, "As 1 Sam 14.50,51
your soul lives, O king, I do not know." 56 The king said, "Inquire whose son the
stripling is." 57 On David's return from killing the Philistine, Abner took him and
brought him before Saul, with the head of the Philistine in his hand. 58 Saul said to **17.58**
him, "Whose son are you, young man?" And David answered, "I am the son of 1 Sam 16.18
your servant Jesse the Bethlehemite."

3. David and Jonathan become friends

Saul is jealous of David

18 When David[f] had finished speaking to Saul, the soul of Jonathan was bound **18.1**
to the soul of David, and Jonathan loved him as his own soul. 2 Saul took him 1 Sam 20.8 23.18
that day and would not let him return to his father's house. 3 Then Jonathan made 2 Sam 1.26; 9.1
a covenant with David, because he loved him as his own soul. 4 Jonathan stripped **18.4**
himself of the robe that he was wearing, and gave it to David, and his armor, and Gen 41.42 Esth 6.8
even his sword and his bow and his belt. 5 David went out and was successful wherever Saul sent him; as a result, Saul set him over the army. And all the people, even
the servants of Saul, approved.
6 As they were coming home, when David returned from killing the Philistine, **18.6**
the women came out of all the towns of Israel, singing and dancing, to meet King Judg 11.34
Saul, with tambourines, with songs of joy, and with musical instruments.[g] 7 And Ps 68.24; 149.3 **18.7**
the women sang to one another as they made merry, 1 Sam 21.11

"Saul has killed his thousands,
 and David his ten thousands." 29.5

8 Saul was very angry, for this saying displeased him. He said, "They have ascribed **18.8**
to David ten thousands, and to me they have ascribed thousands; what more can he 1 Sam 15.28
have but the kingdom?" 9 So Saul eyed David from that day on. 16.13
10 The next day an evil spirit from God rushed upon Saul, and he raved within **18.10**
his house, while David was playing the lyre, as he did day by day. Saul had his 1 Sam 16.14,23
spear in his hand; 11 and Saul threw the spear, for he thought, "I will pin David to
the wall." But David eluded him twice.
12 Saul was afraid of David, because the LORD was with him but had departed **18.13**
from Saul. 13 So Saul removed him from his presence, and made him a commander 2 Sam 5.2 **18.14**
of a thousand; and David marched out and came in, leading the army. 14 David had 1 Sam 14.47
success in all his undertakings; for the LORD was with him. 15 When Saul saw that 16.18; 18.30 2 Sam 5.10

f Heb *he* g Or *triangles,* or *three-stringed instruments*

17.55–58 Although David had played his harp many times in front of Saul, Saul's question to Abner seems to show he didn't know David very well. Perhaps, since David was scheduled to marry Saul's daughter if he was successful (17.25), Saul wanted to know more about his family. Or possibly Saul's unstable mental condition (16.14) may have prevented him from recognizing David.

18.1–4 When David and Jonathan met, they became close friends at once. Their friendship is one of the deepest and closest recorded in the Bible: (1) they based their friendship on commitment to God, not just to each other; (2) they let nothing come between them, not even career or family problems; (3) they drew closer together when their friendship was tested; and (4) they remained friends to the end.

Jonathan, the prince of Israel, later realized that David, and not he, would be the next king (23.17). But that did not weaken his love for David. Jonathan would much rather lose the throne of Israel than lose his closest friend.

18.8 Saul's appreciation for David turned to jealousy as people began to applaud David's exploits. In a jealous rage, Saul attempted to murder David by hurling his spear at him (18.11, 12).

Jealousy may not seem to be a major sin, but in reality, it is one step short of murder. It begins by destroying a person on the inside; then it manifests itself in harmful actions. Beware of letting jealousy get a foothold in your life.

18.10 The note on 16.14 explains what this evil spirit might have been.

18.11, 12 Saul tried to kill David because he was jealous of David's popularity, yet David continued to protect and comfort Saul. Perhaps people have been jealous of you and have even attacked you in some way. They may be intimidated by your strengths, which make them conscious of their own shortcomings. It would be natural to strike back or to avoid them. A better response is to befriend them (Matthew 5.43, 44) and to ask God for the strength to continue to love them, as David kept on loving Saul.

18.15–18 While Saul's popularity made him proud and arrogant, David remained humble even when the entire nation praised him (18.23). Although David succeeded in almost everything he tried and became famous throughout the land, he refused to use his

he had great success, he stood in awe of him. 16 But all Israel and Judah loved
David; for it was he who marched out and came in leading them.

David marries Saul's daughter

18.17 17 Then Saul said to David, "Here is my elder daughter Merab; I will give her
1 Sam 17.25 25.28 to you as a wife; only be valiant for me and fight the LORD's battles." For Saul
thought, "I will not raise a hand against him; let the Philistines deal with him."
18.18 Ex 3.11 18 David said to Saul, "Who am I and who are my kinsfolk, my father's family in
1 Sam 9.21 2 Sam 7.18 Israel, that I should be son-in-law to the king?" 19 But at the time when Saul's
daughter Merab should have been given to David, she was given to Adriel the Me-
18.19 2 Sam 21.8 holathite as a wife.

20 Now Saul's daughter Michal loved David. Saul was told, and the thing
pleased him. 21 Saul thought, "Let me give her to him that she may be a snare for
him and that the hand of the Philistines may be against him." Therefore Saul said
to David a second time,[h] "You shall now be my son-in-law." 22 Saul commanded
his servants, "Speak to David in private and say, 'See, the king is delighted with
18.23 you, and all his servants love you; now then, become the king's son-in-law.' " 23 So
Gen 29.20 34.12 Saul's servants reported these words to David in private. And David said, "Does it
seem to you a little thing to become the king's son-in-law, seeing that I am a poor
man and of no repute?" 24 The servants of Saul told him, "This is what David said."
25 Then Saul said, "Thus shall you say to David, 'The king desires no marriage
present except a hundred foreskins of the Philistines, that he may be avenged on the
king's enemies.' " Now Saul planned to make David fall by the hand of the Philistines. 26 When his servants told David these words, David was well pleased to be
18.27 the king's son-in-law. Before the time had expired, 27 David rose and went, along
2 Sam 3.14 with his men, and killed one hundred[i] of the Philistines; and David brought their
foreskins, which were given in full number to the king, that he might become the
king's son-in-law. Saul gave him his daughter Michal as a wife. 28 But when Saul
realized that the LORD was with David, and that Saul's daughter Michal loved him,
29 Saul was still more afraid of David. So Saul was David's enemy from that time
forward.

18.30 1 Sam 18.14 30 Then the commanders of the Philistines came out to battle; and as often as

[h] Heb *by two* [i] Gk Compare 2 Sam 3.14: Heb *two hundred*

SIMPLE OBJECTS God often uses simple, ordinary objects to accomplish his tasks in the world. It is important only that they be dedicated to him for his use. What do you have that God can use? Anything and everything is a possible "instrument" for him.

Object	*Reference*	*Who used it?*	*How was it used?*
a staff	Exodus 4.2–4	Moses	To work miracles before Pharaoh
trumpets	Joshua 6.3–5	Joshua	To flatten the walls of Jericho
a fleece	Judges 6.36–40	Gideon	To confirm God's will
trumpets, jars, and torches	Judges 7.19–22	Gideon	To defeat the Midianites
jawbone	Judges 15.15	Samson	To kill 1,000 Philistines
small stone	1 Samuel 17.40	David	To slay Goliath
oil	2 Kings 4.1–7	Elisha	To demonstrate God's power to provide
a river	2 Kings 5.9–14	Elisha	To heal a man of leprosy
loincloth	Jeremiah 13.1–11	Jeremiah	As an object lesson of God's wrath
pottery	Jeremiah 19.1–13	Jeremiah	As an object lesson of God's wrath
iron plate, water, and food	Ezekiel 4.1–17	Ezekiel	As an object lesson of judgment
five loaves and two fish	Mark 6.30–44	Jesus	To feed a crowd of over 5,000 people

popular support to his advantage against Saul. Don't allow popularity to twist your perception of your own importance. It's comparatively easy to be humble when you're not on center stage, but how will you react to praise and honor?

they came out, David had more success than all the servants of Saul, so that his
fame became very great.

David escapes from Saul

19 Saul spoke with his son Jonathan and with all his servants about killing Da- **19.1**
vid. But Saul's son Jonathan took great delight in David. 2 Jonathan told 1 Sam 18.1-3
David, "My father Saul is trying to kill you; therefore be on guard tomorrow morning; stay in a secret place and hide yourself. 3 I will go out and stand beside my **19.3**
father in the field where you are, and I will speak to my father about you; if I learn 1 Sam 20.9
anything I will tell you." 4 Jonathan spoke well of David to his father Saul, saying
to him, "The king should not sin against his servant David, because he has not
sinned against you, and because his deeds have been of good service to you; 5 for **19.5**
he took his life in his hand when he attacked the Philistine, and the LORD brought Deut 19.10-13 1 Sam 17.49,50
about a great victory for all Israel. You saw it, and rejoiced; why then will you sin Ps 94.21
against an innocent person by killing David without cause?" 6 Saul heeded the voice
of Jonathan; Saul swore, "As the LORD lives, he shall not be put to death." 7 So **19.7**
Jonathan called David and related all these things to him. Jonathan then brought 1 Sam 16.21
David to Saul, and he was in his presence as before.

8 Again there was war, and David went out to fight the Philistines. He launched
a heavy attack on them, so that they fled before him. 9 Then an evil spirit from the **19.9**
LORD came upon Saul, as he sat in his house with his spear in his hand, while David 1 Sam 16.14 18.10-12
was playing music. 10 Saul sought to pin David to the wall with the spear; but he
eluded Saul, so that he struck the spear into the wall. David fled and escaped that
night.

11 Saul sent messengers to David's house to keep watch over him, planning to **19.11**
kill him in the morning. David's wife Michal told him, "If you do not save your life Judg 16.2 Ps 59 (title),vss
tonight, tomorrow you will be killed." 12 So Michal let David down through the 3,4,6
window; he fled away and escaped. 13 Michal took an idol[j] and laid it on the bed; **19.13**
she put a net[k] of goats' hair on its head, and covered it with the clothes. 14 When Judg 17.4,5 18.14,17
Saul sent messengers to take David, she said, "He is sick." 15 Then Saul sent the
messengers to see David for themselves. He said, "Bring him up to me in the bed,
that I may kill him." 16 When the messengers came in, the idol[l] was in the bed,
with the covering[k] of goats' hair on its head. 17 Saul said to Michal, "Why have you
deceived me like this, and let my enemy go, so that he has escaped?" Michal answered Saul, "He said to me, 'Let me go; why should I kill you?' "

18 Now David fled and escaped; he came to Samuel at Ramah, and told him all **19.18**
that Saul had done to him. He and Samuel went and settled at Naioth. 19 Saul was 1 Sam 7.17 15.34; 19.22
told, "David is at Naioth in Ramah." 20 Then Saul sent messengers to take David. **19.20**
When they saw the company of the prophets in a frenzy, with Samuel standing in Num 11.24,25 1 Sam 10.5,
charge of[k] them, the spirit of God came upon the messengers of Saul, and they also 6,10
fell into a prophetic frenzy. 21 When Saul was told, he sent other messengers, and Joel 2.28
they also fell into a frenzy. Saul sent messengers again the third time, and they also
fell into a frenzy. 22 Then he himself went to Ramah. He came to the great well that **19.22**
is in Secu;[m] he asked, "Where are Samuel and David?" And someone said, "They 1 Sam 19.18
are at Naioth in Ramah." 23 He went there, toward Naioth in Ramah; and the spirit **19.23** 1 Sam 19.20

[j] Heb *took the teraphim* [k] Meaning of Heb uncertain [l] Heb *the teraphim* [m] Gk reads *to the well of the threshing floor on the bare height*

19.1, 2 Is it ever right to disobey your father, as Jonathan did here? It is clearly a principle of Scripture that when a father instructs a son to break God's law, the son should obey God rather than man. This principle assumes that the son is old enough to be accountable and see through any deception. A son's role is to be respectful, helpful, and obedient to his father (Ephesians 6.1–3) but not to follow commands or advice that violate God's law.

19.20–24 This was the second time that Saul surprised everyone by joining a band of prophets and prophesying. The first time (chapter 10) happened right after he was anointed king and did not want to accept the responsibility. This time Saul was consumed with jealousy over David's growing popularity, but the Spirit of God immobilized him so he was unable to harm David. In both cases, Saul spoke God's words (he "prophesied"), although he was far from thinking God's thoughts.

19.23 Jonathan spoke up for David (19.4); Michal helped him escape (19.11–17); Samuel gave him a place to hide (19.18); and the Spirit of God interrupted Saul's manhunt (19.23). Each of these events protected David from harm or death. They were more than coincidence: God was at work. When you are spared from harm, recognize that God may be protecting you because he has a purpose for you.

of God came upon him. As he was going, he fell into a prophetic frenzy, until he
19.24 1 Sam 10.10-12 2 Sam 6.20 Mic 1.8 came to Naioth in Ramah. 24 He too stripped off his clothes, and he too fell into a
frenzy before Samuel. He lay naked all that day and all that night. Therefore it is
said, "Is Saul also among the prophets?"

David and Jonathan's friendship

20.1 1 Sam 24.9, 11,17 **20** David fled from Naioth in Ramah. He came before Jonathan and said,
"What have I done? What is my guilt? And what is my sin against your
father that he is trying to take my life?" 2 He said to him, "Far from it! You shall not
die. My father does nothing either great or small without disclosing it to me; and
20.3 Deut 6.13 2 Kgs 2.6,7 Jer 4.2 why should my father hide this from me? Never!" 3 But David also swore, "Your
father knows well that you like me; and he thinks, 'Do not let Jonathan know this,
or he will be grieved.' But truly, as the LORD lives and as you yourself live, there
is but a step between me and death." 4 Then Jonathan said to David, "Whatever you
20.5 Num 10.10 28.11-17 say, I will do for you." 5 David said to Jonathan, "Tomorrow is the new moon, and
I should not fail to sit with the king at the meal; but let me go, so that I may hide in
20.6 1 Sam 16.2 17.58; 20.28 the field until the third evening. 6 If your father misses me at all, then say, 'David
earnestly asked leave of me to run to Bethlehem his city; for there is a yearly sacri-
fice there for all the family.' 7 If he says, 'Good!' it will be well with your servant;
20.8 1 Sam 18.1-3 23.18 2 Sam 1.26 but if he is angry, then know that evil has been determined by him. 8 Therefore deal
kindly with your servant, for you have brought your servant into a sacred cove-
nant[n] with you. But if there is guilt in me, kill me yourself; why should you bring
20.9 1 Sam 19.2 me to your father?" 9 Jonathan said, "Far be it from you! If I knew that it was decided by my father that evil should come upon you, would I not tell you?" 10 Then
David said to Jonathan, "Who will tell me if your father answers you harshly?"
11 Jonathan replied to David, "Come, let us go out into the field." So they both went
out into the field.

12 Jonathan said to David, "By the LORD, the God of Israel! When I have
sounded out my father, about this time tomorrow, or on the third day, if he is well
20.13 Ruth 1.17 1 Sam 3.17 14.44; 18.11,12 1 Chron 28.20 disposed toward David, shall I not then send and disclose it to you? 13 But if my
father intends to do you harm, the LORD do so to Jonathan, and more also, if I do
not disclose it to you, and send you away, so that you may go in safety. May the
20.15 1 Sam 24.21 2 Sam 9.1; 21.7 LORD be with you, as he has been with my father. 14 If I am still alive, show me the
faithful love of the LORD; but if I die,[o] 15 never cut off your faithful love from my
20.16 Deut 23.21 1 Sam 25.22 house, even if the LORD were to cut off every one of the enemies of David from the
face of the earth." 16 Thus Jonathan made a covenant with the house of David,

[n] Heb *a covenant of the LORD* [o] Meaning of Heb uncertain

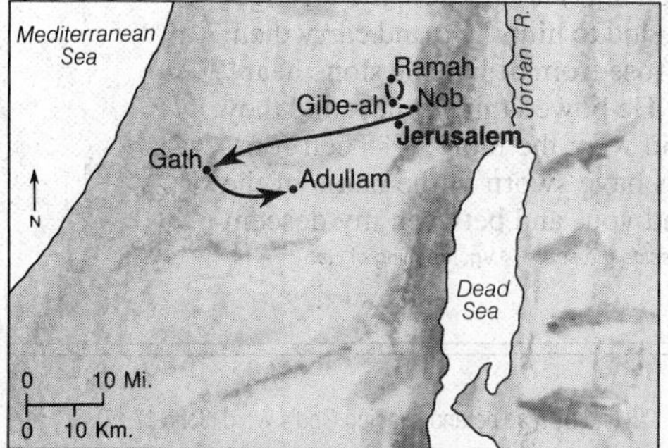

DAVID'S ESCAPE David learned of Saul's plans to kill him, and fled to Samuel at Ramah. Returning to Gibeah to say good-bye to Jonathan, he then escaped to Nob, where he received food and a sword from the priest. He then fled to Gath in Philistine territory. When the Philistines became suspicious, he escaped to a cave near Adullam, where many men joined him.

20.5 At the beginning of each month, the Israelites gathered to celebrate the festival of the new moon. While this was mainly a time to be enjoyed, it was also a way to dedicate the next month to God. Other nations had celebrations during the full moon and worshiped the moon itself. The Israelites, however, celebrated their festival at the time of the new moon, when the moon was not visible in the sky. This was an added precaution against false worship. Nothing in creation is to be worshiped – only the Creator is to be worshiped.

20.15 Jonathan asked David to keep a promise to treat his children kindly in the future. Years later David took great pains to fulfill this promise: he invited Jonathan's son Mephibosheth into his palace to live (2 Samuel 9).

saying, "May the LORD seek out the enemies of David." 17 Jonathan made David
swear again by his love for him; for he loved him as he loved his own life.
18 Jonathan said to him, "Tomorrow is the new moon; you will be missed,
because your place will be empty. 19 On the day after tomorrow, you shall go a long
way down; go to the place where you hid yourself earlier, and remain beside the
stone there.[p] 20 I will shoot three arrows to the side of it, as though I shot at a mark.
21 Then I will send the boy, saying, 'Go, find the arrows.' If I say to the boy, 'Look,
the arrows are on this side of you, collect them,' then you are to come, for, as the
LORD lives, it is safe for you and there is no danger. 22 But if I say to the young man,
'Look, the arrows are beyond you,' then go; for the LORD has sent you away. 23 As **20.23**
for the matter about which you and I have spoken, the LORD is witness[q] between Gen 31.49,53
you and me forever."
24 So David hid himself in the field. When the new moon came, the king sat at
the feast to eat. 25 The king sat upon his seat, as at other times, upon the seat by the
wall. Jonathan stood, while Abner sat by Saul's side; but David's place was empty.
26 Saul did not say anything that day; for he thought, "Something has befallen **20.26**
him; he is not clean, surely he is not clean." 27 But on the second day, the day after Lev 7.21 Num 19.16
the new moon, David's place was empty. And Saul said to his son Jonathan, "Why 1 Sam 16.5
has the son of Jesse not come to the feast, either yesterday or today?" 28 Jonathan **20.28**
answered Saul, "David earnestly asked leave of me to go to Bethlehem; 29 he said, 1 Sam 20.6
'Let me go; for our family is holding a sacrifice in the city, and my brother has
commanded me to be there. So now, if I have found favor in your sight, let me get
away, and see my brothers.' For this reason he has not come to the king's table."
30 Then Saul's anger was kindled against Jonathan. He said to him, "You son **20.30**
of a perverse, rebellious woman! Do I not know that you have chosen the son of Judg 11.1
Jesse to your own shame, and to the shame of your mother's nakedness? 31 For as **20.31**
long as the son of Jesse lives upon the earth, neither you nor your kingdom shall be 1 Sam 26.16
established. Now send and bring him to me, for he shall surely die." 32 Then Jona- 2 Sam 12.5
than answered his father Saul, "Why should he be put to death? What has he done?"
33 But Saul threw his spear at him to strike him; so Jonathan knew that it was the **20.33**
decision of his father to put David to death. 34 Jonathan rose from the table in fierce 1 Sam 18.11
anger and ate no food on the second day of the month, for he was grieved for David, 19.10,11
and because his father had disgraced him.
35 In the morning Jonathan went out into the field to the appointment with David, and with him was a little boy. 36 He said to the boy, "Run and find the arrows **20.36**
that I shoot." As the boy ran, he shot an arrow beyond him. 37 When the boy came 1 Sam 20.20,21
to the place where Jonathan's arrow had fallen, Jonathan called after the boy and
said, "Is the arrow not beyond you?" 38 Jonathan called after the boy, "Hurry, be
quick, do not linger." So Jonathan's boy gathered up the arrows and came to his
master. 39 But the boy knew nothing; only Jonathan and David knew the arrangement. 40 Jonathan gave his weapons to the boy and said to him, "Go and carry them
to the city." 41 As soon as the boy had gone, David rose from beside the stone heap[r]
and prostrated himself with his face to the ground. He bowed three times, and they
kissed each other, and wept with each other; David wept the more.[s] 42 Then Jona- **20.42**
than said to David, "Go in peace, since both of us have sworn in the name of the 1 Sam 20.14,
LORD, saying, 'The LORD shall be between me and you, and between my descen- 15; 23.18

[p] Meaning of Heb uncertain [q] Gk: Heb lacks *witness* [r] Gk: Heb *from beside the south* [s] Vg: Meaning of Heb uncertain

---

20.26 Because the festival of the new moon involved making a sacrifice to God (Numbers 28.11–15), those attending the feast had to be ceremonially clean according to God's law (Exodus 19.10; Leviticus 15; Numbers 19.11–22; also see the note on Joshua 3.5). This cleansing involved washing the body and clothes before approaching God to offer a sacrifice. The outward cleansing was a symbol of the inward desire for a purified heart and right relationship with God. Today our hearts are purified by faith in God through the death of Jesus Christ on our behalf (Hebrews 10.10, 22) and by reading and heeding God's Word (John 17.17).

20.31, 32 Saul was still trying to secure his throne for future generations even though he had already been told his dynasty would end with him (13.13, 14). Even worse, he was trying to do this by sinful human means, because he knew he would get no help from God. Jonathan could have made a move to become the next king by killing his rival, but he bypassed this opportunity because of his love for both God and David (23.16–18).

dants and your descendants, forever.' " He got up and left; and Jonathan went into
the city.[t]

4. Saul pursues David

David asks a priest for bread

21.1 1 Sam 22.19 Neh 11.32 Mk 2.25,26

21 [u] David came to Nob to the priest Ahimelech. Ahimelech came trembling to
meet David, and said to him, "Why are you alone, and no one with you?"

21.2 1 Sam 19.17

2 David said to the priest Ahimelech, "The king has charged me with a matter, and
said to me, 'No one must know anything of the matter about which I send you, and
with which I have charged you.' I have made an appointment[v] with the young men
for such and such a place. 3 Now then, what have you at hand? Give me five loaves

21.4 Ex 19.14,15 Lev 24.5-8 Mt 12.4

of bread, or whatever is here." 4 The priest answered David, "I have no ordinary
bread at hand, only holy bread—provided that the young men have kept themselves from women." 5 David answered the priest, "Indeed women have been kept

[t] This sentence is 21.1 in Heb [u] Ch 21.2 in Heb [v] Q Ms Vg Compare Gk: Meaning of MT uncertain

---

JONATHAN

Loyalty is one of life's most costly qualities; it is the most selfless part of love. To be loyal, you cannot live only for yourself. Loyal people not only stand by their commitments, they are willing to suffer for them. Jonathan is a shining example of loyalty. Sometimes he was forced to deal with conflicting loyalties: to his father Saul and to his friend David. His solution to that conflict teaches us both how to be loyal and what must guide loyalty. In Jonathan, truth always guided loyalty.

Jonathan realized that the source of truth was God, who demanded his ultimate loyalty. It was his relationship with God that gave Jonathan the ability to deal effectively with the complicated situations in his life. He was loyal to Saul because Saul was his father and the king. He was loyal to David because David was his friend. His loyalty to God guided him through the conflicting demands of his human relationships.

The conflicting demands of our relationships challenge us as well. If we attempt to settle these conflicts only at the human level, we will be constantly dealing with a sense of betrayal. But if we communicate to our friends that our ultimate loyalty is to God and his truth, many of our choices will be much clearer. The truth in his Word, the Bible, will bring light to our decisions. Do those closest to you know who has your greatest loyalty?

Strengths and accomplishments:
- Brave, loyal, and a natural leader
- The closest friend David ever had
- Did not put his personal well-being ahead of those he loved
- Depended upon God

Lessons from his life:
- Loyalty is one of the strongest parts of courage
- An allegiance to God puts all other relationships in perspective
- Great friendships are costly

Vital statistics:
- Occupation: Military leader
- Relatives: Father: Saul. Mother: Ahinoam. Brothers: Abinadab and Melchishua. Sisters: Merab and Michal. Son: Mephibosheth

Key verse:
"I am distressed for you, my brother Jonathan; greatly beloved were you to me; your love to me was wonderful, passing the love of women" (2 Samuel 1.26).

His story is told in 1 Samuel 13—31. He is also mentioned in 2 Samuel 9.

21.1ff This is the first time Ahimelech is mentioned. Either he was the Ahijah mentioned in 14.3, 18, or, more likely, he was Ahijah's successor. In either case, Ahimelech had to go against the law to give the holy bread to David, because the bread was supposed to be given only to the priests (Leviticus 24.5–9). But Ahimelech put David's need and life ahead of religious ceremony and fed him the holy food. This upheld a higher law of charity (Leviticus 19.18). Centuries later, Jesus would refer to this incident to show that God's law should not be applied without compassion. To do good and to save life is God's greater law (Matthew 12.1–8; Luke 6.1–5).

21.2 David lied to protect himself from Saul (21.10). Some excuse this lie because a war was going on and it is the duty of a good soldier to deceive the enemy. But nowhere is David's lie condoned. In fact, the opposite is true because his lie led to the death of 85 priests (22.9–19). David's small lie seemed harmless enough, but it led to tragedy. The Bible makes it very clear that lying is wrong (Leviticus 19.11). Lying, like every other sin, is serious in God's sight and may lead to all sorts of harmful consequences. Don't minimize or categorize sins. All sins must be avoided whether or not we can foresee their potential consequences.

21.5 The men's "vessels" (bodies) were ceremonially clean because they had not had sexual intercourse during this journey. Therefore, the priest allowed them to eat the holy bread.

from us as always when I go on an expedition; the vessels of the young men are
holy even when it is a common journey; how much more today will their vessels be
holy?" 6 So the priest gave him the holy bread; for there was no bread there except 21.6
the bread of the Presence, which is removed from before the LORD, to be replaced Mt 12.3,4 Mk 2.25,26
by hot bread on the day it is taken away. Lk 6.4
7 Now a certain man of the servants of Saul was there that day, detained before 21.7
the LORD; his name was Doeg the Edomite, the chief of Saul's shepherds. 1 Sam 22.9 Ps 52.1
8 David said to Ahimelech, "Is there no spear or sword here with you? I did not
bring my sword or my weapons with me, because the king's business required
haste." 9 The priest said, "The sword of Goliath the Philistine, whom you killed in 21.9
the valley of Elah, is here wrapped in a cloth behind the ephod; if you will take that, 1 Sam 17.2, 50,51
take it, for there is none here except that one." David said, "There is none like it;
give it to me."

David pretends insanity

10 David rose and fled that day from Saul; he went to King Achish of Gath. 21.10
11 The servants of Achish said to him, "Is this not David the king of the land? Did 1 Sam 27.1-3 28.1
they not sing to one another of him in dances, 21.11
'Saul has killed his thousands, 1 Sam 18.7
and David his ten thousands'?" 29.5
12 David took these words to heart and was very much afraid of King Achish of
Gath. 13 So he changed his behavior before them; he pretended to be mad when in
their presence.[w] He scratched marks on the doors of the gate, and let his spittle run
down his beard. 14 Achish said to his servants, "Look, you see the man is mad; why
then have you brought him to me? 15 Do I lack madmen, that you have brought this
fellow to play the madman in my presence? Shall this fellow come into my house?"

Saul executes the priests

22 David left there and escaped to the cave of Adullam; when his brothers and 22.1
all his father's house heard of it, they went down there to him. 2 Everyone Josh 15.33-36 2 Sam 23.13
who was in distress, and everyone who was in debt, and everyone who was discon-

[w] Heb *in their hands*

21.6 Once a week on the sabbath, a priest entered the holy place of the tabernacle and placed 12 freshly baked loaves of bread on a small table. This bread, called the bread of the Presence, symbolized God's presence among his people as well as his loving care that met their physical needs. The bread that was replaced was to be eaten only by the priests on duty.

21.7 We don't know why Doeg was "detained" in the sanctuary. Perhaps a vow, suspicion of leprosy, or another impurity kept him there.

21.9 An ephod was a vest worn by the priest (see the second note on 2.18 for a fuller explanation). David didn't know Goliath's sword was there, probably because David was a young man when he killed the giant and he spent much of his time at home.

21.10–15 Why did the Philistines accept their archenemy, David, into their camp? The Philistines may have been initially happy to accept a defector who was a high military leader. Any enemy of Saul would have been a friend of theirs. They could not have known David had been anointed Israel's next king (16.13). Soon, however, the Philistines became nervous about David's presence. After all, he had slain thousands of their own people (18.7). David then protected himself by acting insane, for it was the custom not to harm mentally unstable people.

22.2 Outlaws, malcontents, and troublemakers joined David, who himself was an outlaw. These people were outcasts themselves and could only improve their lot by helping David become king. David's control over this band of men again shows his resourcefulness and ability to lead and motivate others. It is difficult enough to build an army out of good men, but it takes even greater leadership to build one out of the kind of men that followed David. This group eventually formed the core of his military leadership and produced several "mighty men" (2 Samuel 23.8ff).

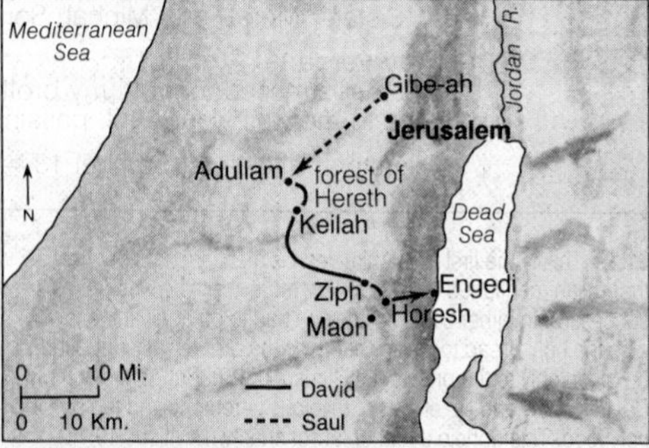

DAVID FLEES FROM SAUL David and his men attacked the Philistines at Keilah from the forest of Hereth. Saul came from Gibeah to attack David, but David escaped into the wilderness of Ziph. At Horesh he met Jonathan, who encouraged him. Then he fled into the wilderness of Maon and into the caves of Engedi.

tented gathered to him; and he became captain over them. Those who were with
him numbered about four hundred.
3 David went from there to Mizpeh of Moab. He said to the king of Moab,
"Please let my father and mother come[x] to you, until I know what God will do for
me." 4 He left them with the king of Moab, and they stayed with him all the time
that David was in the stronghold. 5 Then the prophet Gad said to David, "Do not
remain in the stronghold; leave, and go into the land of Judah." So David left, and
went into the forest of Hereth.
6 Saul heard that David and those who were with him had been located. Saul
was sitting at Gibeah, under the tamarisk tree on the height, with his spear in his
hand, and all his servants were standing around him. 7 Saul said to his servants who
stood around him, "Hear now, you Benjaminites; will the son of Jesse give every
one of you fields and vineyards, will he make you all commanders of thousands and
commanders of hundreds? 8 Is that why all of you have conspired against me? No
one discloses to me when my son makes a league with the son of Jesse, none of you
is sorry for me or discloses to me that my son has stirred up my servant against me,
to lie in wait, as he is doing today." 9 Doeg the Edomite, who was in charge of
Saul's servants, answered, "I saw the son of Jesse coming to Nob, to Ahimelech
son of Ahitub; 10 he inquired of the LORD for him, gave him provisions, and gave
him the sword of Goliath the Philistine."
11 The king sent for the priest Ahimelech son of Ahitub and for all his father's
house, the priests who were at Nob; and all of them came to the king. 12 Saul said,
"Listen now, son of Ahitub." He answered, "Here I am, my lord." 13 Saul said to
him, "Why have you conspired against me, you and the son of Jesse, by giving him
bread and a sword, and by inquiring of God for him, so that he has risen against me,
to lie in wait, as he is doing today?"
14 Then Ahimelech answered the king, "Who among all your servants is so
faithful as David? He is the king's son-in-law, and is quick[y] to do your bidding,
and is honored in your house. 15 Is today the first time that I have inquired of God
for him? By no means! Do not let the king impute anything to his servant or to any
member of my father's house; for your servant has known nothing of all this, much
or little." 16 The king said, "You shall surely die, Ahimelech, you and all your
father's house." 17 The king said to the guard who stood around him, "Turn and kill
the priests of the LORD, because their hand also is with David; they knew that he
fled, and did not disclose it to me." But the servants of the king would not raise
their hand to attack the priests of the LORD. 18 Then the king said to Doeg, "You,
Doeg, turn and attack the priests." Doeg the Edomite turned and attacked the
priests; on that day he killed eighty-five who wore the linen ephod. 19 Nob, the city
of the priests, he put to the sword; men and women, children and infants, oxen,
donkeys, and sheep, he put to the sword.

[x] Syr Vg: Heb *come out* [y] Heb *and turns aside*

22.2 Judg 9.4; 11.3
22.3 Judg 11.29
22.5 2 Sam 24.11; 1 Chron 21.9; 29.29; 2 Chron 29.25, 26
22.6 Judg 4.5; 1 Sam 14.2
22.7 1 Sam 8.14; 1 Chron 12.16
22.8 1 Sam 23.21
22.9 1 Sam 21.1,7; Ps 52.1
22.11 1 Sam 14.3
22.14 1 Sam 19.4; 5; 20.32; 24.11
22.15 2 Sam 5.19,23
22.17 1 Sam 14.45; 2 Kgs 10.25
22.18 1 Sam 2.30-33

22.3, 4 Although Israel was not on friendly terms with Moab (14.47), David may have been able to secure permission from the king because of family ties. His great-grandmother, Ruth, was from Moab (Ruth 1.4; 4.13–22).

22.4, 5 A "stronghold" was a safe and secure place; in this case, probably a cave.

22.7, 8 Why did Saul address his officers as "Benjaminites?" Apparently Saul's key officers were from the tribe of Benjamin, just as he was. David was from the neighboring tribe of Judah. Saul was appealing to tribal loyalty to maintain his hold on the throne.

22.18 Why would Saul have his own priests killed? Saul suspected a conspiracy among Jonathan, David, and the priests. His suspicion came from Doeg's report of seeing David talking to Ahimelech, the high priest, and receiving food and a weapon from him (22.9, 10). Saul's action showed his mental and emotional instability and how far he had strayed from God.

By destroying everything in Nob, Saul was placing the city under the ban (declaring it to be utterly destroyed) described in Deuteronomy 13.12–17, which was supposed to be used only in cases of idolatry and rebellion against God. But it was Saul, not the priests, who had rebelled against God.

22.18, 19 Why did God allow 85 innocent priests to be killed? Their deaths served to dramatize to the nation how a king could become an evil tyrant. Where were Saul's advisors? Where were the elders of Israel? Sometimes God allows evil to develop to teach us not to let evil systems flourish. Serving God is not a ticket to wealth, success, or health. God does not promise to protect good people from evil in this world, but he does promise that ultimately all evil will be abolished. Those who have remained faithful through their trials will experience great rewards in the age to come (Matthew 5.11, 12; Revelation 21.1–7; 22.1–21).

20 But one of the sons of Ahimelech son of Ahitub, named Abiathar, escaped
and fled after David. 21 Abiathar told David that Saul had killed the priests of the
LORD. 22 David said to Abiathar, "I knew on that day, when Doeg the Edomite was
there, that he would surely tell Saul. I am responsible[z] for the lives of all your
father's house. 23 Stay with me, and do not be afraid; for the one who seeks my life
seeks your life; you will be safe with me."

Saul chases David

23 Now they told David, "The Philistines are fighting against Keilah, and are
robbing the threshing floors." 2 David inquired of the LORD, "Shall I go and
attack these Philistines?" The LORD said to David, "Go and attack the Philistines
and save Keilah." 3 But David's men said to him, "Look, we are afraid here in
Judah; how much more then if we go to Keilah against the armies of the Philistines?" 4 Then David inquired of the LORD again. The LORD answered him, "Yes,
go down to Keilah; for I will give the Philistines into your hand." 5 So David and his
men went to Keilah, fought with the Philistines, brought away their livestock, and
dealt them a heavy defeat. Thus David rescued the inhabitants of Keilah.
6 When Abiathar son of Ahimelech fled to David at Keilah, he came down with
an ephod in his hand. 7 Now it was told Saul that David had come to Keilah. And
Saul said, "God has given[a] him into my hand; for he has shut himself in by entering
a town that has gates and bars." 8 Saul summoned all the people to war, to go down
to Keilah, to besiege David and his men. 9 When David learned that Saul was plotting evil against him, he said to the priest Abiathar, "Bring the ephod here." 10 David said, "O LORD, the God of Israel, your servant has heard that Saul seeks to
come to Keilah, to destroy the city on my account. 11 And now, will[b] Saul come
down as your servant has heard? O LORD, the God of Israel, I beseech you, tell
your servant." The LORD said, "He will come down." 12 Then David said, "Will the
men of Keilah surrender me and my men into the hand of Saul?" The LORD said,
"They will surrender you." 13 Then David and his men, who were about six hundred, set out and left Keilah; they wandered wherever they could go. When Saul
was told that David had escaped from Keilah, he gave up the expedition. 14 David
remained in the strongholds in the wilderness, in the hill country of the Wilderness
of Ziph. Saul sought him every day, but the LORD[c] did not give him into his hand.
15 David was in the Wilderness of Ziph at Horesh when he learned that[d] Saul
had come out to seek his life. 16 Saul's son Jonathan set out and came to David at

22.20 1 Sam 2.30-33; 23.9; 30.7; 1 Kgs 2.26,27

23.1 Josh 15.44; Neh 3.17

23.2 1 Sam 22.15; 23.9; 30.8; 2 Sam 5.19,23

23.4 Josh 8.7; Judg 7.7; 2 Sam 5.19; 2 Kgs 3.18

23.9 1 Sam 22.15; 23.2; 30.7

23.13 1 Sam 22.2; 25.13; 2 Sam 15.20

23.14 Josh 15.55; 1 Sam 26.1; 2 Chron 11.8

[z] Gk Vg: Meaning of Heb uncertain [a] Gk Tg: Heb *made a stranger of* [b] Q Ms Compare Gk: MT *Will the men of Keilah surrender me into his hand? Will* [c] Q Ms Gk: MT *God* [d] Or *saw that*

22.20 Abiathar escaped to David with an ephod (23.6), a priestly garment containing the Urim and Thummim, two objects David used to consult God. The ephod was probably the only symbol of the priesthood that survived Saul's raid and made it into David's camp (23.6). Saul destroyed Israel's priesthood, but when David became king, he installed Abiathar as the new high priest. Abiathar remained in that position during David's entire reign.

23.1 The threshing floor was an open, circular area where the grain kernels were separated from their husks. (In order to separate the grain from the husk, farmers would toss their grain into the air. The wind would blow the husks away, leaving only the grain. This process is called *winnowing.*) By robbing the threshing floors, the Philistines were robbing Keilah's citizens of all the results of their farming—that is, of all their food stores. (For more on threshing see the note on Ruth 3.2.)

23.2 Through the Urim and Thummim that Abiathar the priest brought (23.6), David sought the Lord's guidance *before* he took action. He listened to God's directions and then proceeded accordingly. Rather than trying to find God's will *after* the fact or having to ask God to undo the results of our hasty decisions, we should take time to discern God's will beforehand. We can hear him speak through the counsel of others, his Word, and the leading of his Spirit in our hearts, as well as through circumstances.

23.6 An ephod was a sleeveless linen vest worn by priests. The high priest's ephod was brightly colored and had a breastplate with 12 gemstones representing each tribe. The Urim and Thummim were kept in a pouch of the high priest's ephod. (See the second note on 2.18 for a more detailed explanation of the ephod.)

23.7 When Saul heard that David was trapped in a walled city, he thought God was putting David at his mercy. Saul wanted to kill David so badly that he would have interpreted any sign as God's approval to move ahead with his plan. Had Saul known God better, he would have known what God wanted and would not have misread the situation as God's approval for murder.

Not every opportunity is sent from God. We may want something so much that we assume any opportunity to obtain it is from God. As we see from Saul's case, however, this may not be true. An opportunity to do something against God's will can never be from God, because God does not tempt us. When opportunities come your way, double-check your motives. Make sure you are following God's desires, and not just your own.

23.16–18 This may have been the last time David and Jonathan were together. As true friends they were more than just companions who enjoyed each other's company. They encouraged each other's faith in God and trusted each other with their deepest thoughts. These are the marks of true friendship.

23.17 1 Sam 20.31; 24.20 Horesh; there he strengthened his hand through the LORD.[e] 17 He said to him, "Do
not be afraid; for the hand of my father Saul shall not find you; you shall be king
over Israel, and I shall be second to you; my father Saul also knows that this is so."
23.18 1 Sam 20.16 18 Then the two of them made a covenant before the LORD; David remained at Horesh, and Jonathan went home.

23.19 1 Sam 22.6; 26.1 19 Then some Ziphites went up to Saul at Gibeah and said, "David is hiding
among us in the strongholds of Horesh, on the hill of Hachilah, which is south of
Jeshimon. 20 Now, O king, whenever you wish to come down, do so; and our part
23.21 1 Sam 22.8 will be to surrender him into the king's hand." 21 Saul said, "May you be blessed by
the LORD for showing me compassion! 22 Go and make sure once more; find out
exactly where he is, and who has seen him there; for I am told that he is very
cunning. 23 Look around and learn all the hiding places where he lurks, and come
back to me with sure information. Then I will go with you; and if he is in the land,
23.24 Josh 15.55 I will search him out among all the thousands of Judah." 24 So they set out and went
to Ziph ahead of Saul.

David and his men were in the wilderness of Maon, in the Arabah to the south of
Jeshimon. 25 Saul and his men went to search for him. When David was told, he
went down to the rock and stayed in the wilderness of Maon. When Saul heard that,
23.26 Ps 17.9; 22.12 he pursued David into the wilderness of Maon. 26 Saul went on one side of the
mountain, and David and his men on the other side of the mountain. David was
hurrying to get away from Saul, while Saul and his men were closing in on David
and his men to capture them. 27 Then a messenger came to Saul, saying, "Hurry and
come; for the Philistines have made a raid on the land." 28 So Saul stopped pursuing
David, and went against the Philistines; therefore that place was called the Rock of
23.29 Josh 15.62; 2 Chron 20.2 Escape.[f] 29[g] David then went up from there, and lived in the strongholds of En-
gedi.

David spares Saul's life

24 When Saul returned from following the Philistines, he was told, "David is
24.2 1 Sam 13.2; 26.2 in the wilderness of En-gedi." 2 Then Saul took three thousand chosen men
out of all Israel, and went to look for David and his men in the direction of the
Rocks of the Wild Goats. 3 He came to the sheepfolds beside the road, where there
was a cave; and Saul went in to relieve himself.[h] Now David and his men were
24.4 1 Sam 26.8 sitting in the innermost parts of the cave. 4 The men of David said to him, "Here is
the day of which the LORD said to you, 'I will give your enemy into your hand, and
you shall do to him as it seems good to you.' " Then David went and stealthily cut
24.5 2 Sam 24.10 off a corner of Saul's cloak. 5 Afterward David was stricken to the heart because he
24.6 1 Sam 26.11; 2 Sam 1.14 had cut off a corner of Saul's cloak. 6 He said to his men, "The LORD forbid that I
should do this thing to my lord, the LORD's anointed, to raise my hand against him;

[e] Compare Q Ms Gk: MT *God* [f] Or *Rock of Division*; Meaning of Heb uncertain [g] Ch 24.1 in Heb [h] Heb *to cover his feet*

As Jonathan prepared to leave David, he not only promised to be David's friend to the end, but he also encouraged David to remember God's faithfulness. As a friend, remember that you have far more to offer than companionship.

24.3 A sheepfold was a large enclosure with a wall or fence around it which was used at night to protect sheep from thieves and wild animals. Thorn branches were sometimes placed on top of walls that were high enough to prevent most wild animals from getting in. There was only one entrance to the enclosure, and the shepherd often slept in front of it.

24.3 David and his 600 men found the wilderness of En-gedi a good place to hide because of the many caves in the area. These caves were used by local people for housing and as tombs. For David's men they were places of refuge. These caves can still be seen today. Some are large enough to hold thousands of people.

24.4 Scripture does not record that God made any such statement to David or his men. The men were probably offering their own interpretation of some previous event such as David's anointing (16.13) or Jonathan's prediction that David would become king (23.17). When David's men saw Saul entering their cave, they wrongly assumed that this was an indication from God that they should act.

24.5, 6 David had great respect for Saul, in spite of the fact that Saul was trying to kill him. Although Saul was sinning and rebelling against God, David still respected the position he held as God's anointed king. David knew he would one day be king, and he also knew it was not right to strike down the man God had placed on the throne. If he assassinated Saul he would be setting a precedent for his own opponents to remove him someday.

Romans 13.1–7 teaches that God has placed the government and its leaders in power. We may not know why, but, like David, we are to respect the positions and roles of those to whom God has given authority. There is one exception, however. Since God is our highest authority, we should not allow a leader to pressure us to violate God's law.

for he is the LORD's anointed." 7 So David scolded his men severely and did not
permit them to attack Saul. Then Saul got up and left the cave, and went on his
way.
8 Afterwards David also rose up and went out of the cave and called after Saul,
"My lord the king!" When Saul looked behind him, David bowed with his face to
the ground, and did obeisance. 9 David said to Saul, "Why do you listen to the
words of those who say, 'David seeks to do you harm'? 10 This very day your eyes
have seen how the LORD gave you into my hand in the cave; and some urged me to
kill you, but I spared[i] you. I said, 'I will not raise my hand against my lord; for he
is the LORD's anointed.' 11 See, my father, see the corner of your cloak in my hand;
for by the fact that I cut off the corner of your cloak, and did not kill you, you may
know for certain that there is no wrong or treason in my hands. I have not sinned
against you, though you are hunting me to take my life. 12 May the LORD judge
between me and you! May the LORD avenge me on you; but my hand shall not be
against you. 13 As the ancient proverb says, 'Out of the wicked comes forth wickedness'; but my hand shall not be against you. 14 Against whom has the king of Israel
come out? Whom do you pursue? A dead dog? A single flea? 15 May the LORD
therefore be judge, and give sentence between me and you. May he see to it, and
plead my cause, and vindicate me against you."
16 When David had finished speaking these words to Saul, Saul said, "Is this
your voice, my son David?" Saul lifted up his voice and wept. 17 He said to David,
"You are more righteous than I; for you have repaid me good, whereas I have repaid you evil. 18 Today you have explained how you have dealt well with me, in
that you did not kill me when the LORD put me into your hands. 19 For who has ever
found an enemy, and sent the enemy safely away? So may the LORD reward you
with good for what you have done to me this day. 20 Now I know that you shall
surely be king, and that the kingdom of Israel shall be established in your hand.
21 Swear to me therefore by the LORD that you will not cut off my descendants after
me, and that you will not wipe out my name from my father's house." 22 So David
swore this to Saul. Then Saul went home; but David and his men went up to the
stronghold.

Nabal's rudeness angers David

25 Now Samuel died; and all Israel assembled and mourned for him. They buried him at his home in Ramah.
Then David got up and went down to the wilderness of Paran.
2 There was a man in Maon, whose property was in Carmel. The man was very
rich; he had three thousand sheep and a thousand goats. He was shearing his sheep
in Carmel. 3 Now the name of the man was Nabal, and the name of his wife Abigail.
The woman was clever and beautiful, but the man was surly and mean; he was a
Calebite. 4 David heard in the wilderness that Nabal was shearing his sheep. 5 So
David sent ten young men; and David said to the young men, "Go up to Carmel,

24.7 1 Kgs 1.31
24.9 1 Sam 26.19 Ps 7.3,4
24.11 1 Sam 23.14, 23; 26.20
24.12 Gen 31.53 Judg 11.27
24.13 Mt 7.16-20 12.33; 15.19
24.14 1 Sam 26.20
24.15 1 Sam 26.17 Ps 35.1; 84.9
24.17 1 Sam 26.21 Mt 5.44
24.19 1 Sam 26.23
24.20 1 Sam 13.14 20.31; 23.17
24.21 Gen 21.23 1 Sam 20.14-17 2 Sam 21.7
25.1 Num 10.12; 13.3 1 Sam 2.11 7.17; 15.35 28.3
25.2 Josh 15.55 1 Sam 27.2; 3 1 Kgs 18.19
25.3 Gen 24.15,16 29.17 Josh 15.13

[i] Gk Syr Tg Vg: Heb *it* (my eye) *spared*

24.8 To do "obeisance" means to kneel and place one's face on the ground. By this gesture, David was showing his submission to Saul's position of authority.

24.16–19 The means we use to accomplish a goal are just as important as the goal we are trying to accomplish. David's goal was to become king, so his men urged him to kill Saul when he had the chance. David's refusal was not an example of cowardice but of courage – the courage to stand against the group and do what he knew was right. Don't compromise your moral standards by giving in to group pressure or taking the easy way out.

24.21, 22 David kept his promise – he never took revenge on Saul's family or descendants. Most of Saul's sons were killed later, however, by the Philistines (31.2) and the Gibeonites (2 Samuel 21.1–14). David had promised to be kind to the descendants of Saul's son Jonathan (20.14, 15), and he kept this promise when he invited Mephibosheth to live in his palace (2 Samuel 9).

25.1 Saul was king, but Samuel was the nation's spiritual leader. Both as a young boy and as an older man, he was always careful to listen to (3.10; 9.14–17) and obey (3.21; 10.1, 2) the Lord. With Samuel gone, Israel would be without this spiritual leadership until David became king.

25.2–11 Nabal rudely refused David's request to feed his 600 men. If we sympathize with Nabal, it is because customs are so different today. First, simple hospitality demanded that travelers – any number of them – be fed. Nabal was very rich and could have easily afforded to meet David's request. Second, David wasn't asking for a handout. He and his men had been protecting Nabal's work force, and part of Nabal's prosperity was due to David's vigilance.

and go to Nabal, and greet him in my name. 6 Thus you shall salute him: 'Peace be
25.7 to you, and peace be to your house, and peace be to all that you have. 7 I hear that
1 Sam 15.21 you have shearers; now your shepherds have been with us, and we did them no
harm, and they missed nothing, all the time they were in Carmel. 8 Ask your young
men, and they will tell you. Therefore let my young men find favor in your sight;
for we have come on a feast day. Please give whatever you have at hand to your
servants and to your son David.' "

9 When David's young men came, they said all this to Nabal in the name of
25.10 David; and then they waited. 10 But Nabal answered David's servants, "Who is
Ex 5.2 Judg 9.28 David? Who is the son of Jesse? There are many servants today who are breaking
away from their masters. 11 Shall I take my bread and my water and the meat that
I have butchered for my shearers, and give it to men who come from I do not know
where?" 12 So David's young men turned away, and came back and told him all
25.13 this. 13 David said to his men, "Every man strap on his sword!" And every one of
1 Sam 23.13 25.13 them strapped on his sword; David also strapped on his sword; and about four hundred men went up after David, while two hundred remained with the baggage.

14 But one of the young men told Abigail, Nabal's wife, "David sent messengers out of the wilderness to salute our master; and he shouted insults at them.
15 Yet the men were very good to us, and we suffered no harm, and we never missed
anything when we were in the fields, as long as we were with them; 16 they were a
wall to us both by night and by day, all the while we were with them keeping the
sheep. 17 Now therefore know this and consider what you should do; for evil has
been decided against our master and against all his house; he is so ill-natured that
no one can speak to him."

25.18 18 Then Abigail hurried and took two hundred loaves, two skins of wine, five
2 Sam 16.1 1 Chron 12.40 sheep ready dressed, five measures of parched grain, one hundred clusters of rai-
25.19 sins, and two hundred cakes of figs. She loaded them on donkeys 19 and said to her
Gen 32.16,20 young men, "Go on ahead of me; I am coming after you." But she did not tell her
husband Nabal. 20 As she rode on the donkey and came down under cover of the
mountain, David and his men came down toward her; and she met them. 21 Now
David had said, "Surely it was in vain that I protected all that this fellow has in the
wilderness, so that nothing was missed of all that belonged to him; but he has re-
25.22 turned me evil for good. 22 God do so to David[j] and more also, if by morning I
1 Sam 3.17 14.44 leave so much as one male of all who belong to him."

Abigail intercedes for Nabal

23 When Abigail saw David, she hurried and alighted from the donkey, fell

j Gk Compare Syr: Heb *the enemies of David*

LIFE OF DAVID VS. LIFE OF SAUL

Life of David	*Life of Saul*
David was God's kind of king (2 Samuel 7.8–16)	Saul was man's kind of king (1 Samuel 10.23, 24)
David was a man after God's heart (Acts 13.22)	Saul was a man after people's praise (1 Samuel 18.6–8)
David's kingship was eternal (through Jesus) (2 Samuel 7.29)	Saul's kingship was rejected (1 Samuel 15.23)
David was kind and benevolent (2 Samuel 9; 1 Chronicles 19.2)	Saul was cruel (1 Samuel 20.30–34; 22.11–19)
David was forgiving (1 Samuel 26)	Saul was unforgiving (1 Samuel 14.44; 18.9)
David repented (2 Samuel 12.13; 24.10)	When confronted, Saul lied (1 Samuel 15.10–31)
David was courageous (1 Samuel 17; 1 Chronicles 18)	Saul was fearful (1 Samuel 17.11; 18.12)
David was at peace with God (Psalms 4.8; 37.11)	Saul was separated from God (1 Samuel 16.14)

before David on her face, bowing to the ground. 24 She fell at his feet and said,
"Upon me alone, my lord, be the guilt; please let your servant speak in your ears,
and hear the words of your servant. 25 My lord, do not take seriously this ill-natured
fellow, Nabal; for as his name is, so is he; Nabal[k] is his name, and folly is with
him; but I, your servant, did not see the young men of my lord, whom you sent.
26 Now then, my lord, as the LORD lives, and as you yourself live, since the **25.26**
LORD has restrained you from bloodguilt and from taking vengeance with your own 2 Sam 18.32
hand, now let your enemies and those who seek to do evil to my lord be like Nabal.
27 And now let this present that your servant has brought to my lord be given to the **25.27**
young men who follow my lord. 28 Please forgive the trespass of your servant; for Gen 33.11 1 Sam 30.26
the LORD will certainly make my lord a sure house, because my lord is fighting the 2 Kgs 5.15
battles of the LORD; and evil shall not be found in you so long as you live. 29 If **25.28** 2 Sam 7.16
anyone should rise up to pursue you and to seek your life, the life of my lord shall **25.29**
be bound in the bundle of the living under the care of the LORD your God; but the 1 Sam 2.9 Ps 66.9
lives of your enemies he shall sling out as from the hollow of a sling. 30 When the **25.30**
LORD has done to my lord according to all the good that he has spoken concerning Gen 40.14 1 Sam 13.14
you, and has appointed you prince over Israel, 31 my lord shall have no cause of
grief, or pangs of conscience, for having shed blood without cause or for having
saved himself. And when the LORD has dealt well with my lord, then remember
your servant."
32 David said to Abigail, "Blessed be the LORD, the God of Israel, who sent **25.32**
you to meet me today! 33 Blessed be your good sense, and blessed be you, who have Ex 18.10 1 Sam 24.19
kept me today from bloodguilt and from avenging myself by my own hand! 34 For 26.9,10
as surely as the LORD the God of Israel lives, who has restrained me from hurting
you, unless you had hurried and come to meet me, truly by morning there would
not have been left to Nabal so much as one male." 35 Then David received from her **25.35**
hand what she had brought him; he said to her, "Go up to your house in peace; see, Gen 19.21
I have heeded your voice, and I have granted your petition."
36 Abigail came to Nabal; he was holding a feast in his house, like the feast of
a king. Nabal's heart was merry within him, for he was very drunk; so she told him
nothing at all until the morning light. 37 In the morning, when the wine had gone out
of Nabal, his wife told him these things, and his heart died within him; he became
like a stone. 38 About ten days later the LORD struck Nabal, and he died.
39 When David heard that Nabal was dead, he said, "Blessed be the LORD who **25.39**
has judged the case of Nabal's insult to me, and has kept back his servant from evil; 2 Sam 3.28,29
the LORD has returned the evil-doing of Nabal upon his own head." Then David
sent and wooed Abigail, to make her his wife. 40 When David's servants came to
Abigail at Carmel, they said to her, "David has sent us to you to take you to him as
his wife." 41 She rose and bowed down, with her face to the ground, and said,
"Your servant is a slave to wash the feet of the servants of my lord." 42 Abigail got **25.42** Gen 24.61
up hurriedly and rode away on a donkey; her five maids attended her. She went **25.43**
after the messengers of David and became his wife. 1 Sam 27.2,3 30.5
43 David also married Ahinoam of Jezreel; both of them became his wives. 2 Sam 2.2; 3.2
44 Saul had given his daughter Michal, David's wife, to Palti son of Laish, who was **25.44** 1 Sam 18.27
from Gallim. 2 Sam 3.14,15

[k] That is *Fool*

25.24 David was in no mood to listen when he set out for Nabal's ranch (25.13, 22). Nevertheless, he stopped to hear what Abigail had to say. If he had ignored her, he would have been guilty of taking vengeance into his own hands.

25.30 How would Abigail know that David was to be appointed king over all of Israel? Samuel and his students traveled to different parts of the nation from time to time. People would converse and spend time with these prophets as they passed through. Most likely, she found out about his anointing by Samuel and his designation to become the next king from one of the students of the prophets, or perhaps even Samuel himself.

25.36 When Abigail found her husband, he was having a party for himself, "like the feast of a king." Nabal had rejected God's appointed king, David, and instead acted as though he himself were the king. Looking at the story from our perspective, we can see that Nabal was a fool . . . and it cost him his life. But people today make the same mistake. Rejecting God's rule over their lives, they make themselves "king" and indulge themselves with no thought of the consequences. Who is king in your life? Submit to God's authority — then you'll have real cause for celebration.

25.36 Because Nabal was drunk, Abigail waited until morning to tell him what she had done. Abigail knew that in that condition, Nabal wouldn't have understood her or would have reacted foolishly.

David again spares Saul's life

26.1 1 Sam 23.19
26.2 1 Sam 13.2 24.2
26.3 1 Sam 23.19

26 Then the Ziphites came to Saul at Gibeah, saying, "David is in hiding on the
hill of Hachilah, which is opposite Jeshimon."[l] 2 So Saul rose and went
down to the Wilderness of Ziph, with three thousand chosen men of Israel, to seek
David in the Wilderness of Ziph. 3 Saul encamped on the hill of Hachilah, which is
opposite Jeshimon[v] beside the road. But David remained in the wilderness. When
he learned that Saul came after him into the wilderness, 4 David sent out spies, and

[l] Or *opposite the wasteland*

ABIGAIL

Some men don't deserve their wives. Abigail was probably the best woman Nabal could afford, and he got even more than he bargained for when he arranged to marry her. She was beautiful and more suited than he was to manage his wealth. But Nabal took this wife for granted.

In spite of his shortcomings, Nabal's household did what they could to keep him out of trouble. This loyalty must have been inspired by Abigail. Although her culture and her husband placed a low value on her, she made the most of her skills and opportunities. David was impressed with her abilities, and when Nabal died, he married her.

Abigail was an effective counselor to both of the men in her life, working hard to prevent them from making rash moves. By her swift action and skillful negotiation, she kept David from taking vengeance upon Nabal. She saw the big picture and left plenty of room for God to get involved.

Do you, like Abigail, look beyond the present crisis to the big picture? Do you use your skills to promote peace? Are you loyal without being blind? What challenge or responsibility do you face today that needs a person under God's control?

Strengths and accomplishments:
- Sensible and capable manager of a large estate
- A persuasive speaker, able to see beyond herself

Lessons from her life:
- Life's tough situations can bring out the best in people
- One does not need a prestigious title to play a significant role

Vital statistics:
- Where: Carmel
- Occupation: Homemaker, estate manager
- Relatives: First husband: Nabal. Second husband: David. Son: Chileab (Daniel)
- Contemporaries: Saul, Michal, Ahinoam

Key verses:
"David said to Abigail, 'Blessed be the Lord, the God of Israel, who sent you to meet me today! Blessed be your good sense, and blessed be you, who have kept me today from bloodguilt and from avenging myself by my own hand' " (1 Samuel 25.32, 33).

Her story is told in 1 Samuel 25—2 Samuel 2. She is also mentioned in 1 Chronicles 3.1.

When discussing difficult matters with people, especially family members, timing is everything. Ask God for wisdom to know the best time for confrontation and for bringing up touchy subjects.

25.41 When asked if she would become David's wife, Abigail consented without hesitation. Her response was one of gratitude and humility. She said that she was willing to perform even the most menial services for David. While we may prefer a different approach to marriage proposals and weddings, good marriages still require a willingness to serve each other.

26.1 This is the second time that the men of Ziph betrayed David. (See 1 Samuel 23.19 for the first time they told Saul.) There would surely be some kind of reward if Saul was successful in capturing and killing him. David wrote Psalm 54 at this time.

26.2 King Saul was obsessed! David wanted to be loyal to Saul, was the best friend of Saul's son, Jonathan, was married to Saul's daughter, Michal, and had already spared Saul's life once. Despite these facts, Saul took 3000 choice soldiers to find, capture, and kill David and his 400 men. Undoubtedly, Saul had other kingly responsibilities to attend to. But blinded by irrational hatred, he plunged after his obsession. Emotions are like that, often pushing us to do things that make no sense. Consider what people have done for love, hate, greed, or pleasure. What are your potential blind spots? Don't become a "Saul" – live by God's Word and keep an open mind to the advice of clear-thinking friends.

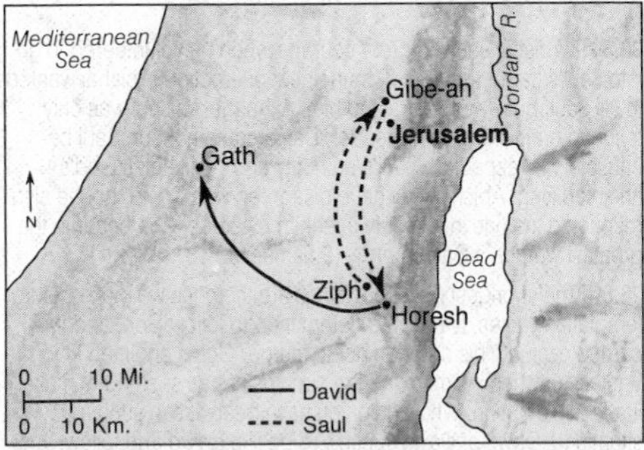

SAUL CHASES DAVID The men of Ziph again betrayed David to Saul, who was in his palace in Gibeah. Saul took 3,000 troops to Horesh in order to find David. David could have killed Saul, but he refused. Saul, feeling foolish at David's kindness, returned to Gibeah, and David went to Gath.

learned that Saul had indeed arrived. 5 Then David set out and came to the place 26.5
where Saul had encamped; and David saw the place where Saul lay, with Abner son Judg 7.10,11 1 Sam 14.50,51
of Ner, the commander of his army. Saul was lying within the encampment, while 2 Sam 3.29 1 Chron 2.15,16
the army was encamped around him.
6 Then David said to Ahimelech the Hittite, and to Joab's brother Abishai son
of Zeruiah, "Who will go down with me into the camp to Saul?" Abishai said, "I
will go down with you." 7 So David and Abishai went to the army by night; there
Saul lay sleeping within the encampment, with his spear stuck in the ground at his
head; and Abner and the army lay around him. 8 Abishai said to David, "God has 26.8
given your enemy into your hand today; now therefore let me pin him to the ground 1 Sam 24.4
with one stroke of the spear; I will not strike him twice." 9 But David said to 26.9
Abishai, "Do not destroy him; for who can raise his hand against the LORD's 1 Sam 24.6 2 Sam 1.14,16
anointed, and be guiltless?" 10 David said, "As the LORD lives, the LORD will strike
him down; or his day will come to die; or he will go down into battle and perish.
11 The LORD forbid that I should raise my hand against the LORD's anointed; but
now take the spear that is at his head, and the water jar, and let us go." 12 So David 26.12
took the spear that was at Saul's head and the water jar, and they went away. No Gen 2.21; 15.12 Isa 29.10
one saw it, or knew it, nor did anyone awake; for they were all asleep, because a
deep sleep from the LORD had fallen upon them.
13 Then David went over to the other side, and stood on top of a hill far away,
with a great distance between them. 14 David called to the army and to Abner son 26.14
of Ner, saying, "Abner! Will you not answer?" Then Abner replied, "Who are you 1 Sam 14.50 17.55
that calls to the king?" 15 David said to Abner, "Are you not a man? Who is like you
in Israel? Why then have you not kept watch over your lord the king? For one of the
people came in to destroy your lord the king. 16 This thing that you have done is not 26.16
good. As the LORD lives, you deserve to die, because you have not kept watch over 2 Sam 12.5
your lord, the LORD's anointed. See now, where is the king's spear, or the water jar
that was at his head?"
17 Saul recognized David's voice, and said, "Is this your voice, my son Da- 26.17
vid?" David said, "It is my voice, my lord, O king." 18 And he added, "Why does 1 Sam 24.16
my lord pursue his servant? For what have I done? What guilt is on my hands?
19 Now therefore let my lord the king hear the words of his servant. If it is the LORD 26.19
who has stirred you up against me, may he accept an offering; but if it is mortals, 1 Sam 24.9 2 Sam 16.11
may they be cursed before the LORD, for they have driven me out today from my
share in the heritage of the LORD, saying, 'Go, serve other gods.' 20 Now therefore,
do not let my blood fall to the ground, away from the presence of the LORD; for the
king of Israel has come out to seek a single flea, like one who hunts a partridge in
the mountains." 26.21
21 Then Saul said, "I have done wrong; come back, my son David, for I will 1 Sam 15.24 24.17

26.5–9 Abishai showed great courage when he volunteered to go into Saul's camp with David. In the heat of emotion, Abishai wanted to kill Saul, but David restrained him. Although Abishai was only trying to protect David, his leader, David could not hurt Saul because of his respect for Saul's authority and position as God's anointed king. Abishai may have disagreed with David, but he also respected the one in authority over him. Eventually he became the greatest warrior in David's army (2 Samuel 23.18, 19).

26.8ff The strongest moral decisions are the ones we make before temptation strikes. David was determined to follow God, and this carried over into his decision not to murder God's anointed king, Saul, even when his men and the circumstances seemed to make it a feasible option. Who would you have been like in such a situation – David or David's men? To be like David and follow God, we must realize that we can't do wrong in order to execute justice. Even when our closest friends counsel us to do something that seems right, we must always put God's commands first.

26.9 Why did David refuse to kill Saul? God had placed Saul in power and had not yet removed him. David did not want to run ahead of God's timing. We are in similar situations when we have leaders in church or government who are unfaithful or incompetent. It may be easy for us to criticize or move against a leader oblivious to God's hidden purposes and timing. Determining not to do wrong, David left Saul's destiny in God's hands. While we should not ignore sin or sit back and allow evil leaders to carry on their wickedness, neither should we take actions that are against God's laws. We should work for righteousness while trusting God.

26.15, 16 David could have killed Saul and Abner, but he would have disobeyed God and set into motion unknown consequences. Instead, he took a water jar and sword, showing that he could have killed the king, but had not done it. And he made the point that he had great respect for both God and God's anointed king. When you need to make a point, look for creative, God-honoring ways to do so. It will have a more significant impact.

26.19 This was David's way of saying he had been driven out of Israel. The whole earth belongs to God, but the tabernacle, the ark of the covenant, and God's people were in Israel. Forced to leave Israel, David could not worship at the tabernacle or participate in the annual festivals. He felt separated, living among people who worshiped strange gods.

never harm you again, because my life was precious in your sight today; I have
been a fool, and have made a great mistake." 22 David replied, "Here is the spear,
26.23 1 Sam 24.19; 2 Sam 22.21
O king! Let one of the young men come over and get it. 23 The LORD rewards everyone for his righteousness and his faithfulness; for the LORD gave you into my hand
26.24 Ps 54.7
today, but I would not raise my hand against the LORD's anointed. 24 As your life
was precious today in my sight, so may my life be precious in the sight of the LORD,
and may he rescue me from all tribulation." 25 Then Saul said to David, "Blessed be
you, my son David! You will do many things and will succeed in them." So David
went his way, and Saul returned to his place.

5. Saul's defeat and death

David lives among the Philistines

27.1 1 Sam 17.52; 28.1
27 David said in his heart, "I shall now perish one day by the hand of Saul;
there is nothing better for me than to escape to the land of the Philistines;
then Saul will despair of seeking me any longer within the borders of Israel, and I
27.2 1 Sam 21.10; 25.42,43; 2 Sam 2.2,3; 1 Kgs 2.39
shall escape out of his hand." 2 So David set out and went over, he and the six
hundred men who were with him, to King Achish son of Maoch of Gath. 3 David
stayed with Achish at Gath, he and his troops, every man with his household, and
David with his two wives, Ahinoam of Jezreel, and Abigail of Carmel, Nabal's
widow. 4 When Saul was told that David had fled to Gath, he no longer sought for
him.
27.6 Josh 15.31; 2 Sam 1.1; Neh 11.28
5 Then David said to Achish, "If I have found favor in your sight, let a place be
given me in one of the country towns, so that I may live there; for why should your
servant live in the royal city with you?" 6 So that day Achish gave him Ziklag;
27.7 1 Sam 29.3
therefore Ziklag has belonged to the kings of Judah to this day. 7 The length of time
that David lived in the country of the Philistines was one year and four months.
27.8 Ex 17.8; Josh 13.2-7,13; 1 Sam 15.7,8
8 Now David and his men went up and made raids on the Geshurites, the Girzites, and the Amalekites; for these were the landed settlements from Telam[m] on
27.9 1 Sam 15.3
the way to Shur and on to the land of Egypt. 9 David struck the land, leaving neither
man nor woman alive, but took away the sheep, the oxen, the donkeys, the camels,

[m] Compare Gk 15.4: Heb *from of old*

26.25 Saul had opportunities to kill David, but he never did. Why? First, every time David and Saul were face to face, David did something generous for Saul. The king did not want to respond to David's kindness with cruelty in front of all his men. Second, David had a large following in Israel. By killing him, Saul would risk his hold on the kingdom. Third, God had appointed David to become king of Israel and was protecting him.

27.2, 3 For the second time, David sought refuge from Saul in Philistine territory (21.10–15). Once the great conqueror of Philistines, he now had permission to live under the protection of King Achish of Gath. Previously David had acted insane in front of this king (21.10–15). Evidently, Achish forgot that incident or overlooked it in light of David's current situation. Achish certainly would have known about the split between Saul and David and would have been glad to shelter this Israelite traitor. In return, Achish would have expected military support from David and his 600 warriors. David further strengthened his position with Achish by conducting fake raids on Israel and by pretending loyalty to the Philistine ruler.

27.4 Saul finally stopped pursuing David. His army was not strong enough to invade Philistine territory just to seek one man. Besides, the immediate threat to Saul's throne was gone while David was out of the country.

27.5–7 Gath was one of five principal cities in Philistia, and Achish was one of five co-rulers. David may have wanted to move out of this important city to avoid potential skirmishes or attacks upon his family. He may also have wanted to escape the close scrutiny of the Philistine officials. Achish let David move to Ziklag, where he lived until Saul's death (2 Samuel 2.1).

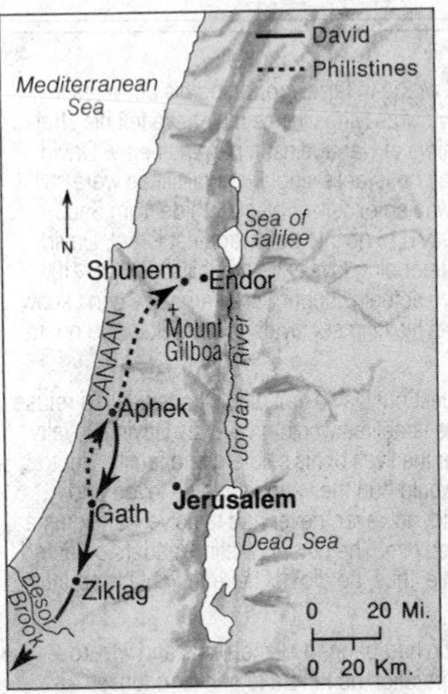

THE BATTLE AT GILBOA
David pretended loyalty to Achish, but when war broke out with Israel, he was sent to Ziklag from Aphek. The Philistines defeated the Israelites at Mount Gilboa. David returned to Ziklag to find that the Amalekites had destroyed Ziklag. So David and his men pursued the Amalekite raiders and slaughtered them, recovering all that was taken.

27.8, 9 David probably conducted these guerrilla-style raids because these three tribes were known for their surprise attacks and cruel treatment of innocent people. These desert tribes were a danger not just to the Philistines, but especially to the Israelites, the people David would one day lead.

and the clothing, and came back to Achish. 10 When Achish asked, "Against
whom[n] have you made a raid today?" David would say, "Against the Negeb of
Judah," or "Against the Negeb of the Jerahmeelites," or, "Against the Negeb of the
Kenites." 11 David left neither man nor woman alive to be brought back to Gath,
thinking, "They might tell about us, and say, 'David has done so and so.'" Such
was his practice all the time he lived in the country of the Philistines. 12 Achish
trusted David, thinking, "He has made himself utterly abhorrent to his people Israel; therefore he shall always be my servant."

27.10 Judg 1.16; 4.11 1 Sam 30.27-31 1 Chron 2.9,25

28 In those days the Philistines gathered their forces for war, to fight against
Israel. Achish said to David, "You know, of course, that you and your men
are to go out with me in the army." 2 David said to Achish, "Very well, then you
shall know what your servant can do." Achish said to David, "Very well, I will
make you my bodyguard for life."

28.1 1 Sam 21.10 27.1-3

Saul consults a witch

3 Now Samuel had died, and all Israel had mourned for him and buried him in
Ramah, his own city. Saul had expelled the mediums and the wizards from the
land. 4 The Philistines assembled, and came and encamped at Shunem. Saul gathered all Israel, and they encamped at Gilboa. 5 When Saul saw the army of the
Philistines, he was afraid, and his heart trembled greatly. 6 When Saul inquired of
the LORD, the LORD did not answer him, not by dreams, or by Urim, or by prophets. 7 Then Saul said to his servants, "Seek out for me a woman who is a medium,
so that I may go to her and inquire of her." His servants said to him, "There is a
medium at Endor."
8 So Saul disguised himself and put on other clothes and went there, he and two
men with him. They came to the woman by night. And he said, "Consult a spirit for
me, and bring up for me the one whom I name to you." 9 The woman said to him,
"Surely you know what Saul has done, how he has cut off the mediums and the
wizards from the land. Why then are you laying a snare for my life to bring about
my death?" 10 But Saul swore to her by the LORD, "As the LORD lives, no punishment shall come upon you for this thing." 11 Then the woman said, "Whom shall I
bring up for you?" He answered, "Bring up Samuel for me." 12 When the woman

28.3 Lev 19.31 Deut 18.10 1 Sam 15.23 25.1

28.4 1 Sam 31.1 2 Sam 1.6

28.5 Ex 28.30,31 Num 12.6

28.7 2 Chron 18.29 35.22 Ps 83.10 Isa 8.19 Acts 16.16

n Q Ms Gk Vg: MT lacks *whom*

27.10–12 Was David wrong in falsely reporting his activities to Achish? No doubt David was lying, but he may have felt his strategy was justified in a time of war against a pagan enemy. David knew he would one day be Israel's king. The Philistines were still his enemies, but this was an excellent place to hide from Saul. When Achish asked David to go into battle against Israel, David agreed, once again pretending loyalty to the Philistines (28.1ff). Whether he would have actually fought Saul's army we can't know, but we can be sure that his ultimate loyalty was to God and not to Achish or Saul.

28.1, 2 Achish's request put David in a difficult position. To refuse to help Achish fight the Israelites would give away David's loyalty to Israel and endanger the lives of his soldiers and family. But to fight his own people would hurt the very people he loved and would soon lead. David, however, never had to solve his dilemma because God protected him. The other Philistine leaders objected to his presence in battle; thus, he did not have to fight his countrymen.

28.3–8 It was Saul who had banned all mediums and wizards from Israel, but in desperation he turned to one for counsel. Although he had removed the sin of witchcraft from the land, he did not remove it from his heart. We may make a great show of renouncing sin, but if our hearts do not change, the sins will return. Knowing what is right and condemning what is wrong does not take the place of *doing* what is right.

28.5, 6 The Urim, along with the Thummim, was used by the high priest to determine God's guidance in certain matters. (See the notes on 2.18 and 10.20 for further information on the use of the Urim and Thummim.)

28.5–7 Saul was overwhelmed at the sight of the Philistine army, and so he turned to the occult. Let life's difficulties and obstacles push you in God's direction and make you depend upon him. As we see from Saul's story, turning to anything or anyone else leads only to disaster.

28.7, 8 God had strictly forbidden the Israelites to have anything to do with black magic, fortune tellers, witches, wizards, or anyone who claimed to bring forth spirits from the dead (Deuteronomy 18.9–14). In fact, sorcerers were to be put to death (Exodus 22.18). Occult practices were carried on in the name of pagan gods, and people turned to the occult for answers that God would not give.

Practitioners of the occult have Satan and demons as the source of their information; God does not reveal his will to them. Instead he speaks through his own channels: prophets, the Holy Spirit, the Bible, and his Son, Jesus Christ.

28.12 Did Samuel really come back from the dead at the medium's call? The medium shrieked at the appearance of Samuel—she knew too well that the spirits she usually contacted were either contrived or satanic. Somehow Samuel's appearance revealed to her that she was dealing with a power far greater than she had known. She did not call up Samuel by trickery or by the power of Satan; God brought Samuel back to give Saul a prediction regarding his fate, a message Saul already knew. This in no way justifies

saw Samuel, she cried out with a loud voice; and the woman said to Saul, "Why
have you deceived me? You are Saul!" 13 The king said to her, "Have no fear; what
do you see?" The woman said to Saul, "I see a divine being[o] coming up out of the
ground." 14 He said to her, "What is his appearance?" She said, "An old man is
coming up; he is wrapped in a robe." So Saul knew that it was Samuel, and he
bowed with his face to the ground, and did obeisance.
28.15 1 Sam 16.13, 14; 28.4-6 — 15 Then Samuel said to Saul, "Why have you disturbed me by bringing me
up?" Saul answered, "I am in great distress, for the Philistines are warring against
me, and God has turned away from me and answers me no more, either by prophets
or by dreams; so I have summoned you to tell me what I should do." 16 Samuel said,
"Why then do you ask me, since the LORD has turned from you and become your
28.17 1 Sam 15.28 16.13 — enemy? 17 The LORD has done to you just as he spoke by me; for the LORD has torn
the kingdom out of your hand, and given it to your neighbor, David. 18 Because you
did not obey the voice of the LORD, and did not carry out his fierce wrath against
28.19 1 Sam 31.2,6 — Amalek, therefore the LORD has done this thing to you today. 19 Moreover the LORD
will give Israel along with you into the hands of the Philistines; and tomorrow you
and your sons shall be with me; the LORD will also give the army of Israel into the
hands of the Philistines."
28.20 1 Sam 25.37,38 — 20 Immediately Saul fell full length on the ground, filled with fear because of
the words of Samuel; and there was no strength in him, for he had eaten nothing all
day and all night. 21 The woman came to Saul, and when she saw that he was terrified, she said to him, "Your servant has listened to you; I have taken my life in my
hand, and have listened to what you have said to me. 22 Now therefore, you also
listen to your servant; let me set a morsel of bread before you. Eat, that you may
28.23 2 Kgs 5.13 — have strength when you go on your way." 23 He refused, and said, "I will not eat."
But his servants, together with the woman, urged him; and he listened to their
28.24 Gen 18.6,7 — words. So he got up from the ground and sat on the bed. 24 Now the woman had a
fatted calf in the house. She quickly slaughtered it, and she took flour, kneaded it,
and baked unleavened cakes. 25 She put them before Saul and his servants, and they
ate. Then they rose and went away that night.

The Philistines distrust David

29.1 Josh 12.18 1 Sam 4.1 2 Kgs 9.30 — **29** Now the Philistines gathered all their forces at Aphek, while the Israelites
were encamped by the fountain that is in Jezreel. 2 As the lords of the Philis-
tines were passing on by hundreds and by thousands, and David and his men were
29.3 1 Sam 27.1-6 1 Chron 12.19, 20 — passing on in the rear with Achish, 3 the commanders of the Philistines said, "What
are these Hebrews doing here?" Achish said to the commanders of the Philistines,
"Is this not David, the servant of King Saul of Israel, who has been with me now
for days and years? Since he deserted to me I have found no fault in him to this
day." 4 But the commanders of the Philistines were angry with him; and the commanders of the Philistines said to him, "Send the man back, so that he may return
to the place that you have assigned to him; he shall not go down with us to battle,
or else he may become an adversary to us in the battle. For how could this fellow
29.5 1 Sam 18.7 21.11 — reconcile himself to his lord? Would it not be with the heads of the men here? 5 Is
this not David, of whom they sing to one another in dances,

[o] Or *a god*; or *gods*

---

efforts to contact the dead today. God is against all such practices (Galatians 5.19–21).

28.14 To do "obeisance" means to kneel and place one's face on the ground in an act of submission.

28.15 God did not answer Saul's appeals, because Saul had not followed God's previous directions. Sometimes people wonder why their prayers are not answered. But if they don't fulfill the responsibilities God has already given them, they should not be surprised when he does not give further guidance.

28.23–25 These verses highlight Saul's grim condition. He was frightened, faint, and depressed by the news Samuel had given him. In his grief over God's rejection, he had gone without food all day and had to be forced to eat. What an unhappy demise for one so gifted and honored by God in the beginning.

29.4 The other Philistine commanders knew that David was the one who, as a young man, had killed their champion, Goliath (17.32–54), had killed hundreds of Philistine soldiers (18.27), and was the hero of Israelite victory songs (21.11). They were afraid that, in the heat of battle, David might turn against them. Although David was upset at this at first, God used the commanders' suspicion to keep him from having to fight against Saul and his countrymen.

'Saul has killed his thousands,
and David his ten thousands'?"

6 Then Achish called David and said to him, "As the LORD lives, you have been **29.6**
honest, and to me it seems right that you should march out and in with me in the 1 Sam 27.12
campaign; for I have found nothing wrong in you from the day of your coming to
me until today. Nevertheless the lords do not approve of you. 7 So go back now; and
go peaceably; do nothing to displease the lords of the Philistines." 8 David said to
Achish, "But what have I done? What have you found in your servant from the day
I entered your service until now, that I should not go and fight against the enemies
of my lord the king?" 9 Achish replied to David, "I know that you are as blameless **29.9**
in my sight as an angel of God; nevertheless, the commanders of the Philistines 2 Sam 14.17, 20; 19.27
have said, 'He shall not go up with us to the battle.' 10 Now then rise early in the
morning, you and the servants of your lord who came with you, and go to the place
that I appointed for you. As for the evil report, do not take it to heart, for you have
done well before me.[p] Start early in the morning, and leave as soon as you have
light." 11 So David set out with his men early in the morning, to return to the land
of the Philistines. But the Philistines went up to Jezreel.

David destroys the Amalekites

30 Now when David and his men came to Ziklag on the third day, the Amalek- **30.1**
ites had made a raid on the Negeb and on Ziklag. They had attacked Ziklag, 1 Sam 15.7 27.6,8; 30.26
burned it down, 2 and taken captive the women and all[q] who were in it, both small
and great; they killed none of them, but carried them off, and went their way.
3 When David and his men came to the city, they found it burned down, and their
wives and sons and daughters taken captive. 4 Then David and the people who were
with him raised their voices and wept, until they had no more strength to weep.
5 David's two wives also had been taken captive, Ahinoam of Jezreel, and Abigail **30.5**
the widow of Nabal of Carmel. 6 David was in great danger; for the people spoke of 1 Sam 25.39, 43; 30.18,19
stoning him, because all the people were bitter in spirit for their sons and daughters. 2 Sam 2.2; 3.2
But David strengthened himself in the LORD his God. **30.6** Ex 17.4

7 David said to the priest Abiathar son of Ahimelech, "Bring me the ephod." So 1 Sam 23.16
Abiathar brought the ephod to David. 8 David inquired of the LORD, "Shall I pursue Ps 18.2
this band? Shall I overtake them?" He answered him, "Pursue; for you shall surely **30.7** 1 Sam 23.9
overtake and shall surely rescue." 9 So David set out, he and the six hundred men **30.8**
who were with him. They came to the Wadi Besor, where those stayed who were Judg 20.18 1 Sam 23.2,4
left behind. 10 But David went on with the pursuit, he and four hundred men; two 2 Sam 5.19
hundred stayed behind, too exhausted to cross the Wadi Besor. **30.9** 1 Sam 27.2

11 In the open country they found an Egyptian, and brought him to David. They **30.11**
gave him bread and he ate, they gave him water to drink; 12 they also gave him a Judg 15.19
piece of fig cake and two clusters of raisins. When he had eaten, his spirit revived;
for he had not eaten bread or drunk water for three days and three nights. 13 Then
David said to him, "To whom do you belong? Where are you from?" He said, "I am
a young man of Egypt, servant to an Amalekite. My master left me behind because **30.14** 1 Sam 30.1
I fell sick three days ago. 14 We had made a raid on the Negeb of the Cherethites and 2 Sam 1.1 15.17,18
on that which belongs to Judah and on the Negeb of Caleb; and we burned Ziklag 1 Chron 18.17

[p] Gk: Heb lacks *and go to the place . . . done well before me* [q] Gk: Heb lacks *and all*

30.6 Faced with the tragedy of losing their families, David's soldiers began to turn against him and even talked about killing him. Instead of planning a rescue, they looked for someone to blame. But David found his strength in God and began looking for a solution instead of a scapegoat. When facing problems, remember that it is useless to look for someone to blame or criticize. Instead, consider how you can help find a solution.

30.7 David couldn't go to the tabernacle to ask the Lord for guidance because it was in Saul's territory. Therefore he called for the ephod, the only tabernacle-related object he possessed. In the presence of the priest and this priestly garment, he asked God for direction. When David called for the ephod, he was really asking the priest to bring him the Urim and Thummim, which were kept in a pouch attached to the ephod. Only the high priest could carry and use the Urim and Thummim. (For more information on the ephod and its contents, see the note on Exodus 39.1–21.)

30.11–15 The Amalekites cruelly left this slave to die, but God used him to lead David and his men to the Amalekite camp. David and his men treated the young man kindly, and he returned the kindness by leading them to the enemy. Treat those you meet with respect and dignity, no matter how insignificant they may seem. You never know how God will use them to help you or haunt you, depending upon your response to them.

30.15 Josh 2.12; 9.19

down." 15 David said to him, "Will you take me down to this raiding party?" He
said, "Swear to me by God that you will not kill me, or hand me over to my master,
and I will take you down to them."

16 When he had taken him down, they were spread out all over the ground,
eating and drinking and dancing, because of the great amount of spoil they had
taken from the land of the Philistines and from the land of Judah. 17 David attacked
them from twilight until the evening of the next day. Not one of them escaped,
except four hundred young men, who mounted camels and fled. 18 David recovered
all that the Amalekites had taken; and David rescued his two wives. 19 Nothing was
missing, whether small or great, sons or daughters, spoil or anything that had been
taken; David brought back everything. 20 David also captured all the flocks and
herds, which were driven ahead of the other cattle; people said, "This is David's
spoil."

30.17 1 Sam 15.3

30.21 1 Sam 30.10,11

21 Then David came to the two hundred men who had been too exhausted to
follow David, and who had been left at the brook Besor. They went out to meet
David and to meet the people who were with him. When David drew near to the
people he saluted them. 22 Then all the corrupt and worthless fellows among the
men who had gone with David said, "Because they did not go with us, we will not
give them any of the spoil that we have recovered, except that each man may take
his wife and children, and leave." 23 But David said, "You shall not do so, my
brothers, with what the LORD has given us; he has preserved us and handed over to
us the raiding party that attacked us. 24 Who would listen to you in this matter? For
the share of the one who goes down into the battle shall be the same as the share of
the one who stays by the baggage; they shall share alike." 25 From that day forward
he made it a statute and an ordinance for Israel; it continues to the present day.

30.24 Num 31.27 Josh 22.7,8

30.26 Gen 33.11 1 Sam 25.27 2 Kgs 5.15

26 When David came to Ziklag, he sent part of the spoil to his friends, the
elders of Judah, saying, "Here is a present for you from the spoil of the enemies of
the LORD"; 27 it was for those in Bethel, in Ramoth of the Negeb, in Jattir, 28 in
Aroer, in Siphmoth, in Eshtemoa, 29 in Racal, in the towns of the Jerahmeelites, in
the towns of the Kenites, 30 in Hormah, in Bor-ashan, in Athach, 31 in Hebron, all
the places where David and his men had roamed.

Saul dies on the battlefield

31.1 1 Sam 28.4 1 Chr 10.1-12

31.3 Judg 9.54 2 Sam 1.6,10

31 Now the Philistines fought against Israel; and the men of Israel fled before
the Philistines, and many fell[r] on Mount Gilboa. 2 The Philistines overtook
Saul and his sons; and the Philistines killed Jonathan and Abinadab and Malchishua, the sons of Saul. 3 The battle pressed hard upon Saul; the archers found him,

[r] Heb *and they fell slain*

30.24, 25 David made a law that those who guarded the equipment were to be treated equally with those who fought in battle. Today it takes several people to provide the support services needed for every soldier in battle. In the church and other organizations, we need to treat those who provide support services equally with those on the front lines. Without bookkeepers, secretaries, trainers, and administrators, those with a public ministry would be unable to do their jobs. Are you on the front lines? Don't forget those who are backing you up. Are you in the support group? Realize that your position, although it may be less glamorous or exciting, is vital to the work of the entire group.

30.26 Why did David send part of the battle spoils to the tribe of Judah? (1) David was from the tribe of Judah. (2) David was recognizing Judah as the largest tribe of Israel representing the greatest authority. (3) After Saul's death, the tribe of Judah split off from the rest of the tribes (2 Samuel 2.4) because they refused to recognize Saul's son as king. David may have anticipated this split. If so, he was preparing the leaders of Judah to accept him as their king.

31.3, 4 The Philistines had a well-earned reputation for torturing their captives. Saul no doubt knew about Samson's fate (Judges 16.18–31) and did not want to risk physical mutilation or other abuse. When his armor-bearer refused to kill him, he took his own life.

31.3, 4 Saul was tall, handsome, strong, rich, and powerful, but all of this was not enough to make him someone we should emulate. He was tall physically, but he was small in God's eyes. He was handsome, but his sin made him ugly. He was strong, but his lack of faith made him weak. He was rich, but he was spiritually bankrupt. He could give orders to many, but he couldn't command their respect or allegiance. Saul looked good on the outside, but he was decaying on the inside. A right relationship with God and a strong character are much more valuable than a good-looking exterior.

31.3, 4 Saul's armor-bearer faced a moral dilemma—should he carry out a sinful order from a man he was supposed to obey? He knew he should obey his master, the king, but he also knew murder was wrong. He decided not to kill Saul.

There is a difference between following an order with which you don't agree and following one you know is wrong. It is never right or ethical to carry out a wrong act, no matter who gives the order or what the consequences for disobedience may be. What shapes your choice when you face a moral dilemma? Have the courage to follow God's law above human commands.

and he was badly wounded by them. 4 Then Saul said to his armor-bearer, "Draw
your sword and thrust me through with it, so that these uncircumcised may not
come and thrust me through, and make sport of me." But his armor-bearer was
unwilling; for he was terrified. So Saul took his own sword and fell upon it. 5 When
his armor-bearer saw that Saul was dead, he also fell upon his sword and died with
him. 6 So Saul and his three sons and his armor-bearer and all his men died together
on the same day. 7 When the men of Israel who were on the other side of the valley
and those beyond the Jordan saw that the men of Israel had fled and that Saul and
his sons were dead, they forsook their towns and fled; and the Philistines came and
occupied them.

8 The next day, when the Philistines came to strip the dead, they found Saul and
his three sons fallen on Mount Gilboa. 9 They cut off his head, stripped off his 31.9
armor, and sent messengers throughout the land of the Philistines to carry the good Judg 16.23,24 2 Sam 1.20
news to the houses of their idols and to the people. 10 They put his armor in the 31.10
temple of Astarte;[s] and they fastened his body to the wall of Beth-shan. 11 But Josh 17.11
when the inhabitants of Jabesh-gilead heard what the Philistines had done to Saul, Judg 2.12-14 1 Sam 7.3
12 all the valiant men set out, traveled all night long, and took the body of Saul and 2 Sam 21.12-14
the bodies of his sons from the wall of Beth-shan. They came to Jabesh and burned 31.11 1 Sam 11.1-13
them there. 13 Then they took their bones and buried them under the tamarisk tree 31.12
in Jabesh, and fasted seven days. 2 Sam 2.4-7

s Heb plural

31.4 Saul faced death the same way he faced life. He took matters into his own hands without thinking of God or asking for his guidance. If our lives aren't the way we would like them to be now, we can't assume that change will come more easily later. When nearing death, we will respond to God the same way we have been responding all along. Coming face to face with death only shows us what we are *really* like. How do you want to face death? Start facing life that way right now.

31.10 Astarte was a goddess of fertility and sex. Beth-shan was a town on the eastern slopes of Mount Gilboa, overlooking the Jordan valley.

31.13 Consider the difference between the last judge of Israel and its first king. Saul, the king, was characterized by inconsistency, disobedience, and self-will. He did not have a heart for God. Samuel, the judge, was characterized by consistency, obedience, and a deep desire for God's will. He had a genuine desire for God.

When God called Samuel, he said, "Speak, for your servant is listening" (3.9). But when God called Saul, he replied, "Why then have you spoken to me in this way?" (9.21). Saul was dedicated to himself; Samuel was dedicated to God.

31.13 Saul's death was also the death of an ideal—Israel could no longer believe that having a king like the other nations would solve all their troubles. The real problem was not the form of government, but the sinful king. Saul tried to please God by spurts of religiosity, but real spirituality takes a lifetime of consistent obedience.

Heroic spiritual lives are built by stacking days of obedience one on top of the other. Like a brick, each obedient act is small in itself, but in time the acts will pile up, and a huge wall of strong character will be built—a great defense against temptation. We should strive for consistent obedience each day.

SAMUEL AND THE JUDGES

Samuel was the last and the greatest of Israel's judges. He provided the transition from the period of the judges to the rule of kings in Israel. While the judges were effective in delivering Israel from their enemies at crucial times, they were unable to unite all of the tribes on a permanent basis. Because the people lacked faith in God to keep them secure from attack, they rejected Samuel as their judge and God as their king. They wanted a king, like the surrounding nations, to unify and lead them.

Judgeship	*Oppressor*	*Reference*
Samuel	Philistines	1 Samuel 7.2
Samson	Philistines	Judges 13.1—16.31
Abdon	Unknown	Judges 12.13-15
Elon	Unknown	Judges 12.11, 12
Ibzan	Unknown	Judges 12.8-10
Jephthah	Ammonites	Judges 10.6—12.7
Jair	Unknown	Judges 10.3-5
Tola	Unknown	Judges 10.1, 2
Abimelech	Civil War	Judges 8.33—9.57
Gideon	Midianites	Judges 6.1—8.32
Deborah	Canaanites	Judges 4.1—5.31
Shamgar	Philistines	Judges 3.31
Ehud	Moabites	Judges 3.12-30

2 SAMUEL

Judges begin to rule 1375 B.C. (1220 B.C.)

Saul becomes king 1050 (1045)

VITAL STATISTICS

PURPOSES:
(1) to record the history of David's reign;
(2) to demonstrate effective leadership under God;
(3) to reveal that one person *can* make a difference;
(4) to show the personal qualities that please God;
(5) to depict David as an ideal leader of an imperfect kingdom, and to foreshadow Christ, who will be the ideal leader of a new and perfect kingdom (chapter 7)

AUTHOR:
Unknown. Some have suggested that Nathan's son Zabud may have been the author (1 Kings 4.5). The book also includes the writings of Nathan and Gad (1 Chronicles 29.29).

DATE WRITTEN:
930 B.C.; written soon after David's reign, 1050–970 B.C.

SETTING:
The land of Israel under David's rule

KEY VERSE:
"David then perceived that the Lord had established him king over Israel, and that he had exalted his kingdom for the sake of his people Israel" (5.12).

SPECIAL FEATURES:
This book was named after the prophet who anointed David and guided him in living for God.

THE CHILD enters the room with long gown flowing, trailing well behind her high-heeled shoes. The wide-brimmed hat rests precariously atop her head, tilted to the right, and the long necklace swings like a pendulum as she walks. Following close is the "man." His fingernails peek out of the coat sleeves that are already pushed upward six inches. With feet shuffling in the double-sized boots, his unsteady steps belie his confident smile. Children at play, dressing up—they copy Mom and Dad, having watched them dress and walk. Models . . . everyone has them . . . people we emulate, people who are our ideals. Unconsciously perhaps, we copy their actions and adopt their ideas.

Among all the godly role models mentioned in the Bible, there is probably no one who stands out more than King David. Born halfway between Abraham and Jesus, he becomes God's leader for all of Israel and the ancestor of the Messiah. David was "a man after [God's] own heart" (1 Samuel 13.14). What are the personal qualities which David possessed that pleased God?

The book of 2 Samuel tells David's story. As you read, you will be filled with excitement as he is crowned king of Judah and then king over all of Israel (5.1–5), praising God as he brings the ark of the covenant back to the tabernacle (6.1–23) and exulting as he leads his armies to victory over all their enemies and completes the conquest of the promised land begun by Joshua (8—10). David was a man who accomplished much.

But David was human, and there were those dark times when he stumbled and fell into sin. The record of lust, adultery, and murder is not easy to read (11—13) and reveals that even great people who try to follow God are susceptible to temptation and sin.

Godliness does not guarantee an easy and carefree life. David had family problems—his own son incited the entire nation to rebellion and crowned himself king (14.1—18.33). And greatness can cause pride, as we see in David's sinful act of taking a census in order to glory in the strength of his nation (24.1–25). But the story of this fallen hero does not end in tragedy. Through repentance, his fellowship and peace with God were restored, but he had to face the consequences of the sins he committed (12—20). These consequences stayed with him the rest of his life as a reminder of his sinful deeds and his need for God.

As you read 2 Samuel, look for David's God-like characteristics—his faithfulness, patience, courage, generosity, commitment, honesty—as well as other God-honoring characteristics such as modesty and penitence. Valuable lessons can be learned from his sins and from his repentance. You, like David, can become a person after God's own heart.

Saul dies; David is king of Judah 1010	David becomes king of all Israel 1003	David and Bathsheba sin 997(?)	Solomon born 991	David's census 980(?)	David dies; Solomon made king 970	The kingdom is divided 930

THE BLUEPRINT

A. DAVID'S SUCCESSES (1.1—10.19)
1. David becomes king of Judah
2. David becomes king of all Israel
3. David conquers the surrounding nations

David took the fractured kingdom which Saul had left behind and built a strong, united power. Forty years later, David would turn this kingdom over to his son Solomon. David had a heart for God. He was a king who governed God's people by God's principles, and God blessed him greatly. We may not have David's earthly success, but following God is, ultimately, the most successful decision we can make.

B. DAVID'S STRUGGLES (11.1—24.25)
1. David and Bathsheba
2. Turmoil in David's family
3. National rebellion against David
4. The later years of David's rule

David sinned with Bathsheba and then tried to cover his sin by having her husband killed. Although he was forgiven for his sin, the consequences remained—he experienced trouble and distress, both with his family and with the nation. God is always ready to forgive, but we must live with the consequences of our actions. Covering up our sin will only multiply sin's painful consequences.

MEGATHEMES

THEME	EXPLANATION	IMPORTANCE
Kingdom Growth	Under David's leadership, Israel's kingdom grew rapidly. With the growth came many changes: from tribal independence to centralized government, from the leadership of judges to a monarchy, from decentralized worship to worship at Jerusalem.	No matter how much growth or how many changes we experience, God provides for us if we love him and highly regard his principles. God's work done in God's way never lacks God's supply of wisdom and energy.
Personal Greatness	David's popularity and influence increased greatly. He realized that the Lord was behind his success because he wanted to pour out his kindness on Israel. David regarded God's interests as more important than his own.	God graciously pours out his favor on us because of what Christ has done. God does not regard personal greatness as something to be used selfishly, but as an instrument to carry out his work among his people. The greatness we should desire is to love others as God loves us.
Justice	King David showed justice, mercy, and fairness to Saul's family, enemies, rebels, allies, and close friends alike. His just rule was grounded in his faith in and knowledge of God. God's perfect moral nature is the standard for justice.	Although David was the most just of all Israel's kings, he was still imperfect. His use of justice offered hope for a heavenly, ideal kingdom. This hope will never be satisfied in the heart of man until Christ, the Son of David, comes to rule in perfect justice forever.
Consequences of Sin	David abandoned his purpose as leader and king in time of war. His desire for prosperity and ease led him from triumph to trouble. Because David committed adultery with Bathsheba, he experienced consequences of his sin that ruined both his family and the nation.	Temptation quite often comes when a person's life is aimless. We sometimes think that sinful pleasures and freedom from God's restraint will bring us a feeling of vitality; but sin creates a cycle of suffering that is not worth the fleeting pleasures it offers.
Feet of Clay	David not only sinned with Bathsheba, he murdered an innocent man. He neglected to discipline his sons when they got involved in rape and murder. This great hero showed a lack of character in some of his most important personal decisions. The man of iron had feet of clay.	Sin should never be considered as a mere weakness or flaw. Sin is fatal and must be eradicated from our lives. David's life teaches us to have compassion for all men, including those whose sinful nature leads them into sinful acts. It serves as a warning to us not to excuse sin in our own lives, even in times of success.

KEY PLACES IN 2 SAMUEL

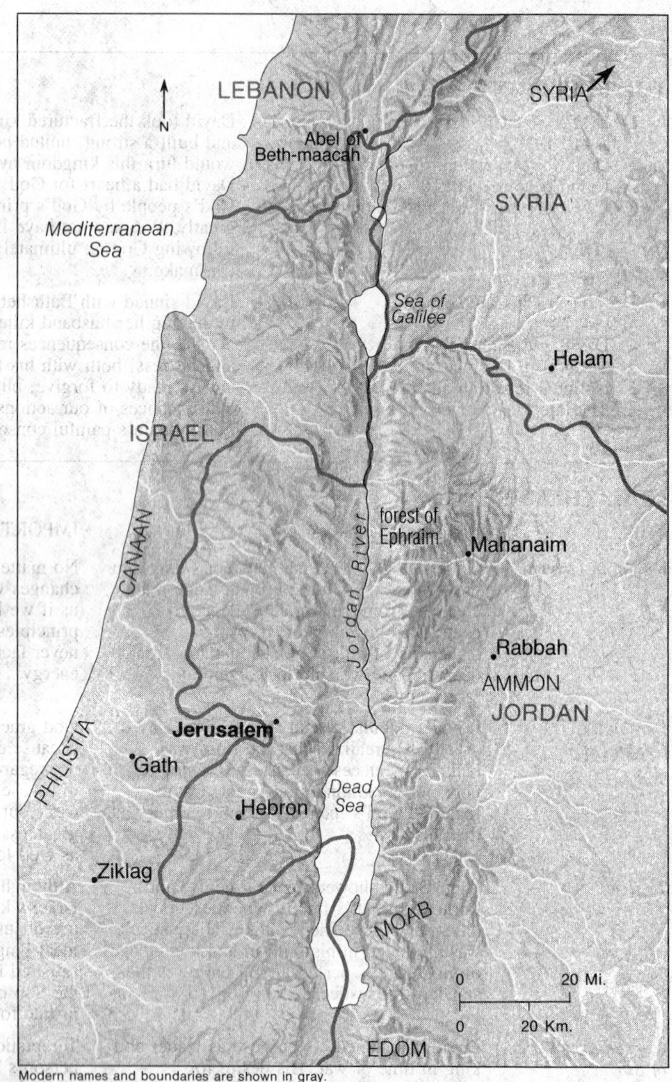

Modern names and boundaries are shown in gray.

1 Hebron After Saul's death, David moved from the Philistine city of Ziklag to Hebron, where the tribe of Judah crowned him king. But the rest of Israel's tribes backed Saul's son Ish-bosheth and crowned him king at Mahanaim. As a result, there was war between Judah and the rest of the tribes of Israel until Ishbaal was assassinated. Then all of Israel pledged loyalty to David as their king (1.1—5.5).

2 Jerusalem One of David's first battles as king occurred at the fortress city of Jerusalem. David and his troops took the city by surprise and it became his capital. It was here that David brought the ark of the covenant and made a special agreement with God (5.6—7.29).

3 Gath The Philistines were Israel's constant enemy, though they did give David sanctuary when he was hiding from Saul (1 Samuel 27). But when Saul died and David became king, the Philistines planned to defeat him. In a battle near Jerusalem, David and his troops routed the Philistines (5.17–25), but they were not completely subdued until David conquered Gath, their largest city (8.1).

4 Moab During the time of the judges, Moab controlled many cities in Israel and demanded heavy taxes (Judges 3.11–30). David conquered Moab and, in turn, levied tribute from them (8.2).

5 Edom Though the Edomites and the Israelites traced their ancestry back to the same man, Isaac (Genesis 25.19–23), they were longstanding enemies. David defeated Edom and forced them to pay tribute also (8.14).

6 Rabbah The Ammonites insulted David's ambassadors and turned a peacemaking mission into angry warfare. The Ammonites called troops from Syria, but David defeated this alliance first at Helam, then at Rabbah, the capital city (9.1—12.31).

7 Mahanaim David had victory in the field, but problems at home. His son, Absalom, incited a rebellion and crowned himself king at Hebron. David and his men fled to Mahanaim. Acting on bad advice, Absalom mobilized his army to fight David (13.1—17.29).

8 Forest of Ephraim The armies of Absalom and David fought in the forest of Ephraim. Absalom's hair got caught in a tree, and Joab, David's general, found and killed him. With Absalom's death, the rebellion died and David was welcomed back to Jerusalem (18.1—19.43).

9 Abel A man named Sheba also incited a rebellion against David. He fled to Abel, but Joab and a small troop besieged the city. The citizens of Abel killed Sheba themselves (20.1–26). David's victories laid the foundation for the peaceful reign of his son, Solomon.

A. DAVID'S SUCCESSES (1.1–10.19)

After years of running from Saul, David is finally crowned king over the tribe of Judah. The rest of Israel, however, followed Ishbaal, Saul's son. David did not attempt to take the tribes by force, but placed the matter in God's hands. After a few years Ishbaal was assassinated and the rest of the tribes finally put their support behind David. David moved the capital to Jerusalem, defeated the surrounding nations, and even showed kindness to Saul's family. We may not understand why God seems to move slowly at times, but we must trust him and be faithful with what he has given us.

1. David becomes king of Judah

David mourns for Saul and Jonathan

1.1 1 Sam 30.1,17, 26; 31.6; 2 Sam 4.9,10 — 1 After the death of Saul, when David had returned from defeating the Amalekites, David remained two days in Ziklag. 2 On the third day, a man came from
Saul's camp, with his clothes torn and dirt on his head. When he came to David, he
fell to the ground and did obeisance. 3 David said to him, "Where have you come
1.4 1 Sam 4.16; 31.2-4; 1 Chron 10.1 — from?" He said to him, "I have escaped from the camp of Israel." 4 David said to
him, "How did things go? Tell me!" He answered, "The army fled from the battle,
but also many of the army fell and died; and Saul and his son Jonathan also died."
5 Then David asked the young man who was reporting to him, "How do you know
1.6 1 Sam 28.4; 31.1 — that Saul and his son Jonathan died?" 6 The young man reporting to him said, "I
happened to be on Mount Gilboa; and there was Saul leaning on his spear, while the
chariots and the horsemen drew close to him. 7 When he looked behind him, he saw
1.8 1 Sam 15.3; 30.1,13 — me, and called to me. I answered, 'Here sir.' 8 And he said to me, 'Who are you?'
I answered him, 'I am an Amalekite.' 9 He said to me, 'Come, stand over me and
1.10 1 Sam 31.3,4 — kill me; for convulsions have seized me, and yet my life still lingers.' 10 So I stood
over him, and killed him, for I knew that he could not live after he had fallen. I took
the crown that was on his head and the armlet that was on his arm, and I have
brought them here to my lord."
1.11 Gen 37.29,34 — 11 Then David took hold of his clothes and tore them; and all the men who were
with him did the same. 12 They mourned and wept, and fasted until evening for Saul
and for his son Jonathan, and for the army of the LORD and for the house of Israel,
because they had fallen by the sword. 13 David said to the young man who had
1.14 1 Sam 24.6; 26.9,11 — reported to him, "Where do you come from?" He answered, "I am the son of a
resident alien, an Amalekite." 14 David said to him, "Were you not afraid to lift

---

1.1 David was a man who had great faith in God. He waited for God to fulfill his promises. The book of 1 Samuel tells of David's struggles as he waited to become king of Israel (Samuel had anointed David as king of Israel many years earlier). King Saul became jealous of David because the people were praising him for his accomplishments. Eventually, Saul's jealousy became so intense that he tried to kill David. As a result, David had to run and hide. For many years David hid from Saul in enemy territory and in the barren wilderness south and east of Jerusalem. David may have wondered when God's promise that he would be king would come true, but his struggles prepared him for the great responsibilities he would later face. The book of 2 Samuel tells how David was finally rewarded for his patience and consistent faith in God.

1.1 When Saul died, David and his men were still living in Ziklag, a Philistine city. Because Saul had driven him out of Israel, David pretended to be loyal to Achish, a Philistine ruler (1 Samuel 27). There he was safe from Saul.

1.2 To do obeisance means to kneel and place one's face on the ground in an act of submission.

1.11, 12 David and his men were visibly shaken over Saul's death: "They mourned and wept, and fasted until evening." This showed their genuine sorrow over the loss of their king, their friend Jonathan, and the other soldiers of Israel who died that day. They were not ashamed to grieve. Today, some people consider expressing emotions to be a sign of weakness. Those who wish to appear strong try to hide their grief. But expressing our grief can help us deal with our intense sorrow when a loved one dies.

1.13 The man identified himself as an Amalekite, but 1.2 states that he was from Saul's camp. Obviously he was lying both about his identity and about what happened on the battlefield. (Compare his story with the account in 1 Samuel 31.3, 4.) Because he had Saul's crown with him, something the Philistines wouldn't have left behind, we can infer that he found Saul dead on the battlefield before the Philistines arrived (1 Samuel 31.8).

A life of deceit leads to disaster. The man lied to gain some personal reward for killing David's rival, but he misread David's character. If David had rewarded him for murdering the king, David would have shared his guilt. Instead, David had the messenger killed. Lying can bring disaster upon the liar, even for something he or she has not done.

1.13 The Amalekites were a fierce nomadic tribe that frequently conducted surprise raids on Canaanite villages. They had been Israel's enemies since Moses' time. David had just destroyed an Amalekite band of raiders who had burned his city and kidnapped its women and children (1 Samuel 30.1–20). This man was probably unaware of David's recent confrontations with Amalekites, or he may not have come. Instead, he incurred David's wrath by posing as an enemy of Israel and claiming to have killed God's chosen king.

1.14–16 Although Saul had been trying to kill David for many years, David did not rejoice upon learning of Saul's death. In spite of all that Saul had done, David maintained respect for Saul's position as God's anointed servant. When looking at our own leaders—religious or civil—we may be tempted to become angry, despairing, or fearful. But despite their shortcomings, we should maintain respect for the positions they hold.

your hand to destroy the LORD's anointed?" 15 Then David called one of the young 1.15 2 Sam 4.10,12
men and said, "Come here and strike him down." So he struck him down and he
died. 16 David said to him, "Your blood be on your head; for your own mouth has 1.16 1 Sam 26.9 2 Sam 1.10
testified against you, saying, 'I have killed the LORD's anointed.' "

David's song for Saul and Jonathan

17 David intoned this lamentation over Saul and his son Jonathan. 18 (He or- 1.17 Josh 10.13 2 Chron 35.27
dered that The Song of the Bow[a] be taught to the people of Judah; it is written in
the Book of Jashar.) He said:

19 Your glory, O Israel, lies slain upon your high places! 1.19 2 Sam 3.38
How the mighty have fallen!
20 Tell it not in Gath, 1.20 1 Sam 6.17 31.8
proclaim it not in the streets of Ashkelon;
or the daughters of the Philistines will rejoice,
the daughters of the uncircumcised will exult.

21 You mountains of Gilboa, 1.21 1 Sam 31.1 Ezek 31.15
let there be no dew or rain upon you,
nor bounteous fields![b]
For there the shield of the mighty was defiled,
the shield of Saul, anointed with oil no more.

22 From the blood of the slain,
from the fat of the mighty,
the bow of Jonathan did not turn back,
nor the sword of Saul return empty.

23 Saul and Jonathan, beloved and lovely! 1.23 Judg 14.18 Prov 31.29-31
In life and in death they were not divided;
they were swifter than eagles,
they were stronger than lions.

24 O daughters of Israel, weep over Saul,
who clothed you with crimson, in luxury,
who put ornaments of gold on your apparel.

25 How the mighty have fallen 1.25 2 Sam 1.19
in the midst of the battle!

Jonathan lies slain upon your high places. 1.26 1 Sam 18.1 19.1; 20.17
26 I am distressed for you, my brother Jonathan;

[a] Heb *that The Bow* [b] Meaning of Heb uncertain

1.15, 16 Why did David consider it a crime to kill the king, even though Saul was his enemy? David believed that God anointed Saul and only God could remove him from office. If it became casual or commonplace to assassinate the king, the whole society would become chaotic. It was God's job, not his, to judge Saul's sins (Leviticus 19.18). We must realize that God has placed rulers in authority over us, and we should respect their positions (Romans 13.1–5).

1.17, 18 David was a talented musician. He played the harp (1 Samuel 16.23), he brought music into the worship services of the temple (1 Chronicles 25), and he wrote many of the psalms. Here we are told that he wrote a poem in memory of Saul and his son Jonathan, David's closest friend. Music played an important role in Israel's history. (For other famous songs in the Bible see the chart in Exodus 16.)

1.17–27 Saul had caused much trouble for David, but when he died, David composed a poem for the king and his son. David had every reason to hate Saul, but he chose not to. Instead, he chose to look at the good Saul had done and ignore the times when Saul had attacked him. It takes courage to lay aside hatred and hurt, and respect the positive side of another person, especially an enemy.

1.21 David pictures Saul's shield as lying on the mountainside, no longer polished or ready to be worn in battle. Instead, it was cast aside, worthless and neglected. Whether made of metal or leather, shields were oiled to keep them in good condition.

1.26 David was not implying that he had a sexual relationship with Jonathan. Homosexual acts were absolutely forbidden in Israel. Leviticus 18.22 calls homosexuality an "abomination," and Leviticus 20.13 decrees the death penalty for those who practice homosexuality. David was simply restating the deep brotherhood and faithful friendship he had with Jonathan. (For more on their friendship, see the note on 1 Samuel 18.1–4.)

greatly beloved were you to me;
your love to me was wonderful,
passing the love of women.

27 How the mighty have fallen,
and the weapons of war perished!

David anointed king over Judah

2.1 Josh 14.13,14 1 Sam 23.2,4,9 2 Sam 5.19

2 After this David inquired of the LORD, "Shall I go up into any of the cities of
Judah?" The LORD said to him, "Go up." David said, "To which shall I go up?"
He said, "To Hebron." 2 So David went up there, along with his two wives, Ahinoam of Jezreel, and Abigail the widow of Nabal of Carmel. 3 David brought up the
men who were with him, every one with his household; and they settled in the
towns of Hebron. 4 Then the people of Judah came, and there they anointed David
king over the house of Judah.
When they told David, "It was the people of Jabesh-gilead who buried Saul,"
5 David sent messengers to the people of Jabesh-gilead, and said to them, "May you
be blessed by the LORD, because you showed this loyalty to Saul your lord, and
buried him! 6 Now may the LORD show steadfast love and faithfulness to you! And

2.3 1 Sam 22.2 2 Sam 3.19; 4.8 1 Chron 12.1

2.4 1 Sam 16.13

2.5 1 Sam 24.19 25.32

CHARACTERS IN THE DRAMA
It can be confusing to keep track of all the characters introduced in the first few chapters of 2 Samuel. Here is some help.

Character	*Relation*	*Position*	*Whose side?*
Joab	Son of Zeruiah, David's half sister	One of David's generals and, later, commander-in-chief	David's
Abner	Saul's cousin	Saul's commander-in-chief	Saul and Ishbaal's, but made overtures to David
Abishai	Joab's brother	High officer in David's army—chief of "The Thirty"	Joab and David's
Asahel	Joab and Abishai's brother	High officer—one of David's 30 select warriors	Joab and David's
Ishbaal (Ish-bosheth)	Saul's son	Saul and Abner's selection as king	Saul's

2.1 Although David knew he would become king (1 Samuel 16.13; 23.17; 24.20), and although the time seemed right now that Saul was dead, David still asked God if he should move back to Judah, the territory of his home tribe. Before moving ahead with what seems obvious, first bring the matter to God, who alone knows the best timing.

2.1 God told David to return to Hebron, where he would soon be crowned king of Judah. David made Hebron his capital because (1) it was the largest city in Judah at that time; (2) it was secure against attack; (3) it was located near the center of Judah's territory, an ideal location for a capital city; and (4) many key trade routes converged at Hebron, making it difficult for supply lines to be cut off in wartime.

2.4 The tribe of Judah publicly anointed David as their king. David had been anointed king by Samuel years earlier (1 Samuel 16.13), but that ceremony had taken place in private. This one was like inaugurating a public official who has already been elected to office. The rest of Israel, however, didn't accept David's kingship for seven and one-half years (2.10, 11).

2.4–7 David sent a message thanking the men of Jabesh-gilead who had risked their lives to bury Saul's body (1 Samuel 31.11–13). In his message, he also suggested that they follow Judah's lead and acknowledge him as their king. Jabesh-gilead was to the north in the land of Gilead, and David was seeking to gain support among the ten remaining tribes who had not yet recognized him as king.

2.5, 6 Despite great danger, the men of Jabesh-gilead took the bodies of their king and his sons and gave them a proper burial. Saul had rescued Jabesh-gilead from certain defeat when Nahash the Ammonite surrounded the city (1 Samuel 11), and now these citizens were showing their gratitude and kindness. Kindness often brings no material reward and sometimes makes us vulnerable as well. But it is a sign of true devotion, friendship, and love.

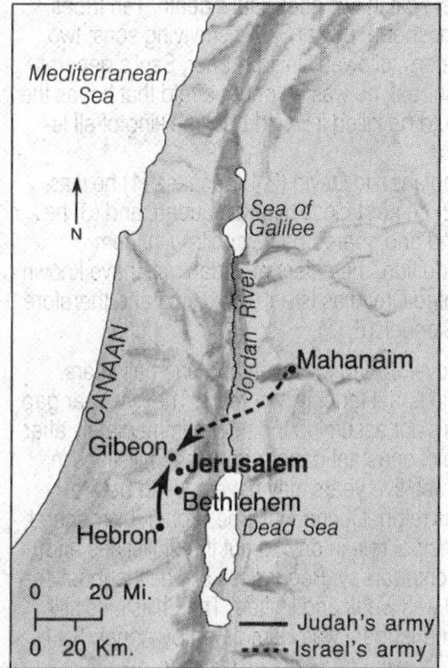

JOAB VS. ABNER
David was crowned king of Judah in Hebron; Ishbaal was crowned king of Israel in Mahanaim. The opposing armies of Judah and Israel met at Gibeon for battle—Judah under Joab, Israel under Abner.

I too will reward you because you have done this thing. 7 Therefore let your hands
be strong, and be valiant; for Saul your lord is dead, and the house of Judah has
anointed me king over them."

2.6 Ex 34.5,6

Abner crowns Ishbaal king

8 But Abner son of Ner, commander of Saul's army, had taken Ishbaal[c] son of
Saul, and brought him over to Mahanaim. 9 He made him king over Gilead, the
Ashurites, Jezreel, Ephraim, Benjamin, and over all Israel. 10 Ishbaal,[c] Saul's son,
was forty years old when he began to reign over Israel, and he reigned two years.
But the house of Judah followed David. 11 The time that David was king in Hebron
over the house of Judah was seven years and six months.

2.8 1 Sam 14.50 17.55; 26.14 2 Sam 2.29 17.24
2.10 2 Sam 5.4,5

Civil war begins

12 Abner son of Ner, and the servants of Ishbaal[c] son of Saul, went out from
Mahanaim to Gibeon. 13 Joab son of Zeruiah, and the servants of David, went out
and met them at the pool of Gibeon. One group sat on one side of the pool, while
the other sat on the other side of the pool. 14 Abner said to Joab, "Let the young men
come forward and have a contest before us." Joab said, "Let them come forward."
15 So they came forward and were counted as they passed by, twelve for Benjamin
and Ishbaal[c] son of Saul, and twelve of the servants of David. 16 Each grasped his
opponent by the head, and thrust his sword in his opponent's side; so they fell down
together. Therefore that place was called Helkath-hazzurim,[d] which is at Gibeon.
17 The battle was very fierce that day; and Abner and the men of Israel were beaten
by the servants of David.

18 The three sons of Zeruiah were there, Joab, Abishai, and Asahel. Now Asahel was as swift of foot as a wild gazelle. 19 Asahel pursued Abner, turning neither
to the right nor to the left as he followed him. 20 Then Abner looked back and said,
"Is it you, Asahel?" He answered, "Yes, it is." 21 Abner said to him, "Turn to your
right or to your left, and seize one of the young men, and take his spoil." But
Asahel would not turn away from following him. 22 Abner said again to Asahel,
"Turn away from following me; why should I strike you to the ground? How then
could I show my face to your brother Joab?" 23 But he refused to turn away. So
Abner struck him in the stomach with the butt of his spear, so that the spear came

2.12 Josh 10.12 2 Sam 19.5 21.5,6
2.13 2 Sam 8.16 1 Chron 2.16 11.5,6
2.17 2 Sam 3.1
2.18 1 Chron 2.16 11.26; 12.8

[c] Gk Compare 1 Chr 8.33; 9.39: Heb *Ish-bosheth,* "man of shame" [d] That is *Field of Sword-edges*

2.8 The nation of Israel split in two after Saul's death. Ten tribes followed Ishbaal (Ish-bosheth), one of Saul's surviving sons; two tribes (Judah and Simeon) followed David. Abner, Saul's general, rallied Israel around Ishbaal; he was no doubt afraid that he, as the opposing general, would be killed if David became king of all Israel.

Judah pledged allegiance to David (2.4) because (1) he was from their own tribe; (2) he kept close ties with Judah; and (3) he had protected their land and shared battle spoils with them (1 Samuel 30.26). In addition, the elders of Judah may have known that Samuel had anointed David as Israel's next king and therefore was God's choice (1 Samuel 16.13).

2.10, 11 David ruled over Judah for seven and one-half years, while Ishbaal reigned in Israel for only two years. The five-year gap may be due to Ishbaal's not assuming the throne immediately after Saul's death. Because of constant danger from the Philistines in the northern part of Israel, five years may have passed before Ishbaal could begin his reign. During that time, Abner, his general, probably played a principal role in driving out the Philistines and leading the northern confederacy. Regardless of when Ishbaal began to rule, his control was weak and limited. The Philistines still dominated the area, and Ishbaal was intimidated by Abner (3.11).

2.12ff With Israel divided, there was constant tension between north and south. David's true rival in the north, however, was not Ishbaal but Abner. In this incident, Abner suggested a "sword game" between the champions of his army and the champions of David's army, led by Joab. The fact that this confrontation occurred at the pool of Gibeon (located in Saul's home territory of Benjamin) suggests that Joab's men were pushing northward, gaining more territory. Abner may have suggested this confrontation hoping to stop Joab's advance.

Twelve men from each side were supposed to fight each other, and the side with the most survivors would be declared the winner. The confrontation between David and Goliath (1 Samuel 17) was a similar battle strategy—a way to avoid terrible bloodshed from an all-out war. In this case, however, all 24 champions were killed before either side could claim victory. Nothing was accomplished, and the civil war continued.

2.14 "Let the young men come forward and have a contest before us" could be translated, "Let's watch some sword play between our young men."

2.21–23 Abner repeatedly warned Asahel to turn back or risk losing his life, but Asahel refused to turn from his self-imposed duty. Persistence is a good trait if it is for a worthy cause. But if the goal is only personal honor or gain, persistence may be no more than stubbornness. Asahel's stubbornness not only cost his life, but also spurred unfortunate disunity in David's army for years to come (3.26, 27; 1 Kings 2.28–35). Before you decide to pursue a goal, make sure it is worthy of your devotion.

out at his back. He fell there, and died where he lay. And all those who came to the
place where Asahel had fallen and died, stood still.
2.24 1 Sam 26.5-7 24 But Joab and Abishai pursued Abner. As the sun was going down they came
2 Sam 10.10 to the hill of Ammah, which lies before Giah on the way to the wilderness of Gib-
2.25 eon. 25 The Benjaminites rallied around Abner and formed a single band; they took
2 Sam 2.9 their stand on the top of a hill. 26 Then Abner called to Joab, "Is the sword to keep
devouring forever? Do you not know that the end will be bitter? How long will it be
before you order your people to turn from the pursuit of their kinsmen?" 27 Joab
said, "As God lives, if you had not spoken, the people would have continued to
pursue their kinsmen, not stopping until morning." 28 Joab sounded the trumpet and
all the people stopped; they no longer pursued Israel or engaged in battle any further.
2.29 29 Abner and his men traveled all that night through the Arabah; they crossed
2 Sam 2.8 the Jordan, and, marching the whole forenoon,[e] they came to Mahanaim. 30 Joab

[e] Meaning of Heb uncertain

ABNER

The honest compliments of an opponent are often the best measure of someone's greatness. Although Abner and David frequently saw each other across battle lines, the Bible gives a glimpse of the respect they had for each other. As a young man, David had served under Abner. But later, Saul's campaign to kill David was carried out by Abner. After Saul's death, Abner temporarily upheld the power of the king's family. But the struggle between Abner and Saul's heir, Ishbaal, brought about Abner's decision to support David's claim to the throne. It was during his efforts to unite the kingdom that Abner was murdered by Joab.

Several years earlier, in a battle between Ishbaal's army under Abner and David's forces under Joab, Abner fled and was pursued by Joab's brother, Asahel. Abner told Asahel twice to stop following him. But the eager young soldier refused, so Abner killed him. Joab was determined to avenge his brother.

Abner realized Saul's family was doomed to defeat and that David would be the next king, so he decided to change sides. He hoped that in exchange for his delivering Saul's kingdom, David would make him commander-in-chief of his army. David's willingness to accept this proposal was probably another reason for Joab's action.

Abner lived by his wits and his will. To him, God was someone with whom he would cooperate if it suited his plans. Otherwise he did what seemed best for him at the time. We can identify with Abner's tendency to give God conditional cooperation. Obedience is easy when the instructions in God's Word fit in with our plans. But our allegiance to God is tested when his plans are contrary to ours. What action should you take today in obedience to God's Word?

Strengths and accomplishments:
- Commander-in-chief of Saul's army and a capable military leader
- Held Israel together for several years under the weak King Ishbaal
- Recognized and accepted God's plan to make David king over all Israel and Judah

Weaknesses and mistakes:
- He had selfish motives in his effort to reunite Judah and Israel rather than godly conviction
- He slept with one of the royal concubines after Saul's death

Lesson from his life:
- God requires more than conditional, half-hearted cooperation

Vital statistics:
- Where: Territory of Benjamin
- Occupation: Commander of the armies under Saul, Ishbaal, and David
- Relatives: Father: Ner. Cousin: Saul. Son: Jaasiel
- Contemporaries: David, Asahel, Joab, Abishai

Key verse:
"And the king said to his servants, 'Do you not know that a prince and a great man has fallen this day in Israel?' " (2 Samuel 3.38).

Abner's story is told in 1 Samuel 14.50—2 Samuel 4.12. He is also mentioned in 1 Kings 2.5, 32; 1 Chronicles 26.28; 27.16–22.

2.28 This battle ended with a victory for Joab's troops (2.17). When casualties were counted, Joab had lost 20 men while Abner had lost 360 men. War in the divided nation continued until David was finally crowned king of all Israel (5.1–5).

returned from the pursuit of Abner; and when he had gathered all the people together, there were missing of David's servants nineteen men besides Asahel. 31 But
the servants of David had killed of Benjamin three hundred sixty of Abner's men.
32 They took up Asahel and buried him in the tomb of his father, which was at 2.32
Bethlehem. Joab and his men marched all night, and the day broke upon them at 1 Sam 17.58
Hebron.

David becomes stronger

3 There was a long war between the house of Saul and the house of David; David 3.1
grew stronger and stronger, while the house of Saul became weaker and 1 Kgs 14.30 15.16,32,33
weaker.
2 Sons were born to David at Hebron: his firstborn was Amnon, of Ahinoam of 3.2 2 Sam 13.1
Jezreel; 3 his second, Chileab, of Abigail the widow of Nabal of Carmel; the third, 1 Chron 3.1
Absalom son of Maacah, daughter of King Talmai of Geshur; 4 the fourth, Adoni- 3.3 1 Sam 25.39
jah son of Haggith; the fifth, Shephatiah son of Abital; 5 and the sixth, Ithream, of 1 Chron 3.2
David's wife Eglah. These were born to David in Hebron. 3.4 1 Chron 3.2,3

Abner negotiates with David

6 While there was war between the house of Saul and the house of David, Abner was making himself strong in the house of Saul. 7 Now Saul had a concubine 3.7
whose name was Rizpah daughter of Aiah. And Ishbaal[f] said to Abner, "Why 2 Sam 21.8
have you gone in to my father's concubine?" 8 The words of Ishbaal[g] made Abner 3.8
very angry; he said, "Am I a dog's head for Judah? Today I keep showing loyalty 1 Sam 24.14 2 Sam 9.8; 16.9
to the house of your father Saul, to his brothers, and to his friends, and have not
given you into the hand of David; and yet you charge me now with a crime concerning this woman. 9 So may God do to Abner and so may he add to it! For just what 3.9
the LORD has sworn to David, that will I accomplish for him, 10 to transfer the king- 1 Sam 3.16,17 14.44
dom from the house of Saul, and set up the throne of David over Israel and over
Judah, from Dan to Beer-sheba." 11 And Ishbaal[f] could not answer Abner another
word, because he feared him.
12 Abner sent messengers to David at Hebron,[h] saying, "To whom does the
land belong? Make your covenant with me, and I will give you my support to bring 3.13
all Israel over to you." 13 He said, "Good; I will make a covenant with you. But one 1 Sam 18.20 1 Chron 15.29

[f] Heb *And he* [g] Gk Compare 1 Chr 8.33; 9.39: Heb *Ish-bosheth*, "man of shame" [h] Gk: Heb *where he was*

3.1 The events of chapter two led to a long war between David's followers and those loyal to Abner and Ishbaal. Civil war rocked the country at great cost to both sides. This war occurred because Israel and Judah had lost sight of God's vision and purpose: to settle the land (Genesis 12.7), to drive out the Canaanites (Deuteronomy 7.1–4), and to obey God's laws (Deuteronomy 8.1). Instead of uniting to accomplish these goals, they fought each other. When you face conflict, step back from the hostilities and consider whether you and your enemy have common goals that are bigger than your differences. Appeal to those interests as you work for a settlement.

3.2–4 David suffered much heartache because of his many wives. Owning a harem was a socially acceptable practice for kings at this time, although God specifically warned against it (Deuteronomy 17.14–17). Sadly, the numerous sons born to David's wives caused him great trouble. Rape (13.14), murder (13.28), rebellion (15.13), and greed (1 Kings 1.5, 6) all resulted from the jealous rivalries among the half brothers. Solomon, one of David's sons and his successor to the throne, also took many wives, and they eventually turned him away from God (1 Kings 11.3, 4).

3.6, 7 To sleep with any of the king's wives or concubines was to make a claim to the throne, and it was considered treason. Because Ishbaal was a weak ruler, Abner was running the country; thus he may have felt justified in sleeping with Saul's concubine. Ishbaal, however, saw that Abner's power was becoming too great.

3.7 Ishbaal may have been right to speak out against Abner's behavior, but he didn't have the moral strength to maintain his authority (3.11). Lack of moral backbone became the root of Israel's troubles over the next four centuries. Only four of the next 40 kings of Israel were called "good." It takes courage and strength to stand firm in your convictions and to confront wrongdoing in the face of opposition. When you believe something is wrong, do not let yourself be talked out of your position. Firmly attack the wrong and uphold the right.

3.8 By saying, "Am I a dog's head?" Abner meant, "Am I a traitor for Judah?" He may have been refuting the accusation that he was trying to take over the throne, or he may have been angry that Ishbaal scolded him after Abner had helped put him on the throne in the first place. Prior to this conversation, Abner realized that he could not keep David from eventually taking over Israel. Because he was angry at Ishbaal, Abner devised a plan to turn over the kingdom of Israel to David in return for being made general of David's army.

3.12 By this time Abner realized that it was useless to fight for the weak ruler, Ishbaal. Nothing could prevent David from becoming king of all Israel, because God was with him (3.18). Abner decided to deal with David to prevent David's men from seeking revenge against him for being the general of both Saul's army (1 Samuel 26.5–7) and the northern confederacy (2.8).

3.13 In an effort to reunite all Israel, David agreed to Abner's deal. Ishbaal was not God's appointed king as Saul had been; therefore,

thing I require of you: you shall never appear in my presence unless you bring
3.14 1 Sam 18.26,27 Saul's daughter Michal when you come to see me." 14 Then David sent messengers
to Saul's son Ishbaal,[i] saying, "Give me my wife Michal, to whom I became en-
3.15 1 Sam 25.44 gaged at the price of one hundred foreskins of the Philistines." 15 Ishbaal[i] sent and
took her from her husband Paltiel the son of Laish. 16 But her husband went with
3.16 2 Sam 16.5 her, weeping as he walked behind her all the way to Bahurim. Then Abner said to
him, "Go back home!" So he went back.

17 Abner sent word to the elders of Israel, saying, "For some time past you
3.18 1 Sam 9.16 15.28 have been seeking David as king over you. 18 Now then bring it about; for the LORD
has promised David: Through my servant David I will save my people Israel from
3.19 1 Sam 10.20 the hand of the Philistines, and from all their enemies." 19 Abner also spoke directly
to the Benjaminites; then Abner went to tell David at Hebron all that Israel and the
whole house of Benjamin were ready to do.

20 When Abner came with twenty men to David at Hebron, David made a feast
for Abner and the men who were with him. 21 Abner said to David, "Let me go and
rally all Israel to my lord the king, in order that they may make a covenant with
you, and that you may reign over all that your heart desires." So David dismissed
Abner, and he went away in peace.

Joab kills Abner

3.22 1 Sam 27.8 22 Just then the servants of David arrived with Joab from a raid, bringing much
spoil with them. But Abner was not with David at Hebron, for David[j] had dismissed him, and he had gone away in peace. 23 When Joab and all the army that was
with him came, it was told Joab, "Abner son of Ner came to the king, and he has
3.24 1 Sam 29.3 dismissed him, and he has gone away in peace." 24 Then Joab went to the king and
said, "What have you done? Abner came to you; why did you dismiss him, so that
he got away? 25 You know that Abner son of Ner came to deceive you, and to learn
your comings and goings and to learn all that you are doing."

26 When Joab came out from David's presence, he sent messengers after Abner, and they brought him back from the cistern of Sirah; but David did not know
3.27 2 Sam 2.23 20.8-10 1 Kgs 2.5 about it. 27 When Abner returned to Hebron, Joab took him aside in the gateway to
speak with him privately, and there he stabbed him in the stomach. So he died for
shedding[k] the blood of Asahel, Joab's[l] brother. 28 Afterward, when David heard
3.29 Lev 13.45,46 Deut 21.7,8 1 Kgs 2.31 of it, he said, "I and my kingdom are forever guiltless before the LORD for the blood
of Abner son of Ner. 29 May the guilt[m] fall on the head of Joab, and on all his
father's house; and may the house of Joab never be without one who has a

[i] Heb *Ish-bosheth* [j] Heb *he* [k] Heb lacks *shedding* [l] Heb *his* [m] Heb *May it*

David accepted Abner's terms of handing Ishbaal over to him.

3.13, 14 Michal had been married to David. Saul had arranged the marriage as a reward for David's acts of bravery (1 Samuel 17.25; 18.24–27). Later, however, in one of his jealous fits, Saul took Michal away from David and forced her to marry Paltiel (called Palti in 1 Samuel 25.44). Now David wanted his wife back before he would begin to negotiate peace with the northern tribes. Perhaps David still loved her (but see 6.20–23 for the tension in their relationship). More likely, he thought that marriage to Saul's daughter would strengthen his claim to rule all Israel and demonstrate that he had no animosity toward Saul's house. Paltiel was the unfortunate victim caught in the web of Saul's jealousy.

3.19 Because Saul, Ishbaal, and Abner were all from the tribe of Benjamin, the support of the elders of that tribe meant that Abner was serious about his offer. There was a strong possibility of overcoming tribal jealousies and uniting the kingdom.

3.26–29 Joab took revenge for the death of his brother instead of leaving justice to God. But that revenge backfired on him (1 Kings 2.31–34). God will repay those who deserve it (Romans 12.19). Refuse to rejoice when your enemies suffer, and don't seek revenge. Seeking revenge will ruin your own peace of mind and increase the chances of further retaliation.

3.27 Abner killed Joab's brother Asahel in self-defense. Joab then killed Abner to avenge his brother's death and also to save his position, since David had agreed to appoint Abner as general. People who killed in self-defense were supposed to be safe in a city of refuge (Numbers 35.22–25). Joab showed his disrespect for God's law by killing Abner out of revenge in Hebron, a city of refuge (Joshua 20.7).

3.29 David was saying that Joab's descendants would be unclean, unhealthy, and in want. (To "hold a spindle" means to walk with a crutch.) Why did David say such harsh words about Joab? David was upset over Abner's death for several reasons. (1) He was grieved over the loss of a skilled military officer. (2) He wanted to place the guilt of Abner's murder on Joab, not himself. (3) He was on the verge of becoming king over the entire nation, and utilizing Abner was the key to winning over the northern tribes. Abner's death could have revived the civil war. (4) Joab violated David's agreement to protect Abner. Joab's murderous act ruined David's plans, and David was especially angry that his own general had committed the crime.

discharge, or who is leprous,[n] or who holds a spindle, or who falls by the sword, or
who lacks food!" 30 So Joab and his brother Abishai murdered Abner because he **3.30**
had killed their brother Asahel in the battle at Gibeon. 2 Sam 2.23

31 Then David said to Joab and to all the people who were with him, "Tear your **3.31**
clothes, and put on sackcloth, and mourn over Abner." And King David followed Gen 37.34 Judg 11.35
the bier. 32 They buried Abner at Hebron. The king lifted up his voice and wept at 2 Sam 1.11
the grave of Abner, and all the people wept. 33 The king lamented for Abner, saying,

"Should Abner die as a fool dies?
34 Your hands were not bound,
your feet were not fettered;
as one falls before the wicked
you have fallen."

And all the people wept over him again. 35 Then all the people came to persuade **3.35**
David to eat something while it was still day; but David swore, saying, "So may 2 Sam 1.12 12.17
God do to me, and more, if I taste bread or anything else before the sun goes
down!" 36 All the people took notice of it, and it pleased them; just as everything the
king did pleased all the people. 37 So all the people and all Israel understood that
day that the king had no part in the killing of Abner son of Ner. 38 And the king said
to his servants, "Do you not know that a prince and a great man has fallen this day
in Israel? 39 Today I am powerless, even though anointed king; these men, the sons **3.39**
of Zeruiah, are too violent for me. The LORD pay back the one who does wickedly 1 Sam 26.5-7 2 Sam 8.16 19.5
in accordance with his wickedness!" 1 Chron 11.5,6

The murder of Ishbaal

4 When Saul's son Ishbaal[o] heard that Abner had died at Hebron, his courage **4.1**
failed, and all Israel was dismayed. 2 Saul's son had two captains of raiding 2 Sam 3.27
bands; the name of the one was Baanah, and the name of the other Rechab. They **4.2** Josh 9.17; 18.25
were sons of Rimmon a Benjaminite from Beeroth—for Beeroth is considered to Neh 11.33
belong to Benjamin. 3 (Now the people of Beeroth had fled to Gittaim and are there
as resident aliens to this day).

4 Saul's son Jonathan had a son who was crippled in his feet. He was five years **4.4**
old when the news about Saul and Jonathan came from Jezreel. His nurse picked 1 Sam 31.1-4 2 Sam 9.3,5,6
him up and fled; and, in her haste to flee, it happened that he fell and became lame. 1 Chron 8.34
His name was Mephibosheth.[p]

5 Now the sons of Rimmon the Beerothite, Rechab and Baanah, set out, and **4.5**
about the heat of the day they came to the house of Ishbaal,[q] while he was taking 2 Sam 2.8
his noonday rest. 6 They came inside the house as though to take wheat, and they **4.6**
struck him in the stomach; then Rechab and his brother Baanah escaped.[r] 7 Now 1 Sam 17.54 31.9 2 Kgs 10.6
they had come into the house while he was lying on his couch in his bedchamber; Mt 14.11

[n] A term for several skin diseases; precise meaning uncertain [o] Heb lacks *Ishbaal* [p] In 1 Chr 8.34 and 9.40, *Merib-baal* [q] Heb *Ish-bosheth* [r] Meaning of Heb of verse 6 uncertain

3.31 By walking behind the bier, or casket, David was leading the mourning.

3.31ff David ordered Joab to mourn, possibly because few people were aware that Joab had committed the crime and because David did not want any further trouble. If this is true, David was thinking more about strengthening his kingdom than about justice.

3.39 Joab and Abishai were the two sons of Zeruiah David mentioned. David had an especially hard time controlling Joab because, although he was intensely loyal, he was strong-willed, preferring to do things his own way. In exchange for his loyalty, however, David was willing to give him the flexibility he craved.

Joab's murder of Abner is an example of his fierce independence. While David opposed the murder, he allowed it to remain unpunished because (1) to punish Joab could cause the troops to rebel; (2) Joab was David's nephew, and any harsh treatment could cause family problems; (3) Joab was from the tribe of Judah, and David didn't want rebellion from his own tribe; (4) to get rid of Joab would mean losing a skilled and competent general who had been invaluable in strengthening his army.

4.1 Ishbaal was a man who took his courage from another man (Abner) rather than from God. When Abner died, Ishbaal was left with nothing. In crisis and under pressure, he collapsed in fear. Fear can paralyze us, but faith and trust in God can overcome fear (2 Timothy 1.6–8; Hebrews 13.6). If we trust in God, we will be free to respond boldly to the events around us.

4.4 The rest of Mephibosheth's story is told in chapter 9; 16.1–4; and 19.24–30.

4.5–11 This situation is similar to the one in 1.1–16 where a man proudly announced to David that he had killed King Saul. Baanah and Rechab undoubtedly were seeking a reward or great recognition for killing David's rival, but they misjudged David's character.

they attacked him, killed him, and beheaded him. Then they took his head and
traveled by way of the Arabah all night long. 8 They brought the head of Ishbaal[s]
to David at Hebron and said to the king, "Here is the head of Ishbaal,[s] son of Saul,
your enemy, who sought your life; the LORD has avenged my lord the king this day
on Saul and on his offspring."
9 David answered Rechab and his brother Baanah, the sons of Rimmon the
Beerothite, "As the LORD lives, who has redeemed my life out of every adversity,
10 when the one who told me, 'See, Saul is dead,' thought he was bringing good
news, I seized him and killed him at Ziklag—this was the reward I gave him for his
news. 11 How much more then, when wicked men have killed a righteous man on
his bed in his own house! And now shall I not require his blood at your hand, and
destroy you from the earth?" 12 So David commanded the young men, and they
killed them; they cut off their hands and feet, and hung their bodies beside the pool
at Hebron. But the head of Ishbaal[s] they took and buried in the tomb of Abner at
Hebron.

4.9 2 Sam 22.20 1 Kgs 1.29
4.10 2 Sam 1.1,2,4,15
4.11 Gen 9.5 1 Kgs 2.32 Ps 9.12
4.12 2 Sam 1.15 3.32

2. David becomes king of all Israel

David anointed king over Israel

5 Then all the tribes of Israel came to David at Hebron, and said, "Look, we are
your bone and flesh. 2 For some time, while Saul was king over us, it was you
who led out Israel and brought it in. The LORD said to you: It is you who shall be
shepherd of my people Israel, you who shall be ruler over Israel." 3 So all the elders
of Israel came to the king at Hebron; and King David made a covenant with them
at Hebron before the LORD, and they anointed David king over Israel. 4 David was
thirty years old when he began to reign, and he reigned forty years. 5 At Hebron he
reigned over Judah seven years and six months; and at Jerusalem he reigned over all
Israel and Judah thirty-three years.

5.1 1 Chron 11.1
5.2 1 Sam 18.5,14
5.3 1 Sam 16.1,13
5.4 1 Kgs 2.11 Lk 3.23

[s] Heb *Ish-bosheth*

4.11 David called Ishbaal a "righteous man." As Saul's son, Ishbaal had reason to think he was in line for the throne. He was not wicked for wanting to be king; rather, he was simply too weak to stand against injustice. Although David knew Ishbaal was not the strong leader needed to unite Israel, he had no intention of killing him. God had promised the kingdom to David, and he knew that God would fulfill his promise.

When David learned of Ishbaal's death, he was angry. He had never harmed Saul, and he thought the assassins' method was cowardly. David wanted to unite Israel, not drive a permanent wedge between him and Ishbaal's supporters. To show that he had nothing to do with the extermination of Saul's royal line, he ordered the assassins killed and gave Ishbaal a proper burial. All the tribes of Israel, recognizing in David the strong leader they needed, pledged their loyalty to him. No doubt the Philistine threat and David's military reputation (1 Samuel 18.7) also helped unify the people.

4.12 David made the punishment of these two men worse than usual. Their hands (that committed the crime) and their feet (that ran for the reward) were cut off. Their bodies were hung in dishonor and disgrace while the head of Ishbaal was given a proper burial. These public actions showed David's concern for justice, and eliminated the need for someone from the tribe of Benjamin to avenge the murder.

5.3–5 This was the third time David was anointed king. First he was privately anointed by Samuel (1 Samuel 16.13). Then he was made king over the tribe of Judah (2.4). Finally he was crowned king over all Israel. As an outlaw, life had looked bleak for him, but God's promise to make him king over all Israel was now being fulfilled. Although the kingdom would be divided again in less than 75 years, David's dynasty would reign over Judah, the southern kingdom, for over 400 years.

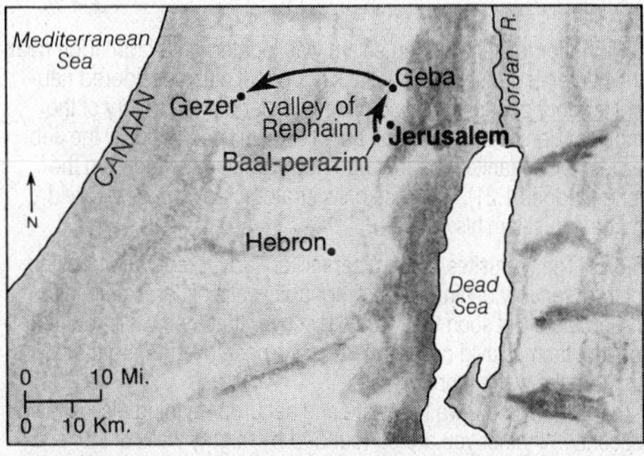

DAVID DEFEATS THE PHILISTINES The Philistines camped in the valley of Rephaim. David defeated them at Baal-perazim, but they remained in the valley. He attacked again, and chased them from Geba to Gezer.

5.4, 5 David did not become king of all Israel until he was 37 years old, although he had been promised the kingdom many years earlier (1 Samuel 16.13). During those years, David had to wait patiently for the fulfillment of God's promise. If you feel pressured to achieve instant results and success, remember David's patience. Just as his time of waiting prepared him for his important task, a waiting period may help prepare you by strengthening your character.

David conquers Jerusalem

6 The king and his men marched to Jerusalem against the Jebusites, the inhabitants of the land, who said to David, "You will not come in here, even the blind and
the lame will turn you back" — thinking, "David cannot come in here." 7 Nevertheless David took the stronghold of Zion, which is now the city of David. 8 David had
said on that day, "Whoever would strike down the Jebusites, let him get up the
water shaft to attack the lame and the blind, those whom David hates."[t] Therefore
it is said, "The blind and the lame shall not come into the house." 9 David occupied
the stronghold, and named it the city of David. David built the city all around from
the Millo inward. 10 And David became greater and greater, for the LORD, the God
of hosts, was with him.

11 King Hiram of Tyre sent messengers to David, along with cedar trees, and
carpenters and masons who built David a house. 12 David then perceived that the
LORD had established him king over Israel, and that he had exalted his kingdom for
the sake of his people Israel.

13 In Jerusalem, after he came from Hebron, David took more concubines and
wives; and more sons and daughters were born to David. 14 These are the names of
those who were born to him in Jerusalem: Shammua, Shobab, Nathan, Solomon,
15 Ibhar, Elishua, Nepheg, Japhia, 16 Elishama, Eliada, and Eliphelet.

David defeats the Philistines

17 When the Philistines heard that David had been anointed king over Israel, all
the Philistines went up in search of David; but David heard about it and went down
to the stronghold. 18 Now the Philistines had come and spread out in the valley of
Rephaim. 19 David inquired of the LORD, "Shall I go up against the Philistines? Will
you give them into my hand?" The LORD said to David, "Go up; for I will certainly
give the Philistines into your hand." 20 So David came to Baal-perazim, and David
defeated them there. He said, "The LORD has burst forth against[u] my enemies before me, like a bursting flood." Therefore that place is called Baal-perazim.[v] 21 The
Philistines abandoned their idols there, and David and his men carried them away.

5.6 Josh 15.63 Judg 1.21 1 Chron 11.4
5.7 1 Kgs 2.10
5.9 1 Kgs 9.15,24
5.10 1 Sam 18.14 2 Sam 3.1
5.11 1 Kgs 5.10,18 1 Chron 14.1
5.12 Deut 7.14 2 Sam 7.15 1 Kgs 10.9
5.13 Deut 17.17 1 Chron 3.9 14.3
5.14 1 Chron 3.5-8 14.4-7
5.18 Josh 15.8; 18.16 2 Sam 23.13
5.19 1 Sam 23.2 30.8
5.20 Num 33.3,4 1 Chron 14.11

[t] Another reading is *those who hate David* [u] Heb *paraz* [v] That is *Lord of Bursting Forth*

5.6 The fortress city of Jerusalem was located on a high ridge near the center of the united Israelite kingdom. It was considered neutral territory because it stood on the border of the territory of the tribes of Benjamin and Judah and it was still occupied by the Jebusites, a Canaanite tribe that had never been expelled from the land (Judges 1.21). Because of its strategic advantages, David made Jerusalem his capital.

5.6, 7 The Jebusites had a clear military advantage and boasted of their security behind the impregnable walls of Jerusalem, also called Zion. But soon they would discover that their walls would not protect them. David caught them by surprise by entering the city through the water tunnel.

Only in God are we truly safe and secure. Anything else is false security. Whether you are surrounded by mighty walls of stone, a comfortable home, or a secure job, no one can predict what tomorrow may bring. Our relationship with God is the only security that cannot be taken away.

5.12 Although the heathen kingdoms based their greatness on conquest, power, armies, and wealth, David knew that his greatness came only from God. To be great means keeping a close relationship with God personally and nationally. To do this, David had to keep his ambition under control. Although he was famous, successful, and well liked, he gave God first place in his life and served the people according to God's purposes. Do you seek greatness from God or from people? In the drive for success, remember to keep your ambition under God's control.

5.13 Although David sincerely sought after God, he had weaknesses like any other person. One of those weaknesses was his desire for many wives. Sadly, the children born to these wives caused David and the kingdom much grief. David also set an unhealthy pattern for his son Solomon. (For more on the problems caused by David's many wives see the note on 3.2–4.)

5.17 The stronghold is the mountain stronghold in the desert of Judah that David used when defending himself against Saul (see 23.14 and 1 Chronicles 12.8).

5.17 The Philistine oppression of Israel began in the days of Samson (Judges 13–16). The Philistines were still Israel's most powerful enemy, although David was once considered a friend and ally (1 Samuel 27, 29). Because they occupied much of Israel's northern territory, they apparently did not bother David while he was king of Judah to the south. But when they learned that David was planning to unite all Israel, they tried to stop him.

5.19 How could David get such a clear message from God? He may have prayed and been urged to action by the Holy Spirit. He may have asked God through a prophet. Most likely, however, he went to the high priest, who consulted God through the Urim and Thummim that God had told the Israelites to use for just such a purpose. (For more on the Urim and Thummim see the notes on Leviticus 8.8 and 1 Samuel 10.20.)

5.19–25 David fought his battles the way God instructed him. In each instance he (1) asked if he should fight or not; (2) followed instructions carefully; and (3) gave God the glory. We can err in our "battles" by ignoring these steps and instead: (1) do what we want without considering God's will; (2) do things our way and ignore advice in the Bible or from other wise people; and (3) take the glory ourselves or give it to someone else without acknowledging the help we received from God. All these responses are sinful.

22 Once again the Philistines came up, and were spread out in the valley of
Rephaim. 23 When David inquired of the LORD, he said, "You shall not go up; go
5.24 around to their rear, and come upon them opposite the balsam trees. 24 When you
Judg 4.14; 7.15 2 Kgs 7.6 hear the sound of marching in the tops of the balsam trees, then be on the alert; for
then the LORD has gone out before you to strike down the army of the Philistines."
5.25 Josh 12.12 25 David did just as the LORD had commanded him; and he struck down the Philis-
21.20-22 tines from Geba all the way to Gezer.

David brings the ark to Jerusalem

6.1 Ex 25.22 **6** David again gathered all the chosen men of Israel, thirty thousand. 2 David and
2 Kgs 19.15 all the people with him set out and went from Baale-judah, to bring up from
1 Chron 13.5,6 there the ark of God, which is called by the name of the LORD of hosts who is

---

MICHAL

Sometimes love is not enough—especially if that love is little more than the strong emotional attraction that grows between a hero and an admirer. To Michal, Saul's daughter, the courageous young David must have seemed like a dream come true. Her feelings about this hero gradually became obvious to others, and eventually, her father heard about her love for David. He saw this as an opportunity to get rid of his rival for the people's loyalty. He promised Michal's hand in marriage in exchange for David's success in the impossible task of killing 100 Philistines. But David was victorious, and so Saul lost a daughter and saw his rival become even more popular with the people.

Michal's love for David did not have time to be tested by the realities of marriage. Instead, she became involved in saving David's life. Her quick thinking helped him escape, but it cost her Saul's anger and her separation from David. Her father gave her to another man, Paltiel, but David eventually took her back.

Unlike her brother, Jonathan, Michal did not have the kind of deep relationship with God that would have helped her through the difficulties in her life. Instead she became bitter. She could not share David's joyful worship of God, so she hated it. As a result, she never bore David any children.

Beyond feeling sorry for her, we need to see Michal as a person mirroring our own tendencies. How quickly and easily we become bitter with life's unexpected turns. But bitterness cannot remove or change the bad things that have happened. Often bitterness only makes a bad situation worse. On the other hand, a willingness to respond to God gives him the opportunity to bring good out of the difficult situations. That willingness has two parts: asking God for his guidance and looking for that guidance in his Word.

Strengths and accomplishments:
- Loved David and became his first wife
- Saved David's life
- Could think and act quickly when it was needed

Weaknesses and mistakes:
- Lied under pressure
- Allowed herself to become bitter over her circumstances
- In her unhappiness, she hated David for loving God

Lessons from her life:
- We are not as responsible for what happens to us as we are for how we respond to our circumstances
- Disobedience to God almost always harms us as well as others

Vital statistics:
- Occupation: Daughter of one king, Saul, and wife of another, David
- Relatives: Parents: Saul and Ahinoam. Brothers: Abinadab, Jonathan, Malchi-shua. Sister: Merab. Husbands: David and Paltiel

Key verse:
"As the ark of the Lord came into the city of David, Michal daughter of Saul looked out of the window, and saw King David leaping and dancing before the Lord; and she despied him in her heart" (2 Samuel 6.16).

Michal's story is told in 1 Samuel 14—2 Samuel 6. She is also mentioned in 1 Chronicles 15.29.

5.25 After David became king, his first order of business was to subdue his enemies – a task the nation had failed to complete when they first entered the land (Judges 2.1–4). David knew this had to be done in order to (1) protect the nation, (2) unify the kingdom, and (3) prepare for building the temple (which would unify religion under God and help abolish idolatrous influences).

enthroned on the cherubim. 3 They carried the ark of God on a new cart, and **6.3**
brought it out of the house of Abinadab, which was on the hill. Uzzah and Ahio,[w] Num 7.9
the sons of Abinadab, were driving the new cart 4 with the ark of God;[x] and Ahio[w]
went in front of the ark. 5 David and all the house of Israel were dancing before the **6.5**
LORD with all their might, with songs[y] and lyres and harps and tambourines and 1 Sam 10.5 16.16
castanets and cymbals. 1 Chron 13.7,8 16.5
6 When they came to the threshing floor of Nacon, Uzzah reached out his hand **6.6**
to the ark of God and took hold of it, for the oxen shook it. 7 The anger of the LORD Num 4.15
was kindled against Uzzah; and God struck him there because he reached out his 1 Chron 13.9 **6.7**
hand to the ark;[z] and he died there beside the ark of God. 8 David was angry be- Lev 10.1,2
cause the LORD had burst forth with an outburst upon Uzzah; so that place is called 1 Sam 6.19
Perez-uzzah,[a] to this day. 9 David was afraid of the LORD that day; he said, "How
can the ark of the LORD come into my care?" 10 So David was unwilling to take the **6.10**
ark of the LORD into his care in the city of David; instead David took it to the house 1 Chron 13.13 26.4; 5
of Obed-edom the Gittite. 11 The ark of the LORD remained in the house of Obed-
edom the Gittite three months; and the LORD blessed Obed-edom and all his household.
12 It was told King David, "The LORD has blessed the household of Obed-edom **6.12**
and all that belongs to him, because of the ark of God." So David went and brought 1 Kgs 8.1 1 Chron 15.1-3, 25
up the ark of God from the house of Obed-edom to the city of David with rejoicing;
13 and when those who bore the ark of the LORD had gone six paces, he sacrificed
an ox and a fatling. 14 David danced before the LORD with all his might; David was **6.14**
girded with a linen ephod. 15 So David and all the house of Israel brought up the ark Ex 15.20 1 Sam 2.18,28
of the LORD with shouting, and with the sound of the trumpet.
16 As the ark of the LORD came into the city of David, Michal daughter of Saul **6.16**
looked out of the window, and saw King David leaping and dancing before the 1 Sam 18.27 2 Sam 3.14
LORD; and she despised him in her heart.
17 They brought in the ark of the LORD, and set it in its place, inside the tent that **6.17**
David had pitched for it; and David offered burnt offerings and offerings of well- 1 Kgs 8.62 1 Chron 15.1
being before the LORD. 18 When David had finished offering the burnt offerings and 2 Chron 1.4
the offerings of well-being, he blessed the people in the name of the LORD of hosts,
19 and distributed food among all the people, the whole multitude of Israel, both

[w] Or *and his brother* [x] Compare Gk: Heb *and brought it out of the house of Abinadab, which was on the hill with the ark of God* [y] Q Ms Gk 1 Chr 13.8: Heb *fir-trees* [z] 1 Chr 13.10 Compare Q Ms: Meaning of Heb uncertain [a] That is *Bursting Out Against Uzzah*

6.3 The ark of the covenant was Israel's national treasure and was ordinarily kept in the tabernacle. When the ark was returned to Israel after a brief Philistine captivity (1 Samuel 4.1–7.2), it was kept in Abinadab's home for 20 years. David saw how God blessed Abinadab, and he wanted to bring the ark to Jerusalem to insure God's blessing on the entire nation. (See the notes on Exodus 37.1 and Joshua 3.2–4 for more information on the ark.)

6.7 Uzzah was only trying to protect the ark, so was God's anger against Uzzah just? According to Numbers 4.5–15, the ark was to be moved only by the Levites, who were to carry it using the carrying poles – they were *never* to touch the ark itself. To touch it was a capital offense under Jewish law. God's action was directed against both David and Uzzah. David placed the ark on a cart, following the Philistines' example (1 Samuel 6.7, 8) rather than God's commands. Uzzah, though sincere in his desire to protect the ark, had to face the consequences of the sin of touching it. Also, Uzzah may not have been a Levite. As David sought to bring Israel back into a relationship with God, God had to remind the nation dramatically that enthusiasm must be accompanied by obedience to his laws. The next time David tried to bring the ark to Jerusalem, he was careful to handle it correctly (1 Chronicles 15.1–15).

6.11–13 David was angry that a well-meaning man had been killed and that his plans for a joyous return of the ark had been spoiled (6.8). He undoubtedly knew that the fault was his own for transporting the ark carelessly. After cooling down, he had the ark put into temporary storage while he waited to see if the Lord would allow him to bring it to Jerusalem. This also gave David time to consider the right way to transport the ark. The fact that God blessed the home of Obed-edom was a sign to David that he could try once again to move the ark to Jerusalem.

6.14 David wore a linen ephod, the priest's apron, possibly because it was a religious celebration.

6.16ff Michal was David's first wife, but here she is simply called Saul's daughter, possibly to show how similar her attitude was to her father's. Her contempt for David probably did not start with David's grand entrance into the city. Perhaps she thought it was undignified to be so concerned with public worship at a time when it was so unimportant in the kingdom. Or maybe she thought it was not fitting for a king to display such emotion. Whatever the reason, this contempt she felt toward her husband escalated into a difficult confrontation, and Michal ended up childless for life. Feelings of bitterness and resentment that go unchecked will destroy a relationship. Deal with your feelings before they escalate into open warfare.

6.17 Only a priest could place the sacrifices on the altar. Leviticus 1.2–13 indicates that anyone who was ceremonially clean could assist a priest in offering the sacrifice (see the notes on Joshua 3.5; 1 Samuel 20.26). Therefore, David probably offered these sacrifices to God with the aid of a priest. Solomon did the same (1 Kings 8.62–65).

men and women, to each a cake of bread, a portion of meat,[b] and a cake of raisins.
Then all the people went back to their homes.
20 David returned to bless his household. But Michal the daughter of Saul came
out to meet David, and said, "How the king of Israel honored himself today, uncovering himself today before the eyes of his servants' maids, as any vulgar fellow
might shamelessly uncover himself!" 21 David said to Michal, "It was before the
LORD, who chose me in place of your father and all his household, to appoint me
as prince over Israel, the people of the LORD, that I have danced before the LORD.
22 I will make myself yet more contemptible than this, and I will be abased in my
own eyes; but by the maids of whom you have spoken, by them I shall be held in
honor." 23 And Michal the daughter of Saul had no child to the day of her death.

God promises eternal blessing to David

7.1 Josh 21.44; 23.1; 1 Kgs 5.4; 2 Chron 14.7
7.2 1 Kgs 8.17,18; 1 Chron 17.1; 29.29; Acts 7.46

7 Now when the king was settled in his house, and the LORD had given him rest
from all his enemies around him, 2 the king said to the prophet Nathan, "See
now, I am living in a house of cedar, but the ark of God stays in a tent." 3 Nathan
said to the king, "Go, do all that you have in mind; for the LORD is with you."
4 But that same night the word of the LORD came to Nathan: 5 Go and tell my
servant David: Thus says the LORD: Are you the one to build me a house to live in?
6 I have not lived in a house since the day I brought up the people of Israel from

[b] Vg: Meaning of Heb uncertain

CRITICIZING GOD'S LEADERS
It is dangerous to criticize God's leaders. Consider the consequences for these men and women.

Person/Situation	*Result*	*Reference*
Miriam: Mocked Moses because he had a Cushite wife	Stricken with leprosy	Numbers 12
Korah and followers: Led the people of Israel to rebel against Moses' leadership	Swallowed by the earth	Numbers 16
Michal: Had contempt for David because he danced before the Lord	Remained childless	2 Samuel 6
Shimei: Cursed and threw stones at David	Executed at Solomon's order	2 Samuel 16 1 Kings 2
Young men: Mocked Elisha and laughed at his baldness	Killed by bears	2 Kings 2
Sanballat and Tobiah: Spread rumors and lies to stop the building of Jerusalem's walls	Frightened and humiliated	Nehemiah 2, 4, 6
Hananiah: Contradicted Jeremiah's prophecies with false predictions	Died two months later	Jeremiah 28
Bar-Jesus, a sorcerer: Lied about Paul in an attempt to turn the governor against him	Stricken with blindness	Acts 13

6.20 Worship had declined in Israel under Saul's rule. His daughter, Michal, was so concerned about David's undignified actions that she did not rejoice in the ark's return to the city. She emphasized outward appearances while David emphasized the inward condition of his heart before God. He was willing to look foolish in the eyes of some in order to worship God fully and honestly. People may worship God in ways that look foolish to us because they have a different culture or tradition. We should accept their heartfelt expressions of worship. We should not be afraid to express our feelings toward God, even when others are present.

7.1ff This chapter records the covenant God made with David, promising to carry on David's line forever. This promise would be fully realized in the birth of Jesus Christ. Although the word *covenant* is not specifically stated here, it is used elsewhere to describe this occasion (23.5; Psalm 89.3, 4, 28, 34–37).

7.2 This is the first time Nathan the prophet is mentioned. God made certain that a prophet was living during the reign of each of the kings of Israel. The prophet's main tasks were to urge the people to follow God and to communicate God's laws and plans to the king. Most of the kings rejected the prophets God sent. But at least God had given them the opportunity to listen and obey. In earlier years, judges and priests had the role of prophets. Samuel served as judge, priest, and prophet, bridging the gap between the period of the judges and the monarchy.

7.5 Why didn't God want David to build a temple for him? God told David that his job was to unify and lead Israel and to destroy its enemies. This huge task would require David to shed a great deal of blood. In 1 Chronicles 28.3, we learn that God did not want his temple built by a warrior. Therefore, David made the plans and collected the materials so that his son Solomon could begin work on the temple as soon as he became king (1 Kings 5–7). David accepted his part in God's plan and did not try to go beyond it. Sometimes God says "no" to our plans. When he does, we should utilize the other opportunities he gives us.

Egypt to this day, but I have been moving about in a tent and a tabernacle. 7 Wherever I have moved about among all the people of Israel, did I ever speak a word
with any of the tribal leaders[c] of Israel, whom I commanded to shepherd my people Israel, saying, "Why have you not built me a house of cedar?" 8 Now therefore
thus you shall say to my servant David: Thus says the LORD of hosts: I took you
from the pasture, from following the sheep to be prince over my people Israel; 9 and
I have been with you wherever you went, and have cut off all your enemies from
before you; and I will make for you a great name, like the name of the great ones
of the earth. 10 And I will appoint a place for my people Israel and will plant them,
so that they may live in their own place, and be disturbed no more; and evildoers
shall afflict them no more, as formerly, 11 from the time that I appointed judges
over my people Israel; and I will give you rest from all your enemies. Moreover the
LORD declares to you that the LORD will make you a house. 12 When your days are
fulfilled and you lie down with your ancestors, I will raise up your offspring after
you, who shall come forth from your body, and I will establish his kingdom. 13 He
shall build a house for my name, and I will establish the throne of his kingdom
forever. 14 I will be a father to him, and he shall be a son to me. When he commits
iniquity, I will punish him with a rod such as mortals use, with blows inflicted by
human beings. 15 But I will not take[d] my steadfast love from him, as I took it from
Saul, whom I put away from before you. 16 Your house and your kingdom shall be
made sure forever before me;[e] your throne shall be established forever. 17 In accordance with all these words and with all this vision, Nathan spoke to David.

7.7 1 Chron 17.6
7.8 1 Sam 16.10; 2 Sam 5.2; Ps 78.70
7.10 1 Sam 12.9-11; Ps 89.22; Isa 60.18
7.12 1 Kgs 2.1; 5.4
7.13 1 Kgs 6.11,12; 8.19; Isa 9.7; Acts 7.46,47
7.14 Ps 89.26; Heb 1.5,6
7.15 1 Sam 15.23; 16.14; Ps 89.35,36
7.16 1 Sam 25.28

David's prayer of acceptance

18 Then King David went in and sat before the LORD, and said, "Who am I,
O Lord GOD, and what is my house, that you have brought me thus far? 19 And yet
this was a small thing in your eyes, O Lord GOD; you have spoken also of your
servant's house for a great while to come. May this be instruction for the people,[f]
O Lord GOD! 20 And what more can David say to you? For you know your servant,
O Lord GOD! 21 Because of your promise, and according to your own heart, you
have wrought all this greatness, so that your servant may know it. 22 Therefore you
are great, O LORD God; for there is no one like you, and there is no God besides
you, according to all that we have heard with our ears. 23 Who is like your people,
like Israel? Is there another[g] nation on earth whose God went to redeem it as a
people, and to make a name for himself, doing great and awesome things for
them,[h] by driving out[i] before his people nations and their gods?[j] 24 And you established your people Israel for yourself to be your people forever; and you,
O LORD, became their God. 25 And now, O LORD God, as for the word that you
have spoken concerning your servant and concerning his house, confirm it forever;
do as you have promised. 26 Thus your name will be magnified forever in the saying, 'The LORD of hosts is God over Israel'; and the house of your servant David
will be established before you. 27 For you, O LORD of hosts, the God of Israel, have
made this revelation to your servant, saying, 'I will build you a house'; therefore
your servant has found courage to pray this prayer to you. 28 And now, O Lord

7.18 1 Sam 18.18; Ps 8.4
7.19 1 Chron 17.17; Isa 55.8,9
7.20 Ps 139.1; Jn 21.17
7.22 Ex 10.2; 15.11; 1 Sam 2.2; Ps 48.1
7.23 Deut 4.32; 10.21; Ps 40.5; 65.5
7.24 Gen 17.7,8; Ex 6.7; Deut 32.6; 1 Chron 17.22
7.26 1 Chron 17.23; Ps 89.35,36
7.28 Ex 34.5,6; Jn 17.17

[c] Or *any of the tribes* [d] Gk Syr Vg 1 Chr 17.13: Heb *shall not depart* [e] Gk Heb Mss: MT *before you*; Compare 2 Sam 7.26, 29 [f] Meaning of Heb uncertain [g] Gk: Heb *one* [h] Heb *you* [i] Gk 1 Chr 17.21: Heb *for your land* [j] Cn: Heb *before your people, whom you redeemed for yourself from Egypt, nations and its gods*

7.8–16 David's request was good, but God said "no." This does not mean that God rejected David. In fact, God was planning to do something even greater in David's life than allowing him the prestige of building the temple. Although God turned down David's request, he promised to continue the house (or dynasty) of David forever. David's earthly dynasty ended four centuries later, but Jesus Christ, a direct descendant of David, was the ultimate fulfillment of this promise (Acts 2.22–36). Christ will reign for eternity—now in his spiritual kingdom and in heaven, and later on earth in the new Jerusalem (Luke 1.30–33; Revelation 21). Have you prayed with good intentions, only to have God say "no"? This is God's way of directing you to a greater purpose in your life. Accepting God's "no" requires as great a faith as carrying out his "yes."

7.18ff This section records David's prayer expressing his humble acceptance of God's promise to extend his dynasty forever. David realized that these blessings were given to him and his descendants in order that Israel might benefit from them. They would help fulfill God's greater purpose and promises for the nation that through it the whole world would be blessed (Genesis 12.1–3).

7.28 David knew that God's words were true, and he based his life on them. People search many places for truth on which to base

GOD, you are God, and your words are true, and you have promised this good thing
7.29 Num 6.24-26 to your servant; 29 now therefore may it please you to bless the house of your servant, so that it may continue forever before you; for you, O Lord GOD, have spoken, and with your blessing shall the house of your servant be blessed forever."

3. David conquers the surrounding nations

Israel's enemies are defeated

8.1 1 Chron 18.1 **8** Some time afterward, David attacked the Philistines and subdued them; David
took Metheg-ammah out of the hand of the Philistines.
8.2 Num 24.15-19 1 Kgs 4.21 2 Kgs 3.4; 17.3 2 He also defeated the Moabites and, making them lie down on the ground,
measured them off with a cord; he measured two lengths of cord for those who were
to be put to death, and one length[k] for those who were to be spared. And the Moabites became servants to David and brought tribute.
8.3 1 Sam 14.47 2 Sam 10.19 1 Kgs 11.23 Ps 60 Title 3 David also struck down King Hadadezer son of Rehob of Zobah, as he went
to restore his monument[l] at the river Euphrates. 4 David took from him one thou-
sand seven hundred horsemen, and twenty thousand foot soldiers. David ham-
8.4 Josh 11.6 strung all the chariot horses, but left enough for a hundred chariots. 5 When the
Arameans of Damascus came to help King Hadadezer of Zobah, David killed
8.6 2 Sam 3.18 2 Chron 17.2 26.8 twenty-two thousand men of the Arameans. 6 Then David put garrisons among the
Arameans of Damascus; and the Arameans became servants to David and brought
8.7 1 Kgs 10.16 14.26 1 Chron 18.7 tribute. The LORD gave victory to David wherever he went. 7 David took the gold
shields that were carried by the servants of Hadadezer, and brought them to Jerusa-
lem. 8 From Betah and from Berothai, towns of Hadadezer, King David took a
8.8 Ezek 47.16 great amount of bronze.
9 When King Toi of Hamath heard that David had defeated the whole
army of Hadadezer, 10 Toi sent his son Joram to King David, to greet him and to

[k] Heb *one full length* [l] Compare 1 Sam 15.12 and 2 Sam 18.18

COVENANTS
A covenant is a legally binding obligation (promise). Throughout history God has made covenants with his people—he would keep his side if they would keep theirs. Here are seven covenants found in the Bible.

Name and Reference	*God's Promise*	*Sign*
In Eden Genesis 3.15	Satan and mankind will be enemies	Pain of childbirth
Noah Genesis 9.8–17	God would never again destroy the earth with a flood	Rainbow
Abraham Genesis 15.12–21; 17.1–14	Abraham's descendants would become a great nation if they obeyed God. God would be their God forever	Smoking fire pot and flaming torch
At Mount Sinai Exodus 19.5, 6	Israel would be God's special people, a holy nation. But they would have to keep their part of the covenant—obedience	The exodus
The Priesthood Numbers 25.10–13	Aaron's descendants would be priests forever	The Aaronic priesthood
David 2 Samuel 7.13; 23.5	Salvation would come through David's line through the birth of the Messiah	David's line continued and the Messiah was born a descendant of David
New Covenant Hebrews 8.6–13	Forgiveness and salvation are available through faith in Christ	Christ's resurrection

their lives. Yet, as David knew, God's Word is the only trustworthy foundation upon which to build a life.

8.1–5 Part of God's covenant with David included the promise that the Israelites' enemies would be brought under control and would no longer oppress them (7.10, 11). God fulfilled this promise by helping David defeat the opposing nations. Several enemies are listed in this chapter: (1) *The Moabites,* descendants of Lot who lived east of the Dead Sea. They posed a constant military and religious threat to Israel (Numbers 25.1–3; Judges 3.12–30; 1 Samuel 14.47). David seemed to have a good relationship with the Moabites at one time (see the note on 1 Samuel 22.3, 4); (2) *King Hadadezer of Zobah.* His defeat at David's hands fulfilled God's promise to Abraham that Israel would control the land as far north as the Euphrates River (Genesis 15.18); (3) *The Edomites,* descendants of Esau (Genesis 36.1) who were also archenemies of Israel (see 2 Kings 8.20; Jeremiah 49.7–22; Ezekiel 25.12–14; and the note on Genesis 36.9).

8.6 The "tribute" was the tax levied on conquered nations. The tax helped to support Israel's government and demonstrated that the conquered nation was under Israel's control.

congratulate him because he had fought against Hadadezer and defeated him. Now
Hadadezer had often been at war with Toi. Joram brought with him articles of silver,
gold, and bronze; 11 these also King David dedicated to the LORD, together with the 8.11
silver and gold that he dedicated from all the nations he subdued, 12 from Edom, 1 Sam 27.8 1 Kgs 7.51
Moab, the Ammonites, the Philistines, Amalek, and from the spoil of King Hadad- 1 Chron 18.11
ezer son of Rehob of Zobah.

13 David won a name for himself. When he returned, he killed eighteen thou- 8.13
sand Edomites[m] in the Valley of Salt. 14 He put garrisons in Edom; throughout all 2 Kgs 14.7 1 Chron 18.12
Edom he put garrisons, and all the Edomites became David's servants. And the 8.14
LORD gave victory to David wherever he went. Gen 27.30,37

15 So David reigned over all Israel; and David administered justice and equity 8.16 2 Sam 3.39
to all his people. 16 Joab son of Zeruiah was over the army; Jehoshaphat son of 19.5 1 Kgs 4.1
Ahilud was recorder; 17 Zadok son of Ahitub and Ahimelech son of Abiathar were 8.18
priests; Seraiah was secretary; 18 Benaiah son of Jehoiada was over[n] the Chereth- 2 Sam 20.7,23 1 Kgs 1.38
ites and the Pelethites; and David's sons were priests. 1 Chron 18.17

David is kind to Mephibosheth

9 David asked, "Is there still anyone left of the house of Saul to whom I may 9.1
show kindness for Jonathan's sake?" 2 Now there was a servant of the house of 1 Sam 20.14, 42; 23.18
Saul whose name was Ziba, and he was summoned to David. The king said to him, 9.2
"Are you Ziba?" And he said, "At your service!" 3 The king said, "Is there anyone 2 Sam 16.1 19.17
remaining of the house of Saul to whom I may show the kindness of God?" Ziba 9.3
said to the king, "There remains a son of Jonathan; he is crippled in his feet." 4 The 2 Sam 4.4
king said to him, "Where is he?" Ziba said to the king, "He is in the house of 9.4 2 Sam 17.27
Machir son of Ammiel, at Lo-debar." 5 Then King David sent and brought him 9.5
from the house of Machir son of Ammiel, at Lo-debar. 6 Mephibosheth[o] son of 2 Sam 19.24 21.7
Jonathan son of Saul came to David, and fell on his face and did obeisance. David 1 Chron 8.34

[m] Gk: Heb *returned from striking down eighteen thousand Arameans* [n] Syr Tg Vg 20.23; 1 Chr 18.17: Heb lacks *was over* [o] Or *Merib-baal*: See 4.4 note

---

DAVID'S ENEMIES
David wanted to complete the conquest of Canaan begun by Joshua. He defeated the Jebusites at Jerusalem and the Philistines at Gath. The Ammonites, Syrians, and Moabites became his subjects. He placed garrisons in Edom and levied a tax upon them.

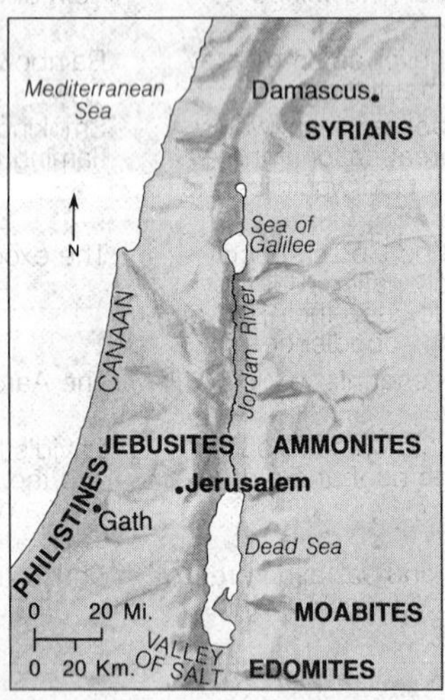

8.15 Everything David did pleased the people (3.35, 36), not because he tried to please them, but because he tried to please God. Often those who try the hardest to become popular never make it. But the praise of people is not that important. Don't spend your time devising ways to become accepted in the public eye. Instead strive to do what is right, and both God and people will respect your convictions.

8.15 King David's reign was characterized by justice. Justice means fairness in interpreting the law, lenience in administering punishment, respect for people's rights, and recognition of people's duty toward God. Is it any wonder that almost everyone trusted and followed him? Why was it good for David to pursue justice? (1) It was God's command (Deuteronomy 16.18–20) and his character (Deuteronomy 32.4). His laws were meant to establish a just society. (2) It was in the nation's best interest because times would arise when each individual would need to rely on it. Justice should characterize the way you relate to others. Make sure you are fair in the way you treat people.

9.1ff Most kings in David's day tried to wipe out the families of their rivals in order to prevent any descendants from seeking the throne. But David showed kindness to Mephibosheth, whose father was Prince Jonathan and whose grandfather was King Saul. David was kind partly because of his loyalty to God's previously anointed king (see the note on 1 Samuel 24.5, 6); partly for political reasons—to unite Judah and Israel (see the notes on 3.13, 14 and 3.29); and mainly because of his vow to show kindness to all of Jonathan's descendants (1 Samuel 20.14–17).

9.3 How Mephibosheth became lame is recorded in 4.4. Mephibosheth was five years old when Saul and Jonathan died.

9.5, 6 Mephibosheth was afraid to visit the king, who was treating him like a prince. Although he feared for his life and may have felt unworthy, that didn't mean he should refuse David's gifts. When God graciously offers us forgiveness of sins and a place in heaven, we may feel unworthy, but we will receive these gifts if we accept them. A reception even warmer than the one David gave Mephibosheth waits for all who receive God's gifts through trusting Jesus Christ—not because we deserve it, but because of God's promise (Ephesians 2.8, 9).

9.6 To do obeisance means to kneel and place one's face on the ground in an act of submission.

9.7 2 Sam 19.28 2 Kgs 25.29

said, "Mephibosheth!"[p] He answered, "I am your servant." [7]David said to him,
"Do not be afraid, for I will show you kindness for the sake of your father Jonathan;
I will restore to you all the land of your grandfather Saul, and you yourself shall eat
at my table always." [8]He did obeisance and said, "What is your servant, that you
should look upon a dead dog such as I?"

9.9 2 Sam 16.4 19.29 9.10 2 Sam 19.28

9 Then the king summoned Saul's servant Ziba, and said to him, "All that belonged to Saul and to all his house I have given to your master's grandson. [10]You
and your sons and your servants shall till the land for him, and shall bring in the
produce, so that your master's grandson may have food to eat; but your master's
grandson Mephibosheth[p] shall always eat at my table." Now Ziba had fifteen sons
and twenty servants. [11]Then Ziba said to the king, "According to all that my lord
the king commands his servant, so your servant will do." Mephibosheth[p] ate at
David's[q] table, like one of the king's sons. [12]Mephibosheth[p] had a young son
whose name was Mica. And all who lived in Ziba's house became Mephibosheth's[r] servants. [13]Mephibosheth[p] lived in Jerusalem, for he always ate at the
king's table. Now he was lame in both his feet.

David defeats the Arameans

10.1 1 Chron 19.1-19

10 Some time afterward, the king of the Ammonites died, and his son Hanun
succeeded him. [2]David said, "I will deal loyally with Hanun son of Nahash,
just as his father dealt loyally with me." So David sent envoys to console him concerning his father. When David's envoys came into the land of the Ammonites,
[3]the princes of the Ammonites said to their lord Hanun, "Do you really think that
David is honoring your father just because he has sent messengers with condo-
lences to you? Has not David sent his envoys to you to search the city, to spy it out,

10.4 Isa 15.2; 20.4 47.2,3 Jer 41.5

and to overthrow it?" [4]So Hanun seized David's envoys, shaved off half the beard
of each, cut off their garments in the middle at their hips, and sent them away.
[5]When David was told, he sent to meet them, for the men were greatly ashamed.
The king said, "Remain at Jericho until your beards have grown, and then return."

10.6 2 Kgs 7.6

6 When the Ammonites saw that they had become odious to David, the Ammonites sent and hired the Arameans of Beth-rehob and the Arameans of Zobah,
twenty thousand foot soldiers, as well as the king of Maacah, one thousand men,

10.7 Judg 11.3

and the men of Tob, twelve thousand men. [7]When David heard of it, he sent Joab
and all the army with the warriors. [8]The Ammonites came out and drew up in battle
array at the entrance of the gate; but the Arameans of Zobah and of Rehob, and the
men of Tob and Maacah, were by themselves in the open country.

[p] Or *Merib-baal*: See 4.4 note [q] Gk: Heb *my* [r] Or *Merib-baal's*: See 4.4 note

DAVID AND THE AMMONITES
Ammon gathered together its troops from the north; Joab brought the Israelite army to attack them near Rabbah. Joab returned to Jerusalem victorious, but the enemy recruited additional forces and regrouped at Helam. David himself led the next victorious attack.

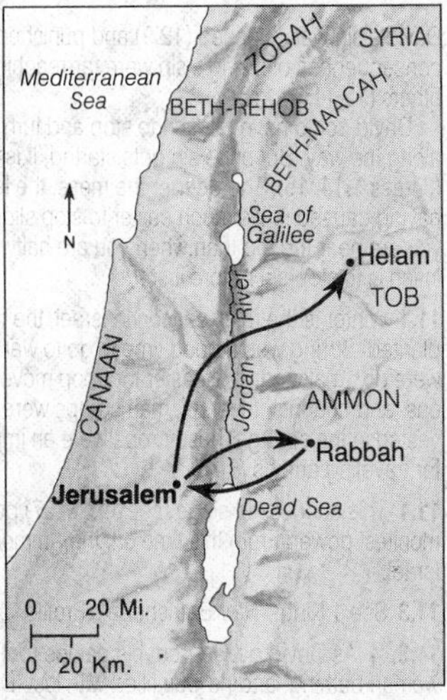

9.7 David's treatment of Mephibosheth shows his integrity as a leader who accepted his obligation to show love and mercy. His generous provision for Saul's son goes beyond any political benefit he might have received. Are you able to forgive those who have wronged you? Can you be generous with those less deserving? Each time we show compassion, our character is strengthened.

10.4, 5 In Israelite culture, all men wore full beards. It was a sign of maturity and authority. Thus when these ambassadors had their beards half-shaved, they suffered great indignity.

10.6 Hanun took the wrong advice, suspected the motives of the ambassadors, humiliated these men, realized David was angry, and immediately marshalled his forces for battle. He should have thought through the advice more carefully; but even if he had not, he should have tried to negotiate with David. Instead, he refused to admit any fault and got ready for war. Often we respond angrily and defensively rather than admitting we made a mistake, apologizing, and trying to defuse the other person's anger. Instead we should be willing to seek peace.

9 When Joab saw that the battle was set against him both in front and in the rear,
he chose some of the picked men of Israel, and arrayed them against the Arameans;
10 the rest of his men he put in the charge of his brother Abishai, and he arrayed **10.10**
them against the Ammonites. 11 He said, "If the Arameans are too strong for me, 2 Sam 2.18; 16.9
then you shall help me; but if the Ammonites are too strong for you, then I will
come and help you. 12 Be strong, and let us be courageous for the sake of our peo- **10.12**
ple, and for the cities of our God; and may the LORD do what seems good to him." Deut 31.6; 1 Sam 3.18
13 So Joab and the people who were with him moved forward into battle against the 1 Cor 16.13
Arameans; and they fled before him. 14 When the Ammonites saw that the Arame- **10.13**
ans fled, they likewise fled before Abishai, and entered the city. Then Joab re- 1 Kgs 20.20; 1 Chron 19.14
turned from fighting against the Ammonites, and came to Jerusalem.
15 But when the Arameans saw that they had been defeated by Israel, they gath- **10.15**
ered themselves together. 16 Hadadezer sent and brought out the Arameans who 2 Sam 8.3; 1 Chron 19.16
were beyond the Euphrates; and they came to Helam, with Shobach the commander
of the army of Hadadezer at their head. 17 When it was told David, he gathered all
Israel together, and crossed the Jordan, and came to Helam. The Arameans arrayed
themselves against David and fought with him. 18 The Arameans fled before Israel; **10.18** 1 Chron 19.17,18
and David killed of the Arameans seven hundred chariot teams, and forty thousand
horsemen,[s] and wounded Shobach the commander of their army, so that he died
there. 19 When all the kings who were servants of Hadadezer saw that they had been **10.19**
defeated by Israel, they made peace with Israel, and became subject to them. So the 2 Sam 8.6
Arameans were afraid to help the Ammonites any more.

B. DAVID'S STRUGGLES (11.1—24.25)

After restoring the nation to peace and great military power, David's personal life becomes entangled in sin. He commits adultery with Bathsheba and then orders her husband killed in an attempted cover-up. David deeply regretted what he had done and sought God's forgiveness, but the child of his sinful act died. We may be forgiven by God for our sins, but we will often experience harsh consequences.

1. David and Bathsheba

David sins with Bathsheba

11 In the spring of the year, the time when kings go out to battle, David sent **11.1**
Joab with his officers and all Israel with him; they ravaged the Ammonites, 1 Chron 20.1; Jer 49.2
and besieged Rabbah. But David remained at Jerusalem. **11.2**
2 It happened, late one afternoon, when David rose from his couch and was 1 Sam 9.25; Acts 10.9,10
walking about on the roof of the king's house, that he saw from the roof a woman **11.3**
bathing; the woman was very beautiful. 3 David sent someone to inquire about the 1 Chron 3.5

s 1 Chr 19.18 and some Gk Mss read *foot soldiers*

10.11 When Joab divided his army in two, he arranged for cooperation ahead of time. The two fronts in battle were clearly divided, but Joab made it clear that both divisions of the army were to help each other if either one ran into trouble. The spirit of interdependency and cooperation should characterize families, church staffs, and your attitude at your place of work.

10.12 There must be a balance in life between our actions and our faith in God. David here says, "Let us be courageous." In other words, do what you can. Plan the battle strategy, use your mind to figure out the best techniques, and use your resources. But he also says, "May the Lord do what seems good to him." He knew that the outcome was in God's hands. We should use our minds and our resources to obey God, while at the same time trusting God for the outcome.

11.1ff In the episode with Bathsheba, David allowed himself to fall deeper and deeper into sin. (1) David abandoned his purpose by staying home from battle (11.1). (2) He focused on his own desires (11.3). (3) When temptation came he looked into it instead of turning away from it (11.4). (4) He sinned deliberately (11.4). (5) He tried to cover up his sin by deceiving others (11.6–15). (6) He committed murder to continue the cover-up (11.15, 17). Eventually David's sin was exposed (12.9) and punished (12.10–14). (7) The consequences of David's sin were far-reaching, affecting many others (12.11, 14, 15).

David could have chosen to stop and turn from evil at any stage along the way. But once sin gets started, it is difficult to stop (James 1.14, 15). The deeper the mess, the less we want to admit having caused it. It's much easier to stop sliding down a hill when you are near the top than when you are halfway down. The best solution is to stop sin before it starts.

11.1 Winter is the rainy season in Israel, the time when crops are planted. Spring was a good time to go to war because the roads were dry, making travel easier for troop movements, supply wagons, and chariots. In Israel, many crops were ready to be harvested in the spring. These crops were an important food source for traveling armies.

11.1 This successful siege (see 12.26, 27) put an end to the Ammonites' power. From this time on, the Ammonites were subject to Israel.

11.3 See 1 Kings 1 for Bathsheba's Profile.

11.3, 4 As David gazed from his palace roof, he saw a beautiful woman bathing, and he was filled with lust. David should have left

11.4 Lev 15.19; 18.19 woman. It was reported, "This is Bathsheba daughter of Eliam, the wife of Uriah
Ps 51 Title the Hittite." 4 So David sent messengers to get her, and she came to him, and he lay
11.5 Lev 20.10 with her. (Now she was purifying herself after her period.) Then she returned to her
Deut 22.22 house. 5 The woman conceived; and she sent and told David, "I am pregnant."

David tries to cover his sin

6 So David sent word to Joab, "Send me Uriah the Hittite." And Joab sent Uriah
to David. 7 When Uriah came to him, David asked how Joab and the people fared,
11.8,9 and how the war was going. 8 Then David said to Uriah, "Go down to your house,
Job 5.12 and wash your feet." Uriah went out of the king's house, and there followed him a
present from the king. 9 But Uriah slept at the entrance of the king's house with all
the servants of his lord, and did not go down to his house. 10 When they told David,
"Uriah did not go down to his house," David said to Uriah, "You have just come
11.11 from a journey. Why did you not go down to your house?" 11 Uriah said to David,
2 Sam 7.2; 20.6 "The ark and Israel and Judah remain in booths;[t] and my lord Joab and the servants
of my lord are camping in the open field; shall I then go to my house, to eat and to
drink, and to lie with my wife? As you live, and as your soul lives, I will not do
such a thing." 12 Then David said to Uriah, "Remain here today also, and tomorrow
I will send you back." So Uriah remained in Jerusalem that day. On the next day,
13 David invited him to eat and drink in his presence and made him drunk; and in the
evening he went out to lie on his couch with the servants of his lord, but he did not
go down to his house.

14 In the morning David wrote a letter to Joab, and sent it by the hand of Uriah.
11.15 15 In the letter he wrote, "Set Uriah in the forefront of the hardest fighting, and then
2 Sam 12.9 draw back from him, so that he may be struck down and die." 16 As Joab was besieging the city, he assigned Uriah to the place where he knew there were valiant
warriors. 17 The men of the city came out and fought with Joab; and some of the
servants of David among the people fell. Uriah the Hittite was killed as well.
11.19 18 Then Joab sent and told David all the news about the fighting; 19 and he instructed
Judg 9.53 the messenger, "When you have finished telling the king all the news about the
fighting, 20 then, if the king's anger rises, and if he says to you, 'Why did you go
so near the city to fight? Did you not know that they would shoot from the wall?
21 Who killed Abimelech son of Jerubbaal?[u] Did not a woman throw an upper millstone on him from the wall, so that he died at Thebez? Why did you go so near the
wall?' then you shall say, 'Your servant Uriah the Hittite is dead too.'"

22 So the messenger went, and came and told David all that Joab had sent him
to tell. 23 The messenger said to David, "The men gained an advantage over us, and
came out against us in the field; but we drove them back to the entrance of the gate.
24 Then the archers shot at your servants from the wall; some of the king's servants
are dead; and your servant Uriah the Hittite is dead also." 25 David said to the

[t] Or *at Succoth* [u] Gk Syr Judg 7.1: Heb *Jerubbesheth*

---

the roof and fled the temptation. Instead, he entertained the temptation by inquiring about Bathsheba. The results were devastating.

To flee temptation, (1) ask God in earnest prayer to help you stay away from people, places, and situations that may tempt you. (2) Memorize and meditate on portions of Scripture that combat your specific weaknesses. At the root of most temptation is a real need or desire that God can fill, but we must trust in his timing. (3) Find another believer with whom you can openly share your struggles, and call this person for help when temptation strikes.

11.4 The phrase "she was purifying herself after her period" means that Bathsheba had just completed the purification rites following menstruation. Thus she could not have already been pregnant by her own husband when David slept with her. Leviticus 15.19–30 gives more information on the purification rites Bathsheba had to perform.

11.15 David put both Bathsheba and Joab in a difficult situation. Bathsheba knew it was wrong to commit adultery, but to refuse a king's request could mean punishment or death. Joab did not know why Uriah had to die, but it was obvious the king wanted him killed. We sometimes face situations with only two apparent choices, and both seem wrong. When that happens, we must not lose sight of what God wants. The answer may be to seek out more choices. By doing this, we are likely to find one that honors God.

11.17 Uriah and several other soldiers died as a result of David's scheme. Sin often hurts innocent bystanders. When you are tempted to do wrong, remember the people who could be hurt by your sin, and resist the temptation.

11.25 David's response to Uriah's death seems flippant and insensitive. Why? David had become callous to his own sin. The only way he could cover up his first sin (adultery) was to sin again, and soon he no longer felt guilty for what he had done. Feelings are not reliable guides for determining right and wrong. Deliberate, repeated sinning had dulled David's sensitivity to God's law and others' rights. Don't become hardened to sin, as David did. Confess your wrong actions to God before you forget they are sins.

messenger, "Thus you shall say to Joab, 'Do not let this matter trouble you, for the
sword devours now one and now another; press your attack on the city, and overthrow it.' And encourage him."
26 When the wife of Uriah heard that her husband was dead, she made lamentation for him. 27 When the mourning was over, David sent and brought her to his
house, and she became his wife, and bore him a son.

Nathan accuses David of sin

12 But the thing that David had done displeased the LORD, 1 and the LORD sent
Nathan to David. He came to him, and said to him, "There were two men in
a certain city, the one rich and the other poor. 2 The rich man had very many flocks
and herds; 3 but the poor man had nothing but one little ewe lamb, which he had
bought. He brought it up, and it grew up with him and with his children; it used to
eat of his meager fare, and drink from his cup, and lie in his bosom, and it was like
a daughter to him. 4 Now there came a traveler to the rich man, and he was loath to
take one of his own flock or herd to prepare for the wayfarer who had come to him,
but he took the poor man's lamb, and prepared that for the guest who had come to
him." 5 Then David's anger was greatly kindled against the man. He said to Nathan, "As the LORD lives, the man who has done this deserves to die; 6 he shall
restore the lamb fourfold, because he did this thing, and because he had no pity."
7 Nathan said to David, "You are the man! Thus says the LORD, the God of
Israel: I anointed you king over Israel, and I rescued you from the hand of Saul; 8 I
gave you your master's house, and your master's wives into your bosom, and gave
you the house of Israel and of Judah; and if that had been too little, I would have
added as much more. 9 Why have you despised the word of the LORD, to do what
is evil in his sight? You have struck down Uriah the Hittite with the sword, and
have taken his wife to be your wife, and have killed him with the sword of the
Ammonites. 10 Now therefore the sword shall never depart from your house, for
you have despised me, and have taken the wife of Uriah the Hittite to be your wife.
11 Thus says the LORD: I will raise up trouble against you from within your own
house; and I will take your wives before your eyes, and give them to your neighbor,
and he shall lie with your wives in the sight of this very sun. 12 For you did it secretly; but I will do this thing before all Israel, and before the sun." 13 David said to
Nathan, "I have sinned against the LORD." Nathan said to David, "Now the LORD
has put away your sin; you shall not die. 14 Nevertheless, because by this deed you

11.26 Gen 50.10 Deut 34.8 1 Sam 31.13
11.27 1 Sam 3.2-5 Ps 51.4,5
12.1 2 Sam 7.2,17 1 Kgs 20.35 Ps 51 Title
12.5 1 Sam 26.16 1 Kgs 20.39
12.6 Ex 22.1
12.7 1 Sam 16.13
12.8 2 Sam 7.2; 9.7
12.9 1 Sam 15.23
12.10 2 Sam 13.29 18.14 1 Kgs 2.23
12.11 2 Sam 16.21 15.6,10
12.13 Lev 20.10; 24.17 2 Sam 11.5 24.10 Prov 28.13 Mic 7.18 Lk 18.13
12.14 Isa 52.5 Rom 2.23

11.27 King David abused his position of authority to get what he wanted. Today we often see abuse of power in government, business, and churches. God is especially hard on leaders who misuse their positions to exploit, manipulate, or compromise those under their authority. This breaks the trust between them and those they serve.

12.1ff As a prophet, Nathan was required to confront sin, even the sin of a king. It took great courage, skill, and tact to speak to David in a way that would make him aware of his wrong actions. When you have to confront someone with unpleasant news, pray for courage, skill, and tact. How you present your message may be as important as what you say.

12.5, 6 It was a year later, and by then David had become so insensitive to his own sins that he didn't realize he was the villain in Nathan's story. The qualities we condemn in others are often our own character flaws. Which friends, associates, or family members do you find easy to criticize and hard to accept? Instead of trying to change them, ask God to help you understand their feelings and see your own flaws more clearly. You may discover that in condemning others, you have been condemning yourself.

12.10–14 The predictions in these verses came true. Because David murdered Uriah and stole his wife, (1) murder was a constant threat in his family (13.26–30; 18.14, 15; 1 Kings 2.23–25); (2) his household rebelled against him (15.13); (3) his wives were given to another in public view (16.20–23); (4) his first child by Bathsheba died (12.18). If David had known the painful consequences of his sin, he might not have pursued the pleasures of the moment. Remember that the consequences of your actions reach farther and deeper than you can ever foresee. God has set up moral guidelines to help us avoid sin in the first place. Be careful to do what God says.

12.13 During this incident, David wrote Psalm 51, giving valuable insight into his character and offering hope for us as well. No matter how miserable guilt makes you feel or how terribly you have sinned, you can pour out your heart to God and seek his forgiveness as David did. There is forgiveness for us when we sin. David also wrote Psalm 32, to express the joy he felt after he was forgiven.

12.14 David confessed and repented of his sin (12.13), but God's judgment was that his child would die. The consequences of David's sin were irreversible. When God forgives us and restores our relationship with him, he doesn't eliminate all the consequences of our wrongdoing. We may be tempted to say, "If this is wrong, I can always apologize to God," but we must remember that we may set into motion events with irreversible consequences.

12.14 Why did this child have to die? This was not a judgment on the child for being conceived out of wedlock, but a judgment on David for his sin. David and Bathsheba deserved to die, but God spared their lives and took the child instead. God still had work for David to do in building the kingdom. Perhaps the child's death was a greater punishment for David than his own death would have been.

have utterly scorned the LORD,[v] the child that is born to you shall die." 15 Then
Nathan went to his house.

David and Bathsheba's baby dies

The LORD struck the child that Uriah's wife bore to David, and it became very ill.
12.16 2 Sam 1.12 13.31 Ps 69.10 16 David therefore pleaded with God for the child; David fasted, and went in and lay
all night on the ground. 17 The elders of his house stood beside him, urging him to
rise from the ground; but he would not, nor did he eat food with them. 18 On the
12.17 2 Sam 3.35 seventh day the child died. And the servants of David were afraid to tell him that
the child was dead; for they said, "While the child was still alive, we spoke to him,
and he did not listen to us; how then can we tell him the child is dead? He may do
himself some harm." 19 But when David saw that his servants were whispering together, he perceived that the child was dead; and David said to his servants, "Is the
child dead?" They said, "He is dead."

20 Then David rose from the ground, washed, anointed himself, and changed
his clothes. He went into the house of the LORD, and worshiped; he then went to his
own house; and when he asked, they set food before him and he ate. 21 Then his
servants said to him, "What is this thing that you have done? You fasted and wept
12.22 Isa 38.1-5 Jonah 3.9 for the child while it was alive; but when the child died, you rose and ate food."
22 He said, "While the child was still alive, I fasted and wept; for I said, 'Who

[v] Ancient scribal tradition: Compare 1 Sam 25.22 note: Heb *scorned the enemies of the LORD*

DAVID'S FAMILY TROUBLES

David's many wives caused him much grief. And as a result of David's sin with Bathsheba, God said that murder would be a constant threat in his family, his family would rebel, and someone else would sleep with his wives. All this happened as the prophet Nathan had predicted. The consequences of sin affect not only us, but those we know and love. Remember that the next time you are tempted to sin.

Wife	*Children*	*What happened*
Michal (Saul's daughter)	She was childless, but adopted five of her sister Merab's sons	David gave her five nephews to the Gibeonites to be killed because of Saul's sins
Ahinoam (from Jezreel)	Amnon, David's firstborn	He raped Tamar, his half sister, and was later murdered by Absalom in revenge
Maacah (daughter of King Talmai of Geshur)	Absalom, third son Tamar, the only daughter mentioned by name	Absalom killed Amnon for raping Tamar, and then fled to Geshur. Later he returned, only to rebel against David. He set up a tent on his roof and slept with ten of his father's wives there. His pride led to his death
Haggith	Adonijah, fourth son. He was very handsome, but it is recorded that he was never disciplined	He set himself up as king before David's death. His plot was exposed and David spared his life, but his half brother Solomon later had him executed
Bathsheba	Unnamed son	Died in fulfillment of God's punishment for David and Bathsheba's adultery
Bathsheba	Solomon	Became the next king of Israel. Ironically, Solomon's many wives caused his downfall

It is also possible that had the child lived, God's name would have been dishonored among Israel's heathen neighbors. What would they have thought of a God who rewards murder and adultery by giving a king a new heir? A baby's death is tragic, but despising God brings death to entire nations. While God readily forgave David's sin, he did not negate all its consequences.

12.15 Nathan, a prophet of great wisdom, bravery, obedience, and loyalty, gave three crucial messages at three critical times in David's life. (1) He told David that his son would build the temple and that David's dynasty would last forever (7.1–17). (2) He confronted David with his sin of adultery (12.1–14). (3) He helped David place Solomon on the throne (1 Kings 1.11–53).

12.20, 21 David did not continue to dwell on his sin. He returned to God, and God forgave him, opening the way to begin life anew. Even the nickname David gave Solomon (*Jedidiah,* "beloved of the Lord"; 12.25) was a reminder of God's grace. When we return to God, accept his forgiveness, and change our ways, he gives us a fresh start. To feel as David did, admit your sins to God and turn to him for forgiveness. Then move ahead with a new and fresh attack on life.

12.22, 23 Perhaps the most bitter experience in life is the death of one's child. For comfort in such difficult circumstances, see Psalms 16.9–11; 17.15; 139; Isaiah 40.11.

knows? The LORD may be gracious to me, and the child may live.' 23 But now he 12.23
is dead; why should I fast? Can I bring him back again? I shall go to him, but he will Job 7.9-10
not return to me."

24 Then David consoled his wife Bathsheba, and went to her, and lay with her; 12.24
and she bore a son, and he named him Solomon. The LORD loved him, 25 and sent 1 Chron 22.9
a message by the prophet Nathan; so he named him Jedidiah,[w] because of the
LORD.

David conquers the Ammonites

26 Now Joab fought against Rabbah of the Ammonites, and took the royal city. 12.26
27 Joab sent messengers to David, and said, "I have fought against Rabbah; more- Deut 3.11 2 Sam 11.1
over, I have taken the water city. 28 Now, then, gather the rest of the people to- 1 Chron 20.1
gether, and encamp against the city, and take it; or I myself will take the city, and
it will be called by my name." 29 So David gathered all the people together and went 12.29
to Rabbah, and fought against it and took it. 30 He took the crown of Milcom[x] from 1 Chron 20.2,3
his head; the weight of it was a talent of gold, and in it was a precious stone; and it
was placed on David's head. He also brought forth the spoil of the city, a very great
amount. 31 He brought out the people who were in it, and set them to work with
saws and iron picks and iron axes, or sent them to the brickworks. Thus he did to
all the cities of the Ammonites. Then David and all the people returned to Jerusalem.

2. Turmoil in David's family

Amnon rapes Tamar

13 Some time passed. David's son Absalom had a beautiful sister whose name 13.1
was Tamar; and David's son Amnon fell in love with her. 2 Amnon was so 2 Sam 3.2,3 1 Chron 3.2,9
tormented that he made himself ill because of his sister Tamar, for she was a virgin
and it seemed impossible to Amnon to do anything to her. 3 But Amnon had a friend
whose name was Jonadab, the son of David's brother Shimeah; and Jonadab was a
very crafty man. 4 He said to him, "O son of the king, why are you so haggard
morning after morning? Will you not tell me?" Amnon said to him, "I love Tamar,
my brother Absalom's sister." 5 Jonadab said to him, "Lie down on your bed, and
pretend to be ill; and when your father comes to see you, say to him, 'Let my sister
Tamar come and give me something to eat, and prepare the food in my sight, so that
I may see it and eat it from her hand.' " 6 So Amnon lay down, and pretended to be
ill; and when the king came to see him, Amnon said to the king, "Please let my
sister Tamar come and make a couple of cakes in my sight, so that I may eat from
her hand."

7 Then David sent home to Tamar, saying, "Go to your brother Amnon's
house, and prepare food for him." 8 So Tamar went to her brother Amnon's house,
where he was lying down. She took dough, kneaded it, made cakes in his sight, and
baked the cakes. 9 Then she took the pan and set them[y] out before him, but he
refused to eat. Amnon said, "Send out everyone from me." So everyone went out
from him. 10 Then Amnon said to Tamar, "Bring the food into the chamber, so that
I may eat from your hand." So Tamar took the cakes she had made, and brought
them into the chamber to Amnon her brother. 11 But when she brought them near
him to eat, he took hold of her, and said to her, "Come, lie with me, my sister." 13.12
12 She answered him, "No, my brother, do not force me; for such a thing is not done Lev 18.9,11 20.17

[w] That is *Beloved of the LORD* [x] Gk See 1 Kings 11.5, 33: Heb *their kings* [y] Heb *and poured*

12.24 Solomon was the fourth son of David and Bathsheba (1 Chronicles 3.5). Therefore several years passed between the death of their first child and Solomon's birth.

12.27 "Taken the water city" refers to defeating the garrison or fort that guarded the city's water supply. Next they would conquer the city.

13.1ff David now faced sins in his family similar to those he had committed. The sin in his life was magnified in the lives of his children. If you are a parent you can't always control what your children do, but you can live by God's standards and give them a good example to follow.

13.3–5 Amnon was encouraged by his cousin Jonadab to commit sexual sin. We may be more vulnerable to the advice of our relatives because we are close to them. However, we must make sure that every piece of advice we are given measures up to God's standards, even when it comes from relatives.

in Israel; do not do anything so vile! 13 As for me, where could I carry my shame?
And as for you, you would be as one of the scoundrels in Israel. Now therefore, I
beg you, speak to the king; for he will not withhold me from you." 14 But he would
not listen to her; and being stronger than she, he forced her and lay with her.
15 Then Amnon was seized with a very great loathing for her; indeed, his loathing was even greater than the lust he had felt for her. Amnon said to her, "Get out!"
16 But she said to him, "No, my brother;[z] for this wrong in sending me away is
13.17 Gen 37.3,32 greater than the other that you did to me." But he would not listen to her. 17 He
called the young man who served him and said, "Put this woman out of my pres-
ence, and bolt the door after her." 18 (Now she was wearing a long robe with
sleeves; for this is how the virgin daughters of the king were clothed in earlier
13.19 Gen 37.29 2 Sam 1.11 Esth 4.1 times.[a]) So his servant put her out, and bolted the door after her. 19 But Tamar put
ashes on her head, and tore the long robe that she was wearing; she put her hand on
her head, and went away, crying aloud as she went.

[z] Cn Compare Gk Vg: Meaning of Heb uncertain [a] Cn: Heb *were clothed in robes*

NATHAN

This prophet lived up to the meaning of his name, "God has given." He was a necessary and helpful gift from God to David. He served as God's spokesman to David and proved himself a fearless friend and counselor, always willing to speak the truth, even when he knew great pain would result.

In confronting David's multiple sin of coveting, theft, adultery, and murder in his affair with Bathsheba, Nathan was able to help David see his own wrongdoing by showing that he would not have tolerated such actions from anyone else. David's repentance allowed Nathan to comfort him with the reality of God's forgiveness, and at the same time remind him of the painful consequences his sin would bring.

Nathan's approach helps us judge our actions. How often do we make choices that we would condemn others for making? It is helpful to ask ourselves how God and others see our actions. Unfortunately, we have a huge capacity to lie to ourselves. God still provides two safeguards against self-deception: his Word, and true friends. In each case, we get a view beyond ourselves. You are holding God's Word. Let it speak to you about yourself, even if the truth is painful. If you don't have a friend like Nathan, ask God for one. And ask God to use you as a suitable Nathan for someone else.

Strengths and accomplishments:
- A trusted adviser to David
- A prophet of God
- A fearless, but careful confronter
- One of God's controls in David's life

Weakness and mistake:
- His eagerness to see David build a temple for God in Jerusalem made him speak without God's instruction

Lessons from his life:
- We should not be afraid to tell the truth to those we care about
- A trustworthy companion is one of God's greatest gifts
- God cares enough to find a way to communicate to us when we are in the wrong

Vital statistics:
- Occupation: Prophet, royal adviser
- Contemporaries: David, Bathsheba, Solomon, Zadok, Adonijah

Key verse:
"In accordance with all these words and with all this vision, Nathan spoke to David" (2 Samuel 7.17).

Nathan's story is told in 2 Samuel 7—1 Kings 1. He is also mentioned in 1 Chronicles 17.15; 2 Chronicles 9.29; 29.25.

13.14, 15 Love and lust are very different. After Amnon raped his half sister, his "love" turned to hate. Although he had claimed to be in love, he was actually overcome by lust. Love is patient; lust requires immediate satisfaction. Love is kind; lust is harsh. Love does not demand its own way; lust does. You can read about the characteristics of real love in 1 Corinthians 13. Lust may feel like love at first, but when physically expressed, it results in self-disgust and hatred of the other person. If you just can't wait, what you feel is not true love.

13.16 Rape was strictly forbidden by God (Deuteronomy 22.28, 29). Why was rejecting Tamar an even greater crime? By throwing her out, Amnon made it look as if Tamar had made a shameful proposition to him, and there were no witnesses on her behalf because he had gotten rid of the servants. His crime destroyed her chances of marriage—because she was no longer a virgin, she could not be given in marriage.

20 Her brother Absalom said to her, "Has Amnon your brother been with you?
Be quiet for now, my sister; he is your brother; do not take this to heart." So Tamar
remained, a desolate woman, in her brother Absalom's house. 21 When King David
heard of all these things, he became very angry, but he would not punish his son
Amnon, because he loved him, for he was his firstborn.[b] 22 But Absalom spoke to
Amnon neither good nor bad; for Absalom hated Amnon, because he had raped his
sister Tamar.

Absalom murders Amnon

23 After two full years Absalom had sheepshearers at Baal-hazor, which is near
Ephraim, and Absalom invited all the king's sons. 24 Absalom came to the king,
and said, "Your servant has sheepshearers; will the king and his servants please go
with your servant?" 25 But the king said to Absalom, "No, my son, let us not all go,
or else we will be burdensome to you." He pressed him, but he would not go but
gave him his blessing. 26 Then Absalom said, "If not, please let my brother Amnon
go with us." The king said to him, "Why should he go with you?" 27 But Absalom
pressed him until he let Amnon and all the king's sons go with him. Absalom made
a feast like a king's feast.[c] 28 Then Absalom commanded his servants, "Watch **13.28**
when Amnon's heart is merry with wine, and when I say to you, 'Strike Amnon,' 2 Sam 3.27
then kill him. Do not be afraid; have I not myself commanded you? Be courageous 11.13
and valiant." 29 So the servants of Absalom did to Amnon as Absalom had com- **13.29**
manded. Then all the king's sons rose, and each mounted his mule and fled. 2 Sam 18.9

30 While they were on the way, the report came to David that Absalom had
killed all the king's sons, and not one of them was left. 31 The king rose, tore his **13.31**
garments, and lay on the ground; and all his servants who were standing by tore 2 Sam 1.11 12.16
their garments. 32 But Jonadab, the son of David's brother Shimeah, said, "Let not **13.32**
my lord suppose that they have killed all the young men the king's sons; Amnon 2 Sam 13.4,14
alone is dead. This has been determined by Absalom from the day Amnon[d] raped
his sister Tamar. 33 Now therefore, do not let my lord the king take it to heart, as if
all the king's sons were dead; for Amnon alone is dead."

34 But Absalom fled. When the young man who kept watch looked up, he saw **13.34**
many people coming from the Horonaim road[e] by the side of the mountain. 35 Jon- 2 Sam 18.24
adab said to the king, "See, the king's sons have come; as your servant said, so it
has come about." 36 As soon as he had finished speaking, the king's sons arrived,
and raised their voices and wept; and the king and all his servants also wept very
bitterly.

37 But Absalom fled, and went to Talmai son of Ammihud, king of Geshur. **13.37**
David mourned for his son day after day. 38 Absalom, having fled to Geshur, stayed 2 Sam 3.3 12.21; 14.23,32
there three years. 39 And the heart of[f] the king went out, yearning for Absalom; for
he was now consoled over the death of Amnon.

A woman intercedes for Absalom

14 Now Joab son of Zeruiah perceived that the king's mind was on Absalom.
2 Joab sent to Tekoa and brought from there a wise woman. He said to her, **14.2**
"Pretend to be a mourner; put on mourning garments, do not anoint yourself with 2 Chron 11.5-10 Amos 1.1
oil, but behave like a woman who has been mourning many days for the dead. 3 Go

[b] Q Ms Gk: MT lacks *but he would not punish . . . firstborn* [c] Gk Compare Q Ms: MT lacks *Absalom made a feast like a king's feast* [d] Heb *he* [e] Cn Compare Gk: Heb *the road behind him* [f] Q Ms Gk: MT *And David*

13.20 Absalom tried to comfort Tamar and persuade her not to turn the incident into a public scandal. Secretly, he planned to take revenge against Amnon himself. This he did two years later (13.23–33). Absalom told Tamar the crime was only a family matter. But God's standards for moral conduct are not suspended when we deal with family matters.

13.21–24 David was angry with Amnon for raping Tamar; however, David did not punish him. David probably hesitated because (1) he didn't want to cross Amnon, who was his eldest son (1 Chronicles 3.1) and therefore next in line to be king, and (2) David was guilty of a similar sin himself in his adultery with Bathsheba. While David was unsurpassed as a king and military leader, he lacked skill and sensitivity as a husband and father.

13.21–24 Hatred leads to disaster. Absalom had reason to be angry with Amnon, but instead of confronting Amnon with his sin, he allowed his anger to turn into hatred. This produced revenge instead of resolution. When wronged or angry at a wrong done to someone else, try to solve the problem, not get even.

13.37–39 Absalom fled to Geshur because King Talmai was his grandfather (1 Chronicles 3.2), and he would be welcomed.

to the king and speak to him as follows." And Joab put the words into her mouth.
14.4 2 Sam 12.1,2
4 When the woman of Tekoa came to the king, she fell on her face to the ground
and did obeisance, and said, "Help, O king!" 5 The king asked her, "What is your
trouble?" She answered, "Alas, I am a widow; my husband is dead. 6 Your servant
had two sons, and they fought with one another in the field; there was no one to part
14.7 Num 35.19 Deut 19.12,13
them, and one struck the other and killed him. 7 Now the whole family has risen
against your servant. They say, 'Give up the man who struck his brother, so that we
may kill him for the life of his brother whom he murdered, even if we destroy the
heir as well.' Thus they would quench my one remaining ember, and leave to my
husband neither name nor remnant on the face of the earth."
8 Then the king said to the woman, "Go to your house, and I will give orders
14.9 Gen 43.9 1 Sam 25.24
concerning you." 9 The woman of Tekoa said to the king, "On me be the guilt, my
lord the king, and on my father's house; let the king and his throne be guiltless."
10 The king said, "If anyone says anything to you, bring him to me, and he shall
14.11 Num 35.19,21 Deut 19.4-10 1 Sam 14.45
never touch you again." 11 Then she said, "Please, may the king keep the LORD
your God in mind, so that the avenger of blood may kill no more, and my son not
be destroyed." He said, "As the LORD lives, not one hair of your son shall fall to the
ground."
12 Then the woman said, "Please let your servant speak a word to my lord the
14.13 2 Sam 12.7 13.37-39 1 Kgs 20.40-42
king." He said, "Speak." 13 The woman said, "Why then have you planned such a
thing against the people of God? For in giving this decision the king convicts himself, inasmuch as the king does not bring his banished one home again. 14 We must
14.14 Job 34.14,15 Heb 9.27
all die; we are like water spilled on the ground, which cannot be gathered up. But
God will not take away a life; he will devise plans so as not to keep an outcast
banished forever from his presence.[g] 15 Now I have come to say this to my lord the
king because the people have made me afraid; your servant thought, 'I will speak
to the king; it may be that the king will perform the request of his servant. 16 For the
king will hear, and deliver his servant from the hand of the man who would cut both
14.17 1 Sam 29.9 2 Sam 19.27
me and my son off from the heritage of God.' 17 Your servant thought, 'The word
of my lord the king will set me at rest'; for my lord the king is like the angel of God,
discerning good and evil. The LORD your God be with you!"
18 Then the king answered the woman, "Do not withhold from me anything I
ask you." The woman said, "Let my lord the king speak." 19 The king said, "Is the
hand of Joab with you in all this?" The woman answered and said, "As surely as
you live, my lord the king, one cannot turn right or left from anything that my lord
the king has said. For it was your servant Joab who commanded me; it was he who
put all these words into the mouth of your servant. 20 In order to change the course
of affairs your servant Joab did this. But my lord has wisdom like the wisdom of the
angel of God to know all things that are on the earth."
21 Then the king said to Joab, "Very well, I grant this; go, bring back the young
man Absalom." 22 Joab prostrated himself with his face to the ground and did obeisance, and blessed the king; and Joab said, "Today your servant knows that I have
found favor in your sight, my lord the king, in that the king has granted the request
14.23 2 Sam 13.37-39
of his servant." 23 So Joab set off, went to Geshur, and brought Absalom to Jerusalem. 24 The king said, "Let him go to his own house; he is not to come into my
presence." So Absalom went to his own house, and did not come into the king's
presence.

Absalom demands to see David

25 Now in all Israel there was no one to be praised so much for his beauty as
Absalom; from the sole of his foot to the crown of his head there was no blemish in

[g] Meaning of Heb uncertain

14.4 To do obeisance means to kneel and place one's face on the ground in an act of submission.

14.11 The law provided for a way to avenge murder. Numbers 35.9–21 records how cities of refuge protected people from revenge and how blood avengers were to pursue murderers. This woman was asking for the king's protection from any claim against her.

him. 26 When he cut the hair of his head (for at the end of every year he used to cut
it; when it was heavy on him, he cut it), he weighed the hair of his head, two
hundred shekels by the king's weight. 27 There were born to Absalom three sons, **14.27**
and one daughter whose name was Tamar; she was a beautiful woman. 2 Sam 13.1
28 So Absalom lived two full years in Jerusalem, without coming into the **14.28**
king's presence. 29 Then Absalom sent for Joab to send him to the king; but Joab 2 Sam 14.24
would not come to him. He sent a second time, but Joab would not come. 30 Then
he said to his servants, "Look, Joab's field is next to mine, and he has barley there;
go and set it on fire." So Absalom's servants set the field on fire. 31 Then Joab rose
and went to Absalom at his house, and said to him, "Why have your servants set my
field on fire?" 32 Absalom answered Joab, "Look, I sent word to you: Come here, **14.32**
that I may send you to the king with the question, 'Why have I come from Geshur? 1 Sam 20.8
It would be better for me to be there still.' Now let me go into the king's presence;
if there is guilt in me, let him kill me!" 33 Then Joab went to the king and told him; **14.33**
and he summoned Absalom. So he came to the king and prostrated himself with his Gen 27.26; 33.4
face to the ground before the king; and the king kissed Absalom. Lk 15.20

3. National rebellion against David

Absalom plots to overthrow David

15 After this Absalom got himself a chariot and horses, and fifty men to run **15.1**
ahead of him. 2 Absalom used to rise early and stand beside the road into the 1 Kgs 1.5
gate; and when anyone brought a suit before the king for judgment, Absalom would
call out and say, "From what city are you?" When the person said, "Your servant
is of such and such a tribe in Israel," 3 Absalom would say, "See, your claims are
good and right; but there is no one deputed by the king to hear you." 4 Absalom said **15.4**
moreover, "If only I were judge in the land! Then all who had a suit or cause might Judg 9.1-3
come to me, and I would give them justice." 5 Whenever people came near to do **15.5**
obeisance to him, he would put out his hand and take hold of them, and kiss them. 2 Sam 14.33
6 Thus Absalom did to every Israelite who came to the king for judgment; so Absalom stole the hearts of the people of Israel.
7 At the end of four[h] years Absalom said to the king, "Please let me go to **15.7**
Hebron and pay the vow that I have made to the LORD. 8 For your servant made a Gen 28.20,21
vow while I lived at Geshur in Aram: If the LORD will indeed bring me back to 2 Sam 13.37-39
Jerusalem, then I will worship the LORD in Hebron."[i] 9 The king said to him, "Go

[h] Gk Syr: Heb *forty* [i] Gk Mss: Heb lacks *in Hebron*

14.27 By naming his daughter Tamar, Absalom was showing his love and respect for his sister Tamar. This was also a reminder to everyone of the Amnon/Tamar incident.

14.30 Already we can see the seeds of rebellion in Absalom. As an independent and scheming young man, he took matters into his own hands and killed his brother (13.22–29). Without his father or anyone else to keep him in check, he probably did whatever he wanted, as evidenced by his setting Joab's field on fire to get his attention (14.30). Undoubtedly his good looks also added to his self-centeredness (14.25). Children need discipline, especially those with natural abilities and beauty. Otherwise, like Absalom, they will grow up thinking they can do whatever they want whenever they want to.

14.33 David made only half-hearted efforts to correct his children. He did not punish Amnon for his sin against Tamar, nor did he deal decisively with Absalom's murder of Amnon. Such indecisiveness became David's undoing. When we ignore sin, we experience greater pain than if we deal with it immediately.

15.1 A group of runners often served as traffic police to clear a path before the chariot of an important person when he was traveling through crowded or narrow streets. Sometimes the runners also announced this person's name.

15.1ff David wrote several psalms during the days of Absalom's rebellion. Some of them are Psalms 39, 41, 55, 61, 62, and 63.

15.2 The city gate was like city hall and a shopping center combined. Because Jerusalem was the nation's capital, both local and national leaders met there daily to transact business and conduct government affairs. The city gate was the perfect spot for this because government and business transactions needed witnesses to be legitimate, and anyone entering or leaving the city had to enter through the gate. Merchants set up their tent-shops near the gate for the same reason. Absalom, therefore, went to the city gate to win the hearts of Israel's leaders as well as those of the common people.

15.5, 6 To do obeisance means to kneel and place one's face on the ground in an act of submission. Absalom's political strategy was to steal the hearts of the people with his good looks, grand entrances, apparent concern for justice, and friendly embraces. Many were fooled and switched their allegiance. Later, however, Absalom proved to be an evil ruler.

We need to evaluate our leaders to make sure their charisma is not a mask covering graft, deception, or hunger for power. Make sure that underneath their style and charm, they are able to make good decisions and handle people wisely.

15.9 Absalom went to Hebron because it was his hometown (3.2, 3). Hebron was David's first capital as well, and there Absalom could expect to find loyal friends who would be proud of him.

15.10 1 Kgs 1.34 2 Kgs 9.13 in peace." So he got up, and went to Hebron. [10]But Absalom sent secret messengers throughout all the tribes of Israel, saying, "As soon as you hear the sound of
the trumpet, then shout: Absalom has become king at Hebron!" [11]Two hundred
men from Jerusalem went with Absalom; they were invited guests, and they went
15.12 2 Sam 16.20 17.14 in their innocence, knowing nothing of the matter. [12]While Absalom was offering
the sacrifices, he sent for[j] Ahithophel the Gilonite, David's counselor, from his
city Giloh. The conspiracy grew in strength, and the people with Absalom kept
increasing.

David flees from Absalom

15.13 Judg 9.3 13 A messenger came to David, saying, "The hearts of the Israelites have gone
15.14 2 Sam 12.11 after Absalom." [14]Then David said to all his officials who were with him at Jerusalem, "Get up! Let us flee, or there will be no escape for us from Absalom. Hurry,
or he will soon overtake us, and bring disaster down upon us, and attack the city

[j] Or *he sent*

ABSALOM

A father's mistakes are often reflected in the lives of his children. In Absalom, David saw a bitter replay and amplification of many of his own past sins. God had predicted that David's family would suffer because of his sin against Bathsheba and Uriah. David's heart was broken as he realized that God's predictions were coming true. God forgave David, but he did not cancel the consequences of his sin. David was horrified as he saw his son's strengths run wild without the controls God had built into his own life.

By most casual evaluations, Absalom would have made an excellent king, and the people loved him. But he lacked the inner character and control needed in a good leader. His appearance, skill, and position did not make up for his lack of personal integrity.

David's sins took him away from God, but repentance brought him back. In contrast, Absalom sinned and kept on sinning. Although he relied heavily on the advice of others, he was not wise enough to evaluate the counsel he received.

Can you identify with Absalom? Do you find yourself on a fast track toward self-destruction? Absalom wasn't able to say, "I was wrong. I need forgiveness." God offers forgiveness, but we will not experience that forgiveness until we genuinely admit our sins and confess them to God. Absalom rejected his father's love and ultimately God's love. How often do you miss entering back into God's love through the door of forgiveness?

Strength and accomplishment:
- Was handsome and charismatic like his father, David

Weaknesses and mistakes:
- Avenged the rape of his sister Tamar by killing his half brother Amnon
- Plotted against his father to take away the throne
- Consistently listened to the wrong advice

Lessons from his life:
- The sins of parents are often repeated and amplified in the children
- A smart man gets a lot of advice; a wise man evaluates the advice he gets
- Actions against God's plans will fail, sooner or later

Vital statistics:
- Where: Hebron
- Occupation: Prince
- Relatives: Father: David. Mother: Maacah. Brothers: Amnon, Chileab, Solomon, and others. Sister: Tamar
- Contemporaries: Nathan, Jonadab, Joab, Ahitophel, Hushai

Key verse:
"But Absalom sent secret messengers throughout all the tribes of Israel, saying, 'As soon as you hear the sound of the trumpet, then shout: Absalom has become king at Hebron!' " (2 Samuel 15.10).

Absalom's story is told in 2 Samuel 3.3; 13—19.

15.14 Had David not escaped from Jerusalem, the ensuing fight might have killed both him and many innocent inhabitants of the city. Some fights that we think necessary can be costly and destructive to those around us. In such cases, it may be wise to back down and save the fight for another day—even if doing so hurts our pride. It takes courage to stand and fight, but it also takes courage to back down for the sake of others.

15.14 Why couldn't David just crush this rebellion? There were several reasons he chose to flee: (1) The rebellion was widespread (15.10–13) and would not have been easily suppressed; (2) David did not want the city of Jerusalem to be destroyed; (3) David still cared for his son and did not want to hurt him. We know that David expected to return to Jerusalem soon, because he left ten of his concubines to keep the palace in order (15.16).

with the edge of the sword.” 15 The king’s officials said to the king, “Your servants
are ready to do whatever our lord the king decides.” 16 So the king left, followed by
all his household, except ten concubines whom he left behind to look after the
house. 17 The king left, followed by all the people; and they stopped at the last
house. 18 All his officials passed by him; and all the Cherethites, and all the Pelethites, and all the six hundred Gittites who had followed him from Gath, passed on
before the king.
19 Then the king said to Ittai the Gittite, “Why are you also coming with us? Go
back, and stay with the king; for you are a foreigner, and also an exile from your
home. 20 You came only yesterday, and shall I today make you wander about with
us, while I go wherever I can? Go back, and take your kinsfolk with you; and may
the LORD show[k] steadfast love and faithfulness to you.” 21 But Ittai answered the
king, “As the LORD lives, and as my lord the king lives, wherever my lord the king
may be, whether for death or for life, there also your servant will be.” 22 David said
to Ittai, “Go then, march on.” So Ittai the Gittite marched on, with all his men and
all the little ones who were with him. 23 The whole country wept aloud as all the
people passed by; the king crossed the Wadi Kidron, and all the people moved on
toward the wilderness.
24 Abiathar came up, and Zadok also, with all the Levites, carrying the ark of
the covenant of God. They set down the ark of God, until the people had all passed
out of the city. 25 Then the king said to Zadok, “Carry the ark of God back into the
city. If I find favor in the eyes of the LORD, he will bring me back and let me see
both it and the place where it stays. 26 But if he says, ‘I take no pleasure in you,’
here I am, let him do to me what seems good to him.” 27 The king also said to the
priest Zadok, “Look,[l] go back to the city in peace, you and Abiathar,[m] with your
two sons, Ahimaaz your son, and Jonathan son of Abiathar. 28 See, I will wait at the
fords of the wilderness until word comes from you to inform me.” 29 So Zadok and
Abiathar carried the ark of God back to Jerusalem, and they remained there.
30 But David went up the ascent of the Mount of Olives, weeping as he went,
with his head covered and walking barefoot; and all the people who were with him
covered their heads and went up, weeping as they went. 31 David was told that
Ahithophel was among the conspirators with Absalom. And David said, “O LORD,
I pray you, turn the counsel of Ahithophel into foolishness.”
32 When David came to the summit, where God was worshiped, Hushai the
Archite came to meet him with his coat torn and earth on his head. 33 David said to
him, “If you go on with me, you will be a burden to me. 34 But if you return to the

15.16 2 Sam 16.21
15.17 1 Sam 23.13 25.13; 30.9 2 Sam 8.18 18.1,2
15.19 1 Sam 23.13 Ruth 1.16
15.23 1 Kgs 15.13 2 Chron 15.16 29.16
15.24 Num 4.15 1 Sam 4.4 2 Sam 8.17 20.25
15.25 1 Sam 3.18
15.27 2 Sam 17.17 18.19
15.28 Judg 3.28; 7.4 12.5 2 Sam 17.16
15.30 Ezek 24.23
15.31 2 Sam 15.12 16.23; 17.14,23
15.32 2 Sam 16.16 17.5
15.33 2 Sam 16.19

[k] Gk Compare 2.6: Heb lacks *may the LORD show* [l] Gk: Heb *Are you a seer* or *Do you see?* [m] Cn: Heb lacks *and Abiathar*

15.17, 18 David had many loyal non-Israelites in his armed forces. The Gittites, from the Philistine city of Gath, were apparently friends David had acquired while hiding from Saul. The Cherethites and Pelethites were also from Philistine territory. Although Israel was supposed to destroy wicked enemies, the nation was to welcome foreigners who came on friendly terms (Exodus 23.9; Deuteronomy 10.19) and to try to show them the importance of obeying God.

15.24, 25 The priests and Levites were also loyal to David. By bringing the ark, the priests wanted the presence of the Lord to leave with David. The ark of God was kept in the tabernacle and contained the two stone tablets of the law (Deuteronomy 10.2-5). But David must have thought it to be unsafe, so he ordered Zadok to carry it back into the city. Earlier in Israel's history, the ark was captured by the Philistines when the ark was brought to the battlefield. (I Samuel 4.11).

15.25, 26 David had the wisdom to know when to take action and when to wait for God to act. His faith and humility are clearly evident when he told the priest that God would bring him back to see the ark if he found favor with the Lord. Yet he also asked him to keep him informed on the events in the city (15.35). Entrusting our lives to God does not mean closing our eyes and ears to the situation. Refusing to take matters into our own hands is living by faith, but refusing to think about our problems at all is living by fear.

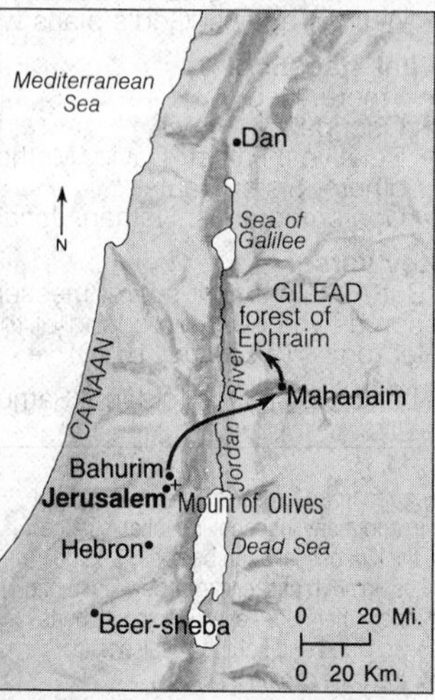

ABSALOM'S REBELLION
Absalom crowned himself king in Hebron. David and his men fled from Jerusalem, crossed the Jordan, and went to Mahanaim. Absalom and his army followed, only to be defeated in the forest of Ephraim, where Absalom was killed.

city and say to Absalom, 'I will be your servant, O king; as I have been your father's servant in time past, so now I will be your servant,' then you will defeat for
15.35 2 Sam 16.15 me the counsel of Ahithophel. 35 The priests Zadok and Abiathar will be with you
17.15 there. So whatever you hear from the king's house, tell it to the priests Zadok and
1 Chron 27.33 Abiathar. 36 Their two sons are with them there, Zadok's son Ahimaaz and Abiathar's son Jonathan; and by them you shall report to me everything you hear." 37 So
Hushai, David's friend, came into the city, just as Absalom was entering Jerusalem.

Ziba joins David

16.1 **16** When David had passed a little beyond the summit, Ziba the servant of Me-
2 Sam 9.2 phibosheth[n] met him, with a couple of donkeys saddled, carrying two hundred loaves of bread, one hundred bunches of raisins, one hundred of summer
16.2 fruits, and one skin of wine. 2 The king said to Ziba, "Why have you brought
Judg 5.10; 10.4 2 Sam 17.28 these?" Ziba answered, "The donkeys are for the king's household to ride, the
bread and summer fruit for the young men to eat, and the wine is for those to drink
16.3 who faint in the wilderness." 3 The king said, "And where is your master's son?"
2 Sam 9.9 19.26,27 Ziba said to the king, "He remains in Jerusalem; for he said, 'Today the house of
Israel will give me back my grandfather's kingdom.' " 4 Then the king said to Ziba,
"All that belonged to Mephibosheth[q] is now yours." Ziba said, "I do obeisance; let
me find favor in your sight, my lord the king."

Shimei curses David

16.5 Ex 22.28 5 When King David came to Bahurim, a man of the family of the house of Saul
1 Sam 17.43 came out whose name was Shimei son of Gera; he came out cursing. 6 He threw
2 Sam 3.16 17.18; 19.16 stones at David and at all the servants of King David; now all the people and all the
1 Kgs 2.8 warriors were on his right and on his left. 7 Shimei shouted while he cursed, "Out!
16.7 2 Sam 12.9 Out! Murderer! Scoundrel! 8 The LORD has avenged on all of you the blood of the
21.1 house of Saul, in whose place you have reigned; and the LORD has given the

[n] Or *Merib-baal*: See 4.4 note

HIGHS AND LOWS OF DAVID'S LIFE

The Bible calls David a man after God's own heart (1 Samuel 13.14; Acts 13.22), but that didn't mean his life was free of troubles. David's life was full of highs and lows. Some of David's troubles were a result of his sins; some were a result of the sins of others. We can't always control our ups and downs, but we can trust God every day. We can be certain that he will help us through our trials, just as he helped David. In the end, he will reward us for our consistent faith.

16.3 Saul was Mephibosheth's grandfather. Most likely Ziba was lying, hoping to receive a reward from David. (See 19.24–30 for Mephibosheth's side of the story.) For the story of Mephibosheth, see chapter nine.

16.4 To do obeisance means to kneel and place one's face on the ground in an act of submission.

16.4 David believed Ziba's charge against Mephibosheth without checking into it or even being skeptical. Don't be hasty to accept someone's condemnation of another, especially when the accuser may profit from the other's downfall. David should have been skeptical of Ziba's comments until he checked them out for himself.

kingdom into the hand of your son Absalom. See, disaster has overtaken you; for
you are a man of blood."
9 Then Abishai son of Zeruiah said to the king, "Why should this dead dog
curse my lord the king? Let me go over and take off his head." 10 But the king said,
"What have I to do with you, you sons of Zeruiah? If he is cursing because the
LORD has said to him, 'Curse David,' who then shall say, 'Why have you done
so?' " 11 David said to Abishai and to all his servants, "My own son seeks my life;
how much more now may this Benjaminite! Let him alone, and let him curse; for
the LORD has bidden him. 12 It may be that the LORD will look on my distress,[o] and
the LORD will repay me with good for this cursing of me today." 13 So David and his
men went on the road, while Shimei went along on the hillside opposite him and
cursed as he went, throwing stones and flinging dust at him. 14 The king and all the
people who were with him arrived weary at the Jordan;[p] and there he refreshed
himself.

The advice of Ahithophel

15 Now Absalom and all the Israelites[q] came to Jerusalem; Ahithophel was
with him. 16 When Hushai the Archite, David's friend, came to Absalom, Hushai
said to Absalom, "Long live the king! Long live the king!" 17 Absalom said to Hushai, "Is this your loyalty to your friend? Why did you not go with your friend?"
18 Hushai said to Absalom, "No; but the one whom the LORD and this people and all
the Israelites have chosen, his I will be, and with him I will remain. 19 Moreover,
whom should I serve? Should it not be his son? Just as I have served your father, so
I will serve you."
20 Then Absalom said to Ahithophel, "Give us your counsel; what shall we
do?" 21 Ahithophel said to Absalom, "Go in to your father's concubines, the ones
he has left to look after the house; and all Israel will hear that you have made yourself odious to your father, and the hands of all who are with you will be strengthened." 22 So they pitched a tent for Absalom upon the roof; and Absalom went in to
his father's concubines in the sight of all Israel. 23 Now in those days the counsel
that Ahithophel gave was as if one consulted the oracle[r] of God; so all the counsel
of Ahithophel was esteemed, both by David and by Absalom.

The advice of Hushai

17 Moreover Ahithophel said to Absalom, "Let me choose twelve thousand
men, and I will set out and pursue David tonight. 2 I will come upon him
while he is weary and discouraged, and throw him into a panic; and all the people
who are with him will flee. I will strike down only the king, 3 and I will bring all the
people back to you as a bride comes home to her husband. You seek the life of only
one man,[s] and all the people will be at peace." 4 The advice pleased Absalom and
all the elders of Israel.
5 Then Absalom said, "Call Hushai the Archite also, and let us hear too what he
has to say." 6 When Hushai came to Absalom, Absalom said to him, "This is what
Ahithophel has said; shall we do as he advises? If not, you tell us." 7 Then Hushai
said to Absalom, "This time the counsel that Ahithophel has given is not good."
8 Hushai continued, "You know that your father and his men are warriors, and that
they are enraged, like a bear robbed of her cubs in the field. Besides, your father is

16.9 Ex 22.28; 1 Sam 26.8; 2 Sam 19.21
16.10 2 Sam 3.39; 19.22; Jn 18.11; Rom 9.20
16.11 Gen 45.5; 1 Sam 26.19; 2 Sam 12.11
16.12 Deut 23.5; Rom 8.28
16.15 2 Sam 15.12,37
16.16 1 Sam 10.24; 2 Sam 15.33; 17.5; 2 Kgs 11.12
16.19 2 Sam 15.33,34
16.21 2 Sam 15.16
16.22 2 Sam 12.11; 20.3
16.23 2 Sam 15.12; 17.14
17.2 2 Sam 16.14; 1 Kgs 22.31
17.5 2 Sam 15.33, 34; 16.16
17.7 2 Sam 16.21
17.8 2 Kgs 2.24; Hos 13.8

[o] Gk Vg: Heb *iniquity* [p] Gk: Heb lacks *at the Jordan* [q] Gk: Heb *all the people, the men of Israel* [r] Heb *word*
[s] Gk: Heb *like the return of the whole (is) the man whom you seek*

16.10–12 Shimei kept up a steady tirade against David. Although his curses were unjustified because David had had no part in Saul's death, David and his followers quietly tolerated the abuse. Maintaining your composure in the face of unjustified criticism can be a trying experience and an emotional drain, but if you can't stop criticism, it is best just to ignore it. Remember that God knows what you are enduring, and he will vindicate you if you are in the right.

16.21, 22 This incident fulfilled Nathan's prediction that because of David's sin, another man would sleep with his wives (12.11, 12). (See the note on 3.6, 7 for the cultural significance of this act. *Odious* means smell or stench.)

16.23 Ahithophel was an adviser to Absalom. Most rulers had advisers to help them make decisions about governmental and political matters. They probably arranged the king's marriages as well, since these were usually politically motivated unions. But God made Ahithophel's advice seem foolish, just as David had prayed (15.31).

expert in war; he will not spend the night with the troops. 9 Even now he has hidden
himself in one of the pits, or in some other place. And when some of our troops[t]
fall at the first attack, whoever hears it will say, 'There has been a slaughter among
the troops who follow Absalom.' 10 Then even the valiant warrior, whose heart is
like the heart of a lion, will utterly melt with fear; for all Israel knows that your
father is a warrior, and that those who are with him are valiant warriors. 11 But my
counsel is that all Israel be gathered to you, from Dan to Beer-sheba, like the sand
by the sea for multitude, and that you go to battle in person. 12 So we shall come
upon him in whatever place he may be found, and we shall light on him as the dew
falls on the ground; and he will not survive, nor will any of those with him. 13 If he
withdraws into a city, then all Israel will bring ropes to that city, and we shall drag
it into the valley, until not even a pebble is to be found there." 14 Absalom and all
the men of Israel said, "The counsel of Hushai the Archite is better than the counsel
of Ahithophel." For the LORD had ordained to defeat the good counsel of Ahithophel, so that the LORD might bring ruin on Absalom.

15 Then Hushai said to the priests Zadok and Abiathar, "Thus and so did Ahithophel counsel Absalom and the elders of Israel; and thus and so I have counseled.
16 Therefore send quickly and tell David, 'Do not lodge tonight at the fords of the
wilderness, but by all means cross over; otherwise the king and all the people who
are with him will be swallowed up.' " 17 Jonathan and Ahimaaz were waiting at
En-rogel; a servant girl used to go and tell them, and they would go and tell King
David; for they could not risk being seen entering the city. 18 But a boy saw them,
and told Absalom; so both of them went away quickly, and came to the house of a
man at Bahurim, who had a well in his courtyard; and they went down into it. 19 The
man's wife took a covering, stretched it over the well's mouth, and spread out grain
on it; and nothing was known of it. 20 When Absalom's servants came to the woman
at the house, they said, "Where are Ahimaaz and Jonathan?" The woman said to
them, "They have crossed over the brook[u] of water." And when they had searched
and could not find them, they returned to Jerusalem.

21 After they had gone, the men came up out of the well, and went and told
King David. They said to David, "Go and cross the water quickly; for thus and so
has Ahithophel counseled against you." 22 So David and all the people who were
with him set out and crossed the Jordan; by daybreak not one was left who had not
crossed the Jordan.

23 When Ahithophel saw that his counsel was not followed, he saddled his donkey and went off home to his own city. He set his house in order, and hanged
himself; he died and was buried in the tomb of his father.

24 Then David came to Mahanaim, while Absalom crossed the Jordan with all
the men of Israel. 25 Now Absalom had set Amasa over the army in the place of
Joab. Amasa was the son of a man named Ithra the Ishmaelite,[v] who had married
Abigal daughter of Nahash, sister of Zeruiah, Joab's mother. 26 The Israelites and
Absalom encamped in the land of Gilead.

27 When David came to Mahanaim, Shobi son of Nahash from Rabbah of the
Ammonites, and Machir son of Ammiel from Lo-debar, and Barzillai the Gileadite
from Rogelim, 28 brought beds, basins, and earthen vessels, wheat, barley, meal,
parched grain, beans and lentils,[w] 29 honey and curds, sheep, and cheese from the
herd, for David and the people with him to eat; for they said, "The troops are hungry and weary and thirsty in the wilderness."

[t] Gk Mss: Heb *some of them* [u] Meaning of Heb uncertain [v] 1 Chr 2.17: Heb *Israelite* [w] Heb *and lentils and parched grain*

17.9 1 Sam 22.2; 23.19
17.11 1 Sam 3.20; 2 Sam 3.9,10; 1 Chron 21.2
17.13 Mic 1.6
17.14 2 Sam 15.33, 34; 16.23
17.15 2 Sam 15.35,36
17.16 2 Sam 15.28; 17.21
17.17 Josh 15.7; 2 Sam 15.27,35, 36; 18.19
17.18 2 Sam 16.5; 19.16
17.19 Josh 2.4-6
17.20 Ex 1.19; Lev 19.11; 1 Sam 19.14
17.23 1 Sam 31.4,5; 2 Sam 15.1,2; 1 Kgs 16.18; 2 Kgs 20.1; Mt 27.5
17.24 2 Sam 2.8; 19.31,32
17.25 2 Sam 19.13; 20.12; 1 Kgs 2.5; 1 Chron 2.16,17
17.27 2 Sam 9.4; 10.1,2; 12.26; 1 Kgs 2.7
17.28 2 Sam 16.2

17.11 Hushai appealed to Absalom through flattery, and Absalom's vanity became his own trap. Hushai predicted great glory for Absalom if he personally led the entire army against David. "Pride goes before destruction" (Proverbs 16.18) is an appropriate comment on Absalom's ambitions.

17.23 Ahithophel hanged himself because he was publically disgraced when his counsel was not followed.

17.25 Joab and Amasa were David's nephews and Absalom's cousins. Because Joab had left Jerusalem with David (see 18.5, 10ff), Amasa took his place as commander of Israel's troops.

Joab kills Absalom

18 Then David mustered the men who were with him, and set over them com- **18.1**
manders of thousands and commanders of hundreds. 2 And David divided Ex 18.25 1 Sam 8.12
the army into three groups:[x] one third under the command of Joab, one third under 22.7
the command of Abishai son of Zeruiah, Joab's brother, and one third under the **18.2** 1 Sam 11.11
command of Ittai the Gittite. The king said to the men, "I myself will also go out 2 Sam 15.19
with you." 3 But the men said, "You shall not go out. For if we flee, they will not **18.3**
care about us. If half of us die, they will not care about us. But you are worth ten 2 Sam 17.2,3 21.17
thousand of us;[y] therefore it is better that you send us help from the city." 4 The 1 Kgs 22.31
king said to them, "Whatever seems best to you I will do." So the king stood at the **18.4** 2 Sam 18.24
side of the gate, while all the army marched out by hundreds and by thousands.
5 The king ordered Joab and Abishai and Ittai, saying, "Deal gently for my sake
with the young man Absalom." And all the people heard when the king gave orders
to all the commanders concerning Absalom.
6 So the army went out into the field against Israel; and the battle was fought in **18.6**
the forest of Ephraim. 7 The men of Israel were defeated there by the servants of Josh 17.15 **18.7**
David, and the slaughter there was great on that day, twenty thousand men. 8 The 2 Sam 2.17
battle spread over the face of all the country; and the forest claimed more victims
that day than the sword.
9 Absalom happened to meet the servants of David. Absalom was riding on his **18.9**
mule, and the mule went under the thick branches of a great oak. His head caught 2 Sam 14.26
fast in the oak, and he was left hanging[z] between heaven and earth, while the mule
that was under him went on. 10 A man saw it, and told Joab, "I saw Absalom hanging in an oak." 11 Joab said to the man who told him, "What, you saw him! Why **18.11**
then did you not strike him there to the ground? I would have been glad to give you 2 Sam 3.27 11.15; 14.20
ten pieces of silver and a belt." 12 But the man said to Joab, "Even if I felt in my
hand the weight of a thousand pieces of silver, I would not raise my hand against
the king's son; for in our hearing the king commanded you and Abishai and Ittai,
saying: For my sake protect the young man Absalom! 13 On the other hand, if I had
dealt treacherously against his life[a] (and there is nothing hidden from the king),
then you yourself would have stood aloof." 14 Joab said, "I will not waste time like
this with you." He took three spears in his hand, and thrust them into the heart of
Absalom, while he was still alive in the oak. 15 And ten young men, Joab's armor-
bearers, surrounded Absalom and struck him, and killed him.
16 Then Joab sounded the trumpet, and the troops came back from pursuing **18.16**
Israel, for Joab restrained the troops. 17 They took Absalom, threw him into a great 2 Sam 2.28 20.22
pit in the forest, and raised over him a very great heap of stones. Meanwhile all the
Israelites fled to their homes. 18 Now Absalom in his lifetime had taken and set up **18.18**
for himself a pillar that is in the King's Valley, for he said, "I have no son to keep 1 Sam 15.12 2 Sam 14.27
my name in remembrance"; he called the pillar by his own name. It is called Absa-
lom's Monument to this day.

David mourns Absalom's death

19 Then Ahimaaz son of Zadok said, "Let me run, and carry tidings to the king **18.19**
that the LORD has delivered him from the power of his enemies." 20 Joab said to 2 Sam 15.35, 36; 17.17
him, "You are not to carry tidings today; you may carry tidings another day, but
today you shall not do so, because the king's son is dead." 21 Then Joab said to a
Cushite, "Go, tell the king what you have seen." The Cushite bowed before Joab,

[x] Gk: Heb *sent forth the army* [y] Gk Vg Symmachus: Heb *for now there are ten thousand such as we* [z] Gk Syr Tg: Heb *was put* [a] Another reading is *at the risk of my life*

18.1 David took command as he had in former days. In recent years, his life had been characterized by indecisiveness and moral paralysis. Now he began to take charge and do his duty.

18.14 This man had caught Joab in his hypocrisy. He knew Joab would have turned on him for killing the man if the king had found out about it. Joab could not answer, but only dismissed him. Those about to do evil often do not take the time to consider what they are about to do. They don't care whether or not it is right or lawful. Don't rush into action without thinking. Consider whether what you are about to do is right or wrong.

18.21–23 Joab wanted Cushi to bring the news of Absalom's death to David, not Ahimaaz, the priest's son. Joab may have been afraid that David would react violently to the dreadful news by killing the messenger (as he did in 1.15 and 4.12).

REBELLION
The Bible records many rebellions. Many were against God's chosen leaders. They were doomed for failure. Others were begun by wicked men against wicked men. While these were sometimes successful, the rebel's life usually came to a violent end. Still other rebellions were made by good people against the wicked or unjust actions of others. This kind of rebellion is sometimes good in freeing the common people from oppression and giving them the freedom to turn back to God.

Who rebelled?	*Who they rebelled against*	*What happened*	*Reference*
Adam and Eve	God	Expelled from Eden	Genesis 3
Israelites	God, Moses	Forced to wander in desert for 40 years	Numbers 14
Korah	Moses	Swallowed by the earth	Numbers 16
Israelites	God	God took away his special promise of protection	Judges 2
Absalom (David's son)	David	Killed in battle	2 Samuel 15—18
Sheba	David	Killed in battle	2 Samuel 20
Adonijah (David's son)	David, Solomon	Killed for treason	1 Kings 1; 2
Joab	David, Solomon	Supported Adonijah's kingship without seeking God's choice. Killed for treason	1 Kings 1; 2
Ten tribes of Israel	Rehoboam	The kingdom was divided. The ten tribes forgot about God, sinned, and were eventually taken into captivity	1 Kings 12.16–20
Baasha, king of Israel	Nadab, king of Israel	Overthrew the throne and became king. God destroyed his descendants	1 Kings15.27—16.7
Zimri, king of Israel	Elah, king of Israel	Overthrew the throne, but killed himself when his rule was not accepted	1 Kings 16.9–16
Jehu, king of Israel	Joram, king of Israel Ahaziah, king of Judah	Killed both kings. Later turned from God and his dynasty was wiped out	2 Kings 9; 10
Joash, king of Judah Jehoida, a priest	Athaliah, queen of Judah	Athaliah, a wicked queen, was overthrown. This was a "good" rebellion	2 Kings 11
Shallum, king of Israel	Zechariah, king of Israel	Overthrew the throne, but then was assassinated	2 Kings 15.8–15
Menahem, king of Israel	Shallum, king of Israel	Overthrew the throne, but then was invaded by Assyrian army	2 Kings 15.16–22
Hoshea, king of Israel	Assyria	The city of Samaria was destroyed, the nation of Israel taken into captivity	2 Kings 17
Zedekiah, king of Judah	Nebuchadnezzar, king of Babylon	The city of Jerusalem destroyed, the nation of Judah taken into captivity	2 Kings 24; 25

and ran. 22 Then Ahimaaz son of Zadok said again to Joab, "Come what may, let
me also run after the Cushite." And Joab said, "Why will you run, my son, seeing
that you have no reward[b] for the tidings?" 23 "Come what may," he said, "I will
run." So he said to him, "Run." Then Ahimaaz ran by the way of the Plain, and
outran the Cushite.

24 Now David was sitting between the two gates. The sentinel went up to the **18.24**
roof of the gate by the wall, and when he looked up, he saw a man running alone. 2 Sam 13.34 18.4; 19.8-10
25 The sentinel shouted and told the king. The king said, "If he is alone, there are 2 Kgs 9.17
tidings in his mouth." He kept coming, and drew near. 26 Then the sentinel saw
another man running; and the sentinel called to the gatekeeper and said, "See, another man running alone!" The king said, "He also is bringing tidings." 27 The sen- **18.27**
tinel said, "I think the running of the first one is like the running of Ahimaaz son of 1 Kgs 1.42
Zadok." The king said, "He is a good man, and comes with good tidings."

28 Then Ahimaaz cried out to the king, "All is well!" He prostrated himself **18.28**
before the king with his face to the ground, and said, "Blessed be the LORD your 1 Sam 17.46 25.23
God, who has delivered up the men who raised their hand against my lord the
king." 29 The king said, "Is it well with the young man Absalom?" Ahimaaz answered, "When Joab sent your servant,[c] I saw a great tumult, but I do not know
what it was." 30 The king said, "Turn aside, and stand here." So he turned aside,
and stood still.

31 Then the Cushite came; and the Cushite said, "Good tidings for my lord the **18.31**
king! For the LORD has vindicated you this day, delivering you from the power of Judg 5.31
all who rose up against you." 32 The king said to the Cushite, "Is it well with the
young man Absalom?" The Cushite answered, "May the enemies of my lord the
king, and all who rise up to do you harm, be like that young man."

33[d] The king was deeply moved, and went up to the chamber over the gate, and **18.33**
wept; and as he went, he said, "O my son Absalom, my son, my son Absalom! 2 Sam 19.4 Rom 9.1-3
Would I had died instead of you, O Absalom, my son, my son!"

19 It was told Joab, "The king is weeping and mourning for Absalom." 2 So the **19.1**
victory that day was turned into mourning for all the troops; for the troops 2 Sam 18.5,14
heard that day, "The king is grieving for his son." 3 The troops stole into the city
that day as soldiers steal in who are ashamed when they flee in battle. 4 The king **19.4**
covered his face, and the king cried with a loud voice, "O my son Absalom, 2 Sam 15.30 18.33
O Absalom, my son, my son!" 5 Then Joab came into the house to the king, and **19.5**
said, "Today you have covered with shame the faces of all your officers who have 2 Sam 3.39 20.8-10
saved your life today, and the lives of your sons and your daughters, and the lives
of your wives and your concubines, 6 for love of those who hate you and for hatred
of those who love you. You have made it clear today that commanders and officers
are nothing to you; for I perceive that if Absalom were alive and all of us were dead
today, then you would be pleased. 7 So go out at once and speak kindly to your
servants; for I swear by the LORD, if you do not go, not a man will stay with you this
night; and this will be worse for you than any disaster that has come upon you from **19.8**
your youth until now." 8 Then the king got up and took his seat in the gate. The 2 Sam 8.1 15.2; 18.24

[b] Meaning of Heb uncertain [c] Heb *the king's servant, your servant* [d] Ch 19.1 in Heb

---

18.29 Although he reached the city first, Ahimaaz was afraid to tell the king the truth about the death of his son Absalom.

18.33 Why was David so upset over the death of his rebel son? (1) David realized that he, in part, was responsible for Absalom's death. Nathan, the prophet, had said that because David had killed Uriah, his own sons would rebel against him. (2) David was angry at Joab and his officers for killing Absalom against his wishes. (3) David truly loved his son, even though Absalom did nothing to deserve his love. It would have been kinder and more loving to deal with Absalom and his runaway ego when he was younger.

19.4–7 At times we must reprove those in authority over us. Joab knew he was risking the king's displeasure by confronting him, but he saw what had to be done. Joab told David that there would be dreadful consequences if he didn't commend the troops for their victory. Joab's actions are a helpful example to us when we must reprove those in authority over us.

19.8 David sat at the city gate because that was where business was conducted and judgment rendered. His presence there showed that he was over his mourning and back in control.

19.8–10 Just a few days before, most of Israel was supporting the rebel ruler Absalom. Now the people wanted David back as their king. Because crowds are often fickle, there must be a higher moral code to follow than the pleasure of the majority. Following the moral principles given in God's Word will help you avoid being swayed by the popular opinions of the crowd.

troops were all told, "See, the king is sitting in the gate"; and all the troops came
before the king.

David returns to Jerusalem

Meanwhile, all the Israelites had fled to their homes. 9 All the people were disputing throughout all the tribes of Israel, saying, "The king delivered us from the
hand of our enemies, and saved us from the hand of the Philistines; and now he has
fled out of the land because of Absalom. 10 But Absalom, whom we anointed over
us, is dead in battle. Now therefore why do you say nothing about bringing the king
back?"
19.11 2 Sam 5.1 11 King David sent this message to the priests Zadok and Abiathar, "Say to the
elders of Judah, 'Why should you be the last to bring the king back to his house?

JOAB

Joab, the great military leader, had two brothers who were also famous soldiers: Abishai and Asahel. Joab proved to be the greatest leader of the three and was the commander of David's army throughout most of David's reign. There is no record that his troops ever lost a battle.

Joab was a fearless fighter like his brothers. Unlike them, he was also a brilliant and ruthless strategist. His plans usually worked, but he was seldom concerned about those hurt or killed by them. He did not hesitate to use treachery or murder to achieve his goals. His career is a story of great accomplishments and shameful acts. He conquered Jerusalem and the surrounding nations, defeated Abner, and reconciled Absalom and David. But he also murdered Abner, Amasa, and Absalom, took part in Uriah's murder, and plotted with Adonijah against Solomon. That plot led to his execution.

Joab set his own standards—he lived by them, and died because of them. There is little evidence that Joab ever acknowledged God's standards. On one occasion he confronted David about the danger of taking a census without God's command, but this may have been little more than a move to protect himself. Joab's self-centeredness eventually destroyed him. He was loyal only to himself, even willing to betray his lifelong relationship with David to preserve his power.

Joab's life illustrates the disastrous results of having no source of direction outside oneself. Brilliance and power are self-destructive without God's guidance. Only God can give the direction we need. For that reason, he has made available his Word, the Bible, and he is willing to be personally present in the lives of those who admit their need for him.

Strengths and accomplishments:
- Brilliant planner and strategist
- Fearless fighter and resourceful commander
- Confident leader who did not hesitate to confront even the king
- Helped reconcile David and Absalom
- Masterminded the conquest of Jerusalem

Weaknesses and mistakes:
- Was repeatedly ruthless, violent, and vengeful
- Carried out David's scheme to have Uriah, Bathsheba's husband, killed
- Avenged his brother's murder by murdering Abner
- Killed Absalom against David's orders
- Plotted with Adonijah against David and Solomon

Lessons from his life:
- Those who live by violence often die by violence
- Even brilliant leaders need guidance

Vital statistics:
- Occupation: Commander-in-chief of David's army
- Relatives: Mother: Zeruiah. Brothers: Abishai, Asahel. Uncle: David
- Contemporaries: Saul, Abner, Absalom

Key verse:
"The king replied to him, 'Do as he has said, strike him down and bury him; and thus take away from me and from my father's house the guilt for the blood that Joab shed without cause' " (1 Kings 2.31).

Joab's story is told in 1 Samuel 22—1 Kings 2. He is also mentioned in 1 Chronicles 2.16; 11.5–9, 20, 26; 19.8–15; 20.1; 21.2–6; 26.28; and in the title of Psalm 60.

19.11, 12 Why was the tribe of Judah hesitant to bring David back as king? Apparently the elders of Judah had consented to Absalom's rebellion. It is not surprising that leaders who had backed Absalom would hesitate before inviting David back.

The talk of all Israel has come to the king.[e] 12 You are my kin, you are my bone and
my flesh; why then should you be the last to bring back the king?' 13 And say to
Amasa, 'Are you not my bone and my flesh? So may God do to me, and more, if
you are not the commander of my army from now on, in place of Joab.' " 14 Amasa[f] swayed the hearts of all the people of Judah as one, and they sent word to the
king, "Return, both you and all your servants." 15 So the king came back to the
Jordan; and Judah came to Gilgal to meet the king and to bring him over the Jordan.
16 Shimei son of Gera, the Benjaminite, from Bahurim, hurried to come down
with the people of Judah to meet King David; 17 with him were a thousand people
from Benjamin. And Ziba, the servant of the house of Saul, with his fifteen sons
and his twenty servants, rushed down to the Jordan ahead of the king, 18 while the
crossing was taking place,[g] to bring over the king's household, and to do his pleasure.

Shimei son of Gera fell down before the king, as he was about to cross the Jordan, 19 and said to the king, "May my lord not hold me guilty or remember how
your servant did wrong on the day my lord the king left Jerusalem; may the king not
bear it in mind. 20 For your servant knows that I have sinned; therefore, see, I have
come this day, the first of all the house of Joseph to come down to meet my lord the
king." 21 Abishai son of Zeruiah answered, "Shall not Shimei be put to death for
this, because he cursed the LORD's anointed?" 22 But David said, "What have I to
do with you, you sons of Zeruiah, that you should today become an adversary to
me? Shall anyone be put to death in Israel this day? For do I not know that I am this
day king over Israel?" 23 The king said to Shimei, "You shall not die." And the king
gave him his oath.
24 Mephibosheth[h] grandson of Saul came down to meet the king; he had not
taken care of his feet, or trimmed his beard, or washed his clothes, from the day the
king left until the day he came back in safety. 25 When he came from Jerusalem to
meet the king, the king said to him, "Why did you not go with me, Mephibosheth?"[h] 26 He answered, "My lord, O king, my servant deceived me; for your
servant said to him, 'Saddle a donkey for me,[i] so that I may ride on it and go with
the king.' For your servant is lame. 27 He has slandered your servant to my lord the
king. But my lord the king is like the angel of God; do therefore what seems good
to you. 28 For all my father's house were doomed to death before my lord the king;
but you set your servant among those who eat at your table. What further right have
I, then, to appeal to the king?" 29 The king said to him, "Why speak any more of
your affairs? I have decided: you and Ziba shall divide the land." 30 Mephibosheth[h]
said to the king, "Let him take it all, since my lord the king has arrived home
safely."
31 Now Barzillai the Gileadite had come down from Rogelim; he went on with
the king to the Jordan, to escort him over the Jordan. 32 Barzillai was a very aged
man, eighty years old. He had provided the king with food while he stayed at Ma-

19.13 2 Sam 8.16 17.25 20.23 1 Chron 2.16,17
19.15 Josh 5.8,9 1 Sam 11.14
19.16 2 Sam 16.5 1 Kgs 2.8
19.17 2 Sam 9.2; 16.1
19.19 1 Sam 26.21 2 Sam 16.6-9 1 Kgs 1.31
19.21 Ex 22.28 1 Sam 24.6 1 Kgs 21.10
19.22 1 Sam 11.13 2 Sam 3.39
19.23 1 Kgs 2.8
19.24 2 Sam 9.5,6 21.7
19.26 2 Sam 9.3,13
19.27 2 Sam 14.17, 20; 16.3,4
19.28 2 Sam 9.7, 10,13
19.31 2 Sam 17.27 1 Kgs 2.7

[e] Gk: Heb *to the king, to his house* [f] Heb *He* [g] Cn: Heb *the ford crossed* [h] Or *Merib-baal*: See 4.4 note [i] Gk Syr Vg: Heb *said, I will saddle a donkey for myself*

19.13 David's appointment of Amasa was a shrewd political move. First, Amasa had been commander of Absalom's army; by making Amasa his commander, David would secure the allegiance of the rebel army. Second, by replacing Joab as commander-in-chief, David punished him for his previous crimes (3.26–29). Third, Amasa had a great deal of influence over the leaders of Judah (19.14). All of these moves would help to unite the kingdom.

19.19, 20 By admitting his wrong and asking David's forgiveness, Shimei was trying to save his own life. His plan worked for a while. This was a day of celebration, not execution. But we read in 1 Kings 2.8, 9 that David advised Solomon to execute Shimei.

19.21ff David showed tremendous mercy and generosity as he returned to Jerusalem. He spared Shimei, restored Mephibosheth, and rewarded faithful Barzillai. David's fairness sets a standard for government that will be fully realized in Christ's righteous rule in the coming kingdom.

19.24–30 David could not be certain if Mephibosheth or Ziba was in the right, and Scripture leaves the question unanswered. (For the whole story on Mephibosheth, see also 9.1–13 and 16.1–4.)

hanaim, for he was a very wealthy man. 33 The king said to Barzillai, "Come over
with me, and I will provide for you in Jerusalem at my side." 34 But Barzillai said
to the king, "How many years have I still to live, that I should go up with the king
19.35 to Jerusalem? 35 Today I am eighty years old; can I discern what is pleasant and
Ps 90.10,13 what is not? Can your servant taste what he eats or what he drinks? Can I still listen
to the voice of singing men and singing women? Why then should your servant be
an added burden to my lord the king? 36 Your servant will go a little way over the
Jordan with the king. Why should the king recompense me with such a reward?
19.37 37 Please let your servant return, so that I may die in my own town, near the graves
1 Kgs 2.7 of my father and my mother. But here is your servant Chimham; let him go over
with my lord the king; and do for him whatever seems good to you." 38 The king
answered, "Chimham shall go over with me, and I will do for him whatever seems
19.39 good to you; and all that you desire of me I will do for you." 39 Then all the people
Gen 31.55 crossed over the Jordan, and the king crossed over; the king kissed Barzillai and
Ruth 1.14
2 Sam 14.33 blessed him, and he returned to his own home. 40 The king went on to Gilgal, and
Chimham went on with him; all the people of Judah, and also half the people of
Israel, brought the king on his way.

41 Then all the people of Israel came to the king, and said to him, "Why have
our kindred the people of Judah stolen you away, and brought the king and his
household over the Jordan, and all David's men with him?" 42 All the people of
Judah answered the people of Israel, "Because the king is near of kin to us. Why
then are you angry over this matter? Have we eaten at all at the king's expense? Or
19.43 has he given us any gift?" 43 But the people of Israel answered the people of Judah,
2 Sam 5.1 "We have ten shares in the king, and in David also we have more than you. Why
then did you despise us? Were we not the first to speak of bringing back our king?"
But the words of the people of Judah were fiercer than the words of the people of
Israel.

Sheba rebels against David

20.1 **20** Now a scoundrel named Sheba son of Bichri, a Benjaminite, happened to be
1 Sam 16.7,8 there. He sounded the trumpet and cried out,
1 Kgs 12.16
2 Chron 10.16 "We have no portion in David,
no share in the son of Jesse!
Everyone to your tents, O Israel!"

20.2 2 So all the people of Israel withdrew from David and followed Sheba son of Bichri;
2 Sam 19.15,41 but the people of Judah followed their king steadfastly from the Jordan to Jerusalem.

20.3 3 David came to his house at Jerusalem; and the king took the ten concubines
2 Sam 15.16
16.21,22 whom he had left to look after the house, and put them in a house under guard, and
provided for them, but did not go in to them. So they were shut up until the day of
their death, living as if in widowhood.

20.4 4 Then the king said to Amasa, "Call the men of Judah together to me within
2 Sam 17.25 three days, and be here yourself." 5 So Amasa went to summon Judah; but he de-
19.13
20.6 layed beyond the set time that had been appointed him. 6 David said to Abishai,
2 Sam 18.2,12 "Now Sheba son of Bichri will do us more harm than Absalom; take your lord's
21.7 servants and pursue him, or he will find fortified cities for himself, and escape from

---

19.37 David was offering to reward Barzillai richly for his aid. This was a very generous offer since it probably included all of his family as well. Why did Barzillai send Chimham in his place? Chimham may have been one of his sons (see 1 Kings 2.7 for a reference to the sons of Barzillai eating at the king's table). Refusing a gift from the king would have been embarrasing for David. But Barzillai used wisdom and tact in graciously declining, while David graciously agreed to give the reward to Chimham instead.

20.1 Although Israel was a united kingdom, it was still made up of 12 separate tribes. These tribes often had difficulty agreeing on the goals of the nation as a whole. Tribal jealousies had originally kept Israel from completely conquering the promised land (read the book of Joshua), and now tribal jealousies were threatening the stability of David's reign by giving Sheba an opportunity to rebel (20.1ff).

us.” 7 Joab’s men went out after him, along with the Cherethites, the Pelethites, and **20.7**
all the warriors; they went out from Jerusalem to pursue Sheba son of Bichri. 2 Sam 8.18; 15.17,18
8 When they were at the large stone that is in Gibeon, Amasa came to meet them. 1 Kgs 1.38
Now Joab was wearing a soldier’s garment and over it was a belt with a sword in **20.8** 2 Sam 2.13
its sheath fastened at his waist; as he went forward it fell out. 9 Joab said to Amasa, 3.27
“Is it well with you, my brother?” And Joab took Amasa by the beard with his right 1 Kgs 2.5; Mt 26.49
hand to kiss him. 10 But Amasa did not notice the sword in Joab’s hand; Joab struck
him in the belly so that his entrails poured out on the ground, and he died. He did
not strike a second blow.
Then Joab and his brother Abishai pursued Sheba son of Bichri. 11 And one of
Joab’s men took his stand by Amasa, and said, “Whoever favors Joab, and whoever is for David, let him follow Joab.” 12 Amasa lay wallowing in his blood on the
highway, and the man saw that all the people were stopping. Since he saw that all
who came by him were stopping, he carried Amasa from the highway into a field,
and threw a garment over him. 13 Once he was removed from the highway, all the
people went on after Joab to pursue Sheba son of Bichri.
14 Sheba[j] passed through all the tribes of Israel to Abel of Beth-maacah;[k] and
all the Bichrites[l] assembled, and followed him inside. 15 Joab’s forces[m] came and **20.15**
besieged him in Abel of Beth-maacah; they threw up a siege-ramp against the city, 2 Kgs 19.32; Ezek 4.2
and it stood against the rampart. Joab’s forces were battering the wall to break it
down. 16 Then a wise woman called from the city, “Listen! Listen! Tell Joab,
‘Come here, I want to speak to you.’ ” 17 He came near her; and the woman said,
“Are you Joab?” He answered, “I am.” Then she said to him, “Listen to the words
of your servant.” He answered, “I am listening.” 18 Then she said, “They used to
say in the old days, ‘Let them inquire at Abel’; and so they would settle a matter.
19 I am one of those who are peaceable and faithful in Israel; you seek to destroy a **20.19** Deut 20.10
city that is a mother in Israel; why will you swallow up the heritage of the LORD?” 2 Sam 14.15,16
20 Joab answered, “Far be it from me, far be it, that I should swallow up or destroy!
21 That is not the case! But a man of the hill country of Ephraim, called Sheba son **20.21**
of Bichri, has lifted up his hand against King David; give him up alone, and I will Josh 24.33; 2 Sam 20.2
withdraw from the city.” The woman said to Joab, “His head shall be thrown over
the wall to you.” 22 Then the woman went to all the people with her wise plan. And **20.22**
they cut off the head of Sheba son of Bichri, and threw it out to Joab. So he blew 2 Sam 2.28; 8.16
the trumpet, and they dispersed from the city, and all went to their homes, while
Joab returned to Jerusalem to the king.
23 Now Joab was in command of all the army of Israel;[n] Benaiah son of Jehoi-

[j] Heb *He* [k] Compare 20.15: Heb *and Beth-maacah* [l] Compare Gk Vg: Heb *Berites* [m] Heb *They* [n] Cn: Heb *Joab to all the army, Israel*

20.7–10 Once again Joab’s murderous act went unpunished, just as it did when he killed Abner (3.26, 27). Eventually, however, justice caught up with him (1 Kings 2.28–35). It may seem that sin and treachery often go unpunished, but God’s justice is not limited to this life’s rewards. Even if Joab had died of old age, he would have to face the Judgment.

20.16ff Joab’s men were attacking the city, and it looked as if it would be destroyed. Though women in that society were usually quiet in public, this woman spoke out. She stopped Joab’s attack not with weapons, but with wise words and a plan of action. Often the courage to speak a few sensible words can prevent great disaster.

20.23 Benaiah was the captain of David’s bodyguard and a famous member of that special group of mighty men called “the Thirty” (23.24). He remained loyal to David during Absalom’s rebellion. Later he helped establish Solomon as king (1 Kings 1.32–40; 2.28–34) and eventually replaced Joab as commander of Israel’s army (1 Kings 2.35).

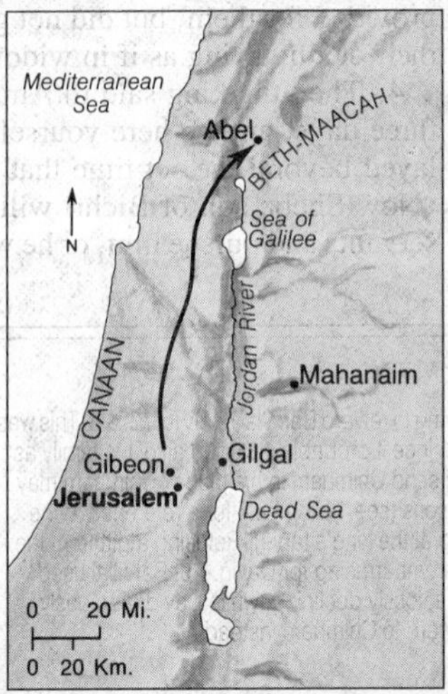

SHEBA’S REBELLION
After defeating Absalom, David returned to Jerusalem from Mahanaim. But Sheba incited a rebellion against David, so David sent Joab, Abishai, and a small army after him. Joab and his troops besieged Abel, Sheba’s hideout, until the people of Abel killed Sheba themselves.

20.24 1 Kgs 12.18 20.26 2 Sam 23.34

ada was in command of the Cherethites and the Pelethites; 24 Adoram was in charge
of the forced labor; Jehoshaphat son of Ahilud was the recorder; 25 Sheva was secretary; Zadok and Abiathar were priests; 26 and Ira the Jairite was also David's priest.

4. The later years of David's rule

The execution of Saul's sons

21.1 Gen 12.10 26.1; 42.5 21.2 Ex 34.11 Josh 9.15-20 1 Sam 7.14

21 Now there was a famine in the days of David for three years, year after year;
and David inquired of the LORD. The LORD said, "There is bloodguilt on
Saul and on his house, because he put the Gibeonites to death." 2 So the king called
the Gibeonites and spoke to them. (Now the Gibeonites were not of the people of
Israel, but of the remnant of the Amorites; although the people of Israel had sworn
to spare them, Saul had tried to wipe them out in his zeal for the people of Israel and

ABISHAI

Most great leaders struggle with a few followers who try too hard. For David, Abishai was that kind of follower. His fierce loyalty to David had to be kept from becoming destructive—he was too willing to leap to his leader's defense. David never put down Abishai's eager loyalty. Instead, he patiently tried to direct its powerful energy. This approach, while not completely successful, saved David's life on at least one occasion. At three other times, however, Abishai would have killed for the king if David had not stopped him.

Abishai was an excellent soldier, but he was better at taking orders than giving them. When he wasn't carrying out David's orders, Abishai was usually under the command of his younger brother Joab. The two brothers helped each other accomplish great military feats as well as shameful acts of violence—Abishai helped Joab murder Abner and Amasa. When he was effective as a leader, he led mostly by example. But all too often he did not think before he acted.

We should be challenged by Abishai's admirable qualities of fearlessness and loyalty, but we should be warned by his tendency to act without thinking. It is not enough to be strong and effective; we must also have the self-control and wisdom that God can give us. We are to follow and obey with our hearts and our minds.

Strengths and accomplishments:
- Known as one of the heroes among David's fighting men
- A fearless and willing volunteer, fiercely loyal to David
- Saved David's life

Weaknesses and mistakes:
- Tended to act without thinking
- Helped Joab murder Abner and Amasa

Lessons from his life:
- The most effective followers combine careful thought and action
- Blind loyalty can cause great evil

Vital statistics:
- Occupation: Soldier
- Relatives: Mother: Zeruiah. Brothers: Joab and Asahel. Uncle: David

Key verses:
"Now Abishai son of Zeruiah, the brother of Joab, was chief of the Thirty. With his spear he fought against three hundred men and killed them, and won a name beside the Three. He was the most renowned of the Thirty, and became their commander; but he did not attain to the Three" (2 Samuel 23.18, 19).

Abishai's story is told in 2 Samuel 2.18—23.19. He is also mentioned in 1 Samuel 26.1–13; 1 Chronicles 2.16; 11.20; 18.12; 19.11, 15.

21.1 Farmers relied heavily on spring and fall rains for their crops. If the rains stopped or came at the wrong time, or if the plants became insect-infested, drastic food shortages could occur in the coming year. Agriculture at that time was completely dependent upon natural conditions. There were no irrigation sprinklers, fertilizers, or pesticides. Even moderate variations in rainfall or insect activity could destroy an entire harvest.

21.1ff The next four chapters are an appendix to the book. The events described are not presented in chronological order. They tell of David's exploits at various times during his reign.

21.1–14 Although the Bible does not record Saul's act of vengeance against the Gibeonites, it was apparently a serious crime, and he was guilty of their blood ("bloodguilt"). Still, why were Saul's sons killed for the murders their father committed? In many Near Eastern cultures, including Israel's, an entire family was held guilty for the crime of the father because the family was considered an indissoluble unit. Saul broke the vow that the Israelites made to the Gibeonites (Joshua 9.16–20). This was a serious offense against God's law (Numbers 30.1, 2). Either David was following the custom of treating the family as a unit, or Saul's sons were guilty of helping Saul kill the Gibeonites.

Judah.) [3]David said to the Gibeonites, "What shall I do for you? How shall I make
expiation, that you may bless the heritage of the LORD?" [4]The Gibeonites said to
him, "It is not a matter of silver or gold between us and Saul or his house; neither
is it for us to put anyone to death in Israel." He said, "What do you say that I should
do for you?" [5]They said to the king, "The man who consumed us and planned to
destroy us, so that we should have no place in all the territory of Israel— [6]let seven
of his sons be handed over to us, and we will impale them before the LORD at
Gibeon on the mountain of the LORD."[o] The king said, "I will hand them over."
7 But the king spared Mephibosheth,[p] the son of Saul's son Jonathan, because
of the oath of the LORD that was between them, between David and Jonathan son of
Saul. [8]The king took the two sons of Rizpah daughter of Aiah, whom she bore to
Saul, Armoni and Mephibosheth;[p] and the five sons of Merab[q] daughter of Saul,
whom she bore to Adriel son of Barzillai the Meholathite; [9]he gave them into the
hands of the Gibeonites, and they impaled them on the mountain before the LORD.
The seven of them perished together. They were put to death in the first days of
harvest, at the beginning of barley harvest.
10 Then Rizpah the daughter of Aiah took sackcloth, and spread it on a rock for
herself, from the beginning of harvest until rain fell on them from the heavens; she
did not allow the birds of the air to come on the bodies[r] by day, or the wild animals
by night. [11]When David was told what Rizpah daughter of Aiah, the concubine of
Saul, had done, [12]David went and took the bones of Saul and the bones of his son
Jonathan from the people of Jabesh-gilead, who had stolen them from the public
square of Beth-shan, where the Philistines had hung them up, on the day the Philistines killed Saul on Gilboa. [13]He brought up from there the bones of Saul and the
bones of his son Jonathan; and they gathered the bones of those who had been
impaled. [14]They buried the bones of Saul and of his son Jonathan in the land of
Benjamin in Zela, in the tomb of his father Kish; they did all that the king commanded. After that, God heeded supplications for the land.

Giants killed by David's men

15 The Philistines went to war again with Israel, and David went down together
with his servants. They fought against the Philistines, and David grew weary.
[16]Ishbi-benob, one of the descendants of the giants, whose spear weighed three
hundred shekels of bronze, and who was fitted out with new weapons,[s] said he
would kill David. [17]But Abishai son of Zeruiah came to his aid, and attacked the
Philistine and killed him. Then David's men swore to him, "You shall not go out
with us to battle any longer, so that you do not quench the lamp of Israel."
18 After this a battle took place with the Philistines, at Gob; then Sibbecai the
Hushathite killed Saph, who was one of the descendants of the giants. [19]Then there
was another battle with the Philistines at Gob; and Elhanan son of Jaare-oregim, the
Bethlehemite, killed Goliath the Gittite, the shaft of whose spear was like a
weaver's beam. [20]There was again war at Gath, where there was a man of great
size, who had six fingers on each hand, and six toes on each foot, twenty-four in
number; he too was descended from the giants. [21]When he taunted Israel, Jonathan
son of David's brother Shimei, killed him. [22]These four were descended from the
giants in Gath; they fell by the hands of David and his servants.

David's song of praise

22 David spoke to the LORD the words of this song on the day when the LORD
delivered him from the hand of all his enemies, and from the hand of Saul.
[2]He said:

21.4 Num 35.31
21.5 Num 25.4; 2 Sam 21.1
21.7 1 Sam 18.1-3; 20.14,15; 23.18; 2 Sam 4.4
21.8 1 Sam 18.19; 2 Sam 3.7
21.10 Deut 21.23; 1 Sam 17.44
21.12 2 Sam 2.4,5; 24.25
21.15 2 Sam 5.17
21.16 Num 13.28; Deut 1.28
21.17 2 Sam 18.2; 20.6
21.18 1 Chron 11.29; 20.4-8; 27.11
21.19 1 Sam 17.4-7
21.22 1 Chron 20.8
22.1 Ex 15.1; Judg 5.1; Ps 18 Title

[o] Cn Compare Gk and 21.9: Heb *at Gibeah of Saul, the chosen of the LORD* [p] Or *Merib-baal*: See 4.4 note [q] Two Heb Mss Syr Compare Gk: MT *Michal* [r] Heb *them* [s] Heb *was belted anew*

21.9, 10 The barley harvest was in late April and early May. Barley was similar to wheat but less suitable for breadmaking. Rizpah guarded the men's bodies during the entire harvest season, which lasted from April to October.

21.18 For more information on giants, see 1 Samuel 17.4–7 and the note on Genesis 6.4.

22.1ff David was a skilled musician who played his harp for Saul (1 Samuel 16.23), instituted the music programs in the temple

22.2 Deut 32.4 1 Sam 2.2 Ps 31.3; 71.3

22.3 Gen 15.1 Deut 33.29 Ps 3.3; 9.9 Lk 1.69

22.4 Ps 66.2,3; 96.4

The LORD is my rock, my fortress, and my deliverer,
3 my God, my rock, in whom I take refuge,
my shield and the horn of my salvation,
my stronghold and my refuge,
my savior; you save me from violence.
4 I call upon the LORD, who is worthy to be praised,
and I am saved from my enemies.

22.5 Ps 69.14; 93.4 Jonah 2.3

22.6 Ps 116.3,4

5 For the waves of death encompassed me,
the torrents of perdition assailed me;
6 the cords of Sheol entangled me,
the snares of death confronted me.

7 In my distress I called upon the LORD;
to my God I called.
From his temple he heard my voice,
and my cry came to his ears.

22.8 Judg 5.4

22.9 Ex 15.7; 19.18 Heb 12.29

22.10 Ex 20.21 1 Kgs 8.12,13 Ps 97.2

22.11 Ps 68.17,18

22.12 Ps 18.11,12

22.14 Ex 19.19 Job 37.2

22.15 Deut 32.23 1 Sam 7.10

22.16 Ex 15.8

8 Then the earth reeled and rocked;
the foundations of the heavens trembled
and quaked, because he was angry.
9 Smoke went up from his nostrils,
and devouring fire from his mouth;
glowing coals flamed forth from him.
10 He bowed the heavens, and came down;
thick darkness was under his feet.
11 He rode on a cherub, and flew;
he was seen upon the wings of the wind.
12 He made darkness around him a canopy,
thick clouds, a gathering of water.
13 Out of the brightness before him
coals of fire flamed forth.
14 The LORD thundered from heaven;
the Most High uttered his voice.
15 He sent out arrows, and scattered them
—lightning, and routed them.
16 Then the channels of the sea were seen,
the foundations of the world were laid bare
at the rebuke of the LORD,
at the blast of the breath of his nostrils.

22.17 Ps 144.7

17 He reached from on high, he took me,
he drew me out of mighty waters.

David reveals many truths about God in his song of praise	*David says, "Jehovah is my . . ."*	Rock, Fortress, Savior, Refuge, Shield, Salvation, High Tower, Light
	David names these characteristics of God. He is:	Saving, Worthy of Praise, Hearing, Wrathful (against enemies), Rescuing, Rewarding, Seeing, Merciful, Showing (revealing) himself, Destroying (evil), Powerful, Strong, Perfect, Pure, True, Shielding (us from enemies), Giving, Gentle, Preserving, Living, Delivering

(1 Chronicles 25), and wrote more of the book of Psalms than anyone else. Writing a song like this was not unusual for David. This royal hymn of thanksgiving is almost identical to Psalm 18. (For other songs in the Bible, see the chart in Exodus 16.)

22.3 David calls God, "the horn of my salvation," referring to the strength and defensive protection animals have in their horns. God had helped David overcome his enemies and rescued him from his foes.

22.11 A cherub is an angel.

18 He delivered me from my strong enemy,
from those who hated me;
for they were too mighty for me.
19 They came upon me in the day of my calamity,
but the LORD was my stay.
20 He brought me out into a broad place;
he delivered me, because he delighted in me.

21 The LORD rewarded me according to my righteousness;
according to the cleanness of my hands he recompensed me.
22 For I have kept the ways of the LORD,
and have not wickedly departed from my God.
23 For all his ordinances were before me,
and from his statutes I did not turn aside.
24 I was blameless before him,
and I kept myself from guilt.
25 Therefore the LORD has recompensed me according to my righteousness,
according to my cleanness in his sight.

26 With the loyal you show yourself loyal;
with the blameless you show yourself blameless;
27 with the pure you show yourself pure,
and with the crooked you show yourself perverse.
28 You deliver a humble people,
but your eyes are upon the haughty to bring them down.
29 Indeed, you are my lamp, O LORD,
the LORD lightens my darkness.
30 By you I can crush a troop,
and by my God I can leap over a wall.
31 This God—his way is perfect;
the promise of the LORD proves true;
he is a shield for all who take refuge in him.

32 For who is God, but the LORD?
And who is a rock, except our God?
33 The God who has girded me with strength[t]
has opened wide my path.[u]
34 He made my[v] feet like the feet of deer,
and set me secure on the heights.
35 He trains my hands for war,
so that my arms can bend a bow of bronze.
36 You have given me the shield of your salvation,
and your help[w] has made me great.
37 You have made me stride freely,
and my feet do not slip;
38 I pursued my enemies and destroyed them,
and did not turn back until they were consumed.
39 I consumed them; I struck them down, so that they did not rise;
they fell under my feet.

22.18 Ps 23.4
22.20 2 Sam 4.9 Ps 31.8; 118.5
22.21 1 Sam 26.23 Ps 24.5; 128.1
22.23 Ps 119.6
22.24 Gen 6.9,10; 7.1 Job 1.8; 9.20
22.26 Mt 5.7 Jas 2.13
22.27 Deut 28.58,59 Ps 125.4,5
22.28 Ex 3.7,8 Ps 72.12,13 Isa 2.11,12,17
22.29 Ps 27.1; 84.11
22.30 Ps 18.29
22.31 Deut 32.4 Ps 12.6 119.140
22.32 1 Sam 2.2 Isa 44.6,8
22.36 2 Sam 22.3 Eph 6.16
22.37 Ps 18.36; 31.8
22.38 2 Sam 8.1,2 Ps 18.37 21.8-10; 110.1
22.39 Mal 4.3

t Q Ms Gk Syr Vg Compare Ps 18.32: MT *God is my strong refuge* u Meaning of Heb uncertain v Another reading is *his* w Q Ms: MT *your answering*

22.22–24 David was not denying that he had ever sinned. Psalm 51 shows his tremendous anguish over his sin against Uriah and Bathsheba. But David understood God's faithfulness and was writing this hymn from God's perspective. He knew that God had made him clean again—"whiter than snow," (Psalm 51.7) with a "clean heart" (Psalm 51.10). Through the death and resurrection of Jesus Christ, we also are made clean and perfect. God replaces our sin with his purity, and he no longer sees our sin.

22.27 "With the crooked you show yourself perverse" means that to those who sin, God is a judge who will punish them for their sins. God destroys those who are evil.

22.40 Ps 18.32

40 For you girded me with strength for the battle;
you made my assailants sink under me.

22.41 Ex 23.27 Ps 18.40,41

41 You made my enemies turn their backs to me,
those who hated me, and I destroyed them.

22.42 1 Sam 28.5,6

42 They looked, but there was no one to save them;
they cried to the LORD, but he did not answer them.

22.43 Ps 18.42 Isa 10.6 Mic 7.10

43 I beat them fine like the dust of the earth,
I crushed them and stamped them down like the mire of the streets.

22.44 2 Sam 3.1; 5.1

44 You delivered me from strife with the peoples;[x]
you kept me as the head of the nations;
people whom I had not known served me.

22.45 Ps 66.3; 72.8-10 Isa 55.5; 60.12

45 Foreigners came cringing to me;
as soon as they heard of me, they obeyed me.
46 Foreigners lost heart,
and came trembling out of their strongholds.

22.47 2 Sam 22.2,32 Ps 89.26

47 The LORD lives! Blessed be my rock,
and exalted be my God, the rock of my salvation,

22.48 1 Sam 24.12 2 Sam 18.19 Ps 94.1; 144.2

48 the God who gave me vengeance
and brought down peoples under me,
49 who brought me out from my enemies;

22.49 Ps 44.5 140.1,4,11

you exalted me above my adversaries,
you delivered me from the violent.

22.50 Ps 18.49 Rom 15.9

50 For this I will extol you, O LORD, among the nations,
and sing praises to your name.

22.51 2 Sam 7.12 Ps 18.50; 89.20

51 He is a tower of salvation for his king,
and shows steadfast love to his anointed,
to David and his descendants forever.

David's last words

23.1 1 Sam 16.12,13 2 Sam 7.8,9 Ps 78.70-72

23 Now these are the last words of David:
The oracle of David, son of Jesse,
the oracle of the man whom God exalted,[y]
the anointed of the God of Jacob,
the favorite of the Strong One of Israel:

23.2 2 Pet 1.20,21

2 The spirit of the LORD speaks through me,
his word is upon my tongue.

23.3 2 Sam 22.2,32 2 Chron 19.7,9 Ps 72.1 Isa 11.3,4

3 The God of Israel has spoken,
the Rock of Israel has said to me:
One who rules over people justly,
ruling in the fear of God,

23.4 Ps 72.6; 110.3

4 is like the light of morning,
like the sun rising on a cloudless morning,
gleaming from the rain on the grassy land.

23.5 2 Sam 7.12 Ps 89.29 Isa 55.3

5 Is not my house like this with God?
For he has made with me an everlasting covenant,
ordered in all things and secure.
Will he not cause to prosper

[x] Gk: Heb *from strife with my people* [y] Q Ms: MT *who was raised on high*

23.3 In the style of a prophet, David spoke of a just and righteous ruler. This will be fulfilled in Jesus Christ when he returns to rule in perfect justice and peace. For similar prophecies see Isaiah 11.1–10; Jeremiah 23.5, 6; 33.15–18; Zechariah 9.9, 10. For the fulfillment of some of these prophecies see Matthew 4.14–16; Luke 24.25–27, 44–49; John 5.45–47; 8.28, 29.

all my help and my desire?

6 But the godless are[z] all like thorns that are thrown away; **23.6** Mt 13.41,42
for they cannot be picked up with the hand;

7 to touch them one uses an iron bar **23.7** Mt 3.10; 13.30
or the shaft of a spear.
And they are entirely consumed in fire on the spot.[a]

David's mighty men

8 These are the names of the warriors whom David had: Josheb-basshebeth a **23.8** 1 Chron 11.11 27.2
Tahchemonite; he was chief of the Three;[b] he wielded his spear[c] against eight
hundred whom he killed at one time.

9 Next to him among the three warriors was Eleazar son of Dodo son of Ahohi. **23.9** 1 Chron 11.12 27.4
He was with David when they defied the Philistines who were gathered there for
battle. The Israelites withdrew,
10 but he stood his ground. He struck down the
Philistines until his arm grew weary, though his hand clung to the sword. The LORD
brought about a great victory that day. Then the people came back to him—but
only to strip the dead.

11 Next to him was Shammah son of Agee, the Hararite. The Philistines gathered together at Lehi, where there was a plot of ground full of lentils; and the army
fled from the Philistines.
12 But he took his stand in the middle of the plot, defended
it, and killed the Philistines; and the LORD brought about a great victory.

13 Towards the beginning of harvest three of the thirty[d] chiefs went down to **23.13** 1 Sam 22.1 2 Sam 5.18
join David at the cave of Adullam, while a band of Philistines was encamped in the
valley of Rephaim.
14 David was then in the stronghold; and the garrison of the
Philistines was then at Bethlehem.
15 David said longingly, "O that someone would
give me water to drink from the well of Bethlehem that is by the gate!"
16 Then the **23.16** Gen 35.13 1 Sam 7.6
three warriors broke through the camp of the Philistines, drew water from the well
of Bethlehem that was by the gate, and brought it to David. But he would not drink
of it; he poured it out to the LORD,
17 for he said, "The LORD forbid that I should do
this. Can I drink the blood of the men who went at the risk of their lives?" Therefore
he would not drink it. The three warriors did these things.

18 Now Abishai son of Zeruiah, the brother of Joab, was chief of the Thirty.[e] **23.18** 2 Sam 10.10 18.2 1 Chron 11.20
With his spear he fought against three hundred men and killed them, and won a
name beside the Three.
19 He was the most renowned of the Thirty,[f] and became
their commander; but he did not attain to the Three.

20 Benaiah son of Jehoiada was a valiant warrior[g] from Kabzeel, a doer of **23.20** Josh 15.21 2 Sam 8.18 20.23 1 Kgs 4.1-6
great deeds; he struck down two sons of Ariel[h] of Moab. He also went down and
killed a lion in a pit on a day when snow had fallen.
21 And he killed an Egyptian,
a handsome man. The Egyptian had a spear in his hand; but Benaiah went against
him with a staff, snatched the spear out of the Egyptian's hand, and killed him with
his own spear.
22 Such were the things Benaiah son of Jehoiada did, and won a
name beside the three warriors.
23 He was renowned among the Thirty, but he did
not attain to the Three. And David put him in charge of his bodyguard.

24 Among the Thirty were Asahel brother of Joab; Elhanan son of Dodo of
Bethlehem;
25 Shammah of Harod; Elika of Harod;
26 Helez the Paltite; Ira son of
Ikkesh of Tekoa;
27 Abiezer of Anathoth; Mebunnai the Hushathite;
28 Zalmon the
Ahohite; Maharai of Netophah;
29 Heleb son of Baanah of Netophah; Ittai son of

[z] Heb *But worthlessness* [a] Heb *in sitting* [b] Gk Vg Compare 1 Chr 11.11: Meaning of Heb uncertain [c] 1 Chr 11.11: Meaning of Heb uncertain [d] Heb adds *head* [e] Two Heb Mss Syr: MT *Three* [f] Syr Compare 1 Chr 11.25: Heb *Was he the most renowned of the Three?* [g] Another reading is *the son of Ish-hai* [h] Gk: Heb lacks *sons of*

23.8–39 These verses tell of some of the exploits that the special corps of David's army carried out. There were two elite groups of men: "the Thirty" and "the Three" (23.18, 23; 1 Chronicles 11.11–25). To become a member of such a group a man had to show unparalleled courage in battle as well as wisdom in leadership. "The Three" was the most elite group. The list of "the Thirty" actually contains 37 names, but it mentions some warriors known to be dead (Uriah, for example, in 23.39). Apparently new members were appointed to replace those who had fallen in battle.

23.16 David poured out the water as an offering to God because he was so moved by the sacrifice it represented. When Hebrews offered sacrifices, they never consumed the blood. It represented life, and they poured it out before God. David would not drink this water which represented the lives of his soldiers. Instead, he offered it to God.

Ribai of Gibeah of the Benjaminites; 30 Benaiah of Pirathon; Hiddai of the torrents
of Gaash; 31 Abi-albon the Arbathite; Azmaveth of Bahurim; 32 Eliahba of Shaalbon; the sons of Jashen: Jonathan 33 son of[i] Shammah the Hararite; Ahiam son of
Sharar the Hararite; 34 Eliphelet son of Ahasbai of Maacah; Eliam son of Ahithophel the Gilonite; 35 Hezro[j] of Carmel; Paarai the Arbite; 36 Igal son of Nathan of
Zobah; Bani the Gadite; 37 Zelek the Ammonite; Naharai of Beeroth, the armor-
bearer of Joab son of Zeruiah; 38 Ira the Ithrite; Gareb the Ithrite; 39 Uriah the
Hittite—thirty-seven in all.

David takes a census

24.1 2 Sam 6.7 1 Kgs 16.33 **24** Again the anger of the LORD was kindled against Israel, and he incited David against them, saying, "Go, count the people of Israel and Judah." 2 So
the king said to Joab and the commanders of the army,[k] who were with him, "Go

[i] Gk: Heb lacks *son of* [j] Another reading is *Hezrai* [k] 1 Chr 21.2 Gk: Heb *to Joab the commander of the army*

DAVID'S MIGHTY MEN

One way to understand David's success is to notice the kind of men who followed him. During the time he was being hunted by Saul, David gradually built a fighting force of several hundred men. Some were relatives, others were outcasts of society, many were in trouble with the law. They all had at least one trait in common—complete devotion to David. Their achievements made them famous. Among these men were elite military groups like "the Three" and "the Thirty." They were true heroes.

Scripture gives the impression that these men were motivated to greatness by the personal qualities of their leader. David inspired them to achieve beyond their goals and meet their true potential. Likewise, the leaders we follow and the causes to which we commit ourselves will affect our lives. David's effectiveness was clearly connected with his awareness of God's leading. He was a good leader when he was following *his* Leader. Do you know whom the people you respect most are following? Your answer should help you decide whether they deserve your loyalty. Do you also recognize God's leading in your life? No one can lead you to excellence as your Creator can.

Strengths and accomplishments:
- Able soldiers and military leaders
- Shared many special skills
- Though frequently outnumbered, were consistently victorious
- Loyal to David

Weakness and mistake:
- Often had little in common beyond their loyalty to David and their military expertise

Lessons from their lives:
- Greatness is often inspired by the quality and character of leadership
- Even a small force of able and loyal men can accomplish great feats

Vital statistics:
- Where: They came from all over Israel (primarily Judah and Benjamin), and from some of the other surrounding nations as well
- Occupations: Various backgrounds—almost all were fugitives

Key verses:
"David left there and escaped to the cave of Adullam; when his brothers and all his father's house heard of it, they went down there to him. Everyone who was in distress, and everyone who was in debt, and everyone who was discontented gathered to him; and he became captain over them. Those who were with him numbered about four hundred" (1 Samuel 22.1, 2).

Their stories are told in 1 Samuel 22—2 Samuel 23.39. They are also mentioned in 1 Chronicles 11; 12.

24.1 Did God cause David to sin? God does not cause people to sin, but he does allow sinners to reveal the sinfulness of their hearts by their actions. God presented the opportunity to David in order to deal with a disastrous national tendency, and he wanted this desire to show itself. First Chronicles 21.1 says Satan incited David to do it. Hebrew writers do not always distinguish between primary and secondary causes. So if God allowed Satan to tempt David, to them it is as if God did it.

24.1–3 What was wrong with taking a census? A census was commanded in Numbers to prepare an army for conquering the promised land (Numbers 1.2; 26.2). A census amounted to a draft or conscription for the army. The land was now at peace, so there was no need to enlist troops. Israel had extended its borders and become a recognized power. David's sin was pride and ambition in counting the people so that he could glory in the size of his nation and army, its power and defenses. By doing this, he put his faith in the size of his army rather than in God's ability to protect them regardless of their number. Even Joab knew a census was wrong, but David did not heed his advice. We sin in a similar way when we place our security in money, possessions, or the might of our nation.

through all the tribes of Israel, from Dan to Beer-sheba, and take a census of the
people, so that I may know how many there are." 3 But Joab said to the king, "May
the LORD your God increase the number of the people a hundredfold, while the eyes
of my lord the king can still see it! But why does my lord the king want to do this?"
4 But the king's word prevailed against Joab and the commanders of the army. So
Joab and the commanders of the army went out from the presence of the king to
take a census of the people of Israel. 5 They crossed the Jordan, and began from[l]
Aroer and from the city that is in the middle of the valley, toward Gad and on to
Jazer. 6 Then they came to Gilead, and to Kadesh in the land of the Hittites;[m] and
they came to Dan, and from Dan[n] they went around to Sidon, 7 and came to the
fortress of Tyre and to all the cities of the Hivites and Canaanites; and they went out
to the Negeb of Judah at Beer-sheba. 8 So when they had gone through all the land,
they came back to Jerusalem at the end of nine months and twenty days. 9 Joab
reported to the king the number of those who had been recorded: in Israel there
were eight hundred thousand soldiers able to draw the sword, and those of Judah
were five hundred thousand.

David submits to judgment

10 But afterward, David was stricken to the heart because he had numbered the
people. David said to the LORD, "I have sinned greatly in what I have done. But
now, O LORD, I pray you, take away the guilt of your servant; for I have done very
foolishly." 11 When David rose in the morning, the word of the LORD came to the
prophet Gad, David's seer, saying, 12 "Go and say to David: Thus says the LORD:
Three things I offer[o] you; choose one of them, and I will do it to you." 13 So Gad
came to David and told him; he asked him, "Shall three[p] years of famine come to
you on your land? Or will you flee three months before your foes while they pursue
you? Or shall there be three days' pestilence in your land? Now consider, and decide what answer I shall return to the one who sent me." 14 Then David said to Gad,
"I am in great distress; let us fall into the hand of the LORD, for his mercy is great;
but let me not fall into human hands."

15 So the LORD sent a pestilence on Israel from that morning until the appointed
time; and seventy thousand of the people died, from Dan to Beer-sheba. 16 But
when the angel stretched out his hand toward Jerusalem to destroy it, the LORD
relented concerning the evil, and said to the angel who was bringing destruction
among the people, "It is enough; now stay your hand." The angel of the LORD was
then by the threshing floor of Araunah the Jebusite. 17 When David saw the angel
who was destroying the people, he said to the LORD, "I alone have sinned, and I
alone have done wickedly; but these sheep, what have they done? Let your hand,
I pray, be against me and against my father's house."

18 That day Gad came to David and said to him, "Go up and erect an altar to the
LORD on the threshing floor of Araunah the Jebusite." 19 Following Gad's instructions, David went up, as the LORD had commanded. 20 When Araunah looked
down, he saw the king and his servants coming toward him; and Araunah went out
and prostrated himself before the king with his face to the ground. 21 Araunah said,
"Why has my lord the king come to his servant?" David said, "To buy the threshing
floor from you in order to build an altar to the LORD, so that the plague may be

24.2 Judg 20.1; 2 Sam 3.9,10
24.3 Deut 1.11
24.5 Num 21.32; 32.34-36; Josh 13.9,16
24.6 Gen 31.21,47; Josh 19.28; 2 Sam 17.26
24.9 Num 1.20-46; 1 Chron 21.5
24.10 1 Sam 24.5; 2 Sam 12.13; 1 Chron 21.8
24.11 1 Sam 22.5; 1 Chron 29.29; 2 Chron 29.25,26
24.13 1 Chron 21.12
24.14 Ps 51.1; 130.3,4
24.15 Num 16.46; 24.9; 1 Sam 6.19; 1 Chron 21.14; 27.24
24.16 Ex 12.23; 32.14; 2 Kgs 19.35; 2 Chron 32.21
24.17 2 Sam 7.8; 1 Kgs 22.17; Ps 74.1
24.18 1 Chron 21.15; 2 Chron 3.1

[l] Gk Mss: Heb *encamped in Aroer south of* [m] Gk: Heb *to the land of Tahtim-hodshi* [n] Cn Compare Gk: Heb *they came to Dan-jaan and* [o] Or *hold over* [p] 1 Chr 21.12 Gk: Heb *seven*

24.12–14 Both David and the Israelites were guilty of sin (24.1). David's sin was pride, but the Bible does not say why God was angry with the people of Israel. Perhaps it was due to their support of the rebellions of Absalom (chapters 15–18) and Sheba (chapter 20), or perhaps they put their security in military and financial prosperity rather than God, as David did. God dealt with the whole nation through David, who exemplified the national sin of pride.

God gave David three choices. Each was a form of punishment God had told the people they could expect if they disobeyed his laws (disease – Deuteronomy 28.20–22; famine – 28.23, 24; war – 28.25, 26). David wisely chose the form of punishment that came most directly from God. He knew how brutal and harsh men in war could be, and he also knew God's great mercy. When you sin greatly, turn back to God. To be punished by him is far better than to take your chances without him.

24.18 Many believe that this threshing floor is the location where Abraham nearly sacrificed his son Isaac (Genesis 22.1–18). After David's death, Solomon built the temple on this spot. Centuries later, Jesus would teach and preach here.

24.22
1 Sam 6.14
1 Kgs 19.21

averted from the people." 22 Then Araunah said to David, "Let my lord the king
take and offer up what seems good to him; here are the oxen for the burnt offering,
and the threshing sledges and the yokes of the oxen for the wood. 23 All this,
O king, Araunah gives to the king." And Araunah said to the king, "May the LORD
your God respond favorably to you."

24.24
Gen 23.16
1 Chron 21.24

24 But the king said to Araunah, "No, but I will buy them from you for a price;
I will not offer burnt offerings to the LORD my God that cost me nothing." So David
bought the threshing floor and the oxen for fifty shekels of silver. 25 David built
there an altar to the LORD, and offered burnt offerings and offerings of well-being.
So the LORD answered his supplication for the land, and the plague was averted
from Israel.

24.25 The book of 2 Samuel describes David's reign. Since the Israelites first entered the promised land under Joshua, they had been struggling to unite the nation and drive out the wicked inhabitants. Now, after more than 400 years, Israel was finally at peace. David had accomplished what no leader before him, judge or king, had done. His administration was run on the principle of dedication to God and to the well-being of the people. Yet David also sinned. Despite his sins, however, the Bible calls David a man after God's own heart (Acts 13.22) because when he sinned, he recognized it and confessed his sins to God. David committed his life to God and remained loyal to him throughout his lifetime. Psalms gives an even deeper insight into David's love for God.

David becomes king 1010 B.C.	Solomon becomes king 970	Temple completed 959	The kingdom divides 930	Shishak invades Jerusalem 925

VITAL STATISTICS

PURPOSE:
To contrast the lives of those who live for God and those who refuse to do so through the history of the kings of Israel and Judah

AUTHOR:
Unknown. Possibly Jeremiah or a group of prophets

SETTING:
The once great nation of Israel turns into a land divided, not only physically, but also spiritually.

KEY VERSES:
"As for you, if you will walk before me, as David your father walked, with integrity of heart and uprightness, doing according to all that I have commanded you, and keeping my statutes and my ordinances, then I will establish your royal throne over Israel forever, as I promised your father David, saying, 'There shall not fail you a successor on the throne of Israel' " (9.4, 5).

KEY PEOPLE:
David, Solomon, Rehoboam, Jeroboam, Elijah, Ahab, Jezebel

SPECIAL FEATURE:
The books of 1 and 2 Kings were originally one book.

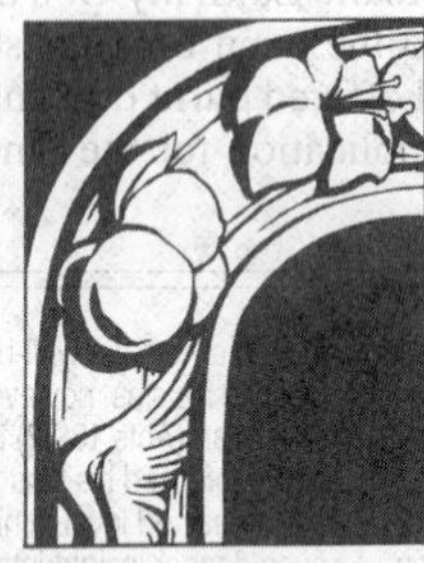

"I DON'T CARE what anyone says, I'm going to do it!" he yells at his mother as he storms out of the house.

This is a familiar scene in our society. The words change, but the essential message is the same . . . the person is *not* open to advice because his mind is closed. Some advice may be sought, but it is heeded only if it reinforces the decision already made or is an easier path to take. It is human nature to reject help and to do things *our* way.

A much wiser approach is to seek, hear, and heed the advice of good counselors. Solomon, the world's wisest man, urges this in Proverbs (see 11.14; 15.22; 24.6). How ironic that his son and successor, Rehoboam, listens instead to foolish advice, with devastating results. At Rehoboam's inauguration, he is petitioned by the people to be a kind and generous ruler. The older men counsel him to "be a servant to this people today and serve them, and speak good words to them" (12.7). But Rehoboam agrees to the cruel words of his peers who urge him to be harsh. As a result, Rehoboam splits the kingdom. Learn from Rehoboam's mistake. Commit yourself to seeking and following wise counsel.

The main events of 1 Kings are David's death, Solomon's reign, the division of the kingdom, and Elijah's ministry. As Solomon ascends the throne, David charges him to obey God's laws and to walk "in his ways" (2.3). This Solomon does; and when given the choice of gifts from God, he humbly asks for wisdom (3.9). As a result, Solomon's reign begins with great success, including the construction of the temple—his greatest achievement. Unfortunately, Solomon takes many pagan wives and concubines who eventually turn his heart away from the Lord to their false gods (11.1–4).

Rehoboam succeeds Solomon and has the opportunity to be a wise, compassionate, and just king. Instead, he accepts the poor advice of his young friends and attempts to rule with an iron hand. But the people rebel, and the kingdom splits with ten tribes in the north (Israel) ruled by Jeroboam, and only Judah and Benjamin remaining with Rehoboam. Both kingdoms weave a path through the reigns of corrupt and idolatrous kings with only the clear voice of the prophets continuing to warn and call the nation back to God.

Elijah is surely one of the greatest prophets, and chapters 17 through 22 feature his conflict with wicked Ahab and Jezebel in Israel. In one of the most dramatic confrontations in history, Elijah defeats the prophets of Baal at Mount Carmel. In spite of incredible opposition, Elijah stands for God and proves that *one plus God* is a majority. If God is on our side, no one can stand against us (Romans 8.31).

Asa becomes king of Judah 910	Elijah begins his ministry 875	Ahab becomes king of Israel 874	Jehoshaphat becomes king of Judah 872	Ben-hadad attacks Samaria 857	Ahab dies in battle 853

THE BLUEPRINT

A. THE UNITED KINGDOM (1.1—11.43) 1. Solomon becomes king 2. Solomon's wisdom 3. Solomon builds the temple 4. Solomon's greatness and downfall	Solomon was a botanist, zoologist, architect, poet, and philosopher. He was the wisest king in the history of Israel, but his wives led to the introduction of false gods and false worship in Israel. It is good for us to have wisdom, but that is not enough. The highest goal in life is to obey the Lord. Patient obedience to God should characterize our lives.
B. THE DIVIDED KINGDOM (12.1—22.53) 1. Revolt of the northern tribes 2. Kings of Israel and Judah 3. Elijah's ministry 4. Kings of Israel and Judah	When the northern kingdom of Israel was being led by wicked kings, God raised up a prophet to proclaim his messages. Elijah single-handedly challenged the priesthood of the state religion and had them removed in one day. Through the dividing of the kingdom and the sending of Elijah, God dealt with the people's sin in powerful ways. Sin in our lives is graciously forgiven by God. However, the sin of an unrepentant person will be handled harshly. We must turn from sin and turn to God to be saved from judgment.

MEGATHEMES

THEME	EXPLANATION	IMPORTANCE
The King	Solomon's wisdom, power, and achievements brought honor to the Israelite nation and to God. All the kings of Israel and Judah were told to obey God and to govern according to his laws. But their tendency to abandon God's Word and to worship other gods led them to change the religion and government to meet their personal desires. This neglect of God's law led to their downfall.	Wisdom, power, and achievement do not ultimately come from any human source; they are from God. No matter what we lead or govern, we can't do well when we ignore God's guidelines. Whether or not we are leaders, effectiveness depends upon listening and obeying God's Word. Don't let your personal desires distort God's Word.
The Temple	Solomon's temple was a beautiful place of worship and prayer. This sanctuary was the center of Jewish religion. It was the place of God's special presence and housed the ark of the covenant containing the ten commandments.	A beautiful house of worship doesn't always guarantee heartfelt worship of God. Providing opportunities for true worship doesn't insure that it will happen. God wants to live in our hearts, not just meet us in a sanctuary.
Other gods	Although the Israelites had God's law and experienced his presence among them, they became attracted to other gods. When this happened, their hearts became cold to God's law, resulting in the ruin of families and government, and eventually leading to the destruction of the nation.	Through the years, the people took on the false qualities of the false gods they worshiped. They became cruel, power-hungry, and sexually perverse. We tend to become what we worship. Unless we serve the true God, we will become slaves to whatever takes his place.
The Prophet's Message	The prophet's responsibility was to confront and correct any deviation from God's law. Elijah was a bolt of judgment against Israel. His messages and miracles were a warning to the evil and rebellious kings and people.	The Bible, the truth in sermons, and the wise counsel of believers are warnings to us. Anyone who points out how we deviate from obeying God's word is a blessing to us. Changing our lives in order to obey God and get back on track often takes painful discipline and hard work.
Sin and Repentance	Each king had God's Word, a priest or prophet, and the lessons of the past to draw him back to God. All the people had the same resources. Whenever they repented and returned to God, God heard their prayers and forgave them.	God hears and forgives us when we pray—if we are willing to trust him and turn from sin. Our desire to forsake our sin must be heartfelt and sincere. Then he will give us a fresh start and a desire to live for him.

KEY PLACES IN 1 KINGS

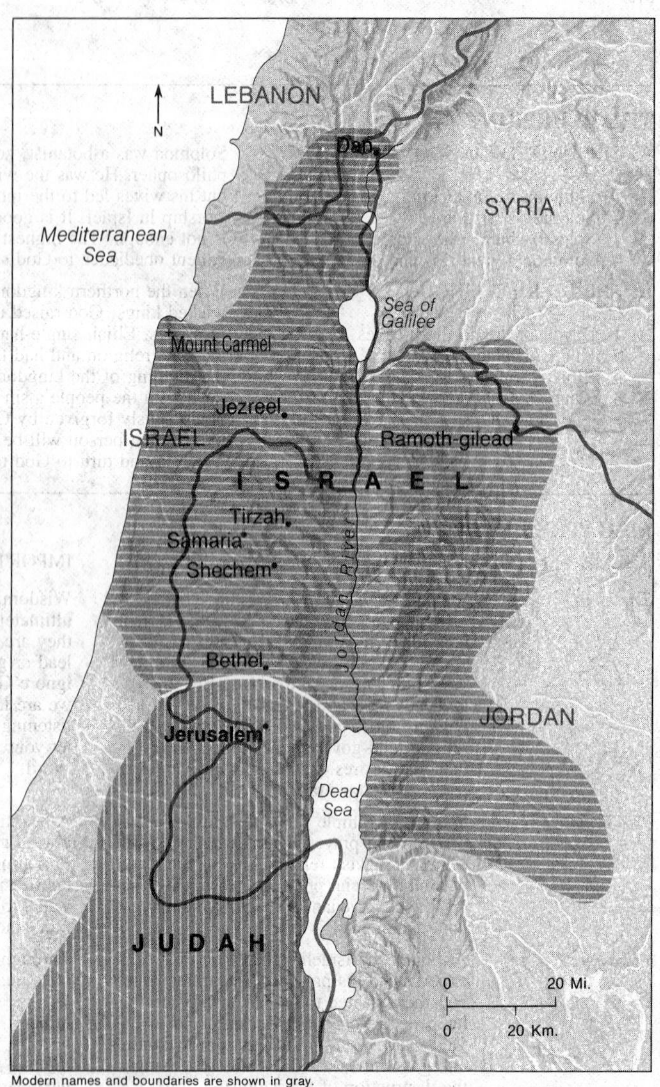

Modern names and boundaries are shown in gray.

Solomon, David's son, brought Israel into its golden age. His wealth and wisdom were acclaimed worldwide. But he ignored God in his later years (1.1—11.25).

1 **Shechem** After Solomon's death, Israel assembled at Shechem to inaugurate his son Rehoboam. However, Rehoboam foolishly angered the people by threatening even higher taxes, causing a revolt (11.26—12.19).

2 **Israel** Jeroboam, leader of the rebels, was made king of Israel, now called the northern kingdom. Jeroboam made Shechem his capital city (12.20, 25).

3 **Judah** Only the tribes of Judah and Benjamin remained loyal to Rehoboam. These two tribes became the southern kingdom. Rehoboam returned to Judah from Shechem and prepared to force the rebels into submission, but a prophet's message halted these plans (12.21–24).

4 **Jerusalem** Jerusalem was the capital city of Judah. Its temple, built by Solomon, was the focal point of Jewish worship. This worried Jeroboam. How could he keep his people loyal if they were constantly going to Rehoboam's capital to worship (12.26, 27)?

5 **Dan** Jeroboam's solution was to set up his own worship centers. Two calf-idols were made and proclaimed to be Israel's gods. One was placed in Dan, and the people were told that they could go there instead of to Jerusalem to worship (12.28, 29).

6 **Bethel** The other idol was placed in Bethel. The people of the northern kingdom had two convenient locations for worship in their own country, but their sin displeased God. In Jerusalem, meanwhile, Rehoboam was also allowing idolatry to creep in. The two nations were constantly at war (12.29—15.26).

7 **Tirzah** Baasha became king of Israel after assassinating Nadab. He moved the capital from Shechem to Tirzah (15.27—16.22).

8 **Samaria** Israel continued to gain and lose kings through plots, assassinations, and warfare. When Omri became king, he bought a hill on which he built a new capital city, Samaria. Omri's son, Ahab, became the most wicked king of Israel. His wife Jezebel worshiped Baal. Ahab erected a temple to Baal in Samaria (16.23–34).

9 **Mount Carmel** Great evil often brings great people who oppose it. Elijah challenged the prophets of Baal and Asherah at Mount Carmel, where he would prove that they were false prophets. There Elijah humiliated these prophets and then executed them (17.1—18.46).

10 **Jezreel** Elijah returned to Jezreel. But Queen Jezebel, furious at the execution of her prophets, vowed to kill Elijah. He ran for his life, but God cared for and encouraged him. During his travels he anointed the future kings of Syria and Israel, as well as Elisha, his own replacement (19.1–21).

11 **Ramoth-gilead** The king of Syria declared war on Israel and was defeated in two battles. But the Syrians occupied Ramoth-gilead. Ahab and Jehoshaphat joined forces to recover the city. In this battle, Ahab was killed. Jehoshaphat later died (20.1—22.53).

A. THE UNITED KINGDOM (1.1 – 11.43)

When Solomon is appointed king, he eliminates all opposition to the throne, builds the temple, establishes a strong army, and becomes the richest and wisest king in the history of Israel. But his heathen wives lead him into idolatry and, as a result, he leads the nation into spiritual decline. No matter what position in life we attain, we are always ripe for a downfall and must never let our guard down against sin and temptation.

1. Solomon becomes king

Adonijah tries to seize the throne

1 King David was old and advanced in years; and although they covered him
with clothes, he could not get warm. 2 So his servants said to him, "Let a young
virgin be sought for my lord the king, and let her wait on the king, and be his

---

BATHSHEBA

Bathsheba was the unlikely link between Israel's two most famous kings—David and Solomon. She was lover and wife to one, mother to the other. Her adultery with David almost brought an end to the family through which God planned to physically enter his world. Out of the ashes of that sin, however, God brought good. Eventually Jesus Christ, the salvation of mankind, was born to a descendant of David and Bathsheba.

David and Bathsheba's story shows that little wrong decisions often lead to big mistakes. It is likely that neither was where he or she should have been. Bathsheba may have been rash in bathing where she might be seen; David should have been at war with his army. Each decision contributed to the beginning of a very sad series of events.

Bathsheba must have been devastated by the chain of events—unfaithfulness to her husband, discovery of pregnancy, death of her husband, death of her child. We are told that David comforted her (2 Samuel 12.24), and she lived to see another son, Solomon, sit on the throne.

From her life we see that the little, day-to-day choices we make are very important. They prepare us to make the right choices when the big decisions come. The wisdom to make right choices in small and large matters is a gift from God. Understanding this should make us more conscious of the decisions we make and more willing to include God in our decision making. Have you asked for his help with today's decisions?

Strengths and accomplishments:
- Became influential in the palace alongside her son, Solomon
- Was the mother of Israel's wisest king and an ancestor of Jesus Christ

Weakness and mistake:
- Committed adultery

Lessons from her life:
- Although we may feel caught up in a chain of events, we are still responsible for the way we participate in those events
- A sin may seem like one small seed, but the harvest of consequences is beyond measure
- In the worst possible situations, God is still able to bring about good when people truly turn to him
- While we must live with the natural consequences of our sins, God's forgiveness of sin is total

Vital statistics:
- Where: Jerusalem
- Occupation: Queen and queen mother
- Relatives: Father: Elim. Husbands: Uriah and David. Son: Solomon
- Contemporaries: Nathan, Joab, Adonijah

Key verses:
"When the wife of Uriah heard that her husband was dead, she made lamentation for him. When the mourning was over, David sent and brought her to his house, and she became his wife, and bore him a son. But the thing that David had done displeased the Lord" (2 Samuel 11.26—12.1).

Her story is told in 2 Samuel 11; 12 and 1 Kings 1; 2. A related passage is Psalm 51.

1.1 Israel was near the end of the golden years of David's reign. The book of 1 Kings begins with a unified kingdom, glorious and God-centered; it ends with a divided kingdom, degraded and idolatrous. The reason for Israel's decline appears simple to us—they failed to obey God. But we are vulnerable to the same forces that brought about Israel's decay—greed, jealousy, lust for power, weakening of marriage vows, and superficiality in our devotion to God. As we read about these tragic events in Israel's history, we must see ourselves in the mirror of their experiences.

attendant; let her lie in your bosom, so that my lord the king may be warm." 3So
they searched for a beautiful girl throughout all the territory of Israel, and found
Abishag the Shunammite, and brought her to the king. 4The girl was very beautiful. She became the king's attendant and served him, but the king did not know her
sexually.
5 Now Adonijah son of Haggith exalted himself, saying, "I will be king"; he
prepared for himself chariots and horsemen, and fifty men to run before him. 6His
father had never at any time displeased him by asking, "Why have you done thus
and so?" He was also a very handsome man, and he was born next after Absalom.
7He conferred with Joab son of Zeruiah and with the priest Abiathar, and they
supported Adonijah. 8But the priest Zadok, and Benaiah son of Jehoiada, and the
prophet Nathan, and Shimei, and Rei, and David's own warriors did not side with
Adonijah.
9 Adonijah sacrificed sheep, oxen, and fatted cattle by the stone Zoheleth,
which is beside En-rogel, and he invited all his brothers, the king's sons, and all the
royal officials of Judah, 10but he did not invite the prophet Nathan or Benaiah or the
warriors or his brother Solomon.
11 Then Nathan said to Bathsheba, Solomon's mother, "Have you not heard
that Adonijah son of Haggith has become king and our lord David does not know
it? 12Now therefore come, let me give you advice, so that you may save your own

1.3 1 Sam 28.4; 1 Kgs 2.17
1.5 2 Sam 3.4; 1 Chron 3.2
1.7 1 Sam 22.20; 2 Sam 20.25; 1 Kgs 2.28
1.8 2 Sam 8.18; 12.1; 20.25; 23.20
1.10 2 Sam 12.24

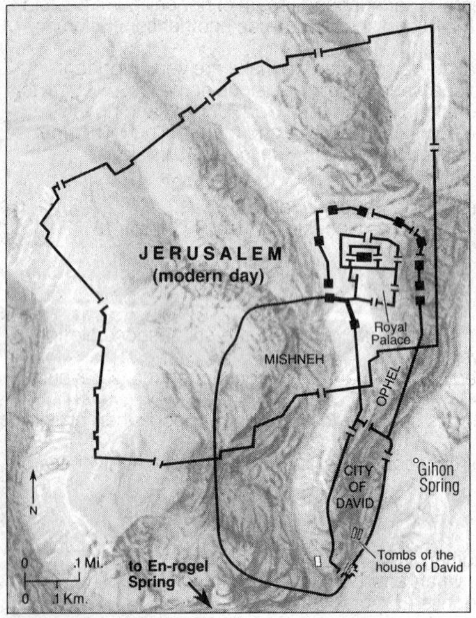

TWO CORONATIONS As David lay on his deathbed, his son Adonijah crowned himself king at the En-rogel Spring outside Jerusalem. When the news reached David, he declared that Solomon was to be the next ruler. Solomon was anointed at Gihon Spring. It may have been more than coincidence that Gihon Spring was not only within shouting distance of En-rogel Spring, but also closer to the palace.

1.4 David was about 70 years old. His health had deteriorated from years of hardship. Abishag served as his nurse and to help keep him warm. In days when polygamy was accepted, this action was not considered offensive.

1.5 Adonijah was David's fourth son and the logical choice to succeed him as king. David's first son, Amnon, had been killed by Absalom for having raped his sister (2 Samuel 13.20–33). His second son, Daniel, is mentioned only in the genealogy of 1 Chronicles 3.1 and had probably died by this time. David's third son, Absalom, died in an earlier rebellion (2 Samuel 18.1–18). Although many people expected Adonijah to be the next king (2.13–25), David — and God — had other plans (1.29, 30).

1.5 Adonijah decided to seize the throne without David's knowledge. He knew that Solomon, not he, was David's first choice to be the next king (1.17). This was why he did not invite Solomon and David's loyal advisors when he declared himself king (1.9, 10). But his deceptive plans to gain the throne were unsuccessful. The proud Adonijah was self-exalted and self-defeated.

1.6 God-fearing people like David and Samuel were used by God to lead nations, but they nevertheless had problems in family relationships. God-fearing leaders cannot take for granted the spiritual well-being of their children. Moral and spiritual character takes years to build, and it requires constant attention and patient discipline.

David served God well as a king, but as a parent he often failed both God and his children. Don't let your service to God even in leadership positions take up so much of your time and energy that you neglect your other God-given responsibilities.

1.6 Because David had never opposed or even questioned his son, Adonijah did not know how to work within limits. The result was that he always wanted his own way, regardless of how it affected others. Adonijah did whatever he wanted and paid no respect to God's wishes. An undisciplined child may look cute to his or her parents, but an undisciplined adult destroys himself and others. Discipline your children carefully while they are young, so that they will grow into self-disciplined adults.

1.7 See Joab's Profile in 2 Samuel 19 for a more complete picture of his life. For more information on Abiathar, see the note on 1 Samuel 22.20.

1.9 Sacrifices were offered when a new king was anointed. A priest had to offer the sacrifices, showing that the king's power was from God. To legitimize his takeover, Adonijah wanted sacrifices offered. But Adonijah was not God's choice to succeed David. Sealing an action with religious ceremony does not make it God's will.

1.11 For more on Bathsheba, David's wife, read 2 Samuel 11, 12. As mother of the king, Bathsheba was highly influential in the palace.

1.11–14 When Nathan learned of Adonijah's conspiracy, he immediately tried to stop it. He was a man of both faith and action. We often know what is right but don't act on it. Perhaps we don't want to get involved, or maybe we are fearful or lazy. Don't stop with prayer,

1.13 1 Chron 22.9 life and the life of your son Solomon. 13 Go in at once to King David, and say to
him, 'Did you not, my lord the king, swear to your servant, saying: Your son Solomon shall succeed me as king, and he shall sit on my throne? Why then is Adonijah
king?' 14 Then while you are still there speaking with the king, I will come in after
you and confirm your words."

15 So Bathsheba went to the king in his room. The king was very old; Abishag
the Shunammite was attending the king. 16 Bathsheba bowed and did obeisance to
the king, and the king said, "What do you wish?" 17 She said to him, "My lord, you
swore to your servant by the LORD your God, saying: Your son Solomon shall
succeed me as king, and he shall sit on my throne. 18 But now suddenly Adonijah
has become king, though you, my lord the king, do not know it. 19 He has sacrificed
oxen, fatted cattle, and sheep in abundance, and has invited all the children of the
king, the priest Abiathar, and Joab the commander of the army; but your servant
1.20 2 Sam 7.12 Solomon he has not invited. 20 But you, my lord the king—the eyes of all Israel are
on you to tell them who shall sit on the throne of my lord the king after him. 21 Otherwise it will come to pass, when my lord the king sleeps with his ancestors, that
my son Solomon and I will be counted offenders."

22 While she was still speaking with the king, the prophet Nathan came in.
23 The king was told, "Here is the prophet Nathan." When he came in before the
king, he did obeisance to the king, with his face to the ground. 24 Nathan said, "My
1.25 1 Sam 10.24 2 Sam 24.24 1 Kgs 1.9 lord the king, have you said, 'Adonijah shall succeed me as king, and he shall
sit on my throne'? 25 For today he has gone down and has sacrificed oxen, fatted
cattle, and sheep in abundance, and has invited all the king's children, Joab the

Who joined Adonijah's conspiracy and who remained loyal to David?
Contrast the fate of those who rebelled and those who remained loyal to David, God's appointed leader. Adonijah, the leader of the conspiracy, met a violent death (2.25). Those who rebel against God's leaders rebel against God.

Joined Adonijah

JOAB (1.7)
Brilliant military general and commander of David's army. He continually demonstrated his belief that cold-blooded murder was as acceptable as a fairly fought battle. Solomon later had him executed.

ABIATHAR (1.7)
One of two high priests under David. He was a son of Ahimelech who had helped David, and David promised to protect him. Abiathar repaid David with his treachery. Solomon later had him banished, fulfilling the prophecy that Eli's priestly line would end (1 Samuel 2.31).

JONATHAN (1.42)
Abiathar's son. He helped David stop Absalom's rebellion (2 Samuel 17.17–22), but supported this rebellion by another of David's sons.

CHARIOTEERS (1.5)
Hired by Adonijah, apparently more loyal to money than to their king.

50 RUNNERS (1.5)
Recruited to give Adonijah a "royal" appearance.

Remained with David

ZADOK (1.8)
The other high priest under David. His loyalty gave him the privilege of crowning Solomon. He became the sole high priest under King Solomon.

BENAIAH (1.8)
Distinguished himself as a great warrior. Commanded a division of David's army—over 24,000 troops. One of The Thirty, he was also placed in charge of David's bodyguard. Solomon later made him chief commander of the army.

NATHAN (1.8)
God's prominent prophet during David's reign. The Bible says he wrote a history of David and Solomon.

SHIMEI (1.8)
This man was probably the Shimei who was rewarded by Solomon and appointed official of the tribe of Benjamin (4.18). (He was not the same person who cursed David at Bahurim and brought on his own death under Solomon.)

REI (1.8)
Only mentioned here. Possibly he was an army officer. The word means "friend."

MIGHTY MEN (1.8, 10)
David's army was highly organized with several different divisions of troops. It is enough to know that many of his leaders remained true to their king.

good intentions, or angry feelings. Take the action needed to correct the situation.

1.13 The Bible does not record David's promise that Solomon would be Israel's next king, but it is clear that Solomon was the choice of both David (1.17, 30) and God (1 Chronicles 22.9, 10).

1.16 *Obeisance* means to bow in submission.

commander[a] of the army, and the priest Abiathar, who are now eating and drinking
before him, and saying, 'Long live King Adonijah!' 26 But he did not invite me,
your servant, and the priest Zadok, and Benaiah son of Jehoiada, and your servant
Solomon. 27 Has this thing been brought about by my lord the king and you have not
let your servants know who should sit on the throne of my lord the king after him?"

David declares Solomon king

28 King David answered, "Summon Bathsheba to me." So she came into the
king's presence, and stood before the king. 29 The king swore, saying, "As the
LORD lives, who has saved my life from every adversity, 30 as I swore to you by the
LORD, the God of Israel, 'Your son Solomon shall succeed me as king, and he shall
sit on my throne in my place,' so will I do this day." 31 Then Bathsheba bowed with
her face to the ground, and did obeisance to the king, and said, "May my lord King
David live forever!"

32 King David said, "Summon to me the priest Zadok, the prophet Nathan, and
Benaiah son of Jehoiada." When they came before the king, 33 the king said to
them, "Take with you the servants of your lord, and have my son Solomon ride on
my own mule, and bring him down to Gihon. 34 There let the priest Zadok and the
prophet Nathan anoint him king over Israel; then blow the trumpet, and say, 'Long
live King Solomon!' 35 You shall go up following him. Let him enter and sit on my
throne; he shall be king in my place; for I have appointed him to be ruler over Israel
and over Judah." 36 Benaiah son of Jehoiada answered the king, "Amen! May the
LORD, the God of my lord the king, so ordain. 37 As the LORD has been with my lord
the king, so may he be with Solomon, and make his throne greater than the throne
of my lord King David."

38 So the priest Zadok, the prophet Nathan, and Benaiah son of Jehoiada, and
the Cherethites and the Pelethites, went down and had Solomon ride on King David's mule, and led him to Gihon. 39 There the priest Zadok took the horn of oil
from the tent and anointed Solomon. Then they blew the trumpet, and all the people
said, "Long live King Solomon!" 40 And all the people went up following him,
playing on pipes and rejoicing with great joy, so that the earth quaked at their noise.

41 Adonijah and all the guests who were with him heard it as they finished
feasting. When Joab heard the sound of the trumpet, he said, "Why is the city in an
uproar?" 42 While he was still speaking, Jonathan son of the priest Abiathar arrived.
Adonijah said, "Come in, for you are a worthy man and surely you bring good
news." 43 Jonathan answered Adonijah, "No, for our lord King David has made
Solomon king; 44 the king has sent with him the priest Zadok, the prophet Nathan,
and Benaiah son of Jehoiada, and the Cherethites and the Pelethites; and they had
him ride on the king's mule; 45 the priest Zadok and the prophet Nathan have
anointed him king at Gihon; and they have gone up from there rejoicing, so that the
city is in an uproar. This is the noise that you heard. 46 Solomon now sits on the
royal throne. 47 Moreover the king's servants came to congratulate our lord King
David, saying, 'May God make the name of Solomon more famous than yours, and
make his throne greater than your throne.' The king bowed in worship on the bed
48 and went on to pray thus, 'Blessed be the LORD, the God of Israel, who today has
granted one of my offspring[b] to sit on my throne and permitted me to witness it.' "

49 Then all the guests of Adonijah got up trembling and went their own ways.

1.29 2 Sam 4.9 22.20
1.32ff 2 Sam 19.19
1.34 1 Sam 10.1 16.3,12 2 Sam 15.10 2 Kgs 9.13 11.13,14
1.37 Josh 1.5,17 1 Sam 20.13 1 Chron 28.20
1.39 1 Sam 16.3,13 1 Kgs 1.34 1 Chron 16.39 29.22
1.40 1 Sam 11.15 2 Kgs 11.13,14
1.42 2 Sam 18.27
1.48 2 Sam 7.12 1 Kgs 3.6
1.49 1 Kgs 2.28

[a] Gk: Heb *the commanders* [b] Gk: Heb *one*

1.33 Today, mules are the brunt of many jokes, but in David's time they were prized animals, ridden by the wealthy and powerful. As a sign that he had been chosen king, Solomon was given David's personal mule to ride. Riding a king's mule was an honor as great as that of traveling in a royal limousine today.

1.39 The sacred oil was used to anoint Israel's kings and high priests, as well as to dedicate certain objects to God. The tent where the oil was kept was probably the tent David set up to shelter the ark of the covenant (2 Samuel 6.17). It was not the tabernacle Moses carried in the wilderness; that tabernacle was still at Gibeon (see the note on 1 Samuel 7.1 for more details). The recipe and uses for the sacred oil are found in Exodus 30.22–33. For more on anointing, see the notes on 1 Samuel 10.1 and 16.13.

1.49, 50 Sometimes it takes getting caught before someone is willing to give up his scheme. When Adonijah learned that his plans had been exposed, he ran in panic to the altar, the place of God's mercy and forgiveness. He went there, however, *after* his plans for treason were exposed. If Adonijah had first considered

50 Adonijah, fearing Solomon, got up and went to grasp the horns of the altar.
51 Solomon was informed, "Adonijah is afraid of King Solomon; see, he has laid
hold of the horns of the altar, saying, 'Let King Solomon swear to me first that he
will not kill his servant with the sword.' " 52 So Solomon responded, "If he proves
to be a worthy man, not one of his hairs shall fall to the ground; but if wickedness
is found in him, he shall die." 53 Then King Solomon sent to have him brought
down from the altar. He came to do obeisance to King Solomon; and Solomon said
to him, "Go home."

David's charge to Solomon

2 When David's time to die drew near, he charged his son Solomon, saying: 2 "I
am about to go the way of all the earth. Be strong, be courageous, 3 and keep
the charge of the LORD your God, walking in his ways and keeping his statutes, his
commandments, his ordinances, and his testimonies, as it is written in the law of
Moses, so that you may prosper in all that you do and wherever you turn. 4 Then the
LORD will establish his word that he spoke concerning me: 'If your heirs take heed
to their way, to walk before me in faithfulness with all their heart and with all their
soul, there shall not fail you a successor on the throne of Israel.'
5 "Moreover you know also what Joab son of Zeruiah did to me, how he dealt
with the two commanders of the armies of Israel, Abner son of Ner, and Amasa son
of Jether, whom he murdered, retaliating in time of peace for blood that had been
shed in war, and putting the blood of war on the belt around his waist, and on the
sandals on his feet. 6 Act therefore according to your wisdom, but do not let his gray
head go down to Sheol in peace. 7 Deal loyally, however, with the sons of Barzillai
the Gileadite, and let them be among those who eat at your table; for with such

2.1 Josh 23.14 Job 16.22; 30.23 Ps 89.48
2.3 Deut 18.18,19 Josh 1.7 1 Chron 22.12
2.4 2 Sam 7.12 1 Kgs 8.25; 9.5 1 Chron 17.11
2.5 2 Sam 3.27 20.10
2.7 2 Sam 17.27

TRAITS OF DAVID, SOLOMON, AND CHRIST

David	*Solomon*	*Christ*
Warlike	Peace-loving	Peace-loving
Faithful	Fell into idol worship	Faithful
Kind	Exploitive	Kind
Obedient to God	Disobedient to God	Obedient to God
A heart after God	A heart after wealth	A heart after God
Served his people	Ruled his people	Serves his people

David and Solomon were two of the most renowned kings in Israel's history. Compare the characteristics of Jesus Christ, the perfect eternal king, to the characteristics of David and Solomon.

what God wanted, he might have avoided trouble. Don't wait until you have made a mess of things to run to God. Seek God's guidance *before* you act.

1.49–51 Both Adonijah and his general, Joab, thought they would be safe by clutching the horns (or corner posts) of the sacred altar of burnt offering in the tabernacle court. They hoped to place themselves under God's protection. Solomon granted Adonijah a reprieve, but he later had Joab killed right at the altar (2.28–34). This punishment was appropriate justice for a cold-blooded murderer such as Joab (Exodus 21.14).

1.52, 53 While Adonijah feared for his life and expected the severest punishment, Solomon simply dismissed his brother and sent him home. As a new king, Solomon had the power to kill his rivals, something Adonijah would have done had his conspiracy succeeded. But Solomon acted as if he had nothing to prove, thus demonstrating his authority and power. Sometimes forgiving a personal attack shows more strength than lashing out in revenge. Trying to prove one's power and authority often proves only one's fear and self-doubt. Only after Adonijah made another attempt to secure royal power was Solomon forced to have him executed (2.13–25).

2.3, 4 David stressed to Solomon the need to make God and his laws the center of personal life and government in order to preserve the kingdom, as God had promised to do (2 Samuel 7). This promise from God had two parts. One part was conditional and depended upon the kings' actions. The other part was unconditional.

God's conditional promise was that David and his descendants would remain in office as kings *only* when they honored and obeyed him. When David's descendants failed to do this, they lost the throne (2 Kings 25). God's unconditional promise was that David's line would go on forever. This was fulfilled in the birth of Jesus Christ, a descendant of David who was also the eternal Son of God (Romans 1.3, 4). David, whose life exemplified obedience, gave well-seasoned advice to his son, the next king. It would be up to Solomon to follow it.

2.5–7 Joab epitomizes those who are ruthless in accomplishing their goals. His strength was his only code, and winning the battle his only law. He wanted to get power for himself and protect it. In contrast, Barzillai stands for those who are loyal to God and live by his standards. When offered glory, for example, he unselfishly asked that it be given to his son. Is your leadership self-serving or God-serving?

2.5–9 David had some harsh advice for Solomon concerning his enemies. This advice was designed to help the young king secure his throne, and it was directed only toward blatant enemies – those who opposed God by opposing God's appointed king. Legally, David was asking Solomon to give his enemies the punishment they deserved. It was against both civil law and God's law for Shimei to curse a king (Exodus 22.28).

2.6 Sheol means the grave or place of the dead.

loyalty they met me when I fled from your brother Absalom. 8 There is also with 2.8
you Shimei son of Gera, the Benjaminite from Bahurim, who cursed me with a 2 Sam 16.5-8 19.16
terrible curse on the day when I went to Mahanaim; but when he came down to
meet me at the Jordan, I swore to him by the LORD, 'I will not put you to death with
the sword.' 9 Therefore do not hold him guiltless, for you are a wise man; you will
know what you ought to do to him, and you must bring his gray head down with 2.10 2 Sam 5.7
blood to Sheol." 1 Chron 29.28 Acts 2.29; 13.36

10 Then David slept with his ancestors, and was buried in the city of David. 2.11
11 The time that David reigned over Israel was forty years; he reigned seven years 2 Sam 5.4,5
in Hebron, and thirty-three years in Jerusalem. 12 So Solomon sat on the throne of 2.12 1 Chron 29.23
his father David; and his kingdom was firmly established. 2 Chron 1.1

Solomon removes the opposition

13 Then Adonijah son of Haggith came to Bathsheba, Solomon's mother. She
asked, "Do you come peaceably?" He said, "Peaceably." 14 Then he said, "May I
have a word with you?" She said, "Go on." 15 He said, "You know that the kingdom
was mine, and that all Israel expected me to reign; however, the kingdom has
turned about and become my brother's, for it was his from the LORD. 16 And now
I have one request to make of you; do not refuse me." She said to him, "Go on."
17 He said, "Please ask King Solomon—he will not refuse you—to give me Abishag the Shunammite as my wife." 18 Bathsheba said, "Very well; I will speak to
the king on your behalf."

19 So Bathsheba went to King Solomon, to speak to him on behalf of Adonijah.
The king rose to meet her, and bowed down to her; then he sat on his throne, and
had a throne brought for the king's mother, and she sat on his right. 20 Then she
said, "I have one small request to make of you; do not refuse me." And the king
said to her, "Make your request, my mother; for I will not refuse you." 21 She said,
"Let Abishag the Shunammite be given to your brother Adonijah as his wife."
22 King Solomon answered his mother, "And why do you ask Abishag the Shunammite for Adonijah? Ask for him the kingdom as well! For he is my elder brother;
ask not only for him but also for the priest Abiathar and for Joab son of Zeruiah!"
23 Then King Solomon swore by the LORD, "So may God do to me, and more also, 2.23 Ruth 1.17
for Adonijah has devised this scheme at the risk of his life! 24 Now therefore as the 1 Sam 14.44
LORD lives, who has established me and placed me on the throne of my father 1 Kgs 20.10
David, and who has made me a house as he promised, today Adonijah shall be put
to death." 25 So King Solomon sent Benaiah son of Jehoiada; he struck him down, 2.25
and he died. 2 Sam 8.18

26 The king said to the priest Abiathar, "Go to Anathoth, to your estate; for you 2.26
deserve death. But I will not at this time put you to death, because you carried the Josh 21.17,18 1 Sam 22.20
ark of the Lord GOD before my father David, and because you shared in all the 26.16 2 Sam 15.24
hardships my father endured." 27 So Solomon banished Abiathar from being priest Jer 1.1
to the LORD, thus fulfilling the word of the LORD that he had spoken concerning the 2.27
house of Eli in Shiloh. 1 Sam 2.30,31

28 When the news came to Joab—for Joab had supported Adonijah though he 2.28 2 Sam 17.25
had not supported Absalom—Joab fled to the tent of the LORD and grasped the 1 Kgs 1.49

2.10 David died at about age 70 (2 Samuel 5.4, 5). See David's Profile in 1 Samuel 17 for more on his life.

2.22 This was not a case of thwarted love, although Adonijah probably hoped Bathsheba would think so. Adonijah wanted Abishag because she had been David's last mistress. To sleep with the king's mistress was equivalent to claiming the throne. Absalom had done the same thing in his rebellion against David (2 Samuel 16.20–23). Solomon well understood what Adonijah was trying to do.

2.23–34 In this plot against Solomon, all the conspirators lost. Adonijah and Joab were killed, and the priest, Abiathar, lost his job. They all thought they would gain something by their alliance: influence, position, recognition, authority. But they had a poor leader and wrong motives. Consider your motives carefully before making alliances with others. Motives are important; be sure you understand yours and those of your leaders and peers.

2.26, 27 As a young man, Abiathar was the only one to escape when King Saul massacred all the priests in the city of Nob (1 Samuel 22.11–23). Abiathar then became the high priest under David and remained loyal to him throughout his reign. When he supported Adonijah's wrongful claim to the throne after David's death (1.7), Solomon forced him to give up the priesthood, fulfilling the prophecy of 1 Samuel 2.27–36 that Eli's descendants would not continue to serve as priests.

2.28 To understand why Joab clutched the horns of the altar, see the note on 1.49–51.

horns of the altar. 29 When it was told King Solomon, "Joab has fled to the tent of
the LORD and now is beside the altar," Solomon sent Benaiah son of Jehoiada,
saying, "Go, strike him down." 30 So Benaiah came to the tent of the LORD and said
to him, "The king commands, 'Come out.' " But he said, "No, I will die here."
Then Benaiah brought the king word again, saying, "Thus said Joab, and thus he
2.31 Ex 21.14 Num 35.33 Deut 19.13
answered me." 31 The king replied to him, "Do as he has said, strike him down and
bury him; and thus take away from me and from my father's house the guilt for the
blood that Joab shed without cause. 32 The LORD will bring back his bloody deeds
2.32 Gen 9.5,6 Judg 9.24,56,57 2 Sam 3.27 20.8-10
on his own head, because, without the knowledge of my father David, he attacked
and killed with the sword two men more righteous and better than himself, Abner
son of Ner, commander of the army of Israel, and Amasa son of Jether, commander
2.33 2 Sam 3.29 Prov 25.5
of the army of Judah. 33 So shall their blood come back on the head of Joab and on
the head of his descendants forever; but to David, and to his descendants, and to his
house, and to his throne, there shall be peace from the LORD forevermore." 34 Then
Benaiah son of Jehoiada went up and struck him down and killed him; and he was
2.35 1 Chron 29.22
buried at his own house near the wilderness. 35 The king put Benaiah son of Jehoiada over the army in his place, and the king put the priest Zadok in the place of
Abiathar.
2.36 2 Sam 16.5 1 Kgs 2.8
36 Then the king sent and summoned Shimei, and said to him, "Build yourself
a house in Jerusalem, and live there, and do not go out from there to any place
whatever. 37 For on the day you go out, and cross the Wadi Kidron, know for certain that you shall die; your blood shall be on your own head." 38 And Shimei said
to the king, "The sentence is fair; as my lord the king has said, so will your servant
do." So Shimei lived in Jerusalem many days.
39 But it happened at the end of three years that two of Shimei's slaves ran
away to King Achish son of Maacah of Gath. When it was told Shimei, "Your
slaves are in Gath," 40 Shimei arose and saddled a donkey, and went to Achish in
Gath, to search for his slaves; Shimei went and brought his slaves from Gath.
41 When Solomon was told that Shimei had gone from Jerusalem to Gath and returned, 42 the king sent and summoned Shimei, and said to him, "Did I not make
you swear by the LORD, and solemnly adjure you, saying, 'Know for certain that on
the day you go out and go to any place whatever, you shall die'? And you said to
me, 'The sentence is fair; I accept.' 43 Why then have you not kept your oath to the
2.44 1 Sam 25.39 2 Sam 16.5
LORD and the commandment with which I charged you?" 44 The king also said to
Shimei, "You know in your own heart all the evil that you did to my father David;
2.45 2 Sam 7.13 Isa 9.7
so the LORD will bring back your evil on your own head. 45 But King Solomon shall
be blessed, and the throne of David shall be established before the LORD forever."
2.46 2 Chron 1.1
46 Then the king commanded Benaiah son of Jehoiada; and he went out and struck
him down, and he died.

So the kingdom was established in the hand of Solomon.

2.31 Joab had spent his life trying to defend his position as David's general. Twice David tried to replace him, and both times Joab treacherously killed his rivals before they could assume command (2 Samuel 3.17–30; 19.13; 20.4–10). Because Joab was in his service, David was ultimately responsible for these senseless deaths. But for political and military reasons (see the note on 2 Samuel 3.39), David decided not to publicly punish Joab. Instead he put a curse on Joab and his family (2 Samuel 3.29). Solomon, in punishing Joab, was publicly declaring that David was not part of Joab's crimes, thus removing the guilt from David and placing it on Joab where it belonged.

2.35 Abiathar the high priest and Joab the army commander were key men in David's kingdom. But when they conspired against Solomon, they were replaced with Zadok and Benaiah. Zadok, a descendant of Aaron, had been a prominent priest during David's reign, and he was also loyal to Solomon after David's death. He was put in charge of the ark of the covenant (2 Samuel 15.24ff). His descendants were in charge of the temple until its destruction. At one time, Benaiah was one of David's mighty men (2 Samuel 23.20–23) and the captain of David's guard.

2.46 Solomon ordered the executions of Adonijah, Joab, and Shimei, forced Abiathar out as priest, and then appointed new men to take their places. He did these things swiftly, and his grip on the kingdom became secure. By executing justice and tying up loose ends that could affect the future stability of his kingdom, Solomon was promoting peace, not bloodshed. He was a man of peace in two ways: he did not go to war, and he put an end to internal rebellion.

2. Solomon's wisdom

Solomon asks for wisdom

3 Solomon made a marriage alliance with Pharaoh king of Egypt; he took Pharaoh's daughter and brought him into the city of David, until he had finished
building his own house and the house of the LORD and the wall around Jerusalem.
2 The people were sacrificing at the high places, however, because no house had yet
been built for the name of the LORD.
3 Solomon loved the LORD, walking in the statutes of his father David; only, he
sacrificed and offered incense at the high places. 4 The king went to Gibeon to sacrifice there, for that was the principal high place; Solomon used to offer a thousand
burnt offerings on that altar. 5 At Gibeon the LORD appeared to Solomon in a dream
by night; and God said, "Ask what I should give you." 6 And Solomon said, "You
have shown great and steadfast love to your servant my father David, because he
walked before you in faithfulness, in righteousness, and in uprightness of heart
toward you; and you have kept for him this great and steadfast love, and have given
him a son to sit on his throne today. 7 And now, O LORD my God, you have made
your servant king in place of my father David, although I am only a little child; I do
not know how to go out or come in. 8 And your servant is in the midst of the people
whom you have chosen, a great people, so numerous they cannot be numbered or
counted. 9 Give your servant therefore an understanding mind to govern your people, able to discern between good and evil; for who can govern this your great
people?"
10 It pleased the Lord that Solomon had asked this. 11 God said to him, "Because you have asked this, and have not asked for yourself long life or riches, or for
the life of your enemies, but have asked for yourself understanding to discern what
is right, 12 I now do according to your word. Indeed I give you a wise and discerning
mind; no one like you has been before you and no one like you shall arise after you.
13 I give you also what you have not asked, both riches and honor all your life; no
other king shall compare with you. 14 If you will walk in my ways, keeping my
statutes and my commandments, as your father David walked, then I will lengthen
your life."
15 Then Solomon awoke; it had been a dream. He came to Jerusalem where he

3.1 1 Kgs 7.8; 9.24
3.2 Lev 17.3-5 Deut 12.13,14 1 Kgs 5.2,3
3.3 1 Kgs 9.4 11.4,6,38 Ps 31.23
3.4 1 Chron 16.39 21.29 2 Chron 1.2,3
3.5 1 Kgs 9.2,3 2 Chron 1.7
3.6 2 Sam 7.8; 12.7 2 Chron 1.8
3.7 1 Chron 22.9 29.1
3.8 Gen 13.16 15.5; 22.17
3.9 2 Sam 14.17 1 Kgs 3.12,13 2 Chron 1.10 Prov 2.3-5,9 Jas 1.5
3.12 1 Kgs 4.29; 5.12
3.13 1 Kgs 3.28 4.20; 10.23
3.14 Deut 5.16 25.13-15
3.15 1 Kgs 8.63

3.1 Marriage between royal families was a common practice in the ancient Near East because it secured peace. Although Solomon's marital alliances built friendships with surrounding nations, they were also the beginning of his downfall. These relationships became inroads for pagan ideas and practices. Solomon's foreign wives brought their idols to Jerusalem and eventually lured him into idolatry (11.1–6).

It is easy to minimize religious differences in order to encourage the development of a friendship, but seemingly small differences can have an enormous impact upon a relationship. God gives us standards to follow for all our relationships, including marriage. If we follow God's will, we will not be lured away from our true focus.

3.2, 3 God's law said that the Israelites could make sacrifices only in specified places (Deuteronomy 12.13, 14). This was to prevent the people from instituting their own methods of worship and allowing heathen practices to creep into their worship. But many Israelites, including Solomon, made sacrifices in the surrounding hills. Solomon loved God, but this act was sin. It took the offerings out of the watchful care of priests and ministers loyal to God and opened the way for false teaching to be tied to these sacrifices. God appeared to Solomon to grant him wisdom, but at night, not during the sacrifice. God honored his prayer but did not condone the sacrifice.

3.6–9 When given a chance to have anything in the world, Solomon asked for wisdom – "an understanding mind" – in order to lead well and to make right decisions. We can ask God for this same wisdom (James 1.5). Notice that Solomon asked for wisdom to carry out his job; he did not ask God to do the job for him. We should not ask God to do *for* us what he wants to do *through* us. Instead we should ask God to give us the wisdom to know what to do and the courage to follow through on it.

3.11–14 Solomon asked for wisdom, not wealth, but God gave him riches and long life as well. While God does not promise riches to those who follow him, he gives us what we need if we put his kingdom, his interests, and his principles first (Matthew 6.31–33). Setting your sights on riches will only leave you dissatisfied, because even if you get the riches you crave, you will still want something more. But if you put God and his work first, he will satisfy your deepest needs.

3.12 Solomon received great wisdom from God, but it was up to him to apply that wisdom to all areas of his life. He was obviously wise in governing the nation, but he was foolish in running his household. Wisdom is both the ability to discern what is best and the strength of character to act upon that knowledge. While Solomon remained wise all his life, he did not always act upon his wisdom (11.6).

3.12 Solomon prayed for wisdom, and God made him wiser than anyone else has ever been. In Proverbs 1.7, Solomon tells us, "The fear of the Lord is the beginning of knowledge." Although no one has equaled Solomon's wisdom, many have remained more faithful to the Lord throughout their lives. We need wisdom, but even more we need a steadfast relationship with God, the source of all wisdom. Not everyone has great wisdom, but all have the opportunity to be faithful to God.

stood before the ark of the covenant of the LORD. He offered up burnt offerings and
offerings of well-being, and provided a feast for all his servants.

Solomon shows great wisdom

16 Later, two women who were prostitutes came to the king and stood before
him. 17 The one woman said, "Please, my lord, this woman and I live in the same
house; and I gave birth while she was in the house. 18 Then on the third day after I
gave birth, this woman also gave birth. We were together; there was no one else
with us in the house, only the two of us were in the house. 19 Then this woman's son
died in the night, because she lay on him. 20 She got up in the middle of the night
and took my son from beside me while your servant slept. She laid him at her
breast, and laid her dead son at my breast. 21 When I rose in the morning to nurse
my son, I saw that he was dead; but when I looked at him closely in the morning,

SOLOMON

Wisdom is only effective when it is put into action. Early in his life, Solomon had the sense to recognize his need for wisdom. But by the time Solomon asked for wisdom to rule his kingdom, he had already started a habit which would make his wisdom ineffective for his own life—he sealed a pact with Egypt by marrying Pharaoh's daughter. She was the first of hundreds of wives married for political reasons. In doing this, Solomon went against not only his father's last words, but also God's direct commands.

It is clear that God's gift of wisdom to Solomon did not mean that he couldn't make mistakes. He had been given great possibilities as the king of God's chosen people, but with them came great responsibilities; unfortunately, he tended to pursue the former and neglect the latter. While becoming famous as the builder of the temple and the palace, he became infamous as a leader who excessively taxed and worked his people. Visitors from distant lands came to admire this wise king, while his own people were gradually alienated from him.

Little is mentioned in the Bible about the last decade of Solomon's reign. Ecclesiastes probably records his last reflections on life. In that book we find a man proving through bitter experience that finding meaning in life apart from God is a vain pursuit. Security and contentment are found only in a personal relationship with God. The contentment we find in the opportunities and successes of this life is temporary. The more we expect our successes to be permanent, the more quickly they are gone. Be sure to balance your pursuit of life's possibilities with reliable fulfillment of your responsibilities.

Strengths and accomplishments:
- Third king of Israel, David's chosen heir
- The wisest man who ever lived
- Author of Ecclesiastes and Song of Solomon, as well as many of the Proverbs and some of the Psalms
- Built God's temple in Jerusalem
- Diplomat, trader, collector, patron of the arts

Weaknesses and mistakes:
- Sealed many foreign agreements by marrying heathen women
- Allowed his wives to affect his loyalty to God
- Excessively taxed his people and drafted them into a labor force

Lessons from his life:
- Effective leadership can be nullified by an ineffective personal life
- Solomon failed to obey God, but did not learn the lesson of repentance until late in life
- Knowing what actions are required of us means little without the will to do those actions

Vital Statistics:
- Where: Jerusalem
- Occupation: King of Israel
- Relatives: Father: David. Mother: Bathsheba. Brothers: Absalom, Adonijah. Sister: Tamar. Son: Rehoboam

Key verse:
"Did not King Solomon of Israel sin on account of such women? Among the many nations there was no king like him, and he was beloved by his God, and God made him king over all Israel; nevertheless, foreign women made even him to sin" (Nehemiah 13.26).

Solomon's story is told in 2 Samuel 12.24—1 Kings 11.43. He is also mentioned in 1 Chronicles 28; 29; 2 Chronicles 1—10; Psalm 72; and Matthew 6.29; 12.42.

clearly it was not the son I had borne." 22But the other woman said, "No, the living
son is mine, and the dead son is yours." The first said, "No, the dead son is yours,
and the living son is mine." So they argued before the king.
23 Then the king said, "The one says, 'This is my son that is alive, and your son
is dead'; while the other says, 'Not so! Your son is dead, and my son is the living
one.' " 24So the king said, "Bring me a sword," and they brought a sword before
the king. 25The king said, "Divide the living boy in two; then give half to the one,
and half to the other." 26But the woman whose son was alive said to the **3.26**
king—because compassion for her son burned within her—"Please, my lord, give Isa 49.15
her the living boy; certainly do not kill him!" The other said, "It shall be neither
mine nor yours; divide it." 27Then the king responded: "Give the first woman the
living boy; do not kill him. She is his mother." 28All Israel heard of the judgment **3.28**
that the king had rendered; and they stood in awe of the king, because they per- 1 Kgs 3.9; 4.29
ceived that the wisdom of God was in him, to execute justice.

Solomon's officials

4 King Solomon was king over all Israel, 2and these were his high officials:
Azariah son of Zadok was the priest; 3Elihoreph and Ahijah sons of Shisha
were secretaries; Jehoshaphat son of Ahilud was recorder; 4Benaiah son of Jehoiada was in command of the army; Zadok and Abiathar were priests; 5Azariah son
of Nathan was over the officials; Zabud son of Nathan was priest and king's friend;
6Ahishar was in charge of the palace; and Adoniram son of Abda was in charge of
the forced labor.
7 Solomon had twelve officials over all Israel, who provided food for the king
and his household; each one had to make provision for one month in the year.
8These were their names: Ben-hur, in the hill country of Ephraim; 9Ben-deker, in
Makaz, Shaalbim, Beth-shemesh, and Elon-beth-hanan; 10Ben-hesed, in Arubboth
(to him belonged Socoh and all the land of Hepher); 11Ben-abinadab, in all
Naphath-dor (he had Taphath, Solomon's daughter, as his wife); 12Baana son of
Ahilud, in Taanach, Megiddo, and all Beth-shean, which is beside Zarethan below
Jezreel, and from Beth-shean to Abel-meholah, as far as the other side of Jok-
meam; 13Ben-geber, in Ramoth-gilead (he had the villages of Jair son of Manasseh, which are in Gilead, and he had the region of Argob, which is in Bashan, sixty
great cities with walls and bronze bars); 14Ahinadab son of Iddo, in Mahanaim;
15Ahimaaz, in Naphtali (he had taken Basemath, Solomon's daughter, as his wife);
16Baana son of Hushai, in Asher and Bealoth; 17Jehoshaphat son of Paruah, in
Issachar; 18Shimei son of Ela, in Benjamin; 19Geber son of Uri, in the land of
Gilead, the country of King Sihon of the Amorites and of King Og of Bashan. And
there was one official in the land of Judah.

Solomon's dominion

20 Judah and Israel were as numerous as the sand by the sea; they ate and drank **4.20**
and were happy. 21[c] Solomon was sovereign over all the kingdoms from the Eu- Gen 32.12 Prov 14.28
phrates to the land of the Philistines, even to the border of Egypt; they brought **4.21**
tribute and served Solomon all the days of his life. 2 Sam 8.2,6 2 Chron 9.26
22 Solomon's provision for one day was thirty cors of choice flour, and sixty Ps 68.29
cors of meal, 23ten fat oxen, and twenty pasture-fed cattle, one hundred sheep, 72.10,11

[c] Ch 5.1 in Heb

4.1ff Solomon was well organized, with 11 princes with specific responsibilities and 12 officers, one for each tribe and a general manager. Each person had a specific responsibility or territory to manage. This organization was essential to maintain the government's effectiveness: it was a wise move by a wise man. It is good stewardship to be well organized. Good organization helps people work together in harmony and insures that the desired goal will be reached.

4.7 During Solomon's reign, each of the 12 tribes was responsible for providing food for the king's household for one month every year. Since Solomon had 700 wives and 300 concubines, not to mention children, servants, and livestock, a lot of food was required. The prophet Samuel had warned the people of heavy taxation when they came to him begging for a king (1 Samuel 8.11–18).

4.20–25 Throughout most of his reign, Solomon applied his wisdom well because he sought after God. The fruits of this wisdom were peace, security, and prosperity for the nation. Solomon's era is often looked upon as the ideal of what any nation can become when united in trust and obedience to God.

4.24 1 Kgs 5.4; 1 Chron 22.9 besides deer, gazelles, roebucks, and fatted fowl. 24 For he had dominion over all
the region west of the Euphrates from Tiphsah to Gaza, over all the kings west of
4.25 Isa 60.18; Jer 23.5,6; Mic 4.4; Zech 3.10 the Euphrates; and he had peace on all sides. 25 During Solomon's lifetime Judah
and Israel lived in safety, from Dan even to Beer-sheba, all of them under their
vines and fig trees. 26 Solomon also had forty thousand stalls of horses for his chari-
4.26 1 Kgs 10.26; 2 Chron 1.14 ots, and twelve thousand horsemen. 27 Those officials supplied provisions for King
Solomon and for all who came to King Solomon's table, each one in his month;
they let nothing be lacking. 28 They also brought to the required place barley and
straw for the horses and swift steeds, each according to his charge.

Solomon's fame

4.29 1 Kgs 3.9,28 29 God gave Solomon very great wisdom, discernment, and breadth of under-
4.30 Isa 19.11; Acts 7.22 standing as vast as the sand on the seashore, 30 so that Solomon's wisdom surpassed
the wisdom of all the people of the east, and all the wisdom of Egypt. 31 He was
wiser than anyone else, wiser than Ethan the Ezrahite, and Heman, Calcol, and
Darda, children of Mahol; his fame spread throughout all the surrounding nations.
4.32 Prov 1.1; Eccles 12.9; Song 1.1 32 He composed three thousand proverbs, and his songs numbered a thousand and
five. 33 He would speak of trees, from the cedar that is in the Lebanon to the hyssop
that grows in the wall; he would speak of animals, and birds, and reptiles, and fish.
4.34 1 Kgs 10.1; 2 Chron 9.23 34 People came from all the nations to hear the wisdom of Solomon; they came from
all the kings of the earth who had heard of his wisdom.

3. Solomon builds the temple

Preparation for the temple

5.1 2 Sam 5.11; 1 Chron 14.1; 2 Chron 14.1 **5** [d] Now King Hiram of Tyre sent his servants to Solomon, when he heard that
they had anointed him king in place of his father; for Hiram had always been
a friend to David. 2 Solomon sent word to Hiram, saying, 3 "You know that my
father David could not build a house for the name of the LORD his God because of
the warfare with which his enemies surrounded him, until the LORD put them under
5.4 1 Kgs 4.24; 1 Chron 22.9 the soles of his feet.[e] 4 But now the LORD my God has given me rest on every side;
there is neither adversary nor misfortune. 5 So I intend to build a house for the name
5.5 2 Sam 7.12,13; 1 Chron 17.12 of the LORD my God, as the LORD said to my father David, 'Your son, whom I will
set on your throne in your place, shall build the house for my name.' 6 Therefore
command that cedars from the Lebanon be cut for me. My servants will join your
servants, and I will give you whatever wages you set for your servants; for you
know that there is no one among us who knows how to cut timber like the Sidonians."

7 When Hiram heard the words of Solomon, he rejoiced greatly, and said,
"Blessed be the LORD today, who has given to David a wise son to be over this great
people." 8 Hiram sent word to Solomon, "I have heard the message that you have

[d] Ch 5.15 in Heb [e] Gk Tg Vg: Heb *my feet* or *his feet*

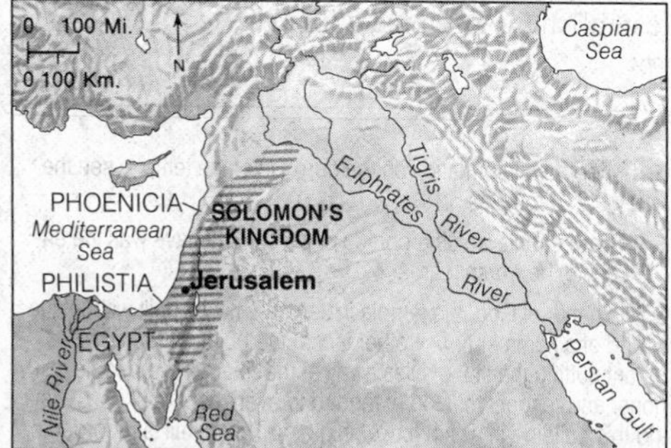

SOLOMON'S KINGDOM Solomon's kingdom spread from the Euphrates River in the north to the borders of Egypt. The entire land was at peace under his rule.

4.22 Thirty cors are about 185 bushels; sixty cors are about 375 bushels.

4.32 The book of Proverbs records many of these 3,000 wise proverbs. Other biblical writings of Solomon include Psalms 72 and 127, and the books of Ecclesiastes and the Song of Solomon.

5.2, 3 When David offered to build a temple, God said "no" through the prophet Nathan (2 Samuel 7.1–17). God wanted a peacemaker, not a warrior, to build his house of prayer (1 Chronicles 28.2, 3).

5.8 Solomon asked Hiram to send cedar and cypress wood for the temple because these were precious woods considered the best for building. They were coarse-grained, very hard, and rot resistant. Equally important, they were beautiful and had a fragrant scent. The logs were tied into rafts and floated down the seacoast from Tyre to a port in Israel, from which they were carried overland to Jerusalem.

sent to me; I will fulfill all your needs in the matter of cedar and cypress timber.
9 My servants shall bring it down to the sea from the Lebanon; I will make it into **5.9** 2 Chron 2.16
rafts to go by sea to the place you indicate. I will have them broken up there for you Ezra 3.7
to take away. And you shall meet my needs by providing food for my household."
10 So Hiram supplied Solomon's every need for timber of cedar and cypress. 11 Solomon in turn gave Hiram twenty thousand cors of wheat as food for his household,
and twenty cors of fine oil. Solomon gave this to Hiram year by year. 12 So the **5.12**
LORD gave Solomon wisdom, as he promised him. There was peace between Hi- 1 Kgs 3.12; 4.29
ram and Solomon; and the two of them made a treaty.

13 King Solomon conscripted forced labor out of all Israel; the levy numbered
thirty thousand men. 14 He sent them to the Lebanon, ten thousand a month in
shifts; they would be a month in the Lebanon and two months at home; Adoniram
was in charge of the forced labor. 15 Solomon also had seventy thousand laborers
and eighty thousand stonecutters in the hill country, 16 besides Solomon's three
thousand three hundred supervisors who were over the work, having charge of the
people who did the work. 17 At the king's command, they quarried out great, costly
stones in order to lay the foundation of the house with dressed stones. 18 So Solomon's builders and Hiram's builders and the Giblites did the stonecutting and prepared the timber and the stone to build the house.

Solomon begins to build the temple

6 In the four hundred eightieth year after the Israelites came out of the land of **6.1** Judg 11.26
Egypt, in the fourth year of Solomon's reign over Israel, in the month of Ziv, 2 Chron 3.1
which is the second month, he began to build the house of the LORD. 2 The house Acts 7.47
that King Solomon built for the LORD was sixty cubits long, twenty cubits wide, **6.2** 1 Chron 28.11
and thirty cubits high. 3 The vestibule in front of the nave of the house was twenty Ezek 40.5
cubits wide, across the width of the house. Its depth was ten cubits in front of the
house. 4 For the house he made windows with recessed frames.[f] 5 He also built a
structure against the wall of the house, running around the walls of the house, both
the nave and the inner sanctuary; and he made side chambers all around. 6 The
lowest story[g] was five cubits wide, the middle one was six cubits wide, and the
third was seven cubits wide; for around the outside of the house he made offsets on
the wall in order that the supporting beams should not be inserted into the walls of
the house.

7 The house was built with stone finished at the quarry, so that neither hammer **6.7** Ex 20.25
nor ax nor any tool of iron was heard in the temple while it was being built. Deut 27.5,6

8 The entrance for the middle story was on the south side of the house: one went
up by winding stairs to the middle story, and from the middle story to the third. 9 So **6.9** 2 Sam 7.7
he built the house, and finished it; he roofed the house with beams and planks of 1 Kgs 6.14,38
cedar. 10 He built the structure against the whole house, each story[h] five cubits
high, and it was joined to the house with timbers of cedar.

11 Now the word of the LORD came to Solomon, 12 "Concerning this house that **6.11** 1 Kgs 3.14
you are building, if you will walk in my statutes, obey my ordinances, and keep all
my commandments by walking in them, then I will establish my promise with you,

[f] Gk: Meaning of Heb uncertain [g] Gk: Heb *structure* [h] Heb lacks *each story*

5.13, 14 Solomon drafted three times the number of workers needed for the temple project and then arranged their schedules so they didn't have to be away from home for long periods of time. This showed his concern for the welfare of his workers and the importance he placed on family life. The strength of a nation is in direct proportion to the strength of its families. Solomon wisely recognized that family should always be a top priority. As you structure your own work or arrange the schedules of others, watch for the impact of your plans on families.

5.18 Giblites were inhabitants of Gebal, also called Byblos, located north of what is now Beirut, near the cedar forest. These men were Phoenicians, probably skilled as shipbuilders, but employed for this project.

6.1ff For more information on the purpose of the temple, see the note on 2 Chronicles 5.1ff.

6.3 The vestibule was the portico or porch. The nave was the entrance into the worship area.

6.7 In honor of God, the temple in Jerusalem was built without the sound of a hammer or any other tool at the building site. This meant cutting the stone miles away at the quarry. The people's honor and respect for God extended to every aspect of constructing this building in which to worship him. This detail is recorded not to teach us how to build a church, but to show us the importance of demonstrating care, concern, honor, and respect for God and his sanctuary.

6.13 Ex 25.8 which I made to your father David. 13 I will dwell among the children of Israel, and
Deut 31.6 will not forsake my people Israel."
Josh 1.5 14 So Solomon built the house, and finished it. 15 He lined the walls of the
house on the inside with boards of cedar; from the floor of the house to the rafters
of the ceiling, he covered them on the inside with wood; and he covered the floor
6.16 of the house with boards of cypress. 16 He built twenty cubits of the rear of the
Ex 26.33 Lev 16.1,2 house with boards of cedar from the floor to the rafters, and he built this within as
2 Chron 3.8 an inner sanctuary, as the most holy place. 17 The house, that is, the nave in front
of the inner sanctuary, was forty cubits long. 18 The cedar within the house had
carvings of gourds and open flowers; all was cedar, no stone was seen. 19 The inner
sanctuary he prepared in the innermost part of the house, to set there the ark of the
covenant of the LORD. 20 The interior of the inner sanctuary was twenty cubits long,
twenty cubits wide, and twenty cubits high; he overlaid it with pure gold. He also
6.21 overlaid the altar with cedar.[i] 21 Solomon overlaid the inside of the house with
Ex 30.1 pure gold, then he drew chains of gold across, in front of the inner sanctuary, and
overlaid it with gold. 22 Next he overlaid the whole house with gold, in order that
the whole house might be perfect; even the whole altar that belonged to the inner
sanctuary he overlaid with gold.
6.23 23 In the inner sanctuary he made two cherubim of olivewood, each ten cubits
Ex 25.20; 37.7 2 Chron 3.10 high. 24 Five cubits was the length of one wing of the cherub, and five cubits the
length of the other wing of the cherub; it was ten cubits from the tip of one wing to
the tip of the other. 25 The other cherub also measured ten cubits; both cherubim had
the same measure and the same form. 26 The height of one cherub was ten cubits,
and so was that of the other cherub. 27 He put the cherubim in the innermost part of
the house; the wings of the cherubim were spread out so that a wing of one was
touching the one wall, and a wing of the other cherub was touching the other wall;
their other wings toward the center of the house were touching wing to wing. 28 He
also overlaid the cherubim with gold.
29 He carved the walls of the house all around about with carved engravings of
cherubim, palm trees, and open flowers, in the inner and outer rooms. 30 The floor
of the house he overlaid with gold, in the inner and outer rooms.
31 For the entrance to the inner sanctuary he made doors of olivewood; the
lintel and the doorposts were five-sided.[i] 32 He covered the two doors of olivewood with carvings of cherubim, palm trees, and open flowers; he overlaid them
with gold, and spread gold on the cherubim and on the palm trees.
33 So also he made for the entrance to the nave doorposts of olivewood, four-
6.34 sided each, 34 and two doors of cypress wood; the two leaves of the one door were
Ezek 41.23 folding, and the two leaves of the other door were folding. 35 He carved cherubim,
palm trees, and open flowers, overlaying them with gold evenly applied upon the
carved work. 36 He built the inner court with three courses of dressed stone to one
course of cedar beams.
6.37 37 In the fourth year the foundation of the house of the LORD was laid, in the
2 Chron 3.3 month of Ziv. 38 In the eleventh year, in the month of Bul, which is the eighth
month, the house was finished in all its parts, and according to all its specifications.
He was seven years in building it.

Solomon builds his palace

7.1 **7** Solomon was building his own house thirteen years, and he finished his entire
1 Kgs 3.1; 9.10 2 Chron 8.1 house.
2 He built the House of the Forest of the Lebanon one hundred cubits long, fifty

[i] Meaning of Heb uncertain

6.13 This verse summarizes the temple's main purpose. God promised that his eternal presence would never leave the temple as long as one condition was met: the Israelites had to obey God's law. Knowing how many laws they had to follow, we may think this condition was difficult. But the Israelites' situation was much like ours today: they were not cut off from God for failing to keep some small subpoint of a law. Forgiveness was amply provided for all their sins, no matter how large or small. As you read the history of the kings, you will see that lawbreaking was the result, not the cause, of estrangement from God. The kings abandoned God in their hearts first and *then* failed to keep his laws. When we close our hearts to God, the power of his presence soon leaves us.

cubits wide, and thirty cubits high, built on four rows of cedar pillars, with cedar 7.2
beams on the pillars. 3 It was roofed with cedar on the forty-five rafters, fifteen in 1 Kgs 10.17 2 Chron 9.16
each row, which were on the pillars. 4 There were window frames in the three rows,
facing each other in the three rows. 5 All the doorways and doorposts had four-sided
frames, opposite, facing each other in the three rows.
6 He made the Hall of Pillars fifty cubits long and thirty cubits wide. There was
a porch in front with pillars, and a canopy in front of them.
7 He made the Hall of the Throne where he was to pronounce judgment, the 7.7
Hall of Justice, covered with cedar from floor to floor. 1 Kgs 6.9
8 His own house where he would reside, in the other court back of the hall, was 7.8
of the same construction. Solomon also made a house like this hall for Pharaoh's 1 Kgs 3.1; 7.8 2 Chron 8.11
daughter, whom he had taken in marriage.
9 All these were made of costly stones, cut according to measure, sawed with
saws, back and front, from the foundation to the coping, and from outside to the
great court. 10 The foundation was of costly stones, huge stones, stones of eight and
ten cubits. 11 There were costly stones above, cut to measure, and cedarwood.
12 The great court had three courses of dressed stone to one layer of cedar beams all
around; so had the inner court of the house of the LORD, and the vestibule of the
house.

Equipment for the temple

13 Now King Solomon invited and received Hiram from Tyre. 14 He was 7.13
the son of a widow of the tribe of Naphtali, whose father, a man of Tyre, had been 1 Kgs 7.40 2 Chron 2.13
an artisan in bronze; he was full of skill, intelligence, and knowledge in working
bronze. He came to King Solomon, and did all his work.
15 He cast two pillars of bronze. Eighteen cubits was the height of the one, and 7.15
a cord of twelve cubits would encircle it; the second pillar was the same.[j] 16 He 2 Kgs 25.13 2 Chron 3.15
also made two capitals of molten bronze, to set on the tops of the pillars; the height 4.12 Jer 52.17
of the one capital was five cubits, and the height of the other capital was five cubits.
17 There were nets of checker work with wreaths of chain work for the capitals on
the tops of the pillars; seven[k] for the one capital, and seven[k] for the other capital.
18 He made the columns with two rows around each latticework to cover the capitals
that were above the pomegranates; he did the same with the other capital. 19 Now
the capitals that were on the tops of the pillars in the vestibule were of lily-work,
four cubits high. 20 The capitals were on the two pillars and also above the rounded
projection that was beside the latticework; there were two hundred pomegranates in
rows all around; and so with the other capital. 21 He set up the pillars at the vestibule
of the temple; he set up the pillar on the south and called it Jachin; and he set up the
pillar on the north and called it Boaz. 22 On the tops of the pillars was lily-work.
Thus the work of the pillars was finished.
23 Then he made the molten sea; it was round, ten cubits from brim to brim,
and five cubits high. A line of thirty cubits would encircle it completely. 24 Under
its brim were panels all around it, each of ten cubits, surrounding the sea; there
were two rows of panels, cast when it was cast. 25 It stood on twelve oxen, three
facing north, three facing west, three facing south, and three facing east; the sea
was set on them. The hindquarters of each were toward the inside. 26 Its thickness
was a handbreadth; its brim was made like the brim of a cup, like the flower of a
lily; it held two thousand baths.[l] 7.27
27 He also made the ten stands of bronze; each stand was four cubits long, four 2 Kgs 16.17

[j] Cn: Heb *and a cord of twelve cubits encircled the second pillar*; Compare Jer 52.21 [k] Heb: Gk *a net* [l] A Heb measure of volume

7.13 This is not King Hiram of Tyre mentioned in chapter 5.

7.14 Hiram was an expert craftsman. Solomon chose only the best.

7.23 This enormous tank, the "molten sea," was also called the *laver*. Designed and used for the priests' ceremonial washings, it was placed in the temple court near the altar of burnt offering. Priests washed themselves before offering sacrifices or entering the temple (Exodus 30.17–21).

7.27–39 These ten basins of water, also called *lavers*, were used for washing the various parts of the animal sacrifices. Each basin was placed on a movable stand so it could be used where needed.

cubits wide, and three cubits high. 28 This was the construction of the stands: they
had borders; the borders were within the frames; 29 on the borders that were set in
the frames were lions, oxen, and cherubim. On the frames, both above and below
the lions and oxen, there were wreaths of beveled work. 30 Each stand had four
bronze wheels and axles of bronze; at the four corners were supports for a basin.
The supports were cast with wreaths at the side of each. 31 Its opening was within
the crown whose height was one cubit; its opening was round, as a pedestal is
made; it was a cubit and a half wide. At its opening there were carvings; its borders
were four-sided, not round. 32 The four wheels were underneath the borders; the
axles of the wheels were in the stands; and the height of a wheel was a cubit and a
half. 33 The wheels were made like a chariot wheel; their axles, their rims, their
spokes, and their hubs were all cast. 34 There were four supports at the four corners
of each stand; the supports were of one piece with the stands. 35 On the top of the
stand there was a round band half a cubit high; on the top of the stand, its stays and
its borders were of one piece with it. 36 On the surfaces of its stays and on its borders
he carved cherubim, lions, and palm trees, where each had space, with wreaths all
around. 37 In this way he made the ten stands; all of them were cast alike, with the
same size and the same form.

7.38 2 Kgs 25.14 2 Chron 4.6 38 He made ten basins of bronze; each basin held forty baths,[m] each basin measured four cubits; there was a basin for each of the ten stands. 39 He set five of the
stands on the south side of the house, and five on the north side of the house; he set
the sea on the southeast corner of the house.

40 Hiram also made the pots, the shovels, and the basins. So Hiram finished all
7.41 2 Chron 4.12 the work that he did for King Solomon on the house of the LORD: 41 the two pillars,
the two bowls of the capitals that were on the tops of the pillars, the two latticeworks to cover the two bowls of the capitals that were on the tops of the pillars;
42 the four hundred pomegranates for the two latticeworks, two rows of pomegranates for each latticework, to cover the two bowls of the capitals that were on the
pillars; 43 the ten stands, the ten basins on the stands; 44 the one sea, and the twelve
oxen underneath the sea.

45 The pots, the shovels, and the basins, all these vessels that Hiram made for
King Solomon for the house of the LORD were of burnished bronze. 46 In the plain
of the Jordan the king cast them, in the clay ground between Succoth and Zarethan.
7.47 1 Chron 22.3,14 47 Solomon left all the vessels unweighed, because there were so many of them; the
weight of the bronze was not determined.

7.48 Ex 37.10,15,16 48 So Solomon made all the vessels that were in the house of the LORD: the
7.49 Ex 25.31; 37.14 golden altar, the golden table for the bread of the Presence, 49 the lampstands of
pure gold, five on the south side and five on the north, in front of the inner sanctu-
7.50 2 Kgs 25.14,15 ary; the flowers, the lamps, and the tongs, of gold; 50 the cups, snuffers, basins,
dishes for incense, and firepans, of pure gold; the sockets for the doors of the innermost part of the house, the most holy place, and for the doors of the nave of the
temple, of gold.

7.51 2 Sam 8.11 2 Chron 5.1 51 Thus all the work that King Solomon did on the house of the LORD was
finished. Solomon brought in the things that his father David had dedicated, the
silver, the gold, and the vessels, and stored them in the treasuries of the house of
the LORD.

[m] A Heb measure of volume

7.40 These other utensils had the same use in the temple as they had in the tabernacle (Exodus 38.3). Kept in the inner court, they were designed to help the priests with all the work connected with the sacrifices.

7.41–46 Hiram's items of bronze would look strange in today's churches, but we use other articles to enhance worship. Stained-glass windows, crosses, pulpits, hymnbooks, baptisteries, and communion tables serve as aids to worship. While the instruments of worship may change, the purpose should never change—to give honor and praise to God.

7.42 A pomegranate is a tasty red fruit, about the size of an orange, which became a symbol of beauty and holiness. Pomegranates were used to decorate the tabernacle of Moses' day as well as the temple. Priests sewed cloth replicas of the fruit onto the hems of their robes.

The ark is brought to the temple

8 Then Solomon assembled the elders of Israel and all the heads of the tribes, the
leaders of the ancestral houses of the Israelites, before King Solomon in Jerusalem, to bring up the ark of the covenant of the LORD out of the city of David,
which is Zion. 2 All the people of Israel assembled to King Solomon at the festival
in the month Ethanim, which is the seventh month. 3 And all the elders of Israel
came, and the priests carried the ark. 4 So they brought up the ark of the LORD, the
tent of meeting, and all the holy vessels that were in the tent; the priests and the
Levites brought them up. 5 King Solomon and all the congregation of Israel, who
had assembled before him, were with him before the ark, sacrificing so many sheep
and oxen that they could not be counted or numbered. 6 Then the priests brought the
ark of the covenant of the LORD to its place, in the inner sanctuary of the house, in
the most holy place, underneath the wings of the cherubim. 7 For the cherubim
spread out their wings over the place of the ark, so that the cherubim made a covering above the ark and its poles. 8 The poles were so long that the ends of the poles
were seen from the holy place in front of the inner sanctuary; but they could not be
seen from outside; they are there to this day. 9 There was nothing in the ark except
the two tablets of stone that Moses had placed there at Horeb, where the LORD made
a covenant with the Israelites, when they came out of the land of Egypt. 10 And
when the priests came out of the holy place, a cloud filled the house of the LORD,
11 so that the priests could not stand to minister because of the cloud; for the glory
of the LORD filled the house of the LORD.

12 Then Solomon said,
"The LORD has said that he would dwell in thick darkness.
13 I have built you an exalted house,
a place for you to dwell in forever."

14 Then the king turned around and blessed all the assembly of Israel, while all
the assembly of Israel stood. 15 He said, "Blessed be the LORD, the God of Israel,
who with his hand has fulfilled what he promised with his mouth to my father
David, saying, 16 'Since the day that I brought my people Israel out of Egypt, I have
not chosen a city from any of the tribes of Israel in which to build a house, that my
name might be there; but I chose David to be over my people Israel.' 17 My father
David had it in mind to build a house for the name of the LORD, the God of Israel.
18 But the LORD said to my father David, 'You did well to consider building a house
for my name; 19 nevertheless you shall not build the house, but your son who shall
be born to you shall build the house for my name.' 20 Now the LORD has upheld the
promise that he made; for I have risen in the place of my father David; I sit on the
throne of Israel, as the LORD promised, and have built the house for the name of the
LORD, the God of Israel. 21 There I have provided a place for the ark, in which is the
covenant of the LORD that he made with our ancestors when he brought them out of
the land of Egypt."

Solomon dedicates the temple

22 Then Solomon stood before the altar of the LORD in the presence of all the
assembly of Israel, and spread out his hands to heaven. 23 He said, "O LORD, God
of Israel, there is no God like you in heaven above or on earth beneath, keeping
covenant and steadfast love for your servants who walk before you with all their

8.1 2 Sam 5.7; 6.17
8.2 2 Chron 5.3; 7.8
8.3 Num 7.9
8.5 1 Kgs 8.62,63 2 Chron 1.5,6
8.8 Ex 25.13,14 37.4,5
8.9 Ex 24.7; 25.16 Deut 4.13,14 10.2 Heb 9.4
8.10 Ex 40.34 2 Chron 7.1
8.12 2 Sam 7.13 22.10 2 Chron 6.1 Ps 97.2; 132.14
8.15 2 Sam 7.12 1 Kgs 8.24 1 Chron 22.10 29.10
8.16 Deut 12.4,5,11 1 Sam 16.1
8.17 2 Sam 7.2,3 1 Chron 17.1
8.19 2 Sam 7.12,13 1 Chron 17.11, 12; 22.8; 28.6
8.20 Neh 9.8 Jer 29.10
8.22 Deut 7.9 1 Sam 2.2 2 Sam 7.22 2 Chron 6.12 Neh 1.5; 9.32

8.1ff Solomon gathered the people not just to dedicate the temple, but to rededicate themselves to God's service. Solomon could well be speaking these words to us today: "Therefore devote yourselves completely to the Lord our God, walking in his statutes and keeping his commandments, as at this day" (8.61).

8.1ff What was the difference between the temple and the tabernacle, and why did the Israelites change from one to the other? The tabernacle was a portable place of worship designed for the people as they were traveling toward the promised land. A tabernacle is a tent. The temple was a permanent place to worship God after the Israelites were at peace in their land.

8.6 Cherubim are mighty angels.

8.16 For 480 years after Israel's escape from Egypt, God did not ask them to build a temple for him. Instead he emphasized the importance of his presence among them and their need for spiritual leaders. It is easy to think of a building as the focus of God's presence and power, but God chooses and uses *people* to do his work. He can use you more than he can use a building of wood and stone. Building or enlarging our place of worship may be necessary, but it should never take priority over developing spiritual leaders.

8.24
1 Kgs 8.15
8.25
2 Sam 7.12,16
1 Kgs 2.4
1 Chron 17.23
8.27
2 Chron 6.18
Ps 139.7
Isa 66.1
Jer 23.24
Acts 7.48,49

heart, [24]the covenant that you kept for your servant my father David as you declared to him; you promised with your mouth and have this day fulfilled with your
hand. [25]Therefore, O LORD, God of Israel, keep for your servant my father David
that which you promised him, saying, 'There shall never fail you a successor before me to sit on the throne of Israel, if only your children look to their way, to walk
before me as you have walked before me.' [26]Therefore, O God of Israel, let your
word be confirmed, which you promised to your servant my father David.
27 "But will God indeed dwell on the earth? Even heaven and the highest

SOLOMON'S TEMPLE
960–586 B.C.
Solomon's temple was a beautiful sight. It took over seven years to build and was a magnificent building containing gold, silver, bronze, and cedar. This house for God was without equal. The description is found in 2 Chronicles 2–4

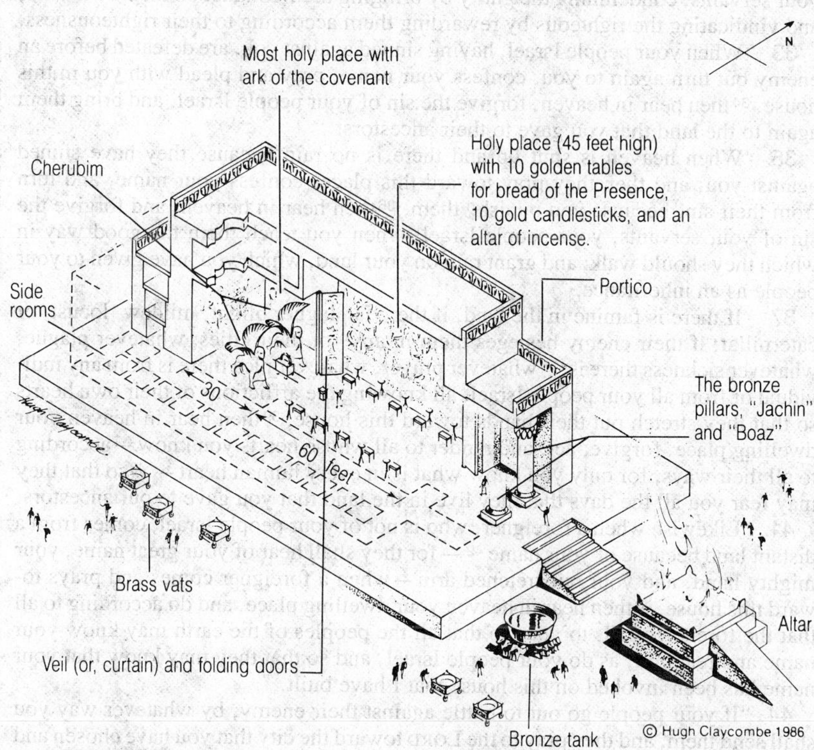

FURNISHINGS

Cherubim: represented heavenly beings, symbolized God's presence and holiness (gold-plated, 15 feet wide)

Ark of the covenant: contained the law written on two tablets, symbolized God's presence with Israel (wood overlaid with gold)

Veil: separated the holy place from the most holy place (fine linen of red and blue, embroidered with depictions of angels)

Folding doors: between holy place and most holy place (wood overlaid with gold)

Golden tables (wood overlaid with gold), *golden candlesticks* (with seven lamps on each stand), and *altar of incense* (wood overlaid with gold): instruments for priestly functions in the holy place

Bronze pillars: named Jachin (meaning "sustainer") and Boaz (meaning "strength")—taken together they could mean "God provides the strength"

Altar: for burning of sacrifices (bronze)

Bronze tank: for priests' washing (had 12,000 gallon capacity)

Brass vats: for washing the sacrifices (tanks on wheeled bases)

This reconstruction uses known archaeological parallels to supplement the text, and assumes interior dimensions from 1 Kings 6.17–20.

8.24 Solomon was referring to the promise God made to David in 2 Samuel 7.12–15 that one of David's sons would build the temple.

8.27 Solomon declared that even the highest heavens cannot contain God. Isn't it amazing that, though the heavens can't contain him, he is willing to live in the hearts of those who love him? The God of the universe takes up residence in his people.

heaven cannot contain you, much less this house that I have built! 28 Regard your
servant's prayer and his plea, O LORD my God, heeding the cry and the prayer that
your servant prays to you today; 29 that your eyes may be open night and day toward
this house, the place of which you said, 'My name shall be there,' that you may
heed the prayer that your servant prays toward this place. 30 Hear the plea of your
servant and of your people Israel when they pray toward this place; O hear in
heaven your dwelling place; heed and forgive.
31 "If someone sins against a neighbor and is given an oath to swear, and comes
and swears before your altar in this house, 32 then hear in heaven, and act, and judge
your servants, condemning the guilty by bringing their conduct on their own head,
and vindicating the righteous by rewarding them according to their righteousness.
33 "When your people Israel, having sinned against you, are defeated before an
enemy but turn again to you, confess your name, pray and plead with you in this
house, 34 then hear in heaven, forgive the sin of your people Israel, and bring them
again to the land that you gave to their ancestors.
35 "When heaven is shut up and there is no rain because they have sinned
against you, and then they pray toward this place, confess your name, and turn
from their sin, because you punish[n] them, 36 then hear in heaven, and forgive the
sin of your servants, your people Israel, when you teach them the good way in
which they should walk; and grant rain on your land, which you have given to your
people as an inheritance.
37 "If there is famine in the land, if there is plague, blight, mildew, locust, or
caterpillar; if their enemy besieges them in any[o] of their cities; whatever plague,
whatever sickness there is; 38 whatever prayer, whatever plea there is from any individual or from all your people Israel, all knowing the afflictions of their own hearts
so that they stretch out their hands toward this house; 39 then hear in heaven your
dwelling place, forgive, act, and render to all whose hearts you know—according
to all their ways, for only you know what is in every human heart— 40 so that they
may fear you all the days that they live in the land that you gave to our ancestors.
41 "Likewise when a foreigner, who is not of your people Israel, comes from a
distant land because of your name 42 —for they shall hear of your great name, your
mighty hand, and your outstretched arm—when a foreigner comes and prays toward this house, 43 then hear in heaven your dwelling place, and do according to all
that the foreigner calls to you, so that all the peoples of the earth may know your
name and fear you, as do your people Israel, and so that they may know that your
name has been invoked on this house that I have built.
44 "If your people go out to battle against their enemy, by whatever way you
shall send them, and they pray to the LORD toward the city that you have chosen and
the house that I have built for your name, 45 then hear in heaven their prayer and
their plea, and maintain their cause.
46 "If they sin against you—for there is no one who does not sin—and you are
angry with them and give them to an enemy, so that they are carried away captive
to the land of the enemy, far off or near; 47 yet if they come to their senses in the land

8.30 Neh 1.5-7
8.31 Ex 22.8 Lev 5.1
8.33 Lev 26.14-17, 40,41 Deut 28.25, 47,48
8.35 Lev 26.19 Deut 11.16,17 28.23 1 Sam 12.23 2 Sam 21.1 1 Kgs 18.41
8.37 Lev 26.16,25 Deut 28.21,31 2 Kgs 6.25
8.39 1 Sam 2.3 1 Chron 28.9 Jer 17.10 Jn 2.24
8.41 1 Kgs 10.1 2 Chron 6.32
8.43 1 Sam 17.46 2 Kgs 19.19
8.44 2 Chron 14.11
8.46 2 Kgs 17.6,18 25.21 2 Chron 6.36 Ps 130.3,4
8.47 Lev 26.40 Ezra 9.5,6 Neh 1.6,7 Ps 106.6,7 Dan 9.5

[n] Or *when you answer* [o] Gk Syr: Heb *in the land*

8.29 Did God really live in the temple? God is everywhere—he does not need a home in which to live. The temple was a visible symbol of the invisible presence of God. Yet God was specially present in the temple. Today God does not need a temple because he lives in his people!

8.33, 34 After Solomon's reign, the people continually turned away from God. The rest of the kingdom era is a vivid fulfillment of Solomon's description in these verses. As a result of the people's sin, God let them be overrun by enemies several times. Then, in desperation, they cried out to God for forgiveness, and God restored them.

8.41–43 God chose Israel to be a blessing to the whole world (Genesis 12.1–3). This blessing found its fulfillment in Jesus—a descendant of Abraham and David (Galatians 3.8, 9)—who became the Messiah for all people, Jews and non-Jews. When the Israelites first entered the promised land, they were ordered to clear out several wicked nations; thus we read in the Old Testament of many wars. But we should not conclude that war was Israel's first duty. After subduing the evil people, Israel was to become a light to the surrounding nations. Sadly, Israel's own sin and spiritual blindness prevented them from reaching out to the rest of the world with God's love. Jesus came to do what the nation of Israel failed to do.

8.46–53 Solomon, who seemed to have prophetic insight into the future captivities of his people (2 Kings 17; 25), asked God to be merciful to them when they cried out to him, to forgive them, and to return them to their homeland. Reference to their return is made in Ezra 1; 2; Nehemiah 1; 2.

to which they have been taken captive, and repent, and plead with you in the land
of their captors, saying, 'We have sinned, and have done wrong; we have acted
wickedly'; 48 if they repent with all their heart and soul in the land of their enemies,
who took them captive, and pray to you toward their land, which you gave to their
ancestors, the city that you have chosen, and the house that I have built for your
name; 49 then hear in heaven your dwelling place their prayer and their plea, maintain their cause 50 and forgive your people who have sinned against you, and all
their transgressions that they have committed against you; and grant them compassion in the sight of their captors, so that they may have compassion on them 51 (for
they are your people and heritage, which you brought out of Egypt, from the midst
of the iron-smelter). 52 Let your eyes be open to the plea of your servant, and to the
plea of your people Israel, listening to them whenever they call to you. 53 For you
have separated them from among all the peoples of the earth, to be your heritage,
just as you promised through Moses, your servant, when you brought our ancestors
out of Egypt, O Lord GOD."

54 Now when Solomon finished offering all this prayer and this plea to the
LORD, he arose from facing the altar of the LORD, where he had knelt with hands
outstretched toward heaven; 55 he stood and blessed all the assembly of Israel with
a loud voice:

56 "Blessed be the LORD, who has given rest to his people Israel according to
all that he promised; not one word has failed of all his good promise, which he
spoke through his servant Moses. 57 The LORD our God be with us, as he was with
our ancestors; may he not leave us or abandon us, 58 but incline our hearts to him,
to walk in all his ways, and to keep his commandments, his statutes, and his ordinances, which he commanded our ancestors. 59 Let these words of mine, with
which I pleaded before the LORD, be near to the LORD our God day and night, and
may he maintain the cause of his servant and the cause of his people Israel, as each
day requires; 60 so that all the peoples of the earth may know that the LORD is God;
there is no other. 61 Therefore devote yourselves completely to the LORD our God,
walking in his statutes and keeping his commandments, as at this day."

62 Then the king, and all Israel with him, offered sacrifice before the LORD.
63 Solomon offered as sacrifices of well-being to the LORD twenty-two thousand
oxen and one hundred twenty thousand sheep. So the king and all the people of
Israel dedicated the house of the LORD. 64 The same day the king consecrated the
middle of the court that was in front of the house of the LORD; for there he offered
the burnt offerings and the grain offerings and the fat pieces of the sacrifices of
well-being, because the bronze altar that was before the LORD was too small to
receive the burnt offerings and the grain offerings and the fat pieces of the sacrifices
of well-being.

65 So Solomon held the festival at that time, and all Israel with him—a great
assembly, people from Lebo-hamath to the Wadi of Egypt—before the LORD our
God, seven days.[p] 66 On the eighth day he sent the people away; and they blessed
the king, and went to their tents, joyful and in good spirits because of all the goodness that the LORD had shown to his servant David and to his people Israel.

4. Solomon's greatness and downfall

God's warning to Solomon

9 When Solomon had finished building the house of the LORD and the king's
house and all that Solomon desired to build, 2 the LORD appeared to Solomon
a second time, as he had appeared to him at Gibeon. 3 The LORD said to him, "I have

[p] Compare Gk: Heb *seven days and seven days, fourteen days*

8.48 Deut 4.29; 1 Sam 7.3; Jer 29.12
8.50 2 Chron 30.9; Ezra 7.6; Neh 1.11; Ps 106.46
8.51 Ex 32.11; Deut 4.20; 9.26; 1 Sam 8.8; Jer 11.4
8.53 Ex 19.5,6; 33.16; Deut 4.34
8.54 1 Kgs 8.22
8.56 Josh 21.45; 23.14; 2 Kgs 10.9,10; Lk 1.54
8.57 Josh 1.5; 1 Sam 12.22; Isa 41.17; Heb 13.5
8.58 Ps 119.36; Jer 31.33
8.59 2 Chron 6.40
8.60 Deut 4.35; 1 Sam 17.46; 1 Kgs 18.39; Jer 10.10
8.61 Deut 18.13; 1 Kgs 20.3
8.62 2 Sam 6.17; 2 Chron 7.4
8.64 2 Chron 7.7
9.1 2 Chron 8.6
9.2 1 Kgs 3.5; 11.9

8.56–60 Solomon blessed the Lord and prayed for the people. His prayer can be a pattern for our prayers. He had five basic requests: (1) for God's presence (8.57); (2) "incline our hearts to him"; for the desire to do God's will in everything (8.58); (3) for help with daily needs (8.59); (4) for the desire and ability to obey God's laws and commandments; (5) for the spread of God's kingdom to the entire world. These prayer requests are just as applicable today as in Solomon's time. When you pray for your church or family, you can make these same requests to God.

8.65 A wadi is a stream or dry stream bed.

heard your prayer and your plea, which you made before me; I have consecrated
this house that you have built, and put my name there forever; my eyes and my
heart will be there for all time. 4 As for you, if you will walk before me, as David
your father walked, with integrity of heart and uprightness, doing according to all
that I have commanded you, and keeping my statutes and my ordinances, 5 then I
will establish your royal throne over Israel forever, as I promised your father David, saying, 'There shall not fail you a successor on the throne of Israel.'
6 "If you turn aside from following me, you or your children, and do not keep
my commandments and my statutes that I have set before you, but go and serve
other gods and worship them, 7 then I will cut Israel off from the land that I have
given them; and the house that I have consecrated for my name I will cast out of my
sight; and Israel will become a proverb and a taunt among all peoples. 8 This house
will become a heap of ruins;[q] everyone passing by it will be astonished, and will
hiss; and they will say, 'Why has the LORD done such a thing to this land and to this
house?' 9 Then they will say, 'Because they have forsaken the LORD their God, who
brought their ancestors out of the land of Egypt, and embraced other gods, worshiping them and serving them; therefore the LORD has brought this disaster upon
them.' "

9.4 1 Kgs 3.14; 11.4
9.5 2 Sam 7.12; 1 Kgs 8.25
9.6 2 Sam 7.14; 1 Chron 28.9; 2 Chron 7.19
9.7 Lev 18.24; Deut 4.26,27; 2 Kgs 17.23; Jer 7.4
9.8 Deut 29.24; 2 Chron 7.21; Jer 22.8
9.9 Deut 29.25; 2 Chron 7.22

Solomon's other achievements

10 At the end of twenty years, in which Solomon had built the two houses, the
house of the LORD and the king's house, 11 King Hiram of Tyre having supplied
Solomon with cedar and cypress timber and gold, as much as he desired, King
Solomon gave to Hiram twenty cities in the land of Galilee. 12 But when Hiram
came from Tyre to see the cities that Solomon had given him, they did not please
him. 13 Therefore he said, "What kind of cities are these that you have given me,
my brother?" So they are called the land of Cabul[r] to this day. 14 But Hiram had
sent to the king one hundred twenty talents of gold.
15 This is the account of the forced labor that King Solomon conscripted to
build the house of the LORD and his own house, the Millo and the wall of Jerusalem, Hazor, Megiddo, Gezer 16 (Pharaoh king of Egypt had gone up and captured
Gezer and burned it down, had killed the Canaanites who lived in the city, and had
given it as dowry to his daughter, Solomon's wife; 17 so Solomon rebuilt Gezer),
Lower Beth-horon, 18 Baalath, Tamar in the wilderness, within the land, 19 as well
as all of Solomon's storage cities, the cities for his chariots, the cities for his cavalry, and whatever Solomon desired to build, in Jerusalem, in Lebanon, and in all

9.10 1 Kgs 6.37
9.11 1 Kgs 5.4; 2 Chron 2.4
9.15 2 Sam 5.9; 1 Kgs 6.38; 7.1; 2 Chron 8.1,2

q Syr Old Latin: Heb *will become high* r Perhaps meaning *a land good for nothing*

9.4–9 For more on the conditions of God's great promise to David and his descendants, see the note on 2.3, 4.

9.11–14 Was Solomon being unfair to Hiram? It is not clear from these verses whether Solomon gave these cities to Hiram, or whether they were collateral until he could repay Hiram for the gold he had lent. Second Chronicles 8.1, 2 implies that the cities were returned to Solomon. In either case, Hiram probably preferred a piece of land on the coast more suitable for trade (the name he gave these cities, *Cabul,* means "dirty" or "displeasing"). But in the end, he was repaid many times over through his trade partnerships with Solomon (2 Chronicles 9.10, 21). Because Phoenicia was on friendly terms with Israel and dependent on it for grain and oil, Hiram's relationship with Solomon was more important than a feud over some cities.

9.16 At this time, Israel and Egypt were the major powers in the Near East. For many years Egypt had retained control of Gezer, even though it was in Israelite territory. In Solomon's time the Pharaoh gave the city to his daughter, whom Solomon married. Thus Gezer fell under Israelite control.

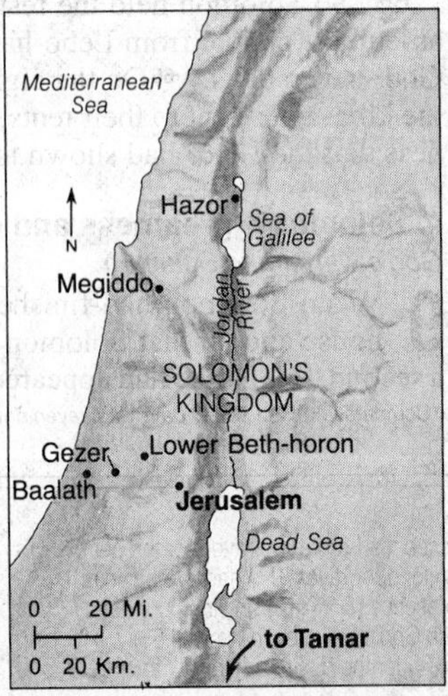

SOLOMON'S BUILDING PROJECTS
Solomon became known as one of the great builders in Israel's history. He built Hazor, Megiddo, and Gezer as fortress cities at key points during his reign. He also rebuilt the cities of Lower Beth-horon, Baalath, and Tamar.

9.20
Gen 9.24,25
Josh 15.63
Judg 1.28,35

the land of his dominion. 20 All the people who were left of the Amorites, the Hittites, the Perizzites, the Hivites, and the Jebusites, who were not of the people of
Israel— 21 their descendants who were still left in the land, whom the Israelites
were unable to destroy completely—these Solomon conscripted for slave labor,
and so they are to this day. 22 But of the Israelites Solomon made no slaves; they
were the soldiers, they were his officials, his commanders, his captains, and the
commanders of his chariotry and cavalry.
23 These were the chief officers who were over Solomon's work: five hundred
fifty, who had charge of the people who carried on the work.

9.24
1 Kgs 3.1; 7.8
11.1,27
2 Chron 32.5

24 But Pharaoh's daughter went up from the city of David to her own house that
Solomon had built for her; then he built the Millo.

9.25
Ex 23.14
Deut 16.16
2 Chron 8.13

25 Three times a year Solomon used to offer up burnt offerings and sacrifices of
well-being on the altar that he built for the LORD, offering incense[s] before the
LORD. So he completed the house.

9.27
1 Kgs 10.11
1 Chron 29.4

26 King Solomon built a fleet of ships at Ezion-geber, which is near Eloth on
the shore of the Red Sea,[t] in the land of Edom. 27 Hiram sent his servants with the
fleet, sailors who were familiar with the sea, together with the servants of Solomon. 28 They went to Ophir, and imported from there four hundred twenty talents
of gold, which they delivered to King Solomon.

The queen of Sheba visits Solomon

10.1
2 Chron 9.1
Ps 72.10,15
Isa 60.6
Mt 12.42

10 When the queen of Sheba heard of the fame of Solomon, (fame due to[u] the
name of the LORD), she came to test him with hard questions. 2 She came to
Jerusalem with a very great retinue, with camels bearing spices, and very much
gold, and precious stones; and when she came to Solomon, she told him all that was
on her mind. 3 Solomon answered all her questions; there was nothing hidden from
the king that he could not explain to her. 4 When the queen of Sheba had observed
all the wisdom of Solomon, the house that he had built, 5 the food of his table, the
seating of his officials, and the attendance of his servants, their clothing, his valets,
and his burnt offerings that he offered at the house of the LORD, there was no more
spirit in her.
6 So she said to the king, "The report was true that I heard in my own land of
your accomplishments and of your wisdom, 7 but I did not believe the reports until
I came and my own eyes had seen it. Not even half had been told me; your wisdom
and prosperity far surpass the report that I had heard. 8 Happy are your wives![v]
Happy are these your servants, who continually attend you and hear your wisdom!

10.9
2 Sam 8.15
23.3
1 Kgs 5.7
2 Chron 2.11

9 Blessed be the LORD your God, who has delighted in you and set you on the throne
of Israel! Because the LORD loved Israel forever, he has made you king to execute
justice and righteousness." 10 Then she gave the king one hundred twenty talents of
gold, a great quantity of spices, and precious stones; never again did spices come
in such quantity as that which the queen of Sheba gave to King Solomon.

[s] Gk: Heb *offering incense with it that was* [t] Or *Sea of Reeds* [u] Meaning of Heb uncertain [v] Gk Syr: Heb *men*

9.24 Millo was an older section of Jerusalem already in use by the Jebusites before David captured the city (2 Samuel 5.9). It was rebuilt by Solomon and again restored by Hezekiah over two centuries later (2 Chronicles 32.5).

9.25 The three times that Solomon offered sacrifices correspond to the three great annual feasts for the nation: passover (as described in Leviticus 23.4–8), the festival of weeks (Leviticus 23.15–21), and the festival of the booths (Leviticus 15.33–43). The burnt offerings were those specified by Moses (Leviticus 1.1–17) and were offered as an atonement for the sin of the nation. The sacrifices of well-being were also specified by Moses (Leviticus 3.1–17). They were offered to express gratitude to God and symbolized fellowship with him. Solomon not only completed the house of the Lord, but he made sure that it was being used for its intended purpose.

10.1–5 The queen of Sheba came to see for herself if everything she had heard about Solomon was true. (A retinue is a group of attendants.) Contests using riddles or proverbs were often used to test wisdom. The queen may have used some of these as she questioned Solomon (10.1, 3). When she realized the extent of his riches and wisdom, there was "no more spirit in her." In other words, she no longer disputed his power or wisdom. No longer a competitor, she became an admirer. Most likely, her experience was repeated by many kings and foreign dignitaries who paid honor to Solomon.

10.8 Because of Solomon's wisdom, the people were happy and the palace aides content. Wisdom's quality is shown by how well it works. In James 3.17 we learn that wisdom is peaceable. Are you seeking the kind of wisdom that establishes peace in your relationships?

11 Moreover, the fleet of Hiram, which carried gold from Ophir, brought from 10.11
Ophir a great quantity of almug wood and precious stones. 12 From the almug wood 1 Kgs 9.27
the king made supports for the house of the LORD, and for the king's house, lyres
also and harps for the singers; no such almug wood has come or been seen to this
day.
13 Meanwhile King Solomon gave to the queen of Sheba every desire that she
expressed, as well as what he gave her out of Solomon's royal bounty. Then she
returned to her own land, with her servants.

Solomon's great riches

14 The weight of gold that came to Solomon in one year was six hundred sixty- 10.14
six talents of gold, 15 besides that which came from the traders and from the busi- 2 Chron 9.13
ness of the merchants, and from all the kings of Arabia and the governors of the
land. 16 King Solomon made two hundred large shields of beaten gold; six hundred 10.16
shekels of gold went into each large shield. 17 He made three hundred shields of 1 Kgs 14.26 2 Chron 9.15
beaten gold; three minas of gold went into each shield; and the king put them in the 12.9
House of the Forest of Lebanon. 18 The king also made a great ivory throne, and
overlaid it with the finest gold. 19 The throne had six steps. The top of the throne
was rounded in the back, and on each side of the seat were arm rests and two lions
standing beside the arm rests, 20 while twelve lions were standing, one on each end
of a step on the six steps. Nothing like it was ever made in any kingdom. 21 All King 10.21
Solomon's drinking vessels were of gold, and all the vessels of the House of the 1 Kgs 7.2
Forest of Lebanon were of pure gold; none were of silver—it was not considered as
anything in the days of Solomon. 22 For the king had a fleet of ships of Tarshish at
sea with the fleet of Hiram. Once every three years the fleet of ships of Tarshish
used to come bringing gold, silver, ivory, apes, and peacocks.[w]
23 Thus King Solomon excelled all the kings of the earth in riches and in wis- 10.23
dom. 24 The whole earth sought the presence of Solomon to hear his wisdom, which 1 Kgs 3.12,13 4.30
God had put into his mind. 25 Every one of them brought a present, objects of silver 2 Chron 9.22
and gold, garments, weaponry, spices, horses, and mules, so much year by year.
26 Solomon gathered together chariots and horses; he had fourteen hundred
chariots and twelve thousand horses, which he stationed in the chariot cities and

w Or *baboons*

10.14ff When Solomon asked for wisdom, God promised him riches and honor as well (3.13). These verses show just how extensive his wealth became. Israel was no longer a second-rate nation, but at the height of its power and wealth. Solomon's riches became legendary. Great men came from many nations to listen to Israel's powerful king. Jesus would later refer to "Solomon in all his glory" (Matthew 6.29).

10.23 Why does the Bible place so much emphasis on Solomon's material possessions? In the Old Testament, riches were considered tangible evidence of God's blessing. Prosperity was seen as a proof of right living. In the books of Ecclesiastes and Job this concept is placed in a broader perspective. In ideal conditions, people prosper when God runs their lives, but prosperity is not guaranteed. Wealth does not prove that a person is living rightly before God, and poverty does not indicate sin.

In fact, a greater evidence that one is living for God is the presence of suffering and persecution (Mark 10.29–31; 13.13). The most important "treasure" is not earthly, but heavenly (Matthew 6.19–21; 19.21; 1 Timothy 6.17–19). The gift of greatest worth has no price tag—it is the gift of salvation freely offered by God to all.

10.26–11.3 In accumulating great horse stables, a huge harem, and incredible wealth, Solomon was violating God's commands for a king (Deuteronomy 17.14–20). Why were they prohibited? God knew how these activities would hurt the nation both politically and spiritually (1 Samuel 8.11–18). The more luxurious Solomon's court became, the more the people were taxed. Excessive taxation created unrest, and soon conditions became ripe for a revolution. When he had everything he wanted, Solomon forgot God and allowed pagan influences to enter his court through his heathen wives, thus accelerating the spiritual corruption of the nation.

10.28 Kue is probably Cilicia, in southern Turkey.

11.2 Although Solomon had clear instructions from God *not* to marry women from foreign nations, he chose to disregard God's commands. He married not one, but many heathen wives, who subsequently led him away from God. God knows our strengths and weaknesses, and his commands are always for our good. Some people ignore God's commands, but negative consequences inevitably result. It is not enough to know God's Word or even to believe it; we must follow it and apply it to our daily activities and decisions. Take God's commands seriously.

10.27 2 Chron 1.15 9.27
10.28 2 Chron 1.16 9.28
10.29 2 Kgs 7.7

with the king in Jerusalem. 27 The king made silver as common in Jerusalem as
stones, and he made cedars as numerous as the sycamores of the Shephelah. 28 Solomon's import of horses was from Egypt and Kue, and the king's traders received
them from Kue at a price. 29 A chariot could be imported from Egypt for six hundred shekels of silver, and a horse for one hundred fifty; so through the king's
traders they were exported to all the kings of the Hittites and the kings of Aram.

Solomon's wives lead him into idolatry

11.1 1 Kgs 3.1; 7.8 9.24 Neh 13.26
11.2 Ex 23.32,33 34.12-14 Deut 7.3,4
11.3 2 Sam 5.13

11 King Solomon loved many foreign women along with the daughter of Pharaoh: Moabite, Ammonite, Edomite, Sidonian, and Hittite women, 2 from the
nations concerning which the LORD had said to the Israelites, "You shall not enter
into marriage with them, neither shall they with you; for they will surely incline
your heart to follow their gods"; Solomon clung to these in love. 3 Among his wives
were seven hundred princesses and three hundred concubines; and his wives turned
away his heart. 4 For when Solomon was old, his wives turned away his heart after
other gods; and his heart was not true to the LORD his God, as was the heart of his

FRIENDS AND ENEMIES
Solomon's reputation brought acclaim and riches from many nations, but he disobeyed God, marrying heathen women and worshiping their idols. So God raised up enemies like Hadad from Edom and Rezin from Zobah (modern-day Syria). Jeroboam from Zeredah was another enemy who would eventually divide this mighty kingdom.

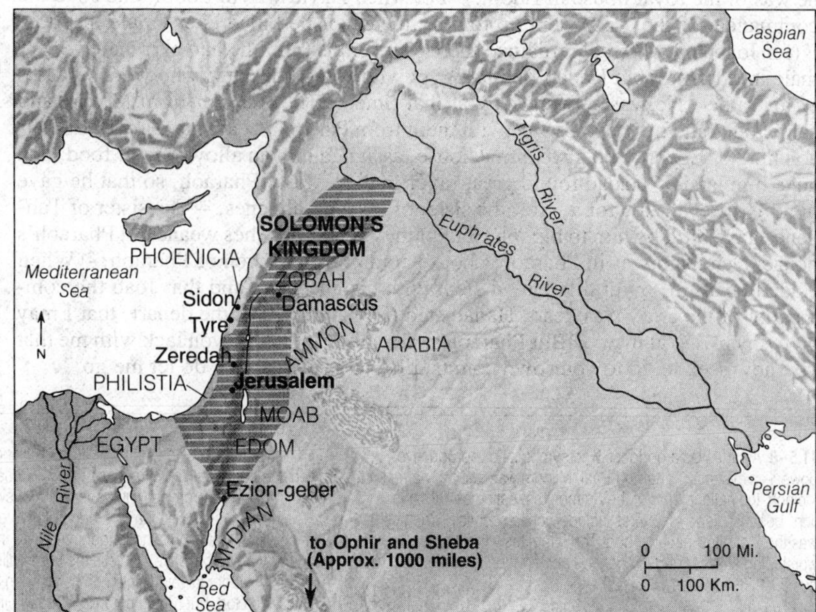

11.3 For all his wisdom, Solomon had some weak spots. He could not say no to compromise or to lustful desires. Whether he married to strengthen political alliances or to gain personal pleasure, these foreign wives led him into idolatry. You may have strong faith, but you also have weak spots—and it is there that temptation usually strikes. Strengthen and protect your weaker areas because a chain is only as strong as its weakest link. If Solomon, the wisest man, could fall, so can you.

11.4 Solomon handled great pressures in running the government, but he could not handle the pressure from his wives who wanted him to worship their gods. In marriage and close friendships, it is difficult to resist pressure to compromise. Our love leads us to identify with the desires of those we care about.

Faced with such pressure, Solomon at first *resisted* it, maintaining pure faith. Then he *tolerated* a more widespread practice of idolatry. Finally he himself became involved in idolatrous worship; he *rationalized* away the potential danger to himself and the kingdom. It is because we naturally wish to please and identify with those we love that God asks us not to marry those who do not share our commitment to him.

father David. 5 For Solomon followed Astarte the goddess of the Sidonians, and
Milcom the abomination of the Ammonites. 6 So Solomon did what was evil in the
sight of the LORD, and did not completely follow the LORD, as his father David had
done. 7 Then Solomon built a high place for Chemosh the abomination of Moab,
and for Molech the abomination of the Ammonites, on the mountain east of Jerusalem. 8 He did the same for all his foreign wives, who offered incense and sacrificed
to their gods.
9 Then the LORD was angry with Solomon, because his heart had turned away
from the LORD, the God of Israel, who had appeared to him twice, 10 and had commanded him concerning this matter, that he should not follow other gods; but he did
not observe what the LORD commanded. 11 Therefore the LORD said to Solomon,
"Since this has been your mind and you have not kept my covenant and my statutes
that I have commanded you, I will surely tear the kingdom from you and give it to
your servant. 12 Yet for the sake of your father David I will not do it in your lifetime;
I will tear it out of the hand of your son. 13 I will not, however, tear away the entire
kingdom; I will give one tribe to your son, for the sake of my servant David and for
the sake of Jerusalem, which I have chosen."

Solomon's adversaries

14 Then the LORD raised up an adversary against Solomon, Hadad the Edomite;
he was of the royal house in Edom. 15 For when David was in Edom, and Joab the
commander of the army went up to bury the dead, he killed every male in Edom
16 (for Joab and all Israel remained there six months, until he had eliminated every
male in Edom); 17 but Hadad fled to Egypt with some Edomites who were servants
of his father. He was a young boy at that time. 18 They set out from Midian and
came to Paran; they took people with them from Paran and came to Egypt, to Pharaoh king of Egypt, who gave him a house, assigned him an allowance of food, and
gave him land. 19 Hadad found great favor in the sight of Pharaoh, so that he gave
him his sister-in-law for a wife, the sister of Queen Tahpenes. 20 The sister of Tahpenes gave birth by him to his son Genubath, whom Tahpenes weaned in Pharaoh's
house; Genubath was in Pharaoh's house among the children of Pharaoh. 21 When
Hadad heard in Egypt that David slept with his ancestors and that Joab the commander of the army was dead, Hadad said to Pharaoh, "Let me depart, that I may
go to my own country." 22 But Pharaoh said to him, "What do you lack with me that
you now seek to go to your own country?" And he said, "No, do let me go."

11.5 Judg 2.12-14
10.6 1 Sam 7.3,4
12.10 1 Kgs 11.33; 2 Kgs 23.13
11.7 Lev 20.2; Num 21.27-30; Judg 11.24; 2 Kgs 23.10,13
11.9 1 Kgs 3.5; 9.2,3
11.11 1 Sam 2.30; 1 Kgs 6.11,12; 11.31
11.12 1 Kgs 21.29
11.15 2 Sam 8.13,14; 1 Chron 18.12
11.16 Num 10.12
11.21 1 Kgs 2.10,34

11.5–8 Astarte was a goddess who symbolized reproductive power—a mistress of the god Baal. Milcom was another name for Molech, the national god of the Ammonites, called an "abomination" because its worship rites included child sacrifice. Chemosh was the Moabites' national god. The Israelites were warned against worshiping all other gods in general and Molech in particular (Exodus 20.1–6; Leviticus 18.21; 20.1–5).

11.6 If Solomon was so wise, why did he turn from God? While Solomon applied his wisdom to political affairs, he did not always apply it to his spiritual life. He knew the right way to live, but he did not always have the will to do it. Many people have enough wisdom to know the difference between right and wrong, but they don't always do right. We need to develop not only the wisdom to do right, but also the *will* to do it.

11.9, 10 Solomon didn't turn away from God all at once or in a brief moment. His spiritual coldness started with a minor departure from God's law (3.1). Over the years, that little sin grew until it resulted in Solomon's downfall. A little sin can be the first step in turning away from God. It is not the sins we don't know about, but the sins we excuse, that cause us the greatest trouble. We must never let any sin go unchallenged. In your life, is an unchallenged sin spreading like a deadly cancer? Don't excuse it. Confess it to God and ask him for strength to resist the temptation.

11.11–13 Solomon's powerful and glorious kingdom could have been blessed for all time; instead, it was approaching its end. Solomon had God's promises, guidance, and answers to prayer, and yet he allowed sin to remain all around him. Eventually it corrupted him so much that he was no longer interested in God. Psalm 127, written by Solomon, says, "Unless the Lord builds the house, those who build it labor in vain." Solomon had begun by laying the foundation with God, but he did not follow through in his later years. As a result he lost everything. It is not enough to get off to a right start in building our marriage, career, or church on God's principles; we must remain faithful to God to the end (Mark 13.13). God must be in control of our lives from start to finish.

11.13 The two tribes of Judah and Benjamin were the only ones to remain loyal to Solomon's son, Rehoboam (12.1ff). Judah and Benjamin were often referred to as one tribe because they shared a border and Benjamin was so small in number.

11.14 God raised up three adversaries against Solomon: Hadad, Rezon, and Jeroboam. Hadad and Rezon were survivors of other armies that David had slaughtered. They were from nations that hated the Israelites. But Jeroboam was from the leading tribe of the norhtern kingdom (Ephraim) and had previously served Solomon in a key position as one of his labor supervisors. The punishment for Solomon's apostasy would not come until after his death, but these opponents served as constant reminders that he owed everything that he accomplished to God.

23 God raised up another adversary against Solomon,[x] Rezon son of Eliada, who had fled from his master, King Hadadezer of Zobah. 24 He gathered followers around him and became leader of a marauding band, after the slaughter by David; they went to Damascus, settled there, and made him king in Damascus. 25 He was an adversary of Israel all the days of Solomon, making trouble as Hadad did; he despised Israel and reigned over Aram.

26 Jeroboam son of Nebat, an Ephraimite of Zeredah, a servant of Solomon, whose mother's name was Zeruah, a widow, rebelled against the king. 27 The following was the reason he rebelled against the king. Solomon built the Millo, and closed up the gap in the wall[y] of the city of his father David. 28 The man Jeroboam was very able, and when Solomon saw that the young man was industrious he gave him charge over all the forced labor of the house of Joseph. 29 About that time, when Jeroboam was leaving Jerusalem, the prophet Ahijah the Shilonite found him on the road. Ahijah had clothed himself with a new garment. The two of them were alone in the open country 30 when Ahijah laid hold of the new garment he was wearing and tore it into twelve pieces. 31 He then said to Jeroboam: Take for yourself ten pieces; for thus says the LORD, the God of Israel, "See, I am about to tear the kingdom from the hand of Solomon, and will give you ten tribes. 32 One tribe will remain his, for the sake of my servant David and for the sake of Jerusalem, the city that I have chosen out of all the tribes of Israel. 33 This is because he has[z] forsaken me, worshiped Astarte the goddess of the Sidonians, Chemosh the god of Moab, and Milcom the god of the Ammonites, and has[z] not walked in my ways, doing what is right in my sight and keeping my statutes and my ordinances, as his father David did. 34 Nevertheless I will not take the whole kingdom away from him but will make him ruler all the days of his life, for the sake of my servant David whom I chose and who did keep my commandments and my statutes; 35 but I will take the kingdom away from his son and give it to you—that is, the ten tribes. 36 Yet to his son I will give one tribe, so that my servant David may always have a lamp before me in Jerusalem, the city where I have chosen to put my name. 37 I will take you, and you shall reign over all that your soul desires; you shall be king over Israel. 38 If you will listen to all that I command you, walk in my ways, and do what is right in my sight by keeping my statutes and my commandments, as David my servant did, I will be with you, and will build you an enduring house, as I built for David, and I will give Israel to you. 39 For this reason I will punish the descendants of David, but not forever." 40 Solomon sought therefore to kill Jeroboam; but Jeroboam promptly fled to Egypt, to King Shishak of Egypt, and remained in Egypt until the death of Solomon.

Solomon's death

41 Now the rest of the acts of Solomon, all that he did as well as his wisdom, are they not written in the Book of the Acts of Solomon? 42 The time that Solomon reigned in Jerusalem over all Israel was forty years. 43 Solomon slept with his ancestors and was buried in the city of his father David; and his son Rehoboam succeeded him.

[x] Heb *him* [y] Heb lacks *in the wall* [z] Gk Syr Vg: Heb *they have*

11.23 2 Sam 8.3 10.15,16
11.24 2 Sam 10.7,8
11.26 1 Kgs 13.1 2 Chron 13.6
11.27 Prov 22.29
11.29 1 Kgs 12.15 14.2 2 Chron 10.15
11.30 1 Sam 15.27
11.31 1 Kgs 11.11
11.33 1 Kgs 11.5,7
11.35 1 Kgs 12.16
11.36 1 Kgs 15.4 2 Kgs 8.19 2 Chron 21.7
11.38 2 Sam 7.11,27 1 Kgs 14.7-9
11.40 1 Kgs 12.2-4 14.25 2 Chron 12.2
11.41 2 Chron 9.29
11.43 2 Chron 9.31

11.29–33 The prophet Ahijah predicted the division of the kingdom of Israel. Ten of Israel's 12 tribes would follow Jeroboam. The other two tribes, Judah and Benjamin, would remain loyal to David. Judah, the largest tribe, and Benjamin, the smallest, were often mentioned as one tribe because they shared the same border. Both Jeroboam and Ahijah were from Ephraim, the most prominent of the ten rebel tribes. (For more on the divided kingdom see the note on 12.20.)

11.40 Why did Solomon want to kill Jeroboam? Evidently, Jeroboam had organized a rebellion against Solomon. While Abijah did say that the Lord would give him 10 of the tribes and that he would rule over them for the rest of his life, this in no way gave him the authority to take the timing of his rule into his own hands. His situation is similar to David's under Saul. While David had been promised the kingdom, he refused to kill Saul, the current king, to get it. But Jerobaom took matters into his own hands, with even less justification than David had. If he had followed the example of Solomon's father, David, he might not have been forced to flee to Egypt.

B. THE DIVIDED KINGDOM (12.1 – 22.53)

After Solomon's death, the northern tribes revolt, forming two separate nations. Each nation experiences disastrous consequences from having evil kings. Elijah appears on the scene, confronting these kings for their sin. God deals with sin in powerful ways. Although judgment may appear to be slow, God will judge evil harshly.

1. Revolt of the northern tribes

Rebellion against Rehoboam

12 Rehoboam went to Shechem, for all Israel had come to Shechem to make 12.1
him king. 2 When Jeroboam son of Nebat heard of it (for he was still in Josh 20.7; 24.1 Judg 9.1,6
Egypt, where he had fled from King Solomon), then Jeroboam returned from[a] 2 Chron 10.1
Egypt. 3 And they sent and called him; and Jeroboam and all the assembly of Israel 12.2 1 Sam 8.18
came and said to Rehoboam, 4 "Your father made our yoke heavy. Now therefore
lighten the hard service of your father and his heavy yoke that he placed on us, and
we will serve you." 5 He said to them, "Go away for three days, then come again to 12.5 1 Kgs 12.12
me." So the people went away.
6 Then King Rehoboam took counsel with the older men who had attended his
father Solomon while he was still alive, saying, "How do you advise me to answer
this people?" 7 They answered him, "If you will be a servant to this people today
and serve them, and speak good words to them when you answer them, then they
will be your servants forever." 8 But he disregarded the advice that the older men
gave him, and consulted with the young men who had grown up with him and now
attended him. 9 He said to them, "What do you advise that we answer this people 12.9
who have said to me, 'Lighten the yoke that your father put on us'?" 10 The young 2 Chron 10.8 18.3-5
men who had grown up with him said to him, "Thus you should say to this people
who spoke to you, 'Your father made our yoke heavy, but you must lighten it for
us'; thus you should say to them, 'My little finger is thicker than my father's loins.
11 Now, whereas my father laid on you a heavy yoke, I will add to your yoke. My
father disciplined you with whips, but I will discipline you with scorpions.' "
12 So Jeroboam and all the people came to Rehoboam the third day, as the king 12.12
had said, "Come to me again the third day." 13 The king answered the people 1 Kgs 12.5
harshly. He disregarded the advice that the older men had given him 14 and spoke 12.15
to them according to the advice of the young men, "My father made your yoke Deut 2.30 Judg 14.4
heavy, but I will add to your yoke; my father disciplined you with whips, but I will 2 Chron 10.15 22.7
discipline you with scorpions." 15 So the king did not listen to the people, because Amos 3.6

[a] Gk Vg Compare 2 Chr 10.2: Heb *lived in*

THE KINGDOM DIVIDES Rehoboam's threat of higher taxes caused a rebellion and divided the nation. Rehoboam ruled the southern kingdom; Jeroboam ruled the northern kingdom. Jeroboam set up idols in Dan and Bethel to discourage worship in Jerusalem. At the same time Syria, Ammon, Moab, and Edom claimed independence from the divided nation.

12.1 Rehoboam was made king at Shechem, about 35 miles north of Jerusalem. It would have been normal to anoint the new king in Jerusalem, the capital city, but Rehoboam saw trouble brewing with Jeroboam and went north to try to maintain good relations with the northern tribes. He probably chose Shechem because it was an ancient location for making covenants (Joshua 24.1). When the kingdom divided, Shechem became the capital of the northern kingdom for a short time (12.25).

12.6–14 Rehoboam asked for advice, but he didn't carefully evaluate that advice. If he had, he would have realized that the advice offered by the older men was wiser than that of his peers. To evaluate advice, ask if it is realistic, workable, and consistent with biblical principles. Determine if the results of following the advice will be fair, make improvements, and give a positive solution or direction. Seek counsel from those more experienced and wiser. Advice is helpful only if we evaluate it with God's standards in mind.

12.15–19 Both Jeroboam and Rehoboam did what was good for themselves, not what was good for their people. Rehoboam was harsh and did not listen to what the people said; Jeroboam established new places of worship to keep his people from traveling to Jerusalem, Rehoboam's capital. Both actions backfired. Rehoboam's move divided the nation, and Jeroboam's turned the people from God. Good leaders put the best interests of the people above their own. Making decisions only for yourself will backfire and cause you to lose more than if you had kept the welfare of others in mind.

it was a turn of affairs brought about by the LORD that he might fulfill his word,
which the LORD had spoken by Ahijah the Shilonite to Jeroboam son of Nebat.
12.16 16 When all Israel saw that the king would not listen to them, the people an-
2 Sam 20.1 swered the king,

"What share do we have in David?
We have no inheritance in the son of Jesse.
To your tents, O Israel!
Look now to your own house, O David."

So Israel went away to their tents. 17 But Rehoboam reigned over the Israelites who
12.18 were living in the towns of Judah. 18 When King Rehoboam sent Adoram, who was
2 Sam 20.24 taskmaster over the forced labor, all Israel stoned him to death. King Rehoboam
12.19 2 Kgs 17.21 then hurriedly mounted his chariot to flee to Jerusalem. 19 So Israel has been in
2 Chron 10.19 rebellion against the house of David to this day.
Isa 7.17 20 When all Israel heard that Jeroboam had returned, they sent and called him
12.20 1 Kgs 12.2-4 to the assembly and made him king over all Israel. There was no one who followed
the house of David, except the tribe of Judah alone.
12.21 21 When Rehoboam came to Jerusalem, he assembled all the house of Judah
2 Chron 11.1 and the tribe of Benjamin, one hundred eighty thousand chosen troops to fight
against the house of Israel, to restore the kingdom to Rehoboam son of Solomon.
12.22 22 But the word of God came to Shemaiah the man of God: 23 Say to King Reho-
2 Chron 11.2 12.5 boam of Judah, son of Solomon, and to all the house of Judah and Benjamin, and
to the rest of the people, 24 "Thus says the LORD, You shall not go up or fight
against your kindred the people of Israel. Let everyone go home, for this thing is
from me." So they heeded the word of the LORD and went home again, according
to the word of the LORD.

Jeroboam leads Israel into idolatry

12.25 25 Then Jeroboam built Shechem in the hill country of Ephraim, and resided
Judg 8.8,17 there; he went out from there and built Penuel. 26 Then Jeroboam said to him-
12.27 Deut 12.4,5 self, "Now the kingdom may well revert to the house of David. 27 If this people

---

TRIBAL JEALOUSIES Although the kingdom of Israel was "united" under David and Solomon, the tensions between north and south were never resolved. The jealousy and animosity behind this civil war didn't begin with Rehoboam and Jeroboam, but had its roots in the days of the judges, when the people were more interested in tribal loyalty than in national unity. Note how easily tension arose between Ephraim, the most prominent tribe in the north, and Judah, the prominent tribe of the south.

- Ephraim claimed the promises in Genesis 48.17–22 and 49.22–26 for its leadership role.
- Joshua, who conquered the promised land, was an Ephraimite (Numbers 13.8).
- Samuel, Israel's greatest judge, was from Ephraim (1 Samuel 1.1ff).
- Ephraim allied with Ishbaal in revolt against David, who was from the tribe of Judah (2 Samuel 2.8–11).
- David, a shepherd from the tribe of Judah, became king over all Israel, including Ephraim, who no longer had a claim to leadership.
- Although David helped to smooth over the bad feelings, the high taxes under Solomon and Rehoboam led the northern tribes to the breaking point.

Such tension developed because Ephraim was the key tribe in the north. They resented Judah's role in leadership under David, and resented that the nation's capital and center of worship were located in Jerusalem.

12.20 This marks the beginning of the division of the kingdom that lasted for centuries. Ten of Israel's 12 tribes followed Jeroboam and called their new nation Israel, or the northern kingdom. The other two tribes remained loyal to Rehoboam and called their nation Judah, or the southern kingdom. The kingdom did not split overnight. It was already dividing as early as the days of the judges because of tribal jealousies, especially between Ephraim, the most influential tribe of the north, and Judah, the chief tribe of the south.

Before the days of Saul and David, the religious center of Israel was located, for the most part, in the territory of Ephraim. When Solomon built the temple, he moved the religious center of Israel to Jerusalem. This eventually brought tribal rivalries to the breaking point. (See Judges 12.1ff; 2 Samuel 2.4ff; 19.41–43.)

continues to go up to offer sacrifices in the house of the LORD at Jerusalem, the heart
of this people will turn again to their master, King Rehoboam of Judah; they will kill
me and return to King Rehoboam of Judah." 28 So the king took counsel, and made **12.28**
two calves of gold. He said to the people,[b] "You have gone up to Jerusalem long Ex 32.4 2 Kgs 10.29
enough. Here are your gods, O Israel, who brought you up out of the land of 2 Chron 11.15 Hos 8.5
Egypt." 29 He set one in Bethel, and the other he put in Dan. 30 And this thing be- **12.29**
came a sin, for the people went to worship before the one at Bethel and before the Gen 28.19; 35.1
other as far as Dan.[c] 31 He also made houses[d] on high places, and appointed priests Judg 20.1
from among all the people, who were not Levites. 32 Jeroboam appointed a festival **12.31** Num 3.10
on the fifteenth day of the eighth month like the festival that was in Judah, and he 2 Kgs 17.32 2 Chron 11.13,
offered sacrifices on the altar; so he did in Bethel, sacrificing to the calves that he 14; 13.9
had made. And he placed in Bethel the priests of the high places that he had made. **12.32** Lev 23.33,34
33 He went up to the altar that he had made in Bethel on the fifteenth day in the
eighth month, in the month that he alone had devised; he appointed a festival for the
people of Israel, and he went up to the altar to offer incense.

2. Kings of Israel and Judah

A prophet dies for disobedience

13 While Jeroboam was standing by the altar to offer incense, a man of God **13.1**
came out of Judah by the word of the LORD to Bethel 2 and proclaimed 2 Kgs 23.17 **13.2**
against the altar by the word of the LORD, and said, "O altar, altar, thus says the 2 Kgs 23.15,16
LORD: 'A son shall be born to the house of David, Josiah by name; and he shall
sacrifice on you the priests of the high places who offer incense on you, and human
bones shall be burned on you.' " 3 He gave a sign the same day, saying, "This is the **13.3**
sign that the LORD has spoken: 'The altar shall be torn down, and the ashes that are 2 Kgs 20.8
on it shall be poured out.' " 4 When the king heard what the man of God cried out
against the altar at Bethel, Jeroboam stretched out his hand from the altar, saying,
"Seize him!" But the hand that he stretched out against him withered so that he
could not draw it back to himself. 5 The altar also was torn down, and the ashes
poured out from the altar, according to the sign that the man of God had given by
the word of the LORD. 6 The king said to the man of God, "Entreat now the favor of **13.6**
the LORD your God, and pray for me, so that my hand may be restored to me." So Ex 8.8,28; 9.28 Jer 37.3
the man of God entreated the LORD; and the king's hand was restored to him, and Acts 8.24
became as it was before. 7 Then the king said to the man of God, "Come home with **13.7** 1 Sam 9.7
me and dine, and I will give you a gift." 8 But the man of God said to the king, "If 2 Kgs 5.15

[b] Gk: Heb *to them* [c] Compare Gk: Heb *went to the one as far as Dan* [d] Gk Vg Compare 13.32: Heb *a house*

12.28 All Jewish men were required to travel to the temple three times each year (Deuteronomy 16.16), but Jeroboam set up his own worship centers and told his people it was too much trouble to travel all the way to Jerusalem. Those who obeyed Jeroboam were disobeying God. Some ideas, though practical, may include suggestions that lead you away from God. Don't let anyone talk you out of doing what is right by telling you that moral actions are not worth the effort. Do what God wants no matter what the cost in time, energy, reputation, or resources.

12.28, 29 Jeroboam shrewdly placed his calf idols in Bethel and Dan, strategic locations. Bethel was just ten miles north of Jerusalem on the main road, enticing the citizens from the north to stop there instead of traveling the rest of the way to Jerusalem. Dan was the northernmost city in Israel, so people living in the north far from Jerusalem were attracted to its convenient location. As leader of the northern kingdom, Jeroboam wanted to establish his own worship centers; otherwise his people would make regular trips to Jerusalem, and his authority would be undermined. Soon this substitute religion had little in common with true faith in God.

12.30 Jeroboam and his advisors did not learn from Israel's previous disaster with a calf idol (Exodus 32). Perhaps they were ignorant of Scripture, or maybe they knew about the event and decided to ignore it. Study the Bible to become aware of God's acts in history, and then apply the important lessons to your life. If you learn from the past, you will not face disaster as a result of repeating others' mistakes (Isaiah 42.23; 1 Corinthians 10.11).

12.32, 33 Jeroboam's feast was probably an imitation of the festival of booths, a harvest celebration. Jeroboam set the feast one month later because the harvest was several weeks later in the far north than in the south. More important, Jeroboam wanted to differentiate Israel's worship from Judah's. He hoped his new feast would replace the feast in Jerusalem and encourage his people to stay in their own land to worship. His real motives were political, not religious. Don't rush to support everything "religious." Unscrupulous leaders still use religious customs for political advantage.

12.32, 33 In the days of Israel's founding fathers, the city of Bethel was a symbol of commitment to God, because it was there that Jacob had rededicated himself to God (Genesis 28.16–22). But Jeroboam turned the city into Israel's chief religious center, intending it to compete with Jerusalem. Bethel's religion, however, centered on an idol, and this led to Israel's eventual downfall. Bethel developed a reputation as a wicked and idolatrous city. The prophets Hosea and Amos recognized the sins of Bethel and condemned the city for its godless ways (Hosea 4.15–17; 10.8; Amos 5.4–6).

13.2 Three hundred years later, this prophecy was fulfilled in every detail when Josiah killed the pagan priests at their own altars. The story is found in 2 Kings 23.1–20.

you give me half your kingdom, I will not go in with you; nor will I eat food or
13.9 Num 22.18 24.13 drink water in this place. [9]For thus I was commanded by the word of the LORD: You
shall not eat food, or drink water, or return by the way that you came." [10]So he
went another way, and did not return by the way that he had come to Bethel.
11 Now there lived an old prophet in Bethel. One of his sons came and told him all that the man of God had done that day in Bethel; the words also that he had spoken to the king, they told to their father.
[12]Their father said to them, "Which

JEROBOAM

Even clear warnings are hard to obey. The Bible is filled with stories of people who had direction from God and yet chose their own way. Their disobedience was rarely due to ignorance of what God wanted; rather, it grew out of stubborn selfishness. Jeroboam was a consistent example of this all-too-human trait.

During the construction of Fort Millo, Solomon noticed young Jeroboam's natural leadership skills and made him a special project foreman. Shortly after this, God contacted Jeroboam through the prophet Ahijah. He told Jeroboam that God would punish David's dynasty by tearing the kingdom from Solomon's son and that Jeroboam would rule the ten northern tribes. And God made it clear that the same fate would destroy Jeroboam's family if they refused to obey God. Apparently Solomon heard about these events and tried to have Jeroboam killed. The future king escaped to Egypt, where he stayed until Solomon died.

When Rehoboam, Solomon's heir, took the throne, Jeroboam returned. He represented the people in demanding that the new king be more lenient than his father. Rehoboam's unwise choice to reject his people's request led to their rejecting him as king. Only Judah and the annexed tribe of Benjamin remained loyal to David's dynasty. The other ten tribes made Jeroboam king.

Rather than seeing this fulfillment of God's promise as motivation to obey God, Jeroboam decided to do whatever he could to secure his position. He led his kingdom away from the God who had allowed him to reign. God had already warned him of the consequences of this action—his family was eventually wiped out. And Jeroboam set into motion events that would lead to the destruction of the northern kingdom.

Sin's consequences are guaranteed in God's Word, but the timing of those consequences is hard to predict. When we do something directly opposed to God's commands and there isn't immediate disaster, we are often fooled into believing we got away with disobedience. But that is a dangerous assumption. Jeroboam's life should make us recognize our frequent need to admit our disobedience and ask God to forgive us.

Strengths and accomplishments:
- An effective leader and organizer
- First king of the ten tribes of Israel in the divided kingdom
- A charismatic leader with much popular support

Weaknesses and mistakes:
- Erected idols in Israel to keep people away from the temple in Jerusalem
- Appointed priests from outside the tribe of Levi
- Depended more on his own cunning than on God's promises

Lessons from his life:
- Great opportunities are often destroyed by small decisions
- Careless efforts to correct another's errors often lead to the same errors
- Mistakes always occur when we attempt to take over God's role in a situation

Vital statistics:
- Where: The northern kingdom of Israel
- Occupation: Project foreman, king of Israel
- Relatives: Father: Nebat. Mother: Zeruah. Sons: Abijah, Nadab
- Contemporaries: Solomon, Nathan, Ahijah, Rehoboam

Key verses:
"Even after this event Jeroboam did not turn from his evil way, but made priests for the high places again from among all the people; any who wanted to be priests he consecrated for the high places. This matter became sin to the house of Jeroboam, so as to cut it off and to destroy it from the face of the earth" (1 Kings 13.33, 34).

Jeroboam's story is told in 1 Kings 11.26—14.20. He is also mentioned in 2 Chronicles 10—13.

13.7–32 This prophet had been given strict orders from God not to eat or drink anything while on his mission (13.9). He died because he listened to a man who claimed to have a message from God, rather than listening to God himself. This prophet should have followed God's Word instead of hearsay. Trust what God's Word says rather than what someone claims is true. Disregard what others claim to be messages from God if their words contradict the Bible.

way did he go?" And his sons showed him the way that the man of God who came
from Judah had gone. 13 Then he said to his sons, "Saddle a donkey for me." So
they saddled a donkey for him, and he mounted it. 14 He went after the man of God,
and found him sitting under an oak tree. He said to him, "Are you the man of God
who came from Judah?" He answered, "I am." 15 Then he said to him, "Come home
with me and eat some food." 16 But he said, "I cannot return with you, or go in with
you; nor will I eat food or drink water with you in this place; 17 for it was said to me
by the word of the LORD: You shall not eat food or drink water there, or return by
the way that you came." 18 Then the other[e] said to him, "I also am a prophet as you
are, and an angel spoke to me by the word of the LORD: Bring him back with you
into your house so that he may eat food and drink water." But he was deceiving
him. 19 Then the man of God[e] went back with him, and ate food and drank water
in his house.

20 As they were sitting at the table, the word of the LORD came to the prophet
who had brought him back; 21 and he proclaimed to the man of God who came from **13.21**
Judah, "Thus says the LORD: Because you have disobeyed the word of the LORD, 1 Sam 15.26
and have not kept the commandment that the LORD your God commanded you,
22 but have come back and have eaten food and drunk water in the place of which
he said to you, 'Eat no food, and drink no water,' your body shall not come to your
ancestral tomb." 23 After the man of God[e] had eaten food and had drunk, they
saddled for him a donkey belonging to the prophet who had brought him back.
24 Then as he went away, a lion met him on the road and killed him. His body was **13.24**
thrown in the road, and the donkey stood beside it; the lion also stood beside the 1 Kgs 20.36
body. 25 People passed by and saw the body thrown in the road, with the lion standing by the body. And they came and told it in the town where the old prophet lived.

26 When the prophet who had brought him back from the way heard of it, he
said, "It is the man of God who disobeyed the word of the LORD; therefore the LORD
has given him to the lion, which has torn him and killed him according to the word
that the LORD spoke to him." 27 Then he said to his sons, "Saddle a donkey for me."
So they saddled one, 28 and he went and found the body thrown in the road, with the
donkey and the lion standing beside the body. The lion had not eaten the body or
attacked the donkey. 29 The prophet took up the body of the man of God, laid it on
the donkey, and brought it back to the city,[f] to mourn and to bury him. 30 He laid
the body in his own grave; and they mourned over him, saying, "Alas, my
brother!" 31 After he had buried him, he said to his sons, "When I die, bury me in **13.31**
the grave in which the man of God is buried; lay my bones beside his bones. 32 For 2 Kgs 23.17
the saying that he proclaimed by the word of the LORD against the altar in Bethel,
and against all the houses of the high places that are in the cities of Samaria, shall
surely come to pass."

33 Even after this event Jeroboam did not turn from his evil way, but made **13.33** 2 Chron 13.9
priests for the high places again from among all the people; any who wanted to be **13.34**
priests he consecrated for the high places. 34 This matter became sin to the house of 1 Kgs 14.10 15.29
Jeroboam, so as to cut it off and to destroy it from the face of the earth. 2 Kgs 17.21

God's judgment on Jeroboam

14 At that time Abijah son of Jeroboam fell sick. 2 Jeroboam said to his wife, **14.2**
"Go, disguise yourself, so that it will not be known that you are the wife of 1 Sam 28.7,8 2 Sam 14.2,3
Jeroboam, and go to Shiloh; for the prophet Ahijah is there, who said of me that I 2 Chron 18.29

[e] Heb *he* [f] Gk: Heb *he came to the town of the old prophet*

13.24, 25 Lions are mentioned frequently in the Old Testament. They were common enough to be a threat both to people and to their flocks. Samson (Judges 14.5, 6), David (1 Samuel 17.34–37), and Benaiah (2 Samuel 23.20) all faced wild lions.

13.33, 34 Under penalty of death, God had forbidden anyone to be a priest who was not from the tribe of Levi (Numbers 3.10). Levites were assured of lifetime support from the tithe, so they did not have to spend time farming, worrying about tribal interests, or fearing for their financial futures. Jeroboam's new priests were financed by the king and his fees. They had to mix priestly and secular duties, and they quickly fell into party politics. Because they didn't have job security, they were easily corrupted by bribes. Jeroboam's disobedience was the downfall of true religion in the northern kingdom.

14.3 1 Sam 9.7,8; 2 Kgs 4.42
14.4 1 Sam 3.2,3; 4.15
14.7 1 Kgs 11.28,31; 12.20
14.8 1 Kgs 11.30,33; 15.5
14.9 Ex 34.17; 1 Kgs 13.33; 2 Chron 11.15; Ps 50.17; Ezek 23.35
14.10 1 Kgs 21.22; 2 Kgs 9.8
14.11 1 Kgs 16.4-7; 21.24
14.12 1 Kgs 14.17
14.14 1 Kgs 15.27,29

should be king over this people. 3 Take with you ten loaves, some cakes, and a jar
of honey, and go to him; he will tell you what shall happen to the child."
4 Jeroboam's wife did so; she set out and went to Shiloh, and came to the house
of Ahijah. Now Ahijah could not see, for his eyes were dim because of his age.
5 But the LORD said to Ahijah, "The wife of Jeroboam is coming to inquire of you
concerning her son; for he is sick. Thus and thus you shall say to her."
When she came, she pretended to be another woman. 6 But when Ahijah heard
the sound of her feet, as she came in at the door, he said, "Come in, wife of Jeroboam; why do you pretend to be another? For I am charged with heavy tidings for
you. 7 Go, tell Jeroboam, 'Thus says the LORD, the God of Israel: Because I exalted
you from among the people, made you leader over my people Israel, 8 and tore the
kingdom away from the house of David to give it to you; yet you have not been like
my servant David, who kept my commandments and followed me with all his
heart, doing only that which was right in my sight, 9 but you have done evil above
all those who were before you and have gone and made for yourself other gods, and
cast images, provoking me to anger, and have thrust me behind your back; 10 therefore, I will bring evil upon the house of Jeroboam. I will cut off from Jeroboam
every male, both bond and free in Israel, and will consume the house of Jeroboam,
just as one burns up dung until it is all gone. 11 Anyone belonging to Jeroboam who
dies in the city, the dogs shall eat; and anyone who dies in the open country, the
birds of the air shall eat; for the LORD has spoken.' 12 Therefore set out, go to your
house. When your feet enter the city, the child shall die. 13 All Israel shall mourn
for him and bury him; for he alone of Jeroboam's family shall come to the grave,
because in him there is found something pleasing to the LORD, the God of Israel, in
the house of Jeroboam. 14 Moreover the LORD will raise up for himself a king over
Israel, who shall cut off the house of Jeroboam today, even right now![g]

g Meaning of Heb uncertain

THE APPEAL OF IDOLS

On the surface, the lives of the kings don't make sense. How could they run to idolatry so fast when they had God's word (at least some of it), prophets, and the example of David? Here are some of the reasons for the enticement of idols:

	The appeal of Idols	*Modern parallel*
POWER	The people wanted freedom from the authority of both God and the priests. They wanted religion to fit their life-style, not have their life-style fit their religion.	People do not want to answer to a greater authority. Instead of having power *over* others, God wants us to have the Holy Spirit's power to *help* others.
PLEASURE	Idol worship exalted sensuality without responsibility or guilt. People acted out the vicious and sensuous personalities of the gods they worshiped, thus gaining approval for their degraded lives.	People deify pleasure, seeking it at the expense of everything else. Instead of seeking pleasure that leads to long-range disaster, God calls us to seek the kind of pleasure that leads to long-range rewards.
PASSION	Mankind was reduced to little more than animals. The people did not have to be viewed as unique individuals, but could be exploited sexually, politically, and economically.	Like animals, people let physical drives and passion rule them. Instead of seeking passion that exploits others, God calls us to redirect our passions to areas that build others up.
PRAISE AND POPULARITY	The high and holy nature of God was replaced by gods who were more a reflection of human nature, thus more culturally suitable to the people. These gods no longer required sacrifice, just a token of appeasement.	Sacrifice is seen as self-inflicted punishment, making no sense. Success is to be sought at all costs. Instead of seeking praise for ourselves, God calls us to praise him and those who honor him.

As societies change, they often throw out norms and values no longer considered necessary or acceptable. Believers must be careful not to follow society's example if it discards God's Word. When society does that, only godlessness and evil remain.

15 "The LORD will strike Israel, as a reed is shaken in the water; he will root up
Israel out of this good land that he gave to their ancestors, and scatter them beyond
the Euphrates, because they have made their sacred poles,[h] provoking the LORD to
anger. 16 He will give Israel up because of the sins of Jeroboam, which he sinned
and which he caused Israel to commit."

17 Then Jeroboam's wife got up and went away, and she came to Tirzah. As
she came to the threshold of the house, the child died. 18 All Israel buried him and
mourned for him, according to the word of the LORD, which he spoke by his servant
the prophet Ahijah.

19 Now the rest of the acts of Jeroboam, how he warred and how he reigned,
are written in the Book of the Annals of the Kings of Israel. 20 The time that Jeroboam reigned was twenty-two years; then he slept with his ancestors, and his son
Nadab succeeded him.

Rehoboam rules Judah

21 Now Rehoboam son of Solomon reigned in Judah. Rehoboam was forty-one
years old when he began to reign, and he reigned seventeen years in Jerusalem, the
city that the LORD had chosen out of all the tribes of Israel, to put his name there.
His mother's name was Naamah the Ammonite. 22 Judah did what was evil in the
sight of the LORD; they provoked him to jealousy with their sins that they committed, more than all that their ancestors had done. 23 For they also built for themselves
high places, pillars, and sacred poles[h] on every high hill and under every green
tree; 24 there were also male temple prostitutes in the land. They committed all the
abominations of the nations that the LORD drove out before the people of Israel.

25 In the fifth year of King Rehoboam, King Shishak of Egypt came up against
Jerusalem; 26 he took away the treasures of the house of the LORD and the treasures
of the king's house; he took everything. He also took away all the shields of gold
that Solomon had made; 27 so King Rehoboam made shields of bronze instead, and
committed them to the hands of the officers of the guard, who kept the door of the
king's house. 28 As often as the king went into the house of the LORD, the guard
carried them and brought them back to the guardroom.

29 Now the rest of the acts of Rehoboam, and all that he did, are they not written in the Book of the Annals of the Kings of Judah? 30 There was war between
Rehoboam and Jeroboam continually. 31 Rehoboam slept with his ancestors and
was buried with his ancestors in the city of David. His mother's name was Naamah
the Ammonite. His son Abijam succeeded him.

Abijam rules Judah

15 Now in the eighteenth year of King Jeroboam son of Nebat, Abijam began
to reign over Judah. 2 He reigned for three years in Jerusalem. His mother's
name was Maacah daughter of Abishalom. 3 He committed all the sins that his father did before him; his heart was not true to the LORD his God, like the heart of his
father David. 4 Nevertheless for David's sake the LORD his God gave him a lamp in

14.15 Ex 34.17 Deut 12.3 1 Sam 12.25 Ps 52.5
14.17 1 Kgs 15.21 16.9
14.19 1 Kgs 14.29 15.7,23,31 16.4-7,14,20 1 Chron 9.1
14.21 1 Kgs 11.32,36 2 Kgs 21.7 2 Chron 12.13
14.22 2 Chron 12.1,14
14.23 Deut 16.22 2 Kgs 17.10 Jer 2.20 Ezek 16.24
14.24 Deut 23.17,18 2 Kgs 23.7
14.25 2 Chron 12.2,9
14.26 1 Kgs 7.51 10.16,17; 15.18
14.30 1 Kgs 15.6 2 Chron 12.15
15.1 2 Chron 13.1
15.3 1 Kgs 11.4
15.4 2 Chron 21.7

[h] Heb *Asherim*

14.15 "Made their sacred poles" refers to idol worship. Wooden images were "planted" for worship of Asherah, a Canaanite mother-goddess.

14.19 Three books are mentioned in 1 and 2 Kings – the chronicles of the kings of Israel (14.19), the chronicles of the kings of Judah (14.29), and the acts of Solomon (11.41). These historical records of Israel and Judah were the main sources of material God directed the author to use to write 1 and 2 Kings. No copies of these books have been found.

14.25 When Rehoboam came to power, he inherited a mighty kingdom. Everything he could ever want was handed over to him. But apparently he did not recognize why he had so much or how it had been obtained. To teach Rehoboam a lesson, God allowed King Shishak of Egypt to invade Judah and Israel. Egypt was no longer the world power it had once been, and Shishak, possibly resenting Solomon's enormous success, was determined to change that. Shishak's army was not strong enough to destroy Judah and Israel, but he weakened them so much that they were never the same again.

14.25 Just five years after Solomon died, the temple and palace were ransacked by foreign invaders. How quickly the glory, power, and money disappeared! When the people became spiritually corrupt and immoral (14.24), it was just a short time until they lost everything. Wealth, idol worship, and immorality had become more important to them than God. When God is gone from our lives, everything else becomes useless, no matter how valuable it seems.

15.1 Abijam is called Abijah in 2 Chronicles 13.1.

15.4 Despite their many sins, the descendants of David were often

Jerusalem, setting up his son after him, and establishing Jerusalem; 5 because David did what was right in the sight of the LORD, and did not turn aside from anything
that he commanded him all the days of his life, except in the matter of Uriah the
Hittite. 6 The war begun between Rehoboam and Jeroboam continued all the days
of his life. 7 The rest of the acts of Abijam, and all that he did, are they not written
in the Book of the Annals of the Kings of Judah? There was war between Abijam
and Jeroboam. 8 Abijam slept with his ancestors, and they buried him in the city of
David. Then his son Asa succeeded him.

Asa rules Judah

9 In the twentieth year of King Jeroboam of Israel, Asa began to reign over
Judah; 10 he reigned forty-one years in Jerusalem. His mother's name was Maacah
daughter of Abishalom. 11 Asa did what was right in the sight of the LORD, as his
father David had done. 12 He put away the male temple prostitutes out of the land,
and removed all the idols that his ancestors had made. 13 He also removed his
mother Maacah from being queen mother, because she had made an abominable
image for Asherah; Asa cut down her image and burned it at the Wadi Kidron.
14 But the high places were not taken away. Nevertheless the heart of Asa was true
to the LORD all his days. 15 He brought into the house of the LORD the votive gifts
of his father and his own votive gifts—silver, gold, and utensils.

16 There was war between Asa and King Baasha of Israel all their days. 17 King
Baasha of Israel went up against Judah, and built Ramah, to prevent anyone from
going out or coming in to King Asa of Judah. 18 Then Asa took all the silver and the

15.5 2 Sam 11.4,15; 1 Kgs 9.4; 14.8
15.7 2 Chron 13.1,2
15.8 1 Chron 3.10-14; 2 Chron 14.1
15.11 2 Chron 14.2; 15.17
15.12 Deut 23.17,18; 1 Kgs 22.46; 2 Chron 15.3
15.13 2 Chron 15.16
15.14 1 Kgs 22.43; 2 Kgs 12.3; 14.4
15.15 1 Kgs 14.27
15.17 2 Chron 16.1

KINGS TO DATE AND THEIR ENEMIES

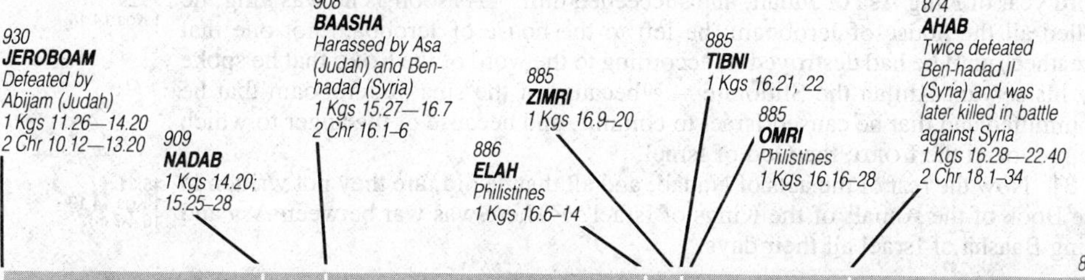

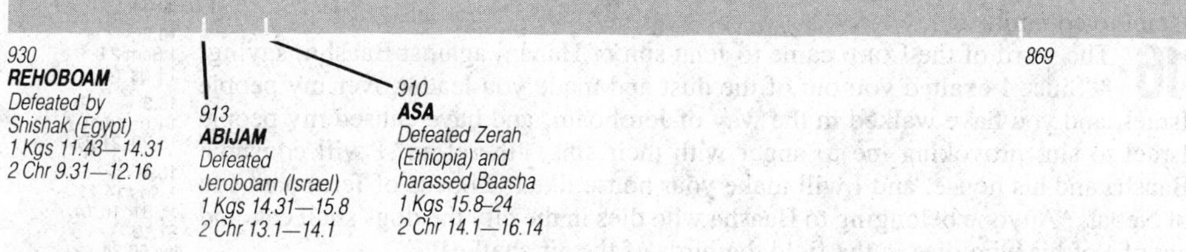

All dates are B.C.
For all the kings of Israel and Judah, see the chart at the end of 1 Kings.

blessed by God "for David's sake." At times we may wonder whether our lives make a difference in the world. After all, life is so short. But there is a ripple effect—our children, grandchildren, and great-grandchildren can be affected by our decisions and actions. Watch how you live and determine to keep your heart in tune with God (15.3) as David did. There's no telling whom your life will affect.

15.5 See 2 Samuel 11 for the story of David and Uriah.

15.9 See Asa's Profile in 2 Chronicles 15 for more information on this king.

15.15 These votive gifts were articles devoted to God as sacred offerings that Abijam (Abijah) had taken in his war with Jeroboam (2 Chronicles 13.16, 17), and Asa had taken when he defeated the Ethiopians (2 Chronicles 14.12, 13).

15.16 Baasha seized the throne from Nadab (15.27, 28), who had replaced his father, Jeroboam, as king.

gold that were left in the treasures of the house of the LORD and the treasures of the 15.18
king's house, and gave them into the hands of his servants. King Asa sent them to 1 Kgs 14.26 20.1-5
King Ben-hadad son of Tabrimmon son of Hezion of Aram, who resided in Damas- 2 Kings 12.18
cus, saying, 19 "Let there be an alliance between me and you, like that between my 15.19 2 Chron 16.7
father and your father: I am sending you a present of silver and gold; go, break your
alliance with King Baasha of Israel, so that he may withdraw from me." 20 Ben-
hadad listened to King Asa, and sent the commanders of his armies against the
cities of Israel. He conquered Ijon, Dan, Abel-beth-maacah, and all Chinneroth,
with all the land of Naphtali. 21 When Baasha heard of it, he stopped building Ra- 15.21
mah and lived in Tirzah. 22 Then King Asa made a proclamation to all Judah, none 2 Chron 16.5
was exempt: they carried away the stones of Ramah and its timber, with which 15.22 2 Chron 16.6
Baasha had been building; with them King Asa built Geba of Benjamin and Mizpah. 23 Now the rest of all the acts of Asa, all his power, all that he did, and the 15.23
cities that he built, are they not written in the Book of the Annals of the Kings of 1 Kgs 15.7,31 2 Chron 16.11
Judah? But in his old age he was diseased in his feet. 24 Then Asa slept with his 15.24
ancestors, and was buried with his ancestors in the city of his father David; his son 1 Kgs 22.41 2 Chron 16.13,
Jehoshaphat succeeded him. 14; 17.1

Nadab rules Israel

25 Nadab son of Jeroboam began to reign over Israel in the second year of King 15.25
Asa of Judah; he reigned over Israel two years. 26 He did what was evil in the sight 1 Kgs 14.20
of the LORD, walking in the way of his ancestor and in the sin that he caused Israel 15.26 1 Kgs 12.28
to commit. 13.33; 14.16
27 Baasha son of Ahijah, of the house of Issachar, conspired against him; and 15.27
Baasha struck him down at Gibbethon, which belonged to the Philistines; for Na- Josh 21.23,24
dab and all Israel were laying siege to Gibbethon. 28 So Baasha killed Nadab[i] in the
third year of King Asa of Judah, and succeeded him. 29 As soon as he was king, he 15.29
killed all the house of Jeroboam; he left to the house of Jeroboam not one that 1 Kgs 14.14
breathed, until he had destroyed it, according to the word of the LORD that he spoke
by his servant Ahijah the Shilonite— 30 because of the sins of Jeroboam that he
committed and that he caused Israel to commit, and because of the anger to which
he provoked the LORD, the God of Israel.
31 Now the rest of the acts of Nadab, and all that he did, are they not written in 15.31
the Book of the Annals of the Kings of Israel? 32 There was war between Asa and 1 Kgs 14.19 16.4-7,14
King Baasha of Israel all their days.

Baasha rules Israel

33 In the third year of King Asa of Judah, Baasha son of Ahijah began to reign
over all Israel at Tirzah; he reigned twenty-four years. 34 He did what was evil in the 16.1
sight of the LORD, walking in the way of Jeroboam and in the sin that he caused 1 Kgs 16.12 2 Chron 19.2
Israel to commit. 20.34
16 The word of the LORD came to Jehu son of Hanani against Baasha, saying, 16.2 1 Sam 2.8
2 "Since I exalted you out of the dust and made you leader over my people 1 Kgs 14.7
Israel, and you have walked in the way of Jeroboam, and have caused my people 16.3 1 Kgs 14.10
Israel to sin, provoking me to anger with their sins, 3 therefore, I will consume 15.29; 21.21
Baasha and his house, and I will make your house like the house of Jeroboam son 16.4 1 Kgs 14.11
of Nebat. 4 Anyone belonging to Baasha who dies in the city the dogs shall eat; and 15.31; 16.14 21.19
anyone of his who dies in the field the birds of the air shall eat." Isa 66.24

[i] Heb *him*

15.29 See 1 Kings 14.12–14 for Ahijah's prediction of this event.

15.30 All the descendants of Jeroboam were killed because he led Israel into sin. Sin is always judged harshly, but the worst sinners are those who lead others into sin. Jesus said it would be better if such people had millstones tied around their necks and were thrown into the sea (Mark 9.42). If you have taken the responsibility of leading others, remember the consequences of leading them astray. Teaching the truth is a responsibility that goes hand in hand with the privilege of leadership.

16.1–7 God destroyed Jeroboam's descendants for their flagrant sins, and yet Baasha repeated the same mistakes. He did not learn from the example of those who went before him; he did not stop to think that his sin would be punished. Make sure you learn the lessons from your own past, the lives of others, and the lives of those whose stories are told in the Bible. Don't repeat mistakes.

5 Now the rest of the acts of Baasha, what he did, and his power, are they not
written in the Book of the Annals of the Kings of Israel? 6 Baasha slept with his
ancestors, and was buried at Tirzah; and his son Elah succeeded him. 7 Moreover
the word of the LORD came by the prophet Jehu son of Hanani against Baasha and
his house, both because of all the evil that he did in the sight of the LORD, provoking him to anger with the work of his hands, in being like the house of Jeroboam,
and also because he destroyed it.

Elah rules Israel

8 In the twenty-sixth year of King Asa of Judah, Elah son of Baasha began to
reign over Israel in Tirzah; he reigned two years. 9 But his servant Zimri, commander of half his chariots, conspired against him. When he was at Tirzah, drinking himself drunk in the house of Arza, who was in charge of the palace at Tirzah,
10 Zimri came in and struck him down and killed him, in the twenty-seventh year of
King Asa of Judah, and succeeded him.
11 When he began to reign, as soon as he had seated himself on his throne, he
killed all the house of Baasha; he did not leave him a single male of his kindred or
his friends. 12 Thus Zimri destroyed all the house of Baasha, according to the word
of the LORD, which he spoke against Baasha by the prophet Jehu— 13 because of all
the sins of Baasha and the sins of his son Elah that they committed, and that they
caused Israel to commit, provoking the LORD God of Israel to anger with their
idols. 14 Now the rest of the acts of Elah, and all that he did, are they not written in
the Book of the Annals of the Kings of Israel?

16.9 2 Kgs 9.31
16.11 1 Kgs 14.10 15.29
16.12 1 Kgs 16.1
16.13 Deut 32.21 1 Kgs 15.30
16.14 1 Kgs 16.4-7,20, 28,30

Zimri rules Israel

15 In the twenty-seventh year of King Asa of Judah, Zimri reigned seven days
in Tirzah. Now the troops were encamped against Gibbethon, which belonged to
the Philistines, 16 and the troops who were encamped heard it said, "Zimri has conspired, and he has killed the king"; therefore all Israel made Omri, the commander
of the army, king over Israel that day in the camp. 17 So Omri went up from Gibbethon, and all Israel with him, and they besieged Tirzah. 18 When Zimri saw that the
city was taken, he went into the citadel of the king's house; he burned down the
king's house over himself with fire, and died— 19 because of the sins that he committed, doing evil in the sight of the LORD, walking in the way of Jeroboam, and for
the sin that he committed, causing Israel to sin. 20 Now the rest of the acts of Zimri,
and the conspiracy that he made, are they not written in the Book of the Annals of
the Kings of Israel?

16.18 1 Sam 31.4,5 2 Sam 17.23
16.19 1 Kgs 12.28 14.6
16.20 1 Kgs 16.14,27

Omri rules Israel

21 Then the people of Israel were divided into two parts; half of the people
followed Tibni son of Ginath, to make him king, and half followed Omri. 22 But the
people who followed Omri overcame the people who followed Tibni son of Ginath;
so Tibni died, and Omri became king. 23 In the thirty-first year of King Asa of
Judah, Omri began to reign over Israel; he reigned for twelve years, six of them in
Tirzah.
24 He bought the hill of Samaria from Shemer for two talents of silver; he fortified the hill, and called the city that he built, Samaria, after the name of Shemer,
the owner of the hill.

16.24 1 Kgs 13.32 18.2 Jn 4.4

16.21, 22 Omri began his reign as political dissension brewed in Israel. After Zimri killed himself, the Israelite army chose Omri, their general, as the next ruler. To eliminate opposition, Omri killed his chief rival to the throne, Tibni, and then began his evil reign. During his 12-year rule over Israel, he was a shrewd and capable leader. He organized the building of his new capital city, Samaria, while strengthening the nation politically and militarily. But he did not care about the nation's spiritual condition (Micah 6.16), and he purposely led Israel farther from God in order to put more power in his own hands.

16.24 Omri's new capital, Samaria, offered some political advantages. The city was his personal property, so he had total control over it. Samaria also commanded a hilltop position, which made it easy to defend. Omri died before completing the city. So his son, Ahab, completed it, building not only the beautiful ivory palace (1 Kings 22.39; Amos 3.13–15), but also a temple to the god Baal. Samaria served as the capital city for the rest of Israel's dynasties until it fell to the Assyrians in 722 B.C. (2 Kings 17.5).

25 Omri did what was evil in the sight of the LORD; he did more evil than all
who were before him. 26 For he walked in all the way of Jeroboam son of Nebat,
and in the sins that he caused Israel to commit, provoking the LORD, the God of
Israel, to anger by their idols. 27 Now the rest of the acts of Omri that he did, and
the power that he showed, are they not written in the Book of the Annals of the
Kings of Israel? 28 Omri slept with his ancestors, and was buried in Samaria; his son
Ahab succeeded him.

16.25 1 Kgs 14.9 Mic 6.16
16.26 1 Kgs 13.33,34
16.27 1 Kgs 16.20 22.39
16.28 2 Chron 18.1

Ahab rules Israel

29 In the thirty-eighth year of King Asa of Judah, Ahab son of Omri began to
reign over Israel; Ahab son of Omri reigned over Israel in Samaria twenty-two
years. 30 Ahab son of Omri did evil in the sight of the LORD more than all who were
before him.
31 And as if it had been a light thing for him to walk in the sins of Jeroboam son
of Nebat, he took as his wife Jezebel daughter of King Ethbaal of the Sidonians,
and went and served Baal, and worshiped him. 32 He erected an altar for Baal in the
house of Baal, which he built in Samaria. 33 Ahab also made a sacred pole.[j] Ahab
did more to provoke the anger of the LORD, the God of Israel, than had all the kings
of Israel who were before him. 34 In his days Hiel of Bethel built Jericho; he laid its
foundation at the cost of Abiram his firstborn, and set up its gates at the cost of his
youngest son Segub, according to the word of the LORD, which he spoke by Joshua
son of Nun.

16.31 Deut 7.3,4 1 Kgs 11.5 2 Kgs 10.18 17.16
16.32 2 Kgs 10.21,26
16.33 1 Kgs 21.19,25 2 Kgs 13.6
16.34 Josh 6.26

3. Elijah's ministry

Elijah predicts drought

17 Now Elijah the Tishbite, of Tishbe[k] in Gilead, said to Ahab, "As the LORD
the God of Israel lives, before whom I stand, there shall be neither dew nor
rain these years, except by my word." 2 The word of the LORD came to him, saying,
3 "Go from here and turn eastward, and hide yourself by the Wadi Cherith, which
is east of the Jordan. 4 You shall drink from the wadi, and I have commanded the

17.1 Judg 12.4 1 Kgs 22.14 Lk 4.25 Jas 5.17
17.4 1 Kgs 19.5

[j] Heb *Asherah* [k] Gk: Heb *of the settlers*

16.31 Ahab's evil wife, Jezebel, came from the Phoenician city of Tyre where her father had been a high priest and eventually king. Jezebel worshiped the god Baal. In order to please her, Ahab built a temple and an altar for Baal (16.32), thus promoting idolatry and leading the entire nation into sin. (For more about Baal, see the note on 18.18.)

17.1 Elijah was one of the first in a long line of important prophets God sent to Israel and Judah. Israel, the northern kingdom, had no faithful kings throughout its history. Each king was wicked, actually leading the people in worshiping heathen gods. There were few priests left from the tribe of Levi (most had gone to Judah), and the priests appointed by Israel's kings were corrupt and ineffective. With no king or priests to bring God's Word to the people, God called prophets to try to rescue Israel from its moral and spiritual decline. For the next 300 years these men and women would play vital roles in both nations, encouraging the people and leaders to turn back to God.

17.1 Those who worshiped Baal believed he was the god who brought the rains and bountiful harvests. So when Elijah walked into the presence of this Baal-worshiping king and told him there would be no rain for several years, Ahab was shocked. Ahab had built a strong military defense, but it would be no help against drought. He had many Baal priests, but they could not bring rain. Elijah bravely confronted the man who led his people into evil, and he told of a power far greater than any heathen god—the Lord God of Israel. When rebellion and heresy were at an all-time high in Israel, God responded not only with words but also with action.

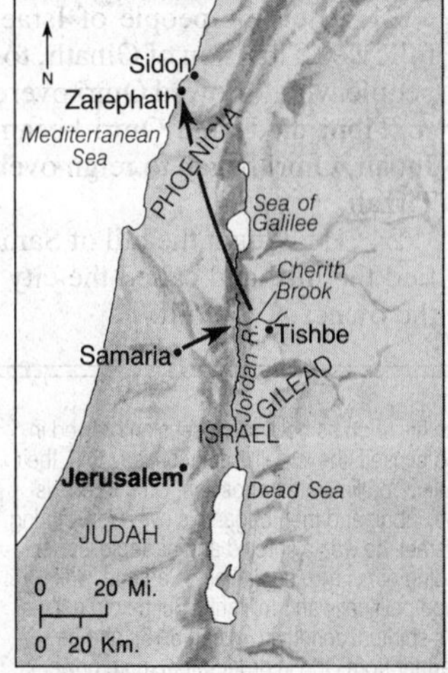

ELIJAH HIDES FROM AHAB
Elijah prophesied a drought and then hid from King Ahab by the Cherith Brook where he was fed by ravens. When the brook dried up, God sent him to Zarephath in Phoenicia where a widow and her son fed him and gave him lodging.

ravens to feed you there." 5 So he went and did according to the word of the LORD;
he went and lived by the Wadi Cherith, which is east of the Jordan. 6 The ravens
brought him bread and meat in the morning, and bread and meat in the evening; and
he drank from the wadi. 7 But after a while the wadi dried up, because there was no
rain in the land.

Elijah miraculously supplies food

17.8 Obad 20 8 Then the word of the LORD came to him, saying, 9 "Go now to Zarephath,
Lk 4.25,26 which belongs to Sidon, and live there; for I have commanded a widow there to
17.10 Gen 24.17 feed you." 10 So he set out and went to Zarephath. When he came to the gate of the
Jn 4.7 town, a widow was there gathering sticks; he called to her and said, "Bring me a
little water in a vessel, so that I may drink." 11 As she was going to bring it, he
17.12 2 Kgs 4.2 called to her and said, "Bring me a morsel of bread in your hand." 12 But she said,
Mt 15.33 "As the LORD your God lives, I have nothing baked, only a handful of meal in a jar,
and a little oil in a jug; I am now gathering a couple of sticks, so that I may go home
and prepare it for myself and my son, that we may eat it, and die." 13 Elijah said to
her, "Do not be afraid; go and do as you have said; but first make me a little cake
of it and bring it to me, and afterwards make something for yourself and your son.
14 For thus says the LORD the God of Israel: The jar of meal will not be emptied and
the jug of oil will not fail until the day that the LORD sends rain on the earth." 15 She
went and did as Elijah said, so that she as well as he and her household ate for many
days. 16 The jar of meal was not emptied, neither did the jug of oil fail, according
to the word of the LORD that he spoke by Elijah.

Elijah restores a boy to life

17 After this the son of the woman, the mistress of the house, became ill; his
illness was so severe that there was no breath left in him. 18 She then said to Elijah,
"What have you against me, O man of God? You have come to me to bring my sin
to remembrance, and to cause the death of my son!" 19 But he said to her, "Give me
your son." He took him from her bosom, carried him up into the upper chamber
where he was lodging, and laid him on his own bed. 20 He cried out to the LORD,
17.21 "O LORD my God, have you brought calamity even upon the widow with whom I
2 Kgs 4.34 Acts 20.10-12 am staying, by killing her son?" 21 Then he stretched himself upon the child three
17.23 times, and cried out to the LORD, "O LORD my God, let this child's life come into
2 Kgs 4.36 Lk 7.15 him again." 22 The LORD listened to the voice of Elijah; the life of the child came
Acts 9.41 Heb 11.35 into him again, and he revived. 23 Elijah took the child, brought him down from the
17.24 upper chamber into the house, and gave him to his mother; then Elijah said, "See,
Jn 2.11; 3.1,2 your son is alive." 24 So the woman said to Elijah, "Now I know that you are a man
11.15 of God, and that the word of the LORD in your mouth is truth."

17.10ff In a nation that was required by law to care for its prophets, it is ironic that God turned to ravens (unclean birds) and a widow (a foreigner from Jezebel's home territory) to care for Elijah. God has help where we least expect it. He provides for us in ways that go beyond our narrow definitions or expectations. No matter how bitter our trials or how seemingly hopeless our situation, we should look for God's caring touch. We may find his providence in some strange places!

17.13–16 When the widow of Zarephath met Elijah, she thought she was preparing her last meal. But a simple act of faith produced a miracle. She trusted Elijah and gave him all she had to eat. Faith is the step between promise and assurance. Miracles seem so out of reach for our feeble faith. But every miracle, large or small, begins with an act of obedience. We may not see the solution until we take the first step of faith.

17.17 Even when God has done a miracle in our lives, our troubles may not be over. The famine was a terrible experience, but the worst was yet to come. God's provision is never given in order to let us rest upon it. We need to depend on him as each new trial faces us.

17.22 This was not a terrible sickness that made it look as if the boy had died, but an actual death. The woman supposed that this was caused by her own sin. But like the man born blind, this tragedy was not the result of the sin of the parents, nor of the son, but happened so that the glory of God might be revealed (John 9.3). By raising this child from the dead, Elijah showed himself as a forerunner of Christ, who will raise all believers from the dead at the resurrection.

17.24 Chapter 17 presents Elijah's credentials in order to establish the authority of his ministry.

Elijah rebukes King Ahab

18 After many days the word of the LORD came to Elijah, in the third year of the 18.1
drought,[l] saying, "Go, present yourself to Ahab; I will send rain on the Jas 5.18
earth." 2So Elijah went to present himself to Ahab. The famine was severe in Sa- 18.2
maria. 3Ahab summoned Obadiah, who was in charge of the palace. (Now Oba- 1 Kgs 16.24
diah revered the LORD greatly; 4when Jezebel was killing off the prophets of the 18.3 1 Kgs 18.16
LORD, Obadiah took a hundred prophets, hid them fifty to a cave, and provided
them with bread and water.) 5Then Ahab said to Obadiah, "Go through the land to
all the springs of water and to all the wadis; perhaps we may find grass to keep the
horses and mules alive, and not lose some of the animals." 6So they divided the
land between them to pass through it; Ahab went in one direction by himself, and
Obadiah went in another direction by himself.
7 As Obadiah was on the way, Elijah met him; Obadiah recognized him, fell on
his face, and said, "Is it you, my lord Elijah?" 8He answered him, "It is I. Go, tell
your lord that Elijah is here." 9And he said, "How have I sinned, that you would
hand your servant over to Ahab, to kill me? 10As the LORD your God lives, there is
no nation or kingdom to which my lord has not sent to seek you; and when they
would say, 'He is not here,' he would require an oath of the kingdom or nation, that
they had not found you. 11But now you say, 'Go, tell your lord that Elijah is here.'
12As soon as I have gone from you, the spirit of the LORD will carry you I know not 18.12
where; so, when I come and tell Ahab and he cannot find you, he will kill me, 2 Kgs 2.16 Ezek 3.12
although I your servant have revered the LORD from my youth. 13Has it not been Acts 8.39
told my lord what I did when Jezebel killed the prophets of the LORD, how I hid a 18.13
hundred of the LORD's prophets fifty to a cave, and provided them with bread and 1 Kgs 18.3,4
water? 14Yet now you say, 'Go, tell your lord that Elijah is here'; he will surely kill
me." 15Elijah said, "As the LORD of hosts lives, before whom I stand, I will surely
show myself to him today." 16So Obadiah went to meet Ahab, and told him; and
Ahab went to meet Elijah.
17 When Ahab saw Elijah, Ahab said to him, "Is it you, you troubler of Israel?" 18.17
18He answered, "I have not troubled Israel; but you have, and your father's house, Josh 7.25
because you have forsaken the commandments of the LORD and followed the Baals. 18.18 1 Kgs 9.9; 21.25
19Now therefore have all Israel assemble for me at Mount Carmel, with the four 2 Chron 15.5
hundred fifty prophets of Baal and the four hundred prophets of Asherah, who eat
at Jezebel's table."

[l] Heb lacks *of the drought*

18.3, 4 Although Elijah was alone in his confrontation with Ahab and Jezebel, he was not the only one in Israel who believed in God. Obadiah had been faithful in hiding 100 prophets still true to the Lord.

18.5 A wadi is a stream or dry streambed.

18.18 Instead of worshiping the true God, Ahab and his wife Jezebel worshiped Baal, the most popular Canaanite god. Baal idols were often made in the shape of a bull, representing strength and fertility and reflecting lust for power and sexual pleasure.

18.19 Ahab brought 850 heathen prophets to Mount Carmel to match wits and power with Elijah. These prophets were also called priests because they were in charge of the heathen religious culture. Evil kings hated God's prophets because they spoke against sin and idolatry and undermined their control over the people. With the wicked kings' backing, many heathen prophets sprang up to counter the words of God's prophets. But Elijah showed the people that speaking a prophecy wasn't enough. One needed the power of a living God to fulfill it.

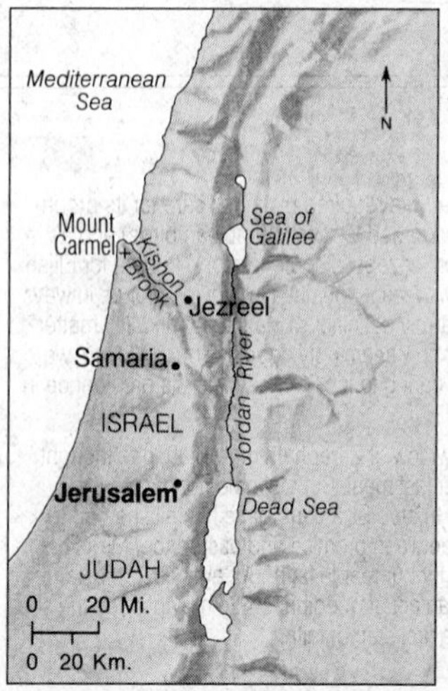

THE SHOWDOWN AT CARMEL
In a showdown with the false prophets of Baal at Mount Carmel, Elijah set out to prove to evil Ahab that only the Lord is God. Elijah then killed the false prophets beside the Kishon Brook and fled back to Jezreel.

Elijah's triumphs over the evil prophets

20 So Ahab sent to all the Israelites, and assembled the prophets at Mount Carmel. 21 Elijah then came near to all the people, and said, "How long will you go
limping with two different opinions? If the LORD is God, follow him; but if Baal,
then follow him." The people did not answer him a word. 22 Then Elijah said to the

18.21 Josh 24.15; 2 Kgs 17.41; Zeph 1.5

ELIJAH

Elijah's single-minded commitment to God shocks and challenges us. He was sent to confront, not comfort, and he spoke God's words to a king who often rejected his message just because he brought it. Elijah chose to carry out his ministry for God alone and paid for that decision by experiencing isolation from others who were also faithful to God.

It is interesting to think about the amazing miracles God accomplished through Elijah, but we would do well to focus on the relationship they shared. All that happened in Elijah's life began with the same miracle that is available to us—he responded to the miracle of being able to know God.

For example, after God worked an overwhelming miracle through Elijah in defeating the prophets of Baal, Queen Jezebel retaliated by threatening Elijah's life. And Elijah ran. He felt afraid, depressed, and abandoned. Despite God's provision of food and shelter in the desert, Elijah wanted to die. So God presented Elijah with an "audio-visual display" and a message he needed to hear. Elijah witnessed a windstorm, an earthquake, and fire. But the Lord was not in any of those powerful things. Instead, God displayed his presence in the sound of silence.

Elijah, like us, struggled with his feelings even after this comforting message from God. So God confronted Elijah's emotions and commanded action. He told Elijah what to do next and informed him that part of his loneliness was based on ignorance: 7,000 others in Israel were still faithful to God.

Even today, God often speaks through the quiet and obvious rather than the spectacular and unusual. God has work for us to do even when we feel fear and failure. And God always has more resources and people than we know about. Although we might wish to do amazing miracles for God, we should instead focus on developing a relationship with him. The real miracle of Elijah's life was his very personal relationship with God. And that miracle is available to us.

Strengths and accomplishments:
- Was the most famous and dramatic of Israel's prophets
- Predicted the beginning and end of a three-year drought
- Was used by God to restore a dead child to his mother
- Represented God in a showdown with priests of Baal and Asherah
- Appeared with Moses and Jesus in the New Testament transfiguration scene

Weaknesses and mistakes:
- Chose to work alone and paid for it with isolation and loneliness
- Fled in fear from Jezebel when she threatened his life

Lessons from his life:
- We are never closer to defeat than in our moments of greatest victory
- We are never as alone as we may feel; God is always there
- God speaks more frequently in persistent whispers than in shouts

Vital statistics:
- Where: Gilead
- Occupation: Prophet
- Contemporaries: Ahab, Jezebel, Ahaziah, Obadiah, Jehu, Hazael

Key verses:
"At the time of the offering of the oblation, the prophet Elijah came near and said, 'O Lord, God of Abraham, Isaac, and Israel, let it be known this day that you are God in Israel, that I am your servant, and that I have done all these things at your bidding. Answer me, O Lord, answer me, so that this people may know that you, O Lord, are God, and that you have turned their hearts back.' Then the fire of the Lord fell and consumed the burnt offering, the wood, the stones, and the dust, and even licked up the water that was in the trench" (1 Kings 18.36–38).

Elijah's story is told in 1 Kings 17.1—2 Kings 2.11. He is also mentioned in 2 Chronicles 21.12–15; Malachi 4.5, 6; Matthew 11.14; 16.14; 17.3–13; 27.47–49; Luke 1.17; 4.25, 26; John 1.19–25; Romans 11.2–4; James 5.17, 18.

18.21 Elijah challenged the people to take a stand – to follow whoever was the true God. Why did so many people waver between the two choices? Perhaps some were not sure. Many, however, knew that the Lord was God, but they enjoyed the sinful pleasures and other benefits that came with following Ahab in his idolatrous worship. It is important to take a stand for the Lord. If we just drift along with whatever is pleasant and easy, we will someday discover that we have been worshiping a false god – ourselves.

people, "I, even I only, am left a prophet of the LORD; but Baal's prophets number
four hundred fifty. 23 Let two bulls be given to us; let them choose one bull for
themselves, cut it in pieces, and lay it on the wood, but put no fire to it; I will
prepare the other bull and lay it on the wood, but put no fire to it. 24 Then you call
on the name of your god and I will call on the name of the LORD; the god who
answers by fire is indeed God." All the people answered, "Well spoken!" 25 Then
Elijah said to the prophets of Baal, "Choose for yourselves one bull and prepare it
first, for you are many; then call on the name of your god, but put no fire to it." 26 So
they took the bull that was given them, prepared it, and called on the name of Baal
from morning until noon, crying, "O Baal, answer us!" But there was no voice,
and no answer. They limped about the altar that they had made. 27 At noon Elijah
mocked them, saying, "Cry aloud! Surely he is a god; either he is meditating, or he
has wandered away, or he is on a journey, or perhaps he is asleep and must be
awakened." 28 Then they cried aloud and, as was their custom, they cut themselves
with swords and lances until the blood gushed out over them. 29 As midday passed,
they raved on until the time of the offering of the oblation, but there was no voice,
no answer, and no response.

30 Then Elijah said to all the people, "Come closer to me"; and all the people
came closer to him. First he repaired the altar of the LORD that had been thrown
down; 31 Elijah took twelve stones, according to the number of the tribes of the sons
of Jacob, to whom the word of the LORD came, saying, "Israel shall be your name";
32 with the stones he built an altar in the name of the LORD. Then he made a trench
around the altar, large enough to contain two measures of seed. 33 Next he put the
wood in order, cut the bull in pieces, and laid it on the wood. He said, "Fill four jars
with water and pour it on the burnt offering and on the wood." 34 Then he said, "Do
it a second time"; and they did it a second time. Again he said, "Do it a third time";
and they did it a third time, 35 so that the water ran all around the altar, and filled the
trench also with water.

36 At the time of the offering of the oblation, the prophet Elijah came near and
said, "O LORD, God of Abraham, Isaac, and Israel, let it be known this day that you
are God in Israel, that I am your servant, and that I have done all these things at
your bidding. 37 Answer me, O LORD, answer me, so that this people may know
that you, O LORD, are God, and that you have turned their hearts back." 38 Then the
fire of the LORD fell and consumed the burnt offering, the wood, the stones, and the

18.22 1 Kgs 19.10,14
18.24 1 Sam 7.5; 1 Chron 21.26
18.26 Ps 115.5; Jer 10.5; 1 Cor 12.2
18.28 Lev 19.28; Deut 14.1
18.30 1 Kgs 19.10,14
18.31 Josh 4.2,3
18.33 Gen 22.9
18.36 Ex 3.6; 4.5; Num 16.28; 1 Sam 17.46; 2 Kgs 19.19; 1 Chron 29.18
18.38 Gen 15.17; Lev 9.24; 10.1; 2 Kgs 1.12; Job 1.16

PROPHETS—FALSE AND TRUE

False Prophets	*True Prophets*
Worked for political purposes to benefit themselves	Worked for spiritual purposes to serve God and the people
Held positions of great wealth	Owned little or nothing
Gave false messages	Spoke only true messages
Spoke only what the people wanted to hear	Spoke only what God told them to say—no matter how unpopular

The false prophets were an obstacle to bringing God's Word to the people. They would bring messages that contradicted the words of the true prophets. They gave "messages" that appealed to the people's sinful natures and comforted their fears. False prophets told people what they wanted to hear. True prophets told God's truth.

18.29 Although the prophets of Baal raved all afternoon, no one answered them. The time of the offering of the oblation was the time of the evening sacrifice. Their god was silent because it was not real. The gods we may be tempted to follow are not idols of wood or stone, but they are just as false and dangerous because they cause us to depend on something other than God. Power, status, appearance, or material possessions can become our gods if we devote our lives to them. But when we reach times of crisis and desperately call out to these gods, there will be only silence. They can offer no true answers, no guidance, and no wisdom.

18.31 Using the 12 stones to build the altar took some courage on Elijah's part. This would have angered some of the people because it was a silent reminder of the split between the tribes. While the tribes of the north called themselves Israel, it was a name originally given to all 12 of the tribes.

18.36–38 Just as God flashed fire from heaven for Elijah, he will help us accomplish what he commands us to do. The proof may not be as dramatic in our lives as in Elijah's, but God will make resources available to us in creative ways to accomplish his purposes. He will give us the wisdom to raise a family, the courage to take a stand for truth, or the means to provide help for someone in need. Like Elijah, we can have faith that, whatever God commands us to do, he will provide what we need to carry it through.

18.39 1 Kgs 8.60 dust, and even licked up the water that was in the trench. 39 When all the people saw
it, they fell on their faces and said, "The LORD indeed is God; the LORD indeed is
18.40 Deut 13.5; 18.20 God." 40 Elijah said to them, "Seize the prophets of Baal; do not let one of them
2 Kgs 10.24 escape." Then they seized them; and Elijah brought them down to the Wadi Kishon, and killed them there.

Elijah prays for rain

18.41-45 Jas 5.18 41 Elijah said to Ahab, "Go up, eat and drink; for there is a sound of rushing
rain." 42 So Ahab went up to eat and to drink. Elijah went up to the top of Carmel;
there he bowed himself down upon the earth and put his face between his knees.
43 He said to his servant, "Go up now, look toward the sea." He went up and
looked, and said, "There is nothing." Then he said, "Go again seven times." 44 At
the seventh time he said, "Look, a little cloud no bigger than a person's hand is
rising out of the sea." Then he said, "Go say to Ahab, 'Harness your chariot and go
down before the rain stops you.' " 45 In a little while the heavens grew black with
clouds and wind; there was a heavy rain. Ahab rode off and went to Jezreel. 46 But
the hand of the LORD was on Elijah; he girded up his loins and ran in front of Ahab
to the entrance of Jezreel.

Elijah flees for his life

19 Ahab told Jezebel all that Elijah had done, and how he had killed all the
19.2 prophets with the sword. 2 Then Jezebel sent a messenger to Elijah, saying,
2 Kgs 6.31 "So may the gods do to me, and more also, if I do not make your life like the life
19.3 of one of them by this time tomorrow." 3 Then he was afraid; he got up and fled for
Gen 21.31 Amos 7.12 his life, and came to Beer-sheba, which belongs to Judah; he left his servant there.
19.4 4 But he himself went a day's journey into the wilderness, and came and sat
Num 11.5 Job 3.20,21 down under a solitary broom tree. He asked that he might die: "It is enough; now,
Jer 20.14 Jonah 4.3,8 O LORD, take away my life, for I am no better than my ancestors." 5 Then he lay
down under the broom tree and fell asleep. Suddenly an angel touched him and said
to him, "Get up and eat." 6 He looked, and there at his head was a cake baked on hot
stones, and a jar of water. He ate and drank, and lay down again. 7 The angel of the
LORD came a second time, touched him, and said, "Get up and eat, otherwise the
19.8 Ex 3.1; 4.27 journey will be too much for you." 8 He got up, and ate and drank; then he went in
24.18; 34.28 Deut 9.9 the strength of that food forty days and forty nights to Horeb the mount of God. 9 At
Mt 4.2 that place he came to a cave, and spent the night there.

God speaks to Elijah

Then the word of the LORD came to him, saying, "What are you doing here,

---

18.46 Elijah ran the six miles back to the city in order to give Ahab a last chance to turn from his sin before joining Jezebel in Jezreel. "Girded up his loins" means he pulled up his robe and tucked it into his belt so that he could run faster. His run also insured that the correct story of what had happened would reach Jezreel.

19.2 Jezebel was enraged about the death of her prophets because they had told her everything *she* wanted to hear, prophesying her future power and glory. Their job was to deify the king and queen and help perpetuate their kingdom. Jezebel was also angry because her supporters had been eliminated and her pride and authority damaged. The money she had invested in these prophets was now lost.

Elijah, who caused the prophets' deaths, was a constant thorn in Jezebel's side because he was always predicting gloom and doom. Because she could not control his actions, she vowed to kill him. As long as God's prophet was around, she could not carry out all the evil she wanted.

19.3ff Elijah experienced the depths of fatigue and discouragement just after his two great spiritual victories: the defeat of the prophets of Baal and the answered prayer for rain. Often discouragement sets in after great spiritual experiences, especially those requiring physical effort or producing emotional excitement. To lead him out of depression, God first let Elijah rest and eat. Then God confronted him with the need to return to his mission – to speak God's words in Israel. Elijah's battles were not over; there was still work for him to do. When you feel let down after a great spiritual experience, remember that God's purpose for your life is not yet over.

19.8 When Elijah fled to Mount Horeb, he was returning to the sacred place where God met Moses and gave his laws to the people. Obviously, God gave Elijah special strength to travel this great distance – over 200 miles – without additional food. Like Moses before him and Jesus after him, Elijah fasted for 40 days and 40 nights (Deuteronomy 9.9; Matthew 4.1, 2). Centuries later, Moses, Elijah, and Jesus would meet together on a mountaintop (Luke 9.28–36).

Elijah?" 10 He answered, "I have been very zealous for the LORD, the God of hosts; **19.10**
for the Israelites have forsaken your covenant, thrown down your altars, and killed Rom 11.2,3
your prophets with the sword. I alone am left, and they are seeking my life, to take
it away."
11 He said, "Go out and stand on the mountain before the LORD, for the LORD **19.11**
is about to pass by." Now there was a great wind, so strong that it was splitting Ex 19.16,19,20 24.12
mountains and breaking rocks in pieces before the LORD, but the LORD was not in Ezek 1.4
the wind; and after the wind an earthquake, but the LORD was not in the earthquake;
12 and after the earthquake a fire, but the LORD was not in the fire; and after the fire **19.12**
a sound of sheer silence. 13 When Elijah heard it, he wrapped his face in his mantle Ex 3.2,6 Deut 4.11
and went out and stood at the entrance of the cave. Then there came a voice to him Job 4.16
that said, "What are you doing here, Elijah?" 14 He answered, "I have been very
zealous for the LORD, the God of hosts; for the Israelites have forsaken your covenant, thrown down your altars, and killed your prophets with the sword. I alone am
left, and they are seeking my life, to take it away." 15 Then the LORD said to him, **19.15**
"Go, return on your way to the wilderness of Damascus; when you arrive, you shall 2 Kgs 8.8
anoint Hazael as king over Aram. 16 Also you shall anoint Jehu son of Nimshi as **19.16**
king over Israel; and you shall anoint Elisha son of Shaphat of Abel-meholah as 2 Kgs 2.9; 9.1
prophet in your place. 17 Whoever escapes from the sword of Hazael, Jehu shall **19.17** 2 Kgs 8.12,13
kill; and whoever escapes from the sword of Jehu, Elisha shall kill. 18 Yet I will 9.14; 13.3
leave seven thousand in Israel, all the knees that have not bowed to Baal, and every **19.18**
mouth that has not kissed him." Hos 13.2 Rom 11.4

Elisha follows Elijah

19 So he set out from there, and found Elisha son of Shaphat, who was plow- **19.19**
ing. There were twelve yoke of oxen ahead of him, and he was with the twelfth. 2 Kgs 2.8,13,14
Elijah passed by him and threw his mantle over him. 20 He left the oxen, ran after
Elijah, and said, "Let me kiss my father and my mother, and then I will follow

---

ELIJAH FLEES FROM JEZEBEL
After killing Baal's prophets, Elijah ran from the furious Queen Jezebel. He fled to Beer-sheba, then into the wilderness, and finally to Mount Horeb (Sinai). There, like Moses centuries earlier, he talked with God.

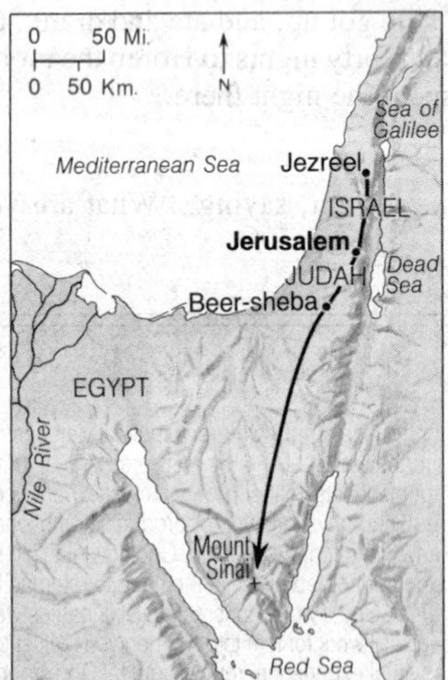

19.10 Elijah thought he was the only person left who was still true to God. He had seen both the king's court and the priesthood become corrupt. After experiencing great victory at Mount Carmel, he had to run for his life. Lonely and discouraged, he forgot that others had remained faithful during the nation's wickedness. When you are tempted to feel you are the only one remaining faithful to a task, don't stop to feel sorry for yourself. Self-pity will dilute the good you are doing. Be assured that even if you don't know who they are, others are faithfully obeying God and fulfilling their duties.

19.11–13 Elijah knew that the sound of sheer silence was God's voice. He realized that God doesn't reveal himself only in powerful, miraculous ways. To look for God only in something big (rallies, churches, conferences, highly visible leaders) may be to miss him, because he is often found gently whispering in the quietness of a humbled heart. Are you listening for God? Step back from the noise and activity of your busy life and listen humbly and quietly for his guidance. It may come when you least expect it.

19.15, 16 God asked Elijah to anoint three different people. The first was Hazael, as king of Syria. Elijah was told to anoint an enemy king because God was going to use Syria as his instrument to punish Israel for its sin. Syria brought Israel's *external* punishment.

Israel's *internal* punishment came from Jehu, the next man Elijah was to anoint. As king of Israel, Jehu would destroy those who worshiped the false god Baal (2 Kings 9; 10).

The third person Elijah was told to anoint was Elisha, the prophet who would succeed him. Elisha's job was to work in Israel, the northern kingdom, and help point the people back to God. The southern kingdom at this time was ruled by Jehoshaphat, a king devoted to God.

19.18 Kissing Baal meant kissing some object representing him to show loyalty to him.

19.19 The mantle, or coat, was the most important article of clothing a person could own. It was used as protection against the weather, as bedding, as a place to sit, and as luggage. It could be given as a pledge for a debt or torn into pieces to show grief. Elijah put his mantle on Elisha's shoulders to show that he would become Elijah's successor. Later, when the transfer of authority was complete, Elijah left his mantle for Elisha (2 Kings 2.11–14).

you." Then Elijah[m] said to him, "Go back again; for what have I done to you?"
21 He returned from following him, took the yoke of oxen, and slaughtered them;
using the equipment from the oxen, he boiled their flesh, and gave it to the people,
and they ate. Then he set out and followed Elijah, and became his servant.

[m] Heb *he*

AHAB

The kings of Israel and Judah, both good and evil, had prophets sent by God to advise, confront, and aid them. King David had a faithful friend in God's prophet, Nathan; Ahab could have had an equally faithful friend in Elijah. But while David listened to Nathan and was willing to repent of his sins, Ahab saw Elijah as his enemy. Why? Because Elijah always brought bad news to Ahab, and Ahab refused to acknowledge that it was his own constant disobedience to God and persistent idol worship, not Elijah's prophecies, that brought the evil on his nation. He blamed Elijah for bringing the prophecies of judgment, rather than taking his advice and changing his evil ways.

Ahab was trapped by his own choices, and he was unwilling to take the right action. As king, he was responsible to God and his prophet Elijah, but he was married to an evil woman who drew him into idol worship. He was a childish man who brooded for days if unable to get his own way. He took his evil wife's advice, listened only to the "prophets" who gave good news, and surrounded himself with people who encouraged him to do whatever he wanted. But the value of advice cannot be judged by the number of people for or against it. Ahab consistently chose to follow the majority opinion of those who surrounded him, and that led to his death.

It may seem nice to have someone encourage us to do whatever we want, because advice that goes against our wishes is difficult to accept. However, our decisions must be based on the quality of the advice, not its attractiveness or the majority opinion of our peers. God encourages us to get advice from wise counselors, but how can we test the advice we receive? Advice that agrees with the principles in God's word is reliable. We must always separate advice from our own desires, the majority opinion, or whatever seems best in our limited perspective, and weigh it against God's commands. He will never lead us to do what he has forbidden in his Word—even in principle. Unlike Ahab, we should trust godly counselors and have the courage to stand against those who would have us do otherwise.

Strengths and accomplishments:
- Seventh king of Israel
- Capable leader and military strategist

Weaknesses and mistakes:
- Was the most evil king of Israel
- Married Jezebel, a heathen woman, and allowed her to promote Baal worship
- Brooded about not being able to get a piece of land, and so his wife had its owner, Naboth, killed
- Was used to getting his own way, and got depressed when he didn't

Lessons from his life:
- The choice of a mate will have a significant effect on life—physically, spiritually, and emotionally
- Selfishness, left unchecked, can lead to great evil

Vital statistics:
- Where: Northern kingdom of Israel
- Occupation: King
- Relatives: Wife: Jezebel. Father: Omri. Sons: Ahaziah, Jehoram
- Contemporaries: Elijah, Naboth, Jehu, Benhadad, Jehoshaphat

Key verses:
"Ahab son of Omri did evil in the sight of the Lord more than all who were before him. . . . He took as his wife Jezebel, daughter of King Ethbaal of the Sidonians, and went and served Baal, and worshiped him. He erected an altar for Baal in the house of Baal, which he built in Samaria. Ahab also made a sacred pole. Ahab did more to provoke the anger of the Lord, the God of Israel, than had all the kings of Israel who were before him" (1 Kings 16.30–33).

Ahab's story is told in 1 Kings 16.28—22.40. He is also mentioned in 2 Chronicles 18—22; Micah 6.16.

19.21 By killing his oxen, Elisha made a strong commitment to follow Elijah. Without them, he could not return to his life as a wealthy farmer. This meal was more than a feast among farmers. It was an offering of thanks to the Lord who chose Elisha to be his prophet.

God gives Israel victory over the Arameans

20 King Ben-hadad of Aram gathered all his army together; thirty-two kings 20.1
were with him, along with horses and chariots. He marched against Sa- 2 Kgs 6.24
maria, laid siege to it, and attacked it. 2 Then he sent messengers into the city to 20.2
King Ahab of Israel, and said to him: "Thus says Ben-hadad: 3 Your silver and gold 1 Kgs 15.18 2 Chron 16.2
are mine; your fairest wives and children also are mine." 4 The king of Israel
answered, "As you say, my lord, O king, I am yours, and all that I have." 5 The
messengers came again and said: "Thus says Ben-hadad: I sent to you, saying,
'Deliver to me your silver and gold, your wives and children'; 6 nevertheless I will
send my servants to you tomorrow about this time, and they shall search your house
and the houses of your servants, and lay hands on whatever pleases them,[n] and
take it away."
7 Then the king of Israel called all the elders of the land, and said, "Look now!
See how this man is seeking trouble; for he sent to me for my wives, my children,
my silver, and my gold; and I did not refuse him." 8 Then all the elders and all the
people said to him, "Do not listen or consent." 9 So he said to the messengers of
Ben-hadad, "Tell my lord the king: All that you first demanded of your servant I
will do; but this thing I cannot do." The messengers left and brought him word
again. 10 Ben-hadad sent to him and said, "The gods do so to me, and more also, if 20.10
the dust of Samaria will provide a handful for each of the people who follow me." 1 Kgs 19.2 2 Kgs 6.31
11 The king of Israel answered, "Tell him: One who puts on armor should not brag 20.11
like one who takes it off." 12 When Ben-hadad heard this message—now he had Prov 27.1
been drinking with the kings in the booths—he said to his men, "Take your positions!" And they took their positions against the city.
13 Then a certain prophet came up to King Ahab of Israel and said, "Thus says 20.13
the LORD, Have you seen all this great multitude? Look, I will give it into your hand 2 Kgs 6.8-10
today; and you shall know that I am the LORD." 14 Ahab said, "By whom?" He said,
"Thus says the LORD, By the young men who serve the district governors." Then he
said, "Who shall begin the battle?" He answered, "You." 15 Then he mustered the
young men who serve the district governors, two hundred thirty-two; after them he
mustered all the people of Israel, seven thousand.
16 They went out at noon, while Ben-hadad was drinking himself drunk in
the booths, he and the thirty-two kings allied with him. 17 The young men who
serve the district governors went out first. Ben-hadad had sent out scouts,[o] and
they reported to him, "Men have come out from Samaria." 18 He said, "If they have

[n] Gk Syr Vg: Heb *you* [o] Heb lacks *scouts*

20.1ff With two evil and two good kings up to this point, the southern kingdom, Judah, wavered between godly and ungodly living. But the northern kingdom, Israel, had eight evil kings in succession. To punish both kingdoms for living their own way instead of following God, God allowed other nations to gain strength and become their enemies. Three main enemies threatened Israel and Judah during the next two centuries—Syria, Assyria, and Babylon. Syria, the first to rise to power, presented an immediate threat to Ahab and Israel.

20.13 God defeated the Syrian army for Ahab so that he would know that "I am the Lord." Despite this great victory and the one to follow on the plains (20.28, 29), Ahab continued to live without God. Evidence of God's greatness surrounds us, but, like Ahab, we can choose to ignore it and go our own way. But when we do, as with this evil king of Israel, disaster will strike. Open your eyes to the evidence—the victories that God is winning for you. And then rededicate yourself to him.

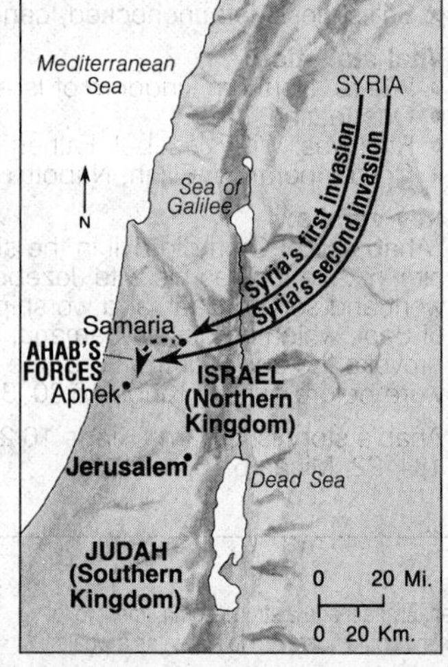

GOD DELIVERS AHAB
Despite Ahab's wickedness, God approached him in love. When Samaria was surrounded by Syrian forces, God miraculously delivered the city. But Ahab refused to give God credit. A year later, the Syrians attacked near Aphek. Again God gave Ahab victory, but again the king refused to acknowledge God's help.

come out for peace, take them alive; if they have come out for war, take them
alive."

19 But these had already come out of the city: the young men who serve the
district governors, and the army that followed them. 20 Each killed his man; the
Arameans fled and Israel pursued them, but King Ben-hadad of Aram escaped on
a horse with the cavalry. 21 The king of Israel went out, attacked the horses and
chariots, and defeated the Arameans with a great slaughter.

22 Then the prophet approached the king of Israel and said to him, "Come,
strengthen yourself, and consider well what you have to do; for in the spring the
king of Aram will come up against you."

23 The servants of the king of Aram said to him, "Their gods are gods of the
hills, and so they were stronger than we; but let us fight against them in the plain,
and surely we shall be stronger than they. 24 Also do this: remove the kings, each
from his post, and put commanders in place of them; 25 and muster an army like the
army that you have lost, horse for horse, and chariot for chariot; then we will fight
against them in the plain, and surely we shall be stronger than they." He heeded
their voice, and did so.

20.26 1 Sam 4.1; 29.1; 2 Kgs 13.17
20.27 Judg 6.5; 1 Sam 13.5

26 In the spring Ben-hadad mustered the Arameans and went up to Aphek to
fight against Israel. 27 After the Israelites had been mustered and provisioned, they
went out to engage them; the people of Israel encamped opposite them like two
little flocks of goats, while the Arameans filled the country. 28 A man of God approached and said to the king of Israel, "Thus says the LORD: Because the Arameans have said, 'The LORD is a god of the hills but he is not a god of the valleys,'
therefore I will give all this great multitude into your hand, and you shall know that
I am the LORD." 29 They encamped opposite one another seven days. Then on the
seventh day the battle began; the Israelites killed one hundred thousand Aramean

20.30 1 Kgs 22.25; 2 Chron 18.24

foot soldiers in one day. 30 The rest fled into the city of Aphek; and the wall fell on
twenty-seven thousand men that were left.

20.31 Gen 37.34; 1 Kgs 21.27; Esth 4.3

Ben-hadad also fled, and entered the city to hide. 31 His servants said to him,
"Look, we have heard that the kings of the house of Israel are merciful kings; let us
put sackcloth around our waists and ropes on our heads, and go out to the king of
Israel; perhaps he will spare your life." 32 So they tied sackcloth around their
waists, put ropes on their heads, went to the king of Israel, and said, "Your servant
Ben-hadad says, 'Please let me live.'" And he said, "Is he still alive? He is my
brother." 33 Now the men were watching for an omen; they quickly took it up from
him and said, "Yes, Ben-hadad is your brother." Then he said, "Go and bring
him." So Ben-hadad came out to him; and he had him come up into the chariot.

20.34 1 Kgs 15.20

34 Ben-hadad[p] said to him, "I will restore the towns that my father took from your
father; and you may establish bazaars for yourself in Damascus, as my father did in
Samaria." The king of Israel responded,[q] "I will let you go on those terms." So he
made a treaty with him and let him go.

A prophet condemns King Ahab

20.35 1 Kgs 13.16,17
20.36 1 Kgs 13.24

35 At the command of the LORD a certain member of a company of prophets[r]
said to another, "Strike me!" But the man refused to strike him. 36 Then he said to
him, "Because you have not obeyed the voice of the LORD, as soon as you have left
me, a lion will kill you." And when he had left him, a lion met him and killed him.

[p] Heb *He* [q] Heb lacks *The king of Israel responded* [r] Heb *of the sons of the prophets*

20.23 Since the days of Joshua, Israel's soldiers had a reputation for being superior fighters in the hills, but ineffective in the open plains and valleys because they did not use chariots in battle. Horse-drawn chariots, useless in hilly terrain and dense forests, could easily run down great numbers of foot soldiers on the plains. What Ben-hadad's officers did not understand was that it was God, not chariots, that made the difference in battle.

20.31 Sackcloth was coarse cloth usually made of goat's hair and was worn as a symbol of mourning for the dead or for natural disaster. Wearing ropes on the head may have been a symbol of putting oneself at another's disposal. In other words, Ahab could have hung them if he wished. Ropes on the head, therefore, were a sign of submission.

20.35, 36 The prophet needed a wound so he would look like an injured soldier and could effectively deliver his prophecy to Ahab. The first man was killed by a lion because he refused to obey the Lord's instructions through the prophet.

37 Then he found another man and said, "Strike me!" So the man hit him, striking
and wounding him. 38 Then the prophet departed, and waited for the king along the **20.38**
road, disguising himself with a bandage over his eyes. 39 As the king passed by, he 2 Sam 14.2,3 1 Kgs 14.2
cried to the king and said, "Your servant went out into the thick of the battle; then 22.30
a soldier turned and brought a man to me, and said, 'Guard this man; if he is miss- **20.39**
ing, your life shall be given for his life, or else you shall pay a talent of silver.' 2 Kgs 10.24
40 While your servant was busy here and there, he was gone." The king of Israel
said to him, "So shall your judgment be; you yourself have decided it." 41 Then he
quickly took the bandage away from his eyes. The king of Israel recognized him as
one of the prophets. 42 Then he said to him, "Thus says the LORD, 'Because you
have let the man go whom I had devoted to destruction, therefore your life shall be
for his life, and your people for his people.' " 43 The king of Israel set out toward
home, resentful and sullen, and came to Samaria.

Ahab takes Naboth's vineyard

21 Later the following events took place: Naboth the Jezreelite had a vineyard **21.1**
in Jezreel, beside the palace of King Ahab of Samaria. 2 And Ahab said to 2 Kgs 9.21
Naboth, "Give me your vineyard, so that I may have it for a vegetable garden,
because it is near my house; I will give you a better vineyard for it; or, if it seems
good to you, I will give you its value in money." 3 But Naboth said to Ahab, "The **21.3**
LORD forbid that I should give you my ancestral inheritance." 4 Ahab went home Lev 25.23 Num 36.6
resentful and sullen because of what Naboth the Jezreelite had said to him; for he Ezek 46.18
had said, "I will not give you my ancestral inheritance." He lay down on his bed,
turned away his face, and would not eat.

5 His wife Jezebel came to him and said, "Why are you so depressed that you
will not eat?" 6 He said to her, "Because I spoke to Naboth the Jezreelite and said
to him, 'Give me your vineyard for money; or else, if you prefer, I will give you
another vineyard for it'; but he answered, 'I will not give you my vineyard.' " 7 His **21.7**
wife Jezebel said to him, "Do you now govern Israel? Get up, eat some food, and 1 Sam 8.14
be cheerful; I will give you the vineyard of Naboth the Jezreelite."

8 So she wrote letters in Ahab's name and sealed them with his seal; she sent the **21.8**
letters to the elders and the nobles who lived with Naboth in his city. 9 She wrote in 2 Sam 11.14 2 Chron 32.17
the letters, "Proclaim a fast, and seat Naboth at the head of the assembly; 10 seat two Esth 3.12; 8.8
scoundrels opposite him, and have them bring a charge against him, saying, 'You **21.10**
have cursed God and the king.' Then take him out, and stone him to death." 11 The Ex 22.28 Lev 24.15,16
men of his city, the elders and the nobles who lived in his city, did as Jezebel had Mt 26.59 Acts 6.11
sent word to them. Just as it was written in the letters that she had sent to them,
12 they proclaimed a fast and seated Naboth at the head of the assembly. 13 The two
scoundrels came in and sat opposite him; and the scoundrels brought a charge
against Naboth, in the presence of the people, saying, "Naboth cursed God and the
king." So they took him outside the city, and stoned him to death. 14 Then they sent
to Jezebel, saying, "Naboth has been stoned; he is dead."

15 As soon as Jezebel heard that Naboth had been stoned and was dead, Jezebel
said to Ahab, "Go, take possession of the vineyard of Naboth the Jezreelite, which
he refused to give you for money; for Naboth is not alive, but dead." 16 As soon as

---

20.41, 42 It is difficult to explain why Ahab let Ben-hadad go, especially after all the trouble Ben-hadad had caused him. God helped Ahab destroy the Syrian army to prove to Ahab and to Syria that he alone was God. But Ahab failed to destroy the king, his greatest enemy. Ben-hadad was under God's judgment to die, and Ahab had no authority to let him live. For this, God told Ahab that he must now die instead. This prophet's message soon came true when Ahab was killed on the battlefield (22.35).

21.4 After hearing God's judgment (20.42), Ahab went home to pout. Driven by anger and rebellion against God, he had a fit of rage when Naboth refused to sell his vineyard. The same feelings that led him to a career of power grabbing drove him to resent Naboth. Rage turned to hatred and led to murder. In stark contrast to Ahab, Naboth wanted to uphold God's laws: it was considered a duty to keep ancestral land in the family. This incident shows the cruel interplay between Ahab and Jezebel, two of the most wicked leaders in Israel's history.

21.13 To get the land for her husband, Jezebel devised a scheme that appeared legal. Two witnesses were required to establish guilt, and the punishment for blasphemy was death by stoning. Those who twist the law and legal procedures to get what they want today may be more sophisticated in how they go about it, but they are still guilty of the same sin.

Ahab heard that Naboth was dead, Ahab set out to go down to the vineyard of
Naboth the Jezreelite, to take possession of it.
17 Then the word of the LORD came to Elijah the Tishbite, saying: 18 Go down
to meet King Ahab of Israel, who rules[s] in Samaria; he is now in the vineyard of
Naboth, where he has gone to take possession. 19 You shall say to him, "Thus says
the LORD: Have you killed, and also taken possession?" You shall say to him,
"Thus says the LORD: In the place where dogs licked up the blood of Naboth, dogs
will also lick up your blood."
20 Ahab said to Elijah, "Have you found me, O my enemy?" He answered, "I
have found you. Because you have sold yourself to do what is evil in the sight of the
LORD, 21 I will bring disaster on you; I will consume you, and will cut off from
Ahab every male, bond or free, in Israel; 22 and I will make your house like the

21.19 1 Kgs 22.38 2 Kgs 9.26

21.21 1 Kgs 14.10 2 Kgs 9.8

21.22 1 Kgs 14.16 15.29. 16.3

[s] Heb *who is*

JEZEBEL

The Bible is as honest about the lives of its heroes as it is about those who rejected God. Some Bible characters found out what God can do with failures when they turned to him. Many, however, neither admitted their failures nor turned to God.

Jezebel ranks as the most evil woman in the Bible. The Bible even uses her name as an example of people who completely reject God (Revelation 2.20, 21). Many heathen women married into Israel without acknowledging the God their husbands worshiped. They brought their religions with them. But no one was as determined as Jezebel to make all Israel worship *her* gods. To the prophet Elijah, she seemed to have succeeded. He felt he was the only one still faithful to God until God told him there were still 7,000 who had not turned from the faith. Jezebel's one outstanding success was in contributing to the cause of the eventual downfall of the northern kingdom—idolatry. God punished the northern tribes for their idolatry by having them carried off into captivity.

Jezebel held great power. She not only managed her husband, Ahab, but she also had 850 assorted pagan priests under her control. She was committed to her gods and to getting what she wanted. She believed that the king had the right to possess anything he wanted. When Naboth refused to sell Ahab his vineyard, Jezebel ruthlessly had Naboth killed and took ownership of the land. Jezebel's plan to wipe out worship of God in Israel led to painful consequences. Before she died, Jezebel suffered the loss of her husband in combat and her son at the hand of Jehu, who took the throne by force. She died in the defiant and scornful way she had lived.

When comparing Jezebel and Elijah, we have to admire each one's strength of commitment. The big difference was *to whom* they were committed. Jezebel was committed to herself and her false gods; Elijah was totally committed to the one true God. In the end, God proved Elijah right. To what or to whom are you most committed? How would God evaluate your commitment?

Weaknesses and mistakes:
- Systematically eliminated the representatives of God in Israel
- Promoted and funded Baal worship
- Threatened to have Elijah killed
- Believed kings could rightfully do or have anything they wanted
- Used her strong convictions to get her own way

Lessons from her life:
- It is not enough to be committed or sincere. Where our commitment lies makes a great difference
- Rejecting God always leads to disaster

Vital statistics:
- Where: Sidon, Samaria
- Occupation: Queen of Israel
- Relatives: Husband: Ahab. Father: Ethbaal. Sons: Jehoram, Ahaziah
- Contemporaries: Elijah, Jehu

Key verse:
"Indeed there was no one like Ahab, who sold himself to do what was evil in the sight of the Lord, urged on by his wife Jezebel" (1 Kings 21.25).

Jezebel's story is told in 1 Kings 16.31—2 Kings 9.37. Her name is used as a synonym for great evil in Revelation 2.20.

21.19, 23 For the fulfillment of these verses, see 22.38 where dogs licked Ahab's blood, and 2 Kings 9.30–10.28 where Jezebel and the rest of Ahab's family were destroyed.

21.20 Ahab still refused to admit his sin against God. Instead he accused Elijah of being his enemy. When we are blinded by envy and hatred, it is almost impossible to see our own sin.

house of Jeroboam son of Nebat, and like the house of Baasha son of Ahijah, because you have provoked me to anger and have caused Israel to sin. 23 Also concerning Jezebel the LORD said, 'The dogs shall eat Jezebel within the bounds of
Jezreel.' 24 Anyone belonging to Ahab who dies in the city the dogs shall eat; and
anyone of his who dies in the open country the birds of the air shall eat."
25 (Indeed, there was no one like Ahab, who sold himself to do what was evil
in the sight of the LORD, urged on by his wife Jezebel. 26 He acted most abominably
in going after idols, as the Amorites had done, whom the LORD drove out before the
Israelites.)
27 When Ahab heard those words, he tore his clothes and put sackcloth over his
bare flesh; he fasted, lay in the sackcloth, and went about dejectedly. 28 Then the
word of the LORD came to Elijah the Tishbite: 29 "Have you seen how Ahab has
humbled himself before me? Because he has humbled himself before me, I will not
bring the disaster in his days; but in his son's days I will bring the disaster on his
house."

21.23 2 Kgs 9.10 33,34
21.24 1 Kgs 14.11 16.4-7
21.26 Gen 15.16 Lev 18.25 Judg 6.10 2 Kgs 21.11
21.27 Gen 37.34 2 Kgs 6.26-30 18.37
21.29 1 Kgs 22.38 2 Kgs 9.25,26 2 Chron 12.7 34.27

4. Kings of Israel and Judah

Jehoshaphat becomes Ahab's ally

22 For three years Aram and Israel continued without war. 2 But in the third
year King Jehoshaphat of Judah came down to the king of Israel. 3 The king
of Israel said to his servants, "Do you know that Ramoth-gilead belongs to us, yet
we are doing nothing to take it out of the hand of the king of Aram?" 4 He said to
Jehoshaphat, "Will you go with me to battle at Ramoth-gilead?" Jehoshaphat replied to the king of Israel, "I am as you are; my people are your people, my horses
are your horses."
5 But Jehoshaphat also said to the king of Israel, "Inquire first for the word of
the LORD." 6 Then the king of Israel gathered the prophets together, about four
hundred of them, and said to them, "Shall I go to battle against Ramoth-gilead, or
shall I refrain?" They said, "Go up; for the LORD will give it into the hand of the
king." 7 But Jehoshaphat said, "Is there no other prophet of the LORD here of whom
we may inquire?" 8 The king of Israel said to Jehoshaphat, "There is still one other
by whom we may inquire of the LORD, Micaiah son of Imlah; but I hate him, for he
never prophesies anything favorable about me, but only disaster." Jehoshaphat
said, "Let the king not say such a thing." 9 Then the king of Israel summoned an
officer and said, "Bring quickly Micaiah son of Imlah." 10 Now the king of Israel
and King Jehoshaphat of Judah were sitting on their thrones, arrayed in their robes,
at the threshing floor at the entrance of the gate of Samaria; and all the prophets
were prophesying before them. 11 Zedekiah son of Chenaanah made for himself
horns of iron, and he said, "Thus says the LORD: With these you shall gore the
Arameans until they are destroyed." 12 All the prophets were prophesying the same
and saying, "Go up to Ramoth-gilead and triumph; the LORD will give it into the
hand of the king."

Micaiah predicts failure

13 The messenger who had gone to summon Micaiah said to him, "Look, the
words of the prophets with one accord are favorable to the king; let your word be
like the word of one of them, and speak favorably." 14 But Micaiah said, "As the
LORD lives, whatever the LORD says to me, that I will speak."

22.2 1 Kgs 15.24
22.3 Deut 4.43 Josh 20.8 2 Kgs 8.28
22.4 2 Kgs 3.6-8
22.5 Num 27.21 Josh 9.14,15 1 Sam 23.2
22.7 2 Kgs 3.11 2 Chron 18.6,7
22.8 1 Kgs 18.17
22.11 2 Chron 18.10
22.14 Num 22.18 24.13 2 Chron 18.13 Jer 23.28 Ezek 2.4

21.29 Ahab was more wicked than any other king of Israel (16.30; 21.25), but when he repented in deep humility, God took notice and reduced his punishment. The same Lord who was merciful to Ahab wants to be merciful to you. No matter how evil you have been, it is never too late to humble yourself, turn to God, and ask for forgiveness.

22.6 These 400 prophets were probably the 400 Asherah priests left alive by Elijah at Carmel, although 450 prophets of Baal were killed (see 18.19–40).

22.7 Jehoshaphat knew there was a difference between these heathen prophets and the "prophet of the Lord," so he asked if one was available. Evidently Jehoshaphat wanted to do what was right although Ahab didn't. However, both kings disregarded God's message and listened only to the heathen prophets.

22.10 Threshing floors were placed in elevated areas to allow the wind to blow away the discarded hulls of grain. This would be a good place to prepare for war.

15 When he had come to the king, the king said to him, "Micaiah, shall we go
to Ramoth-gilead to battle, or shall we refrain?" He answered him, "Go up and
triumph; the LORD will give it into the hand of the king." 16 But the king said to him,
"How many times must I make you swear to tell me nothing but the truth in the
22.17 name of the LORD?" 17 Then Micaiah[t] said, "I saw all Israel scattered on the moun-
Num 27.17 tains, like sheep that have no shepherd; and the LORD said, 'These have no master;
1 Kgs 22.36,37 let each one go home in peace.' " 18 The king of Israel said to Jehoshaphat, "Did I
Jer 23.1 not tell you that he would not prophesy anything favorable about me, but only
disaster?"
22.19 19 Then Micaiah[t] said, "Therefore hear the word of the LORD: I saw the LORD
Isa 6.1 sitting on his throne, with all the host of heaven standing beside him to the right and
Dan 7.9 to the left of him. 20 And the LORD said, 'Who will entice Ahab, so that he may go

[t] Heb *he*

KINGS TO DATE AND THEIR ENEMIES

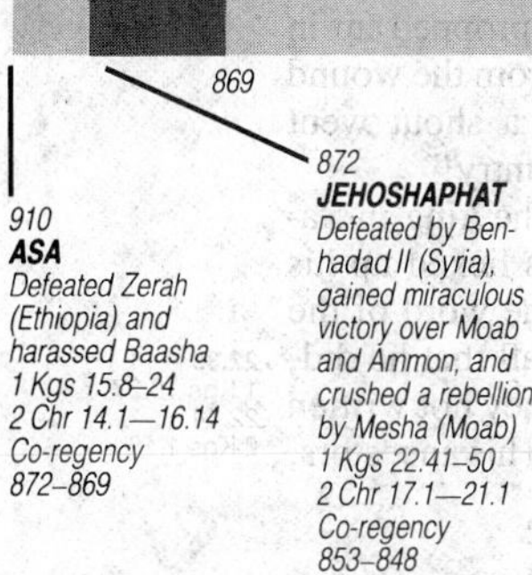

All dates are B.C.
Solid section of the timeline indicates co-regency.
For all the kings of Israel and Judah, see the chart at the end of 1 Kings.

22.15, 16 Why did Micaiah tell Ahab to attack when he had previously vowed to speak only what God had told him? Perhaps he was speaking sarcastically, making fun of the messages from the heathen prophets by showing that they were telling the king only what he wanted to hear. Somehow, Micaiah's tone of voice let everyone know he was mocking the heathen prophets. When confronted, he predicted that the king would die and the battle would be lost. Although Ahab repented temporarily (21.27), he still maintained the system of false prophets. These false prophets would be instrumental in leading him to his own ruin.

22.19–22 The vision Micaiah saw was either a picture of a real incident in heaven, or a parable of what was happening on earth, illustrating that the seductive influence of the false prophets would be part of God's judgment upon Ahab (22.23). Whether or not God sent an angel in disguise, he used the system of false prophets to snare Ahab in his sin. The lying spirit (22.22) symbolized the way of life for these prophets, who told the king only what he wanted to hear.

22.20–22 Does God allow angels to entice people to do evil? To understand evil one must first understand God. (1) God himself is good (Psalm 11.7). (2) God created a good world that fell because of man's sin (Romans 5.12). (3) Someday God will recreate the world and it will be good again (Revelation 21.1). (4) God is stronger than evil (Matthew 13.41–43; Revelation 19.11–21). (5) God allows evil, and thus he has control over it. God did not create evil, and he offers help to those who wish to overcome it (Matthew 11.28–30). (6) God uses everything—both good and evil—for his good purposes (Romans 8.28).

The Bible shows us a God who hates all evil and will one day do away with it completely and forever (Revelation 20.10–15). God does not entice anyone to become evil. Those committed to evil, however, may be used by God to sin even more in order to hurry their deserved judgment (Exodus 11.10). We don't need to understand every detail of how God works in order to have perfect confidence in his absolute power over evil and his total goodness toward us.

up and fall at Ramoth-gilead?' Then one said one thing, and another said another,
21 until a spirit came forward and stood before the LORD, saying, 'I will entice him.'
22 'How?' the LORD asked him. He replied, 'I will go out and be a lying spirit in the **22.22**
mouth of all his prophets.' Then the LORD[u] said, 'You are to entice him, and you 2 Thess 2.11
shall succeed; go out and do it.' 23 So you see, the LORD has put a lying spirit in the **22.23**
mouth of all these your prophets; the LORD has decreed disaster for you." Isa 9.14,15 Ezek 14.9
24 Then Zedekiah son of Chenaanah came up to Micaiah, slapped him on the **22.24**
cheek, and said, "Which way did the spirit of the LORD pass from me to speak to 2 Chron 18.23
you?" 25 Micaiah replied, "You will find out on that day when you go in to hide in
an inner chamber." 26 The king of Israel then ordered, "Take Micaiah, and return **22.27**
him to Amon the governor of the city and to Joash the king's son, 27 and say, 'Thus 2 Chron 16.10 18.25
says the king: Put this fellow in prison, and feed him on reduced rations of bread Jer 20.2
and water until I come in peace.' " 28 Micaiah said, "If you return in peace, the **22.28**
LORD has not spoken by me." And he said, "Hear, you peoples, all of you!" Deut 18.22 Isa 44.26

Ahab dies in battle

29 So the king of Israel and King Jehoshaphat of Judah went up to Ramoth-
gilead. 30 The king of Israel said to Jehoshaphat, "I will disguise myself and go into **22.30**
battle, but you wear your robes." So the king of Israel disguised himself and went 1 Kgs 14.2
into battle. 31 Now the king of Aram had commanded the thirty-two captains of his 2 Chron 35.22 **22.31**
chariots, "Fight with no one small or great, but only with the king of Israel." 2 Chron 18.30
32 When the captains of the chariots saw Jehoshaphat, they said, "It is surely the
king of Israel." So they turned to fight against him; and Jehoshaphat cried out.
33 When the captains of the chariots saw that it was not the king of Israel, they
turned back from pursuing him. 34 But a certain man drew his bow and unknowingly struck the king of Israel between the scale armor and the breastplate; so he
said to the driver of his chariot, "Turn around, and carry me out of the battle, for
I am wounded." 35 The battle grew hot that day, and the king was propped up in
his chariot facing the Arameans, until at evening he died; the blood from the wound
had flowed into the bottom of the chariot. 36 Then about sunset a shout went
through the army, "Every man to his city, and every man to his country!"
37 So the king died, and was brought to Samaria; they buried the king in Samaria. 38 They washed the chariot by the pool of Samaria; the dogs licked up his
blood, and the prostitutes washed themselves in it,[v] according to the word of the
LORD that he had spoken. 39 Now the rest of the acts of Ahab, and all that he did, **22.39**
and the ivory house that he built, and all the cities that he built, are they not written 1 Kgs 16.27 22.44
in the Book of the Annals of the Kings of Israel? 40 So Ahab slept with his ancestors; 2 Kgs 1.18
and his son Ahaziah succeeded him.

Jehoshaphat rules Judah

41 Jehoshaphat son of Asa began to reign over Judah in the fourth year of King **22.41**
Ahab of Israel. 42 Jehoshaphat was thirty-five years old when he began to reign, and 1 Chron 3.10 2 Chron 20.31
he reigned twenty-five years in Jerusalem. His mother's name was Azubah daugh- **22.43**
ter of Shilhi. 43 He walked in all the way of his father Asa; he did not turn aside from 1 Kgs 14.23 15.14
it, doing what was right in the sight of the LORD; yet the high places were not taken 2 Kgs 12.3

[u] Heb *he* [v] Heb lacks *in it*

22.34 Ahab could not escape God's judgment. Ben-hadad sent 32 of his best chariot captains with the sole purpose of killing Ahab. Thinking he could escape, Ahab tried a disguise, but a random arrow struck him while the chariots chased the wrong king, Jehoshaphat. It was foolish for Ahab to think he could escape by wearing a disguise. Sometimes people try to escape reality by disguising themselves—changing jobs, moving to a new town, even changing spouses. Yet when God judges a person, attempted escape is futile.

22.35 Just as the prophet had predicted (20.42), Ahab was killed. See Ahab's Profile in chapter 19 for more of Ahab's sad story.

22.41–50 For more details on Jehoshaphat, see the other account of his reign in 2 Chronicles 17–20.

22.43 Just like his ancestors Solomon and Asa, Jehoshaphat followed God, but he didn't destroy the heathen shrines in the hills (2 Chronicles 20.33). It was against God's law to worship idols in the shrines (Numbers 33.52), and at first Jehoshaphat attempted to destroy them (2 Chronicles 17.6). They were so popular, however, that it proved difficult. In spite of Jehoshaphat's many contributions to the spiritual, moral, and material health of his country, he did not succeed in eradicating the hill shrines.

22.45 1 Kgs 22.39 2 Kgs 1.18
22.46 Deut 23.17 1 Kgs 15.12 2 Kgs 23.7
22.47 2 Sam 8.14 2 Kgs 3.9
22.48 1 Kgs 9.26-28 2 Chron 8.17,18
22.50 2 Kgs 8.16 2 Chron 21.1
22.52 1 Kgs 15.26 16.30

away, and the people still sacrificed and offered incense on the high places. 44 Jehoshaphat also made peace with the king of Israel.
45 Now the rest of the acts of Jehoshaphat, and his power that he showed, and
how he waged war, are they not written in the Book of the Annals of the Kings of
Judah? 46 The remnant of the male temple prostitutes who were still in the land in
the days of his father Asa, he exterminated.
47 There was no king in Edom; a deputy was king. 48 Jehoshaphat made ships
of the Tarshish type to go to Ophir for gold; but they did not go, for the ships were
wrecked at Ezion-geber. 49 Then Ahaziah son of Ahab said to Jehoshaphat, "Let my
servants go with your servants in the ships," but Jehoshaphat was not willing. 50 Jehoshaphat slept with his ancestors and was buried with his ancestors in the city of
his father David; his son Jehoram succeeded him.

Ahaziah rules Israel

51 Ahaziah son of Ahab began to reign over Israel in Samaria in the seventeenth
year of King Jehoshaphat of Judah; he reigned two years over Israel. 52 He did what
was evil in the sight of the LORD, and walked in the way of his father and mother,
and in the way of Jeroboam son of Nebat, who caused Israel to sin. 53 He served
Baal and worshiped him; he provoked the LORD, the God of Israel, to anger, just as
his father had done.

22.52, 53 The book of 1 Kings begins with a nation united under David, the most devout king in Israel's history. The book ends with a divided kingdom and the death of Ahab, the most wicked king of all. What happened? The people forgot to acknowledge God as their ultimate leader; they appointed human leaders who ignored God; and then they conformed to the life-styles of these evil leaders. Occasional wrongdoing gradually turned into a way of life. Their blatant wickedness could be met only with judgment from God, who allowed enemy nations to arise and defeat Israel and Judah in battle as punishment for their sins. Failing to acknowledge God as the ultimate leader of our lives is the first step toward ruin.

DIVIDED KINGDOM OF ISRAEL

AHIJAH 934—909

ELIJAH 8

930
JEROBOAM
(22 years)
Built a capital city (Shechem), set up two golden calf-idols, led the nation into sin, allowed anyone to be a priest
1 Kgs 11.26—14.34
2 Chr 10.12—13.20

909
NADAB
(2 years)
1 Kgs 15.25–28

908
BAASHA
(24 years)
Led people in idol worship
1 Kgs 15.27—16.7
2 Chr 16.1–6

886
ELAH
(2 years)
Continued idol worship
1 Kgs 16.6–14

885
ZIMRI
(7 days)
1 Kgs 16.9–20

885
TIBNI
1 Kgs 16.21, 22

885
OMRI
(12 years)
Built the capital city of Samaria, had great military power, but continued to lead Israel into idolatry
1 Kgs 16.16–28

874
AHAB
(22 years)
Married Jez
(a non-Jew
extremely w
woman), w
Baal, and s
three years
famine cau
by his cons
disobedien
God
1 Kgs 16.2
2 Chr 18.1–

CAPITAL: SHECHEM, THEN TIRZAH, THEN SAMARIA
THE NORTHERN KINGDOM OF ISRAEL (TEN TRIBES)

THE SOUTHERN KINGDOM OF JUDAH (TWO TRIBES)
CAPITAL: JERUSALEM

930
REHOBOAM
(17 years)
Built many fortified cities, strengthened the economy (despite the tribute paid to Egypt), followed God for three years, but then set up idols and shrines to foreign gods
1 Kgs 11.43—14.31
2 Chr 9.31—12.16

913
ABIJAM
(3 years)
Despite his wickedness, he called for God's help to win the battle against Israel
1 Kgs 14.31—15.8
2 Chr 13.1—14.1

910
ASA
(41 years)
Destroyed heathen altars and rebuilt altar of God, built fortified cities, gained much wealth from plunder of foreign conquest, removed the queen-mother for worshiping Asteroth, led the people to worship God with their hearts, provided peace on home soil, was greatly loved, and given a beautiful funeral
1 Kgs 15.8–24
2 Chr 14.1—16.14

872
JEHOSHAPHA
(25 years)
Arranged for th
riage of his son
daughter of Aha
made trouble la
had a strong m
(kept troops in
Israel his father
conquered), col
tribute from the
tines, worshiped
Lord and destro
idols, establishe
cation, and app
judges and cou
1 Kgs 15.24; 22
2 Chr 17.1—21.

All dates are B.C. The total years of reign sometimes include years of co-regency. (See charts, "Kings to Date," throughout 1 and 2 Kings.)

ELISHA 848—797

JONAH
793—753(?)

853
AHAZIAH
(2 years)
Proposed a joint trade venture with Judah
1 Kgs 22.40—2 Kgs 1.18
2 Chr 20.35–37

852
JEHORAM/ JORAM
(12 years)
Suffered famine and war during most of his reign
2 Kgs 3.1—8.25
2 Chr 22.5–7

841
JEHU
(28 years)
Was responsible for the deaths of Joram (king of Judah), Ahaziah (king of Israel), Jezebel (wicked mother of Joram); destroyed the priests and temples of Baal; but did not consistently follow God
2 Kgs 9.1— 10.36
2 Chr 22.7–12

814
JEHOAHAZ
(17 years)
Evil reign included worship of Asheroth, usually called "shameful"
2 Kgs 13.1–9

798
JEHOASH/ JOASH
(16 years)
Even though he was evil, he recognized the authority of Elisha as a prophet of God
2 Kgs 13.10—14.16
2 Chr 25.17–24

793
JEREBOAM II
(41 years)
Very evil but politically powerful, his nation enjoyed economic prosperity and military peace
2 Kgs 14.16–29

853
JEHORAM/ JORAM
(8 years)
Married a wicked daughter of Ahab, compelled the people to worship idols, and killed all his brothers
2 Kgs 8.16–24
2 Chr 21.1–20

841
JEHOAHAZ/ AHAZIAH
(1 year)
Friend of Joram of Israel
2 Kgs 8.24—9.29
2 Chr 22.1–10

841
ATHALIAH (QUEEN)
(6 years)
Killed all her grandchildren except Joash who was hidden by his nurse for six years, and ravaged the Temple to furnish Baal's temple
2 Kgs 11.1–20
2 Chr 22.10—23.21

835
JOASH
(40 years)
Was crowned king at the age of seven by Jehoiada (the High Priest), promoted peace and prosperity, repaired the Temple and smashed the altars to Baal—but after Jehoiada died, Joash abandoned God, and even had Jehoiada's son killed
2 Kgs 11.2—12.21
2 Chr 22.11—24.27

796
AMAZIAH
(29 years)
Was basically good but did not completely wipe out idol worship, organized the army, took a census
2 Kgs 14.1–20
2 Chr 25.1–28

792
UZZIAH/ AZARIAH
(52 years)
Built a city named Elath, owned many farms and vineyards, constructed water reservoirs and forts, reorganized the army (so powerful that his fame spread to Egypt), but violated God's laws for priestly function—so God struck him with leprosy
2 Kgs 15.1–17
2 Chr 26.1–23

OBADIAH 855—840(?)

JOEL 835—796(?)

HOSEA 753—715

AMOS 760—750

752
SHALLUM
(1 month)
2 Kgs 15.10–15

742
PEKAHIAH
(2 years)
Continued idol worship
2 Kgs 15.22–26

732
HOSHEA
(9 years)
Suffered heavy taxation by Assyria and eventual conquest—bringing about Israelite captivity and resettlement of foreigners in Israel
2 Kgs 15.30; 17.1–6

722
END OF THE NORTHERN KINGDOM—Israel taken to Assyria by Shalmaneser

753
ZACHARIAH
(6 months)
Encouraged idol worship
2 Kgs 14.29—15.11

752
MENAHEM
(10 years)
Imposed heavy taxes and oppressed his people
2 Kgs 15.14–22

740
PEKAH
(8 years)
During his reign many of the people were taken captive to Assyria
2 Kgs 15.25–31
2 Chr 28.5–8

ISRAEL

JUDAH

750
JOTHAM
(16 years)
Rebuilt the upper gate of the Temple, rebuilt walls and cities, but still permitted idol worship
2 Kgs 15.32–38
2 Chr 27.1–9

735
AHAZ
(16 years)
Sacrificed his own son to heathen gods, nailed the Temple doors shut
2 Kgs 16.1–20
2 Chr 28.1–27

715
HEZEKIAH
(29 years)
Was a devoted follower of God, reopened Temple doors, cleansed the Temple, reinstated priests and their duties, organized an orchestra to aid worship, destroyed idols (including the bronze serpent of Moses because people had begun to worship it), celebrated Passover and even invited people who were living in the North to participate, constructed large public waterworks, was given 15 extra years of life, foolishly showed ambassadors the wealth in the Temple
2 Kgs 16.20; 18.1—20.21
2 Chr 29.1—32.33

697
MANASSEH
(55 years)
Rebuilt all the heathen shrin[e] sacrificed one [of] his own sons, practiced blac[k] magic, set up [an] idol right in th[e] Temple, murd[ered] many of his o[wn] people, but repented duri[ng] his Assyrian captivity
2 Kgs 21.1–18
2 Chr 33.1–20

MICAH 742—687

ISAIAH 740—681

586
END OF THE SOUTHERN KINGDOM—
carried off captive to Babylon by Nebuchadnezzar

642
AMON
(2 years)
2 Kgs 21.18–26
2 Chr 33.20–25

640
JOSIAH
(31 years)
Loved God with all his heart, repaired the Temple, found a lost scroll of the Law (he promised to obey it, thus God stayed destruction for Judah until after his death), personally oversaw the major project of destroying idol shrines, reinstated the priests of God, celebrated Passover with greater zeal than had been since Samuel's day, was greatly loved by his people
2 Kgs 21.26—23.30
2 Chr 33.25—35.27

609
JEHOAHAZ
(3 months)
Jailed and taken to Egypt where he died
2 Kgs 23.30–34
2 Chr 36.1–4

609
ELIAKIM/ JEHOIAKIM
(11 years)
Burned part of God's Word, was a puppet king for Egypt then Babylon, watched gold and tools taken from the Temple to Babylon, saw first exile (in which Daniel was taken)
2 Kgs 23.34–24.6
2 Chr 36.5–8

598
JEHOIACHIN
(3 months)
Saw next exile to Babylon
2 Kgs 24.6–15; 25.27–30
2 Chr 36.8–10

597
MATTANIAH/ ZEDEKIAH
(11 years)
Saw the Temple burned and Jerusalem destroyed, was tortured and carried away in the final exile to Babylon
2 Kgs 24.17—25.21
2 Chr 36.10–21

HABAKKUK 612—589

–654

ZEPHANIAH 640—621

HULDA 632

JEREMIAH 627—586

2 KINGS

Kingdom divides 930 B.C.	Ahab dies in battle 853	Elijah's ministry transfers to Elisha 848	Jehu becomes king of Israel 841	Joash becomes king of Judah 835	Elisha's ministry ends 797	Jeroboam II becomes king of Israel 793	Amos' ministry begins 760	Hosea's ministry begins 753

VITAL STATISTICS

PURPOSE:
To demonstrate the fate that awaits all who refuse to make God their true leader

AUTHOR:
Unknown. Possibly Jeremiah or a group of prophets

SETTING:
The once-united nation of Israel has been divided into two kingdoms, Israel and Judah, for over a century.

KEY VERSES:
"Yet the Lord warned Israel and Judah by every prophet and every seer, saying, 'Turn from your evil ways and keep my commandments and my statutes, in accordance with all the law that I commanded your ancestors and that I sent to you by my servants the prophets.' They would not listen but were stubborn, as their ancestors had been, who did not believe in the Lord their God" (17.13, 14).

KEY PEOPLE:
Elijah, Elisha, Shunemite woman, Naaman, Jezebel, Jehu, Joash, Hezekiah, Sennacherib, Isaiah, Manasseh, Josiah, Jehoiakim, Zedekiah, Nebuchadnezzar

SPECIAL FEATURES:
The 17 prophetic books at the end of the Old Testament give great insights into the time period of 2 Kings.

SPARKLING as it crashes against boulders along its banks, the river swiftly cascades toward the sea. The current grabs, pushes, and tugs at leaves and logs, carrying them along for the ride. Here and there a sportsman is spotted in a kayak or a canoe, going with the flow. Gravity pulls the water, and the river pulls the rest . . . downward. Suddenly, a silver missile breaks the surface and darts upstream, and then another. Oblivious to the swirling opposition, the shining salmon swim against the stream. They must go upstream, and nothing will stop them from reaching their destination.

The current of society's river is flowing fast and furious, pulling downward everything in its way. It would be easy to float along with the current. But God calls us to swim against the flow. It will not be easy, and we may be alone, but it will be right.

In the book of the Kings, we read of evil rulers, rampant idolatry, and a complacent populace—certainly pulling downward. Despite the pressure to conform, to turn from the Lord and to serve only self, a minority of chosen people move the opposite direction, toward God. The Bethel prophets and others, as well as two righteous kings, speak God's Word and stand for him. As you read 2 Kings, watch these courageous individuals. Catch the strength and force of Elijah and Elisha and the commitment of Hezekiah and Josiah, and determine to be one who swims against the current!

Second Kings continues the history of Israel, halfway between the death of David and the death of the nation. Israel has been divided (1 Kings 12), and the two kingdoms have begun to slide into idolatry and corruption toward collapse and captivity. Second Kings relates the sordid stories of the 12 kings of the northern kingdom (called Israel) and the 16 kings of the southern kingdom (called Judah). For 130 years, Israel endures the succession of evil rulers until they are conquered by Shalmaneser of Assyria and led into captivity in 722 B.C. (17.6). Of all the kings in both the north and south, only two—Hezekiah and Josiah—are called good. Because of their obedience to God and the spiritual revivals during their reigns, Judah stands for an additional 136 years until falling to Nebuchadnezzar and the Babylonians in 586 B.C.

Throughout this dark period, the Bible mentions 30 prophets who proclaim God's message to the people and their leaders. Most notable of these fearless men of God are Elijah and Elisha. As Elijah nears the end of his earthly ministry, Elisha asks for twice the prophetic power as his beloved mentor (2.9). Soon after, Elijah is taken to heaven in a whirlwind (2.11), and Elisha becomes God's spokesman to the northern kingdom. Elisha's life is filled with signs, proclamations, warnings, and miracles. Four of the most memorable are the flowing olive oil (4.1–7), the healing of the Shunemite woman's son (4.8–37), the healing of Naaman's leprosy (5.1–27), and the floating ax head (6.1–7).

Even in the midst of terrible situations, God will have his faithful minority, his remnant (19.31). He desires courageous men and women to proclaim his truth.

Micah's ministry begins 742	Isaiah's ministry begins 740	Israel (northern kingdom) falls 722	Hezekiah becomes king of Judah 715	Josiah becomes king of Judah 640	Jeremiah's ministry begins 627	Book of the law found in the temple 622	First captivity of Judah; Daniel taken 605	Second captivity of Judah; Ezekiel taken 597	Judah (southern kingdom) falls 586

THE BLUEPRINT

A. THE DIVIDED KINGDOM (1.1—17.41)
1. Elisha's ministry
2. Kings of Israel and Judah
3. Israel is exiled to Assyria

Although Israel had the witness and power of Elisha, the nation turned from God and was exiled to Assyria. Assyria filled the northern kingdom with people from other lands. There has been no return from this captivity—it was permanent. Such is the end of all who shut God out of their lives.

B. THE SURVIVING KINGDOM (18.1—25.30)
1. Kings of Judah
2. Judah is exiled to Babylon

The northern kingdom was destroyed, and prophets were predicting the same fate for Judah. What more could cause the nation to repent? Hezekiah and Josiah were able to stem the tide of evil. They both repaired the temple and gathered the people for passover. Josiah eradicated idolatry from the land, but as soon as these good kings were gone, the people returned again to living their own way instead of God's way. Each individual must believe and live for God in his family, church, and nation.

MEGATHEMES

THEME	EXPLANATION	IMPORTANCE
Elisha	The purpose of Elisha's ministry was to restore respect for God and his message, and he stood firmly against the evil kings of Israel. By faith, with courage and prayer, he revealed not only God's judgment on sin, but also his mercy, love, and tenderness toward faithful people.	Elisha's mighty miracles showed that God controls not only great armies, but also events in everyday life. When we listen to and obey God, he shows us his power to transform any situation. God's care is for all who are willing to follow him. He can perform miracles in our lives.
Idolatry	Every evil king in both Israel and Judah encouraged idolatry. These false gods represented war, cruelty, power, and sex. Although they had God's law, priests, and prophets to guide them, these kings sought priests and prophets whom they could manipulate to their own advantage.	An idol is any idea, ability, possession, or person that we regard more highly than God. We condemn Israel and Judah for foolishly worshiping idols, but we also worship other gods—power, money, physical attractiveness. Those who believe in God must resist the lure of these attractive idols.
Evil kings/ good kings	Only 20 percent of Israel and Judah's kings followed God. The evil kings were short-sighted. They thought they could control their nations' destinies by importing other religions, forming alliances with heathen nations, and enriching themselves. The good kings had to spend most of their time undoing the evil done by their predecessors.	Although the evil kings led the people into sin, the priests, princes, heads of families, and military leaders all had to cooperate with the evil plans and practices in order for them to be carried out. We cannot discharge our responsibility to obey God by blaming our leaders. We are responsible to know God's Word and obey it.
God's patience	God told his people that if they obeyed him they would live successfully; if they disobeyed, they would be judged and destroyed. God had been patient with the people for hundreds of years. He sent many prophets to guide them. And he gave ample warning of coming destruction. But even God's patience has limits.	God is patient with us. He gives us many chances to hear his message, to turn from sin, and to believe him. His patience does not mean he is indifferent to how we live, nor does it mean we can ignore his warnings. His patience should make us want to come to him now.
Judgment	After King Solomon's reign, Israel lasted 209 years before the Assyrians destroyed it; Judah lasted 345 years before the Babylonians took Jerusalem. After repeated warnings to his people, God used these evil nations as instruments for his justice.	The consequences of rejecting God's commands and purpose for our lives are severe. He will not ignore unbelief or rebellion. We must believe in him and accept Christ's sacrificial death on our behalf, or we will be judged also.

KEY PLACES IN 2 KINGS

The history of both Israel and Judah was much affected by the prophet Elisha's ministry. He served Israel for 50 years, fighting the idolatry of its kings and calling its people back to God.

1 Jericho Elijah's ministry had come to an end. He touched his cloak to the Jordan River, and he and Elisha crossed on dry land. Elijah was taken by God in a whirlwind, and Elisha returned alone with the cloak. The prophets in Jericho realized that Elisha was Elijah's replacement (1.1—2.25).

2 Wilderness of Edom The king of Moab rebelled against Israel, so the nations of Israel, Judah, and Edom decided to attack from the wilderness of Edom, but ran out of water. The kings consulted Elisha, who said God would send both water and victory (3.1–27).

3 Shunem Elisha cared for individuals and their needs. He helped a woman clear a debt by giving her a supply of olive oil to sell. For another family in Shunem, he raised a son from the dead (4.1–37).

4 Gilgal Elisha cared for the young prophets in Gilgal—he removed poison from a stew, made a small amount of food feed everyone, and even caused an ax head to float so a student could retrieve it. It was to Elisha that Naaman, a commander in the Syrian army, came to be healed of leprosy (4.38—6.7).

5 Dothan Although he cured a Syrian commander's leprosy, Elisha was loyal to Israel. He knew the Syrian army's battle plans and kept Israel's king informed. The Syrian king tracked Elisha down in Dothan and surrounded the city, hoping to kill him. But Elisha prayed that the Syrians would be blinded, then he led the blinded army into Samaria, Israel's capital city (6.8–23).

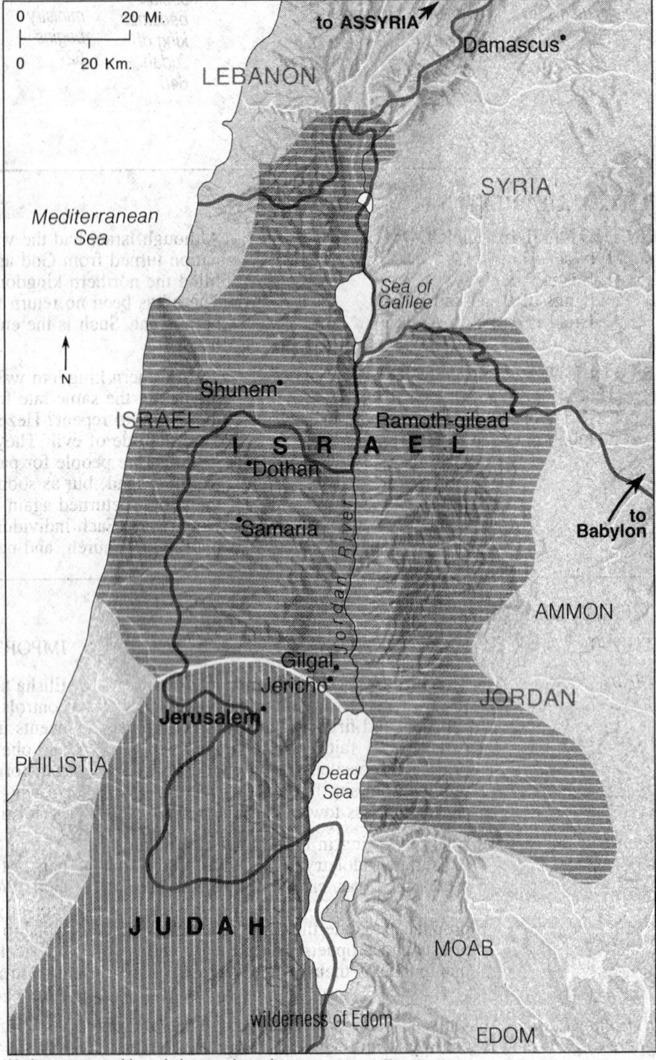

Modern names and boundaries are shown in gray.

6 Samaria But the Syrians didn't learn their lesson. They later besieged Samaria. Ironically, Israel's king thought it was Elisha's fault, but Elisha said food would be available in abundance the next day. True to Elisha's word, the Lord caused panic in the Syrian camp, and the enemy ran, leaving their supplies to Samaria's starving people (6.24—7.20).

7 Damascus Despite Elisha's loyalty to Israel, he obeyed God and traveled to Damascus, the capital of Syria. King Ben-hadad was sick, and he sent Hazael to ask Elisha if he would recover. Elisha knew the king would die, and told this to Hazael. But Hazael then murdered Ben-hadad, making himself king. Later, Israel and Judah joined forces to fight this new Syrian threat (8.1–29).

8 Ramoth-gilead As Israel and Judah warred with Syria, Elisha sent a young prophet to Ramoth-gilead to anoint Jehu as Israel's next king. Jehu set out to destroy the wicked dynasties of Israel and Judah, killing kings Joram and Ahaziah, and wicked Queen Jezebel. He then destroyed King Ahab's family, and all the Baal worshipers in Israel (9.1—11.1).

9 Jerusalem Power-hungry Athaliah became queen of Judah when her son Ahaziah was killed. She had all her grandsons killed except Joash who was hidden by his aunt. Joash was crowned king at the age of seven and overthrew Athaliah. Meanwhile in Samaria, the Syrians continued to harass Israel. Israel's new king met with Elisha and was told that he would be victorious over Syria three times (11.2—13.19).

Following Elisha's death came a series of evil kings in Israel. Their idolatry and rejection of God caused their downfall. The Assyrian Empire captured Samaria and took most of the Israelites into captivity (13.20—17.41). Judah had a short reprieve because of a few good kings who destroyed idols and worshiped God. But many strayed from God. So Jerusalem fell to the next world power, Babylon (18.1—25.30).

A. THE DIVIDED KINGDOM (1.1–17.41)

Elisha begins his ministry to the northern kingdom after Elijah is taken away by a chariot of fire. Elisha performs many miracles and calls Israel to return to God, but they persist in their wickedness. Israel is defeated by Assyria and the people of the northern kingdom are exiled, never to return. Such is the end of all those who ignore God's warnings and demand their own way in their desire to sin.

King Ahaziah's conflict with Elijah

1.1 2 Sam 8.2; 2 Kgs 3.5; 1 Chron 18.2
1.2 1 Kgs 14.3; 2 Kgs 8.7
1.3 1 Kgs 17.1
1.4 2 Kgs 1.16,17

1 After the death of Ahab, Moab rebelled against Israel.
2 Ahaziah had fallen through the lattice in his upper chamber in Samaria, and
lay injured; so he sent messengers, telling them, "Go, inquire of Baal-zebub, the
god of Ekron, whether I shall recover from this injury." 3 But the angel of the LORD
said to Elijah the Tishbite, "Get up, go to meet the messengers of the king of Samaria, and say to them, 'Is it because there is no God in Israel that you are going
to inquire of Baal-zebub, the god of Ekron?' 4 Now therefore thus says the LORD,
'You shall not leave the bed to which you have gone, but you shall surely die.' " So
Elijah went.
5 The messengers returned to the king, who said to them, "Why have you returned?" 6 They answered him, "There came a man to meet us, who said to us, 'Go
back to the king who sent you, and say to him: Thus says the LORD: Is it because
there is no God in Israel that you are sending to inquire of Baal-zebub, the god of
Ekron? Therefore you shall not leave the bed to which you have gone, but shall
surely die.' " 7 He said to them, "What sort of man was he who came to meet you
and told you these things?" 8 They answered him, "A hairy man, with a leather belt
around his waist." He said, "It is Elijah the Tishbite."

1.8 Mt 3.4; Mk 1.6

9 Then the king sent to him a captain of fifty with his fifty men. He went up to
Elijah, who was sitting on the top of a hill, and said to him, "O man of God, the
king says, 'Come down.' " 10 But Elijah answered the captain of fifty, "If I am a
man of God, let fire come down from heaven and consume you and your fifty."
Then fire came down from heaven, and consumed him and his fifty.

1.10 1 Kgs 18.36; 22.28; 2 Chron 36.16; Job 1.16; Lk 9.54

11 Again the king sent to him another captain of fifty with his fifty. He went
up[a] and said to him, "O man of God, this is the king's order: Come down quickly!"
12 But Elijah answered them, "If I am a man of God, let fire come down from
heaven and consume you and your fifty." Then the fire of God came down from
heaven and consumed him and his fifty.
13 Again the king sent the captain of a third fifty with his fifty. So the third
captain of fifty went up, and came and fell on his knees before Elijah, and entreated
him, "O man of God, please let my life, and the life of these fifty servants of yours,
be precious in your sight. 14 Look, fire came down from heaven and consumed the
two former captains of fifty men with their fifties; but now let my life be precious
in your sight." 15 Then the angel of the LORD said to Elijah, "Go down with him; do

1.15 2 Kgs 1.3

[a] Gk Compare verses 9, 13: Heb *He answered*

1.1 Because 1 and 2 Kings were originally one book, 2 Kings continues where 1 Kings ended. The once great nation of Israel is now split in two because the people have forgotten God. The book begins with Elijah, a prophet of God, being carried away to heaven. It ends with the people of Israel and Judah being carried away into captivity. In 1 Kings, the beautiful temple of God was built. In 2 Kings, it is desecrated and destroyed.

Our world is strikingly similar to the world described in 2 Kings. National and local governments do not seek God, and countries are tormented by war. Many people follow the false gods of technology, materialism, and war. True worship of God is rare on the earth.

In our chaotic and corrupt world, we can turn to examples such as David, Elijah, and Elisha, who were devoted to God's high honor and moral law and who brought about renewal and change in their society. More important, we can look to Jesus Christ, the perfect example. For nations to do God's will, they need individuals who will do God's work. If your heart is committed to God, he can work through you to accomplish the work he has called you to do.

1.2 Baal-zebub was not the same god as Baal, the Canaanite god worshiped by Ahab and Jezebel (1 Kings 16.31–33). Baal-zebub was another popular god whose temple was located in the city of Ekron. Because this god was thought to have the power of prophecy, King Ahaziah sent messengers to Ekron to learn of his fate. Supernatural power and mystery were associated with this god. Ahaziah's action showed the king's disrespect for God.

1.8 For more information on Elijah, see his Profile in 1 Kings 18.

1.13–15 Notice how the third captain went to Elijah. Although the first two captains called Elijah "man of God," they were not being genuine – God was not in their hearts. The third captain also called him "man of God," but he humbly begged for mercy. His attitude, which showed respect for God and his power, saved the lives of his men. Effective living begins with a right attitude toward God. Before religious words come to your mouth, make sure they are from your heart. Let respect, humility, and servanthood characterize your attitude toward God and others.

not be afraid of him." So he set out and went down with him to the king, 16 and said
to him, "Thus says the LORD: Because you have sent messengers to inquire of Baal-
zebub, the god of Ekron, — is it because there is no God in Israel to inquire of his
word? — therefore you shall not leave the bed to which you have gone, but you shall
surely die."
17 So he died according to the word of the LORD that Elijah had spoken. His 1.17
brother,[b] Jehoram succeeded him as king in the second year of King Jehoram son 2 Kgs 3.1; 8.16
of Jehoshaphat of Judah, because Ahaziah had no son. 18 Now the rest of the acts of 1.18
Ahaziah that he did, are they not written in the Book of the Annals of the Kings of 2 Kgs 10.34 13.8,12; 14.15
Israel?

1. Elisha's ministry

God takes Elijah to heaven

2 Now when the LORD was about to take Elijah up to heaven by a whirlwind, 2.1
Elijah and Elisha were on their way from Gilgal. 2 Elijah said to Elisha, "Stay Gen 5.23,24 1 Kgs 19.16
here; for the LORD has sent me as far as Bethel." But Elisha said, "As the LORD 2 Kgs 2.11
lives, and as you yourself live, I will not leave you." So they went down to Bethel. Heb 11.5
3 The company of prophets[c] who were in Bethel came out to Elisha, and said to 2.3
him, "Do you know that today the LORD will take your master away from you?" 2 Kgs 2.5,7,15
And he said, "Yes, I know; keep silent."
4 Elijah said to him, "Elisha, stay here; for the LORD has sent me to Jericho." 2.4
But he said, "As the LORD lives, and as you yourself live, I will not leave you." So 1 Kgs 16.34 2 Kgs 2.15
they came to Jericho. 5 The company of prophets[c] who were at Jericho drew near
to Elisha, and said to him, "Do you know that today the LORD will take your master
away from you?" And he answered, "Yes, I know; be silent."
6 Then Elijah said to him, "Stay here; for the LORD has sent me to the Jordan." 2.6
But he said, "As the LORD lives, and as you yourself live, I will not leave you." So Ruth 1.15-17 2 Sam 15.19-21
the two of them went on. 7 Fifty men of the company of prophets[r] also went, and 2 Kgs 2.1,2
stood at some distance from them, as they both were standing by the Jordan. 8 Then 2.8
Elijah took his mantle and rolled it up, and struck the water; the water was parted Ex 14.21 1 Kgs 19.19
to the one side and to the other, until the two of them crossed on dry ground. Ps 114.5
9 When they had crossed, Elijah said to Elisha, "Tell me what I may do for you, 2.9
before I am taken from you." Elisha said, "Please let me inherit a double share of 1 Kgs 3.5 2 Chron 1.7
your spirit." 10 He responded, "You have asked a hard thing; yet, if you see me as
I am being taken from you, it will be granted you; if not, it will not." 11 As they 2.11
continued walking and talking, a chariot of fire and horses of fire separated the two 2 Kgs 2.1; 6.17
of them, and Elijah ascended in a whirlwind into heaven. 12 Elisha kept watching 2.12
and crying out, "Father, father! The chariots of Israel and its horsemen!" But when 2 Kgs 13.14

[b] Gk Syr: Heb lacks *His brother* [c] Heb *sons of the prophets*

1.18 The Book of the Annals of the Kings of Israel and the Book of the Annals of the Kings of Judah (8.23) were history books. The inspired writer of 2 Kings selected facts from these books to retell the story of Israel and Judah from God's perspective. God directed the writer's thoughts and selection process to make sure that the truth, God's Word, would be written.

2.3 At Bethel there was a special school for God's prophets, one of several schools started to help stem the tide of spiritual and moral decline begun under Jeroboam. Most of the schools seem to have been located in Gilgal, Jericho, and Bethel. Those who attended these schools were trained to be spokesmen for God. These schools were gatherings of disciples around certain leaders much as Jesus' disciples gathered around him.

2.8 A mantle was a wraparound garment used both as a cloak and as clothing. It served as a symbol of the prophet's authority.

2.9 Elisha asked for a double share of Elijah's prophetic power. Deuteronomy 21.17 helps explain Elisha's request. According to custom, the firstborn son received a double share of the father's inheritance (see the note on Genesis 25.31). He was asking to be Elijah's heir, or successor, the one who would continue Elijah's work as leader of the prophets. But the decision to grant Elisha's request was up to God. Elijah only told him how he would know if his request had been granted.

2.9 Elisha asked for a double portion of Elijah's spirit. This was a bold request, but God granted it. Why? Because Elisha's motives were pure. His main goal was not to be better or more powerful than Elijah, but to accomplish more for God. If our motives are pure, we don't have to be afraid to ask great things from God. When we ask God for great power or ability, we need to examine our desires and get rid of any selfishness we find. To have the Holy Spirit's help, we must be willing to ask.

2.11 Elijah was taken to heaven without dying. He is the second person mentioned in Scripture to do so. Enoch was the first (Genesis 5.21–24). The other prophets may not have seen God take Elijah, or they may have had a difficult time believing what they saw. In either case, they wanted to search for Elijah (2.16–18). Finding no physical trace of him would confirm what had happened and strengthen their faith. The only other person taken to heaven in bodily form was Jesus after his resurrection from the dead (Acts 1.9).

he could no longer see him, he grasped his own clothes and tore them in two pieces.
13 He picked up the mantle of Elijah that had fallen from him, and went back
and stood on the bank of the Jordan. 14 He took the mantle of Elijah that had fallen
from him, and struck the water, saying, "Where is the LORD, the God of Elijah?"
When he had struck the water, the water was parted to the one side and to the other,
and Elisha went over.
15 When the company of prophets[d] who were at Jericho saw him at a distance,
they declared, "The spirit of Elijah rests on Elisha." They came to meet him and
2.16 bowed to the ground before him. 16 They said to him, "See now, we have fifty
1 Kgs 18.12 Ezek 3.14,15 strong men among your servants; please let them go and seek your master; it may
8.3; 11.24 Acts 8.39 be that the spirit of the LORD has caught him up and thrown him down on some
mountain or into some valley." He responded, "No, do not send them." 17 But when
they urged him until he was ashamed, he said, "Send them." So they sent fifty men
who searched for three days but did not find him. 18 When they came back to him
(he had remained at Jericho), he said to them, "Did I not say to you, Do not go?"

Elisha purifies the water

19 Now the people of the city said to Elisha, "The location of this city is good,
as my lord sees; but the water is bad, and the land is unfruitful." 20 He said, "Bring
2.21 me a new bowl, and put salt in it." So they brought it to him. 21 Then he went to the
Ex 15.25 2 Kgs 4.41 spring of water and threw the salt into it, and said, "Thus says the LORD, I have

[d] Heb *sons of the prophets*

KINGS TO DATE AND THEIR ENEMIES

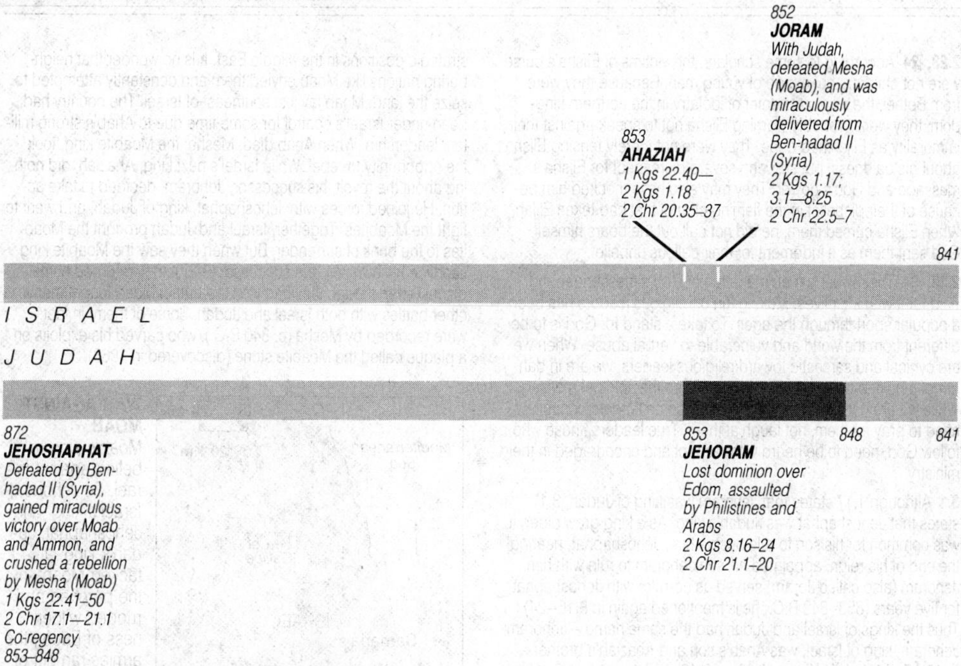

ISRAEL

853 **AHAZIAH** *1 Kgs 22.40— 2 Kgs 1.18 2 Chr 20.35–37*

852 **JORAM** *With Judah, defeated Mesha (Moab), and was miraculously delivered from Ben-hadad II (Syria) 2 Kgs 1.17; 3.1—8.25 2 Chr 22.5–7*

841

JUDAH

872 **JEHOSHAPHAT** *Defeated by Ben-hadad II (Syria), gained miraculous victory over Moab and Ammon, and crushed a rebellion by Mesha (Moab) 1 Kgs 22.41–50 2 Chr 17.1—21.1 Co-regency 853–848*

853 848 841 **JEHORAM** *Lost dominion over Edom, assaulted by Philistines and Arabs 2 Kgs 8.16–24 2 Chr 21.1–20*

All dates are B.C.
Solid section of the timeline indicates co-regency.
For all the kings of Israel and Judah, see the chart at the end of 1 Kings.

2.14 When Elisha struck the water, it was not out of disrespect to God or Elijah. It was a plea by Elisha to God to confirm his appointment as Elijah's successor.

2.14–25 These three incidents were testimonies to Elijah's commission as a prophet of God. They are recorded to demonstrate Elisha's new power and authority as Israel's chief prophet under God's ultimate power and authority.

made this water wholesome; from now on neither death nor miscarriage shall come
from it." 22 So the water has been wholesome to this day, according to the word that
Elisha spoke.

Elisha is mocked

23 He went up from there to Bethel; and while he was going up on the way,
some small boys came out of the city and jeered at him, saying, "Go away, baldhead! Go away, baldhead!" 24 When he turned around and saw them, he cursed 2.24
them in the name of the LORD. Then two she-bears came out of the woods and Judg 9.20,57 1 Kgs 21.19
mauled forty-two of the boys. 25 From there he went on to Mount Carmel, and then 2 Kgs 1.10 Jer 28.16
returned to Samaria.

Jehoram rules Israel

3 In the eighteenth year of King Jehoshaphat of Judah, Jehoram son of Ahab 3.1 1 Kgs 22.51
became king over Israel in Samaria; he reigned twelve years. 2 He did what 2 Kgs 1.17; 8.16
was evil in the sight of the LORD, though not like his father and mother, for he 3.2 1 Kgs 16.31,32
removed the pillar of Baal that his father had made. 3 Nevertheless he clung to the 2 Kgs 10.26
sin of Jeroboam son of Nebat, which he caused Israel to commit; he did not depart 3.3
from it. 1 Kgs 12.28 14.16

Elisha predicts Israel's victory over Moab

4 Now King Mesha of Moab was a sheep breeder, who used to deliver to the 3.4 2 Sam 8.2
king of Israel one hundred thousand lambs, and the wool of one hundred thousand 1 Chron 18.2
rams. 5 But when Ahab died, the king of Moab rebelled against the king of Israel. Ps 60.8 Isa 16.1

2.23, 24 According to some scholars, the victims of Elisha's curse were not children, but a mob of young men. Because they were from Bethel, the religious center of idolatry in the northern kingdom, they were probably warning Elisha not to speak against their immorality as Elijah had done. They were not merely teasing Elisha about his baldness, but showing severe disrespect for Elisha's message and God's power. They may also have mocked him because of their disbelief in the flaming chariot that had taken Elijah. When Elisha cursed them, he did not call out the bears himself. God sent them as a judgment for their callous unbelief.

2.23, 24 These young men made fun of God's messenger and paid for it with their lives. Making fun of religious leaders has been a popular sport through the ages. To take a stand for God is to be different from the world and vulnerable to verbal abuse. When we are cynical and sarcastic toward religious leaders, we are in danger of mocking not just the person, but also the spiritual message. While we are not to condone the sin that some leaders commit, we need to pray for them, not laugh at them. True leaders, those who follow God, need to be heard with respect and encouraged in their ministry.

3.1 Although 1.17 states that Jehoram was king of Judah, 3.1 states that Jehoshaphat was Judah's king. As a king grew older, it was common for his son to rule beside him. Jehoshaphat, nearing the end of his reign, appointed his son Jehoram to rule with him. Jehoram (also called Joram) served as co-ruler with Jehoshaphat for five years (853–848 B.C.; he is mentioned again in 8.16–24). Thus the kings of Israel and Judah had the same name—Jehoram. Jehoram, king of Israel, was Ahab's son and Ahaziah's brother (1.17). Both Ahab (1 Kings 16.29–22.40) and Ahaziah (1.2–18) served as kings before Jehoram.

3.3 The sins of Israel's kings are often compared to "the sin of Jeroboam," the first ruler of the northern kingdom of Israel. His great sin was to institute idol worship throughout his kingdom, causing people to turn away from God (1 Kings 12.25–33). By ignoring God and allowing idol worship, Jehoram clung to Jeroboam's sins.

3.4, 5 Israel and Judah held some of the most fertile land and strategic positions in the Middle East. It is no wonder that neighboring nations like Moab envied them and constantly attempted to seize the land. Moab lay just southeast of Israel. The country had been under Israel's control for some time due to Ahab's strong military leadership. When Ahab died, Mesha, the Moabite king, took the opportunity to rebel. While Israel's next king, Ahaziah, did nothing about the revolt, his successor, Jehoram, decided to take action. He joined forces with Jehoshaphat, king of Judah, and went to fight the Moabites. Together, Israel and Judah brought the Moabites to the brink of surrender. But when they saw the Moabite king sacrifice his own son and successor (3.27), they returned home in disgust even though they had won the battle. Moab fought many other battles with both Israel and Judah. Some of them, in fact, were recorded by Mesha (c. 840 B.C.), who carved his exploits on a plaque called the Moabite stone (discovered in 1868).

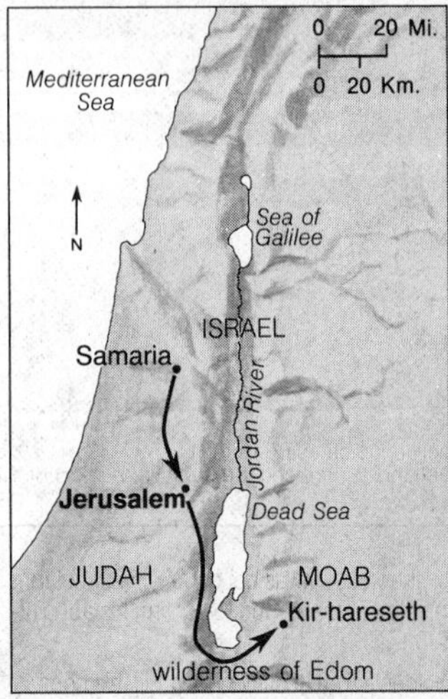

WAR AGAINST MOAB
Moab's king rebelled against Israel. So Jehoram, Israel's king, and Jehoshaphat, Judah's king, attacked Moab. In the parched and rugged wilderness of Edom, the armies ran out of water, but Elisha promised that both water and victory would soon come.

3.5 2 Kgs 1.1 6 So King Jehoram marched out of Samaria at that time and mustered all Israel. 7 As
he went he sent word to King Jehoshaphat of Judah, "The king of Moab has rebelled against me; will you go with me to battle against Moab?" He answered, "I
will; I am with you, my people are your people, my horses are your horses." 8 Then
he asked, "By which way shall we march?" Jehoram answered, "By the way of the
wilderness of Edom."

9 So the king of Israel, the king of Judah, and the king of Edom set out; and
when they had made a roundabout march of seven days, there was no water for the
army or for the animals that were with them. 10 Then the king of Israel said, "Alas!
3.11 1 Kgs 19.21 22.7 The LORD has summoned us, three kings, only to be handed over to Moab." 11 But
Jehoshaphat said, "Is there no prophet of the LORD here, through whom we may
inquire of the LORD?" Then one of the servants of the king of Israel answered,
"Elisha son of Shaphat, who used to pour water on the hands of Elijah, is here."
12 Jehoshaphat said, "The word of the LORD is with him." So the king of Israel and
Jehoshaphat and the king of Edom went down to him.

3.13 1 Kgs 22.6,22 13 Elisha said to the king of Israel, "What have I to do with you? Go to your
father's prophets or to your mother's." But the king of Israel said to him, "No; it is
the LORD who has summoned us, three kings, only to be handed over to Moab."
14 Elisha said, "As the LORD of hosts lives, whom I serve, were it not that I have
regard for King Jehoshaphat of Judah, I would give you neither a look nor a glance.
3.15 1 Sam 10.5 16.23 15 But get me a musician." And then, while the musician was playing, the power of
the LORD came on him. 16 And he said, "Thus says the LORD, 'I will make this wadi
full of pools.' 17 For thus says the LORD, 'You shall see neither wind nor rain, but
the wadi shall be filled with water, so that you shall drink, you, your cattle, and
your animals.' 18 This is only a trifle in the sight of the LORD, for he will also hand

MIRACLES OF ELIJAH & ELISHA

Baal, the false god worshiped by many Israelites, was the god of rain, fire, and farm crops. He also demanded child-sacrifice. Elijah's and Elisha's miracles repeatedly show the power of the true God over the purported realm of Baal, as well as the value God places on the life of a child.

Miracle	*Found where?*	*Factors*
ELIJAH		
1. Food brought by ravens	1 Kings 17.5, 6	Food
2. Widow's food multiplied	1 Kings 17.12–16	Flour and oil
3. Widow's son raised to life	1 Kings 17.17–24	Life of a child
4. Altar and sacrifice consumed	1 Kings 18.16–46	Fire and water
5. Ahaziah's soldiers consumed	2 Kings 1.9–14	Fire
6. Jordan River parted	2 Kings 2.6–8	Water
7. Transported to heaven	2 Kings 2.11, 12	Fire and wind
ELISHA		
1. Jordan River parted	2 Kings 2.13, 14	Water
2. Spring purified at Jericho	2 Kings 2.19–22	Water
3. Widow's oil multiplied	2 Kings 4.1–7	Oil
4. Dead boy raised to life	2 Kings 4.18–37	Life of a child
5. Poison in stew purified	2 Kings 4.38–41	Flour
6. Prophets' food multiplied	2 Kings 4.42–44	Bread and grain
7. Naaman healed of leprosy	2 Kings 5.1–14	Water
8. Gehazi became leprous	2 Kings 5.15–27	Words alone
9. Ax head floated	2 Kings 6.1–7	Water
10. Syrian army blinded	2 Kings 6.8–23	Elisha's prayer

3.10 Edom was under Judah's control, thus they marched with them, making three kings.

3.11–20 Jehoshaphat's request for "a prophet of the Lord" shows how true worship and religious experience in both Israel and Judah had declined. In David's day, both the high priest and the prophets gave the king advice. But most of the priests had left Israel (see the first note on 1 Kings 17.1), and God's prophets were seen as messengers of doom (1 Kings 22.18). This miracle predicted by Elisha affirmed God's power and authority and validated Elisha's ministry. In 2 Chronicles 18, King Jeshoshaphat of Judah and King Ahab of Israel gave the prophet Micaiah a similar request. But they ignored God's advice – with disastrous results.

3.15 The musician probably played a lute, a musical instrument resembling a small guitar. In Old Testament times music often accompanied prophecy (1 Chronicles 25.1).

3.16 A wadi is a stream or dry streambed. In this case, the dry valley would be filled with water.

Moab over to you. 19 You shall conquer every fortified city and every choice city;
every good tree you shall fell, all springs of water you shall stop up, and every good
piece of land you shall ruin with stones." 20 The next day, about the time of the **3.20**
morning offering, suddenly water began to flow from the direction of Edom, until Ex 29.39
the country was filled with water.
21 When all the Moabites heard that the kings had come up to fight against
them, all who were able to put on armor, from the youngest to the oldest, were
called out and were drawn up at the frontier. 22 When they rose early in the morning, and the sun shone upon the water, the Moabites saw the water opposite them
as red as blood. 23 They said, "This is blood; the kings must have fought together, **3.23**
and killed one another. Now then, Moab, to the spoil!" 24 But when they came to 2 Kgs 6.18; 7.6
the camp of Israel, the Israelites rose up and attacked the Moabites, who fled before
them; as they entered Moab they continued the attack.[e] 25 The cities they over- **3.25**
turned, and on every good piece of land everyone threw a stone, until it was cov- Isa 16.7 Jer 48.31,36
ered; every spring of water they stopped up, and every good tree they felled. Only
at Kir-hareseth did the stone walls remain, until the slingers surrounded and attacked it. 26 When the king of Moab saw that the battle was going against him, he
took with him seven hundred swordsmen to break through, opposite the king of
Edom; but they could not. 27 Then he took his firstborn son who was to succeed **3.27**
him, and offered him as a burnt offering on the wall. And great wrath came upon 2 Kgs 16.3 17.17; 21.6
Israel, so they withdrew from him and returned to their own land. Mic 6.7

4 Now the wife of a member of the company of prophets[f] cried to Elisha, "Your **4.1**
servant my husband is dead; and you know that your servant feared the LORD, Lev 25.39,48 Neh 5.2-4
but a creditor has come to take my two children as slaves." 2 Elisha said to her, Jer 34.14
"What shall I do for you? Tell me, what do you have in the house?" She answered, **4.2**
"Your servant has nothing in the house, except a jar of oil." 3 He said, "Go outside, 1 Kgs 17.12
borrow vessels from all your neighbors, empty vessels and not just a few.

Elisha provides oil for a widow

4 Then go in, and shut the door behind you and your children, and start pouring into
all these vessels; when each is full, set it aside." 5 So she left him and shut the door
behind her and her children; they kept bringing vessels to her, and she kept pouring. 6 When the vessels were full, she said to her son, "Bring me another vessel."
But he said to her, "There are no more." Then the oil stopped flowing. 7 She came
and told the man of God, and he said, "Go sell the oil and pay your debts, and you
and your children can live on the rest."

Elisha restores a child to life

8 One day Elisha was passing through Shunem, where a wealthy woman lived, **4.8**
who urged him to have a meal. So whenever he passed that way, he would stop 1 Sam 28.4 1 Kgs 1.3,4
there for a meal. 9 She said to her husband, "Look, I am sure that this man who **4.9**
regularly passes our way is a holy man of God. 10 Let us make a small roof chamber Deut 33.1

[e] Compare Gk Syr: Meaning of Heb uncertain [f] Heb *the sons of the prophets*

3.25 The Israelites scattered stones over the land to make it unfit for farming. They also filled the wells and cut down the fruit trees. Their victory was complete.

4.1ff This chapter records four of God's miracles through Elisha: providing money for a poverty-stricken widow (4.1–7); raising a dead boy to life (4.32–37); purifying poisoned food (4.38–41); and providing food for 100 men (4.42–44). These miracles show God's tenderness and care for those who are faithful to him.

When reading the Old Testament, it is easy to focus on God's harsh judgment of the rebellious and to minimize his tender care for those who love and serve him. To see him at work providing for his followers helps us keep his severe justice toward the unrepentant in proper perspective.

4.1 Poor people and debtors were allowed to pay their debts by selling themselves or their children as slaves. God ordered rich people and creditors not to take advantage of these people during their time of extreme need (see Deuteronomy 15.1–18 for an explanation of these practices). This woman's creditor was not acting in the spirit of God's law. Elisha's kind deed demonstrates that God wants us to go beyond simply keeping the law. We must also show compassion.

4.6 The woman and her sons collected pots and jars from their neighbors, pouring oil into them from their one pot. The oil was olive oil and was used for cooking, for lamps, and for fuel. The oil stopped pouring only when they ran out of containers. The number of jars they gathered was an indication of their faith. God's provision was as large as their faith and willingness to obey. Beware of limiting God's blessings by a lack of faith and obedience. God can and will do even more than we ask or think (Ephesians 3.20).

with walls, and put there for him a bed, a table, a chair, and a lamp, so that he can
stay there whenever he comes to us."
4.11 2 Kgs 4.29 5.20; 8.4 11 One day when he came there, he went up to the chamber and lay down there.
12 He said to his servant Gehazi, "Call the Shunammite woman." When he had
called her, she stood before him. 13 He said to him, "Say to her, Since you have
taken all this trouble for us, what may be done for you? Would you have a word
spoken on your behalf to the king or to the commander of the army?" She answered, "I live among my own people." 14 He said, "What then may be done for
4.15 Gen 18.14 her?" Gehazi answered, "Well, she has no son, and her husband is old." 15 He said,
"Call her." When he had called her, she stood at the door. 16 He said, "At this
season, in due time, you shall embrace a son." She replied, "No, my lord, O man
of God; do not deceive your servant."
17 The woman conceived and bore a son at that season, in due time, as Elisha
had declared to her.
18 When the child was older, he went out one day to his father among the reapers. 19 He complained to his father, "Oh, my head, my head!" The father said to his
servant, "Carry him to his mother." 20 He carried him and brought him to his
mother; the child sat on her lap until noon, and he died. 21 She went up and laid him
on the bed of the man of God, closed the door on him, and left. 22 Then she called
to her husband, and said, "Send me one of the servants and one of the donkeys, so
that I may quickly go to the man of God and come back again." 23 He said, "Why
go to him today? It is neither new moon nor sabbath." She said, "It will be all
right." 24 Then she saddled the donkey and said to her servant, "Urge the animal on;
do not hold back for me unless I tell you." 25 So she set out, and came to the man
of God at Mount Carmel.
When the man of God saw her coming, he said to Gehazi his servant, "Look,
there is the Shunammite woman; 26 run at once to meet her, and say to her, Are you
all right? Is your husband all right? Is the child all right?" She answered, "It is all
4.27 Mt 28.9 right." 27 When she came to the man of God at the mountain, she caught hold of his
feet. Gehazi approached to push her away. But the man of God said, "Let her
alone, for she is in bitter distress; the LORD has hidden it from me and has not told
me." 28 Then she said, "Did I ask my lord for a son? Did I not say, Do not mislead
4.29 Ex 4.17; 7.19 14.16 me?" 29 He said to Gehazi, "Gird up your loins, and take my staff in your hand, and
go. If you meet anyone, give no greeting, and if anyone greets you, do not answer;
and lay my staff on the face of the child." 30 Then the mother of the child said, "As
the LORD lives, and as you yourself live, I will not leave without you." So he rose

THE FAMILY IN SHUNEM
Elisha often stayed with a kind family in Shunem. When the son suddenly died, his mother traveled to Mount Carmel to find Elisha. He returned with her, and raised the boy from the dead. Elisha then went to his home in Gilgal.

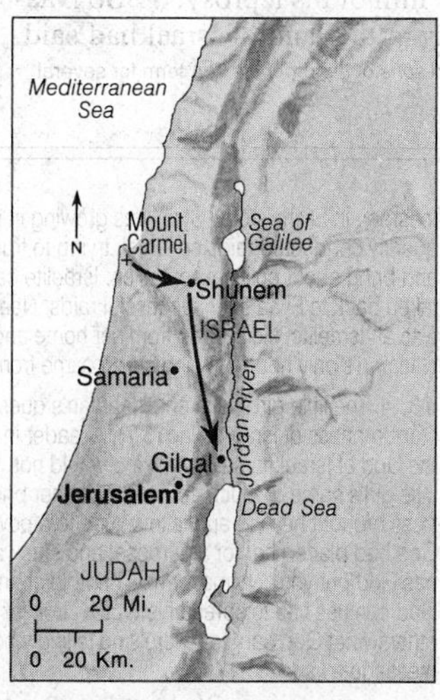

4.9 The Shunammite woman realized that Elisha was a man of God and so she prepared a room for him to use whenever he was in town. She did this out of kindness and because she sensed a need, not for any selfish motives. Soon, however, her kindness would be rewarded far beyond her wildest dreams. How sensitive are you to those who pass by your home and flow through your life – especially those who teach and preach God's Word? What special needs do they have that you could meet? Look for ways to serve and help.

4.16 The Shunammite woman was about to receive the same favor from the Lord as Sarah did many years before. And like Sarah, she reacted in disbelief (Genesis 18.10–15). Perhaps she was afraid to believe after having so many other hopes dashed. Perhaps this just seemed too incredible to possibly come true. Despite her inability to believe, the Lord remained faithful and she did have a child as Elisha had said. Similarly, God remains faithful to us even when his promises are beyond our ability to believe.

up and followed her. 31 Gehazi went on ahead and laid the staff on the face of the
child, but there was no sound or sign of life. He came back to meet him and told
him, "The child has not awakened."
32 When Elisha came into the house, he saw the child lying dead on his bed.
33 So he went in and closed the door on the two of them, and prayed to the LORD.
34 Then he got up on the bed[g] and lay upon the child, putting his mouth upon his 4.34
mouth, his eyes upon his eyes, and his hands upon his hands; and while he lay bent 1 Kgs 17.21
over him, the flesh of the child became warm. 35 He got down, walked once to and
fro in the room, then got up again and bent over him; the child sneezed seven times,
and the child opened his eyes. 36 Elisha[h] summoned Gehazi and said, "Call the
Shunammite woman." So he called her. When she came to him, he said, "Take
your son." 37 She came and fell at his feet, bowing to the ground; then she took her 4.37
son and left. Heb 11.35

Elisha makes a poisonous stew edible

38 When Elisha returned to Gilgal, there was a famine in the land. As the com- 4.38
pany of prophets was[i] sitting before him, he said to his servant, "Put the large pot 2 Sam 21.1
on, and make some stew for the company of prophets."[j] 39 One of them went out 2 Kgs 8.1
into the field to gather herbs; he found a wild vine and gathered from it a lapful of
wild gourds, and came and cut them up into the pot of stew, not knowing what they
were. 40 They served some for the men to eat. But while they were eating the stew,
they cried out, "O man of God, there is death in the pot!" They could not eat it.
41 He said, "Then bring some flour." He threw it into the pot, and said, "Serve the 4.41
people and let them eat." And there was nothing harmful in the pot. Ex 15.25
2 Kgs 2.22

Elisha feeds 100 men

42 A man came from Baal-shalishah, bringing food from the first fruits to the
man of God: twenty loaves of barley and fresh ears of grain in his sack. Elisha said,
"Give it to the people and let them eat." 43 But his servant said, "How can I set this
before a hundred people?" So he repeated, "Give it to the people and let them eat,
for thus says the LORD, 'They shall eat and have some left.'" 44 He set it before 4.44
them, they ate, and had some left, according to the word of the LORD. Mt 14.16,20

The healing of Naaman the leper

5 Naaman, commander of the army of the king of Aram, was a great man and in 5.1
high favor with his master, because by him the LORD had given victory to Lk 4.27
Aram. The man, though a mighty warrior, suffered from leprosy.[k] 2 Now the Ara- 5.2
means on one of their raids had taken a young girl captive from the land of Israel, 2 Kgs 6.23
and she served Naaman's wife. 3 She said to her mistress, "If only my lord were
with the prophet who is in Samaria! He would cure him of his leprosy."[k] 4 So Naaman[h] went in and told his lord just what the girl from the land of Israel had said.

[g] Heb lacks *on the bed* [h] Heb *he* [i] Heb *sons of the prophets were* [j] Heb *sons of the prophets* [k] A term for several skin diseases; precise meaning uncertain

---

4.32–36 Elisha's prayer and method of raising the dead boy show God's personal care for hurting people. We must express genuine concern for others as we carry God's message to them. Only then will we faithfully represent our compassionate Father in heaven.

4.40 "Death in the pot" means that the food was poisonous.

5.1 Leprosy, much like AIDS today, was one of the most feared diseases of the time. Some forms were extremely contagious and, in many cases, incurable. In its worst forms, leprosy led to death. Many lepers were forced out of the cities into quarantined camps. Since Naaman still held his post, he probably had a mild form of the disease, or perhaps it was still in the early stages. In either case, his life would be tragically shortened by his disease. (For more about leprosy in Bible times, see the note on Leviticus 13.1ff.)

5.2 Syria was Israel's neighbor to the northeast, but the two nations were rarely on friendly terms. Under David, Syria paid tribute to Israel. In Elisha's day, Syria was growing in power and frequently conducted raids on Israel, trying to frustrate the people and bring about political confusion. Israelite captives were often taken back to Syria after successful raids. Naaman's servant girl was an Israelite, kidnapped from her home and family. Ironically, Naaman's only hope of being cured came from Israel.

5.3, 4 The little girl's faith and Naaman's quest contrast with the stubbornness of Israel's king (5.7). A leader in mighty Syria sought the God of Israel; Israel's own king would not. We don't know the little girl's name or much about her, but her brief word to her mistress brought healing and faith in God to a powerful Syrian captain. God had placed her for a purpose, and she was faithful. Where has God put you? No matter how humble or small your position, God can use you to spread his Word. Look for opportunities to tell others what God can do. There's no telling who will hear your message!

5 And the king of Aram said, "Go then, and I will send along a letter to the king of
Israel."
He went, taking with him ten talents of silver, six thousand shekels of gold, and
ten sets of garments. 6 He brought the letter to the king of Israel, which read,
"When this letter reaches you, know that I have sent to you my servant Naaman,
that you may cure him of his leprosy."[l] 7 When the king of Israel read the letter, he
tore his clothes and said, "Am I God, to give death or life, that this man sends word
to me to cure a man of his leprosy?[l] Just look and see how he is trying to pick a
quarrel with me."
8 But when Elisha the man of God heard that the king of Israel had torn his
clothes, he sent a message to the king, "Why have you torn your clothes? Let him
come to me, that he may learn that there is a prophet in Israel." 9 So Naaman came
with his horses and chariots, and halted at the entrance of Elisha's house. 10 Elisha
sent a messenger to him, saying, "Go, wash in the Jordan seven times, and your
flesh shall be restored and you shall be clean." 11 But Naaman became angry and
went away, saying, "I thought that for me he would surely come out, and stand and
call on the name of the LORD his God, and would wave his hand over the spot, and
cure the leprosy![l] 12 Are not Abana[m] and Pharpar, the rivers of Damascus, better
than all the waters of Israel? Could I not wash in them, and be clean?" He turned
and went away in a rage. 13 But his servants approached and said to him, "Father,
if the prophet had commanded you to do something difficult, would you not have
done it? How much more, when all he said to you was, 'Wash, and be clean'?"
14 So he went down and immersed himself seven times in the Jordan, according to
the word of the man of God; his flesh was restored like the flesh of a young boy, and
he was clean.
15 Then he returned to the man of God, he and all his company; he came and
stood before him and said, "Now I know that there is no God in all the earth except
in Israel; please accept a present from your servant." 16 But he said, "As the LORD
lives, whom I serve, I will accept nothing!" He urged him to accept, but he refused.
17 Then Naaman said, "If not, please let two mule-loads of earth be given to your
servant; for your servant will no longer offer burnt offering or sacrifice to any god
except the LORD. 18 But may the LORD pardon your servant on one count: when my
master goes into the house of Rimmon to worship there, leaning on my arm, and I

[l] A term for several skin diseases; precise meaning uncertain [m] Another reading is *Amana*

5.5 1 Sam 9.8; 1 Kgs 13.7; 2 Kgs 8.8,9
5.7 Gen 30.2; 37.29; 1 Sam 2.6
5.10 Jn 9.7
5.14 Job 33.23-25; Lk 4.27; 5.13
5.15 Josh 2.9; 9.9; 1 Sam 17.46; 1 Kgs 18.36; Isa 43.10
5.16 Gen 14.22; 2 Kgs 3.14
5.17 Ex 20.24

5.5 The name of Israel's king is not mentioned in this story. Because the events of 2 Kings 1 – 8 are mainly about Elisha's ministry and are not intended to be chronological, we cannot know for sure, but the king was most likely Jehoram (3.1).

5.7 King Ben-hadad of Syria sent Naaman to the king of Israel, thinking the king could order Elisha to cure Naaman. He thought God's gift of healing could be bought. The king of Israel was upset because he knew he had no control over the situation, and he thought the Syrian king was trying to find an excuse to fight. He was completely ignorant of God's power working through Elisha. He did not understand that God's power could transform even Israel's enemies.

5.9–15 Naaman, a great hero, was used to getting respect, and he was outraged when Elisha treated him like an ordinary person. A proud man, he expected royal treatment. To wash in a great river would be one thing, but the Jordan was small and dirty. To wash in the Jordan, Naaman thought, was beneath a man of his position. But Naaman had to humble himself and obey Elisha's commands in order to be healed.

Obedience to God begins with humility. We must believe that his way is better than our own. We may not always understand his ways of working, but by humbly obeying, we will receive his blessings. We must remember that (1) God's ways are best; (2) God wants our obedience more than anything else; and (3) God can use anything to accomplish his purposes.

5.12 Naaman left in a rage because the cure for his disease seemed too simple. He was a hero, and he expected a heroic cure. Full of pride and self-will, he could not accept the simple cure of faith. Sometimes people react to God's offer of forgiveness in the same way. Just to *believe* in Jesus Christ somehow doesn't seem significant enough to bring eternal life. To obey God's commands doesn't seem heroic. What Naaman had to do to have his leprosy washed away is similar to what we must do to have our sin washed away—humbly accept God's mercy. Don't let your reaction to the way of faith keep you from the cure you need the most.

5.16 Elisha refused Naaman's money to show that God's favor cannot be purchased. Our money, like Naaman's, is useless when we face death. No matter how much wealth we accumulate in this life, it will evaporate when we stand before God, our Creator. It will be our faith in Jesus Christ that saves us, not our bank accounts.

5.18, 19 How could Naaman be pardoned for bowing to a heathen idol? Naaman was not asking for permission to worship the god Rimmon, but to do his civil duty, helping the king get down and up as he bowed. Rimmon was short for Hadad-Rimmon, the god of Damascus, who was believed to be a god of rain and thunder. Naaman, unlike most of his contemporaries, showed a keen awareness of God's power. Instead of adding God to his nation's collection of idols, he acknowledged that there was only one true God. He did not intend to worship other gods. His asking for pardon in this one area shows the marked contrast between Naaman and the Israelites, who were continually worshiping many idols.

bow down in the house of Rimmon, when I do bow down in the house of Rimmon,
may the LORD pardon your servant on this one count." 19 He said to him, "Go in
peace."
But when Naaman had gone from him a short distance, 20 Gehazi, the servant of **5.20**
Elisha the man of God, thought, "My master has let that Aramean Naaman off too 2 Kgs 4.11,12,
lightly by not accepting from him what he offered. As the LORD lives, I will run 31,36
after him and get something out of him." 21 So Gehazi went after Naaman. When
Naaman saw someone running after him, he jumped down from the chariot to meet
him and said, "Is everything all right?" 22 He replied, "Yes, but my master has sent
me to say, 'Two members of a company of prophets[n] have just come to me from
the hill country of Ephraim; please give them a talent of silver and two changes of
clothing.' " 23 Naaman said, "Please accept two talents." He urged him, and tied up
two talents of silver in two bags, with two changes of clothing, and gave them to
two of his servants, who carried them in front of Gehazi.[o] 24 When he came to the
citadel, he took the bags[p] from them, and stored them inside; he dismissed the
men, and they left.
25 He went in and stood before his master; and Elisha said to him, "Where have
you been, Gehazi?" He answered, "Your servant has not gone anywhere at all."
26 But he said to him, "Did I not go with you in spirit when someone left his chariot
to meet you? Is this a time to accept money and to accept clothing, olive orchards
and vineyards, sheep and oxen, and male and female slaves? 27 Therefore the lep- **5.27**
rosy[q] of Naaman shall cling to you, and to your descendants forever." So he left Ex 4.6
his presence leprous,[q] as white as snow. Num 12.10

Elisha makes an axhead float

6 Now the company of prophets[n] said to Elisha, "As you see, the place where **6.1**
we live under your charge is too small for us. 2 Let us go to the Jordan, and let 2 Kgs 2.3,5,7
us collect logs there, one for each of us, and build a place there for us to live." He
answered, "Do so." 3 Then one of them said, "Please come with your servants."
And he answered, "I will." 4 So he went with them. When they came to the Jordan,
they cut down trees. 5 But as one was felling a log, his ax head fell into the water;
he cried out, "Alas, master! It was borrowed." 6 Then the man of God said, "Where **6.6**
did it fall?" When he showed him the place, he cut off a stick, and threw it in there, Ex 15.25
and made the iron float. 7 He said, "Pick it up." So he reached out his hand and took 2 Kgs 2.21; 4.41
it.

[n] Heb *sons of the prophets* [o] Heb *him* [p] Heb lacks *the bags* [q] A term for several skin diseases; precise meaning uncertain

Elijah raised a boy from the dead	1 Kings 17.22	**PEOPLE RAISED FROM THE DEAD**
Elisha raised a boy from the dead	2 Kings 4.34–35	God is all-powerful. Nothing in life is beyond his control, not even death.
Elisha's bones raised a man from the dead	2 Kings 13.20–21	
Jesus raised a boy from the dead	Luke 7.14, 15	
Jesus raised a girl from the dead	Luke 8.52–56	
Jesus raised Lazarus from the dead	John 11.38–44	
Peter raised a woman from the dead	Acts 9.40, 41	
Paul raised a man from the dead	Acts 20.9–20	

5.20–27 Gehazi saw a perfect opportunity to get rich by selfishly asking for the reward Elisha had refused. Unfortunately, there were three problems with his plan: (1) he willingly accepted money that had been offered to someone else; (2) he wrongly implied that money could be exchanged for God's free gift of healing and mercy; (3) he lied and tried to cover up his motives for accepting the money. Although Gehazi had been a helpful servant, personal gain had become more important to him than serving God.

This passage is not teaching that money is evil or that ministers should not get paid; instead, it is warning against greed and deceit. True service is motivated by love and devotion to God and seeks no personal gain. As you serve God, check your motives—you can't serve both God and money (Matthew 6.24).

6.1–7 The incident of the floating ax head is recorded to show God's care and provision for those who trust him, even in the insignificant events of everyday life. God is always present. Placed in the Bible between the healing of a Syrian general and the deliverance of Israel's army, this miracle also shows Elisha's personal contact with the students who were learning to be prophets. Although he had the respect of kings, Elisha never forgot to care for the faithful. Don't let the importance of your work drive out your concern for human need.

Elisha captures an army

8 Once when the king of Aram was at war with Israel, he took counsel with his
6.9 1 Kgs 20.13,28 officers. He said, "At such and such a place shall be my camp." 9 But the man of
God sent word to the king of Israel, "Take care not to pass this place, because the
Arameans are going down there." 10 The king of Israel sent word to the place of
which the man of God spoke. More than once or twice he warned such a place[r] so
that it was on the alert.

11 The mind of the king of Aram was greatly perturbed because of this; he
called his officers and said to them, "Now tell me who among us sides with the king
of Israel?" 12 Then one of his officers said, "No one, my lord king. It is Elisha, the
prophet in Israel, who tells the king of Israel the words that you speak in your
6.13 Gen 37.17 bedchamber." 13 He said, "Go and find where he is; I will send and seize him." He
was told, "He is in Dothan." 14 So he sent horses and chariots there and a great
6.14 2 Kgs 1.9 army; they came by night, and surrounded the city.

[r] Heb *warned it*

ELISHA

Few "replacements" in Scripture were as effective as Elisha, who was Elijah's replacement as God's prophet to Israel. But Elisha had a great example to follow in the prophet Elijah. He remained with Elijah until the last moments of his teacher's life on earth. He was willing to follow and learn in order to gain power to do the work to which God had called him.

Both Elijah and Elisha concentrated their efforts on the particular needs of the people around them. The fiery Elijah confronted and exposed idolatry, helping to create an atmosphere where people could freely and publicly worship God. Elisha then moved in to demonstrate God's powerful, yet caring, nature to all who came to him for help. He spent less time in conflict with evil and more in compassionate care of people. The Bible records 18 encounters between Elisha and needy people.

Elisha saw more *in* life than most people because he recognized that with God there was more *to* life. He knew that all we are and have comes to us from God. The miracles that occurred during Elisha's ministry put people in touch with the personal and all-powerful God. Elijah would have been proud of his replacement's work.

We too have great examples to follow—both people in Scripture and those who have positively influenced our lives. We must resist the tendency to think about the limitations that our family background or environment create for us. Instead, we should ask God to use us for his purposes—perhaps, like Elijah, to take a stand against great wrongs or, like Elisha, to show compassion for the daily needs of those around us. Ask him to use you as only he can.

Strengths and accomplishments:
- Was Elijah's successor as a prophet of God
- Had a ministry that lasted over 50 years
- Had a major impact on four nations: Israel, Judah, Moab, and Syria
- Was a man of integrity who did not try to enrich himself at others' expense
- Did many miracles to help those in need

Lessons from his life:
- In God's eyes, one measure of greatness is the willingness to serve the poor as well as the powerful
- An effective replacement not only learns from his master, but also builds upon his master's achievements

Vital statistics:
- Where: From the tribe of Issachar, prophesied to the northern kingdom
- Occupation: Farmer, prophet
- Relatives: Father: Shaphat
- Contemporaries: Elijah, Ahab, Jezebel, Jehu

Key verse:
"When they had crossed, Elijah said to Elisha, 'Tell me what I may do for you, before I am taken from you.' Elisha said, 'Please let me inherit a double share of your spirit' " (2 Kings 2.9).

Elisha's story is told in 1 Kings 19.16—2 Kings 13.20. He is also mentioned in Luke 4.27.

15 When an attendant of the man of God rose early in the morning and went
out, an army with horses and chariots was all around the city. His servant said,
“Alas, master! What shall we do?” 16 He replied, “Do not be afraid, for there are 6.16
more with us than there are with them.” 17 Then Elisha prayed: “O LORD, please Ex 14.13 2 Chron 32.7
open his eyes that he may see.” So the LORD opened the eyes of the servant, and he Ps 3.6; 11.1 Rom 8.31
saw; the mountain was full of horses and chariots of fire all around Elisha. 18 When
the Arameans[s] came down against him, Elisha prayed to the LORD, and said, 6.17 2 Kgs 2.11
“Strike this people, please, with blindness.” So he struck them with blindness as Ps 34.7 Isa 42.7
Elisha had asked. 19 Elisha said to them, “This is not the way, and this is not the Acts 26.18
city; follow me, and I will bring you to the man whom you seek.” And he led them 6.18 Gen 19.11
to Samaria. 6.19
20 As soon as they entered Samaria, Elisha said, “O LORD, open the eyes of 1 Kgs 20.1 2 Kgs 3.1
these men so that they may see.” The LORD opened their eyes, and they saw that
they were inside Samaria. 21 When the king of Israel saw them he said to Elisha, 6.21
“Father, shall I kill them? Shall I kill them?” 22 He answered, “No! Did you capture 1 Sam 24.4,19 26.8
with your sword and your bow those whom you want to kill? Set food and water 6.22
before them so that they may eat and drink; and let them go to their master.” 23 So 2 Chron 28.8 Rom 12.20
he prepared for them a great feast; after they ate and drank, he sent them on their 6.23
way, and they went to their master. And the Arameans no longer came raiding into 2 Kgs 5.2
the land of Israel.

Elisha predicts the end of a famine

24 Some time later King Ben-hadad of Aram mustered his entire army; he 6.24
marched against Samaria and laid siege to it. 25 As the siege continued, famine in 1 Kgs 20.1
Samaria became so great that a donkey's head was sold for eighty shekels of silver, 6.25 2 Kgs 7.12
and one-fourth of a kab of dove's dung for five shekels of silver. 26 Now as the king 6.26
of Israel was walking on the city wall, a woman cried out to him, “Help, my lord Lev 26.29 Deut 28.53
king!” 27 He said, “No! Let the LORD help you. How can I help you? From the 1 Kgs 21.27 Lam 4.10
threshing floor or from the wine press?” 28 But then the king asked her, “What is

[s] Heb *they*

ELISHA AND THE SYRIANS
Elisha knew Syria's battle plans and kept Israel's king informed. The Syrian king tracked down Elisha at Dothan, but Elisha prayed that the Syrian army would be blinded. He then led the blind army into Samaria, Israel's capital city!

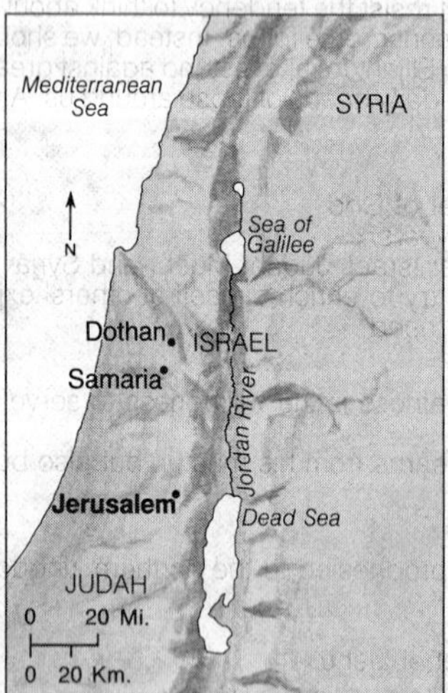

6.15 Elisha's servant is not named in this story, but it may have been Gehazi. Chapters 1 – 8 are not intended to be in chronological order, so this event could have occurred before Gehazi was struck with leprosy (5.27).

6.16, 17 Elisha's servant was no longer afraid when he saw God's mighty heavenly army. Faith reveals that God is doing more for his people than we can ever realize through sight alone. When you face difficulties that seem insurmountable, remember that spiritual resources are there even if you can't see them. Look through the eyes of faith and let God show you his resources. If you don't see God working in your life, the problem may be your spiritual eyesight, not God's power.

6.21, 22 Elisha told the king not to slaughter the Syrians. The king was not to take credit for what God alone had done. In setting food and water before them, he was heaping burning "coals of fire on their heads" (Proverbs 25.21, 22).

6.23 How long the Syrians stayed away from Israel is not known, but a number of years probably passed before the invasion recorded in 6.24 occurred. The Syrians must have forgotten the time their army was supernaturally blinded and sent home.

6.24 This was probably Ben-hadad II, whose father ruled Syria in the days of Baasha (1 Kings 15.18). Elisha constantly frustrated Ben-hadad II in his attempts to take control of Israel.

6.25 When a city like Samaria faced famine, it was no small matter. Although its farmers grew enough food to feed the people for a specific season, they did not have enough to maintain them in prolonged times of emergency when all supplies were cut off. This famine was so severe that mothers resorted to eating their children (6.26–30). Deuteronomy 28.49–57 predicted that this would happen when the people of Israel rejected God's leadership.

your complaint?" She answered, "This woman said to me, 'Give up your son; we
will eat him today, and we will eat my son tomorrow.' 29 So we cooked my son and
ate him. The next day I said to her, 'Give up your son and we will eat him.' But she
has hidden her son." 30 When the king heard the words of the woman he tore his
clothes—now since he was walking on the city wall, the people could see that he
6.31 2 Sam 3.9,10 1 Kgs 2.23,24 19.2 had sackcloth on his body underneath— 31 and he said, "So may God do to me, and
more, if the head of Elisha son of Shaphat stays on his shoulders today." 32 So he
dispatched a man from his presence.
6.32 1 Kgs 18.14 Ezek 8.1; 14.1 20.1 Now Elisha was sitting in his house, and the elders were sitting with him. Before
the messenger arrived, Elisha said to the elders, "Are you aware that this murderer
has sent someone to take off my head? When the messenger comes, see that you
shut the door and hold it closed against him. Is not the sound of his master's feet
6.33 Isa 8.21 behind him?" 33 While he was still speaking with them, the king[t] came down to
him and said, "This trouble is from the LORD! Why should I hope in the LORD any
7 longer?" 1 But Elisha said, "Hear the word of the LORD: thus says the LORD,
Tomorrow about this time a measure of choice meal shall be sold for a shekel,
7.2 Mal 3.10 and two measures of barley for a shekel, at the gate of Samaria." 2 Then the captain
on whose hand the king leaned said to the man of God, "Even if the LORD were to
make windows in the sky, could such a thing happen?" But he said, "You shall see
it with your own eyes, but you shall not eat from it."

Four lepers discover the abandoned camp

7.3 Lev 13.45 Num 5.1,2 2 Kgs 5.1 Mt 8.4 3 Now there were four leprous[u] men outside the city gate, who said to one
another, "Why should we sit here until we die? 4 If we say, 'Let us enter the city,'
the famine is in the city, and we shall die there; but if we sit here, we shall also die.
7.4 2 Kgs 6.24 Therefore, let us desert to the Aramean camp; if they spare our lives, we shall live;
and if they kill us, we shall but die." 5 So they arose at twilight to go to the Aramean
camp; but when they came to the edge of the Aramean camp, there was no one there
7.6 2 Sam 5.24 2 Chron 12.3 at all. 6 For the Lord had caused the Aramean army to hear the sound of chariots,
and of horses, the sound of a great army, so that they said to one another, "The king
of Israel has hired the kings of the Hittites and the kings of Egypt to fight against
us." 7 So they fled away in the twilight and abandoned their tents, their horses, and
their donkeys leaving the camp just as it was, and fled for their lives. 8 When these
leprous[u] men had come to the edge of the camp, they went into a tent, ate and
drank, carried off silver, gold, and clothing, and went and hid them. Then they
came back, entered another tent, carried off things from it, and went and hid them.
9 Then they said to one another, "What we are doing is wrong. This is a day of
good news; if we are silent and wait until the morning light, we will be found
guilty; therefore let us go and tell the king's household." 10 So they came and called

[t] See 7.2: Heb *messenger* [u] A term for several skin diseases; precise meaning uncertain

---

6.31 This verse means, "May God kill me if I don't execute Elisha this very day."

6.31–33 Why did the king blame Elisha for the famine and troubles of the siege? Here are some possible reasons: (1) Some commentators say that Elisha must have told the king to trust God for deliverance. The king did this and even wore sackcloth (6.30), but at this point the situation seemed hopeless. Apparently the king thought Elisha had given him bad advice and not even God could help them. (2) For years there was conflict between the kings of Israel and the prophets of God. The prophets often predicted doom because of the kings' evil, so the kings saw them as troublemakers. Thus Israel's king was striking out in frustration at Elisha. (3) The king may have remembered when Elijah helped bring an end to a famine (1 Kings 18.41–46). Knowing Elisha was a man of God, perhaps the king thought he could do any miracle he wanted and was angry that he had not come to Israel's rescue.

7.1, 2 When Elisha prophesied God's deliverance, the king's officer said it couldn't happen. The officer's faith and hope were gone, but God's words came true anyway (7.14–16)! Sometimes we become preoccupied with problems when we should be looking for opportunities. Instead of focusing on the negatives, develop an attitude of expectancy. To say that God *cannot* rescue someone or that a situation is *impossible* demonstrates a lack of faith.

7.2 "Then the captain on whose hand the king leaned" means an army officer who assisted the king.

7.3 According to the law, lepers were not allowed in the city, but were to depend on charity outside the gate (Leviticus 13.45, 46; Numbers 5.1–4). Because of the famine and the presence of the Syrian army, their situation was desperate.

7.3–10 The lepers discovered the deserted camp and realized their lives had been spared. At first they kept the good news to themselves, forgetting their fellow citizens who were starving in the city. The Good News about Jesus Christ must be shared too, for no news is more important. We must not forget those who are dying without it. We must not become so preoccupied with our own faith that we neglect sharing it with those around us. Our "good news," like that of the lepers, will not "wait until the morning light."

to the gatekeepers of the city, and told them, "We went to the Aramean camp, but
there was no one to be seen or heard there, nothing but the horses tied, the donkeys
tied, and the tents as they were." 11 Then the gatekeepers called out and proclaimed
it to the king's household. 12 The king got up in the night, and said to his servants, **7.12**
"I will tell you what the Arameans have prepared against us. They know that we are Josh 8.6,7 2 Kgs 6.25
starving; so they have left the camp to hide themselves in the open country, thinking, 'When they come out of the city, we shall take them alive and get into the
city.' " 13 One of his servants said, "Let some men take five of the remaining
horses, since those left here will suffer the fate of the whole multitude of Israel that
have perished already;[v] let us send and find out." 14 So they took two mounted
men, and the king sent them after the Aramean army, saying, "Go and find out."
15 So they went after them as far as the Jordan; the whole way was littered with
garments and equipment that the Arameans had thrown away in their haste. So the
messengers returned, and told the king.
16 Then the people went out, and plundered the camp of the Arameans. So a
measure of choice meal was sold for a shekel, and two measures of barley for a
shekel, according to the word of the LORD. 17 Now the king had appointed the cap- **7.17**
tain on whose hand he leaned to have charge of the gate; the people trampled him 2 Kgs 7.2
to death in the gate, just as the man of God had said when the king came down to
him. 18 For when the man of God had said to the king, "Two measures of barley
shall be sold for a shekel, and a measure of choice meal for a shekel, about this time
tomorrow in the gate of Samaria," 19 the captain had answered the man of God,
"Even if the LORD were to make windows in the sky, could such a thing happen?"
And he had answered, "You shall see it with your own eyes, but you shall not eat
from it." 20 It did indeed happen to him; the people trampled him to death in the
gate.

A woman's land is returned

8 Now Elisha had said to the woman whose son he had restored to life, "Get up **8.1**
and go with your household, and settle wherever you can; for the LORD has Gen 41.27 Deut 28.22
called for a famine, and it will come on the land for seven years." 2 So the woman Ps 105.16
got up and did according to the word of the man of God; she went with her household and settled in the land of the Philistines seven years. 3 At the end of the seven
years, when the woman returned from the land of the Philistines, she set out to
appeal to the king for her house and her land. 4 Now the king was talking with **8.4**
Gehazi the servant of the man of God, saying, "Tell me all the great things that 2 Kgs 4.11,12 5.20
Elisha has done." 5 While he was telling the king how Elisha had restored a dead **8.5**
person to life, the woman whose son he had restored to life appealed to the king for 2 Kgs 4.34
her house and her land. Gehazi said, "My lord king, here is the woman, and here
is her son whom Elisha restored to life." 6 When the king questioned the woman,
she told him. So the king appointed an official for her, saying, "Restore all that was
hers, together with all the revenue of the fields from the day that she left the land
until now."

Hazael murders King Ben-hadad

7 Elisha went to Damascus while King Ben-hadad of Aram was ill. When it was **8.7**
told him, "The man of God has come here," 8 the king said to Hazael, "Take a 2 Kgs 6.24; 13.3
present with you and go to meet the man of God. Inquire of the LORD through him, **8.8** 1 Kgs 14.3
whether I shall recover from this illness." 9 So Hazael went to meet him, taking a 19.15
present with him, all kinds of goods of Damascus, forty camel loads. When he
entered and stood before him, he said, "Your son King Ben-hadad of Aram has sent
me to you, saying, 'Shall I recover from this illness?' " 10 Elisha said to him, "Go,

[v] Compare Gk Syr Vg: Meaning of Heb uncertain

8.1–6 This story must have happened before the events recorded in chapter 5, because the seven-year famine must have ended before Gehazi was struck with leprosy. This shows Elijah's long-term concern for this widow and contrasts his miraculous public ministry with his private ministry to this family. Elisha's life exemplifies the kind of concern we should have for others.

say to him, 'You shall certainly recover'; but the LORD has shown me that he shall
8.11 2 Kgs 2.17 certainly die." 11 He fixed his gaze and stared at him, until he was ashamed. Then
the man of God wept. 12 Hazael asked, "Why does my lord weep?" He answered,
8.12 2 Kgs 10.32,33 12.17; 13.3 15.16 "Because I know the evil that you will do to the people of Israel; you will set their
fortresses on fire, you will kill their young men with the sword, dash in pieces their
little ones, and rip up their pregnant women." 13 Hazael said, "What is your ser-
8.13 1 Sam 17.43 2 Sam 9.8 vant, who is a mere dog, that he should do this great thing?" Elisha answered, "The
LORD has shown me that you are to be king over Aram." 14 Then he left Elisha, and
went to his master Ben-hadad,[w] who said to him, "What did Elisha say to you?"
And he answered, "He told me that you would certainly recover." 15 But the next
day he took the bed-cover and dipped it in water and spread it over the king's face,
until he died. And Hazael succeeded him.

2. Kings of Israel and Judah

Jehoram rules Judah

8.16 2 Kgs 1.17; 3.1 16 In the fifth year of King Joram son of Ahab of Israel,[x] Jehoram son of King
Jehoshaphat of Judah began to reign. 17 He was thirty-two years old when he be-
8.17 2 Chron 21.5 came king, and he reigned eight years in Jerusalem. 18 He walked in the way of the
kings of Israel, as the house of Ahab had done, for the daughter of Ahab was his
8.19 1 Kgs 11.36 wife. He did what was evil in the sight of the LORD. 19 Yet the LORD would not
destroy Judah, for the sake of his servant David, since he had promised to give a
8.20 2 Kgs 3.9,26 2 Chron 21.8 lamp to him and to his descendants forever.
20 In his days Edom revolted against the rule of Judah, and set up a king of their
8.22 Gen 27.39,40 own. 21 Then Joram crossed over to Zair with all his chariots. He set out by night
and attacked the Edomites and their chariot commanders who had surrounded
8.23 1 Kgs 15.23 22.45 2 Kgs 12.19 14.18; 15.6 him;[y] but his army fled home. 22 So Edom has been in revolt against the rule of
Judah to this day. Libnah also revolted at the same time. 23 Now the rest of the acts
of Joram, and all that he did, are they not written in the Book of the Annals of the
8.24 1 Kgs 2.10 11.43 Kings of Judah? 24 So Joram slept with his ancestors, and was buried with them in
the city of David; his son Ahaziah succeeded him.

Ahaziah rules Judah

25 In the twelfth year of King Joram son of Ahab of Israel, Ahaziah son of King
8.26 2 Kgs 11.1 Jehoram of Judah began to reign. 26 Ahaziah was twenty-two years old when he
began to reign; he reigned one year in Jerusalem. His mother's name was Athaliah,
8.27 1 Kgs 16.30 a granddaughter of King Omri of Israel. 27 He also walked in the way of the house

[w] Heb lacks *Ben-hadad* [x] Gk Syr: Heb adds *Jehoshaphat being king of Judah,* [y] Meaning of Heb uncertain

8.12, 13 When Elisha told Hazael he would sin greatly, Hazael protested that he would never do that sort of thing. He did not acknowledge his personal potential for evil. In our enlightened society, it is easy to think we are above gross sin and can control our actions. We think that we would never sink so low. Instead, we should take a more biblical and realistic look at ourselves and admit our sinful potential. Then we will ask for God's strength to resist such evil.

8.12–15 Elisha's words about Hazael's treatment of Israel were partially fulfilled in 10.32, 33. Apparently Hazael had known he would be king because Elijah had anointed him (1 Kings 19.15). But he was impatient and, instead of waiting for God's timing, took matters into his own hands, killing Ben-hadad. God used Hazael as an instrument of judgment against the disobedient Israelites.

8.18 King Jehoshaphat arranged the marriage between Jehoram, his son, and Athaliah, the daughter of wicked Ahab and Jezebel. Athaliah followed the idolatrous ways of the northern kingdom, bringing Baal worship into Judah and starting the southern kingdom's decline. When Jehoram died, his son Ahaziah became king. Then, when Ahaziah was killed in battle, Athaliah murdered all her grandsons and made herself queen (11.1–3). Jehoram's marriage may have been politically advantageous, but spiritually it was deadly.

8.20–22 Although Judah and Edom shared a common border and a common ancestor (Isaac), the two nations fought continually. Edom had been a vassal of the united kingdom of Israel and then the southern kingdom of Judah since the days of David (2 Samuel 8.13, 14). Here Edom rebelled against Jehoram (Joram) and declared independence. Immediately Jehoram marched out to attack Edom, but his ambush failed. Thus Jehoram lost some of his borderlands as punishment for his failure to honor God.

8.23 Here King Jehoram of Judah is called Joram, an alternate form of his name (see 8.16). It might be similar to calling someone Bill instead of William. To add to the confusion, the king of Israel during this time was also named Jehoram (and Joram).

8.26 Ahaziah was the only remaining son of Jehoram of Judah. Although he was the youngest son, he took the throne because the rest of his brothers had been taken captive in a raid by the Philistines and Arabians (2 Chronicles 21.16, 17). Ahaziah is also referred to as Jehoahaz.

8.26, 27 Ahaziah's mother was Athaliah, daughter of Ahab and Jezebel, former king and queen of Israel, and granddaughter of Omri, Ahab's father and predecessor. The evil of Ahab and Jezebel spread to Judah through Athaliah.

of Ahab, doing what was evil in the sight of the LORD, as the house of Ahab had
done, for he was son-in-law to the house of Ahab.
28 He went with Joram son of Ahab to wage war against King Hazael of Aram
at Ramoth-gilead, where the Arameans wounded Joram. 29 King Joram returned to **8.29**
be healed in Jezreel of the wounds that the Arameans had inflicted on him at Ra- 2 Kgs 9.14
mah, when he fought against King Hazael of Aram. King Ahaziah son of Jehoram 2 Chron 22.6
of Judah went down to see Joram son of Ahab in Jezreel, because he was wounded.

Jehu is anointed king of Israel

9 Then the prophet Elisha called a member of the company of prophets[z] and **9.1**
said to him, "Gird up your loins; take this flask of oil in your hand, and go to 1 Sam 10.1 16.1
Ramoth-gilead. 2 When you arrive, look there for Jehu son of Jehoshaphat, son of 1 Kgs 1.39
Nimshi; go in and get him to leave his companions, and take him into an inner 2 Kgs 8.28
chamber. 3 Then take the flask of oil, pour it on his head, and say, 'Thus says the **9.2** 1 Kgs 19.16
LORD: I anoint you king over Israel.' Then open the door and flee; do not linger." **9.3**
4 So the young man, the young prophet, went to Ramoth-gilead. 5 He arrived 1 Sam 9.16 2 Chron 22.7
while the commanders of the army were in council, and he announced, "I have a
message for you, commander." "For which one of us?" asked Jehu. "For you, commander." 6 So Jehu[a] got up and went inside; the young man poured the oil on his
head, saying to him, "Thus says the LORD the God of Israel: I anoint you king over
the people of the LORD, over Israel. 7 You shall strike down the house of your mas- **9.7**
ter Ahab, so that I may avenge on Jezebel the blood of my servants the prophets, Deut 32.35 1 Kgs 18.3,4
and the blood of all the servants of the LORD. 8 For the whole house of Ahab shall 21.15,21
perish; I will cut off from Ahab every male, bond or free, in Israel. 9 I will make the 2 Kgs 10.17
house of Ahab like the house of Jeroboam son of Nebat, and like the house of **9.9** 1 Kgs 14.10
Baasha son of Ahijah. 10 The dogs shall eat Jezebel in the territory of Jezreel, and 15.29; 16.3,11
no one shall bury her." Then he opened the door and fled. **9.10** 1 Kgs 21.23
11 When Jehu came back to his master's officers, they said to him, "Is every- 2 Kgs 9.35,36
thing all right? Why did that madman come to you?" He answered them, "You
know the sort and how they babble." 12 They said, "Liar! Come on, tell us!" So he **9.12**
said, "This is just what he said to me: 'Thus says the LORD, I anoint you king over 2 Kgs 9.6
Israel.' " 13 Then hurriedly they all took their cloaks and spread them for him on the **9.13**
bare[b] steps; and they blew the trumpet, and proclaimed, "Jehu is king." 2 Sam 15.10 1 Kgs 1.34,39

Jehu kills Joram and Ahaziah

14 Thus Jehu son of Jehoshaphat son of Nimshi conspired against Joram. Joram

[z] Heb *sons of the prophets* [a] Heb *he* [b] Meaning of Heb uncertain

JEHU TAKES OVER ISRAEL
Elisha sent a prophet to Ramoth-gilead to anoint Jehu as Israel's new king. Jehu immediately rode to Jezreel to find and kill King Joram of Israel and King Ahaziah of Judah. Jehu killed Joram; Ahaziah fled toward Beth-haggan where he was wounded. He later died at Megiddo. Back in Jezreel, Jehu had Jezebel killed.

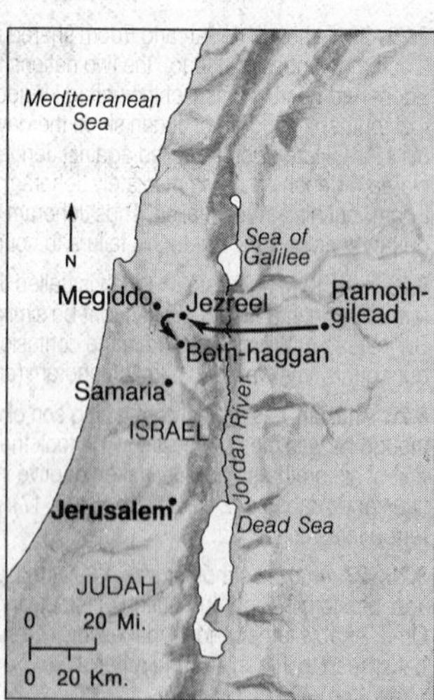

8.29 Jezreel was the location of the summer palace of the kings of Israel.

9.1 "Gird up your loins" meant to tuck the bottom of the robe into the belt so that it would be easier to run.

9.3 Elijah had prophesied that many people would be killed when Jehu became king (1 Kings 19.16, 17). Thus Elisha advised the young prophet to get out of the area as soon as he delivered his message, before the slaughter began. Jehu's actions seem harsh, as he hunted down relatives and friends of Ahab (2 Chronicles 22.8, 9), but unchecked Baal worship was destroying the nation. If Israel was to survive, the followers of Baal had to be eliminated. Jehu fulfilled the need of the hour – justice.

9.7 Elisha's statement fulfilled Elijah's prophecy made 20 years earlier: all of Ahab's family would be killed (1 Kings 21.17–24). Jezebel's death, predicted by Elijah, is described in 9.30–37.

9.9 Ahab's dynasty would end as had those of Jeroboam and Baasha. Ahijah had prophesied the end of Jeroboam's dynasty (1 Kings 14.1–11), and this was fulfilled by Baasha (1 Kings 15.29). The prophet Jehu – not King Jehu – then foretold the end of Baasha's family (1 Kings 16.1–7), and this too was fulfilled (1 Kings 16.11, 12). The end of Ahab's family, therefore, was certain – Elijah had predicted it, and God brought it to pass.

9.14 2 Kgs 8.28 with all Israel had been on guard at Ramoth-gilead against King Hazael of Aram;
15 but King Joram had returned to be healed in Jezreel of the wounds that the Arameans had inflicted on him, when he fought against King Hazael of Aram. So Jehu
said, "If this is your wish, then let no one slip out of the city to go and tell the news
in Jezreel." 16 Then Jehu mounted his chariot and went to Jezreel, where Joram was
lying ill. King Ahaziah of Judah had come down to visit Joram.
9.17 2 Sam 13.34 18.24 Isa 21.6,7 17 In Jezreel, the sentinel standing on the tower spied the company of Jehu
arriving, and said, "I see a company." Joram said, "Take a horseman; send him to
meet them, and let him say, 'Is it peace?' " 18 So the horseman went to meet him;
he said, "Thus says the king, 'Is it peace?' " Jehu responded, "What have you to do
with peace? Fall in behind me." The sentinel reported, saying, "The messenger
reached them, but he is not coming back." 19 Then he sent out a second horseman,
who came to them and said, "Thus says the king, 'Is it peace?' " Jehu answered,

JEHU

Jehu had the basic qualities that could have made him a great success. From a human perspective, in fact, he was a successful king. His family ruled the northern kingdom longer than any other. He was used by God as an instrument of punishment to Ahab's evil dynasty, and he fiercely attacked Baal worship. He came close to being God's kind of king, but he recklessly went beyond God's commands and failed to follow through on the obedient actions that began his reign. Within sight of victory, he settled for mediocrity.

Jehu was a man of immediate action but without ultimate purpose. His kingdom moved, but its destination was unclear. He eliminated one form of idolatry, Baal worship, only to uphold another by continuing to worship the calves Jeroboam had set up. He could have accomplished much for God if he had been obedient to the One who made him king. Even when he was carrying out God's directions, Jehu's style showed he was not fully aware of who was directing him.

As he did with Jehu, God gives each person strengths and abilities that will find their greatest usefulness only under his control. Outside that control, however, they don't accomplish what they could, and often become tools for evil. One way to make sure this does not happen is to tell God of your willingness to be under his control. With his presence in your life, your natural strengths and abilities will be used to their greatest potential for the greatest good.

Strengths and accomplishments:
- Took the throne from Ahab's family and destroyed his evil influence
- Founded the longest-lived dynasty of the northern kingdom
- Was anointed by Elijah and confirmed by Elisha
- Destroyed Baal worship

Weaknesses and mistakes:
- Had a reckless outlook on life that made him bold and prone to error
- Worshiped Jeroboam's golden calves
- Was devoted to God only to the point that obedience served his own interests

Lessons from his life:
- Fierce commitment needs control because it can result in recklessness
- Obedience involves both action and direction

Vital statistics:
- Where: The northern kingdom of Israel
- Occupation: Commander in the army of Jehoram, king of Israel
- Relatives: Grandfather: Nimshi. Father: Jehoshaphat. Son: Jehoahaz
- Contemporaries: Elijah, Elisha, Ahab, Jezebel, Jehoram, Ahaziah

Key verse:
"But Jehu was not careful to follow the law of the Lord the God of Israel with all his heart; he did not turn from the sins of Jeroboam, which he caused Israel to commit" (2 Kings 10.31).

Jehu's story is told in 1 Kings 19.16—2 Kings 10.36. He is also mentioned in 2 Kings 15.12; 2 Chronicles 22.7–9; Hosea 1.4, 5.

9.18, 19 The riders met Jehu and asked if he came in peace. But Jehu responded, "What have you to do with peace?" Peace, properly understood, comes from God. It is not genuine except when rooted in belief in God and love for him. Jehu knew the men represented a disobedient, wicked king. Don't seek peace and friendship with those who are enemies of the good and the true. Lasting peace can come only from knowing God who gives it to us.

9.19 Jehu told the messengers to get behind him so that they could not return to the city and warn the king that his life was in danger. He may also have wanted a clear path when he shot the king.

"What have you to do with peace? Fall in behind me." 20 Again the sentinel reported, "He reached them, but he is not coming back. It looks like the driving of
Jehu son of Nimshi; for he drives like a maniac."
21 Joram said, "Get ready." And they got his chariot ready. Then King Joram **9.21**
of Israel and King Ahaziah of Judah set out, each in his chariot, and went to meet 1 Kgs 21.1
Jehu; they met him at the property of Naboth the Jezreelite. 22 When Joram saw **9.22**
Jehu, he said, "Is it peace, Jehu?" He answered, "What peace can there be, so long 1 Kgs 16.31 18.19
as the many whoredoms and sorceries of your mother Jezebel continue?" 23 Then **9.23**
Joram reined about and fled, saying to Ahaziah, "Treason, Ahaziah!" 24 Jehu drew 2 Kgs 11.14
his bow with all his strength, and shot Joram between the shoulders, so that the **9.24** 1 Kgs 22.34
arrow pierced his heart; and he sank in his chariot. 25 Jehu said to his aide Bidkar, **9.25**
"Lift him out, and throw him on the plot of ground belonging to Naboth the Jezree- 1 Kgs 21.1,19
lite; for remember, when you and I rode side by side behind his father Ahab how
the LORD uttered this oracle against him: 26 'For the blood of Naboth and for the
blood of his children that I saw yesterday, says the LORD, I swear I will repay you
on this very plot of ground.' Now therefore lift him out and throw him on the plot
of ground, in accordance with the word of the LORD."
27 When King Ahaziah of Judah saw this, he fled in the direction of Beth- **9.27**
haggan. Jehu pursued him, saying, "Shoot him also!" And they shot him[c] in the Josh 17.11 Judg 1.27
chariot at the ascent to Gur, which is by Ibleam. Then he fled to Megiddo, and died 2 Chron 22.7
there. 28 His officers carried him in a chariot to Jerusalem, and buried him in his **9.28**
tomb with his ancestors in the city of David. 2 Kgs 8.25 23.30
29 In the eleventh year of Joram son of Ahab, Ahaziah began to reign over **9.29**
Judah. 2 Kgs 8.28

Jezebel's terrible death

30 When Jehu came to Jezreel, Jezebel heard of it; she painted her eyes, and **9.30**
adorned her head, and looked out of the window. 31 As Jehu entered the gate, she Jer 4.30 Ezek 23.40
said, "Is it peace, Zimri, murderer of your master?" 32 He looked up to the window **9.31**
and said, "Who is on my side? Who?" Two or three eunuchs looked out at him. 1 Kgs 16.9,10
33 He said, "Throw her down." So they threw her down; some of her blood spattered on the wall and on the horses, which trampled on her. 34 Then he went in and **9.34**
ate and drank; he said, "See to that cursed woman and bury her; for she is a king's 1 Kgs 16.30 21.20
daughter." 35 But when they went to bury her, they found no more of her than the
skull and the feet and the palms of her hands. 36 When they came back and told him, **9.36**
he said, "This is the word of the LORD, which he spoke by his servant Elijah the 1 Kgs 21.23
Tishbite, 'In the territory of Jezreel the dogs shall eat the flesh of Jezebel; 37 the
corpse of Jezebel shall be like dung on the field in the territory of Jezreel, so that no
one can say, This is Jezebel.' "

Jehu kills Ahab's family

10 Now Ahab had seventy sons in Samaria. So Jehu wrote letters and sent them **10.1**
to Samaria, to the rulers of Jezreel,[d] to the elders, and to the guardians of the Judg 8.30; 12.14 1 Kgs 16.24
sons of[e] Ahab, saying, 2 "Since your master's sons are with you and you have
at your disposal chariots and horses, a fortified city, and weapons, 3 select the son
of your master who is the best qualified, set him on his father's throne, and fight for
your master's house." 4 But they were utterly terrified and said, "Look, two kings

[c] Syr Vg Compare Gk: Heb lacks *and they shot him* [d] Or *of the city*; Vg Compare Gk [e] Gk: Heb lacks *of the sons of*

9.26 Joram of Israel was wicked like his father and mother, Ahab and Jezebel; therefore, his body was thrown into the field that his parents had unlawfully taken. Jezebel had arranged the murder of Naboth, the previous owner, because he would not sell his vineyard—which Ahab wanted for a garden (1 Kings 21.1–24). Little did Ahab know that it would become a burial plot for his evil son.

9.31 Why did Jezebel refer to Zimri? Zimri was an army general who, some 40 years earlier, had killed Elah and then had declared himself king of Israel (1 Kings 16.8–10). Jezebel was accusing Jehu of trying the same treachery.

9.35 Jezebel's skull, feet, and hands were all that remained of her evil life—no power, no money, no prestige, no royal finery, no family, no spiritual heritage. In the end, her life of luxury and treachery amounted to nothing. Power, health, and wealth may make you feel as if you can live forever. But death strips everyone of all external security. The time to set your life's course is now, while you still have time and before your heart becomes hardened. The end comes soon enough.

10.5 Josh 9.8 could not withstand him; how then can we stand?" 5 So the steward of the palace,
and the governor of the city, along with the elders and the guardians, sent word to
Jehu: "We are your servants; we will do anything you say. We will not make any-
10.6 2 Kgs 9.32 one king; do whatever you think right." 6 Then he wrote them a second letter, saying, "If you are on my side, and if you are ready to obey me, take the heads of your
master's sons and come to me at Jezreel tomorrow at this time." Now the king's
sons, seventy persons, were with the leaders of the city, who were charged with
10.7 Judg 9.5 2 Kgs 11.1 their upbringing. 7 When the letter reached them, they took the king's sons and
killed them, seventy persons; they put their heads in baskets and sent them to him
at Jezreel. 8 When the messenger came and told him, "They have brought the heads
of the king's sons," he said, "Lay them in two heaps at the entrance of the gate until
10.9 1 Kgs 8.56 21.19 2 Kgs 9.7 the morning." 9 Then in the morning when he went out, he stood and said to all the
people, "You are innocent. It was I who conspired against my master and killed
him; but who struck down all these? 10 Know then that there shall fall to the earth
nothing of the word of the LORD, which the LORD spoke concerning the house of
10.11 1 Kgs 21.22 2 Kgs 9.8; 10.17 Ahab; for the LORD has done what he said through his servant Elijah." 11 So Jehu
killed all who were left of the house of Ahab in Jezreel, all his leaders, close
friends, and priests, until he left him no survivor.

12 Then he set out and went to Samaria. On the way, when he was at Beth-eked
10.13 2 Chron 22.8 of the Shepherds, 13 Jehu met relatives of King Ahaziah of Judah and said, "Who
are you?" They answered, "We are kin of Ahaziah; we have come down to visit the
royal princes and the sons of the queen mother." 14 He said, "Take them alive."
They took them alive, and slaughtered them at the pit of Beth-eked, forty-two in
all; he spared none of them.

10.15 2 Kgs 10.23 1 Chron 2.55 Jer 35.6 15 When he left there, he met Jehonadab son of Rechab coming to meet him; he
greeted him, and said to him, "Is your heart as true to mine as mine is to yours?"[f]
Jehonadab answered, "It is." Jehu said,[g] "If it is, give me your hand." So he gave
him his hand. Jehu took him up with him into the chariot. 16 He said, "Come with
10.17 2 Kgs 9.8 me, and see my zeal for the LORD." So he[h] had him ride in his chariot. 17 When he
came to Samaria, he killed all who were left to Ahab in Samaria, until he had wiped
them out, according to the word of the LORD that he spoke to Elijah.

Jehu kills the priests of Baal

10.18 1 Kgs 16.31 18.19; 22.6 18 Then Jehu assembled all the people and said to them, "Ahab offered Baal
small service; but Jehu will offer much more. 19 Now therefore summon to me all
the prophets of Baal, all his worshipers, and all his priests; let none be missing, for
I have a great sacrifice to offer to Baal; whoever is missing shall not live." But Jehu
10.20 1 Kgs 16.32 2 Kgs 11.18 was acting with cunning in order to destroy the worshipers of Baal. 20 Jehu decreed,
"Sanctify a solemn assembly for Baal." So they proclaimed it. 21 Jehu sent word
throughout all Israel; all the worshipers of Baal came, so that there was no one left
who did not come. They entered the temple of Baal, until the temple of Baal was
filled from wall to wall. 22 He said to the keeper of the wardrobe, "Bring out the
vestments for all the worshipers of Baal." So he brought out the vestments for
them. 23 Then Jehu entered the temple of Baal with Jehonadab son of Rechab; he
said to the worshipers of Baal, "Search and see that there is no worshiper of the

[f] Gk: Heb *Is it right with your heart, as my heart is with your heart?* [g] Gk: Heb lacks *Jehu said* [h] Gk Syr Tg: Heb *they*

10.7 This fulfilled Elijah's prophecy that not one of Ahab's male descendants would survive (1 Kings 21.17–24).

10.10 "There shall fall to the earth" means that everything will happen just as God said.

10.11 In his zeal, Jehu went far beyond the Lord's command with this bloodbath. The prophet Hosea later announced punishment upon Jehu's dynasty for this senseless slaughter (Hosea 1.4, 5). Many times in history, "religious" people have mixed faith with personal ambition, power, or cruelty, without God's consent or blessing. To use God or the Bible to condone oppression is wrong. When people attack Christianity because of atrocities that "Christians" carried out, help them to see that these men and women were using faith to their own political ends and not following Christ.

10.15 Jehonadab was a man who, like Jehu, was zealous in following God. Jehonadab, however, demonstrated his zeal by separating himself and his family from the materialistic, idol-worshiping culture. He founded a group called the Rechabites (named after his father Rechab), who strove to keep their lives pure by living apart from society's pressures and temptations. Jeremiah 35 gives us an example of their dedication to God. Because of their dedication, God promised that they would always have descendants who would worship him.

LORD here among you, but only worshipers of Baal." 24 Then they proceeded to **10.24**
offer sacrifices and burnt offerings. 1 Kgs 20.40
Now Jehu had stationed eighty men outside, saying, "Whoever allows any of
those to escape whom I deliver into your hands shall forfeit his life." 25 As soon as **10.25**
he had finished presenting the burnt offering, Jehu said to the guards and to the 1 Sam 22.17
officers, "Come in and kill them; let no one escape." So they put them to the sword. 1 Kgs 18.40
The guards and the officers threw them out, and then went into the citadel of the
temple of Baal. 26 They brought out the pillar[i] that was in the temple of Baal, and **10.26**
burned it. 27 Then they demolished the pillar of Baal, and destroyed the temple of 1 Kgs 14.23
Baal, and made it a latrine to this day. 2 Kgs 3.2
28 Thus Jehu wiped out Baal from Israel. 29 But Jehu did not turn aside from the **10.29**
sins of Jeroboam son of Nebat, which he caused Israel to commit—the golden 1 Kgs 12.28
calves that were in Bethel and in Dan. 30 The LORD said to Jehu, "Because you have 13.33,34 **10.30**
done well in carrying out what I consider right, and in accordance with all that was 2 Kgs 13.1
in my heart have dealt with the house of Ahab, your sons of the fourth generation 15.12
shall sit on the throne of Israel." 31 But Jehu was not careful to follow the law of the **10.31**
LORD the God of Israel with all his heart; he did not turn from the sins of Jeroboam, 1 Kgs 12.28,29
which he caused Israel to commit.
32 In those days the LORD began to trim off parts of Israel. Hazael defeated **10.32**
them throughout the territory of Israel: 33 from the Jordan eastward, all the land of Deut 2.36
Gilead, the Gadites, the Reubenites, and the Manassites, from Aroer, which is by 2 Kgs 8.12
the Wadi Arnon, that is, Gilead and Bashan. 34 Now the rest of the acts of Jehu, all 13.22; 14.25 **10.34**
that he did, and all his power, are they not written in the Book of the Annals of the 2 Kgs 1.18; 13.8
Kings of Israel? 35 So Jehu slept with his ancestors, and they buried him in Samaria. 2 Chron 20.34 **10.35**
His son Jehoahaz succeeded him. 36 The time that Jehu reigned over Israel in Sa- 2 Kgs 13.1
maria was twenty-eight years.

Athaliah rules Judah

11 Now when Athaliah, Ahaziah's mother, saw that her son was dead, she set **11.1**
about to destroy all the royal family. 2 But Jehosheba, King Joram's daugh- 2 Kgs 8.26
ter, Ahaziah's sister, took Joash son of Ahaziah, and stole him away from among 2 Chron 22.10
the king's children who were about to be killed; she put[j] him and his nurse in a
bedroom. Thus she[k] hid him from Athaliah, so that he was not killed; 3 he re-

[i] Gk Vg Syr Tg: Heb *pillars* [j] With 2 Chr 22.11: Heb lacks *she put* [k] Gk Syr Vg Compare 2 Chr 22.11: Heb *they*

10.24 Israel was supposed to be intolerant of any religion that did not worship the true God. The religions of surrounding nations were evil and corrupt. They were designed to destroy life, not uphold it. Israel was God's special nation, chosen to be an example of what was right. But Israel's kings, priests, and elders first tolerated then incorporated surrounding pagan beliefs, and thus became apathetic to God's way. We are to be completely intolerant of sin and remove it from our lives. We should be tolerant of people who hold differing views, but we should not condone beliefs or practices that lead people away from God's standards of living.

10.28, 29 Why did Jehu destroy the idols of Baal but not the golden calves in Dan and Bethel? Jehu's motives may have been more political than spiritual. (1) If Jehu had destroyed the golden calves, his people would have traveled to the temple in Jerusalem, in the rival southern kingdom, and worshiped there (which is why Jeroboam set them up in the first place; see 1 Kings 12.25–33). (2) Baal worship was associated with the dynasty of Ahab, so it was politically advantageous to destroy Baal. The golden calves, on the other hand, had a longer history in the northern kingdom and were valued by all political factions. (3) Baal worship was anti-God, but the golden calves were thought by many to be visible representations of God himself, even though God's law stated clearly that such worship was idolatrous (Exodus 20.3–6). Like Jehu, it is easy for us to denounce the sins of others while excusing sin in our own lives.

10.30, 31 Jehu did much of what the Lord told him to, but he did not obey him with all his heart. He had become God's *instrument* for carrying out justice, but he had not become God's *servant*. As a result, he gave only lip service to God while permitting the worship of the golden calves. Check the condition of your heart toward God. We can be very active in our work for God and still not give the heartfelt obedience he desires.

10.34 Jehu is mentioned on an ancient stone monument called the Black Obelisk, inscribed by Shalmaneser III of Assyria. Foreign rulers often recorded their military exploits on stone monuments for everyone to see. Jehu is pictured kneeling before Shalmaneser III in a gesture of submission. He paid tribute to the Assyrians near the beginning of his reign (841 B.C.) to avoid destruction. The Bible does not record Jehu's dealings with Assyria, a nation soon to become a world power.

11.1 This story is continued from 9.27, where Ahaziah, Athaliah's son, had been killed by Jehu. Athaliah's attempt to kill all of Ahaziah's sons was futile, because God had promised that the Messiah would be born through David's descendants (2 Samuel 7).

11.2, 3 Jehosheba was the wife of Jehoiada, the high priest, so the temple was both a practical and natural place to hide baby Joash. Athaliah, who loved idolatry, would have had no interest in the temple.

mained with her six years, hidden in the house of the LORD, while Athaliah reigned
over the land.

Young Joash becomes king

11.4 4 But in the seventh year Jehoiada summoned the captains of the Carites and of
2 Chron 23.1 the guards and had them come to him in the house of the LORD. He made a covenant
with them and put them under oath in the house of the LORD; then he showed them
the king's son. 5 He commanded them, "This is what you are to do: one-third of
you, those who go off duty on the sabbath and guard the king's house 6 (another
third being at the gate Sur and a third at the gate behind the guards), shall guard the
palace; 7 and your two divisions that come on duty in force on the sabbath and guard
the house of the LORD[l] 8 shall surround the king, each with weapons in hand; and
whoever approaches the ranks is to be killed. Be with the king in his comings and
goings."
9 The captains did according to all that the priest Jehoiada commanded; each
brought his men who were to go off duty on the sabbath, with those who were to
11.10 come on duty on the sabbath, and came to the priest Jehoiada. 10 The priest deliv-
2 Sam 8.7 1 Chron 18.7,8 ered to the captains the spears and shields that had been King David's, which were
2 Chron 23.9 in the house of the LORD; 11 the guards stood, every man with his weapons in his
hand, from the south side of the house to the north side of the house, around the
11.12 altar and the house, to guard the king on every side. 12 Then he brought out the
Ex 31.18 1 Sam 10.24 king's son, put the crown on him, and gave him the covenant;[m] they proclaimed
2 Kgs 12.1 him king, and anointed him; they clapped their hands and shouted, "Long live the
king!"
11.13 13 When Athaliah heard the noise of the guard and of the people, she went into
Gen 37.29 44.13 the house of the LORD to the people; 14 when she looked, there was the king stand-
1 Kgs 1.39,40 ing by the pillar, according to custom, with the captains and the trumpeters beside
2 Chron 23.12 the king, and all the people of the land rejoicing and blowing trumpets. Athaliah
tore her clothes and cried, "Treason! Treason!" 15 Then the priest Jehoiada commanded the captains who were set over the army, "Bring her out between the ranks,
and kill with the sword anyone who follows her." For the priest said, "Let her not
be killed in the house of the LORD." 16 So they laid hands on her; she went through
the horses' entrance to the king's house, and there she was put to death.
11.17 17 Jehoiada made a covenant between the LORD and the king and people, that
Josh 24.25 2 Sam 5.3 they should be the LORD's people; also between the king and the people. 18 Then all
2 Chron 15.12 the people of the land went to the house of Baal, and tore it down; his altars and his
11.18 Deut 12.2 images they broke in pieces, and they killed Mattan, the priest of Baal, before the
1 Kgs 18.40 altars. The priest posted guards over the house of the LORD. 19 He took the captains,
2 Kgs 10.24 the Carites, the guards, and all the people of the land; then they brought the king
down from the house of the LORD, marching through the gate of the guards to the
king's house. He took his seat on the throne of the kings. 20 So all the people of the
land rejoiced; and the city was quiet after Athaliah had been killed with the sword
at the king's house.
11.21 2 Chron 24.1 21[n] Jehoash[o] was seven years old when he began to reign.

[l] Heb *the LORD to the king* [m] Or *treaty* or *testimony*; Heb *eduth* [n] Ch 12.1 in Heb [o] Another spelling is *Joash*; see verse 19

11.4 The Carites (or Kerethites) were mercenary troops from Cilicia in southern Turkey.

11.17 This covenant was, in fact, a recommitment to a very old covenant – the one set up in the book of Deuteronomy for the righteous rule of the nation. It was meant to function as a constitution for the people. This covenant, however, had been virtually ignored for over 100 years. Unfortunately, with Jehoiada's death, the reforms were discontinued.

11.18 Baal worship was the most serious threat to Israel among all of the pagan deities in the land. Baal was the most popular god among the Canaanites and was represented by a bull, a symbol of strength and fertility. He was worshiped as the god of the rains and the harvest. Prostitution played a part in the worship of Baal. The worship of Baal had been opposed earlier by Gideon (Judges 6.25–32) and nearly eliminated by Jehu (2 Kings 10.17–29).

11.21 If Jehoash (Joash) became king at only seven years of age, who really ran the country? Although the answer is not spelled out in the Bible, Judah was probably run during the first seven years of Joash's reign by the king's mother, the high priest Jehoiada, and other advisors.

Jehoash rules Judah

12 In the seventh year of Jehu, Jehoash began to reign; he reigned forty years in
Jerusalem. His mother's name was Zibiah of Beer-sheba. 2 Jehoash did what
was right in the sight of the LORD all his days, because the priest Jehoiada instructed
him. 3 Nevertheless the high places were not taken away; the people continued to
sacrifice and make offerings on the high places.
4 Jehoash said to the priests, "All the money offered as sacred donations that is
brought into the house of the LORD, the money for which each person is
assessed — the money from the assessment of persons — and the money from the
voluntary offerings brought into the house of the LORD, 5 let the priests receive from
each of the donors; and let them repair the house wherever any need of repairs is
discovered." 6 But by the twenty-third year of King Jehoash the priests had made no
repairs on the house. 7 Therefore King Jehoash summoned the priest Jehoiada with
the other priests and said to them, "Why are you not repairing the house? Now
therefore do not accept any more money from your donors but hand it over for the
repair of the house." 8 So the priests agreed that they would neither accept more
money from the people nor repair the house.
9 Then the priest Jehoiada took a chest, made a hole in its lid, and set it beside
the altar on the right side as one entered the house of the LORD; the priests who
guarded the threshold put in it all the money that was brought into the house of the
LORD. 10 Whenever they saw that there was a great deal of money in the chest, the
king's secretary and the high priest went up, counted the money that was found in
the house of the LORD, and tied it up in bags. 11 They would give the money that
was weighed out into the hands of the workers who had the oversight of the house
of the LORD; then they paid it out to the carpenters and the builders who worked on
the house of the LORD, 12 to the masons and the stonecutters, as well as to buy
timber and quarried stone for making repairs on the house of the LORD, as well as
for any outlay for repairs of the house. 13 But for the house of the LORD no basins
of silver, snuffers, bowls, trumpets, or any vessels of gold, or of silver, were made
from the money that was brought into the house of the LORD, 14 for that was given
to the workers who were repairing the house of the LORD with it. 15 They did not ask
an accounting from those into whose hand they delivered the money to pay out to
the workers, for they dealt honestly. 16 The money from the guilt offerings and the
money from the sin offerings was not brought into the house of the LORD; it belonged to the priests.
17 At that time King Hazael of Aram went up, fought against Gath, and took it.
But when Hazael set his face to go up against Jerusalem, 18 King Jehoash of Judah

12.1 1 Kgs 19.16 2 Chron 24.1
12.2 2 Kgs 14.3
12.3 1 Kgs 14.23 15.14 2 Kgs 14.4 15.34,35
12.4 Ex 35.5-9,22,29 2 Kgs 22.3-6 1 Chron 29.3
12.9 Mk 12.41 Lk 21.1
12.11 2 Kgs 22.5,6 2 Chron 24.11
12.13 1 Kgs 7.48,50
12.15 2 Kgs 22.7
12.17 2 Kgs 8.12 10.32,33
12.18 1 Kgs 15.18 2 Kgs 16.8 18.15,16

12.2 God's input yields good output. Jehoash had a good teacher in Jehoiada, the high priest. As long as he lived, Jehoiada's faith in God influenced Jehoash for good. Good intent must be fortified with good content. As long as Jehoash heeded Jehoida's good instruction, he fulfilled God's plan for his life. All our plans and actions must be guided by God, and his counsel is made clear to us in his word. Our lives will be productive if we heed God's counsel.

12.2ff Jehoash didn't go far enough in removing sin from the nation, but he did much that was good and right. When we aren't sure if we've gone far enough in correcting our actions, we can ask: (1) Does the Bible expressly prohibit this action? (2) Does this action take me away from loving, worshiping, or serving God? (3) Does it make me its slave? (4) Is it bringing out the best in me, consistent with God's purpose? (5) Does it benefit other believers?

12.3 The Israelites were supposed to offer sacrifices to God only in designated areas under supervision of the priests, not just anywhere (Deuteronomy 12.13, 14). Making sacrifices on the hilltops copied pagan customs and encouraged other pagan practices to enter into their worship. By blending in these beliefs, people were custom-making their religion, and it led them far away from God. (For more information on these shrines in the hills see the note on 1 Kings 22.43.)

12.4, 5 The temple needed repair because it had been damaged and neglected by previous evil leaders, especially Athaliah (2 Chronicles 24.7). The temple was to be a holy place, set apart for worship of God. Thanks to Jehoash's fund-raising program, it could be restored. The dirt and filth that had collected inside over the years were cleaned out; joints were remortared; heathen idols and other traces of idol worship were removed; and the gold and bronze were polished. The neglected condition of the temple reveals how far the people had strayed from God.

12.15 What a contrast between the building superintendents who needed no accounting of their use of the money, and the priests who couldn't be trusted to handle their funds well enough to set some aside for the temple (12.8). As trained men of God, the Levites should have been responsible and concerned. After all, the temple was their life's work. Though the priests were not dishonest, they did not have the commitment or energy needed to finish the work. Sometimes God's work is better accomplished by devoted lay people. Don't let your lack of training or position stop you from contributing to God's kingdom. Everyone's energy is needed to carry out God's work.

12.16 To read more about trespass and sin offerings, see Leviticus 4; 5; 6.24 – 7.10.

took all the votive gifts that Jehoshaphat, Jehoram, and Ahaziah, his ancestors, the
kings of Judah, had dedicated, as well as his own votive gifts, all the gold that was
found in the treasuries of the house of the LORD and of the king's house, and sent
these to King Hazael of Aram. Then Hazael withdrew from Jerusalem.
19 Now the rest of the acts of Joash, and all that he did, are they not written in
the Book of the Annals of the Kings of Judah? 20 His servants arose, devised a
conspiracy, and killed Joash in the house of Millo, on the way that goes down to
Silla. 21 It was Jozacar son of Shimeath and Jehozabad son of Shomer, his servants,
who struck him down, so that he died. He was buried with his ancestors in the city
of David; then his son Amaziah succeeded him.

Jehoahaz rules Israel

13 In the twenty-third year of King Joash son of Ahaziah of Judah, Jehoahaz
son of Jehu began to reign over Israel in Samaria; he reigned seventeen
years. 2 He did what was evil in the sight of the LORD, and followed the sins of
Jeroboam son of Nebat, which he caused Israel to sin; he did not depart from them.
3 The anger of the LORD was kindled against Israel, so that he gave them repeatedly
into the hand of King Hazael of Aram, then into the hand of Ben-hadad son of
Hazael. 4 But Jehoahaz entreated the LORD, and the LORD heeded him; for he saw
the oppression of Israel, how the king of Aram oppressed them. 5 Therefore the
LORD gave Israel a savior, so that they escaped from the hand of the Arameans; and
the people of Israel lived in their homes as formerly. 6 Nevertheless they did not
depart from the sins of the house of Jeroboam, which he caused Israel to sin, but
walked[p] in them; the sacred pole[q] also remained in Samaria. 7 So Jehoahaz was
left with an army of not more than fifty horsemen, ten chariots and ten thousand
footmen; for the king of Aram had destroyed them and made them like the dust at
threshing. 8 Now the rest of the acts of Jehoahaz and all that he did, including his
might, are they not written in the Book of the Annals of the Kings of Israel? 9 So
Jehoahaz slept with his ancestors, and they buried him in Samaria; then his son
Joash succeeded him.

Jehoash rules Israel

10 In the thirty-seventh year of King Joash of Judah, Jehoash son of Jehoahaz
began to reign over Israel in Samaria; he reigned sixteen years. 11 He also did what
was evil in the sight of the LORD; he did not depart from all the sins of Jeroboam son
of Nebat, which he caused Israel to sin, but he walked in them. 12 Now the rest of
the acts of Joash, and all that he did, as well as the might with which he fought
against King Amaziah of Judah, are they not written in the Book of the Annals of
the Kings of Israel? 13 So Joash slept with his ancestors, and Jeroboam sat upon his
throne; Joash was buried in Samaria with the kings of Israel.

p Gk Syr Tg Vg: Heb *he walked* q Heb *Asherah*

12.19 2 Kgs 8.23; 2 Chron 24.27
12.20 2 Sam 5.9; 2 Chron 24.25
12.21 2 Kgs 13.12; 2 Chron 25.1
13.1 2 Kgs 10.35; 2 Chron 25.17
13.2 1 Kgs 12.28; 2 Kgs 10.29
13.3 Judg 2.12-14; 2 Kgs 8.8,9; 10.32,33; 12.17
13.4 2 Kgs 14.26; 2 Chron 33.12
13.5 Judg 2.18,19; Neh 9.27
13.6 2 Kgs 10.29; 17.21
13.8 2 Kgs 10.34; 13.12; 14.15
13.11 1 Kgs 12.28; 2 Kgs 10.29; 13.2
13.12 2 Kgs 10.34; 14.8,15,28; 2 Chron 25.17
13.13 2 Kgs 14.24,27; Amos 7.10

12.18 Votive gifts were sacred gifts dedicated to God. Often they were spoils of war dedicated to the temple.

12.20 The reasons for the officers' plot against Joash are listed in 2 Chronicles 24.17–26. Joash had begun to worship idols, had killed the prophet Zechariah, and had been conquered by the Syrians. When Joash turned away from God, his life began to unravel. Joash's officers didn't kill him because he turned from God; they killed him because his kingdom was now out of control. In the end he became an evil man and was killed by evil people.

13.4–6 The Lord heard Jehoahaz's prayer for help. God delayed his judgment on Israel when they turned to him for help, but they did not sustain their dependence on God for long. Although there were periodic breaks in their idol worship, there was rarely evidence of genuine faith. It is not enough to say no to sin; we must also say yes to a life of commitment to God. An occasional call for help is not a substitute for a daily life of trust in God.

13.5 Syria, which lay to the north of Israel, was always Israel's enemy. This was partly because Israel blocked most of Syria's trade from the south, and Syria cut off most of Israel's from the north. If one nation could conquer the other, all its trade routes would be open and its economy would flourish. Israel and Syria were so busy fighting each other that they didn't notice the rapidly growing strength of the Assyrians to the far north. Soon both nations would be surprised (16.9; 17.6).

13.9, 10 Joash (also called Jehoash) assumed the throne of Israel in 798 B.C. The king of Judah, also named Joash, was nearing the end of his reign. Thus two kings named Joash, one in the south and one in the north, reigned at approximately the same time. While Joash of Judah began as a good king, Joash of Israel was evil.

14 Now when Elisha had fallen sick with the illness of which he was to die, 13.14
King Joash of Israel went down to him, and wept before him, crying, "My father, 2 Kgs 2.12
my father! The chariots of Israel and its horsemen!" 15 Elisha said to him, "Take a
bow and arrows"; so he took a bow and arrows. 16 Then he said to the king of Israel,
"Draw the bow"; and he drew it. Elisha laid his hands on the king's hands. 17 Then
he said, "Open the window eastward"; and he opened it. Elisha said, "Shoot"; and
he shot. Then he said, "The LORD's arrow of victory, the arrow of victory over
Aram! For you shall fight the Arameans in Aphek until you have made an end of
them." 18 He continued, "Take the arrows"; and he took them. He said to the king
of Israel, "Strike the ground with them"; he struck three times, and stopped. 19 Then
the man of God was angry with him, and said, "You should have struck five or six
times; then you would have struck down Aram until you had made an end of it, but
now you will strike down Aram only three times."
20 So Elisha died, and they buried him. Now bands of Moabites used to invade 13.20
the land in the spring of the year. 21 As a man was being buried, a marauding band 2 Kgs 3.7; 5.2 24.2
was seen and the man was thrown into the grave of Elisha; as soon as the man
touched the bones of Elisha, he came to life and stood on his feet.
22 Now King Hazael of Aram oppressed Israel all the days of Jehoahaz. 23 But 13.22 2 Kgs 8.12; 13.3
the LORD was gracious to them and had compassion on them; he turned toward 13.23
them, because of his covenant with Abraham, Isaac, and Jacob, and would not Gen 13.16 17.2-4
destroy them; nor has he banished them from his presence until now. 2 Kgs 14.27
24 When King Hazael of Aram died, his son Ben-hadad succeeded him. 25 Then 13.24 2 Kgs 8.8,9
Jehoash son of Jehoahaz took again from Ben-hadad son of Hazael the towns that 13.3
he had taken from his father Jehoahaz in war. Three times Joash defeated him and 13.25 2 Kgs 10.32
recovered the towns of Israel. 14.25

Amaziah rules Judah

14 In the second year of King Joash son of Joahaz of Israel, King Amaziah son 14.1
of Joash of Judah, began to reign. 2 He was twenty-five years old when he 2 Kgs 13.9,10 14.17
began to reign, and he reigned twenty-nine years in Jerusalem. His mother's name 2 Chron 25.1
was Jehoaddin of Jerusalem. 3 He did what was right in the sight of the LORD, yet 14.3 1 Kgs 11.4; 15.3
not like his ancestor David; in all things he did as his father Joash had done. 4 But 14.4
the high places were not removed; the people still sacrificed and made offerings on 1 Kgs 14.23
the high places. 5 As soon as the royal power was firmly in his hand he killed his 15.14 14.5
servants who had murdered his father the king. 6 But he did not put to death the 2 Kgs 12.20
children of the murderers; according to what is written in the book of the law of 14.6 Deut 24.16
Moses, where the LORD commanded, "The parents shall not be put to death for the 2 Chron 25.4
children, or the children be put to death for the parents; but all shall be put to death Jer 31.30 Ezek 18.4,20
for their own sins."
7 He killed ten thousand Edomites in the Valley of Salt and took Sela by storm; 14.7 2 Sam 8.13 1 Chron 18.12
he called it Jokthe-el, which is its name to this day. 2 Chron 25.11 Isa 16.1
8 Then Amaziah sent messengers to King Jehoash son of Jehoahaz, son of Jehu, 14.8
of Israel, saying, "Come, let us look one another in the face." 9 King Jehoash of 2 Chron 25.17

13.14 Elisha was highly regarded for his prophetic powers and miracles on Israel's behalf. Joash called him, "The chariots of Israel and its horsemen!" This recalls the title Elisha gave to Elijah in 2.12. Joash feared Elisha's death because he ascribed the nation's well-being to Elisha rather than to God. Joash's fear reveals his lack of spiritual understanding. At least 43 years had passed since Elisha was last mentioned in Scripture (9.1), when he anointed Jehu king (841 B.C.). Joash's reign began in 798 B.C.

13.15–19 When Joash was told to strike the floor with the arrows, he did it only halfheartedly. As a result, Elisha told the king that his victory over Syria would not be complete. Receiving the full benefits of God's plan for our lives requires us to receive and obey God's commands fully. If we don't follow God's complete instructions, we should not be surprised that his full benefits and blessings are not present.

13.20, 21 Elisha was dead, but his good influence remained, even causing miracles. This demonstrated that Elisha was indeed a prophet of God. It also attested to God's power—no heathen idol ever raised anyone from the dead. This miracle served as one more reminder to Israel that it had rejected God's word as given through Elisha.

14.7 Sela was the ancient stronghold of Petra, a city carved into a rock cliff. It was not only a stronghold for Edom, but also a wealthy outpost for trade with India.

14.9, 10 In this parable, Judah is compared to a small thorn bush. King Amaziah of Judah had become proud after defeating the Edomites. Here he was trying to pick a fight with Israel because he was sure his army was stronger. Joash tried to warn Amaziah not to attack by comparing his army to a thistle and Israel's army to a cedar tree. Amaziah had overrated his strength; his ambition was

14.9 Judg 9.14,15 Israel sent word to King Amaziah of Judah, "A thorn bush on Lebanon sent to a
cedar on Lebanon, saying, 'Give your daughter to my son for a wife'; but a wild
animal of Lebanon passed by and trampled down the thorn bush. 10 You have indeed defeated Edom, and your heart has lifted you up. Be content with your glory,
and stay at home; for why should you provoke trouble so that you fall, you and
Judah with you?"

14.11 Josh 19.35-39; 1 Sam 6.9 11 But Amaziah would not listen. So King Jehoash of Israel went up; he and
King Amaziah of Judah faced one another in battle at Beth-shemesh, which be-
14.13 2 Chron 25.23; Neh 8.16; 12.39 longs to Judah. 12 Judah was defeated by Israel; everyone fled home. 13 King Jehoash of Israel captured King Amaziah of Judah son of Jehoash, son of Ahaziah, at
Beth-shemesh; he came to Jerusalem, and broke down the wall of Jerusalem from
the Ephraim Gate to the Corner Gate, a distance of four hundred cubits. 14 He
seized all the gold and silver, and all the vessels that were found in the house of the
LORD and in the treasuries of the king's house, as well as hostages; then he returned
to Samaria.

14.15 2 Chron 25.26 15 Now the rest of the acts that Jehoash did, his might, and how he fought with
14.16 2 Kgs 10.35 King Amaziah of Judah, are they not written in the Book of the Annals of the Kings
of Israel? 16 Jehoash slept with his ancestors, and was buried in Samaria with the
14.17 2 Chron 25.25 kings of Israel; then his son Jeroboam succeeded him.

14.18 2 Kgs 12.19 17 King Amaziah son of Joash of Judah lived fifteen years after the death of
King Jehoash son of Jehoahaz of Israel. 18 Now the rest of the deeds of Amaziah,
14.19 2 Kgs 12.20 are they not written in the Book of the Annals of the Kings of Judah? 19 They made
14.20 2 Kgs 8.24,25 a conspiracy against him in Jerusalem, and he fled to Lachish. But they sent after
him to Lachish, and killed him there. 20 They brought him on horses; he was buried
14.21 1 Chron 3.10-14; 2 Chron 26.1; Mt 1.9 in Jerusalem with his ancestors in the city of David. 21 All the people of Judah took
Azariah, who was sixteen years old, and made him king to succeed his father Ama-
14.22 2 Kgs 16.6 ziah. 22 He rebuilt Elath and restored it to Judah, after King Amaziah[r] slept with
his ancestors.

Jeroboam II rules Israel

14.23 2 Kgs 13.13; Hos 1.1; Amos 1.2 23 In the fifteenth year of King Amaziah son of Joash of Judah, King Jeroboam
son of Joash of Israel began to reign in Samaria; he reigned forty-one years. 24 He
14.24 1 Kgs 12.28; 2 Kgs 13.2,6 did what was evil in the sight of the LORD; he did not depart from all the sins of
Jeroboam son of Nebat, which he caused Israel to sin. 25 He restored the border of
Israel from Lebo-hamath as far as the Sea of the Arabah, according to the word

[r] Heb *the king*

GOD OR IDOLS
Why did people continually turn to idols instead of to God?

Idols were:	*God is:*
Tangible	Intangible—no physical form
Morally similar—had human characteristics	Morally dissimilar—had divine characteristics
Comprehensible	Incomprehensible
Able to be manipulated	Not able to be manipulated
Worshiping idols involved:	*Worshiping God involved:*
Materialism	Sacrifice
Sexual immorality	Purity and commitment
Doing whatever a person wanted	Doing what God wants
Focusing on self	Focusing on others

---

greater than his ability. He didn't listen to Joash and was soundly defeated.

14.13 A broken-down city wall disgraced the citizens and left them defenseless against future invasions.

14.25 During this period of history, many prophets – such as Hosea, Amos, Jonah, Micah, and Isaiah – began collecting their prophecies and writing them under God's direction. They continued to preach about the worldwide significance of God's work as they looked forward to the future spiritual kingdom. God would use Israel's moral and spiritual decline to prepare the way for the Messiah's coming. Because the kingdom and military power of Israel was stripped away, many people would be ready to turn to the Good News that Jesus would bring.

14.25 For more information about the prophet Jonah, see the book of Jonah.

of the LORD, the God of Israel, which he spoke by his servant Jonah son of Amittai, **14.25**
the prophet, who was from Gath-hepher. 26 For the LORD saw that the distress of 2 Kgs 13.25 Jonah 1.1
Israel was very bitter; there was no one left, bond or free, and no one to help Israel. **14.26**
27 But the LORD had not said that he would blot out the name of Israel from under 2 Kgs 13.4
heaven, so he saved them by the hand of Jeroboam son of Joash. **14.27** 2 Kgs 13.5,23
28 Now the rest of the acts of Jeroboam, and all that he did, and his might, how **14.28**
he fought, and how he recovered for Israel Damascus and Hamath, which had be- 2 Kgs 14.15
longed to Judah, are they not written in the Book of the Annals of the Kings of
Israel? 29 Jeroboam slept with his ancestors, the kings of Israel; his son Zechariah
succeeded him.

Azariah rules Judah

15 In the twenty-seventh year of King Jeroboam of Israel King Azariah son of **15.1**
Amaziah of Judah began to reign. 2 He was sixteen years old when he began 2 Kgs 14.21 15.13,17
to reign, and he reigned fifty-two years in Jerusalem. His mother's name was Jeco-
liah of Jerusalem. 3 He did what was right in the sight of the LORD, just as his father **15.3** 2 Kgs 14.3
Amaziah had done. 4 Nevertheless the high places were not taken away; the people **15.4**
still sacrificed and made offerings on the high places. 5 The LORD struck the king, Lev 13.46 2 Kgs 12.3; 14.3
so that he was leprous[s] to the day of his death, and lived in a separate house. 2 Chron 26.21
Jotham the king's son was in charge of the palace, governing the people of the land. **15.6** 2 Kgs 14.18
6 Now the rest of the acts of Azariah, and all that he did, are they not written in the 15.36
Book of the Annals of the Kings of Judah? 7 Azariah slept with his ancestors; they **15.7** 2 Kgs 14.20
buried him with his ancestors in the city of David; his son Jotham succeeded him. 15.32,33

Zechariah rules Israel

8 In the thirty-eighth year of King Azariah of Judah, Zechariah son of Jeroboam **15.8**
reigned over Israel in Samaria six months. 9 He did what was evil in the sight of the 2 Kgs 14.29
LORD, as his ancestors had done. He did not depart from the sins of Jeroboam son **15.9** 2 Kgs 10.29
of Nebat, which he caused Israel to sin. 10 Shallum son of Jabesh conspired against 13.2; 14.24

[s] A term for several skin diseases; precise meaning uncertain

---

14.27 Israel was an evil and immoral nation, and its sins would get even worse. God did not want to destroy Israel. Instead, he was warning that judgment was certain if Israel didn't turn back to him. In his mercy, however, he gave Israel yet another chance to turn from its evil ways. But the next five kings of Israel didn't respond to God's mercy. They were so evil that God allowed the nation to be destroyed by Assyria.

14.28 Jeroboam had no devotion to God, yet under his warlike policies and skillful administration Israel enjoyed more national power and material prosperity than at any time since the days of Solomon. The prophets Amos and Hosea, however, tell us what was really happening within the kingdom (Hosea 13.4–8; Amos 6.11–14). Jeroboam's administration ignored policies of justice and fairness. As a result, the rich became richer and the poor, poorer. The people became self-centered, relying more on their power, security, and possessions than on God. The poor were so oppressed that it was hard for them to believe God noticed their plight. Material prosperity is not always an indication of God's blessing. It can also be a result of self-centeredness. If you are experiencing prosperity, remember that God holds us accountable for how we attain success and how we use our wealth. Everything we have really belongs to him. We must use God's gifts with his interests in mind.

15.1 Azariah was also known as Uzziah. His story is given in greater detail in 2 Chronicles 26. He is also mentioned in Isaiah 1.1 and 6.1. Before the beginning of Azariah's reign, Israel broke down 200 yards of Jerusalem's walls after defeating Judah and carrying off their king, Amaziah (2 Chronicles 25.23, 24). But during Azariah's 52-year reign, Judah rebuilt the wall, refortified the city with anti-siege weapons, and gained independence from Israel. Azariah's devotion to God helped Judah enjoy peace and prosperity such as it had not experienced since the days of Solomon. During this time, however, Israel declined drastically and would soon be overthrown.

15.4 Although Azariah accomplished a great deal, he failed to destroy the high places, the location of heathen shrines in Judah, just as his father Amaziah and grandfather Joash had failed to do. Azariah imitated the kings he had heard stories about and watched while growing up. Although Azariah's father and grandfather were basically good kings, they were poor models in some important areas. To rise above the influence of poor models, we must seek better ones. Christ provides a perfect model. No matter how you were raised or who has influenced your life, you can move beyond those limitations by taking Christ as your example and consciously trying to live as he did.

15.5 For 10 years Jotham was the co-ruler with his father, Azariah. A father and son ruled together for any of the following reasons: (1) the father was very old and needed help; (2) the father wanted to train his son in leading the nation; (3) the father was sick or exiled. There were many co-regents during the period of the kings – Asa/Jehoshaphat; Jehoshaphat/Jehoram; Azariah/Jotham; Jehoash/Jeroboam II; Hezekiah/Manasseh.

15.8 Zechariah was an evil king because he encouraged Israel to sin by worshiping idols. Sin in our own lives is serious. But it is even more serious to encourage others to disobey God. We are responsible for the way we influence others. Beware of double sins: ones that not only hurt us, but also hurt others by encouraging them to sin.

15.10 Zechariah was warned by the prophet Amos of his impending death and the subsequent end of Jeroboam's dynasty (Amos 7.9).

15.11 2 Kgs 14.28 15.15,21 him, and struck him down in public and killed him, and reigned in place of him.
11 Now the rest of the deeds of Zechariah are written in the Book of the Annals of
15.12 2 Kgs 10.30 the Kings of Israel. 12 This was the promise of the LORD that he gave to Jehu, "Your
sons shall sit on the throne of Israel to the fourth generation." And so it happened.

Shallum rules Israel

15.13 2 Kgs 15.1 13 Shallum son of Jabesh began to reign in the thirty-ninth year of King Uzziah
of Judah; he reigned one month in Samaria. 14 Then Menahem son of Gadi came up
from Tirzah and came to Samaria; he struck down Shallum son of Jabesh in Sa-
15.15 2 Kgs 15.11,21 maria and killed him; he reigned in place of him. 15 Now the rest of the deeds of
Shallum, including the conspiracy that he made, are written in the Book of the
15.16 2 Kgs 8.12 Annals of the Kings of Israel. 16 At that time Menahem sacked Tiphsah, all who
were in it and its territory from Tirzah on; because they did not open it to him, he
sacked it. He ripped open all the pregnant women in it.

Menahem rules Israel

17 In the thirty-ninth year of King Azariah of Judah, Menahem son of Gadi
15.18 2 Kgs 14.24 began to reign over Israel; he reigned ten years in Samaria. 18 He did what was evil
in the sight of the LORD; he did not depart all his days from any of the sins of
Jeroboam son of Nebat, which he caused Israel to sin. 19 King Pul of Assyria came
against the land; Menahem gave Pul a thousand talents of silver, so that he might

KINGS TO DATE AND THEIR ENEMIES

841 **JEHU** *Lost a large portion of northern Israel to Hazael (Syria) 2 Kgs 9.1—10.36 2 Chr 22.7-9*

814 **JEHOAHAZ** *Continually defeated by Hazael (Syria) 2 Kgs 10.35; 13.1-9*

798 **JEHOASH** *2 Kgs 13.10—14.16 2 Chr 25.17-24 Co-regency 793–782*

793 **JEROBOAM II** *Recaptured Israel's former territories from Syria and Aram, plundered Judah 2 Kgs 14.16-29*

782

753

ISRAEL

JUDAH

767

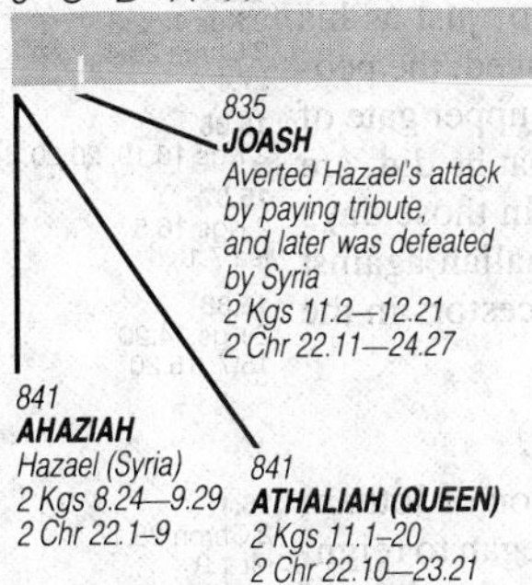

796 **AMAZIAH** *Defeated by Jehoash and Jeroboam II (Israel) 2 Kgs 14.1-20 2 Chr 24.27—25.28*

All dates are B.C.
Solid section of the timeline indicates co-regency.
For all the kings of Israel and Judah, see the chart at the end of 1 Kings.

15.14 Ancient historical documents say that Menahem was the commander-in-chief of Jeroboam's army (see 14.23–29 for an account of Jeroboam II's reign). After Jeroboam's son was assassinated (15.8–10), Menahem probably saw himself, and not Shallum, as the rightful successor to Israel's throne.

15.18 Menahem, like the kings before him, led his people into sin. What a horrible epitaph for a leader! Leaders profoundly affect the people they serve. They can either encourage or discourage devotion to God both by their example and by the structure they give their organization. Good leaders put up no obstacles to faith in God or to right living.

15.19, 20 When King Pul of Assyria (also called Tiglath-pileser in 15.29) took the throne, the Assyrian Empire was becoming a world power, and the nations of Syria, Israel, and Judah were in decline. This is the first mention of Assyria in 2 Kings. Pul's invasion occurred in 743 B.C. Assyria made Israel a vassal, and Menahem was forced to pay tribute to Assyria. This was the first of three Assyrian invasions (15.29 and 17.6 tell of the other ones).

help him confirm his hold on the royal power. 20 Menahem exacted the money from
Israel, that is, from all the wealthy, fifty shekels of silver from each one, to give to
the king of Assyria. So the king of Assyria turned back, and did not stay there in the
land. 21 Now the rest of the deeds of Menahem, and all that he did, are they not
written in the Book of the Annals of the Kings of Israel? 22 Menahem slept with his
ancestors, and his son Pekahiah succeeded him.

Pekahiah rules Israel

23 In the fiftieth year of King Azariah of Judah, Pekahiah son of Menahem
began to reign over Israel in Samaria; he reigned two years. 24 He did what was evil
in the sight of the LORD; he did not turn away from the sins of Jeroboam son of
Nebat, which he caused Israel to sin. 25 Pekah son of Remaliah, his captain, conspired against him with fifty of the Gileadites, and attacked him in Samaria, in the
citadel of the palace along with Argob and Arieh; he killed him, and reigned in
place of him. 26 Now the rest of the deeds of Pekahiah, and all that he did, are
written in the Book of the Annals of the Kings of Israel.

Pekah rules Israel

27 In the fifty-second year of King Azariah of Judah, Pekah son of Remaliah **15.27**
began to reign over Israel in Samaria; he reigned twenty years. 28 He did what was 2 Kgs 15.32
evil in the sight of the LORD; he did not depart from the sins of Jeroboam son of 16.5
Nebat, which he caused Israel to sin.

29 In the days of King Pekah of Israel, King Tiglath-pileser of Assyria came **15.29**
and captured Ijon, Abel-beth-maacah, Janoah, Kedesh, Hazor, Gilead, and Gali- 2 Kgs 17.6
lee, all the land of Naphtali; and he carried the people captive to Assyria. 30 Then **15.30**
Hoshea son of Elah made a conspiracy against Pekah son of Remaliah, attacked 2 Kgs 17.4; 18.1
him, and killed him; he reigned in place of him, in the twentieth year of Jotham son
of Uzziah. 31 Now the rest of the acts of Pekah, and all that he did, are written in the
Book of the Annals of the Kings of Israel.

Jotham rules Judah

32 In the second year of King Pekah son of Remaliah of Israel, King Jotham son **15.32**
of Uzziah of Judah began to reign. 33 He was twenty-five years old when he began 2 Chron 27.1 Mt 1.9
to reign and reigned sixteen years in Jerusalem. His mother's name was Jerusha
daughter of Zadok. 34 He did what was right in the sight of the LORD, just as his **15.34** 2 Kgs 12.2,3
father Uzziah had done. 35 Nevertheless the high places were not removed; the peo- 2 Chron 26.4 27.1,2
ple still sacrificed and made offerings on the high places. He built the upper gate of **15.36**
the house of the LORD. 36 Now the rest of the acts of Jotham, and all that he did, are 2 Kgs 16.19; 20.20
they not written in the Book of the Annals of the Kings of Judah? 37 In those days **15.37** 2 Kgs 16.5
the LORD began to send King Rezin of Aram and Pekah son of Remaliah against Isa 7.1
Judah. 38 Jotham slept with his ancestors, and was buried with his ancestors in the **15.38** 2 Kgs 14.20
city of David, his ancestor; his son Ahaz succeeded him. 15.7; 16.20

Ahaz rules Judah

16 In the seventeenth year of Pekah son of Remaliah, King Ahaz son of Jotham **16.1**
of Judah began to reign. 2 Ahaz was twenty years old when he began to reign; 2 Chron 28.1 Mt 1.9
he reigned sixteen years in Jerusalem. He did not do what was right in the sight of
the LORD his God, as his ancestor David had done, 3 but he walked in the way of the **16.3**
kings of Israel. He even made his son pass through fire, according to the abomina- Lev 18.21 Deut 12.31

15.30 Hoshea was Israel's last king.

15.32 A year after Pekah became king, Uzziah of Judah died, and Isaiah the prophet had a vision of God's holiness and Israel's future destruction. See Isaiah 6 for more details on what Isaiah saw.

15.34, 35 Much good can be said of Jotham and his reign as king of Judah, but he failed in a most critical area: he didn't destroy the shrines to the false gods, although leaving them clearly violated the first commandment (Exodus 20.3). Like Jotham, we may live basically good lives and yet miss doing what is most important. A lifetime of doing good is not enough if we make the crucial mistake of not following God with all our hearts. A true follower of God puts God first in all areas of life.

16.3 "Made his son to pass through fire" is a reference to human sacrifice. Ahaz was so depraved that he sacrificed his own son to the heathen gods. This was a practice of the Canaanites whom the Israelites were supposed to drive out of the land.

ble practices of the nations whom the LORD drove out before the people of Israel.
16.4 Deut 12.2; 14.4 [4]He sacrificed and made offerings on the high places, on the hills, and under every
green tree.
16.5 2 Kgs 15.37 2 Chron 28.5 Isa 7.1 5 Then King Rezin of Aram and King Pekah son of Remaliah of Israel came up
to wage war on Jerusalem; they besieged Ahaz but could not conquer him. [6]At that
16.6 2 Kgs 14.22 2 Chron 26.2 time the king of Edom[t] recovered Elath for Edom,[u] and drove the Judeans from
Elath; and the Edomites came to Elath, where they live to this day. [7]Ahaz sent
16.7 2 Kgs 15.29 2 Chron 28.20 messengers to King Tiglath-pileser of Assyria, saying, "I am your servant and your
son. Come up, and rescue me from the hand of the king of Aram and from the hand
of the king of Israel, who are attacking me." [8]Ahaz also took the silver and gold
16.8 2 Kgs 12.18 18.15 found in the house of the LORD and in the treasures of the king's house, and sent a
present to the king of Assyria. [9]The king of Assyria listened to him; the king of
16.9 Isa 7.15,16 Amos 1.3-5 Assyria marched up against Damascus, and took it, carrying its people captive to
Kir; then he killed Rezin.

[t] Cn: Heb *King Rezin of Aram* [u] Cn: Heb *Aram*

KINGS TO DATE AND THEIR ENEMIES

ISRAEL

793 **JEROBOAM II** *Recaptured Israel's former territories from Syria and Aram, plundered Judah* *2 Kgs 14.16–29*

753 **ZECHARIAH** *2 Kgs 14.29—15.12*

752 **SHALLUM** *2 Kgs 15.10–15*

752 **MENAHEM** *Paid tribute to Tiglath-pileaser (Assyria)* *2 Kgs 15.14–22*

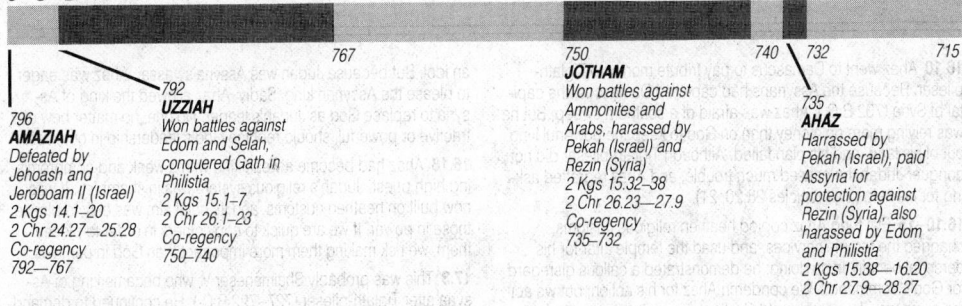

742 **PEKAHIAH** *2 Kgs 15.22–26*

740 **PEKAH** Suffered first conquest by Assyria 2 Kgs 15.25–31 2 Chr 28.5–8

732 **HOSHEA** *Suffered complete conquest by Shalmaneser (Assyria)* *2 Kgs 15.30; 17.1–6*

722 *Captivity*

JUDAH

767 750 740 732 715

796 **AMAZIAH** *Defeated by Jehoash and Jeroboam II (Israel)* *2 Kgs 14.1–20* *2 Chr 24.27—25.28* *Co-regency 792—767*

792 **UZZIAH** *Won battles against Edom and Selah, conquered Gath in Philistia* *2 Kgs 15.1–7* *2 Chr 26.1–23* *Co-regency 750–740*

750 **JOTHAM** *Won battles against Ammonites and Arabs, harassed by Pekah (Israel) and Rezin (Syria)* *2 Kgs 15.32–38* *2 Chr 26.23—27.9* *Co-regency 735–732*

735 **AHAZ** *Harrassed by Pekah (Israel), paid Assyria for protection against Rezin (Syria), also harassed by Edom and Philistia* *2 Kgs 15.38—16.20* *2 Chr 27.9—28.27*

All dates are B.C.
Solid section of the timeline indicates co-regency.
For all the kings of Israel and Judah, see the chart at the end of 1 Kings.

16.5 Israel and Syria were both under Assyria's control. They joined forces against Judah, hoping to force the southern kingdom to join their revolt against Assyria and strengthen their western alliance. But the plan backfired when King Ahaz of Judah unexpectedly asked Assyria to come to his aid (16.8, 9).

10 When King Ahaz went to Damascus to meet King Tiglath-pileser of As- 16.10 2 Chron 28.23
syria, he saw the altar that was at Damascus. King Ahaz sent to the priest Uriah a Isa 8.2
model of the altar, and its pattern, exact in all its details. 11 The priest Uriah built the
altar; in accordance with all that King Ahaz had sent from Damascus, just so did the
priest Uriah build it, before King Ahaz arrived from Damascus. 12 When the king
came from Damascus, the king viewed the altar. Then the king drew near to the
altar, went up on it, 13 and offered his burnt offering and his grain offering, poured
his drink offering, and dashed the blood of his offerings of well-being against the
altar. 14 The bronze altar that was before the LORD he removed from the front of the 16.14 Ex 40.6
house, from the place between his altar and the house of the LORD, and put it on 1 Kgs 8.22,23
the north side of his altar. 15 King Ahaz commanded the priest Uriah, saying, 16.15
"Upon the great altar offer the morning burnt offering, and the evening grain of- Lev 4.14 Num 28.1,2
fering, and the king's burnt offering, and his grain offering, with the burnt offering
of all the people of the land, their grain offering, and their drink offering; then dash
against it all the blood of the burnt offering, and all the blood of the sacrifice; but
the bronze altar shall be for me to inquire by." 16 The priest Uriah did everything that
King Ahaz commanded.
17 Then King Ahaz cut off the frames of the stands, and removed the laver from 16.17
them; he removed the sea from the bronze oxen that were under it, and put it on a 1 Kgs 7.23
pediment of stone. 18 The covered portal for use on the sabbath that had been built
inside the palace, and the outer entrance for the king he removed from[v] the house 16.19
of the LORD. He did this because of the king of Assyria. 19 Now the rest of the acts 2 Kgs 15.36 20.20
of Ahaz that he did, are they not written in the Book of the Annals of the Kings of 16.20
Judah? 20 Ahaz slept with his ancestors, and was buried with his ancestors in the 2 Kgs 18.1
city of David; his son Hezekiah succeeded him. 2 Chron 28.27 29.1

3. Israel is exiled to Assyria

Hoshea rules Israel

17 In the twelfth year of King Ahaz of Judah, Hoshea son of Elah began to reign 17.1
in Samaria over Israel; he reigned nine years. 2 He did what was evil in the 2 Kgs 15.30
sight of the LORD, yet not like the kings of Israel who were before him. 3 King 17.3
Shalmaneser of Assyria came up against him; Hoshea became his vassal, and paid 2 Kgs 18.9
him tribute. 4 But the king of Assyria found treachery in Hoshea; for he had sent 17.4
messengers to King So of Egypt, and offered no tribute to the king of Assyria, as 2 Kgs 18.20,21
he had done year by year; therefore the king of Assyria confined him and imprisoned him.
5 Then the king of Assyria invaded all the land and came to Samaria; for three

[v] Cn: Heb lacks *from*

16.10 Ahaz went to Damascus to pay tribute money to Tiglath-pileser. Because the Assyrians had captured Damascus, the capital of Syria (732 B.C.), Ahaz was afraid of a southern sweep. But he was relying more on money than on God to keep the powerful king out of his land, and his plan failed. Although Tiglath-pileser did not conquer Judah, he caused much trouble, and Ahaz regretted asking for his help (2 Chronicles 28.20, 21).

16.10–15 Evil King Ahaz copied heathen religious customs, changed the temple services, and used the temple altar for his personal benefit. In so doing, he demonstrated a callous disregard for God's commands. We condemn Ahaz for his action, but we act the same way if we try to mold God's message to fit our personal preferences. We must worship God for who he is, not what we would selfishly like him to be.

16.14–18 Ahaz replaced the altar of burnt offering with a replica of the pagan altar he had seen in Damascus. (The original bronze altar was not thrown out, but was kept for use in divination. The laver was where the sacrifices were washed. The sea was a huge reservoir of water for temple use.) This was extremely serious because God had given specific directions on how the altar should look and be used (Exodus 27.1–8). Building this new altar was like installing an idol. But because Judah was Assyria's vassal, Ahaz was eager to please the Assyrian king. Sadly, Ahaz allowed the king of Assyria to replace God as Judah's leader. No one, no matter how attractive or powerful, should replace God's leadership in our lives.

16.18 Ahaz had become a weak king with a weak and compromising high priest. Judah's religious system was in shambles. It was now built on heathen customs, and its chief aim was only to please those in power. If we are quick to copy others in order to please them, we risk making them more important than God in our lives.

17.3 This was probably Shalmaneser V, who became king of Assyria after Tiglath-pileser (727–722 B.C.). He continued to demand heavy tribute from Israel. Israel's King Hoshea decided to rebel against Assyria and join forces with king So of Egypt (17.4). This was not only foolish, but also against God's commands. To destroy this conspiracy, Shalmaneser attacked and besieged Samaria for three years. But just before Samaria fell, Shalmaneser died. His successor, Sargon II, took credit for capturing the city, destroying the nation of Israel, and carrying away its people.

17.5, 6 This was the third and final invasion of Assyria into Israel. (The first two invasions are recorded in 15.19 and 15.29.) The first wave was merely a warning to Israel – to avoid further attack, pay

17.6 Deut 28.64 29.28 1 Chron 5.26 Hos 13.16
17.7 Josh 23.15,16
17.8 Lev 18.3 Deut 18.9 Judg 6.10
17.9 Ex 34.12 1 Kgs 14.23
17.13 Neh 9.29,30 Jer 7.5,6; 18.11 Acts 7.51,52
17.14 Ex 32.9; 33.3 2 Chron 36.15
17.15 Ex 24.7,8 Deut 12.30,31 29.25
17.16 Deut 4.16,17 1 Kgs 12.28 16.31

years he besieged it. 6 In the ninth year of Hoshea the king of Assyria captured
Samaria; he carried the Israelites away to Assyria. He placed them in Halah, on the
Habor, the river of Gozan, and in the cities of the Medes.

Israel exiled for rejecting God

7 This occurred because the people of Israel had sinned against the LORD their
God, who had brought them up out of the land of Egypt from under the hand of
Pharaoh king of Egypt. They had worshiped other gods 8 and walked in the customs
of the nations whom the LORD drove out before the people of Israel, and in the
customs that the kings of Israel had introduced.[w] 9 The people of Israel secretly did
things that were not right against the LORD their God. They built for themselves
high places at all their towns, from watchtower to fortified city; 10 they set up for
themselves pillars and sacred poles[x] on every high hill and under every green tree;
11 there they made offerings on all the high places, as the nations did whom the
LORD carried away before them. They did wicked things, provoking the LORD to
anger; 12 they served idols, of which the LORD had said to them, "You shall not do
this." 13 Yet the LORD warned Israel and Judah by every prophet and every seer,
saying, "Turn from your evil ways and keep my commandments and my statutes,
in accordance with all the law that I commanded your ancestors and that I sent to
you by my servants the prophets." 14 They would not listen but were stubborn, as
their ancestors had been, who did not believe in the LORD their God. 15 They despised his statutes, and his covenant that he made with their ancestors, and the
warnings that he gave them. They went after false idols and became false; they
followed the nations that were around them, concerning whom the LORD had commanded them that they should not do as they did. 16 They rejected all the commandments of the LORD their God and made for themselves cast images of two calves;

[w] Meaning of Heb uncertain [x] Heb *Asherim*

money and don't rebel. The people should have learned their lesson and returned to God. When they didn't, God allowed Assyria to invade again, this time carrying off some captives from the northern border. But the people still did not realize that they had caused their own troubles. Thus Assyria invaded for the third and final time, destroying Israel completely, carrying away most of the people, and resettling the land with foreigners.

God was doing what he had said he would do (Deuteronomy 28). He had given Israel ample warning; they knew what would come, but they still ignored God. Israel was now no better than the heathen nations it had destroyed in the days of Joshua. The nation had turned sour and rejected its original purpose—to honor God and be a light to the world.

17.7–17 The Lord judged the people of Israel because they copied the evil customs of the surrounding nations, worshiping false gods, accommodating pagan customs, and following their own desires. It is not safe to create your own religion; people who do tend to live selfishly. And to live for yourself, as Israel learned, brings serious consequences from God. Sometimes it is difficult and painful to follow God, but consider the alternative. You can live for God or die for yourself. Determine to be God's person and to do what he says regardless of the cost. What God thinks of you is infinitely more important than what those around you think. (See Romans 12.1, 2; 1 John 2.15–17.)

17.9 Ruin came upon Israel for both their public sins and their secret sins. Not only did they condone wickedness and idolatry in public, but they committed even worse sins in private. Secret sins are the ones we don't want others to know about because they are embarrassing or incriminating. Sins done in private are not secret to God, and secret defiance of him is just as damaging as open rebellion.

17.13–15 They "became false" means they became vain and worthless. They took on the characteristics of the idols and imitated the godless nations around them. Israel had forgotten the importance and benefits of obeying God's Word. The king and the people were mired in wickedness. Time and again God sent prophets to warn them of how far they had turned away from him and to call them to turn back.

God's patience and mercy are beyond our ability to understand. He will pursue us until we either respond to him or, by our own choice and hardness of heart, make ourselves unreachable. Then God's judgment is swift and sure. The only safe course is to turn to God before our stubbornness puts us out of his reach.

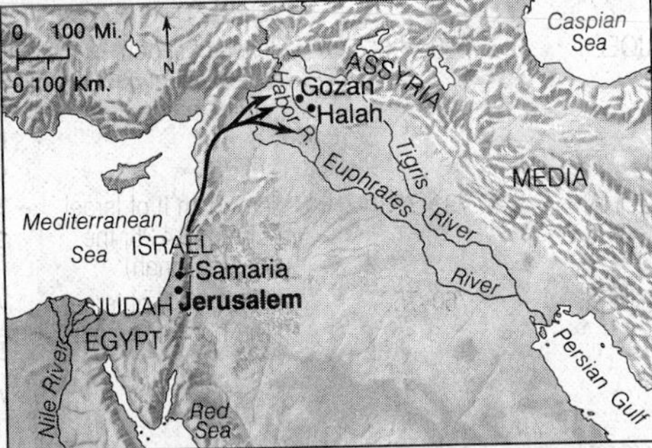

ISRAEL TAKEN CAPTIVE Finally the sins of Israel's people caught up with them. God allowed Assyria to defeat and disperse the people. They were led into captivity, swallowed up by the mighty, evil Assyrian Empire. Sin always brings discipline, and the consequences of that sin are sometimes irreversible.

17.16 The "host of heaven" refers to the Canaanite practice of worshiping the sun, moon, and constellations. These were Assyrian gods that were being added to their religion. (See also 21.1–6; 23.4, 5.)

they made a sacred pole,[y] worshiped all the host of heaven, and served Baal.
17 They made their sons and their daughters pass through fire; they used divination
and augury; and they sold themselves to do evil in the sight of the LORD, provoking
him to anger. 18 Therefore the LORD was very angry with Israel and removed them
out of his sight; none was left but the tribe of Judah alone.
19 Judah also did not keep the commandments of the LORD their God but

[y] Heb *Asherah*

17.17 Lev 19.26 Deut 18.10 2 Kgs 3.27 16.3; 21.6
17.19 1 Kgs 14.24

WHO WERE

Who?	*When? (B.C.)*	*Ministered during the reign of these kings:*	*Main message*	*Significance*
AHIJAH	934–909	Jeroboam of Israel (1 Kings 11.29–39)	Said Israel would split in two and stated that God had chosen Jeroboam to lead the ten tribes. Warned that he should remain obedient to God.	We should not take lightly our God-given responsibilities. Jeroboam did, and lost his kingdom.
ELIJAH	875–848	Ahab of Israel (1 Kings 17.1—2 Kings 2.11)	In fiery style, urged wicked Ahab to turn back to God. On Mount Carmel, he proved who is the one true God (1 Kings 18).	Even giants of faith can't force sinners to change. But those who remain faithful to God have a great impact for him.
MICAIAH	865–853	Ahab of Israel Jehosphaphat of Judah (1 Kings 22.8; 2 Chronicles 18.28)	Ahab would be unsuccessful in fighting the Syrians.	It is foolish to move ahead with plans that are contrary to God's word.
JEHU	853	Jehoshaphat of Judah (2 Chronicles 19.1–3)	Jehoshaphat should never have allied himself with wicked Ahab.	Partnerships with immoral people can lead us into trouble.
OBADIAH	855–840(?)	Jehoram of Judah (The book of Obadiah)	God would judge the Edomites for taking advantage of God's people.	Pride is one of the most dangerous sins because it causes us to take advantage of others.
ELISHA	848–797	Jehoram, Jehu, Jehoahaz, and Jehoash, all of Israel (2 Kings 2.1—9.1; 13.10–21)	Expressed by his actions the importance of helping ordinary people in need.	God is concerned about the everyday needs of his people.
JOEL	835–796(?)	Joash of Judah (The book of Joel)	Because a plague of locusts had come to punish the nation, he called the people to turn back to God before an even greater judgment occurred.	While God judges all people for their sins, he gives eternal salvation only to those who have turned to him.
JONAH	793–753	Jeroboam II of Israel (2 Kings 14.25; the book of Jonah)	Nineveh, the capital of Assyria, should repent of its sins.	God wants all nations to turn to him. His love reaches out to all peoples.
AMOS	760–750	Jeroboam II of Israel (The book of Amos)	Warned against those who exploited or ignored the needy. (In Amos's day, Israel was an affluent and materialistic society.)	Believing in God is more than a personal matter. God calls all believers to work against injustices in society and to aid those less fortunate.
HOSEA	753–715	The last seven kings of Israel; Uzziah, Jotham, Ahaz, and Hezekiah of Judah (The book of Hosea)	Condemned the people of Israel because they had sinned against God as an adulterous woman sins against her husband.	When we sin, we sever our relationship to God, breaking our commitment to him. While all must answer to God for their sins, those who seek God's forgiveness are spared from eternal judgment.

"Yet the Lord warned Israel and Judah by every prophet . . . saying, 'Turn from your evil ways and keep my commandments' " (2 Kings 17.13). Who were these prophets? Here are some of those who tried to turn their nations back to God. Predicting the future as revealed by God was just one part of a prophet's job; his main role was to preach God's Word to the people—

17.20 Jer 6.30 Rom 11.1-3 walked in the customs that Israel had introduced. 20 The LORD rejected all the descendants of Israel; he punished them and gave them into the hand of plunderers,
until he had banished them from his presence.

17.21 1 Kgs 11.11,31 12.20 2 Chron 10.16-19 Isa 7.17 21 When he had torn Israel from the house of David, they made Jeroboam son
of Nebat king. Jeroboam drove Israel from following the LORD and made them
commit great sin. 22 The people of Israel continued in all the sins that Jeroboam
committed; they did not depart from them 23 until the LORD removed Israel out of

THESE PROPHETS?

Who?	*When? (B.C.)*	*Ministered during the reign of these kings:*	*Main message*	*Significance*
MICAH	742–687	Jotham, Ahaz, and Hezekiah of Judah (The book of Micah)	Predicted the fall of both the northern and southern kingdoms. This was God's discipline on the people, actually showing how much he cared for them.	Choosing to live a life apart from God is making a commitment to sin. Sin leads to judgment and death. God alone shows us the way to eternal peace. His discipline often keeps us on the right path.
ISAIAH	740–681	Uzziah, Jotham, Ahaz, Hezekiah, and Manasseh of Judah (The book of Isaiah)	Called the people back to a special relationship with God—although judgment through other nations was inevitable.	Sometimes we must suffer judgment and discipline before we are restored to God.
NAHUM	663–654	Manasseh of Judah (The book of Nahum)	The mighty empire of Assyria that oppressed God's people would soon tumble.	Those who do evil and oppress others will one day meet a bitter end.
ZEPHANIAH	640–621	Josiah of Judah (The book of Zephaniah)	A day will come when God, as Judge, will severely punish all nations; but afterwards, he will show mercy to his people.	We will all be judged for our disobedience to God, but if we remain faithful to him, he will show us mercy.
JEREMIAH	627–586	Josiah, Jehoahaz, Jehoiakim, Jehoiachin, Zedekiah of Judah (The book of Jeremiah)	Repentence would postpone Judah's coming judgment at the hands of Babylon.	Repentance is one of the greatest needs in our world of immorality. God's promises to the faithful shine brightly.
HABAKKUK	612–589	Josiah, Jehoahaz, Jehoiakim, Jehoiachin, Zedekiah of Judah (The book of Habakkuk)	Habakkuk couldn't understand why God seemed to do nothing about the wickedness in society. Then he realized that faith in God alone would one day supply the answer.	Instead of questioning the ways of God, we should realize that he is completely just, and we should have faith that he is in control and that one day evil will be utterly destroyed.
DANIEL	605–536	Prophesied as an exile in Babylon during the reigns of Nebuchadnezzar, Darius the Mede, and Cyrus of Persia (The book of Daniel)	Describes both near and distant future events—throughout all, God is sovereign and triumphant.	We should spend less time wondering when these events will happen and more time learning how we should live *now* so we won't be victims of those events.
EZEKIEL	593–571	Prophesied as an exile in Babylon during the reign of Nebuchadnezzar (The book of Ezekiel)	Sent messages back to Jerusalem urging the people to turn back to God before they were all forced to join him in exile. After Jerusalem fell, Ezekiel urged his fellow exiles to turn back to God so they could eventually return to their homeland.	God disciplines his people to draw them closer to him.

warning, instructing, and encouraging them to live as they ought.

The prophets Haggai, Zechariah, and Malachi were prophets to the people of Judah after they returned from exile. For more information, see the chart in Ezra 5.

his sight, as he had foretold through all his servants the prophets. So Israel was **17.23** 2 Kgs 18.11,12
exiled from their own land to Assyria until this day.

Foreigners resettled in Samaria

24 The king of Assyria brought people from Babylon, Cuthah, Avva, Hamath, **17.24**
and Sepharvaim, and placed them in the cities of Samaria in place of the people of 2 Kgs 18.34
Israel; they took possession of Samaria, and settled in its cities. 25 When they first **17.25**
settled there, they did not worship the LORD; therefore the LORD sent lions among 1 Kgs 13.24,25 20.36
them, which killed some of them. 26 So the king of Assyria was told, "The nations
that you have carried away and placed in the cities of Samaria do not know the law
of the god of the land; therefore he has sent lions among them; they are killing
them, because they do not know the law of the god of the land." 27 Then the king of
Assyria commanded, "Send there one of the priests whom you carried away from
there; let him[z] go and live there, and teach them the law of the god of the land."
28 So one of the priests whom they had carried away from Samaria came and lived
in Bethel; he taught them how they should worship the LORD.
29 But every nation still made gods of its own and put them in the shrines of the **17.29**
high places that the people of Samaria had made, every nation in the cities in which 1 Kgs 12.31 13.32
they lived; 30 the people of Babylon made Succoth-benoth, the people of Cuth made
Nergal, the people of Hamath made Ashima; 31 the Avvites made Nibhaz and Tar- **17.31**
tak; the Sepharvites burned their children in the fire to Adrammelech and Anamme- 2 Kgs 19.37
lech, the gods of Sepharvaim. 32 They also worshiped the LORD and appointed from **17.32**
among themselves all sorts of people as priests of the high places, who sacrificed 1 Kgs 12.31 13.33
for them in the shrines of the high places. 33 So they worshiped the LORD but also
served their own gods, after the manner of the nations from among whom they had
been carried away. 34 To this day they continue to practice their former customs. **17.34**
They do not worship the LORD and they do not follow the statutes or the ordi- Gen 32.28 35.10
nances or the law or the commandment that the LORD commanded the children of
Jacob, whom he named Israel. 35 The LORD had made a covenant with them and **17.35**
commanded them, "You shall not worship other gods or bow yourselves to them or Ex 19.5; 24.7 Judg 6.10
serve them or sacrifice to them, 36 but you shall worship the LORD, who brought
you out of the land of Egypt with great power and with an outstretched arm; you
shall bow yourselves to him, and to him you shall sacrifice. 37 The statutes and the **17.37**
ordinances and the law and the commandment that he wrote for you, you shall Deut 5.32

z Syr Vg: Heb *them*

17.23 Israel was swept away, just as God's prophets had warned. Whatever God predicts will come to pass. This, of course, is good news to those who trust and obey him – they can be confident of his promises; but it is bad news to those who ignore or disobey him. Both the promises and warnings God has given in his word will surely come true.

17.24 Moving the Israelites out and moving foreigners in was Assyria's resettlement policy to prevent revolt. Spreading the captives across Assyria prevented their uniting, and repopulating Israel with foreign captives made it difficult for the remaining Israelites to unite as well. This mixture of peoples resettled in Israel came to be known as *Samaritans.* They were despised by the Jews, and they were still looked down upon during the time of Christ (John 4.9).

17.27–29 The new settlers in Israel worshiped God without giving up their pagan customs. They worshiped God to appease him rather than to please him, treating him as a good luck charm or just another idol to add to their collection. A similar attitude is common today. Many people claim to believe in God while refusing to give up attitudes and actions that God denounces. God cannot be added to the values we already have. He must come first, and his Word must shape all our actions and attitudes.

17.29–31 Israel was conquered because it had lost sight of the only true God and why it was important to follow him. When conquering the land, the Israelites were told to destroy the pagan influences that could lead them away from God. Their failure to do so brought about their ruin. Now they faced an even greater influx of gods from the many heathen peoples moving into the land.

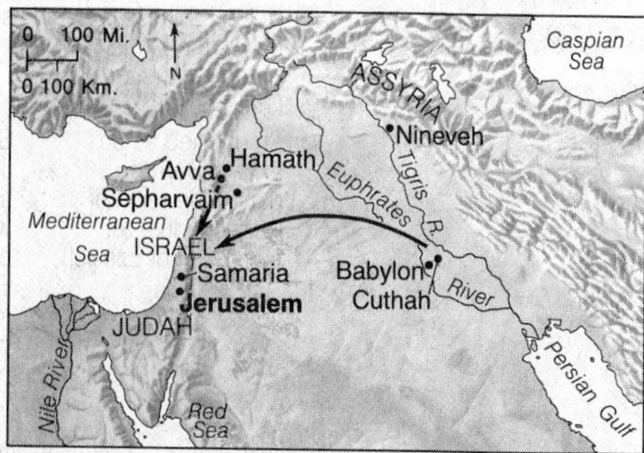

ISRAEL RESETTLED BY FOREIGNERS After the Israelites were deported, foreigners from the Assyrian Empire were sent to resettle the land. This policy helped Assyria keep peace in conquered territories.

17.38 Deut 4.23 6.10-12
17.39 1 Sam 12.24

always be careful to observe. You shall not worship other gods; 38 you shall not
forget the covenant that I have made with you. You shall not worship other gods,
39 but you shall worship the LORD your God; he will deliver you out of the hand of
all your enemies." 40 They would not listen, however, but they continued to practice their former custom.

17.41 Zeph 1.5 Mt 6.24 Acts 7.42

41 So these nations worshiped the LORD, but also served their carved images; to
this day their children and their children's children continue to do as their ancestors did.

B. THE SURVIVING KINGDOM (18.1–25.30)

After seeing their brothers carried away into exile, Judah still lapses into sin. Hezekiah and Josiah begin many reforms, but this is not enough to permanently turn the nation back to God. Judah is defeated by the Babylonians, who exile many of them, but they are not scattered and the land is not repopulated. Sometimes we do not learn from the examples of sin and foolishness around us.

1. Kings of Judah

Hezekiah rules Judah

18.1 2 Kgs 15.30 16.20; 20.3 2 Chron 28.27 31.20
18.4 Num 21.8,9 2 Kgs 12.3 2 Chron 31.1
18.5 2 Kgs 23.25
18.7 Gen 39.2 1 Sam 18.14 2 Chron 15.2 Job 1.10 Dan 6.28
18.8 2 Chron 28.18
18.9 2 Kgs 17.3
18.11 2 Kgs 17.6 19.11
18.12 Num 12.7,8 1 Kgs 8.56 2 Kgs 17.7,13 Neh 9.17 Isa 1.20

18 In the third year of King Hoshea son of Elah of Israel, Hezekiah son of King
Ahaz of Judah began to reign. 2 He was twenty-five years old when he began
to reign; he reigned twenty-nine years in Jerusalem. His mother's name was Abi
daughter of Zechariah. 3 He did what was right in the sight of the LORD just as his
ancestor David had done. 4 He removed the high places, broke down the pillars,
and cut down the sacred pole.[a] He broke in pieces the bronze serpent that Moses
had made, for until those days the people of Israel had made offerings to it; it was
called Nehushtan. 5 He trusted in the LORD the God of Israel; so that there was no
one like him among all the kings of Judah after him, or among those who were
before him. 6 For he held fast to the LORD; he did not depart from following him but
kept the commandments that the LORD commanded Moses. 7 The LORD was with
him; wherever he went, he prospered. He rebelled against the king of Assyria and
would not serve him. 8 He attacked the Philistines as far as Gaza and its territory,
from watchtower to fortified city.

9 In the fourth year of King Hezekiah, which was the seventh year of King
Hoshea son of Elah of Israel, King Shalmaneser of Assyria came up against Samaria, besieged it, 10 and at the end of three years, took it. In the sixth year of
Hezekiah, which was the ninth year of King Hoshea of Israel, Samaria was taken.
11 The king of Assyria carried the Israelites away to Assyria, settled them in Halah,
on the Habor, the river of Gozan, and in the cities of the Medes, 12 because they did
not obey the voice of the LORD their God but transgressed his covenant—all that
Moses the servant of the LORD had commanded; they neither listened nor obeyed.

[a] Heb *Asherah*

18.4 The bronze serpent had been made to cure the Israelites of a deadly plague (Numbers 21.4–9). It demonstrated God's presence and power and reminded the people of his mercy and forgiveness. But it had become an object of worship instead of a reminder of *whom* to worship, so Hezekiah was forced to destroy it. We must be careful that aids to our worship don't become objects of worship themselves. Most objects are not made to be idols—they become idols by the way people use them.

18.5 In dramatic contrast with his father, Ahaz, Hezekiah followed God more closely and sincerely than any other king of Judah or Israel. This statement refers to the kings after the division of the kingdom and so does not include David, considered the king most devoted to God.

18.7 The nation of Judah was sandwiched between two world powers, Egypt and Assyria. Both wanted to control Judah and Israel because they lay at the vital crossroads of all Middle Eastern trade. The nation who controlled Judah would have a military and economic advantage over its rivals. When Hezekiah became king, Assyria controlled Judah. Acting with great courage, Hezekiah rebelled against this mighty empire to whom his father had submitted. He placed his faith in God's strength rather than his own, and he obeyed God's commands in spite of the obstacles and dangers that, from a purely human standpoint, looked overwhelming.

18.9–12 These verses flash back to the days just before Israel's destruction. Hezekiah reigned with his father Ahaz for 14 years (729–715 B.C.), by himself for 18 years (715–697 B.C.), and with his son Manasseh for 11 years (697–686 B.C.)—a total of 43 years. The 29 years listed in 18.2 indicate only those years in which Hezekiah had complete control of the kingdom. While Hezekiah was on the throne, the nation of Israel to the north was destroyed (722 B.C.). Knowing Israel's fate probably caused Hezekiah to reform his own nation. (For more on Hezekiah, see 2 Chronicles 29–32 and Isaiah 36–39.)

Assyria threatens to conquer Judah

13 In the fourteenth year of King Hezekiah, King Sennacherib of Assyria came 18.13
up against all the fortified cities of Judah and captured them. 14 King Hezekiah of 2 Chron 32.1 Isa 36.1
Judah sent to the king of Assyria at Lachish, saying, "I have done wrong; withdraw
from me; whatever you impose on me I will bear." The king of Assyria demanded
of King Hezekiah of Judah three hundred talents of silver and thirty talents of gold.
15 Hezekiah gave him all the silver that was found in the house of the LORD and in 18.15
the treasuries of the king's house. 16 At that time Hezekiah stripped the gold from 1 Kgs 15.18 2 Kgs 12.18
the doors of the temple of the LORD, and from the doorposts that King Hezekiah of
Judah had overlaid and gave it to the king of Assyria. 17 The king of Assyria sent the
Tartan, the Rab-saris, and the Rabshakeh with a great army from Lachish to King
Hezekiah at Jerusalem. They went up and came to Jerusalem. When they arrived,
they came and stood by the conduit of the upper pool, which is on the highway to
the Fuller's Field. 18 When they called for the king, there came out to them Eliakim 18.18
son of Hilkiah, who was in charge of the palace, and Shebnah the secretary, and 2 Kgs 19.2 Isa 22.15,16,
Joah son of Asaph, the recorder. 20; 36.3

19 The Rabshakeh said to them, "Say to Hezekiah: Thus says the great king, the
king of Assyria: On what do you base this confidence of yours? 20 Do you think that 18.20
mere words are strategy and power for war? On whom do you now rely, that you Isa 30.2,7 Ezek 29.2,6
have rebelled against me? 21 See, you are relying now on Egypt, that broken reed of
a staff, which will pierce the hand of anyone who leans on it. Such is Pharaoh king
of Egypt to all who rely on him. 22 But if you say to me, 'We rely on the LORD our
God,' is it not he whose high places and altars Hezekiah has removed, saying to
Judah and to Jerusalem, 'You shall worship before this altar in Jerusalem'? 23 Come
now, make a wager with my master the king of Assyria: I will give you two thousand horses, if you are able on your part to set riders on them. 24 How then can you
repulse a single captain among the least of my master's servants, when you rely on
Egypt for chariots and for horsemen? 25 Moreover, is it without the LORD that I have
come up against this place to destroy it? The LORD said to me, Go up against this
land, and destroy it."

26 Then Eliakim son of Hilkiah, and Shebnah, and Joah said to the Rabshakeh, 18.26
"Please speak to your servants in the Aramaic language, for we understand it; do Ezra 4.7 Isa 36.11,12
not speak to us in the language of Judah within the hearing of the people who are Dan 2.4
on the wall." 27 But the Rabshakeh said to them, "Has my master sent me to speak
these words to your master and to you, and not to the people sitting on the wall,
who are doomed with you to eat their own dung and to drink their own urine?"

28 Then the Rabshakeh stood and called out in a loud voice in the language of
Judah, "Hear the word of the great king, the king of Assyria! 29 Thus says the king:
'Do not let Hezekiah deceive you, for he will not be able to deliver you out of my
hand. 30 Do not let Hezekiah make you rely on the LORD by saying, The LORD will
surely deliver us, and this city will not be given into the hand of the king of Assyria.' 31 Do not listen to Hezekiah; for thus says the king of Assyria: 'Make your 18.31
peace with me and come out to me; then every one of you will eat from your own Deut 8.7-9
vine and your own fig tree, and drink water from your own cistern, 32 until I come
and take you away to a land like your own land, a land of grain and wine, a land of
bread and vineyards, a land of olive oil and honey, that you may live and not die.
Do not listen to Hezekiah when he misleads you by saying, The LORD will deliver

---

18.13 This event occurred in 701 B.C., four years after Sennacherib had become Assyria's king. Sennacherib was the son of Sargon II, the king who had deported Israel's people into captivity (see the note on 17.3). To keep Assyria from attacking, the southern kingdom paid tribute annually. But when Sennacherib became king, Hezekiah stopped paying this money, hoping Assyria would ignore him. When Sennacherib and his army retaliated, Hezekiah realized his mistake and paid the tribute money (18.14), but Sennacherib attacked anyway (18.19ff). Although Sennacherib attacked Judah, he was not as war-hungry as the previous Assyrian kings, preferring to spend most of his time building and beautifying his capital city, Nineveh. With less frequent invasions, Hezekiah was able to institute his many reforms and strengthen the nation.

18.17 The Tartan was the commander-in-chief; the Rabsaris was the chief eunuch; and the Rabshekeh was the chief officer. This would be like sending the vice president, the secretary of state, and the head general of the army to speak to the enemy prior to a battle. All of these men were sent in an effort to impress and discourage the Israelites.

18.33 2 Kgs 19.12 Isa 10.7,9
18.34 2 Kgs 17.24 19.13

us. 33 Has any of the gods of the nations ever delivered its land out of the hand of
the king of Assyria? 34 Where are the gods of Hamath and Arpad? Where are the
gods of Sepharvaim, Hena, and Ivvah? Have they delivered Samaria out of my
hand? 35 Who among all the gods of the countries have delivered their countries out
of my hand, that the LORD should deliver Jerusalem out of my hand?' "
36 But the people were silent and answered him not a word, for the king's command was, "Do not answer him." 37 Then Eliakim son of Hilkiah, who was in
charge of the palace, and Shebna the secretary, and Joah son of Asaph, the

---

HEZEKIAH

The past is an important part of today's actions and tomorrow's plans. The people and kings of Judah had a rich past, filled with God's action, guidance, and commands. But with each passing generation, they also had a growing list of tragedies that occurred when the people forgot that their God, who had cared for them in the past, also cared about the present and the future—and demanded their continued obedience. Hezekiah was one of the few kings of Judah who was constantly aware of God's acts in the past and his interest in the events of every day. The Bible describes him as a king who had a close relationship with God.

As a reformer, Hezekiah was most concerned with present obedience. Judah was filled with visual reminders of the people's lack of trust in God, and Hezekiah boldly cleaned house. Altars, idols, and pagan temples were destroyed. Even the bronze serpent Moses had made in the wilderness was not spared because it had ceased to point the people to God and had also become an idol. The temple in Jerusalem, whose doors had been nailed shut by Hezekiah's own father, was cleaned out and reopened. The passover was reinstituted as a national holiday, and there was revival in Judah.

Although he had a natural inclination to respond to present problems, Hezekiah's life shows little evidence of concern about the future. He took few actions to preserve the effects of his sweeping reforms. His successful efforts made him proud. His unwise display of wealth to the Babylonian delegation got Judah included on Babylon's "Nations to Conquer" list. When Isaiah informed Hezekiah of the foolishness of his act, the king's answer displayed his persistent lack of foresight—he was thankful that any evil consequences would be delayed until after he died. And the lives of three kings who followed him—Manasseh, Amon, and Josiah—were deeply affected by both Hezekiah's accomplishments *and* his weaknesses.

The past affects your decisions and actions today, and these, in turn, affect the future. There are lessons to learn and errors to avoid repeating. Remember that part of the success of your past will be measured by what you do with it now and how well you use it to prepare for the future.

Strengths and accomplishments:
- Was the king of Judah who instigated civil and religious reforms
- Had a personal, growing relationship with God
- Developed a powerful prayer life
- Noted as the patron of several chapters in the book of Proverbs (Proverbs 25.1)

Weaknesses and mistakes:
- Showed little interest or wisdom in planning for the future and protecting for others the spiritual heritage he enjoyed
- Rashly showed all his wealth to messengers from Babylon

Lessons from his life:
- Sweeping reforms are short-lived when little action is taken to preserve them for the future
- Past obedience to God does not remove the possibility of present disobedience
- Complete dependence on God yields amazing results

Vital statistics:
- Where: Jerusalem
- Occupation: 15th king of Judah, the southern kingdom
- Relatives: Father: Ahaz. Mother: Abi. Son: Manasseh
- Contemporaries: Isaiah, Hoshea, Micah, Sennacherib

Key verses:
"He trusted in the Lord the God of Israel; so that there was no one like him among all the kings of Judah after him, or among those who were before him. For he held fast to the Lord; he did not depart from following him but kept the commandments that the Lord commanded Moses" (2 Kings 18.5, 6).

Hezekiah's story is told in 2 Kings 16.20—20.21; 2 Chronicles 28.27—32.33; Isaiah 36.1—39.8. He is also mentioned in Proverbs 25.1; Isaiah 1.1; Jeremiah 15.4; 26.18, 19; Hosea 1.1; Micah 1.1.

recorder, came to Hezekiah with their clothes torn and told him the words of the Rabshakeh.

Isaiah predicts deliverance

19 When King Hezekiah heard it, he tore his clothes, covered himself with
sackcloth, and went into the house of the LORD. 2 And he sent Eliakim, who

19.1 2 Chron 32.20 Isa 37.1

HOW DOES ASSYRIA'S HISTORY COMPARE WITH ISRAEL'S HISTORY?

Era	Date	Assyria	Israel
"Pre-history"	B.C. 5000	Pottery found at Jarmo dates back this far	Tablets with pictographic writing found at Kish and Ur prove writing was used before Flood—gives weight to the biblical record of Genesis as valid.
	3000	Pottery found at Calah, Assur, Nineveh from this date	Genesis 10.8–12 names Nimrod as the founder of these cities.
OLD (not all kings listed)	by 2900	There were Sumerians living at Assur and Erech. Thirty kings are listed in an ancient record discovered nearby. Ziggurat temples were being built then.	The Tower of Babel may have been a ziggurat. Genesis 10.10; 11.1–9
	2350	Sargon I of Akkad conquered Sumer and built a capital in Nineveh. This is the earliest known empire in history.	
	2125	Ur was the seat of the third Dynasty.	Ur was the city of Abraham's forefathers. Genesis 11.26–32
	2025	Ur fell as seat of power.	
	1781	Ishme-dagon was the Assyrian ruler who was contemporary to the famous Hammurabi of Babylon.	Many Assyrian historians suggest that Amraphel of Genesis 14.1 is Hammurabi. If this is true, Abraham knew him.
	1760	Period of lesser importance	The exodus
MIDDLE (not all kings listed)	1365	Ashur-uballit I began to regain the empire.	Period of the Judges
	1274	Shalmaneser I—empire builder	
	1115	Tiglath-pileser I—great fortune and power	
	1050		Saul begins his reign over Israel.
	1010		David begins his reign over Israel.
	970		Solomon begins his reign over Israel.
NEW (complete list of kings after Shalmaneser III)	about 900	Several kings in succession worked to restore Assyria's power.	
	858	Shalmaneser III	Assyrian records say Ahab gave Shalmaneser III 2,000 chariots and over 4,000 men. An Assyrian pillar and obelisk record that Jehu paid tribute to Shalmaneser III.
	824	Shamsi-Adad V	

19.2 Isa 1.1 was in charge of the palace, and Shebna the secretary, and the senior priests, covered with sackcloth, to the prophet Isaiah son of Amoz. 3They said to him, "Thus
says Hezekiah, This day is a day of distress, of rebuke, and of disgrace; children
19.4 2 Kgs 18.35 Isa 1.9 have come to the birth, and there is no strength to bring them forth. 4It may be that
the LORD your God heard all the words of the Rabshakeh, whom his master the king
of Assyria has sent to mock the living God, and will rebuke the words that the LORD

Era	*Date*	*Assyria*	*Israel*
NEW (continued)	805	Followed by his widow	
	783	Adad-nirari III	
	773	Shalmaneser IV	Israel recaptured some lost territory because Shalmaneser IV was putting pressure on Damascus, Israel's oppressors. 2 Kings 14.23–29
	754	Ashurdan III	Jonah probably preached at Nineveh during Ashurdan III's reign.
	727	Tiglath-pileser III—"Pul"	Menahem paid him tribute. 2 Kings 15.19, 20. Ahaz gave him gifts, asked for military aid, and copied an altar design from him. But Pul double-crossed him. 2 Kings 16.7–18; 2 Chronicles 28.16–21; 1 Chronicles 5.23–26; and Isaiah 7.17–25.
	722	Shalmaneser V	He besieged Samaria but died just before it was taken. Fall of the northern kingdom. 2 Kings 17.3–6.
	705	Sargon II	
	681	Sennacherib	Hezekiah had many dealings with Sennacherib: 2 Kings 18.13, 14 and a bas-relief (an illustration carved in stone) in the palace at Nineveh tell of this conquest. 2 Kings 18.14–16 and Assyrian annals tell of tribute and gifts. 2 Kings 19.35–37 and an Assyrian clay tablet relate that the king could not subdue Hezekiah. An Assyrian king would usually not record a defeat.
	669	Esarhaddon	Deported over 27,000 Israelites. 2 Chronicles 33.11.
		Ashurbanipal—He ruled, but was more interested in the arts and his 22,000 tablet library. He gave power to his sons:	Nahum 1.1–8 and Assyrian annals tell that Nineveh's walls were breached by a flood.
	632	Assur-etel-ilani and	
	628	Sin-sar-iskun—Assyrian records say that Sin-sar-iskun died in a fire.	See also Nahum 3.11–19
	612	Nineveh, Assyria's capital, fell to Nabopolassar of Babylon—the end of the great Assyrian Empire.	

your God has heard; therefore lift up your prayer for the remnant that is left."
5 When the servants of King Hezekiah came to Isaiah, 6 Isaiah said to them, "Say to **19.5**
your master, 'Thus says the LORD: Do not be afraid because of the words that you 2 Kgs 18.22
have heard, with which the servants of the king of Assyria have reviled me. 7 I **19.7**
myself will put a spirit in him, so that he shall hear a rumor and return to his own 2 Kgs 19.37
land; I will cause him to fall by the sword in his own land.' "
8 The Rabshakeh returned, and found the king of Assyria fighting against Libnah; for he had heard that the king had left Lachish. 9 When the king[b] heard concerning King Tirhakah of Ethiopia,[c] "See, he has set out to fight against you," he
sent messengers again to Hezekiah, saying, 10 "Thus shall you speak to King Heze- **19.10**
kiah of Judah: Do not let your God on whom you rely deceive you by promising 2 Kgs 18.5,30
that Jerusalem will not be given into the hand of the king of Assyria. 11 See, you
have heard what the kings of Assyria have done to all lands, destroying them ut- **19.12**
terly. Shall you be delivered? 12 Have the gods of the nations delivered them, the 2 Kgs 17.6 18.33
nations that my predecessors destroyed, Gozan, Haran, Rezeph, and the people of Isa 37.12
Eden who were in Telassar? 13 Where is the king of Hamath, the king of Arpad, the **19.13**
king of the city of Sepharvaim, the king of Hena, or the king of Ivvah?" 2 Kgs 17.24 18.34

Hezekiah asks God for help

14 Hezekiah received the letter from the hand of the messengers and read it; **19.14**
then Hezekiah went up to the house of the LORD and spread it before the LORD. Isa 37.14
15 And Hezekiah prayed before the LORD, and said: "O LORD the God of Israel, who **19.15**
are enthroned above the cherubim, you are God, you alone, of all the kingdoms of Ps 80.1 Isa 37.16,17
the earth; you have made heaven and earth. 16 Incline your ear, O LORD, and hear; **19.16**
open your eyes, O LORD, and see; hear the words of Sennacherib, which he has 1 Kgs 8.29,30
sent to mock the living God. 17 Truly, O LORD, the kings of Assyria have laid waste 2 Chron 6.40
the nations and their lands, 18 and have hurled their gods into the fire, though they **19.18**
were no gods but the work of human hands — wood and stone — and so they were Isa 44.9 Acts 17.29
destroyed. 19 So now, O LORD our God, save us, I pray you, from his hand, so that **19.19**
all the kingdoms of the earth may know that you, O LORD, are God alone." 1 Sam 17.46 1 Kgs 8.42,43

God promises safety for Jerusalem

20 Then Isaiah son of Amoz sent to Hezekiah, saying, "Thus says the LORD, the **19.20**
God of Israel: I have heard your prayer to me about King Sennacherib of Assyria. 2 Kgs 20.5 Ps 65.1,2
21 This is the word that the LORD has spoken concerning him: Isa 65.24

She despises you, she scorns you —
virgin daughter Zion;
she tosses her head — behind your back,
daughter Jerusalem.

22 Whom have you mocked and reviled? **19.22**
Against whom have you raised your voice Ex 5.2
and haughtily lifted your eyes? Isa 5.24 30.10,11
Against the Holy One of Israel! Jer 51.5
23 By your messengers you have mocked the Lord,

[b] Heb *he* [c] Or *Nubia*; Heb *Cush*

19.4 The Rabshakeh was the commander of the military for the Assyrians.

19.15 Cherubim are mighty angels.

19.15–19 Although Hezekiah came boldly to God, he did not take him for granted or approach him flippantly. Instead, he acknowledged God's sovereignty and Judah's total dependence upon him. Hezekiah's prayer provides a good model for us. We should not be afraid to approach God with our prayers, but we must come to him with respect for who he is and what he can do.

19.21–34 God replied to Sennacherib's taunting words (18.19–25), indicting him for arrogance. Sennacherib believed his kingdom had grown because of his own efforts and strength. In reality, said God, he succeeded only because of what God had allowed and caused. It is arrogance to think we are solely responsible for our achievements. God, as Creator, rules over nations and people.

and you have said, 'With my many chariots
I have gone up the heights of the mountains,
to the far recesses of Lebanon;
I felled its tallest cedars,
its choicest cypresses;
I entered its farthest retreat,
its densest forest.
24 I dug wells
and drank foreign waters,
I dried up with the sole of my foot
all the streams of Egypt.'
19.25 Isa 10.5-7 37.26; 45.5-7 Hab 1.6
25 Have you not heard
that I determined it long ago?
I planned from days of old
what now I bring to pass,
that you should make fortified cities
crash into heaps of ruins,
19.26 Ps 129.6,7
26 while their inhabitants, shorn of strength,
are dismayed and confounded;
they have become like plants of the field
and like tender grass,
like grass on the housetops,
blighted before it is grown.

19.27 Ps 139.1 Jer 23.23,24
27 "But I know your rising[d] and your sitting,
your going out and coming in,
and your raging against me.
19.28 Ps 32.9 Ezek 29.4 Amos 4.2
28 Because you have raged against me
and your arrogance has come to my ears,
I will put my hook in your nose
and my bit in your mouth;
I will turn you back on the way
by which you came.

19.29 Ex 3.12 2 Kgs 20.8 Isa 7.11
29 "And this shall be the sign for you: This year you shall eat what grows of
itself, and in the second year what springs from that; then in the third year sow,
reap, plant vineyards, and eat their fruit. 30 The surviving remnant of the house of
19.30 2 Chron 32.22, 23 Isa 1.9
Judah shall again take root downward, and bear fruit upward; 31 for from Jerusalem
a remnant shall go out, and from Mount Zion a band of survivors. The zeal of the
LORD of hosts will do this.
32 "Therefore thus says the LORD concerning the king of Assyria: He shall not
19.34 1 Kgs 11.12,13 2 Kgs 20.6 Isa 43.25 48.9,11
come into this city, shoot an arrow there, come before it with a shield, or cast up a
siege-ramp against it. 33 By the way that he came, by the same he shall return; he
shall not come into this city, says the LORD. 34 For I will defend this city to save it,
19.35 2 Chron 32.21 Isa 10.16
for my own sake and for the sake of my servant David."
35 That very night the angel of the LORD set out and struck down one hundred
19.36 Jonah 1.2 Nah 1.1
eighty-five thousand in the camp of the Assyrians; when morning dawned, they
were all dead bodies. 36 Then King Sennacherib of Assyria left, went home, and

[d] Gk Compare Isa 37.27 Q Ms: MT lacks *rising*

19.28 The Assyrians treated captives with cruelty. They tortured them for entertainment by blinding them, cutting them, or pulling off strips of their skin until they died. If they wished to make a captive a slave, they would often put a hook in his nose. God was saying that the Assyrians would be treated the way they had treated others.

19.31 As long as a tiny spark remains, a fire can be rekindled and fanned into a roaring blaze. Similarly, if just the smallest remnant of true believers retains the spark of faith, God can rebuild it into a strong nation. And if only a glimmer of faith remains in a heart, God can use it to restore blazing faith in that believer. If you feel that only a spark of faith remains in you, ask God to use it to rekindle a blazing fire of commitment to him.

lived at Nineveh. 37 As he was worshiping in the house of his god Nisroch, his sons 19.37
Adrammelech and Sharezer killed him with the sword, and they escaped into the Gen 8.4
land of Ararat. His son Esar-haddon succeeded him. Ezra 4.2

Hezekiah's illness

20 In those days Hezekiah became sick and was at the point of death. The 20.1
prophet Isaiah son of Amoz came to him, and said to him, "Thus says the 2 Chron 32.24
LORD: Set your house in order, for you shall die; you shall not recover." 2 Then Isa 38.1
Hezekiah turned his face to the wall and prayed to the LORD: 3 "Remember now, 20.3
O LORD, I implore you, how I have walked before you in faithfulness with a whole 2 Kgs 18.6
heart, and have done what is good in your sight." Hezekiah wept bitterly. 4 Before 2 Chron 17.3
Isaiah had gone out of the middle court, the word of the LORD came to him: 5 "Turn 20.5
back, and say to Hezekiah prince of my people, Thus says the LORD, the God of 2 Kgs 19.20
your ancestor David: I have heard your prayer, I have seen your tears; indeed, I will Ps 39.12
heal you; on the third day you shall go up to the house of the LORD. 6 I will add 20.6
fifteen years to your life. I will deliver you and this city out of the hand of the king 2 Kgs 19.34
of Assyria; I will defend this city for my own sake and for my servant David's
sake." 7 Then Isaiah said, "Bring a lump of figs. Let them take it and apply it to the 20.7
boil, so that he may recover." 2 Kgs 2.20; 4.41
8 Hezekiah said to Isaiah, "What shall be the sign that the LORD will heal me, Isa 38.21
and that I shall go up to the house of the LORD on the third day?" 9 Isaiah said, "This 20.9
is the sign to you from the LORD, that the LORD will do the thing that he has prom- Isa 38.7,8
ised: the shadow has now advanced ten intervals; shall it retreat ten intervals?" Mt 16.1
10 Hezekiah answered, "It is normal for the shadow to lengthen ten intervals; rather
let the shadow retreat ten intervals." 11 The prophet Isaiah cried to the LORD; and he 20.11
brought the shadow back the ten intervals, by which the sun[e] had declined on the Josh 10.12
dial of Ahaz. 2 Chron 32.24, 31

Ambassadors from Babylon visit Hezekiah

12 At that time King Merodach-baladan son of Baladan of Babylon sent envoys
with letters and a present to Hezekiah, for he had heard that Hezekiah had been
sick. 13 Hezekiah welcomed them;[f] he showed them all his treasure house, the 20.13
silver, the gold, the spices, the precious oil, his armory, all that was found in his 2 Chron 32.27
storehouses; there was nothing in his house or in all his realm that Hezekiah did not
show them. 14 Then the prophet Isaiah came to King Hezekiah, and said to him,
"What did these men say? From where did they come to you?" Hezekiah answered,
"They have come from a far country, from Babylon." 15 He said, "What have they
seen in your house?" Hezekiah answered, "They have seen all that is in my house;
there is nothing in my storehouses that I did not show them."
16 Then Isaiah said to Hezekiah, "Hear the word of the LORD: 17 Days are com- 20.17
ing when all that is in your house, and that which your ancestors have stored up 2 Kgs 24.13
until this day, shall be carried to Babylon; nothing shall be left, says the LORD. 25.13 Jer 52.17

[e] Syr See Isa 38.8 and Tg: Heb *it* [f] Gk Vg Syr: Heb *When Hezekiah heard about them*

20.5, 6 Over a 100-year period of Judah's history (732–640 B.C.), Hezekiah was the only faithful king; but what a difference he made! Because of Hezekiah's faith and prayer, God healed him and saved his city from the Assyrians. You can make a difference too, even if your faith puts you in the minority. Faith and prayer, if they are sincere and directed toward the one true God, can bring about change in any situation.

20.11 The dial of Ahaz was a sundial. This is also translated "the steps of Ahaz." Egyptian sundials in this period were sometimes made in the form of miniature staircases so that the shadows moved up and down the steps.

20.12–19 Hezekiah had been a good and faithful king. But when Isaiah asked him what he had shown the ambassadors from Babylon, he replied, "All that is in *my* house." From the account in 2 Chronicles 32.24–31, it appears that Hezekiah's prosperity, success, and deliverance from sickness had made him proud. Rather than giving credit to God for all his blessings, he tried to impress the foreigners. When God helps us, we must not use his blessings to impress others. A testimony of victory can quickly degenerate into vanity and self-congratulations.

20.14 Babylon, a city that had rebelled against the Assyrian Empire, was destroyed by Sennacherib in 689 B.C. This story probably occurred shortly before that date. When Sennacherib died in 681 B.C., his son, Esarhaddon, foolishly rebuilt the city of Babylon. Assyria, whose rulers at that time were weak, allowed Babylon plenty of opportunity to become strong. As the Assyrian army marched off to conquer and oppress faraway lands, the city of Babylon grew and expanded into a small nation. After some years, Babylon was strong enough to rebel again. It eventually crushed Assyria (612 B.C.) and became the next world power.

20.18 2 Kgs 24.12 2 Chron 33.11
20.20 2 Kgs 16.19 21.17
20.21 2 Chron 32.33

18 Some of your own sons who are born to you shall be taken away; they shall be
eunuchs in the palace of the king of Babylon." 19 Then Hezekiah said to Isaiah,
"The word of the LORD that you have spoken is good." For he thought, "Why not,
if there will be peace and security in my days?"
20 The rest of the deeds of Hezekiah, all his power, how he made the pool and
the conduit and brought water into the city, are they not written in the Book of the
Annals of the Kings of Judah? 21 Hezekiah slept with his ancestors; and his son
Manasseh succeeded him.

Manasseh rules Judah

21.1 1 Chron 3.10-14 2 Chron 33.1
21.3 Lev 18.25 Deut 12.31 17.2,3 1 Kgs 16.29-31
21.6 Lev 18.21 19.26,31 Deut 18.10 2 Kgs 3.27 16.3; 17.17
21.7 Deut 16.21 1 Kgs 9.3 2 Kgs 23.6
21.8 2 Kgs 18.12 2 Chron 15.2
21.9 2 Chron 36.16 Ezra 9.10 Neh 9.26 Ps 81.11
21.11 Gen 15.16 1 Kgs 21.26 2 Kgs 21.16 24.3,4
21.12 2 Kgs 22.15,16 Jer 19.3 Mic 3.12

21 Manasseh was twelve years old when he began to reign; he reigned fifty-five
years in Jerusalem. His mother's name was Hephzibah. 2 He did what was
evil in the sight of the LORD, following the abominable practices of the nations that
the LORD drove out before the people of Israel. 3 For he rebuilt the high places that
his father Hezekiah had destroyed; he erected altars for Baal, made a sacred pole,[g]
as King Ahab of Israel had done, worshiped all the host of heaven, and served
them. 4 He built altars in the house of the LORD, of which the LORD had said, "In
Jerusalem I will put my name." 5 He built altars for all the host of heaven in the two
courts of the house of the LORD. 6 He made his son pass through fire; he practiced
soothsaying and augury, and dealt with mediums and with wizards. He did much
evil in the sight of the LORD, provoking him to anger. 7 The carved image of Asherah that he had made he set in the house of which the LORD said to David and to his
son Solomon, "In this house, and in Jerusalem, which I have chosen out of all the
tribes of Israel, I will put my name forever; 8 I will not cause the feet of Israel to
wander any more out of the land that I gave to their ancestors, if only they will be
careful to do according to all that I have commanded them, and according to all the
law that my servant Moses commanded them." 9 But they did not listen; Manasseh
misled them to do more evil than the nations had done that the LORD destroyed
before the people of Israel.
10 The LORD said by his servants the prophets, 11 "Because King Manasseh of
Judah has committed these abominations, has done things more wicked than all that
the Amorites did, who were before him, and has caused Judah also to sin with his
idols; 12 therefore thus says the LORD, the God of Israel, I am bringing upon Jerusalem and Judah such evil that the ears of everyone who hears of it will tingle. 13 I will
stretch over Jerusalem the measuring line for Samaria, and the plummet for the
house of Ahab; I will wipe Jerusalem as one wipes a dish, wiping it and turning it
upside down. 14 I will cast off the remnant of my heritage, and give them into the
hand of their enemies; they shall become a prey and a spoil to all their enemies,

g Heb *Asherah*

20.19 Hezekiah is saying that it is good that these terrible events foretold by Isaiah won't happen during his lifetime. Hezekiah's statement seems selfish, shortsighted, and proud. However, he knew that his nation would be punished for its sins, so he may have been acknowledging and thanking God for choosing not to destroy Judah during his lifetime.

20.20 The pool and the conduit was a 1,777-foot tunnel built from the Gihon Spring to the Pool of Siloam (see 2 Chronicles 32.30). It was from a water source outside the wall of Jerusalem to a secure resevoir inside the city. This was done so the Assyrian army would not cut off the city's water supply.

21.1ff Manasseh followed the example of his grandfather Ahaz more than that of his father. He adopted the wicked practices of the Babylonians and Canaanites including sacrificing his own son (21.6). He did not listen to the words of God's prophets, but willfully led his people into sin. (See his Profile in 2 Chronicles 34 for more information about his life. The "high places" were shrines in the hills for worshiping idols.)

21.6 Manasseh was an evil king, and he angered God with his sin. Listed among his sins are occult practices—fortune-telling, enchantments, and the use of mediums and wizards. "Made his son pass through fire" means he sacrificed his son. God has specific laws against the occult (Leviticus 19.31; Deuteronomy 18.9–13) because it demonstrates a lack of faith in him, involves sinful actions, and opens the door to demonic influences. Today, many books, television shows, and games emphasize fortune-telling, seances, and other occult practices. Don't let desire to know the future or the belief that superstition is harmless lead you into condoning occult practices. They are counterfeits of God's power and have as their root a system of beliefs totally opposed to God.

21.7 Asherah was a Canaanite mother-goddess, a mistress of Baal. Her images were made of wood. In Exodus 34.13 and Deuteronomy 12.3, the Israelites were expressly forbidden to associate with Asherah practices in any way.

21.13 The measuring line and the plummet (level) symbolize destruction. God is saying he will destroy Jerusalem as he did Samaria and the house of Ahab.

15 because they have done what is evil in my sight and have provoked me to anger,
since the day their ancestors came out of Egypt, even to this day."
16 Moreover Manasseh shed very much innocent blood, until he had filled Jerusalem from one end to another, besides the sin that he caused Judah to sin so that
they did what was evil in the sight of the LORD.
17 Now the rest of the acts of Manasseh, all that he did, and the sin that he
committed, are they not written in the Book of the Annals of the Kings of Judah?
18 Manasseh slept with his ancestors, and was buried in the garden of his house, in
the garden of Uzza. His son Amon succeeded him.

21.16 2 Kgs 24.3,4
21.17 2 Kgs 20.20 21.25 2 Chron 33.18
21.18 2 Kgs 21.26 2 Chron 33.20

Amon rules Judah

19 Amon was twenty-two years old when he began to reign; he reigned two
years in Jerusalem. His mother's name was Meshullemeth daughter of Haruz of
Jotbah. 20 He did what was evil in the sight of the LORD, as his father Manasseh had
done. 21 He walked in all the way in which his father walked, served the idols that
his father served, and worshiped them; 22 he abandoned the LORD, the God of his
ancestors, and did not walk in the way of the LORD. 23 The servants of Amon conspired against him, and killed the king in his house. 24 But the people of the land
killed all those who had conspired against King Amon, and the people of the land
made his son Josiah king in place of him. 25 Now the rest of the acts of Amon that
he did, are they not written in the Book of the Annals of the Kings of Judah? 26 He
was buried in his tomb in the garden of Uzza; then his son Josiah succeeded him.

21.21 2 Kgs 21.3-5
21.22 Deut 32.15 2 Kgs 22.17
21.23 2 Kgs 12.20 14.19; 15.25
21.25 2 Kgs 21.17 23.28
21.26 2 Kgs 21.18

Josiah rules Judah

22 Josiah was eight years old when he began to reign; he reigned thirty-one
years in Jerusalem. His mother's name was Jedidah daughter of Adaiah of
Bozkath. 2 He did what was right in the sight of the LORD, and walked in all the way
of his father David; he did not turn aside to the right or to the left.

22.1 Deut 5.32 Josh 1.7 2 Chron 34.1 Jer 1.2 Zeph 1.1

The high priest finds a book of God's law

3 In the eighteenth year of King Josiah, the king sent Shaphan son of Azaliah,
son of Meshullam, the secretary, to the house of the LORD, saying, 4 "Go up to the
high priest Hilkiah, and have him count the entire sum of the money that has been
brought into the house of the LORD, which the keepers of the threshold have collected from the people; 5 let it be given into the hand of the workers who have the
oversight of the house of the LORD; let them give it to the workers who are at the
house of the LORD, repairing the house, 6 that is, to the carpenters, to the builders,
to the masons; and let them use it to buy timber and quarried stone to repair the
house. 7 But no accounting shall be asked from them for the money that is delivered
into their hand, for they deal honestly."
8 The high priest Hilkiah said to Shaphan the secretary, "I have found the book
of the law in the house of the LORD." When Hilkiah gave the book to Shaphan, he
read it. 9 Then Shaphan the secretary came to the king, and reported to the king,
"Your servants have emptied out the money that was found in the house, and have
delivered it into the hand of the workers who have oversight of the house of the

22.3 2 Kgs 12.4,5 2 Chron 34.9
22.5 2 Kgs 12.11,12 Ezra 3.7
22.7 2 Kgs 12.15 2 Chron 34.13
22.8 Deut 31.24-26 2 Chron 34.14-16

21.16 Tradition says that during Manasseh's massive slaughter, Isaiah was sawed in two when trying to hide in a hollow log (see Hebrews 11.37, 38). Other prophets may also have been killed at this time.

22.1, 2 In reading the biblical lists of kings, it is rare to find one who obeyed God completely. Josiah was such a person, and he was only eight years old when he began to reign. For 18 years he reigned obediently; then, when he was 26, he began the reforms based on God's laws. Children are the future leaders of our churches and our world. A person's major work for God may have to wait until he is an adult, but no one is ever too young to take God seriously and obey him. Josiah's early years laid the base for his later task of reforming Judah.

22.4 "The keepers of the threshold" were the doorkeepers. They controlled who entered the temple and supervised the collection of the money.

22.8 This book may have been the entire Pentateuch (Genesis – Deuteronomy) or just the book of Deuteronomy. Because of the long line of evil kings, the record of God's laws had been lost. Josiah, who was about 26 years old at this time, wanted religious reform throughout the nation. When God's Word was found, drastic changes had to be made to bring the kingdom in line with God's commands. Today you have God's Word at your fingertips. How much change must you make in order to bring your life into line with God's Word?

LORD." 10 Shaphan the secretary informed the king, "The priest Hilkiah has given
me a book." Shaphan then read it aloud to the king.
22.11 Josh 7.6 — 11 When the king heard the words of the book of the law, he tore his clothes.
22.12 Deut 29.24,25; 31.17; 2 Kgs 25.22; 2 Chron 34.20; Jer 26.24 — 12 Then the king commanded the priest Hilkiah, Ahikam son of Shaphan, Achbor
son of Micaiah, Shaphan the secretary, and the king's servant Asaiah, saying,
13 "Go, inquire of the LORD for me, for the people, and for all Judah, concerning the
words of this book that has been found; for great is the wrath of the LORD that is
kindled against us, because our ancestors did not obey the words of this book, to do
according to all that is written concerning us."
22.14 2 Chron 34.22 — 14 So the priest Hilkiah, Ahikam, Achbor, Shaphan, and Asaiah went to the
prophetess Huldah the wife of Shallum son of Tikvah, son of Harhas, keeper of the
wardrobe; she resided in Jerusalem in the Second Quarter, where they consulted
her. 15 She declared to them, "Thus says the LORD, the God of Israel: Tell the man
who sent you to me, 16 Thus says the LORD, I will indeed bring disaster on this place
and on its inhabitants—all the words of the book that the king of Judah has read.
22.17 Deut 29.27 — 17 Because they have abandoned me and have made offerings to other gods, so that
they have provoked me to anger with all the work of their hands, therefore my
22.18 Lev 26.31; Ps 51.17; Isa 51.17 — wrath will be kindled against this place, and it will not be quenched. 18 But as to the
king of Judah, who sent you to inquire of the LORD, thus shall you say to him, Thus
says the LORD, the God of Israel: Regarding the words that you have heard, 19 because your heart was penitent, and you humbled yourself before the LORD, when
you heard how I spoke against this place, and against its inhabitants, that they
should become a desolation and a curse, and because you have torn your clothes
22.20 1 Kgs 21.29 — and wept before me, I also have heard you, says the LORD. 20 Therefore, I will
gather you to your ancestors, and you shall be gathered to your grave in peace; your
eyes shall not see all the disaster that I will bring on this place." They took the
message back to the king.

Josiah destroys idol worship

23.1 2 Kgs 22.8; 2 Chron 34.29 — **23** Then the king directed that all the elders of Judah and Jerusalem should be
gathered to him. 2 The king went up to the house of the LORD, and with him
went all the people of Judah, all the inhabitants of Jerusalem, the priests, the prophets, and all the people, both small and great; he read in their hearing all the words
23.3 Ex 24.7; 2 Kgs 11.17 — of the book of the covenant that had been found in the house of the LORD. 3 The
king stood by the pillar and made a covenant before the LORD, to follow the LORD,
keeping his commandments, his decrees, and his statutes, with all his heart and all
his soul, to perform the words of this covenant that were written in this book. All
the people joined in the covenant.
23.4 2 Kgs 22.3,4 — 4 The king commanded the high priest Hilkiah, the priests of the second order,
and the guardians of the threshold, to bring out of the temple of the LORD all the
vessels made for Baal, for Asherah, and for all the host of heaven; he burned them
outside Jerusalem in the fields of the Kidron, and carried their ashes to Bethel.
5 He deposed the idolatrous priests whom the kings of Judah had ordained to make

---

22.11ff When Josiah heard the law, he tore his clothes in grief. He immediately instituted reforms. With just one reading of God's law, he changed the course of the nation. Today many people own Bibles, but few are affected by the truths found in God's Word. The word of God should cause us, like Josiah, to take action immediately to reform our lives and bring them into harmony with God's will.

22.14 Huldah was a prophetess, as were Miriam (Exodus 15.20) and Deborah (Judges 4.4). God freely selects his servants to carry out his will—rich or poor, male or female, king or slave (Joel 2.28–30). Huldah was obviously highly regarded by the people of her time.

22.19 When Josiah realized how corrupt his nation had become, he tore his clothes and wept before God. Then God had mercy on him. Josiah used the customs of his day to show his repentance. When we repent today, we are unlikely to tear our clothing, but weeping, fasting, making restitution or apologies (if our sin has involved others) demonstrate our sincerity when we repent. The hardest part of repentance is changing the attitudes that originally produced the sinful behavior.

23.1, 2 For more about the importance and operation of the temple, see 1 Kings 5–8 and 2 Chronicles 2–7.

23.4–8 When Josiah realized the terrible state of Judah's religious life, he did something about it. It is not enough to say we believe what is right; we must respond with action, doing what faith requires. This is what James was emphasizing when he wrote, "faith apart from works is barren" (James 2.20). This means acting differently at home, school, work, and church. Simply talking about obedience is not enough.

offerings in the high places at the cities of Judah and around Jerusalem; those also
who made offerings to Baal, to the sun, the moon, the constellations, and all the host
of the heavens. 6 He brought out the image of[h] Asherah from the house of the LORD,
outside Jerusalem, to the Wadi Kidron, burned it at the Wadi Kidron, beat it to dust
and threw the dust of it upon the graves of the common people. 7 He broke down the
houses of the male temple prostitutes that were in the house of the LORD, where the
women did weaving for Asherah. 8 He brought all the priests out of the towns of
Judah, and defiled the high places where the priests had made offerings, from Geba
to Beer-sheba; he broke down the high places of the gates that were at the entrance
of the gate of Joshua the governor of the city, which were on the left at the gate of
the city. 9 The priests of the high places, however, did not come up to the altar of
the LORD in Jerusalem, but ate unleavened bread among their kindred. 10 He defiled
Topheth, which is in the valley of Ben-hinnom, so that no one would make a son
or a daughter pass through fire as an offering to Molech. 11 He removed the horses
that the kings of Judah had dedicated to the sun, at the entrance to the house of the
LORD, by the chamber of the eunuch Nathan-melech, which was in the precincts;[i]
then he burned the chariots of the sun with fire. 12 The altars on the roof of the upper
chamber of Ahaz, which the kings of Judah had made, and the altars that Manasseh
had made in the two courts of the house of the LORD, he pulled down from there and
broke in pieces, and threw the rubble into the Wadi Kidron. 13 The king defiled the
high places that were east of Jerusalem, to the south of the Mount of Destruction,
which King Solomon of Israel had built for Astarte the abomination of the Sidonians, for Chemosh the abomination of Moab, and for Milcom the abomination of the
Ammonites. 14 He broke the pillars in pieces, cut down the sacred poles,[j] and covered the sites with human bones.

15 Moreover, the altar at Bethel, the high place erected by Jeroboam son of
Nebat, who caused Israel to sin—he pulled down that altar along with the high
place. He burned the high place, crushing it to dust; he also burned the sacred
pole.[k] 16 As Josiah turned, he saw the tombs there on the mount; and he sent and
took the bones out of the tombs, and burned them on the altar, and defiled it, according to the word of the LORD that the man of God proclaimed,[l] when Jeroboam
stood by the altar at the festival; he turned and looked up at the tomb of the man of
God who had predicted these things. 17 Then he said, "What is that monument that
I see?" The people of the city told him, "It is the tomb of the man of God who came
from Judah and predicted these things that you have done against the altar at
Bethel." 18 He said, "Let him rest; let no one move his bones." So they let his bones
alone, with the bones of the prophet who came out of Samaria. 19 Moreover, Josiah
removed all the shrines of the high places that were in the towns of Samaria, which
kings of Israel had made, provoking the LORD to anger; he did to them just as he had
done at Bethel. 20 He slaughtered on the altars all the priests of the high places who
were there, and burned human bones on them. Then he returned to Jerusalem.

21 The king commanded all the people, "Keep the passover to the LORD your

23.6 2 Kgs 21.7; 2 Chron 34.4
23.7 1 Kgs 14.24; 15.12; 22.46
23.8 1 Kgs 15.22
23.9 Ezek 44.9-11
23.10 Lev 18.21; 1 Kgs 11.7; Jer 7.31,32
23.12 2 Kgs 21.3-5; 2 Chron 33.4,5; Jer 19.13; Zeph 1.5
23.13 1 Kgs 11.5; Jer 48.7
23.14 Deut 7.5,25; 2 Chron 34.3,4
23.15 1 Kgs 12.28; 14.16
23.16 1 Kgs 13.2,32
23.17 1 Kgs 13.1,2,30
23.18 1 Kgs 13.11,31
23.19 2 Kgs 17.19; 2 Chron 34.6,7
23.20 2 Kgs 10.26; 11.18; 2 Chron 34.5
23.21 Num 9.2,3; Deut 16.2; 2 Chron 35.1

[h] Heb lacks *image of* [i] Meaning of Heb uncertain [j] Heb *Asherim* [k] Heb *Asherah* [l] Gk: Heb *proclaimed, who had predicted these things*

23.6 This "image" was the shameful idol of Asherah that the evil King Manasseh had set up in God's temple (21.7). Asherah is most often identified as a sea goddess and the mistress of Baal. She was a chief goddess of the Canaanites. Her worship glorified sex and war and was accompanied by male prostitution.

23.11 These horses were used in processions honoring the sun.

23.13 The Mount of Olives is here called the mount of corruption because it had become a favorite spot to build heathen shrines. Solomon built a heathen shrine and other kings built places of idol worship there. But God-fearing kings such as Hezekiah and Josiah destroyed these heathen worship centers. In New Testament times, Jesus often sat on the Mount of Olives and taught his disciples about serving only God (Matthew 24.3). For more background on Astarte, Chemosh, and Milcom, see the note on 1 Kings 11.5–8.

23.16–18 The prophecies mentioned in this passage appear in 1 Kings 13.20–32.

23.21–23 When Josiah rediscovered the passover in the book of the covenant, he ordered everyone to observe the ceremonies exactly as prescribed. This passover celebration was to have been a yearly holiday celebrated in remembrance of the entire nation's deliverance from slavery in Egypt (Exodus 12), but it had not been kept for many years. As a result, "no such passover had been kept since the days of the judges." It is a common misconception that God is against celebration, wanting to take all the fun out of life. In reality, God wants to give us life in its fullness (John 10.10), and those who love him have the most to celebrate.

23.22 2 Chron 35.18 God as prescribed in this book of the covenant." 22 No such passover had been kept
since the days of the judges who judged Israel, or during all the days of the kings
of Israel or of the kings of Judah; 23 but in the eighteenth year of King Josiah this
passover was kept to the LORD in Jerusalem.
23.24 Lev 19.31 24 Moreover Josiah put away the mediums, wizards, teraphim,[m] idols, and all
Deut 18.10 the abominations that were seen in the land of Judah and in Jerusalem, so that he
2 Kgs 21.6; 22.8 established the words of the law that were written in the book that the priest Hilkiah
23.25 2 Kgs 18.5 had found in the house of the LORD. 25 Before him there was no king like him, who

[m] Or *household gods*

JOSIAH

Josiah never knew his great-grandfather, Hezekiah, but they were alike in many ways. Both had close, personal relationships with God. Both were passionate reformers, making valiant efforts to lead their people back to God. Both were bright flashes of obedience to God among kings with darkened consciences, who seemed bent on outdoing each other in disobedience and evil.

Although Josiah's father and grandfather were exceptionally wicked, his life is an example of God's willingness to provide ongoing guidance to those who set out to be obedient. At a young age, Josiah already understood that there was spiritual sickness in his land. Idols were sprouting in the countryside faster than crops. In a sense, Josiah began his search for God by destroying and cleaning up whatever he recognized as not belonging to the worship of the true God. In the process, God's Word was rediscovered. The king's intentions and the power of God's written revelation were brought together.

As the book of God's law was read to Josiah, he was shocked, frightened, and humbled. He realized what a great gap existed between his efforts to lead his people to God and God's expectations for his chosen nation. He was overwhelmed by God's holiness and immediately tried to expose his people to that holiness. The people did respond, but the Bible makes it clear that their renewed worship of God was much more out of respect for Josiah than out of personal understanding of their own guilt before God.

How would you describe your relationship with God? Are your feeble efforts at holiness based mostly on a desire to "go along" with a well-liked leader or popular opinion? Or are you, like Josiah, deeply humbled by God's Word, realizing that great gap between your life and the kind of life God expects, realizing your deep need to be cleansed and renewed by him? Humble obedience pleases God. Good intentions, even reforms, are not enough. You must allow God's Word to truly humble you and change your life.

Strengths and accomplishments:
- Was king of Judah
- Sought after God and was open to him
- Was a reformer like his great-grandfather, Hezekiah
- Cleaned out the temple and revived obedience to God's law

Weakness and mistake:
- Became involved in a military conflict that he had been warned against

Lessons from his life:
- God consistently responds to those with repentant and humble hearts
- Even sweeping outward reforms are of little lasting value if there are no changes in people's lives

Vital statistics:
- Where: Jerusalem
- Occupation: 18th king of Judah, the southern kingdom
- Relatives: Father: Amon. Mother: Jedidah. Son: Jehoahaz
- Contemporaries: Jeremiah, Huldah, Hilkiah, Zephaniah

Key verse:
"Before him there was no king like him, who turned to the Lord with all his heart, with all his soul, and with all his might, according to all the law of Moses; nor did any like him arise after him" (2 Kings 23.25).

Josiah's story is told in 2 Kings 21.24—23.30; 2 Chronicles 33.25—35.26. He is also mentioned in Jeremiah 1.1–3; 22.11, 17.

23.25 Josiah is remembered as Judah's most obedient king. His obedience followed this pattern: (1) he recognized sin; (2) he eliminated sinful practices; and (3) he attacked the causes of sin. This approach for dealing with sin is still effective today. Not only must we remove sinful actions, but we must also eliminate causes for sin—those situations, relationships, routines, and patterns of life that lead us to the door of temptation.

23.25 Both Josiah and Hezekiah (18.5) are praised for their reverence toward God. Hezekiah was said to be greatest in trusting God (faith), while Josiah is said to be greatest in following the law of God (obedience). May we follow their example through our trust in God and our obedient actions.

turned to the LORD with all his heart, with all his soul, and with all his might,
according to all the law of Moses; nor did any like him arise after him.
26 Still the LORD did not turn from the fierceness of his great wrath, by which **23.26**
his anger was kindled against Judah, because of all the provocations with which 2 Kgs 21.11 22.15,16
Manasseh had provoked him. 27 The LORD said, "I will remove Judah also out of **23.27**
my sight, as I have removed Israel; and I will reject this city that I have chosen, 2 Kgs 17.18 21.13
Jerusalem, and the house of which I said, My name shall be there." Ezek 23.32
28 Now the rest of the acts of Josiah, and all that he did, are they not written in **23.28**
the Book of the Annals of the Kings of Judah? 29 In his days Pharaoh Neco king of 2 Kgs 20.20 24.5
Egypt went up to the king of Assyria to the river Euphrates. King Josiah went to **23.29**
meet him; but when Pharaoh Neco met him at Megiddo, he killed him. 30 His ser- 2 Chron 35.20
vants carried him dead in a chariot from Megiddo, brought him to Jerusalem, and **23.30** 2 Chron 36.1
buried him in his own tomb. The people of the land took Jehoahaz son of Josiah,
anointed him, and made him king in place of his father.

Jehoahaz rules Judah

31 Jehoahaz was twenty-three years old when he began to reign; he reigned **23.31**
three months in Jerusalem. His mother's name was Hamutal daughter of Jeremiah 2 Kgs 21.2 24.18
of Libnah. 32 He did what was evil in the sight of the LORD, just as his ancestors had Jer 22.11
done. 33 Pharaoh Neco confined him at Riblah in the land of Hamath, so that he **23.33**
might not reign in Jerusalem, and imposed tribute on the land of one hundred tal- 2 Kgs 23.29 2 Chron 35.20
ents of silver and a talent of gold. 34 Pharaoh Neco made Eliakim son of Josiah king 36.3
in place of his father Josiah, and changed his name to Jehoiakim. But he took Jeho- **23.34**
ahaz away; he came to Egypt, and died there. 35 Jehoiakim gave the silver and the 1 Chron 3.15 2 Chron 36.4
gold to Pharaoh, but he taxed the land in order to meet Pharaoh's demand for Ezek 19.3
money. He exacted the silver and the gold from the people of the land, from all
according to their assessment, to give it to Pharaoh Neco.

2. Judah is exiled to Babylon

Jehoiakim rules Judah

36 Jehoiakim was twenty-five years old when he began to reign; he reigned **23.36**
eleven years in Jerusalem. His mother's name was Zebidah daughter of Pedaiah of 2 Chron 36.5 Jer 1.3; 26.21
Rumah. 37 He did what was evil in the sight of the LORD, just as all his ancestors had
done.

24 In his days King Nebuchadnezzar of Babylon came up; Jehoiakim became **24.1** 2 Chron 36.6
his servant for three years; then he turned and rebelled against him. 2 The **24.2**
LORD sent against him bands of the Chaldeans, bands of the Arameans, bands of 2 Kgs 13.20,21 23.27

23.29 Pharaoh (or King) Neco of Egypt was marching through Judah to Assyria. Egypt and Assyria had formed an alliance to battle Babylon, which was threatening to become the dominant world power. Josiah may have thought that both nations would turn on him after the battle with Babylon, so he tried to stop Egypt's army from marching through his land. But Josiah was killed, his army was defeated, and the nation of Judah became a vassal of Egypt (609 B.C.). A more detailed account of this story is found in 2 Chronicles 35.20–25.

23.31–34 The people appointed Jehoahaz, one of Josiah's sons, to be Judah's next king. But Neco was not happy with their choice, and he exiled Jehoahaz to Egypt, where he died. Neco then appointed Eliakim, another of Josiah's sons, king of Judah, changing his name to Jehoiakim. Jehoiakim was little more than a puppet ruler. In 605 B.C., Egypt was defeated by Babylon. Judah then became a vassal of Babylon (24.1).

23.36, 37 While Josiah followed God, Jehoiakim, his son, was evil. He killed the prophet Uriah (Jeremiah 26.20–23) and was dishonest, greedy, and unjust with the people (Jeremiah 22.13–19). Jehoiakim also rebelled against Babylon, switching his allegiance to Egypt. This proved to be a crucial mistake. Nebuchadnezzar crushed Jehoiakim's rebellion and took him to Babylon (2 Chronicles 36.6), but he was eventually allowed to return to Jerusalem, where he died. The Bible does not record the cause of his death.

23.37 Many good kings had children who did not turn out to follow God. Perhaps it was neglect, preoccupation with political and military affairs, or because these kings delegated the religious education to others. No doubt many of the children simply rebelled at the way they were raised. Being a strong believer as a parent doesn't guarantee that your children will pick up on your beliefs. Children must be taught about faith and parents dare not leave that task for others to do. Make sure you practice, explain, and teach what you preach.

24.1 Babylon became the new world power after overthrowing Assyria in 612 B.C. and defeating Egypt at the battle of Carchemish in 605 B.C. After defeating Egypt, the Babylonians invaded Judah and brought it under their control. This was the first of three Babylonian invasions of Judah over the next 20 years. The other two invasions occurred in 597 and 586 B.C. With each invasion, captives were taken back to Babylon. Daniel, who wrote the book of Daniel, was one of the captives taken during this first invasion (605 B.C.; Daniel 1.1–6).

24.1 For more information on Nebuchadnezzar, see his Profile in Daniel 4.

the Moabites, and bands of the Ammonites; he sent them against Judah to destroy
it, according to the word of the LORD that he spoke by his servants the prophets.
24.3 3 Surely this came upon Judah at the command of the LORD, to remove them out of
2 Kgs 18.25 21.16; 23.26 his sight, for the sins of Manasseh, for all that he had committed, 4 and also for the
innocent blood that he had shed; for he filled Jerusalem with innocent blood, and
24.5 the LORD was not willing to pardon. 5 Now the rest of the deeds of Jehoiakim, and
2 Kgs 23.28 all that he did, are they not written in the Book of the Annals of the Kings of Judah?
24.6 6 So Jehoiakim slept with his ancestors; then his son Jehoiachin succeeded him.
Jer 22.24,25 24.7 7 The king of Egypt did not come again out of his land, for the king of Babylon had
Jer 37.5,7; 46.2 taken over all that belonged to the king of Egypt from the Wadi of Egypt to the
River Euphrates.

Jehoiachin rules Judah

24.8 8 Jehoiachin was eighteen years old when he began to reign; he reigned three
1 Chron 3.16 months in Jerusalem. His mother's name was Nehushta daughter of Elnathan of
2 Chron 36.9 Jerusalem. 9 He did what was evil in the sight of the LORD, just as his father had
done.
24.10 2 Kgs 25.2 10 At that time the servants of King Nebuchadnezzar of Babylon came up to

KINGS TO DATE AND THEIR ENEMIES

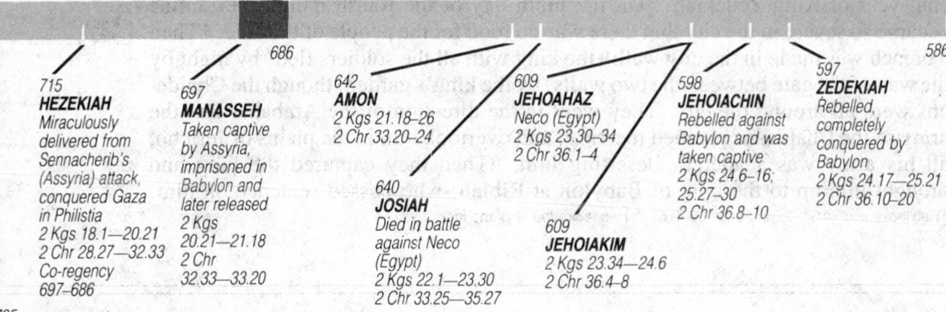

All dates are B.C.
Solid section of the timeline indicates co-regency.
For all the kings of Israel and Judah, see the chart at the end of 1 Kings.

24.1–4 Nebuchadnezzar took control as king of Babylon in 605 B.C. Earlier that year Nebu had defeated the Egyptians led by Pharaoh Neco at Carchemish. Thus Babylon took control of all Egypt's vassals (including Judah). Nebu invaded the land later in order to establish his rule by force.

24.10 Babylonian troops were already on the march to crush Jehoiakim's rebellion when he died. After Jehoiakim's death, his son Jehoiachin became king of Judah, only to face the mightiest army on earth just weeks after he was crowned (597 B.C.). During this second of three invasions, the Babylonians looted the temple and took most of the leaders, including the king, captive. Then Nebuchadnezzar placed Zedekiah, another son of Josiah, on the throne. The Jews, however, didn't recognize him as their true king as long as Jehoiachin was still alive, even though he was a captive in Babylon.

Jerusalem, and the city was besieged. 11 King Nebuchadnezzar of Babylon came to
the city, while his servants were besieging it; 12 King Jehoiachin of Judah gave **24.12**
himself up to the king of Babylon, himself, his mother, his servants, his officers, 2 Chron 36.10 Jer 24.1; 29.1
and his palace officials. The king of Babylon took him prisoner in the eighth year Ezek 17.12,13
of his reign.

13 He carried off all the treasures of the house of the LORD, and the treasures of **24.13**
the king's house; he cut in pieces all the vessels of gold in the temple of the LORD, 1 Kgs 7.48 2 Kgs 20.17
which King Solomon of Israel had made, all this as the LORD had foretold. 14 He 25.13 Isa 39.6
carried away all Jerusalem, all the officials, all the warriors, ten thousand captives, Jer 20.5
all the artisans and the smiths; no one remained, except the poorest people of the **24.14**
land. 15 He carried away Jehoiachin to Babylon; the king's mother, the king's 2 Kgs 25.12 Jer 24.1; 52.28
wives, his officials, and the elite of the land, he took into captivity from Jerusalem
to Babylon. 16 The king of Babylon brought captive to Babylon all the men of valor,
seven thousand, the artisans and the smiths, one thousand, all of them strong and
fit for war. 17 The king of Babylon made Mattaniah, Jehoiachin's uncle, king in his **24.17**
place, and changed his name to Zedekiah. 2 Chron 36.10 Jer 37.1; 52.1

Zedekiah rules Judah

18 Zedekiah was twenty-one years old when he began to reign; he reigned **24.18**
eleven years in Jerusalem. His mother's name was Hamutal daughter of Jeremiah 2 Kgs 23.31
of Libnah. 19 He did what was evil in the sight of the LORD, just as Jehoiakim had
done. 20 Indeed, Jerusalem and Judah so angered the LORD that he expelled them **24.20**
from his presence. 2 Chron 36.13 Jer 27.12

25 Zedekiah rebelled against the king of Babylon. 1 And in the ninth year of his 38.17,21,22 39.1
reign, in the tenth month, on the tenth day of the month, King Nebuchad- **25.1**
nezzar of Babylon came with all his army against Jerusalem, and laid siege to it; 2 Chron 36.17 Jer 39.1
they built siegeworks against it all around. 2 So the city was besieged until the elev- Ezek 24.2
enth year of King Zedekiah. 3 On the ninth day of the fourth month the famine **25.3**
became so severe in the city that there was no food for the people of the land. 4 Then 2 Kgs 6.24,25 Lam 4.9
a breach was made in the city wall;[n] the king with all the soldiers fled[o] by night by
the way of the gate between the two walls, by the king's garden, though the Chaldeans were all around the city. They went in the direction of the Arabah. 5 But the
army of the Chaldeans pursued the king, and overtook him in the plains of Jericho;
all his army was scattered, deserting him. 6 Then they captured the king and **25.6**
brought him up to the king of Babylon at Riblah, who passed sentence on him. Jer 32.4

[n] Heb lacks *wall* [o] Gk Compare Jer 39.4; 52.7: Heb lacks *the king* and lacks *fled*

24.14 The Babylonian policy for taking captives was different from that of the Assyrians, who moved most of the people out and resettled the land with foreigners (see the note on 17.24). The Babylonians took only the strong and skilled, leaving the poor and weak to rule the land, thus elevating them to positions of authority and winning their loyalty. The leaders were taken to Babylonian cities where they were permitted to live together, find jobs, and become an important part of the society. This policy kept the Jews united and faithful to God throughout the captivity and made it possible for their return in the days of Zerubbabel and Ezra as recorded in the book of Ezra.

25.1 Judah was invaded by the Babylonians three times (24.1; 24.10; 25.1), just as Israel was invaded by the Assyrians three times. Once again, God demonstrated his mercy in the face of deserved judgment by giving the people repeated opportunities to repent.

JUDAH EXILED Evil permeated Judah, and God's anger flared against his rebellious people. Babylon conquered Assyria and became the new world power. The Babylonian army marched into Jerusalem, burned the temple, tore down the city's massive walls, and carried off the people into captivity.

25.7 Jer 39.6 Ezek 12.13
25.8 Jer 52.12
25.9 2 Chron 36.19
25.10 Neh 1.3 Jer 52.14
25.11 2 Chron 36.20
25.12 2 Chron 24.14 Jer 40.7; 52.16
25.13 1 Kgs 7.15 2 Chron 36.18
25.14 1 Kgs 7.48-50 Jer 39.10; 42.18
25.17 1 Kgs 7.15 Jer 52.20
25.18 Ezra 7.1 Jer 29.25,26,29

7 They slaughtered the sons of Zedekiah before his eyes, then put out the eyes of
Zedekiah; they bound him in fetters and took him to Babylon.

Jerusalem is demolished

8 In the fifth month, on the seventh day of the month—which was the nineteenth year of King Nebuchadnezzar, king of Babylon—Nebuzaradan, the captain
of the bodyguard, a servant of the king of Babylon, came to Jerusalem. 9 He burned
the house of the LORD, the king's house, and all the houses of Jerusalem; every
great house he burned down. 10 All the army of the Chaldeans who were with the
captain of the guard broke down the walls around Jerusalem. 11 Nebuzaradan the
captain of the guard carried into exile the rest of the people who were left in the city
and the deserters who had defected to the king of Babylon—all the rest of the population. 12 But the captain of the guard left some of the poorest people of the land to
be vinedressers and tillers of the soil.
13 The bronze pillars that were in the house of the LORD, as well as the stands
and the bronze sea that were in the house of the LORD, the Chaldeans broke in
pieces, and carried the bronze to Babylon. 14 They took away the pots, the shovels,
the snuffers, the dishes for incense, and all the bronze vessels used in the temple
service, 15 as well as the firepans and the basins. What was made of gold the captain
of the guard took away for the gold, and what was made of silver, for the silver.
16 As for the two pillars, the one sea, and the stands, which Solomon had made for
the house of the LORD, the bronze of all these vessels was beyond weighing. 17 The
height of the one pillar was eighteen cubits, and on it was a bronze capital; the
height of the capital was three cubits; latticework and pomegranates, all of bronze,
were on the capital all around. The second pillar had the same, with the latticework.
18 The captain of the guard took the chief priest Seraiah, the second priest
Zephaniah, and the three guardians of the threshold; 19 from the city he took an

TEMPLE INVADERS

Who?	Reference	What happened
Shishak, king of Egypt	1 Kings 14.25, 26	Ransacked the temple, carried away certain treasures
Asa, king of Judah	1 Kings 15.18, 19	Took temple treasures and money to buy an alliance with King Ben-hadad of Syria
Athaliah, queen of Judah	2 Kings 11.13–15 2 Chronicles 24.7	Ravaged the temple; Later ran into the temple only to discover that her wicked reign had come to an end
Jehoash (Joash), king of Judah	2 Kings 12.18	Took gold and sacred objects from the temple to stop King Hazael of Syria from attacking
Jehoash (Joash), king of Israel	2 Kings 14.14	Entered the temple, taking gold, silver, and gold cups to get back at Amaziah
Ahaz, king of Judah	2 Kings 16.8–18	Took silver, gold, and various furnishings from the temple to send sufficient tribute to appease Assyria's king
Hezekiah, king of Judah	2 Kings 18.13–16	Took all the silver from the temple and stripped the gold from its doors to persuade Sennacherib, king of Assyria, to call off his attack
Manasseh, king of Judah	2 Kings 21.4–8	Placed heathen altars in the temple
Nebuchadnezzar, king of Babylon	2 Kings 24.13 2 Chronicles 36.10 2 Kings 25.1–17 2 Chronicles 36.18, 19	Nebuchadnezzar raided the temple during his second and third invasions of Judah. In his third invasion, he destroyed the temple and carried away all its treasures.

25.13 The bronze sea was used to contain the huge reservoir of water for temple sacrifices. The pillars, sea, and stands had been made at the request of Solomon (1 Kings 7.13–47). The bronze was so valuable that it was broken up and carried off to Babylon.

officer who had been in command of the soldiers, and five men of the king's council who were found in the city; the secretary who was the commander of the army
who mustered the people of the land; and sixty men of the people of the land who **25.20**
were found in the city. 20 Nebuzaradan the captain of the guard took them, and 2 Kgs 23.33 Jer 52.9
brought them to the king of Babylon at Riblah. 21 The king of Babylon struck them **25.21**
down and put them to death at Riblah in the land of Hamath. So Judah went into 1 Kgs 9.7 Jer 24.9,10
exile out of its land. Ezek 12.25

Leadership after the fall of Jerusalem

22 He appointed Gedaliah son of Ahikam son of Shaphan as governor over the **25.22**
people who remained in the land of Judah, whom King Nebuchadnezzar of Bab- Jer 39.14
ylon had left. 23 Now when all the captains of the forces and their men heard that the **25.23**
king of Babylon had appointed Gedaliah as governor, they came with their men to Jer 40.7
Gedaliah at Mizpah, namely, Ishmael son of Nethaniah, Johanan son of Kareah,
Seraiah son of Tanhumeth the Netophathite, and Jaazaniah son of the Maacathite.
24 Gedaliah swore to them and their men, saying, "Do not be afraid because of the
Chaldean officials; live in the land, serve the king of Babylon, and it shall be well
with you." 25 But in the seventh month, Ishmael son of Nethaniah son of Elishama, **25.25**
of the royal family, came with ten men; they struck down Gedaliah so that he died, Jer 41.1
along with the Judeans and Chaldeans who were with him at Mizpah. 26 Then all the **25.26**
people, high and low[p] and the captains of the forces set out and went to Egypt; for Jer 43.5
they were afraid of the Chaldeans.

Jehoiachin released from prison

27 In the thirty-seventh year of the exile of King Jehoiachin of Judah, in the **25.27**
twelfth month, on the twenty-seventh day of the month, King Evil-merodach of Jer 52.31
Babylon, in the year that he began to reign, released King Jehoiachin of Judah from
prison; 28 he spoke kindly to him, and gave him a seat above the other seats of the
kings who were with him in Babylon. 29 So Jehoiachin put aside his prison clothes.
Every day of his life he dined regularly in the king's presence. 30 For his allowance,
a regular allowance was given him by the king, a portion every day, as long as he
lived.

p Or *young and old*

25.21 Judah, like Israel, was unfaithful to God. So God, as he had warned, allowed Judah to be destroyed and taken away (Deuteronomy 28). The book of Lamentations records the prophet Jeremiah's sorrow at seeing Jerusalem destroyed.

25.22 In place of the king (Zedekiah) who was deported to Babylon, Nebuchadnezzar appointed a governor (Gedaliah) who would faithfully administer the Babylonian policies.

25.22–30 This story shows that Israel's last hope of gaining back her land was gone – even her army captains (now guerrilla rebels) had fled. Judah's earthly kingdom was absolutely demolished, but through prophets like Ezekiel and Daniel, who were also captives, God was able to keep his spiritual kingdom alive in the hearts of many of the exiles.

25.27 Evil-merodach, the son of Nebuchadnezzar, became king of the Babylonian Empire in 562 B.C., 24 years after the beginning of the general captivity and 37 years after Jehoiachin was removed from Jerusalem. The new king treated Jehoiachin with kindness, even allowing him to eat at his table (25.29). Evil-merodach was later killed in a plot by his brother-in-law, Nergal-sharezer, who succeeded him to the throne.

25.30 The book of 2 Kings opens with Elijah being carried to heaven – the destination awaiting those who follow God. But the book ends with the people of Judah being carried off to foreign lands as humiliated slaves – the result of failing to follow God.

Second Kings is an illustration of what happens when we make anything more important than God, when we make ruinous alliances, when our consciences become desensitized to right and wrong, and when we are no longer able to discern God's purpose for our lives. We may fail, like the people of Judah and Israel, but God's promises do not. He is always there to help us straighten out our lives and start over. And that is just what would happen in the book of Ezra. When the people acknowledged their sins, God was ready and willing to help them return to their land and start again.

FIFTEEN EVENTS IN ELISHA'S LIFE

Event	*Reference*
Parting the waters at Jordan	2 Kings 2.14
Purifying the waters at Jericho	2 Kings 2.19-22
Judging some hoodlums at Bethel	2 Kings 2.23,24
Causing some empty ditches to fill with water	2 Kings 3.16-27
Creating oil in empty vessels	2 Kings 4.1-7
Raising a dead boy at Shunem	2 Kings 4.18-21; 32-37
Purifying a poisonous stew at Gilgal	2 Kings 4.38-41
Feeding 100 men by supernaturally increasing twenty loaves of bread and a sack of corn	2 Kings 4.42-44
Healing of Naaman	2 Kings 5.1-14
Recovering a lost axhead from the Jordan	2 Kings 6.1-7
Revealing the secret war plans of Syria to Israel	2 Kings 6.8-12
Praying that his servant could see an invisible angelic army	2 Kings 6.13-17
Blinding the entire Syrian army	2 Kings 6.18-23
Predicting judgment and deliverance	2 Kings 5.20-27; 7.1, 2; 8.1, 7-15; 13.14-19
Raising a man from the dead years after the prophet himself had died	2 Kings 13.20, 21

1 CHRONICLES

Saul becomes king 1050 B.C. (1045 B.C.) — *Saul dies; David becomes king of Judah 1010* — *David becomes king of all Israel 1003* — *David captures Jerusalem 1000* — *David captures Rabbah 997(?)*

VITAL STATISTICS

PURPOSE:
To unify God's people, to trace the Davidic line, and to teach that genuine worship ought to be the center of individual and national life

AUTHOR:
Ezra, according to Jewish tradition

TO WHOM WRITTEN:
All Israel

DATE WRITTEN:
Approximately 430 B.C., recording events which occurred from about 1000–960 B.C.

SETTING:
First Chronicles parallels 2 Samuel and serves as a commentary on it. Written after the exile from a priestly point of view, 1 Chronicles emphasizes the religious history of Judah and Israel.

KEY VERSE:
"David then perceived that the Lord had established him as king over Israel, and that his kingdom was highly exalted for the sake of his people Israel" (14.2).

KEY PEOPLE:
David, Solomon

KEY PLACES:
Hebron, Jerusalem, the temple

IN THE WIDE shade of the ageless oak, a mother watches her toddler discover acorns, leaves, and dandelions. Nearby, her mother, aunt, and uncle spread the checkerboard cloth over park tables and cover it with bowls and platters of fried chicken, potato salad, baked beans, and assorted family recipes. The clanging of Grandpa's and Dad's horseshoes against stakes regularly pierces the air and mixes with cheers, laughs, and shouts of the teenagers' touch football game. A family reunion—a sunny afternoon filled with four generations and miscellaneous kids, parents, and second cousins once-removed.

These meetings are important . . . touching and connecting with other branches of the family tree, tracing one's personal history back through time and culture, seeing physical reflections (her eyes, his nose), remembering warm traditions. Knowing one's genetical and relational path provides a sense of identity, heritage, and destiny.

It is with this same high purpose that the writer of Chronicles begins his unifying work with an extensive genealogy. He traces the roots of the nation in a literary family reunion from Adam onward, recounting its royal line and the loving plan of a personal God. We read 1 Chronicles and gain a glimpse of God at work through his people for generations. If you are a believer, these people are your ancestors too. As you approach this part of God's Word, read their names with awe and respect and gain new security and identity in your relationship with God.

The previous book, 2 Kings, ends with both Israel and Judah in captivity, surely a dark age for God's people. Then follows Chronicles (1 and 2 Chronicles were originally one book). Written after the captivity, it summarizes Israel's history, emphasizing the Jewish people's spiritual heritage in an attempt to unify the nation. The chronicler is selective in his history telling. Instead of writing an exhaustive work, he carefully weaves the narrative, highlighting spiritual lessons and teaching moral truths. In Chronicles the northern kingdom is virtually ignored, David's triumphs—not his sins—are recalled, and the temple is given great prominence as the vital center of national life.

First Chronicles begins with Adam, and, for nine chapters, the writer gives us a "Who's Who" of Israel's history with special emphasis on David's royal line. The rest of the book tells the story of David—the great man of God, Israel's king—who served God and laid out the plans for the construction of and worship in the temple.

First Chronicles is an invaluable supplement to 2 Samuel and a strong reminder of the necessity for tracing our roots, and thus rediscovering our foundation. As you read 1 Chronicles, trace your own godly heritage, thank God for your spiritual forefathers, and recommit yourself to passing on God's truth to the next generation.

David's census 980(?)

Solomon becomes king 970

The kingdom divides 930

THE BLUEPRINT

A. THE GENEALOGIES OF ISRAEL (1.1—9.44) 1. Ancestry of the nation 2. The tribes of Israel 3. Returnees from exile in Babylon	The long list of names that follows presents a history of God's work in the world from Adam through Zerubbabel. Some of these names remind us of stories of great faith, and others of tragic failure. About most of the people named, however, we know nothing. But those who died unknown to us are known by God. God will also remember us when we die.
B. THE REIGN OF DAVID (10.1—29.30) 1. David becomes king over all of Israel 2. David brings the ark to Jerusalem 3. David's military exploits 4. David arranges for the building of the temple	David loved the Lord and wanted to build a temple to replace the tabernacle, but God denied his request. David's greatest contribution to the temple would not be the construction, but the preparation. We may be unable to see the results of our labors for God in our lifetime, but David's example helps us understand that we serve God so *he* will see *his* results, not so we will see ours.

MEGATHEMES

THEME	EXPLANATION	IMPORTANCE
Israel's history	By retelling Israel's history in the genealogies and the stories of the kings, the writer laid down the true spiritual foundation for the nation. God kept his promises and we are reminded of them in the historical record of his people, leaders, prophets, priests, and kings.	Israel's past formed a reliable basis for reconstructing the nation after the exile. Because God's promises are revealed in the Bible, we can know God and trust him to keep his word. Like Israel, we should have no higher goal in life than devoted service to God.
God's people	By listing the names of people in Israel's past, God established Israel's true heritage. They were all one family in Adam, one nation in Abraham, one priesthood under Levi, and one kingdom under David. The national and spiritual unity of the people were important to the rebuilding of the nation.	God is always faithful to his people. He protects them in every generation and provides leaders to guide them. Because God has been at work throughout the centuries, his people can trust him to work in the present. You can rely on his presence today.
David, the king	The story of David's life and his relationship with God showed that he was God's appointed leader. David's devotion to God, the law, the temple, true worship, the people, and justice sets the standard for what God's chosen king should be.	Jesus Christ came to earth as a descendant of David. One day he will rule as king over all the earth. His strength and justice will fulfill God's ideal for the king. He is our hope. We can experience God's kingdom now by giving Christ complete control of our lives.
True worship	David brought the ark of the covenant to the tabernacle at Jerusalem to restore true worship to the people. God gave the plans for building the temple, and David organized the priests to make worship central to all Israel.	The temple stood as the throne of God on earth, the place of true worship. God's true throne is in the hearts of his people. When we acknowledge him as the true king over our lives, true worship takes place.
The priests	God ordained the priests and Levites to guide the people in faithful worship according to his law. By leading the people in worship according to God's design, the priests and Levites were an important safeguard to Israel's faith.	For true worship to remain central in our lives, God's people need to take a firm stand for the ways of God recorded in the Bible. Today, all believers are priests for one another, and we should encourage each other to faithful worship.

KEY PLACES IN 1 CHRONICLES

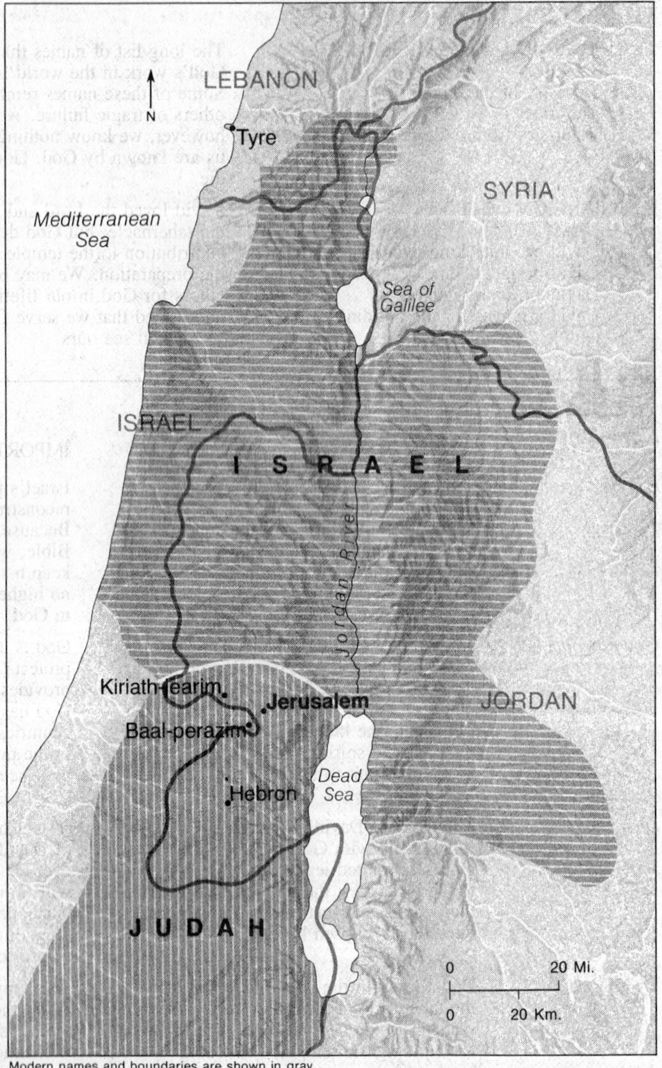

Modern names and boundaries are shown in gray.

The genealogies of 1 Chronicles present an overview of Israel's history. The first nine chapters are filled with genealogies tracing the lineages of people from the creation to the exile in Babylon. Saul's death is recorded in chapter 10. Chapter 11 begins the history of David's reign over Israel.

1 Hebron Although David had been anointed king years earlier, his reign began when the leaders of Israel accepted him as king at Hebron (11.1–3).

2 Jerusalem David set out to complete the conquest of the land begun by Joshua. He attacked Jerusalem, captured it, and made it his capital (11.4—12.40).

3 Kiriath-jearim The ark of the covenant, which had been captured by the Philistines in battle and returned (1 Samuel 4—6), was in safekeeping in Kiriath-jearim. David summoned all Israel to this city to join in bringing the ark to Jerusalem. Unfortunately, it was not moved according to God's instructions, and as a result one man died. David left the ark in the home of Obed-edom until he could discover how to transport it correctly (13.1–14).

4 Tyre David did much building in Jerusalem. King Hiram of Tyre sent workers and supplies to help build David's palace. Cedar, abundant in the mountains north of Israel, was a valuable and hardy wood for the beautiful buildings in Jerusalem (14.1—17.27).

5 Baal-perazim David was not very popular with the Philistines because he had slain Goliath, one of their greatest warriors (1 Samuel 17). When David began to rule over a united Israel, the Philistines set out to capture him. But David and his army attacked the Philistines at Baal-perazim as they approached Jerusalem. His army defeated the mighty Philistines twice, causing all the surrounding nations to fear David's power (14.11–17). After this battle, David moved the ark to Jerusalem (this time in accordance with God's instructions for the transportation of the ark). There was great celebration as the ark was brought into Jerusalem (15.1—17.27). David spent the remainder of his life making preparations for the building of the temple, a central place for the worship of God (18.1—29.30).

A. THE GENEALOGIES OF ISRAEL (1.1 – 9.44)

These genealogies are the official family records of the nation of Israel. They give us an overview of the history of God's work from creation through the captivity of his people. These records served to teach the exiles returning from Babylon about their spiritual heritage as a nation and to inspire them to renew their faithfulness to God. Although these lists show the racial heritage of the Jews, they contain the spiritual heritage for every believer. We are a part of the community of faith which has existed from generation to generation since the dawn of man.

1. Ancestry of the nation

Adam's descendants

1.1 Gen 4.25; 5.3-32; 10.1; Isa 54.9,10; Ezek 14.14; Mt 24.37; Lk 3.38; Heb 11.7
1.5 Gen 10.2-4,6-8; 1 Chron 4.40,42; Ezek 27.13
1.10 Gen 10.8
1.11 Gen 9.22; 10.13-18
1.13 Gen 15.19-21
1.17 Gen 10.21,22; 11.10; Lk 3.36
1.19 Gen 11.16

1 Adam, Seth, Enosh; 2 Kenan, Mahalalel, Jared; 3 Enoch, Methuselah, Lamech; 4 Noah, Shem, Ham, and Japheth.
5 The descendants of Japheth: Gomer, Magog, Madai, Javan, Tubal, Meshech,
and Tiras. 6 The descendants of Gomer: Ashkenaz, Diphath,[a] and Togarmah. 7 The
descendants of Javan: Elishah, Tarshish, Kittim, and Rodanim.[b]
8 The descendants of Ham: Cush, Egypt, Put, and Canaan. 9 The descendants
of Cush: Seba, Havilah, Sabta, Raama, and Sabteca. The descendants of Raamah:
Sheba and Dedan. 10 Cush became the father of Nimrod; he was the first to be a
mighty one on the earth.
11 Egypt became the father of Ludim, Anamim, Lehabim, Naphtuhim, 12 Pathrusim, Casluhim, and Caphtorim, from whom the Philistines come.[c]
13 Canaan became the father of Sidon his firstborn, and Heth, 14 and the Jebusites, the Amorites, the Girgashites, 15 the Hivites, the Arkites, the Sinites, 16 the
Arvadites, the Zemarites, and the Hamathites.
17 The descendants of Shem: Elam, Asshur, Arpachshad, Lud, Aram, Uz,
Hul, Gether, and Meshech.[d] 18 Arpachshad became the father of Shelah; and Shelah became the father of Eber. 19 To Eber were born two sons: the name of the one
was Peleg (for in his days the earth was divided), and the name of his brother Joktan. 20 Joktan became the father of Almodad, Sheleph, Hazarmaveth, Jerah, 21 Hadoram, Uzal, Diklah, 22 Ebal, Abimael, Sheba, 23 Ophir, Havilah, and Jobab; all
these were the descendants of Joktan.

[a] Gen 10.3 *Ripath*; See Gk Vg [b] Gen 10.4 *Dodanim*; See Syr Vg [c] Heb *Casluhim, from which the Philistines come, Caphtorim*; See Am 9.7, Jer 47.4 [d] *Mash* in Gen 10.23

1.1ff This long list of names was compiled after the people of Judah, the southern kingdom, were taken captive to Babylon. As the exiles looked forward to the day when they would return to their homeland, one of their biggest fears was that the records of their heritage would be lost. The Jews placed great importance upon their heritage because each person wanted to be able to prove that he was a descendant of Abraham, the father of the Jewish people. Only then could he enjoy the benefits of the special blessings God promised to Abraham and his descendants (see the notes on Genesis 12.1–3 and 17.2–8 for what these special blessings were).

This list reconstructed the family tree for both Judah, the southern kingdom, and Israel, the northern kingdom, before their captivities and served as proof for those who claimed to be Abraham's descendants. (For more information about why the Bible includes genealogies, read the notes on Genesis 5.1ff, Matthew 1.1, and Luke 3.23–38.)

1.1ff There is more to this long genealogy than meets the eye. It holds importance for us today because it supports the Old Testament promise that Jesus the Messiah would be a descendant of Abraham and David. This promise is recorded in Genesis 12.1–3 and 2 Samuel 7.12, 13.

1.1 This record of names demonstrates that God is interested not only in nations, but also in individuals. Although billions of people have lived since Adam, God knows and remembers the face and name of each person. Each of us is more than a name on a list; we are special persons whom God knows and loves. As we recognize and accept his love, we discover both our uniqueness as individuals and our solidarity with the rest of his family.

1.1, 4 Adam's story and Profile are found in Genesis 1 – 5. Noah's story and Profile are found in Genesis 6 – 9.

1.10 Nimrod is also mentioned in Genesis 10.8, 9.

1.11 *Egypt* is also translated *Mizraim.*

1.11, 12 The Philistines had been Israel's constant enemy from the days of the judges. King David finally weakened them, and by this time they were no longer a threat. (For more information on the Philistines, see the notes on Judges 13.1 and 1 Samuel 4.1.)

1.13–16 Canaan was the ancestor of the Canaanites, who inhabited the promised land (also called Canaan) before the Israelites entered under Joshua's leadership. God helped the Israelites drive out the Canaanites, a wicked and idolatrous people. The land's name was then changed to Israel. The book of Joshua tells this story.

1.19 "The earth was divided" refers to when the earth was divided into different language groups. At one time, everyone spoke a single language. But some people became proud of their accomplishments and gathered to build a monument to themselves – the tower of Babel. The building project was brought to an abrupt conclusion when God caused the people to speak different languages. Without the ability to communicate with one another, the people could not be unified. God showed them that their great efforts were useless without him. Pride in our achievements must not lead us to conclude that we no longer need God. This story is told in Genesis 11.1–9.

24 Shem, Arpachshad, Shelah; 25 Eber, Peleg, Reu; 26 Serug, Nahor, Terah; **1.24** Gen 11.10-26
27 Abram, that is, Abraham. Lk 3.34
28 The sons of Abraham: Isaac and Ishmael. 29 These are their genealogies: the **1.28**
firstborn of Ishmael, Nebaioth; and Kedar, Adbeel, Mibsam, 30 Mishma, Dumah, Gen 16.9-12 17.19; 21.3,9
Massa, Hadad, Tema, 31 Jetur, Naphish, and Kedemah. These are the sons of Ish- 25.9,10
mael. 32 The sons of Keturah, Abraham's concubine: she bore Zimran, Jokshan, **1.32**
Medan, Midian, Ishbak, and Shuah. The sons of Jokshan: Sheba and Dedan. 33 The Gen 25.1,2
sons of Midian: Ephah, Epher, Hanoch, Abida, and Eldaah. All these were the
descendants of Keturah.
34 Abraham became the father of Isaac. The sons of Isaac: Esau and Israel. **1.34**
35 The sons of Esau: Eliphaz, Reuel, Jeush, Jalam, and Korah. 36 The sons of Eli- Gen 25.25,26 32.28
phaz: Teman, Omar, Zephi, Gatam, Kenaz, Timna, and Amalek. 37 The sons of Mal 1.2,3 Mt 1.2
Reuel: Nahath, Zerah, Shammah, and Mizzah. **1.35**
38 The sons of Seir: Lotan, Shobal, Zibeon, Anah, Dishon, Ezer, and Dishan. Gen 36.4-12
39 The sons of Lotan: Hori and Homam; and Lotan's sister was Timna. 40 The sons **1.38** Gen 36.18-21
of Shobal: Alian, Manahath, Ebal, Shephi, and Onam. The sons of Zibeon: Aiah
and Anah. 41 The sons of Anah: Dishon. The sons of Dishon: Hamran, Eshban,
Ithran, and Cheran. 42 The sons of Ezer: Bilhan, Zaavan, and Jaakan.[e] The sons of
Dishan:[f] Uz and Aran.
43 These are the kings who reigned in the land of Edom before any king reigned **1.43** Gen 36.31-39
over the Israelites: Bela son of Beor, whose city was called Dinhabah. 44 When
Bela died, Jobab son of Zerah of Bozrah succeeded him. 45 When Jobab died, Hu- **1.45**
sham of the land of the Temanites succeeded him. 46 When Husham died, Hadad Job 2.11
son of Bedad, who defeated Midian in the country of Moab, succeeded him; and
the name of his city was Avith. 47 When Hadad died, Samlah of Masrekah succeeded him. 48 When Samlah died, Shaul[g] of Rehoboth on the Euphrates succeeded him. 49 When Shaul[g] died, Baal-hanan son of Achbor succeeded him.
50 When Baal-hanan died, Hadad succeeded him; the name of his city was Pai, and
his wife's name Mehetabel daughter of Matred, daughter of Me-zahab. 51 And Hadad died.
The clans[h] of Edom were: clans[h] Timna, Aliah,[i] Jetheth, 52 Oholibamah, Elah,
Pinon, 53 Kenaz, Teman, Mibzar, 54 Magdiel, and Iram; these are the clans[h] of
Edom.

Jacob's descendants

2 These are the sons of Israel: Reuben, Simeon, Levi, Judah, Issachar, Zebulun, **2.1**
2 Dan, Joseph, Benjamin, Naphtali, Gad, and Asher. 3 The sons of Judah: Er, Gen 35.22-26 46.8-25
Onan, and Shelah; these three the Canaanite woman Bath-shua bore to him. Now Rev 7.4-8

[e] Or *and Akan*; See Gen 36.27 [f] See 1.38: Heb *Dishon* [g] Or *Saul* [h] Or *chiefs* [i] Or *Alvah*; See Gen 36.40

1.24-27 *Son* can also mean *descendant;* thus a biblical genealogy may skip several generations. These lists were not meant to be exhaustive, but to give adequate information about the various family lines.

1.24-27 Abraham's story and Profile are found in Genesis 11.26–25.10.

1.28-31 Ishmael's story and Profile are found in Genesis 17 and 21.

1.34 Israel is another name for Jacob because Jacob's 12 sons became the nation of Israel. Esau's descendants became the nation of Edom, a constant enemy of Israel. To learn more about the lives of Isaac and his two sons, Jacob and Esau, read their stories and Profiles in Genesis 21–36 and 46–49.

1.36 Amalek, Esau's grandson, was the son of his father's concubine (Genesis 36.12). He was the ancestor of the wicked tribe known as Amalekites, the first people to attack the Israelites on their way to the promised land. (For more about the Amalekites, read the note on Exodus 17.8.)

1.43-54 Why are we given information in this genealogy about the descendants of Edom who were Israel's enemies? Esau, ancestor of the Edomites, was Isaac's oldest son and thus a direct descendant of Abraham. As Abraham's first grandson, he deserved a place in the Jewish records. It was through Esau's marriages to heathen women, however, that the nation of Edom began. This genealogy shows the ancestry of enemy nations; they were *not* a part of the direct lineage of King David, and thus of the Messiah. This listing further identified Israel's special identity and role.

2.1, 2 The story of Israel's (Jacob's) sons is found in Genesis 29.32–50.26. Profiles of Reuben, Judah, and Joseph are found in the same section.

2.3 This long genealogy not only lists names, but gives us insights into some of the people. Here, almost as an epitaph, the genealogy states that Er "was wicked in the sight of the Lord, and he put him to death." Now, thousands of years later, this is all we know of the man. Each of us is forging a reputation, developing personal qualities by which we will be remembered. How would God summarize your life up to now? Some defiantly claim that how they live is their own business. But Scripture teaches that the way you live

2.3 Gen 38.2-10 — Er, Judah's firstborn, was wicked in the sight of the LORD, and he put him to death.
2.4 Gen 38.13-30 46.8-14 — 4 His daughter-in-law Tamar also bore him Perez and Zerah. Judah had five sons in
all.
5 The sons of Perez: Hezron and Hamul. 6 The sons of Zerah: Zimri, Ethan,
2.7 Josh 7.17; 22.20 — Heman, Calcol, and Dara,[j] five in all. 7 The sons of Carmi: Achar, the troubler of
Israel, who transgressed in the matter of the devoted thing; 8 and Ethan's son was
Azariah.
9 The sons of Hezron, who were born to him: Jerahmeel, Ram, and Chelubai.
2.10 Num 7.12; 10.14 Mt 1.4 Lk 3.32 — 10 Ram became the father of Amminadab, and Amminadab became the father of
Nahshon, prince of the sons of Judah. 11 Nahshon became the father of Salma,
Salma of Boaz, 12 Boaz of Obed, Obed of Jesse. 13 Jesse became the father of Eliab
2.12 Ruth 4.16,17 Mt 1.5 — his firstborn, Abinadab the second, Shimea the third, 14 Nethanel the fourth, Rad-
dai the fifth, 15 Ozem the sixth, David the seventh; 16 and their sisters were Zeruiah
2.13 1 Sam 16.8 — and Abigail. The sons of Zeruiah: Abishai, Joab, and Asahel, three. 17 Abigail bore
2.16 1 Sam 26.5-7 2 Sam 2.13 1 Chron 11.5,6 — Amasa, and the father of Amasa was Jether the Ishmaelite.
18 Caleb son of Hezron had children by his wife Azubah, and by Jerioth; these
were her sons: Jesher, Shobab, and Ardon. 19 When Azubah died, Caleb married
2.17 2 Sam 17.25 19.13 1 Kgs 2.5 — Ephrath, who bore him Hur. 20 Hur became the father of Uri, and Uri became the
father of Bezalel.
21 Afterward Hezron went in to the daughter of Machir father of Gilead, whom
he married when he was sixty years old; and she bore him Segub; 22 and Segub
became the father of Jair, who had twenty-three towns in the land of Gilead. 23 But
Geshur and Aram took from them Havvoth-jair, Kenath and its villages, sixty
towns. All these were descendants of Machir, father of Gilead. 24 After the death of
Hezron, in Caleb-ephrathah, Abijah wife of Hezron bore him Ashhur, father of
Tekoa.
25 The sons of Jerahmeel, the firstborn of Hezron: Ram his firstborn, Bunah,
Oren, Ozem, and Ahijah. 26 Jerahmeel also had another wife, whose name was
Atarah; she was the mother of Onam. 27 The sons of Ram, the firstborn of Jerahmeel: Maaz, Jamin, and Eker. 28 The sons of Onam: Shammai and Jada. The sons
of Shammai: Nadab and Abishur. 29 The name of Abishur's wife was Abihail, and
she bore him Ahban and Molid. 30 The sons of Nadab: Seled and Appaim; and
Seled died childless. 31 The son[k] of Appaim: Ishi. The son[k] of Ishi: Sheshan. The
son[k] of Sheshan: Ahlai. 32 The sons of Jada, Shammai's brother: Jether and Jonathan; and Jether died childless. 33 The sons of Jonathan: Peleth and Zaza. These
were the descendants of Jerahmeel. 34 Now Sheshan had no sons, only daughters;
but Sheshan had an Egyptian slave, whose name was Jarha. 35 So Sheshan gave his
2.36 1 Chron 11.41 — daughter in marriage to his slave Jarha; and she bore him Attai. 36 Attai became the
father of Nathan, and Nathan of Zabad. 37 Zabad became the father of Ephlal, and
Ephlal of Obed. 38 Obed became the father of Jehu, and Jehu of Azariah. 39 Azariah
became the father of Helez, and Helez of Eleasah. 40 Eleasah became the father of
Sismai, and Sismai of Shallum. 41 Shallum became the father of Jekamiah, and
Jekamiah of Elishama.
42 The sons of Caleb brother of Jerahmeel: Mesha[l] his firstborn, who was
father of Ziph. The sons of Mareshah father of Hebron. 43 The sons of Hebron:

[j] Or *Darda*; Compare Syr Tg some Gk Mss; See 1 Kings 4.31 [k] Heb *sons* [l] Gk reads *Mareshah*

---

today will determine how you will be remembered by others and how you will be judged by God. What you do now *does* matter.

2.7 Achar is called Achan in Joshua 7. This was the man who kept for himself some of the booty that was devoted to the Lord for destruction.

2.12 Boaz was Ruth's husband and an ancestor of both David and Jesus. Boaz's story and Profile are found in the book of Ruth.

2.15 David is one of the best-known people of the Bible. He was certainly not perfect, but he exemplified what it means to seek God first in all areas of life. God called David "a man after my heart" (Acts 13.22) because his greatest desire was to serve and worship God. We can please God in the same way by making God our first consideration in all our desires and plans. David's story is found in 1 Samuel 16.1 – 1 Kings 2.10 and 1 Chronicles 10.14 – 29.30. David's Profile is found in 1 Samuel 17.

2.16 Joab's story is found in 2 Samuel 2; 3; 10 – 20; 24; 1 Kings 1 – 3; 1 Chronicles 11.4-9; 19 – 21. His Profile is found in 2 Samuel 19. Abishai's story is found in 1 Samuel 26; 2 Samuel 2; 3; 10; 15 – 21; 23; 1 Chronicles 18.12; 19. Abishai's Profile is found in 2 Samuel 21.

2.18 This is not the Caleb who spied out the promised land with Joshua. Caleb the spy is listed in 4.15.

Korah, Tappuah, Rekem, and Shema. 44 Shema became father of Raham, father of
Jorkeam; and Rekem became the father of Shammai. 45 The son of Shammai:
Maon; and Maon was the father of Beth-zur. 46 Ephah also, Caleb's concubine,
bore Haran, Moza, and Gazez; and Haran became the father of Gazez. 47 The sons
of Jahdai: Regem, Jotham, Geshan, Pelet, Ephah, and Shaaph. 48 Maacah, Caleb's
concubine, bore Sheber and Tirhanah. 49 She also bore Shaaph father of Madmannah, Sheva father of Machbenah and father of Gibea; and the daughter of Caleb was
Achsah. 50 These were the descendants of Caleb.
The sons[m] of Hur the firstborn of Ephrathah: Shobal father of Kiriath-jearim,
51 Salma father of Bethlehem, and Hareph father of Beth-gader. 52 Shobal father of
Kiriath-jearim had other sons: Haroeh, half of the Menuhoth. 53 And the families of
Kiriath-jearim: the Ithrites, the Puthites, the Shumathites, and the Mishraites; from
these came the Zorathites and the Eshtaolites. 54 The sons of Salma: Bethlehem, the
Netophathites, Atroth-beth-joab, and half of the Manahathites, the Zorites. 55 The
families also of the scribes that lived at Jabez: the Tirathites, the Shimeathites, and
the Sucathites. These are the Kenites who came from Hammath, father of the house
of Rechab.

David's descendants

3 These are the sons of David who were born to him in Hebron: the firstborn
Amnon, by Ahinoam the Jezreelite; the second Daniel, by Abigail the Carmel-
ite; 2 the third Absalom, son of Maacah, daughter of King Talmai of Geshur; the
fourth Adonijah, son of Haggith; 3 the fifth Shephatiah, by Abital; the sixth Ithream, by his wife Eglah; 4 six were born to him in Hebron, where he reigned for
seven years and six months. And he reigned thirty-three years in Jerusalem. 5 These
were born to him in Jerusalem: Shimea, Shobab, Nathan, and Solomon, four by
Bath-shua, daughter of Ammiel; 6 then Ibhar, Elishama, Eliphelet, 7 Nogah, Nepheg, Japhia, 8 Elishama, Eliada, and Eliphelet, nine. 9 All these were David's
sons, besides the sons of the concubines; and Tamar was their sister.
10 The descendants of Solomon: Rehoboam, Abijah his son, Asa his son, Jehoshaphat his son, 11 Joram his son, Ahaziah his son, Joash his son, 12 Amaziah his
son, Azariah his son, Jotham his son, 13 Ahaz his son, Hezekiah his son, Manasseh
his son, 14 Amon his son, Josiah his son. 15 The sons of Josiah: Johanan the firstborn, the second Jehoiakim, the third Zedekiah, the fourth Shallum. 16 The descendants of Jehoiakim: Jeconiah his son, Zedekiah his son; 17 and the sons of Jeconiah,
the captive: Shealtiel his son, 18 Malchiram, Pedaiah, Shenazzar, Jekamiah, Hosh-
ama, and Nedabiah; 19 The sons of Pedaiah: Zerubbabel and Shimei; and the sons
of Zerubbabel: Meshullam and Hananiah, and Shelomith was their sister; 20 and
Hashubah, Ohel, Berechiah, Hasadiah, and Jushab-hesed, five. 21 The sons of
Hananiah: Pelatiah and Jeshaiah, his son[n] Rephaiah, his son[n] Arnan, his son[n]
Obadiah, his son[n] Shecaniah. 22 The son[o] of Shecaniah: Shemaiah. And the sons
of Shemaiah: Hattush, Igal, Bariah, Neariah, and Shaphat, six. 23 The sons of Neariah: Elioenai, Hizkiah, and Azrikam, three. 24 The sons of Elioenai: Hodaviah,
Eliashib, Pelaiah, Akkub, Johanan, Delaiah, and Anani, seven.

2.48 Josh 15.17 Judg 1.2
2.53 1 Chron 4.2
2.55 2 Kgs 10.15
3.1 1 Sam 25.42 2 Sam 3.2-5 13.1 1 Chron 2.3
3.2 2 Sam 3.4 13.20; 14.23
3.4 2 Sam 5.4,5
3.5 2 Sam 5.14-16 11.3; 12.24 1 Chron 14.4-7
3.10 1 Kgs 11.43 15.1,8,24 22.50 2 Kgs 8.24,25 11.21; 14.1,21 15.30,32,33 16.1; 18.1 21.1,2,19,20 22.1 2 Chron 9.30 13.1; 14.1 17.1; 21.1,17 24.1; 25.1 26.1; 27.1 28.1; 29.1 33.1,20,21 34.1 Mt 1.7-10
3.15 2 Kgs 23.30,34 2 Chron 36.1,4
3.21 Ezra 8.2-14

[m] Gk Vg: Heb *son* [n] Gk Compare Syr Vg: Heb *sons of* [o] Heb *sons*

3.1 Abigail's story is found in 1 Samuel 25; her Profile is in 1 Samuel 26.

3.2 Absalom's story and Profile are found in 2 Samuel 13 – 18.

3.5 Bath-shua is also called Bathsheba. Her story is found in 2 Samuel 11; 12; 1 Kings 1, and her Profile is in 1 Kings 1. The story of her son, Solomon, who became Israel's third king, is found in 1 Kings 1 – 11 and 2 Chronicles 1 – 9. Solomon's Profile is found in 1 Kings 4.

3.9 The tragic story of Tamar, David's daughter, is found in 2 Samuel 13; 14.

3.10–14 Many of Solomon's descendants ruled the nation of Judah. For Rehoboam's story and Profile see 2 Chronicles 10 – 12. For Jehoshaphat's story and Profile see 2 Chronicles 17 – 20. Azariah's (Uzziah's) story and Profile are found in 2 Chronicles 26. For Hezekiah's story and Profile see 2 Kings 18 – 20. For Josiah's story, see 2 Kings 22; 23. His Profile is in 2 Kings 23.

3.15 Jehoiakim's story is found in Jeremiah 22 – 28; 35; 36. Zedekiah's story is found in Jeremiah 21 – 39.

3.19, 20 Zerubbabel was the leader of the first exiles to return from Babylon. His story and Profile are found in the book of Ezra.

2. The tribes of Israel

Judah's descendants

4.1 Gen 38.29; 46.12; Num 26.19-22; Ruth 4.18; 1 Chron 2.3; Mt 1.3; Lk 3.33
4.2 1 Chron 2.53
4.3 1 Chron 2.19
4.10 Gen 32.26; Ps 72.17; Eph 1.3
4.13 Josh 15.17
4.23 Gen 38.5

4 The sons of Judah: Perez, Hezron, Carmi, Hur, and Shobal. 2 Reaiah son of
Shobal became the father of Jahath, and Jahath became the father of Ahumai
and Lahad. These were the families of the Zorathites. 3 These were the sons[p] of
Etam: Jezreel, Ishma, and Idbash; and the name of their sister was Hazzelelponi,
4 and Penuel was the father of Gedor, and Ezer the father of Hushah. These were the
sons of Hur, the firstborn of Ephrathah, the father of Bethlehem. 5 Ashhur father of
Tekoa had two wives, Helah and Naarah; 6 Naarah bore him Ahuzzam, Hepher,
Temeni, and Haahashtari.[q] These were the sons of Naarah. 7 The sons of Helah:
Zereth, Izhar,[r] and Ethnan. 8 Koz became the father of Anub, Zobebah, and the
families of Aharhel son of Harum. 9 Jabez was honored more than his brothers; and
his mother named him Jabez, saying, "Because I bore him in pain." 10 Jabez called
on the God of Israel, saying, "Oh that you would bless me and enlarge my border,
and that your hand might be with me, and that you would keep me from hurt and
harm!" And God granted what he asked. 11 Chelub the brother of Shuhah became
the father of Mehir, who was the father of Eshton. 12 Eshton became the father of
Beth-rapha, Paseah, and Tehinnah the father of Irnahash. These are the men of
Recah. 13 The sons of Kenaz: Othniel and Seraiah; and the sons of Othniel: Hathath
and Meonothai.[s] 14 Meonothai became the father of Ophrah; and Seraiah became
the father of Joab father of Ge-harashim,[t] so-called because they were artisans.
15 The sons of Caleb son of Jephunneh: Iru, Elah, and Naam; and the son[u] of Elah:
Kenaz. 16 The sons of Jehallelel: Ziph, Ziphah, Tiria, and Asarel. 17 The sons of
Ezrah: Jether, Mered, Epher, and Jalon. These are the sons of Bithiah, daughter of
Pharaoh, whom Mered married;[v] and she conceived and bore[w] Miriam, Shammai,
and Ishbah father of Eshtemoa. 18 And his Judean wife bore Jered father of Gedor,
Heber father of Soco, and Jekuthiel father of Zanoah. 19 The sons of the wife of
Hodiah, the sister of Naham, were the fathers of Keilah the Garmite and Eshtemoa
the Maacathite. 20 The sons of Shimon: Amnon, Rinnah, Ben-hanan, and Tilon.
The sons of Ishi: Zoheth and Ben-zoheth. 21 The sons of Shelah son of Judah: Er
father of Lecah, Laadah father of Mareshah, and the families of the guild of linen
workers at Beth-ashbea; 22 and Jokim, and the men of Cozeba, and Joash, and Sa-
raph, who married into Moab but returned to Lehem[x] (now the records[y] are ancient). 23 These were the potters and inhabitants of Netaim and Gederah; they lived
there with the king in his service.

Simeon's descendants

24 The sons of Simeon: Nemuel, Jamin, Jarib, Zerah, Shaul;[z] 25 Shallum was
his son, Mibsam his son, Mishma his son. 26 The sons of Mishma: Hammuel his
son, Zaccur his son, Shimei his son. 27 Shimei had sixteen sons and six daughters;
but his brothers did not have many children, nor did all their family multiply like
the Judeans. 28 They lived in Beer-sheba, Moladah, Hazar-shual, 29 Bilhah, Ezem,
Tolad, 30 Bethuel, Hormah, Ziklag, 31 Beth-marcaboth, Hazar-susim, Beth-biri,

[p] Gk Compare Vg: Heb *the father* [q] Or *Ahashtari* [r] Another reading is *Zohar* [s] Gk Vg: Heb lacks *and Meonothai*
[t] That is *Valley of artisans* [u] Heb *sons* [v] The clause: *These are . . . married* is transposed from verse 18
[w] Heb lacks *and bore* [x] Vg Compare Gk: Heb *and Jashubi-lahem* [y] Or *matters* [z] Or *Saul*

4.10 Jabez is remembered for a prayer rather than a heroic act. In his prayer, he asked God to (1) bless him, (2) help him in his work, (3) be with him in all he did, and (4) keep him from evil and disaster. Jabez acknowledged God as the true center of his work. When we pray for God's blessing, we should also pray that he will take his rightful position as Lord over our work, our family time, and our recreation. Obeying him in daily responsibilities *is* heroic living.

4.10 Jabez prayed specifically to be protected from hurt and harm. We live in a fallen world filled with sin, and it is important to ask God to keep us safe from the unavoidable evil that comes our way. But we must also avoid evil motives, desires, and actions that begin within us. Therefore, not only must we seek God's protection from evil, we must also ask God to guard our thoughts and actions. We can begin to utilize his protection by filling our minds with positive thoughts and attitudes.

4.13 Othniel was Israel's first judge. He reformed the nation and brought peace to the land. His story is found in Judges 1.9–15 and 3.5–14.

4.15 Caleb was one of the 12 spies sent into the promised land by Moses. He and Joshua were the only two among the spies to return with a positive report, believing in God's promise to help the Israelites conquer the land. Caleb's story is told in Numbers 13; 14 and Joshua 14; 15. His Profile is found in Numbers 15.

and Shaaraim. These were their towns until David became king. 32 And their villages were Etam, Ain, Rimmon, Tochen, and Ashan, five towns, 33 along with all
their villages that were around these towns as far as Baal. These were their settlements. And they kept a genealogical record.
34 Meshobab, Jamlech, Joshah son of Amaziah, 35 Joel, Jehu son of Joshibiah
son of Seraiah son of Asiel, 36 Elioenai, Jaakobah, Jeshohaiah, Asaiah, Adiel, Je-
simiel, Benaiah, 37 Ziza son of Shiphi son of Allon son of Jedaiah son of Shimri son
of Shemaiah— 38 these mentioned by name were leaders in their families, and their
clans increased greatly. 39 They journeyed to the entrance of Gedor, to the east side
of the valley, to seek pasture for their flocks, 40 where they found rich, good pasture, and the land was very broad, quiet, and peaceful; for the former inhabitants
there belonged to Ham. 41 These, registered by name, came in the days of King
Hezekiah of Judah, and attacked their tents and the Meunim who were found there,
and exterminated them to this day, and settled in their place, because there was
pasture there for their flocks. 42 And some of them, five hundred men of the Simeonites, went to Mount Seir, having as their leaders Pelatiah, Neariah, Rephaiah,
and Uzziel, sons of Ishi; 43 they destroyed the remnant of the Amalekites that had
escaped, and they have lived there to this day.

Reuben's descendants

5 The sons of Reuben the firstborn of Israel. (He was the firstborn, but because
he defiled his father's bed his birthright was given to the sons of Joseph son of
Israel, so that he is not enrolled in the genealogy according to the birthright;
2 though Judah became prominent among his brothers and a ruler came from him,
yet the birthright belonged to Joseph.) 3 The sons of Reuben, the firstborn of Israel:
Hanoch, Pallu, Hezron, and Carmi. 4 The sons of Joel: Shemaiah his son, Gog his
son, Shimei his son, 5 Micah his son, Reaiah his son, Baal his son, 6 Beerah his son,
whom King Tilgath-pilneser of Assyria carried away into exile; he was a chieftain
of the Reubenites. 7 And his kindred by their families, when the genealogy of their
generations was reckoned: the chief, Jeiel, and Zechariah, 8 and Bela son of Azaz,
son of Shema, son of Joel, who lived in Aroer, as far as Nebo and Baal-meon. 9 He
also lived to the east as far as the beginning of the desert this side of the Euphrates,
because their cattle had multiplied in the land of Gilead. 10 And in the days of Saul
they made war on the Hagrites, who fell by their hand; and they lived in their tents
throughout all the region east of Gilead.

Gad's descendants

11 The sons of Gad lived beside them in the land of Bashan as far as Salecah:
12 Joel the chief, Shapham the second, Janai, and Shaphat in Bashan. 13 And their
kindred according to their clans: Michael, Meshullam, Sheba, Jorai, Jacan, Zia,
and Eber, seven. 14 These were the sons of Abihail son of Huri, son of Jaroah, son
of Gilead, son of Michael, son of Jeshishai, son of Jahdo, son of Buz; 15 Ahi son of
Abdiel, son of Guni, was chief in their clan; 16 and they lived in Gilead, in Bashan
and in its towns, and in all the pasture lands of Sharon to their limits. 17 All of these
were enrolled by genealogies in the days of King Jotham of Judah, and in the days
of King Jeroboam of Israel.
18 The Reubenites, the Gadites, and the half-tribe of Manasseh had valiant

4.40 Judg 18.7-10
4.42 Gen 36.8
4.43 1 Sam 15.7,8 30.16,17
5.1 Gen 29.32 35.22 48.15-22; 49.4
5.2 Gen 49.8-10 Mic 5.2 Mt 2.6
5.3 Ex 6.14 Num 26.5
5.6 2 Kgs 15.29 16.7
5.7,8 Num 32.34 Josh 12.2
5.9 Josh 22.8,9
5.10 1 Chron 5.18-21
5.11 Num 32.34-36 Josh 13.11,24
5.16 1 Chron 27.29
5.17 2 Kgs 14.16,28 15.5,32,33
5.18 Num 1.3

5.1 Reuben's sin of incest was recorded for all future generations to read. The purpose of this epitaph, however, was not to smear Reuben's name, but to show that painful memories aren't the only results of sin. The real consequences of sin are ruined lives. As the oldest son, Reuben was the rightful heir to both a double portion of his father's estate and the leadership of Abraham's descendants, who had grown into a large tribe. But his sin stripped away his rights and privileges and ruined his family. Before you give in to temptation, take a close look at the disastrous consequences sin may produce in your life and the lives of others.

5.2 This chief ruler from the tribe of Judah refers to David and his royal line, and to Jesus the Messiah, David's greatest descendant.

5.18–22 The armies of Reuben, Gad, and Manasseh succeeded in battle because they trusted God. Although they had instinct and skill as soldiers, they prayed and sought God's direction. The natural and developed abilities God gives us are meant to be used for him, but they should never replace our dependence on him. When we trust in our own cleverness, skill, and strength rather than in God, we open the door for pride. When facing difficult situations, seek God's purpose and ask for his guidance and strength. Psalm 20.7 says, "Some take pride in chariots, and some in horses, but our pride is in the name of the Lord our God."

WHO'S WHO IN THE BIBLE

Here are some of the people mentioned in this genealogy who are also mentioned elsewhere in the Bible. The writer of Chronicles reproduced a thorough history of Israel in one list of people. Many of the people in this list have exciting stories that can be traced through the Bible. Look up some of the names below that intrigue you. You may be surprised what you discover!

Name	*Key life lesson*	*Story told in:*
Adam (1.1)	Our sins have far greater implications than we realize.	Genesis 2; 3
Noah (1.4)	Great rewards come from obeying God.	Genesis 6—9
Abraham (1.27)	Faith alone makes one right in God's eyes.	Genesis 11.26—25.10
Isaac (1.28)	Seeking peace brings true respect.	Genesis 21—35
Esau (1.35)	It is never too late to put away bitterness and forgive.	Genesis 25.20—36.43
Amalek (1.36)	There are evil men and nations who seek to harm God's people.	Exodus 17.8–16
Jacob (2.1)	While our sins may haunt us, God will honor our faith.	Genesis 25.20—50.13
Judah (2.3)	God can change the hearts of even the most wicked people.	Genesis 37—50
Tamar (2.4)	God works his purposes even through sinful events.	Genesis 38
Perez (Pharez) (2.5)	Your background does not matter to God.	Genesis 38.27–30
Boaz (2.12)	Those who are kind to others will receive kindness themselves.	The book of Ruth
Jesse (2.13)	Never take lightly the impact you may have on your children.	1 Samuel 16
David (2.15)	True greatness is having a heart for God.	The books of 1 and 2 Samuel
Joab (2.16)	Those who seek power die with nothing.	2 Samuel 2.13—1 Kings 2.34
Amnon (3.1)	Giving in to lust leads only to tragedy.	2 Samuel 13
Absalom (3.2)	Those seeking to oust a God-appointed leader will have a difficult battle.	2 Samuel 13—18
Adonijah (3.2)	God must determine what is rightfully ours.	1 Kings 1—2
Bathsheba (Bath-shua) (3.5)	One wrong act does not disqualify us from accomplishing things for God.	2 Samuel 11; 12; 1 Kings 1, 2
Solomon (3.5)	Man's wisdom is foolishness without God.	1 Kings 1—11
Reuben (5.1)	What is gained from a moment of passion is only perceived; what is lost is real and permanent.	Genesis 35.22; 37; 49.3, 4
Aaron (6.3)	Don't expect God's leaders to be perfect, but don't let them get away with sin either.	Exodus 4—Numbers 20
Nadab (6.3)	Pretending to be God's representative is dangerous business.	Leviticus 10
Eleazar (6.3)	Those who are consistent in their faith are the best models to follow.	Numbers 20.25–29; 26—34; Joshua 24.33
Korah (6.22)	Rebelling against God's leaders is rebelling against God and will always be unsuccessful.	Numbers 16
Joshua (7.27)	Real courage comes from God.	The book of Joshua
Saul (8.33)	Those who say they follow God but don't live like it waste their God-given potential.	1 Samuel 8—31
Jonathan (8.33)	True friends always think of the other person, not just themselves.	1 Samuel 14—31

warriors, who carried shield and sword, and drew the bow, expert in war, forty-
four thousand seven hundred sixty, ready for service. 19 They made war on the **5.19**
Hagrites, Jetur, Naphish, and Nodab; 20 and when they received help against them, Chron 1.31 5.10
the Hagrites and all who were with them were given into their hands, for they cried **5.20**
to God in the battle, and he granted their entreaty because they trusted in him. Josh 10.42 2 Chron
21 They captured their livestock: fifty thousand of their camels, two hundred fifty 14.11-13
thousand sheep, two thousand donkeys, and one hundred thousand captives. Ps 9.10
22 Many fell slain, because the war was of God. And they lived in their territory **5.22** Josh 23.10 2 Kgs 17.6
until the exile. 2 Chron 32.8

Manasseh's descendants

23 The members of the half-tribe of Manasseh lived in the land; they were very **5.23**
numerous from Bashan to Baal-hermon, Senir, and Mount Hermon. 24 These were Deut 3.9; 4.48
the heads of their clans: Epher,[a] Ishi, Eliel, Azriel, Jeremiah, Hodaviah, and Jah-
diel, mighty warriors, famous men, heads of their clans. 25 But they transgressed **5.25**
against the God of their ancestors, and prostituted themselves to the gods of the Ex 34.15 2 Kgs 17.7
peoples of the land, whom God had destroyed before them. 26 So the God of Israel **5.26**
stirred up the spirit of King Pul of Assyria, the spirit of King Tilgath-pilneser of 2 Kgs 15.19,29
Assyria, and he carried them away, namely, the Reubenites, the Gadites, and the
half-tribe of Manasseh, and brought them to Halah, Habor, Hara, and the river
Gozan, to this day.

Levi's descendants

6 [b] The sons of Levi: Gershom,[c] Kohath, and Merari. 2 The sons of Kohath: Am- **6.1**
ram, Izhar, Hebron, and Uzziel. 3 The children of Amram: Aaron, Moses, and Gen 46.11 Ex 6.16
Miriam. The sons of Aaron: Nadab, Abihu, Eleazar, and Ithamar. 4 Eleazar became Num 3.17
the father of Phinehas, Phinehas of Abishua, 5 Abishua of Bukki, Bukki of Uzzi, **6.3** 1 Chron 23.13
6 Uzzi of Zerahiah, Zerahiah of Meraioth, 7 Meraioth of Amariah, Amariah of Ahi- **6.4**
tub, 8 Ahitub of Zadok, Zadok of Ahimaaz, 9 Ahimaaz of Azariah, Azariah of Joha- 1 Chron 9.20
nan, 10 and Johanan of Azariah (it was he who served as priest in the house that
Solomon built in Jerusalem). 11 Azariah became the father of Amariah, Amariah of
Ahitub, 12 Ahitub of Zadok, Zadok of Shallum, 13 Shallum of Hilkiah, Hilkiah of
Azariah, 14 Azariah of Seraiah, Seraiah of Jehozadak; 15 and Jehozadak went into
exile when the LORD sent Judah and Jerusalem into exile by the hand of Nebuchadnezzar.

16[d] The sons of Levi: Gershom, Kohath, and Merari. 17 These are the names of
the sons of Gershom: Libni and Shimei. 18 The sons of Kohath: Amram, Izhar,
Hebron, and Uzziel. 19 The sons of Merari: Mahli and Mushi. These are the clans **6.19**
of the Levites according to their ancestry. 20 Of Gershom: Libni his son, Jahath his 1 Chron 23.21
son, Zimmah his son, 21 Joah his son, Iddo his son, Zerah his son, Jeatherai his son.
22 The sons of Kohath: Amminadab his son, Korah his son, Assir his son, 23 Elkanah his son, Ebiasaph his son, Assir his son, 24 Tahath his son, Uriel his son, Uz-

[a] Gk Vg: Heb *and Epher* [b] Ch 5.27 in Heb [c] Heb *Gershon*, variant of *Gershom*; See 6.16 [d] Ch 6.1 in Heb

---

5.22 The exile mentioned here refers to the exile of the ten northern tribes (the northern kingdom of Israel) to Assyria in 722 B.C. These tribes never returned to their homeland. This story is found in 2 Kings 15.29 – 17.41.

5.24, 25 As warriors and leaders, these men had established excellent reputations for their great skill and leadership qualities. But in God's eyes they failed in the most important quality – putting God first. If you try to measure up to society's standards for fame and success, you may neglect your true purpose – to please and obey God. In the end, God alone examines our hearts and determines our final standing.

6.1ff The tribe of Levi was set apart to serve God in the tabernacle (Numbers 3; 4), and later in the temple (1 Chronicles 23 – 26). Aaron, Levi's descendant (6.3), became Israel's first high priest. God required all future priests to be descendants of Aaron. The rest of the Levites assisted the priests in the various tabernacle or temple duties and assisted the people by teaching them God's Word and encouraging them to obey it.

6.3 The people listed here played major roles in the drama of the exodus. Aaron's story is found in the books of Exodus, Leviticus, and Numbers. His Profile is found in Exodus 32. Moses was one of the greatest prophets and leaders in Israel's history. His story is found in the books of Exodus, Leviticus, Numbers, and Deuteronomy. His Profile is found in Exodus 15. The story of Miriam, Moses' and Aaron's sister, is found in Exodus 2; 15.20, 21; and Numbers 12; 20.1. Her Profile is found in Numbers 12. Nadab and Abihu were killed for disobeying God (Leviticus 10). Eleazar became Israel's high priest after Aaron (Numbers 20.24–28), and Ithamar played an important role in organizing the worship services of the tabernacle (Numbers 4.28, 33; 7.8).

6.25 1 Sam 1.1
6.28 1 Sam 8.2
6.31 2 Sam 6.17; 1 Chron 15.16, 27; 16.4-6; 25.1
6.49 Ex 29.33,34
6.50 1 Chron 6.4-8
6.54 Josh 21.4,10
6.55-57 Josh 14.13; 15.13; 21.13,19
6.58 Num 35.6; Deut 4.41; 19.2; Josh 20.2

ziah his son, and Shaul his son. 25 The sons of Elkanah: Amasai and Ahimoth,
26 Elkanah his son, Zophai his son, Nahath his son, 27 Eliab his son, Jeroham his
son, Elkanah his son. 28 The sons of Samuel: Joel[e] his firstborn, the second Abijah.[f] 29 The sons of Merari: Mahli, Libni his son, Shimei his son, Uzzah his son,
30 Shimea his son, Haggiah his son, and Asaiah his son.

31 These are the men whom David put in charge of the service of song in the
house of the LORD, after the ark came to rest there. 32 They ministered with song
before the tabernacle of the tent of meeting, until Solomon had built the house of
the LORD in Jerusalem; and they performed their service in due order. 33 These are
the men who served; and their sons were: Of the Kohathites: Heman, the singer,
son of Joel, son of Samuel, 34 son of Elkanah, son of Jeroham, son of Eliel, son of
Toah, 35 son of Zuph, son of Elkanah, son of Mahath, son of Amasai, 36 son of
Elkanah, son of Joel, son of Azariah, son of Zephaniah, 37 son of Tahath, son
of Assir, son of Ebiasaph, son of Korah, 38 son of Izhar, son of Kohath, son of
Levi, son of Israel; 39 and his brother Asaph, who stood on his right, namely, Asaph
son of Berechiah, son of Shimea, 40 son of Michael, son of Baaseiah, son of Malchijah, 41 son of Ethni, son of Zerah, son of Adaiah, 42 son of Ethan, son of Zimmah,
son of Shimei, 43 son of Jahath, son of Gershom, son of Levi. 44 On the left were
their kindred the sons of Merari: Ethan son of Kishi, son of Abdi, son of Malluch,
45 son of Hashabiah, son of Amaziah, son of Hilkiah, 46 son of Amzi, son of Bani,
son of Shemer, 47 son of Mahli, son of Mushi, son of Merari, son of Levi; 48 and
their kindred the Levites were appointed for all the service of the tabernacle of the
house of God.

49 But Aaron and his sons made offerings on the altar of burnt offering and on
the altar of incense, doing all the work of the most holy place, to make atonement
for Israel, according to all that Moses the servant of God had commanded. 50 These
are the sons of Aaron: Eleazar his son, Phinehas his son, Abishua his son, 51 Bukki
his son, Uzzi his son, Zerahiah his son, 52 Meraioth his son, Amariah his son, Ahitub his son, 53 Zadok his son, Ahimaaz his son.

54 These are their dwelling places according to their settlements within their
borders: to the sons of Aaron of the families of Kohathites—for the lot fell to them
first— 55 to them they gave Hebron in the land of Judah and its surrounding pasture
lands, 56 but the fields of the city and its villages they gave to Caleb son of Jephunneh. 57 To the sons of Aaron they gave the cities of refuge: Hebron, Libnah with its
pasture lands, Jattir, Eshtemoa with its pasture lands, 58 Hilen[g] with its pasture

[e] Gk Syr Compare verse 33 and 1 Sam 8.2: Heb lacks *Joel* [f] Heb reads *Vashni, and Abijah* for *the second Abijah*, taking *the second* as a proper name [g] Other readings *Hilez, Holon*; See Josh 21.15

6.28 When Samuel became God's leader and spokesman, Israel was on the brink of collapse. The last few chapters of the book of Judges give a vivid picture of the moral decay and the resulting decline of the nation. But with God's help, Samuel almost single-handedly brought the nation from ruin to revival. He unified the people by showing them that God was their common Leader and that any nation that focused on him would find and fulfill its true purpose. For the rest of Samuel's story, and to see how he set up rules for governing a nation based on spiritual principles, read the book of 1 Samuel and his Profile in chapter 8.

6.31 David did much to bring music into worship. He established songleaders and choirs to perform regularly at the temple (chapter 32). As a young man, David was hired to play the harp for King Saul (1 Samuel 16.15–23). He also wrote many of the songs found in the book of Psalms.

6.31, 32 The builders and craftsmen had completed the temple, and the priests and Levites had been given their responsibilities for taking care of it. Then it was time for another group of people—the choirs—to exercise their talents for God. Some of the songleaders' names are recorded here. You don't have to be an ordained minister to have an important place in the body of believers. Builders, craftsmen, worship assistants, choir members, and songleaders all have significant contributions to make. God has given you a unique combination of talents. Use them to serve and honor him.

6.49 Aaron and his descendants strictly followed the details of worship commanded by God through Moses. They did not choose only those commands they *wanted* to obey. Note what happened to Uzzah when important details in handling the ark of the covenant were neglected (13.6–10). We should not try to obey God selectively, choosing those commands we will obey and those we will ignore. God's Word has authority over every aspect of our lives, not just selected portions.

6.54 The tribe of Levi was not given a specific area of land as were the other tribes. Instead, the Levites were to live throughout the land in order to aid the people of *every* tribe in their worship of God. Thus the Levites were given cities or farmland within the allotted areas of the other tribes (Joshua 13.14, 33).

6.57ff God had told the tribes to designate specific cities to be cities of refuge (Numbers 35). These cities were to provide refuge for a person who accidentally killed someone. This instruction may have seemed unimportant when it was given—the Israelites hadn't even entered the promised land. Sometimes God gives us instructions that do not seem relevant to us at the moment. But later we can see the importance of those instructions. Obey God now—in the future you will have a clearer understanding of the reasons for his instructions.

lands, Debir with its pasture lands, 59 Ashan with its pasture lands, and Beth-
shemesh with its pasture lands. 60 From the tribe of Benjamin, Geba with its pasture
lands, Alemeth with its pasture lands, and Anathoth with its pasture lands. All their
towns throughout their families were thirteen.
61 To the rest of the Kohathites were given by lot out of the family of the tribe, **6.61**
out of the half-tribe, the half of Manasseh, ten towns. 62 To the Gershomites ac- Josh 21.5
cording to their families were allotted thirteen towns out of the tribes of Issachar, 1 Chron 6.66-70
Asher, Naphtali, and Manasseh in Bashan. 63 To the Merarites according to their **6.63**
families were allotted twelve towns out of the tribes of Reuben, Gad, and Zebulun. Josh 21.7,34-40 1 Chron 6.77
64 So the people of Israel gave the Levites the towns with their pasture lands. **6.64**
65 They also gave them by lot out of the tribes of Judah, Simeon, and Benjamin Josh 21.3,41,42 1 Chron 6.57-60
these towns that are mentioned by name.
66 And some of the families of the sons of Kohath had towns of their territory **6.66**
out of the tribe of Ephraim. 67 They were given the cities of refuge: Shechem with Josh 21.20-26 1 Chron 6.61
its pasture lands in the hill country of Ephraim, Gezer with its pasture lands, 68 Jok-
meam with its pasture lands, Beth-horon with its pasture lands, 69 Aijalon with its
pasture lands, Gath-rimmon with its pasture lands; 70 and out of the half-tribe of
Manasseh, Aner with its pasture lands, and Bileam with its pasture lands, for the
rest of the families of the Kohathites.
71 To the Gershomites: out of the half-tribe of Manasseh: Golan in Bashan with
its pasture lands and Ashtaroth with its pasture lands; 72 and out of the tribe of Issachar: Kedesh with its pasture lands, Daberath[h] with its pasture lands, 73 Ramoth
with its pasture lands, and Anem with its pasture lands; 74 out of the tribe of Asher:
Mashal with its pasture lands, Abdon with its pasture lands, 75 Hukok with its pasture lands, and Rehob with its pasture lands; 76 and out of the tribe of Naphtali:
Kedesh in Galilee with its pasture lands, Hammon with its pasture lands, and Kiriathaim with its pasture lands. 77 To the rest of the Merarites out of the tribe of Zebu- **6.77**
lun: Rimmono with its pasture lands, Tabor with its pasture lands, 78 and across the 1 Chron 6.63
Jordan from Jericho, on the east side of the Jordan, out of the tribe of Reuben:
Bezer in the steppe with its pasture lands, Jahzah with its pasture lands, 79 Kedemoth with its pasture lands, and Mephaath with its pasture lands; 80 and out of the
tribe of Gad: Ramoth in Gilead with its pasture lands, Mahanaim with its pasture
lands, 81 Heshbon with its pasture lands, and Jazer with its pasture lands.

Issachar's descendants

7 The sons[i] of Issachar: Tola, Puah, Jashub, and Shimron, four. 2 The sons of **7.1**
Tola: Uzzi, Rephaiah, Jeriel, Jahmai, Ibsam, and Shemuel, heads of their an- Gen 46.13 Num 26.23
cestral houses, namely of Tola, mighty warriors of their generations, their number **7.2**
in the days of David being twenty-two thousand six hundred. 3 The son[j] of Uzzi: 2 Sam 24.1-9 1 Chron 21.1
Izrahiah. And the sons of Izrahiah: Michael, Obadiah, Joel, and Isshiah, five, all of
them chiefs; 4 and along with them, by their generations, according to their ancestral houses, were units of the fighting force, thirty-six thousand, for they had many
wives and sons. 5 Their kindred belonging to all the families of Issachar were in all
eighty-seven thousand mighty warriors, enrolled by genealogy.

Benjamin's descendants

6 The sons of Benjamin: Bela, Becher, and Jediael, three. 7 The sons of Bela: **7.6**
Ezbon, Uzzi, Uzziel, Jerimoth, and Iri, five, heads of ancestral houses, mighty 1 Chron 8.1
warriors; and their enrollment by genealogies was twenty-two thousand thirty-four.
8 The sons of Becher: Zemirah, Joash, Eliezer, Elioenai, Omri, Jeremoth, Abijah,
Anathoth, and Alemeth. All these were the sons of Becher; 9 and their enrollment
by genealogies, according to their generations, as heads of their ancestral houses,

[h] Or *Dobrath* [i] Syr Compare Vg: Heb *And to the sons* [j] Heb *sons*

6.61 The Israelites cast lots in order to take the decision-making process out of man's hands and put it into God's hands. Casting lots was like drawing straws or throwing dice. Lots were cast only after seeking God's guidance in prayer. (For more information on casting lots, see the note on Joshua 18.8.)

mighty warriors, was twenty thousand two hundred. 10 The sons of Jediael: Bilhan.
And the sons of Bilhan: Jeush, Benjamin, Ehud, Chenaanah, Zethan, Tarshish,
and Ahishahar. 11 All these were the sons of Jediael according to the heads of their
ancestral houses, mighty warriors, seventeen thousand two hundred, ready for service in war. 12 And Shuppim and Huppim were the sons of Ir, Hushim the son[k] of
Aher.

Naphtali's descendants

7.13 Gen 46.23-25 13 The descendants of Naphtali: Jahziel, Guni, Jezer, and Shallum, the descendants of Bilhah.

Manasseh's descendants

7.14 Gen 50.23 14 The sons of Manasseh: Asriel, whom his Aramean concubine bore; she bore
Num 26.29 Machir the father of Gilead. 15 And Machir took a wife for Huppim and for Shup-
Josh 13.31 pim. The name of his sister was Maacah. And the name of the second was Zelophehad; and Zelophehad had daughters. 16 Maacah the wife of Machir bore a son, and
she named him Peresh; the name of his brother was Sheresh; and his sons were
Ulam and Rekem. 17 The son[k] of Ulam: Bedan. These were the sons of Gilead son
of Machir, son of Manasseh. 18 And his sister Hammolecheth bore Ishhod, Abiezer, and Mahlah. 19 The sons of Shemida were Ahian, Shechem, Likhi, and Aniam.

Ephraim's descendants

7.20 Num 26.35,36 20 The sons of Ephraim: Shuthelah, and Bered his son, Tahath his son, Eleadah
his son, Tahath his son, 21 Zabad his son, Shuthelah his son, and Ezer and Elead.
Now the people of Gath, who were born in the land, killed them, because they
came down to raid their cattle. 22 And their father Ephraim mourned many days,
and his brothers came to comfort him. 23 Ephraim[l] went in to his wife, and she
conceived and bore a son; and he named him Beriah, because disaster[m] had be-
7.24 Josh 16.3,5 fallen his house. 24 His daughter was Sheerah, who built both Lower and Upper
Beth-horon, and Uzzen-sheerah. 25 Rephah was his son, Resheph his son, Telah his
7.25-27 Ex 17.9-14 son, Tahan his son, 26 Ladan his son, Ammihud his son, Elishama his son, 27 Nun[n]
24.13 his son, Joshua his son. 28 Their possessions and settlements were Bethel and its
towns, and eastward Naaran, and westward Gezer and its towns, Shechem and its
7.29 Josh 17.7-11 towns, as far as Ayyah and its towns; 29 also along the borders of the Manassites,
Beth-shean and its towns, Taanach and its towns, Megiddo and its towns, Dor and
its towns. In these lived the sons of Joseph son of Israel.

Asher's descendants

7.30 Gen 46.17 30 The sons of Asher: Imnah, Ishvah, Ishvi, Beriah, and their sister Serah.
Num 26.44-46 31 The sons of Beriah: Heber and Malchiel, who was the father of Birzaith. 32 Heber
became the father of Japhlet, Shomer, Hotham, and their sister Shua. 33 The sons of
Japhlet: Pasach, Bimhal, and Ashvath. These are the sons of Japhlet. 34 The sons of
Shemer: Ahi, Rohgah, Hubbah, and Aram. 35 The sons of Helem[o] his brother:
Zophah, Imna, Shelesh, and Amal. 36 The sons of Zophah: Suah, Harnepher,
Shual, Beri, Imrah, 37 Bezer, Hod, Shamma, Shilshah, Ithran, and Beera. 38 The
sons of Jether: Jephunneh, Pispa, and Ara. 39 The sons of Ulla: Arah, Hanniel, and
Rizia. 40 All of these were men of Asher, heads of ancestral houses, select mighty
warriors, chief of the princes. Their number enrolled by genealogies, for service in
war, was twenty-six thousand men.

[k] Heb *sons* [l] Heb *He* [m] Heb *beraah* [n] Here spelled *Non*; see Ex 33.11 [o] Or *Hotham*; see 7.32

7.27 Joshua was one of Israel's great leaders, leading the people into the promised land. His story is told in the book of Joshua. His Profile is found in Joshua 2.

7.29 The sons of Joseph were Ephraim and Manasseh. Both were born to him by his wife Asenath, the daughter of an Egyptian priest (Genesis 41.50–52). Jacob (Israel) accepted them as his own sons, thereby making them founders of tribes. Manasseh was older, but Ephraim received the blessing from the right hand of Jacob signifying that he would become the greater tribe (Genesis 48.13–19).

Benjamin's descendants

8 Benjamin became the father of Bela his firstborn, Ashbel the second, Aharah 8.1
the third, 2 Nohah the fourth, and Rapha the fifth. 3 And Bela had sons: Addar, Gen 46.21 1 Chron 7.6-12
Gera, Abihud,[p] 4 Abishua, Naaman, Ahoah, 5 Gera, Shephuphan, and Huram.
6 These are the sons of Ehud (they were heads of ancestral houses of the inhabitants
of Geba, and they were carried into exile to Manahath): 7 Naaman,[q] Ahijah, and
Gera, that is, Heglam,[r] who became the father of Uzza and Ahihud. 8 And Shaharaim had sons in the country of Moab after he had sent away his wives Hushim and
Baara. 9 He had sons by his wife Hodesh: Jobab, Zibia, Mesha, Malcam, 10 Jeuz,
Sachia, and Mirmah. These were his sons, heads of ancestral houses. 11 He also had
sons by Hushim: Abitub and Elpaal. 12 The sons of Elpaal: Eber, Misham, and
Shemed, who built Ono and Lod with its towns, 13 and Beriah and Shema (they
were heads of ancestral houses of the inhabitants of Aijalon, who put to flight the
inhabitants of Gath); 14 and Ahio, Shashak, and Jeremoth. 15 Zebadiah, Arad, Eder,
16 Michael, Ishpah, and Joha were sons of Beriah. 17 Zebadiah, Meshullam, Hizki,
Heber, 18 Ishmerai, Izliah, and Jobab were the sons of Elpaal. 19 Jakim, Zichri,
Zabdi, 20 Elienai, Zillethai, Eliel, 21 Adaiah, Beraiah, and Shimrath were the sons
of Shimei. 22 Ishpan, Eber, Eliel, 23 Abdon, Zichri, Hanan, 24 Hananiah, Elam, An-
thothijah, 25 Iphdeiah, and Penuel were the sons of Shashak. 26 Shamsherai, Sheha-
riah, Athaliah, 27 Jaareshiah, Elijah, and Zichri were the sons of Jeroham. 28 These
were the heads of ancestral houses, according to their generations, chiefs. These
lived in Jerusalem.

29 Jeiel[s] the father of Gibeon lived in Gibeon, and the name of his wife was 8.29
Maacah. 30 His firstborn son: Abdon, then Zur, Kish, Baal,[t] Nadab, 31 Gedor, 1 Chron 9.35-38
Ahio, Zecher, 32 and Mikloth, who became the father of Shimeah. Now these also
lived opposite their kindred in Jerusalem, with their kindred. 33 Ner became the 8.33
father of Kish, Kish of Saul,[u] Saul[u] of Jonathan, Malchishua, Abinadab, and Esh- 1 Sam 9.1 14.50
baal; 34 and the son of Jonathan was Merib-baal; and Merib-baal became the father 1 Chron 9.39-44
of Micah. 35 The sons of Micah: Pithon, Melech, Tarea, and Ahaz. 36 Ahaz became 8.34
the father of Jehoaddah; and Jehoaddah became the father of Alemeth, Azmaveth, 2 Sam 4.4
and Zimri; Zimri became the father of Moza. 37 Moza became the father of Binea;
Raphah was his son, Eleasah his son, Azel his son. 38 Azel had six sons, and these
are their names: Azrikam, Bocheru, Ishmael, Sheariah, Obadiah, and Hanan; all
these were the sons of Azel. 39 The sons of his brother Eshek: Ulam his firstborn,
Jeush the second, and Eliphelet the third. 40 The sons of Ulam were mighty warriors, archers, having many children and grandchildren, one hundred fifty. All
these were Benjaminites. 9.1

9 So all Israel was enrolled by genealogies; and these are written in the Book of 1 Kgs 14.19
the Kings of Israel. And Judah was taken into exile in Babylon because of their 2 Kgs 1.18
unfaithfulness. 2 Now the first to live again in their possessions in their towns were 9.2 Ezra 2.43,58
Israelites, priests, Levites, and temple servants. 8.20 Neh 11.3-22

[p] Or *father of Ehud*; see 8.6 [q] Heb *and Naaman* [r] Or *he carried them into exile* [s] Compare 9.35: Heb lacks *Jeiel*
[t] Gk Ms adds *Ner*; Compare 8.33 and 9.36 [u] Or *Shaul*

8.8–10 These verses list Shaharaim's children by Hodesh after he had divorced (sent away) his first two wives, Hushim and Baara. Divorce and polygamy are sometimes recorded in the Old Testament without critical comments. This does not mean that God takes divorce lightly. Malachi 2.15, 16 says, "Do not let anyone be faithless to the wife of his youth. For I hate divorce, says the Lord, the God of Israel." Jesus explained that although divorce was allowed, it was not God's will: "It was because you were so hard-hearted that Moses allowed you to divorce your wives, but from the beginning it was not so" (Matthew 19.8, 9). Don't assume that God approves of an act because it isn't vigorously condemned in every related Bible reference.

8.33 Saul, Israel's first king, was very inconsistent. His story is found in 1 Samuel 9 – 31, and his Profile is in 1 Samuel 13. Saul's son Jonathan was the opposite. Although Jonathan was the rightful heir to the throne, he realized that David was God's choice to be Israel's next king. Instead of being jealous, Jonathan was David's friend and even helped him escape from Saul's attempts at murder. Jonathan's story is told in 1 Samuel 14 – 31. His Profile is found in 1 Samuel 21.

9.1 Although every person in Judah did not worship idols, the entire nation was carried away into captivity. Everyone was affected by the sin of some. Even if we don't participate in a certain widespread wrongdoing, we will still be affected by those who do. It is not enough to say, "I didn't do it." We must speak out against the sins of our society.

9.1ff Chronologically, this chapter could be placed at the end of 2 Chronicles because it records the names of the exiles who returned from the Babylonian captivity. The writer included it here to show his concern for their need, as a nation, to return to what made them great in the first place – obedience to God.

3. Returnees from exile in Babylon

People living in Jerusalem

3 And some of the people of Judah, Benjamin, Ephraim, and Manasseh lived in
Jerusalem: 4 Uthai son of Ammihud, son of Omri, son of Imri, son of Bani, from
the sons of Perez son of Judah. 5 And of the Shilonites: Asaiah the firstborn, and his
sons. 6 Of the sons of Zerah: Jeuel and their kin, six hundred ninety. 7 Of the Benjaminites: Sallu son of Meshullam, son of Hodaviah, son of Hassenuah, 8 Ibneiah son
of Jeroham, Elah son of Uzzi, son of Michri, and Meshullam son of Shephatiah,
9.9 son of Reuel, son of Ibnijah; 9 and their kindred according to their generations, nine
Neh 11.8 hundred fifty-six. All these were heads of families according to their ancestral
houses.

9.10 10 Of the priests: Jedaiah, Jehoiarib, Jachin, 11 and Azariah son of Hilkiah, son
Neh 11.10-14 Jer 20.1 of Meshullam, son of Zadok, son of Meraioth, son of Ahitub, the chief officer of
the house of God; 12 and Adaiah son of Jeroham, son of Pashhur, son of Malchijah,
and Maasai son of Adiel, son of Jahzerah, son of Meshullam, son of Meshillemith,
son of Immer; 13 besides their kindred, heads of their ancestral houses, one thousand seven hundred sixty, qualified for the work of the service of the house of God.

9.14 14 Of the Levites: Shemaiah son of Hasshub, son of Azrikam, son of Hasha-
Neh 11.15-19 biah, of the sons of Merari; 15 and Bakbakkar, Heresh, Galal, and Mattaniah son of
Mica, son of Zichri, son of Asaph; 16 and Obadiah son of Shemaiah, son of Galal,
son of Jeduthun, and Berechiah son of Asa, son of Elkanah, who lived in the villages of the Netophathites.

9.17 17 The gatekeepers were: Shallum, Akkub, Talmon, Ahiman; and their kin-
Ezek 46.1,2 dred Shallum was the chief, 18 stationed previously in the king's gate on the east
side. These were the gatekeepers of the camp of the Levites. 19 Shallum son of
Kore, son of Ebiasaph, son of Korah, and his kindred of his ancestral house, the
Korahites, were in charge of the work of the service, guardians of the thresholds of
the tent, as their ancestors had been in charge of the camp of the LORD, guardians
9.20 of the entrance. 20 And Phinehas son of Eleazar was chief over them in former
Num 25.7-13 times; the LORD was with him. 21 Zechariah son of Meshelemiah was gatekeeper at
9.21 1 Chron 26.2,14 the entrance of the tent of meeting. 22 All these, who were chosen as gatekeepers at
9.22 1 Chron 26.1 the thresholds, were two hundred twelve. They were enrolled by genealogies in
2 Chron 31.15, 18 their villages. David and the seer Samuel established them in their office of trust.
23 So they and their descendants were in charge of the gates of the house of the
LORD, that is, the house of the tent, as guards. 24 The gatekeepers were on the four
9.25 2 Kgs 11.5,7 sides, east, west, north, and south; 25 and their kindred who were in their villages
2 Chron 23.8 were obliged to come in every seven days, in turn, to be with them; 26 for the four
9.27 1 Chron chief gatekeepers, who were Levites, were in charge of the chambers and the trea-
23.30-32 sures of the house of God. 27 And they would spend the night near the house of God;

9.2 Only two of the original 12 tribes of Israel returned from exile—Judah and Benjamin (Ezra 1.5).

9.10, 11 When we think of doing God's work, usually preaching, teaching, singing, and other kinds of up-front leadership come to mind. Azariah, however, was the temple administrator, and he was singled out for special mention. Whatever role you have in God's church, it is important to God. He appreciates your service and the attitude you have as you do it.

9.17, 18 Gatekeepers guarded the four main entrances to the temple and opened the gates each morning for those who wanted to worship. In addition, they did other day-to-day chores to keep the temple running smoothly—cleaning, preparing the offerings for sacrifice, and accounting for the gifts designated to the temple (9.22–32).

Gatekeepers had to be reliable, honest, and trustworthy. The people in our churches who handle the offerings and care for the materials and functions of the building follow in a great tradition, and we should honor them for their reliability and service.

9.22 The gatekeepers were chosen on the basis of their genealogies. To be eligible to work in the temple, a person had to prove he was descended from Abraham (see the note on 1.1). If his family was listed in the genealogical records, he was then chosen only if he was reliable and trustworthy. We need to follow the principle of choosing church leaders who are reliable and exhibit a deep faith and commitment to God (see also 2 Timothy 2.2–7).

9.22–32 The priests and Levites put a great deal of time and care into worship. Not only did they perform rather complicated tasks (described in Leviticus 1–9), they also took care of many pieces of equipment. Everything relating to worship was carefully prepared and maintained so they and all the people could enter worship with their minds and hearts focused on God.

In our busy world, it is easy to rush into our one-hour-a-week worship services without preparing ourselves for worship beforehand. We reflect and worry about the week's problems; we pray about whatever comes into our minds; and we do not meditate on the words we are singing. But God wants our worship to be conducted "decently and in order" (1 Corinthians 14.40). Just as we prepare to meet a business associate or invited guests, we should carefully prepare to meet our King in worship.

for on them lay the duty of watching, and they had charge of opening it every
morning.

28 Some of them had charge of the utensils of service, for they were required to
count them when they were brought in and taken out. 29 Others of them were ap- **9.29**
pointed over the furniture, and over all the holy utensils, also over the choice flour, 1 Chron 23.29
the wine, the oil, the incense, and the spices. 30 Others, of the sons of the priests, **9.30**
prepared the mixing of the spices, 31 and Mattithiah, one of the Levites, the first- Ex 30.23-25
born of Shallum the Korahite, was in charge of making the flat cakes. 32 Also some **9.32**
of their kindred of the Kohathites had charge of the rows of bread, to prepare them Lev 24.5-8
for each sabbath.

33 Now these are the singers, the heads of ancestral houses of the Levites, liv- **9.33**
ing in the chambers of the temple free from other service, for they were on duty day 1 Chron 6.31-47; 25.1
and night. 34 These were heads of ancestral houses of the Levites, according to their
generations; these leaders lived in Jerusalem.

Saul's genealogy

35 In Gibeon lived the father of Gibeon, Jeiel, and the name of his wife was **9.35**
Maacah. 36 His firstborn son was Abdon, then Zur, Kish, Baal, Ner, Nadab, 37 Ge- 1 Chron 8.29-32
dor, Ahio, Zechariah, and Mikloth; 38 and Mikloth became the father of Shimeam;
and these also lived opposite their kindred in Jerusalem, with their kindred. 39 Ner **9.39**
became the father of Kish, Kish of Saul, Saul of Jonathan, Malchishua, Abinadab, 1 Chron 8.33-38
and Esh-baal; 40 and the son of Jonathan was Merib-baal; and Merib-baal became
the father of Micah. 41 The sons of Micah: Pithon, Melech, Tahrea, and Ahaz;[v] **9.41**
42 and Ahaz became the father of Jarah, and Jarah of Alemeth, Azmaveth, and 1 Chron 8.35-37
Zimri; and Zimri became the father of Moza. 43 Moza became the father of Binea;
and Rephaiah was his son, Eleasah his son, Azel his son. 44 Azel had six sons, and
these are their names: Azrikam, Bocheru, Ishmael, Sheariah, Obadiah, and Hanan;
these were the sons of Azel.

B. THE REIGN OF DAVID (10.1 – 29.30)

David becomes king over all Israel and captures the city of Jerusalem. God promises blessings to him and the nation, but David is not allowed to build the temple. Instead, he begins to make preparations for its construction. Although stumbling and falling occasionally, David walks step by step with God, sincerely wanting to be obedient. Through David's successes and his failures, we learn the importance of giving our whole heart to God and letting him be the focus of our lives, striving each day to be consistent in our obedience to his will.

1. David becomes king over all of Israel

The death of Saul

10 Now the Philistines fought against Israel; and the men of Israel fled before **10.1**
the Philistines, and fell slain on Mount Gilboa. 2 The Philistines overtook 1 Sam 31.1
Saul and his sons; and the Philistines killed Jonathan and Abinadab and Malchi- **10.2**
shua, sons of Saul. 3 The battle pressed hard on Saul; and the archers found him, 1 Sam 31.2
and he was wounded by the archers. 4 Then Saul said to his armor-bearer, "Draw
your sword, and thrust me through with it, so that these uncircumcised may not
come and make sport of me." But his armor-bearer was unwilling, for he was terrified. So Saul took his own sword and fell on it. 5 When his armor-bearer saw that
Saul was dead, he also fell on his sword and died. 6 Thus Saul died; he and his three
sons and all his house died together. 7 When all the men of Israel who were in the

[v] Compare 8.35: Heb lacks *and Ahaz*

9.33, 34 Worship was the primary focus of many Israelites, whose vocation centered on the house of the Lord. Worship (appreciating God for his nature and worth) should occupy the core of our lives and not just a few minutes once a week. We too can worship at all hours if we stay aware of God's presence and guidance in all situations and if we maintain an attitude of serving him. Build your life around the worship of God rather than making worship just another activity in a busy schedule.

10.1 The chronology of chapters 1 – 9 covers Israelite history from creation to the exile in Babylon (586 B.C.). At this point, the narrative goes back to the beginning of Israel's kingdom period, picking up with Israel's first king, Saul. First Chronicles begins with Saul's death; to learn about his reign, read 1 Samuel.

valley saw that the army[w] had fled and that Saul and his sons were dead, they
abandoned their towns and fled; and the Philistines came and occupied them.
8 The next day when the Philistines came to strip the dead, they found Saul and
10.9 his sons fallen on Mount Gilboa. 9 They stripped him and took his head and his
1 Sam 31.9 armor, and sent messengers throughout the land of the Philistines to carry the good
news to their idols and to the people. 10 They put his armor in the temple of their
gods, and fastened his head in the temple of Dagon. 11 But when all Jabesh-gilead
heard everything that the Philistines had done to Saul, 12 all the valiant warriors got
up and took away the body of Saul and the bodies of his sons, and brought them to
Jabesh. Then they buried their bones under the oak in Jabesh, and fasted seven
days.
10.13 1 Sam 13.13,14 13 So Saul died for his unfaithfulness; he was unfaithful to the LORD in that he
15.23; 28.7 did not keep the command of the LORD; moreover, he had consulted a medium,
10.14 1 Sam 15.28 seeking guidance, 14 and did not seek guidance from the LORD. Therefore the
1 Chron 12.23 LORD[x] put him to death and turned the kingdom over to David son of Jesse.

David conquers Jerusalem

11.1 2 Sam 5.1,3,6 **11** Then all Israel gathered together to David at Hebron and said, "See, we are
11.2 your bone and flesh. 2 For some time now, even while Saul was king, it was
2 Sam 5.2; 7.7 you who commanded the army of Israel. The LORD your God said to you: It is you
who shall be shepherd of my people Israel, you who shall be ruler over my people
11.3 Israel." 3 So all the elders of Israel came to the king at Hebron, and David made a
1 Sam 16.1,3, covenant with them at Hebron before the LORD. And they anointed David king over
12,13 Israel, according to the word of the LORD by Samuel.
11.4 Josh 15.8,63 4 David and all Israel marched to Jerusalem, that is Jebus, where the Jebusites
Judg 1.21 were, the inhabitants of the land. 5 The inhabitants of Jebus said to David, "You

[w] Heb *they* [x] Heb *he*

10.10 Dagon, the most important god of the Philistines, was believed to bring rain and provide rich harvests. The Philistines built temples to him when they settled in the grain-producing land of Canaan. In times of drought, people begged Dagon for pity, even to the point of sacrificing their children in his temples. In times of plenty, the temples were used for twisted forms of entertainment, such as the humiliation of captives (see Judges 16.23–30). But Dagon, like the other pagan gods, was powerless against the one true God (1 Samuel 5.1–7).

10.11, 12 The actions of the heroic warriors who brought back and buried the bodies of King Saul and his sons should encourage us to respect our God-given leaders. David showed respect for Saul's position, even when Saul was chasing him down to kill him (1 Samuel 26). How easy it is to be critical of those in authority over us, focusing only on their weaknesses. We cannot excuse sin, but we should respect the position of those in authority, whether at work, at church, or in government. First Thessalonians 5.12, 13 gives instructions for honoring church leaders. Romans 13.1ff gives instructions for relating to government leaders.

10.13, 14 Saul's disobedience was both active and passive; he not only did wrong, but he *failed to do right.* He actively disobeyed by attempting murder, ignoring God's instructions, and seeking guidance from a witch. He passively disobeyed by neglecting to ask God for guidance as he ran the kingdom. Obedience, too, is both passive and active. It is not enough just to avoid what is wrong, we need to actively pursue what is right.

10.13, 14 In the account in 1 Samuel 28, Saul asked the Lord for guidance but received no answer; this account says he "did not seek guidance from the Lord." The answer to this apparent contradiction lies in understanding Saul's motives. His frantic requests to God came only when he had tried everything his own way. He never went to God unless there was nowhere else to turn. When he finally asked, God refused to answer. Saul sought God only when it suited him, and God rejected him for his constant stubbornness and rebellion.

10.14 Throughout much of Saul's reign, David was forced to hide from him (1 Samuel 19–30). During this time David had opportunities to kill Saul (1 Samuel 24; 26) and to assume the throne that God had promised him (1 Samuel 16.1–13). But David trusted in God's promise that he would be king in God's good timing. It was not up to David to decide when Saul's reign would end. During this battle, God ended Saul's reign just as he had promised.

10.14 Why does this verse say that the Lord killed Saul, when Saul took his own life (1 Samuel 31.3, 4)? God had rejected Saul because of his stubbornness and rebellion (1 Samuel 15.22–26) and judged him for his sins (1 Samuel 28.16–19). God arranged a defeat in battle so Saul would die and his kingdom would be taken from his family. If Saul had not taken his own life, the Philistine soldiers would have killed him.

11.1, 2 The details of how David came to power are told more completely in 2 Samuel. Chronicles emphasizes that *God* brought David to power, although he used the efforts of many people, even some of Saul's own family. God is still sovereign over history, directing events to accomplish his will. The books of Chronicles demonstrate that no matter what people may do to hinder God's work, God still controls all events and works his will in them.

11.3, 4 David was king over Judah for seven and a half years before he captured Jerusalem. When David was finally anointed king over all Israel, 20 years had passed since Samuel had anointed him (1 Samuel 16.1–13). God's promises are worth waiting for, even when his timetable doesn't match our expectations or desires.

11.4 David chose Jerusalem as his capital for both political and military reasons. Jerusalem was near the center of the kingdom and, because it rested on a tribal border, was in neutral territory. Thus its location decreased tribal jealousies. Jerusalem also sat on a high ridge, making it difficult to attack. (For more information on the city of Jerusalem, see the note on 2 Samuel 5.6.)

will not come in here." Nevertheless David took the stronghold of Zion, now the
city of David. 6 David had said, "Whoever attacks the Jebusites first shall be chief **11.6**
and commander." And Joab son of Zeruiah went up first, so he became chief. 7 Da- 2 Sam 8.16
vid resided in the stronghold; therefore it was called the city of David. 8 He built the
city all around, from the Millo in complete circuit; and Joab repaired the rest of the **11.9**
city. 9 And David became greater and greater, for the LORD of hosts was with him. 2 Sam 3.1

David's bravest warriors

10 Now these are the chiefs of David's warriors, who gave him strong support **11.10**
in his kingdom, together with all Israel, to make him king, according to the word 2 Sam 23.8-39
of the LORD concerning Israel. 11 This is an account of David's mighty warriors: 1 Chron 11.3 **11.11**
Jashobeam, son of Hachmoni,[y] was chief of the Three;[z] he wielded his spear 2 Sam 23.8
against three hundred whom he killed at one time. 2 Chron 27.2

12 And next to him among the three warriors was Eleazar son of Dodo, the **11.12**
Ahohite. 13 He was with David at Pas-dammim when the Philistines were gathered 1 Chron 27.4 **11.13**
there for battle. There was a plot of ground full of barley. Now the people had fled 2 Sam 23.11,12
from the Philistines, 14 but he and David took their stand in the middle of the plot,
defended it, and killed the Philistines; and the LORD saved them by a great victory.

15 Three of the thirty chiefs went down to the rock to David at the cave of **11.15**
Adullam, while the army of Philistines was encamped in the valley of Rephaim. 1 Chron 14.9
16 David was then in the stronghold; and the garrison of the Philistines was then at **11.16**
Bethlehem. 17 David said longingly, "O that someone would give me water to drink 1 Sam 10.5
from the well of Bethlehem that is by the gate!" 18 Then the Three broke through the
camp of the Philistines, and drew water from the well of Bethlehem that was by the
gate, and they brought it to David. But David would not drink of it; he poured it out
to the LORD, 19 and said, "My God forbid that I should do this. Can I drink the blood
of these men? For at the risk of their lives they brought it." Therefore he would not
drink it. The three warriors did these things.

20 Now Abishai,[a] the brother of Joab, was chief of the Thirty.[b] With his spear
he fought against three hundred and killed them, and won a name beside the Three.
21 He was the most renowned[c] of the Thirty,[b] and became their commander; but he
did not attain to the Three.

22 Benaiah son of Jehoiada was a valiant man[d] of Kabzeel, a doer of great **11.22**
deeds; he struck down two sons of[e] Ariel of Moab. He also went down and killed 2 Sam 8.18
a lion in a pit on a day when snow had fallen. 23 And he killed an Egyptian, a man
of great stature, five cubits tall. The Egyptian had in his hand a spear like a
weaver's beam; but Benaiah went against him with a staff, snatched the spear out
of the Egyptian's hand, and killed him with his own spear. 24 Such were the things
Benaiah son of Jehoiada did, and he won a name beside the three warriors. 25 He
was renowned among the Thirty, but he did not attain to the Three. And David put
him in charge of his bodyguard.

26 The warriors of the armies were Asahel brother of Joab, Elhanan son of

[y] Or *a Hachmonite* [z] Compare 2 Sam 23.8: Heb *Thirty* or *captains* [a] Gk Vg Tg Compare 2 Sam 23.18: Heb *Abshai* [b] Syr: Heb *Three* [c] Compare 2 Sam 23.19: Heb *more renowned among the two* [d] Syr: Heb *the son of a valiant man* [e] See 2 Sam 23.20: Heb lacks *sons of*

11.8 *Millo* means "filling," and may refer to a fortress built to fill a gap in the defenses and complete the "circuit" around Jerusalem.

11.9 David's power and fame increased as a direct result of his consistent trust in God. In contrast, Saul's power and fame decreased because he wanted all the credit for himself and ignored God (1 Samuel 15.17–26). Those who are concerned about building a name for themselves risk losing the very recognition they crave. Like David, we should be concerned for righteousness, honesty, and excellence, and leave the results to God.

11.12–14 Eleazar's action changed the course of a battle. When everyone around him ran, he held his ground and was saved by the Lord. In any struggle, fear can keep us from taking a stand for God and from participating in God's victories. Face your fear head on. If you are grounded in God, victory comes when you hold that ground.

11.15 The 30 chiefs were the most courageous and highest-ranking officers of David's army.

11.15–19 These three men risked their lives just to please David. David recognized that their devotion to him was inspired by their devotion to God, so he poured out the water as a drink offering, demonstrating that only God is worthy of such devotion. They gave the water to David and he, in turn, gave it to God. Just as these men gave of themselves to serve David, we should put aside our own interests to serve other Christians (Romans 12.10). When we serve others, we are also serving God.

11.23 Five cubits is equivalent to 2.3 meters, or over seven feet.

Dodo of Bethlehem, 27 Shammoth of Harod,[f] Helez the Pelonite, 28 Ira son of Ikkesh of Tekoa, Abiezer of Anathoth, 29 Sibbecai the Hushathite, Ilai the Ahohite,
30 Maharai of Netophah, Heled son of Baanah of Netophah, 31 Ithai son of Ribai of
Gibeah of the Benjaminites, Benaiah of Pirathon, 32 Hurai of the wadis of Gaash,
Abiel the Arbathite, 33 Azmaveth of Baharum, Eliahba of Shaalbon, 34 Hashem[g]
the Gizonite, Jonathan son of Shagee the Hararite, 35 Ahiam son of Sachar the Hararite, Eliphal son of Ur, 36 Hepher the Mecherathite, Ahijah the Pelonite, 37 Hezro
of Carmel, Naarai son of Ezbai, 38 Joel the brother of Nathan, Mibhar son of Hagri,
39 Zelek the Ammonite, Naharai of Beeroth, the armor-bearer of Joab son of Zeruiah, 40 Ira the Ithrite, Gareb the Ithrite, 41 Uriah the Hittite, Zabad son of Ahlai,
42 Adina son of Shiza the Reubenite, a leader of the Reubenites, and thirty with
him, 43 Hanan son of Maacah, and Joshaphat the Mithnite, 44 Uzzia the Ashterath-
ite, Shama and Jeiel sons of Hotham the Aroerite, 45 Jediael son of Shimri, and his
brother Joha the Tizite, 46 Eliel the Mahavite, and Jeribai and Joshaviah sons of
Elnaam, and Ithmah the Moabite, 47 Eliel, and Obed, and Jaasiel the Mezobaite.

Warriors join David

12.1 1 Sam 27.2,3 **12** The following are those who came to David at Ziklag, while he could not
move about freely because of Saul son of Kish; they were among the mighty
12.2 Judg 3.15; 20.16 warriors who helped him in war. 2 They were archers, and could shoot arrows and
sling stones with either the right hand or the left; they were Benjaminites, Saul's
kindred. 3 The chief was Ahiezer, then Joash, both sons of Shemaah of Gibeah; also
Jeziel and Pelet sons of Azmaveth; Beracah, Jehu of Anathoth, 4 Ishmaiah of Gibeon, a warrior among the Thirty and a leader over the Thirty; Jeremiah,[h] Jahaziel,
Johanan, Jozabad of Gederah, 5 Eluzai,[i] Jerimoth, Bealiah, Shemariah, Shephatiah the Haruphite; 6 Elkanah, Isshiah, Azarel, Joezer, and Jashobeam, the Korahites; 7 and Joelah and Zebadiah, sons of Jeroham of Gedor.
12.8 2 Sam 2.18 8 From the Gadites there went over to David at the stronghold in the wilderness
mighty and experienced warriors, expert with shield and spear, whose faces were
like the faces of lions, and who were swift as gazelles on the mountains: 9 Ezer the
chief, Obadiah second, Eliab third, 10 Mishmannah fourth, Jeremiah fifth, 11 Attai
sixth, Eliel seventh, 12 Johanan eighth, Elzabad ninth, 13 Jeremiah tenth, Machban-
12.14 Deut 32.30 nai eleventh. 14 These Gadites were officers of the army, the least equal to a hundred and the greatest to a thousand. 15 These are the men who crossed the Jordan in
12.15 Josh 3.15; 4.18 the first month, when it was overflowing all its banks, and put to flight all those in
the valleys, to the east and to the west.
12.16 1 Sam 22.7 16 Some Benjaminites and Judahites came to the stronghold to David. 17 David

[f] Compare 2 Sam 23.25: Heb *the Harorite* [g] Compare Gk and 2 Sam 23.32: Heb *the sons of Hashem* [h] Heb verse 5 [i] Heb verse 6

11.32 A wadi is a stream or dry riverbed.

12.1 Ziklag was a city in Philistia where David had escaped to hide from Saul. Achish, the Philistine ruler of the area, was happy to have a famous Israelite warrior defect to his land. He did not know, however, that David was only pretending loyalty. Achish gave the city of Ziklag to David, his family, and his army (1 Samuel 27.5–7). David's whereabouts were not a great secret, and many loyal followers joined him there.

12.1ff David surrounded himself with great warriors, the best of the Israelite army. What qualities made them worthy to be David's warriors and servants? (1) They had practiced long and hard to perfect their skills (with bow, sling, or spear); (2) they were mentally tough and determined ("whose faces were like the faces of lions," 12.8); (3) they were physically in shape ("swift as gazelles," 12.8); and (4) they were dedicated to serving God and David. Weak leaders are easily threatened by competent subordinates, but strong leaders surround themselves with the best. They are not intimidated by able and competent followers.

12.1–7 All the warriors mentioned here were from the tribe of Benjamin. Even members of Saul's own tribe (1 Samuel 9.1, 2) were deserting him to help David become king of all Israel. It was clear to them that God had chosen David to be Israel's next leader.

12.2 Archers and slingers had special weapons. The sling was unassuming in appearance but deadly in battle. A shallow leather pouch with a cord of leather or goat's hair attached to each side, the sling was whirled around the head and sent a stone to its target. The bow and arrow had been in use for thousands of years. Arrowheads were made of stone, wood, or bone because the Philistines still had a monopoly on metalworking (1 Samuel 13.19, 20). Arrow shafts were made of reed or wood, and bowstrings were made of animal gut.

12.8 While the men of Benjamin were expert archers and slingers, the warriors of Gad were experts with the shield and spear. Israelite spears had wood shafts and spearheads of bone or stone and were often thrown through the air toward their mark. Philistine spears had bronze shafts and iron spearheads, and their shields were made of wood and overlaid with leather. Large shields were often carried by an armor-bearer, whose main task was to protect the warrior.

went out to meet them and said to them, "If you have come to me in friendship, to
help me, then my heart will be knit to you; but if you have come to betray me to my
adversaries, though my hands have done no wrong, then may the God of our ancestors see and give judgment." 18 Then the spirit came upon Amasai, chief of the **12.18**
Thirty, and he said, Judg 3.10; 6.34 1 Chron 2.17

"We are yours, O David;
 and with you, O son of Jesse!
Peace, peace to you,
 and peace to the one who helps you!
 For your God is the one who helps you."

Then David received them, and made them officers of his troops.
19 Some of the Manassites deserted to David when he came with the Philistines **12.19**
for the battle against Saul. (Yet he did not help them, for the rulers of the Philistines 1 Sam 29.3,4
took counsel and sent him away, saying, "He will desert to his master Saul at the
cost of our heads.") 20 As he went to Ziklag these Manassites deserted to him: Adnah, Jozabad, Jediael, Michael, Jozabad, Elihu, and Zillethai, chiefs of the thousands in Manasseh. 21 They helped David against the band of raiders,[j] for they **12.21**
were all warriors and commanders in the army. 22 Indeed from day to day people 1 Sam 30.1
kept coming to David to help him, until there was a great army, like an army of **12.22** Josh 5.13-15
God.
23 These are the numbers of the divisions of the armed troops who came to **12.23**
David in Hebron to turn the kingdom of Saul over to him, according to the word of 2 Sam 2.3,4 1 Chron 10.14
the LORD. 24 The people of Judah bearing shield and spear numbered six thousand 11.10
eight hundred armed troops. 25 Of the Simeonites, mighty warriors, seven thousand **12.24**
one hundred. 26 Of the Levites four thousand six hundred. 27 Jehoiada, leader of the 2 Sam 2.8,9 8.17
house of Aaron, and with him three thousand seven hundred. 28 Zadok, a young 1 Chron 6.8,53 12.2
warrior, and twenty-two commanders from his own ancestral house. 29 Of the Ben- Esth 1.13 Ps 12.2
jaminites, the kindred of Saul, three thousand, of whom the majority had continued
to keep their allegiance to the house of Saul. 30 Of the Ephraimites, twenty thousand
eight hundred, mighty warriors, notables in their ancestral houses. 31 Of the half-
tribe of Manasseh, eighteen thousand, who were expressly named to come and
make David king. 32 Of Issachar, those who had understanding of the times, to
know what Israel ought to do, two hundred chiefs, and all their kindred under their
command. 33 Of Zebulun, fifty thousand seasoned troops, equipped for battle with
all the weapons of war, to help David[k] with singleness of purpose. 34 Of Naphtali,
a thousand commanders, with whom there were thirty-seven thousand armed with
shield and spear. 35 Of the Danites, twenty-eight thousand six hundred equipped for
battle. 36 Of Asher, forty thousand seasoned troops ready for battle. 37 Of the Reu-

[j] Or *as officers of his troops* [k] Gk: Heb lacks *David*

12.18 How did the Holy Spirit work in Old Testament times? When there was an important job to be done, God chose a person to do it, and the Spirit gave that person the needed power and ability. The Spirit gave Bezaleel artistic ability (Exodus 31.1–5), Jephthah military prowess (Judges 11.29), David power to rule (1 Samuel 16.13), and Zechariah an authoritative word of prophecy (2 Chronicles 24.20). Here the Holy Spirit came upon David's warriors. The Spirit came upon individuals in order to accomplish specific goals. Beginning at pentecost, however, the Spirit came upon all believers, not only to empower them to do God's will, but also to dwell in them day by day (Acts 2.14–21).

12.22 David's army was so large and powerful that it was compared to "an army of God." Men were drawn to David by the reputation of his great warriors, the news of their victories, and their desire to see God's will done in making David king. People are often drawn to a great cause and the brave, determined people who support it. As believers, we have the greatest cause—the salvation of mankind. If we are brave, determined, and faithful, others will be drawn to work with us.

12.26–29 In Numbers 1.47–50, God said the Levites were to be exempt from military service. Why then are they listed as part of David's army? Although they were exempt from the draft, they strongly supported David and volunteered their services to help install him as king.

12.32 The 200 leaders from the tribe of Issachar understood the temper of the times. As a result, their knowledge and judgment provided needed help in making decisions for the nation. For leaders today, it is equally necessary to know what is happening in society in order to plan the best course of action for the church. Knowledge of current events, trends, and needs helps one understand people's thoughts and attitudes. This helps leaders make wise decisions for the church and make God's message relevant to people's lives.

benites and Gadites and the half-tribe of Manasseh from beyond the Jordan, one
hundred twenty thousand armed with all the weapons of war.
12.38 2 Sam 5.1-3 1 Chron 12.33
38 All these, warriors arrayed in battle order, came to Hebron with full intent to
make David king over all Israel; likewise all the rest of Israel were of a single mind
to make David king. 39 They were there with David for three days, eating and drink-
12.40 1 Sam 25.18
ing, for their kindred had provided for them. 40 And also their neighbors, from as
far away as Issachar and Zebulun and Naphtali, came bringing food on donkeys,
camels, mules, and oxen—abundant provisions of meal, cakes of figs, clusters of
raisins, wine, oil, oxen, and sheep, for there was joy in Israel.

2. David brings the ark to Jerusalem

Uzza touches the ark and dies

13 David consulted with the commanders of the thousands and of the hundreds,
with every leader. 2 David said to the whole assembly of Israel, "If it seems
good to you, and if it is the will of the LORD our God, let us send abroad to our
kindred who remain in all the land of Israel, including the priests and Levites in the
13.3 1 Sam 7.1,2
cities that have pasture lands, that they may come together to us. 3 Then let us bring
again the ark of our God to us; for we did not turn to it in the days of Saul." 4 The
13.5 1 Sam 6.21; 7.1 2 Sam 6.1 1 Kgs 8.65 1 Chron 15.3
whole assembly agreed to do so, for the thing pleased all the people.
5 So David assembled all Israel from the Shihor of Egypt to Lebo-hamath, to
bring the ark of God from Kiriath-jearim. 6 And David and all Israel went up to
13.6 Josh 15.9 2 Kgs 19.15
Baalah, that is, to Kiriath-jearim, which belongs to Judah, to bring up from there
the ark of God, the LORD, who is enthroned on the cherubim, which is called by
13.7 1 Sam 7.1
his[l] name. 7 They carried the ark of God on a new cart, from the house of Abinadab, and Uzzah and Ahio[m] were driving the cart. 8 David and all Israel were danc-
13.8 1 Chron 15.16
ing before God with all their might, with song and lyres and harps and tambourines
and cymbals and trumpets.
13.9 2 Sam 6.6
9 When they came to the threshing floor of Chidon, Uzzah put out his hand to

[l] Heb lacks *his* [m] Or *and his brother*

12.38 These troops totaled more than 300,000 men. Their goal this day was to show overwhelming support for David and make him king. God had drawn these men together and had focused their energy on a single purpose; they "were of a single mind." Churches and organizations may dilute their energy by trying to go in too many directions. Instead, they should ask God to focus their thoughts on one central purpose—one that will build up the church and glorify God. Like David's army, churches and other Christian groups should be of one mind.

12.40 The people were ready for change. They had suffered under Saul's leadership because of his disobedience of God (see 10.13). They were so overjoyed with David's coronation that they contributed lavishly to the celebration. It is right and proper to give generously for celebration and joyous worship. God is the author of joy, and he will join us in our celebrations.

13.1 David took time to consult with all his officers. As king, he had ultimate authority and could have given orders on his own, but he chose to involve others in leadership. Perhaps this is why there was unanimous support for his decisions (13.1–5). When we are in charge, it is tempting to make unilateral decisions, pushing through our own opinions. But effective leaders listen carefully to others' opinions, and they encourage others to participate in making decisions. However, we should always consult God first. We can run into big problems if we don't talk to God (see the note on 13.10).

13.1ff The parallel account of moving the ark (1 Samuel 5; 6) shows that David's building projects were completed *before* he brought the ark to Jerusalem. The writer of Chronicles puts the moving of the ark first in order to highlight David's spiritual accomplishments and relationship to God.

13.3 The ark of God is also called the ark of the covenant. The most sacred object of the Hebrew faith, it was a large box containing the stone tablets on which God had written the ten commandments (Exodus 25.10–22). David had already made Jerusalem his political capital (11.4–9). Now he brought the ark there in order to make Jerusalem the nation's center for worship.

13.3 The ark of God had been in Kiriath-jearim for many years. The neglect of the ark symbolized Israel's neglect of God. Bringing the ark back to the center of Israel's life reflected David's desire to remind the nation of its true foundation—God. Neglecting those things that remind us of God—the Bible, the church, and contact with Christians—will cause us also to neglect God. We must keep God at the center of our lives.

13.6 Cherubim are mighty angels.

13.8 Worship in the Old Testament was more than a sober religious exercise. David's exuberance as he worshiped God with dancing and music is approved in Scripture. Our worship should reflect a healthy balance: sometimes we should be reflective and serious (see Exodus 19.14ff), and sometimes we should show enthusiasm and jubilation. What do you need—more serious reflection or more joyous celebration?

hold the ark, for the oxen shook it. 10 The anger of the LORD was kindled against **13.10**
Uzzah; he struck him down because he put out his hand to the ark; and he died there Lev 10.2
before God. 11 David was angry because the LORD had burst out against Uzzah; so 1 Chron 15.13, 15
that place is called Perez-uzzah[n] to this day. 12 David was afraid of God that day;
he said, "How can I bring the ark of God into my care?" 13 So David did not take the **13.13**
ark into his care into the city of David; he took it instead to the house of Obed-edom 2 Chron 25.24
the Gittite. 14 The ark of God remained with the household of Obed-edom in his **13.14**
house three months, and the LORD blessed the household of Obed-edom and all that 1 Chron 26.4,5
he had.

David's good fortune

14 King Hiram of Tyre sent messengers to David, along with cedar logs, and **14.1**
masons and carpenters to build a house for him. 2 David then perceived that 2 Sam 5.11
the LORD had established him as king over Israel, and that his kingdom was highly
exalted for the sake of his people Israel.
3 David took more wives in Jerusalem, and David became the father of more
sons and daughters. 4 These are the names of the children whom he had in Jerusa- **14.4**
lem: Shammua, Shobab, and Nathan; Solomon, 5 Ibhar, Elishua, and Elpelet; 6 No- 2 Sam 5.14 1 Chron 3.5-8
gah, Nepheg, and Japhia; 7 Elishama, Beeliada, and Eliphelet.

David conquers the Philistines

8 When the Philistines heard that David had been anointed king over all Israel,
all the Philistines went up in search of David; and David heard of it and went out
against them. 9 Now the Philistines had come and made a raid in the valley of Reph- **14.9**
aim. 10 David inquired of God, "Shall I go up against the Philistines? Will you give 1 Chron 11.15 14.13
them into my hand?" The LORD said to him, "Go up, and I will give them into your
hand." 11 So he went up to Baal-perazim, and David defeated them there. David
said, "God has burst out[o] against my enemies by my hand, like a bursting flood."
Therefore that place is called Baal-perazim.[p] 12 They abandoned their gods there,
and at David's command they were burned.

[n] That is *Bursting Out Against Uzzah* [o] Heb *paraz* [p] That is *Lord of Bursting Out*

13.10 Why did Uzzah die? He touched the ark, and that offense was punishable by death. God had given specific instructions about how the ark was to be moved and carried (Numbers 4.5–15), and these were neglected here. The Levites were responsible to move the ark (there is no record that Uzzah was a Levite), and it was to be carried on their shoulders with poles through its rings (Numbers 7.9). It was *never* to be touched. Bringing the ark on a cart followed the Philistines' example (1 Samuel 6.1ff). Uzzah, though sincere in his desire to protect the ark, had to face the consequences of his sin; and David was reminded that his obedience to God's laws was more important than his enthusiasm. Also David had "consulted with the commanders" (13.1), but he neglected to ask God. The advice of our friends and colleagues is no substitute for God's direction.

13.10–14 Uzzah died instantly for touching the ark, but God blessed Obed-edom's home, where the ark was stored. This demonstrates the two-edged aspect of God's power: he is perfectly loving and perfectly just. Great blessings come to those who obey his commands, but severe punishment comes to those who disobey him. This punishment may come swiftly or over time, but it will come. Sometimes we focus only on the blessings God gives us, while forgetting that when we sin, "It is a fearful thing to fall into the hands of the living God" (Hebrews 10.31). At other times, however, we concentrate so much on doom that we miss his blessings. Don't fall into a one-sided view of God. Along with God's blessings comes the responsibility to live up to his demands for fairness, honesty, and justice.

13.11 David was angry at both God and himself. He knew he had done something wrong in transporting the ark, and he was angry that his plans for the joyous return of the ark had ended in a man's death. But his anger cooled, and he left the ark in Obed-edom's home until he could consider how to get it to Jerusalem. This allowed him to discover God's instructions for transporting the ark. The next trip would be carried out according to God's commands.

14.1 King Hiram also sent lumber and craftsmen to help Solomon build the temple (2 Chronicles 2.1ff).

14.2 God gave David honor and success, but not simply for David's personal gain. David realized that God had prospered him for a special reason – to uplift God's people! Often we are tempted to use our position or possessions only for our own good. Instead, we must remember that God has placed us where we are and given us all we have so that we may encourage and give to others.

14.3 Accumulating wives and concubines was the custom of the day among Middle Eastern royalty, but it was not God's ideal (Genesis 2.24). David's marriages brought him greater power and influence, but they also caused strife, jealousy, and even murder within his family. (See the chart in 2 Samuel 12 for other consequences of polygamy.)

14.8–16 A map of this battle is in 2 Samuel 5.

14.10 Before David went to battle, he talked to God first, asking for his presence and guidance. Too often we wait until we are in trouble before turning to God. By then the consequences of our actions are already unfolding. Do you ask for God's help only as a desperate last resort? Instead, go to him first! Like David, you may receive incredible help and avoid serious trouble.

14.12 David's quick and decisive action against idols helped unify his kingdom and focus the people on worshiping the one true God. He was obeying the law that said, "This is how you must deal with

13 Once again the Philistines made a raid in the valley. 14 When David again
inquired of God, God said to him, "You shall not go up after them; go around and
come on them opposite the balsam trees. 15 When you hear the sound of marching
in the tops of the balsam trees, then go out to battle; for God has gone out before
you to strike down the army of the Philistines." 16 David did as God had commanded him, and they struck down the Philistine army from Gibeon to Gezer.
17 The fame of David went out into all lands, and the LORD brought the fear of him
on all nations.

The Levites carry the ark to Jerusalem

15 David[q] built houses for himself in the city of David, and he prepared a place
for the ark of God and pitched a tent for it. 2 Then David commanded that no
one but the Levites were to carry the ark of God, for the LORD had chosen them to
carry the ark of the LORD and to minister to him forever. 3 David assembled all
Israel in Jerusalem to bring up the ark of the LORD to its place, which he had prepared for it. 4 Then David gathered together the descendants of Aaron and the Levites: 5 of the sons of Kohath, Uriel the chief, with one hundred twenty of his
kindred; 6 of the sons of Merari, Asaiah the chief, with two hundred twenty of his
kindred; 7 of the sons of Gershom, Joel the chief, with one hundred thirty of
his kindred; 8 of the sons of Elizaphan, Shemaiah the chief, with two hundred of his
kindred; 9 of the sons of Hebron, Eliel the chief, with eighty of his kindred; 10 of the
sons of Uzziel, Amminadab the chief, with one hundred twelve of his kindred.
11 David summoned the priests Zadok and Abiathar, and the Levites Uriel,
Asaiah, Joel, Shemaiah, Eliel, and Amminadab. 12 He said to them, "You are the
heads of families of the Levites; sanctify yourselves, you and your kindred, so that
you may bring up the ark of the LORD, the God of Israel, to the place that I have
prepared for it. 13 Because you did not carry it the first time,[r] the LORD our God
burst out against us, because we did not give it proper care." 14 So the priests and
the Levites sanctified themselves to bring up the ark of the LORD, the God of Israel.
15 And the Levites carried the ark of God on their shoulders with the poles, as Moses had commanded according to the word of the LORD.
16 David also commanded the chiefs of the Levites to appoint their kindred as

14.13 1 Chron 14.9
14.17 Ex 15.14 Deut 2.25
15.1 1 Chron 16.1 17.1 Ps 132.2-5
15.2 Num 4.15 Deut 10.8
15.3 2 Sam 6.12,17 1 Kgs 8.1 1 Chron 13.5 15.1,12
15.4 1 Chron 6.16 12.26
15.11 1 Sam 22.20 1 Kgs 2.26,35 1 Chron 12.28
15.12 Ex 19.14,15 2 Chron 35.6
15.15 Ex 25.14 Num 4.5
15.16 1 Chron 13.8 25.1

q Heb *He* r Meaning of Heb uncertain

---

them: break down their altars, smash their pillars, hew down their sacred poles, and burn their idols with fire" (Deuteronomy 7.5). Most of David's successors failed to destroy idols, and this led to unbelievable moral corruption in Israel.

14.12 The soldiers wanted to keep souvenirs from the battle, but David ordered them to burn the idols. The only proper response to sin is to get rid of it completely. You cannot be a follower of God while continuing to hold on to parts of your past life that push God out of the center of your thoughts and actions. Eliminate whatever takes God's rightful place in your life, and follow him with complete devotion.

14.13–16 In almost every new situation, David prayed for guidance. New developments offer us new challenges as well as new risks. We should seek guidance in each new situation. If you seek God's leading in new circumstances, change won't appear as a threat but as an opportunity to let God work in new ways.

15.12 The priests sanctified themselves so they would be prepared to carry the ark. To *sanctify* literally means "to separate," to set apart for sacred purposes, to purify. The priests symbolically separated themselves from sin and evil. This was done by washing themselves and their clothing in a special ceremony (Numbers 8.5–8). While we are not required to carry out this ceremony today, we can purify ourselves by reading God's Word and preparing our hearts to participate in worship.

15.13 David refers to the incident recorded in 13.8–11 and 2 Samuel 6.1–11. As the ark was being brought back to Israel on an ox cart, the oxen stumbled. Uzzah, trying to steady the ark with his hand, was killed instantly for touching it. The mistake was not in David's desire to move the ark, but in his method for its return. David either ignored or was unaware of the specific instructions in God's law about how the ark was to be moved. Obviously he had discovered his mistake and was now preparing to correct it. This incident was a divine object lesson to all Israel that God governed the king and not the other way around. If David were allowed to handle the ark of God carelessly, what would that say to the people about their faith?

15.13–15 When David's first attempt to move the ark failed (13.8–14), he learned an important lesson: when God gives specific instructions, it is wise to follow them precisely. This time David saw to it that the Levites carried the ark (Numbers 4.5–15). We may not fully understand the reasons behind God's instructions, but we do know that his wisdom is complete and his judgment infallible. The way to know God's instructions is to know his Word. But just as children do not understand the reasons for all their parents' instructions until they are older, we may not understand all of God's reasons in this life. It is far better to obey God first, and then discover the reasons. We are never free to disobey God just because we don't understand.

15.16–25 The great musical procession was designed as a worthy accompaniment to the great occasion. It heightened the excitement, elevated the people's hearts and minds, and focused their attention on the event. It also helped seal it in their memory for years to come. Beginning any task by praising God can inspire us to give him our best. Develop the practice of giving praise to God, and you will experience greater joy and strength to face anything.

the singers to play on musical instruments, on harps and lyres and cymbals, to raise
loud sounds of joy. 17 So the Levites appointed Heman son of Joel; and of his kin- **15.17**
dred Asaph son of Berechiah; and of the sons of Merari, their kindred, Ethan son 1 Chron 25.1
of Kushaiah; 18 and with them their kindred of the second order, Zechariah, Jaaziel,
Shemiramoth, Jehiel, Unni, Eliab, Benaiah, Maaseiah, Mattithiah, Eliphelehu,
and Mikneiah, and the gatekeepers Obed-edom and Jeiel. 19 The singers Heman,
Asaph, and Ethan were to sound bronze cymbals; 20 Zechariah, Aziel, Shemira-
moth, Jehiel, Unni, Eliab, Maaseiah, and Benaiah were to play harps according to
Alamoth; 21 but Mattithiah, Eliphelehu, Mikneiah, Obed-edom, Jeiel, and Azaziah
were to lead with lyres according to the Sheminith. 22 Chenaniah, leader of the
Levites in music, was to direct the music, for he understood it. 23 Berechiah and
Elkanah were to be gatekeepers for the ark. 24 Shebaniah, Joshaphat, Nethanel, **15.24**
Amasai, Zechariah, Benaiah, and Eliezer, the priests, were to blow the trumpets 1 Chron 16.6
before the ark of God. Obed-edom and Jehiah also were to be gatekeepers for the
ark.

25 So David and the elders of Israel, and the commanders of the thousands, **15.25**
went to bring up the ark of the covenant of the LORD from the house of Obed-edom 2 Sam 6.12,15
with rejoicing. 26 And because God helped the Levites who were carrying the ark of 1 Chron 13.13 **15.26**
the covenant of the LORD, they sacrificed seven bulls and seven rams. 27 David was Num 23.1,29
clothed with a robe of fine linen, as also were all the Levites who were carrying the
ark, and the singers, and Chenaniah the leader of the music of the singers; and
David wore a linen ephod. 28 So all Israel brought up the ark of the covenant of the
LORD with shouting, to the sound of the horn, trumpets, and cymbals, and made
loud music on harps and lyres.

29 As the ark of the covenant of the LORD came to the city of David, Michal
daughter of Saul looked out of the window, and saw King David leaping and dancing; and she despised him in her heart.

David gives praise to God

16 They brought in the ark of God, and set it inside the tent that David had **16.1**
pitched for it; and they offered burnt offerings and offerings of well-being 2 Sam 6.17 1 Kgs 8.5
before God. 2 When David had finished offering the burnt offerings and the offer- 1 Chron 15.1
ings of well-being, he blessed the people in the name of the LORD; 3 and he distributed to every person in Israel—man and woman alike—to each a loaf of bread, a
portion of meat,[s] and a cake of raisins.

4 He appointed certain of the Levites as ministers before the ark of the LORD, to **16.4**
invoke, to thank, and to praise the LORD, the God of Israel. 5 Asaph was the chief, 1 Chron 15.16
and second to him Zechariah, Jeiel, Shemiramoth, Jehiel, Mattithiah, Eliab, Benaiah, Obed-edom, and Jeiel, with harps and lyres; Asaph was to sound the cymbals,
6 and the priests Benaiah and Jahaziel were to blow trumpets regularly, before the
ark of the covenant of God.

7 Then on that day David first appointed the singing of praises to the LORD by **16.7**
Asaph and his kindred. 2 Sam 22.1

[s] Compare Gk Syr Vg: Meaning of Heb uncertain

15.22 Chenaniah had developed his musical skills, and this led to greater opportunities for service. What natural skills do you have that could be used in God's service? Let Chenaniah's example inspire you to develop and refine them so that you can offer them as valuable gifts to the Lord.

15.29 David was willing to look foolish in the eyes of some people in order to express his thankfulness to God fully and honestly. In contrast, Michal was so disgusted by his undignified actions that she could not rejoice in the ark's return to Jerusalem. Worship had so deteriorated under her father Saul's reign that it had become stilted and ritualistic. Michal could accept David as a military conqueror and as a king, but she could not accept his free and spontaneous expression of praise to God. Some devoted people may look foolish to us in their heartfelt expressions of worship, but we must accept them. In the same way, we should not be afraid to worship God with whatever expressions seem appropriate.

16.4 Certain Levites were appointed to give continual praise and thanks to God. Praise and thanksgiving should be a regular part of our routine, not reserved only for celebrations. Praise God continually, and you will find that you won't take his blessings for granted.

16.7–36 Four elements of true thanksgiving are found in the following song: (1) *remembering* what God has done, (2) *telling* others about it, (3) *showing* God's glory to others, and (4) *offering* gifts of self, time, and resources. Get into the habit of fully expressing your thanks to God.

16.8 1 Kgs 8.43 2 Kgs 19.19 Ps 105.1-15
8 O give thanks to the LORD, call on his name,
make known his deeds among the peoples.
9 Sing to him, sing praises to him,
tell of all his wonderful works.
10 Glory in his holy name;
let the hearts of those who seek the LORD rejoice.
11 Seek the LORD and his strength,
seek his presence continually.
16.12 Ps 78.43; 103.2
12 Remember the wonderful works he has done,
his miracles, and the judgments he uttered,
13 O offspring of his servant Israel,[t]
children of Jacob, his chosen ones.

16.14 Ps 48.10
14 He is the LORD our God;
his judgments are in all the earth.
15 Remember his covenant forever,
the word that he commanded, for a thousand generations,
16.16 Gen 17.2 22.16-18; 26.3
16 the covenant that he made with Abraham,
his sworn promise to Isaac,
16.17 Gen 35.11,12
17 which he confirmed to Jacob as a statute,
to Israel as an everlasting covenant,
16.18 Gen 13.15
18 saying, "To you I will give the land of Canaan
as your portion for an inheritance."

16.19 Gen 34.30 Deut 7.7
19 When they were few in number,
of little account, and strangers in the land,[u]
20 wandering from nation to nation,
from one kingdom to another people,
16.21 Gen 12.17; 20.3 Ex 7.15
21 he allowed no one to oppress them;
he rebuked kings on their account,
16.22 Gen 20.7
22 saying, "Do not touch my anointed ones;
do my prophets no harm."

16.23 Ps 96.1-13
23 Sing to the LORD, all the earth.
Tell of his salvation from day to day.
24 Declare his glory among the nations,
his marvelous works among all the peoples.
16.25 Ps 89.7 144.3,4
25 For great is the LORD, and greatly to be praised;
he is to be revered above all gods.
16.26 Lev 19.4 Ps 102.25
26 For all the gods of the peoples are idols,
but the LORD made the heavens.
27 Honor and majesty are before him;
strength and joy are in his place.

28 Ascribe to the LORD, O families of the peoples,
ascribe to the LORD glory and strength.
16.29 Ps 29.2
29 Ascribe to the LORD the glory due his name;
bring an offering, and come before him.

[t] Another reading is *Abraham* (compare Ps 105.6) [u] Heb *in it*

16.8ff Several parts of this song are parallel to songs in the book of Psalms: 16.8–22 with Psalm 105.1–15; 16.23–33 with Psalm 96; 16.34–36 with Psalm 106.1, 47, 48.

16.15–18 This covenant was given to Abraham (Genesis 15.18–21), and then passed on to Isaac (Genesis 26.24, 25) and Jacob (Genesis 28.13–15). God promised to give the land of Canaan (present-day Israel) to their descendants. He also promised that the Messiah would come from their line.

16.25 The basis of praise is declaring God's character and attributes in the presence of others. When we recognize and affirm his goodness we are holding up his perfect moral nature for all to see. Praise benefits us because it takes our minds off our problems and needs and focuses on God's power, mercy, majesty, and love.

16.29 Genuine praise also involves "ascribing glory" to God. Remember this in your worship – give God all the glory.

Worship the LORD in holy splendor;
30 tremble before him, all the earth.
The world is firmly established; it shall never be moved.
31 Let the heavens be glad, and let the earth rejoice,
and let them say among the nations, "The LORD is king!"
32 Let the sea roar, and all that fills it;
let the field exult, and everything in it.
33 Then shall the trees of the forest sing for joy
before the LORD, for he comes to judge the earth.
34 O give thanks to the LORD, for he is good;
for his steadfast love endures forever.

35 Say also:
"Save us, O God of our salvation,
and gather and rescue us from among the nations,
that we may give thanks to your holy name,
and glory in your praise.
36 Blessed be the LORD, the God of Israel,
from everlasting to everlasting."
Then all the people said "Amen!" and praised the LORD.
37 David left Asaph and his kinsfolk there before the ark of the covenant of the
LORD to minister regularly before the ark as each day required, 38 and also Obed-
edom and his[v] sixty-eight kinsfolk; while Obed-edom son of Jeduthun and Hosah
were to be gatekeepers. 39 And he left the priest Zadok and his kindred the priests
before the tabernacle of the LORD in the high place that was at Gibeon, 40 to offer
burnt offerings to the LORD on the altar of burnt offering regularly, morning and
evening, according to all that is written in the law of the LORD that he commanded
Israel. 41 With them were Heman and Jeduthun, and the rest of those chosen and
expressly named to render thanks to the LORD, for his steadfast love endures forever. 42 Heman and Jeduthun had with them trumpets and cymbals for the music,
and instruments for sacred song. The sons of Jeduthun were appointed to the gate.
43 Then all the people departed to their homes, and David went home to bless
his household.

God promises blessing to David

17 Now when David settled in his house, David said to the prophet Nathan, "I
am living in a house of cedar, but the ark of the covenant of the LORD is
under a tent." 2 Nathan said to David, "Do all that you have in mind, for God is with
you."
3 But that same night the word of the LORD came to Nathan, saying: 4 Go and
tell my servant David: Thus says the LORD: You shall not build me a house to live
in. 5 For I have not lived in a house since the day I brought out Israel to this very
day, but I have lived in a tent and a tabernacle.[w] 6 Wherever I have moved about

[v] Gk Syr Vg: Heb *their* [w] Gk 2 Sam 7.6: Heb *but I have been from tent to tent and from tabernacle*

16.31 Ps 93.1; 96.10 Isa 44.23; 49.13
16.32 Ps 98.7
16.34 Ps 106.1; 136.1
16.35 Ps 106.47,48
16.36 Deut 27.15 1 Kgs 8.15,56 Neh 8.6 Ps 72.18
16.37 2 Chron 8.14 Ezra 3.4
16.38 1 Chron 13.14 26.10
16.39 1 Kgs 3.4 1 Chron 15.11
16.40 Ex 29.38 Num 28.3,4
16.41 1 Chron 6.33 25.1 2 Chron 5.13
16.42 1 Chron 25.7 2 Chron 7.6 29.27
17.1 2 Sam 7.1,2
17.4 1 Chron 28.3 Acts 7.42
17.5 Ex 40.2,3 2 Sam 7.6
17.6 2 Sam 7.7

16.37 Asaph and his fellow Levites ministered in the temple, doing each day whatever was needed. To carry out God's work is not merely to engage in religious exercises. It includes other necessary tasks. Even if you don't have the opportunity to teach or preach, God can use you in the ministry. What needs to be done? Cleaning, serving, singing, planning, administering? Look for ways to minister each day.

16.39 David brought the ark to Jerusalem although the tabernacle was still at Gibeon. His plan was to reunite the tabernacle and ark in a new temple at Jerusalem which would then become Israel's only worship center. The temple, however, was not built until Solomon's time. In the meantime, Israel had two worship centers and two high priests (15.11), one at Gibeon and one at Jerusalem.

17.1 David felt disturbed that the ark, the symbol of God's presence, sat in a tent while he lived in a beautiful palace. David's desire was right, but his timing was wrong. God told David *not* to build a temple (17.3, 4), and David was willing to abide by God's timing. If you live in comparative luxury while God's work, house, or ministers go lacking, perhaps God wants you to change the situation. Like David, take action to correct the imbalance, but be willing to move according to God's timing.

17.3–14 God did not want a warrior to build his temple (28.3; 1 Kings 5.3), and David had shed much blood in unifying the nation as God had commanded. So the honor of building the temple would go to David's son Solomon. David would pass on to Solomon a peaceful and united kingdom, ready to begin work on a beautiful temple.

among all Israel, did I ever speak a word with any of the judges of Israel, whom I
commanded to shepherd my people, saying, Why have you not built me a house of
cedar? 7 Now therefore thus you shall say to my servant David: Thus says the LORD
of hosts: I took you from the pasture, from following the sheep, to be ruler over my
people Israel; 8 and I have been with you wherever you went, and have cut off all
your enemies before you; and I will make for you a name, like the name of the great
ones of the earth. 9 I will appoint a place for my people Israel, and will plant them,
so that they may live in their own place, and be disturbed no more; and evildoers
shall wear them down no more, as they did formerly, 10 from the time that I appointed judges over my people Israel; and I will subdue all your enemies.
17.11 Moreover I declare to you that the LORD will build you a house. 11 When your
2 Sam 7.12 days are fulfilled to go to be with your ancestors, I will raise up your offspring after
1 Kgs 2.4; 5.5 8.25 you, one of your own sons, and I will establish his kingdom. 12 He shall build a
17.13 house for me, and I will establish his throne forever. 13 I will be a father to him, and
1 Chron 10.14 he shall be a son to me. I will not take my steadfast love from him, as I took it from
Heb 1.5 him who was before you, 14 but I will confirm him in my house and in my kingdom
forever, and his throne shall be established forever. 15 In accordance with all these
words and all this vision, Nathan spoke to David.

David's prayer of acceptance

16 Then King David went in and sat before the LORD, and said, "Who am I,
17.17 O LORD God, and what is my house, that you have brought me thus far? 17 And
2 Sam 7.19 even this was a small thing in your sight, O God; you have also spoken of your
servant's house for a great while to come. You regard me as someone of high
rank,[x] O LORD God! 18 And what more can David say to you for honoring your
17.19 servant? You know your servant. 19 For your servant's sake, O LORD, and accord-
2 Sam 7.21 ing to your own heart, you have done all these great deeds, making known all these
Isa 37.35 great things. 20 There is no one like you, O LORD, and there is no God besides you,
according to all that we have heard with our ears. 21 Who is like your people Israel,
one nation on the earth whom God went to redeem to be his people, making for
yourself a name for great and terrible things, in driving out nations before your
17.22 people whom you redeemed from Egypt? 22 And you made your people Israel to be
Ex 19.5,6 your people forever; and you, O LORD, became their God.
23 "And now, O LORD, as for the word that you have spoken concerning your
servant and concerning his house, let it be established forever, and do as you have
17.24 promised. 24 Thus your name will be established and magnified forever in the say-
2 Sam 7.12,16 ing, 'The LORD of hosts, the God of Israel, is Israel's God'; and the house of your
1 Kgs 2.4; 8.25 servant David will be established in your presence. 25 For you, my God, have revealed to your servant that you will build a house for him; therefore your servant
has found it possible to pray before you. 26 And now, O LORD, you are God, and
you have promised this good thing to your servant; 27 therefore may it please you to

[x] Meaning of Heb uncertain

17.10 God promised to subdue David's enemies. Chapters 18–20 tell how God kept that promise.

17.12–14 Why, after this eternal promise, were the Israelites eventually taken from the promised land into captivity? The promise to David had two parts. The first part was conditional: as long as David's descendants followed God's laws and honored him, they would continually be on the throne of Israel. The second part was unconditional: a son of David would occupy his throne forever. This was Jesus the Messiah. The first part of the promise was based on the faithful obedience of David's descendants. The second part would come true regardless of the way his descendants acted.

17.16–20 God told David that Solomon would be given the honor of building the temple. David responded with deep humility, not resentment. This king who had conquered his enemies and was loved by his people said, "Who am I, . . . that you have brought me thus far?" David recognized that God was the *true* king. God has done just as much for us, and he plans to do even more! Like David, we should humble ourselves and give glory to God, saying, "There is no one like you, O Lord." When God chooses someone else to implement your ideas, will you respond with such humility?

17.16–27 David prayed by humbling himself (17.16–18), praising God (17.19, 20), recognizing God's blessings (17.21, 22), and accepting God's decisions, promises, and commands (17.23, 24). Sometimes we are quick to make requests to God and to tell him our troubles, but these other dimensions of prayer can deepen our spiritual life. Take time to praise God, to count his blessings, and to affirm your commitment to do what he has already said to do.

17.21 David's reference to Israel's exodus from Egypt would have had special significance to the original readers of 1 Chronicles who were either beginning or had just completed a second great exodus back to Israel from captivity in Babylon. Remembering God's promises, mercy, and protection during the first exodus would have encouraged the exiles returning once again to Israel, just as God had promised.

bless the house of your servant, that it may continue forever before you. For you,
O LORD, have blessed and are blessed[y] forever."

3. David's military exploits

David conquers many enemies

18 Some time afterward, David attacked the Philistines and subdued them; he 18.1 2 Sam 8.1
took Gath and its villages from the Philistines.
2 He defeated Moab, and the Moabites became subject to David and brought
tribute.
3 David also struck down King Hadadezer of Zobah, toward Hamath,[z] as he
went to set up a monument at the river Euphrates. 4 David took from him one thousand chariots, seven thousand cavalry, and twenty thousand foot soldiers. David
hamstrung all the chariot horses, but left one hundred of them. 5 When the Arameans of Damascus came to help King Hadadezer of Zobah, David killed twenty-two
thousand Arameans. 6 Then David put garrisons[a] in Aram of Damascus; and the
Arameans became subject to David, and brought tribute. The LORD gave victory to
David wherever he went. 7 David took the gold shields that were carried by the
servants of Hadadezer, and brought them to Jerusalem. 8 From Tibhath and from
Cun, cities of Hadadezer, David took a vast quantity of bronze; with it Solomon
made the bronze sea and the pillars and the vessels of bronze.
9 When King Tou of Hamath heard that David had defeated the whole army of
King Hadadezer of Zobah, 10 he sent his son Hadoram to King David, to greet him
and to congratulate him, because he had fought against Hadadezer and defeated
him. Now Hadadezer had often been at war with Tou. He sent all sorts of articles
of gold, of silver, and of bronze; 11 these also King David dedicated to the LORD,
together with the silver and gold that he had carried off from all the nations, from
Edom, Moab, the Ammonites, the Philistines, and Amalek.
12 Abishai son of Zeruiah killed eighteen thousand Edomites in the Valley of
Salt. 13 He put garrisons in Edom; and all the Edomites became subject to David.
And the LORD gave victory to David wherever he went.
14 So David reigned over all Israel; and he administered justice and equity to all
his people. 15 Joab son of Zeruiah was over the army; Jehoshaphat son of Ahilud 18.15
was recorder; 16 Zadok son of Ahitub and Ahimelech son of Abiathar were priests; 1 Chron 11.6
Shavsha was secretary; 17 Benaiah son of Jehoiada was over the Cherethites and the
Pelethites; and David's sons were the chief officials in the service of the king.

[y] Or *and it is blessed* [z] Meaning of Heb uncertain [a] Gk Vg 2 Sam 8.6 Compare Syr: Heb lacks *garrisons*

DAVID SUBDUES HIS ENEMIES
David expanded his kingdom as the Lord continued to give him victory. He subdued the Philistines by taking Gath, conquered Moab, won battles as far north as Zobah and Hamath (conquering Syria when they came to help these enemy nations), and subdued the other surrounding nations of Ammon and Amalek.

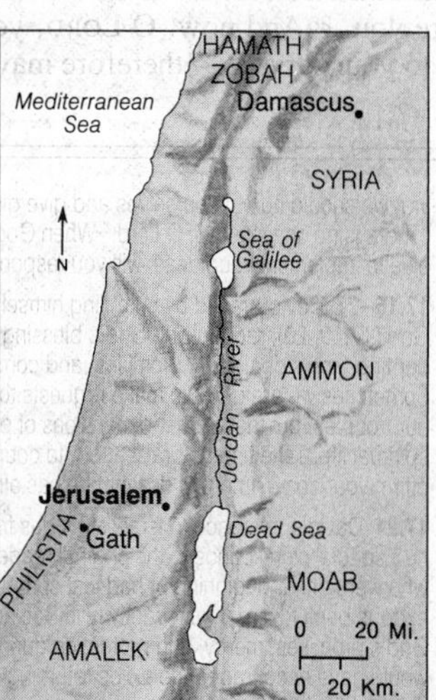

18.2 In 2 Samuel 8.1, 2, it is recorded that David killed two-thirds of the people of Moab. His ancestor, Ruth, was originally from the land of Moab.

18.6, 14 David was a victorious and just ruler. We see in David's glowing success a hint of what Christ's reign will be like—complete victory and justice. If David's glory was great, how much greater will Christ's glory be! The great news for us is that we can be rightly related to Jesus Christ through faith. One day we will share in his glory as we reign with him.

18.9–11 When David received gifts from King Tou, he dedicated them to God, realizing that all had come from him and was to be used for him. It is easy to think that our financial and material blessings are the result of our own skill and hard work rather than coming from a loving God (James 1.17). What has God given you? Dedicate all your gifts and resources to him, and use them for his service. He will lead you in the method you should use. The first step is to be willing.

18.13 The list of battles in this chapter shows how God gave David victory after victory. Unbelieving people think that victory comes from their own skill plus a little luck. Just as David acknowledged God's role in his success, so should we. Don't take personal credit for the work God does.

David's army fights the Ammonites and Arameans

19.1 **19** Some time afterward, King Nahash of the Ammonites died, and his son suc-
2 Sam 10.1 ceeded him. 2 David said, "I will deal loyally with Hanun son of Nahash, for
his father dealt loyally with me." So David sent messengers to console him concerning his father. When David's servants came to Hanun in the land of the Ammonites, to console him, 3 the officials of the Ammonites said to Hanun, "Do you
think, because David has sent consolers to you, that he is honoring your father?
Have not his servants come to you to search and to overthrow and to spy out the
land?" 4 So Hanun seized David's servants, shaved them, cut off their garments in
the middle at their hips, and sent them away; 5 and they departed. When David was
told about the men, he sent messengers to them, for they felt greatly humiliated.
The king said, "Remain at Jericho until your beards have grown, and then return."
6 When the Ammonites saw that they had made themselves odious to David,
Hanun and the Ammonites sent a thousand talents of silver to hire chariots and
19.7 cavalry from Mesopotamia, from Aram-maacah and from Zobah. 7 They hired
Num 21.30 thirty-two thousand chariots and the king of Maacah with his army, who came and
Josh 13.9,16 camped before Medeba. And the Ammonites were mustered from their cities and
came to battle. 8 When David heard of it, he sent Joab and all the army of the warriors. 9 The Ammonites came out and drew up in battle array at the entrance of the
city, and the kings who had come were by themselves in the open country.
10 When Joab saw that the line of battle was set against him both in front and
in the rear, he chose some of the picked men of Israel and arrayed them against the
Arameans; 11 the rest of his troops he put in the charge of his brother Abishai, and
they were arrayed against the Ammonites. 12 He said, "If the Arameans are too
strong for me, then you shall help me; but if the Ammonites are too strong for you,
then I will help you. 13 Be strong, and let us be courageous for our people and for
19.14 the cities of our God; and may the LORD do what seems good to him." 14 So Joab
2 Sam 10.14 and the troops who were with him advanced toward the Arameans for battle; and
they fled before him. 15 When the Ammonites saw that the Arameans fled, they
likewise fled before Abishai, Joab's brother, and entered the city. Then Joab came
to Jerusalem.
19.16 16 But when the Arameans saw that they had been defeated by Israel, they sent
2 Sam 10.15,16 messengers and brought out the Arameans who were beyond the Euphrates, with
Shophach the commander of the army of Hadadezer at their head. 17 When David
was informed, he gathered all Israel together, crossed the Jordan, came to them,
and drew up his forces against them. When David set the battle in array against the
Arameans, they fought with him. 18 The Arameans fled before Israel; and David
killed seven thousand Aramean charioteers and forty thousand foot soldiers, and
also killed Shophach the commander of their army. 19 When the servants of Hadadezer saw that they had been defeated by Israel, they made peace with David, and
became subject to him. So the Arameans were not willing to help the Ammonites
any more.

18.17 The Cherethites and Pelethites were probably a group of foreign soldiers who had joined David during his flight from Saul. They remained loyal to David throughout his reign (2 Samuel 15.17, 18) and became part of his bodyguard.

19.1 The land of Ammon bordered Israel to the east. The nation had a sordid beginning – its founding ancestor, Benammi, was conceived through incest between Lot and his daughter (Genesis 19.30–38). The Ammonites, who were constant enemies of Israel, reached their greatest strength in the days of the judges. David was the first military leader of Israel to crush them. They were unable to cause further trouble for many years.

19.2, 3 Hanun misread David's intentions. Because he was overly suspicious, he brought disaster upon himself. Because of past experiences, it is easy to be overly suspicious of others, questioning every move and second-guessing their motives. But while we should be cautious and wise as we deal with others, we should not assume their every action is ill-intended.

19.4, 5 Jewish men always wore beards. To be forcibly shaven was embarrassing enough, but these men were also left half-naked. Hanun's actions humiliated these men and insulted Israel.

19.6 Rather than admit his mistake and seek forgiveness and reconciliation, Hanun spent an enormous amount of money to cover up his error. His cover-up cost him dearly (20.1–4). It often costs more to cover up an error than to admit it honestly. Rather than compound an error through defensiveness, seek forgiveness and reconciliation as soon as you realize your mistake. You will save yourself and others a lot of pain and trouble.

David's army conquers the Ammonites

20 In the spring of the year, the time when kings go out to battle, Joab led out 20.1
the army, ravaged the country of the Ammonites, and came and besieged 2 Sam 11.1 12.26
Rabbah. But David remained at Jerusalem. Joab attacked Rabbah, and overthrew
it. 2 David took the crown of Milcom[b] from his head; he found that it weighed a 20.2
talent of gold, and in it was a precious stone; and it was placed on David's head. He 2 Sam 12.29,30
also brought out the booty of the city, a very great amount. 3 He brought out the 20.3
people who were in it, and set them to work[c] with saws and iron picks and axes.[d] 2 Sam 12.31
Thus David did to all the cities of the Ammonites. Then David and all the people
returned to Jerusalem.

David fights the Philistines

4 After this, war broke out with the Philistines at Gezer; then Sibbecai the Hu- 20.4
shathite killed Sippai, who was one of the descendants of the giants; and the Philis- 2 Sam 21.18
tines were subdued. 5 Again there was war with the Philistines; and Elhanan son of 20.5
Jair killed Lahmi the brother of Goliath the Gittite, the shaft of whose spear was 1 Sam 17.4-7 2 Sam 21.19
like a weaver's beam. 6 Again there was war at Gath, where there was a man of 1 Chron 11.23
great size, who had six fingers on each hand, and six toes on each foot, twenty-four
in number; he also was descended from the giants. 7 When he taunted Israel, Jonathan son of Shimea, David's brother, killed him. 8 These were descended from the
giants in Gath; they fell by the hand of David and his servants.

David numbers the men of military age

21 Satan stood up against Israel, and incited David to count the people of Is- 21.1
rael. 2 So David said to Joab and the commanders of the army, "Go, number 2 Sam 24.1
Israel, from Beer-sheba to Dan, and bring me a report, so that I may know their 21.2 1 Chron 27.23,
number." 3 But Joab said, "May the LORD increase the number of his people a hun- 24
dredfold! Are they not, my lord the king, all of them my lord's servants? Why then 21.3
should my lord require this? Why should he bring guilt on Israel?" 4 But the king's Deut 1.11
word prevailed against Joab. So Joab departed and went throughout all Israel, and
came back to Jerusalem. 5 Joab gave the total count of the people to David. In all 21.5
Israel there were one million one hundred thousand men who drew the sword, and Num 1.17-19 2 Sam 24.9
in Judah four hundred seventy thousand who drew the sword. 6 But he did not in- 21.6
clude Levi and Benjamin in the numbering, for the king's command was abhorrent 1 Chron 27.24
to Joab.

[b] Gk Vg See 1 Kings 11.5, 33: MT *of their king* [c] Compare 2 Sam 12.31: Heb *and he sawed* [d] Compare 2 Sam 12.31: Heb *saws*

20.1 David's adultery occurred at this time, while he remained in Jerusalem instead of going to battle (2 Samuel 11, 12). This story may have been excluded from 1 Chronicles because the book was written to focus on God's long-term interest in Israel and on the temple as a symbol of God's presence among them. The story of David and Bathsheba did not fit this purpose. The story of Absalom's rebellion, which occurred between this chapter and the next, was probably omitted for the same reason (2 Samuel 15–18).

20.1 Kings went out to battle in early spring. During the winter, they plotted and planned future conquests. Then, when the fair weather permitted it, their armies went to war. But David ignored this opportunity. He stayed home and sent Joab out to lead the army. It was during this time of inactivity that he sinned with Bathsheba. Look for the "springs" in your life, the times when God wants you to respond, take the initiative, and move out to do his will. It is during these critical times that we may be most sensitive to temptation. Resolve to take the action God has prescribed. Don't give temptation a foothold in your inactivity.

21.1 David's census brought disaster because, unlike the census taken in the book of Numbers (Numbers 1, 2) which God had ordered, this census was taken so David could take pride in the strength of his army. In determining his military strength, he was beginning to trust more in military power than in God. There is a thin line between feeling confident because you rely on God's power and becoming proud because you have been used by God for great purposes.

21.1 The Bible text says Satan *incited* David to take a census. Can Satan force people to do wrong? No, Satan only *tempted* David with the idea, but David *decided to act* on the temptation. Ever since the garden of Eden, Satan has been tempting people to sin. David's census was not against God's law, but his reason for the census was wrong – pride in his mighty army while forgetting that his real strength came from God. Even Joab, not known for his high moral ideals, recognized the census as sin. From David's example we learn that an action that may not be wrong in itself can be sinful if it is motivated by greed, arrogance, or selfishness. Often our motives, not the action itself, contain the sin. We must constantly weigh our motives before we act.

21.1–3 David fell to Satan's temptation. God provided a way out in Joab's counsel, but David's curiosity was spurred on by arrogance. His faith was in his own strength rather than in God's. If we feel self-sufficient and put confidence in ourselves apart from God, we soon fall to Satan's schemes. Self-sufficiency pulls us away from God. When you are tempted, examine your inner desires to understand why the external temptation is so appealing. (See 1 Corinthians 10.13 for more about escaping temptation.)

21.8 2 Sam 12.13
21.9 1 Sam 9.9; 2 Sam 24.11; 1 Chron 29.29
21.12 2 Sam 24.13
21.13 Ps 51.1; 130.4,7
21.15 Ex 32.14; 1 Sam 15.11; Jonah 3.10
21.16 1 Kgs 21.27
21.17 2 Sam 7.8; Ps 74.1
21.18 2 Chron 3.1

7 But God was displeased with this thing, and he struck Israel. 8 David said to
God, "I have sinned greatly in that I have done this thing. But now, I pray you, take
away the guilt of your servant; for I have done very foolishly." 9 The LORD spoke
to Gad, David's seer, saying, 10 "Go and say to David, 'Thus says the LORD: Three
things I offer you; choose one of them, so that I may do it to you.' " 11 So Gad came
to David and said to him, "Thus says the LORD, 'Take your choice: 12 either three
years of famine; or three months of devastation by your foes, while the sword of
your enemies overtakes you; or three days of the sword of the LORD, pestilence on
the land, and the angel of the LORD destroying throughout all the territory of Israel.'
Now decide what answer I shall return to the one who sent me." 13 Then David said
to Gad, "I am in great distress; let me fall into the hand of the LORD, for his mercy
is very great; but let me not fall into human hands."
14 So the LORD sent a pestilence on Israel; and seventy thousand persons fell in
Israel. 15 And God sent an angel to Jerusalem to destroy it; but when he was about
to destroy it, the LORD took note and relented concerning the calamity; he said to
the destroying angel, "Enough! Stay your hand." The angel of the LORD was then
standing by the threshing floor of Ornan the Jebusite. 16 David looked up and saw
the angel of the LORD standing between earth and heaven, and in his hand a drawn
sword stretched out over Jerusalem. Then David and the elders, clothed in sackcloth, fell on their faces. 17 And David said to God, "Was it not I who gave the
command to count the people? It is I who have sinned and done very wickedly. But
these sheep, what have they done? Let your hand, I pray, O LORD my God, be
against me and against my father's house; but do not let your people be plagued!"
18 Then the angel of the LORD commanded Gad to tell David that he should go
up and erect an altar to the LORD on the threshing floor of Ornan the Jebusite. 19 So
David went up following Gad's instructions, which he had spoken in the name of
the LORD. 20 Ornan turned and saw the angel; and while his four sons who were with
him hid themselves, Ornan continued to thresh wheat. 21 As David came to Ornan,
Ornan looked and saw David; he went out from the threshing floor, and did obeisance to David with his face to the ground. 22 David said to Ornan, "Give me the
site of the threshing floor that I may build on it an altar to the LORD—give it to me

---

21.7 With leadership comes responsibility. When David made a mistake, his people were affected. In deciding to take the census, David did not consult God or listen to Joab's advice, and the nation suffered terribly. When faced with important decisions, we should ask for God's direction *first.* He may send his answer in a number of ways, often in the form of advice from others. Although advice that goes against our plans is tough to hear, it may save us from tragic consequences.

21.8 When David realized his sin, he took full responsibility, admitted he was wrong, and asked God to forgive him. Many people want to add God and the benefits of Christianity to their lives without acknowledging their personal sin and guilt. But confession and repentance must come before receiving forgiveness. Like David, we must take full responsibility for our actions and confess them to God before we can expect him to forgive us and continue his work in us.

21.13, 14 Sin has a domino effect; once a sin is committed, a series of consequences follows. God will forgive our sin if we ask him, but the consequences of that sin have already been set in motion. David pleaded for mercy, and God responded by stopping the angel before his mission of death was complete. The consequences of David's sin, however, had already caused severe damage. God will always forgive our sins and will often intervene to make their bitter consequences less severe, but the scars will remain. Thinking through the possible consequences before we act can stop us and thus save us much sorrow and suffering.

21.14 Why did 70,000 innocent people die for David's sin? Our society places great emphasis upon the individual. In ancient times, however, the family leaders, tribal leaders, and kings represented the people they led, and all expected to share in their successes as well as in their failures and punishments. David deserved punishment for his sin, but his death could have resulted in political chaos and invasion by enemy armies, leaving hundreds of thousands dead. Instead, God graciously spared David's life. He also put a stop to the plague so that most of the people of Jerusalem were spared.

God made us to work together interdependently. Whether we think it is fair or not, the group usually suffers because of the sins of its leaders. Similarly, our actions always affect other people whether we want them to or not. We cannot fully know the mind of God in this severe judgment. We don't know where the prophets, the tribal leaders, and the other advisers were during this incident and whether or not they chose to go along with the king. We do know that putting confidence in military might alone is idolatry. To allow anything to take God's place is sinful, and it may cause disastrous consequences.

21.20, 21 Ornan is called Araunah in 2 Samuel 24.16. To do *obeisance* means to kneel and place one's face on the ground in a position of submission.

21.22–24 When David wanted to buy Ornan's land to build an altar, Ornan generously offered it as a gift. But David refused, saying, "I will not take for the Lord what is yours, nor offer burnt offerings that cost me nothing." David wanted to offer a sacrifice to God. The word *sacrifice* implies giving something that costs the giver in terms of self, time, or money. To give sacrificially requires more than a token effort or gift. God wants us to give voluntarily, but he wants it to mean something. Giving to God what costs you nothing does not demonstrate commitment.

at its full price—so that the plague may be averted from the people." 23 Then Ornan
said to David, "Take it; and let my lord the king do what seems good to him; see,
I present the oxen for burnt offerings, and the threshing sledges for the wood, and
the wheat for a grain offering. I give it all." 24 But King David said to Ornan, "No; **21.24**
I will buy them for the full price. I will not take for the LORD what is yours, nor 2 Sam 24.24
offer burnt offerings that cost me nothing." 25 So David paid Ornan six hundred
shekels of gold by weight for the site. 26 David built there an altar to the LORD and **21.26**
presented burnt offerings and offerings of well-being. He called upon the LORD, Lev 9.24 Judg 6.21
and he answered him with fire from heaven on the altar of burnt offering. 27 Then
the LORD commanded the angel, and he put his sword back into its sheath.
28 At that time, when David saw that the LORD had answered him at the threshing floor of Ornan the Jebusite, he made his sacrifices there. 29 For the tabernacle **21.29**
of the LORD, which Moses had made in the wilderness, and the altar of burnt offer- 1 Kgs 3.4 1 Chron 16.39
ing were at that time in the high place at Gibeon; 30 but David could not go before
it to inquire of God, for he was afraid of the sword of the angel of the LORD.

22 1 Then David said, "Here shall be the house of the LORD God and here the **22.1**
altar of burnt offering for Israel." 2 Chron 3.1 6.5,6

4. David arranges for the building of the temple

David prepares materials for the temple

2 David gave orders to gather together the aliens who were residing in the land **22.2**
of Israel, and he set stonecutters to prepare dressed stones for building the house of 1 Kgs 5.17,18 9.20,21
God. 3 David also provided great stores of iron for nails for the doors of the gates 2 Chron 2.17
and for clamps, as well as bronze in quantities beyond weighing, 4 and cedar logs **22.4**
without number—for the Sidonians and Tyrians brought great quantities of cedar 1 Kgs 5.6
to David. 5 For David said, "My son Solomon is young and inexperienced, and the **22.5**
house that is to be built for the LORD must be exceedingly magnificent, famous and 1 Kgs 3.7 1 Chron 29.1
glorified throughout all lands; I will therefore make preparation for it." So David
provided materials in great quantity before his death.
6 Then he called for his son Solomon and charged him to build a house for the **22.7**
LORD, the God of Israel. 7 David said to Solomon, "My son, I had planned to build 2 Sam 7.2,3 1 Chron 17.1
a house to the name of the LORD my God. 8 But the word of the LORD came to me, **22.8**
saying, 'You have shed much blood and have waged great wars; you shall not build 1 Chron 28.3 Acts 7.46
a house to my name, because you have shed so much blood in my sight on the earth. **22.9**
9 See, a son shall be born to you; he shall be a man of peace. I will give him peace 2 Sam 12.24,25 1 Kgs 4.20,25
from all his enemies on every side; for his name shall be Solomon,[e] and I will give **22.10**
peace[f] and quiet to Israel in his days. 10 He shall build a house for my name. He 2 Sam 12.24,25 1 Chron 17.12
shall be a son to me, and I will be a father to him, and I will establish his royal **22.11**
throne in Israel forever.' 11 Now, my son, the LORD be with you, so that you may 1 Chron 22.16
succeed in building the house of the LORD your God, as he has spoken concerning **22.12** 1 Kgs 3.9
you. 12 Only, may the LORD grant you discretion and understanding, so that when 2 Chron 1.10

[e] Heb *Shelomoh* [f] Heb *shalom*

22.1 Gibeon was a Benjamite city. After the defeat of Nob by Saul, who was a Benjamite, Saul moved the tabernacle to Gibeon. Gibeon was about a two hour journey northwest of Jerusalem.

22.1 Out of David's tragic mistake came the purchase of a plot of land that would become the site of God's temple, the symbol of God's presence among his people. Every time the people went to the temple they would remember that God is their true King and that everyone, including their human king, is fallible and subject to sin. God can use our sins for good purposes if we are sorry for them and seek his forgiveness. When we confess our sins, the way is opened for God to bring good from a bad situation.

22.5ff David had already chosen Solomon to succeed him as king.

22.7–10 God told David he would not be the one to build the temple. Instead the task would be left to his son Solomon. David graciously accepted this "no" from God. He was not jealous of the fact that his son would have the honor of building God's temple, but instead made preparations for Solomon to carry out his task. Similarly, we should take steps now to prepare the way for our children to find and fulfill God's purpose. Sooner or later our children will have to make their own decisions, but we can help by supplying them with the proper tools: showing them how to pray and study God's Word, teaching them the difference between right and wrong, and emphasizing the importance of church involvement.

22.12, 13 David learned that it takes *total* dedication to please God—obeying with heart and soul (22.19). This requires both right decisions (good judgment), and right attitudes (strength, courage, and enthusiasm). It isn't enough just to understand what God wants; your heart must be totally dedicated to him. Jesus said, "No one who puts a hand to the plow and looks back is fit for the kingdom of God" (Luke 9.62). Remove the distractions that pull you away from God, and serve him wholeheartedly.

he gives you charge over Israel you may keep the law of the LORD your God.
22.13 1 Chron 28.7 Josh 1.6 — [13]Then you will prosper if you are careful to observe the statutes and the ordinances
that the LORD commanded Moses for Israel. Be strong and of good courage. Do not
22.14 1 Chron 22.3 29.4 — be afraid or dismayed. [14]With great pains I have provided for the house of the LORD
one hundred thousand talents of gold, one million talents of silver, and bronze and
iron beyond weighing, for there is so much of it; timber and stone too I have provided. To these you must add more. [15]You have an abundance of workers: stonecutters, masons, carpenters, and all kinds of artisans without number, skilled in
22.16 1 Chron 22.11 — working [16]gold, silver, bronze, and iron. Now begin the work, and the LORD be
with you."
17 David also commanded all the leaders of Israel to help his son Solomon,
22.18 1 Chron 22.9 23.25 — saying, [18]"Is not the LORD your God with you? Has he not given you peace on
every side? For he has delivered the inhabitants of the land into my hand; and the
22.19 1 Kgs 8.6,21 1 Chron 28.9 2 Chron 5.7 — land is subdued before the LORD and his people. [19]Now set your mind and heart to
seek the LORD your God. Go and build the sanctuary of the LORD God so that the
ark of the covenant of the LORD and the holy vessels of God may be brought into a
house built for the name of the LORD."

David assigns duties to the Levites

23.1 1 Chron 28.5 29.22,28 — **23** When David was old and full of days, he made his son Solomon king over
Israel.
2 David assembled all the leaders of Israel and the priests and the Levites. [3]The

DUTIES ASSIGNED IN THE TEMPLE
King David charged all these people to do their jobs with every fiber of their being (1 Chronicles 22.17–19). God needs people of every talent—not just prophets and priests—to obey him.

Duties	Role	Reference
Administrative Duties	Supervisors	1 Chronicles 23.4, 5
	Officers	1 Chronicles 23.4, 5
	Judges	1 Chronicles 23.4, 5
	Public administrators	1 Chronicles 26.29, 30
Ministerial Duties	Priests	1 Chronicles 24.1
	Prophets	1 Chronicles 25.1
	Assistants for sacrifices	1 Chronicles 23.29–31
	Assistants for purification ceremonies	1 Chronicles 23.27–28
Service Duties	Bakers of the bread of the Presence	1 Chronicles 23.29
	Those who checked the weights and measures	1 Chronicles 23.29
	Custodians	1 Chronicles 23.28
Financial Duties	Those who cared for the treasury	1 Chronicles 26.20
	Those who cared for dedicated items	1 Chronicles 26.26-28
Artistic Duties	Musicians	1 Chronicles 25.6
	Singers	1 Chronicles 25.7
Protective Duties	Temple guards	1 Chronicles 23.5
	Gatekeepers	1 Chronicles 26.12–18
Individual Assignments	Recording secretary	1 Chronicles 24.6
	Chaplain to the king	1 Chronicles 25.5
	Private prophet to the king	1 Chronicles 25.2
	Captain of the guard	1 Chronicles 26.1
	Chief officer of the treasury	1 Chronicles 26.23, 24

23.1 For more information on Solomon's coronation and the attempts to seize his throne, see 1 Kings 1; 2.

23.1ff Although David couldn't build the temple, he could make preparations, and he took that job seriously. He not only gathered funds and materials for God's house, he also planned much of the administration and arranged the worship services. The original readers of Chronicles were rebuilding the temple after it had been destroyed by invading armies, and this information about its procedures was invaluable to them. The next five chapters demonstrate that organization is essential for smooth and effective service.

23.3 Why was this census acceptable when the other was not (chapter 21)? This census counted only the Levites—those set apart to serve God—and was used to organize the work in the temple. The census was not based on pride or self-sufficiency as was the previous census of fighting men.

Levites, thirty years old and upward, were counted, and the total was thirty-eight 23.3
thousand. 4 "Twenty-four thousand of these," David said, "shall have charge of the Num 4.3,48 1 Chron 23.24
work in the house of the LORD, six thousand shall be officers and judges, 5 four 23.4
thousand gatekeepers, and four thousand shall offer praises to the LORD with the 1 Chron 15.16 26.29
instruments that I have made for praise." 6 And David organized them in divisions Ezra 3.8,9
corresponding to the sons of Levi: Gershon,[g] Kohath, and Merari. 23.6
7 The sons of Gershon[h] were Ladan and Shimei. 8 The sons of Ladan: Jehiel the 1 Chron 6.1
chief, Zetham, and Joel, three. 9 The sons of Shimei: Shelomoth, Haziel, and Haran, three. These were the heads of families of Ladan. 10 And the sons of Shimei:
Jahath, Zina, Jeush, and Beriah. These four were the sons of Shimei. 11 Jahath was
the chief, and Zizah the second; but Jeush and Beriah did not have many sons, so
they were enrolled as a single family.
12 The sons of Kohath: Amram, Izhar, Hebron, and Uzziel, four. 13 The sons of 23.13
Amram: Aaron and Moses. Aaron was set apart to consecrate the most holy things, Ex 6.20; 28.1 30.6
so that he and his sons forever should make offerings before the LORD, and minister Num 3.25-30 26.58,59
to him and pronounce blessings in his name forever; 14 but as for Moses the man of 23.14
God, his sons were to be reckoned among the tribe of Levi. 15 The sons of Moses: Deut 33.1
Gershom and Eliezer. 16 The sons of Gershom: Shebuel the chief. 17 The sons of
Eliezer: Rehabiah the chief; Eliezer had no other sons, but the sons of Rehabiah
were very numerous. 18 The sons of Izhar: Shelomith the chief. 19 The sons of Hebron: Jeriah the chief, Amariah the second, Jahaziel the third, and Jekameam the
fourth. 20 The sons of Uzziel: Micah the chief and Isshiah the second.
21 The sons of Merari: Mahli and Mushi. The sons of Mahli: Eleazar and Kish. 23.21
22 Eleazar died having no sons, but only daughters; their kindred, the sons of Kish, 1 Chron 6.19-21
married them. 23 The sons of Mushi: Mahli, Eder, and Jeremoth, three.
24 These were the sons of Levi by their ancestral houses, the heads of families 23.24
as they were enrolled according to the number of the names of the individuals from Num 10.17,21 1 Chron 23.3
twenty years old and upward who were to do the work for the service of the house
of the LORD. 25 For David said, "The LORD, the God of Israel, has given rest to his 23.25
people; and he resides in Jerusalem forever. 26 And so the Levites no longer need to 1 Chron 22.18
carry the tabernacle or any of the things for its service"— 27 for according to the last 23.26 Num 4.5,15; 7.9
words of David these were the number of the Levites from twenty years old and
upward— 28 "but their duty shall be to assist the descendants of Aaron for the service of the house of the LORD, having the care of the courts and the chambers, the
cleansing of all that is holy, and any work for the service of the house of God; 29 to 23.29
assist also with the rows of bread, the choice flour for the grain offering, the wafers Lev 6.20,21 19.35,36; 24.5
of unleavened bread, the baked offering, the offering mixed with oil, and all mea- 1 Kgs 7.48 1 Chron 9.31
sures of quantity or size. 30 And they shall stand every morning, thanking and praising the LORD, and likewise at evening, 31 and whenever burnt offerings are offered 23.31
to the LORD on sabbaths, new moons, and appointed festivals, according to the Lev 23.2-4 Isa 1.13,14
number required of them, regularly before the LORD. 32 Thus they shall keep charge 23.32
of the tent of meeting and the sanctuary, and shall attend the descendants of Aaron, Num 1.53 3.6,38
their kindred, for the service of the house of the LORD." 1 Chron 9.27

[g] Or *Gershom*; See 1 Chr 6.1, note, and 23.15 [h] Vg Compare Gk Syr: Heb *to the Gershonite*

23.14 All that is stated here about Moses is that he was "the man of God." What a profound description of a person! A man or woman of God is one whose life reflects God's presence, priorities, and power.

23.24–27 Earlier, the age for entering Levical service was thirty (23.3). To reduce the burden on the Levites, David lowered the minimum age to twenty.

23.28–32 Priests and Levites had different jobs in and around the temple. Priests were authorized to perform the sacrifices. Levites were set apart to help the priests. They did the work of elders, deacons, custodians, assistants, musicians, moving men, and repairmen. Both priests and Levites came from the tribe of Levi, but priests also had to be descendants of Aaron, Israel's first high priest (Exodus 28.1–3). Priests and Levites were supported by Israel's tithes and by revenues from certain cities that had been given to them. Worship in the temple could not have taken place without the combined efforts of the priests and Levites. Their responsibilities were different, but they were equally important to God's plan. No matter what place of service you have in the church, you are important to the healthy functioning of the congregation.

David organizes the priests by duties

24.1 Ex 6.23 **24** The divisions of the descendants of Aaron were these. The sons of Aaron:
Nadab, Abihu, Eleazar, and Ithamar. 2 But Nadab and Abihu died before
24.2 Lev 10.2 their father, and had no sons; so Eleazar and Ithamar became the priests. 3 Along
with Zadok of the sons of Eleazar, and Ahimelech of the sons of Ithamar, David
organized them according to the appointed duties in their service. 4 Since more
chief men were found among the sons of Eleazar than among the sons of Ithamar,
they organized them under sixteen heads of ancestral houses of the sons of Eleazar,
and eight of the sons of Ithamar. 5 They organized them by lot, all alike, for there
were officers of the sanctuary and officers of God among both the sons of Eleazar
24.6 1 Chron 18.16 24.31 and the sons of Ithamar. 6 The scribe Shemaiah son of Nethanel, a Levite, recorded
them in the presence of the king, and the officers, and Zadok the priest, and Ahimelech son of Abiathar, and the heads of ancestral houses of the priests and of the
Levites; one ancestral house being chosen for Eleazar and one chosen for Ithamar.
24.7 Neh 12.4 Lk 1.5 7 The first lot fell to Jehoiarib, the second to Jedaiah, 8 the third to Harim, the
fourth to Seorim, 9 the fifth to Malchijah, the sixth to Mijamin, 10 the seventh to
Hakkoz, the eighth to Abijah, 11 the ninth to Jeshua, the tenth to Shecaniah, 12 the
eleventh to Eliashib, the twelfth to Jakim, 13 the thirteenth to Huppah, the fourteenth to Jeshebeab, 14 the fifteenth to Bilgah, the sixteenth to Immer, 15 the seventeenth to Hezir, the eighteenth to Happizzez, 16 the nineteenth to Pethahiah, the
twentieth to Jehezkel, 17 the twenty-first to Jachin, the twenty-second to Gamul,
24.19 1 Chron 9.25 18 the twenty-third to Delaiah, the twenty-fourth to Maaziah. 19 These had as their
appointed duty in their service to enter the house of the LORD according to the
procedure established for them by their ancestor Aaron, as the LORD God of Israel
had commanded him.
20 And of the rest of the sons of Levi: of the sons of Amram, Shubael; of the
sons of Shubael, Jehdeiah. 21 Of Rehabiah: of the sons of Rehabiah, Isshiah the
24.23 1 Chron 23.19 chief. 22 Of the Izharites, Shelomoth; of the sons of Shelomoth, Jahath. 23 The sons
of Hebron:[i] Jeriah the chief,[j] Amariah the second, Jahaziel the third, Jekameam
the fourth. 24 The sons of Uzziel, Micah; of the sons of Micah, Shamir. 25 The
brother of Micah, Isshiah; of the sons of Isshiah, Zechariah. 26 The sons of Merari:
Mahli and Mushi. The sons of Jaaziah: Beno.[k] 27 The sons of Merari: of Jaaziah,
Beno,[k] Shoham, Zaccur, and Ibri. 28 Of Mahli: Eleazar, who had no sons. 29 Of
Kish, the sons of Kish: Jerahmeel. 30 The sons of Mushi: Mahli, Eder, and Jerimoth. These were the sons of the Levites according to their ancestral houses.
24.31 1 Chron 24.5,6 31 These also cast lots corresponding to their kindred, the descendants of Aaron, in
the presence of King David, Zadok, Ahimelech, and the heads of ancestral houses
of the priests and of the Levites, the chief as well as the youngest brother.

[i] See 23.19: Heb lacks *Hebron* [j] See 23.19: Heb lacks *the chief* [k] Or *his son*: Meaning of Heb uncertain

---

24.1ff The temple service was highly structured, but this did not hinder the Spirit of God. Rather, it provided an orderly context for worship. (Compare 1 Corinthians 14.40.) Sometimes we feel that planning and structure are unspiritual activities that may hinder spontaneity in worship. But order and structure can free us to respond to God. Order brings glory to God as we experience the joy, freedom, and calm that come when we have wisely prepared in advance.

24.3 This Ahimelech was the son of Abiathar and the grandson of another Ahimelech, one of the priests massacred by Saul (1 Samuel 22.11–18). Abiathar and Zadok were co-high priests under David: one was at Jerusalem where the ark of God was kept, and one was at Gibeon serving at the tabernacle. It appears from this verse and 18.16 that Ahimelech began to assume some of Abiathar's duties as his father grew old.

24.4 Eleazar's descendants were divided into 16 groups (as opposed to Ithamar's eight) for three reasons: (1) Eleazar had received the birthright since his two older brothers, Nadab and Abihu, had been killed (Leviticus 10). The birthright included a double portion of the father's estate; (2) His descendants were greater in number than Ithamar's; (3) His descendants had greater leadership ability. These 24 groups gave order to the functioning of the temple.

24.7–18 Each of these 24 groups of priests served two-week shifts each year at the temple. The rest of the time they served in their hometowns. This system was still in place in Jesus' day (Luke 1.5–9). Zacharias was a member of the Abijah division. During his shift at the temple, an angel appeared to him and predicted that he would have a son, John.

24.31 To "cast lots corresponding to their kindred" means that they used this method to determine the order and type of service so it was fair to everyone. See also 6.61.

The duties of the musicians

25 David and the officers of the army also set apart for the service the sons of 25.1 2 Kgs 3.15
Asaph, and of Heman, and of Jeduthun, who should prophesy with lyres, 1 Chron 6.33,
harps, and cymbals. The list of those who did the work and of their duties was: 2 Of 39; 15.16
the sons of Asaph: Zaccur, Joseph, Nethaniah, and Asarelah, sons of Asaph, under
the direction of Asaph, who prophesied under the direction of the king. 3 Of Jedu- 25.3
thun, the sons of Jeduthun: Gedaliah, Zeri, Jeshaiah, Shimei,[l] Hashabiah, and 1 Chron 16.41, 42
Mattithiah, six, under the direction of their father Jeduthun, who prophesied with
the lyre in thanksgiving and praise to the LORD. 4 Of Heman, the sons of Heman: 25.4
Bukkiah, Mattaniah, Uzziel, Shebuel, and Jerimoth, Hananiah, Hanani, Eliathah, 2 Sam 24.11 1 Chron 21.9
Giddalti, and Romamti-ezer, Joshbekashah, Mallothi, Hothir, Mahazioth. 5 All
these were the sons of Heman the king's seer, according to the promise of God to
exalt him; for God had given Heman fourteen sons and three daughters. 6 They 25.6
were all under the direction of their father for the music in the house of the LORD 1 Chron 15.16,
with cymbals, harps, and lyres for the service of the house of God. Asaph, Jedu- 19; 23.5
thun, and Heman were under the order of the king. 7 They and their kindred, who
were trained in singing to the LORD, all of whom were skillful, numbered two hundred eighty-eight. 8 And they cast lots for their duties, small and great, teacher and 25.8
pupil alike. 1 Chron 26.13

9 The first lot fell for Asaph to Joseph; the second to Gedaliah, to him and his
brothers and his sons, twelve; 10 the third to Zaccur, his sons and his brothers,
twelve; 11 the fourth to Izri, his sons and his brothers, twelve; 12 the fifth to Nethaniah, his sons and his brothers, twelve; 13 the sixth to Bukkiah, his sons and his
brothers, twelve; 14 the seventh to Jesarelah,[m] his sons and his brothers, twelve;
15 the eighth to Jeshaiah, his sons and his brothers, twelve; 16 the ninth to Mattaniah,
his sons and his brothers, twelve; 17 the tenth to Shimei, his sons and his brothers,
twelve; 18 the eleventh to Azarel, his sons and his brothers, twelve; 19 the twelfth to
Hashabiah, his sons and his brothers, twelve; 20 to the thirteenth, Shubael, his sons
and his brothers, twelve; 21 to the fourteenth, Mattithiah, his sons and his brothers,
twelve; 22 to the fifteenth, to Jeremoth, his sons and his brothers, twelve; 23 to the
sixteenth, to Hananiah, his sons and his brothers, twelve; 24 to the seventeenth, to
Joshbekashah, his sons and his brothers, twelve; 25 to the eighteenth, to Hanani, his
sons and his brothers, twelve; 26 to the nineteenth, to Mallothi, his sons and his
brothers, twelve; 27 to the twentieth, to Eliathah, his sons and his brothers, twelve;
28 to the twenty-first, to Hothir, his sons and his brothers, twelve; 29 to the twenty-
second, to Giddalti, his sons and his brothers, twelve; 30 to the twenty-third, to
Mahazioth, his sons and his brothers, twelve; 31 to the twenty-fourth, to Romamti-
ezer, his sons and his brothers, twelve.

The duties of the gatekeepers

26 As for the divisions of the gatekeepers: of the Korahites, Meshelemiah son
of Kore, of the sons of Asaph. 2 Meshelemiah had sons: Zechariah the firstborn, Jediael the second, Zebadiah the third, Jathniel the fourth, 3 Elam the fifth,

[l] One Ms: Gk: MT lacks *Shimei* [m] Or *Asarelah*; see 25.2

25.1 There is more to prophesying than predicting the future. Prophecy also involves singing God's praises and preaching God's messages (1 Corinthians 14.1ff). Prophets could be musicians, farmers (Amos 1.1), wives (2 Kings 22.14), or leaders (Deuteronomy 34.10) – anyone who boldly and accurately spoke out for God and tried to bring people back to worshiping him. From a large group of musicians David chose those who showed an unusual ability to tell about God and to encourage others in song.

25.1–7 There were many ways to contribute to the worship in the tabernacle. Some prophesied (25.1), some led in prayer (25.3), and others played instruments and sang (25.6, 7). God wants all his people to participate in worship. You may not be a master musician, a prophet, or a teacher, but God appreciates whatever you have to offer. Develop your special gifts to offer in service to God (Romans 12.3–8; 1 Corinthians 12.29–31).

25.9–31 The singers were divided into 24 groups to match the 24 groups of Levites (24.7–25). This division of labor gave order to the planning of temple work, promoted excellence by making training easier, gave variety to worship because each group worked a term, and provided opportunities for many to be involved.

26.1 There were 4,000 gatekeepers (23.4, 5). They were all Levites and did many other jobs as well. Some of their duties included (1) checking out the equipment and utensils used each day and making sure they were returned, (2) storing, ordering, and maintaining the food supplies for the priests and sacrifices, (3) caring for the furniture, (4) mixing the incense that was burned daily, and (5) accounting for the gifts brought. (For more on gatekeepers, see the note on 9.17, 18.)

Jehohanan the sixth, Eliehoenai the seventh. [4]Obed-edom had sons: Shemaiah the
firstborn, Jehozabad the second, Joah the third, Sachar the fourth, Nethanel the
fifth, [5]Ammiel the sixth, Issachar the seventh, Peullethai the eighth; for God
blessed him. [6]Also to his son Shemaiah sons were born who exercised authority in
their ancestral houses, for they were men of great ability. [7]The sons of Shemaiah:
Othni, Rephael, Obed, and Elzabad, whose brothers were able men, Elihu and
Semachiah. [8]All these, sons of Obed-edom with their sons and brothers, were able
men qualified for the service; sixty-two of Obed-edom. [9]Meshelemiah had sons
and brothers, able men, eighteen. [10]Hosah, of the sons of Merari, had sons: Shimri
the chief (for though he was not the firstborn, his father made him chief), [11]Hilkiah
the second, Tebaliah the third, Zechariah the fourth: all the sons and brothers of
Hosah totaled thirteen.

12 These divisions of the gatekeepers, corresponding to their leaders, had duties, just as their kindred did, ministering in the house of the LORD; [13]and they cast
lots by ancestral houses, small and great alike, for their gates. [14]The lot for the east
fell to Shelemiah. They cast lots also for his son Zechariah, a prudent counselor,
and his lot came out for the north. [15]Obed-edom's came out for the south, and to his
sons was allotted the storehouse. [16]For Shuppim and Hosah it came out for the
west, at the gate of Shallecheth on the ascending road. Guard corresponded to
guard. [17]On the east there were six Levites each day,[n] on the north four each day,
on the south four each day, as well as two and two at the storehouse; [18]and for the
colonnade[o] on the west there were four at the road and two at the colonnade.[o]
[19]These were the divisions of the gatekeepers among the Korahites and the sons of
Merari.

26.10 1 Chron 16.38

26.13 1 Chron 24.5, 31; 25.8

[n] Gk: Heb lacks *each day* [o] Heb *parbar*: meaning uncertain

MUSIC IN BIBLE TIMES
Paul clearly puts forth the Christian's view that things are not good or bad in and of themselves (see Romans 14 and 1 Corinthians 14.7, 8, 26). The point should always be to worship the Lord or help others by means of the things of this world, including music. Music was created by God and can be returned to him in praise. Does the music you play or listen to have a negative or positive impact upon your relationship with God?

Highlights of musical use in Scripture	*References*
Jubal is father of all musicians	Genesis 4.21
Miriam and other women sing and dance to praise God	Exodus 15.1–21
The priest is to have bells on his robes	Exodus 28.34, 35
The ark of the covenant is accompanied by trumpeters	Numbers 31.6
Jericho fell to the sound of trumpets	Joshua 6.4–20
The king's coronation is accompanied by music	1 Kings 1.39, 40
There were musicians for the king's court	Ecclesiastes 2.8
Saul seemed to lean toward the view of music taken by pagan nations	1 Samuel 10.5–8 1 Samuel 16.14–23
From David's time on, the use of music in worship was much more organized. Music for the temple became refined.	1 Chronicles 15.16–24 1 Chronicles 16.4–7 2 Chronicles 5.11–14
Everything was to be used by everyone to praise the Lord	Psalm 150
In the New Testament, worship continued in the synagogues until the Christians became unwelcome there, so there was a rich musical heritage already established. The fact that music is mentioned less often in the New Testament does not mean it was less important.	
Jesus and the disciples sang a hymn	Matthew 26.30
Paul and Silas sang in jail	Acts 16.25
We are to sing to the Lord as a response to what he has done in our lives	Ephesians 5.19, 20 Colossians 3.16 James 5.13

26.5 The status of children in society has fluctuated throughout history; sometimes they are highly esteemed, and sometimes abused and cheated. But Scripture shows no such vacillation – children are called a blessing from God, and God never views them as a burden (Psalm 127.3–5; Mark 10.13–15).

26.12 The gatekeepers *ministered* in God's house – that is, they served there. The word *minister* originally meant "servant." Thus all of us who assist in the Lord's work are ministers. So if we teach, cook, or visit the sick we should do it as though we are doing it for the Lord. He regards what we do even if no one else notices.

The duties of other officials

20 And of the Levites, Ahijah had charge of the treasuries of the house of God **26.20**
and the treasuries of the dedicated gifts. 21 The sons of Ladan, the sons of the Ger- 1 Chron 26.22, 24
shonites belonging to Ladan, the heads of families belonging to Ladan the Gershonite: Jehieli.[p]

22 The sons of Jehieli, Zetham and his brother Joel, were in charge of the treasuries of the house of the LORD. 23 Of the Amramites, the Izharites, the Hebronites,
and the Uzzielites: 24 Shebuel son of Gershom, son of Moses, was chief officer in
charge of the treasuries. 25 His brothers: from Eliezer were his son Rehabiah, his
son Jeshaiah, his son Joram, his son Zichri, and his son Shelomoth. 26 This Shelomoth and his brothers were in charge of all the treasuries of the dedicated gifts that
King David, and the heads of families, and the officers of the thousands and the
hundreds, and the commanders of the army, had dedicated. 27 From booty won in
battles they dedicated gifts for the maintenance of the house of the LORD. 28 Also all
that Samuel the seer, and Saul son of Kish, and Abner son of Ner, and Joab son of
Zeruiah had dedicated — all dedicated gifts were in the care of Shelomoth[q] and his
brothers.

29 Of the Izharites, Chenaniah and his sons were appointed to outside duties for **26.29**
Israel, as officers and judges. 30 Of the Hebronites, Hashabiah and his brothers, one 1 Chron 23.4
thousand seven hundred men of ability, had the oversight of Israel west of the Jor- **26.30** 1 Chron 27.17
dan for all the work of the LORD and for the service of the king. 31 Of the Hebron- **26.31**
ites, Jerijah was chief of the Hebronites. (In the fortieth year of David's reign 1 Chron 19.11 23.19
search was made, of whatever genealogy or family, and men of great ability among
them were found at Jazer in Gilead.) 32 King David appointed him and his brothers,
two thousand seven hundred men of ability, heads of families, to have the oversight
of the Reubenites, the Gadites, and the half-tribe of the Manassites for everything
pertaining to God and for the affairs of the king.

Commanders of the army

27 This is the list of the people of Israel, the heads of families, the commanders
of the thousands and the hundreds, and their officers who served the king in
all matters concerning the divisions that came and went, month after month
throughout the year, each division numbering twenty-four thousand:

2 Jashobeam son of Zabdiel was in charge of the first division in the first month; **27.2**
in his division were twenty-four thousand. 3 He was a descendant of Perez, and was 2 Sam 23.8
chief of all the commanders of the army for the first month. 4 Dodai the Ahohite 1 Chron 11.11
was in charge of the division of the second month; Mikloth was the chief officer of
his division. In his division were twenty-four thousand. 5 The third commander, for
the third month, was Benaiah son of the priest Jehoiada, as chief; in his division
were twenty-four thousand. 6 This is the Benaiah who was a mighty man of the
Thirty and in command of the Thirty; his son Ammizabad was in charge of his
division.[r] 7 Asahel brother of Joab was fourth, for the fourth month, and his son
Zebadiah after him; in his division were twenty-four thousand. 8 The fifth commander, for the fifth month, was Shamhuth, the Izrahite; in his division were
twenty-four thousand. 9 Sixth, for the sixth month, was Ira son of Ikkesh the Tekoite; in his division were twenty-four thousand. 10 Seventh, for the seventh month,
was Helez the Pelonite, of the Ephraimites; in his division were twenty-four thousand. 11 Eighth, for the eighth month, was Sibbecai the Hushathite, of the Zerahites; in his division were twenty-four thousand. 12 Ninth, for the ninth month, was
Abiezer of Anathoth, a Benjaminite; in his division were twenty-four thousand.
13 Tenth, for the tenth month, was Maharai of Netophah, of the Zerahites; in his
division were twenty-four thousand. 14 Eleventh, for the eleventh month, was Be-

[p] The Hebrew text of verse 21 is confused [q] Gk Compare 26.28: Heb *Shelomith* [r] Gk Vg: Heb *Ammizabad was his division*

26.27 War loot (booty) rightfully belonged to the victorious army. These soldiers, however, gave their portion of all the battle spoils to the temple to express their dedication to God. Like these soldiers, we should think of what we *can* give, rather than what we are obligated to give. Is your giving a matter of rejoicing rather than duty? Give as a response of joy and love for God.

naiah of Pirathon, of the Ephraimites; in his division were twenty-four thousand.
15 Twelfth, for the twelfth month, was Heldai the Netophathite, of Othniel; in his
division were twenty-four thousand.

Leaders of the tribes

27.16 1 Chron 28.1

16 Over the tribes of Israel, for the Reubenites, Eliezer son of Zichri was chief
officer; for the Simeonites, Shephatiah son of Maacah; 17 for Levi, Hashabiah son
of Kemuel; for Aaron, Zadok; 18 for Judah, Elihu, one of David's brothers; for
Issachar, Omri son of Michael; 19 for Zebulun, Ishmaiah son of Obadiah; for Naphtali, Jerimoth son of Azriel; 20 for the Ephraimites, Hoshea son of Azaziah; for the
half-tribe of Manasseh, Joel son of Pedaiah; 21 for the half-tribe of Manasseh in
Gilead, Iddo son of Zechariah; for Benjamin, Jaasiel son of Abner; 22 for Dan, Aza-

27.23 Gen 15.5 Num 1.17-19 2 Sam 24.1

rel son of Jeroham. These were the leaders of the tribes of Israel. 23 David did not
count those below twenty years of age, for the LORD had promised to make Israel
as numerous as the stars of heaven. 24 Joab son of Zeruiah began to count them, but

27.24 2 Sam 24.12 1 Chron 21.1

did not finish; yet wrath came upon Israel for this, and the number was not entered
into the account of the Annals of King David.

Administrators of the kingdom

25 Over the king's treasuries was Azmaveth son of Adiel. Over the treasuries in
the country, in the cities, in the villages and in the towers, was Jonathan son of
Uzziah. 26 Over those who did the work of the field, tilling the soil, was Ezri son of
Chelub. 27 Over the vineyards was Shimei the Ramathite. Over the produce of the

27.28 1 Kgs 10.27 2 Chron 1.15

vineyards for the wine cellars was Zabdi the Shiphmite. 28 Over the olive and sycamore trees in the Shephelah was Baal-hanan the Gederite. Over the stores of oil was

27.29 1 Chron 5.16

Joash. 29 Over the herds that pastured in Sharon was Shitrai the Sharonite. Over the
herds in the valleys was Shaphat son of Adlai. 30 Over the camels was Obil the
Ishmaelite. Over the donkeys was Jehdeiah the Meronothite. Over the flocks was

27.31 1 Chron 5.10

Jaziz the Hagrite. 31 All these were stewards of King David's property.

27.33 2 Sam 15.12, 32,37

32 Jonathan, David's uncle, was a counselor, being a man of understanding and
a scribe; Jehiel son of Hachmoni attended the king's sons. 33 Ahithophel was the

27.34 1 Kgs 1.7 1 Chron 11.6 27.5

king's counselor, and Hushai the Archite was the king's friend. 34 After Ahithophel
came Jehoiada son of Benaiah, and Abiathar. Joab was commander of the king's
army.

David instructs Solomon about the temple

28.1 1 Chron 11.10 23.2; 27.1

28 David assembled at Jerusalem all the officials of Israel, the officials of the
tribes, the officers of the divisions that served the king, the commanders of
the thousands, the commanders of the hundreds, the stewards of all the property

28.2 1 Chron 17.1,2 Ps 132.7 Isa 66.1

and cattle of the king and his sons, together with the palace officials, the mighty
warriors, and all the warriors. 2 Then King David rose to his feet and said: "Hear
me, my brothers and my people. I had planned to build a house of rest for the ark

28.3 1 Chron 17.4 22.8 Acts 7.46,47

of the covenant of the LORD, for the footstool of our God; and I made preparations
for building. 3 But God said to me, 'You shall not build a house for my name, for
you are a warrior and have shed blood.' 4 Yet the LORD God of Israel chose me from

28.4 Gen 49.8 1 Sam 16.1,6 1 Chron 5.2 17.23,27

all my ancestral house to be king over Israel forever; for he chose Judah as leader,
and in the house of Judah my father's house, and among my father's sons he took
delight in making me king over all Israel. 5 And of all my sons, for the LORD has

---

27.24 The Annals of King David were historical documents kept in the royal archives with other official records. They no longer exist. See 1 Kings 14.19.

27.33, 34 When Absalom rebelled against David; Ahithophel betrayed David and joined the rebellion. Hushai pretended loyalty to Absalom, and his advice caused Absalom's downfall (2 Samuel 15.31 – 17.23).

28.1 The last two chapters of 1 Chronicles present the transition from David to Solomon as king of Israel. The writer doesn't mention Adonijah's conspiracy or David's frailty (1 Kings 1; 2). Instead, he focuses on the positive – God's plans for Israel and his promise to David's descendants.

28.5 The kingdom of Israel belonged to God, not to David or anyone else. Israel's king, then, was God's deputy, commissioned to carry out God's will for the nation. Thus God could choose the person he wanted as king without following customary lines of succession. David was not Saul's heir, and Solomon was not David's eldest son, but this did not matter, because God appointed them.

given me many, he has chosen my son Solomon to sit upon the throne of the king- **28.5**
dom of the LORD over Israel. 6 He said to me, 'It is your son Solomon who shall 1 Chron 3.1 14.3; 22.9,10
build my house and my courts, for I have chosen him to be a son to me, and I will **28.6**
be a father to him. 7 I will establish his kingdom forever if he continues resolute in 2 Sam 7.13,14
keeping my commandments and my ordinances, as he is today.' 8 Now therefore in **28.7** 1 Chron 22.13
the sight of all Israel, the assembly of the LORD, and in the hearing of our God,
observe and search out all the commandments of the LORD your God; that you may
possess this good land, and leave it for an inheritance to your children after you
forever.

9 "And you, my son Solomon, know the God of your father, and serve him with **28.9**
single mind and willing heart; for the LORD searches every mind, and understands 1 Sam 17.7 1 Kgs 8.61
every plan and thought. If you seek him, he will be found by you; but if you forsake 1 Chron 29.17 2 Chron 15.2
him, he will abandon you forever. 10 Take heed now, for the LORD has chosen you Jer 29.13
to build a house as the sanctuary; be strong, and act." **28.10** 1 Chron 22.13

11 Then David gave his son Solomon the plan of the vestibule of the temple, **28.11**
and of its houses, its treasuries, its upper rooms, and its inner chambers, and of the Ex 25.17,40
room for the mercy seat;[s] 12 and the plan of all that he had in mind: for the courts **28.12**
of the house of the LORD, all the surrounding chambers, the treasuries of the house 1 Chron 26.20,
of God, and the treasuries for dedicated gifts; 13 for the divisions of the priests 28 **28.13**
and of the Levites, and all the work of the service in the house of the LORD; for all 1 Chron 23.6
the vessels for the service in the house of the LORD, 14 the weight of gold for all 24.1
golden vessels for each service, the weight of silver vessels for each service, 15 the **28.15**
weight of the golden lampstands and their lamps, the weight of gold for each lamp- Ex 25.31
stand and its lamps, the weight of silver for a lampstand and its lamps, according to
the use of each in the service, 16 the weight of gold for each table for the rows of
bread, the silver for the silver tables, 17 and pure gold for the forks, the basins, and
the cups; for the golden bowls and the weight of each; for the silver bowls and the
weight of each; 18 for the altar of incense made of refined gold, and its weight; also **28.18**
his plan for the golden chariot of the cherubim that spread their wings and covered Ex 25.18; 30.1
the ark of the covenant of the LORD.

19 "All this, in writing at the LORD's direction, he made clear to me—the plan **28.19**
of all the works." 1 Chron 28.11 12

20 David said further to his son Solomon, "Be strong and of good courage, and **28.20**
act. Do not be afraid or dismayed; for the LORD God, my God, is with you. He will Josh 1.5 1 Sam 20.13
not fail you or forsake you, until all the work for the service of the house of the 1 Kgs 1.37 1 Chron 22.13
LORD is finished. 21 Here are the divisions of the priests and the Levites for all the Heb 13.5
service of the house of God; and with you in all the work will be every volunteer **28.21**
who has skill for any kind of service; also the officers and all the people will be Ex 35.25 36.1,2
wholly at your command."

[s] Or *the cover*

28.8 David told Solomon to seek for and keep every one of God's commands to insure Israel's prosperity and the continuation of David's descendants upon the throne. It was the king's solemn duty to study and obey God's laws. The teachings of Scripture are the keys to security, happiness, and justice, but you'll never discover them unless you search God's Word. If we ignore God's will and neglect his teaching, anything we attempt to build, even if it has God's name on it, is headed for collapse. Get to know God's commands through regular Bible study, and find ways to apply them consistently.

28.9 In 22.18, 19, David told the leaders to obey God, heart and soul. Now he tells Solomon to worship God with a perfect heart and willing mind. God demands complete devotion. He understands our motives, desires, and thoughts. If we desire to know and love him, he responds with more wisdom and guidance than we could ever imagine.

28.9 Nothing can be hidden from God. He sees and understands everything in our hearts. David found this out the hard way when God sent Nathan to expose David's sins of adultery and murder (2 Samuel 12). David told Solomon to be completely open with God and dedicated to him. It makes no sense to try to hide any thoughts or actions from an all-knowing God. This should cause us joy, not fear, for God knows even the worst about us and loves us anyway.

28.13 Some of the instructions about the work of the priests and Levites are found in chapters 23 and 24.

28.20 David advised Solomon not to be frightened about the size of his task as king and builder of the temple. Fear can immobilize us. The size of a job, its risks, or the pressure of the situation can cause us to freeze and do nothing. One remedy for fear is found here—don't focus on the fear; instead, get to work. Getting started is often the most difficult and frightening part of a job.

The people bring gifts for building the temple

29.1 1 Chron 22.5 **29** King David said to the whole assembly, "My son Solomon, whom alone
God has chosen, is young and inexperienced, and the work is great; for the
29.2 1 Chron 22.3 temple[t] will not be for mortals but for the LORD God. 2 So I have provided for the
house of my God, so far as I was able, the gold for the things of gold, the silver for
the things of silver, and the bronze for the things of bronze, the iron for the things
of iron, and wood for the things of wood, besides great quantities of onyx and
stones for setting, antimony, colored stones, all sorts of precious stones, and marble in abundance. 3 Moreover, in addition to all that I have provided for the holy
house, I have a treasure of my own of gold and silver, and because of my devotion
29.4 1 Kgs 9.28 1 Chron 22.14 to the house of my God I give it to the house of my God: 4 three thousand talents of
gold, of the gold of Ophir, and seven thousand talents of refined silver, for overlay-
ing the walls of the house, 5 and for all the work to be done by artisans, gold for the
things of gold and silver for the things of silver. Who then will offer willingly,
consecrating themselves today to the LORD?"

29.6 1 Chron 27.1, 25; 28.1 6 Then the leaders of ancestral houses made their freewill offerings, as did also
the leaders of the tribes, the commanders of the thousands and of the hundreds, and
the officers over the king's work. 7 They gave for the service of the house of God
five thousand talents and ten thousand darics of gold, ten thousand talents of silver,
eighteen thousand talents of bronze, and one hundred thousand talents of iron.
29.8 1 Chron 23.8 8 Whoever had precious stones gave them to the treasury of the house of the LORD,
into the care of Jehiel the Gershonite. 9 Then the people rejoiced because these had
29.9 1 Kgs 8.61 2 Cor 9.7 given willingly, for with single mind they had offered freely to the LORD; King
David also rejoiced greatly.

David praises God

10 Then David blessed the LORD in the presence of all the assembly; David
said: "Blessed are you, O LORD, the God of our ancestor Israel, forever and ever.
29.11 Rev 5.13 11 Yours, O LORD, are the greatness, the power, the glory, the victory, and the
majesty; for all that is in the heavens and on the earth is yours; yours is the king-
29.12 2 Chron 1.12 20.6 dom, O LORD, and you are exalted as head above all. 12 Riches and honor come
from you, and you rule over all. In your hand are power and might; and it is in your

[t] Heb *fortress*

PRINCIPLES TO LIVE BY

King David gave his son Solomon principles to guide him through life (see 1 Chronicles 28.9, 10). These same ideas are ones that any Christian parent would want to present to a child:

1. Get to know God personally.
2. Learn God's commands and discover what he wants you to do.
3. Worship God with a perfect heart.
4. Serve God with a willing mind.
5. Be faithful.
6. Don't become discouraged.

29.1 It is possible to be obsessed with a church building to the neglect of the real church—the people of God. But the opposite response, neglecting the church building, is also wrong. David makes this point when he says that the temple is not "for mortals but for the Lord God." Although we should avoid wasteful extravagance, we must remember that every church building can be a visible witness for God. How can your church building be better used to tell the world about God?

29.3–5 David gave from his personal fortune to the temple. He encouraged others to follow his example, and they willingly did. Both the tabernacle (Exodus 35.5–36.7) and the temple were built from the voluntary gifts of the people. Like David, we can acknowledge that all we have comes from God (29.14–16). We may not have David's wealth, but we can develop his willingness to give. It is not what we have that counts with God, but our willingness to give of it.

29.6–9 These leaders displayed a right attitude toward their money by giving willingly to God's work. This attitude is described by Paul in 2 Corinthians 9.7: "Each of you must give as you have made up your mind, not reluctantly or under compulsion, for God loves a cheerful giver." When we are generous because we are thankful, our attitude inspires others. Give generously to God's work.

29.11, 12 David acknowledged God's greatness. Our constantly changing world is controlled by a constant and unchanging God. During our lifetime, we see objects fade, materials decay, and friends change, but we can depend on God's control. His love and purpose for us never change. Only when we understand this can we have real peace and security.

hand to make great and to give strength to all. 13 And now, our God, we give thanks
to you and praise your glorious name.
14 "But who am I, and what is my people, that we should be able to make this
freewill offering? For all things come from you, and of your own have we given
you. 15 For we are aliens and transients before you, as were all our ancestors; our 29.15
days on the earth are like a shadow, and there is no hope. 16 O LORD our God, all Lev 25.23; Job 14.2,10
this abundance that we have provided for building you a house for your holy name
comes from your hand and is all your own. 17 I know, my God, that you search the 29.17
heart, and take pleasure in uprightness; in the uprightness of my heart I have freely 1 Chron 28.9
offered all these things, and now I have seen your people, who are present here,
offering freely and joyously to you. 18 O LORD, the God of Abraham, Isaac, and 29.18
Israel, our ancestors, keep forever such purposes and thoughts in the hearts of your 1 Kgs 18.36
people, and direct their hearts toward you. 19 Grant to my son Solomon that with 29.19
single mind he may keep your commandments, your decrees, and your statutes, 1 Chron 28.9; Ps 72.1
performing all of them, and that he may build the temple[u] for which I have made
provision."
20 Then David said to the whole assembly, "Bless the LORD your God." And all 29.20
the assembly blessed the LORD, the God of their ancestors, and bowed their heads Josh 22.33
and prostrated themselves before the LORD and the king. 21 On the next day they 29.21
offered sacrifices and burnt offerings to the LORD, a thousand bulls, a thousand 1 Kgs 8.62,63
rams, and a thousand lambs, with their libations, and sacrifices in abundance for all
Israel; 22 and they ate and drank before the LORD on that day with great joy. 29.22
They made David's son Solomon king a second time; they anointed him as the 1 Kgs 1.33; 1 Chron 29.1
LORD's prince, and Zadok as priest. 23 Then Solomon sat on the throne of the LORD,
succeeding his father David as king; he prospered, and all Israel obeyed him. 24 All
the leaders and the mighty warriors, and also all the sons of King David, pledged
their allegiance to King Solomon. 25 The LORD highly exalted Solomon in the sight 29.25
of all Israel, and bestowed upon him such royal majesty as had not been on any king 1 Kgs 3.13; 2 Chron 1.1,12
before him in Israel.

David dies at an old age

26 Thus David son of Jesse reigned over all Israel. 27 The period that he reigned 29.26
over Israel was forty years; he reigned seven years in Hebron, and thirty-three years 2 Sam 5.4,5; 1 Kgs 2.11
in Jerusalem. 28 He died in a good old age, full of days, riches, and honor; and his 1 Chron 18.14
son Solomon succeeded him. 29 Now the acts of King David, from first to last, are 29.28
written in the records of the seer Samuel, and in the records of the prophet Nathan, 1 Chron 23.1; Acts 13.36
and in the records of the seer Gad, 30 with accounts of all his rule and his might and 29.29
of the events that befell him and Israel and all the kingdoms of the earth. 1 Sam 9.9; 22.5; 2 Sam 7.2

[u] Heb *fortress*

29.15 David contrasts God's everlasting nature with the fleeting lives of his people. Nothing lasts unless it is rooted in God's unchanging character. If our most impressive deeds fade as dust before God, where should we place our confidence? Only in a relationship with God can we find anything permanent. His love never fades and nothing can take it away.

29.19 A "single" mind is entirely dedicated to God. This is what David wished for Solomon – a mind that desired, above all else, to serve God. Do you find it hard to do what God wants, or even harder to want to do it? God can give you a single mind. If you have believed in Jesus Christ, this is already happening in you. Paul wrote that God works within us "both to will and to work for his good pleasure" (Philippians 2.13).

29.21 Libations were drink offerings of wine that were poured out as a sacrifice to God to acknowledge his role in providing for us.

29.25 In 29.3–5, we read that David gave of his fortune to the temple. Solomon could have had mixed feelings about his inheritance being diminished. But apparently he approved of his father's gift. In this verse we see that Solomon amassed an even greater fortune than David had. God blessed Solomon, in part because of his attitude toward giving to the Lord's work. An attitude that prizes God's will and work above all else will be rewarded.

29.25 Solomon surpassed his father's wealth and honor. David's legacy resulted from his vital relationship with the Lord, and he passed his spiritual values on to Solomon. Any money or power we leave to our children are far less valuable than the spiritual legacy we pass on. What spiritual inheritance will your children receive?

29.29 A seer was someone who received messages from God for the nation in visions or dreams.

29.30 First Chronicles vividly illustrates the importance of maintaining a relationship with God. The genealogies in chapters 1 – 9 emphasize the importance of a spiritual heritage. The second part of the book details the life of David. Few men or women in the Bible were as close to God as David was. His daily contact with God gave him deep reverence for worship and the desire to build God's temple. David's life shows us the importance of staying close to God – through studying and obeying his Word and communicating with him daily. Second Chronicles, on the other hand, reveals how quickly our lives can deteriorate (spiritually, mentally, and socially) when we fail to stay well grounded in God.

THE KINGS OF THE DAVIDIC THRONE

King	*Began Reign*	*Length of Reign*	*References*
David	1010 (B.C.)	40 years	1 Chronicles 11.1—29.30
Solomon	970	40 years	2 Chronicles 1.1—9.30
Rehoboam	930	17 years	9.31—12.16
Abijam	913	3 years	13.1—14.1
Asa	910	41 years	14.1—16.14
Jehoshaphat	872	25 years	17.1—21.1
Jehoram (Joram)	853	8 years	21.1-20
Jehoahaz (Ahaziah)	841	1 year	22.1-10
Athaliah	841	6 years	22.10—23.21
Joash	835	40 years	22.11—24.27
Amaziah	796	29 years	25.1-28
Uzziah (Azariah)	792	52 years	26.1-23
Jotham	750	16 years	27.1-9
Ahaz	735	16 years	28.1-27
Hezekiah	715	29 years	29.1—32.33
Manasseh	697	55 years	33.1-20
Amon	642	2 years	33.20-25
Josiah	640	31 years	33.25—35.27
Jehoahaz	609	3 months	36.1-4
Jehoiakim	609	11 years	36.5-8
Jehoiachin	598	3 months	36.8-10
Zedekiah	597	11 years	36.10-21

2 CHRONICLES

Solomon becomes king 970 B.C.	Temple built 966–959	The kingdom divides 930	Asa becomes king of Judah 910	Jehoshaphat becomes king of Judah 872	Ahab killed in battle 853	Athaliah seizes the throne 841	Uz... be... kin... Ju... 79...

VITAL STATISTICS

PURPOSE:
To unify the nation around true worship of Jehovah by showing his standard for judging kings. The righteous kings of Judah and the religious revivals under their rule are highlighted, and the sins of the evil kings are exposed.

AUTHOR:
Ezra, according to Jewish tradition

TO WHOM WRITTEN:
All Israel

DATE WRITTEN:
Approximately 430 B.C., recording events from the beginning of Solomon's reign (970 B.C.) to the beginning of the Babylonian captivity (586 B.C.)

SETTING:
Second Chronicles parallels 1 and 2 Kings and serves as their commentary. Originally 1 and 2 Chronicles were one book. It was written after the exile from a priestly perspective, highlighting the importance of the temple and the religious revivals in Judah. The northern kingdom, Israel, is virtually ignored in this history.

KEY VERSE:
"If my people who are called by my name humble themselves, pray, seek my face, and turn from their wicked ways, then I will hear from heaven, and will forgive their sin, and heal their land" (7.14).

KEY PEOPLE:
Solomon, the queen of Sheba, Rehoboam, Asa, Jehoshaphat, Jehoram, Joash, Uzziah, Ahaz, Hezekiah, Manasseh, Josiah

KEY PLACES:
Jerusalem, the temple

SPECIAL FEATURES:
Includes a detailed record of the temple's construction

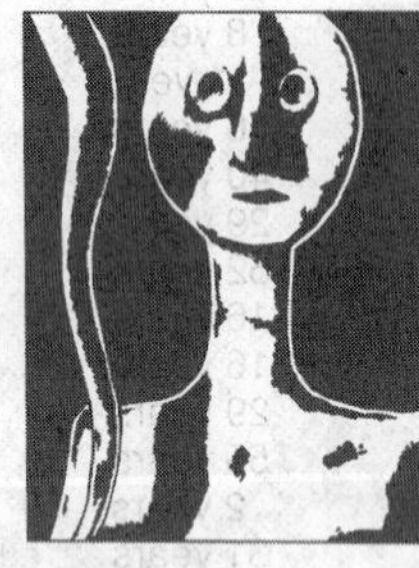

THE slide clicks, and our eyes focus on the image flashed onto the screen in the darkened sanctuary. "This idol," explains the missionary, "is made of stone and is worshiped daily. The natives believe that this will guarantee good crops and healthy children." With condescending smiles, we wonder at their ignorance. How could anyone worship an object? Idols are for the superstitious! Then we return home to *our* idols of wealth, prestige, or self-fulfillment. If we put anything in God's place, we worship it, despite what we profess with our lips.

Our experience parallels Israel's. They were chosen by God to represent him on earth. But too often they forgot the truth and their calling, stumbling blindly after idols as the neighboring nations did. Then prophets, priests, and judgment would push them abruptly back to God, the one true God. Second Chronicles relates this sordid history of Judah's corrupt and idolatrous kings. Here and there a good king arises in Judah, and for a time there is revival, but the downward spiral continues—ending in chaos, destruction, and captivity.

The chronicler writes this volume to bring the nation back to God by reminding them of their past. Only by following God will they prosper! As you read 2 Chronicles you will catch a vivid glimpse of Judah's history (the history of Israel, the northern kingdom, is virtually ignored), and you will see the tragic results of idolatry. Learn the lessons of the past: determine to get rid of any idols in your life and to worship God alone.

Second Chronicles continues the history of 1 Chronicles. David's son, Solomon, is inaugurated as king. Solomon builds the magnificent temple in Jerusalem, thus fulfilling his father's wish and last request (chapters 2—5). Solomon enjoys a peaceful and prosperous reign of 40 years that makes him world famous. After Solomon dies, his son Rehoboam assumes the throne, and his immaturity divides the kingdom.

In Judah, there are a few good kings and many evil ones. The writer of Chronicles faithfully records their achievements and failures, noting how each king measures up to God's standard for success. Clearly a good king obeys God's laws, eliminates the places of idol worship, and makes no alliances with other nations. Judah's good kings include Asa, Jehoshaphat, Uzziah, Hezekiah, and Josiah. Of its many evil ones, Ahaz and Manasseh are perhaps the worst. Eventually the nation is conquered and taken captive, and the temple is destroyed.

The writer's purpose was to reunite the nation around the true worship of God after the captivity. In these pages, he reminds the people of their past. He clearly broadcasts his message through one of the best-known verses in Scripture, "If my people who are called by my name humble themselves, pray, seek my face, and turn from their wicked ways, then I will hear from heaven, and will forgive their sin and heal their land" (7.14). As you read 2 Chronicles, listen to God's voice and obey him; and receive his redemptive, healing touch.

Israel (northern kingdom) falls 722	Hezekiah becomes king of Judah 715	Sennacherib taunts Hezekiah 701	Josiah becomes king 640	Book of the law found 622	Judah (southern kingdom) falls 586	Cyrus' decree 538

THE BLUEPRINT

A. THE REIGN OF SOLOMON (1.1—9.31) 1. Solomon asks God for wisdom 2. Solomon builds the temple 3. Solomon dedicates the temple 4. Solomon's riches and wisdom	Solomon achieved much in business and government, but most important, he was the man God used to build the glorious temple. This beautiful building was the religious center of the nation. It symbolized the unity of all the tribes, the presence of God among them, and the nation's high calling. We may achieve great things in life, but we must not neglect any effort that will help nurture God's people or bring others into God's kingdom. It is easy for us to get the wrong perspective on what's really important in life.
B. THE KINGDOM OF JUDAH (10.1—36.23) 1. The nation of Israel splits apart 2. History of apostasy and reform 3. Judah is exiled to Babylon	Throughout the reigns of 20 kings, the nation of Judah wavered between obedience to God and apostasy. The reigning king's response to God determined the spiritual climate of the nation and whether or not God would send judgment upon his people. Our personal history is shaped by our response to God. Just as Judah's failure to repent brought them captivity in Babylon, so the abuse of our high calling by sinful living will ultimately bring us catastrophe and destruction.

MEGATHEMES

THEME	EXPLANATION	IMPORTANCE
Temple	The temple was the symbol of God's presence and the place set aside for worship and prayer. Built by Solomon from the plans God gave to David, the temple was the spiritual center of the nation.	As Christians meet together to worship God, they experience the presence of God in a way that no individual believer could. For the dwelling place of God is the people of God. The body of Christ is God's temple.
Peace	As Solomon and his descendants were faithful to God, they experienced victory in battle, success in government, and peace with other nations. Peace was the result of the people being unified and loyal to God and his law.	Only God can bring true peace. God is greater than any enemy, army, or nation. Just as Israel's faithful response was key to her peace and survival as a nation, so our obedience to God as individuals and nations is vital to peace today.
Prayer	After Solomon died, David's kingdom was divided. When a king led the Israelites into idolatry, the nation suffered. When the king and his people prayed to God for deliverance and they turned from their sinful ways, God delivered them.	God still answers prayer today. We have God's promise that if we humble ourselves, seek him, turn from our sin, and pray, God will hear, heal, and forgive us. If we are alert, we can pray for God's guidance before we get into trouble.
Reform	Although idolatry and injustice were common, some kings turned to God and led the people in spiritual revival—renewing their commitment to God and reforming their society. Revival included the destruction of idols, obedience to the law, and the restoration of the priesthood.	We must constantly commit ourselves to obeying God. We are never secure in what others have done before us. Each generation of believers must rededicate themselves to the task of carrying out God's will in their own lives as well as in society.
National collapse	In 586 B.C. the Babylonians completely destroyed Solomon's beautiful temple. The formal worship of God was ended. The Israelites had abandoned God. As a result, God brought judgment upon his people and they were carried off into captivity.	Although our disobedience may not be as blatant as Israel's, quite often our commitment to God is insincere and casual. When we forget that all our power, wisdom, and wealth come from God and not ourselves, we are in danger of the same spiritual and moral collapse that Israel experienced.

KEY PLACES IN 2 CHRONICLES

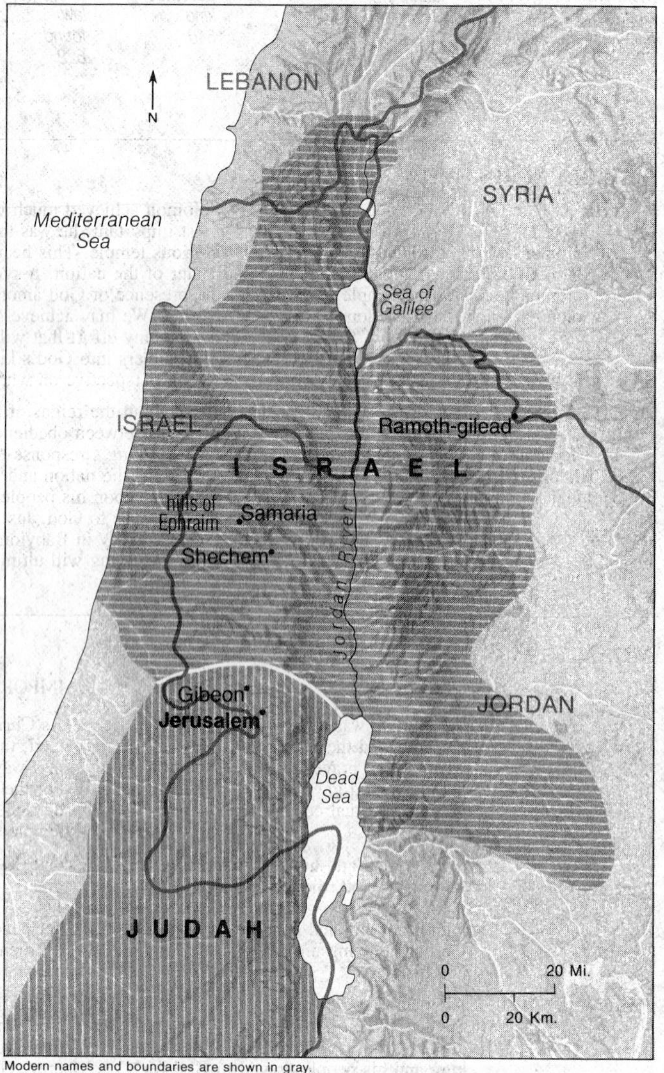

Modern names and boundaries are shown in gray.

1 Gibeon David's son Solomon became king of Israel. He summoned the nation's leaders to a ceremony in Gibeon. Here God told Solomon to ask for whatever he desired. Solomon asked for wisdom and knowledge to rule Israel (1.1–12).

2 Jerusalem After the ceremony in Gibeon, Solomon returned to the capital city, Jerusalem. His reign began a golden age for Israel. Solomon implemented the plans for the temple which had been drawn up by his father, David. It was a magnificent construction. It symbolized Solomon's wealth and wisdom which became known worldwide (1.13—9.31).

3 Shechem After Solomon's death, his son Rehoboam was ready to be crowned in Shechem. However, his promise of higher taxes and harder work for the people led to rebellion. Everyone but the tribes of Judah and Benjamin deserted Rehoboam and set up their own kingdom to the north called Israel. Rehoboam returned to Jerusalem as ruler over the southern kingdom called Judah (10.1—12.16). The remainder of 2 Chronicles records the history of Judah.

4 Hills of Ephraim Abijah became the next king of Judah, and soon war broke out between Israel and Judah. When the armies of the two nations arrived for battle in the hill country of Ephraim, Israel had twice as many troops as Judah. It looked like Judah's defeat was certain. But they cried out to God, and God gave them victory over Israel. In their history as separate nations, Judah had a few godly kings who instituted reforms and brought the people back to God. Israel, however, had a succession of only evil kings (13.1–22).

5 Syria Asa, a godly king, removed every trace of idol worship from Judah and renewed the people's covenant with God in Jerusalem. But King Baasha of Israel built a fortress to control traffic into Judah. Instead of looking to God for guidance, Asa took the silver and gold from the temple and sent it to the king of Syria requesting his help against King Baasha. As a result, God became angry with Judah (14.1—16.14).

6 Samaria Although Jehoshaphat was a godly king, he allied himself with Israel's most evil king, Ahab. Ahab's capital was in Samaria. Ahab wanted help fighting for Ramoth-gilead. Jehoshaphat wanted advice, but rather than listening to God's prophet who had promised defeat, he joined Ahab in battle (17.1—18.27).

7 Ramoth-gilead The alliance with Israel against Ramoth-gilead ended in defeat and Ahab's death. Although shaken by his defeat, Jehoshaphat returned to Jerusalem and to God. But his son Jehoram was a wicked king, as was his son Ahaziah, and history repeated itself. Ahaziah formed an alliance with Israel's King Jehoram (who had the same name as his brother) to do battle with the Syrians at Ramoth-gilead. This led to the death of both kings (18.28—22.9).

8 Jerusalem The rest of Judah's history recorded in 2 Chronicles centers on Jerusalem. Some kings caused Judah to sin by bringing idol worship into their midst. Others cleaned up the idol worship, reopened and restored the temple and, in the case of Josiah, tried to follow God's laws as they were written by Moses. In spite of the few good influences, a series of evil kings sent Judah into a downward spiral that ended with the Babylonian Empire overrunning the country. The temple was burned, the walls of the city were broken down, and the people were deported to Babylon.

A. THE REIGN OF SOLOMON (1.1 – 9.31)

In response to Solomon's request, God gives to Solomon great wisdom. Solomon launches great building programs, including the temple, his greatest achievement. In the midst of the celebration dedicating the temple, fire flashes down from heaven and God's glory fills the temple. God wants to live among his people and to be central in their lives. Today, our bodies are God's temple, the place where God, through his Holy Spirit, lives and reigns.

1. Solomon asks God for wisdom

1.1 1 Kgs 2.12,46 1 Chron 29.25

1 Solomon son of David established himself in his kingdom; the LORD his God
was with him and made him exceedingly great.

1.2 Ex 36.8 1 Kgs 3.4 1 Chron 28.1

2 Solomon summoned all Israel, the commanders of the thousands and of the
hundreds, the judges, and all the leaders of all Israel, the heads of families. 3 Then
Solomon, and the whole assembly with him, went to the high place that was at
Gibeon; for God's tent of meeting, which Moses the servant of the LORD had made

1.4 1 Chron 15.25-28

in the wilderness, was there. 4 (But David had brought the ark of God up from
Kiriath-jearim to the place that David had prepared for it; for he had pitched a tent

1.5 Ex 31.9; 38.1-7 1 Kgs 3.4

for it in Jerusalem.) 5 Moreover the bronze altar that Bezalel son of Uri, son of Hur,
had made, was there in front of the tabernacle of the LORD. And Solomon and the
assembly inquired at it. 6 Solomon went up there to the bronze altar before the
LORD, which was at the tent of meeting, and offered a thousand burnt offerings on
it.

1.7 1 Kgs 3.5-14

7 That night God appeared to Solomon, and said to him, "Ask what I should

1.8 1 Chron 28.5

give you." 8 Solomon said to God, "You have shown great and steadfast love to my
father David, and have made me succeed him as king. 9 O LORD God, let your

1.9 Gen 13.16 22.17 2 Sam 7.12-16

promise to my father David now be fulfilled, for you have made me king over a
people as numerous as the dust of the earth. 10 Give me now wisdom and knowledge to go out and come in before this people, for who can rule this great people of

1.10 2 Sam 5.2

yours?" 11 God answered Solomon, "Because this was in your heart, and you have
not asked for possessions, wealth, honor, or the life of those who hate you, and
have not even asked for long life, but have asked for wisdom and knowledge for

1.12 1 Chron 29.25 2 Chron 9.22

yourself that you may rule my people over whom I have made you king, 12 wisdom
and knowledge are granted to you. I will also give you riches, possessions, and
honor, such as none of the kings had who were before you, and none after you shall

---

1.1 While the book of 1 Chronicles focuses mainly on David's life, 2 Chronicles focuses on the lives of the rest of the kings of Judah, the southern kingdom. Very little is mentioned about Israel, the northern kingdom, because (1) Chronicles was written for Judeans who had returned from captivity in Babylon, and (2) Judah represented David's family, from which the Messiah would come. While Israel was in a state of constant turmoil, anarchy, and rebellion against God, Judah at least made sporadic efforts to follow God.

1.1 More details about Solomon's rise to the throne can be read in 1 Kings 1; 2. Solomon's Profile is found in 1 Kings 3.

1.2–5 The tent of meeting or tabernacle Moses had built centuries earlier (Exodus 35 – 40) was still in operation, although it had been moved several times. When Solomon became king, the tabernacle was located at Gibeon, a town about six miles northwest of Jerusalem. All the tabernacle furniture was kept at Gibeon except the ark of God, which David had moved to Jerusalem (1 Chronicles 13; 15; 16). David wanted the ark, the symbol of God's presence, to reside in the city where he ruled the people. The tabernacle at Gibeon, however, was still considered Israel's main religious center until Solomon built the temple in Jerusalem.

1.10 Wisdom is the ability to make good decisions based on proper discernment and judgment. Knowledge, in this verse, refers to the practical know-how necessary for handling everyday matters. Solomon used his wisdom and knowledge not only to build the temple from his father's plans, but also to put the nation on firm economic footing.

1.10 God's offer to Solomon stretches the imagination: "Ask what I should give you" (1.7). But Solomon put the needs of his people first and asked for wisdom rather than riches. He realized that wisdom would be the most valuable asset he could have as king. Later he wrote that wisdom "is more precious than jewels, and nothing you desire can compare with her" (Proverbs 3.15). The same wisdom that was given to Solomon is available to you; the same God offers it. How can we acquire wisdom? First, we must ask God, who "gives to all generously and ungrudgingly" (James 1.5). Second, we must devote ourselves wholeheartedly to studying and applying God's Word, the source of divine wisdom. (For more on Solomon's wisdom, read the notes on 1 Kings 3.6–9, 12.)

1.11, 12 Solomon could have had anything, but he asked for wisdom to rule the nation. God approved of the way Solomon ordered his priorities, and he gave him riches, wealth, and honor as well. Jesus also spoke about priorities. He said that when we put God first, everything we really need will fall into place (Matthew 6.33). This does not guarantee that we will be wealthy and famous like Solomon, but it means that when we put God first, the wisdom he gives will enable us to have richly rewarding lives. When we have a purpose for living and learn to be content with what we have, we have greater wealth than we could ever accumulate.

1.12 Solomon's wealth was impressive. In this specific case, it symbolized God's blessing in his life and was a reward for seeking God's wisdom. Jesus the Messiah came to fulfill God's promise to David of an eternal kingdom. The spiritual benefits of Jesus' rule are even more impressive than the material benefits of Solomon's. Whereas Solomon's wisdom was limited and his wealth eventually disappeared, Jesus' wisdom is eternal and his treasures can never be taken away.

have the like." 13 So Solomon came from[a] the high place at Gibeon, from the tent 1.13
of meeting, to Jerusalem. And he reigned over Israel. 2 Chron 1.3
14 Solomon gathered together chariots and horses; he had fourteen hundred 1.14
chariots and twelve thousand horses, which he stationed in the chariot cities and 1 Kgs 4.26
with the king in Jerusalem. 15 The king made silver and gold as common in Jerusa- 9.19; 10.26-29
lem as stone, and he made cedar as plentiful as the sycamore of the Shephelah.
16 Solomon's horses were imported from Egypt and Kue; the king's traders received them from Kue at the prevailing price. 17 They imported from Egypt, and
then exported, a chariot for six hundred shekels of silver, and a horse for one hundred fifty; so through them these were exported to all the kings of the Hittites and
the kings of Aram.

2. Solomon builds the temple

Solomon plans the temple

2 [b]Solomon decided to build a temple for the name of the LORD, and a royal 2.1
palace for himself. 2 [c] Solomon conscripted seventy thousand laborers and 1 Kgs 5.5
eighty thousand stonecutters in the hill country, with three thousand six hundred to 2.2 1 Kgs 5.15,16
oversee them. 2 Chron 2.18
3 Solomon sent word to King Huram of Tyre: "Once you dealt with my father 2.3
David and sent him cedar to build himself a house to live in. 4 I am now about to 1 Kgs 5.2-11 1 Chron 14.1
build a house for the name of the LORD my God and dedicate it to him for offering 2.4
fragrant incense before him, and for the regular offering of the rows of bread, and Ex 25.30
for burnt offerings morning and evening, on the sabbaths and the new moons and 29.38-42; 30.7 Num 28.9,10
the appointed festivals of the LORD our God, as ordained forever for Israel. 5 The 2.5
house that I am about to build will be great, for our God is greater than other gods. Ex 15.11 1 Chron 16.25
6 But who is able to build him a house, since heaven, even highest heaven, cannot 2.6
contain him? Who am I to build a house for him, except as a place to make offerings 1 Kgs 8.27
before him? 7 So now send me an artisan skilled to work in gold, silver, bronze, and 2 Chron 6.18

[a] Gk Vg: Heb *to* [b] Ch 1.18 in Heb [c] Ch 2.1 in Heb

2.1 David had wanted to build a temple for God (2 Samuel 7). God denied his request because David had been a warrior, but said that David's son Solomon would build the temple. God allowed David to make the plans and preparations for the temple (1 Chronicles 23–26; 28.11–13). David bought the land (2 Samuel 24.18–25; 1 Chronicles 22.1), gathered most of the construction materials (1 Chronicles 22.14–16), and received the plans from God (1 Chronicles 28.11, 12). It was Solomon's responsibility to make the plans a reality. His job was made easier by his father's exhaustive preparations. God's work can be forwarded when the older generation paves the way for the younger.

2.4 A celebration is an occasion of joy, and remembering God's goodness to his people is certainly a reason to be joyful. God wanted Israel to celebrate certain occasions regularly because the people were so forgetful, so quick to turn to other gods. In church we use celebrations to recall God's goodness. Because we also have short memories, Christmas, Easter, and other special occasions are designed to help us recall what God has done for all his people. We participate in these celebrations by thanking God for how he has worked in the past. Celebrating with thanksgiving adds vitality to our spiritual lives.

2.4–6, 11, 12 Although Huram (called Hiram in the books of Samuel and Kings) was one of David's and Solomon's friendly allies, he was the ruler of a nation that worshiped many different gods. Huram was happy to send materials for the temple, and both David and Solomon used this occasion to testify about the one true God.

2.5, 6 We should try our best to build beautiful and helpful places of worship to be a testimony and credit to God. In so doing, however, we must remember that God cannot be contained in our building or beautiful setting. He is far greater than any building; so we must focus our praise on him and not merely on the place of worship.

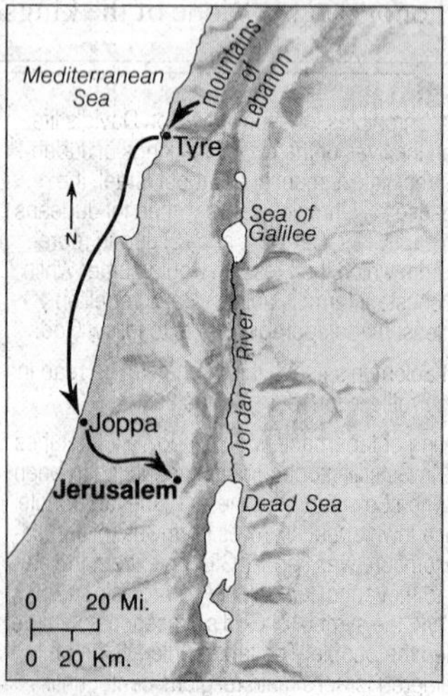

SHIPPING RESOURCES FOR THE TEMPLE
Solomon asked King Huram of Tyre to provide supplies and skilled workmen to help build God's temple in Jerusalem. The plan was to cut the cedar logs in the mountains of Lebanon, float them by sea to Joppa, then bring them inland to Jerusalem by the shortest and easiest route.

2.7 The Israelites had great knowledge of agriculture, but knew little about metalworking. So they found people who were experts in this area. It is not a sin to obtain secular expertise for God's work. He distributes all natural talents as he chooses, and he often chooses to give skill to non-Christians. When we hire secular contractors to build or repair our church buildings, we are recognizing that God gives gifts liberally. We may also be gaining an opportunity to tell the workers about God.

2.7 Ex 31.3-5 1 Chron 22.15 2 Chron 2.13,14 iron, and in purple, crimson, and blue fabrics, trained also in engraving, to join the
skilled workers who are with me in Judah and Jerusalem, whom my father David
provided. 8 Send me also cedar, cypress, and algum timber from Lebanon, for I
2.8 2 Chron 9.10,11 know that your servants are skilled in cutting Lebanon timber. My servants will
work with your servants 9 to prepare timber for me in abundance, for the house I am
about to build will be great and wonderful. 10 I will provide for your servants, those
who cut the timber, twenty thousand cors of crushed wheat, twenty thousand cors
of barley, twenty thousand baths[d] of wine, and twenty thousand baths of oil."

2.11 1 Kgs 10.9 2 Chron 9.8 11 Then King Huram of Tyre answered in a letter that he sent to Solomon,
"Because the LORD loves his people he has made you king over them." 12 Huram
2.12 2 Chron 2.1 Ps 33.6; 102.25 also said, "Blessed be the LORD God of Israel, who made heaven and earth, who
has given King David a wise son, endowed with discretion and understanding, who
will build a temple for the LORD, and a royal palace for himself.

13 "I have dispatched Huram-abi, a skilled artisan, endowed with understand-
2.14 1 Kgs 7.14 ing, 14 the son of one of the Danite women, his father a Tyrian. He is trained to
work in gold, silver, bronze, iron, stone, and wood, and in purple, blue, and crimson fabrics and fine linen, and to do all sorts of engraving and execute any design
that may be assigned him, with your artisans, the artisans of my lord, your father
2.15 2 Chron 2.10 David. 15 Now, as for the wheat, barley, oil, and wine, of which my lord has spo-
2.16 1 Kgs 5.8,9 ken, let him send them to his servants. 16 We will cut whatever timber you need
from Lebanon, and bring it to you as rafts by sea to Joppa; you will take it up to
Jerusalem."

17 Then Solomon took a census of all the aliens who were residing in the land
of Israel, after the census that his father David had taken; and there were found to
2.18 1 Chron 22.2 2 Chron 2.2 be one hundred fifty-three thousand six hundred. 18 Seventy thousand of them he
assigned as laborers, eighty thousand as stonecutters in the hill country, and three
thousand six hundred as overseers to make the people work.

Temple construction begins

3.1 1 Kgs 6.1 1 Chron 21.18 **3** Solomon began to build the house of the LORD in Jerusalem on Mount Moriah,
where the LORD had appeared to his father David, at the place that David had
designated, on the threshing floor of Ornan the Jebusite. 2 He began to build on the
second day of the second month of the fourth year of his reign. 3 These are Solomon's measurements[e] for building the house of God: the length, in cubits of the
3.4 1 Kgs 6.3 old standard, was sixty cubits, and the width twenty cubits. 4 The vestibule in front
of the nave of the house was twenty cubits long, across the width of the house;[f] and
3.5 1 Kgs 6.17 its height was one hundred twenty cubits. He overlaid it on the inside with pure
gold. 5 The nave he lined with cypress, covered it with fine gold, and made palms
3.7 1 Kgs 6.20-22, 29-35 and chains on it. 6 He adorned the house with settings of precious stones. The gold
was gold from Parvaim. 7 So he lined the house with gold—its beams, its thresh-
3.8 Ex 26.33 1 Kgs 6.16 olds, its walls, and its doors; and he carved cherubim on the walls.

8 He made the most holy place; its length, corresponding to the width of the

[d] A Hebrew measure of volume [e] Syr: Heb *foundations* [f] Compare 1 Kings 6.3: Meaning of Heb uncertain

---

2.8, 9 Israel did not have much wood, but Lebanon, a small nation on the seacoast, had some of the finest cedar forests in the Middle East. Lebanon, in turn, imported a great deal of food from Israel. Thus the two kings made a trade agreement that was beneficial to both nations.

2.13 Natural talents are given to all people for God's purposes. We don't know if this craftsman served Yahweh (he was half Jewish), but we know he was gifted by God for a task.

2.17, 18 Why would Solomon force foreigners living in Israel to become slaves? These foreigners were descendants of the heathen nations who had not been driven out of the land in Joshua's day (Judges 1.21–33). Scripture has specific laws about treating slaves fairly (Leviticus 25.39–55), so Solomon would not have treated them harshly as other nations might. Solomon's action was probably only in force during the construction of the temple.

3.1 Solomon built a permanent temple on Mount Moriah to replace the movable tabernacle (now at Gibeon) that had accompanied Israel in the wilderness. Mount Moriah was also the place where God had stopped Abraham from sacrificing Isaac (Genesis 22.1–18). David purchased the land when it was a threshing floor (see 2 Samuel 24.15–25 and the note on 1 Chronicles 21.22–24).

3.1ff Why was the temple decorated so ornately? Although no one can build God a worthy home (2.6), this temple was going to be the best that humans could design. The care and craftsmanship were acts of worship in themselves. Although a simple chapel is an adequate place to pray and meet God, it is not wrong to want to make a beautiful place of worship.

3.3 The old standard was equal to 20.5 inches and was the one used by Ezekiel in the temple he envisioned.

house, was twenty cubits, and its width was twenty cubits; he overlaid it with six
hundred talents of fine gold. 9The weight of the nails was fifty shekels of gold. He **3.9** 1 Chron 28.11
overlaid the upper chambers with gold.
10 In the most holy place he made two carved cherubim and overlaid[g] them **3.10** 1 Kgs 6.23-28
with gold. 11The wings of the cherubim together extended twenty cubits: one wing
of the one, five cubits long, touched the wall of the house, and its other wing, five
cubits long, touched the wing of the other cherub; 12and of this cherub, one wing,
five cubits long, touched the wall of the house, and the other wing, also five cubits
long, was joined to the wing of the first cherub. 13The wings of these cherubim
extended twenty cubits; the cherubim[h] stood on their feet, facing the nave. 14And **3.14** Ex 26.31
Solomon[i] made the curtain of blue and purple and crimson fabrics and fine linen,
and worked cherubim into it.
15 In front of the house he made two pillars thirty-five cubits high, with a capi- **3.15** 1 Kgs 7.15-20
tal of five cubits on the top of each. 16He made encircling[j] chains and put them on
the tops of the pillars; and he made one hundred pomegranates, and put them on the
chains. 17He set up the pillars in front of the temple, one on the right, the other on **3.17** 1 Kgs 7.21
the left; the one on the right he called Jachin, and the one on the left, Boaz.

The temple furnishings are completed

4 He made an altar of bronze, twenty cubits long, twenty cubits wide, and ten **4.1** Ex 27.1,2
cubits high. 2Then he made the molten sea; it was round, ten cubits from rim 2 Kgs 16.14
to rim, and five cubits high. A line of thirty cubits would encircle it completely. **4.2**
3Under it were panels all around, each of ten cubits, surrounding the sea; there 1 Kgs 7.23-26
were two rows of panels, cast when it was cast. 4It stood on twelve oxen, three
facing north, three facing west, three facing south, and three facing east; the sea
was set on them. The hindquarters of each were toward the inside. 5Its thickness **4.5**
was a handbreadth; its rim was made like the rim of a cup, like the flower of a lily; 1 Kgs 7.26
it held three thousand baths.[k] 6He also made ten basins in which to wash, and set **4.6**
five on the right side, and five on the left. In these they were to rinse what was used 1 Kgs 7.38,40
for the burnt offering. The sea was for the priests to wash in.
7 He made ten golden lampstands as prescribed, and set them in the temple, **4.7**
five on the south side and five on the north. 8He also made ten tables and placed 1 Kgs 7.49
them in the temple, five on the right side and five on the left. And he made one
hundred basins of gold. 9He made the court of the priests, and the great court, and **4.9**
doors for the court; he overlaid their doors with bronze. 10He set the sea at the 1 Kgs 6.36 **4.10**
southeast corner of the house. 1 Kgs 7.39
11 And Huram made the pots, the shovels, and the basins. Thus Huram finished the work that he did for King Solomon on the house of God: 12the two pillars, **4.12**
the bowls, and the two capitals on the top of the pillars; and the two latticeworks to 1 Kgs 7.14; 20, 27-43
cover the two bowls of the capitals that were on the top of the pillars; 13the four 2 Chron 2.13
hundred pomegranates for the two latticeworks, two rows of pomegranates for each
latticework, to cover the two bowls of the capitals that were on the pillars. 14He
made the stands, the basins on the stands, 15the one sea, and the twelve oxen underneath it. 16The pots, the shovels, the forks, and all the equipment for these Huram-
abi made of burnished bronze for King Solomon for the house of the LORD. 17In the **4.17**
plain of the Jordan the king cast them, in the clay ground between Succoth and 1 Kgs 7.47

[g] Heb *they overlaid* [h] Heb *they* [i] Heb *he* [j] Cn: Heb *in the inner sanctuary* [k] A Hebrew measure of volume

3.10 Cherubim are mighty angels.

4.6 Why was everything in the temple built on such a grand scale? The great size and numbers were necessary in order to accommodate the crowds of thousands that would visit for the festivals, such as the passover (30.13). The numerous daily sacrifices (5.6) required many priests and a lot of equipment.

4.7 The craftsmen followed God's instructions carefully—with spectacular results. When God gives specific instructions, they must be followed to the letter. There is a time to be creative and put forth our own ideas, but not when they add to, alter, or contradict any specific directions God has already given to us in the Bible. For best results in your spiritual life, carefully seek and follow God's instructions.

4.11–16 Pots, shovels, and basins—these are implements of worship unfamiliar to us. Although the articles we use to aid our worship have changed, the purpose of worship remains the same—to give honor and praise to God. We must never let our worship of God be overshadowed by those helps we use to worship him.

Zeredah. 18 Solomon made all these things in great quantities, so that the weight of
the bronze was not determined.
19 So Solomon made all the things that were in the house of God: the golden
4.20 Ex 25.31-37 altar, the tables for the bread of the Presence, 20 the lampstands and their lamps of
pure gold to burn before the inner sanctuary, as prescribed; 21 the flowers, the
lamps, and the tongs, of purest gold; 22 the snuffers, basins, ladles, and firepans, of
pure gold. As for the entrance to the temple: the inner doors to the most holy place
and the doors of the nave of the temple were of gold.

5 Thus all the work that Solomon did for the house of the LORD was finished.
Solomon brought in the things that his father David had dedicated, and stored
the silver, the gold, and all the vessels in the treasuries of the house of God.

3. Solomon dedicates the temple

The ark is transferred to the temple

2 Then Solomon assembled the elders of Israel and all the heads of the tribes,

CAREFUL OBEDIENCE

Solomon and his workers carefully followed God's instructions. As a result, the temple work was blessed by God and completed in every detail. Here are a few examples of people in the Bible who did *not* carefully follow one of God's instructions, and the resulting consequences. It is not enough to obey God half-heartedly.

Who?	*God's instruction*	*Disobedience*	*Result*
Adam and Eve	Don't eat fruit from the tree of the knowledge of good and evil (Genesis 2.16, 17)	Satan tempted them and they ate (Genesis 3.1–6)	They were banished from the garden of Eden; pain and death were inflicted on all mankind (Genesis 3.24; Romans 5.12)
Nadab and Abihu	Fire for the sacrifice must come from the proper source (Leviticus 6.12, 13)	They used unholy fire for their sacrifice (Leviticus 10.1)	They were struck dead (Leviticus 10.2)
Moses	"Command the rock before their eyes to yield its water" (Numbers 20.8)	He spoke to the rock, but also struck it with his staff (Numbers 20.11)	He was not allowed to enter the promised land (Numbers 20.12)
Saul	Completely destroy the evil Amalekites (1 Samuel 15.3)	He spared the king and kept some of the booty (1 Samuel 15.8, 9)	God promised to end his reign (1 Samuel 15.16–26)
Uzzah	Only a priest can touch the sacred tabernacle furniture (Numbers 4.15)	He touched the ark of the covenant (2 Samuel 6.6)	He died instantly (2 Samuel 6.7)
Uzziah	Only the priests could offer incense in the temple or tabernacle sanctuary (Numbers 16.39, 40; 18.7)	He entered the holy place in the temple where only priests were allowed to go (2 Chronicles 26.16–18)	He became a leper (2 Chronicles 26.19)

4.22 All these details about the temple demonstrated the care Israel gave to acts of worship (see the note on 3.1ff). They also served as a manual to the original readers of 2 Chronicles, those who would rebuild a new temple on its original site (Ezra 3.8–6.15) after Solomon's temple was destroyed by the Babylonians (2 Kings 25).

5.1ff Why is there so much emphasis on the temple in the Old Testament?

(1) *It was a symbol of religious authority.* The temple was God's way of centralizing worship at Jerusalem in order to insure that correct belief would be kept intact through many generations.

(2) *It was a symbol of God's holiness.* The temple's beautiful atmosphere inspired respect and awe for God; it was the setting for many of the great visions of the prophets.

(3) *It was a symbol of God's covenant with Israel.* The temple kept the people focused upon God's law (the tablets of the ten commandments were kept in the temple) rather than on the kings' exploits. It was a place where God was especially present to his people.

(4) *It was a symbol of forgiveness.* The temple's design, furniture, and customs were great object lessons for all the people, reminding them of the seriousness of sin, the penalty that sin incurred, and their need of forgiveness.

(5) *It prepared the people for the Messiah.* In the New Testament, Christ said he came to fulfill the law, not to destroy it. Hebrews 8.1, 2 and 9.11, 12 use temple customs to explain what Christ did when he died for us.

(6) *It was a testimony to human effort and creativity.* Inspired by the beauty of God's character, people devoted themselves to high achievements in engineering, science, and art in order to praise him.

(7) *It was a place of prayer.* In the temple, people could spend time in prayer to God.

5.1–3 The temple took seven years to build. First Kings 6.38 says that the temple was completed in the eighth month (November) of Solomon's eleventh year as king (959 B.C.). Because 5.3 states that the dedication ceremonies were held in the seventh month, they must have occurred either one month before or eleven months after the temple's completion.

the leaders of the ancestral houses of the people of Israel, in Jerusalem, to bring up 5.2
the ark of the covenant of the LORD out of the city of David, which is Zion. 3 And 1 Kgs 8.1-9 2 Chron 1.4
all the Israelites assembled before the king at the festival that is in the seventh
month. 4 And all the elders of Israel came, and the Levites carried the ark. 5 So they 5.4
brought up the ark, the tent of meeting, and all the holy vessels that were in the tent; 2 Chron 5.7
the priests and the Levites brought them up. 6 King Solomon and all the congregation of Israel, who had assembled before him, were before the ark, sacrificing so
many sheep and oxen that they could not be numbered or counted. 7 Then the priests
brought the ark of the covenant of the LORD to its place, in the inner sanctuary of
the house, in the most holy place, underneath the wings of the cherubim. 8 For the
cherubim spread out their wings over the place of the ark, so that the cherubim
made a covering above the ark and its poles. 9 The poles were so long that the ends 5.9
of the poles were seen from the holy place in front of the inner sanctuary; but they 1 Kgs 8.8,9
could not be seen from outside; they are there to this day. 10 There was nothing in 5.10
the ark except the two tablets that Moses put there at Horeb, where the LORD made Deut 10.2-5 Heb 9.4
a covenant[l] with the people of Israel after they came out of Egypt.
11 Now when the priests came out of the holy place (for all the priests who were 5.11
present had sanctified themselves, without regard to their divisions, 12 and all the 1 Chron 13.8 15.16,24
levitical singers, Asaph, Heman, and Jeduthun, their sons and kindred, arrayed in 24.1-5; 25.1-4
fine linen, with cymbals, harps, and lyres, stood east of the altar with one hundred 2 Chron 7.6
twenty priests who were trumpeters). 13 It was the duty of the trumpeters and sing- 5.13
ers to make themselves heard in unison in praise and thanksgiving to the LORD, and 1 Kgs 8.11 1 Chron 16.34,
when the song was raised, with trumpets and cymbals and other musical instru- 42
ments, in praise to the LORD, 2 Chron 7.3

"For he is good,
for his steadfast love endures forever,"

the house, the house of the LORD, was filled with a cloud, 14 so that the priests could
not stand to minister because of the cloud; for the glory of the LORD filled the house
of God.

Solomon's blessing

6 Then Solomon said, "The LORD has said that he would reside in thick dark- 6.1
ness. 2 I have built you an exalted house, a place for you to reside in forever." 1 Kgs 8.12-50
3 Then the king turned around and blessed all the assembly of Israel, while all
the assembly of Israel stood. 4 And he said, "Blessed be the LORD, the God of Israel, who with his hand has fulfilled what he promised with his mouth to my father 6.5
David, saying, 5 'Since the day that I brought my people out of the land of Egypt, 1 Chron 28.4 2 Chron 12.13

[l] Heb lacks *a covenant*

5.3 The festival "that is in the seventh month" was the festival of booths, celebrating God's protection of Israel as they wandered in the wilderness before entering the promised land. The purpose of this annual festival was to renew Israel's commitment to God and their trust in his guidance and protection. The festival beautifully coincided with the dedication of the temple. As the people remembered the wanderings in the wilderness when their ancestors had lived in tents, they were even more thankful for the permanence of this glorious temple.

5.9 Some books of the Bible were compiled and edited under God's inspiration from other sources. Because 1 and 2 Chronicles cover many centuries, they were compiled from several sources by a single person. The phrase "they are there to this day" was taken from material written before Judah's exile in 586 B.C. Although 1 and 2 Chronicles were compiled after the exile and after Solomon's temple was destroyed, the writer thought it best to leave this phrase in the narrative.

5.11, 12 The priests came out of the innermost room of the temple where the ark, the symbol of God's presence among his people, resided. (The Bible sometimes calls this *the most holy place,* sometimes *the holy place. The holy place* usually refers to the outer room, where the bread of the Presence, altar of incense, and lampstand were kept.) Ordinarily the most holy place could be entered only once a year by the high priest on the day of atonement. On this unique occasion, however, several priests had to enter the most holy place in order to carry the ark to its new resting place. The Levites praised God when these priests emerged from the most holy place because they then knew God had accepted this new home for the ark (5.14).

5.13 The first service at the temple began with honoring God and acknowledging his presence and goodness. In the same way, our worship should begin with a recognition of God's love. Praise God first; then you will be prepared to present your needs to him. Recalling God's love and mercy will inspire you to worship him daily. Psalm 107 is an example of how David recalled God's lovingkindness.

6.3 As the people received Solomon's blessing, they stood; as Solomon prayed, he knelt (6.13). Both standing and kneeling are acts of reverence. Acts of reverence make us feel more worshipful, and they let others see that we are honoring God. When you stand or kneel in church or at prayer, make these actions more than mere forms prescribed by tradition. Instead let them indicate your love for God.

I have not chosen a city from any of the tribes of Israel in which to build a house,
so that my name might be there, and I chose no one as ruler over my people Israel;
6 but I have chosen Jerusalem in order that my name may be there, and I have chosen David to be over my people Israel.' 7 My father David had it in mind to build
6.8 a house for the name of the LORD, the God of Israel. 8 But the LORD said to my
1 Kgs 5.3 father David, 'You did well to consider building a house for my name; 9 nevertheless you shall not build the house, but your son who shall be born to you shall build
the house for my name.' 10 Now the LORD has fulfilled his promise that he made; for
I have succeeded my father David, and sit on the throne of Israel, as the LORD
promised, and have built the house for the name of the LORD, the God of Israel.
6.11 11 There I have set the ark, in which is the covenant of the LORD that he made with
2 Chron 5.7,10 the people of Israel."

Solomon's prayer of dedication

6.12 12 Then Solomon[m] stood before the altar of the LORD in the presence of the
1 Kgs 8.54 Neh 8.4 whole assembly of Israel, and spread out his hands. 13 Solomon had made a bronze
platform five cubits long, five cubits wide, and three cubits high, and had set it in
the court; and he stood on it. Then he knelt on his knees in the presence of the whole
6.14 assembly of Israel, and spread out his hands toward heaven. 14 He said, "O LORD,
Ex 15.11 Deut 3.24; 7.9 God of Israel, there is no God like you, in heaven or on earth, keeping covenant in
6.15 steadfast love with your servants who walk before you with all their heart— 15 you
1 Chron 22.9,10 who have kept for your servant, my father David, what you promised to him. Indeed, you promised with your mouth and this day have fulfilled with your hand.
6.16 16 Therefore, O LORD, God of Israel, keep for your servant, my father David, that
1 Kgs 2.4 2 Chron 7.18 which you promised him, saying, 'There shall never fail you a successor before me
to sit on the throne of Israel, if only your children keep to their way, to walk in my
law as you have walked before me.' 17 Therefore, O LORD, God of Israel, let your
word be confirmed, which you promised to your servant David.

6.18 18 "But will God indeed reside with mortals on earth? Even heaven and the
2 Chron 2.6 highest heaven cannot contain you, how much less this house that I have built!
19 Regard your servant's prayer and his plea, O LORD my God, heeding the cry and
6.20 the prayer that your servant prays to you. 20 May your eyes be open day and night
Mic 7.18 toward this house, the place where you promised to set your name, and may you
heed the prayer that your servant prays toward this place. 21 And hear the plea of
your servant and of your people Israel, when they pray toward this place; may you
hear from heaven your dwelling place; hear and forgive.

22 "If someone sins against another and is required to take an oath and comes
and swears before your altar in this house, 23 may you hear from heaven, and act,
and judge your servants, repaying the guilty by bringing their conduct on their own
head, and vindicating those who are in the right by rewarding them in accordance
with their righteousness.

24 "When your people Israel, having sinned against you, are defeated before an

[m] Heb *he*

6.12, 13 It was unusual for a king to kneel before someone else in front of his own people, because kneeling meant submitting to a higher authority. Solomon demonstrated his great love and respect for God by kneeling before him. His action showed that he acknowledged God as the ultimate king and authority, and it encouraged the people to do the same.

6.18 The temple was a place where the people could worship God. God did not *need* a temple to live in, because not even the highest heaven could contain him (2.6). But at the temple God was present in a special way among his people. While it is true that we can praise God and pray anywhere anytime, gathering with others for singing and praise enhances our worship. It also strengthens our resolve to follow God.

6.18 Solomon marveled that the temple could contain the power of God and that God would be willing to live on earth among sinful people. We marvel that God, through his Son, Jesus, lived among us in human form to reveal his eternal purposes to us. In doing so, God was reaching out to us in love. God wants us to reach out to him in return in order to know him and to love him with all our hearts. Don't simply marvel at his power; take time to get to know him.

6.19–42 As Solomon led the people in prayer, he asked God to hear their prayers concerning a variety of situations: (1) crime (6.22, 23); (2) enemy attacks (6.24, 25); (3) drought (6.26, 27); (4) famine (6.28–31); (5) the influx of foreigners (6.32, 33); (6) war (6.34, 35); (7) sin (6.36–39). God is concerned with whatever we face, even the difficult consequences we bring upon ourselves. He wants us to turn to him in prayer. When you pray, remember that God hears you. Don't let the extremity of your situation cause you to doubt his care for you.

enemy but turn again to you, confess your name, pray and plead with you in this
house, 25 may you hear from heaven, and forgive the sin of your people Israel, and
bring them again to the land that you gave to them and to their ancestors.
26 "When heaven is shut up and there is no rain because they have sinned
against you, and then they pray toward this place, confess your name, and turn
from their sin, because you punish them, 27 may you hear in heaven, forgive the sin
of your servants, your people Israel, when you teach them the good way in which
they should walk; and send down rain upon your land, which you have given to
your people as an inheritance.
28 "If there is famine in the land, if there is plague, blight, mildew, locust, or
caterpillar; if their enemies besiege them in any of the settlements of the lands;
whatever suffering, whatever sickness there is; 29 whatever prayer, whatever plea
from any individual or from all your people Israel, all knowing their own suffering
and their own sorrows so that they stretch out their hands toward this house; 30 may **6.30**
you hear from heaven, your dwelling place, forgive, and render to all whose heart 1 Sam 16.7 1 Chron 28.9
you know, according to all their ways, for only you know the human heart. 31 Thus
may they fear you and walk in your ways all the days that they live in the land that
you gave to our ancestors.
32 "Likewise when foreigners, who are not of your people Israel, come from a
distant land because of your great name, and your mighty hand, and your outstretched arm, when they come and pray toward this house, 33 may you hear from
heaven your dwelling place, and do whatever the foreigners ask of you, in order
that all the peoples of the earth may know your name and fear you, as do your
people Israel, and that they may know that your name has been invoked on this
house that I have built.
34 "If your people go out to battle against their enemies, by whatever way you
shall send them, and they pray to you toward this city that you have chosen and the
house that I have built for your name, 35 then hear from heaven their prayer and
their plea, and maintain their cause.
36 "If they sin against you—for there is no one who does not sin—and you are **6.36**
angry with them and give them to an enemy, so that they are carried away captive Job 15.14-16 Jas 3.2
to a land far or near; 37 then if they come to their senses in the land to which they 1 Jn 1.8-10
have been taken captive, and repent, and plead with you in the land of their captivity, saying, 'We have sinned, and have done wrong; we have acted wickedly'; 38 if
they repent with all their heart and soul in the land of their captivity, to which they
were taken captive, and pray toward their land, which you gave to their ancestors,
the city that you have chosen, and the house that I have built for your name, 39 then
hear from heaven your dwelling place their prayer and their pleas, maintain their
cause and forgive your people who have sinned against you. 40 Now, O my God, let **6.40**
your eyes be open and your ears attentive to prayer from this place. 2 Chron 7.15 Neh 1.6,11
41 "Now rise up, O LORD God, and go to your resting place, Ps 17.1
you and the ark of your might. **6.41** Ps 132.8,9
Let your priests, O LORD God, be clothed with salvation,
and let your faithful rejoice in your goodness.

6.26 Why would Solomon assume that drought would come as a result of sin? Sin is not necessarily the direct cause of natural disasters today, but this was a special case. God had made a specific agreement with the Israelites that famine could be a consequence of their sins (Deuteronomy 28.23, 24).

6.30 Have you ever felt far from God, separated by feelings of failure and personal problems? In his prayer, Solomon underscores the fact that God stands ready to hear us, to forgive our sins, and to restore our relationship to him. God is waiting and listening for our confessions of guilt and our recommitment to obey him. He hears us when we pour out our needs and problems to him and is ready to forgive us and restore us to fellowship with him. Don't wait to experience his loving forgiveness.

6.32, 33 A personal testimony is an effective method for convincing people to follow a cause or buy a product. When people see changed lives and watch God's power at work, they will want to worship him. Those close to you should see God at work in your words and actions. What kind of testimony do you give?

6.36 The Bible makes it clear that no one is exempt from sin, not even God's appointed kings. Sin is a condition we all share, and we all should acknowledge it as Solomon did. When we realize we have sinned, we should quickly ask God for forgiveness and restoration. Knowing we have a tendency to sin should keep us close to God, seeking his guidance and strength. This truth is also mentioned in Psalm 14.3, Ecclesiastes 7.20, and Romans 3.23.

42 O LORD God, do not reject your anointed one.
Remember your steadfast love for your servant David."

God's glory fills the temple

7.1 1 Kgs 8.54 18.24,38
7 When Solomon had ended his prayer, fire came down from heaven and consumed the burnt offering and the sacrifices; and the glory of the LORD filled the
temple. 2 The priests could not enter the house of the LORD, because the glory of the
7.3 2 Chron 5.13 20.21
LORD filled the LORD's house. 3 When all the people of Israel saw the fire come
down and the glory of the LORD on the temple, they bowed down on the pavement
with their faces to the ground, and worshiped and gave thanks to the LORD, saying,
"For he is good,
for his steadfast love endures forever."
7.4 1 Kgs 8.62,63
4 Then the king and all the people offered sacrifice before the LORD. 5 King
Solomon offered as a sacrifice twenty-two thousand oxen and one hundred twenty
7.6 1 Chron 15.16-21 2 Chron 5.12
thousand sheep. So the king and all the people dedicated the house of God. 6 The
priests stood at their posts; the Levites also, with the instruments for music to the
LORD that King David had made for giving thanks to the LORD—for his steadfast
love endures forever—whenever David offered praises by their ministry. Opposite
them the priests sounded trumpets; and all Israel stood.
7.7 1 Kgs 8.64-66
7 Solomon consecrated the middle of the court that was in front of the house of
the LORD; for there he offered the burnt offerings and the fat of the offerings of
well-being because the bronze altar Solomon had made could not hold the burnt
offering and the grain offering and the fat parts.
7.8 1 Kgs 8.65
8 At that time Solomon held the festival for seven days, and all Israel with him,
7.9 Lev 23.26
a very great congregation, from Lebo-hamath to the Wadi of Egypt. 9 On the eighth
day they held a solemn assembly; for they had observed the dedication of the altar
seven days and the festival seven days. 10 On the twenty-third day of the seventh
month he sent the people away to their homes, joyful and in good spirits because of
the goodness that the LORD had shown to David and to Solomon and to his people
Israel.
11 Thus Solomon finished the house of the LORD and the king's house; all that
Solomon had planned to do in the house of the LORD and in his own house he
successfully accomplished.

God speaks to Solomon

12 Then the LORD appeared to Solomon in the night and said to him: "I have
heard your prayer, and have chosen this place for myself as a house of sacrifice.
7.13 2 Chron 6.26-28
13 When I shut up the heavens so that there is no rain, or command the locust to
7.14 2 Chron 6.37-39
devour the land, or send pestilence among my people, 14 if my people who are
called by my name humble themselves, pray, seek my face, and turn from their
7.15 2 Chron 6.20,40
wicked ways, then I will hear from heaven, and will forgive their sin and heal their
land. 15 Now my eyes will be open and my ears attentive to the prayer that is made
7.16 2 Chron 7.12
in this place. 16 For now I have chosen and consecrated this house so that my name

---

7.1, 2 God sent fire from heaven to consume the offering and to begin the fire that was to burn continuously under the altar of burnt offering. This symbolized God's presence. God did the same when inaugurating the tabernacle (Leviticus 9.22–24). This was the real dedication of the temple, because only God's purifying power can make something holy.

7.4, 5 The temple was dedicated to God, and Solomon and the people prepared to worship him. Dedication means setting apart a place, object, or person for an exclusive purpose. The purpose of this dedication was to set apart the temple as a place to worship God. Today, our bodies are God's temple (2 Corinthians 6.16). Solomon's dedication of the temple shows us that we should dedicate ourselves to carry out God's special purpose (Ephesians 1.11, 12).

7.12 Months, maybe years, had passed since Solomon's prayer of dedication (chapter 6). Several other building projects were completed after the temple (7.11; 8.1). After all this time God told Solomon that he had heard his prayer. How often do we look for immediate answers to our prayers and, when nothing happens, wonder if God has heard us? God does hear, and he will provide for us, but we must trust that he will answer at the proper time.

7.14 In chapter 6, Solomon asked God to make provisions for the people when they sinned. God answered with four conditions for forgiveness: (1) humble yourself by admitting your sins, (2) pray to God, asking for forgiveness, (3) seek for God continually, and (4) turn from sinful behavior.

7.15 When we are in need, there may be no one with whom we can talk, or we may be afraid to share our need with another person. God assured Solomon, however, that he would not lack assistance if he came to God in humility. God promises to listen to every prayer offered in the right attitude. God is always available.

may be there forever; my eyes and my heart will be there for all time. 17 As for you,
if you walk before me, as your father David walked, doing according to all that I
have commanded you and keeping my statutes and my ordinances, 18 then I will 7.18
establish your royal throne, as I made covenant with your father David saying, 2 Chron 6.16
'You shall never lack a successor to rule over Israel.'

19 "But if you[n] turn aside and forsake my statutes and my commandments that 7.19
I have set before you, and go and serve other gods and worship them, 20 then I will Lev 26.14,33 Deut 28.15
pluck you[o] up from the land that I have given you;[o] and this house, which I have 7.20
consecrated for my name, I will cast out of my sight, and will make it a proverb and Deut 28.37 29.28
a byword among all peoples. 21 And regarding this house, now exalted, everyone 1 Kgs 14.15
passing by will be astonished, and say, 'Why has the LORD done such a thing to this 7.21
land and to this house?' 22 Then they will say, 'Because they abandoned the LORD Deut 29.24,25
the God of their ancestors who brought them out of the land of Egypt, and they
adopted other gods, and worshiped them and served them; therefore he has brought
all this calamity upon them.'"

4. Solomon's riches and wisdom

Solomon's building activities

8 At the end of twenty years, during which Solomon had built the house of the 8.1
LORD and his own house, 2 Solomon rebuilt the cities that Huram had given to 1 Kgs 9.1-28
him, and settled the people of Israel in them.

3 Solomon went to Hamath-zobah, and captured it. 4 He built Tadmor in the
wilderness and all the storage towns that he built in Hamath. 5 He also built Upper 8.5
Beth-horon and Lower Beth-horon, fortified cities, with walls, gates, and bars, 1 Chron 7.24 2 Chron 14.7
6 and Baalath, as well as all Solomon's storage towns, and all the towns for his
chariots, the towns for his cavalry, and whatever Solomon desired to build, in Jerusalem, in Lebanon, and in all the land of his dominion. 7 All the people who were 8.7
left of the Hittites, the Amorites, the Perizzites, the Hivites, and the Jebusites, who Gen 15.18-21 1 Kgs 3.1; 7.8
were not of Israel, 8 from their descendants who were still left in the land, whom the
people of Israel had not destroyed—these Solomon conscripted for forced labor, as
is still the case today. 9 But of the people of Israel Solomon made no slaves for his
work; they were soldiers, and his officers, the commanders of his chariotry and
cavalry. 10 These were the chief officers of King Solomon, two hundred fifty of
them, who exercised authority over the people.

11 Solomon brought Pharaoh's daughter from the city of David to the house 8.11
that he had built for her, for he said, "My wife shall not live in the house of King 1 Kgs 3.1; 7.8
David of Israel, for the places to which the ark of the LORD has come are holy."

12 Then Solomon offered up burnt offerings to the LORD on the altar of the 8.12
LORD that he had built in front of the vestibule, 13 as the duty of each day required, 2 Chron 4.1
offering according to the commandment of Moses for the sabbaths, the new moons, 8.13 Ex 23.14-17
and the three annual festivals—the festival of unleavened bread, the festival of 29.38-42
weeks, and the festival of booths. 14 According to the ordinance of his father David, Num 28.3 8.14
he appointed the divisions of the priests for their service, and the Levites for their 1 Chron 24.1
offices of praise and ministry alongside the priests as the duty of each day required, 25.1; 26.1 Neh 12.24,36

[n] The word *you* in this verse is plural [o] Heb *them*

7.17–22 God plainly set forth certain conditions for Solomon to meet if he wanted the kingdom to continue. If he followed God, Solomon and his descendants would prosper; if he did not, he and the nation would be destroyed. In Deuteronomy 27 and 28, these conditions were outlined before all the people.

But sin is deceptively attractive, and Solomon eventually turned from God. As a result, his son and heir lost most of his kingdom. Following God brings benefits and rewards (not necessarily material). Turning away from him brings suffering, punishment, and ultimately destruction. Today, God's conditions are just as clear as they were in Solomon's day. Will you choose to obey God and live?

7.21, 22 Soon after Solomon's reign, the temple was ransacked (12.9). It is difficult for us to imagine that such a great and wise king could become corrupted by idols—symbols of power, prosperity, and sexuality. But even today these idols lure us into their traps. When we allow any desire to rival God's proper place, we have taken the first step toward moral and spiritual decay.

8.11 Solomon married Pharaoh's daughter to secure a military alliance with Egypt. He did not let the woman live in David's palace, however, where the ark of God had once been kept. This implies that Solomon knew his pagan marriage would not please God. Solomon married many other foreign women, and this was contrary to God's law (Deuteronomy 7.3, 4). These foreign women worshiped false gods and were certain to contaminate Israel with their beliefs and practices. Eventually Solomon's pagan wives caused his downfall (1 Kings 11.1–11).

and the gatekeepers in their divisions for the several gates; for so David the man of
God had commanded. 15 They did not turn away from what the king had commanded the priests and Levites regarding anything at all, or regarding the
treasuries.
16 Thus all the work of Solomon was accomplished from[p] the day the foundation of the house of the LORD was laid until the house of the LORD was finished
completely.
8.17 17 Then Solomon went to Ezion-geber and Eloth on the shore of the sea, in the
1 Kgs 9.26 land of Edom. 18 Huram sent him, in the care of his servants, ships and servants
2 Kgs 14.22 familiar with the sea. They went to Ophir, together with the servants of Solomon,
2 Chron 9.10,13 and imported from there four hundred fifty talents of gold and brought it to King
Solomon.

The queen of Sheba

9.1 **9** When the queen of Sheba heard of the fame of Solomon, she came to Jerusa-
1 Kgs 10.1-13 lem to test him with hard questions, having a very great retinue and camels
Mt 12.42 bearing spices and very much gold and precious stones. When she came to Solo-
Lk 11.31 mon, she discussed with him all that was on her mind. 2 Solomon answered all her
questions; there was nothing hidden from Solomon that he could not explain to her.
3 When the queen of Sheba had observed the wisdom of Solomon, the house that he
had built, 4 the food of his table, the seating of his officials, and the attendance of
his servants, and their clothing, his valets, and their clothing, and his burnt offerings[q] that he offered at the house of the LORD, there was no more spirit left in her.
5 So she said to the king, "The report was true that I heard in my own land of
your accomplishments and of your wisdom, 6 but I did not believe the[r] reports until
I came and my own eyes saw it. Not even half of the greatness of your wisdom had
been told to me; you far surpass the report that I had heard. 7 Happy are your people! Happy are these your servants, who continually attend you and hear your wis-
9.8 dom! 8 Blessed be the LORD your God, who has delighted in you and set you on his
Deut 7.8 throne as king for the LORD your God. Because your God loved Israel and would
1 Chron 28.5 establish them forever, he has made you king over them, that you may execute
29.23 justice and righteousness." 9 Then she gave the king one hundred twenty talents of
2 Chron 2.11 gold, a very great quantity of spices, and precious stones: there were no spices such
as those that the queen of Sheba gave to King Solomon.
9.10 10 Moreover the servants of Huram and the servants of Solomon who brought
2 Chron 8.18 gold from Ophir brought algum wood and precious stones. 11 From the algum
wood, the king made steps[s] for the house of the LORD and for the king's house,
lyres also and harps for the singers; there never was seen the like of them before in
the land of Judah.
12 Meanwhile King Solomon granted the queen of Sheba every desire that she

[p] Gk Syr Vg: Heb *to* [q] Gk Syr Vg 1 Kings 10.5: Heb *ascent* [r] Heb *their* [s] Gk Vg: Meaning of Heb uncertain

---

8.15 Although Solomon carefully followed God's instructions for building the temple and offering sacrifices (8.13), he paid no attention to what God's Word said about marrying heathen women. His sin in marrying a foreign wife (8.11) began his slide away from God. No matter how good or spiritual we are in most areas of life, one unsurrendered area can begin a downfall. Guard carefully *every* area of your life, especially your relationships. Don't give sin any foothold.

9.1–8 The queen of Sheba had heard about Solomon's wisdom, but she was overwhelmed when she saw for herself the fruits of that wisdom. Although Solomon had married Pharaoh's daughter, he still sincerely tried to follow God at this stage in his life. When people get to know you and ask hard questions, will your responses reflect God? Your life can be a powerful witness; let others see God at work in you.

9.2, 6 Ruling a nation is an awesome task. Solomon realized this when he exclaimed, "Who can rule this great people of yours?" (1.10). But God had given him this responsibility, and he also gave Solomon the necessary leadership abilities to carry it out. Following Jesus' example also seems like a difficult task, but God has given you "everything needed for life and godliness" (2 Peter 1.3). Never despair when you think you do not have the ability to solve a problem. God will give you all you need to fulfill the responsibilities he has given you. Then others will be amazed at what they see.

9.8 The queen of Sheba marveled at Solomon, claiming that God must love his people greatly to give them such a king. Israel greatly prospered during Solomon's reign, a witness to God's power and love for his people. The good times are a witness of God's love and faithfulness. But hard times come to believers, too, and our perseverance and steadfast hope during those times will demonstrate our love and faithfulness to God. How we live helps others see our love for God.

9.11 This was probably sandalwood, a smooth, red-colored wood that accepts a high polish. This beautiful wood was extremely expensive.

expressed, well beyond what she had brought to the king. Then she returned to her
own land, with her servants.

Solomon's greatness

13 The weight of gold that came to Solomon in one year was six hundred sixty- **9.13**
six talents of gold, 14 besides that which the traders and merchants brought; and all 1 Kgs 10.14-28
the kings of Arabia and the governors of the land brought gold and silver to Solomon. 15 King Solomon made two hundred large shields of beaten gold; six hundred
shekels of beaten gold went into each large shield. 16 He made three hundred shields
of beaten gold; three hundred shekels of gold went into each shield; and the king put
them in the House of the Forest of Lebanon. 17 The king also made a great ivory
throne, and overlaid it with pure gold. 18 The throne had six steps and a footstool of
gold, which were attached to the throne, and on each side of the seat were arm rests
and two lions standing beside the arm rests, 19 while twelve lions were standing,
one on each end of a step on the six steps. The like of it was never made in any
kingdom. 20 All King Solomon's drinking vessels were of gold, and all the vessels
of the House of the Forest of Lebanon were of pure gold; silver was not considered
as anything in the days of Solomon. 21 For the king's ships went to Tarshish with **9.21**
the servants of Huram; once every three years the ships of Tarshish used to come 2 Chron 20.36,
bringing gold, silver, ivory, apes, and peacocks.[t] 37

22 Thus King Solomon excelled all the kings of the earth in riches and in wis- **9.22**
dom. 23 All the kings of the earth sought the presence of Solomon to hear his wis- 1 Kgs 3.13 2 Chron 1.12
dom, which God had put into his mind. 24 Every one of them brought a present, **9.25**
objects of silver and gold, garments, weaponry, spices, horses, and mules, so Deut 17.16 1 Kgs 4.26
much year by year. 25 Solomon had four thousand stalls for horses and chariots, and 10.26
twelve thousand horses, which he stationed in the chariot cities and with the king 2 Chron 1.14
in Jerusalem. 26 He ruled over all the kings from the Euphrates to the land of the **9.26** 1 Kgs 4.21,24
Philistines, and to the border of Egypt. 27 The king made silver as common in Jeru- **9.27**
salem as stone, and cedar as plentiful as the sycamore of the Shephelah. 28 Horses 2 Chron 1.15-17
were imported for Solomon from Egypt and from all lands. **9.28** 2 Chron 1.16

The death of Solomon

29 Now the rest of the acts of Solomon, from first to last, are they not written **9.29**
in the history of the prophet Nathan, and in the prophecy of Ahijah the Shilonite, 1 Kgs 11.41-43 1 Chron 29.29
and in the visions of the seer Iddo concerning Jeroboam son of Nebat? 30 Solomon
reigned in Jerusalem over all Israel forty years. 31 Solomon slept with his ancestors **9.31**
and was buried in the city of his father David; and his son Rehoboam succeeded 1 Kgs 2.10
him.

B. THE KINGDOM OF JUDAH (10.1 – 36.23)

After Solomon's death, the northern tribes revolt, and we read little more about them in 2 Chronicles. The remainder of 2 Chronicles recounts the alternating periods of apostasy and reform in Judah. In the end, Judah would not turn from its sin, and the tragic result was a 70-year captivity in Babylon. Sin in our lives will also lead to judgment and devastation. Although God's judgment may seem slow, it is nevertheless certain.

1. The nation of Israel splits apart

Rehoboam speaks roughly to the people

10 Rehoboam went to Shechem, for all Israel had come to Shechem to make **10.1**
him king. 2 When Jeroboam son of Nebat heard of it (for he was in Egypt, 1 Kgs 12.1-20
where he had fled from King Solomon), then Jeroboam returned from Egypt. **10.2** 1 Kgs 11.40

[t] Or *baboons*

9.13, 14 God had promised that Israel would prosper if Solomon followed him as David did (7.17, 18). As long as Solomon remained loyal to God, God blessed Israel abundantly. God also honors his promises to us, and his word is the guarantee. But any good guarantee includes certain conditions. God's promises and blessings are guaranteed as long as we keep our agreement with him. We must keep our commitment to him alive and strong.

9.29 For the rest of Solomon's story, see 1 Kings 10.26 – 11.43. In his later years, Solomon turned away from God and led the nation into worshiping idols.

3 They sent and called him; and Jeroboam and all Israel came and said to Rehoboam, 4 "Your father made our yoke heavy. Now therefore lighten the hard service
of your father and his heavy yoke that he placed on us, and we will serve you." 5 He
said to them, "Come to me again in three days." So the people went away.
6 Then King Rehoboam took counsel with the older men who had attended his
father Solomon while he was still alive, saying, "How do you advise me to answer
this people?" 7 They answered him, "If you will be kind to this people and please
them, and speak good words to them, then they will be your servants forever." 8 But
he rejected the advice that the older men gave him, and consulted the young men

REHOBOAM

Settling for cheap imitations in exchange for the real thing is a poor way to live. In every area of his life, Rehoboam consistently traded away what was real for what was counterfeit. Given wise and unwise counsel by his advisers at his coronation, he chose to grab for power and control rather than to take patiently the counsel of those older and wiser than he and treat his people with kindness. Although his position came from God, he chose to abandon God. These unwise decisions made him weaker rather than stronger. As a result, he was invaded by the Egyptians and stripped of the riches he inherited from David and Solomon. To replace them, he had cheap bronze copies made.

Throughout the early part of his reign, Rehoboam fluctuated between obeying God and going his own way. Outward appearances were kept up, but his inward attitudes were evil. Following in the tradition of David gave Rehoboam many opportunities for real greatness. Instead, he ended up with a divided and broken kingdom.

How much of real living have we traded away for the things that do not last? We trade healthy bodies for momentary excitement, personal integrity for fast-fading wealth, honesty for lies, God's wise guidance for our selfish ways. We sin when we willingly give little value to "the real thing" God has already given us.

Our counterfeit lives may fool some people, but they never fool God. Yet in spite of what he sees in us, God offers mercy. Are you a self-managed enterprise, counterfeit at best? Or have you placed yourself in God's care? Do the decisions you must make today need a second consideration in light of Rehoboam's example?

Strengths and accomplishments:
- Third and last king of the united nation of Israel, but only for a short time
- Fortified his kingdom and achieved a measure of popularity

Weaknesses and mistakes:
- Followed unwise advice and divided his kingdom
- Married heathen women, as his father Solomon had done
- Abandoned the worship of God and allowed idolatry to flourish

Lessons from his life:
- Thoughtless decisions often lead to exchanging what is most valuable for something of far less value
- Every choice we make has real and long-lasting consequences

Vital statistics:
- Where: Jerusalem
- Occupation: King of the united kingdom of Israel, and later of the southern kingdom of Judah
- Relatives: Father: Solomon. Mother: Naamah. Son: Abijah. Wife: Maachah
- Contemporaries: Jeroboam, Shishak, Shemaiah

Key verse:
"When the rule of Rehoboam was established and he grew strong, he abandoned the law of the Lord, he and all Israel with him" (2 Chronicles 12.1).

Rehoboam's story is told in 1 Kings 11.43—14.31 and 2 Chronicles 9.31—13.7. He is also mentioned in Matthew 1.7.

10.1 The crowning of an Israelite king would normally have taken place in Jerusalem. But Rehoboam saw that there was the possibility of trouble in the north; so to maintain his hold on the country, he chose Shechem, a city about 35 miles north of Jerusalem. Shechem was an ancient site for making covenants (Joshua 24.1).

10.1–14 Following bad advice can cause disaster. Rehoboam lost the chance to rule a peaceful, united kingdom because he rejected the advice of Solomon's older counselors, preferring that of his peers. Rehoboam made two errors in seeking advice: (1) he did not give extra consideration to the suggestions of those who knew the situation better than he, and (2) he did not ask God for wisdom to discern which was the better option.

It is easy to follow the advice of our peers because they often feel as we do. But their view may be limited. It is important to listen carefully to those who have more experience than we do because they can see the bigger picture.

10.2, 3 Ahijah the prophet had predicted that Israel would split in two and that Jeroboam would become king of the northern section. When Solomon learned of this prophecy, he tried to kill Jeroboam, and Jeroboam was forced to flee to Egypt (1 Kings 11.26–40).

who had grown up with him and now attended him. 9 He said to them, "What do
you advise that we answer this people who have said to me, 'Lighten the yoke that
your father put on us'?" 10 The young men who had grown up with him said to him,
"Thus should you speak to the people who said to you, 'Your father made our yoke
heavy, but you must lighten it for us'; tell them, 'My little finger is thicker than my
father's loins. 11 Now, whereas my father laid on you a heavy yoke, I will add to
your yoke. My father disciplined you with whips, but I will discipline you with
scorpions.' "

12 So Jeroboam and all the people came to Rehoboam the third day, as the king
had said, "Come to me again the third day." 13 The king answered them harshly.
King Rehoboam rejected the advice of the older men; 14 he spoke to them in accordance with the advice of the young men, "My father made your yoke heavy, but I
will add to it; my father disciplined you with whips, but I will discipline you with
scorpions." 15 So the king did not listen to the people, because it was a turn of **10.15**
affairs brought about by God so that the LORD might fulfill his word, which he had 1 Kgs 11.29-39
spoken by Ahijah the Shilonite to Jeroboam son of Nebat.

The northern tribes revolt

16 When all Israel saw that the king would not listen to them, the people an- **10.16**
swered the king, 2 Sam 20.1 2 Chron 10.19

"What share do we have in David?
We have no inheritance in the son of Jesse.
Each of you to your tents, O Israel!
Look now to your own house, O David."

So all Israel departed to their tents. 17 But Rehoboam reigned over the people of
Israel who were living in the cities of Judah. 18 When King Rehoboam sent Hado- **10.18**
ram, who was taskmaster over the forced labor, the people of Israel stoned him to 1 Kgs 4.6; 5.14
death. King Rehoboam hurriedly mounted his chariot to flee to Jerusalem. 19 So
Israel has been in rebellion against the house of David to this day.

Judah is forbidden to reunite the kingdom

11 When Rehoboam came to Jerusalem, he assembled one hundred eighty **11.1**
thousand chosen troops of the house of Judah and Benjamin to fight against 1 Kgs 12.21-24
Israel, to restore the kingdom to Rehoboam. 2 But the word of the LORD came to **11.2**
Shemaiah the man of God: 3 Say to King Rehoboam of Judah, son of Solomon, and 2 Chron 12.5-7, 15
to all Israel in Judah and Benjamin, 4 "Thus says the LORD: You shall not go up or **11.4**
fight against your kindred. Let everyone return home, for this thing is from me." So 2 Chron 10.15 28.8-11
they heeded the word of the LORD and turned back from the expedition against
Jeroboam. **11.5**

5 Rehoboam resided in Jerusalem, and he built cities for defense in Judah. 6 He 2 Chron 8.2-6 11.23

10.14 Rehoboam must have gotten an unbalanced picture of leadership from his father, Solomon. Apparently Rehoboam saw only the difficulty of leading the nation, not the opportunities. He mentioned only the harsher aspects of Solomon's rule, and he himself decided to be very harsh toward the people. As you discuss your responsibilities with your children, be sure that you temper words of complaint with words of joy. Otherwise you may sour their attitudes toward the work you do and those you serve.

10.16–19 In trying to have it all, Rehoboam lost almost everything. Motivated by greed and power, he pressed too hard and divided his kingdom. He didn't need more money or power, because he had inherited the richest kingdom in the world. He didn't need more control, because he was the king. His demands were based on selfishness rather than reason or spiritual discernment. Those who insist on having it all often wind up with little or nothing.

10.16–19 Here is the beginning of the divided kingdom. The peaceful united kingdom under Solomon was now divided into two parts. Ten of the tribes followed Jeroboam and called their nation Israel, or the northern kingdom. The other two tribes, Judah and Benjamin, remained loyal to David's line and accepted Rehoboam's rule. They called their nation Judah, or the southern kingdom.

11.1 Rehoboam's foolishness divided his kingdom, and he tried to reunite it with force. True unity, however, cannot be forced—it must be the free response of willing hearts. If you want the loyalty of employees, children, or anyone else in your charge, win their respect through love instead of trying to gain their submission through force.

11.4 Why would God support this rebellion? It was part of the nation's punishment for turning away from God (1 Kings 11.11). It may also have been God's way of preserving Rehoboam's smaller kingdom from defeat. In doing so, God preserved David's line and kept intact his plan for the Messiah to be a descendant of David (see 2 Samuel 7.16). When we see division, especially in a church that splits, we wonder what God would have us do. God desires unity, and while we should always work toward reconciliation, we must recognize that only God knows the future. He may allow a division in order to fulfill his greater purposes.

built up Bethlehem, Etam, Tekoa, 7 Beth-zur, Soco, Adullam, 8 Gath, Mareshah,
Ziph, 9 Adoraim, Lachish, Azekah, 10 Zorah, Aijalon, and Hebron, fortified cities
that are in Judah and in Benjamin. 11 He made the fortresses strong, and put commanders in them, and stores of food, oil, and wine. 12 He also put large shields and
spears in all the cities, and made them very strong. So he held Judah and Benjamin.

Priests and Levites move to Judah

11.13 Num 35.2-5 1 Kgs 12.28-33 13 The priests and the Levites who were in all Israel presented themselves to
him from all their territories. 14 The Levites had left their common lands and their
holdings and had come to Judah and Jerusalem, because Jeroboam and his sons had
11.15 1 Kgs 12.31 13.33 prevented them from serving as priests of the LORD, 15 and had appointed his own
priests for the high places, and for the goat-demons, and for the calves that he had
11.16 2 Chron 15.9 made. 16 Those who had set their hearts to seek the LORD God of Israel came after
them from all the tribes of Israel to Jerusalem to sacrifice to the LORD, the God of
11.17 2 Chron 12.1 their ancestors. 17 They strengthened the kingdom of Judah, and for three years they
made Rehoboam son of Solomon secure, for they walked for three years in the way
of David and Solomon.

2. History of apostasy and reform

Rehoboam rules Judah

11.18 1 Sam 16.6 18 Rehoboam took as his wife Mahalath daughter of Jerimoth son of David,
and of Abihail daughter of Eliab son of Jesse. 19 She bore him sons: Jeush, Shemariah, and Zaham. 20 After her he took Maacah daughter of Absalom, who bore him
11.21 Deut 17.17 Abijah, Attai, Ziza, and Shelomith. 21 Rehoboam loved Maacah daughter of Absalom more than all his other wives and concubines (he took eighteen wives and sixty
11.22 Deut 21.15-17 concubines, and became the father of twenty-eight sons and sixty daughters). 22 Rehoboam appointed Abijah son of Maacah as chief prince among his brothers, for he
intended to make him king. 23 He dealt wisely, and distributed some of his sons
through all the districts of Judah and Benjamin, in all the fortified cities; he gave
them abundant provisions, and found many wives for them.

Egypt attacks Jerusalem

12.1 2 Chron 11.17 **12** When the rule of Rehoboam was established and he grew strong, he abandoned the law of the LORD, he and all Israel with him. 2 In the fifth year of
12.3 2 Chron 16.8 Nah 3.9 King Rehoboam, because they had been unfaithful to the LORD, King Shishak of
Egypt came up against Jerusalem 3 with twelve hundred chariots and sixty thousand
12.4 2 Chron 11.5-12 cavalry. A countless army came with him from Egypt—Libyans, Sukkiim, and
Ethiopians.[u] 4 He took the fortified cities of Judah and came as far as Jerusalem.
12.5 Deut 28.15 5 Then the prophet Shemaiah came to Rehoboam and to the officers of Judah, who

[u] Or *Nubians*; Heb *Cushites*

11.13, 14 Before the nation split, the center of worship was in Jerusalem, and people flocked there for the three great annual religious festivals. During the rest of the year, other worship services and rituals were conducted in the tribal territories by priests and Levites who lived throughout the land. They offered sacrifices, taught God's laws, and encouraged the people to continue to follow God and avoid pagan influences.

After the nation split, Jeroboam, the new king of Israel, saw these priests and Levites as a threat to his new government because they retained loyalty to Jerusalem, now the capital of Judah. So he appointed his own priests, effectively banning the Levites from their duties and forcing them to move to the southern kingdom. Jeroboam's pagan priests encouraged idol worship. With the absence of spiritual leaders, the new northern kingdom was in danger of abandoning God.

11.16 These laymen obeyed God rather than Jeroboam. By their action, they preserved their integrity and strengthened the southern kingdom. In the future, most of the people in the northern kingdom would cooperate with the evil designs of the kings, hoping to benefit by going along with their plans. We should not rationalize away God's teachings in order to gain earthly reward.

12.1 During his first three years on the throne, Rehoboam made an attempt to obey God, and as a result Judah prospered. But then, at his peak of popularity and power, he abandoned God and the result was destruction. Soon God allowed Judah to be conquered by Egypt. What happened? Often it is more difficult to be a believer in good times than in bad. Tough times push us toward God; but easy times can make us feel self-sufficient and self-satisfied. When everything is going right, guard your faith closely.

12.2 A record of this invasion has been found on an Egyptian stone which says that Shishak's army penetrated as far north as the Sea of Galilee, in the northern kingdom. Egypt was not the world power it had once been, and Shishak wanted to restore his nation to its former greatness. He was not strong enough to conquer both Israel and Judah, but he managed to destroy key cities in Judah in an effort to regain control of the trade routes and create dissension among the people.

had gathered at Jerusalem because of Shishak, and said to them, "Thus says the
LORD: You abandoned me, so I have abandoned you to the hand of Shishak."
6 Then the officers of Israel and the king humbled themselves and said, "The LORD
is in the right." 7 When the LORD saw that they humbled themselves, the word of the
LORD came to Shemaiah, saying: "They have humbled themselves; I will not destroy them, but I will grant them some deliverance, and my wrath shall not be
poured out on Jerusalem by the hand of Shishak. 8 Nevertheless they shall be his
servants, so that they may know the difference between serving me and serving the
kingdoms of other lands."
9 So King Shishak of Egypt came up against Jerusalem; he took away the treasures of the house of the LORD and the treasures of the king's house; he took everything. He also took away the shields of gold that Solomon had made; 10 but King
Rehoboam made in place of them shields of bronze, and committed them to the
hands of the officers of the guard, who kept the door of the king's house. 11 Whenever the king went into the house of the LORD, the guard would come along bearing
them, and would then bring them back to the guardroom. 12 Because he humbled
himself the wrath of the LORD turned from him, so as not to destroy them completely; moreover, conditions were good in Judah.
13 So King Rehoboam established himself in Jerusalem and reigned. Rehoboam was forty-one years old when he began to reign; he reigned seventeen years
in Jerusalem, the city that the LORD had chosen out of all the tribes of Israel to put
his name there. His mother's name was Naamah the Ammonite. 14 He did evil, for
he did not set his heart to seek the LORD.
15 Now the acts of Rehoboam, from first to last, are they not written in the
records of the prophet Shemaiah and of the seer Iddo, recorded by genealogy?
There were continual wars between Rehoboam and Jeroboam. 16 Rehoboam slept
with his ancestors and was buried in the city of David; and his son Abijah succeeded him.

13 In the eighteenth year of King Jeroboam, Abijah began to reign over Judah.
2 He reigned for three years in Jerusalem. His mother's name was Micaiah
daughter of Uriel of Gibeah.

Abijah rules Judah

Now there was war between Abijah and Jeroboam. 3 Abijah engaged in battle,
having an army of valiant warriors, four hundred thousand picked men; and Jeroboam drew up his line of battle against him with eight hundred thousand picked
mighty warriors. 4 Then Abijah stood on the slope of Mount Zemaraim that is in the
hill country of Ephraim, and said, "Listen to me, Jeroboam and all Israel! 5 Do you
not know that the LORD God of Israel gave the kingship over Israel forever to David
and his sons by a covenant of salt? 6 Yet Jeroboam son of Nebat, a servant of Solomon son of David, rose up and rebelled against his lord; 7 and certain worthless

12.6 Ex 9.27; Dan 9.14
12.7 1 Kgs 21.29; 2 Chron 34.25-27; Ps 78.38
12.8 Deut 28.47,48
12.9 1 Kgs 14.26-28; 2 Chron 9.15,16
12.12 2 Chron 12.6,7
12.13 1 Kgs 14.21
12.14 2 Chron 19.3
12.15 1 Kgs 14.29; 2 Chron 9.29; 12.5
12.16 2 Chron 11.20
13.1 1 Kgs 15.1,2,7; 2 Chron 11.20
13.4 Josh 18.22
13.5 Num 18.19; 2 Sam 7.12-16
13.6 1 Kgs 11.26
13.7 2 Chron 12.13

12.6–8 God eased his judgment when Israel's leaders confessed their sins, humbled themselves, and recognized God's justice in punishing them. It's never too late to repent, even in the midst of punishment. Regardless of what we have done, God is willing to receive us back into fellowship. Are you struggling and alone because sin has severed your fellowship with God? Confession and humility will open the door to receiving his mercy.

12.8 "Serving the kingdoms of other lands" was the price Judah had to pay for disobeying God. The nation's leaders thought they could succeed in their own strength, but they were wrong. When we rebel against God, we always pay for it. When we leave God out of our lives, we lose more spiritually than we ever gain financially.

12.10, 11 How ironic that the pure gold of Solomon's temple was replaced by cheaper bronze. Rehoboam tried to maintain the trappings and appearance of former glory, but he couldn't measure up. When God is no longer central in our lives, maintaining the appearance of a Christian life becomes superficial. Outer beauty must come from inner strength.

12.14 Rehoboam's life was a tragedy because he "did not set his heart to seek the Lord." It is dangerous to put off responding to God. God asks us for a firm commitment, and unless we respond by trusting him completely, we will find ourselves alienated from him.

13.1ff In 1 Kings 15.3, Abijah is called a great sinner, but the Chronicles account has only positive comments about him. For the most part, Abijah was no doubt a wicked king. The writer of Chronicles chose to highlight the little good he did in order to show that he was still under God's covenant promise to David. Because of Abijah's stormy speech to Jeroboam (13.4–12), he was spared the immediate consequences of his sin.

scoundrels gathered around him and defied Rehoboam son of Solomon, when Rehoboam was young and irresolute and could not withstand them.

13.8 1 Kgs 12.28; 2 Chron 11.15

8 "And now you think that you can withstand the kingdom of the LORD in the
hand of the sons of David, because you are a great multitude and have with you

13.9 Ex 29.29-33; 2 Chron 11.14; Jer 2.11; 5.7

the golden calves that Jeroboam made as gods for you. 9 Have you not driven out
the priests of the LORD, the descendants of Aaron, and the Levites, and made priests
for yourselves like the peoples of other lands? Whoever comes to be consecrated
with a young bull or seven rams becomes a priest of what are no gods. 10 But as for
us, the LORD is our God, and we have not abandoned him. We have priests ministering to the LORD who are descendants of Aaron, and Levites for their service.

13.11 Ex 25.30-39; 29.38; Lev 24.5-9; 2 Chron 2.4

11 They offer to the LORD every morning and every evening burnt offerings and
fragrant incense, set out the rows of bread on the table of pure gold, and care for the
golden lampstand so that its lamps may burn every evening; for we keep the charge

13.12 Num 10.8,9

of the LORD our God, but you have abandoned him. 12 See, God is with us at our
head, and his priests have their battle trumpets to sound the call to battle against
you. O Israelites, do not fight against the LORD, the God of your ancestors; for you
cannot succeed."

13.13 Josh 8.4-9; 2 Chron 14.11

13 Jeroboam had sent an ambush around to come on them from behind; thus his
troops[v] were in front of Judah, and the ambush was behind them. 14 When Judah
turned, the battle was in front of them and behind them. They cried out to the LORD,

13.15 2 Chron 16.8

and the priests blew the trumpets. 15 Then the people of Judah raised the battle
shout. And when the people of Judah shouted, God defeated Jeroboam and all Israel before Abijah and Judah. 16 The Israelites fled before Judah, and God gave
them into their hands. 17 Abijah and his army defeated them with great slaughter;

13.18 2 Chron 14.11

five hundred thousand picked men of Israel fell slain. 18 Thus the Israelites were
subdued at that time, and the people of Judah prevailed, because they relied on the
LORD, the God of their ancestors. 19 Abijah pursued Jeroboam, and took cities from
him: Bethel with its villages and Jeshanah with its villages and Ephron[w] with its

13.20 1 Sam 25.38; 1 Kgs 14.20

villages. 20 Jeroboam did not recover his power in the days of Abijah; the LORD
struck him down, and he died. 21 But Abijah grew strong. He took fourteen wives,

13.22 2 Chron 9.20; 24.27

and became the father of twenty-two sons and sixteen daughters. 22 The rest of the
acts of Abijah, his behavior and his deeds, are written in the story of the prophet
Iddo.

Asa rules Judah

14.1 1 Kgs 15.8

14 [x] So Abijah slept with his ancestors, and they buried him in the city of David
His son Asa succeeded him. In his days the land had rest for ten years.

14.3 1 Kgs 15.12-14

2[y] Asa did what was good and right in the sight of the LORD his God. 3 He took away
the foreign altars and the high places, broke down the pillars, hewed down the

[v] Heb *they* [w] Another reading is *Ephrain* [x] Ch 13.23 in Heb [y] Ch 14.1 in Heb

---

13.8 Jeroboam's army was cursed because of the golden calves they carried with them. Consider carefully the things you cherish. If you value anything more than God, it becomes your golden calf and will one day drag you down. Let go of anything that interferes with your relationship with God.

13.9 Abijah criticized Jeroboam's low standards in appointing priests. Anyone is qualified to represent a god that is worthless. To represent the Lord God, however, one must live by his standards, not man's. Those appointed to positions of responsibility in your church should not be selected merely because they volunteer, are influential, or are highly educated. Instead they must demonstrate sound doctrine, dedication to God, and strong spiritual character (see 2 Timothy 3).

13.18, 19 Although outnumbered by Israel, Judah won this conflict by depending on God's help. Some kings in Judah's history focused on God, but not one Israelite king consistently followed God—all followed Jeroboam's idolatry or served Baal. As a result, Israel experienced God's judgment years before Judah did.

Judah had an advantage—the temple, with its sacrifices and the loyal priests and prophets, was in the southern kingdom. Many of Judah's kings were good, at least for parts of their reigns. Whenever an idolatrous king reigned, his rule was followed by that of a God-honoring king who reformed religious life. The result was that true faith in God ran stronger and deeper in Judah than in Israel, but it was still not up to God's standards.

14.1–6 Asa's reign was marked by peace because he "did what was good and right in the sight of the Lord his God." This refrain is often repeated in Chronicles—*obedience* to God leads to *peace* with God and others. In the case of Judah's kings, obedience to God led to national peace, just as God had promised centuries earlier. In our case, obedience may not always bring peace with our enemies, but it will bring peace with God and complete peace in his future kingdom. Obeying God is the first step to peace.

14.3–5 Simply attending worship services is not enough to secure God's peace. Like Asa, we must also actively remove anything that is offensive to God. Becoming more active in church attendance or good works will still leave us in turmoil if we have failed to eliminate sinful practices from our lives.

sacred poles,[z] 4 and commanded Judah to seek the LORD, the God of their ancestors, and to keep the law and the commandment. 5 He also removed from all the 14.5
cities of Judah the high places and the incense altars. And the kingdom had rest 2 Chron 15.15; 34.4,7
under him. 6 He built fortified cities in Judah while the land had rest. He had no war 14.6
in those years, for the LORD gave him peace. 7 He said to Judah, "Let us build these 2 Chron 11.5
cities, and surround them with walls and towers, gates and bars; the land is still ours 14.7
because we have sought the LORD our God; we have sought him, and he has given 2 Chron 8.5
us peace on every side." So they built and prospered. 8 Asa had an army of three 14.8
hundred thousand from Judah, armed with large shields and spears, and two hun- 2 Chron 13.3
dred eighty thousand troops from Benjamin who carried shields and drew bows; all
these were mighty warriors.

9 Zerah the Ethiopian[a] came out against them with an army of a million men 14.9
and three hundred chariots, and came as far as Mareshah. 10 Asa went out to meet 2 Chron 11.8; 12.2,3; 16.8
him, and they drew up their lines of battle in the valley of Zephathah at Mareshah.
11 Asa cried to the LORD his God, "O LORD, there is no difference for you between 14.11
helping the mighty and the weak. Help us, O LORD our God, for we rely on you, 2 Chron 13.14, 18
and in your name we have come against this multitude. O LORD, you are our God;
let no mortal prevail against you." 12 So the LORD defeated the Ethiopians[b] before 14.12
Asa and before Judah, and the Ethiopians[b] fled. 13 Asa and the army with him 2 Chron 13.15
pursued them as far as Gerar, and the Ethiopians[b] fell until no one remained alive; 14.13
for they were broken before the LORD and his army. The people of Judah[c] carried Gen 10.19
away a great quantity of booty. 14 They defeated all the cities around Gerar, for the 14.14
fear of the LORD was on them. They plundered all the cities; for there was much 2 Chron 17.10
plunder in them. 15 They also attacked the tents of those who had livestock,[d] and
carried away sheep and goats in abundance, and camels. Then they returned to
Jerusalem.

Asa rebuilds the altar

15 The spirit of God came upon Azariah son of Oded. 2 He went out to meet Asa 15.1
and said to him, "Hear me, Asa, and all Judah and Benjamin: The LORD is 2 Chron 20.14; 24.20
with you, while you are with him. If you seek him, he will be found by you, but if 15.2
you abandon him, he will abandon you. 3 For a long time Israel was without the true 2 Chron 20.17

[z] Heb *Asherim* [a] Or *Nubian*; Heb *Cushite* [b] Or *Nubians*; Heb *Cushites* [c] Heb *They* [d] Meaning of Heb uncertain

14.7 Times of peace are not just for resting. They allow us to prepare for times of trouble. King Asa recognized the period of peace as the right time to build his defenses—the moment of attack would be too late. It is also difficult to withstand spiritual attack unless defenses are prepared beforehand. Decisions about how to face temptations must be made with cool heads long before we feel the heat of temptation. Build your defenses now before temptation strikes.

14.11 If you are facing battles you feel you can't possibly win, don't give up. In the face of vast hordes of enemy soldiers, Asa prayed for God's help, recognizing his powerlessness against such a mighty army. The secret of victory is first to admit the futility of unaided human effort and then to trust God to save. His power works best through those who recognize their limitations (2 Corinthians 12.9). It is those who think they can do it all who are in the greatest danger.

15.1, 2 Asa wisely welcomed people who had a close relationship with God, and he listened to their messages. Azariah gave the armies an important warning and encouraged them to stay close to God. Keep in contact with people who are filled with God's Spirit, and you will learn God's counsel. Spend regular time in discussion and prayer with those who can help explain and apply God's message.

15.3 Azariah said that Israel, the northern kingdom, was "without the true God." Eight kings reigned in Israel during the 41-year rule of Asa, and all eight were evil. Jeroboam, the first ruler of Israel, began this wicked trend by setting up idols and expelling God's priests (11.13–15). Azariah used Israel's problems as an example of the evil that would come to Judah if they turned away from God as their northern brothers had.

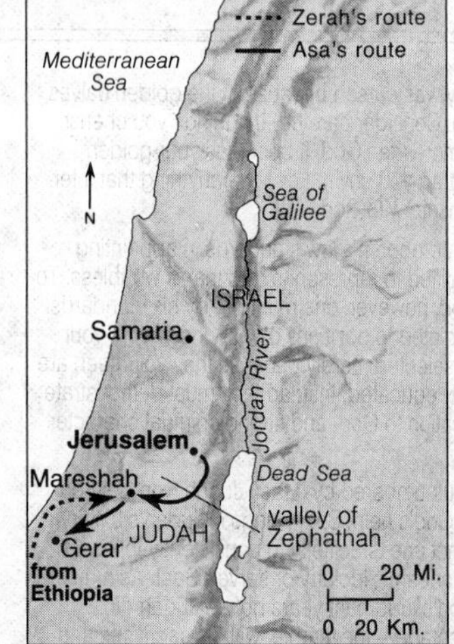

ASA'S BATTLES A huge army from Ethiopia under General Zerah advanced toward Mareshah, greatly outnumbering King Asa's army. Asa sent his troops to meet them, and the battle took place in the valley of Zephathah. Asa prayed to God, and the Ethiopians were defeated and chased as far as Gerar.

15.3 Lev 10.8-11 1 Kgs 12.28-33 2 Chron 17.9
15.4 Deut 4.29
15.7 Josh 1.7,9
15.8 2 Chron 4.1 8.12; 13.19

God, and without a teaching priest, and without law; 4 but when in their distress
they turned to the LORD, the God of Israel, and sought him, he was found by them.
5 In those times it was not safe for anyone to go or come, for great disturbances
afflicted all the inhabitants of the lands. 6 They were broken in pieces, nation
against nation and city against city, for God troubled them with every sort of distress. 7 But you, take courage! Do not let your hands be weak, for your work shall
be rewarded."

8 When Asa heard these words, the prophecy of Azariah son of Oded,[e] he
took courage, and put away the abominable idols from all the land of Judah and

[e] Compare Syr Vg: Heb *the prophecy, the prophet Obed*

God has never accepted the idea that "the ends justify the means." He is just and perfect in all his ways. People, on the other hand, are far from perfect. That a bond can exist between a loving and merciful Creator and a resisting and rebellious creation is as great a miracle as creation itself! As a king, Asa came very close to being good. He traveled a long way with God before getting off track. His sin was not so much deliberate disobedience as choosing the *easy* way rather than the *right* way.

When the odds seemed impossible in the battle with the Ethiopians, Asa recognized his need to depend on God. Following that victory, God's promise of peace based on obedience spurred the king and people to many years of right living. But Asa was to face a tougher test.

Years of animosity between Asa and Israel's king Baasha took an ugly turn. Baasha, king of the rival northern kingdom, was building a fort that threatened both the peace and the economy of Judah. Asa thought he saw a way out—he bribed King Ben-hadad of Syria to break his alliance with King Baasha. The plan worked brilliantly, but it wasn't God's way. When Asa was confronted by God's prophet Hanani, he flew into a rage, jailed Hanani, and took out his anger on his people. Asa rejected correction and refused to admit his error to God. His greatest failure was missing what God could have done with his life if he had been willing to be humble. His pride ruined the health of his reign. He stubbornly held on to his failure until his death.

Does this attitude sound familiar? Can you identify failures in your life that you have continued to rationalize rather than admit them to God and accept his forgiveness? The ends do not justify the means. Such a belief leads to sin and failure. The stubborn refusal to admit a failure due to sin can become a big problem because it makes you spend time rationalizing rather than learning from your mistakes and moving on.

Strengths and accomplishments:
- Obeyed God during the first ten years of his reign
- Carried out a partially successful effort to abolish idolatry
- Deposed his idolatrous mother Maachah
- Defeated Ethiopia's mighty army

Weaknesses and mistakes:
- Responded with rage when confronted about his sin
- Made alliances with heathen nations and evil people

Lessons from his life:
- God not only reinforces good, he confronts evil
- Efforts to follow God's plans and rules yield positive results
- How well a plan works is no measure of its rightness or approval by God

Vital statistics:
- Where: Jerusalem
- Occupation: King of Judah
- Relatives: Mother: Maachah. Father: Abijah. Son: Jehoshaphat
- Contemporaries: Hanani, Ben-hadad, Zerah, Azariah, Baasha

Key verse:
"For the eyes of the Lord range throughout the entire earth, to strengthen those whose heart is true to him. You have done foolishly in this; for from now on you will have wars" (2 Chronicles 16.9).

Asa's story is told in 1 Kings 15.8–24 and 2 Chronicles 14—16. He is also mentioned in Jeremiah 41.9; Matthew 1.7.

15.7 Azariah encouraged the men of Judah to keep up the good work, "for your work shall be rewarded." This is an inspiration for us too. Recognition and reward are great motivators that have two dimensions: (1) *The temporal dimension.* Living by God's standards may result in acclaim here on earth. (2) *The eternal dimension.* Permanent recognition and reward will be given in the next life. Don't be discouraged if you feel your faith in God is going unrewarded here on earth. The best rewards are not in this life, but in the life to come.

Benjamin and from the towns that he had taken in the hill country of Ephraim. He
repaired the altar of the LORD that was in front of the vestibule of the house of the
LORD.[f] 9 He gathered all Judah and Benjamin, and those from Ephraim, Manas- **15.9**
seh, and Simeon who were residing as aliens with them, for great numbers had 2 Chron 11.16
deserted to him from Israel when they saw that the LORD his God was with him.
10 They were gathered at Jerusalem in the third month of the fifteenth year of the
reign of Asa. 11 They sacrificed to the LORD on that day, from the booty that they **15.11**
had brought, seven hundred oxen and seven thousand sheep. 12 They entered into a 2 Chron 14.13-15
covenant to seek the LORD, the God of their ancestors, with all their heart and with **15.12**
all their soul. 13 Whoever would not seek the LORD, the God of Israel, should be put 2 Chron 23.16
to death, whether young or old, man or woman. 14 They took an oath to the LORD **15.13** Ex 22.20
with a loud voice, and with shouting, and with trumpets, and with horns. 15 All Deut 13.6-9
Judah rejoiced over the oath; for they had sworn with all their heart, and had sought **15.15**
him with their whole desire, and he was found by them, and the LORD gave them 2 Chron 14.7
rest all around.

16 King Asa even removed his mother Maacah from being queen mother be- **15.16**
cause she had made an abominable image for Asherah. Asa cut down her image, Ex 34.13 1 Kgs 15.13-15
crushed it, and burned it at the Wadi Kidron. 17 But the high places were not taken 2 Chron 14.2-5
out of Israel. Nevertheless the heart of Asa was true all his days. 18 He brought into
the house of God the votive gifts of his father and his own votive gifts—silver,
gold, and utensils. 19 And there was no more war until the thirty-fifth year of the
reign of Asa.

Asa forgets God

16 In the thirty-sixth year of the reign of Asa, King Baasha of Israel went up **16.1**
against Judah, and built Ramah, to prevent anyone from going out or coming 1 Kgs 15.17-22
into the territory of[g] King Asa of Judah. 2 Then Asa took silver and gold from the
treasures of the house of the LORD and the king's house, and sent them to King
Ben-hadad of Aram, who resided in Damascus, saying, 3 "Let there be an alliance
between me and you, like that between my father and your father; I am sending to
you silver and gold; go, break your alliance with King Baasha of Israel, so that he
may withdraw from me." 4 Ben-hadad listened to King Asa, and sent the command- **16.4**
ers of his armies against the cities of Israel. They conquered Ijon, Dan, Abel- Ex 1.11
maim, and all the store-cities of Naphtali. 5 When Baasha heard of it, he stopped
building Ramah, and let his work cease. 6 Then King Asa brought all Judah, and
they carried away the stones of Ramah and its timber, with which Baasha had been **16.7** 1 Kgs 16.1
building, and with them he built up Geba and Mizpah. 2 Chron 14.11 19.2; 32.7,8

7 At that time the seer Hanani came to King Asa of Judah, and said to him, **16.8**
"Because you relied on the king of Aram, and did not rely on the LORD your God, 2 Chron 12.3 13.16,18; 14.9
the army of the king of Aram has escaped you. 8 Were not the Ethiopians[h] and the **16.9**
Libyans a huge army with exceedingly many chariots and cavalry? Yet because you 2 Chron 15.17
relied on the LORD, he gave them into your hand. 9 For the eyes of the LORD range Prov 15.3 Zech 4.10

[f] Heb *the vestibule of the LORD* [g] Heb lacks *the territory of* [h] Or *Nubians*; Heb *Cushites*

15.14, 15 Many people find it difficult to commit themselves to anything. They are tentative, indecisive, and afraid of responsibility. Asa and his people were different—they had undivided hearts and clearly declared themselves for God. Their oath of allegiance was punctuated with shouts and trumpet blasts! This decisive and wholehearted commitment pleased God and resulted in peace for the nation. If you want peace, check to see if there is some area where you lack total commitment to God. Peace comes as a by-product of committing one's life wholeheartedly to God.

15.16 The ten commandments tell us to honor our fathers and mothers, and yet Asa removed his mother from the throne. While honoring parents is God's command, maintaining loyalty to God is an even higher priority. Jesus warned that respect for parents should never keep us from following him (Luke 14.26). If you have unbelieving parents, you must respect and honor them, but you must make devotion to God an even higher priority.

15.18 Votive offerings were freewill offerings. They were generally those items taken in battle and dedicated to the Lord.

16.7–10 Judah and Israel never learned! Although God had delivered them even when they were outnumbered (13.3ff; 14.9ff), they repeatedly sought help from heathen nations rather than from God. That Asa sought help from Syria was evidence of national spiritual decline. With help from God alone, Asa had defeated Ethiopia in open battle. But his confidence in God had slipped, and now he sought only a human solution to his problem. When confronted by the prophet Hanani, Asa threw him in jail, revealing the true condition of his heart. It is not sin to use human means to solve our problems, but it is sin to trust them more than God, to think they are better than God's ways, or to leave God completely out of the problem-solving process.

throughout the entire earth, to strengthen those whose heart is true to him. You
have done foolishly in this; for from now on you will have wars." 10 Then Asa was
angry with the seer, and put him in the stocks, in prison, for he was in a rage with
him because of this. And Asa inflicted cruelties on some of the people at the same
time.
16.11 11 The acts of Asa, from first to last, are written in the Book of the Kings of
1 Kgs 15.23,24 Judah and Israel. 12 In the thirty-ninth year of his reign Asa was diseased in his feet,
and his disease became severe; yet even in his disease he did not seek the LORD, but
16.13 sought help from physicians. 13 Then Asa slept with his ancestors, dying in the
Gen 50.2 2 Chron 21.19 forty-first year of his reign. 14 They buried him in the tomb that he had hewn out for
Jn 12.1-7 19.39,40 himself in the city of David. They laid him on a bier that had been filled with
various kinds of spices prepared by the perfumer's art; and they made a very great
fire in his honor.

Jehoshaphat rules Judah

17.1 1 Kgs 15.24 **17** His son Jehoshaphat succeeded him, and strengthened himself against Is-
17.2 rael. 2 He placed forces in all the fortified cities of Judah, and set garrisons
2 Chron 11.5 in the land of Judah, and in the cities of Ephraim that his father Asa had taken. 3 The
15.8 LORD was with Jehoshaphat, because he walked in the earlier ways of his father;[i]
17.4 he did not seek the Baals, 4 but sought the God of his father and walked in his
1 Kgs 12.28 commandments, and not according to the ways of Israel. 5 Therefore the LORD es-
17.5 2 Chron 18.1 tablished the kingdom in his hand. All Judah brought tribute to Jehoshaphat, and he
17.6 had great riches and honor. 6 His heart was courageous in the ways of the LORD; and
2 Chron 15.17 furthermore he removed the high places and the sacred poles[j] from Judah.
17.7 7 In the third year of his reign he sent his officials, Ben-hail, Obadiah, Zecha-
Deut 6.4-9 riah, Nethanel, and Micaiah, to teach in the cities of Judah. 8 With them were the
2 Chron 15.3 19.8; 35.3 Levites, Shemaiah, Nethaniah, Zebadiah, Asahel, Shemiramoth, Jehonathan, Adonijah, Tobijah, and Tob-adonijah; and with these Levites, the priests Elishama
and Jehoram. 9 They taught in Judah, having the book of the law of the LORD with
them; they went around through all the cities of Judah and taught among the people.
17.10 10 The fear of the LORD fell on all the kingdoms of the lands around Judah, and
2 Chron 14.14 they did not make war against Jehoshaphat. 11 Some of the Philistines brought Je-
17.11 2 Chron 9.14 hoshaphat presents, and silver for tribute; and the Arabs also brought him seven
26.8 thousand seven hundred rams and seven thousand seven hundred male goats. 12 Jehoshaphat grew steadily greater. He built fortresses and storage cities in Judah.
13 He carried out great works in the cities of Judah. He had soldiers, mighty warriors, in Jerusalem. 14 This was the muster of them by ancestral houses: Of Judah,
the commanders of the thousands: Adnah the commander, with three hundred thousand mighty warriors, 15 and next to him Jehohanan the commander, with two hun-
17.16 dred eighty thousand, 16 and next to him Amasiah son of Zichri, a volunteer for the
Judg 5.2; 9 1 Chron 29.9 service of the LORD, with two hundred thousand mighty warriors. 17 Of Benjamin:
Eliada, a mighty warrior, with two hundred thousand armed with bow and shield,
18 and next to him Jehozabad with one hundred eighty thousand armed for war.

[i] Another reading is *his father David* [j] Heb *Asherim*

16.10 Asa was angry with Hanani's message, so he threw the prophet in jail. God's truth will not always be welcomed with open arms, especially when it reveals people's sins. But we must speak and live by God's truth, no matter how people respond.

16.12 The criticism of Asa's visit to the doctors was not a general indictment of medicine. Asa's problem was that he completely ignored God's help. The medicine practiced at this time was a mixture of superstition and folk remedies. We should certainly avoid any pseudo-medical treatment derived from occult sources. Asa's experience should also encourage us to follow the New Testament practice of receiving prayer for our sickness (James 5.14) as we seek responsible medical help.

16.14 A bier is the stand or platform on which a coffin or corpse is placed.

17.7–9 The people of Judah were biblically illiterate. They had never taken time to listen to and discuss God's Word and understand how it could change them. Jehoshaphat realized that knowing God's Word was the first step to getting people to live as they should, so he initiated a nationwide religious education program. He reversed the religious decline that had occurred at the end of Asa's reign by putting God first in the people's minds and instilling in them a sense of commitment and mission. Because of this action, the nation began to follow God. Churches and Christian schools today need solid Christian education programs. Exposure to good Bible teaching through Sunday school, church, Bible study, and personal and family devotions is essential for living as God intended.

17.14 *Muster* means the military roll call or enrollment.

19 These were in the service of the king, besides those whom the king had placed in 17.19 2 Chron 17.2
the fortified cities throughout all Judah.

Micaiah predicts failure

18 Now Jehoshaphat had great riches and honor; and he made a marriage alli- 18.1 2 Chron. 17.5
ance with Ahab. 2 After some years he went down to Ahab in Samaria. Ahab
slaughtered an abundance of sheep and oxen for him and for the people who were 18.2 1 Kgs 22.2-35
with him, and induced him to go up against Ramoth-gilead. 3 King Ahab of Israel
said to King Jehoshaphat of Judah, "Will you go with me to Ramoth-gilead?" He
answered him, "I am with you, my people are your people. We will be with you in
the war."
4 But Jehoshaphat also said to the king of Israel, "Inquire first for the word of
the LORD." 5 Then the king of Israel gathered the prophets together, four hundred of
them, and said to them, "Shall we go to battle against Ramoth-gilead, or shall I
refrain?" They said, "Go up; for God will give it into the hand of the king." 6 But
Jehoshaphat said, "Is there no other prophet of the LORD here of whom we may
inquire?" 7 The king of Israel said to Jehoshaphat, "There is still one other by whom
we may inquire of the LORD, Micaiah son of Imlah; but I hate him, for he never
prophesies anything favorable about me, but only disaster." Jehoshaphat said, "Let
the king not say such a thing." 8 Then the king of Israel summoned an officer and
said, "Bring quickly Micaiah son of Imlah." 9 Now the king of Israel and King
Jehoshaphat of Judah were sitting on their thrones, arrayed in their robes; and they
were sitting at the threshing floor at the entrance of the gate of Samaria; and all the
prophets were prophesying before them. 10 Zedekiah son of Chenaanah made for
himself horns of iron, and he said, "Thus says the LORD: With these you shall gore
the Arameans until they are destroyed." 11 All the prophets were prophesying the
same and saying, "Go up to Ramoth-gilead and triumph; the LORD will give it into
the hand of the king."
12 The messenger who had gone to summon Micaiah said to him, "Look, the
words of the prophets with one accord are favorable to the king; let your word be

---

18.1ff Although Jehoshaphat was deeply committed to God, he arranged for his son to marry Athaliah, the daughter of wicked King Ahab of Israel, and then made a military alliance with him. Jehoshaphat's popularity and power made him attractive to the cunning and opportunistic Ahab. This alliance had three devastating consequences: (1) Jehoshaphat incurred God's wrath (19.2); (2) when Jehoshaphat died and Athaliah became queen, she seized the throne and almost destroyed all of David's descendants (22.10–12); (3) Athaliah brought the evil practices of Israel into Judah, which eventually led to the nation's downfall.

When believers in leadership positions become allied with unbelievers, values can be compromised and spiritual awareness dulled. The Bible often warns against teaming up with unbelievers (2 Corinthians 6.14). (See the note on 20.37 for more on alliances.)

18.3–8 Evil kings did not like God's prophets bringing messages of doom (18.17; Jeremiah 5.13). Many, therefore, hired prophets who told them only what they wanted to hear (Isaiah 30.10, 11; Jeremiah 14.13–16; 23.16, 21, 30–36). The Bible calls these men false prophets because they extolled the greatness of the king and predicted victory regardless of the real situation.

18.3–8 Wicked Ahab asked Jehoshaphat to join forces with him in battle (18.2, 3). Before making that commitment, Jehoshaphat rightly sought God's advice. However, when God gave his answer through the prophet Micaiah (18.16), Jehoshaphat ignored it (18.28). It does us no good to seek God's advice if we ignore it when it is given. Real love for God is shown not by merely asking for direction, but by following that direction once it is given.

18.5–16 When you want to please or impress someone, it is tempting to lie to make yourself look good. Ahab's 400 prophets did just that, telling Ahab only what he wanted to hear. They were then rewarded for making Ahab happy. Micaiah, however, told the truth and got arrested (18.25, 26). Obeying God doesn't always protect us from evil consequences. Obedience may, in fact, provoke them. But it is better to suffer from man's displeasure than from God's wrath (Matthew 10.28). If you are ridiculed for being honest, remember that this can be a sign that you are indeed doing what is right in God's eyes (Matthew 5.10–12; Romans 8.17, 35–39).

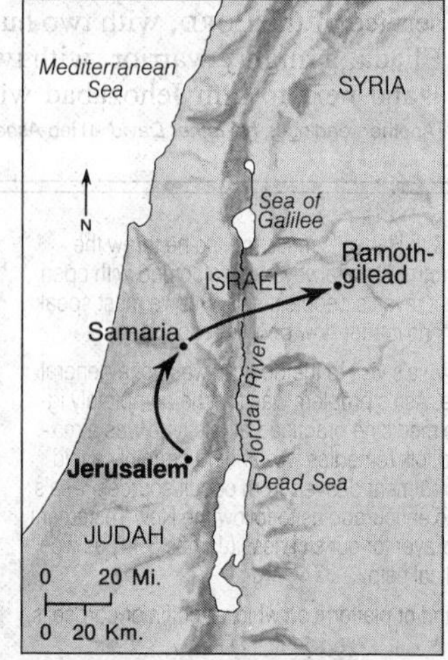

BATTLE WITH SYRIA
King Jehoshaphat made an alliance with evil King Ahab of Israel. Together they decided to attack Ramoth-gilead and rout the Syrians who had occupied the city. But Jehoshaphat first wanted to seek the advice of a prophet. Ahab's prophets predicted victory; but Micaiah predicted defeat. The two kings were defeated and Ahab was killed.

18.13 Num 22.18-20, 35 like the word of one of them, and speak favorably." 13 But Micaiah said, "As the
LORD lives, whatever my God says, that I will speak."
14 When he had come to the king, the king said to him, "Micaiah, shall we go
to Ramoth-gilead to battle, or shall I refrain?" He answered, "Go up and triumph;
they will be given into your hand." 15 But the king said to him, "How many times
must I make you swear to tell me nothing but the truth in the name of the LORD?"
18.16 Num 27.17 Ezek 34.5-8 Mt 9.36 16 Then Micaiah[k] said, "I saw all Israel scattered on the mountains, like sheep
without a shepherd; and the LORD said, 'These have no master; let each one go
home in peace.' " 17 The king of Israel said to Jehoshaphat, "Did I not tell you that
he would not prophesy anything favorable about me, but only disaster?"
18.18 Isa 6.1-5 Dan 7.9,10 18 Then Micaiah[k] said, "Therefore hear the word of the LORD: I saw the LORD
sitting on his throne, with all the host of heaven standing to the right and to the left
of him. 19 And the LORD said, 'Who will entice King Ahab of Israel, so that he may
go up and fall at Ramoth-gilead?' Then one said one thing, and another said another, 20 until a spirit came forward and stood before the LORD, saying, 'I will entice him.' The LORD asked him, 'How?' 21 He replied, 'I will go out and be a lying
spirit in the mouth of all his prophets.' Then the LORD[k] said, 'You are to entice

[k] Heb *he*

JEHOSHAPHAT

Are children more likely to learn from their parents' mistakes or simply to repeat them? In the lives of the people in the Bible, we find that the effects of parental examples are powerful and long-lasting. For much of his life, Jehoshaphat seems to have been a son who learned from his father Asa's mistakes and followed his positive actions. But on several occasions, his decisions reveal the negative aspects of his father's example.

When the challenges were obvious, like the need for religious education of the people or the threat of war with a vast army, Jehoshaphat turned to God for guidance and made the right choices. His dependence on God was consistent when the odds were clearly against him. It was in depending on God for the day-to-day plans and actions that Jehoshaphat was weak. He allowed his son to marry Athaliah, the daughter of the wicked Ahab and Jezebel of Israel. Jehoshaphat was almost killed when, without asking God, he made an alliance with Ahab. Later, he got involved in an unwise shipbuilding venture with Ahab's son, Ahaziah—a venture that was shipwrecked by God.

God's faithfulness when the issues are clear and the enemy overwhelming is more than enough reason to seek his guidance when the issues are unclear and the enemy unseen. Jehoshaphat knew this, yet he made little use of that knowledge.

We repeat Jehoshaphat's error when we relegate God to the background in the "easy" decisions of life. Then, when things get out of hand, we want him to get us out of the mess we got ourselves into. God wants us to give him not only the major decisions, but also our daily lives—the things we are most often fooled into believing we can control. Perhaps there is nothing major facing you today. Have you paused long enough to give your day to God anyway?

Strengths and accomplishments:
- A bold follower of God, he reminded the people of the early years of his father, Asa
- Carried out a national program of religious education
- Had many military victories
- Developed an extensive legal structure throughout the kingdom

Weaknesses and mistakes:
- Failed to recognize the long-term results of his decisions
- Did not completely destroy idolatry in the land
- Became entangled with evil King Ahab through alliances
- Allowed his son Jehoram to marry Athaliah, Ahab's daughter
- Became Ahaziah's business partner in an ill-fated shipping venture

Vital statistics:
- Where: Jerusalem
- Occupation: King of Judah
- Relatives: Father: Asa. Mother: Azubah. Son: Jehoram. Daughter-in-law: Athaliah
- Contemporaries: Ahab, Jezebel, Micaiah, Ahaziah, Jehu

Key verses:
"He walked in the way of his father Asa and did not turn aside from it, doing what was right in the sight of the Lord. Yet the high places were not removed; the people had not yet set their hearts upon the God of their ancestors" (2 Chronicles 20.32, 33).

Jehoshaphat's story is told in 1 Kings 15.24—22.50 and 2 Chronicles 17.1—21.1. He is also mentioned in 2 Kings 3.1–14 and Joel 3.2, 12.

him, and you shall succeed; go out and do it.' 22 So you see, the LORD has put a
lying spirit in the mouth of these your prophets; the LORD has decreed disaster for
you."

23 Then Zedekiah son of Chenaanah came up to Micaiah, slapped him
on the cheek, and said, "Which way did the spirit of the LORD pass from me
to speak to you?" 24 Micaiah replied, "You will find out on that day when you go
in to hide in an inner chamber." 25 The king of Israel then ordered, "Take Micaiah, **18.25**
and return him to Amon the governor of the city and to Joash the king's son; 26 and 2 Chron 18.8 34.8
say, 'Thus says the king: Put this fellow in prison, and feed him on reduced ra- **18.26**
tions of bread and water until I return in peace.' " 27 Micaiah said, "If you return 2 Chron 16.10
in peace, the LORD has not spoken by me." And he said, "Hear, you peoples, all **18.27** Mic 1.2
of you!"

B I B L E

The Persecuted	*The Persecutors*	*Why the Persecution*	*Result*	*Reference*
Isaac	The Philistines	God was blessing Isaac	The Philistines could not subdue Isaac, so they made peace with him	Genesis 26.12–33
Moses	Israelites	The Israelites wanted water	God provided water, thanks to Moses' prayer	Exodus 17.1–7
David	Saul and others	David was becoming a powerful leader, threatening Saul's position as king	David endured the persecution and became king	1 Samuel 20—27 Psalms 31.13; 59.1–4
Priests of Nob	Saul and Doeg	Saul and Doeg thought the priests helped David escape	85 priests were killed	1 Samuel 22
Prophets	Jezebel	Jezebel didn't like to have her evil ways pointed out	Many prophets were killed	1 Kings 18.3, 4
Elijah	Ahab and Jezebel	Elijah confronted their sins	Elijah had to flee for his life	1 Kings 18.10—19.2
Micaiah	Ahab	Ahab thought Micaiah was stirring up trouble rather than prophesying from God	Micaiah was thrown into prison	2 Chronicles 18.12–26
Elisha	A king of Israel	The king thought Elisha had caused the famine	Elisha ignored the threatened persecution and prophesied the famine's end	2 Kings 6.31
Hanani	Asa	Hanani criticized Asa for trusting in Syria's help more than in God's help	Hanani was thrown in jail	2 Chronicles 16.7–10
Zechariah	Joash	Zechariah confronted the people of Judah for disregarding God's Word	Zechariah was executed	2 Chronicles 24.20–22
Uriah (Urijah)	Jehoiakim	Uriah confronted Jehoiakim about his evil ways	Uriah was butchered to death	Jeremiah 26.20–23
Jeremiah	Zedekiah	Zedekiah thought Jeremiah was a traitor for prophesying Jerusalem's fall	Jeremiah was thrown in prison, then into a muddy cistern	Jeremiah 37.1—38.13
Shadrach, Meshach, Abednego	Nebuchadnezzar	The three men refused to bow down to anyone but God	They were thrown into a fiery furnace, but God miraculously saved them	Daniel 3

18.22 God used the seductive influence of false prophets to judge Ahab. They were determined to tell Ahab what he wanted to hear. God confirmed their plans to lie as a means to remove Ahab from the throne. These prophets, supported by Ahab, snared him in his sin. Because he listened to them instead of God, he was killed in battle. The lying spirit is a picture of the prophets' entire way of life – telling the king only what he wanted to hear, not what he needed to hear. Leaders will only find trouble if they surround themselves with advisers whose only thought is to please them.

18.31 Jehoshaphat's troubles began when he joined forces with the evil King Ahab. Almost at once he found himself the target for soldiers who mistakenly identified him as Ahab. He could have accepted this fate because he deserved it, but instead he cried out to God, who miraculously saved him. When we sin and the inevi-

Ahab dies in battle

28 So the king of Israel and King Jehoshaphat of Judah went up to Ramoth-
gilead. 29 The king of Israel said to Jehoshaphat, "I will disguise myself and go into
battle, but you wear your robes." So the king of Israel disguised himself, and they
went into battle. 30 Now the king of Aram had commanded the captains of his chariots, "Fight with no one small or great, but only with the king of Israel." 31 When the
captains of the chariots saw Jehoshaphat, they said, "It is the king of Israel." So
they turned to fight against him; and Jehoshaphat cried out, and the LORD helped
him. God drew them away from him, 32 for when the captains of the chariots saw
that it was not the king of Israel, they turned back from pursuing him. 33 But a
certain man drew his bow and unknowingly struck the king of Israel between the
scale armor and the breastplate; so he said to the driver of his chariot, "Turn

18.31 2 Chron 13.14, 15

PERSECUTIONS

The Persecuted	The Persecutors	Why the Persecution	Result	Reference
Daniel	National leaders	Daniel was praying	Daniel was thrown into a den of lions, but God miraculously saved him	Daniel 6
Job	Satan	Satan wanted to prove that pain and suffering would make a person abandon God	Job remained faithful to God and was restored	Job 1.8–12; 2.3–7
John the Baptist	Herod and Herodias	John confronted King Herod's adultery	John was beheaded	Matthew 14.3–13
Jesus	Religious leaders	Jesus exposed their sinful motives	Jesus was crucified, but rose again from the dead to show his authority over all evil	Mark 7.1–16; Luke 22.63—24.7
Peter and John	Religious leaders	Peter and John preached that Jesus was God's Son and the only way to salvation	They were thrown into prison, but later released	Acts 4.1–31
Stephen	Religious leaders	Stephen exposed their guilt in crucifying Jesus	Stephen was stoned to death	Acts 6—7
The church	Paul and others	The Christians preached Jesus as the Messiah	Believers faced death, prison, torture, exile	Acts 8.1–3; 9.1–9
James	Herod Agrippa I	To please the Jewish leaders	James was executed	Acts 12.1–2
Peter	Herod Agrippa I	To please the Jewish leaders	Peter was thrown into prison	Acts 12.3–17
Paul	Jews, city officials	Paul preached about Jesus and confronted those who made money by manipulating others	Paul was stoned; thrown into prison	Acts 14.19; 16.16–24
Timothy	Unknown	Unknown	Timothy was thrown into prison	Hebrews 13.23
John	Probably the Romans	John told others about Jesus	John was sent into exile on a remote island	Revelation 1.9

Micaiah, like thousands of believers before and after him, was persecuted for his faith. The chart shows that persecution comes from a variety of people and is given in a variety of ways. Sometimes God protects us from it, sometimes he doesn't. But as long as we remain faithful to God *alone*, we must expect persecution (see also Luke 6.22; 2 Corinthians 6.4–10; 2 Timothy 2.9–12; Revelation 2.10). God also seems to have a special reward for those who endure such persecution (Revelation 6.9–11; 20.4).

table consequences follow, we may be tempted to give up. "I chose to sin," we may think, "it's my fault, and I must accept the consequences." While we may deserve what comes to us, that is no reason to avoid calling on God for urgent help. Had Jehoshaphat given up, he might have died. No matter how greatly you have sinned, you can still call upon God.

18.33 Micaiah prophesied death for Ahab (18.16, 27), so Ahab disguised himself to fool the enemy. Apparently the disguise worked, but that didn't change the prophecy. A random Syrian arrow found a crack in his armor and killed him. God fulfills his will despite the defenses people try to erect. God can use anything, even an error, to bring his will to pass. This is good news for God's followers, because we can trust him to work his plans and keep his promises no matter how desperate our circumstances.

around, and carry me out of the battle, for I am wounded." 34 The battle grew hot
that day, and the king of Israel propped himself up in his chariot facing the Arameans until evening; then at sunset he died.

A prophet rebukes Jehoshaphat

19 King Jehoshaphat of Judah returned in safety to his house in Jerusalem.
2 Jehu son of Hanani the seer went out to meet him and said to King Jehosha- **19.2**
phat, "Should you help the wicked and love those who hate the LORD? Because of 1 Kgs 16.1 2 Chron 18.1,3
this, wrath has gone out against you from the LORD. 3 Nevertheless, some good is 20.34; 24.18
found in you, for you destroyed the sacred poles[l] out of the land, and have set your **19.3** 2 Chron 12.12,
heart to seek God." 14; 17.6

Jehoshaphat appoints judges

4 Jehoshaphat resided at Jerusalem; then he went out again among the people, **19.4**
from Beer-sheba to the hill country of Ephraim, and brought them back to the Deut 16.18-20
LORD, the God of their ancestors. 5 He appointed judges in the land in all the fortified cities of Judah, city by city, 6 and said to the judges, "Consider what you are **19.6**
doing, for you judge not on behalf of human beings but on the LORD's behalf; he is Lev 19.15 Deut 1.17
with you in giving judgment. 7 Now, let the fear of the LORD be upon you; take care **19.7**
what you do, for there is no perversion of justice with the LORD our God, or partial- Gen 18.25 Deut 10.17,18
ity, or taking of bribes." 32.4
8 Moreover in Jerusalem Jehoshaphat appointed certain Levites and priests and **19.8**
heads of families of Israel, to give judgment for the LORD and to decide disputed 2 Chron 17.8,9
cases. They had their seat at Jerusalem. 9 He charged them: "This is how you shall
act: in the fear of the LORD, in faithfulness, and with your whole heart; 10 whenever **19.10**
a case comes to you from your kindred who live in their cities, concerning blood- Deut 17.8 2 Chron 19.2
shed, law or commandment, statutes or ordinances, then you shall instruct them, so
that they may not incur guilt before the LORD and wrath may not come on you and
your kindred. Do so, and you will not incur guilt. 11 See, Amariah the chief priest **19.11**
is over you in all matters of the LORD; and Zebadiah son of Ishmael, the governor 1 Chron 28.20 2 Chron 19.8
of the house of Judah, in all the king's matters; and the Levites will serve you as
officers. Deal courageously, and may the LORD be with the good!"

Jehoshaphat defeats Moab and Ammon

20 After this the Moabites and Ammonites, and with them some of the Meunites,[m] came against Jehoshaphat for battle. 2 Messengers[n] came and told **20.2**
Jehoshaphat, "A great multitude is coming against you from Edom,[o] from beyond Gen 14.7
the sea; already they are at Hazazon-tamar" (that is, En-gedi). 3 Jehoshaphat was **20.3**
afraid; he set himself to seek the LORD, and proclaimed a fast throughout all Judah. 1 Sam 7.6 2 Chron 19.3
4 Judah assembled to seek help from the LORD; from all the towns of Judah they Ezra 8.21
came to seek the LORD.
5 Jehoshaphat stood in the assembly of Judah and Jerusalem, in the house of the **20.6**
LORD, before the new court, 6 and said, "O LORD, God of our ancestors, are you not Deut 4.39 1 Chron 29.11

[l] Heb *Asheroth* [m] Compare 26.7: Heb *Ammonites* [n] Heb *They* [o] One Ms: MT *Aram*

19.5–10 Jehoshaphat delegated some of the responsibilities for ruling and judging the people, but he warned his appointees that they were accountable to God for the standards they used to judge others. Jehoshaphat's advice is helpful for all leaders: (1) allow God to help you be just (19.6); (2) be impartial (19.7); (3) be honest (19.9); (4) act only out of fear of God, not men (19.9). God holds us accountable for the authority we exercise.

19.8 Jehoshaphat appointed priests and Levites to help in administering civil laws. In the same way, Moses chose men who were capable, faithful, and honest to help him judge disputes among the people (Exodus 18.21, 22). Obviously the best kind of leader is one who always acts with reverence for God. Effective leaders get the job done; faithful leaders make sure the job is done in God's way with God's timing. They are careful to instill God's wisdom in future leaders and build God's values into the entire community.

20.3 When the nation was faced with disaster, Jehoshaphat called upon the people to get serious with God by going without food for a designated time. By separating themselves from the daily routine of food preparation and eating, they could devote that extra time to considering their sin and praying to God for help. Hunger pangs would reinforce their feelings of penitence and remind them of their weakness and their dependence upon God. Fasting still can be helpful today as we seek God's will in special situations.

20.6ff Jehoshaphat's prayer had several essential ingredients: (1) He committed the situation to God, acknowledging that only God could save the nation. (2) He sought God's favor because his people were God's people. (3) He acknowledged God's sovereignty over the current situation. (4) He praised God's glory and took comfort in his promises. (5) He professed complete dependence on God, not himself, for deliverance. To be God's kind

God in heaven? Do you not rule over all the kingdoms of the nations? In your hand
20.7 Isa 41.8 are power and might, so that no one is able to withstand you. 7 Did you not, O our
God, drive out the inhabitants of this land before your people Israel, and give it
forever to the descendants of your friend Abraham? 8 They have lived in it, and in
20.9 2 Chron 6.20, 28-30 it have built you a sanctuary for your name, saying, 9 'If disaster comes upon us, the
sword, judgment,[p] or pestilence, or famine, we will stand before this house, and
before you, for your name is in this house, and cry to you in our distress, and you
20.10 Num 20.17-21 2 Chron 20.1,22 will hear and save.' 10 See now, the people of Ammon, Moab, and Mount Seir,
whom you would not let Israel invade when they came from the land of Egypt, and
whom they avoided and did not destroy— 11 they reward us by coming to drive us
20.12 Judg 11.27 Ps 25.15 121.1,2 out of your possession that you have given us to inherit. 12 O our God, will you not
execute judgment upon them? For we are powerless against this great multitude
that is coming against us. We do not know what to do, but our eyes are on you."
13 Meanwhile all Judah stood before the LORD, with their little ones, their
20.14 2 Chron 15.1 24.20 wives, and their children. 14 Then the spirit of the LORD came upon Jahaziel son of
Zechariah, son of Benaiah, son of Jeiel, son of Mattaniah, a Levite of the sons of
20.15 Ex 14.13 1 Sam 17.47 2 Chron 32.7,8 Asaph, in the middle of the assembly. 15 He said, "Listen, all Judah and inhabitants
of Jerusalem, and King Jehoshaphat: Thus says the LORD to you: 'Do not fear or be
dismayed at this great multitude; for the battle is not yours but God's. 16 Tomorrow
go down against them; they will come up by the ascent of Ziz; you will find them
20.17 Ex 14.13 2 Chron 15.2 at the end of the valley, before the wilderness of Jeruel. 17 This battle is not for you
to fight; take your position, stand still, and see the victory of the LORD on your
behalf, O Judah and Jerusalem.' Do not fear or be dismayed; tomorrow go out
against them, and the LORD will be with you."
18 Then Jehoshaphat bowed down with his face to the ground, and all Judah
and the inhabitants of Jerusalem fell down before the LORD, worshiping the LORD.
20.19 2 Chron 7.3 19 And the Levites, of the Kohathites and the Korahites, stood up to praise the
LORD, the God of Israel, with a very loud voice.
20.20 Isa 7.9 20 They rose early in the morning and went out into the wilderness of Tekoa;
and as they went out, Jehoshaphat stood and said, "Listen to me, O Judah and
inhabitants of Jerusalem! Believe in the LORD your God and you will be estab-
20.21 1 Chron 16.29, 34 Ps 29.2 lished; believe his prophets." 21 When he had taken counsel with the people, he
appointed those who were to sing to the LORD and praise him in holy splendor, as
they went before the army, saying,
"Give thanks to the LORD,
for his steadfast love endures forever."
20.22 2 Chron 13.13 20.10 22 As they began to sing and praise, the LORD set an ambush against the Ammonites, Moab, and Mount Seir, who had come against Judah, so that they were routed.
20.23 Judg 7.22 1 Sam 14.20 23 For the Ammonites and Moab attacked the inhabitants of Mount Seir, destroying
them utterly; and when they had made an end of the inhabitants of Seir, they all
helped to destroy one another.
24 When Judah came to the watchtower of the wilderness, they looked toward
the multitude; they were corpses lying on the ground; no one had escaped. 25 When
Jehoshaphat and his people came to take the booty from them, they found livestock[q] in great numbers, goods, clothing, and precious things, which they took for
themselves until they could carry no more. They spent three days taking the booty,
because of its abundance. 26 On the fourth day they assembled in the Valley of
Beracah, for there they blessed the LORD; therefore that place has been called the
Valley of Beracah[r] to this day. 27 Then all the people of Judah and Jerusalem, with

[p] Or *the sword of judgment* [q] Gk: Heb *among them* [r] That is *Blessing*

---

of leader today, follow Jehoshaphat's example—focus entirely on God's power rather than your own.

20.15 As the enemy bore down on Judah, God spoke through Jahaziel: "Do not fear; . . . for the battle is not yours but God's." We may not fight an enemy army, but every day we battle temptation, pressure, and "rulers . . . of this present darkness" (Ephesians 6.12) who want us to rebel against God. Remember, as believers, we have God's Spirit in us. If we ask for God's help when we face struggles, God will fight for us. And God always triumphs.

How do we let God fight for us? (1) By realizing the battle is not ours, but God's; (2) by recognizing human limitations and allowing God's strength to work through our fears and weaknesses; (3) by making sure we are pursuing God's interests and not just our own selfish desires; (4) by asking God for help in our daily battles.

Jehoshaphat at their head, returned to Jerusalem with joy, for the LORD had enabled
them to rejoice over their enemies. 28 They came to Jerusalem, with harps and lyres
and trumpets, to the house of the LORD. 29 The fear of God came on all the king- 20.29
doms of the countries when they heard that the LORD had fought against the ene- 2 Chron 14.6,7 15.15
mies of Israel. 30 And the realm of Jehoshaphat was quiet, for his God gave him rest 20.30
all around. 1 Kgs 22.41-43

Summary of Jehoshaphat's reign

31 So Jehoshaphat reigned over Judah. He was thirty-five years old when he 20.31
began to reign; he reigned twenty-five years in Jerusalem. His mother's name was 2 Chron 17.6
Azubah daughter of Shilhi. 32 He walked in the way of his father Asa and did not
turn aside from it, doing what was right in the sight of the LORD. 33 Yet the high 20.33
places were not removed; the people had not yet set their hearts upon the God of 2 Chron 17.6 19.3
their ancestors.
34 Now the rest of the acts of Jehoshaphat, from first to last, are written in the 20.34
Annals of Jehu son of Hanani, which are recorded in the Book of the Kings of 1 Kgs 16.1,7 2 Chron 19.2
Israel.
35 After this King Jehoshaphat of Judah joined with King Ahaziah of Israel, 20.35
who did wickedly. 36 He joined him in building ships to go to Tarshish; they built 1 Kgs 22.48,49
the ships in Ezion-geber. 37 Then Eliezer son of Dodavahu of Mareshah prophesied 20.36 2 Chron 9.21
against Jehoshaphat, saying, "Because you have joined with Ahaziah, the LORD
will destroy what you have made." And the ships were wrecked and were not able
to go to Tarshish.

Jehoram rules Judah

21 Jehoshaphat slept with his ancestors and was buried with his ancestors in the 21.1
city of David; his son Jehoram succeeded him. 2 He had brothers, the sons of 1 Kgs 22.50
Jehoshaphat: Azariah, Jehiel, Zechariah, Azariah, Michael, and Shephatiah; all
these were the sons of King Jehoshaphat of Judah.[s] 3 Their father gave them many 21.3
gifts, of silver, gold, and valuable possessions, together with fortified cities in Ju- 2 Kgs 8.17-22 2 Chron 11.5
dah; but he gave the kingdom to Jehoram, because he was the firstborn. 4 When
Jehoram had ascended the throne of his father and was established, he put all his
brothers to the sword, and also some of the officials of Israel. 5 Jehoram was thirty-
two years old when he began to reign; he reigned eight years in Jerusalem. 6 He 21.6
walked in the way of the kings of Israel, as the house of Ahab had done; for the 1 Kgs 12.28-30 2 Chron 18.1
daughter of Ahab was his wife. He did what was evil in the sight of the LORD. 7 Yet 21.7
the LORD would not destroy the house of David because of the covenant that he had 2 Sam 7.12-17 1 Kgs 11.13

[s] Gk Syr: Heb *Israel*

20.33 This verse says that Jehoshaphat did not destroy the corrupt idol shrines ("high places"), while 17.6 and 19.3 say he destroyed them. Jehoshaphat destroyed most of the Baal and Asherah idols, but he did not succeed in wiping out the corrupt religions practiced at the hilltop shrines.

20.37 Jehoshaphat met disaster when he joined forces with wicked King Ahaziah. He did not learn from his disastrous alliance with Ahab (18.28–34) or from his father's alliance with Syria (16.2–9). The partnership stood on unequal footing because one man served Yahweh and the other worshiped idols. We court disaster when we enter into partnership with unbelievers, because our very foundations differ (2 Corinthians 6.14–18). While one serves the Lord, the other does not recognize God's authority. Inevitably, the one who serves God is faced with the temptation to compromise values. When that happens, spiritual disaster results.

Before entering into partnerships ask: (1) What are my motives? (2) What problems am I avoiding by seeking this partnership? (3) Is this partnership the best solution, or is it only a quick solution to my problem? (4) Have I prayed or asked others to pray for guidance? (5) Are my partner and I really working toward the same goals? (6) Am I willing to settle for less financial gain in order to do God's will?

21.6 Jehoram, the new king of Judah, married Athaliah, one of the daughters of King Ahab of Israel. She became the mother of Judah's next king, Ahaziah (22.2). Athaliah's mother was Jezebel, the most wicked woman Israel had ever known. Jehoram's marriage to Athaliah was Judah's downfall, for Athaliah brought her mother's wicked influence into Judah, causing the nation to forget God and turn to Baal worship (22.3).

21.7 God promised that a descendant of David would always sit on the throne (2 Samuel 7.8–16). What happened to this promise when the nation was destroyed and carried away? There were two parts to God's promise: (1) In the physical sense, as long as there was an actual throne in Judah, a descendant of David would sit upon it. But this part of the promise depended on the obedience of these kings. When they disobeyed, God was not bound to continue David's temporal line. (2) In the spiritual sense, this promise was completely fulfilled in the coming of Jesus the Messiah, a descendant of David, who would sit on the throne of David forever.

made with David, and since he had promised to give a lamp to him and to his
descendants forever.

21.8 2 Chron 20.22, 23; 21.10

8 In his days Edom revolted against the rule of Judah and set up a king of their
own. 9 Then Jehoram crossed over with his commanders and all his chariots. He set
out by night and attacked the Edomites, who had surrounded him and his chariot
commanders. 10 So Edom has been in revolt against the rule of Judah to this day. At
that time Libnah also revolted against his rule, because he had forsaken the LORD,
the God of his ancestors.

21.11 Lev 20.5; 1 Kgs 11.7
21.12 2 Chron 14.2-5; 17.3,4
21.13 1 Kgs 16.31-33; 2 Chron 21.4,6

11 Moreover he made high places in the hill country of Judah, and led the inhabitants of Jerusalem into unfaithfulness, and made Judah go astray. 12 A letter
came to him from the prophet Elijah, saying: "Thus says the LORD, the God of your
father David: Because you have not walked in the ways of your father Jehoshaphat
or in the ways of King Asa of Judah, 13 but have walked in the way of the kings of
Israel, and have led Judah and the inhabitants of Jerusalem into unfaithfulness, as
the house of Ahab led Israel into unfaithfulness, and because you also have killed
your brothers, members of your father's house, who were better than yourself,
14 see, the LORD will bring a great plague on your people, your children, your
wives, and all your possessions, 15 and you yourself will have a severe sickness
with a disease of your bowels, until your bowels come out, day after day, because
of the disease."

21.15 2 Chron 21.18, 19
21.16 2 Chron 17.11; 22.1; 33.11
21.17 2 Chron 25.23

16 The LORD aroused against Jehoram the anger of the Philistines and of the
Arabs who are near the Ethiopians.[t] 17 They came up against Judah, invaded it,
and carried away all the possessions they found that belonged to the king's house,
along with his sons and his wives, so that no son was left to him except Jehoahaz,
his youngest son.

21.18 2 Chron 21.15
21.19 2 Chron 16.14
21.20 2 Chron 24.25; 28.27; Jer 22.18,28

18 After all this the LORD struck him in his bowels with an incurable disease.
19 In course of time, at the end of two years, his bowels came out because of the
disease, and he died in great agony. His people made no fire in his honor, like the
fires made for his ancestors. 20 He was thirty-two years old when he began to reign;
he reigned eight years in Jerusalem. He departed with no one's regret. They buried
him in the city of David, but not in the tombs of the kings.

Ahaziah rules Judah

22.1 2 Kgs 8.24-29; 2 Chron 21.16
22.2 2 Chron 21.6

22 The inhabitants of Jerusalem made his youngest son Ahaziah king as his
successor; for the troops who came with the Arabs to the camp had killed all
the older sons. So Ahaziah son of Jehoram reigned as king of Judah. 2 Ahaziah was
forty-two years old when he began to reign; he reigned one year in Jerusalem. His
mother's name was Athaliah, a granddaughter of Omri. 3 He also walked in the
ways of the house of Ahab, for his mother was his counselor in doing wickedly.
4 He did what was evil in the sight of the LORD, as the house of Ahab had done; for
after the death of his father they were his counselors, to his ruin. 5 He even followed
their advice, and went with Jehoram son of King Ahab of Israel to make war against
King Hazael of Aram at Ramoth-gilead. The Arameans wounded Joram, 6 and he
returned to be healed in Jezreel of the wounds that he had received at Ramah, when
he fought King Hazael of Aram. And Ahaziah son of King Jehoram of Judah went
down to see Joram son of Ahab in Jezreel, because he was sick.

22.7 2 Kgs 9.6,7,21; 2 Chron 10.15

7 But it was ordained by God that the downfall of Ahaziah should come about

[t] Or *Nubians*; Heb *Cushites*

21.8–11 Jehoram's reign was marked by sin and cruelty. He married a woman who worshiped idols; he killed his six brothers; he allowed and even promoted idol worship. Yet he was not killed in battle or by treachery—he died by a lingering and painful disease (21.18, 19). Punishment for sin is not always immediate or dramatic. But if we ignore God's laws, we will eventually suffer the consequences of our sin.

21.12 Chronicles mentions Elijah only here. Much more about this great prophet can be found in 1 Kings 17.1–2 Kings 2.11. Elijah's Profile is found in 1 Kings 18.

22.4, 5 Although it is wise to seek advice, we must also carefully weigh the advice we receive. Ahaziah had advisers, but they were wicked and led him to ruin. When you seek advice, listen carefully and use God's Word to "test everything; hold fast to what is good" (1 Thessalonians 5.21).

22.7 Jehu's Profile and a more complete story of his reign are found in 2 Kings 9.1–10.36.

through his going to visit Joram. For when he came there he went out with Jehoram
to meet Jehu son of Nimshi, whom the LORD had anointed to destroy the house of
Ahab. 8 When Jehu was executing judgment on the house of Ahab, he met the offi- **22.8**
cials of Judah and the sons of Ahaziah's brothers, who attended Ahaziah, and he 2 Kgs 10.11-14
killed them. 9 He searched for Ahaziah, who was captured while hiding in Samaria **22.9**
and was brought to Jehu, and put to death. They buried him, for they said, "He is 2 Kgs 9.27,28 2 Chron 17.4
the grandson of Jehoshaphat, who sought the LORD with all his heart." And the
house of Ahaziah had no one able to rule the kingdom.

Athaliah rules Judah

10 Now when Athaliah, Ahaziah's mother, saw that her son was dead, she set **22.10**
about to destroy all the royal family of the house of Judah. 11 But Jehoshabeath, the 2 Kgs 11.1-3
king's daughter, took Joash son of Ahaziah, and stole him away from among the
king's children who were about to be killed; she put him and his nurse in a bedroom. Thus Jehoshabeath, daughter of King Jehoram and wife of the priest
Jehoiada—because she was a sister of Ahaziah—hid him from Athaliah, so that
she did not kill him; 12 he remained with them six years, hidden in the house of God,
while Athaliah reigned over the land.

Young Joash becomes king

23 But in the seventh year Jehoiada took courage, and entered into a compact **23.1**
with the commanders of the hundreds, Azariah son of Jeroham, Ishmael son 2 Kgs 11.4-20
of Jehohanan, Azariah son of Obed, Maaseiah son of Adaiah, and Elishaphat son
of Zichri. 2 They went around through Judah and gathered the Levites from all the **23.2**
towns of Judah, and the heads of families of Israel, and they came to Jerusalem. 2 Chron 21.7
3 Then the whole assembly made a covenant with the king in the house of God.
Jehoiada[u] said to them, "Here is the king's son! Let him reign, as the LORD promised concerning the sons of David. 4 This is what you are to do: one third of you, **23.4**
priests and Levites, who come on duty on the sabbath, shall be gatekeepers, 5 one 1 Chron 9.25
third shall be at the king's house, and one third at the Gate of the Foundation; and
all the people shall be in the courts of the house of the LORD. 6 Do not let anyone **23.6**
enter the house of the LORD except the priests and ministering Levites; they may 1 Chron 23.28-32
enter, for they are holy, but all the other[v] people shall observe the instructions of Ex 25.16,21
the LORD. 7 The Levites shall surround the king, each with his weapons in his hand; 1 Sam 10.24
and whoever enters the house shall be killed. Stay with the king in his comings and
goings."

8 The Levites and all Judah did according to all that the priest Jehoiada commanded; each brought his men, who were to come on duty on the sabbath, with
those who were to go off duty on the sabbath; for the priest Jehoiada did not dismiss
the divisions. 9 The priest Jehoiada delivered to the captains the spears and the large
and small shields that had been King David's, which were in the house of God;
10 and he set all the people as a guard for the king, everyone with weapon in hand,
from the south side of the house to the north side of the house, around the altar and
the house. 11 Then he brought out the king's son, put the crown on him, and gave
him the covenant;[w] they proclaimed him king, and Jehoiada and his sons anointed
him; and they shouted, "Long live the king!"

12 When Athaliah heard the noise of the people running and praising the king,
she went into the house of the LORD to the people; 13 and when she looked, there

[u] Heb *He* [v] Heb lacks *other* [w] Or *treaty*, or *testimony*; Heb *eduth*

23.1 After seven years of rule by Athaliah, the queen mother, Jehoiada the priest finally got up his courage and took action to get rid of the idolatrous ruler. To confront the king (or queen) with the demands of God's law was supposed to be the role of every priest in every generation. Tragically, many priests shied away from this duty, and thus only a few made a difference in the nation.

23.1 Although it could have cost him his life, this priest "took courage" and did what was right, restoring the temple worship and anointing the new king. There are times when we must correct a wrong or to speak out for what is right. When such a situation arises, gather up your courage and act.

23.12–15 Athaliah thought she had it made. After assuming the throne, she killed all potential heirs to it—so she thought. But even the best plans for evil go sour. When the truth was revealed, she was overthrown immediately. It is much safer to live according to the truth, even if it means not obtaining everything you want.

was the king standing by his pillar at the entrance, and the captains and the trumpeters beside the king, and all the people of the land rejoicing and blowing trumpets,
and the singers with their musical instruments leading in the celebration. Athaliah
tore her clothes, and cried, "Treason! Treason!" 14 Then the priest Jehoiada brought
out the captains who were set over the army, saying to them, "Bring her out between the ranks; anyone who follows her is to be put to the sword." For the priest
23.15 said, "Do not put her to death in the house of the LORD." 15 So they laid hands on
Deut 13.6-9 her; she went into the entrance of the Horse Gate of the king's house, and there they
1 Kgs 18.40 2 Chron 22.10 put her to death.

16 Jehoiada made a covenant between himself and all the people and the king
that they should be the LORD's people. 17 Then all the people went to the house of
Baal, and tore it down; his altars and his images they broke in pieces, and they
23.18 killed Mattan, the priest of Baal, in front of the altars. 18 Jehoiada assigned the care
1 Chron 9.22 23.6,25-31 of the house of the LORD to the levitical priests whom David had organized to be in
2 Chron 5.5 charge of the house of the LORD, to offer burnt offerings to the LORD, as it is written
in the law of Moses, with rejoicing and with singing, according to the order of
David. 19 He stationed the gatekeepers at the gates of the house of the LORD so that
no one should enter who was in any way unclean. 20 And he took the captains, the
nobles, the governors of the people, and all the people of the land, and they brought
the king down from the house of the LORD, marching through the upper gate to the
king's house. They set the king on the royal throne. 21 So all the people of the land
rejoiced, and the city was quiet after Athaliah had been killed with the sword.

Joash repairs the temple

24.1 **24** Joash was seven years old when he began to reign; he reigned forty years in
2 Kgs 11.21 Jerusalem; his mother's name was Zibiah of Beer-sheba. 2 Joash did what
was right in the sight of the LORD all the days of the priest Jehoiada. 3 Jehoiada got
two wives for him, and he became the father of sons and daughters.

24.4 4 Some time afterward Joash decided to restore the house of the LORD. 5 He
2 Chron 24.7 assembled the priests and the Levites and said to them, "Go out to the cities of
Judah and gather money from all Israel to repair the house of your God, year by
24.6 year; and see that you act quickly." But the Levites did not act quickly. 6 So the king
Ex 30.12-16 summoned Jehoiada the chief, and said to him, "Why have you not required the
Levites to bring in from Judah and Jerusalem the tax levied by Moses, the servant
of the LORD, on[x] the congregation of Israel for the tent of the covenant?"[y] 7 For the
children of Athaliah, that wicked woman, had broken into the house of God, and
had even used all the dedicated things of the house of the LORD for the Baals.

8 So the king gave command, and they made a chest, and set it outside the gate
24.9 of the house of the LORD. 9 A proclamation was made throughout Judah and Jerusa-
2 Chron 24.6 36.22 lem to bring in for the LORD the tax that Moses the servant of God laid on Israel in
the wilderness. 10 All the leaders and all the people rejoiced and brought their tax
and dropped it into the chest until it was full. 11 Whenever the chest was brought to
the king's officers by the Levites, when they saw that there was a large amount of
money in it, the king's secretary and the officer of the chief priest would come and
empty the chest and take it and return it to its place. So they did day after day, and
collected money in abundance. 12 The king and Jehoiada gave it to those who had

[x] Compare Vg: Heb *and* [y] Or *treaty*, or *testimony*; Heb *eduth*

23.15–17 Athaliah's life ended as her mother Jezebel's had – by execution. Her life of idolatry and treachery was cut short by God's judgment of her sin. By this time Judah had slipped so far away from God that Baal was worshiped in Jerusalem.

23.18 Jehoiada restored the temple procedures and its worship services according to David's original plans, recorded in 1 Chronicles 24; 25.

24.5 The Levites took their time carrying out the king's order, even though he told them not to delay. A tax for keeping the temple in order was not just the king's order, but God's command (Exodus 30.11–16). The Levites, therefore, were not only disregarding the king, but disregarding God. When it comes to following God's commands, a slow response may be little better than disobedience. Obey God willingly and immediately.

24.10 Evidently the Levites weren't convinced that the people would want to contribute to the rebuilding of the temple (24.5), but the people were glad to give of what they had for this project. Don't underestimate people's desire to be faithful to God. When challenged to do God's work, they will often respond willingly and generously.

charge of the work of the house of the LORD, and they hired masons and carpenters
to restore the house of the LORD, and also workers in iron and bronze to repair the
house of the LORD. 13 So those who were engaged in the work labored, and the
repairing went forward at their hands, and they restored the house of God to its
proper condition and strengthened it. 14 When they had finished, they brought the
rest of the money to the king and Jehoiada, and with it were made utensils for the
house of the LORD, utensils for the service and for the burnt offerings, and ladles,
and vessels of gold and silver. They offered burnt offerings in the house of the
LORD regularly all the days of Jehoiada.

God judges Joash

15 But Jehoiada grew old and full of days, and died; he was one hundred thirty
years old at his death. 16 And they buried him in the city of David among the kings, **24.16**
because he had done good in Israel, and for God and his house. 2 Chron 21.20
17 Now after the death of Jehoiada the officials of Judah came and did obei- **24.17**
sance to the king; then the king listened to them. 18 They abandoned the house of the Ex 34.12-14 Josh 22.20
LORD, the God of their ancestors, and served the sacred poles[z] and the idols. And 2 Chron 24.4
wrath came upon Judah and Jerusalem for this guilt of theirs. 19 Yet he sent proph- **24.19**
ets among them to bring them back to the LORD; they testified against them, but Jer 7.25
they would not listen.
20 Then the spirit of God took possession of[a] Zechariah son of the priest Jehoi- **24.20**
ada; he stood above the people and said to them, "Thus says God: Why do you Num 14.41 2 Chron 20.14
transgress the commandments of the LORD, so that you cannot prosper? Because
you have forsaken the LORD, he has also forsaken you." 21 But they conspired
against him, and by command of the king they stoned him to death in the court of
the house of the LORD. 22 King Joash did not remember the kindness that Jehoiada, **24.22**
Zechariah's father, had shown him, but killed his son. As he was dying, he said, Mt 23.34,35
"May the LORD see and avenge!"
23 At the end of the year the army of Aram came up against Joash. They came **24.23**
to Judah and Jerusalem, and destroyed all the officials of the people from among Gen 9.5
them, and sent all the booty they took to the king of Damascus. 24 Although the **24.24**
army of Aram had come with few men, the LORD delivered into their hand a very 2 Kgs 12.17 2 Chron 16.7,8
great army, because they had abandoned the LORD, the God of their ancestors.
Thus they executed judgment on Joash.
25 When they had withdrawn, leaving him severely wounded, his servants con- **24.25**
spired against him because of the blood of the son[b] of the priest Jehoiada, and they 2 Kgs 12.20,21
killed him on his bed. So he died; and they buried him in the city of David, but they
did not bury him in the tombs of the kings. 26 Those who conspired against him
were Zabad son of Shimeath the Ammonite, and Jehozabad son of Shimrith the
Moabite. 27 Accounts of his sons, and of the many oracles against him, and of the **24.27**
rebuilding[c] of the house of God are written in the Commentary on the Book of 2 Chron 13.22 24.12
the Kings. And his son Amaziah succeeded him.

[z] Heb *Asherim* [a] Heb *clothed itself with* [b] Gk Vg: Heb *sons* [c] Heb *founding*

24.17 To do *obeisance* means to kneel and place one's face on the ground.

24.18 If everything went so well in Judah when the people worshiped God, why did they turn away from him? Prosperity can be both a blessing and a curse. While it can be a sign of God's blessing to those who follow him, it carries with it the potential for moral and spiritual decline. Prosperous people are tempted to become self-sufficient and proud – to take God for granted. In our prosperity, we must not forget that God is the source of our blessings.

24.18–20 When King Joash and the nation of Judah abandoned God, God sent Zechariah to call them to repentance. Before dispensing judgment and punishment, God gave them another chance. In the same way, God does not abandon us or lash out in revenge when we sin. Instead, he aggressively pursues us through his word, his Spirit in us, the words of others, and sometimes discipline. He does not intend to destroy us but to urge us to return to him. When you are moving away from God, remember that he is pursuing you. Stop and listen. Allow him to point out your sin so you can repent and follow him again.

24.19 God sent many prophets to Joash and the people to warn them that they were headed for destruction. Joel may have been one of these prophets. Read the book of Joel for more information about the political and spiritual climate of the times.

24.22 Zechariah asked God to pay the people back for their sins. He was not seeking revenge, but pleading for justice. When we feel like despairing over the wickedness around us, we can rest assured that in the end God will bring complete justice to the earth.

Amaziah rules Judah

25.1 2 Kgs 14.1-6 **25** Amaziah was twenty-five years old when he began to reign, and he reigned
twenty-nine years in Jerusalem. His mother's name was Jehoaddan of Jeru-
salem. 2He did what was right in the sight of the LORD, yet not with a true heart.
3As soon as the royal power was firmly in his hand he killed his servants who had
25.4 Deut 24.16 murdered his father the king. 4But he did not put their children to death, according
to what is written in the law, in the book of Moses, where the LORD commanded,

---

JOASH

All parents want their children to make the right decisions. But to do this, children must first learn to make *their own* decisions. Making bad ones helps them learn to make good ones. If parents make all the decisions for their children, they leave their children without the skills for wise decision making when they are on their own. This problem seriously affected Joash. He had great advice, but he never grew up. He became so dependent on what he was told that his effectiveness was limited to the quality of his advisers.

When Joash was one year old, his grandmother Athaliah decided to slaughter all her descendants in a desperate bid for power. Joash was the only survivor, rescued and hidden by his aunt and uncle, Jehosheba and Jehoiada. Jehoiada's work as a priest made it possible to keep Joash hidden in the temple for six years. At that point, Jehoiada arranged for the overthrow of Athaliah and the crowning of Joash. For many years following, Jehoiada made most of the kingdom's decisions for Joash. When the old priest died, he was buried in the royal cemetery as a tribute to his role.

But after Jehoiada's death, Joash didn't know what to do. He listened to counsel that carried him into evil. Within a short time he even ordered the death of Jehoiada's son Zechariah. After a few months, Joash's army had been soundly defeated by the Syrians. Jerusalem was saved only because Joash stripped the temple of its treasures as a bribe. Finally, the king's own officials assassinated him. In contrast to Jehoiada, Joash was not buried among the kings; he is not even listed in Jesus' genealogy in the New Testament.

As dependent as Joash was on Jehoiada, there is little evidence that he ever established a real dependence on the God Jehoiada obeyed. Like many children, Joash's knowledge of God was secondhand. It was a start, but the king needed his own relationship with God that would outlast and overrule the changes in the advice he received.

It would be easy to criticize Joash's failure were it not for the fact that we often fall into the same traps. How often have we acted on poor advice without considering God's word?

Strengths and accomplishments:
- Carried out extensive repairs on the temple
- Was faithful to God as long as Jehoiada lived

Weaknesses and mistakes:
- Allowed idolatry to continue among his people
- Used the temple treasures to bribe King Hazael of Syria
- Killed Jehoiada's son Zechariah
- Allowed his advisers to lead the people away from God

Lessons from his life:
- A good and hopeful start can be ruined by an evil end
- Even the best counsel is ineffective if it does not help us make wise decisions
- As helpful or hurtful as others may be, we are individually responsible for what we do

Vital statistics:
- Where: Jerusalem
- Occupation: King of Judah
- Relatives: Father: Ahaziah. Mother: Zibiah. Grandmother: Athaliah. Aunt: Jehosheba. Uncle: Jehoiada. Son: Amaziah. Cousin: Zechariah
- Contemporaries: Jehu, Hazael

Key verses:
"Now after the death of Jehoiada the officials of Judah came and did obeisance to the king; then the king listened to them. They abandoned the house of the Lord, the God of their ancestors, and served the sacred poles and the idols. And wrath came upon Judah and Jerusalem for this guilt of theirs" (2 Chronicles 24.17, 18).

Joash's story is told in 2 Kings 11.1—14.23 and 2 Chronicles 22.11—25.25.

25.2 Amaziah did what was right on the outside, but inside he often resented what he had to do. His obedience was at best halfhearted. When the prophet promised God's deliverance, Amaziah first complained about the money that had been lost (25.9). He valued military success more than God's will. We must search our own hearts and root out any resistance to obeying God. Grudging compliance is not true obedience.

"The parents shall not be put to death for the children, or the children be put to
death for the parents; but all shall be put to death for their own sins."
5 Amaziah assembled the people of Judah, and set them by ancestral houses **25.5**
under commanders of the thousands and of the hundreds for all Judah and Benja- Num 1.3 2 Chron 26.13
min. He mustered those twenty years old and upward, and found that they were
three hundred thousand picked troops fit for war, able to handle spear and shield.
6 He also hired one hundred thousand mighty warriors from Israel for one hundred
talents of silver. 7 But a man of God came to him and said, "O king, do not let the **25.7**
army of Israel go with you, for the LORD is not with Israel—all these Ephraimites. 2 Kgs 4.9
8 Rather, go by yourself and act; be strong in battle, or God will fling you down **25.8**
before the enemy; for God has power to help or to overthrow." 9 Amaziah said to 2 Chron 14.11 20.6
the man of God, "But what shall we do about the hundred talents that I have given
to the army of Israel?" The man of God answered, "The LORD is able to give you
much more than this." 10 Then Amaziah discharged the army that had come to him
from Ephraim, letting them go home again. But they became very angry with Judah, and returned home in fierce anger.
11 Amaziah took courage, and led out his people; he went to the Valley of Salt, **25.11**
and struck down ten thousand men of Seir. 12 The people of Judah captured another 2 Kgs 14.7
ten thousand alive, took them to the top of Sela, and threw them down from the top
of Sela, so that all of them were dashed to pieces. 13 But the men of the army whom
Amaziah sent back, not letting them go with him to battle, fell on the cities of Judah
from Samaria to Beth-horon; they killed three thousand people in them, and took
much booty.
14 Now after Amaziah came from the slaughter of the Edomites, he brought the **25.14**
gods of the people of Seir, set them up as his gods, and worshiped them, making 2 Chron 28.23
offerings to them. 15 The LORD was angry with Amaziah and sent to him a prophet, **25.15**
who said to him, "Why have you resorted to a people's gods who could not deliver 2 Chron 25.11, 12
their own people from your hand?" 16 But as he was speaking the king[d] said to him,
"Have we made you a royal counselor? Stop! Why should you be put to death?" So
the prophet stopped, but said, "I know that God has determined to destroy you,
because you have done this and have not listened to my advice."
17 Then King Amaziah of Judah took counsel and sent to King Joash son of **25.17**
Jehoahaz son of Jehu of Israel, saying, "Come, let us look one another in the face." 2 Kgs 14.8-14
18 King Joash of Israel sent word to King Amaziah of Judah, "A thorn bush on **25.18**
Lebanon sent to a cedar on Lebanon, saying, 'Give your daughter to my son for a Judg 9.8-15
wife'; but a wild animal of Lebanon passed by and trampled down the thorn bush.
19 You say, 'See, I have defeated Edom,' and your heart has lifted you up in boast- **25.19**
fulness. Now stay at home; why should you provoke trouble so that you fall, you 2 Chron 26.16 32.25
and Judah with you?"
20 But Amaziah would not listen—it was God's doing, in order to hand them
over, because they had sought the gods of Edom. 21 So King Joash of Israel went

[d] Heb *he*

25.9, 10 Amaziah made a financial agreement with wicked Israelite soldiers, offering to pay them to fight for him (25.6). But before they could go to battle, Amaziah sent them home with their pay because of the prophet's warning. Although it cost him plenty, he wisely realized that the money was not worth the ruin the alliance could cause. Money must never stand in the way of making right decisions. The Lord's favor is worth more than any amount of money.

25.14 After the victory, Amaziah returned and burned incense to idols. We are very susceptible to sin after great victories. It is then that we feel confident, relaxed, and ready to celebrate. If, in that excitement, we let our defenses down, Satan can attack with all sorts of temptations. When you win, watch out. After the mountain peaks come the valleys.

25.15 Amaziah made a foolish mistake by worshiping the gods of the nation he had just conquered. Impressed by the accomplishments of the Edomites, he worshiped their idols! How foolish to serve the gods of a defeated enemy. We make the same mistake as Amaziah when we run after money, power, or recognition. By recognizing the emptiness of these worldly pursuits, we can free ourselves from the desire to follow them.

25.15 The Lord became angry when the king brought idols back to Judah. Yet he responded by sending him a prophet—one more attempt to bring his wandering nation back to him. We should be thankful that God, who loves us very much, cares deeply when his people reject him. When someone we love rejects us or our advice, we should remember how God treats us. Lay aside anger and the sting of rejection even when it may be right to feel that way.

25.18 In this parable, Judah is the thorn bush and Israel's army is the cedar. Ahaziah was proud after defeating Edom. He wanted to defeat Israel, but Joash warned him not to attack. Ahaziah had more ambition than ability, and he paid for it when he was soundly defeated. Don't let ambition and pride into your life for they will cause you to forget God.

up; he and King Amaziah of Judah faced one another in battle at Beth-shemesh,
which belongs to Judah. 22 Judah was defeated by Israel; everyone fled home.
23 King Joash of Israel captured King Amaziah of Judah, son of Joash, son of Ahaziah, at Beth-shemesh; he brought him to Jerusalem, and broke down the wall of
Jerusalem from the Ephraim Gate to the Corner Gate, a distance of four hundred
25.24 cubits. 24 He seized all the gold and silver, and all the vessels that were found in the
1 Chron 26.15 house of God, and Obed-edom with them; he seized also the treasuries of the king's
house, also hostages; then he returned to Samaria.
25.25 25 King Amaziah son of Joash of Judah, lived fifteen years after the death of
2 Kgs 14.17-22 King Joash son of Jehoahaz of Israel. 26 Now the rest of the deeds of Amaziah, from
first to last, are they not written in the Book of the Kings of Judah and Israel?
27 From the time that Amaziah turned away from the LORD they made a conspiracy
against him in Jerusalem, and he fled to Lachish. But they sent after him to Lachish, and killed him there. 28 They brought him back on horses; he was buried with
his ancestors in the city of David.

Uzziah rules Judah

26.1 **26** Then all the people of Judah took Uzziah, who was sixteen years old, and
2 Kgs 15.2,3 made him king to succeed his father Amaziah. 2 He rebuilt Eloth and restored it to Judah, after the king slept with his ancestors. 3 Uzziah was sixteen years

---

UZZIAH

We are never closer to failure than during our greatest successes. If we fail to recognize God's part in our achievements, they are no better than failures. Uzziah was a remarkably successful king. His achievements brought him fame. He was successful in war and peace, in planning and execution, in building and planting.

Uzziah overestimated his own importance in bringing about his great achievements. He did so many things well that a consuming pride gradually invaded his life like the leprous disease that finally destroyed his body. In trying to act as a priest, he took on a role that God did not mean for him to have. He had forgotten not only how much God had given him, but also that God had certain roles for others that he needed to respect.

Uzziah's pride was rooted in his lack of thankfulness. We have no accounts of this king's ever showing appreciation to God for the marvelous gifts he received. Our accomplishments may not compare with Uzziah's, but we still owe a debt of thanksgiving to God for our very lives. If God is not getting the credit for your successes, shouldn't you start looking at your life differently?

Strengths and accomplishments:
- Pleased God during his early years as king
- Successful warrior and city-builder
- Skillful in organizing and delegating
- Reigned for 52 years

Weaknesses and mistakes:
- Developed a prideful attitude due to his great success
- Tried to perform the priests' duties, in direct disobedience to God
- Failed to remove many of the symbols of idolatry in the land

Lessons from his life:
- Lack of thankfulness to God can lead to pride
- Even successful people must acknowledge the role God has for others in their lives

Vital statistics:
- Where: Jerusalem
- Occupation: King of Judah
- Relatives: Father: Amaziah. Mother: Jecoliah. Son: Jotham
- Contemporaries: Isaiah, Amos, Hosea, Jeroboam, Zechariah, Azariah

Key verses:
"In Jerusalem he set up machines, invented by skilled workers, on the towers and the corners for shooting arrows and large stones. And his fame spread far, for he was marvelously helped until he became strong. But when he had become strong he grew proud, to his destruction. For he was false to the Lord his God, and entered the temple of the Lord to make offering on the altar of incense" (2 Chronicles 26.15, 16).

Uzziah's story is told in 2 Kings 15.1–7 (where he is called Azariah), and in 2 Chronicles 26.1–23. He is also mentioned in Isaiah 1.1; 6.1; 7.1; Hosea 1.1; Amos 1.1; Zechariah 14.5.

old when he began to reign, and he reigned fifty-two years in Jerusalem. His
mother's name was Jecoliah of Jerusalem. 4He did what was right in the sight of the
LORD, just as his father Amaziah had done. 5He set himself to seek God in the days **26.5**
of Zechariah, who instructed him in the fear of God; and as long as he sought the 2 Chron 15.2
LORD, God made him prosper.

6 He went out and made war against the Philistines, and broke down the wall of **26.6**
Gath and the wall of Jabneh and the wall of Ashdod; he built cities in the territory Isa 14.29
of Ashdod and elsewhere among the Philistines. 7God helped him against the Phil- **26.7**
istines, against the Arabs who lived in Gur-baal, and against the Meunites. 8The 2 Chron 21.16
Ammonites paid tribute to Uzziah, and his fame spread even to the border of Egypt, **26.8** 2 Chron 17.11
for he became very strong. 9Moreover Uzziah built towers in Jerusalem at the Cor- **26.9**
ner Gate, at the Valley Gate, and at the Angle, and fortified them. 10He built towers 2 Chron 25.23 Neh 3.13
in the wilderness and hewed out many cisterns, for he had large herds, both in the 21.13,15
Shephelah and in the plain, and he had farmers and vinedressers in the hills and in **26.10**
the fertile lands, for he loved the soil. 11Moreover Uzziah had an army of soldiers, Gen 26.18-21
fit for war, in divisions according to the numbers in the muster made by the secretary Jeiel and the officer Maaseiah, under the direction of Hananiah, one of the
king's commanders. 12The whole number of the heads of ancestral houses of
mighty warriors was two thousand six hundred. 13Under their command was an **26.13**
army of three hundred seven thousand five hundred, who could make war with 2 Chron 25.5
mighty power, to help the king against the enemy. 14Uzziah provided for all the
army the shields, spears, helmets, coats of mail, bows, and stones for slinging. 15In
Jerusalem he set up machines, invented by skilled workers, on the towers and the
corners for shooting arrows and large stones. And his fame spread far, for he was
marvelously helped until he became strong.

Uzziah becomes a leper

16 But when he had become strong he grew proud, to his destruction. For he **26.16**
was false to the LORD his God, and entered the temple of the LORD to make offering Deut 32.15 1 Kgs 13.1-4
on the altar of incense. 17But the priest Azariah went in after him, with eighty 2 Chron 25.19
priests of the LORD who were men of valor; 18they withstood King Uzziah, and said **26.17**
to him, "It is not for you, Uzziah, to make offering to the LORD, but for the priests Ex 30.7,8 Num 16.39,40
the descendants of Aaron, who are consecrated to make offering. Go out of the 1 Chron 6.10 2 Chron 19.2
sanctuary; for you have done wrong, and it will bring you no honor from the LORD
God." 19Then Uzziah was angry. Now he had a censer in his hand to make offer- **26.19**
ing, and when he became angry with the priests a leprous[e] disease broke out on his 2 Kgs 5.25-27
forehead, in the presence of the priests in the house of the LORD, by the altar of
incense. 20When the chief priest Azariah, and all the priests, looked at him, he was
leprous[e] in his forehead. They hurried him out, and he himself hurried to get out,
because the LORD had struck him. 21King Uzziah was leprous[e] to the day of his **26.21**
death, and being leprous[e] lived in a separate house, for he was excluded from the Lev 13.46 2 Kgs 15.5-7
house of the LORD. His son Jotham was in charge of the palace of the king, govern- **26.22**
ing the people of the land. Isa 1.1

22 Now the rest of the acts of Uzziah, from first to last, the prophet Isaiah son **26.23**
of Amoz wrote. 23Uzziah slept with his ancestors; they buried him near his ances- 2 Chron 21.20 28.27

[e] A term for several skin diseases; precise meaning uncertain

26.15 These machines were similar to the catapults used by the Romans and were capable of slinging stones or arrows a great distance.

26.16 After God gave Uzziah great prosperity and power, he became proud and corrupt. It is true that "pride goes before destruction" (Proverbs 16.18). If God has given you wealth, influence, popularity, and power, be thankful; but be careful. God hates pride. While it is normal to feel elation when we accomplish something, it is wrong to be disdainful of God or to look down on others. Check your attitudes and remember to give God the credit for what you have. Use your gifts in ways that please him.

26.17–21 When people have power, they often think they can live above the law. But even rulers are subject to God, as Uzziah discovered. No matter what your position in society, God expects you to honor, worship, and obey him.

26.21 For much of his life, Uzziah "did what was right in the sight of the Lord" (26.4). But Uzziah turned away from God and died a leper. He is remembered more for his arrogant act and subsequent punishment than for his great reforms. God requires lifelong obedience. Spurts of obedience are not enough. Only "the one who endures to the end" will be rewarded (Mark 13.13). Be remembered for your consistent faith; otherwise you, too, may become more famous for your downfall than for your success.

tors in the burial field that belonged to the kings, for they said, "He is leprous."[f]
His son Jotham succeeded him.

Jotham rules Judah

27 Jotham was twenty-five years old when he began to reign; he reigned sixteen years in Jerusalem. His mother's name was Jerushah daughter of Zadok. 2 He did what was right in the sight of the LORD just as his father Uzziah had
done—only he did not invade the temple of the LORD. But the people still followed
corrupt practices. 3 He built the upper gate of the house of the LORD, and did extensive building on the wall of Ophel. 4 Moreover he built cities in the hill country of
Judah, and forts and towers on the wooded hills. 5 He fought with the king of the
Ammonites and prevailed against them. The Ammonites gave him that year one
hundred talents of silver, ten thousand cors of wheat and ten thousand of barley.
The Ammonites paid him the same amount in the second and the third years. 6 So
Jotham became strong because he ordered his ways before the LORD his God.
7 Now the rest of the acts of Jotham, and all his wars and his ways, are written in the
Book of the Kings of Israel and Judah. 8 He was twenty-five years old when he
began to reign; he reigned sixteen years in Jerusalem. 9 Jotham slept with his ancestors, and they buried him in the city of David; and his son Ahaz succeeded him.

Ahaz rules Judah

28 Ahaz was twenty years old when he began to reign; he reigned sixteen years
in Jerusalem. He did not do what was right in the sight of the LORD, as his
ancestor David had done, 2 but he walked in the ways of the kings of Israel. He even
made cast images for the Baals; 3 and he made offerings in the valley of the son of
Hinnom, and made his sons pass through fire, according to the abominable practices of the nations whom the LORD drove out before the people of Israel. 4 He
sacrificed and made offerings on the high places, on the hills, and under every
green tree.

5 Therefore the LORD his God gave him into the hand of the king of Aram, who
defeated him and took captive a great number of his people and brought them to
Damascus. He was also given into the hand of the king of Israel, who defeated him
with great slaughter. 6 Pekah son of Remaliah killed one hundred twenty thousand
in Judah in one day, all of them valiant warriors, because they had abandoned the
LORD, the God of their ancestors. 7 And Zichri, a mighty warrior of Ephraim, killed
the king's son Maaseiah, Azrikam the commander of the palace, and Elkanah the
next in authority to the king.

8 The people of Israel took captive two hundred thousand of their kin, women,
sons, and daughters; they also took much booty from them and brought the booty
to Samaria. 9 But a prophet of the LORD was there, whose name was Oded; he went
out to meet the army that came to Samaria, and said to them, "Because the LORD,
the God of your ancestors, was angry with Judah, he gave them into your hand, but
you have killed them in a rage that has reached up to heaven. 10 Now you intend to
subjugate the people of Judah and Jerusalem, male and female, as your slaves. But
what have you except sins against the LORD your God? 11 Now hear me, and send
back the captives whom you have taken from your kindred, for the fierce wrath of

27.1 2 Kgs 15.33-35
27.2 2 Chron 26.16
27.3 2 Chron 33.14; Neh 3.26
27.4 2 Chron 11.5
27.6 2 Chron 26.5
27.7 2 Kgs 15.36
27.8 2 Chron 27.1
28.1 2 Kgs 16.2-4
28.2 Ex 34.17; 2 Chron 22.3
28.3 Lev 18.21; Josh 15.8; 2 Chron 33.2,6
28.5 2 Chron 24.24
28.6 2 Kgs 16.5
28.8 Deut 28.25,41
28.9 2 Chron 25.15; Ezra 9.6; Isa 47.6; Rev 18.5
28.10 2 Chron 28.8

f A term for several skin diseases; precise meaning uncertain

27.2 Jotham was generally a good king (27.6), but his people became corrupt. Those you lead will not always follow your example, but that should not affect the way you live for God. This sinfulness of Jotham's kingdom is vividly portrayed in Isaiah 1–5.

27.5 The tribute he received amounted to 3 3/4 tons of silver and 62,000 bushels each of wheat and barley.

28.1ff During Ahaz's reign the northern kingdom of Israel was conquered by the Assyrians and carried into captivity (2 Kings 17). Chronicles mentions very little about the northern kingdom because the writer was focusing on David's descendants from whom the Messiah would one day come.

28.3 Imagine the monstrous evil of a religion that offers young children as sacrifices. God allowed the nation to be conquered in response to Ahaz's evil practices. Even today the practice hasn't abated. The sacrifice of children to the harsh gods of convenience, economy, and whim continues in sterile medical facilities in numbers that would astound the wicked Ahaz. If we are to allow children to come to Christ (Matthew 19.14), we must first allow them to come into the world.

the LORD is upon you." 12 Moreover, certain chiefs of the Ephraimites, Azariah son
of Johanan, Berechiah son of Meshillemoth, Jehizkiah son of Shallum, and Amasa
son of Hadlai, stood up against those who were coming from the war, 13 and said to
them, "You shall not bring the captives in here, for you propose to bring on us guilt
against the LORD in addition to our present sins and guilt. For our guilt is already
great, and there is fierce wrath against Israel." 14 So the warriors left the captives
and the booty before the officials and all the assembly. 15 Then those who were
mentioned by name got up and took the captives, and with the booty they clothed
all that were naked among them; they clothed them, gave them sandals, provided
them with food and drink, and anointed them; and carrying all the feeble among
them on donkeys, they brought them to their kindred at Jericho, the city of palm
trees. Then they returned to Samaria.

16 At that time King Ahaz sent to the king[g] of Assyria for help. 17 For the
Edomites had again invaded and defeated Judah, and carried away captives. 18 And
the Philistines had made raids on the cities in the Shephelah and the Negeb of Judah, and had taken Beth-shemesh, Aijalon, Gederoth, Soco with its villages, Timnah with its villages, and Gimzo with its villages; and they settled there. 19 For the
LORD brought Judah low because of King Ahaz of Israel, for he had behaved without restraint in Judah and had been faithless to the LORD. 20 So King Tilgath-
pilneser of Assyria came against him, and oppressed him instead of strengthening
him. 21 For Ahaz plundered the house of the LORD and the houses of the king and
of the officials, and gave tribute to the king of Assyria; but it did not help him.

22 In the time of his distress he became yet more faithless to the LORD—this
same King Ahaz. 23 For he sacrificed to the gods of Damascus, which had defeated
him, and said, "Because the gods of the kings of Aram helped them, I will sacrifice
to them so that they may help me." But they were the ruin of him, and of all Israel.
24 Ahaz gathered together the utensils of the house of God, and cut in pieces the
utensils of the house of God. He shut up the doors of the house of the LORD and
made himself altars in every corner of Jerusalem. 25 In every city of Judah he made
high places to make offerings to other gods, provoking to anger the LORD, the God
of his ancestors. 26 Now the rest of his acts and all his ways, from first to last, are
written in the Book of the Kings of Judah and Israel. 27 Ahaz slept with his ancestors, and they buried him in the city, in Jerusalem; but they did not bring him into
the tombs of the kings of Israel. His son Hezekiah succeeded him.

29 Hezekiah began to reign when he was twenty-five years old; he reigned
twenty-nine years in Jerusalem. His mother's name was Abijah daughter of
Zechariah. 2 He did what was right in the sight of the LORD, just as his ancestor
David had done.

Hezekiah rules Judah

3 In the first year of his reign, in the first month, he opened the doors of the
house of the LORD and repaired them. 4 He brought in the priests and the Levites
and assembled them in the square on the east. 5 He said to them, "Listen to me,
Levites! Sanctify yourselves, and sanctify the house of the LORD, the God of your
ancestors, and carry out the filth from the holy place. 6 For our ancestors have been
unfaithful and have done what was evil in the sight of the LORD our God; they have
forsaken him, and have turned away their faces from the dwelling of the LORD, and
turned their backs. 7 They also shut the doors of the vestibule and put out the lamps,
and have not offered incense or made burnt offerings in the holy place to the God
of Israel. 8 Therefore the wrath of the LORD came upon Judah and Jerusalem, and

28.15 Deut 34.3 2 Kgs 6.22 2 Chron 28.12 Prov 25.21,22
28.16 2 Kgs 16.7
28.17 Ezek 16.57
28.20 1 Chron 5.26
28.21 2 Kgs 16.8,9
28.23 2 Chron 25.14 Jer 44.17,18
28.24 2 Kgs 16.17 2 Chron 29.7 30.14; 33.3-5
28.26 2 Kgs 16.19,20
28.27 2 Chron 24.25
29.1 2 Kgs 18.1-3
29.2 2 Chron 28.1 34.2
29.3 2 Chron 28.24 29.7
29.5 2 Chron 29.15, 34; 35.6
29.6 Ezek 8.16
29.8 Deut 28.25 2 Chron 24.18 28.5 Jer 25.9,18

g Gk Syr Vg Compare 2 Kings 16.7: Heb *kings*

28.19 Ahaz ruled two tribes, Judah and Benjamin. Although the northern kingdom (Israel) had split off from them, Judah and Benjamin were two of the original 12 tribes of Israel. Thus Ahaz is called a king of Israel.

28.22 Difficulties and struggles can devastate people, or they can stimulate growth and maturity. For Ahaz, deep trials led to spiritual collapse. We do not need to respond like Ahaz. When facing problems or tragedy, we must remember that rough times give us a chance to grow (James 1.2–4). When you are facing trials, don't turn away from God; turn *to* him. See these times as an opportunity for you to claim God's help.

29.1 Hezekiah's Profile is found in 2 Kings 18.

he has made them an object of horror, of astonishment, and of hissing, as you see
29.9 with your own eyes. 9 Our fathers have fallen by the sword and our sons and our
2 Chron 28.5-8, 17 daughters and our wives are in captivity for this. 10 Now it is in my heart to make
29.10 a covenant with the LORD, the God of Israel, so that his fierce anger may turn away
2 Chron 23.16 from us. 11 My sons, do not now be negligent, for the LORD has chosen you to stand
29.11 Num 3.6; 8.6 in his presence to minister to him, and to be his ministers and make offerings to
him."
29.12 12 Then the Levites arose, Mahath son of Amasai, and Joel son of Azariah, of
Num 3.19,20 2 Chron 31.13 the sons of the Kohathites; and of the sons of Merari, Kish son of Abdi, and Azariah son of Jehallelel; and of the Gershonites, Joah son of Zimmah, and Eden son
of Joah; 13 and of the sons of Elizaphan, Shimri and Jeuel; and of the sons of Asaph,
Zechariah and Mattaniah; 14 and of the sons of Heman, Jehuel and Shimei; and of
29.15 the sons of Jeduthun, Shemaiah and Uzziel. 15 They gathered their brothers, sancti-
1 Chron 23.28 2 Chron 29.5 fied themselves, and went in as the king had commanded, by the words of the
30.12 LORD, to cleanse the house of the LORD. 16 The priests went into the inner part of the
29.16 house of the LORD to cleanse it, and they brought out all the unclean things that they
2 Chron 15.16 found in the temple of the LORD into the court of the house of the LORD; and the
Levites took them and carried them out to the Wadi Kidron. 17 They began to sanctify on the first day of the first month, and on the eighth day of the month they came
to the vestibule of the LORD; then for eight days they sanctified the house of the
LORD, and on the sixteenth day of the first month they finished. 18 Then they went
inside to King Hezekiah and said, "We have cleansed all the house of the LORD, the
altar of burnt offering and all its utensils, and the table for the rows of bread and all
29.19 its utensils. 19 All the utensils that King Ahaz repudiated during his reign when he
2 Chron 28.24 was faithless, we have made ready and sanctified; see, they are in front of the altar
of the LORD."
29.21 20 Then King Hezekiah rose early, assembled the officials of the city, and went
Lev 4.3-14 up to the house of the LORD. 21 They brought seven bulls, seven rams, seven lambs,

GREAT REVIVALS IN THE BIBLE

The Bible records several great revivals where people in great numbers turned to God and gave up their sinful ways of living. Each revival was characterized by a *leader* who recognized his nation's spiritual dryness. And in each case, the leader *took action* and was not afraid to make his desires known to the people.

Leader	*Reference*	*How the People Responded*
Moses	Exodus 32, 33	Accepted God's laws and built the tabernacle
Samuel	1 Samuel 7.1–13	Promised to make God first in their lives by destroying their idols
David	2 Samuel 6	Brought the ark of the covenant to Jerusalem; praised God with singing and musical instruments
Jehoshaphat	2 Chronicles 20	Decided to trust in God alone to help them, and their discouragement turned to joy
Hezekiah	2 Chronicles 29—31	Purified the temple; got rid of idols; brought tithes to God's house
Josiah	2 Chronicles 34, 35	Made a commitment to obey God's Word and remove sinful influences from their lives
Ezra	Ezra 9, 10 Haggai 1	Stopped associating with those who caused them to compromise their faith; renewed their commitment to God's Word
Nehemiah (with Ezra)	Nehemiah 8—10	Fasted, confessed their sins, read God's Word publicly, and promised in writing to again serve God wholeheartedly

29.11 The Levites, chosen by God to serve in the temple, had been kept from their duties by Ahaz's wickedness (28.24). But Hezekiah called them back into service, reminding them that the Lord had chosen them to minister.

We may not have to face a wicked king, but pressures or responsibilities can render us inactive and ineffective. When you have been given the responsibility to minister, don't neglect your duty. If you have become inactive in Christian service, either by choice or by circumstance, look for opportunities (and listen to the "Hezekiahs") God will send your way to help you resume your responsibilities. Then, like the Levites, be ready for action (29.12–15).

29.21 Throughout the Old Testament, the sacrifice was God's appointed way of approaching him and restoring a right relationship with him. The sin offering made by Hezekiah was one such sacrifice, given to ask God's forgiveness for unintentional sins. (For more information on why God required sacrifices and how they were carried out, see the notes in Leviticus 1.)

and seven male goats for a sin offering for the kingdom and for the sanctuary and
for Judah. He commanded the priests the descendants of Aaron to offer them on the
altar of the LORD. 22 So they slaughtered the bulls, and the priests received the 29.22
blood and dashed it against the altar; they slaughtered the rams and their blood was Lev 4.18
dashed against the altar; they also slaughtered the lambs and their blood was dashed
against the altar. 23 Then the male goats for the sin offering were brought to the king 29.23
and the assembly; they laid their hands on them, 24 and the priests slaughtered them Lev 4.15
and made a sin offering with their blood at the altar, to make atonement for all 29.24 Lev 4.26
Israel. For the king commanded that the burnt offering and the sin offering should
be made for all Israel.

25 He stationed the Levites in the house of the LORD with cymbals, harps, and 29.25
lyres, according to the commandment of David and of Gad the king's seer and of 2 Sam 7.2 24.11
the prophet Nathan, for the commandment was from the LORD through his proph- 1 Chron 25.6
ets. 26 The Levites stood with the instruments of David, and the priests with the 2 Chron 5.12 8.14
trumpets. 27 Then Hezekiah commanded that the burnt offering be offered on the 29.27
altar. When the burnt offering began, the song to the LORD began also, and the 2 Chron 23.18
trumpets, accompanied by the instruments of King David of Israel. 28 The whole
assembly worshiped, the singers sang, and the trumpeters sounded; all this continued until the burnt offering was finished. 29 When the offering was finished, the 29.29
king and all who were present with him bowed down and worshiped. 30 King Heze- 2 Chron 20.18
kiah and the officials commanded the Levites to sing praises to the LORD with the
words of David and of the seer Asaph. They sang praises with gladness, and they
bowed down and worshiped.

31 Then Hezekiah said, "You have now consecrated yourselves to the LORD; 29.31
come near, bring sacrifices and thank offerings to the house of the LORD." The Ex 35.5,22
assembly brought sacrifices and thank offerings; and all who were of a willing heart
brought burnt offerings. 32 The number of the burnt offerings that the assembly
brought was seventy bulls, one hundred rams, and two hundred lambs; all these
were for a burnt offering to the LORD. 33 The consecrated offerings were six hundred bulls and three thousand sheep. 34 But the priests were too few and could not 29.34
skin all the burnt offerings, so, until other priests had sanctified themselves, their 2 Chron 35.11
kindred, the Levites, helped them until the work was finished—for the Levites
were more conscientious[h] than the priests in sanctifying themselves. 35 Besides the 29.35
great number of burnt offerings there was the fat of the offerings of well-being, and Num 15.5-10
there were the drink offerings for the burnt offerings. Thus the service of the house 2 Chron 29.32
of the LORD was restored. 36 And Hezekiah and all the people rejoiced because of
what God had done for the people; for the thing had come about suddenly.

Hezekiah reinstates the passover

30 Hezekiah sent word to all Israel and Judah, and wrote letters also to Ephraim 30.2
and Manasseh, that they should come to the house of the LORD at Jerusalem, Num 9.10,11
to keep the passover to the LORD the God of Israel. 2 For the king and his officials 2 Chron 30.13, 15

h Heb *upright in heart*

29.22 The blood dashed upon the altar represented the innocence of the sacrificed animal taking the place of the guilt of the person making the offering. The animal died so the sinner could live. This ritual looked forward to the day when Jesus Christ, God's perfect Son, would sacrifice his innocent life on the cross in order that the sinful and guilty human race might be spared the punishment it deserves (Hebrews 10.1–14).

29.30 A seer was someone who received messages from God for the nation through visions or dreams.

29.31 A thank (or peace) offering was given as an expression of gratitude toward God. It symbolized restored peace and fellowship with God.

29.34 It is ironic that the assistants were more prepared than their leaders, but we sometimes see volunteers in the church today with more zeal to serve God than some professional Christian workers.

30.1 The passover celebration commemorated the time that God spared the lives of Israel's firstborn sons in Egypt. God had promised to send a plague to kill all the firstborn sons except in those homes where the blood of a slain lamb had been painted on the doorposts. The Israelites obeyed, and when the Death Angel saw the blood, he "passed over" the house and did not harm anyone in it (Exodus 12.23). After this plague, Pharaoh freed the Israelites from slavery. This celebration was to be a yearly reminder of how God delivered his people. The careful preparations, both in the temple and for the feast, showed that this was not a temporary or impulsive revival, but a deep-seated change of heart and life.

30.2, 3 God's law had a provision that, under certain circumstances, the passover could be celebrated one month later (Numbers 9.10, 11).

and all the assembly in Jerusalem had taken counsel to keep the passover in the
second month 3 (for they could not keep it at its proper time because the priests had
not sanctified themselves in sufficient number, nor had the people assembled in
30.5 Judg 20.1 Jerusalem). 4 The plan seemed right to the king and all the assembly. 5 So they
decreed to make a proclamation throughout all Israel, from Beer-sheba to Dan, that
the people should come and keep the passover to the LORD the God of Israel, at
30.6 2 Chron 28.20 Jerusalem; for they had not kept it in great numbers as prescribed. 6 So couriers
went throughout all Israel and Judah with letters from the king and his officials, as
the king had commanded, saying, "O people of Israel, return to the LORD, the God
of Abraham, Isaac, and Israel, so that he may turn again to the remnant of you who
30.7 2 Chron 29.8 Ezek 20.13 have escaped from the hand of the kings of Assyria. 7 Do not be like your ancestors
and your kindred, who were faithless to the LORD God of their ancestors, so that he
30.8 Ex 3.29 2 Chron 29.10 made them a desolation, as you see. 8 Do not now be stiff-necked as your ancestors
were, but yield yourselves to the LORD and come to his sanctuary, which he has
sanctified forever, and serve the LORD your God, so that his fierce anger may turn
30.9 Ex 34.6,7 Deut 30.2 Mic 7.18 away from you. 9 For as you return to the LORD, your kindred and your children will
find compassion with their captors, and return to this land. For the LORD your God
is gracious and merciful, and will not turn away his face from you, if you return to
him."

30.10 2 Chron 36.16 10 So the couriers went from city to city through the country of Ephraim and
Manasseh, and as far as Zebulun; but they laughed them to scorn, and mocked
30.11 2 Chron 30.18, 21,35 them. 11 Only a few from Asher, Manasseh, and Zebulun humbled themselves and
came to Jerusalem. 12 The hand of God was also on Judah to give them one heart to
do what the king and the officials commanded by the word of the LORD.

30.13 2 Chron 30.2 13 Many people came together in Jerusalem to keep the festival of unleavened
bread in the second month, a very large assembly. 14 They set to work and removed
30.14 2 Chron 28.24 29.16 the altars that were in Jerusalem, and all the altars for offering incense they took
away and threw into the Wadi Kidron. 15 They slaughtered the passover lamb on the
30.15 2 Chron 29.34 30.2,3 fourteenth day of the second month. The priests and the Levites were ashamed, and
they sanctified themselves and brought burnt offerings into the house of the LORD.
30.16 2 Chron 35.10, 15 16 They took their accustomed posts according to the law of Moses the man of God;
the priests dashed the blood that they received[i] from the hands of the Levites.
30.17 Ex 12.43-49 Num 9.10 2 Chron 19.3 29.34; 30.11,25 17 For there were many in the assembly who had not sanctified themselves; therefore the Levites had to slaughter the passover lamb for everyone who was not clean,
to make it holy to the LORD. 18 For a multitude of the people, many of them from
Ephraim, Manasseh, Issachar, and Zebulun, had not cleansed themselves, yet they
ate the passover otherwise than as prescribed. But Hezekiah prayed for them, saying, "The good LORD pardon all 19 who set their hearts to seek God, the LORD the

[i] Heb lacks *that they received*

30.6–9 Hezekiah was a king dedicated to God and to the spiritual progress of the nation. He sent letters throughout Judah and Israel urging everyone to return to God. He told them not to be stubborn, but to yield themselves to the Lord. To yield means to obey him first, submitting our bodies, minds, wills, and emotions to him. His Holy Spirit must guide and renew every part of us. Only then will we be able to temper our stubborn selfishness.

30.10 The northern kingdom of Israel had recently been conquered by Assyria, and most of the people had been carried away to foreign lands. Hezekiah sent a proclamation to the few people who remained, inviting them to come to the passover (30.1), but they responded with laughter and scorn. People may mock you when you try to promote spiritual renewal and growth. Are you prepared to be ridiculed for your faith? When it comes your way, do not waver. Stand strong in your faith, as Hezekiah did, and God will honor you.

30.11 These people invited to the passover scorned Hezekiah's messengers, but some accepted the invitation. Our efforts to tell others about God often meet with similar reactions. Many people will laugh at an invitation to accept Christ. But this must not stop us from reaching out. If you know and understand that rejecting the gospel is common, you can guard against feelings of personal rejection. Remember that the Holy Spirit convicts and convinces. Our task is to invite others to consider God's actions, his claims, and his promises.

30.14 Just as the priests had cleansed the temple (29.4, 5), so the people cleansed the city of heathen idols and then cleansed themselves to prepare for worship (30.17–19). Even the good kings of Judah found it difficult to get rid of the heathen idols and altars in the high places (2 Kings 14.4; 2 Chronicles 20.33). Finally Hezekiah, with the help of his people, completed this task.

30.15 The people were so zealous to bring gifts and offerings to the temple that the priests and Levites were ashamed they did not share the same enthusiasm. The zeal of the common man's faith motivated the ministers to take action. The devoted faith of laypersons today should motivate professional church staff to rekindle their enthusiasm for God's work. Laypersons should never be shut out of church government or decision making. The church needs their good examples of faith.

God of their ancestors, even though not in accordance with the sanctuary's rules of
cleanness." 20 The LORD heard Hezekiah, and healed the people. 21 The people of **30.21**
Israel who were present at Jerusalem kept the festival of unleavened bread seven Ex 12.15; 13.6
days with great gladness; and the Levites and the priests praised the LORD day by
day, accompanied by loud instruments for the LORD. 22 Hezekiah spoke encourag- **30.22**
ingly to all the Levites who showed good skill in the service of the LORD. So the Ezra 10.11
people ate the food of the festival for seven days, sacrificing offerings of well-
being and giving thanks to the LORD the God of their ancestors.
23 Then the whole assembly agreed together to keep the festival for another **30.23**
seven days; so they kept it for another seven days with gladness. 24 For King Heze- 1 Kgs 8.65 **30.24**
kiah of Judah gave the assembly a thousand bulls and seven thousand sheep for 2 Chron 29.34
offerings, and the officials gave the assembly a thousand bulls and ten thousand 30.3; 35.7,8
sheep. The priests sanctified themselves in great numbers. 25 The whole assembly **30.25**
of Judah, the priests and the Levites, and the whole assembly that came out of 2 Chron 30.11, 18
Israel, and the resident aliens who came out of the land of Israel, and the resident
aliens who lived in Judah, rejoiced. 26 There was great joy in Jerusalem, for since **30.26**
the time of Solomon son of King David of Israel there had been nothing like this in 2 Chron 7.8-10 **30.27**
Jerusalem. 27 Then the priests and the Levites stood up and blessed the people, and Deut 26.15 2 Chron 23.18
their voice was heard; their prayer came to his holy dwelling in heaven. Ps 68.5

Hezekiah restores worship

31 Now when all this was finished, all Israel who were present went out to the **31.1**
cities of Judah and broke down the pillars, hewed down the sacred poles,[j] 2 Kgs 18.4
and pulled down the high places and the altars throughout all Judah and Benjamin,
and in Ephraim and Manasseh, until they had destroyed them all. Then all the people of Israel returned to their cities, all to their individual properties.
2 Hezekiah appointed the divisions of the priests and of the Levites, division by **31.2**
division, everyone according to his service, the priests and the Levites, for burnt 1 Chron 23.28-31; 24.1
offerings and offerings of well-being, to minister in the gates of the camp of the
LORD and to give thanks and praise. 3 The contribution of the king from his own **31.3**
possessions was for the burnt offerings: the burnt offerings of morning and eve- Num 28.1-29,40 2 Chron 35.7
ning, and the burnt offerings for the sabbaths, the new moons, and the appointed
festivals, as it is written in the law of the LORD. 4 He commanded the people who **31.4** Num 18.8
lived in Jerusalem to give the portion due to the priests and the Levites, so that they
might devote themselves to the law of the LORD. 5 As soon as the word spread, the **31.5** Lev 27.30
people of Israel gave in abundance the first fruits of grain, wine, oil, honey, and of Deut 14.28 Neh 13.12
all the produce of the field; and they brought in abundantly the tithe of everything.
6 The people of Israel and Judah who lived in the cities of Judah also brought in the
tithe of cattle and sheep, and the tithe of the dedicated things that had been consecrated to the LORD their God, and laid them in heaps. 7 In the third month they
began to pile up the heaps, and finished them in the seventh month. 8 When Hezekiah and the officials came and saw the heaps, they blessed the LORD and his people **31.10**
Israel. 9 Hezekiah questioned the priests and the Levites about the heaps. 10 The 1 Chron 6.8,9 Mal 3.10

j Heb *Asherim*

30.22 Offerings of well-being, or peace offerings, were given to express gratitude to God for health or for safety in times of crisis.

30.26 It had been more than 200 years since there had been such a celebration in Jerusalem.

31.1ff Why was idol worship so bad? The Israelites had access to the one true God, but they constantly fell into worshiping lifeless idols made of wood or stone. They put aside worshiping the Creator in order to worship the creation. We are just as guilty when God no longer holds first place in our lives. When we think more about wealth, pleasure, prestige, or material possessions than about God, we are actually worshiping them as idols. Because of idol worship, the people of Judah were eventually sent into captivity in foreign lands (36.14–17). We may not be sent into captivity, but discipline awaits all those who continually put earthly desires above spiritual priorities.

31.2–21 The priests had not been supported by the government during the evil kings' reigns. Now that the temple was repaired, Hezekiah organized the priests and resumed the work of the temple according to a plan originally set up by David (1 Chronicles 23.6–23; 24.3–19).

31.4–6 Hezekiah reinstated the practice of tithing – giving a tenth of one's income to the priests and Levites so they could be free to serve God and minister to the people. The people responded immediately and generously. God's work needs the support of God's people. Does God receive a regular percentage of your income? Generosity makes our giving delightful to God (2 Corinthians 8, 9). How different the church would be today if all believers consistently followed this pattern.

chief priest Azariah, who was of the house of Zadok, answered him, "Since they
began to bring the contributions into the house of the LORD, we have had enough to
eat and have plenty to spare; for the LORD has blessed his people, so that we have
this great supply left over."
31.11 1 Kgs 6.5,8 11 Then Hezekiah commanded them to prepare store-chambers in the house of
31.12 2 Chron 31.10 the LORD; and they prepared them. 12 Faithfully they brought in the contributions,
the tithes and the dedicated things. The chief officer in charge of them was Conaniah the Levite, with his brother Shimei as second; 13 while Jehiel, Azaziah, Nahath, Asahel, Jerimoth, Jozabad, Eliel, Ismachiah, Mahath, and Benaiah were
overseers assisting Conaniah and his brother Shimei, by the appointment of King
31.14 Josh 21.9-19 2 Chron 29.12 Hezekiah and of Azariah the chief officer of the house of God. 14 Kore son of Imnah
the Levite, keeper of the east gate, was in charge of the freewill offerings to God,
to apportion the contribution reserved for the LORD and the most holy offerings.
15 Eden, Miniamin, Jeshua, Shemaiah, Amariah, and Shecaniah were faithfully assisting him in the cities of the priests, to distribute the portions to their kindred, old
and young alike, by divisions, 16 except those enrolled by genealogy, males from
three years old and upwards, all who entered the house of the LORD as the duty of
each day required, for their service according to their offices, by their divisions.
31.17 1 Chron 23.24 17 The enrollment of the priests was according to their ancestral houses; that of the
Levites from twenty years old and upwards was according to their offices, by their
divisions. 18 The priests were enrolled with all their little children, their wives, their
sons, and their daughters, the whole multitude; for they were faithful in keeping
31.19 2 Chron 31.12-15 themselves holy. 19 And for the descendants of Aaron, the priests, who were in the
fields of common land belonging to their towns, town by town, the people desig-
nated by name were to distribute portions to every male among the priests and to
everyone among the Levites who was enrolled.
31.20 2 Kgs 20.3; 22.2 20 Hezekiah did this throughout all Judah; he did what was good and right and
faithful before the LORD his God. 21 And every work that he undertook in the service of the house of God, and in accordance with the law and the commandments,
to seek his God, he did with all his heart; and he prospered.

THE DAVIDIC DYNASTY

The Lord promised David that his kingdom would endure and his throne would be established forever (2 Samuel 7.16). As a partial fulfillment of this promise, David and his descendants ruled Judah for over 400 years. Jesus Christ was a direct descendant of David, and was the ultimate fulfillment of this promise (Acts 2.22–36).

David (40 years, 1 Chr. 10—29)
Solomon (40 years, 2 Chr. 1—9)
Rehoboam (17 years, 2 Chr. 10—12)
Abijah (3 years, 2 Chr. 13)
Asa (41 years, 2 Chr. 14—16)
Jehoshaphat (25 years, 2 Chr. 17—20)
Jehoram (8 years, 2 Chr. 21)
Ahaziah (1 years, 2 Chr. 22.1–9)
Athaliah (6 years, 2 Chr. 22.10—23.21)
Joash (40 years, 2 Chr. 24)
Amaziah (29 years, 2 Chr. 25)
Uzziah (52 years, 2 Chr. 26)
Jotham (16 years, 2 Chr. 27)
Ahaz (16 years, 2 Chr. 28)
Hezekiah (29 years, 2 Chr. 29—32)
Manasseh (55 years, 2 Chr. 33.1–20)
Amon (2 years, 2 Chr. 33.21–25)
Josiah (31 years, 2 Chr. 34—35)
Jehoahaz (3 months, 2 Chr. 36.1–4)
Jehoiakim (11 years, 2 Chr. 36.5–8)
Jehoiachin (3 months, 2 Chr. 36.9–10)
Zedekiah (11 years, 2 Chr. 36.11–16)

31.20, 21 Hezekiah led the people of Judah in spiritual renewal. His actions serve as a model of renewal for us: (1) remember God's compassion (30.9); (2) keep going despite ridicule (30.10); (3) aggressively remove evil influences from your life (30.14; 31.1); (4) confess your sin to God (30.22); (5) be open to spontaneity in worship (30.23); (6) contribute generously to God's work (31.4–8). If any of these are lacking in your life, consider how they might apply and renew your commitment to God.

Assyria invades Judah

32 After these things and these acts of faithfulness, King Sennacherib of As- 32.1
syria came and invaded Judah and encamped against the fortified cities, Isa 36.1–37.38
thinking to win them for himself. 2When Hezekiah saw that Sennacherib had come
and intended to fight against Jerusalem, 3he planned with his officers and his war- 32.3
riors to stop the flow of the springs that were outside the city; and they helped him. 2 Kgs 20.20
4A great many people were gathered, and they stopped all the springs and the wadi 32.4
that flowed through the land, saying, "Why should the Assyrian kings come and 2 Chron 32.30
find water in abundance?" 5Hezekiah[k] set to work resolutely and built up the entire 32.5
wall that was broken down, and raised towers on it,[l] and outside it he built another 1 Kgs 9.24 2 Kgs 25.4
wall; he also strengthened the Millo in the city of David, and made weapons and 2 Chron 25.23
shields in abundance. 6He appointed combat commanders over the people, and 32.6
gathered them together to him in the square at the gate of the city and spoke encour- 2 Chron 30.22
agingly to them, saying, 7"Be strong and of good courage. Do not be afraid or 32.7
dismayed before the king of Assyria and all the horde that is with him; for there is 2 Kgs 6.16 1 Chron 22.13
one greater with us than with him. 8With him is an arm of flesh; but with us is the 32.8
LORD our God, to help us and to fight our battles." The people were encouraged by 2 Chron 20.17 Jer 17.5
the words of King Hezekiah of Judah.

9 After this, while King Sennacherib of Assyria was at Lachish with all his
forces, he sent his servants to Jerusalem to King Hezekiah of Judah and to all the
people of Judah that were in Jerusalem, saying, 10"Thus says King Sennacherib of
Assyria: On what are you relying, that you undergo the siege of Jerusalem? 11Is not
Hezekiah misleading you, handing you over to die by famine and by thirst, when
he tells you, 'The LORD our God will save us from the hand of the king of Assyria'?
12Was it not this same Hezekiah who took away his high places and his altars and 32.12
commanded Judah and Jerusalem, saying, 'Before one altar you shall worship, and 2 Chron 31.1
upon it you shall make your offerings'? 13Do you not know what I and my ances-

[k] Heb *He* [l] Vg: Heb *and raised on the towers*

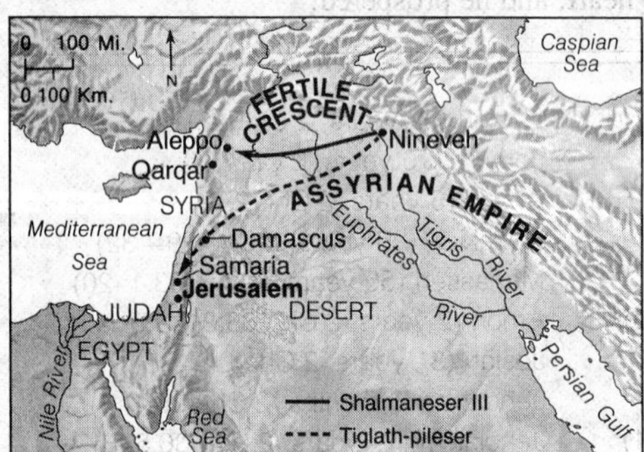

THE ASSYRIAN EMPIRE The mighty Assyrian Empire extended from the Persian Gulf, across the Fertile Crescent, and south to Egypt. Shalmaneser III extended the Empire toward the Mediterranean Sea by conquering cities as far west as Qarqar. Tiglath-pileser extended the Empire south into Syria, Israel, Judah, and Philistia. It was Shalmaneser V who destroyed Samaria, Israel's capital.

32.1 Assyria was a great empire by Hezekiah's time, controlling most of the Middle East. From a small strip of land located in present-day Iran and Iraq, it began to establish its power under Ashurnasirpal II (883–859 B.C.) and his son Shalmaneser III (859–824). Under Tiglath-pileser III (745–727), Assyria's boundaries extended to the borders of Israel, making it one of the largest empires in ancient history. Shalmaneser V destroyed the northern kingdom in 722, and his grandson, Sennacherib (705–681), tried to bring Judah, the southern kingdom, under his control. Less than a century later, Assyria would lie in ruins (612). (For more information on Assyria and its kings, see the chart in 2 Kings 19.)

32.1 Sennacherib wanted to "win them for himself" so he could force them to pay tribute. Forcing captured cities to pay tribute was an excellent way for kings to build their income base. Often Assyria would require an oath of allegiance from a country promising to pay taxes in the form of livestock, wine, battle equipment (horses, chariots, weapons), gold, silver, and anything else that pleased the invading king. Tribute was more important to Assyria than captives, since captives cost money. Thus they were taken only in cases of extreme rebellion or to repopulate cities that had been destroyed.

32.1ff When Hezekiah was confronted with the frightening prospect of an Assyrian invasion, he made two important decisions. He did everything he could to deal with the situation, and he trusted God for the outcome. That is exactly what we must do when faced with difficult or frightening situations. Take all the steps you possibly can to solve the problem or improve the situation. But also commit it to God in prayer and trust him for the solution.

32.3, 4 Cities had to be built near reliable water sources. Natural springs were some of Jerusalem's major sources of water. In a brilliant military move, Hezekiah plugged the springs outside the city and channeled the water through an underground tunnel (32.30); therefore, Jerusalem would have water even through a long siege. Hezekiah's tunnel has been discovered along with an inscription describing how it was built: two groups of workers started digging underground, one in Jerusalem and one at the Gihon Spring, and they met in the middle.

32.7, 8 Hezekiah could see with "eyes of faith." The number of his opponents meant nothing as long as he was on the Lord's side. Victory is "not by might, nor by power, but by my spirit, says the Lord of hosts" (Zechariah 4.6). Hezekiah could confidently encourage his men because he had no doubt about where he stood with God. Are you on the Lord's side? You may never face an enemy army, but the battles you face every day can be won with God's strength.

tors have done to all the peoples of other lands? Were the gods of the nations of
32.14 Isa 10.9-11 those lands at all able to save their lands out of my hand? 14 Who among all the gods
of those nations that my ancestors utterly destroyed was able to save his people
from my hand, that your God should be able to save you from my hand? 15 Now
therefore do not let Hezekiah deceive you or mislead you in this fashion, and do not
believe him, for no god of any nation or kingdom has been able to save his people
from my hand or from the hand of my ancestors. How much less will your God save
you out of my hand!"
16 His servants said still more against the Lord GOD and against his servant
32.17 2 Chron 32.14 Hezekiah. 17 He also wrote letters to throw contempt on the LORD the God of Israel
and to speak against him, saying, "Just as the gods of the nations in other lands did
not rescue their people from my hands, so the God of Hezekiah will not rescue his
people from my hand." 18 They shouted it with a loud voice in the language of
Judah to the people of Jerusalem who were on the wall, to frighten and terrify them,
in order that they might take the city. 19 They spoke of the God of Jerusalem as if
he were like the gods of the peoples of the earth, which are the work of human
hands.
20 Then King Hezekiah and the prophet Isaiah son of Amoz prayed because of
this and cried to heaven. 21 And the LORD sent an angel who cut off all the mighty
warriors and commanders and officers in the camp of the king of Assyria. So he
returned in disgrace to his own land. When he came into the house of his god, some
of his own sons struck him down there with the sword. 22 So the LORD saved Hezekiah and the inhabitants of Jerusalem from the hand of King Sennacherib of Assyria
32.23 2 Sam 8.10 and from the hand of all his enemies; he gave them rest[m] on every side. 23 Many
brought gifts to the LORD in Jerusalem and precious things to King Hezekiah of
Judah, so that he was exalted in the sight of all nations from that time onward.
32.24 2 Kgs 20.1-11 Isa 38.1-8 24 In those days Hezekiah became sick and was at the point of death. He prayed
to the LORD, and he answered him and gave him a sign. 25 But Hezekiah did not
32.25 2 Chron 24.18 26.16 respond according to the benefit done to him, for his heart was proud. Therefore
wrath came upon him and upon Judah and Jerusalem. 26 Then Hezekiah humbled
32.26 Jer 26.18,19 himself for the pride of his heart, both he and the inhabitants of Jerusalem, so that
the wrath of the LORD did not come upon them in the days of Hezekiah.
27 Hezekiah had very great riches and honor; and he made for himself treasuries for silver, for gold, for precious stones, for spices, for shields, and for all kinds
of costly objects; 28 storehouses also for the yield of grain, wine, and oil; and stalls
for all kinds of cattle, and sheepfolds.[n] 29 He likewise provided cities for himself,
and flocks and herds in abundance; for God had given him very great possessions.
32.30 1 Kgs 1.33 2 Kgs 20.20 30 This same Hezekiah closed the upper outlet of the waters of Gihon and directed
them down to the west side of the city of David. Hezekiah prospered in all his
32.31 2 Kgs 20.12 2 Chron 32.24 Isa 38.7,8; 39.1 works. 31 So also in the matter of the envoys of the officials of Babylon, who had
been sent to him to inquire about the sign that had been done in the land, God left
him to himself, in order to test him and to know all that was in his heart.

[m] Gk Vg: Heb *guided them* [n] Gk Vg: Heb *flocks for folds*

32.31 A test can bring out a person's true character. God tested Hezekiah to see what he was really like and to show him his own shortcomings and the attitude of his heart. God did not totally abandon Hezekiah, nor did he tempt him to sin or trick him. The test was meant to strengthen him, develop his character, and prepare him for the tasks ahead. In times of success, most of us can live good lives. But pressure, trouble, or pain quickly removes our thin veneer of goodness unless our strength comes from God. What are you like under pressure or when everything is going wrong? Do you give in or turn to God? Those who are consistently in touch with God don't have to worry what pressure may reveal about them.

32.31 Babylon was slowly and quietly rising to become a world power. At the same time, the Assyrian Empire was slowly declining due to internal strife and a succession of weak kings. When Assyria was finally crushed in 612 B.C., Babylon under Nebuchadnezzar moved into its place of prominence. (For more information on Babylon, see the note on 2 Kings 20.14.)

32.31 Why did God leave Hezekiah to himself? After Hezekiah was healed of his sickness, he developed excessive pride. When envoys came to inquire about his miraculous healing, God stepped back to see how Hezekiah would respond. Unfortunately, Hezekiah's actions revealed his runaway pride. He pointed to his own accomplishments rather than to God. Pride is any attitude that elevates our effort or abilities above God's, or treats with disdain his work in us. It causes us to congratulate ourselves for our success and look down on other people. God does not object to self-confidence, healthy self-esteem, or good feelings about our accomplishments. He objects to the foolish attitude of taking full credit for what he has done or for setting ourselves up as superior to others.

32 Now the rest of the acts of Hezekiah, and his good deeds, are written in the
vision of the prophet Isaiah son of Amoz in the Book of the Kings of Judah and
Israel. 33 Hezekiah slept with his ancestors, and they buried him on the ascent to the
tombs of the descendants of David; and all Judah and the inhabitants of Jerusalem
did him honor at his death. His son Manasseh succeeded him.

Manasseh rules Judah

33 Manasseh was twelve years old when he began to reign; he reigned fifty-five **33.1**
years in Jerusalem. 2 He did what was evil in the sight of the LORD, accord- 2 Kgs 21.1-9
ing to the abominable practices of the nations whom the LORD drove out before the **33.2** 2 Chron 28.3
people of Israel. 3 For he rebuilt the high places that his father Hezekiah had pulled **33.3**
down, and erected altars to the Baals, made sacred poles,[o] worshiped all the host Deut 16.21 2 Kgs 23.5,6
of heaven, and served them. 4 He built altars in the house of the LORD, of which the 2 Chron 31.1
LORD had said, "In Jerusalem shall my name be forever." 5 He built altars for all the **33.4**
host of heaven in the two courts of the house of the LORD. 6 He made his son pass 2 Chron 4.9 7.16; 28.24
through fire in the valley of the son of Hinnom, practiced soothsaying and augury **33.6**
and sorcery, and dealt with mediums and with wizards. He did much evil in the Lev 19.31; 20.27 2 Chron 28.3
sight of the LORD, provoking him to anger. 7 The carved image of the idol that he **33.7**
had made he set in the house of God, of which God said to David and to his son 2 Chron 3.4,15
Solomon, "In this house, and in Jerusalem, which I have chosen out of all the tribes
of Israel, I will put my name forever; 8 I will never again remove the feet of Israel **33.8**
from the land that I appointed for your ancestors, if only they will be careful to do 2 Sam 7.10
all that I have commanded them, all the law, the statutes, and the ordinances given
through Moses." 9 Manasseh misled Judah and the inhabitants of Jerusalem, so that
they did more evil than the nations whom the LORD had destroyed before the people
of Israel.

10 The LORD spoke to Manasseh and to his people, but they gave no heed.
11 Therefore the LORD brought against them the commanders of the army of the king **33.11**
of Assyria, who took Manasseh captive in manacles, bound him with fetters, and Deut 28.36 2 Chron 36.6
brought him to Babylon. 12 While he was in distress he entreated the favor of the **33.12**
LORD his God and humbled himself greatly before the God of his ancestors. 13 He 2 Chron 32.26
prayed to him, and God received his entreaty, heard his plea, and restored him **33.13** Ezra 8.23
again to Jerusalem and to his kingdom. Then Manasseh knew that the LORD indeed Dan 4.32
was God.

14 Afterward he built an outer wall for the city of David west of Gihon, in the **33.14**
valley, reaching the entrance at the Fish Gate; he carried it around Ophel, and 1 Kgs 1.33 Neh 3.3
raised it to a very great height. He also put commanders of the army in all the
fortified cities in Judah. 15 He took away the foreign gods and the idol from the **33.15**
house of the LORD, and all the altars that he had built on the mountain of the house 2 Chron 33.3-7
of the LORD and in Jerusalem, and he threw them out of the city. 16 He also restored
the altar of the LORD and offered on it sacrifices of well-being and of thanksgiving;
and he commanded Judah to serve the LORD the God of Israel. 17 The people, how- **33.17**
ever, still sacrificed at the high places, but only to the LORD their God. 2 Chron 32.12

[o] Heb *Asheroth*

33.6 Sorcery is using power gained from evil spirits. Augury is predicting the future through omens.

33.11 Between 652 and 648 B.C., the city of Babylon rebelled against Assyria. The rebellion was crushed, but Assyria may have suspected that Manasseh supported it. That may explain why Manasseh was taken to Babylon for trial rather than to the Assyrian capital of Nineveh.

33.12, 13 In a list of corrupt kings, Manasseh would rank near the top. His life was a catalog of evil deeds including idol worship, sacrificing his own children, and temple desecration. Eventually, however, he realized his sins and cried out to God for forgiveness. And God listened. If God can forgive Manasseh, surely he can forgive anyone. Are you burdened by overpowering guilt? Do you doubt that anyone could forgive what you have done? Take heart—until death, no one is beyond the reach of God's forgiveness.

33.17 Although the people worshiped God alone, they worshiped him in the wrong way. God had told them to make their sacrifices only in certain places (Deuteronomy 12.13, 14). This kept them from changing their way of worship and protected them against the dangerous influence of pagan religious practices. Unfortunately, the people continued to use these places of worship, not realizing that (1) they were adopting practices God opposed, and (2) these places were against God's law. They were mixing pagan beliefs with worship of God. Blending religious ideas leads to confusion about who God really is. We must take care that subtle secular influences do not distort our worship practices.

33.18 2 Chron 33.10, 12,13
33.19 2 Chron 33.3,13
33.20 2 Kgs 21.19-24

18 Now the rest of the acts of Manasseh, his prayer to his God, and the words
of the seers who spoke to him in the name of the LORD God of Israel, these are in
the Annals of the Kings of Israel. 19 His prayer, and how God received his entreaty,
all his sin and his faithlessness, the sites on which he built high places and set up the
sacred poles[p] and the images, before he humbled himself, these are written in the
records of the seers.[q] 20 So Manasseh slept with his ancestors, and they buried him
in his house. His son Amon succeeded him.

Amon rules Judah

33.22 2 Chron 33.2-7
33.23 2 Chron 33.12, 19
33.24 2 Chron 25.27

21 Amon was twenty-two years old when he began to reign; he reigned two
years in Jerusalem. 22 He did what was evil in the sight of the LORD, as his father
Manasseh had done. Amon sacrificed to all the images that his father Manasseh had
made, and served them. 23 He did not humble himself before the LORD, as his father
Manasseh had humbled himself, but this Amon incurred more and more guilt.
24 His servants conspired against him and killed him in his house. 25 But the people
of the land killed all those who had conspired against King Amon; and the people
of the land made his son Josiah king to succeed him.

Josiah rules Judah

34.1 2 Kgs 22.1,2
34.2 2 Chron 29.2

34 Josiah was eight years old when he began to reign; he reigned thirty-one
years in Jerusalem. 2 He did what was right in the sight of the LORD, and
walked in the ways of his ancestor David; he did not turn aside to the right or to the

p Heb *Asherim* q One Ms Gk: MT *of Hozai*

Even a brief outline of King Manasseh's evil sickens us, and we wonder how God could ever forgive him. Not only did he intentionally offend God by desecrating Solomon's temple with idols, but he also worshiped pagan gods and even sacrificed his children to them! Child sacrifice is a vile act of pagan idolatry, an act against both God and people. Such blatant sins require severe correction.

God showed justice to Manasseh in warning and punishing him. He showed mercy in responding to Manasseh's heartfelt repentance by forgiving and restoring him. Given the nature of Manasseh's rebellion, we are not surprised by God's punishment—defeat and exile at the hands of the Assyrians. But Manasseh's repentance and God's forgiveness are unexpected. Manasseh's life was changed. He was given a new start.

How far has God gone to get your attention? Have you ever, like Manasseh, come to your senses and cried out to God for help? Only your repentance and a prayer for a new attitude stand between you and God's complete forgiveness.

Strengths and accomplishments:
- Despite the bitter consequences of his sins, he learned from them
- Humbly repented of his sins before God

Weaknesses and mistakes:
- Challenged God's authority and was defeated
- Reversed many of the positive effects of his father Hezekiah's rule
- Sacrificed his children to idols

Lessons from his life:
- God will go a long way to get someone's attention
- Forgiveness is limited not by the amount of sin, but by our willingness to repent

Vital statistics:
- Where: Jerusalem
- Occupation: King of Judah
- Relatives: Father: Hezekiah. Mother: Hephzibah. Son: Amon

Key verses:
"While he was in distress he entreated the favor of the Lord his God and humbled himself greatly before the God of his ancestors. He prayed to him, and God received his entreaty, heard his plea, and restored him again to Jerusalem and to his kingdom. Then Manasseh knew that the Lord indeed was God" (2 Chronicles 33.12, 13).

Manasseh's story is told in 2 Kings 21.1–18 and 2 Chronicles 32.33—33.20. He is also mentioned in Jeremiah 15.4.

left. 3 For in the eighth year of his reign, while he was still a boy, he began to seek **34.3**
the God of his ancestor David, and in the twelfth year he began to purge Judah and 2 Chron 33.22
Jerusalem of the high places, the sacred poles,[r] and the carved and the cast images.
4 In his presence they pulled down the altars of the Baals; he demolished the incense **34.4**
altars that stood above them. He broke down the sacred poles[r] and the carved and Ex 32.20 2 Kgs 23.4,5
the cast images; he made dust of them and scattered it over the graves of those who
had sacrificed to them. 5 He also burned the bones of the priests on their altars, and **34.5**
purged Judah and Jerusalem. 6 In the towns of Manasseh, Ephraim, and Simeon, 2 Kgs 23.20
and as far as Naphtali, in their ruins[s] all around, 7 he broke down the altars, beat the **34.6** 2 Kgs 23.15,19
sacred poles[r] and the images into powder, and demolished all the incense altars **34.7**
throughout all the land of Israel. Then he returned to Jerusalem. Chron 31.1

God's law is discovered in the temple

8 In the eighteenth year of his reign, when he had purged the land and the **34.8**
house, he sent Shaphan son of Azaliah, Maaseiah the governor of the city, and Joah 2 Kgs 22.3-20 2 Chron 18.25
son of Joahaz, the recorder, to repair the house of the LORD his God. 9 They came **34.9**
to the high priest Hilkiah and delivered the money that had been brought into the 2 Chron 30.10, 18; 35.8
house of God, which the Levites, the keepers of the threshold, had collected from
Manasseh and Ephraim and from all the remnant of Israel and from all Judah and
Benjamin and from the inhabitants of Jerusalem. 10 They delivered it to the workers
who had the oversight of the house of the LORD, and the workers who were working
in the house of the LORD gave it for repairing and restoring the house. 11 They gave
it to the carpenters and the builders to buy quarried stone, and timber for binders,
and beams for the buildings that the kings of Judah had let go to ruin. 12 The people **34.12**
did the work faithfully. Over them were appointed the Levites Jahath and Obadiah, 1 Chron 25.1
of the sons of Merari, along with Zechariah and Meshullam, of the sons of the
Kohathites, to have oversight. Other Levites, all skillful with instruments of music,
13 were over the burden bearers and directed all who did work in every kind of **34.13**
service; and some of the Levites were scribes, and officials, and gatekeepers. 2 Chron 8.10 Neh 4.10

14 While they were bringing out the money that had been brought into the **34.14**
house of the LORD, the priest Hilkiah found the book of the law of the LORD given 2 Chron 34.9
through Moses. 15 Hilkiah said to the secretary Shaphan, "I have found the book of
the law in the house of the LORD"; and Hilkiah gave the book to Shaphan. 16 Shaphan brought the book to the king, and further reported to the king, "All that was
committed to your servants they are doing. 17 They have emptied out the money that
was found in the house of the LORD and have delivered it into the hand of the overseers and the workers." 18 The secretary Shaphan informed the king, "The priest
Hilkiah has given me a book." Shaphan then read it aloud to the king.

19 When the king heard the words of the law he tore his clothes. 20 Then the **34.19**
king commanded Hilkiah, Ahikam son of Shaphan, Abdon son of Micah, the sec- Josh 7.6
retary Shaphan, and the king's servant Asaiah: 21 "Go, inquire of the LORD for me **34.21**
and for those who are left in Israel and in Judah, concerning the words of the book 2 Chron 29.8
that has been found; for the wrath of the LORD that is poured out on us is great,
because our ancestors did not keep the word of the LORD, to act in accordance with
all that is written in this book."

22 So Hilkiah and those whom the king had sent went to the prophet Huldah,

[r] Heb *Asherim* [s] Meaning of Heb uncertain

34.3 In Josiah's day, boys were considered men at age 12. By 16, Josiah understood the responsibility of his office. Even at this young age, he showed greater wisdom than many of the older kings who came before him, because he had decided to seek the Lord God and his wisdom. If God has given you wisdom and spiritual insight, use it in his service regardless of your age.

34.15, 16 The laws of God that Hilkiah found were probably the book of Deuteronomy, which had been lost during the reigns of the evil kings. Now that it was found, Josiah realized that drastic changes had to be made in order to bring the nation back in line with God's commands. This account is also recorded in 2 Kings 22.8–13.

34.19 It is human nature to treat sin lightly—to make excuses, blame somebody else, or minimize the harm done. Not so with Josiah. He was so appalled at the people's neglect of the law that he tore his clothing to express his grief. True understanding of our sins should lead to "godly grief," which "produces a repentance that leads to salvation" (2 Corinthians 7.10). Are you always excusing your sin, blaming others, and pretending that it's not so bad? God does not take sin lightly, and he wants us to respond as Josiah did.

the wife of Shallum son of Tokhath son of Hasrah, keeper of the wardrobe (who
lived in Jerusalem in the Second Quarter) and spoke to her to that effect. 23 She
declared to them, "Thus says the LORD, the God of Israel: Tell the man who sent
34.24 Deut 28.15-68 you to me, 24 Thus says the LORD: I will indeed bring disaster upon this place and
2 Chron 36.14-20 upon its inhabitants, all the curses that are written in the book that was read before
the king of Judah. 25 Because they have forsaken me and have made offerings to
34.25 2 Chron 33.3 other gods, so that they have provoked me to anger with all the works of their
hands, my wrath will be poured out on this place and will not be quenched. 26 But
as to the king of Judah, who sent you to inquire of the LORD, thus shall you say to
him: Thus says the LORD, the God of Israel: Regarding the words that you have
34.27 heard, 27 because your heart was penitent and you humbled yourself before God
2 Chron 12.7 32.26 when you heard his words against this place and its inhabitants, and you have humbled yourself before me, and have torn your clothes and wept before me, I also have
heard you, says the LORD. 28 I will gather you to your ancestors and you shall be
gathered to your grave in peace; your eyes shall not see all the disaster that I will
bring on this place and its inhabitants." They took the message back to the king.
34.29 29 Then the king sent word and gathered together all the elders of Judah and
2 Kgs 23.1-3 Jerusalem. 30 The king went up to the house of the LORD, with all the people of
34.30 Neh 8.1-3 Judah, the inhabitants of Jerusalem, the priests and the Levites, all the people both
great and small; he read in their hearing all the words of the book of the covenant
34.31 that had been found in the house of the LORD. 31 The king stood in his place and
2 Chron 23.16 29.10 made a covenant before the LORD, to follow the LORD, keeping his commandments, his decrees, and his statutes, with all his heart and all his soul, to perform
the words of the covenant that were written in this book. 32 Then he made all who
were present in Jerusalem and in Benjamin pledge themselves to it. And the inhabitants of Jerusalem acted according to the covenant of God, the God of their ances-
34.33 tors. 33 Josiah took away all the abominations from all the territory that belonged to
2 Chron 34.3-7 the people of Israel, and made all who were in Israel worship the LORD their God.
All his days they did not turn away from following the LORD the God of their
ancestors.

Josiah proclaims a celebration of the passover

35.1 Ex 12.6 **35** Josiah kept a passover to the LORD in Jerusalem; they slaughtered the pass-
Num 9.3 over lamb on the fourteenth day of the first month. 2 He appointed the priests
2 Kgs 23.21 to their offices and encouraged them in the service of the house of the LORD. 3 He
35.2 2 Chron 29.11 said to the Levites who taught all Israel and who were holy to the LORD, "Put the
35.3 holy ark in the house that Solomon son of David, king of Israel, built; you need no
1 Chron 23.26 2 Chron 17.8,9 longer carry it on your shoulders. Now serve the LORD your God and his people
Neh 8.7 Israel. 4 Make preparations by your ancestral houses by your divisions, following
35.4 the written directions of King David of Israel and the written directions of his son
1 Chron 9.10-13 2 Chron 8.14 Solomon. 5 Take position in the holy place according to the groupings of the ancestral houses of your kindred the people, and let there be Levites for each division of
35.6 an ancestral house.[t] 6 Slaughter the passover lamb, sanctify yourselves, and on
2 Chron 29.5 35.1 behalf of your kindred make preparations, acting according to the word of the LORD
by Moses."
7 Then Josiah contributed to the people, as passover offerings for all that were
35.8 present, lambs and kids from the flock to the number of thirty thousand, and three
2 Chron 31.13 thousand bulls; these were from the king's possessions. 8 His officials contributed

[t] Meaning of Heb uncertain

34.31 When Josiah read the scroll that Hilkiah discovered (34.14), he responded with repentance and humility and promised to follow God's commandments. The Bible is God's Word to us, "living and active" (Hebrews 4.12), but we cannot know what God wants us to do if we do not read it. And even reading God's Word is not enough; we must be willing to do what it says. There is not much difference between the scroll hidden in the temple and the Bible hidden on the bookshelf. An unread Bible is as useless as a lost one.

35.3 In Moses' day, one of the duties of the Levites was to carry the ark of the covenant whenever Israel traveled. This was no longer necessary, because the ark was now permanently housed in the temple. Josiah was simply making the Levites aware of the duties God had assigned to them through David when the temple was first being planned (1 Chronicles 24).

willingly to the people, to the priests, and to the Levites. Hilkiah, Zechariah, and
Jehiel, the chief officers of the house of God, gave to the priests for the passover
offerings two thousand six hundred lambs and kids and three hundred bulls. 9 Cona- **35.9**
niah also, and his brothers Shemaiah and Nethanel, and Hashabiah and Jeiel and 2 Chron 31.12
Jozabad, the chiefs of the Levites, gave to the Levites for the passover offerings
five thousand lambs and kids and five hundred bulls.

10 When the service had been prepared for, the priests stood in their place, and **35.10**
the Levites in their divisions according to the king's command. 11 They slaughtered 2 Chron 35.5
the passover lamb, and the priests dashed the blood that they received[u] from them, **35.11** 2 Chron 29.22
while the Levites did the skinning. 12 They set aside the burnt offerings so that they 35.1,6
might distribute them according to the groupings of the ancestral houses of the
people, to offer to the LORD, as it is written in the book of Moses. And they did
the same with the bulls. 13 They roasted the passover lamb with fire according to the **35.13**
ordinance; and they boiled the holy offerings in pots, in caldrons, and in pans, and Ex 12.8,9 Lev 6.25
carried them quickly to all the people. 14 Afterward they made preparations for
themselves and for the priests, because the priests the descendants of Aaron were
occupied in offering the burnt offerings and the fat parts until night; so the Levites
made preparations for themselves and for the priests, the descendants of Aaron.
15 The singers, the descendants of Asaph, were in their place according to the com- **35.15**
mand of David, and Asaph, and Heman, and the king's seer Jeduthun. The gate- 1 Chron 25.1 26.12-19
keepers were at each gate; they did not need to interrupt their service, for their
kindred the Levites made preparations for them.

16 So all the service of the LORD was prepared that day, to keep the passover
and to offer burnt offerings on the altar of the LORD, according to the command of
King Josiah. 17 The people of Israel who were present kept the passover at that **35.17**
time, and the festival of unleavened bread seven days. 18 No passover like it had 2 Chron 30.21 **35.18**
been kept in Israel since the days of the prophet Samuel; none of the kings of Israel 2 Kgs 23.21,22
had kept such a passover as was kept by Josiah, by the priests and the Levites, by 2 Chron 30.5
all Judah and Israel who were present, and by the inhabitants of Jerusalem. 19 In the
eighteenth year of the reign of Josiah this passover was kept.

Josiah dies in battle

20 After all this, when Josiah had set the temple in order, King Neco of Egypt **35.20**
went up to fight at Carchemish on the Euphrates, and Josiah went out against him. 2 Kgs 23.29,30 Isa 10.9
21 But Neco[v] sent envoys to him, saying, "What have I to do with you, king of Jer 46.2
Judah? I am not coming against you today, but against the house with which I am
at war; and God has commanded me to hurry. Cease opposing God, who is with
me, so that he will not destroy you." 22 But Josiah would not turn away from him, **35.22**
but disguised himself in order to fight with him. He did not listen to the words of Judg 5.19 2 Chron 18.29
Neco from the mouth of God, but joined battle in the plain of Megiddo. 23 The 35.21
archers shot King Josiah; and the king said to his servants, "Take me away, for I am
badly wounded." 24 So his servants took him out of the chariot and carried him in

[u] Heb lacks *that they received* [v] Heb *he*

35.15 The temple gatekeepers, who were all Levites, guarded the four main entrances to the temple and opened the gates each morning. They also did other day-to-day chores such as cleaning and preparing the offerings for sacrifice and accounting for the gifts given to the temple. (For more on gatekeepers, see 1 Chronicles 26.1ff.)

35.17 The festival of unleavened bread was a seven-day celebration beginning the day after passover. Like passover, it commemorated the exodus from Egypt. For seven days the people ate bread without yeast just as their ancestors did while leaving Egypt because it could be made quickly in preparation for their swift departure (Exodus 12.14–20). This festival reminded the people that they had left slavery behind and had come to the land God promised them.

35.20 This event occurred in 609 B.C. Nineveh, the Assyrian capital, had been destroyed three years earlier by the Babylonians. The defeated Assyrians regrouped at Haran and Carchemish, but Babylon sent its army to destroy them once and for all. Pharaoh Neco, who wanted to make Egypt a world power, was worried about Babylon's growing strength, so he marched his army north through Judah to help the Assyrians at Carchemish. But King Josiah of Judah tried to prevent Necho from passing through his land on his way to Carchemish. Josiah was killed, and Judah became subject to Egypt. (Second Kings 23.25–30 helps explain the tragedy. Even though Josiah followed the Lord, God did not turn from his judgment on Judah because of Manasseh's sin and Israel's superficial repentance.) Neco went on to Carchemish and held off the Babylonians for four years, but in 605 he was soundly defeated, and Babylon moved into the spotlight as the dominant world power.

his second chariot[w] and brought him to Jerusalem. There he died, and was buried
35.25 Jer 22.10-13 Lam 4.20 Zech 12.11 in the tombs of his ancestors. All Judah and Jerusalem mourned for Josiah. 25 Jeremiah also uttered a lament for Josiah, and all the singing men and singing women
have spoken of Josiah in their laments to this day. They made these a custom in
Israel; they are recorded in the Laments. 26 Now the rest of the acts of Josiah and his
faithful deeds in accordance with what is written in the law of the LORD, 27 and his
acts, first and last, are written in the Book of the Kings of Israel and Judah.

3. Judah is exiled to Babylon

Jehoahaz rules Judah

36.1 Jer 22.11 **36** The people of the land took Jehoahaz son of Josiah and made him king to
36.2 2 Kgs 23.30-34 succeed his father in Jerusalem. 2 Jehoahaz was twenty-three years old when
he began to reign; he reigned three months in Jerusalem. 3 Then the king of Egypt
deposed him in Jerusalem and laid on the land a tribute of one hundred talents of
36.4 Jer 22.10,12 silver and one talent of gold. 4 The king of Egypt made his brother Eliakim king
over Judah and Jerusalem, and changed his name to Jehoiakim; but Neco took his
brother Jehoahaz and carried him to Egypt.

Jehoiakim rules Judah

36.5 Jer 22.13-19 5 Jehoiakim was twenty-five years old when he began to reign; he reigned
eleven years in Jerusalem. He did what was evil in the sight of the LORD his God.
36.6 2 Kgs 24.1 2 Chron 33.11 Jer 22.19,20 6 Against him King Nebuchadnezzar of Babylon came up, and bound him with fetters to take him to Babylon. 7 Nebuchadnezzar also carried some of the vessels of
the house of the LORD to Babylon and put them in his palace in Babylon. 8 Now the
36.7 2 Kgs 24.13 rest of the acts of Jehoiakim, and the abominations that he did, and what was found
36.8 2 Kgs 24.5 against him, are written in the Book of the Kings of Israel and Judah; and his son
Jehoiachin succeeded him.

Jehoiachin rules Judah

36.9 2 Kgs 24.8-17 9 Jehoiachin was eight years old when he began to reign; he reigned three
months and ten days in Jerusalem. He did what was evil in the sight of the LORD.
36.10 2 Sam 11.1 Jer 37.1 10 In the spring of the year King Nebuchadnezzar sent and brought him to Babylon,
along with the precious vessels of the house of the LORD, and made his brother
Zedekiah king over Judah and Jerusalem.

[w] *Or the chariot of his deputy*

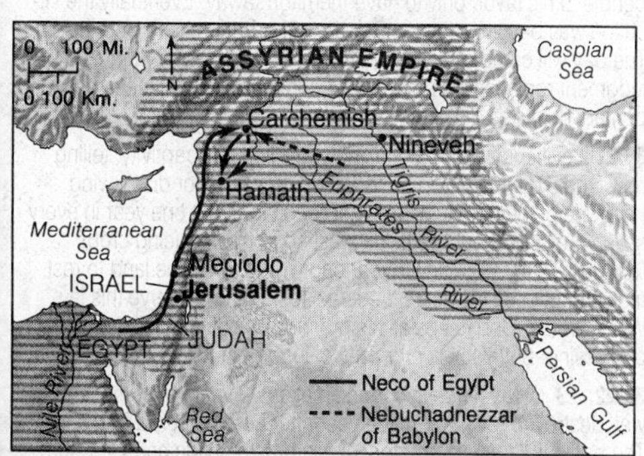

THE BATTLE AT CARCHEMISH A world war was brewing in 609 B.C. when Pharaoh Neco (Necho) of Egypt set out for the city of Carchemish to join the Assyrians in an attempt to defeat the Babylonians, who were rising to great power. Neco marched his armies through Judah, where King Josiah tried to stop him at Megiddo, but was killed. The battle began at Carchemish in 605 B.C. and the Egyptians and Assyrians were soundly defeated, chased to Hamath and defeated again. Babylon was now the new world power.

35.21–23 Josiah ignored Neco's message because of who Neco was—king of a heathen nation. The mistaken assumption that Neco could not be part of God's larger plan cost Josiah his life. While not everyone who claims to have a message from God really does, God's messages may come in unexpected ways. God had spoken to pagan kings in the past (Genesis 12.17–20; 20.3–7; see also Daniel 4.1–3). Don't let prejudice or false assumptions blind you to God's message.

35.25 Though Jeremiah recorded these for the death of Josiah, they are not the same as the book of Lamentations.

36.6 Nebuchadnezzar was the son of the founder of the new Babylonian Empire. In 605 B.C., the year he became king, Nebuchadnezzar won the battle of Carchemish, which crushed Assyria (see the note on 35.20). (For more information about Nebuchadnezzar, read his Profile in Daniel 4.)

36.9, 10 In 2 Kings 24.8, Jehoiachin is listed as 18 years old. Many Hebrew manuscripts list him as 8 years old. The age given in 2 Kings 24.17 is most likely accurate because he had wives (see 2 Kings 24.15).

Zedekiah rules Judah

11 Zedekiah was twenty-one years old when he began to reign; he reigned 36.11
eleven years in Jerusalem. 12 He did what was evil in the sight of the LORD his God. 2 Kgs 24.18-20 Jer 52.1
He did not humble himself before the prophet Jeremiah who spoke from the mouth 36.12
of the LORD. 13 He also rebelled against King Nebuchadnezzar, who had made him Jer 21.3-7
swear by God; he stiffened his neck and hardened his heart against turning to the 36.13 2 Chron 30.8
LORD, the God of Israel. 14 All the leading priests and the people also were exceed- Jer 52.3 Ezek 17.15
ingly unfaithful, following all the abominations of the nations; and they polluted
the house of the LORD that he had consecrated in Jerusalem.

The fall of Jerusalem

15 The LORD, the God of their ancestors, sent persistently to them by his mes- 36.15
sengers, because he had compassion on his people and on his dwelling place; 16 but Jer 7.13; 25.3
they kept mocking the messengers of God, despising his words, and scoffing at his 36.16 2 Chron 30.10
prophets, until the wrath of the LORD against his people became so great that there Ezra 5.12 Prov 1.24-32
was no remedy. Jer 5.12,13
17 Therefore he brought up against them the king of the Chaldeans, who killed 36.17
their youths with the sword in the house of their sanctuary, and had no compassion 2 Kgs 25.1-7
on young man or young woman, the aged or the feeble; he gave them all into his
hand. 18 All the vessels of the house of God, large and small, and the treasures of 36.18 2 Chron 36.7,10
the house of the LORD, and the treasures of the king and of his officials, all these he
brought to Babylon. 19 They burned the house of God, broke down the wall of Jeru- 36.19 2 Kgs 25.9
salem, burned all its palaces with fire, and destroyed all its precious vessels. 20 He Jer 52.13
took into exile in Babylon those who had escaped from the sword, and they became 36.20 2 Kgs 25.11
servants to him and to his sons until the establishment of the kingdom of Persia, Jer 27.7
21 to fulfill the word of the LORD by the mouth of Jeremiah, until the land had made 36.21 Lev 25.4; 26.33
up for its sabbaths. All the days that it lay desolate it kept sabbath, to fulfill seventy Jer 29.10
years.

22 In the first year of King Cyrus of Persia, in fulfillment of the word of the
LORD spoken by Jeremiah, the LORD stirred up the spirit of King Cyrus of Persia so

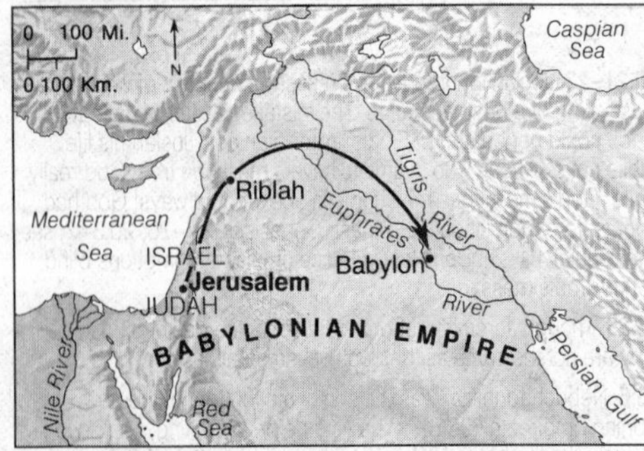

EXILE TO BABYLON Despite Judah's few good kings and timely reforms, the people never truly changed. Their evil continued and finally God used the Babylonian Empire, under Nebuchadnezzar, to conquer Judah, destroy Jerusalem, and take the people captive to Babylon.

36.16 God warned Judah about its sin and continually restored the people to his favor, only to have them turn away. Eventually the situation was beyond remedy. Beware of harboring sin in your heart. The day will come when remedy is no longer possible and God's judgment replaces his mercy. Sin often repeated, but never repented of, invites disaster.

36.21 Leviticus 26.27–45 strikingly predicts the captivity, telling how God's people would be torn from their land for disobeying him. One of the laws they had ignored stated that one year in every seven the land should lie fallow, resting from producing crops (Exodus 23.10, 11). The 70-year captivity allowed the land to rest, making up for all the years the Israelites did not observe this law. We know that God keeps all his promises – not only his promises of blessing, but also his promises of judgment.

36.22, 23 Cyrus made this proclamation 48 years after the temple was destroyed (36.18, 19), the year after he conquered Babylon. The book of Ezra tells the story of this proclamation and the return of the exiles to Judah.

36.22, 23 Second Chronicles focuses on the rise and fall of the worship of God as symbolized by the Jerusalem temple. David planned the temple; Solomon built it and then put on the greatest dedication service the world had ever seen. Worship in the temple was superbly organized.

But several evil kings defiled the temple and degraded worship so that the people revered idols more highly than God. Finally, King Nebuchadnezzar of Babylon destroyed the temple (36.19).

36.22
Ezra 1.1-3
Isa 44.28
Jer 25.12
29.10

that he sent a herald throughout all his kingdom and also declared in a written edict:
23 "Thus says King Cyrus of Persia: The LORD, the God of heaven, has given me all
the kingdoms of the earth, and he has charged me to build him a house at Jerusalem, which is in Judah. Whoever is among you of all his people, may the LORD his
God be with him! Let him go up."

The kings were gone, the temple destroyed, the people removed. The nation was stripped to its very foundation. But fortunately there was a greater foundation – God himself. When everything in life seems stripped away from us, we too still have God – his word, his presence, and his promises.

Jerusalem destroyed; exiles to Babylon 586 B.C.	Babylon overthrown by Cyrus 539	Cyrus's decree to return 538	Exiles return to Jerusalem 537	Temple construction begins 536	Temple work halted 530

VITAL STATISTICS

PURPOSE:
To show God's faithfulness and the way he kept his promise to restore his people to their land

AUTHOR:
Not stated, but probably Ezra

DATE WRITTEN:
Around 450 B.C., recording events from about 538–450 B.C. (omitting 516–458 B.C.); possibly begun earlier in Babylon and finished in Jerusalem

SETTING:
Ezra follows 2 Chronicles as a history of the Jewish people, recording their return to the land after the captivity.

KEY VERSES:
"It was eaten by the people of Israel who had returned from exile, and also by all who had joined them and separated themselves from the pollutions of the nations of the land to worship the Lord, the God of Israel. With joy they celebrated the festival of unleavened bread seven days; for the Lord had made them joyful, and had turned the heart of the king of Assyria to them, so that he aided them in the work on the house of God, the God of Israel" (6.21, 22).

KEY PEOPLE:
Cyrus, Zerubbabel, Haggai, Zechariah, Darius, Artaxerxes I, Ezra

KEY PLACES:
Babylon, Jerusalem

SPECIAL FEATURES:
Ezra and Nehemiah were one book in the Hebrew Bible and, with Esther, comprise the post-captivity historical books. The post-captivity prophetic books are Haggai, Zechariah, and Malachi. Haggai and Zechariah should be studied with Ezra since they prophesied during the period of the reconstruction.

NAME the truly great men and women of your lifetime. Celebrities including politicians, war heroes, sports figures, and maybe your parents and special friends come to mind. You remember them because of certain acts or character qualities. Now, name some biblical heroes—figures etched into your life through countless sermons and Sunday school lessons. This list undoubtedly includes many who served God faithfully and courageously. Does your list include Ezra? Far from being well known, this unheralded man of God deserves to be mentioned in any discussion of greatness.

Ezra was a priest, a scribe, and a great leader. His name means "help," and his whole life was dedicated to serving God and God's people. Tradition says Ezra wrote most of 1 and 2 Chronicles, Ezra, Nehemiah, and Psalm 119, and that he led the council of 120 men who formed the Old Testament canon. He centers the narrative of the book of Ezra around God and his promise that the Jews would return to their land, as promised by Jeremiah (see the note on 1.1). This message formed the core of Ezra's life. The last half of the book gives a very personal glimpse of Ezra. His knowledge of Scripture and his God-given wisdom were so obvious to the king that he appointed Ezra to lead the second emigration to Jerusalem, to teach the people God's Word, and to administer national life (7.14–26).

Ezra not only knew God's Word, he believed and obeyed it. Upon learning of the Israelites' sins of intermarriage and idolatry, Ezra fell in humility before God and prayed for the nation (9.1–15). Their disobedience touched him deeply (10.1). His response helped lead the people back to God.

Second Chronicles ends with Cyrus, king of Persia, asking for volunteers to return to Jerusalem to build a house for God. Ezra continues this account (1.1–3 is almost identical to 2 Chronicles 36.22, 23) as two caravans of God's people return to Jerusalem. Zerubbabel, the leader of the first trip, is joined by over 42,360 pilgrims who journey homeward (chapter 2). After arriving, they begin to build the altar and the temple foundations (chapter 3). But opposition arises from the local inhabitants, and a campaign of accusations and rumors temporarily halts the project (chapter 4). During this time, the prophets Haggai and Zechariah encourage the people (chapter 5). Finally, Darius decrees that the work should proceed unhindered (chapter 6).

After a 58-year gap, Ezra leads a group of Jews from Persia. Armed with decrees and authority from Artaxerxes I, Ezra's task is to administer the affairs of the land (chapters 7, 8). Upon arriving, Ezra learns of intermarriage between God's people and their pagan neighbors. He weeps and prays for the nation (chapter 9). Ezra's example of humble confession leads to national revival (chapter 10). Ezra, a man of God and a true hero, was a model for Israel, and he is a fitting model for us.

Read Ezra, the book, and remember Ezra, the man—a humble, obedient helper. Commit yourself to serving God as he did, with your whole life.

Darius I becomes king of Persia 522	Temple work resumed/ messages of Haggai, Zechariah 520	Temple completed 516	Ezra comes to Jerusalem 458	Nehemiah comes to Jerusalem 445

THE BLUEPRINT

A. THE RETURN LED BY ZERUBBABEL (1.1—6.22) 1. The first group of exiles returns to the land 2. The people rebuild the temple	Finally given the chance to return to their homeland, the people started to rebuild the temple, only to be stopped by opposition from their enemies. God's work in the world is not without opposition. We must not get discouraged and quit, as the returning people did at first, but continue on boldly in the face of difficulties, as they did later with the encouragement from the prophets.
B. THE RETURN LED BY EZRA (7.1—10.44) 1. The second group of exiles returns to the land 2. Ezra opposes intermarriage	Ezra returned to Jerusalem almost 80 years after Zerubbabel, only to discover that the people had married heathen spouses. This polluted the religious purity of the people and endangered the future of the nation. Believers today must be careful not to threaten their walk with God by taking on the practices of unbelievers.

MEGATHEMES

THEME	EXPLANATION	IMPORTANCE
The Jews return	By returning to the land of Israel from Babylon, the Jews showed their faith in God's promise to restore them as a people. They returned not only to their homeland, but also to the place where their forefathers had promised to follow God.	God shows his mercy to every generation. He compassionately restores his people. No matter how difficult our present "captivity," we are never far from his love and mercy. He restores us when we return to him.
Rededication	In 536 B.C., Zerubbabel led the people in rebuilding the altar and laying the temple foundation. They reinstated daily sacrifices and annual festivals, and rededicated themselves to a new spiritual worship of God.	In rededicating the altar, the people were recommitting themselves to God and his service. To grow spiritually, our commitment must be reviewed and renewed often. As we rededicate ourselves to God, our lives become altars to him.
Opposition	Opposition came soon after the altar was built and the temple foundation laid. Enemies of the Jews used deceit to hinder the building for over six years. Finally, there was a decree to stop the building altogether. This opposition severely tested their wavering faith.	There will always be adversaries who oppose God's work. The life of faith is never easy. But God can overrule all opposition to his service. When we face opposition, we must not falter or withdraw, but keep active and patient.
God's Word	When the people returned to the land, they were also returning to the influence of God's Word. The prophets Haggai and Zechariah helped encourage them while Ezra's preaching of Scripture built them up. God's Word gave them what they needed to do God's work.	We also need the encouragement and direction of God's Word. We must make it the basis for our faith and actions to finish God's work and fulfill our obligations. We must never waver in our commitment to hear and obey his Word.
Faith and action	The urging of Israel's leaders motivated the people to complete the temple. Over the years, they had intermarried with idol-worshipers and adopted their pagan practices. Their faith, tested and revived, also led them to remove these sins from their lives.	Faith led them to complete the temple and to remove sin from their society. As we trust God with our hearts and minds, we must also act by completing our daily responsibilities. It is not enough to say we believe; we must make the changes God requires.

A. THE RETURN LED BY ZERUBBABEL (1.1–6.22)

After 70 years in exile, the captives from Judah were allowed to return to their homeland. Nearly 50,000 people made this journey. Upon arrival they began to rebuild the temple, but became discouraged by opposition. After encouragement from Haggai and Zechariah, they returned to the task and completed the temple. The message of the prophets still speaks to us today, encouraging us to continue building up God's church.

1. The first group of exiles returns to the land

King Cyrus releases captive Jews

1 In the first year of King Cyrus of Persia, in order that the word of the LORD by
the mouth of Jeremiah might be accomplished, the LORD stirred up the spirit of
King Cyrus of Persia so that he sent a herald throughout all his kingdom, and also
in a written edict declared:
2 "Thus says King Cyrus of Persia: The LORD, the God of heaven, has given me
all the kingdoms of the earth, and he has charged me to build him a house at Jerusalem in Judah. 3 Any of those among you who are of his people—may their God be
with them!—are now permitted to go up to Jerusalem in Judah, and rebuild the
house of the LORD, the God of Israel—he is the God who is in Jerusalem; 4 and let
all survivors, in whatever place they reside, be assisted by the people of their place
with silver and gold, with goods and with animals, besides freewill offerings for
the house of God in Jerusalem."
5 The heads of the families of Judah and Benjamin, and the priests and the
Levites—everyone whose spirit God had stirred—got ready to go up and rebuild
the house of the LORD in Jerusalem. 6 All their neighbors aided them with silver

1.1 2 Chron 36.22, 23 Ezra 5.13-17 6.3-5 Jer 25.12-14 29.10
1.2 Ezra 3.1,2 Isa 44.28 45.1-13
1.5 2 Chron 36.22

1.1 The book of Ezra opens in 538 B.C., 48 years after Nebuchadnezzar destroyed Jerusalem, defeated the southern kingdom of Judah, and carried the Jews away to Babylon as captives (2 Kings 25; 2 Chronicles 36). Nebuchadnezzar died in 562, and because his successor was not strong, Babylon was overthrown by Persia in 539, just prior to the events recorded in this book. Both the Babylonians and the Persians had a relaxed policy toward their captives, allowing them to own land and homes and to take ordinary jobs. Many Jews such as Daniel, Mordecai, and Esther rose to prominent positions within the nation. King Cyrus of Persia went a step further: he allowed many groups of exiles, including the Jews, to return to their homelands. By doing this, he hoped to win their loyalty and thus provide buffer zones around the borders of his empire. For the Jews this was a day of hope, a new beginning.

1.1 Cyrus, king of Persia (559–530 B.C.), had already begun his rise to power in the Near East by unifying the Medes and Persians into a strong empire. As he conquered cities, he treated the inhabitants with mercy. Although not a servant of Yahweh, Cyrus was used by God to return the Jews to their homeland. Cyrus may have been shown the prophecy of Isaiah 44.28–45.6, written over a century earlier, which predicted that Cyrus himself would help the Jews return to Jerusalem. Daniel, a prominent government official (Daniel 5.29; 6.28), would have been familiar with the prophecy. The book of Daniel has more to say about Cyrus.

1.1 Jeremiah prophesied that the Jews would remain in captivity for 70 years (Jeremiah 25.11; 29.10). The 70-year period has been calculated two different ways: (1) from the first captivity in 605 B.C. (2 Kings 24.1) until the altar was rebuilt by the returned exiles in 536 (Ezra 3.1–6), or (2) from the destruction of the temple in 586 until the exiles finished rebuilding it in 516. Many scholars prefer the second approach because the temple was the focus and heartbeat of the nation. Without it, the Jews did not consider themselves reestablished as a nation.

1.2 Cyrus was not a Jew, but God worked through him to return the exiled Jews to their homeland. Cyrus gave the decree allowing their return, and he gave them protection, money, and the temple vessels taken by Nebuchadnezzar. When you face difficult situations and feel surrounded, outnumbered, overpowered, or outclassed, remember that God's power is not limited to your resources. He is able to use anyone to carry out his plans.

1.3–6 This decree permitted the Jews to work together to accomplish the huge task of rebuilding the temple. Some did the actual building, while others operated the supply lines. Significant ventures require teamwork, with some people serving in the forefront and others providing support. Each function is vital to accomplishing the task. When you're asked to serve, do so faithfully as a team member, no matter who gets the credit.

1.5 Cyrus was king over the entire region that had once been Assyria and Babylon. Assyria had deported the Israelites from the northern kingdom (Israel) in 722 B.C. Babylon, the next world power, had taken Israelites captive from the southern kingdom (Judah) in 586 B.C. Therefore, when the Medo-Persian Empire came to power, King Cyrus's proclamation of freedom went to all the original 12 tribes, but only Judah and Benjamin responded and returned to rebuild God's temple. The ten tribes of the northern kingdom had been so fractured and dispersed by Assyria, and so much time had elapsed since their captivity, that many were unsure of their real heritage. Thus they were unwilling to share in the vision of rebuilding the temple.

1.5 God gave the leaders a great desire to return to Jerusalem and rebuild the temple. Major changes begin on the inside as God works on our attitudes, beliefs, and desires. These inner changes lead to faithful actions. After 48 years of captivity, the arrogant Jewish nation had been humbled. When the people's attitudes and desires changed, God ended their discipline and gave them another opportunity to go home and try again. Paul reminds us that "it is God who is at work in you, enabling you both to will and to work for his good pleasure" (Philippians 2.13). Doing God's will begins with your desires. Are you willing to be humble, to be open to his opportunities, and to move at his direction? Ask God to give you the desire to follow him more closely.

1.7 2 Kgs 24.13; 25.13-16; 2 Chron 36.7-18; Ezra 1.9-11; 6.5
1.8 Ezra 1.11; 5.14-16
1.9 Ezra 1.7
1.11 Ezra 1.8

vessels, with gold, with goods, with animals, and with valuable gifts, besides all
that was freely offered. 7 King Cyrus himself brought out the vessels of the house
of the LORD that Nebuchadnezzar had carried away from Jerusalem and placed in
the house of his gods. 8 King Cyrus of Persia had them released into the charge of
Mithredath the treasurer, who counted them out to Sheshbazzar the prince of Judah. 9 And this was the inventory: gold basins, thirty; silver basins, one thousand;
knives,[a] twenty-nine; 10 gold bowls, thirty; other silver bowls, four hundred ten;
other vessels, one thousand; 11 the total of the gold and silver vessels was five thousand four hundred. All these Sheshbazzar brought up, when the exiles were
brought up from Babylonia to Jerusalem.

[a] Vg: Meaning of Heb uncertain

PROPHECIES FULFILLED BY THE RETURN OF ISRAEL FROM EXILE

Reference	*Prophecy*	*Approximate Date*	*Fulfillment Date*	*Significance*
Isaiah 44.28	Cyrus would be used by God to guarantee the return of a remnant. Jerusalem would be rebuilt and the temple restored.	688 B.C.	539 B.C.	As God named Cyrus even before he was born, God knows what will happen—he is in control.
Jeremiah 25.12	Babylon would be punished for destroying Jerusalem and exiling God's people.	605 B.C.	539 B.C.	Babylon was conquered by Cyrus the Great. God may seem to allow evil to go unpunished, but consequences for wrongdoing are inevitable. God will punish evil.
Jeremiah 29.10	The people would spend 70 years in Babylon, then God would bring them back to their homeland.	594 B.C.	537 B.C.	The 70 years of captivity passed (see the third note on 1.1), and God provided the opportunity for Zerubbabel to lead the first group of captives home. God's plans may allow for hardship, but his desire is for our good.
Daniel 5.17–30	God had judged the Babylonian Empire. It would be given to the Medes and the Persians, forming a new world power.	539 B.C.	539 B.C.	Belshazzar was killed and Babylon was conquered the same night. God's judgment is accurate and swift. God knows the point of no return in each of our lives. Until then he allows the freedom for us to repent and seek his forgiveness.

God, through his faithful prophets, predicted that the people of Judah would be taken into captivity because of their sinfulness. But he also predicted that they would return to Jerusalem and rebuild the city, the temple, and the nation.

1.6 Many Jews chose to remain in Babylon rather than return to their homeland. The journey back to Jerusalem was difficult, dangerous, and expensive, lasting over four months. Travel conditions were poor, Jerusalem and the surrounding countryside were in ruins, and the people living in the area were hostile.

Persian records indicate that many Jews in captivity had accumulated great wealth. Returning to Jerusalem would have meant giving up everything they had and starting over. Many people couldn't bring themselves to do that; they preferred wealth and security to the sacrifice that God's work would require. Their priorities were upside-down (Mark 4.18, 19). We must not let our comfort, security, or material possessions prevent us from doing what God wants.

1.7 When King Nebuchadnezzar ransacked the temple, he took many of the valuable furnishings with him. What he did not take, he burned (2 Chronicles 36.18, 19). Most of the captured items were made of solid gold (1 Kings 7.48–50), and Cyrus kindly returned them to the Jews for the temple they would soon rebuild.

1.8 Either Sheshbazzar was the Babylonian name for Zerubbabel, one of the Jewish leaders during the first return (2.2; 3.8; 4.3), or he was a government official with responsibility for the returning party. The reasons Sheshbazzar may be identified with Zerubbabel are as follows: (1) both were called governors (5.14; Haggai 1.1); (2) both were called leaders of the returning exiles (1.8; 2.2); (3) both laid the temple foundation (3.8; 5.16); and (4) Jews in exile were often given Babylonian names (see Daniel 1.7 where Daniel and his companions were given new names).

1.9–11 Every item of gold and silver was a witness to God's protection and care. Although it had been many years, God delivered them. We may be discouraged by events in life, but we must never give up our hope in God's promises to us. The turning point may be just ahead.

The exiles who returned with Zerubbabel

2 Now these were the people of the province who came from those captive exiles 2.1
whom King Nebuchadnezzar of Babylon had carried captive to Babylonia; 2 Kgs 24.14-16; 25.11
they returned to Jerusalem and Judah, all to their own towns. 2 They came with 2 Chron 36.20
Zerubbabel, Jeshua, Nehemiah, Seraiah, Reelaiah, Mordecai, Bilshan, Mispar, 2.2 Neh 7.7
Bigvai, Rehum, and Baanah.
The number of the Israelite people: 3 the descendants of Parosh, two thousand 2.3
one hundred seventy-two. 4 Of Shephatiah, three hundred seventy-two. 5 Of Arah, 1 Chron 9.1-44; Neh 7.8-38
seven hundred seventy-five. 6 Of Pahath-moab, namely the descendants of Jeshua
and Joab, two thousand eight hundred twelve. 7 Of Elam, one thousand two hundred fifty-four. 8 Of Zattu, nine hundred forty-five. 9 Of Zaccai, seven hundred
sixty. 10 Of Bani, six hundred forty-two. 11 Of Bebai, six hundred twenty-three.
12 Of Azgad, one thousand two hundred twenty-two. 13 Of Adonikam, six hundred
sixty-six. 14 Of Bigvai, two thousand fifty-six. 15 Of Adin, four hundred fifty-four.
16 Of Ater, namely of Hezekiah, ninety-eight. 17 Of Bezai, three hundred twenty-
three. 18 Of Jorah, one hundred twelve. 19 Of Hashum, two hundred twenty-three.
20 Of Gibbar, ninety-five. 21 Of Bethlehem, one hundred twenty-three. 22 The people of Netophah, fifty-six. 23 Of Anathoth, one hundred twenty-eight. 24 The descendants of Azmaveth, forty-two. 25 Of Kiriatharim, Chephirah, and Beeroth,
seven hundred forty-three. 26 Of Ramah and Geba, six hundred twenty-one. 27 The
people of Michmas, one hundred twenty-two. 28 Of Bethel and Ai, two hundred
twenty-three. 29 The descendants of Nebo, fifty-two. 30 Of Magbish, one hundred
fifty-six. 31 Of the other Elam, one thousand two hundred fifty-four. 32 Of Harim,
three hundred twenty. 33 Of Lod, Hadid, and Ono, seven hundred twenty-five. 34 Of
Jericho, three hundred forty-five. 35 Of Senaah, three thousand six hundred thirty.
36 The priests: the descendants of Jedaiah, of the house of Jeshua, nine hundred 2.36
seventy-three. 37 Of Immer, one thousand fifty-two. 38 Of Pashhur, one thousand 1 Chron 9.10, 11; 24.7-18
two hundred forty-seven. 39 Of Harim, one thousand seventeen. Neh 7.39-42
40 The Levites: the descendants of Jeshua and Kadmiel, of the descendants of 2.40
Hodaviah, seventy-four. 41 The singers: the descendants of Asaph, one hundred Neh 7.43-45
twenty-eight. 42 The descendants of the gatekeepers: of Shallum, of Ater, of Talmon, of Akkub, of Hatita, and of Shobai, in all one hundred thirty-nine.
43 The temple servants: the descendants of Ziha, Hasupha, Tabbaoth, 44 Keros, 2.43
Siaha, Padon, 45 Lebanah, Hagabah, Akkub, 46 Hagab, Shamlai, Hanan, 47 Giddel, Neh 7.46-56
Gahar, Reaiah, 48 Rezin, Nekoda, Gazzam, 49 Uzza, Paseah, Besai, 50 Asnah, Meunim, Nephisim, 51 Bakbuk, Hakupha, Harhur, 52 Bazluth, Mehida, Harsha, 53 Barkos, Sisera, Temah, 54 Neziah, and Hatipha.
55 The descendants of Solomon's servants: Sotai, Hassophereth, Peruda, 2.55 Neh 7.57-59

2.2 This is a different Nehemiah from the one who rebuilt Jerusalem's walls 80 years later, and the Mordecai listed here is not the one who appears in the book of Esther.

2.2 This first list is made up of men who were leaders. The same list occurs in Nehemiah 7.7.

2.2–35 These people were from the tribes of Judah and Benjamin (1.5).

2.3–35 This list is the major group of those returning, divided by families (2.3–20) or by cities (2.21–35). Verse 36 begins listing priests, Levites, and other temple servants.

THE JOURNEY HOME The vast Medo-Persian Empire included all the area on this map and more. A group of exiles began the long trip back to their homeland. Many exiles, however, preferred the comfort and security they had in Babylon to the dangerous trip back to Jerusalem, and so they decided to stay in Babylon.

56 Jaalah, Darkon, Giddel, 57 Shephatiah, Hattil, Pochereth-hazzebaim, and Ami.
58 All the temple servants and the descendants of Solomon's servants were
three hundred ninety-two.
2.59 59 The following were those who came up from Tel-melah, Tel-harsha,
Neh 7.61,63-65 Cherub, Addan, and Immer, though they could not prove their families or their
2.60 descent, whether they belonged to Israel: 60 the descendants of Delaiah, Tobiah,
Neh 7.62 and Nekoda, six hundred fifty-two. 61 Also, of the descendants of the priests: the
2.61 2 Sam 17.27 descendants of Habaiah, Hakkoz, and Barzillai (who had married one of the daugh-
2.62 ters of Barzillai the Gileadite, and was called by their name). 62 These looked for
Ex 28.30 Lev 21.21-23 their entries in the genealogical records, but they were not found there, and so they
Num 3.10 16.39,40 were excluded from the priesthood as unclean; 63 the governor told them that they
Ezra 2.59 were not to partake of the most holy food, until there should be a priest to consult
Urim and Thummim.
2.64 64 The whole assembly together was forty-two thousand three hundred sixty,
Neh 7.66,67 65 besides their male and female servants, of whom there were seven thousand three
hundred thirty-seven; and they had two hundred male and female singers. 66 They
had seven hundred thirty-six horses, two hundred forty-five mules, 67 four hundred
thirty-five camels, and six thousand seven hundred twenty donkeys.
2.68 Neh 7.70-72 68 As soon as they came to the house of the LORD in Jerusalem, some of the

THE RETURN FROM EXILE

Year	Number of People Returned	Persian King	Jewish Leader	Main Accomplishment
537 B.C.	50,000	Cyrus	Zerubbabel	They rebuilt the temple, but only after a 20-year struggle. The work was halted for several years, but was finally completed.
458 B.C.	2,000 men and their families	Artaxerxes	Ezra	Ezra confronted the spiritual disobedience of the people and they repented and established worship at the temple. But the wall of Jerusalem remained in ruins.
445 B.C.	Small group	Artaxerxes	Nehemiah	The city was rebuilt and a spiritual awakening followed. But the people still struggled with ongoing disobedience.

Babylon, the once-mighty nation that had destroyed Jerusalem and carried the people of Judah into captivity, had itself become a defeated nation. Persia was the new world power, and under its new foreign policy, captured peoples were allowed to return to their homelands. The people of Judah and Israel returned to their land in three successive waves.

2.59 Genealogies were very important credentials to the Hebrew people. If they could not prove they had descended from Abraham, they were not considered true Jews and were excluded from full participation in Jewish community life. In addition, some privileges were restricted to members of certain tribes. For example, only descendants of Levi (Abraham's great-grandson) could serve in the temple.

2.62, 63 The "governor" mentioned here was probably Zerubbabel. The Urim and Thummim were two objects, probably shaped like flat stones, originally carried in the garment worn by the high priest. They were used to determine God's will in important matters. (For more on the Urim and Thummim, see the note on Leviticus 8.8.)

2.68, 69 As the temple reconstruction progressed, everyone contributed according to his or her ability. Some were able to give huge gifts and did so generously. Everyone's effort and cooperation were required, and the people gave as much as they could. Often we limit our giving to ten percent of our income. The Bible, however, emphasizes that we should give from the heart *all* that we are able (2 Corinthians 8.12; 9.6). Let the amount of your gift be decided by God's call to give generously, not by the amount of your leftovers.

2.69 Darics and minas were gold and silver coins. The money given was enough to start rebuilding the temple. The people put what resources they had to their best use. They were enthusiastic and sincere, but this temple would never match the splendor of Solomon's. The money David gathered to start the building of Solomon's temple was a thousand times more (1 Chronicles 22.14). Some people wept as they remembered the glorious temple that had been destroyed (3.12).

heads of families made freewill offerings for the house of God, to erect it on its site.
69 According to their resources they gave to the building fund sixty-one thousand
darics of gold, five thousand minas of silver, and one hundred priestly robes.
70 The priests, the Levites, and some of the people lived in Jerusalem and its
vicinity;[b] and the singers, the gatekeepers, and the temple servants lived in their
towns, and all Israel in their towns.

2.70 Neh 7.73

2. The people rebuild the temple

The leaders rebuild the altar

3 When the seventh month came, and the Israelites were in the towns, the people
gathered together in Jerusalem. 2 Then Jeshua son of Jozadak, with his fellow
priests, and Zerubbabel son of Shealtiel with his kin set out to build the altar of the
God of Israel, to offer burnt offerings on it, as prescribed in the law of Moses the
man of God. 3 They set up the altar on its foundation, because they were in dread
of the neighboring peoples, and they offered burnt offerings upon it to the LORD,
morning and evening. 4 And they kept the festival of booths,[c] as prescribed, and
offered the daily burnt offerings by number according to the ordinance, as required
for each day, 5 and after that the regular burnt offerings, the offerings at the new
moon and at all the sacred festivals of the LORD, and the offerings of everyone who
made a freewill offering to the LORD. 6 From the first day of the seventh month they
began to offer burnt offerings to the LORD. But the foundation of the temple of the
LORD was not yet laid. 7 So they gave money to the masons and the carpenters, and
food, drink, and oil to the Sidonians and the Tyrians to bring cedar trees from
Lebanon to the sea, to Joppa, according to the grant that they had from King Cyrus
of Persia.

3.1 Lev 1.1-17 6.8-13 Deut 12.4-7 1 Chron 3.17-20 Neh 12.1,8 Hag 1.1 Zech 3.1 4.6-10; 6.10,11
3.3 Ex 29.38-42 Num 28.1-8
3.4 Lev 23.34-36 Num 8.14-17
3.5 Ex 29.42 Lev 1.3 Num 28.11-14 29.39 Deut 12.6,17
3.7 1 Kgs 5.9-11 2 Chron 2.10-16

The people begin to rebuild the temple

8 In the second year after their arrival at the house of God at Jerusalem, in the
second month, Zerubbabel son of Shealtiel and Jeshua son of Jozadak made a beginning, together with the rest of their people, the priests and the Levites and all
who had come to Jerusalem from the captivity. They appointed the Levites, from
twenty years old and upward, to have the oversight of the work on the house of the

3.8 Num 4.3 1 Chron 23.24-32

[b] 1 Esdras 5.46: Heb lacks *lived in Jerusalem and its vicinity* [c] Or *tabernacles*; Heb *succoth*

3.2, 3 The Jews set up the altar as one of their first official acts. It symbolized God's presence and protection. It also demonstrated their purpose as a nation and their commitment to serve God alone. Zerubbabel sacrificed burnt offerings as the laws of Moses instructed (Leviticus 1–7). The sacrifices were essential because they demonstrated that the people were seeking God's guidance, rededicating themselves to living as he commanded, and daily asking him to forgive their sins.

3.3 The Jews were afraid they were going to be attacked by the surrounding people—a mixed group whose ancestors had been conquered by the Assyrians. Foreigners had been forced to resettle in the northern kingdom of Israel after Israel was defeated and her people taken captive in 722 B.C. (4.1, 2). This resettlement procedure was a common tactic of the Assyrians to prevent strong nationalistic uprisings by conquered peoples. Some of the resettled people in Israel had migrated south near Jerusalem, and they thought the returning exiles threatened their claim on the land.

3.4 The festival of booths lasted seven days. During this time the people lived in temporary dwellings (tents, booths, lean-tos) as their ancestors had done years before as they journeyed through the wilderness on their way to the promised land. The feast reminded the people of God's past protection and guidance in the wilderness and of his continued love for them. The festival of booths is described in detail in Leviticus 23.33–36.

3.5 Almost immediately after arriving in the new land, the returning exiles built an altar. The people began worshiping God through sacrifices even before the temple foundations were laid. After many years in captivity, they had learned their lesson—they knew that God does not offer special protection to people who ignore him. They had been carried off by the Babylonians when they were relatively strong; now they were few, weak, and surrounded by enemies. If ever they needed to rely on God's power, it was now. They realized the importance of obeying God from the heart, and not merely out of habit. If we want God's help when we undertake large tasks, we must make staying close to him our top priority.

3.7 When Solomon built the first temple (2 Chronicles 2), he also exchanged food and olive oil—plentiful resources in Israel—for wood, a resource Israel lacked. The wood came from Sidon and Tyre that time too.

3.8 Why was the temple begun first, even before the city wall? The temple was used for spiritual purposes; the wall, for military and political purposes. God had always been the nation's protector, and the Jews knew that the strongest stone wall would not protect them if God was not with them. They knew that putting their spiritual lives in order was a far higher priority than assuring the national defense.

3.8 It took from September (3.1; September was the seventh month because the year began in March) to June just to *prepare* to build the temple. The exiles took time to make plans because the project was important to them. Preparation may not feel heroic or spiritual, but it is vital to any project meant to be done well.

LORD. 9 And Jeshua with his sons and his kin, and Kadmiel and his sons, Binnui and Hodaviah[d] along with the sons of Henadad, the Levites, their sons and kin, together took charge of the workers in the house of God.

[d] Compare 2.40; Neh 7.43; 1 Esdras 5.58: Heb *sons of Judah*

ZERUBBABEL

Sometimes God's ownership of a project is only recognized after *our* best efforts have failed. It is dangerous to think of God as responsible for the insignificant details while we take charge of the larger aspects of a project. Instead, it is God who is in control, and we only play a part in his overall plan. When God gives us important jobs to do, it isn't because he needs our help. Zerubbabel learned this lesson.

God's people had been exiled in Babylon for many years. Many had settled into comfortable life-styles there and wanted to stay. There were, however, almost 60,000 who had not forgotten Judah. When Babylon was defeated in 539 B.C., the Persian ruler, Cyrus, allowed the Jews to return to Jerusalem and rebuild their temple. Zerubbabel led the first and largest group back to the promised land.

Zerubbabel's leadership was by right and recognition. Not only was he a descendant of David, he also had personal leadership qualities. When the people arrived in Judah, they were given time to establish living quarters, and then were called to begin the work. They began not by laying the city walls or constructing government buildings, but by rebuilding the altar, worshiping God together, and celebrating a feast. Under Zerubbabel's leadership, they established a spiritual foundation for their building efforts.

The temple foundation was then quickly completed, and another round of celebration followed. But soon two problems arose. A few old men remembered Solomon's glorious temple and were saddened at how much smaller and less glorious this one was. Also, some enemies of the Jews tried to infiltrate the work force and stop the building with political pressure. Fear caused the work to grind to a halt. The people went to their homes, and 16 years passed.

We do not know what Zerubbabel did during this time. His discouragement, following those first months of excitement and accomplishment, must have been deep. Those feelings eventually hardened into hopelessness. So God sent the prophets Haggai and Zechariah to be Zerubbabel's encouraging companions. They confronted the people's reluctance and comforted their fears. The work began once again with renewed energy and was completed in four years.

Zerubbabel, like many of us, knew how to start well but found it hard to keep going. His successes depended on the quality of encouragement he received. Zerubbabel let discouragement get the better of him. But when he let God take control, the work was finished. God is always in control. We must not let circumstances or lack of encouragement slow us from doing the tasks God has given us.

Strengths and accomplishments:
- Led the first group of Jewish exiles back to Jerusalem from Babylon
- Completed the rebuilding of God's temple
- Demonstrated wisdom in the help he accepted and refused
- Started his building project with worship as the focal point

Weaknesses and mistakes:
- Needed constant encouragement
- Allowed problems and resistance to stop the rebuilding work

Lessons from his life:
- A leader needs to provide not only the initial motivation for a project, but the continued encouragement necessary to keep the project going
- A leader must find his/her own dependable source of encouragement
- God's faithfulness is shown in the way he preserved David's line

Vital statistics:
- Where: Babylon, Jerusalem
- Occupation: Recognized leader of the exiles
- Relatives: Father: Shealtiel. Grandfather: Jehoiachin
- Contemporaries: Cyrus, Darius, Zechariah, Haggai

Key verses:
"He said to me, 'This is the word of the Lord to Zerubbabel: Not by might, nor by power, but by my spirit, says the Lord of hosts. What are you, O great mountain? Before Zerubbabel you shall become a plain; and he shall bring out the top stone amid shouts of "Grace, grace to it!" ' " (Zechariah 4.6, 7).

Zerubbabel's story is told in Ezra 2.2—5.2. He is also mentioned in 1 Chronicles 3.19; Nehemiah 7.7; 12.1, 47; Haggai 1.1, 12, 14; 2.4, 21, 23; Zechariah 4.6–10; Matthew 1.12, 13; Luke 3.27.

10 When the builders laid the foundation of the temple of the LORD, the priests
in their vestments were stationed to praise the LORD with trumpets, and the Levites,
the sons of Asaph, with cymbals, according to the directions of King David of
Israel; 11 and they sang responsively, praising and giving thanks to the LORD,

"For he is good,
for his steadfast love endures forever toward Israel."

And all the people responded with a great shout when they praised the LORD, because the foundation of the house of the LORD was laid. 12 But many of the priests
and Levites and heads of families, old people who had seen the first house on its
foundations, wept with a loud voice when they saw this house, though many
shouted aloud for joy, 13 so that the people could not distinguish the sound of the
joyful shout from the sound of the people's weeping, for the people shouted so
loudly that the sound was heard far away.

3.10 1 Chron 28.11-13,19
3.11 1 Chron 16.34, 41; 29.20 Neh 12.24 Ps 24.7-10 103.17; 106.1 Isa 12.6
3.12 Hag 2.3

Enemies oppose the rebuilding

4 When the adversaries of Judah and Benjamin heard that the returned exiles
were building a temple to the LORD, the God of Israel, 2 they approached Zerubbabel and the heads of families and said to them, "Let us build with you, for we
worship your God as you do, and we have been sacrificing to him ever since the
days of King Esar-haddon of Assyria who brought us here." 3 But Zerubbabel,
Jeshua, and the rest of the heads of families in Israel said to them, "You shall have
no part with us in building a house to our God; but we alone will build to the LORD,
the God of Israel, as King Cyrus of Persia has commanded us."
4 Then the people of the land discouraged the people of Judah, and made them
afraid to build, 5 and they bribed officials to frustrate their plan throughout the reign
of King Cyrus of Persia and until the reign of King Darius of Persia.

4.2 2 Kgs 19.37 Ezra 4.7-10 Neh 4.1-13
4.3 Ezra 1.1-4 6.3-5 Neh 2.20
4.4 Ezra 4.24; 5.5-7 Neh 12.22 Hag 1.1,14,15

3.10, 11 David had given clear instructions concerning the use of music in worship services in the temple (1 Chronicles 16; 25).

3.10, 11 Completing the foundation for the temple required great effort on the part of all involved. But no one tried to get praise for himself and his own hard work. Instead, everyone praised God for what had been done. All good gifts come from God—talents, abilities, strength, and leadership. We should thank God for what has been done in and through us!

3.11 The Bible records many songs and musical events. For a list of such events, see the chart in Exodus 16.

3.12 Fifty years after its destruction, the temple was being rebuilt (536 B.C.). Some of the older people remembered Solomon's temple and were filled with emotion because the new temple would not be as glorious as the first one. But the beauty of the building was not nearly as important to God as were the attitudes of the builders and worshipers. God cares more about who we are than what we accomplish. Our world is always changing, and magnificent accomplishments decay and disappear. Seek to serve God wholeheartedly. Then you won't need to compare your work with anyone else's.

3.12 Because the new temple was built on the foundation of Solomon's temple, the two structures were not that different in size, but the old temple was far more elaborate and ornate, and was surrounded by many buildings and a vast courtyard. Both temples were constructed of imported cedar wood, but Solomon's was decorated with vast amounts of gold and precious stones. Solomon's temple took over seven years to build; Zerubbabel's took about four years. Solomon's temple was at the hub of a thriving city; Zerubbabel's was surrounded by ruins. No wonder the people wept!

3.13 The celebration after laying the temple foundation was marked by contrasts of emotion—weeping and joyful shouting. Both were appropriate. The Holy Spirit can stimulate us both to rejoice over the goodness of his grace and to grieve over the sins that required him to correct us. When we come into the presence of Almighty God, we may feel full of joy and thanksgiving, yet at the same time feel sobered by our shortcomings.

4.1 The enemies of Judah and Benjamin were people who had been relocated in the northern kingdom when Assyria conquered Israel (see 2 Kings 17 and the note on 3.3). In an attempt to infiltrate and disrupt the project, these people offered to help the Jews rebuild the temple. They wanted to keep a close eye on what the Jews were doing. They were hoping to keep Jerusalem from becoming strong again. The Jews, however, saw through their ploy. Such a partnership with unbelievers would have led God's people to compromise their faith.

4.1–6 Believers can expect opposition when they do God's work (2 Timothy 3.12). Unbelievers and evil spiritual forces are always working against God and his people. The opposition may: offer compromising alliances (4.2), attempt to discourage and intimidate us (4.4, 5), or accuse us unjustly (4.6). If you expect these tactics, you won't be halted by them. Move ahead with the work God has planned for you, and trust him to show you how to overcome the obstacles.

4.2 These enemies claimed to worship the same God as Zerubbabel and the rest of the Jews. In one sense, this was true; they worshiped God, but they also worshiped many other gods (see 2 Kings 17.27–29, 32–34, 41). In God's eyes, this was not worship—it was sin and rebellion. True worship involves devotion to God alone (Exodus 20.3–5). To these foreigners, God was just another "idol" to be added to their collection. Their real motive was to disrupt the temple project. Believers today must beware of those who claim to be Christians but whose actions clearly reveal they are using Christianity to serve their own interests.

King Artaxerxes stops the work

6 In the reign of Ahasuerus, in his accession year, they wrote an accusation
against the inhabitants of Judah and Jerusalem.
7 And in the days of Artaxerxes, Bishlam and Mithredath and Tabeel and the
rest of their associates wrote to King Artaxerxes of Persia; the letter was written in
Aramaic and translated.[e] 8 Rehum the royal deputy and Shimshai the scribe wrote
a letter against Jerusalem to King Artaxerxes as follows 9 (then Rehum the royal
deputy, Shimshai the scribe, and the rest of their associates, the judges, the envoys,
the officials, the Persians, the people of Erech, the Babylonians, the people of
Susa, that is, the Elamites, 10 and the rest of the nations whom the great and noble
Osnappar deported and settled in the cities of Samaria and in the rest of the province
Beyond the River wrote—and now 11 this is a copy of the letter that they sent):
"To King Artaxerxes: Your servants, the people of the province Beyond the
River, send greeting. And now 12 may it be known to the king that the Jews who
came up from you to us have gone to Jerusalem. They are rebuilding that rebellious
and wicked city; they are finishing the walls and repairing the foundations. 13 Now
may it be known to the king that, if this city is rebuilt and the walls finished, they
will not pay tribute, custom, or toll, and the royal revenue will be reduced. 14 Now
because we share the salt of the palace and it is not fitting for us to witness the
king's dishonor, therefore we send and inform the king, 15 so that a search may be
made in the annals of your ancestors. You will discover in the annals that this is a
rebellious city, hurtful to kings and provinces, and that sedition was stirred up in it
from long ago. On that account this city was laid waste. 16 We make known to the
king that, if this city is rebuilt and its walls finished, you will then have no possession in the province Beyond the River."
17 The king sent an answer: "To Rehum the royal deputy and Shimshai the
scribe and the rest of their associates who live in Samaria and in the rest of the
province Beyond the River, greeting. And now 18 the letter that you sent to us has
been read in translation before me. 19 So I made a decree, and someone searched
and discovered that this city has risen against kings from long ago, and that rebellion and sedition have been made in it. 20 Jerusalem has had mighty kings who ruled

4.6 Esth 1.1; 2.1,12-14; Dan 9.1
4.7 Ezra 7.1-21; Neh 1.1; 5.14
4.8 Ezra 5.6; 6.13
4.12 Ezra 5.3; Neh 1.3; Dan 9.25
4.13 Ezra 4.20; 7.24; Neh 5.4
4.20 1 Kgs 4.21,24; 1 Chron 18.3,4, 6,13; 19.19; 2 Chron 17.11; Ezra 4.13

[e] Heb adds *in Aramaic,* indicating that 4.8-6.18 is in Aramaic. Another interpretation is *The letter was written in the Aramaic script and set forth in the Aramaic language*

THE PERSIAN KINGS OF EZRA'S DAY

Name	*Date of Reign*	*Relationship to Israel*
Cyrus	559–530 B.C.	Conquered Babylon. Established a policy of returning exiles to their homelands. Sent Zerubbabel to Jerusalem, financed his project, and returned the gold and silver articles that Nebuchadnezzar had taken from the temple. He probably knew Daniel.
Darius	522–486 B.C.	Stopped construction of the temple in Jerusalem.
Ahasuerus (Xerxes)	486–465 B.C.	Was Esther's husband. Allowed the Jews to protect themselves against Haman's attempt to eliminate their people.
Artaxerxes	465–424 B.C.	Had Nehemiah as his cupbearer. Allowed both Ezra and Nehemiah to return to Jerusalem.

4.6 This letter sent to King Ahasuerus may have been inscribed on a clay tablet, a fragment of pottery, or sheets of parchment.

4.6–23 Here Ezra summarizes the entire story of the opposition to building the temple, the walls, and other important buildings in Jerusalem. Chronologically, 4.6 fits between chapters 6 and 7; 4.7–23 refers to the events between Ezra 7 and Nehemiah 1. Ezra grouped them here to highlight the persistent opposition to God's people over the years, and God's ability to overcome it.

4.10 Osnappar was another name for Ashurbanipal (669–626 B.C.), the Assyrian king who completed the relocation of Israelite captives. He was the last of the strong Assyrian kings, and after his death the nation quickly declined. Assyria was conquered by Babylon in 612.

4.14 To "share the salt of the palace" means they were in the king's pay and thus were obligated to him.

4.19, 20 Artaxerxes said that Jerusalem was associated with "rebellion and sedition." By reading the historical records, he learned that mighty kings had come from Jerusalem, and he may have feared that another would arise if the city were rebuilt. Solomon had ruled a huge empire (1 Kings 4.21), and Jerusalem's kings had rebelled against mighty powers—for example, Zedekiah rebelled against Nebuchadnezzar despite his oath of loyalty (2 Chronicles 36.13). Artaxerxes did not want to aid the rebuilding of a rebellious city and nation.

over the whole province Beyond the River, to whom tribute, custom, and toll were
paid. 21 Therefore issue an order that these people be made to cease, and that this
city not be rebuilt, until I make a decree. 22 Moreover, take care not to be slack in
this matter; why should damage grow to the hurt of the king?"
23 Then when the copy of King Artaxerxes' letter was read before Rehum and
the scribe Shimshai and their associates, they hurried to the Jews in Jerusalem and
by force and power made them cease. 24 At that time the work on the house of God **4.24**
in Jerusalem stopped and was discontinued until the second year of the reign of Neh 6.3,9; Hag 1.14,15
King Darius of Persia.

The rebuilding continues

5 Now the prophets, Haggai[f] and Zechariah son of Iddo, prophesied to the Jews **5.1**
who were in Judah and Jerusalem, in the name of the God of Israel who was Ezra 3.2; 6.14; Hag 1.1
over them. 2 Then Zerubbabel son of Shealtiel and Jeshua son of Jozadak set out to Zech 1.1
rebuild the house of God in Jerusalem; and with them were the prophets of God,
helping them.
3 At the same time Tattenai the governor of the province Beyond the River and **5.3**
Shethar-bozenai and their associates came to them and spoke to them thus, "Who Ezra 5.6,9,17; 6.6,13
gave you a decree to build this house and to finish this structure?" 4 They[g] also **5.4**
asked them this, "What are the names of the men who are building this building?" Ezra 5.10
5 But the eye of their God was upon the elders of the Jews, and they did not stop **5.5**
them until a report reached Darius and then answer was returned by letter in reply Ezra 4.4; 6.1; 7.6,12; 8.22; Ps 33.18
to it. 1 Pet 3.12

Enemies inform King Darius

6 The copy of the letter that Tattenai the governor of the province Beyond the **5.6**
River and Shethar-bozenai and his associates the envoys who were in the province Ezra 4.11,23
Beyond the River sent to King Darius; 7 they sent him a report, in which was written
as follows: "To Darius the king, all peace! 8 May it be known to the king that we
went to the province of Judah, to the house of the great God. It is being built of
hewn stone, and timber is laid in the walls; this work is being done diligently and
prospers in their hands. 9 Then we spoke to those elders and asked them, 'Who gave
you a decree to build this house and to finish this structure?' 10 We also asked them **5.10**
their names, for your information, so that we might write down the names of the Ezra 5.4
men at their head. 11 This was their reply to us: 'We are the servants of the God of **5.11** 1 Kgs 6.1-38
heaven and earth, and we are rebuilding the house that was built many years ago, 2 Chron 3.1–5.14
which a great king of Israel built and finished. 12 But because our ancestors had **5.12**
angered the God of heaven, he gave them into the hand of King Nebuchadnezzar of 2 Kgs 24.2,10; 25.1,8-11
Babylon, the Chaldean, who destroyed this house and carried away the people to 2 Chron 36.6-20

[f] Aram adds *the prophet* [g] Gk Syr: Aram *We*

4.24 Ezra resumes his chronological account here. It may have been ten years since the Israelites had worked on the temple. It did not begin again until 520 B.C., the second year of Darius's reign (5.1ff).

5.1 More details about the work and messages of Haggai and Zechariah are found in the books of the Bible that bear their names.

5.1, 2 God sometimes sends prophets to encourage and strengthen his people. To accomplish this, Haggai and Zechariah not only preached, but also got involved in the labor. In the church today, God appoints prophetic voices to help us with our work (Ephesians 4.11–13). Their ministry should have the same effect upon us as Haggai's and Zechariah's had on Israel. "Those who prophesy speak to other people for their upbuilding and encouragement and consolation" (1 Corinthians 14.3). In turn, we should encourage those who bring God's words to us.

5.5 The non-Jews who lived nearby attempted to hinder the construction of the temple. But while the legal debate went on and the decision was under appeal, the Jews continued to rebuild. When we are doing God's work, others may try to delay, confuse, or frustrate us, but we can proceed confidently. God will accomplish his purposes in our world, no matter who attempts to block them. Concentrate on God's purpose, and don't be sidetracked by intrigues or slander.

5.11 While rebuilding the temple, the workers were confronted by the Persia-appointed governor, demanding to know who gave permission for their construction project (5.3). This could have been intimidating, but, as we learn from the letter, they boldly replied, "We are the servants of the God of heaven and earth."

It is not always easy to speak up for our faith in an unbelieving world, but we must. The way to deal with pressure and intimidation is to recognize that we are workers for God. Our allegiance is to him first, people second. When we contemplate the reactions and criticisms of hostile people, we can become paralyzed with fear. If we try to offend no one or please everyone, we won't be effective. God is our leader, and his rewards are most important. So don't be intimidated. Let others know by your words and actions whom you really serve.

5.13 2 Chron 36.22 23 Ezra 1.1-8 6.3-5
5.14 Ezra 1.7,8,11 5.16; 6.3-5
5.17 Ezra 6.1,2

Babylonia. 13 However, King Cyrus of Babylon, in the first year of his reign, made
a decree that this house of God should be rebuilt. 14 Moreover, the gold and silver
vessels of the house of God, which Nebuchadnezzar had taken out of the temple in
Jerusalem and had brought into the temple of Babylon, these King Cyrus took out
of the temple of Babylon, and they were delivered to a man named Sheshbazzar,
whom he had made governor. 15 He said to him, "Take these vessels; go and put
them in the temple in Jerusalem, and let the house of God be rebuilt on its site."
16 Then this Sheshbazzar came and laid the foundations of the house of God in
Jerusalem; and from that time until now it has been under construction, and it is not
yet finished.' 17 And now, if it seems good to the king, have a search made in the
royal archives there in Babylon, to see whether a decree was issued by King Cyrus
for the rebuilding of this house of God in Jerusalem. Let the king send us his pleasure in this matter."

6.1 Ezra 5.17
6.2 Esth 1.1,13-15 10.2 Jer 25.25
6.3 Ezra 1.2-4
6.5 1 Kgs 6.36

King Darius approves the rebuilding

6 Then King Darius made a decree, and they searched the archives where the
documents were stored in Babylon. 2 But it was in Ecbatana, the capital in the
province of Media, that a scroll was found on which this was written: "A record.
3 In the first year of his reign, King Cyrus issued a decree: Concerning the house of
God at Jerusalem, let the house be rebuilt, the place where sacrifices are offered
and burnt offerings are brought;[h] its height shall be sixty cubits and its width sixty
cubits, 4 with three courses of hewn stones and one course of timber; let the cost be
paid from the royal treasury. 5 Moreover, let the gold and silver vessels of the house
of God, which Nebuchadnezzar took out of the temple in Jerusalem and brought to
Babylon, be restored and brought back to the temple in Jerusalem, each to its place;
you shall put them in the house of God."

[h] Meaning of Aram uncertain

THE POST-EXILIC PROPHETS
God used these men to confront and comfort his people after their return to their homeland from exile in Babylon.

Who?	*When?*	*Ministered to These Contemporary Leaders*	*Main Message*	*Significance*
Haggai	520 B.C.	Zerubbabel Joshua	• Encouraged the leaders and the people to continue rebuilding the temple, which God would bless • Challenged the people's careless worship, which God would not bless	Disobedience and careless obedience of God's commands lead to judgment.
Zechariah	520 B.C.	Zerubbabel Joshua	• Emphasized God's command to rebuild his temple • Gave the people another look at God's plan to bless the world through Israel and its coming king—the Messiah (9.9, 10)	Encouragement for today's effort sometimes requires that we remember God has a plan and purpose for tomorrow. Meanwhile, the challenge is to live for him today.
Malachi	430 B.C.	The priests are the only leaders mentioned	• Confronted the people and priests with God's promises of judgment on those who reject him and God's blessing on those who live as he desires	God expects our obedience to him to affect our attitude toward him and our treatment of one another.

5.13–17 Cyrus is called king of Persia in 1.1 and king of Babylon in 5.13. Because Persia had just conquered Babylon, Cyrus was king of both nations. Babylon is more important to this story because it was the location of the Hebrews' 70-year captivity. The Babylon in 5.17 may refer to the city of Babylon which was the capital of the province of Babylon.

6.1, 2 Many clay and papyrus documents recording business transactions and historical data have been discovered in this area (near present-day Syria). A great library and archives with thousands of such records have been discovered at Ebla in Syria.

6 "Now you, Tattenai, governor of the province Beyond the River, Shethar-
bozenai, and you, their associates, the envoys in the province Beyond the River,
keep away; [7]let the work on this house of God alone; let the governor of the Jews
and the elders of the Jews rebuild this house of God on its site. [8]Moreover I make
a decree regarding what you shall do for these elders of the Jews for the rebuilding
of this house of God: the cost is to be paid to these people, in full and without delay,
from the royal revenue, the tribute of the province Beyond the River. [9]Whatever is
needed—young bulls, rams, or sheep for burnt offerings to the God of heaven,
wheat, salt, wine, or oil, as the priests in Jerusalem require—let that be given to
them day by day without fail, [10]so that they may offer pleasing sacrifices to the God
of heaven, and pray for the life of the king and his children. [11]Furthermore I decree — **6.11**
that if anyone alters this edict, a beam shall be pulled out of the house of the perpe- — Ezra 7.26 Dan 2.5; 3.29
trator, who then shall be impaled on it. The house shall be made a dunghill. [12]May — **6.12**
the God who has established his name there overthrow any king or people that shall — Deut 12.4,5,11 1 Kgs 9.2,3
put forth a hand to alter this, or to destroy this house of God in Jerusalem. I, Darius,
make a decree; let it be done with all diligence."

The temple is completed and dedicated

13 Then, according to the word sent by King Darius, Tattenai, the governor of
the province Beyond the River, Shethar-bozenai, and their associates did with all
diligence what King Darius had ordered. [14]So the elders of the Jews built and pros- — **6.14**
pered, through the prophesying of the prophet Haggai and Zechariah son of Iddo. — Ezra 1.1; 5.1 6.12
They finished their building by command of the God of Israel and by decree of — 7.1,7-9,11 Zech 4.9
Cyrus, Darius, and King Artaxerxes of Persia; [15]and this house was finished on the
third day of the month of Adar, in the sixth year of the reign of King Darius.
16 The people of Israel, the priests and the Levites, and the rest of the returned — **6.16**
exiles, celebrated the dedication of this house of God with joy. [17]They offered at — Ezra 3.11,12 6.21,22
the dedication of this house of God one hundred bulls, two hundred rams, four
hundred lambs, and as a sin offering for all Israel, twelve male goats, according to
the number of the tribes of Israel. [18]Then they set the priests in their divisions and — **6.18**
the Levites in their courses for the service of God at Jerusalem, as it is written in the — 2 Chron 35.4,5
book of Moses.

The passover is celebrated

19 On the fourteenth day of the first month the returned exiles kept the pass- — **6.19**
over. [20]For both the priests and the Levites had purified themselves; all of them — Ex 12.6
were clean. So they killed the passover lamb for all the returned exiles, for their — **6.20**
fellow priests, and for themselves. [21]It was eaten by the people of Israel who had — 2 Chron 29.34 30.15-17
returned from exile, and also by all who had joined them and separated themselves — **6.21**
from the pollutions of the nations of the land to worship the LORD, the God of — Ex 19.10,14 Num 9.6,7, 10-14
Israel. [22]With joy they celebrated the festival of unleavened bread seven days; for — Ezra 9.1-15
the LORD had made them joyful, and had turned the heart of the king of Assyria to
them, so that he aided them in the work on the house of God, the God of Israel.

6.14 Ezra carefully pointed out that rebuilding the temple was decreed first by God and then by the kings, who were his instruments. How ironic and wonderful that God's work was carried on by the discovery of a lost paragraph in a pagan library. All the opposition of powerful forces was stopped by a clause in a legal document. God's will is supreme over all rulers, all historical events, and all hostile forces. He can deliver us in ways we can't imagine. If we trust in his power and love, no opposition can deter us.

6.15 The temple was completed in 516 B.C.

6.16–22 Feasting and celebration were in order at the great temple dedication. This celebration was similar to the one that Solomon had when he dedicated the temple in 1 Kings 8.63, although Solomon offered more than 200 times as many oxen and sheep. This "book of Moses" was probably Leviticus. The priests and Levites were organized into groups in order to do "the service of God, . . . as it is written in the book of Moses." There is time to celebrate, but there is also a time to work. Both are proper and necessary when worshiping God; and both are pleasing to him.

B. THE RETURN LED BY EZRA (7.1—10.44)

Ezra returned to the land with a second group of exiles, 80 years after Zerubbabel. Ezra found the temple rebuilt, but the lives of the people in shambles. Intermarriage with foreigners opposed to God threatened the spiritual future of the nation. So Ezra prayed for guidance and then followed through with action. Christians today must also strive to keep their lives pure, refusing to let the sinful allurements of the world around them compromise their life-style.

1. The second group of exiles returns to the land

Ezra's background

7.1 Ezra 7.12,21; 8.1—10.44; Neh 2.1; 8.1-18

7.6 Ezra 7.10,21,25; Neh 8.9,13

7.7 1 Chron 6.31,48,49; Ezra 2.40-58; Neh 7.39-60

7 After this, in the reign of King Artaxerxes of Persia, Ezra son of Seraiah, son
of Azariah, son of Hilkiah, 2 son of Shallum, son of Zadok, son of Ahitub,
3 son of Amariah, son of Azariah, son of Meraioth, 4 son of Zerahiah, son of Uzzi,
son of Bukki, 5 son of Abishua, son of Phinehas, son of Eleazar, son of the chief
priest Aaron— 6 this Ezra went up from Babylonia. He was a scribe skilled in the
law of Moses that the LORD the God of Israel had given; and the king granted him
all that he asked, for the hand of the LORD his God was upon him.
7 Some of the people of Israel, and some of the priests and Levites, the singers
and gatekeepers, and the temple servants also went up to Jerusalem, in the seventh
year of King Artaxerxes. 8 They came to Jerusalem in the fifth month, which was
in the seventh year of the king. 9 On the first day of the first month the journey up

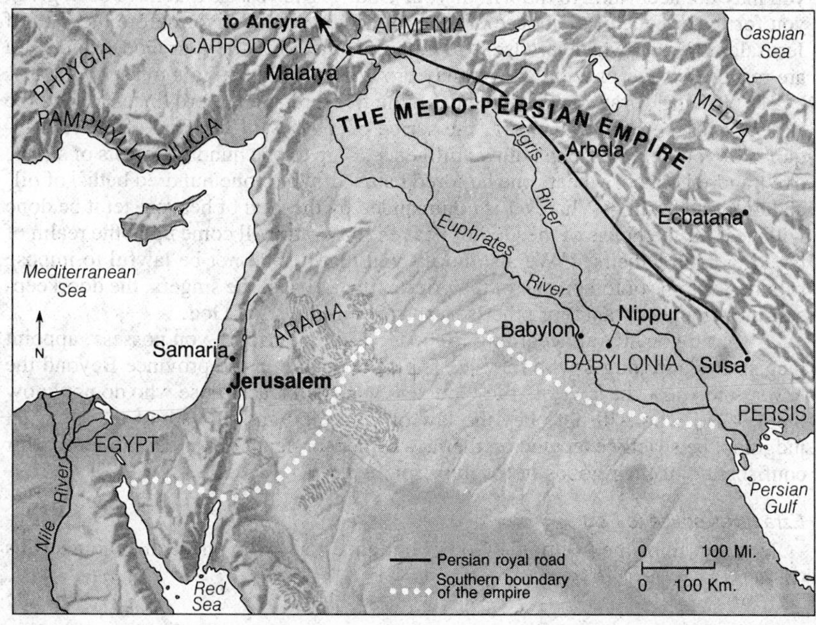

THE MEDO-PERSIAN EMPIRE The Medo-Persian Empire included the lands of Media and Persia, much of the area shown on this map and more. The Jewish exiles were concentrated in the area around Nippur in the Babylonian province. The decree by King Cyrus which allowed the Israelites to return to their homeland and rebuild the temple was discovered in the palace at Ecbatana.

7.1 There is a gap of almost 60 years between the events of chapters six and seven. The story in the book of Esther occurred during this time, in the reign of Ahasuerus (also called Xerxes the Great), who ruled from 486–465 B.C. Artaxerxes, his son, became king in 465, and Ezra returned to Jerusalem in 458.

7.6 Eighty years after the first exiles returned to Jerusalem (2.1), Ezra himself returned. This was his first trip, and it took four months. The temple had been standing for about 58 years. Up to this point in the narrative, Ezra had remained in Babylon, probably compiling a record of the events that had taken place.

Why did he have to ask the king if he could return? Ezra wanted to lead many Jews back to Jerusalem, and he needed a decree from the king stating that any Jew who wanted to return could do so. This decree would be like a passport in case they ran into opposition along the way. The king's generous decree showed that God was blessing Ezra (7.6, 28). It also indicated that Ezra was probably a prominent man in Artaxerxes's kingdom. He was willing to give up this position to return to his homeland and teach the Israelites God's laws.

7.6–10 Ezra demonstrates how a gifted Bible teacher can move God's people forward. He was effective because he was a well-versed student of God's laws and because he was determined to obey those laws. He taught through both his speaking and his example. Like Ezra, we should determine both to study and to obey God's Word.

from Babylon was begun, and on the first day of the fifth month he came to Jerusalem, for the gracious hand of his God was upon him. 10 For Ezra had set his heart **7.10** Ezra 7.6
to study the law of the LORD, and to do it, and to teach the statutes and ordinances
in Israel.

Ezra's letter from King Artaxerxes

11 This is a copy of the letter that King Artaxerxes gave to the priest Ezra, the **7.11**
scribe, a scholar of the text of the commandments of the LORD and his statutes for Ezra 4.11; 5.6
Israel: 12 "Artaxerxes, king of kings, to the priest Ezra, the scribe of the law of the **7.12**
God of heaven: Peace.[i] And now 13 I decree that any of the people of Israel or their Ezek 26.7 Dan 2.37,47
priests or Levites in my kingdom who freely offers to go to Jerusalem may go with
you. 14 For you are sent by the king and his seven counselors to make inquiries **7.14**
about Judah and Jerusalem according to the law of your God, which is in your Ezra 7.28 Esth 1.14
hand, 15 and also to convey the silver and gold that the king and his counselors have
freely offered to the God of Israel, whose dwelling is in Jerusalem, 16 with all the **7.16**
silver and gold that you shall find in the whole province of Babylonia, and with the Deut 16.10 Ezra 1.4,6; 8.28
freewill offerings of the people and the priests, given willingly for the house of
their God in Jerusalem. 17 With this money, then, you shall with all diligence buy **7.17**
bulls, rams, and lambs, and their grain offerings and their drink offerings, and you Ex 30.9 Lev 23.13
shall offer them on the altar of the house of your God in Jerusalem. 18 Whatever Num 6.15 Deut 12.4-11
seems good to you and your colleagues to do with the rest of the silver and gold,
you may do, according to the will of your God. 19 The vessels that have been given
you for the service of the house of your God, you shall deliver before the God of
Jerusalem. 20 And whatever else is required for the house of your God, which you
are responsible for providing, you may provide out of the king's treasury.

21 "I, King Artaxerxes, decree to all the treasurers in the province Beyond the
River: Whatever the priest Ezra, the scribe of the law of the God of heaven, requires of you, let it be done with all diligence, 22 up to one hundred talents of silver,
one hundred cors of wheat, one hundred baths[j] of wine, one hundred baths[j] of oil,
and unlimited salt. 23 Whatever is commanded by the God of heaven, let it be done
with zeal for the house of the God of heaven, or wrath will come upon the realm of
the king and his heirs. 24 We also notify you that it shall not be lawful to impose **7.24**
tribute, custom, or toll on any of the priests, the Levites, the singers, the doorkeep- Gen 47.26
ers, the temple servants, or other servants of this house of God.

25 "And you, Ezra, according to the God-given wisdom you possess, appoint **7.25**
magistrates and judges who may judge all the people in the province Beyond the Ex 18.21-25 Deut 16.18
River who know the laws of your God; and you shall teach those who do not know Ezra 7.6,10
them. 26 All who will not obey the law of your God and the law of the king, let **7.26**
judgment be strictly executed on them, whether for death or for banishment or for Ezra 6.11 Ps 52.5
confiscation of their goods or for imprisonment."

Ezra gives praise to God

27 Blessed be the LORD, the God of our ancestors, who put such a thing as this

[i] Syr Vg 1 Esdras 8.9: Aram *Perfect* [j] A Heb measure of volume

---

7.14 The seven counselors were Artaxerxes's supreme court (see Esther 1.14).

7.14 When Nebuchadnezzar destroyed the temple, he took a vast amount of booty that may have included a copy of the book of the law (2 Chronicles 36.18). It is also possible that this book was brought by the Jews into exile and was confiscated and read by their conquerors. Foreign leaders who worshiped many gods liked to have records of the gods of other nations for both military and political reasons.

7.24 Why did Artaxerxes exempt temple workers from paying taxes? He recognized that the priests and Levites filled an important role in society as spiritual leaders, so he freed them of tax burdens. While the Bible does not teach tax exemption for religious employees, Artaxerxes, a pagan king, recognized and supported the principle. Today, churches have the responsibility to keep worldly burdens off the shoulders of spiritual workers.

7.27 In Ezra's doxology, he acknowledges that only God can change the king's heart (see Proverbs 21.1). When we face life's challenges, we often must work diligently and with extraordinary effort, realizing that God oversees all our work. Recognize his hand in your success and remember to praise him for his help and protection.

7.28 Ezra 7.14

into the heart of the king to glorify the house of the LORD in Jerusalem, 28 and who extended to me steadfast love before the king and his counselors, and before all the king's mighty officers. I took courage, for the hand of the LORD my God was upon me, and I gathered leaders from Israel to go up with me.

It is not personal achievement, but personal commitment to live for God, that is important. Achievements are simply examples of what God can do through someone's life. The most effective leaders spoken of in the Bible had little awareness of the impact their lives had on others. They were too busy obeying God to keep track of their successes. Ezra fits that description.

About 80 years after the rebuilding of the temple under Zerubbabel, Ezra returned to Judah with about 2,000 men and their families. He was given a letter from Artaxerxes instructing him to carry out a program of religious education. Along with the letter came significant power. But long before Ezra's mission began, God had shaped him three important ways so that he would use the power well. First, as a scribe, Ezra dedicated himself to carefully studying God's Word. Second, he intended to apply and obey personally the commands he discovered in God's Word. Third, he was committed to teaching others both God's Word and its application to life.

Knowing Ezra's priorities, it is not surprising to note his actions when he arrived in Jerusalem. The people had disobeyed God's command not to marry women of foreign nations. On a cold and rainy day, Ezra addressed the people and made it clear they had sinned. Because of the sins of many, all were under God's condemnation. Confession, repentance, and action were needed. The people admitted their sin and devised a plan to deal with the problem.

This initial effort on Ezra's part set the stage for what Nehemiah would later accomplish. Ezra continued his ministry under Nehemiah, and the two were used by God to start a spiritual movement that swept the nation following the rebuilding of Jerusalem.

Ezra achieved great things and made a significant impact because he had the right starting place for his actions and his life: God's Word. He studied it seriously and applied it faithfully. He taught others what he learned. He is, therefore, a great model for anyone who wants to live for God.

Strengths and accomplishments:
- Committed to study, follow, and teach God's Word
- Led the second group of exiles from Babylon to Jerusalem
- May have written 1 and 2 Chronicles
- Concerned about keeping the details of God's commands
- Sent by King Artaxerxes to Jerusalem to evaluate the situation, set up a religious education system, and return with a firsthand report
- Worked alongside Nehemiah during the last spiritual awakening recorded in the Old Testament

Lessons from his life:
- A person's willingness to know and practice God's Word will have a direct effect on how God uses his/her life
- The starting place for serving God is a personal commitment to serve him today, even before knowing what that service will be

Vital statistics:
- Where: Babylon, Jerusalem
- Occupation: scribe among the exiles in Babylon, king's envoy, teacher
- Relative: Father; Seriah
- Contemporaries: Nehemiah, Artaxerxes

Key verse:
"For Ezra had set his heart to study the law of the lord, and to do it, and to teach the statutes and ordinances in Israel" (7.10).

Ezra's story is told in Ezra 7.1—10.16 and Nehemiah 8.1—12.36.

7.27, 28 Ezra praised God for all he had done for him and through him. Ezra had honored God throughout his life, and God chose to honor him. Ezra could have assumed that his own greatness and charisma had won over the king and his princes, but he gave the credit to God. We, too, should be grateful to God for our success and not think we did it in our own power.

7.28 The speaker here is Ezra. He writes in the first person for the remainder of the book.

The exiles who returned with Ezra

8 These are their family heads, and this is the genealogy of those who went up
with me from Babylonia, in the reign of King Artaxerxes: 2 Of the descendants
of Phinehas, Gershom. Of Ithamar, Daniel. Of David, Hattush, 3 of the descendants of Shecaniah. Of Parosh, Zechariah, with whom were registered one hundred
fifty males. 4 Of the descendants of Pahath-moab, Eliehoenai son of Zerahiah, and
with him two hundred males. 5 Of the descendants of Zattu,[k] Shecaniah son of
Jahaziel, and with him three hundred males. 6 Of the descendants of Adin, Ebed
son of Jonathan, and with him fifty males. 7 Of the descendants of Elam, Jeshaiah
son of Athaliah, and with him seventy males. 8 Of the descendants of Shephatiah,
Zebadiah son of Michael, and with him eighty males. 9 Of the descendants of Joab,
Obadiah son of Jehiel, and with him two hundred eighteen males. 10 Of the descendants of Bani,[l] Shelomith son of Josiphiah, and with him one hundred sixty males.
11 Of the descendants of Bebai, Zechariah son of Bebai, and with him twenty-eight
males. 12 Of the descendants of Azgad, Johanan son of Hakkatan, and with him one
hundred ten males. 13 Of the descendants of Adonikam, those who came later, their
names being Eliphelet, Jeuel, and Shemaiah, and with them sixty males. 14 Of the
descendants of Bigvai, Uthai and Zaccur, and with them seventy males.

8.1 Ezra 2.2-35,62, 63; 7.1-5

Ezra returns to Jerusalem

15 I gathered them by the river that runs to Ahava, and there we camped three
days. As I reviewed the people and the priests, I found there none of the descendants of Levi. 16 Then I sent for Eliezer, Ariel, Shemaiah, Elnathan, Jarib, Elnathan, Nathan, Zechariah, and Meshullam, who were leaders, and for Joiarib and
Elnathan, who were wise, 17 and sent them to Iddo, the leader at the place called
Casiphia, telling them what to say to Iddo and his colleagues the temple servants at
Casiphia, namely, to send us ministers for the house of our God. 18 Since the gracious hand of our God was upon us, they brought us a man of discretion, of the
descendants of Mahli son of Levi son of Israel, namely Sherebiah, with his sons
and kin, eighteen; 19 also Hashabiah and with him Jeshaiah of the descendants of
Merari, with his kin and their sons, twenty; 20 besides two hundred twenty of the
temple servants, whom David and his officials had set apart to attend the Levites.
These were all mentioned by name.
21 Then I proclaimed a fast there, at the river Ahava, that we might deny ourselves[m] before our God, to seek from him a safe journey for ourselves, our children, and all our possessions. 22 For I was ashamed to ask the king for a band of
soldiers and cavalry to protect us against the enemy on our way, since we had told

8.15 Ezra 8.21,31
8.17 Ezra 2.43-54 8.20 Neh 7.46-56
8.20 Ezra 8.17
8.21 Lev 23.32 2 Chron 7.14 20.3 Ezra 8.15,31 Ps 37.11 Jonah 3.5
8.22 2 Chron 15.2 Ezra 7.6

[k] Gk 1 Esdras 8.32: Heb lacks *of Zattu* [l] Gk 1 Esdras 8.36: Heb lacks *Bani* [m] Or *might fast*

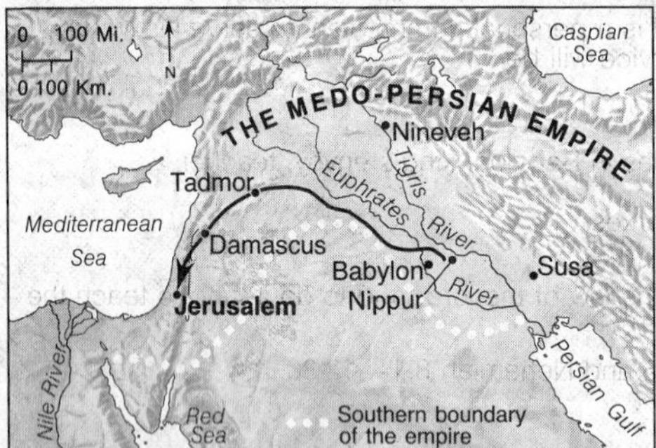

EZRA'S JOURNEY Ezra led a second group of exiles back to Judah and Jerusalem about 80 years after the first group. He traveled the dangerous route without military escort (8.22); but the people prayed and, under Ezra's godly leadership, arrived safely in Jerusalem after several months.

8.15 Ezra's progress back to Jerusalem was halted while he waited to recruit Levites. God had called these men to a special service, and yet they were unwilling to volunteer when their services were needed. God has gifted each of us with abilities so we can make a contribution to his kingdom work (Romans 12.4–8). Don't wait to be recruited, but look for opportunities to volunteer. Don't hinder God's work by holding back. "Like good stewards of the manifold grace of God, serve one another with whatever gift each of you has received" (1 Peter 4.10).

8.21 Ezra and the people traveled approximately 900 miles on foot. The trip took them through dangerous and difficult territory and lasted about four months. They prayed that God would protect them and give them a good journey. Our journeys today may not be as difficult and dangerous as Ezra's, but we should recognize our need to ask God for guidance and protection.

8.21–23 Before making all the physical preparations for the journey, Ezra made spiritual preparations. Their prayers and fasting prepared them spiritually by showing their dependence on God for protection, their faith that God was in control, and their affirmation that they were not strong enough to make the trip without him. When we take time to put God first in any endeavor, we are preparing well for whatever lies ahead.

the king that the hand of our God is gracious to all who seek him, but his power and
his wrath are against all who forsake him. 23 So we fasted and petitioned our God
for this, and he listened to our entreaty.
24 Then I set apart twelve of the leading priests: Sherebiah, Hashabiah, and ten
of their kin with them. 25 And I weighed out to them the silver and the gold and the
vessels, the offering for the house of our God that the king, his counselors, his
lords, and all Israel there present had offered; 26 I weighed out into their hand six
hundred fifty talents of silver, and one hundred silver vessels worth . . . talents,[n]
and one hundred talents of gold, 27 twenty gold bowls worth a thousand darics, and
two vessels of fine polished bronze as precious as gold. 28 And I said to them, "You
are holy to the LORD, and the vessels are holy; and the silver and the gold are a
freewill offering to the LORD, the God of your ancestors. 29 Guard them and keep
them until you weigh them before the chief priests and the Levites and the heads of
families in Israel at Jerusalem, within the chambers of the house of the LORD." 30 So
the priests and the Levites took over the silver, the gold, and the vessels as they
were weighed out, to bring them to Jerusalem, to the house of our God.
31 Then we left the river Ahava on the twelfth day of the first month, to go to
Jerusalem; the hand of our God was upon us, and he delivered us from the hand of
the enemy and from ambushes along the way. 32 We came to Jerusalem and remained there three days. 33 On the fourth day, within the house of our God, the
silver, the gold, and the vessels were weighed into the hands of the priest Meremoth son of Uriah, and with him was Eleazar son of Phinehas, and with them were
the Levites, Jozabad son of Jeshua and Noadiah son of Binnui. 34 The total was
counted and weighed, and the weight of everything was recorded.
35 At that time those who had come from captivity, the returned exiles, offered
burnt offerings to the God of Israel, twelve bulls for all Israel, ninety-six rams,
seventy-seven lambs, and as a sin offering twelve male goats; all this was a burnt
offering to the LORD. 36 They also delivered the king's commissions to the king's
satraps and to the governors of the province Beyond the River; and they supported
the people and the house of God.

8.28 Lev 21.6-8 Ezra 7.16 Isa 52.11

8.31 Ezra 7.15,21

8.36 Ezra 5.3,6

2. Ezra opposes intermarriage

Ezra prays before the people

9 After these things had been done, the officials approached me and said, "The
people of Israel, the priests, and the Levites have not separated themselves
from the peoples of the lands with their abominations, from the Canaanites, the
Hittites, the Perizzites, the Jebusites, the Ammonites, the Moabites, the Egyptians,

9.1 Ex 23.23 Lev 18.3,24-30 Deut 12.30,31 18.9; 20.17,18

[n] The number of talents is lacking

8.23 Ezra knew God's promises to protect his people, but he didn't take them for granted. He also knew that God's blessings are appropriated through prayer; so Ezra and the people humbled themselves by fasting and praying. And their prayers were answered. Fasting humbled them because going without food was a reminder of their complete dependence on God. Fasting also gave them more time to pray and meditate on God.

Too often we pray glibly and superficially. Serious prayer, by contrast, requires concentration. It puts us in touch with God's will and can really change us. Without serious prayer, we reduce God to a quick-service pharmacist with painkillers for our every ailment.

8.26 Six hundred fifty talents of silver would be about 25 tons. Other sources give the amount for the silver vessels as 100 talents, or about 3–3/4 tons. This was a large amount of treasure to transport, with or without a detachment of soldiers for protection.

8.28, 29 Every object used in temple service was set apart for God; each was considered a holy treasure to be guarded carefully. Stewardship means taking special care of whatever God has entrusted to you. This means considering what God has given to you as being from *him* and for *his* use. What has God entrusted to your care?

8.36 *Commissions* means "orders." Satraps were the equivalent of lieutenants.

9.1, 2 Since the time of the judges, Israelite men had married heathen women and then adopted their religious practices (Judges 3.5–7). Even Israel's great King Solomon was guilty of this sin (1 Kings 11.1–8). Although this practice was forbidden in God's law (Exodus 34.11–16; Deuteronomy 7.1–4), it happened in Ezra's day, and again only a generation after him (Nehemiah 13.23–27). Opposition to mixed marriage was not racial prejudice, because Jews and non-Jews of this area were of the same semitic background. The reasons were strictly spiritual. A person who married a heathen was inclined to adopt that person's heathen practices. If the Israelites were insensitive enough to disobey God in something as important as marriage, they wouldn't be strong enough to stand firm against their spouses' idolatry. Until the Israelites finally stopped this practice, idolatry remained a constant problem.

and the Amorites. 2 For they have taken some of their daughters as wives for themselves and for their sons. Thus the holy seed has mixed itself with the peoples of the
lands, and in this faithlessness the officials and leaders have led the way." 3 When
I heard this, I tore my garment and my mantle, and pulled hair from my head and
beard, and sat appalled. 4 Then all who trembled at the words of the God of Israel,
because of the faithlessness of the returned exiles, gathered around me while I sat
appalled until the evening sacrifice.
5 At the evening sacrifice I got up from my fasting, with my garments and my
mantle torn, and fell on my knees, spread out my hands to the LORD my God, 6 and
said,
"O my God, I am too ashamed and embarrassed to lift my face to you, my God,
for our iniquities have risen higher than our heads, and our guilt has mounted up to
the heavens. 7 From the days of our ancestors to this day we have been deep in guilt,
and for our iniquities we, our kings, and our priests have been handed over to the
kings of the lands, to the sword, to captivity, to plundering, and to utter shame, as
is now the case. 8 But now for a brief moment favor has been shown by the LORD
our God, who has left us a remnant, and given us a stake in his holy place, in order
that he[o] may brighten our eyes and grant us a little sustenance in our slavery. 9 For
we are slaves; yet our God has not forsaken us in our slavery, but has extended to
us his steadfast love before the kings of Persia, to give us new life to set up the
house of our God, to repair its ruins, and to give us a wall in Judea and Jerusalem.
10 "And now, our God, what shall we say after this? For we have forsaken your
commandments, 11 which you commanded by your servants the prophets, saying,
'The land that you are entering to possess is a land unclean with the pollutions of
the peoples of the lands, with their abominations. They have filled it from end to
end with their uncleanness. 12 Therefore do not give your daughters to their sons,
neither take their daughters for your sons, and never seek their peace or prosperity,
so that you may be strong and eat the good of the land and leave it for an inheritance
to your children forever.' 13 After all that has come upon us for our evil deeds and
for our great guilt, seeing that you, our God, have punished us less than our iniquities deserved and have given us such a remnant as this, 14 shall we break your commandments again and intermarry with the peoples who practice these
abominations? Would you not be angry with us until you destroy us without remnant or survivor? 15 O LORD, God of Israel, you are just, but we have escaped as a
remnant, as is now the case. Here we are before you in our guilt, though no one can
face you because of this."

9.2 Ex 34.16 Deut 7.3-6 Ezra 10.16-44 Neh 13.23,24
9.3 Josh 7.6 2 Kgs 18.37 19.1 Neh 1.4 Job 2.12,13
9.4 Ex 29.38,39
9.6 2 Chron 28.9
9.7 2 Kgs 24.1-4 2 Chron 36.16-20
9.8 2 Kgs 19.4,30, 31 Isa 1.9 Jer 44.14
9.9 Ex 1.11-14 Neh 9.36,37 Ps 106.45,46 Ezek 11.16
9.12 Deut 7.3 Josh 1.6-9 23.12,13 Ezra 9.2
9.14 Num 16.21,22, 45,46 Deut 9.7,8,13, 14 Ezra 9.2
9.15 Neh 9.33,34 Job 9.2,3 Ps 130.3 Dan 9.7-11 Rom 3.19; 10.3

[o] Heb *our God*

9.2 Some Israelites had married heathen spouses and lost track of God's purpose for them. The New Testament says that believers should not marry unbelievers (2 Corinthians 6.14). Such marriages cannot have unity in the most important issue in life – commitment and obedience to God. Because marriage involves two people becoming one, faith may become an issue, and one spouse may have to compromise beliefs for the sake of unity. Many people discount this problem only to regret it later. Don't allow emotion or passion to blind you to the ultimate importance of marrying someone with whom you can be united spiritually.

9.3 A mantle was a wraparound cloak or coat.

9.5–15 After learning about the sins of the people, Ezra fell to his knees in prayer. His heartfelt prayer provides a good perspective on sin. He recognized: (1) that sin is serious (9.6); (2) that no one sins without affecting others (9.7); (3) that he was not sinless, although he didn't have a heathen wife (9.10ff); (4) that God's love and mercy had spared the nation when they did nothing to deserve it (9.8, 9, 15). It is easy to view sin lightly in a world that sees sin as inconsequential, but we should view sin as seriously as Ezra did.

9.5–15 Ezra's prayer confessed the sins of his people. Although he had not sinned in the way his people had, he identified with their sins. With weeping, he expressed shame for sin, fear of the consequences, and desire that the people would come to their senses and repent. His prayer moved the people to tears (10.1). Ezra demonstrated the need for a holy community around the rebuilt temple. We need a holy community in our local churches too. Even when we sin in the worst imaginable way, we can turn to God with prayers of repentance.

9.9 Building a wall was not only a matter of civic pride or architectural beauty, it was essential for security and defense against robbers and marauders (see 9.7).

9.15 Ezra recognized that if God gave the people the justice they deserved, they would not be able to stand before him. Often we cry out for justice when we feel abused and unfairly treated. In those moments, we forget the reality of our own sin and the righteous judgment we deserve. How fortunate we are that God gives us mercy and grace rather than only justice. The next time you ask God for fair and just treatment, pause to think what would happen if God gave you what you really deserve. Plead instead for his mercy.

The people confess their sin

10 While Ezra prayed and made confession, weeping and throwing himself down before the house of God, a very great assembly of men, women, and children gathered to him out of Israel; the people also wept bitterly. 2 Shecaniah son of Jehiel, of the descendants of Elam, addressed Ezra, saying, "We have broken faith with our God and have married foreign women from the peoples of the land, but even now there is hope for Israel in spite of this. 3 So now let us make a covenant with our God to send away all these wives and their children, according to the counsel of my lord and of those who tremble at the commandment of our God; and let it be done according to the law. 4 Take action, for it is your duty, and we are with you; be strong, and do it." 5 Then Ezra stood up and made the leading priests, the Levites, and all Israel swear that they would do as had been said. So they swore.

6 Then Ezra withdrew from before the house of God, and went to the chamber of Jehohanan son of Eliashib, where he spent the night.[p] He did not eat bread or drink water, for he was mourning over the faithlessness of the exiles. 7 They made a proclamation throughout Judah and Jerusalem to all the returned exiles that they should assemble at Jerusalem, 8 and that if any did not come within three days, by order of the officials and the elders all their property should be forfeited, and they themselves banned from the congregation of the exiles.

9 Then all the people of Judah and Benjamin assembled at Jerusalem within the three days; it was the ninth month, on the twentieth day of the month. All the people sat in the open square before the house of God, trembling because of this matter and because of the heavy rain. 10 Then Ezra the priest stood up and said to them, "You have trespassed and married foreign women, and so increased the guilt of Israel. 11 Now make confession to the LORD the God of your ancestors, and do his will; separate yourselves from the peoples of the land and from the foreign wives." 12 Then all the assembly answered with a loud voice, "It is so; we must do as you have said. 13 But the people are many, and it is a time of heavy rain; we cannot stand in the open. Nor is this a task for one day or for two, for many of us have transgressed in this matter. 14 Let our officials represent the whole assembly, and let all in our towns who have taken foreign wives come at appointed times, and with them the elders and judges of every town, until the fierce wrath of our God on this account is averted from us." 15 Only Jonathan son of Asahel and Jahzeiah son of Tikvah opposed this, and Meshullam and Shabbethai the Levites supported them.

16 Then the returned exiles did so. Ezra the priest selected men,[q] heads of families, according to their families, each of them designated by name. On the first day of the tenth month they sat down to examine the matter. 17 By the first day of the first month they had come to the end of all the men who had married foreign women.

The men who married heathen wives

18 There were found of the descendants of the priests who had married foreign women, of the descendants of Jeshua son of Jozadak and his brothers: Maaseiah,

10.2 Ezra 10.11
10.3 Deut 7.2,3; 24.1; 29.12; Josh 1.17,18; Mt 5.32
10.4 Josh 1.6-9; 1 Chron 28.10
10.5 Ezra 10.3; Neh 5.12; 13.25
10.6 Deut 9.18
10.9 1 Sam 12.17,18; Jer 10.10,13
10.11 Ezra 10.2; Neh 13.3; 2 Cor 6.17
10.14 Num 25.4; Deut 13.17; 2 Chron 29.10; Ezra 9.14

p 1 Esdras 9.2: Heb *where he went* q 1 Esdras 9.16: Syr: Heb *And there were selected Ezra,*

10.3 Why were the people commanded to divorce their wives and leave their children? Although the measure was extreme, intermarriage to heathens was strictly forbidden (Deuteronomy 7.3, 4), and even the priests and Levites had intermarried. This could be compared today to a Christian marrying a devil worshiper. Although a severe solution, it only involved 113 of the approximately 29,000 families.

Ezra's strong act, though very difficult for some, was necessary to preserve Israel as a nation committed to God. Some of the exiles of the northern kingdom of Israel had lost both their spiritual and physical identity through intermarriage. Their heathen spouses had caused the people to worship idols. Ezra did not want this to happen to the exiles of the southern kingdom of Judah.

10.3, 4, 11 Following Ezra's earnest prayer, the people admitted their sin to God. Then they asked for direction in restoring their relationship with God. True repentance does not end with words of confession – that would be mere lip service. It must lead to corrected behavior and changed attitudes. When you sin and are truly sorry, confess this to God, ask his forgiveness, and accept his grace and mercy. Then, as an act of thankfulness for your forgiveness, make the needed corrections.

10.8 To forfeit one's property meant to be disinherited: to lose one's legal right to own land. This was to insure that no pagan children would inherit Israel's land. In addition, the person who refused to come to Jerusalem would be "banned from the congregation" – excluded from the assembly and not allowed to worship in the temple. The Jews considered this a horrible punishment.

Eliezer, Jarib, and Gedaliah. [19]They pledged themselves to send away their wives,
and their guilt offering was a ram of the flock for their guilt. [20]Of the descendants
of Immer: Hanani and Zebadiah. [21]Of the descendants of Harim: Maaseiah, Elijah,
Shemaiah, Jehiel, and Uzziah. [22]Of the descendants of Pashhur: Elioenai, Maaseiah, Ishmael, Nethanel, Jozabad, and Elasah.
23 Of the Levites: Jozabad, Shimei, Kelaiah (that is, Kelita), Pethahiah, Judah,
and Eliezer. [24]Of the singers: Eliashib. Of the gatekeepers: Shallum, Telem, and
Uri.
25 And of Israel: of the descendants of Parosh: Ramiah, Izziah, Malchijah,
Mijamin, Eleazar, Hashabiah,[r] and Benaiah. [26]Of the descendants of Elam: Mattaniah, Zechariah, Jehiel, Abdi, Jeremoth, and Elijah. [27]Of the descendants of
Zattu: Elioenai, Eliashib, Mattaniah, Jeremoth, Zabad, and Aziza. [28]Of the descendants of Bebai: Jehohanan, Hananiah, Zabbai, and Athlai. [29]Of the descendants of Bani: Meshullam, Malluch, Adaiah, Jashub, Sheal, and Jeremoth. [30]Of
the descendants of Pahath-moab: Adna, Chelal, Benaiah, Maaseiah, Mattaniah,
Bezalel, Binnui, and Manasseh. [31]Of the descendants of Harim: Eliezer, Isshijah,
Malchijah, Shemaiah, Shimeon, [32]Benjamin, Malluch, and Shemariah. [33]Of the
descendants of Hashum: Mattenai, Mattattah, Zabad, Eliphelet, Jeremai, Manasseh, and Shimei. [34]Of the descendants of Bani: Maadai, Amram, Uel, [35]Benaiah,
Bedeiah, Cheluhi, [36]Vaniah, Meremoth, Eliashib, [37]Mattaniah, Mattenai, and Ja-
asu. [38]Of the descendants of Binnui:[s] Shimei, [39]Shelemiah, Nathan, Adaiah,
[40]Machnadebai, Shashai, Sharai, [41]Azarel, Shelemiah, Shemariah, [42]Shallum,
Amariah, and Joseph. [43]Of the descendants of Nebo: Jeiel, Mattithiah, Zabad, Ze-
bina, Jaddai, Joel, and Benaiah. [44]All these had married foreign women, and they
sent them away with their children.[t]

[r] 1 Esdras 9.26 Gk: Heb *Malchijah* [s] Gk: Heb *Bani, Binnui* [t] 1 Esdras 9.36; Meaning of Heb uncertain

10.44 The book of Ezra opens with God's temple in ruins and the people of Judah captive in Babylon. Ezra tells of the return of God's people, the rebuilding of the temple, and the restoration of the sacrificial worship system. Similarly, God is able to restore and rebuild the lives of people today. No one is so far away from God that he or she cannot be restored. Repentance is all that is required. No matter how far we have strayed or how long it has been since we have worshiped God, he is able to restore our relationship to him and rebuild our lives.

THE MEDO-PERSIAN EMPIRE

The events in the books of Ezra, Nehemiah, and Esther took place during the rule of the Medes and Persians. These two kingdoms came from the northeast of Mesopotamia (present-day Iran) and joined forces to defeat the Babylonians (Daniel 5.30, 31). The Persians ruled until the rise of the Greek Empire under Alexander the Great. The Persians had a relaxed policy toward their captives, allowing them to own land and homes. King Cyrus of Persia went a step further allowing many groups of exiles, including the Jews, to return to their homelands. In the books of Ezra and Nehemiah, groups of Jewish exiles were allowed to return to Palestine to rebuild their capital city and temple. The first group of returnees led by Zerubbabel arrived in 537 B.C. The second group returned with Ezra in 458 B.C. Nehemiah came in 455 B.C. to encourage the rebuilding of Jerusalem's wall. Esther became queen of the kingdom in 479 B.C., which was between the first and second returns.

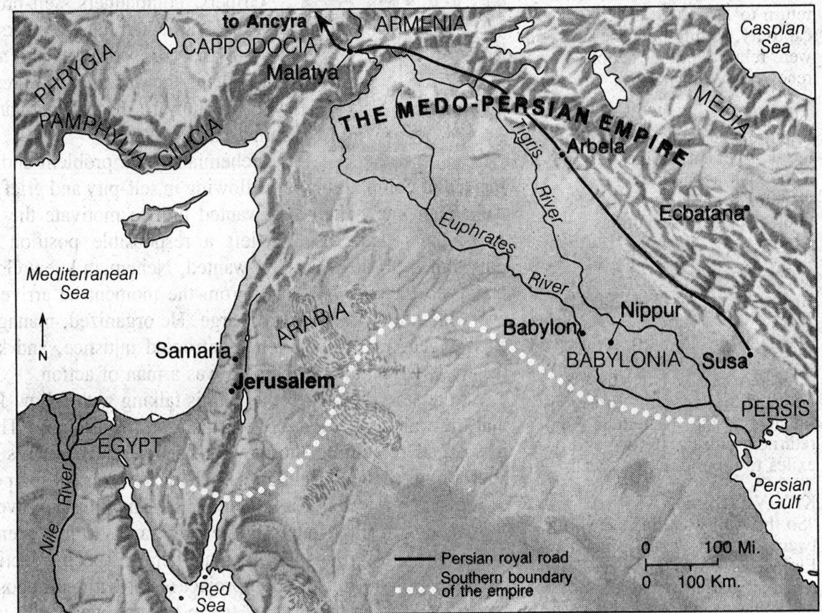

NEHEMIAH

Jerusalem destroyed; exiles go to Babylon 586 B.C.

First exiles return to Jerusalem 537

Temple completed 516

VITAL STATISTICS

PURPOSE:
Nehemiah is the last of the Old Testament historical books. It records the history of the third return to Jerusalem after captivity, telling how the walls were rebuilt and the people renewed in their faith.

AUTHOR:
Much of the book is written in the first person, suggesting Nehemiah as the author. Nehemiah probably wrote the book with Ezra serving as editor.

DATE WRITTEN:
Approximately 445–432 B.C.

SETTING:
Zerubbabel led the first return to Jerusalem in 537 B.C. In 458, Ezra led the second return. Finally, in 445, Nehemiah returned with the third group of exiles to rebuild the city walls.

KEY VERSES:
"So the wall was finished on the twenty-fifth day of the month Elul, in fifty-two days. And when all our enemies heard of it, all the nations around us were afraid and fell greatly in their own esteem; for they perceived that this work had been accomplished with the help of our God" (6.15, 16).

KEY PEOPLE:
Nehemiah, Ezra, Sanballat, Tobiah

KEY PLACE:
Jerusalem

SPECIAL FEATURES:
The book shows the fulfillment of the prophecies of Zechariah and Daniel concerning the rebuilding of Jerusalem's walls.

"WHAT this church needs is . . . !" "I can't believe our government officials. If I were there I would . . . !" "Our schools are really in bad shape. Someone ought to do something!"

Gripers, complainers, self-proclaimed prophets, and "armchair quarterbacks" abound. It is easy to analyze, scrutinze, and *talk* about all the problems in the world. But we really need people who will not just discuss a situation, but will *do* something about it!

Nehemiah saw a problem and was distressed. Instead of complaining or wallowing in self-pity and grief, he took action. Nehemiah knew that God wanted him to motivate the Jews to rebuild Jerusalem's walls, so he left a responsible position in the Persian government to do what God wanted. Nehemiah knew God could use his talents to get the job done. From the moment he arrived in Jerusalem, everyone knew who was in charge. He organized, managed, supervised, encouraged, met opposition, confronted injustice, and kept going until the walls were built. Nehemiah was a man of action.

As the story begins, Nehemiah is talking with fellow Jews who report that the walls and gates of Jerusalem are in disrepair. This is disturbing news, and rebuilding those walls becomes Nehemiah's burden. At the appropriate time, Nehemiah asks King Artaxerxes for permission to go to Jerusalem to rebuild its fallen walls. The king approves.

Armed with royal letters, Nehemiah travels to Jerusalem. He organizes the people into groups and assigns them to specific sections of the wall (chapter 3). The construction project is not without opposition, however. Sanballat, Tobiah, and others try to halt the work with insults, ridicule, threats, and sabotage. Some of the workers become fearful; others become weary. In each case, Nehemiah employs a strategy to frustrate the enemies—prayer, encouragement, guard duty, consolidation (chapter 4). But a different problem arises—an internal one. Rich Jews are profiteering off the plight of their working countrymen. Hearing of their oppression and greed, Nehemiah confronts the extortioners face to face (chapter 5). With the walls almost complete, Sanballat, Tobiah, and company try one last time to stop Nehemiah. But Nehemiah stands firm, and the wall is finished in just 52 days. What a tremendous monument to God's love and faithfulness. Enemies and friends alike knew that God had helped (chapter 6).

After building the walls, Nehemiah continues to organize the people, taking a census and appointing gatekeepers, Levites, and other officials (chapter 7). Ezra leads the city in worship and Bible instruction (chapters 8, 9). This leads to a reaffirmation of faith and religious revival as the people promise to serve God faithfully (chapters 10, 11).

Nehemiah closes with the listing of the clans and their leaders, the dedication of the new wall of Jerusalem, and the purging of sin from the land (chapters 12, 13). As you read this book, watch Nehemiah in action. Then determine to be a person on whom God can depend to *act* for him in the world.

Xerxes becomes king of Persia 486	Artaxerxes I becomes king of Persia 465	Ezra comes to Jerusalem 458	Nehemiah comes to Jerusalem; wall completed 445	Nehemiah returns to Babylon 433	Nehemiah goes back to Jerusalem 432	Malachi begins his ministry 430(?)

THE BLUEPRINT

A. REBUILDING THE WALL (1.1—7.73) 1. Nehemiah returns to Jerusalem 2. Nehemiah leads the people	Nehemiah's life is an example of leadership and organization. Giving up a comfortable and wealthy position in Persia, he returned to the fractured homeland of his ancestors and rallied the people to rebuild Jerusalem's wall. In the face of opposition, he used wise defense measures to care for the people and to keep the project moving. To accomplish more for the sake of God's kingdom, we must pray, persevere, and sacrifice, as did Nehemiah.
B. REFORMING THE PEOPLE (8.1—13.31) 1. Ezra renews the covenant 2. Nehemiah establishes policies	After the wall was rebuilt, Ezra read the law to the people, bringing about national repentance. Nehemiah and Ezra were very different people, yet God used them both to lead the nation. Remember, there is a place for you in God's work even if you're different from most other people. God uses each person in a unique way to accomplish his purposes.

MEGATHEMES

THEME	EXPLANATION	IMPORTANCE
Vision	Although the Jews completed the temple in 516 B.C., the city walls remained in shambles for the next 70 years. These walls represented power, protection, and beauty to the city of Jerusalem. They were also desperately needed to protect the temple from attack and to insure the continuity of worship. God put the desire to rebuild the walls in Nehemiah's heart, giving him a vision for the work.	Does God have a vision for us? Are there "walls" that need to be built today? God still wants his people to be united and trained to do his work. As we recognize deep needs in our world, God can give us the vision and desire to "build." With that vision, we can mobilize others to pray and put together an action plan.
Prayer	Both Nehemiah and Ezra responded to problems with prayer. When Nehemiah began his work, he recognized the problem, immediately prayed, and then acted on the problem.	Prayer is still God's mighty force in solving problems today. Prayer and action go hand in hand. Through prayer, God guides our preparation, teamwork, and diligent efforts to carry out his will.
Leadership	Nehemiah demonstrated excellent leadership. He was spiritually ready to heed God's call. He used careful planning, teamwork, problem solving, and courage to get the work done. Although he had tremendous faith, he never avoided the extra work necessary for good leadership.	Being God's leader is not just gaining recognition, holding a position, or being the boss. It requires planning, hard work, courage, and perseverance. Positive expectations are never a substitute for doing the difficult work. And in order to lead others, you need to listen for God's direction in your own life.
Problems	After the work began, Nehemiah faced scorn, slander, and threats from enemies, as well as fear, conflict, and discouragement from his own workers. Although these problems were difficult, they did not stop Nehemiah from finishing the work.	When difficulties come, there is a tendency for conflict and discouragement to set in. We must recognize that there are no triumphs without troubles. When problems arise, we must face them squarely and press on to complete God's work.
Repentance/ Revival	Although God had enabled them to build the wall, the work wasn't complete until the people rebuilt their lives spiritually. Ezra instructed the people in God's Word. As they listened, they recognized the sin in their lives, admitted it, and took steps to remove it.	Recognizing and admitting sin is not enough; revival must result in reform, or it is merely the expression of enthusiasm. God does not want halfhearted measures. We must not only remove sin from our lives, but also ask God to move into the center of all we do.

A. REBUILDING THE WALL (1.1–7.73)

Despite the fact that the returned exiles had been in Jerusalem for many years, the walls of the city remained unrepaired, leaving its people defenseless and vulnerable. Upon hearing this news, Nehemiah seeks permission from the Persian king to go to Jerusalem. Arriving in Jerusalem, he mobilizes the people to begin rebuilding the wall. Faced with opposition, both from without and from within, Nehemiah perseveres until the project is complete and the city resettled. Seemingly impossible tasks can be accomplished when God is helping those who honor him and when their efforts are united.

1. Nehemiah returns to Jerusalem

Nehemiah receives tragic news about Jerusalem

1 The words of Nehemiah son of Hacaliah. In the month of Chislev, in the twen- **1.1**
tieth year, while I was in Susa the capital, 2 one of my brothers, Hanani, came Neh 2.1; 10.1 Esth 1.2
with certain men from Judah; and I asked them about the Jews that survived, those Zech 7.1
who had escaped the captivity, and about Jerusalem. 3 They replied, "The survivors **1.2** Neh 7.2
there in the province who escaped captivity are in great trouble and shame; the wall **1.3**
of Jerusalem is broken down, and its gates have been destroyed by fire." Neh 2.3,17

Nehemiah prays for the people of Israel

4 When I heard these words I sat down and wept, and mourned for days, fasting **1.4**
and praying before the God of heaven. 5 I said, "O LORD God of heaven, the great and Ezra 9.3; 10.1 Dan 9.3
awesome God who keeps covenant and steadfast love with those who love him
and keep his commandments; 6 let your ear be attentive and your eyes open to hear **1.6**
the prayer of your servant that I now pray before you day and night for your ser- Deut 28.14,15 Ezra 10.1
vants, the people of Israel, confessing the sins of the people of Israel, which we Ps 32.5 Dan 9.8,17-20
have sinned against you. Both I and my family have sinned. 7 We have offended
you deeply, failing to keep the commandments, the statutes, and the ordinances
that you commanded your servant Moses. 8 Remember the word that you com- **1.8** Lev 26.33
manded your servant Moses, 'If you are unfaithful, I will scatter you among the **1.9**
peoples; 9 but if you return to me and keep my commandments and do them, though Deut 12.5 30.2-4
your outcasts are under the farthest skies, I will gather them from there and bring Jer 29.11-14
them to the place at which I have chosen to establish my name.' 10 They are your **1.10** Ex 32.11
servants and your people, whom you redeemed by your great power and your Deut 9.29

1.1 Nehemiah wasn't the first of the exiles to return to Jerusalem. Zerubbabel had led the first group back in 537 B.C., more than 90 years earlier (Ezra 1; 2). Ezra followed with a second group in 458 B.C. (Ezra 7), and now Nehemiah was ready to lead the third major return to Jerusalem (445 B.C.). When he arrived after a three-month journey, he saw the completed temple and became acquainted with others who had returned to their homeland.

But Nehemiah also found a disorganized group of people and a defenseless city with no walls to protect it. Before the exile, Israel had its own language, king, army, and identity. Now it had none of these. What the Jews lacked most was leadership; there was no one to show them where to start and what direction to take as they tried to rebuild their city. As soon as Nehemiah arrived he began a "back to the basics" program. He helped care for the people's physical needs by setting up a fair system of government and rebuilding Jerusalem's walls. He also cared for their spiritual needs by rebuilding broken lives. Nehemiah is a model of committed, God-honoring leadership, and his book contains many lessons that still apply today.

1.2–4 Nehemiah was concerned about Jerusalem because it was the Jews' holy city. As Judah's capital city, it represented Jewish national identity, and it was blessed with God's special presence in the temple. Jewish history centered around the city from the time of Abraham's gifts to Melchizedek, king of Salem (Genesis 14.17–20), to the days when Solomon built the glorious temple (1 Kings 7.51) and throughout the history of the kings. Nehemiah loved his homeland even though he had lived his whole life in Babylon. He wanted to return to Jerusalem to reunite the Jews and to remove the shame of Jerusalem's broken-down walls. This would bring glory to God and restore the reality and power of God's presence among his people.

1.4 Nehemiah broke down and cried when he heard that Jerusalem's walls still had not been rebuilt. Why did this upset him? Walls mean little in most present-day cities, but in Nehemiah's day they were essential. They offered safety from raids and symbolized strength and peace. Nehemiah was also upset for his people, the Jews, who had been stifled by a previous edict that kept them from rebuilding their walls (Ezra 4.6–23).

1.4 Nehemiah was deeply grieved about the condition of Jerusalem, but he didn't just brood about it. After his initial grief, he poured his heart out to God (1.5–11) and looked for ways to improve the situation. He put all his resources of knowledge, experience, and organization into determining what should be done. When tragic news comes to you, first pray. Then seek ways to move beyond grief to specific action that helps those who need it.

1.5ff Nehemiah fasted and prayed for several days, expressing his sorrow for Israel's sin and his desire that Jerusalem again come alive with the worship of the one true God. Nehemiah demonstrates the elements of effective prayer: (1) praise, (2) thanksgiving, (3) repentance, (4) specific request, and (5) commitment.

Heartfelt prayers like Nehemiah's can help clarify (1) any problem you may be facing, (2) God's great power to help you, and (3) the job you have to do. By the end of his prayer time, Nehemiah knew what action he had to take (1.11). When God's people pray, difficult decisions fall into proper perspective, and appropriate actions follow.

1.11 Gen 40.21 Neh 2.1 strong hand. 11 O Lord, let your ear be attentive to the prayer of your servant, and
to the prayer of your servants who delight in revering your name. Give success to
your servant today, and grant him mercy in the sight of this man!"
At the time, I was cupbearer to the king.

The king permits Nehemiah to return

2.1 Neh 1.11 **2** In the month of Nisan, in the twentieth year of King Artaxerxes, when wine
was served him, I carried the wine and gave it to the king. Now, I had never
been sad in his presence before. 2 So the king said to me, "Why is your face sad,
since you are not sick? This can only be sadness of the heart." Then I was very
2.3 Neh 1.3 much afraid. 3 I said to the king, "May the king live forever! Why should my face
not be sad, when the city, the place of my ancestors' graves, lies waste, and its
gates have been destroyed by fire?" 4 Then the king said to me, "What do you request?" So I prayed to the God of heaven. 5 Then I said to the king, "If it pleases the
king, and if your servant has found favor with you, I ask that you send me to Judah,

HOW NEHEMIAH USED PRAYER

Reference	*Occasion*	*Summary of his Prayer*	*What Prayer Accomplished*	*Our Prayers*
1.4–11	After receiving the bad news about the state of Jerusalem's walls	Recognized God's holiness. Asked for a hearing. Confessed sin. Asked for specific help in approaching the king	Included God in Nehemiah's plans and concerns. Prepared Nehemiah's heart and gave God room to work	How often do you pour out your heart to God? How often do you give him a specific request to answer?
2.4	During his conversation with the king	"Here's where you can help, God!"	Put the expected results in God's hands	Giving God the credit keeps us from taking the credit ourselves.
4.4, 5	After being mocked by Tobiah and Sanballat	"They're mocking you, God. You decide what to do with them."	Expressed anger to God, but Nehemiah did not take matters into his own hands	We are prone to do exactly the opposite—take matters into our hands and not tell God how we feel.
4.9	After threats of attack by enemies	"We are in your hands, God. We'll keep our weapons handy in case you want us to use them."	Trusted God and took necessary precautions	Trusting God does not mean we do nothing. Action does not mean we do not trust.
6.9	Responding to threats	"Oh Lord God, please strengthen me!"	Showed Nehemiah's reliance on God for strength and stability	How often do you ask God for help when under pressure?
13.29	Reflecting on the actions of his enemies	Asked God to deal with the enemies and their evil plans	Took away the compulsion to get revenge, and entrusted justice to God	When did you last settle a desire for revenge by turning the matter over to God?
5.19; 13.14, 22, 31	Reflecting on his own efforts to serve God	"Remember me, God."	Kept clear in Nehemiah's mind his own motives for action	How many of your actions today will be done with the purpose of pleasing God?

1.11 Nehemiah was in a unique position to speak to the king. He was the trusted cupbearer who ensured the safety and quality of the king's food and drink. Nehemiah was concerned, prayerful, and prepared as he looked for the right opportunity to tell the king about God's people. Each of us is unique and capable of serving no matter what our position. Just as Nehemiah used his place as the king's trusted servant to intercede for his people, we can use our present positions to serve God.

2.2 Nehemiah was frightened when the king noticed his sad appearance. It was dangerous to show sorrow before the king, who could execute anyone who displeased him. Anyone wearing mourning clothes could not even enter the palace (Esther 4.2).

2.2, 3 Nehemiah wasn't ashamed to admit his fear, but he refused to allow fear to stop him from doing what God had called him to do. When we allow our fears to rule us, we make fear more powerful than God. Is there a task God wants you to do, but fear is holding you back? God is greater than all your fears. To recognize why you are afraid is the first step in committing it to God. Realize that if God has called you to a task, he will help you accomplish it.

2.4 With little time to think, Nehemiah quickly prayed. Eight times in this book we read that he prayed spontaneously (2.4; 4.4–5, 9; 5.19; 6.14; 13.14, 22, 29). Nehemiah prayed at any time, even while talking with others. He knew that God is always in charge, is always present, and hears and answers every prayer. He could confidently pray throughout the day because he had established an intimate relationship with God during times of extended prayer (1.4–7). If we want to reach God with our emergency prayers, we need to take time to cultivate a strong relationship with God through times of in-depth prayer.

2.5, 6 The king asked Nehemiah how long he would be gone. The Bible does not record Nehemiah's immediate answer, but he ended up staying in Jerusalem 12 years (5.14; 13.6).

to the city of my ancestors' graves, so that I may rebuild it." 6The king said to me
(the queen also was sitting beside him), "How long will you be gone, and when will
you return?" So it pleased the king to send me, and I set him a date. 7Then I said **2.7** Ezra 6.6; 7.21 8.36 Neh 2.9
to the king, "If it pleases the king, let letters be given me to the governors of the
province Beyond the River, that they may grant me passage until I arrive in Judah;
8and a letter to Asaph, the keeper of the king's forest, directing him to give me **2.8** Neh 7.2 Eccles 2.5,6
timber to make beams for the gates of the temple fortress, and for the wall of the
city, and for the house that I shall occupy." And the king granted me what I asked,
for the gracious hand of my God was upon me.
9 Then I came to the governors of the province Beyond the River, and gave **2.9** Ezra 8.22 Neh 2.7
them the king's letters. Now the king had sent officers of the army and cavalry with
me. 10When Sanballat the Horonite and Tobiah the Ammonite official heard this, **2.10** Neh 2.19 4.1-3; 6.1
it displeased them greatly that someone had come to seek the welfare of the people
of Israel.

2. Nehemiah leads the people

Nehemiah secretly inspects the wall

11 So I came to Jerusalem and was there for three days. 12Then I got up during
the night, I and a few men with me; I told no one what my God had put into my
heart to do for Jerusalem. The only animal I took was the animal I rode. 13I went **2.13** Neh 1.3; 2.15 3.13; 12.31
out by night by the Valley Gate past the Dragon's Spring and to the Dung Gate, and
I inspected the walls of Jerusalem that had been broken down and its gates that had
been destroyed by fire. 14Then I went on to the Fountain Gate and to the King's **2.14** 2 Kgs 20.20 2 Chron 32.30 Neh 2.13; 3.15
Pool; but there was no place for the animal I was riding to continue. 15So I went up
by way of the valley by night and inspected the wall. Then I turned back and entered by the Valley Gate, and so returned. 16The officials did not know where I had

---

2.7, 8 After his prayer, Nehemiah asked the king for permission to go to Judah. As soon as he got a positive answer, he began asking for additional help. Sometimes when we have needs, we hesitate to ask the right people for help because we are afraid to approach them. Not Nehemiah! He went directly to the person who could help him the most. Don't be reluctant to ask those who are most able to help. They may be more interested and approachable than you think. God's answers to prayer may come as a result of our asking others.

2.9, 10, 19 When Nehemiah arrived in Judah, he was greeted with opposition. Opposition to the rebuilding of Jerusalem had been going on for 90 years by those who settled in the area when the Jews were taken captive. In every generation there are those who hate God's people and try to block God's purpose. When you attempt to do God's work, some will oppose you; some will even hope you fail. If you expect opposition, you will be prepared rather than surprised (1 John 3.13). Knowing that God is behind your task is the best incentive to move ahead in the face of opposition.

2.10 Why were Sanballat and Tobiah, government officials of nearby Samaria, so concerned about the arrival of Nehemiah and his small band of exiles? There are several possible reasons: (1) When Zerubbabel first returned with his group (Ezra 1; 2), his refusal to accept help from the Samaritans had caused bad relations. (2) Nehemiah was no ordinary exile; he was the king's personal adviser and cupbearer, arriving in Jerusalem with the king's approval to build and fortify the city. If anyone could rebuild Jerusalem, he could. A rebuilt Jerusalem was a threat to the authority of the Samaritan officials who had been in charge of the land since Judah's exile. (3) This was the third group to return from exile. The increasing number of people in Jerusalem made Sanballat and Tobiah angry. They did not want returned exiles taking control of the land and threatening their secure position.

2.11–17 Nehemiah arrived quietly in Jerusalem and spent several days carefully observing and assessing the damage to the walls. Following this time of thoughtful consideration, he confidently presented his plan. Nehemiah demonstrated an excellent approach to problem solving. He got firsthand information and carefully considered the situation. Then he presented a realistic strategy. Before jumping into a project, follow Nehemiah's example and plan ahead. Check your information to make sure your ideas will work—be realistic. Then you will be able to present your plan with confidence.

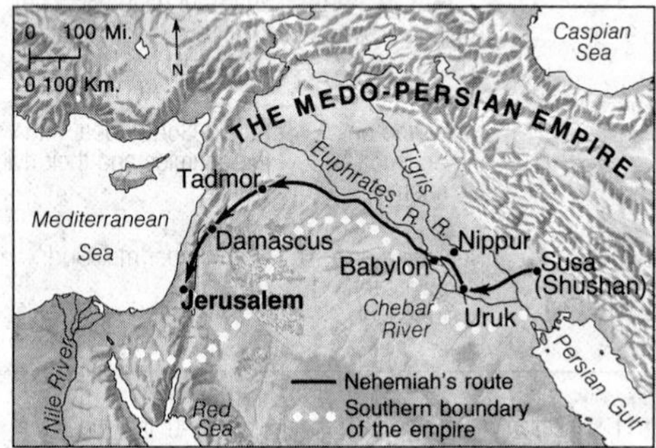

NEHEMIAH GOES TO JERUSALEM Nehemiah worked in Susa as a personal assistant for the king of the vast Medo-Persian Empire. When he heard that the rebuilding projects in Jerusalem were progressing slowly, he asked the king if he could go there to help his people complete the task of rebuilding their city's walls. The king agreed to let him go; so he left as soon as possible, traveling along much the same route Ezra had taken.

2.14 The walls were so broken-down that Nehemiah's animal couldn't get through, so Nehemiah had to inspect that section on foot.

2.16 Nehemiah kept his mission a secret and surveyed the walls by moonlight to avoid unhealthy gossip about his arrival and to prevent enemies from being alerted to his plans. Only after plan-

gone or what I was doing; I had not yet told the Jews, the priests, the nobles, the
officials, and the rest that were to do the work.

Nehemiah calls the people to begin rebuilding

2.17 Neh 1.3; 2.14 17 Then I said to them, "You see the trouble we are in, how Jerusalem lies in
ruins with its gates burned. Come, let us rebuild the wall of Jerusalem, so that we
may no longer suffer disgrace." 18 I told them that the hand of my God had been
gracious upon me, and also the words that the king had spoken to me. Then they
said, "Let us start building!" So they committed themselves to the common good.
2.19 Neh 2.10; 6.6 19 But when Sanballat the Horonite and Tobiah the Ammonite official, and Geshem
the Arab heard of it, they mocked and ridiculed us, saying, "What is this that you
2.20 Ezra 4.3 are doing? Are you rebelling against the king?" 20 Then I replied to them, "The God
of heaven is the one who will give us success, and we his servants are going to start
building; but you have no share or claim or historic right in Jerusalem."

The builders of the city wall

3.1 Neh 3.20,32; 12.39; 13.28; Jer 31.38 **3** Then the high priest Eliashib set to work with his fellow priests and rebuilt the
Sheep Gate. They consecrated it and set up its doors; they consecrated it as far
as the Tower of the Hundred and as far as the Tower of Hananel. 2 And the men of
3.2 Neh 7.36 Jericho built next to him. And next to them[a] Zaccur son of Imri built.
3 The sons of Hassenaah built the Fish Gate; they laid its beams and set up its

[a] Heb *him*

ning carefully would he be ready to go public with his mission from God. A premature announcement could have caused rivalry among the Jews as to the best way to begin. In this case, Nehemiah didn't need tedious planning sessions; he needed one plan that would bring quick action.

2.17, 18 Spiritual renewal often begins with one person's vision. Nehemiah had a vision, and he shared it with enthusiasm, inspiring Jerusalem's leaders to rebuild the walls.

We frequently underestimate people and don't challenge them with our dreams for God's work in the world. When God plants an idea in your mind to accomplish something for him, share it with others and trust the Holy Spirit to impress them with similar thoughts. Don't see yourself as the only one through whom God is working. Often God uses one person to express the vision and others to turn it into reality. When you encourage and inspire others, you put teamwork into action to accomplish God's goals.

2.19 Sanballat and Tobiah labeled the rebuilding of Jerusalem's walls a rebellious act, probably threatening to report the builders as traitors. These enemies also ridiculed Nehemiah, saying the walls could never be rebuilt because the damage was too extensive. Nehemiah did not tell them he already had permission from the king to rebuild. Instead, he simply said he had God's approval—that was enough.

3.1 The high priest is the first person mentioned who pitched in and helped with the work. Spiritual leaders must lead by word and action. The Sheep Gate was the gate used to bring sheep into the city to the temple for sacrifices. Nehemiah had the priests repair this gate and section of the wall, respecting the priests' area of interest and at the same time emphasizing the priority of worship.

3.1ff All the citizens of Jerusalem did their part on the huge job of rebuilding the city wall. Similarly, the work of the church requires every member's effort in order for the body of Christ to function effectively (1 Corinthians 12.12–27). The body needs you! Are you doing your part? Find a place to serve God and start contributing whatever time, talent, and money is needed.

3.1ff Jerusalem was a large city, and because many roads converged there, it required many gates. In times of peace, the city gates were hubs of activity—city council was held there, and shopkeepers set up their wares along the entrance. Building the city walls and gates was not only a military priority, but also a boost for trade.

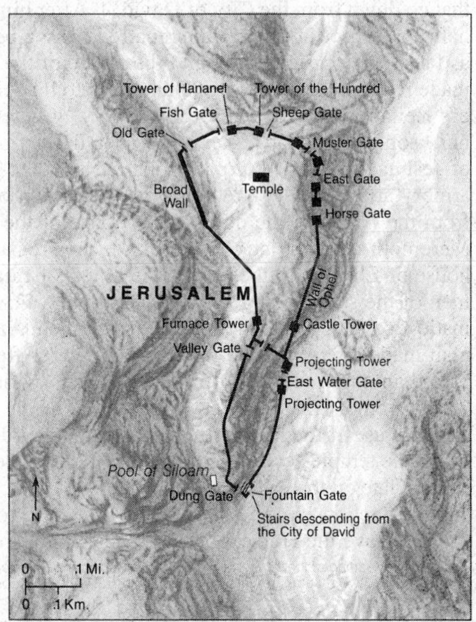

THE RESTORATION OF THE CITY WALLS Nehemiah takes us on a counter-clockwise tour around Jerusalem (beginning with the Sheep Gate). He describes for us each section, gate, and tower on the wall and who worked to rebuild it.

3.3 One of the main roads through Jerusalem entered the city through the Fish Gate (2 Chronicles 33.14). The fish market was near the gate, and merchants from Tyre, the Sea of Galilee, and other fishing areas entered this gate to sell their goods.

doors, its bolts, and its bars. 4 Next to them Meremoth son of Uriah son of Hakkoz **3.3**
made repairs. Next to them Meshullam son of Berechiah son of Meshezabel made Neh 12.39
repairs. Next to them Zadok son of Baana made repairs. 5 Next to them the Tekoites **3.5**
made repairs; but their nobles would not put their shoulders to the work of their Neh 3.27
Lord.[b]
6 Joiada son of Paseah and Meshullam son of Besodeiah repaired the Old Gate; **3.6**
they laid its beams and set up its doors, its bolts, and its bars. 7 Next to them repairs Neh 12.39
were made by Melatiah the Gibeonite and Jadon the Meronothite — the men of Gibeon and of Mizpah — who were under the jurisdiction of[c] the governor of the province Beyond the River. 8 Next to them Uzziel son of Harhaiah, one of the **3.8**
goldsmiths, made repairs. Next to him Hananiah, one of the perfumers, made re- Neh 3.31
pairs; and they restored Jerusalem as far as the Broad Wall. 9 Next to them Repha- **3.9**
iah son of Hur, ruler of half the district of[d] Jerusalem, made repairs. 10 Next to Neh 3.12,17
them Jedaiah son of Harumaph made repairs opposite his house; and next to him
Hattush son of Hashabneiah made repairs. 11 Malchijah son of Harim and Hasshub **3.11**
son of Pahath-moab repaired another section and the Tower of the Ovens. 12 Next Neh 12.38
to him Shallum son of Hallohesh, ruler of half the district of[d] Jerusalem, made **3.12** Neh 3.9
repairs, he and his daughters.
13 Hanun and the inhabitants of Zanoah repaired the Valley Gate; they rebuilt **3.13**
it and set up its doors, its bolts, and its bars, and repaired a thousand cubits of the Neh 2.13
wall, as far as the Dung Gate.
14 Malchijah son of Rechab, ruler of the district of[e] Beth-haccherem, repaired **3.14**
the Dung Gate; he rebuilt it and set up its doors, its bolts, and its bars. Neh 2.13; 3.13
15 And Shallum son of Col-hozeh, ruler of the district of[e] Mizpah, repaired the **3.15**
Fountain Gate; he rebuilt it and covered it and set up its doors, its bolts, and its bars; 2 Kgs 25.4,5 Neh 2.14; 12.37
and he built the wall of the Pool of Shelah of the king's garden, as far as the stairs
that go down from the City of David. 16 After him Nehemiah son of Azbuk, ruler of **3.16**
half the district of[d] Beth-zur, repaired from a point opposite the graves of David, 1 Kgs 14.28 2 Kgs 20.20
as far as the artificial pool and the house of the warriors. 17 After him the Levites 2 Chron 12.10, 11; 16.14
made repairs: Rehum son of Bani; next to him Hashabiah, ruler of half the district Neh 2.14
of[d] Keilah, made repairs for his district. 18 After him their kin made repairs: Binnui,[f] son of Henadad, ruler of half the district of[d] Keilah; 19 next to him Ezer son **3.19**
of Jeshua, ruler[g] of Mizpah, repaired another section opposite the ascent to the Neh 3.16 2 Chron 26.9
armory at the Angle. 20 After him Baruch son of Zabbai repaired another section **3.20**
from the Angle to the door of the house of the high priest Eliashib. 21 After him Neh 3.1
Meremoth son of Uriah son of Hakkoz repaired another section from the door of the
house of Eliashib to the end of the house of Eliashib. 22 After him the priests, the **3.22**
men of the surrounding area, made repairs. 23 After them Benjamin and Hasshub Neh 12.28
made repairs opposite their house. After them Azariah son of Maaseiah son of Ananiah made repairs beside his own house. 24 After him Binnui son of Henadad re- **3.25** Jer 32.2
paired another section, from the house of Azariah to the Angle and to the corner. **3.26**
25 Palal son of Uzai repaired opposite the Angle and the tower projecting from the Neh 3.27; 7.46 8.1,3; 11.21
upper house of the king at the court of the guard. After him Pedaiah son of Parosh 12.37
26 and the temple servants living[h] on Ophel made repairs up to a point opposite the **3.27** Neh 3.5,26
Water Gate on the east and the projecting tower. 27 After him the Tekoites repaired **3.28**
another section opposite the great projecting tower as far as the wall of Ophel. 2 Kgs 11.16 2 Chron 23.15
28 Above the Horse Gate the priests made repairs, each one opposite his own Jer 31.40

[b] Or *lords* [c] Meaning of Heb uncertain [d] Or *supervisor of half the portion assigned to* [e] Or *supervisor of the portion assigned to* [f] Gk Syr Compare verse 24, 10.9: Heb *Bavvai* [g] Or *supervisor* [h] Cn: Heb *were living*

3.5 The Tekoite nobles were lazy and wouldn't help. These men were the only ones who did not support the building project in Jerusalem. Every group, even every church, will have those who think they are too wise or important to work hard. Gentle encouragement doesn't seem to help. Sometimes the best policy is to ignore them. They may think they are getting away with something, but their inactivity will be remembered by all who worked hard.

3.12 Even Shallum's daughters helped with the difficult work of repairing the city walls. Rebuilding Jerusalem's walls was a matter of national emergency for the Jews, not just a civic beautification project. Nearly everyone was dedicated to the task and willing to work at it.

3.14 The Dung Gate was the gate through which the people carried their garbage to be burned in the Valley of Hinnom.

3.28 Each priest also repaired the wall opposite his own house, in addition to other sections. If each person was responsible for the

3.29 Jer 19.2 house. 29 After them Zadok son of Immer made repairs opposite his own house.
After him Shemaiah son of Shecaniah, the keeper of the East Gate, made repairs.
30 After him Hananiah son of Shelemiah and Hanun sixth son of Zalaph repaired
another section. After him Meshullam son of Berechiah made repairs opposite his
3.31 Neh 3.1,8 living quarters. 31 After him Malchijah, one of the goldsmiths, made repairs as far
as the house of the temple servants and of the merchants, opposite the Muster
3.32 Neh 3.1; 12.39 Gate,[i] and to the upper room of the corner. 32 And between the upper room of the
corner and the Sheep Gate the goldsmiths and the merchants made repairs.

Enemies oppose rebuilding the wall

4.1 Ezra 4.9,10 Neh 2.10 4 [j] Now when Sanballat heard that we were building the wall, he was angry and
greatly enraged, and he mocked the Jews. 2 He said in the presence of his associates and of the army of Samaria, "What are these feeble Jews doing? Will they
restore things? Will they sacrifice? Will they finish it in a day? Will they revive the
4.3 Neh 2.10; 4.1 stones out of the heaps of rubbish — and burned ones at that?" 3 Tobiah the Ammonite was beside him, and he said, "That stone wall they are building — any fox going
up on it would break it down!" 4 Hear, O our God, for we are despised; turn their
taunt back on their own heads, and give them over as plunder in a land of captivity.
5 Do not cover their guilt, and do not let their sin be blotted out from your sight; for
they have hurled insults in the face of the builders.
6 So we rebuilt the wall, and all the wall was joined together to half its height;
for the people had a mind to work.
7 [k] But when Sanballat and Tobiah and the Arabs and the Ammonites and the
Ashdodites heard that the repairing of the walls of Jerusalem was going forward
and the gaps were beginning to be closed, they were very angry, 8 and all plotted
4.9 Neh 4.11 together to come and fight against Jerusalem and to cause confusion in it. 9 So we
prayed to our God, and set a guard as a protection against them day and night.
10 But Judah said, "The strength of the burden bearers is failing, and there is
too much rubbish so that we are unable to work on the wall." 11 And our enemies
said, "They will not know or see anything before we come upon them and kill them
and stop the work." 12 When the Jews who lived near them came, they said to us ten
4.13 Neh 4.9,17,18 times, "From all the places where they live[l] they will come up against us."[m] 13 So

[i] Or *Hammiphkad Gate* [j] Ch 3.33 in Heb [k] Ch 4.1 in Heb [l] Cn: Heb *you return* [m] Compare Gk Syr: Meaning of Heb uncertain

part of the wall behind his own house, (1) he would be more motivated to build it quickly and properly, (2) he wouldn't waste time commuting to more distant parts of the wall, (3) he would defend his own home if the wall were attacked, and (4) he would be able to make the building a family effort. Nehemiah blended self-interest with the group's objectives, helping everyone to feel that the wall project was his own. If you are part of a group working on a large project, make sure each person sees the importance and meaning of the job he or she has to do. This will insure high-quality work and personal satisfaction.

4.1 Sanballat was governor of Samaria, the region just north of Judea where Jerusalem was located. Sanballat may have hoped to become governor of Judea as well, but Nehemiah's arrival spoiled his plans. (For his other reasons for opposing Nehemiah, see the note on 2.10.) Sanballat tried to scare Nehemiah away, or at least discourage him by scorn (4.2; 6.6), threats (4.8), and bluffs (6.7).

4.1, 2 Almost 300 years before Nehemiah's time, the northern kingdom of Israel was conquered, and most of the people were carried away captive (722 B.C.). Sargon of Assyria repopulated Israel with captives from other lands. These captives eventually intermarried with the few Israelites who remained in the land, forming a mixed race of people who became known as Samaritans. The Jews who returned to Jerusalem and the southern region of Judea during the days of Ezra and Nehemiah would have nothing to do with Samaritans because they were racially impure. Relations between both groups grew progressively worse — 400 years later, the Jews and Samaritans hated each other (John 4.9).

4.1–5 Ridicule can cut deeply, causing discouragement and despair. Sanballat and Tobiah used ridicule to try to dissuade the Jews from building the wall. Instead of trading insults, however, Nehemiah prayed and the work continued. When you are mocked for your faith or criticized for doing what you know is right, refuse to respond in the same way or to become discouraged. Tell God how you feel and remember his promise to be with you. This will give you encouragement and strength to carry on.

4.6 The work of rebuilding the wall progressed well because the people had set their hearts and minds on accomplishing the task. They did not lose heart or give up, but they persevered in the work. If God has called you to a task, determine to complete it, even if you face opposition or discouragement. The rewards of work well done will be worth the effort.

4.9 Nehemiah constantly combined prayer with preparation. His people trusted God and at the same time kept vigilant watch over what had been entrusted to them. Too often we pray without looking for what God wants us to do. We show God we are serious when we combine prayer with thought, preparation, and effort.

4.10–14 Accomplishing any large task is tiring. There are always pressures that foster discouragement — the task seems impossible, it can never be finished, or too many factors are working against us. The only cure for fatigue and discouragement is focusing on God's purposes. Nehemiah reminded the workers of their calling, their goal, and God's protection. If you are overwhelmed by an assignment, tired and discouraged, remember God's purpose for your life and his special purpose for the project.

in the lowest parts of the space behind the wall, in open places, I stationed the
people according to their families,[n] with their swords, their spears, and their bows.
14 After I looked these things over, I stood up and said to the nobles and the officials 4.14 Num 14.9
and the rest of the people, "Do not be afraid of them. Remember the LORD, who is Deut 1.29,30
great and awesome, and fight for your kin, your sons, your daughters, your wives, 2 Sam 10.12
and your homes."

15 When our enemies heard that their plot was known to us, and that God had
frustrated it, we all returned to the wall, each to his work. 16 From that day on, half
of my servants worked on construction, and half held the spears, shields, bows,
and body-armor; and the leaders posted themselves behind the whole house of Judah, 17 who were building the wall. The burden bearers carried their loads in such
a way that each labored on the work with one hand and with the other held a
weapon. 18 And each of the builders had his sword strapped at his side while he
built. The man who sounded the trumpet was beside me. 19 And I said to the nobles, 4.19 Ex 14.14
the officials, and the rest of the people, "The work is great and widely spread out, Deut 1.30
and we are separated far from one another on the wall. 20 Rally to us wherever you Josh 23.10
hear the sound of the trumpet. Our God will fight for us."

21 So we labored at the work, and half of them held the spears from break of
dawn until the stars came out. 22 I also said to the people at that time, "Let every
man and his servant pass the night inside Jerusalem, so that they may be a guard for
us by night and may labor by day." 23 So neither I nor my brothers nor my servants
nor the men of the guard who followed me ever took off our clothes; each kept his
weapon in his right hand.[o]

Nehemiah defends the poor

5 Now there was a great outcry of the people and of their wives against their 5.1 Lev 25.35
Jewish kin. 2 For there were those who said, "With our sons and our daughters, Deut 15.7
we are many; we must get grain, so that we may eat and stay alive." 3 There were
also those who said, "We are having to pledge our fields, our vineyards, and our
houses in order to get grain during the famine." 4 And there were those who said,
"We are having to borrow money on our fields and vineyards to pay the king's tax.
5 Now our flesh is the same as that of our kindred; our children are the same as their 5.5 Lev 25.39
children; and yet we are forcing our sons and daughters to be slaves, and some of 2 Kgs 4.1
our daughters have been ravished; we are powerless, and our fields and vineyards
now belong to others."

6 I was very angry when I heard their outcry and these complaints. 7 After think- 5.7 Ex 22.25
ing it over, I brought charges against the nobles and the officials; I said to them, Lev 25.36
"You are all taking interest from your own people." And I called a great assembly
to deal with them, 8 and said to them, "As far as we were able, we have bought back 5.8 Lev 25.48
our Jewish kindred who had been sold to other nations; but now you are selling your
own kin, who must then be bought back by us!" They were silent, and could not
find a word to say. 9 So I said, "The thing that you are doing is not good. Should

[n] Meaning of Heb uncertain [o] Cn: Heb *each his weapon the water*

4.16 The workers were spread out along the wall, so Nehemiah devised a plan of defense that would unite and protect his people – half the men worked while the other half stood guard. Christians need to help one another in the same way because we can become so afraid of possible dangers that we can't get anything done. By looking out for each other, we are free to put forth our best efforts, confident that others are ready to offer help when needed. Don't cut yourself off from others; instead, join together for mutual benefit. You need other people as much as they need you.

4.18–20 To further relieve the anxieties of the people, Nehemiah set up a communication system. The man who sounded the trumpet stayed with Nehemiah, and the people knew what to do if they heard it. We have no record that the trumpet was ever used, but simply knowing it would issue a warning when needed was reassuring. The promise of open, immediate communication helped the group accomplish their task.

4.23 Although the exact meaning of the Hebrew phrase, "in his right hand," is unclear (it has been translated, "even when he went for water," or "at his right hand at night"), the point is that each man always had his weapon close at hand. The guards took their responsibilities seriously.

5.1ff Who were these bitterly resented Jews? They were either (1) Jews who had become wealthy in exile and brought this wealth with them to Jerusalem, or (2) descendants of Jews who had arrived almost a century earlier during the first return under Zerubbabel (Ezra 1; 2) and had established lucrative businesses.

5.9–11 Many of the returned exiles were suffering at the hands of some of their rich countrymen. These people would lend large sums of money; then, when the debtors missed a payment, they would take over their fields. Left with no means of income, the

you not walk in the fear of our God, to prevent the taunts of the nations our ene-
5.10 Neh 5.7 Ezek 18.13 mies? 10 Moreover I and my brothers and my servants are lending them money and
grain. Let us stop this taking of interest. 11 Restore to them, this very day, their

NEHEMIAH

God is in the business of working through his people to accomplish seemingly impossible tasks. God often shapes people with personality characteristics, experiences, and training that prepare them for his purpose, and usually the people have no idea what God has in store for them. God prepared and positioned Nehemiah to accomplish one of the Bible's "impossible" tasks.

Nehemiah was a common man in a unique position. He was secure and successful as cupbearer to the Persian King Artaxerxes. Nehemiah had little power, but he had great influence. He was trusted by the king. He was also a man of God, concerned about the fate of Jerusalem.

Seventy years earlier, Zerubbabel had managed to rebuild God's temple. Thirteen years had passed since Ezra had returned to Jerusalem and helped the people with their spiritual needs. Now Nehemiah was needed. Jerusalem's wall was still in ruins, and the news broke his heart. As he talked to God, a plan began to take form in Nehemiah's mind about his own role in the rebuilding of the city walls. He willingly left the security of his home and job in Persia to follow God on an "impossible" mission. And the rest is history.

From beginning to end, Nehemiah prayed for God's help. He never hesitated to ask God to remember him, closing his autobiography with these words: "Remember me, O my God, for good." Throughout the "impossible" task, Nehemiah displayed unusual leadership. The wall around Jerusalem was rebuilt in record time, despite resistance. Even Israel's enemies grudgingly and fearfully admitted that God was with these builders. Not only that, but God worked through Nehemiah to bring about a spiritual awakening among the people of Judah.

You may not have Nehemiah's unique abilities or feel that you are in a position where you can do anything great for God, but there are two ways you can become useful to God. First, be a person who *talks* to God. Welcome him into your thoughts and share yourself with him—your concerns, feelings, and dreams. Second, be a person who *walks* with God. Put what you learn from his Word into action. God may have an "impossible" mission that he wants to do through you.

Strengths and accomplishments:
- A man of character, persistence, and prayer
- Brilliant planner, organizer, and motivator
- Under his leadership, the wall around Jerusalem was rebuilt in 52 days
- As political leader, led the nation to religious reform and spiritual awakening
- Was calm under opposition
- Was capable of being bluntly honest with his people when they were sinning

Lessons from his life:
- The first step in any venture is to pray
- People under God's direction can accomplish impossible tasks
- There are two parts to real service for God: talking with him, and walking with him

Vital statistics:
- Where: Persia, Jerusalem
- Occupation: King's cupbearer, city builder, governor of Judah
- Relative: Father: Hecaliah
- Contemporaries: Ezra, Artaxerxes, Tobiah, Sanballat

Key verse:
"I told them that the hand of my God had been gracious upon me, and also the words that the king had spoken to me. Then they said, 'Let us start building!'" (Nehemiah 2.18).

Nehemiah's story is told in the book of Nehemiah.

debtors were forced to sell their children into slavery, a common practice of this time. Nehemiah was angry with these Jews who were taking advantage of their own people in order to enrich themselves. These practices violated the law set forth in Exodus 22.25.

5.9–11 God's concern for the poor is revealed in almost every book of the Bible. Here, Nehemiah insists that fairness to the poor and oppressed is central to following God. The way we help those in need ought to mirror God's love and concern. The books of Moses clearly spelled out the people's responsibility to care for the poor (Exodus 22.22–27; Leviticus 25.35–37; Deuteronomy 14.28, 29; 15.7–11).

5.10 Nehemiah told the rich Jews to stop charging interest on their loans to their needy brothers. God never intended people to profit from others' misfortunes. In contrast to the values of this world, God says that caring for one another is more important than personal gain. When a Christian brother or sister suffers, we all suffer (1 Corinthians 12.26). We should help needy believers, not exploit them. The Jerusalem church was praised for working together to eliminate poverty (Acts 4.34, 35). Remember, "Whoever gives to the poor will lack nothing" (Proverbs 28.27). Make it a practice to help those in need around you.

fields, their vineyards, their olive orchards, and their houses, and the interest on
money, grain, wine, and oil that you have been exacting from them." 12 Then they **5.12** Ezra 10.5; Neh 10.31
said, "We will restore everything and demand nothing more from them. We will do
as you say." And I called the priests, and made them take an oath to do as they had
promised. 13 I also shook out the fold of my garment and said, "So may God shake
out everyone from house and from property who does not perform this promise.
Thus may they be shaken out and emptied." And all the assembly said, "Amen,"
and praised the LORD. And the people did as they had promised.
14 Moreover from the time that I was appointed to be their governor in the land **5.14** Neh 1.1; 13.6
of Judah, from the twentieth year to the thirty-second year of King Artaxerxes,
twelve years, neither I nor my brothers ate the food allowance of the governor.
15 The former governors who were before me laid heavy burdens on the people, and **5.15** Neh 5.9
took food and wine from them, besides forty shekels of silver. Even their servants
lorded it over the people. But I did not do so, because of the fear of God. 16 Indeed,
I devoted myself to the work on this wall, and acquired no land; and all my servants
were gathered there for the work. 17 Moreover there were at my table one hundred **5.17** 1 Kgs 18.19
fifty people, Jews and officials, beside those who came to us from the nations
around us. 18 Now that which was prepared for one day was one ox and six choice **5.18** 1 Kgs 4.22,23; 2 Thess 3.8
sheep; also fowls were prepared for me, and every ten days skins of wine in abun-
dance; yet with all this I did not demand the food allowance of the governor, because of the heavy burden of labor on the people. 19 Remember for my good, O my **5.19** Neh 13.14,22,31
God, all that I have done for this people.

Continued opposition to rebuilding the wall

6 Now when it was reported to Sanballat and Tobiah and to Geshem the Arab
and to the rest of our enemies that I had built the wall and that there was no gap
left in it (though up to that time I had not set up the doors in the gates), 2 Sanballat **6.2** 1 Chron 8.12
and Geshem sent to me, saying, "Come and let us meet together in one of the
villages in the plain of Ono." But they intended to do me harm. 3 So I sent messengers to them, saying, "I am doing a great work and I cannot come down. Why
should the work stop while I leave it to come down to you?" 4 They sent to me four
times in this way, and I answered them in the same manner. 5 In the same way **6.5** Neh 2.19
Sanballat for the fifth time sent his servant to me with an open letter in his hand. 6 In
it was written, "It is reported among the nations—and Geshem[p] also says it—that
you and the Jews intend to rebel; that is why you are building the wall; and according to this report you wish to become their king. 7 You have also set up prophets to
proclaim in Jerusalem concerning you, 'There is a king in Judah!' And now it will
be reported to the king according to these words. So come, therefore, and let us
confer together." 8 Then I sent to him, saying, "No such things as you say have

p Heb *Gashmu*

5.13 This symbolic act was a curse. Nehemiah shook out the fold of his garment and pronounced that anyone who did not keep his promise would likewise be "shaken out and emptied," losing all he had.

5.14, 15 This comment by Nehemiah was a parenthetical statement, comparing his 12 years as governor with the unjust proceedings in the land before he arrived. The governor was appointed by the Persian king, not elected by the people.

5.16 Nehemiah led the entire construction project, but he also worked on the wall alongside the others. He was not a bureaucrat in a well-guarded office, but a leader who got involved in the day-to-day work. He did not use his position to take advantage of his people. A good leader keeps in touch with the work to be done. Those who lead best lead by what they *do* as well as by what they say.

6.1ff Sanballat and Tobiah were desperate. The wall was almost complete, and their efforts to stop its construction were failing. So they tried a new approach, centering their attacks on Nehemiah's character. They attacked him personally with rumors (6.6), deceit (6.10–13), and false reports (6.17). Personal attacks hurt, and when the criticism is unjustified, it is easy to despair. When you are doing God's work, you may receive attacks on your character. Follow Nehemiah's example by trusting God to accomplish the task and by overlooking unjustified abuse.

6.2 The plain of Ono was about 20 miles northwest of Jerusalem. If Sanballat and Geshem could get Nehemiah to meet them there, they could ambush him on the way.

6.7 During these days, prophets such as Malachi proclaimed the coming of the Messiah (Malachi 3.1–3). Sanballat, with his usual flair for stirring up trouble, tried to turn Nehemiah's people against him by implying that Nehemiah wanted to set himself up as the Messiah. He also tried to turn the local officials against Nehemiah by threatening to report to the king of Persia that Nehemiah was starting a revolt. The fact that Sanballat had an open, or unsealed, letter delivered to Nehemiah shows that he wanted to make sure the letter's contents were made public. But Sanballat's accusations were untrue and did not divert Nehemiah from his task.

been done; you are inventing them out of your own mind" 9 — for they all wanted
to frighten us, thinking, "Their hands will drop from the work, and it will not be
done." But now, O God, strengthen my hands.
10 One day when I went into the house of Shemaiah son of Delaiah son of
Mehetabel, who was confined to his house, he said, "Let us meet together in the
house of God, within the temple, and let us close the doors of the temple, for they
are coming to kill you; indeed, tonight they are coming to kill you." 11 But I said,
"Should a man like me run away? Would a man like me go into the temple to save
6.12 Neh 6.6
his life? I will not go in!" 12 Then I perceived and saw that God had not sent him at
all, but he had pronounced the prophecy against me because Tobiah and Sanballat
had hired him. 13 He was hired for this purpose, to intimidate me and make me sin
by acting in this way, and so they could give me a bad name, in order to taunt me.
6.14 Ezek 13.17; Joel 2.28
14 Remember Tobiah and Sanballat, O my God, according to these things that they
did, and also the prophetess Noadiah and the rest of the prophets who wanted to
make me afraid.

The workers complete the wall

6.15 Neh 4.1,2
15 So the wall was finished on the twenty-fifth day of the month Elul, in fifty-
6.16 Neh 2.10; 4.1,7
two days. 16 And when all our enemies heard of it, all the nations around us were
afraid[q] and fell greatly in their own esteem; for they perceived that this work had
been accomplished with the help of our God. 17 Moreover in those days the nobles
of Judah sent many letters to Tobiah, and Tobiah's letters came to them. 18 For
many in Judah were bound by oath to him, because he was the son-in-law of Shecaniah son of Arah: and his son Jehohanan had married the daughter of Meshullam
son of Berechiah. 19 Also they spoke of his good deeds in my presence, and reported my words to him. And Tobiah sent letters to intimidate me.

Nehemiah gives instructions for guarding the wall

7 Now when the wall had been built and I had set up the doors, and the gatekeep-
7.2 Neh 1.2; 10.23
ers, the singers, and the Levites had been appointed, 2 I gave my brother
Hanani charge over Jerusalem, along with Hananiah the commander of the
citadel — for he was a faithful man and feared God more than many. 3 And I said to
them, "The gates of Jerusalem are not to be opened until the sun is hot; while the

[q] Another reading is *saw*

6.10 Shemaiah was "confined to his house" because he was supposedly receiving a message from God. This false prophet warned Nehemiah of danger and told him to hide in the temple. Nehemiah wisely tested the message, exposing it as another trick of the enemy. People may misuse God's name by saying they know God's will when they have other motives. Examine self-proclaimed "messengers from God" to see if they stand up to the test of being consistent with what is revealed in God's Word.

6.10–13 Nehemiah did not have the full support of the people. Shemaiah (6.10), Noadiah (6.14), and many of the nobles (6.7) were working against him. When Nehemiah was attacked personally, he refused to give in to fear and flee to the temple. According to God's law, it would have been wrong for Nehemiah to go into the temple to hide because he wasn't a priest (Numbers 18.22). If he had run for his life, he would have undermined the courage he was trying to instill in the people. Leaders are targets for attacks. Make it a practice to pray for those in authority (1 Timothy 2.1, 2). Request God to give them strength to stand against personal attacks and temptation. They need God-given courage to overcome fear.

6.15 Daniel, who was among the first group of captives taken from Jerusalem to Babylon (605 B.C.), predicted the rebuilding of the city walls (Daniel 9.25). Here his prophecy comes true. He, like Nehemiah, was a Jew who held a prominent position in the kingdom where he had been exiled (Daniel 5.29 – 6.3).

6.15 They said it couldn't be done. The job was too big, and the problems were too great. But God's men and women, joined together for special tasks, can solve huge problems and accomplish great goals. Don't let the size of a task or the length of time needed to accomplish it keep you from doing it. With God's help, it can be done.

6.16 "Fell greatly in their own esteem" means that they were afraid and humiliated and lost their self-confidence.

7.2 Faithfulness and fear of God (reverence) were the key character traits that qualified these men to govern Jerusalem. Faithful people can be trusted to carry out their work; reverent people can be expected to do so in line with God's priorities. These men had both qualities. If you are in a position of selecting leaders, look for faithfulness and reverence as two of the most important qualifications. Although other qualities may seem more impressive, faithfulness and reverence pass the test of time.

7.3 City gates were usually opened at sunrise, enabling merchants to enter and set up their tent-stores. Nehemiah didn't want Jerusalem to be caught unprepared by an enemy attack, so he ordered the gates closed until well after sunrise when the people were sure to be awake and alert.

7.3, 4 The wall was complete, but the work was not finished. Nehemiah assigned each family the task of protecting the section of wall next to their home. It is tempting to relax our guard and rest on past accomplishments after we have completed a large task. But we must continue to serve and to take care of all that God has entrusted to us. Following through after a project is completed is as vital as doing the project itself.

gatekeepers[r] are still standing guard, let them shut and bar the doors. Appoint
guards from among the inhabitants of Jerusalem, some at their watch posts, and
others before their own houses." 4 The city was wide and large, but the people
within it were few and no houses had been built.

Nehemiah registers the people

5 Then my God put it into my mind to assemble the nobles and the officials and
the people to be enrolled by genealogy. And I found the book of the genealogy of
those who were the first to come back, and I found the following written in it:

6 These are the people of the province who came up out of the captivity of those **7.6**
exiles whom King Nebuchadnezzar of Babylon had carried into exile; they returned Ezra 2.1-70
to Jerusalem and Judah, each to his town. 7 They came with Zerubbabel, Jeshua, **7.7**
Nehemiah, Azariah, Raamiah, Nahamani, Mordecai, Bilshan, Mispereth, Bigvai, Ezra 2.2
Nehum, Baanah.

The number of the Israelite people: 8 the descendants of Parosh, two thousand **7.8**
one hundred seventy-two. 9 Of Shephatiah, three hundred seventy-two. 10 Of Arah, Ezra 2.3-35
six hundred fifty-two. 11 Of Pahath-moab, namely the descendants of Jeshua and
Joab, two thousand eight hundred eighteen. 12 Of Elam, one thousand two hundred
fifty-four. 13 Of Zattu, eight hundred forty-five. 14 Of Zaccai, seven hundred sixty.
15 Of Binnui, six hundred forty-eight. 16 Of Bebai, six hundred twenty-eight. 17 Of
Azgad, two thousand three hundred twenty-two. 18 Of Adonikam, six hundred
sixty-seven. 19 Of Bigvai, two thousand sixty-seven. 20 Of Adin, six hundred fifty-
five. 21 Of Ater, namely of Hezekiah, ninety-eight. 22 Of Hashum, three hundred
twenty-eight. 23 Of Bezai, three hundred twenty-four. 24 Of Hariph, one hundred
twelve. 25 Of Gibeon, ninety-five. 26 The people of Bethlehem and Netophah, one
hundred eighty-eight. 27 Of Anathoth, one hundred twenty-eight. 28 Of Beth-
azmaveth, forty-two. 29 Of Kiriath-jearim, Chephirah, and Beeroth, seven hundred
forty-three. 30 Of Ramah and Geba, six hundred twenty-one. 31 Of Michmas, one
hundred twenty-two. 32 Of Bethel and Ai, one hundred twenty-three. 33 Of the other
Nebo, fifty-two. 34 The descendants of the other Elam, one thousand two hundred
fifty-four. 35 Of Harim, three hundred twenty. 36 Of Jericho, three hundred forty-
five. 37 Of Lod, Hadid, and Ono, seven hundred twenty-one. 38 Of Senaah, three
thousand nine hundred thirty.

39 The priests: the descendants of Jedaiah, namely the house of Jeshua, nine **7.39**
hundred seventy-three. 40 Of Immer, one thousand fifty-two. 41 Of Pashhur, one Ezra 2.36-39
thousand two hundred forty-seven. 42 Of Harim, one thousand seventeen.

43 The Levites: the descendants of Jeshua, namely of Kadmiel of the descen- **7.43**
dants of Hodevah, seventy-four. 44 The singers: the descendants of Asaph, one Ezra 2.40-42
hundred forty-eight. 45 The gatekeepers: the descendants of Shallum, of Ater, of
Talmon, of Akkub, of Hatita, of Shobai, one hundred thirty-eight.

46 The temple servants: the descendants of Ziha, of Hasupha, of Tabbaoth, **7.46**
47 of Keros, of Sia, of Padon, 48 of Lebana, of Hagaba, of Shalmai, 49 of Hanan, Ezra 2.43-54
of Giddel, of Gahar, 50 of Reaiah, of Rezin, of Nekoda, 51 of Gazzam, of Uzza, of
Paseah, 52 of Besai, of Meunim, of Nephushesim, 53 of Bakbuk, of Hakupha, of
Harhur, 54 of Bazlith, of Mehida, of Harsha, 55 of Barkos, of Sisera, of Temah, 56 of
Neziah, of Hatipha.

57 The descendants of Solomon's servants: of Sotai, of Sophereth, of Perida, **7.57**
58 of Jaala, of Darkon, of Giddel, 59 of Shephatiah, of Hattil, of Pochereth- Ezra 2.55-57
hazzebaim, of Amon.

60 All the temple servants and the descendants of Solomon's servants were **7.60** Ezra 2.58
three hundred ninety-two. **7.61**
61 The following were those who came up from Tel-melah, Tel-harsha, Ezra 2.59,60

[r] Heb *while they*

7.5ff Nehemiah says he found the book of the genealogy. Because Nehemiah's genealogy is almost identical to Ezra's (Ezra 2), most likely Ezra's list was stored in the temple archives, and Nehemiah used it as his source.

7.61 Genealogies were greatly valued because it was vitally important for a Jew to be able to prove that he or she was a descendant of Abraham and was, therefore, part of God's people (Genesis 12.1–3; 15; Exodus 19.5, 6; Deuteronomy 11.22–28). A

Cherub, Addon, and Immer, but they could not prove their ancestral houses or their
descent, whether they belonged to Israel: 62 the descendants of Delaiah, of Tobiah,
7.63 Ezra 2.61 of Nekoda, six hundred forty-two. 63 Also, of the priests: the descendants of Hoba-
iah, of Hakkoz, of Barzillai (who had married one of the daughters of Barzillai the
7.64 Ezra 2.62,63 Gileadite and was called by their name). 64 These sought their registration among
those enrolled in the genealogies, but it was not found there, so they were excluded
from the priesthood as unclean; 65 the governor told them that they were not to
partake of the most holy food, until a priest with Urim and Thummim should come.
7.66 Ezra 2.64-67 66 The whole assembly together was forty-two thousand three hundred sixty,
67 besides their male and female slaves, of whom there were seven thousand three
hundred thirty-seven; and they had two hundred forty-five singers, male and female. 68 They had seven hundred thirty-six horses, two hundred forty-five mules,[s]
69 four hundred thirty-five camels, and six thousand seven hundred twenty donkeys.
7.70 Ezra 2.68,69 70 Now some of the heads of ancestral houses contributed to the work. The
governor gave to the treasury one thousand darics of gold, fifty basins, and five
hundred thirty priestly robes. 71 And some of the heads of ancestral houses gave
into the building fund twenty thousand darics of gold and two thousand two hundred minas of silver. 72 And what the rest of the people gave was twenty thousand
darics of gold, two thousand minas of silver, and sixty-seven priestly robes.
7.73 Ezra 2.70 73 So the priests, the Levites, the gatekeepers, the singers, some of the people,
the temple servants, and all Israel settled in their towns.

B. REFORMING THE PEOPLE (8.1—13.31)

When Nehemiah arrived in Jerusalem he found more than just broken walls, he found broken lives. In response, Nehemiah gathers the people together to hear Ezra read God's law. The people repent and promise to change their lives by obeying God's words. No matter where we live, backsliding is an ever-present danger. We must constantly check our behavior against God's standards in the Bible so that we do not slide back into sinful ways of living.

1. Ezra renews the covenant

Ezra reads the law

When the seventh month came—the people of Israel being settled in their
8.1 2 Chron 34.15 Ezra 7.6 Neh 3.26 **8** towns— 1 all the people gathered together into the square before the Water
Gate. They told the scribe Ezra to bring the book of the law of Moses, which
the LORD had given to Israel. 2 Accordingly, the priest Ezra brought the law before
the assembly, both men and women and all who could hear with understanding.
This was on the first day of the seventh month. 3 He read from it facing the square
before the Water Gate from early morning until midday, in the presence of the men
and the women and those who could understand; and the ears of all the people were
attentive to the book of the law. 4 The scribe Ezra stood on a wooden platform that
had been made for the purpose; and beside him stood Mattithiah, Shema, Anaiah,
Uriah, Hilkiah, and Maaseiah on his right hand; and Pedaiah, Mishael, Malchijah,
Hashum, Hash-baddanah, Zechariah, and Meshullam on his left hand. 5 And Ezra

[s] Ezra 2.66 and the margins of some Hebrew Mss: MT lacks *They had . . . forty-five mules*

---

lost genealogy put one's status as a Jew at risk.

7.64, 65 The Urim and Thummim were a means of learning God's will (Exodus 28.30). If someone's name wasn't in the genealogies, he could still be admitted as a priest if the Urim and Thummin proved him to be a Jew. It is not clear whether the Urim and Thummim were the originals which had survived the destruction of Jerusalem or were new.

7.70 Darics were gold coins.

8.1 This is the first mention of Ezra in this book. He had arrived in Jerusalem from Babylon 13 years before Nehemiah (458 B.C., see Ezra 7.6–9).

8.1 Ezra and Nehemiah were contemporaries (8.9), although Ezra was probably much older. Nehemiah, as governor, was the political leader; and Ezra, as priest and scribe, was the religious leader. No doubt the Jews would have liked to set up the kingdom again as in the days of David, but this would have signaled rebellion against the king of Persia to whom they were subject. The best alternative was to divide the leadership between Nehemiah and Ezra.

8.1–5 The people paid close attention to Ezra as he read God's Word, and their lives were changed. Because we hear the Bible so often, we can become dulled to its words and immune to its teachings. Instead, we should *listen carefully* to every verse and ask the Holy Spirit to help us answer the question, "How does this apply to *my* life?"

opened the book in the sight of all the people, for he was standing above all the
people; and when he opened it, all the people stood up. 6 Then Ezra blessed the
LORD, the great God, and all the people answered, "Amen, Amen," lifting up their
hands. Then they bowed their heads and worshiped the LORD with their faces to the
ground. 7 Also Jeshua, Bani, Sherebiah, Jamin, Akkub, Shabbethai, Hodiah, Maaseiah, Kelita, Azariah, Jozabad, Hanan, Pelaiah, the Levites,[t] helped the people
to understand the law, while the people remained in their places. 8 So they read
from the book, from the law of God, with interpretation. They gave the sense, so
that the people understood the reading.

9 And Nehemiah, who was the governor, and Ezra the priest and scribe, and the
Levites who taught the people said to all the people, "This day is holy to the LORD
your God; do not mourn or weep." For all the people wept when they heard the
words of the law. 10 Then he said to them, "Go your way, eat the fat and drink sweet
wine and send portions of them to those for whom nothing is prepared, for this day
is holy to our LORD; and do not be grieved, for the joy of the LORD is your strength."
11 So the Levites stilled all the people, saying, "Be quiet, for this day is holy; do not
be grieved." 12 And all the people went their way to eat and drink and to send portions and to make great rejoicing, because they had understood the words that were
declared to them.

13 On the second day the heads of ancestral houses of all the people, with the
priests and the Levites, came together to the scribe Ezra in order to study the words
of the law. 14 And they found it written in the law, which the LORD had commanded
by Moses, that the people of Israel should live in booths[u] during the festival of the
seventh month, 15 and that they should publish and proclaim in all their towns and
in Jerusalem as follows, "Go out to the hills and bring branches of olive, wild olive,
myrtle, palm, and other leafy trees to make booths,[u] as it is written." 16 So the
people went out and brought them, and made booths[u] for themselves, each on the
roofs of their houses, and in their courts and in the courts of the house of God, and
in the square at the Water Gate and in the square at the Gate of Ephraim. 17 And all
the assembly of those who had returned from the captivity made booths[u] and lived
in them; for from the days of Jeshua son of Nun to that day the people of Israel had
not done so. And there was very great rejoicing. 18 And day by day, from the first
day to the last day, he read from the book of the law of God. They kept the festival
seven days; and on the eighth day there was a solemn assembly, according to the
ordinance.

Ezra leads the people in confession

9 Now on the twenty-fourth day of this month the people of Israel were assembled with fasting and in sackcloth, and with earth on their heads.[v] 2 Then those
of Israelite descent separated themselves from all foreigners, and stood and con-

8.6 Gen 14.22 Ex 4.31 2 Chron 20.18 Neh 5.13 1 Tim 2.8
8.7 Lev 10.11 Deut 33.10
8.9 Deut 12.7,12 Neh 8.2
8.10 Deut 26.11-13 Esth 9.19,22 Ps 28.6-8
8.12 Neh 8.7,8,10 Rom 7.7
8.14 Lev 23.34,40,42
8.16 2 Kgs 14.13 Neh 8.1; 12.39 Jer 32.29
8.17 2 Chron 7.8 8.13; 30.21
8.18 Lev 23.36 Num 29.35 Deut 31.11
9.1 1 Sam 4.12 Ezra 8.23; 10.11 Job 2.12

t 1 Esdras 9.48 Vg: Heb *and the Levites* u Or *tabernacles*; Heb *succoth* v Heb *on them*

8.9 Ezra, not Nehemiah, was the religious leader. It is significant that Nehemiah was a layman, not a member of the religious establishment or a prophet. He was motivated by his relationship with God, and he devoted his life to doing God's will in a secular world. Such people are crucial to God's work in all aspects of life. No matter what your work or role in life, view it as God's special calling to serve him.

8.9, 10 The people wept openly when they heard God's laws and realized how far they were from obeying them. But Ezra told them they should be filled with joy because the day was holy. It was time to celebrate and to give gifts to those in need.

Celebration is not to be self-centered. Ezra connected celebration with giving. This gave those in need an opportunity to celebrate as well. Often when we celebrate and give to others (even when we don't feel like it), we are strengthened spiritually and filled with joy. Enter into celebrations that honor God, and allow him to fill you with his joy.

8.13ff After Ezra read God's laws to the people, they studied them further and then acted upon them. A careful reading of Scripture always calls for a response to these questions: What should I *do* with this knowledge? How should my life change? We must *do* something about what we have learned if it is to have real significance for our lives.

8.14–17 During the seven-day festival of booths, the people lived in booths made of branches. This practice was instituted as a reminder of their rescue from Egypt and the time spent in shelters in the wilderness (Leviticus 23.43). They were to think about God's protection and guidance during their years of wandering and the fact that God would still protect and guide them if they obeyed him. This was a time to remember their origins, where they came from. It is helpful to remember our beginnings in order to appreciate where we are today. Think back on your life to see where God has led you. Then thank God for his continuing work to protect you and provide for your needs.

9.1 Fasting and wearing sackcloth was a public sign of sorrow and repentance.

fessed their sins and the iniquities of their ancestors. 3 They stood up in their place
and read from the book of the law of the LORD their God for a fourth part of the day,
and for another fourth they made confession and worshiped the LORD their God.
4 Then Jeshua, Bani, Kadmiel, Shebaniah, Bunni, Sherebiah, Bani, and Chenani
stood on the stairs of the Levites and cried out with a loud voice to the LORD their
God. 5 Then the Levites, Jeshua, Kadmiel, Bani, Hashabneiah, Sherebiah, Hodiah, Shebaniah, and Pethahiah, said, "Stand up and bless the LORD your God from
everlasting to everlasting. Blessed be your glorious name, which is exalted above
all blessing and praise."
6 And Ezra said:[w] "You are the LORD, you alone; you have made heaven, the
heaven of heavens, with all their host, the earth and all that is on it, the seas and all
that is in them. To all of them you give life, and the host of heaven worships you.
7 You are the LORD, the God who chose Abram and brought him out of Ur of the
Chaldeans and gave him the name Abraham; 8 and you found his heart faithful before you, and made with him a covenant to give to his descendants the land of the
Canaanite, the Hittite, the Amorite, the Perizzite, the Jebusite, and the Girgashite;
and you have fulfilled your promise, for you are righteous.
9 "And you saw the distress of our ancestors in Egypt and heard their cry at the
Red Sea.[x] 10 You performed signs and wonders against Pharaoh and all his servants
and all the people of his land, for you knew that they acted insolently against our
ancestors. You made a name for yourself, which remains to this day. 11 And you
divided the sea before them, so that they passed through the sea on dry land, but
you threw their pursuers into the depths, like a stone into mighty waters.

9.6 Gen 1.1 Deut 6.4 2 Kgs 19.15 Ps 103.21 148.2-4 Col 1.17
9.7 Gen 11.31 12.1; 15.7; 17.5
9.8 Gen 12.1-3 15.18-21 17.2-8 Josh 21.43-45
9.9 Ex 5.2; 7.8-14 14.10-12
9.10 Ex 5.2
9.11 Ex 14.21 15.1,5,10
9.12 Ex 13.21,22 14.19,20

[w] Gk: Heb lacks *And Ezra said* [x] Or *Sea of Reeds*

GOING HOME: TWO GREAT JOURNEYS OF ISRAEL

What about the Journeys?	*The Exodus*	*The Return from Exile*
Where were they?	Egypt (430 years)	Babylon (70 years)
How many?	About 1 million	60,000
How long did the journey take them?	40 years and 2 attempts	100 years and 3 journeys
Who led them?	Moses/Aaron/Joshua	Zerubbabel/Ezra/Nehemiah
What was their purpose?	To reclaim the promised land	To rebuild the temple and city of Jerusalem
What obstacles did they face?	Red Sea/Desert/Enemies	Ruins/Limited Resources/Enemies
What failures did they experience?	Complaining/Disobedience/Retreat—all of which turned a journey of a few weeks into a 40-year epic	Fear/Discouragement/Apathy—all of which turned a project of a few months into one which required a century to complete
What successes did they have?	Eventually entered the promised land	Eventually rebuilt Jerusalem's temple and wall
What lessons did they learn?	God will build his nation. God is both faithful and just. God will accomplish great acts to make his promises come true.	God will preserve his nation. God will continue to have a chosen people, a home for them, and a plan to offer himself to mankind.

9.3 The Hebrews practiced open confession, admitting their sins to one another. Reading and studying God's Word should precede confession (see 8.18) because God can show us where we are sinning. Honest confession should precede worship, because we cannot have a right relationship with God if we hold on to certain sins.

9.6–38 Many prayers and speeches in the Bible include a long summary of Israel's history, because individuals did not have their own copies of the Bible as we do today. This summary of God's past works reminded the people of their great heritage and God's promises.

We should also remember our history to avoid repeating our mistakes so that we can serve God better. Reviewing our past helps us understand how to improve our behavior. It shows us the pattern to our spiritual growth. Learn from your past so that you will become the kind of person God wants you to be.

12 Moreover, you led them by day with a pillar of cloud, and by night with a pillar
of fire, to give them light on the way in which they should go. 13 You came down also
upon Mount Sinai, and spoke with them from heaven, and gave them right ordinances and true laws, good statutes and commandments, 14 and you made known
your holy sabbath to them and gave them commandments and statutes and a law
through your servant Moses. 15 For their hunger you gave them bread from heaven,
and for their thirst you brought water for them out of the rock, and you told them to
go in to possess the land that you swore to give them.
16 "But they and our ancestors acted presumptuously and stiffened their necks
and did not obey your commandments; 17 they refused to obey, and were not mindful of the wonders that you performed among them; but they stiffened their necks
and determined to return to their slavery in Egypt. But you are a God ready to
forgive, gracious and merciful, slow to anger and abounding in steadfast love, and
you did not forsake them. 18 Even when they had cast an image of a calf for themselves and said, 'This is your God who brought you up out of Egypt,' and had
committed great blasphemies, 19 you in your great mercies did not forsake them in
the wilderness; the pillar of cloud that led them in the way did not leave them by
day, nor the pillar of fire by night that gave them light on the way by which they
should go. 20 You gave your good spirit to instruct them, and did not withhold your
manna from their mouths, and gave them water for their thirst. 21 Forty years you
sustained them in the wilderness so that they lacked nothing; their clothes did not
wear out and their feet did not swell. 22 And you gave them kingdoms and peoples,
and allotted to them every corner,[y] so they took possession of the land of King
Sihon of Heshbon and the land of King Og of Bashan. 23 You multiplied their descendants like the stars of heaven, and brought them into the land that you had told
their ancestors to enter and possess. 24 So the descendants went in and possessed the
land, and you subdued before them the inhabitants of the land, the Canaanites, and
gave them into their hands, with their kings and the peoples of the land, to do with
them as they pleased. 25 And they captured fortress cities and a rich land, and took
possession of houses filled with all sorts of goods, hewn cisterns, vineyards, olive
orchards, and fruit trees in abundance; so they ate, and were filled and became fat,
and delighted themselves in your great goodness.
26 "Nevertheless they were disobedient and rebelled against you and cast your
law behind their backs and killed your prophets, who had warned them in order to
turn them back to you, and they committed great blasphemies. 27 Therefore you
gave them into the hands of their enemies, who made them suffer. Then in the time
of their suffering they cried out to you and you heard them from heaven, and according to your great mercies you gave them saviors who saved them from the
hands of their enemies. 28 But after they had rest, they again did evil before you,
and you abandoned them to the hands of their enemies, so that they had dominion
over them; yet when they turned and cried to you, you heard from heaven, and
many times you rescued them according to your mercies. 29 And you warned them
in order to turn them back to your law. Yet they acted presumptuously and did not
obey your commandments, but sinned against your ordinances, by the observance
of which a person shall live. They turned a stubborn shoulder and stiffened their
neck and would not obey. 30 Many years you were patient with them, and warned
them by your spirit through your prophets; yet they would not listen. Therefore you
handed them over to the peoples of the lands. 31 Nevertheless, in your great mercies

9.13 Ex 19.11,18-20 Ps 19.7-9
9.14 Ex 16.23; 20.8
9.15 Ex 16.4,14,15 17.6 Num 20.7-13 Deut 1.8 Josh 1.2-4
9.16 Deut 31.27 Neh 9.10,29
9.17 Num 14.4
9.18 Ex 32.4-8,31
9.19 Neh 9.12
9.20 Num 11.17 Neh 9.15,30 Isa 63.11-14
9.21 Ex 16.35 Deut 2.7
9.22 Num 21.21-35 Deut 2.26-36 3.1-17
9.24 Josh 18.1
9.25 Deut 3.5; 6.11
9.26 Judg 2.11 2 Chron 36.16 Ezek 16.15-21
9.27 Judg 2.16 1 Sam 12.10,11 2 Kgs 13.5
9.29 Lev 18.5 Neh 9.26-30 Zech 7.11
9.30 Neh 9.20
9.31 Neh 9.17 Jer 4.27

y Meaning of Heb uncertain

9.17–21 God's patience is amazing! In spite of our repeated failings, he is always ready to pardon (9.17), and his Spirit is always ready to instruct (9.20). Realizing the extent of God's forgiveness helps us forgive those who fail us, even "seventy times seven" if necessary (Matthew 18.21, 22).

9.28–31 Israel was devastated by times of intense rebellion and sin. Yet when the people repented and returned to God, he delivered them. God puts no limit on the number of times we can come to him to obtain mercy, but we must *come* in order to obtain it, recognizing our need and asking him for help. This miracle of grace should inspire us to say, "You are a gracious and merciful God"! If there is a recurring problem or difficulty in your life, continue to ask God for help, and be willing and ready to make changes in your attitude and behavior that will correct that situation.

you did not make an end of them or forsake them, for you are a gracious and merciful God.
32 "Now therefore, our God—the great and mighty and awesome God, keeping covenant and steadfast love—do not treat lightly all the hardship that has come
upon us, upon our kings, our officials, our priests, our prophets, our ancestors, and
all your people, since the time of the kings of Assyria until today. 33 You have been
just in all that has come upon us, for you have dealt faithfully and we have acted
wickedly; 34 our kings, our officials, our priests, and our ancestors have not kept
your law or heeded the commandments and the warnings that you gave them.
35 Even in their own kingdom, and in the great goodness you bestowed on them,
and in the large and rich land that you set before them, they did not serve you and
did not turn from their wicked works. 36 Here we are, slaves to this day—slaves in
the land that you gave to our ancestors to enjoy its fruit and its good gifts. 37 Its rich
yield goes to the kings whom you have set over us because of our sins; they have
power also over our bodies and over our livestock at their pleasure, and we are in
great distress."

The people agree to obey

38[z] Because of all this we make a firm agreement in writing, and on that sealed
document are inscribed the names of our officials, our Levites, and our priests.
10 [a]Upon the sealed document are the names of Nehemiah the governor, son of
Hacaliah, and Zedekiah; 2 Seraiah, Azariah, Jeremiah, 3 Pashhur, Amariah,
Malchijah, 4 Hattush, Shebaniah, Malluch, 5 Harim, Meremoth, Obadiah, 6 Daniel,
Ginnethon, Baruch, 7 Meshullam, Abijah, Mijamin, 8 Maaziah, Bilgai, Shemaiah;
these are the priests. 9 And the Levites: Jeshua son of Azaniah, Binnui of the sons
of Henadad, Kadmiel; 10 and their associates, Shebaniah, Hodiah, Kelita, Pelaiah,
Hanan, 11 Mica, Rehob, Hashabiah, 12 Zaccur, Sherebiah, Shebaniah, 13 Hodiah,
Bani, Beninu. 14 The leaders of the people: Parosh, Pahath-moab, Elam, Zattu,
Bani, 15 Bunni, Azgad, Bebai, 16 Adonijah, Bigvai, Adin, 17 Ater, Hezekiah, Azzur, 18 Hodiah, Hashum, Bezai, 19 Hariph, Anathoth, Nebai, 20 Magpiash, Meshullam, Hezir, 21 Meshezabel, Zadok, Jaddua, 22 Pelatiah, Hanan, Anaiah, 23 Hoshea,
Hananiah, Hasshub, 24 Hallohesh, Pilha, Shobek, 25 Rehum, Hashabnah, Maaseiah, 26 Ahiah, Hanan, Anan, 27 Malluch, Harim, and Baanah.
28 The rest of the people, the priests, the Levites, the gatekeepers, the singers,
the temple servants, and all who have separated themselves from the peoples of the
lands to adhere to the law of God, their wives, their sons, their daughters, all who
have knowledge and understanding, 29 join with their kin, their nobles, and enter
into a curse and an oath to walk in God's law, which was given by Moses the
servant of God, and to observe and do all the commandments of the LORD our Lord
and his ordinances and his statutes. 30 We will not give our daughters to the peoples

[z] Ch 10.1 in Heb [a] Ch 10.2 in Heb

9.32 2 Kgs 15.19,29; 17.3; Isa 7.17,18
9.33 Gen 18.25; Jer 12.1
9.35 Deut 8.7-10; 32.12-15
9.36 Deut 28.48
9.38 Neh 10.1,29
10.1 Neh 1.1; 9.38; 12.26
10.9 Neh 3.19; 7.43; 8.7; 9.4
10.28 Neh 9.2
10.29 Neh 5.12
10.30 Ex 34.16; Deut 7.3; Ezra 9.1-3, 12-14; 10.10-12

9.35, 36 Sometimes the very blessings God has showered on us make us forget him. We are often tempted to rely on wealth for security rather than on God. Do your blessings make you thankful to God and draw you closer to him, or do they make you feel self-sufficient and forgetful of God?

9.36 The Israelites were in the position of being servants in their own land, having to turn over a part of their resources each year to a foreign king. How ironic, since God had given the land to them.

9.38 This covenant, or promise between the people and God, had six provisions. They agreed to: (1) not marry "peoples of the land" (10.30), (2) observe the sabbath (10.31), (3) observe every seventh year as a sabbath year (10.31), (4) pay a temple tax (10.32, 33), (5) supply wood for the burnt offerings in the temple (10.34), and (6) give dues to the temple (10.35–38). After years of decadence and exile, the people once again took seriously their responsibility to follow God and keep his laws wholeheartedly.

10.28ff The wall was completed, and the covenant God made with his people in the days of Moses was restored (Deuteronomy 8). In this covenant are principles which are important for us today. Our relationship with God should affect our relationships (10.30), our time (10.31), and our material resources (10.32–39). The Israelites had fallen away from their original commitment to follow God. We must be careful not to do the same.

10.30 If God's chosen people were going to witness for him in a heathen world, they needed united, God-fearing families. They also needed to avoid any enticements to worship the idols of the people who lived around them. This was why God prohibited marriage between Israelites and the heathen inhabitants of the land (Deuteronomy 7.3, 4). But Israelites and heathens often intermarried anyway, and the results were disastrous for the families and for the nation. Time after time, marrying foreigners led God's people into idolatry (1 Kings 11.1–11). Whenever the nation turned its back on God, it also lost its prosperity and influence for good.

of the land or take their daughters for our sons; 31 and if the peoples of the land bring
in merchandise or any grain on the sabbath day to sell, we will not buy it from them
on the sabbath or on a holy day; and we will forego the crops of the seventh year and
the exaction of every debt.
32 We also lay on ourselves the obligation to charge ourselves yearly one-third
of a shekel for the service of the house of our God: 33 for the rows of bread, the
regular grain offering, the regular burnt offering, the sabbaths, the new moons, the
appointed festivals, the sacred donations, and the sin offerings to make atonement
for Israel, and for all the work of the house of our God. 34 We have also cast lots
among the priests, the Levites, and the people, for the wood offering, to bring it
into the house of our God, by ancestral houses, at appointed times, year by year, to
burn on the altar of the LORD our God, as it is written in the law. 35 We obligate
ourselves to bring the first fruits of our soil and the first fruits of all fruit of every
tree, year by year, to the house of the LORD; 36 also to bring to the house of our God,
to the priests who minister in the house of our God, the firstborn of our sons and of
our livestock, as it is written in the law, and the firstlings of our herds and of our
flocks; 37 and to bring the first of our dough, and our contributions, the fruit of
every tree, the wine and the oil, to the priests, to the chambers of the house of our
God; and to bring to the Levites the tithes from our soil, for it is the Levites who
collect the tithes in all our rural towns. 38 And the priest, the descendant of Aaron,
shall be with the Levites when the Levites receive the tithes; and the Levites shall
bring up a tithe of the tithes to the house of our God, to the chambers of the storehouse. 39 For the people of Israel and the sons of Levi shall bring the contribution
of grain, wine, and oil to the storerooms where the vessels of the sanctuary are, and
where the priests that minister, and the gatekeepers and the singers are. We will not
neglect the house of our God.

10.31 Ex 23.10 Lev 25.1-7 Deut 15.1,2 Neh 13.15-22
10.32 Ex 30.11-16 Mt 17.24
10.33 Ex 20.8-11 Lev 1.1-17 2.1-16; 6.8-23 23.1-44; 24.5 Num 10.10 28.11-15 Deut 16.1-17 Ezra 3.5
10.34 Neh 11.1; 13.31
10.35 Ex 23.19 Lev 23.17
10.37 Lev 27.30
10.38 Neh 13.12,13 1 Chron 9.26 2 Chron 31.11, 12

2. Nehemiah establishes policies

The people occupy the restored city

11 Now the leaders of the people lived in Jerusalem; and the rest of the people
cast lots to bring one out of ten to live in the holy city Jerusalem, while
nine-tenths remained in the other towns. 2 And the people blessed all those who
willingly offered to live in Jerusalem.
3 These are the leaders of the province who lived in Jerusalem; but in the towns
of Judah all lived on their property in their towns: Israel, the priests, the Levites,
the temple servants, and the descendants of Solomon's servants. 4 And in Jerusalem
lived some of the Judahites and of the Benjaminites. Of the Judahites: Athaiah son
of Uzziah son of Zechariah son of Amariah son of Shephatiah son of Mahalalel, of
the descendants of Perez; 5 and Maaseiah son of Baruch son of Col-hozeh son of
Hazaiah son of Adaiah son of Joiarib son of Zechariah son of the Shilonite. 6 All the

11.1 Neh 7.4; 11.18
11.3 1 Chron 9.2-34 Ezra 2.43-57 8.2-14 Neh 7.57-59 11.20

10.31 Foregoing all debts every seventh year was a part of the law (see Exodus 23.10 and Deuteronomy 15.1, 2). The people were reciting and promising to obey God's law and keep the covenant.

10.31 God recognized that the lure of money would conflict with the need for a day of rest, so trade was forbidden inside the city on the sabbath. By deciding to honor God first, the Israelites would be refusing to make money their god. Our culture often makes us choose between convenience and profit on the one hand, and setting God first on the other. Look at your work and worship habits: is God really first?

10.32 The temple had been rebuilt under Ezra's leadership about 70 years earlier (Ezra 6.14, 15).

10.36 This practice was instituted at the time of the exodus from Egypt (see the note on Exodus 13.12–14). The people needed to relearn the importance of dedicating the firstfruits of their yield to God. Nehemiah was simply reinstating this practice from the early days of the nation (Exodus 13.1, 2; Numbers 3.40–51).

10.37 "The first of our dough" means the first part of the ground meal made from grain.

11.1 The exiles who returned were few in number compared to Jerusalem's population in the days of the kings, and because the walls had been rebuilt on their original foundations, the city seemed sparsely populated. Nehemiah asked one-tenth of the people from the outlying areas to move inside the city walls to keep large areas of the city from being vacant. Apparently these people did not want to move into the city. Only a few people volunteered (11.1, 2), and Nehemiah cast lots to determine who among the remaining people would have to move.

Many of them may not have wanted to live in the city because (1) non-Jews attached a stigma to Jerusalem residents, often excluding them from trade because of their religious beliefs; (2) moving into the city meant rebuilding their homes and reestablishing their businesses, a major investment of time and money; (3) living

descendants of Perez who lived in Jerusalem were four hundred sixty-eight valiant
warriors.
7 And these are the Benjaminites: Sallu son of Meshullam son of Joed son of
Pedaiah son of Kolaiah son of Maaseiah son of Ithiel son of Jeshaiah. 8 And his
brothers[b] Gabbai, Sallai: nine hundred twenty-eight. 9 Joel son of Zichri was their
overseer; and Judah son of Hassenuah was second in charge of the city.
10 Of the priests: Jedaiah son of Joiarib, Jachin, 11 Seraiah son of Hilkiah son of
Meshullam son of Zadok son of Meraioth son of Ahitub, officer of the house of
God, 12 and their associates who did the work of the house, eight hundred twenty-
two; and Adaiah son of Jeroham son of Pelaliah son of Amzi son of Zechariah son
of Pashhur son of Malchijah, 13 and his associates, heads of ancestral houses, two
hundred forty-two; and Amashsai son of Azarel son of Ahzai son of Meshillemoth
son of Immer, 14 and their associates, valiant warriors, one hundred twenty-eight;
their overseer was Zabdiel son of Haggedolim.
11.15 1 Chron 26.29-32 15 And of the Levites: Shemaiah son of Hasshub son of Azrikam son of Hashabiah son of Bunni; 16 and Shabbethai and Jozabad, of the leaders of the Levites,
who were over the outside work of the house of God; 17 and Mattaniah son of Mica
son of Zabdi son of Asaph, who was the leader to begin the thanksgiving in prayer,
and Bakbukiah, the second among his associates; and Abda son of Shammua son of
11.18 Neh 11.3 Galal son of Jeduthun. 18 All the Levites in the holy city were two hundred eighty-
four.
11.19 2 Chron 27.3 33.14 Neh 3.26,27 19 The gatekeepers, Akkub, Talmon and their associates, who kept watch at
the gates, were one hundred seventy-two. 20 And the rest of Israel, and of the priests
and the Levites, were in all the towns of Judah, all of them in their inheritance.
21 But the temple servants lived on Ophel; and Ziha and Gishpa were over the temple servants.
11.22 1 Chron 9.33 25.1-6 Ezra 3.10; 6.8 7.20 Neh 11.17 12.46 22 The overseer of the Levites in Jerusalem was Uzzi son of Bani son of Hashabiah son of Mattaniah son of Mica, of the descendants of Asaph, the singers, in
charge of the work of the house of God. 23 For there was a command from the king
concerning them, and a settled provision for the singers, as was required every day.
24 And Pethahiah son of Meshezabel, of the descendants of Zerah son of Judah, was
at the king's hand in all matters concerning the people.
11.25 Josh 13.9,17 14.15; 15.31 1 Sam 27.6 25 And as for the villages, with their fields, some of the people of Judah lived
in Kiriath-arba and its villages, and in Dibon and its villages, and in Jekabzeel and
its villages, 26 and in Jeshua and in Moladah and Beth-pelet, 27 in Hazar-shual, in
Beer-sheba and its villages, 28 in Ziklag, in Meconah and its villages, 29 in En-
rimmon, in Zorah, in Jarmuth, 30 Zanoah, Adullam, and their villages, Lachish and
its fields, and Azekah and its villages. So they camped from Beer-sheba to the
11.31 Gen 28.19 Josh 18.13 1 Chron 4.14 8.12 Neh 6.2 valley of Hinnom. 31 The people of Benjamin also lived from Geba onward, at
Michmash, Aija, Bethel and its villages, 32 Anathoth, Nob, Ananiah, 33 Hazor, Ra-
mah, Gittaim, 34 Hadid, Zeboim, Neballat, 35 Lod, and Ono, the valley of artisans.
36 And certain divisions of the Levites in Judah were joined to Benjamin.

The priests and Levites

12.1 Ezra 2.36-39 Neh 7.39-42 **12** These are the priests and the Levites who came up with Zerubbabel son of
Shealtiel, and Jeshua: Seraiah, Jeremiah, Ezra, 2 Amariah, Malluch, Hat-
tush, 3 Shecaniah, Rehum, Meremoth, 4 Iddo, Ginnethoi, Abijah, 5 Mijamin, Maa-
diah, Bilgah, 6 Shemaiah, Joiarib, Jedaiah, 7 Sallu, Amok, Hilkiah, Jedaiah. These
were the leaders of the priests and of their associates in the days of Jeshua.
8 And the Levites: Jeshua, Binnui, Kadmiel, Sherebiah, Judah, and Mattaniah,
who with his associates was in charge of the songs of thanksgiving. 9 And Bakbu-
12.10 Ezra 2.2; 7.1-5 Neh 7.7 kiah and Unno their associates stood opposite them in the service. 10 Jeshua was the
father of Joiakim, Joiakim the father of Eliashib, Eliashib the father of Joiada,

[b] Gk Mss: Heb *And after him*

in Jerusalem required stricter obedience to God's Word because of greater social pressure and proximity to the temple.

11.24 "At the king's hand" means that Pethahiah served in the Persian court as the representative for the people.

11 Joiada the father of Jonathan, and Jonathan the father of Jaddua.
12 In the days of Joiakim the priests, heads of ancestral houses, were: of Seraiah, Meraiah; of Jeremiah, Hananiah; 13 of Ezra, Meshullam; of Amariah, Jehohanan; 14 of Malluchi, Jonathan; of Shebaniah, Joseph; 15 of Harim, Adna; of
Meraioth, Helkai; 16 of Iddo, Zechariah; of Ginnethon, Meshullam; 17 of Abijah,
Zichri; of Miniamin, of Moadiah, Piltai; 18 of Bilgah, Shammua; of Shemaiah, Jehonathan; 19 of Joiarib, Mattenai; of Jedaiah, Uzzi; 20 of Sallai, Kallai; of Amok,
Eber; 21 of Hilkiah, Hashabiah; of Jedaiah, Nethanel.
22 As for the Levites, in the days of Eliashib, Joiada, Johanan, and Jaddua,
there were recorded the heads of ancestral houses; also the priests until the reign of
Darius the Persian. 23 The Levites, heads of ancestral houses, were recorded in the
Book of the Annals until the days of Johanan son of Eliashib. 24 And the leaders of
the Levites: Hashabiah, Sherebiah, and Jeshua son of Kadmiel, with their associates over against them, to praise and to give thanks, according to the commandment of David the man of God, section opposite to section. 25 Mattaniah,
Bakbukiah, Obadiah, Meshullam, Talmon, and Akkub were gatekeepers standing
guard at the storehouses of the gates. 26 These were in the days of Joiakim son of
Jeshua son of Jozadak, and in the days of the governor Nehemiah and of the priest
Ezra, the scribe.

The dedication of the city wall

27 Now at the dedication of the wall of Jerusalem they sought out the Levites in
all their places, to bring them to Jerusalem to celebrate the dedication with rejoicing, with thanksgivings and with singing, with cymbals, harps, and lyres. 28 The
companies of the singers gathered together from the circuit around Jerusalem and
from the villages of the Netophathites; 29 also from Beth-gilgal and from the region
of Geba and Azmaveth; for the singers had built for themselves villages around
Jerusalem. 30 And the priests and the Levites purified themselves; and they purified
the people and the gates and the wall.
31 Then I brought the leaders of Judah up onto the wall, and appointed two
great companies that gave thanks and went in procession. One went to the right on
the wall to the Dung Gate; 32 and after them went Hoshaiah and half the officials of
Judah, 33 and Azariah, Ezra, Meshullam, 34 Judah, Benjamin, Shemaiah, and Jeremiah, 35 and some of the young priests with trumpets: Zechariah son of Jonathan
son of Shemaiah son of Mattaniah son of Micaiah son of Zaccur son of Asaph;
36 and his kindred, Shemaiah, Azarel, Milalai, Gilalai, Maai, Nethanel, Judah, and
Hanani, with the musical instruments of David the man of God; and the scribe Ezra
went in front of them. 37 At the Fountain Gate, in front of them, they went straight
up by the stairs of the city of David, at the ascent of the wall, above the house of
David, to the Water Gate on the east.
38 The other company of those who gave thanks went to the left,[c] and I followed them with half of the people on the wall, above the Tower of the Ovens, to
the Broad Wall, 39 and above the Gate of Ephraim, and by the Old Gate, and by the
Fish Gate and the Tower of Hananel and the Tower of the Hundred, to the Sheep
Gate; and they came to a halt at the Gate of the Guard. 40 So both companies of
those who gave thanks stood in the house of God, and I and half of the officials with
me; 41 and the priests Eliakim, Maaseiah, Miniamin, Micaiah, Elioenai, Zechariah,
and Hananiah, with trumpets; 42 and Maaseiah, Shemaiah, Eleazar, Uzzi, Jehohanan, Malchijah, Elam, and Ezer. And the singers sang with Jezrahiah as their
leader. 43 They offered great sacrifices that day and rejoiced, for God had made

12.22 1 Chron 9.1-44 Ezra 4.5,24 5.5; 6.1-15 8.2-14
12.23 Josh 10.13 1 Sam 10.25 1 Chron 29.29 Esth 6.1; 9.32 Jer 32.12
12.24 Neh 11.15
12.25 1 Chron 26.15
12.26 Neh 1.1; 10.1
12.27 1 Chron 15.16, 28 Ezra 3.10,11
12.28 1 Chron 2.54 9.16
12.30 Ezra 10.11 Neh 10.28 13.22,30
12.31 Neh 2.13 3.13,14
12.35 Neh 12.28
12.37 2 Sam 5.7-9 Neh 2.14 3.15,26 8.1,3,16
12.38 Neh 3.8,11
12.39 2 Kgs 14.13 Neh 3.1,3,6,25, 31,32; 8.16 Jer 31.38

c Cn: Heb *opposite*

12.28 "The circuit around Jerusalem" refers to the small towns and villages surrounding Jerusalem.

12.35, 36 How could the priests have used David's original musical instruments? David had instituted music as a part of worship in the temple, and so his instruments had probably been stored there. Although Nebuchadnezzar destroyed the temple, he took many temple items back to Babylon with him (2 Chronicles 36.18). These were most likely preserved in Babylon and given back to the Israelites by Cyrus when they returned to their land (Ezra 1.7–11).

them rejoice with great joy; the women and children also rejoiced. The joy of Jerusalem was heard far away.

Arrangements made for supporting Levites

44 On that day men were appointed over the chambers for the stores, the contributions, the first fruits, and the tithes, to gather into them the portions required by
the law for the priests and for the Levites from the fields belonging to the towns; for
Judah rejoiced over the priests and the Levites who ministered. 45 They performed
the service of their God and the service of purification, as did the singers and the
gatekeepers, according to the command of David and his son Solomon. 46 For in the
days of David and Asaph long ago there was a leader of the singers, and there were
songs of praise and thanksgiving to God. 47 In the days of Zerubbabel and in the
days of Nehemiah all Israel gave the daily portions for the singers and the gatekeepers. They set apart that which was for the Levites; and the Levites set apart that
which was for the descendants of Aaron.

Foreigners are expelled

13 On that day they read from the book of Moses in the hearing of the people;
and in it was found written that no Ammonite or Moabite should ever enter
the assembly of God, 2 because they did not meet the Israelites with bread and water, but hired Balaam against them to curse them—yet our God turned the curse
into a blessing. 3 When the people heard the law, they separated from Israel all
those of foreign descent.
4 Now before this, the priest Eliashib, who was appointed over the chambers of
the house of our God, and who was related to Tobiah, 5 prepared for Tobiah a large
room where they had previously put the grain offering, the frankincense, the vessels, and the tithes of grain, wine, and oil, which were given by commandment to
the Levites, singers, and gatekeepers, and the contributions for the priests. 6 While
this was taking place I was not in Jerusalem, for in the thirty-second year of King
Artaxerxes of Babylon I went to the king. After some time I asked leave of the king
7 and returned to Jerusalem. I then discovered the wrong that Eliashib had done on
behalf of Tobiah, preparing a room for him in the courts of the house of God. 8 And
I was very angry, and I threw all the household furniture of Tobiah out of the room.
9 Then I gave orders and they cleansed the chambers, and I brought back the vessels
of the house of God, with the grain offering and the frankincense.

The people support the Levites once again

10 I also found out that the portions of the Levites had not been given to them;

12.44 Ex 29.26-28 Lev 7.29-34 23.20; 27.30-33 Deut 26.3-10 Neh 10.35-39 Neh 13.5,12,13
12.45 1 Chron 25.1-8 26.1-32
12.46 1 Chron 25.1,7 26.1 2 Chron 29.30
12.47 Num 18.21-29
13.1 Deut 23.3-5 Neh 13.23
13.2 Num 22.3-11
13.3 Ezra 10.11 Neh 9.2; 10.28
13.4 Neh 6.17-19 12.44
13.5 Neh 2.10 6.1,17,18; 13.7
13.6 Ezra 4.11 7.1,11,12,21 Neh 1.1; 5.14
13.7 Neh 13.5
13.9 2 Chron 29.5, 15-19

12.44 Further arrangements were made for supporting those who served at the temple. The storerooms were administrated by men who made sure the tithes and contributions were collected and distributed. These storerooms had to be large to hold all the grain presented by the people. This was an important responsibility.

12.44–47 The dedication of the city wall was characterized by joy, praise, and singing (12.24, 27–29, 35, 36, 40–43). Nehemiah repeatedly mentions David, who began the custom of using choirs in worship. These exiles who had returned wanted their rebuilt Jerusalem to be the hub of a renewed nation, strengthened by God; therefore, they dedicated themselves and their city to God.

13.1 Deuteronomy 23.3–5 states that no Ammonite or Moabite should ever enter the assembly. These people were prohibited because they did not help the Israelites in their journey out of Egypt.

13.3 "All those of foreign descent" refers to the Moabites and Ammonites, two nations who were bitter enemies of Israel (13.1). God's law clearly stated that these two peoples should never be allowed in the temple (Deuteronomy 23.3–5). This had nothing to do with racial prejudice, because God clearly loved all people, including foreigners (Deuteronomy 10.18). He allowed foreigners to make sacrifices (Numbers 15.15, 16), and he desires all nations to know and love him (Isaiah 42.6). But while God wants all to come to him, he warns believers to stay away from those bent on evil (Proverbs 24.1). The relationships established between Jews and heathens had caused their captivity in the first place. In their celebration and rededication, they had to show they were serious about following God's law.

13.5–7 Nehemiah had to return to Babylon in 433 B.C., 12 years after he had arrived in Jerusalem. Either he was recalled by Artaxerxes, or he was fulfilling an agreement to return. It is not known exactly how long he remained in Babylon, but when he returned to Jerusalem (13.7), he found that one of his major opponents in rebuilding the wall, Tobiah, had been given his own room at the temple. Eliashib, the priest, had married Tobiah's daughter, so Tobiah used his influence with his son-in-law to get this special room.

13.10 Because the Levites were no longer supported, they had returned to their farms to fend for themselves, neglecting their temple duties and the spiritual welfare of the people. Spiritual workers deserve their pay, and their support ought to be enough to care for their needs. They shouldn't have to suffer (or leave) because their own people, who claim to be believers, don't adequately assess and meet the needs of their ministers.

so that the Levites and the singers, who had conducted the service, had gone back 13.10
to their fields. 11 So I remonstrated with the officials and said, "Why is the house of Neh 12.28,29
God forsaken?" And I gathered them together and set them in their stations. 12 Then
all Judah brought the tithe of the grain, wine, and oil into the storehouses. 13 And
I appointed as treasurers over the storehouses the priest Shelemiah, the scribe Za- 13.12 Neh 10.37
dok, and Pedaiah of the Levites, and as their assistant Hanan son of Zaccur son of 12.44
Mattaniah, for they were considered faithful; and their duty was to distribute to 13.13 Neh 7.2
their associates. 14 Remember me, O my God, concerning this, and do not wipe out
my good deeds that I have done for the house of my God and for his service.

Nehemiah halts the work on the sabbath

15 In those days I saw in Judah people treading wine presses on the sabbath, 13.15
and bringing in heaps of grain and loading them on donkeys; and also wine, grapes, Ex 20.8-11 34.21
figs, and all kinds of burdens, which they brought into Jerusalem on the sabbath Neh 13.21
day; and I warned them at that time against selling food. 16 Tyrians also, who lived
in the city, brought in fish and all kinds of merchandise and sold them on the sabbath to the people of Judah, and in Jerusalem. 17 Then I remonstrated with the nobles of Judah and said to them, "What is this evil thing that you are doing,
profaning the sabbath day? 18 Did not your ancestors act in this way, and did not our
God bring all this disaster on us and on this city? Yet you bring more wrath on Israel
by profaning the sabbath."

19 When it began to be dark at the gates of Jerusalem before the sabbath, I 13.19
commanded that the doors should be shut and gave orders that they should not be Lev 23.32
opened until after the sabbath. And I set some of my servants over the gates, to
prevent any burden from being brought in on the sabbath day. 20 Then the merchants and sellers of all kinds of merchandise spent the night outside Jerusalem
once or twice. 21 But I warned them and said to them, "Why do you spend the night
in front of the wall? If you do so again, I will lay hands on you." From that time on
they did not come on the sabbath. 22 And I commanded the Levites that they should 13.22
purify themselves and come and guard the gates, to keep the sabbath day holy. 1 Chron 15.12 Neh 12.30
Remember this also in my favor, O my God, and spare me according to the greatness of your steadfast love.

Nehemiah opposes marriage to heathens

23 In those days also I saw Jews who had married women of Ashdod, Ammon, 13.23
and Moab; 24 and half of their children spoke the language of Ashdod, and they Neh 10.30
could not speak the language of Judah, but spoke the language of various peoples. 13.24 Ezra 4.7; 9.2
25 And I contended with them and cursed them and beat some of them and pulled 13.25
out their hair; and I made them take an oath in the name of God, saying, "You shall Deut 25.2 Neh 10.29,30
not give your daughters to their sons, or take their daughters for your sons or for 13.11,17,
yourselves. 26 Did not King Solomon of Israel sin on account of such women?

13.11 To *remonstrate* means to confront and rebuke. After correcting the officials, Nehemiah restored the Levites and singers to their "stations" (places of service).

13.16 Tyrians were people from Tyre, a large Phoenician city and port on the Mediterranean Sea.

13.17 God had commanded Israel not to work on the sabbath, but to rest in remembrance of creation and the exodus (Exodus 20.8–11; Deuteronomy 5.12–15). The sabbath rest, lasting from sunset Friday to sunset Saturday, was to be observed by all Jews, servants, visiting foreigners, and even farm animals. Jerusalem's busy sabbath trade directly violated God's law, so Nehemiah commanded that the city gates be shut and traders be sent home every Friday afternoon as the sabbath hours approached.

13.24 Ashdod was on the Mediterranean coast, in the region controlled by the Philistines. Ammon and Moab were across the Jordan to the east. These nations were abhorrent to those who knew Israel's history.

13.25 Nehemiah was filled with righteous indignation at the blatant way the Jews were breaking God's laws and disregarding the covenant they had previously reaffirmed (10.30). The people had promised not to allow their children to marry heathens. But during Nehemiah's absence, the people had been intermarrying, breaking their solemn covenant with God. Nehemiah's severe treatment of these people shows the contrast between his great faithfulness to God and the people's neglect, disobedience, and disloyalty (see also Ezra 10.3).

13.26 Nehemiah used the example of Solomon's mistakes to teach his people. If one of the greatest kings of Israel fell because of the influence of unbelievers, others could too. Nehemiah saw this principle in Solomon's example: your gifts and strengths won't be of much benefit if you fail to deal with your weaknesses. Although he was a great king, Solomon's marriages to foreign women brought tragedy to the whole kingdom. A tendency to sin must be recognized and dealt with swiftly; otherwise, it may overpower you and

13.26
1 Kgs 11.1-8
Among the many nations there was no king like him, and he was beloved by his
God, and God made him king over all Israel; nevertheless, foreign women made
even him to sin. 27 Shall we then listen to you and do all this great evil and act
treacherously against our God by marrying foreign women?"

13.28
Num 25.13
Neh 2.10,19
28 And one of the sons of Jehoiada, son of the high priest Eliashib, was the
son-in-law of Sanballat the Horonite; I chased him away from me. 29 Remember
them, O my God, because they have defiled the priesthood, the covenant of the
priests and the Levites.

13.30
Neh 10.30
13.31
Neh 10.34
13.14,22
30 Thus I cleansed them from everything foreign, and I established the duties of
the priests and Levites, each in his work; 31 and I provided for the wood offering,
at appointed times, and for the first fruits. Remember me, O my God, for good.

---

bring you down. One of the strongest reasons for reading the Bible is to learn from the mistakes of God's people.

13.31 "Remember me" means "look favorably upon me for all that I have done."

13.31 Nehemiah's life story provides many principles of effective leadership that are still valid today. (1) *Have a clear purpose, and keep evaluating it in light of God's will.* Nothing prevented Nehemiah from staying on track. (2) *Be straightforward and honest.* Everyone knew exactly what Nehemiah needed, and he spoke the truth even when it made his goal harder to achieve. (3) *Live above reproach.* The accusations against Nehemiah were empty and false. (4) *Be a person of constant prayer,* deriving power and wisdom from your contact with God. Everything Nehemiah did glorified God.

Leadership appears glamorous at times, but it is often lonely, thankless, and filled with pressures to compromise values and standards. Nehemiah was able to accomplish a huge task against incredible odds because he learned that there is no success without risk of failure, no reward without hard work, no opportunity without criticism, and no true leadership without trust in God. This book is about rebuilding the wall of a great city, but it is also about spiritual renewal, rebuilding a people's dependence on God. When we take our eyes off of God, our lives begin to crumble.

ESTHER

Jerusalem destroyed/ exiles go to Babylon 586 B.C.	First exiles return to Jerusalem 537	Temple completed 516	Ahasuerus (Xerxes) becomes king of Persia 486	Vashti deposed 483	Esther becomes queen 479	Haman becomes Prime Minister 475

VITAL STATISTICS

PURPOSE:
To demonstrate God's sovereignty and his loving care for his people

AUTHOR:
Unknown. Possibly Mordecai (9.29). Some have suggested Ezra or Nehemiah because of the similarity of the writing style.

DATE WRITTEN:
Approximately 483–471 B.C. (Esther became queen in 479)

SETTING:
Although Esther follows Nehemiah in the Bible, its events are about 30 years prior to those recorded in Nehemiah. The story is set in the Persian Empire, and most of the action takes place in the king's palace in Susa, the Persian capital.

KEY VERSE:
"For if you keep silence at such a time as this, relief and deliverance will rise for the Jews from another quarter, but you and your father's family will perish. Who knows? Perhaps you have come to royal dignity for just such a time as this" (4.14).

KEY PEOPLE:
Esther, Mordecai, King Ahasuerus (Xerxes I), Haman

KEY PLACE:
The king's palace in Susa, Persia

SPECIAL FEATURES:
Esther is one of only two books named for women (Ruth is the other). The book is unusual in that in the original version no name, title, or pronoun for God appears in it (see the note on 4.14). This caused some church fathers to question its inclusion in the canon. But God's presence is clear throughout the book.

DRAMA, power, romance, intrigue—this is the stuff of which best-selling novels are made. But far from a modern piece of fiction, those words describe a true story, lived and written centuries ago. More than entertaining reading, it is a story of the profound interplay of God's sovereignty and human will. God prepared the place and the opportunity, and his people, Esther and Mordecai, chose to act.

The book of Esther begins with Queen Vashti refusing to obey an order from her husband, King Ahasuerus. She is subsequently banished, and the search begins for a new queen. The king sends out a decree to gather together all the beautiful women in the empire and bring them into the royal harem. Esther, a young Jewish woman, is one of those chosen to be in the royal harem. King Ahasuerus is so pleased with Esther that he makes her his queen.

Meanwhile, Mordecai, Esther's older cousin, becomes a government official and during his tenure foils an assassination plot. But the ambitious and self-serving Haman is appointed prime minister—second in command in the empire. When Mordecai refuses to bow in reverence to him, Haman becomes furious and determines to destroy Mordecai and all the Jews along with him.

To accomplish his vengeful deed, Haman deceives the king and persuades him to issue an edict condemning the Jews to death. Mordecai tells Queen Esther about this edict, and she determines to risk her life to save her people. Esther asks King Ahasuerus and Haman to be her guests at a banquet. During the feast, the king asks Esther what she really wants and promises to give her anything. Esther simply invites both men to another banquet the next day.

That night, unable to sleep, the king flips through some records in the royal archives and reads of the assassination plot which Mordecai thwarted. Surprised to learn that Mordecai had never been rewarded for this deed, the king asks Haman what should be done to properly thank a hero. Haman thinks the king must be talking about him, and so he describes a lavish reward. The king agrees, but to Haman's shock and utter humiliation, he learns that Mordecai is the person to be so honored.

During the second banquet, the king again asks Esther what she desires. She replies that someone has plotted to destroy her and her people, and she names Haman as the culprit. Immediately the king sentences Haman to die on the gallows which he had built for Mordecai.

In the final act of this true-life drama, Mordecai is appointed as prime minister, and the Jews are guaranteed protection throughout the land. To celebrate this historic occasion, the feast of Purim is established.

Because of Queen Esther's courageous act, a whole nation is saved. Seeing her God-given opportunity, she seized it! Her life made a difference. Read Esther and watch for God at work in *your* life. Perhaps he has prepared you to act in "such a time as this" (4.14).

Haman's decree to destroy the Jews 474	First feast of Purim 473	Artaxerxes I becomes king 465	Second group of exiles returns to Jerusalem 458	Nehemiah goes to Jerusalem 445

THE BLUEPRINT

1. Esther becomes queen (1.1—2.23)
2. The Jews are threatened (3.1—4.17)
3. Esther intercedes for the Jews (5.1—8.17)
4. The Jews are delivered (9.1—10.3)

The book of Esther is an example of God's divine guidance and care over our lives. God's sovereignty and power are seen throughout this book. Although we may question certain circumstances in our lives, we must have faith that God is in control, working through both the pleasant and difficult times so that we can serve him effectively.

MEGATHEMES

THEME	EXPLANATION	IMPORTANCE
God's sovereignty	The book of Esther tells of the circumstances that were essential to the survival of God's people in Persia. These "circumstances" were not the result of chance, but of God's grand design. God is sovereign over every area of life.	With God in charge, we can take courage. He can guide us through the circumstances we face in our lives. We should expect God to display his power in carrying out his will. As we unite our life's purposes to God's purpose, we benefit from his sovereign care.
Racial hatred	The Jews in Persia had been a minority since their deportation from Judah 100 years earlier. Haman was a descendant of King Agag, an enemy of the Jews. Lust for power and pride drove Haman to hate Mordecai, Esther's cousin. Haman convinced the king to kill all the Jews.	Racial hatred is always sinful. We must never condone it in any form. Every person on earth has intrinsic worth because God created mankind in his image. Therefore, God's people must stand against racism whenever and wherever it occurs.
Deliverance	On February 28th, the Jews celebrate the feast of Purim, which symbolizes God's deliverance. *Purim* means "dice", such as those used by Haman to set the date for the extermination of all Jews from Persia. But God overruled, using Queen Esther to intercede on behalf of the Jews.	Because God is in control of history, he is never frustrated by any turn of events or action of man. He is able to save us from the evil of this world and deliver us from sin and death. Because we trust God, we are not to fear what men may do to us; instead, we are to be confident in God's control.
Action	Faced with death, Esther and Mordecai set aside their own fear and took action. Esther risked her life by asking King Ahasuerus to save the Jews. They were not paralyzed by fear.	When outnumbered and powerless, it is natural for us to feel helpless. Esther and Mordecai resisted this temptation and acted with courage. It is not enough to know that God is in control; we must act with self-sacrifice and courage to follow God's guidance.
Wisdom	The Jews were a minority in a world hostile to them. It took great wisdom for Mordecai to survive. Serving as a faithful official of the king, Mordecai took steps to understand and work with the Persian law. Yet he did not compromise his integrity.	It takes great wisdom to survive in a non-believing world. In a setting which is for the most part hostile to Christianity, we can demonstrate wisdom by giving respect to what is true and good and by humbly standing against what is wrong.

1. Esther becomes queen

Queen Vashti is deposed

1 This happened in the days of Ahasuerus, the same Ahasuerus who ruled over 1.1
one hundred twenty-seven provinces from India to Ethiopia.[a] 2 In those days Ezra 1.2; 4.6 Neh 1.1
when King Ahasuerus sat on his royal throne in the citadel of Susa, 3 in the third Dan 5.28; 8.2
year of his reign, he gave a banquet for all his officials and ministers. The army of
Persia and Media and the nobles and governors of the provinces were present,
4 while he displayed the great wealth of his kingdom and the splendor and pomp of
his majesty for many days, one hundred eighty days in all.
5 When these days were completed, the king gave for all the people present in 1.5
the citadel of Susa, both great and small, a banquet lasting for seven days, in the Esth 7.7,8
court of the garden of the king's palace. 6 There were white cotton curtains and blue
hangings tied with cords of fine linen and purple to silver rings[b] and marble pillars.
There were couches of gold and silver on a mosaic pavement of porphyry, marble, 1.7
mother-of-pearl, and colored stones. 7 Drinks were served in golden goblets, gob- Esth 2.18
lets of different kinds, and the royal wine was lavished according to the bounty of 1.9
the king. 8 Drinking was by flagons, without restraint; for the king had given orders Esth 1.11,12, 16-19; 2.1,4
to all the officials of his palace to do as each one desired. 9 Furthermore, Queen 1.10
Vashti gave a banquet for the women in the palace of King Ahasuerus. Judg 16.25 Esth 2.21
10 On the seventh day, when the king was merry with wine, he commanded 6.2 Dan 1.3-5,18,
Mehuman, Biztha, Harbona, Bigtha and Abagtha, Zethar and Carkas, the seven 19

[a] Or *Nubia*; Heb *Cush* [b] Or *rods*

1.1 Esther's story begins in 483 B.C., 103 years after Nebuchadnezzar had taken the Jews into captivity (2 Kings 25), 54 years after Zerubbabel led the first group of exiles back to Jerusalem (Ezra 1; 2), and 25 years before Ezra led the second group to Jerusalem (Ezra 7). Esther lived in the kingdom of Persia, the dominant kingdom in the Middle East after Babylon's fall in 539 B.C. Esther's parents must have been among those exiles who chose not to return to Jerusalem, even though Cyrus, the Persian king, had issued a decree allowing them to do so. The Jewish exiles had great freedom in Persia, and many remained because they had established themselves there or were fearful of the dangerous journey back to their homeland.

1.1 Ahasuerus, also called Xerxes the Great, was Persia's fifth king (486–465 B.C.). He was proud and impulsive, as we see from the events in chapter 1. His winter palace was in Susa, where he held the banquet described in 1.3–7. Persian kings often held great banquets before going to war. In 481, Ahasuerus launched an attack against Greece. After his fleet won a great victory at Thermopylae, he was defeated at Salamis in 480 and had to return to Persia. In 479, Esther became queen.

1.2 In this context, "citadel" means "palace."

1.4 The celebration lasted six months because its real purpose was to plan the battle strategy for invading Greece and to demonstrate that the king had sufficient wealth to carry it out. Waging war was not for survival; it was a means of acquiring more wealth, territory, and power.

1.5–7 Persia was a world power, and the king, as the center of that power, was one of the wealthiest people in the world. Persian kings loved to flaunt their wealth, even wearing precious gemstones in their beards. Jewelry was a sign of rank for Persian men. Even soldiers wore great amounts of gold jewelry into battle.

1.8 "Drinking was by flagons, without restraint" means that the guests could drink as much or as little as they wished. (Usually the king controlled how much his guests could drink.)

1.9 Ancient Greek documents call Ahasuerus's wife Amestris, probably a Greek form of Vashti. Vashti was deposed in 484/483 B.C., but she is mentioned again in ancient records as the queen mother during the reign of her son, Artaxerxes, who succeeded Ahasuerus. Toward the end of Ahasuerus's reign, either Esther died or Vashti was able through her son to regain the influence she had lost.

1.10, 11 Ahasuerus made a rash, half-drunk decision, based purely on feelings. His self-restraint and practical wisdom were weakened by too much wine, and he later regretted his decision (2.1). Poor decisions are made when people don't think clearly. Base your decisions on careful thinking, not on the emotions of the moment. Impulsive decision making leads to severe complications.

1.12 Queen Vashti refused to parade before the king's all-male party, possibly because it was against Persian custom for a woman to appear before a public gathering of men. This conflict between Persian custom and the king's command put her in a difficult situation, and she chose to refuse her half-drunk husband, hoping he would come to his senses later. Some have suggested that Vashti was pregnant with Artaxerxes, who was born in 483 B.C., and that she did not want to be seen in public in that state.

Whatever the reason, her action was a breach of protocol that also placed Ahasuerus in a difficult situation. Once he made the command, as a Persian king he could not reverse it (see the note on 1.19). While preparing to invade Greece, Ahasuerus had invited

eunuchs who attended him, [11]to bring Queen Vashti before the king, wearing the
royal crown, in order to show the peoples and the officials her beauty; for she was
fair to behold. [12]But Queen Vashti refused to come at the king's command conveyed by the eunuchs. At this the king was enraged, and his anger burned within
him.

1.13 Ezra 7.14 Esth 1.16

13 Then the king consulted the sages who knew the laws[c] (for this was the
king's procedure toward all who were versed in law and custom, [14]and those next
to him were Carshena, Shethar, Admatha, Tarshish, Meres, Marsena, and Memucan, the seven officials of Persia and Media, who had access to the king, and sat
first in the kingdom): [15]"According to the law, what is to be done to Queen Vashti
because she has not performed the command of King Ahasuerus conveyed by the
eunuchs?" [16]Then Memucan said in the presence of the king and the officials, "Not
only has Queen Vashti done wrong to the king, but also to all the officials and all
the peoples who are in all the provinces of King Ahasuerus. [17]For this deed of the
queen will be made known to all women, causing them to look with contempt on

1.16 Esth 1.9; 13

[c] Cn: Heb *times*

THE WORLD OF ESTHER'S DAY
Esther lived in the capital of the vast Medo-Persian Empire, which incorporated the provinces of Media and Persia, as well as the previous empires of Assyria and Babylon. Esther, a Jewess, was chosen by King Ahasuerus to be his queen. The story of how she saved her people takes place in the palace in Susa.

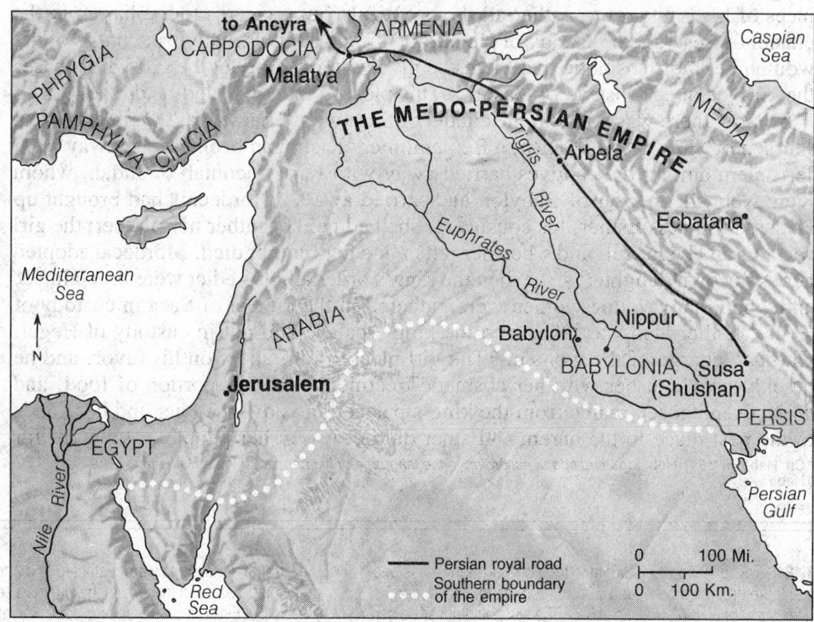

important officials from all over his land to see his power, wealth, and authority. If it was perceived that he had no authority over his own wife, his military credibility would be damaged – the greatest criterion of success for an ancient king.

1.13–15 Ahasuerus, like most rulers past and present, kept a handful of advisers whom he consulted on almost all matters. Often a king's success rose or fell on the wisdom of these men. Daniel was such an adviser under Darius and Cyrus (Daniel 6.28), and perhaps also under the next three Persian kings.

1.15 Oriental kings often did not have close personal relationships with their wives. Ahasuerus demonstrates this because (1) he had a harem (2.3); (2) he showed no respect for Vashti's personhood (1.13–15); (3) Esther, when she became queen, did not see him for long periods of time (4.11).

1.16–21 Perhaps the men's thinking had been clouded by drinking. Obviously this law would not cause the women of the country to respect their husbands. Respect between men and women comes from mutual regard and appreciation for each other as those created in God's image, not from legal pronouncements and orders. Obedience is a poor substitute for the love and respect wives and husbands should have for each other.

their husbands, since they will say, 'King Ahasuerus commanded Queen Vashti to
be brought before him, and she did not come.' 18 This very day the noble ladies of
Persia and Media who have heard of the queen's behavior will rebel against[d] the
king's officials, and there will be no end of contempt and wrath! 19 If it pleases the 1.19
king, let a royal order go out from him, and let it be written among the laws of Esth 8.8 Dan 6.8-15,17
the Persians and the Medes so that it may not be altered, that Vashti is never again
to come before King Ahasuerus; and let the king give her royal position to another
who is better than she. 20 So when the decree made by the king is proclaimed 1.20
throughout all his kingdom, vast as it is, all women will give honor to their hus- Eph 5.33 Col 3.18
bands, high and low alike." 1 Pet 3.1-7
21 This advice pleased the king and the officials, and the king did as Memucan 1.21
proposed; 22 he sent letters to all the royal provinces, to every province in its own Esth 1.13,16
script and to every people in its own language, declaring that every man should be 1.22 Esth 3.12
master in his own house.[e] 8.9,10

The king chooses Esther

2 After these things, when the anger of King Ahasuerus had abated, he remem- 2.1
bered Vashti and what she had done and what had been decreed against her. Esth 1.9
2 Then the king's servants who attended him said, "Let beautiful young virgins be
sought out for the king. 3 And let the king appoint commissioners in all the prov- 2.3
inces of his kingdom to gather all the beautiful young virgins to the harem in the Esth 1.1-3 2.9,15
citadel of Susa under custody of Hegai, the king's eunuch, who is in charge of the
women; let their cosmetic treatments be given them. 4 And let the girl who pleases
the king be queen instead of Vashti." This pleased the king, and he did so.
5 Now there was a Jew in the citadel of Susa whose name was Mordecai son of 2.5
Jair son of Shimei son of Kish, a Benjaminite. 6 Kish[f] had been carried away from Esth 3.2-6; 10.3
Jerusalem among the captives carried away with King Jeconiah of Judah, whom 2.6
King Nebuchadnezzar of Babylon had carried away. 7 Mordecai[g] had brought up 2 Kgs 24.14,15 2 Chron 36.17-20
Hadassah, that is Esther, his cousin, for she had neither father nor mother; the girl 2.7
was fair and beautiful, and when her father and her mother died, Mordecai adopted Dan 1.6,7
her as his own daughter. 8 So when the king's order and his edict were proclaimed,
and when many young women were gathered in the citadel of Susa in custody of
Hegai, Esther also was taken into the king's palace and put in custody of Hegai,
who had charge of the women. 9 The girl pleased him and won his favor, and he
quickly provided her with her cosmetic treatments and her portion of food, and
with seven chosen maids from the king's palace, and advanced her and her maids
to the best place in the harem. 10 Esther did not reveal her people or kindred, for 2.10 Esth 2.20

[d] Cn: Heb *will tell* [e] Heb adds *and speak according to the language of his people* [f] Heb *a Benjamite* [6]*who*
[g] Heb *He*

1.19 A Persian king was thought to be a god by many of his people; therefore, once he issued a law or command, it stood forever (see the note on 8.8 and Daniel 6.8). The law could never be canceled even if it was ill-advised; but if necessary, a new law could be issued to neutralize the effects of the old law.

1.20, 21 One way to rule is to issue edicts that force people to comply. Ahasuerus and his advisers responded this way. But in Matthew 20.25, 26, Jesus reminds us that this is how secular rulers act, lording it over everyone. As believers, we are to act differently. God offers his free gift of salvation to all (Titus 2.11), and he tells us to treat one another with respect and love (1 Corinthians 13).

2.1 The phrase "he remembered Vashti" means that the king began to miss his queen and what she had done for him. But he also remembered that in his anger he had banished her from his presence with a decree that couldn't be rescinded.

2.3, 14–17 Persian kings collected not only vast amounts of jewelry, but also great numbers of women. These young virgins were taken from their homes and required to live in a separate building near the palace, called a harem. Their sole purpose was to serve the king and to await his call for sexual pleasure. They rarely saw the king, and their lives were restricted and boring. If rejected, Esther would be one of many girls the king had seen once and forgotten. But Esther's presence and beauty pleased the king enough that he crowned her queen in place of Vashti. The queen held a more influential position than a concubine, and she was given more freedom and authority than others in the harem. But even as queen, Esther had few rights – especially since she had been chosen to replace a woman who had become too assertive.

2.5, 6 Mordecai was a Jew. The Jewish population had increased since their exile over 100 years earlier. They had been given great freedom and were allowed to run their own businesses and hold positions in government (2.19; Daniel 6.3).

2.6 The Bible says that Mordecai was carried into exile when Jerusalem was destroyed. If this referred to Mordecai himself, he would have been over 100 years old at the time of this story. This conflict can be resolved by understanding that the word *whom,* referring to Mordecai, can also mean *whose family.* It is likely that Mordecai's parents, grandparents, or even great-grandparents were carried into captivity rather than Mordecai himself.

2.6 Jeconiah is also called Jehoiachin in 2 Kings 24.8–17.

Mordecai had charged her not to tell. [11]Every day Mordecai would walk around in front of the court of the harem, to learn how Esther was and how she fared.

12 The turn came for each girl to go in to King Ahasuerus, after being twelve months under the regulations for the women, since this was the regular period of their cosmetic treatment, six months with oil of myrrh and six months with perfumes and cosmetics for women. [13]When the girl went in to the king she was given whatever she asked for to take with her from the harem to the king's palace. [14]In the evening she went in; then in the morning she came back to the second harem in custody of Shaashgaz, the king's eunuch, who was in charge of the concubines; she

MORDECAI

Following Jerusalem's last stand against Nebuchadnezzar, Mordecai's family was deported to the Babylonian Empire. He was probably born in Susa, a city that became one of Persia's capitals after Cyrus conquered Babylon, and inherited an official position among the Jewish captives that kept him around the palace even after the Babylonians were driven out. At one time, when he overheard plans to assassinate Ahasuerus, he reported the plot and saved the king's life.

Mordecai's life was filled with challenges that he turned into opportunities. When his aunt and uncle died, he adopted Esther, their daughter and his young cousin, probably because his own parents were dead and he felt responsible for her. Later, when she was drafted into Ahasuerus's harem and chosen to be queen, Mordecai continued to advise her. Shortly after this, he found himself in conflict with Ahasuerus's recently appointed prime minister, Haman. Although willing to serve the king, Mordecai refused to worship the king's representative. Haman was furious with Mordecai. So he planned to have Mordecai and all the Jews killed. His plan became a law of the Medes and Persians, and it looked as though the Jews were doomed.

Mordecai, willing to be God's servant wherever he was, responded by contacting Esther and telling her that one reason God had allowed her to be queen might well be to save her people from this threat. But God had also placed *him* in the right place years earlier. God revealed to the king through his nighttime reading of historical documents that Mordecai had once saved his life, and the king realized he had never thanked Mordecai. The great honor then given to Mordecai ruined Haman's plan to hang him on the gallows. God had woven an effective counter-strategy against which Haman's plan could not stand.

Later, Mordecai instituted the Jewish feast of Purim. He had a lengthy career of service to the king on behalf of the Jews. In Mordecai's life, God blended both character and circumstances to accomplish great things. He has not changed the way he works. God is using the situations you face each day to weave a pattern of godliness into your character. Pause and ask God to help you respond appropriately to the situations you find yourself in today.

Strengths and accomplishments:
- Exposed an assassination plot against the king
- Cared enough to adopt his cousin
- Refused to bow to anyone except God
- Took Haman's place as prime minister

Lessons from his life:
- The opportunities we have are more important than the ones we wish we had
- We can trust God to weave together the events of life for our best, even though we may not be able to see the overall pattern
- The rewards for doing right are sometimes delayed, but they are guaranteed by God himself

Vital statistics:
- Where: Susa, one of several capital cities in Persia
- Occupation: Jewish official who became prime minister under Ahasuerus
- Relatives: Adopted daughter: Esther. Father: Jair
- Contemporaries: Ahasuerus, Haman

Key verse:
"For Mordecai the Jew was next in rank to King Ahasuerus, and he was powerful among the Jews and popular with his many kindred, for he sought the good of his people and interceded for the welfare of all his descendants" (Esther 10.3).

Mordecai's story is told in the book of Esther.

2.10 With virtually no rights and little access to the king, it was better for Esther not to reveal her identity. While boldness in stating our identity as God's people is our responsibility, at times a good strategy is to keep quiet until we have won the right to be heard. This is especially true when dealing with those in authority over us. But we can always let them see the difference God makes in our lives.

did not go in to the king again, unless the king delighted in her and she was summoned by name.
15 When the turn came for Esther daughter of Abihail the uncle of Mordecai,
who had adopted her as his own daughter, to go in to the king, she asked for nothing
except what Hegai the king's eunuch, who had charge of the women, advised. Now
Esther was admired by all who saw her. 16 When Esther was taken to King Ahasuerus in his royal palace in the tenth month, which is the month of Tebeth, in the
seventh year of his reign, 17 the king loved Esther more than all the other women; **2.17**
of all the virgins she won his favor and devotion, so that he set the royal crown on Esth 1.11 Zech 6.10,11
her head and made her queen instead of Vashti. 18 Then the king gave a great ban- **2.18**
quet to all his officials and ministers — "Esther's banquet." He also granted a holi- Esth 1.5-8
day[h] to the provinces, and gave gifts with royal liberality.
19 When the virgins were being gathered together,[i] Mordecai was sitting at the
king's gate. 20 Now Esther had not revealed her kindred or her people, as Mordecai **2.20**
had charged her; for Esther obeyed Mordecai just as when she was brought up by Esth 2.10
him. 21 In those days, while Mordecai was sitting at the king's gate, Bigthan and **2.21**
Teresh, two of the king's eunuchs, who guarded the threshold, became angry and Esth 1.10; 6.2
conspired to assassinate[j] King Ahasuerus. 22 But the matter came to the knowledge **2.22**
of Mordecai, and he told it to Queen Esther, and Esther told the king in the name Esth 6.1,2
of Mordecai. 23 When the affair was investigated and found to be so, both the men **2.23**
were hanged on the gallows. It was recorded in the book of the annals in the pres- Ezra 6.11 Esth 5.14
ence of the king. 6.1,2; 7.10

2. The Jews are threatened

Haman plans to exterminate the Jews

3 After these things King Ahasuerus promoted Haman son of Hammedatha the **3.1**
Agagite, and advanced him and set his seat above all the officials who were Num 24.3-9 1 Sam 15.8
with him. 2 And all the king's servants who were at the king's gate bowed down and Esth 3.10; 5.11 7.6; 8.2
did obeisance to Haman; for the king had so commanded concerning him. But Mor- 9.24,25; 10.3
decai did not bow down or do obeisance. 3 Then the king's servants who were at the Dan 6.2 **3.2**
king's gate said to Mordecai, "Why do you disobey the king's command?" 4 When Esth 5.9
they spoke to him day after day and he would not listen to them, they told Haman,
in order to see whether Mordecai's words would avail; for he had told them that he
was a Jew. 5 When Haman saw that Mordecai did not bow down or do obeisance to
him, Haman was infuriated. 6 But he thought it beneath him to lay hands on Mordecai alone. So, having been told who Mordecai's people were, Haman plotted to

[h] *Or an amnesty* [i] Heb adds *a second time* [j] Heb *to lay hands on*

2.17 God placed Esther on the throne even before the Jews faced the possibility of complete destruction (3.5ff), so that when trouble came, a person would already be in the position to help. No human effort could thwart God's plan to send the Messiah to earth as a Jew. If you are changing jobs, position, or location and can't see God's purpose in your situation, understand that God is in control. He may be placing you in a position so you can help when the need arises.

3.2 Doing obeisance means to kneel and place one's face on the ground in an act of submission. Mordecai's determination came from his faith in God. He did not first take a poll to determine the safest or most popular course of action; he had the courage to stand alone. Doing what is right will not always make you popular. Those who do right will be in the minority, but to obey God is more important than to obey people (Acts 5.29).

3.2–4 Mordecai refused to bow to Haman. Jews did bow to government authorities, at times, as a sign of respect (Genesis 23.7; 1 Samuel 24.8). But in Persia, kings and their chief officials were considered divine. Mordecai was not about to kneel before wicked Haman and, by his act, acknowledge him as a god. Daniel's three friends had the same convictions (Daniel 3). We must worship God alone. We should never let any person, institution, or government take the place of God. When people demand loyalties or duties from you that do not honor God, don't give in. It may be time to take a stand.

3.5, 6 Haman enjoyed the power and prestige of his position, and he was enraged when Mordecai did not respond with the expected reverential bow. Haman's anger was not directed just toward Mordecai, but toward what Mordecai stood for – the Jews' dedication to God as the only authority worthy of reverence. Haman's attitude was prejudiced: he hated a group of people because of a difference in belief or culture. Prejudice grows out of personal pride – considering oneself better than others. In the end, Haman was punished for his arrogant attitude (7.9, 10). God will harshly judge those who are prejudiced or whose pride causes them to look down on others.

3.5, 6 Why did Haman want to destroy all Jews just because of one man's action? As second in command in the Persian Empire (3.1), Haman loved his power and authority and the reverence shown him. The Jews, however, looked to God as their final authority, not to any man. Haman realized that the only way to fulfill his self-centered desires was to kill all those who disregarded his authority. His quest for personal power led him to an all-consuming racial hatred.

destroy all the Jews, the people of Mordecai, throughout the whole kingdom of
Ahasuerus.
7 In the first month, which is the month of Nisan, in the twelfth year of King
Ahasuerus, they cast Pur—which means "the lot"—before Haman for the day and
for the month, and the lot fell on the thirteenth day[k] of the twelfth month, which
is the month of Adar. 8 Then Haman said to King Ahasuerus, "There is a certain
people scattered and separated among the peoples in all the provinces of your kingdom; their laws are different from those of every other people, and they do not keep
the king's laws, so that it is not appropriate for the king to tolerate them. 9 If it
pleases the king, let a decree be issued for their destruction, and I will pay ten
thousand talents of silver into the hands of those who have charge of the king's
business, so that they may put it into the king's treasuries." 10 So the king took his
signet ring from his hand and gave it to Haman son of Hammedatha the Agagite,
the enemy of the Jews. 11 The king said to Haman, "The money is given to you, and
the people as well, to do with them as it seems good to you."
12 Then the king's secretaries were summoned on the thirteenth day of the first
month, and an edict, according to all that Haman commanded, was written to the
king's satraps and to the governors over all the provinces and to the officials of all
the peoples, to every province in its own script and every people in its own language; it was written in the name of King Ahasuerus and sealed with the king's
ring. 13 Letters were sent by couriers to all the king's provinces, giving orders to
destroy, to kill, and to annihilate all Jews, young and old, women and children, in
one day, the thirteenth day of the twelfth month, which is the month of Adar, and
to plunder their goods. 14 A copy of the document was to be issued as a decree in
every province by proclamation, calling on all the peoples to be ready for that day.
15 The couriers went quickly by order of the king, and the decree was issued in the
citadel of Susa. The king and Haman sat down to drink; but the city of Susa was
thrown into confusion.

3.7 Esth 9.24-26 Prov 16.33 Ezek 21.21,22 Mt 27.35
3.8 Acts 16.20,21
3.9 Esth 4.7
3.10 Esth 8.2,9,10
3.12 1 Kgs 21.8 Esth 1.22 8.8-10
3.13 Esth 1.1,2 8.9-11,14 9.2,7-10,17 Isa 10.5,6
3.14 Esth 4.8 8.13,14
3.15 Esth 1.1-3

Mordecai asks Esther to help

4 When Mordecai learned all that had been done, Mordecai tore his clothes and
put on sackcloth and ashes, and went through the city, wailing with a loud and
bitter cry; 2 he went up to the entrance of the king's gate, for no one might enter the
king's gate clothed with sackcloth. 3 In every province, wherever the king's command and his decree came, there was great mourning among the Jews, with fasting
and weeping and lamenting, and most of them lay in sackcloth and ashes.
4 When Esther's maids and her eunuchs came and told her, the queen was
deeply distressed; she sent garments to clothe Mordecai, so that he might take off
his sackcloth; but he would not accept them. 5 Then Esther called for Hathach, one
of the king's eunuchs, who had been appointed to attend her, and ordered him to go
to Mordecai to learn what was happening and why. 6 Hathach went out to Mordecai
in the open square of the city in front of the king's gate, 7 and Mordecai told him all
that had happened to him, and the exact sum of money that Haman had promised
to pay into the king's treasuries for the destruction of the Jews. 8 Mordecai also
gave him a copy of the written decree issued in Susa for their destruction, that he

4.1 Gen 27.34 2 Sam 1.11 13.19 Isa 15.4 Ezek 27.30 Jonah 3.4-9 Mic 1.8
4.7 Esth 3.9
4.8 Esth 3.14 8.13,14

[k] Cn Compare Gk and verse 13 below: Heb *the twelfth month*

3.7 Haman cast lots (or threw dice) to determine the best day to carry out his decree. Little did he know that he was playing into the hands of God, for the day of death was set for almost a year away, giving Esther time to make her plea to the king. The Persian word for lots or dice was *purim,* which became the name for the holiday celebrated by the Jews when they were delivered, not killed, on the day appointed by Haman.

3.10–12 Officials in the ancient world used signet rings as personal signatures. The ring's surface had a raised imprint made of metal, wood, or bone. Each individual had his own imprint. Letters were sealed by pressing the ring into soft wax, and official documents were certified by using the royal signet. By giving Haman his signet ring, Ahasuerus gave him his personal signature and with it the authority to do whatever he wished. Little did the king realize that his own ring would sign the death warrant for his wife, Esther.

3.13 Haman's death decree was against all Jews in the Persian Empire; thus it would have included the land of Israel. If his decree had been carried out, all of God's chosen people could have been exterminated, and God's plan to send his Son to earth as a Jew could have been ruined. But God's plans cannot be stopped. Haman was doomed to fail.

4.8 "To make supplication to him and entreat him" means to beg and plead for mercy.

might show it to Esther, explain it to her, and charge her to go to the king to make
supplication to him and entreat him for her people.
9 Hathach went and told Esther what Mordecai had said. 10 Then Esther spoke
to Hathach and gave him a message for Mordecai, saying, 11 "All the king's ser- **4.11**
vants and the people of the king's provinces know that if any man or woman goes Esth 5.1,2; 8.4
to the king inside the inner court without being called, there is but one law—all
alike are to be put to death. Only if the king holds out the golden scepter to someone, may that person live. I myself have not been called to come in to the king for
thirty days." 12 When they told Mordecai what Esther had said, 13 Mordecai told
them to reply to Esther, "Do not think that in the king's palace you will escape any
more than all the other Jews. 14 For if you keep silence at such a time as this, relief
and deliverance will rise for the Jews from another quarter, but you and your father's family will perish. Who knows? Perhaps you have come to royal dignity for
just such a time as this." 15 Then Esther said in reply to Mordecai, 16 "Go, gather all **4.16**
the Jews to be found in Susa, and hold a fast on my behalf, and neither eat nor drink 2 Chron 20.3 Joel 2.2-17
for three days, night or day. I and my maids will also fast as you do. After that I will Jonah 3.4-9
go to the king, though it is against the law; and if I perish, I perish." 17 Mordecai
then went away and did everything as Esther had ordered him.

3. Esther intercedes for the Jews

Esther appears before the king

5 On the third day Esther put on her royal robes and stood in the inner court of **5.1**
the king's palace, opposite the king's hall. The king was sitting on his royal Esth 4.11
throne inside the palace opposite the entrance to the palace. 2 As soon as the king **5.2** Esth 4.11; 8.4
saw Queen Esther standing in the court, she won his favor and he held out to her the **5.3**
golden scepter that was in his hand. Then Esther approached and touched the top of 1 Kgs 2.20 Esth 5.6; 7.2
the scepter. 3 The king said to her, "What is it, Queen Esther? What is your request? 9.12 Mt 20.20-22
It shall be given you, even to the half of my kingdom." 4 Then Esther said, "If it Lk 18.41

4.11–5.2 Esther risked her life by coming before the king. Her courageous act gives us a model to follow in approaching a difficult or dangerous task. Like Esther, we can: (1) *Calculate the cost.* Esther realized her life was at stake. (2) *Set priorities.* She believed that the safety of the Jewish race was more important than her life. (3) *Prepare.* She gathered support and fasted. (4) *Determine a course of action and move ahead boldly.* She didn't think too long about it, allowing the interlude to lessen her commitment to what she had to do.

Do you have to face a hostile audience, confront a friend on a delicate subject, or talk to your family about changes to be made? Rather than dreading difficult situations or putting them off, take action with confidence by following Esther's inspiring example.

4.13 Although Esther was the queen and shared some of the king's power and wealth, she still needed God's protection and wisdom. No one is secure in his or her own strength in any political system. It is foolish to believe that wealth or position can make us impervious to danger. Recognize that deliverance comes from God.

4.13, 14 After the decree to kill the Jews was given, Mordecai and Esther could have despaired, decided to save only themselves, or just waited for God's intervention. Instead, they saw that God had placed them in their positions for a purpose, so they seized the moment and acted. When it is within our reach to save others, we must do so. In a life-threatening situation, don't withdraw, behave selfishly, wallow in despair, or wait for God to fix everything. Instead, ask God for his direction, and *act!* God may have placed you where you are "for just such a time as this."

4.13–17 Esther and Mordecai believed that God would deliver his people, but they didn't just sit around and wait. They took action. Although God is sovereign, he works through people. That is why we must *do* his will, not just watch and pray. Many people believe God's promises, but they hesitate to take action. Esther, however, determined to see the king, and Mordecai carried out her instructions. Don't wait for others to do for you what you can do. *Get involved,* and enjoy the results of sharing in God's purposes for mankind.

4.14 It is obvious that Mordecai expected God to deliver his people. While the book of Esther does not mention God directly, his presence fills the pages. Esther and Mordecai believed in God's care, and because they acted at the right time, God used them to save his people.

4.16 By calling for a fast, Esther was asking the Jews to pray for God's help on her dangerous mission. In the Old Testament, prayer always accompanies fasting (see Exodus 34.28; Deuteronomy 9.9; Ezra 8.21–23). An important function of a community of believers is mutual support in difficult times. When you are experiencing struggles, turn to fellow believers for support by sharing your trials with them and gaining strength from the bond that unites you. Ask them to pray for you. And when others need your support, give it willingly.

4.16 "Save your own skin" and "Watch out for number one" are mottoes that reflect the world's selfish outlook on life. Esther's attitude stands in bold contrast to this. She knew what she had to do, and she knew it could cost her her life. And yet she responded, "If I perish, I perish." We should have the same commitment to do what is right despite the possible consequences. Do you try to save your own skin by remaining silent rather than standing up for what is right? Commit yourself to do what God wants, and trust him for the outcome.

4.17–5.1 God was in control, yet Mordecai and Esther had to act. We cannot understand how both can be true at the same time, and yet they are. God chooses to work through those *willing* to act for him. We should pray as if all depended on God and act as if all depended on us. We should avoid two extremes: doing nothing, and feeling that we must do it all.

pleases the king, let the king and Haman come today to a banquet that I have pre-
5.5 Esth 6.14 pared for the king." 5 Then the king said, "Bring Haman quickly, so that we may do
as Esther desires." So the king and Haman came to the banquet that Esther had
prepared. 6 While they were drinking wine, the king said to Esther, "What is your
petition? It shall be granted you. And what is your request? Even to the half of my
kingdom, it shall be fulfilled." 7 Then Esther said, "This is my petition and request:
8 If I have won the king's favor, and if it pleases the king to grant my petition and
fulfill my request, let the king and Haman come tomorrow to the banquet that I will
prepare for them, and then I will do as the king has said."

Haman becomes furious with Mordecai

5.9 Esth 3.2 9 Haman went out that day happy and in good spirits. But when Haman saw
Mordecai in the king's gate, and observed that he neither rose nor trembled before
5.10 Esth 5.14; 6.13 him, he was infuriated with Mordecai; 10 nevertheless Haman restrained himself
and went home. Then he sent and called for his friends and his wife Zeresh, 11 and
Haman recounted to them the splendor of his riches, the number of his sons, all the
promotions with which the king had honored him, and how he had advanced him
above the officials and the ministers of the king. 12 Haman added, "Even Queen
Esther let no one but myself come with the king to the banquet that she prepared.
Tomorrow also I am invited by her, together with the king. 13 Yet all this does me
5.14 Esth 5.10; 7.9 no good so long as I see the Jew Mordecai sitting at the king's gate." 14 Then his
wife Zeresh and all his friends said to him, "Let a gallows fifty cubits high be made,
and in the morning tell the king to have Mordecai hanged on it; then go with the
king to the banquet in good spirits." This advice pleased Haman, and he had the
gallows made.

GOD BEHIND THE SCENES IN ESTHER

Although God's name is not mentioned in the Hebrew text of Esther, he makes himself known in these ways:

Indirect References	2.17	Esther, who worshiped God, became queen
	4.14	In the Hebrew text God's existence and his power over the affairs of men are assumed.
	4.16	Fasting was a distinct spiritual activity usually connected with prayer.
Divine Incidents The book of Esther is filled with divine interventions	2.21, 23	Mordecai overhears a death plot and saves the king's life
	6.1	Ahasuerus can't sleep, decides to read a history book
	6.2	Ahasuerus reads the exact page needed for the moment, reminding him of an unpaid reward to Mordecai
	7.9, 10	Haman's plan is exactly reversed—the intended victims are the victors

Why was God's name hidden in the book of Esther? There were many gods in the Middle East and Persian Empire. Usually, their names were mentioned in official documents in order to control the peoples who worshiped those particular gods. The Jews were unique in being the people of one God. A story about them was naturally a story about God, for even the name "Jew" carried with it the connotation of one who worshiped Jehovah.

5.9 Hatred and bitterness are like weeds with long roots that grow in the heart and corrupt all of life. Haman was so consumed with hatred toward Mordecai that he could not even enjoy the honor of being invited to Esther's party. Hebrews 12.15 warns us to watch out "that no root of bitterness springs up and causes trouble, and through it many become defiled." Don't let hatred and its resulting bitterness build in your heart. Like Haman, you will find it backfiring on you (see 6.13; 7.9, 10). If the mere mention of someone's name provokes you to anger, confess your bitterness as sin. Ignoring bitterness, hiding it from others, or making superficial changes in behavior is not enough. If bitterness isn't completely removed, it will grow back, making matters worse.

5.14 Haman's family and friends, who were as arrogant as he, suggested that the gallows be 50 cubits—75 feet—high, built on the city wall or some prominent building. They wanted to make sure that all the people of the city saw Mordecai's death and would be reminded of the consequences of disobeying Haman. Ironically, these high gallows allowed everyone to see Haman's death.

The king honors Mordecai

6 On that night the king could not sleep, and he gave orders to bring the book of 6.1
records, the annals, and they were read to the king. 2 It was found written how Esth 2.21-23
Mordecai had told about Bigthana and Teresh, two of the king's eunuchs, who
guarded the threshold, and who had conspired to assassinate[l] King Ahasuerus.
3 Then the king said, "What honor or distinction has been bestowed on Mordecai
for this?" The king's servants who attended him said, "Nothing has been done for
him." 4 The king said, "Who is in the court?" Now Haman had just entered the outer
court of the king's palace to speak to the king about having Mordecai hanged on the
gallows that he had prepared for him. 5 So the king's servants told him, "Haman is
there, standing in the court." The king said, "Let him come in." 6 So Haman came
in, and the king said to him, "What shall be done for the man whom the king wishes
to honor?" Haman said to himself, "Whom would the king wish to honor more than
me?" 7 So Haman said to the king, "For the man whom the king wishes to honor, 6.7
8 let royal robes be brought, which the king has worn, and a horse that the king has 1 Kgs 1.33
ridden, with a royal crown on its head. 9 Let the robes and the horse be handed over Zech 9.9 6.9
to one of the king's most noble officials; let him[m] robe the man whom the king Gen 41.43
wishes to honor, and let him[m] conduct the man on horseback through the open 1 Kgs 1.34
square of the city, proclaiming before him: 'Thus shall it be done for the man whom
the king wishes to honor.' " 10 Then the king said to Haman, "Quickly, take the
robes and the horse, as you have said, and do so to the Jew Mordecai who sits at
the king's gate. Leave out nothing that you have mentioned." 11 So Haman took the
robes and the horse and robed Mordecai and led him riding through the open square
of the city, proclaiming, "Thus shall it be done for the man whom the king wishes
to honor."

12 Then Mordecai returned to the king's gate, but Haman hurried to his house, 6.12
mourning and with his head covered. 13 When Haman told his wife Zeresh and all 2 Sam 15.30 Esth 7.8
his friends everything that had happened to him, his advisers and his wife Zeresh Jer 14.3
said to him, "If Mordecai, before whom your downfall has begun, is of the Jewish 6.13
people, you will not prevail against him, but will surely fall before him." Esth 5.10,14

The king hangs Haman

14 While they were still talking with him, the king's eunuchs arrived and hur- 6.14
7 ried Haman off to the banquet that Esther had prepared. 1 So the king and Ha- Esth 5.5-8
man went in to feast with Queen Esther. 2 On the second day, as they were 7.2
drinking wine, the king again said to Esther, "What is your petition, Queen Esther? Esth 5.3,6
It shall be granted you. And what is your request? Even to the half of my kingdom, 7.3-6
it shall be fulfilled." 3 Then Queen Esther answered, "If I have won your fa- 7.3
vor, O king, and if it pleases the king, let my life be given me—that is my Esth 5.7,8; 8.5
petition—and the lives of my people—that is my request. 4 For we have been sold, 7.4
I and my people, to be destroyed, to be killed, and to be annihilated. If we had been Deut 28.68 Esth 3.9,13
sold merely as slaves, men and women, I would have held my peace; but no enemy 4.7,8; 8.6
can compensate for this damage to the king."[n] 5 Then King Ahasuerus said to 7.6
Queen Esther, "Who is he, and where is he, who has presumed to do this?" 6 Esther Esth 8.1

[l] Heb *to lay hands on* [m] Heb *them* [n] Meaning of Heb uncertain

---

6.1, 2 Unable to sleep, the king decided to review the history of his reign, and his servants read to him about Mordecai's good deed. This seems coincidental, but God is *always* at work. God has been working quietly and patiently throughout your life as well. The events that have come together for good are not mere coincidence; they are the result of God's sovereign control over the course of people's lives (Romans 8.28).

6.7–9 Haman had wealth, but he craved something even his money couldn't buy—respect. He could buy the trappings of success and power, but his lust for popularity had become an obsession. Don't let your desire for approval, applause, and popularity drive you to immoral actions.

6.10–13 Mordecai had uncovered a plot to assassinate Ahasuerus—thus he had saved the king's life (2.21–23). Although his good deed was recorded in the history books, Mordecai had gone unrewarded. But God was saving Mordecai's reward for the right time. Just as Haman was about to hang Mordecai unjustly, the king was ready to give the reward. Although God promises to reward our good works, we sometimes feel our "payoff" is too far away. Be patient. God steps in when it will do the most good.

6.12 Just the night before (5.9–14), Haman had bragged about his position and the honor he was about to receive. Now he was humiliated and soon to be marked for death (7.8–10). How quickly the course of life can change. Because we cannot predict what will happen, it is best to avoid bragging (James 4.13–16). God is displeased with this kind of self-reliance.

said, "A foe and enemy, this wicked Haman!" Then Haman was terrified before the
king and the queen. 7The king rose from the feast in wrath and went into the palace
garden, but Haman stayed to beg his life from Queen Esther, for he saw that the
king had determined to destroy him. 8When the king returned from the palace garden to the banquet hall, Haman had thrown himself on the couch where Esther was
reclining; and the king said, "Will he even assault the queen in my presence, in my
own house?" As the words left the mouth of the king, they covered Haman's face.
9Then Harbona, one of the eunuchs in attendance on the king, said, "Look, the
very gallows that Haman has prepared for Mordecai, whose word saved the king,
stands at Haman's house, fifty cubits high." And the king said, "Hang him on

7.9 Esth 5.14

ESTHER

We treasure security, even though we know that security in this life carries no guarantees—possessions can be destroyed, beauty fades, relationships can be broken, death is inevitable. Real security, then, must be found beyond this life. Only when our security rests on God and his unchanging nature can we face the challenges that life is sure to bring our way.

Esther's beauty and character won Ahasuerus's heart, and he made her his queen. Even in her favored position, however, she would risk her life by attempting to see the king when he had not requested her presence. There was no guarantee that the king would even see her. Although she was queen, she was still not secure. But, cautiously and courageously, Esther decided to risk her life by approaching the king on behalf of her people.

She made her plans carefully. The Jews were asked to fast and pray with her before she went to the king. Then on the chosen day she went before him, and he *did* ask her to come forward and speak. But instead of issuing her request directly, she invited him and Haman to a banquet. He was astute enough to realize she had something on her mind, yet she conveyed the importance of the matter by insisting on a second banquet.

In the meantime, God was working behind the scenes. He caused Ahasuerus to read the historical records of the kingdom late one night, and the king discovered that Mordecai had once saved his life. Ahasuerus lost no time in honoring Mordecai for that act. During the second banquet, Esther told the king of Haman's plot against the Jews, and Haman was doomed. There is grim justice in Haman's death on the gallows he had built for Mordecai, and it seems fitting that the day on which the Jews were to be slaughtered became the day their enemies died. Esther's risk confirmed that God was the source of her security.

How much of your security lies in your possessions, position, or reputation? God has not placed you in your present position for your own benefit. He put you there *to serve him.* As in Esther's case, this may involve risking your security. Are you willing to let God be your ultimate security?

Strengths and accomplishments:
- Her beauty and character won the heart of Persia's king
- She combined courage with careful planning
- She was open to advice and willing to act
- She was more concerned for others than for her own security

Lessons from her life:
- Serving God often demands that we risk our own security
- God has a purpose for the situations in which he places us
- Courage, while often vital, does not replace careful planning

Vital statistics:
- Where: Persian Empire
- Occupation: Ahasuerus's wife, queen of Persia
- Relatives: Cousin: Mordecai. Husband: Ahasuerus. Father: Abihail

Key verse:
"Go, gather all the Jews to be found in Susa, and hold a fast on my behalf, and neither eat nor drink for three days, night or day. I and my maids will also fast as you do. After that I will go to the king, though it is against the law; and if I perish, I perish" (Esther 4.16).

Esther's story is told in the book of Esther.

7.6–10 Haman's hatred and evil plotting turned against him as he was hanged on the gallows he had built for someone else. Proverbs 26.27 says that a person who digs a pit for others will fall into it himself. What happened to Haman shows the often violent results of setting any kind of trap for others.

7.8 A veil was placed over the face of someone condemned to death, because Persian kings refused to look upon the face of a condemned person.

that." 10 So they hanged Haman on the gallows that he had prepared for Mordecai. **7.10** Esth 8.7
Then the anger of the king abated. Ps 7.16; 94.23

The king makes a decree for the Jews

8 On that day King Ahasuerus gave to Queen Esther the house of Haman, the **8.1** Esth 7.6
enemy of the Jews; and Mordecai came before the king, for Esther had told
what he was to her. 2 Then the king took off his signet ring, which he had taken **8.2** Esth 3.10
from Haman, and gave it to Mordecai. So Esther set Mordecai over the house of
Haman.
3 Then Esther spoke again to the king; she fell at his feet, weeping and pleading
with him to avert the evil design of Haman the Agagite and the plot that he had
devised against the Jews. 4 The king held out the golden scepter to Esther, 5 and **8.4**
Esther rose and stood before the king. She said, "If it pleases the king, and if I have Esth 4.11; 5.2 **8.5**
won his favor, and if the thing seems right before the king, and I have his approval, Esth 1.22
let an order be written to revoke the letters devised by Haman son of Hammedatha 5.7,8; 7.3 8.9,10
the Agagite, which he wrote giving orders to destroy the Jews who are in all the
provinces of the king. 6 For how can I bear to see the calamity that is coming on my **8.6**
people? Or how can I bear to see the destruction of my kindred?" 7 Then King Ahas- Esth 3.13; 7.4 **8.7**
uerus said to Queen Esther and to the Jew Mordecai, "See, I have given Esther the Esth 7.10; 8.1
house of Haman, and they have hanged him on the gallows, because he plotted to
lay hands on the Jews. 8 You may write as you please with regard to the Jews, in the **8.8**
name of the king, and seal it with the king's ring; for an edict written in the name Esth 1.19 3.2,12
of the king and sealed with the king's ring cannot be revoked." 8.2,9,10,14 Dan 6.8-15,17
9 The king's secretaries were summoned at that time, in the third month, which **8.9**
is the month of Sivan, on the twenty-third day; and an edict was written, according Esth 1.1,2,22
to all that Mordecai commanded, to the Jews and to the satraps and the governors 3.12; 8.8
and the officials of the provinces from India to Ethiopia,[o] one hundred twenty-
seven provinces, to every province in its own script and to every people in its own
language, and also to the Jews in their script and their language. 10 He wrote letters
in the name of King Ahasuerus, sealed them with the king's ring, and sent them by
mounted couriers riding on fast steeds bred from the royal herd.[p] 11 By these letters **8.11**
the king allowed the Jews who were in every city to assemble and defend their Esth 9.2
lives, to destroy, to kill, and to annihilate any armed force of any people or province that might attack them, with their children and women, and to plunder their
goods 12 on a single day throughout all the provinces of King Ahasuerus, on the **8.12**
thirteenth day of the twelfth month, which is the month of Adar. 13 A copy of the Esth 3.13 9.1,17
writ was to be issued as a decree in every province and published to all peoples, and **8.13**
the Jews were to be ready on that day to take revenge on their enemies. 14 So the Esth 3.14; 4.8
couriers, mounted on their swift royal steeds, hurried out, urged by the king's command. The decree was issued in the citadel of Susa.
15 Then Mordecai went out from the presence of the king, wearing royal robes **8.15**
of blue and white, with a great golden crown and a mantle of fine linen and purple, Esth 1.6; 5.1 6.8,11
while the city of Susa shouted and rejoiced. 16 For the Jews there was light and Lk 16.19
gladness, joy and honor. 17 In every province and in every city, wherever the king's **8.17**
command and his edict came, there was gladness and joy among the Jews, a festi- Esth 9.19-31 Zech 8.20-23

[o] Or *Nubia*; Heb *Cush* [p] Meaning of Heb uncertain

8.1–7 While we should not expect earthly rewards for being faithful to God, they often come. Esther and Mordecai were faithful, even to the point of risking their lives to save others. When they were willing to give up everything, God gave them a reward in proportion to their all-out commitment.

8.3 An "evil design" means an evil scheme.

8.8 Haman's message had been sealed with the king's ring and could not be reversed, even by the king. It was part of the famed "law of the Medes and Persians." Now the king gave permission for whatever other decree Mordecai could devise that would offset the first, without actually canceling it.

8.12 This was the day set by Haman for the extermination of the Jews.

8.15 A *mantle* was an outer cloak.

8.15–17 Everyone wants to be a hero and receive praise, honor, and wealth. But few are willing to pay the price. Mordecai served the government faithfully for years, bore Haman's hatred and oppression, and risked his life for his people. The price to be paid by God's heroes is long-term commitment. Are you ready and willing to pay the price?

val and a holiday. Furthermore, many of the peoples of the country professed to be Jews, because the fear of the Jews had fallen upon them.

4. The Jews are delivered

The Jews triumph over their enemies

9.1 Esth 3.13 8.11,12; 9.17

9 Now in the twelfth month, which is the month of Adar, on the thirteenth day,
when the king's command and edict were about to be executed, on the very
day when the enemies of the Jews hoped to gain power over them, but which had
been changed to a day when the Jews would gain power over their foes, 2 the Jews
gathered in their cities throughout all the provinces of King Ahasuerus to lay hands
on those who had sought their ruin; and no one could withstand them, because the
fear of them had fallen upon all peoples. 3 All the officials of the provinces, the
satraps and the governors, and the royal officials were supporting the Jews, because the fear of Mordecai had fallen upon them. 4 For Mordecai was powerful in
the king's house, and his fame spread throughout all the provinces as the man

9.3 Esth 8.17

The most arrogant people are often those who must measure their self-worth by the power or influence they think they have over others. Haman was an extremely arrogant leader. He recognized the king as his superior, but could not accept anyone as an equal. When one man, Mordecai, refused to bow in submission to him, Haman wanted to destroy him. He became consumed with hatred for Mordecai and, in turn, for all the Jewish people. Mordecai's dedication to God and his refusal to give homage to any human person challenged Haman's self-centered religion. Haman saw the Jews as a threat to his power, and he decided to kill them all.

God was preparing Haman's downfall and the protection of his people long before Haman became prime minister under Ahasuerus. Esther, a Jew, became queen, and Mordecai's role in exposing an assassination plot indebted the king to him. Not only was Haman prevented from killing Mordecai, he also had to suffer the humiliation of publicly honoring him. Within hours, Haman died on the gallows he had built to hang Mordecai, and his plan to wipe out the Jews was thwarted. In contrast to Esther, who risked everything for God and won, Haman risked everything for an evil purpose and lost.

Our initial response to the story about Haman is to say that he got what he deserved. But the Bible leads us to ask deeper questions, "How much of Haman is in me?" "Do I desire to control others?" "Am I threatened when others don't appreciate me as I think they should?" "Do I want revenge when my pride is attacked?" Confess these attitudes to God and ask him to replace them with an attitude of forgiveness. Otherwise, God's justice will settle the matter.

Strength and accomplishment:
- Achieved great power, second in command to Persia's King Ahasuerus

Weaknesses and mistakes:
- The desire to control others and receive honor was his highest goal
- Was blinded by arrogance and self-importance
- Planned to murder Mordecai and built a gallows for him
- Orchestrated the plan to slaughter God's people throughout the empire

Lessons from his life:
- Hatred will be punished
- God has an amazing record for making evil plans backfire on the planners
- Pride and self-importance will be punished
- An insatiable thirst for power and prestige is self-destructive

Vital statistics:
- Where: Susa, the capital of Persia
- Occupation: Prime minister
- Relatives: Wife: Zeresh
- Contemporaries: Ahasuerus, Mordecai, Esther

Key verses:
"When Haman saw that Mordecai did not bow down or do obeisance to him, Haman was infuriated. But he thought it beneath him to lay hands on Mordecai alone. So, having been told who Mordecai's people were, Haman plotted to destroy all the Jews, the people of Mordecai, throughout the whole kingdom of Ahasuerus" (Esther 3.5, 6).

Haman's story is told in the book of Esther.

Mordecai grew more and more powerful. 5 So the Jews struck down all their enemies **9.5**
with the sword, slaughtering, and destroying them, and did as they pleased to those Esth 3.13
who hated them. 6 In the citadel of Susa the Jews killed and destroyed five hundred 9.6-16
people. 7 They killed Parshandatha, Dalphon, Aspatha, 8 Poratha, Adalia, Arida- **9.7**
tha, 9 Parmashta, Arisai, Aridai, Vaizatha, 10 the ten sons of Haman son of Hamme- Esth 9.12,13,
datha, the enemy of the Jews; but they did not touch the plunder. 24,25

11 That very day the number of those killed in the citadel of Susa was reported
to the king. 12 The king said to Queen Esther, "In the citadel of Susa the Jews have
killed five hundred people and also the ten sons of Haman. What have they done in
the rest of the king's provinces? Now what is your petition? It shall be granted you.
And what further is your request? It shall be fulfilled." 13 Esther said, "If it pleases
the king, let the Jews who are in Susa be allowed tomorrow also to do according to
this day's edict, and let the ten sons of Haman be hanged on the gallows." 14 So the
king commanded this to be done; a decree was issued in Susa, and the ten sons of
Haman were hanged. 15 The Jews who were in Susa gathered also on the fourteenth
day of the month of Adar and they killed three hundred persons in Susa; but they
did not touch the plunder.

16 Now the other Jews who were in the king's provinces also gathered to defend their lives, and gained relief from their enemies, and killed seventy-five thousand of those who hated them; but they laid no hands on the plunder. 17 This was on **9.17**
the thirteenth day of the month of Adar, and on the fourteenth day they rested and Esth 3.13; 8.12
made that a day of feasting and gladness. 9.1

The feast of Purim is inaugurated

18 But the Jews who were in Susa gathered on the thirteenth day and on the
fourteenth, and rested on the fifteenth day, making that a day of feasting and gladness. 19 Therefore the Jews of the villages, who live in the open towns, hold the **9.19**
fourteenth day of the month of Adar as a day for gladness and feasting, a holiday Neh 8.10 Esth 8.17
on which they send gifts of food to one another. 9.20-31

20 Mordecai recorded these things, and sent letters to all the Jews who were in
all the provinces of King Ahasuerus, both near and far, 21 enjoining them that they
should keep the fourteenth day of the month Adar and also the fifteenth day of the
same month, year by year, 22 as the days on which the Jews gained relief from their
enemies, and as the month that had been turned for them from sorrow into gladness
and from mourning into a holiday; that they should make them days of feasting and
gladness, days for sending gifts of food to one another and presents to the poor.
23 So the Jews adopted as a custom what they had begun to do, as Mordecai had
written to them.

24 Haman son of Hammedatha the Agagite, the enemy of all the Jews, had **9.24**
plotted against the Jews to destroy them, and had cast Pur—that is "the lot"—to Esth 3.1,7 7.9,10; 8.7
crush and destroy them; 25 but when Esther came before the king, he gave orders in 9.12,13
writing that the wicked plot that he had devised against the Jews should come upon
his own head, and that he and his sons should be hanged on the gallows. 26 There- **9.26**
fore these days are called Purim, from the word Pur. Thus because of all that was Esth 3.7
written in this letter, and of what they had faced in this matter, and of what had **9.27**
happened to them, 27 the Jews established and accepted as a custom for themselves Esth 9.20,21

9.5–16 Haman had decreed that on the thirteenth day of the twelfth month anyone could kill the Jews and take their property. Mordecai's decree could not reverse Haman's because no law signed by the king could be repealed. Instead, Mordecai had the king sign a new law giving Jews the right to fight back. When the dreaded day arrived, there was much fighting, but the Jews killed only those who wanted to kill them, and they did not take their enemies' possessions even though they could have (8.11; 9.10, 16). There were no additional riots after the two-day slaughter, so obviously selfish gain or revenge were not primary motives of the Jews. They simply wanted to defend themselves and their families from those who hated them.

9.11 Here the word *citadel* seems to refer to the fortified city of Susa. The king appears to be more concerned about Esther's wishes than the slaughter of his subjects.

9.19–22 People tend to have short memories when it comes to God's faithfulness. To help counter this, Mordecai wrote down these events and encouraged an annual holiday to commemorate the historic day of Purim. Celebrations of feasting, gladness, and gift-giving are important ways to remember God's specific acts. Today the festivities of Christmas and Easter help us remember the birth and resurrection of Jesus Christ. Don't let the celebration or the exchanging of gifts hide the meaning of these great events.

and their descendants and all who joined them, that without fail they would continue to observe these two days every year, as it was written and at the time
9.28 Esth 9.23 appointed. 28 These days should be remembered and kept throughout every generation, in every family, province, and city; and these days of Purim should never fall
into disuse among the Jews, nor should the commemoration of these days cease
among their descendants.
9.29 Esth 1.1,2 8.9,10 9.23,26-28 29 Queen Esther daughter of Abihail, along with the Jew Mordecai, gave full
written authority, confirming this second letter about Purim. 30 Letters were sent
wishing peace and security to all the Jews, to the one hundred twenty-seven provinces of the kingdom of Ahasuerus, 31 and giving orders that these days of Purim
should be observed at their appointed seasons, as the Jew Mordecai and Queen
Esther enjoined on the Jews, just as they had laid down for themselves and for their

HOW GOD WORKS IN THE WORLD

God's will	*What God wants done—He works through . . .*		
	⬇*Natural order*	⬇*Miracles*	⬇*Providence*
God's action	⬇God set into action through creation a normal working of his universe. He also revealed his expectations of man through his Word and man's conscience.	⬇God breaks into the natural order to respond to the expressed needs of people.	⬇God overrules the natural order to accomplish an act which people may or may not have requested.
Examples from Esther	⬇God gave Esther natural beauty.	⬇God allowed Esther to speak to the king.	⬇God allowed Mordecai to overhear a plot.
	⬆Esther planned a way to save her people.	⬆The people prayed and fasted.	⬆Mordecai trusted God to accomplish what was impossible in human terms.
Man's will	*What man wants done—He either . . .*		
	⬆*Plans*	⬆*Prays*	⬆*Trusts & Obeys*
Action we can take	⬆Can make plans based on the order and dependability of God's creation. Know and obey his words.	⬆Can ask God to intervene in certain affairs while realizing that our knowledge and perspective are limited.	⬆Can trust that God is in control even when the circumstances may not seem to indicate that he is.
	or . . .		
Mistakes we can make	⬇*Disobeys*	⬇*Demands*	⬇*Despairs*
	⬇*Can violate the natural order, disobey God's commands.*	⬇Can assume that we understand what is needed and expect God to agree and answer our prayers that way.	⬇Can assume God doesn't answer prayer or respond to our needs and live as though there is nothing but the natural order.

9.29–31 Among Jews, women were expected to be quiet, to serve in the home, and to stay on the fringe of religious and political life. But Esther was a Jewish woman who broke through the cultural norms, stepping outside her expected role to risk her life to help God's people. Whatever your place in life, God can use you. Be open, available, and ready, because God may use you to do what others are afraid even to consider.

descendants regulations concerning their fasts and their lamentations. 32 The command of Queen Esther fixed these practices of Purim, and it was recorded in writing.

Mordecai is given great authority

10 King Ahasuerus laid tribute on the land and on the islands of the sea. 2 All the
acts of his power and might, and the full account of the high honor of Mordecai, to which the king advanced him, are they not written in the annals of the kings
of Media and Persia? 3 For Mordecai the Jew was next in rank to King Ahasuerus,
and he was powerful among the Jews and popular with his many kindred, for he
sought the good of his people and interceded for the welfare of all his descendants.

10.2 Esth 2.23; 6.1

10.3 Gen 41.43,44 Esth 5.11; 8.2 Dan 6.2

10.3 Mordecai enjoyed a good reputation among the Jews because he was still their friend when he rose to a place of power. Corruption and abuse of authority often characterize those in power. But power used to lift the fallen and ease the burden of the oppressed is power used well. People placed by God in positions of power or political influence must not turn their backs on those in need.

10.3 No archeological records of Mordecai's being prime minister have been discovered, but during this time there is a strange gap in ancient Persian records. The records indicate that another man became prime minister in 465 B.C., about seven years after Mordecai was first appointed. One tablet has been discovered naming Mardukaya as an official in the early years of Ahasuerus's reign; some believe this was Mordecai.

10.3 In the book of Esther, we clearly see God at work in the lives of individuals and in the affairs of a nation. Even when it looks as if the world is in the hands of evil men, God is still in control, protecting those who are his. Although we may not understand everything happening around us, we must trust in God's protection and retain our integrity by doing what we know is right. Esther, who risked her life appearing before the king, became a heroine. Mordecai, who was effectively condemned to death, rose to become the prime minister of the nation. No matter how hopeless our condition, or how much we would like to give up, we need not despair. God is in control of our world.

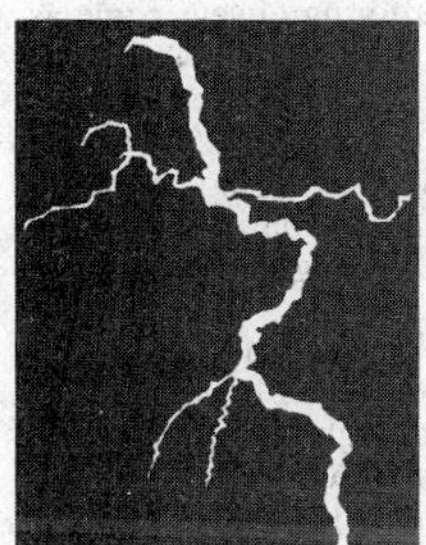

TREES snap like toothpicks or fly upward, wrenched from the earth. Whole rooftops sail, cars tumble like toys, walls collapse, and a mountain of water jumps the shore and engulfs the land. A hurricane cuts and tears, and only solid foundations survive her unbridled fury. But those foundations can be used for rebuilding after the storm.

For any building, the foundation is critical. It must be deep enough and solid enough to withstand the weight of the building and other stresses. Lives are like buildings, and the quality of their foundation will determine the quality of the whole. Too often inferior materials are used, and when tests come, lives crumble.

Job was tested. With a life filled with prestige, possessions, and people, he was suddenly assaulted on every side, devastated, stripped down to his foundation. But his life was built on God, and he endured.

Job, the book, tells the story of Job, the man of God. It is a gripping drama of riches-to-rags-to-riches, a theological treatise about suffering and divine sovereignty, and a picture of faith that endures. As you read Job, analyze your life and check your foundation. And may you be able to say that when all is gone but God, he is enough.

Job is a prosperous farmer living in the land of Uz. He has thousands of sheep, camels, and other livestock, a large family, and many servants. Suddenly Satan, the Accuser, comes before God claiming that Job trusts God only because he is wealthy and everything is going well for him. And so the testing of Job's faith begins.

Satan is allowed to destroy Job's children, servants, livestock, herdsmen, and home; but Job continues to trust in God. Next Satan attacks Job physically, covering him with painful boils. Job's wife tells him to curse God and die (2.9), but Job suffers in silence.

Three of Job's friends, Eliphaz, Bildad, and Zophar, come to visit him. At first they silently grieve with Job. But when they begin to talk about the reasons for Job's tragedies, they tell him that sin caused his suffering. He should confess his sins and turn back to God. But Job maintains his innocence.

Unable to convince Job of his sin, the three men fall silent (32.1). At this point, another voice—the young Elihu—enters the debate. But his argument is similar to that of the three older men, so no one bothers to answer him.

Finally, God speaks out of a mighty whirlwind. Confronted with the great power and majesty of God, Job falls in humble reverence before God—speechless. God rebukes Job's friends, and the drama ends with Job restored to happiness and wealth.

It is easy to think that we have all the answers. In reality, only God knows exactly why things happen as they do, and we must submit to him as our Sovereign. As you read this book, emulate Job and decide to trust God no matter what happens.

VITAL STATISTICS

PURPOSE:
To demonstrate God's sovereignty and the meaning of true faith. It addresses the question, "Why do the righteous suffer?"

AUTHOR:
Possibly Job. Some have suggested Moses, Solomon, or Elihu.

DATE WRITTEN:
Unknown. Records events which probably occurred during the time of the patriarchs, approximately 2000–1800 B.C.

SETTING:
The land of Uz, probably located northeast of Palestine, near desert land between Damascus and the Euphrates River

KEY VERSE:
"The Lord said to Satan, 'Have you considered my servant Job? There is no one like him on earth, a blameless and upright man who fears God and turns away from evil. He still persists in his integrity although you incited me against him, to destroy him for no reason' " (2.3).

KEY PEOPLE:
Job, Eliphaz the Temanite, Bildad the Shuhite, Zophar the Naamathite, Elihu the Buzite

SPECIAL FEATURES:
Job is the first of the poetic books in the Hebrew Bible. Many believe this to be the oldest book in the Bible. The book gives us insights into the work of Satan. Ezekiel 14.14, 20 and James 5.11 mention Job as a historical character.

THE BLUEPRINT

A. JOB IS TESTED (1.1—2.13)	Job, a wealthy and upright man, loses his possessions, his children, and his health. Job did not understand why he was suffering. Why does God allow his children to suffer? Although there is an explanation, we may not know it while we are here on earth. In the meantime, we must always be ready for testing in our lives.
B. THREE FRIENDS ANSWER JOB (3.1—31.40) 1. First round of discussion 2. Second round of discussion 3. Third round of discussion	Job's friends wrongly assumed that suffering always came as a result of sin. With this in mind, they tried to persuade Job to repent of his sin. Because the three friends were wrong, we know that suffering is not always a direct result of personal sin. When we experience severe suffering, it may not be our fault, so we don't have to add to our pain by feeling guilty that some hidden sin is causing our trouble.
C. A YOUNG MAN ANSWERS JOB (32.1—37.24)	A young man named Elihu, who has been listening to the entire conversation, criticizes the three friends for being unable to answer Job. He says that although Job was a good man, he had allowed himself to become proud, and God was punishing him in order to humble him. This answer was partially true because suffering does purify our faith. But God is beyond our comprehension and we cannot know why he allows each instance of suffering to come into our lives. Our part is simply to remain faithful.
D. GOD ANSWERS JOB (38.1—41.34)	God himself finally answers Job. God is in control of the world and only he understands why the good are allowed to suffer. This only becomes clear to us when we see God for who he is. We must courageously accept what God allows to happen in our lives and remain firmly committed to him.
E. JOB IS RESTORED (42.1–17)	Job finally learned that when nothing else was left, he had God, and that was enough. Through suffering, we learn that God is enough for our lives and our future. We must love God regardless of whether he allows blessing or suffering to come to us. Testing is difficult, but the result is often a deeper relationship with God. Those who endure the testing of their faith will experience God's great rewards in the end.

MEGATHEMES

THEME	EXPLANATION	IMPORTANCE
Suffering	Through no fault of his own, Job lost his wealth, children, and health. Even his friends were convinced that Job had brought this suffering upon himself. For Job, the greatest trial was not the pain or the loss; it was not being able to understand why God allowed him to suffer.	Suffering can be, but is not always, a penalty for sin. In the same way, prosperity is not always a reward for being good. Those who love God are not exempt from trouble. Although we may not be able to understand fully the pain we experience, it can lead us to rediscover God.
Satan's attacks	Satan attempted to drive a wedge between Job and God by getting Job to believe that God's governing of the world was not just and good. Satan had to ask God for permission to take Job's wealth, children, and health away. Satan was limited to what God allowed.	We must learn to recognize and not fear Satan's attacks because Satan cannot exceed the limits that God sets. Don't let any experience drive a wedge between you and God. Although you can't control how Satan may attack, you can always choose how you will respond when it happens.
God's goodness	God is all-wise and all-powerful. His will is perfect, yet he doesn't always act in ways that we understand. Job's suffering didn't make sense because everyone believed good people were supposed to prosper. When Job was at the point of despair, God spoke to him, showing him his great power and wisdom.	Although God is present everywhere, at times he may seem far away. This may cause us to feel alone and to doubt his care for us. We should serve God for who he is, not what we feel. He is never insensitive to our suffering. Because God is sufficient, we must hold on to him.

Pride	Job's friends were certain that they were correct in their judgment of him. God rebuked them for their pride and arrogance. Man's wisdom is always partial and temporary, so undue pride in our own conclusions is sin.	We must be careful not to judge others who are suffering. We may be demonstrating the sin of pride. We must be cautious in maintaining the certainty of our own conclusions about how God treats us. When we congratulate ourselves for being right, we become proud.
Trusting	God alone knew the purpose behind Job's suffering, and yet he never explained it to Job. In spite of this, Job never gave up on God—even in the midst of suffering. He never placed his hope in his experience, his wisdom, his friends, or his wealth. Job focused on God.	Job showed the kind of trust we are to have. When everything is stripped away, we are to recognize that God is all we ever really had. We should not demand that God explain everything. God gives us himself, but not all the details of his plans. We must remember that this life, with all its pain, is not our final destiny.

A. JOB IS TESTED (1.1 – 2.13)

Job is portrayed as a wealthy man of upright character who loves God. Yet God allows Satan to destroy his flocks, his possessions, his children, and his health. Job refuses to give up on God, even though he does not understand why this is happening to him. We, too, must trust God when we do not understand the difficulties we face.

Job's character

1.1 Gen 6.9; 17.1; 22.12; Ex 18.21; Job 28.28; 29.25; 42.12; Jer 25.20; Ezek 14.14; Lam 4.21; Jas 5.11
1.2 Job 42.13
1.5 Job 8.4; 42.8

1 There was once a man in the land of Uz whose name was Job. That man was
blameless and upright, one who feared God and turned away from evil. 2There
were born to him seven sons and three daughters. 3He had seven thousand sheep,
three thousand camels, five hundred yoke of oxen, five hundred donkeys, and very
many servants; so that this man was the greatest of all the people of the east. 4His
sons used to go and hold feasts in one another's houses in turn; and they would send
and invite their three sisters to eat and drink with them. 5And when the feast days
had run their course, Job would send and sanctify them, and he would rise early in
the morning and offer burnt offerings according to the number of them all; for Job
said, "It may be that my children have sinned, and cursed God in their hearts." This
is what Job always did.

1.1 As we read the book of Job, we have information that the characters of the story do not. Job, the main character of the book, loses all he has through no fault of his own. As he struggles to understand why all this is happening to him, it becomes clear that he is not meant to know the reasons. He will have to face life with the answers and explanations held back. Only then will his faith fully develop.

We must experience life as Job did – one day at a time and without complete answers to all of life's questions. Will we, like Job, trust God no matter what? Or will we give in to the temptation to say that God doesn't really care?

1.1ff As we see calamity and suffering in the book of Job, we must remember that we live in a fallen world where good behavior is not always rewarded and bad behavior is not always punished. When we see a notorious criminal prospering or an innocent child in pain, we say, "That's wrong." And it is. Sin has twisted justice and made our world unpredictable and ugly.

The book of Job shows a good man suffering for no apparent fault of his own. Sadly, our world is like that. But Job's story does not end in despair. Through Job's life we can see that faith in God is justified even when our situations look hopeless. Faith based on rewards or prosperity is hollow. To be unshakable, faith must be built on the confidence that God's ultimate purpose will come to pass.

1.1 Job was called a blameless and upright man because he feared God; he respected, worshiped, and obeyed him. At the same time, he stayed away from evil. He did not allow sin to creep into his life or temptation to overcome him. Being a good person means both loving God and obeying his laws. Job made the effort to please God. Does your life show this effort?

1.1 The location of the land of Uz is uncertain. We only know that Uz had plentiful pastures and crops (1.3), was located near a desert (1.19), and was close enough to the Sabeans and Chaldeans to be raided (1.14–17). Uz is also mentioned in Jeremiah 25.19, 20. Most scholars believe Uz was located near Canaan (Israel), where the Jews (those to whom God first revealed himself) lived. Job probably knew about God because he knew God's people.

1.5 It is not known for sure, but Job probably lived during the days of the patriarchs (Abraham, Isaac, Jacob) before God gave his written law or appointed priests to be religious leaders. During Job's day, the father was the family's religious leader. Because there were no priests to instruct him in God's laws, Job acted as the priest and offered sacrifices to God to ask for forgiveness for sins he and his family had committed. This demonstrated that Job did not consider himself sinless. Job did this out of conviction and love for God, not just because it was his role as head of the house. Do you carry out your spiritual duties because they are expected, or spontaneously from a heart of devotion?

1.5 Job showed deep concern for the spiritual welfare of his children. Fearful that they might have sinned unknowingly, he offered sacrifices for them as part of their birthday celebrations. Parents today can show the same concern by praying for their children. Regular prayer means "sacrificing" some time each day to ask God to forgive them, to help them grow, to protect them, and to help them please him.

God permits Satan to destroy Job's wealth

6 One day the heavenly beings[a] came to present themselves before the LORD,
and Satan[b] also came among them. 7 The LORD said to Satan,[b] "Where have you 1.7
come from?" Satan[b] answered the LORD, "From going to and fro on the earth, and 1 Pet 5.8
from walking up and down on it." 8 The LORD said to Satan,[b] "Have you consid- 1.8
ered my servant Job? There is no one like him on the earth, a blameless and upright Num 12.7 Josh 1.2,7
man who fears God and turns away from evil." 9 Then Satan[b] answered the LORD, Job 7.8
"Does Job fear God for nothing? 10 Have you not put a fence around him and his 1.10
house and all that he has, on every side? You have blessed the work of his hands, Job 29.2-6 31.25
and his possessions have increased in the land. 11 But stretch out your hand now, Prov 10.22
and touch all that he has, and he will curse you to your face." 12 The LORD said to 1.11
Satan,[b] "Very well, all that he has is in your power; only do not stretch out your Job 2.5; 19.21
hand against him!" So Satan[b] went out from the presence of the LORD.
13 One day when his sons and daughters were eating and drinking wine in the
eldest brother's house, 14 a messenger came to Job and said, "The oxen were plow- 1.14
ing and the donkeys were feeding beside them, 15 and the Sabeans fell on them and Gen 25.3 Job 1.16-19
carried them off, and killed the servants with the edge of the sword; I alone have 6.19
escaped to tell you." 16 While he was still speaking, another came and said, "The 1.16
fire of God fell from heaven and burned up the sheep and the servants, and con- Gen 19.24 Lev 10.2
sumed them; I alone have escaped to tell you." 17 While he was still speaking, an- Num 11.1-3
other came and said, "The Chaldeans formed three columns, made a raid on the 1.17
camels and carried them off, and killed the servants with the edge of the sword; I Gen 11.28,31
alone have escaped to tell you." 18 While he was still speaking, another came and

[a] Heb *sons of God* [b] Or *the Accuser*; Heb *ha-satan*

1.6 The "heavenly beings" may have been angels. The Bible speaks of other heavenly councils where God and the angels plan their activities on earth and where angels are required to give account of themselves (i.e., 1 Kings 22.19–23). Because God is Creator of all angels – both those who serve him and those who rebelled – he has complete power and authority over them.

1.6, 7 Satan, originally an angel of God, became corrupt through his own pride. He has been evil since his rebellion against God (1 John 3.8). Satan considers God as his enemy. He tries to hinder God's work in people, but he is limited by God's power and can do only what he is permitted (Luke 22.31, 32; 1 Timothy 1.19, 20; 2 Timothy 2.23–26). Satan is called the adversary or accuser because he actively looks for people to attack with temptation (1 Peter 5.8, 9) and because he wants to make people hate God. He does this through lies and deception (Genesis 3.1–6). Job, a righteous man who had been greatly blessed, was a perfect target for Satan. Any person who is committed to God should expect Satan's attacks. Satan, who hates God, also hates God's people.

1.6–12 From this conversation, we learn a great deal about Satan. (1) He is accountable to God. All angelic beings, good and evil, are compelled to give an account of themselves before God (1.6). (2) His thoughts are open to God (1.7). God knew Satan was intent on attacking Job. (3) Satan can be at only one place at a time (1.6, 7). His demons aid him in his work; but as a created being, he is limited. (4) Satan cannot see into our minds or foretell the future (1.9–11). If he could, he would have known that Job would not break under pressure. (5) Because Satan can do nothing without God's permission (1.12), God's people can overcome his attacks through God's power. (6) God puts limitations on what Satan can do (1.12; 2.6). Satan's response to the Lord's question (1.7) tells us that Satan is real and active on earth. Knowing this about Satan should cause us to remain close to the One who is greater than Satan – God himself.

1.7ff Some people suggest that this dialogue was made up by the author of this book. Could this conversation between God and Satan really have happened? Other Bible passages tell us that Satan does indeed have access to God (see Revelation 12.10). He even went into God's presence to make accusations against Joshua, the high priest (Zechariah 3.1, 2). If this conversation didn't take place, then the reasons for Job's suffering become meaningless and the book of Job is reduced to fiction rather than fact.

1.8 God called Job his servant. This was a great honor; it placed Job in the same company as Moses and David (Numbers 12.7, 8; 2 Samuel 7.5). God's servants are faithful to him in all they do. They serve him with their whole lives. Are you willing to serve God with such dedication?

1.8, 12 Job was a model of trust and obedience to God; therefore, God permitted Satan to attack him in an especially harsh manner. Although God loves us, believing and obeying him do not shelter us from life's calamities. Setbacks, tragedies, and sorrows strike Christians and non-Christians alike. But in our trials, God expects us to express our faith to the world. How do you respond to your troubles? Do you ask God, "Why me?" or do you say, "Use me!"?

1.9 Satan attacked Job's motives, saying he was righteous only because he had no reason to turn against God. Ever since he had started following God, everything had gone well for Job. Satan wanted to prove that Job worshiped God not out of love, but because God paid him well.

Satan accurately analyzed why many people trust God. They are fair-weather believers, following God only when everything is going well or for what they can get. Adversity destroys this superficial faith. But adversity strengthens real faith by causing believers to dig their roots deeper into God in order to withstand the storms. How deep does your faith go? Put the roots of your faith down deep into God so that you can withstand any storm you may face.

1.12 This conversation between God and Satan teaches us an important fact about God – he is fully aware of every attempt by Satan to bring suffering and difficulty upon us. While God may allow us to suffer for a reason beyond our understanding, he is never caught by surprise by our troubles and is always compassionate.

1.15–17 The Sabeans were from southwest Arabia, while the Chaldeans were from the region north of the Persian Gulf.

1.16 "The fire of God" may be a poetic phrase to describe lightning (1 Kings 18.38; 2 Kings 1.10–14). In this case, it was unusually powerful to kill 7,000 sheep.

said, "Your sons and daughters were eating and drinking wine in their eldest
brother's house, 19 and suddenly a great wind came across the desert, struck the
1.20 Gen 37.29,34; Josh 7.6; Ezra 9.3 — four corners of the house, and it fell on the young people, and they are dead; I alone
have escaped to tell you."
1.21 1 Sam 2.7,8; Job 2.10; Eccles 5.15; 1 Tim 6.7 — 20 Then Job arose, tore his robe, shaved his head, and fell on the ground and
worshiped. 21 He said, "Naked I came from my mother's womb, and naked shall I
return there; the LORD gave, and the LORD has taken away; blessed be the name of
1.22 Job 2.10 — the LORD."
22 In all this Job did not sin or charge God with wrong-doing.

God permits Satan to destroy Job's health

2 One day the heavenly beings[c] came to present themselves before the LORD,
2.1 Job 1.6-8; Isa 6.1,2 — and Satan[d] also came among them to present himself before the LORD. 2 The
LORD said to Satan,[d] "Where have you come from?" Satan[e] answered the LORD,
"From going to and fro on the earth, and from walking up and down on it." 3 The
LORD said to Satan,[d] "Have you considered my servant Job? There is no one like
him on the earth, a blameless and upright man who fears God and turns away from
evil. He still persists in his integrity, although you incited me against him, to de-
2.4 Job 1.11; 19.20,21 — stroy him for no reason." 4 Then Satan[d] answered the LORD, "Skin for skin! All
that people have they will give to save their lives.[f] 5 But stretch out your hand now
and touch his bone and his flesh, and he will curse you to your face." 6 The LORD
2.7 Deut 28.35; Job 7.5; 13.28 — said to Satan,[d] "Very well, he is in your power; only spare his life."
7 So Satan[d] went out from the presence of the LORD, and inflicted loathsome

[c] Heb *sons of God* [d] Or *the Accuser;* Heb *ha-satan* [e] Or *The Accuser;* Heb *ha-satan* [f] Or *All that the man has he will give for his life*

THE SOURCES OF SUFFERING

Sources	*Who is Responsible*	*Who is Affected*	*Needed Response*
My sin	I am	Myself and others	Repentance and confession to God
Others' sin	Person who sinned and others who allowed the sin	Probably many people, including those who sinned	Active resistance to the sinful behavior, while accepting the sinner
Avoidable physical (or natural) disaster	Persons who ignore the facts or refuse to take precautions	Most of those exposed to the cause	Prevent them if possible, be prepared if they can't be prevented
Unavoidable physical (or natural) disaster	God, Satan	Most of those present	Ongoing trust in God's faithfulness

When suffering or troubles happen, do they always come from Satan? In Job's story, his series of tragedies did come from Satan, but this is not always the case. The chart above demonstrates the four main causes of suffering. Any one of these or a combination of them may create suffering. If knowing why we are suffering will teach us to avoid the cause, then the causes are worth knowing. However, it is most important to know how to respond during suffering.

1.20–22 Job did not hide his overwhelming grief. He had not lost his faith in God; instead, his emotions showed that he was human and that he loved his family. God created our emotions, and it is not sinful or inappropriate to express them as Job did. If you have experienced a deep loss, a disappointment, or a heartbreak, admit your feelings to yourself and others, and grieve.

1.20–22 Job lost his possessions and family in this first of Satan's tests, but he reacted rightly toward God by acknowledging God's sovereign authority over everything God had given him.

2.3–6 Can Satan persuade God to change his plans? At first God said he did not want Job harmed physically, but then he decided to allow it. Satan is unable to persuade God to go against his character: God is completely and eternally good. But God was willing to go along with Satan's plan because God knew the eventual outcome of Job's story. God cannot be fooled by Satan. Job's suffering was a test for Job, Satan, and us—not God.

2.4, 5 "Skin for skin" was Satan's comment concerning Job's response to the loss of his family. Satan believed that Job was willing to accept the loss of family and property so long as his own skin was safe. Satan's next step was to inflict physical suffering upon Job to prove his original accusation (1.9).

2.6 Again Satan had to seek permission from God to inflict pain upon Job. God limits Satan, and did not let him destroy Job.

2.7 At times believers may actually suffer more than unbelievers because those who follow God may become Satan's special targets. Believers, therefore, may have to endure hardship, persecution, or testing. This was the case with Job. We must be prepared for Satan's attacks. When we suffer, we must not conclude that God has abandoned us (he did not abandon Job). Consistent faith is the way to defeat Satan.

sores on Job from the sole of his foot to the crown of his head. 8 Job[g] took a potsherd with which to scrape himself, and sat among the ashes.
9 Then his wife said to him, "Do you still persist in your integrity? Curse[h] God,
and die." 10 But he said to her, "You speak as any foolish woman would speak.
Shall we receive the good at the hand of God, and not receive the bad?" In all this
Job did not sin with his lips.

2.8 Job 42.6 Jer 6.26 Jonah 3.6 Mt 11.21
2.10 Job 1.21,22 Mt 12.34-37 Jas 3.2

Job's friends gather

11 Now when Job's three friends heard of all these troubles that had come upon
him, each of them set out from his home — Eliphaz the Temanite, Bildad the Shuhite, and Zophar the Naamathite. They met together to go and console and comfort
him. 12 When they saw him from a distance, they did not recognize him, and they
raised their voices and wept aloud; they tore their robes and threw dust in the air
upon their heads. 13 They sat with him on the ground seven days and seven nights,
and no one spoke a word to him, for they saw that his suffering was very great.

2.12 Josh 7.6 Job 1.20 Lam 2.10 Rev 18.19
2.13 Ezek 3.15

B. THREE FRIENDS ANSWER JOB (3.1 — 31.40)

Job agonizes over his situation. His three friends explain that he must be suffering because of some terrible sin he committed. They try to persuade Job to repent of his sin. When Job argues that he has not sinned enough to deserve such suffering, his friends respond with even harsher accusations. While there are elements of truth in the speeches of Job's three friends, they are based on wrong assumptions. We must be careful what we assume to be true in the lives of others. We cannot assume that suffering is their own fault or a result of their sin.

1. First round of discussion

Job speaks

3 After this Job opened his mouth and cursed the day of his birth. 2 Job said:
3 "Let the day perish in which I was born,
and the night that said,
'A man-child is conceived.'
4 Let that day be darkness!
May God above not seek it,
or light shine on it.
5 Let gloom and deep darkness claim it.
Let clouds settle upon it;
let the blackness of the day terrify it.

3.2 Jer 20.14-18

[g] Heb *He* [h] Heb *Bless*

2.9 Why was Job's wife spared when the rest of his family was killed? It is possible that her very presence caused him even more suffering because of her chiding or her own sorrow over all they had lost.

2.10 Many people think that believing in God protects them from trouble, so when calamity comes, they question God's goodness and justice. But the message of Job is that you should not give up on God just because bad things happen. Faith in God does not guarantee personal prosperity, and lack of faith does not guarantee troubles in this life. If this were so, people would believe in God simply to get rich. God is capable of rescuing us from suffering, but he may also allow suffering to come for reasons we cannot understand. It is Satan's strategy to get us to doubt God at exactly this moment. Here Job shows a perspective broader than seeking his own personal comfort. If we always know why we suffer, our faith will have no room to grow.

2.11 Eliphaz, Bildad, and Zophar were not only Job's friends, they were also known for their wisdom. In the end, however, their wisdom was shown to be narrow-minded and incomplete.

2.11 Upon learning of Job's difficulties, three of his friends came to comfort and console him. Later we learn that their words of comfort were not helpful — but at least they came. While God rebuked them for what they said (42.7), he did not rebuke them for what they did — making the effort to come to someone who was in need. Unfortunately, when they came, they did a poor job of comforting Job because they were proud of their own advice and insensitive to Job's needs. When someone is in need, go to that person, but be sensitive in how you comfort him or her.

2.13 Why did the friends arrive and then just sit quietly? According to Jewish tradition, people who come to comfort someone in mourning should not speak until the mourner speaks. Often the best response to another person's suffering is silence. Job's friends realized that his pain was too deep to be healed with mere words, so they said nothing. (If only they had continued to sit quietly!) Often, we feel we must say something spiritual and insightful to a hurting friend. Perhaps what he or she needs most is just our presence, showing that we care. Pat answers and trite quotations say much less than empathetic silence and loving companionship.

3.1ff Job's response to his second test — physical affliction — contrasts greatly to his attitude after the first test (1.20–22). Job still did not curse God, but he cursed the day of his birth. He felt it would be better never to have been born than to be forsaken by God. Job was struggling emotionally, physically, and spiritually; his misery was pervasive and deep. Never underestimate how vulner-

6 That night — let thick darkness seize it!
let it not rejoice among the days of the year;
let it not come into the number of the months.

Children never tire of asking "Why?" Yet the question produces a bitter taste the older we get. Children wonder about everything; adults wonder about suffering. We notice that the world seems to run by a system of cause and effect, yet there are some effects for which we can't find a clear cause, and some causes that don't lead to the expected effects. We would expect Job's wealth and family to give him a very happy life, and for a while they did. But the loss and pain he experienced shock us. The first two chapters of his story are more than we can bear. To those so quick to ask "Why?" at the smallest misfortune, Job's faithfulness seems incredible. But even Job had something to learn. We can learn with him.

Our age of "instant" everything has caused us to lose the ability to wait. We expect to learn patience instantly, and in our hurry, we miss the contradiction. Of all that we want now, relief from pain is at the top of our list. We want an instant cure for everything from toothaches to heartbreaks.

Although some pains have been cured, we still live in a world where many people suffer. Job was not expecting instant answers for the intense emotional and physical pain he endured. But in the end, what broke Job's patience was not the suffering, but not knowing *why* he suffered.

When Job expressed his frustration, his friends were ready with their answers. They believed that the law of cause and effect applied to all people's experiences. Their view of life boiled down to this: good things happen to good people, and bad things happen to bad people. Because of this, they felt their role was to help Job admit to whatever sin was causing his suffering.

Job actually looked at life almost the same way as his friends. What he couldn't understand was why he was suffering so much when he was sure he had done nothing to deserve such punishment. The last friend, Elihu, did offer another explanation for the pain by pointing out that God might be allowing it to purify Job. But this was only partly helpful. When God finally spoke, he didn't offer Job an answer. Instead, he drove home the point that it is better to know God than to know answers.

Often we suffer consequences for bad decisions and actions. Job's willingness to repent and confess known wrongs is a good guideline for us. Sometimes suffering shapes us for special service to others. Sometimes suffering is an attack by Satan on our lives. And sometimes we don't know why we suffer. At those times, are we willing to trust God in spite of unanswered questions?

Strengths and accomplishments:
- Was a man of faith, patience, and endurance
- Was known as a generous and caring person
- Was very wealthy

Weakness and mistake:
- Allowed his desire to understand why he was suffering overwhelm him and make him question God

Lessons from his life:
- Knowing God is better than knowing answers
- God is not arbitrary or uncaring
- Pain is not always punishment

Vital statistics:
- Where: Land of Uz
- Occupation: Wealthy land and livestock owner
- Relatives: Wife and first ten children not named. Daughters from the second set of children: Jemima, Kezia, Kerenhappuch
- Contemporaries: Eliphaz, Bildad, Zophar, Elihu

Key verses:
"As an example of suffering and patience, beloved, take the prophets who spoke in the name of the Lord. Indeed we call blessed those who showed endurance. You have heard of the endurance of Job, and you have seen the purpose of the Lord, how the Lord is compassionate and merciful" (James 5.10, 11).

Job's story is told in the book of Job. He is also referred to in Ezekiel 14.14, 20 and James 5.11.

able we are during times of suffering and pain. We must hold on to our faith even if there is no relief.

3.6 "Let it not come into the number of the months" means "Don't even let the night I was born be part of the calendar."

7 Yes, let that night be barren;
let no joyful cry be heard[i] in it.
8 Let those curse it who curse the Sea,[j]
those who are skilled to rouse up Leviathan. 3.8 Job 41.25
9 Let the stars of its dawn be dark;
let it hope for light, but have none; 3.9 Job 41.18
may it not see the eyelids of the morning—
10 because it did not shut the doors of my mother's womb,
and hide trouble from my eyes.

11 "Why did I not die at birth,
come forth from the womb and expire? 3.11 Job 10.18,19
12 Why were there knees to receive me,
or breasts for me to suck?
13 Now I would be lying down and quiet;
I would be asleep; then I would be at rest 3.13 Job 3.13-19 6.8,9 14.10-15 19.25-27 Eccles 6.3-5
14 with kings and counselors of the earth
who rebuild ruins for themselves,
15 or with princes who have gold,
who fill their houses with silver.
16 Or why was I not buried like a stillborn child,
like an infant that never sees the light?
17 There the wicked cease from troubling,
and there the weary are at rest.
18 There the prisoners are at ease together;
they do not hear the voice of the taskmaster.
19 The small and the great are there,
and the slaves are free from their masters.

20 "Why is light given to one in misery,
and life to the bitter in soul,
21 who long for death, but it does not come,
and dig for it more than for hidden treasures;
22 who rejoice exceedingly,
and are glad when they find the grave?
23 Why is light given to one who cannot see the way,
whom God has fenced in? 3.23 Job 19.6,8,12
24 For my sighing comes like[k] my bread,
and my groanings are poured out like water. 3.24 Job 6.7; 33.20
25 Truly the thing that I fear comes upon me,
and what I dread befalls me. 3.25 Job 9.28; 30.15
26 I am not at ease, nor am I quiet;
I have no rest; but trouble comes." 3.26 Job 7.13,14

[i] Heb *come* [j] Cn: Heb *day* [k] Heb *before*

3.11 Job was experiencing extreme physical pain as well as grief over the loss of his family and possessions. He can't be blamed for wishing he were dead. Job's grief placed him at the crossroads of his faith, shattering many misconceptions about God (such as: he makes you rich, always keeps you from trouble, or protects your loved ones). Job was driven back to the basics of his faith in God. He had only two choices: (1) he could curse God and give up, or (2) he could trust God and draw strength from him to continue.

3.23–26 Job had been careful not to worship material possessions but to worship God alone. Now he was overwhelmed by calamities that mocked his caution, and he complained about trials that came despite his right living. All the principles by which he had lived were crumbling, and Job began to lose his perspective. Trials and grief, whether temporary or enduring, do not destroy the real purpose of life. Life is not given merely for happiness and personal fulfillment, but for us to serve and honor God. The worth and meaning of life is not based on what we feel, but on the one reality no one can take away—God's love for us. Don't assume that because God truly loves you, he will always prevent suffering. The opposite may be true. God's love cannot be measured or limited by how great or how little we may suffer. Romans 8.38, 39 teaches us that nothing can separate us from God's love.

Eliphaz speaks

4 Then Eliphaz the Temanite answered:
2 "If one ventures a word with you, will you be offended?
But who can keep from speaking?
4.3 Job 29.21,25
3 See, you have instructed many;
you have strengthened the weak hands.
4 Your words have supported those who were stumbling,
and you have made firm the feeble knees.
5 But now it has come to you, and you are impatient;
it touches you, and you are dismayed.
4.6 Prov 3.26; 14.26
6 Is not your fear of God your confidence,
4.7,8 Job 8.20 Ps 37.25 Prov 22.8 Gal 6.7
and the integrity of your ways your hope?

7 "Think now, who that was innocent ever perished?

ADVICE FROM FRIENDS Overwhelmed by suffering, Job was not comforted, but condemned by his friends. Each of their views represents a well-known way to understand suffering. God proves each explanation given by Job's friends has less than the whole answer.

Who they were	*Where they spoke*	*How they helped*	*How they explained Job's pain*	*Their advice to Job*	*Job's response*	*God's response to Job's friends*
Eliphaz the Temanite	Job 4, 5, 15, 22	They sat in silence with Job for seven days (2.11–13)	Job is suffering because he has sinned	Go to God and confess your sins to him. (5.8)	Stop assuming my guilt, for I am righteous. (6.29)	God rebukes Job's friends (42.7)
Bildad the Shuhite	Job 8, 18, 25		Job won't admit he sinned, so he's still suffering	How long will you go on like this? (8.2)	I will say to God, . . . tell me *why* you are doing it. (10.2)	
Zophar the Naamathite	Job 11, 20		Job's sin deserves even more suffering than he's experienced	Get rid of your sins. (11.13, 14)	I know that I will be justified. (13.18)	
Elihu the Buzite	Job 32—37		God is using suffering to mold and train Job	Keep silence and I will teach you wisdom. (33.33)	No response	God does not directly address Elihu.
God	Job 38—41	Confronted Job with the need to be content without knowing why he was suffering	Did not explain the reason for the pain	Do you still want to argue with the Almighty? (40.2)	I was talking about things I knew nothing about. (42.3–5)	

4.1ff Eliphaz claimed to be a man of great knowledge (4.12; 5.27); everything he said was based on his personal experience (4.8; 5.27). He argued that suffering is a direct result of sin, and if Job would only confess his sin, his suffering would end. Eliphaz saw suffering as God's punishment, which should be welcomed in order to bring a person back to God. In some cases, of course, this may be true (Galatians 6.7, 8), but it was not true with Job. Although Eliphaz had many good and true comments, he made three wrong assumptions: (1) a good and innocent person never suffers; (2) those who suffer are being punished for their past sins; and (3) Job, because he was suffering, had done something wrong in God's eyes. (For more about Eliphaz, see the chart in chapter 28.)

4.7, 8 Part of what Eliphaz said is true, and part is false. It is true that those who promote sin and trouble will eventually be punished; it is false that anyone who is good and innocent will never suffer. All the material recorded and quoted in the Bible is there by God's choice. Some is a record of what people said and did, but is not an example to follow. The Bible gives us teachings and examples of what we *should* do as well as what we *should not* do. Eliphaz's comments are an example of what we should try to avoid – making false assumptions about others based on our own experiences.

Or where were the upright cut off?
8 As I have seen, those who plow iniquity
and sow trouble reap the same.
9 By the breath of God they perish,
and by the blast of his anger they are consumed.
10 The roar of the lion, the voice of the fierce lion,
and the teeth of the young lions are broken.
11 The strong lion perishes for lack of prey,
and the whelps of the lioness are scattered.

12 "Now a word came stealing to me,
my ear received the whisper of it.
13 Amid thoughts from visions of the night,
when deep sleep falls on mortals,
14 dread came upon me, and trembling,
which made all my bones shake.
15 A spirit glided past my face;
the hair of my flesh bristled.
16 It stood still,
but I could not discern its appearance.
A form was before my eyes;
there was silence, then I heard a voice:
17 'Can mortals be righteous before[l] God?
Can human beings be pure before[l] their Maker?
18 Even in his servants he puts no trust,
and his angels he charges with error;
19 how much more those who live in houses of clay,
whose foundation is in the dust,
who are crushed like a moth.
20 Between morning and evening they are destroyed;
they perish forever without any regarding it.
21 Their tent-cord is plucked up within them,
and they die devoid of wisdom.'

5 "Call now; is there anyone who will answer you?
To which of the holy ones will you turn?
2 Surely vexation kills the fool,
and jealousy slays the simple.
3 I have seen fools taking root,
but suddenly I cursed their dwelling.
4 Their children are far from safety,
they are crushed in the gate,
and there is no one to deliver them.
5 The hungry eat their harvest,
and they take it even out of the thorns;[m]
and the thirsty[n] pant after their wealth.

[l] Or *more than* [m] Meaning of Heb uncertain [n] Aquila Symmachus Syr Vg: Heb *snare*

4.9 Job 15.30; 2 Thess 2.8
4.11 Job 5.4; 29.17; Jer 4.7; Hos 11.10
4.12 Job 33.15-18
4.17 Gen 18.25; Job 9.2; 25.4; 35.10; 36.3
4.18 Gen 2.7; 3.19; Job 15.15; 22.16; Isa 6.2,3
4.20 Job 14.2,20
4.21 Job 8.22; 36.12
5.2 Prov 12.16; 27.3
5.3 Job 24.18; 31.30
5.5 Job 18.8-10

4.13 Although Eliphaz claimed his vision was divinely inspired, it is doubtful that it came from God, because God criticized Eliphaz for misrepresenting him (42.7). Whatever the vision's source, it is summarized in 4.17. On the surface, this statement is completely true—a mere man cannot compare to God and should not try to question God's motives and actions. Eliphaz, however, took this thought and expounded on it later, expressing his own opinions. His conclusion (5.8) shows a very limited view of the reason Job was suffering. It is easy for teachers, counselors, and well-meaning friends to begin with a portion of God's truth but end with man-made wisdom by drawing their own conclusions.

4.18, 19 Do angels really make mistakes? Remember that Eliphaz was speaking, not God, so we must be careful about building our knowledge of the spiritual world from Eliphaz's opinions. In addition, the word translated "error" is used only here, and its meaning is unclear. We could save Eliphaz's credibility by saying he meant fallen angels, but this passage is not meant to teach about angels. Eliphaz was saying that sinful human beings are far beneath God and the angels. Eliphaz was right about God's greatness, but he did not understand God's greater purposes concerning suffering.

6 For misery does not come from the earth,
nor does trouble sprout from the ground;
7 but human beings are born to trouble
just as sparks[o] fly upward.

5.7 Job 14.1 Eccl 5.15-17

8 "As for me, I would seek God,
and to God I would commit my cause.
9 He does great things and unsearchable,
marvelous things without number.
10 He gives rain on the earth
and sends waters on the fields;
11 he sets on high those who are lowly,
and those who mourn are lifted to safety.
12 He frustrates the devices of the crafty,
so that their hands achieve no success.
13 He takes the wise in their own craftiness;
and the schemes of the wily are brought to a quick end.
14 They meet with darkness in the daytime,
and grope at noonday as in the night.
15 But he saves the needy from the sword of their mouth,
from the hand of the mighty.
16 So the poor have hope,
and injustice shuts its mouth.

5.9 Job 9.10 37.14,16; 42.3
5.10 Job 36.27-29 37.6 Ps 65.9-11 Amos 4.7
5.11 Job 22.29; 36.7
5.14 Deut 28.29 Prov 4.19

17 "How happy is the one whom God reproves;
therefore do not despise the discipline of the Almighty.[p]
18 For he wounds, but he binds up;
he strikes, but his hands heal.
19 He will deliver you from six troubles;
in seven no harm shall touch you.
20 In famine he will redeem you from death,
and in war from the power of the sword.
21 You shall be hidden from the scourge of the tongue,
and shall not fear destruction when it comes.
22 At destruction and famine you shall laugh,
and shall not fear the wild animals of the earth.
23 For you shall be in league with the stones of the field,
and the wild animals shall be at peace with you.
24 You shall know that your tent is safe,
you shall inspect your fold and miss nothing.

5.17 Ps 94.12 Prov 3.1 Heb 12.5-11
5.18 Deut 32.39 Isa 30.26 Hos 6.1
5.20 Ps 33.19 144.10 Prov 10.3
5.23 Isa 11.6-9 65.25

[o] Or *birds*; Heb *sons of Resheph* [p] Traditional rendering of Heb *Shaddai*

5.7 The Bible teaches that everyone has a natural tendency to sin, and Eliphaz supports this view. Those who follow God, however, can decide to resist sin. Eliphaz implied that he had done well at resisting sin while Job had not. This was far from the truth.

5.8 All three of Job's friends made the mistake of assuming that Job had committed some great sin that caused his suffering. Neither they nor Job knew of Satan's conversation with God (1.6–2.8). It is human nature to blame people for their own troubles, but Job's story makes it clear that blame cannot always be attached to those whom trouble strikes.

5.13 Paul later quoted part of this verse (1 Corinthians 3.19) – the only time Job is clearly quoted in the New Testament. Although God rebuked Eliphaz for being wrong in his advice to Job (42.7), not all he said was in error. The part Paul quoted was correct – men are often caught in their own traps. This illustrates how Scripture must be used to explain and comment on itself. We must be familiar with the entire scope of God's Word to properly understand the difficult portions of it.

5.17 Eliphaz was correct – it is a blessing to be disciplined by God when we do wrong. His advice, however, did not apply to Job. As we know from the beginning of the book, Job's suffering was not a result of some great sin. We sometimes give people excellent advice only to learn that it does not apply to them and is therefore not very helpful. All who offer counsel from God's Word should take care to thoroughly understand a person's situation *before* giving advice.

5.17–26 Eliphaz's words in 5.17, 18 show a view of discipline that has been almost forgotten: pain can help us grow. These are good words to remember when we face hardship and loss. Because Job did not understand why he suffered, his faith in God had a chance to grow. On the other hand, we must not make Eliphaz's mistake. God does not eliminate all hardship when we are following him closely, and good behavior is not always rewarded by prosperity. Rewards for good and punishment for evil are in God's hands and given out according to his timetable. Satan's ploy is to get us to doubt God's good will toward us.

25 You shall know that your descendants will be many,
and your offspring like the grass of the earth.
26 You shall come to your grave in ripe old age,
as a shock of grain comes up to the threshing floor in its season.
27 See, we have searched this out; it is true.
Hear, and know it for yourself."

5.26 Gen 15.15 Job 42.17 Prov 9.11; 10.27

Job speaks

6 Then Job answered:
2 "O that my vexation were weighed,
and all my calamity laid in the balances!
3 For then it would be heavier than the sand of the sea;
therefore my words have been rash.
4 For the arrows of the Almighty[q] are in me;
my spirit drinks their poison;
the terrors of God are arrayed against me.
5 Does the wild ass bray over its grass,
or the ox low over its fodder?
6 Can that which is tasteless be eaten without salt,
or is there any flavor in the juice of mallows?[r]
7 My appetite refuses to touch them;
they are like food that is loathsome to me.[r]

6.2 Job 31.6
6.3 Job 23.2
6.4 Job 16.13 21.20; 30.15 Ps 38.2

8 "O that I might have my request,
and that God would grant my desire;
9 that it would please God to crush me,
that he would let loose his hand and cut me off!
10 This would be my consolation;
I would even exult[r] in unrelenting pain;
for I have not denied the words of the Holy One.
11 What is my strength, that I should wait?
And what is my end, that I should be patient?
12 Is my strength the strength of stones,
or is my flesh bronze?
13 In truth I have no help in me,
and any resource is driven from me.

6.8 Num 11.15 1 Kgs 19.4 Job 7.16; 9.21 10.1

14 "Those who withhold[s] kindness from a friend
forsake the fear of the Almighty.[q]
15 My companions are treacherous like a torrent-bed,
like freshets that pass away,
16 that run dark with ice,
turbid with melting snow.
17 In time of heat they disappear;
when it is hot, they vanish from their place.
18 The caravans turn aside from their course;

[q] Traditional rendering of Heb *Shaddai* [r] Meaning of Heb uncertain [s] Syr Vg Compare Tg: Meaning of Heb uncertain

6.1ff Job's reply to Eliphaz has three key points: (1) you are giving me all this advice without sympathizing with my situation, (2) your criticisms are not based on fact but only on your own experience, and (3) you still have not answered my basic question: Why am I suffering like this? Although Job could not understand why he was going through this extreme suffering, while he sought an answer, he was determined to remain true to God (6.10).

6.6, 7 Job said that Eliphaz's advice was like eating the tasteless white of an uncooked egg. When people are going through severe trials, ill-advised counsel is distasteful. They may listen politely, but inside they are upset. Be slow to give advice to those who are hurting. They often need compassion more than they need advice.

6.8, 9 In his grief, Job wanted to give in, to be freed from his discomfort, and to die. But God did not grant Job's request. He had a greater plan for him. Our tendency, like Job's, is to want to give up and get out when the going gets rough. To trust God in the good times is commendable, but to trust him during the difficult times tests us to our limits and exercises our faith. In your struggles, large or small, trust that God is in control (Romans 8.28). He will take care of you.

they go up into the waste, and perish.

6.19
Gen 25.15
Job 1.15
Isa 21.14
Jer 14.3

19 The caravans of Tema look,
the travelers of Sheba hope.
20 They are disappointed because they were confident;
they come there and are confounded.
21 Such you have now become to me;[t]
you see my calamity, and are afraid.
22 Have I said, 'Make me a gift'?
Or, 'From your wealth offer a bribe for me'?
23 Or, 'Save me from an opponent's hand'?
Or, 'Ransom me from the hand of oppressors'?

24 "Teach me, and I will be silent;
make me understand how I have gone wrong.

6.25
Job 8.2; 15.2
16.3
Mt 12.37

25 How forceful are honest words!
But your reproof, what does it reprove?
26 Do you think that you can reprove words,
as if the speech of the desperate were wind?

6.27
Job 22.9; 24.9
Joel 3.3
Nah 3.10
2 Pet 2.3

27 You would even cast lots over the orphan,
and bargain over your friend.

28 "But now, be pleased to look at me;
for I will not lie to your face.

6.29
Job 13.18

29 Turn, I pray, let no wrong be done.
Turn now, my vindication is at stake.

6.30
Job 12.11

30 Is there any wrong on my tongue?
Cannot my taste discern calamity?

7.1
Lev 25.50
Deut 15.18
Mt 20.1-15

7 "Do not human beings have a hard service on earth,
and are not their days like the days of a laborer?
2 Like a slave who longs for the shadow,
and like laborers who look for their wages,
3 so I am allotted months of emptiness,
and nights of misery are apportioned to me.

7.4
Deut 28.67
Job 7.13,14
Isa 54.11

4 When I lie down I say, 'When shall I rise?'
But the night is long,
and I am full of tossing until dawn.

7.5
Ps 38.5-7

5 My flesh is clothed with worms and dirt;
my skin hardens, then breaks out again.
6 My days are swifter than a weaver's shuttle,
and come to their end without hope.[u]

7.7
Job 7.16; 9.25

7 "Remember that my life is a breath;
my eye will never again see good.
8 The eye that beholds me will see me no more;
while your eyes are upon me, I shall be gone.

7.9
Ps 39.13

9 As the cloud fades and vanishes,
so those who go down to Sheol do not come up;
10 they return no more to their houses,
nor do their places know them any more.

[t] Cn Compare Gk Syr: Meaning of Heb uncertain [u] Or *as the thread runs out*

6.29, 30 Job referred to his own righteousness, not because he was sinless, but because he had a right relationship with God. He was not guilty of the sins his friends accused him of (see chapter 31 for his summary of the life he had led). *Righteousness* is not the same as *sinlessness* (Romans 3.23). No one but Jesus Christ has ever been sinless – free from all wrong thoughts and actions. Even Job needed to make some changes in his attitude toward God, as we will see by the end of the book. Nevertheless, Job was righteous (1.8). He carefully obeyed God to the best of his ability in all aspects of his life.

11 "Therefore I will not restrain my mouth;
I will speak in the anguish of my spirit;
I will complain in the bitterness of my soul.
12 Am I the Sea, or the Dragon,
that you set a guard over me?
13 When I say, 'My bed will comfort me,
my couch will ease my complaint,'
14 then you scare me with dreams
and terrify me with visions,
15 so that I would choose strangling
and death rather than this body.
16 I loathe my life; I would not live forever.
Let me alone, for my days are a breath.
17 What are human beings, that you make so much of them,
that you set your mind on them,
18 visit them every morning,
test them every moment?
19 Will you not look away from me for a while,
let me alone until I swallow my spittle?
20 If I sin, what do I do to you, you watcher of humanity?
Why have you made me your target?
Why have I become a burden to you?
21 Why do you not pardon my transgression
and take away my iniquity?
For now I shall lie in the earth;
you will seek me, but I shall not be."

7.13 Ps 6.6; 77.4
7.16 Job 6.9; 7.7 9.21; 10.1
7.17 Job 22.2 Heb 2.6
7.19 Ps 6.3
7.20 Job 35.3,6
7.21 Job 10.9,14

Bildad speaks

8 Then Bildad the Shuhite answered:
2 "How long will you say these things,
and the words of your mouth be a great wind?
3 Does God pervert justice?
Or does the Almighty[v] pervert the right?
4 If your children sinned against him,
he delivered them into the power of their transgression.
5 If you will seek God
and make supplication to the Almighty,[v]
6 if you are pure and upright,
surely then he will rouse himself for you
and restore to you your rightful place.
7 Though your beginning was small,

8.4 Job 1.15-19
8.5 Job 5.17-27
8.6 Job 22.27
8.7 Job 42.12

[v] Traditional rendering of Heb *Shaddai*

7.11 Job felt deep anguish and bitterness, and he spoke honestly to God about it to let out his frustrations. If we express our feelings to God, we can deal with them without exploding in harsh words and actions, possibly hurting ourselves and others. The next time strong emotions threaten to overwhelm you, express them openly to God in prayer. This will help you gain an eternal perspective on the situation, giving you greater ability to deal with it constructively.

7.12 Job stopped talking to Eliphaz and spoke directly to God. Although Job had lived a righteous life, he was beginning to doubt the value of living in such a way. By doing this, he was coming dangerously close to suggesting that God didn't care about him and was not being fair. God later reproved Job for this attitude (38.2). Satan always exploits these thoughts to get us to forsake God. Our suffering, like Job's, may not be the result of our sin, but we must be careful not to sin as a result of our suffering.

7.20 Job refers to God as a watcher or observer of humanity. He is expressing his feeling that God seems like an enemy to him—someone who dispassionately watches him squirm in his misery. We know that God does watch over everything that happens to us. We must never forget that he sees us with compassion, not merely scrutiny. His eyes are eyes of love.

8.1ff Bildad was upset that Job still claimed innocence while questioning God's justice. The basis of Bildad's argument (the justice of God) was correct, but his idea of God's justice was not. Bildad's argument went like this: God could not be unjust, and God would not punish a just man; therefore Job must be unjust. Bildad felt there were no exceptions to his theory. Like Eliphaz, Bildad wrongly assumed that suffering comes only as a result of one's sins. Bildad was even less sensitive and compassionate, saying Job's children died because of *their* wickedness. (For more information about Bildad, see the chart in chapter 28.)

your latter days will be very great.

8.8 Deut 4.32; 32.7

8 "For inquire now of bygone generations,
and consider what their ancestors have found;
9 for we are but of yesterday, and we know nothing,
for our days on earth are but a shadow.
10 Will they not teach you and tell you
and utter words out of their understanding?

8.11 Isa 19.5-7

11 "Can papyrus grow where there is no marsh?
Can reeds flourish where there is no water?
12 While yet in flower and not cut down,
they wither before any other plant.
13 Such are the paths of all who forget God;
the hope of the godless shall perish.
14 Their confidence is gossamer,
a spider's house their trust.

8.15 Job 27.18 Ps 49.11

15 If one leans against its house, it will not stand;
if one lays hold of it, it will not endure.

8.16 Ps 37.35; 80.11

16 The wicked thrive[w] before the sun,
and their shoots spread over the garden.
17 Their roots twine around the stoneheap;
they live among the rocks.[x]
18 If they are destroyed from their place,
then it will deny them, saying, 'I have never seen you.'
19 See, these are their happy ways,[y]
and out of the earth still others will spring.

20 "See, God will not reject a blameless person,
nor take the hand of evildoers.

8.21 Ps 126.1,2

21 He will yet fill your mouth with laughter,
and your lips with shouts of joy.

8.22 Ps 132.18

22 Those who hate you will be clothed with shame,
and the tent of the wicked will be no more."

Job speaks

9 Then Job answered:

9.2 Job 4.17; 25.4

2 "Indeed I know that this is so;
but how can a mortal be just before God?

9.3 Job 10.2; 40.2

3 If one wished to contend with him,
one could not answer him once in a thousand.
4 He is wise in heart, and mighty in strength
—who has resisted him, and succeeded?—

9.5 Job 26.6-14

5 he who removes mountains, and they do not know it,
when he overturns them in his anger;

9.6 Isa 2.19; 13.13

6 who shakes the earth out of its place,
and its pillars tremble;

9.7 Job 38.12-15

7 who commands the sun, and it does not rise;

[w] Heb *He thrives* [x] Gk Vg: Meaning of Heb uncertain [y] Meaning of Heb uncertain

8.14, 15 Bildad wrongly assumed that Job was trusting in something other than God for security, so he pointed out that such supports will collapse. Gossamer is a film of cobwebs that floats through the air. One of man's basic needs is security, and people will do almost anything to feel secure. Eventually, however, our money, possessions, knowledge, and relationships will fail or be gone. Only God can give lasting security. What have you trusted for your security? How lasting is it? If you have a secure foundation with God, then feelings of insecurity cannot undermine you.

9.1ff Bildad said nothing new to Job. Job knew that the wicked ultimately perish, but this confused him. Why, then, was *he* perishing? Job didn't think his life warranted such suffering, so he wanted to present his case before God (9.35). He recognized, however, that arguing with God would be futile and unproductive (9.4). Job didn't claim to be perfect (7.20, 21; 9.20), but he did claim to be good and faithful (6.29, 30). While Job showed impatience toward God, he did not reject or curse God.

who seals up the stars;
8 who alone stretched out the heavens
and trampled the waves of the Sea;[z]
9 who made the Bear and Orion,
the Pleiades and the chambers of the south;
10 who does great things beyond understanding,
and marvelous things without number.
11 Look, he passes by me, and I do not see him;
he moves on, but I do not perceive him.
12 He snatches away; who can stop him?
Who will say to him, 'What are you doing?'

13 "God will not turn back his anger;
the helpers of Rahab bowed beneath him.
14 How then can I answer him,
choosing my words with him?
15 Though I am innocent, I cannot answer him;
I must appeal for mercy to my accuser.[a]
16 If I summoned him and he answered me,
I do not believe that he would listen to my voice.
17 For he crushes me with a tempest,
and multiplies my wounds without cause;
18 he will not let me get my breath,
but fills me with bitterness.
19 If it is a contest of strength, he is the strong one!
If it is a matter of justice, who can summon him?[b]
20 Though I am innocent, my own mouth would condemn me;
though I am blameless, he would prove me perverse.
21 I am blameless; I do not know myself;
I loathe my life.
22 It is all one; therefore I say,
he destroys both the blameless and the wicked.
23 When disaster brings sudden death,
he mocks at the calamity[c] of the innocent.
24 The earth is given into the hand of the wicked;
he covers the eyes of its judges—
if it is not he, who then is it?

25 "My days are swifter than a runner;
they flee away, they see no good.
26 They go by like skiffs of reed,
like an eagle swooping on the prey.
27 If I say, 'I will forget my complaint;
I will put off my sad countenance and be of good cheer,'
28 I become afraid of all my suffering,
for I know you will not hold me innocent.
29 I shall be condemned;
why then do I labor in vain?

9.8 Gen 1.1 Ps 77.19; 104.2
9.9 Job 38.31,32
9.11 Job 23.8,9
9.12 Job 10.7
9.15 Job 8.5; 10.15
9.17 Job 16.12,14
9.18 Job 27.2
9.22 Eccles 9.2
9.24 Job 12.6,17 16.11 Dan 4.17 5.18-21
9.25 2 Sam 1.23 Job 39.29 Isa 18.2 Hab 1.8
9.28 Job 3.25; 7.21 10.14
9.29 Ps 37.33 Jer 2.35

[z] Or *trampled the back of the sea dragon* [a] Or *for my right* [b] Compare Gk: Heb *me* [c] Meaning of Heb uncertain

9.9 The Bear, Orion, and Pleiades are constellations.

9.13 Rahab is the name of a legendary sea monster. According to a Babylonian creation myth, Marduk defeated Tiamat (or Leviaton; both are other names for Rahab), then captured her helpers. Job's friends would have known this myth and understood Job's meaning. God is sovereign over all the forces whether they are real or mythical.

9.20, 21 Job was saying, "In spite of my good life, God is determined to condemn me." As his suffering continued, he became more impatient. Although Job remained loyal to God, he made statements he would later regret. In times of extended sickness or prolonged pain, it is natural for people to doubt, to despair, or to become impatient. During those times, people need someone to listen to them, to help them work through their feelings and frustrations. Your patience with their impatience will help them.

9.30 Job 31.7 Jer 2.22 Rom 10.3 1 Jn 1.8

30 If I wash myself with soap
and cleanse my hands with lye,
31 yet you will plunge me into filth,
and my own clothes will abhor me.

9.32 1 Sam 2.25 Rom 9.20

32 For he is not a mortal, as I am, that I might answer him,
that we should come to trial together.
33 There is no umpire[d] between us,
who might lay his hand on us both.
34 If he would take his rod away from me,
and not let dread of him terrify me,
35 then I would speak without fear of him,
for I know I am not what I am thought to be.[e]

10.1 Job 7.11,16 Isa 38.15,17

10 "I loathe my life;
I will give free utterance to my complaint;
I will speak in the bitterness of my soul.

10.2 Job 9.29 Ps 139.23,24

2 I will say to God, Do not condemn me;
let me know why you contend against me.

10.3 Job 9.22-24 10.8; 19.6 21.16; 22.18

3 Does it seem good to you to oppress,
to despise the work of your hands
and favor the schemes of the wicked?

10.4-7 1 Sam 16.7 Job 9.12; 36.26

4 Do you have eyes of flesh?
Do you see as humans see?
5 Are your days like the days of mortals,
or your years like human years,
6 that you seek out my iniquity
and search for my sin,
7 although you know that I am not guilty,
and there is no one to deliver out of your hand?

10.8 Job 9.22 Ps 119.73 Isa 43.7

8 Your hands fashioned and made me;
and now you turn and destroy me.[f]

10.9 Job 4.19; 7.21

9 Remember that you fashioned me like clay;
and will you turn me to dust again?
10 Did you not pour me out like milk
and curdle me like cheese?
11 You clothed me with skin and flesh,
and knit me together with bones and sinews.

10.12 Job 33.4

12 You have granted me life and steadfast love,
and your care has preserved my spirit.

10.13 Job 7.20,21 9.28; 23.13

13 Yet these things you hid in your heart;
I know that this was your purpose.
14 If I sin, you watch me,
and do not acquit me of my iniquity.

10.15 Job 6.29

15 If I am wicked, woe to me!
If I am righteous, I cannot lift up my head,

[d] Another reading is *Would that there were an umpire* [e] Cn: Heb *for I am not so in myself* [f] Cn Compare Gk Syr: Heb *made me together all around, and you destroy me*

10.1 When we face baffling affliction, a human response is to feel sorry for ourselves. Our pain lures us toward self-pity. At this point we are only one step from self-righteousness, where we keep track of life's injustices and say, "Look what happened to me; how unfair it is!" We may feel like blaming God. Remember that life's trials, whether allowed by God or sent by God, can be the means for development and refinement. When facing trials, ask, "What can I learn and how can I grow?" rather than "Who did this to me and how can I get out of it?"

10.1ff Job was restating his position as both he and God knew it: he was innocent. What Job really wanted was to talk to God personally to plead his case and to have God explain the reasons for this suffering.

10.13, 14 In frustration, Job jumped to the false conclusion that God was out to get him. Wrong assumptions lead to wrong conclusions. We dare not take our limited experiences and jump to conclusions about life in general. If you find yourself doubting God, remember that you don't have all the facts. God wants only the very best for your life. Many people endure great pain, but ultimately they find some greater good came from it. When you're struggling, don't assume the worst.

for I am filled with disgrace
and look upon my affliction.
16 Bold as a lion you hunt me;
you repeat your exploits against me.
17 You renew your witnesses against me,
and increase your vexation toward me;
you bring fresh troops against me.[g]

18 "Why did you bring me forth from the womb?
Would that I had died before any eye had seen me,
19 and were as though I had not been,
carried from the womb to the grave.
20 Are not the days of my life few?[h]
Let me alone, that I may find a little comfort[i]
21 before I go, never to return,
to the land of gloom and deep darkness,
22 the land of gloom[j] and chaos,
where light is like darkness."

10.16 Job 5.9
10.17 Job 7.1; 16.8
10.18 Job 3.11-13
10.20 Job 7.19; 14.1

Zophar speaks

11 Then Zophar the Naamathite answered:
2 "Should a multitude of words go unanswered,
and should one full of talk be vindicated?
3 Should your babble put others to silence,
and when you mock, shall no one shame you?
4 For you say, 'My conduct[k] is pure,
and I am clean in God's[l] sight.'
5 But oh, that God would speak,
and open his lips to you,
6 and that he would tell you the secrets of wisdom!
For wisdom is many-sided.[m]
Know then that God exacts of you less than your guilt deserves.

7 "Can you find out the deep things of God?
Can you find out the limit of the Almighty?[n]
8 It is higher than heaven[o] — what can you do?
Deeper than Sheol — what can you know?
9 Its measure is longer than the earth,
and broader than the sea.
10 If he passes through, and imprisons,
and assembles for judgment, who can hinder him?
11 For he knows those who are worthless;
when he sees iniquity, will he not consider it?

11.2 Job 8.2; 15.2
11.3 Job 17.2; 21.3
11.4 Job 6.10
11.6 Job 22.5
11.7 Job 33.12,13 36.26; 37.5
11.11 Job 24.23 34.21-23

[g] Cn Compare Gk: Heb *toward me; changes and a troop are with me* [h] Cn Compare Gk Syr: Heb *Are not my days few? Let him cease!* [i] Heb *that I may brighten up a little* [j] Heb *gloom as darkness, deep darkness* [k] Gk: Heb *teaching* [l] Heb *your* [m] Meaning of Heb uncertain [n] Traditional rendering of Heb *Shaddai* [o] Heb *The heights of heaven*

10.20–22 Job is expressing the view of death common in Old Testament times – that the dead went to a joyless, dark place called Sheol. There was no punishment or reward in Sheol, and no escape from it. (See the note on 19.26 for a broader picture of Job's view of death.)

11.1ff Zophar was the third of Job's friends to speak, and the least courteous. Full of anger, he lashed out at Job, saying Job deserved more punishment, not less. Zophar took the same position as Eliphaz (chapters 4, 5) and Bildad (chapter 8) – that Job was suffering because of sin – but his speech was by far the most arrogant. Zophar was the kind of person who has an answer for everything; he was totally insensitive to Job's unique situation. (For more on Zophar, see the chart in chapter 28.)

11.11 Zophar incorrectly assumed that Job was hiding secret faults and sins. Although his assumption was wrong, he explained quite accurately that God knows and sees everything. We are often tempted by the thought, "No one will ever know!" Perhaps we can hide some sin from others, but we can do *nothing* without God knowing about it. Because our very thoughts are known to God, of course he will notice our sins. Job understood this as well as Zophar did, but it didn't apply to his current dilemma.

11.12 Ps 62.9
12 But a stupid person will get understanding,
when a wild ass is born human.[p]

11.13 Ps 78.8; 88.9
13 "If you direct your heart rightly,
you will stretch out your hands toward him.
14 If iniquity is in your hand, put it far away,
and do not let wickedness reside in your tents.
11.15 Ps 27.3; 46.2
15 Surely then you will lift up your face without blemish;
you will be secure, and will not fear.
16 You will forget your misery;
you will remember it as waters that have passed away.
11.17 Ps 37.6
17 And your life will be brighter than the noonday;
its darkness will be like the morning.
18 And you will have confidence, because there is hope;
you will be protected[q] and take your rest in safety.
11.19 Lev 26.6
19 You will lie down, and no one will make you afraid;
many will entreat your favor.
11.20 Job 6.9; 34.22
20 But the eyes of the wicked will fail;
all way of escape will be lost to them,
and their hope is to breathe their last."

Job speaks

12 Then Job answered:
12.2 Job 16.1,2 17.10
2 "No doubt you are the people,
and wisdom will die with you.
3 But I have understanding as well as you;
I am not inferior to you.
Who does not know such things as these?
12.4 Job 6.29; 17.6 30.1,9,10
4 I am a laughingstock to my friends;
I, who called upon God and he answered me,
a just and blameless man, I am a laughingstock.
5 Those at ease have contempt for misfortune,[p]
but it is ready for those whose feet are unstable.
12.6 Job 9.24; 21.9
6 The tents of robbers are at peace,
and those who provoke God are secure,
who bring their god in their hands.[r]

7 "But ask the animals, and they will teach you;
the birds of the air, and they will tell you;
8 ask the plants of the earth,[s] and they will teach you;
and the fish of the sea will declare to you.
9 Who among all these does not know
that the hand of the LORD has done this?
10 In his hand is the life of every living thing
and the breath of every human being.
12.11 Job 34.3
11 Does not the ear test words
as the palate tastes food?
12.12 Job 32.7
12 Is wisdom with the aged,
and understanding in length of days?

13 "With God[t] are wisdom and strength;
he has counsel and understanding.

[p] Meaning of Heb uncertain [q] Or *you will look around* [r] Or *whom God brought forth by his hand*; Meaning of Heb uncertain [s] Or *speak to the earth* [t] Heb *him*

12.1ff Job answered Zophar's argument with great sarcasm: "Wisdom will die with you." He went on to say that his three friends didn't need to explain God to him – they were saying nothing he didn't already know (12.7–9; 13.1, 2). Job continued to maintain that his friends had completely misunderstood the reason for his suffering. Job did not know it either, but he was certain that his friends' reasons were both narrow-minded and incorrect. Once again Job appealed to God to give him an answer (13.3).

14 If he tears down, no one can rebuild;
if he shuts someone in, no one can open up.
15 If he withholds the waters, they dry up;
if he sends them out, they overwhelm the land.
16 With him are strength and wisdom;
the deceived and the deceiver are his.
17 He leads counselors away stripped,
and makes fools of judges.
18 He looses the sash of kings,
and binds a waistcloth on their loins.
19 He leads priests away stripped,
and overthrows the mighty.
20 He deprives of speech those who are trusted,
and takes away the discernment of the elders.
21 He pours contempt on princes,
and looses the belt of the strong.
22 He uncovers the deeps out of darkness,
and brings deep darkness to light.
23 He makes nations great, then destroys them;
he enlarges nations, then leads them away.
24 He strips understanding from the leaders[u] of the earth,
and makes them wander in a pathless waste.
25 They grope in the dark without light;
he makes them stagger like a drunkard.

12.14 Job 19.10; 37.7
12.16 Job 13.7,9
12.19 Job 34.24-28
12.20 Job 32.9
12.21 Job 12.18; 34.19
12.22 Dan 2.22 1 Cor 4.5
12.23 Isa 9.3 Zech 10.8
12.24 Dan 4.16,33 Hos 7.11

13 "Look, my eye has seen all this,
my ear has heard and understood it.
2 What you know, I also know;
I am not inferior to you.
3 But I would speak to the Almighty,[v]
and I desire to argue my case with God.
4 As for you, you whitewash with lies;
all of you are worthless physicians.
5 If you would only keep silent,
that would be your wisdom!
6 Hear now my reasoning,
and listen to the pleadings of my lips.
7 Will you speak falsely for God,
and speak deceitfully for him?
8 Will you show partiality toward him,
will you plead the case for God?
9 Will it be well with you when he searches you out?
Or can you deceive him, as one person deceives another?
10 He will surely rebuke you
if in secret you show partiality.
11 Will not his majesty terrify you,
and the dread of him fall upon you?
12 Your maxims are proverbs of ashes,

13.2 Job 12.3
13.3 Job 13.22; 23.4 Jer 12.1,2
13.4 Ps 119.69 Jer 23.32 Hos 5.13
13.5 Job 21.5
13.7 Job 27.4
13.10 Job 32.21
13.11 Job 31.23
13.12 Job 15.3

[u] Heb adds *of the people* [v] Traditional rendering of Heb *Shaddai*

12.24, 25 Job affirms that no leader has any real wisdom apart from God. No research or report can outweigh God's opinion. No scientific discovery or medical advance takes him by surprise. When we look for guidance for our decisions, we must recognize that God's wisdom is superior to any the world has to offer. Don't let earthly advisers dampen your desire to know God better.

13.4 Job compared his three friends to doctors who did not know what they were doing. They were like eye surgeons trying to perform open-heart surgery. Many of their ideas about God were true, but they did not apply to Job's situation. They were right to say that God is just. They were right to say God punishes sin. But they were wrong to assume that Job's suffering was a just punishment for his sin. They took a true principle and applied it wrongly, ignoring the vast differences in human circumstances. We must be careful and compassionate in how we apply biblical condemnations to others; we must be slow to judge.

your defenses are defenses of clay.
13 "Let me have silence, and I will speak,
and let come on me what may.
14 I will take my flesh in my teeth,
and put my life in my hand.[w]
15 See, he will kill me; I have no hope;[x]
but I will defend my ways to his face.
16 This will be my salvation,
that the godless shall not come before him.
17 Listen carefully to my words,
and let my declaration be in your ears.
18 I have indeed prepared my case;
I know that I shall be vindicated.
19 Who is there that will contend with me?
For then I would be silent and die.
20 Only grant two things to me,
then I will not hide myself from your face:
21 withdraw your hand far from me,
and do not let dread of you terrify me.
22 Then call, and I will answer;
or let me speak, and you reply to me.
23 How many are my iniquities and my sins?
Make me know my transgression and my sin.
24 Why do you hide your face,
and count me as your enemy?
25 Will you frighten a windblown leaf
and pursue dry chaff?
26 For you write bitter things against me,
and make me reap[y] the iniquities of my youth.
27 You put my feet in the stocks,
and watch all my paths;
you set a bound to the soles of my feet.
28 One wastes away like a rotten thing,
like a garment that is moth-eaten.

13.15 Job 7.6; 27.5
13.16 Job 34.21-23
13.18 Job 9.21; 23.4
13.19 Job 7.21
13.21 Job 9 34 Ps 39.10
13.22 Job 14.15
13.24 Job 19.11; 33.10
13.25 Job 11.18
13.26 Job 9.18
13.27 Job 2.7

14 "A mortal, born of woman, few of days and full of trouble,
2 comes up like a flower and withers,
flees like a shadow and does not last.
3 Do you fix your eyes on such a one?
Do you bring me into judgment with you?
4 Who can bring a clean thing out of an unclean?
No one can.
5 Since their days are determined,
and the number of their months is known to you,
and you have appointed the bounds that they cannot pass,
6 look away from them, and desist,[z]
that they may enjoy, like laborers, their days.

14.1 Job 5.7
14.2 Job 8.9
14.4 Job 15.14; 25.4
14.5 Job 21.21

[w] Gk: Heb *Why should I take . . . in my hand?* [x] Or *Though he kill me, yet I will trust in him* [y] Heb *inherit* [z] Cn: Heb *that they may desist*

13.21–24 Job was especially upset because God was silent, giving no reasons for his suffering. Job misinterpreted God's silence as rejection, and once again he said that it was not his suffering that bothered him as much as this apparent rejection. If God had given reasons, however, Job's faith might not have been stretched and strengthened.

14.1ff Life is brief and full of trouble, Job laments in his closing remarks. Sickness, loneliness, disappointment, and death cause him to say that life is not fair. Some understand verse 14 to mean that even in his gloom, Job hoped for the resurrection of the dead. If this is true, then Job understood the one truth that could put his suffering in perspective. God's solution to believers who live in an unfair world is to guarantee life with him forever. No matter how unfair your present world seems, God offers the hope of being in his presence eternally. Have you accepted this offer?

7 "For there is hope for a tree,
if it is cut down, that it will sprout again,
and that its shoots will not cease.
8 Though its root grows old in the earth,
and its stump dies in the ground,
9 yet at the scent of water it will bud
and put forth branches like a young plant.
10 But mortals die, and are laid low;
humans expire, and where are they?
11 As waters fail from a lake,
and a river wastes away and dries up,
12 so mortals lie down and do not rise again;
until the heavens are no more, they will not awake
or be roused out of their sleep.
13 Oh that you would hide me in Sheol,
that you would conceal me until your wrath is past,
that you would appoint me a set time, and remember me!
14 If mortals die, will they live again?
All the days of my service I would wait
until my release should come.
15 You would call, and I would answer you;
you would long for the work of your hands.
16 For then you would not[a] number my steps,
you would not keep watch over my sin;
17 my transgression would be sealed up in a bag,
and you would cover over my iniquity.

18 "But the mountain falls and crumbles away,
and the rock is removed from its place;
19 the waters wear away the stones;
the torrents wash away the soil of the earth;
so you destroy the hope of mortals.
20 You prevail forever against them, and they pass away;
you change their countenance, and send them away.
21 Their children come to honor, and they do not know it;
they are brought low, and it goes unnoticed.
22 They feel only the pain of their own bodies,
and mourn only for themselves."

14.10 Job 13.19
14.11 Job 3.13 Isa 19.5
14.13 Isa 26.20
14.16 Job 10.6; 31.4 34.21
14.17 Deut 32.32-34
14.18 Job 7.6
14.20 Job 20.7; 34.20

2. Second round of discussion

Eliphaz speaks

15 Then Eliphaz the Temanite answered:
2 "Should the wise answer with windy knowledge,
and fill themselves with the east wind?

15.2 Job 6.26

[a] Syr: Heb lacks *not*

14.7–22 The Old Testament does not say much about the resurrection of the dead. This is not surprising, because Jesus had not yet conquered death. Job's pessimism about death is understandable. What is remarkable is his budding hope. If only God would hide him with the dead and then bring him out again! If only he could die and live again! When we must endure suffering, we have an advantage over Job. We *know* that the dead will rise. We have hope based on Christ's promise in John 14.19.

14.22 Job's profound speech in this chapter illustrates a great truth: to have a right set of doctrines is not enough. To know what to believe is not all that is required to please God. Truth untested by life's experiences may become static and stagnant. Suffering can bring a dynamic quality to life. Just as drought drives the roots of a tree deeper to find water, so suffering can drive us beyond superficial acceptance of truth to dependence on God for hope and life.

15.1ff With the first round of talks concluded, each friend, in the same order, pressed the argument further. Again Job answered each argument (chapters 15–31). This time Eliphaz was ruder, more intense, and more threatening – but he said nothing new. (See his first speech in chapters 4; 5.) He began by saying Job's words were vain and unprofitable; then he restated his opinion that Job must be a great sinner. According to Eliphaz, the experience and wisdom of their ancestors were more valuable than Job's individual thoughts. Eliphaz assumed that his words were as true as God's. It is easy to spot his arrogance.

3 Should they argue in unprofitable talk,
or in words with which they can do no good?
4 But you are doing away with the fear of God,
and hindering meditation before God.
5 For your iniquity teaches your mouth,
and you choose the tongue of the crafty.
6 Your own mouth condemns you, and not I;
your own lips testify against you.

7 "Are you the firstborn of the human race?
Were you brought forth before the hills?
8 Have you listened in the council of God?
And do you limit wisdom to yourself?
9 What do you know that we do not know?
What do you understand that is not clear to us?
10 The gray-haired and the aged are on our side,
those older than your father.
11 Are the consolations of God too small for you,
or the word that deals gently with you?
12 Why does your heart carry you away,
and why do your eyes flash,[b]
13 so that you turn your spirit against God,
and let such words go out of your mouth?
14 What are mortals, that they can be clean?
Or those born of woman, that they can be righteous?
15 God puts no trust even in his holy ones,
and the heavens are not clean in his sight;
16 how much less one who is abominable and corrupt,
one who drinks iniquity like water!

17 "I will show you; listen to me;
what I have seen I will declare—
18 what sages have told,
and their ancestors have not hidden,
19 to whom alone the land was given,
and no stranger passed among them.
20 The wicked writhe in pain all their days,
through all the years that are laid up for the ruthless.
21 Terrifying sounds are in their ears;
in prosperity the destroyer will come upon them.
22 They despair of returning from darkness,
and they are destined for the sword.
23 They wander abroad for bread, saying, 'Where is it?'
They know that a day of darkness is ready at hand;
24 distress and anguish terrify them;
they prevail against them, like a king prepared for battle.
25 Because they stretched out their hands against God,
and bid defiance to the Almighty,[c]
26 running stubbornly against him
with a thick-bossed shield;
27 because they have covered their faces with their fat,
and gathered fat upon their loins,
28 they will live in desolate cities,

15.4 Job 5.12,13
15.6 Job 9.20
15.7 Job 38.4,21
15.9 Job 12.3; 13.2
15.10 Job 12.12
15.11 Job 6.10
15.12 Job 36.13
15.14 Job 14.4
15.15 Job 4.18; 25.5
15.16 Job 34.7
15.17 Job 8.8; 20.4
15.21 Job 18.11 20.21,25
15.22 Job 15.30 19.29; 27.14
15.25 Job 36.9
15.27 Job 3.14 Ps 73.7; 119.70

[b] Meaning of Heb uncertain [c] Traditional rendering of Heb *Shaddai*

15.15, 16 Eliphaz was repeating his argument that anything created, whether angel or man, is not a sufficient basis for trust and hope. Only in God can we be sure. Remember that Eliphaz was speaking, not God. (See the note on 4.18, 19.)

in houses that no one should inhabit,
houses destined to become heaps of ruins;
29 they will not be rich, and their wealth will not endure,
nor will they strike root in the earth;[d]
30 they will not escape from darkness;
the flame will dry up their shoots,
and their blossom[e] will be swept away[f] by the wind.
31 Let them not trust in emptiness, deceiving themselves;
for emptiness will be their recompense.
32 It will be paid in full before their time,
and their branch will not be green.
33 They will shake off their unripe grape, like the vine,
and cast off their blossoms, like the olive tree.
34 For the company of the godless is barren,
and fire consumes the tents of bribery.
35 They conceive mischief and bring forth evil
and their heart prepares deceit."

15.29 Job 27.16,17
15.30 Job 4.9; 5.14 22.20
15.31 Isa 59.4
15.34 Job 8.13,22
15.35 Ps 7.14 Isa 59.4

Job speaks

16 Then Job answered:
2 "I have heard many such things;
miserable comforters are you all.
3 Have windy words no limit?
Or what provokes you that you keep on talking?
4 I also could talk as you do,
if you were in my place;
I could join words together against you,
and shake my head at you.
5 I could encourage you with my mouth,
and the solace of my lips would assuage your pain.

6 "If I speak, my pain is not assuaged,
and if I forbear, how much of it leaves me?
7 Surely now God has worn me out;
he has[g] made desolate all my company.
8 And he has[i] shriveled me up,
which is a witness against me;
my leanness has risen up against me,
and it testifies to my face.
9 He has torn me in his wrath, and hated me;
he has gnashed his teeth at me;
my adversary sharpens his eyes against me.
10 They have gaped at me with their mouths;
they have struck me insolently on the cheek;
they mass themselves together against me.
11 God gives me up to the ungodly,
and casts me into the hands of the wicked.
12 I was at ease, and he broke me in two;

16.2 Job 13.4; 21.34
16.3 Job 6.26
16.4 Ps 22.7; 109.25
16.6 Job 9.27,28
16.7 Job 7.3 19.13-15
16.8 Job 10.17; 19.20
16.9 Job 13.24; 33.10
16.10 Job 30.12
16.12 Job 7.20; 9.17

[d] Vg: Meaning of Heb uncertain [e] Gk: Heb *mouth* [f] Cn: Heb *will depart* [g] Heb *you have*

16.1ff Job's friends were supposed to be comforting him in his grief. Instead they condemned him for causing his own suffering. Job began his reply to Eliphaz by calling him and his friends "miserable comforters." Job's words reveal several ways to become a better comforter to those in pain: (1) don't talk just for the sake of talking; (2) don't sermonize by giving pat answers; (3) don't accuse or criticize; (4) put yourself in the other person's place; and (5) offer help and encouragement. Try Job's suggestions, knowing that they are given by one who needed great comfort. The best comforters are those who know something about personal suffering.

16.7 First Job's children died, then his friends condemned him, and now he felt that God had deserted him. No wonder he wanted to die! But God still had something important to reveal to him and to us through his experiences.

he seized me by the neck and dashed me to pieces;
he set me up as his target;

16.13 Job 6.4; 19.12

13 his archers surround me.
He slashes open my kidneys, and shows no mercy;
he pours out my gall on the ground.

16.14 Job 9.17

14 He bursts upon me again and again;
he rushes at me like a warrior.

16.15 Job 30.19

15 I have sewed sackcloth upon my skin,
and have laid my strength in the dust.

16.16 Job 16.20; 24.17

16 My face is red with weeping,
and deep darkness is on my eyelids,

16.17 Job 27.4

17 though there is no violence in my hands,
and my prayer is pure.

18 "O earth, do not cover my blood;
let my outcry find no resting place.

16.19 Job 19.25-27 31.2

19 Even now, in fact, my witness is in heaven,
and he that vouches for me is on high.
20 My friends scorn me;
my eye pours out tears to God,
21 that he would maintain the right of a mortal with God,
as[h] one does for a neighbor.

16.22 Job 3.13

22 For when a few years have come,
I shall go the way from which I shall not return.

17 My spirit is broken, my days are extinct,
the grave is ready for me.

17.2 Job 12.4

2 Surely there are mockers around me,
and my eye dwells on their provocation.

17.3 Job 12.20

3 "Lay down a pledge for me with yourself;
who is there that will give surety for me?
4 Since you have closed their minds to understanding,
therefore you will not let them triumph.

17.5 Job 11.20

5 Those who denounce friends for reward—
the eyes of their children will fail.

17.6 Job 30.10

6 "He has made me a byword of the peoples,
and I am one before whom people spit.
7 My eye has grown dim from grief,
and all my members are like a shadow.

17.8 Job 22.19

8 The upright are appalled at this,
and the innocent stir themselves up against the godless.

17.9 Job 22.30

9 Yet the righteous hold to their way,
and they that have clean hands grow stronger and stronger.

17.10 Job 12.2

10 But you, come back now, all of you,
and I shall not find a sensible person among you.

[h] Syr Vg Tg: Heb *and*

16.19 Job was afraid that God hated him. Yet he appealed directly to God (his witness and advocate) and to God's knowledge of his innocence. A *witness* is someone who has seen what has happened, and a *record* can be consulted to prove the facts. By using these terms, Job showed he had cast all his hope for any fair defense upon God. In the New Testament we learn that Jesus Christ witnesses on our behalf (Hebrews 7.25; 1 John 2.1); therefore, we have nothing to fear.

17.10 Job's three friends had a reputation for being wise, but Job said that none of them had shown wisdom. God backed up Job's claim in 42.7, where he condemned these men for their false portrayal of him. Obviously these men had a faulty view of wisdom. They assumed that because they were prosperous and successful, God must be pleased with the way they were living and thinking. Job, however, told his friends that they were starting with the wrong idea, because earthly success and prosperity are not proof of faith in God. Likewise, trouble and affliction do not prove faithlessness. The truly wise man knows that wisdom comes from God alone, not from human successes or failures. And the truly wise man never forsakes God. God's wisdom proved superior to Job and all his friends.

11 My days are past, my plans are broken off,
the desires of my heart.
12 They make night into day;
'The light,' they say, 'is near to the darkness.'[i]
13 If I look for Sheol as my house,
if I spread my couch in darkness,
14 if I say to the Pit, 'You are my father,'
and to the worm, 'My mother,' or 'My sister,'
15 where then is my hope?
Who will see my hope?
16 Will it go down to the bars of Sheol?
Shall we descend together into the dust?"

17.11 Job 7.6
17.13 Job 3.13; 21.26 25.6
17.15 Job 7.6
17.16 Job 3.17; 21.33

Bildad speaks

18 Then Bildad the Shuhite answered:
2 "How long will you hunt for words?
Consider, and then we shall speak.
3 Why are we counted as cattle?
Why are we stupid in your sight?
4 You who tear yourself in your anger—
shall the earth be forsaken because of you,
or the rock be removed out of its place?

5 "Surely the light of the wicked is put out,
and the flame of their fire does not shine.
6 The light is dark in their tent,
and the lamp above them is put out.
7 Their strong steps are shortened,
and their own schemes throw them down.
8 For they are thrust into a net by their own feet,
and they walk into a pitfall.
9 A trap seizes them by the heel;
a snare lays hold of them.
10 A rope is hid for them in the ground,
a trap for them in the path.
11 Terrors frighten them on every side,
and chase them at their heels.
12 Their strength is consumed by hunger,[j]
and calamity is ready for their stumbling.
13 By disease their skin is consumed,[k]
the firstborn of Death consumes their limbs.
14 They are torn from the tent in which they trusted,
and are brought to the king of terrors.
15 In their tents nothing remains;
sulfur is scattered upon their habitations.
16 Their roots dry up beneath,
and their branches wither above.

18.3 Ps 73.22
18.5 Job 21.17
18.6 Job 12.25
18.8 Job 22.10
18.11 Job 15.21; 18.18
18.14 Job 8.22; 15.21 27.18
18.16 Job 15.30,32

[i] Meaning of Heb uncertain [j] Or *Disaster is hungry for them* [k] Cn: Heb *It consumes the limbs of his skin*

17.15 Job gave up hope of any future restoration of wealth and family, and he wrapped himself in thoughts of death and the rest from grief and pain it promised. The rewards that Job's friends described were all related to this present life. They were silent about the possibility of life after death. We must not evaluate life only in terms of this present world, because God promises the faithful a never-ending future.

18.1ff Bildad thought he knew how the universe should be run, and he saw Job as an illustration of the consequences of sin. He rejected Job's side of the story because it did not fit in with his outlook on life. It is easy to condemn Bildad because his errors are obvious; unfortunately, however, we often act the same way when our ideas are threatened.

18.14 The "king of terrors" is a figure of speech referring to death. Bildad viewed death as a great devourer (18.13), but the Bible teaches that God has the power to devour even death (Psalm 49.15; 1 Corinthians 15.55, 56).

18.17
Job 24.20

18.18
Job 5.14
27.21-23

18.19
Job 27.14,15

18.20
Jer 50.27
Obad 12
Lk 19.42,44

17 Their memory perishes from the earth,
and they have no name in the street.
18 They are thrust from light into darkness,
and driven out of the world.
19 They have no offspring or descendant among their people,
and no survivor where they used to live.
20 They of the west are appalled at their fate,
and horror seizes those of the east.
21 Surely such are the dwellings of the ungodly,
such is the place of those who do not know God."

Job speaks

19 Then Job answered:
2 "How long will you torment me,
and break me in pieces with words?
3 These ten times you have cast reproach upon me;
are you not ashamed to wrong me?
4 And even if it is true that I have erred,
my error remains with me.

19.5
Ps 35.26; 38.16

19.6
Job 16.11

19.7
Job 30.20,24

19.8
Job 3.23; 30.26

19.10
Job 7.6; 12.14

19.11
Job 13.24; 16.9

19.12
Job 16.13

5 If indeed you magnify yourselves against me,
and make my humiliation an argument against me,
6 know then that God has put me in the wrong,
and closed his net around me.
7 Even when I cry out, 'Violence!' I am not answered;
I call aloud, but there is no justice.
8 He has walled up my way so that I cannot pass,
and he has set darkness upon my paths.
9 He has stripped my glory from me,
and taken the crown from my head.
10 He breaks me down on every side, and I am gone,
he has uprooted my hope like a tree.
11 He has kindled his wrath against me,
and counts me as his adversary.
12 His troops come on together;
they have thrown up siegeworks[l] against me,
and encamp around my tent.

19.13
Job 16.7,20

13 "He has put my family far from me,
and my acquaintances are wholly estranged from me.
14 My relatives and my close friends have failed me;
15 the guests in my house have forgotten me;
my serving girls count me as a stranger;
I have become an alien in their eyes.
16 I call to my servant, but he gives me no answer;
I must myself plead with him.

[l] Cn: Heb *their way*

18.21 Bildad's second speech was really no different from his first except that it was more harsh, as was Eliphaz's. When we face difficulties, pain, and suffering, we can expect well-meaning Bildads to come along, quoting proverbs and giving advice while not really listening to us or identifying with our pain. Rather than seeking to understand, they give unhelpful, trite answers. When receiving this useless advice, listen politely. Then, in order to sort out the helpful advice from the empty words, talk to God about what was said. When giving advice, avoid empty words. It is more important to convey care and support than to say exactly the right words.

19.3–5 It is easy to point out someone else's faults or sins. Job's friends accused him of sin to make him feel guilty, not to encourage or correct him. If we feel we must admonish someone, we should be sure we are confronting that person because we love him, not because we are annoyed, inconvenienced, or seeking to blame him.

19.6 Job felt that God was treating him as an enemy when, in fact, God was his friend and thought highly of him (1.8; 2.3). In his difficulty, Job pointed at the wrong person. It was Satan, not God, who was Job's enemy. Because they stressed ultimate causes, most Israelites believed that both good and evil came from God; they also thought people were responsible for their own destinies. In verse 7, Job still cries out to be heard by God.

17 My breath is repulsive to my wife;
I am loathsome to my own family.
18 Even young children despise me;
when I rise, they talk against me.
19 All my intimate friends abhor me,
and those whom I loved have turned against me.
20 My bones cling to my skin and to my flesh,
and I have escaped by the skin of my teeth.
21 Have pity on me, have pity on me, O you my friends,
for the hand of God has touched me!
22 Why do you, like God, pursue me,
never satisfied with my flesh?

23 "O that my words were written down!
O that they were inscribed in a book!
24 O that with an iron pen and with lead
they were engraved on a rock forever!
25 For I know that my Redeemer[m] lives,
and that at the last he[n] will stand upon the earth;[o]
26 and after my skin has been thus destroyed,
then in[p] my flesh I shall see God,[q]
27 whom I shall see on my side,[r]
and my eyes shall behold, and not another.
My heart faints within me!
28 If you say, 'How we will persecute him!'
and, 'The root of the matter is found in him';
29 be afraid of the sword,
for wrath brings the punishment of the sword,
so that you may know there is a judgment."

Zophar speaks

20 Then Zophar the Naamathite answered:
2 "Pay attention! My thoughts urge me to answer,
because of the agitation within me.
3 I hear censure that insults me,
and a spirit beyond my understanding answers me.
4 Do you not know this from of old,
ever since mortals were placed on earth,
5 that the exulting of the wicked is short,
and the joy of the godless is but for a moment?
6 Even though they mount up high as the heavens,

19.19 Ps 38.11; 55.13
19.20 Job 33.21
19.21 Job 1.11
19.22 Ps 16.11; 69.26
19.23 Isa 30.8
19.25 Job 16.19 Isa 43.14 Jer 50.34
19.26 Ps 17.15 Mt 5.8 1 Cor 13.12 1 Jn 3.2
20.3 Job 19.3
20.5 Job 8.12,13 Ps 37.35,36
20.6 Isa 14.13,14

[m] Or *Vindicator* [n] Or *that he the Last* [o] Heb *dust* [p] Or *without* [q] Meaning of Heb of this verse uncertain [r] Or *for myself*

19.25–27 At the heart of the book of Job comes his ringing affirmation of confidence: "I know that my Redeemer lives." In ancient Israel a *redeemer* was a family member who bought a slave's way to freedom or who took care of a widow (see the note in Ruth 3.1). What tremendous faith Job had, especially in light of the fact that he was unaware of the conference between God and Satan. Job thought that God had brought all these disasters upon him! Faced with death and decay, Job still expected to see God—and he expected to do so in his body. When the book of Job was written, Israel did not have a well-developed doctrine of the resurrection. Although Job struggled with the idea that God was presently against him, he firmly believed that in the end God would be on his side. This belief was so strong that Job became one of the first to talk about the resurrection of the body (see also Psalm 16.10; Isaiah 26.19; Daniel 12.2, 13).

19.26 Job said: "in my flesh I shall see God." In Job's situation, it seemed unlikely to him that he would, in his flesh, see God. And that's just the point of Job's faith! He was confident that God's justice would triumph, even if it would take a miracle like resurrection to accomplish this.

20.1ff Zophar's speech again revealed his false assumption, because he based his arguments purely on the idea that Job was an evil hypocrite. Zophar said that although Job had it good for a while, he didn't live righteously, so God took his wealth from him. According to Zophar, Job's calamities *proved* his wickedness.

20.6, 7 Although Zophar was wrong in directing this tirade against Job, he was correct in talking about the final end of evil people. At first, sin seems enjoyable and attractive. Lying, stealing, or oppressing others often brings temporary gain to those who practice these sins. Some live a long time with ill-gotten gain. But in the end, God's justice will prevail. What Zophar missed is that judgment for these sins may not come in the lifetime of the sinner.

and their head reaches to the clouds,
7 they will perish forever like their own dung;
those who have seen them will say, 'Where are they?'
8 They will fly away like a dream, and not be found;
they will be chased away like a vision of the night.
9 The eye that saw them will see them no more,
nor will their place behold them any longer.
10 Their children will seek the favor of the poor,
and their hands will give back their wealth.
11 Their bodies, once full of youth,
will lie down in the dust with them.

12 "Though wickedness is sweet in their mouth,
though they hide it under their tongues,
13 though they are loath to let it go,
and hold it in their mouths,
14 yet their food is turned in their stomachs;
it is the venom of asps within them.
15 They swallow down riches and vomit them up again;
God casts them out of their bellies.
16 They will suck the poison of asps;
the tongue of a viper will kill them.
17 They will not look on the rivers,
the streams flowing with honey and curds.
18 They will give back the fruit of their toil,
and will not swallow it down;
from the profit of their trading
they will get no enjoyment.
19 For they have crushed and abandoned the poor,
they have seized a house that they did not build.

20 "They knew no quiet in their bellies;
in their greed they let nothing escape.
21 There was nothing left after they had eaten;
therefore their prosperity will not endure.
22 In full sufficiency they will be in distress;
all the force of misery will come upon them.
23 To fill their belly to the full
God[s] will send his fierce anger into them,
and rain it upon them as their food.[t]
24 They will flee from an iron weapon;
a bronze arrow will strike them through.
25 It is drawn forth and comes out of their body,
and the glittering point comes out of their gall;
terrors come upon them.
26 Utter darkness is laid up for their treasures;
a fire fanned by no one will devour them;
what is left in their tent will be consumed.
27 The heavens will reveal their iniquity,
and the earth will rise up against them.
28 The possessions of their house will be carried away,
dragged off in the day of God's[u] wrath.
29 This is the portion of the wicked from God,
the heritage decreed for them by God."

20.7 Job 4.20; 7.10; 8.18; 14.20
20.9 Job 7.8,10; 8.18
20.10 Job 5.4; 27.16,17
20.11 Job 13.26
20.12 Job 15.16
20.19 Job 24.2-4; 35.9
20.21 Job 15.29
20.22 Job 5.5; 15.21
20.25 Job 16.13; 18.11,14
20.26 Job 15.30; 18.18
20.27 Deut 31.28
20.28 Deut 28.31; Job 21.30
20.29 Job 27.13; 31.2,3

[s] Heb *he* [t] Cn: Meaning of Heb uncertain [u] Heb *his*

Punishment may be deferred until the last judgment, when sinners will be eternally cut off from God. We should not be impressed with the success and power of evil people. God's judgment on them is certain.

Job speaks

21 Then Job answered:
2 "Listen carefully to my words,
and let this be your consolation.
3 Bear with me, and I will speak;
then after I have spoken, mock on.
4 As for me, is my complaint addressed to mortals?
Why should I not be impatient?
5 Look at me, and be appalled,
and lay your hand upon your mouth.
6 When I think of it I am dismayed,
and shuddering seizes my flesh.
7 Why do the wicked live on,
reach old age, and grow mighty in power?
8 Their children are established in their presence,
and their offspring before their eyes.
9 Their houses are safe from fear,
and no rod of God is upon them.
10 Their bull breeds without fail;
their cow calves and never miscarries.
11 They send out their little ones like a flock,
and their children dance around.
12 They sing to the tambourine and the lyre,
and rejoice to the sound of the pipe.
13 They spend their days in prosperity,
and in peace they go down to Sheol.
14 They say to God, 'Leave us alone!
We do not desire to know your ways.
15 What is the Almighty,[v] that we should serve him?
And what profit do we get if we pray to him?'
16 Is not their prosperity indeed their own achievement?[w]
The plans of the wicked are repugnant to me.

17 "How often is the lamp of the wicked put out?
How often does calamity come upon them?
How often does God[x] distribute pains in his anger?
18 How often are they like straw before the wind,
and like chaff that the storm carries away?
19 You say, 'God stores up their iniquity for their children.'
Let it be paid back to them, so that they may know it.
20 Let their own eyes see their destruction,
and let them drink of the wrath of the Almighty.[v]
21 For what do they care for their household after them,
when the number of their months is cut off?
22 Will any teach God knowledge,
seeing that he judges those that are on high?

21.2 Job 11.3; 17.2
21.4 Job 6.11; 7.11
21.6 Ps 55.5
21.7 Ps 73.3
21.8 Ps 17.14
21.9 Job 12.6
21.12 Job 36.11
21.14 Job 22.17
21.15 Job 22.17; 34.9
21.17 Job 18.5,6
21.18 Job 13.25 Ps 1.4; 35.5
21.19 Ex 20.5 Mt 23.31-35
21.22 Job 36.22

[v] Traditional rendering of Heb *Shaddai* [w] Heb *in their hand* [x] Heb *he*

21.1ff Job refuted Zophar's idea that evil people never experience wealth and happiness, pointing out that in the real world the wicked do indeed prosper. God does as he wills to individuals (21.22–25), and people cannot use their circumstances to measure their own goodness or God's – they are sometimes (but not always) related. Success to Job's friends was based on outward performance; success to God, however, is based on a person's heart.

21.22 Although baffled by the reasons for his suffering, Job affirmed God's superior understanding by asking, "Will any teach God knowledge?" The way you respond to your personal struggles shows your attitude toward God. Rather than becoming angry with God, continue to trust him, no matter what your circumstances may be. Although it is sometimes difficult to see, God *is* in control. We must commit ourselves to him so we will not resent his timing.

21.23 Job 20.11

23 One dies in full prosperity,
being wholly at ease and secure,
24 his loins full of milk
and the marrow of his bones moist.
25 Another dies in bitterness of soul,
never having tasted of good.

21.26 Job 3.13; 24.20

26 They lie down alike in the dust,
and the worms cover them.

27 "Oh, I know your thoughts,
and your schemes to wrong me.

21.28 Job 1.3 Ps 37.36 52.5,6

28 For you say, 'Where is the house of the prince?
Where is the tent in which the wicked lived?'
29 Have you not asked those who travel the roads,
and do you not accept their testimony,

21.30 Job 20.29

30 that the wicked are spared in the day of calamity,
and are rescued in the day of wrath?
31 Who declares their way to their face,
and who repays them for what they have done?
32 When they are carried to the grave,
a watch is kept over their tomb.

21.33 Job 3.19,22 17.16; 24.24

33 The clods of the valley are sweet to them;
everyone will follow after,
and those who went before are innumerable.

21.34 Job 16.2; 42.7

34 How then will you comfort me with empty nothings?
There is nothing left of your answers but falsehood."

3. Third round of discussion

Eliphaz speaks

22 Then Eliphaz the Temanite answered:

22.2 Job 35.7

2 "Can a mortal be of use to God?
Can even the wisest be of service to him?
3 Is it any pleasure to the Almighty[y] if you are righteous,
or is it gain to him if you make your ways blameless?

22.4 Job 14.3

4 Is it for your piety that he reproves you,
and enters into judgment with you?

22.5 Job 11.6; 15.5

5 Is not your wickedness great?
There is no end to your iniquities.

22.6 Ex 22.26

6 For you have exacted pledges from your family for no reason,
and stripped the naked of their clothing.

22.7 Job 31.31

7 You have given no water to the weary to drink,
and you have withheld bread from the hungry.

22.8 Job 9.24; 12.19

8 The powerful possess the land,
and the favored live in it.

22.9 Job 6.27 24.3,21

9 You have sent widows away empty-handed,
and the arms of the orphans you have crushed.[z]

22.10 Job 15.21; 18.8

10 Therefore snares are around you,

[y] Traditional rendering of Heb *Shaddai* [z] Gk Syr Tg Vg: Heb *were crushed*

21.24 This verse implies that even the wicked people can experience physical health and well-being.

21.29–32 If wicked people become wealthy despite their sin, why should we try to be good? The wicked may *seem* to get away with sin, but there is a higher Judge and a future Judgment (Revelation 20.11–15). The final settlement of justice will come not in this life, but in the next. What is important is how a person views God in prosperity or poverty, not the prosperity or poverty itself.

22.1ff This is Eliphaz's third and final speech to Job. When he first spoke to Job (chapters 4, 5), he commended Job's good works and gently suggested that Job might need to repent of some sin. While he said nothing new in this speech, he did get more specific. He couldn't shake his belief that suffering is God's punishment for evil deeds, so he suggested several possible sins that Job might have committed. Eliphaz wasn't trying to destroy Job; at the end of his speech he promised that Job would receive peace and restoration if he would only admit his sin and repent.

and sudden terror overwhelms you,
11 or darkness so that you cannot see;
a flood of water covers you.

12 "Is not God high in the heavens?
See the highest stars, how lofty they are!
13 Therefore you say, 'What does God know?
Can he judge through the deep darkness?
14 Thick clouds enwrap him, so that he does not see,
and he walks on the dome of heaven.'
15 Will you keep to the old way
that the wicked have trod?
16 They were snatched away before their time;
their foundation was washed away by a flood.
17 They said to God, 'Leave us alone,'
and 'What can the Almighty[a] do to us?'[b]
18 Yet he filled their houses with good things—
but the plans of the wicked are repugnant to me.
19 The righteous see it and are glad;
the innocent laugh them to scorn,
20 saying, 'Surely our adversaries are cut off,
and what they left, the fire has consumed.'

21 "Agree with God,[c] and be at peace;
in this way good will come to you.
22 Receive instruction from his mouth,
and lay up his words in your heart.
23 If you return to the Almighty,[a] you will be restored,
if you remove unrighteousness from your tents,
24 if you treat gold like dust,
and gold of Ophir like the stones of the torrent-bed,
25 and if the Almighty[a] is your gold
and your precious silver,
26 then you will delight yourself in the Almighty,[a]
and lift up your face to God.
27 You will pray to him, and he will hear you,
and you will pay your vows.
28 You will decide on a matter, and it will be established for you,
and light will shine on your ways.
29 When others are humiliated, you say it is pride;
for he saves the humble.
30 He will deliver even those who are guilty;
they will escape because of the cleanness of your hands."[d]

22.12 Job 11.7-9
22.14 Job 26.9
22.15 Job 14.19
22.17 Job 21.14,15
22.18 Job 12.6; 21.16
22.20 Job 15.30
22.22 Job 6.10; 23.12
22.23 Job 8.5; 11.14
22.24 Job 31.24,25
22.26 Job 27.10
22.27 Job 33.26; 34.28
22.28 Job 11.17
22.29 Job 5.11

Job speaks

23 Then Job answered:
2 "Today also my complaint is bitter;[e]
his[f] hand is heavy despite my groaning.
3 Oh, that I knew where I might find him,

23.2 Job 6.2,3; 7.11

[a] Traditional rendering of Heb *Shaddai* [b] Gk Syr: Heb *them* [c] Heb *him* [d] Meaning of Heb uncertain [e] Syr Vg Tg: Heb *rebellious* [f] Gk Syr: Heb *my*

22.12–14 Eliphaz declared that Job's view of God was too small, and he criticized Job for thinking that God was too far removed from earth to care about him. If Job knew of God's intense, personal interest in him, Eliphaz said, he wouldn't dare take his sins so lightly. Eliphaz had a point—some people do take sin lightly because they think God is far away and doesn't notice all we do. But his point did not apply to Job.

22.21–30 Several times Job's friends showed a partial knowledge of God's truth and character, but they had trouble accurately applying this truth to life. Such was the case with Eliphaz, who gave a beautiful summary of repentance. He was correct in saying that we must ask for God's forgiveness when we sin, but his statement did not apply to Job, who had already sought God's forgiveness (7.20, 21; 9.20; 13.23) and had lived closely in touch with God all along.

that I might come even to his dwelling!

23.4 Job 13.18 Isa 43.26

4 I would lay my case before him,
and fill my mouth with arguments.
5 I would learn what he would answer me,
and understand what he would say to me.

23.6 Job 9.4 2 Cor 12.9,10

6 Would he contend with me in the greatness of his power?
No; but he would give heed to me.

23.7 Job 13.3,16

7 There an upright person could reason with him,
and I should be acquitted forever by my judge.

23.8 Job 9.11

8 "If I go forward, he is not there;
or backward, I cannot perceive him;
9 on the left he hides, and I cannot behold him;
I turn[g] to the right, but I cannot see him.

23.10 Job 7.18 Ps 7.9; 11.5

10 But he knows the way that I take;
when he has tested me, I shall come out like gold.

23.11 Job 31.7 Ps 17.5; 44.18 1 Thess 2.10

11 My foot has held fast to his steps;
I have kept his way and have not turned aside.

23.12 Job 6.10

12 I have not departed from the commandment of his lips;
I have treasured in[h] my bosom the words of his mouth.
13 But he stands alone and who can dissuade him?
What he desires, that he does.
14 For he will complete what he appoints for me;
and many such things are in his mind.
15 Therefore I am terrified at his presence;
when I consider, I am in dread of him.

23.16 Deut 20.3 Job 10.18,19

16 God has made my heart faint;
the Almighty[i] has terrified me;
17 If only I could vanish in darkness,
and thick darkness would cover my face![j]

24

"Why are times not kept by the Almighty,[i]
and why do those who know him never see his days?
2 The wicked[k] remove landmarks;
they seize flocks and pasture them.

24.3 Ex 22.26

3 They drive away the donkey of the orphan;
they take the widow's ox for a pledge.

24.4 Job 29.16; 30.25

4 They thrust the needy off the road;

[g] Syr Vg: Heb *he turns* [h] Gk Vg: Heb *from* [i] Traditional rendering of Heb *Shaddai* [j] Or *But I am not destroyed by the darkness; he has concealed the thick darkness from me* [k] Gk: Heb *they*

23.1–24.25 Job continued his questioning, saying that his suffering would be more bearable if only he knew why it was happening. If there was sin for which he could repent, he would! He knew about the wicked and the fact that they would be punished; he knew God could vindicate him if he so chose. In all his examples of the wicked in the world, his overriding desire was for God to clear his name, prove his righteousness, and explain why he was chosen to receive all this calamity. Job tried to make his friends see that questions about God, life, and justice are not as simple as they assumed.

23.9 Job was saying that God appeared to be avoiding him. In 23.10, however, he expressed confidence that God knew every detail about his situation and would come to his rescue.

23.10 In chapter 22, Eliphaz tried to condemn Job by identifying some secret sin which he may have committed. We are always likely to have hidden sin in our lives, sin we don't even know about because God's standards are so high and our performance is so imperfect. If we are true believers, however, all our sins are forgiven because of what Christ did on the cross in our behalf (Romans 5.1; 8.1). The Bible also teaches that even if our hearts condemn us, God is greater than our hearts (1 John 3.20). His forgiveness and cleansing are sufficient; they overrule our nagging doubts. The Holy Spirit in us is our proof that we are forgiven in God's eyes even though we may *feel* guilty. If we, like Job, are truly seeking God, we can stand up to others' accusations as well as our own nagging doubts. If God has forgiven and accepted us, we are forgiven indeed.

23.14 Job wavered back and forth, first proclaiming loyalty to God and then complaining at being abandoned by him. His friends' words and his own suspicions undermined his confidence in God. When afflictions come, it is natural to blame God and to think our suffering must be divine punishment. But we must not assume that God has rejected us. His purposes go deeper than our ability to grasp all that is really happening. While this sounds like a pat answer, it is the same answer God gave Job in chapters 38–41. We shouldn't demand to know why certain calamities befall us. Often we cannot or are not meant to know.

the poor of the earth all hide themselves.
5 Like wild asses in the desert
they go out to their toil,
scavenging in the wasteland
food for their young.
6 They reap in a field not their own
and they glean in the vineyard of the wicked.
7 They lie all night naked, without clothing,
and have no covering in the cold.
8 They are wet with the rain of the mountains,
and cling to the rock for want of shelter.

9 "There are those who snatch the orphan child from the breast,
and take as a pledge the infant of the poor.
10 They go about naked, without clothing;
though hungry, they carry the sheaves;
11 between their terraces[l] they press out oil;
they tread the wine presses, but suffer thirst.
12 From the city the dying groan,
and the throat of the wounded cries for help;
yet God pays no attention to their prayer.

13 "There are those who rebel against the light,
who are not acquainted with its ways,
and do not stay in its paths.
14 The murderer rises at dusk
to kill the poor and needy,
and in the night is like a thief.
15 The eye of the adulterer also waits for the twilight,
saying, 'No eye will see me';
and he disguises his face.
16 In the dark they dig through houses;
by day they shut themselves up;
they do not know the light.
17 For deep darkness is morning to all of them;
for they are friends with the terrors of deep darkness.

18 "Swift are they on the face of the waters;
their portion in the land is cursed;
no treader turns toward their vineyards.
19 Drought and heat snatch away the snow waters;
so does Sheol those who have sinned.
20 The womb forgets them;
the worm finds them sweet;
they are no longer remembered;
so wickedness is broken like a tree.

21 "They harm[m] the childless woman,
and do no good to the widow.
22 Yet God[n] prolongs the life of the mighty by his power;
they rise up when they despair of life.
23 He gives them security, and they are supported;

24.5 Job 39.5-8
24.8 Lam 4.5; Heb 11.38
24.9 Job 6.27
24.12 Job 9.23,24; Mal 2.17; Rom 2.4,5
24.14 Ps 10.8; Prov 7.9; Mic 2.1
24.16 Ex 22.2; Mt 6.19
24.17 Ps 91.5
24.18 Job 5.3; 22.11,16; 27.20
24.19 Job 6.16,17; 21.13
24.20 Job 18.17; 19.10; 21.26; Prov 10.7; Isa 49.15; Dan 4.14
24.21 Job 22.9
24.22 Job 9.4,10.4; 11.11; 12.6

[l] Meaning of Heb uncertain [m] Gk Tg: Heb *feed on* or *associate with* [n] Heb *he*

24.18–21 Job suddenly seemed to be arguing on his friends' side. For this reason, some commentators think one of Job's friends said these words. But we shouldn't expect Job to present a unified argument. He was confused. He was not arguing that God rewards the wicked and punishes the righteous; he was simply asserting that in his case, a righteous man was suffering.

his eyes are upon their ways.
24 They are exalted a little while, and then are gone;
they wither and fade like the mallow;[o]
they are cut off like the heads of grain.
25 If it is not so, who will prove me a liar,
and show that there is nothing in what I say?"

24.24 Job 14.21 Ps 37.10
24.25 Job 6.28; 27.4

Bildad speaks

25 Then Bildad the Shuhite answered:
2 "Dominion and fear are with God;[p]
he makes peace in his high heaven.
3 Is there any number to his armies?
Upon whom does his light not arise?
4 How then can a mortal be righteous before God?
How can one born of woman be pure?
5 If even the moon is not bright
and the stars are not pure in his sight,
6 how much less a mortal, who is a maggot,
and a human being, who is a worm!"

25.2 Job 9.4; 16.19
25.4 Job 4.17; 9.2
25.5 Job 15.15; 31.26

Job speaks

26 Then Job answered:
2 "How you have helped one who has no power!
How you have assisted the arm that has no strength!
3 How you have counseled one who has no wisdom,
and given much good advice!
4 With whose help have you uttered words,
and whose spirit has come forth from you?
5 The shades below tremble,
the waters and their inhabitants.
6 Sheol is naked before God,
and Abaddon has no covering.
7 He stretches out Zaphon[q] over the void,
and hangs the earth upon nothing.
8 He binds up the waters in his thick clouds,
and the cloud is not torn open by them.
9 He covers the face of the full moon,
and spreads over it his cloud.
10 He has described a circle on the face of the waters,
at the boundary between light and darkness.
11 The pillars of heaven tremble,
and are astounded at his rebuke.
12 By his power he stilled the Sea;

26.5 Job 3.13
26.7 Job 9.8
26.8 Job 37.11
26.9 Job 22.14 Ps 97.2; 105.39
26.10 Job 38.1-11,19, 20,24

[o] Gk: Heb *like all others* [p] Heb *him* [q] Or *the North*

25.1ff Bildad's final reply was weak. It ignored Job's examples of the prosperity of the wicked. Instead of attempting to refute Job, Bildad accused Job of pride because he was claiming that his suffering was not the result of sin. Job never claimed to be without sin, but only that his sin could not have caused his present trouble.

25.6 It is important to understand that Bildad, not God, was calling man a worm. Human beings are created in God's image (Genesis 1.26, 27). Psalm 8.5 says that man is only "a little lower than God." Bildad may have simply been using a poetic description to contrast our worth to the worth and power of God. To come to God, we need not crawl like worms. We can approach him boldly in faith (Hebrews 4.16).

26.1ff Job has the distinction of giving the longest speech in the book – six chapters – weaving together pictures of God's mystery and power in a beautiful poem of trust. Beginning by brushing off Bildad's latest reply as irrelevant (chapter 25), Job then tells Bildad and his friends that they could not possibly know everything about God. Wisdom does not originate from this life or from the human mind – it comes from God (28.27, 28). Job then defends his upright and honest life. He had effectively sought after God's way of living. While admitting that he was not perfect, Job maintains that his motives were right.

26.2–4 With great sarcasm, Job attacked his friends' comments. Their theological explanations failed to bring any relief, because they were unable to turn their knowledge into helpful counsel. When dealing with people, it is more important to love and understand them than to analyze them or give advice. Compassion produces greater results than criticism or blame.

by his understanding he struck down Rahab.
13 By his wind the heavens were made fair;
his hand pierced the fleeing serpent.
14 These are indeed but the outskirts of his ways;
and how small a whisper do we hear of him!
But the thunder of his power who can understand?"

26.13 Job 9.8
26.14 Job 36.29 37.4,5

27

Job again took up his discourse and said:
2 "As God lives, who has taken away my right,
and the Almighty,[r] who has made my soul bitter,
3 as long as my breath is in me
and the spirit of God is in my nostrils,
4 my lips will not speak falsehood,
and my tongue will not utter deceit.
5 Far be it from me to say that you are right;
until I die I will not put away my integrity from me.
6 I hold fast my righteousness, and will not let it go;
my heart does not reproach me for any of my days.

7 "May my enemy be like the wicked,
and may my opponent be like the unrighteous.
8 For what is the hope of the godless when God cuts them off,
when God takes away their lives?
9 Will God hear their cry
when trouble comes upon them?
10 Will they take delight in the Almighty?[r]
Will they call upon God at all times?
11 I will teach you concerning the hand of God;
that which is with the Almighty[r] I will not conceal.
12 All of you have seen it yourselves;
why then have you become altogether vain?

13 "This is the portion of the wicked with God,
and the heritage that oppressors receive from the Almighty:[r]
14 If their children are multiplied, it is for the sword;
and their offspring have not enough to eat.
15 Those who survive them the pestilence buries,
and their widows make no lamentation.
16 Though they heap up silver like dust,
and pile up clothing like clay—
17 they may pile it up, but the just will wear it,
and the innocent will divide the silver.
18 They build their houses like nests,
like booths made by sentinels of the vineyard.
19 They go to bed with wealth, but will do so no more;
they open their eyes, and it is gone.
20 Terrors overtake them like a flood;
in the night a whirlwind carries them off.
21 The east wind lifts them up and they are gone;
it sweeps them out of their place.

27.1 Job 13.12; 29.1
27.2 Job 9.18; 16.11
27.3 Job 32.8; 33.4
27.4 Job 6.28; 33.3
27.6 Job 2.3; 13.18
27.8 Job 8.13; 11.20
27.9 Job 35.12,13
27.10 Job 22.26,27
27.13 Job 20.29
27.17 Job 20.18-21
27.18 Job 8.15
27.19 Job 7.8,21
27.20 Job 15.21; 20.8
27.21 Job 7.10; 21.18

[r] Traditional rendering of Heb *Shaddai*

27.6 In the midst of all the accusations, Job was able to declare that his conscience was clear. Only God's forgiveness and the determination to live rightly before God can bring a clear conscience. How important Job's record became as he was being accused. Like Job, we can't claim sinless lives, but we *can* claim forgiven lives. When we confess our sins to God, he forgives us and we can live with clear consciences (1 John 1.9).

27.13–23 Job agreed with his friends that the end of the wicked will be disaster, but he did not agree that *he* was wicked and deserving of punishment. Most of the punishments Job listed never happened to him, and he certainly never longed to flee from God's hand. So he wasn't including himself as one of the wicked. On the contrary, he continually pleaded for God to vindicate him.

27.22 Job 11.20

22 It[s] hurls at them without pity;
they flee from its[t] power in headlong flight.
23 It[s] claps its[t] hands at them,
and hisses at them from its[t] place.

28 "Surely there is a mine for silver,
and a place for gold to be refined.
2 Iron is taken out of the earth,
and copper is smelted from ore.
3 Miners put[u] an end to darkness,
and search out to the farthest bound
the ore in gloom and deep darkness.
4 They open shafts in a valley away from human habitation;
they are forgotten by travelers,
they sway suspended, remote from people.
5 As for the earth, out of it comes bread;
but underneath it is turned up as by fire.
6 Its stones are the place of sapphires,[v]
and its dust contains gold.

7 "That path no bird of prey knows,
and the falcon's eye has not seen it.
8 The proud wild animals have not trodden it;
the lion has not passed over it.

9 "They put their hand to the flinty rock,
and overturn mountains by the roots.
10 They cut out channels in the rocks,
and their eyes see every precious thing.
11 The sources of the rivers they probe;[w]
hidden things they bring to light.

28.12 Job 28.23,28

12 "But where shall wisdom be found?
And where is the place of understanding?

[s] Or *He* (that is God) [t] Or *his* [u] Heb *He puts* [v] Or *lapis lazuli* [w] Gk Vg: Heb *bind*

WHERE CAN WISDOM BE FOUND?
Job and his friends differed in their ideas of how men become wise.

Person	*His source of wisdom*	*Attitude toward God*
Eliphaz	Wisdom is learned by observing and experiencing life. He based his advice to Job on his confident, firsthand knowledge (4.7, 8; 5.3, 27).	"I have personally observed how God works and have figured him out."
Bildad	Wisdom is inherited from the past. Trustworthy knowledge is secondhand. He based his advice to Job on traditional proverbs and sayings which he frequently quoted (8.8, 9; 18.5–21).	"Those who have gone before us figured God out and all we have to do is use that knowledge."
Zophar	Wisdom belongs to the wise. He based his advice on his wisdom which had no other source than himself (11.6; 20.1–29).	"The wise know what God is like, but there aren't many of us around."
Job	God is the source of wisdom and the first step toward wisdom is to fear God (28.20–28).	"God reveals his wisdom to those who humbly trust him."

28.12 Intelligent people can perform all kinds of technological wonders. They can find stars invisible to the eye, visit space, and store volumes of information on a microchip. But even the greatest scientists, on their own, are at a loss to discover the way to peace with God. There is a vast difference between being intelligent and being wise. Only God can show us where to find wisdom because *he* is the source of wisdom (28.28). True wisdom is having God's perspective on life. As the Creator, only God knows what is best for his creation. It is fruitless for us to try to gain intelligence without seeking God's wisdom, because God alone sees the greater purpose for his world.

13 Mortals do not know the way to it,[x]
and it is not found in the land of the living.
14 The deep says, 'It is not in me,'
and the sea says, 'It is not with me.'
15 It cannot be gotten for gold,
and silver cannot be weighed out as its price.
16 It cannot be valued in the gold of Ophir,
in precious onyx or sapphire.[y]
17 Gold and glass cannot equal it,
nor can it be exchanged for jewels of fine gold.
18 No mention shall be made of coral or of crystal;
the price of wisdom is above pearls.
19 The chrysolite of Ethiopia[z] cannot compare with it,
nor can it be valued in pure gold.

20 "Where then does wisdom come from?
And where is the place of understanding?
21 It is hidden from the eyes of all living,
and concealed from the birds of the air.
22 Abaddon and Death say,
'We have heard a rumor of it with our ears.'

23 "God understands the way to it,
and he knows its place.
24 For he looks to the ends of the earth,
and sees everything under the heavens.
25 When he gave to the wind its weight,
and apportioned out the waters by measure;
26 when he made a decree for the rain,
and a way for the thunderbolt;
27 then he saw it and declared it;
he established it, and searched it out.
28 And he said to humankind,
'Truly, the fear of the Lord, that is wisdom;
and to depart from evil is understanding.' "

28.17 Prov 8.10; 16.16
28.18 Prov 8.11
28.19 Prov 8.19
28.22 Job 26.6
28.23 Ps 11.4 33.13,14 Prov 8.22-36 15.3
28.25 Job 12.15 38.8-11 Ps 135.7
28.26 Job 37.3,6,11, 12; 38.25
28.28 Ps 111.10 Prov 1.7; 9.10

29

Job again took up his discourse and said:
2 "Oh, that I were as in the months of old,
as in the days when God watched over me;
3 when his lamp shone over my head,
and by his light I walked through darkness;
4 when I was in my prime,
when the friendship of God was upon my tent;
5 when the Almighty[a] was still with me,
when my children were around me;

29.3 Job 11.17

[x] Gk: Heb *its price* [y] Or *lapis lazuli* [z] Or *Nubia*; Heb *Cush* [a] Traditional rendering of Heb *Shaddai*

28.13 Job stated that wisdom cannot be found among the living. It is natural for people who do not understand the importance of God's Word to seek wisdom here on earth. They look to philosophers and other leaders to give them direction for living. Yet Job said that wisdom is not found there. No leader or group of leaders can produce enough knowledge or insight to explain the totality of human experience. The ultimate interpretation of life, of who we are and where we are going, must come from outside and above our mortal life. When looking for guidance, seek God's wisdom as made clear in the Bible. To be lifted above and beyond the boundaries of life, we must know and trust the Lord of life.

28.16 Gold of Ophir was considered the finest gold available. Ophir may have been located in Africa, along the Arabian coast, or in India. Wherever it was, it was a good distance from Israel, for it took Solomon's ships three years to make the voyage (1 Kings 10.22).

28.28 "The fear of the Lord" is a key theme in the wisdom literature of the Bible (Job through the Song of Solomon). It means to have respect and reverence for God and to feel in awe of his majesty and power. This is the starting point to finding real wisdom (see Proverbs 1.7–9).

29.6 Deut 32.13 Ps 81.16

6 when my steps were washed with milk,
and the rock poured out for me streams of oil!
7 When I went out to the gate of the city,
when I took my seat in the square,
8 the young men saw me and withdrew,
and the aged rose up and stood;

29.9 Job 21.5

9 the nobles refrained from talking,
and laid their hands on their mouths;
10 the voices of princes were hushed,
and their tongues stuck to the roof of their mouths.

29.11 Job 4.3,4

11 When the ear heard, it commended me,
and when the eye saw, it approved;

29.12 Job 24.4,9 31.17,21; 34.28

12 because I delivered the poor who cried,
and the orphan who had no helper.

29.13 Job 31.19 Isa 27.13

13 The blessing of the wretched came upon me,
and I caused the widow's heart to sing for joy.

29.14 Job 27.5,6 Ps 132.9

14 I put on righteousness, and it clothed me;
my justice was like a robe and a turban.
15 I was eyes to the blind,
and feet to the lame.

29.16 Prov 29.7 Eph 5.1 Jas 1.27

16 I was a father to the needy,
and I championed the cause of the stranger.

29.17 Ps 3.7 Prov 30.14

17 I broke the fangs of the unrighteous,
and made them drop their prey from their teeth.
18 Then I thought, 'I shall die in my nest,
and I shall multiply my days like the phoenix;[b]

29.19 Jer 17.8 Hos 14.5

19 my roots spread out to the waters,
with the dew all night on my branches;

29.20 Gen 49.24 Ps 18.34

20 my glory was fresh with me,
and my bow ever new in my hand.'

29.21 Job 4.3 32.11,12

21 "They listened to me, and waited,
and kept silence for my counsel.
22 After I spoke they did not speak again,
and my word dropped upon them like dew.[c]
23 They waited for me as for the rain;
they opened their mouths as for the spring rain.
24 I smiled on them when they had no confidence;
and the light of my countenance they did not extinguish.[d]

29.25 Job 1.3; 4.4 16.5; 31.37 Isa 61.1-3

25 I chose their way, and sat as chief,
and I lived like a king among his troops,
like one who comforts mourners.

[b] Or *like sand* [c] Heb lacks *like dew* [d] Meaning of Heb uncertain

---

29.6 Milk and olive oil were symbols of material prosperity in an agricultural society. His flocks and olive trees were so plentiful that everything seemed to overflow.

29.7ff Job was walking a fine line between bragging about past accomplishments and recalling good deeds in order to answer the charges against him. Job's one weakness throughout his conversations is that he came dangerously close to pride. Pride is especially deceptive when we are doing right. But it separates us from God by making us think we're better than we really are. Then comes the tendency to trust our own opinions, which leads to other kinds of sin. While it is not wrong to recount past deeds, it is far better to recount God's blessings to us. This will help to keep us from inadvertently falling into pride.

29.7–17 In Job's day, a judge served as both a city councilman and a magistrate, helping to manage the community and settle disputes. In most cases, this was not a full-time position but a part-time post held on the basis of one's respect and standing in the area. Job was a judge.

29.18 To "die in my nest" could also mean "in a ripe old age" or "in honor." The phoenix is a legendary bird that lived 500 years, burned to ashes, then rose youthfully from the ashes to live again.

30 "But now they make sport of me,
those who are younger than I,
whose fathers I would have disdained
to set with the dogs of my flock.
2 What could I gain from the strength of their hands?
All their vigor is gone.
3 Through want and hard hunger
they gnaw the dry and desolate ground,
4 they pick mallow and the leaves of bushes,
and to warm themselves the roots of broom.
5 They are driven out from society;
people shout after them as after a thief.
6 In the gullies of wadis they must live,
in holes in the ground, and in the rocks.
7 Among the bushes they bray;
under the nettles they huddle together.
8 A senseless, disreputable brood,
they have been whipped out of the land.

9 "And now they mock me in song;
I am a byword to them.
10 They abhor me, they keep aloof from me;
they do not hesitate to spit at the sight of me.
11 Because God has loosed my bowstring and humbled me,
they have cast off restraint in my presence.
12 On my right hand the rabble rise up;
they send me sprawling,
and build roads for my ruin.
13 They break up my path,
they promote my calamity;
no one restrains[e] them.
14 As through a wide breach they come;
amid the crash they roll on.
15 Terrors are turned upon me;
my honor is pursued as by the wind,
and my prosperity has passed away like a cloud.

16 "And now my soul is poured out within me;
days of affliction have taken hold of me.
17 The night racks my bones,
and the pain that gnaws me takes no rest.
18 With violence he seizes my garment;[f]
he grasps me by[g] the collar of my tunic.
19 He has cast me into the mire,
and I have become like dust and ashes.
20 I cry to you and you do not answer me;
I stand, and you merely look at me.
21 You have turned cruel to me;
with the might of your hand you persecute me.
22 You lift me up on the wind, you make me ride on it,

30.1 Job 12.4 Isa 3.5
30.9 Job 12.4; 17.6 Ps 35.15,16 69.12
30.10 Isa 50.6 Mt 26.67
30.11 Ruth 1.21 Ps 32.9; 88.7
30.12 Ps 140.4,5 Isa 3.5
30.15 Job 3.25; 7.9 Ps 55.3-5
30.16 Ps 22.14
30.19 Ps 69.2,14
30.20 Job 19.7
30.21 Job 16.9,14
30.22 Job 9.17; 27.21

e Cn: Heb *helps* f Gk: Heb *my garment is disfigured* g Heb *like*

30.1ff To suffer extreme loss, as Job did, was humiliating. But to face abuse at the hands of young upstarts added insult to injury. Job had lost his family, possessions, health, position, and good name. He was not even respected for suffering bravely. Unfortunately, young people sometimes mock and take advantage of older people and those who are limited in some way. Instead, they should realize that their own physical abilities and attributes are short-lived and that God loves all people equally.

30.6 A wadi is a stream or dry streambed.

and you toss me about in the roar of the storm.

30.23 Job 9.22; 10.8

23 I know that you will bring me to death,
and to the house appointed for all living.

30.24 Job 19.7

24 "Surely one does not turn against the needy,[h]
when in disaster they cry for help.[i]
25 Did I not weep for those whose day was hard?
Was not my soul grieved for the poor?

30.26 Job 19.8

26 But when I looked for good, evil came;
and when I waited for light, darkness came.
27 My inward parts are in turmoil, and are never still;
days of affliction come to meet me.

30.28 Job 19.7

28 I go about in sunless gloom;
I stand up in the assembly and cry for help.
29 I am a brother of jackals,
and a companion of ostriches.

30.30 Job 2.7

30 My skin turns black and falls from me,
and my bones burn with heat.
31 My lyre is turned to mourning,
and my pipe to the voice of those who weep.

31.1 Gen 6.2 2 Sam 11.2-4 Mt 5.28

31 "I have made a covenant with my eyes;
how then could I look upon a virgin?
2 What would be my portion from God above,
and my heritage from the Almighty[j] on high?
3 Does not calamity befall the unrighteous,
and disaster the workers of iniquity?

31.4 Job 14.16 28.24; 34.21 Prov 5.21

4 Does he not see my ways,
and number all my steps?

5 "If I have walked with falsehood,
and my foot has hurried to deceit—

31.6 Prov 16.11 Isa 26.7

6 let me be weighed in a just balance,
and let God know my integrity!—

31.7 Lev 26.16 Job 9.30; 23.11 Mic 6.15

7 if my step has turned aside from the way,
and my heart has followed my eyes,
and if any spot has clung to my hands;
8 then let me sow, and another eat;
and let what grows for me be rooted out.

9 "If my heart has been enticed by a woman,
and I have lain in wait at my neighbor's door;

31.10 Deut 28.30 Jer 8.10 Hos 4.13,14

10 then let my wife grind for another,
and let other men kneel over her.

31.11 Lev 20.10 Deut 22.24

11 For that would be a heinous crime;
that would be a criminal offense;

31.12 Job 15.30

12 for that would be a fire consuming down to Abaddon,
and it would burn to the root all my harvest.

13 "If I have rejected the cause of my male or female slaves,

[h] Heb *ruin* [i] Cn: Meaning of Heb uncertain [j] Traditional rendering of Heb *Shaddai*

31.1–4 Job had not only avoided committing the great sin of adultery; he had not even taken the first step toward that sin by looking at a woman with greedy desire. Job said he was innocent of both outward and inward sins. In chapter 29, Job reviewed his good deeds. Here in chapter 31 he listed sins he had not committed—in his heart (31.1–12), against his neighbors (31.13–23), or against God (31.24–34).

31.10 Both parts of this verse possibly imply sexual intercourse. In other words, if I have taken the wife of another, then may my wife be taken away by another man.

when they brought a complaint against me;
14 what then shall I do when God rises up?
When he makes inquiry, what shall I answer him?
15 Did not he who made me in the womb make them?
And did not one fashion us in the womb?

16 "If I have withheld anything that the poor desired,
or have caused the eyes of the widow to fail,
17 or have eaten my morsel alone,
and the orphan has not eaten from it—
18 for from my youth I reared the orphan[k] like a father,
and from my mother's womb I guided the widow[l]—
19 if I have seen anyone perish for lack of clothing,
or a poor person without covering,
20 whose loins have not blessed me,
and who was not warmed with the fleece of my sheep;
21 if I have raised my hand against the orphan,
because I saw I had supporters at the gate;
22 then let my shoulder blade fall from my shoulder,
and let my arm be broken from its socket.
23 For I was in terror of calamity from God,
and I could not have faced his majesty.

24 "If I have made gold my trust,
or called fine gold my confidence;
25 if I have rejoiced because my wealth was great,
or because my hand had gotten much;
26 if I have looked at the sun[m] when it shone,
or the moon moving in splendor,
27 and my heart has been secretly enticed,
and my mouth has kissed my hand;
28 this also would be an iniquity to be punished by the judges,
for I should have been false to God above.

29 "If I have rejoiced at the ruin of those who hated me,
or exulted when evil overtook them—
30 I have not let my mouth sin
by asking for their lives with a curse—
31 if those of my tent ever said,
'O that we might be sated with his flesh!'[n]—
32 the stranger has not lodged in the street;
I have opened my doors to the traveler—
33 if I have concealed my transgressions as others do,[o]
by hiding my iniquity in my bosom,
34 because I stood in great fear of the multitude,
and the contempt of families terrified me,
so that I kept silence, and did not go out of doors—

31.13 Deut 24.14,15
31.15 Job 10.3
31.16 Ex 22.22-24 Job 20.19
31.17 Job 22.7,9
31.19 Job 22.6; 24.4
31.23 Job 13.11
31.24 Job 22.24 Mk 10.24
31.30 Job 5.3

[k] Heb *him* [l] Heb *her* [m] Heb *the light* [n] Meaning of Heb uncertain [o] Or *as Adam did*

31.24–28 In these verses, Job says that depending on wealth for happiness is idolatry and denies the God of heaven. We excuse our society's obsession with money and possessions as a necessary evil or "the way it works" in the modern world. But every society in every age has valued the power and prestige that money brings. True believers must purge themselves of the deep-seated desire for more power, prestige, and possessions. They must also not withhold their resources from neighbors near and far who have desperate physical needs.

31.33, 34 Job declared that he did not try to hide his sin as Adam did (Genesis 3). Adam did not have a crowd watching him, but he tried to hide from God. The fear that our sins will be discovered leads us to patterns of deception. We cover up with lies so that we will appear good to others. But we cannot hide from God. Do you try to keep people from seeing the real you? When you acknowledge your sins, you free yourself to receive forgiveness and a new life.

31.35
Job 19.7; 27.7
30.20,24,28
35.14
Ps 26.1

35 Oh, that I had one to hear me!
(Here is my signature! let the Almighty[p] answer me!)
Oh, that I had the indictment written by my adversary!
36 Surely I would carry it on my shoulder;
I would bind it on me like a crown;
37 I would give him an account of all my steps;
like a prince I would approach him.

31.38
1 Kgs 21.19
Job 24.2,6,
10-12
Hab 2.11
Jas 5.4
31.40
Isa 5.6
Zeph 2.9

38 "If my land has cried out against me,
and its furrows have wept together;
39 if I have eaten its yield without payment,
and caused the death of its owners;
40 let thorns grow instead of wheat,
and foul weeds instead of barley."

The words of Job are ended.

C. A YOUNG MAN ANSWERS JOB (32.1 – 37.24)

Young Elihu rebukes the three friends for being unable to give Job a reasonable answer for why he was suffering. But he only gives a partial answer to Job's question by saying that man cannot understand all that God allows, but must trust him. This was the best answer that man could give, yet it was incomplete. Often the best human answers are incomplete because we do not have all the facts.

32.1
Job 10.7; 13.18
31.6; 33.9

32 So these three men ceased to answer Job, because he was righteous in his
own eyes. 2 Then Elihu son of Barachel the Buzite, of the family of Ram,
became angry. He was angry at Job because he justified himself rather than God;
3 he was angry also at Job's three friends because they had found no answer, though
they had declared Job to be in the wrong.[q] 4 Now Elihu had waited to speak to Job,
because they were older than he. 5 But when Elihu saw that there was no answer in
the mouths of these three men, he became angry.

32.6
Job 15.10
Rom 13.7
1 Tim 5.1
Tit 2.6

6 Elihu son of Barachel the Buzite answered:
"I am young in years,
and you are aged;
therefore I was timid and afraid
to declare my opinion to you.
7 I said, 'Let days speak,
and many years teach wisdom.'

32.8
Job 33.4; 38.36
Prov 2.6
Dan 2.21
Jas 1.5

8 But truly it is the spirit in a mortal,
the breath of the Almighty,[p] that makes for understanding.
9 It is not the old[r] that are wise,
nor the aged that understand what is right.

[p] Traditional rendering of Heb *Shaddai* [q] Another ancient tradition reads *answer, and had put God in the wrong*
[r] Gk Syr Vg: Heb *many*

32.1 If Job was really a good man, his three friends would have to drop their theory that suffering is always God's punishment for evil actions. Instead of considering another viewpoint, however, they cut off the discussion. They were convinced that Job had some hidden fault or sin, so there was no point in talking if Job would not confess it. But Job knew he had lived uprightly before God and others (chapter 29) and had avoided wrong thoughts and actions (chapter 31). He wasn't about to invent a sin to satisfy his friends!

32.2ff When Eliphaz, Bildad, and Zophar had nothing more to say, Elihu became the fourth person to speak to Job. This was the first and only time he spoke. Apparently he was a bystander and much younger than the others (32.6, 7), but he introduced a new viewpoint. While Job's three friends said he was suffering from some past sins, Elihu said Job's suffering would not go away until he realized his *present* sin. He maintained that Job wasn't suffering because of sin, he was sinning because of suffering. Elihu pointed out that Job's attitude had become arrogant as he tried to defend his innocence. Elihu also said that suffering is not meant to punish us as much as it is meant to correct and restore us, to keep us on the right path.

There is much truth in Elihu's speech. He was urging Job to look at his suffering from a different perspective and with a greater purpose in mind. While his speech is on a higher spiritual plateau than the others, Elihu still wrongly assumed that a correct response to suffering always brings prosperity (33.23–30) and that suffering is always in some way connected to sin (34.11).

32.7–9 It is not enough to recognize a great truth; it must be lived out each day. Elihu recognized the truth that God was the only source of real wisdom, but he did not use God's wisdom to help Job. While he recognized where wisdom came from, he did not seek to acquire it. Becoming wise is an ongoing, lifelong pursuit. Don't be content just to know about wisdom; make it part of your life.

10 Therefore I say, 'Listen to me;
let me also declare my opinion.'

11 "See, I waited for your words,
I listened for your wise sayings,
while you searched out what to say. 32.11 Prov 18.17
12 I gave you my attention,
but there was in fact no one that confuted Job,
no one among you that answered his words.
13 Yet do not say, 'We have found wisdom;
God may vanquish him, not a human.'
14 He has not directed his words against me,
and I will not answer him with your speeches.

15 "They are dismayed, they answer no more;
they have not a word to say.
16 And am I to wait, because they do not speak,
because they stand there, and answer no more? 32.16 Prov 17.28 Amos 5.13
17 I also will give my answer;
I also will declare my opinion.
18 For I am full of words;
the spirit within me constrains me.
19 My heart is indeed like wine that has no vent;
like new wineskins, it is ready to burst.
20 I must speak, so that I may find relief;
I must open my lips and answer.
21 I will not show partiality to any person
or use flattery toward anyone. 32.21 Lev 19.15 Job 13.8,10 34.19 Prov 24.23
22 For I do not know how to flatter—
or my Maker would soon put an end to me!

33 "But now, hear my speech, O Job,
and listen to all my words.
2 See, I open my mouth;
the tongue in my mouth speaks.
3 My words declare the uprightness of my heart,
and what my lips know they speak sincerely. 33.3 Job 6.28; 27.4 36.4
4 The spirit of God has made me,
and the breath of the Almighty[s] gives me life.
5 Answer me, if you can;
set your words in order before me; take your stand.
6 See, before God I am as you are;
I too was formed from a piece of clay.
7 No fear of me need terrify you;
my pressure will not be heavy on you.

8 "Surely, you have spoken in my hearing,
and I have heard the sound of your words.
9 You say, 'I am clean, without transgression;
I am pure, and there is no iniquity in me. 33.9 Job 7.21; 9.21 10.7,14
10 Look, he finds occasions against me,
he counts me as his enemy; 33.10 Job 13.23,24 16.17
11 he puts my feet in the stocks,
and watches all my paths.' 33.11 Job 13.27

12 "But in this you are not right. I will answer you:
God is greater than any mortal. 33.13 Job 40.2 Isa 45.9
13 Why do you contend against him,

[s] Traditional rendering of Heb *Shaddai*

saying, 'He will answer none of my[t] words'?

33.14 Job 40.5 Ps 62.11

14 For God speaks in one way,
and in two, though people do not perceive it.

33.15 Job 4.12-17

15 In a dream, in a vision of the night,
when deep sleep falls on mortals,
while they slumber on their beds,

33.16 Job 36.10,15

16 then he opens their ears,
and terrifies them with warnings,

33.17 Job 15.22

17 that he may turn them aside from their deeds,
and keep them from pride,
18 to spare their souls from the Pit,
their lives from traversing the River.

33.19 Job 30.17

19 They are also chastened with pain upon their beds,
and with continual strife in their bones,

33.20 Job 3.24; 6.7 Ps 107.18

20 so that their lives loathe bread,
and their appetites dainty food.

33.21 Job 16.8; 19.20 Ps 22.17

21 Their flesh is so wasted away that it cannot be seen;
and their bones, once invisible, now stick out.
22 Their souls draw near the Pit,
and their lives to those who bring death.

33.23 Job 36.18 Ps 49.7 Isa 38.17

23 Then, if there should be for one of them an angel,
a mediator, one of a thousand,
one who declares a person upright,
24 and he is gracious to that person, and says,
'Deliver him from going down into the Pit;
I have found a ransom;
25 let his flesh become fresh with youth;
let him return to the days of his youthful vigor.'

33.26 Job 22.26,27 34.28

26 Then he prays to God, and is accepted by him,
he comes into his presence with joy,
and God[u] repays him for his righteousness.

33.27 2 Sam 12.13 Lk 15.21 Rom 6.21

27 That person sings to others and says,
'I sinned, and perverted what was right,
and it was not paid back to me.

33.28 Job 22.28

28 He has redeemed my soul from going down to the Pit,
and my life shall see the light.'

33.29 Eph 1.11 Phil 2.13

29 "God indeed does all these things,
twice, three times, with mortals,
30 to bring back their souls from the Pit,
so that they may see the light of life.[v]
31 Pay heed, Job, listen to me;
be silent, and I will speak.
32 If you have anything to say, answer me;
speak, for I desire to justify you.
33 If not, listen to me;
be silent, and I will teach you wisdom."

[t] Compare Gk: Heb *his* [u] Heb *he* [v] Syr: Heb *to be lighted with the light of life*

33.13 Being informed brings a sense of security. It's natural to want to know what's happening in our lives. Job wanted to know what was going on, why he was suffering. In previous chapters, we sense his frustration. Elihu claimed to have the answer for Job's biggest question, "Why doesn't God tell me what is happening?" Elihu told Job that God was trying to answer him, but he was not listening. Elihu misjudged God on this point. If God were to answer all our questions, we would not be adequately tested. What if God had said, "Job, Satan's going to test you and afflict you, but in the end you'll be healed and get everything back"? Job's greatest test was not the pain and suffering, but that he did not know why it happened. Our greatest test may be that we must trust God's goodness even though we don't understand why our lives are going a certain way. We must learn to trust in *God* who is good and not in the goodness of life.

33.14–24 Elihu's point was that God had spoken again and again. He spoke in dreams and visions (33.15–18), through suffering (33.19–22), and by messengers (or mediating angels) who take men's sacrifices to God (33.23, 24). Job already knew that. Elihu accused Job of not listening to God, which was not true.

34 Then Elihu continued and said:
2 "Hear my words, you wise men,
and give ear to me, you who know;
3 for the ear tests words
as the palate tastes food.
4 Let us choose what is right;
let us determine among ourselves what is good.
5 For Job has said, 'I am innocent,
and God has taken away my right;
6 in spite of being right I am counted a liar;
my wound is incurable, though I am without transgression.'
7 Who is there like Job,
who drinks up scoffing like water,
8 who goes in company with evildoers
and walks with the wicked?
9 For he has said, 'It profits one nothing
to take delight in God.'

10 "Therefore, hear me, you who have sense,
far be it from God that he should do wickedness,
and from the Almighty[w] that he should do wrong.
11 For according to their deeds he will repay them,
and according to their ways he will make it befall them.
12 Of a truth, God will not do wickedly,
and the Almighty[w] will not pervert justice.
13 Who gave him charge over the earth
and who laid on him[x] the whole world?
14 If he should take back his spirit[y] to himself,
and gather to himself his breath,
15 all flesh would perish together,
and all mortals return to dust.

16 "If you have understanding, hear this;
listen to what I say.
17 Shall one who hates justice govern?
Will you condemn one who is righteous and mighty,
18 who says to a king, 'You scoundrel!'
and to princes, 'You wicked men!';
19 who shows no partiality to nobles,
nor regards the rich more than the poor,
for they are all the work of his hands?
20 In a moment they die;
at midnight the people are shaken and pass away,
and the mighty are taken away by no human hand.

21 "For his eyes are upon the ways of mortals,
and he sees all their steps.
22 There is no gloom of deep darkness
where evildoers may hide themselves.

34.3 1 Cor 2.15 Heb 5.14
34.7 Ps 50.18
34.9 Job 21.15; 35.3 Mal 3.14
34.10 Ps 92.15
34.14 Ps 104.29
34.15 Gen 3.19; 7.21 Job 9.22; 10.9 Ps 90.3-10
34.17 Job 40.8
34.19 Deut 10.17 Acts 10.34 Rom 2.11 Eph 6.9 1 Pet 1.17
34.20 Ex 12.29 Job 12.19; 36.20
34.21 Prov 52.1; 15.3 Amos 9.8
34.22 Ps 139.11,12 Amos 9.2,3 Heb 4.13

[w] Traditional rendering of Heb *Shaddai* [x] Heb lacks *on him* [y] Heb *his heart his spirit*

34.10–15 God doesn't sin and is never unjust, Elihu claimed. Throughout this book, Eliphaz, Bildad, Zophar, and Elihu all have elements of truth in their speeches. Unfortunately, the nuggets of truth are buried under layers of false assumptions and conclusions. Although we might have a wealth of Bible knowledge and life experiences, we must make sure our conclusions are consistent with all of God's Word, not just parts of it.

34.24 Job 12.19
34.26 Ps 9.5; 11.5 Isa 66.24
34.27 1 Sam 15.11 Zeph 1.6 Lk 17.31,32
34.28 Ex 22.23 Job 22.27; 35.9
34.29 Job 5.15; 20.5

23 For he has not appointed a time[z] for anyone
to go before God in judgment.
24 He shatters the mighty without investigation,
and sets others in their place.
25 Thus, knowing their works,
he overturns them in the night, and they are crushed.
26 He strikes them for their wickedness
while others look on,
27 because they turned aside from following him,
and had no regard for any of his ways,
28 so that they caused the cry of the poor to come to him,
and he heard the cry of the afflicted—
29 When he is quiet, who can condemn?
When he hides his face, who can behold him,
whether it be a nation or an individual?—
30 so that the godless should not reign,
or those who ensnare the people.

34.31 Dan 9.17-14
34.36 Ps 17.3; 26.2

31 "For has anyone said to God,
'I have endured punishment; I will not offend any more;
32 teach me what I do not see;
if I have done iniquity, I will do it no more'?
33 Will he then pay back to suit you,
because you reject it?
For you must choose, and not I;
therefore declare what you know.[a]
34 Those who have sense will say to me,
and the wise who hear me will say,
35 'Job speaks without knowledge,
his words are without insight.'
36 Would that Job were tried to the limit,
because his answers are those of the wicked.
37 For he adds rebellion to his sin;
he claps his hands among us,
and multiplies his words against God."

[z] Cn: Heb *yet* [a] Meaning of Heb of verses 29-33 uncertain

HOW SUFFERING AFFECTS US

Suffering is helpful when:	*Suffering is harmful when:*
We turn to God for understanding, endurance, and deliverance	We become hardened and reject God
We ask important questions we might not take time to think about in our normal routine	We refuse to ask any questions and miss any lessons that might be good for us
We are prepared by it to identify with and comfort others who suffer	We allow it to make us self-centered and selfish
We are open to being helped by others who are obeying God	We withdraw from the help others can give
We are ready to learn from a trustworthy God	We reject the fact that God can bring good out of calamity
We realize we can identify with what Christ suffered on the cross for us	We accuse God of being unjust and perhaps lead others to reject him
We are sensitized to the amount of suffering in the world	We refuse to be open to any changes in our lives

35

Elihu continued and said:
2 "Do you think this to be just?
You say, 'I am in the right before God.'
3 If you ask, 'What advantage have I?
How am I better off than if I had sinned?'
4 I will answer you
and your friends with you.
5 Look at the heavens and see;
observe the clouds, which are higher than you.
6 If you have sinned, what do you accomplish against him?
And if your transgressions are multiplied, what do you do to him?
7 If you are righteous, what do you give to him;
or what does he receive from your hand?
8 Your wickedness affects others like you,
and your righteousness, other human beings.

9 "Because of the multitude of oppressions people cry out;
they call for help because of the arm of the mighty.
10 But no one says, 'Where is God my Maker,
who gives strength in the night,
11 who teaches us more than the animals of the earth,
and makes us wiser than the birds of the air?'
12 There they cry out, but he does not answer,
because of the pride of evildoers.
13 Surely God does not hear an empty cry,
nor does the Almighty[b] regard it.
14 How much less when you say that you do not see him,
that the case is before him, and you are waiting for him!
15 And now, because his anger does not punish,
and he does not greatly heed transgression,[c]
16 Job opens his mouth in empty talk,
he multiplies words without knowledge."

36

Elihu continued and said:
2 "Bear with me a little, and I will show you,
for I have yet something to say on God's behalf.
3 I will bring my knowledge from far away,
and ascribe righteousness to my Maker.
4 For truly my words are not false;
one who is perfect in knowledge is with you.

5 "Surely God is mighty and does not despise any;
he is mighty in strength of understanding.
6 He does not keep the wicked alive,
but gives the afflicted their right.
7 He does not withdraw his eyes from the righteous,
but with kings on the throne
he sets them forever, and they are exalted.
8 And if they are bound in fetters
and caught in the cords of affliction,
9 then he declares to them their work
and their transgressions, that they are behaving arrogantly.

[b] Traditional rendering of Heb *Shaddai* [c] Theodotion Symmachus Compare Vg: Meaning of Heb uncertain

35.2 Job 27.2
35.5 Ps 8.3,4
35.6 Job 7.20
35.7 Job 22.2,3
35.9 Job 27.10; 36.13
35.11 Job 36.33
35.13 Job 27.9
35.14 Job 31.35 Ps 37.5,6
35.16 Job 34.35; 38.2
36.3 Job 8.3; 37.23 Dan 9.7,14
36.4 Job 33.3; 37.16
36.5 Ps 22.24; 69.33 1 Cor 1.24-28
36.6 Job 5.15; 8.22 34.26
36.7 Job 5.11 Ps 33.18; 34.15 113.8
36.9 Job 15.25

35.1ff Sometimes we wonder if being faithful to our convictions really does any good at all. Elihu spoke to this very point. His conclusion was that God is still concerned even though he doesn't intervene immediately in every situation. In the broad scope of time God executes justice. We have his promise on that. Don't lose hope. Wait upon God. He notices your right living and faith.

36.10 Job 33.16; 36.21

10 He opens their ears to instruction,
and commands that they return from iniquity.
11 If they listen, and serve him,
they complete their days in prosperity,
and their years in pleasantness.

36.12 Job 4.21; 15.22

12 But if they do not listen, they shall perish by the sword,
and die without knowledge.

13 "The godless in heart cherish anger;
they do not cry for help when he binds them.
14 They die in their youth,
and their life ends in shame.[d]
15 He delivers the afflicted by their affliction,
and opens their ear by adversity.
16 He also allured you out of distress
into a broad place where there was no constraint,
and what was set on your table was full of fatness.

36.17 Job 22.5,10,11

17 "But you are obsessed with the case of the wicked;
judgment and justice seize you.

36.18 Job 33.24; 34.33

18 Beware that wrath does not entice you into scoffing,
and do not let the greatness of the ransom turn you aside.
19 Will your cry avail to keep you from distress,
or will all the force of your strength?

36.20 Job 34.20,25

20 Do not long for the night,
when peoples are cut off in their place.

36.21 Ps 31.6; 66.18

21 Beware! Do not turn to iniquity;
because of that you have been tried by affliction.

36.22 Job 35.11 Jer 31.33

22 See, God is exalted in his power;
who is a teacher like him?

36.23 Job 8.3

23 Who has prescribed for him his way,
or who can say, 'You have done wrong'?

24 "Remember to extol his work,
of which mortals have sung.
25 All people have looked on it;
everyone watches it from far away.

36.26 Job 11.7-9 Ps 90.2

26 Surely God is great, and we do not know him;
the number of his years is unsearchable.

36.27 Job 5.10 37.6,11

27 For he draws up the drops of water;
he distills[e] his mist in rain,
28 which the skies pour down
and drop upon mortals abundantly.

36.29 Job 26.14

29 Can anyone understand the spreading of the clouds,
the thunderings of his pavilion?
30 See, he scatters his lightning around him
and covers the roots of the sea.

36.31 Job 37.11,13,16

31 For by these he governs peoples;
he gives food in abundance.

36.32 Job 37.11,12,15

32 He covers his hands with the lightning,
and commands it to strike the mark.

d Heb *ends among the temple prostitutes* e Cn: Heb *they distill*

36.26 One theme in the poetic literature of the Bible is that God is incomprehensible; we cannot know him completely. We can have some knowledge about him, for the Bible is full of details about who God is, how we can know him, and how we can have an eternal relationship with him. But we can never know enough to answer all of life's questions (Ecclesiastes 3.11), to predict our own future, or to manipulate God for our own ends. Life always creates more questions than we have answers, and we must constantly go to God for fresh insights into life's dilemmas. (See 37.19–24.)

33 Its crashing[f] tells about him;
he is jealous[f] with anger against iniquity.

36.33 Job 37.2

37

"At this also my heart trembles,
and leaps out of its place.
2 Listen, listen to the thunder of his voice
and the rumbling that comes from his mouth.
3 Under the whole heaven he lets it loose,
and his lightning to the corners of the earth.
4 After it his voice roars;
he thunders with his majestic voice
and he does not restrain the lightnings[g] when his voice is heard.
5 God thunders wondrously with his voice;
he does great things that we cannot comprehend.
6 For to the snow he says, 'Fall on the earth';
and the shower of rain, his heavy shower of rain,
7 serves as a sign on everyone's hand,
so that all whom he has made may know it.[h]
8 Then the animals go into their lairs
and remain in their dens.
9 From its chamber comes the whirlwind,
and cold from the scattering winds.
10 By the breath of God ice is given,
and the broad waters are frozen fast.
11 He loads the thick cloud with moisture;
the clouds scatter his lightning.
12 They turn round and round by his guidance,
to accomplish all that he commands them
on the face of the habitable world.
13 Whether for correction, or for his land,
or for love, he causes it to happen.

14 "Hear this, O Job;
stop and consider the wondrous works of God.
15 Do you know how God lays his command upon them,
and causes the lightning of his cloud to shine?
16 Do you know the balancings of the clouds,
the wondrous works of the one whose knowledge is perfect,
17 you whose garments are hot
when the earth is still because of the south wind?
18 Can you, like him, spread out the skies,
hard as a molten mirror?
19 Teach us what we shall say to him;
we cannot draw up our case because of darkness.
20 Should he be told that I want to speak?
Did anyone ever wish to be swallowed up?
21 Now, no one can look on the light
when it is bright in the skies,
when the wind has passed and cleared them.

37.2 Job 36.33 34.26
37.5 Job 5.9; 26.14 Rom 11.33
37.6 Job 36.27; 38.22
37.7 Job 12.14
37.8 Job 38.40
37.9 Job 9.9
37.10 Job 38.29 Ps 147.17
37.11 Job 36.27,29
37.12 Job 36.32 Ps 148.8 Isa 14.21; 27.6
37.16 Job 36.4
37.18 Gen 1.6-8 Job 9.8,9 Ps 104.2 Isa 45.12

[f] Meaning of Heb uncertain [g] Heb *them* [h] Meaning of Heb of verse 7 uncertain

37.2 Nothing can compare to God. His power and presence are awesome, and when he speaks, we must listen. Too often we presume to speak for God (as did Job's friends), to put words in his mouth, to take him for granted, or to interpret his silence to mean that he is absent or unconcerned. But God cares. He is in control, and he will speak. Be ready to hear what he wants to say to you—in the Bible, in your life through the Holy Spirit, and through circumstances and relationships.

37.21–24 Elihu concluded his speech with the tremendous truth that faith in God is far more important than Job's desire for an explanation for his suffering. He came so close to helping Job but then went down the wrong path. Significantly, it is here that God himself breaks into the discussion to draw the right conclusions from this important truth (38.1ff).

22 Out of the north comes golden splendor;
around God is awesome majesty.
37.23 Isa 63.9 Rom 11.13
23 The Almighty[i] — we cannot find him;
he is great in power and justice,
and abundant righteousness he will not violate.
37.24 Job 5.13 1 Cor 1.26
24 Therefore mortals fear him;
he does not regard any who are wise in their own conceit."

D. GOD ANSWERS JOB (38.1 – 41.34)

Instead of answering Job's question directly, God asks Job a series of questions which no human could possibly answer. Job responds by recognizing that God's ways are best. During difficult times, we, too, must humbly remember our position before the eternal, holy, incompressible God.

38.1 Job 40.6
38.2 Job 35.16; 42.3
38.3 Job 40.7; 42.4

38 Then the LORD answered Job out of the whirlwind:
2 "Who is this that darkens counsel by words without knowledge?
3 Gird up your loins like a man,
I will question you, and you shall declare to me.

38.4 Job 15.7
4 "Where were you when I laid the foundation of the earth?
Tell me, if you have understanding.
5 Who determined its measurements — surely you know!
Or who stretched the line upon it?
38.6 Job 1.6; 26.7
6 On what were its bases sunk,
or who laid its cornerstone

i Traditional rendering of Heb *Shaddai*

GOD SPEAKS
On various occasions in the Old Testament, God chose to communicate audibly with individuals. God will always find a way to make contact with those who want to know him. Some of those occasions are listed here.

Whom he spoke to	*What he said*	*Reference*
Adam and Eve	Confronted them about sin	Genesis 3.8–13
Noah	Gave him directions about building the ark	Genesis 6.13–22; 7.1; 8.15–17
Abraham	Commanded him to follow God's leading and promised to bless him	Genesis 12.1–9
	Tested his obedience by commanding him to sacrifice his son	Genesis 22.1–14
Jacob	Permitted him to go to Egypt	Genesis 46.1–4
Moses	Sent him to lead the people out of Egypt	Exodus 3.1–10
	Gave him the ten commandments	Exodus 19.1—20.20
Moses, Aaron, Miriam	Pronounced judgment on a family argument	Numbers 12.1–15
Joshua	Promised to be with him as he was with Moses	Joshua 1.1–9
Samuel	Chose him to be his spokesman	1 Samuel 3.1–18
Isaiah	Sent him to the people with his message	Isaiah 6.1–13
Jeremiah	Encouraged him to be his prophet	Jeremiah 1.4–10
Ezekiel	Sent him to Israel to warn them of coming judgment	Ezekiel 2.1–8

37.23 Elihu stressed God's sovereignty over all of nature as a reminder of his sovereignty over our lives. God is in control – he directs, preserves, and maintains his created order. Although we can't see it, God is divinely governing the moral and political affairs of people as well. By spending time observing the majestic and intricate parts of God's creation, we can be reminded of his power in every aspect of our lives.

38.1ff From a whirlwind or mighty storm, God spoke. Surprisingly, he didn't answer any of Job's questions; Job's questions were not at the heart of the issue. Instead, God used Job's ignorance of the earth's natural order to reveal his ignorance of God's moral order. If Job did not understand the workings of God's physical creation, how could he possibly understand God's mind and character? There is no standard or criterion higher than God himself by which to judge. God himself is the standard. Our only option is to submit to his authority and rest in his care.

38.3 To "gird up" one's loins means to lift up the bottom of the garment and tuck it into the belt. This is an action that one would do to prepare for a battle or other difficult task.

7 when the morning stars sang together
and all the heavenly beings[j] shouted for joy?

8 "Or who shut in the sea with doors
when it burst out from the womb?—
9 when I made the clouds its garment,
and thick darkness its swaddling band,
10 and prescribed bounds for it,
and set bars and doors,
11 and said, 'Thus far shall you come, and no farther,
and here shall your proud waves be stopped'?

12 "Have you commanded the morning since your days began,
and caused the dawn to know its place,
13 so that it might take hold of the skirts of the earth,
and the wicked be shaken out of it?
14 It is changed like clay under the seal,
and it is dyed[k] like a garment.
15 Light is withheld from the wicked,
and their uplifted arm is broken.

16 "Have you entered into the springs of the sea,
or walked in the recesses of the deep?
17 Have the gates of death been revealed to you,
or have you seen the gates of deep darkness?
18 Have you comprehended the expanse of the earth?
Declare, if you know all this.

19 "Where is the way to the dwelling of light,
and where is the place of darkness,
20 that you may take it to its territory
and that you may discern the paths to its home?
21 Surely you know, for you were born then,
and the number of your days is great!

22 "Have you entered the storehouses of the snow,
or have you seen the storehouses of the hail,
23 which I have reserved for the time of trouble,
for the day of battle and war?
24 What is the way to the place where the light is distributed,
or where the east wind is scattered upon the earth?

25 "Who has cut a channel for the torrents of rain,
and a way for the thunderbolt,
26 to bring rain on a land where no one lives,
on the desert, which is empty of human life,
27 to satisfy the waste and desolate land,
and to make the ground put forth grass?

38.10 Gen 1.9 Ps 33.7 Prov 8.29 Jer 5.22
38.13 Job 37.3 34.25,26
38.15 Job 5.14 Ps 10.15; 37.17
38.16 Gen 7.11; 8.2 Prov 8.24,28 Jer 51.36
38.17 Job 28.24; 34.22
38.20 Job 26.10
38.21 Job 15.7
38.22 Ex 9.18 Job 37.6 Isa 30.30 Ezek 13.11,13
38.24 Job 26.10
38.25 Job 36.27

j Heb *sons of God* k Cn: Heb *and they stand forth*

38.22, 23 God said he was reserving the storehouses of the snow and hail for times of war. God used hail to help Joshua and the Israelites win a battle (Joshua 10.11). Just as armies keep weapons in the armory, God has all the forces of nature in his control. Job can't even begin to know all of God's resources.

38.22–35 God stated that he has all the forces of nature at his command and can unleash or restrain them at will. No one completely understands such common occurrences as rain or snow, and no one can command them—only God who created them has that power. God's point was that if Job could not explain such common events in nature, how could he possibly explain or question God? And if nature is beyond our grasp, God's moral purposes may not be what we imagine either.

38.28 Job 36.27,28

28 "Has the rain a father,
or who has begotten the drops of dew?

38.29 Job 37.10

29 From whose womb did the ice come forth,
and who has given birth to the hoarfrost of heaven?
30 The waters become hard like stone,
and the face of the deep is frozen.

38.31 Job 9.9

31 "Can you bind the chains of the Pleiades,
or loose the cords of Orion?
32 Can you lead forth the Mazzaroth in their season,
or can you guide the Bear with its children?
33 Do you know the ordinances of the heavens?
Can you establish their rule on the earth?

38.34 Job 22.11

34 "Can you lift up your voice to the clouds,
so that a flood of waters may cover you?

38.35 Job 36.32; 37.3

35 Can you send forth lightnings, so that they may go
and say to you, 'Here we are'?

38.36 Job 32.8 Eccles 2.26

36 Who has put wisdom in the inward parts,[l]
or given understanding to the mind?[l]
37 Who has the wisdom to number the clouds?
Or who can tilt the waterskins of the heavens,
38 when the dust runs into a mass
and the clods cling together?

38.39 Job 37.8

39 "Can you hunt the prey for the lion,
or satisfy the appetite of the young lions,
40 when they crouch in their dens,
or lie in wait in their covert?

38.41 Mt 6.26

41 Who provides for the raven its prey,
when its young ones cry to God,
and wander about for lack of food?

39.1 Deut 14.5 Ps 29.9

39

"Do you know when the mountain goats give birth?
Do you observe the calving of the deer?
2 Can you number the months that they fulfill,
and do you know the time when they give birth,

l Meaning of Heb uncertain

GOD'S JUSTICE

Wrong view	*Correct view*
LAW OF FAIRNESS / GOD	GOD / JUSTICE
There is a law of fairness or justice that is higher and more absolute than God. It is binding even for God. God must act in response to that law in order to be fair. Our response is to appeal to that law.	God himself is the standard of justice. He uses his power according to his own moral perfection. Thus, whatever he does is fair, even if we don't understand it. Our response is to appeal directly to him.

38.31, 32 These are constellations.

39.1ff God asked Job several questions about the animal kingdom in order to demonstrate how limited Job's knowledge really was. God was not seeking answers from Job. Instead, he was getting Job to recognize and submit to God's power and sovereignty.

3 when they crouch to give birth to their offspring,
and are delivered of their young?
4 Their young ones become strong, they grow up in the open;
they go forth, and do not return to them.

5 "Who has let the wild ass go free?
Who has loosed the bonds of the swift ass,
6 to which I have given the steppe for its home,
the salt land for its dwelling place?
7 It scorns the tumult of the city;
it does not hear the shouts of the driver.
8 It ranges the mountains as its pasture,
and it searches after every green thing.

9 "Is the wild ox willing to serve you?
Will it spend the night at your crib?
10 Can you tie it in the furrow with ropes,
or will it harrow the valleys after you?
11 Will you depend on it because its strength is great,
and will you hand over your labor to it?
12 Do you have faith in it that it will return,
and bring your grain to your threshing floor?[m]

13 "The ostrich's wings flap wildly,
though its pinions lack plumage.[n]
14 For it leaves its eggs to the earth,
and lets them be warmed on the ground,
15 forgetting that a foot may crush them,
and that a wild animal may trample them.
16 It deals cruelly with its young, as if they were not its own;
though its labor should be in vain, yet it has no fear;
17 because God has made it forget wisdom,
and given it no share in understanding.
18 When it spreads its plumes aloft,[n]
it laughs at the horse and its rider.

19 "Do you give the horse its might?
Do you clothe its neck with mane?
20 Do you make it leap like the locust?
Its majestic snorting is terrible.
21 It paws[o] violently, exults mightily;
it goes out to meet the weapons.
22 It laughs at fear, and is not dismayed;
it does not turn back from the sword.
23 Upon it rattle the quiver,
the flashing spear, and the javelin.
24 With fierceness and rage it swallows the ground;
it cannot stand still at the sound of the trumpet.
25 When the trumpet sounds, it says 'Aha!'
From a distance it smells the battle,
the thunder of the captains, and the shouting.

26 "Is it by your wisdom that the hawk soars,
and spreads its wings toward the south?
27 Is it at your command that the eagle mounts up
and makes its nest on high?
28 It lives on the rock and makes its home

39.5 Job 6.5; 11.12; 24.5; Dan 5.21; Hos 8.9
39.6 Job 24.5; Jer 2.24
39.9 Num 23.22; Deut 33.17; Ps 92.10; Isa 1.3
39.16 Lam 4.3
39.20 Jer 8.16; Joel 2.5
39.21 Prov 21.31; Jer 8.6
39.27 Jer 49.16

[m] Heb *your grain and your threshing floor* [n] Meaning of Heb uncertain [o] Gk Syr Vg: Heb *they dig*

in the fastness of the rocky crag.
29 From there it spies the prey;
its eyes see it from far away.
30 Its young ones suck up blood;
and where the slain are, there it is."

39.29 Job 9.26
39.30 Ezek 39.17-19 Mt 24.28

40 And the LORD said to Job:
2 "Shall a faultfinder contend with the Almighty?[p]
Anyone who argues with God must respond."

40.2 Job 9.3; 10.2 13.3; 23.4 31.35; 33.13

3 Then Job answered the LORD:
4 "See, I am of small account; what shall I answer you?
I lay my hand on my mouth.
5 I have spoken once, and I will not answer;
twice, but will proceed no further."

40.4 Job 21.5; 29.9
40.5 Job 9.3,15

6 Then the LORD answered Job out of the whirlwind:
7 "Gird up your loins like a man;
I will question you, and you declare to me.
8 Will you even put me in the wrong?
Will you condemn me that you may be justified?
9 Have you an arm like God,
and can you thunder with a voice like his?

40.6 Job 38.1
40.7 Job 38.3; 42.4
40.8 Job 10.3,7 13.18; 27.2,6
40.9 Job 37.5 Ps 39.3-9 Isa 45.9

10 "Deck yourself with majesty and dignity;
clothe yourself with glory and splendor.
11 Pour out the overflowings of your anger,
and look on all who are proud, and abase them.
12 Look on all who are proud, and bring them low;
tread down the wicked where they stand.
13 Hide them all in the dust together;
bind their faces in the world below.[q]
14 Then I will also acknowledge to you
that your own right hand can give you victory.

40.11 Isa 2.12; 42.25 Dan 4.37 Nah 1.6,8
40.12 Isa 13.11; 63.3
40.13 Isa 2.10-12 Jn 11.44

[p] Traditional rendering of Heb *Shaddai* [q] Heb *the hidden place*

FOUR VIEWS OF SUFFERING		
	Satan's view	People believe in God only when they are prospering and not suffering. This is wrong.
	The view of Job's three friends	Suffering is God's judgment for sin. This is not always true.
	Elihu's view	Suffering is God's way to teach, discipline, and refine. This is true, but an incomplete explanation.
	God's view	Suffering causes us to trust God for who he is, not what he does.

40.2–5 How do you argue with Almighty God? Do you demand answers when things don't go your way, you lose a job, someone close to you is ill or dies, finances are tight, you fail, or unexpected changes occur? The next time you are tempted to complain to God, consider how much he loves you, and remember Job's reaction when he had his chance to speak. Are you worse off than Job or more righteous than he? Give God a chance to reveal his greater purposes for you, but remember that they may unfold over the course of your life and not at the moment you desire.

40.4 Throughout his time of suffering, Job longed to have an opportunity to plead his innocence before God. Now God appeared to Job and gave him that opportunity. But Job decided to remain quiet because it was no longer necessary for him to speak. God had shown Job that, as a limited human being, he had neither the ability to judge the God who created the universe nor the right to ask why. God's actions do not depend on ours. He will do what he knows is best, regardless of what we think is fair. It is important to note, however, that God came to Job, demonstrating his love and care for him.

40.7 To "gird up" one's loins means to lift up the bottom of the garment and tuck it into the belt. This is an action that one would do to prepare for a battle or other difficult task.

40.15 The Behemoth was a large land animal, possibly an elephant or hippopotamus.

15 "Look at Behemoth,
which I made just as I made you;
it eats grass like an ox.
16 Its strength is in its loins,
and its power in the muscles of its belly.
17 It makes its tail stiff like a cedar;
the sinews of its thighs are knit together.
18 Its bones are tubes of bronze,
its limbs like bars of iron.

19 "It is the first of the great acts of God—
only its Maker can approach it with the sword.
20 For the mountains yield food for it
where all the wild animals play.
21 Under the lotus plants it lies,
in the covert of the reeds and in the marsh.
22 The lotus trees cover it for shade;
the willows of the wadi surround it.
23 Even if the river is turbulent, it is not frightened;
it is confident though Jordan rushes against its mouth.
24 Can one take it with hooks[r]
or pierce its nose with a snare?

41 [s] "Can you draw out Leviathan[t] with a fishhook,
or press down its tongue with a cord?
2 Can you put a rope in its nose,
or pierce its jaw with a hook?
3 Will it make many supplications to you?
Will it speak soft words to you?
4 Will it make a covenant with you
to be taken as your servant forever?
5 Will you play with it as with a bird,
or will you put it on leash for your girls?
6 Will traders bargain over it?
Will they divide it up among the merchants?
7 Can you fill its skin with harpoons,
or its head with fishing spears?
8 Lay hands on it;
think of the battle; you will not do it again!
9[u] Any hope of capturing it[v] will be disappointed;
were not even the gods[w] overwhelmed at the sight of it?
10 No one is so fierce as to dare to stir it up.
Who can stand before it?[x]
11 Who can confront it[x] and be safe?[y]
—under the whole heaven, who?[z]

12 "I will not keep silence concerning its limbs,
or its mighty strength, or its splendid frame.
13 Who can strip off its outer garment?
Who can penetrate its double coat of mail?[a]

40.15 Job 40.19

40.19 Job 41.33 Ps 7.12 Isa 27.1

41.1 Job 3.8

41.8 1 Kgs 20.11 2 Kgs 10.4 Lk 14.31,33

41.10 Job 3.8

41.11 Ex 19.5 Deut 10.14 Ps 24.1; 50.12 1 Cor 10.26

[r] Cn: Heb *in his eyes* [s] Ch 40.25 in Heb [t] Or *the crocodile* [u] Ch 41.1 in Heb [v] Heb *of it* [w] Cn Compare Symmachus Syr: Heb *one is* [x] Heb *me* [y] Gk: Heb *that I shall repay* [z] Heb *to me* [a] Gk: Heb *bridle*

41.1 While *Leviathan* usually refers to a seven-headed sea monster in old Canaanite myths, it probably means crocodile in this usage.

41.9–11 It is foolish for men to think they can stand up against God when they are afraid to confront even a crocodile. How much more powerful is God!

14 Who can open the doors of its face?
There is terror all around its teeth.
15 Its back[b] is made of shields in rows,
shut up closely as with a seal.
16 One is so near to another
that no air can come between them.
17 They are joined one to another;
they clasp each other and cannot be separated.
41.18 Job 3.9
18 Its sneezes flash forth light,
and its eyes are like the eyelids of the dawn.
19 From its mouth go flaming torches;
sparks of fire leap out.
20 Out of its nostrils comes smoke,
as from a boiling pot and burning rushes.
21 Its breath kindles coals,
and a flame comes out of its mouth.
22 In its neck abides strength,
and terror dances before it.
23 The folds of its flesh cling together;
it is firmly cast and immovable.
24 Its heart is as hard as stone,
as hard as the lower millstone.
25 When it raises itself up the gods are afraid;
at the crashing they are beside themselves.
26 Though the sword reaches it, it does not avail,
nor does the spear, the dart, or the javelin.
27 It counts iron as straw,
and bronze as rotten wood.
28 The arrow cannot make it flee;
slingstones, for it, are turned to chaff.
29 Clubs are counted as chaff;
it laughs at the rattle of javelins.
30 Its underparts are like sharp potsherds;
it spreads itself like a threshing sledge on the mire.
31 It makes the deep boil like a pot;
it makes the sea like a pot of ointment.
32 It leaves a shining wake behind it;
one would think the deep to be white-haired.
41.33 Job 40.19
33 On earth it has no equal,
a creature without fear.
41.34 Job 28.8 Ezek 29.3
34 It surveys everything that is lofty;
it is king over all that are proud."

[b] Cn Compare Gk Vg: Heb *pride*

JOB AND JESUS The book of Job is intimately tied to the New Testament because Job's questions and problems are answered perfectly in Jesus Christ.

Subject	*Reference in Job*	*How Jesus is the Answer*
Someone must help us approach God	9.32, 33	1 Timothy 2.5
Is there life after death?	14.14	John 11.25
There is one in heaven working on our behalf	16.19	Hebrews 9.24
There is one who can save us from judgment	19.25	Hebrews 7.24, 25
Where do we find God?	23.3–5	John 14.9
What is important in life?	40.4, 5	Matthew 16.26; John 3.16

E. JOB IS RESTORED (42.1–17)

In response to God's speech, Job humbles himself. God rebukes the three friends for adding to Job's suffering by their false assumptions and critical attitudes. Job's material possessions and family are restored, and he receives even greater blessings than he had before. Those who persist in trusting God will be rewarded.

Job replies to God

42 Then Job answered the LORD:
2 "I know that you can do all things,
and that no purpose of yours can be thwarted.
3 'Who is this that hides counsel without knowledge?'
Therefore I have uttered what I did not understand,
things too wonderful for me, which I did not know.
4 'Hear, and I will speak;
I will question you, and you declare to me.'
5 I had heard of you by the hearing of the ear,
but now my eye sees you;
6 therefore I despise myself,
and repent in dust and ashes."

7 After the LORD had spoken these words to Job, the LORD said to Eliphaz the
Temanite: "My wrath is kindled against you and against your two friends; for you
have not spoken of me what is right, as my servant Job has. 8 Now therefore take
seven bulls and seven rams, and go to my servant Job, and offer up for yourselves
a burnt offering; and my servant Job shall pray for you, for I will accept his prayer
not to deal with you according to your folly; for you have not spoken of me what is
right, as my servant Job has done." 9 So Eliphaz the Temanite and Bildad the Shuhite and Zophar the Naamathite went and did what the LORD had told them; and the
LORD accepted Job's prayer.

God blesses Job more than before

10 And the LORD restored the fortunes of Job when he had prayed for his
friends; and the LORD gave Job twice as much as he had before. 11 Then there came
to him all his brothers and sisters and all who had known him before, and they ate
bread with him in his house; they showed him sympathy and comforted him for all
the evil that the LORD had brought upon him; and each of them gave him a piece of
money[c] and a gold ring. 12 The LORD blessed the latter days of Job more than his
beginning; and he had fourteen thousand sheep, six thousand camels, a thousand
yoke of oxen, and a thousand donkeys. 13 He also had seven sons and three daugh-

[c] Heb *a qesitah*

42.4 Gen 18.27, 30-32; Job 38.3; 40.7
42.5 Job 26.14; Isa 6.5; Jn 1.18; 12.41
42.7 Job 40.3-5
42.8 Job 1.5; 22.30
42.10 Ps 14.7; 85.1-3; 126.1-6
42.11 Job 2.11; 19.13
42.12 Job 1.3,10; Prov 10.22; 1 Tim 6.17
42.13 Job 1.2; Ps 107.41

42.1ff Throughout the book, Job's friends had asked him to admit his sin and ask for forgiveness, and eventually Job did indeed repent. Ironically, Job's repentance was not the kind called for by his friends. He did not ask for forgiveness for committing secret sins, but for questioning God's sovereignty and justice. Job repented of his attitude and acknowledged God's great power and perfect justice. We sin when we angrily ask, "If God is in control, how could he let this happen?" Because we are locked into time, unable to see beyond today, we cannot know the reasons for everything that happens. Thus we must often choose between doubt and trust. Will you trust God with your unanswered questions?

42.2–4 Job is quoting the Lord's earlier questions to him (38.2, 3). He openly and honestly faced God and admitted that he was the one who had been foolish. Are you using what you can't understand as an excuse for your lack of trust? Admit to God that you don't even have enough faith to trust him. True faith begins in such humility.

42.7, 8 God made it clear that Job's friends were wrong. The fact that God did not mention any specific sins shows that God confirmed Job's claim to have led a devout and obedient life. Job's friends had made the error of assuming that Job's suffering was caused by some great sin. They were judging Job without knowing what God was doing. We must be careful to avoid making judgments about a person, because God may be working in ways we know nothing about.

42.8–10 After receiving much criticism, Job was still able to pray for his three friends. It is difficult to forgive someone who has accused you of wrongdoing, but Job did. Are you praying for those who have wronged you? Can you forgive them? Follow the actions of Job, whom God called a good man, and pray for those who have wronged you.

42.10, 11 Would the message of the book of Job change if God had not restored to Job his former blessings? No. God is still sovereign. Jesus said that anyone who gives up something for the kingdom of God will be repaid (Luke 18.29, 30). Our restoration may or may not be the same kind as Job's, which was both spiritual and material. Our complete restoration may not be in this life—but it *will* happen. God loves us, and he is just. He will not only restore whatever we have lost unjustly, but he will give us more than we can imagine as we live with him in eternity. Cling tightly to your faith through all your trials, and you too will be rewarded by God—if not now, in the life to come.

ters. 14 He named the first Jemimah, the second Keziah, and the third Kerenhappuch. 15 In all the land there were no women so beautiful as Job's daughters; and
their father gave them an inheritance along with their brothers. 16 After this Job
lived one hundred and forty years, and saw his children, and his children's children, four generations. 17 And Job died, old and full of days.

42.17
Gen 15.15; 25.8
Job 5.26
Prov 3.16

WHEN WE SUFFER
Here are six questions to ask ourselves when we suffer; and what to do if the answer is yes.

Questions	*Our response*
Am I being punished by God for sin?	Confess known sin.
Is Satan attacking me as I try to survive as a Christian?	Call on God for strength.
Am I being prepared for a special service, learning to be compassionate to those who suffer?	Resist self-pity. Ask God to open up doors of opportunity and help you discover others who suffer as you do.
Am I specifically selected for testing, like Job?	Accept help from the body of believers. Trust God to work his purpose through you.
Is my suffering a result of natural consequences, for which I am not directly responsible?	Recognize that in a sinful world, both good and evil people will suffer. But the good person has a promise from God that his suffering will one day come to an end.
Is my suffering due to some unknown reason?	Don't draw inward from the pain. Proclaim your faith in God, know that he cares, and wait patiently for his aid.

42.17 Job's question is timely: Why do believers experience troubles and suffering? Through a long debate, Job's supposedly wise friends were unable to answer the question. Job's friends made a serious error, for which God rebuked them. They assumed that trouble comes only because people sin. People make the same error today when they assert that sickness or lack of material blessing is a sign of unconfessed sin or lack of faith. Though normally (but not always) following God leads to a happier life, and rebelling against God normally (but not always) leads to an unhappy life, *God is in control.* In our world invaded by sin, calamity and suffering may come to good and bad alike.

This does not mean God is indifferent, uncaring, unjust, or powerless to protect us. Bad things happen because we live in a fallen world where both believers and unbelievers are hit with the tragic consequences of sin. God allows evil for a time, although he often turns it around for our good (Romans 8.28). We may have no answers as to why God allows evil, but we can be sure he is all-powerful and knows what he is doing. The next time you face trials and dilemmas, see them as opportunities to turn to God for strength. You will find a God who only desires to show his love and compassion to you. If you can trust him in pain, confusion, and loneliness, you will win the victory and eliminate doubt, one of Satan's greatest footholds in your life. If God is your foundation, you can never be separated from his love.

VITAL STATISTICS

PURPOSE:
To provide poetry for the expression of praise, worship, and confession to God

AUTHORS:
David wrote 73 psalms; Asaph wrote 12; the sons of Korah wrote nine; Solomon wrote two; Heman (with the sons of Korah), Ethan, and Moses each wrote one; and 51 psalms are anonymous. The New Testament ascribes two of the anonymous psalms (Psalms 2 and 95) to David (see Acts 4.25; Hebrews 4.7).

DATE WRITTEN:
Between the time of Moses (around 1440 B.C.) and the Babylonian captivity (586 B.C.)

SETTING:
For the most part, the psalms were not intended to be narrations of historical events. However, they often parallel events in history, such as David's flight from Saul and his sin with Bathsheba.

KEY VERSE:
"Let everything that breathes praise the Lord! Praise the Lord!" (150.6).

KEY PERSON:
David

KEY PLACE:
God's holy temple

"HI, how are you?" "Fine." Not exactly an "in-depth" discussion, this brief interchange is normal as friends and acquaintances pass and briefly touch each other with a cliché or two. Actually, clichés are a way of life, saturating sentences and permeating paragraphs. But if this is the essence of their communication, the relationship will stall on a superficial plateau. Facts and opinions also fill our verbiage. These words go deeper, but the true person still lies hidden beneath them. In reality, it is only when honest feelings and emotions are shared that real people can be known, loved, and helped.

Often, patterns of superficial communication spill over into our talks with God. We easily slide through well-worn lines recited for decades, or we quickly toss a cliché or two at God and call it prayer. There is no doubt that God hears and understands these feeble attempts, but by limiting the depth of our communication, we become shallow in our relationship with God. But he knows us, and he wants to have genuine communication with us.

At the center of the Bible is the book of Psalms. This great collection of songs and prayers expresses the heart and soul of humanity. In them, the whole range of human experiences is expressed. There are no clichés in this book. Instead, David and the other writers honestly pour out their true feelings, reflecting a dynamic, powerful, and life-changing friendship with God. The psalmists confess their sins, express their doubts and fears, ask God for help in times of trouble, and they praise and worship him.

As you read the book of Psalms, you will hear believers crying out to God from the depths of despair, and you will hear them singing to him in the heights of celebration. But whether despairing or rejoicing, you will always hear them sharing honest feelings with their God. Because of the honesty expressed by the psalmists, men and women throughout history have come, again and again, to the book of Psalms for comfort during times of struggle and distress. And with the psalmists, they have risen from the depths of despair to new heights of joy and praise as they also discovered the power of God's everlasting love and forgiveness. Let the honesty of the psalmists guide you into a more deep and genuine relationship with God.

THE BLUEPRINT

BOOK I
PSALMS 1.1—41.13

While the psalms are not organized by topic, it is helpful to compare the dominant themes in each section of the psalms to the five books of Moses. This first collection of psalms, mainly written by David, is similar to the book of Genesis. Just as Genesis tells how mankind was created, fell into sin, and was then promised redemption, many of these psalms discuss humans as blessed, fallen, and redeemed by God.

BOOK II PSALMS 42.1—72.20	This collection of psalms, mainly written by David and the sons of Korah, is similar to the book of Exodus. Just as Exodus describes the nation of Israel, many of these psalms describe the nation as ruined and then recovered. As God rescued the nation of Israel, he also rescues us. We do not have to work out solutions first, but we can go to God with our problems and ask him to help.
BOOK III PSALMS 73.1—89.52	This collection of psalms, mainly written by Asaph, is similar to the book of Leviticus. Just as Leviticus discusses the tabernacle and God's holiness, many of these psalms discuss the temple and God's enthronement. Because God is almighty, we can turn to him for deliverance. These psalms praise God because he is holy, and his perfect holiness deserves our worship and reverence.
BOOK IV PSALMS 90.1—106.48	This collection of psalms, mainly written by unknown authors, is similar to the book of Numbers. Just as Numbers discusses the relationship of the nation of Israel to surrounding nations, these psalms often mention the relationship of God's overruling kingdom to the other nations. Since we are citizens of the kingdom of God, we can keep the events and troubles of earth in their proper perspective.
BOOK V PSALMS 107.1—150.6	This collection of psalms, mainly written by David, is similar to the book of Deuteronomy. Just as Deuteronomy was concerned with God and his Word, these psalms are anthems of praise and thanksgiving for God and his Word. Most of the psalms were originally set to music and used in worship. We can use these psalms today as they were used in the past, as a hymnbook of praise and worship. This is a book which ought to make our hearts sing.

MEGATHEMES

THEME	EXPLANATION	IMPORTANCE
Praise	Psalms are songs of praise to God as our Creator, Sustainer, and Redeemer. Praise is recognizing, appreciating, and expressing God's greatness.	Focusing our thoughts on God moves us to praise him. The more we know him, the more we can appreciate what he has done for us.
God's power	God is all-powerful; and he always acts at the right time. He is sovereign over every situation. God's power is shown by the ways he reveals himself in creation, history, and his Word.	When we feel powerless, God can help us. His strength can overcome the despair of any pain or trial. We can always pray that he will deliver, protect, and sustain us.
Forgiveness	Many psalms are intense prayers asking God for forgiveness. God forgives us when we confess our sin and turn from it.	Because God forgives us, we can pray to him honestly and directly. When we receive his forgiveness, we move from alienation to intimacy, from guilt to love.
Thankfulness	We are grateful to God for his personal concern, help, and mercy. Not only does he protect, guide, and forgive us, but his creation provides everything we need.	When we realize how we benefit from knowing God, we can fully express our thanks to him. By thanking him often, we develop spontaneity in our prayer life.
Trust	God is faithful and just. When we put our trust in him, he quiets our hearts. Because he has been faithful throughout history, we can trust him in times of trouble.	People can be unfair and friends may desert us. But we can trust God. Knowing God intimately drives away doubt, fear, and loneliness.

BOOK I
Psalms 1.1 – 41.13

In this book, the psalmists praise God for his justice, express confidence in God's compassion, recount the depravity of man, plead for vindication, ask God to deliver them from their enemies, speak of the blessedness of the forgiven sinner, and portray God as a shepherd. We should worship God with the same sense of adoration found in these psalms.

Theme: Life's two roads. The life of the faithful person is contrasted with the life of the faithless person.
Author: Anonymous

PSALM 1

1 Happy are those
who do not follow the advice of the wicked,
or take the path that sinners tread,
or sit in the seat of scoffers;
2 but their delight is in the law of the LORD,
and on his law they meditate day and night.
3 They are like trees
planted by streams of water,
which yield their fruit in its season,
and their leaves do not wither.
In all that they do, they prosper.

4 The wicked are not so,
but are like chaff that the wind drives away.
5 Therefore the wicked will not stand in the judgment,
nor sinners in the congregation of the righteous;

1.1 Ps 17.4; 26.5
1.3 Jer 17.7,8 Ezek 47.12
1.4 Job 21.18 Ps 35.5 Isa 17.13

1.1 The writer began his psalm extolling the joys of obeying God and refusing to listen to those who discredit or ridicule him. Our friends and associates can have a profound influence on us, often in very subtle ways. If we insist on friendships with those who scoff at what God considers important, we might sin by becoming indifferent to God's will. This attitude is the same as scoffing. Do your friends build up your faith, or do they tear it down? True friends should help, not hinder, you to draw closer to God.

1.1 God's advice leads to joy. To obtain God's joy, the psalmist says we should avoid the company of scoffing sinners. In addition, we should seek an understanding of God through his Word. The influence of mockers separates us from the radiance of God's joyful presence, as a dark cloud separates us from the joyful presence of the morning sun.

1.1ff God doesn't judge people on the basis of race, sex, or national origin. He judges them on the basis of their faith in him and their response to his revealed will. Those who diligently try to obey God's will are like healthy, fruit-bearing trees with strong roots (Jeremiah 17.5–8), and God promises to watch over them. God's wisdom guides their lives. In contrast, those who don't obey God have meaningless lives that blow away like dust.

There are only two paths of life before us — God's way of obedience or the way of rebellion and destruction. The path you choose determines how you will spend eternity.

1.2 You can learn how to follow God by meditating on his Word. Meditating means spending time reading and thinking about what you have read. It means asking yourself how you should change so you're living as God wants. Knowing and meditating on God's Word are the first steps toward applying it to your everyday life. If you want to follow God more closely, you must know what he says.

1.2 This "law of the Lord" included all of Scripture: the first five books of Moses, the prophets, and the other writings. The more we know of the whole scope of God's Word, the more resources we will have to guide us in our daily decisions.

1.2, 3 There is a most simple bit of wisdom in these two verses — the more we delight in God's presence, the more fruitful we are. On the other hand, the more we allow those who ridicule God to affect our thoughts and attitudes, the more we separate ourselves from our source of nourishment. We must have contact with unbelievers if we are to witness to them, but we must not join in or imitate their sinful behavior. If you want despair, spend time with scoffing sinners; but if you want joy, make friends with those who love God and his Word.

1.3 When Scripture says, "In all that they do, they prosper," it does not mean immunity from failure or difficulties. Nor is it a guarantee of health, wealth, and happiness. What the Bible means by prosperity is this: when we apply God's wisdom, the fruit (results or by-products) we bear will be good and receive God's approval. As a tree soaks up water and bears luscious fruit, we also are to soak up God's Word, producing actions and attitudes that honor God. To achieve anything worthwhile, we must have God's Word in our hearts.

1.4 Chaff is the outer shell (or husk) that must be removed to get at the valuable kernels of grain inside. Chaff was removed by a process called threshing and winnowing. After the plants were cut, they were crushed, and then the pieces were thrown into the air. Chaff is very light and is carried away by even the slightest wind, while the good grain falls back to the earth. Chaff is a symbol of a faithless life that drifts along without direction. Good grain is a symbol of a faithful life that can be used by God. Unlike grain, we can choose the direction we will take.

1.5 Although evil people may get the upper hand at times, God assures us that a day is coming when their sins will be punished (see Matthew 25.31–46; Revelation 6.16, 17; 20.11–15 for other references to God's judgment). Meanwhile God watches over the plans and purposes of the faithful. So let us remain steadfast in our faith and devotion to him.

1.6 Jn 10.14 2 Tim 2.19
6 for the LORD watches over the way of the righteous,
but the way of the wicked will perish.

Theme: God's ultimate rule. A psalm written to celebrate the coronation of an Israelite king, but also written for the coronation of Christ, the eternal King.
Author: David (see Acts 4.25, 26)

PSALM 2

2.1 Acts 4.25,26
1 Why do the nations conspire,
and the peoples plot in vain?
2 The kings of the earth set themselves,
and the rulers take counsel together,
against the LORD and his anointed, saying,
3 "Let us burst their bonds asunder,
and cast their cords from us."

2.4 Ps 37.12,13 59.8
4 He who sits in the heavens laughs;
the LORD has them in derision.
5 Then he will speak to them in his wrath,

REASONS TO READ PSALMS

When you want . . .	*Read . . .*
to find comfort	Psalm 23
to meet God intimately	Psalm 103
to learn a new prayer	Psalm 136
to learn a new song	Psalm 92
to learn more about God	Psalm 24
to understand yourself more clearly	Psalm 8
to know how to come to God each day	Psalm 5
to be forgiven for your sins	Psalm 51
to feel worthwhile	Psalm 139
to understand why you should read the Bible	Psalm 119
to give praise to God	Psalm 145
to know that God is in control	Psalm 146
to give thanks to God	Psalm 136
to please God	Psalm 15
to know why you should worship God	Psalm 104

God's Word was written to be studied, understood, and applied, and the book of Psalms lends itself most directly to application. We understand Psalms best when we "stand under" them and allow them to flow over us like a rain shower. We may turn to Psalms looking for something, but sooner or later we will meet Someone. As we read and memorize the psalms, we will gradually discover how much they are already part of us. They put into words our deepest hurts, longings, thoughts, and prayers. They gently push us toward being what God designed us to be—people loving and living for him.

2.1ff Several psalms are called *messianic* because of their prophetic descriptions of Jesus the Messiah (Christ)—his life, death, resurrection, and future reign. This psalm describes the rebellion of the nations and the coming of Christ to establish his eternal reign. It is often referred to in the New Testament (see Acts 4.25, 26; 13.33; Hebrews 1.5, 6; 5.5; Revelation 2.26, 27; 12.5; 19.15).

2.1ff David may have written these words during a rebellion by some of the surrounding heathen nations. Chosen and anointed by God, David knew that God would fulfill his promise to bring the Messiah into the world through his bloodline (2 Samuel 7.16; 1 Chronicles 17.11, 12).

2.3 People often think they will be free if they can get away from God. Yet we all inevitably serve somebody or something, whether a ruler, an organization, or even our own selfish desires. Just as a fish is not free when it leaves the water, we are not free when we leave the Lord. We can find the one sure route to freedom by wholeheartedly serving God. He can set you free to be who he created you to be.

2.4 God laughs, not at the nations, but at their confused thoughts about power. It is the laughter of a father when his three-year-old boasts that he or she can outrun him or conquer him in a wrestling match. Every nation is limited, yet he is transcendent. If you have to choose between confidence in God or any nation, choose God!

2.4 God is all-powerful. He created the world, and knew about the empires of the earth long before they came into being (Daniel 2.26–45). Our world has many leaders who boast of their power, who rant and rave against God and his people, who promise to take over and form their own empires. But God laughs, because any power they have comes from him, and he can also take it from them. We need not fear the boasts of tyrants, because they are in God's hands.

2.5–12 David's praise of the Messiah's coronation was prophetic. The rule of Christ described here began after his crucifixion and resurrection, and will be fulfilled when he comes to set up his kingdom on earth.

and terrify them in his fury, saying,
6 "I have set my king on Zion, my holy hill."

7 I will tell of the decree of the LORD:
He said to me, "You are my son;
today I have begotten you.
8 Ask of me, and I will make the nations your heritage,
and the ends of the earth your possession.
9 You shall break them with a rod of iron,
and dash them in pieces like a potter's vessel."

10 Now therefore, O kings, be wise;
be warned, O rulers of the earth.
11 Serve the LORD with fear,
with trembling 12 kiss his feet,[a]
or he will be angry, and you will perish in the way;
for his wrath is quickly kindled.

Happy are all who take refuge in him.

2.6 Ps 3.4; 45.6; 48.1,2
2.7 Acts 13.32,33; Heb 1.5,6; 5.5
2.9 Ps 28.5; 110.5,6; Rev 2.27; 12.5; 19.15
2.11 Ps 5.7; 32.8; 119.119,120; Heb 12.28

Theme: Confidently trusting God for protection and peace.
Author: David

PSALM 3

A Psalm of David, when he fled from his son Absalom.

1 O LORD, how many are my foes!
Many are rising against me;
2 many are saying to me,
"There is no help for you[b] in God." *Selah*

3 But you, O LORD, are a shield around me,
my glory, and the one who lifts up my head.
4 I cry aloud to the LORD,
and he answers me from his holy hill. *Selah*

[a] Cn: Meaning of Heb of verses 11b and 12a is uncertain [b] Syr: Heb *him*

3.1 2 Sam 15.12; Ps 69.4
3.4 Ps 34.4; 99.9

2.11, 12 To "kiss his feet" means to surrender fully and submit to the king. Christ is not only God's chosen King, he is also the rightful King of our hearts and lives. To be ready for his coming, we must submit to his leadership each day.

3.1, 2 David felt like he was in the minority. There may have been as many as 10,000 soldiers surrounding him at this time (3.6). Not only did David's enemies view life differently, they actively sought to harm him. As king, David could have trusted his army to defeat Absalom, but he depended upon God's mercy instead (3.4). Therefore, he was at peace with whatever outcome occurred, knowing that God's great purposes would prevail. We can overcome fear by trusting God for his protection in our darkest hour.

3.1–3 David was not sitting on his throne in a place of power, but running for his life from his rebellious son Absalom and a host of traitors. When circumstances go against us, it is tempting to conclude that God also is against us. But David reminds us that the opposite is true. When everything seems to go against us, God is still for us. If circumstance has turned against you, don't blame God – seek him!

3.2 The word *Selah* occurs 71 times in Psalms and three times in Habakkuk (3.3, 9, 13). Though its precise use is unknown, it was most likely used as a musical sign. Three suggestions are: (1) It was a musical direction to the singers and orchestra to play *forte* or *crescendo*. (2) It was a signal to lift up the hands or voice in worship, or to the priest to give a benediction. (3) It was a phrase like "Amen" or "Hallelujah" meaning "so be it" or "may it ever be true."

3.3 When facing problems, trials, suffering, and death, we may feel like giving up in despair. David ran from his beloved son who threatened to kill him, knowing there was no hope *except* in God. When we feel seriously let down by life, we should remember that we still have *one* hope. God is all the hope we need because he promises to be a shield to protect us. When you focus your thoughts on God, he restores your confidence in him ("lifts up" your head) and in the future he has planned for you.

3.4 God's holy hill was Mount Moriah in Jerusalem, the place where David's son Solomon would build the temple. David knew God could not be confined to any space, but he wrote poetically, expressing confidence that God would hear him when he prayed. God responds to us when we urgently pray to him.

3.5 Sleep does not come easily during a crisis. David could have had sleepless nights when his son Absalom rebelled and gathered an army to kill him. But he slept peacefully, even during the rebellion. What made the difference? David cried out to the Lord, and the Lord heard him. The assurance of answered prayer brings peace. It is easier to sleep well when we have full assurance that

3.5 Lev 26.6 Prov 3.24-26
3.6 Ps 23.4; 27.3
3.8 Isa 43.11

5 I lie down and sleep;
I wake again, for the LORD sustains me.
6 I am not afraid of ten thousands of people
who have set themselves against me all around.

7 Rise up, O LORD!
Deliver me, O my God!
For you strike all my enemies on the cheek;
you break the teeth of the wicked.

8 Deliverance belongs to the LORD;
may your blessing be on your people! *Selah*

PSALMS FROM DAVID'S LIFE

Of the more than 70 psalms attributed to David, at least 14 of them are connected with specific events in his life. From them we see an outline of a growing relationship with God. They are listed here, roughly in chronological order.

Event in David's life	*Reference*	*Psalm*	*What David learned about God*
When Saul sent troops to David's home to capture him	1 Samuel 19	59	You are my high tower of safety, my God of mercy.
While running from Saul	1 Samuel 21	34	I will praise the Lord no matter what happens.
While running from Saul	1 Samuel 21	56	But when I am afraid, I will put my confidence in you.
While hiding in the cave of Adullam	1 Samuel 22	142	You are my only place of refuge. Only you can keep me safe.
After learning Doeg had murdered 85 priests and their families	1 Samuel 22	52	But God will strike you down. See what happens to those who despise God.
When the people of Ziph tried to betray him	1 Samuel 23	54	But God is my helper.
While hiding in a cave	1 Samuel 24	57	I will hide beneath the shadow of your wings until this storm is past.
While hiding in the wilderness of Judea	1 Samuel 24	63	I follow close behind you, protected by your strong right arm.
When Saul's pursuit was over	2 Samuel 22	18	Lord, how merciful you are to those who are merciful. And you do not punish those who run from evil.
After being confronted about his adultery with Bathsheba	2 Samuel 12	51	It is a broken spirit you want—remorse and penitence. A broken and a contrite heart, O God, you will not ignore.
During Absalom's rebellion	2 Samuel 15	3	Salvation comes from God.
During Absalom's rebellion	2 Samuel 15	7	For you, the righteous God, look deep within the hearts of men and examine all their motives and their thoughts.

God is in control of circumstances. If you are lying awake at night worrying about circumstances you can't change, pour out your heart to God, and thank him that he is in control. Then sleep will come.

3.7 This description of God's anger reveals David's desire for justice against his persecutors. David himself was slapped and insulted, and here he simply asked for equal treatment for his enemies. He did this, not out of personal revenge, but for the sake of God's justice. Verse 8 shows the humility behind David's words—he realized that faith in God's timing was the solution to the success the wicked unfairly achieved.

Theme: Rejoicing in God's protection and peace. We can place our confidence in God because he will listen when we call on him.
Author: David

PSALM 4

To the leader: with stringed instruments. A Psalm of David.

1 Answer me when I call, O God of my right!
You gave me room when I was in distress.
Be gracious to me, and hear my prayer.

2 How long, you people, shall my honor suffer shame?
How long will you love vain words, and seek after lies? *Selah*
3 But know that the LORD has set apart the faithful for himself;
the LORD hears when I call to him.

4 When you are disturbed,[c] do not sin;
ponder it on your beds, and be silent. *Selah*
5 Offer right sacrifices,
and put your trust in the LORD.

6 There are many who say, "O that we might see some good!
Let the light of your face shine on us, O LORD!"
7 You have put gladness in my heart
more than when their grain and wine abound.

8 I will both lie down and sleep in peace;
for you alone, O LORD, make me lie down in safety.

4.1 Ps 3.4; 17.6 18.6,18,19
4.2 Ps 3.3 69.7-10,19
4.3 Ps 6.8,9; 17.6 31.23; 50.5
4.4 Ps 33.8; 77.6
4.5 Ps 37.3,5 50.14; 51.19
4.7 Ps 97.11,12 119.14
4.8 Ps 3.5; 16.9

Theme: The lies of enemies. God is able to defend us from lies spoken against us.
Author: David

PSALM 5

To the leader: for the flutes. A Psalm of David.

1 Give ear to my words, O LORD;
give heed to my sighing.
2 Listen to the sound of my cry,
my King and my God,
for to you I pray.
3 O LORD, in the morning you hear my voice;
in the morning I plead my case to you, and watch.
4 For you are not a God who delights in wickedness;

5.1 Ps 54.2; 84.3
5.3 Ps 88.13; 130.5
5.4 Ps 11.5; 34.16

[c] Or *are angry*

4.1ff This psalm may have been written as David was asking his enemies to reconsider their support of Absalom. It was probably written shortly after Psalm 3.

4.3 David knew that God heard his prayers and would answer him. We too can be confident that God listens and answers when we call on him. Sometimes we think God will not hear us because we have fallen short of his high standards for holy living. But God has forgiven us, and he will listen to us. When you feel that your prayers are "bouncing off the ceiling," remember that as a believer you have been set apart by God and that he loves you. He hears and answers (although his answers may not be what you expect). Look at your problems in the light of God's power instead of looking at God in the light of your problems.

4.5 Worship in David's day included animal sacrifices by the priests in the tabernacle. The animal's blood covered or was a remedy for the sins of the one who offered the animal. There were specific rules for offering sacrifices, but more important to God than ceremony was the offerer's attitude of submission and obedience (1 Samuel 15.22, 23). Today, a pleasing sacrifice to God is still the same—he wants our obedience and our praise before our gifts (Hebrews 13.15). Offer him the sacrifice of total obedience and heartfelt praise.

4.7 Two kinds of joy are contrasted here—inward joy that comes from knowing and trusting God and happiness that comes as a result of pleasant circumstances. Inward joy is steady as long as we trust God; happiness is unpredictable. Inward joy defeats discouragement; happiness covers it up. Inward joy is lasting; happiness is temporary.

5.1–3 The secret of a close relationship with God is to pray to him earnestly *each morning.* In the morning, our minds are more free from problems and then we can commit the whole day to God. Regular communication helps any friendship and is certainly necessary for a strong relationship with God. We need to communicate with him daily. Do you have a regular time to pray and read God's Word?

evil will not sojourn with you.

5.5 Ps 1.5; 11.5

5 The boastful will not stand before your eyes;
you hate all evildoers.

5.6 Ps 52.4,5

6 You destroy those who speak lies;
the LORD abhors the bloodthirsty and deceitful.

5.7 Ps 69.13

7 But I, through the abundance of your steadfast love,
will enter your house,
I will bow down toward your holy temple
in awe of you.

5.8 Ps 27.11

8 Lead me, O LORD, in your righteousness
because of my enemies;
make your way straight before me.

5.9 Rom 3.13

9 For there is no truth in their mouths;
their hearts are destruction;
their throats are open graves;
they flatter with their tongues.

5.10 Ps 9.16; 36.12

10 Make them bear their guilt, O God;
let them fall by their own counsels;
because of their many transgressions cast them out,
for they have rebelled against you.

5.11 Ps 2.12; 12.7 33.1; 64.10 Isa 65.13

11 But let all who take refuge in you rejoice;
let them ever sing for joy.
Spread your protection over them,
so that those who love your name may exult in you.

5.12 Ps 29.11 32.7,10

12 For you bless the righteous, O LORD;
you cover them with favor as with a shield.

Theme: Deliverance in trouble. God is able to rescue us.
Author: David

PSALM 6

To the leader: with stringed instruments; according to The Sheminith. A Psalm of David.

6.1 Ps 2.5; 38.1

1 O LORD, do not rebuke me in your anger,
or discipline me in your wrath.

6.2 Ps 22.14

2 Be gracious to me, O LORD, for I am languishing;
O LORD, heal me, for my bones are shaking with terror.

6.3 Ps 88.3; 90.13

3 My soul also is struck with terror,
while you, O LORD—how long?

4 Turn, O LORD, save my life;
deliver me for the sake of your steadfast love.

5.4 God cannot travel ("sojourn") in the company of sin. God cannot condone or excuse even the smallest sin. Therefore we cannot excuse ourselves for sinning "only a little bit." As we grow spiritually, our sensitivity to sin increases. What is your reaction to sin in your life? Are you insensitive, unconcerned, disappointed, or comfortable? As God makes us aware of sin, we must be intolerant toward it and be willing to change. All believers should strive to be more tolerant of people but less tolerant of the sin in others and in themselves.

5.10 When David was in trouble because his enemies were lying about him, he prayed, confident that God's love would not only console him, but defend (5.11) and shield (5.12) him. God would judge these evildoers. We often make the mistake of thinking of love only in terms of gentleness. But God's love is stronger than any evil we might face.

6.1ff This is the first of seven "penitential" psalms, in which the writer humbly realizes his predicament (usually the result of sin), expresses sorrow over it, and demonstrates a fresh commitment to remain close to God. We don't know the cause of David's pain, but whatever the cause, he sought God for the remedy.

6.1–3 David accepted God's punishment, but he begged God not to punish in anger. Jeremiah also asked God to correct him gently and not in anger (Jeremiah 10.24). David recognized that if God treated him with justice alone and not with mercy, he would be wiped out by God's wrath. Often we want God to show mercy to us and justice to everyone else. God in his kindness forgives us instead of giving us what we deserve.

5 For in death there is no remembrance of you;
in Sheol who can give you praise?

6.5 Ps 30.9

6 I am weary with my moaning;
every night I flood my bed with tears;
I drench my couch with my weeping.
7 My eyes waste away because of grief;
they grow weak because of all my foes.

6.6 Ps 42.3; 69.3

6.7 Ps 31.9

8 Depart from me, all you workers of evil,
for the LORD has heard the sound of my weeping.
9 The LORD has heard my supplication;
the LORD accepts my prayer.
10 All my enemies shall be ashamed and struck with terror;
they shall turn back, and in a moment be put to shame.

6.10 Ps 71.24; 73.19

Theme: A request for justice against those who make slanderous comments. God is the perfect judge and will punish those who persecute the innocent.
Author: David

PSALM 7

A Shiggaion of David, which he sang to the LORD concerning Cush, a Benjaminite.

1 O LORD my God, in you I take refuge;
save me from all my pursuers, and deliver me,
2 or like a lion they will tear me apart;
they will drag me away, with no one to rescue.

7.1 Ps 11.1

7.2 Ps 17.12; 57.4

3 O LORD my God, if I have done this,
if there is wrong in my hands,
4 if I have repaid my ally with harm
or plundered my foe without cause,
5 then let the enemy pursue and overtake me,
trample my life to the ground,
and lay my soul in the dust. *Selah*

7.3 1 Sam 24.11

7.4 1 Sam 26.9

6 Rise up, O LORD, in your anger;
lift yourself up against the fury of my enemies;
awake, O my God;[d] you have appointed a judgment.
7 Let the assembly of the peoples be gathered around you,
and over it take your seat[e] on high.
8 The LORD judges the peoples;
judge me, O LORD, according to my righteousness

7.6 Ps 3.7; 35.23

7.7 Ps 18.20; 35.24

[d] Or *awake for me* [e] Cn: Heb *return*

6.5 *Sheol* is the word in the Old Testament for the realm of the dead. It is used to mean the grave, the underworld, or death.

6.6 Pouring out his heart with tears, David was completely honest with God. We can be honest with God even when we are filled with anger or despair, because God knows us thoroughly and wants the very best for us. Anger and despair may result in rash outward acts or turning inward in depression. Because we trust in our all-powerful God, we don't have to be victims of circumstance or be weighed down by the guilt of sin. Be honest with God, and he will help you turn your attention from yourself to his wonderful presence.

6.8–10 David's feelings shifted from fear to confidence. To defend ourselves against the lies and propaganda of our enemies, our best preparation is to be saturated with the knowledge of God and filled with his power. Our daily study of his Word, our prayers, our worship, and our confidence in his power will keep us strong.

7.1 *Shiggaion* is a term derived from the verb "to err" or "to wonder;" it could also mean "wild" or "ecstatic." It is a poem written with intense feeling, a lament to stir the emotions.

7.1–6 Have you ever been falsely accused or so badly hurt that you wanted revenge? David wrote this psalm in response to the slanderous accusations of those who claimed he was trying to kill Saul and seize the throne (1 Samuel 24.9–11). Instead of taking matters into his own hands and striking back, David cried out to God for justice. The proper response to slander is prayer, not revenge, because God says, "Vengeance is mine, I will repay" (Romans 12.19; see also Deuteronomy 32.35, 36; Hebrews 10.30). Instead of striking back, ask God to take your case, bring justice, and restore your reputation.

and according to the integrity that is in me.

9 O let the evil of the wicked come to an end,
but establish the righteous,
you who test the minds and hearts,
O righteous God.

7.10 Ps 18.2,30 97.10,11

10 God is my shield,
who saves the upright in heart.

7.11 Deut 32.41

11 God is a righteous judge,
and a God who has indignation every day.

7.12 Ps 64.7

12 If one does not repent, God[f] will whet his sword;
he has bent and strung his bow;

7.13 Ps 18.14; 45.5

13 he has prepared his deadly weapons,
making his arrows fiery shafts.

7.14 Job 15.35

14 See how they conceive evil,
and are pregnant with mischief,
and bring forth lies.

7.15 Job 4.7,8

15 They make a pit, digging it out,
and fall into the hole that they have made.
16 Their mischief returns upon their own heads,
and on their own heads their violence descends.

7.17 Ps 9.2 66.1,2,4 71.15,16

17 I will give to the LORD the thanks due to his righteousness,
and sing praise to the name of the LORD, the Most High.

Theme: The greatness of God assures the worth of mankind. God, the all-powerful Creator, cares for his most valuable creation—people.
Author: David

PSALM 8

To the leader: according to The Gittith. A Psalm of David.

8.1 Ps 57.5,11 66.2; 113.4 148.13

1 O LORD, our Sovereign,
how majestic is your name in all the earth!

8.2 Mt 21.16

You have set your glory above the heavens.
2 Out of the mouths of babes and infants

[f] Heb *he*

7.9 Nothing is hidden from God—this can be either terrifying or comforting. Our thoughts are an open book to him. Because he knows even our motives, we have no place to hide, no way to pretend we can get away with sin. But that very knowledge also gives us great comfort. We don't have to impress God or put up a false front. Instead, we can trust God to help us work through our weaknesses in order to serve him as he has planned. When we truly follow him, God rewards our effort.

7.11 When evil gets the upper hand, life is unfair. We know that God's justice will ultimately prevail. But not all of God's justice is postponed to the future. He is angry with the wicked every day and often punishes them and rescues the innocent in *this* life. We must never give up our faith in him.

7.14–16 When allowed to run its course, evil destroys itself. Violent people become victims of violence, and liars are victims of others' deceit (9.15, 16). But in the process, innocent people are hurt. Sometimes God intervenes and stops evildoers in their tracks in order to protect his followers. At other times, for reasons known only to him, God allows evil to continue even though innocent people are hurt. It is during these times that we must ask God to protect us. Remember that God will execute final justice, even if he doesn't bring it about during our lifetime.

7.17 During a time of great evil and injustice, David was grateful that God is righteous (see also 7.11). When we wonder if anyone is honest or fair, we can be assured that God will continue to bring justice and fairness when we involve him in our activities. If you ever feel you are being treated unfairly, ask the one who is always fair and just to be with you, and then thank him for his presence (see Isaiah 42.1–6).

8.1ff Portions of this psalm are quoted in the New Testament and applied to Christ (1 Corinthians 15.27; Hebrews 2.6–8). Jesus became human, just a little lower than the angels (8.5), and he will raise all who belong to him above the angels when he comes to reign over the new heavens and new earth. Jesus is the only person who perfectly reflects God's image (Galatians 2.20; Colossians 1.15).

8.2 "Founded a bulwark" can mean he ordained strength or praise. Children are able to trust and praise God without doubts or reservations. As we get older, many of us find this more and more difficult to do. Ask God to give you childlike faith, removing any barriers to having a closer walk with him. Get in touch with this childlike quality in you so that you can be more expressive.

you have founded a bulwark because of your foes,
to silence the enemy and the avenger.

3 When I look at your heavens, the work of your fingers,
the moon and the stars that you have established;
4 what are human beings that you are mindful of them,
mortals[g] that you care for them?

5 Yet you have made them a little lower than God,[h]
and crowned them with glory and honor.
6 You have given them dominion over the works of your hands;
you have put all things under their feet,
7 all sheep and oxen,
and also the beasts of the field,
8 the birds of the air, and the fish of the sea,
whatever passes along the paths of the seas.

9 O LORD, our Sovereign,
how majestic is your name in all the earth!

8.3
Ps 89.11; 136.9

8.4
Job 7.17
Ps 144.3
Heb 2.6-8

8.5
Ps 21.5; 82.6

8.6
Gen 1.26,28

Theme: God never ignores our cries for help.
Author: David, probably written after a victory over the Philistines

PSALM 9

To the leader: according to Muth-labben. A Psalm of David.

1 I will give thanks to the LORD with my whole heart;
I will tell of all your wonderful deeds.
2 I will be glad and exult in you;
I will sing praise to your name, O Most High.

3 When my enemies turned back,
they stumbled and perished before you.
4 For you have maintained my just cause;
you have sat on the throne giving righteous judgment.

5 You have rebuked the nations, you have destroyed the wicked;
you have blotted out their name forever and ever.
6 The enemies have vanished in everlasting ruins;

9.1
Ps 26.7; 86.12

9.2
Ps 66.2,4
92.1; 104.34

9.3
Ps 27.2; 56.9

9.4
Ps 47.8; 140.12

9.5
Ps 69.28
119.21

9.6
Ps 34.16; 40.15

g Heb *ben adam*, lit. *son of man* h Or *than the divine beings* or *angels*: Heb *elohim*

8.3, 4 To respect God's majesty, we must compare ourselves to his greatness. When we look at creation, we often feel small by comparison. To feel small is a healthy way to get back to reality, but God does not want us to dwell on our smallness. Humility means proper respect for God, not self-depreciation.

8.3–5 When we look at the vast expanse of creation, we wonder how God could be concerned for people who constantly disappoint him. Yet God created us only a little lower than God or the angels! The next time you question your worth as a person or feel down about yourself, remember that God considers you highly valuable. We have great worth because we bear the stamp of the Creator. (See Genesis 1.26, 27 for the extent of worth God places on all people.) Because God has already declared how valuable we are to him, we can be set free from feelings of worthlessness.

8.6 God gave human beings tremendous authority – to be in charge of the whole earth. But with great authority comes great responsibility. If we own a pet, we have the legal authority to do with it as we wish, but we also have the responsibility to feed and care for it. How do you treat God's creation? Use your resources wisely because God holds you accountable for your stewardship.

9.1ff Praise is expressing to God our appreciation and understanding of his worth. It is saying "thank you" for each aspect of his divine nature. Our inward attitude becomes outward expression. When we praise God, we help ourselves by expanding our awareness of who he is. In each psalm you read, look for an attribute or characteristic of God for which you can thank him.

9.1, 2 One of the natural results of praising God is witnessing. When we know God is wonderful, we naturally want to tell others and have them praise God with us.

9.4 God maintains our just cause; he is our vindicator (one who clears us from criticism and justifies us before others). In this life, we may face many injustices: (1) we may be falsely accused and misunderstood by friends and enemies; (2) we may not truly be appreciated by others for the love we show; (3) the true value of our work and service may not be duly rewarded; (4) our ideas may be ignored. But God is to be praised, for he sees and remembers all the good we do, and it is up to him to decide the timing and the appropriateness of our rewards. If we do not trust him to vindicate us, then we are susceptible to hatred and self-pity. If we do trust him, we can experience God's peace and be free from the worry of how others perceive us and treat us.

their cities you have rooted out;
the very memory of them has perished.

9.7 Ps 10.16 89.14,15 96.13; 98.8,9

7 But the LORD sits enthroned forever,
he has established his throne for judgment.
8 He judges the world with righteousness;
he judges the peoples with equity.

9.9 Ps 18.2; 37.39 59.9,16,17

9 The LORD is a stronghold for the oppressed,
a stronghold in times of trouble.
10 And those who know your name put their trust in you,
for you, O LORD, have not forsaken those who seek you.

9.11 Ps 76.2; 105.1

11 Sing praises to the LORD, who dwells in Zion.
Declare his deeds among the peoples.

9.12 Gen 9.5,6 Ps 72.14

12 For he who avenges blood is mindful of them;
he does not forget the cry of the afflicted.

9.13 Ps 30.3; 38.19 86.13

13 Be gracious to me, O LORD.
See what I suffer from those who hate me;
you are the one who lifts me up from the gates of death,

9.14 Ps 13.5; 20.5 35.9; 51.12

14 so that I may recount all your praises,
and, in the gates of daughter Zion,
rejoice in your deliverance.

9.15 Ps 7.15; 35.8

15 The nations have sunk in the pit that they made;
in the net that they hid has their own foot been caught.
16 The LORD has made himself known, he has executed judgment;
the wicked are snared in the work of their own hands. *Higgaion. Selah*

9.17 Ps 49.14; 50.22

17 The wicked shall depart to Sheol,
all the nations that forget God.

9.18 Ps 62.5; 71.5

18 For the needy shall not always be forgotten,
nor the hope of the poor perish forever.

19 Rise up, O LORD! Do not let mortals prevail;
let the nations be judged before you.

9.20 Ps 62.9 83.17,18

20 Put them in fear, O LORD;
let the nations know that they are only human. *Selah*

9.10 God will never forsake those who seek and trust him. To forsake someone is to abandon that person. God's promise does not mean that if we trust in him we will escape loss or suffering; it means that God himself will never leave us no matter what we face.

9.11 God does not live only in Zion (another name for Mount Moriah, the hill on which the temple was built); he is everywhere all the time. The focal point of Israelite worship, however, came to be Jerusalem and its beautiful temple. God was present in the tabernacle (Exodus 25.8, 9) and in the temple built by Solomon (2 Chronicles 7.16). From this central place of worship, the Jews were to tell the world about the one true God.

9.13, 14 All of us want God to help us when we are in trouble, but often for different reasons. Some want God's help so that they will be successful and other people will like them. Others want God's help so that they will be comfortable and feel good about themselves. David, however, wanted help from God so that justice would be restored to Israel and so that he could show others God's power. When you call to God for help, consider your motive. Is it to save yourself pain and embarrassment or to bring God glory and honor?

9.15, 16 For more on the boomerang effect of evil, see the note on 7.14–16.

9.16 *Higgaion* is a musical direction and probably means to use the quieter instruments.

9.18 The world may ignore the plight of the needy, crushing any earthly hope they may have. But God, the champion of the weak and needy, promises that this will not be the case forever. The wicked nations who forget the Lord and refuse to help their people will be judged by God. He knows our needs, he knows our tendency to despair, and he has promised to care for us (see also 9.9, 12). Even when others forget us, he will remember.

Theme: Why do the wicked succeed? Although God may seem to be hidden at times, we can be assured that he is aware of every injustice.
Author: Anonymous, but probably David. Many ancient manuscripts combine Psalms 9 and 10, and Psalm 9 was written by David.

PSALM 10

1 Why, O LORD, do you stand far off?
Why do you hide yourself in times of trouble?
2 In arrogance the wicked persecute the poor—
let them be caught in the schemes they have devised.

3 For the wicked boast of the desires of their heart,
those greedy for gain curse and renounce the LORD.
4 In the pride of their countenance the wicked say,
"God will not seek it out";
all their thoughts are, "There is no God."

5 Their ways prosper at all times;
your judgments are on high, out of their sight;
as for their foes, they scoff at them.
6 They think in their heart, "We shall not be moved;
throughout all generations we shall not meet adversity."

7 Their mouths are filled with cursing and deceit and oppression;
under their tongues are mischief and iniquity.
8 They sit in ambush in the villages;
in hiding places they murder the innocent.

Their eyes stealthily watch for the helpless;
9 they lurk in secret like a lion in its covert;
they lurk that they may seize the poor;
they seize the poor and drag them off in their net.

10 They stoop, they crouch,
and the helpless fall by their might.
11 They think in their heart, "God has forgotten,
he has hidden his face, he will never see it."

12 Rise up, O LORD; O God, lift up your hand;
do not forget the oppressed.
13 Why do the wicked renounce God,
and say in their hearts, "You will not call us to account"?

10.1 Ps 13.1; 22.1
10.2 Ps 7.15; 9.16 73.6,8
10.3 Ps 49.6; 94.3,4
10.4 Ps 14.1; 36.1,2
10.5 Ps 28.5; 52.7
10.6 Ps 30.6,7
10.7 Ps 59.12; 73.8 140.3 Rom 3.14
10.8 Ps 11.2; 94.6,7
10.9 Ps 17.12; 59.3
10.11 Ps 10.4
10.12 Ps 9.12; 17.7

10.1 To the psalmist, God seemed far away. "Why do you hide yourself in times of trouble?" he asked God. But even though he had honest doubts, he did not stop praying or conclude that God no longer cared. He was not complaining, but simply asking God to hurry to his aid. It is during those times when we feel most alone or oppressed that we need to keep praying, telling God about our troubles.

10.4–6 Some people succeed in everything they do, and they brag that no one, not even God, can keep them down. We may wonder why God allows these people to amass great wealth while they despise him as they do. But why are we upset when the wicked prosper? Are we angry about the damage they are doing, or just jealous of their success? To answer these questions we must gain the right perspective on wickedness and wealth. The wicked will surely be punished (10.5) because God hates their evil deeds (7.11). Wealth is only temporary. It is not always a sign of God's approval on a person's life; nor is lack of it always a sign of God's disapproval. Don't let wealth or lack of it become your obsession. See Proverbs 30.7, 8 for a prayer you can pray.

10.11 There is an incompatibility between blind arrogance and the presence of God in our hearts. The proud person depends on himself rather than on God. This causes God's guiding influences to leave his life. When God's presence is welcome, there is no room for pride, because he makes us aware of our true selves.

10.12–18 This is the victim's prayer. When evil people are predators and we are their prey, we must remember to trust God for our help. God calls all people to account for their attitudes, so be sure your heart is right toward him.

10.14 God sees and takes note of each evil deed, hears our cries, and comforts our hearts (10.17). His presence is always with us.

10.14 Ps 9.12 22.9-11; 37.5

14 But you do see! Indeed you note trouble and grief,
that you may take it into your hands;
the helpless commit themselves to you;
you have been the helper of the orphan.

10.15 Ps 37.17 140.11

15 Break the arm of the wicked and evildoers;
seek out their wickedness until you find none.

10.16 Ps 29.10

16 The LORD is king forever and ever;
the nations shall perish from his land.

10.17 Ps 9.18; 34.15

17 O LORD, you will hear the desire of the meek;
you will strengthen their heart, you will incline your ear

10.18 Ps 9.9; 74.21 146.9

18 to do justice for the orphan and the oppressed,
so that those from earth may strike terror no more.[i]

Theme: God's rule provides stability in the midst of panic. Because we can trust him, we can face our problems.
Author: David

PSALM 11

To the leader. Of David.

11.1 Ps 56.10,11

1 In the LORD I take refuge; how can you say to me,
"Flee like a bird to the mountains;[j]

11.2 Ps 7.12; 64.3,4

2 for look, the wicked bend the bow,
they have fitted their arrow to the string,
to shoot in the dark at the upright in heart.

11.3 Ps 82.5

3 If the foundations are destroyed,
what can the righteous do?"

11.4 Ps 34.15,16

4 The LORD is in his holy temple;
the LORD's throne is in heaven.
His eyes behold, his gaze examines humankind.

11.5 Ps 5.5; 34.19

5 The LORD tests the righteous and the wicked,
and his soul hates the lover of violence.
6 On the wicked he will rain coals of fire and sulfur;
a scorching wind shall be the portion of their cup.

11.7 Ps 7.9-11

7 For the LORD is righteous;
he loves righteous deeds;
the upright shall behold his face.

[i] Meaning of Heb uncertain [j] Gk Syr Jerome Tg: Heb *flee to your mountain, O bird*

We can face the wicked because we do not face them alone. God is by our side.

11.1–4 David was forced to flee for safety several times. Being God's anointed king did not make him immune to injustice and hatred from others. This psalm may have been written when he was being hunted by Saul (1 Samuel 18 – 31) or during the days of Absalom's rebellion (2 Samuel 15 – 18). In both instances, David fled, but not as if all was lost. He knew God was in control. While David wisely avoided trouble, he did not fearfully run away from his troubles.

11.1–4 David's faith contrasted dramatically with the fear of his advisers. Faith in God keeps us from losing hope and helps us resist fear. David's advisers were afraid because they saw only frightening circumstances and crumbling foundations. David was comforted and optimistic because he knew God was greater than anything his enemies could bring against him (7.10; 16.1; 31.2, 3).

11.4 When law and order collapse and you wish you could hide, remember that God is still in control. His power is not diminished by any turn of events. Nothing happens without his knowledge and permission. When you feel like running away – run to God. He will restore justice and goodness on the earth in his good time.

11.5 God does not preserve believers from difficult circumstances, but he tests both the righteous and the wicked. For some, God's tests become a refining fire, while for others, they become an incinerator for destruction. Don't ignore or defy the tests and challenges that come your way. Use them as opportunities for you to grow.

Theme: The proud and lying words of men versus the true and pure words of God. A call for protection against those who try to manipulate us.
Author: David

PSALM 12

To the leader: according to The Sheminith. A Psalm of David.

1 Help, O LORD, for there is no longer anyone who is godly;
the faithful have disappeared from humankind.
2 They utter lies to each other;
with flattering lips and a double heart they speak. **12.2** Ps 28.3; 41.6

3 May the LORD cut off all flattering lips,
the tongue that makes great boasts, **12.3** Ps 73.8,9
4 those who say, "With our tongues we will prevail;
our lips are our own—who is our master?"

5 "Because the poor are despoiled, because the needy groan, **12.5** Ps 3.7; 9.9 34.6; 35.10
I will now rise up," says the LORD;
"I will place them in the safety for which they long."
6 The promises of the LORD are promises that are pure, **12.6** Ps 19.8-10 119.140
silver refined in a furnace on the ground,
purified seven times.

7 You, O LORD, will protect us;
you will guard us from this generation forever. **12.7** Ps 37.28; 97.10
8 On every side the wicked prowl, **12.8** Ps 55.10,11
as vileness is exalted among humankind.

Theme: Praying for relief from despair. We must continue to trust God even when he doesn't answer us immediately.
Author: David

PSALM 13

To the leader. A Psalm of David.

1 How long, O LORD? Will you forget me forever?
How long will you hide your face from me? **13.1** Ps 44.24; 89.46
2 How long must I bear pain[k] in my soul, **13.2** Ps 42.4,5,9
and have sorrow in my heart all day long?
How long shall my enemy be exalted over me?

3 Consider and answer me, O LORD my God!
Give light to my eyes, or I will sleep the sleep of death,

[k] Syr: Heb *hold counsels*

12.1 Living for God in a deceitful world can be a difficult and lonely battle. At one time the great prophet Elijah felt so lonely he wanted to die. But God told him that there were 7,000 other faithful servants (1 Kings 19.4, 14, 18). We are never alone in our battle against evil. When you feel alone, seek out other believers for strength and support.

12.2–4 We may be tempted to believe that lies are relatively harmless, even useful at times. But God does not overlook deceit, flattery, and boasting. Each of these sins originates from a bad attitude that is eventually expressed in our speech. The tongue can be our greatest enemy because, though small, it can do great damage (James 3.5). Be careful how you use yours.

12.5 God cares for the poor and needy. Here he promises to protect the downtrodden and confront their oppressors. We should identify with God's attitude. His work is not done until we care for the needs of the poor.

12.6 Sincerity and truth are extremely valuable because they are so rare. Many people are deceivers, liars, flatterers; they think they will get what they want by deception. As a king, David certainly faced his share of such people, who hoped to win his favor and gain advancement through flattery. When we feel as though sincerity and truth have nearly gone out of existence, we have one hope—the word of God. God's words are as pure as refined silver. So listen carefully when he speaks.

13.1 Sometimes all we need to do is talk over a problem with a friend to help put it in perspective. In this psalm, the phrase "how long" occurs four times in the first two verses, indicating the depth of David's distress. David expressed his feelings to God and found strength. By the end of his prayer, he was able to express hope and trust in God. Through prayer we can express our feelings and talk our problems out with God. He helps us regain the right perspective, and this gives us peace (Habakkuk 3.17–19).

13.4
Ps 25.2; 38.16

4 and my enemy will say, "I have prevailed";
my foes will rejoice because I am shaken.

13.5
Ps 52.8

5 But I trusted in your steadfast love;
my heart shall rejoice in your salvation.
6 I will sing to the LORD,
because he has dealt bountifully with me.

Theme: Only the fool denies God. How foolish it must seem to God when people say there is no God.
Author: David

PSALM 14

To the leader. Of David.

14.1
Ps 10.4; 53.1
Rom 3.10-12

1 Fools say in their hearts, "There is no God."
They are corrupt, they do abominable deeds;
there is no one who does good.

14.2
Ps 33.13-15
102.19

2 The LORD looks down from heaven on humankind
to see if there are any who are wise,
who seek after God.

TROUBLES AND COMPLAINTS IN PSALMS We can relate to the psalms because they express our feelings. We all face troubles, as did the psalm writers hundreds of years ago, and we often respond as they did. In Psalm 3, David told God how he felt about the odds against him. But within three verses, the king realized that God's presence and care made the odds meaningless. This experience is repeated in many of the psalms. Usually, the hope and confidence in God outweigh the fear and suffering; sometimes they do not. Still, the psalm writers consistently poured out their thoughts and emotions to God. When they felt abandoned by God, they told him so. When they were impatient with how slowly God seemed to be answering their prayers, they also told him so. Because they recognized the difference between themselves and God, they were free to be men and to be honest with their Creator. That is why so many of the dark psalms end in the light. The psalmists started by expressing their feelings and ended up remembering to whom they were speaking!

Although we have much in common with the psalmists, we may differ in two ways: we might not tell God what we are really thinking and feeling; and therefore we also might not recognize, even faintly, who is listening to our prayers!

Notice this pattern as you read Psalms, and put the psalmists' insight to the test. You may well find that your awareness and appreciation of God will grow as you are honest with him. (See Psalms 3; 6; 13; 31; 37; 64; 77; 102; 121; 142.)

13.5 David frequently claimed that God was slow to act on his behalf. We often feel this same impatience. It seems that evil and suffering go unchecked, and we wonder when God is going to stop them. David affirmed that he would continue to trust God no matter how long he had to wait for God's justice to be realized. When you feel impatient, remember David's steadfast faith in God's unfailing mercy.

13.5, 6 David was a faithful man, but he felt the pressure of his problems as much as anyone. His response to pressure, however, stands in stark contrast to that of the people described in Psalm 11, who wanted to give up. David held on to his faith. In times of despair, it is much harder to hold on than to give up. But if you give up on God, you give in to a life of despair.

14.1–3 A fool is not someone who is stupid or uneducated, but a person who rejects God. By rejecting God, the fool rejects the one who made the moral and spiritual laws that make life just and good. A fool is indeed corrupt, because to deny God's existence allows wickedness to prevail. The apostle Paul quotes these verses in Romans 3.10–12 as he mourns the lack of singleheartedness toward God and thus the rampant spread of evil. The wise, however, not only believe there is a God, but also strive to please him. To believe there is a God but refuse to please him is also foolish. Don't be a fool of either sort.

14.1–3 The true atheist is either foolish or wicked—foolish because he ignores the evidence that God exists, or wicked because he refuses to live by God's truths. We become atheists in practice when we rely more on ourselves than on God. The fool mentioned here is someone who is aggressively perverse in his actions. To speak in direct defiance of God is utterly foolish according to the Bible.

3 They have all gone astray, they are all alike perverse;
there is no one who does good,
no, not one.

14.3
Ps 58.3; 143.2

4 Have they no knowledge, all the evildoers
who eat up my people as they eat bread,
and do not call upon the LORD?

5 There they shall be in great terror,
for God is with the company of the righteous.
6 You would confound the plans of the poor,
but the LORD is their refuge.

14.6
Ps 9.9; 40.17

7 O that deliverance for Israel would come from Zion!
When the LORD restores the fortunes of his people,
Jacob will rejoice; Israel will be glad.

14.7
Ps 53.6; 85.1,2
Job 42.10

Theme: Guidelines for living a blameless life.
Author: David

PSALM 15

A Psalm of David.

1 O LORD, who may abide in your tent?
Who may dwell on your holy hill?

15.1
Ps 24.3; 27.5,6

2 Those who walk blamelessly, and do what is right,
and speak the truth from their heart;
3 who do not slander with their tongue,
and do no evil to their friends,
nor take up a reproach against their neighbors;
4 in whose eyes the wicked are despised,
but who honor those who fear the LORD;
who stand by their oath even to their hurt;
5 who do not lend money at interest,

15.2
Ps 24.4

15.3
Ps 28.3

15.5
Ex 22.25; 23.8

14.3 No one but God is perfect; all of us stand guilty before him (see Romans 3.23) and need his forgiveness. No matter how well we perform or what we achieve compared to others, none of us can boast of his or her goodness when compared to God's standard. God not only expects us to obey his guidelines, but he wants us to love him with all our heart. No one except Jesus Christ has done that perfectly. Since we all fall short we must turn to Christ to save us (Romans 10.9–11).

14.3, 4 David applies these observations to his enemies, the godless and fierce people who "eat up my people as they eat bread": "They have all gone astray . . . ; there is no one who does good." By contrast, David said, "If you try my heart, . . . you will find no wickedness in me" (17.3).

There is a clear distinction between those who worship God and those who refuse to worship him. David worshiped God, and under his leadership Israel obeyed God and prospered. Several hundred years later, however, Israel had forgotten God. It was difficult to distinguish between God's followers and those who worshiped idols. When Isaiah called Israel to repentance, he, like David, spoke of people who had strayed away (Isaiah 53.6). But Isaiah was talking about the Israelites themselves. Paul quoted Psalm 14 in Romans 3.10–12. He made the image of straying sheep even more general. The whole human race – Jew and Gentile alike – has strayed from God.

14.5 If God is "with the company of the righteous," then those who attack God's followers may be attacking God. To attack God is utterly futile (see 2.4, 5, 10–12). Thus, while we may feel we are losing the battle, there can be absolutely no doubt that our ultimate victory is in God.

15.1 *Tent* and *holy hill* are interchangeable words describing the focal point of Israelite worship – the dwelling place of God. In Hebrew poetry the repeating pattern is found more in the thought than in the sound or rhythm.

15.1ff God calls his people to be morally upright and, in this psalm, gives us ten standards to determine how we are doing. We live among evil people whose standards and morals are eroding. Our standards for living do not come from our evil society, but from God. Other standards for conduct are found in Isaiah 33.15; 56.1; Micah 6.8; Habakkuk 2.4; and Mark 12.29–31.

15.3, 4 Words are powerful, and how you use them reflects on your relationship with God. Perhaps nothing so identifies Christians as their ability to control their speech – refusing to slander, ignoring gossip, speaking out against sin, and guiding the faithful. Watch out for what you say. (See James 3.1–12 for more on the importance of controlling your tongue.)

15.5 God was against the Jews' charging interest or making a profit on loans to needy fellow Jews (see also Exodus 22.25; Leviticus 25.35–37), although charging interest on loans to foreigners was allowed (Deuteronomy 23.20). Interest was also allowable for business purposes, as long as it wasn't excessive (Proverbs 28.8).

15.5 Some people are so obsessed with money that they will change their God-given standards and life-style to get it. If money

and do not take a bribe against the innocent.

Those who do these things shall never be moved.

Theme: The joys and benefits of a life lived in companionship with God. We enjoy these benefits now and eternally.
Author: David

PSALM 16

A Miktam of David.

16.1 Ps 7.1; 17.8

1 Protect me, O God, for in you I take refuge.
2 I say to the LORD, "You are my Lord;
I have no good apart from you."[l]

16.3 Ps 101.6 119.63

3 As for the holy ones in the land, they are the noble,
in whom is all my delight.

16.4 Ps 32.10 106.37,38

4 Those who choose another god multiply their sorrows;[m]
their drink offerings of blood I will not pour out
or take their names upon my lips.

5 The LORD is my chosen portion and my cup;
you hold my lot.

16.6 Ps 78.55

6 The boundary lines have fallen for me in pleasant places;
I have a goodly heritage.

16.7 Ps 73.24; 77.6

7 I bless the LORD who gives me counsel;
in the night also my heart instructs me.

16.8 Ps 27.8; 73.23 110.5; 123.1,2

8 I keep the LORD always before me;
because he is at my right hand, I shall not be moved.

9 Therefore my heart is glad, and my soul rejoices;
my body also rests secure.

16.10 Ps 49.15; 86.13 Acts 2.27; 13.35

10 For you do not give me up to Sheol,

l Jerome Tg: Meaning of Heb uncertain m Cn: Meaning of Heb uncertain

---

is a controlling force in your life, it must be curbed, or it will harm others and destroy your relationship with God.

15.5 As we grow in our relationship with our Redeemer, we develop a desire to live by his standards. The depth of our eternal relationship with him can often be measured by the way we reflect his standards in our daily activities.

16.1 *Miktam* comes from a term that may mean "to cover." It could mean a covering of the lips, a silent prayer, or a prayer to be covered (a plea for protection).

16.3 At one time or another, we have tried to impress friends by "name-dropping." If we have personally known a famous person, for example, we may casually mention this fact to others. True saints are not necessarily famous, but they live as God desires. Seek the company of those who can build you up spiritually, those who are committed to God and have the right perspective on life.

16.7, 8 It is human nature to make our own plans and *then* ask God to bless them. Instead, we should seek God's will first. By constantly thinking about the Lord and his way of living, we will gain insights that will help us make right decisions and live the way God desires. By communicating with him, we allow him to counsel us and give us wisdom.

16.8 God does not exempt believers from the day-to-day circumstances of life. Believers and unbelievers alike experience pain, trouble, and failure at times (Matthew 5.45). David was talking about the unique sense of security felt by believers. Unbelievers have a sense of hopelessness about life and confusion over their true purpose on earth. Those who seek after God, however, can move ahead confidently with what they know is right and important in God's eyes. They know that God will keep them from being moved off of his chosen path.

16.8–11 This psalm is often called a messianic psalm because it is quoted in the New Testament as referring to the resurrection of Jesus Christ. Both Peter and Paul quoted from this psalm when speaking of Christ's bodily resurrection (see Acts 2.25–28, 31; 13.35–37).

16.9 David found the secret to joy. True joy is far deeper than happiness; we can feel joy even in spite of our deepest troubles. Happiness is temporary because it is based on external circumstances, but joy is lasting because it is based on God's presence within us. As we contemplate his daily presence, we will find contentment. As we understand the future he has for us, we can experience joy.

16.10 David stated confidently that God would not leave him in "Sheol" or the grave. Many people fear death because they can neither control nor understand it. As believers, we can be assured that God will not forget us when we die. He will bring us to life again to live with him forever. This provides *real* security. For other passages about resurrection, see Job 19.25, 26; Isaiah 26.19; Daniel 12.2, 13; Mark 13.27; 1 Corinthians 15.12–58; 1 Thessalonians 4.13–18; Revelation 20.11 – 21.4.

or let your faithful one see the Pit.

11 You show me the path of life.
In your presence there is fullness of joy;
in your right hand are pleasures forevermore.

Theme: A plea for justice in the face of false accusations and persecution. David urges us to realize the true goal of life — to know God — and the true reward of life — to see God one day.
Author: David, written while he was being persecuted by Saul

PSALM 17

A Prayer of David.

1 Hear a just cause, O LORD; attend to my cry;
give ear to my prayer from lips free of deceit.
2 From you let my vindication come;
let your eyes see the right.

3 If you try my heart, if you visit me by night,
if you test me, you will find no wickedness in me;
my mouth does not transgress.
4 As for what others do, by the word of your lips
I have avoided the ways of the violent.
5 My steps have held fast to your paths;
my feet have not slipped.

6 I call upon you, for you will answer me, O God;
incline your ear to me, hear my words.
7 Wondrously show your steadfast love,
O savior of those who seek refuge
from their adversaries at your right hand.

8 Guard me as the apple of the eye;
hide me in the shadow of your wings,
9 from the wicked who despoil me,
my deadly enemies who surround me.
10 They close their hearts to pity;
with their mouths they speak arrogantly.
11 They track me down;[n] now they surround me;
they set their eyes to cast me to the ground.
12 They are like a lion eager to tear,
like a young lion lurking in ambush.

13 Rise up, O LORD, confront them, overthrow them!
By your sword deliver my life from the wicked,

17.1 Ps 61.1; 88.2 142.6
17.2 Ps 98.8,9 99.4; 103.6
17.3 Ps 26.1,2
17.4 Ps 10.5-11 119.9,101
17.5 Ps 18.36 37.30,31; 44.18
17.8 Deut 32.10 Ruth 2.12 Ps 36.7; 91.1,4
17.10 1 Sam 2.3 Ps 31.18 73.7,8
17.12 Ps 7.2; 10.9
17.13 Ps 22.20; 49.6 73.3-7

n One Ms Compare Syr: MT *Our steps*

17.3 Was David saying he was sinless? David's claim was not a proud assumption of purity; it was an understanding of his relationship with God. In Psalms 32 and 51, David freely acknowledged his own sins. Nevertheless, his relationship with God was one of close fellowship and constant repentance and forgiveness. His claim to goodness, therefore, was based on his continual seeking after God.

17.8 Just as we protect the pupils ("apples") of our eyes, it is right to pray, as David did, for God to protect us. We must not conclude, however, that we have somehow missed God's protection if we experience troubles. God's protection has far greater purposes than helping us avoid pain; it is to make us better servants for him. God also protects us by guiding us through painful circumstances, not only by helping us escape them.

17.8 The "shadow of your wings" is a figure of speech symbolizing God's protection. He guards us just as a mother bird protects her young by covering them with her wings. Moses used this same metaphor in Deuteronomy 32.11.

17.13–15 We deceive ourselves when we measure our happiness or contentment in life by the amount of wealth we possess. When we put riches at the top of our value system, we let their power, pleasure, and security overshadow the eternal value of our relationship with God. We think we will be happy or content when we get riches, only to discover that they don't really satisfy and the pleasures fade away. The true measurement of happiness or contentment is found in God's love and in doing his will. You will find true happiness if you put your relationship with God above earthly riches.

14 from mortals—by your hand, O LORD—
from mortals whose portion in life is in this world.
May their bellies be filled with what you have stored up for them;
may their children have more than enough;
may they leave something over to their little ones.

17.15 Ps 4.6,7 16.11; 140.13

15 As for me, I shall behold your face in righteousness;
when I awake I shall be satisfied, beholding your likeness.

Theme: Gratitude for deliverance and victory. The only sure way to be delivered from surrounding evil is to call upon God for help and strength.
Author: David

PSALM 18

To the leader. A Psalm of David the servant of the LORD, who addressed the words of this song to the LORD on the day when the LORD delivered him from the hand of all his enemies, and from the hand of Saul. He said:

18.1 Ps 59.17
18.2 1 Sam 2.2 Ps 28.1; 19.14 59.9,11; 71.3 75.10; 144.2
18.3 Ps 34.6; 96.4

1 I love you, O LORD, my strength.
2 The LORD is my rock, my fortress, and my deliverer,
my God, my rock in whom I take refuge,
my shield, and the horn of my salvation, my stronghold.
3 I call upon the LORD, who is worthy to be praised,
so I shall be saved from my enemies.

18.4 Ps 69.1,2 116.3; 124.2-5

4 The cords of death encompassed me;
the torrents of perdition assailed me;
5 the cords of Sheol entangled me;
the snares of death confronted me.

18.6 Ps 3.4; 34.15

6 In my distress I called upon the LORD;
to my God I cried for help.
From his temple he heard my voice,
and my cry to him reached his ears.

18.7 Ps 114.4,6,7

7 Then the earth reeled and rocked;
the foundations also of the mountains trembled
and quaked, because he was angry.
8 Smoke went up from his nostrils,
and devouring fire from his mouth;
glowing coals flamed forth from him.

18.9 Ex 20.21 Ps 97.2; 144.5
18.10 Ps 80.1; 99.1

9 He bowed the heavens, and came down;
thick darkness was under his feet.
10 He rode on a cherub, and flew;
he came swiftly upon the wings of the wind.
11 He made darkness his covering around him,

17.15 The word *awake* shows that David believed in life after death. Although belief in resurrection was not widespread in Old Testament times, several verses show that it was partially understood. Some of these are Job 19.25–27; Psalms 49.15; 139.17, 18; Isaiah 26.19; and Daniel 12.2, 13.

18.1ff This psalm is almost a duplicate of 2 Samuel 22. It may have been written toward the end of David's life when there was peace. God is praised for his glorious works and blessings through the years.

18.2, 3 God's protection of his people is limitless and can take many forms. David characterized God's care with five military symbols. God is like (1) a *rock* that can't be penetrated by any who would harm us, (2) a *fortress* or place of safety where the enemy can't follow, (3) a *shield* that comes between us and harm, (4) a *horn* of salvation, a symbol of might and power, (5) a *stronghold* high above our enemies. If you need protection, look to God.

18.5 *Sheol* is the word in the Old Testament for the realm of the dead. It is used to mean the grave, the underworld, or death.

18.10 A cherub is a divine being belonging to one of the ranks of angels. One of the functions of the cherubim was to serve as guardians. These mighty angels guarded the entrances to both the tree of life (Genesis 3.24) and the most holy place (Exodus 26.31–33). Two cherubim of beaten gold were part of the ark of the covenant (Exodus 25.18–22). The living creatures carrying God's throne in Ezekiel 1 may have been cherubim.

his canopy thick clouds dark with water.
12 Out of the brightness before him
there broke through his clouds
hailstones and coals of fire.
13 The LORD also thundered in the heavens,
and the Most High uttered his voice.[o]
14 And he sent out his arrows, and scattered them;
he flashed forth lightnings, and routed them.
15 Then the channels of the sea were seen,
and the foundations of the world were laid bare
at your rebuke, O LORD,
at the blast of the breath of your nostrils.

16 He reached down from on high, he took me;
he drew me out of mighty waters.
17 He delivered me from my strong enemy,
and from those who hated me;
for they were too mighty for me.
18 They confronted me in the day of my calamity;
but the LORD was my support.
19 He brought me out into a broad place;
he delivered me, because he delighted in me.

20 The LORD rewarded me according to my righteousness;
according to the cleanness of my hands he recompensed me.
21 For I have kept the ways of the LORD,
and have not wickedly departed from my God.
22 For all his ordinances were before me,
and his statutes I did not put away from me.
23 I was blameless before him,
and I kept myself from guilt.
24 Therefore the LORD has recompensed me according to my righteousness,
according to the cleanness of my hands in his sight.

25 With the loyal you show yourself loyal;
with the blameless you show yourself blameless;
26 with the pure you show yourself pure;
and with the crooked you show yourself perverse.
27 For you deliver a humble people,
but the haughty eyes you bring down.
28 It is you who light my lamp;
the LORD, my God, lights up my darkness.
29 By you I can crush a troop,
and by my God I can leap over a wall.
30 This God—his way is perfect;

18.12 Ps 104.1,2
18.13 Ps 29.3 104.7,8
18.14 Judg 4.15 Ps 144.6
18.15 Ex 15.8 Ps 106.9
18.18 Ps 16.8; 59.16
18.19 Ps 31.8; 37.23 41.1,11; 118.5
18.20 Ps 7.8; 24.4
18.21 Ps 37.34 119.33,102,103
18.25 Ps 62.12
18.27 Ps 72.12; 101.5 Prov 6.16-19
18.28 Ps 27.1
18.29 Ps 118.10-12 2 Cor 12.9
18.30 Ps 12.6; 19.7

[o] Gk See 2 Sam 22.14: Heb adds *hailstones and coals of fire*

18.13 "The Most High" was an important designation for David to make. Heathen idol worship was deeply rooted in the land, and each region had its own deity. But these images of wood and stone were powerless. David was placing the Lord alone in a superior category: he is by far the Highest.

18.16 Our troubles, like "mighty waters," threaten to drown us. David, helpless and weak, knew that God alone had rescued him from his enemies when he was defenseless. How often we wish God would quickly rescue us out of our troubles. Remember that God can either deliver us or help us remain steady as we go through troubles (18.18). Either way, his protection is best for us. When you feel drowned by troubles, ask God to help you, hold you steady, and protect you. In his care, you are never helpless.

18.30 Some people think that belief in God is a crutch for weak people who cannot make it on their own. God is indeed a shield to protect us when we are too weak to face certain trials by ourselves, but he does not want us to remain weak. He strengthens, protects, and guides us in order to send us back into an evil world to fight for him. And then he continues to work with us, because the strongest person on earth is infinitely weaker than God and needs his help. David was not a coward; he was a mighty warrior who, with all his armies and weapons, knew that only God could ultimately protect and save him.

the promise of the LORD proves true;
he is a shield for all who take refuge in him.

18.31 Deut 32.31,39 Ps 62.2; 86.8-10

31 For who is God except the LORD?
And who is a rock besides our God?—
32 the God who girded me with strength,
and made my way safe.

18.33 Hab 3.19

33 He made my feet like the feet of a deer,
and set me secure on the heights.
34 He trains my hands for war,
so that my arms can bend a bow of bronze.

18.35 Ps 33.20; 63.8 119.117

35 You have given me the shield of your salvation,
and your right hand has supported me;
your help[p] has made me great.

18.36 Ps 31.8; 66.9

36 You gave me a wide place for my steps under me,
and my feet did not slip.

18.37 Ps 44.5

37 I pursued my enemies and overtook them;
and did not turn back until they were consumed.

18.38 Ps 36.12; 47.3

38 I struck them down, so that they were not able to rise;
they fell under my feet.
39 For you girded me with strength for the battle;
you made my assailants sink under me.

18.40 Ps 94.23; 21.12

40 You made my enemies turn their backs to me,
and those who hated me I destroyed.

18.41 Ps 50.22

41 They cried for help, but there was no one to save them;
they cried to the LORD, but he did not answer them.
42 I beat them fine, like dust before the wind;
I cast them out like the mire of the streets.

18.43 2 Sam 3.1 Ps 89.27 Isa 55.5 Mic 7.17

43 You delivered me from strife with the peoples;[q]
you made me head of the nations;
people whom I had not known served me.
44 As soon as they heard of me they obeyed me;
foreigners came cringing to me.
45 Foreigners lost heart,
and came trembling out of their strongholds.

46 The LORD lives! Blessed be my rock,
and exalted be the God of my salvation,

18.47 Ps 47.3 94.1,2; 144.2

47 the God who gave me vengeance
and subdued peoples under me;

18.48 Ps 3.7; 27.5,6

48 who delivered me from my enemies;

p Or *gentleness* q Gk Tg: Heb *people*

18.32–34 God promises to give us strength to meet challenges, but he doesn't promise to eliminate them. If he gave us no rough roads to walk, no mountains to climb, and no battles to fight, we would not grow. He does not leave us alone with our challenges, however. Instead he stands beside us, teaches us, and strengthens us to face them.

18.35 David offers an interesting twist to the concept of greatness, saying that God's help or gentleness has made him great. Our society believes that greatness is attained through a combination of opportunity, talent, and aggressiveness. But true greatness comes from living according to God's laws and standards and recognizing that all we have comes not from our own ability and effort, but from the gentleness of God's mercy. Are you seeking his kind of greatness?

18.40–42 David was a merciful man. He spared the lives of Saul (1 Samuel 24.1–8), Nabal (1 Samuel 25.21–35), and Shimei (2 Samuel 16.5–12) and showed great kindness to Mephibosheth (2 Samuel 9). In asking God to destroy his enemies, David was simply asking him to give the wicked the punishment they deserved.

18.43–45 David's great power had become legendary. God gave him victory in every battle. The book of 2 Samuel records victories over the Jebusites (5.6–10), the Philistines (5.17–25; 8.1, 2), Hadadezer of Zobah (8.3, 4), the Syrians (8.5, 6; 10), the Edomites (8.13, 14), and the Ammonites (12.26–31). In addition, the king of Tyre sent supplies and workmen to help David build his palace (5.11). But David did not attribute his victories to himself. He fully realized that the purpose of his position was to bless God's people (1 Chronicles 14.2).

indeed, you exalted me above my adversaries;
you delivered me from the violent.

49 For this I will extol you, O LORD, among the nations,
and sing praises to your name.
50 Great triumphs he gives to his king,
and shows steadfast love to his anointed,
to David and his descendants forever.

18.49 Ps 108.1 Rom 15.9
18.50 Ps 21.1; 28.8 89.4

Theme: Both God's creation and his Word reveal his greatness.
Author: David

PSALM 19

To the leader. A Psalm of David.

1 The heavens are telling the glory of God;
and the firmament[r] proclaims his handiwork.
2 Day to day pours forth speech,
and night to night declares knowledge.
3 There is no speech, nor are there words;
their voice is not heard;
4 yet their voice[s] goes out through all the earth,
and their words to the end of the world.

In the heavens[t] he has set a tent for the sun,
5 which comes out like a bridegroom from his wedding canopy,
and like a strong man runs its course with joy.
6 Its rising is from the end of the heavens,
and its circuit to the end of them;
and nothing is hid from its heat.

7 The law of the LORD is perfect,
reviving the soul;
the decrees of the LORD are sure,
making wise the simple;
8 the precepts of the LORD are right,
rejoicing the heart;
the commandment of the LORD is clear,
enlightening the eyes;
9 the fear of the LORD is pure,
enduring forever;
the ordinances of the LORD are true
and righteous altogether.

19.1 Gen 1.6-8 Rom 1.20
19.2 Ps 74.16
19.6 Ps 113.3
19.7 Ps 36.9
19.9 Ps 119.138,142

[r] Or *dome* [s] Gk Jerome Compare Syr: Heb *line* [t] Heb *In them*

19.1ff David's steps of meditation take him from creation, through God's Word, through his own sinfulness, to salvation. As God reveals himself through nature (19.1–6), we learn about his power and our finiteness. As God reveals himself through Scripture (19.7–11), we learn about his holiness and our sinfulness. As God reveals himself through daily experiences (19.12–14), we learn about his gracious forgiveness and our salvation.

19.1–6 We are surrounded by fantastic displays of God's craftsmanship—the heavens give dramatic evidence of his existence, his power, his love, his care. To say that the universe happened by chance is absurd. Its design, intricacy, and orderliness point to a personally involved Creator. As you look at God's craftsmanship in nature and the heavens, thank him for such magnificent beauty and the truth it reveals about the Creator.

19.3, 4 The apostle Paul referred to this psalm when he explained that everyone knows about God because nature proclaims his existence and power (Romans 1.19, 20). This does not cancel the need for missions, because the message of God's salvation found in his Word, the Bible, must still be told to the ends of the earth. While nature points to the existence of God, the Bible tells us about salvation. God's people must explain to others how they can have a relationship with God. Although people everywhere should already believe in a Creator by just looking at the evidence of nature around them, God needs us to explain his love, mercy, and grace.

19.7–11 When we think of the law, we often think of something that keeps us from having fun. But here we see the opposite—law that revives us, makes us wise, rejoices the heart, enlightens the eyes, warns us, and rewards us. That's because God's laws are guidelines and lights on our path, rather than chains on our hands and feet. They point at danger and warn us, then point at success and guide us.

19.10
Ps 119.127

10 More to be desired are they than gold,
even much fine gold;
sweeter also than honey,
and drippings of the honeycomb.

19.11
Ps 17.4

11 Moreover by them is your servant warned;
in keeping them there is great reward.

19.12
Ps 51.1,2

12 But who can detect their errors?
Clear me from hidden faults.

19.13
Ps 25.11; 32.2

13 Keep back your servant also from the insolent;[u]
do not let them have dominion over me.
Then I shall be blameless,
and innocent of great transgression.

14 Let the words of my mouth and the meditation of my heart
be acceptable to you,
O LORD, my rock and my redeemer.

Theme: A prayer for victory in battle. Such a prayer can help us prepare for any great challenge. David knew that trust should be placed in the Lord more than in human power.
Author: David. The events in 2 Samuel 10 may have prompted this prayer.

PSALM 20

To the leader. A Psalm of David.

20.1
Ps 46.7,11

1 The LORD answer you in the day of trouble!
The name of the God of Jacob protect you!

20.2
Ps 3.4; 110.2
119.28

2 May he send you help from the sanctuary,
and give you support from Zion.

20.3
Ps 51.19
Acts 10.4

3 May he remember all your offerings,
and regard with favor your burnt sacrifices. *Selah*

20.4
1 Sam 1.17
Ps 21.2; 145.19

4 May he grant you your heart's desire,
and fulfill all your plans.

20.5
Ps 9.14; 60.4

5 May we shout for joy over your victory,
and in the name of our God set up our banners.
May the LORD fulfill all your petitions.

6 Now I know that the LORD will help his anointed;
he will answer him from his holy heaven
with mighty victories by his right hand.

20.7
Ps 33.16,17

7 Some take pride in chariots, and some in horses,
but our pride is in the name of the LORD our God.

8 They will collapse and fall,
but we shall rise and stand upright.

[u] Or *from proud thoughts*

19.12, 13 Guilt plagues many Christians. They worry that they may have committed a sin unknowingly, done something good with selfish intentions, failed to put their whole heart into a task, or neglected what they should have done. Guilt can play an important role in bringing us to Christ and in keeping us behaving properly, but it should not cripple us or make us fearful. God fully and completely forgives us—even for those sins we do unknowingly.

19.14 Would you change the way you live if you knew that every word and thought would be examined by God first? David asks that God approve his words and thoughts as though they were sacrifices brought to the altar. As you begin each day, determine that God's love will guide what you say and how you think.

20.2 Zion, the name of the hill on which Jerusalem was built, is also used as another name for the city itself, where David kept the ark of the covenant and Solomon built the great temple for God. God himself chose Zion to represent his presence upon the earth (132.13).

20.6–8 As long as there have been armies and weapons, nations have boasted of their power, but such power does not last. Throughout history, empires and kingdoms have risen to great power only to vanish in the dust. David, however, knew that the true might of his nation was not in weaponry but in worship; not in fire-power but in God's power. Since God alone can preserve a nation or an individual, be sure your confidence is in God, who gives eternal victory. Whom do you trust?

9 Give victory to the king, O LORD;
answer us when we call.[v]

Theme: Praising God after victory in battle. When God answers our prayers for victory, we must quickly and openly thank him for his help.
Author: David

PSALM 21

To the leader. A Psalm of David.

1 In your strength the king rejoices, O LORD,
and in your help how greatly he exults!
2 You have given him his heart's desire,
and have not withheld the request of his lips. *Selah*
3 For you meet him with rich blessings;
you set a crown of fine gold on his head.
4 He asked you for life; you gave it to him—
length of days forever and ever.
5 His glory is great through your help;
splendor and majesty you bestow on him.
6 You bestow on him blessings forever;
you make him glad with the joy of your presence.
7 For the king trusts in the LORD,
and through the steadfast love of the Most High he shall not be moved.

8 Your hand will find out all your enemies;
your right hand will find out those who hate you.
9 You will make them like a fiery furnace
when you appear.
The LORD will swallow them up in his wrath,
and fire will consume them.
10 You will destroy their offspring from the earth,
and their children from among humankind.
11 If they plan evil against you,
if they devise mischief, they will not succeed.
12 For you will put them to flight;
you will aim at their faces with your bows.

13 Be exalted, O LORD, in your strength!
We will sing and praise your power.

21.1 Ps 59.16,17
21.2 Ps 37.4
21.4 Ps 61.6; 91.16 133.3
21.5 Ps 8.5; 96.6
21.7 Ps 112.6; 125.1
21.9 Ps 37.28 Mal 4.1
21.11 Ps 2.1-3
21.12 Ps 7.12,13 18.40
21.13 Ps 59.16; 81.1

[v] Gk: Heb *give victory, O LORD; let the King answer us when we call*

21.1–6 David described all that he had as gifts from God: his "heart's desire," prosperity, a golden crown, long life, honor and majesty, eternal blessings, gladness. We too must look upon all we have—position, family, wealth, talent—as gifts from God. Only then will we use them to give glory back to him.

21.7 Because David trusted in God, God would not let others remove him from the throne. When we trust in God, we have permanence and stability. We may lose a great deal—families, jobs, material possessions—but we cannot be moved out of God's favor. He will be our foundation of solid rock. He will never leave or desert us.

21.7 A good leader trusts God and depends upon his steadfast love. Too often leaders trust in their own cleverness, popular support, or the "god" of military power. But God is above all these gods. If you aspire to leadership, keep the Lord God at the center of your life and depend on him. His wisdom is the best strength you can have.

21.7 One of life's most prized treasures is security—the sure knowledge that no struggle can shake our foundations. David had struggled with enemy forces and won a great victory, not because he was confident in his own uncertain power, but because he trusted in God's unfailing love.

21.11 When you see people getting away with evil, remember that they will not succeed forever. Their power is only temporary, and God's very presence would send them scattering in a moment. God, according to his plan and purpose, will intervene for his people and give the wicked the judgment they deserve. We should not be dismayed when we see the temporary advantage God's enemies have.

Theme: A prayer that carries us from great suffering to great joy. Despite apparent rejection by his friends and God, David believed that God would lead him out of despair. He looked forward to that future day when God would rule over the entire earth.
Author: David

PSALM 22

To the leader: according to The Deer of the Dawn. A Psalm of David.

22.1 Mt 27.46 Mk 15.34
22.2 Ps 42.3; 88.1

1 My God, my God, why have you forsaken me?
Why are you so far from helping me, from the words of my groaning?
2 O my God, I cry by day, but you do not answer;
and by night, but find no rest.

22.3 Ps 99.9; 78.53 107.6; 148.14

3 Yet you are holy,
enthroned on the praises of Israel.
4 In you our ancestors trusted;
they trusted, and you delivered them.
5 To you they cried, and were saved;
in you they trusted, and were not put to shame.

CHRIST IN THE PSALMS

Both the Jewish and Christian faiths have long believed that many psalms referred as much to the promised Messiah as they did to events at the time. Because the Messiah was to be a descendant of David, it was expected that many of the royal psalms would apply to him. Christians noted how many of the passages seemed to describe in detail events from Christ's life and death. Jesus himself frequently quoted from Psalms. Almost everything that happened at the crucifixion and most of Jesus' words during his final hours came directly from Psalms.

The following is a list of the main references in Psalms pertaining to Christ.

Reference in Psalms	*Reference to Christ*	*Fulfillment in the New Testament*
2.7	The Messiah will be God's Son	Hebrews 1.5, 6
16.8–10	He will rise from the dead	Luke 24.5–7
22.1–21	He will be crucified	Matthew 26, 27
22.18	Soldiers gamble for his clothing	Matthew 27.35; John 19.23, 24
22.15	He thirsts while on the cross	John 19.28
22.22	He will speak of his Father	Hebrews 2.12
34.20	His bones would not be broken	John 19.36, 37
40.6–8	He came to do God's will	Hebrews 10.5–7
41.9	One close to him would betray him	Luke 22.48
45.6, 7	His kingdom will last forever	Hebrews 1.8, 9
68.18	He ascended into heaven	Ephesians 4.8–10
69.9	He is zealous for God	John 2.17
69.21	He was offered gall and vinegar for his thirst on the cross	Matthew 27.48
89.3, 4, 35, 36	He will be a descendant of David	Luke 1.31–33
96.13	He will return to judge the world	1 Thessalonians 1.10
110.1	He is David's son and God's Son	Matthew 22.44
110.4	He is the eternal priest-king	Hebrews 6.20
118.22	He is rejected by many but accepted by God	1 Peter 2.7, 8

22.1 David gave an amazingly accurate description of the suffering the Messiah would endure hundreds of years later. David was obviously enduring some great trial, but through his suffering he, like the Messiah to come, gained victory. Jesus, the Messiah, quoted this verse while hanging on the cross carrying our burden of sin (Matthew 27.46). It was not a cry of doubt, but an urgent appeal to God.

6 But I am a worm, and not human;
scorned by others, and despised by the people.
7 All who see me mock at me;
they make mouths at me, they shake their heads;
8 "Commit your cause to the LORD; let him deliver—
let him rescue the one in whom he delights!"

9 Yet it was you who took me from the womb;
you kept me safe on my mother's breast.
10 On you I was cast from my birth,
and since my mother bore me you have been my God.
11 Do not be far from me,
for trouble is near
and there is no one to help.

12 Many bulls encircle me,
strong bulls of Bashan surround me;
13 they open wide their mouths at me,
like a ravening and roaring lion.

14 I am poured out like water,
and all my bones are out of joint;
my heart is like wax;
it is melted within my breast;
15 my mouth[w] is dried up like a potsherd,
and my tongue sticks to my jaws;
you lay me in the dust of death.

16 For dogs are all around me;
a company of evildoers encircles me.
My hands and feet have shriveled;[x]
17 I can count all my bones.
They stare and gloat over me;
18 they divide my clothes among themselves,
and for my clothing they cast lots.

19 But you, O LORD, do not be far away!
O my help, come quickly to my aid!
20 Deliver my soul from the sword,
my life[y] from the power of the dog!
21 Save me from the mouth of the lion!

[w] Cn: Heb *strength* [x] Meaning of Heb uncertain [y] Heb *my only one*

22.6 Job 25.6 Ps 31.11 Isa 41.14
22.7 Isa 53.3 Mt 27.39 Mk 15.29,30
22.9 Ps 71.5,6,12 72.12 Isa 46.3; 49.1
22.13 Job 16.10 Ps 17.12
22.15 Ps 38.10 104.29
22.16 Mt 27.35 Jn 20.25
22.18 Lk 23.34 Jn 19.23,24
22.19 Ps 70.5
22.20 Ps 35.17; 37.14
22.21 Ps 34.4; 118.5 120.1

22.6 When others despise us and heap scorn upon us, they treat us as less than human. After much degradation, we, like David, could begin to feel like worms. When we feel the sting of rejection, we must keep in mind the hope and victory God promises us (22.22ff).

22.9–11 God's loving concern does not begin on the day we are born and conclude on the day we die, but reaches back to those days before we were born, and reaches ahead along the unending path of eternity. Our only sure help comes from a God whose concern for us reaches beyond our earthly existence. When faced with such love, how could anyone reject it?

22.12 The land of Bashan, located east of the Sea of Galilee, was known for its strong and fat cattle (Amos 4.1). Because of its grain fields, it was often called the breadbasket of Palestine.

22.15 A potsherd is a pottery fragment or a piece of sun-baked clay.

22.18 It is a great insult to human dignity to rob a person of everything, even his clothing, leaving him naked and destitute. Jesus the Messiah would suffer this humiliating experience on the cross (Matthew 27.35). Most of us will never know the shame and suffering of being penniless and naked in a public place, as many of the Jews did during the Nazi holocaust. But most of us would feel equally exposed and naked when some sin, secret or not-so-secret, would be uncovered. At that time, we will need to cry out with the psalmist, "O my help, come quickly to my aid!" (22.19).

22.21, 22 The psalmist's private deliverance deserved a public testimony. God wonderfully delivers us in the quiet moments when we are hurting, and we must be prepared to offer public praise for his care.

From the horns of the wild oxen you have rescued[z] me.
22.22 Heb 2.12
22 I will tell of your name to my brothers and sisters;[a]
in the midst of the congregation I will praise you:
22.23 Ps 135.19,20
23 You who fear the LORD, praise him!
All you offspring of Jacob, glorify him;
stand in awe of him, all you offspring of Israel!
22.24 Ps 27.9; 31.22 Heb 5.7
24 For he did not despise or abhor
the affliction of the afflicted;
he did not hide his face from me,[b]
but heard when I[c] cried to him.

22.25 Ps 35.18 40.9,10
25 From you comes my praise in the great congregation;
my vows I will pay before those who fear him.
22.26 Ps 40.16; 69.32
26 The poor[d] shall eat and be satisfied;
those who seek him shall praise the LORD.
May your hearts live forever!

27 All the ends of the earth shall remember
and turn to the LORD;
and all the families of the nations
shall worship before him.[e]
22.28 Ps 47.6,7,8
28 For dominion belongs to the LORD,
and he rules over the nations.

29 To him,[f] indeed, shall all who sleep in[g] the earth bow down;
before him shall bow all who go down to the dust,
and I shall live for him.[h]
22.30 Ps 102.18,28
30 Posterity will serve him;
future generations will be told about the Lord,
31 and[i] proclaim his deliverance to a people yet unborn,
saying that he has done it.

Theme: God is seen as a caring shepherd and a dependable guide. We must follow God and obey his commands. He is our only hope for eternal life and security.
Author: David

PSALM 23

A Psalm of David.

23.1 Jn 10.11 1 Pet 2.25
1 The LORD is my shepherd, I shall not want.
2 He makes me lie down in green pastures;

[z] Heb *answered* [a] Or *kindred* [b] Heb *him* [c] Heb *he* [d] Or *afflicted* [e] Gk Syr Jerome: Heb *you* [f] Cn: Heb *They have eaten and* [g] Cn: Heb *all the fat ones* [h] Compare Gk Syr Vg: Heb *and he who cannot keep himself alive* [i] Compare Gk: Heb *it will be told about the Lord to the generation,* [31]*they will come and*

22.30, 31 If we want future generations to know about God's wonders and miracles, we must teach them to our children. If we want our children to serve the Lord, they must hear about him from us. It is not enough to rely on the church or those with more knowledge to provide all their Christian education. We must reinforce the lessons of the Bible in our homes.

22.30, 31 Unborn generations are depending on our faithfulness today. As we teach our children about the Lord, so they will teach their children and their children's children. If we fail to tell our children about the Lord, we may well be breaking the chain of God's influence in generations to come. We must view our children and all the young people we meet as God's future leaders. If we are faithful in opportunities today, we may well be affecting the future.

23.1 In describing the Lord as a shepherd, David wrote out of his own experience, because he had spent his early years caring for sheep (1 Samuel 16.10, 11). Sheep are completely dependent on the shepherd for provision, guidance, and protection. The New Testament calls Jesus the good shepherd (John 10.11); the great shepherd (Hebrews 13.20, 21); and the chief shepherd (1 Peter 5.4). As the Lord is the good shepherd, so we are his sheep – not dumb, frightened, passive animals, but obedient followers wise enough to follow one who will lead us in the right places and in right ways. This psalm does not focus on the animal-like qualities of sheep, but on the discipleship qualities of those who follow. When you recognize the good shepherd, follow him!

23.2, 3 When we allow God our shepherd to guide us, we have contentment. When we choose to sin, however, we go our own way and cannot blame God for the environment we create for ourselves. Our shepherd knows the "green pastures" and "still waters" that will restore us. We will reach these places only by following him obediently. Rebelling against the shepherd's leading is actually rebelling against our own best interests. We must remember this the next time we are tempted to go our own way rather than the shepherd's way.

he leads me beside still waters;[j]
3 he restores my soul.[k]
He leads me in right paths[l]
for his name's sake.

4 Even though I walk through the darkest valley,[m]
I fear no evil;
for you are with me;
your rod and your staff—
they comfort me.

5 You prepare a table before me
in the presence of my enemies;
you anoint my head with oil;
my cup overflows.
6 Surely[n] goodness and mercy[o] shall follow me
all the days of my life,
and I shall dwell in the house of the LORD
my whole life long.[p]

23.4 Ps 27.1; 107.14

23.5 Ps 16.5; 92.10

23.6 Ps 25.6,7,10

Theme: Everything belongs to God—the glorious eternal king. Let us worship him and welcome his glorious reign.
Author: David

PSALM 24

Of David. A Psalm.

1 The earth is the LORD's and all that is in it,
the world, and those who live in it;
2 for he has founded it on the seas,
and established it on the rivers.

3 Who shall ascend the hill of the LORD?
And who shall stand in his holy place?
4 Those who have clean hands and pure hearts,
who do not lift up their souls to what is false,
and do not swear deceitfully.
5 They will receive blessing from the LORD,
and vindication from the God of their salvation.
6 Such is the company of those who seek him,
who seek the face of the God of Jacob.[q] *Selah*

24.1 Ps 89.11; 1 Cor 10.26

24.3 Ps 15.1; 65.4

24.5 Deut 11.26,27

[j] Heb *waters of rest* [k] Or *life* [l] Or *paths of righteousness* [m] Or *the valley of the shadow of death* [n] Or *Only* [o] Or *kindness* [p] Heb *for length of days* [q] Gk Syr: Heb *your face, O Jacob*

23.4 Death casts a frightening shadow over us because we are entirely helpless in its presence. We can struggle with other enemies—pain, suffering, disease, injury—but strength and courage cannot overcome death. It has the final word. Only one person can walk with us through death's dark valley and bring us safely to the other side—the God of life, our shepherd. Because life is uncertain, we should follow this shepherd who offers us eternal confidence.

23.5, 6 In Middle Eastern culture, when at a banquet, it was customary to anoint a person with fragrant oil as a lotion. Hosts were also expected to protect their guests at all costs. God offers the protection of a host even when enemies surround us. In the final scene of this psalm, we see that believers will dwell with God. God, the perfect shepherd and host, promises to guide and protect us through life to bring us into his home forever.

24.1ff This psalm could have been written to celebrate the moving of the ark of the covenant from Obed-edom's house to Jerusalem (2 Samuel 6.10–12). Tradition says that this psalm was sung on the first day of each week in the temple services. Verses 1–6 tell who is worthy to join in such a celebration of worship.

24.1 Because "the earth is the Lord's," all of us are stewards, or caretakers. We are committed to the proper management of this world and its resources, but we are not to become devoted to anything created or act as sole proprietors because they will all pass away (1 John 2.17).

24.4 Swearing deceitfully means telling lies under oath. How greatly God values honesty! Dishonesty comes easily, especially when complete truthfulness could cost us something, make us uncomfortable, or put us in an unfavorable light. Dishonest communication hinders relationships. Without honesty, a relationship with God is impossible. If we lie to others, we begin to deceive ourselves. God cannot hear us or speak to us if we are building a wall of self-deception.

7 Lift up your heads, O gates!
and be lifted up, O ancient doors!
that the King of glory may come in.

24.8
Ex 15.3,6
Ps 76.3-6

8 Who is the King of glory?
The LORD, strong and mighty,
the LORD, mighty in battle.

24.9
Zech 9.9
Mt 21.5

9 Lift up your heads, O gates!
and be lifted up, O ancient doors!
that the King of glory may come in.

24.10
Josh 5.14

10 Who is this King of glory?
The LORD of hosts,
he is the King of glory. *Selah*

Theme: A prayer for defense, guidance, and pardon. As we trust in God, he grants these same requests for us.
Author: David

PSALM 25

Of David.

1 To you, O LORD, I lift up my soul.
2 O my God, in you I trust;
do not let me be put to shame;
do not let my enemies exult over me.

25.3
Ps 37.9; 40.1

3 Do not let those who wait for you be put to shame;
let them be ashamed who are wantonly treacherous.

25.4
Ps 5.8; 86.11

4 Make me to know your ways, O LORD;

PSALMS TO LEARN AND LOVE

Almost everybody, whether religious or not, has heard Psalm 23 because it is quoted so frequently. Many other psalms are also familiar because they are quoted in music, in literature, or in the words of the worship service.

The psalms we know and love are the ones that come into our minds when we need them. They inspire us, comfort us, correct us just when we need a word from the Lord. If you want to begin memorizing psalms, start with some of these favorites. Memorize the whole psalm or just the verses that speak most directly to you. Or read the psalm aloud several times a day until it is part of you.

Psalms to bring us into God's presence	29; 95.1–7a; 96; 100
Psalms about goodness	1; 19; 24; 133; 136; 139
Psalms of praise	8; 97; 103; 107; 113; 145; 150
Psalms of repentance and forgiveness	32.1–5; 51; 103
Psalms for times of trouble	3; 14; 22; 37.1–11; 42; 46; 53; 116.1–7
Psalms of confidence and trust	23; 40.1–4; 91; 119.11; 121; 127

24.7 Who is the King of glory? The King of glory, identified also as the Lord of hosts, or the commander of heaven's armies, is the Messiah himself, eternal, holy, and mighty (Revelation 19.11–21). This psalm is not only a battle cry for the church, it also looks forward to Christ's future entry into the new Jerusalem to reign forever.

24.7–10 This psalm, often set to music, was probably used in corporate worship. It may have been re-enacted many times at the temple. The people outside would call out to the temple gates to open up and let the King of glory in. From inside, the priests or another group would ask, "Who is the King of glory?" Outside, the people would respond in unison, "The Lord, mighty in battle," proclaiming his great power and strength. The exchange was then repeated (24.9, 10), and the temple gates swung open, symbolizing the people's desire to have God's presence among them. This would have been an important lesson for children who were participating.

25.2 Seventy-two psalms—almost half the book—speak about enemies. Enemies are those who oppose not only us, but also God's way of living. We can view temptations—money, success, prestige, lust—as our enemies. And our greatest enemy is Satan. David asked God to keep his enemies from overcoming him because they opposed what God stood for. If his enemies succeeded, David feared that many would think that living for God was futile. David did not question his own faith—he knew that God would triumph. But he didn't want his enemies' success to be an obstacle to the faith of others.

25.4 David expressed his desire for guidance. How do we receive God's guidance? The first step is to want to be guided and to realize that God's primary guidance system is in his Word, the Bible. Psalm 119 tells of the endless knowledge found in God's Word. By reading it and constantly learning from it, we will gain the wisdom to perceive God's direction for our lives. While we may be tempted to demand answers from God, David asked for direction. When we are willing to seek God, learn from his Word, and obey his commands, then will we receive his specific guidance.

teach me your paths.
5 Lead me in your truth, and teach me,
for you are the God of my salvation;
for you I wait all day long.

6 Be mindful of your mercy, O LORD, and of your steadfast love,
for they have been from of old.
7 Do not remember the sins of my youth or my transgressions;
according to your steadfast love remember me,
for your goodness' sake, O LORD!

8 Good and upright is the LORD;
therefore he instructs sinners in the way.
9 He leads the humble in what is right,
and teaches the humble his way.
10 All the paths of the LORD are steadfast love and faithfulness,
for those who keep his covenant and his decrees.

11 For your name's sake, O LORD,
pardon my guilt, for it is great.
12 Who are they that fear the LORD?
He will teach them the way that they should choose.

13 They will abide in prosperity,
and their children shall possess the land.
14 The friendship of the LORD is for those who fear him,
and he makes his covenant known to them.
15 My eyes are ever toward the LORD,
for he will pluck my feet out of the net.

16 Turn to me and be gracious to me,
for I am lonely and afflicted.
17 Relieve the troubles of my heart,
and bring me[r] out of my distress.
18 Consider my affliction and my trouble,
and forgive all my sins.

19 Consider how many are my foes,
and with what violent hatred they hate me.
20 O guard my life, and deliver me;

[r] Or *The troubles of my heart are enlarged; bring me*

25.5 Ps 24.5; 40.1
25.6 Ps 51.1
25.8 Ps 86.5
25.10 Ps 40.11; 103.17,18
25.11 Ps 79.9
25.12 Ps 31.19
25.13 Ps 37.11; 69.36; Prov 19.23
25.14 Prov 3.32
25.15 Ps 31.4; 123.2
25.16 Ps 69.16
25.17 Ps 40.12; 107.6
25.18 Ps 31.7; 103.3
25.19 Ps 3.1; 9.13
25.20 Ps 25.2; 86.2

25.5–7 These verses suggest that David may have written this psalm toward the end of his life. Despite sinning when he was younger, he had a close relationship with God because he was forgiven. David realized, as we must, that God is unlimited, is all-conquering, and has unrestrained authority over all of creation and over each individual. Therefore, he is the only source of salvation, hope, and true peace. Believing in him is the only way to receive forgiveness of sin.

25.8–11 We are bombarded today with relentless appeals to "go my way." TV advertising alone places hundreds of options before us, in addition to appeals made by political parties, cults, false religions, and dozens of other groups. Numerous organizations, including Christian organizations, seek to motivate us to "support the cause." Add to that the dozens of decisions we must make concerning our job, our family, our money, our society, and we become desperate for someone to show us the right way. If you find yourself pulled in several directions, remember that he teaches the humble his way.

25.12 To fear the Lord is to recognize him for who he is: holy, almighty, righteous, pure, all-knowing, all-powerful, and all-wise. When we regard God correctly, we gain a clearer picture of ourselves: sinful, weak, frail, and needy. When we recognize who God is and who we are, we will fall at his feet in humble respect. Only then can he show us how to choose his way.

25.14 God offers intimate and lasting friendship to those who revere him, who hold him in highest honor. What relationship could ever compare with having the Lord of all creation for a friend? Your everlasting friendship with God will grow as you revere him.

25.16, 17 Do life's problems always seem to go from bad to worse? God is the only one who can reverse this downward spiral. He can take our problems and turn them into glorious victories. There is one necessary requirement – we, like the psalmist, must cry out, "Turn to me and be gracious to me." When you are willing to do that, God can turn the worst into something wonderful. The next step is yours, for God has already made his offer.

do not let me be put to shame, for I take refuge in you.

25.21 Ps 25.3
21 May integrity and uprightness preserve me,
for I wait for you.

22 Redeem Israel, O God,
out of all its troubles.

Theme: Declaring loyalty to God. If we are genuinely committed to God, we can stand up to opposition and cross-examination.
Author: David, possibly written during the days of Absalom's rebellion

PSALM 26

Of David.

26.1 Ps 7.8; 13.5
1 Vindicate me, O LORD,
for I have walked in my integrity,
and I have trusted in the LORD without wavering.

26.2 Ps 7.9; 139.23
2 Prove me, O LORD, and try me;
test my heart and mind.

26.3 Ps 1.2; 48.9
3 For your steadfast love is before my eyes,
and I walk in faithfulness to you.[s]

4 I do not sit with the worthless,
nor do I consort with hypocrites;

26.5 Ps 1.1; 31.6
5 I hate the company of evildoers,
and will not sit with the wicked.

26.6 Ps 43.3,4
6 I wash my hands in innocence,
and go around your altar, O LORD,

26.7 Ps 9.1
7 singing aloud a song of thanksgiving,
and telling all your wondrous deeds.

26.8 Ps 27.4
8 O LORD, I love the house in which you dwell,
and the place where your glory abides.
9 Do not sweep me away with sinners,
nor my life with the bloodthirsty,
10 those in whose hands are evil devices,
and whose right hands are full of bribes.

26.11 Ps 26.1; 44.26
11 But as for me, I walk in my integrity;
redeem me, and be gracious to me.

[s] Or *in your faithfulness*

25.21 If ever we needed two powerful forces to preserve us along life's way, they are integrity and uprightness. The psalmist asks for these to be his bodyguards, to protect him step by step. Uprightness makes us learn God's requirements and strive to fulfill them. Integrity—being what we say we are—keeps us from claiming to be upright while living as if we do not know God. Uprightness says, "This is the Shepherd's way," and integrity says, "I will walk consistently in it."

26.1–3 David was not claiming to be sinless—that is impossible for any human being. But he was consistently in fellowship with God, clearing his record when he sinned by asking for forgiveness. Here he pleads with God to clear his name of the false charges made against him by his enemies. We also can ask God to cross-examine us, trusting him to forgive our sins and clear our record according to his mercy.

26.4, 5 Should we stay away from unbelievers? No. Although there are some places Christians should avoid, Jesus demonstrated that we must go among unbelievers to help them. But there is a difference between being *with* them and being *one of* them. Trying to be one of them harms our witness for God. Ask about the people you enjoy, "If I am with them often, will I become less obedient to God in outlook or action?" If the answer is yes, carefully monitor how you spend your time with them and what effect it has on you.

26.8 God's house in this verse is either the tabernacle in Gibeon (the one constructed in the days of Moses) or the temporary dwelling David built to house the ark of the covenant (2 Samuel 6.17). David exclaimed how he loved to worship God at this place. The goal of all believers should be to worship God with the same love and reverence as David did.

26.12 God does not always prevent us from slipping or falling into sin (although often he does). Instead, David was saying that as long as he trusted in God, he could stand on the firm foundation ("level ground") of God's Word and have God's perspective on life.

26.12 Too often we complain about our problems to anyone who will listen and praise God only in private. How much better it would be to complain privately and praise God publicly.

12 My foot stands on level ground;
in the great congregation I will bless the LORD.

26.12 Ps 22.22; 40.2

Theme: God offers help for today and hope for the future. Unwavering confidence in God is our antidote for fear and loneliness.
Author: David

PSALM 27

Of David.

1 The LORD is my light and my salvation;
whom shall I fear?
The LORD is the stronghold[t] of my life;
of whom shall I be afraid?

27.1 Ps 18.28 118.6,14

2 When evildoers assail me
to devour my flesh—
my adversaries and foes—
they shall stumble and fall.

3 Though an army encamp against me,
my heart shall not fear;
though war rise up against me,
yet I will be confident.

27.3 Ps 3.6,7

4 One thing I asked of the LORD,
that will I seek after:
to live in the house of the LORD
all the days of my life,
to behold the beauty of the LORD,
and to inquire in his temple.

27.4 Ps 23.6; 26.8

5 For he will hide me in his shelter
in the day of trouble;
he will conceal me under the cover of his tent;
he will set me high on a rock.

27.5 Ps 17.8; 31.20

6 Now my head is lifted up
above my enemies all around me,
and I will offer in his tent
sacrifices with shouts of joy;
I will sing and make melody to the LORD.

27.6 Ps 13.6; 107.22

7 Hear, O LORD, when I cry aloud,
be gracious to me and answer me!
8 "Come," my heart says, "seek his face!"
Your face, LORD, do I seek.
9 Do not hide your face from me.

27.7 Ps 13.3; 37.12
27.8 Ps 105.4
27.9 Ps 6.1; 40.17 69.17; 94.14

[t] Or *refuge*

27.1 Fear is a dark shadow that envelops us and ultimately imprisons us within ourselves. Each of us has been a prisoner of fear at one time or another—fear of rejection, misunderstanding, uncertainty, sickness, or even death. If we want to dispel the darkness of fear, let us remember with the psalmist that "the Lord is my light and my salvation."

27.4 David could be referring to the tabernacle in Gibeon, to the sanctuary he had put up to house the ark of the covenant, or to the temple that his son Solomon was to build. David probably had the temple in mind because he made many of the plans for it (1 Chronicles 22). But David may also have used the word *temple* to mean "the presence of the Lord." His greatest desire was to live in God's presence each day of his life. Sadly, this is not the greatest desire of many who claim to be believers. But those who live daily in God's presence now will be able to enjoy that relationship forever.

27.5 We often run to God when we experience difficulties. But David sought God's guiding presence *every day*. When troubles came his way, he was *already* in God's presence and prepared to handle any test. Believers can call to God for help at any time, but how shortsighted to call on God only when troubles come. Many of our problems could be avoided or handled far more easily by seeking God's help and direction beforehand.

Do not turn your servant away in anger,
  you who have been my help.
Do not cast me off, do not forsake me,
  O God of my salvation!

27.10
Isa 40.11; 49.15

10 If my father and mother forsake me,
  the LORD will take me up.

27.11
Ps 5.8; 25.4
86.11

11 Teach me your way, O LORD,
  and lead me on a level path
  because of my enemies.

27.12
Ps 35.11
Jer 11.19

12 Do not give me up to the will of my adversaries,
  for false witnesses have risen against me,
  and they are breathing out violence.

27.13
Ps 116.9; 142.5

13 I believe that I shall see the goodness of the LORD
  in the land of the living.

27.14
Ps 31.24; 37.34

14 Wait for the LORD;
  be strong, and let your heart take courage;
  wait for the LORD!

Theme: Prayer when surrounded by trouble or wickedness. God is our only real source of safety. Prayer is our best help when trials come our way because it keeps us in communion with God.
Author: David

PSALM 28

Of David.

28.1
Ps 18.2; 35.22

1 To you, O LORD, I call;
  my rock, do not refuse to hear me,
for if you are silent to me,
  I shall be like those who go down to the Pit.

28.2
Ps 141.2

2 Hear the voice of my supplication,
  as I cry to you for help,
as I lift up my hands
  toward your most holy sanctuary.[u]

28.3
Ps 26.9,10
55.21; 62.4

3 Do not drag me away with the wicked,
  with those who are workers of evil,
who speak peace with their neighbors,
  while mischief is in their hearts.

28.4
Ps 62.12
2 Tim 4.14
Rev 18.6

4 Repay them according to their work,
  and according to the evil of their deeds;
repay them according to the work of their hands;
  render them their due reward.

[u] Heb *your innermost sanctuary*

27.10 Many have had the sad experience of being forsaken by father or mother. Broken homes, differences of belief, addiction to drugs or alcohol, even psychological isolation can leave children crippled by this loss. Even as adults, the pain may linger. God can take that place in our life, fill that void, and heal that hurt. He can direct us to adults who may take the role of father or mother for us. His love is sufficient for all our needs.

27.13 The "land of the living" simply means this life. David was obviously going through a trial, but he was confident that in this present life God would see him through it.

27.14 David knew from experience what it meant to wait on the Lord. He had been anointed king at age 16, but didn't become king until he was 30. During the interim, he was chased through the wilderness by jealous King Saul. David had to wait on God for the fulfillment of his promise to reign. Later, after becoming king, he was chased by his rebellious son, Absalom.

Waiting on God is not easy. Often it seems that he isn't answering our prayers or doesn't understand the urgency of our situation. That kind of thinking implies that God is not in control or is not fair. But God is worth waiting for. Isaiah 40.27–31 calls us to wait because often God uses waiting to refresh, renew, and teach us. Make good use of your waiting times by discovering what God may be trying to teach you in them.

28.3–5 It's easy to pretend friendship. Wicked people often put on a show of kindness or friendship in order to gain their own ends. David, in his royal position, may have met many who pretended friendship only to meet their own goals. David knew that God would punish them eventually, but he prayed that their punishment would come swiftly. True believers should be straightforward and sincere in all their relationships.

5 Because they do not regard the works of the LORD,
or the work of his hands,
he will break them down and build them up no more.

6 Blessed be the LORD,
for he has heard the sound of my pleadings. **28.6** Ps 116.1
7 The LORD is my strength and my shield;
in him my heart trusts;
so I am helped, and my heart exults,
and with my song I give thanks to him. **28.7** Ps 13.5,6 16.9; 40.3 59.17

8 The LORD is the strength of his people;
he is the saving refuge of his anointed.
9 O save your people, and bless your heritage;
be their shepherd, and carry them forever. **28.9** Deut 9.29; 32.9 Ps 33.12; 80.1 Isa 40.11

Theme: God reveals his great power in nature. We can trust God to give us both the peace and the strength to weather the storms of life.
Author: David

PSALM 29

A Psalm of David.

1 Ascribe to the LORD, O heavenly beings,[v]
ascribe to the LORD glory and strength. **29.1** Ps 96.7-9
2 Ascribe to the LORD the glory of his name;
worship the LORD in holy splendor. **29.2** Ps 110.3

3 The voice of the LORD is over the waters;
the God of glory thunders,
the LORD, over mighty waters.
4 The voice of the LORD is powerful;
the voice of the LORD is full of majesty. **29.4** Ps 104.3

5 The voice of the LORD breaks the cedars;
the LORD breaks the cedars of Lebanon. **29.5** Ps 104.16
6 He makes Lebanon skip like a calf,
and Sirion like a young wild ox.

7 The voice of the LORD flashes forth flames of fire.
8 The voice of the LORD shakes the wilderness;
the LORD shakes the wilderness of Kadesh. **29.8** Num 13.26

9 The voice of the LORD causes the oaks to whirl,[w]
and strips the forest bare;
and in his temple all say, "Glory!" **29.9** Ps 26.8

10 The LORD sits enthroned over the flood; **29.10** Gen 6.17

[v] Heb *sons of gods* [w] Or *causes the deer to calve*

28.7 In the sports world there is a phrase: "The best offense is a good defense." In the spiritual battle around us, God is our strength and shield. He is our defense against all that would harm us. If we trust in him, he will certainly defend us from the vicious attacks of our enemies.

29.5, 6 The cedars of Lebanon were giant trees that could grow to 120 feet tall and 30 feet in circumference. A voice that could split the cedars of Lebanon would be a truly powerful voice – the voice of God. "Sirion" means Mount Hermon. All that was impressive to people was under God's complete control.

29.10 The flood mentioned here is the same Hebrew word for the great flood that covered the earth in Noah's day. The story of the flood is recorded in Genesis 6 – 9.

29.10, 11 Throughout history, God has revealed his power through mighty miracles over nature, such as the great flood (Genesis 6 – 9). He promises to continue to reveal his power. Paul urged us to understand how great God's power is (Ephesians 1.18–23). The same power that raised Christ from the dead is available to help us with our daily problems. When you feel weak and limited, don't despair. Remember that God can give you

the LORD sits enthroned as king forever.

29.11 Ps 37.11; 68.35

11 May the LORD give strength to his people!
May the LORD bless his people with peace!

Theme: A celebration of God's deliverance.
Earthly security is uncertain, but God is always faithful.
Author: David

PSALM 30

A Psalm. A Song at the dedication of the temple. Of David.

30.1 Ps 25.2; 35.19,24; 118.28; 145.1

30.2 Ps 6.2; 88.13

1 I will extol you, O LORD, for you have drawn me up,
and did not let my foes rejoice over me.
2 O LORD my God, I cried to you for help,
and you have healed me.
3 O LORD, you brought up my soul from Sheol,
restored me to life from among those gone down to the Pit.[x]

30.4 Ps 97.12; 149.1

4 Sing praises to the LORD, O you his faithful ones,
and give thanks to his holy name.
5 For his anger is but for a moment;
his favor is for a lifetime.
Weeping may linger for the night,
but joy comes with the morning.

30.6 Ps 10.6; 104.29; 143.7

6 As for me, I said in my prosperity,
"I shall never be moved."
7 By your favor, O LORD,
you had established me as a strong mountain;
you hid your face;
I was dismayed.

30.9 Ps 6.5

8 To you, O LORD, I cried,
and to the LORD I made supplication:
9 "What profit is there in my death,
if I go down to the Pit?
Will the dust praise you?
Will it tell of your faithfulness?

30.10 Ps 4.1; 27.7,9

10 Hear, O LORD, and be gracious to me!
O LORD, be my helper!"

30.11 Ps 6.8; Jer 31.4,13

30.12 Ps 44.8; 57.8; 108.1

11 You have turned my mourning into dancing;
you have taken off my sackcloth
and clothed me with joy,
12 so that my soul[y] may praise you and not be silent.
O LORD my God, I will give thanks to you forever.

[x] *Or that I should not go down to the Pit* [y] *Heb that glory*

---

strength. The power that controls creation and raises the dead is available to you.

30.1ff David may have written this psalm when he dedicated Araunah's threshing floor and after God stopped the great plague he had used to discipline him (2 Samuel 24.18–25). The serious illness mentioned in 30.2, 3 may refer to an illness David experienced or to the plague itself.

30.3 *Sheol* is the word in the Old Testament for the realm of the dead. It is used to mean the grave, the underworld, or death.

30.5 Like a shot given by a doctor, the discomfort of God's anger is momentary, but the good effects go on for a long time. Let God's anger be a sharp pain that warns you to turn from sin.

30.6, 7 Prosperity had made David feel invincible. Although he knew his riches and power had come from God, they had gone to his head, making him proud. Wealth, power, and fame have an intoxicating effect on people, making them feel self-reliant, self-secure, and independent of God. But this false security can be easily shattered. Don't be trapped by the false security of prosperity. Depend on God for your security and you won't be shaken when worldly possessions disappear.

Theme: In times of stress, depending upon God requires complete commitment.
Author: David, although some say Jeremiah

PSALM 31

To the leader. A Psalm of David.

1 In you, O LORD, I seek refuge;
do not let me ever be put to shame;
in your righteousness deliver me.
2 Incline your ear to me;
rescue me speedily.
Be a rock of refuge for me,
a strong fortress to save me.

3 You are indeed my rock and my fortress;
for your name's sake lead me and guide me,
4 take me out of the net that is hidden for me,
for you are my refuge.
5 Into your hand I commit my spirit;
you have redeemed me, O LORD, faithful God.

6 You hate[z] those who pay regard to worthless idols,
but I trust in the LORD.
7 I will exult and rejoice in your steadfast love,
because you have seen my affliction;
you have taken heed of my adversities,
8 and have not delivered me into the hand of the enemy;
you have set my feet in a broad place.

9 Be gracious to me, O LORD, for I am in distress;
my eye wastes away from grief,
my soul and body also.
10 For my life is spent with sorrow,
and my years with sighing;
my strength fails because of my misery,[a]
and my bones waste away.

31.1 Ps 25.2; 71.1-3 143.1
31.2 Ps 71.3; 86.1 102.2
31.3 Ps 18.2; 23.2,3
31.4 Ps 25.15
31.5 Lk 23.46 Acts 7.59
31.9 Ps 6.7; 32.3 38.3,4; 39.11 63.1; 69.17 102.1,3,4

[z] One Heb Ms Gk Syr Jerome: MT *I hate* [a] Gk Syr: Heb *my iniquity*

31.1, 3 David called upon God to deliver him. He wanted God to stop those who were unjustly causing trouble. Therefore, David made his request based upon what he knew of God's name, or character. Because God is righteous and loving, he loves to deliver his people.

31.1–6 We say we have faith in God, but do we really trust him? David's words, "Into your hand I commit my spirit," convey his complete trust in God. Jesus used this phrase as he was dying on the cross—showing his absolute dependence on God the Father (Luke 23.46). Stephen repeated these words as he was being stoned to death (Acts 7.59), confident that in death he was simply passing from God's earthly care to God's eternal care. We should commit our possessions, our families, and our vocations to God. But first and foremost, we should commit *ourselves* completely to him.

31.5, 6 Why did David suddenly bring up the subject of idol worship? He wanted to contrast his total devotion to God with the diluted worship offered by many Israelites. Heathen religious rituals were never completely banished from Israel and Judah, despite the efforts of David and a few other kings. Obviously a person who bowed to idols could not put his spirit in God's hands. When we put today's idols (wealth, material possessions, success) first in our lives, we cannot expect God's Spirit to guide us. He is our highest authority and requires our first allegiance.

31.8 In David's day, armies needed wide open spaces for their military maneuvers. David praised God for the "broad place"—the open spaces that gave his troops and chariots the freedom to move within God's boundaries. If you feel restrained by God's moral boundaries, remember that God has given you much freedom, far more than you need to move within those boundaries. Use the opportunities he gives you to make proper decisions. Use them wisely and they will lead to victory.

31.9–13 In this section, David describes the helplessness and hopelessness we feel when we are hated or rejected. As our feelings overwhelm us, it can seem that everybody is against us. But adversity is easier to accept when we recognize our true relationship with the sovereign God (31.14–18). Although our enemies may temporarily seem to have the upper hand, they are ultimately the helpless and hopeless ones. We know without a doubt that those who are faithful to God will be victorious in the end (31.23). We don't have to live in fear. We can

31.11 Ps 38.11 88.8,18 Isa 53.4

11 I am the scorn of all my adversaries,
a horror[b] to my neighbors,
an object of dread to my acquaintances;
those who see me in the street flee from me.

31.12 Ps 88.5

12 I have passed out of mind like one who is dead;
I have become like a broken vessel.

31.13 Ps 41.7 Jer 20.10 Mt 27.1

13 For I hear the whispering of many—
terror all around!—
as they scheme together against me,
as they plot to take my life.

31.14 Ps 140.6; 143.9

14 But I trust in you, O LORD;
I say, "You are my God."
15 My times are in your hand;
deliver me from the hand of my enemies and persecutors.
16 Let your face shine upon your servant;
save me in your steadfast love.

31.17 1 Sam 2.9 Ps 25.2,3,20

17 Do not let me be put to shame, O LORD,
for I call on you;
let the wicked be put to shame;
let them go dumbfounded to Sheol.

31.18 1 Sam 2.3 Ps 94.4; 120.2

18 Let the lying lips be stilled
that speak insolently against the righteous
with pride and contempt.

19 O how abundant is your goodness
that you have laid up for those who fear you,
and accomplished for those who take refuge in you,
in the sight of everyone!

31.20 Ps 27.5; 31.13

20 In the shelter of your presence you hide them
from human plots;
you hold them safe under your shelter
from contentious tongues.

31.21 Ps 17.7; 28.7

21 Blessed be the LORD,
for he has wondrously shown his steadfast love to me
when I was beset as a city under siege.

31.22 Ps 66.19 116.11,12 145.19 Lam 3.54-56

22 I had said in my alarm,
"I am driven far[c] from your sight."
But you heard my supplications
when I cried out to you for help.

31.23 Deut 32.40,41 Ps 37.28

23 Love the LORD, all you his saints.
The LORD preserves the faithful,
but abundantly repays the one who acts haughtily.

31.24 Ps 27.14

24 Be strong, and let your heart take courage,
all you who wait for the LORD.

[b] Cn: Heb *exceedingly* [c] Another reading is *cut off*

have courage today because God will preserve us.

31.14, 15 In saying, "My times are in your hand," David was expressing his belief that all of life's circumstances are under God's control. Knowing that God loves us and cares for us enables us to keep steady in our faith no matter what our circumstances may be. It keeps us from sinning foolishly by taking matters into our own hands or resenting God's timetable.

Theme: Forgiveness brings true happiness. Only when we ask God to forgive our sins will he give us real happiness and relief from guilt.
Author: David

PSALM 32

Of David. A Maskil.

1 Happy are those whose transgression is forgiven,
whose sin is covered.
2 Happy are those to whom the LORD imputes no iniquity,
and in whose spirit there is no deceit.

3 While I kept silence, my body wasted away
through my groaning all day long.
4 For day and night your hand was heavy upon me;
my strength was dried up[d] as by the heat of summer. *Selah*

5 Then I acknowledged my sin to you,
and I did not hide my iniquity;
I said, "I will confess my transgressions to the LORD,"
and you forgave the guilt of my sin. *Selah*

6 Therefore let all who are faithful
offer prayer to you;
at a time of distress,[e] the rush of mighty waters
shall not reach them.
7 You are a hiding place for me;
you preserve me from trouble;
you surround me with glad cries of deliverance. *Selah*

8 I will instruct you and teach you the way you should go;
I will counsel you with my eye upon you.
9 Do not be like a horse or a mule, without understanding,
whose temper must be curbed with bit and bridle,
else it will not stay near you.

10 Many are the torments of the wicked,
but steadfast love surrounds those who trust in the LORD.
11 Be glad in the LORD and rejoice, O righteous,
and shout for joy, all you upright in heart.

32.1 Ps 85.2; Rom 4.7,8
32.3 Ps 31.10; 39.2
32.4 Ps 22.15; 39.10
32.5 Lev 26.40; Job 31.33; Ps 38.18; 1 Jn 1.9
32.6 Ps 69.13; Isa 43.2
32.7 Ex 15.1; Ps 31.20; 40.3; 121.7
32.8 Ps 25.8; 33.18,19
32.10 Ps 16.4

[d] Meaning of Heb uncertain [e] Cn: Heb *at a time of finding only*

32.1 *Maskil* is a term denoting psalms written to make one wise or prudent, to increase a person's success or skill.

32.1ff This psalm is a sequel to Psalm 51. Here David expresses the joy of forgiveness. God had forgiven him for the sins he had committed against Bathsheba and Uriah (2 Samuel 11, 12). This is another of the penitential (repentance) psalms where the writer confesses his sin to God.

32.1, 2 God *wants* to forgive sinners. Forgiveness has always been part of his loving nature. He announced this to Moses (Exodus 34.7); he revealed it to David; and he dramatically showed it to the world through Jesus Christ. These verses convey several aspects of God's forgiveness: forgives transgression, covers sin, removes guilt from our records and from our spirit. Paul quoted these verses in Romans 4.7, 8 and showed that we can have this joyous experience of forgiveness through faith in Christ.

32.5 What is confession? To confess our sin is to agree with God, to acknowledge that he is right to declare it sin, and that we are wrong to desire or to do it. It is to affirm our intention of abandoning that sin in order to follow him more faithfully.

32.6 When you have hurt someone, it is freeing to receive his or her forgiveness. When God forgives us, he clears the record of our wrongs and takes away our guilt. To experience God's forgiveness, however, we must confess our sins. When we do, we must also make a commitment to change our behavior. A person planning to return to that sin is not sincere in his confession.

32.8, 9 God describes some people as being stubborn as mules. Rather than letting God guide them step by step, they stubbornly leave God only one option. If he wants to keep them useful for him, he must use discipline and punishment, like a bit in a mule's mouth. God longs to guide us with love and wisdom rather than punishment. He offers to guide us along the *best* pathway for our lives. Accept the advice written in God's Word and don't let your stubbornness keep you from obeying God.

Theme: Because God is Creator, Lord, Savior, and Deliverer, he is worthy of our trust and praise. Because he is faithful and his Word is dependable, we can rejoice and sing, giving thanks and praise.
Author: Anonymous

PSALM 33

33.1 Ps 32.11; 147.1
1 Rejoice in the LORD, O you righteous.
Praise befits the upright.
33.2 Ps 92.3
2 Praise the LORD with the lyre;
make melody to him with the harp of ten strings.
33.3 Ps 98.1
3 Sing to him a new song;
play skillfully on the strings, with loud shouts.

33.4 Ps 19.8
4 For the word of the LORD is upright,
and all his work is done in faithfulness.
33.5 Ps 11.7; 119.64
5 He loves righteousness and justice;
the earth is full of the steadfast love of the LORD.

33.6 Gen 1.6,7
6 By the word of the LORD the heavens were made,
and all their host by the breath of his mouth.
33.7 Ex 15.8
7 He gathered the waters of the sea as in a bottle;
he put the deeps in storehouses.

33.8 Ps 67.7; 96.9
8 Let all the earth fear the LORD;
let all the inhabitants of the world stand in awe of him.
33.9 Gen 1.3 Ps 148.5
9 For he spoke, and it came to be;
he commanded, and it stood firm.

33.10 Gen 11.8 Isa 8.9,10
10 The LORD brings the counsel of the nations to nothing;
he frustrates the plans of the peoples.
11 The counsel of the LORD stands forever,
the thoughts of his heart to all generations.

CONFESSION, REPENTANCE, AND FORGIVENESS IN PSALMS

Over the centuries, many believers, overcome by an awareness of their own sins, have found in the words of the penitential (confession) psalms a ray of hope. The psalmists shared with God both the depth of their sorrow and repentance, as well as the height of joy at being forgiven. They rejoiced in the knowledge that God would respond to confession and repentance with complete forgiveness. We, who live on the other side of the cross of Christ, can rejoice even more because we understand more. God has shown us that he is willing to forgive because his judgment on sin was satisfied by Christ's death on the cross.

As you read these psalms, note the pattern followed by the psalmists in responding to God: (1) they recognized their sinfulness and tendency to do wrong; (2) they realized that sin was rebellion against God himself; (3) they admitted their sins to God; (4) they trusted in God's willingness to forgive; and (5) they accepted his forgiveness. Use these psalms as a reminder of how easy it is to drift away from God and fall into sin, and what is needed to reestablish that fellowship.

Selected psalms that emphasize these themes are 6; 14; 31; 32; 38; 41; 51; 102; 130; 143.

33.2, 3 Because David was an accomplished harpist (1 Samuel 16.15–25), he frequently spoke about musical instruments throughout his psalms. He undoubtedly composed music for many of the psalms, and he commissioned music for temple worship (1 Chronicles 25).

33.4 A person's words are measured by the quality of his or her character. If your friends trust what you say, it is because they trust you. If you trust what God says, it is because you trust him to be the God he claims to be. If you doubt his words, you doubt the integrity of God himself. If you believe God is truly God, then believe what he says!

33.4 All God's words are true and trustworthy. God does not lie, forget, change his words, or leave his promises unfulfilled. We can trust the Bible because it contains the words of a holy, trustworthy, and unchangeable God.

33.6–9 This is a poetic summary of the first chapter of Genesis. God is not just the coordinator of natural forces, he is the Lord of creation, the almighty God. Because he is all powerful, we should revere him in all we do.

33.11 God's plan stands forever! Are you frustrated by inconsistencies you see in others, or even in yourself? God is completely trustworthy—his intentions never change. When you wonder if there is anyone in whom you can trust, remember that God is completely consistent. Let him counsel you.

12 Happy is the nation whose God is the LORD,
the people whom he has chosen as his heritage.

33.12
Ex 19.5
Ps 144.15

13 The LORD looks down from heaven;
he sees all humankind.
14 From where he sits enthroned he watches
all the inhabitants of the earth—
15 he who fashions the hearts of them all,
and observes all their deeds.
16 A king is not saved by his great army;
a warrior is not delivered by his great strength.
17 The war horse is a vain hope for victory,
and by its great might it cannot save.

33.16
Ps 44.6; 147.10

18 Truly the eye of the LORD is on those who fear him,
on those who hope in his steadfast love,
19 to deliver their soul from death,
and to keep them alive in famine.

33.18
Ps 34.15; 37.19

20 Our soul waits for the LORD;
he is our help and shield.
21 Our heart is glad in him,
because we trust in his holy name.
22 Let your steadfast love, O LORD, be upon us,
even as we hope in you.

Theme: God pays attention to those who call on him. Whether God offers escape from trouble or help in times of trouble, we can be certain that he always hears and acts on behalf of those who love him.
Author: David, after pretending to be insane in order to escape from King Achish (1 Samuel 21.10–15)

PSALM 34

Of David, when he feigned madness before Abimelech, so that he drove him out, and he went away.

1 I will bless the LORD at all times;
his praise shall continually be in my mouth.
2 My soul makes its boast in the LORD;
let the humble hear and be glad.
3 O magnify the LORD with me,
and let us exalt his name together.

34.1
Ps 71.6

34.2
Jer 9.24

34.3
Lk 1.46

4 I sought the LORD, and he answered me,
and delivered me from all my fears.
5 Look to him, and be radiant;
so your[f] faces shall never be ashamed.
6 This poor soul cried, and was heard by the LORD,

34.4
Mt 7.7

[f] Gk Syr Jerome: Heb *their*

33.16, 17 Because God rules and overrules every nation, leaders should never put their trust in their physical power. Military might is not the ground of our hope. Our hope is in God and in his gracious offer to save us if we will trust in him.

33.18, 19 This is not an ironclad guarantee that all believers will escape starvation or violent death. Thousands of Christian saints have been beaten to death, whipped, fed to lions, or executed (Romans 8.35, 36; Hebrews 11.32–40). God can (and often miraculously does) deliver his followers from pain and death, though sometimes, for purposes known only to him, he chooses not to. When faced with these harsh realities, we must focus on the wise judgments of God. David was pleading for God's watchful care and protection. In times of crisis, we can place our hope in God.

34.1ff God promises great blessings to his people, but many of these blessings require our active participation. He will free us from fear (34.4), deliver us from trouble (34.6), guard us (34.7), show us kindness (34.8), supply our needs (34.9), listen when we talk to him (34.15), and redeem us (34.22), but we must do our part. We can appropriate his blessings when we seek him (34.4, 10), cry out to him (34.6, 17), trust him (34.8), fear him (34.7, 9), keep from lying (34.13), turn from sin, do good, and seek peace (34.14), have humble hearts (34.18), and serve him (34.22).

and was saved from every trouble.

34.7 Ps 91.14

7 The angel of the LORD encamps
around those who fear him, and delivers them.

34.8 Ps 23.1; 1 Pet 2.3

8 O taste and see that the LORD is good;
happy are those who take refuge in him.

34.9 Ps 23.1; 31.23

9 O fear the LORD, you his holy ones,
for those who fear him have no want.

34.10 Ps 84.11

10 The young lions suffer want and hunger,
but those who seek the LORD lack no good thing.

11 Come, O children, listen to me;
I will teach you the fear of the LORD.

34.12 1 Pet 3.10-12

12 Which of you desires life,
and covets many days to enjoy good?

34.13 Jas 1.26

13 Keep your tongue from evil,
and your lips from speaking deceit.

34.14 Rom 14.18,19; Heb 12.14

14 Depart from evil, and do good;
seek peace, and pursue it.

15 The eyes of the LORD are on the righteous,
and his ears are open to their cry.

34.16 Ps 9.6; 109.15

16 The face of the LORD is against evildoers,
to cut off the remembrance of them from the earth.

17 When the righteous cry for help, the LORD hears,
and rescues them from all their troubles.

34.18 Ps 51.17; Isa 57.15

18 The LORD is near to the brokenhearted,
and saves the crushed in spirit.

34.19 Ps 71.20; 2 Tim 3.11,12

19 Many are the afflictions of the righteous,
but the LORD rescues them from them all.

20 He keeps all their bones;

34.8 "Taste and see" does not mean, "Check out God's credentials." Instead it is a warm invitation: "Try this; I know you'll like it." When we take that first step of obedience in following God, we cannot help discovering that he is good and kind. As we trust him daily, we experience how good he is.

34.9 You believe you belong to the Lord, but do you fear—that is, revere—him? To fear the Lord means to show deep respect and honor to him. We demonstrate true reverence by our humble attitude and genuine worship. Reverence was shown by Abraham (Genesis 17.2–4), Moses (Exodus 3.5, 6), and the Israelites (Exodus 19.16–24). Their reactions to God's presence varied, but all deeply respected him.

34.9, 10 At first we may question David's statement, because we seem to lack many good things. This is not a blanket promise that all Christians will have everything they want. Instead, this is David's praise for God's goodness—all those who call upon God in their need will be answered, sometimes in unexpected ways.

Remember, God knows what we need and our deepest needs are spiritual. Many Christians, even though they face unbearable poverty and hardship, still have enough spiritual nourishment to live for God. David was saying that to have God is to have all you really need. God is enough.

If you feel you don't have everything you need, ask: (1) Is this really a need? (2) Is this really good for me? (3) Is this the best time for me to have what I desire? Even if you answer yes to all three questions, God may allow you to go without to help you grow more dependent on him. He may want you to learn that you need *him* more than your immediate desires.

34.11–14 The Bible often connects the fear of the Lord (love and reverence for him) with obedience. "Fear God, and keep his commandments" (Ecclesiastes 12.13); "Those who love me will keep my word" (John 14.23). Reverence means obeying God in the way we speak and the way we treat others.

34.11–14 David encouraged others to trust and fear God, and to exemplify faith, truth, obedience, and goodness in their lives. He feared God, and for the most part he chose the way of goodness and peace. David even treated some of his worst enemies with kindness (see 1 Samuel 24.1–8; 26.5–25). Peter quoted these verses as a strategy for living in a non-Christian environment (1 Peter 3.10–12).

34.14 Somehow we think that peace should come to us with no effort. But David explained that we are to seek and pursue peace. Paul echoed this thought in Romans 12.18. A person who wants peace cannot be argumentative and contentious. Since peaceful relationships come from our efforts at peacemaking, work hard at living in peace with others each day.

34.18, 19 We often wish we could escape troubles—the pain of grief, loss, sorrow, and failure; or even the small daily frustrations that constantly wear us down. God promises to be our source of power, courage, and wisdom to help us through our problems. Sometimes he chooses to deliver us from those problems. When trouble strikes, don't get frustrated with God. Instead, admit that you need his help and thank him for being by your side.

34.20 This is a prophecy about Christ when he was crucified. Although it was the Roman custom to break the legs of the victim to speed death, not one of Jesus' bones was broken (John 19.32–37). Aside from the prophetic meaning, David was pleading for God's protection in times of crisis.

not one of them will be broken.
21 Evil brings death to the wicked,
and those who hate the righteous will be condemned. 34.21 Ps 94.23
22 The LORD redeems the life of his servants;
none of those who take refuge in him will be condemned. 34.22 1 Kgs 1.29 Ps 71.23

Theme: A prayer to God for help against those who try to inflict injury for no reason. When our enemies are unjust and lie about us, even when we do good to them, we can appeal to God who is always just.
Author: David, probably written when he was being hunted by Saul (1 Samuel 24)

PSALM 35

Of David.

1 Contend, O LORD, with those who contend with me;
fight against those who fight against me! 35.1 Ps 56.1,2 Isa 49.25
2 Take hold of shield and buckler,
and rise up to help me!
3 Draw the spear and javelin
against my pursuers;
say to my soul,
"I am your salvation."

4 Let them be put to shame and dishonor
who seek after my life. 35.4 Ps 40.14 70.2,3
Let them be turned back and confounded
who devise evil against me.
5 Let them be like chaff before the wind,
with the angel of the LORD driving them on. 35.5 Ps 1.4; 83.13 Isa 29.5
6 Let their way be dark and slippery,
with the angel of the LORD pursuing them. 35.6 Ps 73.18 Jer 23.12

7 For without cause they hid their net[g] for me;
without cause they dug a pit[h] for my life. 35.7 Ps 69.4; 109.3
8 Let ruin come on them unawares.
And let the net that they hid ensnare them;
let them fall in it—to their ruin. 35.8 Ps 9.15 Isa 47.11 1 Thess 5.3

9 Then my soul shall rejoice in the LORD,
exulting in his deliverance. 35.9 Isa 61.10 Lk 1.47
10 All my bones shall say,
"O LORD, who is like you? 35.10 Ex 15.11,12 Ps 18.17; 37.14
You deliver the weak
from those too strong for them,
the weak and needy from those who despoil them."

11 Malicious witnesses rise up;
they ask me about things I do not know. 35.11 Ps 27.12
12 They repay me evil for good;
my soul is forlorn. 35.12 Ps 38.20 Jn 10.32

[g] Heb *a pit, their net* [h] The word *pit* is transposed from the preceding line

---

35.1ff This is one of the "imprecatory" (cursing) psalms that call upon God to deal with enemies. These psalms sound extremely harsh, but we must remember: (1) David was fleeing from men who were unjustly seeking to kill him. As God's anointed king over a nation called to annihilate the evil people of the land, this was difficult for David to understand. (2) David's call for justice was sincere; it was not a cover for vengeance. He truly wanted to seek God's perfect ideal for his nation. (3) David did not say *he* would take vengeance, but gave the matter to God. These are merely his suggestions. (4) These psalms use hyperbole (or overstatement). They were meant to motivate others to take a strong stand against sin and evil.

Cruelty may be far removed from some people's experience, but it is a daily reality to others. God promises to help the persecuted and bring judgment on unrepentant sinners. When we pray for justice to be done, we are praying as David did. When Christ returns, the wicked will be punished.

35.13 Job 30.25 Jer 18.20

13 But as for me, when they were sick,
I wore sackcloth;
I afflicted myself with fasting.
I prayed with head bowed[i] on my bosom,
14 as though I grieved for a friend or a brother;
I went about as one who laments for a mother,
bowed down and in mourning.

15 But at my stumbling they gathered in glee,
they gathered together against me;
ruffians whom I did not know
tore at me without ceasing;
16 they impiously mocked more and more,[j]
gnashing at me with their teeth.

35.17 Ps 13.1 22.20,21

17 How long, O LORD, will you look on?
Rescue me from their ravages,
my life from the lions!

35.18 Ps 22.23,25

18 Then I will thank you in the great congregation;
in the mighty throng I will praise you.

35.19 Ps 13.4 38.16,19; 69.4

19 Do not let my treacherous enemies rejoice over me,
or those who hate me without cause wink the eye.
20 For they do not speak peace,
but they conceive deceitful words
against those who are quiet in the land.

35.21 Ps 22.13; 40.15

21 They open wide their mouths against me;
they say, "Aha, Aha,
our eyes have seen it."

22 You have seen, O LORD; do not be silent!
O Lord, do not be far from me!
23 Wake up! Bestir yourself for my defense,
for my cause, my God and my Lord!

35.24 Ps 9.4; 43.1

24 Vindicate me, O LORD, my God,
according to your righteousness,
and do not let them rejoice over me.

35.25 Ps 56.1

25 Do not let them say to themselves,
"Aha, we have our heart's desire."
Do not let them say, "We have swallowed you[k] up."

35.26 Ps 38.16; 40.14

26 Let all those who rejoice at my calamity
be put to shame and confusion;
let those who exalt themselves against me
be clothed with shame and dishonor.

35.27 Ps 40.16; 70.4

27 Let those who desire my vindication
shout for joy and be glad,
and say evermore,
"Great is the LORD,

[i] Or *My prayer turned back* [j] Cn Compare Gk: Heb *like the profanest of mockers of a cake* [k] Heb *him*

35.13 "I prayed with head bowed on my bosom" means "my prayer went unanswered." When our deliverance is delayed it is easy to assume God hasn't answered our prayer. God hears our every prayer, but he answers according to his wisdom. Don't let the absence of an immediate answer cause you to doubt or resent God. Instead let it be an occasion to deepen your faith.

35.21–23 David cried out to God to defend him when he was unjustly accused. If you are unjustly accused, your natural reaction may be to lash out in revenge or to give a detailed defense of your every move. Ask God to fight the battle for you. He will clear your name in the eyes of those who really matter.

who delights in the welfare of his servant."
28 Then my tongue shall tell of your righteousness
and of your praise all day long.

35.28
Ps 51.14,15

Theme: God's faithfulness, justice, and love are contrasted with the sinful hearts of men and women. In spite of our fallen condition, God pours out his love on those who know him.
Author: David

PSALM 36

To the leader. Of David, the servant of the LORD.

1 Transgression speaks to the wicked
deep in their hearts;
there is no fear of God
before their eyes.
2 For they flatter themselves in their own eyes
that their iniquity cannot be found out and hated.
3 The words of their mouths are mischief and deceit;
they have ceased to act wisely and do good.
4 They plot mischief while on their beds;
they are set on a way that is not good;
they do not reject evil.

5 Your steadfast love, O LORD, extends to the heavens,
your faithfulness to the clouds.
6 Your righteousness is like the mighty mountains,
your judgments are like the great deep;
you save humans and animals alike, O LORD.

7 How precious is your steadfast love, O God!
All people may take refuge in the shadow of your wings.
8 They feast on the abundance of your house,
and you give them drink from the river of your delights.
9 For with you is the fountain of life;
in your light we see light.

10 O continue your steadfast love to those who know you,
and your salvation to the upright of heart!
11 Do not let the foot of the arrogant tread on me,
or the hand of the wicked drive me away.
12 There the evildoers lie prostrate;
they are thrust down, unable to rise.

36.1
Rom 3.18
36.3
Ps 10.7
36.5
Ps 57.10
103.11; 108.4
36.6
Job 11.8
Ps 104.14,15
145.16,17
Rom 11.33
36.7
Ruth 2.12
Ps 91.4
139.17,18
36.8
Ps 46.4
Isa 25.6
Rev 22.1
36.9
1 Pet 2.9
36.12
Ps 140.10

Theme: Trust in the Lord and wait patiently for him to act. This psalm vividly contrasts the wicked person with the upright.
Author: David

PSALM 37

Of David.

1 Do not fret because of the wicked;
do not be envious of wrongdoers,

36.1 Because the wicked have no fear of God, nothing restrains them from sinning. They plunge ahead as if nothing will happen to them. But God is just and is only delaying their punishment. This knowledge should restrain us from sinning. Let the fear of God do its work in you to keep you from sin. In your gratitude for God's love, don't ignore his justice.

36.5–8 In contrast to evil men and their wicked plots that end in failure, God is merciful, righteous, and kind. His mercy is greater than the heavens; his faithfulness reaches the clouds; his righteousness is as solid as a mountain; and his judgments are as full of wisdom as the oceans with water. We need not fear evil people because we know God loves us, judges evil, and will care for us throughout eternity.

36.9 This metaphor for God – "fountain of life" – gives us a sense of fresh, cleansing water that gives life to the spiritually thirsty. This same picture is used in Jeremiah 2.13, where God is called the "fountain of living water." Jesus spoke of himself as living water that could quench thirst forever and give eternal life (John 4.14).

2 for they will soon fade like the grass,
and wither like the green herb.

37.3 Deut 30.20

3 Trust in the LORD, and do good;
so you will live in the land, and enjoy security.

37.4 Ps 145.19

4 Take delight in the LORD,
and he will give you the desires of your heart.

37.5 Ps 55.22

5 Commit your way to the LORD;
trust in him, and he will act.

37.6 Isa 58.8,10 Mic 7.9

6 He will make your vindication shine like the light,
and the justice of your cause like the noonday.

37.7 Ps 40.1; 62.5 Jer 12.1

7 Be still before the LORD, and wait patiently for him;
do not fret over those who prosper in their way,
over those who carry out evil devices.

37.8 Eph 4.31 Col 3.8

8 Refrain from anger, and forsake wrath.
Do not fret—it leads only to evil.

37.9 Ps 25.13

9 For the wicked shall be cut off,
but those who wait for the LORD shall inherit the land.

37.10 Job 24.24

10 Yet a little while, and the wicked will be no more;
though you look diligently for their place, they will not be there.

37.11 Mt 5.3,5

11 But the meek shall inherit the land,
and delight themselves in abundant prosperity.

37.12 Job 18.20 Ps 2.4; 31.13

12 The wicked plot against the righteous,
and gnash their teeth at them;
13 but the LORD laughs at the wicked,
for he sees that their day is coming.

37.14 Ps 11.2; 35.10

14 The wicked draw the sword and bend their bows
to bring down the poor and needy,
to kill those who walk uprightly;

37.15 Ps 9.16; 46.9

15 their sword shall enter their own heart,
and their bows shall be broken.

37.16 Prov 15.16; 16.8

16 Better is a little that the righteous person has
than the abundance of many wicked.

37.17 Ps 10.15

17 For the arms of the wicked shall be broken,
but the LORD upholds the righteous.

37.1 We should never envy the wicked, even though some may be extremely popular or excessively rich. No matter how much they have, it will fade and vanish like grass that withers and dies. Those who follow God live differently from the wicked and, in the end, have far greater treasures in heaven. What the unbeliever gets may last a lifetime, if he is lucky. What you get from following God lasts forever.

37.4, 5 David calls us to take delight in the Lord and to commit everything we have and do to him. But how do we do this? To *commit* ourselves to the Lord means entrusting everything—our lives, families, jobs, possessions—to his control and guidance. To commit ourselves to the Lord means to trust him (37.5), believing that he can care for us better than we can ourselves. We should be willing to wait (37.7) for him to work out what is best for us.

To *delight* in someone means to experience great pleasure and joy in his or her presence. This happens only when we know that person well. Thus, to delight in the Lord we must know him better. Knowledge of his great love for us will indeed give us delight.

37.8, 9 Anger and worry are two very destructive emotions. They reveal a lack of faith that God loves us and is in control. We should not fret and worry; instead, we should trust in the Lord, giving ourselves to him for his use and safekeeping. When you dwell on your problems, you will become anxious and angry. But if you concentrate on God and his goodness, you will find peace. Where do you focus your attention?

37.11 Meekness hardly seems the proper weapon to deal with enemies. God's warfare must be carried out with calm faith, humility before God, and hope in his deliverance. Jesus likewise promises a sure reward for those with humble attitudes (Matthew 5.5).

18 The LORD knows the days of the blameless,
and their heritage will abide forever;
19 they are not put to shame in evil times,
in the days of famine they have abundance.

37.19 Job 5.20 Ps 33.18,19

20 But the wicked perish,
and the enemies of the LORD are like the glory of the pastures;
they vanish — like smoke they vanish away.

37.20 Ps 68.2; 73.27

21 The wicked borrow, and do not pay back,
but the righteous are generous and keep giving;
22 for those blessed by the LORD shall inherit the land,
but those cursed by him shall be cut off.

37.22 Prov 3.33

23 Our steps[l] are made firm by the LORD,
when he delights in our[m] way;
24 though we stumble,[n] we[o] shall not fall headlong,
for the LORD holds us[p] by the hand.

37.23 Ps 40.2; 147.11

37.24 Ps 145.14

25 I have been young, and now am old,
yet I have not seen the righteous forsaken
or their children begging bread.
26 They are ever giving liberally and lending,
and their children become a blessing.

37.25 Isa 41.17 Heb 13.5

37.26 Ps 147.13

27 Depart from evil, and do good;
so you shall abide forever.
28 For the LORD loves justice;
he will not forsake his faithful ones.

37.27 Ps 34.14

37.28 Ps 11.7

The righteous shall be kept safe forever,
but the children of the wicked shall be cut off.
29 The righteous shall inherit the land,
and live in it forever.

30 The mouths of the righteous utter wisdom,
and their tongues speak justice.
31 The law of their God is in their hearts;
their steps do not slip.

32 The wicked watch for the righteous,
and seek to kill them.
33 The LORD will not abandon them to their power,

37.32 Ps 10.8; 37.14

37.33 Ps 37.22

[l] Heb *a man's steps* [m] Heb *his* [n] Heb *he stumbles* [o] Heb *he* [p] Heb *him*

37.21 You can tell a lot about a person's character by the way he or she handles money. The wicked person steals under the guise of borrowing. The good person gives to the needy. The wicked person, therefore, focuses on himself, while the good person focuses on others.

37.23, 24 A good person is one who follows God, trusts him, and tries to do his will. God watches over and directs every step that person takes. If you would like to have God direct your way, then seek his advice before you step out.

37.25 Since children starve today, as they did in David's time, what did he mean? David is observing God's provision over a lifetime. Though there are unfortunate exceptions to this general principle, God provides for his own people. The children of the righteous need not go hungry, because other believers can help out in their time of need. In David's day, Israel obeyed God's laws, which assured that the poor were treated fairly and mercifully. As long as Israel was obedient, there was enough food for everyone. When Israel forgot God, the rich took care only of themselves and the poor suffered (Amos 2.6, 7).

When we see a Christian brother or sister suffering today, we can respond in one of three ways. (1) We can say, as Job's friends did, that the afflicted person brought this on himself. (2) We can say that this is a test to help the poor develop more patience and trust in God. (3) We can help the person in need. David would approve of only the last option. Although many governments today have their own programs for helping those in need, this is no excuse for ignoring the poor and needy within our reach.

or let them be condemned when they are brought to trial.

37.34 Ps 27.14; 37.9

34 Wait for the LORD, and keep to his way,
and he will exalt you to inherit the land;
you will look on the destruction of the wicked.

35 I have seen the wicked oppressing,
and towering like a cedar of Lebanon.[q]
36 Again I[r] passed by, and they were no more;
though I sought them, they could not be found.

37.37 Ps 7.10 Isa 57.1,2
37.38 Ps 1.4; 73.18

37 Mark the blameless, and behold the upright,
for there is posterity for the peaceable.
38 But transgressors shall be altogether destroyed;
the posterity of the wicked shall be cut off.

37.39 Ps 3.8; 9.9 62.1
37.40 Ps 22.3,4 34.22 Dan 3.17; 6.23

39 The salvation of the righteous is from the LORD;
he is their refuge in the time of trouble.
40 The LORD helps them and rescues them;
he rescues them from the wicked, and saves them,
because they take refuge in him.

Theme: Sorrow for sin brings hope. God alone is the true source of healing and protection for those who confess their sins to him.
Author: David

PSALM 38

A Psalm of David, for the memorial offering.

38.1 Ps 6.1
38.2 Ps 32.4

1 O LORD, do not rebuke me in your anger,
or discipline me in your wrath.
2 For your arrows have sunk into me,
and your hand has come down on me.

38.3 Ps 6.2 31.9,10; 40.12 Isa 1.5,6

3 There is no soundness in my flesh
because of your indignation;
there is no health in my bones
because of my sin.
4 For my iniquities have gone over my head;
they weigh like a burden too heavy for me.

38.5 Ps 42.9; 69.5

5 My wounds grow foul and fester
because of my foolishness;
6 I am utterly bowed down and prostrate;
all day long I go around mourning.

[q] Gk: Meaning of Heb uncertain [r] Gk Syr Jerome: Heb *he*

37.34 It is difficult to wait patiently for God to act when we want change right away. But God promises that if we submit to his timing, he will honor us. Peter said, "Humble yourselves therefore under the mighty hand of God, so that he may exalt you in due time" (1 Peter 5.6). Be patient, steadily doing the work God has given you to do, and allow God to choose the best time to change your circumstances.

38.1ff This is called a penitential psalm because David expressed sorrow for his sin (38.18). He stated that his sin led to health problems (38.1–8) and separated him from God and others, causing extreme loneliness (38.9–14). He then confessed his sin and repented (38.15–22).

38.1 As a child might cry to his father, so David cried to God. David was not saying, "Don't punish me," but "Don't punish me while you are angry." He acknowledged that he deserved to be punished, but asked that God temper his discipline with mercy. Like children, we are free to ask for mercy but should not deny that we deserve punishment.

38.2–4 David saw his anguish as judgment from God for his sins. Although God does not always send physical illness to punish us for sin, this verse and others in Scripture (Acts 12.21–23; 1 Corinthians 11.30–32) indicate that he did so in certain circumstances. Our sin can have physical or mental side-effects that can cause great suffering. Sometimes God has to punish his children in order to bring them back to himself (Hebrews 12.5–11). When we repent of our sin, God promises to forgive us. He delivers us from sin's eternal consequences, although he does not promise to undo all of sin's earthly consequences.

7 For my loins are filled with burning,
and there is no soundness in my flesh.
8 I am utterly spent and crushed;
I groan because of the tumult of my heart.

9 O Lord, all my longing is known to you;
my sighing is not hidden from you.
10 My heart throbs, my strength fails me;
as for the light of my eyes — it also has gone from me.
11 My friends and companions stand aloof from my affliction,
and my neighbors stand far off.

12 Those who seek my life lay their snares;
those who seek to hurt me speak of ruin,
and meditate treachery all day long.

13 But I am like the deaf, I do not hear;
like the mute, who cannot speak.
14 Truly, I am like one who does not hear,
and in whose mouth is no retort.

15 But it is for you, O LORD, that I wait;
it is you, O LORD my God, who will answer.
16 For I pray, "Only do not let them rejoice over me,
those who boast against me when my foot slips."

17 For I am ready to fall,
and my pain is ever with me.
18 I confess my iniquity;
I am sorry for my sin.
19 Those who are my foes without cause[s] are mighty,
and many are those who hate me wrongfully.
20 Those who render me evil for good
are my adversaries because I follow after good.

21 Do not forsake me, O LORD;
O my God, do not be far from me;
22 make haste to help me,
O Lord, my salvation.

38.7 Ps 102.3,4
38.8 Job 3.24 Ps 22.1
38.9 Ps 6.6; 10.17
38.12 Ps 35.20; 54.3
38.15 Ps 17.6; 37.9
38.16 Ps 13.4; 35.26
38.18 2 Cor 7.9,10
38.20 Ps 35.12 1 Jn 3.12
38.21 Ps 22.19; 35.22

Theme: Apart from God, life is fleeting and empty. This is an appeal for God's mercy because life is so brief.
Author: David

PSALM 39

To the leader: to Jeduthun. A Psalm of David.

1 I said, "I will guard my ways
that I may not sin with my tongue;

39.1 Ps 34.13; 141.3

s Q Ms: MT *my living foes*

38.13, 14 It is extremely difficult to be silent when others tear us down, because we want to protect our reputation. We find it difficult to do nothing while they assault something so precious to us. But we don't need to lash back in revenge or justify our position; we can trust God to protect our reputation. Jesus was silent before his accusers (Luke 23.9, 10); he left his case in God's hands (1 Peter 2.21–24). That is a good place to leave our case too!

39.1–3 David resolved not to sin with his tongue; that is, he decided not to complain to other people about God's treatment of him. David certainly had reason to complain. He was the anointed king of Israel, but had to wait many years before taking the throne. Then one of his sons tried to kill him and become king instead. But when David could not keep still any longer, he took his complaints directly to God. We all have complaints about job, money, or situations, but complaining before others may make them think that God cannot take care of us. It may also look as if we blame God for our troubles. Instead, like David, we should take our complaints directly to God.

I will keep a muzzle on my mouth
as long as the wicked are in my presence."

39.2 Ps 38.13-16

2 I was silent and still;
I held my peace to no avail;
my distress grew worse,
3 my heart became hot within me.
While I mused, the fire burned;
then I spoke with my tongue:

39.4 Ps 78.39; 90.12

4 "LORD, let me know my end,
and what is the measure of my days;
let me know how fleeting my life is.

39.5 Job 14.2 Ps 49.10; 62.9 89.47; 144.4

5 You have made my days a few handbreadths,
and my lifetime is as nothing in your sight.
Surely everyone stands as a mere breath. *Selah*
6 Surely everyone goes about like a shadow.
Surely for nothing they are in turmoil;
they heap up, and do not know who will gather.

7 "And now, O Lord, what do I wait for?
My hope is in you.

39.8 Ps 51.9; 79.4,9

8 Deliver me from all my transgressions.
Do not make me the scorn of the fool.

39.9 2 Sam 16.10 Job 2.10

9 I am silent; I do not open my mouth,
for it is you who have done it.

39.10 Job 9.34 Ps 32.4

10 Remove your stroke from me;
I am worn down by the blows[t] of your hand.

39.11 Job 13.27,28 Ps 90.7

11 "You chastise mortals
in punishment for sin,
consuming like a moth what is dear to them;
surely everyone is a mere breath. *Selah*

39.12 2 Chron 29.15 Heb 11.13

12 "Hear my prayer, O LORD,
and give ear to my cry;
do not hold your peace at my tears.
For I am your passing guest,
an alien, like all my forebears.

39.13 Job 10.20; 14.6

13 Turn your gaze away from me, that I may smile again,
before I depart and am no more."

[t] Heb *hostility*

39.4 Life is short no matter how long we live. If there is something important we want to do, we must not put it off for a better day. Ask yourself, "If I had only six months to live, what would I do?" Tell someone that you love him or her? Deal with an undisciplined area in your life? Tell someone about Jesus? Since life is short, don't neglect what is truly important.

39.5, 6 The brevity of life is a theme throughout the books of Psalms, Proverbs, and Ecclesiastes. Christ also spoke about it (Luke 12.20). It is ironic that people spend so much time securing their lives on earth and spend little or no thought on where they will spend eternity. David realized that amassing riches and busily accomplishing worldly tasks would make no difference in eternity. Few people understand that their only hope is in the Lord. (For other verses on the brevity of life, see Ecclesiastes 2.18 and James 4.14.)

39.10 What did David mean when he asked God to stop hitting him? This is a metaphor of parental discipline. It may also be a picture of the difficulties David was facing that caused him to feel as if he was being struck. Just as a loving father carefully disciplines his children, so God corrects us (Hebrews 12.5–9).

39.12 How temporary our lives are! It is as if we were God's guests, visiting with him for a short while before passing on. But while our time here is short, the effects of what we do can be eternal. One well-worn saying states: "Only one life will soon be past; only what's done for Christ will last."

Theme: Doing God's will sometimes means waiting patiently. While we wait, we can love God, serve others, and tell others about him.
Author: David

PSALM 40

To the leader. Of David. A Psalm.

1 I waited patiently for the LORD;
he inclined to me and heard my cry.
2 He drew me up from the desolate pit,[u]
out of the miry bog,
and set my feet upon a rock,
making my steps secure.
3 He put a new song in my mouth,
a song of praise to our God.
Many will see and fear,
and put their trust in the LORD.

4 Happy are those who make
the LORD their trust,
who do not turn to the proud,
to those who go astray after false gods.
5 You have multiplied, O LORD my God,
your wondrous deeds and your thoughts toward us;
none can compare with you.
Were I to proclaim and tell of them,
they would be more than can be counted.

6 Sacrifice and offering you do not desire,
but you have given me an open ear.[v]
Burnt offering and sin offering
you have not required.
7 Then I said, "Here I am;
in the scroll of the book it is written of me.[w]
8 I delight to do your will, O my God;
your law is within my heart."

9 I have told the glad news of deliverance
in the great congregation;
see, I have not restrained my lips,
as you know, O LORD.
10 I have not hidden your saving help within my heart,

40.1 Ps 27.14; 34.15
40.2 Ps 27.5; 69.1,2
40.3 Ps 32.7; 64.9
40.4 Job 37.24 Ps 84.12
40.5 Job 5.9 Ps 136.4 139.17,18
40.6 1 Sam 15.22 Jer 7.22,23 Mic 6.6-8 Heb 10.5-7
40.8 Ps 37.31 2 Cor 3.3 Jn 4.34 Rom 7.22
40.9 Ps 22.25 119.13
40.10 Ps 89.1 Acts 20.20,27

[u] Cn: Heb *pit of tumult* [v] Heb *ears you have dug for me* [w] Meaning of Heb uncertain

40.1–4 Waiting for God to help us is not easy, but David received four benefits from waiting: God (1) lifted him out of his despair, (2) set his feet on firm ground, (3) steadied him as he walked, and (4) gave him a new song. Often blessings cannot be received unless we go through the trial of waiting.

40.6 The religious ritual of David's day involved sacrificing animals in the tabernacle. Today we often make rituals of going to church, taking communion, or paying tithe. These activities are empty if our reasons for doing them are selfish. God doesn't want these sacrifices and offerings without an attitude of devotion to him. The prophet Samuel told Saul, "To obey is better than sacrifice" (1 Samuel 15.22). Make sure you give God the obedience and lifelong service he desires from you.

40.7, 8 Jesus portrayed this attitude of obeying and serving God (John 4.34; 5.30). He came as the prophets foretold, proclaiming the Good News of God's righteousness and forgiveness of sins. Verses 6–8 are applied to Jesus in Hebrews 10.5–10.

40.9, 10 God shows his righteousness and faithfulness to his people in his offer of salvation. David boldly proclaimed this to those around him. When we feel the impact of God's righteousness on our lives, we cannot keep it hidden. We want to tell other people what God has done for us. If God's faithfulness has changed your life, don't be timid. Since it is natural to share a good bargain with others or recommend a skillful doctor, then we should also feel natural sharing what God has done for us.

40.10 When we think of faithfulness, a friend or a spouse may come to mind. People who are faithful to us accept and love us, even when we are unlovable. Faithful people keep their promises, whether promises of support or marriage vows. God's faithfulness is like human faithfulness, only more so. His love is absolute, and his promises irrevocable. He loves us in spite of our constant bent toward sin, and he keeps all the promises he has made to us, even when we break our promises to him.

I have spoken of your faithfulness and your salvation;
I have not concealed your steadfast love and your faithfulness
from the great congregation.

40.11 Ps 43.3; 61.7

11 Do not, O LORD, withhold
your mercy from me;
let your steadfast love and your faithfulness
keep me safe forever.

40.12 Ps 18.5; 38.4 73.26; 116.3

12 For evils have encompassed me
without number;
my iniquities have overtaken me,
until I cannot see;
they are more than the hairs of my head,
and my heart fails me.

40.13 Ps 22.19; 71.12

13 Be pleased, O LORD, to deliver me;
O LORD, make haste to help me.

40.14 Ps 35.4,26 70.2,3

14 Let all those be put to shame and confusion
who seek to snatch away my life;
let those be turned back and brought to dishonor
who desire my hurt.
15 Let those be appalled because of their shame
who say to me, "Aha, Aha!"

40.16 Ps 35.27; 70.4

16 But may all who seek you
rejoice and be glad in you;
may those who love your salvation
say continually, "Great is the LORD!"
17 As for me, I am poor and needy,
but the Lord takes thought for me.
You are my help and my deliverer;
do not delay, O my God.

Theme: A prayer for God's mercy when feeling sick or abandoned. When we're sick or when everyone deserts us, God remains at our side.
Author: David

PSALM 41

To the leader. A Psalm of David.

41.1 Ps 37.19 82.3,4

1 Happy are those who consider the poor;[x]
the LORD delivers them in the day of trouble.

41.2 Ps 27.12 37.22,28

2 The LORD protects them and keeps them alive;
they are called happy in the land.
You do not give them up to the will of their enemies.
3 The LORD sustains them on their sickbed;
in their illness you heal all their infirmities.[y]

41.4 Ps 5.4; 6.2

4 As for me, I said, "O LORD, be gracious to me;
heal me, for I have sinned against you."

41.5 Ps 38.12

5 My enemies wonder in malice
when I will die, and my name perish.

[x] Or *weak* [y] Heb *you change all his bed*

40.17 The leader of your country probably does not know you by name, let alone think about you. But the King of all creation, the Ruler of the universe, is thinking about you right now. Allow this truth to buoy up your self-esteem. If God always has us in his thoughts, perhaps we should keep him in our thoughts more faithfully.

41.1 The Bible often speaks of God's care for the poor and his blessing on those who share this concern. God does not want the poor to suffer. God wants our generosity to reflect his own free giving; as he has blessed us, we should bless others.

6 And when they come to see me, they utter empty words,
while their hearts gather mischief;
when they go out, they tell it abroad.
7 All who hate me whisper together about me;
they imagine the worst for me.

8 They think that a deadly thing has fastened on me,
that I will not rise again from where I lie.
9 Even my bosom friend in whom I trusted,
who ate of my bread, has lifted the heel against me.
10 But you, O LORD, be gracious to me,
and raise me up, that I may repay them.

11 By this I know that you are pleased with me;
because my enemy has not triumphed over me.
12 But you have upheld me because of my integrity,
and set me in your presence forever.

13 Blessed be the LORD, the God of Israel,
from everlasting to everlasting.
Amen and Amen.

41.6 Ps 12.2
41.9 Job 19.19 Ps 55.12,13,20 Jer 20.10 Jn 13.18
41.10 Ps 3.3
41.12 Ps 18.32; 21.6 37.17
41.13 Ps 72.18,19 106.48

BOOK II
Psalms 42.1 – 72.20

These psalms include a prayer for rescue, a call to worship, a confession of sin, an encouragement to trust God, a psalm for those hurt by friends, a prayer for those who have been slandered, and a missionary psalm. These psalms can help us retain a sense of wonder in our worship.

Theme: A thirst for God. When you feel lonely or depressed, meditate on God's kindness and love.
Author: The sons of Korah, who were temple musicians and assistants

PSALM 42

To the leader. A Maskil of the Korahites.

1 As a deer longs for flowing streams,
so my soul longs for you, O God.
2 My soul thirsts for God,
for the living God.
When shall I come and behold
the face of God?
3 My tears have been my food
day and night,

42.1 Ps 63.1
42.2 Ps 43.4; 84.2 143.6 Jer 10.10 Rom 9.26
42.3 Ps 79.10; 80.5 Joel 2.17

41.9 This verse is viewed in the New Testament as a prophecy of Christ's betrayal (John 13.18). Judas, one of Jesus' 12 disciples, had spent three years learning from Jesus, traveling and eating with him (Mark 3.14–19), handling the finances for the group. Eventually Judas, who knew Jesus extremely well, betrayed him (Matthew 26.14–16, 20–25).

41.13 Psalms is divided into five books, and each one ends with a doxology or an expression of praise to God. The first book of the psalms, including chapters 1 through 41, takes us on a journey through suffering, sorrow, and great joy. It teaches us much about God's eternal love and care for us and how we should trust him even in the day-to-day experiences of life.

42.1ff Psalms 42 – 49 were written by the sons of Korah. Korah was a Levite who led a rebellion against Moses (Numbers 16.1–35). He was killed, but his descendants remained faithful to God and continued to serve God in the temple. David appointed men from the clan of Korah to serve as choir leaders (1 Chronicles 6.31–38), and they continued to be temple musicians for hundreds of years (2 Chronicles 20.18, 19).

42.1ff There may come times when, after thirsting for God, weeping for his help, and enduring ridicule, we still do not hear his voice (42.1–3). Such times often lead to depression and discouragement, but the psalmist discovered a remedy. He remembered God's great blessings (42.4, 5); he realized that although God seemed silent, he was present with him (42.4, 5); he gazed upon God's beautiful creation that proclaims his love (42.6). The psalmist had felt billows of sorrow, but he realized that he was never adrift from God's steadfast love (42.7, 8). Finally he faithfully *expected* God to act (42.11). When you cannot seem to find God, use this remedy and you will, once again, find reason to praise him.

42.1, 2 As the life of a deer depends upon water, our lives depend upon God. Those who seek him and long to understand him find never-ending life. Feeling separated from God, this psalmist wouldn't rest until he restored his relationship with God, because he knew that life depended on it.

while people say to me continually,
"Where is your God?"

42.4
Job 30.16
Ps 62.8; 71.14
Isa 30.29
Lam 3.24
Mt 26.38

4 These things I remember,
as I pour out my soul:
how I went with the throng,[z]
and led them in procession to the house of God,
with glad shouts and songs of thanksgiving,
a multitude keeping festival.
5 Why are you cast down, O my soul,
and why are you disquieted within me?
Hope in God; for I shall again praise him,
my help 6 and my God.

42.6
Ps 61.2

My soul is cast down within me;
therefore I remember you
from the land of Jordan and of Hermon,
from Mount Mizar.

42.7
Ps 88.7
Jonah 2.3

7 Deep calls to deep
at the thunder of your cataracts;
all your waves and your billows
have gone over me.

42.8
Ps 16.7; 57.3
77.6; 149.4,5
Job 35.10

8 By day the LORD commands his steadfast love,
and at night his song is with me,
a prayer to the God of my life.

42.9
Ps 17.9; 18.2
38.6

9 I say to God, my rock,
"Why have you forgotten me?
Why must I walk about mournfully
because the enemy oppresses me?"
10 As with a deadly wound in my body,
my adversaries taunt me,
while they say to me continually,
"Where is your God?"

11 Why are you cast down, O my soul,
and why are you disquieted within me?
Hope in God; for I shall again praise him,
my help and my God.

Theme: Hope in a time of discouragement. In the face of discouragement, our only hope is in God.
Author: The sons of Korah (temple assistants). Psalms 42 and 43 are one psalm in many Hebrew manuscripts.

PSALM 43

43.1
1 Sam 24.15
Ps 26.1; 35.24

1 Vindicate me, O God, and defend my cause
against an ungodly people;
from those who are deceitful and unjust

[z] Meaning of Heb uncertain

42.4, 5 The writer of this psalm was discouraged because he was exiled to a place far from Jerusalem and could not worship in the temple. During these God-given holidays, the nation was to remember all that God had done for them. Many of these festivals are explained in the chart in Leviticus 23.

42.6 Hermon refers to Mount Hermon. *Mizar* means smallness, so Mount Mizar could be a smaller mountain in that mountain range.

42.6 Depression is one of the most common emotional ailments. One antidote for depression is to meditate on the record of God's goodness to his people. This will take your mind off the present situation and give hope that it will improve. It focuses your thoughts on God's ability to help you rather than your inability to help yourself. When you feel depressed, take advantage of this psalm's antidepressant. Read the Bible's accounts of God's goodness, and meditate on them.

deliver me!
2 For you are the God in whom I take refuge;
why have you cast me off?
Why must I walk about mournfully
because of the oppression of the enemy?

3 O send out your light and your truth;
let them lead me;
let them bring me to your holy hill
and to your dwelling.
4 Then I will go to the altar of God,
to God my exceeding joy;
and I will praise you with the harp,
O God, my God.

5 Why are you cast down, O my soul,
and why are you disquieted within me?
Hope in God; for I shall again praise him,
my help and my God.

43.2 Ps 28.7; 42.9 44.9

43.3 Ps 36.9 42.4,5; 84.1

43.4 Ps 26.6; 33.2

Theme: A plea for victory by the battle-weary and defeated. When it seems that God has let you down, don't despair. Instead, remember God's past deliverance and be confident that he will restore you.
Author: The sons of Korah (temple assistants)

PSALM 44

To the leader. Of the Korahites. A Maskil.

1 We have heard with our ears, O God,
our ancestors have told us,
what deeds you performed in their days,
in the days of old:
2 you with your own hand drove out the nations,
but them you planted;
you afflicted the peoples,
but them you set free;
3 for not by their own sword did they win the land,
nor did their own arm give them victory;
but your right hand, and your arm,
and the light of your countenance,
for you delighted in them.

4 You are my King and my God;
you command[a] victories for Jacob.
5 Through you we push down our foes;
through your name we tread down our assailants.
6 For not in my bow do I trust,

[a] Gk Syr: Heb *You are my King, O God; command*

44.1 Ps 78.2,3,12, 55; 80.8

44.3 Deut 4.37 Ps 77.15

44.5 Ps 60.12

43.3 The "holy hill" is Mount Zion, in Jerusalem, the city David made Israel's capital. The temple was built on this hill as the place for the people to meet God in worship and prayer.

43.3, 4 The psalmist asked God to send his light and truth to guide him to the temple, where he would meet God. God's truth (see 1 John 2.27) provides the right path to follow, and God's light (see 1 John 1.5) provides the clear vision to follow it. If you feel surrounded by darkness and uncertainty, follow God's light and truth back to him.

44.1ff This psalm may have been sung at an occasion like the one in 2 Chronicles 20.18, 19, where the faithful Jehoshaphat was surrounded by enemies and the Levites sang to the Lord before the battle.

44.1–3 Driving out the heathen refers to the conquest of Canaan (the promised land) described in the book of Joshua. God gave the land to Israel, and they were to enter and drive out anyone who was wicked and determined to oppose God. Israel was told to settle the land and be a witness to the world of God's power and love. Surrounded by enemies, the psalmist remembered what God had done for his people and took heart. We can have this same confidence in God when we feel attacked.

nor can my sword save me.

44.7 Ps 53.5; 136.24

7 But you have saved us from our foes,
and have put to confusion those who hate us.

44.8 Ps 30.12; 34.2

8 In God we have boasted continually,
and we will give thanks to your name forever. *Selah*

44.9 Ps 43.2; 60.10 74.1

9 Yet you have rejected us and abased us,
and have not gone out with our armies.

44.10 Lev 26.33 Josh 7.8,12 Ps 89.42

10 You made us turn back from the foe,
and our enemies have gotten spoil.
11 You have made us like sheep for slaughter,
and have scattered us among the nations.
12 You have sold your people for a trifle,
demanding no high price for them.

13 You have made us the taunt of our neighbors,
the derision and scorn of those around us.

44.14 Ps 17.6; 109.25

14 You have made us a byword among the nations,
a laughingstock[b] among the peoples.
15 All day long my disgrace is before me,
and shame has covered my face
16 at the words of the taunters and revilers,
at the sight of the enemy and the avenger.

44.17 Ps 119.61,83, 109,141,153, 176

17 All this has come upon us,
yet we have not forgotten you,
or been false to your covenant.

44.18 Ps 119.51,157

18 Our heart has not turned back,
nor have our steps departed from your way,

44.19 Ps 51.8; 94.5

19 yet you have broken us in the haunt of jackals,
and covered us with deep darkness.

44.20 Ps 78.11; 81.9

20 If we had forgotten the name of our God,
or spread out our hands to a strange god,
21 would not God discover this?
For he knows the secrets of the heart.

44.22 Isa 53.7 Rom 8.36

22 Because of you we are being killed all day long,
and accounted as sheep for the slaughter.

44.23 Ps 7.6; 77.7 78.65

23 Rouse yourself! Why do you sleep, O Lord?
Awake, do not cast us off forever!

44.24 Ps 42.9; 88.14

24 Why do you hide your face?
Why do you forget our affliction and oppression?
25 For we sink down to the dust;
our bodies cling to the ground.

[b] Heb *a shaking of the head*

44.22 Israel had been defeated despite their faith (44.17) and obedience (44.18) to God. The psalmist could not understand why God allowed this to happen, but he did not give up hope of discovering the answer (44.17–22). Although he felt his suffering was undeserved, he revealed the real reason for it: he suffered because he was *serving God.* Paul quoted the psalmist's complaint (Romans 8.36) to show that we must always be ready to face death for the cause of Christ. Thus, our suffering may not be a punishment, but a battle scar that demonstrates our loyalty.

44.22–26 The writer cried to God to save his people for his mercies' sake; that is, because he is by nature merciful. Nothing can separate us from God's love, not even death (Romans 8.36–39). When you fear for your life, ask God for deliverance, and remember that even death cannot separate you from him.

44.23–25 The psalmist's words suggest that he did not believe God had left him. God was still the Ruler, but he seemed to be asleep, and the psalmist wondered why. In the New Testament, the disciples wondered why Jesus was asleep when they needed his help during a storm (Mark 4.35–41). In both cases, of course, God's power was not asleep. He was ready to help, but he wished first to build faith in his followers.

26 Rise up, come to our help.
Redeem us for the sake of your steadfast love.

Theme: A poem to the king (possibly Solomon) on the occasion of his wedding. While this psalm was written for an historic occasion, it is also seen as a prophecy about Christ and his bride, the church, who will praise him throughout all generations.
Author: The sons of Korah (temple assistants)

PSALM 45

To the leader: according to Lilies. Of the Korahites. A Maskil. A love song.

1 My heart overflows with a goodly theme;
I address my verses to the king;
my tongue is like the pen of a ready scribe.

2 You are the most handsome of men;
grace is poured upon your lips;
therefore God has blessed you forever.
3 Gird your sword on your thigh, O mighty one,
in your glory and majesty.

4 In your majesty ride on victoriously
for the cause of truth and to defend[c] the right;
let your right hand teach you dread deeds.
5 Your arrows are sharp
in the heart of the king's enemies;
the peoples fall under you.

6 Your throne, O God,[d] endures forever and ever.
Your royal scepter is a scepter of equity;
7 you love righteousness and hate wickedness.
Therefore God, your God, has anointed you
with the oil of gladness beyond your companions;
8 your robes are all fragrant with myrrh and aloes and cassia.
From ivory palaces stringed instruments make you glad;
9 daughters of kings are among your ladies of honor;
at your right hand stands the queen in gold of Ophir.

10 Hear, O daughter, consider and incline your ear;
forget your people and your father's house,
11 and the king will desire your beauty.
Since he is your lord, bow to him;
12 the people[e] of Tyre will seek your favor with gifts,
the richest of the people 13 with all kinds of wealth.

45.1 Ezra 7.6
45.2 Ps 21.6 Lk 4.22
45.3 Isa 9.6
45.4 Rev 6.2
45.5 Ps 120.4 Isa 5.28
45.6 Ps 93.2; 98.8,9 Heb 1.8,9
45.7 Ps 11.7; 21.6 33.5
45.8 Song 1.3 4.13,14
45.9 1 Kgs 2.19; 9.28 Song 6.8 Isa 13.12
45.10 Deut 21.13 Isa 54.5 Eph 5.33 1 Pet 3.6
45.12 Ps 22.29 72.10,11
45.13 Isa 61.10

[c] Cn: Heb *and the meekness of* [d] Or *Your throne is a throne of God, it* [e] Heb *daughter*

45.1ff This is called a "messianic" psalm because it prophetically describes the Messiah's future relationship to the church, his body of believers. Verse 2 expresses God's abundant blessing on his Messiah; verses 6–8 find their true fulfillment in Christ (Hebrews 1.8, 9). The church is described as the bride of Christ in Revelation 19.7, 8; 21.9; 22.17.

45.1ff In this royal wedding song, the bridegroom has everything – power, position, wealth, and now a beautiful bride. But the tribute to the king is not because of these things, but because the king pleases God. He defends truth, meekness, and righteousness, loves righteousness and hates wickedness, and for this has earned the praise of many nations. True royalty is characterized not by the robes worn or thrones occupied, but by a faithful obedience to the most royal of all, the King of kings. We have been called to be "a royal priesthood, a holy nation" (1 Peter 2.9), and we portray that royalty by honoring our Lord the King who gave it to us.

45.8, 9 Myrrh is a fragrant gum of an Arabian tree. It is generally used in perfumes. Aloes, a spice, may have come from sandalwood, a close-grained and fragrant wood often used for storage boxes or chests (see also Proverbs 7.14–17; Song of Solomon 4.13, 14). Cassia grows as a thistle; its sweet fragrance comes from the roots of the plant. These expensive fragrances are appropriate for a king's wedding. The location of Ophir is unknown, but believed to be in either Arabia or Africa. It was famous as a source of gold.

45.13–17 In this beautiful poetry we have a picture of Christ's bride, the church, pictured with the richest blessings as she unites forever with him (see Revelation 19.6–8; 21.2).

The princess is decked in her chamber with gold-woven robes;[f]
45.14 Song 1.4 Ezek 16.9-13 14 in many-colored robes she is led to the king;
behind her the virgins, her companions, follow.
15 With joy and gladness they are led along
as they enter the palace of the king.

16 In the place of ancestors you, O king,[g] shall have sons;
you will make them princes in all the earth.
45.17 Ps 138.4 Mal 1.11 17 I will cause your name to be celebrated in all generations;
therefore the peoples will praise you forever and ever.

Theme: God is always there to help, providing refuge, security, and peace. God's power is complete and his ultimate victory is certain. He will not fail to rescue those who love him.
Author: The sons of Korah (temple assistants)

PSALM 46

To the leader. Of the Korahites. According to Alamoth. A Song.

46.1 Ps 9.9; 14.6 62.7,8; 145.18 1 God is our refuge and strength,
a very present[h] help in trouble.
2 Therefore we will not fear, though the earth should change,
though the mountains shake in the heart of the sea;
3 though its waters roar and foam,
though the mountains tremble with its tumult. *Selah*

46.4 Ps 87.3 Isa 60.14 Rev 3.12; 22.1 4 There is a river whose streams make glad the city of God,
the holy habitation of the Most High.
46.5 Isa 12.6; 41.14 Ezek 43.7 5 God is in the midst of the city;[i] it shall not be moved;
God will help it when the morning dawns.
46.6 Ps 2.1 6 The nations are in an uproar, the kingdoms totter;
he utters his voice, the earth melts.

[f] Or *people.* 13*All glorious is the princess within, gold embroidery is her clothing* [g] Heb lacks *O king* [h] Or *well proved* [i] Heb *of it*

PSALMS THAT HAVE INSPIRED HYMNS

Psalm 23	The King of Love My Shepherd Is My Shepherd Shall Supply My Need The Lord Is My Shepherd
Psalm 46	A Mighty Fortress Is Our God
Psalm 61	Hiding in Thee (O Safe to the Rock That Is Higher Than I . . .)
Psalm 87	Glorious Things of Thee Are Spoken
Psalm 90	O God, Our Help in Ages Past
Psalm 100	All People That on Earth Do Dwell Before Jehovah's Awful Throne
Psalm 103	Praise to the Lord, the Almighty
Psalm 104	O Worship the King, All Glorious Above
Psalm 126	Bringing in the Sheaves

46–48 Psalms 46–48 are hymns of praise, celebrating deliverance from some great foe. Psalm 46 may have been written when the Assyrian army invaded the land and surrounded Jerusalem (2 Kings 18.13–19.37).

46.1–3 The fear of mountains or cities suddenly crumbling into the sea as the result of a nuclear blast haunts many people today. But the psalmist says that even if the world ends, we need not fear. In the face of utter destruction, he expressed a quiet confidence in God's ability to save him. It seems impossible to consider the end of the world without fear, but the Bible is clear—God is our refuge even in the face of total destruction. He is not merely a temporary retreat; he is our eternal refuge and can provide strength in any circumstances.

46.4, 5 Many great cities have rivers flowing through them, sustaining people's lives by making agriculture possible and facilitating trade with other cities. Jerusalem had no river, but it had God who, like a river, sustained the people's lives. As long as God lived among the people, the city was invincible. But when the people abandoned him, God no longer protected them, and Jerusalem fell to the Babylonian army.

7 The LORD of hosts is with us;
the God of Jacob is our refuge.[j] *Selah*

8 Come, behold the works of the LORD;
see what desolations he has brought on the earth.
9 He makes wars cease to the end of the earth;
he breaks the bow, and shatters the spear;
he burns the shields with fire.
10 "Be still, and know that I am God!
I am exalted among the nations,
I am exalted in the earth."
11 The LORD of hosts is with us;
the God of Jacob is our refuge.[j] *Selah*

46.7 Num 14.9 Ps 9.9
46.8 Ps 66.5
46.9 Isa 2.4; 9.5
46.10 Ps 100.3

Theme: God is still king of the world. All nations of the earth will eventually recognize his Lordship.
Author: The sons of Korah (temple assistants)

PSALM 47

To the leader. Of the Korahites. A Psalm.

1 Clap your hands, all you peoples;
shout to God with loud songs of joy.
2 For the LORD, the Most High, is awesome,
a great king over all the earth.
3 He subdued peoples under us,
and nations under our feet.
4 He chose our heritage for us,
the pride of Jacob whom he loves. *Selah*

5 God has gone up with a shout,
the LORD with the sound of a trumpet.
6 Sing praises to God, sing praises;
sing praises to our King, sing praises.
7 For God is the king of all the earth;
sing praises with a psalm.[k]

8 God is king over the nations;
God sits on his holy throne.
9 The princes of the peoples gather
as the people of the God of Abraham.
For the shields of the earth belong to God;
he is highly exalted.

47.2 Deut 7.21
47.4 1 Pet 1.4
47.5 Ps 68.18,25,33
47.6 Ps 68.4; 89.18
47.8 1 Chron 16.31
47.9 Ps 72.11 Isa 49.7,23

[j] Or *fortress* [k] Heb *Maskil*

46.10 War and destruction are inevitable, but so is God's final victory. At that time, all will be still before Almighty God. How proper, then, for us to be still now, reverently honoring him and his power and majesty. Take time each day to be still and to exalt God.

47.1ff This psalm was written about the same event as Psalm 46—the Assyrian invasion of Judah by Sennacherib (2 Kings 18.13–19.37).

47.2 The Lord God is awesome beyond words, but this didn't keep Bible writers from trying to describe him. And it shouldn't keep us from talking about him either. We can't describe God completely, but we can tell others what he has done for us. Don't let the indescribable aspects of God's greatness prevent you from telling others what you know about him.

47.9 Abraham was the father of the Israelite nation. The one true God was sometimes called the "God of Abraham" (Exodus 3.6; 1 Kings 18.36). In a spiritual sense, God's promises to Abraham apply to all who believe in God, Jew or Gentile (Romans 4.11, 12; Galatians 3.7–9). Thus the God of Abraham is our God too.

48.2 Why is Mount Zion—Jerusalem—"the city of the great King"? Because the temple was located in Jerusalem, the city was seen as the center of God's presence in the world. The Bible pictures Jerusalem as the place to which believers will flock in the "last days" (Isaiah 2.2ff), and as the spiritual home of all believers where God will live among them (Revelation 21.2, 3).

Theme: God's presence is our joy, security, and salvation. God is praised as the defender of Jerusalem, the holy city of the Jews. He is also our defender and guide forever.
Author: The sons of Korah (temple assistants)

PSALM 48

A Song. A Psalm of the Korahites.

48.1 1 Chron 16.25; Ps 87.1; 96.4; 145.3; Zech 8.3
48.2 Ps 50.2; Lam 2.15; Mt 5.35
48.3 Ps 46.7

1 Great is the LORD and greatly to be praised
in the city of our God.
His holy mountain, 2 beautiful in elevation,
is the joy of all the earth,
Mount Zion, in the far north,
the city of the great King.
3 Within its citadels God
has shown himself a sure defense.

4 Then the kings assembled,
they came on together.
5 As soon as they saw it, they were astounded;
they were in panic, they took to flight;
6 trembling took hold of them there,
pains as of a woman in labor,
7 as when an east wind shatters
the ships of Tarshish.
8 As we have heard, so have we seen
in the city of the LORD of hosts,
in the city of our God,
which God establishes forever. *Selah*

48.6 Isa 13.8
48.8 Ps 87.5

9 We ponder your steadfast love, O God,
in the midst of your temple.
10 Your name, O God, like your praise,
reaches to the ends of the earth.
Your right hand is filled with victory.
11 Let Mount Zion be glad,
let the towns[l] of Judah rejoice
because of your judgments.

48.9 Ps 26.3; 40.10
48.10 Josh 7.9; Mal 1.11
48.11 Ps 97.8

12 Walk about Zion, go all around it,
count its towers,
13 consider well its ramparts;
go through its citadels,
that you may tell the next generation
14 that this is God,
our God forever and ever.
He will be our guide forever.

48.13 Ps 78.5-7

[l] Heb *daughters*

48.8 Since Jerusalem has been destroyed several times since this psalm was written, the phrase, "which God establishes forever" may refer prophetically to the new Jerusalem where God will judge all nations and live with all believers (Revelation 21).

48.11 The people of Judah were from Israel's largest tribe, which settled in the southern part of Canaan where Jerusalem was located (Joshua 15.1–12). David was from Judah, and he made Jerusalem his capital and center of the nation's worship. Jesus was also a member of the tribe of Judah. The psalmist was saying that the day would come when God would bring justice to the land, and his people would get the respect they deserved.

48.12, 13 After an enemy army had unsuccessfully besieged Jerusalem, it was common for the people to make a tour of the city, inspecting its defenses and praising God for the protection it had offered. In times of great joy or after God has brought us through some great trial, we ought to inspect our defenses to make sure that the foundations – God, his Word, and the body of believers – remain strong (Ephesians 2.20–22). Then praise God for his protection!

48.14 We often pray for God's guidance as we struggle with decisions. What we need is both guidance and a guide – a map that gives us landmarks and directions and a constant companion who has an intimate knowledge of the way and will make sure we interpret the map correctly. The Bible will be such a map, and the Holy Spirit will be the constant companion and guide. As you make your way through life, lean upon both the map and the Guide.

Theme: Trusting in worldly possessions is futile. You cannot take possessions with you when you die, and they cannot buy forgiveness from sin.
Author: The sons of Korah (temple assistants)

PSALM 49

To the leader. Of the Korahites. A Psalm.

1 Hear this, all you peoples;
give ear, all inhabitants of the world,
2 both low and high,
rich and poor together.
3 My mouth shall speak wisdom;
the meditation of my heart shall be understanding.
4 I will incline my ear to a proverb;
I will solve my riddle to the music of the harp.

5 Why should I fear in times of trouble,
when the iniquity of my persecutors surrounds me,
6 those who trust in their wealth
and boast of the abundance of their riches?
7 Truly, no ransom avails for one's life,[m]
there is no price one can give to God for it.
8 For the ransom of life is costly,
and can never suffice
9 that one should live on forever
and never see the grave.[n]

10 When we look at the wise, they die;
fool and dolt perish together
and leave their wealth to others.
11 Their graves[o] are their homes forever,
their dwelling places to all generations,
though they named lands their own.
12 Mortals cannot abide in their pomp;
they are like the animals that perish.

13 Such is the fate of the foolhardy,
the end of those[p] who are pleased with their lot. *Selah*
14 Like sheep they are appointed for Sheol;
Death shall be their shepherd;
straight to the grave they descend,[q]

49.1 Ps 78.1
49.3 Ps 39.30 119.130
49.4 2 Kgs 3.15 Ps 78.23
49.5 Ps 23.4; 27.1
49.6 Ps 52.7 Mark 10.24
49.7 Job 36.18 Mt 25.8,9
49.8 Ps 16.10; 89.48 Mt 16.26
49.10 Ps 39.6 Lk 12.20,21
49.11 Deut 3.14
49.14 Ps 9.17 Rev 2.26

[m] Another reading is *no one can ransom a brother* [n] Heb *the pit* [o] Gk Syr Compare Tg: Heb *their inward* (thought) [p] Tg: Heb *after them* [q] Cn: Heb *the upright shall have dominion over them in the morning*

49.1ff The futility of worldliness—riches, pride, fame—resounds from this psalm. Comparable in form to the book of Ecclesiastes, this psalm is one of the few written more to instruct than to give praise.

49.7, 8, 15 In the slave market of the ancient world, a slave had to be redeemed or ransomed (someone paid the price) in order to go free. In Mark 10.45, Ephesians 1.7, and Hebrews 9.12, we learn that Jesus paid such a price so that we could be set free from slavery to sin in order to begin a new life with him.

There is no way for a person to buy eternal life with God. God alone can redeem a soul. Don't count on wealth and physical comforts to keep you happy, because you will never have enough wealth to keep from dying.

49.10–14 The rich and poor have one similarity—when they die, they leave all they own here on earth. At the moment of death (and all of us will face that moment), both rich and poor are naked and empty-handed before God. The only riches we have at that time are those we have already invested in our eternal heritage. At the time of death, each of us will wish we had invested less on earth, where we must leave it, and more in heaven, where we will retain it forever. To have treasure in heaven, we must place our faith in God, pledge ourselves to obey him, and utilize our resources for the good of his kingdom. This is a good time to check up on your investments and see where you have invested the most. Then do whatever it takes to place your investments where they really count.

49.12, 20 We are not like beasts in all ways, but like the animals, we all must face death. It is inevitable and we must be prepared. God will deliver us from the grave and receive us unto himself (49.15) if we trust him, and not our wealth, to save us. Psalm 73.24 also gives us confidence in the afterlife. Let us not be foolish (49.10), but respond to God's offer.

and their form shall waste away;
Sheol shall be their home.[r]

49.15 Ps 16.10,11

15 But God will ransom my soul from the power of Sheol,
for he will receive me. *Selah*

49.16 Ps 37.7

16 Do not be afraid when some become rich,
when the wealth of their houses increases.

49.17 Ps 17.14; 1 Tim 6.7

17 For when they die they will carry nothing away;
their wealth will not go down after them.

49.18 Ps 10.3

18 Though in their lifetime they count themselves happy
—for you are praised when you do well for yourself—
19 they[s] will go to the company of their ancestors,
who will never again see the light.
20 Mortals cannot abide in their pomp;
they are like the animals that perish.

Theme: The contrast between true and false faith. God desires sincere thanks, trust, and praise.
Author: Asaph, one of David's chief musicians

PSALM 50

A Psalm of Asaph.

50.1 Ps 113.3

1 The mighty one, God the LORD,
speaks and summons the earth
from the rising of the sun to its setting.

50.2 Ps 48.2; 80.1

2 Out of Zion, the perfection of beauty,
God shines forth.

50.3 Ps 18.12,13

3 Our God comes and does not keep silence,
before him is a devouring fire,
and a mighty tempest all around him.
4 He calls to the heavens above
and to the earth, that he may judge his people:
5 "Gather to me my faithful ones,
who made a covenant with me by sacrifice!"

50.6 Ps 96.13; 97.6

6 The heavens declare his righteousness,
for God himself is judge. *Selah*

7 "Hear, O my people, and I will speak,
O Israel, I will testify against you.
I am God, your God.
8 Not for your sacrifices do I rebuke you;
your burnt offerings are continually before me.

50.9 Ps 69.31

9 I will not accept a bull from your house,
or goats from your folds.

50.10 Ps 104.24

10 For every wild animal of the forest is mine,

[r] Meaning of Heb uncertain [s] Cn: Heb *you*

50.1ff God judges people for treating him lightly. First, he speaks to the superficially religious people who bring their sacrifices but are only going through the motions (50.1–15). They do not honor God with true praise and thankfulness. Second, he chides evil, hardhearted people for their wicked words and immoral lives (50.16–22). He asks the superficially religious for genuine thanksgiving and trust, and he warns the evil people to consider their deeds, lest he destroy them in his anger.

50.1–4 This psalm begins as though God is finally ready to judge the evil people on earth. But surprisingly, God's great fury is leveled against his own people (or at least those who claim to be his). God's judgment must begin with his own people (1 Peter 4.17).

50.5–9 God's perfect moral nature demands that the penalty for sin be death; but a person could offer an animal to God as a substitute for himself, symbolizing the person's faith in the merciful, forgiving God. However, the people were offering sacrifices and forgetting their significance! The very act of sacrifice showed that they had once agreed to follow God wholeheartedly. But now their hearts were not in it. We may fall into the same pattern when we participate in "religious activities," tithe, or attend church out of habit or conformity rather than out of heartfelt love and obedience. God desires righteousness, not empty ritual. (See the note on 40.6.)

the cattle on a thousand hills.
11 I know all the birds of the air,[t]
and all that moves in the field is mine.

12 "If I were hungry, I would not tell you,
for the world and all that is in it is mine.
13 Do I eat the flesh of bulls,
or drink the blood of goats?
14 Offer to God a sacrifice of thanksgiving,[u]
and pay your vows to the Most High.
15 Call on me in the day of trouble;
I will deliver you, and you shall glorify me."

16 But to the wicked God says:
"What right have you to recite my statutes,
or take my covenant on your lips?
17 For you hate discipline,
and you cast my words behind you.
18 You make friends with a thief when you see one,
and you keep company with adulterers.

19 "You give your mouth free rein for evil,
and your tongue frames deceit.
20 You sit and speak against your kin;
you slander your own mother's child.
21 These things you have done and I have been silent;
you thought that I was one just like yourself.
But now I rebuke you, and lay the charge before you.

22 "Mark this, then, you who forget God,
or I will tear you apart, and there will be no one to deliver.
23 Those who bring thanksgiving as their sacrifice honor me;
to those who go the right way[v]
I will show the salvation of God."

50.13 Hos 6.6
50.14 Deut 23.21 Hos 14.2 Rom 12.1 Heb 13.15
50.16 Isa 29.13
50.17 Rom 2.21,22
50.18 1 Tim 5.22
50.19 Ps 10.7; 36.3
50.20 Mt 10.21
50.21 Ps 90.8
50.23 Ps 91.16

Theme: David's plea for mercy, forgiveness, and cleansing. God wants our hearts to be right with him.
Author: David

PSALM 51

To the leader. A Psalm of David, when the prophet Nathan came to him, after he had gone in to Bathsheba.

1 Have mercy on me, O God,
according to your steadfast love;
according to your abundant mercy
blot out my transgressions.
2 Wash me thoroughly from my iniquity,

51.2 Jer 33.8 Acts 22.16 Heb 9.13,14 1 Jn 1.7,9

[t] Gk Syr Tg: Heb *mountains* [u] Or *make thanksgiving your sacrifice to God* [v] Heb *who set a way*

50.16–22 Some people glibly recite God's laws, but are filled with deceit and evil. They claim his promises, but refuse to obey him. This is sin, and God will judge people for it. We too are hypocrites when we do not believe what we say. To let this inconsistency remain shows we are not true followers of God.

50.21 At times God seems silent. By his silence he is not condoning sin, nor is he indifferent to it, but he is withholding deserved punishment, giving time for people to repent (2 Peter 3.9). God takes no pleasure in the death of the wicked and wants them to turn from evil (Ezekiel 33.11). But his silence does not last forever—a time of punishment will surely come.

51.1–7 David was truly sorry for his adultery with Bathsheba and for murdering her husband to cover it up. He knew his actions had hurt many people. But because David repented of those sins, God mercifully forgave him. No sin is too great to be forgiven! Do you feel that you could never come close to God because you have done something terrible? God can and will forgive you of any sin. While God forgives us, however, he does not always erase the natural consequences of our sin—David's life and family were never the same as a result of his sin (see 2 Samuel 12.1–23).

and cleanse me from my sin.

3 For I know my transgressions,
and my sin is ever before me.
51.4 Rom 3.4
4 Against you, you alone, have I sinned,
and done what is evil in your sight,
so that you are justified in your sentence
and blameless when you pass judgment.
51.5 Job 14.4 Eph 2.3
5 Indeed, I was born guilty,
a sinner when my mother conceived me.

6 You desire truth in the inward being;[w]
therefore teach me wisdom in my secret heart.
51.7 Ex 12.22 Isa 1.18
7 Purge me with hyssop, and I shall be clean;
wash me, and I shall be whiter than snow.
8 Let me hear joy and gladness;
let the bones that you have crushed rejoice.
51.9 Jer 16.17
9 Hide your face from my sins,
and blot out all my iniquities.

51.10 Mt 5.8 Acts 15.9 Eph 2.10
10 Create in me a clean heart, O God,
and put a new and right[x] spirit within me.
51.11 Eph 4.30
11 Do not cast me away from your presence,
and do not take your holy spirit from me.
12 Restore to me the joy of your salvation,
and sustain in me a willing[y] spirit.

51.13 Ps 22.27
13 Then I will teach transgressors your ways,
and sinners will return to you.
51.14 2 Sam 12.9 Ps 9.14; 25.5 71.15
14 Deliver me from bloodshed, O God,
O God of my salvation,
and my tongue will sing aloud of your deliverance.

15 O Lord, open my lips,
and my mouth will declare your praise.
51.16 1 Sam 15.22 Ps 40.6
16 For you have no delight in sacrifice;
if I were to give a burnt offering, you would not be pleased.
51.17 Ps 34.18
17 The sacrifice acceptable to God[z] is a broken spirit;

[w] Meaning of Heb uncertain [x] Or *steadfast* [y] Or *generous* [z] Or *My sacrifice, O God,*

51.4 Although David sinned with Bathsheba, he said he had sinned against God. When someone steals, murders, or slanders, it is against someone else – a victim. According to the world's standards, extramarital sex between two consenting adults is acceptable if nobody gets hurt. But people *do* get hurt – in David's case, a man was murdered and a baby died. All sin hurts us and others, but ultimately it offends God because sin in any form is a rebellion against God's way of living. When tempted to do wrong, remembering that you will be sinning against God may help you stay on the right track.

51.7 Hyssop branches were used by the Israelites to place the blood of a lamb on the doorposts of their homes to keep them safe from death (Exodus 12.22). By this act the Israelites showed their faith and secured their release from slavery in Egypt. This verse calls for cleansing from sin and readiness to serve the Lord.

51.10 Because we are born as sinners (51.5), our natural inclination is to please ourselves rather than God. David followed that inclination when he took another man's wife. We also follow it when we sin in any way. Like David, we must ask God to cleanse us from within (51.7), clearing our hearts and spirits for new thoughts and desires. Right conduct can come only from a clean heart and spirit. Ask God to create in you a clean heart and spirit.

51.12 Do you ever feel stagnant in your faith, as if you are just going through the motions? Has sin driven a wedge between you and God, making him seem distant? David felt this way. He had sinned with Bathsheba and had just been confronted by Nathan the prophet. In his prayer to God he cried, "Restore to me the joy of your salvation." God wants us to be close to him and to experience his full and complete life. But sin that remains unconfessed makes such intimacy impossible. Confess your sin to God. You may still have to face some earthly consequences, as David did, but God will give back the joy of your relationship with him.

51.13 When God forgives our sin and restores us to a relationship with him, we want to reach out to others who need this forgiveness and reconciliation. The more you have felt God's forgiveness, the more you desire to tell others about it.

51.17 God wants a broken spirit and contrite heart. You can never please God by outward actions – no matter how good – if your inward heart attitude is not right. Are you sorry for your sin? Do you genuinely intend to stop? God is pleased by this kind of humility.

a broken and contrite heart, O God, you will not despise.

18 Do good to Zion in your good pleasure;
rebuild the walls of Jerusalem,
19 then you will delight in right sacrifices, **51.19** Ps 4.5 66.13,15
in burnt offerings and whole burnt offerings;
then bulls will be offered on your altar.

Theme: God will judge the evildoer. Our anger must not block our confidence in God's ability to defeat evil.
Author: David

PSALM 52

To the leader. A Maskil of David, when Doeg the Edomite came to Saul and said to him, "David has come to the house of Ahimelech."

1 Why do you boast, O mighty one,
of mischief done against the godly?[a]
All day long 2 you are plotting destruction. **52.2** Ps 5.9; 57.4 59.7
Your tongue is like a sharp razor,
you worker of treachery.
3 You love evil more than good, **52.3** Ps 36.4; 58.3 Jer 9.5
and lying more than speaking the truth. *Selah*
4 You love all words that devour, **52.4** Ps 120.3
O deceitful tongue.

5 But God will break you down forever; **52.5** Prov 2.22 Ps 27.13 Isa 22.18,19
he will snatch and tear you from your tent;
he will uproot you from the land of the living. *Selah*
6 The righteous will see, and fear, **52.6** Job 22.19 Ps 37.34
and will laugh at the evildoer,[b] saying,
7 "See the one who would not take
refuge in God,
but trusted in abundant riches,
and sought refuge in wealth!"[c]

8 But I am like a green olive tree **52.8** Ps 13.5; 128.3 Jer 11.16
in the house of God.
I trust in the steadfast love of God
forever and ever.
9 I will thank you forever,
because of what you have done.
In the presence of the faithful
I will proclaim[d] your name, for it is good.

Theme: All have sinned. Because of sin, no person can find God on his own. Only God can save us.
Author: David

PSALM 53

To the leader: according to Mahalath. A Maskil of David.

1 Fools say in their hearts, "There is no God." **53.1** Ps 14.1-4
They are corrupt, they commit abominable acts;

[a] Cn Compare Syr: Heb *the kindness of God* [b] Heb *him* [c] Syr Tg: Heb *in his destruction* [d] Cn: Heb *wait for*

52.1 Doeg thought he was a great hero—even boasting about his deed. In reality, his deed was evil, an offense to God. It is easy to mistake "accomplishment" with goodness. Just because something is done well or thoroughly doesn't mean it is good (for example, someone may be a great gambler or a skillful liar). Measure all you do by the rule of God's Word, not by how proficiently you do it.

52.8 With God by his side, David compared himself to a green olive tree sheltered in the house of God. Not only is an olive tree one of the longest living trees, but a protected tree has even greater longevity. David was contrasting God's eternal protection of his faithful servants with the sudden destruction of the wicked (52.5–7).

there is no one who does good.

53.2 Ps 33.13-15

2 God looks down from heaven on humankind
to see if there are any who are wise,
who seek after God.

53.3 Rom 3.10,12

3 They have all fallen away, they are all alike perverse;
there is no one who does good,
no, not one.

53.4 Jer 4.22

4 Have they no knowledge, those evildoers,
who eat up my people as they eat bread,
and do not call upon God?

53.5 Lev 26.17,36 Ps 44.7 Prov 28.1 Jer 6.30; 8.1,2 Ezek 6.5

5 There they shall be in great terror,
in terror such as has not been.
For God will scatter the bones of the ungodly;[e]
they will be put to shame,[f] for God has rejected them.

53.6 Ps 14.7

6 O that deliverance for Israel would come from Zion!
When God restores the fortunes of his people,
Jacob will rejoice; Israel will be glad.

Theme: A call for God to overcome enemies. God is our helper, even in times of hurt and betrayal.
Author: David

PSALM 54

To the leader: with stringed instruments. A Maskil of David, when the Ziphites went and told Saul, "David is in hiding among us."

54.1 2 Chron 20.6 Ps 20.1

1 Save me, O God, by your name,
and vindicate me by your might.
2 Hear my prayer, O God;
give ear to the words of my mouth.

54.3 1 Sam 20.1 Ps 36.1; 40.14 86.14; 140.1,4

3 For the insolent have risen against me,
the ruthless seek my life;
they do not set God before them. *Selah*

54.4 Ps 37.17,24,40

4 But surely, God is my helper;
the Lord is the upholder of[g] my life.
5 He will repay my enemies for their evil.
In your faithfulness, put an end to them.

54.6 Ps 50.14
54.7 Ps 34.6; 59.10

6 With a freewill offering I will sacrifice to you;
I will give thanks to your name, O LORD, for it is good.
7 For he has delivered me from every trouble,
and my eye has looked in triumph on my enemies.

[e] Cn Compare Gk Syr: Heb *him who encamps against you* [f] Gk: Heb *you will put to shame* [g] Gk Syr Jerome: Heb *is of those who uphold* or *is with those who uphold*

53.1 Echoing the message of Psalm 14, David proclaimed the foolishness of atheism (see also Romans 3.10). People may say there is no God in order to cover their sin, to have an excuse to continue in sin, and/or to ignore the Judge in order to avoid the judgment. A "fool" does not necessarily lack intelligence; many atheists and unbelievers are highly learned. Fools are people who reject God, the only one who can save them.

54.3, 4 Many of David's psalms follow the pattern found in these two verses – a transition from prayer to praise. He was not afraid to come to God and express his true feelings and needs. Because he did so, his spirit was lifted, and he could not help praising God, his helper, protector, and friend.

54.5 David said that God repays evil to his enemies. Proverbs 26.27 warns that those who set a trap will get caught in it themselves. What we have intended for others may blow up in our own faces. To be honest and straightforward before God and others is simpler, easier, and safer in the long run.

Theme: Expressing deep dismay over the treachery of a close friend. When friends hurt us, the burden is too difficult to carry alone.
Author: David

PSALM 55

To the leader: with stringed instruments. A Maskil of David.

1 Give ear to my prayer, O God;
do not hide yourself from my supplication.
2 Attend to me, and answer me;
I am troubled in my complaint.
I am distraught 3 by the noise of the enemy,
because of the clamor of the wicked.
For they bring[h] trouble upon me,
and in anger they cherish enmity against me.

4 My heart is in anguish within me,
the terrors of death have fallen upon me.
5 Fear and trembling come upon me,
and horror overwhelms me.
6 And I say, "O that I had wings like a dove!
I would fly away and be at rest;
7 truly, I would flee far away;
I would lodge in the wilderness; *Selah*
8 I would hurry to find a shelter for myself
from the raging wind and tempest."

9 Confuse, O Lord, confound their speech;
for I see violence and strife in the city.
10 Day and night they go around it
on its walls,
and iniquity and trouble are within it;
11 ruin is in its midst;
oppression and fraud
do not depart from its marketplace.

12 It is not enemies who taunt me—
I could bear that;
it is not adversaries who deal insolently with me—
I could hide from them.
13 But it is you, my equal,
my companion, my familiar friend,
14 with whom I kept pleasant company;
we walked in the house of God with the throng.
15 Let death come upon them;
let them go down alive to Sheol;
for evil is in their homes and in their hearts.

55.1 Ps 27.9; 61.1
55.2 1 Sam 1.16 Ps 77.3; 86.6,7 Isa 38.14
55.3 2 Sam 16.7,8 Ps 17.9; 71.11
55.4 Ps 116.3
55.6 Job 3.13
55.11 Ps 5.9; 10.7
55.13 Ps 41.9

[h] Cn Compare Gk: Heb *they cause to totter*

55.1ff This psalm was most likely written during the time of Absalom's rebellion and Ahithophel's betrayal (2 Samuel 15–17). Some say verses 12–14 are messianic because they also describe Judas's betrayal of Christ (Matthew 26.14–16, 20–25).

55.6–8 Even those who are especially close to God, as David was, have moments when they want to get away from it all and escape their problems and pressures.

55.9–11 The city that was supposed to be holy was plagued by internal problems: violence, strife, mischief, sorrow, wickedness, deceit, guile. External enemies, though a constant threat, were not nearly as dangerous as the corruption inside. Likewise, churches may expect their troubles to come from the sinful world. Although we defend ourselves against these external pressures, we often fail to see that our own sins cause many of our troubles.

55.12–14 Nothing hurts as much as a wound from a friend. There may be times when friends will lovingly confront you in order to help you. Real friends stick by you in times of trouble and bring healing, love, acceptance, and understanding. What kind of friend are you? Don't betray those you love.

55.16 Ps 57.2,3

16 But I call upon God,
and the LORD will save me.

55.17 Ps 5.3; 88.13 141.2

17 Evening and morning and at noon
I utter my complaint and moan,
and he will hear my voice.

55.18 Ps 103.4

18 He will redeem me unharmed
from the battle that I wage,
for many are arrayed against me.

55.19 Ps 36.1; 90.2 93.2

19 God, who is enthroned from of old, *Selah*
will hear, and will humble them—
because they do not change,
and do not fear God.

55.20 Ps 7.3,4; 89.34

20 My companion laid hands on a friend
and violated a covenant with me[i]

55.21 Ps 12.2; 28.3

21 with speech smoother than butter,
but with a heart set on war;
with words that were softer than oil,
but in fact were drawn swords.

55.22 Ps 37.5; 112.6

22 Cast your burden[j] on the LORD,
and he will sustain you;
he will never permit
the righteous to be moved.

55.23 Ps 5.6; 56.3,4 73.18

23 But you, O God, will cast them down
into the lowest pit;
the bloodthirsty and treacherous
shall not live out half their days.
But I will trust in you.

Theme: Trusting in God's care in the midst of fear. When all seems dark, one truth still shines bright: when God is for us, those against us will never succeed.
Author: David

PSALM 56

To the leader: according to The Dove on Far-off Terebinths. Of David. A Miktam, when the Philistines seized him in Gath.

56.1 Ps 17.9 35.1,25

1 Be gracious to me, O God, for people trample on me;
all day long foes oppress me;
2 my enemies trample on me all day long,
for many fight against me.

56.3 Ps 11.1 56.10,11

O Most High, 3 when I am afraid,
I put my trust in you.
4 In God, whose word I praise,

[i] Heb lacks *with me* [j] Or *Cast what he has given you*

55.17 Praying morning, noon, and night is certainly an excellent way to maintain correct priorities throughout every day. Daniel followed this pattern (Daniel 6.10), as did Peter (Acts 10.9, 10). The prayers of God's people are effective against the overwhelming evil in the world.

55.22 God wants to carry our burdens, but often we continue to bear them ourselves even when we say we are trusting in him. Trust the same strength that sustains you to carry your burdens also.

56.1ff This was probably written on the same occasion as Psalm 34, when David fled from Saul to Philistine territory and had to pretend insanity before Achish when some officials grew suspicious of him (1 Samuel 21.10–15).

56.3, 4 How much harm can people do to us? They can inflict pain, suffering, and death. But no person can rob us of our souls or our future beyond this life. How much harm can we do to ourselves? The worst thing we can do is to reject God and lose our eternal future. Jesus said, "Do not fear those who kill the body but cannot kill the soul" (Matthew 10.28). Instead, we should fear God, who controls this life and the next.

in God I trust; I am not afraid;
what can flesh do to me?

5 All day long they seek to injure my cause; **56.5** Ps 41.7 2 Pet 3.15,16
all their thoughts are against me for evil.
6 They stir up strife, they lurk, **56.6** Ps 17.11; 59.3
they watch my steps.
As they hoped to have my life,
7 so repay[k] them for their crime; **56.7** Ps 36.12; 55.23
in wrath cast down the peoples, O God!

8 You have kept count of my tossings; **56.8** Ps 39.12; 139.3
put my tears in your bottle.
Are they not in your record?
9 Then my enemies will retreat **56.9** Ps 41.11; 118.6
in the day when I call.
This I know, that[l] God is for me.
10 In God, whose word I praise,
in the LORD, whose word I praise,
11 in God I trust; I am not afraid.
What can a mere mortal do to me?

12 My vows to you I must perform, O God;
I will render thank offerings to you.
13 For you have delivered my soul from death, **56.13** Ps 33.19; 86.13
and my feet from falling,
so that I may walk before God
in the light of life.

Theme: God's faithful help and love in times of trouble. When we face trials, God will quiet our hearts and give us confidence.
Author: David

PSALM 57

To the leader: Do Not Destroy. Of David. A Miktam, when he fled from Saul, in the cave.

1 Be merciful to me, O God, be merciful to me, **57.1** Ruth 2.12 Ps 36.7; 91.4
for in you my soul takes refuge;
in the shadow of your wings I will take refuge,
until the destroying storms pass by.
2 I cry to God Most High, **57.2** Ps 138.8
to God who fulfills his purpose for me.
3 He will send from heaven and save me, **57.3** Ps 18.16; 25.10 56.2; 144.5,7
he will put to shame those who trample on me. *Selah*
God will send forth his steadfast love and his faithfulness.

4 I lie down among lions **57.4** Ps 58.6; 64.3
that greedily devour[m] human prey;

[k] Cn: Heb *rescue* [l] Or *because* [m] Cn: Heb *are aflame for*

56.8 Even in our deepest sorrow, God cares! Jesus reminded us further of how much God understands us—he knows even the number of hairs on our heads (Matthew 10.30). Often we waver between faith and fear. When you feel so discouraged that you are sure no one understands, remember that God knows every problem and sees every tear.

56.9–11 Fear can cause physical problems. It can even paralyze us. And what could be more fearful than having an enemy pressing in from all sides! Faced with this situation, David suggested several antidotes for fear: (1) remember that God is with you, (2) trust him, and (3) praise him for fulfilling his promises. When faced with persecution, insecurity, or insurmountable odds, use these to overcome your fear.

57.1ff This psalm was probably written when David was hiding in a cave from Saul (see 1 Samuel 22–24).

57.4 At times, we may be surrounded by people who gossip about us or criticize us. Verbal cruelty can damage us as badly as physical abuse. Rather than throwing back more unacceptable talk, we, like David, can quietly talk with God about the problem.

their teeth are spears and arrows,
their tongues sharp swords.

57.5 Ps 108.5
5 Be exalted, O God, above the heavens.
Let your glory be over all the earth.

57.6 Ps 10.9; 35.7 Prov 26.27
6 They set a net for my steps;
my soul was bowed down.
They dug a pit in my path,
but they have fallen into it themselves. *Selah*

57.7 Ps 108.1-5 112.7
7 My heart is steadfast, O God,
my heart is steadfast.
I will sing and make melody.

57.8 Ps 150.3
8 Awake, my soul!
Awake, O harp and lyre!
I will awake the dawn.
9 I will give thanks to you, O Lord, among the peoples;
I will sing praises to you among the nations.

57.10 Ps 36.5
10 For your steadfast love is as high as the heavens;
your faithfulness extends to the clouds.

11 Be exalted, O God, above the heavens.
Let your glory be over all the earth.

Theme: A prayer for God's justice. When no justice can be found, rejoice in knowing that justice will triumph because there is a God who will judge with complete fairness.
Author: David, at a time when men in authority were twisting justice

PSALM 58

To the leader: Do Not Destroy. Of David. A Miktam.

58.1 Ps 82.2; 94.20
1 Do you indeed decree what is right, you gods?[n]
Do you judge people fairly?
2 No, in your hearts you devise wrongs;
your hands deal out violence on earth.

58.3 Ps 53.3
3 The wicked go astray from the womb;
they err from their birth, speaking lies.

58.4 Ps 81.11; 140.3
4 They have venom like the venom of a serpent,
like the deaf adder that stops its ear,
5 so that it does not hear the voice of charmers
or of the cunning enchanter.

58.6 Ps 3.7
6 O God, break the teeth in their mouths;
tear out the fangs of the young lions, O LORD!

58.7 Ps 64.3
7 Let them vanish like water that runs away;
like grass let them be trodden down[o] and wither.
8 Let them be like the snail that dissolves into slime;
like the untimely birth that never sees the sun.

58.9 Job 27.21
9 Sooner than your pots can feel the heat of thorns,

[n] Or *mighty lords* [o] Cn: Meaning of Heb uncertain

57.7 David's firm faith in God contrasted sharply with his enemies' loud lying and boasting. When confronted with verbal attacks, the best defense is simply to be quiet and praise God, realizing that our confidence is in his kindness, love, and faithfulness (57.10). In times of great suffering, don't turn inward to self-pity or outward to revenge, but upward to God.

58.1ff This is called an "imprecatory" psalm (see the note on 35.1ff). It is a cry for justice so intense that it seems, at first glance, to be a call for revenge upon enemies.

58.1ff The Old Testament is filled with references about justice, and it is a key topic in the psalms. Unfortunately, many judges and rulers in ancient times took justice into their own hands. They had complete authority with no accountability, and the power to make their own laws. When earth's judges are corrupt, there is little hope of justice in this life. But God loves justice, and those who obey him will experience perfect justice in eternity.

whether green or ablaze, may he sweep them away!

10 The righteous will rejoice when they see vengeance done;
they will bathe their feet in the blood of the wicked.
11 People will say, "Surely there is a reward for the righteous;
surely there is a God who judges on earth."

58.10 Ps 32.11; 64.10 68.22,23; 91.8
58.11 Ps 9.8; 18.20 Lk 6.23,35

Theme: Prayer and praise for God's saving help.
God's constant love is our place of safety in a wicked world.
Author: David

PSALM 59

To the leader: Do Not Destroy. Of David. A Miktam, when Saul ordered his house to be watched in order to kill him.

1 Deliver me from my enemies, O my God;
protect me from those who rise up against me.
2 Deliver me from those who work evil;
from the bloodthirsty save me.

3 Even now they lie in wait for my life;
the mighty stir up strife against me.
For no transgression or sin of mine, O LORD,
4 for no fault of mine, they run and make ready.

Rouse yourself, come to my help and see!
5 You, LORD God of hosts, are God of Israel.
Awake to punish all the nations;
spare none of those who treacherously plot evil. *Selah*

6 Each evening they come back,
howling like dogs
and prowling about the city.
7 There they are, bellowing with their mouths,
with sharp words[p] on their lips—
for "Who," they think,[q] "will hear us?"

8 But you laugh at them, O LORD;
you hold all the nations in derision.
9 O my strength, I will watch for you;
for you, O God, are my fortress.
10 My God in his steadfast love will meet me;
my God will let me look in triumph on my enemies.

11 Do not kill them, or my people may forget;
make them totter by your power, and bring them down,
O Lord, our shield.

59.1 Ps 20.1; 143.9
59.2 Ps 14.4; 28.3 94.16; 139.19
59.3 Ps 7.3,4; 56.6 69.4
59.4 Ps 35.19,23
59.5 Ps 9.5; 84.8
59.7 Job 22.13 Ps 10.11; 73.11 94.47
59.8 Ps 2.4; 37.13
59.9 Ps 9.9
59.10 Ps 54.7
59.11 Ps 106.27 144.6

p Heb *with swords* q Heb lacks *they think*

58.11 Of all people, our national leaders should be just and fair. When they are unjust and unfair, people suffer. The rich get richer, the poor get poorer, politicians wrest power from the people, the nation deteriorates, and God is ignored. When right triumphs at last, "the righteous will rejoice" (58.10). Be assured that there will be a day of accountability, and God judges fairly. Be careful that you never side with injustice, lest you find yourself standing before an angry Judge.

59.7, 8 Vile men curse God as if he cannot hear and will not respond. But God listens patiently until that day when those curses will fall back in judgment like stones from heaven. Evil people live as if God cannot see and will not punish. But God watches patiently until that day when their deeds rise up to accuse them. As believers we must be careful not to follow the same foolish practices as evil people. We must remember that God hears and sees all we do.

59.10 David was hunted by those whose love had turned to jealousy, and this was driving them to murder him. Trusted friends, and even his son, turned against him. What changeable love! But David knew that God's love for him was *changeless.* "His steadfast love endures forever" (100.5). God's mercy to all who trust him is just as permanent as his mercy to David. When the love of others fails or disappoints us, we can rest in God's changeless love.

59.12
Ps 10.7; 83.18

12 For the sin of their mouths, the words of their lips,
let them be trapped in their pride.
For the cursing and lies that they utter,
13 consume them in wrath;
consume them until they are no more.
Then it will be known to the ends of the earth
that God rules over Jacob. *Selah*

14 Each evening they come back,
howling like dogs
and prowling about the city.
15 They roam about for food,
and growl if they do not get their fill.

59.16
Ps 21.13; 46.1
101.1

16 But I will sing of your might;
I will sing aloud of your steadfast love in the morning.
For you have been a fortress for me
and a refuge in the day of my distress.

59.17
Ps 59.9,10

17 O my strength, I will sing praises to you,
for you, O God, are my fortress,
the God who shows me steadfast love.

Theme: Real help comes from God alone. When a situation seems out of control, we can trust God to do mighty things.
Author: David, when Israel was away at war with Syria in the north, and Edom invaded Judah from the south (2 Samuel 8)

PSALM 60

To the leader: according to the Lily of the Covenant. A Miktam of David; for instruction; when he struggled with Aram-naharaim and with Aram-zobah, and when Joab on his return killed twelve thousand Edomites in the Valley of Salt.

60.1
Ps 44.9; 79.5
80.3
60.2
2 Chron 7.14
Ps 18.7
60.3
Ps 66.12

1 O God, you have rejected us, broken our defenses;
you have been angry; now restore us!
2 You have caused the land to quake; you have torn it open;
repair the cracks in it, for it is tottering.
3 You have made your people suffer hard things;
you have given us wine to drink that made us reel.

60.4
Ps 11.12; 13.2

4 You have set up a banner for those who fear you,
to rally to it out of bowshot.[r] *Selah*
5 Give victory with your right hand, and answer us,[s]
so that those whom you love may be rescued.

60.6
Gen 33.17
49.10
Josh 13.31; 17.7
Ps 89.35

6 God has promised in his sanctuary:[t]
"With exultation I will divide up Shechem,
and portion out the Vale of Succoth.
7 Gilead is mine, and Manasseh is mine;
Ephraim is my helmet;

[r] Gk Syr Jerome: Heb *because of the truth* [s] Another reading is *me* [t] Or *by his holiness*

60.1ff This psalm gives us information about David's reign not found in the books of 1 and 2 Samuel or 1 and 2 Chronicles. Although the setting of the psalm is found in 2 Samuel 8, that passage makes no reference to the fact that David's forces met stiff resistance (60.1–3) and apparently even a temporary defeat (60.9, 10). The closer we get to God, the stronger our enemies attack us because we become a threat to their evil and selfish way of living.

60.4, 5 God loves truth, and the people who belong to God will rally to truth like soldiers to their flag. The apostle John wrote, "When the Spirit of truth comes, he will guide you into all truth" (John 16.13). Let the truth of God's Word stir you to action and rally you to his cause.

60.6–10 God said the cities and territories of Israel were his, and he knew the future of each of the nations. When the world seems out of control, we must remind ourselves that God owns the cities and knows the future of every nation. God is in control. In him we will gain the victory.

Judah is my scepter.
8 Moab is my washbasin;
on Edom I hurl my shoe;
over Philistia I shout in triumph."

60.8
2 Sam 8.1,2,14

9 Who will bring me to the fortified city?
Who will lead me to Edom?
10 Have you not rejected us, O God?
You do not go out, O God, with our armies.
11 O grant us help against the foe,
for human help is worthless.
12 With God we shall do valiantly;
it is he who will tread down our foes.

60.9
Ps 44.9

60.11
Ps 146.3

60.12
Num 24.15-19
Ps 44.5; 118.16

Theme: Prayer for security and assurance. Wherever we are, we can trust that God will be there to answer our cries for help.
Author: David, written when he was forced to escape during the days of Absalom's rebellion (2 Samuel 15—18), or after he had narrowly escaped one of Saul's efforts to kill him while hiding in the wilderness

PSALM 61

To the leader: with stringed instruments. Of David.

1 Hear my cry, O God;
listen to my prayer.
2 From the end of the earth I call to you,
when my heart is faint.

61.1
Ps 64.1; 86.6

61.2
Ps 18.2; 77.3

Lead me to the rock
that is higher than I;
3 for you are my refuge,
a strong tower against the enemy.

61.3
Ps 62.7

4 Let me abide in your tent forever,
find refuge under the shelter of your wings. *Selah*
5 For you, O God, have heard my vows;
you have given me the heritage of those who fear your name.

61.4
Ps 17.8; 23.6
27.4; 91.4

61.5
Ps 56.12; 86.11

6 Prolong the life of the king;
may his years endure to all generations!
7 May he be enthroned forever before God;
appoint steadfast love and faithfulness to watch over him!

61.7
Ps 40.11; 41.12

8 So I will always sing praises to your name,
as I pay my vows day after day.

61.8
Ps 30.4; 65.1

60.8 David mentioned the enemy nations that surrounded Israel. Moab lay directly to the east, Edom to the south, and Philistia to the west. At the time this psalm was written, David was fighting Syria to the north. Although he was literally surrounded by enemies, David believed that God would help him triumph.

61.1, 2 David must have been far from home when he wrote this psalm. Fortunately, God is not limited to any geographic location. Among unknown people and surroundings, God never changes. His love is always with us.

61.7 David compared the lasting security of living forever with God to the present feelings of uncertainty in his strange surroundings (61.1, 2).

61.8 To pay one's vows means to fulfill an offering or sacrifice that was promised to God. Vows were normally paid for in a single ceremony. This shows a commitment to a debt that could never be paid off, or a recognition that God's blessings are new every morning. David continually praised God through both the good and difficult times of his life. Do you find something to praise God for each day? As you do, you will find your heart elevated from daily distractions to lasting confidence.

Theme: Placing all hope in God. Knowing that God is in control allows us to wait patiently for him to rescue us. True relief does not come when the problem is resolved because more problems are on the way! True relief comes from an enduring hope in God's ultimate salvation. Only then will all trials be resolved.
Author: David, written during the days of Absalom's rebellion (2 Samuel 15—18)

PSALM 62

To the leader: according to Jeduthun. A Psalm of David.

62.1 Ps 33.20; 37.39
62.2 Ps 59.17; 89.26
62.3 Ps 28.3; 55.21
62.7 Ps 46.1
62.8 Lam 2.19
62.9 Isa 40.15
62.10 Mk 10.24; 1 Tim 6.10

1 For God alone my soul waits in silence;
from him comes my salvation.
2 He alone is my rock and my salvation,
my fortress; I shall never be shaken.

3 How long will you assail a person,
will you batter your victim, all of you,
as you would a leaning wall, a tottering fence?
4 Their only plan is to bring down a person of prominence.
They take pleasure in falsehood;
they bless with their mouths,
but inwardly they curse. *Selah*

5 For God alone my soul waits in silence,
for my hope is from him.
6 He alone is my rock and my salvation,
my fortress; I shall not be shaken.
7 On God rests my deliverance and my honor;
my mighty rock, my refuge is in God.

8 Trust in him at all times, O people;
pour out your heart before him;
God is a refuge for us. *Selah*

9 Those of low estate are but a breath,
those of high estate are a delusion;
in the balances they go up;
they are together lighter than a breath.
10 Put no confidence in extortion,
and set no vain hopes on robbery;
if riches increase, do not set your heart on them.

11 Once God has spoken;
twice have I heard this:
that power belongs to God,
12 and steadfast love belongs to you, O Lord.
For you repay to all
according to their work.

62.3–6 Prayer can release our tensions in times of emotional stress. Trusting God to be our rock, salvation, and defense (62.2) changes our entire outlook on life. No longer are we held captive by resentment toward others when they hurt us. We are released to follow an unchanging God.

62.9–12 It is tempting to use honor, power, wealth, or prestige to measure people. We may even feel that such people are really getting ahead in life. But on God's scales, these people are a puff of air. What, then, can tilt the scales when God weighs us? Trusting God and working for him (62.12). Wealth, honor, power, or prestige add nothing to our value in God's eyes, but the faithful work we do for him has eternal value.

62.11, 12 David expressed two lessons he learned about the character of God: 1) God is powerful, and at the same time 2) God is loving. He repays anyone according to what they do. So those who set themselves in opposition to God will feel his powerful judgment, and those who give up their own ways to follow him will experience his steadfast love. Some people think that a loving God would never punish anyone, so they go on living as they please. While they may know something of his love, they have made the tragic mistake of underestimating his mighty power.

Theme: A desire for God's presence, provision, and protection. No matter where we are, our desire should be for God because only he satisfies fully.
Author: David

PSALM 63

A Psalm of David, when he was in the Wilderness of Judah.

1 O God, you are my God, I seek you, **63.1** Ps 42.2; 84.2
my soul thirsts for you;
my flesh faints for you,
as in a dry and weary land where there is no water.
2 So I have looked upon you in the sanctuary, **63.2** Ps 27.4
beholding your power and glory.
3 Because your steadfast love is better than life, **63.3** Ps 69.16
my lips will praise you.
4 So I will bless you as long as I live; **63.4** Ps 28.2; 104.33
I will lift up my hands and call on your name.

5 My soul is satisfied as with a rich feast,[u] **63.5** Ps 36.8; 71.23
and my mouth praises you with joyful lips
6 when I think of you on my bed, **63.6** Ps 4.4; 16.7
and meditate on you in the watches of the night;
7 for you have been my help,
and in the shadow of your wings I sing for joy.
8 My soul clings to you; **63.8** Ps 18.35
your right hand upholds me.

9 But those who seek to destroy my life **63.9** Ps 40.14
shall go down into the depths of the earth;
10 they shall be given over to the power of the sword,
they shall be prey for jackals.
11 But the king shall rejoice in God;
all who swear by him shall exult,
for the mouths of liars will be stopped.

Theme: A complaint against conspiracy. When others conspire against us, we can ask God for protection because he knows everything.
Author: David

PSALM 64

To the leader. A Psalm of David.

1 Hear my voice, O God, in my complaint; **64.1** Ps 56.6; 59.2
preserve my life from the dread enemy.
2 Hide me from the secret plots of the wicked,
from the scheming of evildoers,
3 who whet their tongues like swords, **64.3** Ps 140.3

[u] Heb *with fat and fatness*

63.1ff Psalms 61, 62, and 63 were probably written when David was seeking refuge during Absalom's rebellion (2 Samuel 15–18).

63.1–5 Hiding from his enemies in the barren wilderness of Judea, David was intensely lonely. He longed for a friend he could trust to ease his loneliness. No wonder he cried out, "O God, . . . my flesh faints for you, as in a dry and weary land," as he sought lasting satisfaction. If you are lonely or thirsty for something lasting in your life, remember David's prayer. God alone can satisfy our deepest longings!

63.6 The night was divided into three watches. Someone aware of all three would be having a sleepless night. A cure for sleepless nights is to turn our thoughts to God. There are many reasons we can't sleep – illness, stress, worry – but sleepless nights can be turned into quiet times of reflection and worship. Use them to review how God has guided and helped you.

64.1ff Evil can come in the form of a secret conspiracy or an ambush because Satan wants to catch us unprepared. He tempts us in our weakest areas when we least expect it. But God himself will shoot down our enemies (64.7), whether they be physical or spiritual. Wickedness is widespread and affects us in many ways, but the final victory already belongs to God and those who trust and believe in him.

64.1, 2 We may believe that God wants to hear only certain requests from us. While it is true that we should offer praise, confession, and respectful petitions, it is true also that God is willing to listen to *anything* we want to tell him. David expressed himself honestly, knowing God would hear his voice. God will always listen attentively and will fully understand us.

who aim bitter words like arrows,
64.4 Ps 10.8; 11.2
4 shooting from ambush at the blameless;
they shoot suddenly and without fear.
64.5 Ps 140.5
5 They hold fast to their evil purpose;
they talk of laying snares secretly,
thinking, "Who can see us?[v]
64.6 Ps 49.11
6 Who can search out our crimes?[w]
We have thought out a cunningly conceived plot."
For the human heart and mind are deep.

64.7 Ps 7.12,13
7 But God will shoot his arrow at them;
they will be wounded suddenly.
64.8 Ps 9.3
8 Because of their tongue he will bring them to ruin;[x]
all who see them will shake with horror.
9 Then everyone will fear;
they will tell what God has brought about,
and ponder what he has done.

64.10 Ps 11.1; 32.11
10 Let the righteous rejoice in the LORD
and take refuge in him.
Let all the upright in heart glory.

Theme: God provides abundantly. We can be thankful to God for his many blessings.
Author: David

PSALM 65

To the leader. A Psalm of David. A Song.

65.1 Ps 86.9; 116.18
1 Praise is due to you,
O God, in Zion;
and to you shall vows be performed,
2 O you who answer prayer!
To you all flesh shall come.
65.3 Ps 38.4; 40.12 Heb 9.14
3 When deeds of iniquity overwhelm us,
you forgive our transgressions.
65.4 Ps 33.12; 36.8
4 Happy are those whom you choose and bring near
to live in your courts.
We shall be satisfied with the goodness of your house,
your holy temple.

65.5 Ps 45.4; 48.10
5 By awesome deeds you answer us with deliverance,
O God of our salvation;
you are the hope of all the ends of the earth
and of the farthest seas.
65.6 Ps 93.1; 95.4
6 By your[y] strength you established the mountains;

v Syr: Heb *them* w Cn: Heb *They search out crimes* x Cn: Heb *They will bring him to ruin, their tongue being against them* y Gk Jerome: Heb *his*

65.1, 2 In Old Testament times, vows were taken seriously and fulfilled completely. No one had to make a vow, but once made, it was binding (Deuteronomy 23.21–23). The vow being fulfilled here is to praise God for his answers to prayer.

65.3 Although sinful deeds overwhelm us, God will forgive them all if we ask sincerely. Do you feel as though God could never forgive you, that your sins are too many, or that some of them are too great? The good news is that God can and will forgive them all. Nobody is beyond redemption, and nobody is so full of sin that he or she cannot be made clean.

65.4 Access to God, the joy of living in the tabernacle courts, was a great honor. God had chosen a special group of Israelites, the tribe of Levi, to serve as ministers in the tabernacle (Numbers 3.5–51). They were the only ones who could enter the sacred rooms where God's presence resided. Because of Jesus' death on the cross, all believers today have personal access to God's presence everywhere and any time. We gain this access into God's presence by believing in the death and resurrection of Christ, and turning from our sins to God's way of living.

65.6–13 This harvest psalm glorifies God the Creator as reflected in the beauty of nature. Nature helps us understand something of God's character. The Jews believed that God's care of nature was a sign of his love and provision for them. Nature shows God's generosity – giving us more than we need or deserve. Reflecting on such abundant generosity should produce grateful and generous hearts in us.

you are girded with might.
7 You silence the roaring of the seas,
the roaring of their waves,
the tumult of the peoples.
8 Those who live at earth's farthest bounds are awed by your signs;
you make the gateways of the morning and the evening shout for joy.

9 You visit the earth and water it,
you greatly enrich it;
the river of God is full of water;
you provide the people with grain,
for so you have prepared it.
10 You water its furrows abundantly,
settling its ridges,
softening it with showers,
and blessing its growth.
11 You crown the year with your bounty;
your wagon tracks overflow with richness.
12 The pastures of the wilderness overflow,
the hills gird themselves with joy,
13 the meadows clothe themselves with flocks,
the valleys deck themselves with grain,
they shout and sing together for joy.

65.7 Ps 89.9 Isa 17.12,13
65.8 Ps 139.9,10
65.9 Ps 46.4 104.13,14,24
65.11 Job 38.26,27
65.13 Ps 98.8; 144.13 Isa 30.23; 55.12

Theme: God answers prayer. Individually and as a body of believers, we should praise and worship God.
Author: Anonymous, written after a great victory in battle

PSALM 66

To the leader. A Song. A Psalm.

1 Make a joyful noise to God, all the earth;
2 sing the glory of his name;
give to him glorious praise.
3 Say to God, "How awesome are your deeds!
Because of your great power, your enemies cringe before you.
4 All the earth worships you;
they sing praises to you,
sing praises to your name." *Selah*

5 Come and see what God has done:
he is awesome in his deeds among mortals.
6 He turned the sea into dry land;
they passed through the river on foot.
There we rejoiced in him,
7 who rules by his might forever,
whose eyes keep watch on the nations—
let the rebellious not exalt themselves. *Selah*

8 Bless our God, O peoples,
let the sound of his praise be heard,
9 who has kept us among the living,
and has not let our feet slip.

66.3 Ps 18.44; 47.2
66.4 Ps 22.27; 67.4
66.5 Ps 46.8
66.6 Ex 14.21
66.7 Ps 11.4; 145.13
66.9 Ps 30.3

66.5–7 The writer was referring to the famous story about God's rescue of the Israelites by parting the Red Sea. God saved the Israelites then, and he continues to save his people today.

66.10–12 Just as fire refines silver in the smelting process, trials refine our character. They bring us a new and deeper wisdom, helping us discern truth from falsehood and equipping us with the discipline to carry out what we know is right. These trials help us realize that life is a gift from God not to be taken for granted.

66.10 Ps 17.3

10 For you, O God, have tested us;
you have tried us as silver is tried.
11 You brought us into the net;
you laid burdens on our backs;

66.12 Ps 18.19

12 you let people ride over our heads;
we went through fire and through water;
yet you have brought us out to a spacious place.[z]

66.13 Ps 22.25

13 I will come into your house with burnt offerings;
I will pay you my vows,
14 those that my lips uttered
and my mouth promised when I was in trouble.

66.15 Num 6.14 Ps 51.19

15 I will offer to you burnt offerings of fatlings,
with the smoke of the sacrifice of rams;
I will make an offering of bulls and goats. *Selah*

66.16 Ps 34.11

16 Come and hear, all you who fear God,
and I will tell what he has done for me.
17 I cried aloud to him,
and he was extolled with my tongue.

66.18 Ps 18.41

18 If I had cherished iniquity in my heart,
the Lord would not have listened.

66.19 Ps 116.1,2

19 But truly God has listened;
he has given heed to the words of my prayer.

66.20 Ps 22.24; 68.35

20 Blessed be God,
because he has not rejected my prayer
or removed his steadfast love from me.

Theme: Joy comes from spreading the news about God around the world.
Author: Anonymous, probably written for one of the harvest festivals

PSALM 67

To the leader: with stringed instruments. A Psalm. A Song.

67.1 Num 6.25 Ps 4.6 80.3,7,19

1 May God be gracious to us and bless us
and make his face to shine upon us, *Selah*
2 that your way may be known upon earth,
your saving power among all nations.

67.3 Ps 66.4

3 Let the peoples praise you, O God;
let all the peoples praise you.

67.4 Ps 96.10,13

4 Let the nations be glad and sing for joy,

z Cn Compare Gk Syr Jerome Tg: Heb *to a saturation*

66.12 A spacious place is a place of abundance.

66.13–15 People sometimes make bargains with God, saying, "If you heal me (or get me out of this mess), I'll obey you for the rest of my life." However, soon after they recover, the vow is forgotten and the old life-style resumes. This writer made a promise to God, but he remembered the promise and was prepared to fulfill his vow. God always keeps his promises and wants us to follow his example. Be careful to follow through on whatever you promise to do.

66.16–20 The writer cried to God for help, offering praise while confessing his sins. Confession acknowledges our sin; praise acknowledges God's gracious forgiveness; and crying out to God in prayer acknowledges that we trust God to forgive our sins. No believer's life is complete without daily confession, praise, and prayer.

66.18 We must regularly confess our sins because we continue to do wrong. But true confession requires us to listen to God and be sensitive to our sins. David confessed his sin and prayed, "Clear me from hidden faults. Keep back your servant also from the insolent" (19.12, 13). If we *refuse* to repent, if we harbor and cherish certain sins, then we are placing a wall between us and God. We may not be able to remember *every* sin we have ever committed, but our attitude toward life should be one of confession and obedience.

67.2 Could the psalmist have looked across the years to see the gospel go throughout the earth? This psalm surely speaks of the fulfillment of the great commission (Matthew 28.18–20), when Jesus commanded that the gospel be taken to all nations. Count yourself among that great crowd of believers worldwide who know the Savior; praise him for his Good News; and share that gospel until there is an abundant harvest.

for you judge the peoples with equity
and guide the nations upon earth. *Selah*
5 Let the peoples praise you, O God;
let all the peoples praise you.

6 The earth has yielded its increase;
God, our God, has blessed us.
7 May God continue to bless us;
let all the ends of the earth revere him.

67.6 Lev 26.4 Ps 22.27

Theme: Remembering God's glory and power. Times and cultures change, but God is always majestically present as protector and provider.
Author: David

PSALM 68

To the leader. Of David. A Psalm. A Song.

1 Let God rise up, let his enemies be scattered;
let those who hate him flee before him.
2 As smoke is driven away, so drive them away;
as wax melts before the fire,
let the wicked perish before God.
3 But let the righteous be joyful;
let them exult before God;
let them be jubilant with joy.

68.1 Num 10.35

68.2 Ps 37.20 Isa 9.18

4 Sing to God, sing praises to his name;
lift up a song to him who rides upon the clouds[a]—
his name is the LORD—
be exultant before him.

68.4 Ps 40.3; 68.33

5 Father of orphans and protector of widows
is God in his holy habitation.
6 God gives the desolate a home to live in;
he leads out the prisoners to prosperity,
but the rebellious live in a parched land.

68.5 Deut 10.18

7 O God, when you went out before your people,
when you marched through the wilderness, *Selah*
8 the earth quaked, the heavens poured down rain
at the presence of God, the God of Sinai,
at the presence of God, the God of Israel.
9 Rain in abundance, O God, you showered abroad;
you restored your heritage when it languished;
10 your flock found a dwelling in it;
in your goodness, O God, you provided for the needy.

68.7 Ex 13.21

68.8 Ex 19.18

68.9 Deut 11.11

[a] Or *cast up a highway for him who rides through the deserts*

68.1ff This psalm begins just like Moses' cry in Numbers 10.35 as the Israelites followed the ark of the covenant. Perhaps it was written when David led a joyous procession that brought the ark from the house of Obed-edom to Jerusalem (2 Samuel 6.11–15).

68.3–6 With shouts of praise and the sound of trumpets, David and his people took the holy ark toward Mount Zion. It was a time to sing praises to the Lord, whose presence brings great joy. Only in him is there hope for the orphans, widows, prisoners, and all other lonely people. If you are lonely or disadvantaged, join David in praise and discover great joy from loving God.

68.4–6 David praised God for his protection and provision. When we see God's true majesty, our response should be to praise him. This was a song of faith, since many of these benefits had not yet come true in David's time. It is also our song of faith. We must continue to trust God because, in time, he will fulfill all his promises.

68.8 Mount Sinai, also called Mount Horeb, had a prominent role in Israelite history. It was at Mount Sinai that God met Moses and commissioned him to lead Israel out of Egypt (Exodus 3.1–10). It was to Mount Sinai that the nation of Israel returned and received God's laws (Exodus 19.1–3), and God's presence made the entire mountain quake (Exodus 19.18). This sacred mountain served to remind the people of God's words and promises.

68.11 Ex 15.20

11 The Lord gives the command;
great is the company of those[b] who bore the tidings:
12 "The kings of the armies, they flee, they flee!"
The women at home divide the spoil,
13 though they stay among the sheepfolds—
the wings of a dove covered with silver,
its pinions with green gold.
14 When the Almighty[c] scattered kings there,
snow fell on Zalmon.

68.15 Deut 12.4,5

15 O mighty mountain, mountain of Bashan;
O many-peaked mountain, mountain of Bashan!
16 Why do you look with envy, O many-peaked mountain,
at the mount that God desired for his abode,
where the LORD will reside forever?

68.17 Deut 33.2

17 With mighty chariotry, twice ten thousand,
thousands upon thousands,
the Lord came from Sinai into the holy place.[d]

68.18 Eph 4.8 1 Tim 1.13

18 You ascended the high mount,
leading captives in your train
and receiving gifts from people,
even from those who rebel against the LORD God's abiding there.

68.19 Ps 55.22; 65.5 Isa 46.4

19 Blessed be the Lord,
who daily bears us up;
God is our salvation. *Selah*

68.20 Ps 56.13

20 Our God is a God of salvation,
and to GOD, the Lord, belongs escape from death.

68.21 Ps 110.6 Heb 3.13

21 But God will shatter the heads of his enemies,
the hairy crown of those who walk in their guilty ways.

68.22 Amos 9.1-3

22 The Lord said,
"I will bring them back from Bashan,
I will bring them back from the depths of the sea,

68.23 1 Kgs 21.19 Ps 58.10 Jer 15.3

23 so that you may bathe[e] your feet in blood,
so that the tongues of your dogs may have their share from the foe."

24 Your solemn processions are seen,[f] O God,

68.25 Ex 15.20 1 Chron 13.8

the processions of my God, my King, into the sanctuary—
25 the singers in front, the musicians last,
between them girls playing tambourines:

68.26 Deut 33.28 Ps 22.22,23

26 "Bless God in the great congregation,

[b] Or *company of the women* [c] Traditional rendering of Heb *Shaddai* [d] Cn: Heb *The Lord among them Sinai in the holy* (place) [e] Gk Syr Tg: Heb *shatter* [f] Or *have been seen*

68.13 "Its pinions with green gold" means its feathers are covered with shining gold.

68.15, 16 Bashan, the land northeast of Israel, was the home of mighty mountains, including Mount Hermon, the tallest and most awesome mountain in the region. God's choice of Mount Zion, a foothill by comparison, for the site of the temple led the psalmist to write poetically of the envy of the mountains of Bashan.

68.17 This psalm celebrates the final stages of a journey which began at Mount Sinai with the construction of the ark of the covenant and finally ended appropriately at Mount Zion (site of the holy place), the chosen dwelling place of God among his people. It probably describes the moving of the ark of the covenant into Jerusalem.

68.18 This verse is quoted in Ephesians 4.8 and applied to the ministry of the ascended Christ. It celebrates his victory over evil. It assures all of us who believe in Christ that by trusting him, we can overcome evil.

68.19–21 God frees his people and crushes his enemies. Salvation is freedom from sin and death. Those who refuse to turn to God will be crushed by sin and death. They will be trapped by the sin they loved and destroyed by the death they feared. How much better it is for those who love God and fear the consequences of sin.

68.19–21 Each day we must deal with our share of burdens. As we face these burdens, the Lord is there to help us bear them. Each morning, praise God for the strength he will send you today. It is as sure as the sunrise.

the LORD, O you who are of Israel's fountain!"
27 There is Benjamin, the least of them, in the lead,
the princes of Judah in a body,
the princes of Zebulun, the princes of Naphtali.

28 Summon your might, O God;
show your strength, O God, as you have done for us before.
29 Because of your temple at Jerusalem
kings bear gifts to you.
30 Rebuke the wild animals that live among the reeds,
the herd of bulls with the calves of the peoples.
Trample[g] under foot those who lust after tribute;
scatter the peoples who delight in war.[h]
31 Let bronze be brought from Egypt;
let Ethiopia[i] hasten to stretch out its hands to God.

32 Sing to God, O kingdoms of the earth;
sing praises to the Lord, *Selah*
33 O rider in the heavens, the ancient heavens;
listen, he sends out his voice, his mighty voice.
34 Ascribe power to God,
whose majesty is over Israel;
and whose power is in the skies.
35 Awesome is God in his[j] sanctuary,
the God of Israel;
he gives power and strength to his people.

Blessed be God!

68.28 Ps 29.11; 44.4
68.29 Ps 72.10
68.30 Ps 89.10
68.32 Ps 102.21,22
68.33 Deut 10.14 Ps 18.10; 29.4
68.35 Deut 10.17 Ps 29.11; 47.2

Theme: A cry of distress in a sea of trouble. We may have to suffer severely for our devotion to God, but that should cause us to look forward with joy to the day when evil and injustice will be gone forever.
Author: David

PSALM 69

To the leader: according to Lilies. Of David.

1 Save me, O God,
for the waters have come up to my neck.
2 I sink in deep mire,
where there is no foothold;
I have come into deep waters,
and the flood sweeps over me.
3 I am weary with my crying;
my throat is parched.
My eyes grow dim
with waiting for my God.

69.3 Ps 6.6 119.82,123

[g] Cn: Heb *Trampling* [h] Meaning of Heb of verse 30 is uncertain [i] Or *Nubia*; Heb *Cush* [j] Gk: Heb *from your*

68.34, 35 When we consider all God has done for us, we should feel an overwhelming sense of awe as we kneel before the Lord in his sanctuary. Nature surrounds us with countless signs of his wonderful power. His unlimited power and unspeakable majesty leave us breathless in his presence. How fortunate we are that he cares for us.

69.1ff This is one of the most quoted psalms in the New Testament, and it is often applied to the ministry and suffering of Jesus. Verse 4, like John 15.25, speaks of Jesus' many enemies. The experience of being mocked by his brothers (69.8) is expressed in John 7.5. Verse 9 portrays David's zeal for God; Christ showed great zeal when he threw the money changers out of the temple (John 2.14–17). Paul quoted part of 69.9 in Romans 15.3. Christ's great suffering is portrayed in 69.20, 21 (Matthew 27.24; Mark 15.23; Luke 23.36; John 19.28–30). Verses 22 through 28 are quoted in Romans 11.9, 10; and Peter applied 69.25 to Judas (Acts 1.20).

69.3 David wept until he was physically exhausted, with a dry throat and blurred vision. He wept until he could weep no more, yet he still trusted God to save him. When devastated by death or tragedy, we need not collapse or despair because we can turn to God and ask him to save us and help us. The tears will still come, but we will not be crying in vain.

69.4 Ps 35.11; 59.3 Jn 15.25

4 More in number than the hairs of my head
are those who hate me without cause;
many are those who would destroy me,
my enemies who accuse me falsely.
What I did not steal
must I now restore?

69.5 Ps 44.21

5 O God, you know my folly;
the wrongs I have done are not hidden from you.

69.6 2 Sam 12.14

6 Do not let those who hope in you be put to shame because of me,
O Lord GOD of hosts;
do not let those who seek you be dishonored because of me,
O God of Israel.
7 It is for your sake that I have borne reproach,
that shame has covered my face.

69.8 Ps 31.11; 38.11

8 I have become a stranger to my kindred,
an alien to my mother's children.

69.9 Jn 2.17

9 It is zeal for your house that has consumed me;
the insults of those who insult you have fallen on me.
10 When I humbled my soul with fasting,[k]
they insulted me for doing so.
11 When I made sackcloth my clothing,
I became a byword to them.

69.12 Job 30.9

12 I am the subject of gossip for those who sit in the gate,
and the drunkards make songs about me.

69.13 Ps 32.6

13 But as for me, my prayer is to you, O LORD.
At an acceptable time, O God,
in the abundance of your steadfast love, answer me.

69.14 Ps 144.7

With your faithful help 14 rescue me
from sinking in the mire;
let me be delivered from my enemies
and from the deep waters.

69.15 Ps 124.4,5

15 Do not let the flood sweep over me,
or the deep swallow me up,
or the Pit close its mouth over me.

16 Answer me, O LORD, for your steadfast love is good;
according to your abundant mercy, turn to me.
17 Do not hide your face from your servant,
for I am in distress—make haste to answer me.

69.18 Ps 49.15 119.134

18 Draw near to me, redeem me,
set me free because of my enemies.

69.19 Ps 22.6,7 Isa 53.3

19 You know the insults I receive,
and my shame and dishonor;
my foes are all known to you.
20 Insults have broken my heart,

[k] Gk Syr: Heb *I wept, with fasting my soul,* or *I made my soul mourn with fasting*

69.5–7 Although we want to do God's will, we still make mistakes. But, like David, we should pray that our foolish mistakes will not cause others to stumble. We need to ask God to protect others who look up to us from being harmed by our mistakes and sins. Are you genuinely concerned about those who may copy your actions?

69.13 What problems David faced! He was scoffed at, mocked, insulted, humiliated, and made the object of city-wide gossip. But still he prayed. When we are completely beaten down, we are tempted to turn from God, give up, and quit trusting him. When your situation seems hopeless, determine that no matter how bad things become you will continue to pray. God will hear your prayer, and he will rescue you. When others reject us, we need God most. Don't turn from your most faithful friend.

so that I am in despair.
I looked for pity, but there was none;
and for comforters, but I found none.
21 They gave me poison for food,
and for my thirst they gave me vinegar to drink.

22 Let their table be a trap for them,
a snare for their allies.
23 Let their eyes be darkened so that they cannot see,
and make their loins tremble continually.
24 Pour out your indignation upon them,
and let your burning anger overtake them.
25 May their camp be a desolation;
let no one live in their tents.
26 For they persecute those whom you have struck down,
and those whom you have wounded, they attack still more.[l]
27 Add guilt to their guilt;
may they have no acquittal from you.
28 Let them be blotted out of the book of the living;
let them not be enrolled among the righteous.
29 But I am lowly and in pain;
let your salvation, O God, protect me.

30 I will praise the name of God with a song;
I will magnify him with thanksgiving.
31 This will please the LORD more than an ox
or a bull with horns and hoofs.
32 Let the oppressed see it and be glad;
you who seek God, let your hearts revive.
33 For the LORD hears the needy,
and does not despise his own that are in bonds.

34 Let heaven and earth praise him,
the seas and everything that moves in them.
35 For God will save Zion
and rebuild the cities of Judah;
and his servants shall live[m] there and possess it;
36 the children of his servants shall inherit it,
and those who love his name shall live in it.

69.21 Mt 27.48 Jn 19.29
69.25 Lk 13.35 Acts 1.20
69.26 2 Chron 28.9 Isa 53.4
69.28 Ex 32.33 Lk 10.20 Rev 3.5; 13.8 20.15
69.30 Ps 28.7
69.31 Ps 50.13,14
69.32 Ps 22.26; 34.2
69.34 Ps 148.1-13
69.35 Ps 147.2
69.36 Ps 25.13; 27.29

Theme: An urgent prayer for help. It can be your prayer when you're short on time and long on need.
Author: David

PSALM 70

To the leader. Of David, for the memorial offering.

1 Be pleased, O God, to deliver me.
O LORD, make haste to help me!
2 Let those be put to shame and confusion
who seek my life.

70.1 Ps 40.13-17

[l] Gk Syr: Heb *recount the pain of* [m] Syr: Heb *and they shall live*

69.32 When David says, "Let your hearts revive," he means you will feel glad and joyful. Most people want lasting joy and will try almost anything to obtain it, from scrambling for more money to being involved in sexual escapades. The only genuine source of happiness is God, and we receive lasting joy only by seeking him. How are you trying to find happiness? Seek God and live as he directs you (Matthew 6.33, 34), and true joy will soon follow.

70.1–5 When others disappoint us, we feel empty, as though a vital part of ourselves has been stolen. When others break the trust we have placed in them, they break our spirits as well. At those empty, broken moments, we must join the psalmist in begging God to rush to our aid. He alone can fill our lives with his joy (70.4). With the psalmist we cry out, "O Lord, do not delay!"

Let those be turned back and brought to dishonor
who desire to hurt me.
3 Let those who say, "Aha, Aha!"
turn back because of their shame.

4 Let all who seek you
rejoice and be glad in you.
Let those who love your salvation
say evermore, "God is great!"
70.5 Ps 141.1
5 But I am poor and needy;
hasten to me, O God!
You are my help and my deliverer;
O LORD, do not delay!

Theme: God's constant help—from childhood to old age. Our lives are a testimony of what God has done for us.
Author: Anonymous

PSALM 71

71.1 Ps 31.1-3
1 In you, O LORD, I take refuge;
let me never be put to shame.
2 In your righteousness deliver me and rescue me;
incline your ear to me and save me.
71.3 Deut 33.27 Ps 18.2; 44.4
3 Be to me a rock of refuge,
a strong fortress,[n] to save me,
for you are my rock and my fortress.

4 Rescue me, O my God, from the hand of the wicked,
from the grasp of the unjust and cruel.
71.5 Ps 22.9-11; 39.7 Jer 17.7,13,17
5 For you, O Lord, are my hope,
my trust, O LORD, from my youth.
71.6 Ps 22.9,10
6 Upon you I have leaned from my birth;
it was you who took me from my mother's womb.
My praise is continually of you.

7 I have been like a portent to many,
but you are my strong refuge.
8 My mouth is filled with your praise,
and with your glory all day long.
71.9 Ps 92.14
9 Do not cast me off in the time of old age;
do not forsake me when my strength is spent.
71.10 Mt 27.1
10 For my enemies speak concerning me,
and those who watch for my life consult together.
71.11 Ps 3.2; 7.2
11 They say, "Pursue and seize that person
whom God has forsaken,
for there is no one to deliver."

71.12 Ps 22.9-11
12 O God, do not be far from me;

[n] Gk Compare 31.3: Heb *to come continually you have commanded*

70.4 This short psalm (similar in content to 40.13–17) was David's plea for God to rush to his aid. Yet even in his moment of panic, he did not forget praise. Praise is important because it helps us remember who God is. Often our prayers are filled with requests for ourselves and others, and we forget to thank God for what he has done and to worship him for who he is. Don't take God for granted and treat him as a vending machine. Even when David was afraid, he praised God.

71.1ff The psalmist was old and saw his life as a "portent," a solemn warning or testimony of all God had done for him (71.7, 18). Remembering God's lifetime of blessing will help us to see the consistency of his grace throughout the years, to trust him for the future, and to share with others the benefits of following him.

71.6, 7 God helps us constantly. He is the reason we succeed at anything. He is worthy of our praise and thanks. To take all the credit for our success is dishonest and robs God of the glory due to him.

O my God, make haste to help me!
13 Let my accusers be put to shame and consumed;
let those who seek to hurt me
be covered with scorn and disgrace.
14 But I will hope continually,
and will praise you yet more and more.
15 My mouth will tell of your righteous acts,
of your deeds of salvation all day long,
though their number is past my knowledge.
16 I will come praising the mighty deeds of the Lord GOD,
I will praise your righteousness, yours alone.

17 O God, from my youth you have taught me,
and I still proclaim your wondrous deeds.
18 So even to old age and gray hairs,
O God, do not forsake me,
until I proclaim your might
to all the generations to come.[o]
Your power 19 and your righteousness, O God,
reach the high heavens.

You who have done great things,
O God, who is like you?
20 You who have made me see many troubles and calamities
will revive me again;
from the depths of the earth
you will bring me up again.
21 You will increase my honor,
and comfort me once again.

22 I will also praise you with the harp
for your faithfulness, O my God;
I will sing praises to you with the lyre,
O Holy One of Israel.
23 My lips will shout for joy
when I sing praises to you;
my soul also, which you have rescued.
24 All day long my tongue will talk of your righteous help,
for those who tried to do me harm
have been put to shame, and disgraced.

71.13 Ps 35.4,26
71.15 Ps 35.28; 40.5
71.16 Ps 106.2
71.18 Ps 22.31; 78.4,6
71.19 Deut 3.24; Ps 35.10; 57.10; Lk 1.49
71.20 Ps 23.4; 60.3; 119.25; Hos 6.2
71.22 Ps 33.2; 89.18; 147.7
71.23 Ps 5.11; 103.4

Theme: The perfect king. In this psalm, a king asks God to help his son rule the nation justly and wisely. It looks forward to the endless reign of the Messiah, who alone can rule with perfect justice and whose citizens will enjoy perfect peace.
Author: Solomon

PSALM 72

Of Solomon.

1 Give the king your justice, O God,
and your righteousness to a king's son.

72.1 1 Kgs 3.9; Ps 24.5

o Gk Compare Syr: Heb *to a generation, to all that come*

71.14 As we face the sunset years, we recognize that God has been our constant help in the past. As physical powers wane, we need God even more, and we realize he is still our constant help. We must never despair, but keep on expecting his help no matter how severe our limitations. Hope in him helps us to keep going, to keep serving him.

71.18 A person is never too old to serve God, never too old to pray. Though age may stop us from certain physical activities, it need not end our desire to tell others (especially children) about all we have seen God do in the many years we've lived.

72.1, 2 What qualities do we want most in our rulers? God desires all who rule under him to be righteous and just. As you think of world leaders today, think how the world would change if they would commit themselves to these two qualities. Perhaps we

72.2 Ps 82.3 Isa 9.7; 11.2-5
72.3 Isa 9.5,6 Mic 4.3,4 Zech 9.10
72.5 Ps 89.36,37
72.6 Deut 32.2 Ps 65.10 Hos 6.3
72.8 Ex 23.31 Zech 9.10
72.9 Isa 49.23 Mic 7.17
72.10 Ps 45.12; 68.29 Isa 42.4,10 60.6
72.11 Ps 86.9; 138.4 Isa 49.23
72.12 Job 29.12
72.17 Ps 89.36
72.18 Ex 15.11

2 May he judge your people with righteousness,
and your poor with justice.
3 May the mountains yield prosperity for the people,
and the hills, in righteousness.
4 May he defend the cause of the poor of the people,
give deliverance to the needy,
and crush the oppressor.

5 May he live[p] while the sun endures,
and as long as the moon, throughout all generations.
6 May he be like rain that falls on the mown grass,
like showers that water the earth.
7 In his days may righteousness flourish
and peace abound, until the moon is no more.

8 May he have dominion from sea to sea,
and from the River to the ends of the earth.
9 May his foes[q] bow down before him,
and his enemies lick the dust.
10 May the kings of Tarshish and of the isles
render him tribute,
may the kings of Sheba and Seba
bring gifts.
11 May all kings fall down before him,
all nations give him service.

12 For he delivers the needy when they call,
the poor and those who have no helper.
13 He has pity on the weak and the needy,
and saves the lives of the needy.
14 From oppression and violence he redeems their life;
and precious is their blood in his sight.

15 Long may he live!
May gold of Sheba be given to him.
May prayer be made for him continually,
and blessings invoked for him all day long.
16 May there be abundance of grain in the land;
may it wave on the tops of the mountains;
may its fruit be like Lebanon;
and may people blossom in the cities
like the grass of the field.
17 May his name endure forever,
his fame continue as long as the sun.
May all nations be blessed in him;[r]
may they pronounce him happy.

18 Blessed be the LORD, the God of Israel,

[p] Gk: Heb *may they fear you* [q] Cn: Heb *those who live in the wilderness* [r] Or *bless themselves by him*

should commit ourselves to pray that they will (see 1 Timothy 2.1, 2).

72.12–14 God cares for the helpless and poor because they are precious to him. If God feels so strongly about the poor and loves them so deeply, how can we ignore their plight? Examine what you are doing to reach out with God's love to the poor, weak, and needy. Are you ignoring their plight or are you championing their cause?

72.17 Solomon, David's son, reigned in Israel's golden age. He built the magnificent temple, and the land rested in peace. This psalm, though written by Solomon, looks beyond Solomon's reign to that of Jesus the Messiah, whose kingdom extends "to the ends of the earth" (72.8) and is greater than any human empire. This will be fulfilled when Christ returns to reign forever (Revelation 11.15). When we anticipate his worldwide rule, it fills our hearts with hope.

who alone does wondrous things.
19 Blessed be his glorious name forever;
may his glory fill the whole earth.
Amen and Amen.

20 The prayers of David son of Jesse are ended.

72.19
Num 14.20,21
Neh 9.5

BOOK III
Psalms 73.1 – 89.52

These psalms celebrate the sovereignty of God, God's hand in history, God's faithfulness, and God's covenant with David. These psalms remind us that our worship of the almighty God should be continual.

Theme: The temporary prosperity of the wicked and the lasting rewards of the righteous. We should live holy lives and trust God for our future rewards.
Author: Asaph, a leader of one of the temple choirs (see 1 Chronicles 25.1)

PSALM 73

A Psalm of Asaph.

1 Truly God is good to the upright,[s]
to those who are pure in heart.
2 But as for me, my feet had almost stumbled;
my steps had nearly slipped.
3 For I was envious of the arrogant;
I saw the prosperity of the wicked.

4 For they have no pain;
their bodies are sound and sleek.
5 They are not in trouble as others are;
they are not plagued like other people.
6 Therefore pride is their necklace;
violence covers them like a garment.
7 Their eyes swell out with fatness;
their hearts overflow with follies.
8 They scoff and speak with malice;
loftily they threaten oppression.
9 They set their mouths against heaven,
and their tongues range over the earth.

10 Therefore the people turn and praise them,[t]
and find no fault in them.[u]
11 And they say, "How can God know?
Is there knowledge in the Most High?"
12 Such are the wicked;
always at ease, they increase in riches.
13 All in vain I have kept my heart clean
and washed my hands in innocence.
14 For all day long I have been plagued,
and am punished every morning.

73.1
Ps 24.3,4
51.10
Mt 5.8

73.2
Ps 94.18

73.3
Ps 37.1,7

73.5
Job 21.9,10

73.6
Ps 109.18

73.7
Job 15.27,28

73.8
Ps 1.1; 17.10
Jude 16

73.11
Job 22.13

73.12
Ps 49.6
Ezek 23.42

73.13
Job 21.15; 34.9

73.14
Ps 38.5,6

[s] Or *good to Israel* [t] Cn: Heb *his people return here* [u] Cn: Heb *abundant waters are drained by them*

72.20 Book II ends with "Amen and Amen," as did Psalm 41, which closed Book I. This last verse does not mean that David wrote this psalm, but that he wrote most of the psalms in Book II.

73.1ff Until Asaph entered God's sanctuary, he could not understand the justice of allowing the wicked to thrive while the righteous endured hardship. But when he saw that one day justice would be done, he acknowledged God's wisdom.

73.1–20 Two strong themes wind their way through these verses: (1) the wicked prosper, leaving faithful people wondering why they bother to be good, and (2) the wealth of the wicked looks so inviting that faithful people may wish they could trade places. But these two themes come to unexpected ends, for the wealth of the wicked suddenly loses its power at death and the rewards for the good suddenly take on eternal value. What seemed like wealth is now waste, and what seemed worthless now lasts forever. Don't wish you could trade places with evil people to get their wealth. One day they will wish they could trade places with you and have your eternal wealth.

15 If I had said, "I will talk on in this way,"
I would have been untrue to the circle of your children.

73.16 Eccles 8.16,17

16 But when I thought how to understand this,
it seemed to me a wearisome task,

73.17 Ps 27.4; 77.13

17 until I went into the sanctuary of God;
then I perceived their end.
18 Truly you set them in slippery places;
you make them fall to ruin.

73.19 Num 16.21 Isa 47.11

19 How they are destroyed in a moment,
swept away utterly by terrors!
20 They are[v] like a dream when one awakes;
on awaking you despise their phantoms.

21 When my soul was embittered,
when I was pricked in heart,

73.22 Eccles 3.18

22 I was stupid and ignorant;
I was like a brute beast toward you.
23 Nevertheless I am continually with you;
you hold my right hand.

73.24 Ps 32.8; 48.14

24 You guide me with your counsel,
and afterward you will receive me with honor.[w]
25 Whom have I in heaven but you?
And there is nothing on earth that I desire other than you.

73.26 Ps 16.5; 38.10

26 My flesh and my heart may fail,
but God is the strength[x] of my heart and my portion forever.

73.27 Ex 34.15

27 Indeed, those who are far from you will perish;
you put an end to those who are false to you.

73.28 Ps 40.5

28 But for me it is good to be near God;
I have made the Lord GOD my refuge,
to tell of all your works.

Theme: A plea for God to help his people defend his cause and remember his promises. When we feel devastated or forgotten, we can plead to God for help, knowing that he hears.
Author: Asaph (or one of his descendants, since many believe this to be written after Jerusalem's fall in 586 B.C.)

PSALM 74

A Maskil of Asaph.

74.1 Deut 29.20 Ps 44.9; 89.46

1 O God, why do you cast us off forever?
Why does your anger smoke against the sheep of your pasture?

74.2 Deut 32.6,9 Ps 68.16

2 Remember your congregation, which you acquired long ago,
which you redeemed to be the tribe of your heritage.
Remember Mount Zion, where you came to dwell.

74.3 Ps 79.1 Isa 61.4

3 Direct your steps to the perpetual ruins;
the enemy has destroyed everything in the sanctuary.

4 Your foes have roared within your holy place;

[v] Cn: Heb *Lord* [w] Or *to glory* [x] Heb *rock*

73.20 Asaph realized that the rich who put their hope, joy, and confidence in their wealth are living in a dream. A dream exists only in the mind of the dreamer. Don't let your life's goals be so unreal that you awaken too late and miss the reality of God's truth. Happiness and hope can be a reality, but only when they are based on God, not on riches. Because reality is in God, we should get as close to him as we can in order to be realistic about life.

73.23, 24 From birth to death God has us continually in his grip. But far more we have the hope of the resurrection. Though our courage and strength may fail, we know that one day we will be raised to life to serve him forever. He is our security and we must cling to him.

74.1, 2 God's anger against Israel had grown hot during the many years of their sin and idolatry. His patience endured for generations, but at last it was set aside for judgment. If you fall into sin and quickly seek God's forgiveness, his mercy may come quickly and his anger may leave quickly. But if you persist in sinning against him, don't be surprised if his patience runs out.

they set up their emblems there.
5 At the upper entrance they hacked
the wooden trellis with axes.[y]
6 And then, with hatchets and hammers,
they smashed all its carved work.
7 They set your sanctuary on fire;
they desecrated the dwelling place of your name,
bringing it to the ground.
8 They said to themselves, "We will utterly subdue them";
they burned all the meeting places of God in the land.

9 We do not see our emblems;
there is no longer any prophet,
and there is no one among us who knows how long.
10 How long, O God, is the foe to scoff?
Is the enemy to revile your name forever?
11 Why do you hold back your hand;
why do you keep your hand in[z] your bosom?

12 Yet God my King is from of old,
working salvation in the earth.
13 You divided the sea by your might;
you broke the heads of the dragons in the waters.
14 You crushed the heads of Leviathan;
you gave him as food[a] for the creatures of the wilderness.
15 You cut openings for springs and torrents;
you dried up ever-flowing streams.
16 Yours is the day, yours also the night;
you established the luminaries[b] and the sun.
17 You have fixed all the bounds of the earth;
you made summer and winter.

18 Remember this, O LORD, how the enemy scoffs,
and an impious people reviles your name.
19 Do not deliver the soul of your dove to the wild animals;
do not forget the life of your poor forever.

20 Have regard for your[c] covenant,
for the dark places of the land are full of the haunts of violence.
21 Do not let the downtrodden be put to shame;
let the poor and needy praise your name.
22 Rise up, O God, plead your cause;
remember how the impious scoff at you all day long.
23 Do not forget the clamor of your foes,
the uproar of your adversaries that goes up continually.

74.5 1 Kgs 6.18,29, 32,35 Jer 46.22
74.7 2 Kgs 25.9
74.9 Lev 24.16 Ps 78.43; 79.12
74.11 Ps 59.13
74.12 Ps 44.4
74.13 Ex 14.21
74.15 Ex 14.21,22 17.5,6
74.16 Gen 1.14-18 Ps 136.7,8
74.17 Gen 8.22
74.18 Deut 32.6
74.20 Gen 17.7 Ps 106.45
74.21 Ps 35.10 Isa 41.17
74.22 Ps 43.1

y Cn Compare Gk Syr: Meaning of Heb uncertain z Cn: Heb *do you consume your right hand from* a Heb *food for the people* b Or *moon*; Heb *light* c Gk Syr: Heb *the*

74.8 When enemy armies defeated Israel, they sacked Jerusalem, trying to wipe out every trace of God. This has often been the response of people who hate God. Today many are trying to erase God from traditions in our society and subjects taught in our schools. Do what you can to maintain a Christian influence, but don't become discouraged when others appear to make great strides in eliminating all traces of God, for they cannot eliminate his presence among believers.

74.10–18 From our perspective, God sometimes seems slow to intervene on our behalf. But what might appear slow to us is good timing from God's perspective. It's easy to become impatient for God to act, but never give up waiting on him. When God is silent and we are deep in anguish, follow the method in this psalm. Review the great acts of God throughout biblical history and then review what he has done for you. This will remind you that God is at work not only in history, but in your life today.

74.13, 14 "The dragons in the waters" refers to Egypt (Ezekiel 32.2ff). "Leviathan" refers to the Canaanite, seven-headed serpent, Lotan. In their legends, Baal defeated these creatures. This psalm praised God for doing in reality what the Canaanite gods could only do in legends.

Theme: Because God is the final judge, the tables will be turned upon the wicked. When arrogant people threaten our security, we can be confident that God will ultimately overrule and destroy them.
Author: Asaph

PSALM 75

To the leader: Do Not Destroy. A Psalm of Asaph. A Song.

75.1 Ps 44.1; 71.17

1 We give thanks to you, O God;
we give thanks; your name is near.
People tell of your wondrous deeds.

2 At the set time that I appoint
I will judge with equity.

75.3 1 Sam 2.8 Ps 46.6

3 When the earth totters, with all its inhabitants,
it is I who keep its pillars steady. *Selah*
4 I say to the boastful, "Do not boast,"
and to the wicked, "Do not lift up your horn;
5 do not lift up your horn on high,
or speak with insolent neck."

75.6 1 Sam 2.7 Ps 113.6-8

6 For not from the east or from the west
and not from the wilderness comes lifting up;
7 but it is God who executes judgment,
putting down one and lifting up another.

75.8 Ps 11.6

8 For in the hand of the LORD there is a cup
with foaming wine, well mixed;
he will pour a draught from it,
and all the wicked of the earth
shall drain it down to the dregs.

75.9 Ps 40.10

9 But I will rejoice[d] forever;
I will sing praises to the God of Jacob.

75.10 Ps 89.17 148.14

10 All the horns of the wicked I will cut off,
but the horns of the righteous shall be exalted.

Theme: A call for God to punish evildoers. Even man's angry revolt will be used by God to bring glory to himself.
Author: Asaph

PSALM 76

To the leader: with stringed instruments. A Psalm of Asaph. A Song.

1 In Judah God is known,
his name is great in Israel.

76.2 Ps 48.2,3 132.13; 135.21

2 His abode has been established in Salem,
his dwelling place in Zion.

76.3 Ps 46.9

3 There he broke the flashing arrows,
the shield, the sword, and the weapons of war. *Selah*

[d] Gk: Heb *declare*

75.2 God will act when he is ready. Children have difficulty grasping the concept of time. "It's not time yet" is not a reason they easily understand. They only comprehend the present. As limited human beings, we can't comprehend God's perspective on time. We want everything now, unaware that God's timing is better for us. When God is ready, he will do what needs to be done, not what we would like him to do. We may be impatient as children, but we must not doubt the wisdom of God's timing. Until he reveals his plan, don't take matters into your own hands.

75.8 The cup of wine represents God's judgment. The judgment of God is coming against the wicked. God will pour out his fury on his enemies, and they will be forced to drink it. Drinking the cup of God's judgment is a picture used frequently in Scripture (Isaiah 51.17, 22; Jeremiah 25.15; 49.12; Habakkuk 2.16; Revelation 14.10; 16.19; 18.6). It gives the impression of taking a dose of one's own medicine. To drain it down to the dregs means to suffer complete punishment.

76.1ff This psalm praises God for his awesome power. It was most likely written to celebrate the defeat of Sennacherib's army after he invaded Judah (see 2 Kings 18.13–19, 37).

4 Glorious are you, more majestic
than the everlasting mountains.[e]
5 The stouthearted were stripped of their spoil;
they sank into sleep;
none of the troops
was able to lift a hand.
6 At your rebuke, O God of Jacob,
both rider and horse lay stunned.

7 But you indeed are awesome!
Who can stand before you
when once your anger is roused?
8 From the heavens you uttered judgment;
the earth feared and was still
9 when God rose up to establish judgment,
to save all the oppressed of the earth. *Selah*

10 Human wrath serves only to praise you,
when you bind the last bit of your[f] wrath around you.
11 Make vows to the LORD your God, and perform them;
let all who are around him bring gifts
to the one who is awesome,
12 who cuts off the spirit of princes,
who inspires fear in the kings of the earth.

76.5 Isa 10.12
76.6 Ex 15.1,21 Ps 78.53
76.7 Ps 89.7 Nah 1.6 Rev 6.17
76.8 1 Chron 16.30
76.9 Ps 9.7-9; 72.4

Theme: We are comforted through the hard times by remembering God's help in the past. Recalling God's miracles and previous works can give us courage to continue.
Author: Asaph

PSALM 77

To the leader: according to Jeduthun. Of Asaph. A Psalm.

1 I cry aloud to God,
aloud to God, that he may hear me.
2 In the day of my trouble I seek the Lord;
in the night my hand is stretched out without wearying;
my soul refuses to be comforted.
3 I think of God, and I moan;
I meditate, and my spirit faints. *Selah*

4 You keep my eyelids from closing;
I am so troubled that I cannot speak.
5 I consider the days of old,
and remember the years of long ago.
6 I commune[g] with my heart in the night;
I meditate and search my spirit:[h]
7 "Will the Lord spurn forever,

77.2 Job 11.13 Ps 50.15; 88.9 Isa 26.9
77.3 Ps 43.5; 61.2 142.2,3
77.5 Ps 143.5
77.6 Ps 42.8

[e] Gk: Heb *the mountains of prey* [f] Heb lacks *your* [g] Gk Syr: Heb *My music* [h] Syr Jerome: Heb *my spirit searches*

76.10 How can someone's wrath praise God? Hostility to God and his people gives God the opportunity to do great deeds. For example, the Pharaoh of Egypt refused to free the Hebrew slaves (Exodus 5.1, 2), and this allowed God to work mighty miracles for his people (Exodus 11.9). God turns the tables on evildoers and brings glory to himself from the foolishness of those who deny him or revolt against him.

76.11 To make and perform vows means to promise an offering and then to deliver on your promise. Because God is so great and powerful, he should be revered and feared. Those who take God lightly now will be dealt with severely in the day of wrath. Those who revere him now will find his favor.

77.1–12 Asaph cried out to God for courage during a time of deep distress. His plea was, "I need help." But in 77.13–20, the "I" is gone. As Asaph expressed his requests to God, his focus changed from thinking of himself to worshiping God: "You are the God who works wonders" (77.14). As we pray to God, he shifts our focus from ourselves to him.

77.4–9 The source of Asaph's distress (77.4) was his doubt (77.7–9). Only after he put aside his doubts about God's holiness and care for him (77.13, 14) did he eliminate his distress (77.20).

and never again be favorable?
77.8 Ps 89.49 8 Has his steadfast love ceased forever?
Are his promises at an end for all time?
77.9 Ps 25.6 9 Has God forgotten to be gracious?
Has he in anger shut up his compassion?" *Selah*
77.10 Ps 31.22 10 And I say, "It is my grief
that the right hand of the Most High has changed."

11 I will call to mind the deeds of the LORD;
I will remember your wonders of old.
12 I will meditate on all your work,
and muse on your mighty deeds.
77.13 Ex 15.11 13 Your way, O God, is holy.
What god is so great as our God?
14 You are the God who works wonders;
you have displayed your might among the peoples.
77.15 Ex 6.6 15 With your strong arm you redeemed your people,
the descendants of Jacob and Joseph. *Selah*

77.16 Ex 14.21 16 When the waters saw you, O God,
when the waters saw you, they were afraid;
the very deep trembled.
77.17 Ps 68.33 17 The clouds poured out water;
the skies thundered;
your arrows flashed on every side.
77.18 Judg 5.4 18 The crash of your thunder was in the whirlwind;
your lightnings lit up the world;
the earth trembled and shook.
19 Your way was through the sea,
your path, through the mighty waters;
yet your footprints were unseen.
77.20 Ex 13.21 Ps 78.52 20 You led your people like a flock
by the hand of Moses and Aaron.

Theme: Lessons from history. Asaph retells the history of the Jewish nation from the time of slavery in Egypt to David's reign. It was told over and over to each generation so they would not forget God and make the same mistakes as their ancestors.
Author: Asaph

PSALM 78

A Maskil of Asaph.

1 Give ear, O my people, to my teaching;
incline your ears to the words of my mouth.
78.2 Mt 13.34,35 2 I will open my mouth in a parable;
I will utter dark sayings from of old,
3 things that we have heard and known,
that our ancestors have told us.
78.4 Deut 11.19 4 We will not hide them from their children;
we will tell to the coming generation
the glorious deeds of the LORD, and his might,

77.11, 12 Memories of God's goodness and faithfulness sustained Israel through their difficulties. They knew that God was capable and trustworthy. When you meet new trials, review how good God has been to you, and this will strengthen your faith.

77.16 The miraculous parting of the Red Sea is mentioned many times in the Old Testament (Exodus 14.21, 22; Joshua 24.6; Nehemiah 9.9; Psalm 74.13; 106.9; 136.13–15). The story of this incredible miracle was handed down from generation to generation, reminding the Israelites of God's power, protection, and love.

78.1ff The people of Israel rebelled and refused to give their hearts to God (78.8); forgot about God's miracles (78.11, 12); selfishly complained (78.18); made empty promises to repent (78.37); and were ungrateful (78.42). This is recorded in God's Word so we can avoid the same errors. In 1 Corinthians 10.5–12, Paul uses this classic story to warn the early Christians to be faithful.

and the wonders that he has done.

5 He established a decree in Jacob, 78.5 Deut 6.4-9
and appointed a law in Israel,
which he commanded our ancestors
to teach to their children;
6 that the next generation might know them, 78.6 Deut 11.19
the children yet unborn,
and rise up and tell them to their children,
7 so that they should set their hope in God, 78.7 Deut 4.2,9 Josh 22.5
and not forget the works of God,
but keep his commandments;
8 and that they should not be like their ancestors,
a stubborn and rebellious generation,
a generation whose heart was not steadfast,
whose spirit was not faithful to God.

9 The Ephraimites, armed with[i] the bow, 78.9 Ex 32.9
turned back on the day of battle.
10 They did not keep God's covenant, 78.10 2 Kgs 18.12
but refused to walk according to his law.
11 They forgot what he had done,
and the miracles that he had shown them.
12 In the sight of their ancestors he worked marvels
in the land of Egypt, in the fields of Zoan.
13 He divided the sea and let them pass through it, 78.13 Ex 14.21; 15.18
and made the waters stand like a heap.
14 In the daytime he led them with a cloud, 78.14 Ex 13.21
and all night long with a fiery light.
15 He split rocks open in the wilderness, 78.15 Ex 17.5,6
and gave them drink abundantly as from the deep.
16 He made streams come out of the rock, 78.16 Num 20.8,10,11
and caused waters to flow down like rivers.

17 Yet they sinned still more against him,
rebelling against the Most High in the desert.
18 They tested God in their heart 78.18 Num 11.4,5 1 Cor 10.9,10
by demanding the food they craved.
19 They spoke against God, saying, 78.19 Ex 16.3 Num 21.5
"Can God spread a table in the wilderness?
20 Even though he struck the rock so that water gushed out
and torrents overflowed,
can he also give bread,
or provide meat for his people?"

21 Therefore, when the LORD heard, he was full of rage; 78.21 Num 11.1

[i] Heb *armed with shooting*

78.5 God commanded that the stories of his mighty acts in Israel's history and his laws be passed on from parents to children. This shows the purpose and importance of religious education—to help each generation obey God and set their hope on him. It is important to keep children from repeating the same mistakes as their ancestors. What are you doing to pass on the history of God's work to the next generation?

78.9, 10 Ephraim was the most prominent tribe of Israel from the days of Moses to Saul's time. The tabernacle was set up in its territory. There is no other biblical record of Ephraim's soldiers fleeing in battle, so this is probably a metaphor referring to Ephraim's failure to provide strong leadership during those years. When David became king, the tribe of Judah gained prominence. Because of David's faith and obedience, God chose Jerusalem in Judah to be the place for the new temple and rejected Ephraim (78.67), causing tension between the two tribes. This psalm may have been written because of that tension in order to demonstrate once again why God chose Judah. God works through those who are faithful to him.

a fire was kindled against Jacob,
his anger mounted against Israel,
22 because they had no faith in God,
and did not trust his saving power.
23 Yet he commanded the skies above,
and opened the doors of heaven;
24 he rained down on them manna to eat,
and gave them the grain of heaven.
25 Mortals ate of the bread of angels;
he sent them food in abundance.
26 He caused the east wind to blow in the heavens,
and by his power he led out the south wind;
27 he rained flesh upon them like dust,
winged birds like the sand of the seas;
28 he let them fall within their camp,
all around their dwellings.
29 And they ate and were well filled,
for he gave them what they craved.
30 But before they had satisfied their craving,
while the food was still in their mouths,
31 the anger of God rose against them
and he killed the strongest of them,
and laid low the flower of Israel.

32 In spite of all this they still sinned;
they did not believe in his wonders.
33 So he made their days vanish like a breath,
and their years in terror.
34 When he killed them, they sought for him;
they repented and sought God earnestly.
35 They remembered that God was their rock,
the Most High God their redeemer.
36 But they flattered him with their mouths;
they lied to him with their tongues.
37 Their heart was not steadfast toward him;
they were not true to his covenant.
38 Yet he, being compassionate,
forgave their iniquity,
and did not destroy them;
often he restrained his anger,
and did not stir up all his wrath.
39 He remembered that they were but flesh,
a wind that passes and does not come again.
40 How often they rebelled against him in the wilderness
and grieved him in the desert!
41 They tested God again and again,
and provoked the Holy One of Israel.
42 They did not keep in mind his power,
or the day when he redeemed them from the foe;
43 when he displayed his signs in Egypt,
and his miracles in the fields of Zoan.
44 He turned their rivers to blood,
so that they could not drink of their streams.

78.22 Heb 3.18
78.24 Ex 16.4 Jn 6.30,31
78.26 Num 11.31
78.27 Ex 16.13 Ps 105.40
78.29 Num 11.19,20
78.31 Num 11.33,34
78.32 Num 14.10,11
78.33 Num 14.29,34,35
78.35 Deut 9.26; 32.4
78.38 Ex 34.5,6 Num 14.19
78.42 Judg 8.34
78.43 Ex 7.3
78.44 Ex 7.20 Ps 105.29

78.36, 37 Over and over the children of Israel claimed they would follow God, but then they turned away from him. The problem was that they followed God with words and not with their hearts; thus their repentance was empty. Talk is cheap. God wants our conduct to back up our spiritual claims and promises.

45 He sent among them swarms of flies, which devoured them,
and frogs, which destroyed them.
46 He gave their crops to the caterpillar,
and the fruit of their labor to the locust.
47 He destroyed their vines with hail,
and their sycamores with frost.
48 He gave over their cattle to the hail,
and their flocks to thunderbolts.
49 He let loose on them his fierce anger,
wrath, indignation, and distress,
a company of destroying angels.
50 He made a path for his anger;
he did not spare them from death,
but gave their lives over to the plague.
51 He struck all the firstborn in Egypt,
the first issue of their strength in the tents of Ham.
52 Then he led out his people like sheep,
and guided them in the wilderness like a flock.
53 He led them in safety, so that they were not afraid;
but the sea overwhelmed their enemies.
54 And he brought them to his holy hill,
to the mountain that his right hand had won.
55 He drove out nations before them;
he apportioned them for a possession
and settled the tribes of Israel in their tents.

56 Yet they tested the Most High God,
and rebelled against him.
They did not observe his decrees,
57 but turned away and were faithless like their ancestors;
they twisted like a treacherous bow.
58 For they provoked him to anger with their high places;
they moved him to jealousy with their idols.
59 When God heard, he was full of wrath,
and he utterly rejected Israel.
60 He abandoned his dwelling at Shiloh,
the tent where he dwelt among mortals,
61 and delivered his power to captivity,
his glory to the hand of the foe.
62 He gave his people to the sword,
and vented his wrath on his heritage.
63 Fire devoured their young men,
and their girls had no marriage song.
64 Their priests fell by the sword,
and their widows made no lamentation.
65 Then the Lord awoke as from sleep,
like a warrior shouting because of wine.
66 He put his adversaries to rout;
he put them to everlasting disgrace.

67 He rejected the tent of Joseph,
he did not choose the tribe of Ephraim;
68 but he chose the tribe of Judah,
Mount Zion, which he loves.

78.45 Ex 8.6,24 Ps 105.30,31
78.46 Ex 10.14
78.47 Ex 9.23 Ps 105.32
78.48 Ex 9.19
78.49 Ex 15.7
78.51 Ex 12.29,30 Ps 105.36
78.52 Ps 77.20
78.53 Ex 14.19,20, 27,28
78.54 Ex 15.17
78.55 Josh 23.4,5
78.58 Lev 26.1 Deut 32.16,21
78.59 Lev 26.30 Deut 32.19
78.60 1 Sam 4.11
78.61 1 Sam 4.17
78.62 Judg 20.21 1 Sam 4.10
78.63 Num 11.1 Jer 7.34; 16.9
78.64 1 Sam 22.18

78.51 This was the passover in Exodus 12.29, 30. All the firstborn of the Egyptians were slain. The "tents of Ham" refers to Noah's second son, who was the ancestor of the Egyptians. Ham is sometimes used as a synonym for Egypt.

78.69
1 Kgs 6.1-38

78.70
1 Sam 16.10-12

78.71
2 Sam 5.2; 7.8
1 Kgs 9.4
1 Chron 11.2

69 He built his sanctuary like the high heavens,
like the earth, which he has founded forever.
70 He chose his servant David,
and took him from the sheepfolds;
71 from tending the nursing ewes he brought him
to be the shepherd of his people Jacob,
of Israel, his inheritance.
72 With upright heart he tended them,
and guided them with skillful hand.

Theme: When outraged by injustice, cry out to God, not against him. In times of disaster, our mood may be anger, but our trust must remain in God.
Author: Asaph (or one of his descendants), probably written after the Babylonians had leveled Jerusalem (see 2 Kings 25)

PSALM 79

A Psalm of Asaph.

79.1
Ps 74.2-7
Jer 26.18
Lam 1.10

79.2
Deut 28.26
Jer 7.33; 16.4

79.3
Jer 14.16

1 O God, the nations have come into your inheritance;
they have defiled your holy temple;
they have laid Jerusalem in ruins.
2 They have given the bodies of your servants
to the birds of the air for food,
the flesh of your faithful to the wild animals of the earth.
3 They have poured out their blood like water
all around Jerusalem,
and there was no one to bury them.
4 We have become a taunt to our neighbors,

PRAYER IN THE BOOK OF PSALMS

Prayer is human communication with God. Psalms could be described as a collection of song-prayers. Probably the most striking feature of these prayers is their unedited honesty. The words often express our own feelings—feelings which we would prefer no one, much less God, ever knew. Making these psalms our prayers can teach us a great deal about how God wants us to communicate with him. Too often we give God a watered-down version of our feelings, hoping we won't offend him or make him curious about our motives. As we use the psalms to express our feelings, we learn that honesty, openness, and sincerity are valuable to God.

Following are several types of prayers with examples from Psalms. Note that the psalm writers communicated with God in a variety of ways for a variety of reasons. Each of us is invited to communicate with God. Using the psalms will enrich your personal prayer life.

Prayers of:	*Psalms:*
Praise to God	100; 113; 117
Thanksgiving by a community	67; 75; 136
Thanksgiving by an individual	18; 30; 32
Request by the community	79; 80; 123
Request by an individual	3; 55; 86
Sorrow by the community	44; 74; 137
Sorrow by an individual	5; 6; 120
Anger	35; 109; 140
Confession	6; 32; 51
Faith	11; 16; 23

78.70–72 With love and skill, David the shepherd boy cared for his flocks. As Israel's king, David cared for his people the same way—with skillful hands and a pure heart. Skill and integrity are basic requirements for effective leadership. Those without skill are ineffective. Those without high moral character lead people astray or become easily corrupted. In your pursuit to become more highly skilled, don't neglect integrity.

78.71, 72 Although David had been on the throne when this psalm was written, he is called a shepherd and not a king. Shepherding, a common profession in biblical times, was a highly responsible job. The flocks were completely dependent upon shepherds for guidance, provision, and protection. David had spent his early years as a shepherd (1 Samuel 16.10, 11). This was a training ground for the future responsibilities God had in store for him. When he was ready, God took him from caring for sheep to caring for Israel, God's people. Don't treat your present situation lightly or irresponsibly; it may be God's training ground for your future.

mocked and derided by those around us.

5 How long, O LORD? Will you be angry forever?
Will your jealous wrath burn like fire?
6 Pour out your anger on the nations
that do not know you,
and on the kingdoms
that do not call on your name.
7 For they have devoured Jacob
and laid waste his habitation.

8 Do not remember against us the iniquities of our ancestors;
let your compassion come speedily to meet us,
for we are brought very low.
9 Help us, O God of our salvation,
for the glory of your name;
deliver us, and forgive our sins,
for your name's sake.
10 Why should the nations say,
"Where is their God?"
Let the avenging of the outpoured blood of your servants
be known among the nations before our eyes.

11 Let the groans of the prisoners come before you;
according to your great power preserve those doomed to die.
12 Return sevenfold into the bosom of our neighbors
the taunts with which they taunted you, O Lord!
13 Then we your people, the flock of your pasture,
will give thanks to you forever;
from generation to generation we will recount your praise.

79.6 Jer 10.25
79.7 Ps 53.4
79.8 Ps 106.6; 142.6 Isa 26.5; 64.9
79.9 2 Chron 14.11 Jer 14.7
79.10 Ps 115.2
79.12 Gen 4.15

Theme: A prayer for revival and restoration after experiencing destruction. God is our only hope for salvation.
Author: Asaph (or one of his descendants), probably written after the northern kingdom of Israel was defeated and its people deported to Assyria

PSALM 80

To the leader: on Lilies, a Covenant. Of Asaph. A Psalm.

1 Give ear, O Shepherd of Israel,
you who lead Joseph like a flock!
You who are enthroned upon the cherubim, shine forth
2 before Ephraim and Benjamin and Manasseh.
Stir up your might,
and come to save us!

3 Restore us, O God;
let your face shine, that we may be saved.

80.1 Ex 25.22 Ps 23.1; 77.20
80.2 Ps 35.23
80.3 Num 6.24-26 Ps 31.16; 60.1

79.6 According to the Old Testament, God's wrath and judgment often fell on entire nations because of the sins of people within those nations. Here Asaph pled for judgment on kingdoms who refused to acknowledge God's authority. Ironically, Asaph's own nation of Judah was being judged by God for refusing to do this very thing (2 Chronicles 36.14–20). These were people who had sworn allegiance to God but were now rejecting him. This made their judgment even worse.

79.10 Can we expect God to care for us so others won't scoff at our beliefs? In the end, God's glory will be evident to all people, but in the meantime, we must endure suffering with patience and allow God to strengthen our character through it. For reasons that we do not know, the heathen are allowed to scoff at believers. We should be prepared for criticism, jokes, and unkind remarks because God does not place us beyond the attacks of scoffers.

80.1 Cherubim are mighty angels.

80.3, 7, 19 Three times the writer calls on God to "restore us." Repentance involves humbling ourselves and turning to God to receive his forgiveness and restoration. As we turn to God, he helps us see ourselves, including our sin, more clearly. And as we see our sin, we must repeat the process of repentance.

80.4 Ps 79.5; 84.8

4 O LORD God of hosts,
how long will you be angry with your people's prayers?
5 You have fed them with the bread of tears,
and given them tears to drink in full measure.

80.6 Ps 44.13

6 You make us the scorn[j] of our neighbors;
our enemies laugh among themselves.

7 Restore us, O God of hosts;
let your face shine, that we may be saved.

80.8 2 Chron 20.7; Ps 44.2; Isa 5.2,7; Jer 2.21; 11.17; Ezek 17.6,23; Amos 9.15

80.9 Ex 23.28; Isa 5.2; Hos 14.5

80.11 Ps 72.8

80.12 Ps 89.40; Isa 5.5

80.13 Jer 5.6

8 You brought a vine out of Egypt;
you drove out the nations and planted it.
9 You cleared the ground for it;
it took deep root and filled the land.
10 The mountains were covered with its shade,
the mighty cedars with its branches;
11 it sent out its branches to the sea,
and its shoots to the River.
12 Why then have you broken down its walls,
so that all who pass along the way pluck its fruit?
13 The boar from the forest ravages it,
and all that move in the field feed on it.

80.16 2 Chron 36.19; Jer 52.13

80.17 Ps 89.21

14 Turn again, O God of hosts;
look down from heaven, and see;
have regard for this vine,
15 the stock that your right hand planted.[k]
16 They have burned it with fire, they have cut it down;[l]
may they perish at the rebuke of your countenance.
17 But let your hand be upon the one at your right hand,
the one whom you made strong for yourself.
18 Then we will never turn back from you;
give us life, and we will call on your name.

19 Restore us, O LORD God of hosts;
let your face shine, that we may be saved.

Theme: A holiday hymn. This hymn celebrates the exodus from Egypt—God's goodness versus Israel's waywardness. God is our deliverer in spite of our wanderings.
Author: Asaph, probably written to be used during the festival of booths

PSALM 81

To the leader: according to The Gittith. Of Asaph.

81.1 Ps 46.1; 59.16; 66.1; 95.1,2

81.2 Ps 108.2; 144.9

1 Sing aloud to God our strength;
shout for joy to the God of Jacob.
2 Raise a song, sound the tambourine,
the sweet lyre with the harp.

[j] Syr: Heb *strife* [k] Heb adds from verse 17 *and upon the one whom you made strong for yourself* [l] Cn: Heb *it is cut down*

80.17 The "one at your right hand" is probably not the Messiah, but Israel, whom God calls elsewhere his "firstborn" (Exodus 4.22). The psalmist is making a plea that God would restore his mercy to Israel, the people he chose to bring his message into the world.

81.1–5 Israel's holidays reminded the nation of God's great miracles. They were times of rejoicing and times to renew one's strength for life's daily struggles. At Christmas, do your thoughts revolve mostly around presents? Is Easter only a warm anticipation of spring, and Thanksgiving only a good meal? Remember the spiritual origins of these special days, and use them as opportunities to worship God for his goodness to you, your family, and your nation.

81.2–4 Music and worship go hand in hand. David instituted music for the temple worship services (1 Chronicles 25). Worship involves the whole person, and music helps focus worship by lifting one's thoughts and emotions to God. Through music we can reflect upon our needs and shortcomings as well as celebrate God's greatness.

3 Blow the trumpet at the new moon,
at the full moon, on our festal day.
4 For it is a statute for Israel,
an ordinance of the God of Jacob.
5 He made it a decree in Joseph,
when he went out over[m] the land of Egypt.

I hear a voice I had not known:
6 "I relieved your[n] shoulder of the burden;
your[n] hands were freed from the basket.
7 In distress you called, and I rescued you;
I answered you in the secret place of thunder;
I tested you at the waters of Meribah. *Selah*
8 Hear, O my people, while I admonish you;
O Israel, if you would but listen to me!
9 There shall be no strange god among you;
you shall not bow down to a foreign god.
10 I am the LORD your God,
who brought you up out of the land of Egypt.
Open your mouth wide and I will fill it.

11 "But my people did not listen to my voice;
Israel would not submit to me.
12 So I gave them over to their stubborn hearts,
to follow their own counsels.
13 O that my people would listen to me,
that Israel would walk in my ways!
14 Then I would quickly subdue their enemies,
and turn my hand against their foes.
15 Those who hate the LORD would cringe before him,
and their doom would last forever.
16 I would feed you[o] with the finest of the wheat,
and with honey from the rock I would satisfy you."

81.3 Lev 23.24 Num 10.10
81.5 Ex 11.4
81.7 Ex 2.23; 17.5-7 19.19 Ps 50.15; 95.8
81.9 Ex 20.3 Isa 43.12
81.10 Ex 20.2 Ps 78.25; 103.5
81.11 Ex 32.1
81.12 Rom 1.24,26
81.13 Deut 5.29 Isa 48.18 Jer 7.23
81.16 Deut 32.13,14

Theme: A fair judge. God will judge the wicked who have unfairly treated others.
Author: Asaph

PSALM 82

A Psalm of Asaph.

1 God has taken his place in the divine council;
in the midst of the gods he holds judgment:
2 "How long will you judge unjustly
and show partiality to the wicked? *Selah*
3 Give justice to the weak and the orphan;
maintain the right of the lowly and the destitute.
4 Rescue the weak and the needy;
deliver them from the hand of the wicked."

5 They have neither knowledge nor understanding,
they walk around in darkness;
all the foundations of the earth are shaken.

82.1 Ps 58.11 Isa 3.13
82.2 Deut 1.17
82.3 Deut 24.17

[m] Or *against* [n] Heb *his* [o] Cn Compare verse 16b: Heb *he would feed him*

81.11, 12 God let the Israelites go on blindly, stubbornly, and selfishly, when they should have been obeying and pursuing God's desires. God sometimes lets us continue in our stubbornness to bring us to our senses. He does not keep us from rebelling, because he wants us to learn the consequences of sin. He desires to use these experiences to turn people back from greater sin to faith in him.

82.6
Jn 10.34-36

6 I say, "You are gods,
children of the Most High, all of you;

82.7
Ps 49.12; 83.11

7 nevertheless, you shall die like mortals,
and fall like any prince."[p]

82.8
Ps 2.8; 12.5
Rev 11.15

8 Rise up, O God, judge the earth;
for all the nations belong to you!

Theme: Combatting God's enemies. This psalm is a prayer for God to do whatever it takes to convince the world that he is indeed God. Someday all will recognize and admit that God is in charge.
Author: Asaph (or one of his descendants)

PSALM 83

A Song. A Psalm of Asaph.

1 O God, do not keep silence;
do not hold your peace or be still, O God!

83.2
Ps 2.1

2 Even now your enemies are in tumult;
those who hate you have raised their heads.

83.3
Ps 31.20

3 They lay crafty plans against your people;
they consult together against those you protect.

83.4
Esth 3.5,6

4 They say, "Come, let us wipe them out as a nation;
let the name of Israel be remembered no more."

83.5
Ps 2.2

5 They conspire with one accord;
against you they make a covenant—

83.6
Gen 25.12-16
2 Chron 20.1,10

6 the tents of Edom and the Ishmaelites,
Moab and the Hagrites,

83.7
2 Chron 20.10
1 Sam 4.1; 15.2
Ezek 27.2,3,9

7 Gebal and Ammon and Amalek,
Philistia with the inhabitants of Tyre;
8 Assyria also has joined them;
they are the strong arm of the children of Lot. *Selah*

83.9
Judg 4.22,23

9 Do to them as you did to Midian,
as to Sisera and Jabin at the Wadi Kishon,
10 who were destroyed at En-dor,
who became dung for the ground.

83.11
Judg 7.25; 8.21

11 Make their nobles like Oreb and Zeeb,
all their princes like Zebah and Zalmunna,

83.12
2 Chron 20.11

12 who said, "Let us take the pastures of God
for our own possession."

[p] Or *fall as one man, O princes*

82.6 This psalm calls the judges of Israel "gods" and "children of the Most High." They were called gods because they represented God in executing judgment. In John 10.34–36, Jesus used this passage to defend his claims to be God. His argument was as follows: if God would call mere men gods, why was it blasphemous for him, the Son of God, to declare himself equal with God?

83.5–8 This alliance against God may refer to the gathering of certain kings to fight against Jehoshaphat and the people of Judah (2 Chronicles 20). The psalm's author is called Asaph, but this is an inclusive term meaning Asaph or one of his descendants. A descendant of Asaph named Jahaziel prophesied victory for Judah in the battle against Jehoshaphat (2 Chronicles 20.13–17). The psalmist says the alliance against Judah is really against God. Thus Jahaziel exclaimed, "The battle is not yours but God's" (2 Chronicles 20.15). Because God is in supreme charge of all the earth (83.18), the enemies of Israel were considered God's enemies.

83.6 The Hagrites were the descendants of Hagar (Genesis 21.8–21).

83.8–11 The "children of Lot" refers to the Moabites and Ammonites (Genesis 19.36–38). Sisera was the commander of the army of the oppressive Canaanite King Jabin. He was killed by a woman (see Judges 4 for the complete story). (For the story of Oreb and Zeeb, see Judges 7.25; for Zebah and Zalmunna, see Judges 8.21.)

83.13–18 The rulers of the nations exercise great power, changing the course of history and its peoples. Surrounding Judah were heathen nations that sought its downfall. The psalmist prayed that God would blow his hot breath of judgment upon them until, in their defeat, they recognized that the Lord is above all rulers of the earth. Sometimes we must be humbled by adversity before we will look up and see the Lord; we must be defeated before we can have the ultimate victory. Wouldn't it be better to seek the Lord in times of prosperity than to wait until his judgment is upon us?

13 O my God, make them like whirling dust,[q]
like chaff before the wind.
14 As fire consumes the forest,
as the flame sets the mountains ablaze,
15 so pursue them with your tempest
and terrify them with your hurricane.
16 Fill their faces with shame,
so that they may seek your name, O LORD.
17 Let them be put to shame and dismayed forever;
let them perish in disgrace.
18 Let them know that you alone,
whose name is the LORD,
are the Most High over all the earth.

83.14 Isa 9.18
83.15 Ps 58.9
83.16 Ps 109.29
83.18 Isa 45.21

Theme: God's living presence is our greatest joy. His radiant presence helps us grow in strength, grace, and glory.
Author: The sons of Korah

PSALM 84

To the leader: according to The Gittith. Of the Korahites. A Psalm.

1 How lovely is your dwelling place,
O LORD of hosts!
2 My soul longs, indeed it faints
for the courts of the LORD;
my heart and my flesh sing for joy
to the living God.

3 Even the sparrow finds a home,
and the swallow a nest for herself,
where she may lay her young,
at your altars, O LORD of hosts,
my King and my God.
4 Happy are those who live in your house,
ever singing your praise. *Selah*

5 Happy are those whose strength is in you,
in whose heart are the highways to Zion.[r]
6 As they go through the valley of Baca
they make it a place of springs;
the early rain also covers it with pools.
7 They go from strength to strength;
the God of gods will be seen in Zion.

8 O LORD God of hosts, hear my prayer;
give ear, O God of Jacob! *Selah*
9 Behold our shield, O God;
look on the face of your anointed.

84.1 Ps 27.5
84.2 Ps 42.1,2; 63.1
84.3 Ps 43.4
84.4 Ps 65.4
84.6 Ps 107.35
84.7 Deut 16.16
2 Chron 3.18
Isa 40.31
84.8 Ps 59.5; 81.1
84.9 Gen 15.1
2 Sam 19.21
Ps 115.9-11

[q] Or *a tumbleweed* [r] Heb lacks *to Zion*

84.1, 4 The writer longed to get away from the bustling world and meet God inside his holy temple. We can meet God anywhere at any time, but we know that going into a church building helps us step aside from the busy mainstream of life into a place where we can quietly meditate and pray. We find joy, not only in the beautiful building, but in the praying, singing, teaching, preaching, and fellowship that take place there.

84.5–7 The pilgrimage to the temple passed through the barren valley of Baca. No specific valley has been identified, and it may have been symbolic of the times of struggles and tears through which people must pass on their way to meet God. Growing strong in God's presence is often preceded by our pilgrimage through barren places in our lives. The person who loves to spend time in God's presence will view adversity as an opportunity to re-experience God's faithfulness. If you are walking through your own valley of Baca today, be sure your pilgrimage leads toward God, not away from him.

84.10
1 Chron 23.5
Ps 27.4

10 For a day in your courts is better
than a thousand elsewhere.
I would rather be a doorkeeper in the house of my God
than live in the tents of wickedness.

84.11
Ps 34.10
Isa 60.19,20

11 For the LORD God is a sun and shield;
he bestows favor and honor.
No good thing does the LORD withhold
from those who walk uprightly.
12 O LORD of hosts,
happy is everyone who trusts in you.

Theme: From reverence to restoration. Reverence leads to forgiveness, restoring our love and joy for God.
Author: The sons of Korah

PSALM 85

To the leader. Of the Korahites. A Psalm.

85.1
Jer 30.18
Ezek 39.25
Joel 3.1

1 LORD, you were favorable to your land;
you restored the fortunes of Jacob.
2 You forgave the iniquity of your people;
you pardoned all their sin. *Selah*

85.2
Num 14.19
Jer 31.34
Ps 32.1

3 You withdrew all your wrath;
you turned from your hot anger.

85.3
Ex 32.12
Ps 78.38

4 Restore us again, O God of our salvation,
and put away your indignation toward us.
5 Will you be angry with us forever?
Will you prolong your anger to all generations?
6 Will you not revive us again,
so that your people may rejoice in you?
7 Show us your steadfast love, O LORD,
and grant us your salvation.

85.8
Ps 29.11; 78.57

8 Let me hear what God the LORD will speak,
for he will speak peace to his people,
to his faithful, to those who turn to him in their hearts.[s]

85.9
Ps 34.18; 84.11

9 Surely his salvation is at hand for those who fear him,
that his glory may dwell in our land.

85.10
Ps 89.4

10 Steadfast love and faithfulness will meet;
righteousness and peace will kiss each other.

85.11
Isa 45.8

11 Faithfulness will spring up from the ground,
and righteousness will look down from the sky.
12 The LORD will give what is good,
and our land will yield its increase.
13 Righteousness will go before him,
and will make a path for his steps.

[s] Gk: Heb *but let them not turn back to folly*

84.11 God does not promise to give us everything *we* think is good, but he will not withhold what is permanently good. He will give us the means to walk along his paths, but we must do the walking. When we obey him, he will not hold anything back that will help us to serve him.

85.6, 7 The psalmist was asking God to revive his people. God is capable of reviving both churches and individuals. He can pour out his love on us, bringing us back to loving him. If you need renewal in your church, family, or personal spiritual life, ask God to give you a fresh touch of his love.

85.8–13 What should we do after we pray? This psalm shows us that we should make an effort both to listen and to take action. We learn how to listen by turning to God in our heart (85.8). We learn what to do by following the way of righteousness (85.13). We show that we fear God when we listen and act accordingly after we pray.

Theme: Devoted trust in times of deep trouble
Author: David

PSALM 86

A Prayer of David.

1 Incline your ear, O LORD, and answer me,
for I am poor and needy.
2 Preserve my life, for I am devoted to you;
save your servant who trusts in you. **86.2** Ps 4.3; 25.20
You are my God; 3 be gracious to me, O Lord,
for to you do I cry all day long.
4 Gladden the soul of your servant,
for to you, O Lord, I lift up my soul. **86.4** Ps 25.1
5 For you, O Lord, are good and forgiving,
abounding in steadfast love to all who call on you. **86.5** Ps 103.8; 130.4
6 Give ear, O LORD, to my prayer;
listen to my cry of supplication.
7 In the day of my trouble I call on you,
for you will answer me. **86.7** Ps 50.14,15

8 There is none like you among the gods, O Lord,
nor are there any works like yours. **86.8** Ex 15.11
9 All the nations you have made shall come
and bow down before you, O Lord, **86.9** Isa 66.23
and shall glorify your name.
10 For you are great and do wondrous things;
you alone are God. **86.10** Deut 32.39 Isa 44.6,8 Mk 12.29 1 Cor 8.4
11 Teach me your way, O LORD,
that I may walk in your truth;
give me an undivided heart to revere your name. **86.11** Ps 25.5 Jer 32.39
12 I give thanks to you, O Lord my God, with my whole heart,
and I will glorify your name forever. **86.12** Ps 111.1
13 For great is your steadfast love toward me;
you have delivered my soul from the depths of Sheol.

14 O God, the insolent rise up against me;
a band of ruffians seeks my life, **86.14** Ps 54.3
and they do not set you before them.
15 But you, O Lord, are a God merciful and gracious,
slow to anger and abounding in steadfast love and faithfulness.
16 Turn to me and be gracious to me;
give your strength to your servant;
save the child of your serving girl. **86.17** Ps 112.10 118.13; 119.122
17 Show me a sign of your favor,

86.7 Sometimes our trouble or pain is so great that all we can do is cry out to God, "Preserve my life" (86.2). We feel so poor and needy. Many times when there is no relief in sight, all we can do is acknowledge the greatness of God and wait for better days ahead. The conviction that God answers prayer will sustain us in such difficult times.

86.8–10 The God of the Bible is unique! He is alive and able to work mighty miracles for those who love him. All man-created deities are powerless before him because they are merely inventions of the mind, not living beings. The Lord alone is "worthy . . . to receive glory and honor and power" (Revelation 4.11). Although people believe in many deities, you need never fear that God is only one among many or that you may be worshiping the wrong God. The Lord alone is God.

86.11, 12 To "revere your name" means to give reverence to God, and wholehearted reverence means appreciating God and honoring him in all areas of life. We need to show our loyalty to him in every part of our lives, not just in going to church. If we revere God with our whole heart, then our work, relationships, use of money, and desires will be in keeping with his will.

86.13 *Sheol* is the word used in the Old Testament for the realm of the dead. It is used to mean the grave, underworld, or death.

86.17 It is right to pray for a sign of God's goodness. As David found, it may be just what we need. Let us not overlook the signs he has already given: the support of family and friends, the fellowship of other Christians, the light of each new day. But most of all, God gives us the confidence that he knows our situation no matter how desperate it becomes, and he cares.

so that those who hate me may see it and be put to shame,
because you, LORD, have helped me and comforted me.

Theme: Jerusalem, where all believers will one day gather
Author: The sons of Korah (temple assistants)

PSALM 87

Of the Korahites. A Psalm. A Song.

87.1 Ps 78.68,69 Isa 28.16

1 On the holy mount stands the city he founded;
2 the LORD loves the gates of Zion
more than all the dwellings of Jacob.

87.3 Ps 46.4; 48.8

3 Glorious things are spoken of you,
O city of God. *Selah*

87.4 Ps 45.12; 68.31 Isa 19.23-25

4 Among those who know me I mention Rahab and Babylon;
Philistia too, and Tyre, with Ethiopia[t]—
"This one was born there," they say.

5 And of Zion it shall be said,
"This one and that one were born in it";
for the Most High himself will establish it.

87.6 Isa 4.2-4

6 The LORD records, as he registers the peoples,
"This one was born there." *Selah*

87.7 Ps 30.11; 36.9

7 Singers and dancers alike say,
"All my springs are in you."

Theme: When there is no relief in sight. God understands even our deepest misery.
Author: Heman, one of the sons of Korah (possibly the same man mentioned in 1 Chronicles 15.19; 16.41; 25.4, 5 as the king's prophet)

PSALM 88

A Song. A Psalm of the Korahites. To the leader: according to Mahalath Leannoth. A Maskil of Heman the Ezrahite.

88.1 Ps 22.2; 24.5 Lk 18.7

1 O LORD, God of my salvation,
when, at night, I cry out in your presence,
2 let my prayer come before you;
incline your ear to my cry.

88.3 Ps 107.18 116.3

3 For my soul is full of troubles,
and my life draws near to Sheol.
4 I am counted among those who go down to the Pit;
I am like those who have no help,

88.5 Ps 31.12 Isa 53.8

5 like those forsaken among the dead,
like the slain that lie in the grave,
like those whom you remember no more,
for they are cut off from your hand.

88.6 Ps 32.4; 42.7 69.15; 143.3 Lam 3.55

6 You have put me in the depths of the Pit,
in the regions dark and deep.

[t] Or *Nubia*; Heb *Cush*

87.1ff Jerusalem and its temple here represented the future community of all believers. This psalm looks ahead to the holy city of God described in Revelation 21.10–27. The honor of living there will be granted to all whose names are recorded in the Lamb's book of life (Revelation 21.27). It is God's grace that forms and sustains this wonderful community. How could anyone refuse God's offer to be part of this celebration?

87.4 Rahab is a name for a monster, here used to represent Egypt.

88.1ff Have you ever felt as if you have hit bottom? The psalmist is so low he even despairs of life itself. Although everything is bad and getting worse, he is able to tell it all to God. This is one of the few psalms that gives no answer or hope. Don't think that you must always be cheerful and positive. Grief and depression take time to heal. No matter how low we feel, we can always take our problems to God and express our anguish to him.

88.3 *Sheol* is the word used in the Old Testament for the realm of the dead. It is used to mean the grave, underworld, or death.

7 Your wrath lies heavy upon me,
and you overwhelm me with all your waves. *Selah*

8 You have caused my companions to shun me;
you have made me a thing of horror to them.
I am shut in so that I cannot escape;
9 my eye grows dim through sorrow.
Every day I call on you, O LORD;
I spread out my hands to you.
10 Do you work wonders for the dead?
Do the shades rise up to praise you? *Selah*
11 Is your steadfast love declared in the grave,
or your faithfulness in Abaddon?
12 Are your wonders known in the darkness,
or your saving help in the land of forgetfulness?

13 But I, O LORD, cry out to you;
in the morning my prayer comes before you.
14 O LORD, why do you cast me off?
Why do you hide your face from me?
15 Wretched and close to death from my youth up,
I suffer your terrors; I am desperate.[u]
16 Your wrath has swept over me;
your dread assaults destroy me.
17 They surround me like a flood all day long;
from all sides they close in on me.
18 You have caused friend and neighbor to shun me;
my companions are in darkness.

88.8 Job 19.19; 30.10 Ps 31.11
88.9 Job 11.13 Ps 6.7; 22.2
88.10 Ps 6.5
88.13 Ps 5.3; 119.147
88.14 Ps 13.1
88.17 Ps 22.12,16

Theme: God's promise to preserve David's descendants. God's promise is fulfilled in Jesus Christ, who will reign for eternity. The love and kindness promised to David is ours in Christ.
Author: Ethan (a Levite leader and possibly one of the head musicians in the temple, 1 Chronicles 15.17, 19), or one of his descendants

PSALM 89

A Maskil of Ethan the Ezrahite.

1 I will sing of your steadfast love, O LORD,[v] forever;
with my mouth I will proclaim your faithfulness to all generations.
2 I declare that your steadfast love is established forever;
your faithfulness is as firm as the heavens.

3 You said, "I have made a covenant with my chosen one,
I have sworn to my servant David:
4 'I will establish your descendants forever,
and build your throne for all generations.' " *Selah*

5 Let the heavens praise your wonders, O LORD,

89.1 Ps 40.10; 59.16
89.2 Ps 36.5
89.3 2 Sam 7.16 Ps 132.11 Isa 9.7 Lk 1.31-33

[u] Meaning of Heb uncertain [v] Gk: Heb *the steadfast love of the LORD*

88.13, 14 The psalmist is close to death, debilitated by disease, and forsaken by friends. But he can still pray. Perhaps you are not so afflicted, but you know someone who is. Consider being a prayer companion for that person. This psalm can be a prayer you can lift to God on his or her behalf.

89.1ff This psalm was written to describe the glorious reign of David. God had promised to make David the mightiest king on earth and to keep his descendants on the throne forever (2 Samuel 7.8–16). Because Jerusalem was destroyed and kings no longer reign there, these verses can only look forward prophetically to the future reign of Jesus Christ, David's descendant. Verse 27 is a prophecy concerning David's never-ending dynasty, which will be consummated by Christ's future reign over the world (see Revelation 22.5).

89.5 The assembly of the holy ones generally refers to angels. In the courts of heaven, a myriad of angels praise the Lord. This scene is one of majesty and grandeur to show that God is beyond compare. His power and purity place him high above nature and angels. See Deuteronomy 33.2, Luke 2.13, and Hebrews 12.22 for more about angels.

your faithfulness in the assembly of the holy ones.
89.6 Ps 29.1; 96.4 6 For who in the skies can be compared to the LORD?
Who among the heavenly beings is like the LORD,
89.7 Ps 47.2; 96.4 7 a God feared in the council of the holy ones,
great and awesome[w] above all that are around him?
89.8 Ps 35.10 8 O LORD God of hosts,
who is as mighty as you, O LORD?
Your faithfulness surrounds you.
89.9 Ps 65.7; 107.29 9 You rule the raging of the sea;
when its waves rise, you still them.
89.10 Ps 18.14 10 You crushed Rahab like a carcass;
you scattered your enemies with your mighty arm.
89.11 Gen 1.1 Ps 24.1 11 The heavens are yours, the earth also is yours;
the world and all that is in it—you have founded them.
12 The north and the south[x]—you created them;
Tabor and Hermon joyously praise your name.
13 You have a mighty arm;
strong is your hand, high your right hand.
89.14 Ps 97.2; 98.6 14 Righteousness and justice are the foundation of your throne;
steadfast love and faithfulness go before you.
15 Happy are the people who know the festal shout,
who walk, O LORD, in the light of your countenance;
16 they exult in your name all day long,
and extol[y] your righteousness.
89.17 Ps 44.3; 75.10 148.14 17 For you are the glory of their strength;
by your favor our horn is exalted.
18 For our shield belongs to the LORD,
our king to the Holy One of Israel.

89.19 2 Sam 17.10 1 Kgs 11.34 19 Then you spoke in a vision to your faithful one, and said:
"I have set the crown[z] on one who is mighty,
I have exalted one chosen from the people.
89.20 1 Sam 16.13 Acts 13.22 20 I have found my servant David;
with my holy oil I have anointed him;
21 my hand shall always remain with him;
my arm also shall strengthen him.
89.22 2 Sam 7.10,11 22 The enemy shall not outwit him,
the wicked shall not humble him.
89.23 2 Sam 7.9 23 I will crush his foes before him
and strike down those who hate him.
24 My faithfulness and steadfast love shall be with him;
and in my name his horn shall be exalted.
25 I will set his hand on the sea
and his right hand on the rivers.
89.26 2 Sam 7.14 1 Chron 22.10 26 He shall cry to me, 'You are my Father,
my God, and the Rock of my salvation!'

[w] Gk Syr: Heb *greatly awesome* [x] Or *Zaphon and Yamin* [y] Cn: Heb *are exalted in* [z] Cn: Heb *help*

89.12 This refers to Mount Tabor and Mount Hermon. Mount Tabor, though low in elevation, (1,900 feet) was the scene of Deborah's victory in Judges 4. Mount Hermon (9,000 feet) was tall and majestic. God's power is both strong and majestic. You can depend on him.

89.14, 15 Righteousness and justice, steadfast love and faithfulness surround God on his throne; they are fundamental aspects of the way God rules. As God's ambassadors, we should deal with people similarly. Make sure your actions flow out of righteousness, justice, love, and faithfulness because any unfair, unloving, or dishonest action cannot come from God.

89.17 "By your favor our horn is exalted" means that when we are full of sin we are weak and powerless, inadequate for even the simplest spiritual tasks. But when we are filled with God's Spirit, his power flows through us and our accomplishments will exceed our expectations.

89.19 The faithful one mentioned here may be Samuel, who anointed David as king of Israel (1 Samuel 16.1–13), or Nathan, who was a prophet to Israel when David became king (2 Samuel 7.4–17).

27 I will make him the firstborn,
the highest of the kings of the earth.
28 Forever I will keep my steadfast love for him,
and my covenant with him will stand firm.
29 I will establish his line forever,
and his throne as long as the heavens endure.
30 If his children forsake my law
and do not walk according to my ordinances,
31 if they violate my statutes
and do not keep my commandments,
32 then I will punish their transgression with the rod
and their iniquity with scourges;
33 but I will not remove from him my steadfast love,
or be false to my faithfulness.
34 I will not violate my covenant,
or alter the word that went forth from my lips.
35 Once and for all I have sworn by my holiness;
I will not lie to David.
36 His line shall continue forever,
and his throne endure before me like the sun.
37 It shall be established forever like the moon,
an enduring witness in the skies." *Selah*

38 But now you have spurned and rejected him;
you are full of wrath against your anointed.
39 You have renounced the covenant with your servant;
you have defiled his crown in the dust.
40 You have broken through all his walls;
you have laid his strongholds in ruins.
41 All who pass by plunder him;
he has become the scorn of his neighbors.
42 You have exalted the right hand of his foes;
you have made all his enemies rejoice.
43 Moreover, you have turned back the edge of his sword,
and you have not supported him in battle.
44 You have removed the scepter from his hand,[a]
and hurled his throne to the ground.
45 You have cut short the days of his youth;
you have covered him with shame. *Selah*

46 How long, O LORD? Will you hide yourself forever?
How long will your wrath burn like fire?
47 Remember how short my time is —[b]
for what vanity you have created all mortals!
48 Who can live and never see death?
Who can escape the power of Sheol? *Selah*

49 Lord, where is your steadfast love of old,
which by your faithfulness you swore to David?

89.27 Ps 2.7; 72.11 Rev 19.1,5,16
89.29 1 Kgs 2.4 Isa 9.7 Jer 33.17
89.30 2 Sam 7.14
89.33 2 Sam 7.15
89.34 Num 23.19 Jer 33.20,21
89.38 1 Chron 28.9
89.39 Ps 78.59 Lam 2.7; 5.16
89.40 Ps 80.12 Lam 2.2,5
89.42 Ps 13.2; 80.6
89.43 Ps 44.10
89.44 Ezek 28.7
89.45 Ps 44.15,16
89.46 Ps 13.1; 79.5
89.47 Job 7.7; 14.1 Ps 39.5,6 Eccles 1.2; 2.11
89.48 Ps 22.29 Heb 11.5

[a] Cn: Heb *removed his cleanness* [b] Meaning of Heb uncertain

89.34–37 In light of Israel's continual disobedience throughout history, this is an amazing promise. God promised that David's descendants would always sit on the throne (89.29), but that if the people disobeyed, they would be punished (89.30–32). And yet, even through their disobedience and punishment, God would never break faith with them (89.33). Israel *did* disobey, evil ran rampant, the nation was divided, exile came – but through it all, a remnant of God's people remained faithful. Centuries later, the Messiah arrived, the eternal King from David's line, just as God had promised. All that God promises, he fulfills. He will not take back even one word of what he says. God can also be trusted to save us as he promised he would (Hebrews 6.13–18). God is completely reliable.

50 Remember, O Lord, how your servant is taunted;
how I bear in my bosom the insults of the peoples,[c]
51 with which your enemies taunt, O LORD,
with which they taunted the footsteps of your anointed.

52 Blessed be the LORD forever.
Amen and Amen.

BOOK IV
Psalms 90.1 – 106.48

These psalms include a prayer of Moses, a psalm about oppressors, and a psalm praising God as our King. These psalms remind us that we should remember our place and be submissive before the almighty God.

Theme: God's eternal nature is contrasted with man's frailty. Our time on earth is limited and we are to use it wisely, not living for the moment, but with our eternal home in mind. This psalm is often used in funerals.
Author: Moses, making this the oldest of the psalms. (For more information on Moses, see his Profile in Exodus 16.)

PSALM 90

A Prayer of Moses, the man of God.

90.1 Deut 33.27 Ezek 11.16
1 Lord, you have been our dwelling place[d]
in all generations.
90.2 Gen 1.1 Ps 102.24, 25,27
2 Before the mountains were brought forth,
or ever you had formed the earth and the world,
from everlasting to everlasting you are God.

3 You turn us[e] back to dust,
and say, "Turn back, you mortals."
90.4 Ps 39.5 2 Pet 3.8
4 For a thousand years in your sight
are like yesterday when it is past,
or like a watch in the night.

90.5 Job 14.2; 20.8 Mt 6.30
5 You sweep them away; they are like a dream,
like grass that is renewed in the morning;
6 in the morning it flourishes and is renewed;
in the evening it fades and withers.

7 For we are consumed by your anger;
by your wrath we are overwhelmed.
8 You have set our iniquities before you,
our secret sins in the light of your countenance.

90.9 Ps 78.33
9 For all our days pass away under your wrath;
our years come to an end[f] like a sigh.
90.10 Ps 78.39 Eccles 12.2-7
10 The days of our life are seventy years,
or perhaps eighty, if we are strong;
even then their span[g] is only toil and trouble;
they are soon gone, and we fly away.

90.11 Ps 76.7
11 Who considers the power of your anger?

[c] Cn: Heb *bosom all of many peoples* [d] Another reading is *our refuge* [e] Heb *humankind* [f] Syr: Heb *we bring our years to an end* [g] Cn Compare Gk Syr Jerome Tg: Heb *pride*

90.4 Moses reminds us that a thousand years are like a day to the Lord. God is not limited by time. It's easy to get discouraged when years pass and the world doesn't get better. We sometimes wonder if God is able to see the future. But don't assume that God has our limitations. God is completely unrestricted by time. Because he is eternal, we can depend on him.

90.8 God knows all our sins as if they were spread out before him, even the secret ones. We don't need to cover up our sins before him, because we can talk openly and honestly with him. But while he knows all that terrible information about us, God still loves us and wants to forgive us. This should encourage us to come to him rather than frighten us into covering up our sin.

Your wrath is as great as the fear that is due you.
12 So teach us to count our days
that we may gain a wise heart. 90.12 Ps 39.4

13 Turn, O LORD! How long?
Have compassion on your servants! 90.13 Deut 32.36
14 Satisfy us in the morning with your steadfast love,
so that we may rejoice and be glad all our days. 90.14 Ps 36.8; 103.5 Jer 31.14
15 Make us glad as many days as you have afflicted us,
and as many years as we have seen evil. 90.15 Ps 31.10; 86.4
16 Let your work be manifest to your servants,
and your glorious power to their children. 90.16 Ps 44.1
17 Let the favor of the Lord our God be upon us,
and prosper for us the work of our hands—
O prosper the work of our hands!

Theme: God's protection in the midst of danger. God doesn't promise a world free from danger, but he does promise his help whenever we face danger.
Author: Anonymous

PSALM 91

1 You who live in the shelter of the Most High,
who abide in the shadow of the Almighty,[h] 91.1 Isa 25.4; 32.2
2 will say to the LORD, "My refuge and my fortress;
my God, in whom I trust." 91.2 Ps 18.2; 142.5 Jer 16.19
3 For he will deliver you from the snare of the fowler
and from the deadly pestilence; 91.3 2 Chron 20.9 Ps 124.7
4 he will cover you with his pinions,
and under his wings you will find refuge;
his faithfulness is a shield and buckler. 91.4 Ps 35.2; 57.1 63.7 Isa 51.1-6
5 You will not fear the terror of the night,
or the arrow that flies by day, 91.5 Job 5.19-23 Ps 23.4
6 or the pestilence that stalks in darkness,
or the destruction that wastes at noonday.

7 A thousand may fall at your side,
ten thousand at your right hand,
but it will not come near you.
8 You will only look with your eyes
and see the punishment of the wicked.

9 Because you have made the LORD your refuge,[i]
the Most High your dwelling place,
10 no evil shall befall you,
no scourge come near your tent.

11 For he will command his angels concerning you 91.11 Ps 34.7 Mt 4.6 Lk 4.9-11

[h] Traditional rendering of Heb *Shaddai* [i] Cn: Heb *Because you, LORD, are my refuge; you have made*

90.12 Realizing that life is short helps us use the little time we have more wisely, and for eternal good. Take time to count your days by asking, "What do I want to see happen in my life before I die? What small step could I take toward that purpose today?"

90.15–17 Because God has given us the desire for eternal life (see the note on Ecclesiastes 3.11), we are not satisfied with merely living 70 years (see 90.10). We desire to see God's eternal plan revealed now and for our work to reflect his permanence. If you feel dissatisfied with this life and all its imperfections, remember the desire to see your work established is placed there by God. But it can only be realized in eternity. Until then we must apply ourselves to loving and serving God.

91.5, 6 God is a refuge, a shelter when we are afraid. The writer's faith in God as Protector would carry him through all the dangers and fears of life. This should be a picture of our trust—trading all our fears for faith in him, no matter how intense our fears. To do this we must "live" or "abide" with him (91.1). By consigning ourselves to his protection and pledging our daily devotion to him, we will be kept safely.

91.11 One of the functions of angels is to watch over believers

to guard you in all your ways.
12 On their hands they will bear you up,
so that you will not dash your foot against a stone.
91.13 Judg 14.6 Lk 10.19
13 You will tread on the lion and the adder,
the young lion and the serpent you will trample under foot.

14 Those who love me, I will deliver;
I will protect those who know my name.
91.15 1 Sam 2.30
15 When they call to me, I will answer them;
I will be with them in trouble,
I will rescue them and honor them.
16 With long life I will satisfy them,
and show them my salvation.

Theme: Be thankful and faithful every day.
This psalm was used in temple services on the sabbath.
Author: Anonymous

PSALM 92

A Psalm. A Song for the Sabbath Day.

1 It is good to give thanks to the LORD,
to sing praises to your name, O Most High;
2 to declare your steadfast love in the morning,
and your faithfulness by night,
92.3 1 Sam 10.5 1 Chron 13.8 Neh 12.27
3 to the music of the lute and the harp,
to the melody of the lyre.
4 For you, O LORD, have made me glad by your work;
at the works of your hands I sing for joy.

92.5 Ps 36.6; 40.5 139.17 Rom 11.33
5 How great are your works, O LORD!
Your thoughts are very deep!
6 The dullard cannot know,
the stupid cannot understand this:
92.7 Ps 37.38
7 though the wicked sprout like grass
and all evildoers flourish,
they are doomed to destruction forever,
8 but you, O LORD, are on high forever.
92.9 Ps 37.20; 68.1
9 For your enemies, O LORD,
for your enemies shall perish;
all evildoers shall be scattered.

92.10 Ps 23.5; 45.7 75.10
10 But you have exalted my horn like that of the wild ox;
you have poured over me[j] fresh oil.
11 My eyes have seen the downfall of my enemies;
my ears have heard the doom of my evil assailants.

12 The righteous flourish like the palm tree,

[j] Syr: Meaning of Heb uncertain

(Hebrews 1.14). There are examples of guardian angels in Scripture (1 Kings 19.5; Daniel 6.22; Matthew 18.10; Luke 16.22; Acts 12.7), although there is no indication that one angel is assigned to each believer. Angels can also be God's messengers (Matthew 2.13; Acts 27.23, 24). Verses 11 and 12 were quoted by Satan when he tempted Jesus (Matthew 4.6; Luke 4.10, 11). It is comforting to know that God watches over us even in times of great stress and fear.

92.1, 2 During the Thanksgiving holiday, we focus on our blessings and express our gratitude to God for them. But thanks should be on our lips every day. When thanksgiving becomes an integral part of your life, you will find that your attitude toward life will change. You will become more positive, gracious, loving, and humble.

92.12, 13 Palm trees are known for their long life. The cedars of Lebanon grew to 120 feet in height and up to 30 feet in circumference; thus, they were solid, strong, and immovable. The psalmist saw believers as upright, strong, and unmoved by the winds of circumstance. Those who place their faith firmly in God can have this strength and vitality.

and grow like a cedar in Lebanon.
13 They are planted in the house of the LORD;
they flourish in the courts of our God.
14 In old age they still produce fruit;
they are always green and full of sap,
15 showing that the LORD is upright;
he is my rock, and there is no unrighteousness in him.

92.14
Jn 15.2

92.15
Rom 9.14

Theme: God's unchanging and almighty nature. His creation reminds us of his great power.
Author: Anonymous

PSALM 93

1 The LORD is king, he is robed in majesty;
the LORD is robed, he is girded with strength.
He has established the world; it shall never be moved;
2 your throne is established from of old;
you are from everlasting.

3 The floods have lifted up, O LORD,
the floods have lifted up their voice;
the floods lift up their roaring.
4 More majestic than the thunders of mighty waters,
more majestic than the waves[k] of the sea,
majestic on high is the LORD!

5 Your decrees are very sure;
holiness befits your house,
O LORD, forevermore.

93.1
Isa 51.9

93.3
Ps 98.7,8

93.4
Ps 65.7

Theme: God will keep his people from the severe punishment awaiting the wicked. Since God is holy and just, we can be certain that the wicked will not prevail.
Author: Anonymous

PSALM 94

1 O LORD, you God of vengeance,
you God of vengeance, shine forth!
2 Rise up, O judge of the earth;
give to the proud what they deserve!
3 O LORD, how long shall the wicked,
how long shall the wicked exult?

4 They pour out their arrogant words;
all the evildoers boast.
5 They crush your people, O LORD,
and afflict your heritage.

94.1
Deut 32.35
Isa 35.4
Rom 12.19

[k] Cn: Heb *majestic are the waves*

92.14 Honoring God is not limited to young people who seem to have unlimited strength and energy. Even in old age, devoted believers can produce spiritual fruit. There are many faithful older people who still have a fresh outlook and can teach us from a lifetime experience of serving God. Seek out an elderly friend or relative to tell you about their experiences with the Lord and challenge you to new heights of spiritual growth.

93.1ff Jewish tradition claims that the next seven psalms (93–99) anticipate some of the works of the Messiah. Psalm 93 is said to have been used in post-captivity temple services and may have been written during Sennacherib's invasion (2 Kings 18.13–19.37).

93.5 The key to God's eternal reign is his holiness. God's glory is not mere strength, but his perfect moral character. God will never do anything that is not morally perfect. This reassures us that we can trust him, yet it places a demand on us. Our desire to live holy lives (dedicated to God and morally clean) is our only suitable response. We must never use unholy means to reach a holy goal, for God says, "You shall be holy, for I the Lord your God am holy" (Leviticus 19.1, 2).

94.3–11 For a while the proud and the wicked do seem to get ahead. Both oppressors who command armies and those who abuse their power on the job, at school, or in our neighborhood gain a temporary advantage. We are tempted to conclude that God doesn't hear or care about us. But he does and he will reward and punish in perfect justice. Don't despair. He knows everyone's thoughts and no one can get away with sin.

94.6 Job 22.13 Isa 10.2

6 They kill the widow and the stranger,
they murder the orphan,
7 and they say, "The LORD does not see;
the God of Jacob does not perceive."

8 Understand, O dullest of the people;
fools, when will you be wise?

94.9 Ex 4.11 Prov 20.12

9 He who planted the ear, does he not hear?
He who formed the eye, does he not see?
10 He who disciplines the nations,
he who teaches knowledge to humankind,
does he not chastise?

94.11 1 Cor 3.20

11 The LORD knows our thoughts,[l]
that they are but an empty breath.

94.12 Deut 8.5 Ps 9.15 Heb 12.5,6

12 Happy are those whom you discipline, O LORD,
and whom you teach out of your law,
13 giving them respite from days of trouble,
until a pit is dug for the wicked.

94.14 Rom 11.2

14 For the LORD will not forsake his people;
he will not abandon his heritage;

94.15 Isa 42.3 Mic 7.9

15 for justice will return to the righteous,
and all the upright in heart will follow it.

94.16 Num 10.35

16 Who rises up for me against the wicked?
Who stands up for me against evildoers?
17 If the LORD had not been my help,
my soul would soon have lived in the land of silence.
18 When I thought, "My foot is slipping,"
your steadfast love, O LORD, held me up.

94.19 Isa 57.18; 66.13

19 When the cares of my heart are many,
your consolations cheer my soul.

94.20 Ps 58.2

20 Can wicked rulers be allied with you,
those who contrive mischief by statute?

94.21 Ex 23.7 Mt 27.4

21 They band together against the life of the righteous,
and condemn the innocent to death.

[l] Heb *the thoughts of humankind*

JUSTICE IN THE BOOK OF PSALMS

Justice is a major theme in Psalms. The psalmists praise God because he is just; they plead for him to intervene and bring justice where there is oppression and wickedness; they condemn the wicked who trust in their wealth; they extol the righteous who are just toward their neighbors.

Justice in Psalms is more than honesty. It is active intervention on behalf of the helpless, especially the poor. The psalmists do not merely wish the poor could be given what they need, but they plead with God to destroy those nations that are subverting justice and oppressing God's people.

Here are some examples of psalms that speak about justice. As you read them, ask yourself, "Who is my neighbor? Does my life-style—my work, my play, my buying habits, my giving—help or hurt people who have less than I do? What one thing could I do this week to help a helpless person?"

Selected psalms that emphasize this theme are 7; 9; 15; 37; 50; 72; 75; 82; 94; 145.

94.12, 13 At times, God must punish us to help us. This is similar to a loving parent's disciplining his child. The punishment is not very enjoyable to the child, but is essential to teach him right from wrong. The Bible says that "Discipline always seems painful rather than pleasant at the time, but later it yields the peaceful fruit of righteousness" (Hebrews 12.11). When you feel God's hand of correction, accept it as proof of his love. Realize that he is urging you to follow his paths instead of stubbornly going your own way.

94.19 The psalmist's multitude of thoughts were mostly questions and doubts about God's justice. We have all experienced times when doubts fill our minds. The psalmist saw evil people prospering and oppressing others (94.3–7), corrupt governments (94.20), condemnation of the innocent (94.21) – much as we see in our world today. Because we know that God will not allow evil to continue forever, we must trust his timing and continue to obey him.

22 But the LORD has become my stronghold,
and my God the rock of my refuge.
23 He will repay them for their iniquity
and wipe them out for their wickedness;
the LORD our God will wipe them out.

94.23 Ps 140.9,11

Theme: An invitation to worship God
Author: David

PSALM 95

1 O come, let us sing to the LORD;
let us make a joyful noise to the rock of our salvation!
2 Let us come into his presence with thanksgiving;
let us make a joyful noise to him with songs of praise!
3 For the LORD is a great God,
and a great King above all gods.
4 In his hand are the depths of the earth;
the heights of the mountains are his also.
5 The sea is his, for he made it,
and the dry land, which his hands have formed.

6 O come, let us worship and bow down,
let us kneel before the LORD, our Maker!
7 For he is our God,
and we are the people of his pasture,
and the sheep of his hand.

O that today you would listen to his voice!
8 Do not harden your hearts, as at Meribah,
as on the day at Massah in the wilderness,
9 when your ancestors tested me,
and put me to the proof, though they had seen my work.
10 For forty years I loathed that generation
and said, "They are a people whose hearts go astray,
and they do not regard my ways."
11 Therefore in my anger I swore,
"They shall not enter my rest."

95.4 Ps 135.5,6
95.5 Gen 1.9,10
95.7 Heb 3.7-11,15
95.8 Num 20.13
95.9 Num 14.22
95.10 Acts 7.36; 13.18 Heb 3.17
95.11 Heb 4.3,5

Theme: How to praise God. We can sing about him, tell others about him, worship him, give him glory, bring offerings to him, and live holy lives.
Author: Probably David because this psalm closely resembles David's hymn of praise in 1 Chronicles 16.23–36

PSALM 96

1 O sing to the LORD a new song;
sing to the LORD, all the earth.
2 Sing to the LORD, bless his name;

95.8 A hardened heart is as useless as a hardened lump of clay or a hardened loaf of bread. Nothing can restore it and make it useful. David warns against hardening our hearts as Israel did in the wilderness by continuing to resist God's will (Exodus 17.7). They were so convinced that God couldn't deliver them that they simply lost their faith in him. When someone's heart becomes hardened, that person is so stubbornly set in his ways that he cannot turn to God. This does not happen all at once; it is the result of a series of choices to disregard God's will. If you resist God long enough, he may cast you aside like hardened bread, useless and worthless.

95.8 *Meribah* means "quarrelling," and *Massah* means "testing." This refers to the incident at Rephidim (Exodus 17.1–7) when the Israelites complained to Moses because they had no water (see also Numbers 20.1–13).

95.11 What keeps us from God's ultimate blessings (entering his "rest")? Unthankful hearts (95.2), not listening (95.7), hardening our hearts (95.8), doubt (95.9). In Hebrews 4.5–11, we are encouraged not to harden our hearts, but to reject the glamour of sin and anything that would lead us away from God.

96.1–4 If we believe God is great, we cannot help telling others about him. The best witnessing happens when our hearts are full of appreciation for what he has done. God has chosen to use us to "declare . . . his marvelous works among all the peoples." Praise for our great God overflows from his creation and should overflow from our lips. How well are you doing at telling others about God's greatness?

tell of his salvation from day to day.

96.3 Ps 145.12
3 Declare his glory among the nations,
his marvelous works among all the peoples.
4 For great is the LORD, and greatly to be praised;
he is to be revered above all gods.

96.5 1 Chron 16.26 Isa 42.5
5 For all the gods of the peoples are idols,
but the LORD made the heavens.
6 Honor and majesty are before him;
strength and beauty are in his sanctuary.

7 Ascribe to the LORD, O families of the peoples,
ascribe to the LORD glory and strength.

96.8 Ps 115.1
8 Ascribe to the LORD the glory due his name;
bring an offering, and come into his courts.

96.9 1 Chron 16.29 2 Chron 20.21
9 Worship the LORD in holy splendor;
tremble before him, all the earth.

96.10 Ps 58.11; 67.4
10 Say among the nations, "The LORD is king!
The world is firmly established; it shall never be moved.
He will judge the peoples with equity."

96.11 Isa 49.13
11 Let the heavens be glad, and let the earth rejoice;
let the sea roar, and all that fills it;

96.12 Isa 35.1; 44.23 55.12,13
12 let the field exult, and everything in it.
Then shall all the trees of the forest sing for joy
13 before the LORD; for he is coming,
for he is coming to judge the earth.
He will judge the world with righteousness,
and the peoples with his truth.

Theme: God, our awesome Conqueror, is righteous and just.
Author: Anonymous

PSALM 97

1 The LORD is king! Let the earth rejoice;
let the many coastlands be glad!

97.2 Ex 19.9 Deut 4.11
2 Clouds and thick darkness are all around him;
righteousness and justice are the foundation of his throne.

97.3 Heb 12.29
3 Fire goes before him,
and consumes his adversaries on every side.
4 His lightnings light up the world;
the earth sees and trembles.

97.5 Josh 3.11 Amos 9.5
5 The mountains melt like wax before the LORD,
before the Lord of all the earth.

6 The heavens proclaim his righteousness;
and all the peoples behold his glory.

97.7 Jer 10.14 Heb 1.6
7 All worshipers of images are put to shame,
those who make their boast in worthless idols;

97.8 Ex 18.11 Zeph 3.14
all gods bow down before him.
8 Zion hears and is glad,

96.9 To "worship the Lord in holy splendor" refers to the ceremonial washing of the garments to prepare for worship (Exodus 28.2; Leviticus 11.24–28). While we do not have to wash our clothes in a special way to worship today, we still need to prepare our hearts and minds. Take time to clear away troubling thoughts and preoccupations to be ready to praise God.

97.2 The clouds and darkness that surround God symbolize his unapproachable holiness.

97.7 Although God reveals himself and his love through nature and the Bible, there are many who decide to ignore or reject him and pursue goals they believe are more important. The Bible makes it clear that these people are idol worshipers because they give their highest loyalty to something other than God. One day we will stand before God in all his glory and power. How foolish our earthly pursuits will be then!

and the towns[m] of Judah rejoice,
because of your judgments, O God.
9 For you, O LORD, are most high over all the earth;
you are exalted far above all gods.

10 The LORD loves those who hate[n] evil;
he guards the lives of his faithful;
he rescues them from the hand of the wicked.
11 Light dawns[o] for the righteous,
and joy for the upright in heart.
12 Rejoice in the LORD, O you righteous,
and give thanks to his holy name!

97.10 Dan 3.28 Rom 12.9

Theme: A song of joy and victory. Because God is victorious over evil, all those who follow him will be victorious with him when he judges the earth.
Author: Anonymous

PSALM 98

A Psalm.

1 O sing to the LORD a new song,
for he has done marvelous things.
His right hand and his holy arm
have gotten him victory.
2 The LORD has made known his victory;
he has revealed his vindication in the sight of the nations.
3 He has remembered his steadfast love and faithfulness
to the house of Israel.
All the ends of the earth have seen
the victory of our God.

98.1 Ex 15.6 Isa 52.10

98.2 Lk 1.54,72 Rom 3.25

4 Make a joyful noise to the LORD, all the earth;
break forth into joyous song and sing praises.
5 Sing praises to the LORD with the lyre,
with the lyre and the sound of melody.
6 With trumpets and the sound of the horn
make a joyful noise before the King, the LORD.

98.6 Num 10.10 2 Chron 15.14

7 Let the sea roar, and all that fills it;
the world and those who live in it.
8 Let the floods clap their hands;
let the hills sing together for joy
9 at the presence of the LORD, for he is coming
to judge the earth.
He will judge the world with righteousness,
and the peoples with equity.

98.7 Ps 24.1

98.9 Isa 55.12

[m] Heb *daughters* [n] Cn: Heb *You who love the LORD hate* [o] Gk Syr Jerome: Heb *is sown*

97.10 A sincere desire to please God will result in an alignment of your desires with God's desires. You will love what God loves and hate what God hates. If you love the Lord, you will hate evil. If you do not despise the actions of people who take advantage of others, if you admire people who only look out for themselves, or if you envy those who get ahead using any means to accomplish their ends, then your primary desire in life is not to please God. Learn to love God's ways and hate evil in every form—not only the obvious sins but also the socially acceptable ones.

98.1ff This is a psalm of praise anticipating the coming of God to rule his people. Jesus fulfilled this anticipation when he came to save all people from their sins (98.2, 3), and he will come again to judge the world (98.8, 9). God is both perfectly loving and perfectly just. He is merciful when he punishes, and he overlooks no sin when he loves. Praise him for his promise to save you and to return again.

99.1 Cherubim are mighty angels that comprise one of several ranks of angels. (For more on angels, see the note on 91.11.)

Theme: Praise for God's fairness and holiness. Because God is perfectly just and fair, we can trust him completely.
Author: Anonymous

PSALM 99

99.1 Ex 25.22 1 Sam 4.4
1 The LORD is king; let the peoples tremble!
He sits enthroned upon the cherubim; let the earth quake!
2 The LORD is great in Zion;
he is exalted over all the peoples.
99.3 Deut 28.58 Josh 24.19 1 Sam 2.2
3 Let them praise your great and awesome name.
Holy is he!
99.4 Ps 17.2
4 Mighty King,[p] lover of justice,
you have established equity;
you have executed justice
and righteousness in Jacob.
5 Extol the LORD our God;
worship at his footstool.
Holy is he!

99.6 Ex 15.25 1 Sam 7.9
6 Moses and Aaron were among his priests,
Samuel also was among those who called on his name.
They cried to the LORD, and he answered them.
99.7 Ex 33.9 Num 12.5
7 He spoke to them in the pillar of cloud;
they kept his decrees,
and the statutes that he gave them.

99.8 Num 14.20
8 O LORD our God, you answered them;
you were a forgiving God to them,
but an avenger of their wrongdoings.
9 Extol the LORD our God,
and worship at his holy mountain;
for the LORD our God is holy.

Theme: An invitation to enter joyfully into God's presence. His faithfulness extends to our generation and beyond.
Author: Anonymous

PSALM 100

A Psalm of thanksgiving.

100.2 Deut 12.11,12 28.47
1 Make a joyful noise to the LORD, all the earth.
2 Worship the LORD with gladness;
come into his presence with singing.
100.3 1 Kgs 18.39 Isa 40.11 Ezek 34.30,31 Mk 14.27 Jn 10.11

3 Know that the LORD is God.
It is he that made us, and we are his;[q]

[p] Cn: Heb *And a king's strength* [q] Another reading is *and not we ourselves*

99.3 Everyone should praise God's great and holy name because his name symbolizes his nature, his personage, and his reputation. How easy it is to treat God lightly in everyday life. If you claim him as your father, live worthy of the family name. Respect God's name and give him praise by both your *words* and your *life.*

99.5 God's holiness is terribly frightening for sinners, but a wonderful comfort for believers. God is morally perfect and is set apart from people and sin. He has no weaknesses or shortcomings. For sinners, this is frightening because all their inadequacies and evil are exposed by the light of his holiness. God cannot tolerate, ignore, or excuse sin. For believers, God's holiness gives comfort because, as we worship him, we are lifted from the mire of sin. As we believe in him, we are made holy.

99.6 The Bible records several instances where Moses, Aaron, and Samuel cried out to God for help (Exodus 15.25; 17.4; Numbers 11.11–15; 12.13; 14.13ff; 16.44–48; 1 Samuel 7.5, 9; 15.11).

100.2 Some employees work reluctantly, complaining as they go. Others cheerfully give their best all day long. We are to be faithful employees who serve with gladness. To brood and complain wastes energy. Are you glad to obey the Lord?

100.3 God is our Creator; we did not create ourselves. Many people live as though they are the creator and center of their own little world. This mind-set leads to a greedy possessiveness and, if everything should be taken away, a loss of hope itself. But when we realize that God created us and gives us all we have, we will want to give to others as God gave to us (2 Corinthians 9.8). Then, if all is lost, we still have God and all he gives us.

we are his people, and the sheep of his pasture.

4 Enter his gates with thanksgiving,
and his courts with praise.
Give thanks to him, bless his name.

5 For the LORD is good; 100.5 Ps 25.8
his steadfast love endures forever,
and his faithfulness to all generations.

Theme: A prayer for help to walk a blameless path. To live with integrity, both our efforts and God's help are necessary.
Author: David

PSALM 101

Of David. A Psalm.

1 I will sing of loyalty and of justice; 101.1 Ps 145.7
to you, O LORD, I will sing.
2 I will study the way that is blameless.
When shall I attain it?

I will walk with integrity of heart
within my house;
3 I will not set before my eyes 101.3 Deut 15.9
anything that is base.

I hate the work of those who fall away;
it shall not cling to me.
4 Perverseness of heart shall be far from me; 101.4 Prov 11.20
I will know nothing of evil.

5 One who secretly slanders a neighbor 101.5 Prov 6.16-19
I will destroy.
A haughty look and an arrogant heart
I will not tolerate.

6 I will look with favor on the faithful in the land,
so that they may live with me;
whoever walks in the way that is blameless
shall minister to me.

7 No one who practices deceit
shall remain in my house;
no one who utters lies
shall continue in my presence.

100.4 God is the Creator of all; thus he alone is worthy of being worshiped. What is your attitude toward worship? Do you willingly and joyfully come into God's presence, or are you just going through the motions, reluctantly going to church? This psalm tells us to remember God's goodness and dependability, and then to worship with thanksgiving and praise!

101.1ff David may have written this psalm early in his reign as he set down the standards he wanted to follow. He knew that if he was to walk a blameless path he would need God's help (101.2). We can walk this blameless path if we avoid (1) looking at wickedness ("anything that is base," 101.3), (2) evil associates ("those who fall away," 101.4), (3) slander (101.5), and (4) pride (101.5). While avoiding the wrongs listed above, we must also let God's Word show us the standards to live by.

101.2 Close relationships have great potential for conflict. Our homes can be difficult places to have integrity of heart. Our families usually see us at our worst because we relax and let down our mask of good behavior. Often we do not treat our family members with the same respect and kindness we show to friends and business associates. David must have understood this as he promised to walk within his house with integrity. Because we want to treat those who are closest to us well, let us follow God at home and live as Christian examples.

101.5–8 We can't compartmentalize our ethics. We are accountable to God both in our home life and also in our public responsibilities. We must not tolerate the slanderer, the proud, the deceitful, or the liar. Whenever we have the opportunity, we should encourage and assist the faithful to take public responsibilities.

101.8 Ps 46.4; 75.10

8 Morning by morning I will destroy
all the wicked in the land,
cutting off all evildoers
from the city of the LORD.

Theme: The cure for distress. Because God is living, eternal, and unchanging, we can trust him to help his people in this generation just as he helped his people in past generations.
Author: Anonymous

PSALM 102

A prayer of one afflicted, when faint and pleading before the LORD.

102.1 Ex 2.23 1 Sam 9.16

1 Hear my prayer, O LORD;
let my cry come to you.
2 Do not hide your face from me
in the day of my distress.
Incline your ear to me;
answer me speedily in the day when I call.

102.3 Ezra 10.6 Job 30.30 Jas 4.14

3 For my days pass away like smoke,
and my bones burn like a furnace.
4 My heart is stricken and withered like grass;
I am too wasted to eat my bread.

102.5 Lam 4.8

5 Because of my loud groaning
my bones cling to my skin.
6 I am like an owl of the wilderness,
like a little owl of the waste places.
7 I lie awake;
I am like a lonely bird on the housetop.

102.8 2 Sam 16.5 Isa 65.15 Lk 23.11 Acts 26.11

8 All day long my enemies taunt me;
those who deride me use my name for a curse.
9 For I eat ashes like bread,
and mingle tears with my drink,
10 because of your indignation and anger;
for you have lifted me up and thrown me aside.
11 My days are like an evening shadow;
I wither away like grass.

102.12 Ex 3.15 Lam 5.19

12 But you, O LORD, are enthroned forever;
your name endures to all generations.

102.13 Isa 60.10 Zech 1.12

13 You will rise up and have compassion on Zion,
for it is time to favor it;
the appointed time has come.
14 For your servants hold its stones dear,
and have pity on its dust.

102.15 1 Kgs 8.41,42

15 The nations will fear the name of the LORD,
and all the kings of the earth your glory.

102.16 Isa 60.1,2

16 For the LORD will build up Zion;
he will appear in his glory.

102.1–11 We have the freedom to go directly to God with our laments, our distresses, our complaints. We don't need to cover our real feelings or bring ourselves to a certain point of maturity first. No matter how low we feel, we do not have to be ashamed to turn to God.

102.3, 4 When we face sickness and despair, not only our food but our lives become tasteless. In these times, God alone is our comfort and strength. Even when we are too weak to fight, we can lean on him. It is often when we recognize our weaknesses that God's greatest strength becomes available.

102.6, 7 These birds are pictures of loneliness. While we may need to be alone and solitude may comfort us, we must be careful not to spurn those who reach out to us. Don't take the stance of rejecting help and conversation. "Suffering silently" is neither Christian nor particularly healthy. Try to accept graciously the offers of support from family and friends.

102.16–22 Christ's future reign on earth will encompass two events mentioned in these verses. Jerusalem will be restored, and the entire world will worship God (Revelation 11.15; 21.1–27).

17 He will regard the prayer of the destitute,
and will not despise their prayer.

102.17 Neh 1.6

18 Let this be recorded for a generation to come,
so that a people yet unborn may praise the LORD:
19 that he looked down from his holy height,
from heaven the LORD looked at the earth,
20 to hear the groans of the prisoners,
to set free those who were doomed to die;
21 so that the name of the LORD may be declared in Zion,
and his praise in Jerusalem,
22 when peoples gather together,
and kingdoms, to worship the LORD.

102.18 Deut 31.19 1 Cor 10.11
102.19 Deut 26.15
102.21 Isa 49.22; 23 Zech 8.20-23

23 He has broken my strength in midcourse;
he has shortened my days.
24 "O my God," I say, "do not take me away
at the mid-point of my life,
you whose years endure
throughout all generations."

102.24 Isa 38.10

25 Long ago you laid the foundation of the earth,
and the heavens are the work of your hands.
26 They will perish, but you endure;
they will all wear out like a garment.
You change them like clothing, and they pass away;
27 but you are the same, and your years have no end.
28 The children of your servants shall live secure;
their offspring shall be established in your presence.

102.25 Gen 1.1 Heb 1.10-12
102.26 Mt 24.35 2 Pet 3.10 Rev 20.11
102.27 Mal 3.6 Jas 1.17

Theme: God's great love for us. What God does for us tells us what he is really like.
Author: David

PSALM 103

Of David.

1 Bless the LORD, O my soul,
and all that is within me,
bless his holy name.
2 Bless the LORD, O my soul,
and do not forget all his benefits—
3 who forgives all your iniquity,
who heals all your diseases,
4 who redeems your life from the Pit,
who crowns you with steadfast love and mercy,
5 who satisfies you with good as long as you live[r]
so that your youth is renewed like the eagle's.

103.3 Ex 34.7 Jer 30.17
103.4 Ps 49.15
103.5 Isa 40.31

[r] Meaning of Heb uncertain

102.25–27 The writer of this psalm felt rejected and cast aside because of his great troubles (102.9, 10). Problems and heartaches can overwhelm us and cause us to feel that God has rejected us. But God our Creator is eternally with us and will keep all his promises, even though we may feel alone. Hebrews 1.10–12 quotes these verses to show that Jesus Christ, God's Son, was also present and active at the creation of the world.

103.1ff David's praise focused on God's glorious acts. It is easy to complain about life, but David's list gives us plenty for which to praise God—his forgiveness, healing, redemption, lovingkindness, tender mercies, providence, righteousness, justice, grace, patience. We receive all of these without deserving any of them. No matter how difficult your life's journey, you can always count your blessings—past, present, and future. When you feel as if you have nothing for which to praise God, read David's list.

6 The LORD works vindication
and justice for all who are oppressed.
103.7 Ex 33.13
7 He made known his ways to Moses,
his acts to the people of Israel.
103.8 Num 14.18 Neh 1.3; 9.17 Joel 2.13 Jonah 4.2
8 The LORD is merciful and gracious,
slow to anger and abounding in steadfast love.
9 He will not always accuse,
nor will he keep his anger forever.
103.10 Lam 3.22
10 He does not deal with us according to our sins,
nor repay us according to our iniquities.
11 For as the heavens are high above the earth,
so great is his steadfast love toward those who fear him;
103.12 Isa 38.17 Heb 9.26
12 as far as the east is from the west,
so far he removes our transgressions from us.
103.13 Mal 3.17
13 As a father has compassion for his children,
so the LORD has compassion for those who fear him.
103.14 Gen 3.19 Eccles 12.7
14 For he knows how we were made;
he remembers that we are dust.

103.15 Jas 1.10,11 1 Pet 1.24
15 As for mortals, their days are like grass;
they flourish like a flower of the field;
16 for the wind passes over it, and it is gone,
and its place knows it no more.
17 But the steadfast love of the LORD is from everlasting to everlasting
on those who fear him,
and his righteousness to children's children,
18 to those who keep his covenant
and remember to do his commandments.

19 The LORD has established his throne in the heavens,
and his kingdom rules over all.
103.20 Mt 6.10 Heb 1.14
20 Bless the LORD, O you his angels,
you mighty ones who do his bidding,
obedient to his spoken word.
21 Bless the LORD, all his hosts,
his ministers that do his will.
22 Bless the LORD, all his works,
in all places of his dominion.
Bless the LORD, O my soul.

103.7 God's law was given first to Moses and the people of Israel. God's law presents a clear picture of God's nature and will. It was God's training manual to prepare his people to serve him and to follow his ways. Review the ten commandments (Exodus 20) and the history of how they were given, asking God to show you his will through them.

103.8–10 One of the most frightening prayers we could pray is for God to give us what we deserve. We deserve to be punished for our sins, not forgiven. Fortunately, God is merciful, gracious, and slow to anger. This characteristic of God is clearly stated in numerous places in the Bible (Exodus 34.6, Nehemiah 9.17, Joel 2.13).

103.12 East and west can never meet. This is a symbolic portrait of God's forgiveness—when he forgives our sin, he separates it from us and doesn't even remember it. We need never wallow in the past, for God forgives and forgets. We tend to dredge up the ugly past, but God has wiped our record clean. If we are to follow God, we must model his forgiveness. When we forgive another, we must also forget the sin. Otherwise, we have not truly forgiven.

103.13, 14 We are fragile, but God's care is eternal. Too often we focus on God as Judge and Law-giver, ignoring his compassion and concern for us. When God examines our lives, he remembers our human condition. Our weakness should never be used as a justification for sin. His mercy takes everything into account. Can you trust him to deal with you compassionately?

103.20–22 Everything everywhere is to bless the Lord: all angels—hosts (heavenly armies) and ministers—and all nature! To bless God is to praise him, remembering all he has done for us (103.2), fearing him and obeying his commands (103.17, 18), and doing his will (103.21). Is your life a blessing to the Lord?

Theme: Appreciating God through his creation. He not only creates, but maintains his creation. The Lord's care is the source of our joy.
Author: Anonymous

PSALM 104

1 Bless the LORD, O my soul.
O LORD my God, you are very great.
You are clothed with honor and majesty,
2 wrapped in light as with a garment.
You stretch out the heavens like a tent,
3 you set the beams of your[s] chambers on the waters,
you make the clouds your[s] chariot,
you ride on the wings of the wind,
4 you make the winds your[s] messengers,
fire and flame your[s] ministers.

5 You set the earth on its foundations,
so that it shall never be shaken.
6 You cover it with the deep as with a garment;
the waters stood above the mountains.
7 At your rebuke they flee;
at the sound of your thunder they take to flight.
8 They rose up to the mountains, ran down to the valleys
to the place that you appointed for them.
9 You set a boundary that they may not pass,
so that they might not again cover the earth.

10 You make springs gush forth in the valleys;
they flow between the hills,
11 giving drink to every wild animal;
the wild asses quench their thirst.
12 By the streams[t] the birds of the air have their habitation;
they sing among the branches.
13 From your lofty abode you water the mountains;
the earth is satisfied with the fruit of your work.

14 You cause the grass to grow for the cattle,
and plants for people to use,[u]
to bring forth food from the earth,
15 and wine to gladden the human heart,
oil to make the face shine,
and bread to strengthen the human heart.
16 The trees of the LORD are watered abundantly,
the cedars of Lebanon that he planted.
17 In them the birds build their nests;
the stork has its home in the fir trees.
18 The high mountains are for the wild goats;
the rocks are a refuge for the coneys.
19 You have made the moon to mark the seasons;

104.1 Dan 7.9
104.3 Amos 9.6
104.4 2 Kgs 2.11; 6.17 Heb 1.7
104.5 Job 38.4
104.6 Gen 1.2
104.7 Ps 18.15; 29.3
104.10 Isa 41.18
104.12 Mt 8.20
104.14 Gen 1.29 Job 28.5
104.15 Judg 9.13 19.5,8 Prov 31.6 Eccles 10.19 Lk 7.46
104.18 Lev 11.5 Prov 30.26
104.19 Gen 1.14

[s] Heb *his* [t] Heb *By them* [u] Or *to cultivate*

104.1ff This psalm is a poetic summary of God's creation of the world as found in the first chapter of Genesis. What God created each day is mentioned by the psalmist as a reason to praise God. On day one, God created light (104.1, 2; Genesis 1.3); day two, sky and water (104.1–4; Genesis 1.6); day three, land and vegetation (104.6–18; Genesis 1.9–13); day four, the sun, moon, and stars (104.19–23; Genesis 1.14–16); day five, fish and birds (104.25, 26; Genesis 1.20–23); and on day six, animals, man, and food to sustain them (104.21–24, 27–30; Genesis 1.24–31). God's act of creation deserves the praise of all people.

104.5 The world is built on God's foundations, and he guarantees its permanence. Even though one day the heavens and the earth will be destroyed (2 Peter 3.10), he will create a new heaven and a new earth that will last forever (Isaiah 65.17; Revelation 21.1). The same power that undergirds the world also provides a firm foundation for believers.

the sun knows its time for setting.

104.20 Isa 45.7; 56.9

20 You make darkness, and it is night,
when all the animals of the forest come creeping out.
21 The young lions roar for their prey,
seeking their food from God.

104.22 Job 37.8

22 When the sun rises, they withdraw
and lie down in their dens.

104.23 Gen 3.19

23 People go out to their work
and to their labor until the evening.

104.24 Jer 10.12; 51.15

24 O LORD, how manifold are your works!
In wisdom you have made them all;
the earth is full of your creatures.
25 Yonder is the sea, great and wide,
creeping things innumerable are there,
living things both small and great.

104.26 Job 41.1

26 There go the ships,
and Leviathan that you formed to sport in it.

104.27 Ps 136.25

27 These all look to you
to give them their food in due season;
28 when you give to them, they gather it up;
when you open your hand, they are filled with good things.

104.29 Gen 3.19

29 When you hide your face, they are dismayed;
when you take away their breath, they die
and return to their dust.

104.30 Ezek 37.9

30 When you send forth your spirit,[v] they are created;
and you renew the face of the ground.

[v] Or *your breath*

HOW GOD IS DESCRIBED IN PSALMS

Most of the psalms speak to God or about God. Because they were composed in a variety of situations, various facets of God's character are mentioned. Here is a sample of God's characteristics as understood and experienced by the psalm writers. As you read these psalms, ask yourself if this is the God you know.

God is . . .	*References*
All-knowing and ever-present	Psalm 139
Beautiful and desirable	Psalms 27; 36; 45
Creator	Psalms 8; 104; 148
Good and generous	Psalms 34; 81; 107
Great and sovereign	Psalms 33; 89; 96
Holy	Psalms 66; 99; 145
Loving and faithful	Psalms 23; 42; 51
Merciful and forgiving	Psalms 32; 111; 130
Powerful	Psalms 76; 89; 93
Willing to reveal his will, law, and direction	Psalms 1; 19; 119
Righteous and just	Psalms 71; 97; 113
Spirit	Psalms 104; 139; 143

104.24 Creation is filled with stunning variety, revealing the rich creativity, goodness, and wisdom of our loving God. As you observe your natural surroundings, thank God for his creativity. Take a fresh look at people, seeing each one as his unique creation, each with his or her own special talents, abilities, and gifts.

104.26 Here Leviathan simply means a large and active sea creature.

104.28–30 Psalm 103 expresses God's sovereignty in history; this psalm tells of his sovereignty over all creation. God has supreme, unlimited power over the entire universe. He creates; he preserves; he governs. As we understand God's power, we realize that he is sufficient to handle our lives.

104.30 Many people today are arrogant enough to think they don't need God. But our every breath depends on the Spirit he has breathed into us (Genesis 2.7; 3.19; Job 33.4; 34.14, 15; Daniel 5.23). Not only do we depend on God for our very lives, we must also desire to learn more of his plans for us each day.

31 May the glory of the LORD endure forever;
may the LORD rejoice in his works—
32 who looks on the earth and it trembles,
who touches the mountains and they smoke.
33 I will sing to the LORD as long as I live;
I will sing praise to my God while I have being.
34 May my meditation be pleasing to him,
for I rejoice in the LORD.
35 Let sinners be consumed from the earth,
and let the wicked be no more.
Bless the LORD, O my soul.
Praise the LORD!

104.31 Gen 1.31
104.32 Ex 19.18 Judg 5.5
104.35 Ps 37.10

Theme: God's mighty deeds in bringing Israel to the promised land. Remembering his miracles encourages us to keep living close to him.
Author: David

PSALM 105

1 O give thanks to the LORD, call on his name,
make known his deeds among the peoples.
2 Sing to him, sing praises to him;
tell of all his wonderful works.
3 Glory in his holy name;
let the hearts of those who seek the LORD rejoice.
4 Seek the LORD and his strength;
seek his presence continually.
5 Remember the wonderful works he has done,
his miracles, and the judgments he uttered,
6 O offspring of his servant Abraham,[w]
children of Jacob, his chosen ones.

7 He is the LORD our God;
his judgments are in all the earth.
8 He is mindful of his covenant forever,
of the word that he commanded, for a thousand generations,
9 the covenant that he made with Abraham,
his sworn promise to Isaac,
10 which he confirmed to Jacob as a statute,
to Israel as an everlasting covenant,
11 saying, "To you I will give the land of Canaan
as your portion for an inheritance."

12 When they were few in number,
of little account, and strangers in it,
13 wandering from nation to nation,
from one kingdom to another people,
14 he allowed no one to oppress them;

105.1 1 Chron 16.8-22, 34
105.2 Ps 98.5
105.4 Ps 27.8
105.5 1 Chron 16.13
105.7 Isa 26.9
105.8 Gen 22.16-18 Deut 7.9 Lk 1.72 Gal 3.17
105.10 Gen 28.13-15 Josh 23.4
105.12 Gen 34.30 Heb 11.9
105.14 Gen 12.17 20.7; 35.5

[w] Another reading is *Israel* (compare 1 Chr 16.13)

105.1ff The first 15 verses of this psalm are also found in 1 Chronicles 16.7–22, where they are sung as part of the celebration of David's bringing the ark of the covenant to Jerusalem. Three other psalms are also hymns recounting Israel's history—78, 106, and 136.

105.4 If God seems far away, persist in your search for him. God rewards those who sincerely look for him (Hebrews 11.6). Jesus promised, "Search, and you will find" (Matthew 7.7). David suggested a valuable way to search out God—become familiar with the way he has helped his people in the past. The Bible records the history of God's people. In searching its pages we will discover a loving God who is waiting for us to find him.

105.5, 6 The nation Israel, the people through whom God revealed his laws to mankind, is descended from Abraham. God chose Abraham and promised that his descendants would live in the land of Canaan (now called Israel), and that they would be too numerous to count (Genesis 17.6–8). Abraham's son was Isaac; Isaac's son was Jacob. These three men are considered the patriarchs or founders of Israel. God blessed them because of their faith (see Hebrews 11.8–21).

he rebuked kings on their account,
15 saying, "Do not touch my anointed ones;
do my prophets no harm."

16 When he summoned famine against the land,
and broke every staff of bread,
17 he had sent a man ahead of them,
Joseph, who was sold as a slave.
18 His feet were hurt with fetters,
his neck was put in a collar of iron;
19 until what he had said came to pass,
the word of the LORD kept testing him.
20 The king sent and released him;
the ruler of the peoples set him free.
21 He made him lord of his house,
and ruler of all his possessions,
22 to instruct[x] his officials at his pleasure,
and to teach his elders wisdom.

23 Then Israel came to Egypt;
Jacob lived as an alien in the land of Ham.
24 And the LORD made his people very fruitful,
and made them stronger than their foes,
25 whose hearts he then turned to hate his people,
to deal craftily with his servants.

26 He sent his servant Moses,
and Aaron whom he had chosen.
27 They performed his signs among them,
and miracles in the land of Ham.
28 He sent darkness, and made the land dark;
they rebelled[y] against his words.
29 He turned their waters into blood,
and caused their fish to die.
30 Their land swarmed with frogs,
even in the chambers of their kings.
31 He spoke, and there came swarms of flies,
and gnats throughout their country.
32 He gave them hail for rain,
and lightning that flashed through their land.
33 He struck their vines and fig trees,

105.16 Lev 26.26 Isa 3.1 Ezek 4.16
105.17 Gen 37.28,36 Acts 7.9
105.19 Ps 66.10
105.20 Gen 41.14
105.24 Ex 1.7,9
105.25 Acts 7.19
105.26 Ex 3.10
105.27 Ex 8.10 Ps 78.43-51

[x] Gk Syr Jerome: Heb *to bind* [y] Cn Compare Gk Syr: Heb *they did not rebel*

HISTORY IN THE BOOK OF PSALMS

For the original hearers, the historical psalms were vivid reminders of God's past acts on behalf of Israel. These history songs were written for passing on important lessons to succeeding generations. They celebrated the many promises God had made and faithfully kept; they also recounted the faithlessness of the people.

We cannot read this ancient history without reflecting on how consistently God's people failed to learn from the past. They repeatedly turned from fresh examples of God's faithfulness and forgiveness only to plunge back into sin. God can use these psalms to remind us how often we do exactly the same thing: having every reason to live for God, we choose instead to live for everything but God. If we paid more attention to "his story" we wouldn't make so many mistakes in our own stories.

Selected historical psalms include: 68; 78; 95; 105; 106; 111; 114; 135; 136; 149.

105.23–25 Did God cause the Egyptians to hate the Hebrews? God is not the author of evil, but the Hebrew writers don't always distinguish between God's ultimate action and the intermediate steps. Thus by God blessing the Israelites, the Egyptians came to hate them (Exodus 1.8–22). Because God caused the Israelites' blessing, he is also said to have caused the Egyptians to hate them. God used their animosity as a means to lead the Israelites out of Egypt.

and shattered the trees of their country.
34 He spoke, and the locusts came,
and young locusts without number;
35 they devoured all the vegetation in their land,
and ate up the fruit of their ground.
36 He struck down all the firstborn in their land,
the first issue of all their strength.

105.36 Ex 12.30

37 Then he brought Israel[z] out with silver and gold,
and there was no one among their tribes who stumbled.
38 Egypt was glad when they departed,
for dread of them had fallen upon it.
39 He spread a cloud for a covering,
and fire to give light by night.
40 They asked, and he brought quails,
and gave them food from heaven in abundance.
41 He opened the rock, and water gushed out;
it flowed through the desert like a river.
42 For he remembered his holy promise,
and Abraham, his servant.

105.39 Neh 9.12 Isa 4.5
105.40 Num 11.31 Jn 6.31
105.41 1 Cor 10.4

43 So he brought his people out with joy,
his chosen ones with singing.
44 He gave them the lands of the nations,
and they took possession of the wealth of the peoples,
45 that they might keep his statutes
and observe his laws.
Praise the LORD!

105.43 Ex 15.1
105.44 Josh 13.7
105.45 Deut 4.40

Theme: A song of national repentance as the people return from captivity. God patiently delivers us, in spite of our forgetfulness and self-willed rebellion.
Author: Anonymous

PSALM 106

1 Praise the LORD!
O give thanks to the LORD, for he is good;
for his steadfast love endures forever.
2 Who can utter the mighty doings of the LORD,
or declare all his praise?
3 Happy are those who observe justice,
who do righteousness at all times.

106.1 1 Chron 16.34
106.3 Ps 15.2

4 Remember me, O LORD, when you show favor to your people;
help me when you deliver them;
5 that I may see the prosperity of your chosen ones,
that I may rejoice in the gladness of your nation,
that I may glory in your heritage.

106.4 Ps 44.3
106.5 Ps 1.3

z Heb *them*

105.45 God helps us prepare for the unknown path ahead by providing in his Word a record of his past dealings with people. When we learn about God through the pages of his Word, we learn how to be faithful and obedient, and the future is not as uncertain as it seems at times. We need not fear tomorrow when we know God who will be with us tomorrow.

106.1ff While Psalm 105 is a summary of God's faithfulness, Psalm 106 is a summary of man's sinfulness. Psalm 105 covers events up to the exodus from Egypt, and Psalm 106 covers events from the exodus up to the Babylonian captivity (2 Kings 25).

106.2 If we ever stopped to list all the mighty acts or miracles in the Bible, we would be astounded. They cover every aspect of life. The more we think about what God has done, the more we can appreciate the miracles he has done for us individually—birth, personality development, loving friends and family, specific guidance, healing, salvation—the list goes on and on. If you think you have never seen a miracle, look closer—you will see God's power and loving intervention on your behalf. God still performs great miracles!

106.6 2 Chron 30.7 Ezra 9.7 Neh 1.7 Zech 1.4
106.7 Judg 3.7
106.8 Ezek 20.9
106.9 Ex 14.21 Isa 63.11-13
106.11 Ex 15.5
106.14 Num 11.4
106.15 Ps 78.29-31
106.17 Num 16.32
106.19 Acts 7.41 Rom 1.23
106.21 Deut 10.21
106.23 Ex 32.10-14
106.24 Jer 3.19

6 Both we and our ancestors have sinned;
we have committed iniquity, have done wickedly.
7 Our ancestors, when they were in Egypt,
did not consider your wonderful works;
they did not remember the abundance of your steadfast love,
but rebelled against the Most High[a] at the Red Sea.[b]
8 Yet he saved them for his name's sake,
so that he might make known his mighty power.
9 He rebuked the Red Sea,[b] and it became dry;
he led them through the deep as through a desert.
10 So he saved them from the hand of the foe,
and delivered them from the hand of the enemy.
11 The waters covered their adversaries;
not one of them was left.
12 Then they believed his words;
they sang his praise.

13 But they soon forgot his works;
they did not wait for his counsel.
14 But they had a wanton craving in the wilderness,
and put God to the test in the desert;
15 he gave them what they asked,
but sent a wasting disease among them.

16 They were jealous of Moses in the camp,
and of Aaron, the holy one of the LORD.
17 The earth opened and swallowed up Dathan,
and covered the faction of Abiram.
18 Fire also broke out in their company;
the flame burned up the wicked.

19 They made a calf at Horeb
and worshiped a cast image.
20 They exchanged the glory of God[c]
for the image of an ox that eats grass.
21 They forgot God, their Savior,
who had done great things in Egypt,
22 wondrous works in the land of Ham,
and awesome deeds by the Red Sea.[b]
23 Therefore he said he would destroy them—
had not Moses, his chosen one,
stood in the breach before him,
to turn away his wrath from destroying them.

24 Then they despised the pleasant land,
having no faith in his promise.
25 They grumbled in their tents,
and did not obey the voice of the LORD.

[a] Cn Compare 78.17, 56: Heb *rebelled at the sea* [b] Or *Sea of Reeds* [c] Compare Gk Mss: Heb *exchanged their glory*

106.13–15 In the wilderness, Israel was so intent on getting the food and water *they* wanted that they became blind to what God wanted. They were more concerned about immediate physical gratification than lasting spiritual satisfaction. They did not want what was best for them, and they refused to trust in God's care and provision (Numbers 11.18–33).

If you complain enough, God may give you what you ask for, even if it is not the best for you. If you're not getting what you want, perhaps God knows it is not in your best interest. Trust in his care and provision.

106.22 The land of Ham is Egypt.

106.23 "Stood in the breach" means Moses served as their intercessor. This refers to the time when the Lord wanted to destroy the people for worshiping the golden calf (Exodus 32.7–14).

26 Therefore he raised his hand and swore to them
that he would make them fall in the wilderness,
27 and would disperse[d] their descendants among the nations,
scattering them over the lands.

28 Then they attached themselves to the Baal of Peor,
and ate sacrifices offered to the dead;
29 they provoked the LORD to anger with their deeds,
and a plague broke out among them.
30 Then Phinehas stood up and interceded,
and the plague was stopped.
31 And that has been reckoned to him as righteousness
from generation to generation forever.

32 They angered the LORD[e] at the waters of Meribah,
and it went ill with Moses on their account;
33 for they made his spirit bitter,
and he spoke words that were rash.

34 They did not destroy the peoples,
as the LORD commanded them,
35 but they mingled with the nations
and learned to do as they did.
36 They served their idols,
which became a snare to them.
37 They sacrificed their sons
and their daughters to the demons;
38 they poured out innocent blood,
the blood of their sons and daughters,
whom they sacrificed to the idols of Canaan;
and the land was polluted with blood.
39 Thus they became unclean by their acts,
and prostituted themselves in their doings.

40 Then the anger of the LORD was kindled against his people,
and he abhorred his heritage;
41 he gave them into the hand of the nations,
so that those who hated them ruled over them.
42 Their enemies oppressed them,
and they were brought into subjection under their power.
43 Many times he delivered them,
but they were rebellious in their purposes,
and were brought low through their iniquity.
44 Nevertheless he regarded their distress

106.26 Heb 3.11
106.28 Hos 9.10
106.30 Num 25.7-13
106.32 Ps 78.40
106.34 Judg 1.21,27-36
106.37 Num 35.33; 2 Kgs 17.17
106.39 Hos 4.12
106.40 Judg 2.12-14
106.41 Neh 9.27
106.43 Judg 6.6; Ps 81.12

d Syr Compare Ezek 20.23: Heb *cause to fall* e Heb *him*

106.34–39 Israel constantly turned from their Provider and Protector. How, after the great miracles they saw, could they turn from God and worship the idols of the land? We also have seen God's great miracles, but sometimes find ourselves enticed by the world's gods—power, convenience, fame, sex, and pleasure. As Israel forgot God, so we are susceptible to forgetting him and giving in to the pressures of an evil world. Remember all that God has done for you so you won't be drawn away from him by the world's "pleasures."

106.40–42 Why does God allow his people to be disciplined by pagan forces more evil than they? The tool he uses to discipline his followers is not as important as the discipline itself. When we have turned or drifted away from God, we should not be surprised that he disciplines us. We do not choose his methods of discipline, nor should we complain about them. Our job is to get the message and return to him.

106.40–42 God allowed trouble to come to the Israelites in order to help them. Our troubles can be helpful because they (1) humble us, (2) wean us from the allurements of the world and drive us back to God, (3) vitalize our prayers, (4) allow us to experience more of God's faithfulness, (5) make us more dependent upon God, (6) encourage us to submit to God's purpose for our lives, and (7) make us more compassionate toward others in trouble.

106.44–46 This is a beautiful picture of God's graciousness toward his people who deserved only judgment. Fortunately, God's faithfulness to us is not limited by our faithfulness to him. God was

when he heard their cry.

106.45 Lev 26.42

45 For their sake he remembered his covenant,
and showed compassion according to the abundance of his steadfast love.

106.46 2 Chron 30.9 Ezra 9.9

46 He caused them to be pitied
by all who held them captive.

106.47 Ps 147.2

47 Save us, O LORD our God,
and gather us from among the nations,
that we may give thanks to your holy name
and glory in your praise.

106.48 Ps 41.13

48 Blessed be the LORD, the God of Israel,
from everlasting to everlasting.
And let all the people say, "Amen."
Praise the LORD!

BOOK V
Psalms 107.1–150.6

These psalms praise God's works, recount the blessings of righteous living, thank God for deliverance, and praise God for his wonderful Word. These psalms remind us that the most perfect sacrifice we can offer to God is a faithful and obedient life.

Theme: Thankfulness to God should constantly be on the lips of those whom he has saved. This psalm was written to celebrate the Jews' return from their exile in Babylon.
Author: Anonymous

PSALM 107

1 O give thanks to the LORD, for he is good;
for his steadfast love endures forever.

107.2 Isa 35.9,10

2 Let the redeemed of the LORD say so,
those he redeemed from trouble

107.3 Neh 1.9 Ezek 20.34

3 and gathered in from the lands,
from the east and from the west,
from the north and from the south.[f]

107.4 Josh 5.6

4 Some wandered in desert wastes,
finding no way to an inhabited town;
5 hungry and thirsty,
their soul fainted within them.
6 Then they cried to the LORD in their trouble,
and he delivered them from their distress;

107.7 Jer 31.9

7 he led them by a straight way,
until they reached an inhabited town.
8 Let them thank the LORD for his steadfast love,
for his wonderful works to humankind.

107.9 Mt 5.6 Lk 1.53

9 For he satisfies the thirsty,

[f] Cn: Heb *sea*

---

gracious to us in sending his Son to die for our sins. If he did this while we were yet sinners, how much more gracious will he be now that we are his children?

107.1ff This psalm speaks of four different types of people in distress and how God rescues them: wanderers (107.3–7), prisoners (107.10–16), the sick (107.17–20), and the storm-tossed (107.23–30). No matter how extreme our calamity, God is able to break through to help us. He is loving and kind to those who are distressed.

107.2 God has done so much for us, and we have so much for which to thank him (see Psalm 103). He wants us to proclaim to everyone all that he has done. This verse is not so much a mandate to witness as a declaration of the fact that those who truly live in God's presence will not be able to keep this glorious experience to themselves (see also Acts 1.8; 2 Corinthians 5.18–20). What has God done for you? Is there someone you can tell?

107.5–9 Lost, hungry, thirsty, and exhausted, these wanderers typify the Israelites in exile. But they also typify anyone who has not found the satisfaction that comes from knowing God. Anyone who recognizes his or her own lostness can receive the offer of Jesus to satisfy these needs. Jesus is the way (John 14.6), the bread of life (John 6.33, 35), the water of life (John 4.10–14), and the giver of rest (Matthew 11.28–30). Have you received his life-giving offer?

and the hungry he fills with good things.

10 Some sat in darkness and in gloom,
prisoners in misery and in irons,
11 for they had rebelled against the words of God,
and spurned the counsel of the Most High.
12 Their hearts were bowed down with hard labor;
they fell down, with no one to help.
13 Then they cried to the LORD in their trouble,
and he saved them from their distress;
14 he brought them out of darkness and gloom,
and broke their bonds asunder.
15 Let them thank the LORD for his steadfast love,
for his wonderful works to humankind.
16 For he shatters the doors of bronze,
and cuts in two the bars of iron.

17 Some were sick[g] through their sinful ways,
and because of their iniquities endured affliction;
18 they loathed any kind of food,
and they drew near to the gates of death.
19 Then they cried to the LORD in their trouble,
and he saved them from their distress;
20 he sent out his word and healed them,
and delivered them from destruction.
21 Let them thank the LORD for his steadfast love,
for his wonderful works to humankind.
22 And let them offer thanksgiving sacrifices,
and tell of his deeds with songs of joy.

23 Some went down to the sea in ships,
doing business on the mighty waters;
24 they saw the deeds of the LORD,
his wondrous works in the deep.
25 For he commanded and raised the stormy wind,
which lifted up the waves of the sea.
26 They mounted up to heaven, they went down to the depths;
their courage melted away in their calamity;
27 they reeled and staggered like drunkards,
and were at their wits' end.
28 Then they cried to the LORD in their trouble,
and he brought them out from their distress;
29 he made the storm be still,
and the waves of the sea were hushed.
30 Then they were glad because they had quiet,
and he brought them to their desired haven.
31 Let them thank the LORD for his steadfast love,
for his wonderful works to humankind.
32 Let them extol him in the congregation of the people,
and praise him in the assembly of the elders.

33 He turns rivers into a desert,

107.10 Mic 7.8 Lk 1.79
107.11 Num 15.31
107.12 Ps 22.11
107.14 Acts 12.7
107.16 Isa 45.1,2
107.17 Isa 65.6,7 Ezek 24.23
107.18 Job 33.19-22 Ps 9.13
107.20 2 Kgs 20.5 Mt 8.8
107.22 Lev 7.12 Ps 73.28
107.25 Ps 93.3,4
107.29 Mt 8.26 Lk 8.24
107.32 Ps 22.22,25 Isa 25.1

g Cn: Heb *fools*

107.28–32 Sometimes we feel as though all is hopeless. But trouble can lead us to depend on God as we cry to him for help. When he saves us, we will praise him for the good he has done. Then we understand that God can bring good out of troubles because our afflictions strengthen our faith.

springs of water into thirsty ground,
107.34 Gen 19.24,25
34 a fruitful land into a salty waste,
because of the wickedness of its inhabitants.
107.35 Isa 35.6,7 41.18
35 He turns a desert into pools of water,
a parched land into springs of water.
36 And there he lets the hungry live,
and they establish a town to live in;
107.37 2 Kgs 19.29 Amos 9.14
37 they sow fields, and plant vineyards,
and get a fruitful yield.
107.38 Gen 12.2 Ex 1.7
38 By his blessing they multiply greatly,
and he does not let their cattle decrease.

39 When they are diminished and brought low
through oppression, trouble, and sorrow,
40 he pours contempt on princes
and makes them wander in trackless wastes;
41 but he raises up the needy out of distress,
and makes their families like flocks.
107.42 Job 22.19 Rom 3.19
42 The upright see it and are glad;
and all wickedness stops its mouth.
107.43 Hos 14.9
43 Let those who are wise give heed to these things,
and consider the steadfast love of the LORD.

Theme: Victory in God's strength. With God's help, we can do more than we think.
Author: David

PSALM 108

A Song. A Psalm of David.

108.1 Ps 57.7-11
1 My heart is steadfast, O God, my heart is steadfast;[h]
I will sing and make melody.
Awake, my soul![i]
2 Awake, O harp and lyre!
I will awake the dawn.
3 I will give thanks to you, O LORD, among the peoples,
and I will sing praises to you among the nations.
4 For your steadfast love is higher than the heavens,
and your faithfulness reaches to the clouds.

5 Be exalted, O God, above the heavens,
and let your glory be over all the earth.
6 Give victory with your right hand, and answer me,
so that those whom you love may be rescued.

7 God has promised in his sanctuary:[j]
"With exultation I will divide up Shechem,
and portion out the Vale of Succoth.
8 Gilead is mine; Manasseh is mine;
Ephraim is my helmet;
Judah is my scepter.

[h] Heb Mss Gk Syr: MT lacks *my heart is steadfast* [i] Compare 57.8: Heb *also my soul* [j] Or *by his holiness*

107.43 Those who have never truly suffered may not appreciate God as much as those who have matured under hardship. Those who have seen God work in times of distress have a deeper insight into his lovingkindness. If you have experienced great trials, you have the potential for great praise.

108.1ff The conclusions from two previous psalms have been put together to make this psalm. The first five verses are quoted from Psalm 57.7–11, and the next eight verses (108.6–13) are from Psalm 60.4–12.

108.7 When God speaks, his Word is sacred because he is holy. What he says, he will do, because his Word and his person are inseparable. To violate his own Word would cause him to cease to be God. We can trust his promises.

9 Moab is my washbasin;
on Edom I hurl my shoe;
over Philistia I shout in triumph."

10 Who will bring me to the fortified city?
Who will lead me to Edom?
11 Have you not rejected us, O God?
You do not go out, O God, with our armies.
12 O grant us help against the foe,
for human help is worthless.
13 With God we shall do valiantly;
it is he who will tread down our foes.

108.11 Ps 44.9

Theme: Righteous indignation against liars and slanderers. We can tell God our true feelings and desires.
Author: David

PSALM 109

To the leader. Of David. A Psalm.

1 Do not be silent, O God of my praise.
2 For wicked and deceitful mouths are opened against me,
speaking against me with lying tongues.
3 They beset me with words of hate,
and attack me without cause.
4 In return for my love they accuse me,
even while I make prayer for them.[k]
5 So they reward me evil for good,
and hatred for my love.

6 They say,[l] "Appoint a wicked man against him;
let an accuser stand on his right.
7 When he is tried, let him be found guilty;
let his prayer be counted as sin.
8 May his days be few;
may another seize his position.
9 May his children be orphans,
and his wife a widow.
10 May his children wander about and beg;
may they be driven out of[m] the ruins they inhabit.
11 May the creditor seize all that he has;
may strangers plunder the fruits of his toil.

109.5 Mt 5.44
109.6 Zech 3.1
109.8 Acts 1.20
109.9 Ex 22.24
109.11 Isa 1.7

[k] Syr: Heb *I prayer* [l] Heb lacks *They say* [m] Gk: Heb *and seek*

108.9 Moab, Edom, and Philistia were Israel's enemies to the east, south, and west respectively. They despised the Israelites and Israel's God.

108.13 Do our prayers end with requests for help to make it through stressful situations? David prayed not merely for rescue, but for victory. With God's help we can claim more than just survival, we can claim victory! Look for ways God can use your distress as an opportunity to show his mighty power.

109.1ff David endured many false accusations (1 Samuel 22.7–13; 2 Samuel 15.3, 4), as did Christ centuries later (Matthew 26.59–61; 27.39–44). Verse 8 is quoted in Acts 1.20 as fulfilled by Judas's death.

109.4 David was angry at being attacked by evil people who slandered him and lied. Yet he said he loved his enemies and prayed for them. While we must hate evil and work to overcome it, we must love everyone, including those who do evil, because God loves them. We are called to hate the sin, but love the person. Only through God's strength will we be able to follow David's example.

109.6–20 This is another of the imprecatory psalms, a call for God to judge the wicked. (For an explanation of imprecatory psalms, see the note on 35.1ff.) David was not taking vengeance into his own hands, but was asking that God be swift in his promised judgment of evil people. David's words depict the eventual doom of all God's enemies.

109.17–19 One of the frightening realities of judgment is that people will be filled and covered by what they love. Those who love cursing will have curses heaped upon them. Those who love Christ will be covered by his love. Don't envy sinful people, because one day they will

109.12 Isa 9.17

12 May there be no one to do him a kindness,
nor anyone to pity his orphaned children.
13 May his posterity be cut off;
may his name be blotted out in the second generation.

109.14 Neh 4.5 Isa 65.6,7

14 May the iniquity of his father[n] be remembered before the LORD,
and do not let the sin of his mother be blotted out.

109.15 Jer 16.17

15 Let them be before the LORD continually,
and may his[o] memory be cut off from the earth.

109.16 Ps 37.32

16 For he did not remember to show kindness,
but pursued the poor and needy
and the brokenhearted to their death.

109.17 Mt 7.2

17 He loved to curse; let curses come on him.
He did not like blessing; may it be far from him.

109.18 Ps 73.6

18 He clothed himself with cursing as his coat,
may it soak into his body like water,
like oil into his bones.

109.19 Ezek 7.27

19 May it be like a garment that he wraps around himself,
like a belt that he wears every day."

109.20 Isa 3.11 2 Tim 4.14

20 May that be the reward of my accusers from the LORD,
of those who speak evil against my life.

109.21 Ps 25.11 Ezek 36.22

21 But you, O LORD my Lord,
act on my behalf for your name's sake;
because your steadfast love is good, deliver me.

109.22 Ps 40.17 Prov 18.14

22 For I am poor and needy,
and my heart is pierced within me.
23 I am gone like a shadow at evening;
I am shaken off like a locust.

109.24 Heb 12.12

24 My knees are weak through fasting;
my body has become gaunt.
25 I am an object of scorn to my accusers;
when they see me, they shake their heads.

26 Help me, O LORD my God!
Save me according to your steadfast love.
27 Let them know that this is your hand;
you, O LORD, have done it.

109.28 2 Sam 16.11,12

28 Let them curse, but you will bless.
Let my assailants be put to shame;[p] may your servant be glad.

109.29 Job 8.22 Ps 35.26

29 May my accusers be clothed with dishonor;
may they be wrapped in their own shame as in a mantle.
30 With my mouth I will give great thanks to the LORD;
I will praise him in the midst of the throng.

109.31 Ps 16.8; 37.33

31 For he stands at the right hand of the needy,
to save them from those who would condemn them to death.

[n] Cn: Heb *fathers* [o] Gk: Heb *their* [p] Gk: Heb *They have risen up and have been put to shame*

---

drown in their sin. We can be certain that they will get a taste of their own medicine.

109.21 A name is more than a label, it is a representation of character and reputation. David is pleading for God to live up to his name – to his character of love and mercy. "For your name's sake," then, means "in accordance with your character."

109.22 We will have times in this life when our heart will be pierced. Mary's heart was pierced when her son Jesus was crucified (Luke 2.35). Whether pierced by shame or bitter grief, we can always go to the Lord for help in these troubled times.

109.29 A mantle is a cloak or outer garment.

109.31 In the opening of this psalm the enemies are looking for someone to stand at the psalmist's right hand to accuse him (109.6). Apparently, this was the customary position for the accuser in a court of law. At the end of the psalm we learn that someone is standing at his right hand, but it is the Lord, not a wicked man. The Lord stands at the right hand of the needy, defending rather than accusing (109.31). The Lord is still near to those who call on him.

Theme: The credentials for the Messiah. Jesus is the Messiah.
Author: David

PSALM 110

Of David. A Psalm.

1 The LORD says to my lord,
"Sit at my right hand
until I make your enemies your footstool."

2 The LORD sends out from Zion
your mighty scepter.
Rule in the midst of your foes.
3 Your people will offer themselves willingly
on the day you lead your forces
on the holy mountains.[q]
From the womb of the morning,
like dew, your youth[r] will come to you.
4 The LORD has sworn and will not change his mind,
"You are a priest forever according to the order of Melchizedek."[s]

5 The Lord is at your right hand;
he will shatter kings on the day of his wrath.
6 He will execute judgment among the nations,
filling them with corpses;
he will shatter heads
over the wide earth.
7 He will drink from the stream by the path;
therefore he will lift up his head.

110.1 Mt 22.44 Lk 20.42,43 Acts 2.34,35 Heb 1.13

110.2 Ps 45.6 Dan 7.13,14

110.3 Ps 96.9

110.4 Heb 6.20; 7.21

110.5 Rev 6.17

Theme: All that God does is good. Reverence for God is the beginning of wisdom.
Author: Anonymous

PSALM 111

1 Praise the LORD!
I will give thanks to the LORD with my whole heart,
in the company of the upright, in the congregation.
2 Great are the works of the LORD,
studied by all who delight in them.
3 Full of honor and majesty is his work,
and his righteousness endures forever.
4 He has gained renown by his wonderful deeds;
the LORD is gracious and merciful.
5 He provides food for those who fear him;
he is ever mindful of his covenant.
6 He has shown his people the power of his works,

111.1 Ps 92.5; 138.1

111.3 Ps 96.6; 145.5

111.4 Ps 86.15; 103.8

111.5 Mt 6.31-33

[q] Another reading is *in holy splendor* [r] Cn: Heb *the dew of your youth* [s] Or *forever, a rightful king by my edict*

110.1 This is one of the most-quoted psalms in the New Testament because of its clear references to the Messiah. In Matthew 22.41–45, Jesus recited the words of this verse and applied them to himself. Verses 1 and 6 look forward to Christ's final and total destruction of the wicked (Revelation 6–9); 110.2 prophesies Christ's reign on the earth (Revelation 20.1–7); 110.3, 4 tell of Christ's priestly work for his people (Hebrews 5–8); and 110.5, 6 look forward to the final battle on earth when Christ will overcome the forces of evil (Revelation 19.11–21).

110.1–7 Many people have a vague belief in God, but refuse to accept Jesus as anything more than a great human teacher. But the Bible does not allow that option. Both the Old and New Testaments proclaim the deity of the One who came to save and to reign. Jesus pointed out that this psalm spoke of the Messiah as greater than David, Israel's greatest king (Mark 12.35–37). Peter used this psalm to show that Jesus, the Messiah, sits at God's right hand and is Lord over all (Acts 2.32–35). You can't straddle the fence, calling Jesus "just a good teacher," because the Bible clearly calls him Messiah and Lord.

110.4 For more about Melchizedek, see his Profile at the end of Genesis 16. As a priest like Melchizedek, Christ will never abuse his divine position, and his reign will be forever. Jesus is more fully described as our High Priest in Hebrews 5.

111–118 Psalms 111–118 are called hallelujah psalms. "Hallelujah" means "praise the Lord" and expresses the uplifting and optimistic tone of these songs.

in giving them the heritage of the nations.
7 The works of his hands are faithful and just;
all his precepts are trustworthy.
111.8 Isa 40.8 Mt 5.18
8 They are established forever and ever,
to be performed with faithfulness and uprightness.
111.9 Lk 1.68
9 He sent redemption to his people;
he has commanded his covenant forever.
Holy and awesome is his name.
111.10 Prov 1.7,9 3.4,5; 9.10
10 The fear of the LORD is the beginning of wisdom;
all those who practice it[t] have a good understanding.
His praise endures forever.

Theme: The advantages of having faith in God. God guards the minds and actions of those who follow his commands.
Author: Anonymous

PSALM 112

1 Praise the LORD!
Happy are those who fear the LORD,
who greatly delight in his commandments.
112.2 Ps 25.13
2 Their descendants will be mighty in the land;
the generation of the upright will be blessed.
112.3 Prov 3.16,17 8.18
3 Wealth and riches are in their houses,
and their righteousness endures forever.
112.4 Job 11.17 Ps 97.11
4 They rise in the darkness as a light for the upright;
they are gracious, merciful, and righteous.
5 It is well with those who deal generously and lend,
who conduct their affairs with justice.
112.6 Ps 15.5; 55.22
6 For the righteous will never be moved;
they will be remembered forever.
112.7 Ps 56.4
7 They are not afraid of evil tidings;
their hearts are firm, secure in the LORD.
112.8 Ps 56.10,11
8 Their hearts are steady, they will not be afraid;
in the end they will look in triumph on their foes.
112.9 2 Cor 9.9 Ps 148.14
9 They have distributed freely, they have given to the poor;
their righteousness endures forever;
their horn is exalted in honor.
112.10 Mt 8.12 Lk 13.28
10 The wicked see it and are angry;
they gnash their teeth and melt away;
the desire of the wicked comes to nothing.

[t] Gk Syr: Heb *them*

111.9 The redemption here is the rescue by God of the Israelites from Egypt (see Deuteronomy 7.8; Jeremiah 31.11). *Redemption* means recovery of something or someone upon payment of a ransom. All people were being held in slavery by sin, until Jesus paid the price to free us – giving his life as a perfect sacrifice. Before Jesus offered himself as a sacrifice for sin, people were not permitted into God's presence (the most holy place); now, all believers can freely approach God's throne through prayer and have the presence of the Holy Spirit in their lives.

111.10 The only way to become truly wise is to fear (revere) God. This same thought is expressed in Proverbs 1.7–9. Too often people want to skip this step, thinking they can become wise by life experience and academic knowledge alone. But if we do not acknowledge God as the source of wisdom, then the foundation for making wise decisions is shaky, and we are doomed to mistakes and foolish choices. Always remember that the foundation for wisdom is to recognize that God is the source of wisdom and that to obey his laws is the path to wisdom.

112.1 Many blessings are available to us – honor, prosperity, security, freedom from fear (112.2–9) – if we *fear* the Lord, *trust* in him, and *delight* in obeying his commands. If you expect God's blessings, you must fear him, believe his promises, and gladly obey him.

112.5 Generosity will cure two problems that money can create. The rich man may abuse others in his desire to accumulate wealth. Generosity will eliminate that abuse. Also, the fear of losing money can be a snare. Generosity and respect for God places our trust in him, not our money, for justice and security.

112.7, 8 We all want to live without fear; our heroes are fearless people who take on all dangers and overcome them. The psalmist teaches us that *fear* of God can lead to a *fearless* life. To fear God means to respect and revere him as the almighty Lord. When we trust God completely to take care of us, we will find that our other fears – even of death itself – will subside.

112.9 "Their horn is exalted" means that their dignity is uplifted. The horn was a symbol of power just as the horns of animals represent their strength.

Theme: The scope of God's care. God's great mercy is demonstrated by his concern for the poor and the oppressed.
Author: Anonymous

PSALM 113

1 Praise the LORD!
Praise, O servants of the LORD;
praise the name of the LORD.

2 Blessed be the name of the LORD
from this time on and forevermore.
3 From the rising of the sun to its setting
the name of the LORD is to be praised.
4 The LORD is high above all nations,
and his glory above the heavens.

5 Who is like the LORD our God,
who is seated on high,
6 who looks far down
on the heavens and the earth?
7 He raises the poor from the dust,
and lifts the needy from the ash heap,
8 to make them sit with princes,
with the princes of his people.
9 He gives the barren woman a home,
making her the joyous mother of children.
Praise the LORD!

113.4 Ps 8.1; 97.9
113.5 Ps 89.6; 103.19
113.6 Ps 11.4 Isa 57.15
113.7 1 Sam 2.8

Theme: The mighty God who delivered Israel from Egypt. We can celebrate God's great work in our lives.
Author: Anonymous

PSALM 114

1 When Israel went out from Egypt,
the house of Jacob from a people of strange language,
2 Judah became God's[u] sanctuary,
Israel his dominion.

3 The sea looked and fled;
Jordan turned back.
4 The mountains skipped like rams,
the hills like lambs.

5 Why is it, O sea, that you flee?
O Jordan, that you turn back?
6 O mountains, that you skip like rams?
O hills, like lambs?

7 Tremble, O earth, at the presence of the LORD,

[u] Heb *his*

114.1 Ex 13.3
114.2 Ex 29.45,46
114.3 Ex 14.21
114.4 Ps 29.5,6
114.5 Hab 3.8

113.5–9 In God's eyes, a person's value has no relationship to his or her wealth or position on the social ladder. Many people who have excelled in God's work began in poverty or humble beginnings. God supersedes the social orders of this world, often choosing his future leaders and ambassadors from among social outcasts. Do you treat the unwanted in society as though they have value? Demonstrate by your actions that all people are valuable and useful in God's eyes.

114.7 When God gave the law at Mount Sinai, there was an earthquake (Exodus 19.18). The mountains trembled in God's presence. Even with our great technology, the seas, rivers, and mountains still present us with formidable challenges. But to God, who controls nature, they are as nothing. When observing the power of an ocean wave or the majesty of a mountain peak, think of God's greatness and glory, which are far more awesome than the natural wonders you can see. To tremble at God's presence means to recognize God's complete power and authority and our frailty by comparison.

at the presence of the God of Jacob,
114.8 Ex 17.5,6 Deut 8.15 — 8 who turns the rock into a pool of water,
the flint into a spring of water.

Theme: God is alive. He is thinking about us and caring for us, and we should put him first in our lives.
Author: Anonymous

PSALM 115

115.1 Ps 29.2 Isa 48.11 Ezek 36.22,32 — 1 Not to us, O LORD, not to us, but to your name give glory,
for the sake of your steadfast love and your faithfulness.
2 Why should the nations say,
"Where is their God?"

115.3 Ps 103.19 Dan 4.35 — 3 Our God is in the heavens;
he does whatever he pleases.
115.4 2 Kgs 19.18 — 4 Their idols are silver and gold,
the work of human hands.
5 They have mouths, but do not speak;
eyes, but do not see.
6 They have ears, but do not hear;
noses, but do not smell.
7 They have hands, but do not feel;
feet, but do not walk;
they make no sound in their throats.
8 Those who make them are like them;
so are all who trust in them.

115.9 Ps 33.20; 62.8 — 9 O Israel, trust in the LORD!
He is their help and their shield.
10 O house of Aaron, trust in the LORD!
He is their help and their shield.
115.11 Ps 103.11 135.20 — 11 You who fear the LORD, trust in the LORD!
He is their help and their shield.

115.12 Ps 98.3 128.1,4 — 12 The LORD has been mindful of us; he will bless us;
he will bless the house of Israel;
he will bless the house of Aaron;
13 he will bless those who fear the LORD,
both small and great.

115–118 Psalms 115–118 were traditionally sung at the passover meal, commemorating Israel's escape from slavery in Egypt (Exodus 11, 12).

115.1 The psalmist asked that God's name, not the nation's, be glorified. Too often we ask God to glorify his name *with* ours. For example, we may pray for help to do a good job so that our work will be noticed. Or we may ask that a presentation go well so we will get applause. There is nothing wrong with looking good or impressing others; the problem comes when we want to look good no matter what happens to God's reputation in the process. Before you pray, ask yourself, "Who will get the credit, if God answers my prayer?"

115.1, 2 This may have been written when God was allowing heathen nations to punish his people for their idolatry. Since God's people suffered, the heathen taunted them and said their God was hiding. Nothing has changed. People too often think God is missing because his people appear weak or wounded. The psalmist's people were being refined for God's purposes, and God was very much alive and in control of the refining process. God is presiding over our refinement too.

115.4-8 When the psalms were written, many people worshiped idols—statues of wood, stone, or metal. They took pride in what they could see and had contempt for what they couldn't see. Today, we still put more value in tangible objects (home, clothing, possessions) than in intangible things (spiritual growth, salvation, giving to those in need, spending time with loved ones). Those who give their whole lives to obtaining tangible objects are as foolish and empty as the idols themselves. (For more on the foolishness of idols, see Isaiah 44.9–20.)

115.8 These gods are powerless to do anything because God controls the universe, and those who worship them become just as powerless as their gods. The gods of wealth and power, though they seem strong, are really weak. They can't guarantee immunity from death, and they can't give eternal life.

115.12 "The Lord has been mindful of us" says the psalm writer. What a fantastic truth! There are many times when we feel isolated, alone, and abandoned, even by God. In reality, he sees, understands, and thinks about us. When depressed by problems or struggling with self-worth, be encouraged that God keeps you in his thoughts. If he thinks about you, surely his help is near.

14 May the LORD give you increase,
both you and your children.
15 May you be blessed by the LORD,
who made heaven and earth.

115.15
Gen 1.1; 14.19

16 The heavens are the LORD's heavens,
but the earth he has given to human beings.
17 The dead do not praise the LORD,
nor do any that go down into silence.
18 But we will bless the LORD
from this time on and forevermore.
Praise the LORD!

115.17
Ps 6.5; 31.17

Theme: Praise for being saved from certain death. Worship is a thankful response and not a repayment for what God has done.
Author: Anonymous

PSALM 116

1 I love the LORD, because he has heard
my voice and my supplications.
2 Because he inclined his ear to me,
therefore I will call on him as long as I live.
3 The snares of death encompassed me;
the pangs of Sheol laid hold on me;
I suffered distress and anguish.
4 Then I called on the name of the LORD:
"O LORD, I pray, save my life!"

116.1
Ps 18.1; 66.19

116.2
Ps 17.6; 31.2

116.3
Ps 18.4-6

5 Gracious is the LORD, and righteous;
our God is merciful.
6 The LORD protects the simple;
when I was brought low, he saved me.
7 Return, O my soul, to your rest,
for the LORD has dealt bountifully with you.

116.5
Ex 34.6

116.6
Ps 142.6
Prov 1.4

116.7
Ps 13.6
Mt 11.29

8 For you have delivered my soul from death,
my eyes from tears,
my feet from stumbling.
9 I walk before the LORD
in the land of the living.
10 I kept my faith, even when I said,
"I am greatly afflicted";
11 I said in my consternation,
"Everyone is a liar."

116.8
Ps 49.15

12 What shall I return to the LORD
for all his bounty to me?
13 I will lift up the cup of salvation
and call on the name of the LORD,
14 I will pay my vows to the LORD
in the presence of all his people.
15 Precious in the sight of the LORD

116.12
2 Chron 32.25
1 Thess 3.9

116.14
Ps 22.25; 50.14

116.15
Ps 72.14

116.1, 2 God is so responsive that you can always reach him. He bends down and listens to your prayers. This writer's love for the Lord had grown because he had experienced answers to his prayers. If you are discouraged, remember that God is near, listening carefully to every prayer, and answering each prayer in order to give you his best.

116.15 God stays close to us even in death. When someone we love is nearing death, we may become angry and feel abandoned. But believers are precious to God, and he carefully chooses the time when they are to be called into his presence. Let this truth provide comfort when you've lost a loved one. God notices and each life is valuable to him (see Matthew 10.29).

is the death of his faithful ones.
16 O LORD, I am your servant;
I am your servant, the child of your serving girl.
You have loosed my bonds.
17 I will offer to you a thanksgiving sacrifice
and call on the name of the LORD.
18 I will pay my vows to the LORD
in the presence of all his people,
19 in the courts of the house of the LORD,
in your midst, O Jerusalem.
Praise the LORD!

Theme: Another reason for praise—God's love for the whole world. We should praise God for his unlimited love.
Author: Anonymous

PSALM 117

117.1 Rom 15.11

1 Praise the LORD, all you nations!
Extol him, all you peoples!
2 For great is his steadfast love toward us,
and the faithfulness of the LORD endures forever.
Praise the LORD!

Theme: Confidence in God's eternal love. God's love is unchanging in the midst of changing situations. This gives us security.
Author: Anonymous

PSALM 118

118.1 Ps 136

1 O give thanks to the LORD, for he is good;
his steadfast love endures forever!

2 Let Israel say,
"His steadfast love endures forever."
3 Let the house of Aaron say,
"His steadfast love endures forever."
4 Let those who fear the LORD say,
"His steadfast love endures forever."

118.5 Ps 18.19
118.6 Job 19.27 Heb 13.6
118.7 Ps 54.7
118.8 2 Chron 32.7,8 Isa 57.13

5 Out of my distress I called on the LORD;
the LORD answered me and set me in a broad place.
6 With the LORD on my side I do not fear.
What can mortals do to me?
7 The LORD is on my side to help me;
I shall look in triumph on those who hate me.
8 It is better to take refuge in the LORD
than to put confidence in mortals.
9 It is better to take refuge in the LORD
than to put confidence in princes.

10 All nations surrounded me;
in the name of the LORD I cut them off!

117.1, 2 Psalm 117 is not only the shortest chapter in the Bible, but the middle chapter. Paul quotes from it in Romans 15.11 to show that God's salvation is for *all* people, not just the Jews.

117.1, 2 Have you ever said, "I can't think of anything God has done for me. How can I praise him?" This psalm gives two reasons for praising God: he is merciful, and his truth endures forever. If he did nothing else for us, he would still be worthy of our highest praise.

118.8 Pilots put confidence in their planes. Commuters place confidence in trains, cars, or buses. Each day we must put our confidence in something or someone. If you are willing to trust a plane or car to get you to your destination, are you willing to trust God to guide you here on earth and to your eternal destination? Do you trust him more than any human being? How futile it is to trust anything or anyone more than God.

11 They surrounded me, surrounded me on every side;
in the name of the LORD I cut them off!
12 They surrounded me like bees;
they blazed[v] like a fire of thorns;
in the name of the LORD I cut them off!
13 I was pushed hard,[w] so that I was falling,
but the LORD helped me.
14 The LORD is my strength and my might;
he has become my salvation.

15 There are glad songs of victory in the tents of the righteous:
"The right hand of the LORD does valiantly;
16 the right hand of the LORD is exalted;
the right hand of the LORD does valiantly."
17 I shall not die, but I shall live,
and recount the deeds of the LORD.
18 The LORD has punished me severely,
but he did not give me over to death.

19 Open to me the gates of righteousness,
that I may enter through them
and give thanks to the LORD.

20 This is the gate of the LORD;
the righteous shall enter through it.

21 I thank you that you have answered me
and have become my salvation.
22 The stone that the builders rejected
has become the chief cornerstone.
23 This is the LORD's doing;
it is marvelous in our eyes.
24 This is the day that the LORD has made;
let us rejoice and be glad in it.[x]
25 Save us, we beseech you, O LORD!
O LORD, we beseech you, give us success!

26 Blessed is the one who comes in the name of the LORD.[y]
We bless you from the house of the LORD.
27 The LORD is God,
and he has given us light.
Bind the festal procession with branches,
up to the horns of the altar.[z]

28 You are my God, and I will give thanks to you;
you are my God, I will extol you.

118.12 Deut 1.44
118.14 Ex 15.2 Isa 12.2
118.15 Lk 1.51
118.18 Jer 31.18 1 Cor 11.32 2 Cor 6.9
118.19 Isa 26.2
118.22 Mt 21.42 Mk 12.10,11 Lk 20.17 Acts 4.11 1 Pet 2.7
118.25 Ps 122.6,7
118.26 Mt 21.9 Mk 11.9 Lk 13.35 Jn 12.13
118.27 Isa 25.1 1 Pet 2.9

[v] Gk: Heb *were extinguished* [w] Gk Syr Jerome: Heb *You pushed me hard* [x] Or *in him* [y] Or *Blessed in the name of the LORD is the one who comes* [z] Meaning of Heb uncertain

118.22, 23 Jesus referred to this verse when he spoke of being rejected by his own people (Matthew 21.42; Mark 12.10, 11; Luke 20.17). Although he was rejected, Jesus is now the "cornerstone," the most important part of the church (Acts 4.11; Ephesians 2.20; 1 Peter 2.6, 7).

118.24 There are days when the last thing we want to do is rejoice. Our mood is down, our situation out of hand, our sorrow or guilt overwhelming. We can relate to the writers of the psalms who often felt this way. But no matter how low the psalmists felt, they were always honest with God. And as they talked to God, their prayers ended in praise. When you don't feel like rejoicing, tell God how you truly feel. You will find that God will give you a reason to rejoice.

118.27 "Bind the festal procession" means to join in. The "horns of the altar" were the projections from the four corners of the altar.

29 O give thanks to the LORD, for he is good,
for his steadfast love endures forever.

Theme: God's Word is true and wonderful. Stay true to God and his Word no matter how bad the world becomes. Obedience to God's laws is the only way to achieve real happiness.
Author: Anonymous, some suggest Ezra the priest

PSALM 119

119.1 Prov 11.20; 13.6
119.2 Deut 4.29 10.12; 11.13 30.2
119.4 Deut 4.13

1 Happy are those whose way is blameless,
who walk in the law of the LORD.
2 Happy are those who keep his decrees,
who seek him with their whole heart,
3 who also do no wrong,
but walk in his ways.
4 You have commanded your precepts
to be kept diligently.
5 O that my ways may be steadfast
in keeping your statutes!
6 Then I shall not be put to shame,
having my eyes fixed on all your commandments.
7 I will praise you with an upright heart,
when I learn your righteous ordinances.
8 I will observe your statutes;
do not utterly forsake me.

119.9 1 Kgs 8.25 2 Chron 6.16
119.13 Ps 40.9
119.15 Isa 58.2

9 How can young people keep their way pure?
By guarding it according to your word.
10 With my whole heart I seek you;
do not let me stray from your commandments.
11 I treasure your word in my heart,
so that I may not sin against you.
12 Blessed are you, O LORD;
teach me your statutes.
13 With my lips I declare
all the ordinances of your mouth.
14 I delight in the way of your decrees
as much as in all riches.
15 I will meditate on your precepts,
and fix my eyes on your ways.
16 I will delight in your statutes;
I will not forget your word.

17 Deal bountifully with your servant,

119.1ff This is both the longest psalm and the longest chapter in the Bible. It may have been written by Ezra after the temple was rebuilt (Ezra 6.14, 15) as a repetitive meditation on the beauty of God's Word and how it helps us stay pure and grow in faith. This psalm has 22 carefully constructed sections, each corresponding to a different letter in the Hebrew alphabet and each verse beginning with the letter of its section. Almost every verse mentions God's Word. Such repetition was common in the Hebrew culture. People did not have personal copies of the Scriptures to read as we do, so God's people memorized his Word and passed it along orally. The structure of this psalm allowed for easy memorization. Remember, God's Word, the Bible, is the only sure guide for living a pure life.

119.9 We are drowning in a sea of impurity. Everywhere we look we find temptation to lead impure lives. The psalmist asked a question that troubles us all: how do we keep clean in a filthy environment? We cannot do this on our own, but must have counsel and strength more dynamic than the tempting influences around us. Where can we find that strength and wisdom? By reading God's Word and doing what it says.

119.11 Storing God's Word in our hearts is a deterrent to sin. This alone should inspire us to memorize Scripture. But memorization alone will not keep us from sin; we must also put God's Word to work in our lives, making it a vital guide to everything we do.

119.12–18 Most of us chafe under rules, for we think they restrict us from doing what we want. At first glance, then, it may seem strange to hear the psalmist talk of rejoicing in God's laws as much as in riches. But God's laws were given to free us to be all he wants us to be. They restrict us from doing what might cripple us and keep us from being our best. God's guidelines help us follow his path and avoid paths that lead to destruction.

so that I may live and observe your word.
18 Open my eyes, so that I may behold
wondrous things out of your law.
19 I live as an alien in the land;
do not hide your commandments from me.
20 My soul is consumed with longing
for your ordinances at all times.
21 You rebuke the insolent, accursed ones,
who wander from your commandments;
22 take away from me their scorn and contempt,
for I have kept your decrees.
23 Even though princes sit plotting against me,
your servant will meditate on your statutes.
24 Your decrees are my delight,
they are my counselors.

25 My soul clings to the dust;
revive me according to your word.
26 When I told of my ways, you answered me;
teach me your statutes.
27 Make me understand the way of your precepts,
and I will meditate on your wondrous works.
28 My soul melts away for sorrow;
strengthen me according to your word.
29 Put false ways far from me;
and graciously teach me your law.
30 I have chosen the way of faithfulness;
I set your ordinances before me.
31 I cling to your decrees, O LORD;
let me not be put to shame.
32 I run the way of your commandments,
for you enlarge my understanding.

33 Teach me, O LORD, the way of your statutes,
and I will observe it to the end.
34 Give me understanding, that I may keep your law
and observe it with my whole heart.
35 Lead me in the path of your commandments,
for I delight in it.
36 Turn my heart to your decrees,
and not to selfish gain.
37 Turn my eyes from looking at vanities;
give me life in your ways.
38 Confirm to your servant your promise,

119.19 1 Chron 29.15 Heb 11.13
119.21 Deut 27.26 Ps 37.22
119.25 Ps 44.25
119.28 Ps 22.14 1 Pet 5.10
119.31 Deut 11.22
119.33 1 Chron 22.12 Ezek 44.24
119.35 Ps 25.4; 112.1
119.36 Lk 12.15 Heb 13.5
119.37 Ps 71.20
119.38 2 Sam 7.25

119.19 Almost any long trip requires a map or guide. As we travel through life, the Bible should be our road map, pointing out safe routes, obstacles to avoid, and our final destination. We must recognize ourselves as pilgrims, travelers here on earth who need to study God's map to learn the way. If we ignore the map, we will wander aimlessly through life and risk missing our real destination.

119.25 How can God's Word revive us? Our world is full of evil; God's Word revives us with the promise of victory over evil. Our world says we are worthless without beauty or possessions; God's Word gives us value by telling us that God created us and loves us. Our world is full of discouragement; God's Word encourages us. Our world has no real, lasting answers; God's Word gives satisfying, eternal answers. Read God's Word and be revived.

119.27 Our lives are cluttered with rule books, but the authors never come with us to help us follow the rules. But God does. That is the uniqueness of our Bible. God not only provides the rules and guidelines, but comes with us personally each day to help us live according to those rules. All we must do is invite him and respond to his direction.

119.36 In today's world, people most often covet money. Money represents power, influence, and success. For many people, it is a god. They think about little else. True, money can ease labor, buy certain comforts, and offer some security. But far more valuable than wealth is obedience to God, for it is a heavenly treasure rather than an earthly one (Luke 12.33). We should do what God wants regardless of the financial implications. Make the psalmist's prayer your own, asking God to help you prefer obedience to making money; it's in your own best interest in the long run.

which is for those who fear you.
39 Turn away the disgrace that I dread,
for your ordinances are good.
40 See, I have longed for your precepts;
in your righteousness give me life.

41 Let your steadfast love come to me, O LORD,
your salvation according to your promise.
42 Then I shall have an answer for those who taunt me,
for I trust in your word.
43 Do not take the word of truth utterly out of my mouth,
for my hope is in your ordinances.
119.44 Acts 26.1,2
44 I will keep your law continually,
forever and ever.
45 I shall walk at liberty,
for I have sought your precepts.
46 I will also speak of your decrees before kings,
and shall not be put to shame;
47 I find my delight in your commandments,
because I love them.
48 I revere your commandments, which I love,
and I will meditate on your statutes.

49 Remember your word to your servant,
in which you have made me hope.
50 This is my comfort in my distress,
that your promise gives me life.
119.51 Job 23.11 Jer 20.7
51 The arrogant utterly deride me,
but I do not turn away from your law.
119.52 Ps 103.18
52 When I think of your ordinances from of old,
I take comfort, O LORD.
119.53 Ex 32.19 Neh 13.25
53 Hot indignation seizes me because of the wicked,
those who forsake your law.
54 Your statutes have been my songs
wherever I make my home.
119.55 Ps 42.8; 63.6 92.2 Isa 26.9 Acts 16.25
55 I remember your name in the night, O LORD,
and keep your law.
56 This blessing has fallen to me,
for I have kept your precepts.

119.57 Ps 16.5
57 The LORD is my portion;
I promise to keep your words.
119.58 Ps 41.4
58 I implore your favor with all my heart;
be gracious to me according to your promise.
119.59 Mk 14.72 Lk 15.17
59 When I think of your ways,
I turn my feet to your decrees;
60 I hurry and do not delay
to keep your commandments.
119.61 Ps 140.5
61 Though the cords of the wicked ensnare me,
I do not forget your law.
62 At midnight I rise to praise you,
because of your righteous ordinances.
119.63 Ps 101.6
63 I am a companion of all who fear you,

119.44–46 The psalmist talks about keeping the laws and yet walking at liberty. Contrary to what we often expect, obeying God's laws frees us to be what God designed us to be. By seeking God's salvation and forgiveness, we have freedom from sin and the resulting oppressive guilt. By living God's way, we have freedom to fulfill God's plan for us.

of those who keep your precepts.
64 The earth, O LORD, is full of your steadfast love;
teach me your statutes.

65 You have dealt well with your servant,
O LORD, according to your word.
66 Teach me good judgment and knowledge,
for I believe in your commandments.
67 Before I was humbled I went astray,
but now I keep your word.
68 You are good and do good;
teach me your statutes.
69 The arrogant smear me with lies,
but with my whole heart I keep your precepts.
70 Their hearts are fat and gross,
but I delight in your law.
71 It is good for me that I was humbled,
so that I might learn your statutes.
72 The law of your mouth is better to me
than thousands of gold and silver pieces.

73 Your hands have made and fashioned me;
give me understanding that I may learn your commandments.
74 Those who fear you shall see me and rejoice,
because I have hoped in your word.
75 I know, O LORD, that your judgments are right,
and that in faithfulness you have humbled me.
76 Let your steadfast love become my comfort
according to your promise to your servant.
77 Let your mercy come to me, that I may live;
for your law is my delight.
78 Let the arrogant be put to shame,
because they have subverted me with guile;
as for me, I will meditate on your precepts.
79 Let those who fear you turn to me,
so that they may know your decrees.
80 May my heart be blameless in your statutes,
so that I may not be put to shame.

81 My soul languishes for your salvation;
I hope in your word.
82 My eyes fail with watching for your promise;
I ask, "When will you comfort me?"
83 For I have become like a wineskin in the smoke,
yet I have not forgotten your statutes.
84 How long must your servant endure?
When will you judge those who persecute me?
85 The arrogant have dug pitfalls for me;
they flout your law.
86 All your commandments are enduring;
I am persecuted without cause; help me!
87 They have almost made an end of me on earth;
but I have not forsaken your precepts.
88 In your steadfast love spare my life,
so that I may keep the decrees of your mouth.

89 The LORD exists forever;
your word is firmly fixed in heaven.

119.64 Ps 33.5
119.66 Phil 1.9
119.67 Jer 31.18,19 Heb 12.5-11
119.68 Deut 30.5 Ps 86.5; 125.4
119.70 Isa 6.10 Jer 5.28
119.71 Prov 8.10,11,19
119.73 Job 31.15 Ps 139.15,16
119.74 Ps 35.27
119.75 Heb 12.10
119.82 Isa 38.14 Lam 2.11
119.83 Job 30.30
119.84 Ps 39.4 Rev 6.10
119.85 Ps 35.19; 57.6 Jer 18.22
119.89 Isa 40.8 Mt 24.35 1 Pet 1.25

119.90 Ps 89.1,2 104.2-4; 148.6 Jer 31.35

90 Your faithfulness endures to all generations;
you have established the earth, and it stands fast.
91 By your appointment they stand today,
for all things are your servants.
92 If your law had not been my delight,
I would have perished in my misery.
93 I will never forget your precepts,
for by them you have given me life.
94 I am yours; save me,
for I have sought your precepts.

119.95 Ps 40.14 Isa 32.7

95 The wicked lie in wait to destroy me,
but I consider your decrees.
96 I have seen a limit to all perfection,
but your commandment is exceedingly broad.

97 Oh, how I love your law!
It is my meditation all day long.

119.98 Deut 4.6

98 Your commandment makes me wiser than my enemies,
for it is always with me.
99 I have more understanding than all my teachers,
for your decrees are my meditation.

119.100 Job 32.7-9

100 I understand more than the aged,
for I keep your precepts.
101 I hold back my feet from every evil way,
in order to keep your word.

119.102 Deut 17.20 Josh 23.6 Ps 19.10 Prov 24.13,14

102 I do not turn away from your ordinances,
for you have taught me.
103 How sweet are your words to my taste,
sweeter than honey to my mouth!
104 Through your precepts I get understanding;
therefore I hate every false way.

105 Your word is a lamp to my feet
and a light to my path.
106 I have sworn an oath and confirmed it,
to observe your righteous ordinances.
107 I am severely afflicted;
give me life, O LORD, according to your word.

119.108 Hos 14.2 Heb 13.15

108 Accept my offerings of praise, O LORD,
and teach me your ordinances.
109 I hold my life in my hand continually,
but I do not forget your law.

119.110 Ps 91.3; 140.5

110 The wicked have laid a snare for me,
but I do not stray from your precepts.

119.111 Deut 33.4

111 Your decrees are my heritage forever;
they are the joy of my heart.
112 I incline my heart to perform your statutes
forever, to the end.

119.113 1 Kgs 18.21

113 I hate the double-minded,

119.97–104 God's Word makes us wise. True wisdom goes beyond amassing knowledge, it is *applying* knowledge in a life-changing way. Wisdom comes from allowing what God teaches to guide us.

119.105 To walk safely in the woods at night, we need a light to avoid tripping over tree roots or falling into holes. In this life, we walk through a dark forest of evil. But the Bible can be our light to show us the way ahead so we won't stumble as we walk. It reveals the entangling roots of false values and philosophies.

119.113 Double-minded people cannot make up their minds between good and evil. But when it comes to obeying God, there is no middle ground. Choose to obey God, and say with the psalmist, "I love your law."

but I love your law.
114 You are my hiding place and my shield;
I hope in your word.
115 Go away from me, you evildoers,
that I may keep the commandments of my God.
116 Uphold me according to your promise, that I may live,
and let me not be put to shame in my hope.
117 Hold me up, that I may be safe
and have regard for your statutes continually.
118 You spurn all who go astray from your statutes;
for their cunning is in vain.
119 All the wicked of the earth you count as dross;
therefore I love your decrees.
120 My flesh trembles for fear of you,
and I am afraid of your judgments.

121 I have done what is just and right;
do not leave me to my oppressors.
122 Guarantee your servant's well-being;
do not let the godless oppress me.
123 My eyes fail from watching for your salvation,
and for the fulfillment of your righteous promise.
124 Deal with your servant according to your steadfast love,
and teach me your statutes.
125 I am your servant; give me understanding,
so that I may know your decrees.
126 It is time for the LORD to act,
for your law has been broken.
127 Truly I love your commandments
more than gold, more than fine gold.
128 Truly I direct my steps by all your precepts;[a]
I hate every false way.

129 Your decrees are wonderful;
therefore my soul keeps them.
130 The unfolding of your words gives light;
it imparts understanding to the simple.
131 With open mouth I pant,
because I long for your commandments.
132 Turn to me and be gracious to me,
as is your custom toward those who love your name.
133 Keep my steps steady according to your promise,
and never let iniquity have dominion over me.
134 Redeem me from human oppression,
that I may keep your precepts.
135 Make your face shine upon your servant,
and teach me your statutes.
136 My eyes shed streams of tears
because your law is not kept.

137 You are righteous, O LORD,
and your judgments are right.

119.114 Ps 31.20; 61.4
119.115 Ps 6.8; 139.19 Mt 7.23
119.116 Ps 25.2,20 Rom 5.5; 9.33 Phil 1.20
119.117 Ps 12.5
119.119 Isa 1.22,25 Ezek 22.18,19
119.121 2 Sam 8.15 Job 29.14
119.124 Ps 51.1; 106.45 109.26
119.126 Jer 18.23 Ezek 31.11
119.128 Ps 19.8
119.133 Ps 19.13
119.134 Ps 142.6
119.135 Num 6.25 Ps 67.1
119.136 Jer 9.1,18 14.17 Lam 3.48
119.137 Dan 9.7,14

[a] Gk Jerome: Meaning of Heb uncertain

119.125 Faith comes alive when we apply Scripture to our daily tasks and concerns. With the psalmist, we need the understanding and the desire to apply Scripture where we need help. The Bible is like medicine—it goes to work only when you apply it to the affected areas. As you read the Bible, be on the alert for lessons, commands, or examples that you can put into practice.

138 You have appointed your decrees in righteousness
and in all faithfulness.

119.139
Ps 69.9

139 My zeal consumes me
because my foes forget your words.
140 Your promise is well tried,
and your servant loves it.
141 I am small and despised,
yet I do not forget your precepts.
142 Your righteousness is an everlasting righteousness,
and your law is the truth.
143 Trouble and anguish have come upon me,
but your commandments are my delight.

119.144
Ps 19.9

144 Your decrees are righteous forever;
give me understanding that I may live.

145 With my whole heart I cry; answer me, O LORD.
I will keep your statutes.
146 I cry to you; save me,
that I may observe your decrees.
147 I rise before dawn and cry for help;
I put my hope in your words.
148 My eyes are awake before each watch of the night,
that I may meditate on your promise.
149 In your steadfast love hear my voice;
O LORD, in your justice preserve my life.
150 Those who persecute me with evil purpose draw near;
they are far from your law.

119.151
Ps 34.18
Isa 50.8

151 Yet you are near, O LORD,
and all your commandments are true.
152 Long ago I learned from your decrees
that you have established them forever.

153 Look on my misery and rescue me,
for I do not forget your law.

119.154
Ps 35.1
Mic 7.9

154 Plead my cause and redeem me;
give me life according to your promise.
155 Salvation is far from the wicked,
for they do not seek your statutes.

119.156
2 Sam 24.14

156 Great is your mercy, O LORD;
give me life according to your justice.
157 Many are my persecutors and my adversaries,
yet I do not swerve from your decrees.

119.158
Ps 139.21
Isa 24.16

158 I look at the faithless with disgust,
because they do not keep your commands.
159 Consider how I love your precepts;
preserve my life according to your steadfast love.
160 The sum of your word is truth;
and every one of your righteous ordinances endures forever.

119.161
1 Sam 26.18

161 Princes persecute me without cause,
but my heart stands in awe of your words.

119.162
1 Sam 30.16

162 I rejoice at your word
like one who finds great spoil.

119.163
Ps 31.6

163 I hate and abhor falsehood,

119.160 One of God's characteristics is truthfulness. He embodies perfect truth, and therefore his Word cannot lie. It is true and dependable for guidance and help (see John 17.14–17). The Bible is completely true and trustworthy.

but I love your law.
164 Seven times a day I praise you
for your righteous ordinances.
165 Great peace have those who love your law;
nothing can make them stumble.
166 I hope for your salvation, O LORD,
and I fulfill your commandments. **119.166** Gen 49.18
167 My soul keeps your decrees;
I love them exceedingly.
168 I keep your precepts and decrees,
for all my ways are before you. **119.168** Ps 139.3 Prov 5.21

169 Let my cry come before you, O LORD;
give me understanding according to your word. **119.169** Ps 18.6
170 Let my supplication come before you;
deliver me according to your promise. **119.170** Ps 22.20; 31.2 140.6
171 My lips will pour forth praise,
because you teach me your statutes.
172 My tongue will sing of your promise,
for all your commandments are right.
173 Let your hand be ready to help me,
for I have chosen your precepts. **119.173** Josh 24.22 Lk 10.42
174 I long for your salvation, O LORD,
and your law is my delight.
175 Let me live that I may praise you,
and let your ordinances help me. **119.175** Isa 55.3
176 I have gone astray like a lost sheep; seek out your servant,
for I do not forget your commandments. **119.176** Isa 53.6 Lk 15.4

Theme: A prayer for deliverance from false accusers. All believers must live with the tension of being in the world but not belonging to it.
Author: Anonymous, many suggest Hezekiah

PSALM 120

A Song of Ascents.

1 In my distress I cry to the LORD,
that he may answer me: **120.1ff** Ps 18.6; 66.14 102.2
2 "Deliver me, O LORD,
from lying lips,
from a deceitful tongue."

3 What shall be given to you?
And what more shall be done to you,
you deceitful tongue?
4 A warrior's sharp arrows,
with glowing coals of the broom tree! **120.4** Ps 45.15

5 Woe is me, that I am an alien in Meshech,
that I must live among the tents of Kedar. **120.5** Jer 2.10; 49.28
6 Too long have I had my dwelling

119.165 Modern society longs for peace of mind. Here is clear-cut instruction on how to realize this: if we love God and obey his laws, we will have "great peace." Trust in God who alone stands above the pressures of daily life and gives us full assurance.

120–134 Psalms 120–134 are called "Pilgrim Psalms" or "Songs of Ascent." They were sung by those who journeyed to the temple for the annual festivals. Each psalm is a "step" along the journey. Psalm 120 begins the journey in a distant land in hostile surroundings; Psalm 122 pictures the pilgrims arriving in Jerusalem; and the rest of the psalms move toward the temple and mention the various characteristics of God associated with it.

120.5, 6 Meshech was a nation far to the north of Israel; Kedar a nation to the southeast. Both were known for being warlike and barbarian. Because the psalmist couldn't have been in both places at once, he was lamenting that he felt far from home and surrounded by heathen people.

among those who hate peace.
7 I am for peace;
but when I speak,
they are for war.

Theme: We can depend upon God for help. Pilgrims must travel through lonely country to their destination; they are protected, not by anything created, but by the Creator of everything.
Author: Anonymous, many suggest Hezekiah

PSALM 121

A Song of Ascents.

1 I lift up my eyes to the hills—
from where will my help come?
2 My help comes from the LORD,
who made heaven and earth.

121.3 Ps 66.9
3 He will not let your foot be moved;
he who keeps you will not slumber.
4 He who keeps Israel
will neither slumber nor sleep.

121.5 Ps 91.4
5 The LORD is your keeper;
the LORD is your shade at your right hand.
121.6 Rev 7.16
6 The sun shall not strike you by day,
nor the moon by night.

121.7 Ps 91.10-12
7 The LORD will keep you from all evil;
he will keep your life.
8 The LORD will keep
your going out and your coming in
from this time on and forevermore.

Theme: Stepping into the presence of God. What Jerusalem was for the Israelites, the church is to the believer.
Author: David

PSALM 122

A Song of Ascents. Of David.

122.1 Isa 2.3 Zech 8.21
1 I was glad when they said to me,
"Let us go to the house of the LORD!"
2 Our feet are standing
within your gates, O Jerusalem.

3 Jerusalem—built as a city
that is bound firmly together.
4 To it the tribes go up,
the tribes of the LORD,
as was decreed for Israel,
to give thanks to the name of the LORD.

120.7 Peacemaking is not always popular. Some people prefer to fight for what they believe in. The glory of battle is in the hope of winning, but someone must be a loser. The glory of peacemaking is that it may actually produce two winners. Peacemaking is God's way, so we should carefully and prayerfully attempt to be peacemakers.

121.1ff This song expresses assurance and hope in God's protection day and night. He not only made the hills but heaven and earth as well. We should never trust a lesser power than God himself. But not only is he all-powerful, he also watches over us. Nothing detracts or deters him. We are safe. We never outgrow our need for God's untiring watch over our lives.

122.1 Going to God's house can be a chore or a delight. For the psalmist, it was a delight. As a pilgrim attending one of the three great religious festivals, he was excited to worship with God's people in God's house. We may find worship a chore if we have unconfessed sin or if our love for God has cooled. But if we are close to God and enjoy his presence, we will be eager to worship and praise him. Our attitude toward God will determine our view of worship.

5 For there the thrones for judgment were set up,
the thrones of the house of David.

6 Pray for the peace of Jerusalem:
"May they prosper who love you.
7 Peace be within your walls,
and security within your towers."
8 For the sake of my relatives and friends
I will say, "Peace be within you."
9 For the sake of the house of the LORD our God,
I will seek your good.

122.5 Deut 17.8 2 Chron 19.8

122.6 Ps 102.14

122.7 Isa 62.6

122.8 Ps 133.1

Theme: Look to God for mercy. We are encouraged to be attentive to God's leading.
Author: Anonymous, many suggest Hezekiah

PSALM 123

A Song of Ascents.

1 To you I lift up my eyes,
O you who are enthroned in the heavens!
2 As the eyes of servants
look to the hand of their master,
as the eyes of a maid
to the hand of her mistress,
so our eyes look to the LORD our God,
until he has mercy upon us.

3 Have mercy upon us, O LORD, have mercy upon us,
for we have had more than enough of contempt.
4 Our soul has had more than its fill
of the scorn of those who are at ease,
of the contempt of the proud.

123.1 Ps 11.4; 141.8

123.2 Mal 1.6

123.3 Neh 4.4 Ps 4.1; 51.1 79.4; 119.22

Theme: God delivers us from those who seek to destroy us. God is on the side of those who seek him.
Author: David, probably written after his defeat of the Philistines (2 Samuel 5.17–25)

PSALM 124

A Song of Ascents. Of David.

1 If it had not been the LORD who was on our side
—let Israel now say—
2 if it had not been the LORD who was on our side,
when our enemies attacked us,
3 then they would have swallowed us up alive,
when their anger was kindled against us;
4 then the flood would have swept us away,
the torrent would have gone over us;
5 then over us would have gone
the raging waters.

124.2 Ps 56.1; 138.7

124.4 Ps 18.16; 69.2

122.5 The "thrones for judgment" are the courts of justice by the city gate. In Bible times, the elders in a city sat to hear cases and administer justice at the city gate (Ruth 4.1, 2). Sometimes the king himself would sit at the gate to meet his subjects and make legal decisions (2 Samuel 19.8).

122.6–9 The psalmist was not praying for his own peace and prosperity, but for that of his fellow citizens of Jerusalem. This is intercessory prayer, prayer on behalf of others. Too often we are quick to pray for our own needs and desires, and omit interceding for others. Will you intercede for someone in need today?

122.6–9 The peace sought in these verses is much more than the mere absence of conflict. It suggests completeness, health, justice, prosperity, and protection. The world cannot provide this peace. Real peace comes from faith in God because he alone embodies all the characteristics of peace. To find peace of mind and peace with others, you must find peace with God.

123.1ff The psalmist lifted his eyes to God, waiting and watching for him to send his mercy. The more he waited, the more he cried out to God, because he knew that the evil and proud offered no help—they had only contempt for God.

6 Blessed be the LORD,
who has not given us
as prey to their teeth.

124.7 Ps 91.3; 141.10

7 We have escaped like a bird
from the snare of the fowlers;
the snare is broken,
and we have escaped.

8 Our help is in the name of the LORD,
who made heaven and earth.

Theme: God is our Protector. The mountains around Jerusalem symbolize God's protection for his people.
Author: Anonymous, many suggest Hezekiah

PSALM 125

A Song of Ascents.

125.1 Ps 46.5

1 Those who trust in the LORD are like Mount Zion,
which cannot be moved, but abides forever.
2 As the mountains surround Jerusalem,
so the LORD surrounds his people,
from this time on and forevermore.

125.3 1 Sam 24.10 Prov 22.8 Isa 14.5

3 For the scepter of wickedness shall not rest
on the land allotted to the righteous,
so that the righteous might not stretch out
their hands to do wrong.
4 Do good, O LORD, to those who are good,
and to those who are upright in their hearts.

125.5 Gal 6.16

5 But those who turn aside to their own crooked ways
the LORD will lead away with evildoers.
Peace be upon Israel!

Theme: God does great things. His power not only releases us from sin's captive hold, but brings us back to him.
Author: Anonymous, probably written to celebrate the exiles' return from captivity (Ezra 1)

PSALM 126

A Song of Ascents.

126.1 Jer 29.14

1 When the LORD restored the fortunes of Zion,[b]
we were like those who dream.
2 Then our mouth was filled with laughter,
and our tongue with shouts of joy;
then it was said among the nations,
"The LORD has done great things for them."
3 The LORD has done great things for us,
and we rejoiced.

126.4 Isa 35.6; 43.19

4 Restore our fortunes, O LORD,
like the watercourses in the Negeb.

[b] Or *brought back those who returned to Zion*

124.7, 8 Do you ever feel trapped by overwhelming odds? David compared this feeling to that of a bird outwitted and snared by a hunter. With God, there is always a way out because he is the Creator of all that exists. No problem is beyond his ability to solve; no circumstance is too difficult for him. We can turn to the Creator for help in our time of need, for he is on our side. God will provide a way out; we need only trust him and look for it.

125.1 Have you ever known people who were drawn to every new fad or idea? Such people are inconsistent and therefore unreliable. The secret to consistency is to trust in God, because he never changes. He is completely reliable and will keep us steady.

125.3 Although the psalmist wrote, "The scepter of wickedness shall not rest on the land allotted to the righteous," often in Israel's history the nation had to put up with evil rulers. The psalmist was expressing what will ultimately happen when God executes his final judgment. Human sinfulness often ruins God's ideal on earth, but that doesn't mean God has lost control. Evil prevails only as long as God allows.

5 May those who sow in tears
reap with shouts of joy. 126.5 Ps 80.5 Gal 6.9
6 Those who go out weeping,
bearing the seed for sowing,
shall come home with shouts of joy,
carrying their sheaves.

Theme: Life without God is senseless. All of life's work—building a home, establishing a career, and raising a family—must have God as the foundation.
Author: Solomon

PSALM 127

A Song of Ascents. Of Solomon.

1 Unless the LORD builds the house,
those who build it labor in vain. 127.1 Ps 78.69
Unless the LORD guards the city,
the guard keeps watch in vain.
2 It is in vain that you rise up early
and go late to rest, 127.2 Gen 3.17 Job 11.18,19 Eccles 5.12
eating the bread of anxious toil;
for he gives sleep to his beloved.[c]

3 Sons are indeed a heritage from the LORD,
the fruit of the womb a reward. 127.3 Deut 28.4
4 Like arrows in the hand of a warrior
are the sons of one's youth.
5 Happy is the man who has
his quiver full of them.
He shall not be put to shame
when he speaks with his enemies in the gate.

Theme: God, the true head of the home. This is called the marriage prayer because it was often sung at Israelite marriages. God will reward your devotion to him with inner peace.
Author: Anonymous, many suggest Hezekiah

PSALM 128

A Song of Ascents.

1 Happy is everyone who fears the LORD,
who walks in his ways.
2 You shall eat the fruit of the labor of your hands;
you shall be happy, and it shall go well with you. 128.2 Eccles 8.12

[c] *Or for he provides for his beloved during sleep*

126.5, 6 God's capacity for restoring life is beyond our understanding. Forests burn down and are able to grow back. Broken bones heal. Even grief is not a permanent condition. Our tears can be seeds that will grow into a harvest of joy because God is able to bring good out of tragedy. When burdened by sorrow, know that your times of grief will end and that you will again find joy. We must be patient as we wait. God's great harvest of joy is coming!

127.1 Families establish homes and watchmen guard cities, but both these activities are futile unless God is with them. A family without God can never experience the spiritual bond God brings to relationships. A city without God will crumble from evil and corruption on the inside. Don't make the mistake of leaving God out of your life—if you do, all your accomplishments will be futile. Make God your highest priority, and let him do the building.

127.2 God is not against human effort. Hard work honors God (Proverbs 31.10–29). But working to the exclusion of rest or to the neglect of family may be a cover-up for an inability to trust God to provide for our needs. We all need adequate rest and times of spiritual refreshment. On the other hand, this verse is not an excuse to be lazy (Proverbs 18.9). Be careful to maintain a balance: work while trusting God, and also rest while trusting him.

127.3–5 Children are too often seen as liabilities rather than assets. But the Bible calls children "a heritage from the Lord," a reward. We can learn valuable lessons from their inquisitive minds and trusting spirits. Those who view children as a distraction or nuisance should instead see them as an opportunity to shape the future. We dare not treat them as an inconvenience when God values them so highly.

128.1ff The psalmist wrote that a good family life is a reward for following God. The values outlined in God's Word include love, service, honesty, integrity, and prayer. These help all relationships, and they are especially vital to home life. Is your home life heavenly or hectic? Reading and obeying God's Word is a good place to start to make your family all that it can be.

128.3 Ps 52.8

3 Your wife will be like a fruitful vine
within your house;
your children will be like olive shoots
around your table.
4 Thus shall the man be blessed
who fears the LORD.

128.5 Ps 122.9; 134.3

5 The LORD bless you from Zion.
May you see the prosperity of Jerusalem
all the days of your life.

128.6 Gen 48.11

6 May you see your children's children.
Peace be upon Israel!

Theme: Confidence in times of persecution. God will bring us through the tough times.
Author: Anonymous, many suggest Hezekiah

PSALM 129

A Song of Ascents.

129.1 Ex 1.11; Jer 22.21; Hos 2.15; 11.1
129.2 Jer 15.20; Mt 16.17; 2 Cor 4.8,9

1 "Often have they attacked me from my youth"
—let Israel now say—
2 "often have they attacked me from my youth,
yet they have not prevailed against me.
3 The plowers plowed on my back;
they made their furrows long."
4 The LORD is righteous;
he has cut the cords of the wicked.

129.5 Ps 71.13
129.6 2 Kgs 19.26

5 May all who hate Zion
be put to shame and turned backward.
6 Let them be like the grass on the housetops
that withers before it grows up,
7 with which reapers do not fill their hands
or binders of sheaves their arms,
8 while those who pass by do not say,
"The blessing of the LORD be upon you!
We bless you in the name of the LORD!"

Theme: Assurance of the Lord's forgiveness.
God will surely forgive us if we confess our sins to him.
Author: Anonymous, many suggest Hezekiah

PSALM 130

A Song of Ascents.

130.1 Ps 42.7; 69.2

1 Out of the depths I cry to you, O LORD.
2 Lord, hear my voice!
Let your ears be attentive
to the voice of my supplications!

130.3 Neh 9.17

3 If you, O LORD, should mark iniquities,

129.2 The people of Israel were persecuted from their earliest days, but never destroyed completely. The same is true of the church. Christians have faced times of severe persecution, but the church has never been destroyed. As Jesus said to Peter, "On this rock I will build my church, and the gates of Hades will not prevail against it" (Matthew 16.18). When you face persecution and discrimination, take courage—the church will never be destroyed.

129.3 This verse foreshadows Jesus' unjust punishment before his death. He endured horrible lashes from the whip of his tormentors, which indeed made "furrows" on his back (John 19.1).

130.1, 2 In the depths of despair, the psalmist cried out to God. Despair makes us feel isolated and distant from God, but this is precisely when we need God most. When we feel overwhelmed by a problem, feeling sorry for ourselves will only increase feelings of hopelessness; but crying out to God turns our attention to the only one who can really help.

130.3, 4 Marking iniquities—holding a grudge—is like building a wall between you and another person. God never holds a grudge; when he forgives, he forgives completely, tearing down any wall between us and him. When you pray, realize that God is holding nothing against you. His lines of communication are completely open.

Lord, who could stand?
4 But there is forgiveness with you,
so that you may be revered.

5 I wait for the LORD, my soul waits, 130.5 Isa 8.17
and in his word I hope;
6 my soul waits for the Lord
more than those who watch for the morning,
more than those who watch for the morning.

7 O Israel, hope in the LORD! 130.7 Ps 103.4
For with the LORD there is steadfast love,
and with him is great power to redeem.
8 It is he who will redeem Israel 130.8 Lk 1.68
from all its iniquities.

Theme: Trust and contentment. Quiet trust in God is the basis for our contentment.
Author: David

PSALM 131

A Song of Ascents. Of David.

1 O LORD, my heart is not lifted up, 131.1 Rom 12.16
my eyes are not raised too high;
I do not occupy myself with things
too great and too marvelous for me.
2 But I have calmed and quieted my soul, 131.2 Ps 62.1
like a weaned child with its mother;
my soul is like the weaned child that is with me.[d]

3 O Israel, hope in the LORD
from this time on and forevermore.

Theme: Honor God and he will honor you. The psalmist reflects upon that great day when the ark of the covenant was brought to Jerusalem and praises God for his promise to perpetuate David's line.
Author: Anonymous

PSALM 132

A Song of Ascents.

1 O LORD, remember in David's favor
all the hardships he endured;
2 how he swore to the LORD 132.2 1 Kgs 8.17 1 Chron 22.7 Acts 7.46 Isa 49.26
and vowed to the Mighty One of Jacob,
3 "I will not enter my house
or get into my bed;
4 I will not give sleep to my eyes
or slumber to my eyelids,
5 until I find a place for the LORD,
a dwelling place for the Mighty One of Jacob."

[d] *Or my soul within me is like a weaned child*

131.1, 2 Pride results from overvaluing ourselves and undervaluing others. It leads to restlessness because it makes us dissatisfied with what we have and concerned about what everyone else is doing. It keeps us always hungering for more attention and adoration. By contrast, humility puts others first and allows us to be content with God's leading in our lives. Such contentment gives us security so that we no longer have to prove ourselves to others. Let humility and trust affect your perspective and give you the strength and freedom to serve God and others.

132.2–5 When David became king, he built a beautiful palace, but he was troubled that the ark of the covenant, the symbol of God's presence among his people (Exodus 25.10–22), remained in a tent (2 Samuel 6.17; 7.1–17). This so bothered David that he couldn't sleep until he corrected the situation. He began to lay the plans for the temple to house the ark. We must live so close to God that we become restless until God's will is accomplished through us.

132.6 Gen 35.19; 1 Sam 7.1
132.7 1 Chron 28.2; Ps 5.7; 99.5
132.8 Num 10.35; 2 Chron 6.41; Ps 78.61
132.9 Job 29.14; Ps 149.5
132.11 2 Sam 7.12-16; 2 Chron 6.16
132.12 Lk 1.32; Acts 2.30
132.13 Ps 78.68
132.14 Mt 23.21
132.15 Ps 107.9

6 We heard of it in Ephrathah;
we found it in the fields of Jaar.
7 "Let us go to his dwelling place;
let us worship at his footstool."

8 Rise up, O LORD, and go to your resting place,
you and the ark of your might.
9 Let your priests be clothed with righteousness,
and let your faithful shout for joy.
10 For your servant David's sake
do not turn away the face of your anointed one.

11 The LORD swore to David a sure oath
from which he will not turn back:
"One of the sons of your body
I will set on your throne.
12 If your sons keep my covenant
and my decrees that I shall teach them,
their sons also, forevermore,
shall sit on your throne."

13 For the LORD has chosen Zion;
he has desired it for his habitation:
14 "This is my resting place forever;
here I will reside, for I have desired it.
15 I will abundantly bless its provisions;
I will satisfy its poor with bread.
16 Its priests I will clothe with salvation,
and its faithful will shout for joy.
17 There I will cause a horn to sprout up for David;
I have prepared a lamp for my anointed one.
18 His enemies I will clothe with disgrace,
but on him, his crown will gleam."

Theme: The joy of harmonious relationships
Author: David

PSALM 133

A Song of Ascents.

133.2 Ex 30.25,30; Lev 8.12

1 How very good and pleasant it is
when kindred live together in unity!
2 It is like the precious oil on the head,
running down upon the beard,

132.12 The promise that David's descendants would be on the throne forever is found in 2 Samuel 7.8–29. This promise had two parts: (1) David's descendants would perpetually rule over Israel as long as they followed God, and (2) David's royal line would never end. The first part was conditional; as long as the kings obeyed God, their dynasty continued. The second part of the promise is unconditional. It was fulfilled in Jesus Christ, a descendant of David, who reigns forever.

132.17, 18 The "horn to sprout up for David" refers to one of his mighty descendants. David's son, Solomon, was indeed a glorious king (1 Kings 3.10–14); but these verses look ahead even further to another descendant of David, Jesus the Messiah (Matthew 1.17). The power, might, and glory of the Messiah will last forever.

133.1–3 David stated that unity is pleasant and precious. Unfortunately, unity does not abound in the church as it should. People disagree and cause division over unimportant issues. Some delight in causing tension by discrediting others. Unity is important because (1) it makes the church a positive example to the world and helps draw others to us; (2) it helps us cooperate as a body of believers as God meant us to, giving us a foretaste of heaven; (3) it renews and revitalizes ministry because there is less tension to sap our energy.

Living in unity does not mean we will agree on everything; there will be many opinions just as there are many notes in a musical chord. But we must agree on our purpose in life – to work together for God. Our outward expression of unity will reflect our inward unity of purpose.

133.2 The oil was used by Moses to anoint Aaron the first high priest of Israel (Exodus 29.7) and to dedicate all the priests to God's service. Brotherly unity, like the anointing oil, shows that we are dedicated to serving God wholeheartedly.

on the beard of Aaron,
running down over the collar of his robes.
3 It is like the dew of Hermon,
which falls on the mountains of Zion.
For there the LORD ordained his blessing,
life forevermore.

133.3
Deut 4.48; 28.8

Theme: Worship God and experience the joy of his blessings
Author: Anonymous, some suggest Hezekiah

PSALM 134

A Song of Ascents.

1 Come, bless the LORD, all you servants of the LORD,
who stand by night in the house of the LORD!
2 Lift up your hands to the holy place,
and bless the LORD.

3 May the LORD, maker of heaven and earth,
bless you from Zion.

134.1
Deut 10.8
1 Chron 9.33
2 Chron 29.11

Theme: A hymn of praise. This psalm contrasts the greatness of God with the vanity of idols. The heathen worship idols while God's people worship the living God.
Author: Anonymous

PSALM 135

1 Praise the LORD!
Praise the name of the LORD;
give praise, O servants of the LORD,
2 you that stand in the house of the LORD,
in the courts of the house of our God.
3 Praise the LORD, for the LORD is good;
sing to his name, for he is gracious.
4 For the LORD has chosen Jacob for himself,
Israel as his own possession.

5 For I know that the LORD is great;
our Lord is above all gods.
6 Whatever the LORD pleases he does,
in heaven and on earth,
in the seas and all deeps.
7 He it is who makes the clouds rise at the end of the earth;
he makes lightnings for the rain
and brings out the wind from his storehouses.

8 He it was who struck down the firstborn of Egypt,
both human beings and animals;
9 he sent signs and wonders
into your midst, O Egypt,
against Pharaoh and all his servants.
10 He struck down many nations

135.2
Ps 116.19

135.3
Ps 68.4; 100.5

135.4
Ex 19.5
Deut 7.6; 10.15
1 Pet 2.9

135.5
Ps 48.1; 97.9

135.7
Job 38.25,26
Jer 51.16
Zech 10.1

135.9
Deut 6.22

135.10
Ps 136.17-21

133.3 Mount Hermon is the tallest mountain in Palestine, located northeast of the Sea of Galilee.

134.1–3 Why is an entire psalm aimed directly at a very small group—the temple watchmen? Singing this psalm, the last of the "songs of ascent" (Psalms 120–134), the worshipers ascend the hill where the temple sits and see the guards who protect it day and night. They view the guards' work as an act of praise to God, done reverently and responsibly. Make your job or your responsibility in the church an act of praise by doing it with reverence to God. Honor him by the quality of your work and the attitude of service you bring to it.

134.3 In this verse Zion is another name for Jerusalem.

135.4 That Israel was a chosen people reflects God's commission to the nation in Deuteronomy 7.6–8, and in Peter's sermon to the church in 1 Peter 2.9. God treasures us. He gives his love and mercy to all those who believe in him.

and killed mighty kings—
11 Sihon, king of the Amorites,
and Og, king of Bashan,
and all the kingdoms of Canaan—
12 and gave their land as a heritage,
a heritage to his people Israel.

13 Your name, O LORD, endures forever,
your renown, O LORD, throughout all ages.
14 For the LORD will vindicate his people,
and have compassion on his servants.

15 The idols of the nations are silver and gold,
the work of human hands.
16 They have mouths, but they do not speak;
they have eyes, but they do not see;
17 they have ears, but they do not hear,
and there is no breath in their mouths.
18 Those who make them
and all who trust them
shall become like them.

19 O house of Israel, bless the LORD!
O house of Aaron, bless the LORD!
20 O house of Levi, bless the LORD!
You that fear the LORD, bless the LORD!
21 Blessed be the LORD from Zion,
he who resides in Jerusalem.
Praise the LORD!

135.11 Num 21.33-35 Josh 12.7-24
135.13 Ex 3.15
135.14 Deut 32.36 Ps 106.45
135.15 Ps 115.4-8

Theme: The never-ending story of God's love.
God deserves our praise because his endless love never fails.
Author: Anonymous

PSALM 136

1 O give thanks to the LORD, for he is good,
for his steadfast love endures forever.
2 O give thanks to the God of gods,
for his steadfast love endures forever.
3 O give thanks to the Lord of lords,
for his steadfast love endures forever;

4 who alone does great wonders,
for his steadfast love endures forever;
5 who by understanding made the heavens,
for his steadfast love endures forever;
6 who spread out the earth on the waters,
for his steadfast love endures forever;
7 who made the great lights,
for his steadfast love endures forever;
8 the sun to rule over the day,

136.1 1 Chron 16.41 2 Chron 20.21
136.2 Deut 10.17
136.4 Ps 72.18
136.6 Ps 24.2
136.7 Ps 74.16
136.8 Gen 1.16

135.14–18 Those who worshiped idols were as blind and insensitive as the idols themselves. They couldn't see or hear what God had to say. In subtle, imperceptible ways we become like the idols we worship. If the true God is your God, you will become more like him as you worship him. What are your goals? What takes priority in your life? Choose carefully, because you will take on the characteristics of whatever you worship.

136.1ff Repeated throughout this psalm is the phrase, "for his steadfast love endures forever." This psalm may have been a responsive reading, the congregation saying these words in unison after each sentence. The repetition made this important lesson sink in. "Steadfast love" includes aspects of love, kindness, mercy, and faithfulness. We never have to worry that God will run out of love, because it flows from a well that will never run dry.

for his steadfast love endures forever;
9 the moon and stars to rule over the night,
for his steadfast love endures forever;

10 who struck Egypt through their firstborn,
for his steadfast love endures forever;
11 and brought Israel out from among them,
for his steadfast love endures forever;
12 with a strong hand and an outstretched arm,
for his steadfast love endures forever;
13 who divided the Red Sea[e] in two,
for his steadfast love endures forever;
14 and made Israel pass through the midst of it,
for his steadfast love endures forever;
15 but overthrew Pharaoh and his army in the Red Sea,[e]
for his steadfast love endures forever;
16 who led his people through the wilderness,
for his steadfast love endures forever;
17 who struck down great kings,
for his steadfast love endures forever;
18 and killed famous kings,
for his steadfast love endures forever;
19 Sihon, king of the Amorites,
for his steadfast love endures forever;
20 and Og, king of Bashan,
for his steadfast love endures forever;
21 and gave their land as a heritage,
for his steadfast love endures forever;
22 a heritage to his servant Israel,
for his steadfast love endures forever.

23 It is he who remembered us in our low estate,
for his steadfast love endures forever;
24 and rescued us from our foes,
for his steadfast love endures forever;
25 who gives food to all flesh,
for his steadfast love endures forever.

26 O give thanks to the God of heaven,
for his steadfast love endures forever.

136.10 Ex 12.29 Ps 78.51
136.11 Ex 12.51; 13.3 Deut 9.29 Ps 44.3 Jer 32.17,21
136.13 Ex 14.21 Ps 78.13
136.14 Ps 106.9
136.16 Ex 13.18 Deut 8.15
136.17 Ps 135.10-12
136.22 Ps 105.6 Isa 41.8; 45.4
136.23 Ps 9.12; 106.45
136.24 Judg 6.9
136.25 Ps 104.27

Theme: A person in exile weeps over the bitterness of captivity. Our sorrow can make it difficult to imagine singing joyful songs again.
Author: Anonymous

PSALM 137

1 By the rivers of Babylon —
there we sat down and there we wept
when we remembered Zion.
2 On the willows[f] there
we hung up our harps.
3 For there our captors
asked us for songs,
and our tormentors asked for mirth, saying,
"Sing us one of the songs of Zion!"

4 How could we sing the LORD's song
in a foreign land?

137.1 Neh 1.4 Ezek 1.1,3
137.2 Ezek 26.13
137.3 2 Chron 29.27 Neh 12.46

[e] Or *Sea of Reeds* [f] Or *poplars*

5 If I forget you, O Jerusalem,
let my right hand wither!
6 Let my tongue cling to the roof of my mouth,
if I do not remember you,
if I do not set Jerusalem
above my highest joy.

137.7
Jer 49.7-22
Ezek 25.12-14

7 Remember, O LORD, against the Edomites
the day of Jerusalem's fall,
how they said, "Tear it down! Tear it down!
Down to its foundations!"

137.8
Isa 13.1-22
47.1-15
Jer 50.1-46
51.1-64

8 O daughter Babylon, you devastator![g]
Happy shall they be who pay you back
what you have done to us!
9 Happy shall they be who take your little ones
and dash them against the rock!

Theme: Thanksgiving for answered prayer. God works out his plans for our lives and will bring us through the difficulties we face.
Author: David

PSALM 138

Of David.

1 I give you thanks, O LORD, with my whole heart;
before the gods I sing your praise;

138.2
Ps 5.7
Isa 42.21

2 I bow down toward your holy temple
and give thanks to your name for your steadfast love and your faithfulness;
for you have exalted your name and your word
above everything.[h]
3 On the day I called, you answered me,
you increased my strength of soul.[i]

138.4
Ps 102.15

4 All the kings of the earth shall praise you, O LORD,
for they have heard the words of your mouth.
5 They shall sing of the ways of the LORD,
for great is the glory of the LORD.

138.6
Ps 101.5
113.4-7

6 For though the LORD is high, he regards the lowly;
but the haughty he perceives from far away.

138.7
Ex 15.12
Ezra 9.8,9
Ps 20.6; 23.4

7 Though I walk in the midst of trouble,
you preserve me against the wrath of my enemies;
you stretch out your hand,
and your right hand delivers me.

[g] Or *you who are devastated* [h] Cn: Heb *you have exalted your word above all your name* [i] Syr Compare Gk Tg: Heb *you made me arrogant in my soul with strength*

137.7 Although Israel shared its southern border with Edom, there was bitter hatred between the two nations. The Edomites did not come to help when the city of Jerusalem was besieged by the Babylonian army. In fact, they rejoiced when the city was destroyed (Jeremiah 49.7–22; Joel 3.19; Obadiah 1.1–20).

137.8, 9 God destroyed Babylon and its offspring for their proud assault against God and his kingdom. The Medes and Persians destroyed Babylon in 539 B.C. Many of those who were oppressed lived to see the victory. The psalmist is crying out for judgment: "Treat the Babylonians the way they treated us."

138.1 Thanksgiving should be an integral part of our lives. This theme is woven throughout the psalms. As we thank God for material and spiritual blessings, we should also thank him for answered prayer. Beware of taking God's provision and answered prayer for granted.

138.1 "Before the gods" may mean in the presence of subordinate heavenly beings (angels), or as ridicule of the gods of the heathen nations. God is the highest in the whole earth.

138.8 Each of us dreams and makes plans for our future. We work hard to see those dreams and plans come true. But to make the most of life, we must include God's plan in our plans. He alone knows what is best for us; he alone can "fulfill his purpose" for us. As you make plans and dream dreams, talk with God about them.

8 The LORD will fulfill his purpose for me;
your steadfast love, O LORD, endures forever.
Do not forsake the work of your hands.

138.8 Job 10.3 Ps 27.9; 71.9

Theme: God is all-seeing, all-knowing, all-holy, all-present. God knows us, God is with us, and his greatest gift is to allow us to know him.
Author: David

PSALM 139

To the leader. Of David. A Psalm.

1 O LORD, you have searched me and known me.
2 You know when I sit down and when I rise up;
you discern my thoughts from far away.
3 You search out my path and my lying down,
and are acquainted with all my ways.
4 Even before a word is on my tongue,
O LORD, you know it completely.
5 You hem me in, behind and before,
and lay your hand upon me.
6 Such knowledge is too wonderful for me;
it is so high that I cannot attain it.

7 Where can I go from your spirit?
Or where can I flee from your presence?
8 If I ascend to heaven, you are there;
if I make my bed in Sheol, you are there.
9 If I take the wings of the morning
and settle at the farthest limits of the sea,
10 even there your hand shall lead me,
and your right hand shall hold me fast.
11 If I say, "Surely the darkness shall cover me,
and the light around me become night,"
12 even the darkness is not dark to you;
the night is as bright as the day,
for darkness is as light to you.

13 For it was you who formed my inward parts;
you knit me together in my mother's womb.
14 I praise you, for I am fearfully and wonderfully made.
Wonderful are your works;
that I know very well.
15 My frame was not hidden from you,
when I was being made in secret,
intricately woven in the depths of the earth.
16 Your eyes beheld my unformed substance.
In your book were written
all the days that were formed for me,
when none of them as yet existed.
17 How weighty to me are your thoughts, O God!
How vast is the sum of them!

139.1 Ps 44.21
139.2 Ps 94.11
139.3 Job 14.16
139.4 Heb 4.13
139.7 Jer 23.24
139.8 Prov 15.11 Amos 9.2-4
139.10 Ps 23.2,3
139.11 Job 22.13
139.12 Job 34.22 1 Jn 1.5
139.13 Ps 119.73
139.15 Job 10.8-10 Eccles 11.5
139.16 Job 14.5 Ps 56.8

139.1–5 Sometimes we don't let people get to know us completely because we are afraid they will discover something about us they won't like. But God already knows everything about us, even to the number of hairs on our heads (Matthew 10.30), and still he accepts and loves us. He is with us through every situation, in every trial—protecting, loving, guiding. He knows and loves us completely.

139.7 God is omnipresent—he is present everywhere. Because this is so, you can never be lost to his Spirit. This is good news to those who know and love God, because no matter what we do or where we go, we can never be far from God's comforting presence (see Romans 8.35–39).

139.13–15 God's character goes into the creation of every person. When you feel worthless or even begin to hate yourself, remember that God's Spirit is ready and willing to work within you. God thinks of you constantly (139.17, 18). We should have as much respect for ourselves as our Maker has for us.

18 I try to count them — they are more than the sand;
I come to the end[j] — I am still with you.

139.19 Isa 11.4
19 O that you would kill the wicked, O God,
and that the bloodthirsty would depart from me —
139.20 Ex 20.7 Deut 5.11
20 those who speak of you maliciously,
and lift themselves up against you for evil![k]
21 Do I not hate those who hate you, O LORD?
And do I not loathe those who rise up against you?
22 I hate them with perfect hatred;
I count them my enemies.
139.23 Ps 26.2
23 Search me, O God, and know my heart;
test me and know my thoughts.
24 See if there is any wicked[l] way in me,
and lead me in the way everlasting.[m]

[j] Or *I awake* [k] Cn: Meaning of Heb uncertain [l] Heb *hurtful* [m] Or *the ancient way.* Compare Jer 6.16

ANGER AND VENGEANCE IN THE BOOK OF PSALMS

Several psalms shock those familiar with New Testament teachings. The psalmists didn't hesitate to demand God's justice and make vivid suggestions on how he might carry it out. Apparently, no subject was unsuitable for discussion with God, but our tendency is to avoid the subjects of anger and vengeance in the psalms.

To understand the words of anger and vengeance, we need to understand several things:

(1) The judgments asked for are to be carried out by God, and are written out of intense personal and national suffering. The people are unable or unwilling to take vengeance themselves and are asking God to intervene. Because few of us have suffered intense cruelty on a personal or national level, we find it difficult to grasp these outbursts.

(2) These writers were intimately aware of God's justice. Some of their words are efforts to vividly imagine what God might allow to happen to those who had harmed his people.

(3) If we dared to write down our thoughts while unjustly attacked or suffering cruelty, we might be shocked at our own bold desire for vengeance. We would be surprised at how much we have in common with these men of old. The psalmists did not have Jesus' command to pray for one's enemies, but they did point to the right place to start. We are challenged to return good for evil, but until we respond to this challenge, we will not know how much we need God's help in order to forgive others.

(4) There is a helpful parallel between the psalms of anger and the psalms of vengeance. The "angry" psalms are intense and graphic, but they are directed at God. He is boldly told how disappointing it is when he turns his back on his people or acts too slowly. But while these thoughts and feelings were sincerely expressed, we know from the psalms themselves that these passing feelings were followed by renewed confidence in God's faithfulness. It is reasonable to expect the same of the "vengeance" psalms. We read, for example, David's angry outburst against Saul's pursuit in Psalm 59, yet we know that David never took personal vengeance on Saul. The psalmists freely spoke their minds to God, having confidence that he could sort out what was meant and what was felt. Pray with that same confidence—God can be trusted with your heart.

Selected psalms that emphasize these themes are 10; 23; 28; 35; 59; 69; 109; 137; 139; 140.

139.21–24 David's hatred of his enemies came from his zeal for God. David regarded his enemies as God's enemies, so his hatred was a desire for God's righteous justice and not for personal vengeance. Is it all right to be angry at people who hate God? Yes, but we must remember that it is God who will deal with them, not us. If we truly love God, then we will be deeply hurt if someone hates him. David asked God to search his heart and mind and point out any wrong motives that may have been behind his strong words. But while we seek justice against evil, we must also pray that God's enemies will turn to him before he judges them (see Matthew 5.44).

139.23, 24 David asked God to search for sin and point it out, even to the level of testing his thoughts. This is exploratory surgery for sin. How are we to recognize sin unless God points it out? Then when God shows us, we can repent and be forgiven. Make this verse your prayer. If you ask the Lord to search your heart and your thoughts and to reveal your sin, you will be continuing in God's everlasting way.

Theme: Prayer for protection against those who slander or threaten you. Deliverance begins with concentrating on our future life with God.
Author: David

PSALM 140

To the leader. A Psalm of David.

1 Deliver me, O LORD, from evildoers;
protect me from those who are violent,
2 who plan evil things in their minds
and stir up wars continually.
3 They make their tongue sharp as a snake's,
and under their lips is the venom of vipers. *Selah*

4 Guard me, O LORD, from the hands of the wicked;
protect me from the violent
who have planned my downfall.
5 The arrogant have hidden a trap for me,
and with cords they have spread a net,[n]
along the road they have set snares for me. *Selah*

6 I say to the LORD, "You are my God;
give ear, O LORD, to the voice of my supplications."
7 O LORD, my Lord, my strong deliverer,
you have covered my head in the day of battle.
8 Do not grant, O LORD, the desires of the wicked;
do not further their evil plot.[o] *Selah*

9 Those who surround me lift up their heads;[p]
let the mischief of their lips overwhelm them!
10 Let burning coals fall on them!
Let them be flung into pits, no more to rise!
11 Do not let the slanderer be established in the land;
let evil speedily hunt down the violent!

12 I know that the LORD maintains the cause of the needy,
and executes justice for the poor.
13 Surely the righteous shall give thanks to your name;
the upright shall live in your presence.

140.2 Ps 56.6; Prov 6.14; Isa 59.4
140.3 Rom 3.13; Jas 3.8
140.5 Job 18.9; Ps 35.7; 57.6
140.6 Esth 9.25; Ps 112.10
140.10 Ps 11.6; Mt 3.10
140.11 Ps 34.21; 1 Kgs 8.45,49

Theme: A prayer for help when facing temptation. David asks God to protect him and to give him wisdom in accepting criticism. Be open to honest criticism—God may be speaking to you through others.
Author: David

PSALM 141

A Psalm of David.

1 I call upon you, O LORD; come quickly to me;
give ear to my voice when I call to you.
2 Let my prayer be counted as incense before you,
and the lifting up of my hands as an evening sacrifice.

141.2 Ex 29.41; 30.8; Dan 9.21; Rev 5.8; 8.3,4

[n] *Or they have spread cords as a net* [o] Heb adds *they are exalted* [p] Cn Compare Gk: Heb *those who surround me are uplifted in head*; Heb divides verses 8 and 9 differently

140.12 To whom can the poor turn when they are persecuted? They lack the money to get professional help; they may be unable to defend themselves. But there is always someone on their side—the Lord will stand by them and ultimately bring about justice. This should be a comfort for us all. No matter what our situation may be, the Lord is with us. But it should also call us to responsibility. We as God's people are required to defend the rights of the powerless.

141.3 James wrote that "the tongue is a small member, yet it boasts of great exploits" (James 3.5). On the average, a person

141.3 Ps 39.1 Prov 13.3; 21.23

3 Set a guard over my mouth, O LORD;
keep watch over the door of my lips.

141.4 Ps 119.36 Prov 23.6 Mal 3.15

4 Do not turn my heart to any evil,
to busy myself with wicked deeds
in company with those who work iniquity;
do not let me eat of their delicacies.

141.5 Ps 23.5; 35.14 Prov 19.25; 27.6 Gal 6.1

5 Let the righteous strike me;
let the faithful correct me.
Never let the oil of the wicked anoint my head,[q]
for my prayer is continually[r] against their wicked deeds.
6 When they are given over to those who shall condemn them,
then they shall learn that my words were pleasant.
7 Like a rock that one breaks apart and shatters on the land,
so shall their bones be strewn at the mouth of Sheol.[s]

8 But my eyes are turned toward you, O GOD, my Lord;
in you I seek refuge; do not leave me defenseless.

141.9 Ps 91.3

9 Keep me from the trap that they have laid for me,
and from the snares of evildoers.
10 Let the wicked fall into their own nets,
while I alone escape.

Theme: A prayer when overwhelmed and desperate.
When we feel cornered by our enemies, only God can keep us safe.
Author: David

PSALM 142

A Maskil of David. When he was in the cave. A Prayer.

142.1 Ps 30.8

1 With my voice I cry to the LORD;
with my voice I make supplication to the LORD.
2 I pour out my complaint before him;
I tell my trouble before him.
3 When my spirit is faint,
you know my way.

In the path where I walk
they have hidden a trap for me.

142.4 Ps 88.8,18 Jer 30.17

4 Look on my right hand and see—
there is no one who takes notice of me;
no refuge remains to me;
no one cares for me.

142.5 Ps 91.2,9

5 I cry to you, O LORD;
I say, "You are my refuge,
my portion in the land of the living."

q Gk: Meaning of Heb uncertain r Cn: Heb *for continually and my prayer* s Meaning of Heb of verses 5-7 is uncertain

opens his mouth approximately 700 times a day to speak. David wisely asked God to help him keep his mouth shut—sometimes even as he underwent persecution. Jesus himself was silent before his accusers (Matthew 26.63). Knowing the power of the tongue, we would do well to ask God to guard what we say so that our words will bring honor to his name.

141.4 Evil acts begin with evil desires. It isn't enough to ask God to keep you away from temptation, make you stronger, or change your circumstances. You must ask him to change your desires.

141.5 Nobody really likes criticism, but everybody can benefit from it when it is given wisely and taken humbly. David suggested how to accept criticism: (1) don't refuse it, (2) consider it a kindness, and (3) keep quiet (don't fight back). Putting these suggestions into practice will help you control how you react to criticism, making it productive rather than destructive, no matter how it was originally intended.

141.7 *Sheol* is the word in the Old Testament for the realm of the dead. It is used to mean the grave, the underworld, or death.

142.4, 5 Have you ever felt that no one cared what happened to you? David had good reason to feel that way, and he wrote, "I cry to you, O Lord." Through prayer we can pull out of our tailspin and be reminded that God cares for us deeply.

6 Give heed to my cry,
for I am brought very low.

Save me from my persecutors,
for they are too strong for me.
7 Bring me out of prison,
so that I may give thanks to your name.
The righteous will surround me,
for you will deal bountifully with me.

142.6 Ps 18.17; 79.8
142.7 Ps 13.6

Theme: A prayer in the midst of hopelessness and depression. Our prayers should fit into what we know is consistent with God's character and plans.
Author: David

PSALM 143

A Psalm of David.

1 Hear my prayer, O LORD;
give ear to my supplications in your faithfulness;
answer me in your righteousness.
2 Do not enter into judgment with your servant,
for no one living is righteous before you.

3 For the enemy has pursued me,
crushing my life to the ground,
making me sit in darkness like those long dead.
4 Therefore my spirit faints within me;
my heart within me is appalled.

5 I remember the days of old,
I think about all your deeds,
I meditate on the works of your hands.
6 I stretch out my hands to you;
my soul thirsts for you like a parched land. *Selah*

7 Answer me quickly, O LORD;
my spirit fails.
Do not hide your face from me,
or I shall be like those who go down to the Pit.
8 Let me hear of your steadfast love in the morning,
for in you I put my trust.
Teach me the way I should go,
for to you I lift up my soul.

9 Save me, O LORD, from my enemies;
I have fled to you for refuge.[t]
10 Teach me to do your will,
for you are my God.
Let your good spirit lead me
on a level path.

143.2 1 Kgs 8.46 Job 14.3; 22.4
143.3 Lam 3.6
143.5 Ps 77.5,10,11
143.6 Ps 63.1
143.7 Ps 69.17; 88.4
143.8 Ps 32.8
143.9 Ps 59.1
143.10 Neh 9.20 Ps 23.3; 119.12

[t] One Heb Ms Gk: MT *to you I have hidden*

142.7 This psalm was written when David was hiding from Saul in caves like the ones at Adullam (1 Samuel 22) or Engedi (1 Samuel 24). These may have seemed like prisons to him because of the confinement.

143.7 David was losing hope, caught in a deep depression that was paralyzing him with fear. At times, we feel caught in deepening depression, and we are unable to pull ourselves out. At those times, we can come to the Lord and, like David, express our true feelings. Then he will help us as we remember his miracles (143.5), reach out to him (143.6), trust him (143.8), and decide to do his will (143.10).

143.10 David's prayer was for knowledge to do God's will, not his own. A prayer for guidance is self-centered if it doesn't recognize God's power to redirect our lives. Asking God to restructure our priorities awakens our minds and stirs our wills.

11 For your name's sake, O LORD, preserve my life.
In your righteousness bring me out of trouble.
143.12 Ps 52.5; 116.16
12 In your steadfast love cut off my enemies,
and destroy all my adversaries,
for I am your servant.

Theme: Rejoicing in God's care. Whether in times of prosperity or adversity, happy are those whose God is the Lord.
Author: David

PSALM 144

Of David.

144.1 Ps 18.2
1 Blessed be the LORD, my rock,
who trains my hands for war, and my fingers for battle;
144.2 Ps 84.9
2 my rock[u] and my fortress,
my stronghold and my deliverer,
my shield, in whom I take refuge,
who subdues the peoples[v] under me.

144.3 Ps 8.4
3 O LORD, what are human beings that you regard them,
or mortals that you think of them?
144.4 Job 8.9; 14.2 Ps 39.11 109.23
4 They are like a breath;
their days are like a passing shadow.

144.5 Ex 19.18 Ps 18.9 Isa 64.1
5 Bow your heavens, O LORD, and come down;
touch the mountains so that they smoke.
144.6 Hab 3.11 Zech 9.14
6 Make the lightning flash and scatter them;
send out your arrows and rout them.
144.7 Ps 18.44 69.1,14
7 Stretch out your hand from on high;
set me free and rescue me from the mighty waters,
from the hand of aliens,
144.8 Deut 32.40 Ps 12.2; 41.6 Isa 44.20
8 whose mouths speak lies,
and whose right hands are false.

144.9 Ps 40.3
9 I will sing a new song to you, O God;
upon a ten-stringed harp I will play to you,
144.10 2 Sam 18.7 Ps 140.7
10 the one who gives victory to kings,
who rescues his servant David.
11 Rescue me from the cruel sword,
and deliver me from the hand of aliens,
whose mouths speak lies,
and whose right hands are false.

144.12 2 Kgs 25.10,11 Ps 33.12; 60.2 92.12-14; 128.3 Song 4.4; 7.4 Prov 3.9,10 Isa 24.11 Jer 14.2 Amos 5.3
12 May our sons in their youth
be like plants full grown,
our daughters like corner pillars,
cut for the building of a palace.
13 May our barns be filled,
with produce of every kind;
may our sheep increase by thousands,
by tens of thousands in our fields,
14 and may our cattle be heavy with young.

[u] With 18.2 and 2 Sam 22.2: Heb *my steadfast love* [v] Heb Mss Syr Aquila Jerome: MT *my people*

144.3, 4 Life is short. David reminded us that it is "like a breath" and that our "days are like a passing shadow." James said that our lives are "a mist that appears for a little while and then vanishes" (James 4.14). Because life is short, we should live for God while we have the time. Don't waste your life by selecting an inferior purpose that has no lasting value. Live for God, who alone can make your life worthwhile, purposeful, and meaningful.

May there be no breach in the walls,[w] no exile,
and no cry of distress in our streets.

15 Happy are the people to whom such blessings fall;
happy are the people whose God is the LORD.

Theme: A time will come when all people will join together in recognizing and worshiping God. Because God is full of love, he satisfies all who trust in him.
Author: David

PSALM 145

Praise. Of David.

1 I will extol you, my God and King,
and bless your name forever and ever.
2 Every day I will bless you,
and praise your name forever and ever.
3 Great is the LORD, and greatly to be praised;
his greatness is unsearchable.

145.3 Rom 11.33

4 One generation shall laud your works to another,
and shall declare your mighty acts.
5 On the glorious splendor of your majesty,
and on your wondrous works, I will meditate.
6 The might of your awesome deeds shall be proclaimed,
and I will declare your greatness.
7 They shall celebrate the fame of your abundant goodness,
and shall sing aloud of your righteousness.

145.4 Isa 38.19
145.6 Deut 10.21; 32.3
145.7 Ps 51.14 Isa 63.7

8 The LORD is gracious and merciful,
slow to anger and abounding in steadfast love.
9 The LORD is good to all,
and his compassion is over all that he has made.

145.8 Ex 34.6
145.9 Ps 100.5 Nah 1.7 Mt 19.17 Mk 10.18

10 All your works shall give thanks to you, O LORD,
and all your faithful shall bless you.
11 They shall speak of the glory of your kingdom,
and tell of your power,
12 to make known to all people your[x] mighty deeds,
and the glorious splendor of your[y] kingdom.
13 Your kingdom is an everlasting kingdom,
and your dominion endures throughout all generations.

145.12 Ps 105.1 Isa 2.10,19,21
145.13 2 Pet 1.11

The LORD is faithful in all his words,
and gracious in all his deeds.[z]
14 The LORD upholds all who are falling,
and raises up all who are bowed down.
15 The eyes of all look to you,
and you give them their food in due season.
16 You open your hand,

145.15 Ps 104.27

[w] Heb lacks *in the walls* [x] Gk Jerome Syr: Heb *his* [y] Heb *his* [z] These two lines supplied by Q Ms Gk Syr

145.14 Sometimes our burdens seem more than we can bear, and we wonder how we can go on. The psalmist stands at this bleak intersection of life's road and points toward the Lord, the great burden-bearer. God is able to lift us up because (1) his greatness is unsearchable (145.3); (2) he does mighty acts across many generations (145.4); (3) he is full of glorious honor and majesty (145.5); (4) he does wondrous works and awesome deeds (145.5, 6); (5) he is righteous (145.7); (6) he is gracious, merciful, patient, and compassionate (145.8, 9); (7) he rules over an everlasting kingdom (145.13); (8) he is our source of all our daily needs (145.15, 16); (9) he is just and kind in all his dealings (145.17); (10) he remains near to those who call on him (145.18); (11) he listens to our cries and saves us (145.19, 20). If you are bending under a burden and feel that you are about to fall, turn to God for help. He is ready to lift you up.

satisfying the desire of every living thing.
17 The LORD is just in all his ways,
and kind in all his doings.
145.18 Deut 4.7
18 The LORD is near to all who call on him,
to all who call on him in truth.
145.19 Ps 10.17
19 He fulfills the desire of all who fear him;
he also hears their cry, and saves them.
145.20 Ps 31.23; 37.38
20 The LORD watches over all who love him,
but all the wicked he will destroy.

21 My mouth will speak the praise of the LORD,
and all flesh will bless his holy name forever and ever.

Theme: The help of man versus the help of God. Help from man is temporal and unstable, but help from God is lasting and complete.
Author: Anonymous

PSALM 146

1 Praise the LORD!
Praise the LORD, O my soul!
146.2 Ps 63.4; 104.33
2 I will praise the LORD as long as I live;
I will sing praises to my God all my life long.

146.3 Ps 60.11
3 Do not put your trust in princes,
in mortals, in whom there is no help.
4 When their breath departs, they return to the earth;
on that very day their plans perish.

5 Happy are those whose help is the God of Jacob,
whose hope is in the LORD their God,
146.6 Acts 14.15
6 who made heaven and earth,
the sea, and all that is in them;
who keeps faith forever;
146.7 Ps 68.6
7 who executes justice for the oppressed;
who gives food to the hungry.

The LORD sets the prisoners free;
146.8 Mt 9.30 Jn 9.7
8 the LORD opens the eyes of the blind.
The LORD lifts up those who are bowed down;

PRAISE IN THE BOOK OF PSALMS

Most of the psalms are prayers, and most of the prayers include praise to God. Praise expresses admiration, appreciation, and thanks. Praise in the book of Psalms is often directed to God, and just as often the praise is shared with others. Considering all that God has done and does for us, what could be more natural than outbursts of heartfelt praise?

As you read Psalms, note the praise given to God, not only for what he does—his creation, his blessings, his forgiveness—but also for who he is—loving, just, faithful, forgiving, patient. Note also those times when the praise of God is shared with others, and they too are encouraged to praise him. In what ways have you recently praised God or told others all that he has done for you?

Selected psalms that emphasize this theme are 8; 19; 30; 65; 84; 96; 100; 136; 145; 150.

146–150 These last five psalms overflow with praise. Each begins and ends with "Praise the Lord." They show us where, why, and how to praise God. What does praise do? (1) Praise takes our minds off our problems and shortcomings, and focuses them on God. (2) Praise leads us from individual meditation to corporate worship. (3) Praise causes us to consider and appreciate God's character. (4) Praise lifts our perspective from the earthly to the heavenly.

146.3-8 The psalmist portrays man as an inadequate savior, a false hope; even the princes cannot deliver (146.3). God is the hope and the help of the needy. Jesus affirms his concern for the poor and afflicted in Luke 4.18–21; 7.21–23. He does not separate the social and spiritual needs of people, but attends to both. While God, not the government, is the hope of the needy, *we* are his instruments to help here on earth.

the LORD loves the righteous.
9 The LORD watches over the strangers;
he upholds the orphan and the widow,
but the way of the wicked he brings to ruin.

10 The LORD will reign forever,
your God, O Zion, for all generations.
Praise the LORD!

146.9 Ex 22.21 Lev 19.34 Deut 10.18

146.10 Ps 10.16

Theme: What gives God joy. Although God created everything, his greatest joy comes from our genuine worship and trust.
Author: Anonymous, written when the exiles returned to Jerusalem

PSALM 147

1 Praise the LORD!
How good it is to sing praises to our God;
for he is gracious, and a song of praise is fitting.
2 The LORD builds up Jerusalem;
he gathers the outcasts of Israel.
3 He heals the brokenhearted,
and binds up their wounds.
4 He determines the number of the stars;
he gives to all of them their names.
5 Great is our Lord, and abundant in power;
his understanding is beyond measure.
6 The LORD lifts up the downtrodden;
he casts the wicked to the ground.

7 Sing to the LORD with thanksgiving;
make melody to our God on the lyre.
8 He covers the heavens with clouds,
prepares rain for the earth,
makes grass grow on the hills.
9 He gives to the animals their food,
and to the young ravens when they cry.
10 His delight is not in the strength of the horse,
nor his pleasure in the speed of a runner;[a]
11 but the LORD takes pleasure in those who fear him,
in those who hope in his steadfast love.

12 Praise the LORD, O Jerusalem!
Praise your God, O Zion!
13 For he strengthens the bars of your gates;
he blesses your children within you.
14 He grants peace[b] within your borders;
he fills you with the finest of wheat.

147.2 Isa 11.12; 56.8 Ezek 39.28

147.4 Gen 15.5 Isa 40.26

147.8 Job 5.10; 26.8 38.26

147.10 1 Sam 16.7 Ps 33.17

147.13 Neh 3.3; 7.3 Ps 37.26

147.14 Deut 32.14 Isa 54.13 60.17,18

[a] Heb *legs of a person* [b] Or *prosperity*

146.9 God's plans seem topsy-turvy to our society. Jesus turned society's values upside-down when he proclaimed that "many who are first will be last, and the last will be first" (Matthew 19.30), and that "those who want to save their life will lose it, and those who lose their life for my sake will find it" (Matthew 16.25). Don't be surprised when others don't understand your Christian values, but don't give in to theirs. Instead, be like the early Christians who turned their world "upside down" (Acts 17.6).

147.5 Sometimes we feel as if we don't understand ourselves—what we want, how we feel, what's wrong with us, or what we should do about it. But God's understanding is infinite, and therefore he understands us fully. If you feel troubled and don't understand yourself, remember that God understands you perfectly. Take your mind off yourself and focus it on God. Strive to become more and more like him. The more you learn about God and his ways, the better you will understand yourself.

147.10, 11 We spend much of our lives trying to sharpen our skills or increase our strength. There is nothing wrong with doing so, and, in fact, our gifts can be used to glorify God. But when we use our skills with no regard for God, they are indeed worth little. It is our *fear* (reverence) and hope that God desires. When he has those, then he will use our skills and strengths in ways far greater than we can imagine.

147.15 Job 37.12 Ps 104.4

15 He sends out his command to the earth;
his word runs swiftly.
16 He gives snow like wool;
he scatters frost like ashes.
17 He hurls down hail like crumbs—
who can stand before his cold?
18 He sends out his word, and melts them;
he makes his wind blow, and the waters flow.

147.19 Deut 33.3,4 Mal 4.4
147.20 Deut 4.7,8 Ps 79.6 Jer 10.25

19 He declares his word to Jacob,
his statutes and ordinances to Israel.
20 He has not dealt thus with any other nation;
they do not know his ordinances.
Praise the LORD!

Theme: Let all creation praise and worship the Lord.
Author: Anonymous

PSALM 148

148.1 Ps 102.19 Mt 21.9
148.2 Ps 103.20,21

1 Praise the LORD!
Praise the LORD from the heavens;
praise him in the heights!
2 Praise him, all his angels;
praise him, all his host!

3 Praise him, sun and moon;
praise him, all you shining stars!

148.4 Gen 1.7 Deut 10.14

4 Praise him, you highest heavens,
and you waters above the heavens!

148.5 Gen 1.1
148.6 Job 38.33

5 Let them praise the name of the LORD,
for he commanded and they were created.
6 He established them forever and ever;
he fixed their bounds, which cannot be passed.[c]

148.7 Gen 1.21 Ps 74.13 Hab 3.10

7 Praise the LORD from the earth,
you sea monsters and all deeps,
8 fire and hail, snow and frost,
stormy wind fulfilling his command!

9 Mountains and all hills,
fruit trees and all cedars!
10 Wild animals and all cattle,
creeping things and flying birds!

11 Kings of the earth and all peoples,
princes and all rulers of the earth!
12 Young men and women alike,
old and young together!

[c] Or *he set a law that cannot pass away*

147.19, 20 The nation of Israel was special to God because to its people God brought his laws, and through its people he sent his Son, Jesus Christ. Now any individual who follows God is just as special to him. In fact, the Bible says that the real nation of Israel is not a specific people or geographic place, but the community of all who believe in and obey God (see Galatians 3.28, 29).

148.5 All creation is like a majestic symphony or a great choir composed of many harmonious parts that together offer up songs of praise. Each part (independent, yet part of the whole) is caught up and carried along in the swelling tides of praise. This is a picture of how we as believers should praise God—individually, yet as part of the great choir of believers worldwide. Are you singing your part well in the worldwide choir of praise?

13 Let them praise the name of the LORD,
for his name alone is exalted;
his glory is above earth and heaven.
14 He has raised up a horn for his people,
praise for all his faithful,
for the people of Israel who are close to him.
Praise the LORD!

148.13 Ps 8.1; 113.4 Rev 5.12
148.14 Deut 10.21 1 Sam 2.1 Eph 2.17

Theme: A victory celebration. We have the assurance that God truly enjoys his people.
Author: Anonymous

PSALM 149

1 Praise the LORD!
Sing to the LORD a new song,
his praise in the assembly of the faithful.
2 Let Israel be glad in its Maker;
let the children of Zion rejoice in their King.
3 Let them praise his name with dancing,
making melody to him with tambourine and lyre.
4 For the LORD takes pleasure in his people;
he adorns the humble with victory.
5 Let the faithful exult in glory;
let them sing for joy on their couches.
6 Let the high praises of God be in their throats
and two-edged swords in their hands,
7 to execute vengeance on the nations
and punishment on the peoples,
8 to bind their kings with fetters
and their nobles with chains of iron,
9 to execute on them the judgment decreed.
This is glory for all his faithful ones.
Praise the LORD!

149.1 Ps 33.3; 89.5
149.2 Judg 8.23 Ps 47.6
149.3 Ex 15.20
149.4 Ps 35.27
149.6 Ps 66.17
149.8 Nah 3.10

Theme: A closing hymn of praise. God's creation praises him everywhere in every way. We should join this rejoicing song of praise.
Author: Anonymous

PSALM 150

1 Praise the LORD!
Praise God in his sanctuary;
praise him in his mighty firmament![d]
2 Praise him for his mighty deeds;
praise him according to his surpassing greatness!

3 Praise him with trumpet sound;
praise him with lute and harp!
4 Praise him with tambourine and dance;
praise him with strings and pipe!

150.1 Ps 19.1; 73.17 102.19
150.3 Ps 98.6

[d] Or *dome*

149.3–5 Although the Bible invites us to praise God, we often aren't sure how to go about it. Here, several ways are suggested—in the dance, with the voice, with musical instruments. God enjoys his people, and we should enjoy praising him.

149.6, 7 The two-edged sword symbolizes the completeness of judgment that will be executed by the Messiah when he returns to punish all evildoers (Revelation 1.16).

150.3–5 Music and song were an integral part of Old Testament worship. David introduced music into the tabernacle and temple services (1 Chronicles 16.4–7). The music must have been loud and joyous as evidenced by the list of instruments and the presence of choirs and songleaders. Music was also important in New Testament worship (Ephesians 5.19; Colossians 3.16).

150.6 How could the message be more clear? The writer was telling the individual listeners to praise God. What a fitting way to end this book of praise—with a direct encouragement for *you* to praise

5 Praise him with clanging cymbals;
praise him with loud clashing cymbals!
6 Let everything that breathes praise the LORD!
Praise the LORD!

WHERE TO GET HELP IN THE BOOK OF PSALMS

When you feel . . .

Afraid: 3; 4; 27; 46; 49; 56; 91; 118
Alone: 9; 10; 12; 13; 27; 40; 43
"Burned out": 6; 63
Cheated: 41
Confused: 10; 12; 73
Depressed: 27; 34; 42; 43; 88; 143
Distressed: 13; 25; 31; 40; 107
Elated: 19; 96
Guilty: 19; 32; 38; 51
Hateful: 11
Impatient: 13; 27; 37; 40
Insecure: 3; 5; 12; 91
Insulted: 41; 70
Jealous: 37
Like Quitting: 29; 43; 145
Lost: 23; 139
Overwhelmed: 25; 69; 142
Penitent/Sorry: 32; 51; 66
Proud: 14; 30; 49
Purposeless: 14; 25; 39; 49; 90
Sad: 13
Self-confident: 24
Tense: 4
Thankful: 118; 136; 138
Threatened: 3; 11; 17
Tired/Weak: 6; 13; 18; 28; 29; 40; 86
Trapped: 7; 17; 42; 88; 142
Unimportant: 8; 90; 139
Vengeful: 3; 7; 109
Worried: 37
Worshipful: 8; 19; 27; 29; 150

When you're facing . . .

Atheists: 10; 14; 19; 52; 53; 115
Competition: 133
Criticism: 35; 56; 120
Danger: 11
Death: 6; 71; 90
Decisions: 1; 119
Discrimination: 54
Doubts: 34; 37; 94
Evil people: 10; 35; 36; 49; 52; 109; 140
Enemies: 3; 25; 35; 41; 56; 59
Handicap/Illness: 6; 139
Heresy: 14
Hypocrisy: 26; 28; 40; 50
Lies: 5; 12; 120
Old Age: 71; 92
Persecution: 1; 3; 7; 56
Poverty: 9; 10; 12
Punishment: 6; 38; 39
Slander/Insults: 7; 15; 35; 43; 120
Slaughter: 6; 46; 83
Sorrow: 23; 34
Success: 18; 112; 127; 128
Temptation: 38; 141
Troubles: 34; 55; 86; 102; 142; 145
Verbal Cruelty: 35; 120

When you want . . .

Acceptance: 139
Answers: 4; 17
Confidence: 46; 71
Courage: 11; 42
Fellowship with God: 5; 16; 25; 27; 37; 133
Forgiveness: 32; 38; 40; 51; 69; 86; 103; 130
Friendship: 16
Godliness: 15; 25
Guidance: 1; 5; 15; 19; 25; 32; 48
Healing: 6; 41
Hope: 16; 17; 18; 23; 27
Humility: 19; 147
Illumination: 19
Integrity: 24; 25
Joy: 9; 16; 28; 126
Justice: 2; 7; 14; 26; 37; 49; 58; 82
Knowledge: 2; 8; 18; 19; 25; 29; 97; 103
Leadership: 72
Miracles: 60; 111
Money: 15; 16; 17; 49
Peace: 3; 4
Perspective: 2; 11
Prayer: 5; 17; 27; 61
Protection: 3; 4; 7; 16; 17; 18; 23; 27; 31; 91; 121; 125
Provision: 23
Rest: 23; 27
Salvation: 26; 37; 49; 126
Stability: 11; 33; 46
Vindication: 9; 14; 28; 35; 109
Wisdom: 1; 16; 19; 64; 111

God too. Remember to praise him every day!

150.6 In a way, the book of Psalms parallels our spiritual journey through life. It begins by presenting us with two roads – the way to life and the way to death. If we choose God's way to life, we still face both blessings and troubles, joy and grief, successes and obstacles. As the wise and faithful person's life draws to an end, he or she realizes clearly that God's road is the right road. Knowing this will cause us to praise God for leading us in the right direction and for assuring our place in the perfect world God has in store for those who have faithfully followed him.

VITAL STATISTICS

PURPOSE:
To teach people how to be understanding, just, and fair in everything they do, to make the simple-minded wise, to warn young people about some problems they will face, and to help the wise become good leaders (see 1.2–6)—in short, to apply divine wisdom to daily life and to provide moral instruction

AUTHOR:
Solomon wrote most of this book, with Agur and Lemuel contributing some of the later sections

DATE WRITTEN:
Solomon wrote and compiled most of these proverbs early in his reign

SETTING:
This is a book of wise sayings, a textbook for teaching people how to live godly lives through the repetition of wise thoughts

KEY VERSE:
"The fear of the Lord is the beginning of knowledge; fools despise wisdom and instruction" (1.7).

SPECIAL FEATURES:
The book uses varied *literary forms:* poems, brief parables, pointed questions, and couplets. Other *literary devices* include antithesis, comparison, and personification.

ALPHABET, letters, vowels, and consonants, formed into words, sentences, paragraphs, and books—spoken, lectured, signed, whispered, written, and printed. From friendly advice to impassioned speeches and from dusty volumes to daily tabloids, messages are sent and received with each sender trying to impart knowledge . . . and wisdom.

Woven into human fabric is the desire to learn and understand. Our minds set us apart from animals, and we analyze, conceptualize, theorize, discuss, and debate everything from science to the supernatural. And we build schools, institutes, and universities where learned professors can teach us about the world and about life.

Knowledge is good, but there is a vast difference between "knowledge" (having the facts) and "wisdom" (applying those facts to life). We may amass knowledge, but without wisdom, our knowledge is useless. We must learn how to *live out* what we know.

The wisest man who ever lived, Solomon, left us a legacy of written wisdom in three volumes—Proverbs, Ecclesiastes, and Song of Solomon. In these books, under the inspiration of the Holy Spirit, he gives practical insights and guidelines for life.

In the first of these three volumes, Solomon passes on his practical advice in the form of proverbs. A proverb is a short, concise sentence which conveys moral truth. The book of Proverbs is a collection of these wise statements. The main theme of Proverbs, as we might expect, is the nature of true wisdom. Solomon writes, "The fear of the Lord is the beginning of knowledge; fools despise wisdom and instruction" (1.7). He then proceeds to give hundreds of practical examples of how to live according to godly wisdom.

Proverbs covers a wide range of topics, including youth and discipline, family life, self-control and resisting temptation, business matters, words and the tongue, knowing God, marriage, seeking the truth, wealth and poverty, immorality, and, of course, wisdom. These proverbs are short poems (usually in couplet form), containing a holy mixture of common sense and timely warnings. Although they are not meant to teach doctrine, a person who follows their advice will walk closely with God. The word "proverb" comes from a Hebrew word which means "to rule or to govern," and these sayings, reminders, and admonitions provide profound advice for governing our lives.

As you read Proverbs, understand that knowing God is the key to wisdom. Listen to the thoughts and lessons from the world's wisest man, and apply these truths to your life. Don't just read these proverbs, act on them!

THE BLUEPRINT

A. WISDOM FOR YOUNG PEOPLE (1.1—9.18)	Solomon instructed the young people of his day like a father giving advice to his child. While many of these proverbs are directed toward young people, the principles supporting them are helpful to all believers, male and female, young and old. Anyone beginning their journey to discover more of wisdom will benefit greatly from these wise sayings.
B. WISDOM FOR ALL PEOPLE (10.1—24.34)	Solomon wanted to impart wisdom to all people, regardless of their age, sex, or position in society. These short, wise sayings give us practical wisdom for daily living. We should study them diligently and integrate them into our lives.
C. WISDOM FOR THE LEADERS (25.1—31.31)	In addition to the proverbs which Solomon collected, the men of Hezekiah collected many proverbs that Solomon and others wrote. While most of these are general in nature, many are directed specifically to the king and those who dealt with the king. These are particularly useful for those who are leaders or aspire to be leaders.

MEGATHEMES

THEME	EXPLANATION	IMPORTANCE
Wisdom	God wants his people to be wise. Two kinds of people portray two contrasting paths of life. The fool is the wicked, stubborn person who hates or ignores God. The wise person seeks to know and love God.	When we choose God's way, he grants us wisdom. His Word, the Bible, leads us to live rightly, have right relationships, and make right decisions.
Relationships	Proverbs gives us advice for developing our personal relationships with friends, family members, and co-workers. In every relationship, we must show love, dedication, and high moral standards.	To relate to people, we need consistency, tact, and discipline to use the wisdom God gives us. If we don't treat others according to the wisdom God gives, our relationships will suffer.
Speech	What we say shows our real attitude toward others. How we talk reveals what we're really like. Our speech is a test of how wise we have become.	To be wise in our speech we need to use self-control. Our words should be honest and well-chosen.
Work	God controls the final outcome of all we do. We are accountable to carry out our work with diligence and discipline, not laziness.	Because God evaluates how we live, we should work purposefully. We must never be lax or self-satisfied in using our skills.
Success	Although people work very hard for money and fame, God views success as having a good reputation, moral character, and the spiritual devotion to obey him.	A successful relationship with God counts for eternity. Everything else is perishable. All our resources, time, and talents come from God. We should strive to use them wisely.

A. WISDOM FOR YOUNG PEOPLE (1.1–9.18)

Proverbs begins with a clear statement of its purpose—to impart wisdom for godly living. The first few chapters are Solomon's fatherly advice to young people. Although most of the material in this section is directed toward young people, all who seek wisdom will greatly benefit from these wise words. This is where one can discover the source of wisdom, the value of wisdom, and the benefits of wisdom.

The purpose of Proverbs

1 The proverbs of Solomon son of David, king of Israel:

2 For learning about wisdom and instruction,
for understanding words of insight,
3 for gaining instruction in wise dealing,
righteousness, justice, and equity;
4 to teach shrewdness to the simple,
knowledge and prudence to the young—
5 Let the wise also hear and gain in learning,
and the discerning acquire skill,
6 to understand a proverb and a figure,
the words of the wise and their riddles.

7 The fear of the LORD is the beginning of knowledge;
fools despise wisdom and instruction.

Wisdom keeps a young person from disaster

8 Hear, my child, your father's instruction,
and do not reject your mother's teaching;
9 for they are a fair garland for your head,
and pendants for your neck.
10 My child, if sinners entice you,
do not consent.
11 If they say, "Come with us, let us lie in wait for blood;
let us wantonly ambush the innocent;
12 like Sheol let us swallow them alive
and whole, like those who go down to the Pit.
13 We shall find all kinds of costly things;
we shall fill our houses with booty.

1.1 1 Kgs 4.32 Prov 25.1
1.2 Prov 4.5; 7.4
1.3 Prov 2.9; 19.20
1.4 Prov 8.4; 9.4
1.7 Prov 9.10; 15.33
1.8,9 Prov 6.20
1.10 Ps 1.1 Prov 7.21; 13.20

1.1 What the book of Psalms is to devotional life, the book of Proverbs is to everyday life. Proverbs gives practical suggestions for effective living. This book is not just a collection of homey sayings; it contains deep spiritual insights drawn from experience. A *proverb* is a short, wise, easy-to-learn saying that calls a person to action. It doesn't argue about basic spiritual and moral beliefs; it assumes we already hold them. The book of Proverbs focuses on God—his character, works, and blessings—and it tells how we can live in close relationship to him.

1.1 Solomon, the third king of Israel, son of the great King David, reigned during Israel's golden age. When God said he would give him whatever he wanted, he asked for wisdom (1 Kings 3.5–14). God was pleased with this request, and he not only made Solomon wise but also gave him great riches, power, and peace. Solomon built the glorious temple in Jerusalem (1 Kings 6) and wrote most of the book of Proverbs. His Profile is found in 1 Kings 3.

1.6 A *figure* is an illustration used for teaching. *Riddles* are thought-provoking questions.

1.7 One of the most annoying types of people is a know-it-all, a person who has a dogmatic opinion about everything, is closed to anything new, and refuses to learn. Solomon calls this kind of person a fool. Don't be a know-it-all. Instead, be open to the advice of others, especially those who know you well and can give valuable insight and counsel. Learn how to learn from others. Remember, only God knows it all.

1.7–9 In this age of information, knowledge is plentiful, but wisdom is scarce. Wisdom means far more than simply knowing a lot. It is a basic attitude that affects every aspect of life. The first step to wisdom is to fear the Lord—to honor and respect God, to live in awe of his power. Faith in God should be the foundation for your understanding of the world, your attitudes, and your actions. Trust in God, and he will make you truly wise.

1.8 Our actions speak louder than our words. This is especially true in the home. Children learn values, morals, and priorities by observing how their parents act and react every day. If parents exhibit a deep reverence for and dependence on God, the children will catch these attitudes. Let them see your reverence for God. Teach them right living by giving worship an important place in your family life and by reading the Bible together.

1.10–19 Sin is attractive because it offers a quick route to prosperity and makes us feel like "one of the crowd." When we go along with others and refuse to listen to the truth, our own appetites become our masters, and we'll do anything to satisfy them. But sin, even when attractive, is deadly. We must learn to make choices, not on the basis of flashy appeal or short-range pleasure, but in view of the long-range effects. Sometimes this means steering clear of people who want to draw us into activities that we know are wrong. We can't be friendly with sin and expect our lives to remain unaffected.

14 Throw in your lot among us;
we will all have one purse" —

1.15
Ps 1.1; 26.4
2 Cor 6.17

15 my child, do not walk in their way,
keep your foot from their paths;

1.16
Prov 4.16

16 for their feet run to evil,
and they hurry to shed blood.
17 For in vain is the net baited
while the bird is looking on;

1.18
Prov 5.22; 9.17

18 yet they lie in wait — to kill themselves!
and set an ambush — for their own lives!

1.19
Prov 15.27
28.25

19 Such is the end[a] of all who are greedy for gain;
it takes away the life of its possessors.

The voice of wisdom

20 Wisdom cries out in the street;
in the squares she raises her voice.
21 At the busiest corner she cries out;
at the entrance of the city gates she speaks:

1.22
Prov 9.4; 14.15

22 "How long, O simple ones, will you love being simple?
How long will scoffers delight in their scoffing
and fools hate knowledge?
23 Give heed to my reproof;
I will pour out my thoughts to you;
I will make my words known to you.

1.24
Prov 15.32
Isa 65.12; 66.4

24 Because I have called and you refused,
have stretched out my hand and no one heeded,

1.25
2 Chron 36.16

25 and because you have ignored all my counsel
and would have none of my reproof,
26 I also will laugh at your calamity;
I will mock when panic strikes you,

1.27
Prov 3.25; 10.25

27 when panic strikes you like a storm,
and your calamity comes like a whirlwind,
when distress and anguish come upon you.

1.28
Job 27.9
Ezek 8.18

28 Then they will call upon me, but I will not answer;

a Gk: Heb *ways*

UNDERSTANDING PROVERBS Most often, proverbs are written in the form of couplets. These are constructed in three ways:

Type	*Description*	*Key Word(s)*	*Examples*
Contrasting	Meaning and application come from the difference or contrast between the two statements of the proverb	"but"	10.6; 15.25, 27
Comparing	Meaning and application come from the similarities or comparison between the two statements of the proverb	"as/so" "better/than"	10.26; 15.16, 17; 25.25
Complementing	Meaning and application come from the way the second statement complements the first	"and"	10.18; 15.10, 23

1.19 Being "greedy for gain" is one of Satan's surest traps. It begins when he plants the suggestion that we can't live without some possession or more money. Then that desire fans its own fire until it becomes an all-consuming obsession. Ask God for wisdom to recognize any greedy trap that Satan places in your way. God will help you overcome it (1.23).

1.20 The picture of wisdom shouting in the streets is a personification — a literary device to make wisdom come alive for us. Wisdom is not a separate being; it is the mind of God revealed. By reading about Jesus Christ's earthly ministry, we can see wisdom in action. In order to understand how to become wise, we can listen to wisdom calling and instructing us in the book of Proverbs (see the chart in chapter 14). For New Testament calls to wisdom, see 2 Timothy 1.7 and James 1.5.

1.22 In the book of Proverbs, a "simple one" or a fool is not someone with a *mental* deficiency but someone with a *character* deficiency (such as rebellion, laziness, or anger). The fool is not dumb or stupid, but is unable to tell right from wrong or good from bad.

1.23–28 God is more than willing to pour out his wisdom to us. To receive his advice, we must be willing to listen, refusing to let pride stand in our way. Pride is thinking more highly of our own wisdom and desires than of God's. If we think we know better than God or feel we have no need of God's direction, we have fallen into foolish pride.

they will seek me diligently, but will not find me.
29 Because they hated knowledge
and did not choose the fear of the LORD,
30 would have none of my counsel,
and despised all my reproof,
31 therefore they shall eat the fruit of their way
and be sated with their own devices.
32 For waywardness kills the simple,
and the complacency of fools destroys them;
33 but those who listen to me will be secure
and will live at ease, without dread of disaster."

1.31 Job 4.8 Prov 5.22; 22.8
1.33 Prov 3.24-26

Wisdom is from God

2 My child, if you accept my words
and treasure up my commandments within you,
2 making your ear attentive to wisdom
and inclining your heart to understanding;
3 if you indeed cry out for insight,
and raise your voice for understanding;
4 if you seek it like silver,
and search for it as for hidden treasures—
5 then you will understand the fear of the LORD
and find the knowledge of God.
6 For the LORD gives wisdom;
from his mouth come knowledge and understanding;
7 he stores up sound wisdom for the upright;
he is a shield to those who walk blamelessly,
8 guarding the paths of justice
and preserving the way of his faithful ones.
9 Then you will understand righteousness and justice
and equity, every good path;
10 for wisdom will come into your heart,
and knowledge will be pleasant to your soul;
11 prudence will watch over you;
and understanding will guard you.
12 It will save you from the way of evil,
from those who speak perversely,
13 who forsake the paths of uprightness
to walk in the ways of darkness,
14 who rejoice in doing evil
and delight in the perverseness of evil;
15 those whose paths are crooked,
and who are devious in their ways.

2.1 Prov 3.1; 4.10
2.3 Mt 13.44
2.6 Jas 1.5
2.9 Prov 1.2-6
2.10 Prov 14.33
2.11 Prov 4.19; 6.12
2.14 Prov 10.23

1.31, 32 *Sated* means "filled"; *devices* means "schemes." Many proverbs point out that the "fruit of their way" will be the consequences people will experience in this life. Faced with either choosing God's wisdom or persisting in rebellious independence, many decide to go it alone. The problems such people create for themselves will destroy them.

2.3–6 Wisdom is both a God-given gift and the fruit of an energetic search. Wisdom's starting point is God and his revealed Word, the source of "knowledge and understanding" (2.6). In that sense, it is his gift to us. But he gives it only to those who earnestly seek it. The pathway to wisdom is strenuous. When we are on it, we discover that true wisdom is God's and that we cannot create it by our own efforts. But because God's wisdom is hidden from the rebellious and foolish, it takes effort to find it and use it.

2.9, 10 We gain wisdom through a constant process of growing. First, we must trust and honor God. Second, we must realize that the Bible reveals God's wisdom to us. Third, we must make a lifelong series of right choices. Fourth, when we make sinful or mistaken choices, we must learn from our errors and recover. People don't develop all aspects of wisdom at once. For example, some people have more insight than discretion; others have more knowledge than common sense. But we can pray for all aspects of wisdom and take the steps to develop them in our lives.

2.11 Prudence is discernment, the ability to tell right from wrong. It enables the believer to detect evil motives in men (2.12) and women (2.16). With practice it helps us evaluate courses of action and consequences. For some it is a gift; for most it is developed by using God's truth to make wise choices day by day. Hebrews 5.14 emphasizes that we must discipline ourselves in order to have prudence.

2.16 Prov 6.24; 23.27

16 You will be saved from the loose[b] woman,
from the adulteress with her smooth words,
17 who forsakes the partner of her youth
and forgets her sacred covenant;
18 for her way[c] leads down to death,
and her paths to the shades;
19 those who go to her never come back,
nor do they regain the paths of life.

2.20 Prov 13.20 **2.21** Prov 10.30 **2.22** Deut 28.63

20 Therefore walk in the way of the good,
and keep to the paths of the just.
21 For the upright will abide in the land,
and the innocent will remain in it;
22 but the wicked will be cut off from the land,
and the treacherous will be rooted out of it.

Wisdom is extremely valuable

3.1 Ps 119.93 Prov 9.11; 10.27

3 My child, do not forget my teaching,
but let your heart keep my commandments;
2 for length of days and years of life
and abundant welfare they will give you.

[b] Heb *strange* [c] Cn: Heb *house*

PEOPLE CALLED "WISE" IN THE BIBLE

The special description "wise" is used for 12 significant people in the Bible. They can be helpful models in our own pursuit of wisdom.

The Person	*Their Role*	*Reference*	*How they practiced wisdom*
Joseph	Wise leader	Acts 7.10	Prepared for a major drought. Helped rule Egypt.
Moses	Wise leader	Acts 7.20–22	Learned all the Egyptian wisdom, then graduated to God's lessons in wisdom to lead Israel out of Egypt.
Bezaleel	Wise artist	Exodus 31.1–5	Designed and supervised the construction of the tabernacle and its utensils in the wilderness.
Joshua	Wise leader	Deuteronomy 34.9	Learned by observing Moses, obeyed God, led the people into the promised land.
David	Wise leader	2 Samuel 14.20	Never let his failures keep him from the source of wisdom—reverence for God.
Abigail	Wise wife	1 Samuel 25.3	Managed her household well in spite of an alcoholic husband.
Solomon	Wise leader	1 Kings 3.5–14; 4.29–34	Knew what to do even though he often failed to put his own wisdom into action.
Daniel	Wise counselor	Daniel 5.11, 12	Known as a man in touch with God. A solver of complex problems with God's help
Wise men	Wise learners	Matthew 2.1–12	Not only received special knowledge of God's visit to earth, but checked it out personally.
Stephen	Wise leader	Acts 6.8–10	Organized the distribution of food to the Grecian widows. Preached the gospel to the Jews.
Paul	Wise messenger	2 Peter 3.15, 16	Spent his life communicating God's love to all who would listen.
Christ	Wise youth Wise Savior Wisdom of God	Luke 2.40, 52; 1 Corinthians 1.20–25	Not only lived a perfect life, but died on the cross to save us and make God's wise plan of eternal life available to us.

2.16, 17 A loose woman is a seductive woman or a prostitute. Two of the most difficult sins to resist are pride and sexual immorality. Both are seductive. Pride says, "I deserve it"; sexual desire says, "I need it." In combination, their appeal is deadly. In fact, says Solomon, only by relying on God's strength can we overcome them. Pride appeals to the empty head; sexual enticement to the empty heart. By looking to God, we can fill our heads with his wisdom and our hearts with his love. Don't be fooled – remember what God says about who you are and what you were meant to be. Ask him for strength to resist these temptations.

3 Do not let loyalty and faithfulness forsake you;
bind them around your neck,
write them on the tablet of your heart.
4 So you will find favor and good repute
in the sight of God and of people.

5 Trust in the LORD with all your heart,
and do not rely on your own insight.
6 In all your ways acknowledge him,
and he will make straight your paths.
7 Do not be wise in your own eyes;
fear the LORD, and turn away from evil.
8 It will be a healing for your flesh
and a refreshment for your body.

9 Honor the LORD with your substance
and with the first fruits of all your produce;
10 then your barns will be filled with plenty,
and your vats will be bursting with wine.

11 My child, do not despise the LORD's discipline
or be weary of his reproof,
12 for the LORD reproves the one he loves,
as a father the son in whom he delights.

13 Happy are those who find wisdom,
and those who get understanding,
14 for her income is better than silver,
and her revenue better than gold.
15 She is more precious than jewels,
and nothing you desire can compare with her.
16 Long life is in her right hand;

3.3 Prov 6.21; 7.3
3.4 Prov 8.35; 22.19
3.7 Job 1.1; 28.28 Prov 4.21; 8.13 16.6
3.9 Ex 23.19 Prov 11.24 19.17 Joel 2.24 Mal 3.10
3.11 Deut 8.5 Job 5.17 Ps 94.12 Prov 13.24 Heb 12.5,6
3.13 Job 28.17 Prov 8.10,34 16.16
3.16 Prov 16.7; 22.4

3.3 Two important character qualities are loyalty and faithfulness. Both involve actions as well as attitudes. A loyal person not only feels love; he also acts responsibly. A faithful person not only believes the truth; he also works for justice for others. Thoughts and words are not enough—our lives reveal whether we are truly loyal and faithful. Do your actions measure up to your attitudes?

3.5, 6 When we have an important decision to make, we sometimes feel that we can't trust anyone—not even God. But God knows what is best for us. He is a better judge of what we want than even we are! We must trust him completely in every choice we make. We should not omit careful thinking or belittle our God-given ability to reason; but we should not trust our own ideas to the exclusion of all others. We must not be wise in our own eyes. We should always be willing to listen to and be corrected by God's Word and wise counselors. Bring your decisions to God in prayer; use the Bible as your guide; and then follow God's leading.

3.6 To receive God's guidance, said Solomon, we must acknowledge God in all we do. About a thousand years later, Jesus emphasized this same truth (Matthew 6.33). Look at your values and priorities. What is important to you? Where is God on that list? What is his advice? Make him a vital part of everything you do; then he will guide you because you will be working to accomplish his purposes.

3.9, 10 Many people give God their leftovers. If they can afford to donate anything, they do so. These people may be sincere and contribute willingly, but their attitude is nonetheless backward. It is better to give God the first part of our income. This demonstrates that God, not possessions, has first place in our lives and that our resources belong to him (we are only managers of God's resources). Giving to God first helps us conquer greed, helps us properly manage God's resources, and opens us to God's special blessings.

3.11, 12 *Discipline* means "to teach and to train." Discipline sounds negative to many people because some disciplinarians are not loving. God, however, is the source of all love. He doesn't punish us because he enjoys inflicting pain but because he is deeply concerned about our development. He knows that in order to become morally strong and good, we must learn the difference between right and wrong. His loving discipline enables us to do this.

3.11, 12 It's difficult to know when God has been disciplining us until we look back on the situation later. Not every calamity comes directly from God, of course. But if we rebel against God and refuse to repent when he has identified some sin in our lives, God may use guilt, crises, or bad experiences to bring us back to him. Sometimes, however, difficult times come when there is no flagrant sin in our lives. Our response then should be patience, integrity, and trust that God will show us what to do.

3.13–15 How do people become successful in their family life, in business, or in athletics? By hard work and consistent discipline. The Christian life is much the same. Some people think it's too difficult, but achieving anything worthwhile requires hard work. Being a Christian is not a shortcut to an easy life. When you search for wisdom, working hard at living as God asks, you discover that no worldly success can compare with the joy of knowing God.

3.16, 17 Proverbs contains many strong statements about the benefits of wisdom, including long life, wealth, honor, and peace. If

in her left hand are riches and honor.
17 Her ways are ways of pleasantness,
and all her paths are peace.
18 She is a tree of life to those who lay hold of her;
those who hold her fast are called happy.

3.18 Prov 11.30

19 The LORD by wisdom founded the earth;
by understanding he established the heavens;
20 by his knowledge the deeps broke open,
and the clouds drop down the dew.
21 My child, do not let these escape from your sight:
keep sound wisdom and prudence,
22 and they will be life for your soul
and adornment for your neck.
23 Then you will walk on your way securely
and your foot will not stumble.
24 If you sit down,[d] you will not be afraid;
when you lie down, your sleep will be sweet.
25 Do not be afraid of sudden panic,
or of the storm that strikes the wicked;
26 for the LORD will be your confidence
and will keep your foot from being caught.

3.21 Prov 4.21; 9.11

3.23 Ps 37.23; 91.11 Prov 4.12; 10.9

27 Do not withhold good from those to whom it is due,[e]
when it is in your power to do it.
28 Do not say to your neighbor, "Go, and come again,
tomorrow I will give it" — when you have it with you.

[d] Gk: Heb *lie down* [e] Heb *from its owners*

WISDOM: APPLIED TRUTH
The book of Proverbs tells us about people who have wisdom and enjoy its benefits.

Reference	*The Person Who Has Wisdom*	*Benefits of Wisdom*
Proverbs 3; 4 A father's instructions	Is young Is faithful Trusts in the Lord Puts God first Turns away from evil Knows right from wrong Listens and learns Does what is right	Long, prosperous life Favor with God and people Reputation for good judgment Success Health, vitality Riches, honor, pleasure, peace Protection
Proverbs 8; 9 Wisdom speaks	Possesses knowledge and discernment Hates pride, arrogance, and evil behavior Respects and fears God Gives good advice and has common sense Loves correction and is teachable Knows God	Riches, honor Justice Righteousness Life God's favor Constant learning Understanding

you aren't experiencing them, does this mean you are short on wisdom? Not necessarily. Instead of guarantees, these statements are general principles to make us think. In a perfect world, wise behavior would always lead to these benefits. Even in our troubled world, living wisely usually results in obvious blessings — but not always. Sometimes sin intervenes, and the blessings must be delayed until Jesus returns to establish his eternal kingdom. That is why we must "walk by faith, not by sight" (2 Corinthians 5.7). We can be sure that wisdom ultimately leads to blessing.

3.21 What is the difference between wisdom and prudence? Prudence (or discretion) is the ability God gives to many people to think and make correct choices. Wisdom, however, he gives only to those who follow him. Wisdom includes prudence, but goes beyond it. It also includes the knowledge that comes from instruction, training, and discipline; the understanding that comes through discernment; and the insight that results from knowing and applying God's truths.

3.27, 28 It is easy to get into debt and hard to get out of it. Unfortunately, debt owed to a friend can destroy trust and divide even the best of friends. Delaying the payback is unfair, not just inconvenient. Be as eager to repay your loans as you were to get them, and pay them back ahead of schedule, if possible.

29 Do not plan harm against your neighbor
who lives trustingly beside you.
30 Do not quarrel with anyone without cause,
when no harm has been done to you.
31 Do not envy the violent
and do not choose any of their ways;
32 for the perverse are an abomination to the LORD,
but the upright are in his confidence.
33 The LORD's curse is on the house of the wicked,
but he blesses the abode of the righteous.
34 Toward the scorners he is scornful,
but to the humble he shows favor.
35 The wise will inherit honor,
but stubborn fools, disgrace.

Wisdom can be learned

4 Listen, children, to a father's instruction,
and be attentive, that you may gain[f] insight;
2 for I give you good precepts:
do not forsake my teaching.
3 When I was a son with my father,
tender, and my mother's favorite,
4 he taught me, and said to me,
"Let your heart hold fast my words;
keep my commandments, and live.
5 Get wisdom; get insight: do not forget, nor turn away
from the words of my mouth.
6 Do not forsake her, and she will keep you;
love her, and she will guard you.
7 The beginning of wisdom is this: Get wisdom,
and whatever else you get, get insight.
8 Prize her highly, and she will exalt you;
she will honor you if you embrace her.
9 She will place on your head a fair garland;
she will bestow on you a beautiful crown."

10 Hear, my child, and accept my words,
that the years of your life may be many.
11 I have taught you the way of wisdom;
I have led you in the paths of uprightness.
12 When you walk, your step will not be hampered;

[f] Heb *know*

3.29 Ps 35.20; 55.20 Prov 14.22
3.30 Prov 18.6; 26.17 Rom 12.18
3.31 Ps 37.11; 73.3 Prov 23.17
3.32 Prov 6.16; 11.20
3.34 Jas 4.6
4.1 Prov 1.8; 5.1 6.20
4.4 Prov 3.1; 4.10 9.11
4.6 Prov 2.16; 3.26 8.14,17 2 Thess 2.10
4.7 Ps 119.104 Prov 18.15 23.23
4.12 Ps 37.23; 91.11

3.30 This verse implies that there is a time for quarreling and fighting. Injustice must be combated, sin resisted, and evil confronted wherever it appears. But don't waste time and energy on arguments over trivial matters or personal inconvenience. Save your energy for the real battles against sin and God's enemies.

4.3, 4 One of the greatest responsibilities of parents is to encourage their children to become wise. Here Solomon tells how his father, David, encouraged him to seek after wisdom when he was young ("tender") (see 1 Kings 2.1–9 and 1 Chronicles 28, 29 for David's full charge to his son). This encouragement may have prompted Solomon to ask God for wisdom above everything else (1 Kings 3.9). Wisdom can be passed on from parents to children, from generation to generation. Ultimately, of course, all wisdom comes from God; parents can only urge their children to turn to him. If your parents never taught you in this way, God's Word can function as a loving and compassionate mother or father to you. You can learn from the Scriptures and then create a legacy of wisdom as you rear your own children.

4.5–7 If you want wisdom, you must decide to go after it. It takes resolve – a determination not to abandon the search once you begin no matter how difficult the road may become. This is not a once-in-a-lifetime step, but a daily process of choosing between two paths – the wicked (4.14–17, 19) and the righteous (4.18).

4.7 David taught Solomon as a young boy that seeking God's wisdom was the most important choice he could make. Solomon learned the lesson well. When God appeared to the new king to fulfill any request, Solomon chose wisdom above all else (1 Kings 3.9). We should also make God's wisdom our first choice. We don't have to wait for God to appear to us. We can boldly ask him for wisdom today through prayer (James 1.5). God's wisdom includes insight and understanding.

and if you run, you will not stumble.
4.13 Jn 6.63 13 Keep hold of instruction; do not let go;
guard her, for she is your life.
4.14 Ps 1.1 14 Do not enter the path of the wicked,
and do not walk in the way of evildoers.
15 Avoid it; do not go on it;
turn away from it and pass on.
4.16 Ps 36.4 Mic 2.1 16 For they cannot sleep unless they have done wrong;
they are robbed of sleep unless they have made someone stumble.
17 For they eat the bread of wickedness
and drink the wine of violence.
18 But the path of the righteous is like the light of dawn,
which shines brighter and brighter until full day.
4.19 Jn 1.4,5 19 The way of the wicked is like deep darkness;
they do not know what they stumble over.
20 My child, be attentive to my words;
incline your ear to my sayings.
21 Do not let them escape from your sight;
keep them within your heart.
22 For they are life to those who find them,
and healing to all their flesh.
4.23 Lk 6.45 23 Keep your heart with all vigilance,
for from it flow the springs of life.
4.24 Job 11.14 24 Put away from you crooked speech,
and put devious talk far from you.
4.25 Job 31.1 Mt 6.22 25 Let your eyes look directly forward,
and your gaze be straight before you.
4.26 Prov 5.21; 15.3 Eph 5.15 Heb 12.13 26 Keep straight the path of your feet,
and all your ways will be sure.
4.27 Deut 5.32; 28.14 27 Do not swerve to the right or to the left;
turn your foot away from evil.

Warning against sexual sin

5 My child, be attentive to my wisdom;
incline your ear to my understanding,
2 so that you may hold on to prudence,
and your lips may guard knowledge.

STRATEGY FOR EFFECTIVE LIVING			
	Begins with	God's Wisdom	Respecting and appreciating who God is. Reverence and awe in recognizing the almighty God.
	Requires	Moral Application	Trusting in God and his Word. Allowing his Word to speak to us personally. Willing to obey.
	Requires	Practical Application	Acting on God's direction in daily devotions.
	Results in	Effective Living	Experiencing what God does with our obedience.

4.16, 17 It is difficult for people to accept the fact that friends and aquaintances might be luring them to do wrong. Young people want to be accepted, so they would never want to confront or criticize a friend for wrong plans or actions. Many other people can't even see how their friends' actions could lead to trouble. While we should be accepting of others, we need a healthy scepticism about human behavior. When you feel yourself being heavily influenced, proceed with caution.

4.23–27 Our heart – our feelings of love and desire – dictates to a great extent how we live, because we always find time to do what we enjoy. Solomon tells us to keep our heart with all vigilence, making sure we concentrate on those desires that will keep us on the right path. Make sure your affections push you in the right direction. Put boundaries on your desires: don't go after everything you see. Look straight ahead, keep your eyes fixed on your goal, and don't get sidetracked on detours that lead to sin.

3 For the lips of a loose[g] woman drip honey,
and her speech is smoother than oil;
4 but in the end she is bitter as wormwood,
sharp as a two-edged sword.
5 Her feet go down to death;
her steps follow the path to Sheol.
6 She does not keep straight to the path of life;
her ways wander, and she does not know it.

7 And now, my child,[h] listen to me,
and do not depart from the words of my mouth.
8 Keep your way far from her,
and do not go near the door of her house;
9 or you will give your honor to others,
and your years to the merciless,
10 and strangers will take their fill of your wealth,
and your labors will go to the house of an alien;
11 and at the end of your life you will groan,
when your flesh and body are consumed,
12 and you say, "Oh, how I hated discipline,
and my heart despised reproof!
13 I did not listen to the voice of my teachers
or incline my ear to my instructors.
14 Now I am at the point of utter ruin
in the public assembly."

15 Drink water from your own cistern,
flowing water from your own well.
16 Should your springs be scattered abroad,
streams of water in the streets?
17 Let them be for yourself alone,
and not for sharing with strangers.
18 Let your fountain be blessed,
and rejoice in the wife of your youth,
19 a lovely deer, a graceful doe.
May her breasts satisfy you at all times;
may you be intoxicated always by her love.

5.3 Ps 55.21 Prov 5.20; 7.5
5.4 Eccles 7.26
5.6 Prov 3.23 2 Pet 2.14
5.8 Prov 7.25; 9.14 2 Tim 2.22
5.11 Prov 3.35; 9.13
5.13 Lk 15.18
5.15 Eccles 9.9 Song 4.15
5.18 Eccles 9.9 Mal 2.14
5.19 Song 4.5; 7.3

[g] Heb *strange* [h] Gk Vg: Heb *children*

5.3 This loose woman is a prostitute. Proverbs includes many warnings against illicit sex for several reasons. First, a prostitute's charm is used as an example of any temptation to do wrong or to leave the pursuit of wisdom. Second, sexual immorality of any kind was and still is extremely dangerous. It destroys family life. It erodes a person's ability to love. It degrades human beings and turns them into objects. It can lead to disease. It can result in unwanted children. Third, sexual immorality is against God's law.

5.5 *Sheol* is the word used for the grave or the realm of the dead.

5.13 When temptation strikes, it is too late to ask for advice. When desire is fully activated, people don't want advice – they want satisfaction. The best time to learn the dangers and foolishness of going after forbidden sex (or anything else that is harmful) is long before the temptation comes. Resistance is easier if the decision has already been made. Don't wait to see what happens. Prepare for temptation by deciding *now* how you will act when you face it.

5.15 "Drink water from your own cistern" is a picture of faithfulness in marriage. In desert lands, water is precious, and a well is a family's most important possession. In Old Testament times, it was considered a crime to steal water from someone else's well, just as it was a crime to have intercourse with another man's wife. In both cases, the offender is endangering the family.

5.15–21 In contrast to much of what we read, see, and hear today, this passage urges couples to look to each other for lifelong satisfaction and companionship. Many temptations entice husbands and wives to desert each other for excitement and pleasures to be found elsewhere, when marriage becomes dull. But God designed marriage and sanctified it, and only within this covenant relationship can we find real love and fulfillment. Don't let God's best for you be wasted on the illusion of greener pastures elsewhere. Instead, rejoice with your spouse as you give yourselves to God and to each other.

5.18–20 God does not intend faithfulness in marriage to be boring, lifeless, pleasureless, and dull. Sex is a gift God gives to married people for their mutual enjoyment. Real happiness comes when we decide to find pleasure in the relationship God has given or will give us, and to commit ourselves to making it pleasurable for our spouse. The real danger is in doubting that God knows and cares for us. We then may resent his timing and carelessly pursue sexual pleasure without his blessing.

5.19 See the Song of Solomon, chapter 4, for parallels to this frank expression of the joys of sexual pleasure in marriage.

20 Why should you be intoxicated, my son, by another woman
and embrace the bosom of an adulteress?
5.21 Job 14.16 21 For human ways are under the eyes of the LORD,
and he examines all their paths.
5.22 Num 32.23 22 The iniquities of the wicked ensnare them,
and they are caught in the toils of their sin.
23 They die for lack of discipline,
and because of their great folly they are lost.

Warning against foolish actions

6.1 Prov 17.18 22.26; 27.13 6 My child, if you have given your pledge to your neighbor,
if you have bound yourself to another,[i]
2 you are snared by the utterance of your lips,[j]
caught by the words of your mouth.
3 So do this, my child, and save yourself,
for you have come into your neighbor's power:
go, hurry,[k] and plead with your neighbor.
4 Give your eyes no sleep
and your eyelids no slumber;
5 save yourself like a gazelle from the hunter,[l]
like a bird from the hand of the fowler.

6.6 Prov 10.26 13.4; 30.24,25 6 Go to the ant, you lazybones;
consider its ways, and be wise.
7 Without having any chief
or officer or ruler,
8 it prepares its food in summer,
and gathers its sustenance in harvest.
9 How long will you lie there, O lazybones?
When will you rise from your sleep?
6.10 Prov 24.33,34 10 A little sleep, a little slumber,
a little folding of the hands to rest,
6.11 Prov 23.19 11 and poverty will come upon you like a robber,
and want, like an armed warrior.

6.12 Prov 4.27; 8.13 10.27; 16.27 12 A scoundrel and a villain

[i] Or *a stranger* [j] Cn Compare Gk Syr: Heb *the words of your mouth* [k] Or *humble yourself* [l] Cn: Heb *from the hand*

THINGS GOD HATES
The book of Proverbs notes 14 types of people and actions that God hates. Let these be guidelines of what we are *not* to be and do!

Violent people	Proverbs 3.31
Haughtiness, lying, murdering, scheming, eagerness to do evil, a false witness, stirring up dissension	Proverbs 6.16–19
Those who are untruthful	Proverbs 12.22
The sacrifice of the wicked	Proverbs 15.8
The way of the wicked	Proverbs 15.9
The thoughts of the wicked	Proverbs 15.26
Those who are proud	Proverbs 16.5
Those who judge unjustly	Proverbs 17.15

6.1–5 These verses are not against generosity, but against overextending one's financial resources and acting in irresponsible ways that could lead to poverty. It is important to maintain a balance between generosity and good stewardship. God wants us to help our friends and the needy, but he does not promise to cover the costs of every unwise commitment we make. We should also act responsibly so that our family does not suffer.

6.6–11 Those last few moments of sleep are delicious—we savor them as we resist beginning another workday. But Proverbs warns against giving in to the temptation of laziness, of sleeping instead of working. This does not mean we should never rest: God gave the Jews the sabbath, a weekly day of rest and restoration. But we should not rest when we should be working. If laziness turns us from our responsibilities, poverty will soon bar us from the legitimate rest we should enjoy. (See also the chart in chapter 28.)

goes around with crooked speech,
13 winking the eyes, shuffling the feet,
pointing the fingers,
14 with perverted mind devising evil,
continually sowing discord;
15 on such a one calamity will descend suddenly;
in a moment, damage beyond repair.

16 There are six things that the LORD hates,
seven that are an abomination to him:
17 haughty eyes, a lying tongue,
and hands that shed innocent blood,
18 a heart that devises wicked plans,
feet that hurry to run to evil,
19 a lying witness who testifies falsely,
and one who sows discord in a family.

Warning against adultery

20 My child, keep your father's commandment,
and do not forsake your mother's teaching.
21 Bind them upon your heart always;
tie them around your neck.
22 When you walk, they[m] will lead you;
when you lie down, they[m] will watch over you;
and when you awake, they[m] will talk with you.
23 For the commandment is a lamp and the teaching a light,
and the reproofs of discipline are the way of life,
24 to preserve you from the wife of another,[n]
from the smooth tongue of the adulteress.
25 Do not desire her beauty in your heart,
and do not let her capture you with her eyelashes;
26 for a prostitute's fee is only a loaf of bread,[o]
but the wife of another stalks a man's very life.
27 Can fire be carried in the bosom
without burning one's clothes?
28 Or can one walk on hot coals
without scorching the feet?
29 So is he who sleeps with his neighbor's wife;
no one who touches her will go unpunished.
30 Thieves are not despised who steal only
to satisfy their appetite when they are hungry.
31 Yet if they are caught, they will pay sevenfold;
they will forfeit all the goods of their house.
32 But he who commits adultery has no sense;
he who does it destroys himself.
33 He will get wounds and dishonor,
and his disgrace will not be wiped away.
34 For jealousy arouses a husband's fury,

6.14 Prov 10.32; 17.11
6.16-19 Gen 6.5; Prov 1.16; 6.14; 19.5,9; 21.4; 24.2; 28.17; 30.21; Isa 1.15
6.20 Prov 1.7
6.23 Ps 119.105; Prov 13.9
6.25 2 Kgs 9.30; Prov 21.4; Mt 5.28
6.29 Prov 16.5; Jer 5.8; Ezek 22.11
6.31 Ex 22.7
6.32 Prov 7.7,22,23; 9.14,16
6.33 Ps 51.8; Prov 18.3
6.34 Lev 20.10; Prov 27.4; Song 8.6

[m] Heb *it* [n] Gk: MT *the evil woman* [o] Cn Compare Gk Syr Vg Tg: Heb *for because of a harlot to a piece of bread*

6.20–23 It is natural and good for children, as they grow toward adulthood, to become increasingly independent of their parents. Young adults, however, should take care not to turn a deaf ear to their parents – to reject their advice just when it is needed most. If you are struggling with a decision or looking for insight, check with your parents or other older adults who know you well. Their extra years of experience may have given them the wisdom you seek.

6.25–35 Some people argue that it is all right to break God's law against sexual sin if nobody gets hurt. In truth, somebody always gets hurt. Spouses are devastated. Children are scarred. The partners themselves, even if they escape disease and unwanted pregnancy, lose their ability to fulfill commitments, to feel sexual desire, to trust, and to be entirely open with another person. God's laws are not arbitrary. They do not forbid good, clean fun; rather, they warn us against destroying ourselves through unwise actions or running ahead of God's timetable.

and he shows no restraint when he takes revenge.
35 He will accept no compensation,
and refuses a bribe no matter how great.

Wisdom guards against immorality

7 My child, keep my words
and store up my commandments with you;
2 keep my commandments and live,
keep my teachings as the apple of your eye;
3 bind them on your fingers,
write them on the tablet of your heart.
4 Say to wisdom, "You are my sister,"
and call insight your intimate friend,
5 that they may keep you from the loose[p] woman,
from the adulteress with her smooth words.

6 For at the window of my house
I looked out through my lattice,
7 and I saw among the simple ones,
I observed among the youths,
a young man without sense,
8 passing along the street near her corner,
taking the road to her house
9 in the twilight, in the evening,
at the time of night and darkness.

10 Then a woman comes toward him,
decked out like a prostitute, wily of heart.[q]
11 She is loud and wayward;
her feet do not stay at home;
12 now in the street, now in the squares,
and at every corner she lies in wait.
13 She seizes him and kisses him,
and with impudent face she says to him:
14 "I had to offer sacrifices,
and today I have paid my vows;
15 so now I have come out to meet you,
to seek you eagerly, and I have found you!
16 I have decked my couch with coverings,
colored spreads of Egyptian linen;
17 I have perfumed my bed with myrrh,
aloes, and cinnamon.
18 Come, let us take our fill of love until morning;
let us delight ourselves with love.
19 For my husband is not at home;
he has gone on a long journey.
20 He took a bag of money with him;
he will not come home until full moon."

21 With much seductive speech she persuades him;

7.2 Ps 17.8; Prov 4.4; 9.11; 10.27; 16.22
7.3 Deut 6.8
7.5 Prov 4.24; 22.14
7.7 Prov 1.22; 6.32; 8.5; 22.3
7.8 Prov 4.14,15; 5.8; 7.12,27
7.10 Gen 38.14,15; Isa 3.16; 23.16
7.11 Prov 9.13; 23.28
7.16 Ps 45.8; Prov 31.22; Ezek 27.7
7.21 Prov 5.3; 6.24

[p] Heb *strange* [q] Meaning of Heb uncertain

7.6–23 Although this advice is directed toward young men, young women should heed it as well. The person who has no purpose in life is simpleminded (7.7). Without aim or direction, an empty life is unstable, vulnerable to many temptations. Even though the young man in this passage doesn't know where he is going, the seductress knows where she wants him. Notice her strategies: she is dressed to allure men (7.10); her approach is bold (7.13); she invites him over to her place (7.16–18); she cunningly answers his every objection (7.19, 20); she flatters him (7.21); she traps him (7.23). To combat temptation, make sure your life is full of God's Word and wisdom (7.4). Recognize the strategies of temptation, and run away from them – fast.

with her smooth talk she compels him.
22 Right away he follows her,
and goes like an ox to the slaughter,
or bounds like a stag toward the trap[r]
23 until an arrow pierces its entrails.
He is like a bird rushing into a snare,
not knowing that it will cost him his life.

24 And now, my children, listen to me,
and be attentive to the words of my mouth.
25 Do not let your hearts turn aside to her ways;
do not stray into her paths.
26 for many are those she has laid low,
and numerous are her victims.
27 Her house is the way to Sheol,
going down to the chambers of death.

Wisdom gives good advice

8 Does not wisdom call,
and does not understanding raise her voice?
2 On the heights, beside the way,
at the crossroads she takes her stand;
3 beside the gates in front of the town,
at the entrance of the portals she cries out:
4 "To you, O people, I call,
and my cry is to all that live.
5 O simple ones, learn prudence;
acquire intelligence, you who lack it.
6 Hear, for I will speak noble things,
and from my lips will come what is right;
7 for my mouth will utter truth;
wickedness is an abomination to my lips.
8 All the words of my mouth are righteous;
there is nothing twisted or crooked in them.
9 They are all straight to one who understands
and right to those who find knowledge.
10 Take my instruction instead of silver,
and knowledge rather than choice gold;
11 for wisdom is better than jewels,
and all that you may desire cannot compare with her.
12 I, wisdom, live with prudence,[s]
and I attain knowledge and discretion.
13 The fear of the LORD is hatred of evil.
Pride and arrogance and the way of evil
and perverted speech I hate.

[r] Cn Compare Gk: Meaning of Heb uncertain [s] Meaning of Heb uncertain

7.23 Prov 1.17 Eccles 9.12

7.24 Prov 4.1; 5.7

7.25 Prov 4.23; 5.8

7.27 Prov 2.18; 5.5

8.1 Job 19.7

8.4 Ps 19.7

8.9 Ps 25.12

8.10 Ps 119.72,127

8.11 Prov 3.14,15 16.16; 20.15

8.13 Isa 13.11

7.25 There are definite steps you can take to avoid sexual sins. First, guard your mind. Don't read books, look at pictures, or encourage fantasies that stimulate the wrong desires. Second, keep away from settings and friends that tempt you to sin. Third, don't think only of the moment – focus on the future. Today's thrill may lead to tomorrow's ruin.

7.27 *Sheol* means the grave or the place of the dead.

8.1ff Wisdom's call is contrasted to the call of the seductress in chapter 7. Wisdom is portrayed as a woman who guides us (8.1–13) and makes us succeed (8.14–21). Wisdom was present at the creation and works with the Creator (8.22–31). God approves of those who listen to wisdom's counsel (8.32–35). Those who hate wisdom love death (8.36). Wisdom should affect every aspect of our entire lives, from beginning to end. Be sure to open all corners of your life to God's direction and guidance.

8.3 A portal is an entrance door.

8.13 The more a person respects and fears God, the more he or she will hate evil. Love for God and love for sin cannot coexist. Harboring secret sins means that you are tolerating evil within yourself. Make a clean break with sin and commit yourself completely to God.

8.14 Isa 1.26 Rom 13.1
8.17 1 Sam 2.30 Jn 14.21
8.18 Ps 112.3 Mt 6.33
8.20 Ps 23.3; 25.4 Isa 2.3
8.22 Job 28.27 Ps 104.24 Jn 1.1
8.23 Jn 17.5,24
8.24 Gen 1.9 Job 38.16
8.27 Job 26.10; 38.6 Ps 33.6; 104.5
8.32 Prov 5.7; 29.18
8.34 Ps 27.4 Prov 1.21; 2.3
8.35 Jn 17.3
8.36 Prov 15.32

14 I have good advice and sound wisdom;
I have insight, I have strength.
15 By me kings reign,
and rulers decree what is just;
16 by me rulers rule,
and nobles, all who govern rightly.
17 I love those who love me,
and those who seek me diligently find me.
18 Riches and honor are with me,
enduring wealth and prosperity.
19 My fruit is better than gold, even fine gold,
and my yield than choice silver.
20 I walk in the way of righteousness,
along the paths of justice,
21 endowing with wealth those who love me,
and filling their treasuries.
22 The LORD created me at the beginning[t] of his work,[u]
the first of his acts of long ago.
23 Ages ago I was set up,
at the first, before the beginning of the earth.
24 When there were no depths I was brought forth,
when there were no springs abounding with water.
25 Before the mountains had been shaped,
before the hills, I was brought forth—
26 when he had not yet made earth and fields,[v]
or the world's first bits of soil.
27 When he established the heavens, I was there,
when he drew a circle on the face of the deep,
28 when he made firm the skies above,
when he established the fountains of the deep,
29 when he assigned to the sea its limit,
so that the waters might not transgress his command,
when he marked out the foundations of the earth,
30 then I was beside him, like a master worker;[w]
and I was daily his[x] delight,
rejoicing before him always,
31 rejoicing in his inhabited world
and delighting in the human race.

32 And now, my children, listen to me:
happy are those who keep my ways.
33 Hear instruction and be wise,
and do not neglect it.
34 Happy is the one who listens to me,
watching daily at my gates,
waiting beside my doors.
35 For whoever finds me finds life
and obtains favor from the LORD;
36 but those who miss me injure themselves;
all who hate me love death."

[t] Or *me as the beginning* [u] Heb *way* [v] Meaning of Heb uncertain [w] Another reading is *little child* [x] Gk: Heb lacks *his*

8.22–31 God says wisdom is primary and fundamental. It is the foundation on which all life is built. Paul and John may have alluded to some of Solomon's statements about wisdom to describe Christ's presence at the creation of the world (Colossians 1.15–17; 2.2, 3; Revelation 3.14).

Wisdom is its own reward

9 Wisdom has built her house,
she has hewn her seven pillars.
2 She has slaughtered her animals, she has mixed her wine,
she has also set her table.
3 She has sent out her servant girls, she calls
from the highest places in the town,
4 "You that are simple, turn in here!"
To those without sense she says,
5 "Come, eat of my bread
and drink of the wine I have mixed.
6 Lay aside immaturity,[y] and live,
and walk in the way of insight."

7 Whoever corrects a scoffer wins abuse;
whoever rebukes the wicked gets hurt.
8 A scoffer who is rebuked will only hate you;
the wise, when rebuked, will love you.
9 Give instruction[z] to the wise, and they will become wiser still;
teach the righteous and they will gain in learning.
10 The fear of the LORD is the beginning of wisdom,
and the knowledge of the Holy One is insight.
11 For by me your days will be multiplied,
and years will be added to your life.
12 If you are wise, you are wise for yourself;
if you scoff, you alone will bear it.

13 The foolish woman is loud;
she is ignorant and knows nothing.
14 She sits at the door of her house,
on a seat at the high places of the town,
15 calling to those who pass by,
who are going straight on their way,
16 "You who are simple, turn in here!"
And to those without sense she says,
17 "Stolen water is sweet,
and bread eaten in secret is pleasant."
18 But they do not know that the dead[a] are there,
that her guests are in the depths of Sheol.

9.1 Eph 2.20 Heb 3.5,6 1 Pet 2.5
9.3 Mt 22.3
9.6 Prov 3.22; 4.22 9.11; 16.22
9.9 Prov 1.5; 25.12
9.10 Job 28.28 Ps 111.10
9.12 Job 22.2 Ezek 18.4 Gal 6.5
9.17 Prov 20.17 30.20

[y] Or *simpleness* [z] Heb lacks *instruction* [a] Heb *shades*

9.1 The seven pillars are figurative; they do not represent seven principles of wisdom. In the Bible, the number seven represents completeness and perfection. This verse poetically states that wisdom lacks nothing—it is complete and perfect.

9.1ff Wisdom and foolishness are portrayed in this chapter as rival young women, each preparing a feast and inviting people to it. But wisdom is a responsible woman of character, while foolishness is a prostitute serving stolen food. Wisdom appeals first to the mind; foolishness to the senses. It is easier to excite the senses, but the pleasures of foolishness are temporary. By contrast, the satisfaction that wisdom brings lasts forever.

9.1–5 The banquet described in this chapter has some interesting parallels to the banquet Jesus described in one of his parables (Luke 14.15–24). Many may intend to go, but they never make it because they get sidetracked by other activities that seem more important at the time. Don't let anything become more important than your search for God's wisdom.

9.7–10 Are you a scorner or a wise person? You can tell by the way you respond to criticism. Instead of tossing back a quick put-down or clever retort when rebuked, listen to what is being said. Learn from your critics; this is the path to wisdom. Wisdom begins with knowing God. He gives insight into living because he created life. To know God is not just to know the facts about him, but to stand in awe of him and have a relationship with him. Do you really want to be wise? Get to know God better and better. (See James 1.5, 2 Peter 1.2–4 for more on how to become wise.)

9.14–17 There is something hypnotic and intoxicating about wickedness. One sin leads us to want more; sinful behavior seems more exciting than the "boring" Christian life. That is why many people put aside all thought of wisdom's sumptuous banquet (9.1–5) in order to eat the stolen food of foolishness. Don't be deceived—sin is dangerous. Before reaching for forbidden fruit, take a long look at what happens to those who eat it. (See the chart in chapter 21.)

9.18 *Sheol* means the grave or place of the dead.

B. WISDOM FOR ALL PEOPLE (10.1—24.34)

These short couplets are what we commonly recognize as proverbs. They cover a wide range of topics. The first section was written by Solomon. The next two sections were written by others, but collected by Solomon. These sayings give people practical wisdom for godly living at every stage of life.

Proverbs of Solomon

10.1 Prov 15.20

10 The proverbs of Solomon.

A wise child makes a glad father,
but a foolish child is a mother's grief.
2 Treasures gained by wickedness do not profit,
but righteousness delivers from death.
3 The LORD does not let the righteous go hungry,
but he thwarts the craving of the wicked.
4 A slack hand causes poverty,
but the hand of the diligent makes rich.
5 A child who gathers in summer is prudent,
but a child who sleeps in harvest brings shame.
6 Blessings are on the head of the righteous,
but the mouth of the wicked conceals violence.
7 The memory of the righteous is a blessing,
but the name of the wicked will rot.
8 The wise of heart will heed commandments,
but a babbling fool will come to ruin.
9 Whoever walks in integrity walks securely,
but whoever follows perverse ways will be found out.
10 Whoever winks the eye causes trouble,
but the one who rebukes boldly makes peace.[b]
11 The mouth of the righteous is a fountain of life,
but the mouth of the wicked conceals violence.
12 Hatred stirs up strife,
but love covers all offenses.
13 On the lips of one who has understanding wisdom is found,
but a rod is for the back of one who lacks sense.
14 The wise lay up knowledge,
but the babbling of a fool brings ruin near.
15 The wealth of the rich is their fortress;
the poverty of the poor is their ruin.
16 The wage of the righteous leads to life,
the gain of the wicked to sin.
17 Whoever heeds instruction is on the path to life,
but one who rejects a rebuke goes astray.
18 Lying lips conceal hatred,

10.3 Ps 34.9,10 37.25 Mt 6.33
10.4 Prov 6.6
10.6 Prov 9.11; 28.20
10.7 Ps 9.5,6 109.13; 112.6
10.8 Mt 7.24
10.9 Ps 23.4 Prov 3.23; 26.27 Isa 33.15,16 Mt 10.26
10.10 Prov 6.13
10.11 Ps 37.20 Prov 13.14 18.4; 20.5
10.12 Prov 17.9 1 Cor 13.4-7
10.14 Prov 13.3; 18.7 Jas 3.2,5
10.15 Prov 18.11; 19.7
10.17 Prov 6.23; 12.1 22.17
10.18 Prov 26.24

[b] Gk: Heb *but a babbling fool will come to ruin*

10.2 Some people bring unhappiness on themselves by choosing wrong living. God's principles for right living bring lasting happiness because they guide us into long-term right behavior in spite of our ever-changing feelings.

10.3 Proverbs is full of verses contrasting the good person with the wicked. These statements are not intended to apply universally to all people in every situation. For example, some good people do starve. Rather, they are intended to communicate the general truth that the life of the person who seeks God is better in the long run than the life of the wicked person, which leads to ruin. In addition, a proverb like this assumes a just government that cares for the poor and needy—the kind of government Israel was intended to have (see Deuteronomy 24.17–22). A corrupt government often thwarts the plans of good men and women.

10.4, 5 Every day has 24 hours filled with opportunities to grow, serve, and be productive. Yet it is so easy to waste time, letting life slip from our grasp. See time as God's gift and seize your opportunities to live for him.

10.10 Sin is serious not just because of what it does to us and to others, but because it is personal rebellion against God. He does not take sin lightly, and we dare not either. If there is an area in your life that you have been withholding from God's control, end your rebellion. Boldly confront it and confess it to God, because sin is serious business.

10.18 By hating another person you may become a liar or a fool. If you try to conceal your hate, you end up lying. If you slander the other person and are proven wrong, you are a fool. The only way out is to admit your hateful feelings to God. Ask him to change your heart, to help you love instead of hate.

and whoever utters slander is a fool.
19 When words are many, transgression is not lacking,
but the prudent are restrained in speech.
20 The tongue of the righteous is choice silver;
the mind of the wicked is of little worth.
21 The lips of the righteous feed many,
but fools die for lack of sense.
22 The blessing of the LORD makes rich,
and he adds no sorrow with it.[c]
23 Doing wrong is like sport to a fool,
but wise conduct is pleasure to a person of understanding.
24 What the wicked dread will come upon them,
but the desire of the righteous will be granted.
25 When the tempest passes, the wicked are no more,
but the righteous are established forever.
26 Like vinegar to the teeth, and smoke to the eyes,
so are the lazy to their employers.
27 The fear of the LORD prolongs life,
but the years of the wicked will be short.
28 The hope of the righteous ends in gladness,
but the expectation of the wicked comes to nothing.
29 The way of the LORD is a stronghold for the upright,
but destruction for evildoers.
30 The righteous will never be removed,
but the wicked will not remain in the land.
31 The mouth of the righteous brings forth wisdom,
but the perverse tongue will be cut off.
32 The lips of the righteous know what is acceptable,
but the mouth of the wicked what is perverse.

11 A false balance is an abomination to the LORD,
but an accurate weight is his delight.
2 When pride comes, then comes disgrace;
but wisdom is with the humble.
3 The integrity of the upright guides them,
but the crookedness of the treacherous destroys them.
4 Riches do not profit in the day of wrath,
but righteousness delivers from death.
5 The righteousness of the blameless keeps their ways straight,
but the wicked fall by their own wickedness.
6 The righteousness of the upright saves them,
but the treacherous are taken captive by their schemes.
7 When the wicked die, their hope perishes,
and the expectation of the godless comes to nothing.

10.19 Job 11.2 Prov 18.21
10.21 Prov 12.18; 15.4 Hos 4.6
10.22 Gen 24.35 26.12 Deut 8.18
10.23 Prov 2.14; 15.21
10.24 Job 15.21 Prov 1.27; 15.8
10.25 Ps 15.1-5; 125.1
10.27 Ps 55.23 Prov 14.27
10.28 Job 11.20
10.30 Ps 37.25; 125.1 Prov 2.22
10.31 Ps 37.30
10.32 Prov 6.12 Eccles 12.10
11.1 Deut 25.13-16
11.2 Prov 16.18
11.3 Prov 13.6; 21.7
11.6 Ps 7.15,16 9.15

[c] *Or and toil adds nothing to it*

10.20 A lot of poor advice is worth less than a little good advice. It is easy to get opinions from people who will tell us only what they think will please us, but such advice is not helpful. Instead we should look for those who will speak the truth, even when it hurts. Think about the people to whom you go for advice. What do you expect to hear from them?

10.22 God supplies most people with the personal and financial abilities to respond to the needs of others. If we all realized how God has blessed us, and if we all used our resources to do God's will, hunger and poverty would be wiped out. Wealth is a blessing only if we use it in the way God intended.

10.24 Those who do not believe in God usually fear death, and with good reason. By contrast, believers desire eternal life and God's salvation – their hopes will be rewarded. This verse offers a choice: you can have either your fears or your desires come true. You make that choice by rejecting God and living your own way, or by accepting God and following him.

11.4 "The day of wrath" refers to the time of our death or to the time when God settles accounts with all people. On Judgment Day, each of us will stand alone, accountable for all our deeds. At that time, no amount of riches will buy reconciliation with God. Only our love for and obedience to God will count.

11.8 This verse, like 10.3, contrasts two paths in life, but is not intended to apply universally to all people in all circumstances. It does not exclude God's people from problems or struggles. If a person follows God's wisdom, however, God can rescue him from

11.8 Ps 22.8 51.14,15

8 The righteous are delivered from trouble,
and the wicked get into it instead.
9 With their mouths the godless would destroy their neighbors,
but by knowledge the righteous are delivered.

11.10 Prov 28.28

10 When it goes well with the righteous, the city rejoices;
and when the wicked perish, there is jubilation.
11 By the blessing of the upright a city is exalted,
but it is overthrown by the mouth of the wicked.

11.12 Prov 10.14 13.3; 18.7

12 Whoever belittles another lacks sense,
but an intelligent person remains silent.

11.13 Prov 19.11 20.19 1 Tim 5.13

13 A gossip goes about telling secrets,
but one who is trustworthy in spirit keeps a confidence.

11.14 Prov 15.22 20.18; 24.6

14 Where there is no guidance, a nation[d] falls,
but in an abundance of counselors there is safety.

11.15 Prov 6.1; 27.13

15 To guarantee loans for a stranger brings trouble,
but there is safety in refusing to do so.
16 A gracious woman gets honor,
but she who hates virtue is covered with shame.[e]
The timid become destitute,[f]
but the aggressive gain riches.

11.17 Mt 5.7; 25.34-36

17 Those who are kind reward themselves,
but the cruel do themselves harm.

11.18 Hos 10.12

18 The wicked earn no real gain,
but those who sow righteousness get a true reward.

11.19 Prov 10.16 19.23; 21.16 Rom 6.23

19 Whoever is steadfast in righteousness will live,
but whoever pursues evil will die.
20 Crooked minds are an abomination to the LORD,
but those of blameless ways are his delight.

11.20 Ps 75.5 Prov 13.6; 21.29

21 Be assured, the wicked will not go unpunished,
but those who are righteous will escape.

[d] Or *an army* [e] Compare Gk Syr: Heb lacks *but she . . . shame* [f] Gk: Heb lacks *The timid . . . destitute*

GOD'S ADVICE ABOUT MONEY

Proverbs gives some practical instruction on the use of money, although sometimes it is advice we would rather not hear. It's more comfortable to continue in our habits than to learn how to use money more wisely. The advice includes:

Be generous in giving	11.24, 25; 22.9
Place people's needs ahead of profit	11.26
Be cautious of countersigning for another	17.18; 22.26, 27
Don't accept bribes	17.23
Help the poor	19.17; 21.13
Store up for the future	21.20
Be careful about borrowing	22.7

Other verses to study include: 11.15; 20.16; 25.14; 27.13

trouble. But a wicked person will fall into his or her own traps. Even if a good person suffers, he can be sure he will ultimately be rescued from eternal death.

11.9 Words can be used either as weapons or tools, hurting relationships or building them up. Sadly, it is often easier to destroy than to build, and most people have received more destructive words than words that build up. Every person you meet today is either a demolition site or a construction opportunity. Your words will make a difference. Will they be weapons for destruction or tools for construction?

11.14 A good leader needs and uses wise counselors. One person's perspective and understanding is severely limited; he or she may not have all the facts or may be blinded by bias, emotions, or wrong impressions. To be a wise leader at home, at church, or at work, seek the counsel of others and be open to their advice. Then, after considering all the facts, make your decision. (See the chart in chapter 29.)

11.19 Why does righteousness lead to life? A righteous person finds life because wisdom makes the hours of the day more profitable and the years more fruitful (9.11). He or she lives life more fully each day. He also finds life because people usually live longer when they live right, with proper diet, exercise, and rest. In addition, he need not fear death because eternal life is God's gift to him (John 11.25). By contrast, the evil person not only finds eternal death, but also misses out on real life on earth.

22 Like a gold ring in a pig's snout
is a beautiful woman without good sense.
23 The desire of the righteous ends only in good;
the expectation of the wicked in wrath.
24 Some give freely, yet grow all the richer;
others withhold what is due, and only suffer want.
25 A generous person will be enriched,
and one who gives water will get water.
26 The people curse those who hold back grain,
but a blessing is on the head of those who sell it.
27 Whoever diligently seeks good seeks favor,
but evil comes to the one who searches for it.
28 Those who trust in their riches will wither,[g]
but the righteous will flourish like green leaves.
29 Those who trouble their households will inherit wind,
and the fool will be servant to the wise.
30 The fruit of the righteous is a tree of life,
but violence[h] takes lives away.
31 If the righteous are repaid on earth,
how much more the wicked and the sinner!

12 Whoever loves discipline loves knowledge,
but those who hate to be rebuked are stupid.
2 The good obtain favor from the LORD,
but those who devise evil he condemns.
3 No one finds security by wickedness,
but the root of the righteous will never be moved.
4 A good wife is the crown of her husband,
but she who brings shame is like rottenness in his bones.
5 The thoughts of the righteous are just;
the advice of the wicked is treacherous.
6 The words of the wicked are a deadly ambush,
but the speech of the upright delivers them.

11.22 Ezek 16.15; 1 Pet 3.3
11.23 Rom 2.8,9
11.24 Prov 3.9,10; Mt 5.7; 2 Cor 9.6,7
11.26 Gen 41.56,57; Amos 8.4
11.27 Prov 17.11
11.28 Ps 1.2,3; 92.12; Jer 17.7,8; Mk 10.24,25; 1 Tim 6.17
11.29 Prov 14.19; 15.27
11.30 Jas 5.20
12.1 Prov 25.12
12.3 Ps 15.1-5
12.4 Prov 14.1; 19.13; 21.9; 27.15; 31.10; 1 Cor 11.7
12.5 Prov 16.23; Mt 12.34; 15.18
12.6 Ps 12.5; 35.11; Prov 14.3; 31.8

g Cn: Heb *fall* h Cn Compare Gk Syr: Heb *a wise man*

11.22 Physical attractiveness without strength of character soon wears thin. We are to seek those qualities that help us make wise decisions, not just those that make us look good. Not everyone who looks good is pleasant to live or work with. While taking good care of our body and appearance is not wrong, we also need to develop our ability to think.

11.24, 25 These two verses present a paradox: that we become richer by being generous. The world says to hold on to as much as possible, but God blesses those who give freely of their possessions, time, and energy. When we give, God supplies us with more so that we can give more. In addition, giving helps us gain a right perspective on our possessions. We realize they were never really ours to begin with, but were given to us by God to be used to help others. What then do we gain by giving? Freedom from enslavement to our possessions, the joy of helping others, and God's approval.

11.29 One of the greatest resources God gives us is the family. Families provide acceptance, encouragement, guidance, and counsel. Rejecting your family – whether through anger or through an exaggerated desire for independence – is foolish because you cut yourself off from all they provide. In your family, strive for healing, communication, and understanding.

11.30 A wise person is a model of a meaningful life. His or her sense of purpose attracts others who want to know how they too can find meaning. Gaining wisdom yourself, then, can be the first step in leading people to God. Leading people to God is important because it keeps us in touch with God while offering others eternal life.

11.31 Contrary to popular opinion, no one sins and gets away with it. The faithful are rewarded for their faith. The wicked are punished for their sins. Don't think for a moment that "it won't matter" or "nobody will know" or "we won't get caught" (see also 1 Peter 4.18).

12.1 If you don't want to learn, years of schooling will teach you very little. But if you want to be taught, there is no end to what you can learn. This includes being willing to accept correction and to learn from the wisdom of others. A person who refuses constructive criticism has a problem with pride. Such a person is unlikely to learn very much.

12.3 To find security means to be successful, and Solomon says that real success comes only to those who do what is right. Then, what kind of success does wickedness bring? We all know people who cheat to pass the course or to get a larger tax refund – is this not success? And what about the person who ignores his family commitments and mistreats his workers but gets ahead in business? These apparent successes are only temporary. They are bought at the expense of character. Cheaters grow more and more dishonest, and those who hurt others become callous and cruel. In the long run, evil behavior does not lead to success; it leads only to more evil. Real success does not compromise personal integrity. If you are not a success by God's standards, you have not achieved true success. (See the chart in chapter 20.)

12.7 Isa 3.10,11 Mt 7.24-27

7 The wicked are overthrown and are no more,
but the house of the righteous will stand.
8 One is commended for good sense,
but a perverse mind is despised.

12.9 Lk 14.11

9 Better to be despised and have a servant,
than to be self-important and lack food.
10 The righteous know the needs of their animals,
but the mercy of the wicked is cruel.

12.11 Prov 9.6; 14.24

11 Those who till their land will have plenty of food,
but those who follow worthless pursuits have no sense.

12.12 Prov 1.18,19 11.24,25; 21.10

12 The wicked covet the proceeds of wickedness,[i]
but the root of the righteous bears fruit.

12.13 Prov 25.18

13 The evil are ensnared by the transgression of their lips,
but the righteous escape from trouble.

12.14 Prov 24.12 Isa 3.10

14 From the fruit of the mouth one is filled with good things,
and manual labor has its reward.

12.15 Prov 14.12 16.2; 21.2

15 Fools think their own way is right,
but the wise listen to advice.

12.16 Prov 19.11 29.11

16 Fools show their anger at once,
but the prudent ignore an insult.
17 Whoever speaks the truth gives honest evidence,
but a false witness speaks deceitfully.

12.18 Prov 8.6,7; 15.4

18 Rash words are like sword thrusts,
but the tongue of the wise brings healing.

[i] Or *covet the catch of the wicked*

TEACHING AND LEARNING

Good teaching comes from good learning—and Proverbs has more to say to students than to teachers. Proverbs is concerned with the learning of wisdom. The book makes it clear that there are no good alternatives to learning wisdom. We are either becoming wise learners or refusing to learn and becoming foolish failures. Proverbs encourages us to make the right choice.

Wise Learners	*Proverb(s)*	*Foolish Failures*
Quietly accept instruction and criticism	10.8; 23.12; 25.12	Ignore instruction
Love discipline	12.1	Hate correction
Listen to advice	12.15; 21.11; 24.6	Think they need no advice
Accept parents' discipline	13.1	Mock parents
Lead others to life	10.17	Lead others astray
Receive honor	13.18	End in poverty and shame
Profit from constructive rebuke	15.31, 32; 29.1	Self-destruct by refusing rebuke

Advice to teachers:
Help people avoid traps (13.14).
Use pleasant words (16.21).
Speak at the right time (15.23; 18.20).

12.13 Dishonest people who twist the facts to support the claims they are making are likely to be trapped by their own lies. But for someone who always tells the truth, the facts—plain and unvarnished—give an unshakable defense. If you find you always have to defend yourself to others, maybe your honesty is less than it should be. (See the chart in chapter 21.)

12.16 When someone insults or embarrasses you, it is natural to retaliate. But this solves nothing and only encourages trouble. Instead, answer slowly and quietly. Your positive response will achieve positive results. Proverbs 15.1 says, "A soft answer turns away wrath."

19 Truthful lips endure forever,
but a lying tongue lasts only a moment.
20 Deceit is in the mind of those who plan evil,
but those who counsel peace have joy.
21 No harm happens to the righteous,
but the wicked are filled with trouble.
22 Lying lips are an abomination to the LORD,
but those who act faithfully are his delight.
23 One who is clever conceals knowledge,
but the mind of a fool[j] broadcasts folly.
24 The hand of the diligent will rule,
while the lazy will be put to forced labor.
25 Anxiety weighs down the human heart,
but a good word cheers it up.
26 The righteous gives good advice to friends,[k]
but the way of the wicked leads astray.
27 The lazy do not roast[l] their game,
but the diligent obtain precious wealth.[l]
28 In the path of righteousness there is life,
in walking its path there is no death.

13 A wise child loves discipline,[m]
but a scoffer does not listen to rebuke.
2 From the fruit of their words good persons eat good things,
but the desire of the treacherous is for wrongdoing.
3 Those who guard their mouths preserve their lives;
those who open wide their lips come to ruin.
4 The appetite of the lazy craves, and gets nothing,
while the appetite of the diligent is richly supplied.
5 The righteous hate falsehood,
but the wicked act shamefully and disgracefully.
6 Righteousness guards one whose way is upright,
but sin overthrows the wicked.
7 Some pretend to be rich, yet have nothing;

12.19 Job 20.5 Prov 19.9
12.20 Prov 2.10 26.24-26
12.22 Isa 19.21
12.25 Prov 15.13 17.22
12.26 Prov 18.15
13.3 Prov 18.7,21 20.19; 21.23 Jas 3.2
13.4 Prov 12.11,24 14.11; 22.29
13.5 Prov 3.35
13.6 Ps 15.3
13.7 Lk 12.20,21 Jas 2.5

j Heb *the heart of fools* k Syr: Meaning of Heb uncertain l Meaning of Heb uncertain m Cn: Heb *A wise child the discipline of his father*

12.19 Truth is always timely; it applies today and in the future. Because it is connected with God's changeless character, it is also changeless. Think for a moment about the centuries that have passed since these proverbs were written. Consider the countless hours that have been spent carefully studying every sentence of Scripture. The Bible has withstood the test of time. Because God is truth, you can trust his Word to guide you.

12.21 This is another general, but not universal, truth. Although misfortune does come to good people, they are able to see opportunities in their problems and move ahead. The wicked, without God's wisdom, are unequipped to handle their problems. (See the notes on 3.16, 17; 10.3; 11.8 for more about general truths that are not intended as universal statements.)

12.23 "Clever" or skilled people have a quiet confidence. Insecure or uncertain people feel the need to prove themselves, but skillful people don't have to prove anything. They know they are capable, so they can get on with their work. Beware of showing off. If you are modest, people may not notice you at first, but they will respect you later.

12.27 Waste has become a way of life for many who live in a land of plenty. But waste is a sign of laziness. Waste is poor stewardship. Make good use of everything God has given you, and prize it as "precious wealth."

12.28 For many, death is a darkened door at the end of their lives, a passageway to an unknown and feared destiny. But for God's people, death is a bright doorway to a new and better life. So why do we fear death? Is it because of the pain we expect, the separation from loved ones, its surprise? God can help us deal with those fears. He has shown us that death is just another step in the continuing eternal life we began when we started to follow him. Death is not final; it is the first step into eternity.

13.3 You have not mastered self-control if you do not control what you say. Words can cut and destroy. James recognized this truth when he stated, "The tongue is a small member, yet it boasts of great exploits" (James 3.5). If you want to be self-controlled, begin with your tongue. Stop and think before you react or speak. If you can control this small but powerful member, you can control the rest of your body. (See the chart in chapter 27.)

13.6 Living right is like posting a guard and a guide for your life. Every choice for good sets into motion other opportunities for good. Evil choices follow the same pattern, but in the opposite direction. Each choice you make in obedience to God's Word will bring a greater sense of order to your life, while each choice made in disobedience will bring confusion and destruction. The choices you make will shape your integrity. Obedient choices will bring the greatest safety and security.

13.7 Some rich people are poor because they are spiritually bankrupt, while some poor people are rich in contentment and satisfaction. Money brings opportunities and power, but it also has many negative side effects. A full life of learning, loving, and serving

others pretend to be poor, yet have great wealth.
8 Wealth is a ransom for a person's life,
but the poor get no threats.

13.9 Job 18.5; 29.3 Prov 4.18; 24.20

9 The light of the righteous rejoices,
but the lamp of the wicked goes out.

13.10 Prov 12.15 17.14; 19.20

10 By insolence the heedless make strife,
but wisdom is with those who take advice.
11 Wealth hastily gotten[n] will dwindle,
but those who gather little by little will increase it.
12 Hope deferred makes the heart sick,
but a desire fulfilled is a tree of life.

13.13 2 Chron 36.16 Prov 1.25,30

13 Those who despise the word bring destruction on themselves,
but those who respect the commandment will be rewarded.

13.14 Prov 8.8

14 The teaching of the wise is a fountain of life,
so that one may avoid the snares of death.

13.15 Ps 111.10 Prov 3.4; 8.35

15 Good sense wins favor,
but the way of the faithless is their ruin.[o]

13.16 Prov 16.1,9 27.1

16 The clever do all things intelligently,
but the fool displays folly.

13.17 Prov 26.6

17 A bad messenger brings trouble,
but a faithful envoy, healing.

13.18 Prov 23.12

18 Poverty and disgrace are for the one who ignores instruction,
but one who heeds reproof is honored.
19 A desire realized is sweet to the soul,
but to turn away from evil is an abomination to fools.

13.20 Prov 2.20

20 Whoever walks with the wise becomes wise,
but the companion of fools suffers harm.

13.21 Ps 32.10 Isa 3.10; 47.11

21 Misfortune pursues sinners,
but prosperity rewards the righteous.

13.22 Ezra 9.12 Ps 37.25 Prov 28.8

22 The good leave an inheritance to their children's children,
but the sinner's wealth is laid up for the righteous.
23 The field of the poor may yield much food,
but it is swept away through injustice.

n Gk Vg: Heb *from vanity* o Cn Compare Gk Syr Vg Tg: Heb *is enduring*

---

is better than a life full of money.

13.10 "I was wrong" or "I need help" are difficult phrases to utter because they require humility. Pride is an ingredient in every quarrel. It stirs up conflict and divides people. Humility, by contrast, heals. Guard against pride. If you find yourself constantly arguing, examine your life for pride. Be open to the advice of others, ask for help when you need it, and be willing to admit your mistakes.

13.13 God created us, knows us, and loves us. It only makes sense, then, to listen to his instructions and do what he says. The Bible is his unfailing word to us. It is like an owner's manual for a car. If you obey God's instructions, you will "run right" and find his kind of power to live. If you ignore them, you will have breakdowns, accidents, and failures.

13.17 In Solomon's day, a king had to rely on messengers for information about his country. These messengers had to be trustworthy. Inaccurate information could even lead to bloodshed. Reliable communication is still vital. If the message received is different from the message sent, marriages, businesses, and diplomatic relations can all break down. It is important to choose your words well and to avoid reacting until you clearly understand what the other person means.

13.19 Whether a "desire realized" is good or bad depends on the nature of the desire. It is "sweet to the soul" to achieve worthwhile goals, but not all goals are worth pursuing. When you set your heart on something, you may lose your ability to assess it objectively. Your desire blinds your judgment, and you proceed with an unwise relationship, a wasteful purchase, or a poorly conceived plan. Faithfulness is a virtue, but stubbornness is not.

13.20 The old saying, "A rotten apple spoils the barrel" is often applied to friendships, and with good reason. Our friends and associates affect us, sometimes profoundly. Be careful whom you choose as your closest friends. Spend time with people you want to be like—because you and your friends will surely grow to resemble each other.

13.20 When most people need advice, they go to their friends first because friends accept them and usually agree with them. But that is why they may not be able to help them with difficult problems. Our friends are so much like us that they may not have any answers we haven't already heard. Instead, we should seek out older and wiser people to advise us. Wise people have experienced a lot of life—and succeeded. They are not afraid to tell the truth. Who are the wise, godly people who can warn you of the pitfalls ahead?

13.23 The poor are often victims of an unjust society. A poor man's soil may be good, but unjust laws may rob him of the his own produce. This proverb does not take poverty lightly or wink at injustice; it simply describes what often occurs. We should do what we can to fight injustice of every sort. Our efforts may seem inadequate; but it is comforting to know that in the end God's justice will prevail.

24 Those who spare the rod hate their children,
but those who love them are diligent to discipline them.
25 The righteous have enough to satisfy their appetite,
but the belly of the wicked is empty.

14 The wise woman[p] builds her house,
but the foolish tears it down with her own hands.
2 Those who walk uprightly fear the LORD,
but one who is devious in conduct despises him.
3 The talk of fools is a rod for their backs,[q]
but the lips of the wise preserve them.
4 Where there are no oxen, there is no grain;
abundant crops come by the strength of the ox.
5 A faithful witness does not lie,
but a false witness breathes out lies.
6 A scoffer seeks wisdom in vain,
but knowledge is easy for one who understands.
7 Leave the presence of a fool,
for there you do not find words of knowledge.
8 It is the wisdom of the clever to understand where they go,
but the folly of fools misleads.
9 Fools mock at the guilt offering,[r]
but the upright enjoy God's favor.
10 The heart knows its own bitterness,
and no stranger shares its joy.
11 The house of the wicked is destroyed,
but the tent of the upright flourishes.
12 There is a way that seems right to a person,
but its end is the way to death.[s]
13 Even in laughter the heart is sad,
and the end of joy is grief.
14 The perverse get what their ways deserve,
and the good, what their deeds deserve.[t]
15 The simple believe everything,
but the clever consider their steps.
16 The wise are cautious and turn away from evil,
but the fool throws off restraint and is careless.
17 One who is quick-tempered acts foolishly,
and the schemer is hated.
18 The simple are adorned with[u] folly,
but the clever are crowned with knowledge.
19 The evil bow down before the good,
the wicked at the gates of the righteous.
20 The poor are disliked even by their neighbors,
but the rich have many friends.

13.24 Prov 19.18 22.15; 23.13 Heb 12.6
14.1 Prov 12.4; 21.9 27.15; 31.10
14.2 Ps 92.15
14.3 Prov 24.7,9 26.9
14.5 Prov 14.25; 19.9
14.6 Prov 9.7,8 15.12,14
14.7 Prov 9.6; 23.9
14.8 Prov 1.22; 10.8 12.15; 18.2 28.26
14.11 Prov 12.7,11 13.11; 22.29
14.12 Prov 16.25 Rom 6.21
14.13 Eccles 2.1
14.14 Prov 1.31 12.14,21
14.16 Prov 22.3; 27.12
14.17 Prov 12.16 14.29; 19.19 22.24,25
14.18 Prov 3.35 14.24; 16.22
14.20 Prov 19.4,7

p Heb *Wisdom of women* q Cn: Heb *a rod of pride* r Meaning of Heb uncertain s Heb *ways of death* t Cn: Heb *from upon him* u Or *inherit*

13.24 It is not easy for a loving parent to discipline a child, but it is necessary. The greatest responsibility God gives parents is the nurture and guidance of their children. Lack of discipline puts parents' love in question because it shows a lack of concern for the character development of their children. Disciplining children averts long-range disaster. Without correction, children grow up with no clear understanding of right and wrong and with little direction to their lives. Don't be afraid to discipline your children. It is an act of love. Remember, however, that your efforts cannot make your children wise; they can only encourage your children to seek God's wisdom above all else!

14.6 We all know scoffers, people who mock every word of instruction or advice. They never find wisdom because they don't seek it seriously. Wisdom comes easily only to those who pay attention to experienced people and to God. If the wisdom you need does not come easily to you, perhaps your attitude is the barrier.

14.12 The "way that seems right" may offer many options and require few sacrifices. Easy choices, however, should make us take a second look at the options. Is this solution attractive because it

14.21 Ps 41.1 Prov 19.17; 28.8

14.23 Prov 20.13; 28.19

14.24 Prov 14.18 16.22

14.26 Ps 34.7 Prov 3.7,8, 24-26; 18.10 19.23

14.28 1 Kgs 4.20

21 Those who despise their neighbors are sinners,
but happy are those who are kind to the poor.
22 Do they not err that plan evil?
Those who plan good find loyalty and faithfulness.
23 In all toil there is profit,
but mere talk leads only to poverty.
24 The crown of the wise is their wisdom,[v]
but folly is the garland[w] of fools.
25 A truthful witness saves lives,
but one who utters lies is a betrayer.
26 In the fear of the LORD one has strong confidence,
and one's children will have a refuge.
27 The fear of the LORD is a fountain of life,
so that one may avoid the snares of death.
28 The glory of a king is a multitude of people;

[v] Cn Compare Gk: Heb *riches* [w] Cn: Heb *is the folly*

WISDOM AND FOOLISHNESS
The wise and the foolish are often contrasted in Proverbs. The characteristics, reputation, and results of each are worth knowing if wisdom is our goal.

	The Wise	*The Foolish*	
Characteristics	Help others with good advice	Lack of judgment	10.21
	Enjoy wisdom	Enjoy foolishness	10.23
	Cautious with reason	Gullible	14.15
		Avoid the wise	15.12
	Seek knowledge	Feed on foolishness	15.14
	Value wisdom above riches		16.16
	Receive life	Receive punishment	16.22
	Respond to correction	Respond to punishment	17.10
	Pursue wisdom	Pursue illusive dreams	17.24
		Blame failure on God	19.3
	Profit from correction	Are proud and arrogant	21.24
		Despise advice	23.9
		Make truth useless	26.7
		Repeat their folly	26.11
	Trust in wisdom	Trust in themselves	28.26
	Control their anger	Unleash their anger	29.11
Reputation	Admired as counselors	Beaten as servants	10.13
	Rewarded with knowledge	Inherit folly	14.18
		Cause strife and quarrels	22.10
		Receive no honor	26.1
	Keep peace	Stir up anger	29.8
Results	Stay on straight paths	Go the wrong way	15.21
		Lash out when discovered in folly	17.12
		Endangered by their words	18.6, 7
	Their wisdom conquers others' strength		21.22
	Avoid wicked paths	Walk a rough road as rebels	22.5
	Have great advice		24.5
		Will never be chosen as counselors	24.7
		Must be guided by hardship	26.3
		Persist in foolishness	27.22

allows me to be lazy? Because it doesn't ask me to change my lifestyle? Because it requires no moral restraints? The right choice often requires hard work and self-sacrifice. Don't be enticed by apparent shortcuts that seem right, but end in death.

without people a prince is ruined.
29 Whoever is slow to anger has great understanding,
but one who has a hasty temper exalts folly.
30 A tranquil mind gives life to the flesh,
but passion makes the bones rot.
31 Those who oppress the poor insult their Maker,
but those who are kind to the needy honor him.
32 The wicked are overthrown by their evil-doing,
but the righteous find a refuge in their integrity.[x]
33 Wisdom is at home in the mind of one who has understanding,
but it is not[y] known in the heart of fools.
34 Righteousness exalts a nation,
but sin is a reproach to any people.
35 A servant who deals wisely has the king's favor,
but his wrath falls on one who acts shamefully.

15 A soft answer turns away wrath,
but a harsh word stirs up anger.
2 The tongue of the wise dispenses knowledge,[z]
but the mouths of fools pour out folly.
3 The eyes of the LORD are in every place,
keeping watch on the evil and the good.
4 A gentle tongue is a tree of life,
but perverseness in it breaks the spirit.
5 A fool despises a parent's instruction,
but the one who heeds admonition is prudent.
6 In the house of the righteous there is much treasure,
but trouble befalls the income of the wicked.
7 The lips of the wise spread knowledge;
not so the minds of fools.
8 The sacrifice of the wicked is an abomination to the LORD,
but the prayer of the upright is his delight.
9 The way of the wicked is an abomination to the LORD,
but he loves the one who pursues righteousness.
10 There is severe discipline for one who forsakes the way,
but one who hates a rebuke will die.
11 Sheol and Abaddon lie open before the LORD,
how much more human hearts!
12 Scoffers do not like to be rebuked;
they will not go to the wise.

14.29 Prov 16.32 19.11; 29.11 Jas 1.19
14.31 Ps 12.5 Prov 14.21 17.5; 22.2,16 Eccles 5.8
14.33 Prov 1.20; 8.4
14.34 Deut 4.6 28.1,15
15.1 Judg 8.1-3 1 Sam 25.10-13 Prov 25.10,15
15.3 1 Chron 29.17 Heb 4.13
15.5 1 Sam 2.25 Prov 10.1; 13.1 23.22
15.8 Prov 15.29 21.27 Isa 1.11
15.9,10 Ps 1.6; 146.8,9 Prov 4.18
15.11 Job 26.6 Ps 139.1

[x] Gk Syr: Heb *in their death* [y] Gk Syr: Heb lacks *not* [z] Cn: Heb *makes knowledge good*

14.29 Anger can be like a fire out of control. It can burn us and everything in its path. Anger divides people. It pushes us into hasty decisions that only cause bitterness and guilt. Yet anger, in itself, is not wrong. Anger can be a legitimate reaction to injustice and sin. When you feel yourself getting angry, look for the cause. Are you reacting to an evil situation that you are going to set right? Or are you responding selfishly to a personal insult? Pray that God will help you control your anger, channeling your feelings into effective action and conquering selfish anger through humility and repentance.

14.30 *Passion* here means intense jealousy or envy (as in 6.34). It is not loving life that saps energy and leads to ill health, but allowing yourself to be emotionally driven, wanting what you do not have. How much better to have a passion for God.

14.31 God has a special concern for the poor. He insists that people who have material goods should be generous with those who are needy. Providing for the poor is not just a suggestion in the Bible; it is a command that may require a change of attitude (see Leviticus 23.22; Deuteronomy 15.7, 8; Psalms 113.5–9; 146.5–9; Isaiah 58.7; 2 Corinthians 9.9; James 2.1–9).

15.1 Have you ever tried to argue in a whisper? It is equally hard to argue with someone who insists on answering softly. On the other hand, a rising voice and harsh words almost always trigger an angry response. To turn away wrath and seek peace, quiet words are your best choice.

15.3 At times it seems that God has let evil run rampant in the world; we wonder if he even notices it. But God sees everything clearly – both the evil actions and the evil intentions lying behind them (15.11). He is not an indifferent observer. He cares and is active in our world. Right now, his work may be unseen and unfelt, but don't give up. One day he will wipe out evil and punish the evildoers, just as he will establish the good and reward those who do his will.

15.11 *Sheol* means the realm of the dead or the grave. *Abaddon* is used as a synonym for Sheol and can also mean destruction.

15.13 Prov 17.22 Eccles 8.1

13 A glad heart makes a cheerful countenance,
but by sorrow of heart the spirit is broken.

15.14 Prov 18.15

14 The mind of one who has understanding seeks knowledge,
but the mouths of fools feed on folly.
15 All the days of the poor are hard,
but a cheerful heart has a continual feast.

15.16 Prov 16.8; 28.6

16 Better is a little with the fear of the LORD
than great treasure and trouble with it.

15.17 Prov 17.1

17 Better is a dinner of vegetables where love is
than a fatted ox and hatred with it.

15.18 Prov 14.29 16.28; 26.21

18 Those who are hot-tempered stir up strife,
but those who are slow to anger calm contention.

15.19 Prov 22.13

19 The way of the lazy is overgrown with thorns,
but the path of the upright is a level highway.

15.20 Prov 10.1; 29.3 30.17

20 A wise child makes a glad father,
but the foolish despise their mothers.
21 Folly is a joy to one who has no sense,
but a person of understanding walks straight ahead.

15.22 Prov 11.14; 24.6

22 Without counsel, plans go wrong,
but with many advisers they succeed.

15.23 Prov 12.14 24.26; 25.11

23 To make an apt answer is a joy to anyone,
and a word in season, how good it is!
24 For the wise the path of life leads upward,
in order to avoid Sheol below.

15.25 Ps 68.5; 146.9 Prov 14.11

25 The LORD tears down the house of the proud,
but maintains the widow's boundaries.
26 Evil plans are an abomination to the LORD,
but gracious words are pure.

15.27 Ex 23.8 Prov 20.21 28.16

27 Those who are greedy for unjust gain make trouble for their households,
but those who hate bribes will live.

15.28 Prov 10.19,32 13.16; 16.23

28 The mind of the righteous ponders how to answer,
but the mouth of the wicked pours out evil.
29 The LORD is far from the wicked,
but he hears the prayer of the righteous.
30 The light of the eyes rejoices the heart,
and good news refreshes the body.

15.31 Prov 8.33 13.18; 15.5 23.12

31 The ear that heeds wholesome admonition
will lodge among the wise.
32 Those who ignore instruction despise themselves,
but those who heed admonition gain understanding.

15.14 What we feed our minds is just as important as what we feed our bodies. The kinds of books we read, the people we talk with, the music we listen to, and the films we watch are all part of our mental diet. What you feed your mind influences your total health and well-being. Thus, a strong desire to discover truth is a mark of wisdom.

15.15 Our attitudes color our whole personality. We cannot always choose what happens to us, but we can choose our attitude toward each situation. The secret to a good attitude is filling our minds with thoughts that are true, pure, and lovely; thoughts that dwell on the good things in life (Philippians 4.8). This was Paul's secret as he faced imprisonment, and it can be ours as we face the struggles of daily living. Look at your attitudes and then examine what you allow to enter your mind and what you choose to dwell on. You may need to make some changes.

15.17–19 The "path of the upright" doesn't always seem easy (15.19), but look at the alternatives. Hatred (15.17), strife (15.18), and laziness (15.19) cause problems that the good person does not have to face. By comparison, his life is a smooth, level road because it is built on a solid foundation of love for God.

15.22 Those with tunnel vision, people who are locked into one way of thinking, are likely to miss the right road because they have closed their minds to any new options. We need the help of those who can enlarge our vision and broaden our perspective. Seek out the advice of those who know you and have a wealth of experience. Build a network of counselors. Then be open to new ideas and be willing to weigh their suggestions carefully. Your plans will be stronger and more likely to succeed.

15.28 The righteous ponder their answers; the evil don't wait to speak because they don't care about the effects of their words. It is important to have something to say, but it is equally important to weigh it first. Do you carefully plan your words, or do you pour out your thoughts without concern for their impact?

33 The fear of the LORD is instruction in wisdom,
and humility goes before honor.

15.33 Prov 1.7

16 The plans of the mind belong to mortals,
but the answer of the tongue is from the LORD.
2 All one's ways may be pure in one's own eyes,
but the LORD weighs the spirit.
3 Commit your work to the LORD,
and your plans will be established.
4 The LORD has made everything for its purpose,
even the wicked for the day of trouble.
5 All those who are arrogant are an abomination to the LORD;
be assured, they will not go unpunished.
6 By loyalty and faithfulness iniquity is atoned for,
and by the fear of the LORD one avoids evil.
7 When the ways of people please the LORD,
he causes even their enemies to be at peace with them.
8 Better is a little with righteousness
than large income with injustice.
9 The human mind plans the way,
but the LORD directs the steps.
10 Inspired decisions are on the lips of a king;
his mouth does not sin in judgment.
11 Honest balances and scales are the LORD's;
all the weights in the bag are his work.
12 It is an abomination to kings to do evil,
for the throne is established by righteousness.
13 Righteous lips are the delight of a king,
and he loves those who speak what is right.
14 A king's wrath is a messenger of death,
and whoever is wise will appease it.
15 In the light of a king's face there is life,

16.1 Prov 16.9 19.21; 20.24
16.3 Prov 3.6
16.4 Isa 43.7; 54.16
16.5 Prov 6.16,17
16.7 2 Chron 17.10 Prov 29.25
16.8 Prov 15.16; 21.6 1 Tim 6.8
16.9 Ps 37.23 Prov 16.1 19.21; 20.24
16.10 1 Kgs 3.28
16.12 Prov 14.34 25.5; 29.14
16.13 Prov 22.11
16.14 Prov 19.12; 20.2 Dan 3.13

16.1 "The answer of the tongue is from the Lord" means that the final outcome is in God's hands. If this is so, why make plans? In doing God's will, there must be partnership between our efforts and God's control. He wants us to use our minds, to seek the advice of others, and to plan. Nevertheless, the results are up to him. Planning, then, helps us act God's way. As you live for him, ask for guidance as you plan, and then act on your plan as you trust in him.

16.2 People can rationalize anything if they have no standards for judging right and wrong. We can always prove that we are right. Before putting any plan into action, ask yourself these three questions: (1) Is this plan in harmony with God's truth? (2) Will it work under real-life conditions? (3) Is my attitude pleasing to God?

16.3 There are different ways to fail to commit our work to the Lord. Some people commit their work only superficially. They say the project is being done for the Lord, but in reality they are doing it for themselves. Others give God temporary control of their interests, only to take control back the moment things stop going the way they expect. Still others commit their task fully to the Lord, but put forth no effort themselves, and then they wonder why they do not succeed. We must maintain a delicate balance: trusting God as if everything depended on him, while working as if everything depended on us. Think of a specific effort in which you are involved right now. Have you committed it to the Lord?

16.4 This verse doesn't mean that God created some people to be wicked, but rather that God uses even the activities of wicked people to fulfill his good purposes. God is infinite and we are finite. No matter how great our intellects, we will never be able to understand him completely. But we can accept by faith that he is all-powerful, all-loving, and all-good. We can believe that he is not the cause of evil (James 1.13, 17); and we can trust that there are no loose ends in his system of judgment. Evil is a temporary condition in the universe. One day God will destroy it. In the meantime, he uses even the evil intentions of people for his good purposes (see Genesis 50.20).

16.5 Arrogance (or pride) is the inner voice that whispers, "My way is best." It is resisting God's leadership and believing that you are able to live without his help. Whenever you find yourself wanting to do it your way and looking down on other people, you are being pulled by pride. Only when you eliminate pride can God help you become all he meant you to be. (See the chart in chapter 19.)

16.7 We want other people to like us, and sometimes we will do almost anything to win their approval. But God tells us to put our energy into pleasing him instead. Our effort to be peacemakers will usually make us more attractive to those around us, even our enemies. But even if it doesn't, we haven't lost anything. We are still pleasing God, the only one who truly matters.

16.11 Whether we buy or sell, make a product or offer a service, we know what is fair and what is unfair. Sometimes we feel pressure to be unfair in order to advance ourselves or gain more profit. But if we want to obey God, there is no middle ground: God demands fairness in every business transaction. No amount of rationalizing can cover for an unfair business practice. Fairness is not always easy, but it is what God demands. Ask him for discernment and courage to be consistently fair.

16.16 Ps 119.127

16.18 Jer 49.16

16.20 Ps 2.12; 34.8 Jer 17.7

16.22 Prov 3.22 14.18,24,27

16.23 Ps 37.30 Prov 12.5 15.18,28

16.24 Prov 4.22 17.22; 24.13

and his favor is like the clouds that bring the spring rain.
16 How much better to get wisdom than gold!
To get understanding is to be chosen rather than silver.
17 The highway of the upright avoids evil;
those who guard their way preserve their lives.
18 Pride goes before destruction,
and a haughty spirit before a fall.
19 It is better to be of a lowly spirit among the poor
than to divide the spoil with the proud.
20 Those who are attentive to a matter will prosper,
and happy are those who trust in the LORD.
21 The wise of heart is called perceptive,
and pleasant speech increases persuasiveness.
22 Wisdom is a fountain of life to one who has it,
but folly is the punishment of fools.
23 The mind of the wise makes their speech judicious,
and adds persuasiveness to their lips.
24 Pleasant words are like a honeycomb,
sweetness to the soul and health to the body.
25 Sometimes there is a way that seems to be right,
but in the end it is the way to death.
26 The appetite of workers works for them;

HOW GOD IS DESCRIBED IN PROVERBS
Proverbs is a book about wise living. It often focuses on a person's response and attitude toward God, who is the source of wisdom. And a number of proverbs point out aspects of God's character. Knowing God helps us on the way to wisdom.

God . . .	is aware of all that happens	15.3
	knows the heart of all people	15.11; 16.2; 21.2
	controls all things	16.33
	is a place of safety	18.10
	rescues good people from danger	11.8, 21
	condemns the wicked	11.31
	delights in our prayers	15.8, 29
	loves those who obey him	11.27; 15.9; 22.12
	cares for poor and needy	15.25; 22.22, 23
	purifies hearts	17.3
	hates evil	17.5; 21.27; 28.9
Our Response should be . . .	to fear and reverence God	10.27; 14.26, 27; 15.16; 16.6; 19.23; 28.14
	to obey God's Word	13.13; 19.16
	to please God	21.3
	to trust God	22.17–19; 29.25

16.18 Proud people take little account of their weaknesses and do not anticipate stumbling blocks. They think they are above the frailties of common people. In this state of mind they are easily tripped up. Ironically, proud people seldom realize that pride is their problem, although everyone around them is well aware of it. Ask someone you trust whether self-satisfaction has blinded you to warning signs. He or she may help you avoid a fall.

16.22 For centuries people sought a fountain of youth, a spring that promised to give eternal life and vitality. It was never found. But God's wisdom is a wellspring of life that can make a person happy, healthy, and alive forever. How? When we live by God's Word, he washes away the deadly effects of sin (see Titus 3.4–8), and the hope of eternal life with him gives us a joyful perspective on our present life. The fountain of youth was only a dream, but the wellspring of life is reality. The choice is yours. You can be enlightened by God's wisdom, or you can be dragged down by the weight of your own foolishness.

16.26 "The appetite of workers works for them" means that no matter how much difficulty or drudgery we may find in our work, our appetite is an incentive to keep going. Hunger makes us work to satisfy it.

their hunger urges them on.
27 Scoundrels concoct evil,
and their speech is like a scorching fire.
28 A perverse person spreads strife,
and a whisperer separates close friends.
29 The violent entice their neighbors,
and lead them in a way that is not good.
30 One who winks the eyes plans[a] perverse things;
one who compresses the lips brings evil to pass.
31 Gray hair is a crown of glory;
it is gained in a righteous life.
32 One who is slow to anger is better than the mighty,
and one whose temper is controlled than one who captures a city.
33 The lot is cast into the lap,
but the decision is the LORD's alone.

17 Better is a dry morsel with quiet
than a house full of feasting with strife.
2 A slave who deals wisely will rule over a child who acts shamefully,
and will share the inheritance as one of the family.
3 The crucible is for silver, and the furnace is for gold,
but the LORD tests the heart.
4 An evildoer listens to wicked lips;
and a liar gives heed to a mischievous tongue.
5 Those who mock the poor insult their Maker;
those who are glad at calamity will not go unpunished.
6 Grandchildren are the crown of the aged,
and the glory of children is their parents.
7 Fine speech is not becoming to a fool;
still less is false speech to a ruler.[b]
8 A bribe is like a magic stone in the eyes of those who give it;
wherever they turn they prosper.
9 One who forgives an affront fosters friendship,
but one who dwells on disputes will alienate a friend.
10 A rebuke strikes deeper into a discerning person
than a hundred blows into a fool.
11 Evil people seek only rebellion,

16.27 Jas 3.6
16.28 Prov 6.14,19 18.8; 26.20
16.31 Mt 5.36
16.32 Prov 14.29 15.18; 19.11
17.1 Prov 15.17; 21.9
17.3 1 Chron 29.17
17.4 Prov 1.10; 16.29
17.5 Job 31.29 Prov 24.17 Obad 17
17.6 Gen 48.11 Ps 127.3-5 Prov 13.22
17.7 Prov 12.22; 24.7
17.9 Prov 10.12
17.10 Prov 9.8; 13.1
17.11 Prov 10.32

[a] Gk Syr Vg Tg: Heb *to plan* [b] Or *a noble person*

16.31 The Hebrews believed that a long life was a sign of God's blessing; therefore, gray hair and old age were good. While young people glory in their strength, old people can rejoice in their years of experience and practical wisdom. Gray hair is not a sign of disgrace to be covered over; it is a crown of glory.

16.32 Self-control is superior to conquest. Success in business, school, or home life can be ruined by one who has lost control of his or her anger. So it is a great personal victory to control your temper. When you feel yourself ready to explode, remember losing control may cause you to forfeit what you want the most.

16.33 The lot was almost always used in ceremonial settings and was the common method for determining God's will. Several important events occurred by lot, including the identification of Achan as the man who had sinned (Joshua 7.14), the division of the promised land among the tribes (Joshua 14.2), and the selection of the first king for the nation (1 Samuel 10.16–26).

17.3 It takes intense heat to purify gold and silver. Similarly, it often takes the heat of trials for the Christian to be purified. Through trials, God shows us what is in us and clears out anything that gets in the way of complete trust in him. Peter says, "The genuineness of your faith – being more precious than gold, though perishable, is tested by fire – may be found to result in praise and glory and honor" (1 Peter 1.7). So when tough times come your way, realize that God wants to use them to refine your faith and purify your heart.

17.5 Few acts are as cruel as making fun of the less fortunate, but many people do this because it makes them feel good to be better off or more successful than someone else. Mocking the poor is mocking the God who made them. We also ridicule God when we mock the weak, or those who are different, or anyone else. When you catch yourself putting down others just for fun, stop and think about who created them.

17.8 Solomon is not condoning bribery, but he is making an observation about the way the world operates. Bribes may get people what they want, but the Bible clearly condemns using them (Exodus 23.8; Proverbs 17.23; Matthew 28.11–15).

17.9 This proverb is saying that we should be willing to forgive others' sins against us. Forgetting mistakes is necessary to any relationship. It is tempting, especially in an argument, to bring up all the mistakes the other person has ever made. Love, however, keeps its mouth shut – difficult though that may be. Try never to bring anything into an argument that is unrelated to the topic being discussed. As we grow to be like Christ, we will acquire God's ability to forget the confessed sins of the past.

but a cruel messenger will be sent against them.
12 Better to meet a she-bear robbed of its cubs
than to confront a fool immersed in folly.
17.13 Prov 13.21
13 Evil will not depart from the house
of one who returns evil for good.
17.14 Prov 20.3; 25.8
14 The beginning of strife is like letting out water;
so stop before the quarrel breaks out.
17.15 Prov 24.24
15 One who justifies the wicked and one who condemns the righteous
are both alike an abomination to the LORD.
16 Why should fools have a price in hand
to buy wisdom, when they have no mind to learn?
17.17 Prov 18.24
17 A friend loves at all times,
and kinsfolk are born to share adversity.
17.18 Prov 6.1; 11.15
18 It is senseless to give a pledge,
to become surety for a neighbor.
17.19 Prov 13.2 29.22,23
19 One who loves transgression loves strife;
one who builds a high threshold invites broken bones.
20 The crooked of mind do not prosper,
and the perverse of tongue fall into calamity.
17.21 Prov 10.1 17.25; 19.13
21 The one who begets a fool gets trouble;
the parent of a fool has no joy.
17.22 Prov 15.13
22 A cheerful heart is a good medicine,
but a downcast spirit dries up the bones.
17.23 Ex 23.8
23 The wicked accept a concealed bribe
to pervert the ways of justice.
24 The discerning person looks to wisdom,
but the eyes of a fool to the ends of the earth.
17.25 Prov 10.1
25 Foolish children are a grief to their father
and bitterness to her who bore them.
26 To impose a fine on the innocent is not right,
or to flog the noble for their integrity.
17.27 Prov 10.19 Jas 1.19
27 One who spares words is knowledgeable;
one who is cool in spirit has understanding.
28 Even fools who keep silent are considered wise;
when they close their lips, they are deemed intelligent.

18 The one who lives alone is self-indulgent,
showing contempt for all who have sound judgment.[c]
2 A fool takes no pleasure in understanding,
but only in expressing personal opinion.
3 When wickedness comes, contempt comes also;
and with dishonor comes disgrace.

[c] Meaning of Heb uncertain

17.14 It is difficult to stop a quarrel once it gets started, so it is better not to let it begin.

17.17 What kind of friend are you? There is a vast difference between knowing someone well and being a true friend. The greatest evidence of genuine friendship is loyalty (loving "at all times") (see 1 Corinthians 13.7)—being available to help in times of distress or personal struggles. Too many people are fair-weather friends. They stick around when the friendship helps them and leave when they're not getting anything out of the relationship. Think of your friends and assess your loyalty to them. Be the kind of true friend the Bible encourages.

17.19 If the threshold is high, people will trip over it as they enter the room. In this passage, building a high threshold symbolizes attitudes that lead to destruction.

17.22 To be cheerful is to be ready to greet others with a welcome, a word of encouragement, an enthusiasm for the task at hand, and a positive outlook on the future. Such people are as welcome as pain-relieving medicine.

17.24 While there is something to be said for having big dreams, this proverb points out the folly of chasing fantasies (having eyes "to the ends of the earth"). How much better to align your goals with God's, being the kind of person he wants you to be! Such goals (wisdom, honesty, patience, love) may not seem exciting, but they will determine your eternal future. Take time to think about your dreams and goals, and make sure they cover the really important areas of life.

17.27, 28 This proverb highlights several benefits of keeping quiet: (1) it is the best policy if you have nothing worthwhile to say; (2) it allows you the opportunity to listen and learn; and (3) it gives you something in common with those who are wiser. Make sure to pause to think and to listen so that when you do speak, you will have something important to say.

4 The words of the mouth are deep waters;
the fountain of wisdom is a gushing stream.
5 It is not right to be partial to the guilty,
or to subvert the innocent in judgment.
6 A fool's lips bring strife,
and a fool's mouth invites a flogging.
7 The mouths of fools are their ruin,
and their lips a snare to themselves.
8 The words of a whisperer are like delicious morsels;
they go down into the inner parts of the body.
9 One who is slack in work
is close kin to a vandal.
10 The name of the LORD is a strong tower;
the righteous run into it and are safe.
11 The wealth of the rich is their strong city;
in their imagination it is like a high wall.
12 Before destruction one's heart is haughty,
but humility goes before honor.
13 If one gives answer before hearing,
it is folly and shame.
14 The human spirit will endure sickness;
but a broken spirit—who can bear?
15 An intelligent mind acquires knowledge,
and the ear of the wise seeks knowledge.
16 A gift opens doors;
it gives access to the great.
17 The one who first states a case seems right,
until the other comes and cross-examines.
18 Casting the lot puts an end to disputes
and decides between powerful contenders.
19 An ally offended is stronger than a city;[d]
such quarreling is like the bars of a castle.
20 From the fruit of the mouth one's stomach is satisfied;
the yield of the lips brings satisfaction.
21 Death and life are in the power of the tongue,
and those who love it will eat its fruits.
22 He who finds a wife finds a good thing,
and obtains favor from the LORD.
23 The poor use entreaties,
but the rich answer roughly.

[d] Gk Syr Vg Tg: Meaning of Heb uncertain

18.5 Prov 17.15 24.23
18.6 Prov 10.14; 13.3
18.8 Lev 19.16 Prov 11.13
18.10 2 Sam 22.2 Ps 61.3; 91.2 Prov 29.25
18.11 Prov 10.15
18.12 Prov 11.2 16.18; 29.23
18.13 Prov 20.25 Jn 7.51
18.15 Prov 12.26 15.14; 23.23
18.16 Gen 32.20 Prov 17.8
18.18 Prov 16.33
18.19 2 Cor 6.3
18.21 Prov 13.3
18.22 Prov 12.4 19.14; 31.10-31
18.23 2 Chron 10.13 Prov 19.7 Jas 2.3

18.8 A "whisperer" is a person who spreads gossip. It is as hard to refuse to listen to a rumor as it is to turn down a delicious dessert. Taking just one morsel of either one creates a taste for more. You can resist rumors the same way a determined dieter resists candy—never even open the box. If you don't nibble on the first bite of gossip, you can't take the second and the third.

18.11 In thinking of his wealth as his strongest defense, the rich person is sadly mistaken. Money cannot provide safety—there are too many ways for it to lose its power. The government may cease to back it; thieves may steal it; inflation may rob it of all value. But God never loses his power. He is always dependable. What do you look to for security and safety—uncertain wealth or God who is always faithful?

18.13, 15, 17 In these concise statements, the writer gives three basic principles for making sound decisions: (1) get the facts before deciding; (2) be open to new ideas; (3) make sure you hear both sides of the story before judging. All three principles center around seeking additional information. This is difficult work, but the only alternative is prejudice—judging before getting the facts.

18.22 Today's emphasis on individual freedom is misguided. Strong individuals are important, but so are strong marriages. God created marriage for our enjoyment and he pronounced it good. This is one of many passages in the Bible that show marriage as a joyful and good creation of God (Genesis 2.21–25; Proverbs 5.15–19; John 2.1–11).

18.23 To use entreaties means to plead or beg. This verse does not condone insulting the poor; it is simply recording an unfortunate fact of life. It is wrong for rich people to treat the less fortunate with contempt and arrogance, and God will judge such actions severely (see 14.31).

18.24 Prov 14.20 19.4,6

24 Some[e] friends play at friendship[f]
but a true friend sticks closer than one's nearest kin.

19.1 Prov 11.18; 13.7

19 Better the poor walking in integrity
than one perverse of speech who is a fool.
2 Desire without knowledge is not good,
and one who moves too hurriedly misses the way.

19.3 Isa 8.21

3 One's own folly leads to ruin,
yet the heart rages against the LORD.
4 Wealth brings many friends,
but the poor are left friendless.

19.5 Ex 23.1 Prov 19.9

5 A false witness will not go unpunished,
and a liar will not escape.
6 Many seek the favor of the generous,
and everyone is a friend to a giver of gifts.

19.7 Prov 4.20; 18.23

7 If the poor are hated even by their kin,
how much more are they shunned by their friends!
When they call after them, they are not there.[g]

19.8 Prov 16.20 8.35,36

8 To get wisdom is to love oneself;
to keep understanding is to prosper.
9 A false witness will not go unpunished,
and the liar will perish.

19.10 Prov 26.1

10 It is not fitting for a fool to live in luxury,
much less for a slave to rule over princes.

19.11 Prov 14.29 Col 4.6

11 Those with good sense are slow to anger,
and it is their glory to overlook an offense.

19.12 Prov 16.14,15

12 A king's anger is like the growling of a lion,
but his favor is like dew on the grass.

e Syr Tg: Heb *A man of* f Cn Compare Syr Vg Tg: Meaning of Heb uncertain g Meaning of Heb uncertain

HUMILITY AND PRIDE
Proverbs is direct and forceful in rejecting pride. The proud attitude heads the list of seven things God hates (6.16–17). The harmful results of pride are constantly contrasted with humility and its benefits.

Results of . . .	*Humility*	*Pride*	
	Leads to wisdom	Leads to disgrace	11.2
	Takes advice	Produces quarrels	13.10
	Leads to honor		15.33
		Leads to punishment	16.5
		Leads to destruction	16.18
	Ends in honor	Ends in downfall	18.12
	Bring one to honor	Brings one low	29.23

18.24 Loneliness is everywhere – many people feel cut off and alienated from others. Being in a crowd just makes people more aware of their isolation. We all need friends who will stick close, listen, care, and offer help when it is needed – in good times and bad. It is better to have one such friend than dozens of superficial acquaintances. Instead of wishing you could find a true friend, seek to become one. There are people who need your friendship. Ask God to reveal them to you, and then take on the challenge of being a true friend.

19.1 Integrity is far more valuable than wealth, but most people don't act as if they believe this. Afraid of not getting everything they want, they will pay any price to increase their wealth – cheating on their taxes, stealing from stores or employers, withholding tithes, refusing to give. But when we know and love God, we realize that a lower standard of living – or even poverty – is a small price to pay for personal integrity. Do your actions show that you sacrifice your integrity to increase your wealth? What changes do you need to make in order to get your priorities straight?

19.2 We often move hurriedly through life, rushing headlong into the unknown. Many people marry without knowing what to expect of their partner or of married life. Others try illicit sex or drugs without considering the consequences. Some plunge into jobs without evaluating whether they are suitable to that line of work. Don't rush into the unknown. Be sure you understand what you're getting into and where you want to go before you take the first step. And if it still seems unknown, be sure you're following God.

19.8 Is it good to love yourself? Yes, when your soul is at stake! This proverb does not condone the self-centered person who loves and protects his or her selfish interests and will do anything to serve them. Instead it encourages those who really care about themselves enough to seek wisdom.

13 A stupid child is ruin to a father,
and a wife's quarreling is a continual dripping of rain.
14 House and wealth are inherited from parents,
but a prudent wife is from the LORD.
15 Laziness brings on deep sleep;
an idle person will suffer hunger.
16 Those who keep the commandment will live;
those who are heedless of their ways will die.
17 Whoever is kind to the poor lends to the LORD,
and will be repaid in full.
18 Discipline your children while there is hope;
do not set your heart on their destruction.
19 A violent tempered person will pay the penalty;
if you effect a rescue, you will only have to do it again.[h]
20 Listen to advice and accept instruction,
that you may gain wisdom for the future.
21 The human mind may devise many plans,
but it is the purpose of the LORD that will be established.
22 What is desirable in a person is loyalty,
and it is better to be poor than a liar.
23 The fear of the LORD is life indeed;
filled with it one rests secure
and suffers no harm.
24 The lazy person buries a hand in the dish,
and will not even bring it back to the mouth.
25 Strike a scoffer, and the simple will learn prudence;
reprove the intelligent, and they will gain knowledge.
26 Those who do violence to their father and chase away their mother
are children who cause shame and bring reproach.
27 Cease straying, my child, from the words of knowledge,
in order that you may hear instruction.
28 A worthless witness mocks at justice,
and the mouth of the wicked devours iniquity.
29 Condemnation is ready for scoffers,
and flogging for the backs of fools.

20 Wine is a mocker, strong drink a brawler,
and whoever is led astray by it is not wise.
2 The dread anger of a king is like the growling of a lion;
anyone who provokes him to anger forfeits life itself.

[h] Meaning of Heb uncertain

19.13 Prov 12.4 15.20; 17.25 21.9,19
19.15 Prov 6.9; 16.26 24.33
19.16 Prov 16.17
19.17 Deut 15.7 Prov 14.31 28.27
19.18 Prov 13.24 Heb 12.6
19.19 Prov 12.16 14.17; 15.18
19.23 Ps 25.13 Prov 14.27; 22.3 1 Tim 4.8
19.25 Prov 9.7,8 19.29; 21.11
19.26 Prov 20.20
19.29 Prov 9.12 19.9,25; 26.3
20.1 Prov 31.4
20.2 Prov 16.14

19.16 The commandments we are told to keep are those found in God's Word—both the ten commandments (Exodus 20) and other passages of instruction. To obey what God teaches in the Bible is self-preserving. To disobey is self-destructive.

19.17 Here God identifies with the poor as Jesus does in Matthew 25.31–46. As our Creator, God values all of us, whether we are poor or rich. When we help the poor, we show honor both to the Creator and to his creation. God accepts our help as if we had offered it directly to him.

19.22 What makes a person desirable or attractive, according to this proverb, is loyalty. There is a limit to what you can do with your outward appearance, but you can always develop your character and disposition. You can be as attractive as you want to be inwardly. You can have loyalty, for example, in any amount you choose. You may not be able to do anything more to improve your looks, but you can always take steps to improve your character. What steps are you taking now?

19.23 Those who trust God are spared much harm because of their healthy habits, their beneficial life-style, and sometimes through God's direct intervention. Nevertheless, the fear of the Lord does not always protect us from harm in this life: evil things still happen to people who love God. This verse is not a universal promise, but a general guideline. It describes what would happen if this world were sinless, and what will happen in the new earth, when faithful believers will be under God's protection forever. (See the note on 3.16, 17 for more about this concept.)

19.24 "Buries a hand in the dish" refers to the custom of eating where a dish would be passed and people would reach in and get food for themselves. This proverb is saying that some people are so lazy that they won't even feed themselves.

19.25 There is a great difference between the person who learns from criticism and the person who refuses to accept correction. How we respond to criticism determines whether or not we grow in wisdom. The next time someone criticizes you, listen carefully to all that is said. You might learn something.

20.3 Prov 14.29 16.32; 19.11

3 It is honorable to refrain from strife,
but every fool is quick to quarrel.
4 The lazy person does not plow in season;
harvest comes, and there is nothing to be found.
5 The purposes in the human mind are like deep water,
but the intelligent will draw them out.

20.6 Prov 25.14 Mt 6.2

6 Many proclaim themselves loyal,
but who can find one worthy of trust?

20.7 Ps 37.26; 112.2

7 The righteous walk in integrity—
happy are the children who follow them!

20.8 Prov 16.12 18.13; 23.23

8 A king who sits on the throne of judgment
winnows all evil with his eyes.

20.9 2 Chron 6.36

9 Who can say, "I have made my heart clean;
I am pure from my sin"?

20.10 Prov 11.1; 20.23

10 Diverse weights and diverse measures
are both alike an abomination to the LORD.

20.11 Mt 7.16 Prov 21.8

11 Even children make themselves known by their acts,
by whether what they do is pure and right.
12 The hearing ear and the seeing eye—
the LORD has made them both.

20.13 Prov 6.9,10 19.15; 24.32,33

13 Do not love sleep, or else you will come to poverty;
open your eyes, and you will have plenty of bread.
14 "Bad, bad," says the buyer,
then goes away and boasts.
15 There is gold, and abundance of costly stones;
but the lips informed by knowledge are a precious jewel.

20.16 Ex 22.26 Prov 6.1-5

16 Take the garment of one who has given surety for a stranger;
seize the pledge given as surety for foreigners.

HOW TO SUCCEED IN GOD'S EYES

Proverbs notes two significant by-products of wise living: success and good reputation. Several verses also point out what causes failure and poor reputation.

Qualities that promote success and a good reputation:

Righteousness	10.7; 12.3; 28.12
Hating what is false	13.5
Using words with restraint	16.3
Speaking few words; having a settled mind	17.27, 28
Loving wisdom and understanding	19.8
Humility and fear of the Lord	22.4
Willingness to confess and renounce sin	28.13

Qualities that prevent success and cause a bad reputation:

Wickedness	10.7; 12.3; 28.12
Seeking honor	25.27
Hatred	26.24–26
Praising oneself	27.2
Concealing sin	28.13

Other verses dealing with one's reputation are: 11.10, 16; 14.3; 19.10; 22.1; 23.17, 18; 24.13, 14

20.3 A person who is truly confident of his or her strength does not need to parade it. A truly brave person does not look for chances to prove it. A resourceful woman can find a way out of a fight. A man of endurance will avoid retaliating. Foolish people find it impossible to stay out of fights. Men and women of character can. What kind of person are you?

20.4 You've heard similar warnings: if you don't study, you'll fail the test; if you don't save, you won't have money when you need it. God wants us to anticipate future needs and prepare for them. We can't expect him to come to our rescue when we cause our own problems through lack of planning. He provides for us, but he also expects us to be responsible.

20.9 No one is without sin. As soon as we confess our sin and repent, sinful thoughts and actions begin to creep back into our lives. We all need ongoing cleansing, moment by moment. Thank God for providing forgiveness by his mercy when we ask for it. Make confession and repentance a regular part of your talks with God. Rely on him moment by moment for the cleansing you need.

17 Bread gained by deceit is sweet,
but afterward the mouth will be full of gravel.
18 Plans are established by taking advice;
wage war by following wise guidance.
19 A gossip reveals secrets;
therefore do not associate with a babbler.
20 If you curse father or mother,
your lamp will go out in utter darkness.
21 An estate quickly acquired in the beginning
will not be blessed in the end.
22 Do not say, "I will repay evil";
wait for the LORD, and he will help you.
23 Differing weights are an abomination to the LORD,
and false scales are not good.
24 All our steps are ordered by the LORD;
how then can we understand our own ways?
25 It is a snare for one to say rashly, "It is holy,"
and begin to reflect only after making a vow.
26 A wise king winnows the wicked,
and drives the wheel over them.
27 The human spirit is the lamp of the LORD,
searching every innermost part.
28 Loyalty and faithfulness preserve the king,
and his throne is upheld by righteousness.[i]
29 The glory of youths is their strength,
but the beauty of the aged is their gray hair.
30 Blows that wound cleanse away evil;
beatings make clean the innermost parts.

21 The king's heart is a stream of water in the hand of the LORD;
he turns it wherever he will.
2 All deeds are right in the sight of the doer,
but the LORD weighs the heart.

[i] Gk: Heb *loyalty*

20.18 Prov 11.14 Lk 14.31
20.19 Prov 11.13
20.20 Ex 21.17 Lev 20.9 Prov 19.26
20.21 Prov 15.27 28.16
20.22 Prov 17.23 24.28,29 Mt 5.39 Rom 12.17
20.23 Prov 11.1; 20.10
20.24 Gen 50.20 1 Kgs 12.15 Ps 37.23
20.28 Prov 29.14
20.29 Prov 16.31
21.1 Ezra 6.21,22 Prov 16.1,9
21.2 Prov 16.2 Lk 16.15

20.23 "Differing weights" refers to the loaded scales a merchant might use in order to cheat the customers. Dishonesty is a difficult sin to avoid. It is easy to cheat if we think no one else is looking. But dishonesty affects the very core of a person. It makes him untrustworthy and untrusting. It eventually makes him unable to know himself or relate to others. Don't take dishonesty lightly. Even the smallest portion of dishonesty contains enough of the poison of deceit to kill your spiritual life. If there is any dishonesty in your life, tell God about it now.

20.24 We are often confused by the events around us. Many things we will never understand; others will fall into place in years to come as we look back and see how God was working. This proverb counsels us not to worry if we don't understand everything as it happens. Instead, we should trust that God knows what he's doing, even if his timing or design is not clear to us. See Psalm 37.23 for a reassuring promise of God's direction in your life.

20.25 To declare something holy meant that you intended to give it as an offering to God. *Holy* means set apart or dedicated for religious use. This proverb points out the evil of making a vow and then reconsidering it. God takes vows seriously and requires that they be carried out (Deuteronomy 23.21–23). We often have good intentions when making a vow because we want to show God that we are determined to please him. Jesus, however, says it is better not to make promises to God because he knows how difficult they are to keep (Matthew 5.33–37). If you still feel it is important to make a vow, make sure that you weigh the consequences of breaking that vow. (In Judges 11, Jephthah made a rash promise to sacrifice the first thing he saw on his return home. As it happened, he saw his daughter first.) It is better not to make promises than to make them and then later want to change them. It is better still to count the cost beforehand and then to fulfill them. (For a list of other Bible people who made rash vows, see the chart in Judges 11.)

20.27 God has given each of us a conscience ("human spirit") to tell us right from wrong. Without it, we would be unaware of the harm caused by certain actions, and we would not know how to do good either. The conscience searches us and exposes our hidden motives. Because our consciences are not perfect, we need the additional light of God's Word (see Psalm 119.105). The best way to stay on God's path is to use both lights at once – our conscience exposing our motives and the Bible directing our steps.

21.1 In Solomon's day, kings possessed absolute authority and were often considered like gods. This proverb shows that God, not earthly rulers, has ultimate authority over world politics. Although they may not have realized it, the earth's most powerful kings have always been under God's control. (See Isaiah 10.5–8 for an example of a king who was used for God's purposes.)

21.2 People can find an excuse for doing almost anything, but God looks behind the excuse to the motives of the heart. We often have to make choices in areas where the right action is difficult to discern. We can help ourselves make such decisions by trying to identify our motives first and then asking, "Would God be pleased with my real reasons for doing this?" God is not pleased when we do good deeds only to receive something in return.

21.3 Ps 50.8,9 Prov 15.8

21.4 Prov 6.17; 30.13 Lk 11.34

21.9 Prov 19.13 21.19

21.11 Prov 9.9; 15.14 19.25

3 To do righteousness and justice
is more acceptable to the LORD than sacrifice.
4 Haughty eyes and a proud heart—
the lamp of the wicked—are sin.
5 The plans of the diligent lead surely to abundance,
but everyone who is hasty comes only to want.
6 The getting of treasures by a lying tongue
is a fleeting vapor and a snare[j] of death.
7 The violence of the wicked will sweep them away,
because they refuse to do what is just.
8 The way of the guilty is crooked,
but the conduct of the pure is right.
9 It is better to live in a corner of the housetop
than in a house shared with a contentious wife.
10 The souls of the wicked desire evil;
their neighbors find no mercy in their eyes.
11 When a scoffer is punished, the simple become wiser;
when the wise are instructed, they increase in knowledge.

[j] Gk: Heb *seekers*

HONESTY AND DISHONESTY

Proverbs tells us plainly that God despises all forms of dishonesty. Not only does God hate dishonesty, but we are told that it works against us—others no longer trust us, and we cannot even enjoy our dishonest gains. It is wiser to be honest because "the righteous escape trouble" (12.13).

Others' Opinion	
Leaders value those who speak the truth.	16.13
Most people will appreciate truth in the end more than flattery.	28.23
Quality of life	
The righteous person's plans are just.	12.5
Truthful witnesses never lie; false witnesses always lie.	
Truthful witnesses save lives.	14.25
The children of the righteous are blessed.	20.7
Short-term results	
Ill-gotten treasure is of no value.	10.2
The righteous are rescued from trouble.	11.8
The evil are trapped by sinful talk.	12.13
Fraudulent gain is sweet for awhile.	20.17
Long-term results	
The upright are guided by integrity.	11.3
Truthful lips endure.	12.19
Riches gained quickly don't last.	20.21
Riches gained dishonestly don't last.	21.6
The blameless are kept safe.	28.18
God's Opinion	
God delights in honesty.	11.1
God delights in those who are truthful.	12.22
God detests unjust measures.	20.10
God is pleased when we do what is right and just.	21.3

21.3 Sacrifices and offerings are not bribes to make God overlook our character faults. If our personal and business dealings are not characterized by justice, no amount of generosity when the offering plate is passed will make up for it.

21.5 Faithful completion of mundane tasks is a great accomplishment. Such work is patiently carried out according to a plan. Diligence does not come naturally to most people; it is a result of strong character. Don't look for quick and easy answers. Be a diligent servant of God.

21.11, 12 It is usually better to learn from the mistakes of others than from our own. We can do this by listening to their advice. Take counsel from others instead of plunging ahead and learning the hard way.

12 The Righteous One observes the house of the wicked;
he casts the wicked down to ruin.
13 If you close your ear to the cry of the poor,
you will cry out and not be heard.
14 A gift in secret averts anger;
and a concealed bribe in the bosom, strong wrath.
15 When justice is done, it is a joy to the righteous,
but dismay to evildoers.
16 Whoever wanders from the way of understanding
will rest in the assembly of the dead.
17 Whoever loves pleasure will suffer want;
whoever loves wine and oil will not be rich.
18 The wicked is a ransom for the righteous,
and the faithless for the upright.

21.13 Prov 24.11,12 Mt 18.30-34 Lk 16.19-31 1 Jn 3.17

21.17 Prov 23.19-21

21.18 Prov 11.8 Isa 43.3,4

RIGHTEOUSNESS

Proverbs often compares the life-styles of the wicked and the righteous, and makes a strong case for living by God's pattern. The advantages of righteous living and the disadvantages of wicked living are pointed out. The kind of person we decide to be will affect every area of our lives.

	Righteous	*Wicked*	*References*
Outlook on life	Hopeful	Fearful	10.24
	Concerned about the welfare of God's creation	Even their kindness is cruel	12.10
	Understand justice	Don't understand justice	28.5
Response to life	Covered with blessings	Covered with violence	10.6
		Bent on evil	16.30
	Give thought to their ways	Put up a bold front	21.29
	Persevere against evil	Brought down by calamity	24.15, 16
		Hate those with integrity	29.10
How they are seen by others	Are appreciated	Do not endure	13.15
		Lead others into sin	16.29
	Conduct is upright	Conduct is devious	21.8
	Are not to desire the company of godless people	Plot violence	24.1, 2
	Others are glad when they triumph	Others hide at their rise to power	28.12
	Care for the poor	Unconcerned about the poor	29.7
	Detest the dishonest	Detest the upright	29.27
Quality of life	Stand firm	Swept away	10.25
	Delivered by righteousness	Trapped by evil desires	11.6

21.13 We should work to meet the needs of the poor and protect their rights – we may be in need of such services ourselves someday.

21.20 This proverb is about saving for the future. Easy credit has many people living on the edge of bankruptcy. The desire to keep up and accumulate more pushes them to spend every penny they

21.19 Prov 19.13; 21.9
21.20 Prov 8.21
21.21 Prov 2.10,21 3.16; 11.19
21.22 2 Sam 5.6-9 Prov 24.5
21.23 Prov 13.3 Jas 3.2
21.24 Prov 13.1; 14.6

19 It is better to live in a desert land
than with a contentious and fretful wife.
20 Precious treasure remains[k] in the house of the wise,
but the fool devours it.
21 Whoever pursues righteousness and kindness
will find life[l] and honor.
22 One wise person went up against a city of warriors
and brought down the stronghold in which they trusted.
23 To watch over mouth and tongue
is to keep out of trouble.
24 The proud, haughty person, named "Scoffer,"
acts with arrogant pride.

[k] Gk: Heb *and oil* [l] Gk: Heb *life and righteousness*

AND WICKEDNESS

	Righteous	Wicked	References
Quality of life (cont.)	Income results in treasure	Income results in trouble	15.6
	Avoid evil		16.17
		Fall into constant trouble	17.20
	Are bold as lions	Are fearful constantly	28.1
	Will be safe	Will suddenly fall	28.18
Short-term results	Walk securely	Will be found out	10.9
	Rewarded with prosperity	Pursued by misfortune	13.21
Long-term results	God protects them	God destroys them	10.29
		Will be punished for rebellion	17.11
Eternal expectations	Never uprooted	Never remain	10.30
	Earn a sure reward	Earn deceptive wages	11.18
	Attain life	Go to death	11.19
	End only in good	End only in wrath	11.23
	Shall stand	Shall perish	12.7
	Have a refuge when they die	Will be brought down by calamity	14.32
God's opinion of them	Delight in the good	Detest the perverse	11.20
	Evil people shall bow to them	They shall bow to the righteous	14.19

---

earn, and they stretch their credit to the limit. But anyone who spends all they have is spending more than they can afford. A wise person puts money aside for when they may have less. God approves of foresight and restraint. God's people need to examine their lifestyles to see whether their spending is God-pleasing or merely self-pleasing.

25 The craving of the lazy person is fatal,
for lazy hands refuse to labor.
26 All day long the wicked covet,[m]
but the righteous give and do not hold back.
27 The sacrifice of the wicked is an abomination;
how much more when brought with evil intent.
28 A false witness will perish,
but a good listener will testify successfully.
29 The wicked put on a bold face,
but the upright give thought to[n] their ways.
30 No wisdom, no understanding, no counsel,
can avail against the LORD.
31 The horse is made ready for the day of battle,
but the victory belongs to the LORD.

21.25 Ps 37.26; 112.5 Prov 10.4; 12.24
21.30 Isa 8.9; 14.27 Acts 5.38,39
21.31 Isa 31.1-3

22 A good name is to be chosen rather than great riches,
and favor is better than silver or gold.
2 The rich and the poor have this in common:
the LORD is the maker of them all.
3 The clever see danger and hide;
but the simple go on, and suffer for it.
4 The reward for humility and fear of the LORD
is riches and honor and life.
5 Thorns and snares are in the way of the perverse;
the cautious will keep far from them.
6 Train children in the right way,
and when old, they will not stray.
7 The rich rules over the poor,
and the borrower is the slave of the lender.
8 Whoever sows injustice will reap calamity,
and the rod of anger will fail.
9 Those who are generous are blessed,
for they share their bread with the poor.
10 Drive out a scoffer, and strife goes out;

22.2 Prov 14.31 29.13
22.3 Prov 14.15
22.4 Prov 3.16; 4.4
22.5 Prov 13.9,15
22.6 Ps 78.4 Eph 6.4
22.7 Prov 22.15
22.8 Prov 24.16
22.9 2 Cor 9.6

m Gk: Heb *all day long one covets covetously* n Another reading is *establish*

21.27 The kind of worship ("sacrifice") described in this proverb is no better than a bribe. How do people try to bribe God? They may go to church, tithe, or volunteer, not because of their love and devotion to God, but because they hope God will bless them in return. But God has made it very clear that he desires obedience and love more than religious ritual (see 21.3; 1 Samuel 15.22). God does not want our sacrifices of time, energy, and money alone; he wants our hearts—our complete love and devotion. We may be able to bribe people (21.14), but we cannot bribe God.

21.31 This proverb refers to preparing for battle. All our preparation for any task is useless without God. But even with God's help we still must do our part and prepare. His control of the outcome does not negate our responsibilities. God may want you to produce a great book, but you must learn to write. God may want to use you in foreign missions, but you must learn the language. God will accomplish his purposes, and he will be able to use you if you have done your part by being well prepared.

22.4 This is a general observation that would have been especially applicable to an obedient Israelite living in Solomon's God-fearing kingdom. Nevertheless, some have been martyrs at a young age, and some have given away all their wealth for the sake of God's kingdom. The book of Proverbs describes life the way it should be. It does not dwell on the exceptions. (For more on this concept, see the note on 3.16, 17.)

22.6 "In the right way" is literally, "according to his [the child's] way." It is natural to want to bring up all our children alike or train them the same way. This verse implies that parents should discern the individuality and special strengths that God has given each one. While we should not condone or excuse self-will, each child has natural inclinations that parents can develop. By talking to teachers, other parents, and grandparents, we can better discern and develop the individual capabilities of each child.

22.6 Many parents want to make all the choices for their child, but this hurts him in the long run. When parents teach a child how to make decisions, they don't have to watch every step he takes. They know he will remain on the right path because he has made the choice himself. Train your children to choose the right way.

22.7 Does this mean we should never borrow? No, but it warns us never to take on a loan without carefully examining our ability to repay it. A loan we can handle is enabling; a loan we can't handle is enslaving. The borrower must realize that until the loan is repaid, he is a servant to the individual or institution that made it.

22.8 This proverb is a message of hope to people who must live and work under unjust authoritarian leaders. It is also a warning to those who enjoy ruling with an iron hand. Sometimes God intervenes and directly destroys tyrants. More often, he uses other rulers to overthrow them or their own oppressed people to rebel against them. If you are in a position of authority at church, work, or home, remember what happens to tyrants. Leadership through kindness is more effective and longer-lasting than leadership by force.

quarreling and abuse will cease.

22.11 Prov 14.35 16.15; 22.29 Mt 5.8

11 Those who love a pure heart and are gracious in speech
will have the king as a friend.
12 The eyes of the LORD keep watch over knowledge,
but he overthrows the words of the faithless.
13 The lazy person says, "There is a lion outside!
I shall be killed in the streets!"

22.14 Prov 5.3; 23.26

14 The mouth of a loose[o] woman is a deep pit;
he with whom the LORD is angry falls into it.

22.15 Prov 13.24

15 Folly is bound up in the heart of a boy,
but the rod of discipline drives it far away.

22.16 Job 20.19 Prov 14.31; 28.3

16 Oppressing the poor in order to enrich oneself,
and giving to the rich, will lead only to loss.

Proverbs of the wise

22.17 Prov 1.7; 2.1,2

17 The words of the wise:

Incline your ear and hear my words,[p]
and apply your mind to my teaching;
18 for it will be pleasant if you keep them within you,
if all of them are ready on your lips.
19 So that your trust may be in the LORD,
I have made them known to you today—yes, to you.
20 Have I not written for you thirty sayings
of admonition and knowledge,
21 to show you what is right and true,
so that you may give a true answer to those who sent you?

22 Do not rob the poor because they are poor,
or crush the afflicted at the gate;
23 for the LORD pleads their cause
and despoils of life those who despoil them.

22.24 Prov 1.15; 14.7 29.22

24 Make no friends with those given to anger,
and do not associate with hotheads,
25 or you may learn their ways
and entangle yourself in a snare.

22.26 Ex 22.26 Prov 6.1-5 20.16

26 Do not be one of those who give pledges,
who become surety for debts.
27 If you have nothing with which to pay,
why should your bed be taken from under you?

22.28 Deut 19.14 27.17 Prov 23.10,11

28 Do not remove the ancient landmark
that your ancestors set up.

[o] Heb *strange* [p] Cn Compare Gk: Heb *Incline your ear, and hear the words of the wise*

22.12 *Knowledge* also refers to those who live right and speak the truth. It takes discipline, determination, and hard work to live God's way, but God protects and rewards those who make the commitment to follow him. The wicked may seem to have an easier time of it, but in the long run their plans fail and their lives amount to nothing. Don't resist God and expect lasting success.

22.13 This proverb refers to an excuse a lazy person might use to avoid going to work. The excuse sounds silly to us, but that's often how our excuses sound to others. Don't rationalize laziness. Take your responsibilities seriously and get to work.

22.15 Young children often do foolish and dangerous things simply because they don't understand the consequences. Wisdom and common sense are not transferred by just being a good example. The wisdom a child learns must be taught consciously. "The rod of discipline" stands for all forms of discipline or training. Just as God trains and corrects us to make us better, so parents must discipline their children to make them learn the difference between right and wrong. To see how God corrects us, read 3.11, 12.

22.24, 25 People tend to become like those with whom they spend a lot of time. Even the negative characteristics sometimes rub off. The Bible exhorts us to be cautious in our choice of companions. Choose people with characteristics you would like to develop in your own life.

22.26 This verse is saying that it is wise to be slow to countersign a note or to be liable for another person's debt.

22.28 In Joshua 13–21, the land was divided and the boundaries marked out for each tribe. Moses had already warned the people that when they reached the promised land they shouldn't cheat their neighbors by moving one of the landmarks to give themselves more land and their neighbors less (Deuteronomy 19.14; 27.17).

29 Do you see those who are skillful in their work?
they will serve kings;
they will not serve common people.

22.29 Prov 27.18

23 When you sit down to eat with a ruler,
observe carefully what[q] is before you,
2 and put a knife to your throat
if you have a big appetite.
3 Do not desire the ruler's[r] delicacies,
for they are deceptive food.
4 Do not wear yourself out to get rich;
be wise enough to desist.
5 When your eyes light upon it, it is gone;
for suddenly it takes wings to itself,
flying like an eagle toward heaven.
6 Do not eat the bread of the stingy;
do not desire their delicacies;
7 for like a hair in the throat, so are they.[s]
"Eat and drink!" they say to you;
but they do not mean it.
8 You will vomit up the little you have eaten,
and you will waste your pleasant words.
9 Do not speak in the hearing of a fool,
who will only despise the wisdom of your words.
10 Do not remove an ancient landmark
or encroach on the fields of orphans,
11 for their redeemer is strong;
he will plead their cause against you.
12 Apply your mind to instruction
and your ear to words of knowledge.
13 Do not withhold discipline from your children;
if you beat them with a rod, they will not die.
14 If you beat them with the rod,
you will save their lives from Sheol.
15 My child, if your heart is wise,
my heart too will be glad.
16 My soul will rejoice
when your lips speak what is right.

23.1 Ps 141.4 Prov 23.6 Eccles 7.7

23.4 Prov 15.27 27.23,24; 28.20 Mt 6.19

23.6 Prov 1.15; 4.14

23.9 Prov 14.7; 24.7

23.10 Deut 19.14 27.17 Jer 22.3 Zech 7.10

23.12 Prov 2.2; 5.1 22.17

23.13 Prov 13.24 19.18; 29.15 1 Cor 5.5

23.15 Prov 4.1; 10.1 15.20; 27.11

q Or *who* r Heb *his* s Meaning of Heb uncertain

23.1–3 The point of this proverb is to be careful when eating with a rich person, because he will try to bribe you. No good will come from the meal.

23.4, 5 We have all heard of people who have won millions of dollars and then lost it all. Even the average person can spend an inheritance – or a paycheck – with lightning speed and have little to show for it. Don't spend your time chasing fleeting earthly treasures. Instead store up treasures in heaven, for such treasures will never be lost. (See Luke 12.33, 34 for Jesus' teaching.)

23.6–8 In graphic language, the writer warns us not to envy the life-styles of those who have become rich by being stingy and miserly, and not to gain their favor by fawning over them. Their "friendship" is phony – they will just use you for their own gain.

23.10, 11 The term *redeemer* refers to someone who bought back a family member who had fallen into slavery or who accepted the obligation to marry the widow of a family member (Ruth 4.3–10). God is also called a Redeemer (Exodus 6.6; Job 19.25). (For an explanation of ancient boundary markers, see the note on 22.28.)

23.12 The people most likely to gain knowledge are those who are willing to listen. It is a sign of strength, not weakness, to pay attention to what others have to say. People who are eager to listen continue to learn and grow throughout their lives. If we refuse to become set in our ways, we can always expand the limits of our knowledge.

23.13, 14 The stern tone of correction here is offset by the affection expressed in verse 15. However, many parents are reluctant to discipline their children at all. Some fear they will forfeit their relationship, that their children will resent them, or that they will stifle their children's development. But correction won't kill them, and it may prevent them from foolish moves that will. *Sheol* means death or the grave. Here it is used to emphasize the importance of correction, saving souls from death.

23.17, 18 How easy it is to envy those who get ahead unhampered by Christian responsibility or God's laws. For a time they do seem to get ahead without paying any attention to God's desires. But to those who follow him, God promises a hope and a wonderful

23.17
Ps 19.11; 37.1
73.3
Prov 24.1,14,19

17 Do not let your heart envy sinners,
but always continue in the fear of the LORD.
18 Surely there is a future,
and your hope will not be cut off.

23.19
Prov 20.1; 23.29

19 Hear, my child, and be wise,
and direct your mind in the way.
20 Do not be among winebibbers,
or among gluttonous eaters of meat;
21 for the drunkard and the glutton will come to poverty,
and drowsiness will clothe them with rags.

23.22
Prov 13.1; 15.5
Deut 21.18
23.23
Prov 4.7; 15.14
18.15
Mt 13.44
23.24
Prov 10.1; 23.15

22 Listen to your father who begot you,
and do not despise your mother when she is old.
23 Buy truth, and do not sell it;
buy wisdom, instruction, and understanding.
24 The father of the righteous will greatly rejoice;
he who begets a wise son will be glad in him.
25 Let your father and mother be glad;
let her who bore you rejoice.

23.26
Prov 6.26; 22.14
Eccles 7.26

26 My child, give me your heart,
and let your eyes observe[t] my ways.
27 For a prostitute is a deep pit;
an adulteress[u] is a narrow well.
28 She lies in wait like a robber
and increases the number of the faithless.

23.29
Prov 20.1; 23.19
Isa 5.11,22

29 Who has woe? Who has sorrow?
Who has strife? Who has complaining?
Who has wounds without cause?
Who has redness of eyes?
30 Those who linger late over wine,
those who keep trying mixed wines.
31 Do not look at wine when it is red,
when it sparkles in the cup
and goes down smoothly.

23.32
Ps 140.3

32 At the last it bites like a serpent,
and stings like an adder.
33 Your eyes will see strange things,
and your mind utter perverse things.
34 You will be like one who lies down in the midst of the sea,
like one who lies on the top of a mast.[v]
35 "They struck me," you will say,[w] "but I was not hurt;
they beat me, but I did not feel it.
When shall I awake?
I will seek another drink."

[t] Another reading is *delight in* [u] Heb *an alien woman* [v] Meaning of Heb uncertain [w] Gk Syr Vg Tg: Heb lacks *you will say*

future even if we don't realize it in this life.

23.29, 30 The soothing comfort of alcohol is only temporary. Real relief comes from dealing with the cause of the anguish and sorrow and turning to God for peace. Don't lose yourself in alcohol; find yourself in God.

23.29–35 Israel was a wine-producing country. In the Old Testament, wine presses bursting with new wine were considered a sign of blessing (3.10). Wisdom is even said to have set her table with wine (9.2, 5). But the Old Testament writers were alert to the dangers of wine. It dulls the senses; it limits clear judgment (31.1–9); it lowers the capacity for control (4.17); it destroys one's efficiency (21.17). To make wine an end in itself, a means of self-indulgence, or an escape from life is to misuse it and invite the consequences of the drunkard.

24 Do not envy the wicked,
nor desire to be with them;
2 for their minds devise violence,
and their lips talk of mischief.

3 By wisdom a house is built,
and by understanding it is established;
4 by knowledge the rooms are filled
with all precious and pleasant riches.
5 Wise warriors are mightier than strong ones,[x]
and those who have knowledge than those who have strength;
6 for by wise guidance you can wage your war,
and in abundance of counselors there is victory.
7 Wisdom is too high for fools;
in the gate they do not open their mouths.

8 Whoever plans to do evil
will be called a mischief-maker.
9 The devising of folly is sin,
and the scoffer is an abomination to all.

10 If you faint in the day of adversity,
your strength being small;
11 if you hold back from rescuing those taken away to death,
those who go staggering to the slaughter;
12 if you say, "Look, we did not know this"—
does not he who weighs the heart perceive it?
Does not he who keeps watch over your soul know it?
And will he not repay all according to their deeds?

13 My child, eat honey, for it is good,
and the drippings of the honeycomb are sweet to your taste.
14 Know that wisdom is such to your soul;
if you find it, you will find a future,
and your hope will not be cut off.

15 Do not lie in wait like an outlaw against the home of the righteous;
do no violence to the place where the righteous live;
16 for though they fall seven times, they will rise again;
but the wicked are overthrown by calamity.

24.1 Ps 1.1; 37.3 Prov 1.15

24.5 Prov 21.22

24.6 Prov 11.14

24.7 Prov 14.6

24.8 Prov 6.14; 14.22

24.10 Job 4.5 Heb 12.3

24.11 1 Sam 16.7 Ps 82.4 Eccles 5.8

24.13 Ps 19.10 Prov 25.16

24.15 Job 5.19 Ps 10.9-12 Prov 6.15 14.32; 24.21,22

x Gk Compare Syr Tg: Heb *A wise man is strength*

24.5 The athlete who thinks—who assesses the situation and plans strategies—has an advantage over a physically stronger but unthinking opponent. And wisdom, not muscle, is certainly what has put humankind in charge of the animal kingdom. We exercise reglarly and eat well to build our strength; do we take equal pains to develop wisdom? Because wisdom is a vital part of strength, it pays to work on it.

24.6 In any major decision we make concerning college, marriage, career, children, etc., it is not a sign of weakness to ask for advice. Instead it is foolish not to ask for it. Find good advisers before making any big decision. They can help you expand your alternatives and evaluate your choices.

24.8 Planning to do evil can be as wrong as doing it because what you think determines what you will do. Left unchecked, wrong desires will lead us to sin. God wants pure lives, free from sin; and planning evil spoils the purity even if the evil action has not yet been committed. Should you say, "Then I might as well go ahead and do it, because I've already planned it"? No. You have sinned in your attitude, but you have not yet damaged other people. Stop in your tracks and ask God to forgive you and put you on a different path.

24.10 Adversity can be useful. It shows you who you really are, what kind of character you have developed. In addition, it helps you grow stronger. When Jeremiah questioned God because of the adversity he faced, God asked how he ever expected to face big challenges if the little ones wearied him (Jeremiah 12.5). Don't complain about your problems. The adversity you face today is training you to be strong for the more difficult situations you will face in the future.

24.17, 18 David, Solomon's father, refused to gloat over the death

24.17 Ps 35.15 Rom 11.18-21

17 Do not rejoice when your enemies fall,
and do not let your heart be glad when they stumble,
18 or else the LORD will see it and be displeased,
and turn away his anger from them.

24.19 Job 15.31 Prov 13.9; 24.1

19 Do not fret because of evildoers.
Do not envy the wicked;
20 for the evil have no future;
the lamp of the wicked will go out.

24.21 Prov 24.15,16 Rom 13.4

21 My child, fear the LORD and the king,
and do not disobey either of them;[y]
22 for disaster comes from them suddenly,
and who knows the ruin that both can bring?

More proverbs of the wise

24.23 Prov 18.5; 28.21

23 These also are sayings of the wise:

Partiality in judging is not good.
24 Whoever says to the wicked, "You are innocent,"
will be cursed by peoples, abhorred by nations;
25 but those who rebuke the wicked will have delight,
and a good blessing will come upon them.

24.26 Job 6.25 Prov 15.23 25.12; 27.5

26 One who gives an honest answer
gives a kiss on the lips.

27 Prepare your work outside,
get everything ready for you in the field;
and after that build your house.

24.28 Prov 20.22 25.18 Mt 5.39 Rom 12.17

28 Do not be a witness against your neighbor without cause,
and do not deceive with your lips.
29 Do not say, "I will do to others as they have done to me;
I will pay them back for what they have done."

24.30 Job 4.8 Prov 6.6 Isa 5.6,7

30 I passed by the field of one who was lazy,
by the vineyard of a stupid person;
31 and see, it was all overgrown with thorns;
the ground was covered with nettles,
and its stone wall was broken down.

24.32 Prov 6.10 12.24; 23.21

32 Then I saw and considered it;
I looked and received instruction.
33 A little sleep, a little slumber,
a little folding of the hands to rest,
34 and poverty will come upon you like a robber,
and want, like an armed warrior.

y Gk: Heb *do not associate with those who change*

of his lifelong enemy Saul (see 2 Samuel 1). On the other hand, the nation of Edom rejoiced over Israel's defeat and was punished by God for this (Obadiah 1.12). To gloat over others' misfortune is to make yourself the avenger and to put yourself in the place of God, who alone is the real judge of all the earth (see Deuteronomy 32.35).

24.26 A kiss on the lips was a sign of true friendship. People often think that they should bend the truth to avoid hurting a friend. But one who gives an honest, straightforward answer is a true friend.

24.27 We should carry out our work in its proper order. If a farmer builds his house in the spring, he misses the planting season and goes a year without food. If a businessman invests his money in a house while his business is struggling to grow, he may lose both. It is possible to work hard and still lose everything if the timing is wrong or the resources to carry it out are not in place.

24.29 Here is a reverse version of "the golden rule" (see Luke 6.31). Revenge is the way the world operates, but it is not God's way.

C. WISDOM FOR THE LEADERS (25.1 – 31.31)

These proverbs were collected by Hezekiah's aides. The first section was written by Solomon, and the next two sections were written by others. While we all can learn from these proverbs, many were originally directed toward the king or those who dealt with the king. These are particularly helpful for those who are leaders or aspire to become leaders. The book ends with a description of a truly good wife, who is an example of godly wisdom.

More proverbs by Solomon

25 These are other proverbs of Solomon that the officials of King Hezekiah of Judah copied. **25.1** Prov 1.1

2 It is the glory of God to conceal things,
but the glory of kings is to search things out.
3 Like the heavens for height, like the earth for depth,
so the mind of kings is unsearchable.
4 Take away the dross from the silver,
and the smith has material for a vessel;
5 take away the wicked from the presence of the king,
and his throne will be established in righteousness.
6 Do not put yourself forward in the king's presence
or stand in the place of the great;
7 for it is better to be told, "Come up here,"
than to be put lower in the presence of a noble.

What your eyes have seen
8 do not hastily bring into court;
for[z] what will you do in the end,
when your neighbor puts you to shame?
9 Argue your case with your neighbor directly,
and do not disclose another's secret;
10 or else someone who hears you will bring shame upon you,
and your ill repute will have no end.

11 A word fitly spoken
is like apples of gold in a setting of silver.
12 Like a gold ring or an ornament of gold
is a wise rebuke to a listening ear.
13 Like the cold of snow in the time of harvest
are faithful messengers to those who send them;
they refresh the spirit of their masters.
14 Like clouds and wind without rain
is one who boasts of a gift never given.
15 With patience a ruler may be persuaded,
and a soft tongue can break bones.

25.2 Deut 29.29 Ezra 6.1 Rom 11.33
25.4 Prov 20.8 Ezek 22.18 Mal 3.2,3
25.6 Ps 131.1 Prov 25.27; 27.2 Mt 12.39 Lk 14.7
25.8 Prov 17.14; 18.6 Mt 5.25
25.11 Prov 15.23
25.12 Prov 15.31 26.23
25.15 Prov 15.1 Eccles 10.4

[z] Cn: Heb *or else*

25.1 Hezekiah's story is told in 2 Kings 18 – 20; 2 Chronicles 29 – 32; and Isaiah 36 – 39. He was one of the few kings of Judah who honored the Lord. By contrast, his father Ahaz actually nailed the temple door shut. Hezekiah restored the temple, destroyed idol worship centers, and earned the respect of surrounding nations, many of whom brought gifts to God because of him. It is not surprising that Hezekiah had these proverbs copied and read, for "every work that he undertook in the service of the house of God, and in accordance with the law and the commandments, to seek his God, he did with all his heart; and he prospered" (2 Chronicles 31.21).

25.6, 7 Jesus made this proverb into a parable (see Luke 14.7–11). We should not seek honor for ourselves. It is better to quietly and faithfully accomplish the work God has given us to do. As others notice the quality of our lives then they will draw attention to us.

25.13 It is often difficult to find people you can really trust. A faithful employee ("messenger") is punctual, responsible, honest, and hardworking. This person is invaluable as he/she helps take some of the pressure off his or her employer. Find out what your employer needs from you to make his or her job easier, and do it.

25.14 Most churches, missions organizations, and Christian groups depend on the gifts of people to keep their ministries going. But many who promise to give fail to follow through. The Bible is very clear about the effect this has on those involved in the ministry. If you make a pledge, keep your promise.

25.16 Prov 25.27

16 If you have found honey, eat only enough for you,
or else, having too much, you will vomit it.
17 Let your foot be seldom in your neighbor's house,
otherwise the neighbor will become weary of you and hate you.

25.18 Ps 57.4 Prov 12.18 24.28 Jer 9.8
25.19 Job 6.15
25.20 Prov 27.14

18 Like a war club, a sword, or a sharp arrow
is one who bears false witness against a neighbor.
19 Like a bad tooth or a lame foot
is trust in a faithless person in time of trouble.
20 Like vinegar on a wound[a]
is one who sings songs to a heavy heart.
Like a moth in clothing or a worm in wood,
sorrow gnaws at the human heart.[b]

25.21 Ex 23.4 2 Kgs 6.22 2 Chron 28.15 Mt 5.44; 6.6 Rom 12.20

21 If your enemies are hungry, give them bread to eat;
and if they are thirsty, give them water to drink;
22 for you will heap coals of fire on their heads,
and the LORD will reward you.

25.23 Prov 13.3; 26.20

23 The north wind produces rain,
and a backbiting tongue, angry looks.

25.24 Prov 19.13 21.9; 27.15

24 It is better to live in a corner of the housetop
than in a house shared with a contentious wife.

25.25 2 Cor 7.7 1 Thess 3.5-8

25 Like cold water to a thirsty soul,
so is good news from a far country.

25.26 Ezek 34.18

26 Like a muddied spring or a polluted fountain
are the righteous who give way before the wicked.

25.27 Prov 25.16

27 It is not good to eat much honey,
or to seek honor on top of honor.
28 Like a city breached, without walls,
is one who lacks self-control.

26.1 1 Sam 12.17 Prov 26.8

26 Like snow in summer or rain in harvest,
so honor is not fitting for a fool.

26.2 Num 23.8 2 Sam 16.12 Ps 109.28

2 Like a sparrow in its flitting, like a swallow in its flying,
an undeserved curse goes nowhere.

26.3 Ps 32.9 Prov 10.13

3 A whip for the horse, a bridle for the donkey,
and a rod for the back of fools.

26.4 Prov 23.9; 29.8

4 Do not answer fools according to their folly,
or you will be a fool yourself.
5 Answer fools according to their folly,
or they will be wise in their own eyes.

26.6 Prov 13.17 25.13

6 It is like cutting off one's foot and drinking down violence,
to send a message by a fool.

a Gk: Heb *Like one who takes off a garment on a cold day, like vinegar on lye* b Gk Syr Tg: Heb lacks *Like a moth . . . human heart*

25.18 Lying is vicious. Its effects can be as permanent as those of a stab wound. The next time you are tempted to pass on a bit of gossip, imagine yourself stabbing the victim of your remarks with a sword. This image may shock you into silence.

25.21, 22 God's form of retaliation is most effective and yet difficult to do. Paul quotes this proverb in Romans 12.19–21. In Matthew 5.44, Jesus encourages us to pray for those who hurt us. By returning good for evil, we're acknowledging God as the balancer of all accounts and trusting him to be the judge.

25.26 To "give way" here means setting aside your standards of right and wrong. No one is helped by someone who compromises with the wicked.

25.27 Dwelling on the honors you deserve can only be harmful. It can make you bitter, discouraged, or angry, and it will not bring you the rewards you think should be yours. Pining for what you think you should have received may make you miss the satisfaction of knowing you did your best.

25.28 A "city breached" is one with the defensive walls broken down. Even though city walls restricted the inhabitants' movements, people were happy to have them. Without walls, they would have been vulnerable to attack by any passing group of marauders. Self-control limits us, to be sure, but it is necessary. An out-of-control life is open to all sorts of enemy attack. Think of self-control as a wall for defense and protection.

26.2 "An undeserved curse goes nowhere" means that it has no effect.

26.4, 5 These two verses seem to be in contradiction. But the writer is saying that we shouldn't take a foolish person seriously and try to reason with his or her empty arguments. This will only make him or her proud and determined to win the argument. Instead, we should give light and silly replies.

7 The legs of a disabled person hang limp;
so does a proverb in the mouth of a fool.
8 It is like binding a stone in a sling
to give honor to a fool.
9 Like a thornbush brandished by the hand of a drunkard
is a proverb in the mouth of a fool.
10 Like an archer who wounds everybody
is one who hires a passing fool or drunkard.[c]
11 Like a dog that returns to its vomit
is a fool who reverts to his folly.
12 Do you see persons wise in their own eyes?
There is more hope for fools than for them.
13 The lazy person says, "There is a lion in the road!
There is a lion in the streets!"
14 As a door turns on its hinges,
so does a lazy person in bed.
15 The lazy person buries a hand in the dish,
and is too tired to bring it back to the mouth.
16 The lazy person is wiser in self-esteem
than seven who can answer discreetly.
17 Like somebody who takes a passing dog by the ears
is one who meddles in the quarrel of another.
18 Like a maniac who shoots deadly firebrands and arrows,
19 so is one who deceives a neighbor
and says, "I am only joking!"
20 For lack of wood the fire goes out,
and where there is no whisperer, quarreling ceases.
21 As charcoal is to hot embers and wood to fire,
so is a quarrelsome person for kindling strife.
22 The words of a whisperer are like delicious morsels;
they go down into the inner parts of the body.
23 Like the glaze[d] covering an earthen vessel
are smooth[e] lips with an evil heart.
24 An enemy dissembles in speaking
while harboring deceit within;

26.7 Ps 50.16,17 Prov 17.7
26.11 Ex 8.15 2 Pet 2.22
26.12 Prov 3.7; 28.11
26.13 Prov 15.19
26.14 Prov 6.9; 19.15
26.15 Prov 12.27 Eccles 4.5
26.17 Prov 3.30; 18.6
26.18 Prov 24.12,28
26.20 Prov 16.28 Jas 3.6
26.21 Prov 10.12 15.18; 29.22
26.22 Prov 18.8; 20.19
26.23 Mt 23.28 Lk 11.39
26.24 Prov 12.20

[c] Meaning of Heb uncertain [d] Cn: Heb *silver of dross* [e] Gk: Heb *burning*

26.7 In the mouth of a fool, a parable becomes as useless as a paralyzed leg. Some people are so blind that they won't get much wisdom from reading these proverbs. Only those who want to be wise have the receptive attitude needed to make the most of them. If we want to learn from God, he responds and pours out his wisdom to us (1.23).

26.8 Sometimes when someone in a group causes discord or dissension, the leader tries to make him loyal and productive by giving him a place of privilege or responsibility. This doesn't always work. In fact, it is like tying the stone to the sling – it won't go anywhere and will swing back and hurt you. The dissenter's new power may be just what he needs to manipulate the group.

26.9 Normally the first prick of a thorn alerts us, and we remove the thorn before it damages us. A drunk person, however, may not feel the thorn, and so it works its way into his flesh. Similarly, a fool may not feel the sting of a parable, because he does not see where it touches his life. Instead of taking its point to heart, a fool will apply it to his church, his employer, his spouse, or whomever he is rebelling against. The next time you find yourself saying, "So-and-so should really pay attention to that," stop and ask yourself – "Is there a message in it for me?"

26.13–16 If a person is not willing to work, he can find endless excuses to avoid it. But laziness is more dangerous than a prowling lion. The less you do, the less you want to do, and the more useless you become. To overcome laziness, take a few small steps toward change. Set a concrete, realistic goal. Figure out the steps needed to reach it, and follow those steps. Pray for strength and persistence. To keep your excuses from making you useless, stop making useless excuses.

26.17 Pulling the ears of a stray dog is a good way to get bitten, and interfering in arguments is a good way to get hurt. Many times both arguers will turn on the person who interferes. It is best simply to keep out of arguments that are none of your business. If you must become involved, try to wait until the arguers have stopped fighting and cooled off a bit. Then maybe you can help them mend their differences and their relationship.

26.20 A whisperer is someone who gossips. Talking about every little irritation or piece of gossip only keeps the fires of anger going. Refusing to discuss them cuts the fuel line and makes the fires die out. Does someone continually irritate you? Decide not to complain about the person, and see if your irritation dies from lack of fuel.

26.24–26 To dissemble means to hide under a false appearance, to conceal, or to disguise. This proverb means that a person with hate in their heart may sound pleasant enough, but don't believe what they say.

25 when an enemy speaks graciously, do not believe it,
for there are seven abominations concealed within;
26 though hatred is covered with guile,
the enemy's wickedness will be exposed in the assembly.
27 Whoever digs a pit will fall into it,
and a stone will come back on the one who starts it rolling.
28 A lying tongue hates its victims,
and a flattering mouth works ruin.

27 Do not boast about tomorrow,
for you do not know what a day may bring.
2 Let another praise you, and not your own mouth—
a stranger, and not your own lips.
3 A stone is heavy, and sand is weighty,
but a fool's provocation is heavier than both.
4 Wrath is cruel, anger is overwhelming,
but who is able to stand before jealousy?
5 Better is open rebuke
than hidden love.
6 Well meant are the wounds a friend inflicts,
but profuse are the kisses of an enemy.
7 The sated appetite spurns honey,
but to a ravenous appetite even the bitter is sweet.
8 Like a bird that strays from its nest
is one who strays from home.
9 Perfume and incense make the heart glad,
but the soul is torn by trouble.[f]
10 Do not forsake your friend or the friend of your parent;
do not go to the house of your kindred in the day of your calamity.
Better is a neighbor who is nearby
than kindred who are far away.
11 Be wise, my child, and make my heart glad,
so that I may answer whoever reproaches me.
12 The clever see danger and hide;

26.27 Ps 7.15
26.28 Prov 6.24
27.1 Mt 6.34 Lk 12.19,20 Jas 4.13-16
27.2 Prov 25.27 2 Cor 10.12,18
27.4 Prov 6.34
27.5 Prov 24.26 25.12; 28.23
27.6 Ps 141.5 Mt 26.49
27.8 1 Sam 26.19 Prov 21.16 Heb 11.13
27.10 1 Kgs 12.6 2 Chron 10.6 Prov 17.17
27.11 Prov 10.1; 23.15
27.12 Prov 22.3

[f] Gk: Heb *the sweetness of a friend is better than one's own counsel*

THE FOUR TONGUES What we say probably affects more people than any other action we take. It is not surprising, then, to find that Proverbs gives special attention to words and how they are used. Four common speech patterns are described in Proverbs. The first two should be copied, while the last two should be avoided.

The Controlled Tongue	Those with this speech pattern think before speaking, know when silence is best, and give wise advice.	10.19; 11.12, 13; 12.16; 13.3; 15.1, 4, 28; 16.23; 17.14, 27, 28; 21.23; 24.26
The Caring Tongue	Those with this speech pattern speak truthfully while seeking to encourage.	10.32; 12.18, 25; 15.23; 16.24; 25.15; 27.9
The Conniving Tongue	Those with this speech pattern are filled with wrong motives, gossip, slander, and twist truth.	6.12–14; 8.13; 16.28; 18.8; 25.18; 26.20–28
The Careless Tongue	Those with this speech pattern are filled with lies, curses, quick-tempered words—which can lead to rebellion and destruction.	10.18, 32; 11.9; 12.16, 18; 15.4; 17.9, 14, 19; 20.19; 25.23

Other verses about our speech include: 10.11, 20, 31; 12.6, 17–19; 13.2; 14.3; 19.5, 28; 25.11; 27.2, 5, 14, 17; 29.9

27.6 Who would prefer a friend's wounds to an enemy's kisses? Anyone who considers the source. A friend who has your best interests at heart may have to give you unpleasant advice at times, but you know it is for your own good. An enemy, by contrast, may whisper sweet words and happily send you on your way to ruin. We tend to hear what we want to hear, even if an enemy is the only one who will say it. A friend's advice, no matter how painful, is much better.

but the simple go on, and suffer for it.
13 Take the garment of one who has given surety for a stranger;
seize the pledge given as surety for foreigners.[g]
14 Whoever blesses a neighbor with a loud voice,
rising early in the morning,
will be counted as cursing.
15 A continual dripping on a rainy day
and a contentious wife are alike;
16 to restrain her is to restrain the wind
or to grasp oil in the right hand.[h]
17 Iron sharpens iron,
and one person sharpens the wits[i] of another.
18 Anyone who tends a fig tree will eat its fruit,
and anyone who takes care of a master will be honored.
19 Just as water reflects the face,
so one human heart reflects another.
20 Sheol and Abaddon are never satisfied,
and human eyes are never satisfied.
21 The crucible is for silver, and the furnace is for gold,
so a person is tested[j] by being praised.
22 Crush a fool in a mortar with a pestle
along with crushed grain,
but the folly will not be driven out.

23 Know well the condition of your flocks,
and give attention to your herds;
24 for riches do not last forever,
nor a crown for all generations.
25 When the grass is gone, and new growth appears,
and the herbage of the mountains is gathered,
26 the lambs will provide your clothing,
and the goats the price of a field;
27 there will be enough goats' milk for your food,
for the food of your household
and nourishment for your servant girls.

28 The wicked flee when no one pursues,
but the righteous are as bold as a lion.
2 When a land rebels

27.13 Prov 6.1-5
27.14 Prov 26.18,19
27.15 Prov 19.13 21.9; 25.24
27.18 Lk 12.42 2 Tim 2.6
27.20 Prov 30.15 Eccles 1.8-11 Hab 2.5
27.21 1 Sam 18.7,8 2 Sam 14.25 Ps 12.6 Prov 17.3 Zech 13.9 Lk 6.26
27.22 Prov 23.35 26.11 Jer 5.3
27.23 Job 19.9
28.1 Ps 27.1,2
28.2 1 Kgs 16.8-28 2 Kgs 15.8-15 Hos 7.7; 8.4

[g] Vg and 20.16: Heb *for a foreign woman* [h] Meaning of Heb uncertain [i] Heb *face* [j] Heb lacks *is tested*

27.15, 16 Nagging, a steady stream of unwanted advice, is a form of torture. People nag because they think they're not getting through, but nagging hinders communication more than it helps. When tempted to engage in this destructive habit, stop and examine your motives. Are you more concerned about yourself—getting your way, being right—than about the person you are pretending to help? If you are truly concerned about other people, think of a more effective way to get through to them. Surprise them with words of patience and love, and see what happens.

27.17 There is a mental sharpness that comes from being around good people. And a meeting of minds can help people see their ideas with new clarity, refine them, and shape them into brilliant insights. This requires discussion partners who can challenge each other and stimulate thought—people who focus on the idea without involving their egos in the discussion, people who know how to attack the thought and not the thinker. Two friends who bring their ideas together can help each other become sharper.

27.18 With all the problems and concerns a leader has, it can be easy to overlook the very people who most deserve attention—faithful employees or volunteers (those who tend the fig trees). The people who stand behind you, who work hard and help you get the job done, deserve to share in your success. Be sure that in all your worrying, planning, and organizing, you don't forget the people who are helping you the most.

27.20 *Sheol* means death, the grave, or the realm of the dead. *Abaddon* is used as a synonym for Sheol, meaning the place of the dead or destruction.

27.21 Praise tests a person, just as high temperatures test metal. How does praise affect you? Do you work to get it? Do you work harder after you've gotten it? Your attitude toward praise tells a lot about your character. People of high integrity are not swayed by praise. They are attuned to their inner convictions, and they do what they should whether or not they are praised for it.

27.23–27 Because life is short and our fortunes uncertain, we should be all the more diligent in what we do with our lives. We should act with foresight, giving responsible attention to our homes, our families, and our careers. We should be responsible stewards, like a farmer with his lands and herds. Thinking ahead is a duty, not an option, for God's people.

it has many rulers;
but with an intelligent ruler
there is lasting order.[k]
3 A ruler[l] who oppresses the poor
is a beating rain that leaves no food.
4 Those who forsake the law praise the wicked,
but those who keep the law struggle against them.
5 The evil do not understand justice,
but those who seek the LORD understand it completely.
6 Better to be poor and walk in integrity
than to be crooked in one's ways even though rich.
7 Those who keep the law are wise children,
but companions of gluttons shame their parents.

28.4 Rom 1.32
28.5 Ps 92.6,7 Prov 2.9; 21.15
28.6 Prov 12.9
28.7 Prov 2.1 23.25,26; 29.3

[k] Meaning of Heb uncertain [l] Cn: Heb *A poor person*

DILIGENCE AND LAZINESS
Proverbs makes it clear that diligence—being willing to work hard and do one's best at any job given to him or her—is a vital part of wise living. We work hard not to become rich, famous, or admired (although those may be by-products), but to serve God with our very best during our lives.

The Diligent	*The Lazy*	*References*
Become rich	Are soon poor	10.4
Gather crops early	Sleep during harvest	10.5
	Are an annoyance	10.26
Have abundant food	Chase fantasies	12.11
Hard work returns rewards		12.14
Will rule	Will become slaves	12.24
Prize their possessions	Waste good resources	12.27
Are fully satisfied	Want much but get little	13.4
Bring profit	Experience poverty	14.23
Have an easy path	Have trouble all through life	15.19
	Are like those who destroy	18.9
	Go hungry	19.15
	Won't feed themselves	19.24
	Won't plow in season	20.4
Stay awake and have food to spare	Love sleep and grow poor	20.13
Are steady plodders	Make hasty speculations	21.5
	Love pleasure and become poor	21.17
Give without sparing	Desire things but refuse to work for them	21.25, 26
	Are full of excuses for not working	22.13
Will serve before kings		22.29
	Sleep too much, which leads to poverty	24.30–34
Reap prosperity through hard work	Experience poverty because of laziness	28.19

28.2 For a government or a society to endure, it needs wise, informed leaders—and these are hard to find. "It has many rulers" means that anarchy is prevailing. Each person's selfishness quickly affects others. A selfish employee who steals from his company ruins its productivity. A selfish driver who drinks before taking the wheel makes the state highways unsafe. A selfish spouse who has an adulterous affair often breaks up several families. When enough people live for themselves with little concern for how their actions affect others, the resulting moral rot contaminates the entire nation. Are you part of the problem . . . or the solution?

28.5 Because justice is part of God's character, a person who follows God treats others justly. The beginning of justice is concern for what is happening to others. A Christian cannot be indifferent to human suffering because God isn't. And we certainly must not contribute to human suffering through selfish business practices or unfair government policies. Be sure you are more concerned for justice than for the bottom line.

8 One who augments wealth by exorbitant interest
gathers it for another who is kind to the poor.
9 When one will not listen to the law,
even one's prayers are an abomination.
10 Those who mislead the upright into evil ways
will fall into pits of their own making,
but the blameless will have a goodly inheritance.
11 The rich is wise in self-esteem,
but an intelligent poor person sees through the pose.
12 When the righteous triumph, there is great glory,
but when the wicked prevail, people go into hiding.
13 No one who conceals transgressions will prosper,
but one who confesses and forsakes them will obtain mercy.
14 Happy is the one who is never without fear,
but one who is hard-hearted will fall into calamity.
15 Like a roaring lion or a charging bear
is a wicked ruler over a poor people.
16 A ruler who lacks understanding is a cruel oppressor;
but one who hates unjust gain will enjoy a long life.
17 If someone is burdened with the blood of another,
let that killer be a fugitive until death;
let no one offer assistance.
18 One who walks in integrity will be safe,
but whoever follows crooked ways will fall into the Pit.[m]
19 Anyone who tills the land will have plenty of bread,
but one who follows worthless pursuits will have plenty of poverty.
20 The faithful will abound with blessings,
but one who is in a hurry to be rich will not go unpunished.
21 To show partiality is not good—
yet for a piece of bread a person may do wrong.
22 The miser is in a hurry to get rich
and does not know that loss is sure to come.
23 Whoever rebukes a person will afterward find more favor
than one who flatters with the tongue.
24 Anyone who robs father or mother
and says, "That is no crime,"
is partner to a thug.
25 The greedy person stirs up strife,
but whoever trusts in the LORD will be enriched.

[m] Syr: Heb *fall all at once*

28.8 Ex 22.25 Deut 23.19,20
28.9 Ps 66.18; 109.7 Prov 15.8
28.10 Prov 26.27 Mt 5.19; 18.6
28.11 Prov 18.23 25.27; 26.12
28.13 Ps 32.1-11 1 Jn 1.6-9
28.14 Rom 2.5 Phil 2.12
28.15 Prov 19.12 Mt 2.16 1 Pet 5.8
28.16 Eccles 10.16 Isa 3.12
28.17 Gen 9.6 Ex 21.14 Prov 6.16-19 28.24
28.19 Prov 12.11 14.4; 23.19-21
28.23 Ps 141.5 Prov 29.5,6 Mt 18.15
28.24 Prov 19.26

28.9 God does not listen to our prayers if we intend to go back to our sin as soon as we get off our knees. If we want to forsake our sin and follow him, however, he willingly listens—no matter how bad our sin has been. What closes his ears is not the depth of our sin, but our secret intention to do it again.

28.11 Rich people often think they are wonderful; depending on no one, they take credit for all they do. But that's a hollow self-esteem. Through dependence on God in their struggles, the poor may develop a richness of spirit that no amount of wealth can provide. The rich man can lose all his material wealth, while no one can take away the poor man's character. Don't be jealous of the rich; money may be all they will ever have.

28.13 It is human nature to hide our transgressions or overlook our mistakes. But it is hard to learn from a mistake you don't acknowledge making. And what good is a mistake if it doesn't teach you something? To learn from an error you need to admit it, confess it, analyze it, and make adjustments so that it doesn't happen again. Everybody makes mistakes, but only fools repeat them.

28.13 Something in each of us strongly resists admitting we are wrong. That is why we admire people who openly and graciously admit their mistakes and sins. These people have a strong self-image. They do not always have to be right to feel good about themselves. Be willing to reconsider—to admit you are wrong and to change your plans when necessary. And remember, the first step toward forgiveness is confession.

28.14 *Fear* here refers to fearing the Lord—revering and honoring him.

28.17, 18 A sinner's conscience will drive him either into the "pit" of guilt and on to repentance, or into the Pit of hell itself because of a refusal to repent. It is no act of kindness to try to make him feel better; the more guilt he feels, the more likely he is to turn to God and repent. If we interfere with the natural consequences of his act, we may make it easier for him to continue in sin.

28.26 Job 28.28 Prov 3.5
28.27 Prov 11.24 19.17
29.1 Prov 1.24,25 13.18; 15.31,32
29.2 Esth 8.15,16 Prov 11.10
29.3 Prov 6.26; 10.1 Lk 15.13
29.4 Prov 8.15
29.5 Ps 5.9 Prov 28.23
29.7 Ps 41.1
29.8 Prov 13.2; 17.19 Jas 3.13-18

26 Those who trust in their own wits are fools;
but those who walk in wisdom come through safely.
27 Whoever gives to the poor will lack nothing,
but one who turns a blind eye will get many a curse.
28 When the wicked prevail, people go into hiding;
but when they perish, the righteous increase.

29 One who is often reproved, yet remains stubborn,
will suddenly be broken beyond healing.
2 When the righteous are in authority, the people rejoice;
but when the wicked rule, the people groan.
3 A child who loves wisdom makes a parent glad,
but to keep company with prostitutes is to squander one's substance.
4 By justice a king gives stability to the land,
but one who makes heavy exactions ruins it.
5 Whoever flatters a neighbor
is spreading a net for the neighbor's feet.
6 In the transgression of the evil there is a snare,
but the righteous sing and rejoice.
7 The righteous know the rights of the poor;
the wicked have no such understanding.
8 Scoffers set a city aflame,
but the wise turn away wrath.
9 If the wise go to law with fools,

LEADERSHIP Since many of the proverbs came from King Solomon, it is natural to expect some of his interest to be directed toward leadership.

Qualities of good leadership	*References*
Diligence	12.24
Trustworthy messengers	13.17
Don't penalize people for integrity	17.26
Listen before answering	18.13
Open to new ideas	18.15
Listen to both sides of the story	18.17
Able to stand under adversity	24.10
Able to stand under praise	27.21
What happens without good leadership	
Honoring the wrong people backfires	26.8
A wicked ruler is dangerous	28.15
People despair	29.2
A wicked ruler has wicked aides	29.12
When rulers are wicked, so are the people	29.16

Other verses to study: 24.27; 25.13; 27.18

28.26 For many people, the rugged individualist is a hero. We admire the bold, self-directed men and women who know what they want and fight for it. They are self-reliant, neither giving nor asking advice. What a contrast to God's way. A person can't know the future and can't predict the consequences of his choices with certainty. And so the totally self-reliant person is doomed to failure. The wise person depends on God.

28.27 God wants us to identify with the needy, not ignore them. The second part of this proverb could be restated positively: "those who open their eyes to poor people will be blessed." If we help others when they are in trouble, they will do whatever they can to return the favor (see 11.24, 25). Paul promises that God will supply all our needs (Philippians 4.19); he does this through other people. What can you do today to help God supply someone's need?

29.1 Making the same mistake over and over is an invitation to disaster. Eventually people have to face the consequences of refusing to learn. If their mistake is refusing God's invitations or rejecting his commands, the consequences will be especially serious. In the end, God may have to turn them away ("broken beyond healing"). Make sure you are not hardening your heart.

there is ranting and ridicule without relief.
10 The bloodthirsty hate the blameless,
and they seek the life of the upright.
11 A fool gives full vent to anger,
but the wise quietly holds it back.
12 If a ruler listens to falsehood,
all his officials will be wicked.
13 The poor and the oppressor have this in common:
the LORD gives light to the eyes of both.
14 If a king judges the poor with equity,
his throne will be established forever.
15 The rod and reproof give wisdom,
but a mother is disgraced by a neglected child.
16 When the wicked are in authority, transgression increases,
but the righteous will look upon their downfall.
17 Discipline your children, and they will give you rest;
they will give delight to your heart.
18 Where there is no prophecy, the people cast off restraint,
but happy are those who keep the law.
19 By mere words servants are not disciplined,
for though they understand, they will not give heed.
20 Do you see someone who is hasty in speech?
There is more hope for a fool than for anyone like that.
21 A slave pampered from childhood
will come to a bad end. [n]
22 One given to anger stirs up strife,
and the hothead causes much transgression.
23 A person's pride will bring humiliation,
but one who is lowly in spirit will obtain honor.
24 To be a partner of a thief is to hate one's own life;
one hears the victim's curse, but discloses nothing. [o]
25 The fear of others[p] lays a snare,
but one who trusts in the LORD is secure.
26 Many seek the favor of a ruler,
but it is from the LORD that one gets justice.
27 The unjust are an abomination to the righteous,
but the upright are an abomination to the wicked.

29.11 Prov 14.17,29
29.13 Job 3.19
29.14 Ps 72.4 Prov 16.12; 29.4
29.16 Ps 37.34-38
29.18 Ex 32.25 Ps 1.1,2; 74.9
29.20 Prov 26.12
29.22 Prov 22.24
29.23 Prov 15.33; 22.4 Dan 4.30
29.24 Prov 1.10,11
29.25 Prov 16.7
29.27 Mt 10.22; 24.9 2 Cor 6.14-18

[n] Vg: Meaning of Heb uncertain [o] Meaning of Heb uncertain [p] Or *human fear*

29.13 "The Lord gives light to the eyes of both" means everyone depends on God for light. Both the oppressor and the poor have the gift of light from the same God. God sees and judges both, and his judgment falls on those whose greed or power drives them to oppress the poor.

29.15 As parents, we weary of disciplining our children. It seems that all we do is nag, scold, and punish. When you're tempted to give up and let them do what they want, or when you wonder if you've ruined every chance for a loving relationship with them, remember—kind, firm discipline helps them learn, and learning makes them wise. Consistent, loving discipline will ultimately teach them to discipline themselves.

29.16 In any organization—whether a church, a business, a family, or a government—the climate comes from the top. The people become like their leaders. What kind of climate are you setting for the people you lead?

29.18 *Prophecy* refers to revelation that prophets receive. Where there is ignorance of God, crime and sin run wild. Public morality depends on the knowledge of God, but it also depends on keeping God's laws. In order for both nations and individuals to function well, people must know God's ways and keep his rules.

29.24 *Curse* also means oath, as taken in a courtroom. This proverb is saying that a thief's accomplice won't tell the truth when under oath. Thus, by his perjury, he hurts himself.

29.25 Fear of people can hamper everything you try to do. In extreme forms, it can make you afraid to leave your home. By contrast, fear of God—respect, reverence, and trust—is liberating. Why fear people who can do no eternal harm? Instead, fear God who can turn the harm intended by others into good for those who trust him.

Wise sayings of Agur

30 The words of Agur son of Jakeh. An oracle.

Thus says the man: I am weary, O God,
I am weary, O God. How can I prevail?[q]

30.2 Job 42.3-6

2 Surely I am too stupid to be human;
I do not have human understanding.
3 I have not learned wisdom,
nor have I knowledge of the holy ones.[r]

30.4 Job 26.8 Ps 24.2; 68.18 Isa 45.18

4 Who has ascended to heaven and come down?
Who has gathered the wind in the hollow of the hand?
Who has wrapped up the waters in a garment?
Who has established all the ends of the earth?
What is the person's name?
And what is the name of the person's child?
Surely you know!

30.5 Ps 3.3; 12.6 18.30; 84.11

5 Every word of God proves true;
he is a shield to those who take refuge in him.

30.6 Deut 4.2; 12.32 Rev 22.18

6 Do not add to his words,
or else he will rebuke you, and you will be found a liar.

7 Two things I ask of you;
do not deny them to me before I die:
8 Remove far from me falsehood and lying;
give me neither poverty nor riches;
feed me with the food that I need,

30.9 Deut 8.12; 31.20 Neh 9.25 Hos 13.6

9 or I shall be full, and deny you,
and say, "Who is the LORD?"
or I shall be poor, and steal,
and profane the name of my God.

30.10 Eccles 7.21

10 Do not slander a servant to a master,
or the servant will curse you, and you will be held guilty.

30.11 Ex 21.17 Prov 20.20

11 There are those who curse their fathers
and do not bless their mothers.
12 There are those who are pure in their own eyes
yet are not cleansed of their filthiness.

30.13 Job 29.17 Ps 57.4 Lk 18.11

13 There are those—how lofty are their eyes,
how high their eyelids lift!
14 There are those whose teeth are swords,
whose teeth are knives,
to devour the poor from off the earth,
the needy from among mortals.

[q] Or *I am spent.* Meaning of Heb uncertain [r] Or *Holy One*

30.1 The origin of these sayings is not clear. Nothing is known about Agur except that he was a wise teacher who may have come from Lemuel's kingdom (see the note on 31.1).

30.2–4 Since God is infinite, certain aspects of his nature will always remain a mystery. Compare these questions with the questions God asked Job (Job 38–41).

30.4 Some scholars feel that the child referred to is the Son of God, the preincarnate being of the Messiah who, before the foundation of the earth, participated in the creation. Colossians 1.16, 17 teaches that through Christ the world was created.

30.7–9 Having too much money can be dangerous, but so can having too little. Being poor can, in fact, be hazardous to spiritual as well as physical health. On the other hand, being rich is not the answer. As Jesus pointed out, rich people have trouble getting into God's kingdom (Matthew 19.23, 24). Like Paul, we can learn how to live whether we have little or plenty (Philippians 4.12), but our lives are more likely to be effective if we have "neither poverty nor riches."

30.13 This phrase refers to prideful and haughty people who look down on others. Verses 11–14 contain a fourfold description of arrogance.

15 The leech[s] has two daughters;
"Give, give," they cry.
Three things are never satisfied;
four never say, "Enough":
16 Sheol, the barren womb,
the earth ever thirsty for water,
and the fire that never says, "Enough."[s]

17 The eye that mocks a father
and scorns to obey a mother
will be pecked out by the ravens of the valley
and eaten by the vultures.

18 Three things are too wonderful for me;
four I do not understand:
19 the way of an eagle in the sky,
the way of a snake on a rock,
the way of a ship on the high seas,
and the way of a man with a girl.

20 This is the way of an adulteress:
she eats, and wipes her mouth,
and says, "I have done no wrong."

21 Under three things the earth trembles;
under four it cannot bear up:
22 a slave when he becomes king,
and a fool when glutted with food;
23 an unloved woman when she gets a husband,
and a maid when she succeeds her mistress.

24 Four things on earth are small,
yet they are exceedingly wise:
25 the ants are a people without strength,
yet they provide their food in the summer;
26 the badgers are a people without power,
yet they make their homes in the rocks;
27 the locusts have no king,
yet all of them march in rank;
28 the lizard[t] can be grasped in the hand,
yet it is found in kings' palaces.

29 Three things are stately in their stride;
four are stately in their gait:
30 the lion, which is mightiest among wild animals
and does not turn back before any;
31 the strutting rooster,[u] the he-goat,
and a king striding before[v] his people.

32 If you have been foolish, exalting yourself,
or if you have been devising evil,

30.15 Gen 30.1,2 Prov 27.20

30.17 Gen 9.22 Prov 19.26 20.20

30.18 Job 39.27; 42.3 Ps 139.6

30.20 Prov 7.13

30.21 1 Sam 25.25 Ps 14.1 Prov 17.7,21

30.24 Lev 11.5 Job 12.7-9 Ps 104.18 Prov 6.6-8 Joel 1.6

30.29 Mic 5.8 Prov 20.2

30.32 Job 21.5; 40.4 Prov 17.27,28 Mic 7.16

[s] Meaning of Heb uncertain [t] Or *spider* [u] Gk Syr Tg Compare Vg: Meaning of Heb uncertain

30.15ff "Three things . . . four" is a poetic way of saying the list is not complete. The writer of these proverbs is observing the world with delighted interest. Verses 15–30 are an invitation to look at nature from the perspective of a keen observer.

30.16 *Sheol* means the grave or death.

30.24–28 Ants can teach us about preparation; badgers about wise building; locusts about cooperation and order; and spiders about fearlessness.

put your hand on your mouth.
30.33 Prov 15.18 16.28; 26.21 29.22
33 For as pressing milk produces curds,
and pressing the nose produces blood,
so pressing anger produces strife.

Wise sayings of Lemuel

31 The words of King Lemuel. An oracle that his mother taught him:
2 No, my son! No, son of my womb!
No, son of my vows!
31.3 Prov 5.9; 7.26
3 Do not give your strength to women,
your ways to those who destroy kings.
31.4 Prov 20.1 Eccles 10.16,17
4 It is not for kings, O Lemuel,
it is not for kings to drink wine,
or for rulers to desire[v] strong drink;
31.5 Deut 16.19 Prov 17.15
5 or else they will drink and forget what has been decreed,
and will pervert the rights of all the afflicted.
6 Give strong drink to one who is perishing,
and wine to those in bitter distress;
7 let them drink and forget their poverty,
and remember their misery no more.
31.8 Job 29.12-17
8 Speak out for those who cannot speak,
for the rights of all the destitute.[w]
9 Speak out, judge righteously,
defend the rights of the poor and needy.

A truly good wife

31.10 Ruth 3.11 Prov 8.11; 12.4
10 A capable wife who can find?
She is far more precious than jewels.
31.11 1 Pet 3.1,2
11 The heart of her husband trusts in her,
and he will have no lack of gain.
12 She does him good, and not harm,
all the days of her life.
31.13 Gen 18.6 24.18-20
13 She seeks wool and flax,
and works with willing hands.
14 She is like the ships of the merchant,
she brings her food from far away.
15 She rises while it is still night
and provides food for her household
and tasks for her servant girls.
16 She considers a field and buys it;
with the fruit of her hands she plants a vineyard.

[v] Cn: Heb *where* [w] Heb *all children of passing away*

31.1 Little is known about Lemuel except that he was a king who received wise teachings from his mother. His name means "devoted to God." It is believed that Lemuel and Agur were both from the kingdom of Massa in northern Arabia.

31.4–7 Drunkenness might be understandable among dying people in great pain, but it is inexcusable for national leaders. Alcohol clouds the mind and can lead to injustice and poor decisions. Leaders have better things to do than anesthetize themselves with alcohol.

31.10–31 Proverbs has a lot to say about women. How fitting that the book ends with a picture of a woman of strong character, great wisdom, many skills, and great compassion.

Some people have the mistaken idea that the ideal woman in the Bible is retiring, servile, and entirely domestic. Not so! This woman is an excellent wife and mother. She is also a manufacturer, importer, manager, realtor, farmer, seamstress, upholsterer, and merchant. Her strength and dignity do not come from her amazing achievements, however. They are a result of her reverence for God. In our society where physical appearance counts for so much, it may surprise us to realize that her appearance is never mentioned. Her attractiveness comes entirely from her character.

The woman described in this chapter has outstanding abilities. Her family's social position is high. In fact, she may not be one woman at all – she may be a composite portrait of ideal womanhood. Do not see her as a model to imitate in every detail; your days are not long enough to do everything she does! See her instead as an inspiration to be all you can be. We can't be just like her, but we can learn from her industry, integrity, and resourcefulness.

17 She girds herself with strength,
and makes her arms strong.
18 She perceives that her merchandise is profitable.
Her lamp does not go out at night.
19 She puts her hands to the distaff,
and her hands hold the spindle.
20 She opens her hand to the poor,
and reaches out her hands to the needy.
21 She is not afraid for her household when it snows,
for all her household are clothed in crimson.
22 She makes herself coverings;
her clothing is fine linen and purple.
23 Her husband is known in the city gates,
taking his seat among the elders of the land.
24 She makes linen garments and sells them;
she supplies the merchant with sashes.
25 Strength and dignity are her clothing,
and she laughs at the time to come.
26 She opens her mouth with wisdom,
and the teaching of kindness is on her tongue.
27 She looks well to the ways of her household,
and does not eat the bread of idleness.
28 Her children rise up and call her happy;
her husband too, and he praises her:
29 "Many women have done excellently,
but you surpass them all."
30 Charm is deceitful, and beauty is vain,
but a woman who fears the LORD is to be praised.
31 Give her a share in the fruit of her hands,
and let her works praise her in the city gates.

31.19 Deut 15.11 Job 31.16 Prov 22.9 Rom 12.13
31.22 Ps 45.13,14 Ezek 16.9,10 1 Pet 3.3
31.23 Job 29.7
31.25 Prov 14.26
31.26 Prov 11.16
31.27 Prov 6.6-11
31.30 Prov 1.7; 8.13
31.31 Ps 128.2,3

31.19 The distaff and spindle are two implements used in hand spinning.

31.31 The book of Proverbs begins with the command to trust and reverence the Lord (1.7) and ends with the picture of a woman who fulfills this command. Her qualities are mentioned throughout the book: hard work, fear of God, respect for spouse, foresight, encouragement, care for others, concern for the poor, wisdom in handling money. These qualities, when coupled with fear of God, lead to enjoyment, success, honor, and worth. Proverbs is very practical for our day because it shows us how to become wise, make good decisions, and live according to God's ideal.

ECCLESIASTES

THE MOLDED bunny lies in the basket, surrounded by green paper "grass." His Easter morning eyes wide with anticipation, the little boy carefully lifts the chocolate figure and bites into one of the long ears. But the sweet taste fades quickly, and he looks again at the candy in his hand. It's hollow!

Empty, futile, hollow, nothing . . . the words ring of disappointment and disillusionment. Yet this is the life-experience of many. Grasping the sweet things—possessions, experience, power, and pleasure—they find nothing inside. Life is empty, meaningless . . . and they despair.

Almost 3,000 years ago, Solomon spoke of this human dilemma; but the insights and applications of his message are relevant in our century. Ecclesiastes, Solomon's written sermon, is an analysis of life's experiences and a critical essay about its meaning. In this profound book, Solomon takes us on a mental journey through his life, and he explains how everything he tried, tested, or tasted was "vanity"—useless, irrational, pointless, foolish, and empty—an exercise in futility. And remember, these words are from one who "had it all"—tremendous intellect, power, and wealth. After this biographical tour, Solomon makes his triumphant conclusion: "Fear God, and keep his commandments; for that is the whole duty of everyone. For God will bring every deed into judgment, including every secret thing, whether good or evil" (12.13, 14).

When Solomon became king, he asked God for wisdom (2 Chronicles 1.7–12), and he became the wisest man in the world (1 Kings 4.29–34). He studied, taught, judged, and wrote. Kings and leaders from other nations came to Jerusalem to learn from him. But with all of his practical insight on life, Solomon failed to heed his own advice, and his life began its downward spiral. Near the end of his life, Solomon looked back with an attitude of humility and repentance. He took stock of the world as he had experienced it, hoping to spare his readers the bitterness of learning through personal experience that everything apart from God is empty, hollow, and meaningless.

Although the tone of Ecclesiastes is negative and pessimistic, we must not conclude that the only chapter worth reading and applying is the last where he draws his conclusions. In reality, the entire book is filled with practical wisdom (how to accomplish things in the world and stay out of trouble) and spiritual wisdom (how to find and know eternal values). Solomon had a very honest approach to life. All of his remarks relating to the futility of life are there for a purpose—to lead people to seek true happiness in God alone. He was not trying to destroy all hope, but to direct our hopes to the only One who can truly fulfill them. Solomon affirms the value of knowledge, relationships, work, and pleasure; but only *in their proper place*. All of these temporal things in life must be seen in light of the eternal.

Read Ecclesiastes and learn about life. Hear the stern warnings and dire predictions, and commit yourself to honor your Creator now (12.1).

VITAL STATISTICS

PURPOSE:
To spare future generations the bitterness of learning through their own experience that life is meaningless apart from God

AUTHOR:
Solomon

TO WHOM WRITTEN:
Solomon's subjects in particular, and all people in general

DATE WRITTEN:
Probably around 935 B.C., late in Solomon's life

SETTING:
Solomon looks back on his life, much of which was lived apart from God

KEY VERSE:
"The end of the matter; all has been heard. Fear God, and keep his commandments; for that is the whole duty of everyone" (12.13).

THE BLUEPRINT

1. Solomon's personal experience (1.1—2.26)
2. Solomon's general observations (3.1—5.20)
3. Solomon's practical counsel (6.1—8.17)
4. Solomon's final conclusion (9.1—12.14)

Ecclesiastes shows that certain paths in life lead to emptiness. This profound book also helps us discover true purpose in life. Such wisdom can spare us from the emptiness that results from a life without God. Solomon teaches that people will not find meaning in life in knowledge, money, pleasure, work, or popularity. True satisfaction comes from knowing that what we are doing is part of God's purpose for our lives. This is a book which can help free us from our scramble for power, approval, and money, and draw us closer to God.

MEGATHEMES

THEME	EXPLANATION	IMPORTANCE
Searching	Solomon searched for satisfaction almost as though he was conducting a scientific experiment. Through this process, he discovered that life without God is a long and fruitless search for enjoyment, meaning, and fulfillment. True happiness is not in our power to accumulate or attain because we always want more than we can have. In addition, there are circumstances beyond our control that can snatch away our possessions or attainments.	People are still searching. Yet the more they try to get, the more they realize how little they really have. No pleasure or happiness is possible without God. Without him, satisfaction is a lost search. Above everything we should strive to know and love God. He gives wisdom, knowledge, and joy.
Emptiness	Solomon shows how empty it is to pursue the pleasures that this life has to offer rather than a relationship with an eternal God. The search for pleasure, wealth, and success is ultimately disappointing. Nothing in the world can fill the emptiness and satisfy the deep longings in our restless hearts.	The cure for emptiness is to center on God. His love also can fill the emptiness of human experience. Fear God throughout your life and fill your life with serving God and others rather than with selfish pleasures.
Work	Solomon tried to shake people's confidence in their own efforts, abilities, and wisdom and to direct them to faith in God as the only sound basis for living. Without God, there is no lasting reward or benefit in hard work.	Work done with the wrong attitude will leave us empty. But work accepted as an assignment from God can be seen as a gift. Examine what you expect from your efforts. God gives you abilities and opportunities to work so that you can use your time well.
Death	The certainty of death makes all merely human achievements futile. God has a plan for human destiny that goes beyond life and death. The reality of aging and dying reminds each individual of the end to come when God will judge each person's life.	Because life is short, we need wisdom that is greater than this world can offer. We need the words of God. If we listen to him, his wisdom spares us the bitterness of futile human experience and gives us a hope that goes beyond death.
Wisdom	Human wisdom doesn't contain all the answers. Knowledge and education have their limits. To understand life, we need the wisdom that can be found only in God's Word to us—the Bible.	When we realize that God will evaluate all that we do, we should learn to live wisely, remembering that he is present each day, and obeying his guidelines for living. But in order to have God's wisdom, we must first get to know and honor him.

1. Solomon's personal experience

Everything is futile

1 The words of the Teacher,[a] the son of David, king in Jerusalem.
2 Vanity of vanities, says the Teacher,[a]
vanity of vanities! All is vanity.
3 What do people gain from all the toil
at which they toil under the sun?
4 A generation goes, and a generation comes,
but the earth remains forever.
5 The sun rises and the sun goes down,
and hurries to the place where it rises.
6 The wind blows to the south,
and goes around to the north;
round and round goes the wind,
and on its circuits the wind returns.
7 All streams run to the sea,
but the sea is not full;
to the place where the streams flow,
there they continue to flow.
8 All things[b] are wearisome;
more than one can express;
the eye is not satisfied with seeing,
or the ear filled with hearing.
9 What has been is what will be,
and what has been done is what will be done;
there is nothing new under the sun.
10 Is there a thing of which it is said,
"See, this is new"?
It has already been,
in the ages before us.
11 The people of long ago are not remembered,
nor will there be any remembrance
of people yet to come
by those who come after them.

1.3 Ps 19.4-6 Eccles 2.11 3.9; 5.16
1.6 Eccles 11.5
1.8 Prov 27.20 Eccles 4.8 6.10; 9.5
1.11 Eccles 2.16; 9.5

a Heb *Koheleth*, traditionally rendered *Preacher* b Or *words*

1.1 The author, Solomon (see 1.12), referred to himself as the Teacher, meaning "one who gathers or assembles." He was both assembling people to hear a message and gathering wise sayings (proverbs). Solomon, one person in the Bible who had everything (wisdom, power, riches, honor, reputation, God's favor), is the one who discussed the ultimate emptiness of all that this world has to offer. He tried to destroy people's confidence in their own efforts, abilities, and righteousness and direct them to commitment to God as the only reason for living.

1.1–11 Solomon had a purpose in writing skeptically and pessimistically. Near the end of his life he looked back over everything he had done, and most of it seemed futile. A common belief was that only good people prospered and that only the wicked suffered, but that hadn't proven true in his experience. Solomon wrote this book after he had tried everything and achieved much, only to find that nothing apart from God made him happy. He wanted his readers to avoid these same senseless pursuits. If we try to find meaning in our accomplishments rather than in God, we will never be satisfied, and everything we pursue will become wearying and tiresome.

1.2 *Vanity* means futility or meaninglessness. Solomon's kingdom, Israel, was in its golden age, but Solomon wanted the people to see that success and prosperity can disappear like a vapor of breath on a cold day (Psalm 103.14–16; Isaiah 40.6–8; James 4.14). All human accomplishments will one day disappear, and we must keep this in mind in order to live wisely. If we don't, we can become either proud and self-sufficient when we succeed, or sorely disappointed when we fail. Solomon's goal was to show that earthly possessions and accomplishments are ultimately futile. Only the pursuit of God brings real satisfaction. We should honor him in all we say, think, and do.

1.8–11 Many people feel restless and dissatisfied. They wonder: (1) If I am in God's will, why am I so tired and dissatisfied? (2) What is the meaning of life? (3) When I look back on it all, will I be happy with my accomplishments? (4) Why do I feel burned out, disillusioned, dry? (5) What is to become of me? Solomon tests our faith, challenging us to find true and lasting meaning in God alone. As you take a hard look at your life, as Solomon did his, you will see how important serving God is over all other options. Perhaps God is asking you to rethink your purpose and direction in life as Solomon did in Ecclesiastes.

The king finds wisdom meaningless

12 I, the Teacher,[c] when king over Israel in Jerusalem, 13applied my mind to **1.12**
seek and to search out by wisdom all that is done under heaven; it is an unhappy Eccles 7.27
business that God has given to human beings to be busy with. 14I saw all the deeds **1.13** Eccles 1.17
that are done under the sun; and see, all is vanity and a chasing after wind.[d] 3.10,11; 7.25
15 What is crooked cannot be made straight, **1.14** Eccles 2.11
and what is lacking cannot be counted.
16 I said to myself, "I have acquired great wisdom, surpassing all who were **1.16**
over Jerusalem before me; and my mind has had great experience of wisdom and Eccles 12.12
knowledge." 17And I applied my mind to know wisdom and to know madness and
folly. I perceived that this also is but a chasing after wind.[d]
18 For in much wisdom is much vexation,
and those who increase knowledge increase sorrow.

The king finds pleasures meaningless

2 I said to myself, "Come now, I will make a test of pleasure; enjoy yourself." **2.1**
But again, this also was vanity. 2I said of laughter, "It is mad," and of plea- Prov 14.13
sure, "What use is it?" 3I searched with my mind how to cheer my body with **2.3**
wine—my mind still guiding me with wisdom—and how to lay hold on folly, until Prov 20.1 23.29-35
I might see what was good for mortals to do under heaven during the few days of Eccles 6.12; 8.15; 12.13
their life. 4I made great works; I built houses and planted vineyards for myself; 5I **2.4**
made myself gardens and parks, and planted in them all kinds of fruit trees. 6I made 1 Kgs 7.1-12 Song 8.10,11
myself pools from which to water the forest of growing trees. 7I bought male and **2.5**
female slaves, and had slaves who were born in my house; I also had great posses- Song 4.16; 5.1
sions of herds and flocks, more than any who had been before me in Jerusalem. 8I **2.6** Neh 2.14
also gathered for myself silver and gold and the treasure of kings and of the prov- 3.15,16 **2.7**
inces; I got singers, both men and women, and delights of the flesh, and many 1 Kgs 4.23 9.28
concubines.[e] 10.10,14,21
9 So I became great and surpassed all who were before me in Jerusalem; also **2.9**
my wisdom remained with me. 10Whatever my eyes desired I did not keep from 1 Chron 29.25
them; I kept my heart from no pleasure, for my heart found pleasure in all my toil, **2.10** Eccles 3.22
and this was my reward for all my toil. 11Then I considered all that my hands had 5.18; 6.2; 9.9

[c] Heb *Koheleth*, traditionally rendered *Preacher* [d] *Or a feeding on wind.* See Hos 12.1 [e] Meaning of Heb uncertain

1.12–15 Life's experiences are not always happy. But the world tells us to demand happiness, do all we can to attain it, and make personal satisfaction our chief goal. Solomon, writing about his own life, discovered that his wealth, power, position, wives, and accomplishments did not make him happy. Happiness is an elusive goal because people and circumstances change quickly. True and lasting happiness, however, comes from pleasing God. Thus, happiness cannot be achieved; it can only be received through a right relationship with God, because only God knows what is really best for us. If you are chasing after happiness, you will never find it. If you are seeking after God, you will find endless joy.

1.16–18 After writing that everything is vanity or empty (1.2–11), Solomon recorded that even his great wisdom could not offer the satisfaction he was seeking. Wisdom, in itself, brought grief rather than satisfaction. It analyzed his problem, but it could not solve it. When he discovered his earthbound wisdom could not alter his fate, he became sorrowful. Without God life is no more than repetitive cycles.

1.16–18 The more you understand, the more pain and difficulty you experience. For example, the more you know, the more imperfection you see around you; and the more you observe, the more evil becomes evident. As you set out with Solomon to find the meaning of life, you must be ready to feel more, think more, question more, hurt more, and do more. Are you ready to pay the price for wisdom?

1.16–18 Solomon highlights two kinds of wisdom in the book of Ecclesiastes: (1) human knowledge, reasoning, or philosophy, and (2) the wisdom that comes from God. In these verses Solomon is talking about human knowledge. When human knowledge ignores God, it only highlights our problems because it can't provide answers without God's eternal perspective and solution.

2.1ff Solomon conducted his search for life's meaning as an experiment. He first tried pursuing pleasure. He began grand public works programs, bought slaves, had many wives and concubines, set his mind on complex matters, became extremely wealthy, organized musical groups, and supported the arts. But none of these gave him the satisfaction he was seeking. Some of the pleasures Solomon sought were wrong and some were worthy, but even the worthy pursuits were futile when he pursued them as an end in themselves. We must look beyond our activities to the reasons we do them and the purpose they fulfill. Is your goal in life to search for meaning or to search for God who gives meaning?

2.4–6 Solomon had built a huge home, a temple, a kingdom, a family (see 1 Kings 3–11). In the course of history, it would all be ruined. In Psalm 127 Solomon states, "Unless the Lord builds the house, those who build it labor in vain. Unless the Lord guards the city, the guard keeps watch in vain." These verses are part of his testimony to what happens to a kingdom or family that forgets God. As you examine your projects or goals, what is your starting point, your motivation? Without God as your foundation, all you have lived for will one day be useless to you.

2.11 Solomon summarized all his attempts at finding life's meaning as "chasing after wind." We feel the wind as it passes, but we can't catch hold of it or keep it. In all our accomplishments, even the big ones, our good feelings are only temporary. Security and self-worth

2.11 Eccles 5.16 — done and the toil I had spent in doing it, and again, all was vanity and a chasing
after wind,[f] and there was nothing to be gained under the sun.

The king finds work meaningless

2.12 Eccles 7.25 — 12 So I turned to consider wisdom and madness and folly; for what can the one
do who comes after the king? Only what has already been done. 13 Then I saw that
2.13 Eccles 3.19; 7.2,11,12,19 — wisdom excels folly as light excels darkness.
14 The wise have eyes in their head,
but fools walk in darkness.
2.15 Eccles 6.8,11 — Yet I perceived that the same fate befalls all of them. 15 Then I said to myself,
"What happens to the fool will happen to me also; why then have I been so very
wise?" And I said to myself that this also is vanity. 16 For there is no enduring
remembrance of the wise or of fools, seeing that in the days to come all will have
2.17 Num 11.15; Eccles 4.2 — been long forgotten. How can the wise die just like fools? 17 So I hated life, because
what is done under the sun was grievous to me; for all is vanity and a chasing after
wind.[f]
2.18 Ps 39.6; 49.10; Eccles 2.11; 1 Cor 3.10 — 18 I hated all my toil in which I had toiled under the sun, seeing that I must
leave it to those who come after me 19 —and who knows whether they will be wise
or foolish? Yet they will be master of all for which I toiled and used my wisdom
2.20 Job 5.7; 14.1; Ps 127.2; Eccles 1.18; 5.17 — under the sun. This also is vanity. 20 So I turned and gave my heart up to despair
concerning all the toil of my labors under the sun, 21 because sometimes one who
has toiled with wisdom and knowledge and skill must leave all to be enjoyed by
another who did not toil for it. This also is vanity and a great evil. 22 What do
mortals get from all the toil and strain with which they toil under the sun? 23 For all
their days are full of pain, and their work is a vexation; even at night their minds do
not rest. This also is vanity.

Pleasure is from the hand of God

2.24 Prov 2.6; 13.22; 1 Tim 6.17 — 24 There is nothing better for mortals than to eat and drink, and find enjoyment
in their toil. This also, I saw, is from the hand of God; 25 for apart from him[g] who

[f] Or *a feeding on wind.* See Hos 12.1 [g] Gk Syr: Heb *apart from me*

are not found in these accomplishments, but far beyond them in the love of God. Think about what you consider worthwhile in your life—where you place your time, energy, and money. Will you one day look back and decide that these, too, were a "chasing after wind"?

2.13–16 Solomon concluded that even if life is futile, it is still better to be wise than foolish, to live with good judgment than spend your life in ignorance. Seeking wisdom has definite advantages in this life. The wise man, however, will die like anyone else. Both wealth and wisdom are dead-end pursuits in providing the solution to life. This thought caused Solomon to say that wisdom, while beneficial in this life, is ultimately futile. Because we are limited in our understanding, it is most important that we come to know God who is infinite and all-knowing.

2.16 Solomon realized that wisdom alone cannot guarantee eternal life. Wisdom, riches, and fitness matter very little after death—and everyone must die. We must not build our lives on perishable pursuits, but on the solid foundation of God. Then even if everything we have is taken away, we still have God, who is all we really need anyway. This is the point of the book of Job (see the introduction to Job).

2.16–19 Is death the ultimate equalizer of all people, no matter what they attained in life? While this appears to be true from an earthly perspective, God makes it clear (as Solomon later points out in 12.14) that what we do here has a great impact upon where we will spend our eternal life.

2.17 As king, Solomon had everything a person could want, but here he says he hated his life. What happened? His marvelous accomplishments left him sour because he pursued them as a means to personal satisfaction. Personal satisfaction, by itself, is empty because we are alone in the enjoyment we receive. What is your attitude about what you do? If your goals are to satisfy only yourself, you will find yourself empty, seeking one thing after another, as Solomon did. If your goal is to serve God and others, then you will experience a full life, one that won't leave you sour.

2.18–23 Solomon continued to show that hard work bears no lasting fruit for those who work solely to earn money and gain possessions. Not only will everything be left behind at death, but it may be left to those who have done nothing to earn it. In addition, it may not be well cared for, and all that was gained could be lost. (Solomon's son who inherited the throne was often foolish—see 1 Kings 12.) Hard work done with proper motives (caring for your family, serving God) is not wrong. We must work to survive, and, more important, we are responsible for the physical and spiritual well-being of those under our care. But the fruit of hard work done to glorify only yourself will be passed on to those who may later lose or spoil it all. Such toil often leads to grief, while serving God leads to everlasting joy. Do you know the real reason you are working so hard?

2.24–26 Is Solomon recommending we make life a big, irresponsible party? No, he is encouraging us to take pleasure in what we're doing now and to enjoy life because it comes from God's hand. True enjoyment in life comes only as we follow God's guidelines for living. Without him, satisfaction is a lost search. Those who really know how to enjoy life are the ones who take each day as a gift from God, thanking him for it and serving him in it. Those without God will have no relief from toil and no direction to guide them through life's complications.

can eat or who can have enjoyment? 26 For to the one who pleases him God gives
wisdom and knowledge and joy; but to the sinner he gives the work of gathering
and heaping, only to give to one who pleases God. This also is vanity and a chasing
after wind.[h]

2. Solomon's general observations

A right time for everything

3 For everything there is a season, and a time for every matter under heaven:
2 a time to be born, and a time to die;
a time to plant, and a time to pluck up what is planted;
3 a time to kill, and a time to heal;
a time to break down, and a time to build up;
4 a time to weep, and a time to laugh;
a time to mourn, and a time to dance;
5 a time to throw away stones, and a time to gather stones together;
a time to embrace, and a time to refrain from embracing;
6 a time to seek, and a time to lose;
a time to keep, and a time to throw away;
7 a time to tear, and a time to sew;
a time to keep silence, and a time to speak;
8 a time to love, and a time to hate;
a time for war, and a time for peace.
9 What gain have the workers from their toil? 10 I have seen the business that
God has given to everyone to be busy with. 11 He has made everything suitable for
its time; moreover he has put a sense of past and future into their minds, yet they
cannot find out what God has done from the beginning to the end. 12 I know that
there is nothing better for them than to be happy and enjoy themselves as long as
they live; 13 moreover, it is God's gift that all should eat and drink and take pleasure
in all their toil. 14 I know that whatever God does endures forever; nothing can be
added to it, nor anything taken from it; God has done this, so that all should stand
in awe before him. 15 That which is, already has been; that which is to be, already
is; and God seeks out what has gone by.[i]
16 Moreover I saw under the sun that in the place of justice, wickedness was

3.2 Gen 17.21; 1 Sam 2.5; Job 7.1; Ps 52.5; Heb 9.27
3.4 Ex 15.20; Ps 126.2; Rom 12.15
3.7 Amos 5.13
3.8 Ps 101.3; Prov 5
3.9 Eccles 1.3; 2.11; 5.16
3.10 Eccles 1.13; 2.26
3.11 Eccles 8.17
3.12 Eccles 2.24
3.13 Eccles 5.19
3.14 Eccles 5.7; 7.18; 8.12,13; 12.13
3.15 Eccles 1.9; 6.10
3.16 Eccles 4.1; 5.8; 8.9

[h] Or *a feeding on wind.* See Hos 12.1 [i] Heb *what is pursued*

3.1–5.20 Solomon's point in this section is that God has a plan for all people. Thus he provides cycles of life, each with its work for us to do. Although there are many problems we face that seem to contradict God's plan, these should not be barriers to believing in him, but rather opportunities to discover that, without God, life's problems have no lasting solutions!

3.1–8 Timing is important. All the experiences listed in these verses are appropriate at certain times. The secret to peace with God is to discover, accept, and appreciate God's perfect timing. The danger is to doubt or resent God's timing. This can lead to despair, rebellion, or moving ahead without his advice.

3.8 When is there a time for hating? We shouldn't hate evil people, but we should hate what they do. We should also hate it when people are mistreated, when children are starving, and when God is being dishonored. In addition, we must hate sin in our lives, because this is God's attitude (see Psalm 5.5).

3.9–13 Your ability to enjoy your work depends to a large extent upon your attitude. Work becomes toil when you lose the sense of purpose God intended for it. We can enjoy our work if we (1) remember that God has given us work to do and has equipped us for particular tasks (3.10), and (2) realize that the fruit of our labor is a gift from him (3.13). See your work as a way to serve God.

3.11 God has put a "sense of past and future" into our minds. Many translations say that God has set *eternity* in our hearts. This means that we can never be completely satisfied with earthly pleasures and pursuits. Because we are created in God's image, (1) we have a spiritual thirst, (2) we have eternal value, and (3) nothing but the eternal God can truly satisfy us. He has built in us a restless yearning for the kind of perfect world that can be found only in his perfect rule. He has given us a glimpse of the perfection of his creation. But it is only a glimpse; we cannot see into the future or comprehend everything. So we must trust him now and do his work on earth.

3.12 The ability to rejoice and enjoy life is one of God's most excellent gifts to us, although we can abuse it. God wants us to enjoy life. When we have the proper view of God, we discover that real pleasure is found not in what we accumulate, but in enjoying whatever we have as gifts from God.

3.14 What is the purpose of life? It is that we should fear the all-powerful God. Fear does not mean to cringe in terror, but to respect, revere, and "stand in awe of" God because of who he is. Purpose in life starts with *whom* we know, not what we know or how good we are. It is impossible to fulfill your God-given purpose unless you fear God and give him first place in your life.

3.15 "God seeks out what has gone by" means that God will call back again past events that have been forgotten. They would be used to evaluate the past deeds of people at the Judgment, or as part of God's wise care and oversight of all people's activities.

3.16 There is wickedness in the place of justice. It even affects the legal system. Solomon asked how God's plan can be perfect when there is so much injustice and oppression in the world (4.1). He concluded that God does not ignore injustice, but will bring it to an

3.17 Eccles 3.1; 8.6 there, and in the place of righteousness, wickedness was there as well. 17 I said in
my heart, God will judge the righteous and the wicked, for he has appointed a time
3.18 Ps 49.12,20 for every matter, and for every work. 18 I said in my heart with regard to human
beings that God is testing them to show that they are but animals. 19 For the fate of
humans and the fate of animals is the same; as one dies, so dies the other. They all
3.20 Eccles 12.7 have the same breath, and humans have no advantage over the animals; for all is
3.21 Eccles 12.7 vanity. 20 All go to one place; all are from the dust, and all turn to dust again. 21 Who
knows whether the human spirit goes upward and the spirit of animals goes down-
3.22 Eccles 2.18,24 ward to the earth? 22 So I saw that there is nothing better than that all should enjoy
6.12; 8.7; 10.14 their work, for that is their lot; who can bring them to see what will be after them?

Oppression and sadness in life

4.1 Eccles 3.16; 5.8 **4** Again I saw all the oppressions that are practiced under the sun. Look, the
tears of the oppressed—with no one to comfort them! On the side of their
4.2 Eccles 2.17 oppressors there was power—with no one to comfort them. 2 And I thought the
dead, who have already died, more fortunate than the living, who are still alive;
4.3 Eccles 6.3 3 but better than both is the one who has not yet been, and has not seen the evil deeds
that are done under the sun.

4.4 Eccles 1.14 2.21 4 Then I saw that all toil and all skill in work come from one person's envy of
another. This also is vanity and a chasing after wind.[j]

4.5 Prov 6.10 15.16,17; 16.8 24.33 5 Fools fold their hands
and consume their own flesh.
6 Better is a handful with quiet
than two handfuls with toil,
and a chasing after wind.[j]

4.8 Prov 27.20 Eccles 1.8 2.21; 5.10 7 Again, I saw vanity under the sun: 8 the case of solitary individuals, without
sons or brothers; yet there is no end to all their toil, and their eyes are never satisfied
with riches. "For whom am I toiling," they ask, "and depriving myself of pleasure?" This also is vanity and an unhappy business.

The blessings of companionship

9 Two are better than one, because they have a good reward for their toil. 10 For
if they fall, one will lift up the other; but woe to one who is alone and falls and does
4.11 1 Kgs 1.1 not have another to help. 11 Again, if two lie together, they keep warm; but how can
one keep warm alone? 12 And though one might prevail against another, two will
withstand one. A threefold cord is not quickly broken.

[j] Or *a feeding on wind.* See Hos 12.1

---

end at his appointed time (12.13, 14).

3.16ff Solomon reflects on several apparent contradictions in God's control of the world: (1) there is unfairness where there should be justice (3.16, 17); (2) people created in God's image die just like the animals (3.18–21); (3) no one helps the oppressed (4.1–3); (4) many people are motivated by envy and jealousy (4.4–6); (5) people are lonely (4.7–12); (6) recognition for accomplishments is temporary (4.13–16). It is easy to use such contradictions as excuses not to believe in God. But Solomon used them to show how we can honestly look at life's problems and still keep our faith in God. This life is not all there is, yet even in this life we should not pass judgment on God, because we don't know everything. God's plan is for us to live forever with him. So live with eternal values in view, realizing that all contradictions will one day be cleared up by the Creator himself (12.14).

3.19–22 Our bodies can't live forever in their present state. In that sense, mankind and animals are alike. But Solomon acknowledged that God has given people the hope of eternity (see the note on 3.11), and that we will stand judgment in the next life (12.7, 14)—making us different from animals. Because man has eternity set in his heart, he has a unique purpose in God's overall plan. Yet we cannot discover God's purpose for our lives by our own efforts—only through building a relationship with him and seeking his guidance. Are you now living as God wants? Do you see life as a gift from him?

4.4–6 Some people are lazy while others are workaholics. The lazy person, seeing the futility of dashing about for success, folds his hands and hurts both himself and those who depend on him. The workaholic is driven by envy, greed, and a constant desire to stay ahead of everyone else. Both extremes are foolish and irresponsible. The answer is to work hard but with moderation. Take time to enjoy the other gifts God has given and realize that it is God who gives out the assignments and the rewards, not us.

4.9–12 There are advantages to cooperating with others. Life is designed not for isolation, but companionship; not for loneliness, but intimacy. Some people prefer isolation because they feel they cannot trust anyone. We are not here on earth to serve ourselves, however, but to serve God and others. Don't isolate yourself from others and go it alone. Seek companionship and be a team member.

Success does not last

13 Better is a poor but wise youth than an old but foolish king, who will no
longer take advice. 14 One can indeed come out of prison to reign, even though born
poor in the kingdom. 15 I saw all the living who, moving about under the sun, follow that[k] youth who replaced the king;[l] 16 there was no end to all those people
whom he led. Yet those who come later will not rejoice in him. Surely this also is
vanity and a chasing after wind.[m]

4.13 Eccles 7.19; 9.15
4.14 Gen 41.14, 41-43
4.16 Eccles 1.14

Have respect for God

5 [n] Guard your steps when you go to the house of God; to draw near to listen is
better than the sacrifice offered by fools; for they do not know how to keep
from doing evil.[o] 2[p] Never be rash with your mouth, nor let your heart be quick
to utter a word before God, for God is in heaven, and you upon earth; therefore let
your words be few.
3 For dreams come with many cares, and a fool's voice with many words.
4 When you make a vow to God, do not delay fulfilling it; for he has no pleasure
in fools. Fulfill what you vow. 5 It is better that you should not vow than that you
should vow and not fulfill it. 6 Do not let your mouth lead you into sin, and do not
say before the messenger that it was a mistake; why should God be angry at your
words, and destroy the work of your hands?
7 With many dreams come vanities and a multitude of words;[q] but fear God.
8 If you see in a province the oppression of the poor and the violation of justice
and right, do not be amazed at the matter; for the high official is watched by a
higher, and there are yet higher ones over them. 9 But all things considered, this is
an advantage for a land: a king for a plowed field.[q]
10 The lover of money will not be satisfied with money; nor the lover of wealth,
with gain. This also is vanity.
11 When goods increase, those who eat them increase; and what gain has their
owner but to see them with his eyes?
12 Sweet is the sleep of laborers, whether they eat little or much; but the surfeit
of the rich will not let them sleep.
13 There is a grievous ill that I have seen under the sun: riches were kept by
their owners to their hurt, 14 and those riches were lost in a bad venture; though they
are parents of children, they have nothing in their hands. 15 As they came from their
mother's womb, so they shall go again, naked as they came; they shall take nothing
for their toil, which they may carry away with their hands. 16 This also is a grievous
ill: just as they came, so shall they go; and what gain do they have from toiling for
the wind? 17 Besides, all their days they eat in darkness, in much vexation and sickness and resentment.

5.1 1 Sam 15.22; Prov 15.8; 21.27; Eccles 10.14
5.4 Ps 50.14; 66.13,14; 76.11
5.5 Prov 20.25
5.6 Num 15.25; Eccles 3.14; 7.18; 8.12,13; 12.13
5.8 Ps 12.5; Eccles 4.1
5.10 Eccles 2.10,11
5.11 Eccles 2.9
5.12 Prov 3.24
5.13 Eccles 6.2
5.15 Job 1.21; Ps 49.17
5.16 Prov 11.29; Eccles 1.3; 2.11; 3.9
5.17 Eccles 2.23

To enjoy life is a gift from God

18 This is what I have seen to be good: it is fitting to eat and drink and find

[k] Heb *the second* [l] Heb *him* [m] Or *a feeding on wind.* See Hos 12.1 [n] Ch 4.17 in Heb [o] Cn: Heb *they do not know how to do evil* [p] Ch 5.1 in Heb [q] Meaning of Heb uncertain

4.13–16 Power, popularity, and prestige are poor goals for a life's work. Although many seek them, they are shadows without substance. Many people seek recognition for their accomplishments; but people are fickle, changing quickly and easily. How much better to seek God's approval. His love never changes.

5.1 When we enter the house of God, we should have the attitude of being open and ready to listen to God, not to dictate to him what we think he should do.

5.4, 5 Solomon warns his readers about making foolish promises to God. In Israelite culture, making vows was a serious matter. Vows were voluntary but, once made, were unbreakable (Deuteronomy 23.21–23). It is foolish to make a vow you cannot keep or to play games with God by only partially fulfilling your vow (Proverbs 20.25). It's better not to vow than to make a promise to God and break it. It's better still to make a good promise and keep it. (See the note on Matthew 5.33ff.)

5.9 This verse means that everyone earns money from the fields, even the king. This puts pressure on everyone in the system, but the full weight falls on the poor people who till the ground. They must make it profitable.

5.10, 11 We always want more than we have. Solomon observed that those who love money and seek it obsessively never find the happiness it promises. Wealth also attracts freeloaders and thieves, causes sleeplessness and fear, and ultimately ends in loss because it must be left behind (Mark 10.23–25; Luke 12.16–21). No matter how much you earn, if you try to create happiness by accumulating wealth, you will never have enough. Money in itself is not wrong, but loving money leads to all sorts of sin. Whatever financial situation you are in, don't depend on money to make you happy. Instead, use what you have for the Lord.

5.18 Eccles 2.10,24
5.19 2 Chron 1.12 Eccles 3.13; 6.2
5.20 Deut 28.8-12 Isa 64.5

enjoyment in all the toil with which one toils under the sun the few days of the life
God gives us; for this is our lot. 19 Likewise all to whom God gives wealth and
possessions and whom he enables to enjoy them, and to accept their lot and find
enjoyment in their toil—this is the gift of God. 20 For they will scarcely brood over
the days of their lives, because God keeps them occupied with the joy of their
hearts.

3. Solomon's practical counsel

The king finds life meaningless

6.1 Eccles 5.13
6.2 1 Kgs 3.13 Ps 17.14; 73.7
6.3 Job 3.16 Eccles 4.3
6.6 Eccles 2.14
6.7 Prov 16.26
6.8 Eccles 2.15
6.9 Prov 30.15,16 Eccles 1.14 11.9
6.10 Prov 21.30 Eccles 1.9; 3.15
6.11 Hos 12.1
6.12 Lam 3.24-27 Mic 6.8

6 There is an evil that I have seen under the sun, and it lies heavy upon humankind: 2 those to whom God gives wealth, possessions, and honor, so that they
lack nothing of all that they desire, yet God does not enable them to enjoy these
things, but a stranger enjoys them. This is vanity; it is a grievous ill. 3 A man may
beget a hundred children, and live many years; but however many are the days of
his years, if he does not enjoy life's good things, or has no burial, I say that a
stillborn child is better off than he. 4 For it comes into vanity and goes into darkness, and in darkness its name is covered; 5 moreover it has not seen the sun or
known anything; yet it finds rest rather than he. 6 Even though he should live a
thousand years twice over, yet enjoy no good—do not all go to one place?
7 All human toil is for the mouth, yet the appetite is not satisfied. 8 For what
advantage have the wise over fools? And what do the poor have who know how to
conduct themselves before the living? 9 Better is the sight of the eyes than the wandering of desire; this also is vanity and a chasing after wind.[r]
10 Whatever has come to be has already been named, and it is known what
human beings are, and that they are not able to dispute with those who are stronger.
11 The more words, the more vanity, so how is one the better? 12 For who knows
what is good for mortals while they live the few days of their vain life, which they
pass like a shadow? For who can tell them what will be after them under the sun?

Wise advice for living

7.1 Eccles 4.2; 7.8
7.2 Eccles 2.16 3.19,20; 9.2,3

7 A good name is better than precious ointment,
and the day of death, than the day of birth.
2 It is better to go to the house of mourning
than to go to the house of feasting;

[r] *Or a feeding on wind.* See Hos 12.1

5.19, 20 God wants us to view what we have (whether it is much or little) with the right perspective—our possessions are a gift from God. Although they are not the source of joy, they are a reason to rejoice, because every good thing comes from God. We should focus more on the Giver than on the gift. We can be content with what we have when we realize that with God we have everything we need.

6.1–8.15 Solomon shows that having the right attitude about God can help us deal with present injustices. Prosperity is not always good, nor adversity always bad. But God is always good, and if we live as he wants us to, we will experience contentment.

6.1–6 Many people work hard to improve their physical condition. Yet people don't spend nearly as much time or effort on their spiritual health. How shortsighted it is to work hard to extend this life and not take the steps God requires to gain eternal life.

6.6 "All go to one place" means that everyone dies.

6.9 "The wandering of desire" means wasting time dreaming and wishing for what one doesn't have.

6.10 God knows and directs everything that happens, and he is in complete control over our lives, even though at times it may not seem like it. How foolish it is for us to argue with our Creator, who knows us completely and can see the future. (See also Jeremiah 18.6; Romans 9.19–24.)

6.12 Solomon is stating the profound truth that we do not know what the future holds, but we know who holds the future. He ends with a rhetorical question, the answer to which is God! No human knows the future, so each day must be lived for its own value. Solomon is arguing against the notion that human beings can take charge of their own destiny. In all our plans we should look up to God, not just ahead to the future.

7.1–4 This seems to contradict Solomon's previous advice to eat, drink, and be merry—to enjoy what God has given. We are to enjoy what we have while we can, but realize that adversity also strikes. Adversity reminds us that life is short, teaches us to live wisely, and refines our character. Christianity and Judaism see value in suffering and sorrow. The Greeks and Romans despised it, Eastern religions seek to live above it, but Christians and Jews see it as a refining fire. Most would agree that we learn more about God from difficult times than from happy times. Do you try to avoid sorrow and suffering at all costs? See your struggles as great opportunities to learn from God.

7.2, 4 Many people avoid thinking about death, refuse to face it, and are reluctant to attend funerals. Solomon is not encouraging us to think morbidly, but he knows that it is helpful to think clearly about death. It reminds us that there is still time for change, time to examine the direction of our lives, and time to confess our sins and find forgiveness from God. Because everyone will eventually die, it makes sense to plan ahead to experience God's mercy rather than his justice.

for this is the end of everyone,
and the living will lay it to heart.
3 Sorrow is better than laughter,
for by sadness of countenance the heart is made glad.
4 The heart of the wise is in the house of mourning;
but the heart of fools is in the house of mirth.
5 It is better to hear the rebuke of the wise
than to hear the song of fools.
6 For like the crackling of thorns under a pot,
so is the laughter of fools;
this also is vanity.
7 Surely oppression makes the wise foolish,
and a bribe corrupts the heart.
8 Better is the end of a thing than its beginning;
the patient in spirit are better than the proud in spirit.
9 Do not be quick to anger,
for anger lodges in the bosom of fools.
10 Do not say, "Why were the former days better than these?"
For it is not from wisdom that you ask this.
11 Wisdom is as good as an inheritance,
an advantage to those who see the sun.
12 For the protection of wisdom is like the protection of money,
and the advantage of knowledge is that wisdom gives life to the one who
possesses it.
13 Consider the work of God;
who can make straight what he has made crooked?
14 In the day of prosperity be joyful, and in the day of adversity consider; God
has made the one as well as the other, so that mortals may not find out anything that
will come after them.
15 In my vain life I have seen everything; there are righteous people who perish
in their righteousness, and there are wicked people who prolong their life in their
evil-doing. 16 Do not be too righteous, and do not act too wise; why should you
destroy yourself? 17 Do not be too wicked, and do not be a fool; why should you die
before your time? 18 It is good that you should take hold of the one, without letting
go of the other; for the one who fears God shall succeed with both.
19 Wisdom gives strength to the wise more than ten rulers that are in a city.
20 Surely there is no one on earth so righteous as to do good without ever
sinning.

7.3 Eccles 2.2
7.5 Eccles 9.17
7.6 Eccles 2.2
7.7 Eccles 4.1; 5.8
7.8 Eccles 7.1
7.9 Prov 14.17
7.12 Eccles 9.18
7.13 Eccles 1.15 3.11; 8.17
7.14 Eccles 3.22 9.7; 11.9
7.15 Eccles 6.12 8.12-14; 9.9
7.18 Prov 4.25-27 Eccles 3.14 5.7; 8.12,13
7.20 1 Kgs 8.46 2 Chron 6.36 Ps 143.2

7.5, 6 Have you ever been paid a compliment, knowing it was inappropriate and merely an attempt to flatter you? Some people would rather feel good than know the truth. Pleasant compliments are too often valued above helpful information (Proverbs 27.6). Solomon reminds us that it is far better to face honest criticism than to wallow in the compliments of fools.

7.7 Money talks, and it can confuse those who would otherwise judge fairly. We hear about gifts given to judges, police officers, and witnesses. Bribes are given to hurt those who tell the truth and help those who oppose it. The person who takes a bribe is indeed a fool, no matter how wise he thought he was before. Some say that everyone has a price, but those who are truly wise cannot be bought at any price.

7.8 To finish what we start takes hard work, wise guidance, and self-discipline. Anyone with vision can start a big project. But vision without wisdom often results in unfinished projects and goals.

7.10 The "good old days" are easy to talk about, but they may never have existed. Sometimes we remember only the good things about the past, forgetting that those days also had problems. Instead of living in the past, decide to live today in such a way that you will look back on today as one of the "good old days."

7.14 God allows both adversity and prosperity to come to everyone. He blends them in our lives in such a way that we can't predict the future or count on human wisdom and power. In prosperous times, we love to give ourselves the credit. Then in adversity, we tend to blame God without thanking him for the good that comes out of it. When life appears certain and controllable, don't let pride make you too comfortable, or God may allow adversity to drive you back to him. When life seems uncertain and uncontrollable, don't despair, for God is in control and will bring good results out of tough times.

7.16 How can someone be too good or too wise? This is a warning against religious conceit or false righteousness. Solomon was saying that some people are excessively wise or righteous *in their own eyes.* They become deluded by their own religious acts. They are so rigid or narrow in their views that they lose their sensitivity to the true reason for being good – to honor God. Solomon may be taking to task the wisdom teachers of the day, who often mechanically and coldly applied their teachings to others (Job's three friends did this in the book of Job). Balance is important. God created us to be whole people, not extremists whose specific viewpoints become more important than the people we should love.

21 Do not give heed to everything that people say, or you may hear your servant
cursing you; 22 your heart knows that many times you have yourself cursed others.
23 All this I have tested by wisdom; I said, "I will be wise," but it was far from
me. 24 That which is, is far off, and deep, very deep; who can find it out? 25 I turned
my mind to know and to search out and to seek wisdom and the sum of things, and
to know that wickedness is folly and that foolishness is madness. 26 I found more
bitter than death the woman who is a trap, whose heart is snares and nets, whose
hands are fetters; one who pleases God escapes her, but the sinner is taken by her.
27 See, this is what I found, says the Teacher,[s] adding one thing to another to find
the sum, 28 which my mind has sought repeatedly, but I have not found. One man
among a thousand I found, but a woman among all these I have not found. 29 See,
this alone I found, that God made human beings straightforward, but they have
devised many schemes.

8 Who is like the wise man?
And who knows the interpretation of a thing?
Wisdom makes one's face shine,
and the hardness of one's countenance is changed.

2 Keep[t] the king's command because of your sacred oath. 3 Do not be terrified;
go from his presence, do not delay when the matter is unpleasant, for he does whatever he pleases. 4 For the word of the king is powerful, and who can say to him,
"What are you doing?" 5 Whoever obeys a command will meet no harm, and the
wise mind will know the time and way. 6 For every matter has its time and way,
although the troubles of mortals lie heavy upon them. 7 Indeed, they do not know
what is to be, for who can tell them how it will be? 8 No one has power over the
wind[u] to restrain the wind,[u] or power over the day of death; there is no discharge
from the battle, nor does wickedness deliver those who practice it. 9 All this I observed, applying my mind to all that is done under the sun, while one person exercises authority over another to the other's hurt.

10 Then I saw the wicked buried; they used to go in and out of the holy place,
and were praised in the city where they had done such things.[v] This also is vanity.
11 Because sentence against an evil deed is not executed speedily, the human heart
is fully set to do evil. 12 Though sinners do evil a hundred times and prolong their
lives, yet I know that it will be well with those who fear God, because they stand
in fear before him, 13 but it will not be well with the wicked, neither will they prolong their days like a shadow, because they do not stand in fear before God.

14 There is a vanity that takes place on earth, that there are righteous people
who are treated according to the conduct of the wicked, and there are wicked

7.24 Deut 30.11-14 Job 11.7; 37.23 Rom 11.33
7.25 Eccles 1.7 10.13 Jer 12.1,2
7.26 Prov 5.4 6.23,24; 7.23 22.14
7.28 1 Kgs 11.3
7.29 Gen 1.27
8.1 Deut 28.50
8.2 Eccles 10.4
8.4 Prov 19.12; 20.2
8.5 Eccles 10.2 12.14
8.6 Eccles 3.1,17, 22; 6.12; 7.14
8.8 Eccles 8.13
8.9 Eccles 1.11 2.16; 4.1,16 5.8; 9.5,15
8.12 1 Kgs 2.5-9 Prov 1.33 Eccles 7.15
8.13 Eccles 6.12; 8.8 Isa 3.11
8.14 Job 21.7 Ps 73.3,12 Eccles 2.14 7.15

[s] *Koheleth*, traditionally rendered *Preacher* [t] Heb *I keep* [u] Or *breath* [v] Meaning of Heb uncertain

7.23–25 Solomon, the wisest man in the world, confessed how difficult it had been to act and think wisely. He emphasized that no matter how much we know, there are always mysteries we will never understand. So thinking you have enough wisdom is a sure sign that you don't.

7.27, 28 Did Solomon think women were not capable of having wisdom? No, because in the book of Proverbs he personified wisdom as a responsible woman. The point of Solomon's statement is not that women are unwise, but that hardly anyone, man or woman, is wise before God. In his search, he found that wisdom was almost as scarce among men as among women, even though men were given a religious education program in his culture and women were not. In effect, the verse is saying, "I have found only one in a thousand people who is wise in God's eyes. No. I have found fewer than that!"

7.29 God created human beings to live right and do what is right. Instead, they have left God's path to follow their own downward road.

8.1 Wisdom is the ability to see life from God's perspective and then to know the best course of action to take. Most would agree that wisdom is a valuable asset, but how can we acquire it? In Proverbs 9.10, we learn to find wisdom through respecting and honoring God. Wisdom comes from finding God (knowing and trusting him); it is not merely the way to find God. Knowing God will lead to understanding and to sharing this knowledge with others.

8.10 This verse probably refers to how we quickly forget the evil done by some people after they have died. Returning to the cemetery, we praise them in the very city where they did their evil deeds.

8.11 If God doesn't punish us immediately, we must not assume that he doesn't care or that sin has no consequences, even though it is easy to sin when we don't feel the consequences at once. When a young child does something wrong, and the wrong is not discovered, it will be much easier for him to do it again. But God knows every wrong we commit, and one day we will have to answer for everything we have done (12.14).

8.12, 13 Although Solomon's presentation is pessimistic, it shows that life is ultimately better with God. His presence does not shield us from all trouble, but it guarantees us that we will have his power to meet adversity. Both our eternal destiny and our present trials are in his hands.

people who are treated according to the conduct of the righteous. I said that this
also is vanity. 15 So I commend enjoyment, for there is nothing better for people **8.15**
under the sun than to eat, and drink, and enjoy themselves, for this will go with Eccles 2.24 3.12,13; 5.18
them in their toil through the days of life that God gives them under the sun. 1 Tim 6.17

16 When I applied my mind to know wisdom, and to see the business that is **8.16**
done on earth, how one's eyes see sleep neither day nor night, 17 then I saw all the Eccles 1.13,14 3.11
work of God, that no one can find out what is happening under the sun. However Isa 40.28
much they may toil in seeking, they will not find it out; even though those who are
wise claim to know, they cannot find it out.

4. Solomon's final conclusion

Everyone has a common destiny

9 All this I laid to heart, examining it all, how the righteous and the wise and **9.1**
their deeds are in the hand of God; whether it is love or hate one does not 1 Sam 2.9 Ps 37.5,6
know. Everything that confronts them 2 is vanity,[w] since the same fate comes to all, Prov 16.3
to the righteous and the wicked, to the good and the evil,[x] to the clean and the Eccles 9.6 10.14
unclean, to those who sacrifice and those who do not sacrifice. As are the good, so **9.2**
are the sinners; those who swear are like those who shun an oath. 3 This is an evil Job 9.22
in all that happens under the sun, that the same fate comes to everyone. Moreover, Eccles 2.14 3.19; 6.6; 7.2
the hearts of all are full of evil; madness is in their hearts while they live, and after
that they go to the dead. 4 But whoever is joined with all the living has hope, for a **9.5**
living dog is better than a dead lion. 5 The living know that they will die, but the Job 7.8-10
dead know nothing; they have no more reward, and even the memory of them is Ps 88.12 Eccles 1.11
lost. 6 Their love and their hate and their envy have already perished; never again 2.16; 8.10
will they have any share in all that happens under the sun. **9.6**

7 Go, eat your bread with enjoyment, and drink your wine with a merry heart; Eccles 2.10 3.22
for God has long ago approved what you do. 8 Let your garments always be white; **9.7**
do not let oil be lacking on your head. 9 Enjoy life with the wife whom you love, all Eccles 2.24
the days of your vain life that are given you under the sun, because that is your **9.8** Ps 23.5
portion in life and in your toil at which you toil under the sun. 10 Whatever your **9.10**
hand finds to do, do with your might; for there is no work or thought or knowledge Job 21.13 Eccles 9.5; 11.6
or wisdom in Sheol, to which you are going. **9.11**

11 Again I saw that under the sun the race is not to the swift, nor the battle to 1 Sam 6.9 2 Chron 20.15
the strong, nor bread to the wise, nor riches to the intelligent, nor favor to the Ps 76.5
skillful; but time and chance happen to them all. 12 For no one can anticipate the **9.12** Eccles 8.7

[w] Syr Compare Gk: Heb *Everything that confronts them* [2]*is everything* [x] Gk Syr Vg: Heb lacks *and the evil*

8.15 Solomon recalls the remedy for life's unanswered questions. He recommends joy and contentment as encouragement for us along life's pilgrimage. We must accept each day with its daily measure of work, food, and pleasure. Let us learn to enjoy what God has given us to refresh and strengthen us to continue his work.

8.16, 17 Even if he had access to all the world's wisdom, the wisest man would know very little. There are always more questions than answers. But the unknown should not cast a shadow over our joy, faith, or work, because we know that someone greater is in control and that we can put our trust in him. Don't let what you don't know about the future destroy the joy God wants to give you today.

9.2 "Swear" means to take an oath. Both those who take oaths and those who don't have the same end to their lives – death.

9.5, 10 When Solomon says the dead know nothing, and there is no work, thought, knowledge, or wisdom in death (Sheol), he is not contrasting life with afterlife, but life with death. Once you die, you can't change what you have done. Resurrection to a new life after death was a vague concept for Old Testament believers. It was made clear only after Jesus rose from the dead.

9.7–10 Considering the uncertainties of the future and the certainty of death, Solomon recommends enjoying life as God's gift. He may have been criticizing those who put off all present pleasures in order to accumulate wealth, much like those who get caught up in today's rat race. Solomon asks, "What is your wealth really worth, anyway?" It is important to enjoy God's gifts while we are able, because the future is so uncertain.

9.8 Wearing white clothes and having oil on the head were signs of happiness and celebration.

9.9 Solomon also wrote a proverb about marriage. "He who finds a wife finds a good thing, and obtains favor from the Lord" (Proverbs 18.22). How sad to be married and not appreciate the enjoyment and companionship God has given you.

9.10, 11 It isn't difficult to think of cases where the swiftest or the strongest don't win, the wise remain poor, and the skillful are unknown for their talents. Some see such examples and call life unfair, and they are right. Mankind has twisted life, making it what God did not intend. Solomon is trying to reduce our expectations of this imperfect world. The book of Proverbs emphasizes how life ought to go if everyone acted fairly; Ecclesiastes tells us what often happens in our less-than-perfect world. We must keep our perspective by remembering that we live in a fallen world. Don't let the inequities of life keep you from earnest, dedicated work. We serve God, not people (see Colossians 3.23).

time of disaster. Like fish taken in a cruel net, and like birds caught in a snare, so
mortals are snared at a time of calamity, when it suddenly falls upon them.
13 I have also seen this example of wisdom under the sun, and it seemed great
to me. 14 There was a little city with few people in it. A great king came against it
9.15 Eccles 8.10 — and besieged it, building great siegeworks against it. 15 Now there was found in it
a poor wise man, and he by his wisdom delivered the city. Yet no one remembered
9.16 Eccles 7.12,19 — that poor man. 16 So I said, "Wisdom is better than might; yet the poor man's wisdom is despised, and his words are not heeded."

9.17 Eccles 7.5; 10.12

17 The quiet words of the wise are more to be heeded
than the shouting of a ruler among fools.

9.18 Eccles 9.16

18 Wisdom is better than weapons of war,
but one bungler destroys much good.

Behave wisely

10.1 Ex 30.25

10 Dead flies make the perfumer's ointment give off a foul odor;
so a little folly outweighs wisdom and honor.
2 The heart of the wise inclines to the right,
but the heart of a fool to the left.

10.3 Prov 13.16; 18.2

3 Even when fools walk on the road, they lack sense,
and show to everyone that they are fools.

10.4 1 Sam 25.24-33; Prov 25.15; Eccles 8.3

4 If the anger of the ruler rises against you, do not leave your post,
for calmness will undo great offenses.
5 There is an evil that I have seen under the sun, as great an error as if it pro-
10.6 Prov 28.12; 29.2 — ceeded from the ruler: 6 folly is set in many high places, and the rich sit in a low
10.7 Prov 19.10; 30.22 — place. 7 I have seen slaves on horseback, and princes walking on foot like slaves.

10.8 Ps 7.15; Prov 26.27

8 Whoever digs a pit will fall into it;
and whoever breaks through a wall will be bitten by a snake.
9 Whoever quarries stones will be hurt by them;
and whoever splits logs will be endangered by them.
10 If the iron is blunt, and one does not whet the edge,
then more strength must be exerted;
but wisdom helps one to succeed.
11 If the snake bites before it is charmed,
there is no advantage in a charmer.

10.12 Prov 10.14,32; 22.11; Eccles 7.25

12 Words spoken by the wise bring them favor,
but the lips of fools consume them.
13 The words of their mouths begin in foolishness,
and their talk ends in wicked madness;

10.14 Prov 15.2; Eccles 3.22; 5.3; 6.12; 7.14; 8.7

14 yet fools talk on and on.
No one knows what is to happen,
and who can tell anyone what the future holds?
15 The toil of fools wears them out,
for they do not even know the way to town.

9.13–18 Our society honors wealth, attractiveness, and success above wisdom. Yet wisdom is a greater asset than strength, although it is unrecognized by the masses. Even though it is more effective, wisdom is not always heard, and wise people go unheeded. From this parable we can learn to be receptive to wisdom, no matter who it is from.

10.4 This parable is saying that employees should ride out the temper tantrums of their employer. If we quietly do our work and don't get upset, the employer will probably get over his or her anger and calm down.

10.5–7 By describing these circumstances that aren't fair or don't make sense, Solomon is saying that wisdom alone can't bring justice. Solomon continues to build to his conclusion that everything we have (from wisdom to riches) is nothing without God. But when God uses what little we have, it becomes all we could ever want or need.

10.10 Trying to do anything without the necessary skills or tools is like chopping with a dull axe. If your tool is dull, you sharpen it to do a better job. Similarly, if you lack skills, you should sharpen them through training and practice. In each situation, sharpening the axe means recognizing where a problem exists, acquiring or honing the skills (or tools) to do the job better, and then going out and doing it. Find the areas of your life where your "axe" is dull, and sharpen your skills so you can be more effective for God's work.

16 Alas for you, O land, when your king is a servant,[y]
and your princes feast in the morning!
17 Happy are you, O land, when your king is a nobleman,
and your princes feast at the proper time—
for strength, and not for drunkenness!
18 Through sloth the roof sinks in,
and through indolence the house leaks.
19 Feasts are made for laughter;
wine gladdens life,
and money meets every need.
20 Do not curse the king, even in your thoughts,
or curse the rich, even in your bedroom;
for a bird of the air may carry your voice,
or some winged creature tell the matter.

10.16 2 Chron 13.7 Prov 20.1,2
10.18 Prov 24.30-34
10.19 Ps 104.15 Eccles 2.3; 7.12

Bread upon the waters

11 Send out your bread upon the waters,
for after many days you will get it back.
2 Divide your means seven ways, or even eight,
for you do not know what disaster may happen on earth.
3 When clouds are full,
they empty rain on the earth;
whether a tree falls to the south or to the north,
in the place where the tree falls, there it will lie.
4 Whoever observes the wind will not sow;
and whoever regards the clouds will not reap.
5 Just as you do not know how the breath comes to the bones in the mother's
womb, so you do not know the work of God, who makes everything.
6 In the morning sow your seed, and at evening do not let your hands be idle; for
you do not know which will prosper, this or that, or whether both alike will be
good.

11.5 Ps 139.13-16 Eccles 1.15 3.10; 8.17 Jn 3.8
11.6 Eccles 9.10

Remember your Creator

7 Light is sweet, and it is pleasant for the eyes to see the sun.
8 Even those who live many years should rejoice in them all; yet let them remember that the days of darkness will be many. All that comes is vanity.

11.7 Eccles 6.5; 7.11
11.8 Eccles 9.7; 12.1

[y] *Or a child*

10.16–18 When the Hebrews had immature and irresponsible leaders, their nation fell. The books of 1 and 2 Kings describe the decline of the kingdoms when the leaders were concerned only about themselves. Verse 18 pinpoints the basic problem of these selfish leaders – laziness and self-centeredness.

10.19 Government leaders, businesses, families, even churches get trapped into thinking money is the answer to every problem. We throw money at our problems, but just as the thrill of liquor is only temporary, the soothing effect of the last purchase soon wears off and we have to buy more. Scripture recognizes that money is necessary for survival, but it warns against the love of money (see Matthew 6.24; 1 Timothy 6.10; Hebrews 13.5). Money is dangerous because it deceives us into thinking that wealth is the easiest way to get everything we want. The love of money is sinful because we trust it, rather than God, to solve our problems. Those who pursue its empty promises one day discover that they have nothing, because they are spiritually bankrupt.

11.1–5 In these verses Solomon summarizes that life involves both risk and opportunity. Since life has no guarantees, we must be prepared. Solomon does not support a despairing attitude. Just because life is uncertain does not mean we should do nothing. We need a spirit of trust and adventure. We are to face life's risks and opportunities with God-directed enthusiasm and faith.

11.4 Waiting for perfect conditions can produce inactivity. This practical insight is especially applicable to our spiritual life. If we wait for the perfect time and place for personal Bible reading, we will never begin. If we wait for a perfect church, we will never join. If we wait for the perfect ministry, we will never serve. Take steps now to grow spiritually. Don't wait for conditions that may never exist.

11.7, 8 Solomon is no dreary pessimist in 11.7 – 12.14. He encourages us to rejoice in every day but to remember that eternity is far longer than a person's life span. Psalm 90.12 says, "So teach us to count our days that we may gain a wise heart." The wise person does not think just about the moment and its impact; he takes the long-range view toward eternity. Approach your decisions from God's perspective – consider their impact ten years from now and into eternity. Live with the attitude that although our lives are short, we will live with God forever.

9 Rejoice, young man, while you are young, and let your heart cheer you in the
days of your youth. Follow the inclination of your heart and the desire of your eyes,
but know that for all these things God will bring you into judgment.
10 Banish anxiety from your mind, and put away pain from your body; for
youth and the dawn of life are vanity.

12 Remember your creator in the days of your youth, before the days of trouble
come, and the years draw near when you will say, "I have no pleasure in
them"; 2 before the sun and the light and the moon and the stars are darkened and the
clouds return with[z] the rain; 3 in the day when the guards of the house tremble, and
the strong men are bent, and the women who grind cease working because they are
few, and those who look through the windows see dimly; 4 when the doors on the
street are shut, and the sound of the grinding is low, and one rises up at the sound
of a bird, and all the daughters of song are brought low; 5 when one is afraid of
heights, and terrors are in the road; the almond tree blossoms, the grasshopper
drags itself along[a] and desire fails; because all must go to their eternal home, and
the mourners will go about the streets; 6 before the silver cord is snapped,[b] and the
golden bowl is broken, and the pitcher is broken at the fountain, and the wheel
broken at the cistern, 7 and the dust returns to the earth as it was, and the breath[c]
returns to God who gave it. 8 Vanity of vanities, says the Teacher;[d] all is vanity.

Fear God and obey his commandments

9 Besides being wise, the Teacher[d] also taught the people knowledge, weighing and studying and arranging many proverbs. 10 The Teacher[d] sought to find
pleasing words, and he wrote words of truth plainly.
11 The sayings of the wise are like goads, and like nails firmly fixed are the
collected sayings that are given by one shepherd.[e] 12 Of anything beyond these, my
child, beware. Of making many books there is no end, and much study is a weariness of the flesh.

[z] Or *after*; Heb *'ahar* [a] Or *is a burden* [b] Syr Vg Compare Gk: Heb *is removed* [c] Or *the spirit* [d] *Koheleth*, traditionally rendered *Preacher* [e] Meaning of Heb uncertain

11.9 Job 31.7 Eccles 2.10 3.17; 12.4
12.1 2 Sam 19.35 Ps 63.6; 119.55 Eccles 11.8
12.2 Ezek 32.7,8 Joel 3.5
12.3 1 Sam 3.2 Ps 35.14; 38.6
12.4 2 Sam 19.35 Rev 18.22
12.5 Job 17.13 Zech 4.2,3
12.7 Gen 3.19 Ps 104.29 Eccles 3.20,21
12.8 Eccles 1.2
12.9 1 Kgs 4.32 Prov 10.1; 25.1
12.11 Eccles 7.5 10.12 Isa 22.23
12.12 1 Kgs 4.32,33

11.10 We often hear people say, "It doesn't matter." But many of your choices will be irreversible – they will stay with you for a lifetime. What you do when you're young *does* matter. Enjoy life now, but don't do anything physically, morally, or spiritually that will prevent you from enjoying life when you are old.

12.1 A life without God can produce a bitter, lonely, and hopeless old age. A life centered around God is fulfilling; it makes the "days of trouble" – when disabilities, sickness, and handicaps cause barriers to enjoying life – satisfying because of the hope of eternal life. Being young is exciting. But the excitement of youth can become a barrier to closeness with God if it makes young people focus on passing pleasures instead of eternal values. Make your strength available to God when it is still yours – during your youthful years. Don't waste it on evil or meaningless activities that become bad habits and make you callous. Seek God now.

12.2–5 The imagery in this section is a poetic description of the physical and emotional effects of advancing age. Darkening of the sun, moon, and stars (12.2) refer to the decreased capacity for joy. Clouds (12.2) refer to the sorrows that come in life. Guards of the house (12.3) refer to the arms, and strong men (12.3) refer to the legs. Women who grind (12.3) refer to the teeth, and those who look through the windows (12.3) refer to the eyes. The doors on the street (12.4) refer to loss of hearing, and the blossoming of the almond tree (12.5) refer to the hair turning gray. The grasshopper dragging itself along (12.5) is a picture of the elderly struggling to walk. The reasoon for this inevitable physical decline is then made clear, "all must go to their eternal home."

12.6–8 The silver cord, golden bowl, pitcher, and wheel symbolize life's fragility. How easily death comes to us; how swiftly and unexpectedly we can return to the dust from which we came. Therefore, we should recognize life as a precious resource to be used wisely and not squandered frivolously.

12.7, 8 Stripped of God's Spirit, our bodies return to dust. Stripped of God's purpose, our work is in vain. Stripped of God's love, our service is futile. We must put God first over all we do and in all we do, because without him we have nothing. Knowing that life is futile without God motivates the wise person to seek God first.

12.9 The Teacher is Solomon, who wrote the book of Proverbs. These three characteristics of his teaching – weighing, studying, and arranging – are useful tools for all who teach the Bible. Weighing implies careful evaluation and balance. Studying implies diligent observation, and arranging shows there is an artistic element in presenting truth to others.

12.11 A goad (also called an ox goad) was a sharp metal tip attached to a handle and used to keep oxen or cattle moving. Like a goad, a wise word or important truth might be unpleasant when first applied, but it will keep us moving in God's direction.

12.12 There are endless opinions about life and philosophies about how we should live, and they could be read and studied forever. It is not wrong to study them, but spend the majority of your time feeding on the truth of God's Word. Wisdom should lead to action. Wise students of the Bible will understand and do what they are taught. Because our time on earth is so short, we should use it to learn important truths, for they affect this life and eternity.

13 The end of the matter; all has been heard. Fear God, and keep his commandments; for that is the whole duty of everyone. 14 For God will bring every deed into
judgment, including[f] every secret thing, whether good or evil.

[f] Or *into the judgment on*

12.13 Eccles 3.14
12.14 Mt 10.26

12.13, 14 Solomon presents his antidotes for the two main ailments presented in this book. Those who lack purpose and direction in life should respect God and follow his principles for living. Those who think life is unfair should remember that God will review every person's life to determine how he or she has responded to him. Have you committed your life to him, both present and future? Does your life measure up to his standards?

12.13, 14 The book of Ecclesiastes cannot be interpreted correctly without reading these final verses. No matter what the mysteries and apparent contradictions of life, you must work toward the single purpose of knowing God.

In Ecclesiastes, Solomon shows us that we should enjoy life, but this does not exempt us from obeying God's commands. We should search for purpose and meaning in life, but they cannot be found in human endeavors. We should acknowledge the evil, foolishness, and injustice in life, yet maintain a positive attitude and strong faith in God.

All people will have to stand before God and be judged for what they did in this life. We will not be able to use life's inconsistencies as an excuse for failing to live properly. To live properly, we need to (1) recognize that human effort apart from God is futile; (2) put God first – now; (3) receive everything good as a gift from God; (4) realize that God will judge both evil and good, and (5) know that God will judge the quality of every person's life. How strange that people spend their lives striving for the very enjoyment that God gives freely, as a gift.

THE SONG OF SOLOMON

SATURATED with stories of sexual escapades, secret rendezvous, and extramarital affairs, today's media preach that immorality means freedom, perversion is natural, and commitment is old-fashioned. Sex, created by God and pronounced good in Eden, has been twisted, exploited, and turned into an urgent, illicit, casual, and self-gratifying activity. Love has turned into lust, giving into getting, and lasting commitment into "no strings attached."

In reality, sexual intercourse, the physical and emotional union of male and female, should be a holy means of celebrating love, producing children, and experiencing pleasure, protected by the commitment of marriage.

God thinks sex is important, and Scripture contains numerous guidelines for its use and warnings about its misuse. And sex is always mentioned in the context of a loving relationship between husband and wife. Perhaps the highlight of this is the Song of Solomon, the intimate story of a man and a woman, their love, courtship, and marriage. Solomon probably wrote this "song" in his youth, before being overtaken by his own obsession with women, sex, and pleasure.

A moving story, drama, and poem, the Song of Solomon features the love dialogue between a simple Jewish maiden (the Shulamite woman) and her lover (Solomon, the king). They describe in intimate detail their feelings for each other and their longings to be together. Throughout the dialogue, sex and marriage are put in their proper, God-given perspective.

There has been much debate over the meaning of this song. Some say that it is an allegory of God's love for Israel and/or for the church. Others say it is a literal story about married love. But in reality, it is both—a historical story with two layers of meaning. On one level we learn about love, marriage, and sex; and on the other level we see God's overwhelming love for his people. As you read the Song of Solomon, remember that you are loved by God, and commit yourself to seeing life, sex, and marriage from his point of view.

VITAL STATISTICS

PURPOSE:
To tell of the love between a bridegroom (King Solomon) and his bride, to affirm the sanctity of marriage, and to picture God's love for his people

AUTHOR:
Solomon

DATE WRITTEN:
Probably early in Solomon's reign

SETTING:
Israel—the Shulamite woman's garden and the king's palace

KEY VERSE:
"I am my beloved's and my beloved is mine; he pastures his flock among the lilies" (6.3).

KEY PEOPLE:
King Solomon, the Shulamite woman, the woman's brothers, and the young women of Jerusalem

THE BLUEPRINT

1. The wedding day (1.1—2.7)
2. Memories of courtship (2.8—3.5)
3. Memories of engagement (3.6—5.1)
4. A troubling dream (5.2—6.3)
5. Praising the bride's beauty (6.4—7.9)
6. The bride's tender appeal (7.10—8.4)
7. The power of love (8.5–14)

The Song of Solomon is a wedding song honoring marriage. The most explicit statements on sex in the Bible can be found in this book. It has often been criticized through the centuries because of its sensuous language. The purity and sacredness of love represented here, however, are greatly needed in our day where distorted attitudes about love and marriage are commonplace. God created sex and intimacy, and they are holy and good when enjoyed within the bounds of marriage. A husband and wife honor God when they love and enjoy each other.

MEGATHEMES

THEME	EXPLANATION	IMPORTANCE
Sex	Sex is God's gift to his creatures. He endorses sex, but restricts its expression to those committed to each other in marriage.	God wants sex to be motivated by love and commitment, not lust. It is for mutual pleasure, not selfish enjoyment.
Love	As the relationship developed, the beauty and wonder of a romance unfolded between Solomon and his bride. The intense power of love affected the hearts, minds, and bodies of the two lovers.	Because love is such a powerful expression of feeling and commitment between two people, it is not to be regarded casually. We are not to manipulate others into loving us, and love should not be prematurely encouraged in a relationship.
Commitment	The power of love requires more than the language of feeling to protect it. Sexual expression is such an integral part of our selfhood that we need the boundary of marriage to safeguard our love. Marriage is the celebration of daily commitment to each other.	While romance keeps a marriage interesting, commitment keeps romance from dwindling away. The decision to commit yourself to your spouse alone *begins* at the marriage altar. It must be maintained day by day.
Beauty	The two lovers praise the beauty they see in each other. The language they use shows the spontaneity and mystery of love. Our praise should not be limited to physical beauty; beautiful personality and moral purity should also be praised.	Our love for our spouse makes him or her appear beautiful. It is the inner qualities that keep love alive. Don't just look for physical attractiveness in a spouse. Look for the qualities that don't fade with time—spiritual commitment, integrity, sensitivity, and sincerity.
Problems	Over time, feelings of loneliness, indifference, and isolation came between Solomon and his bride. During those times, love grew cold and barriers were raised.	Through careful communication, lovers can be reconciled, commitment can be renewed and romance refreshed. Don't let walls come between you and your partner. Take care of problems while they are still small.

1. The wedding day

1 The Song of Songs, which is Solomon's. 1.1 1 Kgs 4.32

2 Let him kiss me with the kisses of his mouth! 1.2 Song 4.10
For your love is better than wine,
3 your anointing oils are fragrant, 1.3 Song 4.10
your name is perfume poured out;
therefore the maidens love you.

1.1 Solomon frequently visited the various parts of his kingdom. One day, as he visited some royal vineyards in the north, his royal entourage came by surprise upon a beautiful peasant woman tending the vines. Embarrassed, she ran from them. But Solomon could not forget her. Later, disguised as a shepherd, he returned to the vineyards and won her love. He revealed his true identity and asked her to return to Jerusalem with him. Solomon and his bride are being married in the palace as this book begins.

The Song of Solomon is a series of seven poems, not necessarily in chronological order. It reflects upon the first meeting of Solomon and the peasant woman, their engagement, their wedding, their wedding night, and the growth of their marriage after the wedding.

1.1 Solomon, a son of King David, became king and was chosen by God to build the temple in Jerusalem. God gave him extraordinary wisdom. Much of his reign was characterized by wisdom and reverence for God, although toward the end of his life he became proud and turned from God. Read about Solomon in 1 Kings 1–11 and 1 Chronicles 28–2 Chronicles 9. Solomon wrote more than 3,000 proverbs (see the book of Proverbs) and over 1,000 songs, one of which is this book. His Profile is found in 1 Kings 3.

1.1 There are four characters or groups of characters in this book: the girl, Solomon, the young women ("daughters") of Jerusalem (1.5), and the girl's brothers (8.8). The girl who caught Solomon's attention was from Shulam (thought by many to be Shunem), a farming community about 60 miles north of Jerusalem. Her tanned skin indicates that she worked outside in the vineyards (1.6) – thus she may not have been from the upper class. The women of Jerusalem were either members of Solomon's harem or workers in the palace. In either case, the girl had to live and work with these women in her new surroundings.

1.1–4 This vivid description of a love relationship begins with a picture of love itself. Love is "better than wine"; it makes the lovers rejoice. Acts 10.9–16 teaches that what God has created and cleansed we should not misuse or call common. We can enjoy love. God created it as a gift to us and a treat for all our senses.

1.3 Anointing oil was indispensible in the Middle East. The hot climate made frequent baths necessary. Afterwards, the skin was treated with sweet-smelling oil.

1.4
Song 2.3-5

4 Draw me after you, let us make haste.
The king has brought me into his chambers.
We will exult and rejoice in you;
we will extol your love more than wine;
rightly do they love you.

1.5
Ps 90.17
Song 2.7,14
4.3; 6.4

5 I am black and beautiful,
O daughters of Jerusalem,
like the tents of Kedar,
like the curtains of Solomon.

1.6
Song 8.11

6 Do not gaze at me because I am dark,
because the sun has gazed on me.
My mother's sons were angry with me;
they made me keeper of the vineyards,
but my own vineyard I have not kept!

1.7
Ps 18.1
Song 3.1-4
8.13

7 Tell me, you whom my soul loves,
where you pasture your flock,
where you make it lie down at noon;
for why should I be like one who is veiled
beside the flocks of your companions?

1.8
Song 5.9; 6.1

8 If you do not know,
O fairest among women,
follow the tracks of the flock,
and pasture your kids
beside the shepherds' tents.

1.9
2 Chron 1.16,17
Isa 31.1

9 I compare you, my love,
to a mare among Pharaoh's chariots.

1.10
Song 5.13

10 Your cheeks are comely with ornaments,
your neck with strings of jewels.
11 We will make you ornaments of gold,
studded with silver.

1.12
Song 4.13,14

12 While the king was on his couch,
my nard gave forth its fragrance.
13 My beloved is to me a bag of myrrh
that lies between my breasts.

1.14
1 Sam 23.29
Song 4.13

14 My beloved is to me a cluster of henna blossoms
in the vineyards of En-gedi.

1.15
Song 1.16
2.10,13; 4.1

15 Ah, you are beautiful, my love;
ah, you are beautiful;
your eyes are doves.

1.5 Kedar was a nomadic community in northern Arabia. It was known for its tents that were woven from black goat hair.

1.6 The vineyard mentioned here was apparently owned by Solomon (because he came to visit it) and leased to the girl's stepbrothers (her "mother's sons"), who made her work among the vines in the hot sun. When she was brought to Jerusalem, the young girl was embarrassed about her tanned complexion because the girls in the city had the fair, delicate skin that was considered much more beautiful. But Solomon loved her dark skin.

1.7 The girl felt insecure at being different from the women of Jerusalem (1.6) and at being alone while her lover was away (1.7). She longed for the security of his presence. The basis of true love is commitment, and in a relationship where there is genuine love, there is never any fear of deceit, manipulation, or exploitation.

1.10 These ornaments were probably earrings.

1.12 Nard was a fragrant plant from which was extracted an aromatic oil. It was very precious and highly valued. This sweet-smelling perfume was a symbol of the bride's love.

1.14 En-gedi was an oasis hidden at the base of rugged limestone cliffs west of the Dead Sea. It was known for its fruitful palm trees and fragrant balsam oil. The terrain surrounding En-gedi was some of the most desolate in Palestine, and it had an extremely hot desert climate. The henna blossoms in En-gedi would have appeared all the more beautiful because of their stark surroundings; thus Solomon was complimenting his bride's beauty and comparing her favorably with the women she feared.

16 Ah, you are beautiful, my beloved,
truly lovely.
Our couch is green;
17 the beams of our house are cedar,
our rafters[a] are pine.

2 I am a rose[b] of Sharon,
a lily of the valleys.

2 As a lily among brambles,
so is my love among maidens.

3 As an apple tree among the trees of the wood,
so is my beloved among young men.
With great delight I sat in his shadow,
and his fruit was sweet to my taste.
4 He brought me to the banqueting house,
and his intention toward me was love.
5 Sustain me with raisins,
refresh me with apples;
for I am faint with love.
6 O that his left hand were under my head,
and that his right hand embraced me!
7 I adjure you, O daughters of Jerusalem,
by the gazelles or the wild does:
do not stir up or awaken love
until it is ready!

2. Memories of courtship

8 The voice of my beloved!
Look, he comes,
leaping upon the mountains,
bounding over the hills.
9 My beloved is like a gazelle
or a young stag.
Look, there he stands
behind our wall,
gazing in at the windows,
looking through the lattice.
10 My beloved speaks and says to me:
"Arise, my love, my fair one,
and come away;
11 for now the winter is past,
the rain is over and gone.
12 The flowers appear on the earth;

1.17 2 Chron 3.5

2.3 Song 1.13,16; 8.5

2.4 Ps 63.2-5; Song 1.4; 5.1

2.6 Prov 4.8; Song 8.3

2.7 Song 3.5; 5.8; 8.14

2.9 Prov 6.5; Song 2.17; 3.5; 8.14

[a] Meaning of Heb uncertain [b] Heb *crocus*

1.16, 17 The bride describes her woodland surroundings as a wedding bedroom.

2.1 The rose of Sharon and lily of the valleys are flowers commonly found in Israel. Perhaps the girl was saying, "I'm not so special; I'm just an ordinary flower," to which Solomon replied, "Oh, no, you are extraordinary – a lily among thorns." Solomon used the language of love. There is nothing more vital than encouraging and appreciating the person you love. Be sure to tell your spouse "I love you" every day and show that love by your actions.

2.7 Feelings of love can create intimacy that overpowers reason. Young people are too often in a hurry to develop an intimate relationship based on their strong feelings. But feelings aren't enough to support a lasting relationship. This verse encourages us not to force romance lest the feelings of love grow faster than the commitment needed to make love last. Patiently wait for feelings of love and commitment to develop together. Note: *adjure* means "charge" or "urge."

2.8 – 3.5 In this section Solomon's bride (the girl), reflects on her courtship with Solomon, remembering the first day they met and recalling one of her dreams about their being together.

the time of singing has come,
and the voice of the turtledove
is heard in our land.

2.13 Isa 18.5 Hos 14.6

13 The fig tree puts forth its figs,
and the vines are in blossom;
they give forth fragrance.
Arise, my love, my fair one,
and come away.

2.14 Ps 68.13 Song 5.2; 6.9 Jer 48.28

14 O my dove, in the clefts of the rock,
in the covert of the cliff,
let me see your face,
let me hear your voice;
for your voice is sweet,
and your face is lovely.

2.15 Song 2.13; 7.12

15 Catch us the foxes,
the little foxes,
that ruin the vineyards—
for our vineyards are in blossom."

2.16 Ps 48.14; 63.1 Song 4.5 6.2,3; 7.10

16 My beloved is mine and I am his;
he pastures his flock among the lilies.

2.17 Song 2.8,9; 4.6

17 Until the day breathes
and the shadows flee,
turn, my beloved, be like a gazelle
or a young stag on the cleft mountains.[c]

3.1 Ps 130.1,2 Song 1.7; 5.6

3 Upon my bed at night
I sought him whom my soul loves;
I sought him, but found him not;
I called him, but he gave no answer.[d]
2 "I will rise now and go about the city,
in the streets and in the squares;
I will seek him whom my soul loves."
I sought him, but found him not.

3.3 Song 5.7 Ezek 33.2-9

3 The sentinels found me,
as they went about in the city.
"Have you seen him whom my soul loves?"

3.4 Song 8.2

4 Scarcely had I passed them,
when I found him whom my soul loves.
I held him, and would not let him go

[c] Or *on the mountains of Bether*: meaning of Heb uncertain [d] Gk: Heb lacks this line

2.12, 13 The lovers celebrate their joy in the creation and in their love. God created the world, the beauty we see, the joy of love and sex, and gave us senses to enjoy them. Never let problems, conflicts, or the ravages of time ruin your ability to enjoy God's gifts. Take time to enjoy the world God has created.

2.15 Some believe this verse was spoken by the girl's brothers (see the note on 1.6). Just when the girl and Solomon were enjoying each other's company, the brothers told her that foxes had gotten into the vineyard and she must leave and tend to the problem.

"The little foxes" are an example of the kinds of problems that can disturb or destroy a relationship. The girl wanted anything that could potentially cause problems between her and Solomon to be removed. It is often the "little foxes" that cause the biggest problems in marriage. These irritations must not be minimized or ignored, but identified so that, together, the couple can deal with them.

2.16 Solomon (the beloved) had left the girl for a while, but their commitment to each other kept their relationship strong. It is wonderful to belong to another and have someone belong to you, but belonging to each other is not the same as possessing each other. Togetherness doesn't require us to spend all our time in each other's company. In your love relationship, remember to allow your partner some room. Be willing to release your partner for his or her work or Christian service. Loving someone is like holding sand: close your hand tightly and you lose some; leave your hand open and all the sand remains.

3.1–4 Most scholars agree that in these verses, the girl was recalling a dream in which she became so concerned about her lover's whereabouts that she arose in the middle of the night to search for him. When you love someone, you will do all you can to ensure the safety of that person and care for his or her needs, even at a cost to your personal comfort. This shows up most often in small actions—walking upstairs to get someone you love a glass of water, leaving work early to attend some function your child is involved in, or sacrificing your personal comfort to tend to the needs of the ones you love.

until I brought him into my mother's house,
and into the chamber of her that conceived me.
5 I adjure you, O daughters of Jerusalem,
by the gazelles or the wild does:
do not stir up or awaken love
until it is ready!

3. Memories of engagement

6 What is that coming up from the wilderness,
like a column of smoke,
perfumed with myrrh and frankincense,
with all the fragrant powders of the merchant?
7 Look, it is the litter of Solomon!
Around it are sixty mighty men
of the mighty men of Israel,
8 all equipped with swords
and expert in war,
each with his sword at his thigh
because of alarms by night.
9 King Solomon made himself a palanquin
from the wood of Lebanon.
10 He made its posts of silver,
its back of gold, its seat of purple;
its interior was inlaid with love.[e]
Daughters of Jerusalem,
11 come out.
Look, O daughters of Zion,
at King Solomon,
at the crown with which his mother crowned him
on the day of his wedding,
on the day of the gladness of his heart.

4 How beautiful you are, my love,
how very beautiful!
Your eyes are doves
behind your veil.
Your hair is like a flock of goats,
moving down the slopes of Gilead.
2 Your teeth are like a flock of shorn ewes
that have come up from the washing,
all of which bear twins,
and not one among them is bereaved.
3 Your lips are like a crimson thread,
and your mouth is lovely.
Your cheeks are like halves of a pomegranate
behind your veil.

3.6 Ex 13.21,22 Deut 8.2 Song 1.13 4.12-14 Rev 5.8; 18.13

3.8 Ps 45.3; 91.5 Jer 50.9

3.11 Isa 62.5 Jer 2.2 Hos 2.19

4.1 Ps 45.11 Song 1.15 Ezek 16.14 Mic 7.14

4.3 Prov 10.13,20,21 16.21-24 Song 5.13,16

[e] Meaning of Heb uncertain

3.6–5.1 Here the scene changes. Some believe that the wedding procession is described in 3.6–11, the wedding night in 4.1–5.1, and the consummation of the marriage in 4.16–5.1. Another possible explanation is that the period of Solomon's engagement to the girl is being remembered. In the previous section (2.8–3.5), Solomon and the girl fell in love. In this section, Solomon returns to the girl in all his royal splendor (3.6–11), expresses his great love for her (4.1–5), and then proposes (4.7–15). The girl accepts (4.16), and Solomon responds to her acceptance (5.1).

3.7, 9 A litter, or palanquin, was a covered and curtained couch used for carrying a single passenger on the shoulders of men.

4.1–7 We feel like awkward onlookers when we read this intensely private and intimate exchange. In the ecstasy of their love, the lovers praise each other using beautiful imagery. Their words may seem strange to readers from a different culture, but their intense feelings of love and admiration are universal. Communicating love and expressing admiration in both words and actions can enhance every marriage.

4.4
Song 7.4

4 Your neck is like the tower of David,
built in courses;
on it hang a thousand bucklers,
all of them shields of warriors.

4.5
Song 2.16
6.2,3; 7.3

5 Your two breasts are like two fawns,
twins of a gazelle,
that feed among the lilies.
6 Until the day breathes
and the shadows flee,
I will hasten to the mountain of myrrh
and the hill of frankincense.
7 You are altogether beautiful, my love;
there is no flaw in you.

4.8
1 Kgs 4.33
2 Kgs 5.12
1 Chron 5.23
Song 5.1

8 Come with me from Lebanon, my bride;
come with me from Lebanon.
Depart[f] from the peak of Amana,
from the peak of Senir and Hermon,
from the dens of lions,
from the mountains of leopards.

4.9
Ezek 16.11

9 You have ravished my heart, my sister, my bride,
you have ravished my heart with a glance of your eyes,
with one jewel of your necklace.
10 How sweet is your love, my sister, my bride!
how much better is your love than wine,
and the fragrance of your oils than any spice!

4.11
Song 7.9

11 Your lips distill nectar, my bride;
honey and milk are under your tongue;
the scent of your garments is like the scent of Lebanon.

4.12
Gen 29.3
Prov 5.15-18

12 A garden locked is my sister, my bride,
a garden locked, a fountain sealed.

4.13
Ps 45.8
Song 1.12; 3.6
4.6

13 Your channel[g] is an orchard of pomegranates
with all choicest fruits,
henna with nard,
14 nard and saffron, calamus and cinnamon,
with all trees of frankincense,
myrrh and aloes,
with all chief spices—

4.15
Zech 14.8

15 a garden fountain, a well of living water,
and flowing streams from Lebanon.

4.16
Song 1.13; 2.3
4.13
2 Cor 9.10-15
2 Pet 3.18

16 Awake, O north wind,
and come, O south wind!
Blow upon my garden
that its fragrance may be wafted abroad.
Let my beloved come to his garden,
and eat its choicest fruits.

[f] Or *Look* [g] Meaning of Heb uncertain

4.4 A buckler is a small, round shield held by a handle at arm's length.

4.12 In comparing his bride to a locked garden, Solomon was praising her virginity. Virginity, considered old-fashioned by many in today's culture, has always been God's plan for unmarried people—and with good reason. Sex without marriage is cheap. It cannot compare with the joy of giving yourself completely to the one who is totally committed to you.

4.15 Solomon's bride was as refreshing to him as a fountain or a stream. Sometimes the familiarity that comes with marriage causes us to forget the overwhelming feelings of love we shared at the beginning. Partners in marriage should continually work at refreshing each other by an encouraging word, an unexpected gift, a change of pace, a surprise call or note, or even a withholding of a discussion of some problem until the proper time. Your spouse needs you to be a haven of refreshment, because the rest of the world usually isn't.

5 I come to my garden, my sister, my bride;
I gather my myrrh with my spice,
I eat my honeycomb with my honey,
I drink my wine with my milk.

Eat, friends, drink,
and be drunk with love.

5.1 Prov 9.5 Song 1.13; 4.9 6.2 Isa 55.1 Jn 3.29

4. A troubling dream

2 I slept, but my heart was awake.
Listen! my beloved is knocking.
"Open to me, my sister, my love,
my dove, my perfect one;
for my head is wet with dew,
my locks with the drops of the night."
3 I had put off my garment;
how could I put it on again?
I had bathed my feet;
how could I soil them?
4 My beloved thrust his hand into the opening,
and my inmost being yearned for him.
5 I arose to open to my beloved,
and my hands dripped with myrrh,
my fingers with liquid myrrh,
upon the handles of the bolt.
6 I opened to my beloved,
but my beloved had turned and was gone.
My soul failed me when he spoke.
I sought him, but did not find him;
I called him, but he gave no answer.
7 Making their rounds in the city
the sentinels found me;
they beat me, they wounded me,
they took away my mantle,
those sentinels of the walls.
8 I adjure you, O daughters of Jerusalem,
if you find my beloved,
tell him this:
I am faint with love.

9 What is your beloved more than another beloved,
O fairest among women?
What is your beloved more than another beloved,
that you thus adjure us?

5.3 Gen 19.2

5.5 Song 5.13

5.6 Prov 1.28 Song 3.1; 5.2 6.1

5.7 Song 3.3

5.8 Song 2.7; 3.5

5.9 Song 6.1

5.2ff This new section tells how the couple's marriage grew and matured in spite of problems. Apparently, some time had passed since the wedding, and the girl felt as though some indifference had developed in their relationship. But she quickly moved to correct the problem by searching out her husband (5.6–8).

5.2–7 It is inevitable that, with the passing of time and the growth of familiarity, a marriage will start to lose its initial sparkle. Glances and touches no longer produce the same emotional response. Conflicts and pressures creep in, causing you to lose your tenderness toward your spouse. The world is not a haven for lovers; in fact, external stress often works against the marriage relationship. But spouses can learn to be havens for each other. If intimacy and passion decline, remember that they can be renewed and regenerated. Take time to remember those first thrills, the excitement of sex, your spouse's strengths, and the commitment you made. When you focus on the positives, reconciliation and renewal can result.

5.7 The girl was alone outside during the night. In Old Testament times, she would have been looked upon as a criminal or a prostitute and treated as such. This image symbolizes the pain she felt at being separated from her lover. Note: a *mantle* was a cloak or coat worn as an outer garment.

5.10 1 Sam 16.12 Ps 45.2

10 My beloved is all radiant and ruddy,
distinguished among ten thousand.
11 His head is the finest gold;
his locks are wavy,
black as a raven.

5.12 Song 1.15; 4.1

12 His eyes are like doves
beside springs of water,
bathed in milk,
fitly set.[h]

5.13 Song 2.1; 5.5 6.2

13 His cheeks are like beds of spices,
yielding fragrance.
His lips are lilies,
distilling liquid myrrh.
14 His arms are rounded gold,
set with jewels.
His body is ivory work,[h]
encrusted with sapphires.[i]

5.15 1 Kgs 4.33 Song 7.4

15 His legs are alabaster columns,
set upon bases of gold.
His appearance is like Lebanon,
choice as the cedars.

5.16 2 Sam 1.23 Song 7.9

16 His speech is most sweet,
and he is altogether desirable.
This is my beloved and this is my friend,
O daughters of Jerusalem.

6 Where has your beloved gone,
O fairest among women?
Which way has your beloved turned,
that we may seek him with you?

6.2 Song 1.7; 2.1 4.16; 5.1,13

2 My beloved has gone down to his garden,
to the beds of spices,
to pasture his flock in the gardens,
and to gather lilies.

6.3 Song 2.16; 4.5 7.10

3 I am my beloved's and my beloved is mine;
he pastures his flock among the lilies.

5. Praising the bride's beauty

6.4 1 Kgs 14.17 Song 6.10

4 You are beautiful as Tirzah, my love,
comely as Jerusalem,
terrible as an army with banners.
5 Turn away your eyes from me,
for they overwhelm me!

h Meaning of Heb uncertain i Heb *lapis lazuli*

5.16 The girl calls Solomon her "friend." In a healthy marriage, lovers are also good friends. Too often people are driven into marriage by the exciting feelings of love before they take the time to develop a deep friendship that includes listening, sharing, and showing understanding for the other's likes and dislikes. Friendship takes time, but it makes a love relationship much deeper and far more satisfying.

6.3 The girl said that she and her beloved belonged to each other – they had given themselves to each other unreservedly. No matter how close we may be to our parents or our best friends, it is only in marriage that we realize complete union of mind, heart, and body.

6.4 Tirzah was a city about 35 miles northeast of Jerusalem. Its name means "pleasure" or "beauty." Jeroboam made Tirzah the first capital of the divided northern kingdom (1 Kings 14.17). "Terrible as an army with banners" means that she must have been awe-inspiring, like a mighty army readying for battle.

Your hair is like a flock of goats,
moving down the slopes of Gilead.
6 Your teeth are like a flock of ewes,
that have come up from the washing;
all of them bear twins,
and not one among them is bereaved.
7 Your cheeks are like halves of a pomegranate
behind your veil.
8 There are sixty queens and eighty concubines,
and maidens without number.
9 My dove, my perfect one, is the only one,
the darling of her mother,
flawless to her that bore her.
The maidens saw her and called her happy;
the queens and concubines also, and they praised her.
10 "Who is this that looks forth like the dawn,
fair as the moon, bright as the sun,
terrible as an army with banners?"

11 I went down to the nut orchard,
to look at the blossoms of the valley,
to see whether the vines had budded,
whether the pomegranates were in bloom.
12 Before I was aware, my fancy set me
in a chariot beside my prince.[j]

13[k] Return, return, O Shulammite!
Return, return, that we may look upon you.

Why should you look upon the Shulammite,
as upon a dance before two armies?[l]

7 How graceful are your feet in sandals,
O queenly maiden!
Your rounded thighs are like jewels,
the work of a master hand.
2 Your navel is a rounded bowl
that never lacks mixed wine.
Your belly is a heap of wheat,
encircled with lilies.
3 Your two breasts are like two fawns,
twins of a gazelle.
4 Your neck is like an ivory tower.
Your eyes are pools in Heshbon,
by the gate of Bath-rabbim.
Your nose is like a tower of Lebanon,
overlooking Damascus.

6.8 1 Kgs 11.3 Song 1.3
6.9 Song 2.14; 5.2
6.10 Job 31.26 Song 6.4 Mt 17.2 Rev 1.16
6.11 Song 4.13; 7.12
6.13 Gen 32.2 Judg 21.21 2 Sam 17.24
7.1ff Ps 45.13
7.3 Song 4.5
7.4 Num 21.26 Song 4.4

[j] Cn: Meaning of Heb uncertain [k] Ch 7.1 in Heb [l] Or *dance of Mahanaim*

6.8, 9 Solomon did indeed have many wives and concubines (1 Kings 11.3). Polygamy, though not condoned, was common in Old Testament days. Solomon says his love for this woman has not diminished since their wedding night, even though he has many other women available to him.

7.4, 5 The phrase, "your eyes are pools in Heshbon" suggests sparkling eyes. Heshbon was the ancient capital of the Amorites. Bath-rabbim was a gate of Heshbon. The "tower of Lebanon" was probably a watchtower (evidently a prominent one was seen as very beautiful). Carmel is the mountain range that overlooks the Mediterranean Sea and Palestine.

7.5 Isa 35.2

5 Your head crowns you like Carmel,
and your flowing locks are like purple;
a king is held captive in the tresses.[m]
6 How fair and pleasant you are,
O loved one, delectable maiden![n]
7 You are stately[o] as a palm tree,
and your breasts are like its clusters.

7.8 Song 2.5

8 I say I will climb the palm tree
and lay hold of its branches.
Oh, may your breasts be like clusters of the vine,
and the scent of your breath like apples,

7.9 Prov 23.31 Song 5.16

9 and your kisses[p] like the best wine
that goes down[q] smoothly,
gliding over lips and teeth.[r]

6. The bride's tender appeal

7.10 Ps 45.11 Song 2.16; 6.3

10 I am my beloved's,
and his desire is for me.
11 Come, my beloved,
let us go forth into the fields,
and lodge in the villages;
12 let us go out early to the vineyards,
and see whether the vines have budded,
whether the grape blossoms have opened
and the pomegranates are in bloom.
There I will give you my love.

7.13 Gen 30.14 Song 2.3 4.13,16

13 The mandrakes give forth fragrance,
and over our doors are all choice fruits,
new as well as old,
which I have laid up for you, O my beloved.

8 O that you were like a brother to me,
who nursed at my mother's breast!
If I met you outside, I would kiss you,
and no one would despise me.

8.2 Song 3.4

2 I would lead you and bring you
into the house of my mother,
and into the chamber of the one who bore me.[s]
I would give you spiced wine to drink,
the juice of my pomegranates.

8.3 Song 2.6

3 O that his left hand were under my head,
and that his right hand embraced me!

8.4 Song 2.7; 3.5

4 I adjure you, O daughters of Jerusalem,
do not stir up or awaken love
until it is ready!

[m] Meaning of Heb uncertain [n] Syr: Heb *in delights* [o] Heb *This your stature is* [p] Heb *palate* [q] Heb *down for my lover* [r] Gk Syr Vg: Heb *lips of sleepers* [s] Gk Syr: Heb *my mother; she (or you) will teach me*

7.10–13 As a marriage matures, there should be more love and freedom between marriage partners. Here the girl takes the initiative in lovemaking. Many cultures have stereotypes of the roles men and women play in lovemaking, but the security of true love gives both marriage partners the freedom to initiate acts of love and express their true feelings.

7.13 Mandrakes were a somewhat rare plant often thought to increase fertility. Mandrakes are also mentioned in Genesis 30.14–17.

8.1 In the ancient Near East, it was improper to show public affection except between family members. The girl is wishing she could freely show her lover affection even in public.

7. The power of love

5 Who is that coming up from the wilderness,
leaning upon her beloved?

Under the apple tree I awakened you.
There your mother was in labor with you;
there she who bore you was in labor.

6 Set me as a seal upon your heart,
as a seal upon your arm;
for love is strong as death,
passion fierce as the grave.
Its flashes are flashes of fire,
a raging flame.
7 Many waters cannot quench love,
neither can floods drown it.
If one offered for love
all the wealth of his house,
it would be utterly scorned.

8 We have a little sister,
and she has no breasts.
What shall we do for our sister,
on the day when she is spoken for?
9 If she is a wall,
we will build upon her a battlement of silver;
but if she is a door,
we will enclose her with boards of cedar.
10 I was a wall,
and my breasts were like towers;
then I was in his eyes
as one who brings[t] peace.
11 Solomon had a vineyard at Baal-hamon;
he entrusted the vineyard to keepers;
each one was to bring for its fruit a thousand pieces of silver.
12 My vineyard, my very own, is for myself;
you, O Solomon, may have the thousand,
and the keepers of the fruit two hundred!

13 O you who dwell in the gardens,
my companions are listening for your voice;
let me hear it.

8.5 Song 2.3; 3.6

8.6 Prov 6.34 Isa 49.16 Jer 22.24 Hag 2.23

8.8 Ezek 16.7

8.9 1 Kgs 6.15

8.11 Eccles 2.4 Song 1.6; 8.12 Isa 7.23 Mt 21.33

8.13 Song 1.7

[t] Or *finds*

8.6, 7 In this final description of their love, the girl includes some of its significant characteristics (see also 1 Corinthians 13). Love is as strong as death; it cannot be killed by time or disaster; and it cannot be bought for any price because it is freely given. Love is priceless, and even the richest king cannot buy it. It must be accepted as a gift from God and then shared within the guidelines God provides. Accept the love of your spouse as God's gift, and strive to make your love a reflection of the perfect love that comes from God himself.

8.8, 9 The girl is reflecting on the days when she was younger and under the care of her brothers, who wondered how to help her prepare for marriage. They decided that if she was like a wall, standing firm against sexual temptation, they would praise her. But if she was like a door, open to immorality, they would take steps to guard her from doing something foolish. In 8.10, she testifies that she has been persistent in her morality and thus has found favor in Solomon's eyes.

8.11, 12 The vineyard belongs to the girl and it is her right to assign it, but Solomon will enjoy its fruit. In a good marriage, there is no private property, for everything is shared between the partners. Note: Baal-hamon is mentioned only here in the Bible, and its location is unknown.

8.14
Song 2.7,9,17
4.6

14 Make haste, my beloved,
and be like a gazelle
or a young stag
upon the mountains of spices!

8.14 The love between Solomon and his bride did not diminish in intensity after their wedding night. The lovers relied on each other and kept no secrets from each other. Devotion and commitment were the keys to their relationship, just as they are in our relationships to our spouses and to God. The faithfulness of our marital love should reflect God's perfect faithfulness to us.

Paul shows how marriage represents Christ's relationship to his church (Ephesians 5.22–33), and John pictures the second coming as a great marriage feast for Christ and his bride, his faithful followers (Revelation 19.7, 8; 21.1, 2). Many theologians have thought the Song of Solomon is an allegory showing Christ's love for his church. It makes even better sense to say that it is a love poem about a real human love relationship, and that all loving, committed marriages reflect God's love.

ISAIAH

Amos becomes a prophet 760 B.C.	Hosea becomes a prophet 753	Micah becomes a prophet 742	Isaiah becomes a prophet 740	Ahaz becomes king of Judah 735	Hoshea becomes king of Israel 732	Israel falls to the Assyrians 722	Hezekiah becomes king of Judah 715

VITAL STATISTICS

PURPOSE:
To call the nation of Judah back to God and to tell of God's salvation through the Messiah

AUTHOR:
The prophet Isaiah, son of Amoz

DATE WRITTEN:
The events of chapters 1—39 occurred during Isaiah's ministry, so they were probably written about 700 B.C. Chapters 40—66, however, may have been written near the end of his life, about 681 B.C.

SETTING:
Isaiah is speaking and writing mainly in Jerusalem

KEY VERSE:
"But he was wounded for our transgressions, crushed for our iniquities; upon him was the punishment that made us whole, and by his bruises we are healed" (53.5).

KEY PEOPLE:
Isaiah, his two sons Shear-jashub and Maher-shalal-hash-baz

SPECIAL FEATURES:
The book of Isaiah contains both prose and poetry and uses personification (attributing personal qualities to divine beings or inanimate objects). Also, many of the prophecies in Isaiah contain predictions that foretell a soon-to-occur event and a distant future event at the same time.

SLOWLY he rose, and the crowd fell silent. Those at the back leaned forward, straining to hear. The atmosphere was electric. He spoke, and his carefully chosen words flew like swift arrows and found their mark. The great man, a spokesman for God, was warning . . . and condemning. The crowd became restless—shifting positions, clenching fists, and murmuring. Some agreed with his message, nodding their heads and weeping softly. But most were angry, and they began to shout back insults and threats. Such was the life of a prophet.

The "office" of prophet was instituted during the days of Samuel, the last of the judges. Prophets stood with the priests as God's special representatives. The role of the prophet was to speak for God, confronting the people and their leaders with God's commands and promises. Because of this confrontational stance and the continuing tendency of people to disobey God, true prophets usually were not very popular. Although their message often went unheeded, they faithfully and forcefully proclaimed the truth.

The book of Isaiah is the first of the writings of the Prophets in the Bible; and Isaiah, the author, is generally considered to be the greatest prophet. He was reared in an aristocratic home and married to a prophetess. In the beginning of his ministry he was well-liked. But, like most prophets, he soon became unpopular because his messages were so difficult to hear. He called the people to turn from their lives of sin and warned them of God's judgment and punishment. Isaiah had an active ministry for 60 years before he was executed during Manasseh's reign (according to tradition). As God's special messenger to Judah, Isaiah prophesied during the reigns of several of its rulers, and many of those messages are recorded in his book: Uzziah and Jotham, chapters 1—6; Ahaz, chapters 7—14; and Hezekiah, chapters 15—39.

The first half of the book of Isaiah (chapters 1—39) contains scathing denunciations and pronouncements as he calls Judah, Israel, and the surrounding nations to repent of their sins. However, the last 27 chapters (40—66) are filled with consolation and hope as Isaiah unfolds God's promise of future blessings through his Messiah.

As you read Isaiah, imagine this strong and courageous man of God, fearlessly proclaiming God's Word, and listen to his message in relation to your own life—*return, repent, and be renewed*. Then trust in God's *redemption* through Christ and *rejoice*. Your Savior has come, and he's coming again!

Manasseh becomes king of Judah 697

Isaiah's ministry ends 681

Josiah becomes king of Judah 640

THE BLUEPRINT

A. WORDS OF JUDGMENT (1.1—39.8)
1. The sins of Israel and Judah
2. Judgment against heathen nations
3. God's purpose in judgment
4. Jerusalem's true and false hopes
5. Events during the reign of Hezekiah

The 39 chapters in the first half of Isaiah generally carry the message of judgment for sin. Isaiah brings the message of judgment to Judah, Israel, and the surrounding heathen nations. Judah had a form of godliness, but in their hearts they were corrupt. Isaiah's warnings were intended to purify the people by helping them understand God's true nature and message. However, they ignored the repeated warnings that Isaiah brought. We need not repeat their error; rather, we should heed the prophetic voice.

B. WORDS OF COMFORT (40.1—66.24)
1. Israel's release from captivity
2. The future Redeemer
3. The future kingdom

The 27 chapters in the second half of Isaiah generally bring a message of forgiveness, comfort, and hope. This message of hope looks forward to the coming of the Messiah. Isaiah speaks more about the Messiah than does any other Old Testament prophet. He describes the Messiah as both a suffering servant and a sovereign Lord. The fact that the Messiah was to be both a suffering servant and a sovereign Lord could not be understood clearly until New Testament times. Based on what Jesus Christ has done, God freely offers forgiveness to all who turn to him in faith. This is God's message of comfort to us because those who heed it find eternal peace and fellowship with him.

MEGATHEMES

THEME	EXPLANATION	IMPORTANCE
Holiness	God is highly exalted above all his creatures. His moral perfection stands in contrast to evil people and nations. God is perfect and sinless in all his motives and actions, so he is in perfect control of his power, judgment, love, and mercy. His holy nature is our yardstick for morality.	Because God is without sin, he alone can help us with our sin. It is only right that we regard him as supreme in power and moral perfection. We must never treat God as common or ordinary. He alone deserves our devotion and praise. He is always truthful, fair, and just.
Punishment	Because God is holy, he requires his people to treat others justly. He promised to punish Israel, Judah, and other nations for faithless immorality and idolatry. True faith had degenerated into national pride and empty religious rituals.	We must trust in God alone and fulfill his commands. We cannot forsake justice nor give in to selfishness. If we harden our hearts against his message, punishment will surely come to us.
Salvation	Because God's judgment is coming, we need a Savior. No man or nation can be saved without God's help. Christ's perfect sacrifice for our sins is foretold and portrayed in Isaiah. All who trust God can be freed from their sin and restored to him.	Christ died to save us from our sin. We cannot save ourselves. He is willing to save all those who turn from their sin and come to him. Salvation is from God alone. No amount of good works can earn it.
Messiah	God will send the Messiah to save his people. He will set up his own kingdom as the faithful Prince of Peace who rules with righteousness. He will come as sovereign Lord, but he will do so as a servant who will die to take away sins.	Our trust must be in the Messiah, not in ourselves or in any nation or power. There is no hope unless we believe in him. Trust Christ fully and let him rule in your life as your sovereign Lord.
Hope	God promises comfort, deliverance, and restoration in his future kingdom. The Messiah will rule over his faithful followers in the age to come. Hope is possible because Christ is coming.	We can be refreshed since there is compassion for those who repent. No matter how bleak our situation or how evil the world is, we must continue to be God's faithful people who hope for his return.

A. WORDS OF JUDGMENT (1.1–39.8)

Isaiah begins by bringing a message of divine judgment for both Israel and Judah. Although the advance of the Assyrians poses a problem for Judah, God foretells the destruction of Assyria and other evil surrounding nations through the prophet Isaiah. This section ends with the Assyrian invasion being held off, demonstrating the clear unfolding of God's plan and promises for the nation at this time.

1. The sins of Israel and Judah

Messages to a rebellious people

1 The vision of Isaiah son of Amoz, which he saw concerning Judah and Jerusa- 1.1
lem in the days of Uzziah, Jotham, Ahaz, and Hezekiah, kings of Judah. 2 Kgs 15.1,13 18.1 Isa 2.1; 40.9

2 Hear, O heavens, and listen, O earth;
for the LORD has spoken:
I reared children and brought them up,
but they have rebelled against me.

3 The ox knows its owner,
and the donkey its master's crib;
but Israel does not know,
my people do not understand.

1.2 Deut 32.1 Jer 3.22 Isa 65.2 Mic 1.2
1.3 Jer 8.7

4 Ah, sinful nation,
people laden with iniquity,
offspring who do evil,
children who deal corruptly,
who have forsaken the LORD,
who have despised the Holy One of Israel,
who are utterly estranged!

1.4 Song 2.7,9,17 4.6 Isa 5.24

5 Why do you seek further beatings?
Why do you continue to rebel?
The whole head is sick,
and the whole heart faint.

6 From the sole of the foot even to the head,
there is no soundness in it,
but bruises and sores
and bleeding wounds;
they have not been drained, or bound up,
or softened with oil.

1.5 Ps 38.3

1.1 Isaiah was a prophet while the nation of Israel was divided into two kingdoms–Israel in the north, and Judah in the south. The northern kingdom had sinned greatly against God, and the southern kingdom was headed in the same direction–perverting justice, oppressing the poor, turning from God to idols, and looking for military aid from heathen nations rather than from God. Isaiah came primarily as a prophet to Judah, but his message was also for Israel. Sometimes "Israel" refers to both kingdoms. In fact, Isaiah lived to see the destruction and captivity of the northern kingdom in 722 B.C. Thus, his ministry began as one of warning.

1.2 Isaiah had a vision of what God wanted him to communicate to the people both because he was specially selected for God's use and also because he was receptive to God's messages–he was mentally, morally, and spiritually tuned in to God. He was, therefore, guided by the Holy Spirit in such a way as to convey God's exact thinking to the people. If we are ready to listen to God, we will hear his messages through his Word, other believers, and the Holy Spirit.

1.2–4 The people of Judah were sinning greatly and did not even care. God brought charges against them through Isaiah because they had rebelled, forgotten God, and broken their moral and spiritual contract (the covenant) with him (Deuteronomy 28). By breaking the contract they were bringing God's punishment upon themselves. First God gave them prosperity and they didn't serve him; then he sent them warnings and they refused to listen; now he would bring the fire of his judgment.

1.3 A *crib* is a trough (or manger) for feeding animals.

1.4–9 As long as the people of Judah continued to sin, they cut themselves off from God's help and isolated themselves. Has sin ever made you feel lonely and separated from God? Remember, God does not abandon you–it is your sin that cuts you off from him. The only sure cure for this kind of loneliness is to restore a meaningful relationship with God by confessing your sin, obeying his instructions, and communicating regularly with him (see Psalm 140.13; Isaiah 1.16–19; 1 John 1.9).

1.7 Was this destruction taking place at that time? Judah was attacked many times during Isaiah's lifetime. To be devastated by foreigners was the worst kind of judgment. This verse could be a picture of the results of these invasions or a prediction of the coming invasion of Israel by Assyria. Most likely it pointed to Babylon's

1.7
Lev 26.33
Jer 44.6

7 Your country lies desolate,
your cities are burned with fire;
in your very presence
aliens devour your land;
it is desolate, as overthrown by foreigners.
8 And daughter Zion is left
like a booth in a vineyard,
like a shelter in a cucumber field,
like a besieged city.

1.9
Isa 10.20-22
11.11,16
Rom 9.29

9 If the LORD of hosts
had not left us a few survivors,
we would have been like Sodom,
and become like Gomorrah.

1.10
Ezek 16.46

10 Hear the word of the LORD,
you rulers of Sodom!
Listen to the teaching of our God,
you people of Gomorrah!

1.11
Jer 6.20
Mal 1.10

11 What to me is the multitude of your sacrifices?
says the LORD;
I have had enough of burnt offerings of rams
and the fat of fed beasts;
I do not delight in the blood of bulls,
or of lambs, or of goats.

1.12
1 Chron 23.31
Jer 7.9,10

12 When you come to appear before me,[a]
who asked this from your hand?
Trample my courts no more;
13 bringing offerings is futile;
incense is an abomination to me.

[a] Or *see my face*

ISAIAH served as a prophet to Judah from 740–681 B.C.		
	Climate of the times	Society was in a great upheaval. Under King Ahaz and King Manasseh the people reverted to idolatry, and there was even child sacrifice.
	Main message	Although judgment from other nations was inevitable, the people could still have a special relationship with God.
	Importance of message	Sometimes we must suffer judgment and discipline before we are restored to God.
	Contemporary prophets	Hosea (753–715) Micah (742–687)

future invasion of Judah in 586 B.C.

1.9 Sodom and Gomorrah were two cities that God completely destroyed for their great wickedness (Genesis 19.1–25). They are mentioned elsewhere in the Bible as examples of God's judgment against sin (Jeremiah 50.40; Ezekiel 16.46–63; Matthew 11.23, 24; Jude 1.7). A "few survivors" were spared by God because they were faithful.

1.10 Isaiah compared the leaders of Judah to the leaders of Sodom and Gomorrah. To hear what God wanted to say, the people had to listen and be willing to obey. When we can't hear God's message, perhaps we are not listening carefully or we are not truly willing to do what he says.

1.10–15 God was unhappy with their sacrifices, but he was not revoking the system of sacrifices he had initiated with Moses. Instead, he was calling for their sincere faith and devotion. The leaders were carefully making the traditional sacrifices at holy celebrations, but they were still unfaithful to God in their hearts. Sacrifices were to be an outward sign of their inward faith in God, but the outward signs became empty because no inward faith existed. Why, then, did they continue to offer sacrifices? Like many people today, they had come to place more faith in the rituals of their religion than in the God they worshiped. Examine your own religious practices: do they spring from your faith in the living God? God does not take pleasure in our outward expressions if our inward faith is missing (see Deuteronomy 10.12–16; 1 Samuel 15.22, 23; Psalm 51.16–19).

1.12, 13 "New moon and sabbath" refers to monthly offerings (Numbers 28.11–14) and weekly and special annual sabbaths on the day of atonement and festival of booths (Leviticus 16.31, 23–34, 39). For all the festivals, see the chart in Leviticus 23. Although the people did not feel sorry for their sins, they continued to offer sacrifices for forgiveness. Gifts and sacrifices mean nothing to God when they come from a corrupt heart. God wants us to love him, trust him, and turn from our sin; after that, he will be pleased with our "sacrifices" of time, money, or service.

New moon and sabbath and calling of convocation—
I cannot endure solemn assemblies with iniquity.
14 Your new moons and your appointed festivals
my soul hates;
they have become a burden to me,
I am weary of bearing them.
15 When you stretch out your hands,
I will hide my eyes from you;
even though you make many prayers,
I will not listen;
your hands are full of blood.
16 Wash yourselves; make yourselves clean;
remove the evil of your doings
from before my eyes;
cease to do evil,
17 learn to do good;
seek justice,
rescue the oppressed,
defend the orphan,
plead for the widow.

18 Come now, let us argue it out,
says the LORD:
though your sins are like scarlet,
they shall be like snow;
though they are red like crimson,
they shall become like wool.
19 If you are willing and obedient,
you shall eat the good of the land;
20 but if you refuse and rebel,
you shall be devoured by the sword;
for the mouth of the LORD has spoken.

21 How the faithful city
has become a whore!
She that was full of justice,
righteousness lodged in her—
but now murderers!
22 Your silver has become dross,
your wine is mixed with water.
23 Your princes are rebels
and companions of thieves.
Everyone loves a bribe
and runs after gifts.
They do not defend the orphan,
and the widow's cause does not come before them.

24 Therefore says the Sovereign, the LORD of hosts, the Mighty One of Israel:

1.15
Isa 59.2
Mic 3.4

1.16
Ps 26.6
Isa 52.11
Jer 25.5

1.17
Jer 22.3

1.18
Ps 51.7
Isa 43.26; 44.22
Rev 7.14

1.19
Deut 30.15,16

1.23
Ex 23.8
Jer 5.28
Ezek 22.7
Mic 7.3

1.18 Scarlet was the color of a deep-red permanent dye. Its deep stain was virtually impossible to remove from clothing, and the stain of sin seems equally permanent. But God can remove the stain of sin from our lives as he promised to do for the Israelites. We don't have to go through life permanently soiled. If we are willing and obedient, God's Word assures us that Christ forgives and removes our most indelible stains (Psalm 51.1–7).

1.21, 22 God compares the actions of his people to someone who is unfaithful in marriage. The people had turned from the worship of the true God to worshiping idols. Their faith was defective, impure, and diluted. Idolatry, outward or inward, is spiritual adultery, breaking our commitment to God in order to love something else. Jesus described the people of his day as adulterous, even though they were religiously strict. As the church, we are the "bride" of Christ (Revelation 19.7), and by faith we can be clothed in his righteousness. Has your faith become impure? Ask God to restore you. Keep your devotion to him strong and pure.

Ah, I will pour out my wrath on my enemies,
  and avenge myself on my foes!

1.25 Ezek 22.19-22 Mal 3.3

25 I will turn my hand against you;
  I will smelt away your dross as with lye
  and remove all your alloy.

1.26 Isa 33.5 Zech 8.3

26 And I will restore your judges as at the first,
  and your counselors as at the beginning.
Afterward you shall be called the city of righteousness,
  the faithful city.

27 Zion shall be redeemed by justice,
  and those in her who repent, by righteousness.

1.28 Ps 9.5 2 Thess 1.8,9

28 But rebels and sinners shall be destroyed together,
  and those who forsake the LORD shall be consumed.
29 For you shall be ashamed of the oaks
  in which you delighted;
and you shall blush for the gardens
  that you have chosen.
30 For you shall be like an oak
  whose leaf withers,
  and like a garden without water.

1.31 Isa 33.11-14 Mt 3.12

31 The strong shall become like tinder,
  and their work[b] like a spark;
they and their work shall burn together,
  with no one to quench them.

Walk in the light of the Lord

2 The word that Isaiah son of Amoz saw concerning Judah and Jerusalem.

2.2 Isa 66.20 Mic 4.1,2

2 In days to come
  the mountain of the LORD's house
shall be established as the highest of the mountains,
  and shall be raised above the hills;
all the nations shall stream to it.

2.3 Isa 51.4,5

3 Many peoples shall come and say,
"Come, let us go up to the mountain of the LORD,
  to the house of the God of Jacob;
that he may teach us his ways
  and that we may walk in his paths."
For out of Zion shall go forth instruction,
  and the word of the LORD from Jerusalem.

[b] Or *its makers*

1.25 God promised to refine his people as metal is purged with lye in a smelting pot. This process involves melting the metal and skimming off the impure slag until the worker can see his own image in the liquid metal. We must be willing to submit to God, allowing him to remove our sin so that we might reflect his image.

1.26 Isaiah often speaks with both the present and the future in mind. His prophecies do not necessarily apply to only one event, but may apply to a series of present and future events.

1.29, 30 Throughout history, the oak tree has been a symbol of strength. Ezekiel mentions that groves of oak trees were used as places for idol worship (Ezekiel 6.13). Are you devoted to symbols of strength and power that rival God's place in your life? Do you have interests and commitments where your love for them borders on worship? Make God your first loyalty; everything else will fade in time and burn away under his scrutiny.

1.31 A spark set to tinder ignites a quick, devouring fire. God compares strong men whose evil deeds devour them to burning tinder. Our lives can be destroyed quickly by a small but deadly spark of evil. What potential "fire hazards" do you need to remove?

2.2 The temple was built on Mount Moriah, highly visible to all the people of Jerusalem. For more on the significance of the temple, see the note on 2 Chronicles 5.1ff. In the last days, the temple will be attractive not for its architecture and prominence, but because of God's presence and influence.

2.2–4 God gave Isaiah the gift of seeing the future. Here God showed Isaiah what would eventually happen to Jerusalem. Revelation 21 depicts the glorious fulfillment of this prophecy in the new earth, where only those whose names are written in God's book will be allowed to enter. God made a covenant (promise) with his people and will never break it. God's faithfulness gives us hope for the future.

4 He shall judge between the nations,
and shall arbitrate for many peoples;
they shall beat their swords into plowshares,
and their spears into pruning hooks;
nation shall not lift up sword against nation,
neither shall they learn war any more.

5 O house of Jacob,
come, let us walk
in the light of the LORD!
6 For you have forsaken the ways of[c] your people,
O house of Jacob.
Indeed they are full of diviners[d] from the east
and of soothsayers like the Philistines,
and they clasp hands with foreigners.
7 Their land is filled with silver and gold,
and there is no end to their treasures;
their land is filled with horses,
and there is no end to their chariots.
8 Their land is filled with idols;
they bow down to the work of their hands,
to what their own fingers have made.
9 And so people are humbled,
and everyone is brought low—
do not forgive them!
10 Enter into the rock,
and hide in the dust
from the terror of the LORD,
and from the glory of his majesty.
11 The haughty eyes of people shall be brought low,
and the pride of everyone shall be humbled;
and the LORD alone will be exalted
in that day.
12 For the LORD of hosts has a day
against all that is proud and lofty,
against all that is lifted up and high;[e]
13 against all the cedars of Lebanon,
lofty and lifted up;
and against all the oaks of Bashan;

2.4 Isa 11.6-9 Hos 2.18 Joel 3.10 Zech 9.10

2.5 Isa 60.1,2, 19,20 1 Jn 1.5,7

2.6 2 Kgs 1.2

2.8 Ps 115.4-8 Isa 44.17

2.10 Rev 6.15,16

2.11 Isa 13.11

2.12 Job 40.11,12 Mal 4.1

2.13 Isa 10.33,34 Zech 11.2

[c] Heb lacks *the ways of* [d] Cn: Heb lacks *of diviners* [e] Cn Compare Gk: Heb *low*

2.4 We are told here of a wonderful future of peace when instruments of war will be converted to instruments of farming, when we will be taught God's laws and will obey them. We know that one day God will remove all sin that causes war, conflict, and disruption. Yet we do not need to wait to obey God. In 2.5, we are encouraged along with Judah to obey God now. He has given us his Word to direct and guide us to obey him now. Some benefits of obedience we will receive only in the future. But we may enjoy some benefits now as we apply God's Word to our lives.

2.6 "Diviners from the east" were sorcerers. They were following practices of the Assyrian Empire, which was influencing Judah politically and spiritually. The "soothsayers like the Philistines" were those who claimed to know and control the future by the power of demons or evil spirits. These practices were forbidden by God (see Leviticus 19.26; Deuteronomy 18.10, 14). The Philistines worshiped Dagon, Ashtoreth, and Baal-zebub. During the more sinful periods of their history, the people of Israel worshiped these heathen gods along with Jehovah, and even gave them Hebrew names.

2.8, 9 Under the reign of evil kings, idol worship flourished in both Israel and Judah. A few good kings in Judah stopped it during their reigns. Though very few people worship carved or molded images, worshiping objects that symbolize power still goes on. We worship cars, homes, sports stars, celebrities, and money. Idol worship is bad because (1) it insults God when we worship something he created rather than worshiping him; (2) it keeps us from knowing and serving God when we put our confidence in anything other than him; (3) it causes us to rely on our own efforts rather than on God. (See also Deuteronomy 27.15.)

2.12 The "day" of the Lord of hosts is the day of judgment, the time when God will judge both evil and good. That day will come, and we will want a proper relationship with God when it does. He alone must be exalted (2.11, 17) as the first step toward developing that relationship.

14 against all the high mountains,
and against all the lofty hills;
15 against every high tower,
and against every fortified wall;
2.16 Isa 23.1,14
16 against all the ships of Tarshish,
and against all the beautiful craft.[f]
17 The haughtiness of people shall be humbled,
and the pride of everyone shall be brought low;
and the LORD alone will be exalted on that day.
2.18 Isa 21.9 Mic 1.7
18 The idols shall utterly pass away.
2.19 Ps 18.7 Hag 2.6,7
19 Enter the caves of the rocks
and the holes of the ground,
from the terror of the LORD,
and from the glory of his majesty,
when he rises to terrify the earth.
2.20 Isa 30.22
20 On that day people will throw away
to the moles and to the bats
their idols of silver and their idols of gold,
which they made for themselves to worship,
21 to enter the caverns of the rocks
and the clefts in the crags,
from the terror of the LORD,
and from the glory of his majesty,
when he rises to terrify the earth.
2.22 Ps 8.4; 144.3,4 Jer 17.5
22 Turn away from mortals,
who have only breath in their nostrils,
for of what account are they?

Isaiah warns of judgment on Judah

3.1 Ezek 4.16
3 For now the Sovereign, the LORD of hosts,
is taking away from Jerusalem and from Judah
support and staff—
all support of bread,
and all support of water—
3.2 Isa 9.14,15
2 warrior and soldier,
judge and prophet,
diviner and elder,
3 captain of fifty
and dignitary,
counselor and skillful magician
and expert enchanter.
3.4 Eccles 10.16
4 And I will make boys their princes,
and babes shall rule over them.

[f] Compare Gk: Meaning of Heb uncertain

2.15–17 The "high tower" refers to security based on military fortresses; the "ships of Tarshish" are commercial trade ships referring to economic prosperity; "beautiful craft" are the stately pleasure vessels. Nothing can compare or rival the place God must have in our hearts and minds. To place our hope elsewhere is nothing but false pride. Place your confidence in God alone.

2.19 See Revelation 6.15–17 for a description of the fear of God's enemies in the day of his wrath.

2.22 People seem very limited when compared to God. They can be unreliable, selfish, and short-sighted. Yet we trust our lives and futures more readily to mortal human beings than to the all-knowing God. Beware of people who want you to trust them instead of God. Remember that only God is completely reliable, because only God loves us with an eternal love (Psalm 100.5).

3.1–3 Jerusalem besieged, her leaders destroyed—this unhappy picture would soon become a reality. Disobedience brought the people serious affliction and great destruction, as God had warned (Deuteronomy 28).

3.2 Isaiah was not condoning the use of sorcerers (diviners) by including them on this list. He was showing how far the nation had sunk. See the note on 2.6.

3.5–9 People have a terrible handicap when they become blind to their own sinfulness. The results are broken relationships, authority out of control, lack of concern for the needy, and, worst of all, defiance toward God. Spiritual blindness is a matter of life and death, not merely inconvenience.

5 The people will be oppressed,
everyone by another
and everyone by a neighbor;
the youth will be insolent to the elder,
and the base to the honorable.

6 Someone will even seize a relative,
a member of the clan, saying,
"You have a cloak;
you shall be our leader,
and this heap of ruins
shall be under your rule."
7 But the other will cry out on that day, saying,
"I will not be a healer;
in my house there is neither bread nor cloak;
you shall not make me
leader of the people."
8 For Jerusalem has stumbled
and Judah has fallen,
because their speech and their deeds are against the LORD,
defying his glorious presence.

9 The look on their faces bears witness against them;
they proclaim their sin like Sodom,
they do not hide it.
Woe to them!
For they have brought evil on themselves.
10 Tell the innocent how fortunate they are,
for they shall eat the fruit of their labors.
11 Woe to the guilty! How unfortunate they are,
for what their hands have done shall be done to them.
12 My people — children are their oppressors,
and women rule over them.
O my people, your leaders mislead you,
and confuse the course of your paths.

13 The LORD rises to argue his case;
he stands to judge the peoples.
14 The LORD enters into judgment
with the elders and princes of his people:
It is you who have devoured the vineyard;
the spoil of the poor is in your houses.

3.5 Jer 9.3-8 Mic 7.3-6
3.7 Ezek 34.4
3.8 Isa 65.3,5
3.9 Gen 13.13 Prov 8.36
3.10 Deut 28.1-14
3.11 Deut 28.15-68
3.13 Hos 4.1 Mic 6.2
3.14 Job 24.9,14 Ps 10.9; 14.4 Ezek 18.12 Jas 2.6

3.9–11 Sin is self-destructive. In today's world, sinful living often appears glamorous, exciting, and clever. But sin is wrong, regardless of how society perceives it, because in the long run sin destroys us and makes us miserable. Thus God tries to protect us by warning us about the harm we do to ourselves by sinning. Those who are proud of their sins will receive from God the punishment they deserve. They have rejected God's path to life (see Psalm 1), and the only alternative is the path to destruction.

3.10, 11 Eventually the faithful will receive God's reward and the wicked will receive his punishment. It is disheartening to see the wicked prosper while we get farther behind as we follow God's plan. Yet we must hold on to God's truth and take heart! God will bring about justice in the end, and he will reward those who have been faithful.

3.14 The elders and princes were responsible to help people, but instead they defrauded the poor. Because they were unjust, Isaiah said the leaders would be the first to receive God's wrath. Leaders will be held accountable for how they lead. If you are in a position of leadership, you must lead according to God's just commands. Corruption will bring God's wrath, especially if others follow your example.

3.14 Why is justice so important in the Bible? (1) Justice is part of God's nature; it is the way he runs the universe. (2) It is a desire of every person. Even as sinners, we all want justice for ourselves. (3) When government and church leaders are unjust, the poor and powerless suffer. Thus they are hindered from worshiping God. (4) God holds the poor in high regard. They are the ones most likely to turn to him for help and comfort. Injustice, then, attacks God's children. When we do nothing to help the oppressed we are in fact joining with the oppressor (3.15). Because we follow a just God, we must uphold justice.

3.15 Ps 94.5

15 What do you mean by crushing my people,
by grinding the face of the poor? says the Lord GOD of hosts.

16 The LORD said:
Because the daughters of Zion are haughty
and walk with outstretched necks,
glancing wantonly with their eyes,
mincing along as they go,
tinkling with their feet;
17 the Lord will afflict with scabs
the heads of the daughters of Zion,
and the LORD will lay bare their secret parts.

18 In that day the Lord will take away the finery of the anklets, the headbands,
and the crescents; 19 the pendants, the bracelets, and the scarfs; 20 the headdresses,
the armlets, the sashes, the perfume boxes, and the amulets; 21 the signet rings and
nose rings; 22 the festal robes, the mantles, the cloaks, and the handbags; 23 the garments of gauze, the linen garments, the turbans, and the veils.

3.24 Esth 2.12 Isa 15.3 1 Pet 3.3

24 Instead of perfume there will be a stench;
and instead of a sash, a rope;
and instead of well-set hair, baldness;
and instead of a rich robe, a binding of sackcloth;
instead of beauty, shame.[g]

3.25 Isa 65.12 Lam 2.10

25 Your men shall fall by the sword
and your warriors in battle.
26 And her gates shall lament and mourn;
ravaged, she shall sit upon the ground.

4.1 Isa 54.4

4 Seven women shall take hold of one man in that day, saying,
"We will eat our own bread and wear our own clothes;
just let us be called by your name;
take away our disgrace."

God's holy people will be cleansed

4.2-4 Ex 32.32 Ps 72.16 Isa 28.6; 62.12 Joel 2.32 Obad 17 Lk 10.20

4.5 Num 9.15-23

4.6 Ps 27.5 Isa 32.1,2

2 On that day the branch of the LORD shall be beautiful and glorious, and the
fruit of the land shall be the pride and glory of the survivors of Israel. 3 Whoever is
left in Zion and remains in Jerusalem will be called holy, everyone who has been
recorded for life in Jerusalem, 4 once the Lord has washed away the filth of the
daughters of Zion and cleansed the bloodstains of Jerusalem from its midst by a
spirit of judgment and by a spirit of burning. 5 Then the LORD will create over the
whole site of Mount Zion and over its places of assembly a cloud by day and smoke
and the shining of a flaming fire by night. Indeed over all the glory there will be a
canopy. 6 It will serve as a pavilion, a shade by day from the heat, and a refuge and
a shelter from the storm and rain.

[g] Q Ms: MT lacks *shame*

3.16–26 The women of Judah had placed their emphasis on clothing and jewelry rather than on God. They dressed to be noticed, to gain approval, and to be fashionable. Yet they ignored the real purpose for their lives. Instead of being concerned about the oppression around them (3.14, 15), they were self-serving and self-centered. Those who abuse their possessions will end up with nothing. These verses are not an indictment against clothing and jewelry, but a judgment on those who use them lavishly while remaining blind to the needs of others. When God blesses you with money or position, don't flaunt it. Use what you have to help others, not to impress them.

4.2–4 In the midst of the tribulation predicted by Isaiah, some people will be protected by God's loving grace. Those protected will become God's people when Messiah rules the earth (Jeremiah 23.5, 6; Zechariah 6.12, 13). Their distinctive mark will be their holiness, not wealth or prestige. This holiness comes from a sincere desire to obey God and from wholehearted devotion to him. Evil will not always continue as it does now. God will put an end to all evil, and his faithful followers will share in his glorious reign.

God's people are his vineyard

5 Let me sing for my beloved
my love-song concerning his vineyard:
My beloved had a vineyard
on a very fertile hill.
2 He dug it and cleared it of stones,
and planted it with choice vines;
he built a watchtower in the midst of it,
and hewed out a wine vat in it;
he expected it to yield grapes,
but it yielded wild grapes.

3 And now, inhabitants of Jerusalem
and people of Judah,
judge between me
and my vineyard.
4 What more was there to do for my vineyard
that I have not done in it?
When I expected it to yield grapes,
why did it yield wild grapes?

5 And now I will tell you
what I will do to my vineyard.
I will remove its hedge,
and it shall be devoured;
I will break down its wall,
and it shall be trampled down.
6 I will make it a waste;
it shall not be pruned or hoed,
and it shall be overgrown with briers and thorns;
I will also command the clouds
that they rain no rain upon it.

7 For the vineyard of the LORD of hosts
is the house of Israel,
and the people of Judah
are his pleasant planting;
he expected justice,
but saw bloodshed;
righteousness,
but heard a cry!
8 Ah, you who join house to house,
who add field to field,
until there is room for no one but you,
and you are left to live alone
in the midst of the land!
9 The LORD of hosts has sworn in my hearing:
Surely many houses shall be desolate,
large and beautiful houses, without inhabitant.
10 For ten acres of vineyard shall yield but one bath,

5.1 Ps 80.8 Jer 12.10
5.2 Jer 2.21 Mk 11.13
5.4 Jer 7.25,26 Mt 23.37
5.5 Lam 1.15 Lk 21.24 Rev 11.2
5.6 Jer 14.1-22 25.11
5.8 Jer 22.13-17 Mic 2.2
5.9 Mt 23.38
5.10 Hag 1.6; 2.16

5.1–7 The lesson of the vineyard shows that God's chosen nation was to bear fruit—to carry out his work, to uphold justice. It did bear fruit, but the fruit was wild. This passage uses plays on words: the Hebrew words for *justice* and *bloodshed* sound very much alike, as do those for *righteousness* and *cry*. Jesus said, "You will know them by their fruits" (Matthew 7.20). Have you examined your own "fruit" lately? Is it useful or wild?

5.8–25 God condemns six sins: (1) exploiting others (5.8–10); (2) drunkenness (5.11–17); (3) taking pride in sin (5.18, 19); (4) confusing moral standards (5.20); (5) being conceited (5.21); and (6) perverting justice (5.22–25). Because of these sins, God punished Israel with destruction by Assyria (5.26–30). A similar fate was awaiting Judah if they didn't turn from these sins.

and a homer of seed shall yield a mere ephah.[h]

5.11 Prov 23.29,30 Isa 28.1,3,7,8

11 Ah, you who rise early in the morning
in pursuit of strong drink,
who linger in the evening
to be inflamed by wine,

5.12 Ps 28.5

12 whose feasts consist of lyre and harp,
tambourine and flute and wine,
but who do not regard the deeds of the LORD,
or see the work of his hands!

5.13 Hos 4.6

13 Therefore my people go into exile without knowledge;
their nobles are dying of hunger,
and their multitude is parched with thirst.

14 Therefore Sheol has enlarged its appetite
and opened its mouth beyond measure;
the nobility of Jerusalem[i] and her multitude go down,
her throng and all who exult in her.
15 People are bowed down, everyone is brought low,
and the eyes of the haughty are humbled.

5.16 Isa 33.5,10

16 But the LORD of hosts is exalted by justice,
and the Holy God shows himself holy by righteousness.

5.17 Zeph 2.6

17 Then the lambs shall graze as in their pasture,
fatlings and kids[j] shall feed among the ruins.

5.18 Jer 23.10-14

18 Ah, you who drag iniquity along with cords of falsehood,
who drag sin along as with cart ropes,

5.19 2 Pet 3.3,4

19 who say, "Let him make haste,
let him speed his work
that we may see it;
let the plan of the Holy One of Israel hasten to fulfillment,
that we may know it!"

5.20 Job 17.12 Prov 17.15

20 Ah, you who call evil good
and good evil,
who put darkness for light
and light for darkness,
who put bitter for sweet
and sweet for bitter!

5.21 Prov 3.7 Rom 12.16 1 Cor 3.18-20

21 Ah, you who are wise in your own eyes,
and shrewd in your own sight!

h The Heb *bath, homer,* and *ephah* are measures of quantity i Heb *her nobility* j Cn Compare Gk: Heb *aliens*

5.11–13 These men spent many hours drinking, but Isaiah predicted that many would eventually die of thirst. Ironically, our pleasures – if they do not have God's blessing – may eventually destroy us. Leaving God out of our lives allows sin to come into them. God wants us to enjoy life (1 Timothy 6.17) but to avoid those activities that could lead us away from him.

5.13 This took place when Israel was exiled to Assyria and Judah to Babylon. Where once there were parties with food and music, there would be hunger, thirst, and death. These people brought judgment on themselves. Turning away from God exposes us to judgment.

5.13 The nation's heroes – the "nobles" – would suffer the same humiliation as the common people. Why? Because they lived by their own values rather than God's. Many of today's media and sports heroes are idolized because of their ability to live as they please. Are your heroes those who defy God, or those who defy the world in order to serve God?

5.14 *Sheol* is the word in the Old Testament for the realm of the dead. It is used to mean the grave or state of being dead.

5.18, 19 Some people drag their sins around with them. But their sins become a burden that wears them out. Are you dragging around a cartload of sins that you refuse to give up? Before you find yourself worn-out and useless, turn to the One who promises to take away your burden of sin and replace it with a purpose that is a joy to fulfill (see Matthew 11.28–30).

5.20 When people do not carefully observe the distinction between right and wrong, destruction soon follows. It is easy for people to say, "No one can decide for anyone else what is really right or wrong." They may think getting drunk can't hurt them, extramarital sex isn't really adultery, or money doesn't control them. But when we make excuses for our actions, we break down the distinction between right and wrong. If we do not take God's Word, the Bible, as our standard, soon all moral choices appear fuzzy. Without God, we are headed for a breakdown and much suffering.

22 Ah, you who are heroes in drinking wine
and valiant at mixing drink,
23 who acquit the guilty for a bribe,
and deprive the innocent of their rights!
24 Therefore, as the tongue of fire devours the stubble,
and as dry grass sinks down in the flame,
so their root will become rotten,
and their blossom go up like dust;
for they have rejected the instruction of the LORD of hosts,
and have despised the word of the Holy One of Israel.

25 Therefore the anger of the LORD was kindled against his people,
and he stretched out his hand against them and struck them;
the mountains quaked,
and their corpses were like refuse
in the streets.
For all this his anger has not turned away,
and his hand is stretched out still.

26 He will raise a signal for a nation far away,
and whistle for a people at the ends of the earth;
Here they come, swiftly, speedily!
27 None of them is weary, none stumbles,
none slumbers or sleeps,
not a loincloth is loose,
not a sandal-thong broken;
28 their arrows are sharp,
all their bows bent,
their horses' hoofs seem like flint,
and their wheels like the whirlwind.
29 Their roaring is like a lion,
like young lions they roar;
they growl and seize their prey,
they carry it off, and no one can rescue.
30 They will roar over it on that day,
like the roaring of the sea.
And if one look to the land—
only darkness and distress;
and the light grows dark with clouds.

5.22 Isa 56.12 Hab 2.15
5.23 Mic 3.11 Jas 5.6
5.24 Isa 30.12
5.25 2 Kgs 22.17 Isa 9.12,17,21 10.4; 66.15
5.26 Isa 13.2,3
5.27 Joel 2.7,8
5.28 Jer 4.13
5.29 Isa 42.22 Zeph 3.3
5.30 Jer 4.23-28 6.23 Joel 2.10

God commissions Isaiah

6 In the year that King Uzziah died, I saw the Lord sitting on a throne, high and
lofty; and the hem of his robe filled the temple. 2 Seraphs were in attendance
above him; each had six wings: with two they covered their faces, and with two

6.1 Jn 12.41
6.2 Rev 4.8

5.24 The people suffered because they threw out God's law. It is sad to see so many people today searching for meaning in life while tossing aside God's Word. We can avoid the error of Israel and Judah by making reading the Bible a high priority in our lives.

5.26–30 This passage describes what God said he would do if the people disobeyed him (Deuteronomy 28). Assyria began to torment Israel during the reign of Ahaz (735–715 B.C.). This powerful aggressor destroyed the northern kingdom in 722 B.C. and scattered the people throughout its own empire. Sin has consequences. Although they may not be immediate, they will come to bring judgment on Israel.

6.1 The year of King Uzziah's death was approximately 740 B.C. He died of leprosy for trying to take over the high priest's duties (2 Chronicles 26.18–21). Although he was generally a good king and his reign was long and prosperous, many of his people turned away from God.

6.1ff Isaiah's vision was his call to be God's messenger to his people. Isaiah was given a difficult mission. He had to tell people who believed they were blessed by God that instead God was going to destroy them because of their disobedience.

6.1ff Isaiah's lofty view of God in 6.1–4 gives us a sense of God's greatness, mystery, and power. Isaiah's example of recognizing his sinfulness before God encourages us to confess our sin. His picture of forgiveness reminds us that we, too, are forgiven. When we recognize how great our God is, how sinful we are, and the extent of his forgiveness, we receive power to do his work. How does your concept of the greatness of God measure up to Isaiah's?

6.1–3 The lofty throne, the attending seraphs or angels, and the

6.3 Ps 72.19

they covered their feet, and with two they flew. 3 And one called to another and
said:
"Holy, holy, holy is the LORD of hosts;
the whole earth is full of his glory."
4 The pivots[k] on the thresholds shook at the voices of those who called, and the

[k] Meaning of Heb uncertain

ISAIAH

Trees and prophets share at least one important characteristic—both are planted for the future. Yet seedlings are often overlooked and prophets often ignored. Isaiah is one of the best examples of this. The people of his time could have been rescued by his words. Instead, they refused to believe him. With the passing of centuries, however, Isaiah's words have cast a shadow on all of history.

Isaiah was active as a prophet during the reigns of five kings, but he did not set out to be a prophet. By the time King Uzziah died, Isaiah was established as a scribe in the royal palace in Jerusalem. It was a respectable career, but God had other plans for his servant. Isaiah's account of God's call leaves little doubt about what motivated the prophet for the next half century. His vision of God was unforgettable.

The encounter with God permanently affected Isaiah's character. He reflected the God he represented. Isaiah's messages—some comforting, some confronting—are so distinct that some have guessed they came from different authors. Isaiah's testimony is that the messages came from the only one capable of being perfect in justice as well as in mercy—God himself.

When he called Isaiah as a prophet, God did not encourage him with predictions of great success. God told Isaiah that the people would not listen. But he was to speak and write his messages anyway because eventually some *would* listen. God compared his people to a tree that would have to be cut down so that a new tree could grow from the old roots (Isaiah 6.13).We, who are part of that future, can see that many of the promises God gave through Isaiah have been fulfilled in Jesus Christ. We also gain the hope of knowing that God is active in all of history, including our own.

Strengths and accomplishments:
- Considered the greatest Old Testament prophet
- Quoted at least 50 times in the New Testament
- Had powerful messages of both judgment and hope
- Carried out a consistent ministry even though there was little positive response from his listeners
- His ministry spanned the reigns of five kings of Judah

Lessons from his life:
- God's help is needed in order to effectively confront sin while comforting people
- One result of experiencing forgiveness is the desire to share that forgiveness with others
- God is purely and perfectly holy, just, and loving

Vital statistics:
- Where: Jerusalem
- Occupation: Scribe, prophet
- Relatives: Father: Amoz. Sons: Shear-jashub, Maher-shalal-hash-baz
- Contemporaries: Uzziah, Jotham, Ahaz, Hezekiah, Manasseh, Micah

Key verse:
"Then I heard the voice of the Lord saying, 'Whom shall I send, and who will go for us?' And I said, 'Here am I; send me!' " (Isaiah 6.8).

Isaiah's story is told in 2 Kings 19.2—20.19. He is also mentioned in 2 Chronicles 26.22; 32.20, 32; Matthew 3.3; 8.17; 12.17–21; John 12.38; Romans 10.16, 20.

threefold *holy* all stressed God's holiness. Seraphs were a type of angel whose name is derived from the word for "fire." Perhaps it indicates their burning devotion to God. In a time when moral and spiritual decay had peaked, it was important for Isaiah to see God in his holiness. Holiness means morally perfect, pure, and set apart from all sin. We need to rediscover God's holiness. Our daily frustrations, society's pressures, and our shortcomings reduce and narrow our view of God. We need the Bible's view of God as high and lifted up to empower us to deal with our problems and concerns. God's moral perfection, properly seen, purifies us from sin, cleanses our minds from our problems, and enables us to worship and to serve.

6.2–4 The seraphs are an order of angelic beings created by God. This is the only place in the Bible where they are mentioned. Here they functioned as God's agents in commissioning Isaiah. Isaiah could understand them when they spoke to him and when they praised God. Because they hovered around God's throne, they may have been heavenly attendants. They were awe-inspiring and powerful creatures – their singing shook the temple!

house filled with smoke. 5And I said: "Woe is me! I am lost, for I am a man of 6.5
unclean lips, and I live among a people of unclean lips; yet my eyes have seen the Lk 5.8 Jer 9.3-8
King, the LORD of hosts!"
6 Then one of the seraphs flew to me, holding a live coal that had been taken
from the altar with a pair of tongs. 7The seraph[l] touched my mouth with it and 6.7
said: "Now that this has touched your lips, your guilt has departed and your sin is Isa 40.2 Jer 1.9
blotted out." 8Then I heard the voice of the Lord saying, "Whom shall I send, and Jn 1.7
who will go for us?" And I said, "Here am I; send me!" 9And he said, "Go and say 6.8 Mt 13.14
to this people: Lk 8.10 Acts 26.19

'Keep listening, but do not comprehend; Rom 11.8
keep looking, but do not understand.'

10 Make the mind of this people dull, 6.10 Jer 5.21
and stop their ears,
and shut their eyes,
so that they may not look with their eyes,
and listen with their ears,
and comprehend with their minds,
and turn and be healed."

11 Then I said, "How long, O Lord?" And he said: 6.11
"Until cities lie waste Lev 26.31 Mic 3.12
without inhabitant,
and houses without people,
and the land is utterly desolate;

12 until the LORD sends everyone far away, 6.12 Jer 4.29
and vast is the emptiness in the midst of the land.

13 Even if a tenth part remain in it, 6.13 Job 14.7
it will be burned again,
like a terebinth or an oak
whose stump remains standing
when it is felled."[m]
The holy seed is its stump.

Immanuel—God with us

7 In the days of Ahaz son of Jotham son of Uzziah, king of Judah, King Rezin 7.1
of Aram and King Pekah son of Remaliah of Israel went up to attack Jerusa- 2 Kgs 16.1
lem, but could not mount an attack against it. 2When the house of David heard that

[l] Heb *He* [m] Meaning of Heb uncertain

6.5–8 Listening to the praise of the angels, Isaiah realized he was common and unclean before God, with no hope of measuring up to God's standard of holiness. When his lips were touched with a burning coal, however, he was told his sins were forgiven. It wasn't the coal that cleansed him, but God. In response he submitted himself entirely to God's service. No matter how difficult his task would be, he said, "Here am I; send me." The painful cleansing process was necessary before Isaiah could fulfill the task to which God was calling him. Before we accept God's call to speak for him to those around us, we must be cleansed as Isaiah was. Letting God purify us may be painful, but we must be purified so that we can truly represent God, who is pure and holy.

6.8 The more clearly Isaiah saw God (6.5), the more aware he became of his own powerlessness and inadequacy to do anything of lasting value without him.

6.9–13 God told Isaiah that the people would listen but not learn from his message because their hearts had hardened beyond repentance. God's patience with their chronic rebellion was finally exhausted, and his judgment was to abandon them to their rebellion and hardness of heart. Why did God send Isaiah if he knew the people wouldn't listen? Although the nation itself would not repent and would reap judgment, some individuals would listen. In 6.13 God explains his plan for a remnant of faithful followers. Even in judgment God is merciful. We can gain encouragement from God's promise to preserve his people. If we are faithful to him we can be sure of his mercy.

6.11–13 When would the people listen? Only after they had come to the end and had nowhere to turn but to God. This would happen when the land was destroyed by invading armies and the people taken into captivity. The "tenth part" refers either to those who remained in the land after the captivity or to those who returned from Babylon to rebuild the land. Each group was about a tenth of the total population. When will we listen to God? Must we, like Judah, go through calamities before we will listen to God's words? Consider what God may be telling you, and obey him before time runs out.

7.1 The year was 734 B.C. Ahaz, king of Judah in Jerusalem, was about to be attacked by an alliance of the northern kingdom of Israel and Syria. He was frightened by the possible end of his reign and by the invading armies who killed many people or took them as captives (2 Chronicles 28.5–21). But, as Isaiah predicted, the kingdom of Judah did not come to an end at this time.

7.2 "The house of David" refers to Judah, the southern kingdom. "Ephraim" was another way to indicate Israel, the northern kingdom.

Aram had allied itself with Ephraim, the heart of Ahaz[n] and the heart of his people
shook as the trees of the forest shake before the wind.
3 Then the LORD said to Isaiah, Go out to meet Ahaz, you and your son Shear-
jashub,[o] at the end of the conduit of the upper pool on the highway to the Fuller's
7.4
Field, 4 and say to him, Take heed, be quiet, do not fear, and do not let your heart
Ex 14.13
be faint because of these two smoldering stumps of firebrands, because of the fierce
Isa 10.24; 35.4
Lam 3.26
anger of Rezin and Aram and the son of Remaliah. 5 Because Aram—with Ephraim
and the son of Remaliah—has plotted evil against you, saying, 6 Let us go up
against Judah and cut off Jerusalem[p] and conquer it for ourselves and make the son
7.7
of Tabeel king in it; 7 therefore thus says the Lord GOD:
Ps 2.4-6
It shall not stand,
and it shall not come to pass.
7.8
8 For the head of Aram is Damascus,
Isa 17.1-3
and the head of Damascus is Rezin.
(Within sixty-five years Ephraim will be shattered, no longer a people.)
7.9
9 The head of Ephraim is Samaria,
2 Chron 20.20
Isa 30.12-14
and the head of Samaria is the son of Remaliah.
If you do not stand firm in faith,
you shall not stand at all.
7.11
10 Again the LORD spoke to Ahaz, saying, 11 Ask a sign of the LORD your God;
2 Kgs 19.29
Isa 37.30
let it be deep as Sheol or high as heaven. 12 But Ahaz said, I will not ask, and I will
not put the LORD to the test. 13 Then Isaiah[q] said: "Hear then, O house of David! Is
7.14
it too little for you to weary mortals, that you weary my God also? 14 Therefore the
Isa 8.8,10
Mt 1.23
Lord himself will give you a sign. Look, the young woman[r] is with child and shall
7.15
bear a son, and shall name him Immanuel.[s] 15 He shall eat curds and honey by the
Isa 8.4; 17.3
time he knows how to refuse the evil and choose the good. 16 For before the child
knows how to refuse the evil and choose the good, the land before whose two kings
7.17
you are in dread will be deserted. 17 The LORD will bring on you and on your people
1 Kgs 12.16,17
Isa 10.5,6
and on your ancestral house such days as have not come since the day that Ephraim
departed from Judah—the king of Assyria."
18 On that day the LORD will whistle for the fly that is at the sources of the

[n] Heb *his heart* [o] That is *A remnant shall return* [p] Heb *cut it off* [q] Heb *he* [r] Gk *the virgin* [s] That is *God is with us*

7.3 *Shear-jashub* means "a remnant will return." God told Isaiah to give his son this name as a reminder of his plan for mercy. From the beginning of God's judgment he planned to restore a remnant of his people. Shear-jashub was a reminder to the people of God's faithfulness to them.

7.3 The "conduit of the upper pool" refers to the Gihon Spring, located east of Jerusalem. It was the main source of water for the holy city. This was also the spring that emptied into Hezekiah's famous water tunnel (2 Chronicles 32.30). The Fuller's Field was a well-known place where clothing or newly woven cloth was laid in the sun to dry and whiten (see 36.2).

7.4–8.15 Isaiah predicted the breakup of Israel's alliance with Syria (7.4–7). Because of this alliance, Israel would be destroyed; Assyria would be the instrument God would use to destroy them (7.8–25). But God would not let Assyria destroy Judah (8.1–15). They would be spared because they were trying to follow God.

7.8 Ahaz, one of Judah's worst kings, refused God's help and instead tried to buy aid from the Assyrians with gold from the temple. When the Assyrians came, they brought further trouble instead of help. In 722 B.C., Samaria, the capital of "Ephraim" (another name for Israel, the northern kingdom), fell to the Assyrian armies, thus ending the northern kingdom.

7.10 *Sheol* is the word in the Old Testament for the realm of the dead. It is used to mean the grave or state of being dead.

7.12 Ahaz appeared righteous by saying he would not test God with a sign ("I will not ask, and I will not put the Lord to the test"). In fact, God had told him to ask, but Ahaz didn't really want to know what God would say. Often we use some excuse, such as not wanting to bother God, to keep us from communicating with him. Don't let anything keep you from hearing and obeying God.

7.14–16 "Young woman" or "virgin" is translated from a Hebrew word used for an unmarried woman old enough to be married, one who is sexually mature (see Genesis 24.43; Exodus 2.8; Psalm 68.25; Proverbs 30.19; Song of Solomon 1.3; 6.8). Some have compared this young woman to Isaiah's young wife and newborn son (8.1–4). This is not likely because she had a child, Shear-jashub, and her second child was not named Immanuel. It is more likely that this prophecy had a double fulfillment: (1) a young woman from the house of Ahaz who was not married would marry and have a son. Before three years passed (one year for pregnancy and two for the child to be old enough to talk), the two invading kings would be destroyed; (2) Matthew 1.23 quotes Isaiah 7.14 to show a further fulfillment of this prophecy in that a virgin named Mary conceived and bore a son, Immanuel, the Christ.

7.18 Egypt and Assyria did not at this time devastate Judah. Hezekiah followed Ahaz as king, and he honored God; therefore God held back his hand of judgment. Two more evil kings reigned before Josiah, of whom it was said that no other king turned so completely to the Lord (2 Kings 23.25). However, Judah's doom had been sealed by the extreme evil of Josiah's father. During Josiah's reign, Egypt marched against the Assyrians. Josiah then declared war on Egypt, though God told him not to. After Josiah was killed (2 Chronicles 35.20–27), only weak kings reigned in Judah. The Egyptians carried off Josiah's son after three months. The next king, Jehoiakim, was taken by Nebuchadnezzar to Babylon. Egypt and Assyria had dealt death blows to Judah.

streams of Egypt, and for the bee that is in the land of Assyria. 19 And they will all 7.19
come and settle in the steep ravines, and in the clefts of the rocks, and on all the Jer 16.16
thornbushes, and on all the pastures.
20 On that day the Lord will shave with a razor hired beyond the River—with 7.20
the king of Assyria—the head and the hair of the feet, and it will take off the beard Isa 24.1 Ezek 5.1-4
as well.
21 On that day one will keep alive a young cow and two sheep, 22 and will eat 7.21
curds because of the abundance of milk that they give; for everyone that is left in Jer 39.10
the land shall eat curds and honey.
23 On that day every place where there used to be a thousand vines, worth a
thousand shekels of silver, will become briers and thorns. 24 With bow and arrows
one will go there, for all the land will be briers and thorns; 25 and as for all the hills
that used to be hoed with a hoe, you will not go there for fear of briers and thorns;
but they will become a place where cattle are let loose and where sheep tread.

Isaiah predicts the invasion by Assyria

8 Then the LORD said to me, Take a large tablet and write on it in common char- 8.1
acters, "Belonging to Maher-shalal-hash-baz,"[t] 2 and have it attested[u] for me Hab 2.2
by reliable witnesses, the priest Uriah and Zechariah son of Jeberechiah. 3 And I 8.2 2 Kgs 16.10,11,
went to the prophetess, and she conceived and bore a son. Then the LORD said to 15,16
me, Name him Maher-shalal-hash-baz; 4 for before the child knows how to call
"My father" or "My mother," the wealth of Damascus and the spoil of Samaria will
be carried away by the king of Assyria.
5 The LORD spoke to me again: 6 Because this people has refused the waters of 8.6
Shiloah that flow gently, and melt in fear before[v] Rezin and the son of Remaliah; Isa 30.12
7 therefore, the Lord is bringing up against it the mighty flood waters of the River, 8.7
the king of Assyria and all his glory; it will rise above all its channels and overflow Isa 7.14 17.12,13
all its banks; 8 it will sweep on into Judah as a flood, and, pouring over, it will reach Amos 8.8; 9.5
up to the neck; and its outspread wings will fill the breadth of your land,
O Immanuel.

9 Band together, you peoples, and be dismayed; 8.9
listen, all you far countries; Dan 2.34,35
gird yourselves and be dismayed; Rom 8.31
gird yourselves and be dismayed!
10 Take counsel together, but it shall be brought to naught;
speak a word, but it will not stand,
for God is with us.[w] 8.11

11 For the LORD spoke thus to me while his hand was strong upon me, and Ezek 2.8
warned me not to walk in the way of this people, saying: 12 Do not call conspiracy 8.12 1 Pet 3.13-15

[t] That is *The spoil speeds, the prey hastens* [u] Q Ms Gk Syr: MT *and I caused to be attested* [v] Cn: Meaning of Heb uncertain [w] Heb *immanu el*

7.20 Hiring Assyria to save them would be Israel's downfall (2 Kings 16.7, 8). To "shave" Israel's hair was symbolic of total humiliation. Numbers 6.9 explains that after being defiled, a person who had been set apart for the Lord had to shave his head as part of the cleansing process. Shaving bodily hair was an embarrassment—an exposure of nakedness. For a Hebrew man, having his beard shaved was humiliating.

7.21–25 Israel's rich farmland would be trampled until it became pastureland fit only for grazing. No longer would it be a place of agricultural abundance, a land "flowing with milk and honey" (Exodus 3.8), but a land with only curds and wild honey.

8.1–4 These verses predict the fall of Israel and Syria. Syria fell to Assyria in 732 B.C., and Israel followed in 722 B.C. Isaiah put his message on a large sign in a public place with writing that all could read. God was warning all his people.

8.6–8 "The waters of Shiloah that flow gently" are God's gentle care. Because Judah rejected God's kindness, choosing instead to seek help from other nations, God would punish them. We see two distinct attributes of God—his love and his wrath. To ignore his love and guidance results in sin and invites his wrath. We must recognize the consequences of our choices. God seeks to protect us from bad choices, but he still gives us the freedom to make them.

8.7, 8 The heart of the Assyrian Empire was located between the Tigris and Euphrates Rivers. This flood is a poetic way of describing the overwhelming force of the Assyrian army.

8.9 To "gird" yourself means to prepare as for battle. To "be dismayed" means to lose courage through the pressure of sudden fear.

8.10–15 Isaiah, along with most of the prophets, was viewed as a traitor because he did not support Judah's national policies. He called the people to commit themselves first to God, and then to the king. He even predicted the overthrow of the government.

all that this people calls conspiracy, and do not fear what it fears, or be in dread.
13 But the LORD of hosts, him you shall regard as holy; let him be your fear, and let
him be your dread. 14 He will become a sanctuary, a stone one strikes against; for
both houses of Israel he will become a rock one stumbles over — a trap and a snare
for the inhabitants of Jerusalem. 15 And many among them shall stumble; they shall
fall and be broken; they shall be snared and taken.
16 Bind up the testimony, seal the teaching among my disciples. 17 I will wait
for the LORD, who is hiding his face from the house of Jacob, and I will hope in
him. 18 See, I and the children whom the LORD has given me are signs and portents
in Israel from the LORD of hosts, who dwells on Mount Zion. 19 Now if people say
to you, "Consult the ghosts and the familiar spirits that chirp and mutter; should not
a people consult their gods, the dead on behalf of the living, 20 for teaching and for
instruction?" Surely, those who speak like this will have no dawn! 21 They will pass
through the land,[x] greatly distressed and hungry; when they are hungry, they will
be enraged and will curse[y] their king and their gods. They will turn their faces
upward, 22 or they will look to the earth, but will see only distress and darkness, the
gloom of anguish; and they will be thrust into thick darkness.[z]

8.14 Isa 25.4; Ezek 11.16; Lk 2.34; Rom 9.32,33; 1 Pet 2.8
8.16 Isa 50.4; Dan 12.4
8.17 Deut 31.17; Isa 30.18; 54.8; Hab 2.3
8.18 Heb 2.13
8.19 Lev 20.6; 2 Kgs 21.6
8.22 Jer 13.16; Amos 5.18,20; Zeph 1.14,15

A prophecy about the coming Messiah

9 [a] But there will be no gloom for those who were in anguish. In the former time
he brought into contempt the land of Zebulun and the land of Naphtali, but in
the latter time he will make glorious the way of the sea, the land beyond the Jordan,
Galilee of the nations.

2 [b] The people who walked in darkness
have seen a great light;
those who lived in a land of deep darkness —

9.2 Mt 4.15,16

[x] Heb *it* [y] Or *curse by* [z] Meaning of Heb uncertain [a] Ch 8.23 in Heb [b] Ch 9.1 in Heb

NAMES FOR MESSIAH
Isaiah uses five names to describe the Messiah. These names have special meaning to us.

Wonderful	• He is exceptional, distinguished, and without peer.
Counselor	• He gives the right advice.
The Mighty God	• He is God himself.
The Everlasting Father	• He is timeless; he is God our Father.
The Prince of Peace	• His government is one of justice and peace.

8.16 "Bind up the testimony" means that the words would be written down and preserved for future generations. Because some people faithfully passed on these words from generation to generation, we have the book of Isaiah today. Each of us needs to accept the responsibility to pass on God's Word to our children and grandchildren, encouraging them to love the Bible, read it, and learn from it. Then they will faithfully pass it on to their children and grandchildren.

8.17 Isaiah decided to wait for God's help, though he "is hiding his face from the house of Jacob." Many of the prophecies God gave through the prophets would not come true for 700 years; others still haven't been fulfilled. Are you willing to accept the Lord's timing, not yours?

8.19 "The ghosts and the familiar spirits" refers to the people's practice of consulting wizards and mediums to seek answers from dead people, instead of consulting the living God. God alone knows the future. Only God is eternal, and we can trust him to guide us.

8.21 After rejecting God's plan for them, the people of Judah would blame God for their trials. People continually blame God for their self-induced problems. How do you respond to the unpleasant results of your own choices? Where do you fix the blame? Instead of blaming God, seek ways to grow through your failures.

8.22 Those who consult the forces of darkness will be led onto paths of darkness. The darkness is not necessarily hell; it may mean despair, judgment, trouble, or anguish (see 9.1).

9.1 In our despair, we fear that our sorrows and troubles will never end. But we can take comfort in this certainty: although the Lord may not always take us around our troubles, if we follow him wholeheartedly like Judah, he will lead us safely through them.

9.1–7 This deliverer is the Messiah, Jesus. Matthew quotes these verses in describing Christ's ministry (Matthew 4.15, 16). The territories of Zebulun and Naphtali represent the northern kingdom as a whole. These were also the territories where Jesus grew up and often ministered; this is why they would see "a great light."

9.2 The apostle John also referred to Jesus as the "light" (John 1.9).

9.2–6 In a time of great darkness, God promised to send a light who would shine on everyone living in the shadow of death. He is both "Mighty God" (all-powerful) and "Counselor" (all-loving). This message of hope was fulfilled in the birth of Christ and the establishment of his eternal kingdom. He came to deliver all people from their slavery to sin.

on them light has shined.
3 You have multiplied the nation,
you have increased its joy;
they rejoice before you
as with joy at the harvest,
as people exult when dividing plunder.
4 For the yoke of their burden,
and the bar across their shoulders,
the rod of their oppressor,
you have broken as on the day of Midian.
5 For all the boots of the tramping warriors
and all the garments rolled in blood
shall be burned as fuel for the fire.
6 For a child has been born for us,
a son given to us;
authority rests upon his shoulders;
and he is named
Wonderful Counselor, Mighty God,
Everlasting Father, Prince of Peace.
7 His authority shall grow continually,
and there shall be endless peace
for the throne of David and his kingdom.
He will establish and uphold it
with justice and with righteousness
from this time onward and forevermore.
The zeal of the LORD of hosts will do this.

8 The Lord sent a word against Jacob,
and it fell on Israel;
9 and all the people knew it—
Ephraim and the inhabitants of Samaria—
but in pride and arrogance of heart they said:
10 "The bricks have fallen,
but we will build with dressed stones;
the sycamores have been cut down,
but we will put cedars in their place."
11 So the LORD raised adversaries[c] against them,
and stirred up their enemies,
12 the Arameans on the east and the Philistines on the west,
and they devoured Israel with open mouth.
For all this his anger has not turned away;
his hand is stretched out still.

13 The people did not turn to him who struck them,
or seek the LORD of hosts.
14 So the LORD cut off from Israel head and tail,
palm branch and reed in one day—
15 elders and dignitaries are the head,
and prophets who teach lies are the tail;
16 for those who led this people led them astray,
and those who were led by them were left in confusion.

9.3 Isa 26.15 35.10; 66.10
9.4 Isa 49.26
9.6 Deut 10.17 Neh 9.32 Isa 26.3,12 Mt 28.18 Lk 2.11 1 Cor 15.25
9.7 Dan 2.44 Lk 1.32,33
9.8 Mal 1.4
9.11 Ps 79.7 Jer 10.25
9.13 Jer 5.3 Hos 7.10
9.16 Mt 15.14

c Cn: Heb *the adversaries of Rezin*

9.8–10 Pride made Israel think it would recover and rebuild in its own strength. Even though God made Israel a nation and gave them the land they occupied, the people put their trust in themselves rather than in him. Too often we take pride in our accomplishments, forgetting that it is God who has given us every resource and ability we have. We even become proud of our unique status as Christians. God is not pleased with *any* pride or trust in ourselves because it cuts off our contact with him.

9.17 Isa 32.6 Amos 8.13 Mt 12.34

17 That is why the Lord did not have pity on[d] their young people,
or compassion on their orphans and widows;
for everyone was godless and an evildoer,
and every mouth spoke folly.
For all this his anger has not turned away,
his hand is stretched out still.

9.18 Mal 4.1

18 For wickedness burned like a fire,
consuming briers and thorns;
it kindled the thickets of the forest,
and they swirled upward in a column of smoke.

9.19 Joel 2.3 Mic 7.2,6

19 Through the wrath of the LORD of hosts
the land was burned,
and the people became like fuel for the fire;
no one spared another.
20 They gorged on the right, but still were hungry,
and they devoured on the left, but were not satisfied;
they devoured the flesh of their own kindred;[e]

9.21 Isa 11.13

21 Manasseh devoured Ephraim, and Ephraim Manasseh,
and together they were against Judah.
For all this his anger has not turned away;
his hand is stretched out still.

10.1 Ps 94.20 Isa 59.13,14

10 Ah, you who make iniquitous decrees,
who write oppressive statutes,
2 to turn aside the needy from justice
and to rob the poor of my people of their right,
that widows may be your spoil,
and that you may make the orphans your prey!

10.3 Isa 13.6 Lk 19.43,44

3 What will you do on the day of punishment,
in the calamity that will come from far away?
To whom will you flee for help,
and where will you leave your wealth,

10.4 Isa 34.3; 66.16

4 so as not to crouch among the prisoners
or fall among the slain?
For all this his anger has not turned away;
his hand is stretched out still.

God will punish Assyria

10.5 Isa 13.5 Jer 51.20

5 Ah, Assyria, the rod of my anger—
the club in their hands is my fury!
6 Against a godless nation I send him,
and against the people of my wrath I command him,
to take spoil and seize plunder,
and to tread them down like the mire of the streets.

10.7 Gen 50.20 Mic 4.11,12 Acts 2.23,24

7 But this is not what he intends,
nor does he have this in mind;
but it is in his heart to destroy,

[d] Q Ms: MT *rejoice over* [e] Or *arm*

9.21 Ephraim and Manasseh were tribes in the northern kingdom descended from Joseph's two sons. They fought a civil war because of their selfishness and wickedness.

10.1 God will judge crooked judges and those who make unfair laws. Those who oppress others will be oppressed themselves. It is not enough to live in a land founded on justice; each individual must deal justly with the poor and the powerless. Don't pass your responsibility off to your nation or even your church. You are accountable to God for what you do.

10.7 Although Assyria did not know it was part of God's plan, God used this nation to judge his people. God accomplishes his plans in history despite people or nations who reject him. He did not merely set the world in motion and let it go! Because our all-powerful, sovereign God is still in control today, we have security even in a rapidly changing world.

and to cut off nations not a few:
8 For he says:
"Are not my commanders all kings?
9 Is not Calno like Carchemish?
Is not Hamath like Arpad?
Is not Samaria like Damascus?
10 As my hand has reached to the kingdoms of the idols
whose images were greater than those of Jerusalem and Samaria, 10.10 2 Kgs 19.17,18
11 shall I not do to Jerusalem and her idols
what I have done to Samaria and her images?"

12 When the Lord has finished all his work on Mount Zion and on Jerusalem, 10.12 Jer 50.18
he[f] will punish the arrogant boasting of the king of Assyria and his haughty pride.
13 For he says: 10.13 2 Kgs 19.22-24 Isa 37.24-27 Dan 4.30
"By the strength of my hand I have done it,
and by my wisdom, for I have understanding;
I have removed the boundaries of peoples,
and have plundered their treasures;
like a bull I have brought down those who sat on thrones.
14 My hand has found, like a nest,
the wealth of the peoples;
and as one gathers eggs that have been forsaken,
so I have gathered all the earth;
and there was none that moved a wing,
or opened its mouth, or chirped."

15 Shall the ax vaunt itself over the one who wields it, 10.15 Isa 29.16
or the saw magnify itself against the one who handles it?
As if a rod should raise the one who lifts it up,
or as if a staff should lift the one who is not wood!
16 Therefore the Sovereign, the LORD of hosts,
will send wasting sickness among his stout warriors,
and under his glory a burning will be kindled,
like the burning of fire.
17 The light of Israel will become a fire, 10.17 Isa 27.4; 30.33 31.9; 33.12 37.23 Jer 4.4
and his Holy One a flame;
and it will burn and devour
his thorns and briers in one day.
18 The glory of his forest and his fruitful land
the LORD will destroy, both soul and body,
and it will be as when an invalid wastes away.
19 The remnant of the trees of his forest will be so few 10.19 Isa 21.17
that a child can write them down.

[f] Heb *I*

10.9 Assured of great victories that would enlarge his empire, the king of Assyria gave an arrogant speech. Already Assyria had conquered several cities and thought Judah would be defeated along with the others. Little did the king know that he was under the mightier hand of God.

10.10 Samaria and Jerusalem were filled with idols that were powerless against the Assyrian military machine. Only the God of the universe could and would overthrow Assyria, but not until he had used the Assyrians for his purposes.

10.12 The predicted punishment of the Assyrians soon took place. In 701 B.C., 185,000 Assyrian soldiers were slain by the angel of the Lord (37.36, 37). Later, the Assyrian Empire fell to Babylon, never to rise again as a world power.

10.12 Proud of the victories God permitted, the Assyrians thought they had accomplished them in their own power. Our perspective can be distorted by our successes if we fail to recognize God working his purposes through us. When we think we are strong enough for anything, we are bound to fail because pride has blinded us to the reality that God is ultimately in control.

10.15 The Assyrians were a tool in God's hands, but they failed to recognize it. When a tool boasts of greater power than the one who uses it, it is in danger of being discarded. We are useful only to the extent that we allow God to use us.

10.17 Assyria's downfall came in 612 B.C. when Nineveh, the capital city, was destroyed. Assyria had been God's instrument of judgment against Israel, but it too would be judged for its wickedness. No one escapes God's judgment against sin, not even the most powerful nations (Psalm 2).

10.20 Isa 17.7,8
10.22 Isa 28.22; Rom 9.27,28
10.24 Ex 5.14-16
10.25 Isa 17.14
10.26 Ex 14.16,27; Judg 7.25; Isa 37.36-38
10.27 Isa 14.25

20 On that day the remnant of Israel and the survivors of the house of Jacob will
no more lean on the one who struck them, but will lean on the LORD, the Holy One
of Israel, in truth. 21 A remnant will return, the remnant of Jacob, to the mighty
God. 22 For though your people Israel were like the sand of the sea, only a remnant
of them will return. Destruction is decreed, overflowing with righteousness. 23 For
the Lord GOD of hosts will make a full end, as decreed, in all the earth.[g]
24 Therefore thus says the Lord GOD of hosts: O my people, who live in Zion,
do not be afraid of the Assyrians when they beat you with a rod and lift up their staff
against you as the Egyptians did. 25 For in a very little while my indignation will
come to an end, and my anger will be directed to their destruction. 26 The LORD of
hosts will wield a whip against them, as when he struck Midian at the rock of Oreb;
his staff will be over the sea, and he will lift it as he did in Egypt. 27 On that day his
burden will be removed from your shoulder, and his yoke will be destroyed from
your neck.

He has gone up from Rimmon,[h]
28 he has come to Aiath;
he has passed through Migron,
at Michmash he stores his baggage;
29 they have crossed over the pass,
at Geba they lodge for the night;
Ramah trembles,
Gibeah of Saul has fled.
30 Cry aloud, O daughter Gallim!
Listen, O Laishah!
Answer her, O Anathoth!
31 Madmenah is in flight,
the inhabitants of Gebim flee for safety.

10.32 Isa 19.16; Zech 2.9

32 This very day he will halt at Nob,
he will shake his fist
at the mount of daughter Zion,
the hill of Jerusalem.

10.33 Isa 37.24; Ezek 31.2,3; Amos 2.9

33 Look, the Sovereign, the LORD of hosts,
will lop the boughs with terrifying power;
the tallest trees will be cut down,
and the lofty will be brought low.
34 He will hack down the thickets of the forest with an ax,
and Lebanon with its majestic trees[i] will fall.

A new branch from Jesse

11.1 Jer 23.5
11.2 Isa 61.1

11

A shoot shall come out from the stump of Jesse,
and a branch shall grow out of his roots.
2 The spirit of the LORD shall rest on him,

[g] Or *land* [h] Cn: Heb *and his yoke from your neck, and a yoke will be destroyed because of fatness* [i] Cn Compare Gk Vg: Heb *with a majestic one*

10.20, 21 Once Assyria's army was destroyed, a small remnant of God's people would stop fearing Assyria and start trusting God. This remnant would be but a fraction of Israel's former population (see Ezra 2.64, 65 for the small number who returned to Judah; see also 11.10–16).

10.20, 21 Those who remained faithful to God despite the horrors of the invasion are called the remnant. The key to being a part of the remnant was *faith.* Being a descendant of Abraham, living in the promised land, having trusted God at one time – none of these were good enough. Are you relying on your Christian heritage, the rituals of worship, or past experience to put you in a right relationship with God? The key to being set apart by God is faith in him.

10.28–34 The way these cities are listed approximates the route the Assyrians would take in their invasion of Judah in 701 B.C. They would go from Aiath (Ai) at the northern border to Nob (only two miles from Jerusalem).

11.1–9 Assyria would be like a tree cut down at the height of its power (10.33, 34), never to rise again. Judah (the royal line of David) would be like a tree chopped down to a stump. But from that stump a new branch would grow – the Messiah. He would be greater than the original tree and would bear much fruit. The Messiah is the fulfillment of God's promise that a descendant of David would rule forever (2 Samuel 7.16).

the spirit of wisdom and understanding,
the spirit of counsel and might,
the spirit of knowledge and the fear of the LORD.
3 His delight shall be in the fear of the LORD.

He shall not judge by what his eyes see,
or decide by what his ears hear;
4 but with righteousness he shall judge the poor,
and decide with equity for the meek of the earth;
he shall strike the earth with the rod of his mouth,
and with the breath of his lips he shall kill the wicked.
5 Righteousness shall be the belt around his waist,
and faithfulness the belt around his loins.

6 The wolf shall live with the lamb,
the leopard shall lie down with the kid,
the calf and the lion and the fatling together,
and a little child shall lead them.
7 The cow and the bear shall graze,
their young shall lie down together;
and the lion shall eat straw like the ox.
8 The nursing child shall play over the hole of the asp,
and the weaned child shall put its hand on the adder's den.
9 They will not hurt or destroy
on all my holy mountain;
for the earth will be full of the knowledge of the LORD
as the waters cover the sea.

10 On that day the root of Jesse shall stand as a signal to the peoples; the nations
shall inquire of him, and his dwelling shall be glorious.
11 On that day the Lord will extend his hand yet a second time to recover the
remnant that is left of his people, from Assyria, from Egypt, from Pathros, from
Ethiopia,[j] from Elam, from Shinar, from Hamath, and from the coastlands of the
sea.
12 He will raise a signal for the nations,
and will assemble the outcasts of Israel,
and gather the dispersed of Judah
from the four corners of the earth.

j Or *Nubia*; Heb *Cush*

11.3 Jn 2.24,25
11.4 Isa 30.28; 2 Thess 2.8
11.6 Isa 65.25
11.9 Isa 45.6; Ezek 34.25; Hos 2.18; Hab 2.14
11.10 Lk 2.32; Jn 3.14,15; Rom 15.12
11.11 Isa 60.9; Zech 10.10
11.12 Zeph 3.10

11.3–5 How we long for fair treatment from others, but do we give it? We hate those who base their judgments on appearance, false evidence, or hearsay, but are we quick to judge others using those standards? Only Christ can be the perfectly fair judge. Only as he governs our hearts can we learn to be as fair in our treatment of others as we expect others to be toward us.

11.4, 5 Judah had become corrupt, and now it was surrounded by hostile foreign powers. The nation desperately needed a revival of righteousness, equity, and faithfulness. They needed to turn from selfishness and show justice to the poor and the oppressed. The righteousness that God values is more than refraining from sin. It is actively turning toward others and offering them the help they need.

11.6–8 It is incredible to think of animals normally hostile to each other living at peace. It is even more incredible for hostile people to live at peace with one another. Only in union with Christ can we love enough to overcome our hostilities. And one day the whole world will acknowledge that Christ is Lord.

11.6–10 A golden age is yet to come. Not all of this was fulfilled at Christ's first coming. For example, nature has not returned to its intended balance and harmony (see Romans 8.9–22). Such perfect tranquility is possible only when Christ reigns over the earth.

11.11 When will this remnant of God's people be returned to their land? Old Testament prophecy often applied both to the near future and the distant future. Judah would soon be exiled to Babylon, and a remnant would return to Jerusalem in 537 B.C. at Cyrus's decree. In the ages to come, however, God's people would be dispersed throughout the world. These cities represent the four corners of the known world – Hamath in the north, Egypt in the south, Assyria and Shinar in the east, the coastlands of the sea in the west. Ultimately God's people will be regathered when Christ comes to reign over the earth.

11.13 Ezek 37.16,17,22

13 The jealousy of Ephraim shall depart,
the hostility of Judah shall be cut off;
Ephraim shall not be jealous of Judah,
and Judah shall not be hostile towards Ephraim.
14 But they shall swoop down on the backs of the Philistines in the west,
together they shall plunder the people of the east.
They shall put forth their hand against Edom and Moab,
and the Ammonites shall obey them.

11.15 Isa 51.10

15 And the LORD will utterly destroy
the tongue of the sea of Egypt;
and will wave his hand over the River
with his scorching wind;
and will split it into seven channels,
and make a way to cross on foot;

11.16 Ex 14.26-29 Isa 19.23

16 so there shall be a highway from Assyria
for the remnant that is left of his people,
as there was for Israel
when they came up from the land of Egypt.

Singing God's praise

12.1 Isa 40.1

12 You will say in that day:
I will give thanks to you, O LORD,
for though you were angry with me,
your anger turned away,
and you comforted me.

12.2 Ps 118.14 Isa 26.3; 62.11

2 Surely God is my salvation;
I will trust, and will not be afraid,
for the LORD GOD[k] is my strength and my might;
he has become my salvation.

3 With joy you will draw water from the wells of salvation. 4 And you will say
in that day:
Give thanks to the LORD,
call on his name;
make known his deeds among the nations;
proclaim that his name is exalted.

12.5 Ps 98.1 Isa 44.23

5 Sing praises to the LORD, for he has done gloriously;
let this be known[l] in all the earth.

12.6 Isa 54.1 Zeph 3.14,15-17

6 Shout aloud and sing for joy, O royal[m] Zion,
for great in your midst is the Holy One of Israel.

[k] Heb *for Yah, the* LORD [l] *Or this is made known* [m] *Or O inhabitant of*

11.13 Ephraim is another name for Israel, the northern kingdom.

11.14 Edom, Moab, and Ammon were three countries bordering Judah (along with Philistia). They were the nations who, when Judah was defeated, rejoiced and took their land.

11.15, 16 Isaiah is talking about a new, or second, exodus when God brings his scattered people back to Judah and the Messiah comes to rule the world. The Lord dried up the Red Sea so the Israelites could walk through it on their way to the promised land (Exodus 14). He dried up the Jordan River so the nation could cross into the land (Joshua 3). God will again provide a way of return for his people.

12.1ff This chapter is a hymn of praise – another graphic description of the people's joy when Jesus Christ comes to reign over the earth. Even now we need to express our gratitude to God – thanking him, praising him, and telling others about him. From the depths of our gratitude, we must praise him. As our praise overflows, we must share him with others.

2. Judgment against heathen nations

Prophecy against Babylon

13 The oracle concerning Babylon that Isaiah son of Amoz saw.

2 On a bare hill raise a signal,
cry aloud to them;
wave the hand for them to enter
the gates of the nobles.
3 I myself have commanded my consecrated ones,
have summoned my warriors, my proudly exulting ones,
to execute my anger.

4 Listen, a tumult on the mountains
as of a great multitude!
Listen, an uproar of kingdoms,
of nations gathering together!
The LORD of hosts is mustering
an army for battle.
5 They come from a distant land,
from the end of the heavens,
the LORD and the weapons of his indignation,
to destroy the whole earth.

6 Wail, for the day of the LORD is near;
it will come like destruction from the Almighty![n]
7 Therefore all hands will be feeble,
and every human heart will melt,
8 and they will be dismayed.
Pangs and agony will seize them;
they will be in anguish like a woman in labor.
They will look aghast at one another;
their faces will be aflame.
9 See, the day of the LORD comes,
cruel, with wrath and fierce anger,
to make the earth a desolation,
and to destroy its sinners from it.
10 For the stars of the heavens and their constellations
will not give their light;
the sun will be dark at its rising,
and the moon will not shed its light.
11 I will punish the world for its evil,
and the wicked for their iniquity;
I will put an end to the pride of the arrogant,
and lay low the insolence of tyrants.
12 I will make mortals more rare than fine gold,
and humans than the gold of Ophir.
13 Therefore I will make the heavens tremble,
and the earth will be shaken out of its place,
at the wrath of the LORD of hosts

13.2 Isa 45.1-3
13.4 Isa 5.30
13.5 Isa 5.26
13.6 Isa 34.2,8 Ezek 30.3 Amos 5.18
13.7 Ezek 21.7
13.8 Isa 21.3; 26.17
13.9 Isa 66.15,16
13.10 Mt 24.29
13.11 Dan 5.22,23
13.12 Isa 6.11,12
13.13 Hag 2.6

n Traditional rendering of Heb *Shaddai*

13.1ff Chapters 1 – 6 tell of judgment against the southern kingdom. Chapters 7 – 12 speak of judgment against the northern kingdom. Chapters 13 – 23 are about the judgment on other nations. Chapter 13 is an oracle or message from God concerning Babylon. Long before Babylon became a world power and threatened Judah, Isaiah spoke of its condemnation. Babylon was the rallying point of rebellion against God after the flood (Genesis 11). Revelation 17 and 18 use Babylon as a symbol of God's enemies. Isaiah is trying to tell the people not to fear other nations, but to fear God alone. And he lets them know that their greatest enemies will receive from God the punishment they deserve.

13.12 Ophir was known for its rare and valuable gold. It is thought to have been located on the southwestern coast of Arabia.

in the day of his fierce anger.
13.14 1 Kgs 22.17 Mt 9.36
14 Like a hunted gazelle,
or like sheep with no one to gather them,
all will turn to their own people,
and all will flee to their own lands.
13.15 Jer 51.3,4
15 Whoever is found will be thrust through,
and whoever is caught will fall by the sword.
13.16 Ps 137.8,9 Hos 10.14
16 Their infants will be dashed to pieces
before their eyes;
their houses will be plundered,
and their wives ravished.
13.17 Jer 51.11
17 See, I am stirring up the Medes against them,
who have no regard for silver
and do not delight in gold.
13.18 2 Chron 36.17
18 Their bows will slaughter the young men;
they will have no mercy on the fruit of the womb;
their eyes will not pity children.
13.19 Gen 19.24 Rev 18.11-16,19
19 And Babylon, the glory of kingdoms,
the splendor and pride of the Chaldeans,
will be like Sodom and Gomorrah
when God overthrew them.
13.20 Jer 51.37-43
20 It will never be inhabited
or lived in for all generations;
Arabs will not pitch their tents there,
shepherds will not make their flocks lie down there.
13.21 Isa 34.11-15 Zeph 2.14 Isa 32.14; 34.13
21 But wild animals will lie down there,
and its houses will be full of howling creatures;
there ostriches will live,
and there goat-demons will dance.
22 Hyenas will cry in its towers,
and jackals in the pleasant palaces;
its time is close at hand,
and its days will not be prolonged.

God promises compassion on Israel

14.1 Ps 102.13 Isa 41.8,9 49.13,15 Zech 2.11,12
14.2 Isa 45.14 Dan 7.18,27
14.3 Ezra 9.8,9 Jer 30.10

14 But the LORD will have compassion on Jacob and will again choose Israel,
and will set them in their own land; and aliens will join them and attach
themselves to the house of Jacob. 2 And the nations will take them and bring them
to their place, and the house of Israel will possess the nations[o] as male and female
slaves in the LORD's land; they will take captive those who were their captors, and
rule over those who oppressed them.
3 When the LORD has given you rest from your pain and turmoil and the hard
service with which you were made to serve, 4 you will take up this taunt against the
king of Babylon:
How the oppressor has ceased!

[o] Heb *them*

13.20 Even before Babylon became a world power, Isaiah prophesied that, though it would shine for a while, its destruction would be so complete that the land would never again be inhabited. Babylon, in present-day Iraq, still lies buried in utter ruin.

14.1 God destroyed Babylon to rescue and restore the remnant of his people (i.e., those who remained faithful to him). His patience with his rebellious people followed several steps: (1) Because his chosen people rebelled and sinned against him, God had to use others, even heathen nations, to punish them. (2) But these nations were themselves wicked, and God punished them as well. (3) Because God promised to bless Israel, and God does not break promises, he will restore Israel. (4) God will make Israel an essential ingredient in his work of blessing the Gentile nations.

14.1 A prominent theme in Isaiah is that non-Israelites would join the returning Israelites (56.6, 7; 60.10; 61.5). God's intention was that through his faithful people all the world would be blessed (Genesis 12.3). They would be custodians of his Word, and through the family of David the whole world could be saved by Christ. We must not limit God's love. God loves the whole world.

14.4–11 These verses could have both present and future significance in reference to Babylon. The historical city and empire would be permanently destroyed. Babylon has also been used as a picture of all those who oppose God. Thus, in the end times, all who oppose God will be destroyed along with all evil.

How his insolence[p] has ceased!
5 The LORD has broken the staff of the wicked,
the scepter of rulers,
6 that struck down the peoples in wrath
with unceasing blows,
that ruled the nations in anger
with unrelenting persecution.
7 The whole earth is at rest and quiet;
they break forth into singing.
8 The cypresses exult over you,
the cedars of Lebanon, saying,
"Since you were laid low,
no one comes to cut us down."
9 Sheol beneath is stirred up
to meet you when you come;
it rouses the shades to greet you,
all who were leaders of the earth;
it raises from their thrones
all who were kings of the nations.
10 All of them will speak
and say to you:
"You too have become as weak as we!
You have become like us!"
11 Your pomp is brought down to Sheol,
and the sound of your harps;
maggots are the bed beneath you,
and worms are your covering.

12 How you are fallen from heaven,
O Day Star, son of Dawn!
How you are cut down to the ground,
you who laid the nations low!
13 You said in your heart,
"I will ascend to heaven;
I will raise my throne
above the stars of God;
I will sit on the mount of assembly
on the heights of Zaphon;[q]
14 I will ascend to the tops of the clouds,
I will make myself like the Most High."
15 But you are brought down to Sheol,
to the depths of the Pit.
16 Those who see you will stare at you,
and ponder over you:

14.6 Isa 47.6
14.7 Ps 98.1-9
14.10 Ezek 32.21
14.12 Lk 10.18 Rev 9.1
14.13 Ezek 28.2
14.14 2 Thess 2.4

[p] Q Ms Compare Gk Syr Vg: Meaning of MT uncertain [q] Or *assembly in the far north*

14.5, 6 Power is transitory. God permitted Babylon to have temporary power for a purpose—to chastise his wayward people. When the purpose ended, so did the power. Beware of placing confidence in human power, for one day it will fade no matter how strong it appears now.

14.9 *Sheol* is the word in the Old Testament for the realm of the dead. It is used to mean the grave or state of being dead.

14.12 "Day Star, son of Dawn" could be names used to worship the kings of Assyria and Babylon. More likely, it means that they will fade like the morning star when the sun rises.

14.12–14 There are several interpretations for the tyrant in these verses. (1) It is Satan because the person here is too powerful to be any human king, and also because a parallel is seen between his name "Lucifer" (or light-bearer) and Day Star. Although Satan fits verses 12–14, he does not fit well with the rest of the chapter. (2) This could be Sennacherib or Nebuchadnezzar, kings with supreme power. Their people looked upon them as gods. These kings desired to rule the world. (3) This could refer to both Satan and a great human king, probably Nebuchadnezzar since Babylon is pictured as the seat of evil in Revelation 17, 18. Pride was Satan's sin as well as Babylon's. Common to all three viewpoints is the truth that pride is against God and will result in judgment. Israel made the mistake of being too proud to depend on God, and we are vulnerable to that same mistake.

"Is this the man who made the earth tremble,
who shook kingdoms,
17 who made the world like a desert
and overthrew its cities,
who would not let his prisoners go home?"
18 All the kings of the nations lie in glory,
each in his own tomb;
14.19 Isa 5.25
19 but you are cast out, away from your grave,
like loathsome carrion,[r]
clothed with the dead, those pierced by the sword,
who go down to the stones of the Pit,
like a corpse trampled underfoot.
20 You will not be joined with them in burial,
because you have destroyed your land,
you have killed your people.

May the descendants of evildoers
nevermore be named!
14.21 Ex 20.5 Isa 13.16
21 Prepare slaughter for his sons
because of the guilt of their father.[s]
Let them never rise to possess the earth
or cover the face of the world with cities.

22 I will rise up against them, says the LORD of hosts, and will cut off from
Babylon name and remnant, offspring and posterity, says the LORD. 23 And I will
make it a possession of the hedgehog, and pools of water, and I will sweep it with
the broom of destruction, says the LORD of hosts.

Prophecy against Assyria

14.24 Job 23.13 Isa 46.11
24 The LORD of hosts has sworn:
As I have designed,
so shall it be;
and as I have planned,
so shall it come to pass:
14.25 Isa 9.4 Nah 1.13
25 I will break the Assyrian in my land,
and on my mountains trample him under foot;
his yoke shall be removed from them,
and his burden from their shoulders.
26 This is the plan that is planned
concerning the whole earth;
and this is the hand that is stretched out
over all the nations.
14.27 Isa 43.13 Dan 4.31,35
27 For the LORD of hosts has planned,
and who will annul it?
His hand is stretched out,
and who will turn it back?

Prophecy against Philistia

14.28 2 Kgs 16.20
28 In the year that King Ahaz died this oracle came:

29 Do not rejoice, all you Philistines,

[r] Cn Compare Gk: Heb *like a loathed branch* [s] Syr Compare Gk: Heb *fathers*

14.24–27 This prophecy came true as Isaiah predicted (see 2 Kings 19 and Isaiah 37.21–38).

14.28–31 Isaiah received this message from the Lord in 715 B.C., the year that King Ahaz of Judah died. "Philistia" is the land of the Philistines. "The rod that struck you" was not Ahaz but Shalmaneser V of Assyria. The "smoke" from the north refers to the soldiers of Sargon of Assyria.

that the rod that struck you is broken,
for from the root of the snake will come forth an adder,
and its fruit will be a flying fiery serpent.
30 The firstborn of the poor will graze,
and the needy lie down in safety;
but I will make your root die of famine,
and your remnant I[t] will kill.
31 Wail, O gate; cry, O city;
melt in fear, O Philistia, all of you!
For smoke comes out of the north,
and there is no straggler in its ranks.

32 What will one answer the messengers of the nation?
"The LORD has founded Zion,
and the needy among his people
will find refuge in her."

14.30 Isa 8.21; 11.4
14.31 Isa 3.26 Jer 1.14
14.32 Isa 25.4

Prophecy against Moab

15 An oracle concerning Moab.

Because Ar is laid waste in a night,
Moab is undone;
because Kir is laid waste in a night,
Moab is undone.
2 Dibon[u] has gone up to the temple,
to the high places to weep;
over Nebo and over Medeba
Moab wails.
On every head is baldness,
every beard is shorn;
3 in the streets they bind on sackcloth;
on the housetops and in the squares
everyone wails and melts in tears.
4 Heshbon and Elealeh cry out,
their voices are heard as far as Jahaz;
therefore the loins of Moab quiver;[v]
his soul trembles.
5 My heart cries out for Moab;
his fugitives flee to Zoar,
to Eglath-shelishiyah.
For at the ascent of Luhith
they go up weeping;
on the road to Horonaim
they raise a cry of destruction;
6 the waters of Nimrim
are a desolation;
the grass is withered, the new growth fails,
the verdure is no more.
7 Therefore the abundance they have gained
and what they have laid up
they carry away

15.2 Jer 48.37
15.3 Isa 22.4 Jer 48.38 Jonah 3.6-8
15.5 Jer 31.5
15.6 Jer 48.34 Joel 1.10-12
15.7 Jer 48.36

[t] Q Ms Vg: MT *he* [u] Cn: Heb *the house and Dibon* [v] Cn Compare Gk Syr: Heb *the armed men of Moab cry aloud*

15.1 Moab was east of the Dead Sea. The Moabites were descendants of Lot through his incestuous relationship with his older daughter (Genesis 19.31–38). Moab had always been Israel's enemy. They oppressed Israel and invaded their land (Judges 3.12–14), fought against Saul (1 Samuel 14:47), and fought against David (2 Samuel 8.2, 11, 12). Moab would be punished for its harsh treatment of Israel.

15.7 A wadi is a stream or dry streambed.

over the Wadi of the Willows.
8 For a cry has gone
around the land of Moab;
the wailing reaches to Eglaim,
the wailing reaches to Beer-elim.
15.9 2 Kgs 17.25 Jer 50.17
9 For the waters of Dibon[w] are full of blood;
yet I will bring upon Dibon[w] even more—
a lion for those of Moab who escape,
for the remnant of the land.

16.1 2 Kgs 3.4; 14.7 Isa 42.11
16 Send lambs
to the ruler of the land,
from Sela, by way of the desert,
to the mount of daughter Zion.
16.2 Num 21.13
2 Like fluttering birds,
like scattered nestlings,
so are the daughters of Moab
at the fords of the Arnon.
3 "Give counsel,
grant justice;
make your shade like night
at the height of noon;
hide the outcasts,
do not betray the fugitive;
16.4 Isa 9.6,7; 54.14 Lk 1.32,33
4 let the outcasts of Moab
settle among you;
be a refuge to them
from the destroyer."

When the oppressor is no more,
and destruction has ceased,
and marauders have vanished from the land,
5 then a throne shall be established in steadfast love
in the tent of David,
and on it shall sit in faithfulness
a ruler who seeks justice
and is swift to do what is right.

16.6 Jer 48.29 Zeph 2.8,10
6 We have heard of the pride of Moab
—how proud he is!—
of his arrogance, his pride, and his insolence;
his boasts are false.
16.7 2 Kgs 3.25 Jer 48.31
7 Therefore let Moab wail,
let everyone wail for Moab.
Mourn, utterly stricken,
for the raisin-cakes of Kir-hareseth.

8 For the fields of Heshbon languish,
and the vines of Sibmah,
whose clusters once made drunk
the lords of the nations,
reached to Jazer
and strayed to the desert;

w Q Ms Vg Compare Syr: MT *Dimon*

16.1ff Attacked by the Assyrians, Moabite refugees would flee to Sela, which lay in the country of Edom to the south. Desperate Moabite women would send a tribute of lambs to Jerusalem asking for Judah's protection. Jerusalem would be a safe refuge for a while. Isaiah advised Judah to accept these refugees as a sign of compassion in the enemy's time of devastation.

their shoots once spread abroad
and crossed over the sea.
9 Therefore I weep with the weeping of Jazer
for the vines of Sibmah;
I drench you with my tears,
O Heshbon and Elealeh;
for the shout over your fruit harvest
and your grain harvest has ceased.
10 Joy and gladness are taken away
from the fruitful field;
and in the vineyards no songs are sung,
no shouts are raised;
no treader treads out wine in the presses;
the vintage-shout is hushed.[x]
11 Therefore my heart throbs like a harp for Moab,
and my very soul for Kir-heres.

12 When Moab presents himself, when he wearies himself upon the high place,
when he comes to his sanctuary to pray, he will not prevail.
13 This was the word that the LORD spoke concerning Moab in the past. 14 But
now the LORD says, In three years, like the years of a hired worker, the glory of
Moab will be brought into contempt, in spite of all its great multitude; and those
who survive will be very few and feeble.

16.9 Jer 48.32
16.10 Isa 24.7,8 Jer 48.33 Amos 5.17
16.11 Isa 15.5
16.12 1 Kgs 18.26-29
16.13 Isa 25.10 Jer 48.42

Prophecy against Syria

17 An oracle concerning Damascus.

See, Damascus will cease to be a city,
and will become a heap of ruins.
2 Her towns will be deserted forever;[y]
they will be places for flocks,
which will lie down, and no one will make them afraid.
3 The fortress will disappear from Ephraim,
and the kingdom from Damascus;
and the remnant of Aram will be
like the glory of the children of Israel,
says the LORD of hosts.

4 On that day
the glory of Jacob will be brought low,
and the fat of his flesh will grow lean.
5 And it shall be as when reapers gather standing grain
and their arms harvest the ears,
and as when one gleans the ears of grain
in the Valley of Rephaim.
6 Gleanings will be left in it,

17.1 Isa 10.9; 25.2 Mic 1.6
17.2 Mic 4.4 Zeph 2.6
17.3 Isa 8.4 Hos 9.11
17.5 Jer 51.33
17.6 Deut 4.27 Isa 24.13

x Gk: Heb *I have hushed* y Cn Compare Gk: Heb *the cities of Aroer are deserted*

16.10 The treading of grapes (squeezing the juice from grapes by mashing them with bare feet) climaxed during the harvest season, a time of great joy in the vineyards. But the joy of harvest would soon be ended, because the people ignored God and rebelled against him.

16.12 When the people of Moab experienced God's wrath, they sought their own idols and gods. Nothing happened, however, because there was no one there to save them. We seek our own ways of escape in order to get through our daily troubles. The effect is the same: no pleasure, pastime, or man-made religious idea will come to save us. Our only hope lies in God.

16.13, 14 Tiglath-pileser III invaded Moab in 732 B.C.; Sennacherib invaded Moab the same year that he invaded Judah, 701 B.C. The earlier event occurred three years after Isaiah's prediction, marking Isaiah as a true prophet. In these events, the people of Israel saw prophecy fulfilled before their eyes.

17.1ff The northern kingdom and Syria made an alliance to fight against Assyria. But Tiglath-pileser III captured Damascus, the capital of Syria, in 732 B.C. and annexed the northern kingdom to the Assyrian Empire. Ahaz, king of Judah, then paid tribute to Tiglath-pileser III when he visited the Assyrian king in Damascus.

as when an olive tree is beaten—
two or three berries
in the top of the highest bough,
four or five
on the branches of a fruit tree,
says the LORD God of Israel.

17.7 Isa 10.20 Hos 6.1
17.8 Ex 34.13 Isa 27.9; 30.22

7 On that day people will regard their Maker, and their eyes will look to the
Holy One of Israel; 8 they will not have regard for the altars, the work of their
hands, and they will not look to what their own fingers have made, either the sacred
poles[z] or the altars of incense.
9 On that day their strong cities will be like the deserted places of the Hivites
and the Amorites,[a] which they deserted because of the children of Israel, and there
will be desolation.

17.10 Deut 32.4,18, 30,31 Isa 30.29; 62.11

10 For you have forgotten the God of your salvation,
and have not remembered the Rock of your refuge;
therefore, though you plant pleasant plants
and set out slips of an alien god,

17.11 Hos 10.13

11 though you make them grow on the day that you plant them,
and make them blossom in the morning that you sow;
yet the harvest will flee away
in a day of grief and incurable pain.

17.12 Jer 6.23

12 Ah, the thunder of many peoples,
they thunder like the thundering of the sea!
Ah, the roar of nations,
they roar like the roaring of mighty waters!

17.13 Ps 1.4 Isa 29.5

13 The nations roar like the roaring of many waters,
but he will rebuke them, and they will flee far away,
chased like chaff on the mountains before the wind
and whirling dust before the storm.

17.14 2 Kgs 19.35 Isa 41.11,12

14 At evening time, lo, terror!
Before morning, they are no more.
This is the fate of those who despoil us,
and the lot of those who plunder us.

Prophecy against Ethiopia

18 Ah, land of whirring wings
beyond the rivers of Ethiopia,[b]
2 sending ambassadors by the Nile
in vessels of papyrus on the waters!
Go, you swift messengers,

[z] Heb *Asherim* [a] Cn Compare Gk: Heb *places of the wood and the highest bough* [b] Or *Nubia*; Heb *Cush*

17.7–11 God's message to Damascus is that they will be completely destroyed. The Syrians had turned from the God who could save them, depending instead on their idols and their own strength. No matter how successful they were, God's judgment was sure. Often we depend on the trappings of success (expensive cars, pastimes, clothes, homes) to give us fulfillment. But God says we will reap grief and pain if we have depended on temporal things to give us eternal security. If we don't want the same treatment Damascus received, we must turn from these false allurements and trust in God.

17.8 The sacred poles were images of Asherah, a Canaanite goddess who was the female consort of Baal. Queen Jezebel may have brought the worship of Asherah into the northern kingdom. The cult encouraged immoral sexual practices and attracted many people. The Bible warns against worshiping Asherah, Asherim, or in groves (Exodus 34.13; Deuteronomy 12.3; 16.21), and Manasseh was condemned for putting up an idol that was most likely of her in the temple (2 Kings 21.7). Unlike heathen gods, our God does not try to attract the greatest number of people, but instead seeks the greatest good for all people.

18.1ff This prophecy was probably given in the days of Hezekiah (2 Kings 19, 20). The "land of whirring wings" refers to locusts. The Ethiopian king had heard that Assyria's great army was marching south toward them. He sent messengers up the Nile asking the surrounding nations to form an alliance. Judah was also asked, but Isaiah told the messenger to return home because Judah needed only God's help to repel the Assyrians. Isaiah prophesied that Assyria would be destroyed at the proper time.

to a nation tall and smooth,
to a people feared near and far,
a nation mighty and conquering,
whose land the rivers divide.

3 All you inhabitants of the world,
you who live on the earth,
when a signal is raised on the mountains, look!
When a trumpet is blown, listen!
4 For thus the LORD said to me:
I will quietly look from my dwelling
like clear heat in sunshine,
like a cloud of dew in the heat of harvest.
5 For before the harvest, when the blossom is over
and the flower becomes a ripening grape,
he will cut off the shoots with pruning hooks,
and the spreading branches he will hew away.
6 They shall all be left
to the birds of prey of the mountains
and to the animals of the earth.
And the birds of prey will summer on them,
and all the animals of the earth will winter on them.

7 At that time gifts will be brought to the LORD of hosts from[c] a people tall and
smooth, from a people feared near and far, a nation mighty and conquering, whose
land the rivers divide, to Mount Zion, the place of the name of the LORD of hosts.

18.3 Ps 49.1 Mic 1.2
18.5 Ezek 17.6-10
18.6 Isa 56.9 Ezek 39.17-20
18.7 Zech 14.16,17

Prophecy against Egypt

19 An oracle concerning Egypt.

See, the LORD is riding on a swift cloud
and comes to Egypt;
the idols of Egypt will tremble at his presence,
and the heart of the Egyptians will melt within them.
2 I will stir up Egyptians against Egyptians,
and they will fight, one against the other,
neighbor against neighbor,
city against city, kingdom against kingdom;
3 the spirit of the Egyptians within them will be emptied out,
and I will confound their plans;
they will consult the idols and the spirits of the dead
and the ghosts and the familiar spirits;
4 I will deliver the Egyptians
into the hand of a hard master;
a fierce king will rule over them,
says the Sovereign, the LORD of hosts.

5 The waters of the Nile will be dried up,
and the river will be parched and dry;
6 its canals will become foul,

19.1 Josh 2.11 Jer 43.12
19.2 Judg 7.22 Mt 10.21,36
19.3 Isa 8.19
19.4 Isa 20.4 Ezek 29.19
19.5 Ezek 30.12
19.6 Ex 7.18

[c] Q Ms Gk Vg: MT *of*

18.3 This is the call to all nations to watch for the signal of the fall of Assyria. Ethiopia had been summoning other nations to join an alliance against Assyria. God would stop Assyria in its attempt to overtake the world.

19.1 Egypt, the nation where God's people were enslaved for 400 years (Exodus 1), was a hated memory for the people of Israel, yet Judah was considering an alliance with Egypt against Assyria. But Isaiah warned against this alliance because God would destroy Assyria in his time.

and the branches of Egypt's Nile will diminish and dry up,
reeds and rushes will rot away.
7 There will be bare places by the Nile,
on the brink of the Nile;
and all that is sown by the Nile will dry up,
be driven away, and be no more.
8 Those who fish will mourn;
all who cast hooks in the Nile will lament,
and those who spread nets on the water will languish.
9 The workers in flax will be in despair,
and the carders and those at the loom will grow pale.
10 Its weavers will be dismayed,
and all who work for wages will be grieved.

19.11 Gen 41.38,39 1 Kgs 4.30 Acts 7.22

11 The princes of Zoan are utterly foolish;
the wise counselors of Pharaoh give stupid counsel.
How can you say to Pharaoh,
"I am one of the sages,
a descendant of ancient kings"?

19.12 Rom 9.17

12 Where now are your sages?
Let them tell you and make known
what the LORD of hosts has planned against Egypt.

19.13 Jer 46.14,19

13 The princes of Zoan have become fools,
and the princes of Memphis are deluded;
those who are the cornerstones of its tribes
have led Egypt astray.

19.14 Isa 3.12

14 The LORD has poured into them[d]
a spirit of confusion;
and they have made Egypt stagger in all its doings
as a drunkard staggers around in vomit.
15 Neither head nor tail, palm branch or reed,
will be able to do anything for Egypt.

19.16 Jer 51.30 Heb 10.31

16 On that day the Egyptians will be like women, and tremble with fear before
the hand that the LORD of hosts raises against them. 17 And the land of Judah will

[d] Gk Compare Tg: Heb *it*

ALLIANCES TODAY

Government	We rely on government legislation to protect the moral decisions we want made, but legislation cannot change people's hearts.
Science	We enjoy the benefits of science and technology. We look to scientific predictions and analysis before we look to the Bible.
Education	We act as though education and degrees can guarantee our future and success without considering what God plans for our future.
Medical care	We regard medicine as the way to prolong life and preserve its quality—quite apart from faith and moral living.
Financial systems	We place our faith in financial "security"—making as much money as we can for ourselves—forgetting that, while being wise with our money, we must trust God for our needs.

Isaiah warned Judah not to ally with Egypt. He knew that trust in any nation or any military might was futile. Their only hope was to trust in God. Although we don't consciously put our hope for deliverance in political alliances in quite the same way, we often put our hope in other forces.

19.9 Carders are those who comb the flax to make linen.

19.14, 15 Egypt was noted for its wisdom, but now its wise men and princes were deceived and foolish. True wisdom can come only from God. We must ask him for wisdom to guide our decisions, or we will also be uncertain and misdirected. Are you confused about something in your life now? Ask God for wisdom to deal with it.

become a terror to the Egyptians; everyone to whom it is mentioned will fear be- **19.17** Dan 4.35
cause of the plan that the LORD of hosts is planning against them.
18 On that day there will be five cities in the land of Egypt that speak the language of Canaan and swear allegiance to the LORD of hosts. One of these will be
called the City of the Sun.
19 On that day there will be an altar to the LORD in the center of the land of **19.19**
Egypt, and a pillar to the LORD at its border. 20 It will be a sign and a witness to the Gen 28.18 Josh 22.10,
LORD of hosts in the land of Egypt; when they cry to the LORD because of oppres- 26,27
sors, he will send them a savior, and will defend and deliver them. 21 The LORD will **19.20** Isa 43.3,11
make himself known to the Egyptians; and the Egyptians will know the LORD on 45.15,21; 49.25
that day, and will worship with sacrifice and burnt offering, and they will make **19.21**
vows to the LORD and perform them. 22 The LORD will strike Egypt, striking and Isa 56.7 **19.22**
healing; they will return to the LORD, and he will listen to their supplications and Deut 32.39
heal them. Isa 27.13 Heb 12.11
23 On that day there will be a highway from Egypt to Assyria, and the Assyrian **19.23**
will come into Egypt, and the Egyptian into Assyria, and the Egyptians will wor- Isa 11.16
ship with the Assyrians.
24 On that day Israel will be the third with Egypt and Assyria, a blessing in the
midst of the earth, 25 whom the LORD of hosts has blessed, saying, "Blessed be **19.25**
Egypt my people, and Assyria the work of my hands, and Israel my heritage." Hos 2.23

Prophecy against Egypt and Ethiopia

20 In the year that the commander-in-chief, who was sent by King Sargon of
Assyria, came to Ashdod and fought against it and took it— 2 at that time the **20.2**
LORD had spoken to Isaiah son of Amoz, saying, "Go, and loose the sackcloth from 1 Sam 19.24 Mic 1.8
your loins and take your sandals off your feet," and he had done so, walking naked
and barefoot. 3 Then the LORD said, "Just as my servant Isaiah has walked naked **20.3**
and barefoot for three years as a sign and a portent against Egypt and Ethiopia,[e] Isa 8.18; 43.3
4 so shall the king of Assyria lead away the Egyptians as captives and the Ethiopi- **20.4**
ans[f] as exiles, both the young and the old, naked and barefoot, with buttocks un- Isa 19.4; 47.2,3
covered, to the shame of Egypt. 5 And they shall be dismayed and confounded **20.5**
because of Ethiopia[e] their hope and of Egypt their boast. 6 In that day the inhabi- Isa 31.3
tants of this coastland will say, 'See, this is what has happened to those in whom we Jer 9.23,24
hoped and to whom we fled for help and deliverance from the king of Assyria! And
we, how shall we escape?' "

Prophecy against Babylon

21 The oracle concerning the wilderness of the sea. **21.1** Isa 13.20-22 Jer 51.41 Zech 9.14

As whirlwinds in the Negeb sweep on,
it comes from the desert,

[e] Or *Nubia*; Heb *Cush* [f] Or *Nubians*; Heb *Cushites*

19.19, 23 After Egypt's chastening, it would turn from idols and worship the one true God. Even more amazing is Isaiah's prophecy that the two chief oppressors of Israel, Egypt and Assyria, would unite in worship. This prophecy will come true "on that day," the future day of Christ's reign.

19.20 When Egypt calls to God for help, he will send a Savior to deliver them. Our Savior, Jesus Christ, is available to all who call upon him. We too can pray and receive his saving power (John 1.12).

19.22 Egypt is but one Gentile nation who will bow before the Lord. (Philippians 2.10, 11 says *every* knee shall bow, every tongue confess that Jesus Christ is Lord.) So we shouldn't be surprised that Egyptians and Assyrians are part of the "every." Each of us is part of that "every" too. We may bow now in devotion, or later in submission.

19.23–25 In Jesus Christ, former enemies may unite in love. In Christ, people and nations that are poles apart politically will bow at his feet as brothers and sisters because he breaks down every barrier that threatens relationships (see Ephesians 2.13–19).

20.1ff Sargon II was king of Assyria from 722–705 B.C., and this event happened in 711 B.C. Isaiah graphically reminds Judah that they should not count on foreign alliances to protect them.

20.2 God's command to Isaiah was to walk about naked for three years, a humiliating experience. God was using Isaiah to demonstrate the humiliation that Egypt and Ethiopia would experience at the hands of Assyria. But the message was really for Judah: Don't put your trust in foreign governments, or you will experience this kind of shame and humiliation from your captors.

20.2 God asked Isaiah to do something that seemed shameful and illogical. At times we may be asked to obey God in ways we don't understand. We must obey God in complete faith, for he will never ask us to do something wrong.

from a terrible land.
2 A stern vision is told to me;
the betrayer betrays,
and the destroyer destroys.
Go up, O Elam,
lay siege, O Media;
all the sighing she has caused
I bring to an end.
21.3 Ps 48.6 1 Thess 5.3
3 Therefore my loins are filled with anguish;
pangs have seized me,
like the pangs of a woman in labor;
I am bowed down so that I cannot hear,
I am dismayed so that I cannot see.
21.4 Deut 28.67
4 My mind reels, horror has appalled me;
the twilight I longed for
has been turned for me into trembling.
21.5 Jer 51.39,57
5 They prepare the table,
they spread the rugs,
they eat, they drink.
Rise up, commanders,
oil the shield!
6 For thus the Lord said to me:
"Go, post a lookout,
let him announce what he sees.
7 When he sees riders, horsemen in pairs,
riders on donkeys, riders on camels,
let him listen diligently,
very diligently."
21.8 Isa 13.19 46.1,2 Jer 50.2 Hab 2.1 Rev 14.8
8 Then the watcher[g] called out:
"Upon a watchtower I stand, O Lord,
continually by day,
and at my post I am stationed
throughout the night.
9 Look, there they come, riders,
horsemen in pairs!"
Then he responded,
"Fallen, fallen is Babylon;
and all the images of her gods
lie shattered on the ground."
21.10 Jer 51.33
10 O my threshed and winnowed one,
what I have heard from the LORD of hosts,
the God of Israel, I announce to you.

[g] Q Ms: MT *a lion*

21.1ff "The wilderness of the sea" is Babylon by the Persian Gulf. Some scholars say this prophecy was fulfilled at Babylon's fall in 539 B.C. (see Daniel 5). But others say this was a prophecy of Babylon's revolt against Assyria around 700 B.C.

21.5 If the prophecy refers to the fall of Babylon in 539 B.C., this refers to the feast in Daniel 5.

21.6, 7 Watchmen ("lookouts") often appear in prophetic visions of destruction. They are the first to see trouble coming. The prophet Habakkuk was a watchman (Habakkuk 2.1). The vision of the pair of riders could represent the Medes and Persians attacking Babylon in 539 B.C.

21.8, 9 Babylon was not only a great and powerful city, it was also filled with horrible sin (idolatry, witchcraft, and temple prostitution). Babylon was, and remains, a symbol of all that stands against God. Despite all its glory and power, Babylon would be destroyed with all its idols. They would give no help in time of trouble.

21.10 Threshing and winnowing were two steps in ancient Israel's farming process. The heads of wheat (often used to symbolize Israel) were first trampled to break open the seeds and expose the valued grain inside. The seeds were then thrown into the air, and the worthless chaff blew away while the grain fell back to the ground. Israel would experience this same kind of process – the worthless, sinful, rebellious people would be taken away, but God would keep the good "grain" to replenish Israel.

Prophecy against Edom

11 The oracle concerning Dumah.

One is calling to me from Seir,
"Sentinel, what of the night?
Sentinel, what of the night?"
12 The sentinel says:
"Morning comes, and also the night.
If you will inquire, inquire;
come back again."

Prophecy against Arabia

13 The oracle concerning the desert plain.

In the scrub of the desert plain you will lodge,
O caravans of Dedanites.
14 Bring water to the thirsty,
meet the fugitive with bread,
O inhabitants of the land of Tema.
15 For they have fled from the swords,
from the drawn sword,
from the bent bow,
and from the stress of battle.

16 For thus the Lord said to me: Within a year, according to the years of a hired
worker, all the glory of Kedar will come to an end; 17 and the remaining bows of
Kedar's warriors will be few; for the LORD, the God of Israel, has spoken.

21.11 Gen 32.3
21.15 Isa 13.14,15
21.17 Isa 10.19

Prophecy about Jerusalem

22 The oracle concerning the valley of vision.

What do you mean that you have gone up,
all of you, to the housetops,
2 you that are full of shoutings,
tumultuous city, exultant town?
Your slain are not slain by the sword,
nor are they dead in battle.
3 Your rulers have all fled together;
they were captured without the use of a bow.[h]
All of you who were found were captured,
though they had fled far away.[i]
4 Therefore I said:
Look away from me,

22.1 Jer 21.13
22.2 Isa 23.7 Jer 14.18
22.4 Jer 9.1

[h] Or *without their bows* [i] Gk Syr Vg: Heb *fled from far away*

21.11 Dumah, or Edom, had been a constant enemy of God's people. They rejoiced when Israel fell to the Assyrians, and this sealed Edom's doom. Seir was another name given for Edom because the mountains of Seir were given to Esau and his descendants (see Joshua 24.4). Obadiah foretells, in great detail, the destruction of Edom.

21.13ff The places listed here are all in Arabia. They are border cities that controlled the trade routes through the land. Nabonidus, king of Babylon, would attack Arabia and make the people his servants. He set up court in Tema, leaving Belshazzar in Babylon as regent. This is Isaiah's prediction of disaster. Judah kept trying to make alliances with Arabia against Nabonidus, but Isaiah warned the people against such an alliance and urged them to trust in God alone.

22.1–13 "The valley of vision" refers to the city of Jerusalem because God revealed himself there. Jerusalem would be attacked unless God's people returned to him. Instead they used every means of protection possible except asking God for help. They wanted to trust in their ingenuity, their weapons, and even their pagan neighbors (see 2 Chronicles 32 for the description of a siege of Jerusalem).

22.4 Isaiah had warned his people; but they did not repent, so they would experience God's judgment. Because of his care for them, Isaiah was hurt by their punishment and mourned deeply for them. Sometimes people we care for ignore our attempts to help, so they suffer the very grief we wanted to spare them. At times like that we grieve because of our concern. God expects us to be involved with others, and this may sometimes require us to suffer with them.

let me weep bitter tears;
do not try to comfort me
for the destruction of my beloved people.

22.5 Isa 37.3 Lam 2.2

5 For the Lord GOD of hosts has a day
of tumult and trampling and confusion
in the valley of vision,
a battering down of walls
and a cry for help to the mountains.

22.6 Isa 21.2

6 Elam bore the quiver
with chariots and cavalry,[j]
and Kir uncovered the shield.
7 Your choicest valleys were full of chariots,
and the cavalry took their stand at the gates.
8 He has taken away the covering of Judah.

22.9 2 Kgs 25.4

On that day you looked to the weapons of the House of the Forest, 9 and you saw
that there were many breaches in the city of David, and you collected the waters of
the lower pool. 10 You counted the houses of Jerusalem, and you broke down the
houses to fortify the wall. 11 You made a reservoir between the two walls for the
water of the old pool. But you did not look to him who did it, or have regard for him
who planned it long ago.

22.12 Isa 32.11 Joel 1.13

12 In that day the Lord GOD of hosts
called to weeping and mourning,
to baldness and putting on sackcloth;

22.13 Isa 5.11,22 56.12 1 Cor 15.32

13 but instead there was joy and festivity,
killing oxen and slaughtering sheep,
eating meat and drinking wine.
"Let us eat and drink,
for tomorrow we die."
14 The LORD of hosts has revealed himself in my ears:
Surely this iniquity will not be forgiven you until you die,
says the Lord GOD of hosts.

22.15 2 Chron 16.14 Mt 27.60

15 Thus says the Lord GOD of hosts: Come, go to this steward, to Shebna, who
is master of the household, and say to him: 16 What right do you have here? Who are
your relatives here, that you have cut out a tomb here for yourself, cutting a tomb
on the height, and carving a habitation for yourself in the rock? 17 The LORD is
about to hurl you away violently, my fellow. He will seize firm hold on you,
18 whirl you round and round, and throw you like a ball into a wide land; there you
shall die, and there your splendid chariots shall lie, O you disgrace to your master's

[j] Meaning of Heb uncertain

22.6, 7 Elam and Kir were under Assyrian rule. The entire Assyrian army, including its vassals, joined in the attack against Jerusalem.

22.8–11 The leaders did what they could to prepare for war: they got weapons, inspected the walls, and built a water reservoir. But all their work was pointless because they never asked God for help. Too often we take steps which, though good in themselves, really won't give us the help we need. We must get the weapons and inspect the walls, but God must guide the work.

22.13 National danger should be a call to national repentance. But when these people were threatened, they decided to enjoy what they had instead of gathering together to repent. Seeing the Assyrians should have caused them to realize their sin and helplessness, to heed the prophet's warning, and to repent. Attacked on every side (22.7), they should have repented (22.12), but they chose to feast instead. The root problem was that Judah did not trust God's power or his promises (see 56.12; 1 Corinthians 15.32). When you face difficulties, turn to God.

22.13, 14 The people said, "Let us eat and drink," because they had given up hope. Today we still see people giving up hope. There are two common responses to hopelessness: despair and self-indulgence. But this life is not all there is, so we are not to act as if we have no hope. Our proper response should be to trust God and his promise to include us in a perfect, just new world he will create.

22.15–25 Shebna, a high court steward or official, was just as materialistic as the rest of Jerusalem (22.13). He may have been in the group favoring an alliance with foreigners, thus ignoring Isaiah's advice. Shebna is the peg that will be pulled out of the wall, and everything (his riches, his glory) will fall with it (22.25). The other peg, the secure one, is Eliakim, chosen to replace Shebna. Even his godly influence on the people would not keep Jerusalem from falling, because the people refused to repent.

house! 19 I will thrust you from your office, and you will be pulled down from your 22.19 Ezek 17.24
post.
20 On that day I will call my servant Eliakim son of Hilkiah, 21 and will clothe 22.20 Isa 36.3
him with your robe and bind your sash on him. I will commit your authority to his 22.21 Gen 45.8
hand, and he shall be a father to the inhabitants of Jerusalem and to the house of
Judah. 22 I will place on his shoulder the key of the house of David; he shall open,
and no one shall shut; he shall shut, and no one shall open. 23 I will fasten him like 22.23 Job 36.7 Zech 10.4
a peg in a secure place, and he will become a throne of honor to his ancestral house.
24 And they will hang on him the whole weight of his ancestral house, the offspring
and issue, every small vessel, from the cups to all the flagons. 25 On that day, says 22.25 Esth 9.24,25 Isa 46.11
the LORD of hosts, the peg that was fastened in a secure place will give way; it will
be cut down and fall, and the load that was on it will perish, for the LORD has
spoken.

Prophecy against Tyre

23 The oracle concerning Tyre. 23.1 Ezek 26.1-28

Wail, O ships of Tarshish,
for your fortress is destroyed.[k]
When they came in from Cyprus
they learned of it.
2 Be still, O inhabitants of the coast, 23.2 Ezek 27.3-23
O merchants of Sidon,
your messengers crossed over the sea[l]
3 and were on the mighty waters;
your revenue was the grain of Shihor,
the harvest of the Nile;
you were the merchant of the nations.
4 Be ashamed, O Sidon, for the sea has spoken, 23.4 Gen 10.15,19 Jer 47.4
the fortress of the sea, saying:
"I have neither labored nor given birth,
I have neither reared young men
nor brought up young women."
5 When the report comes to Egypt, 23.5 Josh 2.9-11
they will be in anguish over the report about Tyre.
6 Cross over to Tarshish—
wail, O inhabitants of the coast!
7 Is this your exultant city 23.7 Isa 32.13
whose origin is from days of old,
whose feet carried her
to settle far away?
8 Who has planned this
against Tyre, the bestower of crowns,
whose merchants were princes,
whose traders were the honored of the earth? 23.9 Isa 5.13 Dan 4.37
9 The LORD of hosts has planned it—

[k] Cn Compare verse 14: Heb *for it is destroyed, without houses* [l] Q Ms: MT *crossing over the sea, they replenished you*

22.20–24 Eliakim would be a responsible leader, supporting his followers. Good leaders build up others, not themselves. To do this, they must depend on the Lord.

23.1ff Isaiah's prophecies against other nations began in the east with Babylon (chapter 13) and ended in the west with Tyre in Phoenicia. Tyre was one of the most famous cities of the ancient world, a major trading center with a large seaport. It was a wealthy city and very evil. Tyre was rebuked by Jeremiah (Jeremiah 25.22, 27; 47.4), Ezekiel (Ezekiel 26–28), Joel (Joel 3.4–8), Amos (Amos 1.9, 10), and Zechariah (Zechariah 9.3, 4). This is another warning against political alliances with unstable neighbors.

23.5 Why would Egypt be "in anguish" when Tyre fell? Egypt depended on Tyre's shipping expertise to promote and carry their products around the world. Egypt would lose an important trading partner with the fall of Tyre.

23.9 God destroyed Tyre because he hated its people's pride. Pride separates people from God, and he will not tolerate it. We must examine our lives and remember that all true accomplishment comes from our Creator. We have no reason for pride in ourselves.

to defile the pride of all glory,
to shame all the honored of the earth.
10 Cross over to your own land,
O ships of[m] Tarshish;
this is a harbor[n] no more.
23.11 Isa 50.2 Zech 9.3,4
11 He has stretched out his hand over the sea,
he has shaken the kingdoms;
the LORD has given command concerning Canaan
to destroy its fortresses.
23.12 Rev 18.22
12 He said:
You will exult no longer,
O oppressed virgin daughter Sidon;
rise, cross over to Cyprus—
even there you will have no rest.

23.13 Isa 13.21
13 Look at the land of the Chaldeans! This is the people; it was not Assyria.
They destined Tyre for wild animals. They erected their siege towers, they tore
down her palaces, they made her a ruin.[o]
14 Wail, O ships of Tarshish,
for your fortress is destroyed.
23.15 Jer 25.11
15 From that day Tyre will be forgotten for seventy years, the lifetime of one king.
At the end of seventy years, it will happen to Tyre as in the song about the prostitute:
16 Take a harp,
go about the city,
you forgotten prostitute!
Make sweet melody,
sing many songs,
that you may be remembered.
17 At the end of seventy years, the LORD will visit Tyre, and she will return to her
trade, and will prostitute herself with all the kingdoms of the world on the face of
the earth. 18 Her merchandise and her wages will be dedicated to the LORD; her
profits[p] will not be stored or hoarded, but her merchandise will supply abundant
food and fine clothing for those who live in the presence of the LORD.

3. God's purpose in judgment

God's judgment on the land

24 Now the LORD is about to lay waste the earth and make it desolate,
and he will twist its surface and scatter its inhabitants.
24.2 Lev 25.36,37 Deut 23.19,20
2 And it shall be, as with the people, so with the priest;
as with the slave, so with his master;
as with the maid, so with her mistress;
as with the buyer, so with the seller;
as with the lender, so with the borrower;
as with the creditor, so with the debtor.
3 The earth shall be utterly laid waste and utterly despoiled;
for the LORD has spoken this word.

[m] Cn Compare Gk: Heb *like the Nile, daughter* [n] Cn: Heb *restraint* [o] Meaning of Heb uncertain [p] Heb *it*

23.13 Assyria invaded Tyre in 705 B.C. and again in 681–669 B.C. This message is astounding, however, because it prophesies that the Chaldeans (Babylonians), not yet a world power, would destroy Tyre. They did so in 572 B.C., a century after Isaiah made this prophecy.

23.15, 16 Some scholars believe this is a literal 70 years; some say it is symbolic of a long period of time. If it is literal, this may have occurred between 700–630 B.C. during the Assyrian captivity of Israel, or it may have been during the 70-year captivity of the Jews in Babylon (605–536 B.C.). During the 70 years the Jews would forget about Tyre, but when they returned from captivity they would once again trade with Tyre.

24–27 These four chapters are often called "Isaiah's Apocalypse." They discuss God's judgment on the entire world for its sin. Isaiah's prophecies were first directed to Judah, then to Israel, then to the surrounding nations, and finally to the whole world. These chapters describe the last days when God will judge the whole world. Then he will finally and permanently remove evil.

4 The earth dries up and withers,
the world languishes and withers;
the heavens languish together with the earth.
5 The earth lies polluted
under its inhabitants;
for they have transgressed laws,
violated the statutes,
broken the everlasting covenant.
6 Therefore a curse devours the earth,
and its inhabitants suffer for their guilt;
therefore the inhabitants of the earth dwindled,
and few people are left.
7 The wine dries up,
the vine languishes,
all the merry-hearted sigh.
8 The mirth of the timbrels is stilled,
the noise of the jubilant has ceased,
the mirth of the lyre is stilled.
9 No longer do they drink wine with singing;
strong drink is bitter to those who drink it.
10 The city of chaos is broken down,
every house is shut up so that no one can enter.
11 There is an outcry in the streets for lack of wine;
all joy has reached its eventide;
the gladness of the earth is banished.
12 Desolation is left in the city,
the gates are battered into ruins.
13 For thus it shall be on the earth
and among the nations,
as when an olive tree is beaten,
as at the gleaning when the grape harvest is ended.

14 They lift up their voices, they sing for joy;
they shout from the west over the majesty of the LORD.
15 Therefore in the east give glory to the LORD;
in the coastlands of the sea glorify the name of the LORD, the God of
Israel.
16 From the ends of the earth we hear songs of praise,
of glory to the Righteous One.
But I say, I pine away,
I pine away. Woe is me!
For the treacherous deal treacherously,
the treacherous deal very treacherously.

17 Terror, and the pit, and the snare
are upon you, O inhabitant of the earth!
18 Whoever flees at the sound of the terror
shall fall into the pit;

24.4 Gen 3.17 Num 35.33
24.6 Isa 34.5 Zech 5.3,4
24.7 Joel 1.10,12
24.8 Jer 16.9
24.9 Isa 5.11,22
24.10 Gen 1.2
24.11 Isa 32.13
24.12 Isa 45.2
24.13 Isa 17.6
24.14 Isa 12.6; 52.8
24.15 Isa 42.4,10,12 Jer 5.1
24.18 Gen 7.10-12 Ps 46.2

24.4, 5 Not only the people suffered from their sins; even the land suffered with bad crops and crime. Today we see the results of sin in our own land – pollution, crime, addiction, poverty. Sin affects every aspect of society so extensively that even those faithful to God suffer. We cannot blame God for these conditions, because human sin has brought them about. The more we who are believers renounce sin, speak against immoral practices, and share God's Word with others, the more we slow our society's deterioration. We must not give up: we can make a difference.

24.11 "Joy has reached its eventide" means that the time for joy is over, banished to gloom.

24.14–16 The believers who are left behind after God judges Judah will sing to the glory of God's righteousness. Isaiah grieved because of his world's condition. We too can become depressed by the evil all around us. At those times we need to hold on to God's promises for the future and look forward to singing praises to him when he restores heaven and earth.

and whoever climbs out of the pit
shall be caught in the snare.
For the windows of heaven are opened,
and the foundations of the earth tremble.
24.19 Num 16.31,32
19 The earth is utterly broken,
the earth is torn asunder,
the earth is violently shaken.
24.20 Isa 19.14; 43.27
20 The earth staggers like a drunkard,
it sways like a hut;
its transgression lies heavy upon it,
and it falls, and will not rise again.

24.21 Ps 76.12
21 On that day the LORD will punish
the host of heaven in heaven,
and on earth the kings of the earth.
24.22 Isa 10.4
22 They will be gathered together
like prisoners in a pit;
they will be shut up in a prison,
and after many days they will be punished.
24.23 Mic 4.7 Rev 21.23
23 Then the moon will be abashed,
and the sun ashamed;
for the LORD of hosts will reign
on Mount Zion and in Jerusalem,
and before his elders he will manifest his glory.

Praise to the Lord

25.1 Ex 15.2 Ps 40.5 Eph 1.11
25 O LORD, you are my God;
I will exalt you, I will praise your name;
for you have done wonderful things,
plans formed of old, faithful and sure.
25.2 Isa 17.1
2 For you have made the city a heap,
the fortified city a ruin;
the palace of aliens is a city no more,
it will never be rebuilt.
3 Therefore strong peoples will glorify you;
cities of ruthless nations will fear you.
25.4 Isa 32.2
4 For you have been a refuge to the poor,
a refuge to the needy in their distress,
a shelter from the rainstorm and a shade from the heat.
When the blast of the ruthless was like a winter rainstorm,
25.5 Jer 51.54-56
5 the noise of aliens like heat in a dry place,
you subdued the heat with the shade of clouds;
the song of the ruthless was stilled.

6 On this mountain the LORD of hosts will make for all peoples
a feast of rich food, a feast of well-aged wines,

24.21 "The host of heaven in heaven" refers to spiritual forces that are opposed to God. Nobody, not even the fallen angels, will escape due punishment.

25.1 Isaiah gave honor and praise to God because he realized that God completes his plans as promised. God also fulfills his promises to you. Think of the prayers he has answered, and praise him for his goodness and faithfulness.

25.4 The poor suffered because the rich oppressed them. But God is concerned for the poor and is a refuge for them. When we are disadvantaged or oppressed, we can turn to God for comfort and help. Jesus states in Luke 6.20 that the kingdom of God belongs to the poor.

25.6 Here is a marvelous prophecy of "all peoples" – Gentiles and Jews together – at God's messianic banquet celebrating the overthrow of evil and the joy of eternity with God. It shows that God intended his saving message to go out to the whole world, not just to the Jews. During the feast, God will end death forever (25.7, 8). The people who participate in this great feast will be those who have been living by faith. That is why they say, "This is our God; we have waited for him, so that he might save us" (25.9). See also chapter 55 for another presentation of this great banquet.

of rich food filled with marrow, of well-aged wines strained clear.
7 And he will destroy on this mountain
the shroud that is cast over all peoples,
the sheet that is spread over all nations;
he will swallow up death forever.
8 Then the Lord GOD will wipe away the tears from all faces,
and the disgrace of his people he will take away from all the earth,
for the LORD has spoken.
9 It will be said on that day,
Lo, this is our God; we have waited for him, so that he might save us.
This is the LORD for whom we have waited;
let us be glad and rejoice in his salvation.
10 For the hand of the LORD will rest on this mountain.

The Moabites shall be trodden down in their place
as straw is trodden down in a dung-pit.
11 Though they spread out their hands in the midst of it,
as swimmers spread out their hands to swim,
their pride will be laid low despite the struggle[q] of their hands.
12 The high fortifications of his walls will be brought down,
laid low, cast to the ground, even to the dust.

25.8 Ps 69.9 Isa 65.19 1 Cor 15.54 1 Pet 4.14 Rev 21.4

25.9 Isa 30.18 35.1,2,10; 40.9

25.11 Isa 16.6

25.12 Isa 26.5

The people sing to God

26 On that day this song will be sung in the land of Judah:
We have a strong city;
he sets up victory
like walls and bulwarks.
2 Open the gates,
so that the righteous nation that keeps faith
may enter in.
3 Those of steadfast mind you keep in peace—
in peace because they trust in you.
4 Trust in the LORD forever,
for in the LORD GOD[r]
you have an everlasting rock.
5 For he has brought low
the inhabitants of the height;
the lofty city he lays low.
He lays it low to the ground,
casts it to the dust.
6 The foot tramples it,
the feet of the poor,
the steps of the needy.

26.1 Isa 12.1; 31.9 60.18

26.2 Isa 45.25

26.3 Isa 57.19

26.4 Isa 50.10

26.6 Isa 29.19

[q] Meaning of Heb uncertain [r] Heb *in Yah, the LORD*

25.8 When the Lord speaks, he does what he says. It is comforting to know that God's plans and activities are closely tied to his Word. When we pray according to God's will (as expressed in the Bible) and claim his promises (as recorded in the Bible), he hears us and answers our requests.

25.8 Part of this verse is quoted in 1 Corinthians 15.54 to describe Christ's victory over death. God's ultimate victory is seen when death, our ultimate enemy, is defeated (see also Hosea 13.14). Another part of this verse is quoted in Revelation 21.4, which describes the glorious scene of God's presence with his people.

25.10 Moab was a symbol of all who oppose God and are rebellious to the end.

26.1ff People will praise God on the day of the Lord when Christ establishes his kingdom (see chapter 12). Chapter 26 is a psalm of trust, praise, and meditation. Once more, God revealed the future to Isaiah.

26.2 Isaiah portrays Judah opening the gates of salvation to all who love the Lord. This was accomplished through Christ. Now all who love God are welcome to dwell together as his people. Because God wants to reach all people with his love, we must not exclude anyone who wants to have fellowship with him.

26.3 We can never avoid strife in the world around us, but with God we can know perfect peace even in turmoil. When we are devoted to him, our whole attitude is steady and stable. Supported by God's unchanging love and mighty power, we are not shaken by the surrounding chaos (see Philippians 4.7).

26.7 Ps 25.4,5 Isa 42.16
26.8 Isa 12.4
26.9 Ps 63.1; 77.2 Hos 5.15
26.10 Isa 22.12,13 Jn 5.37,38
26.13 Isa 2.8
26.14 Hab 2.19
26.15 Isa 54.2
26.16 Hos 5.15
26.17 Jn 16.21
26.18 Isa 33.11
26.19 Ezek 37.1-14 Dan 12.2 Eph 5.14

7 The way of the righteous is level;
O Just One, you make smooth the path of the righteous.
8 In the path of your judgments,
O LORD, we wait for you;
your name and your renown
are the soul's desire.
9 My soul yearns for you in the night,
my spirit within me earnestly seeks you.
For when your judgments are in the earth,
the inhabitants of the world learn righteousness.
10 If favor is shown to the wicked,
they do not learn righteousness;
in the land of uprightness they deal perversely
and do not see the majesty of the LORD.
11 O LORD, your hand is lifted up,
but they do not see it.
Let them see your zeal for your people, and be ashamed.
Let the fire for your adversaries consume them.
12 O LORD, you will ordain peace for us,
for indeed, all that we have done, you have done for us.
13 O LORD our God,
other lords besides you have ruled over us,
but we acknowledge your name alone.
14 The dead do not live;
shades do not rise—
because you have punished and destroyed them,
and wiped out all memory of them.
15 But you have increased the nation, O LORD,
you have increased the nation; you are glorified;
you have enlarged all the borders of the land.

16 O LORD, in distress they sought you,
they poured out a prayer[s]
when your chastening was on them.
17 Like a woman with child,
who writhes and cries out in her pangs
when she is near her time,
so were we because of you, O LORD;
18 we were with child, we writhed,
but we gave birth only to wind.
We have won no victories on earth,
and no one is born to inhabit the world.
19 Your dead shall live, their corpses[t] shall rise.
O dwellers in the dust, awake and sing for joy!

[s] Meaning of Heb uncertain [t] Cn Compare Syr Tg: Heb *my corpse*

26.7, 8 At times the "path of the righteous" doesn't seem smooth and it isn't easy to do God's will, but we are never alone when we face tough times. God is there to help us through difficulties, to comfort us, and to lead us. He does this by giving us a purpose (keeping our mind centered on him, 26.3) and giving us provisions as we travel. He provides us with relationships of family, friends, and mentors. He gives us wisdom to make decisions and faith to trust him.

26.10 Even wicked people receive God's benefits, but that doesn't teach them to be good. Sometimes God's judgment teaches us more than God's good gifts. If you have been enriched by God's goodness, will you respond to him with your grateful devotion?

26.16–19 The people realized the pain of being away from God's presence, and yet they are assured that they will live again. God turned his back on his people when they disobeyed, but a small number never lost hope and continued to seek him. No matter how difficult times may be, we have hope when we keep our trust in him. Can you wait patiently for God to act?

26.19 Some people say there is no life after death. Others believe that there is, but it is not physical life. But Isaiah tells us that our bodies shall rise again. According to 1 Corinthians 15.50–53, all the dead believers will arise with new incorruptible bodies—bodies like the one Jesus had when he was resurrected (see Philippians 3.21). Isaiah 26.19 is not the only Old Testament verse to speak about the resurrection; see also Job 19.26; Psalm 16.10; Daniel 12.2, 13.

For your dew is a radiant dew,
and the earth will give birth to those long dead.[u]

20 Come, my people, enter your chambers,
and shut your doors behind you;
hide yourselves for a little while
until the wrath is past.
21 For the LORD comes out from his place
to punish the inhabitants of the earth for their iniquity;
the earth will disclose the blood shed on it,
and will no longer cover its slain.

26.20 Ps 30.5
26.21 Job 16.18 Mic 1.3

The Lord will deliver Israel

27 On that day the LORD with his cruel and great and strong sword will punish
Leviathan the fleeing serpent, Leviathan the twisting serpent, and he will
kill the dragon that is in the sea.

27.1 Job 3.8 Ps 74.14

2 On that day:
A pleasant vineyard, sing about it!
3 I, the LORD, am its keeper;
every moment I water it.
I guard it night and day
so that no one can harm it;
4 I have no wrath.
If it gives me thorns and briers,
I will march to battle against it.
I will burn it up.
5 Or else let it cling to me for protection,
let it make peace with me,
let it make peace with me.

27.3 Jn 10.28
27.4 2 Sam 23.6 Isa 33.12 Rom 5.1

6 In days to come[v] Jacob shall take root,
Israel shall blossom and put forth shoots,
and fill the whole world with fruit.

27.6 Isa 35.1,2

7 Has he struck them down as he struck down those who struck them?
Or have they been killed as their killers were killed?
8 By expulsion,[w] by exile you struggled against them;
with his fierce blast he removed them in the day of the east wind.
9 Therefore by this the guilt of Jacob will be expiated,
and this will be the full fruit of the removal of his sin:
when he makes all the stones of the altars
like chalkstones crushed to pieces,
no sacred poles[x] or incense altars will remain standing.
10 For the fortified city is solitary,

27.7 Isa 10.12,17 Hos 13.15
27.9 Dan 11.35 Isa 17.8

[u] Heb *to the shades* [v] Heb *Those to come* [w] Meaning of Heb uncertain [x] Heb *Asherim*

26.21 When God comes to judge the earth, the guilty will find no place to hide. Jesus said that secret plots will become public information because his truth, like a light shining in a dark corner, will reveal them (Matthew 10.26). Instead of trying to hide your shameful thoughts and actions from God, confess them to him and receive his forgiveness.

27.1 *That day* is a reference to the end of the evil world as we know it. In ancient Syrian (Ugaritic) literature, the dragon (Leviathan) was a seven-headed monster, the enemy of God's created order. Thus Isaiah is comparing God's slaughter of the wicked to the conquering of a great enemy. Although evil is a powerful foe, God will crush it and abolish it from the earth forever.

27.2–6 The trampled vineyard of chapter 5 is restored in God's new earth. God will protect and care for the vineyard, his people. It will no longer produce worthless fruit, but will produce enough good fruit for the whole world. Gentiles will come to know God through Israel.

27.9 *Expiated* means to have it removed, taken away, or atoned for. Only God can take away sin, but to be driven out of the land was considered the penalty that would purify God's people. Deuteronomy 28.49–52, 64 explains God's warning about these consequences.

a habitation deserted and forsaken, like the wilderness;
the calves graze there,
there they lie down, and strip its branches.
27.11 Deut 32.18,28 Isa 43.1,7
11 When its boughs are dry, they are broken;
women come and make a fire of them.
For this is a people without understanding;
therefore he that made them will not have compassion on them,
he that formed them will show them no favor.

27.12 Deut 30.3,4 Isa 11.11
27.13 Zech 14.16 Mt 24.31 Rev 11.15

12 On that day the LORD will thresh from the channel of the Euphrates to the
Wadi of Egypt, and you will be gathered one by one, O people of Israel. 13 And on
that day a great trumpet will be blown, and those who were lost in the land of
Assyria and those who were driven out to the land of Egypt will come and worship
the LORD on the holy mountain at Jerusalem.

4. Jerusalem's true and false hopes

Prophecy against Ephraim

28 Ah, the proud garland of the drunkards of Ephraim,
and the fading flower of its glorious beauty,
which is on the head of those bloated with rich food, of those overcome with wine!
28.2 Isa 8.7; 30.28 Nah 1.8
2 See, the Lord has one who is mighty and strong;
like a storm of hail, a destroying tempest,
like a storm of mighty, overflowing waters;
with his hand he will hurl them down to the earth.
3 Trampled under foot will be
the proud garland of the drunkards of Ephraim.
28.4 Hos 9.10 Nah 3.12
4 And the fading flower of its glorious beauty,
which is on the head of those bloated with rich food,
will be like a first-ripe fig before the summer;
whoever sees it, eats it up
as soon as it comes to hand.

28.5 Isa 41.16
5 In that day the LORD of hosts will be a garland of glory,
and a diadem of beauty, to the remnant of his people;
28.6 2 Chron 32.6-8
6 and a spirit of justice to the one who sits in judgment,
and strength to those who turn back the battle at the gate.

28.7 Hab 2.15,16
7 These also reel with wine
and stagger with strong drink;
the priest and the prophet reel with strong drink,
they are confused with wine,
they stagger with strong drink;
they err in vision,
they stumble in giving judgment.

27.11 Isaiah compares the state of Israel's spiritual life with dead branches that are broken off and used as fuel. Trees in Scripture often represent spiritual life. The trunk is the channel of strength from God; the branches are the people who serve him. Tree branches sometimes waver and blow in the wind. Like Israel, they may dry up from internal rottenness and become useless for anything except building a fire. What kind of branch are you? If you are withering spiritually, check to see if you are firmly attached to God.

27.12 God's purpose in judging the earth is not vengeance, but purging. He wants to correct us and bring us back to him. God does not punish us for our sin just to make us suffer, but to make us better equipped for fruitful service.

27.12 A wadi is a stream or dry streambed.

28.1 Ephraim represents the northern kingdom of Israel, ruled by a line of evil kings. When Israel split into two kingdoms after Solomon's reign, Jerusalem ended up in the southern kingdom. Leaders in the northern kingdom, wishing to stay entirely separate from their relatives to the south, set up idols to keep the people from going to the temple in Jerusalem to worship (see 1 Kings 12). Thus the northern kingdom led the people into idolatry. Isaiah gave this message to Judah to encourage them to repent before being punished as the northern kingdom would be punished only a few years later.

8 All tables are covered with filthy vomit;
no place is clean.

28.8 Jer 48.26

9 "Whom will he teach knowledge,
and to whom will he explain the message?
Those who are weaned from milk,
those taken from the breast?
10 For it is precept upon precept, precept upon precept,
line upon line, line upon line,
here a little, there a little."[y]

28.9 Heb 5.12,13

11 Truly, with stammering lip
and with alien tongue
he will speak to this people,
12 to whom he has said,
"This is rest;
give rest to the weary;
and this is repose";
yet they would not hear.
13 Therefore the word of the LORD will be to them,
"Precept upon precept, precept upon precept,
line upon line, line upon line,
here a little, there a little;"[y]
in order that they may go, and fall backward,
and be broken, and snared, and taken.

28.11 Isa 33.19 1 Cor 14.21

28.12 Jer 6.16 Mt 11.28,29

28.13 Mt 21.44

14 Therefore hear the word of the LORD, you scoffers
who rule this people in Jerusalem.
15 Because you have said, "We have made a covenant with death,
and with Sheol we have an agreement;
when the overwhelming scourge passes through
it will not come to us;
for we have made lies our refuge,
and in falsehood we have taken shelter";
16 therefore thus says the Lord GOD,
See, I am laying in Zion a foundation stone,
a tested stone,
a precious cornerstone, a sure foundation:
"One who trusts will not panic."
17 And I will make justice the line,
and righteousness the plummet;
hail will sweep away the refuge of lies,
and waters will overwhelm the shelter.

28.15 Isa 28.18

28.16 Ps 118.22 Mt 21.42 Acts 4.11 Eph 2.20

28.17 Isa 61.8 Amos 7.7-9

[y] Meaning of Heb of this verse uncertain

28.9–11 These verses characterize the people's reaction to Isaiah. They were saying, "He's speaking to us like a school teacher speaks to small children. We don't need to be taught. We'll make up our own minds." For this attitude, Isaiah prophesied that the Assyrians would teach them in a way they would like even less.

28.13 God used repetition and simple words to get his messages through to the people. Do you find that God has to teach you the same lessons over and over again? The simplicity of God's message can be a stumbling block for some (28.9, 10), leading them to think it must have little value. We must not be too proud to heed God's simple message.

28.15 Judah was afraid of the Assyrians, the "overwhelming scourge." Instead of trusting God, the Judeans turned to other sources for security. God accused them of making a covenant with death. *Sheol* is the word in the Old Testament for the realm of the dead. It is used to mean the grave or state of being dead. This passage probably refers to Hezekiah's alliance with Pharaoh Tirhakah against Assyria. God would cancel this agreement – Egypt would be of no help when Assyria attacked. Is it worth selling out what you believe in for temporary protection against an enemy? If you want lasting protection, turn to the only one able to deliver you from *eternal* death – God.

28.16 If you're building anything, you need a firm base. Isaiah speaks of a *foundation stone*, a *cornerstone*, that will be laid in Zion. This cornerstone is the Messiah, the foundation on whom we build our lives. Is your life built on the flimsy base of your own successes or dreams? Or is it set on a firm foundation (see Psalm 118.22; 1 Peter 2.8)?

18 Then your covenant with death will be annulled,
and your agreement with Sheol will not stand;
when the overwhelming scourge passes through
you will be beaten down by it.
19 As often as it passes through, it will take you;
for morning by morning it will pass through,
by day and by night;
and it will be sheer terror to understand the message.
20 For the bed is too short to stretch oneself on it,
and the covering too narrow to wrap oneself in it.
21 For the LORD will rise up as on Mount Perazim,
he will rage as in the valley of Gibeon;
to do his deed—strange is his deed!
and to work his work—alien is his work!
22 Now therefore do not scoff,
or your bonds will be made stronger;
for I have heard a decree of destruction
from the Lord GOD of hosts upon the whole land.

23 Listen, and hear my voice;
Pay attention, and hear my speech.
24 Do those who plow for sowing plow continually?
Do they continually open and harrow their ground?
25 When they have leveled its surface,
do they not scatter dill, sow cummin,
and plant wheat in rows
and barley in its proper place,
and spelt as the border?
26 For they are well instructed;
their God teaches them.

27 Dill is not threshed with a threshing sledge,
nor is a cart wheel rolled over cummin;
but dill is beaten out with a stick,
and cummin with a rod.
28 Grain is crushed for bread,
but one does not thresh it forever;
one drives the cart wheel and horses over it,
but does not pulverize it.
29 This also comes from the LORD of hosts;
he is wonderful in counsel,
and excellent in wisdom.

28.21 2 Sam 5.20 Lk 19.41-44
28.27 Amos 1.3
28.29 Rom 11.33

Prophecy against Jerusalem

29 Ah, Ariel, Ariel,
the city where David encamped!
Add year to year;
let the festivals run their round.
2 Yet I will distress Ariel,

29.1 2 Sam 5.9
29.2 Lam 2.5

28.21 God fought on Joshua's side at the valley of Gibeon (Joshua 10.1–14) and on David's side at Mount Perazim (2 Samuel 5.20). But now he would fight *against* Israel, his own people, in these same places.

28.23–29 The farmer uses special tools to plant and harvest tender herbs so he will not destroy them. He takes into account how fragile they are. In the same way God will never allow us to be tempted or to suffer more than we can bear. He takes all our individual circumstances and weaknesses into account. He deals with each of us sensitively. We should follow his example when we deal with others. Different people require different treatment. Be sensitive to the needs of those around you and the special treatment they may need.

29.1 *Ariel* is a special name for Jerusalem. It may mean "lion of God" (Jerusalem is strong as a lion) or "altar hearth" (Jerusalem is the place of the altar in the temple. See 29.2; Ezekiel 43.15, 16).

and there shall be moaning and lamentation,
and Jerusalem[z] shall be to me like an Ariel.[a]
3 And like David[b] I will encamp against you;
I will besiege you with towers
and raise siegeworks against you.
4 Then deep from the earth you shall speak,
from low in the dust your words shall come;
your voice shall come from the ground like the voice of a ghost,
and your speech shall whisper out of the dust.

5 But the multitude of your foes[c] shall be like small dust,
and the multitude of tyrants like flying chaff.
And in an instant, suddenly,
6 you will be visited by the LORD of hosts
with thunder and earthquake and great noise,
with whirlwind and tempest, and the flame of a devouring fire.
7 And the multitude of all the nations that fight against Ariel,
all that fight against her and her stronghold, and who distress her,
shall be like a dream, a vision of the night.
8 Just as when a hungry person dreams of eating
and wakes up still hungry,
or a thirsty person dreams of drinking
and wakes up faint, still thirsty,
so shall the multitude of all the nations be
that fight against Mount Zion.

9 Stupefy yourselves and be in a stupor,
blind yourselves and be blind!
Be drunk, but not from wine;
stagger, but not from strong drink!
10 For the LORD has poured out upon you
a spirit of deep sleep;
he has closed your eyes, you prophets,
and covered your heads, you seers.
11 The vision of all this has become for you like the words of a sealed document. If it is given to those who can read, with the command, "Read this," they
say, "We cannot, for it is sealed." 12 And if it is given to those who cannot read,
saying, "Read this," they say, "We cannot read."

13 The Lord said:
Because these people draw near with their mouths
and honor me with their lips,
while their hearts are far from me,
and their worship of me is a human commandment learned by rote;
14 so I will again do
amazing things with this people,
shocking and amazing.
The wisdom of their wise shall perish,
and the discernment of the discerning shall be hidden.

29.3 Lk 19.43,44
29.5 Isa 17.14 41.15,16 1 Thess 5.3
29.6 Lk 21.11 Rev 11.13,19
29.7 Zech 12.9
29.8 Isa 54.17
29.10 Rom 11.8 2 Thess 2.9-12
29.11 Dan 12.4
29.13 Ezek 33.31 Mk 7.6,7
29.14 Isa 44.25 1 Cor 1.19

[z] Heb *she* [a] Probable meaning, *altar hearth*; compare Ezek 43.15 [b] Gk: Meaning of Heb uncertain [c] Cn: Heb *strangers*

29.13, 14 The people claimed to belong to God, but they were disobedient and merely went through the motions; therefore, God would bring vengeance upon them. Religion had become routine instead of real. Jesus quoted Isaiah's condemnation of Israel's hypocrisy when he spoke to the Pharisees, the religious leaders of his day (Matthew 15.7–9; Mark 7.6, 7). We are all capable of hypocrisy. Often we slip into routine forms of worship that mean nothing to us. If we want to be called God's people, we must be obedient and worship him honestly and sincerely.

29.15 Ps 10.11,13 Isa 47.10

15 Ha! You who hide a plan too deep for the LORD,
whose deeds are in the dark,
and who say, "Who sees us? Who knows us?"

29.16 Isa 45.9 Rom 9.19-21

16 You turn things upside down!
Shall the potter be regarded as the clay?
Shall the thing made say of its maker,
"He did not make me";
or the thing formed say of the one who formed it,
"He has no understanding"?

17 Shall not Lebanon in a very little while
become a fruitful field,
and the fruitful field be regarded as a forest?

29.18 Isa 32.3

18 On that day the deaf shall hear
the words of a scroll,
and out of their gloom and darkness
the eyes of the blind shall see.

29.19 Isa 14.30,32 Mt 5.5 Jas 2.5

19 The meek shall obtain fresh joy in the LORD,
and the neediest people shall exult in the Holy One of Israel.
20 For the tyrant shall be no more,
and the scoffer shall cease to be;
all those alert to do evil shall be cut off—

29.21 Amos 5.10,12

21 those who cause a person to lose a lawsuit,
who set a trap for the arbiter in the gate,
and without grounds deny justice to the one in the right.

29.22 Isa 41.8

22 Therefore thus says the LORD, who redeemed Abraham, concerning the
house of Jacob:
No longer shall Jacob be ashamed,
no longer shall his face grow pale.
23 For when he sees his children,
the work of my hands, in his midst,
they will sanctify my name;
they will sanctify the Holy One of Jacob,
and will stand in awe of the God of Israel.

29.24 Isa 30.21; 41.20

24 And those who err in spirit will come to understanding,
and those who grumble will accept instruction.

Prophecy against rebels

30.1 Isa 8.11,12

30 Oh, rebellious children, says the LORD,
who carry out a plan, but not mine;
who make an alliance, but against my will,
adding sin to sin;

29.15 Thinking God couldn't see them and didn't know what was happening, the people of Jerusalem tried to hide their plans from him. How strange that so many people think they can hide from God. In Psalm 139 we learn that God has examined us and knows everything about us. Would you be embarrassed if your best friends knew your personal thoughts? Remember that God knows all of them.

29.17–24 The world described here, under Christ's rule, will be far different from the one we live in today. There will be no more violence or gloom. This new world will be characterized by joy, understanding, justice, and praise to God.

29.21 An arbiter is a person with the power to decide a dispute or judge a matter. Legal matters were often heard and settled at the city gate, where the elders would gather.

30.1 The negotiations were underway, and Isaiah condemned them. The people of Judah sought advice from everyone but God. When we are driven by fear, we tend to search everywhere for comfort, advice, and relief, hoping to find an easy way out of our troubles. Instead, we should consult God. Although he gives emergency help in a crisis, he prefers to be our Guide throughout our lives. By reading his Word and actively seeking to do his will, we can maintain contact that provides stability no matter what the crisis.

30.1–5 God was not happy with his people because they sought power and protection from other kings and nations. He warned them that these alliances, though inviting, would only prove harmful in the long run. Enamored with power or prestige, we also may have sought direction and guidance from sources that are not pleasing to God. Ask God to help you choose wisely.

2 who set out to go down to Egypt
without asking for my counsel,
to take refuge in the protection of Pharaoh,
and to seek shelter in the shadow of Egypt;
3 Therefore the protection of Pharaoh shall become your shame,
and the shelter in the shadow of Egypt your humiliation.
4 For though his officials are at Zoan
and his envoys reach Hanes,
5 everyone comes to shame
through a people that cannot profit them,
that brings neither help nor profit,
but shame and disgrace.

30.2 Isa 8.19; 31.1
30.3 Isa 36.6 Jer 42.18,22
30.5 Isa 31.3 Jer 2.36

6 An oracle concerning the animals of the Negeb.
Through a land of trouble and distress,
of lioness and roaring[d] lion,
of viper and flying serpent,
they carry their riches on the backs of donkeys,
and their treasures on the humps of camels,
to a people that cannot profit them.
7 For Egypt's help is worthless and empty,
therefore I have called her,
"Rahab who sits still."[e]

30.6 Deut 8.15
30.7 Isa 51.9

8 Go now, write it before them on a tablet,
and inscribe it in a book,
so that it may be for the time to come
as a witness forever.
9 For they are a rebellious people,
faithless children,
children who will not hear
the instruction of the LORD;
10 who say to the seers, "Do not see";
and to the prophets, "Do not prophesy to us what is right;
speak to us smooth things,
prophesy illusions,
11 leave the way, turn aside from the path,
let us hear no more about the Holy One of Israel."
12 Therefore thus says the Holy One of Israel:
Because you reject this word,
and put your trust in oppression and deceit,
and rely on them;
13 therefore this iniquity shall become for you
like a break in a high wall, bulging out, and about to collapse,
whose crash comes suddenly, in an instant;
14 its breaking is like that of a potter's vessel
that is smashed so ruthlessly

30.10 1 Kgs 22.8,13 Jer 6.14 Ezek 13.7 Amos 2.12 2 Tim 4.3,4
30.12 Isa 5.24; 59.13
30.14 Ps 2.9 Jer 19.10,11

[d] Cn: Heb *from them* [e] Meaning of Heb uncertain

30.2ff Hezekiah had been seeking a defensive alliance with Egypt against Sennacherib of Assyria (see 2 Kings 18.21).

30.6 This prophecy is titled "to the animals of the Negeb," but directed to those who carried bribes through the desert in the Negeb region to Egypt. "Flying serpent" is probably a reference to a poisonous snake.

30.7 Rahab was a mythological female sea monster associated with Leviathan (see the note on 27.1; also Job 9.13; 26.12). It was a name associated with Egypt where hippopotamuses, perhaps a likeness to Rahab, sat on the Nile River and did nothing.

30.10, 11 Some people in Israel sought refuge in Egypt. Comfortably settled there, they wanted to hear only good news. They did not welcome the truth from God's prophets. Often the truth makes us uncomfortable. We prefer lies and illusions when they make us feel more secure. But Jesus said the truth will set us free (John 8.32). It is much better to face reality than to live a lie. Don't settle for something that makes you feel comfortable but is not true.

that among its fragments not a sherd is found
for taking fire from the hearth,
or dipping water out of the cistern.

30.15 Isa 28.12; 32.17
15 For thus said the Lord GOD, the Holy One of Israel:
In returning and rest you shall be saved;
in quietness and in trust shall be your strength.
30.16 Isa 31.1,3
But you refused 16 and said,
"No! We will flee upon horses"—
therefore you shall flee!
and, "We will ride upon swift steeds"—
therefore your pursuers shall be swift!
30.17 Deut 32.30
17 A thousand shall flee at the threat of one,
at the threat of five you shall flee,
until you are left
like a flagstaff on the top of a mountain,
like a signal on a hill.

30.18 Isa 25.9; 2 Pet 3.9,15
18 Therefore the LORD waits to be gracious to you;
therefore he will rise up to show mercy to you.
For the LORD is a God of justice;
blessed are all those who wait for him.

30.19 Isa 25.8; 65.24
19 Truly, O people in Zion, inhabitants of Jerusalem, you shall weep no more.
He will surely be gracious to you at the sound of your cry; when he hears it, he will
30.20 Ps 80.5
answer you. 20 Though the Lord may give you the bread of adversity and the water
of affliction, yet your Teacher will not hide himself any more, but your eyes shall
30.21 Isa 35.8,9
see your Teacher. 21 And when you turn to the right or when you turn to the left,
your ears shall hear a word behind you, saying, "This is the way; walk in it."
30.22 Ex 32.2,4
22 Then you will defile your silver-covered idols and your gold-plated images. You
will scatter them like filthy rags; you will say to them, "Away with you!"

30.23 Ps 65.9-13
23 He will give rain for the seed with which you sow the ground, and grain, the
produce of the ground, which will be rich and plenteous. On that day your cattle
30.24 Mt 3.12
will graze in broad pastures; 24 and the oxen and donkeys that till the ground will eat
silage, which has been winnowed with shovel and fork. 25 On every lofty mountain
30.25 Isa 41.18
and every high hill there will be brooks running with water—on a day of the great
30.26 Isa 33.24; Hos 6.1,2
slaughter, when the towers fall. 26 Moreover the light of the moon will be like the
light of the sun, and the light of the sun will be sevenfold, like the light of seven
days, on the day when the LORD binds up the injuries of his people, and heals the
wounds inflicted by his blow.

30.27 Isa 66.15
27 See, the name of the LORD comes from far away,
burning with his anger, and in thick rising smoke;[f]
his lips are full of indignation,
and his tongue is like a devouring fire;
30.28 2 Kgs 19.28; Isa 8.7,8
28 his breath is like an overflowing stream
that reaches up to the neck—

[f] Meaning of Heb uncertain

30.15 God warned Judah that turning to Egypt and other nations for military might could not save them. Only God could do that. They must wait for him in quietness and trust. No amount of fast talking or hasty activity could speed up God's grand design. We have nothing but "thank you" to say to God. Salvation comes from God alone. Because he has saved us, we can trust him and be peacefully confident that he will give us strength to face our difficulties. We should lay aside our busy care and endless effort and allow him to act.

30.20 The Lord gave his people the bread of adversity and the water of affliction, but he promised to be with them, teach them, and guide them during hard times. God demands a lot from us, and many times following him can be painful; but he does this out of his love for us. Next time you go through a difficult time, try to appreciate the experience and grow from it, learning what God wants to teach you. God may be showing you his love by patiently walking with you through adversity.

30.21 When the people of Jerusalem left God's path, he would correct them. He will do the same for us. But when we hear his voice of correction, we must be willing to follow it!

to sift the nations with the sieve of destruction,
and to place on the jaws of the peoples a bridle that leads them astray.

29 You shall have a song as in the night when a holy festival is kept; and gladness of heart, as when one sets out to the sound of the flute to go to the mountain
of the LORD, to the Rock of Israel. 30 And the LORD will cause his majestic voice to
be heard and the descending blow of his arm to be seen, in furious anger and a
flame of devouring fire, with a cloudburst and tempest and hailstones. 31 The Assyrian will be terror-stricken at the voice of the LORD, when he strikes with his rod.
32 And every stroke of the staff of punishment that the LORD lays upon him will be **30.32**
to the sound of timbrels and lyres; battling with brandished arm he will fight with 1 Sam 18.6 Jer 31.4
him. 33 For his burning place[g] has long been prepared; truly it is made ready for the **30.33**
king,[h] its pyre made deep and wide, with fire and wood in abundance; the breath Gen 19.24 Isa 34.9
of the LORD, like a stream of sulfur, kindles it.

The futility of trusting in Egypt

31 Alas for those who go down to Egypt for help **31.1**
and who rely on horses, Isa 10.17 Hos 11.9
who trust in chariots because they are many Hab 1.12
and in horsemen because they are very strong,
but do not look to the Holy One of Israel
or consult the LORD!
2 Yet he too is wise and brings disaster; **31.2**
he does not call back his words, Num 23.19 Jer 44.29
but will rise against the house of the evildoers, Rom 16.27
and against the helpers of those who work iniquity.
3 The Egyptians are human, and not God; **31.3**
their horses are flesh, and not spirit. Jer 15.6 Ezek 28.9
When the LORD stretches out his hand,
the helper will stumble, and the one helped will fall,
and they will all perish together.

4 For thus the LORD said to me,
As a lion or a young lion growls over its prey,
and—when a band of shepherds is called out against it—
is not terrified by their shouting
or daunted at their noise,
so the LORD of hosts will come down
to fight upon Mount Zion and upon its hill.
5 Like birds hovering overhead, so the LORD of hosts
will protect Jerusalem;
he will protect and deliver it,
he will spare and rescue it.

6 Turn back to him whom you[i] have deeply betrayed, O people of Israel. 7 For **31.6**
on that day all of you shall throw away your idols of silver and idols of gold, which Isa 55.7 Jer 3.10,14,22
your hands have sinfully made for you.

[g] Or *Topheth* [h] Or *Molech* [i] Heb *they*

31.1 It was wrong for Judah to look to these other nations for military help. (1) They were trusting in man instead of God. Judah sought protection from those who had far less power than God. Both Egypt and Judah would fall as a result of their alliances. (2) They were serving their own interests instead of God's, and thus they did not even consult him. They violated God's stipulation in Deuteronomy 17.16. (3) They did not want to pay the price of looking to God and repenting of their sinful ways. When we have problems it is good to seek help, but we must never bypass God or his previous directions to us.

31.7 Someday these people would throw their idols away, recognizing that they are nothing but man-made objects. Idols such as money, fame, or success are seductive. Instead of contributing to our spiritual development, however, they rob us of our thoughts, time, energy, and devotion to God. At first they seem exciting and promise to "take us places," but in the end we will find that we have become their slaves. We need to recognize their worthlessness now, before they rob us of our freedom.

31.8 Isa 10.12; 14.2
8 "Then the Assyrian shall fall by a sword, not of mortals;
and a sword, not of humans, shall devour him;
he shall flee from the sword,
and his young men shall be put to forced labor.

31.9 Isa 13.2
9 His rock shall pass away in terror,
and his officers desert the standard in panic,"
says the LORD, whose fire is in Zion,
and whose furnace is in Jerusalem.

Prophecy of peace for Israel

32.1 Jer 23.5 Ezek 37.24 Zech 9.9
32.2 Isa 25.4; 35.6

32 See, a king will reign in righteousness,
and princes will rule with justice.
2 Each will be like a hiding place from the wind,
a covert from the tempest,
like streams of water in a dry place,
like the shade of a great rock in a weary land.
3 Then the eyes of those who have sight will not be closed,
and the ears of those who have hearing will listen.

32.4 Isa 29.24
4 The minds of the rash will have good judgment,
and the tongues of stammerers will speak readily and distinctly.
5 A fool will no longer be called noble,
nor a villain said to be honorable.

32.6 Isa 10.2 59.7,13
6 For fools speak folly,
and their minds plot iniquity:
to practice ungodliness,
to utter error concerning the LORD,
to leave the craving of the hungry unsatisfied,
and to deprive the thirsty of drink.

32.7 Isa 5.23 Jer 5.26-28 Mic 7.3
7 The villainies of villains are evil;
they devise wicked devices
to ruin the poor with lying words,
even when the plea of the needy is right.

32.8 2 Cor 9.6-11
8 But those who are noble plan noble things,
and by noble things they stand.

32.9 Isa 47.8
9 Rise up, you women who are at ease, hear my voice;
you complacent daughters, listen to my speech.

32.10 Isa 5.5,6
10 In little more than a year
you will shudder, you complacent ones;
for the vintage will fail,
the fruit harvest will not come.
11 Tremble, you women who are at ease,
shudder, you complacent ones;
strip, and make yourselves bare,
and put sackcloth on your loins.
12 Beat your breasts for the pleasant fields,
for the fruitful vine,

32.1 Judah was hungry for a strong king who would rule effectively. This desire will be fulfilled when Christ reigns. Evil will be banished, and the King will be powerful and just. In the immediate future, Judah would be destroyed and taken into captivity. But one day, God's Son, the King unlike any other king, will reign in righteousness.

32.5, 6 When the righteous King comes, people's motives will become transparent. Scoundrels will not be regarded as heroes. Those who have opposed God's standards of living will be unable to maintain their deception. In the blazing light of the holy Savior, sin cannot disguise itself and appear good. Christ's revealing light shines into the darkest corners of our hearts, showing sin clearly for what it is. When King Jesus reigns in your heart, there is no place for sin, no matter how well hidden you think it is.

32.9–13 The people turned their backs on God and concentrated on their own pleasures. This warning is not just to the women of Judah (see 3.16–4.1), but to all who sit back in their thoughtless ease, enjoying crops, clothes, land, and cities while an enemy approaches. Wealth and luxury bring false security, lulling us into thinking all is well when disaster is around the corner. By abandoning God's purpose for our lives, we also abandon his help.

13 for the soil of my people
growing up in thorns and briers;
yes, for all the joyous houses
in the jubilant city.
14 For the palace will be forsaken,
the populous city deserted;
the hill and the watchtower
will become dens forever,
the joy of wild asses,
a pasture for flocks;
15 until a spirit from on high is poured out on us,
and the wilderness becomes a fruitful field,
and the fruitful field is deemed a forest.
16 Then justice will dwell in the wilderness,
and righteousness abide in the fruitful field.
17 The effect of righteousness will be peace,
and the result of righteousness, quietness and trust forever.
18 My people will abide in a peaceful habitation,
in secure dwellings, and in quiet resting places.
19 The forest will disappear completely,[j]
and the city will be utterly laid low.
20 Happy will you be who sow beside every stream,
who let the ox and the donkey range freely.

32.13 Isa 5.5,6,10,17
32.14 Isa 24.12
32.15 Ps 107.35 Isa 11.2 Joel 2.28
32.16 Isa 33.5
32.17 Isa 2.4 Jas 3.18
32.18 Hos 2.18-23
32.20 Isa 30.23

The Lord is judge

33 Ah, you destroyer,
who yourself have not been destroyed;
you treacherous one,
with whom no one has dealt treacherously!
When you have ceased to destroy,
you will be destroyed;
and when you have stopped dealing treacherously,
you will be dealt with treacherously.

2 O LORD, be gracious to us; we wait for you.
Be our arm every morning,
our salvation in the time of trouble.
3 At the sound of tumult, peoples fled;
before your majesty, nations scattered.
4 Spoil was gathered as the caterpillar gathers;
as locusts leap, they leaped[k] upon it.
5 The LORD is exalted, he dwells on high;
he filled Zion with justice and righteousness;

33.1 Jer 25.12-14 Hab 2.8
33.2 Isa 25.9; 40.10
33.3 Jer 25.30,31
33.5 Ps 97.9

[j] Cn: Heb *And it will hail when the forest comes down* [k] Meaning of Heb uncertain

32.15–17 God acts from above to change man's condition here on earth. Only when God's Spirit is among us can we achieve true peace and prosperity (Ezekiel 36.22–38; Galatians 5.22, 23). This will happen in the end times. We can also have God's Spirit with us now, for he is available to all believers through Christ (John 15.26). But the outpouring mentioned here happens when the worldwide kingdom of God is established for all eternity (see Joel 2.28, 29).

33.1 The Assyrians continually broke their promises, but demanded that others keep theirs. It is easy to put ourselves in the same selfish position, demanding our rights while ignoring the rights of others. Broken promises shatter trust and destroy relationships. Determine to keep your promises; equally important, ask forgiveness for past promises you have broken. Treat others with the same fairness that you demand for yourself.

33.2 "Arm" means strength. These are the words of the righteous remnant who were waiting for God to deliver them from their oppression.

33.4 See 2 Kings 19.20–37 for a description of this victory over Assyria.

33.5 When Christ's kingdom is established, Zion—Jerusalem—will be the home of righteousness and justice because the Messiah reigns there. As a light to the world, the new Jerusalem will be the holy city (Revelation 21.2).

33.6
Ps 112.1-3
Isa 51.6

6 he will be the stability of your times,
abundance of salvation, wisdom, and knowledge;
the fear of the LORD is Zion's treasure.[l]

7 Listen! the valiant[m] cry in the streets;
the envoys of peace weep bitterly.
8 The highways are deserted,
travelers have quit the road.
The treaty is broken,
its oaths[n] are despised,
its obligation[o] is disregarded.

33.9
Isa 10.34; 24.4
35.2

9 The land mourns and languishes;
Lebanon is confounded and withers away;
Sharon is like a desert;
and Bashan and Carmel shake off their leaves.

33.10
Ps 12.5
Isa 2.19

10 "Now I will arise," says the LORD,
"now I will lift myself up;
now I will be exalted.

33.11
Isa 26.18

11 You conceive chaff, you bring forth stubble;
your breath is a fire that will consume you.

33.12
2 Sam 23.6,7
Isa 10.17

12 And the peoples will be as if burned to lime,
like thorns cut down, that are burned in the fire."

33.13
Isa 49.1

13 Hear, you who are far away, what I have done;
and you who are near, acknowledge my might.

33.14
Isa 1.28; 30.27
Heb 12.29

14 The sinners in Zion are afraid;
trembling has seized the godless:
"Who among us can live with the devouring fire?
Who among us can live with everlasting flames?"

33.15
Ps 24.3,4
Isa 58.6-11

15 Those who walk righteously and speak uprightly,
who despise the gain of oppression,
who wave away a bribe instead of accepting it,
who stop their ears from hearing of bloodshed
and shut their eyes from looking on evil,

33.16
Isa 49.10

16 they will live on the heights;
their refuge will be the fortresses of rocks;
their food will be supplied, their water assured.

33.17
Isa 6.5

17 Your eyes will see the king in his beauty;
they will behold a land that stretches far away.
18 Your mind will muse on the terror:
"Where is the one who counted?

[l] Heb *his treasure*; meaning of Heb uncertain [m] Meaning of Heb uncertain [n] Q Ms: MT *cities* [o] Or *everyone*

33.6 In preparation for famine, war, or siege, provisions were stockpiled to be released when conditions required. If Judah would change its direction, attitudes, and actions, God would release his overflowing abundance. God's treasuries have more than we need, and he supplies wisdom and salvation to those who recognize him and respect his authority.

33.8 The Assyrians broke their peace pact (2 Kings 18.14–17).

33.9 These fruitful, productive areas would become deserts. Lebanon was known for its huge cedars. Sharon was very fertile. Bashan was very productive in grain and cattle. Carmel was thickly forested.

33.14–16 These sinners realized that they could not live in the presence of the holy God, for he is like a fire that consumes evil. Only those whose faith produces righteous conduct and upright speech can live with God. Isaiah gives examples of how to demonstrate our righteousness and uprightness: we can reject oppression and bribes, refuse to plot wrong actions, and resist temptation. If we are fair and honest in our relationships, we will dwell with God, and he will supply our needs.

Where is the one who weighed the tribute?
Where is the one who counted the towers?"
19 No longer will you see the insolent people,
the people of an obscure speech that you cannot comprehend,
stammering in a language that you cannot understand.
20 Look on Zion, the city of our appointed festivals!
Your eyes will see Jerusalem,
a quiet habitation, an immovable tent,
whose stakes will never be pulled up,
and none of whose ropes will be broken.
21 But there the LORD in majesty will be for us
a place of broad rivers and streams,
where no galley with oars can go,
nor stately ship can pass.
22 For the LORD is our judge, the LORD is our ruler,
the LORD is our king; he will save us.

23 Your rigging hangs loose;
it cannot hold the mast firm in its place,
or keep the sail spread out.

Then prey and spoil in abundance will be divided;
even the lame will fall to plundering.
24 And no inhabitant will say, "I am sick";
the people who live there will be forgiven their iniquity.

33.19 Deut 28.49,50
33.20 Ps 46.5
33.21 Isa 48.18
33.22 Isa 49.25,26 Zech 9.9
33.24 Mic 7.18,19 1 Jn 1.7-9

God will destroy his enemies

34 Draw near, O nations, to hear;
O peoples, give heed!
Let the earth hear, and all that fills it;
the world, and all that comes from it.
2 For the LORD is enraged against all the nations,
and furious against all their hoards;
he has doomed them, has given them over for slaughter.
3 Their slain shall be cast out,
and the stench of their corpses shall rise;
the mountains shall flow with their blood.
4 All the host of heaven shall rot away,
and the skies roll up like a scroll.
All their host shall wither
like a leaf withering on a vine,
or fruit withering on a fig tree.

5 When my sword has drunk its fill in the heavens,
lo, it will descend upon Edom,
upon the people I have doomed to judgment.
6 The LORD has a sword; it is sated with blood,
it is gorged with fat,
with the blood of lambs and goats,

34.1 Deut 32.1
34.3 Ezek 35.6
34.4 Joel 2.31 Mt 24.29 2 Pet 3.10 Rev 6.12-14
34.5 Isa 24.6
34.6 Isa 63.1

33.21, 22 The presence of the Lord would form an impenetrable defense for Zion, just as natural rivers or deep moats protected other fortified cities. The city of Babylon, for example, was protected from enemy attack by wide rivers. The Lord will shield us, too. The best defense and protection that God's people can have is the presence of the Lord.

34.5 The Edomites shared a common ancestry with Israel. The Israelites were descended from Jacob; the Edomites from Jacob's twin brother, Esau. Edom was always Israel's bitter enemy. The destruction of Edom mentioned here is a picture of the ultimate end of all who oppose God and his people.

with the fat of the kidneys of rams.
For the LORD has a sacrifice in Bozrah,
a great slaughter in the land of Edom.
7 Wild oxen shall fall with them,
and young steers with the mighty bulls.
Their land shall be soaked with blood,
and their soil made rich with fat.

34.8 Isa 13.6; 63.4

8 For the LORD has a day of vengeance,
a year of vindication by Zion's cause.[p]
9 And the streams of Edom[q] shall be turned into pitch,
and her soil into sulfur;
her land shall become burning pitch.

34.10 Isa 1.31 Ezek 29.11 Mal 1.3,4 Rev 14.11; 19.3

10 Night and day it shall not be quenched;
its smoke shall go up forever.
From generation to generation it shall lie waste;
no one shall pass through it forever and ever.

34.11 Lam 2.8

11 But the hawk[r] and the hedgehog[r] shall possess it;
the owl[r] and the raven shall live in it.
He shall stretch the line of confusion over it,
and the plummet of chaos over[s] its nobles.
12 They shall name it No Kingdom There,
and all its princes shall be nothing.

34.13 Jer 9.11; 10.22

13 Thorns shall grow over its strongholds,
nettles and thistles in its fortresses.
It shall be the haunt of jackals,
an abode for ostriches.

34.14 Isa 13.21

14 Wildcats shall meet with hyenas,
goat-demons shall call to each other;
there too Lilith shall repose,
and find a place to rest.
15 There shall the owl nest
and lay and hatch and brood in its shadow;
there too the buzzards shall gather,
each one with its mate.

34.16 Isa 40.5

16 Seek and read from the book of the LORD:
Not one of these shall be missing;
none shall be without its mate.
For the mouth of the LORD has commanded,
and his spirit has gathered them.
17 He has cast the lot for them,
his hand has portioned it out to them with the line;
they shall possess it forever,
from generation to generation they shall live in it.

[p] Or *of recompense by Zion's defender* [q] Heb *her streams* [r] Identification uncertain [s] Heb lacks *over*

34.8 The word *vengeance* usually carries a negative connotation for us. We use it to describe when someone has been hurt by others and wants to get even with them. But this vengeance is an act of God's justice, as when a sentence is pronounced against the guilty party in a courtroom trial. All evil deeds will be punished.

34.10 The fire that will not be quenched and unending smoke refer to the end of the world (Revelation 19.3). The vivid punishment of Edom would also represent the punishment of all nations, and all men who set themselves against God's people.

34.14 "Goat-demons" refers to wild goats. "Lilith" may refer to a female dragon or demon in popular Syrian mythology, who was particularly malicious at night.

34.16 Isaiah referred to his prophecies that God commanded him to write down with the phrase "book of the Lord." Whoever lived to see the time of Edom's destruction would have only to look to these prophecies to find agreement between what happened and what was predicted. Prophecy predicts and history reveals what has been in God's mind for all time.

Streams in the desert

35 The wilderness and the dry land shall be glad,
the desert shall rejoice and blossom;
like the crocus 2 it shall blossom abundantly,
and rejoice with joy and singing.
The glory of Lebanon shall be given to it,
the majesty of Carmel and Sharon.
They shall see the glory of the LORD,
the majesty of our God.

3 Strengthen the weak hands,
and make firm the feeble knees.
4 Say to those who are of a fearful heart,
"Be strong, do not fear!
Here is your God.
He will come with vengeance,
with terrible recompense.
He will come and save you."

5 Then the eyes of the blind shall be opened,
and the ears of the deaf unstopped;
6 then the lame shall leap like a deer,
and the tongue of the speechless sing for joy.
For waters shall break forth in the wilderness,
and streams in the desert;
7 the burning sand shall become a pool,
and the thirsty ground springs of water;
the haunt of jackals shall become a swamp,[t]
the grass shall become reeds and rushes.

8 A highway shall be there,
and it shall be called the Holy Way;
the unclean shall not travel on it,[u]
but it shall be for God's people;[v]
no traveler, not even fools, shall go astray.

35.1 Isa 41.18,19 51.3; 55.12,13
35.3 Job 4.3,4
35.4 Ps 145.19 Isa 63.4
35.5 Jn 9.6,7
35.6 Lk 11.14 Jn 7.38 Acts 3.7,8
35.7 Mt 7.13,14

[t] Cn: Heb *in the haunt of jackals is her resting place* [u] Or *pass it by* [v] Cn: Heb *for them*

35.1ff In chapters 1 – 34, Isaiah has delivered a message of judgment on all nations, including Israel and Judah, for rejecting God. Although there have been glimpses of relief and restoration for the remnant of faithful believers, the climate of wrath, fury, judgment, and destruction has prevailed. Now Isaiah breaks through with a vision of beauty and encouragement. God is just as complete in his mercy as he is severe in his judgment. God's complete moral perfection is revealed by his hatred of all sin, and this leads to judgment. This same moral perfection is revealed in his love for all he has created. This leads to mercy for those who have sinned but who have sincerely loved and obeyed him.

35.1ff This chapter is a beautiful picture of the final kingdom in which God will establish his justice and destroy all evil. This is the world the faithful can anticipate after the Judgment, when creation itself will rejoice in God. Chapter 34 spoke of tribulation, when God will judge all people for their actions. Chapter 35 pictures the days after Judgment, when life will be peaceful at last. Carmel and Sharon were regions of thick vegetation and fertile soil. They were symbols of productivity and plenty.

35.3, 4 Because we all sin, the return of the Lord is frightening to all of us. The Lord will return with vengeance against evil, yet he will save those who have placed their trust in him. We should encourage those who have become weak in their faith. Our fear of judgment can be changed instead to awe at God's salvation.

35.6, 7 The healing of physical defects here is real, and not just a figurative representation of spiritual healing. Our bodies will one day be restored. Similarly, the streams in the desert are not just a mirage. Nature will also be released from the curse of the fall in that day (Genesis 3.17–19).

35.8–10 This highway is the way righteous pilgrims take from the wilderness of suffering to Jerusalem. It is found only by following God. Only the redeemed will travel God's highway; they will be protected from wicked travelers and harmful animals. God is preparing a way for his people to travel to his home, and he will walk with us. God never stops at pointing the way for us to go; he is always beside us as we go.

35.9 Isa 51.10

9 No lion shall be there,
nor shall any ravenous beast come up on it;
they shall not be found there,
but the redeemed shall walk there.

35.10 Rev 21.4

10 And the ransomed of the LORD shall return,
and come to Zion with singing;
everlasting joy shall be upon their heads;
they shall obtain joy and gladness,
and sorrow and sighing shall flee away.

5. Events during the reign of Hezekiah

Sennacherib threatens Judah

36.2 2 Kgs 18.17–20.11 2 Chron 32.9-24

36.4 2 Kgs 18.19

36.5 2 Kgs 18.7

36.6 Ps 146.3 Ezek 29.6,7

36 In the fourteenth year of King Hezekiah, King Sennacherib of Assyria came
up against all the fortified cities of Judah and captured them. 2The king of
Assyria sent the Rabshakeh from Lachish to King Hezekiah at Jerusalem, with a
great army. He stood by the conduit of the upper pool on the highway to the Fuller's
Field. 3And there came out to him Eliakim son of Hilkiah, who was in charge of the
palace, and Shebna the secretary, and Joah son of Asaph, the recorder.
4 The Rabshakeh said to them, "Say to Hezekiah: Thus says the great king, the
king of Assyria: On what do you base this confidence of yours? 5Do you think that
mere words are strategy and power for war? On whom do you now rely, that you
have rebelled against me? 6See, you are relying on Egypt, that broken reed of a

ASSYRIA ADVANCES As Sennacherib beautified his capital city, Nineveh, Hezekiah withheld tribute and prepared for battle. The Assyrians advanced toward their rebellious western border, attacking swiftly down the Mediterranean coast. From Lachish, Sennacherib threatened to take Jerusalem, but Isaiah knew his threats would die with him on his return to Nineveh.

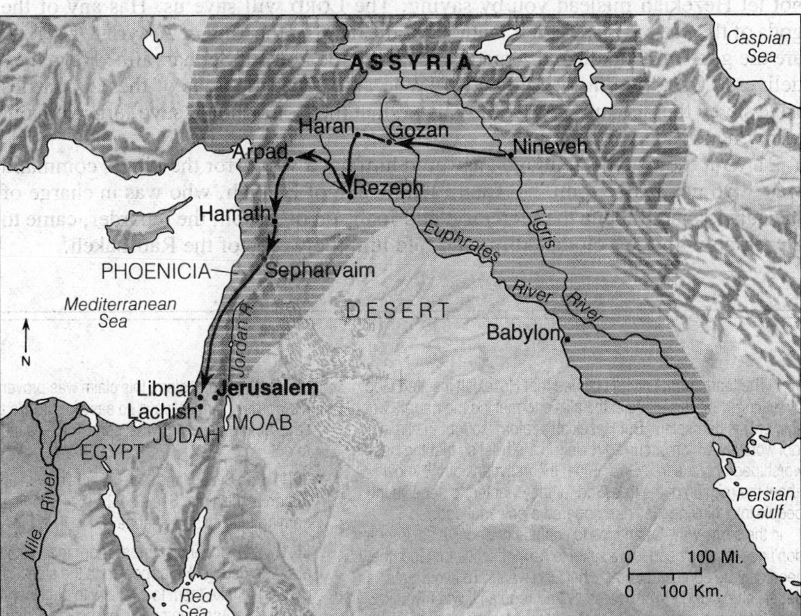

36.4–6 Chapter 19 describes Isaiah's warning to Judah not to ally itself with Egypt in the face of Assyria's impending attack. Sennacherib of Assyria taunts Judah for trusting in Egypt. Even the Assyrians knew that Egypt could not help Judah.

36.5 Hezekiah put great trust in Pharaoh's promise to help Israel against the Assyrians, but promises are only as good as the credibility of the person making them. It was Pharaoh's word against God's. How quickly we organize our lives around human advice while we neglect God's eternal promises. When choosing between God's Word and someone else's, whom will you believe?

staff, which will pierce the hand of anyone who leans on it. Such is Pharaoh king
of Egypt to all who rely on him. 7 But if you say to me, 'We rely on the LORD our **36.7**
God,' is it not he whose high places and altars Hezekiah has removed, saying to Deut 12.2-5 2 Kgs 18.4,5
Judah and to Jerusalem, 'You shall worship before this altar'? 8 Come now, make **36.8**
a wager with my master the king of Assyria: I will give you two thousand horses, Isa 30.2-5,7 31.3
if you are able on your part to set riders on them. 9 How then can you repulse a
single captain among the least of my master's servants, when you rely on Egypt for
chariots and for horsemen? 10 Moreover, is it without the LORD that I have come up **36.10**
against this land to destroy it? The LORD said to me, Go up against this land, and 1 Kgs 13.18
destroy it."

11 Then Eliakim, Shebna, and Joah said to the Rabshakeh, "Please speak to **36.11**
your servants in Aramaic, for we understand it; do not speak to us in the language Ezra 4.7 Dan 2.4
of Judah within the hearing of the people who are on the wall." 12 But the Rabshakeh said, "Has my master sent me to speak these words to your master and to you,
and not to the people sitting on the wall, who are doomed with you to eat their own
dung and drink their own urine?"

13 Then the Rabshakeh stood and called out in a loud voice in the language of **36.13**
Judah, "Hear the words of the great king, the king of Assyria! 14 Thus says the king: 2 Chron 32.18 **36.14**
'Do not let Hezekiah deceive you, for he will not be able to deliver you. 15 Do not Isa 37.10
let Hezekiah make you rely on the LORD by saying, The LORD will surely deliver
us; this city will not be given into the hand of the king of Assyria.' 16 Do not listen **36.16**
to Hezekiah; for thus says the king of Assyria: 'Make your peace with me and come Zech 3.10
out to me; then everyone of you will eat from your own vine and your own fig tree
and drink water from your own cistern, 17 until I come and take you away to a land
like your own land, a land of grain and wine, a land of bread and vineyards. 18 Do
not let Hezekiah mislead you by saying, The LORD will save us. Has any of the
gods of the nations saved their land out of the hand of the king of Assyria? 19 Where **36.19**
are the gods of Hamath and Arpad? Where are the gods of Sepharvaim? Have they 2 Kgs 17.6 Isa 10.9-11
delivered Samaria out of my hand? 20 Who among all the gods of these countries 37.13 Jer 49.23
have saved their countries out of my hand, that the LORD should save Jerusalem out **36.20**
of my hand?'" 1 Kgs 20.23,28

21 But they were silent and answered him not a word, for the king's command
was, "Do not answer him." 22 Then Eliakim son of Hilkiah, who was in charge of
the palace, and Shebna the secretary, and Joah son of Asaph, the recorder, came to
Hezekiah with their clothes torn, and told him the words of the Rabshakeh.

36.7 The team from Assyria claimed that Hezekiah insulted God by tearing down his altars in the hills and making the people worship only in Jerusalem. But Hezekiah's reform sought to eliminate idol worship (which occurred mainly in the hills) so that the people worshiped only the true God. Either the Assyrians didn't know about the religion of the true God, or they wanted to deceive the people into thinking they had angered a powerful god.

In the same way, Satan tries to confuse or deceive us. People don't necessarily need to be sinful to be ineffective for God; they need only be confused about what God wants. To avoid Satan's deceit, study God's Word carefully and regularly. When you know what God says, you will not fall for Satan's lies.

36.10 Sennacherib continued his demoralization campaign by sending the Rabshakeh to try to convince the people of Judah that God had turned against them. The Assyrians hoped to convince the people of Judah to surrender without fighting. But Isaiah had already said that the Assyrians *would not* destroy Jerusalem, so the people did not need to be afraid of them (10.24–27; 29.5–8).

36.10 Did the Lord really tell the king to go against the land and destroy it? How were the Israelites to know whether he was telling them the truth, or just telling a lie to drain their courage? For the residents of Jerusalem, this claim was proven false by the rest of his words. It's not always so easy for us. We should be very cautious before believing what someone tells us God told him or her to do.

36.11 The Syrian language, Aramaic, was an international language at this time. See also 22.15–25 for Isaiah's prophecies concerning Eliakim and Shebna.

36.17 Sennacherib's ambassador tried yet another ploy to demoralize the people. He appealed to the starving city under siege by offering to take them to a land with plenty of food if they surrendered. The Assyrian policy for dealing with conquered nations was to resettle the inhabitants and then to move their own people into the recently conquered area. This provided manpower for their armies and prevented revolts in conquered territories.

36.19, 20 The Rabshakeh said that the gods of the other cities he had conquered had not been able to save their people, so how could the God of Jerusalem save them? Jehovah was supposedly the God of Samaria (the northern kingdom), and it fell. But Jehovah was the God of Samaria in name only, because the people were not worshiping him. That is why prophets foretold the fall of Samaria. But the people in Jerusalem were at this time actively worshiping God, and he would rescue them from the Assyrian army.

God will deliver Jerusalem

37.1 2 Kgs 19.1-37 **37** When King Hezekiah heard it, he tore his clothes, covered himself with
sackcloth, and went into the house of the LORD. 2 And he sent Eliakim, who
was in charge of the palace, and Shebna the secretary, and the senior priests, cov-
37.3 Isa 22.5 26.17,18 ered with sackcloth, to the prophet Isaiah son of Amoz. 3 They said to him, "Thus
says Hezekiah, This day is a day of distress, of rebuke, and of disgrace; children
37.4 Isa 1.9 10.20-22 have come to the birth, and there is no strength to bring them forth. 4 It may be that
the LORD your God heard the words of the Rabshakeh, whom his master the king
of Assyria has sent to mock the living God, and will rebuke the words that the LORD
your God has heard; therefore lift up your prayer for the remnant that is left."
37.6 Isa 7.4; 35.4 5 When the servants of King Hezekiah came to Isaiah, 6 Isaiah said to them,
"Say to your master, 'Thus says the LORD: Do not be afraid because of the words
that you have heard, with which the servants of the king of Assyria have reviled
me. 7 I myself will put a spirit in him, so that he shall hear a rumor, and return to
his own land; I will cause him to fall by the sword in his own land.' "
37.8 Isa 20.5 8 The Rabshakeh returned, and found the king of Assyria fighting against Libnah; for he had heard that the king had left Lachish. 9 Now the king[w] heard concerning King Tirhakah of Ethiopia,[x] "He has set out to fight against you." When he
heard it, he sent messengers to Hezekiah, saying, 10 "Thus shall you speak to King
Hezekiah of Judah: Do not let your God on whom you rely deceive you by promis-
37.11 Isa 10.9-11 ing that Jerusalem will not be given into the hand of the king of Assyria. 11 See, you
have heard what the kings of Assyria have done to all lands, destroying them ut-
37.12 Gen 11.31 2 Kgs 17.6 terly. Shall you be delivered? 12 Have the gods of the nations delivered them, the
nations that my predecessors destroyed, Gozan, Haran, Rezeph, and the people of
Eden who were in Telassar? 13 Where is the king of Hamath, the king of Arpad, the
king of the city of Sepharvaim, the king of Hena, or the king of Ivvah?"

Hezekiah's prayer

14 Hezekiah received the letter from the hand of the messengers and read it;
then Hezekiah went up to the house of the LORD and spread it before the LORD.
37.16 Ex 25.22 Ps 17.6; 74.22 80.1; 86.10 Jer 10.12 15 And Hezekiah prayed to the LORD, saying: 16 "O LORD of hosts, God of Israel,
who are enthroned above the cherubim, you are God, you alone, of all the king-
doms of the earth; you have made heaven and earth. 17 Incline your ear, O LORD,
and hear; open your eyes, O LORD, and see; hear all the words of Sennacherib,
which he has sent to mock the living God. 18 Truly, O LORD, the kings of Assyria
37.19 Isa 17.8; 26.14 have laid waste all the nations and their lands, 19 and have hurled their gods into the
37.20 1 Kgs 18.36,37 Isa 33.22 Ezek 36.23 fire, though they were no gods, but the work of human hands—wood and
stone—and so they were destroyed. 20 So now, O LORD our God, save us from his
hand, so that all the kingdoms of the earth may know that you alone are the LORD."

God will destroy Sennacherib

21 Then Isaiah son of Amoz sent to Hezekiah, saying: "Thus says the LORD, the
God of Israel: Because you have prayed to me concerning King Sennacherib of
37.22 Lam 2.13 Zeph 3.14 Assyria, 22 this is the word that the LORD has spoken concerning him:

She despises you, she scorns you—
    virgin daughter Zion;
she tosses her head—behind your back,
    daughter Jerusalem.

[w] Heb *he* [x] Or *Nubia*; Heb *Cush*

37.3 Judah is compared to a woman trying to give birth to a child who does not come. Too weak to help herself, she wishes for death to end her pain. When the situation seemed hopeless, Hezekiah didn't give up. Instead, he asked the prophet Isaiah to pray that God would help his people.

37.4 Hezekiah did exactly what Isaiah had been calling the people to do (chapters 1–35). He turned to God and watched him come to Judah's aid. Turning to God means believing that God is there and that he is able to help us.

37.8–10 Although the answer to Hezekiah's prayer was already in motion because Ethiopia was poised to attack, Hezekiah did not know it. He persisted in prayer and faith even though he could not see the answer coming. When we pray, we must have faith that God has already prepared the best answer. Our task is to ask in faith and wait.

37.16 Cherubim are mighty angels.

23 Whom have you mocked and reviled?
Against whom have you raised your voice
and haughtily lifted your eyes?
Against the Holy One of Israel!
24 By your servants you have mocked the Lord,
and you have said, 'With my many chariots
I have gone up the heights of the mountains,
to the far recesses of Lebanon;
I felled its tallest cedars,
its choicest cypresses;
I came to its remotest height,
its densest forest.
25 I dug wells
and drank waters,
I dried up with the sole of my foot
all the streams of Egypt.'

26 Have you not heard
that I determined it long ago?
I planned from days of old
what now I bring to pass,
that you should make fortified cities
crash into heaps of ruins,
27 while their inhabitants, shorn of strength,
are dismayed and confounded;
they have become like plants of the field
and like tender grass,
like grass on the housetops,
blighted[y] before it is grown.

28 I know your rising up[z] and your sitting down,
your going out and coming in,
and your raging against me.
29 Because you have raged against me
and your arrogance has come to my ears,
I will put my hook in your nose
and my bit in your mouth;
I will turn you back on the way
by which you came.

30 "And this shall be the sign for you: This year eat what grows of itself, and in
the second year what springs from that; then in the third year sow, reap, plant vineyards, and eat their fruit. 31 The surviving remnant of the house of Judah shall again
take root downward, and bear fruit upward; 32 for from Jerusalem a remnant shall
go out, and from Mount Zion a band of survivors. The zeal of the LORD of hosts
will do this.
33 "Therefore thus says the LORD concerning the king of Assyria: He shall not
come into this city, shoot an arrow there, come before it with a shield, or cast up a
siege ramp against it. 34 By the way that he came, by the same he shall return; he
shall not come into this city, says the LORD. 35 For I will defend this city to save it,
for my own sake and for the sake of my servant David."

37.23 Isa 5.15,21 Ezek 39.7 Hab 1.12
37.24 Isa 14.8
37.26 Isa 25.2 Acts 2.23 4.27,28
37.27 Ps 129.6 Isa 40.7
37.28 Ps 139.1
37.29 Isa 30.28 Ezek 38.4
37.30 Lev 25.5,11
37.31 Isa 10.20; 27.6
37.32 2 Kgs 19.31
37.35 2 Kgs 20.6 Isa 48.9,11

[y] With 2 Kings 19.26: Heb *field* [z] Q Ms Gk: MT lacks *your rising up*

37.29 This was a common torture the Assyrians used on their captives. They were often led away with hooks in their noses or bits in their mouths as signs of humiliation.

37.35 God would defend Jerusalem for his honor and in David's memory. Assyria had insulted God. They would not be his instrument to punish Jerusalem. What Jerusalem could not possibly do, God would do for them. God is prepared to do the impossible if we trust him enough to ask.

37.36 2 Kgs 19.35 Isa 10.12,33,34
37.37 Gen 10.11 Jonah 3.3 Zeph 2.13
37.38 Gen 8.4

36 Then the angel of the LORD set out and struck down one hundred eighty-five
thousand in the camp of the Assyrians; when morning dawned, they were all dead
bodies. 37 Then King Sennacherib of Assyria left, went home, and lived at Nineveh. 38 As he was worshiping in the house of his god Nisroch, his sons Adrammelech and Sharezer killed him with the sword, and they escaped into the land of
Ararat. His son Esar-haddon succeeded him.

Hezekiah's illness

38.1 2 Kgs 20.1-6
38.3 2 Kgs 18.5,6 Neh 13.14 Ps 6.6-8
38.5 2 Kgs 18.2,13
38.6 Isa 31.5
38.7 Isa 7.11,14
38.8 2 Kgs 20.9-11

38 In those days Hezekiah became sick and was at the point of death. The
prophet Isaiah son of Amoz came to him, and said to him, "Thus says the
LORD: Set your house in order, for you shall die; you shall not recover." 2 Then
Hezekiah turned his face to the wall, and prayed to the LORD: 3 "Remember now,
O LORD, I implore you, how I have walked before you in faithfulness with a whole
heart, and have done what is good in your sight." And Hezekiah wept bitterly.
4 Then the word of the LORD came to Isaiah: 5 "Go and say to Hezekiah, Thus
says the LORD, the God of your ancestor David: I have heard your prayer, I have
seen your tears; I will add fifteen years to your life. 6 I will deliver you and this city
out of the hand of the king of Assyria, and defend this city.
7 "This is the sign to you from the LORD, that the LORD will do this thing that
he has promised: 8 See, I will make the shadow cast by the declining sun on the dial
of Ahaz turn back ten steps." So the sun turned back on the dial the ten steps by
which it had declined.[a]

9 A writing of King Hezekiah of Judah, after he had been sick and had recovered from his sickness:

38.10 Ps 102.24
38.11 Ps 27.13
38.12 Job 4.20 2 Cor 5.1
38.14 Ps 119.123 Ezek 7.16
38.15 Job 7.11

10 I said: In the noontide of my days
  I must depart;
I am consigned to the gates of Sheol
  for the rest of my years.
11 I said, I shall not see the LORD
  in the land of the living;
I shall look upon mortals no more
  among the inhabitants of the world.
12 My dwelling is plucked up and removed from me
  like a shepherd's tent;
like a weaver I have rolled up my life;
  he cuts me off from the loom;
from day to night you bring me to an end;[a]
13 I cry for help[b] until morning;
like a lion he breaks all my bones;
  from day to night you bring me to an end.[a]

14 Like a swallow or a crane[a] I clamor,
  I moan like a dove.
My eyes are weary with looking upward.
  O Lord, I am oppressed; be my security!
15 But what can I say? For he has spoken to me,
  and he himself has done it.

[a] Meaning of Heb uncertain [b] Cn: Meaning of Heb uncertain

37.38 The death of Sennacherib was prophesied by Isaiah in 10.12, 33, 34 and in 37.7. His death is also recorded in 2 Kings 19.

38.1ff The events of chapters 38 and 39 happened before those of chapters 36 and 37.

38.1–5 When Isaiah went to Hezekiah, who was extremely ill, and told him of his impending death, Hezekiah immediately turned to God. God responded to his prayer, allowing Hezekiah to live another 15 years. In response to fervent prayer, God may change the course of our lives too. Never hesitate to ask God for radical changes if you will honor him with those changes.

38.1–5 According to 2 Chronicles 32.24–26, Hezekiah had a problem with pride even after this double miracle of healing and deliverance. Eventually he and his subjects humbled themselves, and God's judgment was put off for several more generations.

All my sleep has fled[c]
because of the bitterness of my soul.

16 O Lord, by these things people live,
and in all these is the life of my spirit.[d]
Oh, restore me to health and make me live!
17 Surely it was for my welfare
that I had great bitterness;
but you have held back[e] my life
from the pit of destruction,
for you have cast all my sins
behind your back.
18 For Sheol cannot thank you,
death cannot praise you;
those who go down to the Pit cannot hope
for your faithfulness.
19 The living, the living, they thank you,
as I do this day;
fathers make known to children
your faithfulness.

20 The LORD will save me,
and we will sing to stringed instruments[f]
all the days of our lives,
at the house of the LORD.

21 Now Isaiah had said, "Let them take a lump of figs, and apply it to the boil,
so that he may recover." 22 Hezekiah also had said, "What is the sign that I shall go
up to the house of the LORD?"

38.16 Ps 39.13 119.71,75
38.17 Isa 43.25 Jer 31.34 Jonah 2.6
38.18 Ps 6.5
38.19 Ps 78.5-7 119.175
38.20 Ps 33.1-3 116.17-19 146.2

Messengers from Babylon are welcomed

39 At that time King Merodach-baladan son of Baladan of Babylon sent envoys
with letters and a present to Hezekiah, for he heard that he had been sick and
had recovered. 2 Hezekiah welcomed them; he showed them his treasure house, the
silver, the gold, the spices, the precious oil, his whole armory, all that was found
in his storehouses. There was nothing in his house or in all his realm that Hezekiah
did not show them. 3 Then the prophet Isaiah came to King Hezekiah and said to
him, "What did these men say? From where did they come to you?" Hezekiah
answered, "They have come to me from a far country, from Babylon." 4 He said,
"What have they seen in your house?" Hezekiah answered, "They have seen all that
is in my house; there is nothing in my storehouses that I did not show them."

39.1 2 Kgs 20.12-19
39.2 2 Kgs 18.15,16 2 Chron 32.25, 31
39.3 Jer 5.15

[c] Cn Compare Syr: Heb *I will walk slowly all my years* [d] Meaning of Heb uncertain [e] Cn Compare Gk Vg: Heb *loved*
[f] Heb *my stringed instruments*

38.16–18 Hezekiah realized that his prayer brought deliverance and forgiveness. *Sheol* is the word in the Old Testament for the realm of the dead. His words "death cannot praise you" may reveal that he was unaware of the blessedness of the future life for those who trust in God (57.1, 2), or they may simply mean that dead bodies cannot praise God. In either case, Hezekiah knew God had spared his life, and in his poem he praised him. Hezekiah recognized the good that came from his bitter experience. The next time you pass through a bitter experience, pray for God's help to gain something beneficial from it.

38.19 Hezekiah speaks of the significance of passing the joy of the Lord from father to child, from generation to generation. The heritage of our faith has come to us because of faithful men and women who have carried God's message to us across the centuries. Do you share with your children or other young people the excitement of your relationship with God?

39.1ff Merodach-baladan, a Babylonian prince, was planning a revolt against Assyria and was forming an alliance. He probably hoped to convince Hezekiah to join this alliance against Assyria. Hezekiah, feeling friendly toward this nation that was also an enemy of Assyria, showed the Babylonian envoys his assets. But Isaiah warned the king not to trust Babylon. Someday they would turn on Judah and devour Jerusalem's wealth.

39.4–7 What was so wrong about showing these Babylonians around? Hezekiah failed to see that the Babylonians would become his next threat, and that they, not the Assyrians, would conquer his city. When Isaiah told him Babylon would someday carry it all away, this was an amazing prophecy because Babylon was struggling for independence under Assyria. Hezekiah's self-satisfied display of his earthly wealth brought its own consequences (2 Kings 25; Daniel 1.1, 2). His response (39.8) may seem a bit shortsighted, but he was simply expressing gratitude for the

39.6 2 Kgs 24.13 Jer 20.5

5 Then Isaiah said to Hezekiah, "Hear the word of the LORD of hosts: 6 Days are
coming when all that is in your house, and that which your ancestors have stored up
until this day, shall be carried to Babylon; nothing shall be left, says the LORD.
7 Some of your own sons who are born to you shall be taken away; they shall be
eunuchs in the palace of the king of Babylon." 8 Then Hezekiah said to Isaiah, "The
word of the LORD that you have spoken is good." For he thought, "There will be
peace and security in my days."

39.8 2 Chron 34.28

B. WORDS OF COMFORT (40.1 – 66.24)

Isaiah now speaks of events which will occur after the captivity. This includes the decree by Cyrus to release the remnant captives and allow them to return to Jerusalem after he conquered Babylon. But Isaiah also foretells the coming of the suffering Servant, Jesus Christ, and describes his life and death with incredible detail. Isaiah also speaks about the coming of the new heavens and earth, when God's people will be completely restored. Since all believers will participate in this new world to come, we can have confident hope in the future.

1. Israel's release from captivity

God will feed his flock

40 Comfort, O comfort my people,
says your God.
2 Speak tenderly to Jerusalem,
and cry to her
that she has served her term,
that her penalty is paid,
that she has received from the LORD's hand
double for all her sins.

40.2 Isa 53.5,6,11 Zech 9.12

3 A voice cries out:
"In the wilderness prepare the way of the LORD,
make straight in the desert a highway for our God.
4 Every valley shall be lifted up,
and every mountain and hill be made low;
the uneven ground shall become level,
and the rough places a plain.
5 Then the glory of the LORD shall be revealed,
and all people shall see it together,
for the mouth of the LORD has spoken."

40.3 Mal 3.1 Mt 3.3

40.4 Ezek 17.24

40.5 Hab 2.14

6 A voice says, "Cry out!"
And I said, "What shall I cry?"
All people are grass,

40.6 Job 14.2

---

blessing from God that peace would reign during his lifetime and that God's judgment would not be more severe.

39.8 Hezekiah, one of Judah's most faithful kings, worked hard throughout his reign to stamp out idol worship and to purify the worship of the true God at the Jerusalem temple. Nevertheless, he knew his kingdom was not pure. Powerful undercurrents of evil invited destruction, and only God's miraculous interventions preserved Judah from its enemies. Here Hezekiah expressed gratefulness that God would preserve peace during his reign. As soon as Hezekiah died, the nation rushed back to its sinful ways under the leadership of Manasseh, Hezekiah's son. He actually rebuilt the centers of idolatry his father had destroyed.

40.1 Judah still had 100 years of trouble before Jerusalem would fall, then 70 years of exile. So God tells Isaiah to speak tenderly and to comfort Jerusalem.

The seeds of comfort may take root in the soil of adversity. When your life seems to be falling apart, ask God to comfort you. You may not escape adversity, but you may find God's comfort as you face it. Sometimes, however, the only comfort we have is in the knowledge that someday we will be with God. Appreciate the comfort and encouragement found in his Word, his presence, and his people.

40.1ff The book of Isaiah makes a dramatic shift at this point. The following chapters discuss the majesty of God, who is coming to rule the earth and judge all people. He will reunite Israel and Judah and restore them to glory. Instead of warning the people of impending judgment, Isaiah now comforts them. This foretells the end of time when "Babylon" – the future evil world system – will be destroyed and the persecution of God's people will end.

40.3–5 Preparing a straight, smooth road means removing obstacles and rolling out the red carpet for the coming of the Lord. The wilderness is a picture of life's trials and sufferings. We are not immune to these, but our faith need not be hindered by them. Isaiah told people to prepare to see God work. John the Baptist used these words as he challenged the people to prepare for the coming Messiah (Matthew 3.3).

40.6–8 People are compared here to grass and flowers that fade

their constancy is like the flower of the field.
7 The grass withers, the flower fades,
when the breath of the LORD blows upon it;
surely the people are grass.
8 The grass withers, the flower fades;
but the word of our God will stand forever.
9 Get you up to a high mountain,
O Zion, herald of good tidings;[g]
lift up your voice with strength,
O Jerusalem, herald of good tidings,[h]
lift it up, do not fear;
say to the cities of Judah,
"Here is your God!"
10 See, the Lord GOD comes with might,
and his arm rules for him;
his reward is with him,
and his recompense before him.
11 He will feed his flock like a shepherd;
he will gather the lambs in his arms,
and carry them in his bosom,
and gently lead the mother sheep.

12 Who has measured the waters in the hollow of his hand
and marked off the heavens with a span,
enclosed the dust of the earth in a measure,
and weighed the mountains in scales
and the hills in a balance?
13 Who has directed the spirit of the LORD,
or as his counselor has instructed him?
14 Whom did he consult for his enlightenment,
and who taught him the path of justice?
Who taught him knowledge,
and showed him the way of understanding?
15 Even the nations are like a drop from a bucket,
and are accounted as dust on the scales;
see, he takes up the isles like fine dust.
16 Lebanon would not provide fuel enough,
nor are its animals enough for a burnt offering.
17 All the nations are as nothing before him;
they are accounted by him as less than nothing and emptiness.

18 To whom then will you liken God,
or what likeness compare with him?
19 An idol? —A workman casts it,
and a goldsmith overlays it with gold,
and casts for it silver chains.

40.7 Jas 1.10,11
40.8 Mt 5.18
40.10 Isa 59.16 Rev 22.12
40.11 Ezek 34.12-14, 23,31 Jn 10.11,14-16
40.12 Isa 48.13
40.13 Rom 11.34
40.14 Col 2.3
40.15 Isa 17.13
40.17 Isa 29.7
40.18 Ex 8.10 Isa 46.5 Mic 7.18
40.19 Ps 115.4-8 Hab 2.18,19

[g] Or *O herald of good tidings to Zion* [h] Or *O herald of good tidings to Jerusalem*

away. Our lives are mortal, but God's Word is eternal and unfailing. Public opinion changes and is unreliable, but God's Word is constant. Only in God's eternal Word will we find lasting solutions to our problems and needs.

40.11 God is often pictured as a shepherd, gently caring for and guiding his flock. He is powerful and mighty (40.10), yet careful and gentle. He is called a shepherd (Psalm 23); the good shepherd (John 10.11, 14); the great shepherd (Hebrews 13.20); and the chief shepherd (1 Peter 5.4). Note that the shepherd is caring for the most defenseless members of his society: children and pregnant (or nursing) women. This reinforces the prophetic theme that the truly powerful nation is not the one with a strong military, but rather the one that relies on God's caring strength.

40.12–31 A *span* is the breadth of one hand. Isaiah describes God's power to create, his provision, and his presence to help. God is almighty and all-powerful; but even so, he cares for each of us personally. No person or thing can be compared to God (40.25). We describe God as best we can with our limited knowledge and language, but we only limit our understanding of him and his power when we compare him to what we experience on

40.20 Isa 46.7

20 As a gift one chooses mulberry wood[i]
— wood that will not rot —
then seeks out a skilled artisan
to set up an image that will not topple.

40.21 Isa 51.13 Rom 1.19

21 Have you not known? Have you not heard?
Has it not been told you from the beginning?
Have you not understood from the foundations of the earth?

40.22 Ps 104.2

22 It is he who sits above the circle of the earth,
and its inhabitants are like grasshoppers;
who stretches out the heavens like a curtain,
and spreads them like a tent to live in;

40.23 Ps 107.40 Jer 25.18-27

23 who brings princes to naught,
and makes the rulers of the earth as nothing.

40.24 Isa 17.13

24 Scarcely are they planted, scarcely sown,
scarcely has their stem taken root in the earth,
when he blows upon them, and they wither,
and the tempest carries them off like stubble.

25 To whom then will you compare me,
or who is my equal? says the Holy One.

40.26 Ps 147.4 Isa 42.5

26 Lift up your eyes on high and see:
Who created these?
He who brings out their host and numbers them,
calling them all by name;
because he is great in strength,
mighty in power,
not one is missing.

40.27 Job 34.5,6 Isa 54.8

27 Why do you say, O Jacob,
and speak, O Israel,
"My way is hidden from the LORD,
and my right is disregarded by my God"?

40.28 Ps 90.2; 147.5

28 Have you not known? Have you not heard?
The LORD is the everlasting God,
the Creator of the ends of the earth.
He does not faint or grow weary;
his understanding is unsearchable.

40.29 Jer 31.25

29 He gives power to the faint,
and strengthens the powerless.

40.30 Jer 9.21

30 Even youths will faint and be weary,
and the young will fall exhausted;

40.31 2 Cor 4.8-10,16 Heb 12.3

31 but those who wait for the LORD shall renew their strength,
they shall mount up with wings like eagles,
they shall run and not be weary,
they shall walk and not faint.

[i] Meaning of Heb uncertain

earth. What is your concept of God, especially as revealed in his Son, Jesus Christ? Don't limit his work in your life by underestimating him.

40.29–31 Even the strongest people get tired at times, but God's power and strength never diminish. He is never too tired or too busy to help and listen. His strength is our source of strength. When you feel all of life crushing you and cannot go another step, remember that you can call upon God to renew your strength.

40.31 We all need regular times to listen to God. Waiting for the Lord is expecting that his promise of strength will help us to rise above life's distractions and difficulties. Listening to God helps us to be prepared for when he speaks to us, to be patient when he asks us to wait, and to expect him to fulfill the promises found in his Word.

God will help Israel

41 Listen to me in silence, O coastlands; 41.1 Hab 2.20
let the peoples renew their strength;
let them approach, then let them speak;
let us together draw near for judgment.

2 Who has roused a victor from the east, 41.2 2 Chron 36.23 Isa 46.11
summoned him to his service?
He delivers up nations to him,
and tramples kings under foot;
he makes them like dust with his sword,
like driven stubble with his bow.
3 He pursues them and passes on safely,
scarcely touching the path with his feet.
4 Who has performed and done this, 41.4 Isa 44.7; 48.12 Rev 1.8,17,18
calling the generations from the beginning?
I, the LORD, am first,
and will be with the last.
5 The coastlands have seen and are afraid, 41.5 Josh 5.1 Ezek 26.15,16
the ends of the earth tremble;
they have drawn near and come.
6 Each one helps the other, 41.6 Joel 3.9-11
saying to one another, "Take courage!"
7 The artisan encourages the goldsmith,
and the one who smooths with the hammer encourages the one who strikes the anvil,
saying of the soldering, "It is good";
and they fasten it with nails so that it cannot be moved.
8 But you, Israel, my servant, 41.8 Isa 51.2 Jas 2.23
Jacob, whom I have chosen,
the offspring of Abraham, my friend;
9 you whom I took from the ends of the earth, 41.9 Deut 7.6 Isa 11.11
and called from its farthest corners,
saying to you, "You are my servant,
I have chosen you and not cast you off";
10 do not fear, for I am with you, 41.10 Deut 31.6 Ps 89.13 Rom 8.31
do not be afraid, for I am your God;
I will strengthen you, I will help you,
I will uphold you with my victorious right hand.

11 Yes, all who are incensed against you 41.11 Isa 29.5,7,8
shall be ashamed and disgraced;
those who strive against you

41.1ff The "victor from the east" is Cyrus II of Persia, who would be king within a century and a half (he is also mentioned in 44.28). God could use even a pagan ruler to protect and care for Israel, because God is in control of all world empires and politics.

41.4 Each generation gets caught up in its own problems, but God's plan embraces all generations. When your great-grandparents lived, God worked personally in the lives of his people. When your great-grandchildren live, God will still work personally in the lives of his people. He is the only one who sees 100 years from now as clearly as 100 years ago. When you are concerned about the future, talk with God, who knows the generations of the future as well as he knows the generations of the past.

41.8 God calls Israel his own because of his wonderful friendship with Abraham. He chose Israel, and they had the assurance that God would be with them. God considers us friends when we give ourselves to him as he gives himself to us. When we are God's friends, we know he is always there when we need him. Do you consider God your friend? Are you as devoted to him as he is to you?

41.8–10 God chose Israel through Abraham because he wanted to, not because the people deserved it (Deuteronomy 7.6–8; 9.4–6). Although God chose the Israelites to represent him to the world, they failed to do this; so God punished them and sent them into captivity. Now all believers are God's chosen people, and all share the responsibility of representing him to the world. God will one day bring all his faithful people together. We need not fear, because (1) God's presence is with us ("I am with you"), (2) God has established a relationship with us ("I am your God"), and (3) God's assurance of strength, help, and victory over sin and death is certain.

shall be as nothing and shall perish.
41.12 Job 20.7-9
12 You shall seek those who contend with you,
but you shall not find them;
those who war against you
shall be as nothing at all.
41.13 Isa 45.1
13 For I, the LORD your God,
hold your right hand;
it is I who say to you, "Do not fear,
I will help you."

41.14 Isa 43.14
14 Do not fear, you worm Jacob,
you insect[j] Israel!
I will help you, says the LORD;
your Redeemer is the Holy One of Israel.
41.15 Mic 4.13
15 Now, I will make of you a threshing sledge,
sharp, new, and having teeth;
you shall thresh the mountains and crush them,
and you shall make the hills like chaff.
41.16 Isa 35.10
16 You shall winnow them and the wind shall carry them away,
and the tempest shall scatter them.
Then you shall rejoice in the LORD;
in the Holy One of Israel you shall glory.

41.17 Isa 30.19 42.16; 44.3
17 When the poor and needy seek water,
and there is none,
and their tongue is parched with thirst,
I the LORD will answer them,
I the God of Israel will not forsake them.
41.18 Ps 107.35 Isa 30.25
18 I will open rivers on the bare heights,[k]
and fountains in the midst of the valleys;
I will make the wilderness a pool of water,
and the dry land springs of water.
41.19 Isa 55.13
19 I will put in the wilderness the cedar,
the acacia, the myrtle, and the olive;
I will set in the desert the cypress,
the plane and the pine together,
41.20 Job 12.7-9
20 so that all may see and know,
all may consider and understand,
that the hand of the LORD has done this,
the Holy One of Israel has created it.

21 Set forth your case, says the LORD;
bring your proofs, says the King of Jacob.
41.22 Isa 43.9; 45.21
22 Let them bring them, and tell us
what is to happen.
Tell us the former things, what they are,
so that we may consider them,
and that we may know their outcome;
or declare to us the things to come.
41.23 Jer 10.5 Jn 13.19
23 Tell us what is to come hereafter,
that we may know that you are gods;

[j] Syr: Heb *men of* [k] Or *trails*

41.21–24 Israel was surrounded by many nations whose gods supposedly had special powers, such as raising crops and providing victories in war. These gods, however, failed to deliver. A god with limited or no power at all is not really a god. When we are tempted to put our trust in something other than the living God—money, career, family, or even military power—we should stop and ask some serious questions. Will it deliver? Will it unfailingly provide what I am looking for? God delivers. When he makes a promise, he keeps it. He is the only completely trustworthy God.

do good, or do harm,
that we may be afraid and terrified.
24 You, indeed, are nothing
and your work is nothing at all;
whoever chooses you is an abomination.

25 I stirred up one from the north, and he has come,
from the rising of the sun he was summoned by name.[l]
He shall trample[m] on rulers as on mortar,
as the potter treads clay.
26 Who declared it from the beginning, so that we might know,
and beforehand, so that we might say, "He is right"?
There was no one who declared it, none who proclaimed,
none who heard your words.
27 I first have declared it to Zion,[n]
and I give to Jerusalem a herald of good tidings.
28 But when I look there is no one;
among these there is no counselor
who, when I ask, gives an answer.
29 No, they are all a delusion;
their works are nothing;
their images are empty wind.

41.24 1 Cor 8.4
41.25 Jer 50.3 Mic 7.10
41.26 Isa 44.7
41.27 Isa 40.9
41.28 Isa 63.5
41.29 Jer 5.13

God's chosen servant

42 Here is my servant, whom I uphold,
my chosen, in whom my soul delights;
I have put my spirit upon him;
he will bring forth justice to the nations.
2 He will not cry or lift up his voice,
or make it heard in the street;
3 a bruised reed he will not break,
and a dimly burning wick he will not quench;
he will faithfully bring forth justice.
4 He will not grow faint or be crushed
until he has established justice in the earth;
and the coastlands wait for his teaching.

5 Thus says God, the LORD,
who created the heavens and stretched them out,
who spread out the earth and what comes from it,
who gives breath to the people upon it
and spirit to those who walk in it:
6 I am the LORD, I have called you in righteousness,

42.1 Isa 11.2; 53.11 Mt 3.17 12.18-21
42.3 Ps 72.2,4
42.4 Isa 24.15; 66.19
42.5 Job 33.4 Ps 104.2 Isa 45.18
42.6 Jer 23.5,6 Lk 2.32

[l] Cn Compare Q Ms Gk: MT *and he shall call on my name* [m] Cn: Heb *come* [n] Cn: Heb *First to Zion—Behold, behold them*

42.1–4 These verses are quoted in Matthew 12.18–21 with reference to Christ. The elect or chosen servant reveals a character of gentleness, encouragement, justice, and truth. When you feel broken and bruised or burned out in your spiritual life, God won't step on you or toss you aside as useless, but will gently pick you up. God's loving attributes are desperately needed in the world today. Through God's Spirit, we can show such sensitivity to people around us, reflecting God's goodness and honesty to them.

42.1–17 Sometimes called the Servant Song, these verses are about the Servant-Messiah, not the servant Cyrus (described in chapter 41). Israel and the Messiah are both often called *servant.* Israel, as God's servant, was to help bring the world to a knowledge of God. The Messiah, Jesus, would fulfill this task and show God himself to the world.

42.6 What is righteousness? It is having right actions, right attitudes, and right relationships—all based on our right standing with God. When he forgives us, takes away our sin, and restores us as his children, he not only gives us his righteousness, but he also empowers us to demonstrate it to others.

42.6, 7 Part of Christ's mission on earth was to demonstrate God's righteousness and to be a light to all nations. Through Christ, all people have the opportunity to share in his mission. God calls us to be servants of his Son, demonstrating God's righteousness and bringing his light. What a rare privilege to help the Messiah fulfill his mission! But we must seek his righteousness before we demonstrate it to others, and let his light shine in us before we can be lights ourselves.

I have taken you by the hand and kept you;
I have given you as a covenant to the people,[o]
a light to the nations,
42.7 Isa 35.5; 61.1
7 to open the eyes that are blind,
to bring out the prisoners from the dungeon,
from the prison those who sit in darkness.
42.8 Ex 3.15; 20.3-5
8 I am the LORD, that is my name;
my glory I give to no other,
nor my praise to idols.
9 See, the former things have come to pass,
and new things I now declare;
before they spring forth,
I tell you of them.

42.10 Ps 33.3
10 Sing to the LORD a new song,
his praise from the end of the earth!
Let the sea roar[p] and all that fills it,
the coastlands and their inhabitants.
11 Let the desert and its towns lift up their voice,
the villages that Kedar inhabits;
let the inhabitants of Sela sing for joy,
let them shout from the tops of the mountains.
12 Let them give glory to the LORD,
and declare his praise in the coastlands.
42.13 Isa 59.17; 66.14-16
13 The LORD goes forth like a soldier,
like a warrior he stirs up his fury;
he cries out, he shouts aloud,
he shows himself mighty against his foes.

14 For a long time I have held my peace,
I have kept still and restrained myself;
now I will cry out like a woman in labor,
I will gasp and pant.
42.15 Ezek 38.19,20; Nah 1.4-6
15 I will lay waste mountains and hills,
and dry up all their herbage;
I will turn the rivers into islands,
and dry up the pools.
42.16 Ps 94.14; Isa 40.4; Lk 1.78,79; Eph 5.8
16 I will lead the blind
by a road they do not know,
by paths they have not known

[o] Meaning of Heb uncertain [p] Cn Compare Ps 96.11; 98.7: Heb *Those who go down to the sea*

THE SERVANT IN ISAIAH

The nation Israel is called the servant:	41.8 42.19 43.10 44.1, 2, 21 45.4 48.20
The Messiah is called the Servant:	42.1–17 49.3,5–7 50.10 52.13 53.11

The nation was given a mission to serve God, to be custodian of his Word, and to be a light to the Gentile nations. Because of sin and rebellion; they failed. God sent his Son, Christ, as Messiah to fulfill his mission on earth.

42.10 Look at all the Lord will do for us and through us (42.6–9)! Majestic works prompt majestic responses. Do you really appreciate the good that God does for you and through you? If so, let your praise to him reflect how you really feel.

I will guide them.
I will turn the darkness before them into light,
the rough places into level ground.
These are the things I will do,
and I will not forsake them.
17 They shall be turned back and utterly put to shame—
those who trust in carved images,
who say to cast images,
"You are our gods."

42.17 Ps 97.7 Isa 44.9,11

Blind and deaf toward God

18 Listen, you that are deaf;
and you that are blind, look up and see!
19 Who is blind but my servant,
or deaf like my messenger whom I send?
Who is blind like my dedicated one,
or blind like the servant of the LORD?
20 He sees many things, but does[q] not observe them;
his ears are open, but he does not hear.
21 The LORD was pleased, for the sake of his righteousness,
to magnify his teaching and make it glorious.
22 But this is a people robbed and plundered,
all of them are trapped in holes
and hidden in prisons;
they have become a prey with no one to rescue,
a spoil with no one to say, "Restore!"
23 Who among you will give heed to this,
who will attend and listen for the time to come?
24 Who gave up Jacob to the spoiler,
and Israel to the robbers?
Was it not the LORD, against whom we have sinned,
in whose ways they would not walk,
and whose law they would not obey?
25 So he poured upon him the heat of his anger
and the fury of war;
it set him on fire all around, but he did not understand;
it burned him, but he did not take it to heart.

42.18 Isa 35.5
42.19 Isa 44.26
42.20 Jer 6.10
42.22 Isa 24.18
42.24 Isa 10.5; 48.18
42.25 Isa 5.25

There is no other Savior

43 But now thus says the LORD,
he who created you, O Jacob,
he who formed you, O Israel:
Do not fear, for I have redeemed you;
I have called you by name, you are mine.
2 When you pass through the waters, I will be with you;

43.1 Isa 44.2,21,22, 23,24; 45.3,4
43.2 Deut 31.6,8 Isa 8.7,8 Dan 3.25,27

[q] Heb *You see many things but do*

42.19, 20 How could Israel and Judah be God's servants and yet be so blind? How could they be so close to God and see so little? Jesus condemned the religious leaders of his day for the same disregard of God (John 9.39–41). Yet do we not fail in the same way? Sometimes partial blindness—seeing but not understanding, or knowing what is right but not doing it—can be worse than not seeing at all.

42.23 We may condemn our predecessors for their failures, but we are twice as guilty if we repeat the same mistakes that we recognize as failures. Often we are so ready to direct God's message at others that we can't see how it touches our own lives. Make sure you are willing to take your own advice as you teach or lead.

43.1ff Chapter 42 ends with God's sorrow over the spiritual decay of his people. In chapter 43, God tells the people that despite their spiritual failure, he will show them mercy, bring them back from captivity, and restore them. He would give them an outpouring of love, not wrath. Then the world would know that God alone had done this.

43.1–4 God created Israel and made it special to him. He redeemed it and called it by his name. He protected it in times of trouble. We are important to God, and he calls us by his name! When we bear his wonderful name, we must never do anything that would bring shame to it.

43.2 Going through rivers of difficulty will either cause you to

and through the rivers, they shall not overwhelm you;
when you walk through fire you shall not be burned,
and the flame shall not consume you.
3 For I am the LORD your God,
the Holy One of Israel, your Savior.
I give Egypt as your ransom,
Ethiopia[r] and Seba in exchange for you.
4 Because you are precious in my sight,
and honored, and I love you,
I give people in return for you,
nations in exchange for your life.
5 Do not fear, for I am with you;
I will bring your offspring from the east,
and from the west I will gather you;
6 I will say to the north, "Give them up,"
and to the south, "Do not withhold;
bring my sons from far away
and my daughters from the end of the earth—
7 everyone who is called by my name,
whom I created for my glory,
whom I formed and made."

8 Bring forth the people who are blind, yet have eyes,
who are deaf, yet have ears!
9 Let all the nations gather together,
and let the peoples assemble.
Who among them declared this,
and foretold to us the former things?
Let them bring their witnesses to justify them,
and let them hear and say, "It is true."
10 You are my witnesses, says the LORD,
and my servant whom I have chosen,
so that you may know and believe me
and understand that I am he.
Before me no god was formed,
nor shall there be any after me.
11 I, I am the LORD,
and besides me there is no savior.
12 I declared and saved and proclaimed,
when there was no strange god among you;
and you are my witnesses, says the LORD.
13 I am God, and also henceforth I am He;
there is no one who can deliver from my hand;
I work and who can hinder it?

The promise of victory

14 Thus says the LORD,

43.4 Isa 63.9
43.5 Isa 49.12 Jer 30.10,11
43.6 Ps 107.3 2 Cor 6.17,18
43.7 Ps 100.3 Isa 46.13 Eph 2.10
43.8 Ezek 12.2
43.11 Hos 13.4
43.12 Ps 81.9
43.13 Job 9.12 Ps 90.2

r Or *Nubia*; Heb *Cush*

drown or force you to grow stronger. If you go in your own strength, you are more likely to drown. If you invite the Lord to go with you, he will protect you.

43.3 God gave other nations to Cyrus in exchange for returning the Jews to their homeland. Egypt, Ethiopia, and parts of Arabia (Seba) had attacked Persia, and Cyrus defeated them.

43.5, 6 Isaiah is speaking primarily of Israel's return from Babylon. But there is a broader meaning: all God's people will be regathered when Christ comes to rule in peace over the earth.

43.10, 11 Israel's task was to be a witness (44.8), telling the world who God is and what he has done. Believers today share the responsibility of being God's witnesses. Do people know what God is like through your words and example? They cannot see God directly, but they can see him reflected in you.

43.14 This was fulfilled when the Medo-Persian army dammed up the Euphrates River and literally walked in and took the city of Babylon.

your Redeemer, the Holy One of Israel:
For your sake I will send to Babylon
and break down all the bars,
and the shouting of the Chaldeans will be turned to lamentation.[s]
15 I am the LORD, your Holy One,
the Creator of Israel, your King.
16 Thus says the LORD,
who makes a way in the sea,
a path in the mighty waters,
17 who brings out chariot and horse,
army and warrior;
they lie down, they cannot rise,
they are extinguished, quenched like a wick:
18 Do not remember the former things,
or consider the things of old.
19 I am about to do a new thing;
now it springs forth, do you not perceive it?
I will make a way in the wilderness
and rivers in the desert.
20 The wild animals will honor me,
the jackals and the ostriches;
for I give water in the wilderness,
rivers in the desert,
to give drink to my chosen people,
21 the people whom I formed for myself
so that they might declare my praise.

22 Yet you did not call upon me, O Jacob;
but you have been weary of me, O Israel!
23 You have not brought me your sheep for burnt offerings,
or honored me with your sacrifices.
I have not burdened you with offerings,
or wearied you with frankincense.
24 You have not bought me sweet cane with money,
or satisfied me with the fat of your sacrifices.
But you have burdened me with your sins;
you have wearied me with your iniquities.

25 I, I am He
who blots out your transgressions for my own sake,
and I will not remember your sins.
26 Accuse me, let us go to trial;
set forth your case, so that you may be proved right.
27 Your first ancestor sinned,
and your interpreters transgressed against me.
28 Therefore I profaned the princes of the sanctuary,

43.14 Isa 41.14
43.15 Isa 44.6
43.16 Ex 14.21,22 Josh 3.15,16 Ps 77.19
43.17 Ps 76.5,6
43.18 Jer 16.14
43.19 Deut 8.15 2 Cor 5.17
43.20 Isa 41.17,18
43.22 Mic 6.3
43.23 Ex 30.34 Mal 1.6-8
43.24 Jer 6.20 Mal 2.17
43.25 Isa 55.7 Jer 31.34 Ezek 36.22
43.27 Isa 51.2
43.28 Lam 2.2,6 Ezek 5.15

[s] Meaning of Heb uncertain

43.15–21 The Israelites would be oppressed again, as they had been as slaves in Egypt before the exodus. They would cry to God, and again he would hear and deliver them. A new exodus would take place through a new wilderness. The past miracles were nothing compared to what God would do for his people.

43.22–24 A sacrifice required both giving up a valuable animal and pleading with God for forgiveness. But the people presented God with sins instead of sacrifices. Can you imagine bringing the best of your sins to God's altar? This ironic picture shows the depths to which Israel had sunk. What do you present to God—your sins, or a plea for his forgiveness?

43.22–24 Sin separates the sinner from God. God, however, does not want to be separated from his people, so he instituted the sacrificial system in which sins were symbolically transferred to animals and then destroyed. The people of Judah chose to ignore God's provision for sins, and thus they were in danger of losing his protection. Do you try to "go it on your own," or do you accept God's provision of forgiveness through Christ's sacrifice?

43.25 How tempting it is to remind someone of a past offense! But when God forgives our sins he totally forgets them. We never have to fear that he will remind us of them later. Because God forgives our sin, we need to forgive others.

I delivered Jacob to utter destruction,
and Israel to reviling.

The idols are false gods

44.1 Jer 30.10 **44** But now hear, O Jacob my servant,
Israel whom I have chosen!
2 Thus says the LORD who made you,
who formed you in the womb and will help you:
Do not fear, O Jacob my servant,
Jeshurun whom I have chosen.
44.3 Isa 61.9 Joel 2.28 3 For I will pour water on the thirsty land,
and streams on the dry ground;
I will pour my spirit upon your descendants,
and my blessing on your offspring.
4 They shall spring up like a green tamarisk,
like willows by flowing streams.
5 This one will say, "I am the LORD's,"
another will be called by the name of Jacob,
yet another will write on the hand, "The LORD's,"
and adopt the name of Israel.

44.6 Isa 41.21 45.5,6,21 Rev 1.8,17 6 Thus says the LORD, the King of Israel,
and his Redeemer, the LORD of hosts:
I am the first and I am the last;
besides me there is no god.
7 Who is like me? Let them proclaim it,
let them declare and set it forth before me.
Who has announced from of old the things to come?[t]
Let them tell us[u] what is yet to be.
44.8 Deut 4.35,39 Isa 30.29 8 Do not fear, or be afraid;
have I not told you from of old and declared it?
You are my witnesses!
Is there any god besides me?
There is no other rock; I know not one.

44.9 Ps 97.7 9 All who make idols are nothing, and the things they delight in do not profit;
their witnesses neither see nor know. And so they will be put to shame. 10 Who
44.10 Jer 10.5 Hab 2.18 Acts 19.26 would fashion a god or cast an image that can do no good? 11 Look, all its devotees
shall be put to shame; the artisans too are merely human. Let them all assemble, let
them stand up; they shall be terrified, they shall all be put to shame.
12 The ironsmith fashions it[v] and works it over the coals, shaping it with hammers, and forging it with his strong arm; he becomes hungry and his strength fails,

[t] Cn: Heb *from my placing an eternal people and things to come* [u] Tg: Heb *them* [v] Cn: Heb *an ax*

TODAY'S IDOLATRY

Isaiah tells us, "Who would fashion a god or cast an image that can do no good?" We think of idols as statues of wood or stone, but in reality an idol is anything natural that is given sacred value and power. If your answer to any of the following questions is anything or anyone other than God, you may need to check out who or what you are worshiping.

- Who created me?
- Whom do I ultimately trust?
- Whom do I look to for ultimate truth?
- Whom do I look to for security and happiness?
- Who is in charge of my future?

44.2 Jeshurun ("the upright one") is a poetic name for Israel (Deuteronomy 32.15; 33.5, 26).

44.5 The time will come when Israel will be proud of belonging to God. If we are truly God's, we should be unashamed and delighted to let everyone know about our relationship with him (44.8).

44.9–20 Here Isaiah describes how people make their own gods. How absurd to make a god from the same tree that gives firewood. Do we make our own gods – money, fame, or power? If we make a god of our own choosing, we deceive ourselves. We cannot expect it to empower our lives.

he drinks no water and is faint. 13 The carpenter stretches a line, marks it out with
a stylus, fashions it with planes, and marks it with a compass; he makes it in human
form, with human beauty, to be set up in a shrine. 14 He cuts down cedars or
chooses a holm tree or an oak and lets it grow strong among the trees of the forest.
He plants a cedar and the rain nourishes it. 15 Then it can be used as fuel. Part of it
he takes and warms himself; he kindles a fire and bakes bread. Then he makes a god
and worships it, makes it a carved image and bows down before it. 16 Half of it he
burns in the fire; over this half he roasts meat, eats it and is satisfied. He also warms
himself and says, "Ah, I am warm, I can feel the fire!" 17 The rest of it he makes
into a god, his idol, bows down to it and worships it; he prays to it and says, "Save
me, for you are my god!"

18 They do not know, nor do they comprehend; for their eyes are shut, so that
they cannot see, and their minds as well, so that they cannot understand. 19 No one
considers, nor is there knowledge or discernment to say, "Half of it I burned in the
fire; I also baked bread on its coals, I roasted meat and have eaten. Now shall I
make the rest of it an abomination? Shall I fall down before a block of wood?" 20 He
feeds on ashes; a deluded mind has led him astray, and he cannot save himself or
say, "Is not this thing in my right hand a fraud?"

21 Remember these things, O Jacob,
and Israel, for you are my servant;
I formed you, you are my servant;
O Israel, you will not be forgotten by me.
22 I have swept away your transgressions like a cloud,
and your sins like mist;
return to me, for I have redeemed you.

23 Sing, O heavens, for the LORD has done it;
shout, O depths of the earth;
break forth into singing, O mountains,
O forest, and every tree in it!
For the LORD has redeemed Jacob,
and will be glorified in Israel.

24 Thus says the LORD, your Redeemer,
who formed you in the womb:
I am the LORD, who made all things,
who alone stretched out the heavens,
who by myself spread out the earth;
25 who frustrates the omens of liars,
and makes fools of diviners;
who turns back the wise,
and makes their knowledge foolish;
26 who confirms the word of his servant,
and fulfills the prediction of his messengers;
who says of Jerusalem, "It shall be inhabited,"
and of the cities of Judah, "They shall be rebuilt,
and I will raise up their ruins";
27 who says to the deep, "Be dry—
I will dry up your rivers";

44.13 Ps 115.5-7 Isa 41.7
44.15 2 Chron 25.14
44.17 1 Kgs 18.26,28 Isa 45.20
44.18 Ps 81.12 Isa 6.9,10 29.10 Jer 10.8,14
44.19 Deut 27.15
44.20 Ps 102.9 Hos 4.12
44.22 Ps 51.1,9 Isa 55.7 Acts 3.19 1 Pet 1.18,19
44.23 Ps 69.34 98.7,8
44.24 Isa 40.22
44.25 1 Cor 1.20,27
44.26 Jer 32.15,44
44.27 Isa 50.2

44.21 God said that we should serve our Creator (17.7; 40.28; 43.15; 45.9). Idolaters do the opposite—serving or worshiping what they have made rather than the One who made them. Our Creator paid the price to set us free from our sins against him. By contrast, no idol ever created anybody, and no idol can redeem us from our sins.

44.25, 26 Diviners were people who claimed to bring messages from the gods. Liars were people who would fake omens for their own benefit. Because God is truth, he is the standard for all teachings. We can always trust his Word as absolute truth. His Word is completely accurate, and against it we can measure all other teachings. If you are unsure about a teaching, test it against God's Word. God condemned the false prophets because they gave advice opposite to his.

44.28 2 Chron 36.22, 23 Isa 14.32

28 who says of Cyrus, "He is my shepherd,
and he shall carry out all my purpose";
and who says of Jerusalem, "It shall be rebuilt,"
and of the temple, "Your foundation shall be laid."

Jehovah is the one true God

45.1 Ps 73.23 Jer 51.11,20,24

45 Thus says the LORD to his anointed, to Cyrus,
whose right hand I have grasped
to subdue nations before him
and strip kings of their robes,
to open doors before him—
and the gates shall not be closed:

45.2 Isa 40.4 Jer 51.30

2 I will go before you
and level the mountains,[w]
I will break in pieces the doors of bronze
and cut through the bars of iron,

45.3 Isa 49.1

3 I will give you the treasures of darkness
and riches hidden in secret places,
so that you may know that it is I, the LORD,
the God of Israel, who call you by your name.

45.4 Isa 43.1 Acts 17.23

4 For the sake of my servant Jacob,
and Israel my chosen,
I call you by your name,
I surname you, though you do not know me.
5 I am the LORD, and there is no other;
besides me there is no god.
I arm you, though you do not know me,

45.6 Mal 1.11

6 so that they may know, from the rising of the sun
and from the west, that there is no one besides me;
I am the LORD, and there is no other.

45.7 Ps 104.20 Amos 3.6

7 I form light and create darkness,
I make weal and create woe;
I the LORD do all these things.

45.8 Ps 72.6; 85.11 Isa 61.11

8 Shower, O heavens, from above,
and let the skies rain down righteousness;
let the earth open, that salvation may spring up,[x]
and let it cause righteousness to sprout up also;
I the LORD have created it.

45.9 Rom 9.20,21

9 Woe to you who strive with your Maker,
earthen vessels with the potter![y]
Does the clay say to the one who fashions it, "What are you making"?

[w] Q Ms Gk: MT *the swellings* [x] Q Ms: MT *that they may bring forth salvation* [y] Cn: Heb *with the potsherds*, or *with the potters*

44.28 Isaiah, who lived from about 740–681 B.C., called Cyrus by name almost 150 years before he ruled (559–530 B.C.)! Later historians said that Cyrus read this prophecy and was so moved that he carried it out. Isaiah also predicted that Jerusalem would fall more than 100 years before it happened (586 B.C.) and that the temple would be rebuilt about 200 years before it happened. It is clear these prophecies came from a God who knows the future.

45.1–8 This is the only place in the Bible where a Gentile ruler is said to be "anointed." God is the power over all powers, and he anoints whom he chooses for his special tasks. Cyrus's kingdom spread across 2,000 miles (the largest of any empire then known), including the territories of both the Assyrian and the Babylonian empires. Why did God anoint Cyrus? Because God had a special task for him to do for Israel. Cyrus would allow God's city, Jerusalem, to be rebuilt, and he would set the exiles free without expecting anything in return. Few kings of Israel or Judah had done as much for God's people as Cyrus would.

45.7 God takes no pleasure in evil (Psalm 5.4) so the evil talked about here is physical adversity, not moral evil. God is ruler over light and darkness, over prosperity and adversity. Our lives are sprinkled with both types of experiences, and both are needed for us to grow spiritually. When good times come, thank God and use your prosperity for him. When bad times come, don't resent them, but ask what you can learn from this refining experience to make you a better servant of God.

or "Your work has no handles"?
10 Woe to anyone who says to a father, "What are you begetting?"
or to a woman, "With what are you in labor?"
11 Thus says the LORD,
the Holy One of Israel, and its Maker:
Will you question me[z] about my children,
or command me concerning the work of my hands?
12 I made the earth,
and created humankind upon it;
it was my hands that stretched out the heavens,
and I commanded all their host.
13 I have aroused Cyrus[a] in righteousness,
and I will make all his paths straight;
he shall build my city
and set my exiles free,
not for price or reward,
says the LORD of hosts.
14 Thus says the LORD:
The wealth of Egypt and the merchandise of Ethiopia,[b]
and the Sabeans, tall of stature,
shall come over to you and be yours,
they shall follow you;
they shall come over in chains and bow down to you.
They will make supplication to you, saying,
"God is with you alone, and there is no other;
there is no god besides him."
15 Truly, you are a God who hides himself,
O God of Israel, the Savior.
16 All of them are put to shame and confounded,
the makers of idols go in confusion together.
17 But Israel is saved by the LORD
with everlasting salvation;
you shall not be put to shame or confounded
to all eternity.

18 For thus says the LORD,
who created the heavens
(he is God!),
who formed the earth and made it
(he established it;
he did not create it a chaos,
he formed it to be inhabited!):
I am the LORD, and there is no other.
19 I did not speak in secret,
in a land of darkness;
I did not say to the offspring of Jacob,
"Seek me in chaos."
I the LORD speak the truth,
I declare what is right.

20 Assemble yourselves and come together,

45.11 Ezek 39.7
45.12 Neh 9.6 Jer 27.5
45.13 2 Chron 36.22, 23 Isa 52.3
45.14 Isa 14.1,2 49.23 1 Cor 14.25
45.16 Isa 44.11
45.17 Isa 51.6
45.18 Gen 1.2,26 Ps 115.16 Isa 42.5
45.19 2 Chron 15.2 Isa 43.12 Jer 29.13,14

z Cn: Heb *Ask me of things to come* a Heb *him* b Or *Nubia*; Heb *Cush*

45.14 The Sabeans were people from Seba (or Sheba) in southern Arabia.

45.17 Until this time, Israel had anticipated temporal salvation – God would save them from their enemies. Now Isaiah tells of everlasting salvation with God.

45.18, 19 God's promises are public, and their fulfillment is sure. So why do we ever doubt him? We never have to be uncertain when we have a God of truth and righteousness.

45.20 Isa 44.18,19 46.6,7 Jer 10.5

draw near, you survivors of the nations!
They have no knowledge—
those who carry about their wooden idols,
and keep on praying to a god
that cannot save.

45.21 Isa 43.3,11 44.7

21 Declare and present your case;
let them take counsel together!
Who told this long ago?
Who declared it of old?
Was it not I, the LORD?
There is no other god besides me,
a righteous God and a Savior;
there is no one besides me.

45.22 Num 21.8,9 Isa 52.10 Mic 7.7

22 Turn to me and be saved,
all the ends of the earth!
For I am God, and there is no other.

45.23 Rom 14.11

23 By myself I have sworn,
from my mouth has gone forth in righteousness
a word that shall not return:
"To me every knee shall bow,
every tongue shall swear."

24 Only in the LORD, it shall be said of me,
are righteousness and strength;
all who were incensed against him
shall come to him and be ashamed.

45.25 Isa 53.11

25 In the LORD all the offspring of Israel
shall triumph and glory.

The false gods of Babylon

46.1 Isa 21.9 Jer 43.12,13 51.44

46 Bel bows down, Nebo stoops,
their idols are on beasts and cattle;
these things you carry are loaded
as burdens on weary animals.
2 They stoop, they bow down together;
they cannot save the burden,
but themselves go into captivity.

46.3 Isa 10.21,22

3 Listen to me, O house of Jacob,
all the remnant of the house of Israel,
who have been borne by me from your birth,
carried from the womb;
4 even to your old age I am he,
even when you turn gray I will carry you.
I have made, and I will bear;
I will carry and will save.

46.5 Isa 40.18,25

5 To whom will you liken me and make me equal,

45.22 Salvation is for everyone, not just the Israelites. Many times it seems as though Israel had an inside track on salvation. But God makes it clear that his people include *all* those who follow him. Israel was to be the means through which the whole world would come to know God. Jesus, the Messiah, fulfilled Israel's role and gave all people the opportunity to follow God. (See also Romans 11.11; Galatians 3.28; Ephesians 3.6; Philippians 2.10.)

46.1–4 Cyrus would carry out God's judgment against Babylon. Bel was the chief deity of the Babylonians; Nebo was the god of the royal family. These "gods," however, needed men to carry them around and could not even save themselves from being taken into captivity. They had no power at all. In contrast to gods who must be hauled around by men, our God created us and cares for us. His love is so enduring that he will care for us throughout our lifetime and even through death.

and compare me, as though we were alike?
6 Those who lavish gold from the purse,
and weigh out silver in the scales—
they hire a goldsmith, who makes it into a god;
then they fall down and worship!
7 They lift it to their shoulders, they carry it,
they set it in its place, and it stands there;
it cannot move from its place.
If one cries out to it, it does not answer
or save anyone from trouble.

8 Remember this and consider,[c]
recall it to mind, you transgressors,
9 remember the former things of old;
for I am God, and there is no other;
I am God, and there is no one like me,
10 declaring the end from the beginning
and from ancient times things not yet done,
saying, "My purpose shall stand,
and I will fulfill my intention,"
11 calling a bird of prey from the east,
the man for my purpose from a far country.
I have spoken, and I will bring it to pass;
I have planned, and I will do it.

12 Listen to me, you stubborn of heart,
you who are far from deliverance:
13 I bring near my deliverance, it is not far off,
and my salvation will not tarry;
I will put salvation in Zion,
for Israel my glory.

A prophecy of doom for Babylon

47 Come down and sit in the dust,
virgin daughter Babylon!
Sit on the ground without a throne,
daughter Chaldea!
For you shall no more be called
tender and delicate.
2 Take the millstones and grind meal,
remove your veil,
strip off your robe, uncover your legs,
pass through the rivers.
3 Your nakedness shall be uncovered,
and your shame shall be seen.
I will take vengeance,
and I will spare no one.

[c] Meaning of Heb uncertain

46.6 Isa 44.12-17
46.7 Isa 40.20 Jer 10.5
46.9 Isa 41.26,27 42.9
46.10 Acts 5.39
46.11 Num 23.19
46.12 Zech 7.11,12
46.13 Isa 51.5; 61.3
47.1 Jer 48.18
47.2 Gen 24.65 1 Cor 11.5
47.3 Isa 63.4

46.8–11 Israel was tempted to waver between the Lord God and heathenism. Isaiah affirms the sole lordship of God. God is unique in his knowledge and in his control of the future. His consistent purpose is to carry out what he has planned. If we are tempted to pursue anything that promises pleasure, comfort, peace, or security apart from God, we must not waver.

46.13 Much of the book of Isaiah speaks of a future deliverance when we will all live with God in perfect peace. God offers not only this future hope, but also help for our present needs. His righteousness is near us, and we do not have to wait for his salvation.

47.1ff Isaiah predicted the fall of Babylon more than 150 years before it happened. At this time, Babylon had not yet emerged as the mightiest force on earth, the proud empire that would destroy Judah and Jerusalem. But the Babylonians, Judah's captors, would become captives themselves in 539 B.C. God, not Babylon, has the ultimate power. He used Babylon to punish his sinful people; he would use Medo-Persia to destroy Babylon and free his people.

4 Our Redeemer — the LORD of hosts is his name —
is the Holy One of Israel.

47.5 Lam 2.10 Dan 2.37

5 Sit in silence, and go into darkness,
daughter Chaldea!
For you shall no more be called
the mistress of kingdoms.

47.6 Deut 28.50 Zech 1.15

6 I was angry with my people,
I profaned my heritage;
I gave them into your hand,
you showed them no mercy;
on the aged you made your yoke
exceedingly heavy.
7 You said, "I shall be mistress forever,"
so that you did not lay these things to heart
or remember their end.

47.8 Isa 22.13 32.9,11 Rev 18.7

8 Now therefore hear this, you lover of pleasures,
who sit securely,
who say in your heart,
"I am, and there is no one besides me;
I shall not sit as a widow
or know the loss of children" —

47.9 Isa 13.16 1 Thess 5.2,3 Rev 18.8,10,23

9 both these things shall come upon you
in a moment, in one day:
the loss of children and widowhood
shall come upon you in full measure,
in spite of your many sorceries
and the great power of your enchantments.

47.10 Ps 52.7 Isa 5.21 Ezek 8.12

10 You felt secure in your wickedness;
you said, "No one sees me."
Your wisdom and your knowledge

MAJOR IDOLS MENTIONED IN THE BIBLE

Name	*Where they were worshiped*	*What they stood for*	*What the worship included*
Bel (Marduk)	Babylon	Weather, War, Sun god	Prostitution, child sacrifice
Nebo (Son of Marduk)	Babylon	Learning, astronomy, science	
Ashtoreth (Asherah)	Canaan	Goddess of love, childbirth, and fertility	Prostitution
Chemosh	Moab		Child sacrifice
Molech	Ammon	National god	Child sacrifice
Baal	Canaan	Rain, harvest, symbolized strength and fertility	Prostitution
Dagon	Philistia	Harvest, grain, success in farming	Child sacrifice

47.8, 9 Caught up in the pursuit of power and pleasure, Babylon believed in its own greatness and claimed to be the *only* power on earth. Babylon felt completely secure. Nebuchadnezzar, its king, called himself "god," but the true God taught him a powerful lesson by taking everything away from him (Daniel 4.27–37). Our society is addicted to pleasure and power, but these can quickly pass away. Look at your own life and ask yourself how you can be more responsible with the talents and possessions God has given you. How can you use your life for God's honor rather than your own?

47.10 The wealth that comes from wickedness gives a false sense of security. Knowledge can also deceive people into feeling that they don't need others. In times of plenty we may think we don't even need God. Yet our wisdom and wealth will never give us what God can give. Rely on his wisdom for true wealth.

led you astray,
and you said in your heart,
"I am, and there is no one besides me."
11 But evil shall come upon you,
which you cannot charm away;
disaster shall fall upon you,
which you will not be able to ward off;
and ruin shall come on you suddenly,
of which you know nothing.

12 Stand fast in your enchantments
and your many sorceries,
with which you have labored from your youth;
perhaps you may be able to succeed,
perhaps you may inspire terror.
13 You are wearied with your many consultations;
let those who study[d] the heavens
stand up and save you,
those who gaze at the stars,
and at each new moon predict
what[e] shall befall you.

14 See, they are like stubble,
the fire consumes them;
they cannot deliver themselves
from the power of the flame.
No coal for warming oneself is this,
no fire to sit before!
15 Such to you are those with whom you have labored,
who have trafficked with you from your youth;
they all wander about in their own paths;
there is no one to save you.

47.11 Jer 51.8,43

47.13 Isa 8.19

47.14 Jer 51.30,32,58 Nah 1.10

Israel's stubbornness

48 Hear this, O house of Jacob,
who are called by the name of Israel,
and who came forth from the loins[f] of Judah;
who swear by the name of the LORD,
and invoke the God of Israel,
but not in truth or right.
2 For they call themselves after the holy city,
and lean on the God of Israel;
the LORD of hosts is his name.

3 The former things I declared long ago,
they went out from my mouth and I made them known;
then suddenly I did them and they came to pass.
4 Because I know that you are obstinate,
and your neck is an iron sinew

48.1 Isa 45.23; 52.1 Rom 2.17

48.3 Josh 21.45 Isa 42.9

48.4 Ezek 2.4

[d] Meaning of Heb uncertain [e] Gk Syr Compare Vg: Heb *from what* [f] Cn: Heb *waters*

47.12–15 The people of Babylon sought advice and help from astrologers, stargazers, and fortune-tellers. But like the idols of wood or gold, they could not even deliver themselves. Why rely on those who are powerless? The helpless cannot help us. Alternatives to God are bankrupt. If you want help, find it in God, who has proven his power in creation and in history.

48.1 The people of Judah felt confident because they lived in Jerusalem, the city with God's temple. They depended on their heritage, their city, and their temple—but this was false security because they did not depend on God. Do you feel secure because you go to church or live in a Christian country? Heritage, buildings, or nations cannot give us a relationship with God; we must truly depend on him personally, with all our hearts and minds.

and your forehead brass,
48.5 Jer 44.15-18
5 I declared them to you from long ago,
before they came to pass I announced them to you,
so that you would not say, "My idol did them,
my carved image and my cast image commanded them."

48.6 Isa 43.19
6 You have heard; now see all this;
and will you not declare it?
From this time forward I make you hear new things,
hidden things that you have not known.
7 They are created now, not long ago;
before today you have never heard of them,
so that you could not say, "I already knew them."
48.8 Deut 9.7,24 Ps 58.3
8 You have never heard, you have never known,
from of old your ear has not been opened.
For I knew that you would deal very treacherously,
and that from birth you were called a rebel.

48.9 Ps 103.8-10
9 For my name's sake I defer my anger,
for the sake of my praise I restrain it for you,
so that I may not cut you off.
48.10 1 Kgs 8.51 Ezek 22.18-22
10 See, I have refined you, but not like[g] silver;
I have tested you in the furnace of adversity.
48.11 Deut 32.26,27 Ps 106.8 Isa 42.8
11 For my own sake, for my own sake, I do it,
for why should my name[h] be profaned?
My glory I will not give to another.

48.12 Deut 32.39
12 Listen to me, O Jacob,
and Israel, whom I called:
I am He; I am the first,
and I am the last.
48.13 Ps 102.25
13 My hand laid the foundation of the earth,
and my right hand spread out the heavens;
when I summon them,
they stand at attention.

48.14 Jer 50.21-29
14 Assemble, all of you, and hear!
Who among them has declared these things?
The LORD loves him;
he shall perform his purpose on Babylon,
and his arm shall be against the Chaldeans.
48.15 Isa 41.2; 45.1,2
15 I, even I, have spoken and called him,
I have brought him, and he will prosper in his way.
48.16 Isa 45.19
16 Draw near to me, hear this!

[g] Cn: Heb *with* [h] Gk Old Latin: Heb *for why should it*

48.9–11 There was nothing in Israel's actions, attitudes, or accomplishments to compel God to love and to save them. But for his own sake, to show who he is and what he can do, he saved them. God does not save us because we are good, but because he loves us and because of his forgiving nature.

48.10 Do you find it easy to complain when your life becomes complicated or difficult? Why would a loving God allow all kinds of unpleasant experiences to come to his children? This verse shows us plainly that God tests us in the "furnace of adversity." Rather than complain, our response should be to turn to God in faith for the strength to endure, and rejoice (see James 1.2–4). For without the testing, we never know what we are capable of doing, nor do we grow. And without the refining, we will not become more pure and more like Christ. What kinds of adversity are you facing?

48.14, 15 When Isaiah proclaimed, "The Lord loves him," he was referring to Cyrus. How could the Lord love a pagan king, an enemy? But it was Cyrus whom God would use to free his people from their captivity in Babylon. Cyrus's errand was to set Israel free by conquering Babylon, then to decree that all Jews could return to their homeland.

48.16 God's message has been told plainly and clearly, not in secret. We have a tendency to complicate God's message as we add to it. When God talks through his messenger, whomever he has chosen, our job is to listen. The closer we come to God, the better we can listen to what he says.

From the beginning I have not spoken in secret,
from the time it came to be I have been there.
And now the Lord God has sent me and his spirit.

17 Thus says the LORD,
your Redeemer, the Holy One of Israel:
I am the LORD your God,
who teaches you for your own good,
who leads you in the way you should go.
18 O that you had paid attention to my commandments!
Then your prosperity would have been like a river,
and your success like the waves of the sea;
19 your offspring would have been like the sand,
and your descendants like its grains;
their name would never be cut off
or destroyed from before me.

20 Go out from Babylon, flee from Chaldea,
declare this with a shout of joy, proclaim it,
send it forth to the end of the earth;
say, "The LORD has redeemed his servant Jacob!"
21 They did not thirst when he led them through the deserts;
he made water flow for them from the rock;
he split open the rock and the water gushed out.

22 "There is no peace," says the LORD, "for the wicked."

48.17 Ps 32.8 Isa 41.14

48.18 Deut 5.29 Ps 119.165 Amos 5.24

48.19 Gen 12.17

48.20 Isa 52.9 Jer 31.10

48.21 Ps 78.15,16 Mt 1.20,21

2. The future Redeemer

God's servant will be a light

49 Listen to me, O coastlands,
pay attention, you peoples from far away!
The LORD called me before I was born,
while I was in my mother's womb he named me.
2 He made my mouth like a sharp sword,
in the shadow of his hand he hid me;
he made me a polished arrow,
in his quiver he hid me away.
3 And he said to me, "You are my servant,
Israel, in whom I will be glorified."
4 But I said, "I have labored in vain,
I have spent my strength for nothing and vanity;
yet surely my cause is with the LORD,
and my reward with my God."

5 And now the LORD says,
who formed me in the womb to be his servant,

49.2 Isa 51.16 Heb 4.12 Rev 1.16

49.5 Isa 12.2

48.17, 18 Like a loving parent, God punishes us or corrects us for our own good. We should listen to him, because peace of mind and heart comes to us as we obey his Word. Disobedience invites punishment and threatens the peace of mind and heart we want so much.

48.20 Do you see the captives leaving Babylon many years later? No wonder they are singing, as their ancestors sang after they crossed the Red Sea, free from slavery at last! What is holding you captive? Be free! The Lord has redeemed his servants from the slavery of sin. When you let him free you from your captivity, you will feel like singing.

48.22 Many people cry out for comfort, security, and relief, but they haven't taken the first steps to turn away from sin and open the channels to God. They have not repented and trusted in him. If you want true peace, seek God first. Then you will have it.

49.1–7 Before the servant, the Messiah, was born, God had chosen him to bring the light of the gospel (the message of salvation) to the world (see Acts 13.47). Christ offered salvation to all nations, and his apostles began the missionary movement to take this gospel to the ends of the earth. Missionary work today continues Jesus' great commission (Matthew 28.18–20), taking the light of the gospel to all nations.

to bring Jacob back to him,
and that Israel might be gathered to him,
for I am honored in the sight of the LORD,
and my God has become my strength—
49.6 Ps 37.28 Acts 13.47 26.23
6 he says,
"It is too light a thing that you should be my servant
to raise up the tribes of Jacob
and to restore the survivors of Israel;
I will give you as a light to the nations,
that my salvation may reach to the end of the earth."

49.7 Ps 22.6-8 Isa 53.3
7 Thus says the LORD,
the Redeemer of Israel and his Holy One,
to one deeply despised, abhorred by the nations,
the slave of rulers,
"Kings shall see and stand up,
princes, and they shall prostrate themselves,
because of the LORD, who is faithful,
the Holy One of Israel, who has chosen you."

The Lord will comfort his people

49.8 Ps 69.13 Isa 26.3; 42.7 44.26 Lk 4.18 2 Cor 6.2
8 Thus says the LORD:
In a time of favor I have answered you,
on a day of salvation I have helped you;
I have kept you and given you
as a covenant to the people,[i]
to establish the land,
to apportion the desolate heritages;
9 saying to the prisoners, "Come out,"
to those who are in darkness, "Show yourselves."
They shall feed along the ways,
on all the bare heights[j] shall be their pasture;
49.10 Ps 23.2 Rev 7.16
10 they shall not hunger or thirst,
neither scorching wind nor sun shall strike them down,
for he who has pity on them will lead them,
and by springs of water will guide them.
11 And I will turn all my mountains into a road,
and my highways shall be raised up.
12 Lo, these shall come from far away,
and lo, these from the north and from the west,
and these from the land of Syene.[k]

49.13 Isa 54.7,8,10 Rev 12.12
13 Sing for joy, O heavens, and exult, O earth;
break forth, O mountains, into singing!
For the LORD has comforted his people,
and will have compassion on his suffering ones.

14 But Zion said, "The LORD has forsaken me,
my Lord has forgotten me."
15 Can a woman forget her nursing child,
or show no compassion for the child of her womb?

[i] Meaning of Heb uncertain [j] Or *the trails* [k] Q Ms: MT *Sinim*

49.12 The location of Syene is uncertain; possibly it is the Aswan region of Egypt.

49.14, 15 The people of Israel felt that God had deserted them in Babylon; but Isaiah pointed out that God would never leave them, as a mother would not leave her little child. When we feel that God has deserted us, we must ask if we have deserted God (see Deuteronomy 31.6).

Even these may forget,
yet I will not forget you.
16 See, I have inscribed you on the palms of my hands;
your walls are continually before me.
17 Your builders outdo your destroyers,[l]
and those who laid you waste go away from you.
18 Lift up your eyes all around and see;
they all gather, they come to you.
As I live, says the LORD,
you shall put all of them on like an ornament,
and like a bride you shall bind them on.

19 Surely your waste and your desolate places
and your devastated land—
surely now you will be too crowded for your inhabitants,
and those who swallowed you up will be far away.
20 The children born in the time of your bereavement
will yet say in your hearing:
"The place is too crowded for me;
make room for me to settle."
21 Then you will say in your heart,
"Who has borne me these?
I was bereaved and barren,
exiled and put away—
so who has reared these?
I was left all alone—
where then have these come from?"

22 Thus says the Lord GOD:
I will soon lift up my hand to the nations,
and raise my signal to the peoples;
and they shall bring your sons in their bosom,
and your daughters shall be carried on their shoulders.
23 Kings shall be your foster fathers,
and their queens your nursing mothers.
With their faces to the ground they shall bow down to you,
and lick the dust of your feet.
Then you will know that I am the LORD;
those who wait for me shall not be put to shame.

24 Can the prey be taken from the mighty,
or the captives of a tyrant[m] be rescued?
25 But thus says the LORD:
Even the captives of the mighty shall be taken,
and the prey of the tyrant be rescued;
for I will contend with those who contend with you,
and I will save your children.
26 I will make your oppressors eat their own flesh,
and they shall be drunk with their own blood as with wine.
Then all flesh shall know
that I am the LORD your Savior,
and your Redeemer, the Mighty One of Jacob.

49.16 Song 8.6
49.18 Isa 45.23
49.19 Ps 56.1,2 Isa 1.7 Zech 10.10
49.20 Isa 54.1-3
49.21 Lam 1.1
49.22 Isa 11.10,12 14.2
49.23 Ps 25.3; 72.9 Isa 60.14,16
49.25 Jer 50.33,34
49.26 Isa 14.4 Ezek 39.7

[l] Or *Your children come swiftly; your destroyers* [m] Q Ms Syr Vg: MT *of a righteous person*

49.24, 25 God would prove to the world that he is God by doing the impossible—causing a captor to set his captives free, and even helping them leave. He had done this before at the exodus and would do it again when the exiles returned to Israel. Never should we doubt that God will fulfill his promises. He will even do the impossible to make them come true.

God's servant obeys

50.1 Deut 32.30 Isa 59.2 Jer 3.8

50 Thus says the LORD:
Where is your mother's bill of divorce
with which I put her away?
Or which of my creditors is it
to whom I have sold you?
No, because of your sins you were sold,
and for your transgressions your mother was put away.

50.2 Gen 18.14 Ex 14.21 Josh 3.16

2 Why was no one there when I came?
Why did no one answer when I called?
Is my hand shortened, that it cannot redeem?
Or have I no power to deliver?
By my rebuke I dry up the sea,
I make the rivers a desert;
their fish stink for lack of water,
and die of thirst.[n]

50.3 Rev 6.12

3 I clothe the heavens with blackness,
and make sackcloth their covering.

50.4 Ps 5.3 Jer 31.25

4 The Lord GOD has given me
the tongue of a teacher,[o]
that I may know how to sustain
the weary with a word.
Morning by morning he wakens—
wakens my ear
to listen as those who are taught.

50.5 Mt 26.39 Heb 5.8

5 The Lord GOD has opened my ear,
and I was not rebellious,
I did not turn backward.

50.6 Mk 15.19

6 I gave my back to those who struck me,
and my cheeks to those who pulled out the beard;
I did not hide my face
from insult and spitting.

50.7 Ezek 3.8,9

7 The Lord GOD helps me;
therefore I have not been disgraced;
therefore I have set my face like flint,
and I know that I shall not be put to shame;
8 he who vindicates me is near.
Who will contend with me?
Let us stand up together.
Who are my adversaries?
Let them confront me.

50.9 Isa 54.17

9 It is the Lord GOD who helps me;
who will declare me guilty?
All of them will wear out like a garment;
the moth will eat them up.

10 Who among you fears the LORD

[n] Or *die on the thirsty ground* [o] Cn: Heb *of those who are taught*

50.1, 2 God promised to fight for Israel, but Israel sold itself into sin. Israel had caused its own problems. The phrase "Is my hand shortened . . . ?" means "Am I powerless to help?" The people of Israel forgot God and trusted in other countries to help them. God did not reject Israel, but Israel rejected God.

50.6–11 This is a picture of the ultimate servant, the Messiah. The prophet speaks for God, but the Messiah reveals God perfectly (Hebrews 1.1, 2).

50.10, 11 If we walk by our own lights and reject God's, we become self-sufficient, and the result of self-sufficiency is sorrow. When we place confidence in our own intelligence, appearance, or accomplishments instead of in God, we risk damnation later when these strengths fade.

and obeys the voice of his servant,
who walks in darkness
and has no light,
yet trusts in the name of the LORD
and relies upon his God?
11 But all of you are kindlers of fire,
lighters of firebrands.[p]
Walk in the flame of your fire,
and among the brands that you have kindled!
This is what you shall have from my hand:
you shall lie down in torment.

50.10 Eph 5.8

50.11 Isa 65.13-15

Blessings for God's people

51 Listen to me, you that pursue righteousness,
you that seek the LORD.
Look to the rock from which you were hewn,
and to the quarry from which you were dug.
2 Look to Abraham your father
and to Sarah who bore you;
for he was but one when I called him,
but I blessed him and made him many.
3 For the LORD will comfort Zion;
he will comfort all her waste places,
and will make her wilderness like Eden,
her desert like the garden of the LORD;
joy and gladness will be found in her,
thanksgiving and the voice of song.

4 Listen to me, my people,
and give heed to me, my nation;
for a teaching will go out from me,
and my justice for a light to the peoples.
5 I will bring near my deliverance swiftly,
my salvation has gone out
and my arms will rule the peoples;
the coastlands wait for me,
and for my arm they hope.
6 Lift up your eyes to the heavens,
and look at the earth beneath;
for the heavens will vanish like smoke,
the earth will wear out like a garment,
and those who live on it will die like gnats;[q]
but my salvation will be forever,
and my deliverance will never be ended.

7 Listen to me, you who know righteousness,
you people who have my teaching in your hearts;
do not fear the reproach of others,
and do not be dismayed when they revile you.

51.1 Gen 12.1 17.15-17 Heb 11.11,12

51.3 Gen 2.8 Isa 41.19

51.4 Ps 78.1 Isa 42.4

51.5 Isa 46.13

51.6 Ps 102.25,26 2 Pet 3.10

51.7 Ps 37.30,31 Mt 5.11 Acts 5.40,41

p Syr: Heb *you gird yourselves with firebrands* q Or *in like manner*

51.1, 2 The faithful remnant felt alone because they were few. But God reminded them of their ancestors, the source of their spiritual heritage – Abraham and Sarah. Abraham was only one person, but much came from his faithfulness. If the faithful few would remain faithful, even more could come from them. If we Christians, even a faithful few, remain faithful, think what God can do through us!

51.7 Isaiah encouraged those who follow God's laws. He gave them hope when they faced people's scorn or slander because of their faith. We need not fear when people ridicule us for our faith, because God is with us and truth will prevail. If people make fun of you or dislike you because you believe in God, remember that they are not against you personally, but against God. He will deal with them; you should concentrate on loving and obeying him.

51.8 Isa 14.11

8 For the moth will eat them up like a garment,
and the worm will eat them like wool;
but my deliverance will be forever,
and my salvation to all generations.

51.9 Deut 4.34

9 Awake, awake, put on strength,
O arm of the LORD!
Awake, as in days of old,
the generations of long ago!
Was it not you who cut Rahab in pieces,
who pierced the dragon?

51.10 Ex 14.21,22 Isa 63.11,12

10 Was it not you who dried up the sea,
the waters of the great deep;
who made the depths of the sea a way
for the redeemed to cross over?

51.11 Isa 61.7 Rev 21.4

11 So the ransomed of the LORD shall return,
and come to Zion with singing;
everlasting joy shall be upon their heads;
they shall obtain joy and gladness,
and sorrow and sighing shall flee away.

51.12 Ps 118.6

12 I, I am he who comforts you;
why then are you afraid of a mere mortal who must die,
a human being who fades like grass?

51.13 Deut 8.11 Job 9.8

13 You have forgotten the LORD, your Maker,
who stretched out the heavens
and laid the foundations of the earth.
You fear continually all day long
because of the fury of the oppressor,
who is bent on destruction.
But where is the fury of the oppressor?

51.14 Isa 49.10

14 The oppressed shall speedily be released;
they shall not die and go down to the Pit,
nor shall they lack bread.

51.15 Ps 107.25

15 For I am the LORD your God,
who stirs up the sea so that its waves roar—
the LORD of hosts is his name.

51.16 Ex 33.22 Deut 18.18

16 I have put my words in your mouth,
and hidden you in the shadow of my hand,
stretching out[r] the heavens
and laying the foundations of the earth,
and saying to Zion, "You are my people."

51.17 Jer 25.15

17 Rouse yourself, rouse yourself!
Stand up, O Jerusalem,
you who have drunk at the hand of the LORD

[r] Syr: Heb *planting*

51.9, 10 "Rahab" was a derogatory term used for Egypt (see the note on 30.7). God performed many powerful miracles in founding Israel, perhaps none more exciting than the parting of the Red Sea (Exodus 14). Our God is the very God who made a highway through the sea. His methods may change, but his love and care do not.

51.12–16 Jerusalem feared Assyria, but not God. It had reason to fear Assyria for the harm it wanted to do, but it should also have realized that God's power is much greater than Assyria's. Assyria was interested in making the people captives; God was interested in setting them free. The people had misplaced their fear and their love. Jerusalem should have feared God's power and loved his mercy.

51.17–52.10 Jerusalem was God's holy city, the city with God's temple. But the people of Judah experienced desolation instead of prosperity, destruction instead of liberty. Because of their sins, the people suffered. But God promised to restore Jerusalem as a holy city where sinners cannot enter. "Bared his holy arm" means God has revealed his holy power and justice. God reigns. He is in control.

the cup of his wrath,
who have drunk to the dregs
the bowl of staggering.
18 There is no one to guide her
among all the children she has borne;
there is no one to take her by the hand
among all the children she has brought up.
19 These two things have befallen you
—who will grieve with you?—
devastation and destruction, famine and sword—
who will comfort you?[s]
20 Your children have fainted,
they lie at the head of every street
like an antelope in a net;
they are full of the wrath of the LORD,
the rebuke of your God.

21 Therefore hear this, you who are wounded,[t]
who are drunk, but not with wine:
22 Thus says your Sovereign, the LORD,
your God who pleads the cause of his people:
See, I have taken from your hand the cup of staggering;
you shall drink no more
from the bowl of my wrath.
23 And I will put it into the hand of your tormentors,
who have said to you,
"Bow down, that we may walk on you";
and you have made your back like the ground
and like the street for them to walk on.

51.18 Ps 142.4
51.20 Isa 66.15 Jer 14.16
51.22 Jer 50.34
51.23 Jer 25.15-17, 26,28

The Lord will rescue his people

52 Awake, awake,
put on your strength, O Zion!
Put on your beautiful garments,
O Jerusalem, the holy city;
for the uncircumcised and the unclean
shall enter you no more.
2 Shake yourself from the dust, rise up,
O captive[u] Jerusalem;
loose the bonds from your neck,
O captive daughter Zion!

3 For thus says the LORD: You were sold for nothing, and you shall be redeemed
without money. 4 For thus says the Lord GOD: Long ago, my people went down into
Egypt to reside there as aliens; the Assyrian, too, has oppressed them without
cause. 5 Now therefore what am I doing here, says the LORD, seeing that my people
are taken away without cause? Their rulers howl, says the LORD, and continually,
all day long, my name is despised. 6 Therefore my people shall know my name;
therefore in that day they shall know that it is I who speak; here am I.

52.1 Ex 28.2,40 Neh 11.1 Isa 48.2; 61.10
52.3 Ps 44.12 Isa 63.4
52.5 Ezek 36.20,23

7 How beautiful upon the mountains
are the feet of the messenger who announces peace,
who brings good news,
who announces salvation,
who says to Zion, "Your God reigns."
8 Listen! Your sentinels lift up their voices,
together they sing for joy;

52.7 Ps 93.1 Rom 10.15
52.8 Isa 62.6

[s] Q Ms Gk Syr Vg: MT *how may I comfort you?* [t] Or *humbled* [u] Cn: Heb *rise up, sit*

for in plain sight they see
the return of the LORD to Zion.
52.9 Ps 98.4 Isa 61.4
9 Break forth together into singing,
you ruins of Jerusalem;
for the LORD has comforted his people,
he has redeemed Jerusalem.
52.10 Ps 98.1-3 Lk 3.6
10 The LORD has bared his holy arm
before the eyes of all the nations;
and all the ends of the earth shall see
the salvation of our God.

52.11 Isa 1.16 2 Cor 6.17
11 Depart, depart, go out from there!
Touch no unclean thing;
go out from the midst of it, purify yourselves,
you who carry the vessels of the LORD.
52.12 Ex 12.11,33 14.19,20 Isa 26.7
12 For you shall not go out in haste,
and you shall not go in flight;
for the LORD will go before you,
and the God of Israel will be your rear guard.

God's servant will be despised

52.13 Phil 2.9
13 See, my servant shall prosper;
he shall be exalted and lifted up,
and shall be very high.
52.14 Ps 22.6,7 Rom 15.21
14 Just as there were many who were astonished at him[v]
—so marred was his appearance, beyond human semblance,
and his form beyond that of mortals—
15 so he shall startle[w] many nations;
kings shall shut their mouths because of him;
for that which had not been told them they shall see,
and that which they had not heard they shall contemplate.
53.1 Jn 12.38 Rom 10.16
53 Who has believed what we have heard?
And to whom has the arm of the LORD been revealed?
53.2 Isa 11.1
2 For he grew up before him like a young plant,
and like a root out of dry ground;
he had no form or majesty that we should look at him,
nothing in his appearance that we should desire him.
53.3 Ps 22.6 Lk 18.31-33
3 He was despised and rejected by others;
a man of suffering[x] and acquainted with infirmity;
and as one from whom others hide their faces[y]
he was despised, and we held him of no account.

[v] Syr Tg: Heb *you* [w] Meaning of Heb uncertain [x] Or *a man of sorrows* [y] Or *as one who hides his face from us*

52.12 The people did not leave in fearful haste, because Cyrus, God's anointed (45.1), decreed that the Jewish exiles could return safely to Jerusalem (Ezra 1.1–4). They had the king's approval, his guaranteed protection. God was protecting them.

52.13 The "servant," as the term is used here, is the Messiah, our Lord Jesus. He would be highly exalted because of his sacrifice, described in chapter 53.

52.14, 15 This servant, Christ, would be "marred . . . beyond human semblance"; but through his suffering, he would cleanse the nations (Hebrews 10.14; 1 Peter 1.2).

53.1ff This chapter speaks of the Messiah, Jesus, who would suffer for the sins of all people. Such a prophecy is astounding! Who would believe that God would choose to save the world through a humble, suffering Servant rather than a glorious King? The idea is contrary to human pride and worldly ways. But God often works in ways we don't expect. The Messiah's strength is shown by humility, suffering, and mercy.

53.2 There was nothing attractive in the physical appearance of this Servant. Israel would miscalculate the Servant's importance—they would consider him an ordinary man. But even though Jesus would not attract a large following based on his physical appearance, he would bring salvation and healing. Most people miscalculate the importance of Jesus' life and work. They need faithful Christians to point out his extraordinary nature.

53.3 This man of sorrows was rejected by those around him, and he is still rejected by many today. Some reject him by standing against him. Others ignore him and his great gift of forgiveness. Do you reject him, ignore him, or accept him?

4 Surely he has borne our infirmities
and carried our diseases;
yet we accounted him stricken,
struck down by God, and afflicted.
5 But he was wounded for our transgressions,
crushed for our iniquities;
upon him was the punishment that made us whole,
and by his bruises we are healed.
6 All we like sheep have gone astray;
we have all turned to our own way,
and the LORD has laid on him
the iniquity of us all.

7 He was oppressed, and he was afflicted,
yet he did not open his mouth;
like a lamb that is led to the slaughter,
and like a sheep that before its shearers is silent,
so he did not open his mouth.
8 By a perversion of justice he was taken away.
Who could have imagined his future?
For he was cut off from the land of the living,
stricken for the transgression of my people.
9 They made his grave with the wicked
and his tomb[z] with the rich,[a]
although he had done no violence,
and there was no deceit in his mouth.

10 Yet it was the will of the LORD to crush him with pain.[b]
When you make his life an offering for sin,[c]
he shall see his offspring, and shall prolong his days;
through him the will of the LORD shall prosper.
11 Out of his anguish he shall see light;[d]
he shall find satisfaction through his knowledge.
The righteous one,[e] my servant, shall make many righteous,
and he shall bear their iniquities.
12 Therefore I will allot him a portion with the great,
and he shall divide the spoil with the strong;
because he poured out himself to death,
and was numbered with the transgressors;
yet he bore the sin of many,
and made intercession for the transgressors.

53.4 Mt 8.17; Jn 19.7
53.5 1 Cor 15.3; Heb 5.8; 9.28; 1 Pet 2.24,25
53.7 Mt 27.12-14; Lk 23.9; Acts 8.32,33
53.9 Mt 27.57-60; 1 Pet 2.22
53.10 Ps 22.30; Jn 1.29
53.11 Jn 10.14-18; Rom 5.18,19
53.12 Mt 26.38,39,42; Lk 22.37; 2 Cor 5.21; Phil 2.9-11

z Q Ms: MT *and in his death* a Cn: Heb *with a rich person* b Or *by disease*; meaning of Heb uncertain c Meaning of Heb uncertain d Q Mss: MT lacks *light* e Or *and he shall find satisfaction. Through his knowledge, the righteous one*

53.4, 5 How could an Old Testament person understand the idea of Christ dying for our sins—actually bearing the punishment that we deserved? The sacrifices suggested this idea, but it is one thing to kill a lamb, and something quite different to think of God's chosen Servant as that Lamb. But God was pulling aside the curtain of time to let the people of Isaiah's day look ahead to the suffering of the future Messiah and the resulting forgiveness made available to all mankind.

53.6 Isaiah speaks of Israel straying from God and likens them to wandering sheep. Yet God will send the Messiah to bring them back into the fold. We have the hindsight to see and know the identity of the promised Messiah, who has come and died for our sins. But if we can see all that Jesus did and still reject him, we have a much greater sin than that of the ancient Israelites, who could not see what we have seen. Have you given your life to Jesus Christ, the "good shepherd" (John 10.11–16), or are you still like a wandering sheep?

53.7–12 In the Old Testament, people offered animals as sacrifices for their sins. Here, the sinless servant of the Lord offers himself for our sins. He is the Lamb (53.7) offered for the sins of all people (John 1.29; Revelation 5.6–14). The Messiah suffered for our sakes, bearing our sins to make us acceptable to God. What can we say to such love? How will we respond to him?

53.11 "The righteous one, my servant, shall make many righteous" tells of the enormous family of believers who will become righteous, not by their own works, but by the Messiah's great work on the cross. They are counted righteous because they have claimed Christ, the righteous Servant, as their Savior and Lord (see Romans 10.9; 2 Corinthians 5.21). Their life of sin is stripped away, and they are clothed with Christ's goodness.

Israel will be rebuilt

54.1 Isa 62.4 Gal 4.27

54 Sing, O barren one who did not bear;
burst into song and shout,
you who have not been in labor!
For the children of the desolate woman will be more
than the children of her that is married, says the LORD.
2 Enlarge the site of your tent,
and let the curtains of your habitations be stretched out;
do not hold back; lengthen your cords
and strengthen your stakes.

54.3 Gen 28.14 Isa 14.1,2

3 For you will spread out to the right and to the left,
and your descendants will possess the nations
and will settle the desolate towns.

4 Do not fear, for you will not be ashamed;
do not be discouraged, for you will not suffer disgrace;
for you will forget the shame of your youth,
and the disgrace of your widowhood you will remember no more.

54.5 Hos 2.19

5 For your Maker is your husband,
the LORD of hosts is his name;
the Holy One of Israel is your Redeemer,
the God of the whole earth he is called.

54.6 Isa 62.4

6 For the LORD has called you
like a wife forsaken and grieved in spirit,
like the wife of a man's youth when she is cast off,
says your God.

54.7 Isa 11.12

7 For a brief moment I abandoned you,
but with great compassion I will gather you.

54.8 Isa 49.10,13 60.10

8 In overflowing wrath for a moment
I hid my face from you,
but with everlasting love I will have compassion on you,
says the LORD, your Redeemer.

54.9 Gen 9.9-11 Ezek 39.29

9 This is like the days of Noah to me:
Just as I swore that the waters of Noah
would never again go over the earth,
so I have sworn that I will not be angry with you
and will not rebuke you.

54.10 2 Sam 23.5 Ps 89.34 102.25,26

10 For the mountains may depart
and the hills be removed,
but my steadfast love shall not depart from you,
and my covenant of peace shall not be removed,
says the LORD, who has compassion on you.

54.11 Isa 28.16

11 O afflicted one, storm-tossed, and not comforted,
I am about to set your stones in antimony,

54.1 To be childless ("barren") at that time was a woman's great shame, a disgrace. Families depended on children for survival, especially when the parents became elderly. Israel was unfruitful, like a childless woman, but God would permit her to have many children and change her mourning into singing.

54.6–8 God says that he has forsaken Israel for a brief time, so she is like a young wife abandoned by her husband. But he still calls Israel his own. The God we serve is holy, and he cannot tolerate sin. When Israel blatantly sinned, God in his anger chose to punish her. Sin separates us from God and brings us pain and suffering. But if we confess our sin and repent, God forgives us. Have you ever been separated from a loved one and then experienced joy when that person returned? That is like the joy God experiences when you repent and return to him.

54.9, 10 God made a promise to Noah that he has never broken (Genesis 9.8–17). Likewise, God promised the people of Israel that the time would come when he would cease to rebuke them, would restore their wealth, and would personally teach their children.

54.11 Antimony is a silvery-white, metallic mineral. Here it is used to mean "set in precious stones."

and lay your foundations with sapphires.[f]
12 I will make your pinnacles of rubies,
your gates of jewels,
and all your wall of precious stones.
13 All your children shall be taught by the LORD,
and great shall be the prosperity of your children.
14 In righteousness you shall be established;
you shall be far from oppression, for you shall not fear;
and from terror, for it shall not come near you.
15 If anyone stirs up strife,
it is not from me;
whoever stirs up strife with you
shall fall because of you.
16 See it is I who have created the smith
who blows the fire of coals,
and produces a weapon fit for its purpose;
I have also created the ravager to destroy.
17 No weapon that is fashioned against you shall prosper,
and you shall confute every tongue that rises against you in judgment.
This is the heritage of the servants of the LORD
and their vindication from me, says the LORD.

54.13 Isa 66.12 Jer 31.34
54.14 Isa 9.4,7
54.15 Isa 41.11-16
54.17 Isa 29.8

Blessings for those who seek him

55 Ho, everyone who thirsts,
come to the waters;
and you that have no money,
come, buy and eat!
Come, buy wine and milk
without money and without price.
2 Why do you spend your money for that which is not bread,
and your labor for that which does not satisfy?
Listen carefully to me, and eat what is good,
and delight yourselves in rich food.
3 Incline your ear, and come to me;
listen, so that you may live.
I will make with you an everlasting covenant,
my steadfast, sure love for David.
4 See, I made him a witness to the peoples,
a leader and commander for the peoples.
5 See, you shall call nations that you do not know,
and nations that do not know you shall run to you,
because of the LORD your God, the Holy One of Israel,
for he has glorified you.

6 Seek the LORD while he may be found,
call upon him while he is near;

55.1 Ps 63.1 Mt 10.8 Jn 4.14
55.2 Ps 22.26 Eccles 6.2
55.3 Acts 13.34 Rom 10.5
55.5 Zech 8.22
55.6 Ps 32.6 2 Cor 6.1,2

[f] Or *lapis lazuli*

55.1–6 Food costs money, lasts only a short time, and meets only physical needs. But God offers us *free* nourishment that feeds our soul. How do we get it? We come (55.1), listen (55.3), seek, and call upon God (55.6). God's salvation is freely offered, but to nourish our souls, we must eagerly receive it. We will starve spiritually without this food as surely as we will starve physically without our daily bread.

55.3 God's covenant with David promised a permanent homeland for the Israelites, no threat from heathen nations, and no wars (2 Samuel 7.10, 11). But Israel did not fulfill its part of the covenant by obeying God and staying away from idols. Even so, God was ready to renew his covenant again. He is a forgiving God!

55.6 Isaiah tells us to call upon the Lord while he is near. God is not planning to move away from us, but we often move far from him or erect a barrier between ourselves and him. Don't wait until you have drifted far away from God to seek him. Later in life, turning to him may be far more difficult. Or God may come to judge the earth before you decide to seek him. Do it now while you can, before it is too late.

55.7 Isa 1.16; 44.22

7 let the wicked forsake their way,
and the unrighteous their thoughts;
let them return to the LORD, that he may have mercy on them,
and to our God, for he will abundantly pardon.

55.8 Isa 65.2

8 For my thoughts are not your thoughts,
nor are your ways my ways, says the LORD.

55.9 Ps 103.11

9 For as the heavens are higher than the earth,
so are my ways higher than your ways
and my thoughts than your thoughts.

55.10 2 Cor 9.10

10 For as the rain and the snow come down from heaven,
and do not return there until they have watered the earth,
making it bring forth and sprout,
giving seed to the sower and bread to the eater,

55.11 Isa 46.10

11 so shall my word be that goes out from my mouth;
it shall not return to me empty,
but it shall accomplish that which I purpose,
and succeed in the thing for which I sent it.

55.12 1 Chron 16.33 Jer 29.11

12 For you shall go out in joy,
and be led back in peace;
the mountains and the hills before you
shall burst into song,
and all the trees of the field shall clap their hands.

55.13 Jer 33.9

13 Instead of the thorn shall come up the cypress;
instead of the brier shall come up the myrtle;
and it shall be to the LORD for a memorial,
for an everlasting sign that shall not be cut off.

Blessings for the Gentiles

56.1 Ps 85.9 Isa 1.17

56 Thus says the LORD:
Maintain justice, and do what is right,
for soon my salvation will come,
and my deliverance be revealed.

56.2 Ex 31.13-17 Ps 119.1,2 Ezek 20.12,20

2 Happy is the mortal who does this,
the one who holds it fast,
who keeps the sabbath, not profaning it,
and refrains from doing any evil.

56.3 Acts 8.27,37

3 Do not let the foreigner joined to the LORD say,
"The LORD will surely separate me from his people";
and do not let the eunuch say,
"I am just a dry tree."
4 For thus says the LORD:
To the eunuchs who keep my sabbaths,
who choose the things that please me

55.8, 9 The people of Israel were foolish to act as if they knew what God was thinking and planning. His knowledge and wisdom are far greater than man's. We are foolish to try to fit God into our mold – to make his plans and purposes conform to ours. Instead, we must strive to fit into *his* plans.

56.2 God commanded his people to rest and honor him on the sabbath (Exodus 20.8–11). He wants us to serve him every day, but he wants us to make one day special when we rest and focus our thoughts on him. For the Israelites, this special day was the sabbath (Saturday). A few Christians set Saturday aside as this special day, but most accept Sunday (the day of the week that Jesus rose from the dead) as the "Lord's Day," a day of rest and honor to God.

56.3 Isaiah clearly proclaims the radical message that God's blessings are for *all* people, even Gentiles and eunuchs, who were often not even considered citizens in Israel. Whatever your race, social position, work, or financial situation, God's blessings are as much for you as for anyone else. No one must exclude in any way those God chooses to include.

and hold fast my covenant,
5 I will give, in my house and within my walls,
a monument and a name
better than sons and daughters;
I will give them an everlasting name
that shall not be cut off.

56.5 Isa 2.2,3; 26.1 62.2

6 And the foreigners who join themselves to the LORD,
to minister to him, to love the name of the LORD,
and to be his servants,
all who keep the sabbath, and do not profane it,
and hold fast my covenant—
7 these I will bring to my holy mountain,
and make them joyful in my house of prayer;
their burnt offerings and their sacrifices
will be accepted on my altar;
for my house shall be called a house of prayer
for all peoples.
8 Thus says the Lord GOD,
who gathers the outcasts of Israel,
I will gather others to them
besides those already gathered.[g]

56.7 Isa 65.25 Mic 4.1,2 Mk 11.17 Rom 12.1 Heb 13.15

56.8 Jn 10.16

9 All you wild animals,
all you wild animals in the forest, come to devour!
10 Israel's[h] sentinels are blind,
they are all without knowledge;
they are all silent dogs
that cannot bark;
dreaming, lying down,
loving to slumber.
11 The dogs have a mighty appetite;
they never have enough.
The shepherds also have no understanding;
they have all turned to their own way,
to their own gain, one and all.
12 "Come," they say, "let us[i] get wine;
let us fill ourselves with strong drink.
And tomorrow will be like today,
great beyond measure."

56.9 Jer 12.9

56.10 Jer 14.13,14 Ezek 3.17

56.11 Jer 22.17 Mic 3.5,11

56.12 Lk 12.19,20

The godly shall rest in peace

57 The righteous perish,
and no one takes it to heart;
the devout are taken away,
while no one understands.
For the righteous are taken away from calamity,
2 and they enter into peace;
those who walk uprightly
will rest on their couches.
3 But as for you, come here,

57.1 2 Kgs 22.19,20 Ps 12.1

57.2 Isa 26.7

[g] Heb *besides his gathered ones* [h] Heb *His* [i] Q Ms Syr Vg Tg: MT *me*

56.7 Jesus quoted this verse when he threw the money changers out of the temple (Mark 11.17). See the note on Mark 11.15–17.

56.9–11 The leaders of Israel were blind to every danger. Apathetic about their people's needs, they were more concerned about satisfying their own greed. Leadership's special privileges can cause the leader either to sacrifice for the good of his people or to sacrifice his people for his own greed. If you are in a leadership position, use it for the good of your people.

you children of a sorceress,
you offspring of an adulterer and a whore.[j]
4 Whom are you mocking?
Against whom do you open your mouth wide
and stick out your tongue?
Are you not children of transgression,
the offspring of deceit—

57.5 Ps 106.37,38 Jer 2.20; 7.31
5 you that burn with lust among the oaks,
under every green tree;
you that slaughter your children in the valleys,
under the clefts of the rocks?

57.6 Jer 5.9,29; 7.18 Hab 2.19
6 Among the smooth stones of the valley is your portion;
they, they, are your lot;
to them you have poured out a drink offering,
you have brought a grain offering.
Shall I be appeased for these things?

57.7 Ezek 16.16,28
7 Upon a high and lofty mountain
you have set your bed,
and there you went up to offer sacrifice.
8 Behind the door and the doorpost
you have set up your symbol;
for, in deserting me,[k] you have uncovered your bed,
you have gone up to it,
you have made it wide;
and you have made a bargain for yourself with them,
you have loved their bed,
you have gazed on their nakedness.[l]

57.9 Ezek 23.16,40
9 You journeyed to Molech[m] with oil,
and multiplied your perfumes;
you sent your envoys far away,
and sent down even to Sheol.

57.10 Jer 2.25
10 You grew weary from your many wanderings,
but you did not say, "It is useless."
You found your desire rekindled,
and so you did not weaken.

57.11 Prov 29.25 Jer 2.32
11 Whom did you dread and fear
so that you lied,
and did not remember me
or give me a thought?
Have I not kept silent and closed my eyes,[n]
and so you do not fear me?

57.12 Mic 3.1-4
12 I will concede your righteousness and your works,
but they will not help you.

57.13 Ps 37.3,9 Jer 30.14
13 When you cry out, let your collection of idols deliver you!
The wind will carry them off,

[j] Heb *an adulterer and she plays the whore* [k] Meaning of Heb uncertain [l] Or *their phallus*; Heb *the hand* [m] Or *the king* [n] Gk Vg: Heb *silent even for a long time*

57.7, 8 Marriage is an exclusive relationship in which a man and a woman become one. Adultery breaks this beautiful bond of unity. When the people turned from God and gave their love to idols, God said they were committing adultery—breaking their exclusive commitment to God. How could people give their love to worthless wood and stone instead of to the God who made them and loved them so very much?

57.9 Molech was an Ammonite god whose worship included child sacrifice. *Sheol* is the word in the Old Testament for the realm of the dead. It is used to mean the grave or the state of being dead. Those who went to Molech did not always come back alive.

57.12 God says that he will expose their good works for what they really were—mere pretentions of doing good. Isaiah warned these people that their righteousness and good works would not save them any more than their weak, worthless idols would. We cannot gain our salvation through good works, because our best works are not good enough to outweigh our sins. Salvation is a gift from God. The only way to receive it is through faith in Christ, not good works (Ephesians 2.8, 9).

a breath will take them away.
But whoever takes refuge in me shall possess the land
and inherit my holy mountain.

14 It shall be said,
"Build up, build up, prepare the way,
remove every obstruction from my people's way."
15 For thus says the high and lofty one
who inhabits eternity, whose name is Holy:
I dwell in the high and holy place,
and also with those who are contrite and humble in spirit,
to revive the spirit of the humble,
and to revive the heart of the contrite.
16 For I will not continually accuse,
nor will I always be angry;
for then the spirits would grow faint before me,
even the souls that I have made.
17 Because of their wicked covetousness I was angry;
I struck them, I hid and was angry;
but they kept turning back to their own ways.
18 I have seen their ways, but I will heal them;
I will lead them and repay them with comfort,
creating for their mourners the fruit of the lips.[o]
19 Peace, peace, to the far and the near, says the LORD;
and I will heal them.
20 But the wicked are like the tossing sea
that cannot keep still;
its waters toss up mire and mud.
21 There is no peace, says my God, for the wicked.

57.14 Isa 62.10
57.15 Deut 33.27; Ps 34.18; Isa 66.1
57.16 Mic 7.18
57.17 Isa 1.4
57.18 Isa 53.5; 61.1-3
57.19 Isa 26.12; Eph 2.17
57.20 Job 18.5-14
57.21 Isa 48.22

An admonition to share with the needy

58 Shout out, do not hold back!
Lift up your voice like a trumpet!
Announce to my people their rebellion,
to the house of Jacob their sins.
2 Yet day after day they seek me
and delight to know my ways,
as if they were a nation that practiced righteousness
and did not forsake the ordinance of their God;
they ask of me righteous judgments,
they delight to draw near to God.
3 "Why do we fast, but you do not see?
Why humble ourselves, but you do not notice?"
Look, you serve your own interest on your fast day,
and oppress all your workers.
4 Look, you fast only to quarrel and to fight
and to strike with a wicked fist.
Such fasting as you do today
will not make your voice heard on high.
5 Is such the fast that I choose,

58.2 Isa 29.13; Jer 7.9,10; Titus 1.16
58.3 Zech 7.5,6; Lk 18.12
58.4 1 Kgs 21.9,10

o Meaning of Heb uncertain

57.15–21 Verses 1–14 speak of pride and lust; verses 15–21 tell how God relates to those who are humble and repentant. The high and holy God came down to our level to save us because it is impossible for us go up to his level to save ourselves (see 2 Chronicles 6.18; Psalm 51.1–7; Philippians 2).

58.1ff True worship was more than religious ritual, going to the temple every day, fasting, and listening to Scripture readings. These people missed the point of a living, vital relationship with God. He doesn't want us acting pious when we have unforgiven sin in our hearts and perform sinful practices with our hands. More important even than correct worship and doctrine is genuine compassion for the poor, the helpless, and the oppressed.

a day to humble oneself?
Is it to bow down the head like a bulrush,
and to lie in sackcloth and ashes?
Will you call this a fast,
a day acceptable to the LORD?

58.6 Neh 5.10-12
6 Is not this the fast that I choose:
to loose the bonds of injustice,
to undo the thongs of the yoke,
to let the oppressed go free,
and to break every yoke?

58.7 Deut 22.1-4 Ezek 18.7,16 Lk 3.11 Heb 13.2
7 Is it not to share your bread with the hungry,
and bring the homeless poor into your house;
when you see the naked, to cover them,
and not to hide yourself from your own kin?

58.8 Ps 85.13 Jer 30.17
8 Then your light shall break forth like the dawn,
and your healing shall spring up quickly;
your vindicator[p] shall go before you,
the glory of the LORD shall be your rear guard.
9 Then you shall call, and the LORD will answer;
you shall cry for help, and he will say, Here I am.

If you remove the yoke from among you,
the pointing of the finger, the speaking of evil,

58.10 Deut 15.7
10 if you offer your food to the hungry
and satisfy the needs of the afflicted,
then your light shall rise in the darkness
and your gloom be like the noonday.

58.11 Ps 107.9 Song 4.15 Jn 4.14
11 The LORD will guide you continually,
and satisfy your needs in parched places,
and make your bones strong;
and you shall be like a watered garden,
like a spring of water,
whose waters never fail.

58.12 Ezek 36.10 Amos 9.11
12 Your ancient ruins shall be rebuilt;
you shall raise up the foundations of many generations;
you shall be called the repairer of the breach,
the restorer of streets to live in.

58.13 Ps 84.2,10 Jer 17.21-27
13 If you refrain from trampling the sabbath,
from pursuing your own interests on my holy day;
if you call the sabbath a delight
and the holy day of the LORD honorable;
if you honor it, not going your own ways,
serving your own interests, or pursuing your own affairs;[q]

58.14 Deut 32.13
14 then you shall take delight in the LORD,
and I will make you ride upon the heights of the earth;

[p] Or *vindication* [q] Heb *or speaking words*

58.6–12 We cannot be saved by works of service without faith in Christ, but our faith lacks sincerity if it doesn't reach out to others. Fasting can be beneficial spiritually and physically, but at its best it helps only the person doing it. God says he wants our service to go beyond our own personal growth to acts of kindness, charity, justice, and generosity. Pleasing God is more than what we don't eat or don't do; it is what we do for him and for others.

58.13, 14 The day of rest should also be honored not only because sabbath-keeping is a commandment, but also because it is best for us and because it honors God. Keeping the sabbath honors God, our Creator, who also rested on the seventh day (Genesis 2.3). It also unifies our families and sets priorities for them. Our day of rest refreshes us spiritually and physically – providing time when we can gather together for worship and when we can reflect on God without the stress of our everyday lives.

I will feed you with the heritage of your ancestor Jacob,
for the mouth of the LORD has spoken.

Warnings against sin

59 See, the LORD's hand is not too short to save,
nor his ear too dull to hear.
2 Rather, your iniquities have been barriers
between you and your God,
and your sins have hidden his face from you
so that he does not hear.
3 For your hands are defiled with blood,
and your fingers with iniquity;
your lips have spoken lies,
your tongue mutters wickedness.
4 No one brings suit justly,
no one goes to law honestly;
they rely on empty pleas, they speak lies,
conceiving mischief and begetting iniquity.
5 They hatch adders' eggs,
and weave the spider's web;
whoever eats their eggs dies,
and the crushed egg hatches out a viper.
6 Their webs cannot serve as clothing;
they cannot cover themselves with what they make.
Their works are works of iniquity,
and deeds of violence are in their hands.
7 Their feet run to evil,
and they rush to shed innocent blood;
their thoughts are thoughts of iniquity,
desolation and destruction are in their highways.
8 The way of peace they do not know,
and there is no justice in their paths.
Their roads they have made crooked;
no one who walks in them knows peace.

9 Therefore justice is far from us,
and righteousness does not reach us;
we wait for light, and lo! there is darkness;
and for brightness, but we walk in gloom.
10 We grope like the blind along a wall,
groping like those who have no eyes;
we stumble at noon as in the twilight,
among the vigorous[r] as though we were dead.
11 We all growl like bears;
like doves we moan mournfully.
We wait for justice, but there is none;
for salvation, but it is far from us.
12 For our transgressions before you are many,
and our sins testify against us.
Our transgressions indeed are with us,
and we know our iniquities:

59.1 Jer 32.17 Ezek 8.18
59.2 Isa 1.15
59.3 Jer 2.30,34 Hos 4.2
59.4 Ps 7.14
59.6 Jer 6.7
59.7 Prov 1.16 Mk 7.21,22 Rom 3.15-17
59.9 Isa 5.30
59.10 Deut 28.29 Lam 3.6
59.11 Ezek 7.16
59.12 Ezra 9.6 Hos 5.5

[r] Meaning of Heb uncertain

59.1–12 Sin offends our holy God. Because God is holy, he cannot ignore, excuse, or tolerate sin as though it doesn't matter. Sin cuts people off from him, forming a wall to isolate God from the people he loves. No wonder this long list of wretched sins makes God angry and forces him to look the other way. People who die with their lives of sin unforgiven separate themselves eternally from God. God wants them to live with him forever, but he cannot take them into his holy presence unless their sin is removed. Wouldn't you be angry to see people you love cut themselves off from you and condemn themselves to eternal separation from you?

59.13 Mt 10.33

13 transgressing, and denying the LORD,
and turning away from following our God,
talking oppression and revolt,
conceiving lying words and uttering them from the heart.

59.14 Hab 1.4

14 Justice is turned back,
and righteousness stands at a distance;
for truth stumbles in the public square,
and uprightness cannot enter.

59.15 Isa 1.21-23 5.23

15 Truth is lacking,
and whoever turns from evil is despoiled.

The LORD saw it, and it displeased him
that there was no justice.

59.16 Ezek 22.30

16 He saw that there was no one,
and was appalled that there was no one to intervene;
so his own arm brought him victory,
and his righteousness upheld him.

59.17 Eph 6.14

17 He put on righteousness like a breastplate,
and a helmet of salvation on his head;
he put on garments of vengeance for clothing,
and wrapped himself in fury as in a mantle.
18 According to their deeds, so will he repay;
wrath to his adversaries, requital to his enemies;
to the coastlands he will render requital.

59.19 Isa 30.28

19 So those in the west shall fear the name of the LORD,
and those in the east, his glory;
for he will come like a pent-up stream
that the wind of the LORD drives on.

59.20 Ezek 18.30,31 Acts 2.38 Rom 11.26,27

59.21 Isa 44.3 Jer 31.31-34

20 And he will come to Zion as Redeemer,
to those in Jacob who turn from transgression, says the LORD.
21 And as for me, this is my covenant with them, says the LORD: my spirit that is
upon you, and my words that I have put in your mouth, shall not depart out of your
mouth, or out of the mouths of your children, or out of the mouths of your children's children, says the LORD, from now on and forever.

3. The future kingdom

Promises of glory for God's people

60.1 Eph 5.14

60 Arise, shine; for your light has come,
and the glory of the LORD has risen upon you.

60.2 Col 1.13

2 For darkness shall cover the earth,
and thick darkness the peoples;
but the LORD will arise upon you,
and his glory will appear over you.

59.15 Because of Israel's willful, persistent rebellion (chapters 56–59), the nation became unable to take action against its sins. Sin fills the vacuum left when God's truth no longer fills our lives. Only God can save us.

59.16, 17 God would rescue the nation from enemy armies (Assyria and Babylon). He would also rescue his people from sin. Because this is an impossible task for any human, God himself, as the Messiah, would personally step in to help (Romans 11.26, 27). Whether we sin once or many times, out of rebellion or out of ignorance, our sin separates us from God and will continue to separate us until God forgives it.

59.21 When the Holy Spirit dwells within his people, they change. Their former desires no longer entice them; now their chief aim is to please God. We who are Christians today are the heirs of this prophecy; we are given discernment between right and wrong because the Holy Spirit dwells within us (John 14.26; Philippians 2.13; Hebrews 5.14).

60.1ff As we read these promises, we long for their fulfillment. But we must patiently wait for God's timing. He is in control of history, and he weaves together all our lives into his plan.

60.1–3 God's light will shine on Israel, who will radiate his light to the nations, dispelling the darkness of the surrounding world. God's light alone can dispel the darkness around us. We don't have any light apart from him.

3 Nations shall come to your light,
and kings to the brightness of your dawn.
4 Lift up your eyes and look around;
they all gather together, they come to you;
your sons shall come from far away,
and your daughters shall be carried on their nurses' arms.
5 Then you shall see and be radiant;
your heart shall thrill and rejoice,[s]
because the abundance of the sea shall be brought to you,
the wealth of the nations shall come to you.
6 A multitude of camels shall cover you,
the young camels of Midian and Ephah;
all those from Sheba shall come.
They shall bring gold and frankincense,
and shall proclaim the praise of the LORD.
7 All the flocks of Kedar shall be gathered to you,
the rams of Nebaioth shall minister to you;
they shall be acceptable on my altar,
and I will glorify my glorious house.

8 Who are these that fly like a cloud,
and like doves to their windows?
9 For the coastlands shall wait for me,
the ships of Tarshish first,
to bring your children from far away,
their silver and gold with them,
for the name of the LORD your God,
and for the Holy One of Israel,
because he has glorified you.
10 Foreigners shall build up your walls,
and their kings shall minister to you;
for in my wrath I struck you down,
but in my favor I have had mercy on you.
11 Your gates shall always be open;
day and night they shall not be shut,
so that nations shall bring you their wealth,
with their kings led in procession.
12 For the nation and kingdom
that will not serve you shall perish;
those nations shall be utterly laid waste.
13 The glory of Lebanon shall come to you,
the cypress, the plane, and the pine,
to beautify the place of my sanctuary;
and I will glorify where my feet rest.
14 The descendants of those who oppressed you
shall come bending low to you,
and all who despised you
shall bow down at your feet;
they shall call you the City of the LORD,
the Zion of the Holy One of Israel.
15 Whereas you have been forsaken and hated,
with no one passing through,

60.3 Isa 2.3
60.5 Ps 34.5; Isa 61.6
60.6 Ps 72.10
60.9 Isa 49.22
60.10 Isa 49.23
60.11 Isa 26.2
60.12 Zech 14.17
60.13 Ps 132.7
60.14 Isa 1.26; 14.1,2; Rev 3.9
60.15 Isa 65.18; Jer 30.17

[s] Heb *be enlarged*

60.6, 7 The places mentioned belonged to obscure tribes in the Arabian desert hundreds of miles from Israel. All people would come to Jerusalem because God would be living there and they would be attracted to his light. Don't be discouraged when you look around and see so few people turning to God; one day people throughout the earth will recognize him as the one true God.

I will make you majestic forever,
a joy from age to age.

60.16 Isa 43.3,11 63.16

16 You shall suck the milk of nations,
you shall suck the breasts of kings;
and you shall know that I, the LORD, am your Savior
and your Redeemer, the Mighty One of Jacob.

17 Instead of bronze I will bring gold,
instead of iron I will bring silver;
instead of wood, bronze,
instead of stones, iron.
I will appoint Peace as your overseer
and Righteousness as your taskmaster.

60.18 Isa 26.1

18 Violence shall no more be heard in your land,
devastation or destruction within your borders;
you shall call your walls Salvation,
and your gates Praise.

60.19 Isa 9.2 Zech 2.5 Rev 21.23

19 The sun shall no longer be
your light by day,
nor for brightness shall the moon
give light to you by night;[t]
but the LORD will be your everlasting light,
and your God will be your glory.

60.20 Rev 21.4

20 Your sun shall no more go down,
or your moon withdraw itself;
for the LORD will be your everlasting light,
and your days of mourning shall be ended.

60.21 Ps 37.22 Isa 45.24,25

21 Your people shall all be righteous;
they shall possess the land forever.
They are the shoot that I planted, the work of my hands,
so that I might be glorified.

60.22 Isa 51.2

22 The least of them shall become a clan,
and the smallest one a mighty nation;
I am the LORD;
in its time I will accomplish it quickly.

Good news for those who suffer

61.1 Isa 49.9 Lk 4.18,19

61 The spirit of the Lord GOD is upon me,
because the LORD has anointed me;
he has sent me to bring good news to the oppressed,
to bind up the brokenhearted,
to proclaim liberty to the captives,
and release to the prisoners;

61.2 Mt 5.4

2 to proclaim the year of the LORD's favor,
and the day of vengeance of our God;
to comfort all who mourn;

61.3 Ps 23.5 Jer 17.7,8

3 to provide for those who mourn in Zion—
to give them a garland instead of ashes,
the oil of gladness instead of mourning,
the mantle of praise instead of a faint spirit.

[t] Q Ms Gk Old Latin Tg: MT lacks *by night*

60.19, 20 See Revelation 21.23, 24 where this beautiful reality is also promised.

61.1, 2 Jesus quoted these words in Luke 4.18–21. As he read to the people in the synagogue, he stopped in the middle of 61.2 after the words "to proclaim the year of the Lord's favor." Closing the book, he said, "Today this scripture has been fulfilled in your hearing" (Luke 4.21). The next phrase in 61.2, "and the day of vengeance of our God," will come true when Jesus returns to earth again. We are now under God's favor; his wrath is yet to come.

They will be called oaks of righteousness,
the planting of the LORD, to display his glory.
4 They shall build up the ancient ruins,
they shall raise up the former devastations;
they shall repair the ruined cities,
the devastations of many generations.

5 Strangers shall stand and feed your flocks,
foreigners shall till your land and dress your vines;
6 but you shall be called priests of the LORD,
you shall be named ministers of our God;
you shall enjoy the wealth of the nations,
and in their riches you shall glory.
7 Because their[u] shame was double,
and dishonor was proclaimed as their lot,
therefore they shall possess a double portion;
everlasting joy shall be theirs.

8 For I the LORD love justice,
I hate robbery and wrongdoing;[v]
I will faithfully give them their recompense,
and I will make an everlasting covenant with them.
9 Their descendants shall be known among the nations,
and their offspring among the peoples;
all who see them shall acknowledge
that they are a people whom the LORD has blessed.
10 I will greatly rejoice in the LORD,
my whole being shall exult in my God;
for he has clothed me with the garments of salvation,
he has covered me with the robe of righteousness,
as a bridegroom decks himself with a garland,
and as a bride adorns herself with her jewels.
11 For as the earth brings forth its shoots,
and as a garden causes what is sown in it to spring up,
so the Lord GOD will cause righteousness and praise
to spring up before all the nations.

61.4 Ezek 36.33 Amos 9.14

61.5 Isa 14.2

61.6 Isa 66.21

61.7 Zech 9.12

61.8 Gen 17.7 Isa 5.16

61.10 Isa 51.3; 52.1

Isaiah prays for Jerusalem

62 For Zion's sake I will not keep silent,
and for Jerusalem's sake I will not rest,
until her vindication shines out like the dawn,
and her salvation like a burning torch.

62.1 Isa 46.13

[u] Heb *your* [v] Or *robbery with a burnt offering*

61.6 Under the old covenant, God ordained the priests of Israel to stand between him and his people. They brought God's Word to the people, and the people's needs and sins to God. Under the new covenant, all believers are priests before God, reading God's Word and seeking to understand it, confessing their sins directly to God, and ministering to others.

61.8 We suffer for many reasons – our own mistakes, someone else's mistakes, injustice. When we suffer for our own mistakes, we get what we deserve. When we suffer because of others or injustice, God is angry. God in his mercy says that his people have suffered enough. God will reward those who suffer because of injustice. He will settle all accounts.

61.10 "Me" could refer to the Messiah, the person anointed with the spirit of the Lord (61.1), or to Zion (62.1), which symbolizes God's people. The imagery of the bridegroom is often used in Scripture to depict the Messiah (see Matthew 9.15), while the imagery of the bride is used to depict God's people (see Revelation 19.6–8). We too can be clothed with the righteousness of Christ when we believe in him (2 Corinthians 5.21).

62.1–7 Isaiah's zeal for his people and his desire to see the work of salvation completed caused him to pray without resting, hoping that Israel would be saved. We should have Isaiah's zeal to see God's will done. This is what we mean when we pray, "Your kingdom come. Your will be done, on earth as it is in heaven." It is good to k eep praying persistently for others.

62.2 Isa 56.5

2 The nations shall see your vindication,
and all the kings your glory;
and you shall be called by a new name
that the mouth of the LORD will give.

62.3 Zech 9.16; 1 Thess 2.19

3 You shall be a crown of beauty in the hand of the LORD,
and a royal diadem in the hand of your God.

62.4 Isa 54.6,7; Jer 32.41; Zeph 3.17,18

4 You shall no more be termed Forsaken,[w]
and your land shall no more be termed Desolate;[x]
but you shall be called My Delight Is in Her,[y]
and your land Married;[z]
for the LORD delights in you,
and your land shall be married.
5 For as a young man marries a young woman,
so shall your builder[a] marry you,
and as the bridegroom rejoices over the bride,
so shall your God rejoice over you.

62.6 Jer 14.21; Ezek 33.7; Zeph 3.19,20; Lk 18.1-8

6 Upon your walls, O Jerusalem,
I have posted sentinels;
all day and all night
they shall never be silent.
You who remind the LORD,
take no rest,
7 and give him no rest
until he establishes Jerusalem
and makes it renowned throughout the earth.

62.8 Lev 26.16; Deut 28.31,33

8 The LORD has sworn by his right hand
and by his mighty arm:
I will not again give your grain
to be food for your enemies,
and foreigners shall not drink the wine
for which you have labored;

62.9 Isa 65.13,21-23

9 but those who garner it shall eat it
and praise the LORD,
and those who gather it shall drink it
in my holy courts.

10 Go through, go through the gates,
prepare the way for the people;
build up, build up the highway,
clear it of stones,
lift up an ensign over the peoples.

62.11 Isa 49.6; Zech 9.9

11 The LORD has proclaimed
to the end of the earth:
Say to daughter Zion,
"See, your salvation comes;
his reward is with him,
and his recompense before him."

62.12 Deut 7.6; 1 Pet 2.9

12 They shall be called, "The Holy People,
The Redeemed of the LORD";
and you shall be called, "Sought Out,
A City Not Forsaken."

[w] Heb *Azubah* [x] Heb *Shemamah* [y] Heb *Hephzibah* [z] Heb *Beulah* [a] Cn: Heb *your sons*

62.12 The people of Jerusalem will have new names—"The Holy People" and "The Redeemed of the Lord." Believers today also have new names—Christians. In 1 Peter 2.5, we are called "a holy priesthood."

God's judgment and lovingkindness

63 "Who is this that comes from Edom,
from Bozrah in garments stained crimson?
Who is this so splendidly robed,
marching in his great might?"

"It is I, announcing vindication,
mighty to save."

2 "Why are your robes red,
and your garments like theirs who tread the winepress?"

3 "I have trodden the winepress alone,
and from the peoples no one was with me;
I trod them in my anger
and trampled them in my wrath;
their juice spattered on my garments,
and stained all my robes.
4 For the day of vengeance was in my heart,
and the year for my redeeming work had come.
5 I looked, but there was no helper;
I stared, but there was no one to sustain me;
so my own arm brought me victory,
and my wrath sustained me.
6 I trampled down peoples in my anger,
I crushed them in my wrath,
and I poured out their lifeblood on the earth."

7 I will recount the gracious deeds of the LORD,
the praiseworthy acts of the LORD,
because of all that the LORD has done for us,
and the great favor to the house of Israel
that he has shown them according to his mercy,
according to the abundance of his steadfast love.
8 For he said, "Surely they are my people,
children who will not deal falsely";
and he became their savior
9 in all their distress.
It was no messenger[b] or angel
but his presence that saved them;[c]
in his love and in his pity he redeemed them;
he lifted them up and carried them all the days of old.

10 But they rebelled
and grieved his holy spirit;
therefore he became their enemy;
he himself fought against them.
11 Then they[d] remembered the days of old,
of Moses his servant.[e]

63.1 Jer 49.13 Zeph 3.17

63.2 Rev 19.13,15

63.3 Isa 22.5 Mic 7.10

63.4 Jer 51.6

63.7 1 Kgs 8.66 Ps 25.6,7; 86.5 Eph 2.4

63.8 Ex 6.7

63.9 Ex 23.20-23 Judg 10.16

63.10 Ps 78.40 Eph 4.30

63.11 Num 11.17, 25,29 Isa 51.9,10

[b] Gk: Heb *anguish* [c] Or *savior.* [9]*In all their distress he was distressed; the angel of his presence saved them;* [d] Heb *he* [e] Cn: Heb *his people*

63.1–4 Edom was a constant enemy to Israel despite its common ancestry in Isaac (Genesis 25.23). Edom rejoiced at any trouble Israel faced. The watchman on the wall of Jerusalem, seeing Edom approaching, fears that the Edomite king in his crimson robe is leading an attack. But it turns out to be the Lord, in blood-stained clothes, who has trampled and destroyed Edom. Bozrah is a city in Edom. (For other prophecies against Edom, see Amos 1.11, 12; Obadiah 1.10, 11; Malachi 1.2–4.)

63.10 Grieving the Holy Spirit is willfully thwarting his leading by disobedience or rebellion. Isaiah mentions the work of the Holy Spirit more than any other Old Testament writer. See the note on Ephesians 4.28–32 for more on grieving the Holy Spirit.

Where is the one who brought them up out of the sea
with the shepherds of his flock?
Where is the one who put within them
his holy spirit,
63.12 Ex 6.6 14.21,22
12 who caused his glorious arm
to march at the right hand of Moses,
who divided the waters before them
to make for himself an everlasting name,
63.13 Jer 31.9
13 who led them through the depths?
Like a horse in the desert,
they did not stumble.
63.14 Josh 21.44
14 Like cattle that go down into the valley,
the spirit of the LORD gave them rest.
Thus you led your people,
to make for yourself a glorious name.
63.15 Ps 80.14; 123.1 Jer 31.20
15 Look down from heaven and see,
from your holy and glorious habitation.
Where are your zeal and your might?
The yearning of your heart and your compassion?
They are withheld from me.
63.16 Isa 41.8
16 For you are our father,
though Abraham does not know us
and Israel does not acknowledge us;
you, O LORD, are our father;
our Redeemer from of old is your name.
63.17 Isa 29.13,14
17 Why, O LORD, do you make us stray from your ways
and harden our heart, so that we do not fear you?
Turn back for the sake of your servants,
for the sake of the tribes that are your heritage.
63.18 Ps 74.3-7
18 Your holy people took possession for a little while;
but now our adversaries have trampled down your sanctuary.
63.19 Lam 3.43-45
19 We have long been like those whom you do not rule,
like those not called by your name.

64.1 Ex 19.18 Judg 5.5 Nah 1.5
64 O that you would tear open the heavens and come down,
so that the mountains would quake at your presence—
2[f] as when fire kindles brushwood

[f] Ch 64.1 in Heb

THE SPIRIT IN ISAIAH

Reference	*Main Teaching*
11.2	The Spirit of the Lord brings wisdom, understanding, knowledge, and the fear of God.
32.15	The Spirit of the Lord brings blessings.
34.16	The Spirit of the Lord carries out God's Word.
40.13	The Spirit of the Lord is the Master Counselor.
42.1	The Messiah, God's Servant, will be given the Spirit.
44.3–5	Through the Spirit, God's true children will thrive.
48.16	The Spirit of the Lord sent Isaiah to prophesy.
61.1	God's servants (Isaiah and then Jesus) were anointed by the Spirit to proclaim the Good News.
63.10, 11	The Spirit of the Lord was grieved because of God's people.
63.14	The Spirit of the Lord gives rest.

63.15–64.7 The faithful remnant asks God for two favors: to show compassion to them and to punish their enemies. Before making these requests, these people recited the Lord's past favors, reminding him of his compassion in former days (63.7–14).

64.1-6 God's glory is so intense it is like a consuming fire that burns everything in its path. If we are so impure, how can we be saved? Only by God's mercy. If God were to meet us today, his glory would overwhelm us.

and the fire causes water to boil—
to make your name known to your adversaries,
so that the nations might tremble at your presence!
3 When you did awesome deeds that we did not expect,
you came down, the mountains quaked at your presence.
4 From ages past no one has heard,
no ear has perceived,
no eye has seen any God besides you,
who works for those who wait for him.
5 You meet those who gladly do right,
those who remember you in your ways.
But you were angry, and we sinned;
because you hid yourself we transgressed.[g]
6 We have all become like one who is unclean,
and all our righteous deeds are like a filthy cloth.
We all fade like a leaf,
and our iniquities, like the wind, take us away.
7 There is no one who calls on your name,
or attempts to take hold of you;
for you have hidden your face from us,
and have delivered[h] us into the hand of our iniquity.
8 Yet, O LORD, you are our Father;
we are the clay, and you are our potter;
we are all the work of your hand.
9 Do not be exceedingly angry, O LORD,
and do not remember iniquity forever.
Now consider, we are all your people.
10 Your holy cities have become a wilderness,
Zion has become a wilderness,
Jerusalem a desolation.
11 Our holy and beautiful house,
where our ancestors praised you,
has been burned by fire,
and all our pleasant places have become ruins.
12 After all this, will you restrain yourself, O LORD?
Will you keep silent, and punish us so severely?

The righteousness of God's judgment

65 I was ready to be sought out by those who did not ask,
to be found by those who did not seek me.
I said, "Here I am, here I am,"
to a nation that did not call on my name.
2 I held out my hands all day long
to a rebellious people,
who walk in a way that is not good,
following their own devices;

64.2 Ps 99.1
64.3 Ps 65.5
64.4 Isa 40.31 1 Cor 2.9
64.6 Ps 90.5,6 Isa 1.30; 48.1
64.7 Deut 31.18 Isa 1.15
64.8 Ps 100.3 Isa 45.9
64.9 Ps 79.13 Mic 7.18
64.11 Ps 74.5-7
64.12 Ps 83.1
65.1 Hos 1.10
65.2 Ps 81.11,12 Rom 10.21

[g] Meaning of Heb uncertain [h] Gk Syr Old Latin Tg: Heb *melted*

64.6 Sin makes us unclean so that we cannot approach God (6.5; Romans 3.23) any more than a beggar in rotten rags could dine at a king's table. Our best efforts are still infected with sin. Our only hope, therefore, is faith in Jesus Christ, who can cleanse us and bring us into God's presence (read Romans 3).

This passage can easily be misunderstood. It doesn't mean God will reject us if we come to him in faith, nor that he despises our efforts to please him. It means that if we come to him demanding acceptance on the basis of our "good" conduct, God will point out that our goodness is nothing compared to his infinite goodness. This message is primarily for the unrepentant, not the true follower of God.

65.1 Israel considered itself to be the only people of God, but the time would come when other nations would seek him. Paul mentions Isaiah's statement in Romans 10.20 and points out that these other nations were the Gentiles. God's people today are those who accept Jesus as Savior and Lord, whether they are Jews or Gentiles. The gospel is for every person. Do not ignore or reject anyone when you share the gospel. You may be surprised at how many are sincerely searching for God.

65.3 Job 2.5

3 a people who provoke me
to my face continually,
sacrificing in gardens
and offering incense on bricks;

65.4 Lev 11.7

4 who sit inside tombs,
and spend the night in secret places;
who eat swine's flesh,
with broth of abominable things in their vessels;

65.5 Mt 9.11

5 who say, "Keep to yourself,
do not come near me, for I am too holy for you."
These are a smoke in my nostrils,
a fire that burns all day long.

65.6 Ps 50.3,21 Isa 42.14

6 See, it is written before me:
I will not keep silent, but I will repay;
I will indeed repay into their laps

65.7 Jer 13.25 Ezek 20.27,28 Hos 2.13

7 their[i] iniquities and their[i] ancestors' iniquities together,
says the LORD;
because they offered incense on the mountains
and reviled me on the hills,
I will measure into their laps
full payment for their actions.

8 Thus says the LORD:
As the wine is found in the cluster,
and they say, "Do not destroy it,
for there is a blessing in it,"
so I will do for my servants' sake,
and not destroy them all.

65.9 Amos 9.11-15

9 I will bring forth descendants[j] from Jacob,
and from Judah inheritors[k] of my mountains;
my chosen shall inherit it,
and my servants shall settle there.

65.10 Josh 7.24 Isa 33.9

10 Sharon shall become a pasture for flocks,
and the Valley of Achor a place for herds to lie down,
for my people who have sought me.

65.11 Isa 1.4,28

11 But you who forsake the LORD,
who forget my holy mountain,
who set a table for Fortune
and fill cups of mixed wine for Destiny;

65.12 2 Chron 36.15, 16 Prov 1.24

12 I will destine you to the sword,
and all of you shall bow down to the slaughter;
because, when I called, you did not answer,
when I spoke, you did not listen,
but you did what was evil in my sight,
and chose what I did not delight in.

65.13 Isa 5.13

13 Therefore thus says the Lord GOD:
My servants shall eat,
but you shall be hungry;

[i] Gk Syr: Heb *your* [j] Or *a descendant* [k] Or *an inheritor*

65.3–5 God said these people directly disobeyed his laws when they worshiped idols (Exodus 20.1–6), consulted the dead and evil spirits (Leviticus 19.31), and ate forbidden foods (Leviticus 11). But they were so perverse that they still thought they were holier than others. Jesus called such people hypocrites (Matthew 23.13–36).

65.6 God said he would repay the people for their sins. Judgment is not our job but his, because he alone is just. Who else knows our hearts and minds? Who else knows what is a completely fair reward or punishment?

65.8, 9 God will always preserve a faithful remnant of his people. No matter how bad the world is, there are always a few who remain loyal to him. Jesus made this point in Matthew 13.36–43.

65.10 The Plains of Sharon are in the western part of Israel. The Valley of Achor is in the east near Jericho. The Valley of Achor was also called the Valley of Calamity because Achan was executed there for hiding forbidden spoils of battle (Joshua 7.10–26). Even in this valley there will be peace: the coming restoration will be complete.

my servants shall drink,
but you shall be thirsty;
my servants shall rejoice,
but you shall be put to shame;
14 my servants shall sing for gladness of heart,
but you shall cry out for pain of heart,
and shall wail for anguish of spirit.
15 You shall leave your name to my chosen to use as a curse,
and the Lord GOD will put you to death;
but to his servants he will give a different name.
16 Then whoever invokes a blessing in the land
shall bless by the God of faithfulness,
and whoever takes an oath in the land
shall swear by the God of faithfulness;
because the former troubles are forgotten
and are hidden from my sight.

The new heavens and new earth

17 For I am about to create new heavens
and a new earth;
the former things shall not be remembered
or come to mind.
18 But be glad and rejoice forever
in what I am creating;
for I am about to create Jerusalem as a joy,
and its people as a delight.
19 I will rejoice in Jerusalem,
and delight in my people;
no more shall the sound of weeping be heard in it,
or the cry of distress.
20 No more shall there be in it
an infant that lives but a few days,
or an old person who does not live out a lifetime;
for one who dies at a hundred years will be considered a youth,
and one who falls short of a hundred will be considered accursed.
21 They shall build houses and inhabit them;
they shall plant vineyards and eat their fruit.
22 They shall not build and another inhabit;
they shall not plant and another eat;
for like the days of a tree shall the days of my people be,
and my chosen shall long enjoy the work of their hands.
23 They shall not labor in vain,
or bear children for calamity;[l]
for they shall be offspring blessed by the LORD—
and their descendants as well.
24 Before they call I will answer,
while they are yet speaking I will hear.
25 The wolf and the lamb shall feed together,
the lion shall eat straw like the ox;
but the serpent—its food shall be dust!

65.14 Mt 8.12 Lk 13.28
65.15 Jer 24.9
65.16 Isa 45.23
65.17 2 Pet 3.13
65.18 Ps 98 Isa 35.10
65.19 Jer 32.41
65.20 Eccles 8.12,13
65.21 Deut 32.46,47 Ps 92.12-14 Amos 9.14
65.23 Isa 61.9
65.24 Ps 91.15 Dan 10.12
65.25 Gen 3.14 Isa 11.6,9

[l] Or *sudden terror*

65.17–25 In 65.17–19 we have a pictorial description of the new heaven and the new earth. They are eternal, and in them safety, peace, and plenty will be available to all (see also 66.22, 23; 2 Peter 3.13; Revelation 21.1). Verses 20–25 refer to the reign of Christ on earth because sin and death have not yet been finally destroyed.

They shall not hurt or destroy
on all my holy mountain,
says the LORD.

The world will see God's goodness

66.1 Ps 11.4 Mt 5.34,35 Jn 4.20,21 Acts 7.48-50

66 Thus says the LORD:
Heaven is my throne
and the earth is my footstool;
what is the house that you would build for me,
and what is my resting place?

66.2 Ps 34.18 Lk 18.13,14

2 All these things my hand has made,
and so all these things are mine,[m]
says the LORD.
But this is the one to whom I will look,
to the humble and contrite in spirit,
who trembles at my word.

3 Whoever slaughters an ox is like one who kills a human being;
whoever sacrifices a lamb, like one who breaks a dog's neck;
whoever presents a grain offering, like one who offers swine's blood;[n]
whoever makes a memorial offering of frankincense, like one who
blesses an idol.
These have chosen their own ways,
and in their abominations they take delight;

66.4 Prov 1.31,32 10.24 Jer 7.13,30

4 I also will choose to mock[o] them,
and bring upon them what they fear;
because, when I called, no one answered,
when I spoke, they did not listen;
but they did what was evil in my sight,
and chose what did not please me.

66.5 Ps 38.20 Mt 5.10-12 Jn 9.34

5 Hear the word of the LORD,
you who tremble at his word:
Your own people who hate you
and reject you for my name's sake
have said, "Let the LORD be glorified,
so that we may see your joy";
but it is they who shall be put to shame.

66.6 Joel 3.7

6 Listen, an uproar from the city!
A voice from the temple!
The voice of the LORD,
dealing retribution to his enemies!

7 Before she was in labor
she gave birth;
before her pain came upon her
she delivered a son.

[m] Gk Syr: Heb *these things came to be* [n] Meaning of Heb uncertain [o] Or *to punish*

66.1 Even the beautiful temple in Jerusalem was woefully inadequate for a God who is present everywhere. God cannot be confined to any human structure (see 2 Chronicles 6.18; Acts 7.49, 50). This chapter is a fitting climax to the book. God will lift up the humble, judge all people, destroy the wicked, bring all believers together, and establish a new heaven and a new earth.

66.2, 3 These key verses summarize Isaiah's message. He contrasted two ways of living: that of humble persons who have a profound reverence for God's messages and their application to life, and that of those who choose their own way of living. These sacrifices were only external compliance. In their hearts they were murderers, perverts, and idolaters. God shows mercy to the humble, but he curses the proud and self-sufficient (see Luke 1.51–53). Our society urges us to be assertive and to affirm ourselves. Don't let your freedom and right to choose lead you away from God's pathway to eternal life.

66.7–9 God will not leave his work of national restoration unfinished. In this image of birth, God shows that he will accomplish what he has promised. It is as unstoppable as the birth of a baby. When all the pain is over, the joy begins.

8 Who has heard of such a thing?
Who has seen such things?
Shall a land be born in one day?
Shall a nation be delivered in one moment?
Yet as soon as Zion was in labor
she delivered her children.
9 Shall I open the womb and not deliver?
says the LORD;
shall I, the one who delivers, shut the womb?
says your God.

10 Rejoice with Jerusalem, and be glad for her,
all you who love her;
rejoice with her in joy,
all you who mourn over her—
11 that you may nurse and be satisfied
from her consoling breast;
that you may drink deeply with delight
from her glorious bosom.

12 For thus says the LORD:
I will extend prosperity to her like a river,
and the wealth of the nations like an overflowing stream;
and you shall nurse and be carried on her arm,
and dandled on her knees.
13 As a mother comforts her child,
so I will comfort you;
you shall be comforted in Jerusalem.
14 You shall see, and your heart shall rejoice;
your bodies[p] shall flourish like the grass;
and it shall be known that the hand of the LORD is with his servants,
and his indignation is against his enemies.
15 For the LORD will come in fire,
and his chariots like the whirlwind,
to pay back his anger in fury,
and his rebuke in flames of fire.
16 For by fire will the LORD execute judgment,
and by his sword, on all flesh;
and those slain by the LORD shall be many.

17 Those who sanctify and purify themselves to go into the gardens, following
the one in the center, eating the flesh of pigs, vermin, and rodents, shall come to an
end together, says the LORD.

18 For I know[q] their works and their thoughts, and I am[r] coming to gather all
nations and tongues; and they shall come and shall see my glory, 19 and I will set a
sign among them. From them I will send survivors to the nations, to Tarshish,
Put,[s] and Lud—which draw the bow—to Tubal and Javan, to the coastlands far
away that have not heard of my fame or seen my glory; and they shall declare my
glory among the nations. 20 They shall bring all your kindred from all the nations
as an offering to the LORD, on horses, and in chariots, and in litters, and on mules,
and on dromedaries, to my holy mountain Jerusalem, says the LORD, just as the

66.9 Isa 37.3
66.10 Ps 122.6; Rom 15.10
66.12 Isa 48.18; 60.5
66.14 Prov 3.8; Zech 10.7
66.16 Ezek 38.22
66.17 Lev 11.7
66.19 1 Chron 16.24; Isa 42.12
66.20 Isa 2.2; 43.5,6; 49.22; 52.11; 60.4

p Heb *bones* q Gk Syr: Heb lacks *know* r Gk Syr Vg Tg: Heb *it is* s Gk: Heb *Pul*

66.15–17 This is a vivid picture of the great judgment that will come at Christ's second coming (2 Thessalonians 1.7–9).

66.19 God's people will go out as missionaries to all parts of the earth—to Spain (Tarshish), the Lybians in northern Africa (Put), the Lydians in western Asia Minor (Lud), northeastern Asia Minor (Tubal), and to Greece (Javan).

66.21 Isa 61.6 1 Pet 2.5,9

Israelites bring a grain offering in a clean vessel to the house of the LORD. 21 And I
will also take some of them as priests and as Levites, says the LORD.

66.22 Jn 10.27-29 2 Pet 3.13

22 For as the new heavens and the new earth,
which I will make,
shall remain before me, says the LORD;
so shall your descendants and your name remain.

66.23 Isa. 27.13

23 From new moon to new moon,
and from sabbath to sabbath,
all flesh shall come to worship before me,
says the LORD.

66.24 Isa,1.31 Dan 12.2

24 And they shall go out and look at the dead bodies of the people who have
rebelled against me; for their worm shall not die, their fire shall not be quenched,
and they shall be an abhorrence to all flesh.

66.22–24 Isaiah brings his book to a close with great drama. For the faithless there is a sobering portrayal of judgment. For the faithful, there is a glorious picture of rich reward – "so shall your descendants and your name remain." The contrast is so striking that it would seem that everyone would want to be God's follower. But we are often just as foolish and reluctant to change as the Israelites were. We are just as negligent in feeding the poor, working for justice, and obeying God's Word. Make sure you are among those who will be richly blessed.

JEREMIAH

Zephaniah becomes a prophet 640 B.C.	Jeremiah becomes a prophet 627	Habakkuk becomes a prophet 612	King Josiah killed in battle 609	Daniel/ Ezekiel taken captive 605	Ezekiel begins to prophesy in Babylon 593

VITAL STATISTICS

PURPOSE:
To urge God's people to turn from their sins and back to God

AUTHOR:
Jeremiah

TO WHOM WRITTEN:
Judah (the southern kingdom) and its capital city, Jerusalem

DATE WRITTEN:
During Jeremiah's ministry, approximately 627–586 B.C.

SETTING:
Jeremiah ministered under Judah's last five kings—Josiah, Jehoahaz, Jehoiakim, Jehoiachin, and Zedekiah. The nation was sliding quickly toward destruction and was eventually conquered by Babylon in 586 B.C. (see 2 Kings 21—25). The prophet Zephaniah preceded Jeremiah, and Habakkuk was his contemporary.

KEY VERSE:
"Your wickedness will punish you, and your apostasies will convict you. Know and see that it is evil and bitter for you to forsake the Lord your God; the fear of me is not in you, says the Lord God of hosts" (2.19).

KEY PEOPLE:
Judah's kings (listed above), Baruch, Ebed-melech, King Nebuchadnezzar, the Rechabites

KEY PLACES:
Anathoth, Jerusalem, Ramah, Egypt

SPECIAL FEATURES:
This book is a combination of history, poetry, and biography. Jeremiah often used symbolism to communicate his message.

WHAT is success? Most definitions include references to achieving goals and acquiring wealth, prestige, favor, and power. "Successful" people enjoy the good life—being financially and emotionally secure, being surrounded by admirers, and enjoying the fruits of their labors. They are leaders, opinion makers, trendsetters. Their example is emulated; their accomplishments are noticed. They know who they are and where they are going, and they stride confidently to meet their goals.

By these standards, Jeremiah was a miserable failure. For 40 years he served as God's spokesman to Judah; but when Jeremiah spoke, nobody listened. Consistently and passionately he urged them to act, but nobody moved. And he certainly did not attain material success. He was poor and underwent severe deprivation to deliver his prophecies. He was thrown into prison (chapter 37) and into a well (chapter 38), and he was taken to Egypt against his will (chapter 43). He was rejected by his neighbors (11.19–21), his family (12.6), the false priests and prophets (20.1, 2), friends (20.10), his audience (26.8), and the kings (36.23). Throughout his life, Jeremiah stood alone, declaring God's messages of doom, announcing the new covenant, and weeping over the fate of his beloved country. In the eyes of the world, Jeremiah was not a success.

But in God's eyes, Jeremiah was one of the most successful people in all of history. Success, as measured by God, involves obedience and faithfulness. Regardless of opposition and personal cost, Jeremiah courageously and faithfully proclaimed the word of God. He was obedient to his calling. Jeremiah's book begins with his call to be a prophet. The next 38 chapters are prophecies about Israel (the nation united) and Judah (the southern kingdom). Chapters 2—20 are general and undated, and chapters 21—39 are particular and dated. The basic theme of Jeremiah's message is simple: "Repent and turn to God or he will punish." But then, because the people reject this warning, Jeremiah moves to predicting specifically the destruction of Jerusalem. This terrible event is described in chapter 39. Chapters 40—44 describe events following Jerusalem's fall. The book concludes with prophecies concerning a variety of nations (chapters 45—52).

As you read Jeremiah, feel with him as he agonizes over the message he must deliver, pray with him for those who refuse to respond to the truth, and watch his example of faith and courage. Then commit yourself to being successful in God's eyes.

Judah falls; Jerusalem destroyed; Jeremiah's ministry ends
586

First exiles return to Judah
537

THE BLUEPRINT

A. GOD'S JUDGMENT ON JUDAH (1.1—45.5) 1. God calls Jeremiah 2. Jeremiah condemns Judah for her sins 3. Jeremiah prophesies destruction 4. Jeremiah accuses Judah's leaders 5. Restoration is promised 6. God's promised judgment arrives	Jeremiah confronts many people with their sins: kings, false prophets, those at the temples, and those at the gates. A lack of response made Jeremiah wonder if he was doing any good at all. He often felt discouraged and sometimes bitter. To bring such gloomy messages to these people was a hard task. We too have a responsibility to bring this news to a fallen world: those who continue in their sinful ways are eternally doomed. Although we may feel discouraged at the lack of response, we must press on to tell others about the consequences of sin and the hope that God offers. Those who tell people only what they want to hear are being unfaithful to God's message.
B. GOD'S JUDGMENT ON THE NATIONS (46.1—52.34) 1. Prophecies about foreign nations 2. Details about the fall of Jerusalem	Jeremiah lived to see many of his prophecies come true—most notably the fall of Jerusalem. The fulfillment of this and other prophecies against the foreign nations came as a result of sin. Those who refuse to confess their sin bring judgment upon themselves.

MEGATHEMES

THEME	EXPLANATION	IMPORTANCE
Sin	King Josiah's reformation failed because the people's repentance was shallow. They continued in their selfishness and worship of idols. All the leaders rejected God's law and will for the people. Jeremiah lists all their sins, predicts God's judgment, and begs for repentance.	Judah's deterioration and disaster came from their callous disregard and disobedience of God. When we ignore sin and refuse to listen to God's warning, we invite disaster. Don't settle for half measures in removing sin.
Punishment	Because of sin, Jerusalem was destroyed, the temple was ruined, and the people were captured and carried off to Babylon. The people were responsible for their destruction and captivity because they refused to listen to God's message.	Unconfessed sin brings God's full punishment. It is useless to blame anyone else for our sin—we are accountable to God before anyone else. We must answer to him for how we live.
God is Lord of all	God is the righteous Creator. He is accountable to no one but himself. He wisely and lovingly directs all creation to fulfill his plans, and he brings events to pass according to his timetable. He is Lord over all the world.	Because of God's majestic power and love, our only duty is to submit to his authority. By following his plans, not our own, we can have a loving relationship with him and serve him with our whole hearts.
New hearts	Jeremiah predicted that after the destruction of the nation, God would send a new shepherd, the Messiah. He would lead them into a new future, a new covenant, and a new day of hope. He would accomplish this by changing their sinful hearts into hearts of love for God.	God still restores his people by renewing their hearts. His love can transform the problems created by sin. We can have assurance of a new heart by loving God, trusting Christ to save us, and repenting of our sin.
Faithful service	Jeremiah served God faithfully for 40 years. During that time the people ignored, rejected, and persecuted him. Jeremiah's preaching was unsuccessful by human standards, yet he did not fail in his task. He remained faithful to God.	People's acceptance or rejection of us is not the measure of our success. God's approval alone should be our standard for service. We must bring God's message to others even when we are rejected. We must do God's work even if it means suffering for it.

A. GOD'S JUDGMENT ON JUDAH (1.1 – 45.5)

Jeremiah was called by God to be a prophet to Judah (the southern kingdom). He faithfully confronted the leaders and the people with their sin, prophesied both their 70-year captivity in Babylon and their eventual return from exile. After surviving the fall of Jerusalem, Jeremiah was forcefully taken to Egypt. Yet Jeremiah remained faithful in spite of Jerusalem's destruction. Years of obedience had made him strong and courageous. May we be able to stand through difficult times as did Jeremiah.

1. God calls Jeremiah

1 The words of Jeremiah son of Hilkiah, of the priests who were in Anathoth in
the land of Benjamin, 2 to whom the word of the LORD came in the days of
King Josiah son of Amon of Judah, in the thirteenth year of his reign. 3 It came also
in the days of King Jehoiakim son of Josiah of Judah, and until the end of the
eleventh year of King Zedekiah son of Josiah of Judah, until the captivity of Jerusalem in the fifth month.
4 Now the word of the LORD came to me saying,
5 "Before I formed you in the womb I knew you,
and before you were born I consecrated you;
I appointed you a prophet to the nations."
6 Then I said, "Ah, Lord GOD! Truly I do not know how to speak, for I am only a
boy." 7 But the LORD said to me,
"Do not say, 'I am only a boy';
for you shall go to all to whom I send you,
and you shall speak whatever I command you,
8 Do not be afraid of them,

1.1 1 Kgs 13.2; 2 Kgs 21.24; 2 Chron 36.12; Ezra 1.1; Jer 3.6; 36.2; Dan 9.2
1.3 2 Kgs 23.34; Jer 25.1; 39.2
1.5 Ps 139.15,16; Isa 49.1,5; Jer 25.15-26
1.6 Ex 4.10
1.7 Ezek 2.3,4
1.8 Ezek 2.6

Climate of the times	• Society was deteriorating economically, politically, spiritually. • Wars and captivity. • God's Word was outlawed.	**JEREMIAH** served as a prophet to Judah from 627 B.C. until the exile in 586 B.C.
Main message	Repentance from sin would postpone Judah's coming judgment at the hands of Babylon.	
Importance of message	Repentance is one of the greatest needs in our immoral world. God's promises to the faithful shine brightly by bringing hope for tomorrow and strength for today.	
Contemporary prophets	Habakkuk (612–589) Zephaniah (640–621)	

1.1, 2 After King Solomon's death, the united kingdom of Israel had split into rival northern and southern kingdoms. The northern kingdom was called Israel; the southern, Judah. Jeremiah was from Anathoth, four miles north of Jerusalem. He lived and prophesied during the reigns of the last five kings of Judah. This was a chaotic time politically, morally, and spiritually. As Babylon, Egypt, and Assyria battled for world supremacy, Judah found herself caught in the middle of the triangle. Although Jeremiah prophesied for 40 years, he never saw his people heed his words and turn from their sins.

1.2, 3 God spoke many times to Jeremiah over many years, but Jeremiah's job was to determine what God wanted him to do each day. So it is with us – God has given us his Word with many messages. As we search the Scriptures, we must keep asking, "What do you want me to do for you *today?*"

1.5 God knew you, as he knew Jeremiah, long before you were born or even conceived. He thought about you and planned for you. When you feel discouraged or inadequate, remember that God has always thought of you as valuable and has had a purpose in mind for you.

1.5 Each Christian has a purpose in life, but some are appointed by God for a specific kind of work. Samson (Judges 13.3–5), David (Psalm 139.13), John the Baptist (Luke 1.13–17), and Paul (Galatians 1.15, 16) were each called to do a particular job for God. Whatever work you do should be done for the glory of God. If God gives you a specific task, accept it cheerfully and do it with diligence. If God has not given you a specific assignment, then seek to fulfill the mission common to all believers – to love, obey, and serve God – until such time as his guidance becomes more clear.

1.6–8 Often people struggle with new challenges because they lack self-confidence. They feel they have inadequate ability, training, or experience. Jeremiah thought he was too young and inexperienced to be God's spokesman to the world. But God promised to be with him. We should not allow feelings of inadequacy to keep us from obeying God's call. He will *always* be with us. When you find yourself avoiding something you know you should do, be careful not to use lack of self-confidence as an excuse. If God gives you a job to do, he will provide all you need to do it.

1.7–10 God's message to Jeremiah was like his message to Moses: the God who made our mouths can provide the words he wants us to speak (Exodus 3.10 – 4.12).

1.8 God promised to see Jeremiah through trouble, not to keep trouble from coming. God did not insulate him from jailings, deportation, or insults. God does not keep us from encountering life's storms, but he will see us through them. In fact, he walks through these storms with us.

for I am with you to deliver you,
says the LORD."

1.9 Ex 4.11-16; Deut 18.18

9 Then the LORD put out his hand and touched my mouth; and the LORD said to me,
"Now I have put my words in your mouth.

1.10 Isa 44.26-28; Jer 24.6; 31.28

10 See, today I appoint you over nations and over kingdoms,
to pluck up and to pull down,
to destroy and to overthrow,
to build and to plant."

1.11 Jer 24.3; Amos 7.8

11 The word of the LORD came to me, saying, "Jeremiah, what do you see?"

JEREMIAH

Endurance is not a common quality. Many people lack the long-term commitment, care, and willingness that are vital to sticking with a task despite all odds. But Jeremiah was a prophet who endured.

Jeremiah's call by God teaches how intimately God knows us. He valued us before anyone else knew we would exist. He cared for us while we were in our mother's womb. He planned our lives while our bodies were still being formed. He values us more highly than we value ourselves.

Jeremiah had to depend on God's love as he developed endurance. His audiences were usually antagonistic or apathetic to his messages. He was ignored; his life was often threatened. He saw both the excitement of a spiritual awakening and the sorrow of a national return to idolatry. With the exception of the good King Josiah, Jeremiah watched king after king ignore his warnings and lead the people away from God. He saw fellow prophets murdered. He himself was severely persecuted. Finally, he watched Judah's defeat at the hands of the Babylonians.

Jeremiah responded to all this with God's Word and human tears. He felt firsthand God's love for his people and the people's rejection of that love. But even when he was angry with God and tempted to give up, Jeremiah knew he had to keep going. God had called him to endure. He expressed intense feelings, but he also saw beyond the feelings to the God who was soon to execute justice, but who afterward would administer mercy.

It may be easy for us to identify with Jeremiah's frustrations and discouragement, but we need to realize that this prophet's life is also an encouragement to faithfulness.

Strengths and accomplishments:

- Wrote two Old Testament books, Jeremiah and Lamentations
- Ministered during the reigns of the last five kings of Judah
- Was a catalyst for the great spiritual reformation under King Josiah
- Acted as God's faithful messenger in spite of many attempts on his life
- Was so deeply sorrowful for the fallen condition of Israel that he earned the title "weeping prophet"

Lessons from his life:

- The majority opinion is not necessarily God's will
- Although punishment for sin is severe, there is hope in God's mercy
- God will not accept empty or insincere worship
- Serving God does not guarantee earthly security

Vital statistics:

- Where: Anathoth
- Occupation: Prophet
- Relatives: Father: Hilkiah
- Contemporaries: Josiah, Jehoahaz, Jehoiakim, Jehoiachin, Zedekiah, Baruch

Key verses:

"Then I said, 'Ah, Lord God! Truly I do not know how to speak, for I am only a boy.' But the Lord said to me, 'Do not say, "I am only a boy"; for you shall go to all to whom I send you, and you shall speak whatever I command you, Do not be afraid of them, for I am with you to deliver you,' says the Lord" (Jeremiah 1.6–8).

Jeremiah's story is told in the book of Jeremiah. He is also mentioned in Ezra 1.1; Daniel 9.2; Matthew 2.17; 16.14; 27.9. See also 2 Chronicles 34; 35 for the story of the spiritual revival under Josiah.

1.10 Jeremiah's work was to warn not only the Jews, but all the nations of the world about God's judgment on sin. Don't forget in reading the Old Testament that, while God was consistently working through the people of Judah and Israel, his plan was to communicate to every nation and person. We are included in Jeremiah's message of judgment and hope, and as believers, we are to share God's desire to reach the whole world for him.

1.11–14 The vision of the almond branch reveals the beginning of God's judgment because the almond tree is among the first to blossom in the spring. God sees the sins of Judah and the nations, and he will carry out swift and certain judgment. The boiling pot tipping and spilling over Judah is Babylon delivering God's scalding judgment against Jeremiah's people.

And I said, "I see a branch of an almond tree."[a] 12 Then the LORD said to me, "You
have seen well, for I am watching[b] over my word to perform it." 13 The word of the
LORD came to me a second time, saying, "What do you see?" And I said, "I see a
boiling pot, tilted away from the north."
14 Then the LORD said to me: Out of the north disaster shall break out on all the
inhabitants of the land. 15 For now I am calling all the tribes of the kingdoms of the
north, says the LORD; and they shall come and all of them shall set their thrones at
the entrance of the gates of Jerusalem, against all its surrounding walls and against
all the cities of Judah. 16 And I will utter my judgments against them, for all their
wickedness in forsaking me; they have made offerings to other gods, and worshiped the works of their own hands. 17 But you, gird up your loins; stand up and
tell them everything that I command you. Do not break down before them, or I will
break you before them. 18 And I for my part have made you today a fortified city,
an iron pillar, and a bronze wall, against the whole land—against the kings of
Judah, its princes, its priests, and the people of the land. 19 They will fight against
you; but they shall not prevail against you, for I am with you, says the LORD, to
deliver you.

1.12 Deut 32.35
1.13 Zech 4.2
1.14 Isa 41.25 Jer 4.6; 10.22
1.15 Isa 22.7 Jer 25.9
1.16 Isa 2.8; 37.19 Jer 7.9; 10.3-5 19.4
1.17 Ezek 3.16-18
1.19 Jer 20.11

2. Jeremiah condemns Judah for her sins

Israel turns away from God

2 The word of the LORD came to me, saying: 2 Go and proclaim in the hearing of
Jerusalem, Thus says the LORD:

I remember the devotion of your youth,
your love as a bride,
how you followed me in the wilderness,
in a land not sown.
3 Israel was holy to the LORD,
the first fruits of his harvest.
All who ate of it were held guilty;
disaster came upon them,
says the LORD.

4 Hear the word of the LORD, O house of Jacob, and all the families of the house
of Israel. 5 Thus says the LORD:

What wrong did your ancestors find in me

2.2 Isa 58.1 Ezek 16.8
2.3 Ex 19.5,6 Deut 7.6; 14.2 Isa 41.11 Jer 30.16
2.4 2 Kgs 17.15 Mic 6.3

[a] Heb *shaqed* [b] Heb *shoqed*

1.14–19 The problems we face may not seem as ominous as Jeremiah's problems, but they are critical to us and may overwhelm us! God's promise to Jeremiah and to us is that nothing will defeat us completely; he will help us through the most agonizing problems. Face each day with the assurance that God will be with you and see you through.

1.16 The people of Judah sinned greatly by continuing to worship idols. God had commanded them specifically against this (Exodus 20.3–6) because idolatry places trust in the creation rather than the Creator. Although they belonged to God, they chose to follow false gods. Many "idols" entice us to turn away from God. Material possessions, dreams for the future, approval of others, and vocational goals compete for our total commitment. Striving after these at the expense of our commitment to God puts our heart where Judah's was—and God severely punished Judah.

1.17 To "gird up your loins" means to get ready or prepare yourself.

2.1–3.5 In this section, the marriage analogy sharply contrasts God's love for his people with their love for other gods and reveals Judah's faithlessness. Jeremiah condemns Judah (sometimes called Jerusalem for its capital city) for seeking security in changeable things rather than the unchangeable God. We may be tempted to seek security from possessions, people, or our own abilities, but these will fail us. There is no lasting security apart from the eternal God.

2.2 We appreciate a friend who remains true to his commitment, and we are disappointed with someone who fails to keep a promise. God was pleased when his people obeyed initially, but he became angry with them when they refused to keep their commitment. Temptations distract us from God. Think about your original commitment to obey God, and ask yourself if you are remaining true.

2.3 The first fruits, or the first part of the harvest, were set aside for God (Deuteronomy 26.1–11). That's how Israel was dedicated to him in years gone by. Then Israel had been as eager to please God as if she were his young bride—a holy, committed people. This contrasted greatly with the situation in Jeremiah's time.

2.4–8 Jeremiah knew Israel's history well (the united nation of Israel included both Israel and Judah). The prophets recited history to the people for several reasons: (1) to remind them of God's faithfulness; (2) to make sure the people wouldn't forget (they didn't have Bibles to read); (3) to emphasize God's love for them; and (4) to remind them that there was a time when they *were* close to God. We should learn from history so we can build on the successes and avoid repeating the failures of others.

that they went far from me,
and went after worthless things, and became worthless themselves?
2.6 Deut 8.15; 32.10
6 They did not say, "Where is the LORD
who brought us up from the land of Egypt,
who led us in the wilderness,
in a land of deserts and pits,
in a land of drought and deep darkness,
in a land that no one passes through,
where no one lives?"
2.7 Deut 8.7-9 11.10-12 Jer 3.2; 16.18
7 I brought you into a plentiful land
to eat its fruits and its good things.
But when you entered you defiled my land,
and made my heritage an abomination.
2.8 Jer 10.21; 23.13 Hab 2.18 Mal 2.6,7
8 The priests did not say, "Where is the LORD?"
Those who handle the law did not know me;
the rulers[c] transgressed against me;
the prophets prophesied by Baal,
and went after things that do not profit.

9 Therefore once more I accuse you,
says the LORD,
and I accuse your children's children.
2.10 Ps 106.20 120.5 Isa 23.12; 37.19 Jer 16.20; 49.28 Rom 1.23
10 Cross to the coasts of Cyprus and look,
send to Kedar and examine with care;
see if there has ever been such a thing.
11 Has a nation changed its gods,
even though they are no gods?
But my people have changed their glory
for something that does not profit.
12 Be appalled, O heavens, at this,
be shocked, be utterly desolate,
says the LORD,

[c] Heb *shepherds*

THE KINGS OF JEREMIAH'S LIFETIME

King	*Story of his reign*	*Dates of his reign*	*Character of reign*	*Jeremiah's message to the King*
Josiah	2 Kings 22.1—23.30	640–609 B.C.	Mostly good	3.6–25
Jehoahaz (Shallum)	2 Kings 23.31–33	609 B.C.	Evil	22.11—17
Jehoiakim	2 Kings 23.34—24.7	609–598 B.C.	Evil	22.18–23; 25.1–38; 26.1–24; 27.1–11; 35.1–19; 36.1–32
Jehoiachin (Coniah)	2 Kings 24.8–17	598–597 B.C.	Evil	13.18–27 22.24–30
Zedekiah	2 Kings 24.18—25.26	597–586 B.C.	Evil	21.1–14; 24.8–10; 27.12–22; 32.1–5; 34.1–22; 37.1–21; 38.1–28; 51.59–64

2.8 Baal was the chief male god of the Canaanite religion. He was the god of agriculture. Worship of Baal included animal sacrifice and sacred prostitution (male and female) in the high places. Jezebel, wife of King Ahab, introduced Baal worship into the northern kingdom, and eventually it spread to Judah. The sexual orientation of this worship was a constant temptation to the Israelites, who were called to be holy.

2.9 God's love persists, even when we don't deserve it. Why? God knows how much we will lose if we fail to respond to his love. Eternity is a long, long time without him. Respond to his plea; give yourself wholeheartedly to God.

2.10 God was saying that even pagan nations like Cyprus (in the west) and Kedar (an Arab tribe living in the desert east of Palestine) remained loyal to their national gods. But Israel had abandoned the one and only God for a completely useless object of worship.

13 for my people have committed two evils:
they have forsaken me,
the fountain of living water,
and dug out cisterns for themselves,
cracked cisterns
that can hold no water.

2.13
Ps 36.9
Jer 17.13
Jn 4.14

14 Is Israel a slave? Is he a homeborn servant?
Why then has he become plunder?
15 The lions have roared against him,
they have roared loudly.
They have made his land a waste;
his cities are in ruins, without inhabitant.
16 Moreover, the people of Memphis and Tahpanhes
have broken the crown of your head.
17 Have you not brought this upon yourself
by forsaking the LORD your God,
while he led you in the way?
18 What then do you gain by going to Egypt,
to drink the waters of the Nile?
Or what do you gain by going to Assyria,
to drink the waters of the Euphrates?
19 Your wickedness will punish you,
and your apostasies will convict you.
Know and see that it is evil and bitter
for you to forsake the LORD your God;
the fear of me is not in you,
says the Lord GOD of hosts.

2.15
Jer 4.7

2.16
Jer 44.1
Hos 9.6

2.17
Deut 32.10
Jer 4.18

2.19
Ps 36.1
Isa 3.9
Jer 3.8; 5.24
Hos 11.7
Amos 8.10

20 For long ago you broke your yoke
and burst your bonds,
and you said, "I will not serve!"
On every high hill
and under every green tree
you sprawled and played the whore.
21 Yet I planted you as a choice vine,
from the purest stock.
How then did you turn degenerate
and become a wild vine?
22 Though you wash yourself with lye
and use much soap,
the stain of your guilt is still before me,
says the Lord GOD.
23 How can you say, "I am not defiled,

2.20
Deut 12.2
Isa 57.5
Jer 32.6; 17.2

2.21
Ex 15.17
Ps 80.8
Isa 5.2,4

2.22
Jer 4.14

2.23
Prov 30.12
Jer 7.31

2.13 Who would set aside a sparkling fountain of water for a cistern, a pit that collected rain water? God told the Israelites that was what they were doing when they turned from him, the fountain of living waters, to idols. Not only that, the cisterns they chose were broken and empty. The people had built religious systems to store truth in, but they were worthless. Why should we cling to the broken promises of unstable "cisterns" (money, power, religious systems, or whatever transitory thing we are putting in place of God), when God promises to constantly refresh us with himself, the living water?

2.16, 17 Memphis was near Cairo in lower Egypt, and Tahpanhes was in northeastern Egypt. Jeremiah could be speaking of Pharaoh Shishak's previous invasion of Judah in 925 B.C., or he may have been predicting Pharaoh Neco's invasion in 607 B.C. when King Josiah of Judah would be killed (2 Kings 23.29, 30). His point is that the people brought this on themselves by rebelling against God.

2.22 The stain of sin is more than skin deep. Israel had stains that could not be washed out, even with the strongest cleansers. Spiritual cleansing must reach deep into the heart – and this is a job that God alone can do. We cannot ignore the effects of sin and hope they will go away. Your sin has caused a deep stain that God can and will remove if you are willing to let him cleanse you (Isaiah 1.18).

2.23–27 The people are compared to animals who search for mates in mating season. Unrestrained, they rush for power, money, alliances with foreign powers, and other gods. The idols did not seek the people; the people sought the idols and then ran wildly

I have not gone after the Baals"?
Look at your way in the valley;
know what you have done—
a restive young camel interlacing her tracks,
24 a wild ass at home in the wilderness,
in her heat sniffing the wind!
Who can restrain her lust?
None who seek her need weary themselves;
in her month they will find her.

2.25 Deut 32.16 Jer 18.12

25 Keep your feet from going unshod
and your throat from thirst.
But you said, "It is hopeless,
for I have loved strangers,
and after them I will go."

2.26 Isa 26.16

26 As a thief is shamed when caught,
so the house of Israel shall be shamed—
they, their kings, their officials,
their priests, and their prophets,
27 who say to a tree, "You are my father,"
and to a stone, "You gave me birth."
For they have turned their backs to me,
and not their faces.
But in the time of their trouble they say,
"Come and save us!"

2.28 Deut 32.37 2 Kgs 17.30,31 Isa 45.20 Jer 11.12,13

28 But where are your gods
that you made for yourself?
Let them come, if they can save you,
in your time of trouble;
for you have as many gods
as you have towns, O Judah.

2.29 Dan 9.11

29 Why do you complain against me?
You have all rebelled against me,
says the LORD.

2.30 Neh 9.26 Isa 1.5 Jer 5.3; 7.28 26.20-24

30 In vain I have struck down your children;
they accepted no correction.
Your own sword devoured your prophets
like a ravening lion.

2.31 Deut 32.15

31 And you, O generation, behold the word of the LORD![d]
Have I been a wilderness to Israel,
or a land of thick darkness?
Why then do my people say, "We are free,
we will come to you no more"?

2.32 Isa 17.10 Jer 3.21 Hos 8.14

32 Can a girl forget her ornaments,
or a bride her attire?
Yet my people have forgotten me,
days without number.

[d] Meaning of Heb uncertain

---

after them. Then they became so comfortable in their sin that they could not think of giving it up. Their only shame was in getting caught. If we desire something so much that we'll do anything to get it, this is a sign that we are addicted to it and out of tune with God.

2.30 Being a prophet in those days was risky business. Prophets had to criticize the policies of evil kings, and this made them appear to be traitors. The kings hated the prophets for standing against their policies, and the people often hated them for preaching against their idolatrous life-styles. (See Acts 7.52.)

2.31, 32 Forgetting can be dangerous, whether it is intentional or an oversight. Israel forgot God by focusing its affections on the allurements of the world. The more we focus on the pleasures of the world, the easier it becomes to forget God's care, his love, his dependability, his guidance, and most of all, God himself. What pleases you most? Have you been forgetting God lately?

33 How well you direct your course
to seek lovers!
So that even to wicked women
you have taught your ways.
34 Also on your skirts is found
the lifeblood of the innocent poor,
though you did not catch them breaking in.
Yet in spite of all these things[e]
35 you say, "I am innocent;
surely his anger has turned from me."
Now I am bringing you to judgment
for saying, "I have not sinned."
36 How lightly you gad about,
changing your ways!
You shall be put to shame by Egypt
as you were put to shame by Assyria.
37 From there also you will come away
with your hands on your head;
for the LORD has rejected those in whom you trust,
and you will not prosper through them.

2.34 2 Kgs 21.16 Jer 7.6; 19.4

2.35 Jer 25.31

2.36 2 Chron 28.16, 20,21

2.37 Jer 37.7-10

3

If[f] a man divorces his wife
and she goes from him
and becomes another man's wife,
will he return to her?
Would not such a land be greatly polluted?
You have played the whore with many lovers;
and would you return to me?
says the LORD.
2 Look up to the bare heights,[g] and see!
Where have you not been lain with?
By the waysides you have sat waiting for lovers,
like a nomad in the wilderness.
You have polluted the land
with your whoring and wickedness.
3 Therefore the showers have been withheld,
and the spring rain has not come;
yet you have the forehead of a whore,
you refuse to be ashamed.
4 Have you not just now called to me,

3.1 Deut 24.4 Ezek 16.26, 28,29

3.2 Deut 12.2 Jer 2.7,20 Ezek 16.25

3.3 Jer 6.15; 14.3-6

[e] Meaning of Heb uncertain [f] Q Ms Gk Syr: MT *Saying, If* [g] Or *the trails*

2.36 "Gad about" means to flit or run around. God is not against alliances or working partnerships, but he is against people trusting others for the help that should come from him. This was the problem in Jeremiah's time. After the days of David and Solomon, Israel fell apart because the leaders turned to other nations and gods instead of the true God. They played power politics, thinking that their strong neighbors could protect them. But Judah would soon learn that its alliance with Egypt would be just as disappointing as its former alliance with Assyria (Isaiah 7.13–25).

3.1 This law, found in Deuteronomy 24.1–4, says that a divorced woman who remarries can never be reunited with her first husband. Judah "divorced" God and "married" other gods. God had every right to permanently disown his wayward people, but in his mercy he was willing to take them back again.

3.2 "Like a nomad in the wilderness" means like an Arab thief hiding and waiting to plunder a passing caravan, so did Judah run to idolatry. It was a national preoccupation.

3.2, 3 The words *polluted, whoring,* and *wickedness* reveal a serious problem that had gradually spread until it affected everything. In this situation, even nature had been affected with a drought, which God permitted to bring the people to their senses. Sin brings drastic consequences once it gains a foothold in our lives. Lies lead to more lies and hatred to more hatred. Jeremiah reminded his people repeatedly that sin must not go on unchecked.

3.3 "You have the forehead of a whore" means that Judah had the hardened or brazen look of a prostitute, without shame.

3.4, 5 In spite of their great sin, the people of Israel continued to talk like they were God's children. The only way they could do this was to minimize their sin. When we know we've done something wrong, we want to downplay the error and relieve some of the guilt we feel. As we minimize our sinfulness, we naturally shy away from making changes, and so we keep on sinning. But if we view every wrong attitude and action as a serious offense against God, we will begin to understand what living for God is all about. Is there any

"My Father, you are the friend of my youth—
5 will he be angry forever,
will he be indignant to the end?"
This is how you have spoken,
but you have done all the evil that you could.

Israel is like a faithless wife

3.6 Jer 17.2 Ezek 23.4-10

6 The LORD said to me in the days of King Josiah: Have you seen what she did,
that faithless one, Israel, how she went up on every high hill and under every green
tree, and played the whore there? 7 And I thought, "After she has done all this she

3.8 Isa 50.1 Ezek 16.46,47 23.11

will return to me"; but she did not return, and her false sister Judah saw it. 8 She[h]
saw that for all the adulteries of that faithless one, Israel, I had sent her away with
a decree of divorce; yet her false sister Judah did not fear, but she too went and

3.9 Isa 57.6 Jer 2.7,27

played the whore. 9 Because she took her whoredom so lightly, she polluted the
land, committing adultery with stone and tree. 10 Yet for all this her false sister

3.10 Jer 12.2

Judah did not return to me with her whole heart, but only in pretense, says the
LORD.

3.11 Ezek 16.51

11 Then the LORD said to me: Faithless Israel has shown herself less guilty than

3.12 Ps 86.15 Jer 31.20; 33.26

false Judah. 12 Go, and proclaim these words toward the north, and say:
Return, faithless Israel,
says the LORD.
I will not look on you in anger,
for I am merciful,
says the LORD;
I will not be angry forever.

3.13 Deut 12.2 30.1-3 Jer 14.20

13 Only acknowledge your guilt,
that you have rebelled against the LORD your God,
and scattered your favors among strangers under every green tree,
and have not obeyed my voice,
says the LORD.

3.14 Jer 50.4,5 Hos 2.19

14 Return, O faithless children,
says the LORD,
for I am your master;
I will take you, one from a city and two from a family,
and I will bring you to Zion.

3.15 Jer 23.4 Acts 20.28

3.16 Isa 65.17

15 I will give you shepherds after my own heart, who will feed you with knowledge and understanding. 16 And when you have multiplied and increased in the

[h] Q Ms Gk Mss Syr: MT *I*

sin in your life that you've written off as too small to worry about? God says that we must confess and turn away from *every* sin.

3.6–6.30 The northern kingdom, Israel, had fallen to Assyria, and its people had been taken into captivity. The tragic lesson of their fall should have caused the southern kingdom, Judah, to return to God, but Judah paid no attention. Jeremiah urged Judah to return to God to avoid disaster. This message came between 627 and 621 B.C., during Josiah's reign. Although Josiah obeyed God's commands, his example apparently did not influence the people. If the people didn't repent, God said he would destroy the nation because of the evils of King Manasseh (2 Kings 23.25–27).

3.11–13 Israel was not even trying to look as if it were obeying God, but Judah maintained the appearance of right faith without a true heart. Believing the right doctrines without heart-commitment is like offering sacrifices without true repentance. Judah's false repentance brought Jeremiah's words of condemnation. Being sorry for sin is not enough. Repentance demands a change of mind and heart, which results in changed behavior.

3.12–18 The northern kingdom, Israel, was in captivity, being punished for its sins. The people of Judah looked down on these northern neighbors for their blatant heresy and degraded morals. Even so, Jeremiah promised the remnant of Israel God's blessings if they would turn to him. Judah, still secure, should have turned to God after seeing the destruction of Israel. But the people of Judah refused, so Jeremiah startled them by telling them about God's promise to Israel's remnant if they would repent.

3.15 God promised to give his people leaders ("shepherds") who would follow him, filled with knowledge (wisdom) and understanding. God saw Israel's lack of direction, so he promised to provide the right kind of leadership. We look to and trust our leaders for guidance and direction. But if they do not follow God, they will lead us astray. Pray for God-honoring leaders in our nations, communities, and churches.

3.16, 17 In the days of David and Solomon's reign over a united Israel, the people had a beautiful temple where they worshiped God. The temple housed the ark of the covenant, the symbol of God's presence with the people. The ark held the tablets of the ten commandments (see Exodus 25.10–22). Those days with the ark wouldn't be missed in the future kingdom because God's presence by the Holy Spirit would be there among his people.

land, in those days, says the LORD, they shall no longer say, "The ark of the covenant of the LORD." It shall not come to mind, or be remembered, or missed; nor
shall another one be made. 17 At that time Jerusalem shall be called the throne of the
LORD, and all nations shall gather to it, to the presence of the LORD in Jerusalem,
and they shall no longer stubbornly follow their own evil will. 18 In those days the
house of Judah shall join the house of Israel, and together they shall come from the
land of the north to the land that I gave your ancestors for a heritage.

3.17 Jer 12.15,16 16.19; 17.12 Ezek 43.7
3.18 Isa 60.9 Jer 16.14,15 31.8; 50.4,5 Hos 1.11

19 I thought
how I would set you among my children,
and give you a pleasant land,
the most beautiful heritage of all the nations.
And I thought you would call me, My Father,
and would not turn from following me.
20 Instead, as a faithless wife leaves her husband,
so you have been faithless to me, O house of Israel,
says the LORD.

3.19 Isa 63.16

21 A voice on the bare heights[i] is heard,
the plaintive weeping of Israel's children,
because they have perverted their way,
they have forgotten the LORD their God:
22 Return, O faithless children,
I will heal your faithlessness.

3.21 Isa 15.2 Jer 2.32
3.22 Hos 6.1; 14.4

"Here we come to you;
for you are the LORD our God.
23 Truly the hills are[j] a delusion,
the orgies on the mountains.
Truly in the LORD our God
is the salvation of Israel.

3.23 Ps 3.8; 121.1,2 Jer 17.14

24 "But from our youth the shameful thing has devoured all for which our ancestors had labored, their flocks and their herds, their sons and their daughters.
25 Let us lie down in our shame, and let our dishonor cover us; for we have sinned
against the LORD our God, we and our ancestors, from our youth even to this day;
and we have not obeyed the voice of the LORD our God."

3.25 Jer 22.21 Ezra 9.7

4

If you return, O Israel,
says the LORD,
if you return to me,
if you remove your abominations from my presence,
and do not waver,
2 and if you swear, "As the LORD lives!"
in truth, in justice, and in uprightness,
then nations shall be blessed[k] by him,
and by him they shall boast.

4.1 Jer 7.3,7; 35.15 Joel 2.12
4.2 Deut 10.20 Isa 65.16 Jer 9.24 1 Cor 1.31

3 For thus says the LORD to the people of Judah and to the inhabitants of Jerusalem:

4.3 Hos 10.12 Mt 13.7,22

[i] Or *the trails* [j] Gk Syr Vg: Heb *Truly from the hills is* [k] Or *shall bless themselves*

3.22–25 Jeremiah predicted a day when the nation would be reunited, true worship would be reinstated, and sin would be seen for what it is. Our world glorifies the thrill that comes from wealth, competition, and sexual pleasure, and it ignores the sin that is so often associated with these thrills. Most people can't see this until they are destroyed by the sin they pursue. The advantage of believing God's Word is that we don't have to learn by hard experience the destructive results of sin.

4.3, 4 Jeremiah told the people to break up the hardness of their hearts as a plow breaks up fallow ground—soil that has not been tilled for a season. Good kings like Josiah had tried to turn the people back to God, but the people had continued to worship their idols in secret. Their hearts had become hardened to God's Word. Jeremiah said the people needed to remove the sin that hardened their hearts before the good seed of God's Word could take root.

Break up your fallow ground,
and do not sow among thorns.
4.4 Deut 10.16 Isa 30.27 Jer 9.25,26 Mk 9.43,48 Rom 2.28,29
4 Circumcise yourselves to the LORD,
remove the foreskin of your hearts,
O people of Judah and inhabitants of Jerusalem,
or else my wrath will go forth like fire,
and burn with no one to quench it,
because of the evil of your doings.

Destruction rolls over the land

4.5 Josh 10.20 Jer 6.1
5 Declare in Judah, and proclaim in Jerusalem, and say:
Blow the trumpet through the land;
shout aloud[l] and say,
"Gather together, and let us go
into the fortified cities!"
4.6 Jer 1.14,15 6.1,22
6 Raise a standard toward Zion,
flee for safety, do not delay,
for I am bringing evil from the north,
and a great destruction.
4.7 Isa 1.7; 6.11 Jer 2.15; 5.6 25.9,38
7 A lion has gone up from its thicket,
a destroyer of nations has set out;
he has gone out from his place
to make your land a waste;
your cities will be ruins
without inhabitant.
4.8 Isa 5.25; 10.4 Jer 6.26
8 Because of this put on sackcloth,
lament and wail:
"The fierce anger of the LORD
has not turned away from us."

4.9 Jer 48.41
9 On that day, says the LORD, courage shall fail the king and the officials; the priests
shall be appalled and the prophets astounded. 10 Then I said, "Ah, Lord GOD, how
utterly you have deceived this people and Jerusalem, saying, 'It shall be well with
you,' even while the sword is at the throat!"

11 At that time it will be said to this people and to Jerusalem: A hot wind comes
from me out of the bare heights[m] in the desert toward my poor people, not to winnow or cleanse— 12 a wind too strong for that. Now it is I who speak in judgment
against them.

4.13 Isa 66.15 Lam 4.19
13 Look! He comes up like clouds,
his chariots like the whirlwind;
his horses are swifter than eagles—
woe to us, for we are ruined!
4.14 Isa 1.16 Jer 13.27
14 O Jerusalem, wash your heart clean of wickedness
so that you may be saved.
How long shall your evil schemes
lodge within you?
15 For a voice declares from Dan

[l] Or *shout, take your weapons*: Heb *shout, fill* (your hand) [m] Or *the trails*

Likewise we must remove our heart-hardening sin if we expect God's Word to take root and grow in our lives.

4.6, 7 The destruction from the north would come from Babylon when Nabopolasser and Nebuchadnezzar II attacked (see 2 Chronicles 36).

4.10 Jeremiah, moved by God's words, expressed his deep sorrow to God. Jeremiah was intercessor for the people. They had false expectations because of the past promises of blessings, their blindness to their own sin, and the false prophets who kept telling them that all was well.

4.15 Doom was announced first from Dan and Mount Ephraim because they were located at the northern border of Israel and thus would be the first to see the approaching armies as they invaded from the north. No one would be able to stop the armies because they came as punishment for the people's sin.

and proclaims disaster from Mount Ephraim.
16 Tell the nations, "Here they are!"
Proclaim against Jerusalem,
"Besiegers come from a distant land;
they shout against the cities of Judah.
17 They have closed in around her like watchers of a field,
because she has rebelled against me,
says the LORD.
18 Your ways and your doings
have brought this upon you.
This is your doom; how bitter it is!
It has reached your very heart."

19 My anguish, my anguish! I writhe in pain!
Oh, the walls of my heart!
My heart is beating wildly;
I cannot keep silent;
for I[n] hear the sound of the trumpet,
the alarm of war.
20 Disaster overtakes disaster,
the whole land is laid waste.
Suddenly my tents are destroyed,
my curtains in a moment.
21 How long must I see the standard,
and hear the sound of the trumpet?
22 "For my people are foolish,
they do not know me;
they are stupid children,
they have no understanding.
They are skilled in doing evil,
but do not know how to do good."

23 I looked on the earth, and lo, it was waste and void;
and to the heavens, and they had no light.
24 I looked on the mountains, and lo, they were quaking,
and all the hills moved to and fro.
25 I looked, and lo, there was no one at all,
and all the birds of the air had fled.
26 I looked, and lo, the fruitful land was a desert,
and all its cities were laid in ruins
before the LORD, before his fierce anger.

27 For thus says the LORD: The whole land shall be a desolation; yet I will not
make a full end.
28 Because of this the earth shall mourn,
and the heavens above grow black;
for I have spoken, I have purposed;
I have not relented nor will I turn back.

n Another reading is *for you, O my soul,*

4.16 Ezek 21.22

4.17 2 Kgs 25.1

4.19 Isa 21.3; 22.4

4.20 Jer 10.20 Ezek 7.26

4.22 Jer 5.21; 10.8 13.23 Rom 16.19

4.23 Isa 24.19

4.24 Isa 5.25 Ezek 38.20

4.25 Jer 9.10; 12.4 Zeph 1.3

4.27 Jer 5.10,18 12.11,12 30.11; 46.28

4.28 Num 23.19 Isa 5.30; 50.3 Jer 23.20; 30.24 Hos 4.3 Joel 2.30,31

4.19–31 Jeremiah was overcome by the sure devastation of the coming judgment. This judgment would continue until the people turned from their sin and listened to God. Although this prophecy refers to the future destruction by Babylon, it could also describe the judgment of all sinners at the end of the world.

4.22 Judah was talented at doing wrong and lacked the will and ability to do what was right. Right living is more than simply avoiding sin. It requires decision and discipline. We must develop skills in right living because our behavior attracts attention to our God. We should pursue excellence in Christian living with as much effort as we pursue excellence at work.

4.27 God warned that destruction was certain, but he promised that the faithful remnant would be spared. God is committed to preserving those who are faithful to him.

4.29 Isa 2.19-21 Jer 16.16

29 At the noise of horseman and archer
every town takes to flight;
they enter thickets; they climb among rocks;
all the towns are forsaken,
and no one lives in them.

4.30 2 Kgs 9.30 Jer 22.20,22 Ezek 23.9,10,22

30 And you, O desolate one,
what do you mean that you dress in crimson,
that you deck yourself with ornaments of gold,
that you enlarge your eyes with paint?
In vain you beautify yourself.
Your lovers despise you;
they seek your life.

4.31 Jer 13.21 Lam 1.17

31 For I heard a cry as of a woman in labor,
anguish as of one bringing forth her first child,
the cry of daughter Zion gasping for breath,
stretching out her hands,
"Woe is me! I am fainting before killers!"

No respect for God

5.1 Gen 18.26,32 2 Chron 16.9

5 Run to and fro through the streets of Jerusalem,
look around and take note!
Search its squares and see
if you can find one person
who acts justly
and seeks truth—
so that I may pardon Jerusalem.[o]

5.2 Tit 1.16

2 Although they say, "As the LORD lives,"
yet they swear falsely.

5.3 Jer 7.26,28 8.5; 19.15 Ezek 3.8

3 O LORD, do your eyes not look for truth?
You have struck them,
but they felt no anguish;
you have consumed them,
but they refused to take correction.
They have made their faces harder than rock;
they have refused to turn back.

5.4 Isa 27.11 Jer 4.22 Hos 4.6

4 Then I said, "These are only the poor,
they have no sense;
for they do not know the way of the LORD,
the law of their God.

5.5 Jer 2.20 Mic 3.1

5 Let me go to the rich[p]
and speak to them;
surely they know the way of the LORD,
the law of their God."
But they all alike had broken the yoke,
they had burst the bonds.

[o] Heb *it* [p] Or *the great*

5.1 Jerusalem was the capital city and center of worship for Judah, but God told Jeremiah there might not be *one* fair and honest person in the entire city. God was willing to spare the city if one such person could be found (he made a similar statement about Sodom; see Genesis 18.32). Think how significant your testimony may be in your city or community. You may represent the only witness for God to many people. Are you faithful to that opportunity?

5.3 Nothing but truth is acceptable to God. When we pray, sing, speak, or serve, nothing closes the door of God's acceptance more than hypocrisy, lying, or pretense. God sees through us and refuses to listen. To be close to God, be honest with him.

5.4, 5 Even those who knew God's laws and understood his words of judgment had rejected him. They were supposed to teach and guide the people but instead they led them into sin. Jeremiah observed the poor and ignorant—those who were uninformed of God's ways—and realized they were not learning God's laws from their teachers (the "rich"or "great"). Thus God's search in Jerusalem was complete. There were no true followers in any level of society.

6 Therefore a lion from the forest shall kill them,
a wolf from the desert shall destroy them.
A leopard is watching against their cities;
everyone who goes out of them shall be torn in pieces—
because their transgressions are many,
their apostasies are great.

5.6 Jer 30.14,15 Hos 13.7 Hab 1.8

7 How can I pardon you?
Your children have forsaken me,
and have sworn by those who are no gods.
When I fed them to the full,
they committed adultery
and trooped to the houses of prostitutes.
8 They were well-fed lusty stallions,
each neighing for his neighbor's wife.
9 Shall I not punish them for these things?
says the LORD;
and shall I not bring retribution
on a nation such as this?

5.7 Deut 32.21 Jer 2.11 Gal 4.8

5.8 Jer 29.23 Ezek 22.11

10 Go up through her vine-rows and destroy,
but do not make a full end;
strip away her branches,
for they are not the LORD's.
11 For the house of Israel and the house of Judah
have been utterly faithless to me,
says the LORD.
12 They have spoken falsely of the LORD,
and have said, "He will do nothing.
No evil will come upon us,
and we shall not see sword or famine."
13 The prophets are nothing but wind,
for the word is not in them.
Thus shall it be done to them!

5.10 Jer 4.27

5.11 Jer 3.6,7

5.12 2 Chron 36.16 Jer 43.1-4

5.13 Jer 14.13,15

14 Therefore thus says the LORD, the God of hosts:
Because they[q] have spoken this word,
I am now making my words in your mouth a fire,
and this people wood, and the fire shall devour them.
15 I am going to bring upon you
a nation from far away, O house of Israel,
says the LORD.
It is an enduring nation,
it is an ancient nation,
a nation whose language you do not know,
nor can you understand what they say.
16 Their quiver is like an open tomb;

5.14 Jer 23.29

5.15 Deut 28.49 Isa 5.26; 28.11

5.16 Isa 5.28; 13.18

[q] Heb *you*

5.7 God held these people responsible for the sins of their children because the children had followed their parents' example. The sin of leading others, especially our children, astray by our example is one for which God will hold us accountable.

5.12, 13 The people refused God's message by saying: (1) that it could never come true, (2) that the prophets did not really have authority, and (3) that the punishments would fall on others. This refusal was not because the prophets failed to do their job but because the people failed to listen. The prophet and his people both have responsibilities—the prophet to proclaim God's message faithfully, and the people to apply it to their lives.

5.15 Babylon was indeed an ancient nation. The old Babylonian Empire lasted from about 1900 B.C. to 1550 B.C., and earlier kingdoms had been on her soil as early as 3000 B.C. Babylon in Jeremiah's day would shortly rebel against Assyrian domination, form its own army, conquer Assyria, and become the next dominant world power.

all of them are mighty warriors.
5.17 Lev 26.16 Deut 28.31,33 Jer 8.16 Hos 8.14
17 They shall eat up your harvest and your food;
they shall eat up your sons and your daughters;
they shall eat up your flocks and your herds;
they shall eat up your vines and your fig trees;
they shall destroy with the sword
your fortified cities in which you trust.

18 But even in those days, says the LORD, I will not make a full end of you.
5.19 Deut 29.24-26 28.48 1 Kgs 9.8,9 Jer 16.10-13
19 And when your people say, "Why has the LORD our God done all these things to
us?" you shall say to them, "As you have forsaken me and served foreign gods in
your land, so you shall serve strangers in a land that is not yours."

20 Declare this in the house of Jacob,
proclaim it in Judah:
5.21 Isa 43.8 Ezek 12.2 Mt 13.14
21 Hear this, O foolish and senseless people,
who have eyes, but do not see,
who have ears, but do not hear.
5.22 Deut 28.58 Job 38.8-11 Jer 10.7
22 Do you not fear me? says the LORD;
Do you not tremble before me?
I placed the sand as a boundary for the sea,
a perpetual barrier that it cannot pass;
though the waves toss, they cannot prevail,
though they roar, they cannot pass over it.
5.23 Gen 8.22 Ps 78.8; 147.8 Joel 2.23 Mt 5.45
23 But this people has a stubborn and rebellious heart;
they have turned aside and gone away.
24 They do not say in their hearts,
"Let us fear the LORD our God,
who gives the rain in its season,
the autumn rain and the spring rain,
and keeps for us
the weeks appointed for the harvest."
5.25 Jer 2.17; 4.18
25 Your iniquities have turned these away,
and your sins have deprived you of good.
5.26 Ps 10.9 Jer 18.22
26 For scoundrels are found among my people;
they take over the goods of others.
Like fowlers they set a trap;[r]
they catch human beings.
27 Like a cage full of birds,
their houses are full of treachery;
therefore they have become great and rich,
5.28 Deut 32.15 Isa 1.23 Jer 7.6; 22.3 Zech 7.10
28 they have grown fat and sleek.
They know no limits in deeds of wickedness;
they do not judge with justice
the cause of the orphan, to make it prosper,
and they do not defend the rights of the needy.

[r] Meaning of Heb uncertain

5.21 Have you spoken to someone, only to realize that the person hasn't heard a word you were saying? Jeremiah told the people that their eyes and ears did them no good because they refused to see or hear God's message. The people of Judah and Israel were foolishly deaf when God promised blessings for obedience and destruction for disobedience. When God speaks through his Word or his messengers, we harm ourselves if we fail to listen. God's message will never change us unless we listen to it.

5.22–24 What is your attitude when you come into God's presence? We should come with awe and respect, for God sets the boundaries of the roaring seas and establishes the rains and harvests. God had to strip away all the benefits that Judah and Israel had grown to respect more than him. Without those benefits, the people would turn back to God. Don't wait until God removes your cherished resources before thinking of him as you should.

5.28, 29 People and nations who please God give justice to orphans and care for the needy. Wicked men in Israel treated the defenseless unjustly, which displeased God greatly. Some defenseless people—orphans, the poor, the lonely—are within your reach. What action can you take to help at least one of them?

29 Shall I not punish them for these things?
says the LORD,
and shall I not bring retribution
on a nation such as this?

30 An appalling and horrible thing
has happened in the land:
31 the prophets prophesy falsely,
and the priests rule as the prophets direct;[s]
my people love to have it so,
but what will you do when the end comes?

5.30 Jer 23.14 Hos 6.10
5.31 Jer 14.14 Mic 2.11

Jerusalem's last warning

6 Flee for safety, O children of Benjamin,
from the midst of Jerusalem!
Blow the trumpet in Tekoa,
and raise a signal on Beth-haccherem;
for evil looms out of the north,
and great destruction.
2 I have likened daughter Zion
to the loveliest pasture.[t]
3 Shepherds with their flocks shall come against her.
They shall pitch their tents around her;
they shall pasture, all in their places.
4 "Prepare war against her;
up, and let us attack at noon!"
"Woe to us, for the day declines,
the shadows of evening lengthen!"
5 "Up, and let us attack by night,
and destroy her palaces!"
6 For thus says the LORD of hosts:
Cut down her trees;
cast up a siege ramp against Jerusalem.
This is the city that must be punished;[u]
there is nothing but oppression within her.
7 As a well keeps its water fresh,
so she keeps fresh her wickedness;
violence and destruction are heard within her;
sickness and wounds are ever before me.
8 Take warning, O Jerusalem,
or I shall turn from you in disgust,
and make you a desolation,
an uninhabited land.

9 Thus says the LORD of hosts:
Glean[v] thoroughly as a vine

6.1 Jer 1.14; 4.6
6.2 Deut 28.56
6.3 2 Kgs 25.1 Jer 4.17 Lk 19.43
6.5 Isa 32.14 Jer 52.13
6.6 Deut 20.19,20
6.7 Jer 30.12,13 Ezek 7.11,23 Jas 3.10-12
6.8 Jer 7.28; 17.23 Hos 9.12
6.9 Jer 8.3; 16.16 49.9 Obad 5,6

[s] Or *rule by their own authority* [t] Or *I will destroy daughter Zion, the loveliest pasture* [u] Or *the city of license*
[v] Cn: Heb *They shall glean*

5.31 At this time, the religious climate was chaotic. The priests, God's ministers, were leading by their own authority, not by the truth of God's Word. Many prophets were telling lies and half-truths, not messages from God. The people had turned from truth (God's Word) and heard only what they wanted to hear. No wonder Jeremiah's words had little effect.

6.1 Jeremiah warned his own tribe of Benjamin to flee, not to the security of the great walled city of Jerusalem (for it would be under siege), but to Tekoa, a town about 12 miles south of Jerusalem. The warning smoke signal was lit at Beth-haccherem, halfway between Jerusalem and Bethlehem.

6.3 The shepherds were the leaders of Babylon's armies, and their flocks were their troops.

6.9 The remnant mentioned here is not to be confused with the righteous remnant. This remnant is those left after the first wave of destruction. Like a grape-gatherer, Babylon wouldn't be satisfied until every person was taken. Babylonians invaded Judah three times until they destroyed the nation and its temple completely (2 Kings 24; 25).

the remnant of Israel;
like a grape-gatherer, pass your hand again
over its branches.

10 To whom shall I speak and give warning,
that they may hear?
See, their ears are closed,[w]
they cannot listen.
The word of the LORD is to them an object of scorn;
they take no pleasure in it.
11 But I am full of the wrath of the LORD;
I am weary of holding it in.

Pour it out on the children in the street,
and on the gatherings of young men as well;
both husband and wife shall be taken,
the old folk and the very aged.
12 Their houses shall be turned over to others,
their fields and wives together;
for I will stretch out my hand
against the inhabitants of the land,
says the LORD.

13 For from the least to the greatest of them,
everyone is greedy for unjust gain;
and from prophet to priest,
everyone deals falsely.
14 They have treated the wound of my people carelessly,
saying, "Peace, peace,"
when there is no peace.
15 They acted shamefully, they committed abomination;
yet they were not ashamed,
they did not know how to blush.
Therefore they shall fall among those who fall;
at the time that I punish them, they shall be overthrown,
says the LORD.

16 Thus says the LORD:
Stand at the crossroads, and look,
and ask for the ancient paths,
where the good way lies; and walk in it,
and find rest for your souls.
But they said, "We will not walk in it."
17 Also I raised up sentinels for you:
"Give heed to the sound of the trumpet!"
But they said, "We will not give heed."
18 Therefore hear, O nations,
and know, O congregation, what will happen to them.
19 Hear, O earth; I am going to bring disaster on this people,

6.11 Job 32.18,19 Jer 7.20; 9.21 15.6

6.12 Deut 28.30 Jer 8.10; 38.22

6.13 Isa 56.11; 57.17 Jer 22.17 Mic 3.5,11

6.14 Jer 8.11,12 Ezek 13.10

6.15 Jer 3.3; 8.12

6.16 Jer 18.15; 31.21 Mt 11.29

6.17 Isa 21.11; 58.1 Jer 25.4 Ezek 3.17

6.18 Prov 1.31 Isa 1.2 Jer 8.9; 22.29

[w] Heb *are uncircumcised*

6.10 The people became angry and closed their ears. They wanted no part of God's commands because living for God did not appear very exciting. As in Jeremiah's day, people today dislike God's demand for disciplined living. As unsettling as people's responses might be, we must continue to share God's Word. Our responsibility is to present God's Word; their responsibility is to accept it. We must not let what people want to hear determine what we say.

6.14 "Ignore it and maybe it will go away!" Sound familiar? This was Israel's response to Jeremiah's warnings. They kept listening to predictions of peace because they did not like Jeremiah's condemnation of their sin. But denying the truth never changes it; what God says always happens. Sin is never removed by denying its existence. We must confess to God that we have sinned and ask him to forgive us.

the fruit of their schemes,
because they have not given heed to my words;
and as for my teaching, they have rejected it.
20 Of what use to me is frankincense that comes from Sheba,
or sweet cane from a distant land?
Your burnt offerings are not acceptable,
nor are your sacrifices pleasing to me.
21 Therefore thus says the LORD:
See, I am laying before this people
stumbling blocks against which they shall stumble;
parents and children together,
neighbor and friend shall perish.

22 Thus says the LORD:
See, a people is coming from the land of the north,
a great nation is stirring from the farthest parts of the earth.
23 They grasp the bow and the javelin,
they are cruel and have no mercy,
their sound is like the roaring sea;
they ride on horses,
equipped like a warrior for battle,
against you, O daughter Zion!

24 "We have heard news of them,
our hands fall helpless;
anguish has taken hold of us,
pain as of a woman in labor.
25 Do not go out into the field,
or walk on the road;
for the enemy has a sword,
terror is on every side."

26 O my poor people, put on sackcloth,
and roll in ashes;
make mourning as for an only child,
most bitter lamentation:
for suddenly the destroyer
will come upon us.

27 I have made you a tester and a refiner[x] among my people
so that you may know and test their ways.
28 They are all stubbornly rebellious,
going about with slanders;
they are bronze and iron,
all of them act corruptly.
29 The bellows blow fiercely,
the lead is consumed by the fire;
in vain the refining goes on,
for the wicked are not removed.
30 They are called "rejected silver,"
for the LORD has rejected them.

6.20 Ps 40.6; 50.7-9 Isa 1.11; 60.6 66.3 Amos 5.21

6.21 Isa 8.14 9.14-17 Jer 9.21,22

6.22 Jer 1.15; 10.22

6.23 Isa 5.30 Jer 4.29; 50.42

6.24 Isa 28.19 Jer 4.19-21

6.25 Jer 12.12; 14.18

6.26 Jer 4.8 Amos 8.10 Mic 1.10

6.27 Jer 1.18; 15.20

6.28 Ezek 22.18

6.30 Ps 119.119 Isa 1.22

[x] Or *a fortress*

6.29, 30 Metal is purified by fire. As it is heated, impurities are burned away and only the pure metal remains. As God tested the people of Judah, however, he could find no purity in their lives. They continued in their sinful ways. Do you see impurities in your life that should be burned away? Confess these to God and allow him to purify you as he sees fit. Take time right now to reflect on the areas of your life that he has already refined; then thank him for what he is doing.

The people indulge in false worship

7.2 Jer 17.19
7.3 Jer 4.1; 18.11; 26.13
7.4 Mic 3.11
7.5 Isa 1.19; Jer 21.12; 22.3
7.6 Ex 22.21-24; Deut 6.14,15; Jer 5.28; 13.10
7.7 Deut 4.40
7.9 Jer 11.13,17
7.11 Isa 56.7; Jer 29.23; Mt 21.13; Mk 11.17; Lk 19.46
7.12 Josh 18.1,10; Jer 26.6
7.13 1 Kgs 9.7; Jer 4.1,2; 18.11; 26.13
7.15 Deut 6.14,15; 2 Kgs 17.23
7.16 Deut 4.40; Jer 11.14; 15.1
7.18 Deut 32.16; Jer 11.17; 44.17

7 The word that came to Jeremiah from the LORD: 2Stand in the gate of the
LORD's house, and proclaim there this word, and say, Hear the word of the
LORD, all you people of Judah, you that enter these gates to worship the LORD.
3Thus says the LORD of hosts, the God of Israel: Amend your ways and your doings, and let me dwell with you[y] in this place. 4Do not trust in these deceptive
words: "This is[z] the temple of the LORD, the temple of the LORD, the temple of the
LORD."

5 For if you truly amend your ways and your doings, if you truly act justly one
with another, 6if you do not oppress the alien, the orphan, and the widow, or shed
innocent blood in this place, and if you do not go after other gods to your own hurt,
7then I will dwell with you in this place, in the land that I gave of old to your
ancestors forever and ever.

8 Here you are, trusting in deceptive words to no avail. 9Will you steal, murder, commit adultery, swear falsely, make offerings to Baal, and go after other
gods that you have not known, 10and then come and stand before me in this house,
which is called by my name, and say, "We are safe!"—only to go on doing all these
abominations? 11Has this house, which is called by my name, become a den of
robbers in your sight? You know, I too am watching, says the LORD. 12Go now to
my place that was in Shiloh, where I made my name dwell at first, and see what I
did to it for the wickedness of my people Israel. 13And now, because you have done
all these things, says the LORD, and when I spoke to you persistently, you did not
listen, and when I called you, you did not answer, 14therefore I will do to the house
that is called by my name, in which you trust, and to the place that I gave to you and
to your ancestors, just what I did to Shiloh. 15And I will cast you out of my sight,
just as I cast out all your kinsfolk, all the offspring of Ephraim.

16 As for you, do not pray for this people, do not raise a cry or prayer on their
behalf, and do not intercede with me, for I will not hear you. 17Do you not see what
they are doing in the towns of Judah and in the streets of Jerusalem? 18The children
gather wood, the fathers kindle fire, and the women knead dough, to make cakes
for the queen of heaven; and they pour out drink offerings to other gods, to provoke
me to anger. 19Is it I whom they provoke? says the LORD. Is it not themselves, to

[y] *Or and I will let you dwell* [z] Heb *They are*

7.1—10.25 As this section opens, God sends Jeremiah to the temple gates to confront the false belief that God will not let harm come to the temple and those who live near it. Jeremiah rebukes the people for their empty religion, their idolatry, and the shameless behavior of the people and their leaders. Judah, he says, is ripe for judgment and exile. This happened during the reign of Jehoiakim, a puppet of Egypt. The nation, in shock over the death of Josiah, was going through a spiritual reversal that removed much of the good Josiah had done. The themes of this section are false religion, idolatry, and hypocrisy. Jeremiah was almost put to death for this sermon, but he was saved by the princes.

7.2 The temple entrance was the perfect place to confront people about their biggest problem—hypocrisy. The people believed that having the temple in their city would protect them and that their religious ritual would save them. God may let Judah fall, but he would never let his temple be destroyed, they thought. But Jeremiah proclaimed that the temple and its rituals were worthless if the people's hearts were not right with God.

7.8 The people followed a worship ritual but maintained a sinful life-style. It was religion without personal commitment to God. We can easily fall into this snare. Attending church, taking communion, teaching Sunday school, singing in the choir—all are empty exercises unless we are truly doing them for God. It is good to do these activities, not because we ought to do them for the church, but because we want to do them for God.

7.8–11 There are several parallels between how the people of Judah viewed their temple and how many today view their churches. (1) *They didn't take the temple home with them.* We go to beautiful churches well-prepared for worship, but often we don't take the presence of God with us through the week. (2) *The image of the temple became more important than the substance of faith.* The image of going to church and belonging to a group can become more important than a life changed for God. (3) *The people used their temple as a refuge.* Many use religious affiliation as a hideout, thinking it will protect them from evil and problems.

7.11, 12 Jesus used these words in cleansing the temple (Mark 11.17; Luke 19.46). This passage applied to the evil in the temple in his day as well as in Jeremiah's. God's tabernacle had been at Shiloh, but Shiloh had been abandoned (Psalm 78.60; Jeremiah 26.6). If God did not preserve Shiloh because the tabernacle was there, why would he preserve Jerusalem because of the temple?

7.15 Ephraim is another name for Israel, the northern kingdom, which had been taken into captivity by Assyria in 722 B.C.

7.18 The queen of heaven was a name for Ishtar, the Mesopotamian goddess of love and war. After the fall of Jerusalem, the refugees from Judah who fled to Egypt continued to worship her (chapter 44). A papyrus dating from the 5th century B.C., found at Hermopolis in Egypt, mentions the queen of heaven among the gods honored by the Jewish community living there.

7.19 This verse answers the question, Who gets hurt when we turn away from God? We do! Separating ourselves from God is like keeping a green plant away from sunlight or water. God is our only source of spiritual strength. Cut yourself off from him, and you cut off life itself.

their own hurt? 20 Therefore thus says the Lord GOD: My anger and my wrath shall
be poured out on this place, on human beings and animals, on the trees of the field
and the fruit of the ground; it will burn and not be quenched.

21 Thus says the LORD of hosts, the God of Israel: Add your burnt offerings to
your sacrifices, and eat the flesh. 22 For in the day that I brought your ancestors out
of the land of Egypt, I did not speak to them or command them concerning burnt
offerings and sacrifices. 23 But this command I gave them, "Obey my voice, and I
will be your God, and you shall be my people; and walk only in the way that I
command you, so that it may be well with you." 24 Yet they did not obey or incline
their ear, but, in the stubbornness of their evil will, they walked in their own counsels, and looked backward rather than forward. 25 From the day that your ancestors
came out of the land of Egypt until this day, I have persistently sent all my servants
the prophets to them, day after day; 26 yet they did not listen to me, or pay attention,
but they stiffened their necks. They did worse than their ancestors did.

27 So you shall speak all these words to them, but they will not listen to you.
You shall call to them, but they will not answer you. 28 You shall say to them: This
is the nation that did not obey the voice of the LORD their God, and did not accept
discipline; truth has perished; it is cut off from their lips.

29 Cut off your hair and throw it away;
  raise a lamentation on the bare heights,[a]
for the LORD has rejected and forsaken
  the generation that provoked his wrath.

30 For the people of Judah have done evil in my sight, says the LORD; they have
set their abominations in the house that is called by my name, defiling it. 31 And
they go on building the high place[b] of Topheth, which is in the valley of the son of
Hinnom, to burn their sons and their daughters in the fire—which I did not command, nor did it come into my mind. 32 Therefore, the days are surely coming, says
the LORD, when it will no more be called Topheth, or the valley of the son of Hinnom, but the valley of Slaughter: for they will bury in Topheth until there is no
more room. 33 The corpses of this people will be food for the birds of the air, and
for the animals of the earth; and no one will frighten them away. 34 And I will bring
to an end the sound of mirth and gladness, the voice of the bride and bridegroom in
the cities of Judah and in the streets of Jerusalem; for the land shall become a waste.

8 At that time, says the LORD, the bones of the kings of Judah, the bones of its
officials, the bones of the priests, the bones of the prophets, and the bones of
the inhabitants of Jerusalem shall be brought out of their tombs; 2 and they shall be
spread before the sun and the moon and all the host of heaven, which they have
loved and served, which they have followed, and which they have inquired of and
worshiped; and they shall not be gathered or buried; they shall be like dung on the
surface of the ground. 3 Death shall be preferred to life by all the remnant that remains of this evil family in all the places where I have driven them, says the LORD
of hosts.

[a] Or *the trails* [b] Gk Tg: Heb *high places*

7.21 Isa 1.11; Jer 6.20; 14.12; Hos 8.13; Amos 5.21
7.22 1 Sam 15.22; Ps 51.16; Hos 6.6
7.23 Isa 3.10; Jer 11.4; 38.20
7.24 Jer 11.8; Ezek 20.8,13, 16,21
7.26 Jer 16.12; 17.23; Mt 23.32
7.27 Isa 65.12; Jer 26.2
7.28 Jer 11.10
7.29 Isa 15.2; 22.12; Jer 6.30; 14.19
7.30 2 Kgs 21.4; 2 Chron 33.4, 5,7; Jer 32.34
7.31 2 Kgs 16.17; Jer 19.5
7.33 Deut 28.26; Ps 79.2; Jer 12.9
7.34 Isa 1.7; 24.7; Jer 4.27; 16.9; Ezek 26.13; Hos 2.11
8.2 2 Kgs 23.5; Jer 22.19; 36.30; Zeph 1.5; Acts 7.42
8.3 Deut 30.1,4; Job 3.21,22; Jonah 4.3; Rev 9.6

7.21–23 God had set up a system of sacrifices to encourage the people to obey him (see the book of Leviticus). He required the people to make these sacrifices, not because the sacrifices themselves pleased him, but because they caused the people to recognize their sin and refocus on living for God. They faithfully made the sacrifices but forgot the reason they were offering them, and thus they disobeyed God. Jeremiah reminded the people that acting out religious rituals is meaningless unless they were prepared to obey God in all areas of life. (See the chart in Hosea 7.)

7.25 From the time of David to the end of the Old Testament period, God sent many prophets to Israel and Judah. No matter how bad the circumstances, God always had a prophet to speak against their stubborn spiritual attitudes.

7.31 The high place (or altar) of Topheth (meaning "fireplace") was set up in the Hinnom Valley, where debris and rubbish from the city was thrown away. This altar was used to worship Molech—a god who required child sacrifice (2 Kings 23.10). At the place where the people had killed their children in sinful idol worship, they themselves would be slain.

8.1, 2 The threat that the graves of Judah's people would be opened was horrible to a people who highly honored the dead and believed it the highest insult to open graves. This would be an ironic punishment for idol worshipers—their bodies would be laid out before the sun, moon, and stars—the gods they thought could save them.

The people are deceived by false teachers

8.4 Jer 7.24,27; 9.6 Mic 7.8

4 You shall say to them, Thus says the LORD:
When people fall, do they not get up again?
If they go astray, do they not turn back?
5 Why then has this people[c] turned away
in perpetual backsliding?
They have held fast to deceit,
they have refused to return.

8.6 Job 39.21-25 Mal 3.16

6 I have given heed and listened,
but they do not speak honestly;
no one repents of wickedness,
saying, "What have I done!"
All of them turn to their own course,
like a horse plunging headlong into battle.

8.7 Prov 6.6-8 Isa 1.3

7 Even the stork in the heavens
knows its times;
and the turtledove, swallow, and crane[d]
observe the time of their coming;
but my people do not know
the ordinance of the LORD.

8.8 Jer 4.22 Rom 1.22; 2.17

8 How can you say, "We are wise,
and the law of the LORD is with us,"
when, in fact, the false pen of the scribes
has made it into a lie?

8.9 Jer 6.15 1 Cor 1.27

9 The wise shall be put to shame,
they shall be dismayed and taken;
since they have rejected the word of the LORD,
what wisdom is in them?

8.10 Deut 28.30 Isa 56.11 Jer 6.12,13

10 Therefore I will give their wives to others
and their fields to conquerors,
because from the least to the greatest
everyone is greedy for unjust gain;
from prophet to priest
everyone deals falsely.

8.11 Jer 6.14 14.13,14 Lam 2.14 Ezek 13.10

11 They have treated the wound of my people carelessly,
saying, "Peace, peace,"
when there is no peace.

8.12 Deut 32.35 Isa 3.9; 9.14 Jer 6.15 Zeph 3.5

12 They acted shamefully, they committed abomination;
yet they were not at all ashamed,
they did not know how to blush.
Therefore they shall fall among those who fall;
at the time when I punish them, they shall be overthrown,
says the LORD.

8.13 Mt 21.19

13 When I wanted to gather them, says the LORD,
there are[e] no grapes on the vine,
nor figs on the fig tree;
even the leaves are withered,

[c] One Ms Gk: MT *this people, Jerusalem,* [d] Meaning of Heb uncertain [e] Or *I will make an end of them, says the* LORD. *There are*

8.4–6 When people fall or realize that they are headed in the wrong direction, it only makes sense for them to get up or change directions. But as God watched the nation, he saw people living sinful lives by choice, deceiving themselves that there would be no consequences. They had lost perspective concerning God's will for their lives and were trying to minimize their sin. Are there some indicators that you have fallen or are heading the wrong way? What are you doing to get back on the right path?

8.8–11 The scribes, prophets, and priests were giving false assurances rather than correction. How can we correct a fault or turn from a sin if our leaders tell us all is well? Beware of people who are always agreeable. At best, they give you no help; at worst, they may be trying to manipulate you.

and what I gave them has passed away from them.[f]

14 Why do we sit still?
Gather together, let us go into the fortified cities
and perish there;
for the LORD our God has doomed us to perish,
and has given us poisoned water to drink,
because we have sinned against the LORD.
15 We look for peace, but find no good,
for a time of healing, but there is terror instead.

16 The snorting of their horses is heard from Dan;
at the sound of the neighing of their stallions
the whole land quakes.
They come and devour the land and all that fills it,
the city and those who live in it.
17 See, I am letting snakes loose among you,
adders that cannot be charmed,
and they shall bite you,
says the LORD.

Jeremiah weeps for the people

18 My joy is gone, grief is upon me,
my heart is sick.
19 Hark, the cry of my poor people
from far and wide in the land:
"Is the LORD not in Zion?
Is her King not in her?"
("Why have they provoked me to anger with their images,
with their foreign idols?")
20 "The harvest is past, the summer is ended,
and we are not saved."
21 For the hurt of my poor people I am hurt,
I mourn, and dismay has taken hold of me.

22 Is there no balm in Gilead?
Is there no physician there?
Why then has the health of my poor people
not been restored?

9 [g] O that my head were a spring of water,
and my eyes a fountain of tears,
so that I might weep day and night
for the slain of my poor people!
2 [h] O that I had in the desert
a traveler's lodging place,

8.14 Deut 29.18 Ps 69.21 Jer 3.25; 4.5 9.15; 14.20
8.15 Jer 14.19
8.19 Deut 32.21 Ps 31.6 Isa 13.4,5 Jer 9.16
8.21 Jer 4.19; 9.1 14.17
8.22 Gen 37.25 Jer 30.13; 46.11
9.1 Jer 8.18; 13.17

[f] Meaning of Heb uncertain [g] Ch 8.23 in Heb [h] Ch 9.1 in Heb

8.16 Dan was the northernmost tribe in Israel.

8.21, 22 These words vividly portray Jeremiah's emotion as he watches his people reject God. He responds with anguish to a world dying in sin. We watch that same world still dying in sin, still rejecting God. But how often are our hearts broken for our lost friends and neighbors, our lost world? Only when we have Jeremiah's kind of concern will we be moved to help. We must begin by asking God to break our hearts for the world he loves.

8.22 Gilead was famous for its healing balm (medicine). This is a rhetorical question. The obvious answer is "Yes, God," but Israel was not applying the "balm"; they were not obeying the Lord. Although the people's spiritual sickness was still very deep, it could be cured. But the people refused the medicine. God could heal their self-inflicted wounds, but he would not force his healing on them.

9.1–4 Jeremiah felt conflicting emotions concerning his people. Lying, deceit, treachery, adultery, and idolatry had become common sins. He was angered by their sin, but he had compassion too. He was set apart from them by his work for God, but he was also one of them. Jesus had similar feelings when he stood before Jerusalem, the city that would reject him (Matthew 23.37).

that I might leave my people
and go away from them!
For they are all adulterers,
a band of traitors.

9.3 Ps 64.3 Isa 59.4 Hos 4.1

3 They bend their tongues like bows;
they have grown strong in the land for falsehood, and not for truth;
for they proceed from evil to evil,
and they do not know me, says the LORD.

9.4 Gen 27.35 Jer 12.6

4 Beware of your neighbors,
and put no trust in any of your kin;[i]
for all your kin[j] are supplanters,
and every neighbor goes around like a slanderer.
5 They all deceive their neighbors,
and no one speaks the truth;
they have taught their tongues to speak lies;
they commit iniquity and are too weary to repent.[k]

9.6 Jer 5.27; 11.10

6 Oppression upon oppression, deceit[l] upon deceit!
They refuse to know me, says the LORD.

9.7 Isa 1.25 Mal 3.3

7 Therefore thus says the LORD of hosts:
I will now refine and test them,
for what else can I do with my sinful people?[m]

9.8 Ps 28.3 Jer 5.26

8 Their tongue is a deadly arrow;
it speaks deceit through the mouth.
They all speak friendly words to their neighbors,
but inwardly are planning to lay an ambush.

9.9 Isa 1.24 Jer 5.9,29

9 Shall I not punish them for these things? says the LORD;
and shall I not bring retribution
on a nation such as this?

9.10 Jer 4.24,25 Ezek 29.11 Hos 4.3

10 Take up[n] weeping and wailing for the mountains,
and a lamentation for the pastures of the wilderness,
because they are laid waste so that no one passes through,
and the lowing of cattle is not heard;
both the birds of the air and the animals
have fled and are gone.

9.11 Isa 25.2; 34.13 Jer 26.9

11 I will make Jerusalem a heap of ruins,
a lair of jackals;
and I will make the towns of Judah a desolation,
without inhabitant.

9.12 Jer 23.10,16 Hos 14.9
9.13 2 Chron 7.19,20 Ps 89.30 Jer 5.19; 22.9
9.14 Jer 2.8; 7.24 Rom 1.21-24 1 Pet 1.18
9.15 Jer 8.14; 23.15
9.16 Deut 28.64 Jer 13.24; 44.27 Ezek 5.2,12

12 Who is wise enough to understand this? To whom has the mouth of the LORD
spoken, so that they may declare it? Why is the land ruined and laid waste like a
wilderness, so that no one passes through? 13 And the LORD says: Because they
have forsaken my law that I set before them, and have not obeyed my voice, or
walked in accordance with it, 14 but have stubbornly followed their own hearts and
have gone after the Baals, as their ancestors taught them. 15 Therefore thus says the
LORD of hosts, the God of Israel: I am feeding this people with wormwood, and
giving them poisonous water to drink. 16 I will scatter them among nations that
neither they nor their ancestors have known; and I will send the sword after them,
until I have consumed them.

9.17 Isa 22.4 Jer 9.1; 14.17

17 Thus says the LORD of hosts:
Consider, and call for the mourning women to come;
send for the skilled women to come;

[i] Heb *in a brother* [j] Heb *for every brother* [k] Cn Compare Gk: Heb *they weary themselves with iniquity.* [6] *Your dwelling* [l] Cn: Heb *Your dwelling in the midst of deceit* [m] Or *my poor people* [n] Gk Syr: Heb *I will take up*

18 let them quickly raise a dirge over us,
so that our eyes may run down with tears,
and our eyelids flow with water.
19 For a sound of wailing is heard from Zion:
"How we are ruined!
We are utterly shamed,
because we have left the land,
because they have cast down our dwellings."

9.19 Jer 7.15,29; 15.1

20 Hear, O women, the word of the LORD,
and let your ears receive the word of his mouth;
teach to your daughters a dirge,
and each to her neighbor a lament.
21 "Death has come up into our windows,
it has entered our palaces,
to cut off the children from the streets
and the young men from the squares."
22 Speak! Thus says the LORD:
"Human corpses shall fall
like dung upon the open field,
like sheaves behind the reaper,
and no one shall gather them."

9.21 2 Chron 36.17 Jer 6.11; 18.21

9.22 Isa 5.25 Jer 8.2; 16.4

23 Thus says the LORD: Do not let the wise boast in their wisdom, do not let the
mighty boast in their might, do not let the wealthy boast in their wealth; 24 but let
those who boast boast in this, that they understand and know me, that I am the
LORD; I act with steadfast love, justice, and righteousness in the earth, for in these
things I delight, says the LORD.
25 The days are surely coming, says the LORD, when I will attend to all those
who are circumcised only in the foreskin: 26 Egypt, Judah, Edom, the Ammonites,
Moab, and all those with shaven temples who live in the desert. For all these nations are uncircumcised, and all the house of Israel is uncircumcised in heart.

9.23 1 Kgs 20.10,11 Ezek 28.3-7

9.24 Ex 34.6,7 Isa 61.8 Mic 7.18 1 Cor 1.31 2 Cor 10.17 Gal 6.14

9.25 Jer 4.4 Ezek 44.7 Rom 2.8,9, 28,29

The Lord is the God of creation

10 Hear the word that the LORD speaks to you, O house of Israel. 2 Thus says the
LORD:
Do not learn the way of the nations,
or be dismayed at the signs of the heavens;
for the nations are dismayed at them.
3 For the customs of the peoples are false:
a tree from the forest is cut down,
and worked with an ax by the hands of an artisan;
4 people deck it with silver and gold;
they fasten it with hammer and nails
so that it cannot move.
5 Their idols[o] are like scarecrows in a cucumber field,

10.2 Lev 18.3 Isa 44.9-20 47.12-14

10.4 Isa 40.19; 41.7

10.5 Isa 41.23,24 46.1,7

[o] Heb *They*

9.23, 24 People tend to admire three qualities in others: human wisdom, power, and riches. But God puts a higher priority on knowing him personally and living a life that reflects his justice, righteousness, and love. What do you want people to admire most about you?

9.25, 26 Circumcision went back to the time of Abraham. For the people of Israel it was a symbol of their covenant relationship to God (Genesis 17.9–14). Circumcision was also practiced by heathen nations, but not as the sign of a covenant with God. By Jeremiah's time, the Israelites had forgotten the spiritual significance of circumcision even though they continued to do it.

10.2, 3 Most people would like to know the future. Decisions would be easier, failures avoided, and success assured. The people of Judah wanted to know the future too, and they tried to discern it in horoscopes—"signs of the heavens." Jeremiah's response applies today: God made the stars that people consult (10.12). No one will discover the future in made-up charts of God's stars. But God, who promises to guide you, knows your future and will be with you all the way. He may not reveal your future to you, but he will walk with you as the future unfolds. Don't trust the stars; trust the One who made the stars.

and they cannot speak;
they have to be carried,
for they cannot walk.
Do not be afraid of them,
for they cannot do evil,
nor is it in them to do good.

10.6 Deut 33.26 Ps 48.1; 96.4 Isa 12.6 Jer 10.16

6 There is none like you, O LORD;
you are great, and your name is great in might.

10.7 Ps 22.28 Dan 2.27,28 1 Cor 1.19,20

7 Who would not fear you, O King of the nations?
For that is your due;
among all the wise ones of the nations
and in all their kingdoms
there is no one like you.
8 They are both stupid and foolish;
the instruction given by idols
is no better than wood![p]
9 Beaten silver is brought from Tarshish,
and gold from Uphaz.
They are the work of the artisan and of the hands of the goldsmith;
their clothing is blue and purple;
they are all the product of skilled workers.

10.10 Ps 10.16; 29.10 76.7 Isa 65.16

10 But the LORD is the true God;
he is the living God and the everlasting King.
At his wrath the earth quakes,
and the nations cannot endure his indignation.

10.11 Ps 96.5 Isa 2.18

11 Thus shall you say to them: The gods who did not make the heavens and the
earth shall perish from the earth and from under the heavens.[q]

10.12 Job 9.8; 38.4-7 Isa 40.22; 45.18 Jer 51.15

12 It is he who made the earth by his power,
who established the world by his wisdom,
and by his understanding stretched out the heavens.

10.13 Job 36.27-29 Ps 29.3-9; 135.7

13 When he utters his voice, there is a tumult of waters in the heavens,
and he makes the mist rise from the ends of the earth.
He makes lightnings for the rain,
and he brings out the wind from his storehouses.
14 Everyone is stupid and without knowledge;
goldsmiths are all put to shame by their idols;
for their images are false,
and there is no breath in them.

10.15 Isa 41.24 Jer 8.12; 14.22

15 They are worthless, a work of delusion;
at the time of their punishment they shall perish.

10.16 Deut 32.9 Isa 45.7 Jer 31.35 32.18; 51.19

16 Not like these is the LORD,[r] the portion of Jacob,
for he is the one who formed all things,
and Israel is the tribe of his inheritance;
the LORD of hosts is his name.

10.17 Ezek 12.3-12

17 Gather up your bundle from the ground,
O you who live under siege!

[p] Meaning of Heb uncertain [q] This verse is in Aramaic [r] Heb lacks *the LORD*

10.8 Those who put their trust in a chunk of wood, even though it is carved well and clothed beautifully, are foolish. The simplest person who worships God is wiser than the wisest person who worships a worthless substitute, because this person has discerned who God really is. In what or whom do you place your trust?

10.9 Tarshish was located at the westward limit of the ancient world, perhaps in what is now Spain. It was a source of silver, tea, lead, and iron for Tyre. The location of Uphaz is unknown. Instead, it may be a metallurgical term for "refined gold." No matter how well made or how beautiful idols are, they can never have the power and life of God.

18 For thus says the LORD:
I am going to sling out the inhabitants of the land
at this time,
and I will bring distress on them,
so that they shall feel it.

19 Woe is me because of my hurt!
My wound is severe.
But I said, "Truly this is my punishment,
and I must bear it."
20 My tent is destroyed,
and all my cords are broken;
my children have gone from me,
and they are no more;
there is no one to spread my tent again,
and to set up my curtains.
21 For the shepherds are stupid,
and do not inquire of the LORD;
therefore they have not prospered,
and all their flock is scattered.

22 Hear, a noise! Listen, it is coming—
a great commotion from the land of the north
to make the cities of Judah a desolation,
a lair of jackals.

23 I know, O LORD, that the way of human beings is not in their control,
that mortals as they walk cannot direct their steps.
24 Correct me, O LORD, but in just measure;
not in your anger, or you will bring me to nothing.

25 Pour out your wrath on the nations that do not know you,
and on the peoples that do not call on your name;
for they have devoured Jacob;
they have devoured him and consumed him,
and have laid waste his habitation.

10.19 Jer 4.31 Mic 7.9
10.20 Isa 51.18 Jer 4.20; 31.15 Lam 1.5; 2.4
10.21 Jer 23.2
10.22 Jer 9.11; 49.33
10.23 Isa 26.7
10.25 Jer 8.16; 50.7 Zeph 1.6; 3.8

3. Jeremiah prophesies destruction

Remember the covenant

11 The word that came to Jeremiah from the LORD: 2 Hear the words of this
covenant, and speak to the people of Judah and the inhabitants of Jerusalem.
3 You shall say to them, Thus says the LORD, the God of Israel: Cursed be anyone
who does not heed the words of this covenant, 4 which I commanded your ancestors
when I brought them out of the land of Egypt, from the iron-smelter, saying, Listen
to my voice, and do all that I command you. So shall you be my people, and I will

11.1 Ex 19.5 Deut 27.26
11.4 Ex 24.3,7 Deut 4.20 1 Kgs 8.51 Zech 8.8

10.19–21 In this section, Jeremiah uses the picture of nomads, wandering in the desert, trying to pitch their tents. The shepherds of the nation are the evil leaders responsible for the calamity. The flock is the people of Judah. When the leaders should have been guiding the people to God, they were leading them astray.

10.23, 24 God's ability to plan our lives well is infinitely beyond our ability. Sometimes we are afraid of God's power and God's plans because we know his power would easily crush us if he used it against us. Don't be afraid to let God correct your plans. He will give you wisdom if you are willing.

11.1–13.27 This section concerns the broken covenant, a rebuke for those who returned to idols after Josiah's reform. Jeremiah's rebuke prompted a threat against his life by his own countrymen. As Jeremiah suffered, he pondered the prosperity of the wicked. As he brought these words to a close, he used a ruined linen loincloth and clay wine jars as object lessons of God's coming judgment (see the note on 13.1–11).

11.1–8 God tells Jeremiah to remind the people of their history—specifically what God had done for them as a result of their obedience or disobedience to his Word. Obeying God's Word was like finding the single safe passageway on the sea through treacherous rocks. Disobeying brought ultimate disaster. We have the freedom to obey and find the refuge God has waiting for us; we also have the freedom to sail any other direction into disaster. The choice is ours.

be your God, 5 that I may perform the oath that I swore to your ancestors, to give
them a land flowing with milk and honey, as at this day. Then I answered, "So be
it, LORD."
6 And the LORD said to me: Proclaim all these words in the cities of Judah, and
in the streets of Jerusalem: Hear the words of this covenant and do them. 7 For I
solemnly warned your ancestors when I brought them up out of the land of Egypt,
warning them persistently, even to this day, saying, Obey my voice. 8 Yet they did
not obey or incline their ear, but everyone walked in the stubbornness of an evil
will. So I brought upon them all the words of this covenant, which I commanded
them to do, but they did not.
9 And the LORD said to me: Conspiracy exists among the people of Judah and
the inhabitants of Jerusalem. 10 They have turned back to the iniquities of their ancestors of old, who refused to heed my words; they have gone after other gods to
serve them; the house of Israel and the house of Judah have broken the covenant
that I made with their ancestors. 11 Therefore, thus says the LORD, assuredly I am
going to bring disaster upon them that they cannot escape; though they cry out to
me, I will not listen to them. 12 Then the cities of Judah and the inhabitants of Jerusalem will go and cry out to the gods to whom they make offerings, but they will
never save them in the time of their trouble. 13 For your gods have become as many
as your towns, O Judah; and as many as the streets of Jerusalem are the altars you
have set up to shame, altars to make offerings to Baal.
14 As for you, do not pray for this people, or lift up a cry or prayer on their
behalf, for I will not listen when they call to me in the time of their trouble. 15 What
right has my beloved in my house, when she has done vile deeds? Can vows[s] and
sacrificial flesh avert your doom? Can you then exult? 16 The LORD once called you,
"A green olive tree, fair with goodly fruit"; but with the roar of a great tempest he
will set fire to it, and its branches will be consumed. 17 The LORD of hosts, who
planted you, has pronounced evil against you, because of the evil that the house of
Israel and the house of Judah have done, provoking me to anger by making offerings to Baal.

18 It was the LORD who made it known to me, and I knew;
  then you showed me their evil deeds.
19 But I was like a gentle lamb
  led to the slaughter.
And I did not know it was against me
  that they devised schemes, saying,
"Let us destroy the tree with its fruit,
  let us cut him off from the land of the living,
  so that his name will no longer be remembered!"
20 But you, O LORD of hosts, who judge righteously,
  who try the heart and the mind,
let me see your retribution upon them,
  for to you I have committed my cause.
21 Therefore thus says the LORD concerning the people of Anathoth, who seek
your life, and say, "You shall not prophesy in the name of the LORD, or you will die

11.5 Ex 13.5 Deut 7.12 Jer 32.22
11.6 Jer 3.12; 7.2
11.7 Ex 15.26 Jer 7.25; 11.4
11.8 Lev 26.14-43 Jer 7.24; 9.14 Ezek 20.8
11.9 Ezek 22.25
11.10 Judg 2.11-13 Jer 3.6-9; 13.10 Ezek 16.59
11.11 Jer 6.19; 25.35
11.12 Deut 32.37 Jer 44.17
11.13 Jer 2.28; 7.9,10
11.14 Ps 66.18 Jer 7.16; 14.11 Hos 5.6
11.16 Ps 52.8; 83.2 Isa 27.11 Jer 21.14
11.17 Jer 2.21; 32.29
11.18 1 Sam 23.11,12 2 Kgs 6.9,10 Ezek 8.6
11.19 Ps 52.5; 83.4 109.13
11.20 Ps 7.9 Jer 17.10; 20.12
11.21 2 Chron 36.17 Jer 1.1; 12.5,6 18.21; 20.10 26.8; 38.4

[s] Gk: Heb *Can many*

11.14 At first glance this command is shocking—God tells Jeremiah not to pray and says he won't listen to the people if they pray. A time comes when God must dispense justice. Sin brings its own bitter reward. If the people were unrepentant and continued in their sin, neither their prayers nor Jeremiah's would prevent God's judgment. Their only hope was repentance—sorrow for sin, turning from it, and turning to God. How can we keep praying for God's help if we haven't committed our lives to him? His blessings come when we are committed to him, not when we selfishly hang on to our sinful ways.

11.18–23 To Jeremiah's surprise, the people of Anathoth, his hometown, were plotting to kill him. They wanted to silence his message for several reasons: (1) economic—this would hurt the business of the idol-makers; (2) religious—the message of doom and gloom made the people feel guilty; (3) political—he openly rebuked their hypocritical politics; and (4) personal—the people hated him for showing them that they were wrong. Jeremiah had two options: run and hide, or call on God. Jeremiah called, and God answered. Like Jeremiah, we can either run and hide when we face threats because of our faithfulness to God, or we can call on God for help. Hiding compromises our message; calling on God lets him reinforce it.

by our hand" — 22 therefore thus says the LORD of hosts: I am going to punish them;
the young men shall die by the sword; their sons and their daughters shall die by
famine; 23 and not even a remnant shall be left of them. For I will bring disaster
upon the people of Anathoth, the year of their punishment.

11.23 Jer 6.9; 23.12 Hos 9.7 Mic 7.4

Jeremiah complains to God

12 You will be in the right, O LORD,
when I lay charges against you;
but let me put my case to you.
Why does the way of the guilty prosper?
Why do all who are treacherous thrive?
2 You plant them, and they take root;
they grow and bring forth fruit;
you are near in their mouths
yet far from their hearts.
3 But you, O LORD, know me;
You see me and test me — my heart is with you.
Pull them out like sheep for the slaughter,
and set them apart for the day of slaughter.
4 How long will the land mourn,
and the grass of every field wither?
For the wickedness of those who live in it
the animals and the birds are swept away,
and because people said, "He is blind to our ways."[t]

12.1 Ezra 9.15 Job 13.3 Jer 5.27,28 Hab 1.4

12.2 Isa 29.13 Ezek 17.5-10 Tit 1.16

12.3 Ps 7.9; 139.1-4 Jer 11.20

12.4 Jer 5.31 Hos 4.3 Joel 1.10-17

God answers Jeremiah

5 If you have raced with foot-runners and they have wearied you,
how will you compete with horses?
And if in a safe land you fall down,
how will you fare in the thickets of the Jordan?
6 For even your kinsfolk and your own family,
even they have dealt treacherously with you;
they are in full cry after you;
do not believe them,
though they speak friendly words to you.

12.6 Gen 37.4-11 Ps 69.8 Prov 26.25

7 I have forsaken my house,
I have abandoned my heritage;
I have given the beloved of my heart
into the hands of her enemies.
8 My heritage has become to me
like a lion in the forest;
she has lifted up her voice against me —
therefore I hate her.
9 Is the hyena greedy[u] for my heritage at my command?
Are the birds of prey all around her?
Go, assemble all the wild animals;

12.7 Jer 7.29; 11.15 Hos 11.1-4

12.8 Amos 6.8

12.9 Jer 7.33; 15.3

[t] Gk: Heb *to our future* [u] Cn: Heb *Is the hyena, the bird of prey*

12.1–6 Many people have asked, "Why does the way of the guilty prosper?" (See, for example, Job 21.4–21 and Habakkuk 1.1–4.) Jeremiah knows that God's ultimate justice will come, but he is impatient because he wants justice to come quickly. God doesn't give a doctrinal answer; instead he gives a challenge – if Jeremiah can't handle this, how will he handle the injustices ahead? It is natural for us to demand fair play and cry for justice against those who take advantage of others. But when we call for justice, we must realize that we ourselves would be in big trouble if God gave each of us what we truly deserve.

12.5, 6 Life was extremely difficult for Jeremiah despite his love for and obedience to God. When he called to God for relief, God's reply in effect was, "If you think this is bad, how are you going to cope when it gets really tough?" Not all of God's answers to prayer are nice or easy to handle. Any Christian who has experienced war, bereavement, or a serious illness knows this. But we are to be committed to God even when the going gets tough and when his answers to our prayers don't bring immediate relief.

bring them to devour her.

12.10 Ps 80.8-16 Isa 5.1-7

10 Many shepherds have destroyed my vineyard,
they have trampled down my portion,
they have made my pleasant portion
a desolate wilderness.

12.11 Jer 4.20,27

11 They have made it a desolation;
desolate, it mourns to me.
The whole land is made desolate,
but no one lays it to heart.
12 Upon all the bare heights[v] in the desert
spoilers have come;
for the sword of the LORD devours
from one end of the land to the other;
no one shall be safe.

12.13 Jer 4.26; 17.10 25.37,38

13 They have sown wheat and have reaped thorns,
they have tired themselves out but profit nothing.
They shall be ashamed of their[w] harvests
because of the fierce anger of the LORD.

12.14 Jer 2.3; 49.1 50.11,12 Zech 2.8
12.15 Isa11.11-16 Jer 49.6,39
12.16 Isa 49.6 Jer 16.19
12.17 Ps 2.8-12 Isa 60.12

14 Thus says the LORD concerning all my evil neighbors who touch the heritage
that I have given my people Israel to inherit: I am about to pluck them up from their
land, and I will pluck up the house of Judah from among them. 15 And after I have
plucked them up, I will again have compassion on them, and I will bring them
again to their heritage and to their land, everyone of them. 16 And then, if they will
diligently learn the ways of my people, to swear by my name, "As the LORD lives,"
as they taught my people to swear by Baal, then they shall be built up in the midst
of my people. 17 But if any nation will not listen, then I will completely uproot it
and destroy it, says the LORD.

The people threatened with captivity

13.1 Jer 13.11
13.2 Isa 20.2
13.4 Jer 51.63
13.5 Ex 39.42,43 40.16

13 Thus said the LORD to me, "Go and buy yourself a linen loincloth, and put
it on your loins, but do not dip it in water." 2 So I bought a loincloth according to the word of the LORD, and put it on my loins. 3 And the word of the LORD
came to me a second time, saying, 4 "Take the loincloth that you bought and are
wearing, and go now to the Euphrates,[x] and hide it there in a cleft of the rock." 5 So
I went, and hid it by the Euphrates,[y] as the LORD commanded me. 6 And after many
days the LORD said to me, "Go now to the Euphrates,[x] and take from there the
loincloth that I commanded you to hide there." 7 Then I went to the Euphrates,[x]
and dug, and I took the loincloth from the place where I had hidden it. But now the
loincloth was ruined; it was good for nothing.

13.8 Lev 26.19 Isa 2.10-17 23.9
13.11 Ex 19.5,6 Deut 32.10,11 Ps 81.11 Isa 43.21 Jer 7.24; 33.9

8 Then the word of the LORD came to me: 9 Thus says the LORD: Just so I will
ruin the pride of Judah and the great pride of Jerusalem. 10 This evil people, who
refuse to hear my words, who stubbornly follow their own will and have gone after
other gods to serve them and worship them, shall be like this loincloth, which is
good for nothing. 11 For as the loincloth clings to one's loins, so I made the whole
house of Israel and the whole house of Judah cling to me, says the LORD, in order

[v] Or *the trails* [w] Heb *your* [x] Or *to Parah*; Heb *perath* [y] Or *by Parah*; Heb *perath*

12.14–17 God speaks to the nations surrounding Judah with a message that contains both judgment and hope. They will be punished by the same enemy that punishes Judah, and like Judah they will be deported from their homelands. If they repent and turn to God, they will be permitted to return. The nations that led Judah into idolatry may share Judah's true God – but only if they repent. The same offer is made to us. If we repent and turn to God, we will share in the same God who makes these promises.

13.1 A "loincloth" was one of the more intimate pieces of clothing, clinging close to the body. It was often dipped in water to make it soft and pliable. And, of course, it would also have to be soaked with water to be washed properly. Jeremiah's action showed how God would ruin Judah just as Jeremiah had ruined the loincloth.

13.1–11 Actions speak louder than words. Jeremiah often used vivid object lessons to arouse the people's curiosity and get his point across. This lesson of the linen loincloth illustrated Judah's destiny. Although the people had once been close to God, their pride had made them useless. Proud people may look important, but God says their pride makes them good for nothing. Pride rots our hearts until we lose our usefulness to God.

that they might be for me a people, a name, a praise, and a glory. But they would
not listen.

12 You shall speak to them this word: Thus says the LORD, the God of Israel:
Every wine-jar should be filled with wine. And they will say to you, "Do you think
we do not know that every wine-jar should be filled with wine?" 13 Then you shall
say to them: Thus says the LORD: I am about to fill all the inhabitants of this
land—the kings who sit on David's throne, the priests, the prophets, and all the
inhabitants of Jerusalem—with drunkenness. 14 And I will dash them one against
another, parents and children together, says the LORD. I will not pity or spare or
have compassion when I destroy them.

13.13 Ps 60.3; 75.8 Jer 25.27

13.14 Isa 27.11 Jer 6.21; 16.5 19.9-11

15 Hear and give ear; do not be haughty,
for the LORD has spoken.
16 Give glory to the LORD your God
before he brings darkness,
and before your feet stumble
on the mountains at twilight;
while you look for light,
he turns it into gloom
and makes it deep darkness.
17 But if you will not listen,
my soul will weep in secret for your pride;
my eyes will weep bitterly and run down with tears,
because the LORD's flock has been taken captive.

13.16 Ps 96.8 Isa 5.30; 59.9 Amos 5.18

13.17 Jer 9.1; 23.1,2 Mal 2.2 Lk 19.41,42

18 Say to the king and the queen mother;
"Take a lowly seat,
for your beautiful crown
has come down from your head."[z]
19 The towns of the Negeb are shut up
with no one to open them;
all Judah is taken into exile,
wholly taken into exile.

13.18 2 Kgs 24.12,15

20 Lift up your eyes and see
those who come from the north.
Where is the flock that was given you,
your beautiful flock?
21 What will you say when they set as head over you
those whom you have trained
to be your allies?
Will not pangs take hold of you,
like those of a woman in labor?
22 And if you say in your heart,
"Why have these things come upon me?"
it is for the greatness of your iniquity
that your skirts are lifted up,

13.20 Jer 1.15; 6.22 13.17; 23.2 Hab 1.6

13.21 Isa 13.8 Jer 4.31; 38.22

13.22 Jer 2.17-19 9.2-9

z Gk Syr Vg: Meaning of Heb uncertain

13.15 While it is good to respect our country and our church, our loyalties always carry a hidden danger—pride. When is pride harmful? When it causes us to (1) look down on others; (2) be selfish with our resources; (3) force our solutions on others' problems; (4) think God is blessing us because of our own merits; (5) be content with our plans rather than seeking God's plans.

13.18 The king is Jehoiachin, and the queen mother is Nehushta. The king's father, Jehoiakim, had surrendered to Nebuchadnezzar but later rebelled. During Jehoiachin's reign, Nebuchadnezzar's armies besieged Jerusalem, and both Jehoiachin and Nehushta surrendered. Jehoiachin was sent to Babylon and imprisoned (2 Kings 24.1–12). Jeremiah's prophecy came true.

13.19 The Negeb region was south of the Gaza to Beer-sheba road. The towns in this area would be closed to any refugees fleeing the invading army.

and you are violated.
13.23 Prov 27.22 Jer 4.22 Mt 19.24
23 Can Ethiopians[a] change their skin
or leopards their spots?
Then also you can do good
who are accustomed to do evil.
13.24 Lev 26.33 Ps 9.17 Jer 2.32; 9.16 18.17 Ezek 5.2,12
24 I will scatter you[b] like chaff
driven by the wind from the desert.
25 This is your lot,
the portion I have measured out to you, says the LORD,
because you have forgotten me
and trusted in lies.
13.26 Lam 1.8
26 I myself will lift up your skirts over your face,
and your shame will be seen.
13.27 Prov 1.22 Jer 2.20; 5.7,8 11.15
27 I have seen your abominations,
your adulteries and neighings, your shameless prostitutions
on the hills of the countryside.
Woe to you, O Jerusalem!
How long will it be
before you are made clean?

God pronounces doom for Jerusalem

14 The word of the LORD that came to Jeremiah concerning the drought:
14.2 Jer 11.11 Zech 7.13
2 Judah mourns
and her gates languish;
they lie in gloom on the ground,
and the cry of Jerusalem goes up.
14.3 2 Sam 15.30 1 Kgs 18.5
3 Her nobles send their servants for water;
they come to the cisterns,
they find no water,
they return with their vessels empty.
They are ashamed and dismayed
and cover their heads,
14.4 Joel 1.11,19,20
4 because the ground is cracked.
Because there has been no rain on the land
the farmers are dismayed;
they cover their heads.
5 Even the doe in the field forsakes her newborn fawn
because there is no grass.
14.6 Job 39.5,6
6 The wild asses stand on the bare heights,[c]
they pant for air like jackals;
their eyes fail
because there is no herbage.

14.7 Isa 59.12 Hos 5.5
7 Although our iniquities testify against us,
act, O LORD, for your name's sake;
14.8 Ps 9.9 Isa 43.3; 63.8 Jer 17.13
our apostasies indeed are many,
and we have sinned against you.
8 O hope of Israel,

[a] Or *Nubians*; Heb *Cushites* [b] Heb *them* [c] Or *the trails*

13.23 The people had become so accustomed to doing evil that they had lost their ability to change. God never rejects those who sincerely turn to him. God is warning them to repent before it becomes impossible to change. We must never put off until tomorrow those changes God wants us to make. Our attitudes and patterns for living can become so set that we will lose all desire to change and will no longer fear the consequences.

14.1–15.21 This section opens with God sending a drought on Judah and refusing to answer their prayers for rain. It continues with Jeremiah's description of judgment to come.

14.1ff Drought was a judgment with devastating consequences. As usual, when their backs were to the wall, the people cried out to God. But God rejected their plea because they did not repent; they merely wanted his rescue. Not even Jeremiah's prayers would help. Their only hope was to turn to God.

its savior in time of trouble,
why should you be like a stranger in the land,
like a traveler turning aside for the night?
9 Why should you be like someone confused,
like a mighty warrior who cannot give help?
Yet you, O LORD, are in the midst of us,
and we are called by your name;
do not forsake us!

10 Thus says the LORD concerning this people:
Truly they have loved to wander,
they have not restrained their feet;
therefore the LORD does not accept them,
now he will remember their iniquity
and punish their sins.

11 The LORD said to me: Do not pray for the welfare of this people. 12 Although
they fast, I do not hear their cry, and although they offer burnt offering and grain
offering, I do not accept them; but by the sword, by famine, and by pestilence I
consume them.
13 Then I said: "Ah, Lord GOD! Here are the prophets saying to them, 'You
shall not see the sword, nor shall you have famine, but I will give you true peace in
this place.' " 14 And the LORD said to me: The prophets are prophesying lies in my
name; I did not send them, nor did I command them or speak to them. They are
prophesying to you a lying vision, worthless divination, and the deceit of their own
minds. 15 Therefore thus says the LORD concerning the prophets who prophesy in
my name though I did not send them, and who say, "Sword and famine shall not
come on this land": By sword and famine those prophets shall be consumed. 16 And
the people to whom they prophesy shall be thrown out into the streets of Jerusalem,
victims of famine and sword. There shall be no one to bury them—themselves,
their wives, their sons, and their daughters. For I will pour out their wickedness
upon them.

17 You shall say to them this word:
Let my eyes run down with tears night and day,
and let them not cease,
for the virgin daughter—my people—is struck down with a crushing
blow,
with a very grievous wound.
18 If I go out into the field,
look—those killed by the sword!
And if I enter the city,
look—those sick with[d] famine!
For both prophet and priest ply their trade throughout the land,
and have no knowledge.

19 Have you completely rejected Judah?

14.9 Num 11.23 Ps 46.5 Isa 50.2; 63.19 Jer 8.19; 15.16

14.10 Ps 119,101 Jer 2.25 44.21-23

14.11 Jer 7.16; 11.14

14.12 Isa 1.15 Jer 8.13

14.13 Jer 5.12; 6.14 8.11; 23.17

14.14 Jer 5.31 23.16,25,26 27.9,10

14.15 Ezek 14.10

14.16 Ps 79.2,3 Prov 1.31 Jer 7.33; 15.2,3

14.17 Jer 8.21; 9.1 Lam 2.13

14.18 Jer 6.25 Lam 1.20 Ezek 7.15

14.19 Job 30.26 Jer 8.15; 30.13 1 Thess 5.3

[d] Heb *look—the sicknesses of*

14.11, 12 The people of Judah had stretched God's patience. Their false repentance and empty rituals had continued long enough, and God turned deaf ears to their cries. For a third time, God told Jeremiah not to pray for the people. Why should people pray to God when he was less important to them than handmade idols of wood or stone? Why not let the idols answer their prayers? If you are trusting something more than God when all is going well, will you still trust in this false god when trouble comes?

14.14 What made the people listen to and encourage the false prophets? These "prophets" said what the people wanted to hear. False teachers earn fame and money by giving people what they want to hear, but they lead people away from God. If we encourage them, we are as guilty as they are.

14.17 Was this Jeremiah or God crying? Actually it was both. Jeremiah was so in tune with God that he expressed God's great compassion and sorrow for his chosen people in his own tears. This was a symbol the people could understand.

14.19–22 Interceding for the people, Jeremiah asks God if

Does your heart loathe Zion?
Why have you struck us down
so that there is no healing for us?
We look for peace, but find no good;
for a time of healing, but there is terror instead.

14.20 Ps 32.5 Jer 3.25

20 We acknowledge our wickedness, O LORD,
the iniquity of our ancestors,
for we have sinned against you.

14.21 Ps 25.11 Jer 3.17; 14.7 17.12

21 Do not spurn us, for your name's sake;
do not dishonor your glorious throne;
remember and do not break your covenant with us.

14.22 1 Kgs 17.1 Isa 41.29 Jer 5.24; 10.3 Lam 3.26

22 Can any idols of the nations bring rain?
Or can the heavens give showers?
Is it not you, O LORD our God?
We set our hope on you,
for it is you who do all this.

Jerusalem is persecuted

15.1 Ex 32.11-14 1 Sam 7.9 Jer 10.18; 52.3

15.2 Jer 14.12 24.10; 43.11

15 Then the LORD said to me: Though Moses and Samuel stood before me, yet
my heart would not turn toward this people. Send them out of my sight, and
let them go! 2 And when they say to you, "Where shall we go?" you shall say to
them: Thus says the LORD:

Those destined for pestilence, to pestilence,
and those destined for the sword, to the sword;
those destined for famine, to famine,
and those destined for captivity, to captivity.

15.3 Lev 26.16,22,25

15.4 2 Kgs 23.26,27 24.3,4 Jer 24.9; 29.18

3 And I will appoint over them four kinds of destroyers, says the LORD: the sword
to kill, the dogs to drag away, and the birds of the air and the wild animals of the
earth to devour and destroy. 4 I will make them a horror to all the kingdoms of the
earth because of what King Manasseh son of Hezekiah of Judah did in Jerusalem.

15.5 Ps 69.20 Jer 13.14

5 Who will have pity on you, O Jerusalem,
or who will bemoan you?
Who will turn aside
to ask about your welfare?

15.6 Isa 1.4 Jer 6.11 7.16,24 Zeph 1.4

6 You have rejected me, says the LORD,
you are going backward;
so I have stretched out my hand against you and destroyed you—
I am weary of relenting.

15.7 Jer 18.21; 51.2 Hos 9.12-16

7 I have winnowed them with a winnowing fork
in the gates of the land;
I have bereaved them, I have destroyed my people;
they did not turn from their ways.

15.8 Isa 3.25,26; 4.1

8 Their widows became more numerous
than the sand of the seas;
I have brought against the mothers of youths
a destroyer at noonday;

Judah's repentance will bring his help. But God refuses to come to their aid (15.1) because the people are insincere, wicked, and stubborn. They know he wants to bless them, and they know what they need to do to receive that blessing. They want God to do his part, but they do not want to do theirs. It's easy to express sorrow for wrong actions, especially when we want something, but we must be willing to stop doing what is wrong. God will forgive the truly repentant, but not the hypocrite.

15.1 Moses and Samuel were two of God's greatest prophets. Like Jeremiah, both interceded between God and the people (Exodus 32.11; Numbers 14.11–20; 1 Samuel 7.9; 12.17; Psalm 99.6). Intercession is often effective. In this case, however, the people were so wicked and stubborn that God knew they would not turn to him.

15.3, 4 The goal of these destroyers was to destroy the living and consume the dead. This would happen because of Manasseh's evil reign and the people's sin (2 Kings 21.1–16; 23.26; 24.3), and the destruction would be total. The people may have argued that they should not be responsible for Manasseh's sins, but they continued what Manasseh began. If we follow corrupt leaders knowingly, we can't excuse ourselves by blaming their bad example.

I have made anguish and terror
fall upon her suddenly.
9 She who bore seven has languished;
she has swooned away;
her sun went down while it was yet day;
she has been shamed and disgraced.
And the rest of them I will give to the sword
before their enemies,
says the LORD.

15.9 1 Sam 2.5 Isa 47.9 Amos 8.9

10 Woe is me, my mother, that you ever bore me, a man of strife and contention
to the whole land! I have not lent, nor have I borrowed, yet all of them curse me.
11 The LORD said: Surely I have intervened in your life[e] for good, surely I have
imposed enemies on you in a time of trouble and in a time of distress.[f] 12 Can iron
and bronze break iron from the north?
13 Your wealth and your treasures I will give as plunder, without price, for all
your sins, throughout all your territory. 14 I will make you serve your enemies in a
land that you do not know, for in my anger a fire is kindled that shall burn forever.
15 O LORD, you know;
remember me and visit me,
and bring down retribution for me on my persecutors.
In your forbearance do not take me away;
know that on your account I suffer insult.
16 Your words were found, and I ate them,
and your words became to me a joy
and the delight of my heart;
for I am called by your name,
O LORD, God of hosts.
17 I did not sit in the company of merrymakers,
nor did I rejoice;
under the weight of your hand I sat alone,
for you had filled me with indignation.
18 Why is my pain unceasing,
my wound incurable,
refusing to be healed?
Truly, you are to me like a deceitful brook,
like waters that fail.

15.10 Deut 23.19 Job 3.3 Jer 1.18,19 20.7,8,14
15.11 Isa 41.10
15.12 Jer 17.3; 20.5
15.14 Deut 28.64 Jer 16.13; 17.4
15.15 Ps 69.7-9 Jer 20.8
15.16 Job 23.12 Ps 119.103 Jer 14.9
15.17 Job 6.15,20 Ps 102.7 Jer 13.17; 16.8 30.12,15 2 Cor 6.17

19 Therefore thus says the LORD:
If you turn back, I will take you back,
and you shall stand before me.
If you utter what is precious, and not what is worthless,
you shall serve as my mouth.
It is they who will turn to you,
not you who will turn to them.
20 And I will make you to this people
a fortified wall of bronze;
they will fight against you,
but they shall not prevail over you,
for I am with you

15.19 Ezek 44.23
15.20 Jer 1.8,18,19 Ps 46.7 Isa 41.10 Ezek 3.9

e Heb *intervened with you* f Meaning of Heb uncertain

15.17–21 Jeremiah accused God of not helping him when he really needed it. Jeremiah had taken his eyes off God's purposes and was feeling sorry for himself. He was angry, hurt, and afraid. In response, God didn't get angry at Jeremiah; he answered by reorienting Jeremiah's priorities. As God's mouthpiece, he was to influence the people, not let them influence him. There are three important lessons in this passage: (1) in prayer we can reveal our deepest thoughts to God; (2) God expects us to trust him, no matter what; and (3) we are here to influence others for God.

to save you and deliver you,
says the LORD.
21 I will deliver you out of the hand of the wicked,
and redeem you from the grasp of the ruthless.

A prophecy of disaster

16 The word of the LORD came to me: 2 You shall not take a wife, nor shall you
have sons or daughters in this place. 3 For thus says the LORD concerning the
sons and daughters who are born in this place, and concerning the mothers who
bear them and the fathers who beget them in this land: 4 They shall die of deadly
diseases. They shall not be lamented, nor shall they be buried; they shall become
like dung on the surface of the ground. They shall perish by the sword and by
famine, and their dead bodies shall become food for the birds of the air and for the
wild animals of the earth.
5 For thus says the LORD: Do not enter the house of mourning, or go to lament,
or bemoan them; for I have taken away my peace from this people, says the LORD,
my steadfast love and mercy. 6 Both great and small shall die in this land; they shall
not be buried, and no one shall lament for them; there shall be no gashing, no
shaving of the head for them. 7 No one shall break bread[g] for the mourner, to offer
comfort for the dead; nor shall anyone give them the cup of consolation to drink for
their fathers or their mothers. 8 You shall not go into the house of feasting to sit with
them, to eat and drink. 9 For thus says the LORD of hosts, the God of Israel: I am
going to banish from this place, in your days and before your eyes, the voice of
mirth and the voice of gladness, the voice of the bridegroom and the voice of the
bride.
10 And when you tell this people all these words, and they say to you, "Why
has the LORD pronounced all this great evil against us? What is our iniquity? What
is the sin that we have committed against the LORD our God?" 11 then you shall say
to them: It is because your ancestors have forsaken me, says the LORD, and have
gone after other gods and have served and worshiped them, and have forsaken me
and have not kept my law; 12 and because you have behaved worse than your ancestors, for here you are, everyone of you, following your stubborn evil will, refusing
to listen to me. 13 Therefore I will hurl you out of this land into a land that neither
you nor your ancestors have known, and there you shall serve other gods day and
night, for I will show you no favor.
14 Therefore, the days are surely coming, says the LORD, when it shall no longer be said, "As the LORD lives who brought the people of Israel up out of the land
of Egypt," 15 but "As the LORD lives who brought the people of Israel up out of the
land of the north and out of all the lands where he had driven them." For I will bring
them back to their own land that I gave to their ancestors.
16 I am now sending for many fishermen, says the LORD, and they shall catch
them; and afterward I will send for many hunters, and they shall hunt them from
every mountain and every hill, and out of the clefts of the rocks. 17 For my eyes are
on all their ways; they are not hidden from my presence, nor is their iniquity

g Two Mss Gk: MT *break for them*

15.21 Isa 49.26 Jer 39.11,12
16.4 Ps 79.2 Isa 18.6 Jer 15.2,3
16.5 Ps 25.6 Isa 27.11 Jer 12.12 Ezek 24.16-23
16.6 Deut 14.1 Ezek 9.6
16.8 Eccles 7.2-4 Isa 22.12-14 Jer 15.17
16.9 Jer 7.34; 25.10 Hos 2.11
16.10 Deut 29.24,25 1 Kgs 9.8,9 Jer 5.19; 13.22
16.11 Neh 9.26-29 Ps 106.35-41 1 Pet 4.3
16.12 Jer 7.24; 9.14 Mk 7.21
16.13 Deut 4.26,27 Jer 5.19; 15.14
16.14 Deut 15.15 Ps 106.47 Isa 11.11-16 Jer 23.7,8 Hos 3.4,5
16.16 Isa 2.21 Amos 4.2; 9.1-3 Hab 1.14,15
16.17 Ps 90.8 Jer 23.24; 32.19 Lk 12.2 1 Cor 4.5 Heb 4.13

16.1–17.18 This section begins by showing Jeremiah's loneliness. He is a social outcast because of his harsh messages and his celibate life-style. He must not marry, have children, or take part in funerals or festivals. The section concludes with another appeal to avoid judgment by turning to God. The people did not heed Jeremiah's words, however, and the first wave of destruction came almost immediately, in 605 B.C. (2 Kings 24.8–12). The second wave came in 597 B.C., and Judah was completely destroyed in 586 B.C.

16.5–7 In Jeremiah's culture, it was unthinkable not to show grief publicly. The absence of mourning showed the people how complete their devastation would be. So many people would die that it would be impossible to carry out mourning rituals for all of them.

16.14, 15 The book of Exodus records God's miraculous rescue of his people from Egyptian slavery (Exodus 1–15). The people's return from exile would be so momentous that it would overshadow even the exodus from Egypt. Even though his people had been so stubborn, he would once again show his great mercy.

16.17 Small children think that if they can't see you, then you can't see them. The people of Israel may have wished that hiding from God were as simple as closing their eyes. Although they closed their eyes to their sinful ways, their sins certainly weren't hidden from God. He who sees all cannot be deceived. Do you have a sinful attitude or action that you hope God won't notice? He knows about it. The first step of repentance is to acknowledge that God knows about our sins.

concealed from my sight. 18 And[h] I will doubly repay their iniquity and their sin,
because they have polluted my land with the carcasses of their detestable idols,
and have filled my inheritance with their abominations.

16.18 Num 35.34 Jer 2.7; 3.9 Rev 18.6

19 O LORD, my strength and my stronghold,
my refuge in the day of trouble,
to you shall the nations come
from the ends of the earth and say:
Our ancestors have inherited nothing but lies,
worthless things in which there is no profit.
20 Can mortals make for themselves gods?
Such are no gods!

16.19 Isa 25.4 Jer 3.17; 4.2

16.20 Ps 115.4-8 Jer 5.7 Hos 8.4-6

21 "Therefore I am surely going to teach them, this time I am going to teach
them my power and my might, and they shall know that my name is the LORD."

16.21 Isa 43.3 Amos 5.8

Jeremiah warns the people

17 The sin of Judah is written with an iron pen; with a diamond point it is engraved on the tablet of their hearts, and on the horns of their altars, 2 while
their children remember their altars and their sacred poles,[i] beside every green
tree, and on the high hills, 3 on the mountains in the open country. Your wealth and
all your treasures I will give for spoil as the price of your sin[j] throughout all your
territory. 4 By your own act you shall lose the heritage that I gave you, and I will
make you serve your enemies in a land that you do not know, for in my anger a fire
is kindled[k] that shall burn forever.

17.1 Prov 3.3; 7.3 2 Cor 3.3

17.2 Ex 34.13 Isa 39.4-6 Jer 3.6; 15.13 20.5

17.4 Deut 28.48 Isa 5.25 Jer 7.20; 12.7 15.14

5 Thus says the LORD:
Cursed are those who trust in mere mortals
and make mere flesh their strength,
whose hearts turn away from the LORD.
6 They shall be like a shrub in the desert,
and shall not see when relief comes.
They shall live in the parched places of the wilderness,
in an uninhabited salt land.

17.5 Ps 146.3 Isa 30.1; 31.3 Ezek 29.6,7

17.6 Deut 29.23 Jer 48.6

7 Blessed are those who trust in the LORD,
whose trust is the LORD.
8 They shall be like a tree planted by water,
sending out its roots by the stream.
It shall not fear when heat comes,
and its leaves shall stay green;
in the year of drought it is not anxious,

17.7 Ps 34.8; 40.4 84.12

17.8 Ps 1.3; 92.12-14

[h] Gk: Heb *And first* [i] Heb *Asherim* [j] Cn: Heb *spoil your high places for sin* [k] Two Mss Theodotion: *you kindled*

16.19 In this prayer, Jeremiah approaches God with three descriptive names: strength, stronghold, and refuge. Each name gives a slightly different glimpse of how Jeremiah experienced God's presence, and each is a picture of security. Let God be your strength when you feel weak, your stronghold when enemies come against you, and your refuge when you need to retreat from life's pressures.

16.20 God will be number one in your life or not in your life at all. To put God in second place is to make someone or something greater than the Creator of all the universe. How can the created ever be greater than the Creator?

17.1 Why did God's people continue to sin even though they had the law, the prophets of God, and history filled with God's miracles? Why do we continue to cherish sin even though we understand the eternal consequences? Jeremiah says the heart is devious (17.9). The Hebrews symbolized the various aspects of a person by locating them in certain physical organs. The heart was the organ of reason, intelligence, and will. So deep is our tendency to sin that only God's redemption can deliver us.

17.5–8 Two kinds of people are contrasted here: the wicked and the righteous. The wicked, specifically Judah, trust false gods and military alliances instead of God, and thus are barren and unfruitful. The righteous place their confidence in God, so they flourish like trees planted by water (see Psalm 1). In times of trouble, the wicked are already impoverished and spiritually weak, so they have no strength to draw on. But the righteous have abundant strength, not only for their own needs, but even for the needs of others. Are you satisfied with being unfruitful, or do you, like a well-watered tree, have strength for the time of crisis and even some to share?

and it does not cease to bear fruit.

17.9 Eccles 9.3 Mt 13.15 Mk 2.17 Rom 1.21

9 The heart is devious above all else;
it is perverse—
who can understand it?

17.10 1 Sam 16.7 Jer 11.20 Rom 8.27

10 I the LORD test the mind
and search the heart,
to give to all according to their ways,
according to the fruit of their doings.

11 Like the partridge hatching what it did not lay,
so are all who amass wealth unjustly;
in mid-life it will leave them,
and at their end they will prove to be fools.

17.12 Jer 14.21

12 O glorious throne, exalted from the beginning,
shrine of our sanctuary!

17.13 Jer 14.8

13 O hope of Israel! O LORD!
All who forsake you shall be put to shame;
those who turn away from you[l] shall be recorded in the underworld,[m]
for they have forsaken the fountain of living water, the LORD.

17.14 Deut 10.21 Ps 54.1 Jer 33.6

14 Heal me, O LORD, and I shall be healed;
save me, and I shall be saved;
for you are my praise.

17.15 Isa 5.19 Amos 5.18

15 See how they say to me,
"Where is the word of the LORD?
Let it come!"
16 But I have not run away from being a shepherd[n] in your service,
nor have I desired the fatal day.
You know what came from my lips;
it was before your face.

17.17 Jer 16.19 Nah 1.7

17 Do not become a terror to me;
you are my refuge in the day of disaster;

17.18 Ps 35.4,26 Jer 20.11

18 Let my persecutors be shamed,
but do not let me be shamed;
let them be dismayed,
but do not let me be dismayed;
bring on them the day of disaster;
destroy them with double destruction!

God will burn the city gates

17.21 Ex 16.23-29 Num 15.32-36 Neh 13.15-21 Isa 56.2; 58.13 Ezek 20.12 Mk 4.24 Jn 5.9-12

19 Thus said the LORD to me: Go and stand in the People's Gate, by which the
kings of Judah enter and by which they go out, and in all the gates of Jerusalem,
20 and say to them: Hear the word of the LORD, you kings of Judah, and all Judah,
and all the inhabitants of Jerusalem, who enter by these gates. 21 Thus says the
LORD: For the sake of your lives, take care that you do not bear a burden on the

[l] Heb *me* [m] Or *in the earth* [n] Meaning of Heb uncertain

17.9, 10 Our hearts have been inclined toward sin from the time we were born. It is easy to fall into the routine of forgetting and forsaking God. But we can still choose whether or not to continue in sin. We can yield to a specific temptation, or we can ask God to help us resist.

17.11 There is a right way and a wrong way to do any task. Jeremiah says that the man who becomes wealthy through deceit will end up foolish and poor. Whether at work, school, or play, we should strive to be honest in all our dealings. Getting a promotion, passing an exam, or gaining prestige through deceit will never bring God's blessing or lasting happiness.

17.19–27 The people were using the sabbath, their day of rest (Exodus 20.8–11), to work. They considered making money more important than keeping God's law. If they would repent and put God first in their lives, God promised them honor among the nations. Over a century later, when Nehemiah led the exiles who were returning to Jerusalem, one of his most important reforms was to reinstitute sabbath observance (Nehemiah 13.15–22).

sabbath day or bring it in by the gates of Jerusalem. 22 And do not carry a burden out
of your houses on the sabbath or do any work, but keep the sabbath day holy, as I
commanded your ancestors. 23 Yet they did not listen or incline their ear; they stiffened their necks and would not hear or receive instruction.
24 But if you listen to me, says the LORD, and bring in no burden by the gates
of this city on the sabbath day, but keep the sabbath day holy and do no work on it,
25 then there shall enter by the gates of this city kings[o] who sit on the throne of
David, riding in chariots and on horses, they and their officials, the people of Judah
and the inhabitants of Jerusalem; and this city shall be inhabited forever. 26 And
people shall come from the towns of Judah and the places around Jerusalem, from
the land of Benjamin, from the Shephelah, from the hill country, and from the
Negeb, bringing burnt offerings and sacrifices, grain offerings and frankincense,
and bringing thank offerings to the house of the LORD. 27 But if you do not listen to
me, to keep the sabbath day holy, and to carry in no burden through the gates of
Jerusalem on the sabbath day, then I will kindle a fire in its gates; it shall devour the
palaces of Jerusalem and shall not be quenched.

The people try to silence Jeremiah

18 The word that came to Jeremiah from the LORD: 2 "Come, go down to the
potter's house, and there I will let you hear my words." 3 So I went down to
the potter's house, and there he was working at his wheel. 4 The vessel he was
making of clay was spoiled in the potter's hand, and he reworked it into another
vessel, as seemed good to him.
5 Then the word of the LORD came to me: 6 Can I not do with you, O house of
Israel, just as this potter has done? says the LORD. Just like the clay in the potter's
hand, so are you in my hand, O house of Israel. 7 At one moment I may declare
concerning a nation or a kingdom, that I will pluck up and break down and destroy
it, 8 but if that nation, concerning which I have spoken, turns from its evil, I will
change my mind about the disaster that I intended to bring on it. 9 And at another
moment I may declare concerning a nation or a kingdom that I will build and plant
it, 10 but if it does evil in my sight, not listening to my voice, then I will change my
mind about the good that I had intended to do to it. 11 Now, therefore, say to the
people of Judah and the inhabitants of Jerusalem: Thus says the LORD: Look, I am
a potter shaping evil against you and devising a plan against you. Turn now, all of
you from your evil way, and amend your ways and your doings.
12 But they say, "It is no use! We will follow our own plans, and each of us will
act according to the stubbornness of our evil will."

13 Therefore thus says the LORD:
Ask among the nations:
  Who has heard the like of this?
The virgin Israel has done
  a most horrible thing.
14 Does the snow of Lebanon leave
  the crags of Sirion?[p]
Do the mountain[q] waters run dry,[r]

17.23 Jer 7.26; 19.15
17.24 Ex 15.26; 20.8-11; Deut 11.13; Ezek 20.20
17.25 2 Sam 7.16; Ps 132.13,14; Jer 22.4; Lk 1.32
17.26 Ps 107.22; Jer 33.11
17.27 Jer 39.8; Ezek 20.47; Amos 2.5
18.2 Jer 19.1,2
18.6 Isa 45.9; 64.8; Rom 9.21
18.7 Jer 1.10
18.8 Jer 7.3-7; Ezek 18.21
18.9 Jer 31.28; Amos 9.11-15
18.10 1 Sam 2.30; Jer 7.24-28; Ezek 33.18
18.11 2 Kgs 17.13; Isa 1.16-19; Jer 4.6; 11.11; Acts 28.20
18.12 Deut 29.19; Jer 2.25; 16.12
18.13 Jer 2.10,11; 23.14; Hos 6.10

[o] Cn: Heb *kings and officials* [p] Cn: Heb *of the field* [q] Cn: Heb *foreign* [r] Cn: Heb *Are . . . plucked up?*

17.26 The Shephelah are the hills in western Palestine. The Negeb is the southern part of Judah.

18.1–19.15 The parables in these chapters, probably written during the early years of Jehoiakim's reign, illustrate God's sovereignty over the nation. God has power over the clay (Judah), and he continues to work with it to make it a useful vessel. But Judah must soon repent, or the clay will harden the wrong way. Then it will be worth nothing and will be broken and destroyed.

18.6 As the potter molded or shaped a clay pot on the potter's wheel, defects often appeared. The potter had power over the clay, to allow the defects or to reshape the pot. Likewise, God had power to reshape the nation to conform to his purposes. Our strategy is not to become mindless and passive – one aspect of clay – but to be willing and receptive to God's impact on us. When we yield to God, he begins reshaping us into valuable vessels.

18.12 Our society admires assertiveness, independence, and defiance of authority. In a relationship with God these qualities become stubbornness, self-importance, and refusal to listen or change. Unchecked, stubborness becomes a way of life hostile to God.

the cold flowing streams?
18.15 Isa 62.10 Jer 2.32; 6.16 7.9; 44.17
15 But my people have forgotten me,
they burn offerings to a delusion;
they have stumbled[s] in their ways,
in the ancient roads,
and have gone into bypaths,
not the highway,
18.16 Jer 25.9; 48.27 50.13 Ezek 33.28,29
16 making their land a horror,
a thing to be hissed at forever.
All who pass by it are horrified
and shake their heads.
18.17 Jer 13.24
17 Like the wind from the east,
I will scatter them before the enemy.
I will show them my back, not my face,
in the day of their calamity.

18.18 Ps 52.2 Jer 2.8; 5.13 8.8; 11.19 18.11; 20.10
18 Then they said, "Come, let us make plots against Jeremiah — for instruction
shall not perish from the priest, nor counsel from the wise, nor the word from the
prophet. Come, let us bring charges against him,[t] and let us not heed any of his
words."

19 Give heed to me, O LORD,
and listen to what my adversaries say!
18.20 Ps 35.7; 57.6 Jer 5.26
20 Is evil a recompense for good?
Yet they have dug a pit for my life.
Remember how I stood before you
to speak good for them,
to turn away your wrath from them.

[s] Gk Syr Vg: Heb *they made them stumble* [t] Heb *strike him with the tongue*

GOD'S OBJECT LESSONS IN JEREMIAH

Reference	Object Lesson	Significance
1.11, 12	Whip from the almond tree	God will carry out his threats of punishment.
1.13	Pot of boiling water tipping southward	God will punish Judah.
13.1–11	A ruined loincloth	Because the people refused to listen to God they had become useless, good for nothing, like a ruined belt (or loincloth).
18.1–17	Potter's clay	God could destroy his sinful people if he so desired. This is a warning to them to repent before he is forced to bring judgment.
19.1–12	Broken clay jars	God would smash Judah just as Jeremiah smashed the clay jars.
24.1–10	Two baskets of figs	Good figs represent God's remnant. Bad figs are the people left behind.
27.2–11	Yoke	Any nation who refused to submit to Babylon's yoke of control would be punished.
43.8–13	Large stones	The stones marked the place where Nebuchadnezzar would set his throne when God allowed him to conquer Egypt.
51.59–64	Book sunk in the river	Babylon would sink, to rise no more.

18.18 Jeremiah's words and actions challenged the people's social and moral behavior. He had openly spoken against the priests, wise men, and prophets (4.9; 8.8, 9). He wasn't afraid to give unpopular criticism. The people could either obey him or silence him. They chose the latter. They did not think they needed Jeremiah; their false prophets told them what they wanted to hear.

21 Therefore give their children over to famine;
hurl them out to the power of the sword,
let their wives become childless and widowed.
May their men meet death by pestilence,
their youths be slain by the sword in battle.
22 May a cry be heard from their houses,
when you bring the marauder suddenly upon them!
For they have dug a pit to catch me,
and laid snares for my feet.
23 Yet you, O LORD, know
all their plotting to kill me.
Do not forgive their iniquity,
do not blot out their sin from your sight.
Let them be tripped up before you;
deal with them while you are angry.

18.21 Ps 109.9-20 Jer 9.21; 11.22 14.16
18.22 Ps 140.5 Jer 6.26
18.23 Jer 6.15,21 7.20; 17.4

God will shatter Jerusalem

19 Thus said the LORD: Go and buy a potter's earthenware jug. Take with you[u]
some of the elders of the people and some of the senior priests, 2 and go out
to the valley of the son of Hinnom at the entry of the Potsherd Gate, and proclaim
there the words that I tell you. 3 You shall say: Hear the word of the LORD, O kings
of Judah and inhabitants of Jerusalem. Thus says the LORD of hosts, the God of
Israel: I am going to bring such disaster upon this place that the ears of everyone
who hears of it will tingle. 4 Because the people have forsaken me, and have profaned this place by making offerings in it to other gods whom neither they nor their
ancestors nor the kings of Judah have known; and because they have filled this
place with the blood of the innocent, 5 and gone on building the high places of Baal
to burn their children in the fire as burnt offerings to Baal, which I did not command or decree, nor did it enter my mind. 6 Therefore the days are surely coming,
says the LORD, when this place shall no more be called Topheth, or the valley of the
son of Hinnom, but the valley of Slaughter. 7 And in this place I will make void the
plans of Judah and Jerusalem, and will make them fall by the sword before their
enemies, and by the hand of those who seek their life. I will give their dead bodies
for food to the birds of the air and to the wild animals of the earth. 8 And I will make
this city a horror, a thing to be hissed at; everyone who passes by it will be horrified
and will hiss because of all its disasters. 9 And I will make them eat the flesh of their
sons and the flesh of their daughters, and all shall eat the flesh of their neighbors in
the siege, and in the distress with which their enemies and those who seek their life
afflict them.
10 Then you shall break the jug in the sight of those who go with you, 11 and
shall say to them: Thus says the LORD of hosts: So will I break this people and this
city, as one breaks a potter's vessel, so that it can never be mended. In Topheth
they shall bury until there is no more room to bury. 12 Thus will I do to this place,
says the LORD, and to its inhabitants, making this city like Topheth. 13 And the
houses of Jerusalem and the houses of the kings of Judah shall be defiled like the
place of Topheth—all the houses upon whose roofs offerings have been made to
the whole host of heaven, and libations have been poured out to other gods.
14 When Jeremiah came from Topheth, where the LORD had sent him to proph-

19.1 Num 11.16 Josh 15.8 Jer 7.31,32
19.4 2 Kgs 21.6,16 Isa 65.11 Jer 2.34; 7.6,9 11.13; 17.13 Dan 11.31
19.5 2 Kgs 7.17 Ps 106.37,38 Jer 32.35
19.7 Ps 33.10,11 79.2,3 Isa 28.17,18
19.8 1 Kgs 9.8 2 Chron 7.21 Jer 18.16
19.9 Deut 28.53,55 Ezek 5.10 Lam 4.10
19.11 Ps 2.9 Isa 30.14 Jer 7.32 Rev 2.27
19.13 Deut 4.19 2 Kgs 17.16 Jer 8.2; 32.29 52.13 Ezek 20.28 Zeph 1.5
19.14 Jer 26.2

u Syr Tg Compare Gk: Heb lacks *take with you*

19.6 The valley of the son of Hinnom was the garbage dump of Jerusalem and the place where children were sacrificed to the god Molech. It is also mentioned in 7.31, 32. Topheth is a location in the valley and means "fire place." This is where the child sacrifices were made.

19.7–13 The horrible carnage that Jeremiah predicted happened twice, during the Babylonian invasion under Nebuchadnezzar in 586 B.C. and in A.D. 70 when Titus destroyed Jerusalem. During the Babylonian siege, food became so scarce that people became cannibals, even eating their own children. (See Leviticus 26.29 and Deuteronomy 28.53–57 for prophecies concerning this; and see 2 Kings 6.28, 29; Lamentations 2.20; 4.10 for accounts of actual occurrences.)

19.8 "Hissing" could be a reference to the sound made by people who are so horrified that they suck in their breath. Or it could be a sound of mockery and scorn.

19.15 Neh 9.17,29 Jer 7.26; 17.23

esy, he stood in the court of the LORD's house and said to all the people: 15Thus
says the LORD of hosts, the God of Israel: I am now bringing upon this city and
upon all its towns all the disaster that I have pronounced against it, because they
have stiffened their necks, refusing to hear my words.

Jeremiah is put in stocks

20.1 1 Chron 24.14 Ezra 2.37,38
20.2 1 Kgs 22.27 2 Chron 16.10 Jer 1.19; 37.13 Zech 14.10
20.4 Jer 29.21 39.6,7 Ezek 26.21
20.5 2 Kgs 20.17 2 Chron 36.10 Jer 15.13; 17.3 27.21,22
20.6 Jer 14.14,15 Lam 2.14

20 Now the priest Pashhur son of Immer, who was chief officer in the house of
the LORD, heard Jeremiah prophesying these things. 2Then Pashhur struck
the prophet Jeremiah, and put him in the stocks that were in the upper Benjamin
Gate of the house of the LORD. 3The next morning when Pashhur released Jeremiah
from the stocks, Jeremiah said to him, The LORD has named you not Pashhur but
"Terror-all-around." 4For thus says the LORD: I am making you a terror to yourself
and to all your friends; and they shall fall by the sword of their enemies while you
look on. And I will give all Judah into the hand of the king of Babylon; he shall
carry them captive to Babylon, and shall kill them with the sword. 5I will give all
the wealth of this city, all its gains, all its prized belongings, and all the treasures
of the kings of Judah into the hand of their enemies, who shall plunder them, and
seize them, and carry them to Babylon. 6And you, Pashhur, and all who live in
your house, shall go into captivity, and to Babylon you shall go; there you shall die,
and there you shall be buried, you and all your friends, to whom you have prophesied falsely.

20.7 Ps 22.7 Lam 3.14 Ezek 3.14 Mic 3.8

7 O LORD, you have enticed me,
and I was enticed;
you have overpowered me,
and you have prevailed.
I have become a laughingstock all day long;
everyone mocks me.
8 For whenever I speak, I must cry out,
I must shout, "Violence and destruction!"
For the word of the LORD has become for me
a reproach and derision all day long.

20.9 Ps 39.3 Jer 4.19 Acts 4.20

9 If I say, "I will not mention him,
or speak any more in his name,"
then within me there is something like a burning fire
shut up in my bones;
I am weary with holding it in,
and I cannot.

20.10 1 Kgs 19.2 22.27 Neh 6.6-13 Ps 41.9

10 For I hear many whispering:
"Terror is all around!
Denounce him! Let us denounce him!"
All my close friends
are watching for me to stumble.
"Perhaps he can be enticed,
and we can prevail against him,

20.1ff This event took place during the reign of Jehoiakim of Judah. Jeremiah preached at the valley of Hinnom, the center of idolatry in the city. He also preached in the temple, which should have been the center of true worship. Both places attracted many people; both were places of false worship.

20.1–3 Pashhur was the official in charge of maintaining order in the temple (see 29.26 for a description of the responsibility). He was also a priest and a prophet. Pashhur heard Jeremiah's words and locked Jeremiah up instead of taking his message to heart and acting upon it. The truth sometimes stings, but our reaction to the truth shows what we are made of. We can deny the charges and destroy evidence of our misdeeds, or we can take the truth humbly to heart and let it change us. Pashhur may have thought he was a strong leader, but he was really a coward.

20.4–6 This prophecy of destruction came true in three waves of invasion by Babylon. The first wave happened within the year (605 B.C.). Pashhur was probably exiled to Babylon during the second wave in 597 B.C., when Jehoiachin was taken captive. The third invasion occurred in 586 B.C.

20.7–18 Jeremiah cried out in despair mixed with praise, unburdening his heart to God. He had faithfully proclaimed God's Word and had received nothing in return but persecution and sorrow. Yet when he withheld God's Word for a while, it became fire in his bones until he could withhold it no longer. When God's living Word becomes fire in your bones, you also will feel compelled to share it with others, whatever the results.

and take our revenge on him."
11 But the LORD is with me like a dread warrior;
therefore my persecutors will stumble,
and they will not prevail.
They will be greatly shamed,
for they will not succeed.
Their eternal dishonor
will never be forgotten.
12 O LORD of hosts, you test the righteous,
you see the heart and the mind;
let me see your retribution upon them,
for to you I have committed my cause.

13 Sing to the LORD;
praise the LORD!
For he has delivered the life of the needy
from the hands of evildoers.

14 Cursed be the day
on which I was born!
The day when my mother bore me,
let it not be blessed!
15 Cursed be the man
who brought the news to my father, saying,
"A child is born to you, a son,"
making him very glad.
16 Let that man be like the cities
that the LORD overthrew without pity;
let him hear a cry in the morning
and an alarm at noon,
17 because he did not kill me in the womb;
so my mother would have been my grave,
and her womb forever great.
18 Why did I come forth from the womb
to see toil and sorrow,
and spend my days in shame?

20.11 Deut 32.35,36 Jer 1.8; 15.20

20.12 Ps 7.9; 17.3 139.23 Jer 11.20; 17.10

20.13 Ps 34.6; 69.33 Jer 15.21

20.14 Job 3.3-6

20.17 Job 3.10,11,16 10.18,19

20.18 Job 3.20; 14.1 Ps 102.3 Jer 15.10 1 Cor 4.9-13

4. Jeremiah accuses Judah's leaders

God refuses the king's request

21 This is the word that came to Jeremiah from the LORD, when King Zedekiah
sent to him Pashhur son of Malchiah and the priest Zephaniah son of Maaseiah, saying, 2"Please inquire of the LORD on our behalf, for King Nebuchadrezzar

21.1 2 Kgs 25.18-21 Jer 29.25,29

21.1 Chapters 21 – 28 are Jeremiah's messages concerning Nebuchadnezzar's attacks on Jerusalem between 588 and 586 B.C. (see also 2 Kings 25). King Zedekiah decided to rebel against Nebuchadnezzar, and the nobles advised allying with Egypt. Jeremiah pronounced judgment on the kings (21.1 – 23.8) and false prophets (23.9–40) for leading the people astray. In this section, *Nebuchadnezzar* is spelled *Nebuchadrezzar,* another Hebrew form of the Babylonian name and closer to the Babylonian form of the name.

21.1, 2 King Zedekiah probably referred to God's deliverance of Jerusalem from Sennacherib, king of Assyria, in the days of Hezekiah (Isaiah 36, 37). But Zedekiah's hopes were dashed. He was Judah's last ruler before the exile of 597 B.C.

21.1, 2 Pashhur's abuse had driven Jeremiah to the point of despondency and depression, but now Pashhur came to the prophet for help. God still had work for Jeremiah to do. In living out our faith, we may find that rejection, disappointment, or hard work has brought us to the point of despondency. But we are still needed. God has important work for us as well.

21.1–14 Jeremiah had foretold Jerusalem's destruction. The city's leaders had denied his word and mocked his announcements. In desperation, King Zedekiah turned to God for help, but without acknowledging God's warnings or admitting his sin. Too often we expect God to help us in our time of trouble even though we have ignored him in our time of prosperity. But God wants a lasting relationship. Are you trying to build a lasting friendship with God, or are you merely using him occasionally to escape trouble? What would you think of your family or friends if they thought of you only as a temporary resource?

of Babylon is making war against us; perhaps the LORD will perform a wonderful
deed for us, as he has often done, and will make him withdraw from us."
3 Then Jeremiah said to them: 4 Thus you shall say to Zedekiah: Thus says the
LORD, the God of Israel: I am going to turn back the weapons of war that are in your
hands and with which you are fighting against the king of Babylon and against the
Chaldeans who are besieging you outside the walls; and I will bring them together
into the center of this city. 5 I myself will fight against you with outstretched hand
and mighty arm, in anger, in fury, and in great wrath. 6 And I will strike down the
inhabitants of this city, both human beings and animals; they shall die of a great
pestilence. 7 Afterward, says the LORD, I will give King Zedekiah of Judah, and his
servants, and the people in this city—those who survive the pestilence, sword, and
famine—into the hands of King Nebuchadrezzar of Babylon, into the hands of
their enemies, into the hands of those who seek their lives. He shall strike them
down with the edge of the sword; he shall not pity them, or spare them, or have
compassion.
8 And to this people you shall say: Thus says the LORD: See, I am setting before
you the way of life and the way of death. 9 Those who stay in this city shall die by
the sword, by famine, and by pestilence; but those who go out and surrender to the
Chaldeans who are besieging you shall live and shall have their lives as a prize of
war. 10 For I have set my face against this city for evil and not for good, says the
LORD: it shall be given into the hands of the king of Babylon, and he shall burn it
with fire.
11 To the house of the king of Judah say: Hear the word of the LORD, 12 O house
of David! Thus says the LORD:

Execute justice in the morning,
and deliver from the hand of the oppressor
anyone who has been robbed,
or else my wrath will go forth like fire,
and burn, with no one to quench it,
because of your evil doings.

13 See, I am against you, O inhabitant of the valley,
O rock of the plain,
says the LORD;
you who say, "Who can come down against us,
or who can enter our places of refuge?"
14 I will punish you according to the fruit of your doings,
says the LORD;
I will kindle a fire in its forest,
and it shall devour all that is around it.

God decrees judgment on evil kings

22 Thus says the LORD: Go down to the house of the king of Judah, and speak
there this word, 2 and say: Hear the word of the LORD, O King of Judah
sitting on the throne of David—you, and your servants, and your people who enter
these gates. 3 Thus says the LORD: Act with justice and righteousness, and deliver
from the hand of the oppressor anyone who has been robbed. And do no wrong or
violence to the alien, the orphan, and the widow, or shed innocent blood in this
place. 4 For if you will indeed obey this word, then through the gates of this house
shall enter kings who sit on the throne of David, riding in chariots and on horses,

21.2 2 Kgs 25.1,2; Ps 44.1-4
21.3 Jer 32.5; 33.5; 37.8-10; 38.17,18; 39.3; Lam 2.5,7; Zech 14.2
21.5 Isa 5.25; 63.10; Jer 6.12
21.7 2 Chron 36.17; Jer 13.14; Ezek 7.9; Hab 1.6-10
21.9 Jer 38.2; 39.18
21.10 2 Chron 36.19; Jer 32.28,29; 39.8; 44.11,27; 52.13
21.12 Isa 1.17; Jer 4.5; Ezek 20.47,48; Zech 7.9,10
21.14 2 Chron 36.19; Jer 52.13
22.2 Isa 9.7; Jer 17.25; Lk 1.32
22.3 Ex 22.21-24; Ps 72.4; Jer 7.6; 19.4; 21.12; 22.17

21.13 "Inhabitant of the valley" and "rock of the plain" refer to Jerusalem. Jerusalem was built on a plateau with valleys on three sides. Because of its strategic location, the inhabitants thought they were safe.

22.1ff Chapters 22–25 are not in chronological order. In 21.9 God says it is too late for repentance. In 22.4 God says there is still time to change. The events of this chapter occurred before those of chapter 21. This message was probably given during the reign of Jehoiakim (22.13), about ten years before Zedekiah.

22.3 God gave the king the basis for rebuilding the nation—turn from evil and do right. Doing right is more than simply believing all the right doctrines about God. It is living obediently to God. Good works do not save us, but they display our faith (James 2.17–26).

they, and their servants, and their people. 5 But if you will not heed these words, I
swear by myself, says the LORD, that this house shall become a desolation. 6 For
thus says the LORD concerning the house of the king of Judah:

You are like Gilead to me,
  like the summit of Lebanon;
but I swear that I will make you a desert,
  an uninhabited city.[v]
7 I will prepare destroyers against you,
  all with their weapons;
they shall cut down your choicest cedars
  and cast them into the fire.

8 And many nations will pass by this city, and all of them will say one to another, "Why has the LORD dealt in this way with that great city?" 9 And they will
answer, "Because they abandoned the covenant of the LORD their God, and worshiped other gods and served them."

10 Do not weep for him who is dead,
  nor bemoan him;
weep rather for him who goes away,
  for he shall return no more
  to see his native land.

11 For thus says the LORD concerning Shallum son of King Josiah of Judah,
who succeeded his father Josiah, and who went away from this place: He shall
return here no more, 12 but in the place where they have carried him captive he shall
die, and he shall never see this land again.

13 Woe to him who builds his house by unrighteousness,
  and his upper rooms by injustice;
who makes his neighbors work for nothing,
  and does not give them their wages;
14 who says, "I will build myself a spacious house
  with large upper rooms,"
and who cuts out windows for it,
  paneling it with cedar,
  and painting it with vermilion.
15 Are you a king
  because you compete in cedar?
Did not your father eat and drink
  and do justice and righteousness?
  Then it was well with him.
16 He judged the cause of the poor and needy;
  then it was well.
Is not this to know me?
  says the LORD.
17 But your eyes and heart
  are only on your dishonest gain,
for shedding innocent blood,
  and for practicing oppression and violence.

22.5 Amos 6.8 Heb 6.13
22.6 Isa 6.11 Jer 7.34
22.7 Isa 10.3-6, 33,34 Jer 4.6,7
22.8 Deut 29.24-26 1 Kgs 9.8,9 2 Chron 7.20,22 Jer 16.10
22.9 2 Chron 34.25 Jer 11.3
22.12 2 Kgs 23.34
22.13 Jer 17.11 Hab 2.9
22.14 Isa 5.8,9 Hab 1.4
22.15 2 Kgs 23.25 Jer 21.12; 42.6
22.16 Ps 72.1-4,12,13 Jer 9.24
22.17 Jer 6.13; 8.10 Lk 12.15-20

v Cn: Heb *uninhabited cities*

22.10–12 Good King Josiah had died at the battle of Megiddo; his son Shallum (Jehoahaz) reigned for only three months in 609 B.C. before being taken away to Egypt by Pharaoh Neco. He would be the first ruler to die in exile. The people were told not to waste their tears on the death of Josiah, but to cry for the king who was taken into exile and would never return.

22.15, 16 God passed judgment on King Jehoiakim. His father, Josiah, had been one of Judah's great kings, but Jehoiakim was evil. Josiah had been faithful with his responsibility to teach his son and model right living, but Jehoiakim had been unfaithful with his responsibility to imitate his father. God's judgment was on unfaithful Jehoiakim. He could not claim his father's blessings when he had not followed his father's God. We may inherit our parents' money, but we cannot inherit their faith. A great heritage, a good education, or a beautiful home doesn't guarantee a strong character. We must have our own relationship with God.

18 Therefore thus says the LORD concerning King Jehoiakim son of Josiah of
Judah:

They shall not lament for him, saying,
"Alas, my brother!" or "Alas, sister!"
They shall not lament for him, saying,
"Alas, lord!" or "Alas, his majesty!"
22.19 Jer 36.30
19 With the burial of a donkey he shall be buried—
dragged off and thrown out beyond the gates of Jerusalem.

22.20 Deut 32.49
20 Go up to Lebanon, and cry out,
and lift up your voice in Bashan;
cry out from Abarim,
for all your lovers are crushed.
21 I spoke to you in your prosperity,
but you said, "I will not listen."
This has been your way from your youth,
for you have not obeyed my voice.
22.22 Jer 30.14
22 The wind shall shepherd all your shepherds,
and your lovers shall go into captivity;
then you will be ashamed and dismayed
because of all your wickedness.
23 O inhabitant of Lebanon,
nested among the cedars,
how you will groan[w] when pangs come upon you,
pain as of a woman in labor!

22.24 2 Kgs 24.15,16 Jer 21.7 34.20,21 Hag 2.23
24 As I live, says the LORD, even if King Coniah son of Jehoiakim of Judah
were the signet ring on my right hand, even from there I would tear you off 25 and
give you into the hands of those who seek your life, into the hands of those of whom
you are afraid, even into the hands of King Nebuchadrezzar of Babylon and into the
hands of the Chaldeans. 26 I will hurl you and the mother who bore you into another
country, where you were not born, and there you shall die. 27 But they shall not
return to the land to which they long to return.

22.28 Jer 15.1 Hos 8.8
28 Is this man Coniah a despised broken pot,
a vessel no one wants?
Why are he and his offspring hurled out
and cast away in a land that they do not know?
22.29 Jer 6.19 Mic 1.2
29 O land, land, land,
hear the word of the LORD!
22.30 Jer 36.30 Mt 1.12
30 Thus says the LORD:
Record this man as childless,
a man who shall not succeed in his days;
for none of his offspring shall succeed
in sitting on the throne of David,
and ruling again in Judah.

[w] Gk Vg Syr: Heb *will be pitied*

22.21 Jehoiakim had been hardheaded and hardhearted since childhood. God warned him, but he refused to listen. His prosperity always took a higher priority than his relationship with God. If you ever find yourself so comfortable that you don't have time for God, stop and ask which is more important—the comforts of this life or a close relationship with God.

22.24, 25 Coniah is an abbreviation for Jeconiah (another name for Jehoiachin). A signet ring was extremely valuable because a king used it to authenticate important documents. Jehoiachin's sins spoiled his usefulness to God. Even if he was God's own signet ring, God would depose him because of his sins (see 24.1).

22.30 Zedekiah reigned after Jehoiachin but died before him (52.10, 11). Jehoiachin (Coniah) was the last king of David's line through Solomon, and his line died with him (1 Chronicles 3.15–20). Jehoiachin adopted the seven sons of Neri, a descendant of Solomon's brother Nathan, and Jehoiachin's grandson Zerubbabel ruled after the return from exile (Ezra 2.2). He was only a governor, not a king. But through Zerubbabel, David's line was continued until the time of Christ's birth.

A righteous king will come

23 Woe to the shepherds who destroy and scatter the sheep of my pasture! says
the LORD. 2 Therefore thus says the LORD, the God of Israel, concerning the
shepherds who shepherd my people: It is you who have scattered my flock, and
have driven them away, and you have not attended to them. So I will attend to you
for your evil doings, says the LORD. 3 Then I myself will gather the remnant of my
flock out of all the lands where I have driven them, and I will bring them back to
their fold, and they shall be fruitful and multiply. 4 I will raise up shepherds over
them who will shepherd them, and they shall not fear any longer, or be dismayed,
nor shall any be missing, says the LORD.
5 The days are surely coming, says the LORD, when I will raise up for David a
righteous Branch, and he shall reign as king and deal wisely, and shall execute
justice and righteousness in the land. 6 In his days Judah will be saved and Israel
will live in safety. And this is the name by which he will be called: "The LORD is
our righteousness."
7 Therefore, the days are surely coming, says the LORD, when it shall no longer
be said, "As the LORD lives who brought the people of Israel up out of the land of
Egypt," 8 but "As the LORD lives who brought out and led the offspring of the house
of Israel out of the land of the north and out of all the lands where he[x] had driven
them." Then they shall live in their own land.

Warning against false prophets

9 Concerning the prophets:
My heart is crushed within me,
all my bones shake;
I have become like a drunkard,
like one overcome by wine,
because of the LORD
and because of his holy words.
10 For the land is full of adulterers;
because of the curse the land mourns,
and the pastures of the wilderness are dried up.
Their course has been evil,
and their might is not right.
11 Both prophet and priest are ungodly;
even in my house I have found their wickedness,
says the LORD.
12 Therefore their way shall be to them
like slippery paths in the darkness,
into which they shall be driven and fall;
for I will bring disaster upon them
in the year of their punishment,
says the LORD.
13 In the prophets of Samaria

[x] Gk: Heb *I*

23.1 Isa 56.9-12
23.2 Ex 32.34; Jer 44.22
23.3 Isa 11.11-16; Jer 31.7,8
23.4 Jer 3.15; 31.10; Jn 6.39; 10.28; 1 Pet 1.5
23.5 Isa 9.6; 11.1-5; 53.2; Jer 33.15,16; Zech 3.8; 6.12,13; Mt 1.21-23; Rom 3.21,22; 1 Cor 1.30
23.7 Isa 43.18,19; Jer 16.14,15
23.10 Ps 107.34; Jer 5.7,8; 9.10
23.11 Jer 6.13; 7.9-10; 8.10
23.12 Isa 8.22; Jer 13.16; Jn 12.35
23.13 1 Kgs 18.18-21; Jer 2.8

23.1–4 After his indictment of Israel's civil leaders, Jeremiah lashed out at the religious leaders. Those responsible to lead Israel in God's path were the very ones responsible for Israel's present plight, and so God had decreed harsh judgment against them. Leaders are held responsible for those entrusted to their care. Whom has God placed in your care? Remember that you are accountable to God for those you influence and lead.

23.5, 6 Jeremiah contrasted the present corrupt leaders with the coming Messiah, the perfect King who would come from David's line to reign over Israel. He is called a righteous Branch because he will sprout up from the roots of David's fallen dynasty. This new growth will have God's own characteristics. Like the Creator, the Branch will be righteous.

23.9–14 How did the nation become so corrupt? A major factor was false prophecy. The false prophets had a large, enthusiastic audience and were very popular because they made the people believe that all was well. By contrast, Jeremiah's message from God was unpopular because it showed the people how bad they were.

There are four warning signs of false prophets – characteristics we need to watch for even today. (1) They may appear to speak God's message, but they do not live according to his principles. (2) They water down God's message in order to make it more palatable. (3) They encourage their listeners, often subtly, to disobey

I saw a disgusting thing:
they prophesied by Baal
and led my people Israel astray.

23.14 Isa 1.9,10 Jer 5.30,32 Ezek 13.22,23 Mt 11.24

14 But in the prophets of Jerusalem
I have seen a more shocking thing:
they commit adultery and walk in lies;
they strengthen the hands of evildoers,
so that no one turns from wickedness;
all of them have become like Sodom to me,
and its inhabitants like Gomorrah.

23.15 Deut 29.18 Jer 8.14; 9.15

15 Therefore thus says the LORD of hosts concerning the prophets:
"I am going to make them eat wormwood,
and give them poisoned water to drink;
for from the prophets of Jerusalem
ungodliness has spread throughout the land."

23.16 Jer 14.14 Ezek 13.2,3,6 Mt 7.15 2 Cor 11.13-15 Gal 1.8,9 1 Jn 4.1
23.17 Jer 5.12; 8.11 Amos 9.10 Mic 2.11; 3.11

16 Thus says the LORD of hosts: Do not listen to the words of the prophets who
prophesy to you; they are deluding you. They speak visions of their own minds, not
from the mouth of the LORD. 17 They keep saying to those who despise the word of
the LORD, "It shall be well with you"; and to all who stubbornly follow their own
stubborn hearts, they say, "No calamity shall come upon you."

18 For who has stood in the council of the LORD
so as to see and to hear his word?
Who has given heed to his word so as to proclaim it?

23.19 Jer 30.23 Amos 1.14

19 Look, the storm of the LORD!
Wrath has gone forth,
a whirling tempest;
it will burst upon the head of the wicked.

23.20 Isa 55.11 Jer 30.24 Zech 1.5,6

20 The anger of the LORD will not turn back
until he has executed and accomplished
the intents of his mind.
In the latter days you will understand it clearly.

21 I did not send the prophets,
yet they ran;
I did not speak to them,
yet they prophesied.

23.22 Jer 35.15 Zech 1.4 1 Thess 1.9,10

22 But if they had stood in my council,
then they would have proclaimed my words to my people,
and they would have turned them from their evil way,
and from the evil of their doings.

23.23 Ps 139.1-10
23.24 Job 22.13,14 Ps 139.7-12 Isa 29.15,16
23.25 Jer 8.6; 29.8
23.26 1 Tim 4.1,2
23.27 Deut 13.1-3 Judg 3.12 8.33,34

23 Am I a God near by, says the LORD, and not a God far off? 24 Who can hide
in secret places so that I cannot see them? says the LORD. Do I not fill heaven and
earth? says the LORD. 25 I have heard what the prophets have said who prophesy lies
in my name, saying, "I have dreamed, I have dreamed!" 26 How long? Will the
hearts of the prophets ever turn back — those who prophesy lies, and who prophesy
the deceit of their own heart? 27 They plan to make my people forget my name by
their dreams that they tell one another, just as their ancestors forgot my name for

God. (4) They tend to be arrogant and self-serving, appealing to the desires of their audience instead of being true to God's Word.

23.14 Sodom and Gomorrah were sinful cities destroyed by God (Genesis 19.23, 24). In the Bible they typify the ultimate in degrading, sinful behavior and rebellion toward God.

23.20 "The latter days" means the days to come. The people will see the truth of this prophecy when Jerusalem falls.

Baal. 28 Let the prophet who has a dream tell the dream, but let the one who has my
word speak my word faithfully. What has straw in common with wheat? says the
LORD. 29 Is not my word like fire, says the LORD, and like a hammer that breaks a
rock in pieces? 30 See, therefore, I am against the prophets, says the LORD, who
steal my words from one another. 31 See, I am against the prophets, says the LORD,
who use their own tongues and say, "Says the LORD." 32 See, I am against those
who prophesy lying dreams, says the LORD, and who tell them, and who lead my
people astray by their lies and their recklessness, when I did not send them or appoint them; so they do not profit this people at all, says the LORD.

33 When this people, or a prophet, or a priest asks you, "What is the burden of
the LORD?" you shall say to them, "You are the burden,[y] and I will cast you off,
says the LORD." 34 And as for the prophet, priest, or the people who say, "The
burden of the LORD," I will punish them and their households. 35 Thus shall you say
to one another, among yourselves, "What has the LORD answered?" or "What has
the LORD spoken?" 36 But "the burden of the LORD" you shall mention no more, for
the burden is everyone's own word, and so you pervert the words of the living God,
the LORD of hosts, our God. 37 Thus you shall ask the prophet, "What has the LORD
answered you?" or "What has the LORD spoken?" 38 But if you say, "the burden of
the LORD," thus says the LORD: Because you have said these words, "the burden of
the LORD," when I sent to you, saying, You shall not say, "the burden of the
LORD," 39 therefore, I will surely lift you up[z] and cast you away from my presence,
you and the city that I gave to you and your ancestors. 40 And I will bring upon you
everlasting disgrace and perpetual shame, which shall not be forgotten.

Jeremiah's vision of the figs

24 The LORD showed me two baskets of figs placed before the temple of the
LORD. This was after King Nebuchadrezzar of Babylon had taken into exile
from Jerusalem King Jeconiah son of Jehoiakim of Judah, together with the officials of Judah, the artisans, and the smiths, and had brought them to Babylon. 2 One
basket had very good figs, like first-ripe figs, but the other basket had very bad figs,
so bad that they could not be eaten. 3 And the LORD said to me, "What do you see,
Jeremiah?" I said, "Figs, the good figs very good, and the bad figs very bad, so bad
that they cannot be eaten."

4 Then the word of the LORD came to me: 5 Thus says the LORD, the God of
Israel: Like these good figs, so I will regard as good the exiles from Judah, whom
I have sent away from this place to the land of the Chaldeans. 6 I will set my eyes

23.28 1 Cor 3.12,13
23.29 Jer 5.14; 20.9; 2 Cor 10.4,5
23.30 Ezek 13.8
23.33 Nah 1.1; Hab 1.1; Zech 9.1
23.34 Zech 13.3
23.35 Jer 33.3; 42.4
23.36 2 Kgs 19.4; Jer 10.10; 2 Pet 3.16
23.38 Jer 7.14,15; Ezek 8.18
23.40 Jer 20.11; Ezek 5.14,15
24.1 2 Kgs 24.10-16; 2 Chron 36.10; Jer 27.19-21
24.4 Nah 1.7; Zech 13.9
24.6 Jer 29.10; 31.4; 32.37,41; 33.7; Ezek 11.17

y Gk Vg: Heb *What burden* z Heb Mss Gk Vg: MT *forget you*

23.28 True prophets and false prophets are as different as straw (chaff) and wheat (grain). Worthless chaff blows away with the wind, while the grain remains to nourish many. To share God's Word is a great responsibility, because the way we present it and live it will encourage people either to accept it or to reject it. Whether we speak from a pulpit, teach in a class, or share with friends, we are entrusted with accurately communicating and living out God's Word. As you share God's Word with friends and neighbors, they will look for its effectiveness in your life. Unless it has changed you, why should they let it change them? If you preach it, make sure you live it!

23.33–40 People mocked Jeremiah by saying sarcastically, "What is the burden of the Lord?" ("burden" meaning "utterance"). Jeremiah says that *they* were God's burden, or "weight," which he will cast off. The people mocked Jeremiah and God because it seemed that Jeremiah brought nothing but God's sad news of condemnation. But this sad news was the truth. If they accepted it, they would have to repent and turn to God. Because they did not want to do this, they rejected Jeremiah's message. Have you ever rejected a message or made fun of it because it would require you to change your ways? Before dismissing someone who brings sad news, look carefully at your motives.

24.1 This happened in 597 B.C. Jeconiah (also known as Jehoiachin) was taken to Babylon, and Zedekiah became king. Princes were exiled to keep them from exerting power and starting a rebellion. Skilled tradesmen were taken because they were valuable for Babylon's building program. Jeremiah foretold this event in 22.24–28.

24.2–10 The good figs represented the exiles to Babylon—not because they themselves were good, but because their hearts would respond to God. He would preserve them and bring them back to the land. The bad figs represented those who remained in Judah or ran away to Egypt. The people believed they would be blessed if they remained in the land, but the opposite was true, because God would use the captivity to refine the exiles. We may assume we are blessed when life goes well and cursed when it does not. But trouble is a blessing when it makes us stronger, and prosperity is a curse if it entices us away from God. If you are facing trouble, ask God to help you grow stronger for him. If things are going your way, ask God to help you use your prosperity for him.

24.6 The exiles in Babylon were treated well. Although they were moved to a foreign land, their captivity was not enslavement. The people could function in business and own homes. Some, like Daniel, even held high positions in the government (see Daniel 2.48).

upon them for good, and I will bring them back to this land. I will build them up,
and not tear them down; I will plant them, and not pluck them up. 7 I will give them
a heart to know that I am the LORD; and they shall be my people and I will be their
God, for they shall return to me with their whole heart.
8 But thus says the LORD: Like the bad figs that are so bad they cannot be eaten,
so will I treat King Zedekiah of Judah, his officials, the remnant of Jerusalem who
remain in this land, and those who live in the land of Egypt. 9 I will make them a
horror, an evil thing, to all the kingdoms of the earth—a disgrace, a byword, a
taunt, and a curse in all the places where I shall drive them. 10 And I will send
sword, famine, and pestilence upon them, until they are utterly destroyed from the
land that I gave to them and their ancestors.

Jeremiah prophesies captivity

25 The word that came to Jeremiah concerning all the people of Judah, in the
fourth year of King Jehoiakim son of Josiah of Judah (that was the first year
of King Nebuchadrezzar of Babylon), 2 which the prophet Jeremiah spoke to all the
people of Judah and all the inhabitants of Jerusalem: 3 For twenty-three years, from
the thirteenth year of King Josiah son of Amon of Judah, to this day, the word of
the LORD has come to me, and I have spoken persistently to you, but you have not
listened. 4 And though the LORD persistently sent you all his servants the prophets,
you have neither listened nor inclined your ears to hear 5 when they said, "Turn
now, everyone of you, from your evil way and wicked doings, and you will remain
upon the land that the LORD has given to you and your ancestors from of old and
forever; 6 do not go after other gods to serve and worship them, and do not provoke
me to anger with the work of your hands. Then I will do you no harm." 7 Yet you
did not listen to me, says the LORD, and so you have provoked me to anger with the
work of your hands to your own harm.
8 Therefore thus says the LORD of hosts: Because you have not obeyed my
words, 9 I am going to send for all the tribes of the north, says the LORD, even for
King Nebuchadrezzar of Babylon, my servant, and I will bring them against this
land and its inhabitants, and against all these nations around; I will utterly destroy
them, and make them an object of horror and of hissing, and an everlasting disgrace.[a] 10 And I will banish from them the sound of mirth and the sound of gladness, the voice of the bridegroom and the voice of the bride, the sound of the
millstones and the light of the lamp. 11 This whole land shall become a ruin and a
waste, and these nations shall serve the king of Babylon seventy years. 12 Then after
seventy years are completed, I will punish the king of Babylon and that nation, the
land of the Chaldeans, for their iniquity, says the LORD, making the land an everlasting waste. 13 I will bring upon that land all the words that I have uttered against
it, everything written in this book, which Jeremiah prophesied against all the nations. 14 For many nations and great kings shall make slaves of them also; and I will
repay them according to their deeds and the work of their hands.

The cup of God's wrath

15 For thus the LORD, the God of Israel, said to me: Take from my hand this cup

[a] Gk Compare Syr: Heb *and everlasting desolations*

24.7 Jer 31.33; 32.40 Zech 8.8 Heb 8.10
24.8 Jer 29.17; 39.5 44.26-30 Ezek 12.13
24.9 1 Kgs 9.7 Ps 44.13,14 Isa 65.15
24.10 Isa 51.19 Jer 27.8 Ezek 5.12-17
25.1 2 Kgs 24.1,2 Jer 36.1; 46.2
25.2 Jer 1.2 7.25,26 11.7,8; 26.5 36.2,3
25.5 Gen 17.8-10 Isa 55.6,7 Jer 4.1; 7.7 35.15
25.6 Deut 6.14; 8.19 2 Kgs 17.35
25.7 2 Kgs 17.17 21.15 Jer 7.19 32.30-33
25.8 Jer 27.6; 43.10
25.10 Isa 24.8-11 Jer 16.9 Ezek 26.13
25.11 Dan 9.2 Zech 7.5
25.12 Ezra 1.1 Isa 13.14 Jer 29.10, 50,51
25.13 Jer 36.4,29,32
25.14 Jer 27.7

25.1ff Jeremiah gave this message in 605 B.C., the year Nebuchadnezzar came to power. From verse 3 we learn that the beginning of Jeremiah's ministry was in 627 B.C. He predicted the 70 years of captivity a full 20 years before it began.

25.2–6 Imagine preaching the same message for 23 years and continually being rejected! Jeremiah faced this; but because he had committed his life to God, he continued to proclaim the message—"Turn now, everyone of you, from your evil way and wicked doings." Regardless of the people's response, Jeremiah did not give up. God never stops loving us, even when we reject him. We can thank God that he won't give up on us; and like Jeremiah, we can commit ourselves to never giving him up. No matter how people respond when you tell them about God, remain faithful to God's high call and continue to witness for him.

25.12 This event is further described in Daniel 5. The troops of Cyrus the Great entered Babylon in 539 B.C. and killed Belshazzar, the last Babylonian ruler.

25.15–38 Judah would not be the only nation to drink the cup of God's wrath. Jeremiah listed other wicked nations who would experience God's wrath at the hand of Babylon. Finally, Babylon itself (called Sheshach in 25.26) would be destroyed because of its sin.

of the wine of wrath, and make all the nations to whom I send you drink it. 16 They
shall drink and stagger and go out of their minds because of the sword that I am
sending among them.

17 So I took the cup from the LORD's hand, and made all the nations to whom
the LORD sent me drink it: 18 Jerusalem and the towns of Judah, its kings and officials, to make them a desolation and a waste, an object of hissing and of cursing,
as they are today; 19 Pharaoh king of Egypt, his servants, his officials, and all his
people; 20 all the mixed people;[b] all the kings of the land of Uz; all the kings of the
land of the Philistines—Ashkelon, Gaza, Ekron, and the remnant of Ashdod;
21 Edom, Moab, and the Ammonites; 22 all the kings of Tyre, all the kings of Sidon,
and the kings of the coastland across the sea; 23 Dedan, Tema, Buz, and all who
have shaven temples; 24 all the kings of Arabia and all the kings of the mixed peoples[b] that live in the desert; 25 all the kings of Zimri, all the kings of Elam, and all
the kings of Media; 26 all the kings of the north, far and near, one after another, and
all the kingdoms of the world that are on the face of the earth. And after them the
king of Sheshach[c] shall drink.

27 Then you shall say to them, Thus says the LORD of hosts, the God of Israel:
Drink, get drunk and vomit, fall and rise no more, because of the sword that I am
sending among you.

28 And if they refuse to accept the cup from your hand to drink, then you shall
say to them: Thus says the LORD of hosts: You must drink! 29 See, I am beginning
to bring disaster on the city that is called by my name, and how can you possibly
avoid punishment? You shall not go unpunished, for I am summoning a sword
against all the inhabitants of the earth, says the LORD of hosts.

30 You, therefore, shall prophesy against them all these words, and say to
them:

The LORD will roar from on high,
  and from his holy habitation utter his voice;
he will roar mightily against his fold,
  and shout, like those who tread grapes,
  against all the inhabitants of the earth.
31 The clamor will resound to the ends of the earth,
  for the LORD has an indictment against the nations;
he is entering into judgment with all flesh,
  and the guilty he will put to the sword,
says the LORD.

32 Thus says the LORD of hosts:
See, disaster is spreading
  from nation to nation,
and a great tempest is stirring
  from the farthest parts of the earth!

33 Those slain by the LORD on that day shall extend from one end of the earth
to the other. They shall not be lamented, or gathered, or buried; they shall become
dung on the surface of the ground.

34 Wail, you shepherds, and cry out;
  roll in ashes, you lords of the flock,
for the days of your slaughter have come—and your dispersions,[b]
  and you shall fall like a choice vessel.
35 Flight shall fail the shepherds,
  and there shall be no escape for the lords of the flock.
36 Hark! the cry of the shepherds,
  and the wail of the lords of the flock!
For the LORD is despoiling their pasture,
37 and the peaceful folds are devastated,
  because of the fierce anger of the LORD.
38 Like a lion he has left his covert;

25.15 Jer 51.7
25.17 Jer 1.10
25.19 Jer 46.2-28 Lam 4.21
25.21 Jer 48.1-47 49.1-22 Amos 1.13-15 2.1-3
25.22 Jer 47.4 Zech 9.2-4
25.23 Jer 49.7,8
25.25 Jer 49.34
25.26 Jer 50.9; 51.41
25.29 Prov 11.31 1 Pet 4.17
25.30 Joel 2.11 Amos 1.2
25.31 Isa 66.16
25.32 Isa 30.30 34.2,3
25.33 Isa 5.25 Jer 16.4 Ezek 39.4,7
25.34 Isa 34.7 Jer 50.27
25.38 Jer 4.7; 5.6 Hos 5.14 13.7,8

b Meaning of Heb uncertain c *Sheshach* is a cryptogram for *Babel*, Babylon

for their land has become a waste
because of the cruel sword,
and because of his fierce anger.

Jeremiah narrowly escapes death

26 At the beginning of the reign of King Jehoiakim son of Josiah of Judah, this
word came from the LORD: 2 Thus says the LORD: Stand in the court of the
LORD's house, and speak to all the cities of Judah that come to worship in the house
of the LORD; speak to them all the words that I command you; do not hold back a
word. 3 It may be that they will listen, all of them, and will turn from their evil way,
that I may change my mind about the disaster that I intend to bring on them because
of their evil doings. 4 You shall say to them: Thus says the LORD: If you will not
listen to me, to walk in my law that I have set before you, 5 and to heed the words
of my servants the prophets whom I send to you urgently—though you have not
heeded— 6 then I will make this house like Shiloh, and I will make this city a curse
for all the nations of the earth.
7 The priests and the prophets and all the people heard Jeremiah speaking these
words in the house of the LORD. 8 And when Jeremiah had finished speaking all that
the LORD had commanded him to speak to all the people, then the priests and the
prophets and all the people laid hold of him, saying, "You shall die! 9 Why have
you prophesied in the name of the LORD, saying, 'This house shall be like Shiloh,
and this city shall be desolate, without inhabitant'?" And all the people gathered
around Jeremiah in the house of the LORD.
10 When the officials of Judah heard these things, they came up from the king's
house to the house of the LORD and took their seat in the entry of the New Gate of
the house of the LORD. 11 Then the priests and the prophets said to the officials and
to all the people, "This man deserves the sentence of death because he has prophesied against this city, as you have heard with your own ears."
12 Then Jeremiah spoke to all the officials and all the people, saying, "It is the
LORD who sent me to prophesy against this house and this city all the words you
have heard. 13 Now therefore amend your ways and your doings, and obey the voice
of the LORD your God, and the LORD will change his mind about the disaster that he
has pronounced against you. 14 But as for me, here I am in your hands. Do with me
as seems good and right to you. 15 Only know for certain that if you put me to death,
you will be bringing innocent blood upon yourselves and upon this city and its
inhabitants, for in truth the LORD sent me to you to speak all these words in your
ears."
16 Then the officials and all the people said to the priests and the prophets,
"This man does not deserve the sentence of death, for he has spoken to us in the
name of the LORD our God." 17 And some of the elders of the land arose and said to

26.2 Deut 4.2 Jer 7.2; 19.14 42.4 Acts 20.20,27
26.3 Isa 1.16-19 Jer 36.3-7
26.4 Lev 26.14 1 Kgs 9.6 Isa 1.20 Jer 17.27; 22.5 44.10,23
26.5 Ezra 9.11 Jer 25.4
26.6 Ps 78.60,61 Jer 7.12,14 25.8
26.7 Jer 5.31; 11.19 Lam 4.13,14 Mic 3.11 Mt 23.34,35
26.10 Acts 21.31,32
26.11 Jer 18.23; 38.4 Mt 26.66 Acts 6.11-14
26.13 Jer 7.3,5; 18.11
26.15 Num 35.33
26.16 Jer 36.19,25 38.7,13 Acts 5.34-39 23.9,29; 25.25 26.31

26.1ff The events described in this chapter took place in 609–608 B.C., following the events described in chapter 25. Jehoiakim was a materialistic and self-centered king who persecuted and murdered innocent people (36.22–32; 2 Kings 23.36–24.6). Chapter 26 describes how and why Jeremiah was on trial for his life.

26.2 God reminded Jeremiah that he wanted his entire message given—"Do not hold back a word." Jeremiah may have been tempted to leave out the parts that would turn his audience against him, would sound too harsh (the "burden of the Lord" he had been accused of giving, 23.33–40), or would make him sound like a traitor. But by God's command, he was not to delete parts of God's message to suit himself, his audience, or the circumstances in which he found himself. Like Jeremiah, we must never ignore or repress important parts of God's Word to please anyone.

26.2–9 When Jeremiah said that Jerusalem, the city of God, would become a curse word and the temple would be destroyed (26.6), the priests and false prophets were infuriated. The temple was important to them because the people's reverence for it brought them power. By saying that the temple would be destroyed, Jeremiah undermined their authority. Jesus also infuriated the religious leaders of his time by foretelling the destruction of Jerusalem and the temple (Matthew 24.2).

26.16–24 Jeremiah's life was in serious danger, but God used officials and wise men to protect the prophet. God spared Jeremiah because his work for God was not done. Believers, even some of God's prophets, are permitted to die painful deaths. God does not promise to keep every follower from suffering. But he does promise to be with us through every trial, even death.

26.17–19 The elders remembered the words of the prophet Micah (Micah 3.12), similar to the words Jeremiah spoke. When Micah called the people to repent, they did not kill him but turned from their wickedness. Although because of this story the people did not kill Jeremiah, they missed the main point—that the application of the story was for them. They spared Jeremiah, but they did not spare themselves by repenting of their sins. As you recall a great story of the Bible, ask how it can be applied to your life.

all the assembled people, 18 “Micah of Moresheth, who prophesied during the days
of King Hezekiah of Judah, said to all the people of Judah: ‘Thus says the LORD of
hosts,

Zion shall be plowed as a field;
Jerusalem shall become a heap of ruins,
and the mountain of the house a wooded height.’

19 Did King Hezekiah of Judah and all Judah actually put him to death? Did he not
fear the LORD and entreat the favor of the LORD, and did not the LORD change his
mind about the disaster that he had pronounced against them? But we are about to
bring great disaster on ourselves!”

20 There was another man prophesying in the name of the LORD, Uriah son of
Shemaiah from Kiriath-jearim. He prophesied against this city and against this land
in words exactly like those of Jeremiah. 21 And when King Jehoiakim, with all his
warriors and all the officials, heard his words, the king sought to put him to death;
but when Uriah heard of it, he was afraid and fled and escaped to Egypt. 22 Then
King Jehoiakim sent[d] Elnathan son of Achbor and men with him to Egypt, 23 and
they took Uriah from Egypt and brought him to King Jehoiakim, who struck him
down with the sword and threw his dead body into the burial place of the common
people.

24 But the hand of Ahikam son of Shaphan was with Jeremiah so that he was
not given over into the hands of the people to be put to death.

Jeremiah urges submission to Babylon

27 In the beginning of the reign of King Zedekiah[e] son of Josiah of Judah, this
word came to Jeremiah from the LORD. 2 Thus the LORD said to me: Make
yourself a yoke of straps and bars, and put them on your neck. 3 Send word[f] to the
king of Edom, the king of Moab, the king of the Ammonites, the king of Tyre, and
the king of Sidon by the hand of the envoys who have come to Jerusalem to King
Zedekiah of Judah. 4 Give them this charge for their masters: Thus says the LORD
of hosts, the God of Israel: This is what you shall say to your masters: 5 It is I who
by my great power and my outstretched arm have made the earth, with the people
and animals that are on the earth, and I give it to whomever I please. 6 Now I have
given all these lands into the hand of King Nebuchadnezzar of Babylon, my servant, and I have given him even the wild animals of the field to serve him. 7 All the
nations shall serve him and his son and his grandson, until the time of his own land
comes; then many nations and great kings shall make him their slave.

8 But if any nation or kingdom will not serve this king, Nebuchadnezzar of
Babylon, and put its neck under the yoke of the king of Babylon, then I will punish
that nation with the sword, with famine, and with pestilence, says the LORD, until
I have completed its[g] destruction by his hand. 9 You, therefore, must not listen to
your prophets, your diviners, your dreamers,[h] your soothsayers, or your sorcerers,
who are saying to you, ‘You shall not serve the king of Babylon.’ 10 For they are
prophesying a lie to you, with the result that you will be removed far from your
land; I will drive you out, and you will perish. 11 But any nation that will bring its

26.18 Mic 1.1
26.19 2 Chron 29.6-11; 32.26 Isa 37.1,15-20
26.21 1 Kgs 19.2-4 2 Chron 16.10 Jer 36.26 Mt 10.23,28
26.22 Jer 36.12
26.23 Jer 2.30
26.24 2 Kgs 22.12-14 Jer 1.18,19 39.14; 40.5,6
27.2 Jer 28.10,13
27.3 Jer 25.21,22
27.5 Jer 10.12 32.17; 51.15
27.6 Jer 21.7; 22.25 28.14; 43.10 Ezek 29.18-20
27.7 Isa 14.4-6 Jer 25.12; 44.30
27.8 Jer 24.10 29.17; 42.15,16 Ezek 14.21 17.19-21
27.9 Deut 18.10 Isa 8.19
27.11 Jer 21.9; 38.2 40.9-12

[d] Heb adds *men to Egypt* [e] Another reading is *Jehoiakim* [f] Cn: Heb *send them* [g] Heb *their* [h] Gk Syr Vg: Heb *dreams*

26.20 Uriah is an otherwise unknown prophet who was executed for faithfully proclaiming God's words. This shows us that God has had other prophets whose words are not included in the Bible.

27.1ff The year was 597 B.C., and Nebuchadnezzar had already invaded Judah once and taken many captives. Jeremiah wore a yoke (a wooden frame used to fasten a team of animals to a plow) as a symbol of bondage. This was an object lesson, telling the people they must put themselves under Babylon's yoke or be destroyed.

27.5, 6 God punished the people of Judah in an unusual way, by appointing a sinful foreign ruler to be his deputy. Nebuchadnezzar was not used to proclaim God's Word, but to fulfill God's promise of judgment on sin. Because God is in control of all events, he uses whomever he wants. God may use unexpected people or circumstances to correct you. Be ready to accept God's improvement, even if it comes from unexpected sources.

27.9–11 The false prophets told the people what they wanted to hear, even though they knew it was not true. The people needed a true friend like Jeremiah, who brought God's painful, corrective word. A true friend speaks the truth no matter how much it hurts to hear. Seek friends who speak truthfully, even though their correction is painful. Someone who flatters you by telling you lies is not a true friend.

neck under the yoke of the king of Babylon and serve him, I will leave on its own
land, says the LORD, to till it and live there.
12 I spoke to King Zedekiah of Judah in the same way: Bring your necks under
the yoke of the king of Babylon, and serve him and his people, and live. 13 Why
should you and your people die by the sword, by famine, and by pestilence, as the
LORD has spoken concerning any nation that will not serve the king of Babylon?
14 Do not listen to the words of the prophets who are telling you not to serve the king
of Babylon, for they are prophesying a lie to you. 15 I have not sent them, says the
LORD, but they are prophesying falsely in my name, with the result that I will drive
you out and you will perish, you and the prophets who are prophesying to you.
16 Then I spoke to the priests and to all this people, saying, Thus says the
LORD: Do not listen to the words of your prophets who are prophesying to you,
saying, "The vessels of the LORD's house will soon be brought back from Babylon," for they are prophesying a lie to you. 17 Do not listen to them; serve the king
of Babylon and live. Why should this city become a desolation? 18 If indeed they
are prophets, and if the word of the LORD is with them, then let them intercede with
the LORD of hosts, that the vessels left in the house of the LORD, in the house of the
king of Judah, and in Jerusalem may not go to Babylon. 19 For thus says the LORD
of hosts concerning the pillars, the sea, the stands, and the rest of the vessels that
are left in this city, 20 which King Nebuchadnezzar of Babylon did not take away
when he took into exile from Jerusalem to Babylon King Jeconiah son of Jehoiakim
of Judah, and all the nobles of Judah and Jerusalem— 21 thus says the LORD of
hosts, the God of Israel, concerning the vessels left in the house of the LORD, in the
house of the king of Judah, and in Jerusalem: 22 They shall be carried to Babylon,
and there they shall stay, until the day when I give attention to them, says the LORD.
Then I will bring them up and restore them to this place.

27.13 Jer 38.23 Ezek 18.31
27.14 2 Chron 11.13-15 Ezek 13.22
27.15 2 Chron 25.16 Jer 23.21,25 29.9
27.16 2 Kgs 24.13 2 Chron 36.7,10 Jer 28.3
27.18 1 Kgs 18.24
27.19 1 Kgs 7.15 2 Kgs 25.13,17 Jer 22.28; 24.1 52.17-23
27.22 Ezra 5.13-15 7.9 Jer 29.10; 32.5 34.2,3

Jeremiah rebukes a false prophet

28 In that same year, at the beginning of the reign of King Zedekiah of Judah,
in the fifth month of the fourth year, the prophet Hananiah son of Azzur,
from Gibeon, spoke to me in the house of the LORD, in the presence of the priests
and all the people, saying, 2 "Thus says the LORD of hosts, the God of Israel: I have
broken the yoke of the king of Babylon. 3 Within two years I will bring back to this
place all the vessels of the LORD's house, which King Nebuchadnezzar of Babylon
took away from this place and carried to Babylon. 4 I will also bring back to this
place King Jeconiah son of Jehoiakim of Judah, and all the exiles from Judah who
went to Babylon, says the LORD, for I will break the yoke of the king of Babylon."
5 Then the prophet Jeremiah spoke to the prophet Hananiah in the presence of
the priests and all the people who were standing in the house of the LORD; 6 and the
prophet Jeremiah said, "Amen! May the LORD do so; may the LORD fulfill
the words that you have prophesied, and bring back to this place from Babylon the
vessels of the house of the LORD, and all the exiles. 7 But listen now to this word
that I speak in your hearing and in the hearing of all the people. 8 The prophets who
preceded you and me from ancient times prophesied war, famine, and pestilence
against many countries and great kingdoms. 9 As for the prophet who prophesies

28.1 Jer 27.12
28.3 2 Chron 36.10 Jer 27.16 Dan 1.2
28.4 2 Kgs 25.27 Jer 22.10; 27.8
28.5 Ps 41.13 Jer 11.5; 17.16
28.7 1 Kgs 22.28
28.8 1 Kgs 14.15 17.1; 22.17 Isa 5.5-7 Joel 1.20 Amos 1.2 Nah 1.2
28.9 Deut 18.22

27.12–18 Zedekiah was in a tough spot. Jeremiah called upon him to surrender to Nebuchadnezzar, while many of the other leaders wanted him to form an alliance and fight. It would be disgraceful for a king to surrender, and he would look like a coward. This was a great opportunity for the false prophets, who kept saying that the Babylonians would not defeat the great city of Jerusalem and that God would never allow the magnificent, holy temple to be destroyed.

27.19–22 When Nebuchadnezzar invaded Judah, first in 605 and then in 597 B.C., he took away many important people living in Jerusalem – including Ezekiel and Daniel. Although these men were captives, they had a profound impact on the exiles and leaders in Babylon. Jeremiah predicted that more people and even the precious objects in the temple would be taken. This happened in 586 B.C. during Babylon's third and last invasion.

28.8–17 Jeremiah spoke the truth, but it was unpopular; Hananiah spoke lies, but his deceitful words brought false hope and comfort to the people. God had already outlined the marks of a true prophet (Deuteronomy 13; 18.20–22): a true prophet's predictions always come true and his words never contradict previous revelation. Jeremiah's predictions were already coming true, from Hananiah's death to the Babylonian invasions. But the people still preferred to listen to comforting lies rather than painful truth.

peace, when the word of that prophet comes true, then it will be known that the
LORD has truly sent the prophet."
10 Then the prophet Hananiah took the yoke from the neck of the prophet Jere-
miah, and broke it. 11 And Hananiah spoke in the presence of all the people, saying,
"Thus says the LORD: This is how I will break the yoke of King Nebuchadnezzar of
Babylon from the neck of all the nations within two years." At this, the prophet
Jeremiah went his way.
12 Sometime after the prophet Hananiah had broken the yoke from the neck of
the prophet Jeremiah, the word of the LORD came to Jeremiah: 13 Go, tell Hananiah,
Thus says the LORD: You have broken wooden bars only to forge iron bars in place
of them! 14 For thus says the LORD of hosts, the God of Israel: I have put an iron
yoke on the neck of all these nations so that they may serve King Nebuchadnezzar
of Babylon, and they shall indeed serve him; I have even given him the wild animals. 15 And the prophet Jeremiah said to the prophet Hananiah, "Listen, Hananiah, the LORD has not sent you, and you made this people trust in a lie. 16 Therefore
thus says the LORD: I am going to send you off the face of the earth. Within this year
you will be dead, because you have spoken rebellion against the LORD."
17 In that same year, in the seventh month, the prophet Hananiah died.

Jeremiah warns the people against false prophets

29 These are the words of the letter that the prophet Jeremiah sent from Jerusalem to the remaining elders among the exiles, and to the priests, the prophets, and all the people, whom Nebuchadnezzar had taken into exile from Jerusalem
to Babylon. 2 This was after King Jeconiah, and the queen mother, the court officials, the leaders of Judah and Jerusalem, the artisans, and the smiths had departed
from Jerusalem. 3 The letter was sent by the hand of Elasah son of Shaphan and
Gemariah son of Hilkiah, whom King Zedekiah of Judah sent to Babylon to King
Nebuchadnezzar of Babylon. It said: 4 Thus says the LORD of hosts, the God of
Israel, to all the exiles whom I have sent into exile from Jerusalem to Babylon:
5 Build houses and live in them; plant gardens and eat what they produce. 6 Take
wives and have sons and daughters; take wives for your sons, and give your daughters in marriage, that they may bear sons and daughters; multiply there, and do not
decrease. 7 But seek the welfare of the city where I have sent you into exile, and
pray to the LORD on its behalf, for in its welfare you will find your welfare. 8 For
thus says the LORD of hosts, the God of Israel: Do not let the prophets and the
diviners who are among you deceive you, and do not listen to the dreams that they
dream,[i] 9 for it is a lie that they are prophesying to you in my name; I did not send
them, says the LORD.
10 For thus says the LORD: Only when Babylon's seventy years are completed
will I visit you, and I will fulfill to you my promise and bring you back to this place.
11 For surely I know the plans I have for you, says the LORD, plans for your welfare
and not for harm, to give you a future with hope. 12 Then when you call upon me

i Cn: Heb *your dreams that you cause to dream*

28.10 1 Kgs 22.11,24 Jer 27.2
28.11 Jer 14.15; 27.10
28.12 Jer 1.2
28.13 Ps 107.16
28.14 Deut 28.48 Jer 25.11 27.6,8
28.15 Jer 29.31 Ezek 13.2,3,22 22.28 Lam 2.14
28.16 Gen 7.4 Deut 6.15; 13.5 1 Kgs 13.34 Jer 20.6; 29.32
29.1 2 Kgs 24.12 Jer 22.24-28 24.1; 27.20
29.6 Jer 16.1-4
29.7 Ezra 6.10 Dan 4.27 1 Tim 2.1,2
29.8 Jer 14.14 23.21,25,27
29.9 Jer 27.15; 29.31
29.10 2 Chron 36.21-23 Jer 24.6,7 Dan 9.2
29.11 Isa 40.9-11 Jer 23.5,6 30.9,10,18-22 Hos 2.15
29.12 Jer 33.3

29.4-7 Jeremiah wrote to the captives in Babylon (29.4–23 is the letter) instructing them to move ahead with their lives and to pray for the heathen nation that enslaved them. Life cannot grind to a halt during troubled times. In an unpleasant or distressing situation, we must adjust and keep moving. You may find it difficult to pray for those in authority if they are evil, but that is when your prayers are most needed (1 Timothy 2.1, 2). When you enter times of trouble or sudden change, pray diligently and move ahead, doing whatever you can rather than giving up because of uncertainty.

29.10 Scholars differ on the exact dates of this 70-year period in Babylon. Some say it refers to the years 605 – 535 B.C., from the first deportation to Babylon to the arrival of the first exiles back in Jerusalem after Cyrus's freedom decree. Others point to the years 586 – 516 B.C., from the last deportation to Babylon and the destruction of the temple until its rebuilding. A third possibility is that 70 years is an approximate number meaning a lifetime. All agree that God sent his people to Babylon for a long time, not the short captivity predicted by the false prophets.

29.11 We're all encouraged by a leader who stirs us to move ahead, someone who believes we can do the task he has given and who will be with us all the way. God is that kind of leader. He knows the future, and his plans for us are good and full of hope. As long as the God who knows the future provides our agenda and goes with us as we fulfill his mission, we can have boundless hope. This does not mean we will be spared pain, suffering, or hardship, but that God will see us through to a glorious conclusion.

29.12-14 God did not forget his people, even though they were captive in Babylon. He planned to give them a new beginning with a new purpose – to turn them into new people. In times of deep trouble, it may seem that God has forgotten you. But he may be

and come and pray to me, I will hear you. 13 When you search for me, you will find
me; if you seek me with all your heart, 14 I will let you find me, says the LORD, and
I will restore your fortunes and gather you from all the nations and all the places
where I have driven you, says the LORD, and I will bring you back to the place from
which I sent you into exile.
15 Because you have said, "The LORD has raised up prophets for us in
Babylon,"— 16 Thus says the LORD concerning the king who sits on the throne of
David, and concerning all the people who live in this city, your kinsfolk who did
not go out with you into exile: 17 Thus says the LORD of hosts, I am going to let
loose on them sword, famine, and pestilence, and I will make them like rotten figs
that are so bad they cannot be eaten. 18 I will pursue them with the sword, with
famine, and with pestilence, and will make them a horror to all the kingdoms of the
earth, to be an object of cursing, and horror, and hissing, and a derision among all
the nations where I have driven them, 19 because they did not heed my words, says
the LORD, when I persistently sent to you my servants the prophets, but they[j]
would not listen, says the LORD. 20 But now, all you exiles whom I sent away from
Jerusalem to Babylon, hear the word of the LORD: 21 Thus says the LORD of hosts,
the God of Israel, concerning Ahab son of Kolaiah and Zedekiah son of Maaseiah,
who are prophesying a lie to you in my name: I am going to deliver them into the
hand of King Nebuchadrezzar of Babylon, and he shall kill them before your eyes.
22 And on account of them this curse shall be used by all the exiles from Judah in
Babylon: "The LORD make you like Zedekiah and Ahab, whom the king of Babylon roasted in the fire," 23 because they have perpetrated outrage in Israel and have
committed adultery with their neighbors' wives, and have spoken in my name lying
words that I did not command them; I am the one who knows and bears witness,
says the LORD.
24 To Shemaiah of Nehelam you shall say: 25 Thus says the LORD of hosts, the
God of Israel: In your own name you sent a letter to all the people who are in
Jerusalem, and to the priest Zephaniah son of Maaseiah, and to all the priests, saying, 26 The LORD himself has made you priest instead of the priest Jehoiada, so that
there may be officers in the house of the LORD to control any madman who plays
the prophet, to put him in the stocks and the collar. 27 So now why have you not
rebuked Jeremiah of Anathoth who plays the prophet for you? 28 For he has actually
sent to us in Babylon, saying, "It will be a long time; build houses and live in them,
and plant gardens and eat what they produce."
29 The priest Zephaniah read this letter in the hearing of the prophet Jeremiah.
30 Then the word of the LORD came to Jeremiah: 31 Send to all the exiles, saying,
Thus says the LORD concerning Shemaiah of Nehelam: Because Shemaiah has
prophesied to you, though I did not send him, and has led you to trust in a lie,
32 therefore thus says the LORD: I am going to punish Shemaiah of Nehelam and his
descendants; he shall not have anyone living among this people to see[k] the good
that I am going to do to my people, says the LORD, for he has spoken rebellion
against the LORD.

29.13 Jer 24.7
29.14 Deut 30.1-10 Isa 43.5,6 Jer 12.15 16.14,15; 30.3
29.16 Jer 24.3,8-10
29.18 Isa 65.15 Jer 25.9; 42.18 Lam 2.15,16
29.19 Jer 6.19; 26.5
29.20 Jer 24.5 Ezek 11.9
29.21 Jer 14.14,15 Lam 2.14
29.22 Isa 65.15
29.23 2 Sam 13.12 Prov 5.21 Jer 5.8; 7.11
29.25 2 Kgs 25.18 Jer 21.1; 37.3
29.26 Deut 13.1-5 Jer 20.1,2 Hos 9.7 Zech 13.1-5 Jn 10.20 Acts 16.24 26.24,25 2 Cor 5.13
29.27 Jer 1.1
29.31 Jer 14.14,15 28.15 Ezek 13.8,16, 22,23
29.32 Deut 13.5 1 Sam 2.30-34 Jer 22.30 28.16; 36.31

[j] Syr: Heb *you* [k] Gk: Heb *and he shall not see*

---

preparing you, as he did the people of Judah, for a new beginning with God at the center.

29.13 According to God's wise plan, his people were to have hope and a future, so they should call upon him. Although the exiles were in a difficult place and time, they should not despair, because they had God's presence, the privilege of prayer, and God's grace. God can be sought and found when we seek him wholeheartedly. Neither strange lands, sorrows, frustration, nor physical problems can break that communion.

29.21 These false prophets, Ahab and Zedekiah, should not be confused with the kings who had the same names. Their family connections clearly identify them.

29.24–28 These verses describe the reaction of Shemaiah, a prophet exiled in 597 B.C., who had protested about Jeremiah's letter. To discredit Jeremiah, Shemaiah accused him of false prophecy. Although Jeremiah's message was true and his words were from God, the people hated him because he told them to make the most of the exile. But Jeremiah's truth from God offered temporary correction and long-range benefit, while the false teachers' lies offered only temporary comfort and long-range punishment.

5. Restoration is promised

Restoration will follow punishment

30 The word that came to Jeremiah from the LORD: 2 Thus says the LORD, the
God of Israel: Write in a book all the words that I have spoken to you. 3 For
the days are surely coming, says the LORD, when I will restore the fortunes of my
people, Israel and Judah, says the LORD, and I will bring them back to the land that
I gave to their ancestors and they shall take possession of it.

4 These are the words that the LORD spoke concerning Israel and Judah:

5 Thus says the LORD:
We have heard a cry of panic,
of terror, and no peace.
6 Ask now, and see,
can a man bear a child?
Why then do I see every man
with his hands on his loins like a woman in labor?
Why has every face turned pale?
7 Alas! that day is so great
there is none like it;
it is a time of distress for Jacob;
yet he shall be rescued from it.

8 On that day, says the LORD of hosts, I will break the yoke from off his[l] neck,
and I will burst his[l] bonds, and strangers shall no more make a servant of him.
9 But they shall serve the LORD their God and David their king, whom I will raise
up for them.

10 But as for you, have no fear, my servant Jacob, says the LORD,
and do not be dismayed, O Israel;
for I am going to save you from far away,
and your offspring from the land of their captivity.
Jacob shall return and have quiet and ease,
and no one shall make him afraid.
11 For I am with you, says the LORD, to save you;
I will make an end of all the nations
among which I scattered you,
but of you I will not make an end.
I will chastise you in just measure,
and I will by no means leave you unpunished.

12 For thus says the LORD:
Your hurt is incurable,
your wound is grievous.
13 There is no one to uphold your cause,
no medicine for your wound,
no healing for you.
14 All your lovers have forgotten you;
they care nothing for you;

30.2 Jer 25.13 36.4,28,32
30.3 Jer 3.18; 16.15 23.7,8; 25.13 29.10; 30.18 36.4,28
30.6 Jer 4.31; 6.24 22.23
30.7 Isa 2.12 Jer 2.27; 50.19
30.8 Isa 9.4 Ezek 34.27
30.9 Ezek 34.23,24 37.24 Hos 3.5 Lk 1.69 Acts 2.30 13.23,24
30.10 Isa 35.9; 43.5 44.2 Jer 23.3; 29.14 46.27,28 Mic 4.4
30.11 Jer 1.8,19 4.27; 5.10,18 10.24; 46.28
30.13 Jer 14.19; 46.11
30.14 Jer 22.20,22

[l] Cn: Heb *your*

30.1ff Chapters 30 and 31 show that Jeremiah spoke of hope as well as trouble and gloom. The people would one day be restored to their land, and God would make a new contract with them to replace the one they broke. Where once they sinned and disobeyed, they would one day repent and obey.

30.8, 9 Like Isaiah, Jeremiah associates events of the near future and those of the distant future. Reading these prophecies is like looking at several mountain peaks in a range. From a distance they look as though they are next to each other, when actually they are miles apart. Jeremiah presents near and distant events as if they will all happen soon. He sees the exile, but he sees also the future day when Christ will reign forever. The reference to David is not to King David, but to his famous descendant, the Messiah (Luke 1.69).

30.12, 13, 17 The medical language here conveys the idea that sin is terminal. It cannot be cured by being good or being religious. Beware of putting your confidence in useless cures while your sin spreads and causes you pain. God alone can cure the disease of sin, but you must be willing to let him do it.

for I have dealt you the blow of an enemy,
the punishment of a merciless foe,
because your guilt is great,
because your sins are so numerous.
15 Why do you cry out over your hurt?
Your pain is incurable.
Because your guilt is great,
because your sins are so numerous,
I have done these things to you.

30.16 Isa 14.2 Jer 2.3; 10.25

16 Therefore all who devour you shall be devoured,
and all your foes, everyone of them, shall go into captivity;
those who plunder you shall be plundered,
and all who prey on you I will make a prey.

30.17 Ps 107.20 Isa 56.8 Jer 8.22 33.6,24

17 For I will restore health to you,
and your wounds I will heal,
says the LORD,
because they have called you an outcast:
"It is Zion; no one cares for her!"

30.18 1 Chron 29.1,19 Ps 48.3; 122.7 Jer 31.38-40

18 Thus says the LORD:
I am going to restore the fortunes of the tents of Jacob,
and have compassion on his dwellings;
the city shall be rebuilt upon its mound,
and the citadel set on its rightful site.

30.19 Isa 12.1; 51.3 55.5; 60.9 Jer 17.26; 33.11

19 Out of them shall come thanksgiving,
and the sound of merrymakers.
I will make them many, and they shall not be few;
I will make them honored, and they shall not be disdained.

30.20 Isa 54.14

20 Their children shall be as of old,
their congregation shall be established before me;
and I will punish all who oppress them.

30.21 Ex 3.5 Num 16.5

21 Their prince shall be one of their own,
their ruler shall come from their midst;
I will bring him near, and he shall approach me,
for who would otherwise dare to approach me?
says the LORD.

30.22 Ex 6.7 Jer 32.38 Hos 2.23 Zech 13.9

22 And you shall be my people,
and I will be your God.

30.23 Jer 23.19,20

23 Look, the storm of the LORD!
Wrath has gone forth,
a whirling[m] tempest;
it will burst upon the head of the wicked.
24 The fierce anger of the LORD will not turn back
until he has executed and accomplished
the intents of his mind.
In the latter days you will understand this.

[m] One Ms: Meaning of MT uncertain

30.15 Judah protested its punishment, even though the sin that caused it was scandalous. But punishment is an opportunity for growth, because it makes us aware of sin's consequences. The people should have asked how they could profit from their mistakes. Remember this the next time you are corrected.

30.18 This prophecy that Jerusalem would be rebuilt was not completely fulfilled by the work of Ezra, Nehemiah, and Zerubbabel. The city was indeed rebuilt after the captivity, but the final restoration will occur when all believers are gathered in Christ's kingdom. This will include buildings (30.18), people (30.19), and rulers (30.21).

30.21 This verse refers to the restoration after the Babylonian captivity (the rulers of the Maccabean period were both priests and kings), as well as to the final restoration under Christ.

God promises to rebuild the nation

31 At that time, says the LORD, I will be the God of all the families of Israel, and they shall be my people.

2 Thus says the LORD:
The people who survived the sword
found grace in the wilderness;
when Israel sought for rest,
3 the LORD appeared to him[n] from far away.[o]
I have loved you with an everlasting love;
therefore I have continued my faithfulness to you.
4 Again I will build you, and you shall be built,
O virgin Israel!
Again you shall take[p] your tambourines,
and go forth in the dance of the merrymakers.
5 Again you shall plant vineyards
on the mountains of Samaria;
the planters shall plant,
and shall enjoy the fruit.
6 For there shall be a day when sentinels will call
in the hill country of Ephraim:
"Come, let us go up to Zion,
to the LORD our God."

7 For thus says the LORD:
Sing aloud with gladness for Jacob,
and raise shouts for the chief of the nations;
proclaim, give praise, and say,
"Save, O LORD, your people,
the remnant of Israel."
8 See, I am going to bring them from the land of the north,
and gather them from the farthest parts of the earth,
among them the blind and the lame,
those with child and those in labor, together;
a great company, they shall return here.
9 With weeping they shall come,
and with consolations[q] I will lead them back,
I will let them walk by brooks of water,
in a straight path in which they shall not stumble;
for I have become a father to Israel,
and Ephraim is my firstborn.

10 Hear the word of the LORD, O nations,
and declare it in the coastlands far away;
say, "He who scattered Israel will gather him,
and will keep him as a shepherd a flock."
11 For the LORD has ransomed Jacob,
and has redeemed him from hands too strong for him.
12 They shall come and sing aloud on the height of Zion,
and they shall be radiant over the goodness of the LORD,
over the grain, the wine, and the oil,
and over the young of the flock and the herd;

31.1 Rom 11.26-28
31.2 Ex 33.14
31.3 Deut 4.37; 7.8 Ps 25.6
31.4 Isa 30.32 Jer 24.6; 33.7
31.5 Ps 107.37 Isa 65.21 Ezek 28.26
31.7 Ps 14.7; 28.9 Isa 37.31; 61.9 Jer 20.13; 23.3
31.8 Deut 30.64 Isa 40.11; 43.6 Ezek 34.16 Mic 4.6
31.9 Isa 49.10; 63.13
31.10 Isa 40.11; 66.19
31.12 Isa 2.2; 35.10 58.11; 60.20 65.19 Hos 2.22 Joel 3.18 Mic 4.1 Jn 16.22

[n] Gk: Heb *me* [o] Or *to him long ago* [p] Or *adorn yourself with* [q] Gk Compare Vg Tg: Heb *supplications*

31.1 This promise is to all the families of Israel, not only to the tribe of Judah. The restoration will include all people who trust God.

31.3 God reaches toward his people with kindness motivated by deep and everlasting love. He is eager to do the best for them if they will only let him. After many words of warning about sin, this reminder of God's magnificent love is a breath of fresh air. Rather than thinking of God with dread, look carefully and see him lovingly drawing us toward himself.

their life shall become like a watered garden,
and they shall never languish again.

31.13 Ps 30.11 Isa 51.11; 61.3 Zech 8.4,5

13 Then shall the young women rejoice in the dance,
and the young men and the old shall be merry.
I will turn their mourning into joy,
I will comfort them, and give them gladness for sorrow.

31.14 Jer 50.19

14 I will give the priests their fill of fatness,
and my people shall be satisfied with my bounty,
says the LORD.

31.15 Ps 77.2 Jer 10.20

15 Thus says the LORD:
A voice is heard in Ramah,
lamentation and bitter weeping.
Rachel is weeping for her children;
she refuses to be comforted for her children,
because they are no more.

31.16 Isa 25.8; 30.19 Jer 30.3 Ezek 11.17

16 Thus says the LORD:
Keep your voice from weeping,
and your eyes from tears;
for there is a reward for your work,
says the LORD:
they shall come back from the land of the enemy;

31.17 Jer 29.11

17 there is hope for your future,
says the LORD:
your children shall come back to their own country.

31.18 Job 5.17 Ps 80.3,7,19 94.12 Jer 17.14 Hos 4.16

18 Indeed I heard Ephraim pleading:
"You disciplined me, and I took the discipline;
I was like a calf untrained.
Bring me back, let me come back,
for you are the LORD my God.

31.19 Ezek 36.31 Lk 18.13

19 For after I had turned away I repented;
and after I was discovered, I struck my thigh;
I was ashamed, and I was dismayed
because I bore the disgrace of my youth."

31.20 Isa 55.7 Hos 11.8; 14.4

20 Is Ephraim my dear son?
Is he the child I delight in?
As often as I speak against him,
I still remember him.
Therefore I am deeply moved for him;
I will surely have mercy on him,
says the LORD.

31.21 Isa 48.20; 52.11

21 Set up road markers for yourself,
make yourself guideposts;
consider well the highway,
the road by which you went.
Return, O virgin Israel,
return to these your cities.

31.14 This means that many sacrifices will be made at the temple, so the priests will have a feast with their portion.

31.15 Rachel, Jacob's favorite wife, was the symbolic mother of the northern tribes, who were taken away by the Assyrians as slaves. Rachel is pictured crying for the exiles at Ramah, a staging point of deportation. This verse is quoted in Matthew 2.18 to describe the sadness of the mothers of Bethlehem as their children were killed. The weeping was great in both cases.

31.18–20 "I struck my thigh" was an expression that meant to demonstrate grief. Ephraim was one of the major tribes of the northern kingdom. Although the northern kingdom had sunk into the most degrading sins, God still loved the people. A remnant would turn to God, repenting of their sins, and God would forgive. God still loves you, despite anything you may have done. He will forgive you if you turn back to him.

22 How long will you waver,
O faithless daughter?
For the LORD has created a new thing on the earth:
a woman encompasses[r] a man.

23 Thus says the LORD of hosts, the God of Israel: Once more they shall use
these words in the land of Judah and in its towns when I restore their fortunes:
"The LORD bless you, O abode of righteousness,
O holy hill!"
24 And Judah and all its towns shall live there together, and the farmers and those
who wander[s] with their flocks.
25 I will satisfy the weary,
and all who are faint I will replenish.
26 Thereupon I awoke and looked, and my sleep was pleasant to me.
27 The days are surely coming, says the LORD, when I will sow the house of
Israel and the house of Judah with the seed of humans and the seed of animals.
28 And just as I have watched over them to pluck up and break down, to overthrow,
destroy, and bring evil, so I will watch over them to build and to plant, says the
LORD. 29 In those days they shall no longer say:
"The parents have eaten sour grapes,
and the children's teeth are set on edge."
30 But all shall die for their own sins; the teeth of everyone who eats sour grapes
shall be set on edge.
31 The days are surely coming, says the LORD, when I will make a new covenant with the house of Israel and the house of Judah. 32 It will not be like the covenant that I made with their ancestors when I took them by the hand to bring them out
of the land of Egypt—a covenant that they broke, though I was their husband,[t]
says the LORD. 33 But this is the covenant that I will make with the house of Israel
after those days, says the LORD: I will put my law within them, and I will write it
on their hearts; and I will be their God, and they shall be my people. 34 No longer
shall they teach one another, or say to each other, "Know the LORD," for they shall
all know me, from the least of them to the greatest, says the LORD; for I will forgive
their iniquity, and remember their sin no more.

35 Thus says the LORD,
who gives the sun for light by day
and the fixed order of the moon and the stars for light by night,
who stirs up the sea so that its waves roar—
the LORD of hosts is his name:
36 If this fixed order were ever to cease
from my presence, says the LORD,
then also the offspring of Israel would cease
to be a nation before me forever.

31.23 Ps 48.1; 87.1 Isa 1.26
31.24 Ezek 36.10 Zech 8.4-8
31.27 Ezek 36.9-11 Hos 2.23
31.28 Dan 9.14
31.29 Ezek 18.2 Lam 5.7
31.30 Deut 24.16 Isa 3.11 Ezek 18.4,20
31.31 Ezek 37.26 Lk 22.20 1 Cor 11.25 Heb 8.8-12
31.32 Deut 1.31; 5.2,3 Isa 63.12
31.33 Heb 10.16,17
31.34 Isa 11.9; 43.25 Jer 50.20 Mic 7.18 1 Thess 4.9 1 Jn 2.27
31.35 Gen 1.14-18
31.36 Isa 54.9,10 Jer 33.20-26 Amos 9.8,9

[r] Meaning of Heb uncertain [s] Cn Compare Syr Vg Tg: Heb *and they shall wander* [t] Or *master*

31.22 This idea reflects a turnaround in the land when God rules. The weaker partner will surround and sustain the stronger one. God will provide for everyone's safety.

31.29, 30 The people tried to blame God's judgment on the sins of their fathers. One person's sin does indeed affect other people, but all people are still held personally accountable for the sin in their own lives (Deuteronomy 24.16; Ezekiel 18.2).

31.33 God would write his law upon their hearts rather than upon tablets of stone as were the ten commandments. In 17.1 their sin was engraved on their hearts so that they wanted above all to disobey. This change seems to describe an experience very much like the new birth—and God is taking the initiative. When we turn our lives over to God, he, by his Holy Spirit, builds into us the desire to obey him.

31.33 The old covenant, broken by the people, would be replaced by a new covenant. The foundation of this new covenant is Christ (Hebrews 8.6). It is revolutionary, involving not only Israel and Judah, but even the Gentiles. It offers a uniquely personal relationship with God himself, with his laws inscribed on hearts instead of on stone. Jeremiah looked forward to the day when Jesus would come to establish this covenant. But for us today, this covenant is here. We have the wonderful opportunity to make a fresh start and establish a permanent, personal relationship with God (see 29.11; 32.38–40).

31.35–37 God has the power to do away with the laws of nature or his people. But he will do neither. This is not a prediction, but a promise. It is God's way of saying he will not reject Israel any more than he will do away with nature's laws. Neither will happen!

31.37 Rom 11.2-5, [37] Thus says the LORD:
26,27 If the heavens above can be measured,
  and the foundations of the earth below can be explored,
then I will reject all the offspring of Israel
  because of all they have done,
    says the LORD.

31.38 2 Chron 26.9 38 The days are surely coming, says the LORD, when the city shall be rebuilt for
Neh 3.1; 12.39 the LORD from the tower of Hananel to the Corner Gate. [39] And the measuring line
Zech 14.10 shall go out farther, straight to the hill Gareb, and shall then turn to Goah. [40] The
31.40 2 Kgs 23.6 whole valley of the dead bodies and the ashes, and all the fields as far as the Wadi
Joel 3.17 Kidron, to the corner of the Horse Gate toward the east, shall be sacred to the
Zech 14.20 LORD. It shall never again be uprooted or overthrown.

Jeremiah buys land in Judah

32.1 2 Kgs 25.1,2 **32** The word that came to Jeremiah from the LORD in the tenth year of King
Jer 39.1,2 Zedekiah of Judah, which was the eighteenth year of Nebuchadrezzar. [2] At
that time the army of the king of Babylon was besieging Jerusalem, and the prophet
Jeremiah was confined in the court of the guard that was in the palace of the king
32.3 Jer 21.4-7 of Judah, [3] where King Zedekiah of Judah had confined him. Zedekiah had said,
26.8,9; 34.2,3 "Why do you prophesy and say: Thus says the LORD: I am going to give this city
32.4 2 Kgs 25.4-7 into the hand of the king of Babylon, and he shall take it; [4] King Zedekiah of Judah
Jer 37.17 shall not escape out of the hands of the Chaldeans, but shall surely be given into the
hands of the king of Babylon, and shall speak with him face to face and see him eye
32.5 Ezek 12.12,13 to eye; [5] and he shall take Zedekiah to Babylon, and there he shall remain until I
attend to him, says the LORD; though you fight against the Chaldeans, you shall not
succeed?"
32.6 Lev 25.25 6 Jeremiah said, The word of the LORD came to me: [7] Hanamel son of your
Ruth 4.3,4 uncle Shallum is going to come to you and say, "Buy my field that is at Anathoth,
32.8 1 Sam 9.16,17 for the right of redemption by purchase is yours." [8] Then my cousin Hanamel came
to me in the court of the guard, in accordance with the word of the LORD, and said
to me, "Buy my field that is at Anathoth in the land of Benjamin, for the right of
possession and redemption is yours; buy it for yourself." Then I knew that this was
the word of the LORD.
9 And I bought the field at Anathoth from my cousin Hanamel, and weighed out
32.10 Ruth 4.1,9 the money to him, seventeen shekels of silver. [10] I signed the deed, sealed it, got
Isa 8.1,2 witnesses, and weighed the money on scales. [11] Then I took the sealed deed of
purchase, containing the terms and conditions, and the open copy; [12] and I gave the
deed of purchase to Baruch son of Neriah son of Mahseiah, in the presence of my
cousin Hanamel, in the presence of the witnesses who signed the deed of purchase,
and in the presence of all the Judeans who were sitting in the court of the guard.
[13] In their presence I charged Baruch, saying, [14] Thus says the LORD of hosts, the
32.15 Amos 9.14,15 God of Israel: Take these deeds, both this sealed deed of purchase and this open
Zech 3.10 deed, and put them in an earthenware jar, in order that they may last for a long time.
32.16 Gen 32.9-12 [15] For thus says the LORD of hosts, the God of Israel: Houses and fields and vine-
Jer 12.1 yards shall again be bought in this land.
Phil 4.6,7 16 After I had given the deed of purchase to Baruch son of Neriah, I prayed to

---

31.38–40 These points mark the boundaries of restored Jerusalem in the days of Nehemiah. Gareb and Goah are unknown. The valley of the dead bodies and the ashes is the valley of the son of Hinnom where children were sacrified in pagan worship. A wadi is a stream or dry streambed.

32.1–12 God told Jeremiah to buy a field outside Jerusalem. The city had been under siege for a year, and Jeremiah bought land that the soldiers occupied—certainly a poor investment. In addition, Jeremiah was a prisoner in the palace. But Jeremiah was demonstrating his faith in God's promises to return his people and rebuild Jerusalem.

32.6–17 Trust doesn't come easy. It wasn't easy for Jeremiah to publicly buy land already captured by the enemy. But he trusted God. It wasn't easy for David to believe that he would become king, even after he was anointed. But he trusted God (1 Samuel 16–31). It wasn't easy for Moses to believe that he and his people would escape Egypt, even after God spoke to him from a burning bush. But he trusted God (Exodus 3.1–4.20). It isn't easy for us to believe that God can fulfill his "impossible" promises, either, but we must trust him. God, who worked in the lives of biblical heroes, offers to work in our lives too, if we will let him.

the LORD, saying: 17 Ah Lord GOD! It is you who made the heavens and the earth by
your great power and by your outstretched arm! Nothing is too hard for you. 18 You
show steadfast love to the thousandth generation,[u] but repay the guilt of parents
into the laps of their children after them, O great and mighty God whose name is
the LORD of hosts, 19 great in counsel and mighty in deed; whose eyes are open to
all the ways of mortals, rewarding all according to their ways and according to the
fruit of their doings. 20 You showed signs and wonders in the land of Egypt, and to
this day in Israel and among all humankind, and have made yourself a name that
continues to this very day. 21 You brought your people Israel out of the land of
Egypt with signs and wonders, with a strong hand and outstretched arm, and with
great terror; 22 and you gave them this land, which you swore to their ancestors to
give them, a land flowing with milk and honey; 23 and they entered and took possession of it. But they did not obey your voice or follow your law; of all you commanded them to do, they did nothing. Therefore you have made all these disasters
come upon them. 24 See, the siege-ramps have been cast up against the city to take
it, and the city, faced with sword, famine, and pestilence, has been given into the
hands of the Chaldeans who are fighting against it. What you spoke has happened,
as you yourself can see. 25 Yet you, O Lord GOD, have said to me, "Buy the field
for money and get witnesses"—though the city has been given into the hands of the
Chaldeans.

26 The word of the LORD came to Jeremiah: 27 See, I am the LORD, the God of
all flesh; is anything too hard for me? 28 Therefore, thus says the LORD: I am going
to give this city into the hands of the Chaldeans and into the hand of King Nebuchadrezzar of Babylon, and he shall take it. 29 The Chaldeans who are fighting
against this city shall come, set it on fire, and burn it, with the houses on whose
roofs offerings have been made to Baal and libations have been poured out to other
gods, to provoke me to anger. 30 For the people of Israel and the people of Judah
have done nothing but evil in my sight from their youth; the people of Israel have
done nothing but provoke me to anger by the work of their hands, says the LORD.
31 This city has aroused my anger and wrath, from the day it was built until this day,
so that I will remove it from my sight 32 because of all the evil of the people of Israel
and the people of Judah that they did to provoke me to anger—they, their kings and
their officials, their priests and their prophets, the citizens of Judah and the inhabitants of Jerusalem. 33 They have turned their backs to me, not their faces; though I
have taught them persistently, they would not listen and accept correction. 34 They
set up their abominations in the house that bears my name, and defiled it. 35 They
built the high places of Baal in the valley of the son of Hinnom, to offer up their
sons and daughters to Molech, though I did not command them, nor did it enter my
mind that they should do this abomination, causing Judah to sin.

36 Now therefore thus says the LORD, the God of Israel, concerning this city of
which you say, "It is being given into the hand of the king of Babylon by the sword,
by famine, and by pestilence": 37 See, I am going to gather them from all the lands
to which I drove them in my anger and my wrath and in great indignation; I will
bring them back to this place, and I will settle them in safety. 38 They shall be my
people, and I will be their God. 39 I will give them one heart and one way, that they
may fear me for all time, for their own good and the good of their children after

u Or *to thousands*

32.17 Gen 18.14 2 Kgs 19.15 Isa 40.26-29 Jer 27.5
32.18 Ex 34.6,7 Deut 7.9,10 1 Kgs 16.1-3 Jer 10.16 20.11; 31.35 Mt 23.32-36
32.19 Isa 28.29 Jer 17.10 21.14; 23.24 Mt 16.27 Jn 5.29
32.20 Ps 78.43 105.27 Isa 63.12,14 Dan 9.15
32.21 Deut 4.34; 26.8 1 Chron 17.21
32.22 Ex 13.5 Deut 1.8 Ps 105.9-11 Jer 11.5
32.23 Ezra 9.7 Ps 44.2,3 78.54,55 Lam 1.18 Dan 9.11,12
32.24 Josh 23.15,16 Ezek 14.21 Zech 1.6
32.28 Jer 19.7-12
32.29 2 Chron 36.19 Jer 44.17-19,25
32.31 1 Kgs 11.7,8 2 Kgs 21.4-7, 15; 23.27 Mt 23.37
32.32 Jer 2.26
32.33 Jer 25.3; 26.5
32.35 Lev 18.21 20.2-5 2 Chron 28.2,3 33.6 Acts 7.43
32.37 Deut 30.3 Isa 11.11-16 Ezek 11.17 34.25,28 Amos 9.14,15 Hos 1.11 Zech 14.11

32.17–25 After Jeremiah bought the field, he began to wonder if such a move was wise. He sought relief in prayer from his nagging doubts. He affirmed that God is Creator (32.17), the wise Judge of all the ways of people (32.19), and Redeemer (32.21). God loves us and sees our situation. Whenever we doubt his wisdom or wonder if it is practical to obey him, we can review what we already know about him. Such thoughts and prayers will quiet our doubts and calm our fears.

32.29 Libations were drink offerings, liquids poured out as a sacrifice. Drink offerings were used in the worship of the Lord (Leviticus 23.13).

32.35 These high places were where the most important and grotesque part of Molech worship took place. Children were offered in sacrifice to this pagan god.

32.36–42 God uses his power to accomplish *his* purposes through *his* people. God doesn't give you power to be all you want to be, but he gives you power to be all he wants you to be. The people of Israel had to learn that trusting God meant radically realigning their purposes and desires toward God. He gave them "one heart" toward him (32.39). We must develop that singleness of purpose to love him above anything else.

32.39 Deut 11.18-21; Ezek 37.25; Jn 17.21; Acts 4.32
32.40 Isa 55.3
32.41 Deut 30.9; Isa 65.19; Jer 31.28; Amos 9.15
32.42 Jer 31.28; Zech 8.14,15
32.43 Ezek 37.11-14

them. 40 I will make an everlasting covenant with them, never to draw back from doing good to them; and I will put the fear of me in their hearts, so that they may not turn from me. 41 I will rejoice in doing good to them, and I will plant them in this land in faithfulness, with all my heart and all my soul.

42 For thus says the LORD: Just as I have brought all this great disaster upon this people, so I will bring upon them all the good fortune that I now promise them. 43 Fields shall be bought in this land of which you are saying, It is a desolation, without human beings or animals; it has been given into the hands of the Chaldeans. 44 Fields shall be bought for money, and deeds shall be signed and sealed and witnessed, in the land of Benjamin, in the places around Jerusalem, and in the cities of Judah, of the hill country, of the Shephelah, and of the Negeb; for I will restore their fortunes, says the LORD.

God promises peace and prosperity

33.2 Ex 3.15
33.3 Ps 50.15; Isa 48.6; 55.6,7
33.4 Isa 32.13,14
33.5 Jer 21.10
33.6 Isa 66.12; Jer 17.14; Gal 5.22,23
33.7 Ps 85.1; Jer 30.18; Amos 9.14,15
33.8 Ps 51.2; Jer 50.20; Heb 9.11-14
33.9 Ps 40.3; Isa 62.2,4; Jer 16.19; 24.6; Hos 3.5
33.10 Isa 35.10

33 The word of the LORD came to Jeremiah a second time, while he was still confined in the court of the guard: 2 Thus says the LORD who made the earth,[v] the LORD who formed it to establish it—the LORD is his name: 3 Call to me and I will answer you, and will tell you great and hidden things that you have not known. 4 For thus says the LORD, the God of Israel, concerning the houses of this city and the houses of the kings of Judah that were torn down to make a defense against the siege-ramps and before the sword:[w] 5 The Chaldeans are coming in to fight[x] and to fill them with the dead bodies of those whom I shall strike down in my anger and my wrath, for I have hidden my face from this city because of all their wickedness. 6 I am going to bring it recovery and healing; I will heal them and reveal to them abundance[w] of prosperity and security. 7 I will restore the fortunes of Judah and the fortunes of Israel, and rebuild them as they were at first. 8 I will cleanse them from all the guilt of their sin against me, and I will forgive all the guilt of their sin and rebellion against me. 9 And this city[y] shall be to me a name of joy, a praise and a glory before all the nations of the earth who shall hear of all the good that I do for them; they shall fear and tremble because of all the good and all the prosperity I provide for it.

10 Thus says the LORD: In this place of which you say, "It is a waste without human beings or animals," in the towns of Judah and the streets of Jerusalem that are desolate, without inhabitants, human or animal, there shall once more be heard 11 the voice of mirth and the voice of gladness, the voice of the bridegroom and the voice of the bride, the voices of those who sing, as they bring thank offerings to the house of the LORD:

"Give thanks to the LORD of hosts,
for the LORD is good,
for his steadfast love endures forever!"

For I will restore the fortunes of the land as at first, says the LORD.

33.12 Ezek 34.12-14; Zeph 2.6,7
33.14 Hag 2.6-9

12 Thus says the LORD of hosts: In this place that is waste, without human beings or animals, and in all its towns there shall again be pasture for shepherds resting their flocks. 13 In the towns of the hill country, of the Shephelah, and of the Negeb, in the land of Benjamin, the places around Jerusalem, and in the towns of Judah, flocks shall again pass under the hands of the one who counts them, says the LORD.

14 The days are surely coming, says the LORD, when I will fulfill the promise

[v] Gk: Heb *it* [w] Meaning of Heb uncertain [x] Cn: Heb *They are coming in to fight against the Chaldeans* [y] Heb *And it*

32.44 The Shephelah are the low hills in western Palestine. The Negeb is the southern part of Judah.

33.1ff God would restore Jerusalem, not because the people cried, but because it was part of his ultimate plan. The Babylonian disaster did not change God's purposes for his people. Although Jerusalem would be destroyed, it would be restored (after the 70-year captivity and in the end times when the Messiah will rule). God's justice is always tempered by his mercy.

33.3 God assures Jeremiah that he has only to ask (see also Psalm 145.18; Isaiah 58.9; Matthew 7.7). God is ready to answer our prayers, but we must ask for his assistance. Surely he could take care of our needs without our asking. But when we ask, we are acknowledging that he alone is God and that we cannot accomplish in our own strength all that is his domain to do. When we ask, we must humble ourselves, lay aside our willfulness and worry, and determine to obey him.

I made to the house of Israel and the house of Judah. 15 In those days and at that time
I will cause a righteous Branch to spring up for David; and he shall execute justice
and righteousness in the land. 16 In those days Judah will be saved and Jerusalem
will live in safety. And this is the name by which it will be called: "The LORD is our
righteousness."
17 For thus says the LORD: David shall never lack a man to sit on the throne of
the house of Israel, 18 and the levitical priests shall never lack a man in my presence
to offer burnt offerings, to make grain offerings, and to make sacrifices for all time.
19 The word of the LORD came to Jeremiah: 20 Thus says the LORD: If any of you
could break my covenant with the day and my covenant with the night, so that day
and night would not come at their appointed time, 21 only then could my covenant
with my servant David be broken, so that he would not have a son to reign on his
throne, and my covenant with my ministers the Levites. 22 Just as the host of heaven
cannot be numbered and the sands of the sea cannot be measured, so I will increase
the offspring of my servant David, and the Levites who minister to me.
23 The word of the LORD came to Jeremiah: 24 Have you not observed how
these people say, "The two families that the LORD chose have been rejected by
him," and how they hold my people in such contempt that they no longer regard
them as a nation? 25 Thus says the LORD: Only if I had not established my covenant
with day and night and the ordinances of heaven and earth, 26 would I reject the
offspring of Jacob and of my servant David and not choose any of his descendants
as rulers over the offspring of Abraham, Isaac, and Jacob. For I will restore their
fortunes, and will have mercy upon them.

33.15 Ps 72.1-5 Isa 11.1-5
33.16 Isa 45.24,25 Jer 23.6 2 Cor 5.21 Phil 3.9
33.17 1 Kgs 2.4 Ps 89.29-37
33.18 Deut 18.1 Ezek 44.15 Heb 13.15
33.20 2 Sam 23.5 2 Chron 21.7 Ps 104.19-23 Isa 54.9
33.22 Gen 22.17
33.24 Neh 4.2-4 Ps 44.13,14 Isa 11.13 Jer 3.7,8,10,18 Ezek 36.2
33.25 Gen 49.10 Ezek 39.25 Hos 2.23

6. God's promised judgment arrives

Zedekiah will be exiled to Babylon

34 The word that came to Jeremiah from the LORD, when King Nebuchadrezzar of Babylon and all his army and all the kingdoms of the earth and all the
peoples under his dominion were fighting against Jerusalem and all its cities:
2 "Thus says the LORD, the God of Israel: Go and speak to King Zedekiah of Judah
and say to him: Thus says the LORD: I am going to give this city into the hand of the
king of Babylon, and he shall burn it with fire. 3 And you yourself shall not escape
from his hand, but shall surely be captured and handed over to him; you shall see
the king of Babylon eye to eye and speak with him face to face; and you shall go to
Babylon. 4 Yet hear the word of the LORD, O King Zedekiah of Judah! Thus says
the LORD concerning you: You shall not die by the sword; 5 you shall die in peace.

34.1 Jer 1.15 Dan 2.37,38
34.2 2 Chron 36.11, 12 Jer 37.1-4
34.3 2 Kgs 25.4-7 Jer 21.7
34.5 2 Chron 16.14

33.15, 16 These verses refer to both the first and second comings of Christ. At his first coming he would set up his reign in the hearts of believers; at his second coming he will execute justice and righteousness throughout the whole earth. Christ is the "righteousness Branch" growing from David, the man after God's own heart.

33.18 As Christ fulfills the role of King, he also fulfills the role of Priest, maintaining constant fellowship with God and mediating for the people (see the note on 22.30). This verse does not mean that actual priests will perform sacrifices, for they will no longer be necessary (Hebrews 7.24, 25). Now that Christ is our High Priest, all believers are priests of God, and we can come before him personally.

33.22 The promise of countless descendants was also given to Abraham (Genesis 15.5; 22.17). Not only is God remembering his promises to the nation's forefathers, he is also giving an even greater promise during the nation's darkest hour.

34.1ff This chapter describes the fulfillment of many of Jeremiah's predictions. In the book of Jeremiah, many prophecies are both given and quickly fulfilled.

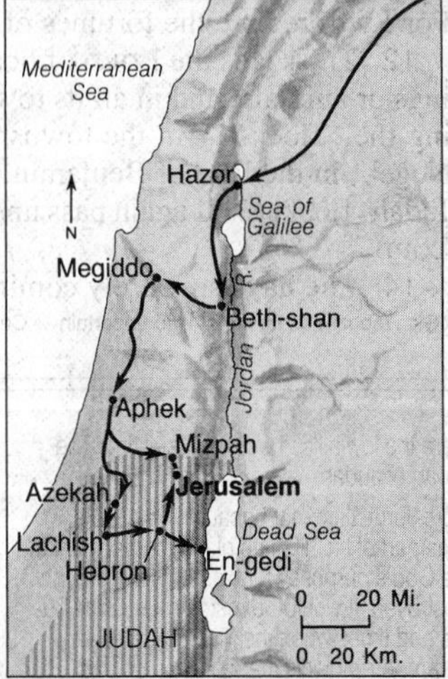

BABYLON ATTACKS JUDAH
Zedekiah incurred Babylon's wrath in allying with Egypt and not surrendering as God told him through Jeremiah. Nebuchadnezzar attacked Judah for the third and final time, moving systematically until all its cities fell. Jerusalem withstood siege for several months but was burned, as Jeremiah predicted.

And as spices were burned[z] for your ancestors, the earlier kings who preceded
you, so they shall burn spices[a] for you and lament for you, saying, "Alas, lord!"
For I have spoken the word, says the LORD.
6 Then the prophet Jeremiah spoke all these words to Zedekiah king of Judah,
in Jerusalem, 7when the army of the king of Babylon was fighting against Jerusalem and against all the cities of Judah that were left, Lachish and Azekah; for these
were the only fortified cities of Judah that remained.

God proclaims freedom for slaves

8 The word that came to Jeremiah from the LORD, after King Zedekiah had
made a covenant with all the people in Jerusalem to make a proclamation of liberty
to them, 9that all should set free their Hebrew slaves, male and female, so that no
one should hold another Judean in slavery. 10And they obeyed, all the officials and
all the people who had entered into the covenant that all would set free their slaves,
male or female, so that they would not be enslaved again; they obeyed and set them
free. 11But afterward they turned around and took back the male and female slaves
they had set free, and brought them again into subjection as slaves. 12The word of
the LORD came to Jeremiah from the LORD: 13Thus says the LORD, the God of
Israel: I myself made a covenant with your ancestors when I brought them out of the
land of Egypt, out of the house of slavery, saying, 14"Every seventh year each of
you must set free any Hebrews who have been sold to you and have served you six
years; you must set them free from your service." But your ancestors did not listen
to me or incline their ears to me. 15You yourselves recently repented and did what
was right in my sight by proclaiming liberty to one another, and you made a covenant before me in the house that is called by my name; 16but then you turned around
and profaned my name when each of you took back your male and female slaves,
whom you had set free according to their desire, and you brought them again into
subjection to be your slaves. 17Therefore, thus says the LORD: You have not obeyed
me by granting a release to your neighbors and friends; I am going to grant a release
to you, says the LORD—a release to the sword, to pestilence, and to famine. I will
make you a horror to all the kingdoms of the earth. 18And those who transgressed
my covenant and did not keep the terms of the covenant that they made before me,
I will make like[b] the calf when they cut it in two and passed between its parts: 19the
officials of Judah, the officials of Jerusalem, the eunuchs, the priests, and all the
people of the land who passed between the parts of the calf 20shall be handed over
to their enemies and to those who seek their lives. Their corpses shall become food
for the birds of the air and the wild animals of the earth. 21And as for King Zedekiah of Judah and his officials, I will hand them over to their enemies and to those
who seek their lives, to the army of the king of Babylon, which has withdrawn from
you. 22I am going to command, says the LORD, and will bring them back to this
city; and they will fight against it, and take it, and burn it with fire. The towns of
Judah I will make a desolation without inhabitant.

[z] Heb *as there was burning* [a] Heb *shall burn* [b] Cn: Heb lacks *like*

34.7 Josh 10.3,10 2 Kgs 14.19 2 Chron 11.5-10
34.8 Lev 25.39-46 Neh 5.1-13
34.9 Gen 14.13
34.11 Ps 78.34-36 Hos 6.4
34.13 Deut 5.2,3,27 Jer 31.32
34.14 Ex 21.2 1 Kgs 9.22 2 Kgs 17.13,14
34.15 Neh 10.29
34.16 Ex 20.7 1 Sam 15.11 Ezek 18.24
34.17 Lev 26.34,35 Deut 28.25,64 Mt 7.2
34.18 Gen 15.10 Hos 6.7 Mic 7.1-5
34.20 1 Sam 17.46 Jer 19.7
34.21 2 Kgs 25.18-21 Ezek 17.16
34.22 Jer 44.22

34.8, 9 Babylon had laid siege to Jerusalem, and the city was about to fall. Zedekiah finally decided to listen to Jeremiah and to try to appease God—so he freed the slaves. He thought he could win God's favor with a kind act, but what he needed was a change of heart. The people had been disobeying God's law from the beginning (Exodus 21.2–11; Leviticus 25.39–55; Deuteronomy 15.12–18). When the siege was temporarily lifted, the people became bold and returned to their sins (34.11–17).

34.15, 16 The people of Israel had a hard time keeping their promises to God. In the temple, they would solemnly promise to obey God, but back in their homes and at work they wouldn't do it. God expressed his great displeasure. If you want to please him, make sure you keep your promises. God wants promises lived out, not just piously made.

34.18, 19 Cutting a calf in two and walking between the halves was a customary way to ratify a contract (Genesis 15.9, 10). This action symbolized the judgment on anyone who broke the contract. God was saying, "You have broken the contract you made with me, so you know the judgment awaiting you!"

The Rechabites demonstrate obedience

35 The word that came to Jeremiah from the LORD in the days of King Jehoiakim son of Josiah of Judah: 2 Go to the house of the Rechabites, and speak
with them, and bring them to the house of the LORD, into one of the chambers; then
offer them wine to drink. 3 So I took Jaazaniah son of Jeremiah son of Habazziniah,
and his brothers, and all his sons, and the whole house of the Rechabites. 4 I
brought them to the house of the LORD into the chamber of the sons of Hanan son
of Igdaliah, the man of God, which was near the chamber of the officials, above the
chamber of Maaseiah son of Shallum, keeper of the threshold. 5 Then I set before
the Rechabites pitchers full of wine, and cups; and I said to them, "Have some
wine." 6 But they answered, "We will drink no wine, for our ancestor Jonadab son
of Rechab commanded us, 'You shall never drink wine, neither you nor your children; 7 nor shall you ever build a house, or sow seed; nor shall you plant a vineyard,
or even own one; but you shall live in tents all your days, that you may live many
days in the land where you reside.' 8 We have obeyed the charge of our ancestor
Jonadab son of Rechab in all that he commanded us, to drink no wine all our days,
ourselves, our wives, our sons, or our daughters, 9 and not to build houses to live
in. We have no vineyard or field or seed; 10 but we have lived in tents, and have
obeyed and done all that our ancestor Jonadab commanded us. 11 But when King
Nebuchadrezzar of Babylon came up against the land, we said, 'Come, and let us
go to Jerusalem for fear of the army of the Chaldeans and the army of the Arameans.' That is why we are living in Jerusalem."
12 Then the word of the LORD came to Jeremiah: 13 Thus says the LORD of
hosts, the God of Israel: Go and say to the people of Judah and the inhabitants of
Jerusalem, Can you not learn a lesson and obey my words? says the LORD. 14 The
command has been carried out that Jonadab son of Rechab gave to his descendants
to drink no wine; and they drink none to this day, for they have obeyed their ancestor's command. But I myself have spoken to you persistently, and you have not
obeyed me. 15 I have sent to you all my servants the prophets, sending them persistently, saying, 'Turn now everyone of you from your evil way, and amend your
doings, and do not go after other gods to serve them, and then you shall live in the
land that I gave to you and your ancestors.' But you did not incline your ear or obey
me. 16 The descendants of Jonadab son of Rechab have carried out the command
that their ancestor gave them, but this people has not obeyed me. 17 Therefore, thus
says the LORD, the God of hosts, the God of Israel: I am going to bring on Judah and
on all the inhabitants of Jerusalem every disaster that I have pronounced against
them; because I have spoken to them and they have not listened, I have called to
them and they have not answered.
18 But to the house of the Rechabites Jeremiah said: Thus says the LORD of
hosts, the God of Israel: Because you have obeyed the command of your ancestor
Jonadab, and kept all his precepts, and done all that he commanded you, 19 therefore thus says the LORD of hosts, the God of Israel: Jonadab son of Rechab shall not
lack a descendant to stand before me for all time.

35.1 2 Kgs 23.34-36 Dan 1.1
35.2 1 Kgs 6.5,6,8 1 Chron 2.55
35.5 2 Cor 2.9
35.6 Lev 10.9 Num 6.2-4 2 Kgs 10.15,23 1 Chron 2.55 Lk 1.15
35.7 Ex 20.12 1 Chron 16.19 Heb 11.9
35.8 Prov 4.1,2,10 6.20 Col 3.20
35.9 Ps 37.16 1 Tim 6.6
35.11 2 Kgs 24.1,2 Dan 1.1,2
35.13 Isa 28.9-12
35.14 2 Chron 36.15 Isa 30.9
35.15 Deut 6.14 Jer 29.19 Ezek 18.30-32 Acts 26.20
35.16 Mal 1.6
35.17 Prov 1.24,25 Mic 3.12 Lk 13.34,35 Rom 10.21
35.18 Ex 20.12 Jer 15.19 Eph 6.1-3

35.1ff The Rechabites' code of conduct resembled that of the nazirites, who took a special vow of dedication to God (Numbers 6). For 200 years, they had obeyed their ancestors' vow to abstain from wine. While the rest of the nation was breaking its covenant with God, these people were steadfast in their commitment. God wanted the rest of his people to remain as committed to their covenant with him as the Rechabites were to their vow.

35.6 Jonadab (Jehonadab), son of Rechab, had joined Jehu in purging the northern kingdom of Baal worship (2 Kings 10.15–28).

35.13–17 There is a vivid contrast between the Rechabites and the other Israelites: (1) The Rechabites kept their vows to a fallible human leader; the people of Israel broke their covenant with their infallible divine Leader. (2) Jonadab told his family one time not to drink, and they obeyed; God commanded Israel constantly to turn from sin, and they refused. (3) The Rechabites obeyed laws that dealt with temporal issues; Israel refused to obey God's laws that dealt with eternal issues. (4) The Rechabites had obeyed for hundreds of years; Israel had disobeyed for hundreds of years. (5) The Rechabites would be rewarded; Israel would be punished. We often are willing to observe customs merely for the sake of tradition; how much more should we obey God's Word because it is eternal.

Baruch reads God's messages

36 In the fourth year of King Jehoiakim son of Josiah of Judah, this word came
to Jeremiah from the LORD: 2 Take a scroll and write on it all the words that
I have spoken to you against Israel and Judah and all the nations, from the day I
spoke to you, from the days of Josiah until today. 3 It may be that when the house
of Judah hears of all the disasters that I intend to do to them, all of them may turn
from their evil ways, so that I may forgive their iniquity and their sin.

4 Then Jeremiah called Baruch son of Neriah, and Baruch wrote on a scroll at
Jeremiah's dictation all the words of the LORD that he had spoken to him. 5 And
Jeremiah ordered Baruch, saying, "I am prevented from entering the house of the
LORD; 6 so you go yourself, and on a fast day in the hearing of the people in the
LORD's house you shall read the words of the LORD from the scroll that you have
written at my dictation. You shall read them also in the hearing of all the people of
Judah who come up from their towns. 7 It may be that their plea will come before
the LORD, and that all of them will turn from their evil ways, for great is the anger
and wrath that the LORD has pronounced against this people." 8 And Baruch son of
Neriah did all that the prophet Jeremiah ordered him about reading from the scroll
the words of the LORD in the LORD's house.

9 In the fifth year of King Jehoiakim son of Josiah of Judah, in the ninth month,
all the people in Jerusalem and all the people who came from the towns of Judah to
Jerusalem proclaimed a fast before the LORD. 10 Then, in the hearing of all the people, Baruch read the words of Jeremiah from the scroll, in the house of the LORD,
in the chamber of Gemariah son of Shaphan the secretary, which was in the upper
court, at the entry of the New Gate of the LORD's house.

11 When Micaiah son of Gemariah son of Shaphan heard all the words of the
LORD from the scroll, 12 he went down to the king's house, into the secretary's
chamber; and all the officials were sitting there: Elishama the secretary, Delaiah
son of Shemaiah, Elnathan son of Achbor, Gemariah son of Shaphan, Zedekiah
son of Hananiah, and all the officials. 13 And Micaiah told them all the words that
he had heard, when Baruch read the scroll in the hearing of the people. 14 Then all
the officials sent Jehudi son of Nethaniah son of Shelemiah son of Cushi to say to
Baruch, "Bring the scroll that you read in the hearing of the people, and come." So
Baruch son of Neriah took the scroll in his hand and came to them. 15 And they said
to him, "Sit down and read it to us." So Baruch read it to them. 16 When they heard
all the words, they turned to one another in alarm, and said to Baruch, "We certainly must report all these words to the king." 17 Then they questioned Baruch,
"Tell us now, how did you write all these words? Was it at his dictation?" 18 Baruch
answered them, "He dictated all these words to me, and I wrote them with ink on
the scroll." 19 Then the officials said to Baruch, "Go and hide, you and Jeremiah,
and let no one know where you are."

20 Leaving the scroll in the chamber of Elishama the secretary, they went to the
court of the king; and they reported all the words to the king. 21 Then the king sent
Jehudi to get the scroll, and he took it from the chamber of Elishama the secretary;
and Jehudi read it to the king and all the officials who stood beside the king. 22 Now
the king was sitting in his winter apartment (it was the ninth month), and there was

36.1 Jer 25.1-3; 45.1
36.2 Jer 1.2,3,5,9,10; 25.9-29; Zech 5.1,2
36.3 Isa 55.7; Jer 18.8,11; Mk 4.12; Acts 3.19
36.4 Jer 32.12; Ezek 2.9
36.5 Jer 32.2
36.6 Zech 8.19
36.7 1 Kgs 8.33; 2 Kgs 22.13; Jer 26.3
36.10 Jer 26.10
36.12 Jer 26.22
36.13 2 Kgs 22.9,10
36.16 Amos 7.10,11; Acts 24.25
36.18 Jer 43.2,3
36.19 1 Kgs 17.3; 18.4; Jer 26.20-24
36.21 2 Kgs 22.9,10; 2 Chron 34.18; Ezek 2.4,5
36.22 Amos 3.15

36.1ff This happened in the summer of 605 B.C., shortly after Nebuchadnezzar's victory over the Egyptian army at Carchemish, before the events recorded in chapters 34 and 35.

36.2–4 Most people in ancient times could neither read nor write, so those who could were extremely valuable. They held positions of great importance and were very respected for their knowledge. Writing was often done on vellum or papyrus sheets that were sewn or glued together and stored in long rolls called scrolls. After the exile, scribes became teachers of the law. In New Testament times, the scribes formed a powerful political party.

36.9 Days of fasting (when people abstained from eating food to show their humility and repentance) were often called at times of national emergency. Babylon was destroying city after city and closing in on Jerusalem. As the people came to the temple, Baruch told them how to avert the coming tragedy. But they refused to listen.

36.10–32 God told Jeremiah to write his words on a scroll. Because he was not allowed to go to the temple, Jeremiah asked his scribe, Baruch, to whom he had dictated the scroll, to read it to the people gathered there. Baruch then read it to the officials, and finally Jehudi read it to the king himself. Although the king burned the scroll, he could not destroy God's Word. Today many people try to put God's Word aside or say that it contains errors and therefore cannot be trusted. People may reject God's Word, but they cannot destroy it. God's Word will stand forever (Psalm 119.89).

36.22 A brazier is a pan for holding burning coals.

a fire burning in the brazier before him. 23 As Jehudi read three or four columns, the
king[c] would cut them off with a penknife and throw them into the fire in the brazier, until the entire scroll was consumed in the fire that was in the brazier. 24 Yet
neither the king, nor any of his servants who heard all these words, was alarmed,
nor did they tear their garments. 25 Even when Elnathan and Delaiah and Gemariah
urged the king not to burn the scroll, he would not listen to them. 26 And the king
commanded Jerahmeel the king's son and Seraiah son of Azriel and Shelemiah son
of Abdeel to arrest the secretary Baruch and the prophet Jeremiah. But the LORD
hid them.

27 Now, after the king had burned the scroll with the words that Baruch wrote
at Jeremiah's dictation, the word of the LORD came to Jeremiah: 28 Take another
scroll and write on it all the former words that were in the first scroll, which King
Jehoiakim of Judah has burned. 29 And concerning King Jehoiakim of Judah you
shall say: Thus says the LORD, You have dared to burn this scroll, saying, Why
have you written in it that the king of Babylon will certainly come and destroy this
land, and will cut off from it human beings and animals? 30 Therefore thus says the
LORD concerning King Jehoiakim of Judah: He shall have no one to sit upon the
throne of David, and his dead body shall be cast out to the heat by day and the frost
by night. 31 And I will punish him and his offspring and his servants for their iniquity; I will bring on them, and on the inhabitants of Jerusalem, and on the people
of Judah, all the disasters with which I have threatened them — but they would not
listen.

32 Then Jeremiah took another scroll and gave it to the secretary Baruch son of
Neriah, who wrote on it at Jeremiah's dictation all the words of the scroll that King
Jehoiakim of Judah had burned in the fire; and many similar words were added to
them.

Jeremiah is put in prison

37 Zedekiah son of Josiah, whom King Nebuchadrezzar of Babylon made king
in the land of Judah, succeeded Coniah son of Jehoiakim. 2 But neither he
nor his servants nor the people of the land listened to the words of the LORD that he
spoke through the prophet Jeremiah.

3 King Zedekiah sent Jehucal son of Shelemiah and the priest Zephaniah son of
Maaseiah to the prophet Jeremiah saying, "Please pray for us to the LORD our
God." 4 Now Jeremiah was still going in and out among the people, for he had not
yet been put in prison. 5 Meanwhile, the army of Pharaoh had come out of Egypt;
and when the Chaldeans who were besieging Jerusalem heard news of them, they
withdrew from Jerusalem.

6 Then the word of the LORD came to the prophet Jeremiah: 7 Thus says the
LORD, God of Israel: This is what the two of you shall say to the king of Judah, who
sent you to me to inquire of me, Pharaoh's army, which set out to help you, is going
to return to its own land, to Egypt. 8 And the Chaldeans shall return and fight
against this city; they shall take it and burn it with fire. 9 Thus says the LORD: Do not

36.23 Prov 1.29,30 Isa 5.18,19 28.14,22
36.24 2 Kgs 19.1,2 Ps 36.1 Isa 26.10,11 Acts 5.34-39
36.26 1 Kgs 19.1-3, 10,14 Jer 15.20,21
36.28 Jer 28.13,14 44.28 Zech 1.5,6
36.29 Deut 29.19 Isa 30.10,11 45.9 Jer 25.8-11 26.9
36.30 2 Kgs 24.12-15 Jer 22.30
36.31 Deut 28.15-19 Prov 29.1 Jer 19.15
36.32 Ex 34.1
37.1 2 Chron 36.9,10 Jer 22.24,28
37.2 2 Kgs 24.18-20 2 Chron 36.12 Prov 29.12
37.3 Jer 2.26,27 21.1,2; 52.24
37.5 Ezek 17.15,16
37.7 Isa 30.1-3 31.1-3 Jer 21.1,2 Ezek 17.17
37.8 Jer 34.22
37.9 Jer 29.8 Obad 3 Eph 5.6

[c] Heb *he*

36.25 Only three leaders protested this evil act of burning God's Word. This shows how complacent and insensitive to God the people had become.

36.30 Jehoiakim's son, Jehoiachin, was king for three months before he was taken into captivity, but this did not qualify as sitting "upon the throne of David" – an expression that implied permanence. Jehoiakim did not secure a dynasty. Zedekiah, the next ruler, was Jehoiachin's uncle. Thus the line of mortal human kings descended from David's son Solomon was finished, but in less than 600 years the eternal King would come through Solomon's brother Nathan (see also the note on 22.30).

37.1ff The people of Jerusalem assassinated King Jehoiakim and appointed his son Coniah (Jehoiachin) king, but he was taken captive to Babylon three months later. Nebuchadnezzar then appointed Zedekiah as his vassal in Judah.

37.2, 3 King Zedekiah and his officials did not want to listen to Jeremiah's words, but they wanted the blessings of his prayers. They wanted a superficial religion that wouldn't cost anything. But God is not pleased with those who come to him only for what they can get rather than seeking to establish or deepen a relationship with him. We would not accept that kind of relationship with someone else, and we shouldn't expect God to accept it from us.

37.5 When Nebuchadnezzar besieged Jerusalem in 589 B.C., Pharaoh Hophra marched against him at Zedekiah's invitation. Jerusalem looked to Egypt for help in spite of Jeremiah's warnings. But the Egyptians were no help, for as soon as the Babylonians turned on them, they retreated. Jeremiah's warnings had been correct.

37.10 Lev 26.36-38 Isa 30.17 Joel 2.11
37.12 Jer 32.8
37.13 Jer 18.18; 20.10 Zech 14.10 Acts 24.5-9,13
37.14 Ps 27.12 Jer 40.4-6 Mt 5.11,12
37.15 Jer 18.23; 38.6 Mt 21.35 Acts 5.18
37.17 Jer 21.7 38.14-16,24-27 Ezek 12.12,13 17.19-21
37.18 1 Sam 24.9 26.18 Jn 10.32 Acts 25.8,10,11
37.19 Deut 32.37,38
37.20 Jer 38.26
37.21 Job 5.20 Ps 33.18,19 Isa 33.16 Jer 52.6

deceive yourselves, saying, "The Chaldeans will surely go away from us," for they
will not go away. 10 Even if you defeated the whole army of Chaldeans who are
fighting against you, and there remained of them only wounded men in their tents,
they would rise up and burn this city with fire.
11 Now when the Chaldean army had withdrawn from Jerusalem at the approach of Pharaoh's army, 12 Jeremiah set out from Jerusalem to go to the land of
Benjamin to receive his share of property[d] among the people there. 13 When he
reached the Benjamin Gate, a sentinel there named Irijah son of Shelemiah son of
Hananiah arrested the prophet Jeremiah saying, "You are deserting to the Chaldeans." 14 And Jeremiah said, "That is a lie; I am not deserting to the Chaldeans." But
Irijah would not listen to him, and arrested Jeremiah and brought him to the officials. 15 The officials were enraged at Jeremiah, and they beat him and imprisoned
him in the house of the secretary Jonathan, for it had been made a prison. 16 Thus
Jeremiah was put in the cistern house, in the cells, and remained there many days.
17 Then King Zedekiah sent for him, and received him. The king questioned
him secretly in his house, and said, "Is there any word from the LORD?" Jeremiah
said, "There is!" Then he said, "You shall be handed over to the king of Babylon."
18 Jeremiah also said to King Zedekiah, "What wrong have I done to you or your
servants or this people, that you have put me in prison? 19 Where are your prophets
who prophesied to you, saying, 'The king of Babylon will not come against you
and against this land'? 20 Now please hear me, my lord king: be good enough to
listen to my plea, and do not send me back to the house of the secretary Jonathan
to die there." 21 So King Zedekiah gave orders, and they committed Jeremiah to the
court of the guard; and a loaf of bread was given him daily from the bakers' street,
until all the bread of the city was gone. So Jeremiah remained in the court of the
guard.

Jeremiah is rescued

38.1 Jer 21.8
38.2 Jer 21.9; 42.17
38.3 Jer 21.10 32.3-5
38.4 1 Kgs 18.17,18 Jer 26.11 Amos 7.10 Acts 16.20,21
38.5 1 Sam 15.24 29.9
38.6 Ps 40.2 69.1,2,14 Jer 37.15,16 Zech 9.11

38 Now Shephatiah son of Mattan, Gedaliah son of Pashhur, Jucal son of Shelemiah, and Pashhur son of Malchiah heard the words that Jeremiah was
saying to all the people, 2 Thus says the LORD, Those who stay in this city shall die
by the sword, by famine, and by pestilence; but those who go out to the Chaldeans
shall live; they shall have their lives as a prize of war, and live. 3 Thus says the
LORD, This city shall surely be handed over to the army of the king of Babylon and
be taken. 4 Then the officials said to the king, "This man ought to be put to death,
because he is discouraging the soldiers who are left in this city, and all the people,
by speaking such words to them. For this man is not seeking the welfare of this
people, but their harm." 5 King Zedekiah said, "Here he is; he is in your hands; for
the king is powerless against you." 6 So they took Jeremiah and threw him into the
cistern of Malchiah, the king's son, which was in the court of the guard, letting
Jeremiah down by ropes. Now there was no water in the cistern, but only mud, and
Jeremiah sank in the mud.

[d] Meaning of Heb uncertain

37.16 Jeremiah seems to have been placed in an underground dungeon, in solitary confinement.

37.17 Zedekiah teetered between surrender and resistance. Too frightened and weak to exercise authority, he asked Jeremiah to come secretly to the palace, perhaps hoping for some better news from God. Zedekiah was desperate; he wanted to hear God's Word, but he feared the political ramifications of being caught talking to Jeremiah.

38.4, 5 No wonder Judah was in turmoil: the king agreed with everybody. He listened to Jeremiah (37.21); then he agreed Jeremiah should be killed (38.5); and finally he rescued Jeremiah (38.10). Jeremiah was not popular; his words undermined the morale of the army and the people. Zedekiah couldn't decide between public opinion and God's Word.

38.6 Officials put Jeremiah in a cistern to kill him. A cistern was a large hole in the ground lined with rocks to collect rain water. The bottom would have been dark, damp, and, in this case, full of mud. Jeremiah could drown, die of exposure, or starve to death in the cistern.

38.6 Judah's leaders persecuted Jeremiah repeatedly for faithfully proclaiming God's messages. For 40 years of faithful ministry, he received no acclaim, no love, no popular following. He was beaten, jailed, threatened, and even forced to leave his homeland. Only the heathen Babylonians showed him any respect. God does not guarantee that his servants will escape persecution, even when they are faithful. But God does promise that he will be with them and will give them strength to endure (2 Corinthians 1.3–7). As you minister to others, recognize that your service is for God and not just for human approval. God rewards our faithfulness, but not always during our stay on earth.

7 Ebed-melech the Ethiopian,[e] a eunuch in the king's house, heard that they
had put Jeremiah into the cistern. The king happened to be sitting at the Benjamin
Gate, 8 So Ebed-melech left the king's house and spoke to the king, 9 "My lord
king, these men have acted wickedly in all they did to the prophet Jeremiah by
throwing him into the cistern to die there of hunger, for there is no bread left in the
city." 10 Then the king commanded Ebed-melech the Ethiopian,[e] "Take three men
with you from here, and pull the prophet Jeremiah up from the cistern before he
dies." 11 So Ebed-melech took the men with him and went to the house of the king,
to a wardrobe of[f] the storehouse, and took from there old rags and worn-out
clothes, which he let down to Jeremiah in the cistern by ropes. 12 Then Ebed-
melech the Ethiopian[e] said to Jeremiah, "Just put the rags and clothes between
your armpits and the ropes." Jeremiah did so. 13 Then they drew Jeremiah up by the
ropes and pulled him out of the cistern. And Jeremiah remained in the court of the
guard.

14 King Zedekiah sent for the prophet Jeremiah and received him at the third
entrance of the temple of the LORD. The king said to Jeremiah, "I have something
to ask you; do not hide anything from me." 15 Jeremiah said to Zedekiah, "If I tell
you, you will put me to death, will you not? And if I give you advice, you will not
listen to me." 16 So King Zedekiah swore an oath in secret to Jeremiah, "As the
LORD lives, who gave us our lives, I will not put you to death or hand you over to
these men who seek your life."

17 Then Jeremiah said to Zedekiah, "Thus says the LORD, the God of hosts, the
God of Israel, If you will only surrender to the officials of the king of Babylon, then
your life shall be spared, and this city shall not be burned with fire, and you and
your house shall live. 18 But if you do not surrender to the officials of the king of
Babylon, then this city shall be handed over to the Chaldeans, and they shall burn
it with fire, and you yourself shall not escape from their hand." 19 King Zedekiah
said to Jeremiah, "I am afraid of the Judeans who have deserted to the Chaldeans,
for I might be handed over to them and they would abuse me." 20 Jeremiah said,
"That will not happen. Just obey the voice of the LORD in what I say to you, and it
shall go well with you, and your life shall be spared. 21 But if you are determined
not to surrender, this is what the LORD has shown me— 22 a vision of all the women
remaining in the house of the king of Judah being led out to the officials of the king
of Babylon and saying,

"Your trusted friends have seduced you
  and have overcome you;
Now that your feet are stuck in the mud,
  they desert you.'

23 All your wives and your children shall be led out to the Chaldeans, and you yourself shall not escape from their hand, but shall be seized by the king of Babylon;
and this city shall be burned with fire."

24 Then Zedekiah said to Jeremiah, "Do not let anyone else know of this conversation, or you will die. 25 If the officials should hear that I have spoken with you,
and they should come and say to you, 'Just tell us what you said to the king; do not
conceal it from us, or we will put you to death. What did the king say to you?'
26 then you shall say to them, 'I was presenting my plea to the king not to send me
back to the house of Jonathan to die there.' " 27 All the officials did come to Jere-

[e] Or *Nubian*; Heb *Cushite* [f] Cn: Heb *to under*

38.8 Job 29.7
38.9 Jer 37.21
38.13 Jer 37.21 39.14,15
38.14 1 Kgs 22.16 Jer 21.1,2 37.17
38.15 Jer 42.2-5,20 Lk 22.67,68
38.17 2 Kgs 25.27-30 Ps 80.7,14 Jer 21.8-10 27.12,17
38.18 2 Kgs 25.4-10 Jer 27.8; 37.8
38.19 Isa 51.12,13 57.11 Jer 39.9 Jn 12.42
38.20 Isa 55.3 Jer 7.23 11.4,8; 26.13
38.21 Jer 6.12; 8.10 43.6
38.23 2 Kgs 25.7 Jer 39.6; 41.10
38.26 Jer 37.15,16,20
38.27 1 Sam 10.15, 16; 16.2-5

38.7, 8 The Benjamin Gate was one of Jerusalem's city gates where legal matters were handled. A palace official, Ebed-melech, had access to the king. When he heard of Jeremiah's plight, he went immediately to deal with the injustice.

38.9–13 Ebed-melech feared God more than man. He alone among the palace officials stood up against the murder plot. His obedience could have cost him his life. Because he obeyed, however, he was spared when Jerusalem fell (39.15–18). You can either go along with the crowd or speak up for God. When someone is treated unkindly or unjustly, for example, reach out to that person with God's love. You may be the only one who does. And, when you're being treated unkindly yourself, be sure to thank God when he sends an "Ebed-melech" your way.

38.27 The officials wanted accurate information, but not God's truth. They wanted to use this information against God, his prophet, and the king. But Jeremiah told the officials only what the king ordered him to say. We must not withhold God's truth from others, but we should withhold information that will be used for evil.

miah and questioned him; and he answered them in the very words the king had
commanded. So they stopped questioning him, for the conversation had not been
overheard. 28 And Jeremiah remained in the court of the guard until the day that
Jerusalem was taken.

Nebuchadnezzar captures Jerusalem

39 In the ninth year of King Zedekiah of Judah, in the tenth month, King Nebuchadrezzar of Babylon and all his army came against Jerusalem and besieged it; 2 in the eleventh year of Zedekiah, in the fourth month, on the ninth day
of the month, a breach was made in the city. 3 When Jerusalem was taken,[g] all the
officials of the king of Babylon came and sat in the middle gate: Nergal-sharezer,
Samgar-nebo, Sarsechim the Rab-saris, Nergal-sharezer the Rab-mag, with all the
rest of the officials of the king of Babylon. 4 When King Zedekiah of Judah and all
the soldiers saw them, they fled, going out of the city at night by way of the king's
garden through the gate between the two walls; and they went toward the Arabah.
5 But the army of the Chaldeans pursued them, and overtook Zedekiah in the plains
of Jericho; and when they had taken him, they brought him up to King Nebuchadrezzar of Babylon, at Riblah, in the land of Hamath; and he passed sentence on
him. 6 The king of Babylon slaughtered the sons of Zedekiah at Riblah before his
eyes; also the king of Babylon slaughtered all the nobles of Judah. 7 He put out the
eyes of Zedekiah, and bound him in fetters to take him to Babylon. 8 The Chaldeans
burned the king's house and the houses of the people, and broke down the walls of
Jerusalem. 9 Then Nebuzaradan the captain of the guard exiled to Babylon the rest
of the people who were left in the city, those who had deserted to him, and the
people who remained. 10 Nebuzaradan the captain of the guard left in the land of
Judah some of the poor people who owned nothing, and gave them vineyards and
fields at the same time.

11 King Nebuchadrezzar of Babylon gave command concerning Jeremiah
through Nebuzaradan, the captain of the guard, saying, 12 "Take him, look after
him well and do him no harm, but deal with him as he may ask you." 13 So Nebuzaradan the captain of the guard, Nebushazban the Rab-saris, Nergal-sharezer the
Rab-mag, and all the chief officers of the king of Babylon sent 14 and took Jeremiah
from the court of the guard. They entrusted him to Gedaliah son of Ahikam son of
Shaphan to be brought home. So he stayed with his own people.

15 The word of the LORD came to Jeremiah while he was confined in the court
of the guard: 16 Go and say to Ebed-melech the Ethiopian:[h] Thus says the LORD of
hosts, the God of Israel: I am going to fulfill my words against this city for evil and
not for good, and they shall be accomplished in your presence on that day. 17 But I
will save you on that day, says the LORD, and you shall not be handed over to those

38.28 Ps 23.4; Jer 37.20,21; 39.13,14
39.1 2 Kgs 25.1-12
39.3 Jer 21.3,4
39.4 2 Kgs 25.4; Isa 30.15,16; Jer 52.7; Amos 2.14
39.5 Jer 32.4,5; 52.9; Lam 4.20; 52.8
39.6 Jer 24.8-10; 34.18-21; 52.10
39.7 2 Kgs 25.7; Jer 52.11; Ezek 12.13
39.8 2 Kgs 25.9,10; Neh 1.3
39.9 2 Kgs 25.11,20; Jer 52.12-16,26
39.10 2 Kgs 25.12
39.11 Job 5.15,16; Prov 16.7; 21.1; Jer 1.8; 15.20,21
39.14 2 Kgs 22.12,14; Jer 26.24; 40.1-6
39.16 Jer 21.10; Dan 9.12; Zech 1.6
39.17 Ps 41.1,2; 50.14,15

[g] This clause has been transposed from 38.28 [h] Or *Nubian*; Heb *Cushite*

39.1 Zedekiah, son of Josiah and last king of Judah, ruled 11 years, from 597 to 586 B.C. Zedekiah's two older brothers, Jehoahaz and Jehoiakim, and his nephew Coniah (also called Jehoiachin) ruled before him. When Coniah was exiled to Babylon, Nebuchadnezzar made 21-year-old Mattaniah the king, changing his name to Zedekiah. Zedekiah rebelled against Nebuchadnezzar, who captured him, killed his sons before him, and then blinded him and took him back to Babylon where he later died (see 2 Kings 24, 25; 2 Chronicles 36; and Jeremiah 52).

39.5 Riblah was 200 miles north of Jerusalem. This was the Babylonian headquarters for ruling the region.

39.10 Babylon had a shrewd foreign policy toward conquered lands. They deported the rich and powerful, leaving only the very poor in charge, thus making them grateful to their conquerors. This policy assured that conquered populations would be too loyal and too weak to revolt.

39.11, 12 God had promised to see Jeremiah through his trouble (1.8). The superstitious Babylonians, who highly respected magicians and fortune-tellers, treated Jeremiah as a seer. Because he had been imprisoned by his own people, they assumed he was a traitor and on their side. They undoubtedly knew he had counseled cooperation with Babylon and predicted a Babylonian victory. So the Babylonians freed Jeremiah and protected him.

39.14 What a difference between Jeremiah's fate and Zedekiah's. Jeremiah was freed, Zedekiah was imprisoned. Jeremiah was saved because of his faith, Zedekiah was destroyed because of his fear. Jeremiah was treated with respect, Zedekiah was treated with contempt. Jeremiah was concerned for the people, Zedekiah was concerned for himself.

39.17, 18 Ebed-melech risked his life to save God's prophet Jeremiah (38.7–13). When Babylon conquered Jerusalem, God protected Ebed-melech from the Babylonians. God has special rewards for his faithful people, but not everyone will receive them in this life (see the note on 38.6).

whom you dread. 18 For I will surely save you, and you shall not fall by the sword; 39.18 Ps 34.22
but you shall have your life as a prize of war, because you have trusted in me, says Jer 17.7,8
the LORD.

Jeremiah stays in the occupied land

40 The word that came to Jeremiah from the LORD after Nebuzaradan the cap- 40.1 Jer 31.15
tain of the guard had let him go from Ramah, when he took him bound in
fetters along with all the captives of Jerusalem and Judah who were being exiled to
Babylon. 2 The captain of the guard took Jeremiah and said to him, "The LORD your 40.2
God threatened this place with this disaster; 3 and now the LORD has brought it Deut 29.24-28 Jer 22.8,9; 50.7
about, and has done as he said, because all of you sinned against the LORD and did Dan 9.11 Rom 2.5
not obey his voice. Therefore this thing has come upon you. 4 Now look, I have just 40.4
released you today from the fetters on your hands. If you wish to come with me to Gen 20.15
Babylon, come, and I will take good care of you; but if you do not wish to come Jer 39.11,12
with me to Babylon, you need not come. See, the whole land is before you; go
wherever you think it good and right to go. 5 If you remain,[i] then return to Geda- 40.5
liah son of Ahikam son of Shaphan, whom the king of Babylon appointed governor 2 Kgs 25.23
of the towns of Judah, and stay with him among the people; or go wherever you
think it right to go." So the captain of the guard gave him an allowance of food and
a present, and let him go. 6 Then Jeremiah went to Gedaliah son of Ahikam at Mizpah, and stayed with him among the people who were left in the land.
7 When all the leaders of the forces in the open country and their troops heard 40.7 2 Kgs 25.23,24
that the king of Babylon had appointed Gedaliah son of Ahikam governor in the Jer 39.10; 52.16
land, and had committed to him men, women, and children, those of the poorest of
the land who had not been taken into exile to Babylon, 8 they went to Gedaliah at 40.8
Mizpah—Ishmael son of Nethaniah, Johanan son of Kareah, Seraiah son of Tan- 2 Kgs 25.23 Jer 41.1
humeth, the sons of Ephai the Netophathite, Jezaniah son of the Maacathite, they
and their troops. 9 Gedaliah son of Ahikam son of Shaphan swore to them and their 40.9
troops, saying, "Do not be afraid to serve the Chaldeans. Stay in the land and serve 2 Kgs 25.24 Jer 27.11
the king of Babylon, and it shall go well with you. 10 As for me, I am staying at 40.10
Mizpah to represent you before the Chaldeans who come to us; but as for you, Jer 35.19; 39.10
gather wine and summer fruits and oil, and store them in your vessels, and live in
the towns that you have taken over." 11 Likewise, when all the Judeans who were 40.11
in Moab and among the Ammonites and in Edom and in other lands heard that the 1 Sam 11.1 Isa 11.14
king of Babylon had left a remnant in Judah and had appointed Gedaliah son of 16.4,5
Ahikam son of Shaphan as governor over them, 12 then all the Judeans returned 40.12
from all the places to which they had been scattered and came to the land of Judah, Jer 43.5
to Gedaliah at Mizpah; and they gathered wine and summer fruits in great abundance.
13 Now Johanan son of Kareah and all the leaders of the forces in the open 40.13
country came to Gedaliah at Mizpah 14 and said to him, "Are you at all aware that Jer 25.21; 41.10
Baalis king of the Ammonites has sent Ishmael son of Nethaniah to take your life?"
But Gedaliah son of Ahikam would not believe them. 15 Then Johanan son of Ka- 40.15
reah spoke secretly to Gedaliah at Mizpah, "Please let me go and kill Ishmael son 1 Sam 26.8 2 Sam 21.17
of Nethaniah, and no one else will know. Why should he take your life, so that all Jer 42.1,2

[i] Syr: Meaning of Heb uncertain

40–45 These six chapters cover events following Jerusalem's fall to Babylon.

40.2, 3 The Babylonian captain, who did not know God, acknowledged that God had given the Babylonians victory. It is strange when people recognize that God exists and does miracles, but still they do not personally accept him. Knowing God is more than knowing about him. Be sure you know him personally.

40.4 Jeremiah was free to go anywhere. In Babylon he would have had great comfort and power. In Judah he would continue to face hardship. In Babylon he would have been favored by the Babylonians, but hated by the Judean exiles. In Judah he would remain poor and unwanted, but the Judean remnant would know he was not a traitor. He returned to Judah.

40.6 Mizpah was a few miles north of Jerusalem. Not thoroughly destroyed by the Babylonians, Mizpah served as a refuge after the destruction of Jerusalem.

40.13–41.3 Gedaliah, appointed governor of Judah, foolishly ignored the warnings of assassination. Ishmael, in the line of David, may have been angry that he had been passed over for leadership. This is similar to the chaotic political situation Ezra and Nehemiah faced when they returned to rebuild the temple and the city.

the Judeans who are gathered around you would be scattered, and the remnant of
40.16 Mt 10.16 Judah would perish?” 16 But Gedaliah son of Ahikam said to Johanan son of Kareah, “Do not do such a thing, for you are telling a lie about Ishmael.”

Gedaliah is assassinated

41.1 2 Kgs 25.25 Jer 39.14 40.5,6,8,13,14 **41** In the seventh month, Ishmael son of Nethaniah son of Elishama, of the
royal family, one of the chief officers of the king, came with ten men to
Gedaliah son of Ahikam, at Mizpah. As they ate bread together there at Mizpah,
41.2 2 Sam 3.27 20.8-10 Ps 41.9; 109.5 Jn 13.18 2 Ishmael son of Nethaniah and the ten men with him got up and struck down Gedaliah son of Ahikam son of Shaphan with the sword and killed him, because the king
of Babylon had appointed him governor in the land. 3 Ishmael also killed all the
Judeans who were with Gedaliah at Mizpah, and the Chaldean soldiers who happened to be there.

41.5 Deut 14.1 Josh 18.1 1 Kgs 16.24 Ps 78.60 Jer 16.6 4 On the day after the murder of Gedaliah, before anyone knew of it, 5 eighty
men arrived from Shechem and Shiloh and Samaria, with their beards shaved and
their clothes torn, and their bodies gashed, bringing grain offerings and incense to
present at the temple of the LORD. 6 And Ishmael son of Nethaniah came out from
41.6 Jer 50.4 Mizpah to meet them, weeping as he came. As he met them, he said to them,
41.7 Isa 59.7 Ezek 22.27 33.24,26 “Come to Gedaliah son of Ahikam.” 7 When they reached the middle of the
city, Ishmael son of Nethaniah and the men with him slaughtered them, and threw
them[j] into a cistern. 8 But there were ten men among them who said to Ishmael,
“Do not kill us, for we have stores of wheat, barley, oil, and honey hidden in the
fields.” So he refrained, and did not kill them along with their companions.

41.9 1 Sam 13.6 1 Kgs 15.17-22 2 Chron 16.1-6 Heb 11.37,38 9 Now the cistern into which Ishmael had thrown all the bodies of the men
whom he had struck down was the large cistern[k] that King Asa had made for de-
fense against King Baasha of Israel; Ishmael son of Nethaniah filled that cistern
41.10 Jer 40.11,12 43.6 with those whom he had killed. 10 Then Ishmael took captive all the rest of the
people who were in Mizpah, the king’s daughters and all the people who were left
at Mizpah, whom Nebuzaradan, the captain of the guard, had committed to Gedaliah son of Ahikam. Ishmael son of Nethaniah took them captive and set out to
cross over to the Ammonites.

41.11 Jer 40.7,8, 13-16 11 But when Johanan son of Kareah and all the leaders of the forces with him
heard of all the crimes that Ishmael son of Nethaniah had done, 12 they took all their
41.12 2 Sam 2.13 men and went to fight against Ishmael son of Nethaniah. They came upon him at
the great pool that is in Gibeon. 13 And when all the people who were with Ishmael
saw Johanan son of Kareah and all the leaders of the forces with him, they were
glad. 14 So all the people whom Ishmael had carried away captive from Mizpah
41.15 Prov 28.17 turned around and came back, and went to Johanan son of Kareah. 15 But Ishmael
son of Nethaniah escaped from Johanan with eight men, and went to the Ammon-
41.16 2 Sam 19.37, 38,40 Jer 42.8,14 43.4-7 ites. 16 Then Johanan son of Kareah and all the leaders of the forces with him took
all the rest of the people whom Ishmael son of Nethaniah had carried away captive[l]
from Mizpah after he had slain Gedaliah son of Ahikam—soldiers, women, children, and eunuchs, whom Johanan brought back from Gibeon.[m] 17 And they set
out, and stopped at Geruth Chimham near Bethlehem, intending to go to Egypt
41.18 Isa 57.11 Lk 12.4,5 18 because of the Chaldeans; for they were afraid of them, because Ishmael son of
Nethaniah had killed Gedaliah son of Ahikam, whom the king of Babylon had
made governor over the land.

[j] Syr: Heb lacks *and threw them*; compare verse 9 [k] Gk: Heb *whom he had killed by the hand of Gedaliah* [l] Cn: Heb *whom he recovered from Ishmael son of Nethaniah* [m] Meaning of Heb uncertain

41.4–9 The 80 men came from three cities of the northern kingdom to worship in Jerusalem. Ishmael probably killed them for the money and food they were carrying. Without a king, with no law and no loyalty to God, Judah was subjected to complete anarchy.

41.12 The great pool that is in Gibeon is mentioned in 2 Samuel 2.13. This was the location of the beginning of the battle of Gibeon, where Joab and Abner each sent 12 men to fight each other. The great pool was a cistern that was dug down 35 feet into the rock. Steps led down a tunnel another 40 feet to a water chamber.

41.16, 17 Johanan and his group were already on their way to Egypt, headed south from Gibeon, stopping first at Chimham, near Bethlehem. Their visit to Jeremiah (42.1–6) was deceptive, as Jeremiah later told them (42.20).

God warns against going to Egypt

42 Then all the commanders of the forces, and Johanan son of Kareah and Azariah[n] son of Hoshaiah, and all the people from the least to the greatest,
approached 2 the prophet Jeremiah and said, "Be good enough to listen to our plea,
and pray to the LORD your God for us—for all this remnant. For there are only a
few of us left out of many, as your eyes can see. 3 Let the LORD your God show us
where we should go and what we should do." 4 The prophet Jeremiah said to them,
"Very well: I am going to pray to the LORD your God as you request, and whatever
the LORD answers you I will tell you; I will keep nothing back from you." 5 They in
their turn said to Jeremiah, "May the LORD be a true and faithful witness against us
if we do not act according to everything that the LORD your God sends us through
you. 6 Whether it is good or bad, we will obey the voice of the LORD our God to
whom we are sending you, in order that it may go well with us when we obey the
voice of the LORD our God."
7 At the end of ten days the word of the LORD came to Jeremiah. 8 Then he
summoned Johanan son of Kareah and all the commanders of the forces who were
with him, and all the people from the least to the greatest, 9 and said to them, "Thus
says the LORD, the God of Israel, to whom you sent me to present your plea before
him: 10 If you will only remain in this land, then I will build you up and not pull you
down; I will plant you, and not pluck you up; for I am sorry for the disaster that I
have brought upon you. 11 Do not be afraid of the king of Babylon, as you have
been; do not be afraid of him, says the LORD, for I am with you, to save you and to
rescue you from his hand. 12 I will grant you mercy, and he will have mercy on you
and restore you to your native soil. 13 But if you continue to say, 'We will not stay
in this land,' thus disobeying the voice of the LORD your God 14 and saying, 'No,
we will go to the land of Egypt, where we shall not see war, or hear the sound of
the trumpet, or be hungry for bread, and there we will stay,' 15 then hear the word
of the LORD, O remnant of Judah. Thus says the LORD of hosts, the God of Israel:
If you are determined to enter Egypt and go to settle there, 16 then the sword that
you fear shall overtake you there, in the land of Egypt; and the famine that you
dread shall follow close after you into Egypt; and there you shall die. 17 All the
people who have determined to go to Egypt to settle there shall die by the sword,
by famine, and by pestilence; they shall have no remnant or survivor from the disaster that I am bringing upon them.
18 "For thus says the LORD of hosts, the God of Israel: Just as my anger and my
wrath were poured out on the inhabitants of Jerusalem, so my wrath will be poured
out on you when you go to Egypt. You shall become an object of execration and
horror, of cursing and ridicule. You shall see this place no more. 19 The LORD has
said to you, O remnant of Judah, Do not go to Egypt. Be well aware that I have
warned you today 20 that you have made a fatal mistake. For you yourselves sent me
to the LORD your God, saying, 'Pray for us to the LORD our God, and whatever the
LORD our God says, tell us and we will do it.' 21 So I have told you today, but you
have not obeyed the voice of the LORD your God in anything that he sent me to tell
you. 22 Be well aware, then, that you shall die by the sword, by famine, and by
pestilence in the place where you desire to go and settle."

The people refuse to believe

43 When Jeremiah finished speaking to all the people all these words of the
LORD their God, with which the LORD their God had sent him to them, 2 Azariah son of Hoshaiah and Johanan son of Kareah and all the other insolent men said

42.1 Jer 40.8,12,13
42.2 Deut 28.62 Isa 1.9
42.4 Ps 40.10 Jer 23.28
42.5 Jer 43.2 Mic 1.2
42.6 Ex 24.7 Deut 5.29 Jer 7.23
42.7 Ps 27.14
42.10 Jer 31.28 Hos 11.8 Joel 2.13
42.11 Ps 46.7,11 Isa 43.5 Jer 41.18 Rom 8.31
42.12 Ps 106.45,46 Prov 16.7
42.13 Isa 31.1 Jer 41.16,17
42.15 Jer 44.12
42.16 Jer 44.13,27
42.17 Jer 44.13,14,28
42.18 2 Chron 36.16-19 Jer 29.18,19 39.1-9
42.19 Deut 17.16 Ezek 2.5
42.20 Ezek 14.3
42.21 Deut 11.26 Ezek 2.7
42.22 Jer 43.11
43.2 Jer 5.12,13 36.4,10,32 38.4; 42.5

[n] Gk: Heb *Jezaniah*

42.5, 6 Johanan and his associates spoke their own curse; Jeremiah merely elaborated on it. It was a tragic mistake to ask for God's guidance with no intention of following it. Be sure never to ask God for something if you know in your heart that you do not want it. It is better not to pray than to pray deceptively. God cannot be deceived.

43.1–3 Johanan and his tiny band had come to Jeremiah for God's approval of their plan, not for his direction. This is a recurring problem for most of us—seeking God's approval of our desires rather than asking him for guidance. It's not good to make plans unless we are willing to have God change them, and it is not good to pray unless we are willing to accept God's answer.

to Jeremiah, “You are telling a lie. The LORD our God did not send you to say, ‘Do
not go to Egypt to settle there’; 3 but Baruch son of Neriah is inciting you against us,
to hand us over to the Chaldeans, in order that they may kill us or take us into exile
in Babylon.” 4 So Johanan son of Kareah and all the commanders of the forces and
all the people did not obey the voice of the LORD, to stay in the land of Judah. 5 But
Johanan son of Kareah and all the commanders of the forces took all the remnant of
Judah who had returned to settle in the land of Judah from all the nations to which
they had been driven— 6 the men, the women, the children, the princesses, and
everyone whom Nebuzaradan the captain of the guard had left with Gedaliah son of
Ahikam son of Shaphan; also the prophet Jeremiah and Baruch son of Neriah.
7 And they came into the land of Egypt, for they did not obey the voice of the LORD.
And they arrived at Tahpanhes.

8 Then the word of the LORD came to Jeremiah in Tahpanhes: 9 Take some large
stones in your hands, and bury them in the clay pavement[o] that is at the entrance
to Pharaoh’s palace in Tahpanhes. Let the Judeans see you do it, 10 and say to them,
Thus says the LORD of hosts, the God of Israel: I am going to send and take my
servant King Nebuchadrezzar of Babylon, and he[p] will set his throne above these
stones that I have buried, and he will spread his royal canopy over them. 11 He shall
come and ravage the land of Egypt, giving

> those who are destined for pestilence, to pestilence,
> and those who are destined for captivity, to captivity,
> and those who are destined for the sword, to the sword.

12 He[q] shall kindle a fire in the temples of the gods of Egypt; and he shall burn them
and carry them away captive; and he shall pick clean the land of Egypt, as a shepherd picks his cloak clean of vermin; and he shall depart from there safely. 13 He
shall break the obelisks of Heliopolis, which is in the land of Egypt; and the temples
of the gods of Egypt he shall burn with fire.

God’s judgment because of idolatry

44 The word that came to Jeremiah for all the Judeans living in the land of
Egypt, at Migdol, at Tahpanhes, at Memphis, and in the land of Pathros,
2 Thus says the LORD of hosts, the God of Israel: You yourselves have seen all the
disaster that I have brought on Jerusalem and on all the towns of Judah. Look at
them; today they are a desolation, without an inhabitant in them, 3 because of the
wickedness that they committed, provoking me to anger, in that they went to make
offerings and serve other gods that they had not known, neither they, nor you, nor

43.4 Jer 42.5,6, 10-12
43.5 Jer 40.11,12
43.6 Jer 40.7
43.8 Ps 139.7; Jer 44.1; 46.14; Ezek 30.18; 2 Tim 2.9
43.10 Ps 18.11; Jer 25.8,9,11; 27.6; 46.13
43.11 Isa 19.1-25; 44.13
43.12 Jer 46.25; Ezek 29.19; 30.13
44.2 Isa 6.11; Jer 6.11; Mic 3.12
44.3 Deut 32.17; Jer 32.30-32

[o] Meaning of Heb uncertain [p] Gk Syr: Heb *I* [q] Gk Syr Vg: Heb *I*

ESCAPE TO EGYPT
With Judah in turmoil after the murder of Gedaliah, the people turned to Jeremiah for guidance. Jeremiah had God’s answer, “Stay in the land.” But the leaders disobeyed and went to Egypt, taking Jeremiah with them. In Egypt, Jeremiah told them they were not safe.

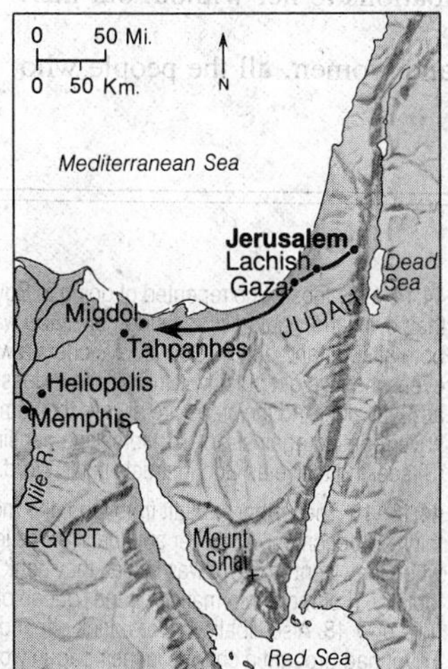

43.6 Afraid to obey, the people headed for Egypt, even forcing Jeremiah to go with them. (They thought that perhaps God would spare them if Jeremiah was with them.) Jeremiah had served as a prophet for 40 years. Many of his words had already come true, and he had turned down an offer to live comfortably in Babylon, returning instead to his beloved people. But the people still rejected Jeremiah’s advice. The response of our audience is not necessarily a measure of our success. Jeremiah was doing all God asked, but he had been called to minister to a very stubborn group of people.

43.11 Nebuchadnezzar invaded Egypt in 568–567 B.C. Like Judah, Egypt rebelled against him and was quickly crushed. So much for the great empire on which Judah had constantly placed its hopes!

44.1ff This message, given in 580 B.C. while Jeremiah was in Egypt against his will, reminded the people that their following other gods had brought destruction on their land. Jeremiah told them they would never return to Judah because the escape to Egypt had been against God’s advice (42.9ff). But the people refused to learn any lessons from all the destruction their sins had caused.

your ancestors. 4 Yet I persistently sent to you all my servants the prophets, saying,
"I beg you not to do this abominable thing that I hate!" 5 But they did not listen or
incline their ear, to turn from their wickedness and make no offerings to other gods.
6 So my wrath and my anger were poured out and kindled in the towns of Judah and
in the streets of Jerusalem; and they became a waste and a desolation, as they still
are today. 7 And now thus says the LORD God of hosts, the God of Israel: Why are
you doing such great harm to yourselves, to cut off man and woman, child and
infant, from the midst of Judah, leaving yourselves without a remnant? 8 Why do
you provoke me to anger with the works of your hands, making offerings to other
gods in the land of Egypt where you have come to settle? Will you be cut off and
become an object of cursing and ridicule among all the nations of the earth? 9 Have
you forgotten the crimes of your ancestors, of the kings of Judah, of their[r] wives,
your own crimes and those of your wives, which they committed in the land of
Judah and in the streets of Jerusalem? 10 They have shown no contrition or fear to
this day, nor have they walked in my law and my statutes that I set before you and
before your ancestors.
11 Therefore thus says the LORD of hosts, the God of Israel: I am determined to
bring disaster on you, to bring all Judah to an end. 12 I will take the remnant of
Judah who are determined to come to the land of Egypt to settle, and they shall
perish, everyone; in the land of Egypt they shall fall; by the sword and by famine
they shall perish; from the least to the greatest, they shall die by the sword and by
famine; and they shall become an object of execration and horror, of cursing and
ridicule. 13 I will punish those who live in the land of Egypt, as I have punished
Jerusalem, with the sword, with famine, and with pestilence, 14 so that none of the
remnant of Judah who have come to settle in the land of Egypt shall escape or
survive or return to the land of Judah. Although they long to go back to live there,
they shall not go back, except some fugitives.
15 Then all the men who were aware that their wives had been making offerings
to other gods, and all the women who stood by, a great assembly, all the people
who lived in Pathros in the land of Egypt, answered Jeremiah: 16 "As for the word
that you have spoken to us in the name of the LORD, we are not going to listen to
you. 17 Instead, we will do everything that we have vowed, make offerings to the
queen of heaven and pour out libations to her, just as we and our ancestors, our
kings and our officials, used to do in the towns of Judah and in the streets of Jerusalem. We used to have plenty of food, and prospered, and saw no misfortune. 18 But
from the time we stopped making offerings to the queen of heaven and pouring out
libations to her, we have lacked everything and have perished by the sword and by
famine." 19 And the women said,[s] "Indeed we will go on making offerings to the
queen of heaven and pouring out libations to her; do you think that we made cakes
for her, marked with her image, and poured out libations to her without our husbands' being involved?"
20 Then Jeremiah said to all the people, men and women, all the people who

44.4 Jer 32.34,35; 35.15; Ezek 8.10; Zech 7.7
44.6 Isa 51.17-20; Jer 7.17,34
44.7 Jer 9.21; Ezek 33.11
44.8 1 Kgs 9.7,8; 2 Kgs 17.15-17; 2 Chron 7.19,20; Jer 11.12,17; 1 Cor 10.21,22
44.9 Jer 7.9,10, 17,18
44.10 Jer 6.15; 8.12
44.11 Lev 26.17; Jer 21.10
44.12 Isa 65.15; Jer 42.15-18,22
44.13 Jer 24.10
44.14 Isa 10.20; Rom 9.27
44.15 Jer 5.1-5
44.16 Jer 8.6; 13.10
44.17 Ex 16.3; 2 Kgs 17.16; Jer 7.18; Phil 3.19
44.18 Num 11.5,6; Mal 3.13-15
44.19 Num 30.6,7

[r] Heb *his* [s] Compare Syr: Heb lacks *And the women said*

44.7 "Why are you doing such great harm to yourselves?" These people took an oath of obedience (42.5, 6) and yet still refused to listen to God's clear directions. They feared the Babylonians, who would have been kind to them, and destroyed themselves. Self-destruction, whether through foolish decisions, dangerous habits, or blatant disobedience to God, is worse than destruction by an enemy. There is no honor whatsoever in self-destruction.

44.9, 10 When we forget a lesson or refuse to learn it, we risk repeating our mistakes. The people of Judah struggled with this; to forget their former sins was to repeat them. To fail to learn from failure is to assure future failure. Your past is your school of experience. Let your past mistakes point you to God's way.

44.14 Only those who repented of going to Egypt and returned to their own land would escape judgment. God wanted a change of both attitude and action. God always offers a way of escape—even when we get ourselves in so deep it doesn't look as if there is any way out. And the steps are always the same: (1) admitting we have rebelled against God, (2) forsaking our sinful direction, and (3) seeking to live as God instructs in his Word.

44.16–18 The farther we drift from God, the more confused our thinking becomes. Whatever spiritual life was left in the Israelites when they went to Egypt was lost as they sank into the depths of idolatry. (For more information on the "queen of heaven," see the note on 7.18. Also, libations were drink offerings.) The escape to Egypt had brought a change in their pagan worship habits, and

were giving him this answer: 21 "As for the offerings that you made in the towns of
Judah and in the streets of Jerusalem, you and your ancestors, your kings and your
officials, and the people of the land, did not the LORD remember them? Did it not
come into his mind? 22 The LORD could no longer bear the sight of your evil doings,
the abominations that you committed; therefore your land became a desolation and
a waste and a curse, without inhabitant, as it is to this day. 23 It is because you
burned offerings, and because you sinned against the LORD and did not obey the
voice of the LORD or walk in his law and in his statutes and in his decrees, that this
disaster has befallen you, as is still evident today."
24 Jeremiah said to all the people and all the women, "Hear the word of the
LORD, all you Judeans who are in the land of Egypt, 25 Thus says the LORD of hosts,
the God of Israel: You and your wives have accomplished in deeds what you declared in words, saying, 'We are determined to perform the vows that we have
made, to make offerings to the queen of heaven and to pour out libations to her.' By
all means, keep your vows and make your libations! 26 Therefore hear the word of
the LORD, all you Judeans who live in the land of Egypt: Lo, I swear by my great
name, says the LORD, that my name shall no longer be pronounced on the lips of
any of the people of Judah in all the land of Egypt, saying, 'As the Lord GOD lives.'
27 I am going to watch over them for harm and not for good; all the people of Judah
who are in the land of Egypt shall perish by the sword and by famine, until not one
is left. 28 And those who escape the sword shall return from the land of Egypt to the
land of Judah, few in number; and all the remnant of Judah, who have come to the
land of Egypt to settle, shall know whose words will stand, mine or theirs! 29 This
shall be the sign to you, says the LORD, that I am going to punish you in this place,
in order that you may know that my words against you will surely be carried out:
30 Thus says the LORD, I am going to give Pharaoh Hophra, king of Egypt, into the
hands of his enemies, those who seek his life, just as I gave King Zedekiah of Judah
into the hand of King Nebuchadrezzar of Babylon, his enemy who sought his life."

A message to Baruch

45 The word that the prophet Jeremiah spoke to Baruch son of Neriah, when he
wrote these words in a scroll at the dictation of Jeremiah, in the fourth year
of King Jehoiakim son of Josiah of Judah: 2 Thus says the LORD, the God of Israel,
to you, O Baruch: 3 You said, "Woe is me! The LORD has added sorrow to my pain;
I am weary with my groaning, and I find no rest." 4 Thus you shall say to him,
"Thus says the LORD: I am going to break down what I have built, and pluck up
what I have planted—that is, the whole land. 5 And you, do you seek great things
for yourself? Do not seek them; for I am going to bring disaster upon all flesh, says
the LORD; but I will give you your life as a prize of war in every place to which you
may go."

44.21 Jer 11.13; 14.10 Ezek 8.10,11 16.24 Hos 7.2
44.22 Isa 7.13 Jer 4.4 25.11,18,38 30.14
44.23 1 Kgs 9.9 Jer 7.13-15 40.3 Dan 9.11,12
44.24 Jer 43.7
44.25 Ezek 20.39 Jas 1.14,15
44.26 Deut 32.40 Ps 50.16,17 Heb 6.13,18
44.27 Jer 1.10
44.28 Isa 14.27 46.9,10 Zech 1.5,6
44.29 Isa 40.8 Mt 24.15,16,32
44.30 2 Kgs 25.4-7 Jer 46.25
45.1 Jer 25.1 36.4,18,32
45.3 Ps 6.6 2 Cor 4.1,16 Gal 6.9
45.5 Isa 66.16 Mt 6.25; 31,32 Rom 12.16

---

they blamed their troubles on their neglect of their idols. But idol worship had started all their problems in the first place. They refused to recognize the true source of their problems—departure from God's leading. When calamity forces you to examine your life, take a close look at God's instructions for you.

44.28 After Jeremiah's forced move to Egypt, there is no word in the Bible about the rest of his life.

44.30 Pharaoh Hophra ruled Egypt from 588 to 568 B.C. and was killed by Ahmose, one of his generals, who was then crowned in his place.

45.1ff The event relating to this chapter is recorded in 36.1–8. The chapter was written in 605–604 B.C. Baruch was the scribe who recorded Jeremiah's words on a scroll.

45.5 Baruch had long been serving this unpopular prophet, writing his book of struggles and judgments, and now he was upset. God told Baruch to take his eyes off himself and whatever rewards he thought he deserved. If he did this, God would protect him. It is easy to lose the joy of serving our God when we take our eyes off him. The more we look away from God's purposes toward our own sacrifices, the more frustrated we become. As you serve God, beware of focusing on what you are giving up. When this happens, ask God's forgiveness; then look at him rather than at yourself.

B. GOD'S JUDGMENT ON THE NATIONS (46.1—52.34)

All of Jeremiah's prophecies against foreign nations have been grouped together. Many of the people in these nations assumed that they were free from judgment and punishment for their sin. Following these prophecies is an historical appendix recounting the fall of Jerusalem. Just as Jerusalem received its punishment, these nations were certain to receive theirs as well. Those today who think that judgment will never touch them are forewarned.

1. Prophecies about foreign nations

Judgment on the Egyptians

46 The word of the LORD that came to the prophet Jeremiah concerning the nations. **46.1** Jer 1.10 Ezek 29-32

2 Concerning Egypt, about the army of Pharaoh Neco, king of Egypt, which **46.2** 2 Kgs 23.29 2 Chron 35.20
was by the river Euphrates at Carchemish and which King Nebuchadrezzar of Bab-
ylon defeated in the fourth year of King Jehoiakim son of Josiah of Judah:

3 Prepare buckler and shield, **46.3** Joel 3.9
and advance for battle!
4 Harness the horses; **46.4** Ezek 21.9-11
mount the steeds!
Take your stations with your helmets,
whet your lances,
put on your coats of mail!
5 Why do I see them terrified? **46.5** Isa 42.17 Jer 6.25; 49.29 Ezek 39.18
They have fallen back;
their warriors are beaten down,
and have fled in haste.
They do not look back—
terror is all around!
says the LORD.

6 The swift cannot flee away, **46.6** Isa 30.16 Dan 11.18
nor can the warrior escape;
in the north by the river Euphrates
they have stumbled and fallen.

7 Who is this, rising like the Nile,
like rivers whose waters surge?
8 Egypt rises like the Nile, **46.8** Isa 10.13
like rivers whose waters surge.
It said, Let me rise, let me cover the earth,
let me destroy cities and their inhabitants.
9 Advance, O horses, **46.9** Nah 3.9
and dash madly, O chariots!
Let the warriors go forth:
Ethiopia[t] and Put who carry the shield,
the Ludim, who draw[u] the bow.
10 That day is the day of the Lord GOD of hosts, **46.10** Isa 31.8; 34.6 Zeph 1.7
a day of retribution,
to gain vindication from his foes.
The sword shall devour and be sated,

[t] Or *Nubia*; Heb *Cush* [u] Cn: Heb *who grasp, who draw*

46.1ff In this chapter, we gain several insights about God and his plan for this world. (1) Although God chose Israel for a special purpose, he loves all people and wants all to come to him. (2) God is holy and will not tolerate sin. (3) God's judgments are not based on prejudice and a desire for revenge, but on fairness and justice. (4) God does not delight in judgment, but in salvation. (5) God is impartial—he judges everyone by the same standard.

46.2 At the battle of Carchemish in 605 B.C., Babylon and Egypt, the two major world powers after Assyria's fall, clashed. The Babylonians entered Carchemish by surprise and defeated Egypt. This battle, which passed world leadership to Babylon, was Nebuchadnezzar's (here he is called Nebuchadrezzar) first victory, establishing him in his new position as king of the Babylonian Empire. With Egypt's power declining, it was both poor strategy and disobedience to God for Judah to form an alliance with Egypt.

46.3 A buckler was a small, round shield used in battle.

46.9 The soldiers from Ethiopia and Put were from eastern and northern Africa. The Ludim were from Greece.

and drink its fill of their blood.
For the Lord GOD of hosts holds a sacrifice
in the land of the north by the river Euphrates.

46.11 Jer 8.22; 30.13 Ezek 30.21-26 Nah 3.19

11 Go up to Gilead, and take balm,
O virgin daughter Egypt!
In vain you have used many medicines;
there is no healing for you.

46.12 Jer 2.36 Nah 3.8-10

12 The nations have heard of your shame,
and the earth is full of your cry;
for warrior has stumbled against warrior;
both have fallen together.

13 The word that the LORD spoke to the prophet Jeremiah about the coming of
King Nebuchadrezzar of Babylon to attack the land of Egypt:

46.14 Jer 44.1 Nah 2.13

14 Declare in Egypt, and proclaim in Migdol;
proclaim in Memphis and Tahpanhes;
Say, "Take your stations and be ready,
for the sword shall devour those around you."

46.15 Ps 18.39 68.1,2

15 Why has Apis fled?[v]
Why did your bull not stand?
—because the LORD thrust him down.

46.16 Jer 51.9

16 Your multitude stumbled[w] and fell,
and one said to another,[x]
"Come, let us go back to our own people
and to the land of our birth,
because of the destroying sword."

46.17 Ex 15.9,10 1 Kgs 20.10,11 Isa 19.11-16

17 Give Pharaoh, king of Egypt, the name
"Braggart who missed his chance."

46.18 1 Kgs 18.42 Ps 89.12 Jer 48.15

18 As I live, says the King,
whose name is the LORD of hosts,
one is coming
like Tabor among the mountains,
and like Carmel by the sea.

46.19 Isa 20.4 Ezek 30.13

19 Pack your bags for exile,
sheltered daughter Egypt!
For Memphis shall become a waste,
a ruin, without inhabitant.

46.20 Isa 34.7 Jer 48.44 Obad 13

20 A beautiful heifer is Egypt—
a gadfly from the north lights upon her.
21 Even her mercenaries in her midst
are like fatted calves;
they too have turned and fled together,
they did not stand;
for the day of their calamity has come upon them,
the time of their punishment.

46.22 Isa 10.34

22 She makes a sound like a snake gliding away;
for her enemies march in force,
and come against her with axes,
like those who fell trees.

[v] Gk: Heb *Why was it swept away* [w] Gk: Meaning of Heb uncertain [x] Gk: Heb *and fell one to another and they said*

46.17 In 589 B.C. when Nebuchadnezzar besieged Jerusalem, Pharaoh-hophra marched against him at Zedekiah's invitation. But when the Babylonians stood up to the Egyptians, Pharaoh Hophra and his troops retreated. Jeremiah had prophesied that Pharaoh Hophra would be killed by his enemies (44.30). This was fulfilled nearly 20 years later when his co-regent Ahmose led a revolt.

23 They shall cut down her forest,
says the LORD,
though it is impenetrable,
because they are more numerous
than locusts;
they are without number.
24 Daughter Egypt shall be put to shame;
she shall be handed over to a people from the north.

25 The LORD of hosts, the God of Israel, said: See, I am bringing punishment
upon Amon of Thebes, and Pharaoh, and Egypt and her gods and her kings, upon
Pharaoh and those who trust in him. 26 I will hand them over to those who seek their
life, to King Nebuchadrezzar of Babylon and his officers. Afterward Egypt shall be
inhabited as in the days of old, says the LORD.

46.25 Isa 20.5,6 Jer 43.12,13 Ezek 30.13-16
46.26 Jer 44.30 Ezek 29.8-14 32.11

27 But as for you, have no fear, my servant Jacob,
and do not be dismayed, O Israel;
for I am going to save you from far away,
and your offspring from the land of their captivity.
Jacob shall return and have quiet and ease,
and no one shall make him afraid.
28 As for you, have no fear, my servant Jacob,
says the LORD,
for I am with you.
I will make an end of all the nations
among which I have banished you,
but I will not make an end of you!
I will chastise you in just measure,
and I will by no means leave you unpunished.

46.27 Isa 41.13,14 Jer 23.3,4
46.28 Ps 46.7 Isa 43.2 Jer 10.24 Amos 9.8,9

Judgment on the Philistines

47 The word of the LORD that came to the prophet Jeremiah concerning the
Philistines, before Pharaoh attacked Gaza:
2 Thus says the LORD:
See, waters are rising out of the north
and shall become an overflowing torrent;
they shall overflow the land and all that fills it,
the city and those who live in it.
People shall cry out,
and all the inhabitants of the land shall wail.
3 At the noise of the stamping of the hoofs of his stallions,
at the clatter of his chariots, at the rumbling of their wheels,
parents do not turn back for children,
so feeble are their hands,
4 because of the day that is coming
to destroy all the Philistines,
to cut off from Tyre and Sidon
every helper that remains.
For the LORD is destroying the Philistines,
the remnant of the coastland of Caphtor.
5 Baldness has come upon Gaza,

47.1 Jer 25.17,20
47.2 Isa 14.31
47.3 Jer 8.16
47.4 Isa 14.31
47.5 Jer 25.19,20 Amos 1.7,8 Zeph 2.4,7; 9.5

46.28 God punished his people in order to bring them back to himself, and he punishes us to correct and purify us. No one welcomes punishment, but we should all welcome its results: correction and purity.

47.1 Located on the coastal plain next to Judah, Philistia had always been a thorn in Israel's side. The two nations battled constantly. Other prophets who spoke against Philistia include Isaiah (14.28–32), Ezekiel (25.15–17), Amos (1.6–8), and Zephaniah (2.4–7).

Ashkelon is silenced.
O remnant of their power![y]
How long will you gash yourselves?
47.6 Jer 12.12
6 Ah, sword of the LORD!
How long until you are quiet?
Put yourself into your scabbard,
rest and be still!
47.7 Mic 6.9
7 How can it[z] be quiet,
when the LORD has given it an order?
Against Ashkelon and against the seashore—
there he has appointed it.

Judgment on the Moabites

48.1 Num 32.37,38 Ezek 25.9,10
48 Concerning Moab.

Thus says the LORD of hosts, the God of Israel:
Alas for Nebo, it is laid waste!
Kiriathaim is put to shame, it is taken;
the fortress is put to shame and broken down;
48.2 Isa 15.4,5 16.13,14
2 the renown of Moab is no more.
In Heshbon they planned evil against her:
"Come, let us cut her off from being a nation!"
You also, O Madmen, shall be brought to silence;[a]
the sword shall pursue you.

3 Hark! a cry from Horonaim,
"Desolation and great destruction!"
4 "Moab is destroyed!"
her little ones cry out.
48.5 Isa 15.5
5 For at the ascent of Luhith
they go[b] up weeping bitterly;
for at the descent of Horonaim
they have heard the distressing cry of anguish.
6 Flee! Save yourselves!
Be like a wild ass[c] in the desert!

48.7 Num 21.29 Jer 9.23
7 Surely, because you trusted in your strongholds[d] and your treasures,
you also shall be taken;
Chemosh shall go out into exile,
with his priests and his attendants.
48.8 Josh 13.10, 17,21
8 The destroyer shall come upon every town,
and no town shall escape;
the valley shall perish,
and the plain shall be destroyed,
as the LORD has spoken.

48.9 Isa 16.2
9 Set aside salt for Moab,
for she will surely fall;
her towns shall become a desolation,

[y] Gk: Heb *their valley* [z] Gk Vg: Heb *you* [a] The place-name *Madmen* sounds like the Hebrew verb *to be silent*
[b] Cn: Heb *he goes* [c] Gk Aquila: Heb *like Aroer* [d] Gk: Heb *works*

48.1 The Moabites were descendants of Lot through an incestuous relationship with one of his daughters (Genesis 19.30–37). They led the Israelites into idolatry (Numbers 25.1–3) and joined the bands of raiders Nebuchadnezzar sent into Judah in 602 B.C. They were later conquered by Babylon and disappeared as a nation.

48.7 Chemosh was the main god of the nation of Moab (Numbers 21.29), and child sacrifice was an important part of his worship (2 Kings 3.26, 27).

48.9 Putting salt on a city was a symbolic act to show that it was totally destroyed (see Judges 9.45).

with no inhabitant in them.

10 Accursed is the one who is slack in doing the work of the LORD; and accursed is the one who keeps back the sword from bloodshed.

11 Moab has been at ease from his youth,
settled like wine[e] on its dregs;
he has not been emptied from vessel to vessel,
nor has he gone into exile;
therefore his flavor has remained
and his aroma is unspoiled.
12 Therefore, the time is surely coming, says the LORD, when I shall send to
him decanters to decant him, and empty his vessels, and break his[f] jars in pieces.
13 Then Moab shall be ashamed of Chemosh, as the house of Israel was ashamed of
Bethel, their confidence.

14 How can you say, "We are heroes
and mighty warriors"?
15 The destroyer of Moab and his towns has come up,
and the choicest of his young men have gone down to slaughter,
says the King, whose name is the LORD of hosts.
16 The calamity of Moab is near at hand
and his doom approaches swiftly.
17 Mourn over him, all you his neighbors,
and all who know his name;
say, "How the mighty scepter is broken,
the glorious staff!"

18 Come down from glory,
and sit on the parched ground,
enthroned daughter Dibon!
For the destroyer of Moab has come up against you;
he has destroyed your strongholds.
19 Stand by the road and watch,
you inhabitant of Aroer!
Ask the man fleeing and the woman escaping;
say, "What has happened?"
20 Moab is put to shame, for it is broken down;
wail and cry!
Tell it by the Arnon,
that Moab is laid waste.

21 Judgment has come upon the tableland, upon Holon, and Jahzah, and Mephaath, 22 and Dibon, and Nebo, and Beth-diblathaim, 23 and Kiriathaim, and Beth-
gamul, and Beth-meon, 24 and Kerioth, and Bozrah, and all the towns of the land of
Moab, far and near. 25 The horn of Moab is cut off, and his arm is broken, says the
LORD.
26 Make him drunk, because he magnified himself against the LORD; let Moab
wallow in his vomit; he too shall become a laughingstock. 27 Israel was a laughingstock for you, though he was not caught among thieves; but whenever you spoke of
him you shook your head!

[e] Heb lacks *like wine* [f] Gk Aquila: Heb *their*

48.10 1 Kgs 20.42 Jer 47.6,7
48.11 Zech 1.15
48.13 1 Kgs 12.29 Isa 45.16 Hos 10.6
48.14 Ps 33.16,17 Isa 10.13-16
48.18 Josh 13.9,17 Isa 47.1
48.19 Josh 12.2
48.20 Num 21.13 Isa 16.7
48.21 Josh 13.18 Isa 15.4
48.23 Josh 13.19
48.24 Amos 2.2
48.25 Ps 10.15; 75.10 Zech 1.19-21
48.26 Jer 25.15,27
48.27 Lam 2.15-17 Zeph 2.8

48.12 To "decant" means to pour from one vessel to another. When making wine, the grapes are crushed, and after 40 days the wine is poured off (decanted) from the dregs in the bottom of the jar. If this is not done, the wine will spoil. The prophet is saying that the people have become too complacent.

48.13 After Israel divided into northern and southern kingdoms, the northern kingdom set up golden calf-idols in Bethel and Dan to keep people from going to worship in Jerusalem, capital of the southern kingdom (1 Kings 12.25–29).

48.28 Ps 55.6 Song 2.14 Isa 2.19 28 Leave the towns, and live on the rock,
O inhabitants of Moab!
Be like the dove that nests
on the sides of the mouth of a gorge.
48.29 Ps 138.6 Isa 16.6 Zeph 2.8 29 We have heard of the pride of Moab—
he is very proud—
of his loftiness, his pride, and his arrogance,
and the haughtiness of his heart.
30 I myself know his insolence, says the LORD;
his boasts are false,
his deeds are false.
48.31 Isa 15.5 16.7,11 31 Therefore I wail for Moab;
I cry out for all Moab;
for the people of Kir-heres I mourn.
48.32 Isa 16.8,9 32 More than for Jazer I weep for you,
O vine of Sibmah!
Your branches crossed over the sea,
reached as far as Jazer;[g]
upon your summer fruits and your vintage
the destroyer has fallen.
48.33 Isa 16.10 33 Gladness and joy have been taken away
from the fruitful land of Moab;
I have stopped the wine from the wine presses;
no one treads them with shouts of joy;
the shouting is not the shout of joy.

48.34 Gen 13.10 Isa 15.4-6 34 Heshbon and Elealeh cry out;[h] as far as Jahaz they utter their voice, from
Zoar to Horonaim and Eglath-shelishiyah. For even the waters of Nimrim have
become desolate. 35 And I will bring to an end in Moab, says the LORD, those who
48.36 Isa 16.11 offer sacrifice at a high place and make offerings to their gods. 36 Therefore my
heart moans for Moab like a flute, and my heart moans like a flute for the people of
Kir-heres; for the riches they gained have perished.
48.37 Isa 15.2,3 37 For every head is shaved and every beard cut off; on all the hands there are
48.38 Jer 25.34 gashes, and on the loins sackcloth. 38 On all the housetops of Moab and in the
squares there is nothing but lamentation; for I have broken Moab like a vessel that
no one wants, says the LORD. 39 How it is broken! How they wail! How Moab has
turned his back in shame! So Moab has become a derision and a horror to all his
neighbors.

48.40 Jer 49.22 40 For thus says the LORD:
Look, he shall swoop down like an eagle,
and spread his wings against Moab;
48.41 Jer 30.6; 49.22 41 the towns[i] shall be taken
and the strongholds seized.
The hearts of the warriors of Moab, on that day,
shall be like the heart of a woman in labor.
48.42 Ps 83.4 Jer 48.26 42 Moab shall be destroyed as a people,
because he magnified himself against the LORD.
48.43 Isa 24.17 Lam 3.47 43 Terror, pit, and trap
are before you, O inhabitants of Moab!
says the LORD.

[g] Two Mss and Isa 16.8: MT *the sea of Jazer* [h] Cn: Heb *From the cry of Heshbon to Elealeh* [i] Or *Kerioth*

48.29 Moab was condemned for its pride. God cannot tolerate pride, for it is a created person elevating himself above the Creator. Pride is taking personal credit for what God has done or looking down on others. God does not condemn our taking satisfaction in what we do (Ecclesiastes 3.22), but he stands against false pride, the overestimate of our own importance. Romans 12.3 teaches us to have an honest estimate of ourselves.

48.31 Kir-heres was a stronghold city in Moab. God's compassion reaches to all creation, even to his enemies.

44 Everyone who flees from the terror
shall fall into the pit,
and everyone who climbs out of the pit
shall be caught in the trap.
For I will bring these things[j] upon Moab
in the year of their punishment,
says the LORD.

48.44 1 Kgs 19.17 Amos 5.19

45 In the shadow of Heshbon
fugitives stop exhausted;
for a fire has gone out from Heshbon,
a flame from the house of Sihon;
it has destroyed the forehead of Moab,
the scalp of the people of tumult.[k]
46 Woe to you, O Moab!
The people of Chemosh have perished,
for your sons have been taken captive,
and your daughters into captivity.
47 Yet I will restore the fortunes of Moab
in the latter days, says the LORD.
Thus far is the judgment on Moab.

48.45 Num 21.27-30 Ps 135.10,11
48.46 Num 21.27-30
48.47 Jer 12.14-17

Judgment on the Ammonites

49 Concerning the Ammonites.

Thus says the LORD:
Has Israel no sons?
Has he no heir?
Why then has Milcom dispossessed Gad,
and his people settled in its towns?
2 Therefore, the time is surely coming,
says the LORD,
when I will sound the battle alarm
against Rabbah of the Ammonites;
it shall become a desolate mound,
and its villages shall be burned with fire;
then Israel shall dispossess those who dispossessed him,
says the LORD.

49.1 1 Kgs 11.5 Ezek 25.2
49.2 2 Sam 11.1 Isa 14.2 Ezek 21.28

3 Wail, O Heshbon, for Ai is laid waste!
Cry out, O daughters[l] of Rabbah!
Put on sackcloth,
lament, and slash yourselves with whips![m]
For Milcom shall go into exile,
with his priests and his attendants.
4 Why do you boast in your strength?
Your strength is ebbing,
O faithless daughter.
You trusted in your treasures, saying,
"Who will attack me?"
5 I am going to bring terror upon you,
says the Lord GOD of hosts,

49.3 Josh 7.2-5 8.1-29 Jer 48.2
49.4 Ps 62.10,11 Ezek 28.4,5 1 Tim 6.17
49.5 Jer 16.16 Lam 4.15

[j] Gk Syr: Heb *bring upon it* [k] Or *of Shaon* [l] Or *villages* [m] Cn: Meaning of Heb uncertain

49.1 The Ammonites were descendants of Lot through an incestuous relationship with one of his daughters (as were the Moabites; see Genesis 19.30–38). They were condemned for stealing land from God's people and for worshiping the idol Milcom (Molech), to whom they made child sacrifices.

from all your neighbors,
and you will be scattered, each headlong,
with no one to gather the fugitives.

49.6 Jer 48.47; 49.39

6 But afterward I will restore the fortunes of the Ammonites, says the LORD.

Judgment on the Edomites

7 Concerning Edom.

Thus says the LORD of hosts:
Is there no longer wisdom in Teman?
Has counsel perished from the prudent?
Has their wisdom vanished?

49.8 Isa 21.13 Jer 25.23

8 Flee, turn back, get down low,
inhabitants of Dedan!
For I will bring the calamity of Esau upon him,
the time when I punish him.

49.9 Isa 17.14 Jer 13.26 Obad 5

9 If grape-gatherers came to you,
would they not leave gleanings?
If thieves came by night,
even they would pillage only what they wanted.
10 But as for me, I have stripped Esau bare,
I have uncovered his hiding places,
and he is not able to conceal himself.
His offspring are destroyed, his kinsfolk
and his neighbors; and he is no more.

49.11 Ps 68.5 Zech 7.10

11 Leave your orphans, I will keep them alive;
and let your widows trust in me.

49.12 Jer 25.15,28,29 1 Pet 4.17

49.13 Isa 34.6,9-15

12 For thus says the LORD: If those who do not deserve to drink the cup still
have to drink it, shall you be the one to go unpunished? You shall not go unpunished; you must drink it. 13 For by myself I have sworn, says the LORD, that Bozrah
shall become an object of horror and ridicule, a waste, and an object of cursing; and
all her towns shall be perpetual wastes.

49.14 Jer 50.14 Obad 1-4

14 I have heard tidings from the LORD,
and a messenger has been sent among the nations:
"Gather yourselves together and come against her,
and rise up for battle!"

49.15 Lk 1.51

15 For I will make you least among the nations,
despised by humankind.

49.16 Isa 14.13-15 Amos 9.2

16 The terror you inspire
and the pride of your heart have deceived you,
you who live in the clefts of the rock,[n]
who hold the height of the hill.
Although you make your nest as high as the eagle's,
from there I will bring you down,
says the LORD.

49.17 Jer 51.37 Ezek 35.7

49.18 Gen 19.24,25

17 Edom shall become an object of horror; everyone who passes by it will be
horrified and will hiss because of all its disasters. 18 As when Sodom and Gomorrah

[n] Or *of Sela*

49.7 Since the Israelites descended from Jacob and the Edomites from his twin brother, Esau, both nations descended from their father, Isaac. There was constant conflict between these nations, and Edom rejoiced at the fall of Jerusalem (see the book of Obadiah). Teman, a town in the northern part of Edom, was known for its wisdom and was the hometown of Eliphaz, one of Job's friends (Job 2.11). But even the wisdom of Teman could not save Edom from God's wrath.

49.8 Dedan was a flourishing city supporting caravan travel. God told its inhabitants to flee to the desert or they would also be destroyed. Teman and Dedan were at opposite ends of the country, so this shows the completeness of God's destruction of Edom. Bozrah (49.13) is a town in northern Edom.

49.16 Edom was destroyed because of her pride. Pride destroys individuals as well as nations. It makes us think we can take care of ourselves without God's help. Even serving God and others can lead us into pride. Take inventory of your life and service for God; ask God to point out and remove any pride you may be harboring.

and their neighbors were overthrown, says the LORD, no one shall live there, nor
shall anyone settle in it. 19 Like a lion coming up from the thickets of the Jordan
against a perennial pasture, I will suddenly chase Edom[o] away from it; and I will
appoint over it whomever I choose.[p] For who is like me? Who can summon me?
Who is the shepherd who can stand before me? 20 Therefore hear the plan that the
LORD has made against Edom and the purposes that he has formed against the inhabitants of Teman: Surely the little ones of the flock shall be dragged away; surely
their fold shall be appalled at their fate. 21 At the sound of their fall the earth shall
tremble; the sound of their cry shall be heard at the Red Sea.[q] 22 Look, he shall
mount up and swoop down like an eagle, and spread his wings against Bozrah, and
the heart of the warriors of Edom in that day shall be like the heart of a woman in
labor.

49.19 Isa 46.9 Jer 50.44
49.20 Isa 14.24,27 Jer 50.45
49.21 Jer 50.46
49.22 Isa 13.8 Jer 48.40,41

Judgment on the Syrians

23 Concerning Damascus.

49.23 Ex 15.15 Isa 10.9; 57.20 Jer 39.5 Amos 6.2

Hamath and Arpad are confounded,
for they have heard bad news;
they melt in fear, they are troubled like the sea[r]
that cannot be quiet.
24 Damascus has become feeble, she turned to flee,
and panic seized her;
anguish and sorrows have taken hold of her,
as of a woman in labor.
25 How the famous city is forsaken,[s]
the joyful town![t]
26 Therefore her young men shall fall in her squares,
and all her soldiers shall be destroyed in that day,
says the LORD of hosts.
27 And I will kindle a fire at the wall of Damascus,
and it shall devour the strongholds of Ben-hadad.

49.25 Jer 51.41
49.27 1 Kgs 15.18-20 Amos 1.3-5

Judgment on Kedar and Hazor

28 Concerning Kedar and the kingdoms of Hazor that King Nebuchadrezzar of
Babylon defeated.

49.28 Isa 21.16,17

Thus says the LORD:
Rise up, advance against Kedar!
Destroy the people of the east!
29 Take their tents and their flocks,
their curtains and all their goods;
carry off their camels for yourselves,
and a cry shall go up: "Terror is all around!"
30 Flee, wander far away, hide in deep places,
O inhabitants of Hazor!
says the LORD.
For King Nebuchadrezzar of Babylon
has made a plan against you
and formed a purpose against you.

49.30 Jer 25.8,9,24 27.6

31 Rise up, advance against a nation at ease,

49.31 Judg 18.7 Isa 47.8

[o] Heb *him* [p] Or *and I will single out the choicest of his rams*: Meaning of Heb uncertain [q] Or *Sea of Reeds*
[r] Cn: Heb *there is trouble in the sea* [s] Vg: Heb *is not forsaken* [t] Syr Vg Tg: Heb *the town of my joy*

49.23–26 Damascus was the capital of Syria, north of Israel. This city was defeated by both Assyria and Babylon. Nebuchadnezzar attacked and defeated Damascus in 605 B.C. (Amos 1.4, 5). It is difficult to attribute the defeat of the army to a particular event, but God utterly destroyed Syria.

49.28 Kedar and Hazor were nomadic tribes east of Israel and south of Syria, in the desert. In 599 B.C. Nebuchadnezzar destroyed them.

that lives secure,

says the LORD,

that has no gates or bars,
that lives alone.

49.32 Jer 9.25,26 25.23

32 Their camels shall become booty,
their herds of cattle a spoil.
I will scatter to every wind
those who have shaven temples,
and I will bring calamity
against them from every side,

says the LORD.

49.33 Isa 13.20-22 Zeph 2.9,13-15

33 Hazor shall become a lair of jackals,
an everlasting waste;
no one shall live there,
nor shall anyone settle in it.

Judgment on the Elamites

49.34 Gen 10.22 2 Kgs 24.17,18 Isa 11.11 Dan 8.2
49.36 Ezek 5.10 Rev 7.1
49.37 Jer 6.19; 30.24

34 The word of the LORD that came to the prophet Jeremiah concerning Elam,
at the beginning of the reign of King Zedekiah of Judah.
35 Thus says the LORD of hosts: I am going to break the bow of Elam, the
mainstay of their might; 36 and I will bring upon Elam the four winds from the four
quarters of heaven; and I will scatter them to all these winds, and there shall be no
nation to which the exiles from Elam shall not come. 37 I will terrify Elam before
their enemies, and before those who seek their life; I will bring disaster upon them,
my fierce anger, says the LORD. I will send the sword after them, until I have consumed them; 38 and I will set my throne in Elam, and destroy their king and officials, says the LORD.
39 But in the latter days I will restore the fortunes of Elam, says the LORD.

Judgment on the Babylonians

50 The word that the LORD spoke concerning Babylon, concerning the land of
the Chaldeans, by the prophet Jeremiah:

50.2 Isa 46.1 Jer 51.31

2 Declare among the nations and proclaim,
set up a banner and proclaim,
do not conceal it, say:
Babylon is taken,
Bel is put to shame,
Merodach is dismayed.
Her images are put to shame,
her idols are dismayed.

50.3 Zeph 1.3
50.4 Isa 11.12,13 Ezra 3.12,13 Hos 1.11 Jer 31.9
50.5 Isa 55.3 Jer 6.16; 32.40

3 For out of the north a nation has come up against her; it shall make her land
a desolation, and no one shall live in it; both human beings and animals shall flee
away.

4 In those days and in that time, says the LORD, the people of Israel shall come,
they and the people of Judah together; they shall come weeping as they seek the
LORD their God. 5 They shall ask the way to Zion, with faces turned toward it, and

---

49.34 Elam lay east of Babylon and was attacked by Nebuchadnezzar in 597 B.C. Later it became the nucleus of the Persian Empire (Daniel 8.2) and the residence of Darius.

49.38 The throne represents God's judgment and sovereignty. He would preside over Elam's destruction. He is the King over all kings, including Elam's.

50.1ff Babylon is another name for the land of the Chaldeans. At the height of its power, this empire seemed immovable. But when Babylon had finished serving God's purpose of punishing Judah for her sins, it would be punished and crushed for its own sins. Babylon was destroyed in 539 B.C. by the Medo-Persians (Daniel 5.30, 31). Babylon is also used in Scripture as a symbol of all evil. This message can thus apply to the end times when God wipes out all evil, once and for all.

50.3 The nation from the north was Medo-Persia, an alliance of Media and Persia that would become the next world power. Cyrus took the city of Babylon by surprise and brought the nation to its knees in 539 B.C. (Daniel 5.30, 31). The complete destruction of the city was accomplished by later Persian kings.

they shall come and join[u] themselves to the LORD by an everlasting covenant that
will never be forgotten.

6 My people have been lost sheep; their shepherds have led them astray, turning **50.6** Isa 53.6
them away on the mountains; from mountain to hill they have gone, they have Jer 13.16
forgotten their fold. 7 All who found them have devoured them, and their enemies Ezek 34.15,16 Mt 9.36
have said, "We are not guilty, because they have sinned against the LORD, the true **50.7**
pasture, the LORD, the hope of their ancestors." Jer 17.13

8 Flee from Babylon, and go out of the land of the Chaldeans, and be like male
goats leading the flock. 9 For I am going to stir up and bring against Babylon a
company of great nations from the land of the north; and they shall array themselves against her; from there she shall be taken. Their arrows are like the arrows
of a skilled warrior who does not return empty-handed. 10 Chaldea shall be plun- **50.10**
dered; all who plunder her shall be sated, says the LORD. Jer 51.24,35

11 Though you rejoice, though you exult,
O plunderers of my heritage,
though you frisk about like a heifer on the grass,
and neigh like stallions,
12 your mother shall be utterly shamed, **50.12** Jer 22.6
and she who bore you shall be disgraced.
Lo, she shall be the last of the nations,
a wilderness, dry land, and a desert.
13 Because of the wrath of the LORD she shall not be inhabited, **50.13**
but shall be an utter desolation; Jer 18.16
everyone who passes by Babylon shall be appalled
and hiss because of all her wounds.
14 Take up your positions around Babylon, **50.14**
all you that bend the bow; Hab 2.8,17
shoot at her, spare no arrows,
for she has sinned against the LORD.
15 Raise a shout against her from all sides, **50.15**
"She has surrendered; Ps 137.8
her bulwarks have fallen,
her walls are thrown down."
For this is the vengeance of the LORD:
take vengeance on her,
do to her as she has done.
16 Cut off from Babylon the sower, **50.16**
and the wielder of the sickle in time of harvest; Jer 46.16
because of the destroying sword
all of them shall return to their own people,
and all of them shall flee to their own land.

50.17
17 Israel is a hunted sheep driven away by lions. First the king of Assyria de- 2 Kgs 18.9-13 24.1,10-12
voured it, and now at the end King Nebuchadrezzar of Babylon has gnawed its Jer 4.7
bones. 18 Therefore, thus says the LORD of hosts, the God of Israel: I am going to **50.18** Isa 10.12
punish the king of Babylon and his land, as I punished the king of Assyria. 19 I will Nah 1.1
restore Israel to its pasture, and it shall feed on Carmel and in Bashan, and on the 3.7,18,19 **50.19**
hills of Ephraim and in Gilead its hunger shall be satisfied. 20 In those days and at Jer 31.10

u Gk: Heb *toward it. Come! They shall join*

50.17–20 God would punish wicked Babylon as he punished Assyria for what they had done to Israel. Assyria was crushed by Babylon, over which it had once ruled. Babylon, in turn, would be crushed by Medo-Persia, formerly under its authority. These verses also look to the time when the Messiah will rule and Israel will be fully restored. No sin will then be found in Israel because those who sought God will be forgiven.

50.20 Jer 31.34 Mic 7.19

that time, says the LORD, the iniquity of Israel shall be sought, and there shall be none; and the sins of Judah, and none shall be found; for I will pardon the remnant that I have spared.

21 Go up to the land of Merathaim;[v]
go up against her,
and attack the inhabitants of Pekod[w]
and utterly destroy the last of them,[x]
says the LORD;
do all that I have commanded you.

50.22 Jer 4.19-21

22 The noise of battle is in the land,
and great destruction!

50.23 Jer 51.20-24

23 How the hammer of the whole earth
is cut down and broken!
How Babylon has become
a horror among the nations!

50.24 Job 9.4; 40.2,9 Jer 48.43

24 You set a snare for yourself and you were caught, O Babylon,
but you did not know it;
you were discovered and seized,
because you challenged the LORD.

50.25 Isa 13.4,5

25 The LORD has opened his armory,
and brought out the weapons of his wrath,
for the Lord GOD of hosts has a task to do
in the land of the Chaldeans.

50.26 Isa 14.23

26 Come against her from every quarter;
open her granaries;
pile her up like heaps of grain, and destroy her utterly;
let nothing be left of her.

50.27 Ps 37.13 Ezek 7.7

27 Kill all her bulls,
let them go down to the slaughter.
Alas for them, their day has come,
the time of their punishment!

50.28 Ps 149.6-9 Isa 48.20 Lam 1.10

28 Listen! Fugitives and refugees from the land of Babylon are coming to declare in Zion the vengeance of the LORD our God, vengeance for his temple.

50.29 Ex 10.3 Ps 137.8
50.30 Jer 18.21

29 Summon archers against Babylon, all who bend the bow. Encamp all around
her; let no one escape. Repay her according to her deeds; just as she has done, do
to her — for she has arrogantly defied the LORD, the Holy One of Israel. 30 Therefore
her young men shall fall in her squares, and all her soldiers shall be destroyed on
that day, says the LORD.

50.31 Nah 2.13

31 I am against you, O arrogant one,
says the Lord GOD of hosts;
for your day has come,
the time when I will punish you.

50.32 Isa 10.12-15 Jer 21.14

32 The arrogant one shall stumble and fall,
with no one to raise him up,
and I will kindle a fire in his cities,
and it will devour everything around him.

[v] Or *of Double Rebellion* [w] Or *of Punishment* [x] Tg: Heb *destroy after them*

50.21 Merathaim was located in southern Babylonia; Pekod was in eastern Babylonia.

50.32 Pride (arrogance) was Babylon's characteristic sin. Pride comes from feeling self-sufficient, or believing that we don't need God. Proud nations or persons, however, will eventually fail, because they refuse to recognize God as the ultimate power. Getting rid of pride is not easy, but we can admit it and ask God to forgive us and help us struggle against it. The best antidote to pride is to focus our attention on the greatness and goodness of God.

33 Thus says the LORD of hosts: The people of Israel are oppressed, and so too
are the people of Judah; all their captors have held them fast and refuse to let them
go. 34 Their Redeemer is strong; the LORD of hosts is his name. He will surely plead
their cause, that he may give rest to the earth, but unrest to the inhabitants of Babylon.

50.33 Isa 14.17
50.34 Isa 14.3-7 43.14 Mic 7.9

35 A sword against the Chaldeans, says the LORD,
and against the inhabitants of Babylon,
and against her officials and her sages!
36 A sword against the diviners,
so that they may become fools!
A sword against her warriors,
so that they may be destroyed!
37 A sword against her[y] horses and against her[y] chariots,
and against all the foreign troops in her midst,
so that they may become women!
A sword against all her treasures,
that they may be plundered!
38 A drought[z] against her waters,
that they may be dried up!
For it is a land of images,
and they go mad over idols.

50.35 Jer 47.6
50.36 Isa 44.25
50.37 Ps 20.7,8 Jer 25.19,20 48.41

39 Therefore wild animals shall live with hyenas in Babylon,[a] and ostriches
shall inhabit her; she shall never again be peopled, or inhabited for all generations.
40 As when God overthrew Sodom and Gomorrah and their neighbors, says the
LORD, so no one shall live there, nor shall anyone settle in her.

50.39 Isa 13.20
50.40 Lk 17.28-30 2 Pet 2.6 Jude 7

41 Look, a people is coming from the north;
a mighty nation and many kings
are stirring from the farthest parts of the earth.
42 They wield bow and spear,
they are cruel and have no mercy.
The sound of them is like the roaring sea;
they ride upon horses,
set in array as a warrior for battle,
against you, O daughter Babylon!
43 The king of Babylon heard news of them,
and his hands fell helpless;
anguish seized him,
pain like that of a woman in labor.

50.41 Isa 13.2-5
50.42 Isa 13.17,18 Hab 1.8
50.43 Jer 30.6

44 Like a lion coming up from the thickets of the Jordan against a perennial
pasture, I will suddenly chase them away from her; and I will appoint over her
whomever I choose.[b] For who is like me? Who can summon me? Who is the shepherd who can stand before me? 45 Therefore hear the plan that the LORD has made
against Babylon, and the purposes that he has formed against the land of the Chaldeans: Surely the little ones of the flock shall be dragged away; surely their[c] fold
shall be appalled at their fate. 46 At the sound of the capture of Babylon the earth
shall tremble, and her cry shall be heard among the nations.

50.44 Num 16.5 Job 41.10 Isa 46.9
50.46 Jer 10.10 Ezek 26.18

[y] Cn: Heb *his* [z] Another reading is *A sword* [a] Heb lacks *in Babylon* [b] Or *and I will single out the choicest of her rams*: Meaning of Heb uncertain [c] Syr Gk Tg Compare 49.20: Heb lacks *their*

50.39 Babylon remains a wasteland to this day. See also Isaiah 13.19–22.

50.44–46 The invader was Cyrus, who attacked Babylon by surprise and overthrew it. The world was shocked that its greatest empire was overthrown so quickly. No earthly power, no matter how great, can last forever.

Jeremiah predicts the fall of Babylon

51.1 Jer 4.11,12

51 Thus says the LORD:
I am going to stir up a destructive wind[d]
against Babylon
and against the inhabitants of Leb-qamai;[e]

51.2 Jer 15.7 Mt 3.12

2 and I will send winnowers to Babylon,
and they shall winnow her.
They shall empty her land
when they come against her from every side
on the day of trouble.
3 Let not the archer bend his bow,
and let him not array himself in his coat of mail.
Do not spare her young men;
utterly destroy her entire army.
4 They shall fall down slain in the land of the Chaldeans,
and wounded in her streets.

51.5 Isa 54.7,8 Jer 33.24-26

5 Israel and Judah have not been forsaken
by their God, the LORD of hosts,
though their land is full of guilt
before the Holy One of Israel.

51.6 Num 16.26

6 Flee from the midst of Babylon,
save your lives, each of you!
Do not perish because of her guilt,
for this is the time of the LORD's vengeance;
he is repaying her what is due.

51.7 Jer 25.15 Rev 14.8; 18.3

7 Babylon was a golden cup in the LORD's hand,
making all the earth drunken;
the nations drank of her wine,
and so the nations went mad.
8 Suddenly Babylon has fallen and is shattered;
wail for her!
Bring balm for her wound;
perhaps she may be healed.

51.9 Jer 46.16

9 We tried to heal Babylon,
but she could not be healed.
Forsake her, and let each of us go
to our own country;
for her judgment has reached up to heaven
and has been lifted up even to the skies.

51.10 Isa 40.2 Mic 7.9

10 The LORD has brought forth our vindication;
come, let us declare in Zion
the work of the LORD our God.

51.11 Joel 3.9,10

11 Sharpen the arrows!
Fill the quivers!
The LORD has stirred up the spirit of the kings of the Medes, because his purpose concerning Babylon is to destroy it, for that is the vengeance of the LORD, vengeance for his temple.

51.12 Jer 4.28

12 Raise a standard against the walls of Babylon;

[d] Or *stir up the spirit of a destroyer* [e] *Leb-qamai* is a cryptogram for *Kasdim*, Chaldea

51.2 Winnowers worked to separate the wheat from the chaff. When they threw the mixture into the air, the wind blew away the worthless chaff while the wheat settled to the ground. Babylon would be blown away like chaff in the wind. (See also Matthew 3.12.)

51.11 Cyrus, king of Persia, had allied with Babylon to defeat Nineveh (capital of the Assyrian Empire) in 612 B.C. Then the Medes joined Persia to defeat Babylon (539 B.C.).

make the watch strong;
post sentinels;
prepare the ambushes;
for the LORD has both planned and done
what he spoke concerning the inhabitants of Babylon.
13 You who live by mighty waters,
rich in treasures,
your end has come,
the thread of your life is cut.
14 The LORD of hosts has sworn by himself:
Surely I will fill you with troops like a swarm of locusts,
and they shall raise a shout of victory over you.

15 It is he who made the earth by his power,
who established the world by his wisdom,
and by his understanding stretched out the heavens.
16 When he utters his voice there is a tumult of waters in the heavens,
and he makes the mist rise from the ends of the earth.
He makes lightnings for the rain,
and he brings out the wind from his storehouses.
17 Everyone is stupid and without knowledge;
goldsmiths are all put to shame by their idols;
for their images are false,
and there is no breath in them.
18 They are worthless, a work of delusion;
at the time of their punishment they shall perish.
19 Not like these is the LORD,[f] the portion of Jacob,
for he is the one who formed all things,
and Israel is the tribe of his inheritance;
the LORD of hosts is his name.

20 You are my war club, my weapon of battle:
with you I smash nations;
with you I destroy kingdoms;
21 with you I smash the horse and its rider;
with you I smash the chariot and the charioteer;
22 with you I smash man and woman;
with you I smash the old man and the boy;
with you I smash the young man and the girl;
23 with you I smash shepherds and their flocks;
with you I smash farmers and their teams;
with you I smash governors and deputies.

24 I will repay Babylon and all the inhabitants of Chaldea before your very eyes for all the wrong that they have done in Zion, says the LORD.

25 I am against you, O destroying mountain,
says the LORD,
that destroys the whole earth;
I will stretch out my hand against you,
and roll you down from the crags,
and make you a burned-out mountain.

51.13 Hab 2.9-11
51.14 Nah 3.15
51.15 Ps 146.5,6 Jer 10.12-16 Rom 1.20
51.16 Job 37.2-5 Ps 18.13; 135.7 Jonah 1.4
51.17 Ps 73.22 Isa 44.18-20 Hab 2.18,19
51.19 Jer 10.16
51.20 Mic 4.12,13
51.21 Ex 15.1 Isa 43.17
51.22 Isa 13.15,16,18 Rev 8.8
51.25 Rev 8.8

f Heb lacks *the* LORD

51.17–19 It is foolish to trust in man-made images rather than God. It is easy to think that things we see and touch will bring us more security than God will. But things rust, rot, and decay. God is eternal. Why put your trust in something that will disappear within a few years?

51.26 Isa 13.19-22

26 No stone shall be taken from you for a corner
and no stone for a foundation,
but you shall be a perpetual waste,
says the LORD.

51.27 Gen 8.4; 10.3 2 Kgs 19.37 Isa 13.2-5

27 Raise a standard in the land,
blow the trumpet among the nations;
prepare the nations for war against her,
summon against her the kingdoms,
Ararat, Minni, and Ashkenaz;
appoint a marshal against her,
bring up horses like bristling locusts.
28 Prepare the nations for war against her,
the kings of the Medes, with their governors and deputies,
and every land under their dominion.

51.29 Jer 10.10 Amos 8.8

29 The land trembles and writhes,
for the LORD's purposes against Babylon stand,
to make the land of Babylon a desolation,
without inhabitant.

51.30 Isa 13.7,8; 45.1

30 The warriors of Babylon have given up fighting,
they remain in their strongholds;
their strength has failed,
they have become women;
her buildings are set on fire,
her bars are broken.
31 One runner runs to meet another,
and one messenger to meet another,
to tell the king of Babylon
that his city is taken from end to end:
32 the fords have been seized,
the marshes have been burned with fire,
and the soldiers are in panic.

51.33 Isa 21.10 Joel 3.13

33 For thus says the LORD of hosts, the God of Israel:
Daughter Babylon is like a threshing floor
at the time when it is trodden;
yet a little while
and the time of her harvest will come.

51.34 Job 20.15 Ps 137.8 Isa 24.1-3

34 "King Nebuchadrezzar of Babylon has devoured me,
he has crushed me;
he has made me an empty vessel,
he has swallowed me like a monster;
he has filled his belly with my delicacies,
he has spewed me out.
35 May my torn flesh be avenged on Babylon,"
the inhabitants of Zion shall say.
"May my blood be avenged on the inhabitants of Chaldea,"
Jerusalem shall say.

51.33 Grain was threshed on a threshing floor, where sheaves were brought from the field. The stalks of grain were distributed on the floor, a large level section of hard ground. There the grain was crushed to separate the kernels from the stalk; then the kernels were beaten with a wooden tool. Sometimes a wooden sledge was pulled over the grain by animals to break the kernels loose. Babylon would soon be "threshed" as God judged it for its sins.

51.36 This verse may refer to an event accomplished by Cyrus, who took Babylon by surprise by diverting the river that ran through the city far upstream and walking in on the dry river bed. More likely it is saying that Babylon will be deprived of life-giving water. Unlike Jerusalem, Babylon will not be restored.

36 Therefore thus says the LORD:
I am going to defend your cause
and take vengeance for you.
I will dry up her sea
and make her fountain dry;
37 and Babylon shall become a heap of ruins,
a den of jackals,
an object of horror and of hissing,
without inhabitant.

38 Like lions they shall roar together;
they shall growl like lions' whelps.
39 When they are inflamed, I will set out their drink
and make them drunk, until they become merry
and then sleep a perpetual sleep
and never wake, says the LORD.
40 I will bring them down like lambs to the slaughter,
like rams and goats.

41 How Sheshach[g] is taken,
the pride of the whole earth seized!
How Babylon has become
an object of horror among the nations!
42 The sea has risen over Babylon;
she has been covered by its tumultuous waves.
43 Her cities have become an object of horror,
a land of drought and a desert,
a land in which no one lives,
and through which no mortal passes.
44 I will punish Bel in Babylon,
and make him disgorge what he has swallowed.
The nations shall no longer stream to him;
the wall of Babylon has fallen.

45 Come out of her, my people!
Save your lives, each of you,
from the fierce anger of the LORD!
46 Do not be faint-hearted or fearful
at the rumors heard in the land—
one year one rumor comes,
the next year another,
rumors of violence in the land
and of ruler against ruler.

47 Assuredly, the days are coming
when I will punish the images of Babylon;
her whole land shall be put to shame,
and all her slain shall fall in her midst.
48 Then the heavens and the earth,
and all that is in them,
shall shout for joy over Babylon;
for the destroyers shall come against them out of the north,
says the LORD.
49 Babylon must fall for the slain of Israel,
as the slain of all the earth have fallen because of Babylon.

51.36 Ps 140.12 Rom 12.19
51.39 Ps 76.5 Jer 25.27
51.43 Isa 13.20
51.44 Isa 2.2 Ezra 1.7
51.45 Gen 19.12-16 Isa 48.20 Acts 2.40
51.46 Isa 19.2
51.47 Isa 21.9; 46.1,2
51.48 Isa 44.23

g *Sheshach* is a cryptogram for *Babel*, Babylon

50 You survivors of the sword,
go, do not linger!
Remember the LORD in a distant land,
and let Jerusalem come into your mind:
51.51 Lam 1.10
51 We are put to shame, for we have heard insults;
dishonor has covered our face,
for aliens have come
into the holy places of the LORD's house.

52 Therefore the time is surely coming, says the LORD,
when I will punish her idols,
and through all her land
the wounded shall groan.
51.53 Job 20.6,7
53 Though Babylon should mount up to heaven,
and though she should fortify her strong height,
from me destroyers would come upon her,
says the LORD.

54 Listen!—a cry from Babylon!
A great crashing from the land of the Chaldeans!
51.55 Ps 69.2
55 For the LORD is laying Babylon waste,
and stilling her loud clamor.
Their waves roar like mighty waters,
the sound of their clamor resounds;
51.56 Ps 76.3; 94.1,2
56 for a destroyer has come against her,
against Babylon;
her warriors are taken,
their bows are broken;
for the LORD is a God of recompense,
he will repay in full.
51.57 Ps 76.5,6
57 I will make her officials and her sages drunk,
also her governors, her deputies, and her warriors;
they shall sleep a perpetual sleep and never wake,
says the King, whose name is the LORD of hosts.

51.58 Isa 45.1,2 Hab 2.13
58 Thus says the LORD of hosts:
The broad wall of Babylon
shall be leveled to the ground,
and her high gates
shall be burned with fire.
The peoples exhaust themselves for nothing,
and the nations weary themselves only for fire.[h]

59 The word that the prophet Jeremiah commanded Seraiah son of Neriah son
of Mahseiah, when he went with King Zedekiah of Judah to Babylon, in the fourth
year of his reign. Seraiah was the quartermaster. 60 Jeremiah wrote in a[i] scroll all
the disasters that would come on Babylon, all these words that are written concerning Babylon. 61 And Jeremiah said to Seraiah: "When you come to Babylon, see

[h] Gk Syr Compare Hab 2.13: Heb *and the nations for fire, and they are weary* [i] Or *one*

51.51 The people were paralyzed with guilt over their past. The Babylonian armies had desecrated the temple, and the people were ashamed to return to Jerusalem. But God told them to return to the city, for he would destroy Babylon for its sins.

51.59 Jeremiah could not visit Babylon, so he sent the message with Seraiah, the officer who cared for the comforts of the army. Seriah was probably Baruch's brother (32.12).

51.60–64 In this last of Jeremiah's messages, we find again the twin themes of God's sovereignty and his judgment. Babylon has been allowed to oppress the people of Israel, but now Babylon itself would be judged. Although God brings good out of evil, he does not allow evil to remain unpunished. The wicked may succeed for a while, but resist the temptation to follow them or you may share in their judgment.

that you read all these words, [62]and say, 'O LORD, you yourself threatened to 51.62
destroy this place so that neither human beings nor animals shall live in it, and it Isa 13.19-22 Ezek 35.9
shall be desolate forever.' [63]When you finish reading this scroll, tie a stone to it, 51.63
and throw it into the middle of the Euphrates, [64]and say, 'Thus shall Babylon sink, Rev 18.21
to rise no more, because of the disasters that I am bringing on her.' "[j] 51.64 Nah 1.8,9
Thus far are the words of Jeremiah.

2. Details about the fall of Jerusalem

52 Zedekiah was twenty-one years old when he began to reign; he reigned 52.1
eleven years in Jerusalem. His mother's name was Hamutal daughter of Jer- 2 Kgs 8.22 24.18-20
emiah of Libnah. [2]He did what was evil in the sight of the LORD, just as Jehoiakim 52.2
had done. [3]Indeed, Jerusalem and Judah so angered the LORD that he expelled them Jer 36.30,31
from his presence. 52.3 2 Chron 36.13
Zedekiah rebelled against the king of Babylon. [4]And in the ninth year of his 52.4
reign, in the tenth month, on the tenth day of the month, King Nebuchadrezzar of 2 Kgs 25.1-7 Jer 39.1
Babylon came with all his army against Jerusalem, and they laid siege to it; they
built siegeworks against it all around. [5]So the city was besieged until the eleventh
year of King Zedekiah. [6]On the ninth day of the fourth month the famine became 52.6
so severe in the city that there was no food for the people of the land. [7]Then a Jer 38.9
breach was made in the city wall;[k] and all the soldiers fled and went out from the 52.7 Jer 39.2,4-7
city by night by the way of the gate between the two walls, by the king's garden,
though the Chaldeans were all around the city. They went in the direction of the
Arabah. [8]But the army of the Chaldeans pursued the king, and overtook Zedekiah 52.8
in the plains of Jericho; and all his army was scattered, deserting him. [9]Then they Jer 21.7; 38.23
captured the king, and brought him up to the king of Babylon at Riblah in the land 52.9 2 Kgs 25.6
of Hamath, and he passed sentence on him. [10]The king of Babylon killed the sons Jer 39.5
of Zedekiah before his eyes, and also killed all the officers of Judah at Riblah. [11]He 52.10 Jer 39.6
put out the eyes of Zedekiah, and bound him in fetters, and the king of Babylon 52.11
took him to Babylon, and put him in prison until the day of his death. Ezek 12.13
12 In the fifth month, on the tenth day of the month—which was the nineteenth 52.12
year of King Nebuchadrezzar, king of Babylon—Nebuzaradan the captain of the 2 Kgs 25.8-21
bodyguard who served the king of Babylon, entered Jerusalem. [13]He burned the 52.13
house of the LORD, the king's house, and all the houses of Jerusalem; every great 2 Chron 36.19 Ps 74.6-8
house he burned down. [14]All the army of the Chaldeans, who were with the captain Jer 39.8
of the guard, broke down all the walls around Jerusalem. [15]Nebuzaradan the cap- 52.14 2 Kgs 25.10
tain of the guard carried into exile some of the poorest of the people and the rest of
the people who were left in the city and the deserters who had defected to the king
of Babylon, together with the rest of the artisans. [16]But Nebuzaradan the captain of
the guard left some of the poorest people of the land to be vinedressers and tillers
of the soil.
17 The pillars of bronze that were in the house of the LORD, and the stands and 52.17
the bronze sea that were in the house of the LORD, the Chaldeans broke in pieces, 1 Kgs 7.15-36
and carried all the bronze to Babylon. [18]They took away the pots, the shovels, the 52.18
snuffers, the basins, the ladles, and all the vessels of bronze used in the temple 1 Kgs 7.40,45
service. [19]The captain of the guard took away the small bowls also, the firepans,
the basins, the pots, the lampstands, the ladles, and the bowls for libation, both
those of gold and those of silver. [20]As for the two pillars, the one sea, the twelve 52.20
bronze bulls that were under the sea, and the stands,[l] which King Solomon had 1 Kgs 7.47
made for the house of the LORD, the bronze of all these vessels was beyond weigh-

[j] Gk: Heb *on her. And they shall weary themselves* [k] Heb lacks *wall* [l] Cn: Heb *that were under the stands*

52.1ff This chapter provides more detail about the destruction of Jerusalem recorded in chapter 39 (similar material is found in 2 Kings 24.18–25.21). This appendix shows that Jeremiah's prophecies concerning the destruction of Jerusalem and the Babylonian captivity happened just as he predicted. For more information on Zedekiah, see the note on 39.1.

52.9 Riblah was 200 miles north of Jerusalem. This was the Babylonian headquarters for ruling the region. Hamath was the district of Syria containing the nation's capital.

52.19 Libations were drink offerings made to the Lord. (For an example, see Leviticus 23.13.)

52.21 A cubit was a measure equal to 17 to 20 inches.

52.22 ing. 21 As for the pillars, the height of the one pillar was eighteen cubits, its circum-
1 Kgs 7.20,42 ference was twelve cubits; it was hollow and its thickness was four fingers. 22 Upon
it was a capital of bronze; the height of the one capital was five cubits; latticework
and pomegranates, all of bronze, encircled the top of the capital. And the second
pillar had the same, with pomegranates. 23 There were ninety-six pomegranates on
52.24 the sides; all the pomegranates encircling the latticework numbered one hundred.
2 Kgs 25.18 Ezra 7.1 24 The captain of the guard took the chief priest Seraiah, the second priest
Esth 1.14 Zephaniah, and the three guardians of the threshold; 25 and from the city he took an
officer who had been in command of the soldiers, and seven men of the king's
council who were found in the city; the secretary of the commander of the army
who mustered the people of the land; and sixty men of the people of the land who
52.27 were found inside the city. 26 Then Nebuzaradan the captain of the guard took them,
Jer 13.19 Mic 4.10 and brought them to the king of Babylon at Riblah. 27 And the king of Babylon
struck them down, and put them to death at Riblah in the land of Hamath. So Judah
52.28 went into exile out of its land.
2 Kgs 24.2,3, 12-16 28 This is the number of the people whom Nebuchadrezzar took into exile: in
the seventh year, three thousand twenty-three Judeans; 29 in the eighteenth year of
Nebuchadrezzar he took into exile from Jerusalem eight hundred thirty-two persons; 30 in the twenty-third year of Nebuchadrezzar, Nebuzaradan the captain of the
guard took into exile of the Judeans seven hundred forty-five persons; all the per-
52.31 sons were four thousand six hundred.
2 Kgs 25.27-30 Ps 3.3 31 In the thirty-seventh year of the exile of King Jehoiachin of Judah, in the
twelfth month, on the twenty-fifth day of the month, King Evil-merodach of Babylon, in the year he began to reign, showed favor to King Jehoiachin of Judah and
52.33 brought him out of prison; 32 he spoke kindly to him, and gave him a seat above the
2 Sam 9.7,13 seats of the other kings who were with him in Babylon. 33 So Jehoiachin put aside
his prison clothes, and every day of his life he dined regularly at the king's table.
34 For his allowance, a regular daily allowance was given him by the king of Babylon, as long as he lived, up to the day of his death.

52.31 Babylon's king showed kindness to Jehoiachin. In 560 B.C. he was released from prison and allowed to eat with the king. God continued to show kindness to the descendants of King David, even in exile.

52.34 In the world's eyes, Jeremiah looked totally unsuccessful. He had no money, family, or friends. He prophesied the destruction of the nation, the capital city, and the temple, but the political and religious leaders would not accept or follow his advice. No group of people liked him or listened to him. Yet as we look back, we see that he successfully completed the work God gave him to do. Success must never be measured by popularity, fame, or fortune, for these are temporal measures. Zedekiah, for example, lost everything by pursuing selfish goals. God measures our success with the yardsticks of obedience, faithfulness, and righteousness. If you are faithfully doing the work God gives you, you are successful in his eyes.

LAMENTATIONS

VITAL STATISTICS

PURPOSE:
To teach people that to disobey God is to invite disaster and to show that God suffers when his people suffer

AUTHOR:
Jeremiah

DATE WRITTEN:
Soon after the fall of Jerusalem in 586 B.C.

SETTING:
Jerusalem had been destroyed by Babylon and her people killed, tortured, or taken captive.

KEY VERSE:
"My eyes are spent with weeping; my stomach churns; my bile is poured out on the ground because of the destruction of my people, because infants and babes faint in the streets of the city" (2.11).

KEY PEOPLE:
Jeremiah, the people of Jerusalem

KEY PLACE:
Jerusalem

SPECIAL FEATURES:
Three strands of Hebrew thought meet in Lamentations—prophecy, ritual, and wisdom. Lamentations is written in the rhythm and style of ancient Jewish funeral songs or chants. It contains five poems corresponding to the five chapters (see the note on 3.1ff).

TEARS are defined simply as "drops of salty fluid flowing from the eyes." They can be caused by irritation or laughter but are usually associated with weeping, sorrow, and grief. When we cry, friends wonder what's wrong and try to console us. Babies cry for food, children at the loss of a pet, and adults when confronted with trauma and death.

Jeremiah's grief ran deeper. Called the "weeping prophet," his tears flowed from a broken heart. As God's spokesman, he knew what lay ahead for Judah, his country, and for Jerusalem, the capital and "city of God." God's judgment would fall and destruction would come. And Jeremiah wept. His tears were not self-centered, mourning over personal suffering or loss. He wept because the people had rejected their God—the God who had made them, loved them, and sought repeatedly to bless them. His heart was broken because he knew that the selfishness and sinfulness of the people would bring them much suffering and an extended exile. Jeremiah's tears were tears of empathy and sympathy. His heart was broken with those things that break God's heart.

Jeremiah's two books focus on one event—the destruction of Jerusalem. The book of Jeremiah predicts it, and Lamentations looks back on it. Known as the book of tears, Lamentations is a dirge, a funeral song written for the fallen city of Jerusalem.

What makes a person cry says a lot about that person—whether he or she is self-centered or God-centered. The book of Lamentations allows us to see what made Jeremiah sorrowful. As one of God's choice servants, he stands alone in the depth of his emotions, his care for the people, his love for the nation, and his devotion to God.

What causes your tears? Do you weep because your selfish pride has been wounded, or because the people around you sin against and reject the God who loves them dearly? Do you weep because you have lost something that gives you pleasure, or because people all around you will suffer for their sinfulness? Our world is filled with injustice, poverty, war, and rebellion against God, all of which should move us to tears and to action. Read Lamentations and learn what it means to grieve with God.

THE BLUEPRINT

1. Jeremiah mourns for Jerusalem (1.1–22)
2. God's anger at sin (2.1–22)
3. Hope in the midst of affliction (3.1–66)
4. God's anger is satisfied (4.1–22)
5. Jeremiah pleads for restoration (5.1–22)

Jeremiah grieves deeply because of the destruction of Jerusalem and the devastation of his nation. But in the middle of the book, in the depths of his grief, there shines a ray of hope. God's compassion is ever-present. His faithfulness is great. Jeremiah realizes that it is only the Lord's mercy that has prevented total annihilation. This book shows us the serious consequences of human sin and how we can still have hope in the midst of tragedy because God is able to turn it around for good. We see the timeless importance of prayer and confession of sin. We will all face tragedy in our lives. But in the midst of our afflictions, there is hope in God.

MEGATHEMES

THEME	EXPLANATION	IMPORTANCE
Destruction of Jerusalem	Lamentations is a sad funeral song for the great capital city of the Jews. The temple has been destroyed, the king is gone, and the people are in exile. God had warned that he would destroy them if they abandoned him. Now, afterwards, the people realize their condition and confess their sin.	God's warnings are justified. He does what he says he will do. His punishment for sin is certain. Only by confessing and renouncing our sin can we turn to him for deliverance. How much better to do so before his warnings are fulfilled.
God's mercy	God's compassion was at work even when the Israelites were experiencing the affliction of their Babylonian conquerors. Although the people had been unfaithful, God's faithfulness was great. He used this affliction to bring his people back to him.	God will always be faithful to his people. His merciful, refining work is evident even in affliction. At those times, we must pray for forgiveness and then turn to him for deliverance.
Sin's consequences	God was angry at the prolonged rebellion by his people. Sin is the cause of their misery and destruction is the result of their sin. The destruction of the nation shows the vanity of human glory and pride.	To continue in rebellion against God is to invite disaster. We must never trust our own leadership, resources, intelligence, or power more than God. If we do, we will experience consequences similar to Jerusalem's.
Hope	God's mercy in sparing some of the people offers hope for better days. One day, the people will be restored to a true and fervent relationship with God.	Only God can deliver us from sin. Without him there is no comfort or hope for the future. Because of Christ's death for us and his promise to return, we have a bright hope for tomorrow.

1. Jeremiah mourns for Jerusalem

1.1 Isa 22.2 Jer 31.7; 40.9

1 How lonely sits the city
that once was full of people!
How like a widow she has become,
she that was great among the nations!
She that was a princess among the provinces
has become a vassal.

1.2 Jer 2.25 22.20-22 Mic 7.5

2 She weeps bitterly in the night,
with tears on her cheeks;
among all her lovers
she has no one to comfort her;
all her friends have dealt treacherously with her,
they have become her enemies.

1.3 Lev 26.39 Deut 28.64-67 2 Kgs 25.4,5

3 Judah has gone into exile with suffering
and hard servitude;

1.1 This is the prophet Jeremiah's song of sorrow for Jerusalem's destruction. The nation of Judah had been utterly defeated, the temple destroyed, and captives taken away to Babylon. Jeremiah's tears were for the suffering and humiliation of the people, but they went even deeper. He cried because God had rejected the people for their rebellious ways. Each year this book was read aloud to remind all the Jews that their great city fell because of their stubborn sinfulness.

1.2 The term *lovers* refers to nations such as Egypt to whom Judah kept turning for help. As the Babylonians closed in on Jerusalem, the nation of Judah turned away from God and sought help and protection from other nations instead.

she lives now among the nations,
and finds no resting place;
her pursuers have all overtaken her
in the midst of her distress.

4 The roads to Zion mourn,
for no one comes to the festivals;
all her gates are desolate,
her priests groan;
her young girls grieve,[a]
and her lot is bitter.

1.4 Jer 9.11; 10.22 Lam 2.6,7 Joel 1.8-13

5 Her foes have become the masters,
her enemies prosper,
because the LORD has made her suffer
for the multitude of her transgressions;
her children have gone away,
captives before the foe.

1.5 Ps 90.7,8 Ezek 8.17,18 9.9,10

6 From daughter Zion has departed
all her majesty.
Her princes have become like stags
that find no pasture;
they fled without strength
before the pursuer.

1.6 Ps 132.13 Jer 13.18

7 Jerusalem remembers,
in the days of her affliction and wandering,
all the precious things
that were hers in days of old.
When her people fell into the hand of the foe,
and there was no one to help her,
the foe looked on mocking
over her downfall.

1.7 Jer 37.7 Lam 4.17

8 Jerusalem sinned grievously,
so she has become a mockery;
all who honored her despise her,
for they have seen her nakedness;
she herself groans,
and turns her face away.

1.8 Isa 59.2-13 Lam 1.15

9 Her uncleanness was in her skirts;
she took no thought of her future;
her downfall was appalling,
with none to comfort her.
"O LORD, look at my affliction,
for the enemy has triumphed!"

1.9 Ps 74.23 Isa 3.8 Jer 13.17,18

10 Enemies have stretched out their hands
over all her precious things;

1.10 Ps 74.4-8 Isa 64.10,11 Jer 51.51

[a] Meaning of Heb uncertain

1.9 The warning was loud and clear: If Judah played with fire, its people would get burned. Jerusalem foolishly took a chance and lost, refusing to believe that immoral living brings God's punishment. The ultimate consequence of sin is punishment (Romans 6.23). We can choose to ignore God's warnings, but as surely as judgment came upon Jerusalem, so will it come upon those who defy God. Are you listening to God's Word? Are you obeying it? Obedience is a sure sign of your love for him.

she has even seen the nations
invade her sanctuary,
those whom you forbade
to enter your congregation.

1.11
1 Sam 30.12
Jer 15.19

11 All her people groan
as they search for bread;
they trade their treasures for food
to revive their strength.
Look, O LORD, and see
how worthless I have become.

1.12
Isa 13.13
Jer 4.8; 18.16
48.27

12 Is it nothing to you,[b] all you who pass by?
Look and see
if there is any sorrow like my sorrow,
which was brought upon me,
which the LORD inflicted
on the day of his fierce anger.

1.13
Job 19.6; 30.30
Ps 22.14
Jer 44.6
Hab 3.16

13 From on high he sent fire;
it went deep into my bones;
he spread a net for my feet;
he turned me back;
he has left me stunned,
faint all day long.

1.14
Prov 5.22
Isa 47.6
Jer 32.3,5
Ezek 25.4,7

14 My transgressions were bound[b] into a yoke;
by his hand they were fastened together;
they weigh on my neck,
sapping my strength;
the Lord handed me over
to those whom I cannot withstand.

1.15
Isa 41.2
Jer 13.24; 37.10

15 The LORD has rejected
all my warriors in the midst of me;
he proclaimed a time against me
to crush my young men;
the Lord has trodden as in a wine press
the virgin daughter Judah.

1.16
Ps 69.20
Eccles 4.1
Lam 1.2

16 For these things I weep;
my eyes flow with tears;
for a comforter is far from me,
one to revive my courage;
my children are desolate,
for the enemy has prevailed.

1.17
2 Kgs 24.2-4
Isa 1.15
Jer 4.31

17 Zion stretches out her hands,
but there is no one to comfort her;
the LORD has commanded against Jacob

[b] Meaning of Heb uncertain

1.14 At first, sin seems to offer freedom. But the liberty to do anything we want gradually becomes a desire to do everything. Then we become captive to sin. Freedom from sin's captivity comes only from God. He gives us freedom, not to do anything we want, but to do what he knows is best for us. Strange as it may seem, true freedom comes in obeying God—following his guidance so that we can receive his best.

1.16 God is the comforter, but because of the people's sins, he had to turn away from them and become their judge.

that his neighbors should become his foes;
Jerusalem has become
a filthy thing among them.

18 The LORD is in the right,
for I have rebelled against his word;
but hear, all you peoples,
and behold my suffering;
my young women and young men
have gone into captivity.

1.18 Deut 28.32,41; 1 Sam 12.14,15; Ps 119.75; Jer 12.1

19 I called to my lovers
but they deceived me;
my priests and elders
perished in the city
while seeking food
to revive their strength.

1.19 Job 19.13-19; Jer 14.15; Lam 1.2; 2.20

20 See, O LORD, how distressed I am;
my stomach churns,
my heart is wrung within me,
because I have been very rebellious.
In the street the sword bereaves;
in the house it is like death.

1.20 Isa 16.11; Jer 4.19

21 They heard how I was groaning,
with no one to comfort me.
All my enemies heard of my trouble;
they are glad that you have done it.
Bring on the day you have announced,
and let them be as I am.

1.21 Ps 35.15; Isa 14.5,6; 47.6; Jer 30.16

22 Let all their evil doing come before you;
and deal with them
as you have dealt with me
because of all my transgressions;
for my groans are many
and my heart is faint.

1.22 Neh 4.4,5; Ps 137.7,8

2. God's anger at sin

2 How the Lord in his anger
has humiliated[c] daughter Zion!
He has thrown down from heaven to earth
the splendor of Israel;
he has not remembered his footstool
in the day of his anger.

2.1 Ps 99.5; 132.7; Isa 64.11; Ezek 28.14-16

[c] Meaning of Heb uncertain

1.19 Jerusalem's "lovers," her allies, could not come to her aid because, like Jerusalem, they failed to seek God. Though these allies appeared strong, they were actually weak because God was not with them. Dependable assistance can come only from an ally whose power is from God. When you seek wise counsel, go to Christians who get their wisdom from all-knowing God.

1.22 Babylon, although sinful, was God's instrument for punishing Judah and its capital, Jerusalem. The people of Jerusalem pleaded for God to punish sinful Babylon as he had punished them. God would do this, for he had already passed judgment on Babylon (see Jeremiah 50.1–27).

2.1ff While chapter 1 described Jerusalem's desolation and called for God's revenge on his enemies, chapter 2 calls for God's people to repent if they expect mercy from him. The people must turn from their sins; they must sincerely mourn over their wrongs against God. The people had much to cry about. Because of their stubborn rebellion against God, they had brought great suffering to all, especially to the innocent. Was this suffering God's fault? No, it was the fault of the wayward people. Sinful people brought destruction on themselves, but, tragically, sin's consequences affected everyone – good and evil alike.

2.2
Ps 21.9
89.39,40
Lam 3.43

2 The Lord has destroyed without mercy
all the dwellings of Jacob;
in his wrath he has broken down
the strongholds of daughter Judah;
he has brought down to the ground in dishonor
the kingdom and its rulers.

2.3
Ps 75.5,10
Isa 42.25
Jer 21.14

3 He has cut down in fierce anger
all the might of Israel;
he has withdrawn his right hand from them
in the face of the enemy;
he has burned like a flaming fire in Jacob,
consuming all around.

2.4
Job 6.4; 16.13
Jer 7.20

4 He has bent his bow like an enemy,
with his right hand set like a foe;
he has killed all in whom we took pride
in the tent of daughter Zion;
he has poured out his fury like fire.

2.5
Jer 52.13
Lam 2.2

5 The Lord has become like an enemy;
he has destroyed Israel;
He has destroyed all its palaces,
laid in ruins its strongholds,
and multiplied in daughter Judah
mourning and lamentation.

2.6
Lam 1.4
Zeph 3.18

6 He has broken down his booth like a garden,
he has destroyed his tabernacle;
the LORD has abolished in Zion
festival and sabbath,
and in his fierce indignation has spurned
king and priest.

2.7
Ps 74.3-8
Isa 64.11
Ezek 7.20-22

7 The Lord has scorned his altar,
disowned his sanctuary;
he has delivered into the hand of the enemy
the walls of her palaces;
a clamor was raised in the house of the LORD
as on a day of festival.

2.8
2 Kgs 21.13
Isa 34.11
Amos 7.7-9

8 The LORD determined to lay in ruins
the wall of daughter Zion;
he stretched the line;
he did not withhold his hand from destroying;
he caused rampart and wall to lament;
they languish together.

2.6 King Solomon's temple (here called God's tabernacle) in Jerusalem represented God's presence with the people (1 Kings 8.1–11). The temple was the central place of worship. Its destruction symbolized God's rejection of his people—that he no longer lived among them.

2.7 Our place of worship is not as important to God as our pattern of worship. A church may be beautiful, but if its people don't sincerely follow God, it decays from within. The people of Judah, despite their beautiful temple, had rejected in their daily lives what they proclaimed by their worship rituals. Thus their worship turned into a mocking lie. When you worship, are you saying words you don't really mean? Do you pray for help you don't really believe will come? Do you express love for God you don't really have? Earnestly seek God and catch a fresh vision of his love and care. Then worship him wholeheartedly.

9 Her gates have sunk into the ground;
he has ruined and broken her bars;
her king and princes are among the nations;
guidance is no more,
and her prophets obtain
no vision from the LORD.

2.9
Neh 1.3
Jer 23.16

10 The elders of daughter Zion
sit on the ground in silence;
they have thrown dust on their heads
and put on sackcloth;
the young girls of Jerusalem
have bowed their heads to the ground.

2.10
Job 2.13
Isa 3.26
Amos 8.3
Jonah 3.6-8

11 My eyes are spent with weeping;
my stomach churns;
my bile is poured out on the ground
because of the destruction of my people,
because infants and babes faint
in the streets of the city.

2.11
Job 16.13
Jer 4.19
Lam 2.19

12 They cry to their mothers,
"Where is bread and wine?"
as they faint like the wounded
in the streets of the city,
as their life is poured out
on their mothers' bosom.

2.12
Job 30.16
Ps 42.4

13 What can I say for you, to what compare you,
O daughter Jerusalem?
To what can I liken you, that I may comfort you,
O virgin daughter Zion?
For vast as the sea is your ruin;
who can heal you?

2.13
Lam 1.12

14 Your prophets have seen for you
false and deceptive visions;
they have not exposed your iniquity
to restore your fortunes,
but have seen oracles for you
that are false and misleading.

2.14
Ezek 22.25,28
23.36
Mic 3.8

15 All who pass along the way
clap their hands at you;
they hiss and wag their heads

2.15
Job 27.23
Ps 48.2; 50.2
Jer 18.16

2.9 Four powerful symbols and sources of security are lost: the protection of the *city* ("gates"), the leadership of the *monarchy*, the guidance of *God's law*, and the vision of his *prophets*. With those four factors present, the people were lulled into a false sense of security and felt comfortable with their sins. But now that they are removed, the people are confronted with the choice of repenting and returning to God or continuing on this path of suffering. Don't substitute symbols, even good ones, for the reality of a living, personal relationship with God himself.

2.11 Jeremiah's tears were sincere and full of compassion. Sorrow does not mean we lack faith or strength. There is nothing wrong with crying—Jesus himself felt sorrow and even wept (John 11.35). How do we react to the tearing down of our society and to moral degradation? This may not be as obvious as an invading enemy army, but the destruction is just as certain. We too should be deeply moved when we see the moral decay that surrounds us.

2.14 False prophets were everywhere in Jeremiah's day. They faked "oracles" (messages to people from God). While Jeremiah warned the people of coming destruction and lengthy captivity, the false prophets said all was well and the people need not fear. All of Jeremiah's words came true because he was a true prophet of God (Jeremiah 14.14–16).

2.15 Clapping hands, hissing, and wagging heads were all signs of derision and mockery. They were contemptuous gestures.

at daughter Jerusalem;
"Is this the city that was called
the perfection of beauty,
the joy of all the earth?"

2.16 Ps 56.2 Lam 3.46 Obad 12-15

16 All your enemies
open their mouths against you;
they hiss, they gnash their teeth,
they cry: "We have devoured her!
Ah, this is the day we longed for;
at last we have seen it!"

2.17 Deut 28.43,44 Ps 89.42 Lam 1.5

17 The LORD has done what he purposed,
he has carried out his threat;
as he ordained long ago,
he has demolished without pity;
he has made the enemy rejoice over you,
and exalted the might of your foes.

2.18 Ps 119.145 Lam 2.8 Hos 7.14 Hab 2.11

18 Cry aloud[d] to the Lord!
O wall of daughter Zion!
Let tears stream down like a torrent
day and night!
Give yourself no rest,
your eyes no respite!

2.19 1 Sam 1.15 Ps 42.3,4 Isa 51.20

19 Arise, cry out in the night,
at the beginning of the watches!
Pour out your heart like water
before the presence of the Lord!
Lift your hands to him
for the lives of your children,
who faint for hunger
at the head of every street.

2.20 Ex 32.11 Deut 9.26 Ps 78.64 Jer 23.11,12 Lam 4.13,16

20 Look, O LORD, and consider!
To whom have you done this?
Should women eat their offspring,
the children they have borne?
Should priest and prophet be killed
in the sanctuary of the Lord?

2.21 2 Chron 36.17 Jer 6.11

21 The young and the old are lying
on the ground in the streets;
my young women and my young men
have fallen by the sword;
in the day of your anger you have killed them,
slaughtering without mercy.

22 You invited my enemies from all around

[d] Cn: Heb *Their heart cried*

2.19 The people's suffering and sin should have brought them to the Lord, weeping for forgiveness. Only when sin breaks our hearts can God come to our rescue. Just feeling sorry about experiencing sin's consequences does not bring forgiveness. But if we cry out to God, he will forgive us.

2.21, 22 This horrible scene could have been avoided. Jeremiah had warned the people for years that this would happen, and it broke his heart to see it fulfilled. We are always shocked when we hear of tragedy striking the innocent. But often innocent bystanders are victims of judgment on a nation. Sin has a way of causing great sorrow and devastation to many.

as if for a day of festival;
and on the day of the anger of the LORD
no one escaped or survived;
those whom I bore and reared
my enemy has destroyed.

2.22 Ps 31.13 Isa 24.17,18 Jer 16.2-4

3. Hope in the midst of affliction

3 I am one who has seen affliction
under the rod of God's[e] wrath;
2 he has driven and brought me
into darkness without any light;
3 against me alone he turns his hand,
again and again, all day long.

4 He has made my flesh and my skin waste away,
and broken my bones;
5 he has besieged and enveloped me
with bitterness and tribulation;
6 he has made me sit in darkness
like the dead of long ago.

7 He has walled me about so that I cannot escape;
he has put heavy chains on me;
8 though I call and cry for help,
he shuts out my prayer;
9 he has blocked my ways with hewn stones,
he has made my paths crooked.

10 He is a bear lying in wait for me,
a lion in hiding;
11 he led me off my way and tore me to pieces;
he has made me desolate;
12 he bent his bow and set me
as a mark for his arrow.

13 He shot into my vitals
the arrows of his quiver;
14 I have become the laughingstock of all my people,
the object of their taunt-songs all day long.
15 He has filled me with bitterness,
he has sated me with wormwood.

16 He has made my teeth grind on gravel,
and made me cower in ashes;
17 my soul is bereft of peace;
I have forgotten what happiness is;
18 so I say, "Gone is my glory,
and all that I had hoped for from the LORD."

3.2 Jer 4.23
3.4 Jer 50.17
3.5 Job 19.8 Ps 69.21 Jer 23.15
3.6 Ps 88.5,6
3.7 Jer 40.4
3.8 Ps 22.2
3.11 Job 16.12,13 Hos 6.1
3.14 Lam 3.63
3.17 Isa 59.11 Jer 12.12
3.18 Job 17.15 Ezek 37.11

[e] Heb *his*

3.1ff In Jeremiah's darkest moment, his hope was strengthened with this assurance: God had been faithful and would continue to be faithful. Jeremiah saw both God's judgment and God's steadfast love. In the time of judgment, Jeremiah could still cling to God's love just as in times of prosperity he had warned of his judgment.

3.1ff In the original Hebrew, the chapters in Lamentations are acrostic poems. Each verse in each chapter begins with a successive letter of the Hebrew alphabet. Chapter 3 has 66 verses rather than 22 because it is a triple acrostic: the first three verses begin with the equivalent of "A," the next three with "B," and so on. This was a typical form of Hebrew poetry. Other examples of acrostics are Psalm 119, Psalm 145, and Proverbs 31.

3.15 Wormwood was a bitter plant.

19 The thought of my affliction and my homelessness
is wormwood and gall!

3.20 Ps 42.5,6,11 43.5

20 My soul continually thinks of it
and is bowed down within me.
21 But this I call to mind,
and therefore I have hope:

3.22 Ps 78.38 Jer 3.12 Mal 3.6

22 The steadfast love of the LORD never ceases,[f]
his mercies never come to an end;
23 they are new every morning;
great is your faithfulness.

3.24 Ps 73.26

24 "The LORD is my portion," says my soul,
"therefore I will hope in him."

3.25 Isa 25.9; 26.9

25 The LORD is good to those who wait for him,
to the soul that seeks him.
26 It is good that one should wait quietly
for the salvation of the LORD.
27 It is good for one to bear
the yoke in youth,
28 to sit alone in silence
when the Lord has imposed it,
29 to put one's mouth to the dust
(there may yet be hope),

3.30 Job 16.10 Isa 50.6 Mt 5.39

30 to give one's cheek to the smiter,
and be filled with insults.

3.31 Isa 54.7-10

31 For the Lord will not
reject forever.
32 Although he causes grief, he will have compassion
according to the abundance of his steadfast love;
33 for he does not willingly afflict
or grieve anyone.

34 When all the prisoners of the land
are crushed under foot,
35 when human rights are perverted
in the presence of the Most High,

3.36 Jer 22.3 Hab 1.13

36 when one's case is subverted
—does the Lord not see it?

37 Who can command and have it done,
if the Lord has not ordained it?

3.38 Job 2.10 Jer 32.42

38 Is it not from the mouth of the Most High
that good and bad come?

[f] Syr Tg: Heb *LORD, we are not cut off*

3.21, 22 Jeremiah saw one ray of hope in all the sin and sorrow surrounding him: *God's steadfast love never ceases, his mercies never come to an end.* God willingly responds with help when we ask. Perhaps there is some sin in your life that you thought God would not forgive. God's steadfast love and mercy are greater than any sin, and he promises forgiveness.

3.23 Jeremiah knew about God's faithfulness. God had promised that punishment would follow disobedience, and it did. But God also promised future restoration and blessing, and Jeremiah knew that God would keep that promise also. Trusting in God's faithfulness day by day makes us confident in his great promises for the future.

3.27–33 To "bear the yoke" means willingly coming under God's discipline and learning what he wants to teach. This involves several important factors: (1) silent reflection on what God wants, (2) repentant humility, (3) self-control in the face of adversity, and (4) confident patience, depending on the Teacher to bring about loving lessons in our lives. God has several long-term and short-term lessons for you right now. Are you doing your homework?

3.30 To "give one's cheek to the smiter" means to submit to physical abuse without defending yourself or fighting back. Jesus taught his followers to turn the other cheek (Matthew 5.39), and he exemplified this at the highest level just before his crucifixion.(Matthew 27.27–31; Luke 22.64; John 18.22; 19.3).

39 Why should any who draw breath complain
about the punishment of their sins?

40 Let us test and examine our ways,
and return to the LORD.
41 Let us lift up our hearts as well as our hands
to God in heaven.
42 We have transgressed and rebelled,
and you have not forgiven.

43 You have wrapped yourself with anger and pursued us,
killing without pity;
44 you have wrapped yourself with a cloud
so that no prayer can pass through.
45 You have made us filth and rubbish
among the peoples.

46 All our enemies
have opened their mouths against us;
47 panic and pitfall have come upon us,
devastation and destruction.
48 My eyes flow with rivers of tears
because of the destruction of my people.

49 My eyes will flow without ceasing,
without respite,
50 until the LORD from heaven
looks down and sees.
51 My eyes cause me grief
at the fate of all the young women in my city.

52 Those who were my enemies without cause
have hunted me like a bird;
53 they flung me alive into a pit
and hurled stones on me;
54 water closed over my head;
I said, "I am lost."

55 I called on your name, O LORD,
from the depths of the pit;
56 you heard my plea, "Do not close your ear
to my cry for help, but give me relief!"
57 You came near when I called on you;
you said, "Do not fear!"

58 You have taken up my cause, O Lord,
you have redeemed my life.
59 You have seen the wrong done to me, O LORD;
judge my cause.
60 You have seen all their malice,
all their plots against me.

3.39 Mic 7.2 Heb 12.5,6

3.40 Ps 119.59 139.23,24 2 Cor 13.5

3.42 Neh 9.26 Jer 14.20

3.47 Isa 24.17,18 Jer 48.43,44

3.50 Isa 63.15

3.54 Jonah 2.3-5

3.56 Job 34.28 Ps 55.1; 116.12

3.57 Josh 1.6 Isa 41.10,14

3.58 Ps 34.22 Jer 50.34; 51.36

3.39–42 Parents discipline children to produce right behavior. God disciplined Judah to produce right living and worship. We must not complain about discipline but learn from it, trusting God and being willing to change. We must allow God's correction to bring about the kind of behavior in our lives that pleases him.

3.52–57 At one point in his ministry, Jeremiah was thrown into an empty cistern, and he was left to die in the mire at the bottom (Jeremiah 38.6–13). But God rescued him. Jeremiah used this experience as a picture of the nation sinking into sin. If they turned to God, he would rescue them.

61 You have heard their taunts, O LORD,
all their plots against me.
3.62 Ezek 36.3
62 The whispers and murmurs of my assailants
are against me all day long.
63 Whether they sit or rise — see,
I am the object of their taunt-songs.

3.64 Jer 51.24
64 Pay them back for their deeds, O LORD,
according to the work of their hands!
3.65 Deut 2.30
65 Give them anguish of heart;
your curse be on them!
66 Pursue them in anger and destroy them
from under the LORD's heavens.

4. God's anger is satisfied

4.1 2 Kgs 25.9,10
4 How the gold has grown dim,
how the pure gold is changed!
The sacred stones lie scattered
at the head of every street.

4.2 Isa 30.14 Jer 19.1,11
2 The precious children of Zion,
worth their weight in fine gold —
how they are reckoned as earthen pots,
the work of a potter's hands!

3 Even the jackals offer the breast
and nurse their young,
but my people has become cruel,
like the ostriches in the wilderness.

4 The tongue of the infant sticks
to the roof of its mouth for thirst;
the children beg for food,
but no one gives them anything.

5 Those who feasted on delicacies
perish in the streets;
those who were brought up in purple
cling to ash heaps.

4.6 Gen 19.25 Jer 20.16 Ezek 16.48
6 For the chastisement[g] of my people has been greater
than the punishment[h] of Sodom,
which was overthrown in a moment,
though no hand was laid on it.[i]

7 Her princes were purer than snow,

[g] Or *iniquity* [h] Or *sin* [i] Meaning of Heb uncertain

4.1ff This chapter contrasts the situation before the siege of Jerusalem with the situation after the siege. The sights and sounds of prosperity were gone because of the people's sin. This chapter warns us not to assume that when life is going well, it will always stay that way. We must be careful not to glory in our prosperity and fall into spiritual bankruptcy.

4.1–10 When a city was under siege, the city wall — built for protection — sealed the people inside. They could not get out to the fields to get food and water because the enemy was camped around the city. As food in the city ran out, the people watched their enemies harvest and eat the food in the fields. The siege was a test of wills to see who could outlast the other. Jerusalem was under siege for two years. Life became so harsh that people even ate their own children, and dead bodies were left to rot in the streets. All hope was gone.

4.6 Sodom, destroyed by fire from heaven because of its wickedness (Genesis 18.20 – 19.29), became a symbol of God's ultimate judgment. Yet the sin of Jerusalem was even greater than the sin of Sodom!

whiter than milk;
their bodies were more ruddy than coral,
their hair[j] like sapphire.[k]

8 Now their visage is blacker than soot;
they are not recognized in the streets.
Their skin has shriveled on their bones;
it has become as dry as wood.

9 Happier were those pierced by the sword
than those pierced by hunger,
whose life drains away, deprived
of the produce of the field.

10 The hands of compassionate women
have boiled their own children;
they became their food
in the destruction of my people.

11 The LORD gave full vent to his wrath;
he poured out his hot anger,
and kindled a fire in Zion
that consumed its foundations.

12 The kings of the earth did not believe,
nor did any of the inhabitants of the world,
that foe or enemy could enter
the gates of Jerusalem.

13 It was for the sins of her prophets
and the iniquities of her priests,
who shed the blood of the righteous
in the midst of her.

14 Blindly they wandered through the streets,
so defiled with blood
that no one was able
to touch their garments.

15 "Away! Unclean!" people shouted at them;
"Away! Away! Do not touch!"
So they became fugitives and wanderers;
it was said among the nations,
"They shall stay here no longer."

16 The LORD himself has scattered them,
he will regard them no more;
no honor was shown to the priests,
no favor to the elders.

17 Our eyes failed, ever watching

4.8 Ps 102.5 Lam 5.10
4.9 Lev 26.39
4.10 Deut 28.53-55 2 Kgs 6.26-30
4.11 Deut 32.22
4.12 Jer 21.13
4.13 Jer 2.30; 26.8,9
4.14 Deut 28.28,29 Isa 29.10 56.10; 59.9,10
4.15 Lev 13.45,46 Jer 45.5
4.16 Isa 9.14-16 Jer 52.24-27

j Meaning of Heb uncertain k Or *lapis lazuli*

4.13–15 To be defiled or unclean meant to be unfit to enter the temple or to worship before God. The priests and prophets should have been the most careful to maintain ceremonial purity so they could continue to perform their duties before God. But many priests and prophets did evil and were defiled. As the nation's leaders, their example led the people into sin and caused the ultimate downfall of the nation and its capital city, Jerusalem.

4.17 Judah asked Egypt to help them fight the Babylonian army.

4.17
Jer 37.7
Lam 1.7
Ezek 29.16

vainly for help;
we were watching eagerly
for a nation that could not save.

18 They dogged our steps
so that we could not walk in our streets;
our end drew near; our days were numbered;
for our end had come.

4.19
Deut 28.49
Jer 4.13

19 Our pursuers were swifter
than the eagles in the heavens;
they chased us on the mountains,
they lay in wait for us in the wilderness.

4.20
Jer 39.5
Ezek 12.12,13
Dan 4.12

20 The LORD's anointed, the breath of our life,
was taken in their pits—
the one of whom we said, "Under his shadow
we shall live among the nations."

4.21
Isa 34.7
Amos 1.11

21 Rejoice and be glad, O daughter Edom,
you that live in the land of Uz;
but to you also the cup shall pass;
you shall become drunk and strip yourself bare.

4.22
Isa 40.2
Jer 49.10

22 The punishment of your iniquity, O daughter Zion, is accomplished,
he will keep you in exile no longer;
but your iniquity, O daughter Edom, he will punish,
he will uncover your sins.

5. Jeremiah pleads for restoration

5 Remember, O LORD, what has befallen us;
look, and see our disgrace!

5.2
Isa 1.7
Hos 8.7,8

2 Our inheritance has been turned over to strangers,
our homes to aliens.

5.3
Jer 15.8; 18.21

3 We have become orphans, fatherless;
our mothers are like widows.

5.4
Isa 3.1

4 We must pay for the water we drink;
the wood we get must be bought.
5 With a yoke[l] on our necks we are hard driven;
we are weary, we are given no rest.
6 We have made a pact with[m] Egypt and Assyria,
to get enough bread.

5.7
Jer 14.20; 16.12

7 Our ancestors sinned; they are no more,
and we bear their iniquities.

[l] Symmachus: Heb lacks *With a yoke* [m] Heb *have given the hand to*

Egypt gave Judah false hope—they started to help, but then retreated (Jeremiah 37.5–7). Jeremiah warned Judah not to ally itself with Egypt. He told the leaders to rely on God, but they refused to listen.

4.20 King Zedekiah, although called "the Lord's anointed," had little spiritual depth and leadership power. Instead of putting his faith in God and listening to God's true prophet, Jeremiah, he listened to the false prophets. To make matters worse, the people chose to follow and trust in their king (2 Chronicles 36.11–23). They chose the path of false confidence and complacency, wanting to feel secure rather than follow the directives God was giving his people through Jeremiah. But the object of their confidence—King Zedekiah—was captured.

4.21, 22 Edom was Judah's archenemy, even though they had a common ancestor, Isaac (see Genesis 25.19–26; 36.1). Edom actively aided Babylon in the siege of Jerusalem. As a reward, Nebuchadnezzar gave the outlying lands of Judah to Edom. Jeremiah said that Edom would be judged for her treachery against her brothers. (See also Jeremiah 49.7–22; Ezekiel 25.12–14; Amos 9.12; Obadiah 1.1–21.)

5.1ff After expressing the full extent of his or her grief, the true believer should turn to God in prayer. Here Jeremiah prayed for mercy for his people. At the end of his prayer he wondered if God was "angry with us beyond measure." But God would not stay angry with them forever—as it says in Micah 7.18, "He does not retain his anger forever, because he delights in showing clemency."

8 Slaves rule over us;
there is no one to deliver us from their hand.
9 We get our bread at the peril of our lives,
because of the sword in the wilderness.
10 Our skin is black as an oven
from the scorching heat of famine.
11 Women are raped in Zion,
virgins in the towns of Judah.
12 Princes are hung up by their hands;
no respect is shown to the elders.
13 Young men are compelled to grind,
and boys stagger under loads of wood.
14 The old men have left the city gate,
the young men their music.
15 The joy of our hearts has ceased;
our dancing has been turned to mourning.
16 The crown has fallen from our head;
woe to us, for we have sinned!
17 Because of this our hearts are sick,
because of these things our eyes have grown dim:
18 because of Mount Zion, which lies desolate;
jackals prowl over it.

19 But you, O LORD, reign forever;
your throne endures to all generations.
20 Why have you forgotten us completely?
Why have you forsaken us these many days?
21 Restore us to yourself, O LORD, that we may be restored;
renew our days as of old—
22 unless you have utterly rejected us,
and are angry with us beyond measure.

5.9 Jer 40.9-12
5.11 Isa 13.16 Zech 14.2
5.12 Isa 47.6 Lam 4.16
5.14 Isa 24.8 Jer 7.34
5.15 Jer 25.10
5.17 Job 17.7 Ps 6.7
5.19 Ps 45.6
5.20 Ps 13.1; 44.24
5.21 Jer 31.18

5.14 During peace and prosperity, the leaders and older men of the city would sit at the city gate and talk over politics, theology, and philosophy, and conduct business.

5.22 A high calling flouted by low living results in deep suffering. Lamentations gives us a portrait of the bitter suffering the people of Jerusalem experienced when sin caught up with them and God turned his back on them. Every material goal they had lived for collapsed. But although God turned away from them because of their sin, he did not abandon them—that was their great hope. Despite their sinful past, God would restore them if they returned to him. Hope is found only in the Lord. Thus our grief should turn us toward him, not away from him.

PROPHECIES AGAINST THE NATIONS

The Old Testament prophets usually targeted Israel and Judah in their messages. But other surrounding nations also received warnings of impending judgment. Ezekiel prophesied against six of the nations that surrounded Israel. But Ezekiel was not the only one. These nations were also condemned by other prophets of God.

AMMON	The nation of Ammon was located east of the Jordan River. They were related to the Israelites because they were descendants of Lot. Ezekiel said that God would make them slaves of the Babylonians because they rejoiced at Israel's fall (Ezekiel 25.1-7).	Other prophets that spoke against Ammon included Jeremiah (49.1-6), Amos (1.13-15), and Zephaniah (2.8-11).
EDOM	The nation of Edom was located south of the Dead Sea. They were related to the Israelites as descendants of Esau. Ezekiel said Israel would someday conquer the land of Edom because the Edomites had acted revengefully against them (Ezekiel 25.12-14).	Other prophets that spoke against Edom included Jeremiah (49.7-22), Joel (3.19), Amos (9.11, 12), and Obadiah (1.10-21).
EGYPT	The Egyptians lived along the Nile River. The Israelites had lived in Egypt for over 400 years, and were delivered from slavery there by Moses. Ezekiel promised that the Babylonians would plunder Egypt because the Egyptians did not respect the Lord (Ezekiel 29.1—32.32).	Other prophets that spoke against Egypt included Moses (Exodus 5.1—12.42), Isaiah (19.1—20.6), Jeremiah (46.1-28), Daniel (11.42-43), Joel (3.19), and Zechariah (10.11; 14.18, 19).
MOAB	The nation of Moab was located to the south of Ammon and east of the Dead Sea. They were related to the Israelites as they were descended from Lot. Because Moab said that Judah is just like any other nation, God would sell them with Ammon into the Babylonians' hands (Ezekiel 25.8-11).	Other prophets that spoke against Moab included Isaiah (15.1—16.14), Jeremiah (9.26; 25.21; 27.3; 48.1-47), Amos (2.1-3), and Zephaniah (2.8-11).
PHILISTIA	The Philistines lived in southwestern Palestine, along the Mediterranean coast. They were constant enemies of the Israelites from the time of Joshua to Solomon. Ezekiel said they would be destroyed because of their unending hostilities toward God's people (Ezekiel 25.15-17).	Other prophets that spoke against Philistia included Jeremiah (47.5-7), Amos (1.6-8; 6.2), Obadiah (1.19), Zephaniah (2.4, 5), and Zechariah (9.5-7).
PHOENICIA (TYRE AND SIDON)	The Phoenicians lived on the Mediterranean coast, north of Palestine. They had always been good (though often competing) trading partners with the Israelites. Ezekiel said that they would be destroyed because they had rejoiced at Israel's demise (Ezekiel 26.1—28.24).	Other prophets that spoke against Tyre and Sidon included Amos (1.9,10), Jeremiah (25.22, 27.1-11), and Zechariah (9.2-4).

EZEKIEL

Jeremiah becomes a prophet to Judah 627 B.C.	*Daniel taken captive to Babylon 605*	*Ezekiel taken captive to Babylon 597*	*Ezekiel becomes a prophet to exiles 593*	*Judah falls; Jerusa destro 586*

VITAL STATISTICS

PURPOSE:
To announce God's judgment on Israel and other nations and to foretell the eventual salvation for God's people

AUTHOR:
Ezekiel—the son of Buzi, a Zadokite priest

TO WHOM WRITTEN:
The Jews in captivity in Babylon and God's people everywhere

DATE WRITTEN:
Approximately 571 B.C.

SETTING:
Ezekiel was a younger contemporary of Jeremiah. While Jeremiah ministered to the people still in Judah, Ezekiel prophesied to those already exiled in Babylon after the defeat of Jehoiachin. He was taken there in 597 B.C.

KEY VERSES:
"I will take you from the nations, and gather you from all the countries, and bring you into your own land. I will sprinkle clean water upon you, and you shall be clean from all your uncleannesses, and from all your idols I will cleanse you. A new heart I will give you, and a new spirit I will put within you; and I will remove from your body the heart of stone and give you a heart of flesh" (36.24–26).

KEY PEOPLE:
Ezekiel, Israel's leaders, Ezekiel's wife, Nebuchadnezzar, the "Prince"

KEY PLACES:
Jerusalem, Babylon, and Egypt

A computer can be programmed to respond at your command. And by conditioning a dog with rewards and punishments, you can teach him to obey. But as every parent knows, children are not so easily taught. People have wills and must choose to submit, to follow the instructions of their parents and leaders. Surely discipline is part of the process—boys and girls should know the consequences of disobedience—but there is a choice. They are not machines or animals.

God's children must learn to obey their heavenly Father. Created in his image, they have a choice, and God allows them to choose.

Ezekiel was a man who chose to obey God. Although he was a priest (1.3), he served as a Jewish "street preacher" in Babylon for 22 years, telling everyone about God's judgment and salvation, and calling them to repentance and obedience. And Ezekiel *lived* what he preached. During his ministry God told him to illustrate his messages with dramatic object lessons. Some of these acts included (1) lying on his side for 390 days during which he could eat only one eight-ounce meal a day cooked over manure, (2) shaving his head and beard, and (3) showing no sorrow when his wife died. He obeyed and faithfully proclaimed God's Word.

God may not ask you to do anything quite so dramatic or difficult; but if he did, would you do it?

The book of Ezekiel chronicles the prophet's life and ministry. Beginning with his call as a prophet and commissioning as a "watchman for Israel" (chapters 1—3), Ezekiel immediately begins to preach and demonstrate God's truth, as he predicts the approaching siege and destruction of Jerusalem (chapters 4—24). This devastation would be God's judgment for the people's idolatry. Ezekiel challenges them to turn from their wicked ways. In the next section, he speaks to the surrounding nations, prophesying that God will judge them for their sins as well (chapters 25—32). The book concludes with a message of hope, as Ezekiel proclaims the faithfulness of God and foretells the future blessings for God's people (chapters 33—48).

As you read this exciting record, watch Ezekiel fearlessly preach the word of God to the exiled Jews in the streets of Babylon and hear the timeless truth of God's love and power. Think about each person's responsibility to trust God, and about the inevitability of God's judgment against idolatry, rebellion, and indifference. Then commit yourself to obey God, whatever, wherever, and whenever he asks.

THE BLUEPRINT

A. MESSAGES OF DOOM
(1.1—24.27)
1. Ezekiel's call and commission
2. Visions of sin and judgment
3. Punishment is certain

While Jeremiah was prophesying in Jerusalem that the city would soon fall to the Babylonians, Ezekiel was giving the same message to the captives who were already in Babylon. Like those in Jerusalem, the captives stubbornly believed that Jerusalem would not fall and that they would soon return to their land. Ezekiel warned them that punishment was certain because of their sins and that God was purifying his people. God will always punish sin, whether we believe it or not.

Ezekiel's ministry ends 571

Babylon overthrown by Cyrus 539

First exiles return to Judah 537

B. MESSAGES AGAINST FOREIGN NATIONS (25.1—32.32)	Ezekiel condemns the sinful actions of seven nations. The people in these nations were saying that God was obviously too weak to defend his people and the city of Jerusalem. But God was allowing them to be defeated in order to punish them for their sins. These heathen nations, however, would face a similar fate and then they would know that God is all-powerful. Those who dare to mock God today will also face a terrible fate.
C. MESSAGES OF HOPE (33.1—48.35) 1. Restoring the people of God 2. Restoring the worship of God	After the fall of Jerusalem, Ezekiel delivered messages of future restoration and hope for the people. God is holy, but Jerusalem and the temple had become defiled. The nation had to be cleansed through 70 years of captivity. Ezekiel gives a vivid picture of the unchangeable holiness of God. We too must gain a vision of the glory of God, a fresh sense of his greatness as we face the struggles of daily life.

MEGATHEMES

THEME	EXPLANATION	IMPORTANCE
God's holiness	Ezekiel had a vision that revealed God's absolute moral perfection. God was spiritually and morally superior to Israel's corrupt and compromising society. Ezekiel wrote to let the people know that God was also present in Babylon, not just in Jerusalem.	Because God is morally perfect, he can help us live above our tendency to compromise with this world. When we focus on his greatness, he gives us the power to overcome sin and to reflect his holiness.
Sin	Israel had sinned, and God's punishment came. The fall of Jerusalem and the Babylonian exile were used by God to correct the rebels and draw them back from their sinful way of life. Ezekiel warned them that not only was the nation responsible for sin, but each individual was also accountable to God.	We cannot excuse ourselves from our responsibilities before God. We are accountable to God for our choices. Rather than neglect him, we must recognize sin for what it is—rebellion against God—and choose to follow him instead.
Restoration	Ezekiel consoles the people by telling them that the day will come when God will restore those who turn from sin. God will be their King and Shepherd. He will give his people a new heart to worship him, and he will establish a new government and a new temple.	The certainty of future restoration encourages believers in times of trial. But we must be faithful to God because we love him, not merely for what he can do for us. Is our faith in *him* or merely in our future benefits?
Leaders	Ezekiel condemned the shepherds (unfaithful priests and leaders) who led the people astray. By contrast, he served as a caring shepherd and a watchful sentry to warn the people about their sin. One day God's perfect Shepherd, the Messiah, will lead his people.	Jesus is our perfect leader. If we truly want him to lead us, our devotion must be more than talk. If we are given the responsibility of leading others, we must take care of them even if it means sacrificing personal pleasure, happiness, time, or money. We are responsible for those we lead.
Worship	An angel gave Ezekiel a vision of the temple in great detail. God's holy presence had departed from Israel and the temple because of sin. The building of a future temple portrays the return of God's presence. God will cleanse his people and restore true worship.	All of God's promises will be fulfilled under the rule of the Messiah. The faithful followers will be restored to perfect fellowship with God and with one another. To be prepared for this time, we must focus on God. We do this through regular worship. Through worship we learn about God's holiness and the changes we must make in how we live.

A. MESSAGES OF DOOM (1.1 – 24.27)

Ezekiel prophesied to the exiles in Babylon. He had to dispel the false hope that Israel's captivity would be short, explain the reasons for the severe judgments on their nation, and bring a message of future hope. Although the people did not respond positively, they heard the messages and knew the truth. God's people were not without explanation and direction, and neither are we.

1. Ezekiel's call and commission

A vision of living beings

1 In the thirtieth year, in the fourth month, on the fifth day of the month, as I was **1.1** Ezek 40.2
among the exiles by the river Chebar, the heavens were opened, and I saw
visions of God. 2On the fifth day of the month (it was the fifth year of the exile of
King Jehoiachin), 3the word of the LORD came to the priest Ezekiel son of Buzi, in
the land of the Chaldeans by the river Chebar; and the hand of the LORD was on him **1.4**
there. Ezek 13.11,13
4 As I looked, a stormy wind came out of the north: a great cloud with bright- **1.5** Ezek 10.15-17, 20
ness around it and fire flashing forth continually, and in the middle of the fire,
something like gleaming amber. 5In the middle of it was something like four living **1.6** Ezek 10.14,21
creatures. This was their appearance: they were of human form. 6Each had four **1.7**
faces, and each of them had four wings. 7Their legs were straight, and the soles of Rev 1.15; 2.18

1.1 Ezekiel, born and raised in the land of Judah, was preparing to become a priest in God's temple when the Babylonians attacked in 597 B.C. and carried him away along with 10,000 other captives (2 Kings 24.10–14). The nation was on the brink of complete destruction. Five years later, when Ezekiel was 30 (the normal age for becoming a priest), God called him to be a prophet. During the first six years when Ezekiel ministered in Babylon ("the land of the Chaldeans," 1.3), Jeremiah was preaching to the Jews still in Judah, and Daniel was serving in Nebuchadnezzar's court. The river Chebar connected to the Euphrates in Babylonia and was the location of a Jewish settlement of exiles.

1.1 Why did the Jewish exiles in Babylon need a prophet? God wanted Ezekiel to (1) help the exiles understand why they had been taken captive, (2) dispel the false hope that captivity was going to be short, (3) bring a new message of hope, and (4) call the people to a new awareness of their dependence upon God.

1.1 God communicated to Ezekiel in visions. A vision is a miraculous revelation of God's truth. These visions seem strange to us because they are *apocalyptic*. This means that Ezekiel saw symbolic pictures that vividly convey an idea. Daniel and John were others in the Bible who used apocalyptic imagery. The people in exile had lost their perspective of God's purpose and presence, and Ezekiel came to them with a vision from God to warn them of sin's consequences before it was too late.

1.1ff Ezekiel's latest dated message from God (29.17) was given in 571 B.C. He was taken captive during the second Babylonian invasion of Judah in 597 B.C. The Babylonians invaded Judah a third and final time in 586 B.C., completely destroying Jerusalem, burning the temple, and deporting the rest of the people (see 2 Kings 25). Ezekiel dates all his messages from the year he was taken captive (597). His first prophecy to the exiles occurred four years after he arrived in the land of Babylon (593 B.C.).

1.3 The name *Ezekiel* means "God is strong" or "God makes strong." In a very real sense, this sums up the basic message of the book – that in spite of the captivity, God's sovereign strength prevails and he will judge his enemies and restore his true people.

1.4ff In this first vision, God calls Ezekiel to be a prophet (see 2.5). Nothing in his previous experience had prepared him for such a display of God's presence and power. The stormy wind from the north was a symbol of the great armies of Babylon approaching Jerusalem to be God's instrument of judgment upon the nation of Judah. Around the great cloud shone a brilliant light; from the midst of the cloud came four living creatures. They showed Ezekiel that Jerusalem's coming destruction was God's punishment of Judah for its sins. The Babylonian attack was certainly a physical disaster, but the four living creatures dramatically portrayed the truth that it was also a spiritual judgment. (These living creatures are also seen in Revelation 4.6, 7.)

Ezekiel was far away from the temple in Jerusalem, the physical symbol of God's presence, when he received this vision. Through this vision he learned that God is present everywhere, and his activities in heaven are shaping the events on earth.

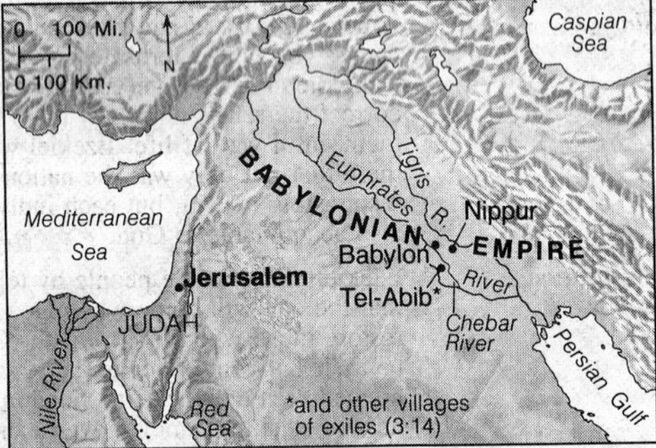

EXILE IN BABYLON Ezekiel worked for God right where he was—among the exiles in various colonies near the Chebar River in Babylonia. Jerusalem and its temple lay over 500 miles away, but Ezekiel helped the people understand that although they were far from home, they did not need to be far from God.

1.5 Each of the four living creatures had four faces, symbolizing God's perfect nature. Some believe that the lion represented strength; the ox, diligent service; the human, intelligence; and the eagle, divinity. Others see these as the most majestic of God's creatures and say that they therefore represent God's whole creation. The early church fathers saw a connection between these beings and the four Gospels: the lion with Matthew, presenting Christ as the Lion of Judah; the ox with Mark, portraying Christ as the Servant; the human with Luke, portraying Christ as the perfect human; the eagle with John, portraying Christ as the Son of God, high and divine. The vision of John in Revelation 4 parallels Ezekiel's vision.

their feet were like the sole of a calf's foot; and they sparkled like burnished bronze.
8 Under their wings on their four sides they had human hands. And the four had
their faces and their wings thus: 9 their wings touched one another; each of them
moved straight ahead, without turning as they moved. 10 As for the appearance of
their faces: the four had the face of a human being, the face of a lion on the right
side, the face of an ox on the left side, and the face of an eagle; 11 such were their
faces. Their wings were spread out above; each creature had two wings, each of
which touched the wing of another, while two covered their bodies. 12 Each moved
straight ahead; wherever the spirit would go, they went, without turning as they
went. 13 In the middle of[a] the living creatures there was something that looked like
burning coals of fire, like torches moving to and fro among the living creatures; the
fire was bright, and lightning issued from the fire. 14 The living creatures darted to
and fro, like a flash of lightning.
15 As I looked at the living creatures, I saw a wheel on the earth beside the
living creatures, one for each of the four of them.[b] 16 As for the appearance of the
wheels and their construction: their appearance was like the gleaming of beryl; and
the four had the same form, their construction being something like a wheel within
a wheel. 17 When they moved, they moved in any of the four directions without
veering as they moved. 18 Their rims were tall and awesome, for the rims of all four
were full of eyes all around. 19 When the living creatures moved, the wheels moved
beside them; and when the living creatures rose from the earth, the wheels rose.
20 Wherever the spirit would go, they went, and the wheels rose along with them;
for the spirit of the living creatures was in the wheels. 21 When they moved, the
others moved; when they stopped, the others stopped; and when they rose from the
earth, the wheels rose along with them; for the spirit of the living creatures was in
the wheels.
22 Over the heads of the living creatures there was something like a dome,
shining like crystal,[c] spread out above their heads. 23 Under the dome their wings
were stretched out straight, one toward another; and each of the creatures had two
wings covering its body. 24 When they moved, I heard the sound of their wings like
the sound of mighty waters, like the thunder of the Almighty,[d] a sound of tumult
like the sound of an army; when they stopped, they let down their wings. 25 And
there came a voice from above the dome over their heads; when they stopped, they
let down their wings.
26 And above the dome over their heads there was something like a throne,
in appearance like sapphire;[e] and seated above the likeness of a throne was

1.8 Ezek 10.8,21
1.9 Ezek 10.22
1.10 Ezek 10.14; Rev 4.7
1.11 Isa 6.2; Ezek 10.16,19
1.13 Ps 104.4; Dan 10.5,6; Rev 4.5
1.14 Zech 4.10; Mt 24.27
1.16 Ezek 10.9-13
1.18 Prov 15.3; Ezek 10.9-13; Zech 4.10; Rev 4.6,8
1.19 Ezek 10.16, 17,19
1.22 Ex 24.10; Job 37.22; Ezek 10.1; Rev 4.6; 22.1
1.24 Ezek 10.5; 43.2; Dan 10.6; Rev 1.15; 19.6
1.26 Ex 24.10; Isa 6.1; 54.11; Ezek 10.1; 24.10; 43.6; Dan 7.9; Rev 1.13

[a] Gk OL: Heb *And the appearance of* [b] Heb *of their faces* [c] Gk: Heb *like the awesome crystal* [d] Traditional rendering of Heb *Shaddai* [e] Or *lapis lazuli*

EZEKIEL served as a prophet to the exiles in Babylon from 593–571 B.C.

Climate of the times	• Ezekiel and his people are taken to Babylon as captives. • The Jews become foreigners in a strange land ruled by an authoritarian government.
Main message	Because of the people's sins, God allowed the nation of Judah to be destroyed. But there was still hope—God promised to restore the land to those who remained faithful to him.
Importance of message	God never forgets those who faithfully seek to obey him. They have a glorious future ahead.
Contemporary Prophets	Daniel (605–536) Habakkuk (612–589) Jeremiah (627–586)

1.16–18 The "wheel within a wheel" is probably a picture of two wheels at right angles to each other, one on a north-south and the other on an east-west axis. Thus able to move anywhere, these wheels show that God is present everywhere and is able to see all things (1.18). God rules all of life and history. Though the exiles had experienced great change, God was still in control.

1.26 This human revealed God's holiness and prepared Ezekiel for what God was about to tell him. He represented God himself on the throne. In a similar way, Christ revealed God in human form and prepared us for his message of salvation. Christ came into history in a real, human body.

something that seemed like a human form. 27 Upward from what appeared like the
loins I saw something like gleaming amber, something that looked like fire enclosed all around; and downward from what looked like the loins I saw something
that looked like fire, and there was a splendor all around. 28 Like the bow in a cloud
on a rainy day, such was the appearance of the splendor all around. This was the
appearance of the likeness of the glory of the LORD.
When I saw it, I fell on my face, and I heard the voice of someone speaking.

God calls Ezekiel

2 He said to me: O mortal,[f] stand up on your feet, and I will speak with you.
2 And when he spoke to me, a spirit entered into me and set me on my feet; and
I heard him speaking to me. 3 He said to me, Mortal, I am sending you to the people
of Israel, to a nation[g] of rebels who have rebelled against me; they and their ancestors have transgressed against me to this very day. 4 The descendants are impudent
and stubborn. I am sending you to them, and you shall say to them, "Thus says the
Lord GOD." 5 Whether they hear or refuse to hear (for they are a rebellious house),
they shall know that there has been a prophet among them. 6 And you, O mortal, do
not be afraid of them, and do not be afraid of their words, though briers and thorns
surround you and you live among scorpions; do not be afraid of their words, and do
not be dismayed at their looks, for they are a rebellious house. 7 You shall speak my
words to them, whether they hear or refuse to hear; for they are a rebellious house.
8 But you, mortal, hear what I say to you; do not be rebellious like that rebellious house; open your mouth and eat what I give you. 9 I looked, and a hand was
stretched out to me, and a written scroll was in it. 10 He spread it before me; it had
writing on the front and on the back, and written on it were words of lamentation
and mourning and woe.

3 He said to me, O mortal, eat what is offered to you; eat this scroll, and go,
speak to the house of Israel. 2 So I opened my mouth, and he gave me the scroll
to eat. 3 He said to me, Mortal, eat this scroll that I give you and fill your stomach
with it. Then I ate it; and in my mouth it was as sweet as honey.

1.27 Gen 9.13 Ezek 3.23; 8.2 2 Thess 1:7 Rev 1.17; 4.3 10.1
2.2 Ezek 3.24 Dan 8.18
2.3 Dan 9.5-13
2.5 Ezek 3.11,27 Mt 10.12-15 Lk 10.10,11 Jn 15.22 Acts 13.46
2.6 2 Sam 23.6,7 Isa 51.12 Jer 1.8
2.7 Ezek 3.17
2.8 1 Tim 4.14-16 Rev 10.9
2.9 Dan 5.5; 10.10 Rev 5.1-5; 8.13 10.8-11
3.2 Jer 25.17 Acts 26.19
3.3 Ps 19.10 119.102,103 Jer 6.11; 15.16 Rev 10.9,10

[f] Or *son of man*; Heb *ben adam* (and so throughout the book when Ezekiel is addressed) [g] Syr: Heb *to nations*

1.27, 28 The four living creatures and the four wheels are powerful pictures of judgment, yet the rainbow ("bow in a cloud on a rainy day") over the throne symbolizes God's never-ending faithfulness to his people. Just as God sent a rainbow to Noah to symbolize his promise never again to destroy the earth by a flood (Genesis 9.8–17), so this rainbow symbolizes his promise to preserve those who remain faithful to him. The purpose of God's judgment is to correct us and, ultimately, to allow perfect peace and righteousness to reign on the earth forever.

1.27, 28 The glory of the Lord appeared like a bright light and a dazzling fire to Ezekiel. He fell to the ground, overwhelmed by the contrast between God's holiness and his own sinfulness and insignificance. Eventually every person will fall before God, either out of reverence and awe for his mercy or out of fear of his judgment. Based on the way you are living today, how will you respond?

2.1 The immortal God addressed Ezekiel by calling him *mortal*, emphasizing the distance between them. It is amazing that God chooses to work his divine will on earth through finite, imperfect beings. We are made from dust, yet God chooses to place within us his life and breath, and asks us to serve him.

2.2 We can only imagine what it was like for Ezekiel to experience this vision. Certainly there was much he did not understand, but he knew that each part had significance because it came from God. When God saw Ezekiel's open and obedient attitude, he filled him with his Spirit and gave him power for the job ahead. God doesn't expect us to understand everything about him, but to be willing and obedient servants, faithful to what we know is true and right.

2.3–5 Business defines success in terms of giving customers what they want. Ezekiel, however, was to give God's message to the people whether they would listen or not. The measure of Ezekiel's success would not be how well the people responded, but how well he obeyed God and thus fulfilled God's purpose for him. Isaiah and Jeremiah also prophesied with little positive response (see Isaiah 6.9–12; Jeremiah 1.17–19). God's truth does not depend on how people respond. God will not judge us for how well others respond to our faith, but for how faithful we have been. God always gives us the strength to accomplish what he asks us to do.

2.4, 5 God called the people "impudent and stubborn" because they refused to admit their sin. Rebellion was the nation's primary characteristic at this time. Even when God pointed out their wrongdoing, the people ignored the truth. Is God pointing at sin in your life? Don't be stubborn – confess your sin and begin to live for God. By obeying him now you will be ready for God's final review of your life.

2.6–8 God gave Ezekiel the difficult responsibility of presenting his message to ungrateful and abusive people. Sometimes we must be an example or share our faith with unkind people. The Lord told Ezekiel not to be afraid and join the rebels, but to speak his words whether or not the people would listen. He also wants us to tell the Good News "whether the time is favorable or unfavorable" (2 Timothy 4.2).

2.6–10 Four times God told Ezekiel not to be afraid or dismayed. When God's Spirit is within us, we can lay aside our fears of rejection or ridicule. God's strength is powerful enough to help us live for him even under the heaviest criticism.

2.9, 10 Ancient books were usually scrolls, one page (up to 30 feet long) rolled up simultaneously from both ends. Normally, scrolls had writing on only one side. But in this case, the warnings overflowed to the scroll's other side, showing the full measure of judgment about to come down upon Judah.

3.5 Ps 81.5 Jonah 1.2; 3.2-4 Acts 26.17,18
3.6 Isa 28.11
3.7 Ezek 2.4 Lk 10.16 Jn 5.40-47
3.8 Jer 1.18

4 He said to me: Mortal, go to the house of Israel and speak my very words to
them. 5 For you are not sent to a people of obscure speech and difficult language,
but to the house of Israel— 6 not to many peoples of obscure speech and difficult
language, whose words you cannot understand. Surely, if I sent you to them, they
would listen to you. 7 But the house of Israel will not listen to you, for they are not
willing to listen to me; because all the house of Israel have a hard forehead and a
stubborn heart. 8 See, I have made your face hard against their faces, and your
forehead hard against their foreheads. 9 Like the hardest stone, harder than flint, I
have made your forehead; do not fear them or be dismayed at their looks, for they

---

EZEKIEL

Although Ezekiel's visions and prophecies were clear and vivid, very little is known about the prophet's personal life. He was among the thousands of young men deported from Judah to Babylon when King Jehoiakim surrendered. Until those tragic days, Ezekiel was being trained for the priesthood. But during the exile in Babylon, God called Ezekiel to be his prophet during one of Israel's darkest times.

Ezekiel experienced the same kind of shocking encounter with God that Isaiah had reported 150 years earlier. Like Isaiah, Ezekiel was never the same after his personal encounter with God. Although God's messages through both these prophets had many points in common, the conditions in which they lived were very different. Isaiah warned of the coming storm; Ezekiel spoke in the midst of the storm of national defeat that devastated his people. He announced that even Jerusalem would not escape destruction. In addition, during this time Ezekiel had to endure the pain of his wife's death.

God's description of Ezekiel as a watchman (sentinel) on the walls of the city captures the personal nature of his ministry. A watchman's job was dangerous. If he failed at his post, he and the entire city might be destroyed. His own safety depended on the quality of his work. The importance of each person's accountability before God was a central part of Ezekiel's message. He taught the exiles that God expected personal obedience and worship from each of them.

As in Ezekiel's day, it is easy for us today to forget that God has a personal interest in each one of us. We may feel insignificant or out of control when we look at world events. But knowing that God is ultimately in control, that he cares, and that he is willing to be known by us can bring a new sense of purpose to our lives. How do you measure your worth? Are you valuable because of your achievements and potential, or because God, your Creator and Designer, declares you valuable?

Strengths and accomplishments:
- Was a priest by training, a prophet by God's call
- Received vivid visions and delivered powerful messages
- Served as God's messenger during Israel's captivity in Babylon
- God shaped his character to fit his mission—a tough and stalwart man to reach a hard and stubborn people (Ezekiel 3.8)

Lessons from his life:
- Even the repeated failures of his people will not prevent God's plan for the world from being fulfilled
- Each person's response to God determines his or her eternal destiny
- In seemingly hopeless situations God still has people through whom he can work

Vital statistics:
- Where: Babylon
- Occupation: Prophet to the captives in Babylon
- Relatives: Father: Buzi. Wife: Unknown
- Contemporaries: Jehoiachin, Jeremiah, Jehoiakim, Nebuchadnezzar

Key verses:
"He said to me: Mortal, all my words that I shall speak to you receive in your heart and hear with your ears; then go to the exiles, to your people, and speak to them. Say to them, 'Thus says the Lord God'; whether they hear or refuse to hear" (Ezekiel 3.10, 11).

Ezekiel's story is told in the book of Ezekiel and 2 Kings 24.14–17.

3.1–3 In his vision, Ezekiel ate God's message and found this spiritual food not only good for him, but also sweet as honey (see Revelation 10.8–10 for a similar use of this image). If you "digest" God's Word, you will find that not only does it make you stronger in your faith, but its wisdom sweetens your life. You need to feed yourself spiritually just as you do physically. This means doing more than simply giving God's message a casual glance. You must make digesting God's Word a regular part of your life.

3.8, 9 Belief in God is not a crutch for those too weak to stand on their own. God makes his followers strong enough to stand against anything or anyone, including those who hate what is right. Just as God gave Ezekiel tough love (a hard face) and tough faith (a hard forehead), he wants to give you the stability, perseverance, and insight you need to live up to the great task he has given you. Give yourself over to God's conditioning, and let him get your life in shape.

are a rebellious house. 10He said to me: Mortal, all my words that I shall speak to
you receive in your heart and hear with your ears; 11then go to the exiles, to your
people, and speak to them. Say to them, "Thus says the Lord GOD"; whether they
hear or refuse to hear.

3.10 Ezek 2.8 Lk 8.15 1 Thess 2.13
3.11 Ezek 2.5,7

God appoints Ezekiel to be a watchman

12 Then the spirit lifted me up, and as the glory of the LORD rose[h] from its
place, I heard behind me the sound of loud rumbling; 13it was the sound of the
wings of the living creatures brushing against one another, and the sound of the
wheels beside them, that sounded like a loud rumbling. 14The spirit lifted me up
and bore me away; I went in bitterness in the heat of my spirit, the hand of the LORD
being strong upon me. 15I came to the exiles at Tel-abib, who lived by the river
Chebar.[i] And I sat there among them, stunned, for seven days.
16 At the end of seven days, the word of the LORD came to me: 17Mortal, I have
made you a sentinel for the house of Israel; whenever you hear a word from my
mouth, you shall give them warning from me. 18If I say to the wicked, "You shall
surely die," and you give them no warning, or speak to warn the wicked from their
wicked way, in order to save their life, those wicked persons shall die for their
iniquity; but their blood I will require at your hand. 19But if you warn the wicked,
and they do not turn from their wickedness, or from their wicked way, they shall
die for their iniquity; but you will have saved your life. 20Again, if the righteous
turn from their righteousness and commit iniquity, and I lay a stumbling block
before them, they shall die; because you have not warned them, they shall die for
their sin, and their righteous deeds that they have done shall not be remembered;
but their blood I will require at your hand. 21If, however, you warn the righteous
not to sin, and they do not sin, they shall surely live, because they took warning;
and you will have saved your life.
22 Then the hand of the LORD was upon me there; and he said to me, Rise up,
go out into the valley, and there I will speak with you. 23So I rose up and went out
into the valley; and the glory of the LORD stood there, like the glory that I had seen

3.12 Ezek 8.3 Acts 2.2; 8.39
3.13 Ezek 1.15,24 10.5,16,17
3.14 Ezek 8.1
3.17 Isa 52.8; 58.1 Ezek 33.7-9
3.18 Ezek 33.6,8
3.19 Ezek 33.3,9
3.20 Ezek 18.24
3.21 Acts 20.31
3.22 Acts 9.6
3.23 Ezek 1.28; 8.4 Acts 7.55

h Cn: Heb *and blessed be the glory of the* LORD i Two Mss Syr: Heb *Chebar, and to where they lived.* Another reading is *Chebar, and I sat where they sat*

3.10, 11 Ezekiel was to receive God's words in his heart before preaching them to others. God's message must sink deep into your heart and show in your actions before you can effectively help others understand and apply it.

3.14, 15 Ezekiel was angry, not at God, but at the sins and attitudes of the people. His extraordinary vision had ended, and now he had to begin the tedious job of prophesying among his people, who cared little about God's messages. Before the exile, the people had heard Jeremiah, but they would not listen. Now Ezekiel had to give a similar message, and he expected to be rejected as well. But he had the vision of the living creatures and the rumbling wheels on his side. He had nothing to fear, because God was with him. Despite the probable outcome, Ezekiel obeyed God.

As we grow, we will have times of great joy when we feel close to God, and times when sins, struggles, or everyday tasks overwhelm us. Like Ezekiel, we should obey God even when we don't feel like it. Don't let feelings hinder your obedience.

3.14, 15 Ezekiel sat quietly among the people for seven days. This was the customary period of mourning for the dead (Genesis 50.10; 1 Samuel 31.13; Job 2.13). Ezekiel was mourning for those who were spiritually dead. Tel-abib was a settlement of Jews who were exiled from Jerusalem.

3.17, 18 A watchman ("sentinel") stood on the city wall and warned the people of approaching danger. Ezekiel's role was to be a spiritual watchman, warning the people of coming judgment. Just as a watchman on the wall would pay with his life if he failed to warn the city of approaching enemies, some think that Ezekiel would have been punished by death if he had refused to warn the people of coming judgment. Others believe it simply means that God would hold Ezekiel responsible for those lost.

3.18 God had already told Ezekiel that the people would not listen, so why should he bother to tell them God's message? God wanted the people to know they had been warned. Ezekiel's job was to obey God. We are responsible to tell others about God's judgment and his message of salvation, although we are not held responsible for how they respond. But if we refuse to tell others what we know, God will judge us. Remember God's words to Ezekiel when you are tempted to remain silent among those who don't believe.

3.18–21 In these verses, God is not talking about loss of salvation but rather about physical death. If the people back in Judah continued in their sins, they and their land and cities would be destroyed by Nebuchadnezzar's armies. If, on the other hand, they turned to God, he would spare them. God would hold Ezekiel responsible for his fellow Jews if he failed to warn them of the consequences of their sins. All people are individually responsible to God, but believers have a special responsibility to warn unbelievers of the consequences of rejecting God. If we fail to do this, God will hold us responsible for what happens to them. This should motivate us to begin sharing our faith with others – by both word and deed – and to avoid becoming callous or unconcerned in our attitude.

3.23 Ezekiel recognized his helplessness before God. Sometimes our prosperity, popularity, or physical strength blind us to our spiritual helplessness. But nothing we do on our own can accomplish much for God. Only when God is in control of our wills can we accomplish great tasks for him. The first step to being God's person is to admit that you need his help; then you can begin to see what God can really do in your life.

3.24 Ezek 2.2
3.25 Ezek 4.8 Hos 4.17
3.26 Amos 8.11,12
3.27 Ezek 33.22

by the river Chebar; and I fell on my face. 24 The spirit entered into me, and set me
on my feet; and he spoke with me and said to me: Go, shut yourself inside your
house. 25 As for you, mortal, cords shall be placed on you, and you shall be bound
with them, so that you cannot go out among the people; 26 and I will make your
tongue cling to the roof of your mouth, so that you shall be speechless and unable
to reprove them; for they are a rebellious house. 27 But when I speak with you, I will
open your mouth, and you shall say to them, "Thus says the Lord GOD"; let those
who will hear, hear; and let those who refuse to hear, refuse; for they are a rebellious house.

2. Visions of sin and judgment

A symbol of the coming siege

4.1 Isa 20.2 Jer 6.6; 13.1 19.1 Ezek 21.22
4.3 Isa 8.18; 20.3 Jer 39.1,2 Ezek 12.6,11 24.24-27
4.4 Num 14.34
4.6 Dan 9.24-26 26.11,12 Rev 11.2,3
4.7 Ezek 21.2
4.8 Ezek 3.25

4 And you, O mortal, take a brick and set it before you. On it portray a city,
Jerusalem; 2 and put siegeworks against it, and build a siege-wall against it,
and cast up a ramp against it; set camps also against it, and plant battering rams
against it all around. 3 Then take an iron plate and place it as an iron wall between
you and the city; set your face toward it, and let it be in a state of siege, and press
the siege against it. This is a sign for the house of Israel.
4 Then lie on your left side, and place the punishment of the house of Israel
upon it; you shall bear their punishment for the number of the days that you lie
there. 5 For I assign to you a number of days, three hundred ninety days, equal to
the number of the years of their punishment; and so you shall bear the punishment
of the house of Israel. 6 When you have completed these, you shall lie down a second time, but on your right side, and bear the punishment of the house of Judah;
forty days I assign you, one day for each year. 7 You shall set your face toward the
siege of Jerusalem, and with your arm bared you shall prophesy against it. 8 See, I

EZEKIEL'S ACTS OF OBEDIENCE		
	2.1	Stood and received God's message
	3.24–27	Imprisoned himself in his house
	3.27	Faithfully proclaimed God's message
	4.1ff	Drew a map of the city of Jerusalem on a large stone
	4.4, 5	Lay on his left side for 390 days
	4.6	Lay on his right side for 40 days
	4.9–17	Followed specific cooking instructions
	5.1–4	Shaved his head and beard
	12.2–7	Left home to demonstrate exile
	13.1ff	Spoke against false prophets
	19.1ff	Sang a lamentation for the leaders
	21.2	Prophesied against Israel and the temple
	21.19–23	Made a map
	24.16, 17	Could not mourn his wife's death

3.24, 25 God called Ezekiel "mortal" to contrast his frail humanity with God's own power. Whenever Ezekiel saw God for who he really is, he fell down in respect and submission and did whatever God asked. Then God's Spirit empowered him (see 2.2; 3.12). Although we may not have a task like Ezekiel's, we have the same Spirit of power that God gives to all who live for him.

3.24–27 Ezekiel was allowed to speak only when God had a message for the people. Thus the people knew that whatever Ezekiel said was God's message. They did not have to wonder whether Ezekiel was speaking by God's authority or his own.

4.1ff Ezekiel enacted the coming siege and fall of Jerusalem before it actually happened. God gave Ezekiel specific instructions about what to say and how to say it. Each detail had a specific meaning. Often we ignore or disregard the smaller details of God's Word, thinking God probably doesn't care. Like Ezekiel, we should want to obey God completely, even in the details.

4.4–17 Ezekiel's unusual actions symbolically portrayed the fate of Jerusalem. He lay on his left side for 390 days to show that Israel would be punished for 390 years; he lay on his right side for 40 days to show that Judah would be punished for 40 years. Ezekiel was not allowed to move, symbolizing the fact that the people of Jerusalem would be imprisoned within the walls of the city. We know that Ezekiel did not have to lie on his side all day, because these verses tell of other tasks God asked him to do during this time. The small amount of food he was allowed to eat was the normal ration provided to those living in a city under siege by enemy armies. The food cooked over human dung was a symbol of Judah's spiritual uncleanness.

Certainly many people came to view these spectacles and, in the process, heard Ezekiel's occasional speeches (3.27). How many of us would be willing to so dramatically portray the sins of our nation? We need to pray for greater boldness in our witness.

am putting cords on you so that you cannot turn from one side to the other until you
have completed the days of your siege.
9 And you, take wheat and barley, beans and lentils, millet and spelt; put them
into one vessel, and make bread for yourself. During the number of days that you
lie on your side, three hundred ninety days, you shall eat it. 10 The food that you eat
shall be twenty shekels a day by weight; at fixed times you shall eat it. 11 And you
shall drink water by measure, one-sixth of a hin; at fixed times you shall drink.
12 You shall eat it as a barley-cake, baking it in their sight on human dung. 13 The
LORD said, "Thus shall the people of Israel eat their bread, unclean, among the
nations to which I will drive them." 14 Then I said, "Ah Lord GOD! I have never
defiled myself; from my youth up until now I have never eaten what died of itself
or was torn by animals, nor has carrion flesh come into my mouth." 15 Then he said
to me, "See, I will let you have cow's dung instead of human dung, on which you
may prepare your bread."
16 Then he said to me, Mortal, I am going to break the staff of bread in Jerusalem; they shall eat bread by weight and with fearfulness; and they shall drink water
by measure and in dismay. 17 Lacking bread and water, they will look at one another in dismay, and waste away under their punishment.

Jerusalem will be a public example

5 And you, O mortal, take a sharp sword; use it as a barber's razor and run it
over your head and your beard; then take balances for weighing, and divide the
hair. 2 One third of the hair you shall burn in the fire inside the city, when the days
of the siege are completed; one third you shall take and strike with the sword all
around the city;[j] and one third you shall scatter to the wind, and I will unsheathe
the sword after them. 3 Then you shall take from these a small number, and bind
them in the skirts of your robe. 4 From these, again, you shall take some, throw
them into the fire and burn them up; from there a fire will come out against all the
house of Israel.
5 Thus says the Lord GOD: This is Jerusalem; I have set her in the center of the
nations, with countries all around her. 6 But she has rebelled against my ordinances
and my statutes, becoming more wicked than the nations and the countries all
around her, rejecting my ordinances and not following my statutes. 7 Therefore thus
says the Lord GOD: Because you are more turbulent than the nations that are all
around you, and have not followed my statutes or kept my ordinances, but have
acted according to the ordinances of the nations that are all around you; 8 therefore
thus says the Lord GOD: I, I myself, am coming against you; I will execute judgments among you in the sight of the nations. 9 And because of all your abominations, I will do to you what I have never yet done, and the like of which I will never
do again. 10 Surely, parents shall eat their children in your midst, and children shall
eat their parents; I will execute judgments on you, and any of you who survive I
will scatter to every wind. 11 Therefore, as I live, says the Lord GOD, surely, be-

j Heb *it*

4.9 Ex 9.32 Isa 28.25
4.10 Ezek 45.12
4.12 Isa 36.12
4.13 Dan 1.8 Hos 9.3
4.14 Lev 17.15; 22.8 Deut 14.3-5 Isa 66.17 Ezek 20.49 Acts 10.14
4.16 Lev 26.26 Isa 3.1 Lam 5.4 Ezek 5.16 12.18,19; 14.13
4.17 Ezek 24.23 33.10
5.1 Lev 21.5 Ezek 44.20 Dan 5.27
5.2 Lev 26.33 Jer 39.1,2 Ezek 4.1-8
5.3 2 Kgs 25.15 Jer 39.10
5.5 2 Kgs 17.8-20 Ezek 4.1 16.47,48,51
5.8 Jer 24.9 Ezek 5.15; 15.7 Zech 14.2
5.9 Dan 9.12 Mt 24.21
5.11 Jer 7.9-11 Ezek 8.5,6, 16,18

4.12–14 Ezekiel asked God not to make him use human dung for fuel because it violated the laws for purity (Leviticus 21, 22; Deuteronomy 23.12–14). As a priest, Ezekiel would have been careful to keep all these laws. To use human dung for fuel would paint a dramatic picture of ruin. If nothing was left in the city that could be burned, it would be impossible to continue to follow God's laws for sacrifices.

5.1–10 Shaving one's head signified mourning, humiliation, and repentance. Ezekiel was directed to shave his head and beard, and then to divide the hair into three parts symbolizing what was going to happen to the people in Jerusalem (see 5.12). Along with verbal prophecies, God asked Ezekiel to use visual images to command the people's attention and to burn an indelible impression on their minds. Just as God gave Ezekiel creative means to communicate his message to the exiles, we can creatively communicate the good news about God to a lost generation.

5.3, 4 The tiny bit of hair Ezekiel put in his robe symbolized the small remnant of faithful people God would preserve. But even some from this remnant would be judged and destroyed because their faith was not genuine. Where will you stand in the coming judgment? Matthew 7.22, 23 warns that many who believe they are safe are not. Make sure your commitment is heartfelt.

5.7 *Turbulent* means unruly or rebellious. Their wickedness was so great that they couldn't even keep the laws of the heathen nations around them, not to mention God's laws.

5.11 It was a serious sin to defile the temple, God's sanctuary, by worshiping idols and practicing evil within its very walls. In the New Testament, we learn that God now makes his home *within* those who are his. Our bodies are his temple (see 1 Corinthians 6.19). We defile God's temple today by allowing gossip, bitterness, love

cause you have defiled my sanctuary with all your detestable things and with all
your abominations—therefore I will cut you down;[k] my eye will not spare, and I
5.12 Ezek 6.11,12; 12.14; 15.2
will have no pity. 12 One third of you shall die of pestilence or be consumed by
famine among you; one third shall fall by the sword around you; and one third I will
scatter to every wind and will unsheathe the sword after them.
13 My anger shall spend itself, and I will vent my fury on them and satisfy
myself; and they shall know that I, the LORD, have spoken in my jealousy, when I
5.14 Ps 74.3-10; 79.1-4; Ezek 22.4
spend my fury on them. 14 Moreover I will make you a desolation and an object of
mocking among the nations around you, in the sight of all that pass by. 15 You shall
be[l] a mockery and a taunt, a warning and a horror, to the nations around you, when
5.15 Isa 66.15,16; Jer 22.8,9; Ezek 25.17; 1 Cor 10.11
I execute judgments on you in anger and fury, and with furious punishments—I,
the LORD, have spoken— 16 when I loose against you[m] my deadly arrows of famine, arrows for destruction, which I will let loose to destroy you, and when I bring
5.16 Deut 32.23,24
more and more famine upon you, and break your staff of bread. 17 I will send fam-
5.17 Ezek 14.21
ine and wild animals against you, and they will rob you of your children; pestilence
and bloodshed shall pass through you; and I will bring the sword upon you. I, the
LORD, have spoken.

Ezekiel prophesies against the mountains of Israel

6.2 Ezek 36.1
6 The word of the LORD came to me: 2 O mortal, set your face toward the moun-
6.3 Ezek 36.4
tains of Israel, and prophesy against them, 3 and say, You mountains of Israel,
hear the word of the Lord GOD! Thus says the Lord GOD to the mountains and the
hills, to the ravines and the valleys: I, I myself will bring a sword upon you, and I
6.4 2 Chron 14.5; Isa 27.9; Ezek 6.6; Mic 1.7
will destroy your high places. 4 Your altars shall become desolate, and your incense
stands shall be broken; and I will throw down your slain in front of your idols. 5 I
will lay the corpses of the people of Israel in front of their idols; and I will scatter
your bones around your altars. 6 Wherever you live, your towns shall be waste and
your high places ruined, so that your altars will be waste and ruined,[n] your idols
broken and destroyed, your incense stands cut down, and your works wiped out.
7 The slain shall fall in your midst; then you shall know that I am the LORD.
6.8 Jer 44.14,28; Ezek 7.16; 14.22
8 But I will spare some. Some of you shall escape the sword among the nations
and be scattered through the countries. 9 Those of you who escape shall remember
6.9 Deut 30.2; Isa 7.13; 43.24; Ezek 20.43; Hos 11.8
me among the nations where they are carried captive, how I was crushed by their
wanton heart that turned away from me, and their wanton eyes that turned after
their idols. Then they will be loathsome in their own sight for the evils that they
have committed, for all their abominations. 10 And they shall know that I am the
6.11 Ezek 5.12; 7.15; 9.4; 25.6
LORD; I did not threaten in vain to bring this disaster upon them.
11 Thus says the Lord GOD: Clap your hands and stamp your foot, and say,
6.12 Lam 4.11,12; Ezek 5.13
Alas for all the vile abominations of the house of Israel! For they shall fall by the
sword, by famine, and by pestilence. 12 Those far off shall die of pestilence; those

[k] Another reading is *I will withdraw* [l] Gk Syr Vg Tg: Heb *It shall be* [m] Heb *them* [n] Syr Vg Tg: Heb *and be made guilty*

---

of money, lies, or any other wrong actions or attitudes to be a part of our lives. By asking the Holy Spirit's help, we can keep from defiling his temple.

5.13 Have you ever seen someone try to discipline a child by saying, "If you do that one more time . . ."? If the parent doesn't follow through, the child learns not to listen. Empty threats backfire. God was going to punish the Israelites for their blatant sins, and he wanted them to know that he would do what he said. The people learned the hard way that God always follows through on his word. Too many people ignore God's warnings, treating them as empty threats. But what God threatens, he does. Don't make the mistake of thinking God doesn't really mean what he says.

6.1ff This is the beginning of a two-part message. Remember that Ezekiel could speak only when giving messages from God. The message in chapter 6 is that Judah's idolatry will surely call down God's judgment. The message in chapter 7 describes the nature of that judgment—utter destruction of the nation. The nature of the people's sins laid them wide open to invasion. Nevertheless, God in his mercy saved a remnant.

6.8–10 A ray of light appears in this prophecy of darkness—God would spare a remnant of people, but only after they had learned some hard lessons. God sometimes has to break a person in order to bring him or her to true repentance. The people needed new attitudes, but they wouldn't change until God broke their hearts with humiliation, pain, suffering, and defeat. Does your heart long for God enough to change those areas displeasing him? Or will God have to break your heart?

6.11 Prophets often used this threefold description of judgment upon Jerusalem—sword, famine, and pestilence—as a way of saying that the destruction would be complete. The sword meant death in battle, famine came when enemies besieged a city, and disease was always a danger during famine. Don't make the mistake of underestimating the extent of God's judgment. If you ignore the biblical warnings and turn away from God, eternal judgment awaits you.

nearby shall fall by the sword; and any who are left and are spared shall die of
famine. Thus I will spend my fury upon them. 13 And you shall know that I am the
LORD, when their slain lie among their idols around their altars, on every high hill,
on all the mountain tops, under every green tree, and under every leafy oak, wherever they offered pleasing odor to all their idols. 14 I will stretch out my hand
against them, and make the land desolate and waste, throughout all their settlements, from the wilderness to Riblah.[o] Then they shall know that I am the LORD.

6.13 1 Kgs 14.23; 2 Kgs 16.4; Isa 57.5-7; Ezek 20.27,28
6.14 Ezek 14.13

God will pour out his anger

7 The word of the LORD came to me: 2 You, O mortal, thus says the Lord GOD to
the land of Israel:

An end! The end has come
upon the four corners of the land.
3 Now the end is upon you,
I will let loose my anger upon you;
I will judge you according to your ways,
I will punish you for all your abominations.
4 My eye will not spare you, I will have no pity.
I will punish you for your ways,
while your abominations are among you.
Then you shall know that I am the LORD.

5 Thus says the Lord GOD:
Disaster after disaster! See, it comes.
6 An end has come, the end has come.
It has awakened against you; see, it comes!
7 Your doom[p] has come to you,
O inhabitant of the land.
The time has come, the day is near—
of tumult, not of reveling on the mountains.
8 Soon now I will pour out my wrath upon you;
I will spend my anger against you.
I will judge you according to your ways,
and punish you for all your abominations.
9 My eye will not spare; I will have no pity.
I will punish you according to your ways,
while your abominations are among you.
Then you shall know that it is I the LORD who strike.

10 See, the day! See, it comes!
Your doom[p] has gone out.
The rod has blossomed, pride has budded.
11 Violence has grown into a rod of wickedness.
None of them shall remain,
not their abundance, not their wealth;
no pre-eminence among them.[p]
12 The time has come, the day draws near;
let not the buyer rejoice, nor the seller mourn,

7.2 Ezek 11.13; Amos 8.2,10
7.4 Ezek 11.21
7.5 2 Kgs 21.12,13
7.7 Ezek 12.23-25, 28
7.8 Ezek 9.8; 14.19; 33.20; 36.19
7.10 Isa 10.5; 59.6-8
7.12 Isa 5.13,14; Ezek 6.11,12; 1 Cor 7.29-31; Jas 5.8,9

o Another reading is *Diblah* p Meaning of Heb uncertain

6.14 The phrase "then they shall know that I am the Lord" occurs 70 times in the book of Ezekiel. The purpose of all God's punishment was not to take revenge, but to impress upon the people the truth that the Lord is the only true and living God. Many people in Ezekiel's day were worshiping man-made idols and calling them gods. Today money, sex, and power have become idols for many. Punishment will come upon all who put other things ahead of God. It is easy to forget that the Lord alone is God, the supreme authority and the only source of eternal love and life. Remember that God may use the difficulties of your life to remind you that he alone is God.

7.10, 11 In chapter 7, Ezekiel predicts the complete destruction of Judah. The wicked and proud will finally get what they deserve. If it seems that God ignores the evil and proud of our day, be assured that a day of judgment will come, just as it came for the people of Judah. God is waiting patiently for sinners to repent (see 2 Peter 3.9), but when his judgment comes, "none of them shall remain." What you decide about God now will determine your fate then.

7.12, 13 The nation of Judah trusted in its prosperity instead of in God. So God planned to destroy the basis of its prosperity. Whenever we begin to trust in jobs, the economy, a political system, or military might for our security, we put God in the back seat.

for wrath is upon all their multitude.

7.13 Lev 25.24-28,31

13 For the sellers shall not return to what has been sold as long as they remain alive.
For the vision concerns all their multitude; it shall not be revoked. Because of their
iniquity, they cannot maintain their lives.[q]

7.14 Num 10.9 Jer 4.5

14 They have blown the horn and made everything ready;
but no one goes to battle,
for my wrath is upon all their multitude.

7.15 Jer 14.18 Ezek 6.11,12

15 The sword is outside, pestilence and famine are inside;
those in the field die by the sword;
those in the city — famine and pestilence devour them.

7.16 Isa 38.14; 59.11 Ezek 6.8; 14.22 Nah 2.7

16 If any survivors escape,
they shall be found on the mountains
like doves of the valleys,
all of them moaning over their iniquity.

7.17 Isa 13.7 Ezek 21.7; 22.14 Heb 12.12

17 All hands shall grow feeble,
all knees turn to water.

7.18 Job 21.6 Isa 15.3 Ezek 27.31 Amos 8.10

18 They shall put on sackcloth,
horror shall cover them.
Shame shall be on all faces,
baldness on all their heads.

7.19 Prov 11.4 Isa 2.20; 30.22 Zeph 1.8

19 They shall fling their silver into the streets,
their gold shall be treated as unclean.
Their silver and gold cannot save them on the day of the wrath of the LORD. They
shall not satisfy their hunger or fill their stomachs with it. For it was the stumbling
block of their iniquity. 20 From their[r] beautiful ornament, in which they took pride,
they made their abominable images, their detestable things; therefore I will make of
it an unclean thing to them.

7.21 2 Kgs 24.13 Ps 74.2-8 Jer 7.30

21 I will hand it over to strangers as booty,
to the wicked of the earth as plunder;
they shall profane it.

7.22 Ezek 39.23,24

22 I will avert my face from them,
so that they may profane my treasured[s] place;
the violent shall enter it,
they shall profane it.

7.23 Ezek 8.17; 9.9

23 Make a chain![q]
For the land is full of bloody crimes;
the city is full of violence.

7.24 Ezek 21.31 28.7; 33.28

24 I will bring the worst of the nations
to take possession of their houses.
I will put an end to the arrogance of the strong,
and their holy places shall be profaned.

25 When anguish comes, they will seek peace,
but there shall be none.

7.26 Ezek 21.7 22.26; 26.16

26 Disaster comes upon disaster,
rumor follows rumor;
they shall keep seeking a vision from the prophet;

[q] Meaning of Heb uncertain [r] Syr Symmachus: Heb *its* [s] Or *secret*

7.19 God's people had allowed their love of money to lead them into sin. And for this, God would destroy them. Money has a strange power to lead people into sin. Paul said that "the love of money is a root of all kinds of evil" (1 Timothy 6.10). How ironic that we use money — a gift of God — to buy things that separate us from him. How tragic it is that we spend so much money seeking to satisfy ourselves, and so little time seeking God, the true source of satisfaction.

7.20 God gave the people gold to decorate the temple, but they used it to make idols. The resources God gives us should be used to do his work and carry out his will, but too often we consume them to satisfy our own desires. When we abuse God's gifts or use resources selfishly, we have missed the real purpose God had in mind. To do so is as shortsighted as idolatry.

7.24 The people of Jerusalem took great pride in their buildings. The temple itself was a source of pride (see 24.20, 21). This pride would be crushed when the evil and godless Babylonians destroyed Jerusalem's houses, fortifications, and holy places. If you are going through a humiliating experience, God may be using that experience to weed out pride in your life.

instruction shall perish from the priest,
and counsel from the elders.
27 The king shall mourn,
the prince shall be wrapped in despair,
and the hands of the people of the land shall tremble.
According to their way I will deal with them;
according to their own judgments I will judge them.
And they shall know that I am the LORD.

The sins of the people

8 In the sixth year, in the sixth month, on the fifth day of the month, as I sat in
my house, with the elders of Judah sitting before me, the hand of the Lord GOD
fell upon me there. 2 I looked, and there was a figure that looked like a human **8.2** Ezek 1.4,27,28
being;[t] below what appeared to be its loins it was fire, and above the loins it was
like the appearance of brightness, like gleaming amber. 3 It stretched out the form **8.3** Jer 7.30 Ezek 3.12; 11.1 Dan 5.5
of a hand, and took me by a lock of my head; and the spirit lifted me up between
earth and heaven, and brought me in visions of God to Jerusalem, to the entrance
of the gateway of the inner court that faces north, to the seat of the image of jealousy, which provokes to jealousy. 4 And the glory of the God of Israel was there, **8.4** Ezek 1.27,28
like the vision that I had seen in the valley.
5 Then God[u] said to me, "O mortal, lift up your eyes now in the direction of the **8.5** Ps 78.58 Jer 3.2; 7.30 32.34 Ezek 8.3 Zech 5.5
north." So I lifted up my eyes toward the north, and there, north of the altar gate,
in the entrance, was this image of jealousy. 6 He said to me, "Mortal, do you see
what they are doing, the great abominations that the house of Israel are committing
here, to drive me far from my sanctuary? Yet you will see still greater abomina- **8.6** 2 Kgs 23.4,5 Ezek 5.11 8.9,17
tions."
7 And he brought me to the entrance of the court; I looked, and there was a hole
in the wall. 8 Then he said to me, "Mortal, dig through the wall"; and when I dug **8.8** Job 34.22 Isa 29.15
through the wall, there was an entrance. 9 He said to me, "Go in, and see the vile
abominations that they are committing here." 10 So I went in and looked; there, **8.10** Ex 20.4 Isa 29.15
portrayed on the wall all around, were all kinds of creeping things, and loathsome
animals, and all the idols of the house of Israel. 11 Before them stood seventy of the **8.11** Num 11.16,25 16.17,35 Jer 19.1 Lk 10.1
elders of the house of Israel, with Jaazaniah son of Shaphan standing among them.
Each had his censer in his hand, and the fragrant cloud of incense was ascending.
12 Then he said to me, "Mortal, have you seen what the elders of the house of Israel **8.12** Ezek 9.9
are doing in the dark, each in his room of images? For they say, 'The LORD does not
see us, the LORD has forsaken the land.' " 13 He said also to me, "You will see still
greater abominations that they are committing."
14 Then he brought me to the entrance of the north gate of the house of the **8.14** Ezek 44.4; 46.9
LORD; women were sitting there weeping for Tammuz. 15 Then he said to me,
"Have you seen this, O mortal? You will see still greater abominations than these."

[t] Gk: Heb *like fire* [u] Heb *he*

8.1ff This prophecy's date corresponds to 592 B.C. The message of chapters 8–11 is directed specifically toward Jerusalem and its leaders. In chapter 8 Ezekiel is taken by means of a vision from Babylon to the temple in Jerusalem to see the great wickedness being practiced there. The people and their religious leaders are thoroughly corrupt. While Ezekiel's first vision showed that judgment was from God; this vision shows their sin was the reason for judgment.

8.2 This fiery person could have been an angel or a manifestation of God himself. In Ezekiel's previous vision, such a man was pictured as God on his throne (1.26–28).

8.3–5 This "image of jealousy" could be of Asherah, the Canaanite goddess of fertility, whose character encouraged sexual immorality and self-gratification. King Manasseh had placed such an idol in the temple (2 Kings 21.7). King Josiah burned it (2 Kings 23.6), but there were certainly many other idols around.

8.6ff In scene after scene, God reveals to Ezekiel the extent to which the people have embraced idolatry and wickedness. God's Spirit works with us in a similar way, revealing sin that lurks in our lives. How comfortable would you feel if God held an open house in your life today?

8.14 Tammuz was the Babylonian god of spring. He was the husband or lover of the goddess, Ishtar. The followers of this cult believed that the green vegetation shriveled and died in the hot summer because Tammuz had died and descended into the underworld. Thus, the worshipers wept and mourned his death. In the springtime when the new vegetation appeared they rejoiced, believing he had come back to life. God was showing Ezekiel that many people were no longer worshiping the *true* God of life and vegetation. We must also be careful not to spend so much time thinking about the benefits of creation that we lose sight of the Creator.

16 And he brought me into the inner court of the house of the LORD; there, at the
entrance of the temple of the LORD, between the porch and the altar, were about
twenty-five men, with their backs to the temple of the LORD, and their faces toward
the east, prostrating themselves to the sun toward the east. 17 Then he said to me,
"Have you seen this, O mortal? Is it not bad enough that the house of Judah commits the abominations done here? Must they fill the land with violence, and provoke my anger still further? See, they are putting the branch to their nose!
18 Therefore I will act in wrath; my eye will not spare, nor will I have pity; and
though they cry in my hearing with a loud voice, I will not listen to them."

The death of idolaters

9 Then he cried in my hearing with a loud voice, saying, "Draw near, you execu-
tioners of the city, each with his destroying weapon in his hand." 2 And six
men came from the direction of the upper gate, which faces north, each with his
weapon for slaughter in his hand; among them was a man clothed in linen, with a
writing case at his side. They went in and stood beside the bronze altar.
3 Now the glory of the God of Israel had gone up from the cherub on which it
rested to the threshold of the house. The LORD called to the man clothed in linen,
who had the writing case at his side; 4 and said to him, "Go through the city,
through Jerusalem, and put a mark on the foreheads of those who sigh and groan
over all the abominations that are committed in it." 5 To the others he said in my
hearing, "Pass through the city after him, and kill; your eye shall not spare, and you
shall show no pity. 6 Cut down old men, young men and young women, little children and women, but touch no one who has the mark. And begin at my sanctuary."
So they began with the elders who were in front of the house. 7 Then he said to
them, "Defile the house, and fill the courts with the slain. Go!" So they went out
and killed in the city. 8 While they were killing, and I was left alone, I fell prostrate
on my face and cried out, "Ah Lord GOD! will you destroy all who remain of Israel
as you pour out your wrath upon Jerusalem?" 9 He said to me, "The guilt of the
house of Israel and Judah is exceedingly great; the land is full of bloodshed and the
city full of perversity; for they say, 'The LORD has forsaken the land, and the LORD
does not see.' 10 As for me, my eye will not spare, nor will I have pity, but I will
bring down their deeds upon their heads."

8.16 Deut 4.19; 17.3; 2 Chron 29.6; Job 31.26-28; Jer 2.27; 44.17
8.17 Jer 7.18,19; Amos 3.10; Mic 2.2
8.18 Isa 1.15; Jer 11.11; Mic 3.4; Zech 7.13
9.2 Ezek 10.2
9.3 Ezek 10.4; 11.22,23
9.4 Ex 12.7,13; Ps 119.53,136; 2 Cor 1.22; 2 Tim 2.19; Rev 7.2,3
9.6 Ex 12.23; 2 Chron 36.17; Rev 9.4
9.7 Ezek 7.20-22
9.8 1 Chron 21.16; Ezek 11.13; Amos 7.2-6
9.9 2 Kgs 21.16; Ps 10.11; 94.7; Isa 29.15; Ezek 7.23; 8.12; 22.2,3,29; Mic 3.1-3; 7.3
9.10 Isa 65.6; Ezek 7.4; 24.14; Hos 9.7

8.17 The branch to the nose could refer either to a cultic worship practice, or to the fact that Judah's sins had become a stench to God.

9.1ff This chapter presents a picture of coming judgment. Once Ezekiel had seen how corrupt Jerusalem had become, God called one man to spare the small minority who had been faithful. Then he called six men to slaughter the wicked of the city. This judgment was ordered by God himself (9.5–7).

9.2 The writing case was a common object in Ezekiel's day. It included a long narrow board with a groove to hold the reed brush used to write on parchment, papyrus, or dried clay. The board had hollowed out areas that held cakes of black and red ink which had to be moistened before use.

9.3 What is God's glory? It is the manifestation of God's character—his ultimate power, transcendence, and moral perfection. He is completely above man and his limitations. Yet he reveals himself to us so that we can worship and follow him.

9.3 Cherubim ("cherub" is singular) are an order of powerful angelic beings created to glorify God. They are associated with God's absolute holiness and moral perfection. God placed cherubim at the entrance of Eden to keep Adam and Eve out after they sinned (Genesis 3.24). Representations of cherubim were used to decorate the tabernacle and temple. The lid of the ark of the covenant, called the mercy seat, was adorned with two gold cherubim (Exodus 37.6–9). It was a symbol of the very presence of God. The cherubim seen by Ezekiel left the temple along with the glory of God. Ezekiel then recognized them as the divine beings he had seen in his first vision (see chapter 1).

9.4, 5 The man with the writing case was to put a mark on those who were faithful to God. Their faithfulness was determined by their sensitivity to and sorrow over their nation's sin. Those with the mark were spared when the six men began to destroy the wicked people. During the exodus, the Israelites put a mark of blood on their doorposts to save them from death. In the final days, God will mark the foreheads of those destined for salvation (Revelation 7.3), and Satan will mark his followers (Revelation 13.16, 17), who, like him, are destined for destruction. When God punishes sin, he won't forget his promise to preserve his people.

9.7 The spiritual leaders ("elders") of Israel blatantly promoted their idolatrous beliefs, and the people abandoned God and followed them. Spiritual leaders are especially accountable to God because they are entrusted with the task of teaching the truth (see James 3.1). When they pervert the truth, they can lead countless people away from God and even cause a nation to fall. It is not surprising, then, that when God began to judge the nation, he started at the temple and worked outward (see 1 Peter 4.17). How sad that in the temple, the one place where they should be teaching God's truth, they were teaching lies.

9.9, 10 The people said that the Lord had forsaken the land and wouldn't see their sin. People have many convenient explanations to make it easier to sin: "It doesn't matter," "Everybody's doing it," or "Nobody will ever know." Do you find yourself making excuses for sin? Rationalizing sin makes it easier to commit, but rationalization does not convince God or cancel the punishment.

11 Then the man clothed in linen, with the writing case at his side, brought back
word, saying, "I have done as you commanded me."

Burning coals are scattered over Jerusalem

10 Then I looked, and above the dome that was over the heads of the cherubim 10.1 Ex 24.10
there appeared above them something like a sapphire,[v] in form resembling Ezek 1.22,26
a throne. 2 He said to the man clothed in linen, "Go within the wheelwork under- Rev 4.2,3
neath the cherubim; fill your hands with burning coals from among the cherubim,
and scatter them over the city." He went in as I looked on. 3 Now the cherubim were 10.3
standing on the south side of the house when the man went in; and a cloud filled the Ezek 8.3,16
inner court. 4 Then the glory of the LORD rose up from the cherub to the threshold 10.4
of the house; the house was filled with the cloud, and the court was full of the Ex 40.34,35 Isa 6.1-4
brightness of the glory of the LORD. 5 The sound of the wings of the cherubim was Ezek 1.27,28
heard as far as the outer court, like the voice of God Almighty[w] when he speaks. 9.3; 11.22,23
6 When he commanded the man clothed in linen, "Take fire from within the 10.5 Job 40.9
wheelwork, from among the cherubim," he went in and stood beside a wheel. 7 And Ezek 1.24 Rev 10.3
a cherub stretched out his hand from among the cherubim to the fire that was among 10.7
the cherubim, took some of it and put it into the hands of the man clothed in linen, Ezek 1.8
who took it and went out. 8 The cherubim appeared to have the form of a human
hand under their wings.
9 I looked, and there were four wheels beside the cherubim, one beside each 10.9
cherub; and the appearance of the wheels was like gleaming beryl. 10 And as for Ezek 1.16,17 Rev 21.18-20
their appearance, the four looked alike, something like a wheel within a wheel.
11 When they moved, they moved in any of the four directions without veering as
they moved; but in whatever direction the front wheel faced, the others followed
without veering as they moved. 12 Their entire body, their rims, their spokes, their
wings, and the wheels—the wheels of the four of them—were full of eyes all
around. 13 As for the wheels, they were called in my hearing "the wheelwork."
14 Each one had four faces: the first face was that of the cherub, the second face was 10.14
that of a human being, the third that of a lion, and the fourth that of an eagle. 1 Kgs 7.27-30, 36
15 The cherubim rose up. These were the living creatures that I saw by the river Ezek 1.6,10 10.21
Chebar. 16 When the cherubim moved, the wheels moved beside them; and when Rev 4.7
the cherubim lifted up their wings to rise up from the earth, the wheels at their side 10.15
did not veer. 17 When they stopped, the others stopped, and when they rose up, the Ezek 1.3-6, 19-21
others rose up with them; for the spirit of the living creatures was in them. 10.17
18 Then the glory of the LORD went out from the threshold of the house and Ezek 1.12
stopped above the cherubim. 19 The cherubim lifted up their wings and rose up from 10.18 Ps 18.10
the earth in my sight as they went out with the wheels beside them. They stopped
at the entrance of the east gate of the house of the LORD; and the glory of the God
of Israel was above them.
20 These were the living creatures that I saw underneath the God of Israel by the 10.20 Ezek 1.5,26 10.15
river Chebar; and I knew that they were cherubim. 21 Each had four faces, each four 10.21
wings, and underneath their wings something like human hands. 22 As for what Ezek 1.6,8 10.14; 41.18-20
their faces were like, they were the same faces whose appearance I had seen by the 10.22
river Chebar. Each one moved straight ahead. Ezek 1.10,12

[v] Or *lapis lazuli* [w] Traditional rendering of Heb *El Shaddai*

10.1ff Chapters 8–11 depict God's glory departing from the temple. In 8.3, 4, his glory was over the northern gate. It then moved to the door (the "threshold," 9.3), the south side of the temple (10.3, 4), the eastern gate (10.18, 19; 11.1), and finally the mountain east of the temple (11.23), probably the Mount of Olives. Because of the nation's sins, God's glory had departed.

10.2 God's perfect holiness demands judgment for sin. The cherubim are mighty angels. The coals of fire scattered over the city represent the purging of sin. For Jerusalem, this meant the destruction of all the people who blatantly sinned and refused to repent. Shortly after this prophecy, the Babylonians destroyed Jerusalem by fire (2 Kings 25.9; 2 Chronicles 36.19).

10.18 God's glory departed from the temple and was never completely present again until Christ himself visited it in New Testament times. God's holiness required that he leave the temple because the people had so defiled it. God had to completely destroy what people had perverted in order for true worship to be revived. We must commit ourselves, our families, our churches, and our nation to follow God faithfully so that we never have to experience God's abandoning us.

Judgment against the leaders

11 The spirit lifted me up and brought me to the east gate of the house of the
LORD, which faces east. There, at the entrance of the gateway, were twenty-
five men; among them I saw Jaazaniah son of Azzur, and Pelatiah son of Benaiah,
officials of the people. 2 He said to me, "Mortal, these are the men who devise
iniquity and who give wicked counsel in this city; 3 they say, 'The time is not near
to build houses; this city is the pot, and we are the meat.' 4 Therefore prophesy
against them; prophesy, O mortal."
5 Then the spirit of the LORD fell upon me, and he said to me, "Say, Thus says
the LORD: This is what you think, O house of Israel; I know the things that come
into your mind. 6 You have killed many in this city, and have filled its streets with
the slain. 7 Therefore thus says the Lord GOD: The slain whom you have placed
within it are the meat, and this city is the pot; but you shall be taken out of it. 8 You
have feared the sword; and I will bring the sword upon you, says the Lord GOD. 9 I
will take you out of it and give you over to the hands of foreigners, and execute
judgments upon you 10 You shall fall by the sword; I will judge you at the border
of Israel. And you shall know that I am the LORD. 11 This city shall not be your pot,
and you shall not be the meat inside it; I will judge you at the border of Israel.
12 Then you shall know that I am the LORD, whose statutes you have not followed,
and whose ordinances you have not kept, but you have acted according to the ordinances of the nations that are around you."
13 Now, while I was prophesying, Pelatiah son of Benaiah died. Then I fell
down on my face, cried with a loud voice, and said, "Ah Lord GOD! will you make
a full end of the remnant of Israel?"

God will regather Israel

14 Then the word of the LORD came to me: 15 Mortal, your kinsfolk, your own
kin, your fellow exiles,[x] the whole house of Israel, all of them, are those of whom
the inhabitants of Jerusalem have said, "They have gone far from the LORD; to us
this land is given for a possession." 16 Therefore say: Thus says the Lord GOD:
Though I removed them far away among the nations, and though I scattered them
among the countries, yet I have been a sanctuary to them for a little while[y] in the
countries where they have gone. 17 Therefore say: Thus says the Lord GOD: I will
gather you from the peoples, and assemble you out of the countries where you have

11.1 1 Kgs 18.12; 2 Kgs 2.16; Isa 30.1; Jer 5.5; Ezek 8.3; 43.5; Mic 2.1
11.3 Jer 1.13; Ezek 24.3,6; 2 Pet 3.4
11.4 Ezek 3.4,17
11.6 Ezek 7.23; 22.2-6,9,12,27
11.7 2 Kgs 25.18-22; Jer 52.24-27
11.9 Rom 13.4
11.10 Num 34.8,9; Josh 13.5
11.12 Lev 26.40; Deut 12.30,31; 2 Kgs 16.3-12; Ezek 8.10,14, 16; 18.8,9
11.13 Ezek 9.8
11.15 Jer 24.1-5; Ezek 33.24
11.17 Isa 11.11-16; Hos 1.10,11; Amos 9.14,15

[x] Gk Syr: Heb *people of your kindred* [y] Or *to some extent*

11.1–4 God had abandoned his altar and temple (chapters 9—11); now his judgment was complete as he left Jerusalem. The city gate was where merchants and politicians conducted business, so the 25 men may have represented the nation's rulers. Because of their leadership positions, they were responsible for leading the people astray. They had wrongly said that Jerusalem was secure from another attack by the Babylonians. "This city is the pot, and we are the meat" means they believed the city was a sure fortress, an iron shield, and would protect them from all harm. Without God our situation is always precarious.

11.5 God knew everything about the Israelites, even their thoughts. And he knows everything about us, even the sins we try to hide. It's pointless to worry about people noticing how we look or what we do, unless we also care what God thinks, for he sees everything. Trying to hide our thoughts and actions from God is futile. "Secret" sins are never secret from God. The only effective way to deal with sin is to confess it and ask God to help us overcome it.

11.12 From the time they entered the promised land, the Israelites were warned not to copy the customs and religious practices of other nations. Disobeying this command and following heathen customs instead of God's laws always got them into trouble. Today, believers are still tempted to copy the ways of the world. But we must get our standards of right and wrong from God, not from the popular trends of society.

11.14ff God promised the exiles in Babylon that he would continue to be with them even though they were not in Jerusalem. This was a major concern to the Jews because they believed God was present primarily in the temple. But God assured them that he would continue to be their God regardless of where they were. In the midst of Ezekiel's burning message of judgment stands a cool oasis—God's promise to restore the faithful few to their homeland. His arms are now open to receive those who will repent of their sins.

11.15–21 God's messages through Ezekiel are full of irony. Here he says that the Jews in captivity are the faithful ones, and those in Jerusalem are the sinful and wicked ones. This was the opposite of the people's perception. Appearances can be deceiving. God will evaluate your life by your faith and obedience, not by your apparent earthly success. Furthermore, we cannot judge others by outward appearance.

11.16 God was a sanctuary for the righteous remnant. Idolatrous people, even though they worshiped in the Jerusalem temple (11.15), would find no true sanctuary; but the faithful exiles, even though they were far from home, would be protected by God. Likewise, our external circumstances do not truly indicate our standing with God. Those who appear safe and secure may be far from him, while those going through difficult times may be safely under God's spiritual protection. We can depend on God to keep us safe if we pledge ourselves to his care.

been scattered, and I will give you the land of Israel. 18 When they come there, they
will remove from it all its detestable things and all its abominations. 19 I will give
them one[z] heart, and put a new spirit within them; I will remove the heart of stone
from their flesh and give them a heart of flesh, 20 so that they may follow my statutes and keep my ordinances and obey them. Then they shall be my people, and I
will be their God. 21 But as for those whose heart goes after their detestable things
and their abominations,[a] I will bring their deeds upon their own heads, says the
Lord GOD.

22 Then the cherubim lifted up their wings, with the wheels beside them; and
the glory of the God of Israel was above them. 23 And the glory of the LORD ascended from the middle of the city, and stopped on the mountain east of the city.
24 The spirit lifted me up and brought me in a vision by the spirit of God into Chaldea, to the exiles. Then the vision that I had seen left me. 25 And I told the exiles all
the things that the LORD had shown me.

11.18 Ezek 5.11; 37.23
11.19 Deut 30.6; 2 Kgs 22.19; Jer 24.7; 32.39; 2 Cor 3.3
11.20 Hos 2.23
11.21 Jer 16.18
11.22 Ezek 10.19
11.23 Ezek 8.4
11.24 2 Cor 12.2-4; Acts 10.16
11.25 Ezek 2.7

3. Punishment is certain

Ezekiel demonstrates the exile

12 The word of the LORD came to me: 2 Mortal, you are living in the midst of a
rebellious house, who have eyes to see but do not see, who have ears to hear
but do not hear; 3 for they are a rebellious house. Therefore, mortal, prepare for
yourself an exile's baggage, and go into exile by day in their sight; you shall go like
an exile from your place to another place in their sight. Perhaps they will understand, though they are a rebellious house. 4 You shall bring out your baggage by
day in their sight, as baggage for exile; and you shall go out yourself at evening in
their sight, as those do who go into exile. 5 Dig through the wall in their sight, and
carry the baggage through it. 6 In their sight you shall lift the baggage on your
shoulder, and carry it out in the dark; you shall cover your face, so that you may not
see the land; for I have made you a sign for the house of Israel.

7 I did just as I was commanded. I brought out my baggage by day, as baggage
for exile, and in the evening I dug through the wall with my own hands; I brought
it out in the dark, carrying it on my shoulder in their sight.

8 In the morning the word of the LORD came to me: 9 Mortal, has not the house
of Israel, the rebellious house, said to you, "What are you doing?" 10 Say to them,
"Thus says the Lord GOD: This oracle concerns the prince in Jerusalem and all the
house of Israel in it." 11 Say, "I am a sign for you: as I have done, so shall it be done
to them; they shall go into exile, into captivity." 12 And the prince who is among
them shall lift his baggage on his shoulder in the dark, and shall go out; he[b] shall
dig through the wall and carry it through; he shall cover his face, so that he may not
see the land with his eyes. 13 I will spread my net over him, and he shall be caught
in my snare; and I will bring him to Babylon, the land of the Chaldeans, yet he shall
not see it; and he shall die there. 14 I will scatter to every wind all who are around

12.2 Deut 29.4; Isa 6.9,10; Jer 5.21; Mt 13.13,14; Jn 9.39-41
12.3 Deut 5.29; Ps 18.13; Jer 26.3; Lk 20.13; 2 Tim 2.25
12.4 2 Kgs 25.4; Jer 39.4; 52.7
12.6 Isa 20.3; Ezek 4.3
12.7 Ezek 24.18
12.9 Ezek 2.5-8; 17.12; 24.19
12.10 2 Kgs 9.25; Isa 13.1; 14.28
12.11 Jer 15.2,28-30
12.12 2 Kgs 25.4; Jer 39.4; 52.7
12.13 Isa 24.17; Jer 39.7; Hos 7.12

[z] Another reading is *a new* [a] Cn: Heb *And to the heart of their detestable things and their abominations their heart goes* [b] Gk Syr: Heb *they*

11.18, 19 "One heart" indicates a unanimous singleness of purpose. No longer will God's people seek many gods, they will be content with God. The new heart is a radical transplant of the hard, deaf, immovable one for a tender, receptive, and responsive one (see Jeremiah 32.39; Ezekiel 18.31; 36.26). This new life can only be the work of the Holy Spirit. It is God's work, but we must recognize and turn from our sin. When we do, God gives us new motives, new guidelines, and new purpose. Have you received your new heart?

11.23 God's glory left Jerusalem and stood above a mountain on the east side of the city—almost certainly the Mount of Olives. Ezekiel 43.1–4 implies that God will return the same way he left, when he comes back to earth to set up his perfect kingdom.

12.1ff Ezekiel played the role of a captive being led away to exile, portraying what was about to happen to King Zedekiah and the people remaining in Jerusalem. The exiles knew exactly what Ezekiel was doing because only six years earlier they had made similar preparations as they left Jerusalem for Babylon. This was to show the people that they should not trust the king or the capital city to save them from the Babylonian army—only God could do that. And the exiles who hoped for an early return from exile would be disappointed. Ezekiel's graphic demonstration was proven correct to the last detail. But many refused to listen.

12.10–12 Zedekiah, Judah's last king (597–586 B.C.), was reigning in Jerusalem when Ezekiel gave these oracles or messages from God. Ezekiel showed the people what would happen to Zedekiah. Jerusalem would be attacked again, and Zedekiah would join the exiles already in Babylon. Zedekiah would be unable to see because Nebuchadnezzar would have his eyes gouged out (2 Kings 25.3–7; Jeremiah 52.10, 11).

him, his helpers and all his troops; and I will unsheathe the sword behind them.
15 And they shall know that I am the LORD, when I disperse them among the nations
and scatter them through the countries. 16 But I will let a few of them escape from
the sword, from famine and pestilence, so that they may tell of all their abominations among the nations where they go; then they shall know that I am the LORD.
17 The word of the LORD came to me: 18 Mortal, eat your bread with quaking,
and drink your water with trembling and with fearfulness; 19 and say to the people
of the land, Thus says the Lord GOD concerning the inhabitants of Jerusalem in the
land of Israel: They shall eat their bread with fearfulness, and drink their water in
dismay, because their land shall be stripped of all it contains, on account of the
violence of all those who live in it. 20 The inhabited cities shall be laid waste, and
the land shall become a desolation; and you shall know that I am the LORD.
21 The word of the LORD came to me: 22 Mortal, what is this proverb of yours
about the land of Israel, which says, "The days are prolonged, and every vision
comes to nothing"? 23 Tell them therefore, "Thus says the Lord GOD: I will put an
end to this proverb, and they shall use it no more as a proverb in Israel." But say to
them, The days are near, and the fulfillment of every vision. 24 For there shall no
longer be any false vision or flattering divination within the house of Israel. 25 But
I the LORD will speak the word that I speak, and it will be fulfilled. It will no longer
be delayed; but in your days, O rebellious house, I will speak the word and fulfill
it, says the Lord GOD.
26 The word of the LORD came to me: 27 Mortal, the house of Israel is saying,
"The vision that he sees is for many years ahead; he prophesies for distant times."
28 Therefore say to them, Thus says the Lord GOD: None of my words will be delayed any longer, but the word that I speak will be fulfilled, says the Lord GOD.

Judgment against false prophets

13 The word of the LORD came to me: 2 Mortal, prophesy against the prophets
of Israel who are prophesying; say to those who prophesy out of their own
imagination: "Hear the word of the LORD!" 3 Thus says the Lord GOD, Alas for the
senseless prophets who follow their own spirit, and have seen nothing! 4 Your
prophets have been like jackals among ruins, O Israel. 5 You have not gone up into
the breaches, or repaired a wall for the house of Israel, so that it might stand in
battle on the day of the LORD. 6 They have envisioned falsehood and lying divination; they say, "Says the LORD," when the LORD has not sent them, and yet they
wait for the fulfillment of their word! 7 Have you not seen a false vision or uttered
a lying divination, when you have said, "Says the LORD," even though I did not
speak?
8 Therefore thus says the Lord GOD: Because you have uttered falsehood and
envisioned lies, I am against you, says the Lord GOD. 9 My hand will be against the
prophets who see false visions and utter lying divinations; they shall not be in the
council of my people, nor be enrolled in the register of the house of Israel, nor shall
they enter the land of Israel; and you shall know that I am the Lord GOD. 10 Because, in truth, because they have misled my people, saying, "Peace," when there

12.14 Ezek 5.2; 17.21
12.16 Deut 29.24-28; 1 Kgs 9.6-9; Jer 22.8,9
12.19 Isa 6.11; Mic 7.13; Zech 7.14
12.20 Isa 7.23,24; Jer 25.9; Dan 9.17
12.22 Jer 5.12; Amos 6.3; 2 Pet 3.3,4
12.24 1 Kgs 22.11-13; Prov 26.28; Jer 14.13-16; Zech 13.2-4
12.25 Num 14.28-34
12.27 Dan 10.14
13.2 Isa 9.15; 56.9-12; Jer 37.19; Zech 11.15; 2 Pet 2.1-3
13.5 Ps 106.23; Isa 58.12; Eph 6.13,14; Rev. 16.14
13.6 Jer 28.15; 29.8; Mk 13.22,23; 2 Thess 2.11
13.8 Nah 2.13
13.9 Ex 32.32,33; Ezra 2.59-63; Ps 69.28; Jer 20.3-6; Dan 12.1; Phil 4.3

12.21–28 These two short messages were warnings that God's words would come true—*soon!* Less than six years later, Jerusalem was destroyed. Yet the people were skeptical. Unbelief and false security led them to believe it would never happen. The apostle Peter dealt with this problem in the church (2 Peter 3.9). It is dangerous to say Christ will never return or to regard his coming as so far in the future as to be irrelevant today. All that God says is sure to happen. Don't dare assume you have plenty of time to get right with God.

13.1ff This warning was directed against false prophets whose messages were not from God, but were lies intended to win popularity by saying whatever made the people happy. False prophets did not care about the truth as Ezekiel did. They lulled people into a false sense of security, making Ezekiel's job even more difficult. Beware of leaders who bend the truth in their quest for popularity and power.

13.2, 3 The false prophets had a large following because they comforted the people and approved of their sinful actions. Lies are often attractive, and liars may have large followings. Today, for example, some leaders assure us that God promises his followers health and material success. This is comforting, but is it true? God's own Son did not have an easy life on earth. Make sure the messages you believe are consistent with what God teaches in his Word.

13.10–12 These false prophets covered their lies with "whitewash"—a pleasing front. Such superficiality can't hold up under God's scrutiny.

is no peace; and because, when the people build a wall, these prophets[c] smear
whitewash on it. 11 Say to those who smear whitewash on it that it shall fall. There
will be a deluge of rain,[d] great hailstones will fall, and a stormy wind will break
out. 12 When the wall falls, will it not be said to you, "Where is the whitewash you
smeared on it?" 13 Therefore thus says the Lord GOD: In my wrath I will make a
stormy wind break out, and in my anger there shall be a deluge of rain, and hailstones in wrath to destroy it. 14 I will break down the wall that you have smeared
with whitewash, and bring it to the ground, so that its foundation will be laid bare;
when it falls, you shall perish within it; and you shall know that I am the LORD.
15 Thus I will spend my wrath upon the wall, and upon those who have smeared it
with whitewash; and I will say to you, The wall is no more, nor those who smeared
it— 16 the prophets of Israel who prophesied concerning Jerusalem and saw visions
of peace for it, when there was no peace, says the Lord GOD.
17 As for you, mortal, set your face against the daughters of your people, who
prophesy out of their own imagination; prophesy against them 18 and say, Thus says
the Lord GOD: Woe to the women who sew bands on all wrists, and make veils for
the heads of persons of every height, in the hunt for human lives! Will you hunt
down lives among my people, and maintain your own lives? 19 You have profaned
me among my people for handfuls of barley and for pieces of bread, putting to
death persons who should not die and keeping alive persons who should not live, by
your lies to my people, who listen to lies.
20 Therefore thus says the Lord GOD: I am against your bands with which you
hunt lives;[e] I will tear them from your arms, and let the lives go free, the lives that
you hunt down like birds. 21 I will tear off your veils, and save my people from your
hands; they shall no longer be prey in your hands; and you shall know that I am the
LORD. 22 Because you have disheartened the righteous falsely, although I have not
disheartened them, and you have encouraged the wicked not to turn from their
wicked way and save their lives; 23 therefore you shall no longer see false visions or
practice divination; I will save my people from your hand. Then you will know that
I am the LORD.

Idolatry is condemned

14 Certain elders of Israel came to me and sat down before me. 2 And the word
of the LORD came to me: 3 Mortal, these men have taken their idols into their
hearts, and placed their iniquity as a stumbling block before them; shall I let myself
be consulted by them? 4 Therefore speak to them, and say to them, Thus says the
Lord GOD: Any of those of the house of Israel who take their idols into their hearts
and place their iniquity as a stumbling block before them, and yet come to the
prophet—I the LORD will answer those who come with the multitude of their idols,
5 in order that I may take hold of the hearts of the house of Israel, all of whom are
estranged from me through their idols.
6 Therefore say to the house of Israel, Thus says the Lord GOD: Repent and turn

13.10 Jer 8.11; 50.6 1 Tim 4.1 2 Tim 3.13
13.13 Ex 9.24,25 Ps 18.12,13 Rev 11.19 16.21
13.14 Mic 1.6 1 Cor 3.11-15
13.16 Isa 57.21
13.17 Judg 4.4 2 Kgs 22.14 Lk 2.36 Acts 21.9 Rev 2.20
13.19 Jer 23.14,17
13.21 Ps 91.3; 124.7
13.22 Amos 5.12 2 Pet 2.18,19
13.23 Mic 3.6 Zech 13.3
14.1 2 Kgs 6.32
14.3 Isa 1.15 Zeph 1.3
14.4 1 Kgs 21.20-24 2 Kgs 1.16 Isa 66.4
14.5 Deut 32.14,15 Jer 2.11 Hos 10.2 Zech 7.12

[c] Heb *they* [d] Heb *rain and you* [e] Gk Syr: Heb *lives for birds*

13.17 In the Bible, prophecy was open to women as well as men. Miriam (Exodus 15.20), Deborah (Judges 4.4), and Huldah (2 Kings 22.14) were prophetesses. But the women mentioned here are more like the witch of 1 Samuel 28.7, and are condemned for disheartening the people (13.22).

13.18 These bands and veils were charms used in witchcraft practices. They were advertised as good luck charms, but were used to ensnare the people in idolatry.

14.3 God condemned the elders for worshiping idols in their hearts and then daring to come to God's prophet for advice. On the outside, they appeared to worship God. They made regular visits to the temple where they offered sacrifices, but they were not sincere. It is easy for us to criticize the Israelites for worshiping idols when they so clearly needed God. But we have idols in our hearts when we pursue reputation, acceptance, wealth, or sensual pleasure with the intensity and commitment that we should have for serving God.

14.3–5 For Hebrew writers, important functions of life were assigned to different physical organs. The heart was considered the core of a person's intellectual and spiritual function. Because all people have someone or something as the object of their heart's dependence, they have a type of idolatry. God wants to recapture the hearts of his people. We must never let anything captivate our allegiance or imagination in such a way to replace or weaken our devotion to God.

14.6–11 The people of Judah, though eager to accept the messages of false prophets, considered the presence of a few God-fearing men in the nation an insurance policy against disaster. In a pinch, they could always ask God's prophets for advice. But merely having God's people around doesn't help. We must remem-

away from your idols; and turn away your faces from all your abominations. 7 For
any of those of the house of Israel, or of the aliens who reside in Israel, who separate themselves from me, taking their idols into their hearts and placing their iniquity as a stumbling block before them, and yet come to a prophet to inquire of me
by him, I the LORD will answer them myself. 8 I will set my face against them; I will
make them a sign and a byword and cut them off from the midst of my people; and
you shall know that I am the LORD.

9 If a prophet is deceived and speaks a word, I, the LORD, have deceived that
prophet, and I will stretch out my hand against him, and will destroy him from the
midst of my people Israel. 10 And they shall bear their punishment—the punishment of the inquirer and the punishment of the prophet shall be the same— 11 so
that the house of Israel may no longer go astray from me, nor defile themselves any
more with all their transgressions. Then they shall be my people, and I will be their
God, says the Lord GOD.

12 The word of the LORD came to me: 13 Mortal, when a land sins against me by
acting faithlessly, and I stretch out my hand against it, and break its staff of bread
and send famine upon it, and cut off from it human beings and animals, 14 even if
Noah, Daniel,[f] and Job, these three, were in it, they would save only their own
lives by their righteousness, says the Lord GOD. 15 If I send wild animals through
the land to ravage it, so that it is made desolate, and no one may pass through
because of the animals; 16 even if these three men were in it, as I live, says the Lord
GOD, they would save neither sons nor daughters; they alone would be saved, but
the land would be desolate. 17 Or if I bring a sword upon that land and say, 'Let a
sword pass through the land,' and I cut off human beings and animals from it;
18 though these three men were in it, as I live, says the Lord GOD, they would save
neither sons nor daughters, but they alone would be saved. 19 Or if I send a pestilence into that land, and pour out my wrath upon it with blood, to cut off humans
and animals from it; 20 even if Noah, Daniel,[f] and Job were in it, as I live, says the
Lord GOD, they would save neither son nor daughter; they would save only their
own lives by their righteousness.

21 For thus says the Lord GOD: How much more when I send upon Jerusalem
my four deadly acts of judgment, sword, famine, wild animals, and pestilence, to
cut off humans and animals from it! 22 Yet, survivors shall be left in it, sons and
daughters who will be brought out; they will come out to you. When you see their
ways and their deeds, you will be consoled for the evil that I have brought upon
Jerusalem, for all that I have brought upon it. 23 They shall console you, when you
see their ways and their deeds; and you shall know that it was not without cause that
I did all that I have done in it, says the Lord GOD.

Jerusalem is a useless vine

15 The word of the LORD came to me:
2 O mortal, how does the wood of the vine surpass all other wood—
the vine branch that is among the trees of the forest?
3 Is wood taken from it to make anything?
Does one take a peg from it on which to hang any object?
4 It is put in the fire for fuel;

14.6 1 Sam 7.3 Neh 1.9 Isa 30.22 55.6,7
14.8 Isa 65.15 Jer 24.9 Rom 11.22
14.9 Jer 6.14,15
14.11 Deut 13.11 19.20 Isa 9.16 Ezek 44.10,15
14.13 Ezek 15.8; 20.27
14.14 Gen 6.8 8.20,21 Job 1.1,5 Dan 10.11 Heb 11.7
14.16 Gen 19.29 Acts 27.24
14.19 Jer 14.12 Ezek 5.12
14.21 Amos 4.6-10 Rev 6.4-8
14.22 Ezek 36.20
15.2 Ps 80.8-16 Isa 5.1-7 Hos 10.1 Jn 15.1-6
15.4 Isa 27.11 Heb 6.8

[f] Or, as otherwise read, *Danel*

---

ber that the relationship our pastor, family, or friends have with God will not protect us from the consequences of our own sins. Each person is responsible for his or her own relationship with God. Is your faith personal and real, or are you resting in what others have done?

14.14 Noah, Daniel, and Job were great men in Hebrew history, renowned for their relationships with God and their wisdom (see Genesis 6.8, 9; Daniel 2.47, 48; Job 1.1). Daniel had been taken into captivity during Babylon's first invasion of Judah in 605 B.C., eight years before Ezekiel was taken captive. At the time of Ezekiel's message, Daniel occupied a high government position in Babylon. But even these great men of God could not have saved the people of Judah, because God had already passed judgment on the nation's pervasive evil.

15.1ff The messages given to Ezekiel in chapters 15–17 provided further evidence that God was going to destroy Jerusalem. The first message was about a vine, useless at first and even more useless after being burned. The people of Jerusalem were useless to God because of their idol worship, and so they would be destroyed and their cities burned. Have you also become dormant and unfruitful to God? How can you begin fulfilling his plan for you?

when the fire has consumed both ends of it
and the middle of it is charred,
is it useful for anything?
5 When it was whole it was used for nothing;
how much less—when the fire has consumed it,
and it is charred—
can it ever be used for anything!

6 Therefore thus says the Lord GOD: Like the wood of the vine among the trees
of the forest, which I have given to the fire for fuel, so I will give up the inhabitants
of Jerusalem. 7 I will set my face against them; although they escape from the fire,
the fire shall still consume them; and you shall know that I am the LORD, when I set
my face against them. 8 And I will make the land desolate, because they have acted
faithlessly, says the Lord GOD.

Israel's loathsome sins

16 The word of the LORD came to me: 2 Mortal, make known to Jerusalem her
abominations, 3 and say, Thus says the Lord GOD to Jerusalem: Your origin
and your birth were in the land of the Canaanites; your father was an Amorite, and
your mother a Hittite. 4 As for your birth, on the day you were born your navel cord
was not cut, nor were you washed with water to cleanse you, nor rubbed with salt,
nor wrapped in cloths. 5 No eye pitied you, to do any of these things for you out of
compassion for you; but you were thrown out in the open field, for you were abhorred on the day you were born.

6 I passed by you, and saw you flailing about in your blood. As you lay in your
blood, I said to you, "Live! 7 and grow up[g] like a plant of the field." You grew up
and became tall and arrived at full womanhood;[h] your breasts were formed, and
your hair had grown; yet you were naked and bare.

8 I passed by you again and looked on you; you were at the age for love. I
spread the edge of my cloak over you, and covered your nakedness: I pledged myself to you and entered into a covenant with you, says the Lord GOD, and you
became mine. 9 Then I bathed you with water and washed off the blood from you,
and anointed you with oil. 10 I clothed you with embroidered cloth and with sandals
of fine leather; I bound you in fine linen and covered you with rich fabric.[i] 11 I
adorned you with ornaments: I put bracelets on your arms, a chain on your neck,
12 a ring on your nose, earrings in your ears, and a beautiful crown upon your head.
13 You were adorned with gold and silver, while your clothing was of fine linen,
rich fabric,[i] and embroidered cloth. You had choice flour and honey and oil for
food. You grew exceedingly beautiful, fit to be a queen. 14 Your fame spread
among the nations on account of your beauty, for it was perfect because of my
splendor that I had bestowed on you, says the Lord GOD.

15 But you trusted in your beauty, and played the whore because of your fame,
and lavished your whorings on any passer-by.[j] 16 You took some of your garments, and made for yourself colorful shrines, and on them played the whore; noth-

15.7 Lev 26.17; 1 Kgs 19.17; Amos 5.19; 9.1-4
16.2 Isa 58.1; Hos 8.1
16.5 Deut 32.10; Isa 49.15; Jer 9.21,22; 22.19
16.6 Ex 1.7; Deut 1.10; Ps 105.10-15
16.8 Gen 22.16-18; Ex 24.7,8; Deut 4.31; Hos 2.18-20
16.9 Ex 26.36; Ezek 26.16; 27.7,16
16.11 Gen 24.22,47; Isa 3.18,19
16.12 Jer 13.18
16.13 Deut 32.13,14; Ps 45.13,14
16.14 Deut 4.6-8, 32-38; 1 Kgs 10.1,24; Ps 50.2
16.15 Ezek 27.3

[g] Gk Syr: Heb *Live! I made you a myriad* [h] Cn: Heb *ornament of ornaments* [i] Meaning of Heb uncertain
[j] Heb adds *let it be his*

16.1ff Using the imagery of a young baby growing to mature womanhood, God reminded Jerusalem that he raised her from a lowly state to great glory as his bride. However, she betrayed God's trust and prostituted herself by seeking alliances with pagan nations and adopting their customs. If we push God aside for anything, even education, family, career, or pleasure, we are abandoning him in the same way.

16.3 *Canaan* was the ancient name of the territory taken over by the children of Israel. The Bible often uses this name to refer to all the corrupt heathen nations of the region. The Amorites and Hittites, two Canaanite nations, were known for their wickedness. But now God says his people are no better than the Canaanites.

16.8–14 God chose Israel to be the channel to communicate his message of salvation to the entire world. He gave Israel special privileges and trained the nation to do his work. But these resources and advantages became its source of pride and vanity. We must remember that it is God who made us what we are. To use our resources and opportunities only for our own selfish pursuits is both dangerous and foolish.

16.15 God cared for and loved Judah, only to have it turn away to other nations and their false gods. The nation had grown to maturity and became famous; but it forgot who had helped (16.22). This is a picture of spiritual adultery (called *apostasy*—turning from the one true God). As you become wise and more mature, don't turn away from the One who truly loves you. It is a mistake to confuse maturity with rebellion against God.

ing like this has ever been or ever shall be.[k] 17 You also took your beautiful jewels
of my gold and my silver that I had given you, and made for yourself male images,
and with them played the whore; 18 and you took your embroidered garments to
cover them, and set my oil and my incense before them. 19 Also my bread that I
gave you — I fed you with choice flour and oil and honey — you set it before them
as a pleasing odor; and so it was, says the Lord GOD. 20 You took your sons and
your daughters, whom you had borne to me, and these you sacrificed to them to be
devoured. As if your whorings were not enough! 21 You slaughtered my children
and delivered them up as an offering to them. 22 And in all your abominations and
your whorings you did not remember the days of your youth, when you were naked
and bare, flailing about in your blood.

23 After all your wickedness (woe, woe to you! says the Lord GOD), 24 you built
yourself a platform and made yourself a lofty place in every square; 25 at the head
of every street you built your lofty place and prostituted your beauty, offering yourself to every passer-by, and multiplying your whoring. 26 You played the whore
with the Egyptians, your lustful neighbors, multiplying your whoring, to provoke
me to anger. 27 Therefore I stretched out my hand against you, reduced your rations, and gave you up to the will of your enemies, the daughters of the Philistines,
who were ashamed of your lewd behavior. 28 You played the whore with the Assyrians, because you were insatiable; you played the whore with them, and still you
were not satisfied. 29 You multiplied your whoring with Chaldea, the land of merchants; and even with this you were not satisfied.

30 How sick is your heart, says the Lord GOD, that you did all these things, the
deeds of a brazen whore; 31 building your platform at the head of every street, and
making your lofty place in every square! Yet you were not like a whore, because
you scorned payment. 32 Adulterous wife, who receives strangers instead of her
husband! 33 Gifts are given to all whores; but you gave your gifts to all your lovers,
bribing them to come to you from all around for your whorings. 34 So you were
different from other women in your whorings: no one solicited you to play the
whore; and you gave payment, while no payment was given to you; you were different.

35 Therefore, O whore, hear the word of the LORD: 36 Thus says the Lord GOD,
Because your lust was poured out and your nakedness uncovered in your whoring
with your lovers, and because of all your abominable idols, and because of the
blood of your children that you gave to them, 37 therefore, I will gather all your
lovers, with whom you took pleasure, all those you loved and all those you hated;
I will gather them against you from all around, and will uncover your nakedness to
them, so that they may see all your nakedness. 38 I will judge you as women who
commit adultery and shed blood are judged, and bring blood upon you in wrath and
jealousy. 39 I will deliver you into their hands, and they shall throw down your
platform and break down your lofty places; they shall strip you of your clothes and
take your beautiful objects and leave you naked and bare. 40 They shall bring up a
mob against you, and they shall stone you and cut you to pieces with their swords.
41 They shall burn your houses and execute judgments on you in the sight of many
women; I will stop you from playing the whore, and you shall also make no more
payments. 42 So I will satisfy my fury on you, and my jealousy shall turn away from
you; I will be calm, and will be angry no longer. 43 Because you have not remembered the days of your youth, but have enraged me with all these things; therefore,
I have returned your deeds upon your head, says the Lord GOD.

16.17 Ex 32.3,4 Hos 2.13; 10.1
16.20 Ex 13.2,12 Ps 106.37,38 Jer 7.31
16.21 2 Kgs 17.17 21.6
16.24 2 Kgs 21.3-7 23.5-7 Ps 78.58 Isa 57.5-7
16.26 Jer 7.18,19
16.27 Isa 9.12
16.28 Judg 10.6 2 Kgs 16.7-18 2 Chron 28.16-23 Hos 10.6
16.30 Prov 7.11-13 9.13 Isa 3.9 Rev 17.1-6
16.31 Isa 52.3 Hos 12.11
16.33 Hos 8.9,10 Joel 3.3 Lk 15.30
16.36 Jer 19.5 Ezek 20.31 23.37
16.37 Isa 47.3 Nah 3.5,6
16.38 Ps 79.3,5 Zeph 1.17 Rev 16.6
16.40 2 Kgs 25.9 Jer 39.8
16.42 2 Sam 24.25 Isa 40.1,2 54.9,10
16.43 Ps 78.42 Isa 63.10

[k] Meaning of Heb uncertain

16.20, 21 Child sacrifice had been practiced by the Canaanites long before Israel invaded their land. But it was strictly forbidden by God (Leviticus 20.1–3). By Ezekiel's time, however, the people were openly sacrificing their own children (2 Kings 16.3; 21.6). Jeremiah confirmed that this was a common practice (Jeremiah 7.31; 32.35). Because of such vile acts among the people and priesthood, the temple became unfit for God to inhabit. When God left the temple, he was no longer Judah's guide and protector.

16.27 The actions of the Jews were so disgusting that even those who worshiped other gods, including their great enemy the Philistines, would have been ashamed to behave that way. The Jews outdid them in doing evil.

Have you not committed lewdness beyond all your abominations? 44 See, everyone who uses proverbs will use this proverb about you, “Like mother, like daughter.” 45 You are the daughter of your mother, who loathed her husband and her
children; and you are the sister of your sisters, who loathed their husbands and their
children. Your mother was a Hittite and your father an Amorite. 46 Your elder sister
is Samaria, who lived with her daughters to the north of you; and your younger
sister, who lived to the south of you, is Sodom with her daughters. 47 You not only
followed their ways, and acted according to their abominations; within a very little
time you were more corrupt than they in all your ways. 48 As I live, says the Lord
GOD, your sister Sodom and her daughters have not done as you and your daughters
have done. 49 This was the guilt of your sister Sodom: she and her daughters had
pride, excess of food, and prosperous ease, but did not aid the poor and needy.
50 They were haughty, and did abominable things before me; therefore I removed
them when I saw it. 51 Samaria has not committed half your sins; you have committed more abominations than they, and have made your sisters appear righteous by
all the abominations that you have committed. 52 Bear your disgrace, you also, for
you have brought about for your sisters a more favorable judgment; because of your
sins in which you acted more abominably than they, they are more in the right than
you. So be ashamed, you also, and bear your disgrace, for you have made your
sisters appear righteous.

53 I will restore their fortunes, the fortunes of Sodom and her daughters and the
fortunes of Samaria and her daughters, and I will restore your own fortunes along
with theirs, 54 in order that you may bear your disgrace and be ashamed of all that
you have done, becoming a consolation to them. 55 As for your sisters, Sodom and
her daughters shall return to their former state, Samaria and her daughters shall
return to their former state, and you and your daughters shall return to your former
state. 56 Was not your sister Sodom a byword in your mouth in the day of your
pride, 57 before your wickedness was uncovered? Now you are a mockery to the
daughters of Aram[l] and all her neighbors, and to the daughters of the Philistines,
those all around who despise you. 58 You must bear the penalty of your lewdness
and your abominations, says the LORD.

59 Yes, thus says the Lord GOD: I will deal with you as you have done, you who
have despised the oath, breaking the covenant; 60 yet I will remember my covenant
with you in the days of your youth, and I will establish with you an everlasting
covenant. 61 Then you will remember your ways, and be ashamed when I[m] take
your sisters, both your elder and your younger, and give them to you as daughters,
but not on account of my[n] covenant with you. 62 I will establish my covenant with
you, and you shall know that I am the LORD, 63 in order that you may remember and
be confounded, and never open your mouth again because of your shame, when I
forgive you all that you have done, says the Lord GOD.

[l] Another reading is *Edom* [m] Syr: Heb *you* [n] Heb lacks *my*

16.45 Isa 1.4 Zech 11.8
16.46 Gen 13.11-13 Deut 32.32 Jer 3.8-11
16.47 1 Kgs 16.31 2 Kgs 21.9 Jn 15.21,22 1 Cor 5.1
16.48 Mt 11.23,24
16.49 Gen 13.10 Ps 138.6 Isa 22.13 Lk 12.16-20
16.50 Gen 19.24,25
16.51 Jer 3.8-11 Mt 12.41,42 Rom 3.9-20
16.53 Isa 19.24,25
16.54 Jer 2.26
16.57 2 Kgs 16.5-7 2 Chron 28.5,6, 18-23 Hos 2.10; 7.1
16.59 Isa 24.5 Jer 32.38-41
16.62 Jer 24.7
16.63 Ezra 9.6 Ps 39.9 Dan 9.7,8 Rom 3.19

16.44–52 The city of Sodom, a symbol of total corruption, was completely destroyed by God for its wickedness (Genesis 19.24, 25). Samaria, the capital of what had been the northern kingdom (Israel), was despised and rejected by the Jews in Judah. To be called a sister to Samaria and Sodom was bad enough, but to be called *worse* than that meant that Judah's sins were an unspeakable abomination and that its doom was inevitable. The reason it was considered worse was not that its sins were worse, but that it knew better. In that light, we, who live in an age when God's message is made clear to us through the Bible, are worse than Judah if we continue in sin! (See also Matthew 11.20–24.)

16.49 It is easy to point our finger at Sodom, especially for its terrible sexual sins. Ezekiel reminded Judah, however, that Sodom was destroyed because of pride, laziness, gluttony, and ignoring the needy within its reach. It is easy to be selective in what we consider gross sin. If we do not commit such horrible sins as adultery, homosexuality, stealing, and murder, we may think we are living well enough. But what about sins like pride, laziness, gluttony, and ignoring the needy? These sins may not be as shocking to you as the others, but they are also forbidden by God.

16.59–63 Although the people had broken their promises and did not deserve anything but punishment, God would not break his promises. If the people turned back to him, he would again forgive them and renew his covenant. This covenant was put into effect when Jesus paid for the sins of all mankind by his death on the cross (Hebrews 10.8–10). No one is beyond the reach of God's forgiveness. Although we don't deserve anything but punishment for our sins, God's arms are still outstretched. He will not break his promise to give us salvation and forgiveness if we repent and turn to him.

The riddle of the great eagle

17.2 Ezek 20.49; 24.3
17.3 Jer 48.40 Dan 4.22

17 The word of the LORD came to me: 2 O mortal, propound a riddle, and speak
an allegory to the house of Israel. 3 Say: Thus says the Lord GOD:
A great eagle, with great wings and long pinions,
rich in plumage of many colors,
came to the Lebanon.
He took the top of the cedar,
4 broke off its topmost shoot;
He carried it to a land of trade,
set it in a city of merchants.

17.5 Deut 8.7-9 Isa 44.4 Jer 37.1

5 Then he took a seed from the land,
placed it in fertile soil;
A plant° by abundant waters,
he set it like a willow twig.
6 It sprouted and became a vine
spreading out, but low;
Its branches turned toward him,
its roots remained where it stood.
So it became a vine;
it brought forth branches,
put forth foliage.

17.7 Ezek 31.4

7 There was another great eagle,
with great wings and much plumage.
And see! This vine stretched out
its roots toward him;
It shot out its branches toward him,
so that he might water it.
From the bed where it was planted
8 it was transplanted
to good soil by abundant waters,
so that it might produce branches
and bear fruit
and become a noble vine.
9 Say: Thus says the Lord GOD:
Will it prosper?
Will he not pull up its roots,
cause its fruit to rot° and wither,
its fresh sprouting leaves to fade?
No strong arm or mighty army will be needed
to pull it from its roots.

17.10 Ezek 19.12-14 Hos 13.15 Mt 21.19

10 When it is transplanted, will it thrive?
When the east wind strikes it,
will it not utterly wither,
wither on the bed where it grew?

17.12 2 Kgs 24.10-17 2 Chron 36.13 Jer 22.24-28

11 Then the word of the LORD came to me: 12 Say now to the rebellious house:
Do you not know what these things mean? Tell them: The king of Babylon came to
Jerusalem, took its king and its officials, and brought them back with him to Bab-
ylon. 13 He took one of the royal offspring and made a covenant with him, putting

° Meaning of Heb uncertain

17.1ff The first eagle in this chapter represents King Nebuchadnezzar of Babylon (see 17.12), who appointed or "placed" or planted Zedekiah as king in Jerusalem. Zedekiah rebelled against this arrangement and tried to ally with Egypt, the second eagle, to battle against Babylon. This took place while Ezekiel, miles away in Babylon, was describing these events. Jeremiah, a prophet in Judah, was also warning Zedekiah not to form this alliance (Jeremiah 2.36, 37). Although miles apart, the prophets had the same message because both spoke for God. God still directs his chosen spokesmen to speak his truth all around the world.

17.10 This east wind was the hot, dry wind blowing off the desert, a wind that could wither a flourishing crop. The hot wind of Nebuchadnezzar's armies was about to overcome the nation of Judah.

him under oath (he had taken away the chief men of the land), 14 so that the kingdom might be humble and not lift itself up, and that by keeping his covenant it
might stand. 15 But he rebelled against him by sending ambassadors to Egypt, in
order that they might give him horses and a large army. Will he succeed? Can one
escape who does such things? Can he break the covenant and yet escape? 16 As I
live, says the Lord GOD, surely in the place where the king resides who made him
king, whose oath he despised, and whose covenant with him he broke—in Babylon
he shall die. 17 Pharaoh with his mighty army and great company will not help him
in war, when ramps are cast up and siege-walls built to cut off many lives. 18 Because he despised the oath and broke the covenant, because he gave his hand and
yet did all these things, he shall not escape. 19 Therefore thus says the Lord GOD: As
I live, I will surely return upon his head my oath that he despised, and my covenant
that he broke. 20 I will spread my net over him, and he shall be caught in my snare;
I will bring him to Babylon and enter into judgment with him there for the treason
he has committed against me. 21 All the pick[p] of his troops shall fall by the sword,
and the survivors shall be scattered to every wind; and you shall know that I, the
LORD, have spoken.

22 Thus says the Lord GOD:
I myself will take a sprig
from the lofty top of a cedar;
I will set it out.
I will break off a tender one
from the topmost of its young twigs;
I myself will plant it
on a high and lofty mountain.
23 On the mountain height of Israel
I will plant it,
in order that it may produce boughs and bear fruit,
and become a noble cedar.
Under it every kind of bird will live;
in the shade of its branches will nest
winged creatures of every kind.
24 All the trees of the field shall know
that I am the LORD.
I bring low the high tree,
I make high the low tree;
I dry up the green tree
and make the dry tree flourish.
I the LORD have spoken;
I will accomplish it.

17.14 Jer 27.12-17 38.17
17.15 Deut 29.12-15 2 Kgs 24.20 2 Chron 36.13 Jer 38.18,23
17.16 Jer 52.11 Hos 10.4
17.17 Isa 36.6 Jer 37.7
17.18 1 Chron 29.24 2 Chron 30.8
17.21 2 Kgs 25.5,11 Jer 48.44 Amos 9.1-10
17.22 Ps 72.16; 80.15 Isa 27.6 Zech 3.8 4.12-14
17.24 Isa 37.12,13 55.12 Amos 9.11 1 Cor 1.27,28

Each person is responsible for his own sin

18 The word of the LORD came to me: 2 What do you mean by repeating this
proverb concerning the land of Israel, "The parents have eaten sour grapes,
and the children's teeth are set on edge"? 3 As I live, says the Lord GOD, this prov-

18.2 Jer 31.29 Mt 23.36 Rom 9.20

[p] Another reading is *fugitives*

17.22, 23 Ezekiel's prophecy of judgment ends in hope. When the people put their hope in foreign alliances, they were disappointed. Only God could give them true hope. God said he would plant a tender twig, the Messiah, whose kingdom would grow and become a shelter for all who come to him (see Isaiah 11.1–5). This prophecy was fulfilled at the coming of Jesus Christ.

18.1ff The people of Judah believed they were being punished for the sins of their ancestors, not their own, and rightly so, for this was the teaching of the ten commandments (Exodus 20.5). Ezekiel taught also that the destruction of Jerusalem was due to the spiritual decay in previous generations. Their belief in the corporate life of Israel led to fatalism and irresponsibility. So Ezekiel gave God's new policy for this new land since the people misconstrued the old one. God judges each person individually. Although we often suffer from the effects of sins committed by those who came before us, God does not punish us for someone else's sins, and we can't use their mistakes as an excuse for our sins. Each person is accountable to God for his or her actions.

In addition, some people of Judah used the corporate umbrella of God's blessing as an excuse for disobeying God. They thought that because of their righteous ancestors (18.5–9), they would live. God told them that they would not; they were the evil sons of righteous parents and, as such, would die (18.10–13). If, however, anyone returned to God, he or she would live (18.14–18).

erb shall no more be used by you in Israel. 4 Know that all lives are mine; the life
of the parent as well as the life of the child is mine: it is only the person who sins
that shall die.
5 If a man is righteous and does what is lawful and right— 6 if he does not eat
upon the mountains or lift up his eyes to the idols of the house of Israel, does not
defile his neighbor's wife or approach a woman during her menstrual period, 7 does
not oppress anyone, but restores to the debtor his pledge, commits no robbery,
gives his bread to the hungry and covers the naked with a garment, 8 does not take
advance or accrued interest, withholds his hand from iniquity, executes true justice
between contending parties, 9 follows my statutes, and is careful to observe my
ordinances, acting faithfully—such a one is righteous; he shall surely live, says the
Lord GOD.
10 If he has a son who is violent, a shedder of blood, 11 who does any of these
things (though his father[q] does none of them), who eats upon the mountains, defiles his neighbor's wife, 12 oppresses the poor and needy, commits robbery, does
not restore the pledge, lifts up his eyes to the idols, commits abomination, 13 takes
advance or accrued interest; shall he then live? He shall not. He has done all these
abominable things; he shall surely die; his blood shall be upon himself.
14 But if this man has a son who sees all the sins that his father has done, considers, and does not do likewise, 15 who does not eat upon the mountains or lift up
his eyes to the idols of the house of Israel, does not defile his neighbor's wife,
16 does not wrong anyone, exacts no pledge, commits no robbery, but gives his
bread to the hungry and covers the naked with a garment, 17 withholds his hand
from iniquity,[r] takes no advance or accrued interest, observes my ordinances, and
follows my statutes; he shall not die for his father's iniquity; he shall surely live.
18 As for his father, because he practiced extortion, robbed his brother, and did
what is not good among his people, he dies for his iniquity.
19 Yet you say, "Why should not the son suffer for the iniquity of the father?"
When the son has done what is lawful and right, and has been careful to observe all
my statutes, he shall surely live. 20 The person who sins shall die. A child shall not
suffer for the iniquity of a parent, nor a parent suffer for the iniquity of a child; the
righteousness of the righteous shall be his own, and the wickedness of the wicked
shall be his own.
21 But if the wicked turn away from all their sins that they have committed and
keep all my statutes and do what is lawful and right, they shall surely live; they
shall not die. 22 None of the transgressions that they have committed shall be remembered against them; for the righteousness that they have done they shall live.
23 Have I any pleasure in the death of the wicked, says the Lord GOD, and not rather
that they should turn from their ways and live? 24 But when the righteous turn away
from their righteousness and commit iniquity and do the same abominable things
that the wicked do, shall they live? None of the righteous deeds that they have done
shall be remembered; for the treachery of which they are guilty and the sin they
have committed, they shall die.
25 Yet you say, "The way of the Lord is unfair." Hear now, O house of Israel:

[q] Heb *he* [r] Gk: Heb *the poor*

18.4 Num 16.22; 27.16; Isa 57.16; Zech 12.1; Rom 6.23
18.6 Deut 4.19; Mt 5.28; 1 Cor 6.9-11; 10.20
18.7 Lev 19.13; 1 Sam 12.3,4; Mt 25.35-40; Lk 3.11
18.8 Ex 22.25; Zech 8.16
18.9 Hab 2.4; Rom 1.17
18.12 2 Kgs 21.11; Hos 12.7; Amos 4.1
18.14 2 Chron 29.6-10; 34.21; Prov 17.21; Mt 23.32
18.16 Job 31.16; Ps 41.1
18.19 Zech 1.3-6
18.20 Deut 24.16; 1 Kgs 14.13; Isa 53.11; Mt 16.27; Rom 2.6-9
18.22 Ps 18.20-24; Mic 7.19
18.23 Ps 147.11; 2 Pet 3.9
18.24 1 Sam 15.11; Prov 21.16; Gal 3.3,4
18.25 Gen 18.25; Deut 32.4; Zeph 3.5; Mal 3.13-15

18.8 The law of Moses had rules about charging interest (Exodus 22.25; Leviticus 25.36; Deuteronomy 23.19, 20) to prevent Jews from taking advantage of the poor or of fellow Israelites.

18.12 "Restore the pledge" referred to the lender letting the debtor use the cloak each night that he has placed as security on his loan. Without the cloak, the debtor would be cold at night. (See Exodus 22.26 and Deuteronomy 24.10–13 for the giving of this law.)

18.14–18 Family traditions were very important to the Jews, but God made it clear that people should not follow a tradition of sin. You may have come from an unbelieving family, but you can choose to believe in God and you will be saved. It is far better to begin a new spiritual heritage than to hold on to patterns of unbelief.

18.23 God is a God of love, but he is also a God of perfect justice. His perfect love causes him to be merciful to those who recognize their sin and turn back to him, but he cannot wink at those who willfully sin. Wicked people die both physically and spiritually. God takes no joy in their deaths; he would prefer that they turn to him and have eternal life. Likewise, we should not rejoice in the misfortunes of nonbelievers. Instead, we should do all in our power to bring them to faith.

18.25 A typical childish response to punishment is to say, "That isn't fair!" In reality, God is fair, but *we* have broken the rules. It is not God who must live up to our ideas of fairness; instead, we must live up to his.

Is my way unfair? Is it not your ways that are unfair? 26 When the righteous turn
away from their righteousness and commit iniquity, they shall die for it; for the
iniquity that they have committed they shall die. 27 Again, when the wicked turn
away from the wickedness they have committed and do what is lawful and right,
they shall save their life. 28 Because they considered and turned away from all the
transgressions that they had committed, they shall surely live; they shall not die.
29 Yet the house of Israel says, "The way of the Lord is unfair." O house of Israel,
are my ways unfair? Is it not your ways that are unfair?

30 Therefore I will judge you, O house of Israel, all of you according to your **18.30** Ezek 14.6; 33.11
ways, says the Lord GOD. Repent and turn from all your transgressions; otherwise Hos 12.6
iniquity will be your ruin.[s] 31 Cast away from you all the transgressions that you **18.31** Ps 51.10
have committed against me, and get yourselves a new heart and a new spirit! Why Jer 32.39
will you die, O house of Israel? 32 For I have no pleasure in the death of anyone, Acts 3.19 Rom 8.13
says the Lord GOD. Turn, then, and live. Jas 4.8

A lamentation for Israel's leaders

19 As for you, raise up a lamentation for the princes of Israel, 2 and say: **19.1** 2 Kgs 25.5-7 2 Chron 36.3-10 Jer 22.10-12, 28-30

What a lioness was your mother
among lions!
She lay down among young lions,
rearing her cubs.
3 She raised up one of her cubs; **19.3** 2 Kgs 23.31-34 2 Chron 36.1-4
he became a young lion,
and he learned to catch prey;
he devoured humans.
4 The nations sounded an alarm against him;
he was caught in their pit;
and they brought him with hooks
to the land of Egypt.
5 When she saw that she was thwarted, **19.5** 2 Kgs 24.8-12 2 Chron 36.9,10
that her hope was lost,
she took another of her cubs
and made him a young lion.
6 He prowled among the lions;
he became a young lion,
and he learned to catch prey;
he devoured people.
7 And he ravaged their strongholds,[t]
and laid waste their towns;
the land was appalled, and all in it,
at the sound of his roaring.
8 The nations set upon him
from the provinces all around;
they spread their net over him;
he was caught in their pit.
9 With hooks they put him in a cage, **19.9** 2 Kgs 24.15

[s] *Or so that they shall not be a stumbling block of iniquity to you* [t] *Heb his widows*

18.30–32 Ezekiel's solution to the problem of inherited guilt is for each person to have a changed life. This is God's work in us and not something we can do for ourselves. The Holy Spirit does it (Psalm 51.10–12). If we renounce our life's direction of sin and rebellion and turn to God, he gives us a new direction, new love, and a new power to change. You can begin by faith, trusting in his power to change your heart and mind. Then determine to live each day with him in control (Ephesians 4.22–24).

19.1ff Ezekiel used illustrations to communicate many of his messages. With the picture of the lioness and her cubs, he raised the curiosity of his listeners. The lioness symbolized the nation of Judah, and the two cubs were two of its kings. The first cub was King Jehoahaz, who was taken captive to Egypt in 609 B.C. by Pharaoh Neco (2 Kings 23.31–33). The second cub was either King Jehoiachin, who had already been taken into captivity in Babylon (2 Kings 24.8ff), or King Zedekiah, who soon would be (2 Kings 25.7). This illustration showed that for Judah, there was no hope for a quick return from exile, and no escape from the approaching Babylonian armies.

and brought him to the king of Babylon;
they brought him into custody,
so that his voice should be heard no more
on the mountains of Israel.

19.10 Ps 80.8-11

10 Your mother was like a vine in a vineyard[u]
transplanted by the water,
fruitful and full of branches
from abundant water.
11 Its strongest stem became
a ruler's scepter;[v]
it towered aloft
among the thick boughs;
it stood out in its height
with its mass of branches.

19.12 Hos 13.15 Mt 3.10 Jn 15.6

12 But it was plucked up in fury,
cast down to the ground;
the east wind dried it up;
its fruit was stripped off,
its strong stem was withered;
the fire consumed it.

19.13 2 Kgs 24.12-16

13 Now it is transplanted into the wilderness,
into a dry and thirsty land.
14 And fire has gone out from its stem,
has consumed its branches and fruit,
so that there remains in it no strong stem,
no scepter for ruling.

This is a lamentation, and it is used as a lamentation.

A reminder of rebellion

20.1 Ezek 8.1,11,12

20 In the seventh year, in the fifth month, on the tenth day of the month, certain
elders of Israel came to consult the LORD, and sat down before me. 2 And the
word of the LORD came to me: 3 Mortal, speak to the elders of Israel, and say to
them: Thus says the Lord GOD: Why are you coming? To consult me? As I live,

20.4 Ezek 16.2; 22.2

says the Lord GOD, I will not be consulted by you. 4 Will you judge them, mortal,
will you judge them? Then let them know the abominations of their ancestors, 5 and

20.5 Ezek 6.2-9; 33.3 Deut 7.6; 14.2 Jer 33.24 Mk 13.20

say to them: Thus says the Lord GOD: On the day when I chose Israel, I swore to the
offspring of the house of Jacob—making myself known to them in the land of
Egypt—I swore to them, saying, I am the LORD your God. 6 On that day I swore to
them that I would bring them out of the land of Egypt into a land that I had searched
out for them, a land flowing with milk and honey, the most glorious of all lands.

20.7 Deut 29.16,18

7 And I said to them, Cast away the detestable things your eyes feast on, every one
of you, and do not defile yourselves with the idols of Egypt; I am the LORD your

20.8 Isa 63.10

God. 8 But they rebelled against me and would not listen to me; not one of them cast
away the detestable things their eyes feasted on, nor did they forsake the idols of
Egypt.

20.9 Ex 32.11-14 Num 14.13 Deut 9.28 32.26,27

Then I thought I would pour out my wrath upon them and spend my anger against
them in the midst of the land of Egypt. 9 But I acted for the sake of my name, that
it should not be profaned in the sight of the nations among whom they lived, in

[u] Cn: Heb *in your blood* [v] Heb *Its strongest stems became rulers' scepters*

19.11, 12 Not even the political and military might of Judah's kings could save the nation. Like branches of a vine, they would be cut off and uprooted by "the east wind"—the powerful Babylonian army.

20.1ff Here Ezekiel gives a panoramic view of Israel's history of rebellion. The emphasis is upon God's attempts to bring the nation back to himself and his mercy on his constantly rebellious and disobedient people. Ezekiel gives the message that the people alone are responsible for the troubles and judgments they have experienced. Those who continue to rebel he will "purge out" (20.38), while he promises to bring the faithful "into the land of Israel, the country that I swore to give to your ancestors" (20.42). The reason: that "you shall know that I am the Lord."

whose sight I made myself known to them in bringing them out of the land of
Egypt. 10 So I led them out of the land of Egypt and brought them into the wilderness. 11 I gave them my statutes and showed them my ordinances, by whose observance everyone shall live. 12 Moreover I gave them my sabbaths, as a sign between
me and them, so that they might know that I the LORD sanctify them. 13 But the
house of Israel rebelled against me in the wilderness; they did not observe my statutes but rejected my ordinances, by whose observance everyone shall live; and my
sabbaths they greatly profaned.

Then I thought I would pour out my wrath upon them in the wilderness, to make
an end of them. 14 But I acted for the sake of my name, so that it should not be
profaned in the sight of the nations, in whose sight I had brought them out. 15 Moreover I swore to them in the wilderness that I would not bring them into the land that
I had given them, a land flowing with milk and honey, the most glorious of all
lands, 16 because they rejected my ordinances and did not observe my statutes, and
profaned my sabbaths; for their heart went after their idols. 17 Nevertheless my eye
spared them, and I did not destroy them or make an end of them in the wilderness.

18 I said to their children in the wilderness, Do not follow the statutes of your
parents, nor observe their ordinances, nor defile yourselves with their idols. 19 I the
LORD am your God; follow my statutes, and be careful to observe my ordinances,
20 and hallow my sabbaths that they may be a sign between me and you, so that you
may know that I the LORD am your God. 21 But the children rebelled against me;
they did not follow my statutes, and were not careful to observe my ordinances, by
whose observance everyone shall live; they profaned my sabbaths.

Then I thought I would pour out my wrath upon them and spend my anger against
them in the wilderness. 22 But I withheld my hand, and acted for the sake of my
name, so that it should not be profaned in the sight of the nations, in whose sight I
had brought them out. 23 Moreover I swore to them in the wilderness that I would
scatter them among the nations and disperse them through the countries, 24 because
they had not executed my ordinances, but had rejected my statutes and profaned my
sabbaths, and their eyes were set on their ancestors' idols. 25 Moreover I gave them
statutes that were not good and ordinances by which they could not live. 26 I defiled
them through their very gifts, in their offering up all their firstborn, in order that I
might horrify them, so that they might know that I am the LORD.

27 Therefore, mortal, speak to the house of Israel and say to them, Thus says
the Lord GOD: In this again your ancestors blasphemed me, by dealing treacherously with me. 28 For when I had brought them into the land that I swore to give
them, then wherever they saw any high hill or any leafy tree, there they offered
their sacrifices and presented the provocation of their offering; there they sent up
their pleasing odors, and there they poured out their drink offerings. 29 (I said to
them, What is the high place to which you go? So it is called Bamah[w] to this day.)
30 Therefore say to the house of Israel, Thus says the Lord GOD: Will you defile

[w] That is *High Place*

20.11 Ex 20.1-23,33 Lev 18.5 Neh 9.13,14
20.13 Num 14.11 Isa 56.6
20.16 Ezek 11.21 14.3-7
20.17 Jer 4.27; 5.18 Nah 1.8,9
20.18 Deut 4.3,4 Ps 78.6,8
20.19 Ex 6.7; 20.2
20.21 Num 25.1-3
20.22 Job 13.21 Ps 78.38 Isa 48.9-11
20.23 Deut 28.64-68 32.26,27 Jer 15.4
20.25 Ps 81.12 Rom 1.21-25,28 2 Thess 2.9-11
20.26 Rom 11.8
20.27 1 Kgs 14.23
20.30 Judg 2.19

20.12, 13 The sabbath, instituted by God at creation, was entrusted to Israel as a sign that God had created and redeemed them (Exodus 20.8–11; Deuteronomy 5.12–15). This day of rest was a gift from a loving God, not a difficult obligation. But the people repeatedly desecrated the sabbath and ignored their God (see also 20.20, 21). It was meant to be a memory device but they ignored it. While most Christians celebrate the Lord's day, Sunday, as their sabbath, we must be careful to fulfill God's purpose in it. He wants us to rest, refocus, and remember him.

20.23, 24 At the very beginning of Israel's history, God clearly warned the people about the consequences of disobedience (Deuteronomy 28.15ff). When the people disobeyed, God let them experience those devastating consequences to remind them of the seriousness of their sins. If you choose to live for yourself, apart from God, you may experience similar destructive consequences. However, even through such consequences, God may be drawing you to himself. Let your misfortunes bring you to your senses and to the merciful God before it is too late.

20.25 Why would God give them laws that weren't good? This isn't talking about any aspect of the Mosaic law because Ezekiel reinforces that (20.11, 13, 21). Evidently the Jews had taken Exodus 13.12 and 22.29, the dedication of firstborn animals and children, as a justification for child sacrifice to the Canaanite god Molech. God was giving them over to this delusion to speed up their judgment (20.26), and to allow them to fall away in order to jar their consciences and revitalize their faith.

20.30 Water containing contaminants, even in small amounts, is polluted. Likewise, our lives are polluted when we accept the immoral values of this world. If we love money, we become greedy. If we lust, we become sexually immoral. Remaining pure in a polluted world is difficult, to say the least. But a heart filled with God's Holy Spirit leaves no room for pollution (see Titus 1.15).

yourselves after the manner of your ancestors and go astray after their detestable
20.31 Ps 106.37-39 things? 31 When you offer your gifts and make your children pass through the fire,
you defile yourselves with all your idols to this day. And shall I be consulted by
you, O house of Israel? As I live, says the Lord GOD, I will not be consulted
by you.
32 What is in your mind shall never happen—the thought, "Let us be like the
nations, like the tribes of the countries, and worship wood and stone."
33 As I live, says the Lord GOD, surely with a mighty hand and an outstretched
20.34 Lam 2.4 arm, and with wrath poured out, I will be king over you. 34 I will bring you out from
the peoples and gather you out of the countries where you are scattered, with a
20.35 Deut 32.10 1 Cor 10.5-10 mighty hand and an outstretched arm, and with wrath poured out; 35 and I will bring
you into the wilderness of the peoples, and there I will enter into judgment with you
face to face. 36 As I entered into judgment with your ancestors in the wilderness of
the land of Egypt, so I will enter into judgment with you, says the Lord GOD. 37 I
will make you pass under the staff, and will bring you within the bond of the cove-
20.38 Ps 95.11 Ezek 34.17-22 Heb 4.3 nant. 38 I will purge out the rebels among you, and those who transgress against me;
I will bring them out of the land where they reside as aliens, but they shall not enter
the land of Israel. Then you shall know that I am the LORD.
20.39 Isa 1.12-15 39 As for you, O house of Israel, thus says the Lord GOD: Go serve your idols,
everyone of you now and hereafter, if you will not listen to me; but my holy name
you shall no more profane with your gifts and your idols.
20.40 Ezek 43.12,27 40 For on my holy mountain, the mountain height of Israel, says the Lord GOD,
there all the house of Israel, all of them, shall serve me in the land; there I will
accept them, and there I will require your contributions and the choicest of your
20.41 Isa 27.12,13 Amos 9.14 gifts, with all your sacred things. 41 As a pleasing odor I will accept you, when I
bring you out from the peoples, and gather you out of the countries where you have
been scattered; and I will manifest my holiness among you in the sight of the nations. 42 You shall know that I am the LORD, when I bring you into the land of
20.43 Zech 12.10-14 Lk 18.13 2 Cor 7.11 Israel, the country that I swore to give to your ancestors. 43 There you shall remember your ways and all the deeds by which you have polluted yourselves; and you
shall loathe yourselves for all the evils that you have committed. 44 And you shall
know that I am the LORD, when I deal with you for my name's sake, not according
to your evil ways, or corrupt deeds, O house of Israel, says the Lord GOD.
20.46 Jer 13.19 45[x] The word of the LORD came to me: 46 Mortal, set your face toward the south,
20.47 Isa 9.18 preach against the south, and prophesy against the forest land in the Negeb; 47 say
to the forest of the Negeb, Hear the word of the LORD: Thus says the Lord GOD, I
will kindle a fire in you, and it shall devour every green tree in you and every dry
20.48 Jer 17.27 tree; the blazing flame shall not be quenched, and all faces from south to north shall
be scorched by it. 48 All flesh shall see that I the LORD have kindled it; it shall not
20.49 Mt 13.12,13 Jn 16.25 be quenched. 49 Then I said, "Ah Lord GOD! they are saying of me, 'Is he not a
maker of allegories?' "

[x] Ch 21.1 in Heb

20.35, 36 When the Israelites disobeyed God by refusing to enter the promised land the first time, God chose to purify his people by forcing them to wander in the wilderness until that entire generation died (Numbers 14.26–35). Here he promises to purge the nation of its rebellious people again as they cross the vast wilderness from their captivity in Babylon. Only those who faithfully follow God will be able to return to their land. The purpose of this desert judgment will be to purge all those who worship idols.

20.39 The Israelites were worshiping idols and giving gifts to God at the same time! They did not believe in their God as the one true God; instead, they worshiped him along with the other gods of the land. Perhaps they enjoyed the immoral pleasures of idol worship; or perhaps they didn't want to miss out on the benefits the idols might give them. Often people believe in God and give him gifts of church attendance or service, while still holding on to their idols of money, power, or pleasure. They don't want to miss out on any possible benefits. But God wants all of our lives and all of our devotion; he will not share it because devotion to anything else is idol worship. Beware of trying to keep God pleased while you also pursue the pleasures of sin. You must choose one or the other.

20.45 The Negeb is the southern part of Judah.

20.49 Ezekiel was exasperated and discouraged. Many Israelites complained that he spoke only in riddles ('allegories"), so they refused to listen. No matter how important our work or how significant our ministry, we will have moments of discouragement. Apparently God did not answer Ezekiel's plea; instead, he gave Ezekiel another message to proclaim. What has been discouraging you? Have you felt like giving up? Instead, continue doing what God has told you to do. He promises to reward the faithful (Mark 13.13). God's cure for discouragement may be another assignment. In serving others, we may find the renewal we need.

Babylon will attack Judah

21 [y]The word of the LORD came to me: 2 Mortal, set your face toward Jerusalem
and preach against the sanctuaries; prophesy against the land of Israel 3 and
say to the land of Israel, Thus says the LORD: I am coming against you, and will
draw my sword out of its sheath, and will cut off from you both righteous and
wicked. 4 Because I will cut off from you both righteous and wicked, therefore my
sword shall go out of its sheath against all flesh from south to north; 5 and all flesh
shall know that I the LORD have drawn my sword out of its sheath; it shall not be
sheathed again. 6 Moan therefore, mortal; moan with breaking heart and bitter grief
before their eyes. 7 And when they say to you, "Why do you moan?" you shall say,
"Because of the news that has come. Every heart will melt and all hands will be
feeble, every spirit will faint and all knees will turn to water. See, it comes and it
will be fulfilled," says the Lord GOD.
8 And the word of the LORD came to me: 9 Mortal, prophesy and say: Thus says
the Lord; Say:

A sword, a sword is sharpened,
 it is also polished;
10 It is sharpened for slaughter,
 honed to flash like lightning!
How can we make merry?
 You have despised the rod,
 and all discipline.[z]
11 The sword[a] is given to be polished,
 to be grasped in the hand;
It is sharpened, the sword is polished,
 to be placed in the slayer's hand.
12 Cry and wail, O mortal,
 for it is against my people;
it is against all Israel's princes;
 they are thrown to the sword,
 together with my people.
 Ah! Strike the thigh!

13 For consider: What! If you despise the rod, will it not happen?[z] says the Lord
GOD.

14 And you, mortal, prophesy;
 Strike hand to hand.
Let the sword fall twice, thrice;
 it is a sword for killing.
A sword for great slaughter—
 it surrounds them;
15 therefore hearts melt
 and many stumble.
At all their gates I have set
 the point[z] of the sword.
Ah! It is made for flashing,
 it is polished[b] for slaughter.
16 Attack to the right!
 Engage to the left!
 Wherever your edge is directed.
17 I too will strike hand to hand,

21.3 Isa 57.1; Jer 21.13; Nah 2.13; 3.5
21.4 Jer 12.12; Ezek 7.2
21.5 1 Sam 3.12; Neh 1.9
21.7 Isa 13.7; Ezek 7.26
21.9 Ps 110.5,6; Isa 34.5,6
21.12 Joel 1.13
21.15 Josh 2.11; 2 Sam 17.10; Jer 17.27
21.17 Ezek 5.13

[y] Ch 21.6 in Heb [z] Meaning of Heb uncertain [a] Heb *It* [b] Tg: Heb *wrapped up*

21.1ff The short message in 20.45–48 introduces the first of four messages about the judgments that would come upon Jerusalem: (1) the sword of the Lord (20.45–21.7); (2) the sharpened sword (21.8–17); (3) the sword of Nebuchadnezzar (21.18–22); (4) the sword of conquest (21.28–32). The city would be destroyed because it was defiled. According to Jewish law, defiled objects were to be passed through fire in order to purify them (see Numbers 31.22, 23; Psalm 66.10–12; Proverbs 17.3). God's judgment is designed to purify; destruction is often a necessary part of that process.

21.12 To strike the thigh was a gesture of grief, similar to beating the chest or pulling the hair today.

I will satisfy my fury;
I the LORD have spoken.

21.19 Deut 3.11 Amos 1.14

18 The word of the LORD came to me: 19 Mortal, mark out two roads for the
sword of the king of Babylon to come; both of them shall issue from the same land.
And make a signpost, make it for a fork in the road leading to a city; 20 mark out the
road for the sword to come to Rabbah of the Ammonites or to Judah and to[c] Jerusalem the fortified. 21 For the king of Babylon stands at the parting of the way, at the
fork in the two roads, to use divination; he shakes the arrows, he consults the teraphim,[d] he inspects the liver. 22 Into his right hand comes the lot for Jerusalem, to
set battering rams, to call out for slaughter, for raising the battle cry, to set battering
rams against the gates, to cast up ramps, to build siege-towers. 23 But to them it will
seem like a false divination; they have sworn solemn oaths; but he brings their guilt
to remembrance, bringing about their capture.

21.21 Prov 16.33; 21.1 Hos 4.12 Zech 10.2
21.22 Ezek 4.2; 26.9
21.23 Num 5.15 Ezek 17.16,18

24 Therefore thus says the Lord GOD: Because you have brought your guilt to
remembrance, in that your transgressions are uncovered, so that in all your deeds
your sins appear—because you have come to remembrance, you shall be taken in
hand.[e]

21.25 Ps 37.13 Ezek 7.2-7

25 As for you, vile, wicked prince of Israel,
you whose day has come,
the time of final punishment,

21.26 Ps 75.7 Jer 13.18

26 thus says the Lord GOD:
Remove the turban, take off the crown;
things shall not remain as they are.
Exalt that which is low,
abase that which is high.

21.27 Ps 2.6 Jer 23.56 Hag 2.21,22

27 A ruin, a ruin, a ruin—
I will make it!
(Such has never occurred.)
Until he comes whose right it is;
to him I will give it.

21.28 Jer 12.12 Zeph 2.8-10

28 As for you, mortal, prophesy, and say, Thus says the Lord GOD concerning
the Ammonites, and concerning their reproach; say:
A sword, a sword! Drawn for slaughter
Polished to consume,[f] to flash like lightning.

21.29 Jer 27.9 Ezek 13.6-9

29 Offering false visions for you,
divining lies for you,
they place you over the necks
of the vile, wicked ones—
those whose day has come,
the time of final punishment.

21.30 Jer 47.6,7 Ezek 25.5

30 Return it to its sheath!
In the place where you were created,
in the land of your origin,

[c] Gk Syr: Heb *Judah in* [d] Or *the household gods* [e] Or *be taken captive* [f] Cn: Heb *to contain*

21.19 Nebuchadnezzar had three ways to get advice on the future. One was shaking the arrows, much like drawing straws, to see which course of action was right; the second was consulting a household god to see if some spirit might direct him; the third was having priests inspect the liver of a sacrificed animal to see if its shape and size would indicate a decision.

21.19–23 In 589 B.C., the nations of Judah and Ammon made a peace treaty, conspiring against Babylon. Ezekiel gave this message to the exiles who had heard the news and were again filled with hope of returning to their homeland. Ezekiel said that Babylon's king would march his armies into the region to stop the rebellion. Traveling from the north, he would stop at a fork in the road, one leading to Rabbah, the capital of Ammon, and the other leading to Jerusalem, the capital of Judah. He had to decide which city to destroy. Just as Ezekiel predicted, King Nebuchadnezzar went to Jerusalem and besieged it.

21.27 Instead of using exclamation points for emphasis, the Hebrew language used repetition. The repetition of *a ruin* shows the certainty of the end of the old order—the world as it is now. The new order—the world as God intends it—will come when he "whose right it is" (the Messiah) returns and sets up his righteous kingdom.

21.28 The Ammonites and Israelites were usually at odds with each other. God told the Israelites not to ally with foreign nations, but Judah and Ammon allied against Babylon in 589 B.C. God first judged Judah as Nebuchadnezzar first went to Jerusalem (21.22); but Ammon will also be judged, not for allying with Judah, but for watching Jerusalem's destruction with delight.

I will judge you.
31 I will pour out my indignation upon you,
with the fire of my wrath
I will blow upon you.
I will deliver you into brutish hands,
those skillful to destroy.
32 You shall be fuel for the fire;
your blood shall enter the earth;
You shall be remembered no more,
for I the LORD have spoken.

God lists Jerusalem's sins

22 The word of the LORD came to me: 2 You, mortal, will you judge, will you
judge the bloody city? Then declare to it all its abominable deeds. 3 You
shall say, Thus says the Lord GOD: A city! Shedding blood within itself; its time has
come; making its idols, defiling itself. 4 You have become guilty by the blood that
you have shed, and defiled by the idols that you have made; you have brought your
day near, the appointed time of your years has come. Therefore I have made you a
disgrace before the nations, and a mockery to all the countries. 5 Those who are
near and those who are far from you will mock you, you infamous one, full of
tumult.
6 The princes of Israel in you, everyone according to his power, have been bent
on shedding blood. 7 Father and mother are treated with contempt in you; the alien
residing within you suffers extortion; the orphan and the widow are wronged in
you. 8 You have despised my holy things, and profaned my sabbaths. 9 In you are
those who slander to shed blood, those in you who eat upon the mountains, who
commit lewdness in your midst. 10 In you they uncover their fathers' nakedness; in
you they violate women in their menstrual periods. 11 One commits abomination
with his neighbor's wife; another lewdly defiles his daughter-in-law; another in you
defiles his sister, his father's daughter. 12 In you, they take bribes to shed blood;
you take both advance interest and accrued interest, and make gain of your neighbors by extortion; and you have forgotten me, says the Lord GOD.
13 See, I strike my hands together at the dishonest gain you have made, and at
the blood that has been shed within you. 14 Can your courage endure, or can your
hands remain strong in the days when I shall deal with you? I the LORD have spoken, and I will do it. 15 I will scatter you among the nations and disperse you
through the countries, and I will purge your filthiness out of you. 16 And I[g] shall be
profaned through you in the sight of the nations; and you shall know that I am the
LORD.
17 The word of the LORD came to me: 18 Mortal, the house of Israel has become
dross to me; all of them, silver,[h] bronze, tin, iron, and lead. In the smelter they
have become dross. 19 Therefore thus says the Lord GOD: Because you have all
become dross, I will gather you into the midst of Jerusalem. 20 As one gathers silver, bronze, iron, lead, and tin into a smelter, to blow the fire upon them in order
to melt them; so I will gather you in my anger and in my wrath, and I will put you
in and melt you. 21 I will gather you and blow upon you with the fire of my wrath,
and you shall be melted within it. 22 As silver is melted in a smelter, so you shall be

21.31 Ps 18.15 Nah 1.6 Hab 1.6,10
21.32 Mal 4.1 Mt 3.10
22.3 Ezek 23.37,45
22.4 2 Kgs 21.16 Ps 44.13,14 Ezek 5.14,15 Dan 9.16
22.6 Isa 1.23 Mic 3.1-3,9-11
22.7 Ex 22.22; 23.9 Deut 27.19 Prov 22.22,23
22.9 Judg 20.6 Hos 4.2,10,14
22.10 Lev 18.8,19 Deut 27.20-23 1 Cor 5.1
22.11 Lev 18.15 2 Sam 13.14
22.12 Lev 19.13; 25.36 Deut 27.25 Ps 106.21
22.13 Num 24.10 Prov 28.8 Isa 33.15 Amos 2.6-8
22.15 Deut 4.27
22.16 Ezek 6.4-7
22.22 Ezek 20.8,33 Hos 5.10

[g] Gk Syr Vg: Heb *you* [h] Transposed from the end of the verse; compare verse 20

22.1ff Chapter 22 explains why Jerusalem's judgment would come (22.2–16), how it would come (22.17–22), and who would be judged by it (22.23–31).

22.6–13 The leaders were especially responsible for the moral climate of the nation because God chose them to lead. The same is true today (see James 3.1). Unfortunately, many of the sins mentioned here have been committed in recent years by Christian leaders. We are living in a time of unprecedented attacks by Satan. It is vital that we uphold our leaders in prayer; and it is vital for leaders to seek accountability to help them keep their moral and spiritual integrity.

22.17–22 Precious metals are refined with intense heat to remove the impurities. When heated, the dross (impurities) rises to the top of the molten metal and is skimmed off and thrown away. The purpose of the invasion of Jerusalem was to refine the people, but the refining process showed that the people, like worthless dross, had nothing good in them.

melted in it; and you shall know that I the LORD have poured out my wrath upon
you.
23 The word of the LORD came to me: 24 Mortal, say to it: You are a land that is
not cleansed, not rained upon in the day of indignation. 25 Its princes[i] within it are
like a roaring lion tearing the prey; they have devoured human lives; they have
taken treasure and precious things; they have made many widows within it. 26 Its
priests have done violence to my teaching and have profaned my holy things; they
have made no distinction between the holy and the common, neither have they
taught the difference between the unclean and the clean, and they have disregarded
my sabbaths, so that I am profaned among them. 27 Its officials within it are like
wolves tearing the prey, shedding blood, destroying lives to get dishonest gain.
28 Its prophets have smeared whitewash on their behalf, seeing false visions and
divining lies for them, saying, "Thus says the Lord GOD," when the LORD has not
spoken. 29 The people of the land have practiced extortion and committed robbery;
they have oppressed the poor and needy, and have extorted from the alien without
redress. 30 And I sought for anyone among them who would repair the wall and
stand in the breach before me on behalf of the land, so that I would not destroy it;
but I found no one. 31 Therefore I have poured out my indignation upon them; I
have consumed them with the fire of my wrath; I have returned their conduct upon
their heads, says the Lord GOD.

A parable of adultery

23 The word of the LORD came to me: 2 Mortal, there were two women, the
daughters of one mother; 3 they played the whore in Egypt; they played the
whore in their youth; their breasts were caressed there, and their virgin bosoms
were fondled. 4 Oholah was the name of the elder and Oholibah the name of her
sister. They became mine, and they bore sons and daughters. As for their names,
Oholah is Samaria, and Oholibah is Jerusalem.
5 Oholah played the whore while she was mine; she lusted after her lovers the
Assyrians, warriors[j] 6 clothed in blue, governors and commanders, all of them
handsome young men, mounted horsemen. 7 She bestowed her favors upon them,
the choicest men of Assyria all of them; and she defiled herself with all the idols of
everyone for whom she lusted. 8 She did not give up her whorings that she had
practiced since Egypt; for in her youth men had lain with her and fondled her virgin
bosom and poured out their lust upon her. 9 Therefore I delivered her into the hands
of her lovers, into the hands of the Assyrians, for whom she lusted. 10 These uncovered her nakedness; they seized her sons and her daughters; and they killed her with
the sword. Judgment was executed upon her, and she became a byword among
women.

22.24 2 Chron 28.22; Isa 9.13; Jer 2.30; Zeph 3.2
22.25 Jer 2.34; 15.8; Hos 6.9
22.26 1 Sam 2.12-17; Hag 2.11-14
22.28 Jer 23.25-32; Ezek 13.6
22.29 Isa 5.7; Amos 3.10; Jas 5.4
22.30 Ps 106.23; Isa 59.16; 63.5; Jer 5.1; Ezek 13.5
22.31 Isa 10.5; Ezek 7.3-9; 16.43; Rom 2.8,9
23.2 Jer 3.7-10
23.4 2 Kgs 15.19; 16.7; 17.3; Hos 5.13; 8.9,10; 10.6
23.7 Hos 5.3; 6.10
23.8 Ex 32.4; 1 Kgs 12.28; 2 Kgs 17.16
23.9 Ezek 16.37; Hos 11.5; Rev 17.12-16

[i] Gk: Heb *indignation. 25A conspiracy of its prophets* [j] Meaning of Heb uncertain

22.26 The priests were supposed to keep God's worship pure and teach the people right living. But God had become commonplace to them, they ignored the sabbath, and they refused to teach the people. They no longer carried out their God-given duties (Leviticus 10.10, 11; Ezekiel 44.23). When doing God's work becomes no more important than any mundane task, we are no longer giving God the reverence he deserves. Instead of bringing God down to our level, we should live up to his level.

22.28–30 The wall spoken of here is not made of stones, but of faithful people united in their efforts to resist evil. This wall was in disrepair because there was no one who could lead the people back to God. The feeble attempts to repair it – through religious rituals or messages based on opinion rather than God's Word – were as worthless as whitewash, which only covers up problems. What the people really needed was total spiritual reconstruction! When we give the appearance of loving God without living his way, we are covering up sins which could eventually damage us beyond repair. Don't use religion as a whitewash; repair your life by applying the principles of God's Word. Then you can join with others to "stand in the breach" and make a difference for God in the world.

23.1ff Ezekiel continues his discussion of the reasons for God's judgment upon the nation by telling a further allegory. He compared the northern and southern kingdoms to two sisters giving themselves to adultery. The proud citizens of Jerusalem had long scorned their sister city of Samaria, thinking that they were superior. But God called both of these cities filthy whores – a shock to the people of Jerusalem who thought that they were righteous. Just as the imagery of this message was shocking and distasteful to the people, so our sins are repugnant to God.

23.4–6 Oholah (meaning, "her tent"), the northern kingdom of Israel, was lured away from God by the dashing Assyrians – their handsome clothes and powerful positions. The people coveted youth, strength, power, wealth, and pleasure – the same qualities people think will bring happiness today. But the charming Assyrians drew Israel away from God.

11 Her sister Oholibah saw this, yet she was more corrupt than she in her lusting
and in her whorings, which were worse than those of her sister. 12 She lusted after
the Assyrians, governors and commanders, warriors[k] clothed in full armor,
mounted horsemen, all of them handsome young men. 13 And I saw that she was
defiled; they both took the same way. 14 But she carried her whorings further; she
saw male figures carved on the wall, images of the Chaldeans portrayed in vermilion, 15 with belts around their waists, with flowing turbans on their heads, all of
them looking like officers—a picture of Babylonians whose native land was Chaldea. 16 When she saw them she lusted after them, and sent messengers to them in
Chaldea. 17 And the Babylonians came to her into the bed of love, and they defiled
her with their lust; and after she defiled herself with them, she turned from them in
disgust. 18 When she carried on her whorings so openly and flaunted her nakedness,
I turned in disgust from her, as I had turned from her sister. 19 Yet she increased her
whorings, remembering the days of her youth, when she played the whore in the
land of Egypt 20 and lusted after her paramours there, whose members were like
those of donkeys, and whose emission was like that of stallions. 21 Thus you longed
for the lewdness of your youth, when the Egyptians[l] fondled your bosom and caressed[m] your young breasts.

22 Therefore, O Oholibah, thus says the Lord GOD: I will rouse against you
your lovers from whom you turned in disgust, and I will bring them against you
from every side: 23 the Babylonians and all the Chaldeans, Pekod and Shoa and
Koa, and all the Assyrians with them, handsome young men, governors and commanders all of them, officers and warriors,[n] all of them riding on horses. 24 They
shall come against you from the north[o] with chariots and wagons and a host of
peoples; they shall set themselves against you on every side with buckler, shield,
and helmet, and I will commit the judgment to them, and they shall judge you
according to their ordinances. 25 I will direct my indignation against you, in order
that they may deal with you in fury. They shall cut off your nose and your ears, and
your survivors shall fall by the sword. They shall seize your sons and your daughters, and your survivors shall be devoured by fire. 26 They shall also strip you of
your clothes and take away your fine jewels. 27 So I will put an end to your lewdness
and your whoring brought from the land of Egypt; you shall not long for them, or
remember Egypt any more. 28 For thus says the Lord GOD: I will deliver you into
the hands of those whom you hate, into the hands of those from whom you turned
in disgust; 29 and they shall deal with you in hatred, and take away all the fruit of
your labor, and leave you naked and bare, and the nakedness of your whorings shall
be exposed. Your lewdness and your whorings 30 have brought this upon you, because you played the whore with the nations, and polluted yourself with their idols.
31 You have gone the way of your sister; therefore I will give her cup into your
hand. 32 Thus says the Lord GOD:

You shall drink your sister's cup,
deep and wide;

23.11 Jer 3.8-11
23.13 Hos 12.1,2
23.14 Ezek 8.10
23.16 Prov 6.25 Mt 5.28 2 Pet 2.14
23.17 2 Kgs 24.17
23.18 Deut 32.19 Ps 78.59 106.40 Jer 8.12
23.20 Ezek 17.15
23.21 Jer 3.9
23.22 Isa 10.5,6 Hab 1.6-10
23.23 Gen 25.18 2 Kgs 20.14-17 Job 1.17
23.24 Jer 39.5,6
23.26 Isa 3.16-24
23.28 Jer 21.7-10
23.29 Deut 28.48 2 Sam 13.15
23.31 1 Kgs 21.8-14 2 Kgs 21.13 Dan 9.12
23.32 Ps 60.3 Ezek 5.14,15

[k] Meaning of Heb uncertain [l] Two Mss: MT *from Egypt* [m] Cn: Heb *for the sake of* [n] Compare verses 6 and 12: Heb *officers and called ones* [o] Gk: Meaning of Heb uncertain

23.11ff Oholibah (meaning, "my tent is in her") is now shown to be worse because she did not learn from the judgment upon her sister, but continued in her lust for the Assyrians and Babylonians. Therefore, her judgment was equally certain. Just as Oholibah was privileged and should have known better, so we are privileged because we know about Christ. We need to be doubly sure we follow him.

23.12 "She lusted after the Assyrians" (excessively tried to please) probably refers to Ahaz paying protection money to Tiglath-pileser III (2 Kings 16.7, 8).

23.16 This invitation to Chaldea (Babylon) was given by Hezekiah to the envoys from Babylon (Isaiah 38, 39).

23.17 At first, Judah made an alliance with Babylon (Chaldea), but then changed its mind. During the reigns of the last two Judean kings, Jehoiakim and Zedekiah, it looked to Egypt for help. Judah's faithlessness (its alliances with godless nations) cost it the only real protection it ever had—God.

23.21 "Lewdness" is promiscuity (see also 23.27, 49)—giving sexual favors instead of being faithful to a spouse or to God. We don't think of ourselves as being spiritually promiscuous, but we often spend more time seeking the advice of magazines, television commercials, and non-Christian experts than we do God and his Word.

23.22–26 This predicts the last attack on Jerusalem, which would destroy the city and bring to Babylon the third wave of captives in 586 B.C. (2 Kings 25; Jeremiah 52). The first attack came in 605 B.C., the second in 597 B.C. Pekod, Shoa, and Koa were regions within Chaldea. A buckler was a small, round shield used in battle.

you shall be scorned and derided,
it holds so much.

23.33 Jer 25.15,16,27

33 You shall be filled with drunkenness and sorrow.
A cup of horror and desolation
is the cup of your sister Samaria;

23.34 Ps 75.8 Isa 51.17

34 you shall drink it and drain it out,
and gnaw its sherds,
and tear out your breasts;

23.35 1 Kgs 14.9 Neh 9.26 Hos 13.6

for I have spoken, says the Lord GOD. 35 Therefore thus says the Lord GOD: Because you have forgotten me and cast me behind your back, therefore bear the
consequences of your lewdness and whorings.

23.36 Isa 58.1 Jer 1.10 Mt 23.13-35

36 The LORD said to me: Mortal, will you judge Oholah and Oholibah? Then
declare to them their abominable deeds. 37 For they have committed adultery, and
blood is on their hands; with their idols they have committed adultery; and they
have even offered up to them for food the children whom they had borne to me.

23.38 2 Kgs 21.4,7 Neh 13.17,18 Jer 17.27

38 Moreover this they have done to me: they have defiled my sanctuary on the same
day and profaned my sabbaths. 39 For when they had slaughtered their children for
their idols, on the same day they came into my sanctuary to profane it. This is what

23.39 Jer 7.9-11

they did in my house.

23.40 2 Kgs 9.30 20.13-15 Ezek 16.13-16

40 They even sent for men to come from far away, to whom a messenger was
sent, and they came. For them you bathed yourself, painted your eyes, and decked
yourself with ornaments; 41 you sat on a stately couch, with a table spread before it

23.41 Esth 1.6 Jer 44.17

on which you had placed my incense and my oil. 42 The sound of a raucous multitude was around her, with many of the rabble brought in drunken from the wilder-

23.42 Gen 24.30 Amos 6.3-6

ness; and they put bracelets on the arms[p] of the women, and beautiful crowns upon
their heads.

23.43 Ezra 9.7

43 Then I said, Ah, she is worn out with adulteries, but they carry on their
sexual acts with her. 44 For they have gone in to her, as one goes in to a whore. Thus
they went in to Oholah and to Oholibah, wanton women. 45 But righteous judges
shall declare them guilty of adultery and of bloodshed; because they are adulter-
esses and blood is on their hands.
46 For thus says the Lord GOD: Bring up an assembly against them, and make

23.47 Jer 24.9; 29.18

them an object of terror and of plunder. 47 The assembly shall stone them and with
their swords they shall cut them down; they shall kill their sons and their daughters,
and burn up their houses. 48 Thus will I put an end to lewdness in the land, so that

23.49 Isa 59.18 Ezek 9.10

all women may take warning and not commit lewdness as you have done. 49 They
shall repay you for your lewdness, and you shall bear the penalty for your sinful
idolatry; and you shall know that I am the Lord GOD.

The parable of the cooking pot

24 In the ninth year, in the tenth month, on the tenth day of the month, the word

24.2 2 Kgs 25.1 Jer 39.1; 52.4 Hab 2.2,3

of the LORD came to me: 2 Mortal, write down the name of this day, this very
day. The king of Babylon has laid siege to Jerusalem this very day. 3 And utter an
allegory to the rebellious house and say to them, Thus says the Lord GOD:

24.3 Jer 1.13,14

Set on the pot, set it on,
pour in water also;

24.4 Mic 3.2,3

4 put in it the pieces,
all the good pieces, the thigh and the shoulder;

p Heb *hands*

23.39 The Israelites went so far as to sacrifice their own children to idols, and then sacrifice to the Lord the same day. This made a mockery of worship. We cannot praise God and willfully sin at the same time. That would be like celebrating one's wedding anniversary and then going to bed with a neighbor.

24.1–14 Ezekiel gave this illustration in 588 B.C., three years after the first of the previous messages (see 20.1, 2). The people in Judah thought they were the choice meat because they hadn't been taken into captivity in 597 when the Babylonians last invaded the land. Ezekiel used this illustration before (chapter 11) to show that though the people thought they were safe and secure inside the pot, this pot would actually be the place of their destruction. This message was given to the exiles in Babylon the very day that the Babylonians attacked Jerusalem (24.2), beginning a siege that lasted over two years and resulted in the city's destruction. When God's judgment comes, it is relentless.

fill it with choice bones.
5 Take the choicest one of the flock,
pile the logs[q] under it;
boil its pieces,[r]
seethe[s] also its bones in it.

6 Therefore thus says the Lord GOD:
Woe to the bloody city,
the pot whose rust is in it,
whose rust has not gone out of it!
Empty it piece by piece,
making no choice at all.[t]
7 For the blood she shed is inside it;
she placed it on a bare rock;
she did not pour it out on the ground,
to cover it with earth.
8 To rouse my wrath, to take vengeance,
I have placed the blood she shed
on a bare rock,
so that it may not be covered.
9 Therefore thus says the Lord GOD:
Woe to the bloody city!
I will even make the pile great.
10 Heap up the logs, kindle the fire;
boil the meat well, mix in the spices,
let the bones be burned.
11 Stand it empty upon the coals,
so that it may become hot, its copper glow,
its filth melt in it, its rust be consumed.
12 In vain I have wearied myself;[u]
its thick rust does not depart.
To the fire with its rust![v]
13 Yet, when I cleansed you in your filthy lewdness,
you did not become clean from your filth;
you shall not again be cleansed
until I have satisfied my fury upon you.
14 I the LORD have spoken; the time is coming, I will act. I will not refrain, I will not
spare, I will not relent. According to your ways and your doings I will judge you,
says the Lord GOD.
15 The word of the LORD came to me: 16 Mortal, with one blow I am about to
take away from you the delight of your eyes; yet you shall not mourn or weep, nor
shall your tears run down. 17 Sigh, but not aloud; make no mourning for the dead.
Bind on your turban, and put your sandals on your feet; do not cover your upper lip
or eat the bread of mourners.[w] 18 So I spoke to the people in the morning, and at
evening my wife died. And on the next morning I did as I was commanded.

24.5 Jer 52.10; 24-27
24.6 2 Kgs 24.3,4 Rev 11.7,8 17.6; 18.24
24.7 Lev 17.13 Deut 12.16
24.8 Isa 26.21 Jer 22.8,9
24.9 Lk 13.34,35 Rev 14.20 16.6,19
24.12 Jer 6.28-30 Dan 9.13,14
24.13 Ezek 8.18 Rom 2.8,9
24.16 Job 23.2 Song 7.10 Jer 22.10
24.17 Lev 21.10-12 2 Sam 15.30 Jer 16.7

[q] Compare verse 10: Heb *the bones* [r] Two Mss: Heb *its boilings* [s] Cn: Heb *its bones seethe* [t] Heb *piece, no lot has fallen on it* [u] Cn: Meaning of Heb uncertain [v] Meaning of Heb uncertain [w] Vg Tg: Heb *of men*

24.6–13 The city of Jerusalem was like a pot so encrusted with sin that it would not come clean, even in the hottest fire. God wanted to cleanse the lives of those who lived in Jerusalem, and he wants to cleanse our lives today. Sometimes he tries to purify us through difficulties and troublesome circumstances. When you face tough times, allow the sin to be burned from your life. Look at your problems as an opportunity for your faith to grow. When these times come, unnecessary priorities and diversions are purged away. We can re-examine our life to do what really counts.

24.15–18 God told Ezekiel that his wife would die and he was not to grieve for her. Ezekiel obeyed God fully, even as Hosea did when he was told to marry an unfaithful woman (Hosea 1.2, 3). In both cases, these unusual events were intended as symbolic acts to picture God's relationship with his people. Obeying God can carry a high cost. The only grief more excruciating than losing your spouse and not being allowed to grieve would be to lose eternal life because you did not obey God. Ezekiel always obeyed God wholeheartedly. We should be wholehearted in our obedience. We can begin by doing all that God commands us to do, even when we don't feel like it. Are you willing to serve God as completely as Ezekiel did?

24.20 Ps 27.4; 84.1 Jer 16.3,4 Dan 11.31
24.24 Ezek 4.3 Lk 11.29,30 Jn 13.19; 14.29
24.25 Ps 48.2; 122.1-9 Jer 7.4; 11.22
24.26 1 Sam 4.12 Job 1.15-19 Ezek 33.21,22
24.27 Ex 6.11,12 Ps 51.15 Eph 6.19

19 Then the people said to me, "Will you not tell us what these things mean for
us, that you are acting this way?" 20 Then I said to them: The word of the LORD
came to me: 21 Say to the house of Israel, Thus says the Lord GOD: I will profane my
sanctuary, the pride of your power, the delight of your eyes, and your heart's desire; and your sons and your daughters whom you left behind shall fall by the
sword. 22 And you shall do as I have done; you shall not cover your upper lip or eat
the bread of mourners.[x] 23 Your turbans shall be on your heads and your sandals on
your feet; you shall not mourn or weep, but you shall pine away in your iniquities
and groan to one another. 24 Thus Ezekiel shall be a sign to you; you shall do just
as he has done. When this comes, then you shall know that I am the Lord GOD.
25 And you, mortal, on the day when I take from them their stronghold, their
joy and glory, the delight of their eyes and their heart's affection, and also[y] their
sons and their daughters, 26 on that day, one who has escaped will come to you to
report to you the news. 27 On that day your mouth shall be opened to the one who
has escaped, and you shall speak and no longer be silent. So you shall be a sign to
them; and they shall know that I am the LORD.

B. MESSAGES AGAINST FOREIGN NATIONS (25.1 – 32.32)

These messages were given concerning seven nations which surrounded Judah. The Ammonites were judged because of their joy over the profaning of the temple, the Moabites because they scorned Judah as special people, the Edomites because of their special hatred of the Jews, and the Philistines because of their vengeance. All these nations would soon realize that God is supreme. Nations today are also under limits imposed by God.

A prophecy against Ammon

25.3 Ps 70.2,3 Ezek 21.28 26.2; 36.2
25.4 Deut 28.33,51 Judg 6.3,33
25.5 2 Sam 12.26 Jer 49.2 Zeph 2.14,15

25 The word of the LORD came to me: 2 Mortal, set your face toward the Ammonites and prophesy against them. 3 Say to the Ammonites, Hear the word
of the Lord GOD: Thus says the Lord GOD, Because you said, "Aha!" over my
sanctuary when it was profaned, and over the land of Israel when it was made
desolate, and over the house of Judah when it went into exile; 4 therefore I am handing you over to the people of the East for a possession. They shall set their encampments among you and pitch their tents in your midst; they shall eat your fruit, and
they shall drink your milk. 5 I will make Rabbah a pasture for camels and Ammon

x Vg Tg: Heb *of men* y Heb lacks *and also*

24.20–24 Ezekiel was not allowed to mourn for his dead wife in order to show his fellow exiles that they were not to mourn over Jerusalem when it was destroyed. Any personal sorrow felt would soon be eclipsed by national sorrow over the horror of the city's total destruction. The individuals would mourn for their sins which caused the city's destruction.

24.27 For some time Ezekiel had not been allowed to speak except when God gave him a message to deliver to the people (3.25–27). This restriction would soon end when Jerusalem was destroyed and all Ezekiel's prophecies about Judah and Jerusalem had come true (33.21, 22).

24.27 God gave these messages to Ezekiel so the people would know that he is the Lord. How would they know this? (1) The judgments God pronounced on Jerusalem (chapters 1 – 24) were all about to come true; (2) the judgments God pronounced on the other nations (chapters 25 – 32) would all come true; and (3) the remnant of faithful people God promised to preserve was still present.

25.1ff Chapters 25 – 32 are God's word concerning the seven nations surrounding Judah. The judgments in these chapters are not simply the vengeful statements of Jews against their enemies; they are God's judgments on nations who failed to acknowledge the one true God and fulfill the good purposes God intended for them. The Ammonites were judged because of their joy over the desecration of the temple (25.1–7), the Moabites because they found pleasure in Judah's wickedness (25.8–11), the Edomites because of their racial hatred for the Jews (25.12–14), and the Philistines because they sought revenge against Judah for defeating them in battle (25.15–17).

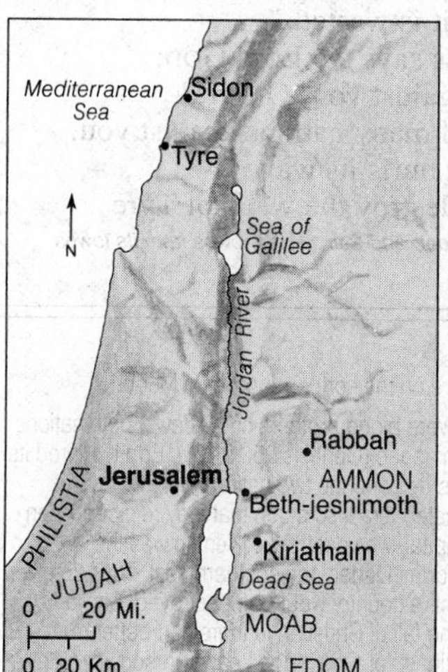

JUDAH'S ENEMIES Ammon, Moab, Edom, and Philistia, although once allied to Judah against Babylon, had abandoned Judah and rejoiced to see its ruin. But these nations were as sinful as Judah and would also feel the sting of God's judgment.

25.5 Rabbah was the capital city of the Ammonites.

a fold for flocks. Then you shall know that I am the LORD. 6 For thus says the Lord 25.6 Job 27.23 Obad 12
GOD: Because you have clapped your hands and stamped your feet and rejoiced
with all the malice within you against the land of Israel, 7 therefore I have stretched 25.7 Amos 1.14,15
out my hand against you, and will hand you over as plunder to the nations. I will cut
you off from the peoples and will make you perish out of the countries; I will destroy you. Then you shall know that I am the LORD.

A prophecy against Moab

8 Thus says the Lord GOD: Because Moab[z] said, The house of Judah is like all
the other nations, 9 therefore I will lay open the flank of Moab from the towns[a] on 25.9 Num 32.37,38 Josh 13.17-20 1 Chron 5.8 Jer 48.23
its frontier, the glory of the country, Beth-jeshimoth, Baal-meon, and Kiriathaim.
10 I will give it along with Ammon to the people of the East as a possession. Thus
Ammon shall be remembered no more among the nations, 11 and I will execute
judgments upon Moab. Then they shall know that I am the LORD.

A prophecy against Edom

12 Thus says the Lord GOD: Because Edom acted revengefully against the
house of Judah and has grievously offended in taking vengeance upon them,
13 therefore thus says the Lord GOD, I will stretch out my hand against Edom, and 25.13 Gen 36.34 Mal 1.3,4
cut off from it humans and animals, and I will make it desolate; from Teman even
to Dedan they shall fall by the sword. 14 I will lay my vengeance upon Edom by the 25.14 Ezek 34.11 Nah 1.2-4 Heb 10.30,31
hand of my people Israel; and they shall act in Edom according to my anger and
according to my wrath; and they shall know my vengeance, says the Lord GOD.

A prophecy against Philistia

15 Thus says the Lord GOD: Because with unending hostilities the Philistines 25.15 Isa 14.29-31 Amos 1.6-8 Zeph 2.4-7 Zech 9.5-8
acted in vengeance, and with malice of heart took revenge in destruction; 16 there-
fore thus says the Lord GOD, I will stretch out my hand against the Philistines, cut
off the Cherethites, and destroy the rest of the seacoast. 17 I will execute great ven- 25.16 1 Sam 30.14
geance on them with wrathful punishments. Then they shall know that I am the
LORD, when I lay my vengeance on them.

A prophecy against Tyre

26 In the eleventh year, on the first day of the month, the word of the LORD
came to me: 2 Mortal, because Tyre said concerning Jerusalem, 26.2 Isa 23.1 Jer 25.22 Joel 3.4

"Aha, broken is the gateway of the peoples;
it has swung open to me;
I shall be replenished,
now that it is wasted."

3 Therefore, thus says the Lord GOD: 26.3 Jer 50.42; 51.42 Lk 21.25

See, I am against you, O Tyre!
I will hurl many nations against you,
as the sea hurls its waves. 26.4 Isa 23.11 Amos 1.10
4 They shall destroy the walls of Tyre

[z] Gk Old Latin: Heb *Moab and Seir* [a] Heb *towns from its towns*

25.9 These towns were on the northern border of Moab.

25.13 The Edomites were blood brothers of the Jews, both nations being descended from Isaac (Genesis 25.19–26). Edom shared its northern border with Israel, and the two nations were always at odds. The Edomites hated Israel so much that they rejoiced when Jerusalem, Israel's capital, was destroyed. Teman was the northernmost city in Edom; Dedan, the southernmost. Thus, Ezekiel was saying that the entire country would be destroyed. Similarly, those who rejoice at the fall of Christian leaders had better re-examine their own actions, for God judges each person impartially.

25.16 The Cherethites was another name for the Philistines. The word was probably derived from the word "Crete."

26.1ff This message came to Ezekiel in 586 B.C. Chapters 26 and 27 are a prophecy against Tyre, the capital of Phoenicia just north of Israel. Part of the city was on the coastline, and part was on a beautiful island. Tyre rejoiced when Jerusalem fell, because Tyre and Judah always competed for the lucrative trade which came through their lands from Egypt in the south and Mesopotamia to the north. Tyre dominated the sea trading routes while Judah dominated the caravan routes. Now that Judah was defeated, Tyre thought it had all the trade routes to itself. But this gloating didn't last long. In 585 B.C., Nebuchadnezzar (Nebuchadrezzar) attacked the city of Tyre. It took him 13 years to capture the city because its back side lay on the sea and fresh supplies could be shipped in daily.

and break down its towers.
I will scrape its soil from it
and make it a bare rock.
5 It shall become, in the midst of the sea,
a place for spreading nets.
I have spoken, says the Lord GOD.
It shall become plunder for the nations,
26.6 Jer 47.4; 49.2
6 and its daughter-towns in the country
shall be killed by the sword.
Then they shall know that I am the LORD.

26.7 Dan 2.37,47 Nah 2.3,4
7 For thus says the Lord GOD: I will bring against Tyre from the north King
Nebuchadrezzar of Babylon, king of kings, together with horses, chariots, cavalry,
and a great and powerful army.

26.8 Jer 6.6; 32.24
8 Your daughter-towns in the country
he shall put to the sword.
He shall set up a siege-wall against you,
cast up a ramp against you,
and raise a roof of shields against you.
9 He shall direct the shock of his battering rams against your walls
and break down your towers with his axes.
26.10 Jer 39.3
10 His horses shall be so many
that their dust shall cover you.
At the noise of cavalry, wheels, and chariots
your very walls shall shake,
when he enters your gates
like those entering a breached city.
26.11 Isa 5.28; 26.5 Hab 1.8
11 With the hoofs of his horses
he shall trample all your streets.
He shall put your people to the sword,
and your strong pillars shall fall to the ground.
26.12 2 Chron 32.27 Isa 23.8,18 Dan 11.8 Amos 5.11
12 They will plunder your riches
and loot your merchandise;
they shall break down your walls
and destroy your fine houses.
Your stones and timber and soil
they shall cast into the water.
26.13 Isa 24.8,9 Amos 6.5 Jas 5.1-5 Rev 18.22,23
13 I will silence the music of your songs;
the sound of your lyres shall be heard no more.
26.14 Deut 13.16 Isa 14.27
14 I will make you a bare rock;
you shall be a place for spreading nets.
You shall never again be rebuilt,
for I the LORD have spoken,
says the Lord GOD.

26.15 Jer 49.21 Heb 12.26,27
15 Thus says the Lord GOD to Tyre: Shall not the coastlands shake at the sound
of your fall, when the wounded groan, when slaughter goes on within you? 16 Then
26.16 Ps 35.26 Jonah 3.6
all the princes of the sea shall step down from their thrones; they shall remove their
robes and strip off their embroidered garments. They shall clothe themselves with
trembling, and shall sit on the ground; they shall tremble every moment, and be
26.17 Isa 14.12 Jer 48.39; 50.23 Mic 2.4
appalled at you. 17 And they shall raise a lamentation over you, and say to you:
How you have vanished[b] from the seas,
O city renowned,

[b] Gk OL Aquila: Heb *have vanished, O inhabited one,*

26.14 After a 13-year siege, Nebuchadnezzar (Nebuchadrezzar) could not conquer the part of Tyre located on the island; thus certain aspects of the description in 26.12, 14 exceed the actual damage done to Tyre by Nebuchadnezzar and predicted what would happen to the island settlement later during the conquests of Alexander the Great. Alexander threw the rubble of the mainland city into the sea until it made a bridge to the island. Today the island city is still a pile of rubble, a testimony to God's judgment.

once mighty on the sea,
you and your inhabitants,[c]
who imposed your[d] terror
on all the mainland![e]
18 Now the coastlands tremble
on the day of your fall;
the coastlands by the sea
are dismayed at your passing.

19 For thus says the Lord GOD: When I make you a city laid waste, like cities
that are not inhabited, when I bring up the deep over you, and the great waters
cover you, 20 then I will thrust you down with those who descend into the Pit, to the
people of long ago, and I will make you live in the world below, among primeval
ruins, with those who go down to the Pit, so that you will not be inhabited or have
a place[f] in the land of the living. 21 I will bring you to a dreadful end, and you shall
be no more; though sought for, you will never be found again, says the Lord GOD.

26.18 Isa 23.5-7, 10-15
26.19 Isa 8.7,8 Dan 9.26; 11.40 Rev 17.15
26.20 Ps 88.6 Jonah 2.2,6 Zech 2.8

The greatness of Tyre

27 The word of the LORD came to me: 2 Now you, mortal, raise a lamentation
over Tyre, 3 and say to Tyre, which sits at the entrance to the sea, merchant
of the peoples on many coastlands, Thus says the Lord GOD:
O Tyre, you have said,
"I am perfect in beauty."
4 Your borders are in the heart of the seas;
your builders made perfect your beauty.
5 They made all your planks
of fir trees from Senir;
they took a cedar from Lebanon
to make a mast for you.
6 From oaks of Bashan
they made your oars;
they made your deck of pines[g]
from the coasts of Cyprus,
inlaid with ivory.
7 Of fine embroidered linen from Egypt
was your sail,
serving as your ensign;
blue and purple from the coasts of Elishah
was your awning.
8 The inhabitants of Sidon and Arvad
were your rowers;
skilled men of Zemer[h] were within you,
they were your pilots.
9 The elders of Gebal and its artisans were within you,
caulking your seams;
all the ships of the sea with their mariners were within you,
to barter for your wares.
10 Paras[i] and Lud and Put
were in your army,
your mighty warriors;

27.2 Jer 7.20
27.5 Isa 14.8
27.6 Num 21.33 Jer 22.20
27.7 Ex 25.4 1 Kgs 10.28 Jer 10.9
27.8 Gen 10.18 1 Kgs 9.27 1 Chron 1.16
27.10 Ezek 38.5

[c] Heb *it and its inhabitants* [d] Heb *their* [e] Cn: Heb *its inhabitants* [f] Gk: Heb *I will give beauty* [g] Or *boxwood*
[h] Cn Compare Gen 10.18: Heb *your skilled men, O Tyre* [i] Or *Persia*

27.1ff Chapter 27 is a funeral lament over Tyre's fall. It compares the city to a ship (27.1–9), mentions many of its trading partners (27.10–25), and then describes how the ship sank (27.26–36). Jesus spoke of Tyre in Matthew 11.22 as a city worthy of God's judgment.

27.3, 4 The beauty of Tyre was the source of its pride, and its pride guaranteed its judgment. Unwarranted conceit or pride in our own accomplishments should be a danger signal to us (see James 4.13–17). God is not against our finding pleasure or satisfaction in what we do; he is against arrogant, inflated self-esteem that looks down on others. We must acknowledge God as the basis and source of our life.

they hung shield and helmet in you;
  they gave you splendor.
11 Men of Arvad and Helech[j]
  were on your walls all around;
  men of Gamad were at your towers.
They hung their quivers all around your walls;
  they made perfect your beauty.

12 Tarshish did business with you out of the abundance of your great wealth;
silver, iron, tin, and lead they exchanged for your wares. 13 Javan, Tubal, and Meshech traded with you; they exchanged human beings and vessels of bronze for
your merchandise. 14 Beth-togarmah exchanged for your wares horses, war horses,
and mules. 15 The Rhodians[k] traded with you; many coastlands were your own
special markets; they brought you in payment ivory tusks and ebony. 16 Edom[l] did
business with you because of your abundant goods; they exchanged for your wares
turquoise, purple, embroidered work, fine linen, coral, and rubies. 17 Judah and the
land of Israel traded with you; they exchanged for your merchandise wheat from
Minneth, millet,[m] honey, oil, and balm. 18 Damascus traded with you for your
abundant goods—because of your great wealth of every kind—wine of Helbon,
and white wool. 19 Vedan and Javan from Uzal[m] entered into trade for your wares;
wrought iron, cassia, and sweet cane were bartered for your merchandise. 20 Dedan
traded with you in saddlecloths for riding. 21 Arabia and all the princes of Kedar
were your favored dealers in lambs, rams, and goats; in these they did business
with you. 22 The merchants of Sheba and Raamah traded with you; they exchanged
for your wares the best of all kinds of spices, and all precious stones, and gold.
23 Haran, Canneh, Eden, the merchants of Sheba, Asshur, and Chilmad traded with
you. 24 These traded with you in choice garments, in clothes of blue and embroidered work, and in carpets of colored material, bound with cords and made secure;
in these they traded with you.[n] 25 The ships of Tarshish traveled for you in your
trade.

So you were filled and heavily laden
  in the heart of the seas.
26 Your rowers have brought you
  into the high seas.
The east wind has wrecked you
  in the heart of the seas.
27 Your riches, your wares, your merchandise,
  your mariners and your pilots,
your caulkers, your dealers in merchandise,
  and all your warriors within you,
with all the company
  that is with you,
sink into the heart of the seas
  on the day of your ruin.
28 At the sound of the cry of your pilots
  the countryside shakes,
29 and down from their ships
  come all that handle the oar.
The mariners and all the pilots of the sea
  stand on the shore
30 and wail aloud over you,
  and cry bitterly.
They throw dust on their heads
  and wallow in ashes;
31 they make themselves bald for you,
  and put on sackcloth,
and they weep over you in bitterness of soul,

27.13 Gen 10.2,3 1 Chron 1.5,7 Isa 66.19 Dan 8.21; 10.20 Rev 18.13
27.14 1 Kgs 10.22
27.16 Ezek 16.13,18
27.17 Judg 11.33 1 Kgs 5.9 Ezra 3.7 Acts 12.20
27.18 Gen 14.15 Ezek 47.16-18
27.21 Gen 25.13 Isa 21.13; 60.7 Gal 4.25
27.22 Gen 10.7; 43.11 1 Kgs 10.2 Ezek 38.13
27.23 2 Kgs 19.12 Isa 37.12 Amos 1.5; 6.2
27.26 Ps 48.7 Jer 18.17 Acts 27.14,41 Rev 17.15
27.29 Rev 18.17-19
27.30 1 Sam 4.12 2 Sam 1.2 Isa 23.1-6 Jonah 3.6 Mic 1.10
27.31 Isa 16.9 Ezek 7.18

j Or *and your army* k Gk: Heb *The Dedanites* l Another reading is *Aram* m Meaning of Heb uncertain n Cn: Heb *in your market*

with bitter mourning.
32 In their wailing they raise a lamentation for you,
and lament over you:
"Who was ever destroyed[o] like Tyre
in the midst of the sea?
33 When your wares came from the seas,
you satisfied many peoples;
with your abundant wealth and merchandise
you enriched the kings of the earth.
34 Now you are wrecked by the seas,
in the depths of the waters;
your merchandise and all your crew
have sunk with you.
35 All the inhabitants of the coastlands
are appalled at you;
and their kings are horribly afraid,
their faces are convulsed.
36 The merchants among the peoples hiss at you;
you have come to a dreadful end
and shall be no more forever."

The king of Tyre is condemned

28 The word of the LORD came to me: 2 Mortal, say to the prince of Tyre, Thus
says the Lord GOD:
Because your heart is proud
and you have said, "I am a god;
I sit in the seat of the gods,
in the heart of the seas,"
yet you are but a mortal, and no god,
though you compare your mind
with the mind of a god.
3 You are indeed wiser than Daniel;[p]
no secret is hidden from you;
4 by your wisdom and your understanding
you have amassed wealth for yourself,
and have gathered gold and silver
into your treasuries.
5 By your great wisdom in trade
you have increased your wealth,
and your heart has become proud in your wealth.
6 Therefore thus says the Lord GOD:
Because you compare your mind
with the mind of a god,
7 therefore, I will bring strangers against you,
the most terrible of the nations;
they shall draw their swords against the beauty of your wisdom
and defile your splendor.
8 They shall thrust you down to the Pit,

o Tg Vg: Heb *like silence* p Or, as otherwise read, *Danel*

27.32 Lam 2.13 Rev 18.18
27.34 Zech 9.3,4
27.36 Ps 37.10,36 Jer 49.17 Zeph 2.15
28.2 2 Thess 2.4
28.3 Dan 2.20-23
28.4 Prov 18.11 23.4,5 Zech 9.2-4
28.5 Job 31.24,25 Ps 52.7 Hos 12.7,8
28.6 Ex 9.17 1 Cor 10.22 Jas 1.11
28.7 Dan 7.7 Hab 1.6-8

28.1ff Previously Ezekiel prophesied against the city of Tyre (chapters 26, 27). Now he focuses his prophecy on Tyre's leader. The chief sin of Tyre's king was pride – believing himself to be a god. But Ezekiel also made a broader spiritual application, speaking about the spiritual king of Tyre, Satan, whom the people were really following.

28.2, 3 Daniel, an important official in Nebuchadnezzar's kingdom (14.14), was already renowned for his wisdom. Daniel proclaimed that all his wisdom came from God (Daniel 2.20–23). By contrast, the king of Tyre thought that he himself *was* a god. When truly wise people get closer to God, they recognize their need to depend on him for guidance.

28.6–10 The enemy army ("strangers") that attacked Tyre was the Babylonian army under Nebuchadnezzar. This attack occurred in 573 or 572 B.C.

and you shall die a violent death
in the heart of the seas.
9 Will you still say, "I am a god,"
in the presence of those who kill you,
though you are but a mortal, and no god,
in the hands of those who wound you?

28.10 1 Sam 17.26,36 Acts 7.51 Phil 3.3

10 You shall die the death of the uncircumcised
by the hand of foreigners;
for I have spoken, says the Lord GOD.

11 Moreover the word of the LORD came to me: 12 Mortal, raise a lamentation
over the king of Tyre, and say to him, Thus says the Lord GOD:
You were the signet of perfection,[q]
full of wisdom
and perfect in beauty.

28.13 Gen 2.8 Ex 28.17-20 39.10-21 Isa 51.3 54.11,12

13 You were in Eden, the garden of God;
every precious stone was your covering,
carnelian, chrysolite, and moonstone,
beryl, onyx, and jasper,
sapphire,[r] turquoise, and emerald;
and worked in gold were your settings
and your engravings.[q]
On the day that you were created
they were prepared.

28.14 Ex 25.17-20 Ezek 20.40 Dan 2.37,38 5.18-23 Rev 18.16

14 With an anointed cherub as guardian I placed you;[q]
you were on the holy mountain of God;
you walked among the stones of fire.

28.15 Isa 14.12 Rom 7.9

15 You were blameless in your ways
from the day that you were created,
until iniquity was found in you.

28.16 Ezek 8.17 Hab 2.8,17

16 In the abundance of your trade
you were filled with violence, and you sinned;
so I cast you as a profane thing from the mountain of God,
and the guardian cherub drove you out
from among the stones of fire.

28.17 Isa 19.11 Jer 8.9

17 Your heart was proud because of your beauty;
you corrupted your wisdom for the sake of your splendor.
I cast you to the ground;
I exposed you before kings,
to feast their eyes on you.

28.18 Amos 1.9,10 Mal 4.3

18 By the multitude of your iniquities,
in the unrighteousness of your trade,
you profaned your sanctuaries.
So I brought out fire from within you;
it consumed you,
and I turned you to ashes on the earth
in the sight of all who saw you.

28.19 Jer 51.64 Rev 18.21

19 All who know you among the peoples
are appalled at you;
you have come to a dreadful end
and shall be no more forever.

[q] Meaning of Heb uncertain [r] Or *lapis lazuli*

28.12–19 Some of the phrases in this passage describing the human king of Tyre may describe Satan. Great care must be taken to interpret these verses with discernment. It is clear that, at times, Ezekiel describes this king in terms that could not apply to a mere man. This king had been in the garden of Eden (28.13), had been a guardian angel ("the anointed cherub") (28.14), and had access to the holy mountain of God (28.14), but was cast down from there (28.16, 17). Ezekiel, therefore, may have been condemning not only the king of Tyre, but Satan, who had motivated the king to sin.

A prophecy against Sidon

20 The word of the LORD came to me: 21 Mortal, set your face toward Sidon,
and prophesy against it, 22 and say, Thus says the Lord GOD:
I am against you, O Sidon,
and I will gain glory in your midst.
They shall know that I am the LORD
when I execute judgments in it,
and manifest my holiness in it;
23 for I will send pestilence into it,
and bloodshed into its streets;
and the dead shall fall in its midst,
by the sword that is against it on every side.
And they shall know that I am the LORD.

28.21 Gen 10.15-19 Isa 23.2-4,12 Jer 25.22; 27.3 Joel 3.4-8

24 The house of Israel shall no longer find a pricking brier or a piercing thorn
among all their neighbors who have treated them with contempt. And they shall
know that I am the Lord GOD.

28.24 Num 33.35 Josh 23.13

25 Thus says the Lord GOD: When I gather the house of Israel from the peoples
among whom they are scattered, and manifest my holiness in them in the sight of
the nations, then they shall settle on their own soil that I gave to my servant Jacob.
26 They shall live in safety in it, and shall build houses and plant vineyards. They
shall live in safety, when I execute judgments upon all their neighbors who have
treated them with contempt. And they shall know that I am the LORD their God.

28.25 Ps 106.47 Isa 11.12,13 Jer 23.8

28.26 Jer 32.15,43,44 Amos 9.13,14

A prophecy against Egypt

29 In the tenth year, in the tenth month, on the twelfth day of the month, the
word of the LORD came to me: 2 Mortal, set your face against Pharaoh king
of Egypt, and prophesy against him and against all Egypt; 3 speak, and say, Thus
says the Lord GOD:
I am against you,
Pharaoh king of Egypt,
the great dragon sprawling
in the midst of its channels,
saying, "My Nile is my own;
I made it for myself."
4 I will put hooks in your jaws,
and make the fish of your channels stick to your scales.
I will draw you up from your channels,
with all the fish of your channels
sticking to your scales.
5 I will fling you into the wilderness,
you and all the fish of your channels;
you shall fall in the open field,

29.2 Isa 19.1-17 Jer 43.8-13 46.2-16 Joel 3.19

29.3 Ps 74.13 Isa 27.1

29.4 2 Kgs 19.28 Isa 37.29 Ezek 38.4

29.5 Jer 7.33; 34.20

28.20, 21 Sidon was another famous seaport, located a few miles north of Tyre. God charged this city with contempt for his people. Sidon's economy was bound to Tyre's, so when Tyre fell to Nebuchadnezzar, Sidon was doomed to follow.

28.24–26 This promise that God's people will live in complete safety has yet to be fulfilled. While many were allowed to return from exile under Zerubbabel, Ezra, and Nehemiah, and although the political nation is restored today, the inhabitants do not yet live in complete safety (28.26). Therefore, this promise will have its ultimate fulfillment when Christ sets up his eternal kingdom. Then all people who have been faithful to God will dwell together in harmony and complete safety.

29.1ff There are seven prophecies in chapters 29 – 32, all dealing with judgment on Egypt. This is probably the first prophecy which was given by Ezekiel in 587 B.C. Hezekiah, Jehoiakim, and Zedekiah (kings of Judah) had all sought help from Egypt despite God's warnings.

There are three key reasons for this prophecy: (1) Egypt was an ancient enemy of the Jews, having once enslaved them for 400 years; (2) Egypt worshiped many gods; (3) Egypt's wealth and power made it seem like a good ally. Egypt offered to help Judah only because of the benefits it hoped to receive from such an alliance. When the Egyptians didn't get what they hoped for, they bailed out of their agreement without regard to any promises they had made.

29.2ff Egypt had great artistic treasures, a flourishing civilization, and world-renowned military power. Unfortunately, it was also evil, egotistical, idolatrous, and treated slaves cruelly. And for those sins God condemned Egypt. At the battle of Carchemish in 605 B.C., Babylon crushed Egypt along with Assyria, its rivals for the position of world ruler.

and not be gathered and buried.
To the animals of the earth and to the birds of the air
I have given you as food.
6 Then all the inhabitants of Egypt shall know
that I am the LORD
because you[s] were a staff of reed
to the house of Israel;
7 when they grasped you with the hand, you broke,
and tore all their shoulders;
and when they leaned on you, you broke,
and made all their legs unsteady.[t]

8 Therefore, thus says the Lord GOD: I will bring a sword upon you, and will cut
off from you human being and animal; 9 and the land of Egypt shall be a desolation
and a waste. Then they shall know that I am the LORD.
Because you[u] said, "The Nile is mine, and I made it," 10 therefore, I am against
you, and against your channels, and I will make the land of Egypt an utter waste
and desolation, from Migdol to Syene, as far as the border of Ethiopia.[v] 11 No
human foot shall pass through it, and no animal foot shall pass through it; it shall
be uninhabited forty years. 12 I will make the land of Egypt a desolation among
desolated countries; and her cities shall be a desolation forty years among cities that
are laid waste. I will scatter the Egyptians among the nations, and disperse them
among the countries.

13 Further, thus says the Lord GOD: At the end of forty years I will gather the
Egyptians from the peoples among whom they were scattered; 14 and I will restore
the fortunes of Egypt, and bring them back to the land of Pathros, the land of their
origin; and there they shall be a lowly kingdom. 15 It shall be the most lowly of the
kingdoms, and never again exalt itself above the nations; and I will make them so
small that they will never again rule over the nations. 16 The Egyptians[w] shall never
again be the reliance of the house of Israel; they will recall their iniquity, when they
turned to them for aid. Then they shall know that I am the Lord GOD.

17 In the twenty-seventh year, in the first month, on the first day of the month,
the word of the LORD came to me: 18 Mortal, King Nebuchadrezzar of Babylon
made his army labor hard against Tyre; every head was made bald and every shoulder was rubbed bare; yet neither he nor his army got anything from Tyre to pay for
the labor that he had expended against it. 19 Therefore thus says the Lord GOD: I will
give the land of Egypt to King Nebuchadrezzar of Babylon; and he shall carry off
its wealth and despoil it and plunder it; and it shall be the wages for his army. 20 I
have given him the land of Egypt as his payment for which he labored, because they
worked for me, says the Lord GOD.

21 On that day I will cause a horn to sprout up for the house of Israel, and I will
open your lips among them. Then they shall know that I am the LORD.

[s] Gk Syr Vg: Heb *they* [t] Syr: Heb *stand* [u] Gk Syr Vg: Heb *he* [v] Or *Nubia*; Heb *Cush* [w] Heb *It*

29.6 Isa 36.6 Jer 2.36
29.7 Prov 25.19 Jer 37.5-11 Ezek 17.15-17
29.9 Prov 18.12 29.23
29.11 Jer 43.11,12 Dan 9.2
29.12 Jer 25.15-19 27.6-11
29.14 Isa 11.11 Jer 44.1
29.15 Dan 11.42,43 Nah 3.8,9 Zech 10.11
29.16 Isa 30.1-3; 64.9 Hos 5.13; 8.13 9.9
29.17 Ezek 24.1; 30.20
29.18 Jer 25.9; 27.6 Ezek 26.7-12
29.19 Jer 43.10-13 Ezek 30.10-12
29.20 Isa 10.6,7 45.1-3
29.21 1 Sam 2.10 Ps 92.10 Amos 3.7,8 Lk 21.15

29.9, 10 The Nile was Egypt's pride and joy, a life-giving river cutting through the middle of the desert. Rather than thanking God, however, Egypt declared, "The Nile is mine, and I made it." We do the same when we say "This house is mine; I built it," or "I have brought myself to the place where I am today," or "I have built this church, business, or reputation, from the ground up." These statements reveal our pride. We sometimes take for granted what God has given us, thinking we have made it ourselves. Of course, we have put forth a lot of hard effort, but God supplied the resources, gave us the abilities, and provided us with the opportunities to make it happen. Instead of claiming our own greatness, as the Egyptians did, we should proclaim God's greatness and give him the credit. (Migdol is in the far north of Egypt, and Syene in the far south. Thus, this meant all of Egypt.)

29.11–15 This 40-year period of desolation in Egypt is hard to pinpoint. Nebuchadnezzar attacked Egypt around 572 B.C. and carried many people off to Babylon, while others fled for safety to surrounding nations. Approximately 33 years later, Cyrus, king of the Persian Empire, conquered Babylon and allowed the nations which Babylon had conquered to return to their homelands. Adding a possible seven-year regrouping and travel period, this could then make up that 40-year time period. And since that time, Egypt has never returned to its previous dominance as a world power. Pathros was upper Egypt, the region south of the Nile delta.

29.17, 18 This prophecy was given in 571 B.C. and is actually the latest prophecy in Ezekiel. Nebuchadnezzar (Nebuchadrezzar) had finally conquered Tyre after a long and costly 13-year siege (587–574 B.C.). He had not counted on such an expense, so he went south and conquered Egypt to make up for all he had lost in taking Tyre. Ezekiel placed this prophecy here to describe *who* would bring this punishment to Egypt. God was using Nebuchadnezzar, an evil man, as an instrument of his judgment on Tyre, Judah, and Egypt—evil nations themselves. When Babylon didn't recognize God's help, he judged it too.

Egypt faces doom

30 The word of the LORD came to me: 2Mortal, prophesy, and say, Thus says the Lord GOD:
Wail, "Alas for the day!"
3 For a day is near,
the day of the LORD is near;
it will be a day of clouds,
a time of doom[x] for the nations.
4 A sword shall come upon Egypt,
and anguish shall be in Ethiopia,[y]
when the slain fall in Egypt,
and its wealth is carried away,
and its foundations are torn down.
5Ethiopia,[y] and Put, and Lud, and all Arabia, and Libya,[z] and the people of the
allied land[a] shall fall with them by the sword.

6 Thus says the LORD:
Those who support Egypt shall fall,
and its proud might shall come down;
from Migdol to Syene
they shall fall within it by the sword,
says the Lord GOD.
7 They shall be desolated among other desolated countries,
and their cities shall lie among cities laid waste.
8 Then they shall know that I am the LORD,
when I have set fire to Egypt,
and all who help it are broken.
9 On that day, messengers shall go out from me in ships to terrify the unsuspecting Ethiopians;[b] and anguish shall come upon them on the day of Egypt's doom;[c]
for it is coming!

10 Thus says the Lord GOD:
I will put an end to the hordes of Egypt,
by the hand of King Nebuchadrezzar of Babylon.
11 He and his people with him, the most terrible of the nations,
shall be brought in to destroy the land;
and they shall draw their swords against Egypt,
and fill the land with the slain.
12 I will dry up the channels,
and will sell the land into the hand of evildoers;
I will bring desolation upon the land and everything in it
by the hand of foreigners;
I the LORD have spoken.

13 Thus says the Lord GOD:
I will destroy the idols
and put an end to the images in Memphis;
there shall no longer be a prince in the land of Egypt;
so I will put fear in the land of Egypt.
14 I will make Pathros a desolation,

30.2 Isa 13.6; 65.14 Joel 1.5,11, 13,15 Jas 5.1
30.5 Isa 18.1; 20.4 Jer 25.20,24 Nah 3.8,9
30.6 Isa 20.3-6
30.8 Ps 58.11 Amos 1.4,7, 10-14 Nah 1.5,6
30.9 Isa 23.6 Jer 49.21 Zech 11.2,3
30.12 Ezek 29.3,9
30.13 Isa 2.18 Jer 44.1; 46.14 Hos 9.6
30.14 Ps 78.12,43 Isa 19.11,13 Nah 3.8

[x] Heb lacks *of doom* [y] Or *Nubia*; Heb *Cush* [z] Compare Gk Syr Vg: Heb *Cub* [a] Meaning of Heb uncertain
[b] Or *Nubians*; Heb *Cush* [c] Heb *the day of Egypt*

30.1–19 This is a prophecy against Egypt and its allies. Because of the pride and idolatry of the Egyptians, they would be brought down.

30.12 Egypt's pharaohs claimed they had made the Nile – the river on which the entire nation depended. If God dried up the Nile, the nation would be doomed.

30.13–19 The list of cities to be destroyed shows the breadth of the destruction; the drying up of the Nile (30.12) shows its depth. Egypt would be completely incapacitated. This was a clear message to Judah not to trust Egypt for help against the Babylonians.

and will set fire to Zoan,
and will execute acts of judgment on Thebes.
15 I will pour my wrath upon Pelusium,
the stronghold of Egypt,
and cut off the hordes of Thebes.
16 I will set fire to Egypt;
Pelusium shall be in great agony;
Thebes shall be breached,
and Memphis face adversaries by day.

30.17 Gen 41.45

17 The young men of On and of Pi-beseth shall fall by the sword;
and the cities themselves[d] shall go into captivity.

30.18 Lev 26.13 Jer 43.8-13 46.20-26

18 At Tehaphnehes the day shall be dark,
when I break there the dominion of Egypt,
and its proud might shall come to an end;
the city[e] shall be covered by a cloud,
and its daughter-towns shall go into captivity.

30.19 Num 33.4 Ps 9.16 Ezek 5.8,15

19 Thus I will execute acts of judgment on Egypt.
Then they shall know that I am the LORD.

30.20 Ezek 26.1
30.21 Ps 10.15; 37.17 Jer 30.13; 46.11 Nah 3.16
30.22 2 Kgs 24.7 Jer 37.7 46.1-12,21-25
30.24 Isa 10.5,6 45.1,5 Zech 10.12
30.25 Josh 8.18 1 Chron 21.16 Ps 9.16

20 In the eleventh year, in the first month, on the seventh day of the month, the
word of the LORD came to me: 21 Mortal, I have broken the arm of Pharaoh king of
Egypt; it has not been bound up for healing or wrapped with a bandage, so that it
may become strong to wield the sword. 22 Therefore thus says the Lord GOD: I am
against Pharaoh king of Egypt, and will break his arms, both the strong arm and the
one that was broken; and I will make the sword fall from his hand. 23 I will scatter
the Egyptians among the nations, and disperse them throughout the lands. 24 I will
strengthen the arms of the king of Babylon, and put my sword in his hand; but I will
break the arms of Pharaoh, and he will groan before him with the groans of one
mortally wounded. 25 I will strengthen the arms of the king of Babylon, but the
arms of Pharaoh shall fall. And they shall know that I am the LORD, when I put my
sword into the hand of the king of Babylon. He shall stretch it out against the land
of Egypt, 26 and I will scatter the Egyptians among the nations and disperse them
throughout the countries. Then they shall know that I am the LORD.

Egypt's pride

31.2 Isa 10.33,34 Dan 4.20-23 Nah 3.8,9

31 In the eleventh year, in the third month, on the first day of the month, the
word of the LORD came to me: 2 Mortal, say to Pharaoh king of Egypt and to
his hordes:
Whom are you like in your greatness?
3 Consider Assyria, a cedar of Lebanon,
with fair branches and forest shade,
and of great height,
its top among the clouds.[f]

31.4 Ezek 17.5,8 Rev 17.1,15

4 The waters nourished it,
the deep made it grow tall,

[d] Heb *and they* [e] Heb *she* [f] Gk: Heb *thick boughs*

30.20, 21 This message came in 587 B.C. while Jerusalem was under attack from Babylon. Judah had rebelled against Babylon and made an alliance with Egypt in spite of God's warnings (Jeremiah 2.36, 37). Pharaoh Hophra made a halfhearted attempt to help Jerusalem; but when Nebuchadnezzar's army turned on him, he fled back to Egypt (Jeremiah 37.5–7). This defeat is what Ezekiel meant when he said God would break the arm of Pharaoh.

30.21–26 This prophecy was given to Ezekiel in 587 B.C. God destroyed Egypt's military superiority and gave it to Babylon. God allows nations to rise to power to accomplish a particular purpose, often beyond our immediate understanding. When you read about armies and wars, don't despair. Remember that God is sovereign and in charge of everything, even military might. Besides praying for your military and government leaders, pray that God's greater purposes be carried out and that his will be done "on earth as it is in heaven" (see Matthew 6.10).

31.1ff This message was given in 587 B.C. Ezekiel compared Egypt to Assyria, calling Assyria a great cedar tree. The Egyptians were to look at the fall of the mighty nation of Assyria (whose demise they had seen) as an example of what would happen to them. Just like Assyria, Egypt took pride in its strength and beauty; this would be its downfall. She would crash like a mighty tree and be sent to the place of the dead. There is no permanence apart from God, even for a great society with magnificent culture and military power.

making its rivers flow[g]
around the place it was planted,
sending forth its streams
to all the trees of the field.
5 So it towered high
above all the trees of the field;
its boughs grew large
and its branches long,
from abundant water in its shoots.

31.5 Ps 1.3

6 All the birds of the air
made their nests in its boughs;
under its branches all the animals of the field
gave birth to their young;
and in its shade
all great nations lived.

31.6 Ezek 17.23 Dan 4.12,21 Mt 13.23

7 It was beautiful in its greatness,
in the length of its branches;
for its roots went down
to abundant water.
8 The cedars in the garden of God could not rival it,
nor the fir trees equal its boughs;
the plane trees were as nothing
compared with its branches;
no tree in the garden of God
was like it in beauty.

31.8 Gen 2.8,9 13.10 Ps 80.10 Isa 51.3

9 I made it beautiful
with its mass of branches,
the envy of all the trees of Eden
that were in the garden of God.

10 Therefore thus says the Lord GOD: Because it[h] towered high and set its top
among the clouds,[i] and its heart was proud of its height, 11 I gave it into the hand
of the prince of the nations; he has dealt with it as its wickedness deserves. I have
cast it out. 12 Foreigners from the most terrible of the nations have cut it down and
left it. On the mountains and in all the valleys its branches have fallen, and its
boughs lie broken in all the watercourses of the land; and all the peoples of the earth
went away from its shade and left it.

31.10 2 Chron 32.25 Isa 14.13,14 Dan 5.20

31.11 Deut 18.12 Dan 5.18,19 Nah 3.18

31.12 Dan 4.14 Hab 1.6

13 On its fallen trunk settle
all the birds of the air,
and among its boughs lodge
all the wild animals.

31.13 Isa 18.6 Rev 19.17,18

14 All this is in order that no trees by the waters may grow to lofty height or set their
tops among the clouds,[i] and that no trees that drink water may reach up to them in
height.

For all of them are handed over to death,
to the world below;
along with all mortals,
with those who go down to the Pit.

15 Thus says the Lord GOD: On the day it went down to Sheol I closed the deep
over it and covered it; I restrained its rivers, and its mighty waters were checked.
I clothed Lebanon in gloom for it, and all the trees of the field fainted because of it.
16 I made the nations quake at the sound of its fall, when I cast it down to Sheol with
those who go down to the Pit; and all the trees of Eden, the choice and best of

31.15 Nah 2.8-10 Rev 18.9-11,16,19

31.16 Isa 14.8 Hag 2.7 Heb 12.26,27 Rev 18.9

[g] Gk: Heb *rivers going* [h] Syr Vg: Heb *you* [i] Gk: Heb *thick boughs*

31.9 "All the trees of Eden" may refer to all the other nations of the world who were jealous of Assyria's power and grandeur.

31.11 The "prince of the nations" is the Babylonian king Nebuchadnezzar (see Daniel 2.37, 38).

31.15 *Sheol* is the word in the Old Testament for the realm of the dead. It is used to mean the grave or the state of being dead.

31.17 Ps 9.17 Dan 4.11,12 Nah 3.17

Lebanon, all that were well watered, were consoled in the world below. 17They
also went down to Sheol with it, to those killed by the sword, along with its allies,[j]
those who lived in its shade among the nations.

31.18 Ps 52.7 Jer 9.25,26 Mt 13.19

18 Which among the trees of Eden was like you in glory and in greatness? Now
you shall be brought down with the trees of Eden to the world below; you shall lie
among the uncircumcised, with those who are killed by the sword. This is Pharaoh
and all his horde, says the Lord GOD.

All of Israel's enemies will perish

32.2 Jer 46.7,8 Nah 2.11-13

32 In the twelfth year, in the twelfth month, on the first day of the month, the
word of the LORD came to me: 2Mortal, raise a lamentation over Pharaoh
king of Egypt, and say to him:

You consider yourself a lion among the nations,
but you are like a dragon in the seas;
you thrash about in your streams,
trouble the water with your feet,
and foul your[k] streams.
3 Thus says the Lord GOD:
In an assembly of many peoples
I will throw my net over you;
and I[l] will haul you up in my dragnet.

32.4 1 Sam 17.44-46 Isa 34.2-7 Jer 8.2

4 I will throw you on the ground,
on the open field I will fling you,
and will cause all the birds of the air to settle on you,
and I will let the wild animals of the whole earth gorge themselves with you.
5 I will strew your flesh on the mountains,
and fill the valleys with your carcass.[m]

32.6 Ex 7.17 Isa 34.3,7 Rev 14.20; 16.6

6 I will drench the land with your flowing blood
up to the mountains,
and the watercourses will be filled with you.

32.7 Ex 10.21-23 Prov 13.9 Amos 8.9

7 When I blot you out, I will cover the heavens,
and make their stars dark;
I will cover the sun with a cloud,
and the moon shall not give its light.

32.8 Gen 1.14

8 All the shining lights of the heavens
I will darken above you,
and put darkness on your land,
says the Lord GOD.

32.9 Ex 15.14-16 Jer 25.15-26 Rev 18.10-15

9 I will trouble the hearts of many peoples,
as I carry you captive[n] among the nations,
into countries you have not known.
10 I will make many peoples appalled at you;
their kings shall shudder because of you.
When I brandish my sword before them,
they shall tremble every moment
for their lives, each one of them,
on the day of your downfall.

[j] Heb *its arms* [k] Heb *their* [l] Gk Vg: Heb *they* [m] Symmachus Syr Vg: Heb *your height* [n] Gk: Heb *bring your destruction*

32.1ff This prophecy was given in 585 B.C., two months after the news of Jerusalem's fall reached the exiles in Babylon. Ezekiel prophesied numerous judgments upon many wicked nations. These judgments served a positive purpose: they showed that evil forces are continually being overcome and that one day God will overthrow all evil, making the world the perfect place he intended. They also serve as warnings that only God is sovereign. Even the mightiest rulers, like Pharaoh, will fall before God. All are accountable to him.

32.2 Although Pharaoh thought of himself as a strong lion, in God's eyes he was nothing but a crocodile ("dragon") muddying the water. God's judgment would reduce Pharaoh to his true size. Anyone who defies God will face his judgment.

11 For thus says the Lord GOD:
The sword of the king of Babylon shall come against you.
12 I will cause your hordes to fall
by the swords of mighty ones,
all of them most terrible among the nations.
They shall bring to ruin the pride of Egypt,
and all its hordes shall perish.
13 I will destroy all its livestock
from beside abundant waters;
and no human foot shall trouble them any more,
nor shall the hoofs of cattle trouble them.
14 Then I will make their waters clear,
and cause their streams to run like oil, says the Lord GOD.
15 When I make the land of Egypt desolate
and when the land is stripped of all that fills it,
when I strike down all who live in it,
then they shall know that I am the LORD.
16 This is a lamentation; it shall be chanted.
The women of the nations shall chant it.
Over Egypt and all its hordes they shall chant it,
says the Lord GOD.

17 In the twelfth year, in the first month,[o] on the fifteenth day of the month, the
word of the LORD came to me:
18 Mortal, wail over the hordes of Egypt,
and send them down,
with Egypt[p] and the daughters of majestic nations,
to the world below,
with those who go down to the Pit.
19 "Whom do you surpass in beauty?
Go down! Be laid to rest with the uncircumcised!"
20 They shall fall among those who are killed by the sword. Egypt[q] has been handed
over to the sword; carry away both it and its hordes. 21 The mighty chiefs shall
speak of them, with their helpers, out of the midst of Sheol: "They have come
down, they lie still, the uncircumcised, killed by the sword."
22 Assyria is there, and all its company, their graves all around it, all of them
killed, fallen by the sword. 23 Their graves are set in the uttermost parts of the Pit.
Its company is all around its grave, all of them killed, fallen by the sword, who
spread terror in the land of the living.
24 Elam is there, and all its hordes around its grave; all of them killed, fallen by
the sword, who went down uncircumcised into the world below, who spread terror
in the land of the living. They bear their shame with those who go down to the Pit.

32.15 Ex 7.5; 14.4,18 Ps 83.17,18 Ezek 8.7
32.16 2 Sam 3.33,34 2 Chron 35.25 Jer 9.17
32.18 Jer 1.10 Hos 6.5
32.19 Jer 9.25,26
32.20 Ps 28.3 Prov 24.11 Jer 22.19
32.21 Isa 14.9-12 Lk 16.23,24
32.22 Ps 83.8-10 Isa 37.36-38 Nah 1.7-12
32.24 Gen 10.22 Job 28.13 Ps 52.5 Jer 49.32-39

o Gk: Heb lacks *in the first month* p Heb *it* q Heb *It*

32.18 The Hebrews believed in an afterlife (Sheol or the grave) for all people, good and bad. Ezekiel's message assumed that the evil nations had already been sent there (to the "Pit"), and Egypt would share their fate. The words here are more poetic than doctrinal (see Job 24.19; Psalm 16.10; Isaiah 38.10, and the note on Matthew 25.46). The Egyptians had a preoccupation with the afterlife (the pyramids were built solely to ensure the Pharaohs' comfort in the next life). This message should remind us that any attempt to control our afterlife and ignore God is foolish. God alone controls the future and life after death.

32.19, 24 "Laid to rest with the uncircumcised" and "went down uncircumcised" means they were idolators, people who did not believe in the one true God and thus were not circumcised as part of his covenant. There is no spiritual hope outside of God's covenant. Although these people were physically circumcised, they were not spiritually circumcised—they did not have pure hearts set apart to worship God alone (Deuteronomy 10.16; 30.6).

32.21–32 In these verses, Ezekiel conducts a guided tour of Sheol, the region of the afterlife. In Sheol all of God's enemies are condemned in judgment; many of them experience the fate they so quickly imposed on others. Though Babylon is not mentioned, Ezekiel's readers would have concluded that if all the other nations would be judged for their rebellion against God, Babylon would be judged as well. These words would comfort the captives.

32.24–26 Meshech and Tubal were territories located in the eastern region of Asia Minor, now eastern and central Turkey. In chapters 38 and 39 they are described as allies of Gog, the chief prince of a confederacy. They are included with the evil nations who will be judged for fighting against God's people. Elam was a nation of fierce warriors from the region east of Babylonia. They were conquered by Nebuchadnezzar (Jeremiah 49.34–39) and eventually rebuilt themselves and became part of Persia.

[25]They have made Elam[r] a bed among the slain with all its hordes, their graves all
around it, all of them uncircumcised, killed by the sword; for terror of them was
spread in the land of the living, and they bear their shame with those who go down
to the Pit; they are placed among the slain.
26 Meshech and Tubal are there, and all their multitude, their graves all around
them, all of them uncircumcised, killed by the sword; for they spread terror in the
land of the living. [27]And they do not lie with the fallen warriors of long ago[s] who
went down to Sheol with their weapons of war, whose swords were laid under their
heads, and whose shields[t] are upon their bones; for the terror of the warriors was
in the land of the living. [28]So you shall be broken and lie among the uncircumcised,
with those who are killed by the sword.
29 Edom is there, its kings and all its princes, who for all their might are laid
with those who are killed by the sword; they lie with the uncircumcised, with those
who go down to the Pit.
30 The princes of the north are there, all of them, and all the Sidonians, who
have gone down in shame with the slain, for all the terror that they caused by their
might; they lie uncircumcised with those who are killed by the sword, and bear
their shame with those who go down to the Pit.
31 When Pharaoh sees them, he will be consoled for all his hordes—Pharaoh
and all his army, killed by the sword, says the Lord GOD. [32]For he[u] spread terror
in the land of the living; therefore he shall be laid to rest among the uncircumcised,
with those who are slain by the sword—Pharaoh and all his multitude, says the
Lord GOD.

32.25 Ps 139.8
32.26 Gen 10.2; Isa 66.19
32.27 Prov 14.32; Isa 14.18,19; Jn 8.24
32.29 Isa 34.5-15; Jer 49.7-22; Ezek 25.13
32.30 Jer 1.15; 25.26; Ezek 28.21-23; 38.15
32.31 Lam 2.13; Ezek 31.16

C. MESSAGES OF HOPE (33.1–48.35)

This begins a new direction in Ezekiel's prophecies. Ezekiel is reminded that he is the nation's watchman. Before Jerusalem's fall, he told the people of their punishment and dispersion. Now he is to proclaim the hope of restoration, but even this message does not improve the people's response. They listen to him with curiosity and then live as they please. Today we have the good news of forgiveness, but how easy it is to ignore the message and continue to live sinful lives.

1. Restoring the people of God

God reminds Ezekiel that he is a watchman

33 The word of the LORD came to me: [2]O Mortal, speak to your people and say
to them, If I bring the sword upon a land, and the people of the land take one
of their number as their sentinel; [3]and if the sentinel sees the sword coming upon
the land and blows the trumpet and warns the people; [4]then if any who hear the
sound of the trumpet do not take warning, and the sword comes and takes them
away, their blood shall be upon their own heads. [5]They heard the sound of the
trumpet and did not take warning; their blood shall be upon themselves. But if they
had taken warning, they would have saved their lives. [6]But if the sentinel sees the
sword coming and does not blow the trumpet, so that the people are not warned,

33.2 Jer 12.12
33.3 Neh 4.18-20
33.4 Ezek 18.13
33.5 Ex 9.19-21,25
33.6 Ezek 3.18,20

[r] Heb *it* [s] Gk Old Latin: Heb *of the uncircumcised* [t] Cn: Heb *iniquities* [u] Cn: Heb *I*

32.30 The princes of the north were probably the princes of the Phoenician city-states.

32.32 After reading Ezekiel's prophecies against all these foreign nations, we may wonder if he was blindly loyal to his own nation. But Ezekiel spoke only when God gave him a message (3.27). Besides, God's prophets pronounced judgment on God's sinful people just as much as on God's enemies. But if Babylon was God's enemy, why isn't it mentioned in Ezekiel's judgments? Perhaps because (1) God wanted to foster a spirit of cooperation between the exiles and Babylon in order to preserve his people; (2) God was still using Babylon to refine his own people; (3) God wanted to use Daniel, a powerful official in Babylon, to draw the Babylonians to him.

33.1ff This chapter sets forth a new direction for Ezekiel's prophecies. Up to this point, Ezekiel has pronounced judgment upon Judah (chapters 1–24) and the surrounding evil nations (chapters 25–32) for their sins. Now that Jerusalem has fallen, he turns from messages of doom and judgment to messages of comfort, hope, and future restoration for God's people (chapters 33–48). God previously appointed Ezekiel to be a watchman warning the nation of coming judgment (see 3.17–21). Here God appoints him to be a watchman ("sentinel") again, but this time to preach a message of hope. There are still sections full of warnings (33.23–34.10; 36.1–7), but these are part of the larger picture of hope. God will remember to bless those who are faithful to him. We must pay attention to both aspects of Ezekiel's message: warning and promise. Those who persist in rebelling against God should take warning. Those faithful to God should find encouragement and hope.

and the sword comes and takes any of them, they are taken away in their iniquity,
but their blood I will require at the sentinel's hand.
7 So you, mortal, I have made a sentinel for the house of Israel; whenever you
hear a word from my mouth, you shall give them warning from me. 8 If I say to the
wicked, "O wicked ones, you shall surely die," and you do not speak to warn the
wicked to turn from their ways, the wicked shall die in their iniquity, but their
blood I will require at your hand. 9 But if you warn the wicked to turn from their
ways, and they do not turn from their ways, the wicked shall die in their iniquity,
but you will have saved your life.
10 Now you, mortal, say to the house of Israel, Thus you have said: "Our transgressions and our sins weigh upon us, and we waste away because of them; how
then can we live?" 11 Say to them, As I live, says the Lord GOD, I have no pleasure
in the death of the wicked, but that the wicked turn from their ways and live; turn
back, turn back from your evil ways; for why will you die, O house of Israel?
12 And you, mortal, say to your people, The righteousness of the righteous shall not
save them when they transgress; and as for the wickedness of the wicked, it shall
not make them stumble when they turn from their wickedness; and the righteous
shall not be able to live by their righteousness[v] when they sin. 13 Though I say to
the righteous that they shall surely live, yet if they trust in their righteousness and
commit iniquity, none of their righteous deeds shall be remembered; but in the
iniquity that they have committed they shall die. 14 Again, though I say to the
wicked, "You shall surely die," yet if they turn from their sin and do what is lawful
and right— 15 if the wicked restore the pledge, give back what they have taken by
robbery, and walk in the statutes of life, committing no iniquity—they shall surely
live, they shall not die. 16 None of the sins that they have committed shall be remembered against them; they have done what is lawful and right, they shall surely
live.
17 Yet your people say, "The way of the Lord is not just," when it is their own
way that is not just. 18 When the righteous turn from their righteousness, and commit iniquity, they shall die for it.[w] 19 And when the wicked turn from their wickedness, and do what is lawful and right, they shall live by it.[w] 20 Yet you say, "The
way of the Lord is not just." O house of Israel, I will judge all of you according to
your ways!

The fall of Jerusalem

21 In the twelfth year of our exile, in the tenth month, on the fifth day of the
month, someone who had escaped from Jerusalem came to me and said, "The city
has fallen." 22 Now the hand of the LORD had been upon me the evening before the
fugitive came; but he had opened my mouth by the time the fugitive came to me in
the morning; so my mouth was opened, and I was no longer unable to speak.
23 The word of the LORD came to me: 24 Mortal, the inhabitants of these waste
places in the land of Israel keep saying, "Abraham was only one man, yet he got
possession of the land; but we are many; the land is surely given us to possess."
25 Therefore say to them, Thus says the Lord GOD: You eat flesh with the blood,
and lift up your eyes to your idols, and shed blood; shall you then possess the land?

33.7 Isa 62.6,7 Jer 26.2
33.8 Ezek 18.4,13, 18-20 Acts 20.26,27
33.9 Ezek 3.19,21 Acts 13.40-46 Gal 5.19-21
33.10 Ezek 24.23
33.11 1 Tim 2.4 2 Pet 3.9
33.12 Ezek 3.20 Mt 21.28-31
33.13 Ezek 18.26 2 Pet 2.20,21
33.14 Ezek 18.27
33.15 Lev 6.4,5
33.16 Isa 1.18; 43.25 Ezek 18.22 Rom 5.16,21 1 Jn 2.1-3
33.17 Ezek 18.24-29
33.21 Jer 39.1,2 Ezek 24.1,2,26
33.22 Ezek 3.26,27
33.24 Isa 51.1,2 Rom 4.12; 9.7
33.25 Lev 17.10-14 Deut 12.16,23 Jer 7.9,10

[v] Heb *by it* [w] Heb *them*

33.10-12 The exiles were discouraged by their past sins. This is an important turning point in this book—elsewhere in Ezekiel the people had refused to face their sins. Now, they felt heavy guilt for rebelling against God for so many years. Therefore, God assured them of forgiveness if they repented. God *wants* everyone to turn to him. He looks at what we are and will become, not what we have been. God gives you the opportunity to turn to him, if you will take it. Sincerely follow him, and ask him to forgive you when you fail.

33.13 Past good deeds will not save a person who decides to turn to a life of sin. Some people think they have done enough good deeds to overshadow the sins they don't want to give up. But it's useless to try to be good in some areas so you can be deliberately bad in others. God wants wholehearted love and obedience.

33.15 While good deeds will not save us, our salvation must lead to righteous actions (see Ephesians 2.10; James 2.14–17). This includes restitution for past sins (as exemplified in the story of Zacchaeus, see Luke 19.1–10). God expects us to make restitution, whenever necessary, for the wrongs we have committed.

33.21, 22 Near the beginning of his ministry, Ezekiel was unable to speak except to give specific messages from God (3.26, 27). Now that his prophecies have come true and the false prophets have been exposed, Ezekiel is again able to talk freely. No longer needing to prove himself, he is free to offer God's message of restoration and hope.

26 You depend on your swords, you commit abominations, and each of you defiles
his neighbor's wife; shall you then possess the land? 27 Say this to them, Thus says
the Lord GOD: As I live, surely those who are in the waste places shall fall by the
sword; and those who are in the open field I will give to the wild animals to be
devoured; and those who are in strongholds and in caves shall die by pestilence. 28 I
will make the land a desolation and a waste, and its proud might shall come to an
end; and the mountains of Israel shall be so desolate that no one will pass through.
29 Then they shall know that I am the LORD, when I have made the land a desolation
and a waste because of all their abominations that they have committed.
30 As for you, mortal, your people who talk together about you by the walls,
and at the doors of the houses, say to one another, each to a neighbor, "Come and
hear what the word is that comes from the LORD." 31 They come to you as people
come, and they sit before you as my people, and they hear your words, but they will
not obey them. For flattery is on their lips, but their heart is set on their gain. 32 To
them you are like a singer of love songs,[x] one who has a beautiful voice and plays
well on an instrument; they hear what you say, but they will not do it. 33 When this
comes—and come it will!—then they shall know that a prophet has been among
them.

Israel is God's flock

34 The word of the LORD came to me: 2 Mortal, prophesy against the shepherds
of Israel: prophesy, and say to them—to the shepherds: Thus says the Lord
GOD: Ah, you shepherds of Israel who have been feeding yourselves! Should not
shepherds feed the sheep? 3 You eat the fat, you clothe yourselves with the wool,
you slaughter the fatlings; but you do not feed the sheep. 4 You have not strengthened the weak, you have not healed the sick, you have not bound up the injured,
you have not brought back the strayed, you have not sought the lost, but with force
and harshness you have ruled them. 5 So they were scattered, because there was no
shepherd; and scattered, they became food for all the wild animals. 6 My sheep

[x] Cn: Heb *like a love song*

33.26 Mic 2.1,2
33.27 Isa 2.19; Jer 15.2-4; Ezek 5.12-14
33.28 Jer 44.22; Ezek 6.14; 36.34; Mic 7.13
33.29 Ezek 23.33,35
33.30 Ezek 14.3; 29.13
33.31 Ps 78.36,37; Isa 29.13; Mt 13.22; Lk 12.15; Jas 2.14-16; 1 Jn 3.18
33.32 Mk 6.20
33.33 Ezek 2.5; 33.29
34.2 Jer 10.21; 23.1; Mic 3.1-3; Jn 10.11; 21.15-17
34.3 Isa 56.11
34.4 Mt 9.36; 18.12,13; 1 Pet 5.3
34.5 Zech 10.2

BAD SHEPHERDS VS. GOOD SHEPHERDS

Bad Shepherds	*Good Shepherds*
Feed themselves	Feed their flock
Worry about their own health	Tend for the weak and sick, search for the lost
Rule with force and cruelty	Rule with love
Abandon and scatter the sheep	Gather and protect the sheep
Keep the best for themselves	Give their best to the sheep

33.30–32 The people refused to act upon Ezekiel's message. When people mock your witness for Christ or fail to act upon your advice, don't give up. You are not witnessing for them alone, but out of faithfulness to God. You cannot make them accept your message; you can only be faithful in delivering it.

33.31 In your heart, do you really love God? These people gave the appearance of following God, but they loved their money more. Many today also give the outward impression of being religious while remaining inwardly greedy. Jesus warned that we cannot love God and money at the same time (Matthew 6.24). It's easy to say "I surrender all" when we don't have much. It's when we start gaining some money that it becomes difficult to avoid loving it.

33.32 The people were coming to listen to Ezekiel in order to be entertained. They weren't interested in hearing a message from the Lord. Many people see church as entertainment. They enjoy the music, the people, and the activities; but they don't take the messages to heart. They don't seek to be challenged or to serve. Have you reduced church services to the level of entertainment, or does your worship truly have an impact on your life?

34.1ff Ezekiel called the exiles "Israel," referring to all Jews in captivity from both the northern and southern kingdoms. Ezekiel criticized Israel's leaders for taking care of themselves rather than taking care of their people. He outlined their sins (34.1–6) and pronounced judgment upon them (34.7–10). Then he promised that a true shepherd (the Messiah) would come who would take care of the people as the other leaders were supposed to do (34.11–31). This beautiful message portrays the fate of the present shepherds, the work of the new shepherd, and the future of the sheep.

34.2 Ezekiel prophesied against the religious leaders ("shepherds") of Israel who took care of themselves while exploiting and even abusing their people. Jeremiah also accused these leaders of neglecting the people (Jeremiah 23.1–4). Leaders in the church today must not fall into the trap of spending time and money to promote or enjoy themselves when they should use resources to provide for the needs of those they serve. To avoid this, leaders must stay close to their flocks.

34.4–6 God would judge the religious leaders because they were caught up in their own concerns and were neglecting their service to others. Spiritual leaders must be careful not to pursue self-development at the expense of broken, scattered people. When we give too much attention to our own needs and ideas, we may push God aside and abandon those who depend upon us.

were scattered, they wandered over all the mountains and on every high hill; my
sheep were scattered over all the face of the earth, with no one to search or seek for
them.
7 Therefore, you shepherds, hear the word of the LORD: 8As I live, says the
Lord GOD, because my sheep have become a prey, and my sheep have become food
for all the wild animals, since there was no shepherd; and because my shepherds
have not searched for my sheep, but the shepherds have fed themselves, and have
not fed my sheep; 9therefore, you shepherds, hear the word of the LORD: 10Thus
says the Lord GOD, I am against the shepherds; and I will demand my sheep at their
hand, and put a stop to their feeding the sheep; no longer shall the shepherds feed
themselves. I will rescue my sheep from their mouths, so that they may not be food
for them.
11 For thus says the Lord GOD: I myself will search for my sheep, and will seek
them out. 12As shepherds seek out their flocks when they are among their scattered
sheep, so I will seek out my sheep. I will rescue them from all the places to which
they have been scattered on a day of clouds and thick darkness. 13I will bring them
out from the peoples and gather them from the countries, and will bring them into
their own land; and I will feed them on the mountains of Israel, by the watercourses, and in all the inhabited parts of the land. 14I will feed them with good
pasture, and the mountain heights of Israel shall be their pasture; there they shall lie
down in good grazing land, and they shall feed on rich pasture on the mountains of
Israel. 15I myself will be the shepherd of my sheep, and I will make them lie down,
says the Lord GOD. 16I will seek the lost, and I will bring back the strayed, and I
will bind up the injured, and I will strengthen the weak, but the fat and the strong
I will destroy. I will feed them with justice.
17 As for you, my flock, thus says the Lord GOD: I shall judge between sheep
and sheep, between rams and goats: 18Is it not enough for you to feed on the good
pasture, but you must tread down with your feet the rest of your pasture? When you
drink of clear water, must you foul the rest with your feet? 19And must my sheep
eat what you have trodden with your feet, and drink what you have fouled with your
feet?
20 Therefore, thus says the Lord GOD to them: I myself will judge between the
fat sheep and the lean sheep. 21Because you pushed with flank and shoulder, and
butted at all the weak animals with your horns until you scattered them far and
wide, 22I will save my flock, and they shall no longer be ravaged; and I will judge
between sheep and sheep.
23 I will set up over them one shepherd, my servant David, and he shall feed
them: he shall feed them and be their shepherd. 24And I, the LORD, will be their
God, and my servant David shall be prince among them; I, the LORD, have spoken.
25 I will make with them a covenant of peace and banish wild animals from the
land, so that they may live in the wild and sleep in the woods securely. 26I will
make them and the region around my hill a blessing; and I will send down the
showers in their season; they shall be showers of blessing. 27The trees of the field
shall yield their fruit, and the earth shall yield its increase. They shall be secure on
their soil; and they shall know that I am the LORD, when I break the bars of their
yoke, and save them from the hands of those who enslaved them. 28They shall no

34.6 1 Pet 2.25
34.8 1 Sam 2.29,30; Ps 72.12-14; Zech 10.3; Acts 20.29
34.11 Ezek 11.17; Mt 13.11,12; Jn 10.16
34.12 Jer 23.3; 31.10; Ezek 30.3; Lk 19.10
34.13 Isa 30.25; Ps 23.1-3; Ezek 36.29,30
34.14 Isa 49.26; Mt 18.11; Lk 5.32; Jn 10.9
34.16 Isa 10.16; 49.26
34.17 Ezek 20.38; Zech 10.3; Mal 4.1; Mt 25.32
34.18 Num 16.9,13; Mt 23.13,14; Lk 11.52
34.21 Lk 13.14-16
34.22 Ps 72.12-14; Jer 23.2,3; Zech 11.7-9
34.23 Isa 40.11; Jer 23.4-6; 30.9; Jn 10.11; Heb 13.20
34.24 Jer 30.9; Ezek 37.24,25
34.25 Isa 11.6-9; Ezek 37.26
34.26 Gen 12.2; Deut 28.12; Isa 32.15; 44.3; Zech 8.13; Mal 3.10
34.27 Isa 52.2,3; Jn 15.5-8

34.9, 10 Those shepherds who failed their flock would be removed from office and held responsible for what happened to the people they were supposed to lead. Christian leaders must heed this warning and care for their flock or total failure and judgment will be the result (see 1 Corinthians 9.24–27). True leadership focuses on helping others, not just getting ahead.

34.11–16 God promises to take over as shepherd of his scattered flock. When our leaders fail us, we must not despair, but remember that God is in control and that he promises to one day return and care for his flock. Thus we know we can turn to him for help. He is still in control and can transform any tragic situation to produce good for his kingdom (see Romans 8.28).

34.18–20 A bad shepherd is not only selfish but destructive. A minister who muddies the waters for others by raising unnecessary doubts, teaching false ideas, and acting sinfully is destroying his flock's spiritual nourishment.

34.23–25 In contrast to the present evil shepherds (leaders) of God's people (34.1–6), God will send a perfect shepherd, the Messiah ("my servant David"), who will take care of every need his people have and set up a kingdom of perfect peace and justice (see Psalm 23; Jeremiah 23.5, 6; John 10.11; Hebrews 13.20, 21; Revelation 21).

more be plunder for the nations, nor shall the animals of the land devour them; they
shall live in safety, and no one shall make them afraid. 29 I will provide for them a
splendid vegetation so that they shall no more be consumed with hunger in the land,
and no longer suffer the insults of the nations. 30 They shall know that I, the LORD
their God, am with them, and that they, the house of Israel, are my people, says the
Lord GOD. 31 You are my sheep, the sheep of my pasture[y] and I am your God, says
the Lord GOD.

Edom will be wiped out

35 The word of the LORD came to me: 2 Mortal, set your face against Mount
Seir, and prophesy against it, 3 and say to it, Thus says the Lord GOD:

I am against you, Mount Seir;
  I stretch out my hand against you
  to make you a desolation and a waste.
4 I lay your towns in ruins;
  you shall become a desolation,
  and you shall know that I am the LORD.

5 Because you cherished an ancient enmity, and gave over the people of Israel to the
power of the sword at the time of their calamity, at the time of their final punishment; 6 therefore, as I live, says the Lord GOD, I will prepare you for blood, and
blood shall pursue you; since you did not hate bloodshed, bloodshed shall pursue
you. 7 I will make Mount Seir a waste and a desolation; and I will cut off from it all
who come and go. 8 I will fill its mountains with the slain; on your hills and in your
valleys and in all your watercourses those killed with the sword shall fall. 9 I will
make you a perpetual desolation, and your cities shall never be inhabited. Then you
shall know that I am the LORD.

10 Because you said, "These two nations and these two countries shall be mine,
and we will take possession of them,"—although the LORD was there— 11 therefore, as I live, says the Lord GOD, I will deal with you according to the anger and
envy that you showed because of your hatred against them; and I will make myself
known among you,[z] when I judge you. 12 You shall know that I, the LORD, have
heard all the abusive speech that you uttered against the mountains of Israel, saying, "They are laid desolate, they are given us to devour." 13 And you magnified
yourselves against me with your mouth, and multiplied your words against me; I
heard it. 14 Thus says the Lord GOD: As the whole earth rejoices, I will make you
desolate. 15 As you rejoiced over the inheritance of the house of Israel, because it
was desolate, so I will deal with you; you shall be desolate, Mount Seir, and all
Edom, all of it. Then they shall know that I am the LORD.

God promises that good times will return

36 And you, mortal, prophesy to the mountains of Israel, and say: O mountains
of Israel, hear the word of the LORD. 2 Thus says the Lord GOD: Because the
enemy said of you, "Aha!" and, "The ancient heights have become our possession," 3 therefore prophesy, and say: Thus says the Lord GOD: Because they
made you desolate indeed, and crushed you from all sides, so that you became the

[y] Gk OL: Heb *pasture, you are people* [z] Gk: Heb *them*

34.29 Isa 53.2; 60.21 Ezek 36.6,15,29 Zech 3.8; 6.12
34.30 Ezek 36.28
34.31 Ps 100.2 Jn 10.11
35.2 Gen 36.6-8 Ezek 25.12
35.3 Jer 49.13,17,18 Ezek 25.13
35.4 Ps 137.7 Ezek 6.6 Amos 1.11 Mal 1.2-4
35.8 Isa 34.5,6 Ezek 31.12 32.4,5
35.9 Jer 49.13 Ezek 25.13
35.10 Ps 48.1-3 Ezek 36.2,5
35.11 Ps 9.16; 137.7 Ezek 25.14
35.12 Ezek 36.2
35.13 Isa 10.13,14 Ezek 36.3
35.14 Isa 44.23; 49.13
35.15 Isa 34.5,6
36.1 Ezek 6.2,3 37.22
36.2 Deut 32.13 Ps 78.69 Isa 58.14

35.1ff Ezekiel gave another prophecy against Edom (also called Seir); his first prophecy against Edom is found in 25.12–14. In this prophecy, Ezekiel is probably using Edom to represent *all* the nations opposed to God's people. Chapter 36 says that Israel will be restored, while this chapter says that Edom (God's enemies) will be made "a desolation and a waste."

35.2 Edom offered to help destroy Jerusalem and rejoiced when the city fell. Edom's long-standing hostility against God's people resulted in God's judgment.

35.6–8 Ezekiel prophesied not only against the people of Edom, but also against their mountains and land. Their home territory was Mount Seir. Mountains, symbols of strength and power, represent the pride of these people who thought they could get away with evil. Edom's desire for revenge turned against it. They received the punishment they were so hasty to give out. God has a way of turning our treatment of others into a boomerang. So we must be careful in our judgment of others (Matthew 7.1, 2).

36.1ff In this chapter, Ezekiel said that Israel would be restored as a nation and would return to its own land. To the exiles in Babylon, this seemed impossible. This message again emphasizes God's sovereignty and trustworthiness. He would first judge the nations used to punish Israel (36.1–7) and then restore his people (36.8–15).

possession of the rest of the nations, and you became an object of gossip and
slander among the people; [4]therefore, O mountains of Israel, hear the word of the
Lord GOD: Thus says the Lord GOD to the mountains and the hills, the watercourses
and the valleys, the desolate wastes and the deserted towns, which have become
a source of plunder and an object of derision to the rest of the nations all around;
[5]therefore thus says the Lord GOD: I am speaking in my hot jealousy against the rest
of the nations, and against all Edom, who, with wholehearted joy and utter contempt, took my land as their possession, because of its pasture, to plunder it.
[6]Therefore prophesy concerning the land of Israel, and say to the mountains and
hills, to the watercourses and valleys, Thus says the Lord GOD: I am speaking in my
jealous wrath, because you have suffered the insults of the nations; [7]therefore thus
says the Lord GOD: I swear that the nations that are all around you shall themselves
suffer insults.

8 But you, O mountains of Israel, shall shoot out your branches, and yield your
fruit to my people Israel; for they shall soon come home. [9]See now, I am for you;
I will turn to you, and you shall be tilled and sown; [10]and I will multiply your
population, the whole house of Israel, all of it; the towns shall be inhabited and the
waste places rebuilt; [11]and I will multiply human beings and animals upon you.
They shall increase and be fruitful; and I will cause you to be inhabited as in your
former times, and will do more good to you than ever before. Then you shall know
that I am the LORD. [12]I will lead people upon you—my people Israel—and they
shall possess you, and you shall be their inheritance. No longer shall you bereave
them of children.

13 Thus says the Lord GOD: Because they say to you, "You devour people, and
you bereave your nation of children," [14]therefore you shall no longer devour people and no longer bereave your nation of children, says the Lord GOD; [15]and no
longer will I let you hear the insults of the nations, no longer shall you bear the
disgrace of the peoples; and no longer shall you cause your nation to stumble, says
the Lord GOD.

16 The word of the LORD came to me: [17]Mortal, when the house of Israel lived
on their own soil, they defiled it with their ways and their deeds; their conduct in
my sight was like the uncleanness of a woman in her menstrual period. [18]So I
poured out my wrath upon them for the blood that they had shed upon the land, and
for the idols with which they had defiled it. [19]I scattered them among the nations,
and they were dispersed through the countries; in accordance with their conduct
and their deeds I judged them. [20]But when they came to the nations, wherever they
came, they profaned my holy name, in that it was said of them, "These are the
people of the LORD, and yet they had to go out of his land." [21]But I had concern for
my holy name, which the house of Israel had profaned among the nations to which
they came.

22 Therefore say to the house of Israel, Thus says the Lord GOD: It is not for
your sake, O house of Israel, that I am about to act, but for the sake of my holy
name, which you have profaned among the nations to which you came. [23]I will
sanctify my great name, which has been profaned among the nations, and which
you have profaned among them; and the nations shall know that I am the LORD,
says the Lord GOD, when through you I display my holiness before their eyes. [24]I
will take you from the nations, and gather you from all the countries, and bring you
into your own land. [25]I will sprinkle clean water upon you, and you shall be clean

36.3 Jer 2.15; 51.34 Ezek 35.13
36.4 Ezek 34.28
36.5 Isa 66.15,16 Ezek 35.15
36.8 Ezek 17.22,23 34.26-29
36.10 Isa 27.6 49.17-22 Jer 31.27,28 Ezek 37.21,22
36.11 Jer 30.18 Ezek 16.55
36.12 Jer 32.44 Ezek 34.13,14 47.14
36.15 Isa 54.4 Jer 18.15 Ezek 22.4; 34.29
36.17 Jer 2.7
36.18 2 Chron 34.21 Lam 2.4; 4.11 Ezek 22.18-20
36.19 Ezek 22.15 Rom 2.6 Rev 20.12-15
36.20 Isa 52.5 Ezek 12.16 Rom 2.24
36.21 Ezek 20.44
36.22 Deut 9.5-7
36.24 Deut 30.3-5 Isa 43.5,6 Ezek 34.13
36.25 Jn 3.5 Tit 3.5,6 Heb 10.22

36.8 The growth prophesied here is in contrast to the desolation earlier prophesied for Israel (6.2, 3). Only through *God's* mercy would this be possible. God's restoration was intended to show that he is the Lord (36.11).

36.21–23 Why did God want to protect his holy name—his reputation—among the nations of the world? God was concerned about the salvation not only of his people, but also of the whole world. To allow his people to remain in sin and be permanently destroyed by their enemies would lead other nations to conclude that their heathen gods were more powerful than Israel's God (Isaiah 48.11). Thus, to protect his holy name, he would return a remnant of his people to their land. God will not share his glory with false gods—he alone is the one true God. The people had the responsibility to represent God properly to the rest of the world. Believers today have that same responsibility. How do you represent God to the world?

36.25–27 God promised to restore Israel not only physically, but spiritually. To accomplish this, he would give them a new heart for

from all your uncleannesses, and from all your idols I will cleanse you. 26 A new
heart I will give you, and a new spirit I will put within you; and I will remove from
your body the heart of stone and give you a heart of flesh. 27 I will put my spirit
within you, and make you follow my statutes and be careful to observe my ordinances. 28 Then you shall live in the land that I gave to your ancestors; and you shall
be my people, and I will be your God. 29 I will save you from all your uncleannesses, and I will summon the grain and make it abundant and lay no famine upon
you. 30 I will make the fruit of the tree and the produce of the field abundant, so that
you may never again suffer the disgrace of famine among the nations. 31 Then you
shall remember your evil ways, and your dealings that were not good; and you shall
loathe yourselves for your iniquities and your abominable deeds. 32 It is not for your
sake that I will act, says the Lord GOD; let that be known to you. Be ashamed and
dismayed for your ways, O house of Israel.

33 Thus says the Lord GOD: On the day that I cleanse you from all your iniquities, I will cause the towns to be inhabited, and the waste places shall be rebuilt.
34 The land that was desolate shall be tilled, instead of being the desolation that it
was in the sight of all who passed by. 35 And they will say, "This land that was
desolate has become like the garden of Eden; and the waste and desolate and ruined
towns are now inhabited and fortified." 36 Then the nations that are left all around
you shall know that I, the LORD, have rebuilt the ruined places, and replanted that
which was desolate; I, the LORD, have spoken, and I will do it.

37 Thus says the Lord GOD: I will also let the house of Israel ask me to do this
for them: to increase their population like a flock. 38 Like the flock for sacrifices,[a]
like the flock at Jerusalem during her appointed festivals, so shall the ruined towns
be filled with flocks of people. Then they shall know that I am the LORD.

The valley of dried bones

37 The hand of the LORD came upon me, and he brought me out by the spirit of
the LORD and set me down in the middle of a valley; it was full of bones. 2 He
led me all around them; there were very many lying in the valley, and they were
very dry. 3 He said to me, "Mortal, can these bones live?" I answered, "O Lord
GOD, you know." 4 Then he said to me, "Prophesy to these bones, and say to them:

a Heb *flock of holy things*

36.26 Ps 51.10; Ezek 11.19; 2 Cor 5.17
36.27 Ezek 11.20
36.28 Ezek 14.11; 37.23,27; 2 Cor 6.16-18
36.29 Ezek 34.27,29
36.30 Deut 29.23-28
36.31 Ezek 6.9; 16.61-63; 20.43
36.32 Dan 9.18,19
36.35 Isa 51.3; Joel 2.3
36.36 Hos 14.4-7; Mic 7.15-17; Mt 24.35
36.37 1 Kgs 8.62,63; 2 Chron 35.7-9; Zech 11.17; Jn 10.9,16
37.1 Jer 7.32—8.2; Ezek 33.22; 40.1
37.3 Jn 6.5,6; Rom 4.17

OLD AND NEW COVENANTS

Old Covenant	*New Covenant*
Placed upon stone	Placed upon people's hearts
Based on the law	Based on desire to love and serve God
Must be taught	Known by all
Legal relationship with God	Personal relationship with God

following him and put his Spirit within them (see 11.19, 20; Psalm 51.7–11) to transform them and empower them to do his will. Again the new covenant is promised (16.61–63; 34.23–25), ultimately to be fulfilled in Christ. No matter how impure your life is right now, God offers you a fresh start. You can have your sins washed away, receive a new heart from God, and have his Spirit within you—if you accept God's promise. Why try to patch up your old life when you can have a new one?

36.32 The people had become so callous that they had lost all sensitivity to sin. First they had to "remember" (36.31) their sins, then despise them, and finally repent of them (see James 4.8, 9). As we examine our lives, we may find that we too have lost our sensitivity to certain sins. To regain sensitivity we must recognize our sin for what it is, feel sorry for displeasing God, and ask his forgiveness. The Holy Spirit will guide us, making us responsive and receptive to God's truth (John 14.26; 16.8, 13).

36.37, 38 God said that if the people asked, he would come to their aid. We cannot expect his mercy, however, until we have sought a new heart from him (36.26). We can be thankful that his invitation is open to all.

37.1ff This vision illustrates the promise of chapter 36—new life and a nation restored, both physically and spiritually. The dry bones are a picture of the Jews in captivity—scattered and dead. The two sticks (37.15–17) represent the reunion of the entire nation of Israel which had divided into northern and southern kingdoms after Solomon. The scattered exiles of both Israel and Judah would be released from the "graves" of captivity and one day regathered in their homeland, with the Messiah as their leader. This vision has yet to be fulfilled. Ezekiel felt he was speaking to the dead as he preached to the exiles because they rarely responded to his message. But these bones responded! And just as God brought life to the bones, he would bring life to his spiritually dead people.

37.4, 5 The dry bones represented the people's spiritually dead condition. Your church may seem like a heap of dried-up bones to you, spiritually dead with no hope of vitality. But just as God promised to restore his nation, he can restore any church, no matter how dry or dead it may be. Rather than give up, pray for renewal, for God can restore it to life. The hope and prayer of every church should be that God will put his Spirit into it (37.14). God is always at work calling his people back to himself.

O dry bones, hear the word of the LORD. 5 Thus says the Lord GOD to these bones:
I will cause breath[b] to enter you, and you shall live. 6 I will lay sinews on you, and
will cause flesh to come upon you, and cover you with skin, and put breath[b] in
you, and you shall live; and you shall know that I am the LORD."
7 So I prophesied as I had been commanded; and as I prophesied, suddenly
there was a noise, a rattling, and the bones came together, bone to its bone. 8 I
looked, and there were sinews on them, and flesh had come upon them, and skin
had covered them; but there was no breath in them. 9 Then he said to me, "Prophesy
to the breath, prophesy, mortal, and say to the breath:[c] Thus says the Lord GOD:
Come from the four winds, O breath,[c] and breathe upon these slain, that they may
live." 10 I prophesied as he commanded me, and the breath came into them, and
they lived, and stood on their feet, a vast multitude.
11 Then he said to me, "Mortal, these bones are the whole house of Israel. They
say, 'Our bones are dried up, and our hope is lost; we are cut off completely.'
12 Therefore prophesy, and say to them, Thus says the Lord GOD: I am going to
open your graves, and bring you up from your graves, O my people; and I will
bring you back to the land of Israel. 13 And you shall know that I am the LORD,
when I open your graves, and bring you up from your graves, O my people. 14 I will
put my spirit within you, and you shall live, and I will place you on your own soil;
then you shall know that I, the LORD, have spoken and will act," says the LORD.

The kingdom will be reunited

15 The word of the LORD came to me: 16 Mortal, take a stick and write on it,
"For Judah, and the Israelites associated with it"; then take another stick and write
on it, "For Joseph (the stick of Ephraim) and all the house of Israel associated with
it"; 17 and join them together into one stick, so that they may become one in your
hand. 18 And when your people say to you, "Will you not show us what you mean
by these?" 19 say to them, Thus says the Lord GOD: I am about to take the stick of
Joseph (which is in the hand of Ephraim) and the tribes of Israel associated with it;
and I will put the stick of Judah upon it,[d] and make them one stick, in order that
they may be one in my hand. 20 When the sticks on which you write are in your hand
before their eyes, 21 then say to them, Thus says the Lord GOD: I will take the people of Israel from the nations among which they have gone, and will gather them
from every quarter, and bring them to their own land. 22 I will make them one nation in the land, on the mountains of Israel; and one king shall be king over them
all. Never again shall they be two nations, and never again shall they be divided
into two kingdoms. 23 They shall never again defile themselves with their idols and
their detestable things, or with any of their transgressions. I will save them from all
the apostasies into which they have fallen,[e] and will cleanse them. Then they shall
be my people, and I will be their GOD.
24 My servant David shall be king over them; and they shall all have one shepherd. They shall follow my ordinances and be careful to observe my statutes.
25 They shall live in the land that I gave to my servant Jacob, in which your ancestors lived; they and their children and their children's children shall live there forever; and my servant David shall be their prince forever. 26 I will make a covenant
of peace with them; it shall be an everlasting covenant with them; and I will bless[f]

37.4 Num 20.8 Isa 42.18 Jer 22.29
37.5 Ps 104.29,30 Jn 20.22
37.6 Joel 2.27
37.9 Ps 104.30 Hos 13.14
37.10 Rev 11.11
37.11 Num 17.12,13 Ps 141.7 Isa 49.14
37.12 Deut 32.39 Isa 26.19 Ezek 36.24 Amos 9.14,15
37.14 Ezek 11.19 36.27 Joel 2.28,29
37.16 1 Kgs 12.16-20
37.17 Isa 11.13; 50.4
37.18 Ezek 20.49 24.19
37.21 Ezek 39.27
37.22 Ezek 34.23,24
37.23 Ezek 11.18 36.25 Zech 13.1,2 14.21
37.24 Isa 40.11 Ezek 34.23,24
37.25 Isa 11.1
37.26 Isa 55.3 Ezek 43.7 Heb 13.20,21

[b] Or *spirit* [c] Or *wind* or *spirit* [d] Heb *I will put them upon it* [e] Another reading is *from all the settlements in which they have sinned* [f] Tg: Heb *give*

37.16 The first stick was for Judah, being the leading tribe in the southern kingdom. The other was for Joseph, because he was the father of Ephraim, the leading tribe in the northern kingdom.

37.24, 25 The Messiah is often called David because he is David's descendant. David was a good king, but the Messiah will be the perfect King (Revelation 17.14; 19.16; 21.1ff).

37.26, 27 God's promise here goes beyond the physical and geographical restoration of Israel. He promises to breathe new spiritual life into his people so that their hearts and attitudes will be right with him and united with one another. This same process is described throughout God's Word as the cleansing of our hearts by God's Spirit (Titus 3.4–6; 1 John 2.27).

37.26–28 The restoration of the temple meant far more than repairing what had been damaged. The "sanctuary" and "dwelling place" symbolized God's presence on earth and his rule in the heart of every person who obeys him. People will know God is not dead and that he loves them. Even now, our witness to God's power and provision for us will draw others to him.

them and multiply them, and will set my sanctuary among them forevermore. 27 My
dwelling place shall be with them; and I will be their God, and they shall be my
people. 28 Then the nations shall know that I the LORD sanctify Israel, when my
sanctuary is among them forevermore.

A prophecy against Gog

38 The word of the LORD came to me: 2 Mortal, set your face toward Gog, of
the land of Magog, the chief prince of Meshech and Tubal. Prophesy against
him 3 and say: Thus says the Lord GOD: I am against you, O Gog, chief prince of
Meshech and Tubal; 4 I will turn you around and put hooks into your jaws, and I
will lead you out with all your army, horses and horsemen, all of them clothed in
full armor, a great company, all of them with shield and buckler, wielding swords.
5 Persia, Ethiopia,[g] and Put are with them, all of them with buckler and helmet;
6 Gomer and all its troops; Beth-togarmah from the remotest parts of the north with
all its troops—many peoples are with you.
7 Be ready and keep ready, you and all the companies that are assembled
around you, and hold yourselves in reserve for them. 8 After many days you shall
be mustered; in the latter years you shall go against a land restored from war, a land
where people were gathered from many nations on the mountains of Israel, which
had long lain waste; its people were brought out from the nations and now are living
in safety, all of them. 9 You shall advance, coming on like a storm; you shall be like
a cloud covering the land, you and all your troops, and many peoples with you.
10 Thus says the Lord GOD: On that day thoughts will come into your mind, and
you will devise an evil scheme. 11 You will say, "I will go up against the land of
unwalled villages; I will fall upon the quiet people who live in safety, all of them
living without walls, and having no bars or gates"; 12 to seize spoil and carry off
plunder; to assail the waste places that are now inhabited, and the people who were
gathered from the nations, who are acquiring cattle and goods, who live at the
center[h] of the earth. 13 Sheba and Dedan and the merchants of Tarshish and all its
young warriors[i] will say to you, "Have you come to seize spoil? Have you assembled your horde to carry off plunder, to carry away silver and gold, to take away
cattle and goods, to seize a great amount of booty?"
14 Therefore, mortal, prophesy, and say to Gog: Thus says the Lord GOD: On
that day when my people Israel are living securely, you will rouse yourself[j] 15 and
come from your place out of the remotest parts of the north, you and many peoples
with you, all of them riding on horses, a great horde, a mighty army; 16 you will
come up against my people Israel, like a cloud covering the earth. In the latter days
I will bring you against my land, so that the nations may know me, when through
you, O Gog, I display my holiness before their eyes.
17 Thus says the Lord GOD: Are you he of whom I spoke in former days by my
servants the prophets of Israel, who in those days prophesied for years that I would
bring you against them? 18 On that day, when Gog comes against the land of Israel,
says the Lord GOD, my wrath shall be aroused. 19 For in my jealousy and in my
blazing wrath I declare: On that day there shall be a great shaking in the land of
Israel; 20 the fish of the sea, and the birds of the air, and the animals of the field, and

[g] Or *Nubia*; Heb *Cush* [h] Heb *navel* [i] Heb *young lions* [j] Gk: Heb *will you not know?*

37.27 Lev 26.11,12; Jn 1.14; 2 Cor 6.16
38.2 Ezek 39.1,9; Rev 20.8,9
38.4 Isa 43.17; Ezek 39.2; Dan 11.40
38.5 Gen 10.6,7; Ezek 27.10
38.6 Gen 10.2,3; Ezek 27.14
38.8 Ezek 34.13; Amos 9.14,15
38.9 Isa 5.28; Jer 4.13; Dan 11.40; Joel 2.2
38.12 Ezek 29.19
38.13 Isa 10.5-7; Ezek 32.2; Nah 2.11-13
38.14 Jer 23.5,6; Zech 2.5,8
38.15 Isa 8.13; Ezek 28.22
38.17 Isa 5.26-30; Dan 11.40-45; Zech 12.2-8
38.19 Ezek 36.5,6; Hag 2.6,7; Heb 12.26-29
38.20 Zech 14.4,5

38.1ff In chapter 37, Ezekiel revealed how Israel (God's people) would be restored to their land from many parts of the world. Once Israel became strong, a confederacy of nations from the north would attack, led by Gog (see also Revelation 20.8). Their purpose would be to destroy God's people. Gog's allies came from the mountainous area southeast of the Black Sea and southwest of the Caspian Sea (central Turkey), as well as from the area that is present-day Iran, Ethiopia, Libya, and possibly the Soviet Union. Gog could be a person, but from the context Gog could also be a symbol of all evil in the world. Whether symbolic or literal, he represents the aggregate military might of all the forces opposed to God.

Many say that the battle Ezekiel described will occur at the end of human history, but there are nevertheless many differences between the events described here and those in Revelation 20. God will deliver his people. No enemy can stand before his mighty power.

38.4 A buckler is a small, round shield used in battle.

38.13 Sheba and Dedan, great trading centers in Arabia, would say to Gog, "Who are you to usurp our position as the world's trade leaders?" Sheba and Dedan would then join this confederacy. Tarshish was the leading trade center in the west; many believe it was in Spain.

all creeping things that creep on the ground, and all human beings that are on the
face of the earth, shall quake at my presence, and the mountains shall be thrown
down, and the cliffs shall fall, and every wall shall tumble to the ground. 21 I will
summon the sword against Gog[k] in[l] all my mountains, says the Lord GOD; the
swords of all will be against their comrades. 22 With pestilence and bloodshed I will
enter into judgment with him; and I will pour down torrential rains and hailstones,
fire and sulfur, upon him and his troops and the many peoples that are with him.
23 So I will display my greatness and my holiness and make myself known in the
eyes of many nations. Then they shall know that I am the LORD.

God's holiness will be vindicated

39 And you, mortal, prophesy against Gog, and say: Thus says the Lord GOD:
I am against you, O Gog, chief prince of Meshech and Tubal! 2 I will turn
you around and drive you forward, and bring you up from the remotest parts of the
north, and lead you against the mountains of Israel. 3 I will strike your bow from
your left hand, and will make your arrows drop out of your right hand. 4 You shall
fall upon the mountains of Israel, you and all your troops and the peoples that are
with you; I will give you to birds of prey of every kind and to the wild animals to
be devoured. 5 You shall fall in the open field; for I have spoken, says the Lord
GOD. 6 I will send fire on Magog and on those who live securely in the coastlands;
and they shall know that I am the LORD.

7 My holy name I will make known among my people Israel; and I will not let
my holy name be profaned any more; and the nations shall know that I am the
LORD, the Holy One in Israel. 8 It has come! It has happened, says the Lord GOD.
This is the day of which I have spoken.

9 Then those who live in the towns of Israel will go out and make fires of the
weapons and burn them—bucklers and shields, bows and arrows, handpikes and
spears—and they will make fires of them for seven years. 10 They will not need to
take wood out of the field or cut down any trees in the forests, for they will make
their fires of the weapons; they will despoil those who despoiled them, and plunder
those who plundered them, says the Lord GOD.

11 On that day I will give to Gog a place for burial in Israel, the Valley of the
Travelers[m] east of the sea; it shall block the path of the travelers, for there Gog and
all his horde will be buried; it shall be called the Valley of Hamon-gog.[n] 12 Seven
months the house of Israel shall spend burying them, in order to cleanse the land.
13 All the people of the land shall bury them; and it will bring them honor on the day
that I show my glory, says the Lord GOD. 14 They will set apart men to pass through
the land regularly and bury any invaders[o] who remain on the face of the land, so
as to cleanse it; for seven months they shall make their search. 15 As the searchers[o]
pass through the land, anyone who sees a human bone shall set up a sign by it, until
the buriers have buried it in the Valley of Hamon-gog.[n] 16 (A city Hamonah[p] is
there also.) Thus they shall cleanse the land.

17 As for you, mortal, thus says the Lord GOD: Speak to the birds of every kind
and to all the wild animals: Assemble and come, gather from all around to the
sacrificial feast that I am preparing for you, a great sacrificial feast on the moun-

38.21 2 Chron 20.23
38.22 Zech 14.12-15; Rev 16.21
38.23 Ezek 36.23; Rev 15.3,4
39.1 Ezek 38.2-4; Nah 2.13; 3.5
39.2 Ezek 38.15; Dan 11.40
39.3 Jer 21.4,5; Ezek 30.21-24
39.4 Isa 14.24,25; Ezek 29.5; 32.4,5
39.6 Jer 25.22; Ezek 30.8,16; Amos 1.4-10
39.7 Ex 20.7; Isa 6.9,14; Ezek 20.39
39.9 Zech 9.10
39.10 Isa 14.2; Mt 7.2
39.11 Ezek 47.18
39.13 Ezek 28.22; Zeph 3.19,20; 1 Pet 1.7
39.17 Isa 34.6,7; Jer 46.10; Zeph 1.7; Rev 19.17,18

[k] Heb *him* [l] Heb *to* or *for* [m] Or *of the Abarim* [n] That is, *the Horde of Gog* [o] Heb *travelers* [p] That is *The Horde*

38.21 God will directly intervene in the defense of Israel, unleashing severe natural disasters on the invaders from the north. In the end the stricken heathen nations will turn upon themselves in confusion and panic. All those who set themselves against God will be destroyed.

39.1ff The story of the battle continues. The defeat of the evil forces will be final and complete; they will be destroyed by divine intervention. Because of this victory, God's name will be known throughout the world. His glory will be evident, and the nations will understand that he alone is in charge of human history. God will clearly show his love for his people by restoring them to their homeland.

39.12–16 Two themes are intertwined: God's total victory over his enemies, and the need to purify the land to make it holy. After the final battle, teams will be used to give proper burial to the bodies of the dead enemies in order for the land to be cleansed. The land would be defiled by unburied corpses. Those who would come in contact with the corpses out in the open would become ceremonially unclean (according to Numbers 19.14–16). Yet there will be so many that the carrion birds will be called to the "feast" in order to help dispose of the corpses (39.17–20). The message for us is an exciting one: with God on our side, we are assured of ultimate victory over his foes, for God will fight on our behalf (see also Zephaniah 3.14–17; Romans 8.38, 39).

39.18 Deut 32.14 Ps 22.12
39.20 Ps 75.5,6 Ezek 38.4 Hag 2.22
39.21 Ex 9.16; 14.4 Ezek 38.16,23
39.23 Isa 59.2 Jer 22.8,9 Ezek 36.18,19
39.24 2 Kgs 17.7 Jer 2.17,19 4.18 Ezek 36.19
39.25 Jer 33.7 Ezek 34.13 36.10
39.26 Dan 9.16
39.27 Ezek 28.25,26 37.21
39.28 Deut 30.3,4 Neh 1.8-10 Rom 9.6-8 11.1-7
39.29 Joel 2.28 Acts 2.17

tains of Israel, and you shall eat flesh and drink blood. 18 You shall eat the flesh of
the mighty, and drink the blood of the princes of the earth—of rams, of lambs, and
of goats, of bulls, all of them fatlings of Bashan. 19 You shall eat fat until you are
filled, and drink blood until you are drunk, at the sacrificial feast that I am preparing for you. 20 And you shall be filled at my table with horses and charioteers,[q]
with warriors and all kinds of soldiers, says the Lord God.
21 I will display my glory among the nations; and all the nations shall see my
judgment that I have executed, and my hand that I have laid on them. 22 The house
of Israel shall know that I am the LORD their God, from that day forward. 23 And the
nations shall know that the house of Israel went into captivity for their iniquity,
because they dealt treacherously with me. So I hid my face from them and gave
them into the hand of their adversaries, and they all fell by the sword. 24 I dealt with
them according to their uncleanness and their transgressions, and hid my face
from them.
25 Therefore thus says the Lord God: Now I will restore the fortunes of Jacob,
and have mercy on the whole house of Israel; and I will be jealous for my holy
name. 26 They shall forget[r] their shame, and all the treachery they have practiced
against me, when they live securely in their land with no one to make them afraid,
27 when I have brought them back from the peoples and gathered them from their
enemies' lands, and through them have displayed my holiness in the sight of many
nations. 28 Then they shall know that I am the LORD their God because I sent them
into exile among the nations, and then gathered them into their own land. I will
leave none of them behind; 29 and I will never again hide my face from them, when
I pour out my spirit upon the house of Israel, says the Lord God.

2. Restoring the worship of God

The temple area

40.1 2 Kgs 25.1-7 Jer 39.1-9
40.3 Dan 10.5,6 Zech 2.1,2 Rev 11.1; 21.15

40 In the twenty-fifth year of our exile, at the beginning of the year, on the
tenth day of the month, in the fourteenth year after the city was struck down,
on that very day, the hand of the LORD was upon me, and he brought me there. 2 He
brought me, in visions of God, to the land of Israel, and set me down upon a very
high mountain, on which was a structure like a city to the south. 3 When he brought

[q] Heb *chariots* [r] Another reading is *They shall bear*

39.29 Both in this prophecy and in Joel 2.28, 29, God promises to pour out his Spirit on mankind. The early church believed this began to be fulfilled at pentecost, when God's Holy Spirit came to dwell in all believers (Acts 2.1–18).

40.1ff The building of the temple conveys a time of complete restoration to the exiles, a time when God would return to his people. The temple was built in 520–515 B.C. (see Ezra 5, 6), but fell short of Ezekiel's plan (Haggai 2.3; Zechariah 4.10). This vision of the temple has been interpreted in four main ways: (1) This is the temple Zerubbabel should have built in 520–515 B.C. This is the actual blueprint Ezekiel intended, but due to disobedience (43.2–10) and noncompliance, it was never followed. (2) This is a literal temple to be rebuilt during the millennial reign of Christ. (3) This temple is symbolic of the true worship of God by the Christian church right now. (4) This temple is symbolic of the future and eternal reign of God when his presence and blessing fill the earth.

Whether the temple is literal or symbolic, it seems clear that this is a vision of God's final perfect kingdom. This gave hope to the people of Ezekiel's time who had just seen their nation and its temple destroyed with no hope of rebuilding it in the near future. The details given in this vision gave the people even more hope that what Ezekiel saw had come from God and would come to pass.

40.1ff One argument against the view that Ezekiel's temple is a literal building of the future is that sacrifices are mentioned (40.38–43). If the sacrifices were to be reinstituted in the last days, then Christ's sacrifice would be meaningless. The New Testament makes it clear that Christ died once and for all (Romans 6.10; Hebrews 9.12; 10.10, 18).

In Ezekiel's day, however, the only kind of worship the people knew was the kind that revolved around the sacrifices and ceremonies described in Exodus through Deuteronomy. Ezekiel had to explain the new order of worship in terms the people would understand. The next nine chapters tell how the temple is the focal point of everything, showing that all of life centers on God.

40.1ff Ezekiel explained God's dwelling place in words and images the people could understand. God wanted them to see the great splendor he had planned for those who lived faithfully. This temple was never built, but was a vision intended to typify God's perfect plan for his people, the centrality of worship, the presence of the Lord, the blessings flowing from it, and the orderliness of worship and duties. Don't let the details obscure the point of this vision—one day all those who have been faithful to God will enjoy eternal life with him.

40.1–43.27 This vision came to Ezekiel in 573 B.C. Chapters 40–43 give the temple's measurements and then describe how it is filled with God's glory. Because Ezekiel was a priest, he would have been familiar with the furnishings and ceremonies of Solomon's temple. As in Revelation 11.1, 2, the command to "measure" defines the areas God has marked out for special use. In all these details, the important point to remember is that God is sovereign.

40.3, 4 Who was this man? He was obviously not a human being, so he was probably the angel in 9.1–11 or one like him. Some say he may have been Christ himself, because he speaks as God had been speaking to Ezekiel, calling him "Mortal."

me there, a man was there, whose appearance shone like bronze, with a linen cord
and a measuring reed in his hand; and he was standing in the gateway. 4 The man
said to me, "Mortal, look closely and listen attentively, and set your mind upon all
that I shall show you, for you were brought here in order that I might show it to you;
declare all that you see to the house of Israel."

5 Now there was a wall all around the outside of the temple area. The length of
the measuring reed in the man's hand was six long cubits, each being a cubit and a
handbreadth in length; so he measured the thickness of the wall, one reed; and the
height, one reed. 6 Then he went into the gateway facing east, going up its steps,
and measured the threshold of the gate, one reed deep.[s] There were 7 recesses, and
each recess was one reed wide and one reed deep; and the space between the recesses, five cubits; and the threshold of the gate by the vestibule of the gate at the
inner end was one reed deep. 8 Then he measured the inner vestibule of the gateway, one cubit. 9 Then he measured the vestibule of the gateway, eight cubits; and
its pilasters, two cubits; and the vestibule of the gate was at the inner end. 10 There
were three recesses on either side of the east gate; the three were of the same size;
and the pilasters on either side were of the same size. 11 Then he measured the width
of the opening of the gateway, ten cubits; and the width of the gateway, thirteen
cubits. 12 There was a barrier before the recesses, one cubit on either side; and the
recesses were six cubits on either side. 13 Then he measured the gate from the back[t]
of the one recess to the back[t] of the other, a width of twenty-five cubits, from wall
to wall.[u] 14 He measured[v] also the vestibule, twenty cubits; and the gate next to the
pilaster on every side of the court.[w] 15 From the front of the gate at the entrance to
the end of the inner vestibule of the gate was fifty cubits. 16 The recesses and their
pilasters had windows, with shutters[w] on the inside of the gateway all around, and
the vestibules also had windows on the inside all around; and on the pilasters were
palm trees.

17 Then he brought me into the outer court; there were chambers there, and a
pavement, all around the court; thirty chambers fronted on the pavement. 18 The
pavement ran along the side of the gates, corresponding to the length of the gates;
this was the lower pavement. 19 Then he measured the distance from the inner front
of[x] the lower gate to the outer front of the inner court, one hundred cubits.[y]

20 Then he measured the gate of the outer court that faced north—its depth and
width. 21 Its recesses, three on either side, and its pilasters and its vestibule were of
the same size as those of the first gate; its depth was fifty cubits, and its width
twenty-five cubits. 22 Its windows, its vestibule, and its palm trees were of the same
size as those of the gate that faced toward the east. Seven steps led up to it; and its
vestibule was on the inside.[z] 23 Opposite the gate on the north, as on the east, was
a gate to the inner court; he measured from gate to gate, one hundred cubits.

24 Then he led me toward the south, and there was a gate on the south; and he
measured its pilasters and its vestibule; they had the same dimensions as the others.
25 There were windows all around in it and in its vestibule, like the windows of the
others; its depth was fifty cubits, and its width twenty-five cubits. 26 There were
seven steps leading up to it; its vestibule was on the inside.[z] It had palm trees on
its pilasters, one on either side. 27 There was a gate on the south of the inner court;
and he measured from gate to gate toward the south, one hundred cubits.

28 Then he brought me to the inner court by the south gate, and he measured the
south gate; it was of the same dimensions as the others. 29 Its recesses, its pilasters,
and its vestibule were of the same size as the others; and there were windows all
around in it and in its vestibule; its depth was fifty cubits, and its width twenty-five
cubits. 30 There were vestibules all around, twenty-five cubits deep and five cubits

40.4 Jer 26.2 Ezek 43.10; 44.5
40.5 Ezek 42.20
40.6 Ezek 8.16; 11.1 43.1
40.7 1 Kgs 6.5-10 2 Chron 31.11 Jer 35.4
40.14 Ex 27.9 1 Chron 28.6 Ps 100.4 Isa 62.4 Ezek 42.1
40.16 1 Kgs 6.4 Ezek 41.26 1 Cor 13.12
40.17 1 Chron 9.26 2 Chron 31.11 Ezek 46.21 Rev 11.2
40.18 Ezek 46.1,2
40.22 1 Kgs 6.29-35 7.36 2 Chron 3.5 Rev 7.9
40.23 Ex 27.9-18 38.9-12
40.24 Ezek 46.9

[s] Heb *deep, and one threshold, one reed deep* [t] Gk: Heb *roof* [u] Heb *opening facing opening* [v] Heb *made* [w] Meaning of Heb uncertain [x] Compare Gk: Heb *from before* [y] Heb adds *the east and the north* [z] Gk: Heb *before them*

40.5 The long cubit was about 21 inches, compared with the ordinary cubit of about 18 inches.

40.16 The *pilasters* were the supporting columns that projected from the walls.

wide. 31 Its vestibule faced the outer court, and palm trees were on its pilasters, and
its stairway had eight steps.
32 Then he brought me to the inner court on the east side, and he measured the
gate; it was of the same size as the others. 33 Its recesses, its pilasters, and its vestibule were of the same dimensions as the others; and there were windows all around
in it and in its vestibule; its depth was fifty cubits, and its width twenty-five cubits.
34 Its vestibule faced the outer court, and it had palm trees on its pilasters, on either
side; and its stairway had eight steps.

40.35 Ezek 44.4; 47.2

35 Then he brought me to the north gate, and he measured it; it had the same
dimensions as the others. 36 Its recesses, its pilasters, and its vestibule were of the
same size as the others;[a] and it had windows all around. Its depth was fifty cubits,
and its width twenty-five cubits. 37 Its vestibule[b] faced the outer court, and it had
palm trees on its pilasters, on either side; and its stairway had eight steps.

40.38 1 Kgs 6.8; 1 Chron 28.12; Ezek 41.10; 42.13; Neh 13.5,9
40.39 Lev 1.2-17; 4.2,3; 5.6; 6.6; 7.1,2; Ezek 46.2
40.42 Ex 20.25

38 There was a chamber with its door in the vestibule of the gate,[c] where the
burnt offering was to be washed. 39 And in the vestibule of the gate were two tables
on either side, on which the burnt offering and the sin offering and the guilt offering
were to be slaughtered. 40 On the outside of the vestibule[d] at the entrance of the
north gate were two tables; and on the other side of the vestibule of the gate were
two tables. 41 Four tables were on the inside, and four tables on the outside of the
side of the gate, eight tables, on which the sacrifices were to be slaughtered.
42 There were also four tables of hewn stone for the burnt offering, a cubit and a half
long, and one cubit and a half wide, and one cubit high, on which the instruments
were to be laid with which the burnt offerings and the sacrifices were slaughtered.
43 There were pegs, one handbreadth long, fastened all around the inside. And on
the tables the flesh of the offering was to be laid.

40.44 1 Chron 6.31, 32; 16.41-43; 25.1-7
40.45 Lev 8.35; Num 3.27-32; 18.5; 1 Chron 9.23; Mal 2.4-7
40.46 1 Kgs 2.35; Ezek 43.19; 48.11

44 On the outside of the inner gateway there were chambers for the singers in
the inner court, one[e] at the side of the north gate facing south, the other at the side
of the east gate facing north. 45 He said to me, "This chamber that faces south is for
the priests who have charge of the temple, 46 and the chamber that faces north is for
the priests who have charge of the altar; these are the descendants of Zadok, who
alone among the descendants of Levi may come near to the LORD to minister to
him." 47 He measured the court, one hundred cubits deep, and one hundred cubits
wide, a square; and the altar was in front of the temple.

The temple

40.48 1 Kgs 6.3; 2 Chron 3.17; Jer 52.17-23; Rev 3.12

48 Then he brought me to the vestibule of the temple and measured the pilasters
of the vestibule, five cubits on either side; and the width of the gate was fourteen
cubits; and the sidewalls of the gate were three cubits[f] on either side. 49 The depth
of the vestibule was twenty cubits, and the width twelve[g] cubits; ten steps led up[h]
to it; and there were pillars beside the pilasters on either side.

41.1 Ezek 40.2,3,17; Zech 6.12,13; Eph 2.20-22; Rev 11.1,2; 21.3,15
41.2 1 Kgs 6.2,17
41.4 Ex 26.33,34; Heb 9.3-8

41

Then he brought me to the nave, and measured the pilasters; on each side six
cubits was the width of the pilasters.[i] 2 The width of the entrance was ten
cubits; and the sidewalls of the entrance were five cubits on either side. He measured the length of the nave, forty cubits, and its width, twenty cubits. 3 Then he
went into the inner room and measured the pilasters of the entrance, two cubits; and
the width of the entrance, six cubits; and the sidewalls[j] of the entrance, seven
cubits. 4 He measured the depth of the room, twenty cubits, and its width, twenty
cubits, beyond the nave. And he said to me, This is the most holy place.

[a] One Ms: Compare verses 29 and 33: MT lacks *were of the same size as the others* [b] Gk Vg Compare verses 26, 31, 34: Heb *pilasters* [c] Cn: Heb *at the pilasters of the gates* [d] Cn: Heb *to him who goes up* [e] Heb lacks *one* [f] Gk: Heb *and the width of the gate was three cubits* [g] Gk: Heb *eleven* [h] Gk: Heb *and by steps that went up* [i] Compare Gk: Heb *tent* [j] Gk: Heb *width*

40.38, 39 The washing of the sacrifices was done according to the standards of preparation established in Leviticus 1.6–9. This washing was part of the process of presenting an acceptable sacrifice to God.

41.1 The nave was the main part of the interior of the temple.

41.4 God's holiness is a central theme throughout both the Old and New Testaments. The most holy place was the innermost room in the temple (Exodus 26.33, 34). This was where the ark of the covenant was kept and where God's glory was said to dwell. This room was entered only once a year by the high priest, who performed a ceremony to atone for the nation's sins.

5 Then he measured the wall of the temple, six cubits thick; and the width of the 41.5
side chambers, four cubits, all around the temple. 6 The side chambers were in three 1 Kgs 6.5
stories, one over another, thirty in each story. There were offsets[k] all around the 41.6 1 Kgs 6.6,10
wall of the temple to serve as supports for the side chambers, so that they should not
be supported by the wall of the temple. 7 The passageway[l] of the side chambers 41.7
widened from story to story; for the structure was supplied with a stairway all 1 Kgs 6.8
around the temple. For this reason the structure became wider from story to story.
One ascended from the bottom story to the uppermost story by way of the middle
one. 8 I saw also that the temple had a raised platform all around; the foundations of 41.8
the side chambers measured a full reed of six long cubits. 9 The thickness of the Ezek 40.5 Rev 21.16
outer wall of the side chambers was five cubits; and the free space between the side
chambers of the temple 10 and the chambers of the court was a width of twenty 41.10
cubits all around the temple on every side. 11 The side chambers opened onto the Ezek 40.17
area left free, one door toward the north, and another door toward the south; and the
width of the part that was left free was five cubits all around.

12 The building that was facing the temple yard on the west side was seventy 41.12
cubits wide; and the wall of the building was five cubits thick all around, and its Ezek 42.1 Rev 21.27
depth ninety cubits. 22.14,15

13 Then he measured the temple, one hundred cubits deep; and the yard and the 41.13
building with its walls, one hundred cubits deep; 14 also the width of the east front Ezek 40.47
of the temple and the yard, one hundred cubits.

15 Then he measured the depth of the building facing the yard at the west, to- 41.15
gether with its galleries[m] on either side, one hundred cubits. 1 Kgs 6.4,15 Isa 6.4

The nave of the temple and the inner room and the outer[n] vestibule 16 were pan- Zech 3.7
eled,[o] and, all around, all three had windows with recessed[p] frames. Facing the
threshold the temple was paneled with wood all around, from the floor up to the
windows (now the windows were covered), 17 to the space above the door, even to 41.17
the inner room, and on the outside. And on all the walls all around in the inner room 1 Kgs 6.29,32 2 Chron 3.5
and the nave there was a pattern.[q] 18 It was formed of cherubim and palm trees, a Ezek 10.18
palm tree between cherub and cherub. Each cherub had two faces: 19 a human face 41.19
turned toward the palm tree on the one side, and the face of a young lion turned Ezek 1.10; 10.14
toward the palm tree on the other side. They were carved on the whole temple all
around; 20 from the floor to the area above the door, cherubim and palm trees were
carved on the wall.[r] 41.21

21 The doorposts of the nave were square. In front of the holy place was some- 1 Kgs 6.33
thing resembling 22 an altar of wood, three cubits high, two cubits long, and two 41.22 Ex 25.23,30
cubits wide;[s] its corners, its base,[t] and its walls were of wood. He said to me, 30.1-3,8 Ezek 44.16
"This is the table that stands before the LORD." 23 The nave and the holy place had Mal 1.7,12 Rev 8.3
each a double door. 24 The doors had two leaves apiece, two swinging leaves for 41.23
each door. 25 On the doors of the nave were carved cherubim and palm trees, such 1 Kgs 6.31-35
as were carved on the walls; and there was a canopy of wood in front of the vesti- 41.24
bule outside. 26 And there were recessed windows and palm trees on either side, on 1 Kgs 6.34 41.26
the sidewalls of the vestibule.[u] Ezek 40.7-12

Rooms for the priests

42 Then he led me out into the outer court, toward the north, and he brought me 42.1
to the chambers that were opposite the temple yard and opposite the building Ezek 40.2,3,17 41.9,12-15
on the north. 2 The length of the building that was on the north side[v] was[w] one 42.2
hundred cubits, and the width fifty cubits. 3 Across the twenty cubits that belonged Ezek 41.13
to the inner court, and facing the pavement that belonged to the outer court, the

[k] Gk Compare 1 Kings 6.6: Heb *they entered* [l] Cn: Heb *it was surrounded* [m] Cn: Meaning of Heb uncertain
[n] Gk: Heb *of the court* [o] Gk: Heb *the thresholds* [p] Cn Compare Gk 1 Kings 6.4: Meaning of Heb uncertain
[q] Heb *measures* [r] Cn Compare verse 25: Heb *and the wall* [s] Gk: Heb lacks *two cubits wide* [t] Gk: Heb *length*
[u] Cn: Heb *vestibule. And the side chambers of the temple and the canopies* [v] Gk: Heb *door* [w] Gk: Heb *before the length*

41.18 *Cherubim* are mighty angels. The cherubim and palms were sculpted or carved. Consequently, only two faces could be shown rather than four, as in the vision.

41.22 The dimensions given would fit either the table of the bread of the Presence (Exodus 25.30) or the altar of incense (Exodus 30.1–3).

42.3 Ezek 40.17 41.10 chambers rose[x] gallery[y] by gallery[y] in three stories. 4 In front of the chambers was
a passage on the inner side, ten cubits wide and one hundred cubits deep,[z] and its[a]
42.4 Ezek 46.19 entrances were on the north. 5 Now the upper chambers were narrower, for the
galleries[y] took more away from them than from the lower and middle chambers in
42.6 1 Kgs 6.8 Ezek 41.6 the building. 6 For they were in three stories, and they had no pillars like the pillars
of the outer[b] court; for this reason the upper chambers were set back from the
42.7 Ezek 41.13,14 ground more than the lower and the middle ones. 7 There was a wall outside parallel
to the chambers, toward the outer court, opposite the chambers, fifty cubits long.
8 For the chambers on the outer court were fifty cubits long, while those opposite
42.9 Ezek 44.5; 46.19 the temple were one hundred cubits long. 9 At the foot of these chambers ran a
passage that one entered from the east in order to enter them from the outer court.
10 The width of the passage[c] is fixed by the wall of the court.

On the south[d] also, opposite the vacant area and opposite the building, there
were chambers 11 with a passage in front of them; they were similar to the chambers
on the north, of the same length and width, with the same exits[e] and arrangements
and doors. 12 So the entrances of the chambers to the south were entered through the
entrance at the head of the corresponding passage, from the east, along the match-
ing wall.[y]

42.13 Lev 6.25,29 7.6; 10.13-17 Num 18.9,10 13 Then he said to me, "The north chambers and the south chambers opposite
the vacant area are the holy chambers, where the priests who approach the LORD
shall eat the most holy offerings; there they shall deposit the most holy
offerings—the grain offering, the sin offering, and the guilt offering, for the place
42.14 Ex 29.4-9 Isa 61.10 Ezek 22.26 Zech 3.4,5 is holy. 14 When the priests enter the holy place, they shall not go out of it into the
outer court without laying there the vestments in which they minister, for these are
holy; they shall put on other garments before they go near to the area open to the
people."

15 When he had finished measuring the interior of the temple area, he led me
42.16 Ezek 40.3,5 45.2 Zech 2.5 Rev 11.1,2 out by the gate that faces east, and measured the temple area all around. 16 He measured the east side with the measuring reed, five hundred cubits by the measuring
reed. 17 Then he turned and measured[f] the north side, five hundred cubits by the
measuring reed. 18 Then he turned and measured[f] the south side, five hundred cubits by the measuring reed. 19 Then he turned to the west side and measured, five
hundred cubits by the measuring reed. 20 He measured it on the four sides. It had a
wall around it, five hundred cubits long and five hundred cubits wide, to make a
separation between the holy and the common.

Sacrifices in the temple

43.1 Ezek 10.19 **43** Then he brought me to the gate, the gate facing east. 2 And there, the glory
43.2 Isa 6.3 Hab 2.14; 3.3 of the God of Israel was coming from the east; the sound was like the sound
of mighty waters; and the earth shone with his glory. 3 The[g] vision I saw was like
43.3 Ezek 1.4,27,28 the vision that I had seen when he came to destroy the city, and[h] like the vision that
I had seen by the river Chebar; and I fell upon my face. 4 As the glory of the LORD

[x] Heb lacks *the chambers rose* [y] Meaning of Heb uncertain [z] Gk Syr: Heb *a way of one cubit* [a] Heb *their* [b] Gk: Heb lacks *outer* [c] Heb lacks *of the passage* [d] Gk: Heb *east* [e] Heb *and all their exits* [f] Gk: Heb *measuring reed all around. He measured* [g] Gk: Heb *Like the vision* [h] Syr: Heb *and the visions*

42.14 Approaching our holy God must not be taken lightly. The holy robes the priests were required to wear may symbolize the importance of having a holy heart when approaching God. The priests had to wear these special robes in order to minister in the inner rooms of the temple. Because the robes were holy, the priests had to change their clothes before going back out to the public.

42.16–20 The perfect symmetry of Ezekiel's temple may represent the order and harmony in God's future kingdom.

43.1ff This is the culmination of chapters 40–42, for God's glory returns to the temple. It reverses the negative cast of the book and concludes all the passages dealing with the blessings reserved for the restored remnant. All true believers should long for that moment when God's name will finally be glorified and he will live among his people forever.

43.2 In 11.23, God's glory stopped over the Mount of Olives, to the east of Jerusalem, before leaving the city. This prophecy states that his glory would also return from the east.

43.2–4 Just as it was completely devastating when God's glory departed (11.23) from his temple, so it was overwhelming beyond expression when Ezekiel saw God's glory return.

43.3 The river Chebar connected to the Euphrates River and was the location of a Jewish settlement of exiles in Babylonia.

entered the temple by the gate facing east, 5 the spirit lifted me up, and brought me
into the inner court; and the glory of the LORD filled the temple.
6 While the man was standing beside me, I heard someone speaking to me out
of the temple. 7 He said to me: Mortal, this is the place of my throne and the place
for the soles of my feet, where I will reside among the people of Israel forever. The
house of Israel shall no more defile my holy name, neither they nor their kings, by
their whoring, and by the corpses of their kings at their death.[i] 8 When they placed
their threshold by my threshold and their doorposts beside my doorposts, with only
a wall between me and them, they were defiling my holy name by their abominations that they committed; therefore I have consumed them in my anger. 9 Now let
them put away their idolatry and the corpses of their kings far from me, and I will
reside among them forever.
10 As for you, mortal, describe the temple to the house of Israel, and let them
measure the pattern; and let them be ashamed of their iniquities. 11 When they are
ashamed of all that they have done, make known to them the plan of the temple, its
arrangement, its exits and its entrances, and its whole form—all its ordinances and
its entire plan and all its laws; and write it down in their sight, so that they may
observe and follow the entire plan and all its ordinances. 12 This is the law of the
temple: the whole territory on the top of the mountain all around shall be most holy.
This is the law of the temple.
13 These are the dimensions of the altar by cubits (the cubit being one cubit and
a handbreadth): its base shall be one cubit high,[j] and one cubit wide, with a rim of
one span around its edge. This shall be the height of the altar: 14 From the base on
the ground to the lower ledge, two cubits, with a width of one cubit; and from the
smaller ledge to the larger ledge, four cubits, with a width of one cubit; 15 and the
altar hearth, four cubits; and from the altar hearth projecting upward, four horns.
16 The altar hearth shall be square, twelve cubits long by twelve wide. 17 The ledge
also shall be square, fourteen cubits long by fourteen wide, with a rim around it half
a cubit wide, and its surrounding base, one cubit. Its steps shall face east.
18 Then he said to me: Mortal, thus says the Lord GOD: These are the ordinances for the altar: On the day when it is erected for offering burnt offerings upon
it and for dashing blood against it, 19 you shall give to the levitical priests of the
family of Zadok, who draw near to me to minister to me, says the Lord GOD, a bull
for a sin offering. 20 And you shall take some of its blood, and put it on the four
horns of the altar, and on the four corners of the ledge, and upon the rim all around;
thus you shall purify it and make atonement for it. 21 You shall also take the bull of
the sin offering, and it shall be burnt in the appointed place belonging to the temple,
outside the sacred area.
22 On the second day you shall offer a male goat without blemish for a sin
offering; and the altar shall be purified, as it was purified with the bull. 23 When you
have finished purifying it, you shall offer a bull without blemish and a ram from the
flock without blemish. 24 You shall present them before the LORD, and the priests
shall throw salt on them and offer them up as a burnt offering to the LORD. 25 For
seven days you shall provide daily a goat for a sin offering; also a bull and a ram
from the flock, without blemish, shall be provided. 26 Seven days shall they make
atonement for the altar and cleanse it, and so consecrate it. 27 When these days are

43.4 Ezek 44.2
43.5 1 Kgs 8.10,11 Hag 2.7-9
43.6 Ezek 1.26; 40.3
43.7 Ezek 6.4-7 37.26-28
43.8 2 Kgs 21.4-7 Ezek 8.3
43.9 Ezek 18.30,31
43.10 Ezek 40.4
43.11 Ezek 11.20 36.27; 44.5
43.12 Ezek 40.2
43.13 Ex 27.1-8 2 Chron 4.1
43.15 Lev 9.9 1 Kgs 1.49,50 Ps 118.27
43.16 Ex 27.1; 38.1,2 Ezra 3.3
43.17 Neh 9.4
43.18 Ex 40.29 Lev 1.5,11 Heb 9.21,22
43.19 1 Kgs 2.35 Heb 7.27
43.20 Lev 8.15; 9.9
43.21 Lev 4.11,12 Heb 13.11
43.22 Lev 8.18-21
43.23 Ex 29.1
43.24 Lev 2.13 Num 18.19 Mk 9.49,50 Col 4.6
43.25 Ex 29.35-37 Lev 8.33,35

[i] Or *on their high places* [j] Gk: Heb lacks *high*

43.9–11 When God departed from the city, it was a signal for the destruction of the city and the temple. For God to return, his conditions had to be met; they had to get rid of the idolatry and the dead bodies of their kings. Many feel these verses indicate that Ezekiel was commanding the people of his day to build this temple according to the designs and regulations the angelic architect had given. But the people never repented, the conditions were not met, so the fulfillment was postponed.

43.12 The basic law of God's temple was holiness. In all he does, God is holy. There is no trace of evil or sin in him. Just as God is holy, so we are to be holy (Leviticus 19.1; 1 Peter 1.15, 16). People are holy when they are devoted to God and separated from sin. If we do not understand the basic concept of holiness, we will never progress very far in our Christian growth.

43.18–27 This vision was simultaneously flashing back to Mount Sinai and forward to Mount Calvary. When the people returned from exile, they would seek forgiveness through the sacrificial system instituted in Moses' day. Today, Christ's death has made the forgiveness of our sins possible, making us acceptable to God (Hebrews 9.9–15). God stands ready to forgive those who come to him in faith.

over, then from the eighth day onward the priests shall offer upon the altar your
burnt offerings and your offerings of well-being; and I will accept you, says the
Lord GOD.

Requirements for the priests

44 Then he brought me back to the outer gate of the sanctuary, which faces
east; and it was shut. 2 The LORD said to me: This gate shall remain shut; it
shall not be opened, and no one shall enter by it; for the LORD, the God of Israel,
has entered by it; therefore it shall remain shut. 3 Only the prince, because he is a
prince, may sit in it to eat food before the LORD; he shall enter by way of the vestibule of the gate, and shall go out by the same way.
4 Then he brought me by way of the north gate to the front of the temple; and
I looked, and lo! the glory of the LORD filled the temple of the LORD; and I fell upon
my face. 5 The LORD said to me: Mortal, mark well, look closely, and listen attentively to all that I shall tell you concerning all the ordinances of the temple of the
LORD and all its laws; and mark well those who may be admitted to[k] the temple and
all those who are to be excluded from the sanctuary. 6 Say to the rebellious house,[l]
to the house of Israel, Thus says the Lord GOD: O house of Israel, let there be an
end to all your abominations 7 in admitting foreigners, uncircumcised in heart and
flesh, to be in my sanctuary, profaning my temple when you offer to me my food,
the fat and the blood. You[m] have broken my covenant with all your abominations.
8 And you have not kept charge of my sacred offerings; but you have appointed
foreigners[n] to act for you in keeping my charge in my sanctuary.
9 Thus says the Lord GOD: No foreigner, uncircumcised in heart and flesh, of
all the foreigners who are among the people of Israel, shall enter my sanctuary.
10 But the Levites who went far from me, going astray from me after their idols
when Israel went astray, shall bear their punishment. 11 They shall be ministers in
my sanctuary, having oversight at the gates of the temple, and serving in the temple; they shall slaughter the burnt offering and the sacrifice for the people, and they
shall attend on them and serve them. 12 Because they ministered to them before
their idols and made the house of Israel stumble into iniquity, therefore I have
sworn concerning them, says the Lord GOD, that they shall bear their punishment.
13 They shall not come near to me, to serve me as priest, nor come near any of my
sacred offerings, the things that are most sacred; but they shall bear their shame,
and the consequences of the abominations that they have committed. 14 Yet I will
appoint them to keep charge of the temple, to do all its chores, all that is to be done
in it.
15 But the levitical priests, the descendants of Zadok, who kept the charge of
my sanctuary when the people of Israel went astray from me, shall come near to me
to minister to me; and they shall attend me to offer me the fat and the blood, says
the Lord GOD. 16 It is they who shall enter my sanctuary, it is they who shall approach my table, to minister to me, and they shall keep my charge. 17 When they
enter the gates of the inner court, they shall wear linen vestments; they shall have
nothing of wool on them, while they minister at the gates of the inner court, and

[k] Cn: Heb *the entrance of* [l] Gk: Heb lacks *house* [m] Gk Syr Vg: Heb *They* [n] Heb lacks *foreigners*

43.27 Lev 3.1; 9.1 Ezek 20.40 Hos 8.13 1 Pet 2.5
44.1 Ezek 40.6
44.2 Ezek 43.4
44.3 Ex 24.9-11 Deut 12.7,17,18 Ezek 37.25 Zech 6.12,13
44.4 Isa 6.3,4 Ezek 1.28; 3.23 Hag 2.7
44.5 Ezek 40.4 43.10,11
44.6 Ezek 2.5-7; 3.9 1 Pet 4.3
44.7 Gen 17.14 Ex 12.43-49 Jer 4.4; 9.26 Heb 8.9
44.8 Num 18.7 Acts 7.53 1 Tim 6.13
44.10 Num 18.23 2 Kgs 23.8,9 Ezek 22.26
44.11 Num 3.5-37 4.1-33; 16.8,9
44.12 2 Kgs 16.10-16 Ezek 14.3,4 Hos 4.6; 5.1
44.13 Num 18.3 2 Kgs 23.9 Ezek 16.61,63
44.14 Num 18.4,6 Ezek 40.45
44.15 Jer 33.18-22 Ezek 48.11 Zech 3.7
44.16 Ezek 41-22
44.17 Ex 28.39-43 39.27-29

44.2 Why was this east gate to remain closed? Several reasons have been suggested. (1) This was the gate through which God entered the temple, and no one else could walk where God had (43.2); (2) the closed gate indicated that God would never again leave the temple; (3) it would prevent people from worshiping the sun from within the temple grounds (8.16).

44.3 Although Christ is called a prince (37.25), this prince is probably not Christ, because he offers a sacrifice to God (46.4) and he can enter only by the "vestibule of the gate." They say he is a princely ruler of the city, but he is distinguished from other princes because he will be just and fair (see 45.8). Another view is that this picture anticipates Christ offering a sacrifice of his own life to God.

44.9 Unbelievers would not be allowed to enter the temple. Ezekiel's vision was for a restored, purified worship where only those who prepared themselves physically and spiritually could participate. In 47.22, 23, we find that aliens are allowed to join in worship by accepting the standards of faith and practice declared in the law (see Leviticus 24.22; Numbers 15.29).

44.15 Zadok's descendants are mentioned because the priests in Zadok's line remained faithful to God, while others became corrupt. Zadok supported God's choice of Solomon to succeed David, and was therefore appointed high priest during his reign (1 Kings 1.32–35; 2.27, 35). His descendants were considered the true priestly line throughout the time between the Old and New Testaments.

within. 18 They shall have linen turbans on their heads, and linen undergarments on
their loins; they shall not bind themselves with anything that causes sweat. 19 When
they go out into the outer court to the people, they shall remove the vestments in
which they have been ministering, and lay them in the holy chambers; and they
shall put on other garments, so that they may not communicate holiness to the people with their vestments. 20 They shall not shave their heads or let their locks grow
long; they shall only trim the hair of their heads. 21 No priest shall drink wine when
he enters the inner court. 22 They shall not marry a widow, or a divorced woman,
but only a virgin of the stock of the house of Israel, or a widow who is the widow
of a priest. 23 They shall teach my people the difference between the holy and the
common, and show them how to distinguish between the unclean and the clean.
24 In a controversy they shall act as judges, and they shall decide it according to my
judgments. They shall keep my laws and my statutes regarding all my appointed
festivals, and they shall keep my sabbaths holy. 25 They shall not defile themselves
by going near to a dead person; for father or mother, however, and for son or
daughter, and for brother or unmarried sister they may defile themselves. 26 After
he has become clean, they shall count seven days for him. 27 On the day that he goes
into the holy place, into the inner court, to minister in the holy place, he shall offer
his sin offering, says the Lord GOD.

28 This shall be their inheritance: I am their inheritance; and you shall give
them no holding in Israel; I am their holding. 29 They shall eat the grain offering,
the sin offering, and the guilt offering; and every devoted thing in Israel shall be
theirs. 30 The first of all the first fruits of all kinds, and every offering of all kinds
from all your offerings, shall belong to the priests; you shall also give to the priests
the first of your dough, in order that a blessing may rest on your house. 31 The
priests shall not eat of anything, whether bird or animal, that died of itself or was
torn by animals.

The holy district

45 When you allot the land as an inheritance, you shall set aside for the LORD
a portion of the land as a holy district, twenty-five thousand cubits long and
twenty[o] thousand cubits wide; it shall be holy throughout its entire extent. 2 Of this,
a square plot of five hundred by five hundred cubits shall be for the sanctuary, with
fifty cubits for an open space around it. 3 In the holy district you shall measure off
a section twenty-five thousand cubits long and ten thousand wide, in which shall be
the sanctuary, the most holy place. 4 It shall be a holy portion of the land; it shall be
for the priests, who minister in the sanctuary and approach the LORD to minister to
him; and it shall be both a place for their houses and a holy place for the sanctuary.
5 Another section, twenty-five thousand cubits long and ten thousand cubits wide,
shall be for the Levites who minister at the temple, as their holding for cities to
live in.[p]

6 Alongside the portion set apart as the holy district you shall assign as a holding for the city an area five thousand cubits wide, and twenty-five thousand cubits
long; it shall belong to the whole house of Israel.

7 And to the prince shall belong the land on both sides of the holy district and
the holding of the city, alongside the holy district and the holding of the city, on the
west and on the east, corresponding in length to one of the tribal portions, and
extending from the western to the eastern boundary 8 of the land. It is to be his

44.18 Ex 28.40,42
44.19 Lev 16.23,24; Ezek 42.14; Mt 23.17-19
44.20 Lev 21.5
44.21 Lev 10.8,9
44.22 Lev 21.7,13-15
44.23 Lev 10.10; Deut 33.10; Ezek 22.26
44.24 2 Chron 19.8-10; Ezek 20.12,20
44.25 Lev 21.1-3
44.26 Num 19.13-19; Heb 9.13,14
44.27 Num 6.9-11
44.28 1 Pet 5.2-4
44.29 Lev 27.21,28; Num 18.9,14,15; Josh 13.14
44.30 Num 18.12; Neh 10.35-37
44.31 Lev 22.8; Ezek 4.14
45.1 Josh 13.7; 14.2; Ps 16.5,6; Ezek 47.21; 48.8,9
45.2 Ezek 42.16-20
45.3 Ezek 48.10
45.4 Num 16.5; Ezek 40.45; 44.13,14; 48.10,11
45.5 Ezek 48.12-14
45.6 Ezek 48.15,16
45.7 Ezek 46.16-18; 48.21,22
45.8 Isa 11.3-5; Jer 23.5,6; Ezek 22.27

o Gk: Heb *ten* p Gk: Heb *as their holding, twenty chambers*

44.20–31 These laws were originally given to God's people in the wilderness. They are recorded in the books of Exodus and Leviticus. They reveal the importance of approaching God respectfully, and they give guidelines for the priests to live above reproach so they could carry out their responsibility to teach the people "the difference between the holy and the common" (44.23).

44.23 Teaching people the difference between right and wrong is one of the responsibilities of ministers (see also Leviticus 10.8–11; Philippians 1.10). Ministers are God's representatives and spokesmen. Support your minister by encouraging him to speak out on moral issues, praying for him to have wisdom in his personal life, and standing beside him if he faces criticism for speaking the truth.

45.1–7 The land allotted to the temple was in the center of the nation. God is central to life. He must be our first priority.

45.8–12 Greed and extortion were two of the major social sins of

property in Israel. And my princes shall no longer oppress my people; but they shall
let the house of Israel have the land according to their tribes.
9 Thus says the Lord GOD: Enough, O princes of Israel! Put away violence and
oppression, and do what is just and right. Cease your evictions of my people, says
the Lord GOD.
10 You shall have honest balances, an honest ephah, and an honest bath.[q]
11 The ephah and the bath shall be of the same measure, the bath containing one-
tenth of a homer, and the ephah one-tenth of a homer; the homer shall be the standard measure. 12 The shekel shall be twenty gerahs. Twenty shekels, twenty-five
shekels, and fifteen shekels shall make a mina for you.

Special offerings in the temple

13 This is the offering that you shall make: one-sixth of an ephah from each
homer of wheat, and one-sixth of an ephah from each homer of barley, 14 and as the
fixed portion of oil,[r] one-tenth of a bath from each cor (the cor,[s] like the homer,
contains ten baths); 15 and one sheep from every flock of two hundred, from the
pastures of Israel. This is the offering for grain offerings, burnt offerings, and offerings of well-being, to make atonement for them, says the Lord GOD. 16 All the
people of the land shall join with the prince in Israel in making this offering. 17 But
this shall be the obligation of the prince regarding the burnt offerings, grain offerings, and drink offerings, at the festivals, the new moons, and the sabbaths, all the
appointed festivals of the house of Israel: he shall provide the sin offerings, grain
offerings, the burnt offerings, and the offerings of well-being, to make atonement
for the house of Israel.
18 Thus says the Lord GOD: In the first month, on the first day of the month,
you shall take a young bull without blemish, and purify the sanctuary. 19 The priest
shall take some of the blood of the sin offering and put it on the doorposts of the
temple, the four corners of the ledge of the altar, and the posts of the gate of the
inner court. 20 You shall do the same on the seventh day of the month for anyone
who has sinned through error or ignorance; so you shall make atonement for the
temple.
21 In the first month, on the fourteenth day of the month, you shall celebrate the
festival of the passover, and for seven days unleavened bread shall be eaten. 22 On
that day the prince shall provide for himself and all the people of the land a young
bull for a sin offering. 23 And during the seven days of the festival he shall provide
as a burnt offering to the LORD seven young bulls and seven rams without blemish,
on each of the seven days; and a male goat daily for a sin offering. 24 He shall
provide as a grain offering an ephah for each bull, an ephah for each ram, and a hin
of oil to each ephah. 25 In the seventh month, on the fifteenth day of the month and
for the seven days of the festival, he shall make the same provision for sin offerings, burnt offerings, and grain offerings, and for the oil.

46 Thus says the Lord GOD: The gate of the inner court that faces east shall
remain closed on the six working days; but on the sabbath day it shall be
opened and on the day of the new moon it shall be opened. 2 The prince shall enter
by the vestibule of the gate from outside, and shall take his stand by the post of the

45.9 Jer 6.7; 22.3 Nah 5.1-5 Zech 8.16
45.10 Lev 19.35,36 Deut 25.13-15 Prov 11.1; 16.11 Mic 6.10,11
45.12 Ex 30.13 Lev 27.25 Num 3.47
45.15 Lev 1.4; 6.30 Dan 9.24
45.17 Lev 23.1-44 1 Kgs 8.62-64 Ezek 43.27 46.4-12
45.18 Ex 12.2 Heb 9.14
45.19 Lev 16.18-20 Ezek 43.20
45.20 Rom 16.18,19 Heb 5.2
45.21 Ex 1.24 Lev 23.5-8 Num 9.2,3 28.16,17
45.22 Lev 4.14 2 Cor 5.21
45.23 Lev 23.8 Num 28.16-25 Heb 10.8-12
45.24 Num 28.12-15 Ezek 46.5-7
45.25 Lev 23.33-36 Num 29.12-38
46.1 Ex 20.9,10 Isa 66.23 Ezek 44.1,2
46.2 Ezek 44.3 Jn 10.1-3

[q] A Heb measure of volume [r] Cn: Heb *oil, the bath the oil* [s] Vg: Heb *homer*

the nation during this time (see Amos 5.10–13). In the new economy there would be plenty of land for the "princes" (45.7, 8) and no longer any basis for greed. Therefore, God commands the princes and the people to be fair and honest, especially when they do business. Consider the ways you measure goods, money, or services. If you are paid for an hour of work, be sure you work for a full hour. If you sell a bushel of apples, make sure it is a full bushel. God is completely trustworthy and his followers should be too.

45.17 The conditions and regulations for these offerings are described in detail in Leviticus 1–7.

45.21 The passover was an annual seven-day festival instituted by God so that his people would remember when he brought them out of slavery in Egypt. On that first passover night, the angel of death passed over the homes marked by lamb's blood; he struck only the unmarked homes (see Exodus 11; 12).

45.25 This annual festival celebrated in October is called the festival of booths. It commemorates God's protection of his people as they traveled through the wilderness from Egypt to the promised land (see Leviticus 23.33–43; Deuteronomy 16.13–17).

46.1–15 Ezekiel continues to describe various aspects of daily worship. While allowing for diversity in worship, God prescribed order and continuity. This continuity gave a healthy rhythm to the spiritual life of his people.

gate. The priests shall offer his burnt offering and his offerings of well-being, and
he shall bow down at the threshold of the gate. Then he shall go out, but the gate
shall not be closed until evening. 3 The people of the land shall bow down at the **46.3**
entrance of that gate before the LORD on the sabbaths and on the new moons. 4 The Lk 1.10 Jn 10.9
burnt offering that the prince offers to the LORD on the sabbath day shall be six Heb 10.19-22
lambs without blemish and a ram without blemish; 5 and the grain offering with the **46.4** Ezek 45.17
ram shall be an ephah, and the grain offering with the lambs shall be as much as he **46.5**
wishes to give, together with a hin of oil to each ephah. 6 On the day of the new Ezek 45.24
moon he shall offer a young bull without blemish, and six lambs and a ram, which
shall be without blemish; 7 as a grain offering he shall provide an ephah with the **46.7**
bull and an ephah with the ram, and with the lambs as much as he wishes, together Deut 16.17
with a hin of oil to each ephah. 8 When the prince enters, he shall come in by the **46.8**
vestibule of the gate, and he shall go out by the same way. Ezek 44.1-3 Col 1.18
9 When the people of the land come before the LORD at the appointed festivals, **46.9**
whoever enters by the north gate to worship shall go out by the south gate; and Ex 23.14-17 Deut 16.16
whoever enters by the south gate shall go out by the north gate: they shall not return Ps 84.7 Heb 10.38
by way of the gate by which they entered, but shall go out straight ahead. 10 When 2 Pet 2.20,21
they come in, the prince shall come in with them; and when they go out, he shall go **46.10**
out. 2 Chron 6.3; 7.4 Ps 42.4
11 At the festivals and the appointed seasons the grain offering with a young **46.11**
bull shall be an ephah, and with a ram an ephah, and with the lambs as much as one Ezek 45.17
wishes to give, together with a hin of oil to an ephah. 12 When the prince provides **46.12**
a freewill offering, either a burnt offering or offerings of well-being as a freewill Lev 23.38 2 Chron 29.31
offering to the LORD, the gate facing east shall be opened for him; and he shall offer Ezek 44.3; 45.17
his burnt offering or his offerings of well-being as he does on the sabbath day. Then
he shall go out, and after he has gone out the gate shall be closed.
13 He shall provide a lamb, a yearling, without blemish, for a burnt offering to **46.13**
the LORD daily; morning by morning he shall provide it. 14 And he shall provide a Ex 29.38 Num 28.3,4
grain offering with it morning by morning regularly, one-sixth of an ephah, and Isa 50.4
one-third of a hin of oil to moisten the choice flour, as a grain offering to the LORD; Dan 8.11-13 **46.14**
this is the ordinance for all time. 15 Thus the lamb and the grain offering and the oil Ex 29.42
shall be provided, morning by morning, as a regular burnt offering. Num 28.5,6
16 Thus says the Lord GOD: If the prince makes a gift to any of his sons out of
his inheritance,[t] it shall belong to his sons, it is their holding by inheritance. 17 But **46.17**
if he makes a gift out of his inheritance to one of his servants, it shall be his to the Lev 25.10 Mt 25.14-29
year of liberty; then it shall revert to the prince; only his sons may keep a gift from Lk 19.25,26
his inheritance. 18 The prince shall not take any of the inheritance of the people, Gal 4.30,31 **46.18**
thrusting them out of their holding; he shall give his sons their inheritance out of his Isa 11.3,4
own holding, so that none of my people shall be dispossessed of their holding. Ezek 45.8 Mic 2.1,2
19 Then he brought me through the entrance, which was at the side of the gate, **46.19**
to the north row of the holy chambers for the priests; and there I saw a place at the Lev 2.4-7 2 Chron 35.13
extreme western end of them. 20 He said to me, "This is the place where the priests Ezek 42.9; 44.19
shall boil the guilt offering and the sin offering, and where they shall bake the grain
offering, in order not to bring them out into the outer court and so communicate
holiness to the people."
21 Then he brought me out to the outer court, and led me past the four corners
of the court; and in each corner of the court there was a court — 22 in the four corners
of the court were small[u] courts, forty cubits long and thirty wide; the four were of
the same size. 23 On the inside, around each of the four courts[v] was a row of ma-
sonry, with hearths made at the bottom of the rows all around. 24 Then he said to **46.24**
me, "These are the kitchens where those who serve at the temple shall boil the Lev 44.10,11 1 Pet 5.2
sacrifices of the people."

The river of healing

47 Then he brought me back to the entrance of the temple; there, water was **47.1** Ps 46.4
flowing from below the threshold of the temple toward the east (for the tem- Joel 2.13
ple faced east); and the water was flowing down from below the south end of the Rev 22.1,17

[t] Gk: Heb *it is his inheritance* [u] Gk Syr Vg: Meaning of Heb uncertain [v] Heb *the four of them*

threshold of the temple, south of the altar. 2 Then he brought me out by way of the
north gate, and led me around on the outside to the outer gate that faces toward the
east;[w] and the water was coming out on the south side.
3 Going on eastward with a cord in his hand, the man measured one thousand
cubits, and then led me through the water; and it was ankle-deep. 4 Again he measured one thousand, and led me through the water; and it was knee-deep. Again he
measured one thousand, and led me through the water; and it was up to the waist.
5 Again he measured one thousand, and it was a river that I could not cross, for the
water had risen; it was deep enough to swim in, a river that could not be crossed.
6 He said to me, "Mortal, have you seen this?"
Then he led me back along the bank of the river. 7 As I came back, I saw on the
bank of the river a great many trees on the one side and on the other. 8 He said to
me, "This water flows toward the eastern region and goes down into the Arabah;
and when it enters the sea, the sea of stagnant waters, the water will become fresh.
9 Wherever the river goes,[x] every living creature that swarms will live, and there
will be very many fish, once these waters reach there. It will become fresh; and
everything will live where the river goes. 10 People will stand fishing beside the
sea[y] from En-gedi to En-eglaim; it will be a place for the spreading of nets; its fish
will be of a great many kinds, like the fish of the Great Sea. 11 But its swamps and
marshes will not become fresh; they are to be left for salt. 12 On the banks, on both
sides of the river, there will grow all kinds of trees for food. Their leaves will not
wither nor their fruit fail, but they will bear fresh fruit every month, because the
water for them flows from the sanctuary. Their fruit will be for food, and their
leaves for healing."

The boundaries of the nation

13 Thus says the Lord GOD: These are the boundaries by which you shall divide
the land for inheritance among the twelve tribes of Israel. Joseph shall have two
portions. 14 You shall divide it equally; I swore to give it to your ancestors, and this
land shall fall to you as your inheritance.
15 This shall be the boundary of the land: On the north side, from the Great Sea
by way of Hethlon to Lebo-hamath, and on to Zedad,[z] 16 Berothah, Sibraim (which
lies between the border of Damascus and the border of Hamath), as far as Hazer-
hatticon, which is on the border of Hauran. 17 So the boundary shall run from the
sea to Hazar-enon, which is north of the border of Damascus, with the border of
Hamath to the north.[w] This shall be the north side.
18 On the east side, between Hauran and Damascus; along the Jordan between
Gilead and the land of Israel; to the eastern sea and as far as Tamar.[a] This shall be
the east side.
19 On the south side, it shall run from Tamar as far as the waters of Meribath-
kadesh, from there along the Wadi of Egypt[b] to the Great Sea. This shall be the
south side.
20 On the west side, the Great Sea shall be the boundary to a point opposite
Lebo-hamath. This shall be the west side.
21 So you shall divide this land among you according to the tribes of Israel.
22 You shall allot it as an inheritance for yourselves and for the aliens who reside

47.2 Ezek 44.1-4
47.3 Ezek 40.3; Zech 2.1; Rev 11.1; 21.15
47.5 Isa 11.9; Hab 2.14
47.6 Ezek 40.4; 44.5
47.7 Isa 60.21; 61.3; Rev 22.2
47.8 Isa 35.6,7; 41.17-19; 44.3; Jer 31.9
47.9 Zech 2.11; 8.21-23; Jn 4.14; 7.37,38; Rev 21.6
47.10 Ps 104.25; Lk 5.5-9
47.12 Gen 2.9; Jer 17.8; Rev 22.2
47.13 Num 34.1-13
47.14 Gen 12.7; Deut 1.8; Ezek 20.5,6
47.15 Num 34.7-9; Ezek 48.1
47.16 Num 13.21; 1 Kgs 8.65; Amos 6.14; Zech 9.2
47.17 Num 34.9; Ezek 48.1
47.18 Gen 13.10,11; Num 34.10-12; Judg 10.8; Job 40.23
47.19 Num 34.3-5; Deut 32.51; Isa 27.12
47.20 Num 34.6

w Meaning of Heb uncertain x Gk Syr Vg Tg: Heb *the two rivers go* y Heb *it* z Gk: Heb *Lebo-zedad, 16Hamath*
a Compare Syr: Heb *you shall measure* b Heb lacks *of Egypt*

47.1–12 This river (or stream) is similar to the river mentioned in Revelation 22.1, 2. The river symbolizes life from God and the blessings that flow from his throne. It is a gentle, safe, deep river, expanding as it flows.

47.8, 9 The Arabah is the geological depression in which the Dead Sea lies. The sea that will "become fresh" refers to the Dead Sea, a body of water so salty that nothing can live in it. The river will freshen the Dead Sea's water so it can support life. This is another picture of the life-giving nature of the water that flows from God's temple. God's power can transform us no matter how lifeless or corrupt we may be. Even when we feel messed up and beyond hope, his power can heal us.

47.10 En-gedi and En-eglaim were on the western shore of the Dead Sea.

47.22, 23 In the restoration there will be room for foreigners ("aliens"). The regulations of Leviticus 24.22 and Numbers 15.29 provided for this. Isaiah also taught it (Isaiah 56.3–8). Anyone who accepts the standards and is willing to obey may enjoy the blessings of God's rule.

among you and have begotten children among you. They shall be to you as citizens
of Israel; with you they shall be allotted an inheritance among the tribes of Israel.
23 In whatever tribe aliens reside, there you shall assign them their inheritance, says
the Lord GOD.

The land divided among the tribes

48 These are the names of the tribes: Beginning at the northern border, on the
Hethlon road,[c] from Lebo-hamath, as far as Hazar-enon (which is on the
border of Damascus, with Hamath to the north), and[d] extending from the east side
to the west,[e] Dan, one portion. 2 Adjoining the territory of Dan, from the east side
to the west, Asher, one portion. 3 Adjoining the territory of Asher, from the east
side to the west, Naphtali, one portion. 4 Adjoining the territory of Naphtali, from
the east side to the west, Manasseh, one portion. 5 Adjoining the territory of Manasseh, from the east side to the west, Ephraim, one portion. 6 Adjoining the territory
of Ephraim, from the east side to the west, Reuben, one portion. 7 Adjoining the
territory of Reuben, from the east side to the west, Judah, one portion.
8 Adjoining the territory of Judah, from the east side to the west, shall be the
portion that you shall set apart, twenty-five thousand cubits in width, and in length
equal to one of the tribal portions, from the east side to the west, with the sanctuary
in the middle of it. 9 The portion that you shall set apart for the LORD shall be
twenty-five thousand cubits in length, and twenty[f] thousand in width. 10 These
shall be the allotments of the holy portion: the priests shall have an allotment measuring twenty-five thousand cubits on the northern side, ten thousand cubits in
width on the western side, ten thousand in width on the eastern side, and twenty-
five thousand in length on the southern side, with the sanctuary of the LORD in the
middle of it. 11 This shall be for the consecrated priests, the descendants[g] of Zadok,
who kept my charge, who did not go astray when the people of Israel went astray,
as the Levites did. 12 It shall belong to them as a special portion from the holy
portion of the land, a most holy place, adjoining the territory of the Levites.
13 Alongside the territory of the priests, the Levites shall have an allotment twenty-
five thousand cubits in length and ten thousand in width. The whole length shall be
twenty-five thousand cubits and the width twenty[h] thousand. 14 They shall not sell
or exchange any of it; they shall not transfer this choice portion of the land, for it
is holy to the LORD.
15 The remainder, five thousand cubits in width and twenty-five thousand in
length, shall be for ordinary use for the city, for dwellings and for open country. In
the middle of it shall be the city; 16 and these shall be its dimensions: the north side
four thousand five hundred cubits, the south side four thousand five hundred, the
east side four thousand five hundred, and the west side four thousand and five hundred. 17 The city shall have open land: on the north two hundred fifty cubits, on the
south two hundred fifty, on the east two hundred fifty, on the west two hundred
fifty. 18 The remainder of the length alongside the holy portion shall be ten thousand
cubits to the east, and ten thousand to the west, and it shall be alongside the holy
portion. Its produce shall be food for the workers of the city. 19 The workers of the
city, from all the tribes of Israel, shall cultivate it. 20 The whole portion that you
shall set apart shall be twenty-five thousand cubits square, that is, the holy portion
together with the property of the city.
21 What remains on both sides of the holy portion and of the property of the city
shall belong to the prince. Extending from the twenty-five thousand cubits of the
holy portion to the east border, and westward from the twenty-five thousand cubits
to the west border, parallel to the tribal portions, it shall belong to the prince. The
holy portion with the sanctuary of the temple in the middle of it, 22 and the property

47.22 Isa 14.1; 56.6,7 Acts 11.18 Rom 10.12 Eph 2.12-14 Col 3.11

48.1 Ex 1.1 Josh 19.40-48 2 Sam 24.2 1 Kgs 12.28,29

48.2 Gen 30.12,13 Josh 19.24-31

48.3 Gen 30.7,8 Josh 19.32-39

48.4 Gen 30.22-24 41.51 48.5,14-20 Josh 13.29-31 17.1-11

48.5 Josh 13.15-23 15.1-63 16.5-10 17.8-10,14-18 19.9

48.8 Ezek 45.1-6 Zech 2.11,12 2 Cor 6.16 Rev 21.3,22

48.10 Ezek 44.28; 45.4

48.11 Ezek 44.10-15

48.14 Lev 25.32-34 Mal 3.8-10

48.15 Ezek 42.20; 45.6

48.16 Rev 21.16

48.21 Ezek 34.24; 45.7

[c] Compare 47.15: Heb *by the side of the way* [d] Cn: Heb *and they shall be his* [e] Gk Compare verses 2-8: Heb *the east side the west* [f] Compare 45.1: Heb *ten* [g] One Ms Gk: Heb *of the descendants* [h] Gk: Heb *ten*

48.1ff The land would be divided into 13 parallel portions (one for each tribe plus a holy district) that would stretch from the Jordan River or Dead Sea to the Mediterranean Sea. The division of the land shows that in God's kingdom there is a place for all who believe in and obey the one true God (see John 14.1–6).

of the Levites and of the city, shall be in the middle of that which belongs to the
prince. The portion of the prince shall lie between the territory of Judah and the
territory of Benjamin.

48.23 Josh 18.21-28
48.24 Gen 49.5-7; Josh 19.1-9
48.25 Gen 30.14-18; Josh 19.17-23
48.26 Gen 30.19,20; Josh 19.10-16
48.27 Gen 30.10,11

23 As for the rest of the tribes: from the east side to the west, Benjamin, one
portion. 24 Adjoining the territory of Benjamin, from the east side to the west, Simeon, one portion. 25 Adjoining the territory of Simeon, from the east side to the
west, Issachar, one portion. 26 Adjoining the territory of Issachar, from the east side
to the west, Zebulun, one portion. 27 Adjoining the territory of Zebulun, from the
east side to the west, Gad, one portion. 28 And adjoining the territory of Gad to the
south, the boundary shall run from Tamar to the waters of Meribath-kadesh, from
there along the Wadi of Egypt[i] to the Great Sea. 29 This is the land that you shall
allot as an inheritance among the tribes of Israel, and these are their portions, says
the Lord God.

The city gates

48.30 Rev 21.12,13

30 These shall be the exits of the city: On the north side, which is to be four
thousand five hundred cubits by measure, 31 three gates, the gate of Reuben, the
gate of Judah, and the gate of Levi, the gates of the city being named after the tribes
of Israel. 32 On the east side, which is to be four thousand five hundred cubits, three
gates, the gate of Joseph, the gate of Benjamin, and the gate of Dan. 33 On the south
side, which is to be four thousand five hundred cubits by measure, three gates, the
gate of Simeon, the gate of Issachar, and the gate of Zebulun. 34 On the west side,
which is to be four thousand five hundred cubits, three gates,[j] the gate of Gad, the
gate of Asher, and the gate of Naphtali. 35 The circumference of the city shall be
eighteen thousand cubits. And the name of the city from that time on shall be, The
Lord is There.

48.35 Isa 12.6; 24.23; Jer 23.6; Joel 3.21; Zech 2.10; Rev 21.3; 22.3

[i] Heb lacks *of Egypt* [j] One Ms Gk Syr: MT *their gates three*

48.28 The Great Sea is the Mediterranean.

48.35 The book of Ezekiel begins by describing the holiness of God, which Israel had despised and ignored. As a result, God's presence departed from the temple, the city, and the people. The book ends with a detailed vision of the new temple, the new city, and the new people – all demonstrating God's holiness. The pressures of everyday life can persuade us to focus on the here and now and thus forget God. That is why worship is so important; it takes our eyes off our current worries, gives us a glimpse of God's holiness, and allows us to look toward his future kingdom. God's presence makes everything glorious, and worship brings us into his presence.

DANIEL

Habakkuk becomes a prophet to Judah 612 B.C.	Jehoiakim becomes king of Judah 609	Daniel taken captive to Babylon 605	Daniel becomes a Babylonian official; fiery furnace 600?	Nebuchad-nezzar takes more captives 597	Ezekiel becomes a prophet to exiles 593	Judah falls; Jerusalem is destroyed; Jeremiah's ministry ends 586

VITAL STATISTICS

PURPOSE:
To give an historical account of the faithful Jews who lived in captivity and to show how God is in control of heaven and earth, directing the forces of nature, the destiny of nations, and the care of his people

AUTHOR:
Daniel

TO WHOM WRITTEN:
The other captives in Babylon and God's people everywhere

DATE WRITTEN:
Approximately 535 B.C., recording events which occurred from about 605–535 B.C.

SETTING:
Daniel had been taken captive and deported to Babylon by Nebuchadnezzar in 605 B.C. There he served in the government for about 60 years during the reigns of Nebuchadnezzar, Belshazzar, Darius, and Cyrus.

KEY VERSE:
"He [God] reveals deep and hidden things; he knows what is in the darkness, and light dwells with him" (2.22).

KEY PEOPLE:
Daniel, Nebuchadnezzar, Shadrach, Meshach, Abednego, Belshazzar, Darius

KEY PLACES:
Nebuchadnezzar's palace, the fiery furnace, Belshazzar's banquet, the den of lions

SPECIAL FEATURES:
Daniel's apocalyptic visions (chapters 8—12) give a glimpse of God's plan for the ages, including a direct prediction of the Messiah.

AN EARTHQUAKE shakes the foundation of our security; a tornado blows away a lifetime of mementoes; an assassin's bullet changes national history; a drunk driver claims an innocent victim; a divorce shatters a home. International and personal tragedies make our world seem a fearful place, overflowing with evil and seemingly out of control. And the litany of bombings, coups, murders, and natural disasters could cause us to think that God is absent or impotent. "Where is God?" we cry, engulfed by sorrow and despair.

Twenty-five centuries ago, Daniel could have despaired. He and thousands of his countrymen were deported to a foreign land after Judah was conquered. Daniel found himself facing an egocentric despot and surrounded by idolaters. Instead of giving in or giving up, this courageous young man held fast to his faith in his God. Daniel knew that despite the circumstances, God was sovereign and was working out his plan for nations and individuals. The book of Daniel centers around this profound truth—the sovereignty of God.

After a brief account of Nebuchadnezzar's siege and defeat of Jerusalem, the scene quickly shifts to Daniel and his three friends, Hananiah, Mishael, and Azariah (Shadrach, Meshach, and Abednego). These men held prominent positions within the Babylonian government. Daniel, in particular, held such a position because of his ability to interpret the king's dreams that tell of God's unfolding plan (chapters 2 and 4). Sandwiched between the dreams is the fascinating account of Daniel's three friends and the furnace (chapter 3). Because they refused to bow to a golden idol, they were condemned to a fiery death. But God intervened and spared their lives.

Belshazzar ruled Babylon after Nebuchadnezzar, and chapter 5 tells of his encounter with God's message written on a wall. Daniel, who was summoned to interpret the message, predicted Babylon's fall to the Medes and Persians. This prediction came true that very night, and Darius the Mede conquered the Babylonian kingdom.

Daniel became one of Darius's most trusted advisers. His privileged position angered other administrators who plotted his death by convincing the king to outlaw prayer. In spite of the law, Daniel continued to pray to his sovereign Lord. As a result, he was condemned to die in a den of hungry lions. Again, God intervened and saved him, shutting the mouths of the lions (chapter 6).

The book concludes with a series of visions that Daniel had during the reigns of Belshazzar (chapters 7, 8), Darius (chapter 9), and Cyrus (chapters 10—12). These dreams dramatically outline God's future plans, beginning with Babylon and continuing to the end of the age. They give a preview of God's redemption and have been called the key to all biblical prophecy.

God is sovereign. He was in control in Babylon, and he has been moving in history, controlling the destinies of people ever since. And he is here now! Despite news reports or personal stress, we can be confident that God is in control. As you read Daniel, watch God work and find your security in his sovereignty.

Nebuchadnezzar dies 562 | Daniel's first vision 553 | Babylon overthrown; Daniel thrown to lions 539 | First exiles return to Judah 537 | Daniel's ministry ends 536

THE BLUEPRINT

A. DANIEL'S LIFE (1.1—6.28)

Daniel and his three friends chose not to eat the king's food. They did not bow down to the king's idol even under penalty of death. Daniel continued to pray even though he knew he might be noticed and sentenced to death. These men are inspiring examples for us of living a faithful life in a sinful world. When we face trials, we can expect God to remain present with us through our trials. May God grant us the same courage to remain faithful under pressure.

B. DANIEL'S VISIONS (7.1—12.13)

These visions gave the captives added confidence that God is in control of history. They were to wait patiently and in faith and not to worship the gods of Babylon or accept their way of life. God still rules over human activities. Evil will be overcome, so we should wait patiently and not give in to the temptations and pressures of the sinful way of life around us.

MEGATHEMES

THEME	EXPLANATION	IMPORTANCE
God is in control	God is all-knowing, and he is in charge of world events. God overrules and removes rebellious leaders who defy him. God will overcome evil; no one is exempt. But he will deliver the faithful who follow him.	Although nations vie for world control now, one day Christ's kingdom will replace and surpass the kingdoms of this world. Our faith is sure because our future is secure in Christ. We must have courage and put our faith in God who controls everything.
Purpose in life	Daniel and his three friends are examples of dedication and commitment. They determined to serve God regardless of the consequences. They did not give in to pressures from an ungodly society because they had a clear purpose in life.	It is wise to make trusting and obeying God alone our true purpose in life. This will give us direction and peace in spite of the circumstances or consequences. We should disobey anyone who asks us to disobey God. Our first allegiance must be to God.
Perseverance	Daniel served in a foreign land that was hostile to God for 70 years, yet he did not compromise his faith in God. He was truthful, persistent in prayer, and disinterested in power for personal glory.	In order to fulfill your life's purpose, you need staying power. Don't let your Christian distinctives become blurred. Be relentless in your prayers, stay firm in your integrity, and be content to serve God wherever he puts you.
God's faithfulness	God was faithful in Daniel's life. He delivered him from prison, from a den of lions, and from enemies who hated him. God cares for his people and deals patiently with them.	We can trust God to be with us through any trial because he promises to be there. Because he has been faithful to us, we should remain faithful to him.

A. DANIEL'S LIFE (1.1–6.28)

While Ezekiel was ministering to the captives in Babylon, Daniel was drafted as a counselor to King Nebuchadnezzar. With God's help, Daniel interpreted two of the king's dreams, Daniel's three friends were rescued from certain death in the fiery furnace, and Daniel was rescued from a lions' den. Daniel's life is a picture of the triumph of faith. May God grant us this type of faith so that we may also live courageously each day.

Daniel becomes the king's counselor

1 In the third year of the reign of King Jehoiakim of Judah, King Nebuchadnez- **1.1**
zar of Babylon came to Jerusalem and besieged it. 2 The Lord let King Jehoia- 2 Chron 36.5-7
kim of Judah fall into his power, as well as some of the vessels of the house of God.
These he brought to the land of Shinar,[a] and placed the vessels in the treasury of **1.3** 2 Kgs 24.14
his gods. Isa 39.7 Dan 5.7,11,30
3 Then the king commanded his palace master Ashpenaz to bring some of the 9.1
Israelites of the royal family and of the nobility, 4 young men without physical de- **1.5** 1 Sam 16.22
fect and handsome, versed in every branch of wisdom, endowed with knowledge Dan 1.19
and insight, and competent to serve in the king's palace; they were to be taught the **1.6** Ezek 14.14,20
literature and language of the Chaldeans. 5 The king assigned them a daily portion 28.3
of the royal rations of food and wine. They were to be educated for three years, so Mt 24.15
that at the end of that time they could be stationed in the king's court. 6 Among them **1.7** Dan 2.49
were Daniel, Hananiah, Mishael, and Azariah, from the tribe of Judah. 7 The pal- 3.12-30; 4.8
ace master gave them other names: Daniel he called Belteshazzar, Hananiah he **1.8** Lev 11.47
called Shadrach, Mishael he called Meshach, and Azariah he called Abednego. Deut 32.38 Ezek 4.13,14
8 But Daniel resolved that he would not defile himself with the royal rations of Hos 9.3

[a] Gk Theodotion: Heb adds *to the house of his own gods*

1.1, 2 Daniel was born during the middle of Josiah's reign (2 Kings 22, 23) and grew up during the king's reforms. During this time he probably heard Jeremiah, a prophet he quoted in 9.2. In 609 B.C., Josiah was killed in a battle against Egypt, and within four years, the southern kingdom of Judah had returned to its evil ways.

In 605 B.C. Nebuchadnezzar became king of Babylonia. In September of that year, he swept into Palestine and surrounded Jerusalem, making Judah his vassal state. To demonstrate his dominance, he took many of Jerusalem's wisest men and most beautiful women to Babylon as captives. Daniel was among this group.

1.1, 2 Nebuchadnezzar, the supreme leader of Babylonia, was feared throughout the world. When he invaded a country, defeat was certain. After a victory, the Babylonians usually took the most valuable people back to Babylonia and left the poor behind to take whatever land they wanted and live peacefully there. This system fostered great loyalty from conquered lands and insured a steady supply of wise and talented people for their civil service.

1.2 The land of Shinar is another name for Babylonia.

1.3, 4 The language of Chaldea (Babylonia) was Aramaic (Syriac). The academic program would have included mathematics, astronomy, history, science, and magic. These young men demonstrated not only aptitude, but also discipline. These character traits, combined with integrity, served them well in their new culture.

1.7 Nebuchadnezzar changed the names of Daniel and his friends because he wanted to make them Babylonian – in their own eyes and in the eyes of the Babylonian people. The king thought new names would help them assimilate into the culture. *Daniel* means "God is my judge" in Hebrew; his name was changed to *Belteshazzar* meaning "he whom Bel favors" (Bel was the chief Babylonian god). *Hananiah* means "mercy of God"; his new name, *Shadrach,* means "under the command of Aku" (the moon god). *Mishael* means "who is like God?"; his new name, *Meshach,* means "who is like Aku?" *Azariah* means "whom God helps"; his new name, *Abednego,* means "one who serves Nebo" (the fire god). This was how the king attempted to change the religious loyalty of these young men from Judah's God to Babylonia's gods.

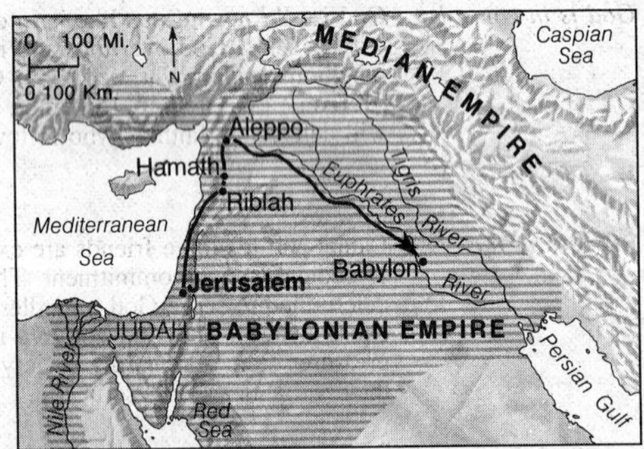

TAKEN TO BABYLON Daniel, as a captive of Babylonian soldiers, faced a long and difficult march to a new land. The 500–mile trek, under harsh conditions, certainly tested his faith in God.

1.8 Daniel resolved not to eat this food either because the meat was some food forbidden by Jewish law, like pork (see Leviticus 11), or because accepting the king's rich food was the first step toward depending on his gifts and favors. Although Daniel was in a culture that did not follow God's laws, he still obeyed them himself.

1.8 *Resolve* is a strong word that means to be devoted to principle and to be committed to a course of action. When Daniel resolved not to defile himself, he was following through on a lifelong determination to do what is right and not to give in to the pressures around him. We too are often assaulted by pressures to compromise our standards and live more like the world around us. Merely wanting or preferring God's will and way is not enough to stand against the onslaught of temptation. Like Daniel, we must resolve to obey God.

1.8 It is easier to resist temptation if you have thought through your convictions well before the temptation arises. Daniel and his

food and wine; so he asked the palace master to allow him not to defile himself.
9 Now God allowed Daniel to receive favor and compassion from the palace master. 10 The palace master said to Daniel, "I am afraid of my lord the king; he has
appointed your food and your drink. If he should see you in poorer condition than
the other young men of your own age, you would endanger my head with the king."
11 Then Daniel asked the guard whom the palace master had appointed over Daniel,
Hananiah, Mishael, and Azariah: 12 "Please test your servants for ten days. Let us
be given vegetables to eat and water to drink. 13 You can then compare our appearance with the appearance of the young men who eat the royal rations, and deal with
your servants according to what you observe." 14 So he agreed to this proposal and
tested them for ten days. 15 At the end of ten days it was observed that they appeared
better and fatter than all the young men who had been eating the royal rations. 16 So
the guard continued to withdraw their royal rations and the wine they were to drink,
and gave them vegetables. 17 To these four young men God gave knowledge and
skill in every aspect of literature and wisdom; Daniel also had insight into all visions and dreams.

18 At the end of the time that the king had set for them to be brought in, the
palace master brought them into the presence of Nebuchadnezzar, 19 and the king
spoke with them. And among them all, no one was found to compare with Daniel,
Hananiah, Mishael, and Azariah; therefore they were stationed in the king's court.
20 In every matter of wisdom and understanding concerning which the king inquired
of them, he found them ten times better than all the magicians and enchanters in his
whole kingdom. 21 And Daniel continued there until the first year of King Cyrus.

1.9 Ezra 7.27,28 Neh 1.11 Ps 106.46 Prov 16.7
1.12 Ex 23.25 Prov 10.22
1.15 Ex 23.25 Prov 10.22
1.17 1 Kgs 3.12,28 Job 32.8 Dan 1.20; 2.21 7.1; 8.1
1.19 Gen 41.46 1 Kgs 17.1 Prov 22.29 Jer 15.1 Dan 1.5
1.20 Num 14.22 Isa 19.3 Dan 1.17; 2.2 4.18; 5.7
1.21 Dan 6.28; 10.1

DANIEL served as a prophet to the exiles in Babylon from 605–536 B.C.

Climate of the times	The people of Judah were captives in a strange land, feeling hopeless.
Main message	God is sovereign over all of human history, past, present, and future.
Importance of message	We should spend less time wondering when future events will happen and more time learning how we should live now.
Contemporary prophets	Jeremiah (627–586) Habakkuk (612–589) Ezekiel (593–571)

friends made their decision to be faithful to the laws of their religion before they were faced with the king's delicacies, so they did not hesitate to stick with their convictions. We will get into trouble if we have not previously decided where to draw the line. Before such situations arise, decide on your commitments. Then when temptation comes, you will be ready to say no.

1.12 The Babylonians were trying to change the *thinking* of these Jews by giving them a Chaldean education, their *loyalty* by changing their names, and their *life-style* by changing their diet. Without compromising, Daniel found a way to live by God's standards in a culture that did not honor God. Wisely choosing to negotiate rather than to rebel, he suggested an experimental ten-day diet of vegetables and water, instead of the choice foods and wine the king offered. Without compromising, Daniel thought of a practical, creative solution that saved both their lives. As God's people, we may adjust to our culture as long as we do not compromise God's laws.

1.15 "Better and fatter" means better nourished or healthier.

1.17 Daniel and his friends learned all they could about their new culture so they could do their work with excellence. But while they learned, they maintained steadfast allegiance to God. Culture need not be God's enemy. If it does not violate his commands, it can aid in accomplishing his purpose. We who follow God are free to be competent leaders in our culture, but we are required to pledge our allegiance to God first.

1.20 Nebuchadnezzar put Daniel and his friends on his staff of advisers. This staff included many "magicians and enchanters." They were astrologers who claimed to be able to tell the future through occult practices. They were masters at communicating their message so that it sounded authoritative—as if it came directly from their gods. In addition to knowledge, Daniel and his three friends had wisdom and understanding, given to them by God. Thus the king was far more pleased with them than with his magicians and enchanters. As we serve others, we must not merely imitate or pretend to have God's wisdom. Our wisdom must be real because we are truly connected to God.

1.20 How did the captives survive in an alien culture? They learned about the culture, achieved excellence in their work, served the people, prayed for God's help, and maintained their integrity. We may feel like aliens whenever we experience change. Alien cultures come in many forms: a new job, a new school, a new neighborhood. We can use the same principles to help us adapt to our new surroundings without abandoning God.

1.21 Daniel was one of the first captives taken to Babylonia, and he lived to see the first exiles return to Jerusalem in 538 B.C. Throughout this time he honored God, and God honored him. While serving as a counselor to the kings of Babylonia, Daniel was God's spokesman to the Babylonian Empire. Babylonia was a wicked nation, but it would have been much worse without Daniel's influence.

Daniel interprets the king's dream

2 In the second year of Nebuchadnezzar's reign, Nebuchadnezzar dreamed such
dreams that his spirit was troubled and his sleep left him. 2 So the king commanded that the magicians, the enchanters, the sorcerers, and the Chaldeans be
summoned to tell the king his dreams. When they came in and stood before the
king, 3 he said to them, "I have had such a dream that my spirit is troubled by the
desire to understand it." 4 The Chaldeans said to the king (in Aramaic),[b] "O king,
live forever! Tell your servants the dream, and we will reveal the interpretation."
5 The king answered the Chaldeans, "This is a public decree: if you do not tell me
both the dream and its interpretation, you shall be torn limb from limb, and your
houses shall be laid in ruins. 6 But if you do tell me the dream and its interpretation,
you shall receive from me gifts and rewards and great honor. Therefore tell me the
dream and its interpretation." 7 They answered a second time, "Let the king first tell
his servants the dream, then we can give its interpretation." 8 The king answered,
"I know with certainty that you are trying to gain time, because you see I have
firmly decreed: 9 if you do not tell me the dream, there is but one verdict for you.
You have agreed to speak lying and misleading words to me until things take a turn.
Therefore, tell me the dream, and I shall know that you can give me its interpretation." 10 The Chaldeans answered the king, "There is no one on earth who can reveal what the king demands! In fact no king, however great and powerful, has ever
asked such a thing of any magician or enchanter or Chaldean. 11 The thing that the
king is asking is too difficult, and no one can reveal it to the king except the gods,
whose dwelling is not with mortals."

12 Because of this the king flew into a violent rage and commanded that all the
wise men of Babylon be destroyed. 13 The decree was issued, and the wise men
were about to be executed; and they looked for Daniel and his companions, to execute them. 14 Then Daniel responded with prudence and discretion to Arioch, the
king's chief executioner, who had gone out to execute the wise men of Babylon;
15 he asked Arioch, the royal official, "Why is the decree of the king so urgent?"
Arioch then explained the matter to Daniel. 16 So Daniel went in and requested that
the king give him time and he would tell the king the interpretation.

17 Then Daniel went to his home and informed his companions, Hananiah,
Mishael, and Azariah, 18 and told them to seek mercy from the God of heaven concerning this mystery, so that Daniel and his companions with the rest of the wise

2.1 Gen 40.5-8 41.1 Job 33.15-17 Dan 2.3; 4.5 6.18
2.4 Ezra 4.7 Isa 36.11
2.5 Deut 13.16 Ezra 6.11 Dan 2.12; 3.29
2.6 Dan 2.48 5.7,16,29
2.7 Dan 2.26; 4.8 5.12
2.8 Isa 41.23 Dan 3.15
2.11 Gen 41.39 Ex 29.45 1 Kgs 8.27 Isa 57.15 Dan 5.11
2.12 Ps 76.10 Dan 2.5; 3.13
2.18 Gen 18.28 Esth 4.15 Ps 50.15 Isa 37.4 Ezek 36.27 Dan 2.23

[b] The text from this point to the end of chapter 7 is in Aramaic

---

2.1–11 Dreams were considered messages from the gods, and the wise men were expected to interpret them. Usually these wise men could give some sort of interpretation as long as they knew what the dream was about. This time, however, Nebuchadnezzar demanded to be told the dream also because he could not remember it. God sent a series of dreams to Nebuchadnezzar with prophetic messages that could be revealed and understood only by a servant of God. People from other time periods who received dreams from God include Jacob (Genesis 28.10–15), Joseph (Genesis 37.5–11), Pharaoh's cupbearer and his baker (Genesis 40), Pharaoh (Genesis 41), Solomon (1 Kings 3.5–15), and Joseph (Matthew 1.20–24).

2.10, 11 The Chaldeans told the king that "no one on earth" could know the dreams of another person. What the king demanded was humanly impossible. But Daniel could tell the king what he had dreamed, and he could give the interpretation because God was working through him. In daily life, we face many apparently impossible situations that would be hopeless if we had to handle them with our limited human strength. But God specializes in working through us to achieve the impossible.

2.11 The Chaldeans said that the gods were not there to help (their "dwelling is not with mortals"). Of course they weren't—they didn't even exist! This exposed the limitations of the astrologers and wise men. They could invent interpretations of dreams, but they could not tell Nebuchadnezzar *what* he had dreamed. Although his request was unreasonable, Nebuchadnezzar was furious when his advisers couldn't fulfill it. He was probably already suspicious of them because of his previous experience with them. It was typical of the times for astrologers to be in conflict with the king. They used their craft to gain power.

2.11 The astrologers answered that the gods don't dwell with mortals. This betrayed their concept of the gods. Theirs was a hollow religion, a religion of convenience. They believed in the gods, but that belief made no difference in their conduct. Today many people say they believe in God, but this is also a hollow belief. In essence, they are practical atheists because they don't listen to God or do what he says. Do you believe in God? He *does* dwell among people, and he wants to change your life.

2.16–18 Daniel was at a crisis point. Imagine going to see the powerful, temperamental king who had just angrily ordered your death! Daniel did not shrink back in fear, but confidently believed God would tell him all the king wanted to know. When the king gave Daniel time to find the answer, Daniel found his three friends and they prayed. When you find yourself in a tight spot, share your needs with trusted friends who also believe in God's power. Prayer is more effective than panic. Panic confirms your hopelessness; prayer confirms your hope in God. Daniel's trust in God saved himself, his three friends, and all the other wise men.

2.19 Num 12.6 2 Kgs 6.8-12 Job 33.15,16 Dan 7.2,7
2.20 1 Chron 29.11, 12 Job 12.13 Ps 103.1,2 Dan 2.21-23 Mt 6.13
2.21 1 Sam 2.7,8 1 Kgs 3.9,10 4.29 Jas 1.5
2.22 Gen 37.5-9 Job 12.22; 26.6 Isa 45.7 Dan 2.19,28 1 Jn 1.5
2.23 Ex 3.15 Ps 21.2,4 Dan 2.21
2.25 Dan 1.6; 5.13 6.13
2.27 Dan 2.2,10,11 5.7,8
2.28 Gen 40.8; 41.16 Isa 41.21 Dan 2.22,45 Hos 3.5

men of Babylon might not perish. 19 Then the mystery was revealed to Daniel in a
vision of the night, and Daniel blessed the God of heaven.
20 Daniel said:
"Blessed be the name of God from age to age,
for wisdom and power are his.
21 He changes times and seasons,
deposes kings and sets up kings;
he gives wisdom to the wise
and knowledge to those who have understanding.
22 He reveals deep and hidden things;
he knows what is in the darkness,
and light dwells with him.
23 To you, O God of my ancestors,
I give thanks and praise,
for you have given me wisdom and power,
and have now revealed to me what we asked of you,
for you have revealed to us what the king ordered."
24 Therefore Daniel went to Arioch, whom the king had appointed to destroy
the wise men of Babylon, and said to him, "Do not destroy the wise men of Babylon; bring me in before the king, and I will give the king the interpretation."
25 Then Arioch quickly brought Daniel before the king and said to him: "I have
found among the exiles from Judah a man who can tell the king the interpretation."
26 The king said to Daniel, whose name was Belteshazzar, "Are you able to tell me
the dream that I have seen and its interpretation?" 27 Daniel answered the king, "No
wise men, enchanters, magicians, or diviners can show to the king the mystery that
the king is asking, 28 but there is a God in heaven who reveals mysteries, and he has
disclosed to King Nebuchadnezzar what will happen at the end of days. Your
dream and the visions of your head as you lay in bed were these: 29 To you, O king,

THE FULFILLMENT OF DANIEL'S INTERPRETATION

The large statue in Nebuchadnezzar's dream (2.24–45) represented the four kingdoms that would dominate as world powers. We recognize these as the Babylonian Empire, the Medo-Persian Empire, the Grecian Empire, and the Roman Empire. All of these will be crushed and brought to an end by the kingdom of God, which will continue forever.

Part	*Material*	*Empire*	*Period of Domination*
Head	Gold	Babylonian	606 B.C.—539 B.C.
Chest and Arms	Silver	Medo-Persian	539 B.C.—331 B.C.
Belly and Thighs	Bronze	Grecian	331 B.C.—146 B.C.
Legs and Feet	Iron and Clay	Roman	146 B.C.—A.D. 476

2.19–23 After Daniel asked God to reveal Nebuchadnezzar's dream to him, he saw a vision of the dream. His prayer was answered. Before rushing to Arioch with the news, Daniel took time to give God credit for all wisdom and power, thanking him for answering his request. How do you feel when your prayers are answered? Excited, surprised, relieved? There are times when we seek God in prayer and, after having been answered, dash off in our excitement, forgetting to give God credit for the answer. Match your persistence in prayer with gratitude when your requests are answered.

2.21 When we see evil leaders who live long and good leaders who die young, we may wonder if God controls world events. Daniel saw evil rulers with almost limitless power, but he knew and proclaimed that God controls everything that happens. The world is moving according to God's purposes and toward his specified ends. Let this knowledge give you confidence and peace no matter what happens.

2.24 Daniel did not use his success merely to promote his own self-interest. He also thought of others. When striving to succeed or survive, remember the needs of others.

2.27–30 Before Daniel told the king anything else, he gave credit to God, explaining that he did not know the dream through his own wisdom but only because God revealed it. How easily we take credit for what God does through us! This robs God of the honor that he alone deserves. Instead, like Daniel, we should give God the glory.

as you lay in bed, came thoughts of what would be hereafter, and the revealer of
mysteries disclosed to you what is to be. 30 But as for me, this mystery has not been
revealed to me because of any wisdom that I have more than any other living being,
but in order that the interpretation may be known to the king and that you may
understand the thoughts of your mind.
31 "You were looking, O king, and lo! there was a great statue. This statue was
huge, its brilliance extraordinary; it was standing before you, and its appearance
was frightening. 32 The head of that statue was of fine gold, its chest and arms of
silver, its middle and thighs of bronze, 33 its legs of iron, its feet partly of iron and
partly of clay. 34 As you looked on, a stone was cut out, not by human hands, and
it struck the statue on its feet of iron and clay and broke them in pieces. 35 Then the
iron, the clay, the bronze, the silver, and the gold, were all broken in pieces and
became like the chaff of the summer threshing floors; and the wind carried them
away, so that not a trace of them could be found. But the stone that struck the statue
became a great mountain and filled the whole earth.
36 "This was the dream; now we will tell the king its interpretation. 37 You,
O king, the king of kings—to whom the God of heaven has given the kingdom, the
power, the might, and the glory, 38 into whose hand he has given human beings,
wherever they live, the wild animals of the field, and the birds of the air, and whom
he has established as ruler over them all—you are the head of gold. 39 After you
shall arise another kingdom inferior to yours, and yet a third kingdom of bronze,
which shall rule over the whole earth. 40 And there shall be a fourth kingdom,
strong as iron; just as iron crushes and smashes everything,[c] it shall crush and
shatter all these. 41 As you saw the feet and toes partly of potter's clay and partly of
iron, it shall be a divided kingdom; but some of the strength of iron shall be in it,
as you saw the iron mixed with the clay. 42 As the toes of the feet were part iron and
part clay, so the kingdom shall be partly strong and partly brittle. 43 As you saw the
iron mixed with clay, so will they mix with one another in marriage,[d] but they will
not hold together, just as iron does not mix with clay. 44 And in the days of those
kings the God of heaven will set up a kingdom that shall never be destroyed, nor
shall this kingdom be left to another people. It shall crush all these kingdoms and
bring them to an end, and it shall stand forever; 45 just as you saw that a stone was
cut from the mountain not by hands, and that it crushed the iron, the bronze, the
clay, the silver, and the gold. The great God has informed the king what shall be
hereafter. The dream is certain, and its interpretation trustworthy."
46 Then King Nebuchadnezzar fell on his face, worshiped Daniel, and commanded that a grain offering and incense be offered to him. 47 The king said to
Daniel, "Truly, your God is God of gods and Lord of kings and a revealer of mysteries, for you have been able to reveal this mystery!" 48 Then the king promoted
Daniel, gave him many great gifts, and made him ruler over the whole province of
Babylon and chief prefect over all the wise men of Babylon. 49 Daniel made a re-

2.30 Gen 41.16 Ps 139.2 Isa 43.3 Dan 1.17 Acts 3.12 1 Cor 3.21-23

2.34 Dan 8.25 Zech 4.6

2.35 Ps 1.4 Isa 17.13 Hos 13.3

2.37 1 Kgs 4.24 Ezra 7.12 Isa 10.8; 47.5 Jer 27.6,7 Ezek 26.7 Hos 8.10 Rev 1.5; 17.14

2.38 Ps 50.10

2.44 Gen 49.10 Ps 2.9; 21.8,9 145.13 Isa 9.6,7 Ezek 37.25 Mic 4.7

2.45 Gen 41.28,32 Deut 10.17 2 Sam 7.22 Dan 2.29 Rev 1.19; 4.1

2.46 Lev 26.31 Dan 3.5,7 Acts 10.25 Rev 19.10; 22.8

2.47 Deut 10.17 Dan 3.15; 4.25 Amos 3.7

2.48 Gen 41.39-43 Dan 2.6 3.1,12,30; 5.16

2.49 Esth 2.19,21 Dan 3.12-30 Amos 5.15

c Gk Theodotion Syr Vg: Aram adds *and like iron that crushes* d Aram *by human seed*

2.31ff The head of gold on the image in the dream represented Nebuchadnezzar, ruler of the Babylonian Empire. The silver chest and two arms represented the Medo-Persian Empire, which conquered Babylonia in 539 B.C. The middle and thighs of brass were Greece and Macedonia under Alexander the Great, who conquered the Medo-Persian Empire in 334–330 B.C. The legs of iron represented Rome, which conquered the Greeks in 63 B.C. The feet and toes of clay and iron represented the breakup of the Roman Empire, when the territory Rome ruled divided into a mixture of strong and weak nations. The type of metal in each part depicted the strength of the political power it represented. The stone cut from the mountain depicted God's kingdom which would be ruled eternally by the Messiah, the King of kings. Daniel revealed his God as the power behind all earthly kingdoms.

2.36 When Daniel says "we," he is referring to himself and his three friends. Just as he involved them in praying for God's help, he gave them credit when he presented the interpretation.

2.44 God's kingdom will never be destroyed. If you are upset by threats of war and the prosperity of evil leaders, remember that God, not world leaders, decides the outcome of history. Under God's protection, his kingdom is indestructible. Those who believe in him are members of his kingdom and are secure in him.

2.47 Nebuchadnezzar honored Daniel and Daniel's God. If Daniel had taken the credit himself, the king would have honored only Daniel. Because Daniel gave God the credit, the king honored both of them. Part of our mission in this world is to show nonbelievers what God is like. We can do that by giving God credit for what he does in our lives. Our acts of love and compassion may impress people, and if we give God credit for our actions, they will want to know more about him. Give thanks to God for what he is doing in and through you.

2.49 After being named ruler over the whole province of Babylon

quest of the king, and he appointed Shadrach, Meshach, and Abednego over the affairs of the province of Babylon. But Daniel remained at the king's court.

Four men in the fiery furnace

3.1 Isa 46.6 Jer 16.20 Dan 2.31 Hab 2.19

3.2 Dan 3.3,27 6.1-7

3 King Nebuchadnezzar made a golden statue whose height was sixty cubits and whose width was six cubits; he set it up on the plain of Dura in the province of Babylon. 2 Then King Nebuchadnezzar sent for the satraps, the prefects, and the governors, the counselors, the treasurers, the justices, the magistrates, and all the officials of the provinces to assemble and come to the dedication of the statue that King Nebuchadnezzar had set up. 3 So the satraps, the prefects, and the governors, the counselors, the treasurers, the justices, the magistrates, and all the officials of

---

DANIEL

Daniel's early life demonstrates that there is more to being young than making mistakes. No characteristic wins the hearts of adults more quickly than wisdom in the words and actions of a young person. Daniel and his friends had been taken from their homes in Judah and exiled. Their futures were in doubt, but they all had personal traits that qualified them for jobs as servants in the king's palace. They took advantage of the opportunity without letting the opportunity take advantage of them.

Our first hint of Daniel's greatness comes in his quiet refusal to give up his convictions. He had applied God's Word to his own life, and he resisted changing the habits he had formed from that application. Both his physical and spiritual diets were an important part of his relationship with God. He ate carefully and lived prayerfully. One of the benefits of being in training for royal service was eating food from the king's table. Daniel tactfully chose a simpler menu and proved it was a healthy choice. As with Daniel, mealtimes are obvious and regular tests of our efforts to control our appetites.

While Daniel limited his food intake, he indulged in prayer. He was able to communicate with God because he made it a habit. He put into practice his convictions, even when that meant being thrown into a den of hungry lions. His life proved he made the right choice.

Do you hold so strongly to your faith in God that whatever happens you will do what God says? Such conviction keeps you a step ahead of temptation; such conviction gives you wisdom and stability in changing circumstances. Prayerfully live out your convictions in everyday life and trust God for the results.

Strengths and accomplishments:
- Although young when deported, remained true to his faith
- Served as a counselor to two Babylonian kings and two Medo-Persian kings
- Was a man of prayer and a statesman with the gift of prophecy
- Survived the lions' den

Lessons from his life:
- Quiet convictions often earn long-term respect
- Don't wait until you are in a tough situation to learn about prayer
- God can use people wherever they are

Vital statistics:
- Where: Judah and the courts of both Babylon and Persia
- Occupation: A captive from Israel who became a counselor of kings
- Contemporaries: Hananiah, Mishael, Azariah, Nebuchadnezzar, Belshazzar, Darius, Cyrus

Key verse:
"Because an excellent spirit, knowledge, and understanding to interpret dreams, explain riddles, and solve problems were found in this Daniel, whom the king named Belteshazzar. Now let Daniel be called, and he will give the interpretation" (Daniel 5.12).

Daniel's story is told in the book of Daniel. He is also mentioned in Matthew 24.15.

---

and chief over the wise men, Daniel requested that his companions, Shadrach, Meshach, and Abednego, be appointed his assistants. Daniel knew he could not handle such an enormous responsibility without capable assistants, so he chose the best men he knew—his three Hebrew companions. A competent leader never does all the work alone; he knows how to delegate. Moses, Israel's greatest leader, shared the burden of administration with dozens of assistants. (See this story in Exodus 18.13–27.)

3.1 In Babylon's religious culture, statues were frequently worshiped. Nebuchadnezzar hoped to use this huge statue (90 feet tall by 9 feet wide) as a strategy to unite the nation and solidify his power. This gold image may have been inspired by his dream. Instead of having only a head of gold, however, it was gold from head to toe: Nebuchadnezzar wanted his kingdom to last forever. When he made the statue, he showed that his devotion to Daniel's God was short-lived. He neither feared nor obeyed the God who was behind the dream.

3.2 Satraps served as the chief representatives of the king. Prefects were the military commanders. Governors were civil administrators.

the provinces, assembled for the dedication of the statue that King Nebuchadnezzar
had set up. When they were standing before the statue that Nebuchadnezzar had set
up, 4 the herald proclaimed aloud, "You are commanded, O peoples, nations, and
languages, 5 that when you hear the sound of the horn, pipe, lyre, trigon, harp,
drum, and entire musical ensemble, you are to fall down and worship the golden
statue that King Nebuchadnezzar has set up. 6 Whoever does not fall down and
worship shall immediately be thrown into a furnace of blazing fire." 7 Therefore, as
soon as all the peoples heard the sound of the horn, pipe, lyre, trigon, harp, drum,
and entire musical ensemble, all the peoples, nations, and languages fell down and
worshiped the golden statue that King Nebuchadnezzar had set up.

8 Accordingly, at this time certain Chaldeans came forward and denounced the
Jews. 9 They said to King Nebuchadnezzar, "O king, live forever! 10 You, O king,
have made a decree, that everyone who hears the sound of the horn, pipe, lyre,
trigon, harp, drum, and entire musical ensemble, shall fall down and worship the
golden statue, 11 and whoever does not fall down and worship shall be thrown into
a furnace of blazing fire. 12 There are certain Jews whom you have appointed over
the affairs of the province of Babylon: Shadrach, Meshach, and Abednego. These
pay no heed to you, O King. They do not serve your gods and they do not worship
the golden statue that you have set up."

13 Then Nebuchadnezzar in furious rage commanded that Shadrach, Meshach,
and Abednego be brought in; so they brought those men before the king. 14 Nebuchadnezzar said to them, "Is it true, O Shadrach, Meshach, and Abednego, that
you do not serve my gods and you do not worship the golden statue that I have set
up? 15 Now if you are ready when you hear the sound of the horn, pipe, lyre, trigon,
harp, drum, and entire musical ensemble to fall down and worship the statue that I
have made, well and good.[e] But if you do not worship, you shall immediately be
thrown into a furnace of blazing fire, and who is the god that will deliver you out
of my hands?"

16 Shadrach, Meshach, and Abednego answered the king, "O Nebuchadnezzar, we have no need to present a defense to you in this matter. 17 If our God whom
we serve is able to deliver us from the furnace of blazing fire and out of your hand,
O king, let him deliver us.[f] 18 But if not, be it known to you, O king, that we will
not serve your gods and we will not worship the golden statue that you have set up."

3.4 Dan 3.7; 4.1
3.5 Dan 3.7,10
3.6 Dan 3.11,15, 21; 6.7 Mt 13.42 Rev 9.2; 14.11
3.8 Ezra 4.12-16 Esth 3.8,9 Dan 6.12,13
3.10 Esth 3.12-14 Dan 3.4-6
3.13 Dan 2.12; 3.19
3.14 Ex 21.13,14 Isa 46.1 Dan 3.1; 4.8
3.15 Ex 5.2 Isa 36.18-20 Dan 2.47
3.16 Dan 1.7; 3.12
3.17 1 Sam 17.37 Ps 27.1,2 Isa 26.3,4 Jer 1.8
3.18 Josh 24.15 1 Kgs 19.14 Dan 3.28 Lk 12.3-9 Rev 12.11

[e] Aram lacks *well and good* [f] Or *If our God whom we serve is able to deliver us, he will deliver us from the furnace of blazing fire and out of your hand, O king.*

3.6 This blazing furnace was not a small oven for cooking dinner or heating a house; it was a huge industrial furnace that could have been used for baking bricks or smelting metals. The temperatures were hot enough to assure that no one could survive its heat. The roaring flames could be seen leaping from its top opening, and a fiery blast killed the soldiers who went up to the large opening (3.22).

3.12 We don't know if other Jews refused to bow to the statue, but these three were singled out as public examples. Why didn't the three men just bow to the image and tell God that they didn't mean it? They had determined never to worship another god, and they courageously took their stand. As a result, they were condemned and led away to be executed. They did not know whether they would be delivered from the fire; all they knew was that they would not bow to an idol. Are you ready to take a stand for God no matter what? When you stand for God, you will stand out. It may be painful, and it may not always have a happy ending. Be prepared to say, "If he delivers me, or if he doesn't, I will serve only God."

3.13 Nebuchadnezzar had lost control. As the supreme ruler of his country, he expected absolute obedience. But his pride had caused him to go beyond his own authority. His demands were unjust and his reactions extreme. If you find yourself angered when people don't follow your directions, ask yourself, "Why am I reacting?" Is your ego overly involved with your authority?

3.15 The three men had one more chance. Here are eight excuses they could have used to bow to the statue and save their lives: (1) We will bow down but not actually *worship* the idol. (2) We won't become idol worshipers, but will do this one time, then ask God for forgiveness. (3) The king has absolute power and we must obey him. God will understand. (4) The king appointed us—we owe this to him. (5) This is a foreign land so God will excuse us for following the customs of the land. (6) Our ancestors set up idols in God's temple! This isn't half as bad! (7) We're not hurting anybody. (8) If we get ourselves killed and some heathens take our high positions, they won't help our people in exile!

Although all these excuses sound sensible at first, they are dangerous. To bow to the image would violate God's command in Exodus 20.3, "You shall have no other gods before me." It would also erase their testimony for God forever. Never again could they talk about the power of their God above all other gods. What excuses do you use for not standing up for God?

3.16–18 Shadrach, Meshach, and Abednego were pressured to deny God, but they chose to be faithful to him no matter what happened! They trusted God to deliver them, but they were determined to be faithful regardless of the consequences. If God always rescued those who are true to him, Christians would not need faith. Their religion would be a great insurance policy, and there would be lines of selfish people ready to sign up. We should be faithful to God whether he intervenes on our behalf or not. Our eternal reward is worth any suffering we may have to endure first.

3.19 Lev 26.18-28 Dan 3.13 — 19 Then Nebuchadnezzar was so filled with rage against Shadrach, Meshach,
and Abednego that his face was distorted. He ordered the furnace heated up seven
times more than was customary, 20 and ordered some of the strongest guards in his
army to bind Shadrach, Meshach, and Abednego and throw them into the furnace
of blazing fire. 21 So the men were bound, still wearing their tunics,[g] their trou-
sers,[g] their hats, and their other garments, and they were thrown into the furnace
3.22 Dan 2.15 — of blazing fire. 22 Because the king's command was urgent and the furnace was so
overheated, the raging flames killed the men who lifted Shadrach, Meshach, and
Abednego. 23 But the three men, Shadrach, Meshach, and Abednego, fell down,
bound, into the furnace of blazing fire.
3.25 Ps 91.3-9 Jer 1.8,19 — 24 Then King Nebuchadnezzar was astonished and rose up quickly. He said to
his counselors, "Was it not three men that we threw bound into the fire?" They
3.26 Deut 4.20 1 Kgs 8.51 Dan 3.17; 4.2 — answered the king, "True, O king." 25 He replied, "But I see four men unbound,
walking in the middle of the fire, and they are not hurt; and the fourth has the
appearance of a god."[h] 26 Nebuchadnezzar then approached the door of the furnace

[g] Meaning of Aram word uncertain [h] Aram *a son of the gods*

Shadrach/Meshach/Abednego

Friendships make life enjoyable and difficult times bearable. They are strengthened by hardships. Such was the relationship between three young Jewish men deported to Babylon along with Daniel. Shadrach, Meshach, and Abednego help us think about the real meaning of friendship. As much as these friends meant to each other, they never allowed their friendship to usurp God's place in their lives—not even in the face of death.

Together they silently defied King Nebuchadnezzar's order to bow to and worship the idol he had made of himself. They shared a courageous act, while others, eager to get rid of them, told the king that the three Jews were being disloyal. While this was not true, Nebuchadnezzar could not spare them without shaming himself.

This was the moment of truth. Death was about to end their friendship. A small compromise would have allowed them to live and go on enjoying each other, serving God, and serving their people while in this foreign land. But they were wise enough to see that compromise would have poisoned the very conviction that bound them so closely—each had a higher allegiance to God. So they did not hesitate to place their lives in the hands of God. The rest was victory!

When we leave God out of our most important relationships, we tend to expect those relationships to meet needs in us that only God can meet. Friends are helpful, but they cannot meet our deepest spiritual needs. Leaving God out of our relationships indicates how unimportant he really is in our own lives. Our relationship with God should be important enough to touch our other relationships—especially our closest friendships.

Strengths and accomplishments:
- Stood with Daniel against eating food from the king's table
- Shared a friendship that stood the tests of hardship, success, wealth, and possible death
- Unwilling to compromise their convictions even in the face of death
- Survived the fiery furnace

Lessons from their lives:
- There is great strength in real friendship
- It is important to stand with others with whom we share convictions
- God can be trusted even when we can't predict the outcome

Vital statistics:
- Where: Babylon
- Occupations: King's servants and counselors
- Contemporaries: Daniel, Nebuchadnezzar

Key verses:
"Shadrach, Meshach, and Abednego answered the king, 'O Nebuchadnezzar, we have no need to present a defense to you in this matter. If our God whom we serve is able to deliver us from the furnace of blazing fire and out of your hand, O king, let him deliver us. But if not, be it known to you, O king, that we will not serve your gods and we will not worship the golden statue that you have set up' " (3.16–18).

The story of Shadrach (Hananiah), Meshach (Mishael), and Abednego (Azariah) is told in the book of Daniel.

3.25 It was obvious to those watching that this fourth person was supernatural. We cannot be certain who the fourth man was. It could have been an angel or a pre-incarnate appearance of Christ. In either case, God sent a heavenly visitor to accompany these faithful men during their time of great trial.

of blazing fire and said, “Shadrach, Meshach, and Abednego, servants of the Most
High God, come out! Come here!” So Shadrach, Meshach, and Abednego came
out from the fire. 27 And the satraps, the prefects, the governors, and the king’s **3.27**
counselors gathered together and saw that the fire had not had any power over the Dan 3.21 Heb 11.34
bodies of those men; the hair of their heads was not singed, their tunics[i] were not
harmed, and not even the smell of fire came from them. 28 Nebuchadnezzar said, **3.28**
“Blessed be the God of Shadrach, Meshach, and Abednego, who has sent his angel Ps 34.7,8 Isa 37.36
and delivered his servants who trusted in him. They disobeyed the king’s command Dan 3.25; 6.22 Acts 5.19; 12.7
and yielded up their bodies rather than serve and worship any god except their own
God. 29 Therefore I make a decree: Any people, nation, or language that utters blas- **3.29**
phemy against the God of Shadrach, Meshach, and Abednego shall be torn limb Ezra 6.11 Dan 3.12,15
from limb, and their houses laid in ruins; for there is no other god who is able to
deliver in this way.” 30 Then the king promoted Shadrach, Meshach, and Abednego **3.30**
in the province of Babylon. Dan 2.49; 3.12

The king dreams about a tree

4 [j] King Nebuchadnezzar to all peoples, nations, and languages that live throughout the earth: May you have abundant prosperity! 2 The signs and wonders that
the Most High God has worked for me I am pleased to recount.

3 How great are his signs, **4.3**
how mighty his wonders! Deut 4.34 Isa 25.1
His kingdom is an everlasting kingdom, Dan 2.44; 4.34 6.26
and his sovereignty is from generation to generation.

4[k] I, Nebuchadnezzar, was living at ease in my home and prospering in my pal- **4.4**
ace. 5 I saw a dream that frightened me; my fantasies in bed and the visions of my Isa 47.7,8 Zeph 1.12
head terrified me. 6 So I made a decree that all the wise men of Babylon should be **4.5**
brought before me, in order that they might tell me the interpretation of the dream. Job 7.13,14 Dan 4.10,13
7 Then the magicians, the enchanters, the Chaldeans, and the diviners came in, and **4.7**
I told them the dream, but they could not tell me its interpretation. 8 At last Daniel Isa 44.25 Jer 27.9,10
came in before me—he who was named Belteshazzar after the name of my god, Dan 2.7
and who is endowed with a spirit of the holy gods[l]—and I told him the dream: **4.8**
9 “O Belteshazzar, chief of the magicians, I know that you are endowed with a Num 11.17 Isa 63.11
spirit of the holy gods[l] and that no mystery is too difficult for you. Hear[m] the Dan 1.7; 4.9,18
dream that I saw; tell me its interpretation.

10[n] Upon my bed this is what I saw;
there was a tree at the center of the earth,
and its height was great.
11 The tree grew great and strong,
its top reached to heaven,
and it was visible to the ends of the whole earth. **4.12**
12 Its foliage was beautiful, Jer 27.6,7 Ezek 31.7

[i] Meaning of Aram word uncertain [j] Ch 3.31 in Aram [k] Ch 4.1 in Aram [l] Or *a holy, divine spirit* [m] Theodotion: Aram *The visions of* [n] Theodotion Syr Compare Gk: Aram adds *The visions of my head*

3.27 These young men were completely untouched by the fire and heat. No scorch marks were found on them, and they didn’t even smell of smoke! Only the rope that bound them had been burned. No human can bind us if God wants us to be free. The power available to us is the same that delivered Shadrach, Meshach, and Abednego and raised Christ from the dead (Ephesians 1.18–20). Trust God in every situation. There are eternal reasons for temporary trials; so let us be thankful that our destiny is in God’s hands, not man’s.

3.28, 29 Nebuchadnezzar was not making a commitment here to serve the Hebrews’ God alone. Instead, he acknowledged that God is powerful, and he commanded his people not to speak against him. He didn’t say the people should throw away all the other gods, but that they should add this one to the list.

3.30 Where was Daniel in this story? The Bible doesn’t say, but there are several possibilities. (1) He may have been on official business in another part of the kingdom. (2) He may have been present, but because he was a ruler, the officials didn’t accuse him of not bowing down to the idol. (3) He could have been in the capital city handling the administration while Nebuchadnezzar was away. (4) He could have been considered exempt from bowing to the idol because of his reputation for interpreting dreams through his God. Whether Daniel was there or not, we can be sure that he would not have bowed to the idol.

4.2, 3 Although Nebuchadnezzar praised Daniel’s God, he still did not believe in him completely or submit to him (4.8). Many people attend church and use spiritual language, but they really don’t believe in God or obey him. Profession doesn’t always mean possession. How do your beliefs match with your obedience?

4.7 “Diviners” were those who foretold future events and claimed to have secret knowledge. Also, the priests and astronomers who advised the king were called “Chaldeans.”

its fruit abundant,
and it provided food for all.
The animals of the field found shade under it,
the birds of the air nested in its branches,
and from it all living beings were fed.

4.13 Deut 33.2 Dan 8.13
4.14 Jer 51.5,6 Ezek 31.10-14 Rev 10.3; 18.2

13 I continued looking, in the visions of my head as I lay in bed, and there was a holy
watcher, coming down from heaven. 14 He cried aloud and said:
'Cut down the tree and chop off its branches,
strip off its foliage and scatter its fruit.
Let the animals flee from beneath it
and the birds from its branches.

NEBUCHADNEZZAR

Nebuchadnezzar was one world leader who decided he could get more cooperation from the people he conquered by letting them keep their gods. Their lands he took, but their idols he allowed them to worship. Nebuchadnezzar's plan worked well, with one glaring exception. When he conquered the little nation of Judah, he met a God who demanded *exclusive* worship—not just his share among many gods. In a sense, Nebuchadnezzar had always been able to rule the gods. This new God was different; this God dared to claim that he had made Nebuchadnezzar all that he was. One of the great conquerors in history was himself conquered by his Creator.

The Bible allows us to note the ways in which God worked on Nebuchadnezzar. God allowed him victories, but he was accomplishing God's purposes. God allowed him to deport the best young Jewish leaders as his palace servants, while placing close to him a young man named Daniel who would change the king's life. God allowed Nebuchadnezzar to attempt to kill three of his servants to teach the king that he did not really have power over life and death. God warned him of the dangers in his pride, then allowed Nebuchadnezzar to live through seven years of mental illness before restoring him to the throne. God showed the king who was really in control!

These lessons are clear to us today because of our place in history. When our attention shifts to our own lives, we find ourselves unable to see how God is working today. But we do have the advantage of God's Word as our guide for today's challenges. We are commanded to obey God; we are also commanded to trust him. Trusting him covers those times when we are not sure about the outcome. God has entrusted us with this day; have we trusted him with our lives?

Strengths and accomplishments:
- Greatest of the Babylonian kings
- Known as a builder of cities
- Described in the Bible as one of the foreign rulers God used for his purposes

Weaknesses and mistakes:
- Thought of himself as a god and was persuaded to build a statue of himself that all were to worship
- Became extremely proud, which led to a bout of mental illness
- Tended to forget the demonstrations of God's power he had witnessed

Lessons from his life:
- History records the actions of God's willing servants and those who were his unwitting tools
- A leader's greatness is affected by the quality of his counselors
- Uncontrolled pride is self-destructive

Vital statistics:
- Where: Babylon
- Occupation: King
- Relatives: Father: Nabopolassar. Son: Evil-Merodach. Grandson: Belshazzar
- Contemporaries: Jeremiah, Ezekiel, Daniel, Jehoiakim, Jehoiachin

Key verse:
"Now I, Nebuchadnezzar, praise and extol and honor the King of heaven, for all his works are truth, and his ways are justice; and he is able to bring low those who walk in pride" (4.37).

Nebuchadnezzar's story is told in 2 Kings 24; 25; 2 Chronicles 36; Jeremiah 21—52; Daniel 1—4.

4.13, 17 Babylonians believed in *watchers.* They thought there were mighty spiritual beings who watched over the universe. Nebuchadnezzar explained that these messengers were announcing what would happen to him and why.

15 But leave its stump and roots in the ground,
with a band of iron and bronze,
in the tender grass of the field.
Let him be bathed with the dew of heaven.
and let his lot be with the animals of the field
in the grass of the earth.
16 Let his mind be changed from that of a human,
and let the mind of an animal be given to him.
And let seven times pass over him.
17 The sentence is rendered by decree of the watchers,
the decision is given by order of the holy ones,
in order that all who live may know
that the Most High is sovereign over the kingdom of mortals;
he gives it to whom he will
and sets over it the lowliest of human beings.'

18 This is the dream that I, King Nebuchadnezzar, saw. Now you, Belteshazzar,
declare the interpretation, since all the wise men of my kingdom are unable to tell
me the interpretation. You are able, however, for you are endowed with a spirit of
the holy gods."[o]
19 Then Daniel, who was called Belteshazzar, was severely distressed for a
while. His thoughts terrified him. The king said, "Belteshazzar, do not let the
dream or the interpretation terrify you." Belteshazzar answered, "My lord, may the
dream be for those who hate you, and its interpretation for your enemies! 20 The tree
that you saw, which grew great and strong, so that its top reached to heaven and
was visible to the end of the whole earth, 21 whose foliage was beautiful and its fruit
abundant, and which provided food for all, under which animals of the field lived,
and in whose branches the birds of the air had nests — 22 it is you, O king! You have
grown great and strong. Your greatness has increased and reaches to heaven, and
your sovereignty to the ends of the earth. 23 And whereas the king saw a holy
watcher coming down from heaven and saying, 'Cut down the tree and destroy it,
but leave its stump and roots in the ground, with a band of iron and bronze, in the
grass of the field; and let him be bathed with the dew of heaven, and let his lot be
with the animals of the field, until seven times pass over him' — 24 this is the interpretation, O king, and it is a decree of the Most High that has come upon my lord
the king: 25 You shall be driven away from human society, and your dwelling shall
be with the wild animals. You shall be made to eat grass like oxen, you shall be
bathed with the dew of heaven, and seven times shall pass over you, until you have
learned that the Most High has sovereignty over the kingdom of mortals, and gives
it to whom he will. 26 As it was commanded to leave the stump and roots of the tree,
your kingdom shall be reestablished for you from the time that you learn that
Heaven is sovereign. 27 Therefore, O king, may my counsel be acceptable to you:

4.15 Job 14.7-9
4.16 1 Chron 29.30; Isa 6.10; Dan 4.23-25; 7.25; Heb 1.11
4.17 Ex 9.16; 1 Sam 2.8; Ps 9.16; Dan 4.25; 11.21
4.18 Gen 41.8; 1 Kgs 14.2,3; Dan 4.7; 5.8
4.19 1 Sam 3.17; 2 Sam 18.32; 1 Kgs 18.7; Dan 7.15,28; 8.27
4.22 Jer 27.6,7; Dan 2.37,38
4.25 Job 40.11,12; Ps 75.7; 107.40; Jer 27.5; Dan 4.17,33; 5.21
4.26 Dan 4.31
4.27 Gen 41.33-37; 2 Sam 12.7; 1 Kgs 21.29; Ps 41.1-3; 119.46; Prov 28.13; Isa 55.6,7; Jonah 3.9

[o] *Or a holy, divine spirit*

4.17 One of the most difficult lessons to learn is that God is sovereign. He is above all of those who are above us. He limits the power and authority of all the government, business, and religious leaders in the world. Those who live in freedom and with a relatively high degree of autonomy find this difficult to understand. While we may feel that we are free to do what we please, God is sovereign over all our plans and desires.

4.19 When Daniel understood Nebuchadnezzar's dream, he was stunned. He told the king that he wished what the dream foreshadowed would happen to the king's enemies and not to him. How could he be so deeply grieved at the fate of Nebuchadnezzar, the king who was responsible for the destruction of his home and nation? Daniel had forgiven him, and so God was able to use Daniel. Often when we have been wronged by someone, we find it difficult to forgive and forget. We may even be glad if that person suffers. Forgiveness means putting the past behind us. Can you love someone who has hurt you? Can you serve someone who mistreated you? Ask God to help you forgive, forget, and love. God may use you in an extraordinary way in that person's life!

4.23ff Although much of the world thought that Nebuchadnezzar was a mighty (even divine) king, God demonstrated that he was an ordinary man. Nebuchadnezzar would go insane and become like an animal for seven years ("seven times"). God humiliated Nebuchadnezzar to show that he, not Nebuchadnezzar, was Lord of the nations. No matter how powerful a person may become, self-centered pride will push God from his or her life. Pride may be one of the most dangerous temptations you will face. Don't let your accomplishments cause you to forget God.

4.27 "Atone for" may also be translated "break off." Daniel was urging Nebuchadnezzar to demonstrate his acceptance of

atone for[p] your sins with righteousness, and your iniquities with mercy to the oppressed, so that your prosperity may be prolonged."
4.28 Num 23.19 Zech 1.6 28 All this came upon King Nebuchadnezzar. 29 At the end of twelve months he
was walking on the roof of the royal palace of Babylon, 30 and the king said, "Is this
4.29 2 Pet 3.9 not magnificent Babylon, which I have built as a royal capital by my mighty power
and for my glorious majesty?" 31 While the words were still in the king's mouth, a
4.30 Hab 2.4 voice came from heaven: "O King Nebuchadnezzar, to you it is declared: The kingdom has departed from you! 32 You shall be driven away from human society, and
your dwelling shall be with the animals of the field. You shall be made to eat grass
like oxen, and seven times shall pass over you, until you have learned that the Most
High has sovereignty over the kingdom of mortals and gives it to whom he will."
4.33 Dan 4.25; 5.21 33 Immediately the sentence was fulfilled against Nebuchadnezzar. He was driven
away from human society, ate grass like oxen, and his body was bathed with the
dew of heaven, until his hair grew as long as eagles' feathers and his nails became
like birds' claws.
4.34 Jer 10.10 Dan 4.2 5.18,21 34 When that period was over, I, Nebuchadnezzar, lifted my eyes to heaven,
and my reason returned to me.

I blessed the Most High,
  and praised and honored the one who lives forever.
For his sovereignty is an everlasting sovereignty,
  and his kingdom endures from generation to generation.
4.35 Job 42.2 Isa 43.13 Dan 6.27 Acts 4.28 35 All the inhabitants of the earth are accounted as nothing,
  and he does what he wills with the host of heaven
  and the inhabitants of the earth.
There is no one who can stay his hand
  or say to him, "What are you doing?"

4.36 Dan 4.22,34 2 Cor 4.17 36 At that time my reason returned to me; and my majesty and splendor were restored to me for the glory of my kingdom. My counselors and my lords sought me
out, I was reestablished over my kingdom, and still more greatness was added to
4.37 Ex 18.11 1 Sam 2.3 Mt 11.25 me. 37 Now I, Nebuchadnezzar, praise and extol and honor the King of heaven,
for all his works are truth,
  and his ways are justice;
and he is able to bring low
  those who walk in pride.

Daniel interprets the writing on the wall

5.1 Esth 1.3 Isa 22.12-14 **5** King Belshazzar made a great festival for a thousand of his lords, and he was
drinking wine in the presence of the thousand.
2 Under the influence of the wine, Belshazzar commanded that they bring in the
vessels of gold and silver that his father Nebuchadnezzar had taken out of the temple in Jerusalem, so that the king and his lords, his wives, and his concubines might

[p] Aram *break off*

God's will by changing his life-style.

4.27–33 Daniel pleaded with Nebuchadnezzar to change his ways, and God gave him 12 months in which to do it. Unfortunately, there was no repentance in the heart of this proud king, and so the dream was fulfilled.

4.34 Nebuchadnezzar's pilgrimage with God is one of the themes of this book. In 2.47, he acknowledged that God revealed dreams to Daniel. In 3.28, 29 he praised the God who delivered the three Hebrews. Despite Nebuchadnezzar's recognition that God exists and works great miracles, in 4.30 we see that he still did not acknowledge God as his Lord. We may recognize that God exists and does wonderful miracles, but God will not work in us until we acknowledge him as Lord.

4.34 Ancient kings tried to avoid mentioning their weaknesses or defeats in their monuments and official records. From Nebuchadnezzar's records, however, we can infer that for a time during his 43-year reign he did not rule. The Bible explains Nebuchadnezzar's pride and punishment.

5.1 Sixty-six years have elapsed since chapter 1, which tells of Nebuchadnezzar's strike against Jerusalem in 605 B.C. Nebuchadnezzar died in 562 B.C. after a reign of 43 years. His son, Awel-Marduk (Evil-Merodach), ruled from 562–560 B.C.; his brother-in-law Neriglissar reigned four years from 560–556 B.C. After a two-month reign by Labashi-Marduk in 556 B.C., the Babylonian Empire continued from 556–539 B.C. under the command of Nabonidus. Belshazzar was the son of Nabonidus. He co-reigned with his father from 553–539 B.C.

5.1 Archeologists have recently discovered Belshazzar's name on several documents. He ruled with his father, Nabonidus, staying home to administer the affairs of the kingdom while his father tried to reopen trade routes taken over by Cyrus and the Persians. Belshazzar was in charge of the city of Babylon when it was captured.

drink from them. 3 So they brought in the vessels of gold and silver[q] that had been
taken out of the temple, the house of God in Jerusalem, and the king and his lords,
his wives, and his concubines drank from them. 4 They drank the wine and praised
the gods of gold and silver, bronze, iron, wood, and stone.
5 Immediately the fingers of a human hand appeared and began writing on the
plaster of the wall of the royal palace, next to the lampstand. The king was watching the hand as it wrote. 6 Then the king's face turned pale, and his thoughts terrified him. His limbs gave way, and his knees knocked together. 7 The king cried
aloud to bring in the enchanters, the Chaldeans, and the diviners; and the king said
to the wise men of Babylon, "Whoever can read this writing and tell me its interpretation shall be clothed in purple, have a chain of gold around his neck, and rank
third in the kingdom." 8 Then all the king's wise men came in, but they could not
read the writing or tell the king the interpretation. 9 Then King Belshazzar became
greatly terrified and his face turned pale, and his lords were perplexed.
10 The queen, when she heard the discussion of the king and his lords, came
into the banqueting hall. The queen said, "O king, live forever! Do not let your
thoughts terrify you or your face grow pale. 11 There is a man in your kingdom who
is endowed with a spirit of the holy gods.[r] In the days of your father he was found
to have enlightenment, understanding, and wisdom like the wisdom of the gods.
Your father, King Nebuchadnezzar, made him chief of the magicians, enchanters,
Chaldeans, and diviners,[s] 12 because an excellent spirit, knowledge, and understanding to interpret dreams, explain riddles, and solve problems were found in this
Daniel, whom the king named Belteshazzar. Now let Daniel be called, and he will
give the interpretation."
13 Then Daniel was brought in before the king. The king said to Daniel, "So
you are Daniel, one of the exiles of Judah, whom my father the king brought from
Judah? 14 I have heard of you that a spirit of the gods[t] is in you, and that enlightenment, understanding, and excellent wisdom are found in you. 15 Now the wise men,
the enchanters, have been brought in before me to read this writing and tell me its
interpretation, but they were not able to give the interpretation of the matter. 16 But
I have heard that you can give interpretations and solve problems. Now if you are
able to read the writing and tell me its interpretation, you shall be clothed in purple,
have a chain of gold around your neck, and rank third in the kingdom."
17 Then Daniel answered in the presence of the king, "Let your gifts be for
yourself, or give your rewards to someone else! Nevertheless I will read the writing
to the king and let him know the interpretation. 18 O king, the Most High God gave
your father Nebuchadnezzar kingship, greatness, glory, and majesty. 19 And because of the greatness that he gave him, all peoples, nations, and languages trembled and feared before him. He killed those he wanted to kill, kept alive those he
wanted to keep alive, honored those he wanted to honor, and degraded those he
wanted to degrade. 20 But when his heart was lifted up and his spirit was hardened
so that he acted proudly, he was deposed from his kingly throne, and his glory was
stripped from him. 21 He was driven from human society, and his mind was made

5.2 2 Kgs 24.13 2 Chron 36.10, 18 Ezra 1.7-11 Jer 27.7 Dan 1.2; 3.1 Hab 2.19
5.6 Ps 69.23 Dan 7.28 Nah 2.10
5.7 Gen 41.42-44 Isa 44.25 Ezek 16.11 Dan 5.11,16, 29; 6.2,3
5.9 Job 18.11-14 Ps 18.14 Isa 21.2-4 Jer 6.24 Dan 5.6 Mt 2.3
5.10 Dan 3.9; 6.6
5.11 Gen 41.11-15 2 Sam 14.17 Dan 2.47 4.8,9; 5.14 Acts 16.16
5.12 Dan 5.14; 6.3
5.13 Dan 1.1; 2.25
5.15 Isa 47.12 Dan 5.8
5.17 2 Kgs 5.16
5.18 Deut 32.8 Dan 2.37 4.2,17; 5.21
5.19 Prov 16.14 Dan 2.12; 3.6 11.3
5.20 Ex 9.17 Prov 16.5,18 Isa 14.13-15 Jer 13.18 Dan 4.30 Lk 18.14
5.21 Ex 9.14-16 Ezek 17.24

[q] Theodotion Vg: Aram lacks *and silver* [r] Or *a holy, divine spirit* [s] Aram adds *the king your father* [t] Or *a divine spirit*

5.7 Belshazzar served as co-regent with his father Nabonidus. Thus, Nabonidus was first ruler and his son Belshazzar, the second. The person who could read the writing would be given third place, the highest position and honor he could offer.

5.8 Although the writing on the wall was only three words in Aramaic, a language understood by Babylonians (see 2.4), the people could not understand its prophetic significance. God gave Daniel alone the ability to interpret the message of doom to Babylon. The wise men of the kingdom were ignorant of God's wisdom, no matter how great the reward. Daniel did not come with them. His loyalty was to God, not money.

5.10 This queen was either Nabonidus's wife or the wife of one of his predecessors, possibly even of Nebuchadnezzar. She was not Belshazzar's wife, because his wives were with him in the banquet hall.

5.17 The king offered Daniel beautiful gifts and great power if he would explain the writing, but Daniel turned him down. Daniel was not motivated by material rewards. His entire life was characterized by doing right. He was not showing disrespect in refusing the gifts, but he knew they would be short-lived. Daniel wanted to show the king that he was giving an unbiased interpretation. Doing right should be our first priority, not gaining power or rewards. Do you love God enough to do what is right even if it means giving up personal rewards?

5.21–23 Belshazzar knew Babylonian history, and so he knew how God had humbled Nebuchadnezzar. Nevertheless, his ban-

like that of an animal. His dwelling was with the wild asses, he was fed grass like
oxen, and his body was bathed with the dew of heaven, until he learned that the
Most High God has sovereignty over the kingdom of mortals, and sets over it
whomever he will. 22 And you, Belshazzar his son, have not humbled your heart,
even though you knew all this! 23 You have exalted yourself against the Lord of
heaven! The vessels of his temple have been brought in before you, and you and
your lords, your wives and your concubines have been drinking wine from them.
You have praised the gods of silver and gold, of bronze, iron, wood, and stone,
which do not see or hear or know; but the God in whose power is your very breath,
and to whom belong all your ways, you have not honored.

24 "So from his presence the hand was sent and this writing was inscribed.
25 And this is the writing that was inscribed: MENE, MENE, TEKEL, and PARSIN.
26 This is the interpretation of the matter: MENE, God has numbered the days of[u]
your kingdom and brought it to an end; 27 TEKEL, you have been weighed on the
scales and found wanting; 28 PERES,[v] your kingdom is divided and given to the
Medes and Persians."

29 Then Belshazzar gave the command, and Daniel was clothed in purple, a
chain of gold was put around his neck, and a proclamation was made concerning
him that he should rank third in the kingdom.

30 That very night Belshazzar, the Chaldean king, was killed. 31[w] And Darius
the Mede received the kingdom, being about sixty-two years old.

Daniel in the lions' den

6 It pleased Darius to set over the kingdom one hundred twenty satraps, stationed throughout the whole kingdom, 2 and over them three presidents, including Daniel; to these the satraps gave account, so that the king might suffer no
loss. 3 Soon Daniel distinguished himself above all the other presidents and satraps
because an excellent spirit was in him, and the king planned to appoint him over the
whole kingdom. 4 So the presidents and the satraps tried to find grounds for complaint against Daniel in connection with the kingdom. But they could find
no grounds for complaint or any corruption, because he was faithful, and no

5.22 Ex 10.3 2 Chron 33.23 36.12 Acts 4.8-13
5.23 2 Kgs 14.10 Job 12.10 Jer 50.29 Dan 5.3,4 Hab 2.18,19 1 Cor 8.4
5.26 Job 14.14 Isa 13.6,17 Jer 25.11 Acts 15.18
5.28 Isa 21.2; 45.1,2 Dan 5.31; 6.28
5.30 Isa 21.4-9 Jer 51.11,31, 39,57
6.2 Ezra 4.22 Esth 7.4 Dan 2.48,49 5.16,29 Mt 18.23
6.3 Gen 41.40 Eccles 2.13 Dan 5.12

u Aram lacks *the days of* v The singular of *Parsin* w Ch 6.1 in Aram

quet was a rebellious challenge to God's authority as he took the sacred vessels from God's temple and drank from them. No one who understands that God is the Creator of the universe would be foolish enough to challenge him.

5.22 Often kings would kill the bearer of bad news. But Daniel was not afraid to tell the truth to the king even though it was not what the king wanted to hear. We should be just as courageous in telling the truth under pressure.

5.24 Belshazzar used the goblets from the temple for his party, and God condemned him for this act. We must not use what has been dedicated to God for sinful purposes. Today this would include church buildings, financial donations, and anything else that has been set apart for God. Be careful how you use what belongs to God.

5.27 The handwriting on the wall was a message for all those who defy God. Although Belshazzar had power and wealth, his kingdom was totally corrupt and he could not withstand the judgment of God. God's time of judgment comes for all people. If you have forgotten God and slipped into a sinful way of life, turn away from your sin now. Ask God to forgive you, and begin to live by his standards.

5.28 The Medes and Persians joined forces to overthrow Babylon. This event began the second phase of Nebuchadnezzar's dream in chapter 2—the silver chest and arms.

5.31 Darius and his soldiers entered Babylon by diverting the river that ran through the city, then walking in on the dry river bed.

5.31 This Darius is not to be confused with Darius I, mentioned in Ezra, Haggai, and Zechariah, or Darius II (the Persian), mentioned in Nehemiah. Darius the Mede is named only in the book of Daniel. Other records name no king between Belshazzar and Cyrus. Thus, Darius may have been (1) appointed by Cyrus to rule over Babylonia as a province of Persia, (2) another name for Cyrus himself or for his son, Cambyses, or (3) a descendant of Xerxes I (Ahasuerus in Hebrew).

6.1–3 At this time, Daniel was over 80 years old and one of Darius's top three administrators. He was working with those who did not believe in his God, but he worked more efficiently and capably than all the rest. Thus, he attracted the attention of the pagan king and earned a place of respect. One of the best ways to influence non-Christian employers is to work diligently and responsibly. How do you represent God to your employer?

6.3, 4 Daniel made enemies at work by doing a good job. Perhaps you have had a similar experience. When you begin to excel, you may find that some co-workers look for ways to hold you back and tear you down. How should you deal with those who would celebrate your downfall and even try to bring it about? Conduct your whole life above reproach. Then you will have nothing to hide, and your enemies will have a difficult time finding legitimate charges against you. Of course this may not save you from all attacks. Like Daniel, you will have to rely on God for protection.

6.4, 5 The jealous officials couldn't find anything about Daniel's life to criticize, so they attacked his religion. If you face jealous critics because of your faith, be glad they're criticizing that part of your life—perhaps they had to focus on your religion as a last resort! Respond by continuing to believe and live as you should. Then remember that God is in control, fighting this battle for you.

negligence or corruption could be found in him. 5 The men said, "We shall not
find any ground for complaint against this Daniel unless we find it in connection
with the law of his God."
6 So the presidents and satraps conspired and came to the king and said to him,
"O King Darius, live forever! 7 All the presidents of the kingdom, the prefects and
the satraps, the counselors and the governors are agreed that the king should establish an ordinance and enforce an interdict, that whoever prays to anyone, divine or
human, for thirty days, except to you, O king, shall be thrown into a den of lions.
8 Now, O king, establish the interdict and sign the document, so that it cannot be
changed, according to the law of the Medes and the Persians, which cannot be
revoked." 9 Therefore King Darius signed the document and interdict.
10 Although Daniel knew that the document had been signed, he continued to
go to his house, which had windows in its upper room open toward Jerusalem, and
to get down on his knees three times a day to pray to his God and praise him, just
as he had done previously. 11 The conspirators came and found Daniel praying and
seeking mercy before his God. 12 Then they approached the king and said concerning the interdict, "O king! Did you not sign an interdict, that anyone who prays to
anyone, divine or human, within thirty days except to you, O king, shall be thrown
into a den of lions?" The king answered, "The thing stands fast, according to the
law of the Medes and Persians, which cannot be revoked." 13 Then they responded
to the king, "Daniel, one of the exiles from Judah, pays no attention to you, O king,
or to the interdict you have signed, but he is saying his prayers three times a day."
14 When the king heard the charge, he was very much distressed. He was determined to save Daniel, and until the sun went down he made every effort to rescue
him. 15 Then the conspirators came to the king and said to him, "Know, O king,
that it is a law of the Medes and Persians that no interdict or ordinance that the king
establishes can be changed."
16 Then the king gave the command, and Daniel was brought and thrown into
the den of lions. The king said to Daniel, "May your God, whom you faithfully
serve, deliver you!" 17 A stone was brought and laid on the mouth of the den, and
the king sealed it with his own signet and with the signet of his lords, so that nothing might be changed concerning Daniel. 18 Then the king went to his palace and
spent the night fasting; no food was brought to him, and sleep fled from him.
19 Then, at break of day, the king got up and hurried to the den of lions.
20 When he came near the den where Daniel was, he cried out anxiously to Daniel,
"O Daniel, servant of the living God, has your God whom you faithfully serve been
able to deliver you from the lions?" 21 Daniel then said to the king, "O king, live
forever! 22 My God sent his angel and shut the lions' mouths so that they would not
hurt me, because I was found blameless before him; and also before you, O king,
I have done no wrong." 23 Then the king was exceedingly glad and commanded that
Daniel be taken up out of the den. So Daniel was taken up out of the den, and no

6.5 1 Sam 24.17 Jn 19.6,7 Acts 24.13-16
6.7 Ps 62.4; 64.2-6 Dan 6.16 Mt 12.14
6.8 Esth 3.12; 8.10 Isa 10.1 Dan 6.12,13 Mt 24.35
6.9 Ps 62.9,10 118.9
6.10 1 Kgs 8.48,49 2 Chron 6.38 Ps 34.1 Dan 9.4-19 Col 3.17 1 Thess 5.17,18
6.11 Ps 37.32,33 Dan 6.6
6.12 Esth 1.19 Dan 3.8-12; 6.8
6.13 Esth 3.8 Dan 3.12 Acts 5.29; 17.7
6.14 Mk 6.26
6.15 Esth 8.8 Ps 94.20,21 Dan 6.8,12
6.16 Job 5.19 Ps 37.39,40 Jer 38.5 Dan 6.20
6.17 Lam 3.53 Mt 27.66 Acts 12.4
6.18 2 Sam 12.16,17 Rev 18.22
6.20 Jer 32.17 Dan 3.17 Hos 12.6
6.22 Num 20.16 Ps 91.11-13 Acts 12.11 2 Tim 4.17 Heb 11.33

6.8, 9 An "interdict" is a prohibitory decree. In Babylonia, the king's word *was* the law. In the Medo-Persian Empire, however, when a law was made, even the king couldn't change it. Darius was an effective government administrator, but he had a fatal flaw – pride. By appealing to his vanity, the men talked him into signing a law effectively making himself a god for 30 days. This law could not be broken – not even by an important official like Daniel. (Another example of the irrevocable nature of the laws of the Medes and Persians appears in Esther 8.8.)

6.10 Daniel stood alone. He knew about the law against praying to anyone except the king, yet he still prayed three times a day as he always had. Daniel had a disciplined prayer life. Our prayers are usually interrupted not by threats, but simply by the pressure of our schedules. Don't let threats or pressures cut into your prayer time. Pray regularly, no matter what, because prayer is your lifeline to God.

6.10 Daniel made no attempt to hide his daily prayer routine from his enemies in government, even though he knew this would be disobeying the new law. Hiding his daily prayers would have been futile since the officials surely would have caught him at something else during the month. Also, hiding would have demonstrated that he was afraid of the officials. Daniel continued to pray because he could not look to the king for the guidance and strength that he needed during this difficult time. Only God could provide what he really needed.

6.16 Lions roamed the countryside and forests in Mesopotamia, and the people feared them and had great respect for their power. Some kings hunted lions for sport. The Persians captured lions, keeping them in large parks where they were fed and attended. Lions were also used for executing people. But God has ways of delivering his people (6.22) that none of us can imagine. It is always premature to give up and give in to the pressure of unbelievers. God can even shut the lions' mouths.

that all peoples, nations, and languages
should serve him.
His dominion is an everlasting dominion
that shall not pass away,
and his kingship is one
that shall never be destroyed.

7.15 Dan 4.19; 7.28
15 As for me, Daniel, my spirit was troubled within me,[d] and the visions of my
7.16 Dan 8.13-16 10.5,6,11,12 Zech 1.8-11 Rev 5.5 7.13,14
head terrified me. 16 I approached one of the attendants to ask him the truth concerning all this. So he said that he would disclose to me the interpretation of the
matter: 17 "As for these four great beasts, four kings shall arise out of the earth.
7.18 Dan 7.22,25,27 2 Tim 2.11,12 Rev 2.26,27 20.4
18 But the holy ones of the Most High shall receive the kingdom and possess the
kingdom forever — forever and ever."
19 Then I desired to know the truth concerning the fourth beast, which was
different from all the rest, exceedingly terrifying, with its teeth of iron and claws of
bronze, and which devoured and broke in pieces, and stamped what was left with
its feet; 20 and concerning the ten horns that were on its head, and concerning the
other horn, which came up and to make room for which three of them fell out — the
horn that had eyes and a mouth that spoke arrogantly, and that seemed greater than
7.21 Rev 13.7
the others. 21 As I looked, this horn made war with the holy ones and was prevailing
7.22 Dan 7.10 1 Cor 6.2,3
over them, 22 until the Ancient One[e] came; then judgment was given for the holy
ones of the Most High, and the time arrived when the holy ones gained possession
of the kingdom.

23 This is what he said: "As for the fourth beast,
there shall be a fourth kingdom on earth
that shall be different from all the other kingdoms;
it shall devour the whole earth,
and trample it down, and break it to pieces.
24 As for the ten horns,
out of this kingdom ten kings shall arise,
and another shall arise after them.
This one shall be different from the former ones,
and shall put down three kings.
7.25 Dan 4.2; 11.36 12.7,14 Rev 12.14 13.6,7
25 He shall speak words against the Most High,
shall wear out the holy ones of the Most High,
and shall attempt to change the sacred seasons and the [illegible]
and they shall be given into his power
for a time, two times,[f] and half a time.
7.26 Rev 17.14; 19.2
26 Then the court shall sit in judgment,
and his dominion shall be taken away,
to be consumed and totally destroyed.
7.27 Isa 60.12 Dan 2.44; 4.34 7.14,18,22 Rev 11.1; 20.4
27 The kingship and dominion
and the greatness of the kingdoms under the whole heaven
shall be given to the people of the holy ones of the Most High;
their kingdom shall be an everlasting kingdom,
and all dominions shall serve and obey them."

[d] Aram *troubled in its sheath* [e] Aram *the Ancient of Days* [f] Aram *a time, times*

7.15 If you feel as Daniel did about these prophecies — troubled and confused — recognize with him that God has not yet revealed their full meaning. The full implications of these prophecies will not be known until God reveals them to his people.

7.18 The "holy ones of the Most High" are the true Israel, the people ruled by the Messiah. Jesus Christ gave the kingdom to the new Israel, his church made up of all believers. His coming ushered in the kingdom of God, and all believers are its citizens (see also 7.22, 27). Although God may allow persecution to continue for a while, the destiny of his followers will be to possess the kingdom and be with him forever.

7.24 The ten horns, or ten kings, are again mentioned in Revelation 17.12. There were also ten toes in Nebuchadnezzar's vision (2.41, 42). While all do not agree on the identity of these ten kings, we are reminded in Revelation 17.12–14 that these kings will war against Christ, but as the King of kings, he will conquer them. The other king mentioned is the future antichrist of 2 Thessalonians 2.3, 4.

7.25 While the exact nature of this "time, two times, and half a time" is debated, we do know that God conveyed to Daniel that persecution will continue only a relatively short while. Ultimately God will deliver his people.

28 Here the account ends. As for me, Daniel, my thoughts greatly terrified me,
and my face turned pale; but I kept the matter in my mind.

Daniel dreams of a ram and goat

8 In the third year of the reign of King Belshazzar a vision appeared to me,
Daniel, after the one that had appeared to me at first. 2 In the vision I was **8.2**
looking and saw myself in Susa the capital, in the province of Elam,[g] and I was by Gen 10.22; 14.1
the river Ulai.[h] 3 I looked up and saw a ram standing beside the river.[i] It had two
horns. Both horns were long, but one was longer than the other, and the longer one
came up second. 4 I saw the ram charging westward and northward and southward. **8.4**
All beasts were powerless to withstand it, and no one could rescue from its power; Deut 33.17 1 Kgs 22.11
it did as it pleased and became strong. Ezek 34.21 Mic 5.8
5 As I was watching, a male goat appeared from the west, coming across the
face of the whole earth without touching the ground. The goat had a horn[j] between
its eyes. 6 It came toward the ram with the two horns that I had seen standing beside
the river,[i] and it ran at it with savage force. 7 I saw it approaching the ram. It was **8.8**
enraged against it and struck the ram, breaking its two horns. The ram did not have 2 Chron 26.16 Dan 5.20; 7.2
power to withstand it; it threw the ram down to the ground and trampled upon it, Rev 7.1
and there was no one who could rescue the ram from its power. 8 Then the male goat **8.9**
grew exceedingly great; but at the height of its power, the great horn was broken, Dan 8.23 11.16,41
and in its place there came up four prominent horns toward the four winds of **8.10**
heaven. Jer 48.26,42 Ezek 46.14
9 Out of one of them came another[k] horn, a little one, which grew exceedingly Dan 7.7; 8.7 11.31
great toward the south, toward the east, and toward the beautiful land. 10 It grew as Rev 12.4
high as the host of heaven. It threw down to the earth some of the host and some of **8.12**
the stars, and trampled on them. 11 Even against the prince of the host it acted arro- Isa 59.14
gantly; it took the regular burnt offering away from him and overthrew the place of **8.13** Deut 33.2
his sanctuary. 12 Because of wickedness, the host was given over to it together with Isa 63.18 Dan 4.13,23
the regular burnt offering;[l] it cast truth to the ground, and kept prospering in what 12.6,8
it did. 13 Then I heard a holy one speaking, and another holy one said to the one that Lk 10.22; 21.24 Heb 10.29
spoke, "For how long is this vision concerning the regular burnt offering, the trans- Rev 6.10; 11.2
gression that makes desolate, and the giving over of the sanctuary and host to be **8.14** Dan 7.25
trampled?"[l] 14 And he answered him,[m] "For two thousand three hundred evenings 12.7,11 Rev 11.2,3
and mornings; then the sanctuary shall be restored to its rightful state." 12.14; 13.5
15 When I, Daniel, had seen the vision, I tried to understand it. Then someone **8.15** Dan 7.13
appeared standing before me, having the appearance of a man, 16 and I heard a 10.16,18

[g] Gk Theodotion: MT Q Ms repeat *in the vision I was looking* [h] Or *the Ulai Gate* [i] Or *gate* [j] Theodotion: Gk *one horn*; Heb *a horn of vision* [k] Cn Compare 7.8: Heb *one* [l] Meaning of Heb uncertain [m] Gk Theodotion Syr Vg: Heb *me*

8.1 As with chapter 7, this chapter precedes chapter 5 chronologically: the dream probably occurred in 551 B.C. when Daniel was about 70 years old. Chapters 7 and 8 correspond to the first and third years of Belshazzar's reign and belong chronologically between chapters 4 and 5. Chapter 9 takes place at approximately the same time as chapter 6. It gives us more details about the Medo-Persian and Greek Empires, the two world powers that ruled after Babylonia.

8.2 Susa was one of the capitals of the Babylonian Empire at this time. Located in what is now Iran, it was a well-developed city. The earliest known code of law, the Code of Hammurabi, was found there. Susa rivaled Babylon itself in cultural sophistication.

8.3 The two horns were the kings of Media and Persia (8.20). The longer horn represented the growing dominance of Persia in the Medo-Persian Empire.

8.5–7 The goat represents Greece, and its large horn, Alexander the Great (8.21). This is an amazing prediction, because Greece was not considered a world power when this prophecy was given. Alexander the Great conquered the world with great speed, indicated by the goat's rapid movement. Breaking off both horns symbolized Alexander breaking both parts of the Medo-Persian Empire.

8.8 Alexander the Great died in his thirties at the height of his power. His kingdom was split into four parts under four generals: Ptolemy I of Egypt and Palestine; Seleucus of Babylonia and Syria; Lysimachus of Asia Minor; and Cassander of Macedonia and Greece.

8.9 Israel ("the beautiful land") was attacked by Antiochus IV Epiphanes (the little horn) in the second century B.C. He was the eighth ruler of the Seleucid Empire. He overthrew the high priest, looted the temple, and replaced worship of God with a Greek form of worship. A further fulfillment of this prophecy will occur in the future with the coming of the antichrist (see 8.17, 19, 23).

8.11 The "prince of the host" here refers to a heavenly authority, perhaps an angel. (See also Joshua 5.13–15.)

8.14 The 2,300 "evenings and mornings" refers to the total number of evening and morning sacrifices that would take place from the desecration of the altar in the temple by Antiochus IV Epiphanes to the restoration of temple worship under Judas Maccabees in 165 B.C.

human voice by the Ulai, calling, "Gabriel, help this man understand the vision."
17 So he came near where I stood; and when he came, I became frightened and fell
prostrate. But he said to me, "Understand, O mortal,[n] that the vision is for the time
of the end."
18 As he was speaking to me, I fell into a trance, face to the ground; then he
touched me and set me on my feet. 19 He said, "Listen, and I will tell you what will
take place later in the period of wrath; for it refers to the appointed time of the end.
20 As for the ram that you saw with the two horns, these are the kings of Media and
Persia. 21 The male goat[o] is the king of Greece, and the great horn between its eyes
is the first king. 22 As for the horn that was broken, in place of which four others
arose, four kingdoms shall arise from his[p] nation, but not with his power.

23 At the end of their rule,
when the transgressions have reached their full measure,
a king of bold countenance shall arise,
skilled in intrigue.
24 He shall grow strong in power,[q]
shall cause fearful destruction,
and shall succeed in what he does.
He shall destroy the powerful
and the people of the holy ones.
25 By his cunning
he shall make deceit prosper under his hand,
and in his own mind he shall be great.
Without warning he shall destroy many
and shall even rise up against the Prince of princes.
But he shall be broken, and not by human hands.

26 The vision of the evenings and the mornings that has been told is true. As for you,
seal up the vision, for it refers to many days from now."
27 So I, Daniel, was overcome and lay sick for some days; then I arose and
went about the king's business. But I was dismayed by the vision and did not understand it.

8.17 Gen 17.3 Ezek 1.28; 6.2 44.4 Dan 2.46; 8.19 11.35,40
8.18 Ezek 2.2 Dan 10.9,10, 16,18 Lk 9.32
8.19 Dan 8.15-17
8.24 Dan 8.11-13 12.7 Rev 13.3-9 16.6; 17.12-17
8.25 Job 34.20 Dan 2.34,45
8.27 Dan 7.28; 8.17 Hab 3.16

Daniel prays for his people

9 In the first year of Darius son of Ahasuerus, by birth a Mede, who became king
over the realm of the Chaldeans— 2 in the first year of his reign, I, Daniel,
perceived in the books the number of years that, according to the word of the LORD
to the prophet Jeremiah, must be fulfilled for the devastation of Jerusalem, namely,
seventy years.

9.1 Dan 5.31; 11.1
9.2 2 Chron 36.21 Ezra 1.1 Jer 25.11; 29.10 Zech 7.5

[n] Heb *son of man* [o] Or *shaggy male goat* [p] Gk Theodotion Vg: Heb *the* [q] Theodotion and one Gk Ms: Heb repeats (from 8.22) *but not with his power*

8.16 Gabriel is an angel, the heavenly messenger God used to explain Daniel's visions (9.21). He also announced the birth of John the Baptist (Luke 1.11) and the Messiah (Luke 1.26).

8.17 The "time of the end," in this case, refers to the whole period from the end of the exile until the second coming of Christ. Many of the events that would happen under Antiochus IV Epiphanes would be repeated on a broader scale just before Christ's second coming. During these times, God deals with Israel in a radically different way, with divine discipline coming through Gentile nations. This period is sometimes referred to as the "times of the Gentiles."

8.23 This stern king ("of bold countenance") may symbolize both Antiochus IV Epiphanes and the antichrist at the end of human history.

8.25 This "Prince of princes" is God himself. No human power could defeat the king whom Daniel saw in his vision; but God would bring him down. Antiochus IV Epiphanes went insane and died in Persia in 163 B.C. God's power and justice will prevail. Never give up or lose hope, no matter how powerful God's enemies may seem.

9.1 The vision in chapter 9 was given to Daniel during the same time period of chapter 6. This Darius is the person mentioned in chapter 6. The Ahasuerus mentioned here is not Esther's husband. The events described in the book of Esther happened about 50 years later.

9.2, 3 Daniel pleaded with God to bring about the promised return of his people to their land. The prophet Jeremiah had written that God would not allow the captives to return to their land for 70 years (Jeremiah 25.11, 12; 29.10). Daniel knew of this prophecy and realized that this 70-year period was coming to an end.

3 Then I turned to the Lord God, to seek an answer by prayer and supplication
with fasting and sackcloth and ashes. 4 I prayed to the LORD my God and made
confession, saying,
"Ah, Lord, great and awesome God, keeping covenant and steadfast love with
those who love you and keep your commandments, 5 we have sinned and done
wrong, acted wickedly and rebelled, turning aside from your commandments and
ordinances. 6 We have not listened to your servants the prophets, who spoke in your
name to our kings, our princes, and our ancestors, and to all the people of the land.
7 "Righteousness is on your side, O Lord, but open shame, as at this day, falls
on us, the people of Judah, the inhabitants of Jerusalem, and all Israel, those who
are near and those who are far away, in all the lands to which you have driven them,
because of the treachery that they have committed against you. 8 Open shame,
O LORD, falls on us, our kings, our officials, and our ancestors, because we have
sinned against you. 9 To the Lord our God belong mercy and forgiveness, for we
have rebelled against him, 10 and have not obeyed the voice of the LORD our God by
following his laws, which he set before us by his servants the prophets.
11 "All Israel has transgressed your law and turned aside, refusing to obey your
voice. So the curse and the oath written in the law of Moses, the servant of God,
have been poured out upon us, because we have sinned against you. 12 He has confirmed his words, which he spoke against us and against our rulers, by bringing
upon us a calamity so great that what has been done against Jerusalem has never
before been done under the whole heaven. 13 Just as it is written in the law of Moses, all this calamity has come upon us. We did not entreat the favor of the LORD
our God, turning from our iniquities and reflecting on his[r] fidelity. 14 So the LORD
kept watch over this calamity until he brought it upon us. Indeed, the LORD our God
is right in all that he has done; for we have disobeyed his voice.
15 "And now, O Lord our God, who brought your people out of the land of
Egypt with a mighty hand and made your name renowned even to this day—we
have sinned, we have done wickedly. 16 O Lord, in view of all your righteous acts,
let your anger and wrath, we pray, turn away from your city Jerusalem, your holy
mountain; because of our sins and the iniquities of our ancestors, Jerusalem and
your people have become a disgrace among all our neighbors. 17 Now therefore,
O our God, listen to the prayer of your servant and to his supplication, and for your
own sake, Lord,[s] let your face shine upon your desolated sanctuary. 18 Incline your
ear, O my God, and hear. Open your eyes and look at our desolation and the city

9.4 Deut 7.9,21 Neh 9.32 Nah 1.2-7 Jas 2.5 1 Jn 5.2,3
9.5 Isa 53.6 Lam 1.18,20 Dan 9.11
9.6 Jer 44.4,5,21
9.7 Ezra 9.6,7 Jer 2.26,27 3.25; 23.6 33.16 Dan 9.18
9.9 Neh 9.17 Dan 9.5,6
9.10 2 Kgs 17.13-15 18.12
9.12 Isa 44.26 Jer 44.2-6 Zech 1.6
9.13 Lev 26.14-45 Deut 28.15-68 Isa 9.13 Jer 2.30; 5.3 Dan 9.11
9.14 Jer 31.28; 44.27 Dan 9.7
9.15 Deut 5.15 Neh 9.10 Jer 32.20 2 Cor 1.10
9.16 Ezek 5.14 Dan 9.20 Joel 3.17 Zech 8.3 Mt 23.31,32
9.17 Num 6.24-26 Ps 80.3,7,19 Lam 5.18

[r] Heb *your* [s] Theodotion Vg Compare Syr: Heb *for the Lord's sake*

9.3ff In Daniel's prayer for the nation, he used the pronoun "we" throughout. In times of adversity, it's easy to blame others and excuse our own actions. If anyone in Israel was righteous, it was Daniel; and yet he confessed his sinfulness and need for God's forgiveness. Instead of looking for others to blame, first look inside and confess your own sins to God.

9.3–19 Daniel knew how to pray. As he prayed, he fasted, confessed his sins, and pleaded that God would reveal his will. He prayed with complete surrender to God and with complete openness to what God was saying to him. When you pray, do you speak honestly with God? Examine your attitude. Talk to God with openness, vulnerability, and honesty.

9.4ff The captives from Judah had rebelled against God. Their sins had led to their captivity. But God is merciful, even to rebels, if they confess their sins and return to him. Don't let your past disobedience keep you from returning to God. He is waiting for you with open arms.

9.6 Through the years, God had sent many prophets to speak to his people, but their messages were ignored. The truth was too painful to hear. God still speaks clearly and accurately through the Bible, and he also speaks through preachers, teachers, and concerned friends. Sometimes the truth hurts, and we would rather hear words that soothe, even if they are false. If you are unwilling to accept God's Word, maybe you are trying to avoid making a painful change. Don't settle for a soothing lie that will bring harsh judgment. Accepting the truth even if it is painful can only help you.

9.11–13 Daniel mentioned the blessings and curses outlined in Deuteronomy 28. God had given the people of Israel a choice: obey me and receive blessings, or disobey me and face curses. The affliction was meant to turn the people to God. When we face difficult circumstances, we should ask ourselves if God has reason to send judgment. If we think so, we must urgently seek his forgiveness. Then we can ask him to help us through our troubles. "Reflecting on his fidelity" means accepting and obeying God's truth.

9.17–19 It would be a mistake to read the Bible as history and miss the deep personal feelings. In this section, Daniel is crying out to the Lord. He has a deep concern for his nation and his people. So often our prayers are without passion and true compassion for others. Are you willing to pray by pouring out your deep feelings to God?

9.18 Daniel begged for mercy, not for help, because he knew his people deserved God's wrath and punishment. God sends his help, not because we deserve it, but because he wants to show great mercy. If God refused to help us because of our sin, how could we complain? But when he sends mercy when we deserve punishment, how can we withhold our praise?

9.18 Ps 80.14 Isa 37.17 Jer 7.12; 36.7 Ezek 36.22
9.20 Isa 6.5; 58.9 Dan 9.3; 10.12
9.22 Dan 8.16; 10.21 Zech 1.9,14 Rev 4.1
9.24 Lev 25.8 Num 14.34 2 Chron 29.24 Isa 51.6,8 53.10 Rom 3.21; 5.10 2 Cor 5.18-20
9.25 Ezra 4.24 6.1-15 Neh 2.1-8; 3.1 Isa 9.6 Jn 1.41; 4.25
9.26 Isa 53.8 Nah 1.8 Mt 24.2 Mk 9.12; 13.2 Lk 24.26
9.27 Dan 11.31 Mt 24.15 Mk 13.14 Lk 21.20

that bears your name. We do not present our supplication before you on the ground
of our righteousness, but on the ground of your great mercies. 19 O Lord, hear;
O Lord, forgive; O Lord, listen and act and do not delay! For your own sake, O my
God, because your city and your people bear your name!"
20 While I was speaking, and was praying and confessing my sin and the sin of
my people Israel, and presenting my supplication before the LORD my God on behalf of the holy mountain of my God— 21 while I was speaking in prayer, the man
Gabriel, whom I had seen before in a vision, came to me in swift flight at the time
of the evening sacrifice. 22 He came[t] and said to me, "Daniel, I have now come out
to give you wisdom and understanding. 23 At the beginning of your supplications a
word went out, and I have come to declare it, for you are greatly beloved. So consider the word and understand the vision:
24 "Seventy weeks are decreed for your people and your holy city: to finish the
transgression, to put an end to sin, and to atone for iniquity, to bring in everlasting
righteousness, to seal both vision and prophet, and to anoint a most holy place.[u]
25 Know therefore and understand: from the time that the word went out to restore
and rebuild Jerusalem until the time of an anointed prince, there shall be seven
weeks; and for sixty-two weeks it shall be built again with streets and moat, but in
a troubled time. 26 After the sixty-two weeks, an anointed one shall be cut off and
shall have nothing, and the troops of the prince who is to come shall destroy the city
and the sanctuary. Its[v] end shall come with a flood, and to the end there shall be
war. Desolations are decreed. 27 He shall make a strong covenant with many for one
week, and for half of the week he shall make sacrifice and offering cease; and in
their place[w] shall be an abomination that desolates, until the decreed end is poured
out upon the desolator."

Daniel sees a heavenly messenger

10.1 Dan 1.17,21 2.21; 6.28
10.2 Ezra 9.4 Neh 1.4
10.4 Ezek 1.3
10.5 Jer 10.9 Rev 1.13; 15.6
10.7 2 Kgs 6.17 Ezek 12.18 Acts 9.7 Heb 12.21

10 In the third year of King Cyrus of Persia a word was revealed to Daniel, who
was named Belteshazzar. The word was true, and it concerned a great conflict. He understood the word, having received understanding in the vision.
2 At that time I, Daniel, had been mourning for three weeks. 3 I had eaten no
rich food, no meat or wine had entered my mouth, and I had not anointed myself at
all, for the full three weeks. 4 On the twenty-fourth day of the first month, as I was
standing on the bank of the great river (that is, the Tigris), 5 I looked up and saw a
man clothed in linen, with a belt of gold from Uphaz around his waist. 6 His body
was like beryl, his face like lightning, his eyes like flaming torches, his arms and
legs like the gleam of burnished bronze, and the sound of his words like the roar of
a multitude. 7 I, Daniel, alone saw the vision; the people who were with me did not

[t] Gk Syr: Heb *He made to understand* [u] Or *thing* or *one* [v] Or *His* [w] Cn: Meaning of Heb uncertain

---

9.24, 25 Each day of these 70 weeks may represent one year. Scripture often uses round numbers to make a point, not to give an exact count. For example, Jesus said we are to forgive others "seventy times seven" times. He did not mean a literal 490 times only, but that we should be abundantly forgiving. Similarly, some scholars see this figure of 70 weeks as a figurative time period. Others, however, interpret this time period as a literal 70 weeks or 490 years, observing that Christ's death came at the end of the 69 weeks (i.e., 483 years later). One interpretation places the 70th week as the seven years of the great tribulation, still in the future.

9.26, 27 The Messiah would be rejected by his own people. His perfect eternal kingdom would come later. There has been much discussion on the numbers, times, and events in these verses, and there are three basic views: (1) this was fulfilled in the past at the desecration of the temple by Antiochus IV Epiphanes in 168–167 B.C.; (2) this was fulfilled at the destruction of the temple by the Roman general Titus Vespasian in 70 A.D. when one million Jews were killed; or (3) this is still to be fulfilled in the future under the antichrist.

10.1ff This is Daniel's final vision (536 B.C.). In it, he is given further insight into the great spiritual battle between those who protect God's people and those who want to destroy them. There is also more detailed information on the future, specifically the struggles between the Ptolemies (kings of the south) and the Seleucids (kings of the north).

10.1ff Prior to this vision, Cyrus allowed the Jews to return to Jerusalem, but Daniel stayed in Babylonia. Why didn't Daniel return to Jerusalem? He may have been too old to make the long, hazardous journey (he was over 80); his government duties could have prevented him; or God may have told him to stay behind to complete the work he was called to do.

10.3 Daniel refrained from eating choice foods and using lotions because these were signs of feasting and rejoicing.

10.5, 6 The person seen by Daniel was a heavenly being. This is believed by some commentators to be an appearance of Christ (see Revelation 1.13–15), while others contend it is an angel (because he required Michael's help – 10.13). In either case, Daniel caught a glimpse of the battle between good and evil supernatural powers.

see the vision, though a great trembling fell upon them, and they fled and hid themselves. 8 So I was left alone to see this great vision. My strength left me, and my
complexion grew deathly pale, and I retained no strength. 9 Then I heard the sound
of his words; and when I heard the sound of his words, I fell into a trance, face to
the ground.
10 But then a hand touched me and roused me to my hands and knees. 11 He said
to me, "Daniel, greatly beloved, pay attention to the words that I am going to speak
to you. Stand on your feet, for I have now been sent to you." So while he was
speaking this word to me, I stood up trembling. 12 He said to me, "Do not fear,
Daniel, for from the first day that you set your mind to gain understanding and to
humble yourself before your God, your words have been heard, and I have come
because of your words. 13 But the prince of the kingdom of Persia opposed me
twenty-one days. So Michael, one of the chief princes, came to help me, and I left
him there with the prince of the kingdom of Persia,[x] 14 and have come to help you
understand what is to happen to your people at the end of days. For there is a further
vision for those days."
15 While he was speaking these words to me, I turned my face toward the
ground and was speechless. 16 Then one in human form touched my lips, and I
opened my mouth to speak, and said to the one who stood before me, "My lord,
because of the vision such pains have come upon me that I retain no strength.
17 How can my lord's servant talk with my lord? For I am shaking,[y] no strength
remains in me, and no breath is left in me."
18 Again one in human form touched me and strengthened me. 19 He said, "Do
not fear, greatly beloved, you are safe. Be strong and courageous!" When he spoke
to me, I was strengthened and said, "Let my lord speak, for you have strengthened
me." 20 Then he said, "Do you know why I have come to you? Now I must return
to fight against the prince of Persia, and when I am through with him, the prince of
Greece will come. 21 But I am to tell you what is inscribed in the book of truth.
There is no one with me who contends against these princes except Michael, your
11 prince. 1 As for me, in the first year of Darius the Mede, I stood up to support
and strengthen him.

The messenger predicts the future

2 "Now I will announce the truth to you. Three more kings shall arise in Persia.
The fourth shall be far richer than all of them, and when he has become strong
through his riches, he shall stir up all against the kingdom of Greece. 3 Then a
warrior king shall arise, who shall rule with great dominion and take action as he

10.8 Gen 32.34 Ex 3.3 Dan 7.28; 8.27 Hab 3.16 Rev 1.17
10.11 Ezek 2.1 Dan 8.16,17
10.12 Dan 9.20-23 10.2,3,19
10.13 Dan 10.21; 12.1 Zech 3.1 Eph 6.12 Jude 9 Rev 12.7
10.14 Dan 2.28; 8.26 12.4,9 Hos 3.5 2 Thess 3.1
10.15 Ezek 24.27 33.22 Lk 1.20
10.16 Ex 4.10 Josh 5.14 Isa 6.7 Jer 1.9 Dan 7.15 8.17,27; 10.8,9
10.17 Ex 24.10,11 Isa 6.1-5 Mt 22.43,44
10.19 Josh 1.6-9 Isa 35.4; 43.1 Dan 10.12
11.3 Dan 5.19 8.4,5,21 11.16,36

x Gk Theodotion: Heb *I was left there with the kings of Persia* y Gk: Heb *from now*

10.9–18 Daniel was frightened by this vision and fell into a "trance" (frozen by fear). But the messenger reassured him. Daniel lost his speech, but the messenger's touch restored it; Daniel felt weak, but the messenger's words strengthened him. God can bring us healing when we are hurt, peace when we are troubled, and strength when we are weak. Ask God to minister to you as he did to Daniel.

10.12, 13 Although God sent a messenger to Daniel, powerful spiritual beings detained the messenger for three weeks. Daniel faithfully continued praying and fasting, and God's messenger eventually arrived. Answers to our prayers may be hindered by unseen obstacles. Don't expect God's answers to come too easily or too quickly. Prayer may be challenged by evil forces, so pray fervently and pray earnestly. Then expect God to answer at the right time.

10.20, 21 The heavenly warfare was to be directed against Persia, and then Greece. Each of these nations was to have power over God's people. They were represented by evil angelic "princes"or demons. But God is in control of the past, present, and future, and he has all events recorded in his "book of truth."

11.1ff Babylon was defeated by Medo-Persia. Persia was defeated by Greece under Alexander the Great, who conquered most of the Mediterranean and Middle Eastern lands. After Alexander's death, the empire was divided into four parts. The Ptolemies gained control of the southern section of Palestine, and the Seleucids took the northern part. Verses 1–20 show the conflict between the Ptolemies and Seleucids over control of Palestine in 300–200 B.C. Verses 21–39 describe the persecution of Israel under Antiochus IV Epiphanes. In verses 40–45 the prophecy shifts to the end times. Antiochus IV fades from view, and the antichrist of the last days becomes the center of attention.

11.1, 2 The angelic messenger was revealing Israel's future (see 10.20, 21). Only God can reveal future events so clearly. God's work not only deals with the sweeping panorama of history, but also focuses on the intricate details of people's lives. And his plans – whether for nations or individuals – are unshakable.

11.2 The fourth Persian king may be Xerxes I, also known as Ahasuerus in the book of Esther (486–465 B.C.), who launched an all-out effort against Greece.

11.3 This mighty king of Greece is Alexander the Great who conquered Medo-Persia and built a huge empire in only four years.

pleases. 4 And while still rising in power, his kingdom shall be broken and divided
toward the four winds of heaven, but not to his posterity, nor according to the
dominion with which he ruled; for his kingdom shall be uprooted and go to others
besides these.
5 "Then the king of the south shall grow strong, but one of his officers shall
grow stronger than he and shall rule a realm greater than his own realm. 6 After
some years they shall make an alliance, and the daughter of the king of the south
shall come to the king of the north to ratify the agreement. But she shall not retain
her power, and his offspring shall not endure. She shall be given up, she and her
attendants and her child and the one who supported her.
"In those times 7 a branch from her roots shall rise up in his place. He shall come
against the army and enter the fortress of the king of the north, and he shall take
action against them and prevail. 8 Even their gods, with their idols and with their
precious vessels of silver and gold, he shall carry off to Egypt as spoils of war. For
some years he shall refrain from attacking the king of the north; 9 then the latter
shall invade the realm of the king of the south, but will return to his own land.
10 "His sons shall wage war and assemble a multitude of great forces, which
shall advance like a flood and pass through, and again shall carry the war as far as
his fortress. 11 Moved with rage, the king of the south shall go out and do battle
against the king of the north, who shall muster a great multitude, which shall, however, be defeated by his enemy. 12 When the multitude has been carried off, his
heart shall be exalted, and he shall overthrow tens of thousands, but he shall not
prevail. 13 For the king of the north shall again raise a multitude, larger than the
former, and after some years[z] he shall advance with a great army and abundant
supplies.
14 "In those times many shall rise against the king of the south. The lawless
among your own people shall lift themselves up in order to fulfill the vision, but
they shall fail. 15 Then the king of the north shall come and throw up siegeworks,
and take a well-fortified city. And the forces of the south shall not stand, not even
his picked troops, for there shall be no strength to resist. 16 But he who comes
against him shall take the actions he pleases, and no one shall withstand him. He
shall take a position in the beautiful land, and all of it shall be in his power. 17 He
shall set his mind to come with the strength of his whole kingdom, and he shall
bring terms of peace[a] and perform them. In order to destroy the kingdom,[b] he
shall give him a woman in marriage; but it shall not succeed or be to his advantage.
18 Afterward he shall turn to the coastlands, and shall capture many. But a commander shall put an end to his insolence; indeed,[c] he shall turn his insolence back
upon him. 19 Then he shall turn back toward the fortresses of his own land, but he
shall stumble and fall, and shall not be found.
20 "Then shall arise in his place one who shall send an official for the glory of
the kingdom; but within a few days he shall be broken, though not in anger or in
battle. 21 In his place shall arise a contemptible person on whom royal majesty had

11.4 Jer 49.36 Ezek 37.9 Dan 7.2; 8.8 Zech 2.6 Lk 12.20 Rev 7.1
11.6 Dan 11.7,13,15, 40
11.7 Dan 11.19,38, 39
11.8 Isa 37.19 46.1,2 Jer 43.12,13
11.10 Isa 8.8 Jer 46.7,8 51.42 Dan 11.26,40
11.13 Dan 4.16; 12.7
11.15 Jer 6.6 Ezek 4.2; 17.17
11.16 Josh 1.5 Dan 5.19; 8.9 11.3,36,41
11.17 2 Kgs 12.17 Ezek 4.3,7 Lk 9.51; 11.23 Rom 8.31
11.18 Gen 10.5 Zeph 2.11
11.19 Ps 27.2; 37.36 Jer 46.6 Ezek 26.21

[z] Heb *and at the end of the times years* [a] Gk: Heb *kingdom, and upright ones with him* [b] Heb *it* [c] Meaning of Heb uncertain

11.4, 5 Alexander the Great's empire was eventually divided into four nations. These four weaker nations were comprised of the following regions: (1) Egypt, (2) Babylonia and Syria, (3) Asia Minor, and (4) Macedonia and Greece. The king of Egypt ("the king of the south") was Ptolemy I.

11.6, 7 These prophecies seem to have been fulfilled many years later in the Seleucid wars between Egypt and Syria. In 252 B.C., Ptolemy II of Egypt ("the south") gave his daughter Berenice in marriage to Antiochus II of Syria ("the north") to conclude a peace treaty between their two lands. But Berenice was murdered in Antioch by Antiochus II's former wife, Laodice. Berenice's brother, Ptolemy III, ascended the Egyptian throne and declared war against the Seleucids to avenge his sister's murder.

11.9–11 The king of Syria ("the north") is Seleucus II, and the king of Egypt ("the south") is Ptolemy IV.

11.13 This Syrian king is possibly Antiochus III (the Great). He defeated many Egyptian cities (11.15), and pillaged Israel ("the beautiful land," 11.16). He was later defeated by the Romans at Magnesia (11.18).

11.20 The successor to Antiochus III is Seleucus IV. He sent Heliodorus to rob and desecrate the temple in Jerusalem.

11.21 Seleucus IV was succeeded by his brother, Antiochus IV Epiphanes, who ingratiated himself with the Romans and took over after his brother's death.

11.21, 22 All opposition against this "contemptible person" will be broken. The "prince of the covenant" may be the high priest Onias III who was assassinated by Menelaus in 171 B.C.

not been conferred; he shall come in without warning and obtain the kingdom
through intrigue. 22 Armies shall be utterly swept away and broken before him, and
the prince of the covenant as well. 23 And after an alliance is made with him, he
shall act deceitfully and become strong with a small party. 24 Without warning he
shall come into the richest parts[d] of the province and do what none of his predecessors had ever done, lavishing plunder, spoil, and wealth on them. He shall devise
plans against strongholds, but only for a time. 25 He shall stir up his power and
determination against the king of the south with a great army, and the king of the
south shall wage war with a much greater and stronger army. But he shall not succeed, for plots shall be devised against him 26 by those who eat of the royal rations.
They shall break him, his army shall be swept away, and many shall fall slain.
27 The two kings, their minds bent on evil, shall sit at one table and exchange lies.
But it shall not succeed, for there remains an end at the time appointed. 28 He shall
return to his land with great wealth, but his heart shall be set against the holy covenant. He shall work his will, and return to his own land.

29 "At the time appointed he shall return and come into the south, but this time
it shall not be as it was before. 30 For ships of Kittim shall come against him, and
he shall lose heart and withdraw. He shall be enraged and take action against the
holy covenant. He shall turn back and pay heed to those who forsake the holy covenant. 31 Forces sent by him shall occupy and profane the temple and fortress. They
shall abolish the regular burnt offering and set up the abomination that makes desolate. 32 He shall seduce with intrigue those who violate the covenant; but the people
who are loyal to their God shall stand firm and take action. 33 The wise among the
people shall give understanding to many; for some days, however, they shall fall by
sword and flame, and suffer captivity and plunder. 34 When they fall victim, they
shall receive a little help, and many shall join them insincerely. 35 Some of the wise
shall fall, so that they may be refined, purified, and cleansed,[e] until the time of the
end, for there is still an interval until the time appointed.

36 "The king shall act as he pleases. He shall exalt himself and consider himself
greater than any god, and shall speak horrendous things against the God of gods.
He shall prosper until the period of wrath is completed, for what is determined shall
be done. 37 He shall pay no respect to the gods of his ancestors, or to the one beloved by women; he shall pay no respect to any other god, for he shall consider
himself greater than all. 38 He shall honor the god of fortresses instead of these; a

11.24 Num 13.20 Neh 9.25 Ezek 34.14
11.27 Jer 9.3-5 Dan 11.35,40 Hab 2.3 Acts 17.31
11.31 Ezek 24.21,24 Dan 8.11-13 9.27; 12.11 Mt 24.15 Mk 13.14
11.32 Dan 11.21,34 Zech 9.13-16 10.3-6 Rev 12.7-11
11.33 Zech 8.20-23 Mt 24.9 Jn 16.2 Heb 11.36-38 Rev 1.9; 6.9 7.14
11.34 Dan 11.21,32 Mt 7.15 Rom 16.18 Rev 2.20 13.11-14
11.35 Deut 8.16 Prov 17.3 Dan 12.10 Zech 13.9 Rev 14.15 17.17
11.36 Deut 10.17 Isa 10.25 14.13; 26.20 Dan 2.47; 5.20 7.8,11; 8.11 9.27; 11.3 Acts 4.28 Rev 10.7 13.5,6

[d] Or *among the richest men* [e] Heb *made them white*

11.27 These two treacherous kings are probably Antiochus IV of Syria and Ptolemy VI of Egypt. Treachery and deceit are a power broker's way to position himself over another. But when two power brokers try to do this to each other, it is a mutually weakening and self-destructive process. It is also futile, because God ultimately holds all power in his hands.

11.29–31 Antiochus IV would again turn his armies southward, but enemy ships would cause him to retreat. On his way back, he pillaged Jerusalem, polluted the temple, and stopped the Jews' daily sacrifices. The sanctuary was polluted when he sacrificed pigs on an altar erected in honor of Zeus. According to Jewish law, pigs were unclean and were not to be touched or eaten. To sacrifice a pig in the temple was the worst kind of insult an enemy could level against the Jews. This happened in 168–167 B.C.

11.32 This reference may be to Menelaus, the high priest, who was won over by Antiochus and conspired with him against Jews who were "loyal to their God." These Jews could be the Maccabees and their sympathizers, but a further fulfillment may lie in the future.

11.33, 34 Those who are wise will teach many, but they will also face great persecution. Difficult times remind us of our weaknesses and our inability to cope. We want answers, leadership, and clear direction. During these times, God's Word begins to interest even those who would never look at it. We should be ready to use our opportunities to share God's Word in needy times. We must also be prepared to face persecution and rejection as we teach and preach.

11.35 God's messenger describes a time of trial when even wise believers may stumble. This could mean (1) falling into sin, (2) being fearful and losing faith, (3) mistakenly following wrong teaching, or (4) experiencing severe suffering and martyrdom. If we persevere in our faith, any such experience will only refine us and make us stronger. Are you facing trials? Recognize them as opportunities to strengthen your faith. If we remain steadfast in these experiences, we will be stronger in our faith and closer to God.

11.36–39 These verses could refer to Antiochus IV Epiphanes, Titus Vespasian, or the antichrist. Some of these events seem to have been fulfilled in the past, and some have yet to be fulfilled.

11.37 The "one beloved by women" refers to Tammuz, a Babylonian fertility god. Tammuz is also mentioned in Ezekiel 8.14. In other words, this person won't recognize any deity or religions at all, not even pagan ones. Instead, he will proclaim himself as divine and the ultimate power.

11.38 The "god of fortresses" is sometimes believed to be Jupiter or Zeus. The implication is that this king will make *war* his god. More than all his predecessors, he will wage war and glorify its horrors.

god whom his ancestors did not know he shall honor with gold and silver, with
precious stones and costly gifts. 39 He shall deal with the strongest fortresses by the
help of a foreign god. Those who acknowledge him he shall make more wealthy,
and shall appoint them as rulers over many, and shall distribute the land for a price.
40 "At the time of the end the king of the south shall attack him. But the king
of the north shall rush upon him like a whirlwind, with chariots and horsemen, and
with many ships. He shall advance against countries and pass through like a flood.
41 He shall come into the beautiful land, and tens of thousands shall fall victim, but
Edom and Moab and the main part of the Ammonites shall escape from his power.
42 He shall stretch out his hand against the countries, and the land of Egypt shall not
escape. 43 He shall become ruler of the treasures of gold and of silver, and all the
riches of Egypt; and the Libyans and the Ethiopians[f] shall follow in his train. 44 But
reports from the east and the north shall alarm him, and he shall go out with great
fury to bring ruin and complete destruction to many. 45 He shall pitch his palatial
tents between the sea and the beautiful holy mountain. Yet he shall come to his end,
with no one to help him.

A prophecy of the last days

12 "At that time Michael, the great prince, the protector of your people, shall
arise. There shall be a time of anguish, such as has never occurred since
nations first came into existence. But at that time your people shall be delivered,
everyone who is found written in the book. 2 Many of those who sleep in the dust
of the earth[g] shall awake, some to everlasting life, and some to shame and everlasting contempt. 3 Those who are wise shall shine like the brightness of the sky,[h] and
those who lead many to righteousness, like the stars forever and ever. 4 But you,
Daniel, keep the words secret and the book sealed until the time of the end. Many
shall be running back and forth, and evil[i] shall increase."
5 Then I, Daniel, looked, and two others appeared, one standing on this bank of
the stream and one on the other. 6 One of them said to the man clothed in linen, who
was upstream, "How long shall it be until the end of these wonders?" 7 The man
clothed in linen, who was upstream, raised his right hand and his left hand toward
heaven. And I heard him swear by the one who lives forever that it would be for a
time, two times, and half a time,[j] and that when the shattering of the power of the
holy people comes to an end, all these things would be accomplished. 8 I heard but
could not understand; so I said, "My lord, what shall be the outcome of these
things?" 9 He said, "Go your way, Daniel, for the words are to remain secret and

11.40 Jer 4.13 Dan 11.27,35 12.4,9 Zech 9.14
11.41 Jer 48.47; 49.6
11.43 Ezek 30.4,5 Nah 3.9
12.1 Jer 30.7 Ezek 5.9 Dan 7.10; 9.12 10.21; 12.4 Mk 13.19
12.2 Isa 26.19 Jn 5.28,29
12.3 Isa 53.11 Jn 5.35
12.4 Isa 8.16; 11.9
12.6 Ezek 9.2 Dan 8.13,16 10.5; 12.8 Zech 1.12,13 Mt 24.3 Mk 13.4
12.7 Ezek 20.5 Dan 7.25; 8.24 Lk 21.24 Rev 10.7 11.7-15; 12.14

[f] Or *Nubians;* Heb *Cushites* [g] Or *the land of dust* [h] Or *dome* [i] Cn Compare Gk: Heb *knowledge* [j] Heb *a time, times, and a half*

11.40 The prophecy takes a turn here. Antiochus IV fades from view, and the antichrist of the last days becomes the center of attention from this point through the rest of the book of Daniel.

11.45 "The beautiful holy mountain" is Mount Zion or the city of Jerusalem.

12.1 Great suffering is in store for God's people throughout the years ahead. This way of describing the future is also used by Jeremiah (Jeremiah 30.7) and Jesus (Matthew 24.21ff). Yet the great suffering is tempered by a great promise of hope for true believers.

12.2 This is a clear reference to the resurrection of both the righteous and the wicked, although the eternal fates of each will be quite different. Up to this point in time, teaching about the resurrection was not common, although every Israelite believed that one day he or she would be included in the restoration of the new kingdom. This reference to a bodily resurrection of both the saved and the lost was a sharp departure from common belief. (See also Job 19.25, 26; Psalm 16.10; and Isaiah 26.19 for other Old Testament references to the resurrection.)

12.3 Many people try to be stars in the world of entertainment, only to find their stardom temporary. God tells us how we can be eternal "stars" – by being wise and leading "many to *God's* righteousness." If we share our Lord with others, we can be true stars – radiantly beautiful in God's sight!

12.4 Closing up and sealing the words of the scroll meant that it was to be kept safe and preserved. This was to be done so that believers of all times could look back on God's work in history and find hope. Daniel did not understand the exact meaning of the times and events in his vision. We can see events as they unfold, for we are in the end times. The whole book will not be understood until the climax of earth's history.

12.7 "Time, two times, and half a time" means three and a half years, and may be taken as literal or figurative.

12.7 "The power of the holy people" seems to be broken again and again throughout history. God's recurring purpose in this is to break the pride and self-sufficiency of his rebellious people and to bring them to accept him as their Lord.

sealed until the time of the end. 10Many shall be purified, cleansed, and refined,
but the wicked shall continue to act wickedly. None of the wicked shall understand,
but those who are wise shall understand. 11From the time that the regular burnt
offering is taken away and the abomination that desolates is set up, there shall be
one thousand two hundred ninety days. 12Happy are those who persevere and attain
the thousand three hundred thirty-five days. 13But you, go your way,[k] and rest;
you shall rise for your reward at the end of the days."

[k] Gk Theodotion: Heb adds *to the end*

12.10 Isa 32.6,7 Rev 3.18 9.20,21; 16.11
12.11 Mt 24.15 Mk 13.14 Rev 11.2; 12.6
12.13 Ps 16.5

12.10 Trials and persecutions make very little sense to us when we experience them. But they can purify us if we are willing to learn from them. After you survive a difficult time, seek to learn from it so that it can help you in the future. See Romans 5.3–5 for more on God's purpose in trials.

12.11 "The abomination" set up in the temple refers to the altar of Zeus where Antiochus IV Epiphanes sacrificed a pig. Some think it will have a double fulfillment and refer to the antichrist or one of his horrible acts of evil. More likely, this and the predictions at the early part of the chapter refer specifically to Antiochus IV Epiphanes, and then the prophecy shifts to the end times.

12.11, 12 Either these are further calculations relating to the persecution of the Jews under Antiochus IV Epiphanes, or they refer to the end times. The abolishing of the daily sacrifices means the removal of worship of the true God and the oppression of believers. There is much speculation about these numbers. The point is that this time of persecution has an end, God is in control of it, and he will be victorious over evil.

12.13 The promise of resurrection is reaffirmed to Daniel. He would one day see the fulfillment of his words, but he was not to spend the rest of his life wondering what his visions might mean. Instead, he was to rest in the comfort of God's sovereignty and look forward to the time when he would rise to receive and share eternal life with God. God does not reveal everything to us in this life. We must be content with the partial picture until he wants us to see more. He will tell us all we need to know.

12.13 Daniel stands tall in the gallery of God's remarkable servants. Born of royal heritage, yet taken into captivity when only a teenager, Daniel determined to remain faithful to God in the land of his captivity. Even at great personal cost, Daniel spent his entire lifetime advising his captors with unusual wisdom. God chose him as his servant to record some of the events of the captivity and some significant events concerning the future. As an old man, having been faithful to God throughout his years, Daniel is assured by God that he will be resurrected from the dead and receive his portion in God's eternal kingdom. Faithfulness to God has a rich reward, not necessarily in this life, but most certainly in the life to come.

THE MESSAGE OF THE MINOR PROPHETS

The twelve books from Hosea to Malachi are called the minor prophets. They are called "minor" because they are shorter in length than Isaiah, Jeremiah, and Ezekiel—not because they have any less value or authority. Their prophecies were directed to the Northern Kingdom of Israel, the Southern Kingdom of Judah, as well as other surrounding nations. The minor prophets made a major contribution to the Bible.

Prophet	*Contemporary Kings*	*Historical Setting*	*Main Message*
Hosea	Jeroboam II, Zechariah, Shallum, Menahem, Pekahiah, Pekah, Hoshea	2 Kings 14.23—18.23	The people of Israel had sinned against God. Judgment was sure to come for living in total disregard for God and fellow man.
Joel	Joash (Jehoash), Amaziah, Uzziah (Azariah)	2 Kings 11.1—15.7; 2 Chronicles 22.11—26.23	A plague of locusts had come to discipline the nation of Judah. Joel called the people to turn back to God before an even greater judgment occurred.
Amos	Uzziah (Azariah), Jeroboam II	2 Kings 14.23—15.7	Amos spoke against those who exploited or ignored the needy.
Obadiah	possibly Jehoram (Joram)	2 Kings 8.16-24; 2 Chronicles 21.1-20	God would judge Edom for its evil actions toward God's people.
Jonah	Jeroboam II	2 Kings 14.23-29	Jonah was called by God to warn those living in Nineveh that they would receive judgment if they did not repent.
Micah	Jotham, Ahaz, Hezekiah	2 Kings 15.1—20.21; 2 Chronicles 27.1—32.33	Micah predicted the fall of both Israel and Judah. This was to warn of judgment and to offer pardon to all who repent. Israel's destruction was swift, but Hezekiah's good reign helped postpone Judah's punishment.
Nahum	Manasseh	2 Kings 21.1-18; 2 Chronicles 33.1-20	The nation of Assyria made Judah one of its vassal states. Nahum predicted that Assyria would soon tumble.
Habakkuk	Jehoiakim	2 Kings 23.36—24.7; 2 Chronicles 36.5-8	Habakkuk couldn't understand why God seemed to do nothing about the wickedness in society. He soon learned that God is still in control of the world despite the apparent triumph of evil.
Zephaniah	Josiah	2 Kings 22.1—23.30; 2 Chronicles 34.1—36.1	A day will come when God, as Judge, will severly punish all nations. But after judgment, he will show mercy to the faithful.
Haggai	Darius	Ezra 5.1—6.22	The people returned to Jerusalem to begin rebuilding the temple, but the work was halted. Haggai's message encouraged the people to finish the work.
Zechariah	Darius	Ezra 5.1—6.22	Zechariah encouraged the people to finish building the temple. He told them of a future king who would one day establish an eternal kingdom.
Malachi	Artaxerxes I	Nehemiah 13.1-31	The people had become complacent in their worship of God. They would soon be punished for their sin, but those who repented would receive God's blessing.

HOSEA

Jeroboam II becomes King of Israel 793 B.C.

Amos becomes a prophet 760

VITAL STATISTICS

PURPOSE:
To illustrate God's love for his sinful people

AUTHOR:
Hosea, son of Beeri ("Hosea" means "salvation")

TO WHOM WRITTEN:
Israel (the northern kingdom) and God's people everywhere

DATE WRITTEN:
Approximately 715 B.C., recording events from about 753–715 B.C.

SETTING:
Hosea began his ministry during the end of the prosperous but morally declining reign of Jeroboam II of Israel (the upper classes were doing well, but they were oppressing the poor). He prophesied until shortly after the fall of Samaria in 722 B.C.

KEY VERSE:
"The Lord said to me again, 'Go, love a woman who has a lover and is an adulteress, just as the Lord loves the people of Israel, though they turn to other gods and love raisin cakes' " (3.1).

KEY PEOPLE:
Hosea, Gomer, their children

KEY PLACES:
The northern kingdom (Israel), Samaria, Ephraim

SPECIAL FEATURES:
Hosea employs many images from daily life—God is depicted as husband, father, lion, leopard, she-bear, dew, rain, moth, and others; Israel is pictured as wife, sick person, grapevine, grapes, early fig, olive tree, woman in labor, oven, morning mist, chaff, and smoke, to name a few.

GROOMSMEN stand at attention as the music swells and the bride begins her long walk down the aisle, arm in arm with her father. The smiling, but nervous, husband-to-be follows every step, his eyes brimming with love. Happy tears are shed, vows stated, and families merged. A wedding is a joyous celebration of love. It is the holy mystery of two becoming one, of beginning life together, and of commitment. Marriage is ordained by God and illustrates his relationship with his people. There is perhaps no greater tragedy, therefore, than the violation of those sacred vows.

God told Hosea to find a wife, and told him ahead of time that she would be unfaithful to him. Although she would bear many children, some of these offspring would be fathered by others. In obedience to God, Hosea married Gomer. His relationship with her, her adultery, and their children became living, prophetic examples to Israel.

The book of Hosea is a love story—real, tragic, and true. Transcending the tale of young man and wife, it tells of God's love for his people and the response of his "bride." A covenant had been made and God had been faithful. His love was steadfast and his commitment unbroken. But Israel, like Gomer, was adulterous and unfaithful, spurning God's love and turning instead to false gods. After warning of judgment, God reaffirms his love and offers reconciliation. His love and mercy overflow, but justice will be served.

The book begins with God's marriage instructions to Hosea. After Hosea's marriage, children are born, and each given a name signifying a divine message (chapter 1). Then, as predicted, Gomer leaves Hosea to pursue her lusts (chapter 2). But Hosea (whose name means "salvation") finds her, redeems her, and brings her home again, fully reconciled (chapter 3). Images of God's love, judgment, grace, and mercy are woven into their relationship. Next, God outlines his case against the people of Israel—their sins will ultimately cause their destruction (chapters 4, 6, 7, 12), and will rouse his anger, resulting in punishment (chapters 5, 8—10, 12, 13). But even in the midst of Israel's immorality, God is merciful and offers hope, expressing his infinite love for his people (chapter 11) and the fact that their repentance will bring about blessing (chapter 14).

The book of Hosea dramatically portrays our God's constant and persistent love. As you read this book, watch the prophet submit himself willingly to his Lord's direction; grieve with him over the unfaithfulness of his wife and his people; and hear the clear warning of judgment. Then reaffirm your commitment to being God's person, faithful in your love and true to your vows.

Hosea becomes a prophet; Zechariah is killed 753	King Shallum of Israel is killed 752	Tiglath-pileser III invades Israel 743	Micah becomes a prophet to Judah 742	Isaiah becomes a prophet to Judah 740	Israel (northern kingdom) falls 722	Hosea's ministry ends 715

THE BLUEPRINT

A. HOSEA'S WAYWARD WIFE (1.1—3.5)	Hosea was commanded by God to marry a woman who was faithless in marriage and would cause him many heartaches. Just as Gomer lost interest in Hosea and ran after other lovers, we too can easily lose appreciation for our special relationship with God and pursue dreams and goals that do not include him. When we compromise our Christian lifestyles and adopt the ways of the world, we are being faithless.
B. GOD'S WAYWARD PEOPLE (4.1—14.9) 1. Israel's sinfulness 2. Israel's punishment 3. God's love for Israel	God wanted the people in the northern kingdom to turn from their sin and return to worshiping him alone, but they persisted in their wickedness. Throughout the book, Israel is described as ignorant of God, with no desire to please him. Israel did not understand God at all, just as Gomer did not understand Hosea. Like a loving husband or patient father, God wants people to know him and to turn to him daily.

MEGATHEMES

THEME	EXPLANATION	IMPORTANCE
The nation's sin	Just as Hosea's wife, Gomer, was unfaithful to him, so the nation of Israel had been unfaithful to God. Israel's idolatry was like adultery. They sought "illicit" relationships with Assyria and Egypt to give them military might, and they mixed Baal worship with the worship of God.	Like Gomer, we can chase after other loves—love of power, pleasure, money, or recognition. The temptations in this world can be very seductive. Are we loyal to God, remaining completely faithful, or have other loves taken his rightful place?
God's judgment	Hosea was solemnly warning Judah against following Israel's example. Because Judah broke the covenant, turned away from God, and forgot her maker, she experienced a devastating invasion and exile. Sin has terrible consequences.	Disaster surely follows ingratitude toward God and rebellion. The Lord is our only true refuge. If we harden our hearts against him, there is no safety or security anywhere else. We cannot escape God's judgment.
God's love	Just as Hosea went after his unfaithful wife to bring her back, so the Lord pursues us with his love. His love is tender, loyal, unchanging, and undying. No matter what, God still loves us.	Have you forgotten God and become disloyal to him? Don't let prosperity diminish your love for him or let success blind you to your need for his love.
Restoration	Although God will discipline his people for sin, he encourages and restores those who have repented. True repentance opens the way to a new beginning. God forgives and restores.	There is still hope for those who turn back to God. No loyalty, achievement, or honor can be compared to loving him. Turn to the Lord while the offer is still good. No matter how far you have strayed, God is willing to bring you back.

A. HOSEA'S WAYWARD WIFE (1.1–3.5)

Hosea highlights the parallels between his relationship with Gomer and God's relationship with the nation of Israel. Although Israel made a covenant with the one true God, she sought after other false gods. In the same way, Hosea married Gomer, knowing ahead of time that she would leave him. Hosea tenderly dealt with his wife in spite of her sin. And God was merciful toward the people of Israel despite their sins. God has not changed, he is still merciful and forgiving.

Hosea's wife and children

1 The word of the LORD that came to Hosea son of Beeri, in the days of Kings
Uzziah, Jotham, Ahaz, and Hezekiah of Judah, and in the days of King Jeroboam son of Joash of Israel.
2 When the LORD first spoke through Hosea, the LORD said to Hosea, "Go, take
for yourself a wife of whoredom and have children of whoredom, for the land commits great whoredom by forsaking the LORD." 3 So he went and took Gomer daughter of Diblaim, and she conceived and bore him a son.
4 And the LORD said to him, "Name him Jezreel;[a] for in a little while I will
punish the house of Jehu for the blood of Jezreel, and I will put an end to the kingdom of the house of Israel. 5 On that day I will break the bow of Israel in the valley
of Jezreel."
6 She conceived again and bore a daughter. Then the LORD said to him, "Name
her Lo-ruhamah,[b] for I will no longer have pity on the house of Israel or forgive
them. 7 But I will have pity on the house of Judah, and I will save them by the LORD
their God; I will not save them by bow, or by sword, or by war, or by horses, or by
horsemen."
8 When she had weaned Lo-ruhamah, she conceived and bore a son. 9 Then the

1.1 1 Kgs 13.1-34 2 Kgs 15.32-38 16.1; 18.1 2 Chron 10.12-16 26.1-23 Mic 1.1
1.2 Hos 3.1
1.4 Josh 17.16 Judg 6.33 2 Kgs 9.14-36 10.1-28 2 Chron 22.8,9
1.7 Ps 44.3-7 Isa 30.18

[a] That is *God sows* [b] That is *Not pitied*

1.1 Hosea was a prophet assigned to the northern kingdom of Israel. He served from 753 to 715 B.C. Under the reign of Jeroboam II, the northern kingdom had prospered materially but had decayed spiritually. The people were greedy and had adopted the moral behavior and idolatrous religion of the surrounding Canaanites.

Hosea's role was to show how the northern kingdom had been unfaithful to God, their "husband" and provider, and had married themselves to Baal and the gods of Canaan. He warned that unless they repented of their sin and turned back to God they were headed for destruction. Hosea spoke of God's characteristics—his powerful love and fierce justice—and how these should affect their lives and make them return to him. Unfortunately, the people had broken their covenant with God, and they would receive the punishments God had promised (Deuteronomy 27, 28).

1.2, 3 Did God really order his prophet to marry a prostitute? Some who find it difficult to believe God could make such a request view this story as an illustration, not an historial event. Many, however, think the story is historical and give one of these explanations: (1) According to God's law, a priest could not marry a prostitute (Leviticus 21.7). However, Hosea was not a priest. (2) It is possible that Gomer was not a prostitute when Hosea married her, and that God was letting Hosea know that Gomer would later turn to adultery and prostitution. In any case, Hosea knew ahead of time that his wife would be unfaithful and that their married life would become a living object lesson to the adulterous northern kingdom. Hosea's marriage to an unfaithful woman would illustrate God's relationship to the unfaithful nation of Israel.

1.2, 3 It is hard to imagine Hosea's feelings when God told him to marry a woman who would be unfaithful to him. He may not have wanted to do it, but he obeyed. God often required extraordinary obedience from his prophets who were facing extraordinary times. He may ask you to do something difficult and extraordinary too. If he does, how will you respond? Will you obey him, trusting that he who knows everything has a special purpose for his request? Will you be able to accept the fact that the pain involved in obedience may benefit those you serve, and not you personally?

1.4, 5 Elijah had predicted that the family of Israel's King Ahab would be destroyed because of their evil (1 Kings 21.20–22), but Jehu went too far in carrying out God's command (2 Kings 10.1–11). Therefore, Jehu's dynasty would also be punished—in Jezreel, the very place where he carried out the massacre of Ahab's family. God's promise to put an end to Israel as an independent kingdom ("break the bow of Israel") came true 25 years later when the Assyrians conquered the northern kingdom and carried the people into captivity.

1.6, 8 In 1.3, we read that Gomer "bore him [Hosea] a son." In 1.6 and 1.8, we learn that Gomer gave birth to two more children, but there is no indication that Hosea was their natural father, and some translations imply that he was not. Whether or not they were his, the key to this part of the story is found in the names God chose for the children, showing his reaction to Israel's unfaithfulness. His reaction to unfaithfulness is no different today. He desires our complete devotion.

1.7 Israel and Judah had been a united kingdom under David and Solomon. After Solomon's death a civil dispute arose, and the land was divided into a northern kingdom (Israel, whose capital was Samaria) and a southern kingdom (Judah, whose capital was Jerusalem). Although Hosea spoke mainly to the northern kingdom, his concern, like God's, was for the entire nation of Israelites including those from the kingdom of Judah. Just as Hosea prophesied, God helped Judah because Judah had a few kings who honored him. Shortly after defeating Israel, the Assyrian Emperor Sennacherib invaded Judah and beseiged Jerusalem. He was driven off by an angel's powerful and dramatic intervention (Isaiah 36, 37).

1.7 God said he would personally rescue the people of Judah from their enemies with no help from their armies or weapons. Although God asks us to do our part, we should remember that he is not limited to human effort. He often chooses to work through people, but only because it is good for *them.* He can accomplish all his purposes without any help from us if he so chooses. You are very important to God, but on your own you have neither the ability to fulfill nor the power to disrupt God's plans.

1.9 Here God is basically dissolving the covenant (Jeremiah 7.23).

LORD said, "Name him Lo-ammi,[c] for you are not my people and I am not your God."[d]

1.10 Gen 22.17 Isa 63.16; 64.8 Jer 33.22

10[e] Yet the number of the people of Israel shall be like the sand of the sea, which
can be neither measured nor numbered; and in the place where it was said to them,
"You are not my people," it shall be said to them, "Children of the living God."

1.11 Jer 30.21 Hos 3.5

11 The people of Judah and the people of Israel shall be gathered together, and they
shall appoint for themselves one head; and they shall take possession of[f] the land,
for great shall be the day of Jezreel.

2.1 Hos 1.4,5,11

2 [g] Say to your brother,[h] Ammi,[i] and to your sister,[j] Ruhamah.[k]

Punishment and restoration

2 Plead with your mother, plead—
for she is not my wife,
and I am not her husband—
that she put away her whoring from her face,
and her adultery from between her breasts,

2.3 Isa 20.2,3 32.13,14 Jer 14.3 Ezek 16.7,22,29 Hos 13.15 Amos 8.11-13

3 or I will strip her naked
and expose her as in the day she was born,
and make her like a wilderness,
and turn her into a parched land,

[c] That is *Not my people* [d] Heb *I am not yours* [e] Ch 2.1 in Heb [f] Heb *rise up from* [g] Ch 2.3 in Heb [h] Gk: Heb *brothers* [i] That is *My People* [j] Gk Vg: Heb *sisters* [k] That is *Pitied*

HOSEA served as a prophet to Israel (the northern kingdom) from 753–715 B.C.

Climate of the times	Israel's last six kings were especially wicked; they promoted heavy taxes, oppression of the poor, idol worship, and total disregard for God. Israel was subjected to Assyria and was forced to pay tribute, which robbed its few remaining resources.
Main message	The people of Israel had sinned against God, as an adulterous woman sins against her husband. Judgment was sure to come for living in total disregard for God and fellow man. Israel fell to Assyria in 722 B.C.
Importance of message	When we sin we sever our relationship with God, breaking our commitment to him. While all must answer to God for their sins, those who seek God's forgiveness are spared eternal judgment.
Contemporary prophets	Jonah (793–753) Amos (760–750) Micah (742–687) Isaiah (740–681)

The name of the third child conveys the finality of God's judgment. God's warnings recorded in Deuteronomy 28.15–68 were beginning to come true: Israel was abandoning him, and in turn, he was leaving them alone and without his blessings.

1.10 The Old Testament prophetic books sometimes use the word "Israel" to refer to the united kingdom (north and south) and sometimes just to the northern kingdom. In talking about past events, Hosea usually thought of Israel as the northern kingdom with its capital in Samaria. But when Hosea spoke about future events relating to God's promises of restoration, it is difficult to understand his words as applying only to the northern kingdom because the exiled northerners became hopelessly interbred with their conquerors. Thus the promises of return are seen by most as either: (1) conditional—the Israelites chose not to return to God and therefore were not entitled to the blessings included in the promises of restoration, or (2) unconditional—God's promises of restoration are fulfilled in Jesus Christ and therefore the church (the new Israel) receives his blessings.

1.10, 11 Although Israel was unfaithful, God's commitment remained unchanged. This promise of a future reuniting reiterates the covenant made with Moses (Deuteronomy 30.1–10) and foreshadows the prophecies of Jeremiah (Jeremiah 29.11–14; 31.31–40) and Ezekiel (Ezekiel 11.16–21). It is a prediction of the day when all the people of God will be united under Christ. Today all believers everywhere are God's chosen people, a nation of priests (see 1 Peter 2.9).

1.11 Just as the children's names carried significance, so did Jezreel. Before it meant "place of judgment" (1.4); now it will mean "God plants," a sign of a new day and a new relationship between God and Israel.

2.1ff Israel's punishment and restoration are the themes of this chapter. As in a court case, the adulteress is brought to trial and found guilty. But after her punishment, she is joyfully and tenderly restored to God.

2.3 Hosea had supplied his wife with clothing, and God had provided Israel with plenty of rain for their crops. Whether the picture is of Hosea and Gomer or of God and Israel, it warns of the punishment that results from unfaithfulness.

and kill her with thirst.
4 Upon her children also I will have no pity,
because they are children of whoredom.
5 For their mother has played the whore;
she who conceived them has acted shamefully.
For she said, "I will go after my lovers;
they give me my bread and my water,
my wool and my flax, my oil and my drink."
6 Therefore I will hedge up her[l] way with thorns;
and I will build a wall against her,
so that she cannot find her paths.
7 She shall pursue her lovers,
but not overtake them;
and she shall seek them,
but shall not find them.
Then she shall say, "I will go
and return to my first husband,
for it was better with me then than now."
8 She did not know
that it was I who gave her
the grain, the wine, and the oil,
and who lavished upon her silver
and gold that they used for Baal.
9 Therefore I will take back
my grain in its time,
and my wine in its season;
and I will take away my wool and my flax,
which were to cover her nakedness.
10 Now I will uncover her shame
in the sight of her lovers,
and no one shall rescue her out of my hand.
11 I will put an end to all her mirth,
her festivals, her new moons, her sabbaths,
and all her appointed festivals.
12 I will lay waste her vines and her fig trees,
of which she said,
"These are my pay,
which my lovers have given me."
I will make them a forest,
and the wild animals shall devour them.
13 I will punish her for the festival days of the Baals,

2.5 Jer 2.25 3.1,2 Ezek 23.16,17, 40-45

2.6 Job 19.8

2.7 2 Chron 28.20-22 Jer 2.2; 3.1 Ezek 23.4 Hos 2.5; 5.13

2.8 Hos 2.13; 8.4 13.2

2.10 Ezek 16.37 Hos 2.3

2.11 Jer 7.34; 16.9

2.12 Jer 5.17; 8.13

2.13 Jer 7.9 Ezek 23.40-42 Hos 4.13; 11.2

[l] Gk Syr: Heb *your*

2.5–7 The Israelites were thanking false gods (specifically Baal, the god whom they believed controlled weather and thus farming) for their food, shelter, and clothing, instead of the true God who gave those blessings. Therefore, God would hedge Israel's "way with thorns; and . . . build a wall," by making the rewards of idol worship so disappointing that the people would be persuaded to turn back to God. Despite Israel's unfaithfulness, God was still faithful and merciful. He would continue to seek out his people, even to the point of placing obstacles in their wayward path to turn them back to him.

2.7 Just as Gomer would return to her husband if she thought she would be better off with him, so people often return to God when they find life's struggle too difficult to handle. Returning to God out of desperation is better than rebelling against him, but it is better yet to turn to him out of gratitude for his care.

2.8 Material possessions are success symbols in most societies. Israel was a wealthy nation at this time, and Gomer had acquired gold and silver. But Gomer didn't realize that Hosea gave her all she owned, and Israel did not recognize God as the Giver of blessings. Both Gomer and Israel used their possessions irresponsibly as they ran after other lovers and other gods. How do you use your possessions? Use what God has given you to honor him.

2.12 The Israelites were so immersed in idolatry that they actually believed heathen gods gave them their orchards and vineyards. They had forgotten that the entire land was a gift from God (Deuteronomy 32.49). Today many people give credit to everything but God for their prosperity – luck, hard work, quick thinking, the right contacts. When you succeed, who gets the credit?

2.13 Baal was the most important of the Canaanite gods, but his name came to be used to describe all the local deities worshiped throughout the land occupied by Israel. Unfortunately, Israel did not get rid of the idols and heathen worship centers as they had

when she offered incense to them
and decked herself with her ring and jewelry,
and went after her lovers,
and forgot me, says the LORD.

2.14
Ezek 20.33-38

14 Therefore, I will now allure her,
and bring her into the wilderness,
and speak tenderly to her.

2.15
Josh 7.26
Isa 65.10
Jer 2.1-3
Ezek 16.8,22

15 From there I will give her her vineyards,
and make the Valley of Achor a door of hope.
There she shall respond as in the days of her youth,
as at the time when she came out of the land of Egypt.

2.16
Isa 54.5
Hos 2.7
2.18
Lev 26.5,6
Isa 2.4
Jer 33.16
Ezek 34.25
39.1-10
Mic 4.3

16 On that day, says the LORD, you will call me, "My husband," and no longer will
you call me, "My Baal."[m] 17 For I will remove the names of the Baals from her
mouth, and they shall be mentioned by name no more. 18 I will make for you[n] a
covenant on that day with the wild animals, the birds of the air, and the creeping
things of the ground; and I will abolish[o] the bow, the sword, and war from the land;
and I will make you lie down in safety. 19 And I will take you for my wife forever;
I will take you for my wife in righteousness and in justice, in steadfast love, and in

[m] That is, *"My master"* [n] Heb *them* [o] Heb *break*

SPIRITUAL UNFAITHFULNESS

Spiritual adultery and physical adultery are alike in many ways and both are dangerous. God was disappointed with his people because they had committed spiritual adultery against him, as Gomer had committed physical adultery against Hosea.

Parallels	*The danger*
Both spiritual and physical adultery are against God's law.	When we break God's law in full awareness of what we're doing, our hearts become hardened to the sin and our relationship with God is broken.
Both spiritual and physical adultery begin with disappointment and dissatisfaction—either real or imagined—with an already existing relationship.	The feeling that God disappoints can lead you away from him. Feelings of disappointment and dissatisfaction are normal and, when endured, will pass.
Both spiritual and physical adultery begin with diverting affection from one object of devotion to another.	The diverting of our affection is the first step in the blinding process that leads into sin.
Both spiritual and physical adultery involve a process of deterioration; it is not usually an impulsive decision.	The process is dangerous because you don't always realize it is happening until it is too late.
Both spiritual and physical adultery involve the creation of a fantasy about what a new object of love can do for you.	Such fantasy creates unrealistic expectations of what a new relationship can do and only leads to disappointment in all existing and future relationships.

been commanded. Instead, they tolerated and frequently joined Baal worshipers, often through the influence of corrupt kings. One Israelite king noted for his Baal worship was Ahab. The prophet Elijah, in a dramatic showdown with Ahab's hired prophets, proved God's power far superior to Baal's (1 Kings 18).

2.14 God would court Israel in the wilderness of captivity, far away from Canaan's tempting idols. In his great mercy, God spoke tenderly to his people who had forsaken him to worship Baal, wanting to restore his relationship with them.

2.14, 15 God was promising: (1) to bring the people to the wilderness where there were no distractions so he could clearly communicate with them, and (2) to change what had been a time of difficulty into a day of hope. The Valley of Achor ("trouble") is the site where Achan sinned by keeping forbidden war treasures (see Joshua 7). He brought great disaster to Joshua's army when they were attempting to conquer the land. God uses even our negative experiences to create opportunities for us to turn back to him. As you face problems and trials, remember that God speaks to you in the desert, not just in times of prosperity.

2.16 Not until Judah's exile would the entire nation begin to come to its senses, give up its idols, and turn back to God; and not until God rules through Jesus the Messiah will the relationship between God and his people be restored. In that day, God will no longer be like a master or owner to them ("Baal"); he will be like a husband. The relationship will be deep and personal, the kind of relationship we can know, though imperfectly, in marriage (Isaiah 54.4–8).

2.19, 20 The time will come when unfaithfulness will be impossible—God will bind us to himself in his perfect righteousness, love, and mercy. Betrothal in Hosea's time was more than a simple agreement to marry. It was a binding engagement, a deep commitment between two families for a future, permanent relationship. God was promising a fresh new beginning, not just a repair job on a tired old agreement. (See Jeremiah 31.31–34.)

2.19, 20 God's wedding gift to his people, both in Hosea's day and in our own, is his mercy. Through no merit of our own, he forgives us and makes us right with him. There is no way for us by our own efforts to reach God's high standard for moral and spiritual life, but he graciously accepts us, forgives us, and draws us into a relationship with himself. In that relationship we have personal and intimate communion with him.

mercy. 20 I will take you for my wife in faithfulness; and you shall know the LORD.
21 On that day I will answer, says the LORD,
I will answer the heavens
and they shall answer the earth;
22 and the earth shall answer the grain, the wine, and the oil,
and they shall answer Jezreel;[p]
23 and I will sow him[q] for myself in the land.
And I will have pity on Lo-ruhamah,[r]
and I will say to Lo-ammi,[s] "You are my people";
and he shall say, "You are my God."

2.20 Jer 31.34 Hos 6.6; 13.4
2.21 Isa 55.10 Jer 31.27 Zech 8.12
2.23 Hos 1.6,9

Hosea is reconciled to his wife

3 The LORD said to me again, "Go, love a woman who has a lover and is an
adulteress, just as the LORD loves the people of Israel, though they turn to other
gods and love raisin cakes." 2 So I bought her for fifteen shekels of silver and a
homer of barley and a measure of wine.[t] 3 And I said to her, "You must remain as
mine for many days; you shall not play the whore, you shall not have intercourse
with a man, nor I with you." 4 For the Israelites shall remain many days without
king or prince, without sacrifice or pillar, without ephod or teraphim. 5 Afterward
the Israelites shall return and seek the LORD their God, and David their king; they
shall come in awe to the LORD and to his goodness in the latter days.

3.1 2 Sam 6.19 Song 2.5
3.2 Ruth 4.10
3.4 Judg 17.5 18.17-24
3.5 Isa 55.3,4 Jer 50.4,5 Amos 9.11 Acts 15.16-18

B. GOD'S WAYWARD PEOPLE (4.1—14.9)

The rest of the book deals with Israel's sin and her impending judgment. Hosea points out the moral and spiritual decay of the nation. He describes the punishment awaiting them and pleads with them to return to God. Although judgment and condemnation of sin are prevalent in the book, a strand of love and restoration runs throughout. Even in the midst of judgment, God is merciful and will restore those who repent and turn to him.

1. Israel's sinfulness

God charges Israel with sins

4 Hear the word of the LORD, O people of Israel;
for the LORD has an indictment against the inhabitants of the land.
There is no faithfulness or loyalty,

4.1 Isa 50.4 Jer 7.28 Mic 6.2

[p] That is *God sows* [q] Cn: Heb *her* [r] That is *Not pitied* [s] That is *Not my people* [t] Gk: Heb *a homer of barley and a lethech of barley*

2.20–23 Although Israel was unfaithful and was condemned for its idolatry, God—unchanging in his love—would offer forgiveness and a renewed relationship with himself, one even better than any it had previously experienced. Why? Because he loved Israel with an everlasting love. Have you been unfaithful to God? God loves you still. If you turn back to him, he will forgive you. He wants you to know him as you never have before.

3.1 God is asking Hosea to do something almost unthinkable—to buy back his adulterous, unrepentant wife and continue to love her! When those who knew about Gomer's adultery heard Hosea say that God loved idolatrous Israel as much as he loved Gomer, they must have been amazed. The people had heard God's words many times, but they felt the impact of those words when they saw them acted out in Hosea's troubled home life.

3.1 Here Hosea may be talking about the entire nation—Judah and Israel. This short chapter pictures the nation's exile and return. Israel would experience a time of purification in a foreign land, but God would still love the people and would be willing to accept them back. He commanded Hosea to show the same forgiving spirit to Gomer. Although Hosea had good reason to divorce her, he was told to buy her back and love her.

3.2 Gomer apparently was on her own for a while. Needing to support herself, she must have either sold herself into slavery or become the mistress of another man. In either case, Hosea had to pay to get her back—although the required amount was pitifully small. Gomer was no longer worth much to anyone except Hosea, but he loved her just as God loved Israel. No matter how low we sink, God is willing to "buy us back"—to redeem us—and to lift us up again.

3.3 After this, Gomer is no longer mentioned by Hosea. This is explained in 3.4. Gomer's absence and isolation show how God will deal with the northern kingdom (5.6, 15). It is dangerous to rebel against God. If he were ever to withdraw his love and mercy, we would be without hope.

3.4 God would separate the Israelites from their treasured idolatrous practices. Pillars were used in idol worship; the ephod is not the official vest of the priest, but a cultic garment used to tell the future; the teraphim were household gods that were strictly forbidden to God's people.

3.4, 5 The northern kingdom rebelled against David's dynasty and took Jeroboam as their king (1 Kings 12, 13). Their rebellion was both political and religious. At that time, they reverted back to the worship of golden idols. "David their king" refers to the time of Messiah's rule when all people will stand before him in humility and submission. Those who won't accept his blessings now will face his power and judgment later. How much better to love and follow him now than face his angry judgment later.

4.1ff In this chapter, God brings a charge of disobedience against Israel. The religious leaders had failed to turn the people to God, and ritual prostitution had replaced right worship. The nation had declined spiritually and morally, breaking the laws God had given them. The people found it easy to condemn Hosea's wife for her

and no knowledge of God in the land.
2 Swearing, lying, and murder,
and stealing and adultery break out;
bloodshed follows bloodshed.
4.3 Isa 24.4; 33.9
3 Therefore the land mourns,
and all who live in it languish;
together with the wild animals
and the birds of the air,
even the fish of the sea are perishing.

4.4 Deut 17.12 Ezek 3.26 Amos 5.10,13
4 Yet let no one contend,
and let none accuse,
for with you is my contention, O priest.[u]
4.5 Ezek 14.3,7 Hos 5.5
5 You shall stumble by day;
the prophet also shall stumble with you by night,
and I will destroy your mother.
4.6 Hos 4.14 Zech 11.8,9, 15-17
6 My people are destroyed for lack of knowledge;
because you have rejected knowledge,
I reject you from being a priest to me.
And since you have forgotten the law of your God,
I also will forget your children.

4.7 Hos 2.16; 10.1 13.6 Rom 1.21-23
7 The more they increased,
the more they sinned against me;
they changed[v] their glory into shame.
8 They feed on the sin of my people;
they are greedy for their iniquity.
4.9 Isa 24.2 Jer 5.31 Mt 15.13,14
9 And it shall be like people, like priest;
I will punish them for their ways,
and repay them for their deeds.

[u] Cn: Meaning of Heb uncertain [v] Ancient Heb tradition: MT *I will change*

adultery. They were not so quick to see that *they* were faithless to God.

4.1–3 God explains the reasons for Israel's suffering. Their lawless behavior had brought the twin judgments of increased violence and ecological crisis. There is not always a direct cause-and-effect relationship between our actions and the problems we face. Nevertheless, when we are surrounded with difficulties, we should seriously ask, "Have I done anything sinful or irresponsible that has caused my suffering?" If we discover we are at fault, even partially, we must change our ways before God will help us.

4.2 This verse may allude to the assassinations of kings during Hosea's lifetime. Shallum killed Zechariah (the king, not the prophet) and took the throne. Then Menahem killed Shallum and destroyed an entire city because it refused to accept him as king (2 Kings 15.8–16). God pointed out that even murder was being taken casually in Israel.

4.4 We often blame others if we fear punishment for wrongdoing. Hosea warned the priests not to blame anyone else; the nation's sins were largely their fault. Israel's priests pointed out the people's sins, but God would not allow them to overlook their own irresponsible actions. Instead of instructing the nation in religion and morality, they had led the way toward idolatry and immorality. Their failure to lead the people in God's ways placed most of the blame for Israel's destruction on them. Knowing that God will not allow us to blame others for our mistakes should cause us to admit our own sins. We are responsible for our own sinful actions. Beware of the tendency to blame others because it can keep you from feeling the need to repent.

4.4–10 Hosea leveled his charges against the religious leaders. Who were these religious leaders? When Jeroboam I rebelled against Solomon's son Rehoboam and set up a rival kingdom in the north, he also set up his own religious system (see 1 Kings 12.25–33). In violation of God's law, he made two gold calf-idols and told the people to worship them. He also appointed his own priests, who were not descendants of Aaron. At first the residents of the northern kingdom continued to worship God, even though they were doing it in the wrong way; but very soon they also began to worship Canaanite gods. Before long they substituted Baal for God and no longer worshiped God at all. It is not surprising that Jeroboam's false priests were unable to preserve the true worship of God.

4.6–9 God accused the religious leaders of keeping the people from knowing him. They were supposed to be spiritual leaders, but they became leaders in wrongdoing. The people may have said to one another, "It must be OK if the priests do it." Spiritual leadership is a heavy responsibility. Whether you teach a Sunday school class, hold a church office, or lead a Bible study, don't take your leadership responsibilities lightly. Be a leader who leads others to God.

4.8 The priests rejoiced in the people's sins. Every time a person brought a sin offering, the priest received a portion of it. The more the people sinned, the more the priests received. Since they couldn't eat all of the offerings themselves, they sold some and gave some to their relatives. The priests profited from the continuation of sin; it gave them power and position in the community. So instead of trying to lead the people out of sin, they encouraged it to increase their profits.

10 They shall eat, but not be satisfied;
they shall play the whore, but not multiply;
because they have forsaken the LORD
to devote themselves to 11 whoredom.

Wine and new wine
take away the understanding.
12 My people consult a piece of wood,
and their divining rod gives them oracles.
For a spirit of whoredom has led them astray,
and they have played the whore, forsaking their God.
13 They sacrifice on the tops of the mountains,
and make offerings upon the hills,
under oak, poplar, and terebinth,
because their shade is good.

Therefore your daughters play the whore,
and your daughters-in-law commit adultery.
14 I will not punish your daughters when they play the whore,
nor your daughters-in-law when they commit adultery;
for the men themselves go aside with whores,
and sacrifice with temple prostitutes;
thus a people without understanding comes to ruin.

15 Though you play the whore, O Israel,
do not let Judah become guilty.
Do not enter into Gilgal,
or go up to Beth-aven,
and do not swear, "As the LORD lives."
16 Like a stubborn heifer,
Israel is stubborn;
can the LORD now feed them
like a lamb in a broad pasture?

17 Ephraim is joined to idols—
let him alone.
18 When their drinking is ended, they indulge in sexual orgies;
they love lewdness more than their glory.[w]
19 A wind has wrapped them[x] in its wings,
and they shall be ashamed because of their altars.[y]

[w] Cn Compare Gk: Meaning of Heb uncertain [x] Heb *her* [y] Gk Syr: Heb *sacrifices*

4.11
Isa 5.12; 28.7

4.12
1 Chron 10.13
Isa 19.3
Ezek 21.21

4.13
Jer 2.20; 3.6
Ezek 6.13
Hos 2.13; 11.2

4.14
Deut 23.17

4.16
Ps 23.2,3; 78.8
Isa 5.17; 7.25

4.19
Hos 12.1; 13.15
Zech 5.9-11

4.10 The chief Canaanite gods, Baal and Asherah, represented the power of fertility and sexual reproduction. Not surprisingly, their worship included rituals with vile sexual practices. Male worshipers had sex with female temple prostitutes, or priestesses, and young women wishing to bear children had sex with male priests. But their efforts to increase fertility would not succeed.

4.12–14 This section is an attack on the Baal cult. The stick or divining rod was a way of attempting to tell the future. By divorcing themselves from God's authoritative religion centered in Jerusalem, inhabitants of the northern kingdom had effectively cut themselves off from his Word and from his way of forgiveness. The drive to be free and independent from all restrictions can move us completely out of God's will.

4.15 God sent a warning to the southern kingdom of Judah and its priests not to become like Israel. Israel's priests who remained in the north had forgotten their spiritual heritage and sold out to Baal. They now promoted idol worship and ritual prostitution. Israel would not escape punishment, but Judah could if it refused to follow Israel's example.

4.17 Ephraim is another name for Israel, the northern kingdom, because Ephraim was the most powerful of the ten tribes in the north. In the same way, the southern kingdom was called Judah after its most powerful tribe.

4.19 The wind that would sweep Israel away refers to the Assyrian invasion that destroyed the nation about 20 years later.

God's judgment against Israel

5 Hear this, O priests!
Give heed, O house of Israel!
Listen, O house of the king!
For the judgment pertains to you;
for you have been a snare at Mizpah,
and a net spread upon Tabor,
2 and a pit dug deep in Shittim;[z]
but I will punish all of them.

5.3 Amos 5.12 Heb 4.13
3 I know Ephraim,
and Israel is not hidden from me;
for now, O Ephraim, you have played the whore;
Israel is defiled.
5.4 Hos 4.6,14
4 Their deeds do not permit them
to return to their God.
For the spirit of whoredom is within them,
and they do not know the LORD.

5.5 2 Kgs 17.19,20 Ezek 23.31-35
5 Israel's pride testifies against him;
Ephraim[a] stumbles in his guilt;
Judah also stumbles with them.
5.6 Ezek 8.6
6 With their flocks and herds they shall go
to seek the LORD,
but they will not find him;
he has withdrawn from them.
5.7 Hos 2.4
7 They have dealt faithlessly with the LORD;
for they have borne illegitimate children.
Now the new moon shall devour them along with their fields.

8 Blow the horn in Gibeah,
the trumpet in Ramah.
Sound the alarm at Beth-aven;
look behind you, Benjamin!
5.9 Isa 28.1-4; 37.3 Hos 9.11-17 Amos 3.14,15
9 Ephraim shall become a desolation
in the day of punishment;
among the tribes of Israel
I declare what is sure.
5.10 Deut 27.17 Ps 32.6; 93.3,4 Prov 22.28 Ezek 7.8
10 The princes of Judah have become
like those who remove the landmark;
on them I will pour out
my wrath like water.
11 Ephraim is oppressed, crushed in judgment,
5.12 Ps 39.11 Isa 51.8
because he was determined to go after vanity.[b]
12 Therefore I am like maggots to Ephraim,

[z] Cn: Meaning of Heb uncertain [a] Heb *Israel and Ephraim* [b] Gk: Meaning of Heb uncertain

5.1, 2 Mizpah and Tabor were sites used in the false worship of Baal. The leaders had even encouraged the people to sin at these places. With both civil and religious leaders hopelessly corrupt, the people of Israel did not have much of a chance. They looked to their leaders for guidance, and in God's plan they should have found it. Today we can often choose our own leaders, but we still need to be aware of whether they are taking us toward or away from God. God held the people responsible for what they did. Similarly, he holds us responsible for our actions and choices.

5.4 Persistent sin hardens a person's heart and makes it difficult to repent. Deliberately choosing to disobey God can sear the conscience; each sin makes the next one easier to commit. Don't allow sin to wear down a hard path deep within you. Steer as far away from sinful practices as possible.

5.8 Gibeah and Ramah were Israelite cities near Jerusalem. Hosea prophesies that these cities will sound the alarm of the coming judgment.

5.10 Those who "remove the landmark" are the lowest sort of thieves. The princes of Judah were like those who cheat people by moving the boundary marker on their land (see Deuteronomy 19.14).

and like rottenness to the house of Judah.
13 When Ephraim saw his sickness,
and Judah his wound,
then Ephraim went to Assyria,
and sent to the great king.[c]
But he is not able to cure you
or heal your wound.
14 For I will be like a lion to Ephraim,
and like a young lion to the house of Judah.
I myself will tear and go away;
I will carry off, and no one shall rescue.
15 I will return again to my place
until they acknowledge their guilt and seek my face.
In their distress they will beg my favor:
6 "Come, let us return to the LORD;
for it is he who has torn, and he will heal us;
he has struck down, and he will bind us up.
2 After two days he will revive us;
on the third day he will raise us up,
that we may live before him.
3 Let us know, let us press on to know the LORD;
his appearing is as sure as the dawn;
he will come to us like the showers,
like the spring rains that water the earth."

5.14 Ps 7.2 Hos 13.7

6.1 Isa 30.26; 61.1 Zeph 2.1-3

6.3 Isa 2.3; 5.6 Hos 14.5 Mic 4.2

2. Israel's punishment

Israel is like a crooked bow

4 What shall I do with you, O Ephraim?
What shall I do with you, O Judah?
Your love is like a morning cloud,
like the dew that goes away early.
5 Therefore I have hewn them by the prophets,
I have killed them by the words of my mouth,
and my[d] judgment goes forth as the light.
6 For I desire steadfast love and not sacrifice,
the knowledge of God rather than burnt offerings.

7 But at[e] Adam they transgressed the covenant;

6.4 Ps 78.34-37 Hos 13.3

6.5 Isa 49.2 Heb 4.12

6.6 Mt 9.13; 12.7

[c] Cn: Heb *to a king who will contend* [d] Gk Syr: Heb *your* [e] Cn: Heb *like*

5.13 During the reigns of Menahem and Hoshea, Israel turned to Assyria for help (2 Kings 15.19, 20; 17.3, 4). But even the great world powers of that time could not help Israel, for God himself had determined to judge the nation. If we neglect God's call to repentance, how can we escape? (See Hebrews 2.3.)

6.1–3 This is presumption, not genuine repentance. The people did not understand the depth of their sins. They did not turn from idols, pledge to change, or regret their sins. They thought God's wrath would last only a few days; little did they know that their nation would soon be taken into exile. Israel was interested in God only for the material benefits he provided; they did not value the eternal benefits that come from worshiping him. Before judging them, however, consider your attitude. What do you hope to gain from your religion? Do you "repent" easily, without seriously considering what changes need to take place in your life?

6.3 God had shown his faithfulness to Israel many times. They knew that if they sought to know him and his ways, he would reveal himself to them, and they were right (see 2.20 for a promise of God's faithfulness). The problem was that they were so deep in sin, they did not really want to know him. They wanted the benefits, but not his discipline or guidance.

6.4 God answered his people, pointing out that their profession of loyalty, like dew, easily evaporated and had no substance. Many find it easy and comfortable to maintain the appearance of being committed, but is their loyalty deep and sincere? If you profess loyalty to God, back it up with your words and actions.

6.6 Religious rituals can help people understand God and nourish their relationship with him. That is why God instituted circumcision and the sacrificial system in the Old Testament and baptism and the Lord's Supper in the New. But a religious ritual is helpful only if it is carried out with an attitude of love and obedience to God. If one's heart is far from God, ritual becomes empty mockery. God didn't want the Israelites' rituals; he wanted their hearts. Why do you worship? What is the motive behind your "offerings" and "sacrifices"?

6.7 One of Hosea's key themes is that Israel had broken the treaty, or covenant, they had made with God at Mount Sinai (Exodus 19, 20). God wanted to make Israel a light to all the nations, and if they obeyed him and proclaimed him to the world, he would give them special blessings. If they broke the covenant, however, they would

there they dealt faithlessly with me.
8 Gilead is a city of evildoers,
tracked with blood.
9 As robbers lie in wait[f] for someone,
so the priests are banded together;[g]
they murder on the road to Shechem,
they commit a monstrous crime.
10 In the house of Israel I have seen a horrible thing;
Ephraim's whoredom is there, Israel is defiled.

11 For you also, O Judah, a harvest is appointed.

When I would restore the fortunes of my people,
7 1 when I would heal Israel,
the corruption of Ephraim is revealed,
and the wicked deeds of Samaria;
for they deal falsely,
the thief breaks in,
and the bandits raid outside.
2 But they do not consider
that I remember all their wickedness.
Now their deeds surround them,
they are before my face.
3 By their wickedness they make the king glad,
and the officials by their treachery.
4 They are all adulterers;
they are like a heated oven,
whose baker does not need to stir the fire,
from the kneading of the dough until it is leavened.
5 On the day of our king the officials
became sick with the heat of wine;

6.9 Jer 7.9 Hos 4.2

6.11 Jer 51.33 Joel 3.13

7.1 Jer 51.9 Ezek 24.13 Hos 7.13

7.3 Hos 7.5 Mic 7.3

7.4 Jer 9.2; 23.10

7.5 Prov 20.1 Isa 5.11,22,23 28.1

[f] Cn: Meaning of Heb uncertain [g] Syr: Heb *are a company*

OBEDIENCE VS. SACRIFICES

God says many times that he doesn't want our gifts and sacrifices when we give them out of ritual or hypocrisy. God wants us first to love and obey him.

Reference	
1 Samuel 15.22, 23	Obedience is far better than sacrifice.
Psalm 40.6–8	God doesn't want burnt animals; he wants our lifelong service.
Psalm 51.16–19	God isn't interested in penance; he wants a broken and contrite heart.
Jeremiah 7.21–23	It isn't offerings God wants; he desires our obedience and promises that he will be our God and we shall be his people.
Hosea 6.6	God doesn't want sacrifices, he wants love; he doesn't want offerings, he wants us to know him.
Amos 5.21–24	God hates pretense and hypocrisy; he wants to see a flood of justice.
Micah 6.6–8	God is not satisfied with sacrifices; he wants us to be fair and just and merciful, and to walk humbly with him.
Matthew 9.13	God doesn't want gifts; he wants us to be merciful.

suffer severe penalties, as they should have known (see Deuteronomy 28.15–68). Sadly, the people broke the treaty and proved themselves unfaithful to God. How about us? Have we also broken faith with God? What about our forgotten promises to serve him?

6.8, 9 Gilead was once a sacred place, but now it was corrupt. Shechem and Gilead both were once cities of refuge designated by Joshua (Joshua 20.1, 2, 7, 8). Now they were associated with murder and crime.

6.11 So that Judah would not become proud as they saw the northern kingdom's destruction, Hosea interjected a solemn warning. God's temple was in Judah (Jerusalem), and the people thought that what happened in Israel could never happen to them. But when they had become utterly corrupt, they too were led off into captivity (see 2 Kings 25).

7.1, 2 God sees and knows everything. Like Israel we often forget this. Thoughts like "No one will ever know," or "No one is watching," may tempt us to try to get away with sin. If you are facing difficult temptations, you will be less likely to give in if you remind yourself that God is watching. When faced with the opportunity to sin, remember that God sees everything.

he stretched out his hand with mockers.
6 For they are kindled[h] like an oven, their heart burns within them;
all night their anger smolders;
in the morning it blazes like a flaming fire.
7 All of them are hot as an oven,
and they devour their rulers.
All their kings have fallen;
none of them calls upon me.

8 Ephraim mixes himself with the peoples;
Ephraim is a cake not turned.
9 Foreigners devour his strength,
but he does not know it;
gray hairs are sprinkled upon him,
but he does not know it.
10 Israel's pride testifies against[i] him;
yet they do not return to the LORD their God,
or seek him, for all this.

11 Ephraim has become like a dove,
silly and without sense;
they call upon Egypt, they go to Assyria.
12 As they go, I will cast my net over them;
I will bring them down like birds of the air;
I will discipline them according to the report made to their assembly.[j]
13 Woe to them, for they have strayed from me!
Destruction to them, for they have rebelled against me!
I would redeem them,
but they speak lies against me.

14 They do not cry to me from the heart,
but they wail upon their beds;
they gash themselves for grain and wine;
they rebel against me.
15 It was I who trained and strengthened their arms,
yet they plot evil against me.
16 They turn to that which does not profit;[k]
they have become like a defective bow;
their officials shall fall by the sword

7.6 Ps 21.9 Dan 3.6
7.9 Isa 57.1-11
7.12 Job 19.6 Ezek 12.13
7.15 Ps 2.1 Nah 1.9
7.16 Hos 8.13; 9.3,6 Lk 8.13

h Gk Syr: Heb *brought near* i Or *humbles* j Meaning of Heb uncertain k Cn: Meaning of Heb uncertain

7.7 "Hot as an oven" refers to the lust for power and intrigue burning in these leaders' hearts. Three Israelite kings were assassinated during Hosea's lifetime—Zechariah, Shallum, and Pekahiah (2 Kings 15.8–26). Their foreign relations and domestic lives were ruined because they ignored God and his Word.

7.8 Israel had intermarried with heathen people and had picked up their evil ways. When we spend a lot of time with people, we can easily pick up their attitudes and begin to imitate their actions. When you work, live, or play with unbelievers, beware of the influence they may have on you. Instead of drifting into bad habits, see if you can have a positive influence and point them to God.

7.10 Pride keeps a person from returning to God, because pride acknowledges no need of help from anyone, human or divine. To be proud of an idol means to value an object you have made rather than the One who made you. Pride intensifies all our other sins, because we cannot repent of any of them without first giving up our pride.

7.11 Israel's King Menahem had paid Assyria to support him in power (2 Kings 15.19, 20); King Hoshea turned against Assyria and went to Egypt for help (2 Kings 17.4). Israel's kings went back and forth allying themselves with different nations when they should have allied themselves with God.

7.14 Baal worshipers would often wail and cut themselves as part of their ritual and as a way to get the attention of their god (1 Kings 18.28). This was forbidden for God's people (Deuteronomy 14.1).

7.16 A defective bow is unreliable. Its arrows miss the target. Life without God is as unreliable as a warped bow. Without God's direction, our thoughts are filled with lust, cheating, selfishness, and deceit. As long as we are warped by sin, we will never reach our true potential.

7.16 People look everywhere except to God for happiness and fulfillment, pursuing possessions, activities, and relationships. In reality, only God can truly satisfy the deep longings of the soul. Look first to heaven, to the Most High God. He will meet your spiritual needs, but not all your materialistic wants.

because of the rage of their tongue.
So much for their babbling in the land of Egypt.

Israel will reap the whirlwind

8.1 Jer 48.40 Hab 1.8

8 Set the trumpet to your lips!
One like a vulture[l] is over the house of the LORD,
because they have broken my covenant,
and transgressed my law.
2 Israel cries to me,
"My God, we—Israel—know you!"
3 Israel has spurned the good;
the enemy shall pursue him.

4 They made kings, but not through me;
they set up princes, but without my knowledge.
With their silver and gold they made idols
for their own destruction.

8.5 Jer 13.27

5 Your calf is rejected, O Samaria.
My anger burns against them.
How long will they be incapable of innocence?
6 For it is from Israel,
an artisan made it;
it is not God.
The calf of Samaria
shall be broken to pieces.[m]

8.7 Job 38.1 Nah 1.3 Zech 7.14; 9.14

7 For they sow the wind,
and they shall reap the whirlwind.
The standing grain has no heads,
it shall yield no meal;
if it were to yield,
foreigners would devour it.

8.8 Isa 30.14 Jer 48.38

8 Israel is swallowed up;
now they are among the nations
as a useless vessel.

8.9 Job 39.5-8 Jer 2.24 Ezek 16.33

9 For they have gone up to Assyria,
a wild ass wandering alone;
Ephraim has bargained for lovers.

8.10 Hos 10.10

10 Though they bargain with the nations,
I will now gather them up.
They shall soon writhe
under the burden of kings and princes.

11 When Ephraim multiplied altars to expiate sin,

[l] Meaning of Heb uncertain [m] Or *shall go up in flames*

8.1–4 "One like a vulture is over the house of the Lord" refers to Assyria coming to attack Israel and take the people into captivity (2 Kings 15.28, 29). The people will call to God, but it will be too late because they had stubbornly refused to give up their idols. We, like Israel, often call upon God to ease our pain without wanting him to change our behavior. We, like Israel, may repent after it is too late to avoid the painful consequences of sin.

8.5 Samaria was the capital of the northern kingdom and sometimes it stands for the whole kingdom. Jeroboam I had set up worship of calf-idols at Bethel and Dan and had encouraged the people to worship them (1 Kings 12.25–33). Thus the people were worshiping the image of a created animal rather than the Creator.

8.7 Crop yield is the result of good seed planted in good soil and given the proper proportions of sunlight, moisture, and fertilizer. A single seed can produce multiple fruit in good conditions. Israel, however, had sown its spiritual seed to the wind—it had invested itself in activities without substance. Like the wind that comes and goes, its idolatry and foreign alliances offered no protection. In seeking self-preservation apart from God, it brought about its own destruction. Like a forceful whirlwind, God's judgment would come upon Israel by means of the Assyrians. When we seek security in anything besides God, we expose ourselves to great danger. Without God there is no lasting security.

8.11 To expiate means to remove, cleanse, or forgive. The altars which were supposed to remove sin were actually increasing sin because of their being misused to worship Baal.

they became to him altars for sinning.
12 Though I write for him the multitude of my instructions,
they are regarded as a strange thing.
13 Though they offer choice sacrifices,[n]
though they eat flesh,
the LORD does not accept them.
Now he will remember their iniquity,
and punish their sins;
they shall return to Egypt.
14 Israel has forgotten his Maker,
and built palaces;
and Judah has multiplied fortified cities;
but I will send a fire upon his cities,
and it shall devour his strongholds.

8.13 Hos 7.2; 9.9 1 Cor 4.5

8.14 2 Sam 7.2 1 Kgs 7.1-12 2 Kgs 18.13 Neh 1.1 Jer 17.27 Dan 4.29; 8.2 Hos 2.13; 4.6

Wandering aimlessly without God

9 Do not rejoice, O Israel!
Do not exult[o] as other nations do;
for you have played the whore, departing from your God.
You have loved a prostitute's pay
on all threshing floors.
2 Threshing floor and winevat shall not feed them,
and the new wine shall fail them.
3 They shall not remain in the land of the LORD;
but Ephraim shall return to Egypt,
and in Assyria they shall eat unclean food.

4 They shall not pour drink offerings of wine to the LORD,
and their sacrifices shall not please him.
Such sacrifices shall be like mourners' bread;
all who eat of it shall be defiled;
for their bread shall be for their hunger only;
it shall not come to the house of the LORD.

5 What will you do on the day of appointed festival,
and on the day of the festival of the LORD?
6 For even if they escape destruction,

9.1 Isa 17.11 22.12,13

9.3 Ezek 4.13 Dan 1.8 Acts 10.14

9.4 Ex 29.40 Lev 22.4-9 23.13 Hag 2.14

9.5 Hos 2.11 Joel 1.13

9.6 Prov 24.31 Isa 5.6; 7.23 Hos 10.8

n Cn: Meaning of Heb uncertain o Gk: Heb *To exultation*

8.12 It is easy to listen to a sermon and think of all the people we know who should be listening, or to read the Bible and think of those who should do what the passage teaches. The Israelites did this constantly, applying God's laws to others but not to themselves. This is just another way to deflect God's Word and avoid making needed changes. As you think of others who need to apply what you are hearing or reading, check to see if the same application could fit you. Apply the lessons to your own life first because often our own faults are the very first ones we see in others.

8.13 The people's sacrifices became mere ritual, and God refused to accept them. We have rituals too – attending church, observing a regular quiet time, celebrating Christian holidays, praying before meals. Rituals give us security in a changing world. Because they are repeated often, they drive God's lessons deep within us. But rituals can be abused. Beware if you find yourself observing a religious ritual for any of the following reasons: (1) to gain community approval, (2) to avoid the risks of doing something different, (3) to make thought unnecessary, (4) to substitute for personal relationships, (5) to make up for bad behavior, (6) to earn God's favor. We should not reject the rituals of our worship, but we must be careful with them. Think about why you do them; focus on God; and perform every act with sincere devotion.

8.13 In Egypt, the Israelites had been slaves (Exodus 1.11). The people would not literally return to Egypt, but they would return to slavery – this time scattered throughout the Assyrian Empire.

8.14 Israel put its confidence in military strength, strong defenses, and economic stability, just as nations do today. But because of the people's inner moral decay, their apparent sources of strength were inadequate. There is a tendency in many nations toward removing all traces of God from daily life. But if a nation forgets its Maker, its strengths may prove worthless when put to the test.

9.1 A threshing floor was a flat area, often built on a hilltop, where harvesters beat the wheat and separated it from the chaff. Often men would stay overnight at the threshing floor to protect their grain, so this was a natural gathering place. Because of their elevation, threshing floors began to be used as places to sacrifice to false gods.

9.1ff Hosea probably spoke these words at a national festival, the festival of booths, when it was customary to live in tents to commemorate God's care for his people in the wilderness (Leviticus 23.33–44).

Egypt shall gather them,
Memphis shall bury them.
Nettles shall possess their precious things of silver;[p]
thorns shall be in their tents.

9.7 Isa 10.3 Jer 10.15 Jer 29.26 Lam 2.14 Ezek 7.2-7 13.3,10 Amos 8.2

7 The days of punishment have come,
the days of recompense have come;
Israel cries,[q]
"The prophet is a fool,
the man of the spirit is mad!"
Because of your great iniquity,
your hostility is great.
8 The prophet is a sentinel for my God over Ephraim,
yet a fowler's snare is on all his ways,
and hostility in the house of his God.

9.9 Isa 24.4,5; 31.6 Hos 7.2; 8.13

9 They have deeply corrupted themselves
as in the days of Gibeah;
he will remember their iniquity,
he will punish their sins.

9.10 Num 13.21-23 25.1-9 Josh 22.17,18 Jer 24.2 Mic 7.1

10 Like grapes in the wilderness,
I found Israel.
Like the first fruit on the fig tree,
in its first season,
I saw your ancestors.
But they came to Baal-peor,
and consecrated themselves to a thing of shame,
and became detestable like the thing they loved.

9.11 Hos 4.7

11 Ephraim's glory shall fly away like a bird—
no birth, no pregnancy, no conception!
12 Even if they bring up children,
I will bereave them until no one is left.
Woe to them indeed
when I depart from them!
13 Once I saw Ephraim as a young palm planted in a lovely meadow,[p]
but now Ephraim must lead out his children for slaughter.
14 Give them, O LORD—
what will you give?

[p] Meaning of Heb uncertain [q] Cn Compare Gk: Heb *shall know*

9.6 Israel's leaders vacillated between alliances with Egypt and alliances with Assyria. Hosea was saying that both were wrong. Breaking an alliance with untrustworthy Assyria and fleeing for help to the equally untrustworthy Egypt would cause Israel's destruction. Their only hope was to return to God.

9.7 By the time Israel began to experience the consequences of its sins, it was no longer listening to God's messengers. Refusing to hear the truth from prophets who spoke out so clearly about its sins, the nation did not hear God's warnings about what was soon to happen. We all listen and read selectively—focusing on what seems to support our present life-style, ignoring what demands a radical reordering of our priorities. In doing this, we are likely to miss the warnings we need most. Listen to people who think your approach is all wrong. Read articles that present viewpoints you would be unlikely to take. Ask yourself, "Is God speaking to me through these speakers and writers? Is there something I need to change?"

9.9 A couple had stopped to stay overnight in Gibeah when a gang of sex perverts gathered around the house and demanded that the man come out. Instead, the traveler gave them his wife. They raped and abused her all night and then left her dead on the doorstep (Judges 19.14–30). That horrible act revealed the depths to which the people had sunk. Gibeah was destroyed for its evil (Judges 20.8–48), but Hosea said that the whole nation was now as evil as that city. Just as the city didn't escape punishment, neither would the nation.

9.10 Baal-peor was the god of Peor, a city in Moab. In Numbers 22, Balaam, a freelance prophet, was hired by King Balak of Moab to curse the Israelites as they were coming through his land. The Moabites enticed the Israelites into sexual sin and Baal worship. Before long, they became as corrupt as the gods they worshiped. People can take on the characteristics of what or whom they love. What do you worship? Are you becoming more like God, or are you becoming more like someone or something else?

9.14 Hosea prayed this prayer when he foresaw the destruction that Israel's sins would bring (2 Kings 17). This vision of Israel's terrible fate moved him to pray that women would not get pregnant and that children would die as infants so they would not have to experience the tremendous suffering and pain that lay ahead.

Give them a miscarrying womb
and dry breasts.

15 Every evil of theirs began at Gilgal;
there I came to hate them.
Because of the wickedness of their deeds
I will drive them out of my house.
I will love them no more;
all their officials are rebels.

16 Ephraim is stricken,
their root is dried up,
they shall bear no fruit.
Even though they give birth,
I will kill the cherished offspring of their womb.
17 Because they have not listened to him,
my God will reject them;
they shall become wanderers among the nations.

9.15 Hos 5.2 Amos 4.4; 5.5

9.16 Ezek 24.21

Hosea predicts punishment

10 Israel is a luxuriant vine
that yields its fruit.
The more his fruit increased
the more altars he built;
as his country improved,
he improved his pillars.
2 Their heart is false;
now they must bear their guilt.
The LORD[r] will break down their altars,
and destroy their pillars.

3 For now they will say:
"We have no king,
for we do not fear the LORD,
and a king—what could he do for us?"
4 They utter mere words;
with empty oaths they make covenants;
so litigation springs up like poisonous weeds
in the furrows of the field.
5 The inhabitants of Samaria tremble
for the calf[s] of Beth-aven.

10.1 1 Kgs 14.23 Isa 5.1-7 Ezek 15.1-5

10.2 1 Kgs 18.21 Mic 5.13 Zeph 1.5

10.3 Mic 4.9

10.4 Ezek 17.13-19

10.5 1 Kgs 12.28-32 2 Chron 11.15 Hos 10.6

[r] Heb *he* [s] Gk Syr: Heb *calves*

9.15 At Gilgal, both the political and the religious failure of the nation began. Here idols and kings were substituted for God. Saul, the united nation's first king, was crowned at Gilgal (1 Samuel 11.15), but by Hosea's time, Baal worship flourished there (4.15; 12.11).

10.1 Israel prospered under Jeroboam II, gaining military and economic strength. But the more prosperous the nation became, the more it lavished on idols. It seems as if the more God gives, the more we spend. We want bigger houses, better cars, finer clothes, and more expensive education. But the finest things the world offers line the pathway to destruction. As you prosper, consider where your money is going. Is it being used for God's purposes, or are you consuming it all on yourself?

10.3 This statement shows Israel's unrepentant attitude. First they put their confidence in a king. When their king was taken away, however, they did not turn back to God. Instead, they said in effect, "So what?" and continued in their sinful ways.

10.4 God was angry with the people of Israel for their insincere promises, and in response he said that punishment would come. Because the people did not keep their word, there were many lawsuits (litigation). People break their promises, but God always keeps his. Are you remaining true to your promises, both to other people and to God? If not, ask God for forgiveness and help to get back on track. Then be careful about the promises you make. Never make a promise unless you are sure you can keep it.

10.5 Beth-aven means "house of wickedness" and it refers to Bethel ("house of God") where their false worship took place. If the Israelites' idols were really gods, they should have been able to protect the people. How ironic that the people were fearing for their gods' safety! For more information on this "calf," see the notes on 3.4, 5 and 8.5.

Its people shall mourn for it,
and its idolatrous priests shall wail[t] over it,
over its glory that has departed from it.
10.6 Hos 10.5
6 The thing itself shall be carried to Assyria
as tribute to the great king.[u]
Ephraim shall be put to shame,
and Israel shall be ashamed of his idol.[v]

7 Samaria's king shall perish
like a chip on the face of the waters.
10.8 Hos 5.8; 9.6 10.5
8 The high places of Aven, the sin of Israel,
shall be destroyed.
Thorn and thistle shall grow up
on their altars.
They shall say to the mountains, Cover us,
and to the hills, Fall on us.

9 Since the days of Gibeah you have sinned, O Israel;
there they have continued.
Shall not war overtake them in Gibeah?
10 I will come[w] against the wayward people to punish them;
and nations shall be gathered against them
when they are punished[x] for their double iniquity.

10.11 Deut 28.48 Jer 28.14
11 Ephraim was a trained heifer
that loved to thresh,
and I spared her fair neck;
but I will make Ephraim break the ground;
Judah must plow;
Jacob must harrow for himself.
10.12 Prov 11.18 Isa 32.20
12 Sow for yourselves righteousness;
reap steadfast love;
break up your fallow ground;
for it is time to seek the LORD,
that he may come and rain righteousness upon you.

10.13 Ps 33.16 Eccles 9.11
13 You have plowed wickedness,
you have reaped injustice,
you have eaten the fruit of lies.
Because you have trusted in your power
10.14 2 Kgs 17.6 18.9,10
and in the multitude of your warriors,
14 therefore the tumult of war shall rise against your people,

[t] Cn: Heb *exult* [u] Cn: Heb *to a king who will contend* [v] Cn: Heb *counsel* [w] Cn Compare Gk: Heb *In my desire* [x] Gk: Heb *bound*

10.9, 10 For information on "the days of Gibeah" see the notes on 9.9 and 9.15 or read Judges 19 and 20. Gibeah stands for cruelty and sensuality as in Judges, and for rebellion as in Saul's day.

10.12 Hosea repeatedly uses illustrations about fields and crops. Here he speaks of a plowed field, ground that is ready to receive seeds. It is no longer stony and hard; it has been carefully prepared, and it is available. Is your life ready for God to work in it? You can plow the hard ground of your heart by acknowledging your sins and receiving God's forgiveness and guidance.

10.12, 13 When we think of reaping what we sow, we usually think of negative results. Here we see that the results can be positive or negative. Just as small seeds eventually produce large crops, our small everyday actions can produce far-reaching results for good or for evil. What kind of crop are you sowing today? What might be the long-term effects of some of your actions?

10.13 The Israelites trusted in the lie that military power could keep them safe. Believers today are also capable of falling for lies. Those who want to lead others astray often follow these rules for effective lying: make it big; keep it simple; repeat it often. Believers can avoid falling for lies by asking: (1) Am I believing this because there is personal gain in it for me? (2) Am I discounting important facts? (3) Does it conflict with a direct command of Scripture? (4) Are there any biblical parallels to the situation I'm facing that would help me know what to believe?

10.14 Shalman was Salaman, king of Moab, who invaded Gilead around 740 B.C. Shalman destroyed the city of Beth-arbel, killing many people, including women and children. Hosea was saying that Israel's fate will be like the fate of Beth-arbel.

and all your fortresses shall be destroyed,
as Shalman destroyed Beth-arbel on the day of battle
when mothers were dashed in pieces with their children.
15 Thus it shall be done to you, O Bethel,
because of your great wickedness.
At dawn the king of Israel
shall be utterly cut off.

3. God's love for Israel

God's fatherly love

11 When Israel was a child, I loved him,
and out of Egypt I called my son.
2 The more I[y] called them,
the more they went from me;[z]
they kept sacrificing to the Baals,
and offering incense to idols.

3 Yet it was I who taught Ephraim to walk,
I took them up in my[a] arms;
but they did not know that I healed them.
4 I led them with cords of human kindness,
with bands of love.
I was to them like those
who lift infants to their cheeks.[b]
I bent down to them and fed them.

5 They shall return to the land of Egypt,
and Assyria shall be their king,
because they have refused to return to me.
6 The sword rages in their cities,
it consumes their oracle-priests,
and devours because of their schemes.
7 My people are bent on turning away from me.
To the Most High they call,
but he does not raise them up at all.[c]

8 How can I give you up, Ephraim?

11.1 Ex 4.22

11.4 Ex 16.32 Jer 31.2,3

11.6 Isa 9.14; 18.5

11.7 Jer 8.5 Hos 4.16

[y] Gk: Heb *they* [z] Gk: Heb *them* [a] Gk Syr Vg: Heb *his* [b] Or *who ease the yoke on their jaws* [c] Meaning of Heb uncertain

10.15 Israel put its confidence in military might rather than in God, and as a result, it would be destroyed by military power. Israel's king, who had led the people into idol worship, would be the first to fall. Divine judgment is *sometimes* swift, but it is *always* sure.

11.1ff In the final four chapters, Hosea shifts to the theme of God's intense love for Israel. God had always loved Israel as a parent loves a stubborn child, and that is why he would not release it from the consequences of its behavior. The Israelites were sinful, and they would be punished like a wayward son brought by his parents before the elders (Deuteronomy 21.18–21). All through Israel's sad history, God repeatedly offered to restore the nation if it would only turn to him. By stubbornly refusing his invitation, the northern kingdom sealed its doom. It would be destroyed, never to rise again. Even so, Israel as a nation was not finished. A remnant of faithful Israelites would return to Jerusalem, where one day the Messiah would come, offering pardon and reconciliation to all who would faithfully follow him.

11.3 God had consistently provided for his people, but they refused to see what he had done, and they showed no interest in thanking him. Ungratefulness is a common human fault. For example, when was the last time you thanked your parents for caring for you? Your pastor for the service he gives your church? Your child's teacher for the care taken with each day's activities? Your heavenly Father for his guidance? Many of the benefits and privileges we enjoy are the result of loving actions done long ago. Look for hidden acts of nurturing, and thank those who make the world better through their love. But begin by thanking God for all his blessings.

11.4 God's discipline requires times of leading and times of feeding. Sometimes the rope is taut, sometimes it is slack. It is always loving, and its object is always the well-being of the beloved. When you are called to discipline others – children, students, employees, or church members – do not be rigid. Vary your approach according to the goals you are seeking to accomplish. In each case, ask yourself: does this person need guidance, or does he or she need to be nurtured?

11.5 The northern kingdom survived only two centuries after the break with Jerusalem. Its spiritual and political leaders did not help the people learn the way to God, so as a nation they would never repent. Hosea prophesied its downfall, which happened when Shalmaneser of Assyria conquered Israel in 722 B.C. Judah also would go into captivity, but a remnant would return to their homeland.

11.8
Gen 14.8
Deut 29.23
Hos 6.4; 7.1

How can I hand you over, O Israel?
How can I make you like Admah?
How can I treat you like Zeboiim?
My heart recoils within me;
my compassion grows warm and tender.

11.9
Ex 32.10-14
Deut 13.17
Isa 5.24; 12.6
Jer 31.1-3

9 I will not execute my fierce anger;
I will not again destroy Ephraim;
for I am God and no mortal,
the Holy One in your midst,
and I will not come in wrath.[d]

11.10
Isa 66.2,5
Jer 5.22; 25.30
Joel 3.16
Amos 1.2; 3.4

10 They shall go after the LORD,
who roars like a lion;
when he roars,
his children shall come trembling from the west.

11.11
Isa 11.11; 60.8
Zech 10.10

11 They shall come trembling like birds from Egypt,
and like doves from the land of Assyria;
and I will return them to their homes, says the LORD.

12[e] Ephraim has surrounded me with lies,
and the house of Israel with deceit;
but Judah still walks[f] with God,
and is faithful to the Holy One.

12.1
Jer 22.22
Ezek 17.10

12 Ephraim herds the wind,
and pursues the east wind all day long;
they multiply falsehood and violence;
they make a treaty with Assyria,
and oil is carried to Egypt.

God invites his people to return to him

2 The LORD has an indictment against Judah,
and will punish Jacob according to his ways,
and repay him according to his deeds.

12.3
Gen 25.26
Rom 9.11

3 In the womb he tried to supplant his brother,
and in his manhood he strove with God.

12.4
Gen 28.13-15
32.24-30
35.10-15

4 He strove with the angel and prevailed,
he wept and sought his favor;
he met him at Bethel,
and there he spoke with him.[g]
5 The LORD the God of hosts,
the LORD is his name!

[d] Meaning of Heb uncertain [e] Ch 12.1 in Heb [f] Heb *roams* or *rules* [g] Gk Syr: Heb *us*

11.8 Admah and Zeboiim were cities of the plain that perished with Sodom and Gomorrah (Genesis 14.8; Deuteronomy 29.23).

11.9 "I am God and no mortal." It is easy for us to define God in terms of our own expectations and behavior. In so doing, we make him just slightly larger than ourselves. In reality, he is infinitely greater than we are. We should seek to become like him rather than attempting to remake him in our image.

11.12 Unlike Israel, Judah had some fairly good kings—Asa, Jehoshaphat, Joash, Amaziah, Azariah, Jotham, and especially Hezekiah and Josiah. Under some of these kings, God's law was dusted off and taught to the people. The priests continued to serve in God's appointed temple in Jerusalem, and the festivals were celebrated at least some of the time. Unfortunately, the political or religious leaders were unable to completely wipe out idol worship and pagan rites (although Hezekiah and Josiah came close), which continued to fester until they eventually erupted and infected the whole country. Still, the influence of the good kings enabled Judah to survive more than 150 years longer than Israel, and it fortified a small group—a remnant—of faithful people who would one day return and restore their land and temple.

12.2-5 Jacob, whose name was later changed to Israel, was the common ancestor of all 12 tribes of Israel (both northern and southern kingdoms). Like the nations that descended from him, Jacob practiced deceit. Unlike Israel and Judah, however, he constantly searched for God. Jacob wrestled with the Angel in order to be blessed, but his descendants thought their blessings came from their own successes. Jacob purged his house of idols (Genesis 35.2), but his descendants could not seem to banish idol worship from their midst.

6 But as for you, return to your God,
hold fast to love and justice,
and wait continually for your God.

7 A trader, in whose hands are false balances,
he loves to oppress.
8 Ephraim has said, "Ah, I am rich,
I have gained wealth for myself;
in all of my gain
no offense has been found in me
that would be sin."[h]
9 I am the LORD your God
from the land of Egypt;
I will make you live in tents again,
as in the days of the appointed festival.

10 I spoke to the prophets;
it was I who multiplied visions,
and through the prophets I will bring destruction.
11 In Gilead[i] there is iniquity,
they shall surely come to nothing.
In Gilgal they sacrifice bulls,
so their altars shall be like stone heaps
on the furrows of the field.
12 Jacob fled to the land of Aram,
there Israel served for a wife,
and for a wife he guarded sheep.[j]
13 By a prophet the LORD brought Israel up from Egypt,
and by a prophet he was guarded.
14 Ephraim has given bitter offense,
so his Lord will bring his crimes down on him
and pay him back for his insults.

12.6 Mic 7.7
12.7 Prov 11.1 Hos 7.14 Amos 8.5 Mic 6.11
12.8 Ps 62.10 Zech 11.5
12.10 Isa 20.2-5 Jer 25.4
12.12 Gen 28.5; 29.20
12.13 Ex 12.50
12.14 1 Kgs 2.33,34 2 Kgs 17.7-18 Ezek 18.13 23.2-10

God expresses his anger against Israel

13 When Ephraim spoke, there was trembling;
he was exalted in Israel;
but he incurred guilt through Baal and died.

[h] Meaning of Heb uncertain [i] Compare Syr: Heb *Gilead* [j] Heb lacks *sheep*

12.6 The two principles Hosea called his nation to live by, love and justice, are at the very foundation of God's character. They are essential to his followers, but they are not easy to keep in balance. Some people are loving to the point that they excuse wrongdoing. Others are just to the extent that they forget love. Love without justice, because it is not aiming at a higher standard, leaves people in their sins. Justice without love, because it has no heart, drives people away from God. To specialize in one at the expense of the other is to distort our witness. Today's church, just like Hosea's nation, must live by both principles.

12.7, 8 In Israel, dishonesty had become an accepted means of attaining wealth. Israelites who were financially successful could not imagine that God would consider them sinful. They thought their wealth was a sign of his approval, and they didn't bother to consider how they had gotten it. But God said Israel's riches would not make up for its sin. Remember that God's measure of success is different from ours. He calls us to faithfulness, not to affluence. Our character is more important to him than our pocketbook.

12.8 Rich people and nations often claim that their material success is due to their own hard work, initiative, and intelligence. Because they have every possession they want, they don't feel the need for God. They believe that their riches are their own, and they feel they have the right to use them any way they please. If you find yourself feeling proud of your accomplishments, remember that all your opportunities, abilities, and resources come from God, and that you hold them in sacred trust for him.

12.9 Once a year the Israelites spent a week living in tents during the festival of booths, which commemorated God's protection as they wandered in the wilderness for 40 years (see Deuteronomy 1.19–2.1). Now, because of their sin, God would cause them to live in tents again—this time not as part of a festival, but in actual bondage.

12.12 Hosea was using this reference to Jacob to say "Don't forget your humble beginnings. What you have is not a result of your own efforts, but is yours because God has been gracious to you."

12.13 The prophet who led Israel out of Egypt was Moses (Exodus 13.17–19).

13.1 Israel had been great, but by Hosea's time the people had rebelled against God and lost their authority among the nations. Greatness in the past is no guarantee of greatness in the future. It is good to remember what God has done for you and through you, but it is equally important to keep your relationship with him up to

13.2 1 Kgs 19.18 Isa 44.17-20 Jer 10.2-5

2 And now they keep on sinning
and make a cast image for themselves,
idols of silver made according to their understanding,
all of them the work of artisans.
"Sacrifice to these," they say.[k]
People are kissing calves!

13.3 Ps 68.2 Isa 17.13 Hos 6.4

3 Therefore they shall be like the morning mist
or like the dew that goes away early,
like chaff that swirls from the threshing floor
or like smoke from a window.

13.4 Ex 20.3 Isa 43.11

4 Yet I have been the LORD your God
ever since the land of Egypt;
you know no God but me,
and besides me there is no savior.

13.5 Deut 2.7; 8.15 32.10

5 It was I who fed[l] you in the wilderness,
in the land of drought.

13.6 Hos 2.13; 4.6

6 When I fed[m] them, they were satisfied;
they were satisfied, and their heart was proud;
therefore they forgot me.
7 So I will become like a lion to them,
like a leopard I will lurk beside the way.
8 I will fall upon them like a bear robbed of her cubs,
and will tear open the covering of their heart;
there I will devour them like a lion,
as a wild animal would mangle them.

9 I will destroy you, O Israel;
who can help you?[n]

13.10 2 Kgs 17.4 Hos 8.4

10 Where now is[o] your king, that he may save you?
Where in all your cities are your rulers,
of whom you said,
"Give me a king and rulers"?

13.11 1 Sam 8.7 1 Kgs 14.7-10

11 I gave you a king in my anger,
and I took him away in my wrath.

13.12 Deut 32.34,35

12 Ephraim's iniquity is bound up;
his sin is kept in store.

13.13 Mic 4.9,10

13 The pangs of childbirth come for him,
but he is an unwise son;

[k] Cn Compare Gk: Heb *To these they say sacrifices of people* [l] Gk Syr: Heb *knew* [m] Cn: Heb *according to their pasture* [n] Gk Syr: Heb *for in me is your help* [o] Gk Syr Vg: Heb *I will be*

CYCLES OF JUDGMENT/ SALVATION IN HOSEA

Judgment	1.2–9; 2.2–13; 4.1—5.14; 6.4—11.7; 11.12—13.16
Salvation	1.10—2.1; 2.14—3.5; 5.15—6.3; 11.8–11; 14.1–9

God promises to judge, but he also promises mercy. Here you can see the cycles of judgment and salvation in Hosea. Prophecies of judgment are consistently followed by prophecies of forgiveness.

date. Commit yourself to God moment by moment.

13.4–6 When Israel's possessions made it feel self-sufficient, it turned its back on God and forgot him. Self-sufficiency is as destructive today as it was in Hosea's time. Do you see your constant need of God's presence and help? Learn to rely on him both in good times and bad. If you are traveling along a smooth and easy path right now, beware of forgetting who gave you your good fortune. Don't depend on your gifts; depend on the Giver. See Deuteronomy 6.10–12 and 8.7–20 for God's warning.

13.11 God had warned Israel that kings would cause more problems than they would solve, and he reluctantly gave them Saul as their first king (1 Samuel 8.4–22). David was a good king, and Solomon had his strengths, but once the nation divided in two, the northern kingdom never had another good ruler. Evil kings led the nations deeper into idolatry and unwise political alliances. Eventually the evil kings destroyed the nation, and with Hoshea, the northern kingdom's kings were cut off (2 Kings 17.1–6).

13.12 Ephraim's (Israel's) sins were recorded for later punishment. All our sins are known and will be revealed at the day of Judgment (2 Corinthians 5.10; Revelation 20.11–15).

for at the proper time he does not present himself
at the mouth of the womb.

14 Shall I ransom them from the power of Sheol?
Shall I redeem them from Death?
O Death, where are[p] your plagues?
O Sheol, where is[p] your destruction?
Compassion is hidden from my eyes.

13.14 Isa 25.8 Ezek 37.12,13 1 Cor 15.55

15 Although he may flourish among rushes,[q]
the east wind shall come, a blast from the LORD,
rising from the wilderness;
and his fountain shall dry up,
his spring shall be parched.
It shall strip his treasury
of every precious thing.
16[r] Samaria shall bear her guilt,
because she has rebelled against her God;
they shall fall by the sword,
their little ones shall be dashed in pieces,
and their pregnant women ripped open.

13.15 Jer 51.36 Hos 12.1

13.16 2 Kgs 15.16

Repentance will bring restoration

14 Return, O Israel, to the LORD your God,
for you have stumbled because of your iniquity.
2 Take words with you
and return to the LORD;
say to him,
"Take away all guilt;
accept that which is good,
and we will offer
the fruit[s] of our lips.
3 Assyria shall not save us;
we will not ride upon horses;
we will say no more, 'Our God,'
to the work of our hands.
In you the orphan finds mercy."

4 I will heal their disloyalty;
I will love them freely,

14.2 Mic 7.18,19

14.3 Ps 68.5 Mic 5.10-14

14.4 Isa 57.18 Jer 3.22 Zeph 3.17

p Gk Syr: Heb *I will be* q Or *among brothers* r Ch 14.1 in Heb s Gk Syr: Heb *bulls*

13.14 God cannot save those who refuse to repent. Saying no to God can become a stubborn habit. Before time runs out or you become completely hardened to his voice, come to him for forgiveness and new direction for your life.

13.14 "Sheol" is the Old Testament word for the realm of the dead. It is used to mean the grave or the state of being dead.

14.1ff Verses 1–3 are Hosea's call to repent. Verses 4–8 are God's promise of restoration. God must punish Israel for its gross and repeated violations of his law, but he does so with a heavy heart. What he really wants to do is restore the nation and make it prosper.

14.1, 2 The people could return to God by asking him to take away their sins. The same is true for us: we can pray Hosea's prayer and know our sins are forgiven because Christ died for them on the cross (John 3.16).

Forgiveness begins when we see the destructiveness of sin and the futility of life without God. Then we must admit we cannot save ourselves; our only hope is in God's mercy. When we request forgiveness, we must recognize that we do not deserve it and therefore cannot demand it. Our appeal must be for God's love and mercy, not for his justice. Although we cannot demand forgiveness, we can be confident we have received it, because God is gracious and loving and wants to restore us to himself, just as he wanted to restore Israel.

14.4–8 When our will is weak, when our reason is confused, when our conscience is burdened with a load of guilt, we must remember that God cares for us continually, his mercies never fail. When friends and family desert us, when co-workers don't understand us, when we are tired of being good, God's mercies never fail. When we can't see the way or seem to hear God's voice, when we lack courage to go on, God's mercies never fail. When our shortcomings beset us and awareness of our sins overcomes us, God's mercies never fail.

for my anger has turned from them.
5 I will be like the dew to Israel;
he shall blossom like the lily,
he shall strike root like the forests of Lebanon.[t]

14.6 Ps 52.8 Jer 11.16

6 His shoots shall spread out;
his beauty shall be like the olive tree,
and his fragrance like that of Lebanon.

14.7 Ps 91.1 Isa 32.1,2

7 They shall again live beneath my[u] shadow,
they shall flourish as a garden;[v]
they shall blossom like the vine,
their fragrance shall be like the wine of Lebanon.

14.8 Isa 41.19

8 O Ephraim, what have I[w] to do with idols?
It is I who answer and look after you.[x]
I am like an evergreen cypress;
your faithfulness[y] comes from me.

14.9 Job 34.10-12 Prov 1.5,6; 4.18 Rom 9.32

9 Those who are wise understand these things;
those who are discerning know them.
For the ways of the LORD are right,
and the upright walk in them,
but transgressors stumble in them.

[t] Cn: Heb *like Lebanon* [u] Heb *his* [v] Cn: Heb *they shall grow grain* [w] Or *What more has Ephraim* [x] Heb *him* [y] Heb *your fruit*

14.9 Hosea closes with an appeal to listen, learn, and benefit from God's Word. To those receiving the Lord's message through Hosea, this meant the difference between life and death. For you, the reader of the book of Hosea, the choice is similar: either listen to the book's message and follow God's ways, or refuse to walk along the Lord's path. But people who insist on following their own direction without God's guidance are "like deep darkness; they do not know what they stumble over" (Proverbs 4.19). If you are lost, you can find the way by turning from your sin and following God.

14.9 God's concern for *justice* that requires faithfulness and *love* that offers forgiveness can be seen in his dealings with Hosea. We can err by forgetting God's love and feeling that our sins are hopeless; but we can also err by forgetting his wrath against our sins and thinking he will continue to accept us no matter how we act. *Forgiveness* is a key word: when God forgives us, he judges the sin but shows mercy to the sinner. We should never be afraid to come to God for a clean slate and a renewed life.

JOEL

King Ahab dies in battle 853 B.C.

Elisha becomes a prophet 848

Jehu becomes king of Israel; Athaliah siezes Judah's throne 841

Joel becomes a prophet; Joash becomes king of Judah 835

VITAL STATISTICS

PURPOSE:
To warn Judah of God's impending judgment because of their sins and to urge them to turn back to God

AUTHOR:
Joel, son of Pethuel

TO WHOM WRITTEN:
The people of Judah, the southern kingdom, and God's people everywhere

DATE WRITTEN:
Probably during the time Joel prophesied, from about 835 to 796 B.C.

SETTING:
The people of Judah had become prosperous and complacent. Taking God for granted, they had turned to self-centeredness, idolatry, and sin. Joel warns them that this kind of life-style will inevitably bring down God's judgment.

KEY VERSES:
"Yet even now, says the Lord, return to me with all your heart, with fasting, with weeping, and with mourning; rend your hearts and not your clothing. Return to the Lord, your God, for he is gracious and merciful, slow to anger, and abounding in steadfast love, and relents from punishing" (2.12, 13).

KEY PEOPLE:
Joel, the people of Judah

KEY PLACE:
Jerusalem

A single bomb devastates a city and the world is ushered into the nuclear age. A split atom . . . power and force such as we have never seen.

At a launch site, rockets roar and a payload is thrust into space. Discoveries dreamed of for centuries are ours as we begin to explore the edge of the universe.

Volcanos, earthquakes, tidal waves, hurricanes, and tornados unleash uncontrollable and unstoppable force. And we can only avoid them and then pick up the pieces.

Power, strength, might—we stand in awe at the natural and man-made display. But these forces cannot touch the power of omnipotent God. Creator of galaxies, atoms, and natural laws, the sovereign Lord rules all there is and ever will be. How silly to live without him; how foolish to run and hide from him; how ridiculous to disobey him. But we do. Since Eden, we have sought independence from his control, as though we were gods and could control our destiny. And he has allowed our rebellion. But soon *the day of the Lord* will come.

It is about this day that the prophet Joel spoke, and it is the theme of his book. On this day God will judge all unrighteousness and disobedience—all accounts will be settled and the crooked made straight.

We know very little about Joel, only that he was a prophet and the son of Pethuel. He may have lived in Jerusalem, because his audience was Judah, the southern kingdom. Whoever he was, Joel speaks forthrightly and forcefully in this short and powerful book. His message is one of foreboding and warning, but it is also filled with hope. Joel states that our Creator, the omnipotent Judge, is also merciful, and he wants to bless all those who trust him.

Joel begins by describing a terrible plague of locusts that covers the land and devours the crops. The devastation wrought by these creatures is but a foretaste of the coming judgment of God, the "day of the Lord." Joel, therefore, urges the people to turn from their sin and turn back to God. Woven into this message of judgment and repentance is an affirmation of God's kindness and the blessings he promises for all who follow him. In fact, "everyone who calls on the name of the Lord shall be saved" (2.32).

As you read Joel, catch his vision of the power and might of God and of his ultimate judgment of sin. Choose to follow, obey, and worship God alone as your sovereign Lord.

Jehoahaz becomes king of Israel 814	*Jehoash becomes king of Israel 798* · *Joel's ministry ends 796?*

THE BLUEPRINT

1. The day of the locusts (1.1—2.27)
2. The day of the Lord (2.28—3.21)

The locust plague was only a foretaste of the judgment to come in the day of the Lord. This is a timeless call to repentance with the promise of blessing. Just as the people faced the tragedy of their crops being destroyed, we too will face tragic judgment if we live in sin. But God's grace is available to us both now and in that coming day.

MEGATHEMES

THEME	EXPLANATION	IMPORTANCE
Punishment	Like a destroying army of locusts, God's punishment for sin is overwhelming, dreadful, and unavoidable. When it comes, there will be no food, no water, no protection, and no escape. The day for settling accounts with God for how we have lived is fast approaching.	God is the one with whom we all must reckon—not nature, the economy, or a foreign invader. We can't ignore or offend God forever. We must pay attention to his message now, or we will face his anger later.
Forgiveness	God stood ready to forgive and restore all those who would come to him and turn away from sin. God wanted to shower his people with his love and restore them to a proper relationship with him.	Forgiveness comes by turning from sin and turning toward God. It is not too late to receive God's forgiveness. God's greatest desire is for you to come to him.
Promise of the Holy Spirit	Joel predicts the time when God will pour out his Holy Spirit on all people. It will be the beginning of new and fresh worship of God by those who believe in him, but also the beginning of judgment on all who reject him.	God is in control. Justice and restoration are in his hands. The Holy Spirit confirms God's love for us just as he did for the first Christians (Acts 2). We must be faithful to God and place our lives under the guidance and power of his Holy Spirit.

1. The day of the locusts

Joel predicts a plague of locusts

1 The word of the LORD that came to Joel son of Pethuel:

1.2 Jer 30.7

2 Hear this, O elders,
give ear, all inhabitants of the land!
Has such a thing happened in your days,
or in the days of your ancestors?

1.3 Ex 10.2 Deut 6.4-9

3 Tell your children of it,
and let your children tell their children,
and their children another generation.

1.1 Joel was a prophet to the nation of Judah, also known as the southern kingdom. The book does not mention when he lived, but it is likely he prophesied during the reign of King Joash (835–796 B.C.). But the date of Joel's book is not nearly so important as its timeless message. Sin brings God's judgment. Yet with God's justice there is also great mercy.

1.3 God urged adults to pass their history down to their children, telling over and over the important lessons they learned. One of the greatest gifts you can give younger people is your life's story to help them repeat your successes and avoid your mistakes.

4 What the cutting locust left,
the swarming locust has eaten.
What the swarming locust left,
the hopping locust has eaten,
and what the hopping locust left,
the destroying locust has eaten.

5 Wake up, you drunkards, and weep;
and wail, all you wine-drinkers,
over the sweet wine,
for it is cut off from your mouth.
6 For a nation has invaded my land,
powerful and innumerable;
its teeth are lions' teeth,
and it has the fangs of a lioness.
7 It has laid waste my vines,
and splintered my fig trees;
it has stripped off their bark and thrown it down;
their branches have turned white.

8 Lament like a virgin dressed in sackcloth
for the husband of her youth.
9 The grain offering and the drink offering are cut off
from the house of the LORD.
The priests mourn,
the ministers of the LORD.
10 The fields are devastated,
the ground mourns;
for the grain is destroyed,
the wine dries up,
the oil fails.

11 Be dismayed, you farmers,
wail, you vinedressers,
over the wheat and the barley;
for the crops of the field are ruined.
12 The vine withers,
the fig tree droops.
Pomegranate, palm, and apple—
all the trees of the field are dried up;
surely, joy withers away
among the people.

Joel calls the people to repent

13 Put on sackcloth and lament, you priests;
wail, you ministers of the altar.

1.4 Isa 33.4; Jer 51.14; Joel 2.25
1.6 Joel 1.4
1.7 Amos 4.9
1.9 Hos 9.4; Joel 1.13; 2.14
1.11 Ezra 9.3; Amos 5.16
1.12 Song 2.3; Joel 1.7; Hab 3.17,18; Hag 2.19
1.13 1 Kgs 21.27; Jer 4.8

1.4 A locust plague can be as devastating as an invading army. Locusts gather in swarms too great to number (1.6) and fly several feet above the ground, seeming to darken the sun as they pass by (2.2). When they land, they devour almost every piece of vegetation (1.7–12), covering and entering everything in their path (2.9).

1.4 Joel's detailed description has caused many to believe that he was referring to an actual locust plague that had come or was about to come upon the land. Another view is that the locusts symbolize an invading enemy army. Regardless of which view is correct, Joel's point was that God would punish the people because of their sin. Joel calls this judgment the "day of the Lord" (see the note on 1.15).

1.5 The people's moral senses were dulled, making them oblivious to sin. Joel called them to awaken from their complacency and admit their sins before it was too late. Otherwise, everything would be destroyed, even the grapes and wine that caused their drunkenness. Our times of peace and prosperity can lull us to sleep. We must never let material abundance hinder our spiritual readiness.

1.9 Because of the devastation, there was no grain or grapes for the grain or drink offerings (see Leviticus 1 and 2 for a detailed explanation of these offerings).

Come, pass the night in sackcloth,
  you ministers of my God!
Grain offering and drink offering
  are withheld from the house of your God.

14 Sanctify a fast,
  call a solemn assembly.
Gather the elders
  and all the inhabitants of the land
to the house of the LORD your God,
  and cry out to the LORD.

1.15 Isa 13.9 Ezek 7.2-13 Joel 2.1

15 Alas for the day!
For the day of the LORD is near,
  and as destruction from the Almighty[a] it comes.

1.16 Isa 3.7 Amos 4.6,7

16 Is not the food cut off
  before our eyes,
joy and gladness
  from the house of our God?

1.17 Isa 17.10,11

17 The seed shrivels under the clods,[b]
  the storehouses are desolate;
the granaries are ruined
  because the grain has failed.
18 How the animals groan!
  The herds of cattle wander about
because there is no pasture for them;
  even the flocks of sheep are dazed.[c]

1.19 Ps 50.15; 91.15 Mic 7.7

19 To you, O LORD, I cry.
For fire has devoured

a Traditional rendering of Heb *Shaddai* b Meaning of Heb uncertain c Compare Gk Syr Vg: Meaning of Heb uncertain

JOEL served as a prophet to Judah from 835–796 B.C.

Climate of the times	Wicked Queen Athaliah seized power in a bloody coup, but was overthrown after a few years. Joash was crowned king, but he was only seven years old and in great need of spiritual guidance. Joash followed God in his early years, but then turned away from him.
Main message	A plague of locusts had come to discipline the nation. Joel called the people to turn back to God before an even greater judgment occurred.
Importance of message	God judges all people for their sins, but is merciful to those who turn to him and offers them eternal salvation.
Contemporary prophets	Elisha (848–797) Jonah (793–753)

1.14 A fast was a period of time when no food was eaten and people approached God with humility, sorrow for sin, and urgent prayer. In the Old Testament, people often would fast during times of calamity in order to focus their attention on God and to demonstrate their change of heart and true devotion (see, for example, Judges 20.26; 1 Kings 21.27; Ezra 8.21; Jonah 3.5). The solemn assembly was a public religious gathering called so that everyone could repent and pray to God for mercy.

1.15 The "day of the Lord" is a common phrase in the Old Testament and in the book of Joel (see 2.1, 11, 31; 3.14). It always refers to some extraordinary happening, whether a present event (like a locust plague), an event in the near future (like the destruction of Jerusalem or the defeat of enemy nations), or the final period of history when God will defeat all the forces of evil.

Even when the day of the Lord refers to a present event, it also pictures the *final* day of the Lord. This final event of history has two aspects to it: (1) the last judgment on all evil and sin and (2) the final reward for faithful believers. Righteousness and truth will prevail, but not before much suffering (Zechariah 14.1–3). If you trust the Lord, this final day will be a time of hope, because all who are faithful will be united forever with God.

1.15–19 Without God, destruction is sure. Those who have not personally accepted God's love and forgiveness will stand before him with no appeal. Be sure to call upon God's love and mercy while you have the opportunity (2.32).

the pastures of the wilderness,
and flames have burned
all the trees of the field.
20 Even the wild animals cry to you
because the watercourses are dried up,
and fire has devoured
the pastures of the wilderness.

1.20 1 Kgs 17.7; 18.5

Joel warns of the approaching judgment

2 Blow the trumpet in Zion;
sound the alarm on my holy mountain!
Let all the inhabitants of the land tremble,
for the day of the LORD is coming, it is near—
2 a day of darkness and gloom,
a day of clouds and thick darkness!
Like blackness spread upon the mountains
a great and powerful army comes;
their like has never been from of old,
nor will be again after them
in ages to come.

2.1 Joel 1.15 2.11,15,31 3.14

2.2 Dan 9.12 Joel 1.2 2.5,10,11,15

3 Fire devours in front of them,
and behind them a flame burns.
Before them the land is like the garden of Eden,
but after them a desolate wilderness,
and nothing escapes them.

2.3 Gen 2.8 Isa 51.3 Amos 7.4

4 They have the appearance of horses,
and like war-horses they charge.
5 As with the rumbling of chariots,
they leap on the tops of the mountains,
like the crackling of a flame of fire
devouring the stubble,
like a powerful army
drawn up for battle.

2.5 Isa 5.24; 30.30 Nah 2.3; 3.2

6 Before them peoples are in anguish,
all faces grow pale.[d]
7 Like warriors they charge,
like soldiers they scale the wall.
Each keeps to its own course,
they do not swerve from[e] their paths.
8 They do not jostle one another,
each keeps to its own track;
they burst through the weapons
and are not halted.
9 They leap upon the city,
they run upon the walls;
they climb up into the houses,
they enter through the windows like a thief.

2.6 Jer 30.6

2.9 Ex 10.6 Jer 9.21 Jn 10.1

[d] Meaning of Heb uncertain [e] Gk Syr Vg: Heb *they do not take a pledge along*

2.1ff Joel was still describing the devastating effects of the locust plague (see 2.25). The alarm showed that the crisis was at hand. However, Joel implied that the locust plague would be only the forerunner of an even greater crisis if the people didn't turn from their sins.

2.3 The garden of Eden was Adam and Eve's first home (Genesis 2.8). Known for its beauty, here it is used to describe the beauty of the land prior to the devastation.

2.10 Isa 13.10; Joel 2.31; 3.15; Nah 1.5; Mt 24.29; 27.51; Acts 2.20

10 The earth quakes before them,
the heavens tremble.
The sun and the moon are darkened,
and the stars withdraw their shining.

2.11 Ps 46.6; Isa 42.13; Joel 2.1; 3.16

11 The LORD utters his voice
at the head of his army;
how vast is his host!
Numberless are those who obey his command.
Truly the day of the LORD is great;
terrible indeed — who can endure it?

Return to the Lord your God

2.12 Deut 4.29,30

12 Yet even now, says the LORD,
return to me with all your heart,
with fasting, with weeping, and with mourning;

2.13 Ex 34.6; Num 14.18; Ps 106.45; Amos 7.2-6

13 rend your hearts and not your clothing.
Return to the LORD, your God,
for he is gracious and merciful,
slow to anger, and abounding in steadfast love,
and relents from punishing.

2.14 Hag 2.19

14 Who knows whether he will not turn and relent,
and leave a blessing behind him,
a grain offering and a drink offering
for the LORD, your God?

2.15 Joel 2.1

15 Blow the trumpet in Zion;
sanctify a fast;
call a solemn assembly;
16 gather the people.
Sanctify the congregation;
assemble the aged;
gather the children,
even infants at the breast.
Let the bridegroom leave his room,
and the bride her canopy.

2.17 Ps 44.13; 79.10; Isa 37.20; Mic 7.10

17 Between the vestibule and the altar
let the priests, the ministers of the LORD, weep.
Let them say, "Spare your people, O LORD,
and do not make your heritage a mockery,
a byword among the nations.
Why should it be said among the peoples,
'Where is their God?' "

2.18 Deut 32.36; Isa 60.10

18 Then the LORD became jealous for his land,
and had pity on his people.

2.19 Ezek 34.29; 39.29

19 In response to his people the LORD said:
I am sending you

2.12, 13 God told the people to turn to him while there was still time. Destruction would soon be upon them. Time is also running out for us. Because we don't know when our lives will end, we should trust and obey God now, while we can. Don't let anything hold you back from turning to him.

2.13 Deep remorse was often shown by tearing (rending) one's clothes. But God didn't want an outward display of penitence without true inward repentance (1 Samuel 16.7; Matthew 23.1–36). Be sure your attitude toward God is correct, not just your actions.

2.18 Joel reaches a turning point in his prophecy, moving from prophesying about an outpouring of God's judgment to prophesying about an outpouring of God's forgiveness and blessing. But this would come only if the people began to live as God wanted them to, giving up their sins. Where there is repentance, there is hope. This section of the book feeds that hope. Without it, Joel's prophecy could bring only despair. This promise of forgiveness should have encouraged the people to repent.

grain, wine, and oil,
and you will be satisfied;
and I will no more make you
a mockery among the nations.

20 I will remove the northern army far from you,
and drive it into a parched and desolate land,
its front into the eastern sea,
and its rear into the western sea;
its stench and foul smell will rise up.
Surely he has done great things!

21 Do not fear, O soil;
be glad and rejoice,
for the LORD has done great things!
22 Do not fear, you animals of the field,
for the pastures of the wilderness are green;
the tree bears its fruit,
the fig tree and vine give their full yield.

23 O children of Zion, be glad
and rejoice in the LORD your God;
for he has given the early rain[f] for your vindication,
he has poured down for you abundant rain,
the early and the later rain, as before.
24 The threshing floors shall be full of grain,
the vats shall overflow with wine and oil.

25 I will repay you for the years
that the swarming locust has eaten,
the hopper, the destroyer, and the cutter,
my great army, which I sent against you.

26 You shall eat in plenty and be satisfied,
and praise the name of the LORD your God,
who has dealt wondrously with you.
And my people shall never again be put to shame.
27 You shall know that I am in the midst of Israel,
and that I, the LORD, am your God and there is no other.
And my people shall never again
be put to shame.

[f] Meaning of Heb uncertain

2.20 Deut 11.24; Jer 1.14,15; Zech 14.8

2.23 Ps 28.6; 72.6; 95.1-3; Hos 6.3; Zech 10.1; Phil 3.1; 1 Thess 5.16

2.26 Ps 67.5-7; Isa 45.17; Rom 10.11

2.27 Lev 26.11,12; Isa 45.5,6,18; Ezek 39.22,28; Joel 3.17,21

2.20 Joel visualizes the invasion from the north by the armies of Assyria and Babylon, typified by the locusts.

2.21 Joel contrasts the fear of God's judgment (2.1) with the joy of God's intervention (2.21). On the day of the Lord, sin will bring judgment, and only God's forgiveness will bring rejoicing. Unless you repent, your sin will result in punishment. Let God intervene in your life. Then you will be able to rejoice in that day because you will have nothing to fear. Before, there were fasting, plagues, and dirges; then, there will be feasting, harvesting, and songs of praise. When God rules, his restoration is complete. In the meantime, we must remember that God does not promise that all his followers will be prosperous now. When God pardons, he restores our relationship with him, but this does not guarantee individual wealth. Instead, God promises to meet the deepest needs of those who love him – by loving us, forgiving us, giving us purpose in life, and giving us a caring Christian community.

2.26, 27 If the Jews would never again experience a disaster like this locust plague ("never again be put to shame"), how do we explain the captivity in Babylon, the Jews' slavery under the Greeks and Romans, and their persecution under Hitler? It is important not to take these verses out of context. This is still part of the "blessings" section of Joel's prophecy. Only if the people truly repented would they avoid a disaster like the one Joel had described. God's blessings are promised only to those who sincerely and consistently follow him. God does promise that after the final day of Judgment, his people will never again experience this kind of disaster (Zechariah 14.9–11; Revelation 21).

2. The day of the Lord

God will pour out his Spirit

2.28 Isa 32.15 Acts 2.16-18

28[g] Then afterward
I will pour out my spirit on all flesh;
your sons and your daughters shall prophesy,
your old men shall dream dreams,
and your young men shall see visions.

2.29 1 Cor 12.13

29 Even on the male and female slaves,
in those days, I will pour out my spirit.

2.31 Joel 2.1,10 3.15
2.32 Isa 4.2 Acts 2.21 Rom 10.13

30 I will show portents in the heavens and on the earth, blood and fire and
columns of smoke. 31 The sun shall be turned to darkness, and the moon to blood,
before the great and terrible day of the LORD comes. 32 Then everyone who calls on
the name of the LORD shall be saved; for in Mount Zion and in Jerusalem there shall
be those who escape, as the LORD has said, and among the survivors shall be those
whom the LORD calls.

3.2 Isa 66.18 Joel 3.12,14 Zeph 3.8
3.3 Obad 11 Nah 3.10

3 [h] For then, in those days and at that time, when I restore the fortunes of Judah
and Jerusalem, 2 I will gather all the nations and bring them down to the valley
of Jehoshaphat, and I will enter into judgment with them there, on account of my
people and my heritage Israel, because they have scattered them among the nations. They have divided my land, 3 and cast lots for my people, and traded boys for
prostitutes, and sold girls for wine, and drunk it down.

3.5 2 Kgs 12.18 Dan 5.2,3

4 What are you to me, O Tyre and Sidon, and all the regions of Philistia? Are
you paying me back for something? If you are paying me back, I will turn your
deeds back upon your own heads swiftly and speedily. 5 For you have taken my
silver and my gold, and have carried my rich treasures into your temples.[i] 6 You
have sold the people of Judah and Jerusalem to the Greeks, removing them far from
their own border. 7 But now I will rouse them to leave the places to which you have
sold them, and I will turn your deeds back upon your own heads. 8 I will sell your
sons and your daughters into the hand of the people of Judah, and they will sell
them to the Sabeans, to a nation far away; for the LORD has spoken.

The day of the Lord is near

9 Proclaim this among the nations:

[g] Ch 3.1 in Heb [h] Ch 4.1 in Heb [i] Or *palaces*

2.28–32 Peter quoted this passage (see Acts 2.16–21)—the outpouring of the Spirit predicted by Joel occurred on pentecost. While in the past, God's Spirit seemed available to kings, prophets, and judges, Joel visualizes a time when the Spirit will be available to every believer. Ezekiel also spoke of an outpouring of the Spirit (Ezekiel 39.28, 29), which some think will come after Christ returns. God's Spirit is available now to anyone who calls upon the Lord (2.32).

2.30 A portent is something that gives a hint or a picture of a coming event.

2.31, 32 Judgment and mercy go hand in hand. Joel had said that if the people repented, the Lord would save them from judgment (2.12–14). In this judgment and catastrophe, therefore, some will be saved. God's intention is not to destroy but to heal. However, we must accept his salvation or we will certainly perish with the unrepentant.

3.1, 2 The phrase "at that time" refers to the time when those who call upon the Lord will be saved (2.32). God will not only bless believers with everything they need; he will bless them by destroying all evil, ending the pain and suffering on earth. This prophecy had three fulfillments: immediate, ongoing, and final. Its immediate interpretation could apply to King Jehoshaphat's recent battle against several enemy nations, including Moab and Ammon (2 Chronicles 20). Its ongoing fulfillment could be the partial restoration of the people to their land after the exile to Babylon. The final fulfillment will come in the great battle that precedes the Messiah's reign over the earth (Revelation 20.7–9).

3.2 The geographic location of the valley of Jehoshaphat is not known. Some think it is a future valley created by the splitting of the Mount of Olives when the Messiah returns (Zechariah 14.4). The most important fact for us is that the name means "the Lord judges."

3.4 Tyre and Sidon were major cities in Phoenicia to the north of Israel; Philistia was the nation southwest of Judah. Phoenicia and Philistia were small countries who rejoiced at the fall of Judah and Israel because they would benefit from the increased trade. God would judge them for their wrong attitude.

3.6 Jews were sold to Greeks, a heathen and unclean people. Some think this verse and 3.1 indicate that Joel lived after the captivity in Babylon (586 B.C.), when the Greek culture began to flourish. But archaeological studies have shown that the Greeks were trading with Phoenicia as early as 800 B.C. Also 3.4 mentions Tyre, Sidon, and Philistia. These nations were contemporary nations of Judah before their captivity.

3.8 The Sabeans came from Sheba, a nation in southwest Arabia. One of Sheba's queens had visited Solomon over a century earlier (1 Kings 10.1–13). They controlled the eastern trade routes.

Prepare war,[j]
stir up the warriors.
Let all the soldiers draw near,
let them come up.
10 Beat your plowshares into swords,
and your pruning hooks into spears;
let the weakling say, "I am a warrior."

11 Come quickly,[k]
all you nations all around,
gather yourselves there.
Bring down your warriors, O LORD.
12 Let the nations rouse themselves,
and come up to the valley of Jehoshaphat;
for there I will sit to judge
all the neighboring nations.

13 Put in the sickle,
for the harvest is ripe.
Go in, tread,
for the wine press is full.
The vats overflow,
for their wickedness is great.

14 Multitudes, multitudes,
in the valley of decision!
For the day of the LORD is near
in the valley of decision.
15 The sun and the moon are darkened,
and the stars withdraw their shining.

16 The LORD roars from Zion,
and utters his voice from Jerusalem,
and the heavens and the earth shake.
But the LORD is a refuge for his people,
a stronghold for the people of Israel.

17 So you shall know that I, the LORD your God,
dwell in Zion, my holy mountain.
And Jerusalem shall be holy,
and strangers shall never again pass through it.

18 In that day
the mountains shall drip sweet wine,
the hills shall flow with milk,
and all the stream beds of Judah

3.9 Isa 34.1; Jer 46.3; 51.27; Zech 14.2,3
3.10 Isa 2.4; Mic 4.3
3.12 Ps 76.8,9; Isa 3.13; Rev 19.11
3.13 Hos 6.11; Mt 13.39; Mk 4.29
3.14 Isa 34.2-8; Ezek 38.8-23; Joel 2.1; 3.2,12
3.15 Joel 12.10,31
3.16 Ps 18.2; 19.21; Hos 11.10; Amos 1.2; 3.8; Zech 12.5-9
3.17 Isa 11.9; Ezek 20.40; Zech 8.3
3.18 Ex 3.8; Isa 55.12,13; Amos 9.13

j Heb *sanctify war* k Meaning of Heb uncertain

3.14 Joel described multitudes waiting in the "valley of decision" (also translated the "valley of Judgment"). Billions of people have lived on earth, and every one of them – dead, living, and yet to be born – will face judgment. Look around you. See your friends, those with whom you work and live. Have they received God's forgiveness? Have they been warned about sin's consequences? If we understand the severity of God's final judgment, we will want to take God's offer of hope to those we know.

3.17 The last word will be God's; his ultimate sovereignty will be revealed in the end. We cannot predict when that end will come, but we can have confidence in his control over the world's events. The world's history, as well as our own, is in God's hands. We can be secure in his love and trust him to guide our decisions.

3.18 The picture of this restored land is one of perfect beauty, similar to the garden of Eden. The life-giving fountain flowing from the temple illustrates the blessings that come from God. Those who attach themselves to him will be forever fruitful. (See also Ezekiel 47.1–12; Revelation 22.1, 2.)

3.18 A wadi is a stream or dry streambed.

shall flow with water;
a fountain shall come forth from the house of the LORD
and water the Wadi Shittim.

3.19 Amos 1.11 Obad 10

19 Egypt shall become a desolation
and Edom a desolate wilderness,
because of the violence done to the people of Judah,
in whose land they have shed innocent blood.

3.20 Ezek 37.25 Amos 9.15

20 But Judah shall be inhabited forever,
and Jerusalem to all generations.

3.21 Isa 4.4 Ezek 36.25,29 Mt 27.25

21 I will avenge their blood, and I will not clear the guilty,[l]
for the LORD dwells in Zion.

[l] Gk Syr: Heb *I will hold innocent their blood that I have not held innocent*

3.19 Egypt and Edom were two of Israel's most persistent enemies. They represent all the nations hostile to God's people. God's promise that they would be destroyed is also a promise that all evil in the world will one day be destroyed.

3.20, 21 The word *Judah* is used here to refer to all God's people – anyone who has called on the name of the Lord. There is full assurance of victory and peace for those who trust in God (2.32).

3.21 Joel began with a prophecy about the destruction of the land and ended with a prophecy about its restoration. He began by stressing the need for repentance and ended with the promise of forgiveness that repentance brings. Joel was trying to convince the people to wake up (1.5), get rid of their complacency, and realize the danger of living apart from God. His message to us is that there is still time; anyone who calls on God's name can be saved (2.12–14, 32). Those who turn to God will enjoy the blessings mentioned in Joel's prophecy; those who refuse will face destruction.

AMOS

Jeroboam II becomes king of Israel 793 B.C.

VITAL STATISTICS

PURPOSE:
To pronounce God's judgment upon Israel, the northern kingdom, for their complacency, idolatry, and oppression of the poor

AUTHOR:
Amos

TO WHOM WRITTEN:
Israel, the northern kingdom, and God's people everywhere

DATE WRITTEN:
Probably during the reigns of Jeroboam II of Israel and Uzziah of Judah (about 760–750 B.C.)

SETTING:
The wealthy people of Israel were enjoying peace and prosperity. They were quite complacent and were oppressing the poor, even selling them into slavery. Soon, however, Israel would be conquered by Assyria, and the rich would themselves be made slaves.

KEY VERSE:
"But let justice roll down like waters, and righteousness like an everflowing stream" (5.24).

KEY PEOPLE:
Amos, Amaziah, Jeroboam II

KEY PLACES:
Bethel, Samaria

SPECIAL FEATURES:
Amos uses striking metaphors from his shepherding and farming experience—an overloaded cart (2.13), a roaring lion (3.8), a torn lamb (3.12), fat cows (4.1), and a basket of fruit (8.1, 2).

WHEN we hear, "he's a man of God," the images that most often come to mind are some famous evangelist, a "Reverend," or the campus minister—professionals, Christian workers, those who preach and teach the Word as a vocation.

Surely Amos was a man of God—a person whose life was devoted to serving the Lord and whose life-style reflected this devotion—but he was a layman. Herding sheep and tending sycamore-fig trees in the Judean countryside, Amos was not the son of a prophet; he was not the son of a priest. As a humble herdsman, he could have stayed in Tekoa, doing his job, providing for his family, and worshiping his God. But God gave Amos a vision of the future (1.2), and told him to take his message to Israel, the northern kingdom (7.15). Amos obeyed, and thus proved he was a man of God.

Amos means *burden* or *burden-bearer.* He carried the heavy burden of God's message to Israel. Amos's message has had an impact upon God's people throughout the centuries, and it needs to be heard today, by individuals and nations. Although they were divided from their southern brothers and sisters in Judah, the northern Israelites were still God's people. But they were living beneath a pious veneer of religion, worshiping idols, and oppressing the poor. Amos, a fiery, fearless, and honest shepherd from the south, confronted them with their sin and warned them of the impending judgment.

The book of Amos opens with this humble herdsman watching his sheep. God then gives him a vision of what was about to happen to the nation of Israel. God condemns all the nations who have sinned against him and harmed his people. Beginning with Syria, he moves quickly through Philistia, Tyre, Edom, Ammon, and Moab. All are condemned, and we can almost hear the Israelites shouting, "Amen!" And then, even Judah, Amos's homeland, is included in God's scathing denunciation (2.4, 5). How Amos's listeners must have enjoyed hearing those words! Suddenly, however, Amos turns to the people of Israel and pronounces God's judgment on *them.* The next four chapters enumerate and describe their sins. It is no wonder that Amaziah, the priest, intervenes and tries to stop the preaching (7.10–13). Fearlessly, Amos continues to relate the visions of future judgment which God gave to him (chapters 8, 9). After all the chapters on judgment, the book concludes with a message of hope. Eventually God will restore his people and make them great again (9.8–15).

As you read Amos's book, put yourself in the place of those Israelites and listen to God's message. Have you grown complacent? Have other concerns taken God's place in your life? Do you ignore those in need or oppress the poor? Picture yourself as Amos, faithfully doing what God calls you to do. You, too, can be God's person. Listen for his clear call and do what he says, wherever it leads.

Amos becomes a prophet to Israel 760	Hosea becomes a prophet to Israel 753	King Shallum of Israel is assassinated 752	Amos's ministry ends 750	Isaiah becomes a prophet to Judah 740

THE BLUEPRINT

1. Announcement of judgment (1.1—2.16)
2. Reasons for judgment (3.1—6.14)
3. Visions of judgment (7.1—9.15)

Amos speaks with brutal frankness in denouncing sin. He collided with the false religious leaders of his day and was not intimidated by priest or king. He continued to speak his message boldly. God requires truth and goodness from all people and nations today as well. Many of the conditions in Israel during Amos's time are evident in today's societies. We need Amos's courage to ignore danger and stand against sin.

MEGATHEMES

THEME	EXPLANATION	IMPORTANCE
Everyone answers to God	Amos pronounced judgment from God on all the surrounding nations. Then he included Judah and Israel. God is in supreme control of all the nations. Everyone is accountable to him.	All people will have to account for their sin. When those who reject God seem to get ahead, don't envy their prosperity or feel sorry for yourself. Remember that we all must answer to God for how we live.
Complacency	Everyone was optimistic, business was booming, people were happy (except for the poor and oppressed). With all the comfort and luxury came self-sufficiency and a false sense of security. But prosperity brought corruption and destruction.	A complacent present leads to a disastrous future. Don't congratulate yourself for the blessings and benefits you now enjoy. They are from God. If you are more satisfied with yourself than with God, remember everything is meaningless without him. A self-sufficient attitude may be your downfall.
Oppressing the poor	The wealthy and powerful people of Samaria, the capital of Israel, had become prosperous, greedy, and unfair. Illegal and immoral slavery came as the result of over-taxation and land-grabbing. There was also cruelty and indifference towards the poor. God is weary of greed and will not tolerate injustice.	God made all people; therefore, to ignore the poor is to ignore those whom God loves and whom Christ came to save. We must go beyond feeling bad for the poor and oppressed. We must act compassionately to stop injustice and to help care for those in need.
Superficial religion	Although many people had abandoned real faith in God, they still pretended to be religious. They were carrying on nominal religious performances instead of having spiritual integrity and practicing heartfelt obedience toward God.	Merely participating in ceremony or ritual falls short of true religion. God wants simple trust in him, not showy external motions. Don't settle for impressing others with external rituals when God wants heartfelt obedience and commitment.

1. Announcement of judgment

God will punish the surrounding nations

1 The words of Amos, who was among the shepherds of Tekoa, which he saw concerning Israel in the days of King Uzziah of Judah and in the days of King Jeroboam son of Joash of Israel, two years[a] before the earthquake.

1.1 2 Sam 14.2 2 Chron 11.6

2 And he said:

The LORD roars from Zion,
and utters his voice from Jerusalem;
the pastures of the shepherds wither,
and the top of Carmel dries up.

1.2 Isa 42.13 Jer 12.4; 14.2 Joel 3.16 Zech 14.5

3 Thus says the LORD:
For three transgressions of Damascus,
and for four, I will not revoke the punishment;[b]
because they have threshed Gilead
with threshing sledges of iron.
4 So I will send a fire on the house of Hazael,
and it shall devour the strongholds of Ben-hadad.
5 I will break the gate bars of Damascus,
and cut off the inhabitants from the Valley of Aven,
and the one who holds the scepter from Beth-eden;
and the people of Aram shall go into exile to Kir,
says the LORD.

1.3 Isa 8.4 Amos 1.6,9,11, 13; 2.1,4,6

1.5 Jer 50.36; 51.30 Lam 2.9 Nah 3.13

6 Thus says the LORD:
For three transgressions of Gaza,
and for four, I will not revoke the punishment;[b]
because they carried into exile entire communities,
to hand them over to Edom.
7 So I will send a fire on the wall of Gaza,

1.6 1 Sam 6.17 2 Chron 28.16 Ezek 35.5 Amos 1.9,11

a Or *during two years* b Heb *cause it to return*

1.1 Amos was a shepherd and fig grower from the southern kingdom (Judah), but he prophesied to the northern kingdom (Israel). Israel was politically at the height of its power with a prosperous economy, but the nation was spiritually corrupt. Idols were worshiped throughout the land, and especially at Bethel, which was supposed to be the nation's religious center. Like Hosea, Amos was sent by God to denounce this social and religious corruption. About 30 or 40 years after Amos prophesied, Assyria destroyed the capital city, Samaria, and conquered the nation (722 B.C.). Uzziah reigned in Judah from 792–750; Jeroboam II reigned in Israel from 793–753.

1.1 Tekoa, Amos's hometown, was located in the rugged sheep country of Judah, ten miles south of Jerusalem. Long before Amos was born, a woman of Tekoa helped reconcile David and his rebellious son, Absalom (2 Samuel 14.1–23).

1.1 All day long Amos took care of sheep—not a particularly "spiritual" job—yet he became a channel of God's message to others. Your job may not cause you to feel spiritual or successful, but it is a vital work if you are in the place God wants you to be. God can work through you to do extraordinary things, no matter how ordinary your occupation.

1.1 The prophet Zechariah and other historical records from this period mention an earthquake at this time (Zechariah 14.5).

1.2 In the Bible, God is often pictured as a shepherd and his people as sheep. As a shepherd, he leads and protects his flock. But here he is depicted as a ferocious lion ready to devour those who are evil or unfaithful. (See also Hosea 11.10.)

1.2 *Carmel* means "garden land," and it was a very fertile area. A drought that would dry up this area would be quite severe.

1.3 Damascus was the capital of Syria. In the past, Syria had been one of Israel's formidable enemies. After the defeat of Syria by Assyria in 802 B.C., Damascus was no longer a real threat.

1.3–2.6 Amos pronounced God's judgment on nation after nation around Israel's borders—even Judah. Perhaps the people of Israel cheered when they heard the rebukes leveled against those nations. But then Amos proclaimed God's judgment on Israel. They could not excuse their own sin, because they thought the sins of their neighbors were worse. God is no respecter of persons. He judges all people fairly and equally.

1.3–2.6 The accusation, "For three transgressions . . . and for four" means that these nations have sinned again and again. This phrase echoes through these verses as God evaluates nation after nation. Each had persistently refused to follow God's commands. A sinful practice can become a way of life. Ignoring or denying the problem will not help us. We must begin the process of correction by confessing our sins to God and asking him to forgive us. Otherwise, we have no hope but to continue our pattern of sin.

1.4 The "house of Hazael" refers to the king of Damascus. Ben-hadad was Hazael's son.

1.5 The Syrians are called "people of Aram" because those who lived in Damascus were Aramean. The Syrians had been slaves in Kir and were now free (9.7). Decreeing that the Syrians should go back to Kir was like saying the Israelites should go back to Egypt as slaves (Exodus 1).

1.7, 8 Gaza, Ashdod, Ashkelon, and Ekron were four of the five major city-states of Philistia, which often threatened Israel. The fifth city-state, Gath, had already been destroyed. Amos was saying that the nation of Philistia would be destroyed for its sins.

fire that shall devour its strongholds.

1.8 Isa 14.29-31 Jer 47.1-7 Ezek 25.16 Zeph 2.4-7

8 I will cut off the inhabitants from Ashdod,
and the one who holds the scepter from Ashkelon;
I will turn my hand against Ekron,
and the remnant of the Philistines shall perish,
says the Lord GOD.

1.9 2 Sam 5.11 1 Kgs 5.1 9.11-14 Isa 23.1-18 Zech 9.2-4

9 Thus says the LORD:
For three transgressions of Tyre,
and for four, I will not revoke the punishment;[c]
because they delivered entire communities over to Edom,
and did not remember the covenant of kinship.
10 So I will send a fire on the wall of Tyre,
fire that shall devour its strongholds.

1.11 Gen 27.40 Num 20.14-21 Isa 34.1-17 63.1-3 Jer 49.7-22 Ezek 25.12-14

11 Thus says the LORD:
For three transgressions of Edom,
and for four, I will not revoke the punishment;[c]
because he pursued his brother with the sword
and cast off all pity;
he maintained his anger perpetually,[d]
and kept his wrath[e] forever.

1.12 Gen 36.11 Jer 49.7,20

12 So I will send a fire on Teman,
and it shall devour the strongholds of Bozrah.

1.13 Jer 49.1-6 Hos 13.16

13 Thus says the LORD:
For three transgressions of the Ammonites,
and for four, I will not revoke the punishment;[c]
because they have ripped open pregnant women in Gilead
in order to enlarge their territory.

1.14 Isa 9.5; 30.30 Dan 11.40 Zech 7.14

14 So I will kindle a fire against the wall of Rabbah,
fire that shall devour its strongholds,
with shouting on the day of battle,
with a storm on the day of the whirlwind;

[c] Heb *cause it to return* [d] Syr Vg: Heb *and his anger tore perpetually* [e] Gk Syr Vg: Heb *and his wrath kept*

AMOS served as a prophet to Israel (the northern kingdom) from 760–750 B.C.

Climate of the times	Israel was enjoying economic prosperity and peace. But this had caused her to become a selfish, materialistic society. Those who were well-off ignored the needs of those less fortunate. The people were self-centered and indifferent toward God.
Main message	Amos spoke against those who exploited or ignored the needy.
Importance of message	Believing in God is more than a personal matter. God calls all believers to work against injustices in society and to aid those less fortunate.
Contemporary prophets	Jonah (793–753) Hosea (753–715)

1.9 Tyre was one of two major cities in Phoenicia. Several treaties had been made with this city because it supplied the cedar used to build David's palace and God's temple (2 Samuel 5.11; 1 Kings 5).

1.11, 12 Edom and Israel both descended from Isaac: Edom from Isaac's son Esau, and Israel from Esau's twin brother, Jacob (Genesis 25.19–28; 27). But these two nations, like the two brothers, were always at odds. Edom rejoiced at Israel's misfortunes. As a result, God promised to destroy Edom completely, from Teman in the north to Bozrah in the south.

1.13–15 The Ammonites descended from an incestuous relationship between Lot and his younger daughter (Genesis 19.30–38). They were hostile to Israel, and although Israel began to worship their idols, they still attacked (Judges 10.6–8). After Saul was anointed Israel's king, his first victory in battle was against the Ammonites (1 Samuel 11). Rabbah was Ammon's capital city. Amos's prophecy of Ammon's destruction was fulfilled through the Assyrian invasion.

15 then their king shall go into exile,
he and his officials together,
says the LORD.

1.15 Jer 49.3

2 Thus says the LORD:
For three transgressions of Moab,
and for four, I will not revoke the punishment;[f]
because he burned to lime
the bones of the king of Edom.
2 So I will send a fire on Moab,
and it shall devour the strongholds of Kerioth,
and Moab shall die amid uproar,
amid shouting and the sound of the trumpet;
3 I will cut off the ruler from its midst,
and will kill all its officials with him,
says the LORD.

2.1 Isa 15.1-9 Zech 2.8,9
2.2 Isa 9.5 Jer 48.24,41,45

4 Thus says the LORD:
For three transgressions of Judah,
and for four, I will not revoke the punishment;[f]
because they have rejected the law of the LORD,
and have not kept his statutes,
but they have been led astray by the same lies
after which their ancestors walked.
5 So I will send a fire on Judah,
and it shall devour the strongholds of Jerusalem.

2.4 Lev 26.14,15 Judg 2.17-20 2 Kgs 17.19 Hos 6.11
2.5 Jer 17.27 37.8-10 Hos 8.14

God will punish Israel

6 Thus says the LORD:
For three transgressions of Israel,
and for four, I will not revoke the punishment;[f]
because they sell the righteous for silver,
and the needy for a pair of sandals—
7 they who trample the head of the poor into the dust of the earth,
and push the afflicted out of the way;
father and son go in to the same girl,
so that my holy name is profaned;
8 they lay themselves down beside every altar

2.6 Joel 3.3,6 Mic 3.2,3
2.7 Lev 18.8,15 Prov 28.21 Ezek 22.11

[f] Heb *cause it to return*

2.1–3 The Moabites descended from an incestuous relationship between Lot and his older daughter (Genesis 19.30–38). Balak, king of Moab, tried to hire the seer, Balaam, to curse the Israelites so they could be defeated (Numbers 22—24). Balaam refused, but some of the Moabites succeeded in getting Israel to worship Baal (Numbers 25.1–3). The Moabites were known for their atrocities (2 Kings 3.26, 27). An archaeological artifact, the Moabite stone, reveals that Moab was always ready to profit from the downfall of others.

2.4–6 After Solomon's reign, the kingdom divided, and the tribes of Judah and Benjamin became the southern kingdom (Judah) under Solomon's son, Rehoboam. The other ten tribes became the northern kingdom (Israel) and followed Jeroboam, who had rebelled against Rehoboam.

God punished other nations harshly for their evil actions and atrocities. But God also promised to judge both Israel and Judah because they ignored the revealed word of God. The other nations were ignorant, but Judah and Israel, God's people, knew what God wanted. Still they ignored him and joined pagan nations in worshiping idols. If we know God's Word and refuse to obey it, like Israel we will carry a greater guilt.

2.4–6 Amos won his audience as he proclaimed God's judgment against the evil nations surrounding Israel. He even spoke against his own nation, Judah, before focusing on God's indictment of Israel.

2.6ff God condemned Israel for five specific sins: (1) selling the poor as slaves (see Deuteronomy 15.7–11; Amos 8.6), (2) exploiting the poor (see Exodus 23.6; Deuteronomy 16.19), (3) engaging in perverse sexual sins, (4) taking illegal collateral for loans (see Exodus 22.26, 27; Deuteronomy 24.6, 12, 13), and (5) worshiping false gods (see Exodus 20.3–5).

2.6, 7 Amos spoke to the upper class. There was no middle class in the country—only the very rich and the very poor. The rich kept religious rituals. They gave extra tithes, went to places of worship, and offered sacrifices. But they were greedy and unjust, and they took advantage of the helpless. Be sure that you do not neglect the needs of the poor while you faithfully attend church and fulfill religious rituals. God expects us to live out our faith, and this means responding to those in need.

on garments taken in pledge;
and in the house of their God they drink
wine bought with fines they imposed.

2.9 Josh 11.21,22

9 Yet I destroyed the Amorite before them,
whose height was like the height of cedars,
and who was as strong as oaks;
I destroyed his fruit above,
and his roots beneath.

2.10 Num 14.34 Deut 2.7; 8.2-4

10 Also I brought you up out of the land of Egypt,
and led you forty years in the wilderness,
to possess the land of the Amorite.

2.11 Num 6.1-21 1 Kgs 17.1; 22.8

11 And I raised up some of your children to be prophets
and some of your youths to be nazirites.[g]
Is it not indeed so, O people of Israel?
says the LORD.

2.12 Jer 11.21 Amos 7.13,16

12 But you made the nazirites[g] drink wine,
and commanded the prophets,
saying, "You shall not prophesy."

2.13 Joel 13.13

13 So, I will press you down in your place,
just as a cart presses down
when it is full of sheaves.[h]

2.14 Isa 30.16,17 Jer 9.23 Amos 9.1-3

14 Flight shall perish from the swift,
and the strong shall not retain their strength,
nor shall the mighty save their lives;

2.15 Ps 33.16,17 Isa 31.3

15 those who handle the bow shall not stand,
and those who are swift of foot shall not save themselves,
nor shall those who ride horses save their lives;
16 and those who are stout of heart among the mighty
shall flee away naked in that day,
says the LORD.

2. Reasons for judgment

Sin separates the people from God

3.1 Jer 8.3 33.24-26 Ezek 37.16

3 Hear this word that the LORD has spoken against you, O people of Israel,
against the whole family that I brought up out of the land of Egypt:
2 You only have I known
of all the families of the earth;

[g] That is, *those separated* or *those consecrated* [h] Meaning of Heb uncertain

2.9–11 The prophets were constantly challenging people to remember what God had done! When we read a list like this one, we are amazed at Israel's forgetfulness. But what would the prophets say about us? God's past faithfulness should have reminded the Israelites to obey him; likewise, what he has done for us should remind us to live for him.

2.11 The nazirites took a vow of service to God. The vow included abstaining from wine and never cutting their hair. But instead of being respected for their disciplined and temperate lives, they were being urged to break their vows. If the nazirites were corrupted, there would remain little influence for good among the Israelites.

2.13 This verse means that God would cause Israel to be pressed down or crushed as a wagon is pressed when it is loaded with wheat. Their sins were leading to God's punishment.

2.16 "That day" refers to when Assyria would attack Israel, destroy Samaria, and take the people captive (722 B.C.). This military defeat came only a few decades after this pronouncement.

2.16 Television and movies are filled with images of people who seem to have no fear. Many today have modeled their lives after these images – they want to be tough. But God is not impressed with bravado. He says that even the toughest of men will run in fear when God's judgment comes. Can you think of people who think they can make it through life without God? Don't be swayed by their self-assured rhetoric. Recognize that God fears no one, and one day all people will fear him.

3.2 God chose Israel to be the people through whom all other nations of the world could know God. He made this promise to Abraham, father of the Israelites (Genesis 12.1–3). Israel didn't have to do anything to be chosen; God gave them this special privilege because he wanted to, not because they deserved special treatment (Deuteronomy 9.4–6). Pride in their privileged position, however, ruined Israel's sensitivity to the word of God and to the plight of others.

therefore I will punish you
for all your iniquities.

3.2
Ex 19.5,6
Deut 7.6

3 Do two walk together
unless they have made an appointment?
4 Does a lion roar in the forest,
when it has no prey?
Does a young lion cry out from its den,
if it has caught nothing?
5 Does a bird fall into a snare on the earth,
when there is no trap for it?
Does a snare spring up from the ground,
when it has taken nothing?
6 Is a trumpet blown in a city,
and the people are not afraid?
Does disaster befall a city,
unless the LORD has done it?
7 Surely the Lord GOD does nothing,
without revealing his secret
to his servants the prophets.
8 The lion has roared;
who will not fear?
The Lord GOD has spoken;
who can but prophesy?

3.4
Ps 104.21
Hos 11.10

3.6
Isa 14.24-27
Jer 4.5
Ezek 33.3
Hos 5.8
Zeph 1.16

3.7
Gen 18.17
Dan 9.22-27

3.8
Jer 20.9

9 Proclaim to the strongholds in Ashdod,
and to the strongholds in the land of Egypt,
and say, "Assemble yourselves on Mount[i] Samaria,
and see what great tumults are within it,
and what oppressions are in its midst."
10 They do not know how to do right, says the LORD,
those who store up violence and robbery in their strongholds.
11 Therefore thus says the Lord GOD:
An adversary shall surround the land,
and strip you of your defense;
and your strongholds shall be plundered.

3.10
Hab 2.8-11
Zeph 1.9
Zech 5.3,4

12 Thus says the LORD: As the shepherd rescues from the mouth of the lion two

[i] Gk Syr: Heb *the mountains of*

3.3–6 With a series of seven rhetorical questions, Amos shows how two events are linked together in each case (two people walk together because they have agreed on an appointment). Once one event takes place, the second will surely follow. Amos was showing that God's revelation to him was the sure sign that judgment would follow.

3.6 This verse means that God himself would be sending disaster to Israel.

3.7 Even in anger, God is merciful; he always warned his people through prophets before punishing them. Warnings about sin and judgment apply to people today just as they did to Israel. Because we have been warned about our sin, we have no excuse when punishment comes. God had warned his people through his prophets, so they could not rationalize or complain when God punished them for refusing to repent. Do not take lightly the warnings in God's Word about judgment. His warnings are a way of showing mercy to you.

3.9 Ashdod was a Philistine city that may have been under Assyrian domination by this time. Ashdod was also the location of the temple of Dagon, a pagan god. Amos pictured Assyria and Egypt coming to witness Israel's great sins. Even Israel's most wicked and idolatrous neighbors would see God judge Israel.

3.10 Israel no longer knew how to do what was right. The more they sinned, the harder it was to remember what God wanted. The same is true for us. The longer we wait to deal with sin, the greater its hold on us becomes. Finally, we forget what it means to do right. Are you on the verge of forgetting?

3.11, 12 The approaching adversary was Assyria, who conquered the nation and did just as Amos predicted. The people were scattered to foreign lands, and foreigners were placed in the land to keep the peace. Israel's leaders had robbed their defenseless fellow countrymen, and now they would be rendered defenseless by the Assyrians. Amos added that even if they tried to repent then, it would be too late. The destruction would be so complete that nothing of value would be left.

3.12 1 Sam 17.34-37 legs, or a piece of an ear, so shall the people of Israel who live in Samaria be
rescued, with the corner of a couch and part[j] of a bed.

3.13 Ezek 2.7 13 Hear, and testify against the house of Jacob,
says the Lord GOD, the God of hosts:
3.14 Amos 4.4 5.5,6; 7.10,13 14 On the day I punish Israel for its transgressions,
I will punish the altars of Bethel,
and the horns of the altar shall be cut off
and fall to the ground.
3.15 Judg 3.20 1 Kgs 22.39 Jer 36.22 15 I will tear down the winter house as well as the summer house;
and the houses of ivory shall perish,
and the great houses[j] shall come to an end,
says the LORD.

The people refuse to turn to God

4.1 Deut 32.14,15 **4** Hear this word, you cows of Bashan
who are on Mount Samaria,
who oppress the poor, who crush the needy,
who say to their husbands, "Bring something to drink!"
4.2 Isa 37.29 Jer 16.16 Ezek 29.4; 38.4 2 The Lord GOD has sworn by his holiness:
The time is surely coming upon you,
when they shall take you away with hooks,
even the last of you with fishhooks.
4.3 2 Kgs 25.4 Ezek 12.5,12 3 Through breaches in the wall you shall leave,
each one straight ahead;
and you shall be flung out into Harmon,[k]
says the LORD.

4 Come to Bethel — and transgress;
to Gilgal — and multiply transgression;
bring your sacrifices every morning,
your tithes every three days;
4.5 Lev 7.13 22.18-21 5 bring a thank-offering of leavened bread,
and proclaim freewill offerings, publish them;
for so you love to do, O people of Israel!
says the Lord GOD.

4.6 Lev 26.26 Deut 28.38 6 I gave you cleanness of teeth in all your cities,
and lack of bread in all your places,

j Or *many houses* k Meaning of Heb uncertain

3.14 God's judgment against Israel's altars showed that he was rejecting Israel's entire religious system, because it was so polluted. God's altar in Jerusalem was a place of protection (1 Kings 1.49–53); and the false altars would soon be gone. Then the people would have no sanctuary, protection, or refuge (see 4.4) when judgment came.

4.1 Israel's wealthy women were compared to the cows of Bashan — pampered, sleek, and well-fed (see Psalm 22.12). These women selfishly pushed their husbands to oppress the helpless in order to support their lavish life-styles. Be careful not to desire material possessions so much that you are willing to oppress others and displease God to get them.

4.4 Amos sarcastically invited the people to sin in Bethel and Gilgal where they worshiped idols instead of God. Bethel was where God had renewed his covenant to Abraham with Jacob (Genesis 28.10–22). Now Bethel was the religious center of the northern kingdom, and Jeroboam had placed an idol there to discourage the people from traveling to Jerusalem in the southern kingdom to worship (1 Kings 12.26–29). Gilgal was Israel's first campground after entering the promised land (Joshua 4.19). Here Joshua renewed the covenant and the rite of circumcision, and the people celebrated the passover (Joshua 5.2–11). Saul was crowned Israel's first king in Gilgal (1 Samuel 11.15).

4.4, 5 The Israelites were tithing and thanking God for the wealth they had achieved by oppressing the poor. Wealth is not necessarily a blessing from God. It is good to thank God for prosperity, but God must also be involved in the process leading to prosperity.

4.6 "Cleanness of teeth" means lack of food, or hunger.

4.6–13 No matter how God warned the people — through famine, drought, blight, locusts, plagues, or war — they still ignored him. Because they didn't get the message, they would have to meet him face to face in judgment. No longer would they ignore God; they would have to face the One they had rejected, the One they had refused to obey when he commanded them to care for the poor. One day each of us will meet God face to face to account for what we have done or refused to do. Have you listened to his Word that tells you how to prepare yourself to meet him?

yet you did not return to me,
says the LORD.

7 And I also withheld the rain from you
when there were still three months to the harvest;
I would send rain on one city,
and send no rain on another city;
one field would be rained upon,
and the field on which it did not rain withered;
8 so two or three towns wandered to one town
to drink water, and were not satisfied;
yet you did not return to me,
says the LORD.

9 I struck you with blight and mildew;
I laid waste[l] your gardens and your vineyards;
the locust devoured your fig trees and your olive trees;
yet you did not return to me,
says the LORD.

10 I sent among you a pestilence after the manner of Egypt;
I killed your young men with the sword;
I carried away your horses;[m]
and I made the stench of your camp go up into your nostrils;
yet you did not return to me,
says the LORD.

11 I overthrew some of you,
as when God overthrew Sodom and Gomorrah,
and you were like a brand snatched from the fire;
yet you did not return to me,
says the LORD.

12 Therefore thus I will do to you, O Israel;
because I will do this to you,
prepare to meet your God, O Israel!

13 For lo, the one who forms the mountains, creates the wind,
reveals his thoughts to mortals,
makes the morning darkness,
and treads on the heights of the earth—
the LORD, the God of hosts, is his name!

4.7 1 Kgs 8.35,36
4.8 1 Kgs 18.5 Isa 41.17,18 Jer 14.3,4
4.9 Deut 28.22,42 1 Kgs 8.37 Joel 2.25
4.10 Ex 9.3-6 Jer 11.22; 18.21 Isa 9.13
4.11 Gen 19.24,25 Jer 23.14
4.12 Isa 47.3 Ezek 13.5
4.13 Deut 32.13 Job 38.4-11 Dan 2.28,30 Hab 3.19

Amos mourns for Israel

5 Hear this word that I take up over you in lamentation, O house of Israel:
2 Fallen, no more to rise,
is maiden Israel;
forsaken on her land,
with no one to raise her up.

3 For thus says the Lord GOD:
The city that marched out a thousand
shall have a hundred left,

5.1 Jer 9.10 Ezek 19.1,14 Mic 2.4

[l] Cn: Heb *the multitude of* [m] Heb *with the captivity of your horses*

5.1 Amos shocked his listeners by singing a lamentation or song of grief for them as if they had already been destroyed. The Israelites believed their wealth and religious ritual made them secure, but Amos lamented their sure destruction.

and that which marched out a hundred
shall have ten left.[n]

5.4 Deut 4.29 30.1-8 32.46,47

4 For thus says the LORD to the house of Israel:
Seek me and live;
5 but do not seek Bethel,
and do not enter into Gilgal
or cross over to Beer-sheba;
for Gilgal shall surely go into exile,
and Bethel shall come to nothing.

5.6 Ex 22.6 Deut 4.24

6 Seek the LORD and live,
or he will break out against the house of Joseph like fire,
and it will devour Bethel, with no one to quench it.

5.7 Amos 2.3; 5.12

7 Ah, you that turn justice to wormwood,
and bring righteousness to the ground!

5.8 Gen 7.11-20 Job 9.9; 12.22 37.13; 38.31-34 Amos 9.6

8 The one who made the Pleiades and Orion,
and turns deep darkness into the morning,
and darkens the day into night,
who calls for the waters of the sea,
and pours them out on the surface of the earth,
the LORD is his name,

5.9 Amos 2.14 Mic 5.11

9 who makes destruction flash out against the strong,
so that destruction comes upon the fortress.

5.10 Jer 17.16,17 Amos 5.15 Jn 7.7; 8.45-47

10 They hate the one who reproves in the gate,
and they abhor the one who speaks the truth.

5.11 Deut 28.30 Isa 65.21,23 Mic 6.15

11 Therefore because you trample on the poor
and take from them levies of grain,
you have built houses of hewn stone,
but you shall not live in them;
you have planted pleasant vineyards,
but you shall not drink their wine.

5.12 Ps 26.9,10 Isa 1.23 Mic 3.11; 7.3

12 For I know how many are your transgressions,
and how great are your sins—
you who afflict the righteous, who take a bribe,
and push aside the needy in the gate.

[n] Heb adds *to the house of Israel*

5.4 There is one sure remedy for a world that is sick and dying in sin—seek God and live. Sin seeks to destroy, but hope is found in seeking God. In times of difficulty, seek God. In personal discomfort and struggle, seek God. When others are struggling, encourage them to seek God too.

5.7 The law courts should have been places of justice where the poor and oppressed could find relief. Instead, they had become places of greed and injustice. Wormwood was a bitter, poisonous herb.

5.8 Pleiades and Orion are star constellations. For thousands of years, navigators have staked lives and fortunes on the reliability of the stars. The constancy of the heavens challenges us to look beyond them to their Creator.

5.10–12 "One who reproves in the gate" refers to an honest judge. The city gate was where justice was administered. A society is in trouble when those who try to do right are hated for their justice. Any society that exploits the poor and defenseless or hates the truth is bent on destroying itself.

5.12 Why does God put so much emphasis on the way we treat the needy? How we treat the rich, or those of equal station, often reflects what we hope to get from them. But because the poor can give us nothing, how we treat them reflects our true character. Do we, like Christ, give without thought of gain? We should treat the poor as we would like God to treat us.

5.12 Here are eight common excuses for not helping the poor and needy: (1) They don't deserve help. They got themselves into poverty; let them get themselves out. (2) God's call to help the poor applies to another time. (3) We don't have any people like this. (4) I have my own needs. (5) Any money I give will be wasted, stolen, or spent on other things. The poor will never see it. (6) I may become a victim myself. (7) I don't know where to start, and I don't have time. (8) My little bit won't make any difference.

Instead of making lame excuses, ask what can be done to help. Does your church have programs that help the needy? Could you volunteer to work with a community group that fights poverty? As one individual, you may not be able to accomplish much, but join up with similarly motivated people and watch mountains begin to move.

13 Therefore the prudent will keep silent in such a time;
for it is an evil time.

14 Seek good and not evil,
that you may live;
and so the LORD, the God of hosts, will be with you,
just as you have said.
15 Hate evil and love good,
and establish justice in the gate;
it may be that the LORD, the God of hosts,
will be gracious to the remnant of Joseph.

5.15 1 Kgs 20.31 Ps 34.14; 97.10 Joel 2.14 Jonah 3.9

16 Therefore thus says the LORD, the God of hosts, the Lord:
In all the squares there shall be wailing;
and in all the streets they shall say, "Alas! alas!"
They shall call the farmers to mourning,
and those skilled in lamentation, to wailing;
17 in all the vineyards there shall be wailing,
for I will pass through the midst of you,
says the LORD.

5.16 Isa 15.2-5 Amos 8.3,10 Joel 1.8,11

5.17 Isa 16.10 32.10-12

18 Alas for you who desire the day of the LORD!
Why do you want the day of the LORD?
It is darkness, not light;
19 as if someone fled from a lion,
and was met by a bear;
or went into the house and rested a hand against the wall,
and was bitten by a snake.
20 Is not the day of the LORD darkness, not light,
and gloom with no brightness in it?

5.18 Isa 5.30 Jer 30.7 2 Pet 3.10

5.19 Amos 9.1,2

5.20 Amos 5.18

21 I hate, I despise your festivals,
and I take no delight in your solemn assemblies.
22 Even though you offer me your burnt offerings and grain offerings,
I will not accept them;
and the offerings of well-being of your fatted animals
I will not look upon.
23 Take away from me the noise of your songs;
I will not listen to the melody of your harps.
24 But let justice roll down like waters,
and righteousness like an everflowing stream.

5.21 Isa 1.11-16

5.22 Lev 6.9-23 7.11-21

5.24 Jer 22.3 Amos 5.7 Mic 6.8

25 Did you bring to me sacrifices and offerings the forty years in the wilder-

5.15 If Israel swept away the corrupt system of false accusations, bribery, and corruption, and insisted that only just decisions be given, this would show their change of heart. We dare not read this passage lightly or write it off simply as encouragement to be good. Instead, it is a command to reform our own legal and social system.

5.16 Failure to honor the dead was considered horrible in Israel, so loud weeping was common at funerals. Paid mourners ("those skilled in lamentation"), usually women, cried and mourned loudly with dirges and eulogies. Amos said there would be so many funerals that there would be a shortage of professional mourners, so farmers would be called from the fields to help. (See also Jeremiah 9.17–20.)

5.18 Here "the day of the Lord" means the imminent destruction by the Assyrian army as well as the future day of the Lord's judgment. For the faithful, that day will be glorious; but for the unfaithful it will be darkness and doom. (See Joel 1.15 for more discussion of the day of the Lord.)

5.18–24 These people were calling for the day of the Lord, thinking it would bring an end to their troubles. But God says, "You don't know what you are asking for." This "day of the Lord" will bring "judgment" (justice), and justice would bring the punishment they deserved for their sins.

5.21–23 God hates false worship ("festivals" and "solemn assemblies") by people who do it out of pretense or for show. If we are living sinful lives and use religious ritual and traditions to make ourselves look good, God will despise our worship and will not accept what we offer. He wants sincere hearts, not the songs of hypocrites. When we worship at church, are we more concerned about our image or our attitude toward God?

ness, O house of Israel? 26 You shall take up Sakkuth your king, and Kaiwan your
star-god, your images,[o] which you made for yourselves; 27 therefore I will take you
into exile beyond Damascus, says the LORD, whose name is the God of hosts.

God despises Israel's pride

6.1 Judg 18.7 Isa 32.9-11

6 Alas for those who are at ease in Zion,
and for those who feel secure on Mount Samaria,
the notables of the first of the nations,
to whom the house of Israel resorts!

6.2 Gen 10.10 1 Sam 17.23 2 Kgs 17.24,30 19.13 Isa 10.9

2 Cross over to Calneh, and see;
from there go to Hamath the great;
then go down to Gath of the Philistines.
Are you better[p] than these kingdoms?
Or is your[q] territory greater than their[r] territory,

6.3 Amos 5.18; 9.10

3 O you that put far away the evil day,
and bring near a reign of violence?

6.4 Ezek 34.2,3

4 Alas for those who lie on beds of ivory,
and lounge on their couches,
and eat lambs from the flock,
and calves from the stall;

6.5 1 Chron 15.16 23.5

5 who sing idle songs to the sound of the harp,
and like David improvise on instruments of music;
6 who drink wine from bowls,
and anoint themselves with the finest oils,
but are not grieved over the ruin of Joseph!
7 Therefore they shall now be the first to go into exile,
and the revelry of the loungers shall pass away.

6.8 Lev 26.11 Zech 11.8

8 The Lord GOD has sworn by himself
(says the LORD, the God of hosts):
I abhor the pride of Jacob
and hate his strongholds;
and I will deliver up the city and all that is in it.

6.10 1 Sam 31.12 Amos 5.13; 8.3

9 If ten people remain in one house, they shall die. 10 And if a relative, one who
burns the dead,[s] shall take up the body to bring it out of the house, and shall say
to someone in the innermost parts of the house, "Is anyone else with you?" the
answer will come, "No." Then the relative[t] shall say, "Hush! We must not mention the name of the LORD."

[o] Heb *your images, your star-god* [p] Or *Are they better* [q] Heb *their* [r] Heb *your* [s] Or *who makes a burning for him* [t] Heb *he*

5.26 Sakkuth and Kaiwan were heathen gods associated with Saturn. Israel had turned to worshiping stars and planets, preferring nature over nature's God. Heathen religion allowed them to indulge themselves in sexual immorality and to become wealthy through any means. Because they refused to worship and obey the one true God, they would cause their own destruction.

5.27 Israel's captivity was indeed beyond Damascus—the people were taken to Assyria. God's punishment was more than defeat; it was complete exile from their homeland.

6.1–6 Amos leveled his attack at those living in ease and luxury in both Israel and Judah. Great wealth and comfortable life-styles may make people think they are secure; but God is not pleased if we isolate ourselves from others' needs. God wants us to care for others as he cares for us. His kingdom has no place for selfishness or indifference. We must learn to put the needs of others before our wants. Using our wealth to help others is one way to guard against pride and complacency.

6.2 Great cities to the east, north, and west had been destroyed because of their pride. What happened to them would happen to Israel, because its sin was just as great as theirs.

6.4 Ivory was an imported luxury, rare and extremely expensive. Even a small amount of ivory symbolized wealth. Something as extravagant as an ivory bed shows the gross waste of resources that should have been used to help the poor.

6.8–11 The people had built luxurious homes to flaunt their achievements. While it is not wrong to live in comfortable houses, we must not let them become sources of inflated pride and self-glorification. God gave our homes to us, and they are to be used for service, not just for show.

6.10 Amos gives us a picture of God's fearful judgment: the people will be afraid even to speak God's name, even during a time of grief, lest they attract his attention and be judged also.

11 See, the LORD commands,
and the great house shall be shattered to bits,
and the little house to pieces.
12 Do horses run on rocks?
Does one plow the sea with oxen?[u]
But you have turned justice into poison
and the fruit of righteousness into wormwood—
13 you who rejoice in Lo-debar,[v]
who say, "Have we not by our own strength
taken Karnaim[w] for ourselves?"
14 Indeed, I am raising up against you a nation,
O house of Israel, says the LORD, the God of hosts,
and they shall oppress you from Lebo-hamath
to the Wadi Arabah.

6.12 Amos 5.7,11,12

6.14 Num 34.7,8; 2 Kgs 14.25

3. Visions of judgment

Amos sees a swarm of locusts

7 This is what the Lord GOD showed me: he was forming locusts at the time the
latter growth began to sprout (it was the latter growth after the king's mow-
ings). 2 When they had finished eating the grass of the land, I said,
"O Lord GOD, forgive, I beg you!
How can Jacob stand?
He is so small!"
3 The LORD relented concerning this;
"It shall not be," said the LORD.

7.1 Ex 10.12-16; Nah 3.15-17

7.2 Ex 10.15; Num 14.17-19; Jer 14.7; 42.2; Ezek 9.8; Rev 9.4

Amos sees a great fire

4 This is what the Lord GOD showed me: the Lord GOD was calling for a shower
of fire,[x] and it devoured the great deep and was eating up the land. 5 Then I said,
"O Lord GOD, cease, I beg you!
How can Jacob stand?
He is so small!"
6 The LORD relented concerning this;
"This also shall not be," said the Lord GOD.

7.4 Isa 66.15,16; Amos 2.5

7.6 Amos 7.3

Amos sees a plumb line

7 This is what he showed me: the Lord was standing beside a wall built with a
plumb line, with a plumb line in his hand. 8 And the LORD said to me, "Amos, what
do you see?" And I said, "A plumb line." Then the Lord said,
"See, I am setting a plumb line
in the midst of my people Israel;
I will never again pass them by;
9 the high places of Isaac shall be made desolate,
and the sanctuaries of Israel shall be laid waste,
and I will rise against the house of Jeroboam with the sword."

7.8 Isa 28.17; 34.11

7.9 2 Kgs 15.8-10

10 Then Amaziah, the priest of Bethel, sent to King Jeroboam of Israel, saying,

[u] Or *Does one plow them with oxen* [v] Or *in a thing of nothingness* [w] Or *horns* [x] Or *for a judgment by fire*

6.13, 14 Karnaim was a city northeast of Israel, an insignificant border town compared to the nation they were about to face, Assyria. Lebo-hamath was to the north, and Wadi Arabah to the south. The entire nation would be destroyed by Assyria (2 Kings 17).

7.1ff The following series of visions conveyed God's message to the people using images that were familiar to them—insects, fire, tools.

7.1–6 Twice Amos was shown a vision of Israel's impending punishment, and his immediate response was to pray that God would spare Israel. Prayer is a powerful privilege. Amos's prayers should remind us to pray for our nation.

7.7–9 A plumb line is a device used to ensure the straightness of a wall. A wall that is not straight will eventually collapse. God wants people to be right with him; he wants the sin that makes us crooked removed immediately. God's Word is the plumb line that helps us be aware of our sin. How do you measure up to this plumb line?

7.10 1 Kgs 12.31 18.17 2 Kgs 14.23,24

"Amos has conspired against you in the very center of the house of Israel; the land
is not able to bear all his words. 11 For thus Amos has said,
'Jeroboam shall die by the sword,
and Israel must go into exile
away from his land.' "

7.12 1 Sam 9.9 2 Chron 16.10
7.13 1 Kgs 12.29,32 13.1 Amos 2.12
7.14 1 Kgs 20.35 2 Kgs 2.3-7 2 Chron 16.7
7.15 Jer 1.7 Ezek 2.3,4
7.16 Isa 31.10 Mic 2.6
7.17 Isa 13.16 Jer 14.16; 20.6 Hos 4.13,14

12 And Amaziah said to Amos, "O seer, go, flee away to the land of Judah, earn
your bread there, and prophesy there; 13 but never again prophesy at Bethel, for it
is the king's sanctuary, and it is a temple of the kingdom."
14 Then Amos answered Amaziah, "I am[y] no prophet, nor a prophet's son; but
I am[y] a herdsman, and a dresser of sycamore trees, 15 and the LORD took me from
following the flock, and the LORD said to me, 'Go, prophesy to my people Israel.'
16 "Now therefore hear the word of the LORD.
You say, 'Do not prophesy against Israel,
and do not preach against the house of Isaac.'
17 Therefore thus says the LORD:
'Your wife shall become a prostitute in the city,
and your sons and your daughters shall fall by the sword,
and your land shall be parceled out by line;
you yourself shall die in an unclean land,
and Israel shall surely go into exile away from its land.' "

Amos sees a basket of fruit

8.2 Isa 28.4 Jer 24.1-3

8 This is what the Lord GOD showed me—a basket of summer fruit.[z] 2 He said,
"Amos, what do you see?" And I said, "A basket of summer fruit."[z] Then the
LORD said to me,
The end[a] has come upon my people Israel;
I will never again pass them by.

8.3 Hos 10.5,6 Amos 5.23

3 The songs of the temple[b] shall become wailings in that day,"
says the Lord GOD;
"the dead bodies shall be many,
cast out in every place. Be silent!"

[y] Or *was* [z] Heb *qayits* [a] Heb *qets* [b] Or *palace*

AMOS'S VISIONS

Vision	*Reference*	*Significance*
Swarm of locusts	7.1–3	God was preparing punishment which he delayed only because of Amos's intervention.
Fire	7.4–6	God was preparing to devour the land, but Amos intervened on behalf of the people.
Wall and plumb line	7.7–9	God would see if the people were crooked and, if they were, he would punish them.
Basket of ripe fruit	8.1ff	The people were ripe for punishment; though once beautiful, they were now rotten.
God standing beside the altar	9.1ff	Punishment was executed.

Amos had a series of visions concerning God's judgment on Israel. God was planning to judge Israel by sending a swarm of locusts or fire. In spite of Amos's intercession on Israel's behalf, God would still carry out his judgment because Israel persisted in her disobedience.

7.10 Prophets like Amos were often seen as traitors because they spoke out against the king and his advisors, undermining their authority and exposing their sin. The kings often saw the prophets as enemies rather than as God's spokesmen who were really trying to help him and the nation.

7.10ff Amaziah was the chief priest in Bethel, representing Israel's official religion. He was not concerned about hearing God's message; he was only worried about his own position. Maintaining his position was more important than listening to the truth. Don't let your desire for prestige, authority, or money keep you tied to a job or position you should leave. Don't let anything come between you and obeying God.

7.14, 15 Without any special preparation, education, or upbringing, Amos obeyed God's call to "Go, prophesy to my people Israel." Obedience is the test of a faithful servant of God. Are you obeying God's Word?

4 Hear this, you that trample on the needy,
and bring to ruin the poor of the land,
5 saying, "When will the new moon be over
so that we may sell grain;
and the sabbath,
so that we may offer wheat for sale?
We will make the ephah small and the shekel great,
and practice deceit with false balances,
6 buying the poor for silver
and the needy for a pair of sandals,
and selling the sweepings of the wheat."

7 The LORD has sworn by the pride of Jacob:
Surely I will never forget any of their deeds.
8 Shall not the land tremble on this account,
and everyone mourn who lives in it,
and all of it rise like the Nile,
and be tossed about and sink again, like the Nile of Egypt?

9 On that day, says the Lord GOD,
I will make the sun go down at noon,
and darken the earth in broad daylight.
10 I will turn your feasts into mourning,
and all your songs into lamentation;
I will bring sackcloth on all loins,
and baldness on every head;
I will make it like the mourning for an only son,
and the end of it like a bitter day.

11 The time is surely coming, says the Lord GOD,
when I will send a famine on the land;
not a famine of bread, or a thirst for water,
but of hearing the words of the LORD.
12 They shall wander from sea to sea,
and from north to east;
they shall run to and fro, seeking the word of the LORD,
but they shall not find it.

13 In that day the beautiful young women and the young men
shall faint for thirst.
14 Those who swear by Ashimah of Samaria,
and say, "As your god lives, O Dan,"
and, "As the way of Beer-sheba lives"—
they shall fall, and never rise again.

8.5 Ex 20.8-10 Neh 13.15-21 Hos 12.7

8.7 Deut 33.26-29 Ps 10.11; 47.4 68.34 Hos 7.2; 8.13

8.8 Isa 8.7,8 Jer 4.24-26 46.8 Hag 2.6,7

8.9 Ex 10.21-23 Amos 4.13; 5.8 Mic 3.6 Mt 24.29; 27.45

8.10 Isa 15.2,3 Ezek 7.18

8.12 Ezek 20.3,31

8.13 Isa 41.17 Hos 2.3

8.14 1 Kgs 12.28,29 2 Kgs 10.29 Hos 8.5

8.5, 6 An ephah was a measure of volume, and a shekel was a measure of weight. These merchants kept the religious holidays, but not in spirit. They couldn't wait for the holidays and sabbaths to be over so they could go back to making money. Their real interest was in enriching themselves, even if that meant cheating (short-changing the quantity while boosting the price, or even selling chaff as wheat). Do you take a day to rest and worship God at least once a week, or is making money more important to you than anything else? When you give time to God, is your heart in your worship, or is your religion only a front for unethical practices?

8.11–13 The people had no appetite for God's Word when prophets like Amos brought it. Because of their apathy, God said he would take away even the opportunity to hear his Word. We have God's Word, the Bible. But many still look everywhere for answers to life's problems *except* in Scripture. You can help them by directing them to the Bible, showing them the parts that speak to their special needs and questions. God's Word is available to us. Let us help people know it before a time comes when they cannot find it.

8.14 *Ashimah* means guilt or shame and it was used instead of the name of the pagan goddess worshiped in Samaria. Swearing by these false gods was like worshiping them.

Israel will be destroyed

9.1 2 Chron 18.18 Zeph 2.14

9 I saw the LORD standing beside[c] the altar, and he said:
Strike the capitals until the thresholds shake,
and shatter them on the heads of all the people;[d]
and those who are left I will kill with the sword;
not one of them shall flee away,
not one of them shall escape.

9.2 Job 26.6 Ps 139.7-10 Isa 14.13-16

2 Though they dig into Sheol,
from there shall my hand take them;
though they climb up to heaven,
from there I will bring them down.

9.3 Job 34.22 Ps 139.9-11

3 Though they hide themselves on the top of Carmel,
from there I will search out and take them;
and though they hide from my sight at the bottom of the sea,
there I will command the sea-serpent, and it shall bite them.

9.4 Lev 26.33,36-39 Deut 28.63-65 Jer 24.6; 44.11

4 And though they go into captivity in front of their enemies,
there I will command the sword, and it shall kill them;
and I will fix my eyes on them
for harm and not for good.

9.5 Ps 46.6 Isa 64.1 Rev 20.11

5 The Lord, GOD of hosts,
he who touches the earth and it melts,
and all who live in it mourn,
and all of it rises like the Nile,
and sinks again, like the Nile of Egypt;

9.6 Ps 104.3,6,13

6 who builds his upper chambers in the heavens,
and founds his vault upon the earth;
who calls for the waters of the sea,
and pours them out upon the surface of the earth—
the LORD is his name.

9.7 2 Chron 14.9,12 Isa 20.4; 43.3

7 Are you not like the Ethiopians[e] to me,
O people of Israel? says the LORD.
Did I not bring Israel up from the land of Egypt,
and the Philistines from Caphtor and the Arameans from Kir?

9.8 Deut 4.31; 6.15 1 Kgs 13.34 Jer 5.10 Hos 9.11-17 Joel 2.32

8 The eyes of the Lord GOD are upon the sinful kingdom,
and I will destroy it from the face of the earth
—except that I will not utterly destroy the house of Jacob,
says the LORD.

[c] *Or on* [d] *Heb all of them* [e] *Or Nubians; Heb Cushites*

9.1 Judgment would begin at the altar, the center of the nation's life, the place where the people expected protection and blessing. This judgment would cover all 12 tribes. Commentators disagree concerning this altar—some think it was the altar at Bethel; more likely it was the altar in the temple in Jerusalem. God would destroy their base of security in order to bring them to himself. But in 9.11 he promises to restore his renewed people.

9.2–4 Sheol was the place of the dead, and Carmel is a mountain. Both were symbols of inaccessibility. No one can escape God's judgment. This was good news for the faithful but bad news for the unfaithful. Whether we go to the mountaintops or the bottom of the sea, God will find us and judge us for our deeds. Amos pictured the judgment of the wicked as a sea-serpent, relentlessly pursuing the condemned. For God's faithful followers, however, the judgment brings a new earth of peace and prosperity. Does God's judgment sound like good news or bad news to you?

9.7 Ethiopia, south of Egypt, was a remote and exotic land to the Israelites. Caphtor is Crete, where the Philistines originally lived. God would judge Israel no differently than he judges foreign nations. He is not just the God of Israel; he is God of the universe and he controls all nations.

9.8 Amos assured the Israelites that God would not "utterly destroy" Israel—in other words, the punishment would not be permanent or total. God wants to redeem, not punish. But when punishment is necessary he doesn't withhold it. Like a loving father, God disciplines those he loves in order to correct them. If he disciplines you, accept it as a sign of his love.

9.8, 9 Although Assyria would destroy Israel and take the people into exile, some would be preserved. This exile had been predicted hundreds of years earlier (Deuteronomy 28.63–68). Although the nation was purified through this invasion and captivity, not one true believer would be eternally lost. Our system of justice is not always perfect, but God is. Sinners will not get away, and the faithful will not be forgotten. True believers will not be lost.

9 For lo, I will command,
and shake the house of Israel among all the nations
as one shakes with a sieve,
but no pebble shall fall to the ground.
10 All the sinners of my people shall die by the sword,
who say, "Evil shall not overtake or meet us."

Israel will be restored

11 On that day I will raise up
the booth of David that is fallen,
and repair its[f] breaches,
and raise up its[g] ruins,
and rebuild it as in the days of old;
12 in order that they may possess the remnant of Edom
and all the nations who are called by my name,
says the LORD who does this.

13 The time is surely coming, says the LORD,
when the one who plows shall overtake the one who reaps,
and the treader of grapes the one who sows the seed;
the mountains shall drip sweet wine,
and all the hills shall flow with it.
14 I will restore the fortunes of my people Israel,
and they shall rebuild the ruined cities and inhabit them;
they shall plant vineyards and drink their wine,
and they shall make gardens and eat their fruit.
15 I will plant them upon their land,
and they shall never again be plucked up
out of the land that I have given them,
says the LORD your God.

9.9 Lev 26.33 Deut 28.64

9.11 Isa 9.6,7 16.5; 63.11 Ezek 21.25-27

9.13 Isa 55.13 Ezek 36.35 Hos 2.21-23 Joel 3.18,20

9.14 Ps 53.6 Isa 61.4 Jer 30.3 Ezek 36.33-36

[f] Gk: Heb *their* [g] Gk: Heb *his*

9.11, 12 In the punishment, the "house of David" was reduced to a "booth." God's covenant with David stated that one of David's descendants would always sit on his throne (2 Samuel 7.12–16). The exile made this seem impossible. But "on that day" God will raise and restore the kingdom to its promised glory. This was a promise to both Israel and Judah, not to be fulfilled by an earthly, political ruler, but by the Messiah, who would renew the spiritual kingdom and rule forever.

James quoted this verse (Acts 15.16, 17), finding its fulfillment in Christ's resurrection and in the presence of both Jews and Gentiles in the church. "Possess the remnant of Edom" means that the Messianic kingdom will be universal and include Gentiles. When God brings in the Gentiles, he is repairing the broken down "tabernacle." After the Gentiles are called together, God will renew and restore the fortunes of the new Israel. All the land that was once under David's rule will again be part of God's nation.

9.13 This verse describes a time of such an abundance of crops that they won't be able to harvest them all.

9.13–15 The Jews of Amos's day had lost sight of God's care and love for them. The rich were carefree and comfortable, refusing to help others in need. They observed their religious rituals in hopes of appeasing God, but they did not truly love him. Amos announced God's warnings of destruction for their evil ways.

We must not assume that going to church and being good is enough. God expects our belief in him to penetrate all areas of our conduct and extend to all people and circumstances. We should let Amos's words inspire us to live faithfully according to God's desires.

OBADIAH

WRINKLED face, tiny hands with fingernail chips, rolls of new skin, and miniature eyes, nose, and mouth—she's a newborn. After months of formation, she burst forth into the world and into her family. "She has her mother's eyes," "I can sure tell who her parents are," "Now that's your nose" . . . relatives and friends gaze into the little face and see her mom and dad. Mother and father rejoice in their daughter, a miracle, a new member of the family. As loving parents, they will protect, nurture, feed, guide, and discipline her. This is their duty and joy.

God too has children—men and women whom he has chosen as his very own. There have always been individuals marked as his, but with Abraham he promised to build a nation. Israel was to be God's country and her people, the Jews, his very own sons and daughters. Through the following centuries, there was discipline and punishment, but always love and mercy. God, the eternal Father, protected and cared for his children.

Obadiah, the shortest book in the Old Testament, is a dramatic example of God's response to anyone who would harm his children. Edom was a mountainous nation, occupying the region southeast of the Dead Sea including Petra, the spectacular city discovered by archaeologists a few decades ago. As descendants of Esau (Genesis 25.19—27.45), the Edomites were blood relatives of Israel and, like their father, they were rugged, fierce, and proud warriors with a seemingly invincible mountain home. Of all people, they should have rushed to the aid of their northern brothers. Instead, however, they gloated over Israel's problems, captured and delivered fugitives to the enemy, and even looted Israel's countryside.

Obadiah gives God's message to Edom. Because of their indifference and defiance of God, their cowardice and pride, and their treachery toward their brothers in Judah, they stand condemned and will be destroyed. The book begins with the announcement that disaster is coming to Edom (1.1–9). Despite their "impregnable" cliffs and mountains, they will not be able to escape God's judgment. Obadiah then gives the reasons for their destruction (1.10–14)—their blatant arrogance toward God and their persecution of his children. This concise prophecy ends with a description of the "day of the Lord," when judgment will fall on all who have harmed God's people (1.15–21).

Today, God's holy nation is his church—all who have trusted Christ for their salvation and have given their lives to him. These men and women are his born again and adopted children. As you read Obadiah, catch a glimpse of what it means to be God's child, under his love and protection. See how the heavenly Father responds to all who would attack those whom he loves.

VITAL STATISTICS

PURPOSE:
To show that God judges those who have harmed his people

AUTHOR:
Obadiah. Very little is known about this man whose name means "servant of the Lord" or "worshiper of Jehovah."

TO WHOM WRITTEN:
The Edomites, the Jews in Judah, and God's people everywhere

DATE WRITTEN:
Possibly during the reign of Jehoram in Judah, 853–841 B.C.

SETTING:
Historically, Edom had constantly harassed the Jews. Prior to the time this book was written, they had participated in attacks against Judah. Given the dates above, this prophecy comes after the division of Israel into the northern and southern kingdoms and before the conquering of Judah by Nebuchadnezzar in 586 B.C.

KEY VERSE:
"For the day of the Lord is near against all the nations. As you have done, it shall be done to you; your deeds shall return on your own head" (1.15).

KEY PEOPLE:
The Edomites

KEY PLACES:
Edom, Jerusalem

SPECIAL FEATURES:
The book of Obadiah uses vigorous poetic language and is written in the form of a dirge of doom.

THE BLUEPRINT

1. Edom's destruction (1.1–16)
2. Israel's restoration (1.17–21)

The book of Obadiah shows the end of the ancient feud between Edom and Israel. Edom was proud of its high position, but God would bring her down. Those who are high and powerful today should not be overconfident in themselves, whether they are a nation, a corporation, a church, or a family. Just as Edom was destroyed for its pride, so will anyone who lives in defiance of God.

MEGATHEMES

THEME	EXPLANATION	IMPORTANCE
Justice	Obadiah predicted that God would destroy Edom as punishment for helping Babylon invade Judah. Because of their treachery, Edom's land would be given to Judah in the day when God rights the wrongs against his people.	God will judge and fiercely punish all who harm his people. We can be confident in God's final victory. He is our champion and we can trust him to bring about true justice.
Pride	Because of their seemingly invincible rock fortress, the Edomites were proud and self-confident. But God humbled them and their nation disappeared from the face of the earth.	All those who defy God will meet their doom as Edom did. Any nation who trusts in its power, wealth, technology, or wisdom more than in God will be brought low. All who are proud will one day be shocked to discover that no one is exempt from God's justice.

1. Edom's destruction

1 The vision of Obadiah.

Thus says the Lord GOD concerning Edom:
We have heard a report from the LORD,
and a messenger has been sent among the nations:
"Rise up! Let us rise against it for battle!"
2 I will surely make you least among the nations;
you shall be utterly despised.
3 Your proud heart has deceived you,
you that live in the clefts of the rock,[a]
whose dwelling is in the heights.
You say in your heart,
"Who will bring me down to the ground?"
4 Though you soar aloft like the eagle,

[a] Or *clefts of Sela*

1.1 Isa 34.5-15; 63.1-6; Jer 49.7-22; Ps 137.7; Ezek 25.12-14; Amos 1.11,12

1.2 Num 24.15-19

1.3 Jer 49.15,16

1.4 Job 39.26-30; Isa 14.12-15

1.1 Obadiah was a prophet from Judah who told of God's judgment against the nation of Edom. Two commonly accepted dates for this prophecy are (1) between 848 and 841 B.C., when King Jehoram and Jerusalem were attacked by a Philistine/Arab coalition (2 Chronicles 21.16ff), or (2) 586 B.C., when Jerusalem was completely destroyed by the Babylonians (2 Kings 25; 2 Chronicles 36). Edom had rejoiced over the misfortunes of both Israel and Judah, and yet the Edomites and Jews descended from two brothers – Esau and Jacob (Genesis 25.19–26). But just as these two brothers were constantly at odds, Israel and Edom were rarely at peace. God pronounced judgment on Edom for their callous and malicious actions toward his people.

1.3 Edom was Judah's southern neighbor, sharing a common boundary. But neighbors are not always friends, and Edom liked nothing about Judah. Edom's capital at this time was Petra, a city considered impregnable because it was cut into a solid rock cliff and set in a canyon that could be entered only through a narrow gap. What Edom perceived as its strengths would be its downfall: (1) safety in their city (1.3, 4) – God would send them plummeting from the heights; (2) pride in their self-sufficiency (1.4) – God would humble them; (3) wealth (1.5, 6) – thieves would steal all they had; (4) allies (1.7) – God would cause them to turn against Edom; (5) wisdom (1.8, 9) – they would be confused.

1.3 The Edomites felt secure, and they were proud of their self-sufficiency. But they were fooling themselves because there is no lasting security apart from God. Is your security in objects or people? Ask yourself how much lasting security they really offer. Possessions and people can disappear in a moment, but God does not change. Only he can supply true security.

1.4 The Edomites were proud of their city carved right into the rock. Today it is considered one of the marvels of the ancient world, but only as a tourist attraction. The Bible warns that pride is

though your nest is set among the stars,
from there I will bring you down,
says the LORD.

1.5
Jer 49.9,10

5 If thieves came to you,
if plunderers by night
—how you have been destroyed!—
would they not steal only what they wanted?
If grape-gatherers came to you,
would they not leave gleanings?
6 How Esau has been pillaged,
his treasures searched out!
7 All your allies have deceived you,
they have driven you to the border;
your confederates have prevailed against you;
those who ate[b] your bread have set a trap for you—
there is no understanding of it.
8 On that day, says the LORD,
I will destroy the wise out of Edom,
and understanding out of Mount Esau.
9 Your warriors shall be shattered, O Teman,
so that everyone from Mount Esau will be cut off.
10 For the slaughter and violence done to your brother Jacob,
shame shall cover you,
and you shall be cut off forever.
11 On the day that you stood aside,
on the day that strangers carried off his wealth,
and foreigners entered his gates
and cast lots for Jerusalem,

1.7
Ps 55.12-14
Isa 19.11-14
Jer 4.30

1.8
Job 5.12-14
Isa 19.3,13,14
29.14

1.9
Jer 49.20-22
Amos 2.16

1.10
Num 20.14-22
Ps 83.5-8
109.29
Ezek 7.18
25.12-14

1.11
2 Kgs 25.8-21
2 Chron 36.19,
20
Jer 52.12-30

[b] Cn: Heb lacks *those who ate*

HISTORY OF THE CONFLICT BETWEEN ISRAEL AND EDOM

The nation of Israel descended from Jacob; the nation of Edom descended from Esau	Genesis 25.23
Jacob and Esau struggled in their mother's womb	Genesis 25.19–26
Esau sold his birthright and blessing to Jacob	Genesis 25.29–34
Edom refused to let the Israelites pass through their land	Numbers 20.14–22
Israel's kings had constant conflict with Edom	
• Saul	1 Samuel 14.47
• David	2 Samuel 8.13, 14
• Solomon	1 Kings 11.14–22
• Jehoram	2 Kings 8.20–22; 2 Chronicles 21.8ff
• Ahaz	2 Chronicles 28.16
Edom encouraged Babylon to destroy Jerusalem	Psalm 137.7

the surest route to self-destruction (Proverbs 16.18). Just as Petra and Edom fell, so will proud people fall. A humble person is more secure than a proud person, because humility gives one a more accurate perspective of oneself and the world.

1.4–9 Esau is named (1.6) because he was the father of the nation of Edom. God did not pronounce these harsh judgments against Edom out of vengeance but in order to bring about justice. God is morally perfect and demands complete justice and fairness. The Edomites were simply getting what they deserved. Because they murdered, they would be murdered. Because they robbed, they would be robbed. Because they took advantage of others, they would be used. Don't talk yourself into sin, thinking that "nobody will know" or "I won't get caught." God knows all our sins, and he will be just.

1.8 Edom was noted for its wise men. There is a difference, however, between man's wisdom and God's wisdom. The Edomites may have been wise in the ways of the world, but they were foolish because they ignored and even mocked God.

1.9 Eliphaz, one of Job's three friends (Job 2.11), was from Teman, five miles east of Petra. Teman was named after Esau's grandson (Genesis 36.11).

1.10, 11 The Israelites descended from Jacob, and the Edomites from his brother, Esau (Genesis 25.19–26). Instead of helping Israel and Judah when they were in need, Edom let them be destroyed and even plundered what was left behind. Edom, therefore, was an enemy and would be punished. Anyone who does not help God's people is God's enemy. If you have withheld your help from someone in a time of need, this is sin (James 4.17). Sin includes not only what we do, but also what we refuse to do. Don't ignore or refuse to help those in need.

you too were like one of them.
12 But you should not have gloated[c] over[d] your brother
on the day of his misfortune;
you should not have rejoiced over the people of Judah
on the day of their ruin;
you should not have boasted
on the day of distress.
13 You should not have entered the gate of my people
on the day of their calamity;
you should not have joined in the gloating over Judah's[e] disaster
on the day of his calamity;
you should not have looted his goods
on the day of his calamity.
14 You should not have stood at the crossings
to cut off his fugitives;
you should not have handed over his survivors
on the day of distress.

15 For the day of the LORD is near against all the nations.
As you have done, it shall be done to you;
your deeds shall return on your own head.
16 For as you have drunk on my holy mountain,
all the nations around you shall drink;
they shall drink and gulp down,[f]
and shall be as though they had never been.

2. Israel's restoration

17 But on Mount Zion there shall be those that escape,
and it shall be holy;
and the house of Jacob shall take possession of those who dispossessed
them.
18 The house of Jacob shall be a fire,
the house of Joseph a flame,
and the house of Esau stubble;
they shall burn them and consume them,
and there shall be no survivor of the house of Esau;
for the LORD has spoken.
19 Those of the Negeb shall possess Mount Esau,
and those of the Shephelah the land of the Philistines;
they shall possess the land of Ephraim and the land of Samaria,
and Benjamin shall possess Gilead.
20 The exiles of the Israelites who are in Halah[g]

1.12 Ps 22.17 Mic 4.11

1.13 2 Kgs 24.13-16 2 Chron 36.18

1.15 Jer 9.25,26 25.15 Joel 1.15

1.17 Isa 14.1,2 Joel 3.19-21 Amos 9.11-15

1.19 Num 24.15-19 Jer 31.5; 32.44 Ezek 36.6-12 47.13-20

1.20 1 Kgs 17.9

[c] Heb *But do not gloat* (and similarly through verse 14) [d] Heb *on the day of* [e] Heb *his* [f] Meaning of Heb uncertain
[g] Cn: Heb *in this army*

1.12 Edom was glad to see Judah in trouble. Their hatred made them want the nation destroyed. For this wrong, God obliterated Edom. How often do you find yourself rejoicing at the misfortunes of others? Because God alone is the judge, we must never be happy about others' misfortunes, even if we think they deserve them (see Proverbs 24.17).

1.12–14 Of all Israel and Judah's neighbors, Edom was the only one not promised any mercy from God. This was because they looted Jerusalem and rejoiced at the misfortunes of Israel and Judah. They betrayed their blood brothers in times of crisis and aided their brothers' enemies. (See also Psalm 137.7; Jeremiah 49.7–22; Ezekiel 25.12–14; Amos 1.11, 12.)

1.15 Why will God's vengeance fall on the Gentile nations? Edom was not the only nation to rejoice at Judah's fall. All nations and individuals will be judged for the way they treat God's people. Some nations today treat God's people favorably, while others are hostile toward them. God will judge all people according to the way they treat others, especially believers (Revelation 20.12, 13). Jesus talked about this in Matthew 25.31–46.

1.17–21 The Edomites were routed by Judas Maccabeus in 185 B.C. The nation no longer existed by the first century A.D. At the time of Obadiah's prophecy, Edom may have seemed more likely to survive than Judah. Yet Edom has vanished and Judah still exists. This demonstrates the absolute certainty of God's Word and of the punishment awaiting all who have mistreated God's people.

1.19 The Negeb was the southern part of Judah, a dry, hot region. The Shephelah was the land of low hills in the western part of Judah.

shall possess[h] Phoenicia as far as Zerephath;
and the exiles of Jerusalem who are in Sepharad
shall possess the towns of the Negeb.
21 Those who have been saved[i] shall go up to Mount Zion
to rule Mount Esau;
and the kingdom shall be the LORD's.

1.21 Zech 9.11-17 Lk 1.32,33 Rev 11.15; 19.6

[h] Cn: Meaning of Heb uncertain [i] Or *Saviors*

OBADIAH served as a prophet to Judah around 853 B.C.

Climate of the times	Edom was a constant thorn in Judah's side. They often participated in attacks initiated by other enemies.
Main message	God will judge Edom for its evil actions toward God's people.
Importance of message	Just as Edom was destroyed and disappeared as a nation, so God will destroy proud and wicked people.
Contemporary prophets	Elijah (875–848) Micaiah (865–853) Jehu (855–840?)

1.20 The boundaries of the kingdom would be extended to include the Canaanites (Phoenicians) as far south as Zarephath, located between Tyre and Sidon on the Mediterranean coast. Sepharad was most likely Sardis.

1.21 Obadiah brought God's message of judgment on Edom. God was displeased with both their inward and their outward rebellion. People today are much the same as those in Obadiah's time. We see arrogance, envy, and dishonesty, and we wonder where it will all end. Regardless of sin's effects, however, God is in control. As you struggle, don't despair or give up hope. Know that when all is said and done, the Lord will still be King, and the confidence you place in him will not be in vain.

1.21 Edom is an example to all the nations who are hostile to God. Nothing can break God's promise to protect his people from complete destruction. In the book of Obadiah we see four aspects of God's message of judgment: (1) evil will certainly be punished; (2) those faithful to God have hope for a new future; (3) God is sovereign in human history; (4) God's ultimate purpose is to establish his eternal kingdom. The Edomites had been cruel to God's people. They were arrogant and proud, and they took advantage of others' misfortunes. Any nation who mistreats people who obey God will be punished, regardless of how invincible they appear. Similarly we, as individuals, cannot allow ourselves to feel so comfortable with our wealth or security that we fail to help God's people. This is sin. And because God is just, they will be punished.

JONAH

Jeroboam II becomes king; Jonah becomes a prophet 793 B.C.	*Uzziah becomes king of Judah 792*	*Shalmaneser IV becomes king of Assyria 783*	*Ashur-dan III becomes king of Assyria 772*	*Amos becomes a prophet 760*	*Jona[h] prea[c]h[es] to Ni[neveh] 759?*

VITAL STATISTICS

PURPOSE:
To show the extent of God's grace—the message of salvation is for *all* people

AUTHOR:
Jonah, son of Amittai

TO WHOM WRITTEN:
Israel and God's people everywhere

DATE WRITTEN:
Approximately 785–760 B.C.

SETTING:
Jonah preceded Amos and ministered under Jeroboam II, Israel's most powerful king (793–753 B.C., see 2 Kings 14.23–25). Assyria was Israel's great enemy, and Israel was conquered by them in 722 B.C. Nineveh's repentance must have been short-lived.

KEY VERSE:
"And should I not be concerned about Nineveh, that great city, in which there are more than a hundred and twenty thousand persons who do not know their right hand from their left?" (4.11).

KEY PEOPLE:
Jonah, the boat's captain and crew

KEY PLACES:
Joppa, Nineveh

SPECIAL FEATURES:
This book is different from the other prophetic books because it tells the story of the prophet and does not center on his prophecies. In fact, only one verse summarizes his message to the people of Nineveh (3.4). Jonah is an historical narrative. It is also mentioned by Jesus as a picture of his death and resurrection (Matthew 12.38–42).

SIN runs rampant in society—daily headlines and overflowing prisons bear dramatic witness to that fact. With child abuse, pornography, serial killings, terrorism, anarchy, and ruthless dictatorships, the world seems to be filled to overflowing with violence, hatred, and corruption. Reading, hearing, and perhaps even experiencing these tragedies, we begin to understand the necessity of God's judgment. We may even find ourselves wishing for vengeance by any means upon the violent perpetrators. Surely they are beyond redemption! But suppose that in the midst of such thoughts, God told you to take the gospel to the worst of these offenders—how would you respond?

Jonah was given such a task. Assyria—a great, but evil empire—was Israel's most dreaded enemy. The Assyrians flaunted their power before God and the world through numerous acts of heartless cruelty. So when Jonah heard God tell him to go to Assyria and call the people to repentance, he ran in the opposite direction.

The book of Jonah tells the story of this prophet's flight and how God stopped him and turned him around. But it is much more than a story of a man and a great fish—Jonah's story is a profound illustration of God's mercy and grace. No one deserved God's favor less than the people of Nineveh, Assyria's capital. Jonah knew this. But he knew that God would forgive and bless them if they turned from their sin and worshiped him. He also knew the power of God's message, that even through his weak preaching, they would respond and be spared God's judgment. But Jonah hated the Assyrians, and he wanted vengeance, not mercy, and so he ran. Eventually, Jonah obeyed and preached in the streets of Nineveh, and the people repented and were delivered from judgment. Then Jonah sulked and complained to God, "I knew that you are a gracious God and merciful, slow to anger, and abounding in steadfast love, and ready to relent from punishing" (4.2). In the end, God confronted Jonah about his self-centered values and lack of compassion, saying, "And should I not be concerned about Nineveh, that great city, in which there are more than a hundred and twenty thousand persons who do not know their right hand from their left?" (4.11).

As you read Jonah, see the full picture of God's love and compassion and realize that no one is beyond redemption. The gospel is for all who will repent and believe. Begin to pray for those who seem to be farthest from the kingdom, and look for ways to tell them about God. Learn from the story of this reluctant prophet and determine to obey God, doing whatever and going wherever he leads.

shur-nirari V
comes
ng of
ssyria
54

Jonah's
ministry
ends
753

Israel
falls to
Assyria
722

THE BLUEPRINT

1. Jonah forsakes his mission (1.1—2.10)
2. Jonah fulfills his mission (3.1—4.11)

Jonah was a reluctant prophet given a mission which he found distasteful. He chose to run away from God rather than obey him. Like Jonah, we may have to do things in life which we don't want to do. Sometimes, we find ourselves wanting to turn and run. But it is better to obey God than to defy him or run away. Often, in spite of our defiance, God in his mercy will give us another chance to serve him when we return to him.

MEGATHEMES

THEME	EXPLANATION	IMPORTANCE
God's sovereignty	Although the prophet Jonah tried to run away from God, God was in control. By controlling the stormy seas and a great fish, God displayed his absolute, yet loving guidance.	Rather than running from God, trust him with your past, present, and future. Saying "no" to God quickly leads to disaster. Saying "yes" brings new understanding of God and his purpose in the world.
God's message to all the world	God had given Jonah a purpose—to preach to the great Assyrian city of Nineveh. Jonah hated Nineveh, and so he responded with anger and indifference. Jonah had yet to learn that God loves all people. Through Jonah, God reminded Israel of their missionary purpose.	We must not limit our focus to our own people. God wants his people to proclaim his love in words and actions to the whole world. He wants us to be his missionaries wherever we are, wherever he sends us.
Repentance	When the reluctant preacher went to Nineveh, there was a great response. The people repented and turned to God. This was a powerful rebuke to Israel who thought themselves better and yet refused to respond to God's message. God will forgive all those who turn from their sin.	God doesn't honor sham or pretense. He wants the sincere devotion of each person. It is not enough to share the privileges of Christianity; we must ask God to forgive us and to remove our sin. Refusing to repent is the same as loving our sin.
God's compassion	God's message of love and forgiveness was not for the Jews alone. God loves all the people of the world. The Assyrians didn't deserve it, but God spared them when they repented. In his mercy, God did not reject Jonah for aborting his mission. God has great love, patience, and forgiveness.	God loves each of us even when we fail him. But he also loves other people, including those not of our group, background, race, or denomination. When we accept his love, we must also learn to accept all those whom he loves. We will find it much easier to love others when we love God.

1. Jonah forsakes his mission

Jonah runs away from God

1 Now the word of the LORD came to Jonah son of Amittai, saying, 2“Go at once
to Nineveh, that great city, and cry out against it; for their wickedness has
come up before me.” 3But Jonah set out to flee to Tarshish from the presence of the
LORD. He went down to Joppa and found a ship going to Tarshish; so he paid his
fare and went on board, to go with them to Tarshish, away from the presence of the
LORD.
4 But the LORD hurled a great wind upon the sea, and such a mighty storm came
upon the sea that the ship threatened to break up. 5Then the mariners were afraid,
and each cried to his god. They threw the cargo that was in the ship into the sea, to
lighten it for them. Jonah, meanwhile, had gone down into the hold of the ship and
had lain down, and was fast asleep. 6The captain came and said to him, “What are
you doing sound asleep? Get up, call on your god! Perhaps the god will spare us a
thought so that we do not perish.”
7 The sailors[a] said to one another, “Come, let us cast lots, so that we may know
on whose account this calamity has come upon us.” So they cast lots, and the lot
fell on Jonah. 8Then they said to him, “Tell us why this calamity has come upon us.
What is your occupation? Where do you come from? What is your country? And of
what people are you?” 9“I am a Hebrew,” he replied. “I worship the LORD, the God

1.1 2 Kgs 14.25 Mt 12.39-41
1.2 2 Kgs 19.36 Jonah 3.3
1.3 Gen 3.8; 4.16 2 Chron 2.16 9.21 Isa 23.6 Acts 9.36
1.5 1 Kgs 18.26 Isa 44.17-20 Acts 27.18,19, 38
1.6 Ps 107.28 Jer 2.28
1.7 Judg 20.9,10 Esth 3.7 Prov 16.33
1.8 Gen 47.3

[a] Heb *They*

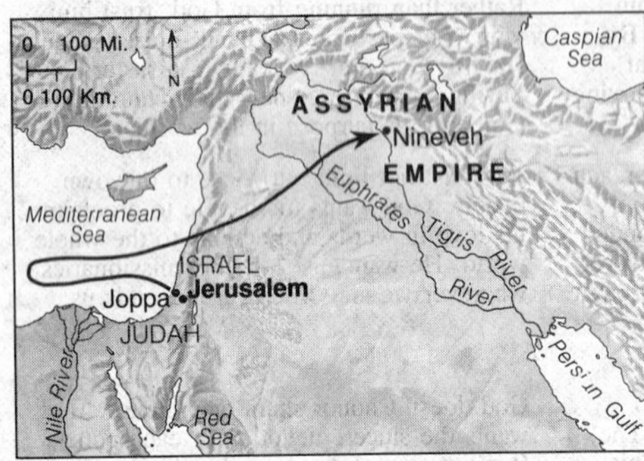

JONAH'S ROUNDABOUT JOURNEY God told Jonah to go to Nineveh, the capital of the Assyrian Empire. Many of Jonah's countrymen had experienced the atrocities of these fierce people. The last place Jonah wanted to go on a missionary trip was to Nineveh! So he went in the opposite direction. He boarded a ship in Joppa which was headed for Tarshish in Spain. But Jonah could not run from God.

1.1, 2 Jonah is mentioned in 2 Kings 14.25. He prophesied during the reign of Jeroboam II, the king of Israel from 793–753 B.C. He may have been one of the young prophets of the school mentioned in connection with Elisha's ministry (2 Kings 2.3).

God called Jonah to preach to Nineveh, the most important city in Assyria, the rising world power of Jonah's day. Within 50 years, Nineveh would become the capital of the vast Assyrian Empire. Jonah doesn't say much about Nineveh's wickedness, but the prophet Nahum gives us more insight. He says that Nineveh was guilty of (1) evil plots against God (Nahum 1.9), (2) exploitation of the helpless (Nahum 2.12), (3) cruelty in war (Nahum 2.12, 13), (4) idolatry, prostitution, and witchcraft (Nahum 3.4). God told Jonah to go to Nineveh, about 500 miles northeast of Israel, to warn of judgment and to declare that the people could receive mercy and forgiveness if they repented.

1.3 Nineveh was a powerful and wicked city. Jonah grew up hating the Assyrians and fearing their atrocities. His hatred was so strong that he didn't want them to receive God's mercy. Jonah was actually afraid the people would repent (4.2, 3). Jonah's attitude is representative of Israel's reluctance to share God's love and mercy with others, even though this was their God-given mission (Genesis 12.3). They, like Jonah, did not want non-Jews (Gentiles) to obtain God's favor.

1.3 Jonah was afraid. He knew God had a specific job for him, but he didn't want to do it. Tarshish could refer to any of a number of Phoenicia's western ports. Nineveh was toward the east. Jonah decided to go as far west as he could. When God gives us directions through his Word, sometimes we run in fear, claiming that God is asking too much. Fear made Jonah run. But running got him into worse trouble. In the end, he understood it is best to do what God asks in the first place. But by then he had paid a costly price for running. It is far better to obey from the start.

1.4 Before settling in the promised land, the Israelites had been nomads. They wandered from place to place, seeking good pastureland for their flocks. Although they were not a seafaring people, their location along the Mediterranean Sea and near the neighboring maritime powers of Phoenicia and Philistia allowed much contact with ships and sailors. The ship Jonah sailed on was probably a large trading vessel with a deck.

1.4 Jonah's disobedience to God endangered the lives of the ship's crew. We have a great responsibility to obey God's Word because our sin and disobedience will hurt others around us.

1.4, 5 While the storm raged, Jonah was sound asleep in the ship's hold. Even as he ran from God, he apparently didn't have a guilty conscience. But the absence of guilt isn't always a barometer of whether we are doing right. Because we can deny reality, we cannot measure obedience by our feelings. Instead, we must compare what we do with God's standards for living.

1.7 The crew cast lots (like drawing straws) to find the guilty person, relying on their superstitions to give them the answer. Their system worked, but only because God intervened to let Jonah know he couldn't run away.

1.9–12 You cannot seek God's love and run from him at the same time. Jonah soon realized that no matter where he went, he couldn't get away from God. But before Jonah could return to God, he first had to stop going in the opposite direction. What has God told you to do? If you want more of God's love and power, you must be willing to carry out the responsibilities he gives you. You

1.9 Gen 1.9,10 Ezra 1.2; 5.11 Neh 1.4; 9.6

of heaven, who made the sea and the dry land." 10 Then the men were even more
afraid, and said to him, "What is this that you have done!" For the men knew that
he was fleeing from the presence of the LORD, because he had told them so.
11 Then they said to him, "What shall we do to you, that the sea may quiet

1.12 Jn 11.50

down for us?" For the sea was growing more and more tempestuous. 12 He said to
them, "Pick me up and throw me into the sea; then the sea will quiet down for you;
for I know it is because of me that this great storm has come upon you." 13 Nevertheless the men rowed hard to bring the ship back to land, but they could not, for
the sea grew more and more stormy against them. 14 Then they cried out to the
LORD, "Please, O LORD, we pray, do not let us perish on account of this man's life.

1.15 Ps 89.9 Mk 4.34

Do not make us guilty of innocent blood; for you, O LORD, have done as it pleased
you." 15 So they picked Jonah up and threw him into the sea; and the sea ceased

1.16 Gen 28.20 Ps 66.13,14

from its raging. 16 Then the men feared the LORD even more, and they offered a
sacrifice to the LORD and made vows.

1.17 Jonah 1.1; 2.1

17[b] But the LORD provided a large fish to swallow up Jonah; and Jonah was in
the belly of the fish three days and three nights.

Jonah prays inside the fish

2.1 Ps 130.1 Jonah 1.17

2.2 Ps 18.4-6; 22.24

2 Then Jonah prayed to the LORD his God from the belly of the fish, 2 saying,
"I called to the LORD out of my distress,
and he answered me;

[b] Ch 2.1 in Heb

JONAH served as a prophet to Israel and Assyria from 793–753 B.C.

Climate of the times	Nineveh was the most important city in Assyria and would soon become the capital of the huge Assyrian Empire. But Nineveh was also a very wicked city.
Main message	Jonah, who hated the powerful and wicked Assyrians, was called by God to warn the Assyrians that they would receive judgment if they did not repent.
Importance of message	Jonah didn't want to go to Nineveh, so he tried to run from God. But God has ways of teaching us to obey and follow him. When Jonah preached, the city repented and God withheld his judgment. Even the most wicked will be saved if they truly repent of their sins and turn to God.
Contemporary prophets	Joel (853–796?) Amos (760–750)

---

cannot say that you truly believe in God if you don't do what he says.

1.12 Jonah knew he had disobeyed and that the storm was his fault, but he didn't say anything until the crew cast lots and the lot fell to him (1.7). Then he was willing to give his life to save the sailors (although he had refused to do the same for the people of Nineveh). Jonah's hatred for the Assyrians had affected his perspective.

1.13 By trying to save Jonah's life, the heathen sailors showed more compassion than Jonah, because Jonah did not want to warn the Ninevites of the coming judgment of God. Believers should be ashamed when unbelievers show more concern and compassion than they do. God wants us to be concerned for all of his people, lost and saved.

1.14–16 Jonah had disobeyed God. While he was running away, he stopped and submitted to God. Then the ship's crew began to worship God, because they saw the storm quiet down. God is able to use even our mistakes to help others come to know him. It may be painful, but admitting our sins can be a powerful example to those who don't know God. Ironically, the pagan sailors did what the entire nation of Israel would not do – prayed to God and vowed to serve him.

1.17 Many have tried to dismiss this miraculous event as fiction, but the Bible does not describe it as a dream or a legend. We should not explain away this miracle as if we could pick and choose which of the miracles in the Bible we want to believe and which ones we don't. This kind of attitude allows us to question any part of the Bible, causing us to lose our trust in it as God's true and reliable Word. Jonah's experience was used by Christ himself as an illustration of his death and resurrection (Matthew 12.39, 40).

2.1ff This is a prayer of thanksgiving, not a prayer for deliverance. Jonah was simply thankful that he had not been drowned. He was delivered in a most spectacular way and was overwhelmed that he had escaped certain death. Even from inside the fish, Jonah's prayer was heard by God. We can pray anywhere and at any time, and God will hear us. Your sin is never too great nor your predicament ever too difficult for God.

2.1–7 Jonah said, "As my life was ebbing away, I remembered the Lord" (2.7). Often we act the same way. When life is going well, we tend to take God for granted; but when we lose hope, we cry out to him. This kind of relationship with God can result only in an inconsistent, up-and-down spiritual life. A consistent, daily commitment to God promotes a solid relationship with him. Look to God during both the good and bad times, and you will have a stronger spiritual life.

2.2 *Sheol* means the grave or place of the dead. Jonah pictured his predicament in the belly of the fish as though he had been buried alive.

out of the belly of Sheol I cried,
and you heard my voice.
3 You cast me into the deep,
into the heart of the seas,
and the flood surrounded me;
all your waves and your billows
passed over me.
4 Then I said, 'I am driven away
from your sight;
how[c] shall I look again
upon your holy temple?'
5 The waters closed in over me;
the deep surrounded me;
weeds were wrapped around my head
6 at the roots of the mountains.
I went down to the land
whose bars closed upon me forever;
yet you brought up my life from the Pit,
O LORD my God.
7 As my life was ebbing away,
I remembered the LORD;
and my prayer came to you,
into your holy temple.
8 Those who worship vain idols
forsake their true loyalty.
9 But I with the voice of thanksgiving
will sacrifice to you;
what I have vowed I will pay.
Deliverance belongs to the LORD!"
10 Then the LORD spoke to the fish, and it spewed Jonah out upon the dry land.

2.3 Ps 42.7
2.4 1 Kgs 8.38 Ps 5.7 77.1-7 Isa 38.10-14
2.6 Ps 30.3; 65.6 Isa 38.17; 40.12
2.7 2 Chron 30.27 Ps 18.6; 142.3
2.9 Lev 27.1-33 Deut 23.21 Ps 50.14; 68.20

2. Jonah fulfills his mission

Jonah preaches at Nineveh

3 The word of the LORD came to Jonah a second time, saying, 2"Get up, go to
Nineveh, that great city, and proclaim to it the message that I tell you." 3So
Jonah set out and went to Nineveh, according to the word of the LORD. Now Nine-
veh was an exceedingly large city, a three days' walk across. 4Jonah began to go

3.2 Jer 1.17 Ezek 2.7; 3.17 Mt 3.8
3.3 Jonah 1.2; 4.11

[c] Theodotion: Heb *surely*

2.8 Those who worship false gods are abandoning any hope for mercy from the Lord. Any object of our devotion that replaces God is a lying vanity. We deceive ourselves with something that is ultimately empty and foolish. Make sure nothing takes God's rightful place in your life.

2.9 Jonah was obviously not in a position to bargain with God. Instead, he simply thanked God for saving his life. Our troubles should cause us to cling tightly to God, not make an attempt at bargaining our way out of the pain. We can thank and praise him for what he has already done for us, for his love and mercy.

2.9 It took a miracle of deliverance to get Jonah to do as God had commanded. As a prophet, he was obligated to obey God's Word, but he had tried to escape his responsibilities. He now pledged to keep his vows. Jonah's story began with a tragedy, but a greater tragedy would have happened if God had allowed him to keep running. When you know God wants you to do something, don't run. God may not stop you as he did Jonah.

3.1, 2 Jonah had ignored God and rebelled against him, but God still showed him compassion. When we ignore God, he may punish us, but he will show compassion and forgive us if we turn from our sins.

3.1, 2 Jonah ran away from God, but he was given a second chance to participate in God's work. You may feel you are disqualified from serving God because of past mistakes. But serving God is not an earned position. No one qualifies for God's service, but he still asks us to carry out his work. You may yet have another chance.

3.1, 2 Jonah was to preach only what God told him – a message of doom to the most powerful city in the world. This was not the most desirable assignment, but those who bring God's Word to others should not let social pressures or fear of people dictate their words. They are called to preach God's message and his truth, no matter how unpopular it may be.

3.3 The Hebrew text makes no distinction between the city proper (the walls of which were only about eight miles in circumference, accomodating a population of about 175,000 persons) and the administrative district of Nineveh, which was about 30 to 60 miles across. An "exceedingly large city," it took three days just to walk through it.

3.4–9 God's message is for everyone. Despite the wickedness of the Ninevite people, they were open to God's message and repented immediately. If we simply proclaim what we know about

3.4 2 Kgs 20.1,6 2 Chron 20.3 Ezra 8.21 Dan 9.3 Mt 12.41 Lk 11.32
3.7 2 Chron 30.1-10
3.8 Ps 130.1,2 Isa 1.16-19 Jonah 1.6,14 Acts 3.19
3.9 2 Sam 12.22 Joel 2.14
3.10 1 Kgs 21.27-29

into the city, going a day's walk. And he cried out, "Forty days more, and Nineveh
shall be overthrown!" 5 And the people of Nineveh believed God; they proclaimed
a fast, and everyone, great and small, put on sackcloth.
6 When the news reached the king of Nineveh, he rose from his throne, removed his robe, covered himself with sackcloth, and sat in ashes. 7 Then he had a
proclamation made in Nineveh: "By the decree of the king and his nobles: No human being or animal, no herd or flock, shall taste anything. They shall not feed, nor
shall they drink water. 8 Human beings and animals shall be covered with sackcloth, and they shall cry mightily to God. All shall turn from their evil ways and
from the violence that is in their hands. 9 Who knows? God may relent and change
his mind; he may turn from his fierce anger, so that we do not perish."
10 When God saw what they did, how they turned from their evil ways, God
changed his mind about the calamity that he had said he would bring upon them;
and he did not do it.

God's mercy makes Jonah angry

4.2 Jer 20.7 Hos 11.8,9
4.3 1 Kgs 19.4 Job 6.8,9

4 But this was very displeasing to Jonah, and he became angry. 2 He prayed to
the LORD and said, "O LORD! Is not this what I said while I was still in my own
country? That is why I fled to Tarshish at the beginning; for I knew that you are a
gracious God and merciful, slow to anger, and abounding in steadfast love, and
ready to relent from punishing. 3 And now, O LORD, please take my life from me,
for it is better for me to die than to live." 4 And the LORD said, "Is it right for you
to be angry?" 5 Then Jonah went out of the city and sat down east of the city, and
made a booth for himself there. He sat under it in the shade, waiting to see what
would become of the city.

MIRACLES IN THE BOOK OF JONAH

God caused a great storm	1.4
God arranged a great fish to swallow Jonah	1.17
God ordered the fish to spit up Jonah	2.10
God made a vine (bush) to shade Jonah	4.6
God prepared a worm to eat the vine	4.7
God ordered a scorching wind to blow on Jonah	4.8

God, we may be surprised at how many people will listen.

3.10 The heathen people of Nineveh believed Jonah's message and repented. What a miraculous effect God's words had on these evil people! Their repentance stood in stark contrast to Israel's stubbornness. The people of Israel heard many messages from the prophets, but they refused to repent. The people of Nineveh only needed to hear God's message once. Jesus said that at the Judgment Day, these Ninevites will rise up to condemn the Israelites for their failure to repent (Matthew 12.39–41). It is not our hearing God's Word that pleases him, but our responding obediently to it.

3.10 God responded in mercy by canceling his threatened punishment. God himself said that any nation on which he pronounced judgment would be saved if they repented (Jeremiah 18.7, 8). God forgave Nineveh just as he had forgiven Jonah. The purpose of God's judgment is correction, not revenge. He is always ready to show compassion to anyone willing to seek him.

4.1 Why did Jonah become angry when God spared Nineveh? The Jews did not want to share God's message with Gentile nations in Jonah's day, just as in Paul's day (1 Thessalonians 2.14–16). They forgot their original purpose as a nation – to be a blessing to the rest of the world by sharing God's message with other nations (Genesis 22.18). Jonah thought God should not freely give his salvation to a wicked heathen nation. Yet this is exactly what he does for all who come to him today in faith.

4.1 Jonah was angry that God had spared Nineveh. He forgot that God forgave his own sin of disobedience and spared his life. How much better it would have been if he had rejoiced that sinners had repented (compare Luke 15.10)!

4.1, 2 Jonah reveals the reason for his reluctance to go to Nineveh (1.3). He didn't want the Ninevites forgiven; he wanted them destroyed. Jonah did not understand that the God of Israel is also the God of the whole world. Are you surprised when some unexpected person turns to God? Is it possible that your view is as narrow as Jonah's? We must not forget that, in reality, *we* do not deserve to be forgiven by God.

4.3 Jonah had run from the job of delivering God's message of destruction to Nineveh (1.2, 3); now he wanted to die because the destruction wouldn't happen. How quickly Jonah had forgotten God's mercy on him when he was in the fish (2.9, 10). He was happy when God saved him, but angry when Nineveh was saved. But Jonah was learning a valuable lesson about God's mercy and forgiveness. God's forgiveness was not only for Jonah or for Israel alone, it extends to all who repent and believe.

4.3 Jonah was more concerned about his own reputation than God's. He knew that if the people repented, none of his warnings to Nineveh would come true. This would embarrass him, although it would give glory to God. Are you more interested in getting glory for God or for yourself?

4.5–11 God ministered tenderly to Jonah just as he did to Nineveh and to Israel, and just as he does to us. He could have destroyed Jonah for his defiant anger, but instead he gently taught him a lesson. If we will obey God's Word he will lead us. His harsh judgment is reserved for those who persist in rebellion.

6 The LORD God appointed a bush,[d] and made it come up over Jonah, to give
shade over his head, to save him from his discomfort; so Jonah was very happy
about the bush. 7 But when dawn came up the next day, God appointed a worm that **4.7**
attacked the bush, so that it withered. 8 When the sun rose, God prepared a sultry Joel 1.12 **4.8**
east wind, and the sun beat down on the head of Jonah so that he was faint and Isa 49.10
asked that he might die. He said, "It is better for me to die than to live." Ezek 19.12 Hos 13.15
9 But God said to Jonah, "Is it right for you to be angry about the bush?" And Rev 7.16
he said, "Yes, angry enough to die." 10 Then the LORD said, "You are concerned
about the bush, for which you did not labor and which you did not grow; it came
into being in a night and perished in a night. 11 And should I not be concerned about **4.11**
Nineveh, that great city, in which there are more than a hundred and twenty thou- Jonah 3.10
sand persons who do not know their right hand from their left, and also many animals?"

[d] Heb *qiqayon,* possibly *the castor bean plant*

4.9 Jonah was angry at the death of the plant, but not over what could have happened to Nineveh. Most of us have cried at the death of a pet or when an object with sentimental value is broken, but have we cried over the fact that a friend does not know God? How easy it is to be more sensitive to our own interests than to the spiritual needs of people around us.

4.10, 11 Sometimes people wish that judgment and destruction would come upon sinful people whose wickedness seems to demand immediate punishment. But God is more merciful than we can imagine. He feels compassion for the sinners we want judged, and he devises plans to bring them to himself. What is your attitude toward those who are especially wicked? Do you want them destroyed? Or do you wish that they could experience God's mercy and forgiveness?

4.11 God spared the sailors when they pleaded for mercy. God saved Jonah when he prayed from the belly of the fish. God saved the people of Nineveh when they responded to Jonah's preaching. God answers the prayers of those who call upon him. God will always work his will, and he desires that all come to him, trust in him, and be saved. We can be saved if we heed God's warnings to us through his Word. If we respond in obedience, he will be gracious, and we will receive his mercy, not his judgment.

THE SIGN OF JONAH

Jonah was sent by God to the Assyrians in Nineveh to warn them of coming judgment. In running from his commission, he was swallowed by a great fish and delivered after three days. Then he went to Nineveh and the Ninevites responded with repentance. These events in the life of Jonah were cited by Jesus at least three different times during his ministry. The religious leaders demanded that Jesus give them a sign to prove his authority, but Jesus said the only sign they would receive was the sign of Jonah: They would see Jesus swallowed by death and delivered after three days.

"Then some of the scribes and Pharisees said to him, 'Teacher, we wish to see a sign from you.' But he answered them, 'An evil and adulterous generation asks for a sign, but no sign will be given to it except the sign of the prophet Jonah. For just as Jonah was three days and three nights in the belly of the sea monster, so for three days and three nights the Son of Man will be in the heart of the earth. The people of Nineveh will rise up at the judgment with this generation and condemn it, because they repented at the proclamation of Jonah, and see, something greater than Jonah is here!'" (Matthew 12.38-41)

"An evil and adulterous generation asks for a sign, but no sign will be given to it except the sign of Jonah." Then he left them and went away. (Matthew 16.4)

When the crowds were increasing, he began to say, "This generation is an evil generation; it asks for a sign, but no sign will be given to it except the sign of Jonah. For just as Jonah became a sign to the people of Nineveh, so the Son of Man will be to this generation. The queen of the South will rise at the judgment with the people of this generation and condemn them, because she came from the ends of the earth to listen to the wisdom of Solomon, and see, something greater than Solomon is here!" (Luke 11.29-31)

The queen of Sheba respected the wisdom of Solomon. The Ninevites responded to God's Word through Jonah. Yet, the religious leaders of Jesus' day refused to believe the word of God spoken by his very own Son. The queen of Sheba and the Ninevites, though Gentiles, would rise up and condemn the leaders of God's chosen people for their unbelief. Often, people in our generation demand a sign from God, but the only sign they will receive is the sign of Jonah—the death and resurrection of Christ.

MICAH

Hosea becomes a prophet 753 B.C.	Jotham becomes king of Judah 750	Tiglath-pileser III invades Israel 743	Micah becomes a prophet; Pekahiah becomes king 742	Isaiah becomes a prophet 740	Ahaz becomes king of Judah 735

VITAL STATISTICS

PURPOSE:
To warn God's people that judgment is coming and to offer pardon to all who repent

AUTHOR:
Micah, a native of Moresheth, near Gath, about 20 miles southwest of Jerusalem

TO WHOM WRITTEN:
The people of Israel (the northern kingdom) and of Judah (the southern kingdom)

DATE WRITTEN:
Possibly during the reigns of Jotham, Ahaz, and Hezekiah (742–687 B.C.)

SETTING:
The political situation is described in 2 Kings 15—20 and 2 Chronicles 26—30. Micah was a contemporary of Isaiah and Hosea.

KEY VERSE:
"He has told you, O mortal, what is good; and what does the Lord require of you but to do justice, and to love kindness, and to walk humbly with your God?" (6.8).

KEY PEOPLE:
The people of Samaria and Jerusalem

KEY PLACES:
Samaria, Jerusalem, Bethlehem

SPECIAL FEATURES:
This is a beautiful example of classical Hebrew poetry. There are three parts, each beginning with "Hear" or "Listen" (1.2; 3.1; 6.1) and closing with a promise.

"I HATE YOU!" she screams, and runs from the room. Words from a child, thrown as emotional darts. Perhaps she learned the phrase from Mom and Dad, or maybe it just burst forth from that inner well of "sinful nature." Whatever the case, hate and love have become society's by-words, almost tired clichés, tossed carelessly at objects, situations, and even people.

The casual use of such words as "love" and "hate" has emptied them of their meaning. We no longer understand statements which describe a loving God who hates sin. So we picture God as gentle and kind—a cosmic "pushover"; and our concept of what he hates is tempered by our misconceptions and wishful thinking.

The words of the prophets stand in stark contrast to such misconceptions. God's hatred is real—burning, consuming, and destroying. He hates sin, and he stands as the righteous judge, ready to mete out just punishment to all who defy his rule. God's love is also real. So real that he sent his Son, the Messiah to save and accept judgment in the sinner's place. Love and hate are together—both unending, irresistible, and unfathomable.

In seven short chapters, Micah presents this true picture of God—the Almighty Lord who hates sin and loves the sinner. Much of the book is devoted to describing God's judgment on Israel (the northern kingdom), on Judah (the southern kingdom), and on all the earth. This judgment will come "for the transgression of Jacob, and for the sins of the house of Israel" (1.5). And the prophet lists their despicable sins, including fraud (2.2), theft (2.8), greed (2.9), debauchery (2.11), oppression (3.3), hypocrisy (3.4), heresy (3.5), injustice (3.9), extortion and lying (6.12), murder (7.2), and other offenses. God's judgment will come.

In the midst of this overwhelming prediction of destruction, Micah gives hope and consolation, because he also describes God's love. The truth is that judgment comes only after countless opportunities to repent, to turn back to true worship and obedience—"to do justice, and to love kindness, and to walk humbly with your God" (6.8). But even in the midst of judgment, God promises to deliver the small minority who have continued to follow him. He states, "Their king will pass on before them, the Lord at their head" (2.13). The king, of course, is Jesus; and we read in 5.2 that he will be born as a baby in Bethlehem, an obscure Judean village.

As you read Micah, catch a glimpse of God's anger in action as he judges and punishes sin. See God's love in action as he offers eternal life to all who repent and believe. And then determine to join the faithful remnant of God's people who live according to his will.

Israel (the northern kingdom) falls 722	*Hosea's ministry ends; Hezekiah becomes king of Judah 715*	*Sennacherib surrounds Jerusalem 701*	*Micah's ministry ends 687*

THE BLUEPRINT

1. The trial of the capitals (1.1—2.13)
2. The trial of the leaders (3.1—5.15)
3. The trial of the people (6.1—7.20)

Micah emphasized the need for justice and peace. Like a lawyer, he set forth God's case against Israel and Judah, their leaders, and their people. Throughout the book are prophecies about Jesus the Messiah who will gather the people into one nation. He will be their king and ruler, acting mercifully toward them. Micah makes it clear that God hates unkindness, idolatry, injustice, and empty ritual—and he still hates these today. But God is very willing to pardon the sins of any who repent.

MEGATHEMES

THEME	EXPLANATION	IMPORTANCE
Perverting faith	God will judge the false prophets, dishonest leaders, and selfish priests in Israel and Judah. While they publicly carried out religious ceremonies, they were privately seeking to gain money and influence. To mix selfish motives with an empty display of religion is to pervert faith.	Don't try to mix your own selfish desires with true faith in God. One day God will reveal how foolish it is to substitute anything for loyalty to him. Coming up with your own private blend of religion will pervert your faith.
Oppression	Micah predicted ruin for all nations and leaders who were oppressive towards others. The upper classes oppressed and exploited the poor. Yet no one was speaking against them or doing anything to stop them. God will not put up with such injustice.	We dare not ask God to help us while we ignore those who are needy and oppressed, or silently condone the actions of those who oppress them.
The Messiah—King of Peace	God promised to provide a new king to bring strength and peace to his people. Hundreds of years before Christ's birth, God promised that the eternal king would be born in Bethlehem. It was God's great plan to restore his people through the Messiah.	Christ our king leads us just as God promised. But until his final judgment, his leadership is only visible among those who welcome his authority. We can have God's peace now by giving up our sins and welcoming him as king.
Pleasing God	Micah preached that God's greatest desire was not the offering of sacrifices at the temple. God delights in faith that produces fairness, love to others, and obedience to him.	True faith in God generates kindness, compassion, justice, and humility. We can please God by seeking these results in our work, our family, our church, and our neighborhood.

1. The trial of the capitals

1 The word of the LORD that came to Micah of Moresheth in the days of Kings Jotham, Ahaz, and Hezekiah of Judah, which he saw concerning Samaria and Jerusalem.

1.1 Jer 26.18

Judgment against Samaria and Jerusalem

2 Hear, you peoples, all of you;
listen, O earth, and all that is in it;
and let the Lord GOD be a witness against you,
the Lord from his holy temple.
3 For lo, the LORD is coming out of his place,
and will come down and tread upon the high places of the earth.
4 Then the mountains will melt under him
and the valleys will burst open,
like wax near the fire,
like waters poured down a steep place.
5 All this is for the transgression of Jacob
and for the sins of the house of Israel.
What is the transgression of Jacob?
Is it not Samaria?
And what is the high place[a] of Judah?
Is it not Jerusalem?
6 Therefore I will make Samaria a heap in the open country,
a place for planting vineyards.
I will pour down her stones into the valley,
and uncover her foundations.
7 All her images shall be beaten to pieces,
all her wages shall be burned with fire,
and all her idols I will lay waste;
for as the wages of a prostitute she gathered them,
and as the wages of a prostitute they shall again be used.

8 For this I will lament and wail;
I will go barefoot and naked;
I will make lamentation like the jackals,
and mourning like the ostriches.
9 For her wound[b] is incurable.
It has come to Judah;
it has reached to the gate of my people,
to Jerusalem.

10 Tell it not in Gath,

1.2 Deut 32.1 Ps 50.7 Jer 6.19
1.3 Isa 26.21 64.1-3
1.4 Ps 97.5 Amos 9.5
1.5 2 Chron 34.3,4
1.6 Jer 51.25 Lam 4.1 Ezek 13.14
1.7 Lev 26.30 Deut 9.21; 23.18 Joel 3.3
1.8 Job 30.29 Isa 13.21,22
1.9 Isa 1.5,6; 3.26 Jer 15.18 30.11-15 Mic 1.11

a Heb *what are the high places* b Gk Syr Vg: Heb *wounds*

1.1 Micah and Isaiah lived at the same time, about 750–680 B.C., and undoubtedly knew of each other. Micah directed his message mainly to Judah, the southern kingdom, but he also had some words for Israel, the northern kingdom. Judah enjoyed great prosperity at this time. Of the three kings mentioned, Jotham (750–735) and Hezekiah (715–686) tried to follow God (2 Kings 15.32–38; 18–20), but Ahaz (735–715) was one of the most evil kings ever to reign in Judah (2 Kings 16). Moresheth was a Judean village, near Gath on the border with Philistia.

1.3 "High places" could simply mean "mountaintops" or may refer to the altars to various idols (see also 1.5).

1.3–7 Jerusalem was the capital city of Judah (the southern kingdom); Samaria was the capital city of Israel (the northern kingdom). The destruction of Samaria was literally fulfilled during Micah's lifetime, in 722 B.C. (2 Kings 17.1–18), just as he had predicted.

1.5 There are two sins identified in Micah's message—the perversion of worship (1.7; 3.5–7, 11; 5.12, 13) and injustice toward others (2.1, 2, 8, 9; 3.2, 3, 9–11; 7.2–6). Rampant in the capital cities, these sins infiltrated and infected the entire country.

1.9 Samaria's sins were beyond healing, and God's judgment on the city had already begun. This sin was not like a gash in the skin, but more like a stab wound in a vital organ, causing an injury that would soon prove fatal (Samaria was, in fact, destroyed early in Micah's ministry). Tragically, Samaria's sin had influenced Jerusalem, and judgment would come to its very gates. This probably refers to Sennacherib's siege in 701 B.C. (see 2 Kings 18, 19).

1.10–16 Micah declares God's judgment on city after city because of the people's sins. There is a clever word play in the Hebrew of 1.11. Micah bitterly denounces each town by using puns. *Shaphir* sounds like the Hebrew word for "beauty"; *Zaanan* sounds

weep not at all;
in Beth-leaphrah
roll yourselves in the dust.

1.11 Mic 1.8

11 Pass on your way,
inhabitants of Shaphir,
in nakedness and shame;
the inhabitants of Zaanan
do not come forth;
Beth-ezel is wailing
and shall remove its support from you.

1.12 Isa 59.9-11 Jer 8.15; 14.19

12 For the inhabitants of Maroth
wait anxiously for good,
yet disaster has come down from the LORD
to the gate of Jerusalem.

1.13 Josh 10.3; 15.39 Amos 2.14

13 Harness the steeds to the chariots,
inhabitants of Lachish;
it was the beginning of sin
to daughter Zion,
for in you were found
the transgressions of Israel.

1.14 Josh 15.44

14 Therefore you shall give parting gifts
to Moresheth-gath;
the houses of Achzib shall be a deception
to the kings of Israel.

1.15 Josh 15.35 2 Chron 11.7

15 I will again bring a conqueror upon you,
inhabitants of Mareshah;
the glory of Israel
shall come to Adullam.

1.16 Deut 28.32,41 2 Kgs 17.6 Isa 22.12 Jer 7.29

16 Make yourselves bald and cut off your hair
for your pampered children;
make yourselves as bald as the eagle,
for they have gone from you into exile.

MICAH served as a prophet to Judah from 742–687 B.C.

Climate of the times	King Ahaz set up pagan idols in the temple and finally nailed the temple door shut. Four different nations harassed Judah. When Hezekiah became king, the nation began a slow road to recovery and economic strength. Hezekiah probably heeded much of Micah's advice.
Main message	Predicted the fall of both the northern kingdom of Israel and the southern kingdom of Judah. This was God's discipline upon the people, actually showing how much he cared for them. Hezekiah's good reign helped postpone Judah's punishment.
Importance of message	Choosing to live a life apart from God is making a commitment to sin. Sin leads to judgment and death. God alone shows us the way to eternal peace. His discipline often keeps us on the right path.
Contemporary prophets	Hosea (753–715) Isaiah (740–681)

like the verb meaning "to go forth"; and *Beth-ezel* sounds like a word for "foundation." Read 1.11 aloud, substituting the meaning for each city's name, and you will realize the effect of Micah's word choice. Lachish was on the border with Philistia and took the brunt of the Assyrian invasion.

1.13 The people of Lachish influenced many to follow their evil example. We often do the same when we sin. Regardless of whether you consider yourself a leader, your daily actions and words are observed by others, and they may choose to follow your example, whether you know it or not.

1.14 Moresheth-gath was Micah's hometown (1.1).

1.15 The terrain surrounding Adullam had numerous caves. Micah was warning that when the enemy approached, Judah's proud princes would be forced to flee and hide in these caves.

1.16 Micah pictured the devastating sorrow of parents seeing their children taken away to be slaves in a distant land. This happened frequently in both Israel and Judah, most horribly when each nation was completely conquered – Israel in 722 B.C. and Judah in 586 B.C.

God will remove injustice

2 Alas for those who devise wickedness
and evil deeds[c] on their beds!
When the morning dawns, they perform it,
because it is in their power.
2 They covet fields, and seize them;
houses, and take them away;
they oppress householder and house,
people and their inheritance.
3 Therefore thus says the LORD:
Now, I am devising against this family an evil
from which you cannot remove your necks;
and you shall not walk haughtily,
for it will be an evil time.
4 On that day they shall take up a taunt song against you,
and wail with bitter lamentation,
and say, "We are utterly ruined;
the LORD[d] alters the inheritance of my people;
how he removes it from me!
Among our captors[e] he parcels out our fields."
5 Therefore you will have no one to cast the line by lot
in the assembly of the LORD.

6 "Do not preach"—thus they preach—
"one should not preach of such things;
disgrace will not overtake us."
7 Should this be said, O house of Jacob?
Is the LORD's patience exhausted?
Are these his doings?
Do not my words do good
to one who walks uprightly?
8 But you rise up against my people[f] as an enemy;
you strip the robe from the peaceful,[g]
from those who pass by trustingly
with no thought of war.
9 The women of my people you drive out
from their pleasant houses;
from their young children you take away
my glory forever.
10 Arise and go;

2.1 Isa 32.7 Hos 7.6,7 Rom 1.30
2.3 Deut 28.32-35 Isa 2.11,12 28.14-18 Jer 11.8
2.4 Isa 14.4 Jer 6.12; 8.10 Hab 2.6
2.5 Deut 32.8 Josh 18.4,10
2.6 Isa 30.10 Jer 26.8,9 Amos 2.12
2.7 Jer 15.16 Rom 7.13
2.8 Isa 9.21 Jer 12.8 Mic 3.2,3
2.9 Mt 23.14 Mk 12.40
2.10 Lev 18.24-28 Ps 106.38

[c] Cn: Heb *work evil* [d] Heb *he* [e] Cn: Heb *the rebellious* [f] Cn: Heb *But yesterday my people rose* [g] Cn: Heb *from before a garment*

2.1, 2 Micah warned against those who use their position to take advantage of others. Less than a century earlier, King Ahab of Israel had pouted because he couldn't get Naboth's vineyard. So his wife, Jezebel, had Naboth killed in order to give the garden to Ahab (1 Kings 21.1–16). This kind of immorality had spread throughout Judah and, like a disease, was destroying the nation from the inside out.

There are many victims of unethical attempts to take what little they have and give it to those who are more powerful. Some of these actions may be legally permissible, but they are not morally acceptable to God. Being legal doesn't necessarily mean being right.

2.1, 2 Micah spoke out against those who planned evil deeds at night and rose at dawn to do them. A person's thoughts reflect his or her character. What do you think about as you lie down to sleep? Do your desires involve greed or stepping on others to achieve your goals? Evil thoughts lead to evil deeds.

2.5 Those who have been oppressing others will find the tables turned. They will end up not having any share in the decisions to divide the land because they won't have any surviving relatives.

2.6, 7 If these messages seem harsh, remember that God did not want to take revenge on Israel; he wanted to get them back on the right path. The people had rejected what was true and right, and they needed stern discipline. Children may think discipline is harsh, but it helps keep them going in the right direction. If we only want God's comforting messages, we may miss what he has for us. Listen whenever God speaks, even when the message is hard to take.

for this is no place to rest,
because of uncleanness that destroys
with a grievous destruction.[h]

2.11 Mic 3.5,11

11 If someone were to go about uttering empty falsehoods,
saying, "I will preach to you of wine and strong drink,"
such a one would be the preacher for this people!

2.12 Isa 11.11

12 I will surely gather all of you, O Jacob,
I will gather the survivors of Israel;
I will set them together
like sheep in a fold,
like a flock in its pasture;
it will resound with people.
13 The one who breaks out will go up before them;
they will break through and pass the gate,
going out by it.
Their king will pass on before them,
the LORD at their head.

2. The trial of the leaders

Wicked rulers and Prophets

3.1 Deut 16.18 Ps 14.4

3 And I said:
Listen, you heads of Jacob
and rulers of the house of Israel!
Should you not know justice?—
2 you who hate the good and love the evil,
who tear the skin off my people,[i]
and the flesh off their bones;

3.3 Ps 14.4; 27.2

3 who eat the flesh of my people,

[h] Meaning of Heb uncertain [i] Heb *from them*

MICAH'S CHARGES OF INJUSTICE
Micah charged the people with injustice of many kinds.

Plotting wickedness	2.1
Fraud, threats, violence	2.2
Stealing, dishonesty	2.8
Driving out widows	2.9
Hating good, loving evil	3.1, 2
Hating justice, loving unfairness	3.9
Murder	3.10
Taking bribes	3.11

2.11 The people liked the false prophets who told them only what they wanted to hear. Micah spoke against prophets who encouraged the people to feel comfortable in their sin. Preachers are popular when they don't ask too much of us, when they tell us our greed or lust might even be good for us. But a true teacher of God speaks the truth, regardless of what the listeners want to hear.

2.12, 13 Micah's prophecy telescopes two great events—Judah's return from captivity in Babylon, and the great gathering of all believers when the Messiah returns. God gave his prophets visions of various future events, but not necessarily the ability to discern when these events would happen. For example, they could not see the long period of time between the Babylonian captivity and the coming of the Messiah, but they could clearly see that the Messiah was coming. The purpose of this prophecy was not to predict exactly *how* this would occur, but *that* it would. This gave the people hope and helped them turn from sin.

3.1ff Micah denounced the sins of the leaders, priests, and prophets ("heads of Jacob" and "rulers")—those responsible for teaching the people right from wrong. Elders, who were supposed to live among the people, had moved into Jerusalem and become an elite ruling class. The leaders, who should have known the law and taught it to the people, had set the law aside and become the worst of sinners. They took advantage of the very people they were supposed to serve. All sin is bad, but the sin that leads others astray is the worst of all.

3.1 The dividing line between right and wrong often seems blurred, but spiritual leaders are supposed to help others see it. The Bible is God's guidebook to show us how to distinguish right and wrong. Leaders must understand the Bible's principles and teach them to others. Leaders cannot force people to do right, but they should point them in that direction by their teaching and example.

3.2–4 The leaders had no compassion or respect for those they were supposed to serve. They treated the people miserably in order to satisfy their own desires, and then had the gall to ask for God's help when they found themselves in trouble. We, like the leaders, should not treat God like a light switch to be turned on only as needed. Instead, we should always rely on him.

flay their skin off them,
break their bones in pieces,
and chop them up like meat[j] in a kettle,
like flesh in a caldron.

4 Then they will cry to the LORD,
but he will not answer them;
he will hide his face from them at that time,
because they have acted wickedly.

3.4 Jer 33.5

5 Thus says the LORD concerning the prophets
who lead my people astray,
who cry "Peace"
when they have something to eat,
but declare war against those
who put nothing into their mouths.
6 Therefore it shall be night to you, without vision,
and darkness to you, without revelation.
The sun shall go down upon the prophets,
and the day shall be black over them;
7 the seers shall be disgraced,
and the diviners put to shame;
they shall all cover their lips,
for there is no answer from God.
8 But as for me, I am filled with power,
with the spirit of the LORD,
and with justice and might,
to declare to Jacob his transgression
and to Israel his sin.

3.5 Isa 9.15 Jer 6.14

3.6 Ps 74.9 Isa 8.20-22 29.10; 59.10 Amos 8.9,10

3.7 1 Sam 28.6,15 Zech 13.4

3.8 Isa 58.1; 61.1,2 Ezek 16.2 Mt 3.7-12

9 Hear this, you rulers of the house of Jacob
and chiefs of the house of Israel,
who abhor justice
and pervert all equity,
10 who build Zion with blood
and Jerusalem with wrong!
11 Its rulers give judgment for a bribe,
its priests teach for a price,
its prophets give oracles for money;
yet they lean upon the LORD and say,
"Surely the LORD is with us!
No harm shall come upon us."
12 Therefore because of you

3.10 Jer 22.13-17 Ezek 22.25-28 Hab 2.9-12

3.11 Jer 7.8-12 Mic 7.3

j Gk: Heb *as*

3.5–7 Micah remained true to his calling and proclaimed God's words. In contrast, the false prophets' messages were geared to the favors they received. Not all those who claim to have messages from God really do. Micah prophesied that one day the false prophets would be shamed by their actions.

3.8 Micah attributed the power of his ministry to God's Spirit. Our power comes from the same source. Jesus told his followers they would receive power to witness about him when the Holy Spirit came to them (Acts 1.8). You can't witness effectively by relying on your own strength, because fear will keep you from speaking out for God. Only by relying on the power of the Holy Spirit can you live and witness for him.

3.11 An oracle is a message from God. Micah severely condemned religious leaders who ministered only if they got paid for it. Jesus came to serve, not to promote a big-business gospel. When people "minister" for what they can get, servanthood is lost. Preaching and teaching should never be motivated by the promise of personal gain. When God calls you to do something, obey him, even if there is no monetary reward.

3.11 Micah warned the ministers of his day to avoid bribes. Pastors today accept bribes when they allow those who contribute much to control the church. When fear of losing money or members influences a pastor to remain silent when he should speak up for what is right, his church is in danger. We should remember that Judah was finally destroyed because of the behavior of its religious leaders. A similar warning must be directed at those who have money—*never* use your resources to influence or manipulate God's ministers—that is bribery.

Zion shall be plowed as a field;
Jerusalem shall become a heap of ruins,
and the mountain of the house a wooded height.

The Lord will be king

4.1 Ps 22.27; 86.9 Dan 2.28; 10.14 Mic 3.12 Zeph 3.9,10

4 In days to come
the mountain of the LORD's house
shall be established as the highest of the mountains,
and shall be raised up above the hills.
Peoples shall stream to it,
2 and many nations shall come and say:
"Come, let us go up to the mountain of the LORD,
to the house of the God of Jacob;
that he may teach us his ways
and that we may walk in his paths."
For out of Zion shall go forth instruction,
and the word of the LORD from Jerusalem.

4.2 Deut 6.1 Ps 25.8-12 Isa 2.3; 42.1-4 Jer 31.6 Hos 6.3 Zech 8.20-23 Acts 1.8 Rom 15.19

3 He shall judge between many peoples,
and shall arbitrate between strong nations far away;
they shall beat their swords into plowshares,
and their spears into pruning hooks;
nation shall not lift up sword against nation,
neither shall they learn war any more;

4.3 Ps 82.8; 98.9 Isa 11.3-5

4 but they shall all sit under their own vines and under their own fig trees,
and no one shall make them afraid;
for the mouth of the LORD of hosts has spoken.

4.4 Isa 1.20; 40.5 58.14

5 For all the peoples walk,
each in the name of its god,
but we will walk in the name of the LORD our God
forever and ever.

4.5 2 Kgs 17.29,34 Jer 2.10,11

6 In that day, says the LORD,
I will assemble the lame
and gather those who have been driven away,
and those whom I have afflicted.

4.6 Isa 35.3-7 Zeph 3.19

7 The lame I will make the remnant,
and those who were cast off, a strong nation;
and the LORD will reign over them in Mount Zion
now and forevermore.

4.7 Isa 9.6,7; 24.23

8 And you, O tower of the flock,
hill of daughter Zion,
to you it shall come,
the former dominion shall come,
the sovereignty of daughter Jerusalem.

4.8 Ps 48.12 Dan 7.18

3.12 Jerusalem would be destroyed just as Samaria was (1.6). This happened in 586 B.C. when Nebuchadnezzar and the Babylonian army attacked the city (2 Kings 25). Although Micah blamed the corrupt leaders, the people were not without fault. They allowed the corruption to continue without turning to God or calling for justice.

4.1ff The phrase, "in days to come," describes the days when God will reign over his perfect kingdom (see 4.1–8). This will be an era of peace and blessing, when war will be forever ended. We cannot pinpoint its date, but God has promised that it *will* arrive (see also Isaiah 2.2; Jeremiah 16.15; Joel 3.1ff; Zechariah 14.9–11; Malachi 3.17, 18; Revelation 19–22).

Verses 9–13 predict the Babylonian captivity in 586 B.C., even before Babylon became a powerful empire. Just as God promises a time of peace and prosperity, he also promises judgment and punishment for all who refuse to follow him. Both results are certain.

9 Now why do you cry aloud?
Is there no king in you?
Has your counselor perished,
that pangs have seized you like a woman in labor?
10 Writhe and groan,[k] O daughter Zion,
like a woman in labor;
for now you shall go forth from the city
and camp in the open country;
you shall go to Babylon.
There you shall be rescued,
there the LORD will redeem you
from the hands of your enemies.

11 Now many nations
are assembled against you,
saying, "Let her be profaned,
and let our eyes gaze upon Zion."
12 But they do not know
the thoughts of the LORD;
they do not understand his plan,
that he has gathered them as sheaves to the threshing floor.
13 Arise and thresh,
O daughter Zion,
for I will make your horn iron
and your hoofs bronze;
you shall beat in pieces many peoples,
and shall[l] devote their gain to the LORD,
their wealth to the Lord of the whole earth.

5 [m] Now you are walled around with a wall;[n]
siege is laid against us;
with a rod they strike the ruler of Israel
upon the cheek.

A ruler will come from Bethlehem

2[o] But you, O Bethlehem of Ephrathah,
who are one of the little clans of Judah,
from you shall come forth for me
one who is to rule in Israel,
whose origin is from of old,

4.9 Jer 4.21; 8.19
4.10 2 Kgs 20.18 2 Chron 36.20 Hos 2.14 Mic 7.8-12
4.12 Ps 147.19,20 Isa 55.8
4.13 Isa 18.7 41.15,16; 60.9 Jer 51.33 Mic 5.8-15 Rom 15.25-28
5.1 Jer 5.7 Lam 3.30
5.2 Jer 30.21 Zech 9.9 Mt 2.6 Jn 1.1-3; 7.42

[k] Meaning of Heb uncertain [l] Gk Syr Tg: Heb *and I will* [m] Ch 4.14 in Heb [n] Cn Compare Gk: Meaning of Heb uncertain [o] Ch 5.1 in Heb

4.9–13 Micah predicted the end of the kings — a drastic statement to the people of Judah who thought their kingdom would last forever. He also said that Babylon would destroy the land of Judah and carry away its king, but that after a while God would help his people return to their land. This all happened just as Micah prophesied, and these events are recorded in 2 Chronicles 36.9–23 and Ezra 1, 2.

4.12 When God reveals the future, his purpose goes beyond satisfying our curiosity. He wants us to change our present behavior because of what we know about the future. Forever begins now; and a glimpse of God's plan for his followers should motivate us to serve him, no matter what the rest of the world may do.

5.1 This judge was probably King Zedekiah who was reigning in Jerusalem when Nebuchadnezzar conquered the city (2 Kings 25.1, 2). Zedekiah was the last of the kings in David's line to sit on the throne in Jerusalem. Micah said that the next king in David's line would be the Messiah, who would establish a kingdom that would never end.

5.1ff Jerusalem's leaders were obsessed with wealth and position, but Micah prophesied that mighty Jerusalem, with all its wealth and power, would be besieged and destroyed. Its king could not save it. In contrast, Bethlehem, a tiny town, would be the birthplace of the only king who could save his people. This deliverer, the Messiah, would be born as a baby in Bethlehem (Luke 2.4–7), and eventually would reign as the eternal King (Revelation 19—22).

5.2 Ephrathah was the district in which Bethlehem was located.

5.2 This ruler is Jesus, the Messiah. Micah accurately predicted Christ's birthplace hundreds of years before he was born. The promised eternal King in David's line, who would come to live as a man, had been alive forever — "from of old, from ancient days." Although eternal, he entered human history as the man, Jesus of Nazareth.

from ancient days.
5.3 Isa 10.20-22 Mic 4.10; 5.7,8 7.13
3 Therefore he shall give them up until the time
when she who is in labor has brought forth;
then the rest of his kindred shall return
to the people of Israel.
5.4 Ps 72.8 Isa 52.10 Mic 7.14
4 And he shall stand and feed his flock in the strength of the LORD,
in the majesty of the name of the LORD his God.
5.5 Isa 8.7,8 37.31-36 Jer 33.15
And they shall live secure, for now he shall be great
to the ends of the earth;
5 and he shall be the one of peace.

If the Assyrians come into our land
and tread upon our soil,[p]
we will raise against them seven shepherds
and eight installed as rulers.
5.6 Gen 10.8-11 2 Kgs 19.32-35 Nah 2.11-13
6 They shall rule the land of Assyria with the sword,
and the land of Nimrod with the drawn sword;[q]
they[r] shall rescue us from the Assyrians
if they come into our land
or tread within our border.

5.7 Deut 32.2 Ps 72.6
7 Then the remnant of Jacob,
surrounded by many peoples,
shall be like dew from the LORD,
like showers on the grass,
which do not depend upon people
or wait for any mortal.
5.8 Gen 49.9 Zech 9.15
8 And among the nations the remnant of Jacob,
surrounded by many peoples,
shall be like a lion among the animals of the forest,
like a young lion among the flocks of sheep,
which, when it goes through, treads down
and tears in pieces, with no one to deliver.
9 Your hand shall be lifted up over your adversaries,
and all your enemies shall be cut off.

10 In that day, says the LORD,
I will cut off your horses from among you
and will destroy your chariots;
5.11 Isa 2.12-17 Ezek 38.11 Amos 5.9
11 and I will cut off the cities of your land
and throw down all your strongholds;
5.12 Deut 18.10-12
12 and I will cut off sorceries from your hand,
and you shall have no more soothsayers;

[p] Gk: Heb *in our palaces* [q] Cn: Heb *in its entrances* [r] Heb *he*

5.5 Micah's prophecy of seven shepherds and eight rulers is a figurative way of saying that the Messiah will raise up many good leaders when he returns to reign. This contrasts with Micah's words in chapter three about Judah's corrupt leaders. "Assyria" symbolically refers to all nations in every age that oppose God's people. These good leaders will help Christ defeat all evil in the world.

5.5 This chapter provides one of the clearest Old Testament prophecies of Christ's coming. The key descriptive phrase is "and he shall be the one of peace." In one of Christ's closing talks he said, "Peace I leave with you; my peace I give to you. I do not give to you as the world gives. Do not let your hearts be troubled, and do not let them be afraid" (John 14.27). With Christ's first coming we have the opportunity for peace with God. No more fear of judgment, no more conflict and guilt. Christ's peace gives us assurance even though wars continue. With Christ's second coming all wars and weapons will be destroyed (4.3–5).

5.6 The land of Nimrod is another name for Assyria, which, in this case, is a symbol of all the evil nations in the world.

5.10 When God rules in his eternal kingdom, our strength will not be found in military might but in God's almighty power. He will destroy all the weapons that people use for security. There will be no need for armies because God will rule in the heart of every person. Our hearts should not be ruled by fear of invasion or nuclear attack. Our confidence should be in God.

5.12–14 Soothsayers were fortune-tellers. Images, pillars, and sacred poles were all part of pagan worship.

13 and I will cut off your images
and your pillars from among you,
and you shall bow down no more
to the work of your hands;
14 and I will uproot your sacred poles[s] from among you
and destroy your towns.
15 And in anger and wrath I will execute vengeance
on the nations that did not obey.

3. The trial of the people

God has a complaint against his people

6 Hear what the LORD says:
Rise, plead your case before the mountains,
and let the hills hear your voice.
2 Hear, you mountains, the controversy of the LORD,
and you enduring foundations of the earth;
for the LORD has a controversy with his people,
and he will contend with Israel.

6.2 Hos 4.1; 12.2

3 "O my people, what have I done to you?
In what have I wearied you? Answer me!
4 For I brought you up from the land of Egypt,
and redeemed you from the house of slavery;
and I sent before you Moses,
Aaron, and Miriam.
5 O my people, remember now what King Balak of Moab devised,
what Balaam son of Beor answered him,
and what happened from Shittim to Gilgal,
that you may know the saving acts of the LORD."

6.3 Jer 2.5,31
6.4 Ex 20.1,2 Ps 77.20
6.5 Num 22.5,6

6 "With what shall I come before the LORD,
and bow myself before God on high?
Shall I come before him with burnt offerings,
with calves a year old?
7 Will the LORD be pleased with thousands of rams,
with ten thousands of rivers of oil?
Shall I give my firstborn for my transgression,
the fruit of my body for the sin of my soul?"
8 He has told you, O mortal, what is good;

6.6 Lev 1.3,6.9-13
6.7 Lev 18.21 20.1-5 Ps 50.9 Isa 40.16
6.8 Lev 26.41 Deut 10.12,13 Isa 57.15

[s] Heb *Asherim*

6.1ff Here Micah pictures a courtroom. God, the judge, tells his people what he requires of them and recites all the ways they have wronged both him and others. Chapters 4 and 5 are full of hope; chapters 6 and 7 proclaim judgment and appeal to the people to repent.

6.1, 2 God called to the mountains to confirm the people's guilt. The mountains would serve as excellent witnesses, for it was in the high places that the people had built pagan altars and sacrificed to false gods (1 Kings 14.23; Jeremiah 17.2, 3; Ezekiel 20.28).

6.3 The people would never be able to answer this question because God had done nothing wrong. In fact, he had been exceedingly patient with them, had always lovingly guided them, and had given them every opportunity to return to him. If God asked you this question, how would you reply?

6.5 The story of Balak and Balaam is found in Numbers 22 – 24. Shittim (Acacia) was the Israelites' campsite east of the Jordan River just before they entered the promised land (Joshua 2.1). There the people received many of God's instructions about how to live. Gilgal, their first campsite after crossing the Jordan (Joshua 4.19), was where the people renewed their covenant with God (Joshua 5.3–9). These two places represent God's loving care for his people: his willingness both to protect them and to warn them about potential troubles. In Micah's day, the people had forgotten this covenant and its benefits and had turned away from God.

6.5 God continued to be kind to his forgetful people, but their short memory and lack of thankfulness condemned them. When people refuse to see how fortunate they are and begin to take God's gifts for granted, they become self-centered. Regularly remember God's goodness and thank him. Remembering God's past protection will help you see his present provision.

6.6–8 Israel responded to God's request by trying to appease him with sacrifices, hoping he would then leave them alone. But sacrifices and other religious rituals aren't enough; God wants changed lives. He wants his people to be fair, just, merciful, and humble. God wants us to become *living* sacrifices (Romans 12.1, 2), not just doing religious deeds, but living rightly (Jeremiah 4.4; Hebrews 9.14). It is impossible to follow God consistently without his transforming love in our hearts.

and what does the LORD require of you
but to do justice, and to love kindness,
and to walk humbly with your God?

9 The voice of the LORD cries to the city
(it is sound wisdom to fear your name):
Hear, O tribe and assembly of the city![t]
10 Can I forget[u] the treasures of wickedness in the house of the wicked,
and the scant measure that is accursed?
11 Can I tolerate wicked scales
and a bag of dishonest weights?
12 Your[v] wealthy are full of violence;
your[w] inhabitants speak lies,
with tongues of deceit in their mouths.
13 Therefore I have begun[x] to strike you down,
making you desolate because of your sins.
14 You shall eat, but not be satisfied,
and there shall be a gnawing hunger within you;
you shall put away, but not save,
and what you save, I will hand over to the sword.
15 You shall sow, but not reap;
you shall tread olives, but not anoint yourselves with oil;
you shall tread grapes, but not drink wine.
16 For you have kept the statutes of Omri[y]
and all the works of the house of Ahab,
and you have followed their counsels.
Therefore I will make you a desolation, and your[z] inhabitants an object of hissing;
so you shall bear the scorn of my people.

6.10 Prov 10.2; 11.1 20.10,23; 21.6 Jer 5.26,27 Amos 3.10
6.11 Mic 6.10
6.12 Isa 3.10
6.13 Lev 26.16 Isa 1.5,6 Jer 14.18 Acts 12.23
6.14 Lev 26.26 Isa 9.20; 30.6
6.15 Deut 28.38-40 Isa 62.8,9
6.16 1 Kgs 16.29-33 Jer 18.15,16 Ezek 8.17,18

God promises eventual restoration

7 Woe is me! For I have become like one who,
after the summer fruit has been gathered,
after the vintage has been gleaned,
finds no cluster to eat;
there is no first-ripe fig for which I hunger.
2 The faithful have disappeared from the land,
and there is no one left who is upright;
they all lie in wait for blood,
and they hunt each other with nets.
3 Their hands are skilled to do evil;
the official and the judge ask for a bribe,
and the powerful dictate what they desire;

7.1 Ps 12.1 Mic 3.10
7.3 Prov 4.16,17 Jer 3.5 Mic 3.11

[t] Cn Compare Gk: Heb *tribe, and who has appointed it yet?* [u] Cn: Meaning of Heb uncertain [v] Heb *Whose* [w] Heb *whose* [x] Gk Syr Vg: Heb *have made sick* [y] Gk Syr Vg Tg: Heb *the statutes of Omri are kept* [z] Heb *its*

6.8 People have tried all kinds of ways to please God (6.6, 7), but God has made his wishes clear: he wants his people to be fair, just, and merciful, and to walk humbly with him. In your efforts to please God, examine these areas on a regular basis. Are you fair in your dealings with people? Do you show mercy to those who wrong you? Are you learning humility?

6.16 Omri reigned over Israel and led the people into idol worship (1 Kings 16.21–26). Ahab, his son, was Israel's most wicked king (1 Kings 16.29–33). If the people were following only the commands and examples of these kings, they were in bad shape. Such pervasive evil was ripe for punishment.

7.1ff This chapter begins in gloom (7.1–6) and ends in hope (7.7–20). Micah watched as society rotted around him. Rulers demanded gifts; judges accepted bribes; corruption was universal. But God promised to lead the people out of the darkness of sin and into his light. Then the people would praise him for his faithfulness. God alone is perfectly faithful.

7.1–4 Micah could not find an honest ("faithful") person anywhere in the land. Even today, real honesty is difficult to find. Society rationalizes sin, and even Christians sometimes compromise Christian principles in order to do what they want. It is easy to convince ourselves that we deserve a few breaks, especially when "everyone else" is doing it. But the standards for honesty come from God, not society. We are honest because God is truth, and we are to be like him.

thus they pervert justice.[a]
4 The best of them is like a brier,
the most upright of them a thorn hedge.
The day of their[b] sentinels, of their[b] punishment, has come;
now their confusion is at hand.
5 Put no trust in a friend,
have no confidence in a loved one;
guard the doors of your mouth
from her who lies in your embrace;
6 for the son treats the father with contempt,
the daughter rises up against her mother,
the daughter-in-law against her mother-in-law;
your enemies are members of your own household.
7 But as for me, I will look to the LORD,
I will wait for the God of my salvation;
my God will hear me.

8 Do not rejoice over me, O my enemy;
when I fall, I shall rise;
when I sit in darkness,
the LORD will be a light to me.
9 I must bear the indignation of the LORD,
because I have sinned against him,
until he takes my side
and executes judgment for me.
He will bring me out to the light;
I shall see his vindication.
10 Then my enemy will see,
and shame will cover her who said to me,
"Where is the LORD your God?"
My eyes will see her downfall;[c]
now she will be trodden down
like the mire of the streets.

11 A day for the building of your walls!
In that day the boundary shall be far extended.
12 In that day they will come to you
from Assyria to[d] Egypt,
and from Egypt to the River,
from sea to sea and from mountain to mountain.
13 But the earth will be desolate
because of its inhabitants,
for the fruit of their doings.

7.4 Isa 10.3; 22.5 55.13 Jer 8.12; 10.15 Ezek 2.6 Nah 1.10 Lk 21.25
7.5 Jer 9.4,5 Mt 10.16
7.6 Mt 10.36
7.7 Ps 4.3; 34.5,6 Hab 3.17-19
7.8 Prov 24.15,16 Isa 9.2; 50.11 Amos 9.11
7.9 Jer 50.34 51.35,36 Mic 7.8
7.10 Isa 25.10-12 Zech 10.5
7.12 Isa 11.16 19.23-25
7.13 Mic 6.13

[a] Cn: Heb *they weave it* [b] Heb *your* [c] Heb lacks *downfall* [d] One Ms: MT *Assyria and cities of*

7.5, 6 Sin had affected the government leaders and society in general. Deceit had even ruined the family, the core of society. As a result, the only way left to purify the people was God's judgment. This would draw the nation back to him and restore them from the inside out.

7.7–9 Micah showed great faith in God as he proclaimed that (1) he would wait upon God, because God hears and saves when help is needed, (2) God would bring him through when times were tough, (3) he would be patient in punishment because God would bring him out of the darkness, and (4) his enemies would be punished. We too can have a relationship with God that can allow us to have confidence like Micah's. It doesn't take unusual talent; it simply takes faith in God and a willingness to act on that faith.

7.9 Micah realized that if the people would be patient and obedient while they were being punished, God would forgive them and show his goodness again (Lamentations 3.39–41). Punishment does not mean rejection. The nation of Judah was being punished in order to bring the people to God, not to send them away from him. When you face trials because of your sin, do not be angry with God or be afraid that he has rejected you. Instead, turn away from your sin and turn to God.

7.14 Bashan and Gilead were fertile areas east of the Jordan, pre-

7.14
Lev 27.32
Ps 77.5-11
110.2

14 Shepherd your people with your staff,
the flock that belongs to you,
which lives alone in a forest
in the midst of a garden land;
let them feed in Bashan and Gilead
as in the days of old.

7.15
Ex 3.20

15 As in the days when you came out of the land of Egypt,
show us[e] marvelous things.

7.16
Mic 3.7

16 The nations shall see and be ashamed
of all their might;
they shall lay their hands on their mouths;
their ears shall be deaf;

7.17
Gen 3.14,15
Josh 2.9-11

17 they shall lick dust like a snake,
like the crawling things of the earth;
they shall come trembling out of their fortresses;
they shall turn in dread to the LORD our God,
and they shall stand in fear of you.

7.18
Ex 34.7
Num 14.18,19
Jer 4.2; 32.41
Eph 2.4,5

18 Who is a God like you, pardoning iniquity
and passing over the transgression
of the remnant of your[f] possession?
He does not retain his anger forever,
because he delights in showing clemency.

7.19
Jer 50.20

19 He will again have compassion upon us;
he will tread our iniquities under foot.
You will cast all our[g] sins
into the depths of the sea.

7.20
Gen 24.27
32.10

20 You will show faithfulness to Jacob
and unswerving loyalty to Abraham,
as you have sworn to our ancestors
from the days of old.

[e] Cn: Heb *I will show him* [f] Heb *his* [g] Gk Syr Vg Tg: Heb *their*

---

viously the territory of Reuben, Gad, and the half tribe of Manasseh.

7.18 God loves to be merciful! He does not forgive grudgingly, but is glad when we repent and offers forgiveness to all who come back to him. Today you can confess your sins and receive his loving forgiveness. Don't be too proud to accept God's free offer.

7.20 In an age when religion was making little difference in people's lives, Micah said that God expected his people to be fair, just, and merciful (6.8). He requires the same of Christians today. In a world that is unfair, we must act justly. In a world of tough breaks, we must be merciful. In a world of pride and self-sufficiency, we must walk humbly with God. Only when we live God's way will we begin to affect our homes, our society, and our world.

NAHUM

Manasseh becomes king of Judah 697 B.C.

Ashurbanipal becomes king of Assyria 669

The fall of Thebes; Nahum becomes a prophet 663

VITAL STATISTICS

PURPOSE:
To pronounce God's judgment on Assyria and to comfort Judah with this truth

AUTHOR:
Nahum

TO WHOM WRITTEN:
The people of Nineveh and Judah

DATE WRITTEN:
Sometime during Nahum's prophetic ministry (probably between 663 and 654 B.C.)

SETTING:
This particular prophecy takes place after the fall of Thebes in 663 B.C. (see 3.8–10)

KEY VERSES:
"The Lord is good, a stronghold in a day of trouble; he protects those who take refuge in him, even in a rushing flood. He will make a full end of his adversaries, and will pursue his enemies into darkness. Why do you plot against the Lord? He will make an end; no adversary will rise up twice" (1.7–9).

KEY PLACE:
Nineveh, the capital of Assyria

THE SHRILL whistle pierces the air and all the action on the court abruptly stops. Pointing to the offending player, the referee shouts, "Foul!"

Rules, fouls, and penalties are part of any game and are regulated and enforced vigorously by referees, umpires, judges, and other officials. Every participant knows that boundaries must be set and behavior monitored, or the game will degenerate into chaos.

There are laws in the world as well—boundaries and rules for living established by God. But men and women regularly flaunt these regulations, hiding their infractions or overpowering others, declaring that "might makes right." God calls this sin—willful disobedience, rebellion against his control, or apathy. And, at times, it seems as though the violators succeed—no whistles blow, no fouls are called, and individual despots rule. The truth is, however, that ultimately justice will be served in the world. God will settle all accounts.

Assyria was the most powerful nation on earth. Proud in their self-sufficiency and military might, they plundered, oppressed, and slaughtered their victims. One hundred years earlier, Jonah had preached in the streets of the capital city, Nineveh; the people heard God's message and turned from their evil. But generations later, evil is again reigning, and the prophet Nahum pronounces judgment on this wicked nation. Nineveh is called a "city of bloodshed" (3.1), a city of cruelty (3.19), and the Assyrians are judged for their arrogance (1.11), idolatry (1.14), murder, lies, treachery, and social injustice (3.1–19). Because of their sins, Nahum predicts that this proud and powerful nation will be utterly destroyed. The end came within 50 years.

In this judgment of Assyria and its capital city, Nineveh, God is judging a sinful world. And the message is clear—disobedience, rebellion, and injustice will not prevail but will be punished severely by a righteous and holy God who rules over all the earth.

As you read Nahum, sense God's wrath as he avenges sin and brings about justice. Decide to live under his guidance and within his rules, commands, and guidelines for life.

THE BLUEPRINT

1. Nineveh's judge (1.1–15)
2. Nineveh's judgment (2.1—3.19)

Nineveh, the capital of the Assyrian Empire, is the subject of Nahum's prophecy. The news of its coming destruction was a relief for Judah, who was subject to Assyrian domination. No longer would Judah be forced to pay tribute as insurance against invasions. Judah was comforted to know that God was still in control. Nineveh is an example to all rulers and nations of the world today. God is sovereign over even those who are seemingly invincible. We can be confident that God's power and justice will one day conquer all evil.

Josiah becomes king of Judah; Zephaniah becomes a prophet 640	Jeremiah becomes a prophet 627	Nineveh falls 612	Assyria completely conquered 609	Babylonians win battle of Carchemish 605	Judah falls to Babylon 586

MEGATHEMES

THEME	EXPLANATION	IMPORTANCE
God judges	God would judge the city of Nineveh for its idolatry, arrogance, and oppression. Although Assyria was the leading military power in the world, God would completely destroy this "invincible" nation. God allows no person or power to assume or scoff at his authority.	Anyone who remains arrogant and resists God's authority will face his anger. No ruler or nation will get away from rejecting him. No individual will be able to hide from his judgment. Yet those who keep trusting God will be kept safe forever.
God rules	God rules over all the earth, even over those who don't acknowledge him. God is all-powerful and no one can thwart his plans. God will overcome any who attempt to defy him. Human power is futile against God.	If you are impressed by or afraid of any weapons, armies, or powerful people, remember that God alone can truly rescue you from fear or oppression. We must place our confidence in God because he alone rules all of history, all the earth, and our lives.

1. Nineveh's judge

God's patience and power

1.1 Isa 13.1; Ezek 40.2; Zeph 2.13
1.2 Ex 20.5; Deut 4.24; 32.35

1 An oracle concerning Nineveh. The book of the vision of Nahum of Elkosh.

2 A jealous and avenging God is the LORD,
the LORD is avenging and wrathful;
the LORD takes vengeance on his adversaries
and rages against his enemies.

NAHUM served as a prophet to Judah and Assyria from 663–654 B.C.

Climate of the times	Manasseh, one of Judah's most wicked kings, ruled the land. He openly defied God and persecuted God's people. Assyria, the world power at that time, made Judah one of its vassal states. The people of Judah wanted to be like the Assyrians, who seemed to have all the power and possessions they wanted.
Main message	The mighty empire of Assyria that oppressed God's people would soon tumble.
Importance of message	Those who do evil and oppress others will one day meet a bitter end.
Contemporary prophet	Zephaniah (640–621)

1.1 Nahum, like Jonah, was a prophet to Nineveh, the capital of the Assyrian Empire, and he prophesied between 663 and 654 B.C. Jonah had seen the city repent a century earlier (see the book of Jonah), but it had fallen back into wickedness. Assyria, the world power controlling the Fertile Crescent, seemed unstoppable. Its ruthless and savage warriors had already conquered Israel, the northern kingdom, and were causing great suffering in Judah. So Nahum proclaimed God's anger against Assyria's evil. Within a few decades, the mighty Assyrian Empire would be toppled by Babylon. An *oracle* is a message from God.

1.2 God alone has the right to be jealous and to carry out vengeance. Jealousy and vengeance may be surprising terms to associate with God. When humans are jealous and take vengeance, they are usually acting in a spirit of selfishness. But it is appropriate for God to insist on our complete allegiance, and it is just for him to punish unrepentant evildoers. His jealousy and vengeance are unmixed with selfishness. Their purpose is to remove sin and restore peace to the world (Deuteronomy 4.24; 5.9).

3 The LORD is slow to anger but great in power,
and the LORD will by no means clear the guilty.

His way is in whirlwind and storm,
and the clouds are the dust of his feet.
4 He rebukes the sea and makes it dry,
and he dries up all the rivers;
Bashan and Carmel wither,
and the bloom of Lebanon fades.
5 The mountains quake before him,
and the hills melt;
the earth heaves before him,
the world and all who live in it.

6 Who can stand before his indignation?
Who can endure the heat of his anger?
His wrath is poured out like fire,
and by him the rocks are broken in pieces.
7 The LORD is good,
a stronghold in a day of trouble;
he protects those who take refuge in him,
8 even in a rushing flood.
He will make a full end of his adversaries,[a]
and will pursue his enemies into darkness.
9 Why do you plot against the LORD?
He will make an end;
no adversary will rise up twice.
10 Like thorns they are entangled,
like drunkards they are drunk;
they are consumed like dry straw.
11 From you one has gone out
who plots evil against the LORD,
who counsels wickedness.

God will rescue Judah

12 Thus says the LORD,
"Though they are at full strength and many,[b]
they will be cut off and pass away.
Though I have afflicted you,

1.5 Ps 68.8; 97.5 Isa 2.12-18

1.6 Mal 3.2 Rev 6.17

1.7 Ps 25.8; 100.5

1.8 Isa 8.7,8

1.9 Job 9.4 Ps 2.1-4; 21.11 Prov 21.30

1.10 Isa 9.18; 10.17 Mal 4.1 Rev 14.10,11

a Gk: Heb *of her place* b Meaning of Heb uncertain

1.3 God is slow to get angry, but when he is ready to punish, even the earth trembles. Often people avoid God because they see evildoers in the world and hypocrites in the church. They don't realize that because God is slow to anger, he gives his true followers time to share his love and truth with evildoers. But judgment *will* come; God will not allow sin to go unchecked forever. When people wonder why God doesn't punish evil immediately, help them remember that if he did, none of us would be here. We can all be thankful that God gives people time to turn to him.

1.4 Bashan and Carmel were very fertile areas.

1.6 No person on earth can safely defy God, the Almighty, the Creator of all the universe. God, who controls the sun, the galaxies, and the vast stretches beyond, also controls the rise and fall of nations. How could a small, temporal kingdom like Assyria, no matter how powerful, challenge his awesome power? If only Assyria could have looked ahead to see the desolate mound of rubble that it would become – and yet God would still be alive and well! Don't defy God; he will be here forever with greater power than that of all armies and nations combined.

1.6–8 To those who refuse to believe, God's punishment is like an angry fire. To those who love him, his mercy is security and peace, supplying all our needs without diminishing his supply. But to his enemies he is a flood that will sweep them away. The relationship we have is up to us. Which kind of relationship will you choose?

1.11 The one "who plots evil against the Lord, who counsels wickedness" could have been (1) Ashurbanipal (669–627 B.C.), king of Assyria during much of Nahum's life and the one who brought Assyria to the zenith of its power; (2) Sennacherib (705–681), who openly defied God (2 Kings 18.13–35), epitomizing rebellion against God; or (3) no one king in particular, but the entire evil monarchy. The point is that Nineveh would be destroyed for rebelling against God.

1.12–15 The good news for Judah, whom Assyria destroyed, was that its conquerors and tormentors would be destroyed and would never rise to torment it again. Nineveh was so completely wiped out that its ruins were not identified until 1845.

1.13 Ps 107.14 Isa 9.4 Jer 2.20

I will afflict you no more.
13 And now I will break off his yoke from you
and snap the bonds that bind you."

1.14 Nah 3.4-6

14 The LORD has commanded concerning you:
"Your name shall be perpetuated no longer;
from the house of your gods I will cut off
the carved image and the cast image.
I will make your grave, for you are worthless."

1.15 Ps 107.15, 21,22 Isa 29.7,8 Lk 2.10,14 Rom 10.15-17

15[c] Look! On the mountains the feet of one
who brings good tidings,
who proclaims peace!
Celebrate your festivals, O Judah,
fulfill your vows,
for never again shall the wicked invade you;
they are utterly cut off.

2. Nineveh's judgment

The city will fall

2.1 Isa 10.12 37.36,37 Zeph 2.13-15

2 A shatterer[d] has come up against you.
Guard the ramparts;
watch the road;
gird your loins;
collect all your strength.

2.2 Hos 2.14-23 11.11

2 (For the LORD is restoring the majesty of Jacob,
as well as the majesty of Israel,
though ravagers have ravaged them
and ruined their branches.)

3 The shields of his warriors are red;
his soldiers are clothed in crimson.
The metal on the chariots flashes
on the day when he musters them;
the chargers[e] prance.

2.4 Nah 3.2

4 The chariots race madly through the streets,
they rush to and fro through the squares;
their appearance is like torches,
they dart like lightning.
5 He calls his officers;
they stumble as they come forward;
they hasten to the wall,
and the mantelet[f] is set up.
6 The river gates are opened,
the palace trembles.
7 It is decreed[f] that the city[g] be exiled,
its slave women led away,
moaning like doves

[c] Ch 2.1 in Heb [d] Cn: Heb *scatterer* [e] Cn Compare Gk Syr: Heb *cypresses* [f] Meaning of Heb uncertain [g] Heb *it*

2.1ff This chapter predicts the events of 612 B.C., when the combined armies of the Babylonians and the Medes sacked the impregnable Nineveh. Ramparts were fortified walls. "Gird your loins" means "get ready."

2.2 Assyria had plundered and crushed the northern kingdom and deported its people in 722 B.C. (2 Kings 17.3–6; 18.9–11). Assyria had also attacked the southern kingdom and forced it to pay tribute.

2.6 This reference to the opening of river gates could refer either to the enemy flowing into Nineveh like a flood (1.8) or to an actual flood of water. Some scholars suggest that dam gates, which have been found in archaeological excavations, were closed to dam up the river. When an enormous amount of water had been accumulated, the gates were opened, allowing the water to flood Nineveh.

and beating their breasts.
8 Nineveh is like a pool
whose waters[h] run away.
"Halt! Halt!"—
but no one turns back.
9 "Plunder the silver,
plunder the gold!
There is no end of treasure!
An abundance of every precious thing!"

10 Devastation, desolation, and destruction!
Hearts faint and knees tremble,
all loins quake,
all faces grow pale!
11 What became of the lions' den,
the cave[i] of the young lions,
where the lion goes,
and the lion's cubs, with no one to disturb them?
12 The lion has torn enough for his whelps
and strangled prey for his lionesses;
he has filled his caves with prey
and his dens with torn flesh.

13 See, I am against you, says the LORD of hosts, and I will burn your[j] chariots
in smoke, and the sword shall devour your young lions; I will cut off your prey
from the earth, and the voice of your messengers shall be heard no more.

The people will be scattered

3 Ah! City of bloodshed,
utterly deceitful, full of booty—
no end to the plunder!
2 The crack of whip and rumble of wheel,
galloping horse and bounding chariot!
3 Horsemen charging,
flashing sword and glittering spear,
piles of dead,
heaps of corpses,
dead bodies without end—
they stumble over the bodies!
4 Because of the countless debaucheries of the prostitute,
gracefully alluring, mistress of sorcery,
who enslaves[k] nations through her debaucheries,
and peoples through her sorcery,
5 I am against you,
says the LORD of hosts,

2.8 Nah 3.3
2.9 Gen 14.21,24; Ex 15.9; 2 Chron 25.13; Isa 33.4
2.10 Lev 26.33; Isa 24.1; 34.10; Jer 4.23
2.13 Ps 46.9
3.1 Ezek 22.2-5; 24.6-9; Zeph 3.13
3.2 Nah 2.4
3.3 Nah 2.3,6,8
3.4 Rev 17.1-6; 18.2,3
3.5 Rev 18.3-7

[h] Cn Compare Gk: Heb *a pool, from the days that she has become, and they* [i] Cn: Heb *pasture* [j] Heb *her*
[k] Heb *sells*

2.12–3.1 The major source of the Assyrian economy was the plunder taken from other nations. The Assyrians had taken the food of innocent people to maintain their luxurious standard of living, depriving others to supply their excesses. Depriving innocent people to support the luxury of a few is a sin that angers God. As Christians we must stand firm against this common but evil practice.

2.13 God had given the people of Nineveh a chance to repent, which they did after hearing Jonah (see the book of Jonah). But now they had returned to their sin, and its consequences were destroying them. There is a point for people, cities, and nations after which there is no turning back; Assyria had crossed that point. We must warn others to repent while there is still time.

3.4 Nineveh used its beauty, prestige, and power to seduce other nations. Like a prostitute, she enticed them into false friendships. Then when the other nations relaxed, thinking Assyria was a friend, Assyria destroyed and plundered them. Beautiful and impressive on the outside, Nineveh was vicious and deceitful on the inside. Beneath beautiful facades sometimes lie seduction and death. Don't let an attractive institution, company, movement, or person seduce you into lowering your standards or compromising your moral principles.

and will lift up your skirts over your face;
and I will let nations look on your nakedness
and kingdoms on your shame.

3.6 Lam 3.15

6 I will throw filth at you
and treat you with contempt,
and make you a spectacle.

3.7 Isa 51.19

7 Then all who see you will shrink from you and say,
"Nineveh is devastated; who will bemoan her?"
Where shall I seek comforters for you?

3.8 Jer 46.25 Ezek 30.14-16

8 Are you better than Thebes[l]
that sat by the Nile,
with water around her,
her rampart a sea,
water her wall?

3.9 Isa 20.5,6 Jer 46.9

9 Ethiopia[m] was her strength,
Egypt too, and that without limit;
Put and the Libyans were her[n] helpers.

3.10 2 Kgs 8.12 Ps 137.9 Hos 13.16 Nah 3.8 Mt 2.16-18

10 Yet she became an exile,
she went into captivity;
even her infants were dashed in pieces
at the head of every street;
lots were cast for her nobles,
all her dignitaries were bound in fetters.

3.11 Isa 29.9; 49.26 Jer 25.15-27 51.57

11 You also will be drunken,
you will go into hiding;[o]
you will seek
a refuge from the enemy.
12 All your fortresses are like fig trees
with first-ripe figs—
if shaken they fall
into the mouth of the eater.

3.13 Isa 19.16 Jer 50.37; 51.30

13 Look at your troops:
they are women in your midst.
The gates of your land
are wide open to your foes;
fire has devoured the bars of your gates.

3.14 2 Chron 32.3, 4,11 Isa 8.9,10 22.9-11; 37.25 Nah 2.1

14 Draw water for the siege,
strengthen your forts;
trample the clay,
tread the mortar,
take hold of the brick mold!

3.15 Isa 66.15,16

15 There the fire will devour you,
the sword will cut you off.
It will devour you like the locust.

Multiply yourselves like the locust,
multiply like the grasshopper!

[l] Heb *No-amon* [m] Or *Nubia*; Heb *Cush* [n] Gk: Heb *your* [o] Meaning of Heb uncertain

3.8–10 Thebes was a city in Egypt, the previous world power, which stood in the path of Assyria's expansion in the south. The Assyrians conquered Thebes 51 years before this prophecy was given. To Judah, surrounded to the north and south by Assyria, the situation appeared hopeless. But God said that the same atrocities done in Thebes would happen in Nineveh.

3.8–10 No power on earth can protect us from God's judgment or be a suitable substitute for his power in our lives. Thebes and Assyria put their trust in alliances and military power, but history would show these inadequate. Don't insist on learning through personal experience; instead, learn the lessons history has already taught. Put your trust in God above all else.

16 You increased your merchants
more than the stars of the heavens.
The locust sheds its skin and flies away.
17 Your guards are like grasshoppers,
your scribes like swarms[p] of locusts
settling on the fences
on a cold day—
when the sun rises, they fly away;
no one knows where they have gone.

18 Your shepherds are asleep,
O king of Assyria;
your nobles slumber.
Your people are scattered on the mountains
with no one to gather them.
19 There is no assuaging your hurt,
your wound is mortal.
All who hear the news about you
clap their hands over you.
For who has ever escaped
your endless cruelty?

3.18
Jer 50.18
Ezek 32.22,23

3.19
Job 27.23
Jer 30.13-15
Ezek 25.6
Nah 2.2

p Meaning of Heb uncertain

3.19 All the nations hated to be ruled by the merciless Assyrians, but they wanted to be like Assyria—powerful, wealthy, prestigious—and they courted its friendship. In the same way, we don't like the idea of being ruled harshly, so we do what we can to stay on good terms with a powerful leader. And deep down, we would like to have that kind of power. The thought of being on top can be captivating. But power is seductive, so we should not scheme to get it or hold on to it. Those who lust after power will be powerfully destroyed, as was the mighty Assyrian Empire.

MEMORABLE WORDS FROM THE MINOR PROPHETS

Prophet	Date (B.C.)	Key Verse
Hosea	753-715	The Lord said to me again, "Go, love a woman who has a lover and is an adulteress, just as the Lord loves the people of Israel, though they turn to other gods and love raisin cakes" (3.1).
Joel	835-796	Yet even now, says the Lord, return to me with all your heart, with fasting, with weeping, and with mourning; rend your hearts and not your clothing. Return to the Lord, your God, for he is gracious and merciful, slow to anger, and abounding in steadfast love, and relents from punishing (2.12, 13).
Amos	760-750	But let justice roll down like waters, and righteousness like an everflowing stream (5.24).
Obadiah	855-840	For the day of the Lord is near against all the nations. As you have done, it shall be done to you; for your deeds shall return on your own head (1.15).
Jonah	793-753	"And should I not be concerned about Nineveh, that great city, in which there are more than a hundred and twenty thousand persons who do not know their right hand from their left, and also many animals?" (4.11).
Micah	742-687	He has told you, O mortal, what is good; and what does the Lord require of you but to do justice, and to love kindness, and to walk humbly with your God? (6.8).
Nahum	633-654	The Lord is good, a stronghold in a day of trouble; he protects those who take refuge in him, even in a rushing flood. He will make a full end of his adversaries, and will pursue his enemies into darkness (1.7, 8).
Habakkuk	612-589	O Lord, I have heard of your renown, and I stand in awe, O Lord, of your work. In our own time revive it; in our own time make it known; in wrath may you remember mercy (3.2).
Zephaniah	640-621	Seek the Lord, all you humble of the land, who do his commands; seek righteousness, seek humility; perhaps you may be hidden on the day of the Lord's wrath (2.3).
Haggai	520	Is it a time for you yourselves to live in your paneled houses, while this house lies in ruins? (1.4).
Zechariah	520-480	Rejoice greatly, O daughter Zion! Shout aloud, O daughter Jerusalem! Lo, your king comes to you; triumphant and victorious is he, humble and riding on a donkey, on a colt, the foal of a donkey. He will cut off the chariot from Ephraim and the war horse from Jerusalem; and the battle bow shall be cut off, and he shall command peace to the nations; his dominion shall be from sea to sea, and from the River to the ends of the earth (9.9, 10).
Malachi	430	See, the day is coming, burning like an oven, when all the arrogant and all evildoers will be stubble; the day that comes shall burn them up, says the Lord of hosts, so that it will leave them neither root nor branch. But for you who revere my name the sun of righteousness shall rise, with healing in its wings. You shall go out leaping like calves from the stall (4.1, 2).

HABAKKUK

Sennacherib surrounds Jerusalem 701

VITAL STATISTICS

PURPOSE:
To show that God is still in control of the world despite the apparent triumph of evil

AUTHOR:
Habakkuk

TO WHOM WRITTEN:
Judah (the southern kingdom), and God's people everywhere

DATE WRITTEN:
Between 612 and 589 B.C.

SETTING:
Babylon was becoming the dominant world power and Judah would soon feel Babylon's destructive force

KEY VERSE:
"O Lord, I have heard of your renown, and I stand in awe, O Lord, of your work. In our own time revive it; in our own time make it known; in wrath may you remember mercy" (3.2).

KEY PEOPLE:
Habakkuk, the Chaldeans (Babylonians)

KEY PLACE:
Judah

FROM innocent childhood queries to complex university discussions, life is filled with questions. Asking how and why and when, we probe beneath the surface to find satisfying answers. But not all questions have answers wrapped and neatly tied. These unanswered interrogations beget more questions and nagging, spirit-destroying doubt. Some choose to live with their doubts, ignoring them and moving on with life. Others become cynical and hardened. But there are those who reject those options and continue to ask, looking for answers.

Habakkuk was such a man. Troubled by what he observed, he asked difficult questions. These questions were not merely intellectual exercises or bitter complaints. Habakkuk saw a dying world, and it broke his heart. Why is there evil in the world? Why do the wicked seem to be winning? He boldly and confidently took his complaints directly to God. And God answered . . . with an avalanche of proof and prediction.

The prophet's questions and God's answers are recorded in this book. As we turn the pages, we are immediately confronted with his urgent cries, "O Lord, how long shall I cry for help, and you will not listen? Or cry to you 'Violence!' and you will not save?" (1.2). In fact, most of the first chapter is devoted to his questions. As chapter two begins, Habakkuk declares that he will wait to hear God's answers to his complaints. Then God begins to speak, telling the prophet to write his answer in large letters so that all will see and understand. It may seem, God says, as though the wicked triumph, but eventually they will be judged, and righteousness will prevail. It may not come quickly, but it will happen. God's answers fill chapter two. Then Habakkuk concludes his book with a prayer of triumph. With questions answered and a new understanding of God's power and love, Habakkuk rejoices in who God is and in what he will do. "Yet I will rejoice in the Lord; I will exult inthe God of my salvation. God, the Lord, is my strength; he makes my feet like the feet of a deer, and makes me tread upon the heights" (3.18, 19).

Listen to Habakkuk's profound questions which he boldly brings to God, and realize that you can also bring your doubts and inquiries to him. Listen to God's answers and rejoice that he is at work in the world and in your life.

THE BLUEPRINT

1. Habakkuk's doubt (1.1—2.20)
2. Habakkuk's prayer (3.1–19)

When Habakkuk was troubled he brought his concerns directly to God. After receiving God's answers, he responded with a prayer of faith. Habakkuk's example is one that should encourage us as we struggle to move from doubt to faith. We don't have to be afraid to ask questions of God. The problem is not with God's ways, but with our limited understanding of him.

Jeremiah becomes a prophet 627 B.C.	*Habakkuk becomes a prophet 612*	*King Josiah dies in battle 609*	*Daniel taken captive to Babylon 605*	*Ezekiel a captive in Babylon; Zedekiah becomes king 597*	*Habakkuk's ministry ends 589*	*Fall of Judah; Jerusalem destroyed 586*

MEGATHEMES

THEME	EXPLANATION	IMPORTANCE
Struggle and doubt	Habakkuk asked God why the people of Judah were not being punished for their sin. He couldn't understand why a just God would allow such evil to exist. God promised to use the Babylonians to punish Judah. When Habakkuk cried out for answers in his time of struggle, God answered him with words of hope.	God wants us to come to him with our struggles and doubts. But his answers may not be what we expect. God sustains us by revealing himself to us. Trusting him leads to quiet hope, not bitter resignation.
God's sovereignty	Habakkuk asked God why he would use the wicked Babylonians to punish his people. God said that he would also punish the Babylonians after they had fulfilled his purpose.	God is still in control of this world in spite of the apparent triumph of evil. God doesn't overlook sin. One day he will rule the whole earth with perfect justice.
Hope	God is the Creator; he is all-powerful. He has a plan and he will carry it out. He will punish sin. He is our strength and our place of safety. We can have confidence that he will love us and guard our relationship with him forever.	Hope means going beyond our unpleasant daily experiences to the joy of knowing God. We live by trusting in him, not in the benefits, happiness, or success we may experience in this life. Our hope comes from God.

1. Habakkuk's doubt

Habakkuk's first question

1 The oracle that the prophet Habakkuk saw.

2 O LORD, how long shall I cry for help,
and you will not listen?
Or cry to you "Violence!"
and you will not save?
3 Why do you make me see wrong-doing
and look at trouble?
Destruction and violence are before me;
strife and contention arise.
4 So the law becomes slack
and justice never prevails.
The wicked surround the righteous—
therefore judgment comes forth perverted.

1.4
2 Kgs 24.1-5
2 Chron 36.4-8

1.1 Habakkuk lived in Judah during the reign of Jehoiakim (2 Kings 23.36–24.5). He prophesied between the fall of Nineveh (the capital of Assyria) in 612 B.C. and the invasion of Judah in 589 B.C. With Assyria in disarray, Babylon was becoming the dominant world power. This book records the prophet's dialogue with God concerning the questions, "Why does God often seem indifferent in the face of evil? Why do evil people seem to go unpunished?" While other prophetic books brought God's Word to people, this brought people's questions to God. An oracle is a message from God.

1.2–4 Saddened by the violence and corruption he saw around him, Habakkuk poured out his heart to God. Today injustice is still rampant, but don't let your concern cause you to doubt God or rebel against him. Instead, consider the message God gave Habakkuk and recognize God's long-range plans and purposes. Realize that God is doing right, even if you do not understand why he works as he does.

The Lord's answer

5 Look at the nations, and see!
Be astonished! Be astounded!
For a work is being done in your days
that you would not believe if you were told.
6 For I am rousing the Chaldeans,
that fierce and impetuous nation,
who march through the breadth of the earth
to seize dwellings not their own.
7 Dread and fearsome are they;
their justice and dignity proceed from themselves.
8 Their horses are swifter than leopards,
more menacing than wolves at dusk;
their horses charge.
Their horsemen come from far away;
they fly like an eagle swift to devour.
9 They all come for violence,
with faces pressing[a] forward;
they gather captives like sand.
10 At kings they scoff,
and of rulers they make sport.
They laugh at every fortress,
and heap up earth to take it.
11 Then they sweep by like the wind;
they transgress and become guilty;
their own might is their god!

Habakkuk's second question

12 Are you not from of old,
O LORD my God, my Holy One?
You[b] shall not die.
O LORD, you have marked them for judgment;
and you, O Rock, have established them for punishment.
13 Your eyes are too pure to behold evil,
and you cannot look on wrongdoing;
why do you look on the treacherous,
and are silent when the wicked swallow

1.6 Deut 28.49-57 2 Kgs 24.2, 10-20; 25.1-23 2 Chron 36.6-13

1.7 Jer 39.5-9

1.8 Deut 28.49 Isa 5.26-30 Lam 4.19

1.9 2 Kgs 24.14,15 2 Chron 36.18

1.10 2 Kgs 25.6,7 2 Chron 36.6 Jer 32.24 33.4,5; 52.4-7 Ezek 26.7-11

1.12 Deut 32.4,30,31 2 Kgs 19.25 Isa 10.5-7 Jer 25.8-14

1.13 Job 15.15 Ps 5.4; 11.7 1 Pet 1.15,16

[a] Meaning of Heb uncertain [b] Ancient Heb tradition: MT *We*

1.5 God responds to Habakkuk's questions and concerns by stating that he will yet do unbelievable acts that will glorify himself. When circumstances around us become almost unbearable, we wonder if God has forgotten us. But remember, he is in control. He has a plan and will judge evildoers in his time. If we are truly humble, we will be willing to accept God's answers and await his timing.

1.5 God told the inhabitants of Jerusalem that they would be astounded at what he was about to do. The people would see a series of unbelievable events: (1) their own independent and prosperous kingdom, Judah, would suddenly become a vassal nation; (2) Egypt, a world power for centuries, would be crushed almost overnight; (3) Nineveh, the capital of the Assyrian Empire, would be so completely ransacked that people would forget where it had been; and (4) the Chaldeans (Babylonians) would rise to power. Though these words were indeed astounding, the people saw them fulfilled during their lifetime.

1.6 The Chaldeans (Babylonians), who lived northwest of the Persian Gulf, made a rapid rise to power around 630 B.C. They began to assert themselves against the Assyrian Empire, and by 605 B.C. had conquered Assyria to become the strongest world power. But they were as wicked as the Assyrians, for they loved to collect captives (1.9), were proud of their warfare tactics (1.10), and trusted in their idols and military strength (1.11).

1.10 Armies were able to take walled cities by heaping mounds of earth against the walls.

1.11 Babylon was proud of its military might, strategies, armies, and weapons. With no regard for humanity, the armies brought home riches, booty, slaves, and tribute from the nations they plundered. Such is the essence of idolatry—asking the gods we make to help us get all we want. The essence of Christianity is asking the God *who made us* to help us give all we can in service to him. The goal of idolatry is self-glory; the aim of Christianity is God's glory.

1.13 Judah's forthcoming punishment would be at the hands of the Babylonians. Habakkuk was appalled that God would use a nation more wicked than Judah to punish Judah. But the Babylonians did not know they were being used by God to help Judah return to him, and Babylon's pride in its victories would be its fall. Evil is self-destructive, and it is never beyond God's control. God may use whatever unusual instrument he chooses to correct or punish us. When we deserve punishment or correction, how can we complain about the kind of "rod" God uses on us?

those more righteous than they?
14 You have made people like the fish of the sea,
like crawling things that have no ruler.

1.15 Jer 16.16 Ezek 29.4,5

15 The enemy[c] brings all of them up with a hook;
he drags them out with his net,
he gathers them in his seine;
so he rejoices and exults.

1.16 Jer 7.18 44.17,18 Hab 1.11

16 Therefore he sacrifices to his net
and makes offerings to his seine;
for by them his portion is lavish,
and his food is rich.
17 Is he then to keep on emptying his net,
and destroying nations without mercy?

The Lord's answer

2 I will stand at my watchpost,
and station myself on the rampart;
I will keep watch to see what he will say to me,
and what he[d] will answer concerning my complaint.

2.2 Deut 27.8 Isa 8.1 Rev 1.19; 14.13

2 Then the LORD answered me and said:
Write the vision;
make it plain on tablets,
so that a runner may read it.

2.3 Dan 8.17-19 9.24-27 2 Thess 2.6-14

3 For there is still a vision for the appointed time;
it speaks of the end, and does not lie.
If it seems to tarry, wait for it;
it will surely come, it will not delay.

[c] Heb *He* [d] Syr: Heb *I*

HABAKKUK served as a prophet to Judah from 612–589 B.C.

Climate of the times	Judah's last four kings were wicked men who rejected God and oppressed their own people. Babylon invaded Judah twice before finally destroying it in 586. It was a time of fear, oppression, persecution, lawlessness, and immorality.
Main message	Habakkuk couldn't understand why God seemed to do nothing about the wickedness in society. Then he realized that faith in God alone would supply the answers to his questions.
Importance of message	Instead of questioning the ways of God, we should realize that he is totally just, and we should have faith that he is in control and that one day evil will be utterly destroyed.
Contemporary prophets	Jeremiah (627–586) Daniel (605–536) Ezekiel (593–571)

2.1 The watchman and watchtower ("watchpost"), often used by the prophets to show an attitude of expectation (Isaiah 21.8, 11; Jeremiah 6.17; Ezekiel 3.17), are pictures of Habakkuk's attitude of patient waiting and watching for God's response. Stone watchtowers were built on city walls or ramparts so watchmen could see people (enemies or messengers) approaching their city while they were still at a distance. Watchtowers were also erected in vineyards to help guard the ripening grapes. Habakkuk wanted to be in the best position to receive God's message.

2.2ff This chapter records God's answers to Habakkuk's questions: (1) How long would evil prevail (1.2, 3)? (2) Why was Babylon chosen to punish Judah (1.13)? God said that the judgment, though slow to come, was certain. Although God used Babylon against Judah, he was aware of Babylon's sins and would punish it in due time.

2.3 Evil seems to have the upper hand in the world. Like Habakkuk, Christians often feel angry and discouraged as they see what goes on. Habakkuk complained vigorously to God about it. God's answer to him is the same answer he would give us, "Be patient! I will work out my plans in my perfect timing." It isn't easy to be patient, but it helps to remember that God hates sin even more than we do. Punishment of sin will certainly come. As God told Habakkuk, "Don't despair." To trust God fully means to trust him even when we don't understand why events occur as they do.

4 Look at the proud!
Their spirit is not right in them,
but the righteous live by their faith.[e]
5 Moreover, wealth[f] is treacherous;
the arrogant do not endure.
They open their throats wide as Sheol;
like Death they never have enough.
They gather all nations for themselves,
and collect all peoples as their own.

2.4 Prov 3.6; 16.3 Rom 1.17 Gal 3.11 Heb 10.38

6 Shall not everyone taunt such people and, with mocking riddles, say about
them,
"Alas for you who heap up what is not your own!"
How long will you load yourselves with goods taken in pledge?
7 Will not your own creditors suddenly rise,
and those who make you tremble wake up?
Then you will be booty for them.
8 Because you have plundered many nations,
all that survive of the peoples shall plunder you—
because of human bloodshed, and violence to the earth,
to cities and all who live in them.

2.6 Mic 2.4,5 Hab 2.9,12, 15,19

2.8 Isa 13.16-18 Jer 27.7,8 50.10,34-46

9 "Alas for you who get evil gain for your houses,
setting your nest on high
to be safe from the reach of harm!"
10 You have devised shame for your house
by cutting off many peoples;
you have forfeited your life.
11 The very stones will cry out from the wall,
and the plaster[g] will respond from the woodwork.

2.9 Ps 10.3-11; 52.7

2.11 Josh 24.27 Lk 19.40

12 "Alas for you who build a town by bloodshed,
and found a city on iniquity!"
13 Is it not from the LORD of hosts
that peoples labor only to feed the flames,
and nations weary themselves for nothing?
14 But the earth will be filled
with the knowledge of the glory of the LORD,
as the waters cover the sea.

2.12 Mic 3.10 Hab 2.9,15,19

2.14 Ps 22.27; 86.9 Isa 6.3 Zech 14.9 Rev 11.15 15.3,4

15 "Alas for you who make your neighbors drink,
pouring out your wrath[h] until they are drunk,
in order to gaze on their nakedness!"
16 You will be sated with contempt instead of glory.
Drink, you yourself, and stagger![i]

2.15 Hos 7.5 Hab 2.9,12,19

2.16 Isa 51.21-23 Jer 25.15,16 Rev 14.10; 18.6

[e] Or *faithfulness* [f] Other Heb Mss read *wine* [g] Or *beam* [h] Or *poison* [i] Q Ms Gk: MT *be uncircumcised*

2.4 The wicked Babylonians trusted in themselves and would fall; but the righteous live because of their faith and trust in God. This verse has inspired countless Christians. Paul quotes it in Romans 1.17 and Galatians 3.11. The writer of Hebrews quotes it in 10.38, just before the famous chapter on faith. And it is helpful to all Christians who must live through difficult times without seeing signs of hope. Christians must trust that God is directing all things according to his purposes.

2.4–8 Babylon was proud, trusted in itself and its military might, and lived to satisfy its own lusts at the expense of captives. But these very sins would rise up to judge it, and the captives it wronged would strip and taunt Babylon. Justice would come slowly, but it would come.

2.5 *Sheol* means death, the grave, or the place of the dead.

2.9–13 Babylon's riches came from the misfortunes of others, and these riches would turn to worthless ashes in its hands. The victims and their cities would cry out against Babylon. Money is not evil, but God condemns the love of riches and all evil means of acquiring it (1 Timothy 6.10). Be careful not to hunger for wealth so much that you lose your appetite for God. Do not allow money to take the place of family, friends, or God.

The cup in the LORD's right hand
will come around to you,
and shame will come upon your glory!

2.17 Lev 26.16,17 Deut 28.25,28, 29,66-68

17 For the violence done to Lebanon will overwhelm you;
the destruction of the animals will terrify you—[j]
because of human bloodshed and violence to the earth,
to cities and all who live in them.

2.18 1 Kgs 18.26-27 Isa 42.17 Jer 2.28; 50.2

18 What use is an idol
once its maker has shaped it—
a cast image, a teacher of lies?
For its maker trusts in what has been made,
though the product is only an idol that cannot speak!

2.19 Ex 32.2-4 Isa 40.19; 46.6 Jer 10.4,5 Acts 17.29

19 Alas for you who say to the wood, "Wake up!"
to silent stone, "Rouse yourself!"
Can it teach?
See, it is gold and silver plated,
and there is no breath in it at all.

2.20 Zeph 1.7 Zech 2.13

20 But the LORD is in his holy temple;
let all the earth keep silence before him!

2. Habakkuk's prayer

3 A prayer of the prophet Habakkuk according to Shigionoth.

3.2 Hab 3.16 Heb 11.7

2 O LORD, I have heard of your renown,
and I stand in awe, O LORD, of your work.
In our own time revive it;
in our own time make it known;
in wrath may you remember mercy.

3.3 Ex 24.15-17 Ps 48.10; 113.4 Rev 5.13,14

3 God came from Teman,
the Holy One from Mount Paran. *Selah*
His glory covered the heavens,
and the earth was full of his praise.

3.4 Ex 14.20 Ps 18.12; 104.1 1 Tim 6.16

4 The brightness was like the sun;
rays came forth from his hand,

[j] Gk Syr: Meaning of Heb uncertain

2.18 Idolatry may seem like a sin that modern people need not fear. But idolatry is not just bowing down to idols; it is trusting in what one has made, and therefore, in one's own power as creator and sustainer. If we say we worship God, but we put our trust in bank accounts, homes, businesses, and organizations, then we are idolaters. Do you trust God more than you trust what your hands have made?

2.20 Idols have no life, no personhood, no power; they are empty chunks of wood or stone. Temples built to idols are equally empty; no one lives there. But the Lord *is* in his temple. He is real, alive, and powerful. He is truly and fully God. Idolaters command their idols to save them, but we who worship the living God come to him in silent awe, great respect, and reverence. We acknowledge that he is in control and knows what he is doing. Idols remain silent, because they cannot answer. The living God, by contrast, speaks through his Word. Approach God reverently and wait silently to hear what he has to say.

3.1 *Shigionoth* is the plural of *Shiggaion* (Psalm 7.1). It comes from the verb "to err" or "to wander." It could also mean "wild" or "ecstatic." Using this term shows that this was written with intense feeling.

3.1ff Habakkuk praised God for answering his questions. Evil will not triumph forever; God is in control, and he can be completely trusted to vindicate those who are faithful to him. We must quietly wait for him to act (3.16).

3.2 Habakkuk knew that God was going to discipline the people of Judah, and that it wasn't going to be a pleasant experience. But he accepted God's will, asking for help and mercy. Habakkuk did not ask to escape the discipline, but accepted the truth that Judah needed to learn a lesson. God still disciplines in love to bring his children back to him (Hebrews 12.5, 6). Accept his discipline gladly, and ask him to help you change.

3.3 The word *Selah* occurs 71 times in Psalms and three times in Habakkuk. Although its precise meaning is unknown, it most likely was a musical term. It could be a signal to lift up the hands or voice in worship, or it could be an exclamation like "Amen!" or "Hallelujah!" affirming the truth of the passage.

3.3–16 In these verses, Habakkuk paints the picture of God delivering his people out of Egypt in the dramatic exodus (see Exodus 14). God's awesome power is not restricted to creating scenic wonders; he also uses it to execute righteousness and justice. It is not enough to be awed by God's power. We need discipline in order to learn how to obey and live for him.

where his power lay hidden.
5 Before him went pestilence, **3.5** Deut 32.24,25
and plague followed close behind.
6 He stopped and shook the earth; **3.6** Josh 10.40-42 Neh 9.22-25
he looked and made the nations tremble.
The eternal mountains were shattered;
along his ancient pathways
the everlasting hills sank low.
7 I saw the tents of Cushan under affliction; **3.7** 1 Chron 1.5-9
the tent-curtains of the land of Midian trembled.
8 Was your wrath against the rivers,[k] O LORD? **3.8** Ex 14.21,22 Josh 3.12-17 2 Kgs 2.11,12
Or your anger against the rivers,[k]
or your rage against the sea,[l]
when you drove your horses,
your chariots to victory?
9 You brandished your naked bow,
sated[m] were the arrows at your command.[n] *Selah*
You split the earth with rivers.
10 The mountains saw you, and writhed; **3.10** Ps 93.3; 96.11
a torrent of water swept by;
the deep gave forth its voice.
The sun[o] raised high its hands;
11 the moon[p] stood still in its exalted place, **3.11** Josh 10.12-14
at the light of your arrows speeding by,
at the gleam of your flashing spear.
12 In fury you trod the earth, **3.12** Hab 3.6
in anger you trampled nations.
13 You came forth to save your people, **3.13** Ps 18.38; 68.21
to save your anointed.
You crushed the head of the wicked house,
laying it bare from foundation to roof.[n] *Selah*
14 You pierced with his own arrows the head[q] of his warriors,[r] **3.14** Judg 7.22 Dan 11.40
who came like a whirlwind to scatter us,[s]
gloating as if ready to devour the poor who were in hiding.
15 You trampled the sea with your horses, **3.15** Hab 3.8
churning the mighty waters.

16 I hear, and I tremble within; **3.16** Isa 6.5
my lips quiver at the sound.
Rottenness enters into my bones,
and my steps tremble[t] beneath me.
I wait quietly for the day of calamity
to come upon the people who attack us.

17 Though the fig tree does not blossom, **3.17** Deut 28.15-19 Jer 14.2-6 Joel 1.10,12 Hag 2.16,17 Mt 21.19,20
and no fruit is on the vines;
though the produce of the olive fails
and the fields yield no food;
though the flock is cut off from the fold
and there is no herd in the stalls,

[k] Or *against River* [l] Or *against Sea* [m] Cn: Heb *oaths* [n] Meaning of Heb uncertain [o] Heb *It* [p] Heb *sun, moon* [q] Or *leader* [r] Vg Compare Gk Syr: Meaning of Heb uncertain [s] Heb *me* [t] Cn Compare Gk: Meaning of Heb uncertain

---

3.17–19 Crop failure and the death of flocks would devastate Judah. But Habakkuk affirmed that even in the times of starvation, he would still rejoice in the Lord. Habakkuk's feelings were not controlled by the events around him but by faith in God's ability to give him strength. When nothing makes sense, and when troubles seem more than you can bear, remember that God gives strength. Take your eyes off your difficulties and look to God.

3.18
Ps 25.5; 27.1
Isa 12.2
Phil 4.4
3.19
Ps 18.2,3; 46.1
Phil 4.13

18 yet I will rejoice in the LORD;
I will exult in the God of my salvation.
19 GOD, the Lord, is my strength;
he makes my feet like the feet of a deer,
and makes me tread upon the heights.[u]

To the choirmaster: with stringed[v] instruments.

[u] Heb *my heights* [v] Heb *my stringed*

3.19 God will give his followers surefooted confidence through difficult times. They will run like deer across rough and dangerous terrain. At the proper time, God will bring about his justice and completely rid the world of evil. In the meantime, God's people need to live in the strength of his Spirit, confident in his ultimate victory over evil.

3.19 The note to the choirmaster was to be used when this passage was sung as a psalm in temple worship.

3.19 Habakkuk had asked God why evil people prosper while the righteous suffer. God's answer: they don't, not in the long run. Habakkuk saw his own limitations in contrast to God's unlimited control of all the world's events. God is alive and in control of the world and its events. We cannot see all that God is doing, and we cannot see all that God will do. But we can be assured that he is God and will do what is right. Knowing this can give us confidence and hope in a confusing world.

ZEPHANIAH

Zephaniah becomes a prophet; Josiah becomes king of Judah 640 B.C.	Jeremiah becomes a prophet 627	Book of the law found in the temple 622	Zephaniah's ministry ends 621	Habakkuk becomes a prophet 612

VITAL STATISTICS

PURPOSE:
To shake the people of Judah out of their complacency and urge them to return to God

AUTHOR:
Zephaniah

TO WHOM WRITTEN:
Judah and all nations

DATE WRITTEN:
Probably near the end of Zephaniah's ministry (640–621 B.C.), when King Josiah's great reforms began

SETTING:
King Josiah of Judah was attempting to reverse the evil trends set by the two previous kings of Judah—Manasseh and Amon. Josiah was able to extend his influence because there wasn't a strong superpower dominating the world at that time (Assyria was declining rapidly). Zephaniah's prophecy may have been the motivating factor in Josiah's reform. Zephaniah was a contemporary of Jeremiah.

KEY VERSE:
"Seek the Lord, all you humble of the land, who do his commands; seek righteousness, seek humility; perhaps you may be hidden on the day of the Lord's wrath" (2.3).

KEY PLACE:
Jerusalem

OVERWHELMING grief, prolonged distress, incessant abuse, continual persecution, and imminent punishment breed hopelessness and despair. "If only," we cry as we search our minds for a way out and look to the skies for rescue. With just a glimmer of hope, we would take courage and carry on, enduring until the end.

Hope is the silver shaft of sun breaking through the storm-darkened sky, words of comfort in the intensive care unit, a letter from across the sea, the first spring bird perched on a snow-covered twig, and the finish line in sight. It is a rainbow, a song, a loving touch. Hope is knowing God and resting in his love.

As God's prophet, Zephaniah was bound to speak the truth—this he did clearly, thundering certain judgment and horrible punishment for all who would defy the Lord. God's awful wrath would sweep away everything in the land and destroy it. "I will sweep away humans and animals; I will sweep away the birds of the air and the fish of the sea. I will make the wicked stumble. I will cut off humanity from the face of the earth, says the Lord" (1.3). No living thing in the land would escape. And that terrible day was coming soon: "The great day of the Lord is near, near and hastening fast; the sound of the day of the Lord is bitter, the warrior cries aloud there. That day will be a day of wrath, a day of distress and anguish, a day of ruin and devastation, a day of darkness and gloom, a day of clouds and thick darkness" (1.14, 15). One can sense the oppression and depression his listeners must have felt. They were judged guilty and doomed.

But in the midst of this terrible pronouncement, there is hope. Chapter one of Zephaniah's prophecy is filled with terror. In chapter two, however, a whispered promise appears. "Seek the Lord, all you humble of the land, who do his commands; seek righteousness, seek humility; perhaps you may be hidden on the day of the Lord's wrath" (2.3). And a few verses later we read of a "remnant of the house of Judah" (2.7) who will be restored.

Finally in chapter three, the quiet refrain grows to a crescendo as God's salvation and deliverance for those who are faithful to him is declared. "Sing aloud, O daughter Zion; shout, O Israel! Rejoice and exult with all your heart, O daughter Jerusalem! The Lord has taken away the judgments against you, he has turned away your enemies. The king of Israel, the Lord, is in your midst; you shall fear disaster no more" (3.14, 15). This is true hope, grounded in the knowledge of God's justice and his love for his people.

As you read Zephaniah, listen carefully to the words of judgment. God does not take sin lightly, and it will be punished. But be encouraged by the words of hope—our God reigns, and he will rescue his own. Decide to be part of that faithful remnant of souls who humbly worship and obey the living Lord.

Josiah dies in battle 609	First captives taken to Babylon 605	Babylon's second attack on Judah 597	Judah (the southern kingdom) falls 586

THE BLUEPRINT

1. The day of wrath (1.1—3.8)
2. The day of hope (3.9–20)

Zephaniah warned the people of Judah that if they refused to repent, the entire nation, including Jerusalem, would be lost. The people knew that God would eventually bless them, but Zephaniah made it clear that there would be judgment first, then blessing. This judgment would not be merely punishment for sin, but also a process of purifying the people. Though we live in a fallen world surrounded by evil, we can hope in the perfect kingdom of God to come and we can allow any punishment that touches us now to purify us from sin.

MEGATHEMES

THEME	EXPLANATION	IMPORTANCE
Day of judgment	Destruction was coming because Judah had forsaken the Lord. The people worshiped Baal, Milcom (Molech), and nature. Even the priests mixed pagan practices with faith in God. God's punishment for sin was on the way.	To escape God's judgment we must listen to him, accept his correction, trust him, and seek his guidance. If we accept him as our Lord, we can escape his condemnation.
Indifference to God	Although there had been occasional attempts at renewal, Judah had no sorrow for her sins. The people were prosperous and they no longer cared about God. God's demands for righteous living seemed irrelevant to Judah, whose security and wealth made her complacent.	Don't let material comfort be a barrier to your commitment to God. Prosperity can produce an attitude of proud self-sufficiency. The only antidote is to admit that money won't save us and that we cannot save ourselves. Only God can save us and cure our indifference to spiritual matters.
Day of cheer	The day of Judgment will also be a day of cheer. God will judge all those who mistreat his people. He will purify his people, purging away all sin and evil. God will restore his people and give them hope.	When people are purged of sin, there is great relief and hope. No matter how difficult our experience now, we can look forward to the day of celebration when God will completely restore us. It will truly be our day of cheer.

1. The day of wrath

Zephaniah predicts the destruction of Judah

1.1 2 Kgs 22.1–23.28 2 Chron 34.1–35.26

1 The word of the LORD that came to Zephaniah son of Cushi son of Gedaliah
son of Amariah son of Hezekiah, in the days of King Josiah son of Amon of
Judah.

2 I will utterly sweep away everything

1.1 Zephaniah prophesied in the days of Josiah, king of Judah (640–609 B.C.). Josiah followed God, and during his reign the books of the law were discovered in the temple. After reading them, Josiah began a great religious revival in Judah (2 Kings 22.1–23.25). Zephaniah helped the revival by warning the people that judgment would come if they did not turn from their sins. Although this great revival turned the nation back to God, it did not fully eliminate idolatry and lasted only a short time. Twelve years later Judah was conquered by Babylon and sent into exile.

1.2ff The people of Judah were clearly warned by the highest authority of all – God. They refused to listen, either because they doubted God's prophet and thus did not believe the message was from God, or because they doubted God himself and thus did not believe he would do what he said. If we refuse to listen to God's Word, the Bible, we are as shortsighted as the people of Judah; and like them, we will be punished.

from the face of the earth, says the LORD.
3 I will sweep away humans and animals;
I will sweep away the birds of the air
and the fish of the sea.
I will make the wicked stumble.[a]
I will cut off humanity
from the face of the earth, says the LORD.
4 I will stretch out my hand against Judah,
and against all the inhabitants of Jerusalem;
and I will cut off from this place every remnant of Baal
and the name of the idolatrous priests;[b]
5 those who bow down on the roofs
to the host of the heavens;
those who bow down and swear to the LORD,
but also swear by Milcom;[c]
6 those who have turned back from following the LORD,
who have not sought the LORD or inquired of him.

7 Be silent before the Lord GOD!
For the day of the LORD is at hand;
the LORD has prepared a sacrifice,
he has consecrated his guests.
8 And on the day of the LORD's sacrifice
I will punish the officials and the king's sons
and all who dress themselves in foreign attire.
9 On that day I will punish
all who leap over the threshold,
who fill their master's house
with violence and fraud.

10 On that day, says the LORD,
a cry will be heard from the Fish Gate,
a wail from the Second Quarter,
a loud crash from the hills.
11 The inhabitants of the Mortar wail,
for all the traders have perished;
all who weigh out silver are cut off.

1.2 2 Kgs 22.15-20; Isa 6.11; Ezek 33.27-29
1.4 2 Kgs 21.12-15; 23.4-7; 2 Chron 34.3-7
1.5 Lev 20.2-5; 2 Kgs 21.3-5; Acts 7.42
1.6 Isa 43.22; Rom 3.11
1.7 Ezek 39.17-21
1.8 Isa 10.12; 24.21-23
1.9 Neh 5.15
1.10 2 Chron 33.14; Neh 3.3; 12.39
1.11 Ezek 22.12; Hos 12.7,8

[a] Cn: Heb *sea, and those who cause the wicked to stumble* [b] Compare Gk: Heb *the idolatrous priests with the priests* [c] Gk Mss Syr Vg: Heb *Malcam* (or, *their king*)

1.4 When the Israelites arrived in the promised land, God had commanded that they completely rid the land of its heathen inhabitants who worshiped idols. But the Israelites failed to do so, and gradually they began to worship the Canaanites' gods. The Canaanites believed in many gods that represented many aspects of life, and the chief god was Baal, symbolizing strength and fertility. God was extremely angry when his people turned from him to Baal.

1.4–6 History is littered with idols and their worship. More than just a stone statue, an idol can be anything reverenced more than God. Thus idol worship is prevalent even today as people trust in themselves, money, or power and not in God. But ultimately all idols will prove worthless, and the true God will prevail. Seek God first (Matthew 6:33), and put no other gods before him (Exodus 20.3).

1.5 The people had become polytheistic, worshiping the Lord *and* all the other gods of the land. They added the "best" of pagan worship to true faith in God. But God commands that he alone be worshiped (Exodus 20.1–5), thus the people committed a horrible sin. One of these other gods was Molech (Milcom), the national god of the Ammonites. Molech worship included child sacrifice, an abominable sin. From the time of Moses, the Israelites had been warned about worshiping this false god (Leviticus 18.21; 20.5), but they refused to take heed. Because of their sins, God would destroy them.

1.7 A day of judgment and a great slaughter occurred during the lifetime of these people when Babylon invaded the land. The prophet saw these prophecies as future events, but he could not see when or in what order these events would take place. Many think these prophecies have a double fulfillment – one for the near future (soon after the prophecy was made) and another for the distant future (possibly during the end times). Some scholars understand these prophecies of judgment to refer to events entirely in the future.

1.8, 9 Wearing heathen clothing ("foreign attire") showed a desire for foreign gods and foreign ways. Leaders who should have been good examples to the people were adopting foreign practices and thus showing their contempt for the Lord by ignoring his commands against adopting pagan culture. To "leap over the threshold" was a pagan observance (see 1 Samuel 5.5).

1.11 The Mortar was the lower town or market district.

1.12 Jer 16.16 Amos 9.1-3 Obad 6

12 At that time I will search Jerusalem with lamps,
and I will punish the people
who rest complacently[d] on their dregs,
those who say in their hearts,
"The LORD will not do good,
nor will he do harm."

1.13 Deut 28.30 Isa 5.8,9 Amos 5.11

13 Their wealth shall be plundered,
and their houses laid waste.
Though they build houses,
they shall not inhabit them;
though they plant vineyards,
they shall not drink wine from them.

The great day of the Lord is near

1.14 Ezek 7.16-18

14 The great day of the LORD is near,
near and hastening fast;
the sound of the day of the LORD is bitter,
the warrior cries aloud there.

1.15 Joel 2.2

15 That day will be a day of wrath,
a day of distress and anguish,
a day of ruin and devastation,
a day of darkness and gloom,
a day of clouds and thick darkness,

1.16 Isa 2.12-15

16 a day of trumpet blast and battle cry
against the fortified cities
and against the lofty battlements.

1.17 Deut 28.28,29 Ps 79.3; 83.10 Jer 8.2; 9.22 Mt 15.13,14

17 I will bring such distress upon people
that they shall walk like the blind;
because they have sinned against the LORD,
their blood shall be poured out like dust,
and their flesh like dung.
18 Neither their silver nor their gold

[d] Heb *who thicken*

ZEPHANIAH served as a prophet to Judah from 640–621 B.C.	*Climate of the times*	Josiah was the last good king in Judah. His bold attempts to reform the nation and turn it back to God were probably influenced by Zephaniah.
	Main message	A day will come when God, as Judge, will severely punish all nations. But after judgment, he will show mercy to all who have been faithful to him.
	Importance of message	We will all be judged for our disobedience to God; but if we remain faithful to him, he will show us mercy.
	Contemporary prophet	Jeremiah (627–586)

1.12 God would search the city with lamps and punish the deserving people. Because they did not search their own hearts, and because they were content with their sins ("dregs") and indifferent to God, God would use the Babylonians to judge them. Within 20 years, the Babylonians would enter Jerusalem, drag people out of hiding, and take them captive or kill them. No one would escape.

1.12–14 Some people think of God as an indulgent heavenly grandfather–nice to have around, but not a real force in shaping modern life. They don't believe in his power or his coming judgment. When people are indifferent to God, they tend to think he is indifferent to them and their sin. But God is holy, and therefore he will actively judge and justly punish everyone who is content to live in sin, indifferent to him, or unconcerned about justice.

1.14–18 The great day of the Lord was near; the Babylonians would soon come and destroy Jerusalem. The day of the Lord is also near to us. God promises a final judgment, a day of worldwide destruction (Revelation 20.12–15). The Babylonian conquest occurred just as surely and horribly as Zephaniah predicted. And God's final day of Judgment is also sure – but so is his ability to save. To be spared from judgment, recognize that you have sinned, that your sin will bring judgment, that you cannot save yourself, and that God alone can save you.

1.18 Money is not evil in itself, but it is useless to save us. In this life, money can warp our perspective, giving us feelings of security and power. Just as the Israelites' wealth could not save them from the Babylonian invasion, so at the final judgment, our riches will be worthless. Only Christ's redemptive work on our behalf matters for eternity. He alone will ransom us if we believe in him.

will be able to save them
on the day of the LORD's wrath;
in the fire of his passion
the whole earth shall be consumed;
for a full, a terrible end
he will make of all the inhabitants of the earth.

1.18 Deut 32.21-25 Ps 49.6-9 Zeph 3.8

Judgment will come to the surrounding nations

2 Gather together, gather,
O shameless nation,
2 before you are driven away
like the drifting chaff,[e]
before there comes upon you
the fierce anger of the LORD,
before there comes upon you
the day of the LORD's wrath.
3 Seek the LORD, all you humble of the land,
who do his commands;
seek righteousness, seek humility;
perhaps you may be hidden
on the day of the LORD's wrath.
4 For Gaza shall be deserted,
and Ashkelon shall become a desolation;
Ashdod's people shall be driven out at noon,
and Ekron shall be uprooted.

5 Ah, inhabitants of the seacoast,
you nation of the Cherethites!
The word of the LORD is against you,
O Canaan, land of the Philistines;
and I will destroy you until no inhabitant is left.
6 And you, O seacoast, shall be pastures,
meadows for shepherds
and folds for flocks.
7 The seacoast shall become the possession
of the remnant of the house of Judah,
on which they shall pasture,
and in the houses of Ashkelon
they shall lie down at evening.

2.2 Ezek 33.11 Rom 2.4 2 Pet 3.9

2.3 2 Kgs 22.18,19 2 Chron 7.14,15 Ps 25.8,9 Zeph 3.12

2.4 Jer 25.19,20 47.1-7 Amos 1.6-8

2.5 Isa 14.29,31

2.7 Ps 85.1-3 Amos 9.14 Zeph 3.20

e Cn Compare Gk Syr: Heb *before a decree is born; like chaff a day has passed away*

2.1–3 There was still time for the people to avert God's judgment. They simply had to turn from their sins, humble themselves, and obey God. The Old Testament prophets announced news of destruction, but they also offered the only means of escape and protection—turning from sin and walking with God (see also Micah 6.8).

2.1–3 God's judgment against Judah came with ample warning, so the people had no excuse. God told them to (1) "gather together," (2) "seek righteousness," and (3) "seek humility." As God warned Judah, so he also warns us concerning the final day of Judgment. We must (1) pray for forgiveness of sin, (2) ask God to bring us into his heavenly kingdom, and (3) humbly obey him. At the end of time, when God comes to judge, you cannot say, "But no one told me." Turn to God today for salvation.

2.4 The four cities mentioned are in Philistia, the nation southwest of Judah on the coast of the Mediterranean Sea. Age-old enemies of Israel from the days of Joshua, they were known for their cruelty. God judged them for their idolatry and their constant taunting of Israel. These four cities were four of the five capitals. The fifth (Gath) had already been destroyed.

2.4–3.8 God's judgment on the nations is universal—no one will escape. He punishes his own people for their sin; but he also punishes the surrounding nations for their wickedness, their idolatry, and their treatment of his people.

2.5 The Cherethites were people of the island of Crete.

2.7 All the prophets, even while prophesying doom and destruction, speak of a "remnant"—a small group of God's people who remain faithful to him and whom God will restore to the land. Although God said he would destroy Judah, he also promised to save a remnant, thus keeping his original covenant to preserve Abraham's descendants (Genesis 17.4–8). God is holy, and he cannot allow sin to continue. But he is also faithful to his promises. He cannot stay angry forever with Israel, or with you, if you are his child, because he loves his children and always seeks their good.

For the LORD their God will be mindful of them
and restore their fortunes.

2.8 Ps 83.4-8 Zeph 2.10

8 I have heard the taunts of Moab
and the revilings of the Ammonites,
how they have taunted my people
and made boasts against their territory.
9 Therefore, as I live, says the LORD of hosts,
the God of Israel,
Moab shall become like Sodom
and the Ammonites like Gomorrah,
a land possessed by nettles and salt pits,
and a waste forever.
The remnant of my people shall plunder them,
and the survivors of my nation shall possess them.

2.10 Isa 16.6-10 Jer 48.28-31 Dan 5.20,21 Obad 3,4 Zeph 2.8

10 This shall be their lot in return for their pride,
because they scoffed and boasted
against the people of the LORD of hosts.

2.11 Joel 2.11

11 The LORD will be terrible against them;
he will shrivel all the gods of the earth,
and to him shall bow down,
each in its place,
all the coasts and islands of the nations.

2.12 Isa 20.3,4; 43.3

12 You also, O Ethiopians,[f]
shall be killed by my sword.

2.13 Nah 3.7

13 And he will stretch out his hand against the north,
and destroy Assyria;
and he will make Nineveh a desolation,
a dry waste like the desert.

2.14 Lev 11.13-19 Deut 14.11-18 Ps 102.6 Isa 14.23; 34.11

14 Herds shall lie down in it,
every wild animal;[g]
the desert owl[h] and the screech owl[h]
shall lodge on its capitals;
the owl[i] shall hoot at the window,

[f] Or *Nubians*; Heb *Cushites* [g] Tg Compare Gk: Heb *nation* [h] Meaning of Heb uncertain [i] Cn: Heb *a voice*

2.8 The Moabites and Ammonites lived to the east of Judah, and they often ridiculed and attacked Judah. These nations worshiped Chemosh and Molech (1 Kings 11.7). Moab's king once sacrificed his son on the city wall to stop an invasion (2 Kings 3.26, 27). God would judge them for their wickedness and for their treatment of his people.

2.8–11 Judah had been taunted and mocked by the neighboring nations, Moab and Ammon, but God reminded them that he had "heard the taunts . . . and the revilings" (2.8), and that they would be punished for their pride (2.10). At times the whole world seems to mock God and those who have faith in him. When you are ridiculed, remember that God hears and will answer. Eventually, in God's timing, justice will be served.

2.9 The nations of Moab and Ammon began with Lot's incest with his daughters after they escaped the destruction of evil Sodom and Gomorrah (Genesis 19). Ironically, Moab and Ammon would face the same kind of perpetual desolation that God sent those evil cities. Sodom and Gomorrah were so completely destroyed that their exact location is still unknown.

2.12 Ethiopia, at the southern end of the Red Sea, controlled Egypt at this time. No one can escape deserved judgment. The Ethiopians were "killed by *God's* sword" when the Assyrians invaded Egypt in 670 B.C. (See Isaiah 18 and Ezekiel 30.9 for other prophecies concerning Ethiopia.)

2.13 Zephaniah mentioned the large nation to the south and then moved to the nation of the north, Assyria. Though declining, Assyria was still the strongest military power of the day, dominating the world for three centuries and destroying anyone in its path. Nineveh, the large capital city, was considered impregnable. However, just as Zephaniah predicted, it was wiped out in 612 B.C. by the Babylonians, who would become the next world power.

2.14, 15 To predict the destruction of Nineveh ten years before it happened would be equivalent to predicting the destruction of Tokyo, Moscow, or New York. Nineveh was the Middle Eastern center for culture, technology, and beauty. It had great libraries, buildings, and a vast irrigation system that created lush gardens in the city. The city wall was 60 miles long, 100 feet high, and over 30 feet wide and was fortified with 1,500 towers. Yet the entire city was destroyed so completely that its very existence was questioned until it was discovered, with great difficulty, by 19th-century archaeologists. Nineveh had indeed become a pastureland.

the raven[j] croak on the threshold;
for its cedar work will be laid bare.
15 Is this the exultant city
that lived secure,
that said to itself,
"I am, and there is no one else"?
What a desolation it has become,
a lair for wild animals!
Everyone who passes by it
hisses and shakes the fist.

2.15 1 Kgs 9.7,8 Isa 10.12-14 22.2-7 Lam 2.15,16 Mt 27.39

Judgment will come to Jerusalem

3 Ah, soiled, defiled,
oppressing city!
2 It has listened to no voice;
it has accepted no correction.
It has not trusted in the LORD;
it has not drawn near to its God.

3.1 Jer 6.6

3.2 Jer 32.33

3 The officials within it
are roaring lions;
its judges are evening wolves
that leave nothing until the morning.
4 Its prophets are reckless,
faithless persons;
its priests have profaned what is sacred,
they have done violence to the law.
5 The LORD within it is righteous;
he does no wrong.
Every morning he renders his judgment,
each dawn without fail;
but the unjust knows no shame.

3.3 Ps 10.8-10 Ezek 22.6-12

3.4 Hos 4.5,6 Mal 2.7-9

3.5 Jer 3.3; 6.15

6 I have cut off nations;
their battlements are in ruins;
I have laid waste their streets
so that no one walks in them;
their cities have been made desolate,
without people, without inhabitants.

3.6 Isa 10.1-33 15.1-9; 16.1-14 Zeph 2.4,5

j Gk Vg: Heb *desolation*

3.1ff After predicting the destruction of the surrounding nations, Zephaniah returned to the problem at hand—sin in Jerusalem. The city of God and God's people had become "soiled, defiled"—as sinful as their heathen neighbors. The people pretended worship and devotion to God, but in their hearts they had rejected him and continued to be complacent about their sins. They no longer cared about the consequences of turning away from God.

3.2 Do you know people who refuse to listen when someone disagrees with their opinions? Their root problem is pride—inflated self-esteem. God's people had become so proud that they would not hear or accept God's correction. Do you find it difficult to listen to the spiritual counsel of others or God's words from the Bible? Don't let pride make you unable or unwilling to let God work in your life. You will be more willing to listen when you consider how weak and sinful you really are compared to God.

3.3, 4 Leading God's people is a privilege and a responsibility. Through Zephaniah, God rebukes all types of leadership in Jerusalem—princes, judges, prophets, and priests—because of their callous disobedience, irresponsibility, and sin. If you are a leader in the church, consider yourself in a privileged position, but be careful. God holds you responsible for the purity of your actions, the quality of your example, and the truth of your words.

3.5 Jerusalem's citizens, of all people, had no excuse for their sins. Jerusalem, where the temple was located, was the religious center of the nation. But even though the people didn't follow God, he was "within it," present in the midst of corruption, persecution, and unbelief. No matter how spiritually desolate the world seems, God is here, and he is at work. Ask yourself, "What is he doing now, and how can I be part of his work?"

3.7 We may wonder how the Israelites could have such clear warnings and still not turn to God. The problem was that they had allowed sin to so harden them that they no longer cared to follow God. They refused to heed God's warnings and they refused to repent. The more God punished them, the more they sinned. If you disobey God now, your heart may grow hard, and you may lose your desire for God.

3.7 When God teaches, he expects us to listen and learn. If we do not learn, he must punish us in order to teach us. God doesn't want

7 I said, "Surely the city[k] will fear me,
it will accept correction;
it will not lose sight[l]
of all that I have brought upon it."
But they were the more eager
to make all their deeds corrupt.

2. The day of hope

3.8 Ezek 38.14-23 Zeph 1.18

8 Therefore wait for me, says the LORD,
for the day when I arise as a witness.
For my decision is to gather nations,
to assemble kingdoms,
to pour out upon them my indignation,
all the heat of my anger;
for in the fire of my passion
all the earth shall be consumed.

3.9 Isa 19.18

9 At that time I will change the speech of the peoples
to a pure speech,
that all of them may call on the name of the LORD
and serve him with one accord.

3.10 Isa 11.11

10 From beyond the rivers of Ethiopia[m]
my suppliants, my scattered ones,
shall bring my offering.

3.11 Num 16.3 Isa 11.9 48.1,2; 54.4 Dan 9.16,20 Mt 3.9 Rom 2.17-20 9.33 1 Pet 2.6

11 On that day you shall not be put to shame
because of all the deeds by which you have rebelled against me;
for then I will remove from your midst
your proudly exultant ones,
and you shall no longer be haughty
in my holy mountain.

3.12 Nah 1.7 Zeph 2.3 1 Pet 1.21

12 For I will leave in the midst of you
a people humble and lowly.
They shall seek refuge in the name of the LORD—

3.13 Lev 26.6 Hos 2.18

13 the remnant of Israel;
they shall do no wrong
and utter no lies,
nor shall a deceitful tongue
be found in their mouths.
Then they will pasture and lie down,
and no one shall make them afraid.

[k] Heb *it* [l] Gk Syr: Heb *its dwelling will not be cut off* [m] Or *Nubia*; Heb *Cush*

us to suffer, but he will continue to chasten us until we learn the lesson he has for us. Be teachable, not unreachable.

3.8 In the last days, God will judge all people according to their deeds (Revelation 20.12). Justice will prevail; evildoers will be punished, and the obedient will be blessed. Don't try to avenge yourself. Be patient, and God's justice will come.

3.9 God will purify and unify language so that all his people from all nations will be able to worship him in unison. In the new earth, all believers will speak the same language; the confusion of languages at the tower of Babel will be reversed (Genesis 11). God will purify our hearts, so that the words coming from our lips will be pure as well.

3.9 Throughout Scripture, prophets who mention judgment for God's people follow it with the promise of restoration. There is hope for those who obey and trust God. Today, as in Bible times, God offers restoration to those who turn to him.

3.10 The "scattered ones" refers to Jews dispersed beyond the rivers of Ethiopia. It symbolizes that all Jews, no matter how far they have been scattered, will return to worship God.

3.11, 12 God will remove the proud people and leave the poor and humble. God is opposed to the proud and haughty of every generation. But those who are poor and humble, both physically and spiritually, will be rewarded because they trust in God. Self-reliance and arrogance have no place among God's people or in his kingdom.

14 Sing aloud, O daughter Zion;
shout, O Israel!
Rejoice and exult with all your heart,
O daughter Jerusalem!
15 The LORD has taken away the judgments against you,
he has turned away your enemies.
The king of Israel, the LORD, is in your midst;
you shall fear disaster no more.
16 On that day it shall be said to Jerusalem:
Do not fear, O Zion;
do not let your hands grow weak.
17 The LORD, your God, is in your midst,
a warrior who gives victory;
he will rejoice over you with gladness,
he will renew you[n] in his love;
he will exult over you with loud singing
18 as on a day of festival.[o]
I will remove disaster from you,[p]
so that you will not bear reproach for it.
19 I will deal with all your oppressors
at that time.
And I will save the lame
and gather the outcast,
and I will change their shame into praise
and renown in all the earth.
20 At that time I will bring you home,
at the time when I gather you;
for I will make you renowned and praised
among all the peoples of the earth,
when I restore your fortunes
before your eyes, says the LORD.

3.15 Ps 21.1-7 24.1-10 Isa 33.22

3.16 Isa 35.3,4 43.1-4 Hag 2.4,5 Heb 12.12,13

3.17 Isa 63.1 Heb 7.25

3.19 Isa 61.7 Ezek 39.26-29

3.20 Zeph 2.7

n Gk Syr: Heb *he will be silent* o Gk Syr: Meaning of Heb uncertain p Cn: Heb *I will remove from you; they were*

3.14–18 The Lord himself would remove his hand of judgment, disperse Israel's enemies, and come to live among his people. He would give them gladness. We sin when we pursue happiness by cutting ourselves off from fellowship with God – the only person who can make us truly happy. Zephaniah points out that gladness results when we allow God to be with us. We do that by faithfully following him and obeying his Word. Then God rejoices over us in song. If you want to be happy, draw close to the source of happiness by obeying God.

3.20 "Before your eyes" does not mean this promise will be fulfilled during Zephaniah's generation. Rather, it means that the restoration will be an obvious work of the Lord.

3.20 The message of doom in the beginning of the book becomes a message of hope by the end. There will be a new day when God will bless his people. If the leaders in the church today were to hear a message from a prophet of God, the message would probably resemble the book of Zephaniah. Under Josiah's religious reforms, the people did return to God *outwardly*, but their hearts were far from him. Zephaniah encouraged the nation to gather together and pray for salvation. We must also ask ourselves: Is our reform merely an outward show, or is it changing our hearts and lives? We need to gather together and pray, to walk humbly with God, to do what is right, and to hear the message of hope regarding the new world to come.

TIME TO REBUILD

Haggai and Zechariah prophesied under the rule of the Medo-Persian Empire. At this time the Jews were allowed to return to Jerusalem to rebuild the temple. Zerubbabel, Ezra, and Nehemiah led the people in the work. During the difficult times when the work stopped, they encouraged the people and their leaders to continue. They also called the people to remove sin from their lives. When others around us become discouraged or want to give up, we can be a voice to encourage them to continue in God's ways.

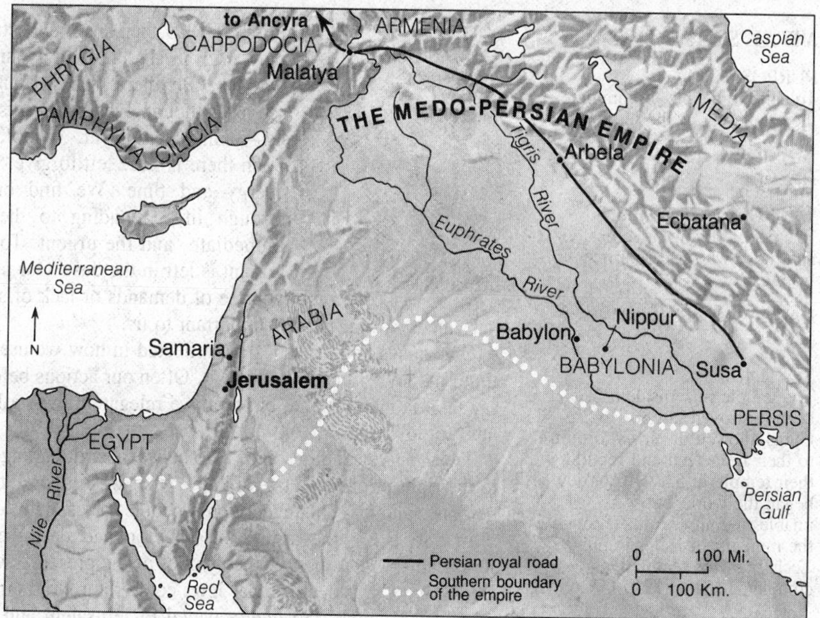

HAGGAI

Daniel taken to Babylon 605 B.C.	Ezekiel taken to Babylon 597	Jerusalem falls 586	Babylon overthrown by Cyrus 539	Cyrus's decree allowing the exiles to return 538	Exiles return to Jerusalem 537	Temple constr begins 536

VITAL STATISTICS

PURPOSE:
To call the people to complete the rebuilding of the temple

AUTHOR:
Haggai

TO WHOM WRITTEN:
The people living in Jerusalem and those who had returned from exile

DATE WRITTEN:
520 B.C.

SETTING:
The temple in Jerusalem had been destroyed in 586 B.C. Cyrus allowed the Jews to return to their homeland and rebuild their temple in 538 B.C. They began the work, but were unable to complete it. Through the ministry of Haggai and Zechariah, the temple was completed (520–515 B.C.).

KEY VERSE:
"Is it a time for you yourselves to live in your paneled houses, while this house lies in ruins?" (1.4).

KEY PEOPLE:
Haggai, Zerubbabel, Joshua

KEY PLACE:
Jerusalem

SPECIAL FEATURES:
Haggai was the first of the post-exilic prophets. The other two were Zechariah and Malachi. The literary style of this book is simple and direct.

PRESSURES, demands, expectations, and tasks push in from all sides and assault our schedules. Do this! Be there! Finish that! Call them! It seems as though everyone wants something from us—family, employer, school, church, clubs. Soon there is little left to give, as we run out of energy and time. We find ourselves rushing through life, attending to the necessary, the immediate, and the urgent. Too often, the important is left in the dust. Our problem is not the volume of demands or lack of scheduling skills, but values—what is *truly* important to us.

Our values and priorities are reflected in how we use our resources—time, money, strength, and talent. Often our actions belie our words. We say God is number one, but then we relegate him to a lesser number on our "to do" lists.

Twenty-five centuries ago, a voice was heard, calling men and women to the right priorities. Haggai knew what was important and what had to be done, and he challenged God's people to respond.

In 586 B.C., the armies of Babylon had destroyed the temple in Jerusalem—God's house, the symbol of his presence with them. In 538 B.C. King Cyrus decreed that Jews could return to their beloved city and rebuild the temple. So they traveled to Jerusalem and began the work. But then they forgot their purpose and lost their priorities, as opposition and apathy brought the work to a standstill (Ezra 4.4, 5). Then Haggai speaks, calling them back to God's values. "Is it a time for you yourselves to live in your paneled houses, while this house lies in ruins?" (1.4) The people were more concerned with their own needs than with doing God's will and, as a result, they suffered. Then Haggai calls them to action, "Thus says the Lord of hosts: Consider how you have fared. Go up to the hills and bring wood and build the house, so that I may take pleasure in it and be honored, says the Lord" (1.7, 8). And God's message through his servant Haggai became the catalyst for finishing the work.

Although Haggai is a small book, it is filled with challenge and promise, reminding us of God's claim on our lives and our priorities. As you read Haggai, imagine him walking the streets and alleys of Jerusalem, urging the people to get back to doing God's work. And listen to Haggai speaking to you, urging you to reorder your priorities in accordance with God's will. What has God told you to do? Put all aside and obey him.

Temple work halted 530	Haggai, Zechariah become prophets; temple work resumed 520	Temple completed 516	Ezra comes to Jerusalem 458	Nehemiah comes to Jerusalem 445

THE BLUEPRINT

1. The call to rebuild the temple (1.1–15)
2. Encouragement to complete the temple (2.1–23)

When the exiles first returned from Babylon, they set about rebuilding the temple right away. Although they began with the right attitudes, they slipped back into wrong behavior and the work came to a standstill. In the same way, we need to be on guard to keep our priorities straight. Remain active in your service to God and continue to put first things first.

MEGATHEMES

THEME	EXPLANATION	IMPORTANCE
Right priorities	God had given the Jews the assignment to finish the temple in Jerusalem when they returned from captivity. After 15 years, they still had not completed it. They were more concerned about building their own homes than finishing God's work. Haggai told them to get their priorities straight.	It is easy to make other priorities more important than doing God's work. But God wants us to follow through and build up his kingdom. Don't stop and don't make excuses. Set your heart on what is right and do it. Get your priorities straight.
God's encouragement	Haggai encouraged the people as they worked. He assured them of the divine presence of the Holy Spirit, of final victory, and of the Messiah's reign.	If God gives you a task, don't be afraid to get started. His resources are infinite. God will help you complete it by giving you encouragement from others along the way.

1. The call to rebuild the temple

1.1 Ezra 2.2; 3.8; 4.1-3,24; 5.1,2; 6.6-14; Neh 12.1-7

1 In the second year of King Darius, in the sixth month, on the first day of the
month, the word of the LORD came by the prophet Haggai to Zerubbabel son
of Shealtiel, governor of Judah, and to Joshua son of Jehozadak, the high priest:
2 Thus says the LORD of hosts: These people say the time has not yet come to rebuild

HAGGAI served as a prophet to Judah about 520 B.C. after the return from exile.

Climate of the times	The people of Judah had been exiled to Babylon in 586 B.C. and Jerusalem and the temple had been destroyed. Under Cyrus, king of Persia, the Jews were allowed to return to Judah and rebuild their temple.
Main message	The people returned to Jerusalem to begin rebuilding the temple, but they never finished. Haggai's message encouraged the people to finish rebuilding God's temple.
Importance of message	The temple lay half-finished while the people lived in beautiful homes. Haggai warned them against putting their possessions and jobs ahead of God. We must put God first in our lives.
Contemporary prophets	Zechariah (520–480)

1.1 Zerubbabel, governor of Judah, and Joshua, the high priest, were key leaders in rebuilding the temple. They had already reestablished the altar, but work had slowed. Haggai sent a letter to these outstanding leaders and to the exiles who had returned from Babylon, encouraging them to complete the rebuilding of the temple in Jerusalem.

1.1ff The Jews who had returned from Babylon in 537 B.C. to rebuild the temple in Jerusalem were not able to finish their work because they were hindered by their enemies. There was no further work done on the temple for over 15 years. In August, 520 B.C., Haggai delivered a message to encourage the people to rebuild the temple!

1.2–15 Haggai encouraged the people to finish rebuilding the temple. Opposition from hostile neighbors had caused them to feel discouraged, neglect the temple, and thus neglect God. But Haggai's message turned them around and motivated them to pick up their tools and continue the work they had begun.

the LORD's house. 3 Then the word of the LORD came by the prophet Haggai, saying: 4 Is it a time for you yourselves to live in your paneled houses, while this house
lies in ruins? 5 Now therefore thus says the LORD of hosts: Consider how you have
fared. 6 You have sown much, and harvested little; you eat, but you never have
enough; you drink, but you never have your fill; you clothe yourselves, but no one
is warm; and you that earn wages earn wages to put them into a bag with holes.
7 Thus says the LORD of hosts: Consider how you have fared. 8 Go up to the hills
and bring wood and build the house, so that I may take pleasure in it and be honored, says the LORD. 9 You have looked for much, and, lo, it came to little; and
when you brought it home, I blew it away. Why? says the LORD of hosts. Because
my house lies in ruins, while all of you hurry off to your own houses. 10 Therefore
the heavens above you have withheld the dew, and the earth has withheld its produce. 11 And I have called for a drought on the land and the hills, on the grain, the
new wine, the oil, on what the soil produces, on human beings and animals, and on
all their labors.
12 Then Zerubbabel son of Shealtiel, and Joshua son of Jehozadak, the high
priest, with all the remnant of the people, obeyed the voice of the LORD their God,
and the words of the prophet Haggai, as the LORD their God had sent him; and the
people feared the LORD. 13 Then Haggai, the messenger of the LORD, spoke to the
people with the LORD's message, saying, I am with you, says the LORD. 14 And the
LORD stirred up the spirit of Zerubbabel son of Shealtiel, governor of Judah, and
the spirit of Joshua son of Jehozadak, the high priest, and the spirit of all the remnant of the people; and they came and worked on the house of the LORD of hosts,
their God, 15 on the twenty-fourth day of the month, in the sixth month.

1.6 Lev 26.14-20 Deut 28.15-19, 22,24,30-34 Hag 1.9; 2.16
1.8 Ezra 3.7-13
1.9 Hag 1.6
1.10 Deut 28.24 1 Kgs 8.35,36 17.1 Joel 1.18-20
1.11 Lev 26.18-22 Deut 28.22-24 Jer 14.1-6
1.12 Ps 112.1 Eccles 12.13 Isa 50.10 Hag 1.1
1.13 2 Chron 20.15-17 Ps 46.7 Isa 8.9,10; 43.2 Hag 2.4,5
1.14,15 Ezra 3.1; 4.24 Neh 4.6; 11.2 Hag 1.1; 2.10

2. Encouragement to complete the temple

2 In the second year of King Darius, 1 in the seventh month, on the twenty-first
day of the month, the word of the LORD came by the prophet Haggai, saying:
2 Speak now to Zerubbabel son of Shealtiel, governor of Judah, and to Joshua son
of Jehozadak, the high priest, and to the remnant of the people, and say, 3 Who is
left among you that saw this house in its former glory? How does it look to you
now? Is it not in your sight as nothing? 4 Yet now take courage, O Zerubbabel, says
the LORD; take courage, O Joshua, son of Jehozadak, the high priest; take courage,
all you people of the land, says the LORD; work, for I am with you, says the LORD

2.3 Ezra 3.12

1.3–6 God asked his people how they could live in luxury when his house was lying in ruins. The temple was the focal point of Judah's relationship with God, but it was still demolished. Instead of rebuilding it, the people put their energies into beautifying their own homes. However, the harder the people worked for themselves, the less they had, because they ignored their spiritual lives. The same happens to us. If we put God first, he will provide for our deepest needs. If we put him in any other place, all our efforts will be futile. Caring only for your physical needs while ignoring your relationship with God leads to ruin.

1.6 Because the people had not given God first place in their lives, their work was not fruitful or productive, and their material possessions did not satisfy. They concentrated on building and beautifying their own homes, but God's blessing was withheld, because they no longer put him in first place. Moses predicted that this would be the result if the people neglected God (Deuteronomy 28.38–45).

1.9 Judah's problem was confused priorities. Like Judah, our priorities involving job, family, and God's work are often confused. Jobs, homes, vacations, and leisure activities may rank higher on our list of importance than God. What is most important to you? Where does God rank?

1.11 Grain, grapes, and olives were Israel's major crops. The people depended on these for security while neglecting the worship of God. As a result, God would send a drought to destroy their livelihood and call them back to himself.

1.14, 15 The people began rebuilding the temple just 23 days after Haggai's first message. Rarely did a prophet's message produce such a quick response. How often we hear a sermon and respond, "That was an excellent point – I ought to do that," only to leave church and forget to act. These people put their words into action. When you hear a good sermon or lesson, ask what you should *do* about it, and then make plans to put it into practice.

2.1–9 This is Haggai's second message, given during the festival of booths, October, 520 B.C. The older people could remember the incredible beauty of Solomon's temple, destroyed 66 years earlier. Many were discouraged because the rebuilt temple was inferior to Solomon's. But Haggai encouraged them with God's message that the splendor of this temple would surpass that of its predecessor. The most important part of the temple is God's presence. Five hundred years later, Jesus Christ would walk in the temple courts.

2.4 "Take courage . . . work, for I am with you." Judah's people had already returned to worshiping God, and he promised to bless their efforts. Now it was time for them to *work*. We must be people of prayer, Bible study, and worship; but eventually we must get out and *do* what God has in mind for us. He wants to change the world through us. God has given you a job to do in the church, at your place of employment, and at home. The time has come to be strong and work, because God is with you!

2.5 Ex 29.45,46 2 Chron 20.15-17 Jn 14.15-17
2.6 Isa 13.10; 34.4 Ezek 38.20 Mt 24.29 Mk 13.24,25 Lk 21.25,26 Rev 6.12-17
2.7 1 Kgs 8.11 Ps 80.1 Rom 15.9-13 Gal 3.8,9
2.8,9 Ps 84.8 Isa 9.6 Lk 2.14
2.10 Hag 1.14
2.12 Ex 29.37 Ezek 44.19
2.13 Lev 11.28,40 22.4-6 Num 19.11,12, 22
2.14 Prov 21.4,24 Isa 1.11-15 Tit 1.15
2.15 Ezra 4.24
2.16 Hag 1.9
2.18 Hag 2.10
2.21 Hag 2.6

of hosts, 5 according to the promise that I made you when you came out of Egypt.
My spirit abides among you; do not fear. 6 For thus says the LORD of hosts: Once
again, in a little while, I will shake the heavens and the earth and the sea and the dry
land; 7 and I will shake all the nations, so that the treasure of all nations shall come,
and I will fill this house with splendor, says the LORD of hosts. 8 The silver is mine,
and the gold is mine, says the LORD of hosts. 9 The latter splendor of this house shall
be greater than the former, says the LORD of hosts; and in this place I will give
prosperity, says the LORD of hosts.

10 On the twenty-fourth day of the ninth month, in the second year of Darius,
the word of the LORD came by the prophet Haggai, saying: 11 Thus says the LORD
of hosts: Ask the priests for a ruling: 12 If one carries consecrated meat in the fold
of one's garment, and with the fold touches bread, or stew, or wine, or oil, or any
kind of food, does it become holy? The priests answered, "No." 13 Then Haggai
said, "If one who is unclean by contact with a dead body touches any of these, does
it become unclean?" The priests answered, "Yes, it becomes unclean." 14 Haggai
then said, So is it with this people, and with this nation before me, says the LORD;
and so with every work of their hands; and what they offer there is unclean. 15 But
now, consider what will come to pass from this day on. Before a stone was placed
upon a stone in the LORD's temple, 16 how did you fare?[a] When one came to a heap
of twenty measures, there were but ten; when one came to the winevat to draw fifty
measures, there were but twenty. 17 I struck you and all the products of your toil
with blight and mildew and hail; yet you did not return to me, says the LORD.
18 Consider from this day on, from the twenty-fourth day of the ninth month. Since
the day that the foundation of the LORD's temple was laid, consider: 19 Is there any
seed left in the barn? Do the vine, the fig tree, the pomegranate, and the olive tree
still yield nothing? From this day on I will bless you.

20 The word of the LORD came a second time to Haggai on the twenty-fourth
day of the month: 21 Speak to Zerubbabel, governor of Judah, saying, I am about to
shake the heavens and the earth, 22 and to overthrow the throne of kingdoms; I am
about to destroy the strength of the kingdoms of the nations, and overthrow the

[a] Gk: Heb *since they were*

2.5 The Israelites had been led from captivity in Egypt to their promised land. They were God's chosen people, guided and cared for by his Holy Spirit. Although God punished them for their sins, he kept his promise and never left them (Exodus 29.45, 46). No matter what difficulties we face or how frustrating our work may be, God's Spirit is with us.

2.6–9 The focus shifts from the local temple being rebuilt in Jerusalem to the worldwide reign of the Messiah on earth. The words "in a little while" are not limited to the immediate historical context; they refer to God's control of history—he can act any time he chooses. God will act *in his time* (see also Hebrews 12.26, 27).

2.7 When God promised to shake all the nations with his judgment, he was speaking of both present judgment on evil nations and future judgment during the last days.

2.7–9 The "treasure of all nations" has two possible meanings: (1) It could refer to the Messiah, Jesus, who, 500 years later, would enter the temple and fill it with his glory and his peace. (2) It could also refer to the riches that would flow into the temple, given as offerings to God's people.

2.8, 9 God wanted the temple to be rebuilt, and he had the gold and silver to do it, but he needed willing hands. God has chosen to do his work through people. He provides the resources, but willing hands must do the work. Are your hands available for God's work in the world?

2.10–19 The example given in this message (delivered in December, 520 B.C.) makes it clear that holiness will not rub off on others, but contamination will. ("Consecrated meat" is meat made holy for the sacrifice.) Now that the people were beginning to obey God, he promised to encourage and prosper them. But they needed to understand that activities in the temple would not clean up their sin; only repentance and obedience could do that. If we insist on harboring wrong attitudes and sins or on maintaining close relationships with sinful people, we will be contaminated. Holy living will come only when we are empowered by God's Holy Spirit.

2.14 When a child eats spaghetti sauce, it isn't long before face, hands, and clothes are red. Sin and selfish attitudes produce the same result: they stain everything they touch. Even good works done for God can be tainted by sinful attitudes. The only remedy is God's cleansing.

2.16 A "heap" refers to a stack of grain at the harvest. For many years, the grain had only given a 50 percent yield, and wine had done even worse.

2.18, 19 The people relaid the temple foundation, and immediately God blessed them. He did not wait for the project to be completed. God often sends his encouragement and approval with our first few obedient steps. He is eager to bless us!

2.20–23 Haggai's final message acknowledges that he is merely the messenger who brings the word of the Lord. It is addressed to Zerubbabel, the governor of Judah.

chariots and their riders; and the horses and their riders shall fall, every one by the
sword of a comrade. 23 On that day, says the LORD of hosts, I will take you,
O Zerubbabel my servant, son of Shealtiel, says the LORD, and make you like a
signet ring; for I have chosen you, says the LORD of hosts.

2.23 A signet ring was used to guarantee the authority and authenticity of a letter. It served as a signature when pressed in soft wax on a written document. God was reaffirming and guaranteeing his promise of a Messiah through David's line (Matthew 1:12).

2.23 God closes his message to Zerubbabel with this tremendous affirmation: "I have chosen you." Such a proclamation is ours as well—each of us has been chosen by God (Ephesians 1:4). This truth should make us see our value in God's eyes and motivate us to work for him. When you feel down, remind yourself, "God has chosen me!"

2.23 Haggai's message to the people sought to get their priorities straight, help them quit worrying, and motivate them to rebuild the temple. Like them, we often place a higher priority on our personal comfort than on God's work and true worship. But God is pleased and promises strength and guidance when we give him first place in our lives.

HOW GOD USED FOREIGN KINGS TO REBUILD THE TEMPLE

King	*Date (B.C.)*	*Event*	*Reference*
Cyrus the Great	539-530	Persia conquers Babylon. Jewish captives are allowed to return under Zerubbabel.	Daniel 5; Ezra 1—6
Smerdis	522-520	When political leaders send letters objecting to the work on the temple, he stops the work.	Ezra 4.1-23
Darius	520-486	Darius allows the work on the temple to continue.	Ezra 4.24; 6.1-22
		Haggai and Zechariah deliver their messages to continue rebuilding the temple.	Haggai 1.1—2.23; Zechariah 1.1—8.23
Ahasuerus (Xerxes)	486-465	He makes Esther his queen. The Jews are protected from their enemies.	Esther 1.1—10.3
Artaxerxes	465-424	He allows Ezra to return with a large group of Jewish exiles.	Ezra 7.1—10.44
		Nehemiah is allowed to take a leave of absence as his royal cupbearer to rebuild the walls of Jerusalem.	Nehemiah 1.1—13.31

Despite the suffering of God's people in the exile, God's promises of restoration would come true. Under the rule of the seemingly invincible Babylonians, the rebuilding of the temple and the city of Jerusalem appeared impossible. God's people had little hope. Through the decrees of these pagan kings, God fulfilled his promises of restoration.

ZECHARIAH

Daniel taken to Babylon 605 B.C.

Ezekiel taken to Babylon 597

Jerusalem falls 586

Babylon overthrown by Cyrus 539

Cyrus's decree allowing the exiles to return 538

Exiles return Jerusa 537

VITAL STATISTICS

PURPOSE:
To give hope to God's people by revealing God's future deliverance through the Messiah

AUTHOR:
Zechariah

TO WHOM WRITTEN:
The Jews in Jerusalem who had returned from their captivity in Babylon and to God's people everywhere

DATE WRITTEN:
Chapters 1—8 were written about 520-518 B.C. Chapters 9—14 were written around 480 B.C.

SETTING:
The exiles had returned from Babylon to rebuild the temple, but the work had been thwarted and stalled. Haggai and Zechariah confronted the people with their task and encouraged them to complete it.

KEY VERSES:
"Rejoice greatly, O daughter Zion! Shout aloud, O daughter Jerusalem! Lo, your king comes to you; triumphant and victorious is he, humble and riding on a donkey, on a colt, the foal of a donkey. . . . and he shall command peace to the nations; his dominion shall be from sea to sea, and from the River to the ends of the earth" (9.9, 10).

KEY PEOPLE:
Zerubbabel, Joshua

KEY PLACE:
Jerusalem

SPECIAL FEATURES:
This book is the most apocalyptic and messianic of all the minor prophets.

THE FUTURE—that vast uncharted sea of unknown, holding joy or terror, comfort or pain, love or loneliness. Some people fear the days to come, wondering what evils lurk in their shadows; others consult seers and future-telling charlatans, trying desperately to discover its secrets. But tomorrow's story is known only to God and to those special messengers, called prophets, to whom he has revealed a chapter or two.

A prophet's primary task was to proclaim the word of the Lord, pointing out sin, explaining its consequences, and calling men and women to repentance and obedience. Elijah, Elisha, Isaiah, Jeremiah, Ezekiel, Hosea, and Amos stand with scores of others who faithfully delivered God's message despite rejection, ridicule, and persecution. And at times they were given prophetic visions foretelling coming events.

Nestled near the end of the Old Testament, among what are known as "minor prophets," is the book of Zechariah. As one of three post-exilic prophets, along with Haggai and Malachi, Zechariah ministered to the small remnant of Jews who had returned to Judah to rebuild the temple and their nation. Like Haggai, he encouraged them to finish rebuilding the temple, but his message went far beyond those physical walls and contemporary issues. With spectacular apocalyptic imagery and graphic detail, Zechariah told of the Messiah, the one whom God would send to rescue his people and to reign over all the earth. Zechariah is one of our most important prophetic books, giving detailed messianic references which were clearly fulfilled in the life of Jesus Christ. The rebuilding of the temple, he says, was just the first act in the drama of the end and the ushering in of the messianic age. Zechariah proclaimed a stirring message of hope to these ex-captives and exiles—their King was coming!

Jesus is Messiah, the promised "great deliverer" of Israel. Unlike Zechariah's listeners, we can look back at his ministry and mission. As you study his prophecy, you will see details of Christ's life which were written 500 years before their fulfillment. Read and stand in awe of our God who keeps his promises. But there is also a future message which has not yet been fulfilled—the return of Christ at the end of the age. As you read Zechariah, therefore, think through the implications of this promised event. *Your King is coming,* and he will reign forever and ever.

God knows and controls the future. We may never see a moment ahead, but we can be secure if we trust in him. Read Zechariah and strengthen your faith in God—he alone is your hope and security.

nple struction ins	Temple work halted 530	Haggai, Zechariah become prophets; temple work resumed 520	Temple completed 516	Ezra comes to Jerusalem 458	Nehemiah comes to Jerusalem 445

THE BLUEPRINT

A. MESSAGES WHILE REBUILDING THE TEMPLE (1.1—8.23)
1. Zechariah's night visions
2. Zechariah's words of encouragement

Zechariah encouraged the people to put away the sin in their lives and to continue rebuilding the temple. His visions described the judgment of Israel's enemies, the blessings to Jerusalem, and the need for God's people to remain pure—avoiding hypocrisy, superficiality, and sin. Zechariah's visions provided hope for the people. We also need to carefully follow the instruction to remain pure until Christ returns again.

B. MESSAGES AFTER COMPLETING THE TEMPLE (9.1—14.21)

Besides encouragement and hope, Zechariah's messages were also a warning that God's messianic kingdom would not begin as soon as the temple was complete. Israel's enemies would be judged and the King would come, but they would face many difficult circumstances before experiencing the blessing of the messianic kingdom. We too may face much sorrow, disappointment, and tribulation before coming into Christ's eternal kingdom.

MEGATHEMES

THEME	EXPLANATION	IMPORTANCE
God's jealousy	God was angry at his people for neglecting his prophets through the years, and he was concerned that they not follow the careless and false leaders who exploited them. Disobedience was the root of their problems and the cause of their misery. God was jealous for their devotion to him.	God is jealous for our devotion. To avoid Israel's ruin, don't walk in their steps. Don't reject God, follow false teachers, or lead others astray. Turn to God, faithfully obey his Word, and make sure you are leading others correctly.
Rebuild the temple	The Jews were discouraged. They were free from exile, yet the temple was not completed. Zechariah encouraged them to rebuild it. God would both protect his workmen and also empower them by his Holy Spirit to carry out his work.	More than the rebuilding of the temple was at stake—the people were staging the first act in God's wonderful drama of the end times. Those of us who believe in God must complete his work. To do so we must have the Holy Spirit's help. God will empower us with his Spirit.
The King is coming	The Messiah will come both to rescue people from sin and to reign as king. He will establish his kingdom, conquer all his enemies, and rule over all the earth. Everything will one day be under his loving and powerful control.	The Messiah came as a servant to die for us. He will return as a victorious king. At that time, he will usher in peace throughout the world. Submit to his leadership now to be ready for the King's triumphant return.
God's protection	There was opposition to God's plan in Zechariah's day, and he prophesied future times of trouble. But God's Word endures. God remembers the agreements he makes with his people. He cares for his people and will deliver them from all the world powers that oppress them.	Although evil is still present, God's infinite love and personal care have been demonstrated through the centuries. God keeps his promises. Although our bodies may be destroyed, we need never fear our ultimate destiny if we love and obey him.

A. MESSAGES WHILE REBUILDING THE TEMPLE (1.1—8.23)

Zechariah begins by describing eight visions that came to him at night. Then he gives a collection of messages about the crowning of Joshua, answers about feasting and fasting, and encouragment to continue rebuilding the temple. We, too, can be inspired to continue following God in faithfulness throughout our lives.

1. Zechariah's night visions

Return to the Lord

1 In the eighth month, in the second year of Darius, the word of the LORD came 1.1
to the prophet Zechariah son of Berechiah son of Iddo, saying: 2 The LORD was Ezra 5.1 Neh 12.4,16
very angry with your ancestors. 3 Therefore say to them, Thus says the LORD of 1.2
hosts: Return to me, says the LORD of hosts, and I will return to you, says the LORD 2 Kgs 23.26
of hosts. 4 Do not be like your ancestors, to whom the former prophets proclaimed, 1.3 2 Chron 15.4
"Thus says the LORD of hosts, Return from your evil ways and from your evil Neh 9.28 Isa 31.6
deeds." But they did not hear or heed me, says the LORD. 5 Your ancestors, where Joel 2.12
are they? And the prophets, do they live forever? 6 But my words and my statutes, 1.4
which I commanded my servants the prophets, did they not overtake your ances- Ezra 9.7
tors? So they repented and said, "The LORD of hosts has dealt with us according to 1.5 Deut 28.45
our ways and deeds, just as he planned to do." Jer 12.16 Amos 9.10

Zechariah sees a man among the myrtle trees

7 On the twenty-fourth day of the eleventh month, the month of Shebat, in the 1.8
second year of Darius, the word of the LORD came to the prophet Zechariah son of Neh 8.15 Isa 41.19; 55.13
Berechiah son of Iddo; and Zechariah[a] said, 8 In the night I saw a man riding on a 1.10
red horse! He was standing among the myrtle trees in the glen; and behind him were Job 2.1,2 Zech 1.19
red, sorrel, and white horses. 9 Then I said, "What are these, my lord?" The angel 4.4,5,13; 6.4
who talked with me said to me, "I will show you what they are." 10 So the man who 1.11
was standing among the myrtle trees answered, "They are those whom the LORD Zech 1.15 1 Thess 5.3
has sent to patrol the earth." 11 Then they spoke to the angel of the LORD who was 1.12
standing among the myrtle trees, "We have patrolled the earth, and lo, the whole 2 Chron 36.21 Ps 74.10; 69.5
earth remains at peace." 12 Then the angel of the LORD said, "O LORD of hosts, how Isa 64.9-12 Jer 25.11,12
long will you withhold mercy from Jerusalem and the cities of Judah, with which Dan 9.2
you have been angry these seventy years?" 13 Then the LORD replied with gracious Rev 6.10
and comforting words to the angel who talked with me. 14 So the angel who talked 1.13 Isa 40.1,2
with me said to me, Proclaim this message: Thus says the LORD of hosts; I am very Zech 1.17
jealous for Jerusalem and for Zion. 15 And I am extremely angry with the nations 1.14 Zech 1.17

[a] Heb *and he*

1.1 Born in Babylon during the exile, Zechariah was a fairly young man when he returned to Jerusalem in 538 B.C. King Cyrus of Persia had defeated Babylon in 539 and decreed that captives in exile could return to their homelands. Zechariah and Haggai were among the first to leave. Zechariah, a prophet and a priest, began ministering at the same time as the prophet Haggai (520–518 B.C.). His first prophecy was delivered two months after Haggai's first prophecy.

Like Haggai, Zechariah encouraged the people to continue rebuilding the temple, whose reconstruction had been halted for nearly 15 years. Zechariah combated the people's spiritual apathy, despair over pressures from their enemies, and discouragement about the smaller scale of the new temple foundation. Neglect of our spiritual priorities can be just as devastating today to fulfilling God's purpose.

1.2–6 The familiar phrase, "Like father, like son," implies that children turn out like their parents. But God warned Israel *not* to be like their fathers who disobeyed him and reaped the consequences—his judgment. We are responsible before God for our actions. We aren't trapped by our heredity or environment, and we can't use these as excuses for our sins. We can choose, and individually we must return to God and follow him.

1.5, 6 The words God had spoken through his prophets a century earlier, before the captivity, also applied to Zechariah's generation, and they are still relevant for us. Because God's Word endures, we must read, study, and apply it. Learn the lessons of God's Word so you will not have to repeat the mistakes of others.

1.7–17 The horses and their colors were symbols of God's involvement in world governments. The full meaning of the colors is unknown, although the red horse is often associated with war and the white horse with final victory. *Sorrel* (1.8) means light brown or chestnut colored.

1.11 The angel saw that all the nations were prosperous and at peace while Israel was still conquered and despised. But God was planning a change. He had released his people, and he would allow them to return and rebuild his temple.

1.12 Seventy years was the time God had decreed for Israel to remain in captivity (Jeremiah 25.11; 29.10). This time was now completed, and the angel asked God to act swiftly to complete the promised return of his people to Jerusalem.

1.13 God's people had lived under his judgment for 70 years during their captivity in Babylon. But now God spoke words of comfort and assurance. God promises that when we return to him, he will heal us (Hosea 6.1). If you feel wounded and torn by the events of your life, turn to God so he can heal and comfort you.

1.15 Although the heathen nations afflicted God's people beyond

that are at ease; for while I was only a little angry, they made the disaster worse.
16 Therefore, thus says the LORD, I have returned to Jerusalem with compassion;
my house shall be built in it, says the LORD of hosts, and the measuring line shall
be stretched out over Jerusalem. 17 Proclaim further: Thus says the LORD of hosts:
My cities shall again overflow with prosperity; the LORD will again comfort Zion
and again choose Jerusalem.

Zechariah sees four horns and four blacksmiths

18[b] And I looked up and saw four horns. 19 I asked the angel who talked with me,
"What are these?" And he answered me, "These are the horns that have scattered
Judah, Israel, and Jerusalem." 20 Then the LORD showed me four blacksmiths.
21 And I asked, "What are they coming to do?" He answered, "These are the horns
that scattered Judah, so that no head could be raised; but these have come to terrify
them, to strike down the horns of the nations that lifted up their horns against the
land of Judah to scatter its people."[c]

Zechariah sees a man with a measuring line

2 [d] I looked up and saw a man with a measuring line in his hand. 2 Then I asked,
"Where are you going?" He answered me, "To measure Jerusalem, to see what
is its width and what is its length." 3 Then the angel who talked with me came
forward, and another angel came forward to meet him, 4 and said to him, "Run, say
to that young man: Jerusalem shall be inhabited like villages without walls, because
of the multitude of people and animals in it. 5 For I will be a wall of fire all around
it, says the LORD, and I will be the glory within it."
6 Up, up! Flee from the land of the north, says the LORD; for I have spread you
abroad like the four winds of heaven, says the LORD. 7 Up! Escape to Zion, you that
live with daughter Babylon. 8 For thus said the LORD of hosts (after his glory[e] sent
me) regarding the nations that plundered you: Truly, one who touches you touches
the apple of my eye.[f] 9 See now, I am going to raise[g] my hand against them, and
they shall become plunder for their own slaves. Then you will know that the LORD
of hosts has sent me. 10 Sing and rejoice, O daughter Zion! For lo, I will come and
dwell in your midst, says the LORD. 11 Many nations shall join themselves to the

1.16 Ezra 6.14,15; Isa 12.1; 54.8-10; Zech 2.10
1.17 Isa 52.9; 54.8
1.19 1 Kgs 22.11
1.21 Zech 1.18,19; 9.12-16; 10.3-5; 12.2-6
2.1 Ezek 40.3,5
2.2 Jer 31.39; Rev 21.15-17
2.4 Jer 1.6; Dan 1.17; 1 Tim 4.12
2.5 Isa 60.18,19
2.6 Num 16.26; Deut 28.64; Rev 18.4
2.9 Isa 10.32
2.11 Ex 19.5,6; Mic 4.2

[b] Ch 2.1 in Heb [c] Heb *it* [d] Ch 2.5 in Heb [e] Cn: Heb *after glory he* [f] Heb *his eye* [g] Or *wave*

ZECHARIAH served as a prophet to Judah about 520 B.C., after the return from exile.

Climate of the times	The exiles had returned from captivity to rebuild their temple. But work on the temple had stalled and the people were neglecting their service to God.
Main message	Zechariah, like Haggai, encouraged the people to finish rebuilding the temple. His visions gave the people hope. He told the people of a future king who would one day establish an eternal kingdom.
Importance of message	Even in times of discouragement and despair, God is working out his plan. God protects and guides us; we must trust and follow him.
Contemporary prophets	Haggai (about 520 B.C.)

his intentions, he was not powerless to stop them. God used these nations to punish his sinful people. When they went beyond his plans by trying to destroy Israel as a nation, he intervened.

1.18–21 The horns were the four world powers who oppressed Israel – Egypt, Assyria, Babylon, and Medo-Persia. The blacksmiths (1.20) were the nations used to overthrow Israel's enemies.

2.6, 7 Many of the captive Israelites did not return to Jerusalem because they preferred to stay with the wealth they had accumulated in Babylon. But Zechariah instructed them to leave Babylon quickly. This was an urgent request, because Babylon would be destroyed and because its decadent culture would cause his people to forget their spiritual priorities. About 90 percent of the Israelites rejected these warnings and remained in Babylon.

2.8 Believers are precious to God (Psalm 116.15); they are his very own children (Psalm 103.13). Treating any believer unkindly is the same as treating God that way. As Jesus told his disciples, when we help others we are helping him; when we neglect them, we are neglecting him (Matthew 25.34–46).

2.9–12 *Me* (2.9) may refer to the Messiah who, in the end, will judge all who have oppressed God's people. God promises to live among his people, and he says that many nations will come to know him (John 1.14; Revelation 21.3).

2.11, 12 God did not forget his words to Abraham, "In you all the families of the earth shall be blessed" (Genesis 12.3). Abraham, the father of the nation of Israel, was promised that his descendants would bless the whole world. Since the coming of Jesus, the Messiah, this promise is being fulfilled – people from all nations are coming to God through him.

LORD on that day, and shall be my people; and I will dwell in your midst. And you
shall know that the LORD of hosts has sent me to you. 12 The LORD will inherit Judah
as his portion in the holy land, and will again choose Jerusalem.
13 Be silent, all people, before the LORD; for he has roused himself from his
holy dwelling.

2.13 Deut 26.15 2 Chron 30.27 Hab 2.20

Zechariah sees the high priest

3 Then he showed me the high priest Joshua standing before the angel of the
LORD, and Satan[h] standing at his right hand to accuse him. 2 And the LORD
said to Satan,[h] "The LORD rebuke you, O Satan![h] The LORD who has chosen Jerusalem rebuke you! Is not this man a brand plucked from the fire?" 3 Now Joshua
was dressed with filthy clothes as he stood before the angel. 4 The angel said to
those who were standing before him, "Take off his filthy clothes." And to him he
said, "See, I have taken your guilt away from you, and I will clothe you with festal
apparel." 5 And I said, "Let them put a clean turban on his head." So they put a
clean turban on his head and clothed him with the apparel; and the angel of the
LORD was standing by.
6 Then the angel of the LORD assured Joshua, saying 7 "Thus says the LORD of
hosts: If you will walk in my ways and keep my requirements, then you shall rule
my house and have charge of my courts, and I will give you the right of access
among those who are standing here. 8 Now listen, Joshua, high priest, you and your
colleagues who sit before you! For they are an omen of things to come: I am going
to bring my servant the Branch. 9 For on the stone that I have set before Joshua, on
a single stone with seven facets, I will engrave its inscription, says the LORD of
hosts, and I will remove the guilt of this land in a single day. 10 On that day, says
the LORD of hosts, you shall invite each other to come under your vine and fig tree."

3.1 Ezra 5.2 Job 1.6-12 2.1-8 Hag 1.1
3.3 Ezra 9.15 Dan 9.18
3.4 Isa 43.25; 61.10 Mt 22.11-13 Lk 15.22 Rev 7.14
3.5 Ex 28.37-40 Lev 8.9 Ezek 44.18
3.7 1 Kgs 3.14 Isa 62.9
3.8 Isa 4.2; 8.18 11.1; 53.2 Jer 33.15 Ezek 12.11
3.10 1 Kgs 4.25 Mic 4.4

Zechariah sees the golden lampstand

4 The angel who talked with me came again, and wakened me, as one is wakened from sleep. 2 He said to me, "What do you see?" And I said, "I see a
lampstand all of gold, with a bowl on the top of it; there are seven lamps on it, with
seven lips on each of the lamps that are on the top of it. 3 And by it there are two

4.2 Ex 25.31,37 37.17-24 Zech 5.2 Rev 4.5

[h] Or *the Accuser*; Heb *the Adversary*

3.1 Joshua was Israel's high priest when the remnant returned to Jerusalem and began rebuilding the walls (Haggai 1.1, 12; 2.4).

3.1, 2 Satan accused Joshua, who here represents the nation of Israel. The accusations were accurate – Joshua stood in "filthy clothes" (sins). Yet God revealed his mercy, stating that he chose to save his people anyway. Satan is always accusing people of their sins before God (Job 1.6). But he greatly misunderstands the breadth of God's mercy and forgiveness toward those who believe in him. Satan the Accuser will ultimately be destroyed (Revelation 12.10), while everyone who is a believer will be saved (John 3.16). To be prepared, we can ask God to remove our clothing of sin and dress us with his goodness.

3.2 God punished Judah through the fire of great trials, but he rescued the nation before it was completely destroyed, like "a brand plucked from the fire."

3.2–4 Zechariah's vision graphically portrays how we obtain God's mercy. We do nothing ourselves. It is at God's initiative that our filthy clothes (sins) are removed, and God provides us with new, clean clothes (the righteousness of God – 2 Corinthians 5.21; Revelation 19.8). All we need to do is repent and ask God to forgive us. When Satan tries to make you feel dirty and unworthy, remember that the clean clothes of Christ's righteousness make you worthy to draw near to God.

3.5–7 The Greek name for Joshua is *Jesus,* meaning "Jehovah saves." This Joshua should not be confused with the warrior of the book of Joshua. Both the warrior Joshua and the high priest Joshua have been seen as symbols of Jesus, the Messiah.

3.7–10 There was no priesthood during the exile, so it had to be reinstated upon the return to the land. In this vision, Joshua was installed as high priest. One of the high priest's duties was to offer a sacrifice on the day of atonement to make amends for all the sins of the people. The priest was the mediator between God and the nation. Thus, he represented the coming Messiah (Isaiah 11.1), who would change the entire order of God's dealing with people's sin (Hebrews 10.8–14 explains this in detail). Jesus, the Messiah, was the High Priest who offered, once for all, the sacrifice of himself to take away our sins. In his new order, every Christian is a priest offering a holy, cleansed life to God (1 Peter 2.9; Revelation 5.10).

3.8, 9 The "Branch" refers to the Messiah. The meaning of the stone with seven facets is unclear. It could mean (1) the Branch himself as the foundation stone of the temple, (2) the rock struck by Moses that produced water for the Israelites (Numbers 20.7–11), or (3) the renewed spiritual priesthood of the church. These verses were fulfilled hundreds of years later by Jesus Christ. God said, "I will remove the guilt of this land in a single day," and this was fulfilled in Christ who "suffered for sins once for all, the righteous for the unrighteous, in order to bring you to God" (1 Peter 3.18). You cannot remove your sins by your own effort. You must allow God to remove them through Christ.

3.10 God promises that each person will have his own home during Christ's reign (see also Micah 4.4). This is a symbol of peace and prosperity.

ZECHARIAH'S VISIONS

Vision	Reference	Significance
Zechariah sees scouts reporting to God that the surrounding nations who have oppressed Judah are living in careless and sinful ease.	1.7–17	Israel was asking, "Why isn't God punishing the wicked?" Wicked nations may prosper, but not forever. God will bring upon them the judgment they deserve.
Zechariah sees four animal horns, representing the four world powers that oppressed and scattered the people of Judah and Israel. Then he sees four blacksmiths who will pound the horns.	1.18–21	God will do what he promised. After the evil nations have carried out his will in punishing his people, God will destroy those nations for their sin.
Zechariah sees a man measuring the city of Jerusalem. The city will one day be full of people and God himself will be a wall around the city.	2.1–13	The city will be restored in God's future kingdom. God will keep his promise to protect his people.
Zechariah sees Joshua, the high priest, standing before God. His filthy rags are exchanged for clean clothes; Satan's accusations against him are rejected by God.	3.1–10	Joshua's position as high priest pictures how the filthy rags of sin are replaced with the pure linen of God's righteousness. Christ has taken our rags of sin and replaced them with God's righteousness. (See Ephesians 4.24; 1 John 1.9.)
Zechariah sees a lampstand that is continually kept burning by an unlimited reservoir of oil. This picture reminds the people that it is only through God's Spirit that they will succeed, not by their own might and resources.	4.1–14	The Spirit of God is given without measure. Human effort does not make a difference. The work of God is not accomplished in human strength.
Zechariah sees a flying scroll which represents God's curse.	5.1–4	By God's Word and Spirit every person will be judged. The individual's sin is the focus here, not the sins of the nation. Each person is responsible for his or her deeds; no one has an excuse. God's curse is a symbol of destruction; all sin will be judged and removed.
Zechariah sees a vision of a woman in a basket. She represents the wickedness of the nations. The angel packed the woman back into the basket and sent her back to Babylon.	5.5–11	Sins of the individual were judged in the last vision (5.1–4); now sin is being removed from society. Sin has to be eradicated in order to clean up the nation and the individual.
Zechariah sees a vision of four horses and chariots. The horses represent God's judgment on the world—one is sent north, the direction from which most of Judah's enemies came. The other horses are patrolling the world, ready to execute judgment at God's command.	6.1–8	Judgment will come upon those who oppress God's people—it will come in God's time and at his command.

olive trees, one on the right of the bowl and the other on its left." 4 I said to the angel
who talked with me, "What are these, my lord?" 5 Then the angel who talked with
me answered me, "Do you not know what these are?" I said, "No, my lord." 6 He
said to me, "This is the word of the LORD to Zerubbabel: Not by might, nor by
power, but by my spirit, says the LORD of hosts. 7 What are you, O great mountain?
Before Zerubbabel you shall become a plain; and he shall bring out the top stone
amid shouts of 'Grace, grace to it!' "
8 Moreover the word of the LORD came to me, saying, 9 "The hands of Zerubbabel have laid the foundation of this house; his hands shall also complete it. Then
you will know that the LORD of hosts has sent me to you. 10 For whoever has despised the day of small things shall rejoice, and shall see the plummet in the hand
of Zerubbabel.
"These seven are the eyes of the LORD, which range through the whole earth."
11 Then I said to him, "What are these two olive trees on the right and the left of the
lampstand?" 12 And a second time I said to him, "What are these two branches of
the olive trees, which pour out the oil[i] through the two golden pipes?" 13 He said
to me, "Do you not know what these are?" I said, "No, my lord." 14 Then he said,
"These are the two anointed ones who stand by the Lord of the whole earth."

4.3 Zech 4.11,12, 14; Rev 11.4
4.6 2 Chron 14.11; Ezra 3.1,2; Isa 11.2-4; Hag 2.4,5; Eph 6.17
4.7 Ezra 3.11-13; 6.15-17; Rev 5.9-13
4.9 Ezra 3.8-10; 5.16; Zech 6.12,13
4.10 Amos 7.2,7,8; Hag 2.3; Zech 3.9
4.14 Dan 9.24-26

Zechariah sees a flying scroll

5 Again I looked up and saw a flying scroll. 2 And he said to me, "What do you
see?" I answered, "I see a flying scroll; its length is twenty cubits, and its width
ten cubits." 3 Then he said to me, "This is the curse that goes out over the face of
the whole land; for everyone who steals shall be cut off according to the writing on
one side, and everyone who swears falsely[j] shall be cut off according to the writing on the other side. 4 I have sent it out, says the LORD of hosts, and it shall enter
the house of the thief, and the house of anyone who swears falsely by my name; and
it shall abide in that house and consume it, both timber and stones."

5.1 Ezek 2.9,10; Rev 10.2,8-11
5.3 Ex 20.15; Isa 24.6; Jer 26.6
5.4 Lev 14.34-45; Deut 7.26; Hab 2.9-11

Zechariah sees a flying basket

5 Then the angel who talked with me came forward and said to me, "Look up
and see what this is that is coming out." 6 I said, "What is it?" He said, "This is a
basket[k] coming out." And he said, "This is their iniquity[l] in all the land." 7 Then
a leaden cover was lifted, and there was a woman sitting in the basket![k] 8 And he
said, "This is Wickedness." So he thrust her back into the basket,[k] and pressed the
leaden weight down on its mouth. 9 Then I looked up and saw two women coming

5.6 Lev 19.36; Amos 8.5
5.8 Hos 12.7; Mic 6.11

[i] Cn: Heb *gold* [j] The word *falsely* added from verse 4 [k] Heb *ephah* [l] Gk Compare Syr: Heb *their eye*

4.6 Zerubbabel was given the responsibility of rebuilding the temple in Jerusalem (Ezra 3.2, 8; Haggai 1.1; 2.23). While the prophets Haggai and Zechariah gave the moral and spiritual encouragement to resume work on the temple, Zerubbabel saw that the task was carried out. As the work was being completed, the prophets encouraged Zerubbabel and told him of a time when spiritual apathy and foreign oppression would forever be abolished.

4.6 Many people believe that to survive in this world a person must be tough, strong, unbending, and harsh. But God says, "Not by might, nor by power, but by my spirit." The key words are "by my spirit." It is *only* through God's Spirit that anything of lasting value is accomplished. The returned exiles were indeed weak—harassed by their enemies, tired, discouraged, and poor. But actually they had God on their side! As you live for God, determine not to trust in your own strength or abilities. Instead, depend on God and work in the power of his Spirit! (See also Hosea 1.7.)

4.9 The temple was completed in 516 B.C. (Ezra 6.14, 15).

4.10 *Plummet* probably means the last ceremonial stone to be placed in building the temple. Many of the older Jews were disheartened when they realized this new temple would not match the size and splendor of the previous temple built during King Solomon's reign. But bigger and more beautiful is not always better. What you do for God may seem small and insignificant at the time, but God rejoices in what is right, not necessarily in what is big. Be faithful in the small opportunities. Begin where you are and do what you can, and leave the results to God.

4.14 The two anointed ones may be Joshua and Zerubbabel, dedicated for this special task. Also note that in Revelation 11.3, two prophets (witnesses) arise to prophesy to the nations during the time of tribulation. They will be killed but will rise again.

5.1–9 The flying scroll was about 30 feet long and 15 feet wide. The judgment of the flying scroll was leveled against those who violated God's law, specifically by stealing and lying (5.1–4). The woman in the basket personified wickedness, and so this vision showed that wickedness would be not only severely punished (the vision of the flying scroll), but also banished (the vision of the woman in the basket, 5.6–9).

5.9–11 The woman in the basket was carried away to "the land of Shinar" (Babylon), which had become a symbol, the center of world idolatry and wickedness. This woman was a picture to Zechariah that wickedness and sin would be taken away from Israel; and one day sin will be removed from the entire earth. When Christ died, he removed sin's power and penalty. When we trust him to forgive us, he removes the penalty of sin and gives us the power to overcome sin in our lives. When he returns, he will remove all sin from the earth and people will live in safety and security.

5.9 Lev 11.13-19; Ps 104.17; Jer 8.7 forward. The wind was in their wings; they had wings like the wings of a stork, and
they lifted up the basket[m] between earth and sky. 10 Then I said to the angel who
talked with me, "Where are they taking the basket?"[m] 11 He said to me, "To the land
5.11 Isa 11.11; Dan 1.2 of Shinar, to build a house for it; and when this is prepared, they will set the basket[m] down there on its base."

Zechariah sees four chariots

6.1 Zech 6.5 **6** And again I looked up and saw four chariots coming out from between two
mountains — mountains of bronze. 2 The first chariot had red horses, the second chariot black horses, 3 the third chariot white horses, and the fourth chariot
6.5 Dan 7.2; 11.4; Zech 6.1; Mt 24.31; Rev 7.1 dappled gray[n] horses. 4 Then I said to the angel who talked with me, "What are
these, my lord?" 5 The angel answered me, "These are the four winds[o] of heaven
going out, after presenting themselves before the LORD of all the earth. 6 The char-
6.6 Jer 1.14,15; 25.9; Ezek 1.4; Dan 11.5,6, 9,40 iot with the black horses goes toward the north country, the white ones go toward
the west country,[p] and the dappled ones go toward the south country." 7 When the
steeds came out, they were impatient to get off and patrol the earth. And he said,
"Go, patrol the earth." So they patrolled the earth. 8 Then he cried out to me, "Lo,
6.8 Zech 1.15 those who go toward the north country have set my spirit at rest in the north country."

2. Zechariah's words of encouragement

The symbolic crowning of Joshua

6.10 Ezra 7.14-16; 8.26-30; Ps 21.3; Song 3.11; Zech 3.1 9 The word of the LORD came to me: 10 Collect silver and gold[q] from the
exiles — from Heldai, Tobijah, and Jedaiah — who have arrived from Babylon; and
go the same day to the house of Josiah son of Zephaniah. 11 Take the silver and gold
and make a crown,[r] and set it on the head of the high priest Joshua son of Jehoza-
6.12 Isa 4.2,3; 11.1; Jer 23.5,6; Zech 3.8; 4.6-9 dak; 12 say to him: Thus says the LORD of hosts: Here is a man whose name is
Branch: for he shall branch out in his place, and he shall build the temple of the
6.13 Ps 110.4; Isa 9.6; 11.10; Dan 7.13,14; Heb 3.1; 4.14-16; 10.12,13 LORD. 13 It is he that shall build the temple of the LORD; he shall bear royal honor,
and shall sit and rule on his throne. There shall be a priest by his throne, with
peaceful understanding between the two of them. 14 And the crown[s] shall be in the
care of Heldai,[t] Tobijah, Jedaiah, and Josiah[u] son of Zephaniah, as a memorial in
the temple of the LORD.
6.15 Isa 56.6-8; 60.10; Zech 3.7 15 Those who are far off shall come and help to build the temple of the LORD;
and you shall know that the LORD of hosts has sent me to you. This will happen if
you diligently obey the voice of the LORD your God.

The people urged to be just and merciful

7.2 Zech 8.21 **7** In the fourth year of King Darius, the word of the LORD came to Zechariah on
the fourth day of the ninth month, which is Chislev. 2 Now the people of Bethel

m Heb *ephah* n Compare Gk: Meaning of Heb uncertain o Or *spirits* p Cn: Heb *go after them* q Cn Compare verse 11: Heb lacks *silver and gold* r Gk Mss Syr Tg: Heb *crowns* s Gk Syr: Heb *crowns* t Syr Compare verse 10: Heb *Helem* u Syr Compare verse 10: Heb *Hen*

6.8 The black horse that went north executed God's judgment in the north country. Zechariah said the execution of judgment had quieted God's anger. God is angry with sin and with the wicked (Psalm 7.11), and his anger is expressed in judgment. Much as we like to concentrate on God's love and mercy, anger and judgment are also part of his righteous character. If you have unconfessed or habitual sin in your life, confess it and turn away from it. Confession releases God's mercy, but refusing to repent invites his judgment.

6.9–15 This vision is about the Messiah, the King-Priest. In the days of the kings and during the exile, Judah's government was to be ruled by two distinct persons — the king, ruling the nation's political life, and the high priest, ruling its religious life. Kings and priests had often been corrupt. God was telling Zechariah that someone would come who would rule as both king ("rule on his throne") and priest ("a priest by his throne" — this could also be translated, "upon his throne"). This was an unlikely combination for that day. This King-Priest, the Messiah, would rule both over his people and in the hearts of those who believe in him.

6.15 Some of God's promises are conditional — we must obey him to receive them. The rebuilding of the temple required careful obedience. God would protect the people as long as they obeyed. Casual or occasional obedience, the result of a halfhearted or divided commitment, would not lead to blessing. Many of God's blessings come to us as a result of diligent obedience. Inconsistent obedience can't produce consistent blessing.

7.1ff The fourth year of King Darius's reign was 518 B.C. For the previous 70 years, the people had been holding a fast in August to remember the destruction of Jerusalem. Now that Jerusalem was being rebuilt, they came to the temple to ask if they had to continue this annual fast. God did not answer their question directly. Instead, he told them that their behavior was more important than their religious actions. What he wanted from his people was honesty in business and compassion for the weak.

had sent Sharezer and Regem-melech and their men, to entreat the favor of the
LORD, 3 and to ask the priests of the house of the LORD of hosts and the prophets,
"Should I mourn and practice abstinence in the fifth month, as I have done for so
many years?" 4 Then the word of the LORD of hosts came to me: 5 Say to all the
people of the land and the priests: When you fasted and lamented in the fifth month
and in the seventh, for these seventy years, was it for me that you fasted? 6 And
when you eat and when you drink, do you not eat and drink only for yourselves?
7 Were not these the words that the LORD proclaimed by the former prophets, when
Jerusalem was inhabited and in prosperity, along with the towns around it, and
when the Negeb and the Shephelah were inhabited?
8 The word of the LORD came to Zechariah, saying: 9 Thus says the LORD of
hosts: Render true judgments, show kindness and mercy to one another; 10 do not
oppress the widow, the orphan, the alien, or the poor; and do not devise evil in your
hearts against one another. 11 But they refused to listen, and turned a stubborn
shoulder, and stopped their ears in order not to hear. 12 They made their hearts
adamant in order not to hear the law and the words that the LORD of hosts had sent
by his spirit through the former prophets. Therefore great wrath came from the
LORD of hosts. 13 Just as, when I[v] called, they would not hear, so, when they
called, I would not hear, says the LORD of hosts, 14 and I scattered them with a
whirlwind among all the nations that they had not known. Thus the land they left
was desolate, so that no one went to and fro, and a pleasant land was made desolate.

Judah will be blessed

8 The word of the LORD of hosts came to me, saying: 2 Thus says the LORD of
hosts: I am jealous for Zion with great jealousy, and I am jealous for her with
great wrath. 3 Thus says the LORD: I will return to Zion, and will dwell in the midst
of Jerusalem; Jerusalem shall be called the faithful city, and the mountain of the
LORD of hosts shall be called the holy mountain. 4 Thus says the LORD of hosts: Old
men and old women shall again sit in the streets of Jerusalem, each with staff in
hand because of their great age. 5 And the streets of the city shall be full of boys and
girls playing in its streets. 6 Thus says the LORD of hosts: Even though it seems
impossible to the remnant of this people in these days, should it also seem impossible to me, says the LORD of hosts? 7 Thus says the LORD of hosts: I will save my
people from the east country and from the west country; 8 and I will bring them to

v Heb *he*

7.3 Ezra 3.10-12
7.5 Isa 1.11,12; Zech 1.12; Mt 5.16-18; 6.2,5,16; 23.5
7.7 Deut 34.3; Jer 17.26; 22.21; Zech 1.4
7.8 2 Sam 9.7; Mic 6.8; Zech 8.16
7.10 Ex 22.22; Deut 24.14-18; Prov 22.22,23; Zech 8.17
7.11 Neh 9.29; Acts 7.57
7.12 2 Chron 36.16; Jer 17.1; 26.19
7.13 Prov 1.24-28; Isa 1.15; 50.2; Jer 11.10,14
7.14 Jer 12.10; 44.6
8.4 Isa 65.20-22; Lam 2.20
8.5 Jer 30.19,20; Zech 2.4
8.6 Jer 32.17,27
8.7 Ps 107.2,3; Amos 9.14,15
8.8 Zech 10.10

7.3 To practice abstinence meant to keep the fast days, one of the religious practices that the Israelites had been able to keep alive through the captivity.

7.5–7 The Israelites had lost their sincere desire for God. Zechariah told them that they had been fasting without a proper attitude of repentance or worship. They fasted and mourned during their exile with no thought of God or their sins that had caused the exile in the first place. When you go to church, pray, or fellowship with other believers, are you doing these from habit or for what you get out of it? God says that an attitude of worship without a sincere desire for him will lead to ruin.

7.7 The Negev was the southern part of Judah, and the Shephelah was the western part.

7.8–10 God is just, and he wants his people to reflect his justice in their lives. Here God tells Zechariah what he expects of his people: (1) give true judgments; (2) be merciful and kind; (3) don't oppress others; (4) don't plan evil against others. This sounds like a good prescription for judges, but are you fair and just in *all* your dealings – the small as well as the large?

7.11, 12 Zechariah explained to the people that their ancestors brought God's great wrath on themselves by hardening their hearts. Any sin seems more natural the second time – as we become hardened, each repetition is easier. Ignoring or refusing God's warning hardens you each time you do wrong. Read God's Word and apply it to your life. Sensitivity and submission to God's Word can soften your heart and allow you to live as you should.

8.3 One day Christ will reign in his kingdom on earth. There all his people will live with him. This truth encourages us to look forward to the Messiah's reign.

8.4, 5 In troubled times, the very old and very young are the first to suffer and die. But both groups are plentiful in this vision, filling the streets with their normal everyday activities. This is a sign of the complete peace and prosperity of God's new earth.

8.6 The remnant was the small group of exiles who had returned from Babylon to rebuild Jerusalem and the temple. Struggling to survive in the land, they became discouraged over the opposition they often faced from hostile neighbors. It was hard to believe that one day God himself would reign from this city and that their land would enjoy great peace and plenty.

8.6 This verse could also be translated, "What seems unbelievable to you is no great thing for me." God reminded Zechariah of this truth when predicting his deliverance of Jerusalem. Our God is all-

live in Jerusalem. They shall be my people and I will be their God, in faithfulness
and in righteousness.
9 Thus says the LORD of hosts: Let your hands be strong — you that have recently been hearing these words from the mouths of the prophets who were present
when the foundation was laid for the rebuilding of the temple, the house of the
LORD of hosts. 10 For before those days there were no wages for people or for animals, nor was there any safety from the foe for those who went out or came in, and
I set them all against one other. 11 But now I will not deal with the remnant of this
people as in the former days, says the LORD of hosts. 12 For there shall be a sowing
of peace; the vine shall yield its fruit, the ground shall give its produce, and the
skies shall give their dew; and I will cause the remnant of this people to possess all
these things. 13 Just as you have been a cursing among the nations, O house of
Judah and house of Israel, so I will save you and you shall be a blessing. Do not be
afraid, but let your hands be strong.
14 For thus says the LORD of hosts: Just as I purposed to bring disaster upon
you, when your ancestors provoked me to wrath, and I did not relent, says the LORD
of hosts, 15 so again I have purposed in these days to do good to Jerusalem and to
the house of Judah; do not be afraid. 16 These are the things that you shall do: Speak
the truth to one another, render in your gates judgments that are true and make for
peace, 17 do not devise evil in your hearts against one another, and love no false
oath; for all these are things that I hate, says the LORD.
18 The word of the LORD of hosts came to me, saying: 19 Thus says the LORD of
hosts: The fast of the fourth month, and the fast of the fifth, and the fast of the
seventh, and the fast of the tenth, shall be seasons of joy and gladness, and cheerful
festivals for the house of Judah: therefore love truth and peace.
20 Thus says the LORD of hosts: Peoples shall yet come, the inhabitants of many
cities; 21 the inhabitants of one city shall go to another, saying, "Come, let us go to
entreat the favor of the LORD, and to seek the LORD of hosts; I myself am going."
22 Many peoples and strong nations shall come to seek the LORD of hosts in Jerusalem, and to entreat the favor of the LORD. 23 Thus says the LORD of hosts: In those
days ten men from nations of every language shall take hold of a Jew, grasping his
garment and saying, "Let us go with you, for we have heard that God is with you."

8.9 Ezra 5.1; 6.14
8.10 Isa 19.2 Amos 3.6; 9.4 Hag 1.6-11 2.16-19
8.12 Gen 27.28 1 Kgs 17.1 Hag 1.10
8.13 Deut 28.37 Ps 72.17 Jer 29.18 Dan 9.11 Mic 5.7 Zech 10.6-9 14.11
8.14 Jer 4.28 29.11-14 Mic 4.10-13
8.16 Zech 8.3
8.17 Jer 4.2 Zech 5.3,4 7.10 Mal 3.5
8.19 Esth 8.17 Isa 12.1 Zech 7.3-5; 8.16 Lk 1.74,75
8.20 Zech 2.11 14.16
8.22 Isa 49.6,22,23 52.15; 60.3-12
8.23 Isa 45.14; 60.14

---

powerful; he can do anything! When confronting seemingly impossible tasks or situations, remember that "for God all things are possible" (Matthew 19.26).

8.8 The covenant relationship will be renewed and the whole community will be filled with the presence of God. This promise of forgiveness and restoration refers to all God's people wherever they may be found. (For other references to this promise, see Exodus 6.6, 7; 19.5, 6; 29.45; Leviticus 26.12; Deuteronomy 7.6; Jeremiah 31.1, 33.)

8.9 God had to give the temple workers a little push to get them moving. They had heard the prophets' words of encouragement; now they needed to stop just listening and get to work. We need to listen to what God says, but after he has made our course of action plain, we need to "be strong" and do what he wants.

8.13–15 For more than 15 years, God and his prophets had been urging the people to finish building the temple. Once more God encouraged them with visions of the future. We are tempted to slow down for many reasons: people aren't responding; we feel physically or emotionally drained; the workers are uncooperative; the work is distasteful, too difficult, or not worth the effort. God's promises about the future should encourage us *now*. He knows what the results of our labors will be, and thus he can give us a perspective that will help us continue in our work for him.

8.14–17 God promised to give his people rich rewards. He reassured them that despite the punishments they had endured, he would not change his mind to now bless them. But he also said they had a job to do — "These are the things that you shall do." God will be faithful, but we also have responsibilities: to tell the truth, be fair, and live peacefully. If you expect God to do his part, be sure to do yours.

8.19–22 There will come a time when fasting for sins will be replaced by feasting and joy. People from all nations will "go to entreat the favor of the Lord." This is also promised in 2.11.

8.23 In the past, Jerusalem had often borne the brunt of cruel jokes from other nations (8.13). The city was not respected; its citizens had sinned so much that God let them be "kicked around" by their enemies. But eventually, says Zechariah, Jerusalem will be a holy place — respected highly throughout the world because its people will have a change of heart toward God. People from other nations will see how God has rewarded his people for their faithfulness and will want to be included in their great blessings.

B. MESSAGES AFTER COMPLETING THE TEMPLE (9.1—14.21)

After the temple was completed, Zechariah gave several prophecies about Israel's future, which describe the first and second comings of Jesus Christ. This book contains more about the person, work, and future glory of Christ than the other minor prophets combined. Israel's King would come, but he would be rejected by his people. They would later repent and be restored to God. The King who is coming is our king. May we be found faithful and pure in his sight when we meet him face to face.

Israel's enemies will be judged

9

An Oracle.

The word of the LORD is against the land of Hadrach
and will rest upon Damascus.
For to the LORD belongs the capital[w] of Aram,[x]
as do all the tribes of Israel;
2 Hamath also, which borders on it,
Tyre and Sidon, though they are very wise.
3 Tyre has built itself a rampart,
and heaped up silver like dust,
and gold like the dirt of the streets.
4 But now, the Lord will strip it of its possessions
and hurl its wealth into the sea,
and it shall be devoured by fire.

5 Ashkelon shall see it and be afraid;
Gaza too, and shall writhe in anguish;
Ekron also, because its hopes are withered.
The king shall perish from Gaza;
Ashkelon shall be uninhabited;
6 a mongrel people shall settle in Ashdod,
and I will make an end of the pride of Philistia.
7 I will take away its blood from its mouth,
and its abominations from between its teeth;
it too shall be a remnant for our God;
it shall be like a clan in Judah,
and Ekron shall be like the Jebusites.
8 Then I will encamp at my house as a guard,
so that no one shall march to and fro;
no oppressor shall again overrun them,
for now I have seen with my own eyes.

The coming of the King

9 Rejoice greatly, O daughter Zion!
Shout aloud, O daughter Jerusalem!

[w] Heb *eye* [x] Cn: Heb *of Adam* (or *of humankind*)

9.1 Gen 14.15 Amos 1.3-5 3.12
9.2 Num 13.21 1 Kgs 17.9 2 Kgs 25.21 Isa 23.1-18 Ezek 28.3-5 12.21-26
9.3 1 Kgs 10.27 Isa 23.8 Ezek 27.33
9.4 Isa 23.1-7 Ezek 27.26-36 28.16,18 Joel 3.8
9.5 Jer 47.4-7 Zeph 2.4
9.8 Isa 54.14 Zech 14.11

9.1–17 An oracle is a message from God. Hadrach was probably a city in northern Syria. The last six chapters of the book are two messages delivered late in Zechariah's life which point to the Messiah and his second coming. Some of these prophecies were fulfilled before the Messiah came, perhaps by Alexander the Great; others were fulfilled during the Messiah's time on earth; and others will be fulfilled when he returns. Those who oppressed Jerusalem—Syria, Philistia, Phoenicia—would be crushed. The promised King would come—first as a servant on a donkey's colt, then as a powerful ruler and judge.

9.5–7 Zechariah mentions four key cities in Philistia: Ashkelon, Gaza, and Ekron would be destroyed; and Ashdod would be overtaken by foreigners. This would happen because of their great evil and idolatry. But those who are left in the land would be adopted into Israel as a new clan, as the Jebusites were (when David conquered Jerusalem, he did not wipe out the Jebusites, but absorbed them into Judah).

9.8 Several centuries after Zechariah's day, Antiochus IV Epiphanes invaded Israel; and in A.D. 70, Titus, a Roman general, completely destroyed the temple. This promise, therefore, may have been conditional upon the people's obedience. The day will come, however, when God's people will never again have to worry about invading enemies (Joel 3.17).

9.9 The triumphal entry of Jesus riding into Jerusalem (Matthew 21.1–11) is predicted here 500 years before it happened. Just as this prophecy was fulfilled when Jesus came to earth, so the prophecies of his second coming are just as certain to come true. We are to be ready for his return, for he is coming!

9.9 Isa 9.6,7; 12.6 57.15 Jer 23.5,6 Zeph 3.5 Mt 11.29

Lo, your king comes to you;
triumphant and victorious is he,
humble and riding on a donkey,
on a colt, the foal of a donkey.

9.10 Ps 72.17 Isa 57.18,19 Mic 4.2-10; 5.4

10 He[y] will cut off the chariot from Ephraim
and the war horse from Jerusalem;
and the battle bow shall be cut off,
and he shall command peace to the nations;
his dominion shall be from sea to sea,
and from the River to the ends of the earth.

9.11 Ex 24.8 Heb 9.10-26

11 As for you also, because of the blood of my covenant with you,
I will set your prisoners free from the waterless pit.

9.12 Isa 40.2; 52.2 Joel 3.16

12 Return to your stronghold, O prisoners of hope;
today I declare that I will restore to you double.

9.13 Dan 11.32-34 Joel 3.6-8 Mic 4.2,3

13 For I have bent Judah as my bow;
I have made Ephraim its arrow.
I will arouse your sons, O Zion,
against your sons, O Greece,
and wield you like a warrior's sword.

9.14 Josh 6.4,5 Isa 18.3; 27.13

14 Then the LORD will appear over them,
and his arrow go forth like lightning;
the Lord GOD will sound the trumpet
and march forth in the whirlwinds of the south.
15 The LORD of hosts will protect them,
and they shall devour and tread down the slingers;[z]
they shall drink their blood[a] like wine,
and be full like a bowl,
drenched like the corners of the altar.

9.16 Ps 27.4 Isa 40.10; 62.3 Jer 31.12,14 Ezek 34.22-26 Hag 2.23

16 On that day the LORD their God will save them
for they are the flock of his people;
for like the jewels of a crown
they shall shine on his land.
17 For what goodness and beauty are his!
Grain shall make the young men flourish,
and new wine the young women.

Israel and Judah are lost sheep

10.1 Deut 11.14 Hos 6.3

10 Ask rain from the LORD
in the season of the spring rain,
from the LORD who makes the storm clouds,
who gives showers of rain to you,[b]

[y] Gk: Heb *I* [z] Cn: Heb *the slingstones* [a] Gk: Heb *shall drink* [b] Heb *them*

9.10 Ephraim is another name for the northern kingdom of Israel. When we view two distant mountains, they appear to be close together, perhaps even to touch each other. But as we approach them, we can see that they are in fact far apart, even separated by a huge valley. This is the situation with many Old Testament prophecies. Verse 9 was clearly fulfilled in Christ's first coming, but verse 10 can now be seen to refer to his second coming. At that time all nations will be subject to Christ; and his reign will cover the whole earth. In Philippians 2.9, 10, we are told that at that time every knee will bow to Christ and every tongue confess him as Lord.

9.11 Covenants in Old Testament times were sealed or confirmed with blood, much as we would sign our name to a contract. The old covenant was sealed by the blood of sacrifices, pointing ahead to the blood Christ would shed at Calvary, his "signature" that confirmed God's new covenant with his people. Because God had made a covenant with these people, he delivered them from the "waterless pit," the cistern-like prison of exile.

9.13–17 After Solomon's reign, the kingdom was divided into the northern kingdom (called Israel or Ephraim) and the southern kingdom (called Judah). This prophecy says that all Israel, north and south, will someday be reunited. The first part of this chapter tells how God will help his people avoid war; now God explains that he will help his people when war is inevitable. Verses 14–16 explain how the Jews will win over the Greeks, but it is also a figurative picture of the ultimate future victory over evil by God's people.

the vegetation in the field to everyone.
2 For the teraphim[c] utter nonsense,
and the diviners see lies;
the dreamers tell false dreams,
and give empty consolation.
Therefore the people wander like sheep;
they suffer for lack of a shepherd.

3 My anger is hot against the shepherds,
and I will punish the leaders;[d]
for the LORD of hosts cares for his flock, the house of Judah,
and will make them like his proud war horse.
4 Out of them shall come the cornerstone,
out of them the tent peg,
out of them the battle bow,
out of them every commander.
5 Together they shall be like warriors in battle,
trampling the foe in the mud of the streets;
they shall fight, for the LORD is with them,
and they shall put to shame the riders on horses.

6 I will strengthen the house of Judah,
and I will save the house of Joseph.
I will bring them back because I have compassion on them,
and they shall be as though I had not rejected them;
for I am the LORD their God and I will answer them.
7 Then the people of Ephraim shall become like warriors,
and their hearts shall be glad as with wine.
Their children shall see it and rejoice,
their hearts shall exult in the LORD.

8 I will signal for them and gather them in,
for I have redeemed them,
and they shall be as numerous as they were before.
9 Though I scattered them among the nations,
yet in far countries they shall remember me,
and they shall rear their children and return.
10 I will bring them home from the land of Egypt,
and gather them from Assyria;
I will bring them to the land of Gilead and to Lebanon,
until there is no room for them.
11 They[e] shall pass through the sea of distress,

10.2 Jer 23.25-27 Ezek 21.29 Mic 3.6-11 Mt 9.36

10.3 Isa 10.12 Ezek 34.2,7,12

10.5 2 Sam 22.8

10.6 Isa 54.8 Zech 1.16; 8.11

10.7 Isa 38.19; 54.13

10.8 Isa 5.26 7.18,19 Jer 33.22

10.9 Deut 30.1-4 1 Kgs 8.47,48 Jer 51.50

10.10 Isa 11.11-16 49.19-21 Mic 7.11,12

c *Or household gods* d *Or male goats* e Gk: Heb *He*

10.2 Teraphim were household idols. We often create idols of money, power, fame, or success, and then expect them to give us happiness and security. But these idols can't supply what we need any more than a stone image can make it rain. How foolish it is to trust in idols. Instead, trust God's promises for your future.

10.4 Zechariah's prophecy, 500 years before Christ's first coming, calls him a "cornerstone" (see also Isaiah 28.16), a "tent peg" (Isaiah 22.23), a "bow" that wins the battle, and a "commander" who was a man of action (see also Genesis 49.10; Micah 5.2). This Messiah would be strong, stable, victorious, and trustworthy – in all, the answer to Israel's problems. Only in the Messiah will all the promises to God's people be fulfilled.

10.6 The "house of Judah" refers to the southern kingdom, and the "house of Joseph" refers to the northern kingdom. Ephraim, the leading tribe of the northern kingdom, was the son of Joseph. One day God will unite all his people. This verse tells about his reuniting the Jews (see also Jeremiah 31.10). This was a startling idea: the people of the northern kingdom of Israel were so completely absorbed into other cultures after their captivity in 722 B.C. that a regathering could not be done by human means, but only by God.

10.6, 12 God promises to strengthen his people. When we stay closely connected to God, his Spirit enables us to do his will, despite the obstacles. When we stray away from God, we are cut off from our power source.

10.10 This pictured return from Egypt and Assyria was a symbolic way of saying that the people would be returned from all the countries where they had been dispersed. Egypt and Assyria evoked memories of slavery and separation. "Until there is no room for them" could also be translated, "there will scarcely be room for all of them."

10.11 Ps 66.10-12 Isa 11.15,16 19.5-7 Zeph 2.13 Ezek 30.13
10.12 Isa 2.5 Mic 4.5

and the waves of the sea shall be struck down,
and all the depths of the Nile dried up.
The pride of Assyria shall be laid low,
and the scepter of Egypt shall depart.
12 I will make them strong in the LORD,
and they shall walk in his name,
says the LORD.

11.1 Ezek 31.3

11 Open your doors, O Lebanon,
so that fire may devour your cedars!
2 Wail, O cypress, for the cedar has fallen,
for the glorious trees are ruined!
Wail, oaks of Bashan,
for the thick forest has been felled!

11.3 Jer 2.15 25.34-36; 50.44

3 Listen, the wail of the shepherds,
for their glory is despoiled!
Listen, the roar of the lions,
for the thickets of the Jordan are destroyed!

The two shepherds

11.5 Jer 50.7 Ezek 34.2-6 Hos 12.8
11.6 Isa 9.19-21 Jer 13.14

4 Thus said the LORD my God: Be a shepherd of the flock doomed to slaughter.
5 Those who buy them kill them and go unpunished; and those who sell them say,
"Blessed be the LORD, for I have become rich"; and their own shepherds have no
pity on them. 6 For I will no longer have pity on the inhabitants of the earth, says the
LORD. I will cause them, every one, to fall each into the hand of a neighbor, and
each into the hand of the king; and they shall devastate the earth, and I will deliver
no one from their hand.

11.7 Lev 27.32 Ps 27.4; 90.17 Ezek 37.16-23 Jn 17.21-23
11.8 Hos 5.7
11.9 Ps 69.22-28 Jer 15.2,3
11.12 1 Kgs 3.5 Mt 26.15 27.9,10 Jn 13.2,27-30

7 So, on behalf of the sheep merchants, I became the shepherd of the flock
doomed to slaughter. I took two staffs; one I named Favor, the other I named Unity,
and I tended the sheep. 8 In one month I disposed of the three shepherds, for I had
become impatient with them, and they also detested me. 9 So I said, "I will not be
your shepherd. What is to die, let it die; what is to be destroyed, let it be destroyed;
and let those that are left devour the flesh of one another!" 10 I took my staff Favor
and broke it, annulling the covenant that I had made with all the peoples. 11 So it
was annulled on that day, and the sheep merchants, who were watching me, knew
that it was the word of the LORD. 12 I then said to them, "If it seems right to you,
give me my wages; but if not, keep them." So they weighed out as my wages thirty
shekels of silver. 13 Then the LORD said to me, "Throw it into the treasury"[f]—this

[f] Syr: Heb *it to the potter*

10.11 The "sea of distress" refers to the Red Sea through which the Israelites were miraculously delivered from Egypt. As the Israelites returned once again from Egypt and other lands, they would be protected by God's miraculous power.

11.1–17 In this message, God asks Zechariah to act out the roles of two different kinds of shepherds. The first shepherd was to demonstrate how God would reject his people (the sheep) because they rejected him (11.1–14). The second shepherd was to demonstrate how God would give over his people to evil shepherds (11.15–17). (See Ezekiel 34 for a detailed portrayal of the evil shepherds of Israel.)

11.4 God told Zechariah to take a job as shepherd of a flock of sheep being fattened for butchering. The Messiah would shepherd God's people during a time of spiritual and political confusion. The flock represented the people feeding on their own greed and evil desires until they were ripe for God's judgment.

11.7 Zechariah took two shepherd's staffs and named them "Favor" and "Unity." He broke the first one ("Favor") to show that God's gracious covenant with his people was broken. He broke the second one ("Unity") to show that "the family ties between Judah and Israel" were broken (11.14).

11.8 The identity of the three evil shepherds is not known. But God knew they were unfit to shepherd his people, and so he removed them.

11.10, 11 Because Israel had rejected the good shepherd, God broke the staff called "Favor," thereby revoking his agreement to protect his people.

11.12 To pay this shepherd 30 shekels of silver was an insult—this was the price paid to an owner for a slave gored by an ox (Exodus 21.32). This is also the amount Judas received for betraying Jesus (Matthew 27.3–10). The priceless Messiah was sold for the price of a slave.

11.13 The word *treasury* could also be translated "potter." Potters were in the lowest social class. The "goodly price" (a sarcastic comment) was so little that it could be thrown to the potter. It is significant that the 30 pieces of silver paid to Judas for betraying Jesus were returned to the temple and used to buy a potter's field (Matthew 27.3–10).

lordly price at which I was valued by them. So I took the thirty shekels of silver and
threw them into the treasury[g] in the house of the LORD. 14 Then I broke my second
staff Unity, annulling the family ties between Judah and Israel.
15 Then the LORD said to me: Take once more the implements of a worthless
shepherd. 16 For I am now raising up in the land a shepherd who does not care for
the perishing, or seek the wandering,[h] or heal the maimed, or nourish the
healthy,[i] but devours the flesh of the fat ones, tearing off even their hoofs.

17 Oh, my worthless shepherd,
who deserts the flock!
May the sword strike his arm
and his right eye!
Let his arm be completely withered,
his right eye utterly blinded!

God will destroy his people's enemies

12

An Oracle.

The word of the LORD concerning Israel: Thus says the LORD, who stretched out
the heavens and founded the earth and formed the human spirit within: 2 See, I am
about to make Jerusalem a cup of reeling for all the surrounding peoples; it will be
against Judah also in the siege against Jerusalem. 3 On that day I will make Jerusalem a heavy stone for all the peoples; all who lift it shall grievously hurt themselves. And all the nations of the earth shall come together against it. 4 On that day,
says the LORD, I will strike every horse with panic, and its rider with madness. But
on the house of Judah I will keep a watchful eye, when I strike every horse of the
peoples with blindness. 5 Then the clans of Judah shall say to themselves, "The
inhabitants of Jerusalem have strength through the LORD of hosts, their God."
6 On that day I will make the clans of Judah like a blazing pot on a pile of wood,
like a flaming torch among sheaves; and they shall devour to the right and to the left
all the surrounding peoples, while Jerusalem shall again be inhabited in its place,
in Jerusalem.
7 And the LORD will give victory to the tents of Judah first, that the glory of the
house of David and the glory of the inhabitants of Jerusalem may not be exalted
over that of Judah. 8 On that day the LORD will shield the inhabitants of Jerusalem
so that the feeblest among them on that day shall be like David, and the house of
David shall be like God, like the angel of the LORD, at their head. 9 And on that day
I will seek to destroy all the nations that come against Jerusalem.

11.13 Mt 27.3-10,12 Acts 1.18,19
11.14 Zech 11.6
11.15 Jer 2.26,27 Ezek 13.3 Zech 11.17
11.16 Jer 23.2,22 Ezek 34.2-6
11.17 Zech 10.2 11.15
12.1 Gen 2.7 Ps 102.23,26 Isa 57.16 Jer 51.15
12.2 Isa 51.17,22,23 Jer 49.12
12.3 Dan 2.34,35 Mt 21.44
12.6 Isa 10.16-18 Obad 18
12.7 Isa 2.11-17 Amos 9.11 Zech 4.6; 11.11
12.8 Gen 22.15-17 Ex 14.19 Lev 26.8 Ps 82.6 Mic 7.8 Zech 9.14,15

[g] Syr: Heb *it to the potter* [h] Syr Compare Gk Vg: Heb *the youth* [i] Meaning of Heb uncertain

---

11.14 Because the people rejected the Messiah, God would reject them – symbolized by Zechariah breaking the staff called "Unity." Not long after Zechariah's time, the Jews began to divide into numerous factions – Pharisees, Sadducees, Essenes, Herodians, and Zealots. The discord among these groups was a key factor leading to the destruction of Jerusalem in A.D. 70.

11.15–17 Israel would not only reject the true shepherd; they would accept instead a worthless shepherd. This shepherd would serve his own concerns rather than the concerns of his flock and would destroy rather than defend them. Condemnation is his rightful fate because he trusted his arm (military might) and his eye (intellect). God would destroy both areas.

11.17 It is a great tragedy for God's people when their leaders fail to care for them adequately. God holds leaders particularly accountable for the condition of his people. The New Testament tells church leaders, "Not many of you should become teachers, . . . for you know that we who teach will be judged with greater strictness" (James 3.1). If God puts you in a position of leadership, remember that it is also a place of great responsibility.

12.1–14 This chapter pictures the final siege against the people of Jerusalem.

12.3, 4 This speaks of a great future battle against Jerusalem. Some say it is Armaggedon, the last great battle on earth. Those who go against God's people will not prevail forever. Evil, pain, and oppression will one day be abolished once and for all.

12.7 As water flows downhill, so a city's influence usually flows to its surrounding countryside. But this time, the countryside of Judah (the "tents") would have priority over Jerusalem so that the people of Jerusalem would not become proud. Don't think you have to witness first to the "important" people – professional athletes, movie stars, and top businessmen. Christ came to seek and save the lost, even the "down-and-out" lost. We must be careful to avoid spiritual pride or we, like Jerusalem, may be the last to know what God is doing.

Mourning for the one they pierced

12.10 Ps 22.16,17 Isa 32.15 Joel 2.28,29 Jn 19.34-37 Heb 12.2 Rev 1.7
12.11 Jer 6.26 Amos 8.10 Mt 24.30; 26.75

10 And I will pour out a spirit of compassion and supplication on the house of
David and the inhabitants of Jerusalem, so that, when they look on the one[j] whom
they have pierced, they shall mourn for him, as one mourns for an only child, and
weep bitterly over him, as one weeps over a firstborn. 11 On that day the mourning
in Jerusalem will be as great as the mourning for Hadad-rimmon in the plain of
Megiddo. 12 The land shall mourn, each family by itself; the family of the house of
David by itself, and their wives by themselves; the family of the house of Nathan
by itself, and their wives by themselves; 13 the family of the house of Levi by itself,
and their wives by themselves; the family of the Shimeites by itself, and their wives
by themselves; 14 and all the families that are left, each by itself, and their wives by
themselves.

13.1 Lev 15.2 Num 19.9-22

13 On that day a fountain shall be opened for the house of David and the inhabitants of Jerusalem, to cleanse them from sin and impurity.

Idolatry is removed

13.2 Ex 23.13 Deut 12.3 Jer 8.10-12
13.3 Deut 13.6-11 Jer 23.25
13.4 Isa 20.2 Jer 2.26; 6.15 Mic 3.6,7 Mt 3.4; 11.8,9
13.5 Amos 7.14

2 On that day, says the LORD of hosts, I will cut off the names of the idols from
the land, so that they shall be remembered no more; and also I will remove from the
land the prophets and the unclean spirit. 3 And if any prophets appear again, their
fathers and mothers who bore them will say to them, "You shall not live, for you
speak lies in the name of the LORD"; and their fathers and their mothers who bore
them shall pierce them through when they prophesy. 4 On that day the prophets will
be ashamed, every one, of their visions when they prophesy; they will not put on a
hairy mantle in order to deceive, 5 but each of them will say, "I am no prophet, I am
a tiller of the soil; for the land has been my possession[k] since my youth." 6 And if
anyone asks them, "What are these wounds on your chest?"[l] the answer will be
"The wounds I received in the house of my friends."

The sheep are scattered

13.7 Isa 9.6; 40.11 53.4,5,10 Hos 12.3-5
13.8 Zech 11.6-9

7 "Awake, O sword, against my shepherd,
against the man who is my associate,"
says the LORD of hosts.
Strike the shepherd, that the sheep may be scattered;
I will turn my hand against the little ones.
8 In the whole land, says the LORD,
two-thirds shall be cut off and perish,
and one-third shall be left alive.

[j] Heb *on me* [k] Cn: Heb *for humankind has caused me to possess* [l] Heb *wounds between your hands*

12.10 The Holy Spirit was poured out at pentecost, 50 days after Christ's resurrection (see Acts 2). Zechariah calls the Spirit "a spirit of compassion and supplication." It is this Spirit who convicts us of sin, reveals to us God's righteousness and judgment, and helps us as we pray. "Likewise the Spirit helps us in our weakness; for we do not know how to pray as we ought, but that very Spirit intercedes with sighs too deep for words" (Romans 8.26). Ask God to fill you with his Spirit.

12.10–14 Eventually *all* people will realize that Jesus, the man who was pierced and killed, is indeed the Messiah. There will be an awakening and a revival. The crucified Messiah will be clearly revealed (Philippians 2.10; Revelation 5.13).

12.11 Hadad-rimmon could refer to King Josiah who was killed in the valley of Megiddo. He was greatly mourned by his people (see 2 Chronicles 35.22–25).

13.1ff There will be a never-ending supply of God's mercy, forgiveness, and cleansing power. This picture of a fountain is similar to the never-ending stream flowing out of the temple (Ezekiel 47.1). The fountain is used in Scripture to symbolize God's forgiveness. In John 4, Jesus tells of his "living water" that satisfies completely. Are you spiritually thirsty? Do you need to experience God's forgiveness? Drink from the fountain – ask Jesus to forgive you and give you his salvation.

13.2–6 This chapter pictures the final days of the earth as we know it. For God's new era to begin, there must be a cleansing – all evil must be abolished. Therefore, idols will be "cut off," and false prophets will be ashamed of themselves and will no longer try to deceive God's people.

13.7 Just before his arrest, Jesus quoted from this verse, referring to himself and his disciples (Matthew 26.31, 32). He knew beforehand that his disciples would scatter when he was arrested. The Roman "sword" was the military power that put Christ to death.

13.9 A remnant is a small part of the whole. Throughout the history of Israel, whenever the whole nation seemed to turn against God, God said that a righteous remnant still trusted and followed him. These believers were refined like silver and gold through the fire of their difficult circumstances. Determine to be part of God's remnant, that small part of the whole that is obedient to him. Obey him no matter what the rest of the world does. This may mean trials and troubles at times; but as fire purifies gold and silver, you will be purified and made more like Christ.

9 And I will put this third into the fire,
refine them as one refines silver,
and test them as gold is tested.
They will call on my name,
and I will answer them.
I will say, "They are my people";
and they will say, "The LORD is our God."

The Lord will rule

14 See, a day is coming for the LORD, when the plunder taken from you will be
divided in your midst. 2 For I will gather all the nations against Jerusalem to
battle, and the city shall be taken and the houses looted and the women raped; half
the city shall go into exile, but the rest of the people shall not be cut off from the
city. 3 Then the LORD will go forth and fight against those nations as when he fights
on a day of battle. 4 On that day his feet shall stand on the Mount of Olives, which
lies before Jerusalem on the east; and the Mount of Olives shall be split in two from
east to west by a very wide valley; so that one half of the Mount shall withdraw
northward, and the other half southward. 5 And you shall flee by the valley of the
LORD's mountain,[m] for the valley between the mountains shall reach to Azal;[n] and
you shall flee as you fled from the earthquake in the days of King Uzziah of Judah.
Then the LORD my God will come, and all the holy ones with him.
6 On that day there shall not be[o] either cold or frost.[p] 7 And there shall be
continuous day (it is known to the LORD), not day and not night, for at evening time
there shall be light.
8 On that day living waters shall flow out from Jerusalem, half of them to the
eastern sea and half of them to the western sea; it shall continue in summer as in
winter.
9 And the LORD will become king over all the earth; on that day the LORD will
be one and his name one.
10 The whole land shall be turned into a plain from Geba to Rimmon south of
Jerusalem. But Jerusalem shall remain aloft on its site from the Gate of Benjamin
to the place of the former gate, to the Corner Gate, and from the Tower of Hananel
to the king's wine presses. 11 And it shall be inhabited, for never again shall it be
doomed to destruction; Jerusalem shall abide in security.
12 This shall be the plague with which the LORD will strike all the peoples that
wage war against Jerusalem: their flesh shall rot while they are still on their feet;
their eyes shall rot in their sockets, and their tongues shall rot in their mouths. 13 On
that day a great panic from the LORD shall fall on them, so that each will seize the
hand of a neighbor, and the hand of the one will be raised against the hand of the
other; 14 even Judah will fight at Jerusalem. And the wealth of all the surrounding
nations shall be collected—gold, silver, and garments in great abundance. 15 And
a plague like this plague shall fall on the horses, the mules, the camels, the donkeys, and whatever animals may be in those camps.

[m] Heb *my mountains* [n] Meaning of Heb uncertain [o] Cn: Heb *there shall not be light* [p] Compare Gk Syr Vg Tg: Meaning of Heb uncertain

13.9 Zech 12.10
14.1 Isa 2.12 Mal 4.1 Rev 16.14
14.4 Ezek 47.1-10 Zech 4.7
14.5 Isa 29.6
14.6 Isa 60.1-3 Acts 2.16,19
14.7 Amos 8.9 Rev 21.23; 22.5
14.8 Lk 24.47 Jn 4.10,14
14.9 Deut 6.4 Zech 9.9 14.16,17
14.10 Josh 15.32 21.17 2 Kgs 14.13 2 Chron 25.23 Neh 12.39 Jer 31.8
14.11 Jer 31.40 Rev 22.3
14.14 Zech 14.1

14.1 Many times in the Bible we are encouraged to look for the day of the Lord, which is coming soon. What if you knew exactly when this would happen? Would you live differently? Christ could return at any moment. Be ready for him by studying the Scriptures carefully and making sure you live as he intends—in obedience and spiritual readiness.

14.1ff The eventual triumph of the Messiah over all the earth and his reign over God's people are pictured in this chapter.

14.1–21 This chapter portrays important future events, but their chronological order is not clear. They show that God has various ways of dealing with his people. Now we are to watch (14.1) as the events unfold and God provides an escape for his people.

14.4 On the Mount of Olives, Jesus spoke with his disciples about the end times (Matthew 24). Near this same mount, an angel promised that Jesus would return in the same manner as he had left (Acts 1.11; see also Ezekiel 11.23).

14.5 Only God's people will escape God's punishment (Matthew 24.16–20). In this time of confusion, God will clearly know who his people are.

14.8 The eastern sea and the western sea refer to the Dead Sea and the Mediterranean Sea respectively.

14.10 Jerusalem is honored as the city of God and the focal point of all the world's worship. Jerusalem's elevation is a dramatic way of showing God's supremacy.

14.16 This festival of booths is the only feast still appropriate in

14.16 Lev 23.34-44 Isa 60.6-9 66.18-21

14.17 1 Kgs 17.1 Jer 14.3-6

14.20 Ex 28.36; 39.30 Lev 6.28 Ezek 46.20-24 Rev 20.6

14.21 Deut 12.7,12 Neh 8.10 Rom 14.6,7 1 Cor 10.31 1 Tim 4.3-5

16 Then all who survive of the nations that have come against Jerusalem shall
go up year after year to worship the King, the LORD of hosts, and to keep the festival of booths.[q] 17 If any of the families of the earth do not go up to Jerusalem to
worship the King, the LORD of hosts, there will be no rain upon them. 18 And if the
family of Egypt do not go up and present themselves, then on them shall[r] come the
plague that the LORD inflicts on the nations that do not go up to keep the festival of
booths.[q] 19 Such shall be the punishment of Egypt and the punishment of all the
nations that do not go up to keep the festival of booths.[q]

20 On that day there shall be inscribed on the bells of the horses, "Holy to the
LORD." And the cooking pots in the house of the LORD shall be as holy as[s] the
bowls in front of the altar; 21 and every cooking pot in Jerusalem and Judah shall be
sacred to the LORD of hosts, so that all who sacrifice may come and use them to boil
the flesh of the sacrifice. And there shall no longer be traders[t] in the house of the
LORD of hosts on that day.

[q] Or *tabernacles*; Heb *succoth* [r] Gk Syr: Heb *shall not* [s] Heb *shall be like* [t] Or *Canaanites*

Messiah's reign. The passover was fulfilled in Christ's death; the day of atonement, in acceptance of Christ's salvation; the festival of first fruits, in his resurrection; and pentecost, with the arrival of the Holy Spirit. But the festival of booths, a festival of thanksgiving, celebrates the harvest of human souls for the Lord. Jesus may have alluded to it in John 4.35.

14.20, 21 In the future, even such common objects as horses' bells and cooking pots will be holy. This vision of a restored, holy Jerusalem stands in contrast to its broken walls and unpleasant living conditions. One day God would fulfill the people's dreams for Jerusalem beyond what they could imagine. God still wants to do much more for us than we can imagine (Ephesians 3.20). When we walk with him, we discover this more deeply each day.

14.21 Zechariah was speaking to a people enduring hardships—they were being harassed by neighbors; they were discouraged over their small numbers and inadequate temple; and their worship was apathetic. But God said, "I am very jealous for Jerusalem" (1.14). He promised to restore their land, their city, and their temple. Like other prophets, Zechariah blended prophecies of the present, near future, and final days into one sweeping panorama. Through his message we learn that our hope is found in God and his Messiah, who are in complete control of the world.

MALACHI

Jerusalem is destroyed 586 B.C.	First exiles return to Jerusalem 537	Temple reconstruction begins 536	Haggai, Zechariah become prophets 520	Temple completed 516

VITAL STATISTICS

PURPOSE:
To confront the people with their sins and to restore their relationship with God

AUTHOR:
Malachi

TO WHOM WRITTEN:
The Jews in Jerusalem and God's people everywhere

DATE WRITTEN:
About 430 B.C.

SETTING:
Malachi, Haggai, and Zechariah were post-exilic prophets to Judah (the southern kingdom). Haggai and Zechariah rebuked the people for their failure to rebuild the temple. Malachi confronted them with their neglect of the temple and their false and profane worship.

KEY VERSES:
"See, the day is coming, burning like an oven; . . . But for you who revere my name the sun of righteousness shall rise, with healing in its wings. You shall go out leaping like calves from the stall" (4.1, 2).

KEY PEOPLE:
Malachi, the priests

KEY PLACES:
Jerusalem, the temple

SPECIAL FEATURES:
Malachi's literary style displays a continual use of questions asked by God and his people (for example, see 3.7, 8).

A VASE shatters, brushed by a careless elbow; a toy breaks, pushed beyond its limit by young fingers; and fabric rips, pulled by strong and angry hands. Spills and tears take time to clean up or repair and money to replace, but far more costly are shattered relationships. Unfaithfulness, untruths, hateful words, and forsaken vows tear and rip delicate personal bonds and inflict wounds not easily healed. Most tragic, however, are broken relationships with God.

God loves perfectly and completely. And his love is a love of action—giving, guiding, and guarding. He is altogether faithful, true to his promises to his chosen people. But consistently they spurn their loving God, breaking the covenant, following other gods, and living for themselves. So the relationship is shattered.

But the breach is not irreparable; all hope is not lost. God can heal and mend and reweave the fabric. Forgiveness is available. And that is grace.

This is the message of Malachi, God's prophet in Jerusalem. His words reminded the Jews, God's chosen nation, of their willful disobedience, beginning with the priests (1.1—2.9) and then including every person (2.10—3.15). They had dishonored God's name (1.6), offered false worship (1.7–14), led others into sin (2.7–9), broken God's laws (2.11–16), called evil "good" (2.17), kept God's tithes and offerings for themselves (3.8–12), and become arrogant and proud (3.13–15). The relationship was broken, and judgment and punishment would be theirs. In the midst of this wickedness, however, there were a faithful few—the remnant—who loved and honored God. God would shower his blessings upon these men and women (3.16–18).

This litany of unfaithfulness is terrible and surely worthy of punishment; but woven throughout this message is hope—the possibility of forgiveness. This is beautifully expressed in 4.2—"But for you who revere my name the sun of righteousness shall rise, with healing in its wings. You shall go out leaping like calves from the stall" (4.1, 2).

Malachi concludes with a promise of the coming of "the prophet Elijah" who will offer God's forgiveness to all people through repentance and faith (4.5, 6).

The book of Malachi forms a bridge between the Old Testament and the New Testament. As you read Malachi, see yourself as the recipient of this word of God to his people. Evaluate the depth of your commitment, the sincerity of your worship, and the direction of your life. Then allow God to restore your relationship with him through his love and forgiveness.

Esther becomes queen of Persia 479	Artaxerxes I becomes king of Persia 465	Ezra comes to Jerusalem 458	Nehemiah comes to Jerusalem 445	Malachi becomes a prophet 430

THE BLUEPRINT

1. The sinful priests (1.1—2.9)
2. The sinful people (2.10—3.15)
3. The faithful few (3.16—4.6)

Malachi rebuked the people and the priests for neglecting the worship of God and failing to live according to God's Word. If the priests were unfaithful, how could they lead the people? They had become stumbling blocks instead of spiritual leaders. If the people were divorcing their wives and marrying heathen women, how could they lead their children? Their relationship to God had become inconsequential. When our relationship with God becomes less important than it should be, we can strengthen it by setting aside our sinful habits, thinking often of our Lord, and giving God our best each day.

MEGATHEMES

THEME	EXPLANATION	IMPORTANCE
God's love	God loves his people even when they neglect or disobey him. He has great blessings to bestow on those who are faithful to him. His love never ends.	Because God loves us so much, he hates hypocrisy and careless living. This kind of living denies him the relationship he wants to have with us. What we give and how we live reflects the sincerity of our love for God.
The sin of the priests	Malachi singled out the priests for condemnation. They knew what God required, yet their sacrifices were unworthy, their service was insincere, and they were lazy, arrogant, and insensitive. They had a casual attitude toward the worship of God and observance of God's standards.	If religious leaders go wrong, how will the people be led? We are all leaders in some capacity. Don't neglect your responsibilities or be ruled by what is convenient. Neglect and insensitivity are acts of disobedience. God wants leaders who are faithful and sincere.
The sin of the people	The people had not learned the lesson of the exile nor listened to the prophets. Men were callously divorcing their faithful wives to marry younger, pagan women. This was against God's law because it disobeyed his commands about marriage and threatened the religious training of the children. But pride had hardened the hearts of the people.	God deserves our very best honor, respect, and faithfulness. But sin hardens our hearts to our true condition. Pride is unwarranted self-esteem; setting your own judgment above God's and looking down on others. Don't let pride keep you from giving God your devotion, money, marriage, and family.
The Lord's coming	God's love for his faithful people is demonstrated by the Messiah's coming. The Messiah will lead the people to the realization of all their fondest hopes. It will be a day of comfort and healing for a faithful few, and a day of judgment for those who reject him.	Christ's coming the first time refined and purified all those who believe in him. His return will expose and condemn those who are proud, insensitive, or unprepared. Yet God can heal and mend. Forgiveness is available to all who come to him for it.

1. The sinful priests

God's love for his people

1 An oracle. The word of the LORD to Israel by Malachi.[a] 1.1 Zech 9.1

2 I have loved you, says the LORD. But you say, "How have you loved us?" Is 1.2 Rom 9.13
not Esau Jacob's brother? says the LORD. Yet I have loved Jacob 3 but I have hated
Esau; I have made his hill country a desolation and his heritage a desert for jackals.
4 If Edom says, "We are shattered but we will rebuild the ruins," the LORD of hosts 1.4 Isa 9.9
says: They may build, but I will tear down, until they are called the wicked country, 1.5
the people with whom the LORD is angry forever. 5 Your own eyes shall see this, Ps 35.27 58.10,11
and you shall say, "Great is the LORD beyond the borders of Israel!" Mic 5.4

God rejects the imperfect sacrifice

6 A son honors his father, and servants their master. If then I am a father, where 1.6
is the honor due me? And if I am a master, where is the respect due me? says the Ex 20.12 Deut 1.31
LORD of hosts to you, O priests, who despise my name. You say, "How have we Prov 30.11,17 Isa 1.2
despised your name?" 7 By offering polluted food on my altar. And you say, "How Jer 31.9
have we polluted it?"[b] By thinking that the LORD's table may be despised. 8 When 1.7
you offer blind animals in sacrifice, is that not wrong? And when you offer those Lev 21.6,8 Deut 15.21
that are lame or sick, is that not wrong? Try presenting that to your governor; will 1.8
he be pleased with you or show you favor? says the LORD of hosts. 9 And now Lev 22.19-25 Mal 1.14
implore the favor of God, that he may be gracious to us. The fault is yours. Will he 1.9
show favor to any of you? says the LORD of hosts. 10 Oh, that someone among you Jer 27.18 Joel 1.13,14
would shut the temple[c] doors, so that you would not kindle fire on my altar in vain! 1.10
I have no pleasure in you, says the LORD of hosts, and I will not accept an offering Isa 1.13

[a] Or *by my messenger* [b] Gk: Heb *you* [c] Heb lacks *temple*

1.1 An oracle is a message from God. Malachi, the last Old Testament prophet, preached after Haggai, Zechariah, and Nehemiah—about 430 B.C. The temple had been rebuilt for almost a century, and the people were losing their enthusiasm for worship. Apathy and disillusionment had set in because the exciting messianic prophecies of Isaiah, Jeremiah, and Micah had not been fulfilled. Many of the sins that brought the downfall of Jerusalem in 586 B.C. were still being practiced in Judah. Malachi confronted the hypocrites with their sin by portraying a graphic dialogue between a righteous God and his hardened people.

1.2 God's first message through Malachi was "I have loved you." Although this message applied specifically to Israel, it is a message of hope for all people in all times. Unfortunately, many people are cynical about God's love, using political and economic progress as a measure of success. Because the government was corrupt and the economy poor, the Israelites assumed that God didn't love them. They were wrong. God loves all people because he made them; however, his *eternal* rewards go only to those who are faithful to him.

1.2–5 The phrase "I have hated Esau" does not refer to Esau's eternal destiny. It simply means that God chose Jacob, not his brother Esau, to be the one through whom the nation of Israel and the Messiah would come. God allowed Esau to father a nation, but this nation, Edom, later became one of Israel's chief enemies. The story is found in Genesis 25.19–26. Because God chose Jacob and his descendants as the nation through whom the world would be blessed, God cared for them in a special way. Ironically, they rejected God after he chose them.

1.6ff God charged the priests with failing to honor him (to the point of despising his name) and failing to be good spiritual examples to the people. The temple had been rebuilt in 516 B.C., and worship was being conducted there, but the priests did not worship God properly—they did not follow his laws for the sacrifices. Ezra, the priest, had sparked a great revival around 458 B.C. However, by Malachi's time, the nation's leaders had once again fallen away from God, and the people with them. The worship of God was no longer from heartfelt adoration; instead it was simply a job for the priests.

1.6–8 God's law required that only perfect animals be offered to God (see for example, Leviticus 1.3). But these priests were allowing the people to offer blind, lame, and sick animals to God. God accused them of dishonoring him by offering imperfect sacrifices, and he was greatly displeased. The New Testament says that our lives are living sacrifices to God (Romans 12.1). If we give God only our leftover time, money, and energy, we repeat the same sin as these worshipers who didn't want to bring anything valuable to God. What we give God reflects our true attitude toward him.

1.7, 8 From a practical standpoint, it made sense for the Jews to keep the best animals for themselves and to sacrifice the unwanted ones. But these sacrifices were to God, and God requires and deserves the very best. By giving our best to him, we honor him and demonstrate our trust in his provision. To give second best to God implies that he is second-rate in our lives. What are you giving to God?

1.7, 8 The people sacrificed to God wrongly through (1) expedience—being as cheap as possible, (2) neglect—not caring how they offered the sacrifice, and (3) outright disobedience—sacrificing their own way and not as God had commanded. Their methods of giving showed their real attitudes toward God. How about your attitude? Do expedience, neglect, or disobedience characterize your giving?

1.10 As intermediaries between God and the people, priests were responsible for reflecting God's attitudes and character. By accepting imperfect sacrifices, they led the people to believe that God accepted those sacrifices as well. But God says, "I have no pleasure in you." As Christians, we are often in the same position as these priests because we reflect God to our friends and family. What image of God's character and attitudes do they see in you? If you casually accept sin, you are like these priests in Malachi's day; and God will have "no pleasure in you."

1.11 Ps 50.1; 141.2 Isa 45.6; 60.6 Jer 10.6,7

1.13 Lev 6.4 22.19-23 Isa 43.22; 61.8

1.14 Ps 47.2; 68.35 Zeph 2.11 Zech 14.9 Mal 1.13

from your hands. 11 For from the rising of the sun to its setting my name is great
among the nations, and in every place incense is offered to my name, and a pure
offering; for my name is great among the nations, says the LORD of hosts. 12 But
you profane it when you say that the Lord's table is polluted, and the food for it[d]
may be despised. 13 "What a weariness this is," you say, and you sniff at me,[e] says
the LORD of hosts. You bring what has been taken by violence or is lame or sick,
and this you bring as your offering! Shall I accept that from your hand? says the
LORD. 14 Cursed be the cheat who has a male in the flock and vows to give it, and
yet sacrifices to the Lord what is blemished; for I am a great King, says the LORD
of hosts, and my name is reverenced among the nations.

God warns his priests

2.1 Lev 26.14-17 Deut 28.15-20

2.4 Num 3.45; 18.21

2.5 Num 25.7,8,13

2.6 Ps 37.30 119.142

2 And now, O priests, this command is for you. 2 If you will not listen, if you
will not lay it to heart to give glory to my name, says the LORD of hosts, then
I will send the curse on you and I will curse your blessings; indeed I have already
cursed them,[f] because you do not lay it to heart. 3 I will rebuke your offspring, and
spread dung on your faces, the dung of your offerings, and I will put you out of my
presence.[g]
4 Know, then, that I have sent this command to you, that my covenant with
Levi may hold, says the LORD of hosts. 5 My covenant with him was a covenant of
life and well-being, which I gave him; this called for reverence, and he revered me
and stood in awe of my name. 6 True instruction was in his mouth, and no wrong

[d] Compare Syr Tg: Heb *its fruit, its food* [e] Another reading is *at it* [f] Heb *it* [g] Cn Compare Gk Syr: Heb *and he shall bear you to it*

MALACHI served as a prophet to Judah about 430 B.C. He was the last of the Old Testament prophets.

Climate of the times	The city of Jerusalem and the temple had been rebuilt for almost a century, but the people had become complacent in their worship of God.
Main message	The people's relationship with God was broken because of their sin and they would soon be punished. But the few who repented would receive God's blessing, illustrated in his promise to send a Messiah.
Importance of message	Hypocrisy, neglecting God, and careless living have devastating consequences. Serving and worshiping God must be the primary focus of our lives, both now and in eternity.
Contemporary prophets	None

1.11 A theme that can be heard throughout the Old Testament is affirmed in this book—"my name is great among the nations." God had a chosen people, the Jews, through whom he planned to save and bless the entire world. Today God still wants to save and bless the world through all who believe in him—Jews and Gentiles. Christians are now his chosen people, and our pure offering to the Lord is our new life in Christ. Are you available to God to be used in making his name great to the nations? This mission begins in your home and in your neighborhood, but doesn't stop there. We must work and pray for God's worldwide mission.

1.13 "You sniff at me" means "you look with contempt at me."

1.13 Worship was a "weariness" to these priests. Too many think that following God is supposed to make life easy and more comfortable. They are looking for a God of convenience. The truth is that it often takes hard work to live by God's high standards. He may call us to face poverty or suffering. But if serving God is more important to us than anything else, what we must give up is of little importance compared to what we gain—eternal life with God.

2.1, 2 God warned the priests that if they did not "give glory" to his name, he would punish them. Like these priests, we too are called to give glory to God's name—to worship him. This means acknowledging God for who he is—the almighty Creator of the universe who alone is perfect and who reaches down to sinful mankind with perfect love. According to this definition, are you giving glory to God's name?

2.1, 2 The priests didn't take seriously ("lay it to heart") God's priority, even though he had reminded them through his Word many times. How do you find out what is most important to God? Begin by loving him with all your heart, soul, and might (Deuteronomy 6.5). This means listening to what he says in his Word and then setting your heart, mind, and will on doing what he says. When we love God, his Word is a shining light that guides our daily activities. The priests in Malachi's day had stopped loving God, and thus they did not know nor care what he wanted.

2.4–6 Levi "walked with [God] . . . and he turned many from iniquity" (2.6). He was the ancestor of the tribe of Levites, the tribe set apart for service to God (Numbers 1.47–54). The Levites became God's ministers, first in the tabernacle, then in the temple. In these verses, God was addressing the priests who were from this tribe, saying they should listen to the laws he gave their ancestor Levi, and follow his example.

was found on his lips. He walked with me in integrity and uprightness, and he
turned many from iniquity. 7 For the lips of a priest should guard knowledge, and
people should seek instruction from his mouth, for he is the messenger of the LORD
of hosts. 8 But you have turned aside from the way; you have caused many to stumble by your instruction; you have corrupted the covenant of Levi, says the LORD of
hosts, 9 and so I make you despised and abased before all the people, inasmuch as
you have not kept my ways but have shown partiality in your instruction.

2.7 Lev 10.11 Num 27.21 Deut 17.8-11 Ezra 7.10 Neh 8.2-8
2.8 Neh 13.29 Isa 9.16 Jer 18.15 Ezek 44.10

2. The sinful people

Treachery in Jerusalem

10 Have we not all one father? Has not one God created us? Why then are we
faithless to one another, profaning the covenant of our ancestors? 11 Judah has been
faithless, and abomination has been committed in Israel and in Jerusalem; for Judah
has profaned the sanctuary of the LORD, which he loves, and has married the
daughter of a foreign god. 12 May the LORD cut off from the tents of Jacob anyone
who does this—any to witness[h] or answer, or to bring an offering to the LORD of
hosts.

13 And this you do as well: You cover the LORD's altar with tears, with weeping
and groaning because he no longer regards the offering or accepts it with favor at
your hand. 14 You ask, "Why does he not?" Because the LORD was a witness between you and the wife of your youth, to whom you have been faithless, though she
is your companion and your wife by covenant. 15 Did not one God make her?[i] Both
flesh and spirit are his.[j] And what does the one God[k] desire? Godly offspring. So
look to yourselves, and do not let anyone be faithless to the wife of his youth. 16 For
I hate[l] divorce, says the LORD, the God of Israel, and covering one's garment with
violence, says the LORD of hosts. So take heed to yourselves and do not be faithless.

17 You have wearied the LORD with your words. Yet you say, "How have we
wearied him?" By saying, "All who do evil are good in the sight of the LORD, and
he delights in them." Or by asking, "Where is the God of justice?"

2.10 Ex 19.4-6 Josh 24.3 Isa 63.16 Jer 9.4
2.11 Lev 20.26 Ezra 9.1,2 Jer 3.7-9 Ezek 18.13
2.12 Lev 18.29 Num 15.30,31
2.13 Isa 1.11-15 Jer 11.14; 14.12
2.15 Ex 20.14 Lev 20.10 Hos 1.10 Mal 2.14
2.16 Deut 24.1 Mt 5.31; 19.6-8
2.17 Isa 5.19 43.22,24 Jer 17.15 Zeph 1.12

[h] Cn Compare Gk: Heb *arouse* [i] Or *Has he not made one?* [j] Cn: Heb *and a remnant of spirit was his* [k] Heb *he*
[l] Cn: Heb *he hates*

2.7, 8 Malachi was angry at the priests because, though they were to be God's "messengers," they did not know God's Word. And this lack of knowledge caused them to lead God's people astray. Their ignorance was willful and inexcusable. Pastors and leaders of God's people *must* know God's Word—what it says, what it means, and how it applies to daily life. How much time do you spend in God's Word?

2.9 The priests had allowed influential and favored people to break the law. They were so dependent on these people for support that they could not afford to confront them when they did wrong. In your church, are certain people allowed to do wrong without criticism? There should be no double standard based on wealth or position. Let your standards be those presented in God's Word. Playing favorites is contemptible in God's sight (see James 2.1–9).

2.10–16 The people were being unfaithful. Though not openly saying they rejected God, they were living as if he did not exist. Men were marrying heathen women who worshiped idols. Divorce was common, occurring for no reason other than a desire for change. People acted as if they could do anything without being punished. And they wondered why God refused to accept their offerings and bless them (2.13)! We cannot successfully separate our dealings with God from the rest of our lives. He must be Lord of all.

2.11, 12 After the temple had been rebuilt and the walls completed, the people were excited to see past prophecies coming true. But as time passed, the prophecies about the destruction of God's enemies and a coming Messiah were not fulfilled. The people became discouraged, and they grew complacent about obeying all of God's laws. This complacency gradually led to blatant sin, such as marriage to those who worshiped idols. Ezra and Nehemiah also confronted this problem years earlier (Ezra 9, 10; Nehemiah 13.23–31).

2.14 The people were complaining about their adverse circumstances when they had only themselves to blame. People often try to avoid guilt feelings by shifting the blame. But this doesn't solve the problem. When you face problems, look first at yourself. If you changed your attitude or behavior, would the problem be solved?

2.14, 15 Divorce in these times was practiced exclusively by men. They broke faith with their wives and ignored the bonding between a husband and a wife that God instills (the two become one person) and his purpose for them (raising children who love the Lord, "godly offspring"). Not only were men breaking faith with their wives, they were ignoring the bonding relationship and spiritual purpose of being united with God.

2.15, 16 "Take heed to yourselves and do not be faithless" means to have the same commitment to marriage that God has to his promises with his people. We need passion in the marriage relationship to keep the commitment and intimacy satisfying, but this passion should be focused exclusively on our spouse.

2.17–3.6 God was tired of the way the people twisted his truths. He would punish those who insisted that because God was silent, he approved of their actions or at least would never punish them. God would also punish those who professed a counterfeit faith while acting sinfully (see 3.5).

3.1 Isa 63.9
3.2 Isa 4.4 Ezek 22.14 Zech 13.9 Mt 3.10-12
3.3 Ps 51.19 Ezek 22.18-22 Dan 12.10
3.4 2 Chron 7.1-3 Ps 51.17-19 Jer 2.2 Zech 8.3
3.5 Ex 22.22-24 Deut 5.11 18.10; 27.19 Jer 5.2; 7.9 Ezek 22.9-11
3.7 Zech 1.3

The coming of the Lord

3 See, I am sending my messenger to prepare the way before me, and the Lord
whom you seek will suddenly come to his temple. The messenger of the covenant in whom you delight—indeed, he is coming, says the LORD of hosts. 2 But
who can endure the day of his coming, and who can stand when he appears?
For he is like a refiner's fire and like fullers' soap; 3 he will sit as a refiner and
purifier of silver, and he will purify the descendants of Levi and refine them like
gold and silver, until they present offerings to the LORD in righteousness.[m] 4 Then
the offering of Judah and Jerusalem will be pleasing to the LORD as in the days of
old and as in former years.
5 Then I will draw near to you for judgment; I will be swift to bear witness
against the sorcerers, against the adulterers, against those who swear falsely,
against those who oppress the hired workers in their wages, the widow and the
orphan, against those who thrust aside the alien, and do not fear me, says the LORD
of hosts.
6 For I the LORD do not change; therefore you, O children of Jacob, have not
perished. 7 Ever since the days of your ancestors you have turned aside from my
statutes and have not kept them. Return to me, and I will return to you, says the
LORD of hosts. But you say, "How shall we return?"

3.8 Lev 5.15,16 Neh 13.11
3.10 Ps 78.23-29 Ezek 34.26
3.11 Joel 1.4; 2.25
3.12 Deut 8.7-10 Ps 72.17 Isa 61.9; 62.4 Zech 8.23
3.14,15 Ps 73.8-13 Isa 58.3 Jer 7.10 Zeph 1.12

God's people rob him

8 Will anyone rob God? Yet you are robbing me! But you say, "How are we
robbing you?" In your tithes and offerings! 9 You are cursed with a curse, for you
are robbing me—the whole nation of you! 10 Bring the full tithe into the storehouse,
so that there may be food in my house, and thus put me to the test, says the LORD
of hosts; see if I will not open the windows of heaven for you and pour down for you
an overflowing blessing. 11 I will rebuke the locust[n] for you, so that it will not
destroy the produce of your soil; and your vine in the field shall not be barren, says
the LORD of hosts. 12 Then all nations will count you happy, for you will be a land
of delight, says the LORD of hosts.
13 You have spoken harsh words against me, says the LORD. Yet you say,
"How have we spoken against you?" 14 You have said, "It is vain to serve God.
What do we profit by keeping his command or by going about as mourners before

[m] Or *right offerings to the LORD* [n] Heb *devourer*

3.1 There are two messengers in this verse. The first is usually understood to be John the Baptist (Matthew 11.10; Luke 7.27). The second messenger is Jesus, the Messiah, for whom both Malachi and John the Baptist prepared the way.

3.2, 3 In the process of refining metals, the raw metal is heated with fire until it melts. The impurities separate from it and rise to the surface. They are skimmed off, leaving the pure metal. Without this heating and melting, there could be no purifying. As the impurities are skimmed off the top, the reflection of the worker appears in the smooth, pure surface. As we are purified by God, his reflection in our lives will become more and more clear to those around us. God says that leaders (here the Levites) should be especially open to his purification process in their lives. Fullers' soap was alkali used to whiten cloth. It is also used here as a symbol of the purifying process.

3.7 God's patience seems endless! Throughout history, his people have disobeyed, even scorned, his laws; but he has always been willing to accept them back. Here, however, they have the nerve to say they never disobeyed ("How shall we return?")! Many people have turned their backs on forgiveness and restoration because they have refused to admit their sin. Don't follow their example. God is ready to return to us if we are willing to return to him.

3.8–12 Malachi urged the people to stop holding back their tithes, to stop keeping from God what he deserved. The tithing system began during the time of Moses (Leviticus 27.30–34; Deuteronomy 14.22). The Levites received some of the tithe, because they could not possess land of their own (Numbers 18.20, 21). During Malachi's day, the people were not giving tithes, so the Levites went to work to earn a living, thereby neglecting their God-given responsibilities to care for the temple and worship. Everything we have is from God; so when we refuse to return to him a part of what he has given, we rob him. Do you selfishly want to keep 100 percent of what God gives, or are you willing to return at least 10 percent for advancing God's kingdom?

3.8–12 The people of Malachi's day ignored God's command to give a tithe of their income to his temple. They may have feared losing what they had worked so hard to get, but in this they misjudged God. "Give, and it will be given to you" he says (Luke 6.38). When we give, we must remember that the blessings God promises are not always material and may not be experienced completely here on earth, but we will certainly receive them in our future life with him.

3.10 The "storehouse" was a place in the temple for storing grain and other food given as tithes. The priests lived off these gifts.

3.13–15 These verses describe the people's arrogant attitude toward God. When we ask, "What good does it do to worship God?" we are really asking, "What good does it do for *me?*" Our focus is selfish. Our real question should be, "What good does it do for God?" We must worship God just because he is God and deserves to be worshiped.

the LORD of hosts? 15 Now we count the arrogant happy; evildoers not only prosper,
but when they put God to the test they escape."

3. The faithful few

The book of remembrance

16 Then those who revered the LORD spoke with one another. The LORD took **3.16**
note and listened, and a book of remembrance was written before him of those who Isa 4.2,3 Dan 12.1
revered the LORD and thought on his name. 17 They shall be mine, says the LORD of **3.17**
hosts, my special possession on the day when I act, and I will spare them as parents Neh 13.22 1 Pet 1.13-16
spare their children who serve them. 18 Then once more you shall see the difference **3.18**
between the righteous and the wicked, between one who serves God and one who Ps 58.10,11 Amos 5.15
does not serve him.

The great judgment day of the Lord

4 [o] See, the day is coming, burning like an oven, when all the arrogant and all **4.1**
evildoers will be stubble; the day that comes shall burn them up, says the LORD Isa 5.24 9.18,19
of hosts, so that it will leave them neither root nor branch. 2 But for you who revere Mt 3.12
my name the sun of righteousness shall rise, with healing in its wings. You shall go **4.2** 2 Sam 23.4
out leaping like calves from the stall. 3 And you shall tread down the wicked, for Isa 30.26; 35.6 Jer 30.17; 33.6
they will be ashes under the soles of your feet, on the day when I act, says the LORD **4.4**
of hosts. Ex 20.3 Deut 4.5,6
4 Remember the teaching of my servant Moses, the statutes and ordinances that **4.5**
I commanded him at Horeb for all Israel. Mt 11.14 Mk 9.11-13
5 Lo, I will send you the prophet Elijah before the great and terrible day of the **4.6**
LORD comes. 6 He will turn the hearts of parents to their children and the hearts of Isa 24.6 Mt 11.21
children to their parents, so that I will not come and strike the land with a curse. [p] Rev 19.15

[o] Ch 4.1-6 are Ch 3.19-24 in Heb [p] Or *a ban of utter destruction*

3.16 The "book of remembrance" may or may not be an actual book. The point is that God will remember those who remain faithful to him, and who love, fear, honor, and respect him.

4.2 At the day of Judgment, God's wrath toward the wicked will be like the blasting heat of an oven (4.1). But he will be like the healing warmth of the sun to those who love and obey him. John the Baptist prophesied that with the coming of Jesus, the dawn was about to break with light for those in sin's darkness (Luke 1.76–79). In Isaiah 60.20 and Revelation 21.23, 24 we learn that no light will be needed in God's holy city because God himself will be the light.

4.2ff These last verses of the Old Testament are filled with hope. Regardless of how life looks now, God controls the future and everything will be made right. We who have loved and served God look forward to a joyful celebration. This hope for the future is ours as soon as we trust God with our lives.

4.4 These laws, given to Moses on Mount Horeb (Sinai), are the foundation of the nation's civil, moral, and ceremonial life (Exodus 20; Deuteronomy 4.5, 6). We still must obey these moral laws for they apply to all generations.

4.5, 6 Elijah was one of the greatest prophets who ever lived (his story is recorded in 1 Kings 17 – 2 Kings 2). With Malachi's death, the voice of God's prophets would be silent for 400 years. Then a prophet would come, like Elijah, to herald Christ's coming (Matthew 17.10–13; Luke 1.17). This prophet was John the Baptist. He prepared people's hearts for Jesus by urging people to repent of their sins. This would bring unity and peace, but also judgment on those who refused to turn from their sins.

4.6 Malachi gives us practical guidelines about commitment to God. God deserves the best we have to offer (1.7–10). We must be willing to change our wrong ways of living (2.1, 2). We should make family a lifelong priority (2.13–16). We should welcome God's refining process in our lives (3.3). We should tithe our income (3.8–12). There is no room for pride (3.13–15).

Malachi closes his messages by pointing to that great final day of Judgment. For those who are committed to God, it will be a day of joy, because it will usher in eternity in God's presence. Those who have ignored God will be "stubble," to be burned up (4.1). To help the people prepare for that day, God would send a prophet like Elijah (John the Baptist) who would prepare the way for Jesus, the Messiah. The New Testament begins with this prophet calling the people to turn from their sins and turn toward God. Such a commitment to God demands great sacrifice on our part, but we can be sure it will be worth it all in the end.

THE NEW COVENANT

commonly called

THE NEW TESTAMENT

of

OUR LORD AND SAVIOR

JESUS CHRIST

The Gospel according to MATTHEW

Herod the Great begins to rule 37 B.C.	Jesus is born 6/5 B.C.	Escape to Egypt 5/4 B.C.	Herod the Great dies 4 B.C.	Return to Nazareth 4/3 B.C.	Judea becomes a Roman province A.D. 6	Je vis te as 6/

VITAL STATISTICS

PURPOSE:
To prove that Jesus is the Messiah, the eternal King

AUTHOR:
Matthew (Levi)

TO WHOM WRITTEN:
Matthew wrote especially to the Jews

DATE WRITTEN:
Probably between A.D. 60–65

SETTING:
Matthew was a Jewish tax collector who became one of Jesus' disciples. This Gospel forms the connecting link between the Old and New Testaments because of its emphasis on the fulfillment of prophecy.

KEY VERSE:
"Do not think that I have come to abolish the law or the prophets; I have come not to abolish but to fulfill" (5.17).

KEY PEOPLE:
Jesus, Mary, Joseph, John the Baptist, the disciples, the religious leaders, Caiaphas, Pilate, Mary Magdalene

KEY PLACES:
Bethlehem, Jerusalem, Capernaum, Galilee, Judea

SPECIAL FEATURES:
Matthew is filled with messianic language ("Son of David" is used throughout) and Old Testament references (53 quotes and 76 other references). This gospel is not written as a chronological account; its purpose is to present the clear evidence that Jesus is the Messiah, the Savior.

MOTORCADES herald the approach of heads of state. Pomp and ceremony are symbols of their position and importance. Whether they are leaders by birth or election, we honor and respect them.

The Jews waited for a leader who had been promised centuries before by prophets. They believed that this leader—the Messiah (''anointed one'')—would rescue them from their Roman oppressors and establish a new kingdom. As their king, he would rule the world with justice. However, many Jews overlooked prophecies which also spoke of this king as a suffering servant who would be rejected and killed. It is no wonder, then, that few recognized Jesus as the Messiah. How could this humble teacher from Nazareth be their king? But Jesus was and is the King of all the earth!

Matthew (Levi) was one of Jesus' 12 disciples. Once he was a despised tax collector, but his life was changed by this man from Galilee. Matthew wrote this Gospel to his fellow Jews to prove that Jesus is the Messiah and to explain God's kingdom.

Matthew begins his account by giving Jesus' genealogy. He then tells of Jesus' birth and early years, including the family's escape to Egypt from the murderous Herod and their return to Nazareth. Following his baptism by John (3.17) and his defeat of Satan in the desert, Jesus begins his public ministry by calling his first disciples and giving the ''Sermon on the Mount'' (chapters 5—7). Matthew shows Christ's authority by reporting his miracles of healing the sick and the demon-possessed, and even raising the dead.

Despite opposition from the Pharisees and others in the religious establishment (chapters 12—15), Jesus continued to teach concerning the kingdom of heaven (chapters 16—20). During this time, Jesus spoke with his disciples about his imminent death and resurrection (16.21), and revealed his true identity to Peter, James, and John (17.1–5). Near the end of his ministry, Jesus entered Jerusalem in a triumphant procession (21.1–11). But soon opposition mounted and Jesus realized that his death was near. So he taught his disciples about the future—what they could expect before his return (chapter 24) and how to live until then (chapter 25).

In Matthew's finale (chapters 26—28), he focuses on Jesus' final days on earth—the last supper, his prayer in Gethsemane, the betrayal by Judas, the flight of the disciples, Peter's denial, the trials before Caiaphas and Pilate, Jesus' final words on the cross, and his burial in a borrowed tomb. But the story does not end there, for the Messiah rose from the dead—conquering death and then telling his followers to continue his work by making disciples in all nations.

As you read this Gospel, listen to Matthew's clear message: Jesus is the Christ, the King of kings and Lord of lords. Celebrate his victory over evil and death, and make Jesus the Lord of your life.

Tiberius Caesar becomes emperor 14	Pontius Pilate appointed governor 26	Jesus begins his ministry 26/27	Jesus chooses twelve disciples 28	Jesus feeds 5,000 29	Jesus is crucified, rises again, and ascends 30

THE BLUEPRINT

A. BIRTH AND PREPARATION OF JESUS, THE KING (1.1—4.11)

The people of Israel were waiting for the Messiah, their king. Matthew begins his book by showing how Jesus Christ was a descendant of David. But Matthew goes on to show that God did not send Jesus to be an earthly king, but a heavenly king. His kingdom would be much greater than David's, because it would never end. Even at his birth, many recognized Jesus as a king. Herod, the ruler, as well as Satan, was afraid of Jesus' kingship and tried to stop him, but others worshiped him and brought royal gifts. We must be willing to recognize Jesus for who he really is and worship him as king of our lives.

B. MESSAGE AND MINISTRY OF JESUS, THE KING (4.12—25.46)

1. Jesus begins his ministry
2. Jesus gives the Sermon on the Mount
3. Jesus performs many miracles
4. Jesus teaches about the kingdom
5. Jesus encounters differing reactions to his ministry
6. Jesus faces conflict with the religious leaders
7. Jesus teaches on the Mount of Olives

Jesus gave the Sermon on the Mount, directions for living in his kingdom. He also told many parables about the difference between his kingdom and the kingdoms of earth. Forgiveness, peace, and putting others first are some of the characteristics that make one great in the future kingdom of God. And to be great in God's kingdom, we must live by God's standards right now. Jesus came to show us how to live as faithful subjects in his kingdom.

C. DEATH AND RESURRECTION OF JESUS, THE KING (26.1—28.20)

Jesus was formally presented to the nation of Israel, but rejected. How strange for the king to be accused, arrested, and crucified. But Jesus demonstrated his power even over death through his resurrection, and gained access for us into his Kingdom. With all this evidence that Jesus is God's Son, we, too, should accept him as our Lord.

MEGATHEMES

THEME	EXPLANATION	IMPORTANCE
Jesus Christ, the King	Jesus is revealed as the King of kings. His miraculous birth, his life and teaching, his miracles, and his triumph over death show his true identity.	Jesus cannot be equated with any person or power. He is the supreme ruler of time and eternity, heaven and earth, men and angels. We should give him his rightful place as king of our lives.
The Messiah	Jesus was the Messiah, the one for whom the Jews had waited to deliver them from Roman oppression. Yet tragically, they didn't recognize him when he came because his kingship was not what they expected. The true purpose of God's anointed deliverer was to die for all people to free them from sin's oppression.	Because Jesus was sent by God, we can trust him with our lives. It is worth everything we have to recognize him and give ourselves to him because he came to be our Messiah, our Savior.
Kingdom of God	Jesus came to earth to begin his kingdom. His full kingdom will be realized at his return and will be made up of anyone who has faithfully followed him.	The way to enter God's kingdom is by faith—believing in Christ to save us from sin and change our lives. We must do the work of his kingdom now to be prepared for his return.
Teachings	Jesus taught the people through sermons, illustrations, and parables. Through them, he showed the true ingredients of faith and how to guard against a fruitless and hypocritical life.	Jesus' teachings show us how to prepare for life in his kingdom by living properly right now. His life was an example of his teachings, as our lives should be.

Resurrection	When Jesus rose from the dead, he rose in power as the true king. In his victory over death, he established his credentials as king and his power and authority over evil.	The resurrection shows Jesus' all-powerful life for us—not even death could stop his plan of offering eternal life. Those who believe in Jesus can hope for a resurrection like his. Our role is to tell his story to all the earth so that everyone may share in his victory.

KEY PLACES IN MATTHEW

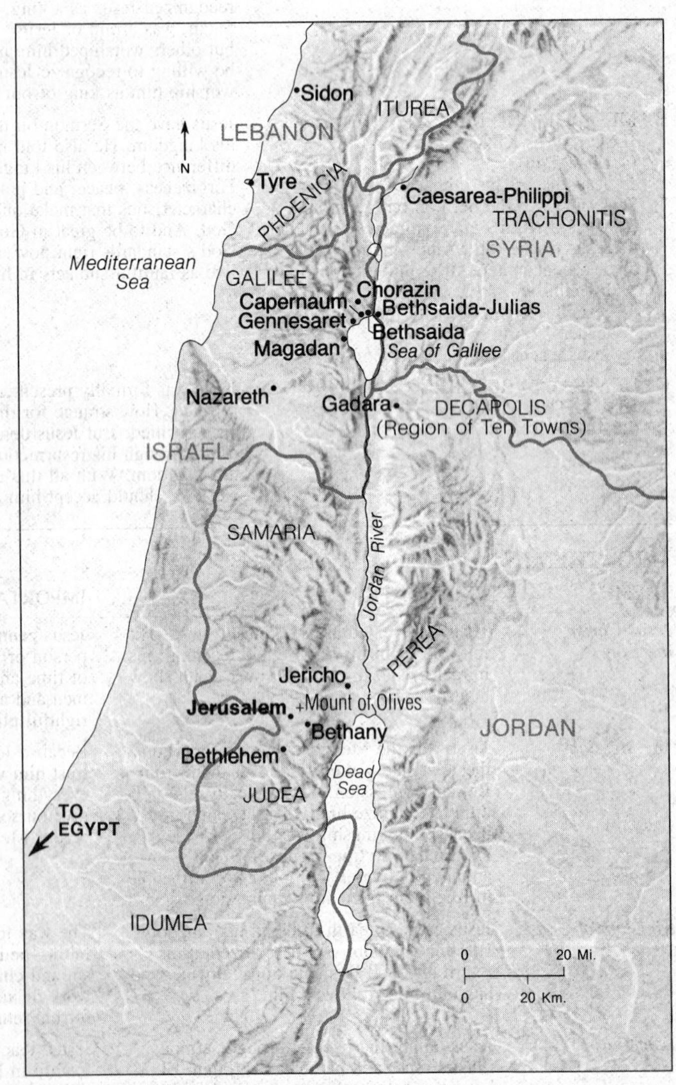

Jesus' earthly story begins in the town of Bethlehem in the Roman province of Judea (2.1). A threat to kill the infant king led Joseph to take his family to Egypt (2.14). When they returned, God led them to settle in Nazareth in Galilee (2.22, 23). At about age 30, Jesus was baptized in the Jordan River and was tempted by Satan in the Judean wilderness (3.13; 4.1). He set up his base of operations in Capernaum (4.12, 13) and from there ministered throughout Israel, telling parables, teaching about the kingdom, and healing the sick. He traveled to the country of the Gadarenes and healed two demon-possessed men (8.28ff); fed over 5,000 people with five small loaves and two fish on the shores of Galilee near Bethsaida-Julias (14.15ff); healed the sick in Gennesaret (14.34ff); ministered to the Gentiles in Tyre and Sidon (15.21ff); visited Caesarea-Philippi where Peter declared him as the Messiah (16.13ff); and taught in Perea, across the Jordan (19.1). As he set out on his last visit to Jerusalem, he told the disciples what would happen to him there (20.17ff). He spent some time in Jericho (20.29) and then stayed in Bethany at night as he went back and forth into Jerusalem during his last week (21.17ff). In Jerusalem he would be crucified, but he would rise again.

A. BIRTH AND PREPARATION OF JESUS, THE KING (1.1–4.11)

Matthew opens his Gospel with a genealogy to prove that Jesus is the descendant of both King David and Abraham, just as the Old Testament had predicted. Jesus' birth didn't go unnoticed, for both shepherds and wise kings came to worship him. The Jewish people were waiting for the Messiah to appear. Finally, he was born, but the Jews didn't recognize him because they were looking for a different kind of king.

The ancestors of Jesus
(3/Luke 3.23–38)

1 An account of the genealogy[a] of Jesus the Messiah,[b] the son of David, the son
of Abraham.
2 Abraham was the father of Isaac, and Isaac the father of Jacob, and Jacob the
father of Judah and his brothers, 3 and Judah the father of Perez and Zerah by Tamar, and Perez the father of Hezron, and Hezron the father of Aram, 4 and Aram the
father of Aminadab, and Aminadab the father of Nahshon, and Nahshon the father
of Salmon, 5 and Salmon the father of Boaz by Rahab, and Boaz the father of Obed
by Ruth, and Obed the father of Jesse, 6 and Jesse the father of King David.
And David was the father of Solomon by the wife of Uriah, 7 and Solomon the
father of Rehoboam, and Rehoboam the father of Abijah, and Abijah the father of
Asaph,[c] 8 and Asaph[c] the father of Jehoshaphat, and Jehoshaphat the father of
Joram, and Joram the father of Uzziah, 9 and Uzziah the father of Jotham, and Jotham the father of Ahaz, and Ahaz the father of Hezekiah, 10 and Hezekiah the
father of Manasseh, and Manasseh the father of Amos,[d] and Amos[d] the father of
Josiah, 11 and Josiah the father of Jechoniah and his brothers, at the time of the
deportation to Babylon.
12 And after the deportation to Babylon: Jechoniah was the father of Salathiel,
and Salathiel the father of Zerubbabel, 13 and Zerubbabel the father of Abiud, and
Abiud the father of Eliakim, and Eliakim the father of Azor, 14 and Azor the father
of Zadok, and Zadok the father of Achim, and Achim the father of Eliud, 15 and
Eliud the father of Eleazar, and Eleazar the father of Matthan, and Matthan the
father of Jacob, 16 and Jacob the father of Joseph the husband of Mary, of whom
Jesus was born, who is called the Messiah.[e]
17 So all the generations from Abraham to David are fourteen generations; and
from David to the deportation to Babylon, fourteen generations; and from the deportation to Babylon to the Messiah,[e] fourteen generations.

1.1 Gen 22.18; Lk 3.23-28; Acts 2.30; Rom 1.3
1.3 Ruth 4.18; 1 Chron 2.5,9
1.4 Num 1.2-15
1.5 Josh 6.25; Heb 11.31
1.6 1 Sam 16.1
1.7 1 Chron 3.10-14
1.10 2 Kgs 20.21
1.11 Jer 27.20; 52.11; Dan 1.1
1.12 Ezra 3.2; Hag 1.1
1.16 Gen 3.15; Isa 9.6; 53.2; Lk 2.11; Jn 3.14; 4.25; Rom 9.5; 1 Tim 3.16
1.17 Jer 27.20

a Or *birth* b Or *Jesus Christ* c Other ancient authorities read *Asa* d Other ancient authorities read *Amon* e Or *the Christ*

1.1 This genealogy was one of the most interesting ways Matthew could begin a book for a Jewish audience. Because a person's family line proved his or her standing as one of God's chosen people, Matthew begins by showing that Jesus was a descendant of Abraham, the father of all Jews, and a direct descendant of David, fulfilling Old Testament prophecies about the Messiah's line. The facts of this ancestry were carefully preserved. This is the first of many proofs recorded by Matthew to show that Jesus is the true Messiah.

1.1ff More than 400 years had passed since the last Old Testament prophecies, and faithful Jews all over the world were still awaiting the Messiah (Luke 3.15). Matthew wrote this book to Jews to present Jesus as King and Messiah, the promised descendant of David who would reign forever (Isaiah 11.1–5). The Gospel of Matthew links the Old and New Testaments and contains many references showing how Jesus fulfilled Old Testament prophecy.

1.1ff Jesus entered history when the land of Israel was controlled by Rome and considered an insignificant outpost of the vast and mighty Roman Empire. The presence of Roman soldiers in Israel gave the Jews military peace, but at the price of oppression, slavery, injustice, and immorality. Into this kind of world came the promised Messiah.

1.1–17 In the first 17 verses we meet 46 people spanning 2,000 years. All were ancestors of Jesus, but they varied considerably in personality, spirituality, and experience. Some were heroes of faith—like Abraham, Isaac, Ruth, and David. Some had shady reputations—like Rahab and Tamar. Many were very ordinary—like Hezron, Aram, Nahshon, and Achim. And others were evil—like Manasseh and Abijah. God's work in history is not limited by human failures or sins, and he works through ordinary people. Just as God used all kinds of people to bring his Son into the world, he uses all kinds today to accomplish his will. And God wants to use you.

1.11 The deportation (exile or captivity) occurred in 586 B.C. when Nebuchadnezzar, king of Babylonia, conquered Judah, destroyed Jerusalem, and took thousands of captives to Babylonia.

1.16 Because Mary was a virgin when she became pregnant, Matthew lists Joseph only as the husband of Mary, not the father of Jesus. Matthew's genealogy gives Jesus' legal (or royal) lineage through Joseph. Mary's ancestral line is recorded in Luke 3.23–38. Both Mary and Joseph were direct descendants of David.

Matthew traced the genealogy back to Abraham, while Luke traced it back to Adam. Matthew wrote to the Jews, so Jesus was shown as a descendant of their father, Abraham. Luke wrote to the Gentiles and emphasized Jesus as the Savior of all people.

1.17 Matthew breaks Israel's history into three sets of 14 generations, but there were probably more than those listed here. Genealogies often compressed history, meaning that not every generation of ancestors was specifically listed. Thus the phrase *the father of* can also be translated "was the ancestor of."

An angel appears to Joseph
(8)

18 Now the birth of Jesus the Messiah[f] took place in this way. When his
mother Mary had been engaged to Joseph, but before they lived together, she was
found to be with child from the Holy Spirit. 19 Her husband Joseph, being a righteous man and unwilling to expose her to public disgrace, planned to dismiss her
quietly. 20 But just when he had resolved to do this, an angel of the Lord appeared
to him in a dream and said, "Joseph, son of David, do not be afraid to take Mary as
your wife, for the child conceived in her is from the Holy Spirit. 21 She will bear a
son, and you are to name him Jesus, for he will save his people from their sins."
22 All this took place to fulfill what had been spoken by the Lord through the
prophet:
23 "Look, the virgin shall conceive and bear a son,
and they shall name him Emmanuel,"
which means, "God is with us." 24 When Joseph awoke from sleep, he did as the
angel of the Lord commanded him; he took her as his wife, 25 but had no marital
relations with her until she had borne a son;[g] and he named him Jesus.

1.18 Lk 1.27,35 Gal 4.4 Heb 10.5
1.19 Deut 24.1
1.20 Lk 1.35
1.21 Dan 9.24 Lk 1.31; 2.11,21 Jn 1.29 Acts 5.31; 13.23 Heb 7.25 Rev 1.5
1.23 Isa 7.14; 9.6 Jn 1.14 1 Tim 3.16

[f] Or *Jesus Christ* [g] Other ancient authorities read *her firstborn son*

1.18 There were three steps in a Jewish marriage. First, the two families agreed to the union. Second, a public announcement was made. At this point, the couple was engaged. This was similar to engagement today except that their relationship could be broken only through death or divorce (even though sexual relations were not yet permitted). Third, the couple was married and began living together. Because Mary and Joseph were engaged, Mary's apparent unfaithfulness carried a severe social stigma. According to Jewish civil law, Joseph had a right to divorce her, and the Jewish authorities could have her stoned to death (Deuteronomy 22.23, 24).

1.18 Why is the virgin birth important to the Christian faith? Jesus Christ, God's Son, had to be free from the sinful nature passed on to all other human beings by Adam. Because he was born of a woman, he was a human being; but because he was the Son of God, he was born without any trace of human sin. He was both fully human and fully divine.

Because Jesus lived as a man, we know that he fully understands our experiences and struggles (Hebrews 4.15, 16). Because he is God, he has the power and authority to deliver us from sin (Colossians 2.13–15). We can tell him all our thoughts, feelings, and needs. He has been where we are now, and he has the ability to help.

1.18–25 Joseph was faced with a difficult choice after discovering that Mary was pregnant. Although he knew that taking Mary as his wife could be humiliating, he chose to obey the angel's command to marry her. His action revealed four admirable qualities: (1) stern principle (1.19), (2) discretion and sensitivity (1.19), (3) responsiveness to God (1.24), and (4) self-discipline (1.25).

1.19 Perhaps Joseph thought he had only two options: divorce Mary quietly ("dismiss her") or have her stoned. But God had a third option – marry her (1.20–23). In view of the circumstances, this had not occurred to Joseph. But God often shows us that there are more options available than we think. Although Joseph seemed to be doing right by breaking the engagement, only God's guidance helped him make the best decision. When our decisions affect the lives of others, we must always seek God's wisdom.

1.20 The conception and birth of Jesus Christ are supernatural events beyond human logic or reasoning. Because of this, God sent angels to help certain people understand the significance of what was happening (see 2.13, 19; Luke 1.11, 26; 2.9).

1.20–23 The angel declared to Joseph that Mary's child was conceived by the Holy Spirit and that it would be a son. This reveals an important truth about Jesus – he is both God and human. God took on the limitations of humanity so he could live and die for the salvation of all who would believe in him.

Angels are spiritual beings created by God who help carry out his work on earth. They bring God's messages to people (Luke 1.26), protect God's people (Daniel 6.22), offer encouragement (Genesis 16.7ff), give guidance (Exodus 14.19), bring punishment (2 Samuel 24.16), patrol the earth (Zechariah 1.9–14), and fight the forces of evil (2 Kings 6.16–18; Revelation 20.1, 2). There are both good and bad angels (Revelation 12.7), but because bad angels are allied with the devil or Satan, they have considerably less power and authority. Eventually the main role of angels will be to offer continuous praise to God (Revelation 19.1–3).

1.21 *Jesus* means "Savior." Jesus came to earth to save us because we can't save ourselves from sin and its consequences. No matter how good we are, we can't eliminate the sinful nature present in all of us. Only Jesus can do that. Jesus didn't come to help people save themselves; he came to be their Savior from the power and penalty of sin. Thank Christ for his death on the cross for your sin, and then ask him to take control of your life. Your new life begins from that moment.

1.23 Jesus was to be called *Emmanuel* ("God with us"), as predicted by Isaiah the prophet (Isaiah 7.14). Jesus was God in the flesh; thus God was literally among us. Through the Holy Spirit, Christ is present today in the life of every believer. Perhaps not even Isaiah understood how far-reaching the meaning of "Emmanuel" would be.

JOSEPH

The strength of what we believe is measured by how much we are willing to suffer for those beliefs. Joseph was a man with strong beliefs. He was prepared to do what was right despite the pain he knew it would cause. But Joseph had another trait—he not only tried to do what was right, he tried to do it in the right way.

When Mary told Joseph about her pregnancy, Joseph knew the child was not his. His respect for Mary's character and the story she told him, as well as her attitude toward the expected child, must have made it hard to think his bride had done something wrong. Still, someone else was the child's father—and it was difficult to accept that the "someone else" was God.

Joseph decided he had to break the engagement, but he was determined to do it in a way that would not cause public shame to Mary. He intended to act with justice and love.

At this point, God sent a messenger to Joseph to confirm Mary's story and open another way of obedience for Joseph—to take Mary as his wife. Joseph obeyed God, married Mary, and honored her virginity until the baby was born.

We do not know how long Joseph lived his role as Jesus' earthly father—he is last mentioned when Jesus was 12 years old. But Joseph trained his son in the trade of carpentry, made sure he had good spiritual training in Nazareth, and took the whole family on the yearly trip to Jerusalem for the Passover, which Jesus continued to observe during his adult years.

Joseph knew Jesus was someone special from the moment he heard the angel's words. His strong belief in that fact, and his willingness to follow God's leading, enabled him to be Jesus' chosen earthly father.

Strengths and accomplishments:
- A man of integrity
- A descendant of King David
- Jesus' legal and earthly father
- A person sensitive to God's guidance and willing to do God's will no matter what the consequence

Lessons from his life:
- God honors integrity
- Social position is of little importance when God chooses to use us
- Being obedient to the guidance we have from God leads to more guidance from him
- Feelings are not accurate measures of the rightness or wrongness of an action

Vital statistics:
- Where: Nazareth, Bethlehem
- Occupation: Carpenter
- Relatives: Wife: Mary. Children: Jesus, James, Joses, Judas, Simon, and daughters
- Contemporaries: Herod the Great, John the Baptist, Simeon, Anna

Key verses:

"Her husband Joseph, being a righteous man and unwilling to expose her to public disgrace, planned to dismiss her quietly. But just when he had resolved to do this, an angel of the Lord appeared to him in a dream and said, 'Joseph, son of David, do not be afraid to take Mary as your wife, for the child conceived in her is from the Holy Spirit' " (Matthew 1.19, 20).

"Now after they had left, an angel of the Lord appeared to Joseph in a dream and said, 'Get up, take the child and his mother, and flee to Egypt, and remain there until I tell you; for Herod is about to search for the child, to destroy him.' Then Joseph got up, took the child and his mother by night, and went to Egypt, and remained there until the death of Herod" (Matthew 2.13–15).

"When Herod died, an angel of the Lord suddenly appeared in a dream to Joseph in Egypt and said, 'Get up, take the child and his mother, and go to the land of Israel, for those who were seeking the child's life are dead.' Then Joseph got up, took the child and his mother, and went to the land of Israel. But when he heard that Archelaus was ruling over Judea in place of his father Herod, he was afraid to go there. And after being warned in a dream, he went away to the district of Galilee. There he made his home in a town called Nazareth, so that what had been spoken through the prophets might be fulfilled, 'He will be called a Nazorean' " (Matthew 2.19–23).

Joseph's story is told in Matthew 1.16—2.23; Luke 1.26—2.52.

1.24 Joseph changed his plans quickly after learning that Mary had not been unfaithful to him (1.19). He obeyed God and proceeded with the marriage plans. Although others may have disapproved of his decision, Joseph went ahead with what he knew was right. Sometimes we avoid doing right because of what others might think. Like Joseph, we must choose to obey God rather than seek the approval of others.

Visitors arrive from eastern lands
(12)

2 In the time of King Herod, after Jesus was born in Bethlehem of Judea, wise men[h] from the East came to Jerusalem, 2 asking, "Where is the child who has 2.1 1 Kgs 4.30 Lk 2.4
been born king of the Jews? For we observed his star at its rising,[i] and have come 2.2 Jer 23.5; 30.9
to pay him homage." 3 When King Herod heard this, he was frightened, and all
Jerusalem with him; 4 and calling together all the chief priests and scribes of the 2.4 Ps 2.1 Mal 2.7
people, he inquired of them where the Messiah[j] was to be born. 5 They told him,
"In Bethlehem of Judea; for so it has been written by the prophet: 2.5 Jn 7.42 Rev 2.27

6 'And you, Bethlehem, in the land of Judah,
are by no means least among the rulers of Judah; 2.6 Mic 5.2
for from you shall come a ruler

[h] Or *astrologers*; Gk *magi* [i] Or *in the East* [j] Or *the Christ*

2.1 Bethlehem is a small town five miles south of Jerusalem. It sits on a high ridge over 2,000 feet above sea level. It is mentioned in more detail in the Gospel of Luke. Luke also explains why Joseph and Mary were in Bethlehem when Jesus was born, rather than in Nazareth, their hometown.

2.1 The land of Israel was divided into four political districts and several lesser territories. Judea was to the south, Samaria in the middle, Galilee to the north, and Idumea to the southeast. Bethlehem of Judea (Judah) had been prophesied as the Messiah's birthplace (Micah 5.2). Jerusalem was also in Judea and was the seat of government for Herod the Great, king over all four political districts. After Herod's death, the districts were divided among three separate rulers (see the note on 2.19–22). Although he was a ruthless, evil man who murdered many in his own family, Herod the Great supervised the renovation of the temple, making it much larger and more beautiful. This made him popular with many Jews. Jesus would visit Jerusalem many times because the great Jewish festivals were held there.

2.1, 2 Not much is known about these wise men. We don't know where they came from or how many there were. Tradition says they were men of high position from Parthia, near the site of ancient Babylon. How did they know the star represented the Messiah? (1) They could have been Jews who remained in Babylon after the exile and knew the Old Testament predictions of the Messiah's coming. (2) They may have been Eastern astrologers who studied ancient manuscripts from around the world. Because of the Jewish exile centuries earlier, they would have had copies of the Old Testament in their land. (3) They may have had a special message from God directing them to the Messiah. Some scholars say these wise men were each from a different land, representing the entire world bowing before Jesus. These men from faraway lands recognized Jesus as the Messiah when most of God's chosen people in Israel did not. Matthew pictures Jesus as King over the whole world, not just Judea.

2.1, 2 The wise men traveled thousands of miles to see the King of the Jews. When they finally found him, they responded with joy, worship ("pay him homage"), and gifts. How different from the approach people often take today. We expect God to come looking for us, to explain himself, prove who he is, and give *us* gifts. But those who are wise still seek and worship Jesus today, not for what they can get, but for who he is.

2.2 The wise men said they saw Jesus' star. Balaam referred to a coming "star . . . out of Jacob" (Numbers 24.17). Some say this star may have been a conjunction of Jupiter, Saturn, and Mars in 6 B.C., and others offer other explanations. But couldn't God, who created the heavens, have created a special star to announce the arrival of his Son? Whatever the nature of the star, these wise men traveled thousands of miles searching for a king, and they found him.

2.3 Herod the Great was quite disturbed when the wise men asked about a newborn king of the Jews because (1) Herod was not the rightful heir to the throne of David; therefore many Jews hated him as a usurper. If Jesus really was an heir, trouble would arise. (2) Herod was ruthless and, because of his many enemies, he was suspicious that someone would try to overthrow him. (3) Herod didn't want the Jews, a religious people, to unite around a religious figure. (4) If these astrologers were of Jewish descent and from Parthia (the most powerful region next to Rome), they would have welcomed a Jewish king who could swing the balance of power away from Rome. The land of Israel, far from Rome, would have been easy prey for a nation trying to gain more control.

THE FLIGHT TO EGYPT
Herod planned to kill the baby Jesus, whom he perceived to be a future threat to his position. Warned of this treachery in a dream, Joseph took his family to Egypt until Herod's death, which occurred a year or two later. They then planned to return to Judea, but God led them instead to Nazareth in Galilee.

2.4 The chief priests and scribes were aware of Micah 5.2 and other prophecies about the Messiah. The wise men's news troubled Herod because he knew the Jewish people expected the Messiah to come soon (Luke 3.15). Most Jews expected the Messiah to be a great military and political deliverer, like Alexander the Great. Herod's counselors would have told Herod this. No wonder this ruthless man took no chances and ordered all the babies in Bethlehem killed!

2.5, 6 Matthew often quoted Old Testament prophets. This prophecy, paraphrasing Micah 5.2, was delivered seven centuries earlier. Matthew changed the words slightly as he applied the prophecy to Christ. New Testament writers often combined similar verses when quoting the Old Testament.

2.6 Most religious leaders believed in a literal fulfillment of all Old Testament prophecy; therefore, they believed the Messiah would be born in Bethlehem. Ironically, when Jesus was born, these same religious leaders became his greatest enemies. When the Messiah for whom they had been waiting finally came, they didn't recognize him.

who is to shepherd[k] my people Israel.' "
7 Then Herod secretly called for the wise men[l] and learned from them the exact time when the star had appeared. 8 Then he sent them to Bethlehem, saying,
"Go and search diligently for the child; and when you have found him, bring me
word so that I may also go and pay him homage." 9 When they had heard the king,
they set out; and there, ahead of them, went the star that they had seen at its rising,[m]
2.11 until it stopped over the place where the child was. 10 When they saw that the star
Ps 2.12; 22.29 had stopped,[n] they were overwhelmed with joy. 11 On entering the house, they saw
72.10 the child with Mary his mother; and they knelt down and paid him homage. Then,
Isa 49.7; 60.6 Jn 5.23 opening their treasure chests, they offered him gifts of gold, frankincense, and
2.12 Job 33.14,15 myrrh. 12 And having been warned in a dream not to return to Herod, they left for
Mt 1.20; 2.19,20 their own country by another road.

The escape to Egypt

(13)

13 Now after they had left, an angel of the Lord appeared to Joseph in a dream
and said, "Get up, take the child and his mother, and flee to Egypt, and remain
there until I tell you; for Herod is about to search for the child, to destroy him."
14 Then Joseph[o] got up, took the child and his mother by night, and went to Egypt,
2.15 15 and remained there until the death of Herod. This was to fulfill what had been
Ex 4.22,23 Hos 11.1 spoken by the Lord through the prophet, "Out of Egypt I have called my son."
16 When Herod saw that he had been tricked by the wise men,[l] he was infuriated, and he sent and killed all the children in and around Bethlehem who were two
years old or under, according to the time that he had learned from the wise men.[l]
17 Then was fulfilled what had been spoken through the prophet Jeremiah:
2.18 Jer 31.15 18 "A voice was heard in Ramah,
wailing and loud lamentation,
Rachel weeping for her children;
she refused to be consoled, because they are no more."

[k] Or *rule* [l] Or *astrologers*; Gk *magi* [m] Or *in the East* [n] Gk *saw the star* [o] Gk *he*

2.8 Herod did not want to worship Christ ("pay him homage")—he was lying. This was a trick to get the wise men to return to him and reveal the whereabouts of the newborn king. Herod's plan was to kill him.

2.11 Jesus was probably one or two years old when the wise men found him. By this time, Mary and Joseph were married, living in a house, and intending to stay in Bethlehem for a while. For more on why Joseph and Mary stayed, see the note on Luke 2.39.

2.11 The wise men gave these expensive gifts because they were worthy presents for a future king. Bible students have seen in the gifts symbols of Christ's identity and what he would accomplish. Gold was a gift for a king; frankincense, a gift for deity; myrrh, a spice for a man who was going to die. These gifts may have provided the financial resources for the trip to Egypt and back.

2.11 The wise men brought gifts and worshiped Jesus for who he was. This is the essence of true worship—honoring Christ for who he is and being willing to give him what is valuable to you. Worship God because he is the perfect, just, and almighty Creator of the universe, worthy of the best you have to give.

2.12 After finding Jesus and worshiping him, the wise men were warned by God not to return through Jerusalem as they had intended. Finding Jesus may mean that your life must take a different direction, one that is responsive and obedient to God's Word. Are you willing to be led a different way?

2.13 This is the second dream or vision that Joseph received from God. His first dream revealed that Mary's child would be the Messiah (1.20, 21). His second dream told him how to protect the child's life. Although Joseph was not Jesus' natural father, he was his legal father and was responsible for his safety and well-being. Divine guidance comes only to prepared hearts. Joseph remained receptive to God's guidance.

2.14, 15 Going to Egypt was not unusual because there were colonies of Jews in several major cities there. These colonies developed during the time of the great captivity (see Jeremiah 43, 44). There is an interesting parallel between this flight to Egypt and Israel's history. When Israel was an infant nation, it went to Egypt, as Jesus did as a child. God led Israel out (Hosea 11.1); God brought Jesus back. Both events show God working to save his people.

2.16 Herod, the king of the Jews, killed all the boys under two years of age in an obsessive attempt to kill Jesus, the newborn King. He stained his hands with blood, but he did not harm Jesus. Herod was king by a human appointment; Jesus was King by a divine appointment. No one can thwart God's plans.

2.16 Herod was afraid that this newborn king would one day take his throne. He completely misunderstood the reason for Christ's coming. Jesus didn't want Herod's throne; he wanted to be king of Herod's life. He wanted to give him eternal life, not take away his present life. Today people are often afraid that Christ wants to take things away when, in reality, he wants to give them real freedom, peace, and joy. Don't fear Christ—give him the throne of your life.

2.17, 18 Rachel was the wife of Jacob, one of the great men of God in the Old Testament. From Jacob's 12 sons came the 12 tribes of Israel. Rachel was buried near Bethlehem (Genesis 35.19). For more about the significance of this verse see Jeremiah 31.15, from which this verse was quoted.

The return to Nazareth
(14)
19 When Herod died, an angel of the Lord suddenly appeared in a dream to
Joseph in Egypt and said, 20 "Get up, take the child and his mother, and go to the
land of Israel, for those who were seeking the child's life are dead." 21 Then Joseph[p] got up, took the child and his mother, and went to the land of Israel. 22 But
when he heard that Archelaus was ruling over Judea in place of his father Herod, he
was afraid to go there. And after being warned in a dream, he went away to the 2.23
district of Galilee. 23 There he made his home in a town called Nazareth, so that Judg 13.5 Isa 11.1
what had been spoken through the prophets might be fulfilled, "He will be called a Lk 2.39 Jn 1.45,46
Nazorean." Acts 4.10; 24.5

John the Baptist prepares the way for Jesus
(16/Mark 1.1–8; Luke 3.1–17)
3 In those days John the Baptist appeared in the wilderness of Judea, proclaim- 3.1
ing, 2 "Repent, for the kingdom of heaven has come near."[q] 3 This is the one Mal 3.1
of whom the prophet Isaiah spoke when he said, 3.3 Isa 40.3

"The voice of one crying out in the wilderness:
'Prepare the way of the Lord,
make his paths straight.' "

[p] Gk *he* [q] Or *is at hand*

2.19–22 Herod the Great died in 4 B.C. of an incurable disease. Rome trusted him, but didn't trust his sons. Herod knew Rome wouldn't give his successor as much power, so he divided his kingdom into three parts, one for each son. Archelaus got Judea, Samaria, and Idumea; Herod Antipas received Galilee and Peraea; Herod Philip II got Trachonitis. Archelaus, a violent man, began his reign by slaughtering 3,000 influential people. He was banished nine years later. God didn't want Joseph's family to go into the region of this evil ruler.

2.23 Nazareth sat in the hilly area of southern Galilee near the crossroads of great caravan trade routes. The people of Nazareth had constant contact with people from all over the world, so world news reached them quickly. The town itself was rather small. The Roman garrison in charge of Galilee was housed there, making Nazareth despised by many Jews. This may have been why Nathanael commented (John 1.46), "Can anything good come out of Nazareth?"

2.23 The Old Testament does not record this specific statement, "He will be called a Nazorean." Many scholars believe, however, that Matthew was referring to Isaiah 11.1 where the Hebrew word for "branch" is similar to the word for Nazarene. Or he may have been referring to a prophecy unrecorded in the Bible. In any case, Matthew painted the picture of Jesus as the true Messiah announced by God through the prophets; and he made the point that Jesus, the Messiah, had unexpectedly humble beginnings, just as the Old Testament predicted (see Micah 5.2).

3.1, 2 Almost 30 years had passed since the events of chapter 2. Now John the Baptist burst onto the scene. His theme was "Repent!" Repentance means doing an about-face – a 180-degree turn – from the kind of self-centeredness that leads to wrong actions such as lying, cheating, stealing, gossiping, revenge, abuse, and sexual immorality. A person who repents stops rebelling and begins following God's way of living prescribed in his Word. The first step in turning to God is to admit your sin, as John urged. Then God will receive you and help you live the way he wants. Remember that only God can get rid of sin. He doesn't expect us to clean up our lives *before* we come to him.

3.1, 2 John the Baptist's Profile is found in John 1.

3.2 The kingdom of heaven began when God himself entered human history as a man. Today Jesus Christ reigns in the hearts of believers, but the kingdom of heaven will not be fully realized until all evil in the world is judged and removed. Christ came to earth first as a suffering servant; he will come again as King and Judge to rule victoriously over all the earth.

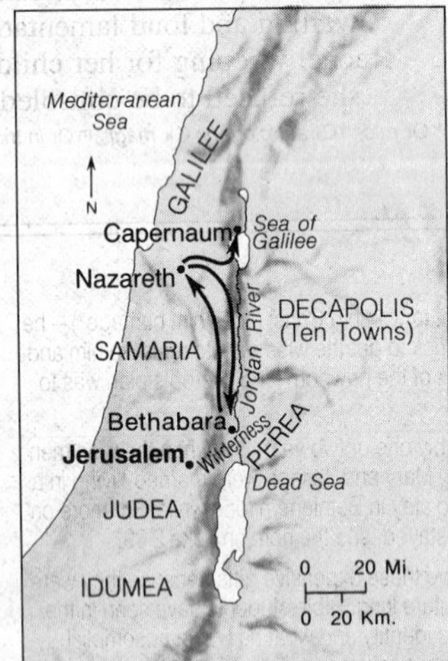

JESUS BEGINS HIS MINISTRY
From his childhood home, Nazareth, Jesus set out to begin his earthly ministry. He was baptized by John the Baptist in the Jordan River, tempted by Satan in the wilderness, and then returned to Galilee. Between the temptation and his move to Capernaum (4.12, 13), he ministered in Judea, Samaria, and Galilee (see John 1–4).

3.3 The prophet quoted is Isaiah (40.3), one of the greatest prophets of the Old Testament and one of the most quoted in the New. Like Isaiah, John was a prophet who urged the people to confess their sins and live for God. Both prophets taught that the message of repentance is good news to those who listen and seek the healing forgiveness of God's love, but terrible news to those who refuse to listen and cut off their only hope.

3.3 John the Baptist *prepared* the way for Jesus. People who do not know Jesus need to be prepared to meet him. We can prepare them by explaining their need for forgiveness, demonstrating Christ's teachings by our conduct, and telling them how Christ can give their lives meaning. We can "make his paths straight" by correcting misconceptions that might be hindering them from approaching Christ. Someone you know may be open to a relationship with Christ. What can you do to prepare the way for this person?

3.4 Lev 11.22; 2 Kgs 1.8
3.7 Jn 8.44; Rom 5.9; 1 Thess 1.10; 1 Jn 3.8,10
3.9 Rom 4.1
3.10 Jn 15.6; Heb 6.8

4 Now John wore clothing of camel's hair with a leather belt around his waist, and
his food was locusts and wild honey. 5 Then the people of Jerusalem and all Judea
were going out to him, and all the region along the Jordan, 6 and they were baptized
by him in the river Jordan, confessing their sins.
7 But when he saw many Pharisees and Sadducees coming for baptism, he said
to them, "You brood of vipers! Who warned you to flee from the wrath to come?
8 Bear fruit worthy of repentance. 9 Do not presume to say to yourselves, 'We have
Abraham as our ancestor'; for I tell you, God is able from these stones to raise up
children to Abraham. 10 Even now the ax is lying at the root of the trees; every tree
therefore that does not bear good fruit is cut down and thrown into the fire.

GOSPEL ACCOUNTS FOUND ONLY IN MATTHEW

Passage	*Subject*
1.20–24	Joseph's vision*
2.1–12	The visit of the wise men
2.13–15	Escape to Egypt*
2.16–18	Slaughter of the children*
27.3–10	The death of Judas*
27.19	The dream of Pilate's wife
27.52	The extra resurrections
28.11–15	The bribery of the guards
28.19, 20	The baptism emphasis in the great commission*

Matthew records nine special events that are not mentioned in any of the other Gospels. In each case, the most apparent reason for Matthew's choice has to do with his purpose in communicating the gospel to Jewish people. Five cases are fulfillments of Old Testament prophecies (marked with asterisks above). The other four would have been of particular interest to the Jews of Matthew's day.

3.4 John was markedly different from other religious leaders of his day. While many were greedy, selfish, and preoccupied with winning the praise of the people, John was concerned only with the praise of God. Having separated himself from the evil and hypocrisy of his day, he lived differently from other people to show that his message was new. John not only preached God's law, he *lived* it. Do you practice what you preach? Could people discover what you believe by observing the way you live?

3.4–6 John must have presented a strange image! Many people came to hear this preacher who wore odd clothes and ate unusual food. Some probably came simply out of curiosity and ended up repenting of their sins as they listened to his powerful message. People may be curious about your Christian life-style and values. You can use their simple curiosity as an opener to share how Christ makes a difference in you.

3.5 Why did John attract so many people? He was the first true prophet in 400 years. He blasted both Herod and the religious leaders, a daring act that fascinated the common people. But John also had strong words for them—they too were sinners and needed to repent. His message was powerful and true. The people were expecting a prophet like Elijah (Malachi 4.5), and John seemed to be the one!

3.6 When you wash dirty hands, the results are immediately visible. But repentance happens inside with a cleansing that isn't immediately seen. So John used a symbolic action that people could see: baptism. The Jews used baptism to initiate converts, so John's audience was familiar with the rite. Here, baptism was used as a sign of repentance and forgiveness. *Repent* means "to turn," implying a change in behavior. It is turning from sin toward God. Have you repented of sin in your life? Can others see the difference it makes in you? A changed life with new and different behavior makes your repentance real and visible.

3.6 The Jordan River is about 70 miles long, its main section stretching between the Sea of Galilee and the Dead Sea. Jerusalem lies about 20 miles west of it. This river was Israel's eastern border, and many significant events in the nation's history took place there. It was by the Jordan River that the Israelites renewed their covenant with God before entering the promised land (Joshua 1, 2). Here John the Baptist calls them to renew their covenant with God again, this time through baptism.

3.7 The Jewish religious leaders were divided into several groups. Two of the most prominent were the Pharisees and the Sadducees. The Pharisees separated themselves from anything non-Jewish and carefully followed both the Old Testament laws and the oral traditions handed down through the centuries. The Sadducees believed the Pentateuch alone (Genesis–Deuteronomy) to be God's Word. They were descended mainly from priestly nobility, while the Pharisees came from all classes of people. The two groups disliked each other greatly, and both opposed Jesus. John the Baptist criticized the Pharisees for being legalistic and hypocritical, following the letter of the law while ignoring its true intent. He criticized the Sadducees for using religion to advance their political position. For more information on these two groups, see the chart in chapter 4.

3.8 John the Baptist called people to more than words or ritual; he told them to change their behavior. "Bear fruit worthy of repentance" means that God looks beyond our words and religious activities to see if our conduct backs up what we say, and he judges our words by the actions that accompany them. Do your actions match your words?

3.9, 10 Just as a fruit tree is expected to bear fruit, God's people should produce a crop of good deeds. God has no use for those who call themselves Christians but do nothing about it. Like many people in John's day who were God's people in name only, we are of no value if we are Christians in name only. If others can't see our faith in the way we treat them, we may not be God's people at all.

3.10 God's message hasn't changed since the Old Testament—people will be judged for their unproductive lives. God calls us to be *active* in our obedience. John compared people who claim they believe God but don't live for God to unproductive trees that will be chopped down. To be productive for God, we must obey his teachings, resist temptation, actively serve and help others, and share our faith. How productive are you for God?

11 "I baptize you with[r] water for repentance, but one who is more powerful 3.11
than I is coming after me; I am not worthy to carry his sandals. He will baptize you Jn 1.26,33 Acts 1.5; 2.3,4
with[r] the Holy Spirit and fire. 12 His winnowing fork is in his hand, and he will 3.12
clear his threshing floor and will gather his wheat into the granary; but the chaff he Mal 3.2,3; 4.1
will burn with unquenchable fire."

John baptizes Jesus
(17/Mark 1.9–11; Luke 3.21, 22)

13 Then Jesus came from Galilee to John at the Jordan, to be baptized by him.
14 John would have prevented him, saying, "I need to be baptized by you, and do
you come to me?" 15 But Jesus answered him, "Let it be so now; for it is proper for 3.16
us in this way to fulfill all righteousness." Then he consented. 16 And when Jesus Isa 11.2
had been baptized, just as he came up from the water, suddenly the heavens were 3.17
opened to him and he saw the Spirit of God descending like a dove and alighting on Mt 12.18; 17.5 Mk 9.7
him. 17 And a voice from heaven said, "This is my Son, the Beloved,[s] with whom Isa 42.1 Lk 9.35
I am well pleased." Jn 12.28

Satan tempts Jesus in the wilderness
(18/Mark 1.12, 13; Luke 4.1–13)

4 Then Jesus was led up by the Spirit into the wilderness to be tempted by the 4.1
devil. 2 He fasted forty days and forty nights, and afterwards he was famished. Ezek 3.14 Mk 1.12,13
3 The tempter came and said to him, "If you are the Son of God, command these Acts 8.39

[r] Or *in* [s] Or *my beloved Son*

3.11 John baptized people as a sign that they had asked God to forgive their sins and had decided to live as he wanted them to. Baptism was an *outward* sign of commitment. To be effective, it had to be accompanied by an *inward* change of attitude leading to a changed life – the work of the Holy Spirit. John said that Jesus would baptize with the Holy Spirit and fire. This looks ahead to pentecost (Acts 2), when the Holy Spirit would be sent by Jesus in the form of tongues of fire, empowering his followers to preach the gospel. It also symbolizes the work of the Holy Spirit in bringing God's judgment on those who refuse to repent. Everyone will one day be baptized – either now by God's Holy Spirit, or later by the fire of his judgment.

3.12 A winnowing fork is a pitchfork used to toss wheat in the air to separate wheat from chaff. The wheat is the part of the plant that is useful; chaff is the worthless outer shell. Because it is useless, chaff is burned; wheat, however, is stored. Unrepentant people will be judged and discarded because they are worthless in God's work; those who repent and believe will be saved and used by God.

3.13–15 John had been explaining that Jesus' baptism would be much greater than his, when suddenly Jesus came to him and asked to be baptized! John felt unqualified. He wanted Jesus to baptize him. Why did Jesus ask to be baptized? It was not for repentance for sin, because he never sinned. "To fulfill all righteousness" means to accomplish God's mission. Jesus saw his baptism as advancing God's work. Jesus was baptized because (1) he was personally confessing sin on behalf of the nation, as Nehemiah, Ezra, Moses, and Daniel had done; (2) he was showing support for what John was doing; (3) he was inaugurating his public ministry; (4) he was identifying with the penitent people of God, not with the critical Pharisees who were only watching. Jesus, the perfect man, didn't need baptism for sin, but he accepted it in obedient service to the Father, and God showed his approval.

3.15 Put yourself in John's shoes. Your work is going well, people are taking notice, everything is growing. But you know that the purpose of your work is to prepare the people for Jesus (John 1.35–37). Now Jesus has arrived, and his coming tests your integrity. Will you be able to turn your followers over to him? John passed the test by publicly baptizing Jesus. Soon he would say, "He must increase, but I must decrease" (John 3.30). Can we, like John, put our egos and profitable work aside in order to point others to Jesus? Are we willing to lose some of our status so that everyone will benefit?

3.16, 17 The doctrine of the trinity means that God is three persons and yet one in essence. In this passage, all three persons of the trinity are present and active. God the Father speaks; God the Son is baptized; God the Holy Spirit descends on Jesus. God is one, yet in three persons at the same time. This is one of God's incomprehensible mysteries. Other Bible references that speak of the Father, Son, and Holy Spirit are Matthew 28.19; John 15.26; 1 Corinthians 12.4–13; 2 Corinthians 13.14; Ephesians 2.18; 1 Thessalonians 1.2–5; and 1 Peter 1.2.

4.1 This time of testing showed that Jesus really was the Son of God, able to overcome the devil and his temptations. A person has not shown true obedience if he or she has never had an opportunity to disobey. We read in Deuteronomy 8.2 that God led Israel into the wilderness to humble and prove them. He wanted to find out whether or not they would really obey him. We too will be tested. Because we know that testing will come, we should be alert and ready for it. Remember, your convictions are only as strong as they hold up under pressure!

4.1 The devil, also called Satan, tempted Eve in the garden of Eden, and here he tempts Jesus in the wilderness. Satan is a fallen angel. He is *real,* not symbolic, and is constantly fighting against those who follow and obey God. Satan's temptations are real, and he is always trying to get us to do things his way or ours rather than God's way. Jesus will one day reign over all creation, but Satan tried to force his hand and get him to declare his kingship prematurely. If Jesus had given in, his mission on earth – to die for our sins and give us the opportunity to have eternal life – would have been lost. When temptations seem especially strong, or when you think you can rationalize giving in, consider whether Satan may be trying to block God's purposes for your life or someone else's.

4.1ff This temptation by the devil shows us that Jesus was human, and it gave Jesus the opportunity to reaffirm God's plan for his ministry. It also gives us an example to follow when we are

4.4 Deut 8.3 Eph 6.17 stones to become loaves of bread." 4 But he answered, "It is written,
'One does not live by bread alone,
but by every word that comes from the mouth of God.' "

HEROD

The Bible records history. It has proven itself an accurate and reliable record of people, events, and places. Independent historical accounts back up the Bible's descriptions and details of many famous lives. One of these was the father of the Herodian family, Herod the Great.

Herod is remembered as a builder of cities and lavish rebuilder of the temple in Jerusalem. But he also destroyed people. He showed little greatness in either his personal actions or his character. He was ruthless in ruling his territory. His suspicions and jealousy led to the murder of several of his children and the death of his wife Mariamne.

Herod's title, king of the Jews, was granted by Rome but never accepted by the Jewish people. He was not part of the Davidic family line, and he was only partly Jewish. Although Israel benefited from Herod's lavish efforts to repair the temple in Jerusalem, he won little admiration because he also rebuilt various pagan temples. Herod's costly attempt to gain the loyalty of the people failed because it was superficial. His only loyalty was to himself.

Because his royal title was not genuine, Herod was constantly worried about losing his position. His actions when hearing from the wise men about their search for the new king are consistent with all that we know about Herod. He planned to locate and kill the child before he could become a threat. The murder of innocent children that followed is a tragic lesson in what can happen when actions are motivated by selfishness. Herod's suspicions did not spare even his own family. His life was self-destructive.

Strengths and accomplishments:
- Was given the title king of the Jews by the Romans
- Held onto his power for more than 30 years
- Was an effective, though ruthless, ruler
- Sponsored a great variety of large building projects

Weaknesses and mistakes:
- Tended to treat those around him with fear, suspicion, and jealousy
- Had several of his own children and at least one wife killed
- Ordered the killing of the infants in Bethlehem
- Although claiming to have become Jewish, he was still involved in many forms of pagan religion

Lessons from his life:
- Great power brings neither peace nor security
- No one can prevent God's plans from being carried out
- Superficial loyalty does not impress people or God

Vital statistics:
- Occupation: King of Judaea from 37 to 4 B.C.
- Relatives: Father: Antipater. Sons: Archelaus, Antipater, Antipas, Philip, and others. Wives: Doris, Mariamne, and others
- Contemporaries: Zacharias, Elizabeth, Mary, Joseph, Mark Antony, Augustus

Notes about Herod the Great are found in Matthew 2.1–22 and Luke 1.5.

tempted. Jesus' temptation was an important demonstration of his sinlessness. He would face temptation and not give in.

4.1ff Jesus wasn't tempted in the temple or at his baptism but in the wilderness where he was tired, alone, and hungry, and thus most vulnerable. The devil often tempts us when we are vulnerable – when we are under physical or emotional stress (for example, lonely, tired, weighing big decisions, or faced with uncertainty). But he also likes to tempt us through our strengths where we are susceptible to pride (see the note on Luke 4.3ff). We must guard at all times against his attacks.

4.1–10 The devil's temptations focused on three crucial areas: (1) physical desires, (2) possessions and power, and (3) pride (see 1 John 2.15, 16 for a similar list). But Jesus did not give in. Hebrews 4.15 says that Jesus "in every respect has been tested as we are, yet without sin." He knows firsthand what we are experiencing, and he is willing and able to help us in our struggles. When you are tempted, turn to him for strength.

4.3, 4 Jesus was hungry and weak after fasting for 40 days, but he chose not to use his divine power to satisfy his natural desire for food. Food, hunger, and eating are good, but the timing was wrong, because Jesus had given up the unlimited, independent use of his divine power in order to experience humanity fully. We also may be tempted to satisfy a perfectly normal desire in a wrong way or at the wrong time. If we indulge in sex before marriage or if we steal to get food, we are trying to satisfy God-given desires in wrong ways. Remember, many of your desires are normal and good, but God wants you to satisfy them in the right way and at the right time.

4.3, 4 Jesus was able to resist all of the devil's temptations because he not only knew Scripture, he obeyed it. Ephesians 6.17 says that God's Word is a sword to use in spiritual combat. Knowing Bible verses is an important step in helping us resist the devil's attacks, but we must also obey the Bible. Note that the devil had memorized Scripture, but he failed to obey it. Knowing and obeying the Bible helps us follow God's desires rather than the devil's.

5 Then the devil took him to the holy city and placed him on the pinnacle of the
temple, [6]saying to him, "If you are the Son of God, throw yourself down; for it is 4.6 Ps 91.11
written,

'He will command his angels concerning you,'
and 'On their hands they will bear you up,
so that you will not dash your foot against a stone.' "

[7]Jesus said to him, "Again it is written, 'Do not put the Lord your God to the test.' " 4.7 Deut 6.16
8 Again, the devil took him to a very high mountain and showed him all the
kingdoms of the world and their splendor; [9]and he said to him, "All these I will give
you, if you will fall down and worship me." [10]Jesus said to him, "Away with you, 4.10 Deut 6.13
Satan! for it is written,

'Worship the Lord your God,
and serve only him.' "

4.11 Heb 1.14 Jas 4.7
[11]Then the devil left him, and suddenly angels came and waited on him.

B. MESSAGE AND MINISTRY OF JESUS, THE KING (4.12—25.46)

Matthew features Jesus' sermons. The record of his actions are woven around great passages of his teaching. This section of Matthew, then, is topical rather than chronological. Matthew records for us the Sermon on the Mount, the parables of the kingdom, Jesus' teachings on forgiveness, and parables about the end of the age.

1. Jesus begins his ministry

Jesus preaches in Galilee

(30/Mark 1.14, 15; Luke 4.14, 15; John 4.43–45)

12 Now when Jesus[t] heard that John had been arrested, he withdrew to Gali- 4.12 Mark 1.14
lee. [13]He left Nazareth and made his home in Capernaum by the sea, in the territory
of Zebulun and Naphtali, [14]so that what had been spoken through the prophet Isaiah might be fulfilled:

[t] Gk *he*

4.5 The temple was the religious center of the Jewish nation and the place where the people expected the Messiah to arrive (Malachi 3.1). Herod the Great had renovated the temple in hopes of gaining the Jews' confidence. The temple was the tallest building in the area, and this pinnacle was probably the corner wall that jutted out of the hillside, overlooking the valley below. From this spot, Jesus could see all of Jerusalem behind him and the country for miles in front of him.

4.5–7 God is not our magician in the sky. In response to Satan's temptations, Jesus said not to put God to a foolish test (Deuteronomy 6.16). You may want to ask God to do something to prove his existence or his love for you. A man once asked Jesus for a special sign to be sent to help people believe. Jesus told him that people who don't believe through what is written in the Bible won't believe if someone comes back from the dead to warn them (Luke 16.31)! God wants us to live by faith, not by magic. Don't try to manipulate God by asking for signs.

4.6 The devil used Scripture to try to convince Jesus to sin! Sometimes friends or associates will present attractive and convincing reasons why you should try something you know is wrong. They may even find Bible verses that *seem* to support their viewpoint. Study the Bible carefully, especially the broader contexts of specific verses, so that you understand God's principles for living and what he wants for your life. Only if you really understand what the *whole* Bible says, can you recognize errors of interpretation when people take verses out of context and twist them to say what they want them to say.

4.8, 9 Did the devil have the power to give Jesus the kingdoms of the world? Didn't God, the Creator of the world, have control over them? The devil may have been lying about his implied power, or he may have based his offer on his temporary control and free rein over the earth because of humanity's sinfulness. Jesus' temptation was to take the world as a political ruler right then, without carrying out his plan to save the world from sin. Satan was trying to distort Jesus' perspective by making him focus on worldly power and not on God's plans.

4.8–10 The devil offered all the world to Jesus if he would only kneel and worship him. Today the devil offers us the world by trying to entice us with materialism and power. We can resist temptations the same way Jesus did. If you find yourself craving something that the world offers, quote Jesus' words to the devil: "Worship the Lord your God, and serve only him."

4.11 Angels, like these who waited on Jesus, have a significant role as God's messengers. These spiritual beings were involved in Jesus' life on earth by (1) announcing his birth to Mary, (2) reassuring Joseph, (3) naming Jesus, (4) announcing his birth to the shepherds, (5) protecting Jesus by sending his family to Egypt, (6) ministering to him in Gethsemane. For more on angels, see the note on 1.20.

4.12, 13 Jesus moved from Nazareth, his hometown, to Capernaum, about 20 miles farther north. Capernaum became Jesus' home base during his ministry in Galilee. He probably moved (1) to get away from intense opposition in Nazareth, (2) to have an impact on the greatest number of people (Capernaum was a busy city and Jesus' message could reach more people and spread more quickly), and (3) to utilize extra resources and support for his ministry.

Jesus' move fulfilled the prophecy of Isaiah 9.1, 2, which states that the Messiah will be a light to the land of Zebulun and Naphtali, the region of Galilee where Capernaum was located. Zebulun and Naphtali were two of the original 12 tribes of Israel.

4.14–16 By quoting from the book of Isaiah, Matthew continues to tie Jesus' ministry to the Old Testament. This was helpful for his Jewish listeners, who were familiar with these scriptures. In addition, it shows the unity of God's purposes as he works with his people throughout all ages.

4.15,16 Isa 9.1,2; 42.6,7 Lk 2.32
15 "Land of Zebulun, land of Naphtali,
on the road by the sea, across the Jordan, Galilee of the Gentiles—
16 the people who sat in darkness
have seen a great light,
and for those who sat in the region and shadow of death
light has dawned."

4.17 Mt 10.7
17 From that time Jesus began to proclaim, "Repent, for the kingdom of heaven has
come near."[u]

Four fishermen follow Jesus
(33/Mark 1.16–20)

4.18 Lk 5.1-11
18 As he walked by the Sea of Galilee, he saw two brothers, Simon, who is
called Peter, and Andrew his brother, casting a net into the sea—for they were
4.19 Jn 1.42
fishermen. 19 And he said to them, "Follow me, and I will make you fish for people." 20 Immediately they left their nets and followed him. 21 As he went from there,

[u] Or *is at hand*

THE PHARISEES AND SADDUCEES
The Pharisees and Sadducees were the two major religious groups in Israel at the time of Christ. The Pharisees were more religiously minded while the Sadducees were more politically minded. Although the groups disliked and distrusted each other, they became allies in their common hatred for Jesus.

Name	*Positive Characteristics*	*Negative Characteristics*
PHARISEES	• Were committed to obeying all of God's Word • Were admired by the common people for their apparent piety • Believed in a bodily resurrection and eternal life • Believed in angels and demons	• Behaved as though their own religious rules were just as important as God's rules for living • Their piety was often hypocritical and their efforts often forced others to try to live up to standards they themselves could not live up to • Believed that salvation came from perfect obedience to the law and was not based on forgiveness of sins • Became so obsessed with obeying their legal interpretations in every detail that they completely ignored God's message of mercy and grace • Were more concerned with appearing to be good than obeying God
SADDUCEES	• Believed God's Word was limited to the first five books of the Bible: Genesis to Deuteronomy • Were more practically minded than the Pharisees	• Relied on logic while placing little importance on faith • Did not believe all the Old Testament was God's Word • Did not believe in a bodily resurrection or eternal life • Did not believe in angels or demons • Were often willing to compromise their values with the Romans and others in order to maintain their status and influential positions

4.17 The "kingdom of heaven" has the same meaning as the "kingdom of God" in Mark and Luke. Matthew uses this phrase because the Jews, out of their intense reverence and respect, did not pronounce God's name. The kingdom of heaven is still near, because it has arrived in our hearts. See the note on 3.2 for more on the kingdom of heaven.

4.17 Jesus started his ministry with the very word people had heard John the Baptist say: "Repent." The message is the same today as when Jesus and John gave it. Becoming a follower of Christ means turning away from our self-centeredness and "self" control and turning our lives over to Christ's direction and control.

4.18 The Sea of Galilee is really a large lake. About 30 fishing towns surrounded it during Jesus' day, and Capernaum was the largest.

4.18–20 Jesus told Peter and Andrew to leave their fishing business and "fish for people," to help others find God. Jesus was calling them from their productive trades to be productive spiritually. We all need to fish for souls. If we practice Christ's teachings and share the gospel with others, we will be able to draw those around us to Christ like a fisherman who pulls fish into his boat with nets.

4.19, 20 These men already knew Jesus. He had talked to Peter and Andrew previously (John 1.40–42) and had been preaching in the area. When Jesus called them, they knew what kind of man he was and were willing to follow him. They were not in a hypnotic trance when they followed, but instead were thoroughly convinced that following him would change their lives forever.

4.21, 22 James and his brother, John, along with Peter and Andrew, were the first disciples Jesus called to work with him. Jesus' call motivated these men to get up and leave their jobs—immediately. They didn't make excuses about why it wasn't a good time. They left at once and followed. Jesus calls each of us to follow him. When Jesus asks us to serve him, we must be like the disciples and do it at once.

he saw two other brothers, James son of Zebedee and his brother John, in the boat
with their father Zebedee, mending their nets, and he called them. 22 Immediately
they left the boat and their father, and followed him.

Jesus preaches throughout Galilee
(36/Mark 1.35–39; Luke 4.42–44)

23 Jesus[v] went throughout Galilee, teaching in their synagogues and proclaim- **4.23** Mt 9.35 Mk 1.39 Lk 4.15
ing the good news[w] of the kingdom and curing every disease and every sickness
among the people. 24 So his fame spread throughout all Syria, and they brought to
him all the sick, those who were afflicted with various diseases and pains, demoniacs, epileptics, and paralytics, and he cured them. 25 And great crowds followed
him from Galilee, the Decapolis, Jerusalem, Judea, and from beyond the Jordan.

2. Jesus gives the Sermon on the Mount

Jesus gives the beatitudes
(49/Luke 6.17–26)

5 When Jesus[x] saw the crowds, he went up the mountain; and after he sat down, **5.1** Lk 6.20-23
his disciples came to him. 2 Then he began to speak, and taught them, saying:
3 "Blessed are the poor in spirit, for theirs is the kingdom of heaven. **5.3** Ps 37.11; 51.17 Isa 57.15; 66.2
4 "Blessed are those who mourn, for they will be comforted.

[v] Gk *He* [w] Gk *gospel* [x] Gk *he*

4.23 Jesus was teaching, preaching, and healing. These were the three main aspects of his ministry. *Teaching* shows Jesus' concern for understanding; *proclaiming* or *preaching* shows his concern for commitment; and *curing* shows his concern for wholeness. His miracles of healing authenticated his teaching and preaching, showing that he truly was from God.

4.23 Jesus soon developed a powerful preaching ministry and often spoke in the synagogues. Most towns that had ten or more Jewish families had a synagogue. The building served as a religious gathering place on the sabbath and as a school during the week. The leader of the synagogue was not a preacher as much as an administrator. His job was to find and invite rabbis to teach and preach. It was customary to invite visiting rabbis like Jesus to speak.

4.23, 24 Jesus preached the gospel—the good news—to everyone who wanted to hear it. The gospel is that the kingdom of heaven has come, that God is with us, and that he cares for us. He can heal us, not just of physical sickness, but of spiritual sickness as well. There's no sin or problem too great or too small for him to handle. Jesus' words were good news because they offered freedom, hope, peace of heart, and eternal life with God.

4.25 Decapolis was a league of ten Gentile cities east of the Sea of Galilee, joined together for better trade and mutual defense. The word about Jesus was out, and Jews and Gentiles were coming long distances to hear him.

5.1ff Matthew 5—7 is called the Sermon on the Mount because Jesus gave it on a hillside near Capernaum. This "sermon" probably covered several days of preaching. In it, Jesus proclaimed his attitude toward the law. Position, authority, and money are not important in his kingdom—what matters is faithful obedience from the heart. The Sermon on the Mount challenged the proud and legalistic religious leaders of the day. It called them back to the messages of the Old Testament prophets who, like Jesus, taught that heartfelt obedience is more important than legalistic observance.

5.1, 2 Enormous crowds were following Jesus—he was the talk of the town and everyone wanted to see him. The disciples, who were the closest associates of this popular man, were certainly tempted to feel important, proud, and possessive. Being with Jesus gave them not only prestige, but also opportunity for receiving money.
The crowds were gathering once again. But before speaking to them, Jesus pulled his disciples aside and warned them about the temptations they would face as his associates. Don't expect fame and fortune, Jesus was saying, but mourning, hunger, and persecution. Nevertheless, Jesus assured his disciples, they would be rewarded—but perhaps not in this life. There may be times when following Jesus will bring us great popularity. If we don't live by Jesus' words in this sermon, we will find ourselves using God's message only to promote our personal interests.

5.3–5 Jesus began his sermon with words that seem to contradict each other. But God's way of living usually contradicts the world's. If you want to live for God you must be ready to say and do what seems strange to the world. You must be willing to give when others take, to love when others hate, to help when others abuse. By giving up your own rights in order to serve others, you will one day receive everything God has in store for you.

5.3–12 There are at least four ways to understand the beatitudes: (1) They are a code of ethics for the disciples and a standard of conduct for all believers. (2) They contrast kingdom values (what is eternal) with worldly values (what is temporary). (3) They contrast the superficial "faith" of the Pharisees with the real faith Christ wants. (4) They show how the Old Testament expectations will be fulfilled in the new kingdom. These beatitudes are not multiple choice—pick what you like and leave the rest. They must be taken as a whole. They describe what we should be like as Christ's followers.

5.3–12 Each beatitude tells how to be *blessed.* Other translations use the words *fortunate* or *happy.* These words don't promise laughter, pleasure, or earthly prosperity. Jesus turns the world's idea of happiness upside down. To Jesus, happiness means hope and joy, independent of outward circumstances. To find hope and joy, the deepest form of happiness, follow Jesus no matter what the cost.

5.3–12 With Jesus' announcement that the kingdom was near (4.17), people were naturally asking, "How do I qualify to be in God's kingdom?" Jesus said that God's kingdom is organized differently from worldly kingdoms. In the kingdom of heaven, wealth and power and authority are unimportant. Kingdom people seek different blessings and benefits, and they have different attitudes. Are your attitudes a carbon copy of the world's selfishness, pride, and lust for power, or do they reflect the humility and self-sacrifice of Jesus, your King?

5.5 1 Pet 3.4 5 "Blessed are the meek, for they will inherit the earth.
6 "Blessed are those who hunger and thirst for righteousness, for they will be
filled.
5.7 Ps 41.1 7 "Blessed are the merciful, for they will receive mercy.
5.8 1 Jn 3.2,3 8 "Blessed are the pure in heart, for they will see God.
9 "Blessed are the peacemakers, for they will be called children of God.
5.10 2 Tim 2.12 1 Pet 3.13,14 10 "Blessed are those who are persecuted for righteousness' sake, for theirs is
the kingdom of heaven.
11 "Blessed are you when people revile you and persecute you and utter all
5.12 2 Chron 36.16 Mt 23.37 Acts 7.52 kinds of evil against you falsely[y] on my account. 12 Rejoice and be glad, for your
reward is great in heaven, for in the same way they persecuted the prophets who
were before you.

Jesus teaches about salt and light
(50)

13 "You are the salt of the earth; but if salt has lost its taste, how can its saltiness
be restored? It is no longer good for anything, but is thrown out and trampled under
foot.
5.14 Phil 2.15 14 "You are the light of the world. A city built on a hill cannot be hid. 15 No one
after lighting a lamp puts it under the bushel basket, but on the lampstand, and it
5.16 Jn 15.8 gives light to all in the house. 16 In the same way, let your light shine before others,
so that they may see your good works and give glory to your Father in heaven.

[y] Other ancient authorities lack *falsely*

THE TEMPTATIONS	*Temptation*	*Real needs used as basis for temptation*	*Possible doubts that made the temptations real*	*Potential weaknesses Satan sought to exploit*	*Jesus' answer*
	Make bread	Physical need: Hunger	Would God provide food?	Hunger, impatience, need to "prove his Sonship"	Deuteronomy 8.3 "Depend on God" Focus: God's purpose
	Dare God to rescue you (based on misapplied Scripture, Psalm 91.11, 12)	Emotional need: Security	Would God protect?	Pride, insecurity, need to test God	Deuteronomy 6.16 "Don't test God" Focus: God's plan
	Worship me! (Satan)	Psychological need: Significance, power, achievement	Would God direct?	Desire for quick power, easy solutions, need to prove equality with God	Deuteronomy 6.13 "No compromise with evil" Focus: God's person

As if going through a final test of preparation, Jesus was tempted by Satan in the wilderness. Three specific parts of the temptation are listed by Matthew. They are familiar because we face the same kinds of temptations. As the chart shows, temptation is often the combination of a real need and a possible doubt that create an inappropriate desire. Jesus demonstrates both the importance and effectiveness of knowing and applying Scripture to combat temptation.

5.11, 12 Jesus said to rejoice when we're persecuted. Persecution can be good because (1) it takes our eyes off earthly rewards, (2) it strips away superficial believers, (3) it strengthens the faith of those who endure, and (4) it serves as an example to others who follow. We can be comforted to know that God's greatest prophets were persecuted (Elijah, Jeremiah, Daniel). Our persecution means we have shown ourselves faithful. In the future God will reward the faithful by receiving them into his eternal kingdom, where there is no more persecution.

5.13 If a seasoning has no flavor, it has no value. If Christians make no effort to affect the world around them, they are of little value to God. If we are too much like the world, we are worthless. Christians should not blend in with everyone else. Instead, we should affect them positively, just as seasoning brings out the best flavor in food.

5.14–16 Can you hide a city that is sitting on top of a hill? Its light at night can be seen for miles. If we live for Christ, we will glow like lights, showing others what Christ is like. We hide our light by (1) being quiet when we should speak, (2) going along with the crowd, (3) denying the light, (4) letting sin dim our light, (5) not explaining our light to others, or (6) ignoring the needs of others. Be a beacon of truth – don't shut your light off from the rest of the world.

Jesus teaches about the law
(51)

17 "Do not think that I have come to abolish the law or the prophets; I have
come not to abolish but to fulfill. 18 For truly I tell you, until heaven and earth pass **5.18**
away, not one letter,[z] not one stroke of a letter, will pass from the law until all is Lk 16.17
accomplished. 19 Therefore, whoever breaks[a] one of the least of these command- **5.19**
ments, and teaches others to do the same, will be called least in the kingdom of Jas 2.10
heaven; but whoever does them and teaches them will be called great in the kingdom of heaven. 20 For I tell you, unless your righteousness exceeds that of the **5.20**
scribes and Pharisees, you will never enter the kingdom of heaven. Rom 10.3

Jesus teaches about anger
(52)

21 "You have heard that it was said to those of ancient times, 'You shall not **5.21**
murder'; and 'whoever murders shall be liable to judgment.' 22 But I say to you that Ex 20.13 Deut 5.17
if you are angry with a brother or sister,[b] you will be liable to judgment; and if you
insult[c] a brother or sister,[d] you will be liable to the council; and if you say, 'You
fool,' you will be liable to the hell[e] of fire. 23 So when you are offering your gift at
the altar, if you remember that your brother or sister[f] has something against you,
24 leave your gift there before the altar and go; first be reconciled to your brother or

[z] Gk *one iota* [a] Or *annuls* [b] Gk *a brother*; other ancient authorities add *without cause* [c] Gk *say Raca to* (an obscure term of abuse) [d] Gk *a brother* [e] Gk *Gehenna* [f] Gk *your brother*

5.17 God's moral and ceremonial laws were given to help people love God with all their hearts and minds. Throughout Israel's history, however, these laws were often misquoted and misapplied. By Jesus' time, religious leaders had turned the laws into a confusing mass of rules. When Jesus talked about a new way to understand God's law, he was actually trying to bring people back to its *original* purpose. He did not speak against the law itself, but against the abuses and excesses to which it had been subjected. (See John 1.17.)

5.17–20 If Jesus did not come to cancel the law, does that mean all the Old Testament laws still apply to us today? In the Old Testament, there were three categories of law: ceremonial, civil, and moral.

(1) The *ceremonial law* related specifically to Israel's worship (see Leviticus 1.2, 3, for example). Its primary purpose was to point forward to Jesus Christ; these laws, therefore, were no longer necessary after Jesus' death and resurrection. While we are no longer bound by ceremonial laws, the principles behind them – to worship and love a holy God – still apply. Jesus was often accused by the Pharisees of violating ceremonial law.

(2) The *civil law* applied to daily living in Israel (see Deuteronomy 24.10, 11, for example). Because modern society and culture are so radically different from that time, all of these guidelines cannot be followed specifically. But the principles behind the commands are timeless and should guide our conduct. Jesus fulfilled these by example.

(3) The *moral law* (such as the ten commandments) is the direct command of God, and it requires strict obedience (see Exodus 20.13, for example). It reveals the nature and will of God, and it still applies today. Jesus obeyed the moral law completely.

5.19 Some of those in the crowd were experts at telling others what to do, but they missed the central point of God's laws themselves. Jesus made it clear, however, that obeying God's law is more important than explaining it. It's much easier to study God's laws and tell others to obey them than to put them into practice. How are you doing at obeying God *yourself*?

5.20 The Pharisees were exacting and scrupulous in their attempts to follow their laws. So how could Jesus reasonably call us to a greater righteousness than theirs? The Pharisees' weakness was that they were content to obey the laws outwardly without allowing God to change their hearts (or attitudes). Jesus was saying, therefore, that the *quality* of our goodness should be greater than that of the Pharisees. They looked pious, but they were far from the kingdom of God. God judges our hearts as well as our deeds, for it is in the heart where our real allegiance lies. Be just as concerned about your attitudes, which people don't see, as your actions, which are seen by all.

5.20 Jesus was saying that his listeners needed a different kind of goodness altogether (love and obedience), not just a more intense version of the Pharisees' goodness (legal compliance). Our goodness must (1) come from what God does in us, not what we can do by ourselves, (2) be God-centered, not self-centered, (3) be based on reverence for God, not approval from people, and (4) go beyond keeping the law to living by the principles behind it.

5.21, 22 When Jesus said, "But I say to you," he was not doing away with the law or adding his own beliefs. Rather, he was giving a fuller understanding of why God made that law in the first place. For example, when Moses said, "You shall not murder" (Exodus 20.13), Jesus taught, "Don't even become angry enough to murder, for then you have already committed murder in your heart." The Pharisees read this law and, not having murdered, felt righteous. Yet they were angry enough with Jesus that they would soon plot his murder, though they would not do the dirty work themselves. We miss the intent of God's Word when we read his rules for living without trying to understand why he made them. When do you keep God's rules but close your eyes to his intent?

5.21, 22 Killing is a terrible sin, but *anger* is a great sin too because it also violates God's command to love. Anger in this case refers to a seething, brooding bitterness against someone. It is a dangerous emotion that always threatens to leap out of control, leading to violence, emotional hurt, increased mental stress, and spiritual damage. Anger keeps us from developing a spirit pleasing to God. Have you ever been proud that you didn't strike out and say what was really on your mind? Self-control is good, but Christ wants us to practice thought-control as well. Jesus said we will be held accountable even for our attitudes.

5.23, 24 Broken relationships can hinder our relationship with God. If we have a problem or grievance with a friend, we should resolve the problem as soon as possible. We are hypocrites if we claim to love God while we hate others. Our attitudes toward others reflect our relationship with God (1 John 4.20).

5.25 Prov 25.8 Lk 12.58

sister,[g] and then come and offer your gift. 25 Come to terms quickly with your
accuser while you are on the way to court[h] with him, or your accuser may hand you
over to the judge, and the judge to the guard, and you will be thrown into prison.
26 Truly I tell you, you will never get out until you have paid the last penny.

Jesus teaches about lust
(53)

5.27 Ex 20.17 Deut 5.18

27 "You have heard that it was said, 'You shall not commit adultery.' 28 But I
say to you that everyone who looks at a woman with lust has already committed
adultery with her in his heart. 29 If your right eye causes you to sin, tear it out and

[g] Gk *your brother* [h] Gk lacks *to court*

KEY LESSONS FROM THE SERMON ON THE MOUNT

Beatitude	*Old Testament anticipation*	*Clashing worldly values*	*God's reward*	*How to develop this attitude*
Humility (5.3)	Isaiah 57.15	Pride and personal independence	Kingdom of heaven	James 4.7–10
Mourning (5.4)	Isaiah 61.1, 2	Happiness at any cost	Comfort (2 Corinthians 1.4)	Psalm 51 James 4.7–10
Meekness and lowliness (5.5)	Psalm 37.5–11	Power	Wide world belongs to you	Matthew 11.27–30
Justice and goodness (5.6)	Isaiah 11.4, 5; 42.1–4	Pursuing personal needs	Complete satisfaction	John 16.5–11 Philippians 3.7–11
Kindness and mercy (5.7)	Psalm 41.1	Strength without feeling	Receive mercy	Ephesians 5.1, 2
Hearts that are pure (5.8)	Psalm 24.3, 4; 51.10	Deception is acceptable	To see God	1 John 3.1–3
Peace (5.9)	Isaiah 57.18, 19; 60.17	Personal peace is pursued without concern for the world's chaos	Be called sons of God	Romans 12.9–21 Hebrews 12.10, 11
Faithfulness (5.10)	Isaiah 52.13; 53.12	Weak commitments	Will inherit the kingdom of God	2 Timothy 3.12

In his longest recorded sermon, Jesus began by describing the traits he was looking for in his followers. He called those who lived out those traits fortunate because God had something special in store for them. Each beatitude is an almost direct contradiction of society's typical way of life. In the last beatitude, Jesus even points out that a serious effort to develop these traits is bound to create opposition. The best example of each trait is found in Jesus himself. If our goal is to become like him, the beatitudes will challenge the way we live each day.

5.25, 26 In Jesus' day, someone who couldn't pay a debt was thrown into prison until the debt was paid. Unless someone came to pay the debt for the prisoner, he would probably die there. It is practical advice to resolve our differences with our enemies before their anger causes more trouble (Proverbs 25.8–10). You may not get into a disagreement that takes you to court, but even small conflicts mend more easily if you try to make peace right away. In a broader sense, these verses advise us to get things right with our fellow man before we have to stand before God.

5.27, 28 The Old Testament law said that it is wrong for a person to have sex with someone other than his or her spouse (Exodus 20.14). But Jesus said that the *desire* to have sex with someone other than your spouse is mental adultery and thus sin. Jesus emphasized that if the *act* is wrong, then so is the *intention.* To be faithful to your spouse with your body but not your mind is to break the trust so vital to a strong marriage. Jesus is not condemning natural interest in the opposite sex or even healthy sexual desire, but the deliberate and repeated filling of one's mind with fantasies that would be evil if acted out.

5.27, 28 Some think, if lustful thoughts are sin, why shouldn't a person go ahead and do the lustful actions too? Acting out sinful desires is harmful in several ways: (1) it causes people to excuse sin rather than stop doing it; (2) it destroys marriages; (3) it is deliberate rebellion against God's Word; and (4) it always hurts someone else in addition to the sinner. Sinful action is more dangerous than sinful desire, and that is why desires should not be acted out. Nevertheless, sinful desire is just as damaging to righteousness. Left unchecked, wrong desires result in wrong actions and turn people away from God.

5.29, 30 When Jesus said to get rid of your hand or your eye, he was speaking figuratively. He didn't mean literally to pluck out your eye, because even a blind person can lust. But if that were the only choice, it would be better to go into heaven with one eye or hand than to go to hell with two. We sometimes tolerate sins in our lives that, unchecked, could eventually destroy us. It is better to experience the pain of removal (getting rid of a bad habit or something we treasure, for instance) than to allow the sin to bring judgment and condemnation. Examine your life for anything that causes you to sin, and take every necessary action to remove it.

throw it away; it is better for you to lose one of your members than for your whole 5.29 Mt 18.9
body to be thrown into hell.[i] 30 And if your right hand causes you to sin, cut it off Mk 9.43-47
and throw it away; it is better for you to lose one of your members than for your 5.30
whole body to go into hell.[i] Mt 18.8

Jesus teaches about divorce
(54)

31 "It was also said, 'Whoever divorces his wife, let him give her a certificate 5.31
of divorce.' 32 But I say to you that anyone who divorces his wife, except on the Deut 24.1 5.32
ground of unchastity, causes her to commit adultery; and whoever marries a di- Rom 7.3
vorced woman commits adultery. 1 Cor 7.10

Jesus teaches about vows
(55)

33 "Again, you have heard that it was said to those of ancient times, 'You shall
not swear falsely, but carry out the vows you have made to the Lord.' 34 But I say 5.34
to you, Do not swear at all, either by heaven, for it is the throne of God, 35 or by the Isa 66.1 Jas 5.12
earth, for it is his footstool, or by Jerusalem, for it is the city of the great King. 5.35
36 And do not swear by your head, for you cannot make one hair white or black. Ps 48.2 Isa 66.1
37 Let your word be 'Yes, Yes' or 'No, No'; anything more than this comes from 5.37
the evil one.[j] Col 4.6

Jesus teaches about retaliation
(56)

38 "You have heard that it was said, 'An eye for an eye and a tooth for a tooth.' 5.38
39 But I say to you, Do not resist an evildoer. But if anyone strikes you on the right Lev 24.20
cheek, turn the other also; 40 and if anyone wants to sue you and take your coat, give 5.39 Rom 12.17
your cloak as well; 41 and if anyone forces you to go one mile, go also the second 1 Cor 6.7 1 Pet 3.9
mile. 42 Give to everyone who begs from you, and do not refuse anyone who wants 5.42
to borrow from you. Deut 15.8

[i] Gk *Gehenna* [j] Or *evil*

5.31, 32 Divorce is as hurtful and destructive today as in Jesus' day. God intends marriage to be a lifetime commitment (Genesis 2.24). When entering into marriage, people should never consider divorce an option for solving problems or a way out of a relationship that seems dead. In these verses, Jesus is also attacking those who purposefully abuse the marriage contract, using divorce to satisfy their lustful desire to marry someone else. Are your actions today helping your marriage grow stronger, or are you tearing it apart?

5.32 Jesus said that divorce is not permissible except for unchastity. This does not mean that divorce should automatically occur when a spouse commits adultery. The word translated "unchastity" implies a sexually immoral life-style, not a confessed and repented act of adultery. Those who discover that their partner has been unfaithful should first attempt to forgive, reconcile, and restore their relationship. We are always to look for reasons to restore the marriage relationship rather than for excuses to leave it.

5.33ff In this passage, Jesus is emphasizing the importance of telling the truth. People were breaking promises and using sacred language casually and carelessly. Keeping vows and promises is important; it builds trust and makes committed human relationships possible. The Bible condemns making vows or taking oaths casually, giving your word knowing you won't keep it, or swearing falsely in God's name (Exodus 20.7; Leviticus 19.12; Numbers 30.1, 2; Deuteronomy 19.16–20). Oaths are needed in certain situations only because we live in a sinful society that breeds distrust.

5.33–37 Oaths, or vows, were common, but Jesus told his followers not to use them—their word alone should be enough (see James 5.12). Are you known as a person of your word? Truthfulness seems so rare that we feel we must end our statements with "I promise." If we tell the truth all the time, we will have less pressure to back up our words with an oath or promise.

5.38 God's purpose for this law was mercy. It was given to judges and said, in effect, "Make the punishment fit the crime." It was not a guide for personal revenge (Exodus 21.23–25; Leviticus 24.19, 20; Deuteronomy 19.21). These laws were given to *limit* vengeance and help the court administer punishment that was neither too strict nor too lenient. Some people, however, were using this phrase to justify their vendettas against others. People still try to excuse their acts of revenge by saying, "I was just doing to him what he did to me."

5.38–42 When we are wronged, often our first reaction is to get even. Instead Jesus said we should do *good* to those who wrong us! Our desire should not be to keep score, but to love and forgive. This is not natural—it is supernatural. Only God can give us the strength to love as he does. Instead of planning vengeance, pray for those who hurt you.

5.39–44 To many Jews of Jesus' day, these statements were offensive. Any Messiah who would turn the other cheek was not the military leader they wanted to lead a revolt against Rome. Under Roman oppression, they wanted retaliation against their enemies, whom they hated. But Jesus suggested a new, radical response to injustice: instead of demanding rights, give them up freely! According to Jesus, it is more important to *give* justice and mercy than to receive it.

Jesus teaches about loving enemies (57/Luke 6.27–36)

43 "You have heard that it was said, 'You shall love your neighbor and hate
your enemy.' 44 But I say to you, Love your enemies and pray for those who persecute you, 45 so that you may be children of your Father in heaven; for he makes his
sun rise on the evil and on the good, and sends rain on the righteous and on the
unrighteous. 46 For if you love those who love you, what reward do you have? Do
5.48 not even the tax collectors do the same? 47 And if you greet only your brothers and
Lev 19.1 Col 1.28 sisters,[k] what more are you doing than others? Do not even the Gentiles do the
1 Pet 1.15 same? 48 Be perfect, therefore, as your heavenly Father is perfect.

Jesus teaches about giving to the needy (58)

6.1 2 Cor 9.9 **6** "Beware of practicing your piety before others in order to be seen by them; for
then you have no reward from your Father in heaven.
6.2 Mt 23.5 2 "So whenever you give alms, do not sound a trumpet before you, as the hypocrites do in the synagogues and in the streets, so that they may be praised by others.

[k] Gk *your brothers*

SIX WAYS TO THINK LIKE CHRIST

Reference	*Example*	*It's not enough to:*	*We must also:*
5.21, 22	Murder	Avoid killing	Avoid anger and hatred
5.23–26	Sacrifices	Offer regular sacrifices	Have right relationships with God and others
5.27–30	Adultery	Avoid adultery	Keep our hearts from lusting and be faithful
5.31, 32	Divorce	Be legally married	Live out our marriage commitments
5.33–37	Vows	Make a vow	Avoid casual and irresponsible commitments to God
5.38–47	Revenge	Seek justice for ourselves	Show mercy and love to others

We are, more often than not, guilty of avoiding the extreme sins while regularly committing the types of sins with which Jesus was most concerned. In these six examples, our real struggle with sin is exposed. Jesus pointed out what kind of lives would be required of his followers. Are you living as Jesus taught?

5.43, 44 By calling us not to retaliate, Jesus keeps us from taking the law into our own hands. By loving and praying for our enemies, we can overcome evil with good.

The Pharisees interpreted Leviticus 19.18 as teaching that they should love only those who love in return, and Psalm 139.19–22 and 140.9–11 as meaning that they should hate their enemies. But Jesus says we are to love our enemies. If you love your enemies and treat them well, you will truly show that Jesus is Lord of your life. This is possible only for those who give themselves fully to God, because only he can deliver people from natural selfishness. We must trust the Holy Spirit to help us *show* love to those for whom we may not *feel* love.

5.48 How can we be perfect? (1) *In character.* In this life we cannot be flawless, but we can aspire to be as much like Christ as possible, demonstrating moral perfection and sinless behavior. (2) *In holiness.* Like the Pharisees, we are to separate ourselves from the world's sinful values. But unlike the Pharisees, we are to be devoted to God's desires rather than our own, and carry his love and mercy into the world. (3) *In maturity.* We can't achieve Christlike character and holy living all at once, but must grow toward wholeness. Just as we expect different behavior from a baby, a child, a teenager, and an adult, so God expects different behavior from us depending on our stage of spiritual development. (4) *In love.* We can seek to love others as completely as God loves us. We can be perfect if our behavior is appropriate for our maturity level—perfect, yet with much room to grow. Our tendency to sin must never deter us from striving to be more like Christ. Christ calls all of his disciples to excel, to rise above mediocrity and to mature in every area, becoming like him. Those who strive to become perfect will one day be perfect even as he is perfect (1 John 3.2, 3).

6.2 The term *hypocrite,* as used here, means a person who does good acts for appearances only—not out of compassion or other good motives. His actions may be good, but his motives are hollow. These empty acts are his only reward, while God will reward those who are sincere in their faith.

6.3 When Jesus says not to let your left hand know what your right hand is doing, he is teaching that our motives for giving to God and to others must be pure. It is easy to give with mixed motives, to do something for someone if it will benefit us in return. But believers should avoid all scheming and give for the sake of giving and as a response to God's love. Why do *you* give?

6.3, 4 It's easy to do what's right for recognition and praise. To be sure our motives are not selfish, we should do our good deeds quietly or in secret, with no thought of reward. Jesus says we should check our motives in three areas: generosity (6.4), prayer (6.6), and fasting (6.18). Those acts should not be self-centered, but God-centered; done not to make us look good, but to make God look good. The reward God promises is not material, and it is never given to those who seek it. Doing something only for ourselves is not a loving sacrifice. With your next good deed, ask, "Would I still do this if no one would ever know I did it?"

Truly I tell you, they have received their reward. 3 But when you give alms, do not 6.4 Mt 6.6,18
let your left hand know what your right hand is doing, 4 so that your alms may be
done in secret; and your Father who sees in secret will reward you.[l]

Jesus teaches about prayer
(59)

5 "And whenever you pray, do not be like the hypocrites; for they love to stand 6.5 Lk 18.11,12
and pray in the synagogues and at the street corners, so that they may be seen by
others. Truly I tell you, they have received their reward. 6 But whenever you pray, 6.6 Jer 17.10
go into your room and shut the door and pray to your Father who is in secret; and
your Father who sees in secret will reward you.[l]

7 "When you are praying, do not heap up empty phrases as the Gentiles do; for 6.7 1 Kgs 18.26
they think that they will be heard because of their many words. 8 Do not be like
them, for your Father knows what you need before you ask him.

9 "Pray then in this way: 6.9 Mt 23.9 Lk 11.2 Rom 8.15,16
Our Father in heaven,
hallowed be your name.
10 Your kingdom come. 6.10 Ps 103.20
Your will be done,
on earth as it is in heaven.
11 Give us this day our daily bread.[m] 6.11 Prov 30.8
12 And forgive us our debts,
as we also have forgiven our debtors.
13 And do not bring us to the time of trial,[n] 6.13 Lk 22.40,46 Jn 17.15
but rescue us from the evil one.[o]

14 For if you forgive others their trespasses, your heavenly Father will also forgive
you; 15 but if you do not forgive others, neither will your Father forgive your tres- 6.14 Eph 4.32 Col 3.13
passes.

[l] Other ancient authorities add *openly* [m] Or *our bread for tomorrow* [n] Or *us into temptation* [o] Or *from evil.* Other ancient authorities add, in some form, *For the kingdom and the power and the glory are yours forever. Amen.*

6.5, 6 Some people, especially the religious leaders, wanted to be seen as "holy," and public prayer was one way to get attention. Jesus saw through their self-righteous acts, however, and taught that the essence of prayer is not public style but private communication with God. There is a place for public prayer, but to pray only where others will notice you is an indication that your real audience is not God.

6.5–15 Jesus also teaches about prayer in Luke 11.1–13.

6.7, 8 Repeating the same words over and over like a magic incantation is no way to insure that God will hear them. It's not wrong to come to God many times with the same requests – Jesus encourages *persistent* prayer. But he condemns the shallow repetition of words that are not offered with a sincere heart. We can never pray too much if our prayers are honest and sincere.

6.9 This is often called the Lord's prayer because Christ gave it to the disciples. It can be a pattern for our prayers. We should praise God, pray for his work in the world, pray for our daily needs, and pray for help in our daily struggles.

6.9 The phrase "Our Father in heaven" indicates that God is not only majestic and holy, but also personal and loving. The first line of this model prayer is a statement of praise and a commitment to honor God's holy name. We can honor God's name by being careful to use it respectfully. If we use God's name lightly, we aren't remembering God's holiness.

6.10 The phrase "Your kingdom come" is a reference to God's spiritual reign, not Israel's freedom from Rome. God's kingdom was announced in the covenant with Abraham (8.11; Luke 13.28), is present in Christ's reign in believers' hearts (Luke 17.21), and will be complete when all evil is destroyed and God establishes the new heaven and earth (Revelation 21.1).

6.10 When we pray "Your will be done," we are not resigning ourselves to fate, but praying that God's perfect purpose will be accomplished in this world as well as in the next.

6.11 When we pray, "Give us this day our daily bread," we are acknowledging that God is our Sustainer and Provider. It is a misconception to think that we provide for our needs ourselves. We must trust God *daily* to provide what he knows we need.

6.13 God doesn't lead us into temptations, but sometimes he allows us to be tested by them. As disciples, we should pray to be delivered from these trying times and for deliverance from Satan ("the evil one") and his deceit. All Christians struggle with temptation. Sometimes it is so subtle that we don't even realize what is happening to us. God has promised that he won't allow us to be tempted beyond our endurance (1 Corinthians 10.13). Ask God to help you recognize temptation and to give you strength to overcome it and choose God's way. For more on temptation, see the notes on 4.1.

6.14, 15 Jesus gives a startling warning about forgiveness: if we refuse to forgive others, God will also refuse to forgive us. Why? Because when we don't forgive others, we are denying our common ground as sinners in need of God's forgiveness. God's forgiveness of sin is not the direct result of our forgiving others, but it is based on our realizing what forgiveness means (see Ephesians 4.32). It is easy to ask God for forgiveness but difficult to grant it to others. Whenever we ask God to forgive us for sin, we should ask ourselves, "Have I forgiven the people who have wronged me?"

Jesus teaches about fasting
(60)

6.16 Isa 58.5,6 16 "And whenever you fast, do not look dismal, like the hypocrites, for they
disfigure their faces so as to show others that they are fasting. Truly I tell you, they
have received their reward. 17 But when you fast, put oil on your head and wash
your face, 18 so that your fasting may be seen not by others but by your Father who
is in secret; and your Father who sees in secret will reward you.[p]

Jesus teaches about money
(61)

6.19 Prov 23.4,5 19 "Do not store up for yourselves treasures on earth, where moth and rust[q]
6.20 Mt 19.21 Lk 12.33,34 consume and where thieves break in and steal; 20 but store up for yourselves treasures in heaven, where neither moth nor rust[q] consumes and where thieves do not
break in and steal. 21 For where your treasure is, there your heart will be also.
22 "The eye is the lamp of the body. So, if your eye is healthy, your whole body
6.23 Rom 1.21 2 Cor 3.15; 4.4 will be full of light; 23 but if your eye is unhealthy, your whole body will be full of
darkness. If then the light in you is darkness, how great is the darkness!
6.24 1 Jn 2.15 24 "No one can serve two masters; for a slave will either hate the one and love
the other, or be devoted to the one and despise the other. You cannot serve God and
wealth.[r]

[p] Other ancient authorities add *openly* [q] Gk *eating* [r] Gk *mammon*

JESUS AND THE OLD TESTAMENT LAW

Reference	*Examples of Old Testament mercy in justice:*
Leviticus 19.18	"You shall not take vengeance or bear a grudge against any of your people, but you shall love your neighbor as yourself; I am the Lord."
Proverbs 24.28, 29	"Do not be a witness against your neighbor without cause, and do not deceive with your lips. Do not say, 'I will do to others as they have done to me; I will pay them back for what they have done.'"
Proverbs 25.21, 22	"If your enemies are hungry, give them bread to eat; and if they are thirsty, give them water to drink; for you will heap coals of fire on their heads, and the Lord will reward you."
Lamentations 3.27-31	"It is good for one . . . to give one's cheek to the smiter, and be filled with insults. For the Lord will not reject forever."

What seems to be a case of Jesus contradicting the laws of the Old Testament deserves a careful look. It is too easy to overlook how much mercy was written into the Old Testament laws. Above are several examples. What God designed as a system of justice with mercy had been distorted over the years into a license for revenge. It was this misapplication of the law that Jesus attacked.

6.16 Fasting—going without food in order to spend time in prayer—is noble *and* difficult. It gives us time to pray, teaches self-discipline, reminds us that we can live with a lot less, and helps us appreciate God's gifts. Jesus was not condemning fasting, but hypocrisy—fasting in order to gain public approval. Fasting was mandatory for the Jewish people once a year, on the day of atonement (Leviticus 23.32). The Pharisees voluntarily fasted twice a week to impress the people with their "holiness." Jesus commended acts of self-sacrifice done quietly and sincerely. He wanted people to adopt spiritual disciplines for the right reasons, not from a selfish desire for praise.

6.17 Olive oil was used as a common cosmetic like a lotion. Jesus was saying, 'Go about your normal daily routine when you fast. Don't make a show of it.'

6.20 Storing up treasures in heaven is not limited to tithing but is accomplished by all acts of obedience to God. There is a sense in which giving our money to God's work is like investing in heaven, but our intention should be to seek the fulfillment of God's purposes in all we do, not merely what we do with our money.

6.22, 23 Spiritual vision is our capacity to see clearly what God wants us to do and to see the world from his point of view. But this spiritual insight can be easily clouded. Self-serving desires, interests, and goals block that vision. Serving God is the best way to restore it. A "healthy" eye is one that is fixed on God.

6.24 Jesus says we can have only one master. We live in a materialistic society where many people serve money. They spend all their lives collecting and storing it, only to die and leave it behind. Their desire for money and what it can buy far outweighs their commitment to God and spiritual matters. Whatever you store up, you will spend much of your time and energy thinking about. Don't fall into the materialistic trap, because "the love of money is a root of all kinds of evil" (1 Timothy 6.10). Can you honestly say that God, and not money, is your Master? One test is to ask which one occupies more of your thoughts, time, and efforts.

6.24 Jesus contrasted heavenly values with earthly values when he explained that our first loyalty should be to those things that do not fade, cannot be stolen or used up, and never wear out. We should not be fascinated with our possessions lest *they* possess *us*. This means we may have to do some cutting back if our possessions are becoming too important to us. Jesus is calling for a decision that allows us to live contentedly with whatever we have because we have chosen what is eternal and lasting.

Jesus teaches about worry
(62)

25 “Therefore I tell you, do not worry about your life, what you will eat or what — **6.25**
you will drink,[s] or about your body, what you will wear. Is not life more than — Lk 12.22-31 Phil 4.6,19
food, and the body more than clothing? 26 Look at the birds of the air; they neither — 1 Pet 5.7
sow nor reap nor gather into barns, and yet your heavenly Father feeds them. Are — **6.26**
you not of more value than they? 27 And can any of you by worrying add a single — Job 38.41 Ps 39.5,6
hour to your span of life?[t] 28 And why do you worry about clothing? Consider the
lilies of the field, how they grow; they neither toil nor spin, 29 yet I tell you, even — **6.29**
Solomon in all his glory was not clothed like one of these. 30 But if God so clothes — 1 Kgs 10.4-7
the grass of the field, which is alive today and tomorrow is thrown into the oven, — **6.30** Mt 8.26
will he not much more clothe you—you of little faith? 31 Therefore do not worry, — 16.8
saying, ‘What will we eat?’ or ‘What will we drink?’ or ‘What will we wear?’ 32 For — **6.31** Ps 23.1
it is the Gentiles who strive for all these things; and indeed your heavenly Father
knows that you need all these things. 33 But strive first for the kingdom of God[u] and — **6.33**
his[v] righteousness, and all these things will be given to you as well. — Ps 34.9; 37.25 Mk 10.29,30

34 “So do not worry about tomorrow, for tomorrow will bring worries of its
own. Today’s trouble is enough for today.

Jesus teaches about criticizing others
(63/Luke 6.37–42)

7 “Do not judge, so that you may not be judged. 2 For with the judgment you — **7.1**
make you will be judged, and the measure you give will be the measure you — Lk 6.37,38 Rom 2.1-3; 14.4
get. 3 Why do you see the speck in your neighbor’s[w] eye, but do not notice the log — 1 Cor 4.5 Jas 4.11
in your own eye? 4 Or how can you say to your neighbor,[x] ‘Let me take the speck — **7.3**
out of your eye,’ while the log is in your own eye? 5 You hypocrite, first take the log — Lk 6.41,42
out of your own eye, and then you will see clearly to take the speck out of your
neighbor’s[w] eye.

6 “Do not give what is holy to dogs; and do not throw your pearls before swine,
or they will trample them under foot and turn and maul you.

Jesus teaches about asking, seeking, knocking
(64)

7 “Ask, and it will be given you; search, and you will find; knock, and the door

[s] Other ancient authorities lack *or what you will drink* [t] Or *add one cubit to your height* [u] Other ancient authorities lack *of God* [v] Or *its* [w] Gk *brother’s* [x] Gk *brother*

6.25 Because of the ill effects of worry, Jesus tells us not to worry about those needs that God promises to supply. Worry may (1) damage your health, (2) cause the object of your worry to consume your thoughts, (3) disrupt your productivity, (4) negatively affect the way you treat others, and (5) reduce your ability to trust in God. How many ill effects of worry are you experiencing? Here is the difference between worry and genuine concern—worry immobilizes, but concern moves you to action.

6.33 To “strive first for the kingdom of God and his righteousness” means to turn to him first for help, to fill your thoughts with his desires, to take his character for your pattern, and to serve and obey him in everything. What is really important to you? People, objects, goals, and other desires all compete for priority. Any of these can quickly bump God out of first place if you don’t actively choose to give him first place in *every* area of your life.

6.34 Planning for tomorrow is time well spent; worrying about tomorrow is time wasted. Sometimes it’s difficult to tell the difference. Careful planning is thinking ahead about goals, steps, and schedules, and trusting in God’s guidance. When done well, planning can help alleviate worry. The worrier, by contrast, is consumed by fear and finds it difficult to trust God. The worrier lets his plans interfere with his relationship with God. Don’t let worries about tomorrow affect your relationship with God today.

7.1, 2 Jesus tells us to examine our own motives and conduct instead of judging others. The traits that bother us in others are often the habits we dislike in ourselves. Our unbroken bad habits and behavior patterns are the very ones we most want to change in others. Do you find it easy to magnify others’ faults while excusing your own? If you are ready to criticize someone, check to see if you deserve the same criticism. Judge yourself first, and then lovingly forgive and help your neighbor.

7.1–5 Jesus’ statement, “Do not judge” is against the kind of hypercritical, judgmental attitude that tears others down in order to build oneself up. It is not a blanket statement against all critical thinking, but a call to be *discerning* rather than negative. Jesus said to discern false teachers (7.15–23), and Paul taught that we should exercise church discipline (1 Corinthians 5.1, 2), and trust God to be the final Judge (1 Corinthians 4.3–5).

7.6 Pigs (swine) were unclean animals according to God’s law (Deuteronomy 14.8). Anyone who touched an unclean animal became “ceremonially unclean” and could not go to the temple to worship until the uncleanness was removed. Jesus says that we should not entrust holy teachings to unholy or unclean people. It is futile to try to teach holy concepts to people who don’t want to listen and will only tear apart what we say. We should not stop giving God’s Word to unbelievers, but we should be wise and discerning in what we teach to whom so we will not be wasting our time.

7.7, 8 Jesus tells us to persist in pursuing God. People often give

7.7 Mt 21.22 Mk 11.24 Lk 11.9-13 Jn 14.13,14 15.7; 16.23 Jas 1.5,6 1 Jn 3.21,22 5.14,15
7.12 Lk 6.31 Rom 13.8-10 Gal 5.14

will be opened for you. 8 For everyone who asks receives, and everyone who
searches finds, and for everyone who knocks, the door will be opened. 9 Is there
anyone among you who, if your child asks for bread, will give a stone? 10 Or if the
child asks for a fish, will give a snake? 11 If you then, who are evil, know how to
give good gifts to your children, how much more will your Father in heaven give
good things to those who ask him!
12 "In everything do to others as you would have them do to you; for this is the
law and the prophets.

Jesus teaches about the way to heaven
(65)

7.13 Lk 13.24
7.14 Jn 14.6

13 "Enter through the narrow gate; for the gate is wide and the road is easy[y]
that leads to destruction, and there are many who take it. 14 For the gate is narrow
and the road is hard that leads to life, and there are few who find it.

Jesus teaches about fruit in people's lives
(66/Luke 6.43–45)

7.15 Deut 13.1-4 Jer 23.16 Acts 20.29 2 Pet 2.1 1 Jn 4.1
7.16-20 Mt 12.33 Lk 6.43-49

15 "Beware of false prophets, who come to you in sheep's clothing but inwardly are ravenous wolves. 16 You will know them by their fruits. Are grapes
gathered from thorns, or figs from thistles? 17 In the same way, every good tree
bears good fruit, but the bad tree bears bad fruit. 18 A good tree cannot bear bad
fruit, nor can a bad tree bear good fruit. 19 Every tree that does not bear good fruit
is cut down and thrown into the fire. 20 Thus you will know them by their fruits.

[y] Other ancient authorities read *for the road is wide and easy*

SEVEN REASONS NOT TO WORRY		
	6.25	The same God who created life in you can be trusted with the details of your life.
	6.26	Worrying about the future hampers your efforts for today.
	6.27	Worrying is more harmful than helpful.
	6.28–30	God does not ignore those who depend on him.
	6.31, 32	Worry shows a lack of faith and understanding of God.
	6.33	There are real challenges God wants us to pursue, and worrying keeps us from them.
	6.34	Living one day at a time keeps us from being consumed with worry.

up after a few halfhearted efforts and conclude that God cannot be found. But knowing God takes faith, focus, and follow-through, and Jesus assures us that our efforts will be rewarded. Don't give up seeking God. Continue to ask him for more knowledge, patience, wisdom, love, and understanding. He will give them to you.

7.9, 10 The child in Jesus' example asked his father for bread and fish—good and necessary items. If the child had asked for a poisonous snake, would the wise father have granted his request? Sometimes God knows we are praying for "snakes" and does not give us what we ask for, even though we persist in our prayers. As we learn to know God better as a loving Father, we learn to ask for what is good for us, and then he grants it.

7.11 Christ is showing us the heart of God the Father. He is not selfish, begrudging, or stingy, and we don't have to beg or grovel as we come with our requests. He is a loving Father who understands, cares, and comforts. If humans can be kind, imagine how kind God, the Creator of kindness, can be.

7.11 Jesus used the expression, "If you then, who are evil" to contrast sinful, fallible human beings with the holy, perfect God.

7.12 This is commonly known as the Golden Rule. In many religions, it is stated negatively: "Don't do to others what you don't want done to you." By stating it positively, Jesus made it more significant. It is not so hard to refrain from harming others; it is much more difficult to take the initiative in doing something good for them. The Golden Rule as Jesus formulated it is the foundation of active goodness and mercy—the kind God shows to us every day. Think of a good and merciful action you can take today.

7.13, 14 The gateway to eternal life (John 10.7–9) is called "narrow." There is only *one* way to live eternally with God and only a few that decide to follow it. Believing in Jesus is the only way to heaven, because he alone died for our sins and made us right before God. Living his way may not be popular, but it is true and right. Thank God there is one way!

7.15 False prophets were common in Old Testament times. They prophesied only what the king and the people wanted to hear, claiming it was God's message. False teachers are just as common today. Jesus says to beware of those whose words sound religious but who are motivated by money, fame, or power. You can tell who they are because in their teaching they minimize Christ and glorify themselves.

7.20 We should evaluate teachers' words by examining their lives. Just as trees are consistent in the kind of fruit they produce, good teachers consistently exhibit good behavior and high moral character as they attempt to live out the truths of Scripture. This does not mean we should have witch hunts, throwing out Sunday school teachers, pastors, and others who are less than perfect. Every one of us is subject to sin, and we must show the same mercy to others that we need for ourselves. We must examine the teachers' motives, the direction they are taking, and the results they are seeking.

Jesus teaches about those who build houses on rock and sand
(67/Luke 6.46–49)

21 “Not everyone who says to me, ‘Lord, Lord,’ will enter the kingdom of 7.21 Lk 6.46
heaven, but only the one who does the will of my Father in heaven. 22 On that day Jas 1.22
many will say to me, ‘Lord, Lord, did we not prophesy in your name, and cast out 7.22
demons in your name, and do many deeds of power in your name?’ 23 Then I will Acts 19.13-15
declare to them, ‘I never knew you; go away from me, you evildoers.’ 7.23 Mt 25.11,12,41
24 “Everyone then who hears these words of mine and acts on them will be like Lk 13.24-27
a wise man who built his house on rock. 25 The rain fell, the floods came, and the 7.24 2 Tim 2.19
winds blew and beat on that house, but it did not fall, because it had been founded Jas 1.22-24
on rock. 26 And everyone who hears these words of mine and does not act on them
will be like a foolish man who built his house on sand. 27 The rain fell, and the
floods came, and the winds blew and beat against that house, and it fell—and great
was its fall!” 7.28
28 Now when Jesus had finished saying these things, the crowds were as- Isa 50.4 Mt 13.54
tounded at his teaching, 29 for he taught them as one having authority, and not as Mk 1.22; 6.2 Lk 4.32
their scribes. Jn 7.46

3. Jesus performs many miracles

Jesus heals a man with leprosy
(38/Mark 1.40–45; Luke 5.12–16)

8 When Jesus[z] had come down from the mountain, great crowds followed
him; 2 and there was a leper[a] who came to him and knelt before him, saying, 8.2
“Lord, if you choose, you can make me clean.” 3 He stretched out his hand and Lev 14.3 Mk 1.40-44
touched him, saying, “I do choose. Be made clean!” Immediately his leprosy[a] was Lk 5.12-14

[z] Gk *he* [a] The terms *leper* and *leprosy* can refer to several diseases

---

7.21 Some self-professed athletes can “talk” a great game, but that tells you nothing about their athletic skills. And not everyone who talks about heaven belongs to God’s kingdom. Jesus is more concerned about our *walk* than our *talk*. He wants us to *do* right, not just *say* the right words. Your house (which represents your life, 7.24) will withstand the storms of life only if you do what is right instead of just talking about it. What you do cannot be separated from what you believe.

7.21–23 Jesus exposed those people who sounded religious but had no personal relationship with him. On “that day” (the day of Judgment), only our relationship with Christ—our acceptance of him as Savior and our obedience to him—will matter. Many people think that if they are “good” and sound religious, they will be rewarded with eternal life. In reality, faith in Christ is what will count at the judgment.

7.22 “That day” is the final day of reckoning when God will settle all accounts, judging sin and rewarding faith.

7.24 To build “on rock” means to be a hearing, responding disciple, not a phony, superficial one. Practicing obedience becomes the solid foundation to weather the storms of life. See James 1.22–27 for more on practicing what we hear.

7.26 Like a house of cards, the fool’s life crumbles. Most people do not deliberately seek to build upon a false or inferior foundation; instead, they just don’t think about their life’s purpose. Many people are headed for destruction, not out of stubbornness but out of thoughtlessness. Part of our responsibility as believers is to help others stop and think about where their lives are headed and to point out the consequences of ignoring Christ’s message.

7.29 The scribes (religious scholars) often cited traditions and quoted authorities to support their arguments and interpretations. But Jesus spoke with a new authority—his own. He didn’t need to quote anyone, because he was the original Word (John 1.1).

8.2, 3 Leprosy, like AIDS, was a terrifying disease because there was no known cure. In Jesus’ day, the word *leprosy* was used for a variety of similar diseases, and some forms were contagious. If a person contracted the contagious type, a priest declared him a leper and banished him from his home and city. He was sent to live in a community with other lepers until he either got better or died. Yet when the leper begged Jesus to heal him, Jesus reached out and touched him, even though his skin was covered with the dread disease.

Sin is also an incurable disease—and we all have it. Only Christ’s healing touch can miraculously take away our sins and restore us to real living. But first, just like the leper, we must realize our inability to cure ourselves and ask for Christ’s saving help.

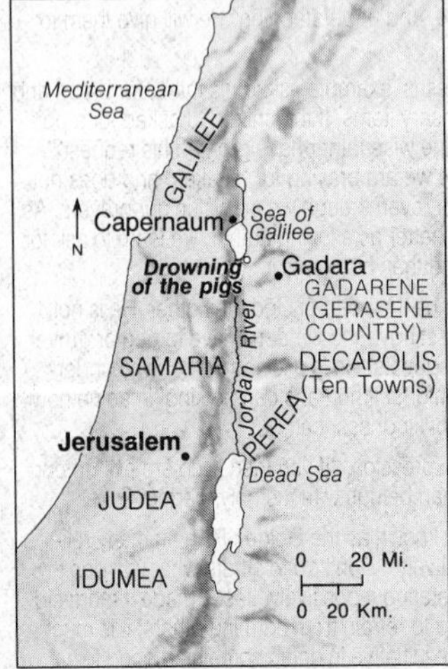

JESUS’ MIRACULOUS POWER DISPLAYED
Jesus finished the sermon he had given on a hillside near Galilee and returned to Capernaum. As he and his disciples crossed the Sea of Galilee, Jesus calmed a fierce storm. Then, in the Gentile Gadarene country, Jesus commanded demons to come out of two men.

8.4 Mk 1.43,44 Lk 5.14; 17.14
cleansed. 4 Then Jesus said to him, "See that you say nothing to anyone; but go,
show yourself to the priest, and offer the gift that Moses commanded, as a testimony to them."

A Roman soldier demonstrates faith
(68/Luke 7.1–10)

8.5 Lk 7.1-10
5 When he entered Capernaum, a centurion came to him, appealing to him 6 and
saying, "Lord, my servant is lying at home paralyzed, in terrible distress." 7 And he
said to him, "I will come and cure him." 8 The centurion answered, "Lord, I am not
worthy to have you come under my roof; but only speak the word, and my servant
8.9 Ps 107.20
will be healed. 9 For I also am a man under authority, with soldiers under me; and
I say to one, 'Go,' and he goes, and to another, 'Come,' and he comes, and to my
slave, 'Do this,' and the slave does it." 10 When Jesus heard him, he was amazed
8.11 Isa 2.2; 11.10 Lk 13.28,29 Acts 10.45 11.18; 14.27 Eph 3.6
and said to those who followed him, "Truly I tell you, in no one[b] in Israel have I
found such faith. 11 I tell you, many will come from east and west and will eat with
Abraham and Isaac and Jacob in the kingdom of heaven, 12 while the heirs of the
kingdom will be thrown into the outer darkness, where there will be weeping and
8.12 Mt 13.41,42 21.43
gnashing of teeth." 13 And to the centurion Jesus said, "Go; let it be done for you
according to your faith." And the servant was healed in that hour.

Jesus heals Peter's mother-in-law and many others
(35/Mark 1.29–34; Luke 4.38–41)

14 When Jesus entered Peter's house, he saw his mother-in-law lying in bed
with a fever; 15 he touched her hand, and the fever left her, and she got up and began
to serve him. 16 That evening they brought to him many who were possessed with
8.17 1 Pet 2.24
demons; and he cast out the spirits with a word, and cured all who were sick. 17 This
was to fulfill what had been spoken through the prophet Isaiah, "He took our infirmities and bore our diseases."

[b] Other ancient authorities read *Truly I tell you, not even*

8.4 The law required a healed leper to be examined by the priest (Leviticus 14). Jesus wanted this man to give his story firsthand to the priest to prove that his leprosy was completely gone so that he could be restored to his community.

8.5, 6 The centurion could have let many obstacles stand between him and Jesus—pride, doubt, money, language, distance, time, self-sufficiency, power, race. But he didn't. If he did not let these barriers block his approach to Jesus, we don't need to either. What keeps you from Christ?

8.8–12 A centurion was a career military officer in the Roman army with control over 100 soldiers. Roman soldiers, of all people, were hated by the Jews for their oppression, control, and ridicule. Yet this man's genuine faith amazed Jesus! This hated Gentile's faith put to shame the stagnant piety of many of the Jewish religious leaders.

8.10–12 Jesus told the crowd that many religious Jews who should be in the kingdom would be excluded because of their lack of faith. Entrenched in their religious traditions, they could not accept Christ and his new message. We must be careful not to become so set in our religious habits that we expect God to work only in specified ways. Don't limit God by your mindset and lack of faith.

8.11, 12 "East and west" stands for the four corners of the earth. All the faithful people of God will be gathered to feast with the Messiah (Isaiah 6, 55). The Jews should have known that when the Messiah came, his blessings would be for Gentiles too (see Isaiah 66.12, 19). But this message came as a shock because they were too wrapped up in their own affairs and destiny. In claiming God's promises, we must not apply them so personally that we forget to see what God wants to do to reach *all* the people he loves.

8.11, 12 Matthew emphasizes this universal theme—Jesus' message is for everyone. The Old Testament prophets knew this (see Isaiah 56.3, 6–8; 66.12, 19; Malachi 1.11), but many New Testament Jewish leaders chose to ignore it. Each individual has to choose to accept or reject the gospel, and no one can become part of God's kingdom on the basis of heritage or connections. Having a Christian family is a wonderful blessing, but it won't guarantee you eternal life. *You* must believe in and follow Christ.

8.14 Peter was one of Jesus' 12 disciples. His Profile is found in chapter 27.

8.14, 15 Peter's mother-in-law gives us a beautiful example to follow. Her response to Jesus' touch was to serve Jesus and his disciples—immediately. Has God ever helped you through a dangerous or difficult situation? If so, you should ask, "How can I express my gratitude to him?" Because God has promised us all the rewards of his kingdom, we should look for ways to serve him and his followers now.

8.16, 17 Matthew continues to show Jesus' kingly nature. Through a single touch, he heals (8.3, 15); when he speaks a single word, evil spirits flee his presence (8.16). Jesus has authority over all evil powers and all earthly disease. He also has power and authority to conquer sin. Sickness and evil are consequences of living in a fallen world. But in the future, when God cleanses the earth from sin, there will be no more sickness and death. Jesus' healing miracles were a taste of what the whole world will one day experience in God's kingdom.

Jesus teaches about the cost of following him
(122/Luke 9.51–62)

18 Now when Jesus saw great crowds around him, he gave orders to go over to 8.19 Lk 9.57-60
the other side. 19 A scribe then approached and said, "Teacher, I will follow you 8.20
wherever you go." 20 And Jesus said to him, "Foxes have holes, and birds of the air Dan 7.13,14 Jn 1.11
have nests; but the Son of Man has nowhere to lay his head." 21 Another of his Acts 7.56
disciples said to him, "Lord, first let me go and bury my father." 22 But Jesus said 8.22 Mk 2.14
to him, "Follow me, and let the dead bury their own dead." Jn 1.43; 21.19

Jesus calms the storm
(87/Mark 4.35–41; Luke 8.22–25)

23 And when he got into the boat, his disciples followed him. 24 A windstorm 8.23 Mk 4.35-41
arose on the sea, so great that the boat was being swamped by the waves; but he was Lk 8.22-25
asleep. 25 And they went and woke him up, saying, "Lord, save us! We are perishing!" 26 And he said to them, "Why are you afraid, you of little faith?" Then he got 8.26
up and rebuked the winds and the sea; and there was a dead calm. 27 They were Job 38.8-11 Ps 65.7; 89.9
amazed, saying, "What sort of man is this, that even the winds and the sea obey 107.29 Prov 30.4
him?" Phil 4.6

Jesus sends demons into a herd of pigs
(88/Mark 5.1–20; Luke 8.26–39)

28 When he came to the other side, to the country of the Gadarenes,[c] two de-

[c] Other ancient authorities read *Gergesenes*; others, *Gerasenes*

8.19, 20 Following Jesus is not always easy or comfortable. Often it means great cost and sacrifice, with no earthly rewards or security. Jesus didn't have a place to call home. You may find that following Christ costs you popularity, friendships, leisure time, or treasured habits. But while the cost of following Christ is high, the value of being Christ's disciple is even higher. Discipleship is an investment that lasts for eternity and yields incredible rewards.

8.21, 22 This disciple was not asking permission to go to his father's funeral, but rather to put off following Jesus until his elderly father died. Perhaps he was the firstborn son and wanted to be sure to claim his inheritance. Perhaps he didn't want to face his father's wrath if he left the family business to follow an itinerant preacher. Whether his concern was financial security, family approval, or something else, he did not want to commit himself to Jesus just yet. Jesus, however, would not accept his excuse.

8.21, 22 Jesus was always direct with those who wanted to follow him. He made sure they counted the cost and set aside any conditions they might have for following him. As God's Son, Jesus did not hesitate to demand complete loyalty. Even family loyalty was not to take priority over the demands of obedience. His direct challenge forces us to ask ourselves about our own priorities in following him. The decision to follow Christ should not be put off, even though other loyalties compete for our attention. Nothing should be placed above a total commitment to living for Christ.

8.23 This would have been a fishing boat, because many of Jesus' disciples were fishermen. Josephus, an ancient historian, wrote that there were usually more than 300 fishing boats on the Sea of Galilee at one time. This boat was large enough to hold Jesus and his 12 disciples and was powered by both oars and sails. During a storm, however, the sails were taken down to keep them from ripping and to make the boat easier to control.

8.24 The Sea of Galilee is an unusual body of water. It is relatively small (13 miles long, 7 miles wide), but it is 150 feet deep, and the shoreline is 680 feet below sea level. Sudden storms can appear over the surrounding mountains with little warning, stirring the water into violent 20-foot waves. The disciples had not foolishly set out in a storm. They had been caught without warning, and their danger was great.

8.25 Although the disciples had witnessed many miracles, they panicked in this storm. As experienced sailors, they knew its danger; what they did not know was that Christ could control the forces of nature. There is often a stormy area of our human nature where we feel God can't or won't work. When we truly understand who he is, however, we will realize that he controls both the storms of nature and the storms of the troubled heart. Jesus' power that calmed this storm can also help us deal with the problems we face. He is willing to help if we only ask him. We should never discount his power even in terrible trials.

8.28 The country of the Gadarenes is located southeast of the Sea of Galilee, near the town of Gadara, the capital of the region (see map). Gadara was a member of the Decapolis (see the note on Mark 5.20). These ten cities with independent governments were largely inhabited by Gentiles, which explains the herd of swine (8.30). The Jews did not raise pigs because they were considered unclean and thus unfit to eat.

8.28 A demoniac is a person under the control of a demon. Demons were fallen angels who joined Satan in his rebellion against God and are now evil spirits under Satan's control. They help Satan tempt people to sin and have great destructive powers. But whenever they are confronted by Jesus, they lose their power. These demons recognized Jesus as God's Son (8.29), but they didn't think they had to obey him. Just believing is not enough (see James 2.19 for a discussion of belief and devils). Faith is more than belief. By faith, you accept what Jesus has done for you, receive him as the only one who can save you from sin, and live out your faith by obeying his Word.

8.28 Matthew says there were two demoniacs, while Mark and Luke refer only to one. Apparently Mark and Luke mention only the man who did the talking.

8.28 According to Jewish ceremonial laws, the men Jesus encountered were unclean in three ways: they were Gentiles (non-Jews), they were demon-possessed, and they lived in a graveyard. Jesus helped them anyway. We should not turn our backs on people who are "unclean" or repulsive to us, or who violate our moral standards and religious beliefs. Instead, we must realize that every human individual is a unique creation of God who needs to be touched by his love.

moniacs coming out of the tombs met him. They were so fierce that no one could
8.29 Mk 1.23,24 pass that way. 29 Suddenly they shouted, "What have you to do with us, Son of
Lk 4.33,34 God? Have you come here to torment us before the time?" 30 Now a large herd of
2 Pet 2.4 swine was feeding at some distance from them. 31 The demons begged him, "If you
8.30 Deut 14.8 cast us out, send us into the herd of swine." 32 And he said to them, "Go!" So they
came out and entered the swine; and suddenly, the whole herd rushed down the
steep bank into the sea and perished in the water. 33 The swineherds ran off, and on
going into the town, they told the whole story about what had happened to the
8.34 Lk 5.8 demoniacs. 34 Then the whole town came out to meet Jesus; and when they saw
9 him, they begged him to leave their neighborhood. 1 And after getting into a
boat he crossed the sea and came to his own town.

Jesus heals a paralyzed man
(39/Mark 2.1–12; Luke 5.17–26)

9.2 Mk 2.2-12 2 And just then some people were carrying a paralyzed man lying on a bed.
Lk 5.17-26 When Jesus saw their faith, he said to the paralytic, "Take heart, son; your sins are
9.3 Eph 1.7 forgiven.' 3 Then some of the scribes said to themselves, "This man is blasphem-
9.4 Mt 12.25 ing." 4 But Jesus, perceiving their thoughts, said, "Why do you think evil in your
Lk 6.8; 9.47 hearts? 5 For which is easier, to say, 'Your sins are forgiven,' or to say, 'Stand up
11.17 and walk'? 6 But so that you may know that the Son of Man has authority on earth
9.5 Acts 5.31 to forgive sins"—he then said to the paralytic—"Stand up, take your bed and go to
9.8 Mt 15.31 your home." 7 And he stood up and went to his home. 8 When the crowds saw it,
Mk 2.12 they were filled with awe, and they glorified God, who had given such authority to
Lk 7.16 human beings.

Jesus eats with sinners at Matthew's house
(40/Mark 2.13–17; Luke 5.27–32)

9.9 Lk 15.1,2 9 As Jesus was walking along, he saw a man called Matthew sitting at the tax
Acts 1.14 booth; and he said to him, "Follow me." And he got up and followed him.

8.29 The Bible tells us that at the end of the world, the devil and his angels will be thrown into the lake of fire (Revelation 20.10). When the demons asked if Jesus had come to torment them "before the time," they showed they knew their ultimate fate.

8.32 When the demons entered the pigs, they drove the animals into the sea. The devils' action proves their destructive intent—if they could not destroy the men, they would destroy the pigs. Jesus' action, by contrast, shows the value he places on each human life.

8.33 The swineherds were those who watched over the pigs.

8.34 Why did the people ask Jesus to leave? Unlike their own pagan gods, Jesus could not be contained, controlled, or appeased. They feared Jesus' supernatural power, a power they had never before witnessed. And they were upset about losing a herd of pigs more than they were glad about the deliverance of the demon-possessed men. Are you more concerned about property and programs than people? Human beings are created in God's image and have eternal value. How foolish and yet how easy to value possessions, investments, and even animals above human life. Would you rather have Jesus leave than finish his work in you?

9.1 "His own town" was Capernaum, a good choice for Jesus' base of operations. It was a wealthy city due to fishing and trade. Situated on the Sea of Galilee in a densely populated area, it housed the Roman garrison that kept peace in the region. The city was a cultural melting pot, greatly influenced by Greek and Roman manners, dress, architecture, and politics.

9.2 The first words Jesus said to the paralyzed man were "Your sins are forgiven." Then he healed the man. We must be careful not to concentrate on God's power to heal physical sickness more than on his power to forgive spiritual sickness in the form of sin. Jesus saw that in addition to physical health, this man needed spiritual health. Spiritual health comes only from Jesus' healing touch.

9.2 Both the man's body and his spirit were paralyzed—he could not walk and he did not know Jesus. But the man's spiritual state was Jesus' first concern. If God does not heal us or someone we love, we need to remember that physical healing is not Christ's only concern. We will all be completely healed in Christ's coming kingdom; but first we have to come to know Jesus.

9.3 Blasphemy is claiming to be God and applying his characteristics to yourself. The religious leaders rightly saw that Jesus was claiming to be God. What they did not understand was that he *is* God and thus has the authority to heal and to forgive sins.

9.5, 6 It's easy to tell someone his sins are forgiven; it's a lot more difficult to reverse a case of paralysis! Jesus backed up his words by healing the man's legs. His action showed that his words were true; he had the power to forgive as well as to heal. Talk is cheap, but our words lack meaning if our actions do not back them up. We can say we love God or others, but if we are not taking practical steps to demonstrate that love, our words are empty and meaningless. How well do your actions back up what you say?

9.9 Matthew was a Jew who was appointed by the Romans to be the area's tax collector. He collected taxes from the citizens as well as from merchants passing through town. Tax collectors were expected to take a commission on the taxes they collected, but most of them overcharged and kept the profits. Tax collectors were thus hated by the Jews because of their reputation for cheating and their support of Rome.

9.9 When Jesus called Matthew to be one of his disciples, Matthew jumped up and followed, leaving a lucrative career. When God calls you to follow or obey him, do you do it with as much abandon as Matthew? Sometimes the decision to follow Christ requires difficult or painful choices. Like Matthew, we must decide to leave behind those things that would keep us from following Christ.

10 And as he sat at dinner[d] in the house, many tax collectors and sinners came 9.11
and were sitting[e] with him and his disciples. 11 When the Pharisees saw this, they Mt 11.19 Mk 2.16
said to his disciples, "Why does your teacher eat with tax collectors and sinners?" Lk 5.30; 15.2
12 But when he heard this, he said, "Those who are well have no need of a physi- 9.13
cian, but those who are sick. 13 Go and learn what this means, 'I desire mercy, not Hos 6.6 Mic 6.6-8
sacrifice.' For I have come to call not the righteous but sinners." Mt 12.7; 18.11

Religious leaders ask Jesus about fasting
(41/Mark 2.18–22; Luke 5.33–39)

14 Then the disciples of John came to him, saying, "Why do we and the Phari- 9.14
sees fast often,[f] but your disciples do not fast?" 15 And Jesus said to them, "The Mk 2.18-22 Lk 5.33-39
wedding guests cannot mourn as long as the bridegroom is with them, can they? 18.12
The days will come when the bridegroom is taken away from them, and then they 9.15 Jn 3.29
will fast. 16 No one sews a piece of unshrunk cloth on an old cloak, for the patch Acts 13.2; 14.23
pulls away from the cloak, and a worse tear is made. 17 Neither is new wine put into
old wineskins; otherwise, the skins burst, and the wine is spilled, and the skins are
destroyed; but new wine is put into fresh wineskins, and so both are preserved."

Jesus heals a bleeding woman and restores a girl to life
(89/Mark 5.21–43; Luke 8.40–56)

18 While he was saying these things to them, suddenly a leader of the syna- 9.18 Mk 5.22-43
gogue[g] came in and knelt before him, saying, "My daughter has just died; but Lk 8.41-56
come and lay your hand on her, and she will live." 19 And Jesus got up and followed
him, with his disciples. 20 Then suddenly a woman who had been suffering from
hemorrhages for twelve years came up behind him and touched the fringe of his 9.22 Mt 9.29; 15.28
cloak, 21 for she said to herself, "If I only touch his cloak, I will be made well." Mk 10.52 Lk 7.50; 17.19
22 Jesus turned, and seeing her he said, "Take heart, daughter; your faith has made 18.42

[d] Gk *reclined* [e] Gk *were reclining* [f] Other ancient authorities lack *often* [g] Gk lacks *of the synagogue*

9.10–13 When he visited Matthew, Jesus hurt his reputation. Matthew was cheating the people, but Jesus found and changed him. We should not be afraid to reach out to people who are living in sin, because God's message can change anyone.

9.11, 12 The Pharisees constantly tried to trap Jesus, and they thought his association with these "low lives" was the perfect opportunity. They were more concerned with their own appearance of holiness than with helping people, with criticism than encouragement, with outward respectability than practical help. But God is concerned for all people, including the sinful and hurting ones. The Christian life is not a popularity contest! Following Jesus' example, we should share the gospel with the poor, immoral, lonely, and outcast, not just the rich, moral, popular, and powerful.

9.13 Those who are sure they are righteous can't be saved, because the first step in following Jesus is acknowledging our need and admitting that we don't have all the answers. For more on "I desire mercy, not sacrifice," see the chart in Hosea 7.

9.14 John's disciples fasted (went without food) to repent of sin and prepare for the Messiah's coming. Jesus' disciples did not need to fast, because he is the Messiah and he was with them! Jesus did not condemn fasting—he himself fasted (4.2). He emphasized that fasting must be done for the right reasons.

9.14 John the Baptist's message was harsh, and it focused on law. When people look at God's law and compare themselves to it, they realize how far they fall short and that they must repent. Jesus' message focused on life, the result of turning from sin and turning to him. John's disciples had the right start, but they needed to take the next step and trust in Jesus. Where is your focus—on law or on Christ?

9.15 The arrival of the kingdom of heaven was like a wedding feast with Jesus as the bridegroom. His disciples, therefore, were filled with joy. It would not be right to mourn or fast when the bridegroom was present.

9.17 In Bible times, wine was not kept in glass bottles but in goatskins sewn around the edges to form watertight bags. New wine expanded as it fermented, stretching its wineskin. After the wine had aged, the stretched skin would burst if more new wine was poured into it. New wine was always put into *new* wine skins.

9.17 Jesus did not come to "patch up" the old religious system of Judaism with its rules and traditions. If he had, his message would have damaged it. His purpose was to bring in something new, though it had been prophesied for centuries. This new message, the gospel, said that Jesus Christ, God's Son, came to earth to offer all people forgiveness of sins and reconciliation with God. The gospel did not fit into the old rigid legalistic system of religion. It needed a fresh start. The message will always remain "new" because it must be accepted and applied in every generation. When we follow Christ, we must be prepared for new ways to live, new ways to look at people, and new ways to serve.

9.18 Mark and Luke say this man's name was Jairus (Mark 5.22; Luke 8.41). As leader of the synagogue, he was responsible for administration—looking after the building, supervising worship, running the school on weekdays, and finding rabbis to teach on the sabbath.

9.20–22 This woman had suffered for 12 years with "hemorrhages" (a menstrual disorder). In our times of desperation, we don't have to worry about the correct way to reach out to God. Like this woman, we can simply reach out in faith. He will respond.

9.22 God changed a situation that had been a problem for years. Like the leper and the demoniacs (see the notes on 8.3 and 8.28), this diseased woman was considered unclean. For 12 years, she too had been one of the "untouchables" and had not been able to lead a normal life. But Jesus changed that and restored her. Sometimes we are tempted to give up on people or situations that have not changed for many years. God can change what seems unchangeable, giving new purpose and hope.

9.23 2 Chron 35.25 Jer 9.17,18
9.24 Jn 11.11-13 Acts 20.10

you well." And instantly the woman was made well. 23 When Jesus came to the
leader's house and saw the flute players and the crowd making a commotion, 24 he
said, "Go away; for the girl is not dead but sleeping." And they laughed at him.
25 But when the crowd had been put outside, he went in and took her by the hand,
and the girl got up. 26 And the report of this spread throughout that district.

Jesus heals the blind and mute
(90)

9.27 Mk 10.47

27 As Jesus went on from there, two blind men followed him, crying loudly,
"Have mercy on us, Son of David!" 28 When he entered the house, the blind men

---

MATTHEW

More than any other disciple, Matthew had a clear idea of how much it would cost to follow Jesus, yet he did not hesitate a moment. When he left his tax-collecting booth, he guaranteed himself unemployment. For several of the other disciples, there was always fishing to return to, but for Matthew, there was no turning back.

Two changes happened to Matthew when he decided to follow Jesus. First, Jesus gave him a new life. He not only belonged to a new group; he belonged to the Son of God. He was not just accepting a different way of life; he was now an accepted person. For a despised tax collector, that change must have been wonderful! Second, Jesus gave Matthew a new purpose for his skills. When he followed Jesus, the only tool from his past job that he carried with him was his pen. From the beginning, God had made him a record-keeper. Jesus' call eventually allowed him to put his skills to their finest work. Matthew was a keen observer, and he must have recorded what he saw going on around him. The Gospel that bears his name came as a result.

Matthew's experience points out that each of us, from the beginning, is one of God's works in progress. Much of what God has for us he gives long before we are able to consciously respond to him. He trusts us with skills and abilities ahead of schedule. He has made us each capable of being his servant. When we trust him with what he has given us, we begin a life of real adventure. Matthew couldn't have known that God would use the very skills he had sharpened as a tax collector to record the greatest story ever lived. And God has no less meaningful a purpose for each one of us. Have you recognized Jesus saying to you, "Follow me"? What has been your response?

Strengths and accomplishments:
- Was one of Jesus' 12 disciples
- Responded immediately to Jesus' call
- Invited many friends to his home to meet Jesus
- Compiled the Gospel of Matthew
- Clarified for his Jewish audience Jesus' fulfillment of Old Testament prophecies

Lessons from his life:
- Jesus consistently accepted people from every level of society
- Matthew was given a new life, and his God-given skills of record-keeping and attention to detail were given new purpose
- Having been accepted by Jesus, Matthew immediately tried to bring others into contact with Jesus

Vital statistics:
- Where: Capernaum
- Occupation: Tax collector, disciple of Jesus
- Relatives: Father: Alphaeus
- Contemporaries: Jesus, Pilate, Herod, other disciples

Key verse:
"As he was walking along, he saw Levi son of Alphaeus sitting at the tax booth, and he said to him, 'Follow me.' And he got up and followed him" (Mark 2.14).

Matthew's story is told in the Gospels. He is also mentioned in Acts 1.13.

9.23–26 The synagogue leader didn't come to Jesus until his daughter was dead – it was too late for anyone else to help. But Jesus raised her! In our lives, Christ can make a difference when it seems too late for anyone else to help. He can bring healing to broken relationships, release from addicting habits, and forgiveness and healing of emotional scars. If your situation looks hopeless, remember that Christ can do the impossible.

9.27–30 Jesus didn't respond immediately to the blind men's pleas. He waited to see if they had faith. Not everyone who says he wants help really believes God can help. Jesus may have waited and questioned these men to emphasize and increase their faith. When you think that God is slow in answering your prayers, consider that he might be testing you as he did the blind men. Do you believe God can help you? Do you *really* want his help?

9.27 "Son of David" was a popular way of addressing Jesus as the Messiah, because it was known that the Messiah would be a descendant of David (Isaiah 9.7).

9.28 These blind men were persistent. They knew Jesus could heal them, and they would let nothing stop them from finding him. If you believe Jesus is the answer to your every need, don't let anything or anyone stop you from reaching him.

came to him; and Jesus said to them, “Do you believe that I am able to do this?” 9.30 Ps 146.8
They said to him, “Yes, Lord.” 29 Then he touched their eyes and said, “According Lk 5.14
to your faith let it be done to you.” 30 And their eyes were opened. Then Jesus 9.31
sternly ordered them, “See that no one knows of this.” 31 But they went away and Mk 7.36
spread the news about him throughout that district. 9.32 Lk 11.14,15
32 After they had gone away, a demoniac who was mute was brought to him.
33 And when the demon had been cast out, the one who had been mute spoke; and 9.34 Mt 12.24
the crowds were amazed and said, “Never has anything like this been seen in Is- Mk 3.22
rael.” 34 But the Pharisees said, “By the ruler of the demons he casts out the de- Lk 11.15 Jn 7.20
mons.”[h]

Jesus urges the disciples to pray for workers
(92)

35 Then Jesus went about all the cities and villages, teaching in their synagogues, and proclaiming the good news of the kingdom, and curing every disease
and every sickness. 36 When he saw the crowds, he had compassion for them, be- 9.37 Lk 10.2
cause they were harassed and helpless, like sheep without a shepherd. 37 Then he Jn 4.35
said to his disciples, “The harvest is plentiful, but the laborers are few; 38 therefore 9.38 Acts 13.2
ask the Lord of the harvest to send out laborers into his harvest.” 2 Thess 3.1

Jesus sends out the twelve disciples
(93/Mark 6.7–13; Luke 9.1–6)

10 Then Jesus[i] summoned his twelve disciples and gave them authority over 10.1 Mk 3.13; 6.7
unclean spirits, to cast them out, and to cure every disease and every sick- Lk 6.13; 9.1
ness. 2 These are the names of the twelve apostles: first, Simon, also known as 10.2
Peter, and his brother Andrew; James son of Zebedee, and his brother John; 3 Philip Jn 1.42
and Bartholomew; Thomas and Matthew the tax collector; James son of Alphaeus,
and Thaddaeus;[j] 4 Simon the Cananaean, and Judas Iscariot, the one who betrayed 10.4 Jn 13.26
him.

[h] Other ancient authorities lack this verse [i] Gk *he* [j] Other ancient authorities read *Lebbaeus,* or *Lebbaeus called Thaddaeus*

9.30 Jesus told the people to keep quiet about his healings because he did not want to be known only as a miracle worker. He healed because he had compassion on people, but he also wanted to bring *spiritual* healing to a sin-sick world.

9.32 While Jesus was on earth, demonic forces seemed especially active. Although we cannot always be sure why or how demon possession occurs, it causes both physical and mental problems. In this case, the demon made the man unable to talk. For more on demons and demon possession, read the notes on 8.28 and Mark 1.23.

9.34 In chapter 9, the Pharisees accuse Jesus of four different sins: blasphemy, immorality, impiety, and demon possession. Matthew shows how Jesus was maligned by those who should have received him most gladly. Why did the Pharisees do this? (1) Jesus bypassed their religious authority. (2) He weakened their control over the people. (3) He challenged their cherished beliefs. (4) He exposed their insincere motives.

9.34 While the Pharisees questioned, debated, and dissected Jesus, people were being healed and lives changed right in front of them. Their skepticism was based not on insufficient evidence but on jealousy of Jesus' popularity.

9.35 The good news of the kingdom was that the promised and long-awaited Messiah had finally come. His healing miracles were a sign that his teaching was true.

9.35–38 Jesus needs workers who know how to deal with people's problems. We can comfort others and show them the way to live because we have been helped with our problems by God and his laborers (2 Corinthians 1.3–7).

9.36 Ezekiel also compared Israel to sheep without a shepherd (Ezekiel 34.5, 6). Jesus came to be the Shepherd, the one who could show people how to avoid life's pitfalls (see John 10.14).

9.37, 38 Jesus looked at the crowds following him and referred to them as a field ripe for harvest. Many people are ready to give their lives to Christ if someone will show them how. Jesus commands us to pray that people will respond to this need for laborers. Often, when we pray for something, God answers our prayers by using *us.* Be prepared for God to use you to show another person the way to him.

10.1 Jesus *called* his 12 disciples. He didn't draft them, force them, or ask them to volunteer; he chose them to serve him in a special way. Christ calls us today. He doesn't twist our arms and make us do something we don't want to do. We can choose to join him or remain behind. When Christ calls you to follow him, how do you respond?

10.2–4 The list of Jesus' 12 disciples doesn't give us many details—probably because there weren't many impressive details to tell. Jesus called people from all walks of life—fishermen, political activists, tax collectors. He called common men and leaders; rich and poor; educated and uneducated. Today, many people think only certain people are fit to follow Christ, but this was not the attitude of the Master himself. God can use anyone, no matter how insignificant he appears. When you feel small and useless, remember that God uses ordinary people to do his extraordinary work.

10.3 Bartholomew is probably another name for Nathanael, whom we meet in John 1.45–51. Thaddaeus is also known as Judas, brother of James. The disciples are also listed in Mark 3.16–19; Luke 6.14–16; and Acts 1.13.

10.4 Simon the Cananaean was a member of the Zealots, a radical

10.5 2 Kgs 17.24 Jn 4.9
10.6 Isa 53.6 Jer 50.6,17 Mt 15.24 Acts 3.25,26 13.46
10.9,10 1 Cor 9.7-10 1 Tim 5.17,18
10.14 Acts 13.51
10.15 Mt 11.23,24

5 These twelve Jesus sent out with the following instructions: "Go nowhere
among the Gentiles, and enter no town of the Samaritans, 6 but go rather to the lost
sheep of the house of Israel. 7 As you go, proclaim the good news, 'The kingdom
of heaven has come near.'[k] 8 Cure the sick, raise the dead, cleanse the lepers,[l] cast
out demons. You received without payment; give without payment. 9 Take no gold,
or silver, or copper in your belts, 10 no bag for your journey, or two tunics, or
sandals, or a staff; for laborers deserve their food. 11 Whatever town or village you
enter, find out who in it is worthy, and stay there until you leave. 12 As you enter the
house, greet it. 13 If the house is worthy, let your peace come upon it; but if it is not
worthy, let your peace return to you. 14 If anyone will not welcome you or listen to
your words, shake off the dust from your feet as you leave that house or town.
15 Truly I tell you, it will be more tolerable for the land of Sodom and Gomorrah on
the day of judgment than for that town.

Jesus prepares the disciples for persecution
(94)

10.16 Mk 13.8-13 1 Cor 14.20
10.17 Acts 5.40
10.18 Acts 12.1; 24.10
10.20 2 Sam 23.2

16 "See, I am sending you out like sheep into the midst of wolves; so be wise
as serpents and innocent as doves. 17 Beware of them, for they will hand you over
to councils and flog you in their synagogues; 18 and you will be dragged before
governors and kings because of me, as a testimony to them and the Gentiles.
19 When they hand you over, do not worry about how you are to speak or what you
are to say; for what you are to say will be given to you at that time; 20 for it is not
you who speak, but the Spirit of your Father speaking through you. 21 Brother will

[k] Or *is at hand* [l] The terms *leper* and *leprosy* can refer to several diseases

---

political party working for the violent overthrow of Roman rule in Israel. Luke calls him Simon the Zealot (Luke 6.15; Acts 1.13).

10.5, 6 Why didn't Jesus send the disciples to the Gentiles or the Samaritans? A Gentile is anyone who is not a Jew. The Samaritans were a race that resulted from intermarriage between Jews and Gentiles after the Old Testament captivities (see 2 Kings 17.24). Jesus asked his disciples to go only to the Jews because he came *first* to the Jews. God chose them to tell the rest of the world about him. Jewish disciples and apostles preached the gospel of the risen Christ all around the Roman Empire, and soon Gentiles were pouring into the church. The Bible clearly teaches that God's message of salvation is for *all* people, regardless of race, sex, or national origin (Genesis 12.3; Isaiah 25.6; 56.3–7; Malachi 1.11; Acts 10.34, 35; Romans 3.29, 30; Galatians 3.28).

10.7 The Jews were waiting for the Messiah to usher in his kingdom. They hoped for a political and military kingdom that would free them from Roman rule and bring back the days of glory under David and Solomon. But Jesus was talking about a spiritual kingdom. The gospel today is that the kingdom is still *near.* Jesus, the Messiah, has already begun his kingdom on earth in the hearts of his followers. One day the kingdom will be fully realized. Then evil will be destroyed and all people will live in peace with one another.

10.8 Jesus gave the disciples a principle to guide their actions as they ministered to others: "You received without payment; give without payment." Because God has showered us with his blessings, we should give generously to others of our time, love, and possessions.

10.10 Jesus said that those who minister are to be cared for. The disciples could expect food and shelter in return for the spiritual service they provided. Who ministers to you? Make sure you take care of the pastors, missionaries, and teachers who serve God by serving you (see 1 Corinthians 9.9, 10; 1 Timothy 5.17).

10.10 Mark (6.8) says to take a staff (walking stick), and Matthew and Luke (9.3) say not to. Jesus may have meant that they were not to take an *extra* pair of sandals, staff, and bag. In any case, the principle was that they were to go out ready for duty and travel, unencumbered by excess material goods.

10.14 Why did Jesus tell his disciples to shake the dust off their feet if a city or home didn't welcome them? When leaving Gentile cities, pious Jews often shook the dust from their feet to show their separation from Gentile practices. If the disciples shook the dust of a *Jewish* town from their feet, it would show their separation from Jews who rejected their Messiah. This gesture was to show the people that they were making a wrong choice—that the opportunity to choose Christ might not present itself again. Are you receptive to teaching from God? If you ignore the Spirit's prompting, you may not get another chance.

10.15 The cities of Sodom and Gomorrah were destroyed by fire from heaven because of their wickedness (Genesis 19.24, 25). Those who reject the gospel when they hear it will be worse off than the wicked people of these destroyed cities, who never heard it at all.

10.16 The opposition of the Pharisees would be like ravaging wolves. The disciples' only hope would be to look to their Shepherd for protection. We may face similar hostility. Like the disciples, we are not to be sheeplike in our attitude but sensible and prudent. We are not to be gullible pawns, but neither are we to be conniving. We must find a balance between wisdom and vulnerability to accomplish God's work.

10.17, 18 Later the disciples experienced these hardships (Acts 5.40; 12.1–3), not only from without (governments, courts), but also from within (friends, family; 10.21). Living for God often brings on persecution, but with it comes the opportunity to tell the good news of salvation. In times of persecution, we can be confident because Jesus has "conquered the world" (John 16.33). And those who endure to the end will be saved (10.22).

10.19, 20 Jesus told the disciples that when arrested for preaching the gospel, they should not worry about what to say in their defense—God's Spirit would speak through them. This promise was fulfilled in Acts 4.8–14 and elsewhere. Some mistakenly think this means we don't have to prepare to present the gospel because God will take care of everything. Scripture teaches, however, that we are to make carefully prepared, thoughtful statements (Colossians 4.6). Jesus is not telling us to stop preparing, but to stop worrying.

betray brother to death, and a father his child, and children will rise against parents
and have them put to death; 22 and you will be hated by all because of my name. But
the one who endures to the end will be saved. 23 When they persecute you in one
town, flee to the next; for truly I tell you, you will not have gone through all the
towns of Israel before the Son of Man comes.
24 "A disciple is not above the teacher, nor a slave above the master; 25 it is
enough for the disciple to be like the teacher, and the slave like the master. If they
have called the master of the house Beelzebul, how much more will they malign
those of his household!
26 "So have no fear of them; for nothing is covered up that will not be uncovered, and nothing secret that will not become known. 27 What I say to you in the
dark, tell in the light; and what you hear whispered, proclaim from the housetops.
28 Do not fear those who kill the body but cannot kill the soul; rather fear him who
can destroy both soul and body in hell.[m] 29 Are not two sparrows sold for a penny?
Yet not one of them will fall to the ground apart from your Father. 30 And even the
hairs of your head are all counted. 31 So do not be afraid; you are of more value than
many sparrows.
32 "Everyone therefore who acknowledges me before others, I also will acknowledge before my Father in heaven; 33 but whoever denies me before others, I
also will deny before my Father in heaven.
34 "Do not think that I have come to bring peace to the earth; I have not come
to bring peace, but a sword.
35 For I have come to set a man against his father,
and a daughter against her mother,
and a daughter-in-law against her mother-in-law;
36 and one's foes will be members of one's own household.
37 Whoever loves father or mother more than me is not worthy of me; and whoever
loves son or daughter more than me is not worthy of me; 38 and whoever does not
take up the cross and follow me is not worthy of me. 39 Those who find their life
will lose it, and those who lose their life for my sake will find it.
40 "Whoever welcomes you welcomes me, and whoever welcomes me wel-

10.21 Mic 7.6
10.22 Gal 6.9
10.23 Mt 16.28 Acts 14.6
10.24 Jn 13.16; 15.20
10.26 Lk 12.1-9
10.27 Lk 12.3
10.28 Isa 8.13 Jer 1.8 Heb 10.31
10.29 Lk 12.6
10.30 Lk 21.18 Acts 27.34
10.32 Lk 12.8 Rom 10.9 Rev 3.5
10.33 Lk 9.26 2 Tim 2.12
10.34 Lk 12.51-53
10.36 Mic 7.6
10.37 Lk 14.26
10.38 Mt 16.24 Mk 8.34 Lk 9.23; 14.27
10.39 Mk 8.35 Lk 9.24; 17.33 Jn 12.25

m Gk *Gehenna*

10.22 Enduring to the end is not a way to be saved but the evidence that you are really committed to Jesus. Persistence is not a means to earn salvation, but the by-product of a truly devoted life.

10.23 Christ warned them against premature martyrdom. They were to leave before the persecution got too great. We have plenty of work to do and many people to reach. Our work won't be finished until Christ returns. And only after he returns will the whole world discover who he is (see 24.14).

10.25 Beelzebul was also known as the lord of the flies and the prince of the demons. The Pharisees accused Jesus of using Beelzebul's power to cast out demons (see 12.24). Good is sometimes labeled evil. If Jesus, who is perfect, was called evil, his followers can expect similar accusations directed at them. But those who endure will be vindicated (10.22).

10.29–31 Jesus said that God is aware of everything that happens even to sparrows, and you are far more valuable to him than they are. You are so valuable that God sent his only Son to die for you (John 3.16). Because he places such value on you, you need never fear personal threats or difficult trials. These can't shake God's love or dislodge his Spirit from within you.

But this doesn't mean God will take away all your troubles (see 10.16). The real test of value is how well something holds up under the wear, tear, and abuse of everyday life. Those who stand up for Christ in spite of their troubles truly have lasting value and will receive great rewards (see 5.11, 12).

10.34 Jesus did not come to bring the kind of peace that glosses over deep differences just for the sake of superficial harmony. Conflict and disagreement will arise between those who choose to follow Christ and those who don't. Yet we can look forward to the day when all conflict will be resolved. For more on Jesus as peacemaker, see Isaiah 9.6; Matthew 5.9; John 14.27.

10.34–39 Christian commitment may separate friends and loved ones. In saying this, Jesus was not encouraging disobedience to parents or conflict at home. Rather, he was showing that his presence demands a decision. Because some will follow him and some won't, conflict will inevitably arise. As we take up our cross and follow him, our different values, morals, goals, and purposes will set us apart from others. Don't neglect your family, but remember that your commitment to God is even more important than they are. God should be your first priority.

10.37 Christ calls us to a higher mission than to find comfort and tranquility in this life. Love of family is a law of God, but even this love can be self-serving and used as an excuse not to serve God or do his work.

10.38 To take up our cross and follow Jesus means being willing to publicly identify with him, face almost certain opposition, and be committed to face even suffering and death for his sake.

10.39 This verse is a positive and negative statement of the same truth: clinging to this life may cause us to forfeit the best from Christ in this world *and* in the next. The more we love this life's rewards (leisure, power, popularity, financial security), the more we discover how empty they really are. The best way to enjoy life, therefore, is to loosen our greedy grasp on earthly rewards to be free to follow Christ. In doing so, we will inherit eternal life and begin at once to experience the benefits of following him.

10.40 Jn 12.44; 13.20
10.41 2 Kgs 4.8

comes the one who sent me. 41 Whoever welcomes a prophet in the name of a
prophet will receive a prophet's reward; and whoever welcomes a righteous person
in the name of a righteous person will receive the reward of the righteous; 42 and
whoever gives even a cup of cold water to one of these little ones in the name of a
disciple—truly I tell you, none of these will lose their reward."

4. Jesus teaches about the kingdom

Jesus eases John's doubt
(70/Luke 7.18–35)

11.2 Mt 14.3; Lk 7.18-35
11.3 Num 24.17; Deut 18.15; Mal 3.1; Jn 6.14
11.5 Isa 42.7; 61.1; Lk 4.18,19; Jn 5.36; Jas 2.5
11.6 Mt 13.57; 1 Pet 2.8
11.9 Lk 1.76
11.10 Isa 40.3; Mal 3.1; Mk 1.2

11 Now when Jesus had finished instructing his twelve disciples, he went on
from there to teach and proclaim his message in their cities.
2 When John heard in prison what the Messiah[n] was doing, he sent word by
his[o] disciples 3 and said to him, "Are you the one who is to come, or are we to wait
for another?" 4 Jesus answered them, "Go and tell John what you hear and see: 5 the
blind receive their sight, the lame walk, the lepers[p] are cleansed, the deaf hear, the
dead are raised, and the poor have good news brought to them. 6 And blessed is
anyone who takes no offense at me."
7 As they went away, Jesus began to speak to the crowds about John: "What did
you go out into the wilderness to look at? A reed shaken by the wind? 8 What then
did you go out to see? Someone[q] dressed in soft robes? Look, those who wear soft
robes are in royal palaces. 9 What then did you go out to see? A prophet?[r] Yes, I
tell you, and more than a prophet. 10 This is the one about whom it is written,
'See, I am sending my messenger ahead of you,
who will prepare your way before you.'
11 Truly I tell you, among those born of women no one has arisen greater than John

[n] Or *the Christ* [o] Other ancient authorities read *two of his* [p] The terms *leper* and *leprosy* can refer to several diseases [q] Or *Why then did you go out? To see someone* [r] Other ancient authorities read *Why then did you go out? To see a prophet?*

COUNTING THE COST OF FOLLOWING CHRIST
Jesus helped his disciples prepare for the rejection many of them would experience by being Christians. Being God's person will usually create reactions from others who are resisting him.

Who may oppose us?	*Natural response*	*Possible pressures*		*Needed truth*
GOVERNMENT 10.18–19		*THREATS 10.26*	→	The truth will be revealed (10.26)
		PHYSICAL HARM 10.28	→	Our soul cannot be harmed (10.28)
RELIGIOUS PEOPLE 10.17	*FEAR AND WORRY*	*PUBLIC RIDICULE (10.22)*	→	God himself will acknowledge us if we acknowledge him (10.32)
FAMILY 10.21		*REJECTION BY LOVED ONES 10.34–37*	→	God's love can sustain us (10.31)

10.42 How much we love God can be measured by how well we treat others. Jesus' example of giving a cup of cold water to a thirsty child is a good model of unselfish service. A child usually can't or won't return a favor. God notices every good deed we do or don't do as if he were the one receiving it. Is there something unselfish you can do for someone else today? Although no one else may see you, God will notice.

11.1 This verse could be included with Jesus' instructions in chapter 10. Jesus may have visited the cities where the disciples had first announced his coming.

11.2, 3 John had been put in prison by Herod. Herod had married his own sister-in-law, and John publicly rebuked Herod's flagrant sin (14.3–5). John's Profile is found in John 1. Herod's Profile is found in Mark 6.

11.4–6 As John sat in prison, he began to have some doubts about whether Jesus really was the Messiah. If John's purpose was to prepare people for the coming Messiah (3.3), and if Jesus really was that Messiah, then why was John in prison when he could have been preaching to the crowds, preparing their hearts?

Jesus answered John's doubts by pointing to his acts of healing the blind, lame, and deaf, curing the lepers, raising the dead, and preaching the good news to the poor. With so much evidence, Jesus' identity was obvious. If you sometimes doubt your salvation, the forgiveness of your sins, or God's work in your life, look at the evidence in Scripture and the changes in your life. When you doubt, don't turn away from Christ, turn *to* him.

11.11 No man ever fulfilled his God-given purpose better than John. Yet in God's coming kingdom all members would have a greater spiritual heritage than John because they would have seen and known Christ and his finished work on the cross.

the Baptist; yet the least in the kingdom of heaven is greater than he. 12 From the
days of John the Baptist until now the kingdom of heaven has suffered violence,[s]
and the violent take it by force. 13 For all the prophets and the law prophesied until
John came; 14 and if you are willing to accept it, he is Elijah who is to come. 15 Let
anyone with ears[t] listen!

16 "But to what will I compare this generation? It is like children sitting in the
marketplaces and calling to one another,

17 'We played the flute for you, and you did not dance;
we wailed, and you did not mourn.'

18 For John came neither eating nor drinking, and they say, 'He has a demon'; 19 the
Son of Man came eating and drinking, and they say, 'Look, a glutton and a drunkard, a friend of tax collectors and sinners!' Yet wisdom is vindicated by her
deeds."[u]

11.12 Lk 16.16
11.14 Mal 4.5 Mt 17.11-13 Mk 9.11-13 Lk 1.17 Jn 1.23
11.15 Mt 13.9,43 Mk 4.9,23 Lk 8.8 Rev 2.7,11,17, 29; 3.6,13,22
11.18 Mt 3.4 Lk 1.15
11.19 Lk 15.2

Jesus promises rest for the soul
(71)

20 Then he began to reproach the cities in which most of his deeds of power had
been done, because they did not repent. 21 "Woe to you, Chorazin! Woe to you,
Bethsaida! For if the deeds of power done in you had been done in Tyre and Sidon,
they would have repented long ago in sackcloth and ashes. 22 But I tell you, on the
day of judgment it will be more tolerable for Tyre and Sidon than for you. 23 And
you, Capernaum,
will you be exalted to heaven?
No, you will be brought down to Hades.
For if the deeds of power done in you had been done in Sodom, it would have
remained until this day. 24 But I tell you that on the day of judgment it will be more
tolerable for the land of Sodom than for you."

25 At that time Jesus said, "I thank[v] you, Father, Lord of heaven and earth,
because you have hidden these things from the wise and the intelligent and have
revealed them to infants; 26 yes, Father, for such was your gracious will.[w] 27 All
things have been handed over to me by my Father; and no one knows the Son
except the Father, and no one knows the Father except the Son and anyone to whom
the Son chooses to reveal him.

28 Come to me, all you that are weary and are carrying heavy burdens, and I

11.20 Lk 10.12-15
11.21 Mk 8.22,23 Lk 6.17,18; 9.10, 11; 10.13-15
11.22 Ezek 26.19,20 Mt 10.15
11.23 Isa 14.13,15 Ezek 31.14
11.25 Lk 10.21-22 Eph 1.17,18
11.27 Mt 28.18 Jn 1.18; 3.35 6.46; 10.15 17.2,26

[s] Or *has been coming violently* [t] Other ancient authorities add *to hear* [u] Other ancient authorities read *children*
[v] Or *praise* [w] Or *for so it was well-pleasing in your sight*

11.12 There are three common views about the meaning of this verse. (1) Jesus may have been referring to a vast movement toward God, the momentum that began with John's preaching. (2) He may have been reflecting the Jewish activists' expectation that God's kingdom would come through a violent overthrow of Rome. (3) Or he may have meant that entering God's kingdom takes courage, unwavering faith, determination, and endurance because of the growing opposition leveled at Jesus' followers.

11.14 John was not a resurrected Elijah, but he took Elijah's prophetic role – boldly confronting sin and pointing people to God (Malachi 3.1). See Elijah's Profile in 1 Kings 18.

11.16–19 Jesus condemned the attitude of his generation. No matter what he said or did, they took the opposite view. They were cynical and skeptical because he challenged their comfortable, secure, and self-centered lives. Too often we justify our inconsistencies because listening to God may require us to change the way we live.

11.21–24 Tyre, Sidon, and Sodom were ancient cities with a long-standing reputation for wickedness (Genesis 18; 19; Ezekiel 27; 28). Each was destroyed by God for its evil. The people of Bethsaida, Chorazin, and Capernaum saw Jesus firsthand, and yet they stubbornly refused to repent of their sins and believe in him. Jesus said that if some of the wickedest cities in the world had seen him, they would have repented. Because Bethsaida, Chorazin, and Capernaum saw Jesus and didn't believe, they would suffer even greater punishment than that of the wicked cities who didn't see Jesus. Similarly, nations and cities with churches on every corner and Bibles in every home will have no excuse on Judgment Day if they do not repent and believe.

11.23 *Hades* was the Greek word used for the Hebrew word *Sheol*. It stood for the place of the dead.

11.25 Jesus mentions two kinds of people in his prayer: the "wise" – arrogant in their own knowledge – and the "infants" – humbly open to receive the truth of God's Word. Are you wise in your own knowledge, or do you seek the truth in childlike faith, realizing that only God holds all the answers?

11.27 In the Old Testament, "know" means more than knowledge. It implies intimate relationship. The communion between God the Father and God the Son is the core of their relationship. For anyone else to know God, God must reveal himself to that person, by the Son's choice. How fortunate we are that Jesus has clearly revealed to us God, his truth, and how we can know him.

11.28–30 A yoke is a heavy wooden harness that fits over the shoulders of an ox or oxen. It is attached to a piece of equipment the oxen are to pull. A person may be carrying heavy burdens of (1) sin, (2) excessive demands of religious leaders (23.4; Acts 15.10), (3) oppression and persecution, or (4) weariness in the search for God.

11.29,30 Jn 13.15 Eph 4.20 Phil 2.5-8 1 Pet 2.21

will give you rest. 29 Take my yoke upon you, and learn from me; for I am gentle
and humble in heart, and you will find rest for your souls. 30 For my yoke is easy,
and my burden is light."

The disciples pick wheat on the sabbath
(45/Mark 2.23–28; Luke 6.1–5)

12.2 Ex 20.10 Deut 5.14
12.3 1 Sam 21.6
12.4 Ex 25.30
12.5 Num 28.9
12.6 Mal 3.1
12.7 1 Sam 15.22 Hos 6.6 Mic 6.6-8

12 At that time Jesus went through the grainfields on the sabbath; his disciples
were hungry, and they began to pluck heads of grain and to eat. 2 When the
Pharisees saw it, they said to him, "Look, your disciples are doing what is not
lawful to do on the sabbath." 3 He said to them, "Have you not read what David did
when he and his companions were hungry? 4 He entered the house of God and ate
the bread of the Presence, which it was not lawful for him or his companions to eat,
but only for the priests. 5 Or have you not read in the law that on the sabbath the
priests in the temple break the sabbath and yet are guiltless? 6 I tell you, something
greater than the temple is here. 7 But if you had known what this means, 'I desire
mercy and not sacrifice,' you would not have condemned the guiltless. 8 For the
Son of Man is lord of the sabbath."

Jesus heals a man's hand on the sabbath
(46/Mark 3.1–6; Luke 6.6–11)

12.9 Mk 3.1-6
12.10 Jn 9.16
12.11 Deut 22.4

9 He left that place and entered their synagogue; 10 a man was there with a withered hand, and they asked him, "Is it lawful to cure on the sabbath?" so that they
might accuse him. 11 He said to them, "Suppose one of you has only one sheep and
it falls into a pit on the sabbath; will you not lay hold of it and lift it out? 12 How
much more valuable is a human being than a sheep! So it is lawful to do good on the

---

Jesus frees people from all these burdens. The rest Jesus promises is love, healing, and peace with God, not the end of all effort. A relationship with God changes meaningless toil into spiritual productivity and purpose.

12.1, 2 The Pharisees had established 39 categories of actions forbidden on the sabbath, based on interpretations of God's law and on Jewish custom. Harvesting was one of those forbidden actions. By picking wheat and rubbing it in their hands, the disciples were technically harvesting, according to the religious leaders. Jesus and the disciples were picking grain because they were hungry, not because they wanted to harvest the grain for a profit. They were not working on the sabbath. The Pharisees, however, could not (and did not want to) see beyond their law's technicalities.

12.4 This story is recorded in 1 Samuel 21.1–6. The bread of the Presence was replaced every week, and the old loaves were eaten by the priests. The loaves given to David were the old loaves that had just been replaced with fresh ones. Although the priests were the only ones allowed to eat this bread, God did not punish David, because his need for food was more important than the legal technicalities. Jesus was saying, "If you condemn me, you must also condemn David," something the religious leaders could never do without causing a great uproar among the people. Jesus was not condoning disobedience to God's laws. Instead he was emphasizing discernment and compassion in enforcing the laws.

12.5 The ten commandments prohibit work on the sabbath (Exodus 20.8–11). That was the *letter* of the law. But because the *purpose* of the sabbath is to rest and to worship God, the priests were allowed to work by performing sacrifices and conducting worship services. This "sabbath work" was serving and worshiping God. Jesus always emphasized the intent of the law, the meaning behind the letter. The Pharisees had lost the spirit of the law and rigidly demanded that the letter (and their interpretation of it) be obeyed.

12.6 The Pharisees were so concerned about religious rituals that they missed the whole purpose of the temple – to bring people to God. And because Jesus Christ is even greater than the temple, how much better can he bring people to God. God is far more important than the created instruments of worship. If we become more concerned with the means of worship than with the One we worship, we will miss God even as we think we are worshiping him.

12.7 Jesus repeated to the Pharisees words the Jewish people had heard time and again throughout their history (1 Samuel 15.22, 23; Psalm 40.6–8; Isaiah 1.11–17; Jeremiah 7.21–23; Hosea 6.6). Our heart attitude toward God comes first. Only then can we properly obey and observe religious regulations and rituals.

12.8 When Jesus said he is lord of the sabbath, he claimed to be greater than and above the law. To the Pharisees, this was heresy. They did not realize that Jesus, the divine Son of God, created the sabbath. The Creator is always greater than the creation; thus Jesus had the authority to overrule their traditions and regulations.

12.9 For more information on synagogues, read the notes on Mark 1.21 and 5.22.

12.10 As they pointed to the man with the deformed ("withered") hand, the Pharisees tried to trick Jesus by asking him if it was legal to heal on the sabbath. Their sabbath rules said that people could be helped on the sabbath only if their lives were in danger. Jesus healed on the sabbath several times, and none of those healings were in response to emergencies. If Jesus had waited until another day, he would have been submitting to the Pharisees' authority, showing that their petty rules were equal to God's law. If he healed the man on the sabbath, the Pharisees could claim that because he broke their rules, his power was not from God. But Jesus made it clear how ridiculous and petty their rules were. God is a God of people, not rules. The best time to reach out to someone is when he or she needs help.

12.10–12 The Pharisees placed their laws above human need. They were so concerned about Jesus' breaking one of their rules that they did not care about the man's deformed hand. What is your attitude toward others? If your convictions don't allow you to help certain people, your convictions may not be in tune with God's Word. Don't allow dogma to blind you to human need.

sabbath." 13 Then he said to the man, "Stretch out your hand." He stretched it out, 12.12 Mt 10.31
and it was restored, as sound as the other. 14 But the Pharisees went out and conspired against him, how to destroy him.

Huge crowds follow Jesus
(47/Mark 3.7–12)

15 When Jesus became aware of this, he departed. Many crowds[x] followed 12.15 Mk 3.7
him, and he cured all of them, 16 and he ordered them not to make him known. Heb 4.13
17 This was to fulfill what had been spoken through the prophet Isaiah:
18 "Here is my servant, whom I have chosen, 12.18-21 Isa 42.1-4
my beloved, with whom my soul is well pleased.
I will put my Spirit upon him,
and he will proclaim justice to the Gentiles.
19 He will not wrangle or cry aloud,
nor will anyone hear his voice in the streets.
20 He will not break a bruised reed
or quench a smoldering wick
until he brings justice to victory.
21 And in his name the Gentiles will hope."

Religious leaders accuse Jesus of being Satan
(74/Mark 3.20–30)

22 Then they brought to him a demoniac who was blind and mute; and he cured 12.22 Mk 3.20-30
him, so that the one who had been mute could speak and see. 23 All the crowds were Lk 11.14-23
amazed and said, "Can this be the Son of David?" 24 But when the Pharisees heard 12.24
it, they said, "It is only by Beelzebul, the ruler of the demons, that this fellow casts Mt 9.34
out the demons." 25 He knew what they were thinking and said to them, "Every 12.25
kingdom divided against itself is laid waste, and no city or house divided against Ps 139.2 Mt 9.4
itself will stand. 26 If Satan casts out Satan, he is divided against himself; how then Jn 2.25
will his kingdom stand? 27 If I cast out demons by Beelzebul, by whom do your own 12.27
exorcists[y] cast them out? Therefore they will be your judges. 28 But if it is by the Mt 9.34 12.28
Spirit of God that I cast out demons, then the kingdom of God has come to you. Lk 1.33
29 Or how can one enter a strong man's house and plunder his property, without first 17.20,21
tying up the strong man? Then indeed the house can be plundered. 30 Whoever is

x Other ancient authorities lack *crowds* y Gk *sons*

12.14 The Pharisees plotted Jesus' death because they were outraged. Jesus had overruled their authority (Luke 6.11) and had exposed their evil attitudes in front of the entire crowd in the synagogue. Jesus had showed that the Pharisees were more loyal to their religious system than to God.

12.15 Up to this point, Jesus had been aggressively confronting the Pharisees' hypocrisy. Here he decided to withdraw from the synagogue before a major confrontation developed because it was not time for him to die. Jesus had many lessons still to teach.

12.16 Jesus did not want those he healed to tell others about his miracles because he didn't want the people coming to him for the wrong reasons. This would hinder his teaching ministry and arouse false hopes about an earthly kingdom. But the news of his miracles spread, and many came to see for themselves (see Mark 3.7, 8).

12.17–21 Matthew quoted the Old Testament often because he wanted to prove to his Jewish audience that Jesus was the Messiah. The Jews held the Bible as their highest authority. They believed it pointed to a coming Messiah, but they didn't believe Jesus was the one. Matthew showed that Jesus was the Messiah prophesied by Old Testament prophets. This particular prophecy teaches that the Messiah was to be not the high-profile conqueror the Jews expected but a gentle Judge instead (Isaiah 42.1–7).

12.20 The people expected the Messiah to be a king. This quotation from Isaiah's prophecy shows he is indeed a king, but illustrates what *kind* of king – a quiet, gentle ruler who brings justice to the Gentiles. Like the crowd in Jesus' day, we may want Christ to rule as a king and bring great and visible victories in our lives. But often his work is quiet, and it happens according to *his* perfect timing, not ours.

12.24 The Pharisees had already accused Jesus of being in league with the ruler of the demons (9.34). They were trying to discredit him by using an emotional argument. Refusing to believe he came from God, they said he was in league with Satan. Jesus easily exposed the foolishness of their argument.

12.25 As a man, Jesus did not have supernatural ability to know everything, but he still had profound insight into human nature. His discernment stopped the religious leaders' attempts to trick him. The resurrected Christ knows all our thoughts. This can be comforting because he knows what we really mean when we speak to him. It can be threatening because we cannot hide from him, and he knows our selfish motives.

12.29 At Jesus' birth, Satan's power and control were disrupted. In the wilderness, Jesus overcame the devil's temptations, and at the resurrection, he defeated Satan's ultimate weapon, death. Eventually Satan will be constrained forever (Revelation 20.10), and evil will no longer pervade the earth. Jesus has complete power and authority over Satan and all his forces.

12.30 It is impossible to be neutral about Christ. Anyone who is not actively following him has chosen to reject him. Any person who tries to remain neutral in the struggle of good against evil is choos-

12.30 Mk 9.40 not with me is against me, and whoever does not gather with me scatters. 31 There-
Lk 9.50; 11.23 fore I tell you, people will be forgiven for every sin and blasphemy, but blasphemy
12.31,32 Mt 11.19 against the Spirit will not be forgiven. 32 Whoever speaks a word against the Son of
Lk 12.10 Man will be forgiven, but whoever speaks against the Holy Spirit will not be for-
1 Jn 5.16 given, either in this age or in the age to come.
33 "Either make the tree good, and its fruit good; or make the tree bad, and its
12.33 fruit bad; for the tree is known by its fruit. 34 You brood of vipers! How can you
Mt 7.15-20 Lk 6.43-45 speak good things, when you are evil? For out of the abundance of the heart the
12.34 mouth speaks. 35 The good person brings good things out of a good treasure, and
Mt 3.7; 23.33 the evil person brings evil things out of an evil treasure. 36 I tell you, on the day of
12.36 judgment you will have to give an account for every careless word you utter; 37 for
Eph 5.4 by your words you will be justified, and by your words you will be condemned."

Religious leaders ask Jesus for a miracle
(75)

12.38 38 Then some of the scribes and Pharisees said to him, "Teacher, we wish to
Mt 16.1-4 Mk 8.11,12 see a sign from you." 39 But he answered them, "An evil and adulterous generation
Lk 11.16,29-32 Jn 2.18 asks for a sign, but no sign will be given to it except the sign of the prophet Jonah.
1 Cor 1.22 40 For just as Jonah was three days and three nights in the belly of the sea monster,
12.39 Jn 4.48 so for three days and three nights the Son of Man will be in the heart of the earth.
12.40 41 The people of Nineveh will rise up at the judgment with this generation and con-
Jonah 1.17 demn it, because they repented at the proclamation of Jonah, and see, something
12.41 Jonah 3.5 greater than Jonah is here! 42 The queen of the South will rise up at the judgment
Rom 9.5 with this generation and condemn it, because she came from the ends of the earth
12.42 1 Kgs 10.1 to listen to the wisdom of Solomon, and see, something greater than Solomon is
2 Chron 9.1 Mt 12.6 here!
12.43 43 "When the unclean spirit has gone out of a person, it wanders through water-
Lk 11.24-26 1 Pet 5.8 less regions looking for a resting place, but it finds none. 44 Then it says, 'I will
12.45 return to my house from which I came.' When it comes, it finds it empty, swept,
2 Pet 2.20 and put in order. 45 Then it goes and brings along seven other spirits more evil than

---

ing to be separated from God, who alone is good. To refuse to follow Christ is to choose to be on Satan's team.

12.31, 32 Blasphemy against the Spirit is denying that the Holy Spirit convicts us of sin. Because a person can be saved only through the Holy Spirit's work, to refuse to repent or even to acknowledge our sin is to refuse God's forgiveness. Sometimes believers worry that they have accidently committed this unforgivable sin. But only those who have turned their backs on God and rejected all faith have any need to worry. Jesus said they can't be forgiven—not because their sin is worse than any other, but because they will never ask for forgiveness. Whoever rejects the prompting of the Holy Spirit removes himself from the only force that can lead him to repentance and restoration to God.

12.34–36 Jesus reminds us that what we say reveals what is in our hearts. What kinds of words come from your mouth? That is an indication of what your heart is really like. You can't solve your heart problem, however, just by cleaning up your speech. You must allow the Holy Spirit to fill you with new attitudes and motives; then your speech will be cleansed at its source.

12.38–40 The Pharisees were asking for another miracle, but they were not sincerely seeking to know Jesus. Jesus knew they had already seen enough miraculous proof to convince them that he was the Messiah, if they would just open their hearts. But they had already decided not to believe in him, and more miracles would not change that.

Many people have thought, "If I could just see a real miracle, then I could really believe in God." But Jesus' response to the Pharisees applies to us. We have plenty of evidence—Jesus' death, resurrection, and ascension, and centuries of his work in believers around the world. Instead of looking for additional evidence or miracles, accept what God has already given and move forward. He may use your life as evidence to reach another person.

12.39–41 Jonah was a prophet sent to the Assyrian city of Nineveh (see the book of Jonah). Because Assyria was such a cruel and warlike nation, Jonah tried to run from his assignment and ended up spending three days in the belly of a great fish (sea monster). When he got out, he grudgingly went to Nineveh, preached God's message, and saw the city repent. By contrast, when Jesus came to his people, they refused to repent. Here he is clearly saying that his resurrection will prove he is the Messiah. Three days after his death he will come back to life, just as Jonah was given a new chance at life after three days in the fish.

12.41, 42 In Jonah's day, Nineveh was the capital of the Assyrian Empire, and it was as powerful as it was evil (Jonah 1.2). But the entire city repented at Jonah's preaching. The queen of the South traveled far to see Solomon, king of Israel, and learn about his great wisdom (1 Kings 10.1–10; also see the note on Luke 11.31, 32 for more on the Queen of Sheba). These Gentiles recognized the truth about God when it was presented to them, unlike the religious leaders who ignored the truth even though it stared them in the face. How have you responded to the evidence and truth that you have?

12.43–45 Jesus was describing the attitude of the nation of Israel and the religious leaders in particular. Just cleaning up one's life without filling it with God leaves plenty of room for Satan to enter. The book of Ezra records how the people rid themselves of idolatry, but failed to replace it with God's love and obedience to him. Ridding our lives of sin is the first step. We must also take the second step: filling our lives with God's Word and the Holy Spirit. Unfilled and inactive people are easy targets for Satan.

itself, and they enter and live there; and the last state of that person is worse than the
first. So will it be also with this evil generation."

Jesus describes his true family
(76/Mark 3.31–35; Luke 8.19–21)

46 While he was still speaking to the crowds, his mother and his brothers were 12.46
standing outside, wanting to speak to him. 47 Someone told him, "Look, your Mk 3.31-35; 6.3
mother and your brothers are standing outside, wanting to speak to you."[z] 48 But to Lk 8.19-21 Jn 7.3-5
the one who had told him this, Jesus[a] replied, "Who is my mother, and who are my Acts 1.14 1 Cor 9.5
brothers?" 49 And pointing to his disciples, he said, "Here are my mother and my Gal 1.19
brothers! 50 For whoever does the will of my Father in heaven is my brother and
sister and mother."

Jesus tells the parable of the four soils
(77/Mark 4.1–9; Luke 8.4–8)

13 That same day Jesus went out of the house and sat beside the sea. 2 Such 13.1
great crowds gathered around him that he got into a boat and sat there, while Mk 4.1-20 Lk 8.4-15
the whole crowd stood on the beach. 3 And he told them many things in parables,
saying: "Listen! A sower went out to sow. 4 And as he sowed, some seeds fell on
the path, and the birds came and ate them up. 5 Other seeds fell on rocky ground,
where they did not have much soil, and they sprang up quickly, since they had no
depth of soil. 6 But when the sun rose, they were scorched; and since they had no
root, they withered away. 7 Other seeds fell among thorns, and the thorns grew up
and choked them. 8 Other seeds fell on good soil and brought forth grain, some a
hundredfold, some sixty, some thirty. 9 Let anyone with ears[b] listen!"

Jesus explains the parable of the four soils
(78/Mark 4.10–25; Luke 8.9–18)

10 Then the disciples came and asked him, "Why do you speak to them in para- 13.11
bles?" 11 He answered, "To you it has been given to know the secrets[c] of the king- 1 Cor 2.10 Col 1.26,27
dom of heaven, but to them it has not been given. 12 For to those who have, more 1 Jn 2.27
will be given, and they will have an abundance; but from those who have nothing, 13.12 Lk 19.26
even what they have will be taken away. 13 The reason I speak to them in parables 13.13
is that 'seeing they do not perceive, and hearing they do not listen, nor do they Jer 5.21
understand.' 14 With them indeed is fulfilled the prophecy of Isaiah that says: 13.14 Isa 6.9,10
'You will indeed listen, but never understand, Acts 28.26,27 Rom 11.8
and you will indeed look, but never perceive. 2 Cor 3.14

[z] Other ancient authorities lack verse 47 [a] Gk *he* [b] Other ancient authorities add *to hear* [c] Or *mysteries*

12.46–50 Jesus was not denying his responsibility to his earthly family. On the contrary, he had earlier criticized the religious leaders for not following the Old Testament command to honor their parents. He provided for his mother's security as he hung on the cross (John 19.25–27). His mother and brothers were present in the upper room at Pentecost (Acts 1.14). Instead Jesus was pointing out that spiritual relationships are as binding as physical ones, and he was paving the way for a new community of believers (the universal church), our spiritual family.

13.2, 3 Jesus used many illustrations, or *parables,* when speaking to the crowds. A parable compares something familiar to something unfamiliar. It helps us understand spiritual truth by using everyday objects and relationships. Parables compel the listener to discover truth, while at the same time concealing the truth from those too lazy or too stubborn to see it. To those who are honestly searching, the truth becomes clear. We must be careful not to read too much into parables, forcing them to say what they don't mean. All parables have one meaning unless otherwise specified by Jesus.

13.8 This parable should encourage spiritual "sowers"—those who teach, preach, and lead others. The man sowed good seed, but not all the seed sprouted, and even the plants that grew had varying yields. Don't be discouraged if you do not always see results as you faithfully teach the Word. Belief cannot be forced to follow a mathematical formula (i.e., a 4:1 ratio of seeds planted to seeds sprouted). Rather, it is a miracle of God's Holy Spirit as he uses your words to lead others to him.

13.9 Human ears hear many sounds, but there is a deeper kind of listening that results in spiritual understanding. If you honestly seek God's will, you have spiritual hearing, and these parables will give you new perspectives.

13.10 When speaking in parables, Jesus was not hiding truth from sincere seekers, because those who were receptive to spiritual truth understood the illustrations. To others they were only stories without meaning. This allowed Jesus to give spiritual food to those who hungered for it while preventing his enemies from trapping him sooner than they might otherwise have done.

13.12 This phrase means we are responsible to use well what we have. When people reject Jesus, their hardness of heart drives away or renders useless even the little understanding they had.

13.14–16 This prophecy is found in Isaiah 6.9, 10.

15 For this people's heart has grown dull,
and their ears are hard of hearing,
and they have shut their eyes;
so that they might not look with their eyes,
and listen with their ears,
and understand with their heart and turn—
and I would heal them.'

13.17 Lk 10.23,24 Jn 8.56 Heb 11.13 1 Pet 1.10-12

16 But blessed are your eyes, for they see, and your ears, for they hear. 17 Truly I tell
you, many prophets and righteous people longed to see what you see, but did not
see it, and to hear what you hear, but did not hear it.

13.19 Ezek 11.19 2 Cor 4.3,4 Eph 4.17,18

18 "Hear then the parable of the sower. 19 When anyone hears the word of the
kingdom and does not understand it, the evil one comes and snatches away what is
sown in the heart; this is what was sown on the path. 20 As for what was sown on
rocky ground, this is the one who hears the word and immediately receives it with
13.21 Col 2.7
joy; 21 yet such a person has no root, but endures only for a while, and when trouble
13.22 Jer 4.3 Ezek 33.31 Mt 19.23 Eph 2.2 1 Tim 6.9,10,17 2 Tim 4.4,10
or persecution arises on account of the word, that person immediately falls away.[d]
22 As for what was sown among thorns, this is the one who hears the word, but the
cares of the world and the lure of wealth choke the word, and it yields nothing.
23 But as for what was sown on good soil, this is the one who hears the word and
13.23 Gen 26.12
understands it, who indeed bears fruit and yields, in one case a hundredfold, in
another sixty, and in another thirty."

Jesus tells the parable of the weeds
(80)

13.24 Mk 4.26-29

24 He put before them another parable: "The kingdom of heaven may be compared to someone who sowed good seed in his field; 25 but while everybody was
asleep, an enemy came and sowed weeds among the wheat, and then went away.
26 So when the plants came up and bore grain, then the weeds appeared as well.
27 And the slaves of the householder came and said to him, 'Master, did you not
sow good seed in your field? Where, then, did these weeds come from?' 28 He
answered, 'An enemy has done this.' The slaves said to him, 'Then do you want us
to go and gather them?' 29 But he replied, 'No; for in gathering the weeds you
13.30 Mt 3.12
would uproot the wheat along with them. 30 Let both of them grow together until the
harvest; and at harvest time I will tell the reapers, Collect the weeds first and bind
them in bundles to be burned, but gather the wheat into my barn.'"

Jesus tells the parable of the mustard seed
(81/Mark 4.30–34)

13.31,32 Gen 1.11,12 Ezek 17.22,23

31 He put before them another parable: "The kingdom of heaven is like a mustard seed that someone took and sowed in his field; 32 it is the smallest of all the

[d] Gk *stumbles*

13.22 How easy it is to agree with Christ with no intention of obeying. It is easy to denounce cares of this life (anxiety and worry) and the deceitfulness of riches, and still do nothing to change our ways. In light of eternal life with God, are your present worries justified? If you had everything you could want and forfeited eternal life with God, would those things be so desireable?

13.23 The four types of soil represent different responses to God's message. People respond differently because they are in different states of readiness. Some are hardened, others are shallow, others are contaminated by distracting cares, and some are receptive. How has God's Word taken root in your life? What kind of soil are you?

13.24ff Jesus gives the meaning of this parable in verses 36–43. All the parables in this chapter teach us about God and his kingdom. They explain what the kingdom is really like as opposed to our expectations of it. The kingdom of heaven is not a geographic location, but a spiritual realm in which God rules and in which we share in his eternal life. We join that kingdom when we trust in Christ as Savior.

13.30 The young weeds and the young blades of wheat look the same and can't be distinguised until they are grown and ready for harvest. Weeds (unbelievers) and wheat (believers) must live side by side in this world. God allows unbelievers to remain for a while just as a farmer allows weeds to remain in his field so the surrounding wheat isn't uprooted with them. At the harvest, however, the weeds will be uprooted and thrown away. God's harvest (judgment) of all people is coming. We are to make ourselves ready by making sure our faith is sincere.

13.31, 32 The mustard seed was the smallest seed a farmer used. Jesus used this parable to show that the kingdom has small beginnings but will grow and produce great results.

seeds, but when it has grown it is the greatest of shrubs and becomes a tree, so that
the birds of the air come and make nests in its branches."

Jesus tells the parable of the yeast
(82)

33 He told them another parable: "The kingdom of heaven is like yeast that a 13.33 Lev 7.13; 23.17
woman took and mixed in with[e] three measures of flour until all of it was leav- Mt 16.6,12 Lk 13.20,21
ened." 1 Cor 5.6-8
34 Jesus told the crowds all these things in parables; without a parable he told Gal 5.8,9
them nothing. 35 This was to fulfill what had been spoken through the prophet:[f] 13.34,35 Ps 78.2,3

"I will open my mouth to speak in parables; Mk 4.34
I will proclaim what has been hidden from the foundation of the Jn 10.6; 16.25 Rom 16.25
world."[g] 1 Cor 2.7

Jesus explains the parable of the weeds
(83)

36 Then he left the crowds and went into the house. And his disciples ap- 13.36
proached him, saying, "Explain to us the parable of the weeds of the field." 37 He Mt 15.15
answered, "The one who sows the good seed is the Son of Man; 38 the field is the 13.38 Lk 24.27
world, and the good seed are the children of the kingdom; the weeds are the chil- Jn 8.44
dren of the evil one, 39 and the enemy who sowed them is the devil; the harvest is 13.39 Joel 3.13
the end of the age, and the reapers are angels. 40 Just as the weeds are collected and Rev 14.15
burned up with fire, so will it be at the end of the age. 41 The Son of Man will send 13.41 Mt 24.31
his angels, and they will collect out of his kingdom all causes of sin and all evildo- 25.31-46
ers, 42 and they will throw them into the furnace of fire, where there will be weeping 13.42 Mt 13.50; 22.13
and gnashing of teeth. 43 Then the righteous will shine like the sun in the kingdom 13.43
of their Father. Let anyone with ears[h] listen! Dan 12.3

Jesus tells the parable of the hidden treasure
(84)

44 "The kingdom of heaven is like treasure hidden in a field, which someone 13.44 1 Cor 6.20
found and hid; then in his joy he goes and sells all that he has and buys that field. Phil 3.7

Jesus tells the parable of the pearl merchant
(85)

45 "Again, the kingdom of heaven is like a merchant in search of fine pearls;
46 on finding one pearl of great value, he went and sold all that he had and bought
it.

Jesus tells the parable of the fishing net
(86)

47 "Again, the kingdom of heaven is like a net that was thrown into the sea and

[e] Gk *hid in* [f] Other ancient authorities read *the prophet Isaiah* [g] Other ancient authorities lack *of the world* [h] Other ancient authorities add *to hear*

13.33 In other Bible passages, yeast is used as a symbol of evil or uncleanness. Here it is a positive symbol of growth. Although yeast looks like a minor ingredient, it permeates the whole loaf. Although the kingdom began small and was nearly invisible, it would soon grow and have a great impact on the world.

13.40–43 At the end of the world, angels will separate the evil from the good. There are true and false believers in churches today, but we should be cautious in our judgments because only Christ is qualified to make the final separation. If you start judging, you may damage some of the good "plants." It's more important to judge our own response to God than to analyze others' responses.

13.42 Jesus often uses these terms to refer to the coming judgment. The weeping indicates sorrow or remorse, and gnashing of teeth shows extreme anxiety or pain. Those who say they don't care what happens to them after they die don't realize what they are saying. They will be punished for living in selfishness and indifference to God.

13.43 Those who receive God's favor stand in bright contrast to those who receive his judgment. A similiar illustration is used in Daniel 12.3.

13.44–46 The kingdom of heaven is more valuable than anything else we can have, and a person must be willing to give up everything to obtain it. The man who discovered the treasure in the field stumbled upon it by accident but knew its value when he found it. The merchant was earnestly searching for the choice pearl and, when he found it, sold everything he had to purchase it.

13.47–49 The parable of the fishing net has the same meaning as the parable of the wheat and weeds. We are to obey God and tell others about his grace and goodness, but we are not to dictate who is part of the kingdom of heaven and who is not. This sorting

13.47,48 Mt 22.10 caught fish of every kind; 48 when it was full, they drew it ashore, sat down, and put
the good into baskets but threw out the bad. 49 So it will be at the end of the age. The
13.50 Mt 8.12 angels will come out and separate the evil from the righteous 50 and throw them into
the furnace of fire, where there will be weeping and gnashing of teeth.
51 "Have you understood all this?" They answered, "Yes." 52 And he said to
13.53 Mt 2.23 Mk 6.1-6 Lk 3.23; 4.16-24 them, "Therefore every scribe who has been trained for the kingdom of heaven is
like the master of a household who brings out of his treasure what is new and what
is old." 53 When Jesus had finished these parables, he left that place.

5. Jesus encounters differing reactions to his ministry

The people of Nazareth refuse to believe in Jesus
(91/Mark 6.1–6)

54 He came to his hometown and began to teach the people[i] in their synagogue, so that they were astounded and said, "Where did this man get this wisdom
13.55 Ps 69.8 Mt 12.46 Mk 15.40 Jn 6.42 and these deeds of power? 55 Is not this the carpenter's son? Is not his mother called
Mary? And are not his brothers James and Joseph and Simon and Judas? 56 And are
not all his sisters with us? Where then did this man get all this?" 57 And they took
13.57 Ps 6 Isa 53.2,3 Jn 4.44 offense at him. But Jesus said to them, "Prophets are not without honor except in
their own country and in their own house." 58 And he did not do many deeds of
power there, because of their unbelief.

Herod kills John the Baptist
(95/Mark 6.14–29; Luke 9.7–9)

14.1 Mk 6.14-29 Lk 9.7-9 3.19,20 **14** At that time Herod the ruler[j] heard reports about Jesus; 2 and he said to his
servants, "This is John the Baptist; he has been raised from the dead, and for
this reason these powers are at work in him." 3 For Herod had arrested John, bound

[i] Gk *them* [j] Gk *tetrarch*

---

will be done at the last Judgment by those infinitely more qualified than we.

13.52 There is a double benefit for those who understand and use both Old and New Testaments. The Old Testament points the way to Jesus, the Messiah. Jesus always upheld its authority and relevance. The New Testament reveals Christ himself, who is now available to anyone who accepts his spiritual kingship. Both the Old and New teach about God and give practical guidelines for living in the world. The religious leaders, however, were trapped in the Old and blind to the New. They were looking for a future kingdom *preceded* by judgment. Jesus, however, taught that the kingdom was *now* and the judgment was future. The religious leaders were looking for a physical and temporal kingdom (via military rebellion and physical rule), but were blind to the spiritual significance of the kingdom Christ brought.

13.55 The residents of Jesus' hometown had known him since he was a young child and were acquainted with his family, and they could not bring themselves to believe in his message. They were too close to the situation. Jesus had come to them as a prophet, one who challenged them to respond to unpopular spiritual truth. They did not listen to the timeless message because they could not see beyond the man.

13.57 Jesus was not the first prophet to be rejected in his own country. Jeremiah experienced rejection in his hometown, even by members of his own family (Jeremiah 12.5, 6).

13.58 Jesus did few miracles in his hometown "because of their unbelief." Lack of faith blinds people to the truth and robs them of hope. These people missed the Messiah. How does your faith measure up? If you can't see God work in your life, perhaps it is because of your unbelief. Believe, ask God for a mighty work in your life, and expect him to act. Look with the eyes of faith.

14.1 Herod was one of four rulers over the four districts of Palestine. His territory included the regions of Galilee and Peraea. This is the son of Herod the Great who ordered the killing of the babies (2.16). Also known as Herod Antipas, he judged Jesus before his crucifixion (Luke 23.6–12). His Profile is found in Mark 6.

NAZARETH REJECTS JESUS
Chronologically, this return to Nazareth occurred after Jesus was in the Gadarene country and healed the demon-possessed men (8.28–34), then recrossed the sea to Capernaum. From there he traveled to Nazareth, where he had grown up, only to discover that the people refused to believe he was Christ.

14.2 For more information on John the Baptist, see his Profile in John 1.

14.3 Philip, Herod's half brother, was another of Palestine's four rulers. His territories were Ituraea and Trachonitis, northeast of the Sea of Galilee (Luke 3.1). Philip's wife, Herodias, left him to live with Herod Antipas. John the Baptist condemned the two for living immorally (see Mark 6.17, 18).

him, and put him in prison on account of Herodias, his brother Philip's wife,[k]
4 because John had been telling him, "It is not lawful for you to have her." 5 Though
Herod[l] wanted to put him to death, he feared the crowd, because they regarded
him as a prophet. 6 But when Herod's birthday came, the daughter of Herodias
danced before the company, and she pleased Herod 7 so much that he promised on
oath to grant her whatever she might ask. 8 Prompted by her mother, she said,
"Give me the head of John the Baptist here on a platter." 9 The king was grieved,
yet out of regard for his oaths and for the guests, he commanded it to be given; 10 he
sent and had John beheaded in the prison. 11 The head was brought on a platter and
given to the girl, who brought it to her mother. 12 His disciples came and took the
body and buried it; then they went and told Jesus.

14.4 Lev 18.16; 20.21 Eph 5.11 2 Tim 4.2
14.5 Mt 21.26 Lk 20.6

Jesus feeds five thousand
(96/Mark 6.30–44; Luke 9.10–17; John 6.1–15)

13 Now when Jesus heard this, he withdrew from there in a boat to a deserted
place by himself. But when the crowds heard it, they followed him on foot from the
towns. 14 When he went ashore, he saw a great crowd; and he had compassion for
them and cured their sick. 15 When it was evening, the disciples came to him and
said, "This is a deserted place, and the hour is now late; send the crowds away so
that they may go into the villages and buy food for themselves." 16 Jesus said to
them, "They need not go away; you give them something to eat." 17 They replied,
"We have nothing here but five loaves and two fish." 18 And he said, "Bring them
here to me." 19 Then he ordered the crowds to sit down on the grass. Taking the five
loaves and the two fish, he looked up to heaven, and blessed and broke the loaves,
and gave them to the disciples, and the disciples gave them to the crowds. 20 And
all ate and were filled; and they took up what was left over of the broken pieces,
twelve baskets full. 21 And those who ate were about five thousand men, besides
women and children.

14.13 Mk 6.30-45 Lk 9.10-17 Jn 6.1-13
14.14 Mt 9.36 Mk 1.41 Heb 2.17,18 4.15; 5.1-3
14.16 2 Kgs 4.42-44
14.19 Mt 15.35-38 Lk 22.19

Jesus walks on water
(97/Mark 6.45–52; John 6.16–21)

22 Immediately he made the disciples get into the boat and go on ahead to the
other side, while he dismissed the crowds. 23 And after he had dismissed the

14.23 Mk 6.46-56 Jn 6.15-21

[k] Other ancient authorities read *his brother's wife* [l] Gk *he*

14.9 Herod did not want to kill John the Baptist, but he gave the order so he wouldn't be embarrassed in front of his guests. How easy it is to give in to the crowd and to let ourselves be pressured into doing wrong. Don't get in a situation where it will be too embarrassing to do what is right. Determine to do what is right no matter how embarrassing or painful it may be.

14.13, 14 Jesus sought solitude after the news of John's death. Sometimes we may need to deal with our grief alone. Jesus did not dwell on his grief, but then returned to the ministry he came to do.

14.14 Jesus performed some miracles as signs of his identity. Others he used to teach important truths. But here we read that he healed people because he was "had compassion for them." Jesus was and is a loving, caring, and feeling person. When you are suffering, remember that Jesus hurts with you. He "has compassion" for you.

14.19–22 Jesus multiplied five loaves and two fish to feed over 5,000 people. What he was originally given seemed insufficient, but in his hands it became more than enough. We often feel that our contribution to Jesus is meager, but he can use and multiply whatever we give him, whether it is talent, time, or treasure. It is when we give them to Jesus that our resources are multiplied.

14.21 The text states that there were 5,000 men present, *besides* women and children. Therefore, the total number of people Jesus fed could have been 10 to 15 thousand. The number of men is listed separately because in the Jewish culture of the day, men and women usually ate separately.

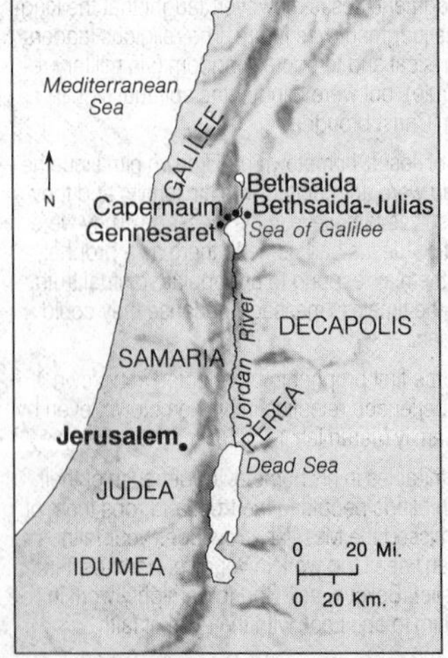

JESUS WALKS ON THE SEA
The miraculous feeding of the 5,000 occurred on the shores of the Sea of Galilee near Bethsaida-Julias. Jesus then sent his disciples across the lake. Several hours later, they encountered a storm, and Jesus came to them—walking on the water. The boat then landed at Gennesaret.

14.23 Seeking solitude was an important priority for Jesus (see also 14.13). He made room in his busy schedule to be alone with

crowds, he went up the mountain by himself to pray. When evening came, he was
there alone, 24 but by this time the boat, battered by the waves, was far from the
14.25 Job 9.8
land,[m] for the wind was against them. 25 And early in the morning he came walking
toward them on the sea. 26 But when the disciples saw him walking on the sea, they
were terrified, saying, "It is a ghost!" And they cried out in fear. 27 But immediately
Jesus spoke to them and said, "Take heart, it is I; do not be afraid."
14.32 Ps 107.29
28 Peter answered him, "Lord, if it is you, command me to come to you on the
14.33 Ps 2.7 Mt 16.16; 26.63 Mk 1.1 Lk 4.41 Jn 1.49; 6.69 11.27 Acts 8.37 Rom 1.4
water." 29 He said, "Come." So Peter got out of the boat, started walking on the
water, and came toward Jesus. 30 But when he noticed the strong wind,[n] he became
frightened, and beginning to sink, he cried out, "Lord, save me!" 31 Jesus immediately reached out his hand and caught him, saying to him, "You of little faith, why
did you doubt?" 32 When they got into the boat, the wind ceased. 33 And those in the
boat worshiped him, saying, "Truly you are the Son of God."

Jesus heals all who touch him
(98/Mark 6.53–56)

34 When they had crossed over, they came to land at Gennesaret. 35 After the
people of that place recognized him, they sent word throughout the region and
brought all who were sick to him, 36 and begged him that they might touch even the
fringe of his cloak; and all who touched it were healed.

Jesus teaches about inner purity
(102/Mark 7.1–23)

15.1 Mk 7.1-23
15.2 Lk 11.37,38 Gal 1.14
15 Then Pharisees and scribes came to Jesus from Jerusalem and said, 2 "Why
do your disciples break the tradition of the elders? For they do not wash their
hands before they eat." 3 He answered them, "And why do you break the commandment of God for the sake of your tradition? 4 For God said,[o] 'Honor your father and

[m] Other ancient authorities read *was out on the sea* [n] Other ancient authorities read *the wind* [o] Other ancient authorities read *commanded, saying*

---

the Father. Spending time with God in prayer nurtures a vital relationship and equips us to meet life's challenges and struggles. Develop the discipline of spending time alone with God—it will help you grow spiritually and become more and more like Christ.

14.28 Peter was not testing Jesus, something we are told not to do (4.7). Instead he was the only one in the boat to react in faith. His impulsive request led him to experience a rather unusual demonstration of God's power. Peter started to sink because he took his eyes off Jesus and focused on the high waves around him. His faith wavered when he realized what he was doing. We may not walk on water, but we do walk through tough situations. If we focus on the waves of difficult circumstances around us without looking to Christ for help, we too may despair and sink. To maintain your faith when situations are difficult, keep your eyes on Christ's power rather than on your inadequacies.

14.30, 31 Although we start out with good intentions, sometimes our faith falters. This doesn't necessarily mean we have failed. When Peter's faith faltered, he reached out to Christ, the only one who could help. He was afraid, but he still looked to Christ. When you are apprehensive about the troubles around you and doubt Christ's presence or ability to help, you must remember that he is the *only* one who can really help.

14.34 Gennesaret was located on the west side of the Sea of Galilee in a fertile, well-watered area.

14.35, 36 The people recognized Jesus as a great healer, but how many understood who he truly was? They came to Jesus for physical healing, but did they come for spiritual healing? They came to prolong their lives on earth, but did they come to secure their eternal lives? People may seek Jesus to learn valuable lessons from his life or in hopes of finding relief from pain. But we miss Jesus' whole message if we seek him only to heal our bodies but not our souls; if we look to him for help only in this life, rather than for his eternal plan for us. Only when we understand the real Jesus Christ can we appreciate how he can truly change our lives.

14.36 Jewish men wore fringe on the lower edges of their robes according to God's command (Deuteronomy 22.12). By Jesus' day, these were seen as signs of holiness (23.5). It was natural that people seeking healing should reach out and touch these, but as one sick woman learned, healing came from faith and not from Jesus' cloak (9.19–22).

15.1, 2 The scribes and Pharisees came from Jerusalem, the center of Jewish authority, to scrutinize Jesus' activities. Over the centuries since the Jews' return from Babylonian captivity, hundreds of religious traditions had been added to God's laws. The scribes and Pharisees considered them all equally important. Many traditions are not bad in themselves. Certain religious traditions can add richness and meaning to life. But we must not assume that because our traditions have been practiced for years they should be elevated to a sacred standing. God's principles never change, and his law doesn't need additions. Traditions should help us understand God's laws better, not become laws themselves.

your mother,' and, 'Whoever speaks evil of father or mother must surely die.' 5 But
you say that whoever tells father or mother, 'Whatever support you might have had
from me is given to God,'[p] then that person need not honor the father.[q] 6 So, for
the sake of your tradition, you make void the word[r] of God. 7 You hypocrites!
Isaiah prophesied rightly about you when he said:

8 'This people honors me with their lips,
but their hearts are far from me;
9 in vain do they worship me,
teaching human precepts as doctrines.' "

10 Then he called the crowd to him and said to them, "Listen and understand:
11 it is not what goes into the mouth that defiles a person, but it is what comes out
of the mouth that defiles." 12 Then the disciples approached and said to him, "Do
you know that the Pharisees took offense when they heard what you said?" 13 He
answered, "Every plant that my heavenly Father has not planted will be uprooted.
14 Let them alone; they are blind guides of the blind.[s] And if one blind person
guides another, both will fall into a pit." 15 But Peter said to him, "Explain this
parable to us." 16 Then he said, "Are you also still without understanding? 17 Do you
not see that whatever goes into the mouth enters the stomach, and goes out into the
sewer? 18 But what comes out of the mouth proceeds from the heart, and this is what
defiles. 19 For out of the heart come evil intentions, murder, adultery, fornication,
theft, false witness, slander. 20 These are what defile a person, but to eat with un-
washed hands does not defile."

Jesus sends a demon out of a girl
(103/Mark 7.24–30)

21 Jesus left that place and went away to the district of Tyre and Sidon. 22 Just

15.4 Ex 20.12; 21.17 Lev 19.2; 20.9 Deut 5.16; 27.16 Prov 20.20 30.17 Eph 6.2
15.7,8 Ezek 33.31
15.9 Col 2.8,18,22 1 Tim 1.6,7 Tit 1.13,14
15.11 Acts 10.15 Rom 14.14 1 Tim 4.4
15.13 Isa 60.21; 61.3 Jn 15.2 1 Cor 3.9
15.14 Isa 9.16 Mal 2.8 Lk 6.39
15.16 Mt 16.9
15.18 Jas 3.6
15.19 Prov 6.14 Jer 17.9 Gal 5.19-21

[p] Or *is an offering* [q] Other ancient authorities add *or the mother* [r] Other ancient authorities read *law*; others, *commandment* [s] Other ancient authorities lack *of the blind*

MINISTRY IN PHOENICIA
After preaching again in Capernaum, Jesus left Galilee for Phoenicia, where he preached in Tyre and Sidon. On his return, he traveled through the region of the Decapolis (Ten Towns), fed the 4,000 beside the sea, then crossed to Magadan.

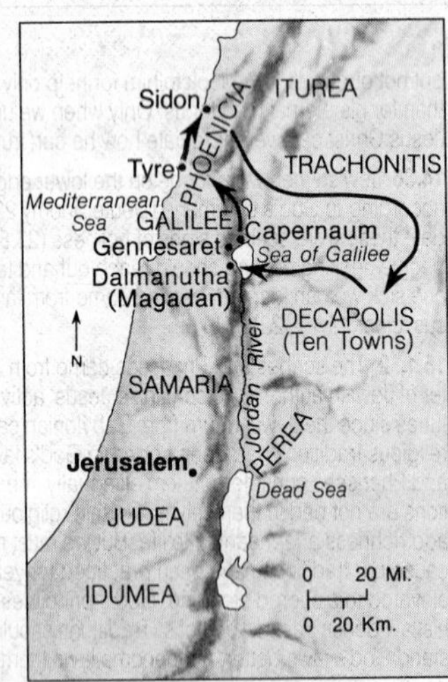

15.5, 6 This was known as the law of *Corban.* Anyone who made a Corban vow was required to dedicate money that otherwise would have gone to support his parents to a worthy cause, usually the temple. Corban had become a religiously acceptable way to neglect parents, circumventing the child's responsibility to them. Although the action – giving money to God – seemed worthy and no doubt conferred prestige on the giver, many people who took the Corban vow were neglecting God's command to care for needy parents. These Pharisees were ignoring God's clear command to honor their parents.

15.8, 9 The prophet Isaiah also criticized hypocrites (Isaiah 29.13), and Jesus applied his words to these religious leaders. When we claim to honor God while our hearts are far from him, our worship means nothing. It is not enough to act religious. Our actions and our attitudes must be sincere. If they are not, Isaiah's words also describe us.

15.9 The Pharisees knew a lot about God, but they didn't know God. It is not enough to study about religion or even to study the Bible. We must respond to God himself.

15.11 Jesus was referring to the Jewish regulations concerning food and drink. This verse could be translated: "You aren't made unholy by eating non-kosher food! It is what you *say* and *think* that makes you unclean!" This statement offended the Pharisees, who were very concerned about what people ate and drank.

15.13, 14 Jesus told his disciples to let the Pharisees alone because they were blind to God's truth. Anyone who listened to their teaching would risk spiritual blindness as well. Not all religious leaders clearly see God's truth. Make sure those you listen to and learn from are those with good spiritual eyesight – those who teach and follow the principles of Scripture.

15.15 Later Peter would be faced with the issue of non-kosher food (see the note on 15.11 and Acts 10.9–17). Then he would learn that nothing should be a barrier to proclaiming the gospel to the Gentiles (non-Jews).

15.16–20 We work hard to keep our outward appearance attractive, but what is in our hearts is even more important. The way we are deep down (where others can't see) matters much to God. What are you like inside? When people become Christians, God makes them different on the inside. He will continue the change process inside them if they only ask. God wants us to seek healthy thoughts and motives, not just healthy food and exercise.

15.22 This woman is called a Syrophoenician in Mark's Gospel

then a Canaanite woman from that region came out and started shouting, "Have
mercy on me, Lord, Son of David; my daughter is tormented by a demon." 23 But
he did not answer her at all. And his disciples came and urged him, saying, "Send
15.24 Isa 53.6 her away, for she keeps shouting after us." 24 He answered, "I was sent only to the
Mt 10.5,6 lost sheep of the house of Israel." 25 But she came and knelt before him, saying,
Acts 3.25,26 13.46 "Lord, help me." 26 He answered, "It is not fair to take the children's food and
15.26 throw it to the dogs." 27 She said, "Yes, Lord, yet even the dogs eat the crumbs that
Mt 7.6 Eph 2.12 fall from their masters' table." 28 Then Jesus answered her, "Woman, great is your
faith! Let it be done for you as you wish." And her daughter was healed instantly.

The crowd marvels at Jesus' healings
(104/Mark 7.31–37)

15.29 Mk 7.31 29 After Jesus had left that place, he passed along the Sea of Galilee, and he
15.30 went up the mountain, where he sat down. 30 Great crowds came to him, bringing
Isa 35.5,6 Mt 4.23; 11.5 with them the lame, the maimed, the blind, the mute, and many others. They put
Lk 7.22 them at his feet, and he cured them, 31 so that the crowd was amazed when they saw
the mute speaking, the maimed whole, the lame walking, and the blind seeing. And
they praised the God of Israel.

Jesus feeds four thousand
(105/Mark 8.1–10)

15.32 Ps 103.13 32 Then Jesus called his disciples to him and said, "I have compassion for the
111.4-5 crowd, because they have been with me now for three days and have nothing to eat;
Mk 1.41; 8.1,10 Heb 2.17; 4.15 and I do not want to send them away hungry, for they might faint on the way."
5.1-3 33 The disciples said to him, "Where are we to get enough bread in the desert to feed
15.33 so great a crowd?" 34 Jesus asked them, "How many loaves have you?" They said,
Num 11.21,22 2 Kgs 4.43 "Seven, and a few small fish." 35 Then ordering the crowd to sit down on the
15.36 1 Sam 9.13 ground, 36 he took the seven loaves and the fish; and after giving thanks he broke
Lk 22.19 them and gave them to the disciples, and the disciples gave them to the crowds.
15.37 37 And all of them ate and were filled; and they took up the broken pieces left over,
Ps 104.28 145.15 seven baskets full. 38 Those who had eaten were four thousand men, besides
15.39 women and children. 39 After sending away the crowds, he got into the boat and
Mk 8.10 went to the region of Magadan.[t]

[t] Other ancient authorities read *Magdala* or *Magdalan*

(7.26), indicating she was from the territory northwest of Galilee where the cities of Tyre and Sidon were located. Matthew calls her a Canaanite, naming her ancient ancestors who were enemies of Israel. Matthew's Jewish audience would have immediately understood the significance of Jesus helping this woman.

15.23 The disciples asked Jesus to get rid of the woman because she was bothering them with her begging. They showed no compassion for her or sensitivity to her needs. It is possible to become so occupied with spiritual matters that we miss real needs right around us. This is especially likely if we are prejudiced against the needy people or if they cause us inconvenience. Instead of being bothered, be aware of the opportunities that surround you. Be open to the beauty of God's message for *all* people, and make an effort not to shut out those who are different from you.

15.24 Jesus' words do not contradict the truth that God's message is for all people (Psalm 22.27; Isaiah 56.7; Matthew 28.19; Romans 15.9–12). After all, when Jesus said these words he was in Gentile territory on a mission to Gentile people. He ministered to Gentiles on many other occasions also. Jesus was simply telling the woman that Jews were to have the first opportunity to accept him as the Messiah because God wanted them to present the message of salvation to the rest of the world (see Genesis 12.3). Jesus was not rejecting the Canaanite woman. He may have wanted to test her faith, or he may have wanted to use the situation as another opportunity to teach that faith is available to all people.

15.26–28 *Dog* was a term the Jews commonly applied to Gentiles, because the Jews considered these pagan people no more likely than dogs to receive God's blessing. Jesus was not degrading the woman by using this term, he was reflecting the Jews' attitude so as to contrast it with his own. The woman did not argue. Instead, using Jesus' choice of words, she agreed to be considered a dog as long as she could receive God's blessing for her daughter. Ironically, many Jews would lose God's blessing and salvation because they rejected Jesus, and many Gentiles would find salvation because they recognized and accepted him.

15.29–31 A vast crowd was brought to Jesus to be healed, and he healed them all. Jesus is still able to heal broken lives, and we can be the ones who bring the suffering to him. Who do you know that needs Christ's healing touch? You can bring them to Jesus through prayer or by explaining to them the reason for your faith. Then let Christ do the healing.

15.32ff This feeding of 4,000 is a separate event from the feeding of the 5,000 (14.13–21), confirmed by Mark 8.19, 20. This was the beginning of Jesus' expanded ministry to the Gentiles.

15.33 Jesus had already fed more than 5,000 people with five loaves and two fish. Now, in a similar situation, the disciples were again perplexed. How easily we throw up our hands in despair when faced with difficult situations. Like the disciples, we often forget that if God has cared for us in the past, he will do the same now. When facing a difficult situation, remember how God cared for you and trust him to work faithfully again.

Religious leaders ask for a sign in the sky
(106/Mark 8.11–13)

16 The Pharisees and Sadducees came, and to test Jesus[u] they asked him to 16.1
show them a sign from heaven. 2 He answered them, "When it is evening, Mt 12.38 Mk 8.11-21
you say, 'It will be fair weather, for the sky is red.' 3 And in the morning, 'It will Lk 11.16
be stormy today, for the sky is red and threatening.' You know how to interpret the 16.2 Isa 7.14
appearance of the sky, but you cannot interpret the signs of the times.[v] 4 An evil Lk 12.54-56
and adulterous generation asks for a sign, but no sign will be given to it except the 16.4 Mt 12.39
sign of Jonah." Then he left them and went away.

Jesus warns against wrong teaching
(107/Mark 8.14–21)

5 When the disciples reached the other side, they had forgotten to bring any
bread. 6 Jesus said to them, "Watch out, and beware of the yeast of the Pharisees 16.6
and Sadducees." 7 They said to one another, "It is because we have brought no Mt 7.15 Lk 12.1
bread." 8 And becoming aware of it, Jesus said, "You of little faith, why are you Rom 16.17,18 Phil 3.2
talking about having no bread? 9 Do you still not perceive? Do you not remember Col 2.8
the five loaves for the five thousand, and how many baskets you gathered? 10 Or the 2 Pet 3.17
seven loaves for the four thousand, and how many baskets you gathered? 11 How 16.9 Mt 14.19; 15.36
could you fail to perceive that I was not speaking about bread? Beware of the yeast 16.11
of the Pharisees and Sadducees!" 12 Then they understood that he had not told them Lk 12.1
to beware of the yeast of bread, but of the teaching of the Pharisees and Sadducees.

Peter says Jesus is the Messiah
(109/Mark 8.27–30; Luke 9.18–20)

13 Now when Jesus came into the district of Caesarea Philippi, he asked his 16.14
disciples, "Who do people say that the Son of Man is?" 14 And they said, "Some say Mal 4.5
John the Baptist, but others Elijah, and still others Jeremiah or one of the proph- 16.16 Jn 6.69; 11.27
ets." 15 He said to them, "But who do you say that I am?" 16 Simon Peter answered, 16.17
"You are the Messiah,[w] the Son of the living God." 17 And Jesus answered him, Gal 1.16
"Blessed are you, Simon son of Jonah! For flesh and blood has not revealed this to 16.18 Jn 1.42
you, but my Father in heaven. 18 And I tell you, you are Peter,[x] and on this rock[y] 1 Cor 3.11 Eph 2.20-22
I will build my church, and the gates of Hades will not prevail against it. 19 I will 4.15-16
give you the keys of the kingdom of heaven, and whatever you bind on earth will 1 Pet 2.4,5
be bound in heaven, and whatever you loose on earth will be loosed in heaven." 16.19 Jn 20.23

[u] Gk *him* [v] Other ancient authorities lack *2When it is . . . of the times* [w] Or *the Christ* [x] Gk *Petros* [y] Gk *petra*

16.1 The Pharisees and Sadducees were Jewish religious leaders of two different parties, and their views were diametrically opposed on many issues. The Pharisees carefully followed their religious rules and traditions, believing that this was the way to God. They also believed in the authority of all Scripture and in the resurrection of the dead. The Sadducees accepted only the books of Moses as Scripture and did not believe in life after death. In Jesus, however, these two groups had a common enemy, and they joined forces to try to kill him. For more information on the Pharisees and Sadducees, see the charts in Matthew 4 and Mark 3.

16.1 The Pharisees and Sadducees demanded a sign *from heaven.* They tried to explain away Jesus' other miracles as sleight of hand, coincidence, or use of evil power, but they believed only God could do a sign in the sky. This, they were sure, would be a feat beyond Jesus' power. Although Jesus could have easily impressed them, he refused. He knew that even a miracle in the sky would not convince them he was the Messiah, because they had already decided not to believe in him.

16.4 In using the sign of Jonah, who was inside a great fish for three days, Jesus was predicting his death and resurrection (see also 12.38–42).

16.4 Many people, like these Jewish leaders, say they want to see a miracle so they can believe. But Jesus knew that miracles never convince the skeptical. Jesus had been healing, raising people from the dead, and feeding thousands, and still people wanted him to prove himself. Do you doubt Christ because you haven't *seen* a miracle? Do you expect God to prove himself to you personally before you believe? Jesus says, "Blessed are those who have not seen and yet have come to believe" (John 20.29). We have all the miracles recorded in the Old and New Testaments, 2,000 years of church history, and the witness of thousands. With all this evidence, those who won't believe are either too proud or too stubborn. If you simply step forward in faith and believe, then you will begin to see the miracles God can do with your own life!

16.12 Yeast is put into bread to make it rise, and it takes only a little to affect a whole batch of dough. Jesus used yeast as an example of how a small amount of evil can affect a large group of people. The wrong teachings of the Pharisees and Sadducees were leading many people astray. Beware of the tendency to say, "How can this little wrong possibly affect anyone?"

16.13 Caesarea Philippi was located several miles north of the Sea of Galilee, in the territory ruled by Philip. The influence of Greek and Roman culture was everywhere, and pagan temples and idols abounded. When Philip became ruler, he rebuilt and renamed the city after the emperor (Caesar) and himself. The city was originally called Caesarea, the same name as the capital city of his brother Herod's territory.

[20]Then he sternly ordered the disciples not to tell anyone that he was[z] the Messiah.[a]

Jesus predicts his death the first time
(110/Mark 8.31–9.1; Luke 9.21–27)

16.21 Mk 8.31–9.1 Lk 9.22-27
21 From that time on, Jesus began to show his disciples that he must go to
Jerusalem and undergo great suffering at the hands of the elders and chief priests
and scribes, and be killed, and on the third day be raised. [22]And Peter took him
aside and began to rebuke him, saying, "God forbid it, Lord! This must never hap-
16.23 Rom 8.7
pen to you." [23]But he turned and said to Peter, "Get behind me, Satan! You are a
stumbling block to me; for you are setting your mind not on divine things but on
16.24 1 Thess 3.3 2 Tim 3.12
human things."
24 Then Jesus told his disciples, "If any want to become my followers, let them

[z] Other ancient authorities add *Jesus* [a] Or *the Christ*

JOURNEY TO CAESAREA-PHILIPPI
Jesus left Magadan, crossed the lake, and landed in Bethsaida-Julias. There he healed a man who had been born blind. From there, he and his disciples went to Caesarea-Philippi, where Peter confessed Jesus as indeed the Messiah and Son of God.

16.13–17 The disciples answered Jesus' question with the common view—that Jesus was one of the great prophets come back to life. This belief may have stemmed from Deuteronomy 18.18, where God said he would raise up a prophet from among the people. (John the Baptist's Profile is in John 1; Elijah's Profile is in 1 Kings 18; and Jeremiah's Profile is in Jeremiah 1.) Peter, however, confessed Jesus as divine and as the promised and long-awaited Messiah. If Jesus asked you this question, how would you answer? Is he your Lord and Messiah?

16.18 The rock upon which Jesus would build his church has been identified as: (1) Jesus himself (his work of salvation by dying for us on the cross); (2) Peter (the first great leader in the church at Jerusalem); (3) the confession of faith that Peter gave and that all subsequent true believers would give. It seems most likely that the rock refers to Peter as the leader of the church (for his function, not necessarily his character). Just as Peter had revealed the true identity of Christ, so Jesus revealed Peter's identity and role.

Later, Peter reminds Christians that they are the church built on the foundation of the apostles and prophets with Jesus Christ as the cornerstone (1 Peter 2.4–6). All believers are joined into this church by faith in Jesus Christ as Savior, the same faith that Peter expressed here (see also Ephesians 2.20, 21). Jesus praised Peter for his confession of faith. It is faith like Peter's that is the foundation of Christ's kingdom.

16.19 This verse has been a subject of debate for centuries. Some say the keys represent the authority to carry out church discipline, legislation, and administration (18.15–18), while others say the keys give the authority to announce the forgiveness of sins (John 20.23). Still others say the keys may be the opportunity to bring people to the kingdom of heaven by presenting them with the message of salvation found in God's Word (Acts 15.7–9). The religious leaders thought they held the keys to the kingdom, and they tried to shut some out. We cannot decide to open or close the kingdom of heaven for others, but God uses us to help others find the way inside. To all who believe in Christ and obey his words, the kingdom doors are swung wide open.

16.20 Jesus warned the disciples not to publicize Peter's confession, because they did not yet fully understand the kind of Messiah he had come to be—not a military commander but a suffering servant. They needed to come to a full understanding of Jesus and their mission as disciples before they could proclaim it to others in a way that would not precipitate rebellion. They would have a difficult time understanding what Jesus came to do until his earthly mission was complete.

16.21 The phrase, "From that time on" marks a turning point. In 4.17 it signals Jesus' announcement of the kingdom of heaven. Here it points to his new emphasis on his death and resurrection. Still, the disciples didn't grasp Jesus' true purpose because of their preconceived notions about what the Messiah should be. This is the first of three times Jesus predicted his death (see 17.22, 23; 20.18 for others).

16.21–28 This passage corresponds to Daniel's prophecies: the Messiah would be cut off (Daniel 9.26); there would be a period of trouble (9.27); and the king would come in glory (7.13, 14). The disciples would endure the same suffering as their King and, like him, would be rewarded in the end.

16.22 Peter, Jesus' friend and devoted follower who had just eloquently proclaimed his true identity, sought to protect him from the suffering he prophesied. But if Jesus hadn't suffered and died, Peter would have died in his sins. Great temptations can come from those who love us and seek to protect us. Be cautious of advice from a friend who says, "Surely God doesn't want you to face this." Often our most difficult temptations come from those who are only trying to protect us from discomfort.

16.23 In his wilderness temptations, Jesus heard the message that he could achieve greatness without dying (4.6). Now he heard the same message from Peter. Peter had just recognized Jesus as Messiah; now, however, he forsook God's perspective and evaluated the situation from a human one. Satan is always trying to get us to leave God out of the picture. Jesus rebuked Peter for this attitude.

16.24 When Jesus used this picture of his followers taking up their crosses to follow him, the disciples knew what he meant. Crucifixion was a common Roman method of execution, and condemned criminals had to carry their crosses through the streets to the execution site. Following Jesus, therefore, meant a true commitment, the risk of death, and no turning back (see 10.39).

deny themselves and take up their cross and follow me. 25 For those who want to
save their life will lose it, and those who lose their life for my sake will find it.
26 For what will it profit them if they gain the whole world but forfeit their life? Or 16.26
what will they give in return for their life? Ps 49.7-9
27 "For the Son of Man is to come with his angels in the glory of his Father, and 16.27
then he will repay everyone for what has been done. 28 Truly I tell you, there are Mt 25.31 2 Cor 5.10
some standing here who will not taste death before they see the Son of Man coming Jude 14,15 Rev 22.12
in his kingdom."

Jesus is transfigured on the mountain
(111/Mark 9.2–13; Luke 9.28–36)

17 Six days later, Jesus took with him Peter and James and his brother John and 17.1
led them up a high mountain, by themselves. 2 And he was transfigured be- Mk 9.2-8 Lk 9.28-36
fore them, and his face shone like the sun, and his clothes became dazzling white.
3 Suddenly there appeared to them Moses and Elijah, talking with him. 4 Then Peter
said to Jesus, "Lord, it is good for us to be here; if you wish, I[b] will make three
dwellings[c] here, one for you, one for Moses, and one for Elijah." 5 While he was 17.5 Deut 18.15
still speaking, suddenly a bright cloud overshadowed them, and from the cloud a Isa 42.1 Mk 1.11
voice said, "This is my Son, the Beloved;[d] with him I am well pleased; listen to Lk 3.22
him!" 6 When the disciples heard this, they fell to the ground and were overcome by Acts 3.22 Heb 12.25
fear. 7 But Jesus came and touched them, saying, "Get up and do not be afraid." 2 Pet 1.17,18
8 And when they looked up, they saw no one except Jesus himself alone. 17.9 Mk 9.9-13
9 As they were coming down the mountain, Jesus ordered them, "Tell no one 17.10
about the vision until after the Son of Man has been raised from the dead." 10 And Mal 4.5
the disciples asked him, "Why, then, do the scribes say that Elijah must come 17.11 Lk 1.17
first?" 11 He replied, "Elijah is indeed coming and will restore all things; 12 but I tell 17.12
you that Elijah has already come, and they did not recognize him, but they did to Mt 14.3

[b] Other ancient authorities read *we* [c] Or *tents* [d] Or *my beloved Son*

16.25 The possibility of losing their lives was very real for the disciples as well as for Jesus. Real discipleship implies real commitment – pledging our whole existence to his service. If we try to save our physical life from death, pain, or discomfort, we may risk losing our true eternal life. If we protect ourselves from pain, we begin to die spiritually and emotionally. Our lives turn inward, and we lose our intended purpose. When we give our lives in service to Christ, however, we discover the real purpose of living.

16.26 When we don't know Christ, we make choices as though this life were all we have. In reality, this life is just the introduction to eternity. How we live this brief span, however, determines our eternal state. What we accumulate on earth has no value in purchasing eternal life. Even the highest social or civic honors cannot earn our way to heaven. Evaluate all that happens from an eternal perspective, and you will find your values and decisions changing.

16.27 Jesus Christ has been given the authority to judge all the earth (Philippians 2.9–11). Although his judgment is already working in our lives, there is a future, final judgment when Christ returns (25.31–46) and everyone's life is reviewed and evaluated. This will not be confined to unbelievers; Christians too will face a judgment. Their eternal destiny is secure, but Jesus will look at how they handled gifts, opportunities, and responsibilities in order to determine their heavenly rewards. At the time of judgment, God will deliver the righteous and condemn the wicked. We should not judge others' salvation; that is God's work.

16.28 Since all the disciples died *before* Christ's return, many believe Jesus' words were fulfilled at the transfiguration when Peter, James, and John saw his glory (17.1–3). Others say they refer to Pentecost (Acts 2) and the beginning of Christ's church. In either case, certain disciples were eyewitnesses to the power and glory of Christ's kingdom.

17.1ff The transfiguration was a vision, a brief glimpse of the true glory of the King (16.27, 28). This was a special revelation of Jesus' divinity to three of the disciples, and it was God's divine affirmation of everything Jesus had done and was about to do.

17.3–5 Moses and Elijah were the two greatest prophets in the Old Testament. Moses represents the law. He wrote the Pentateuch, and he predicted the coming of a great Prophet (Deuteronomy 18.15–19). Elijah represents the prophets who foretold the coming of the Messiah (Malachi 4.5, 6). Moses' and Elijah's presence with Jesus confirms his messianic mission – to fulfill God's law and the words of God's prophets. Just as God's voice in the cloud over Mount Sinai gave authority to his law (Exodus 19.9), God's voice at the transfiguration gave authority to Jesus' words.

17.4 Peter wanted to build a place for these three great men to stay. But he had the wrong idea. He wanted to act, but this was a time for worship and adoration. He wanted to capture the moment, but he was supposed to learn and move on. He saw Christ as equal to the others, but Christ is infinitely greater and not to be equated with anyone.

17.5 Jesus is more than just a great leader, a good example, a good influence, or a great prophet. He is the Son of God. When you understand this profound truth, the only adequate response is worship. When you have a correct understanding of Christ, you will obey him.

17.9 Jesus told Peter, James, and John not to tell what they had seen until after his resurrection, because Jesus knew that they didn't fully understand it and could not explain what they didn't understand. Their questions (17.10ff) revealed their misunderstandings. They knew that he was the Messiah, but they had much more to learn about the significance of his death and resurrection.

17.11, 12 Jesus was referring to John the Baptist, not to the Old Testament prophet Elijah. John the Baptist took Elijah's prophetic role – boldly confronting sin and pointing people to God. Malachi had prophesied that a prophet like Elijah would come (Malachi 4.5).

him whatever they pleased. So also the Son of Man is about to suffer at their
hands." 13 Then the disciples understood that he was speaking to them about John
the Baptist.

Jesus heals the demon-possessed boy
(112/Mark 9.14–29; Luke 9.37–43)

17.14 Mk 9.14-29 14 When they came to the crowd, a man came to him, knelt before him, 15 and
Lk 9.37-43 said, "Lord, have mercy on my son, for he is an epileptic and he suffers terribly; he
often falls into the fire and often into the water. 16 And I brought him to your disciples, but they could not cure him." 17 Jesus answered, "You faithless and perverse
generation, how much longer must I be with you? How much longer must I put up
with you? Bring him here to me." 18 And Jesus rebuked the demon,[e] and it[f] came
out of him, and the boy was cured instantly. 19 Then the disciples came to Jesus
17.20 Mt 21.21 privately and said, "Why could we not cast it out?" 20 He said to them, "Because of
Mk 11.22,23 your little faith. For truly I tell you, if you have faith the size of a[g] mustard seed,
Lk 17.6 Jn 11.40 you will say to this mountain, 'Move from here to there,' and it will move; and
1 Cor 13.2 nothing will be impossible for you."[h]

Jesus predicts his death the second time
(113/Mark 9.30–32; Luke 9.44, 45)

17.22 Mk 9.30-32 22 As they were gathering[i] in Galilee, Jesus said to them, "The Son of Man is
Lk 9.22,43-45 going to be betrayed into human hands, 23 and they will kill him, and on the third
day he will be raised." And they were greatly distressed.

Peter finds the coin in the fish's mouth
(114)

24 When they reached Capernaum, the collectors of the temple tax[j] came to

[e] Gk *it* or *him* [f] Gk *the demon* [g] Gk *faith as a grain of* [h] Other ancient authorities add verse 21, *But this kind does not come out except by prayer and fasting* [i] Other ancient authorities read *living* [j] Gk *didrachma*

17.17 The disciples had been given the authority to do the healing, but they had not yet learned how to appropriate the power of God. Jesus' frustration is with the unbelieving and unresponsive generation. His disciples were merely a reflection of that attitude in this instance. Jesus' purpose was not to criticize the disciples, but to encourage them to greater faith.

17.17–20 The disciples were unable to cast out this demon, and they asked Jesus why. He pointed to their lack of faith. It is the power of God, not our faith, that moves mountains, but faith must be present to do so. The mustard seed was the smallest particle imaginable. Even small or undeveloped faith would have been sufficient. Perhaps they had tried to cast out the devil with their own ability rather than God's. There is great power in even a little faith when God is with us. If we feel weak or powerless as Christians, we should examine our faith, making sure we are trusting not in our own abilities to produce results, but in God's.

17.20 Jesus wasn't condemning the disciples for substandard faith; he was trying to show how important faith would be in their future ministry. If you are facing a problem that seems as big and immovable as a mountain, turn your eyes from the mountain and look to Christ for more faith. Only then will your work for him become useful and vibrant.

17.21 Jesus was teaching that some work for God is more difficult than others and requires a greater than usual dependence on God. This verse means that prayer and fasting alone would not have accomplished the miracle. Prayer and fasting indicate faith, discipline, and humility before God, without which there can be no hope of success.

17.22, 23 Once again Jesus predicted his death (see also 16.21); but more important, he told of his resurrection. Unfortunately, the disciples heard only the first part of Jesus' words and became discouraged. They couldn't understand why Jesus wanted to go back to Jerusalem where he would walk right into trouble.

The disciples didn't fully comprehend the purpose of Jesus' death and resurrection until Pentecost (Acts 2). We shouldn't get upset at ourselves for being slow to understand everything about Jesus. After all, the disciples were with him, saw his miracles, heard his words, and still had difficulty understanding. Despite their questions and doubts, however, they believed. We should do no less.

17.22, 23 The disciples didn't understand why Jesus kept talking about his death because they expected him to set up a political kingdom. His death, they thought, would dash their hopes. They didn't know that Jesus' death and resurrection would make his kingdom possible.

17.24 All Jewish males had to pay a temple tax to support temple upkeep (Exodus 30.11–16). Tax collectors set up booths to collect these taxes. Only Matthew records this incident—perhaps because he had been a tax collector himself.

17.24–27 As usual, Peter answered a question without really knowing the answer, putting Jesus and the disciples in an awkward position. Jesus used this situation, however, to emphasize his kingly role. Just as kings pay no taxes and collect none from their family, Jesus, the King, owed no taxes. But Jesus supplied the tax payment for both himself and Peter rather than offend those who didn't understand his kingship. Although Jesus supplied the tax money, Peter had to go and get it. Ultimately all that we have comes to us from God's supply, but he may want us to be active in the process.

17.24–27 As God's people, we are foreigners on earth because our loyalty is always to our real King—Jesus. Still we have to cooperate with the authorities and be responsible citizens. An ambassador to another country keeps the local laws in order to represent well the one who sent him. We are Christ's ambassadors. Are you being a good foreign ambassador for him to this world?

Peter and said, “Does your teacher not pay the temple tax?”[k] 25 He said, “Yes, he 17.24
does.” And when he came home, Jesus spoke of it first, asking, “What do you Mk 12.14-17
think, Simon? From whom do kings of the earth take toll or tribute? From their
children or from others?” 26 When Peter[l] said, “From others,” Jesus said to him,
“Then the children are free. 27 However, so that we do not give offense to them, go 17.27
to the sea and cast a hook; take the first fish that comes up; and when you open its Mt 18.6-9
mouth, you will find a coin;[m] take that and give it to them for you and me.” 1 Cor 8.13; 10.32

The disciples argue about who would be the greatest
(115/Mark 9.33–37; Luke 9.46–48)

18 At that time the disciples came to Jesus and asked, “Who is the greatest in 18.3
the kingdom of heaven?” 2 He called a child, whom he put among them, Mk 10.14
3 and said, “Truly I tell you, unless you change and become like children, you will Lk 18.16,17
never enter the kingdom of heaven. 4 Whoever becomes humble like this child is 1 Cor 14.20
the greatest in the kingdom of heaven. 5 Whoever welcomes one such child in my 1 Pet 2.2
name welcomes me. 18.4 1 Pet 5.5,6 18.5 Mt 10.42

Jesus warns against temptation
(117/Mark 9.42–50)

6 “If any of you put a stumbling block before one of these little ones who be- 18.6
lieve in me, it would be better for you if a great millstone were fastened around Lk 17.1-3
your neck and you were drowned in the depth of the sea. 7 Woe to the world because 1 Cor 8.12,13
of stumbling blocks! Occasions for stumbling are bound to come, but woe to the
one by whom the stumbling block comes!

8 “If your hand or your foot causes you to stumble, cut it off and throw it away; 18.8
it is better for you to enter life maimed or lame than to have two hands or two feet Mt 5.29,30
and to be thrown into the eternal fire. 9 And if your eye causes you to stumble, tear
it out and throw it away; it is better for you to enter life with one eye than to have
two eyes and to be thrown into the hell[n] of fire.

Jesus warns against looking down on others
(118)

10 “Take care that you do not despise one of these little ones; for, I tell you, in 18.10
heaven their angels continually see the face of my Father in heaven.[o] 12 What do Ps 34.7
you think? If a shepherd has a hundred sheep, and one of them has gone astray, Lk 1.19
does he not leave the ninety-nine on the mountains and go in search of the one that Acts 12.15
went astray? 13 And if he finds it, truly I tell you, he rejoices over it more than over Heb 1.14 18.12 Lk 15.3-7

[k] Gk *didrachma* [l] Gk *he* [m] Gk *stater*; the stater was worth two didrachmas [n] Gk *Gehenna* [o] Other ancient authorities add verse 11, *For the Son of Man came to save the lost*

18.1–4 Jesus used a child to help his self-centered disciples get the point. We are not to be *childish* (like the disciples, arguing over petty issues), but rather *childlike,* with humble and sincere hearts. Are you being childlike or childish?

18.3, 4 The disciples had become so preoccupied with the organization of Jesus' earthly kingdom, they had lost sight of its divine purpose. Instead of seeking a place of service, they sought positions of advantage. How easy it is to lose our eternal perspective and compete for promotions or status in the church. How hard it is to identify with the “children” – weak and dependent people with no status or influence.

18.6 Children are trusting by nature. They trust adults, and through that trust their capacity to trust God grows. Parents and other adults who influence young children are held accountable by God for how they affect these little ones' ability to trust. Jesus warned that anyone who turns little children away from faith will receive severe punishment.

18.7ff Jesus warned the disciples about three ways to cause “little ones” to lose faith: tempting them (18.7–9), neglecting or demeaning them (18.10–14), and teaching false doctrine to them (18.15–26). As leaders, we are to help young or new believers avoid anything or anyone that could cause them to stumble in their faith and lead them to sin. We must never take lightly the spiritual education and protection of the young in age and in the faith.

18.8, 9 We must remove stumbling blocks that cause us to sin. This does not mean to cut off a part of the body; it means that any person, program, or teaching in the church that threatens the spiritual growth of the body must be removed. For the individual, any relationship, practice, or activity that leads us to sin should be stopped. Jesus says it would be better to go to heaven with one hand than to hell with both. Sin, of course, affects more than our hands; it affects our minds and hearts.

18.10 Our concern for children must parallel God's treatment of them. Certain angels are assigned to watch over children, and they have direct access to God. These words ring out sharply in cultures where children are taken lightly, ignored, or aborted. If their angels have constant access to God, the least we can do is to allow children to approach us easily in spite of our far too busy schedules.

the ninety-nine that never went astray. 14 So it is not the will of your[p] Father in
heaven that one of these little ones should be lost.

Jesus teaches about how to treat a believer who sins
(119)

18.15 Lk 17.3; Gal 6.1; 2 Thess 3.15; Jas 5.19,20
18.16 Deut 19.15
18.17 Rom 16.17; 1 Cor 6.1-8; 1 Tim 5.20
18.18 Mt 16.19; Jn 20.23

15 "If another member of the church[q] sins against you,[r] go and point out the
fault when the two of you are alone. If the member[s] listens to you, you have regained that one. 16 But if you are not listened to, take one or two others along with
you, so that every word may be confirmed by the evidence of two or three witnesses. 17 If the member[s] refuses to listen to them, tell it to the church; and if the
offender[s] refuses to listen even to the church, let such a one be to you as a Gentile
and a tax collector. 18 Truly I tell you, whatever you bind on earth will be bound in
heaven, and whatever you loose on earth will be loosed in heaven. 19 Again, truly
I tell you, if two of you agree on earth about anything you ask, it will be done for
you by my Father in heaven. 20 For where two or three are gathered in my name, I
am there among them."

Jesus tells the parable of the unforgiving debtor
(120)

18.21 Lk 17.4
18.22 Col 3.13
18.23 Mt 25.19

21 Then Peter came and said to him, "Lord, if another member of the church[t]
sins against me, how often should I forgive? As many as seven times?" 22 Jesus said
to him, "Not seven times, but, I tell you, seventy-seven[u] times.
23 "For this reason the kingdom of heaven may be compared to a king who
wished to settle accounts with his slaves. 24 When he began the reckoning, one who
owed him ten thousand talents[v] was brought to him; 25 and, as he could not pay, his

[p] Other ancient authorities read *my* [q] Gk *If your brother* [r] Other ancient authorities lack *against you* [s] Gk *the brother* [t] Gk *if my brother* [u] Or *seventy times seven* [v] A talent was worth more than fifteen years' wages of a laborer

JESUS AND FORGIVENESS

Jesus forgave	*Reference*
the paralyzed man lowered on a stretcher through the roof.	Matthew 9.2–8
the woman caught in adultery.	John 8.3–11
the woman who anointed his feet with oil.	Luke 7.47–50
Peter, for denying he knew Jesus.	John 18.15–18, 25–27; 21.15–19
the thief on the cross.	Luke 23.39–43
the people who crucified him.	Luke 23.34

Jesus not only taught frequently about forgiveness, he also demonstrated his own willingness to forgive. Here are several examples that should be an encouragement to recognize his willingness to forgive us also.

18.14 Just as a shepherd is concerned enough for one lost sheep to go search the hills for it, so God is concerned about every human being he creates (he is "not wanting any to perish," 2 Peter 3.9). You come in contact with children who need Christ at home, at school, in church, and in the neighborhood. Steer them toward Christ by your example, your words, and your acts of kindness.

18.15–17 These are Jesus' guidelines for dealing with those who sin against us. They were meant for (1) Christians, not unbelievers, (2) sins against *you* and not others, and (3) conflict resolution in the context of the church, not the community at large. Jesus' words are not a license for a frontal attack on every person who hurts or slights us. They are not a license to start a destructive gossip campaign or to call for a church trial. They are designed to reconcile those who disagree so that all Christians can live in harmony.

When someone wrongs us, we often do the opposite of what Jesus recommends. We turn away in hatred or resentment, seek revenge, or gossip. By contrast, we should go to that person *first,* as difficult as that may be. Then we should forgive that person as often as he or she needs it (18.21, 22). This creates a much better chance of restoring the relationship.

18.18 This *binding* and *loosing* refers to the decisions of the church in conflicts. Among believers, there is no court of appeals beyond the church. Ideally, the church's decisions should be God-guided and based on discernment of his Word. Believers have the responsibility, therefore, to bring their problems to the church, and the church has the responsibility to use God's guidance in seeking to resolve conflicts. Handling problems God's way will have an impact now and for eternity.

18.19, 20 Jesus looks ahead to a new day when he will be present with his followers not in body, but through his Holy Spirit. In the body of believers (the church), the sincere agreement of two people is more powerful than the superficial agreement of thousands, because Christ's Holy Spirit is with them. Two or more believers, *filled with the Holy Ghost,* will pray according to God's will, not their own; and thus their requests will be granted.

18.22 The rabbis taught that people should forgive those who offend them three times. Peter, trying to be especially generous, asked Jesus if seven (the "perfect" number) was enough times to forgive someone. But Jesus answered, "Seventy-seven times" (the number of eternity), meaning that we shouldn't even keep track of how many times we forgive someone. We should always forgive those who are truly repentant, no matter how many times they ask.

lord ordered him to be sold, together with his wife and children and all his posses- **18.25** Ex 21.2
sions, and payment to be made. 26 So the slave fell on his knees before him, saying, Lev 25.39
'Have patience with me, and I will pay you everything.' 27 And out of pity for him, 2 Kings 4.1 Neh 5.5
the lord of that slave released him and forgave him the debt. 28 But that same slave,
as he went out, came upon one of his fellow slaves who owed him a hundred denarii;[w] and seizing him by the throat, he said, 'Pay what you owe.' 29 Then his
fellow slave fell down and pleaded with him, 'Have patience with me, and I will
pay you.' 30 But he refused; then he went and threw him into prison until he would
pay the debt. 31 When his fellow slaves saw what had happened, they were greatly
distressed, and they went and reported to their lord all that had taken place. 32 Then
his lord summoned him and said to him, 'You wicked slave! I forgave you all that **18.33** Mt 7.2
debt because you pleaded with me. 33 Should you not have had mercy on your fel- Eph 4.32; 5.2
low slave, as I had mercy on you?' 34 And in anger his lord handed him over to be Col 3.13
tortured until he would pay his entire debt. 35 So my heavenly Father will also do to **18.34** Mk 11.25
every one of you, if you do not forgive your brother or sister[x] from your heart." Jas 2.13

6. Jesus faces conflict with the religious leaders

Jesus teaches about marriage and divorce

(173/Mark 10.1–12)

19 When Jesus had finished saying these things, he left Galilee and went to the
region of Judea beyond the Jordan. 2 Large crowds followed him, and he
cured them there. **19.3** Mk 10.2-12
3 Some Pharisees came to him, and to test him they asked, "Is it lawful for a **19.4** Gen 1.27; 5.2
man to divorce his wife for any cause?" 4 He answered, "Have you not read that the
one who made them at the beginning 'made them male and female,' 5 and said, 'For **19.5** Gen 2.24
this reason a man shall leave his father and mother and be joined to his wife, and the Mal 2.15 1 Cor 6.16
two shall become one flesh'? 6 So they are no longer two, but one flesh. Therefore Eph 5.31
what God has joined together, let no one separate." 7 They said to him, "Why then **19.7** Deut 24.1
did Moses command us to give a certificate of dismissal and to divorce her?" 8 He Mt 5.31,32

[w] The denarius was the usual day's wage for a laborer [x] Gk *brother*

18.30 In Bible times, serious consequences awaited those who could not pay their debts. A person lending money could seize the borrower who couldn't pay him back and force him or his family to work until the debt was paid. The debtor could also be thrown into prison, or his family could be sold into slavery to help pay off the debt. It was hoped that the debtor, while in prison, would sell off his landholdings or that relatives would pay the debt. If not, the debtor could remain in prison for life.

18.35 Because God has forgiven all our sins, we should not withhold forgiveness from others. Realizing how completely Christ has forgiven us should produce a free and generous attitude of forgiveness toward others. When we don't forgive others, we are setting ourselves outside and above Christ's law of love.

19.3–12 John was put in prison and killed for his public opinions on marriage and divorce, and the Pharisees hoped to trap Jesus too. They were trying to trick Jesus by having him choose sides in a theological controversy. Two main groups had two opposing views of divorce. One group supported divorce for almost any reason. The other believed divorce could be allowed only for marital unfaithfulness. This conflict hinged on how each group interpreted Deuteronomy 24.1–4. But in his answer, Jesus focused on marriage rather than divorce. He pointed out that God intended marriage to be permanent, and he gave four reasons for the importance of marriage (19.4–6).

19.7, 8 This law is found in Deuteronomy 24.1–4. In Moses' day, as well as in Jesus' day, the practice of marriage fell far short of God's intention. The same is true today. Jesus said that Moses gave this law only because of the people's hard hearts. Permanent marriage was God's intention, but because sinful human nature made divorce inevitable, Moses instituted some laws to help its victims. These were civil laws designed especially to protect the women who, in that culture, were quite vulnerable when living alone. With Moses' law, a man could no longer just throw his wife out—he had to write a formal letter of dismissal. This was a radical step toward civil rights, for it made men think twice about divorce. God designed marriage to be indissoluble. Instead of looking for reasons to leave each other, married couples should concentrate on how to stay together (19.3–9).

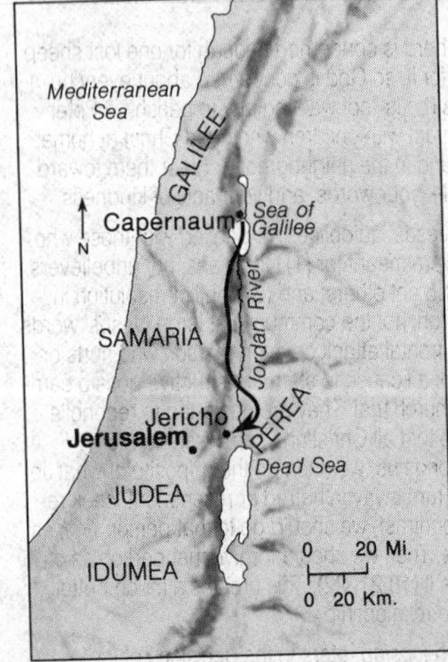

JESUS TRAVELS TOWARD JERUSALEM Jesus left Galilee for the last time—heading toward his death in Jerusalem. He again crossed the Jordan, spending some time in Perea before going on to Jericho.

said to them, "It was because you were so hard-hearted that Moses allowed you to
19.9 divorce your wives, but from the beginning it was not so. [9]And I say to you, who-
Lk 16.18 1 Cor 7.10,11 ever divorces his wife, except for unchastity, and marries another commits adultery."[y]
10 His disciples said to him, "If such is the case of a man with his wife, it is
19.11 1 Cor 7.7-9,17 better not to marry." [11]But he said to them, "Not everyone can accept this teaching,
19.12 but only those to whom it is given. [12]For there are eunuchs who have been so from
1 Cor 7.32,34 birth, and there are eunuchs who have been made eunuchs by others, and there are
eunuchs who have made themselves eunuchs for the sake of the kingdom of
heaven. Let anyone accept this who can."

Jesus blesses little children
(174/Mark 10.13–16; Luke 18.15–17)

19.13 13 Then little children were being brought to him in order that he might lay his
Mk 10.13-16 Lk 18.15-17 hands on them and pray. The disciples spoke sternly to those who brought them;
19.14 Mt 18.3 [14]but Jesus said, "Let the little children come to me, and do not stop them; for it is
to such as these that the kingdom of heaven belongs." [15]And he laid his hands on
them and went on his way.

Jesus speaks to the rich young man
(175/Mark 10.17–31; Luke 18.18–30)

19.16 16 Then someone came to him and said, "Teacher, what good deed must I do
Mk 10.17-31 Lk 10.25 to have eternal life?" [17]And he said to him, "Why do you ask me about what is
18.18-30 good? There is only one who is good. If you wish to enter into life, keep the com-
19.18 Ex 20.12-17 mandments." [18]He said to him, "Which ones?" And Jesus said, "You shall not
Deut 5.16-21 murder; You shall not commit adultery; You shall not steal; You shall not bear false
19.19 Lev 19.18 witness; [19]Honor your father and mother; also, You shall love your neighbor as
Mt 15.4; 22.39 Mk 12.31 yourself." [20]The young man said to him, "I have kept all these;[z] what do I still
19.21 lack?" [21]Jesus said to him, "If you wish to be perfect, go, sell your possessions,
Lk 12.33 and give the money[a] to the poor, and you will have treasure in heaven; then come,
Acts 2.45 4.34,35 follow me." [22]When the young man heard this word, he went away grieving, for he
1 Tim 6.18 had many possessions.

[y] Other ancient authorities read *except on the ground of unchastity, causes her to commit adultery*; others add at the end of the verse *and he who marries a divorced woman commits adultery* [z] Other ancient authorities add *from my youth* [a] Gk lacks *the money*

19.10–12 Although divorce was relatively easy in Old Testament times (19.7), it is not what God originally intended. Couples should decide against divorce from the start and build their marriage on mutual commitment. There are also many good reasons for not marrying, one being to have more time to work for God's kingdom. Don't assume that God wants everyone to marry. For many it may be better if they don't. Be sure you prayerfully seek God's will before you plunge into the lifelong commitment of marriage.

19.12 A eunuch is an emasculated male—a man with no testicles.

19.12 Some have physical limitations that prevent their marrying, while others choose not to marry because, in their particular situation, they can serve God better as single people. Jesus was not teaching us to avoid marriage because it is inconvenient or takes away our freedom. That would be selfishness. A good reason to remain single is to use the time and freedom to serve God. Paul elaborates on this in 1 Corinthians 7.

19.13–15 The disciples must have forgotten what Jesus had said about children (18.4–6). Jesus wanted little children to come because he loves them and because they have the kind of attitude needed to approach God. He didn't mean that heaven is only for children, but that people need childlike attitudes of trust in God. The receptiveness of little children was a great contrast to the stubbornness of the religious leaders who let their education and sophistication stand in the way of the simple faith needed to believe in Jesus.

19.16 To this man seeking assurance of eternal life, Jesus pointed out that salvation does not come from good deeds unaccompanied by love for God. The man needed a whole new starting point. Instead of adding another commandment to keep or good deed to perform, he needed to submit humbly to the lordship of Christ.

19.17 In response to the young man's question about how to have eternal life, Jesus told him to keep God's ten commandments. Jesus then listed six of them, all referring to relationships with others. When the young man replied that he had kept them, Jesus told him he must do something more—sell everything and give the money to the poor. This showed the man's weakness. In reality, his wealth was his god, his idol, and he would not give it up. Thus he violated the first and greatest commandment (Exodus 20.3; Matthew 22.36–40).

19.21 When Jesus told this young man that he would "be perfect" if he gave everything he had to the poor, he wasn't speaking in the temporal, human sense. Jesus was explaining how to be "justified," made whole or complete, in God's sight.

19.21 Should all believers sell everything they own? No. We are responsible to care for our own needs and the needs of our families so as not to be a burden on others. We should, however, be willing to give up anything if God asks us to do so. This kind of attitude allows nothing to come between us and God and keeps us from using our God-given wealth selfishly. If you are comforted by the fact that Christ did not tell all his followers to sell all their possessions, then you may be too attached to what you have.

23 Then Jesus said to his disciples, "Truly I tell you, it will be hard for a rich
person to enter the kingdom of heaven. 24 Again I tell you, it is easier for a camel
to go through the eye of a needle than for someone who is rich to enter the kingdom
of God." 25 When the disciples heard this, they were greatly astounded and said,
"Then who can be saved?" 26 But Jesus looked at them and said, "For mortals it is
impossible, but for God all things are possible."
27 Then Peter said in reply, "Look, we have left everything and followed you.
What then will we have?" 28 Jesus said to them, "Truly I tell you, at the renewal of
all things, when the Son of Man is seated on the throne of his glory, you who have
followed me will also sit on twelve thrones, judging the twelve tribes of Israel.
29 And everyone who has left houses or brothers or sisters or father or mother or
children or fields, for my name's sake, will receive a hundredfold,[b] and will inherit eternal life. 30 But many who are first will be last, and the last will be first.

19.23 Job 31.24-28 Mt 13.22 1 Cor 1.26 1 Tim 6.9
19.26 Gen 18.14 Job 42.2 Jer 32.17 Zech 8.6
19.27 Mt 4.20 Lk 5.11
19.28 Lk 22.28-30 1 Cor 6.2,3 Rev 2.26
19.30 Mt 20.16

Jesus tells the parable of the workers paid equally
(176)

20 "For the kingdom of heaven is like a landowner who went out early in the
morning to hire laborers for his vineyard. 2 After agreeing with the laborers
for the usual daily wage,[c] he sent them into his vineyard. 3 When he went out about
nine o'clock, he saw others standing idle in the marketplace; 4 and he said to them,
'You also go into the vineyard, and I will pay you whatever is right.' So they went.
5 When he went out again about noon and about three o'clock, he did the same.
6 And about five o'clock he went out and found others standing around; and he said
to them, 'Why are you standing here idle all day?' 7 They said to him, 'Because no
one has hired us.' He said to them, 'You also go into the vineyard.' 8 When evening
came, the owner of the vineyard said to his manager, 'Call the laborers and give
them their pay, beginning with the last and then going to the first.' 9 When those
hired about five o'clock came, each of them received the usual daily wage.[c]
10 Now when the first came, they thought they would receive more; but each of
them also received the usual daily wage.[c] 11 And when they received it, they grumbled against the landowner, 12 saying, 'These last worked only one hour, and you
have made them equal to us who have borne the burden of the day and the scorching
heat.' 13 But he replied to one of them, 'Friend, I am doing you no wrong; did you
not agree with me for the usual daily wage?[c] 14 Take what belongs to you and go;
I choose to give to this last the same as I give to you. 15 Am I not allowed to do what

20.1 Song 1.6; 8.11,12
20.2
20.8 Lev 19.13
20.12 Mt 4.8 Lk 1.11
20.15 Rom 9.21

[b] Other ancient authorities read *manifold* [c] Gk *a denarius*

19.24 Because it is impossible for a camel to go through the eye of a needle, it appears impossible for a rich person to get into heaven. Jesus explained, however, that "for God all things are possible" (19.26). Even rich men can enter the kingdom if God brings them in. Faith in him, not in self or riches, is what counts. On what are you counting for salvation?

19.25, 26 The disciples were confused. They thought that if anyone could be saved it would be the rich, whom their culture considered especially blessed by God.

19.27 In the Bible, God gives rewards to his people according to his justice. In the Old Testament, obedience often brought reward in this life (Deuteronomy 28), but obedience and immediate reward are not always linked. If they were, good people would always be rich, and suffering would always be a sign of sin. As believers, our true reward is God's presence and power through the Holy Spirit. Later, in eternity, we will be rewarded for our faith and service. If material rewards in this life came to us for every faithful deed, we would be tempted to boast about our achievements and soil our motives.

19.29 Jesus assured the disciples that anyone who gives up something valuable for his sake will be repaid many times over in this life, although not necessarily in the same form. For example, a person may be rejected by his family for accepting Christ, but he will gain the larger family of believers.

19.30 Jesus turned the world's values upside down. Consider the most powerful or well-known people in our world—how many got where they are by being mild-tempered, self-effacing, and gentle? Not many! But in the life to come, the last will be first—if they got in last place by choosing to follow Jesus. Don't forfeit eternal rewards for temporary benefits. Be willing to make sacrifices now for greater rewards later. Be willing to accept man's disapproval for God's approval.

20.1ff Jesus further clarified the membership rules of the kingdom of heaven—entrance is by God's grace alone. In this parable, God is the landowner, and believers are the laborers. This parable is especially for those who feel superior because of heritage or favored position, to those who feel superior because they have spent so much time with Christ, and to new believers as reassurance of God's grace.

20.15 This parable is not about rewards but about salvation. It is a strong teaching about *grace*, God's generosity. We shouldn't begrudge those who turn to God in the last moments of life because, in reality, *no one* deserves eternal life.

Many people we don't expect to see in the kingdom will be there. The thief who repented as he was dying (Luke 23.40–43) will be there along with people who have believed and served God for many years. Do you resent God's gracious acceptance of the despised, the outcast, and the sinners who have turned to him for

20.16 Mt 19.30

I choose with what belongs to me? Or are you envious because I am generous?'[d]
16 So the last will be first, and the first will be last."[e]

Jesus predicts his death the third time
(177/Mark 10.32–34; Luke 18.31–34)

20.17 Mk 10.32-34 Lk 18.31-33
20.19 Mt 16.21; 27.2 Jn 18.28 Acts 2.23; 3.13

17 While Jesus was going up to Jerusalem, he took the twelve disciples aside by
themselves, and said to them on the way, 18 "See, we are going up to Jerusalem,
and the Son of Man will be handed over to the chief priests and scribes, and they
will condemn him to death; 19 then they will hand him over to the Gentiles to be
mocked and flogged and crucified; and on the third day he will be raised."

Jesus teaches about serving others
(178/Mark 10.35–45)

20.20 Mk 10.35-45 15.40
20.21 Jas 4.3
20.22 Mk 14.36 Jn 18.11
20.23 Acts 12.2 Rom 8.17 Rev 1.9
20.24 Lk 22.24
20.26 Mk 9.35 1 Pet 5.3
20.28 Phil 2.7 1 Pet 1.19

20 Then the mother of the sons of Zebedee came to him with her sons, and
kneeling before him, she asked a favor of him. 21 And he said to her, "What do you
want?" She said to him, "Declare that these two sons of mine will sit, one at your
right hand and one at your left, in your kingdom." 22 But Jesus answered, "You do
not know what you are asking. Are you able to drink the cup that I am about to
drink?"[f] They said to him, "We are able." 23 He said to them, "You will indeed
drink my cup, but to sit at my right hand and at my left, this is not mine to grant,
but it is for those for whom it has been prepared by my Father."
24 When the ten heard it, they were angry with the two brothers. 25 But Jesus
called them to him and said, "You know that the rulers of the Gentiles lord it over
them, and their great ones are tyrants over them. 26 It will not be so among you; but
whoever wishes to be great among you must be your servant, 27 and whoever
wishes to be first among you must be your slave; 28 just as the Son of Man came not
to be served but to serve, and to give his life a ransom for many."

[d] Gk *is your eye evil because I am good?* [e] Other ancient authorities add *for many are called but few are chosen*
[f] Other ancient authorities add *or to be baptized with the baptism that I am baptized with?*

---

forgiveness? Are you ever jealous of what God has given to another person? Instead, focus on God's gracious benefits to you, and be thankful for what you have.

20.17–19 Jesus predicted his death and resurrection for the third time (see 16.21 and 17.22, 23 for the first two times). But the disciples still didn't understand what he meant. They continued to argue greedily over their positions in Christ's kingdom (20.20–28).

20.20 James' and John's mother came to Jesus and "kneeling before him, she asked a favor of him." She gave Jesus worship, but her real motive was to get something from him. Too often this happens in our churches and in our lives. We play religious games expecting God to give us something in return. True worship, however, adores and praises Christ for who he is and for what he has done.

20.20 The mother of James and John asked Jesus to give her sons special positions in his kingdom. Parents naturally want to see their children promoted and honored, but this desire is dangerous if it causes them to lose sight of God's specific will for their children. God may have different work for them—not as glamorous, but just as important. Thus parents' desires for their children's advancement must be held in check as they pray that God's will be done in their children's lives.

20.20 According to 27.56, the mother of James and John was at the cross when Jesus was crucified. Some have suggested she was the sister of Mary, the mother of Jesus. A close family relationship could have prompted her to make this request for her sons.

20.22 James, John, and their mother failed to grasp Jesus' previous teachings on rewards (19.16–30) and eternal life (20.1–16). They failed to understand the suffering they would face before living in the glory of God's kingdom. The "cup" was the suffering and crucifixion Christ faced. Both James and John would also face great suffering. James would be put to death for his faith, and John would be exiled.

20.23 Jesus was showing that he was under the authority of the Father, who alone makes the decisions about leadership in heaven. Such rewards are not granted as favors. They are for those who have maintained their commitment to Jesus in spite of severe trials.

20.24 The other disciples were upset with James and John for trying to grab the top positions. *All* the disciples wanted to be the greatest (18.1), but Jesus taught them that the greatest person in God's kingdom is the servant of all. Authority is given not for self-importance, ambition, or respect, but for useful service to God and his creation.

20.27 Jesus described leadership from a new perspective. Instead of using people, we are to serve them. Jesus' mission was to serve others and to give his life away. A real leader has a servant's heart. He appreciates others' worth and realizes he's not above any job. If you see something that needs to be done, don't wait to be asked. Take the initiative and do it like a faithful servant.

20.28 A ransom was the price paid to release a slave from bondage. Jesus often told his disciples that he must die, but here he told them why—to redeem all people from the bondage of sin and death. The disciples thought that as long as Jesus was alive, he could save them. But Jesus revealed that only his death would save them and the world.

Jesus heals a blind beggar
(179/Mark 10.46–52; Luke 18.35–43)

29 As they were leaving Jericho, a large crowd followed him. 30 There were two 20.29 Mk 10.46-52
blind men sitting by the roadside. When they heard that Jesus was passing by, they Lk 18.35-43
shouted, "Lord,[g] have mercy on us, Son of David!" 31 The crowd sternly ordered
them to be quiet; but they shouted even more loudly, "Have mercy on us, Lord, Son
of David!" 32 Jesus stood still and called them, saying, "What do you want me to do
for you?" 33 They said to him, "Lord, let our eyes be opened." 34 Moved with compassion, Jesus touched their eyes. Immediately they regained their sight and followed him.

Jesus rides into Jerusalem on a donkey
(183/Mark 11.1–11; Luke 19.28–44; John 12.12–19)

21 When they had come near Jerusalem and had reached Bethphage, at the 21.1 Zech 14.4
Mount of Olives, Jesus sent two disciples, 2 saying to them, "Go into the Mk 11.1-10
village ahead of you, and immediately you will find a donkey tied, and a colt with Lk 19.28-40 Jn 12.12-19
her; untie them and bring them to me. 3 If anyone says anything to you, just say this, 21.3
'The Lord needs them.' And he will send them immediately.[h]" 4 This took place to Ps 24.1
fulfill what had been spoken through the prophet, saying,

5 "Tell the daughter of Zion, 21.5 Zech 9.9
Look, your king is coming to you,
humble, and mounted on a donkey,
and on a colt, the foal of a donkey."

6 The disciples went and did as Jesus had directed them; 7 they brought the donkey
and the colt, and put their cloaks on them, and he sat on them. 8 A very large
crowd[i] spread their cloaks on the road, and others cut branches from the trees and
spread them on the road. 9 The crowds that went ahead of him and that followed 21.9 Ps 118.26 Mt 22.42
were shouting, Mk 12.35-37 Rom 1.3

"Hosanna to the Son of David!
Blessed is the one who comes in the name of the Lord!
Hosanna in the highest heaven!"

10 When he entered Jerusalem, the whole city was in turmoil, asking, "Who is

[g] Other ancient authorities lack *Lord* [h] Or *'The Lord needs them and will send them back immediately.'* [i] Or *Most of the crowd*

20.29–34 Matthew records that there were two blind men, while Mark and Luke mention only one. This is probably the same event, but Mark and Luke singled out the more vocal of the two men.

20.30 The blind men called Jesus "Son of David" because the Jews knew that the Messiah would be a descendant of David (see Isaiah 9.6, 7; 11.1; Jeremiah 23.5, 6). These blind beggars could *see* that Jesus was the long-awaited Messiah, while the religious leaders who witnessed Jesus' miracles were blind to his identity, refusing to open their eyes to the truth. Seeing with your eyes doesn't guarantee seeing with your heart.

20.32, 33 Although Jesus was concerned about the coming events in Jerusalem, he demonstrated what he had just told the disciples about service (20.28) by stopping to care for the blind men.

21.2–5 Matthew mentions a donkey and a colt, while the other Gospels mention only the colt. This was the same event, but Matthew focuses on the prophecy in Zechariah 9.9, where a donkey and a colt are mentioned. He shows how Jesus' actions fulfilled the prophet's words, thus giving another indication that Jesus was indeed the Messiah. Jesus entering Jerusalem on a donkey's colt affirmed his messianic royalty as well as his humility.

21.8 This is one of the few places where the Gospels record that Jesus' glory is recognized on earth. Jesus boldly declared himself King, and the crowd gladly joined him. But these same people would bow to political pressure and desert him in just a few days. Today we celebrate this event on Palm Sunday. It should remind us to guard against superficial acclaim for Christ.

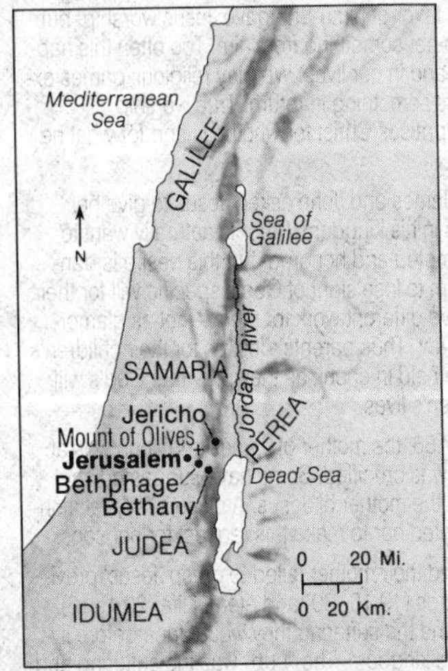

PREPARATION FOR THE TRIUMPHAL ENTRY
On their way from Jericho, Jesus and the disciples neared Bethphage, on the slope of the Mount of Olives just outside Jerusalem. Two disciples went into the village, as Jesus told them, to bring back a donkey and its colt. Jesus rode into Jerusalem on the donkey, an unmistakable sign of his kingship.

21.11 Lk 7.16 Jn 6.14; 7.40 this?" 11 The crowds were saying, "This is the prophet Jesus from Nazareth in
Galilee."

Jesus clears the temple again
(184/Mark 11.12–19; Luke 19.45–48)

21.12 Deut 14.24-26 Mk 11.15-19 Lk 19.45-48 Jn 2.13-16 12 Then Jesus entered the temple[j] and drove out all who were selling and buying in the temple, and he overturned the tables of the money changers and the seats
of those who sold doves. 13 He said to them, "It is written,

21.13 Isa 56.7 Jer 7.11 'My house shall be called a house of prayer';
but you are making it a den of robbers."

21.14 Isa 35.5,6 14 The blind and the lame came to him in the temple, and he cured them. 15 But
when the chief priests and the scribes saw the amazing things that he did, and
21.15 Ps 8.2 heard[k] the children crying out in the temple, "Hosanna to the Son of David," they
became angry 16 and said to him, "Do you hear what these are saying?" Jesus said
to them, "Yes; have you never read,

'Out of the mouths of infants and nursing babies
21.17 Mk 11.11 Jn 11.18 you have prepared praise for yourself'?"

17 He left them, went out of the city to Bethany, and spent the night there.

Jesus says the disciples can pray for anything
(188/Mark 11.20–26)

21.18 Mk 11.12-14 18 In the morning, when he returned to the city, he was hungry. 19 And seeing
21.21 Lk 17.6 1 Cor 13.2 Jas 1.6 a fig tree by the side of the road, he went to it and found nothing at all on it but
leaves. Then he said to it, "May no fruit ever come from you again!" And the fig
tree withered at once. 20 When the disciples saw it, they were amazed, saying,
21.22 Mt 7.7 Mk 11.24 Lk 11.9 Jas 5.16 1 Jn 3.22; 5.14 "How did the fig tree wither at once?" 21 Jesus answered them, "Truly I tell you, if
you have faith and do not doubt, not only will you do what has been done to the fig
tree, but even if you say to this mountain, 'Be lifted up and thrown into the sea,' it
will be done. 22 Whatever you ask for in prayer with faith, you will receive."

Religious leaders challenge Jesus' authority
(189/Mark 11.27–33; Luke 20.1–8)

23 When he entered the temple, the chief priests and the elders of the people

[j] Other ancient authorities add *of God* [k] Gk lacks *heard*

21.12 This is the second time Jesus cleared the temple (see John 2.13–17). Merchants and money changers set up their booths in the court of the Gentiles in the temple, crowding out the Gentiles who had come from all over the civilized world to worship God. The merchants sold sacrificial animals at high prices, taking advantage of those who had come long distances. The money changers exchanged all international currency for the special temple coins—the only money the merchants would accept. They often deceived foreigners who didn't know the exchange rates. Their commercialism in God's house frustrated people's attempts at worship. This, of course, greatly angered Jesus. Any practice that interferes with worshiping God should be stopped.

21.19 Why did Jesus curse the fig tree? This was not a thoughtless, angry act, but an acted-out parable. Jesus was showing his anger at religion without substance. Just as the fig tree looked good from a distance but was fruitless at close examination, so the temple looked impressive at first glance, but its sacrifices and other activities were hollow because they were not done to worship God sincerely (see 21.43). If you only appear to have faith without putting it to work in your life, you are like the fig tree that withered and died because it bore no fruit. Genuine faith means bearing fruit for God's kingdom. For more information about the fig tree, see the note on Mark 11.13–26.

21.21 Many have wondered about Jesus' statement that if we have faith and don't doubt, we can move mountains. Jesus, of course, was not suggesting that his followers use prayer as "magic" and perform capricious mountain-moving acts. Instead, he was making a strong point about the disciples' (and our) lack of faith. What kinds of mountains do you face? Have you talked to God about them? How strong is your faith?

21.22 This is not a guarantee that we can get *anything* we want simply by asking Jesus and believing. God does not grant requests that would hurt us or others or that violate his own nature or will. Jesus' statement is not a blank check. To be fulfilled, our requests must be in harmony with the principles of God's kingdom. The stronger our belief, the more likely our prayers will be in line with God's will, and then God will be happy to grant them.

21.23–25 In Jesus' world, as in ours, people looked for the outward sign of authority—education, title, position, connections. But Jesus' authority came from who he was, not from any outward and superficial trappings. As followers of Christ, God has given us authority—we can confidently speak and act on his behalf because he has authorized us. Are you exercising your authority?

21.23–27 The Pharisees demanded to know where Jesus got his authority. If Jesus said his authority came from God, they would accuse him of blasphemy. If he said he acted on his own authority, the crowds would be convinced that the Pharisees had the greater authority. But Jesus answered them with a seemingly unrelated question that exposed their real motives. They didn't really want an answer to their question; they only wanted to trap him. Jesus showed that the Pharisees wanted the truth only if it supported their own views and causes.

came to him as he was teaching, and said, "By what authority are you doing these 21.23 Mk 11.26-33
things, and who gave you this authority?" 24 Jesus said to them, "I will also ask you Lk 20.1-8
one question; if you tell me the answer, then I will also tell you by what authority Acts 4.7; 7.27 21.24
I do these things. 25 Did the baptism of John come from heaven, or was it of human Job 5.13
origin?" And they argued with one another, "If we say, 'From heaven,' he will say
to us, 'Why then did you not believe him?' 26 But if we say, 'Of human origin,' we 21.26 Mt 14.5
are afraid of the crowd; for all regard John as a prophet." 27 So they answered Jesus, Mk 6.20
"We do not know." And he said to them, "Neither will I tell you by what authority
I am doing these things.

Jesus tells the parable of the two sons
(190)

28 "What do you think? A man had two sons; he went to the first and said, 'Son,
go and work in the vineyard today.' 29 He answered, 'I will not'; but later he
changed his mind and went. 30 The father[l] went to the second and said the same;
and he answered, 'I go, sir'; but he did not go. 31 Which of the two did the will of
his father?" They said, "The first." Jesus said to them, "Truly I tell you, the tax
collectors and the prostitutes are going into the kingdom of God ahead of you.
32 For John came to you in the way of righteousness and you did not believe him, 21.32 Mt 3.2
but the tax collectors and the prostitutes believed him; and even after you saw it, Lk 3.3,12
you did not change your minds and believe him. 7.29,30

Jesus tells the parable of the wicked farmers
(191/Mark 12.1–12; Luke 20.9–19)

33 "Listen to another parable. There was a landowner who planted a vineyard, 21.33 Mk 12.1-12
put a fence around it, dug a wine press in it, and built a watchtower. Then he leased Lk 20.9-19
it to tenants and went to another country. 34 When the harvest time had come, he
sent his slaves to the tenants to collect his produce. 35 But the tenants seized his 21.35 2 Chron 36.15,
slaves and beat one, killed another, and stoned another. 36 Again he sent other 16
slaves, more than the first; and they treated them in the same way. 37 Finally he sent Mt 23.34 Acts 7.52
his son to them, saying, 'They will respect my son.' 38 But when the tenants saw the 21.37
son, they said to themselves, 'This is the heir; come, let us kill him and get his Gal 4.4
inheritance.' 39 So they seized him, threw him out of the vineyard, and killed him. 21.38 Jn 11.53
40 Now when the owner of the vineyard comes, what will he do to those tenants?"
41 They said to him, "He will put those wretches to a miserable death, and lease the 21.41
vineyard to other tenants who will give him the produce at the harvest time." Lk 21.24

42 Jesus said to them, "Have you never read in the scriptures: 21.42
'The stone that the builders rejected Ps 118.22,23
has become the cornerstone;[m] Isa 28.16 Acts 4.11
this was the Lord's doing, Eph 2.20 1 Pet 2.6,7
and it is amazing in our eyes'?
43 Therefore I tell you, the kingdom of God will be taken away from you and given
to a people that produces the fruits of the kingdom.[n] 44 The one who falls on this 21.44 Isa 8.14,15
stone will be broken to pieces; and it will crush anyone on whom it falls."[o] Dan 2.44,45

l Gk *He* m Or *keystone* n Gk *the fruits of it* o Other ancient authorities lack verse 44

21.25 For more information on John the Baptist, see chapter 3 and his Profile in John 1.

21.30 The son who said he would obey and then didn't represented the nation of Israel in Jesus' day. They said they wanted to do God's will, but they constantly disobeyed. They were phony, just going through the motions. It is dangerous to pretend to obey God when our hearts are far from him, because God knows our true intentions. Our actions must match our words.

21.33ff The main elements in this parable are (1) the landowner—God, (2) the vineyard—Israel, (3) the tenants—the Jewish religious leaders, (4) the householder's slaves—the prophets and priests who remained faithful to God and preached to Israel, (5) the son—Jesus (21.38), and (6) the other tenants—the Gentiles. Jesus was exposing the religious leaders' murderous plot (21.45).

21.37 In trying to reach us with his love, God finally sent his own Son. His perfect life, his words of truth, and his sacrifice of love are meant to cause us to listen to Christ and to follow him as Lord. If we ignore God's gracious gift of his Son, we reject God.

21.42 Jesus refers to himself as "the stone that the builders rejected." Though rejected by many of his people, he would become the cornerstone of his new building, the church (see Acts 4.11).

21.44 Jesus is quoting from several Old Testament texts: Isaiah 8.14, 15; 28.16; Daniel 2.34, 44, 45. He uses this metaphor to show that one stone can affect people different ways, depending on how they relate to it. Ideally they will build on it; many, however, will trip

45 When the chief priests and the Pharisees heard his parables, they realized
21.46 Jn 7.40-44 that he was speaking about them. 46 They wanted to arrest him, but they feared the
crowds, because they regarded him as a prophet.

Jesus tells the parable of the wedding feast
(192)

22.1 Lk 14.15-24 **22** Once more Jesus spoke to them in parables, saying: 2 "The kingdom of
heaven may be compared to a king who gave a wedding banquet for his son.
3 He sent his slaves to call those who had been invited to the wedding banquet, but
they would not come. 4 Again he sent other slaves, saying, 'Tell those who have
been invited: Look, I have prepared my dinner, my oxen and my fat calves have
been slaughtered, and everything is ready; come to the wedding banquet.' 5 But
they made light of it and went away, one to his farm, another to his business,
22.7 Dan 9.26 6 while the rest seized his slaves, mistreated them, and killed them. 7 The king was
enraged. He sent his troops, destroyed those murderers, and burned their city.
22.8 Acts 13.46 8 Then he said to his slaves, 'The wedding is ready, but those invited were not
worthy. 9 Go therefore into the main streets, and invite everyone you find to the
wedding banquet.' 10 Those slaves went out into the streets and gathered all whom
they found, both good and bad; so the wedding hall was filled with guests.
22.12 Rom 3.19 11 "But when the king came in to see the guests, he noticed a man there who
22.13 Mt 8.12; 25.30 was not wearing a wedding robe, 12 and he said to him, 'Friend, how did you get in
here without a wedding robe?' And he was speechless. 13 Then the king said to the
22.14 Mt 24.22 2 Pet 1.10 Rev 17.14 attendants, 'Bind him hand and foot, and throw him into the outer darkness, where
there will be weeping and gnashing of teeth.' 14 For many are called, but few are
chosen."

Religious leaders question Jesus about paying taxes
(193/Mark 12.13–17; Luke 20.20–26)

15 Then the Pharisees went and plotted to entrap him in what he said. 16 So they
sent their disciples to him, along with the Herodians, saying, "Teacher, we know
that you are sincere, and teach the way of God in accordance with truth, and show
22.17 Mt 17.24 deference to no one; for you do not regard people with partiality. 17 Tell us, then,
what you think. Is it lawful to pay taxes to the emperor, or not?" 18 But Jesus, aware
of their malice, said, "Why are you putting me to the test, you hypocrites? 19 Show
22.21 Rom 13.7 me the coin used for the tax." And they brought him a denarius. 20 Then he said to
them, "Whose head is this, and whose title?" 21 They answered, "The emperor's."

---

over it. And at the last Judgment God's enemies will be crushed by it. Christ, the "building block," will in the end become the "crushing stone." He offers mercy and forgiveness *now* and promises judgment later. We should not wait to make our choice.

22.1–14 In this culture, two invitations were expected when banquets were given. The first asked the guests to attend; the second announced that all was ready. In this story the king invited his guests three times – and each time they rejected his invitation. God wants us to join him at his banquet, which will last for eternity. That's why he sends us invitations again and again. Have you accepted his invitation?

22.11, 12 It was customary for wedding guests to be given a robe to wear to the banquet. It was unthinkable to refuse to wear it. This would insult the host, who could only assume that the guest was arrogant and thought he didn't need a robe, or that he did not want to take part in the wedding celebration. The wedding robe is a picture of the righteousness needed to enter God's kingdom – the total acceptance in God's eyes that Christ gives every believer. Christ has provided this robe of righteousness for everyone, but each person must choose to put it on in order to enter the King's banquet (eternal life).

22.15–17 The Pharisees, a religious group, opposed the Roman occupation of Palestine. The Herodians, a political party, supported Herod Antipas and the policies instituted by Rome. Normally these two groups were bitter enemies, but here they united against Jesus. Thinking they had a foolproof plan to corner him, together their representatives asked Jesus about paying Roman taxes. If Jesus agreed that it was right to pay taxes to Caesar, the Pharisees would say he was opposed to God, the only King they recognized. If Jesus said the taxes should not be paid, the Herodians would hand him over to Herod for rebellion. In this case the Pharisees were not motivated by love for God's laws, and the Herodians were not motivated by love for Roman justice. Jesus' answer exposed their evil motives and embarrassed them.

22.17 The Jews were required to pay taxes to support the Roman government. They hated this taxation because the money went directly into Caesar's treasury, where some of it went to support the pagan temples and decadent life-style of the Roman aristocracy. Caesar's image on the coins was a constant reminder of Israel's subjection to Rome.

22.19 The denarius was the usual day's wage for a laborer.

22.21 Jesus avoided this trap by showing that we have dual citizenship (1 Peter 2.17). Our citizenship in the state requires that we pay money for the services and benefits we receive. Our citizenship in the kingdom of heaven requires that we pledge to God our primary obedience and commitment.

Then he said to them, “Give therefore to the emperor the things that are the emperor’s, and to God the things that are God’s.” 22 When they heard this, they were 22.22 Job 5.12,13
amazed; and they left him and went away.

Religious leaders question Jesus about the resurrection
(194/Mark 12.18–27; Luke 20.27–40)

23 The same day some Sadducees came to him, saying there is no resurrec- 22.23 Mk 12.18-27 Lk 10.27-40 Acts 23.8 1 Cor 15.12
tion;[p] and they asked him a question, saying, 24 “Teacher, Moses said, ‘If a man
dies childless, his brother shall marry the widow, and raise up children for his
brother.’ 25 Now there were seven brothers among us; the first married, and died 22.24 Gen 38.8 Deut 25.5
childless, leaving the widow to his brother. 26 The second did the same, so also the
third, down to the seventh. 27 Last of all, the woman herself died. 28 In the resurrection, then, whose wife of the seven will she be? For all of them had married her.”
29 Jesus answered them, “You are wrong, because you know neither the scrip- 22.29 Jn 20.9
tures nor the power of God. 30 For in the resurrection they neither marry nor are
given in marriage, but are like angels[q] in heaven. 31 And as for the resurrection of 22.32 Ex 3.6,15 Acts 7.32
the dead, have you not read what was said to you by God, 32 ‘I am the God of
Abraham, the God of Isaac, and the God of Jacob’? He is God not of the dead, but
of the living.” 33 And when the crowd heard it, they were astounded at his teaching.

Religious leaders question Jesus about the greatest commandment
(195/Mark 12.28–34)

34 When the Pharisees heard that he had silenced the Sadducees, they gathered 22.34 Mk 12.28-31
together, 35 and one of them, a lawyer, asked him a question to test him. 22.35 Lk 10.25
36 “Teacher, which commandment in the law is the greatest?” 37 He said to him,
“ ‘You shall love the Lord your God with all your heart, and with all your soul, and 22.37 Deut 6.5 10.12,13; 30.6
with all your mind.’ 38 This is the greatest and first commandment. 39 And a second
is like it: ‘You shall love your neighbor as yourself.’ 40 On these two command- 22.38 Lev 19.18 Rom 13.9
ments hang all the law and the prophets.”

Religious leaders cannot answer Jesus’ question
(196/Mark 12.35–37; Luke 20.41–44)

41 Now while the Pharisees were gathered together, Jesus asked them this

[p] Other ancient authorities read *who say that there is no resurrection* [q] Other ancient authorities add *of God*

22.23ff After the Pharisees and Herodians failed to trap Jesus, the Sadducees smugly stepped in to try. They did not believe in the resurrection because the Pentateuch (Genesis – Deuteronomy) has no direct teaching on it. The Pharisees had never been able to come up with a convincing argument from the Pentateuch for the resurrection, and the Sadducees thought they had trapped Jesus for sure. But he was about to show them otherwise (see 22.31, 32 for Jesus’ answer).

22.24 For more information on Moses, see his Profile in Exodus 15.

22.24 The law said that when a woman’s husband died without having a son, the man’s brother had a responsibility to marry and care for the widow (Deuteronomy 25.5, 6). This protected women who were left alone, because in that culture they usually had no other means to live.

22.29, 30 The Sadduces asked Jesus what marriage would be like in heaven. Jesus said it was more important to understand God’s power than know what heaven will be like. In every generation and culture, ideas of eternal life tend to be based upon images and experiences of present life. Jesus answered that these faulty ideas are caused by ignorance of God’s Word. We must not make up our own ideas about eternity and heaven by thinking of it and God in human terms. We should concentrate more on our relationship with God than about what heaven will look like. Eventually we will find out, and it will be far beyond our greatest expectations.

22.31, 32 Because the Sadducees accepted only the Pentateuch as God’s divine Word, Jesus answered them from the book of Exodus (3.6). God would not have said, “I *am* the God of Abraham, the God of Isaac, and the God of Jacob” if God thought of Abraham, Isaac, and Jacob as dead. From God’s perspective, they are alive. Jesus’ use of the present tense pointed to the resurrection and the eternal life that all believers enjoy in him.

22.33, 34 We might think the Pharisees would have been glad to see the Sadducees silenced. The question that the Sadducees had always used to trap them was finally answered by Jesus. But the Pharisees were too proud to be impressed. Jesus’ answer gave them a theological victory over the Sadducees, but they were more interested in trapping and stopping Jesus than in learning truth.

22.35–40 A lawyer, as used here, refers to an expert in religious law. The Pharisees, who had classified over 600 laws, often tried to distinguish the more important from the less important. So they asked Jesus to identify the most important law. Jesus quoted from Deuteronomy 6.5 and Leviticus 19.18. By fulfilling these two commands, a person keeps all the others. They summarize the ten commandments and the other Old Testament moral laws.

22.37–40 Jesus says that if we truly love God and our neighbor, we will naturally keep the commandments. This is looking at God’s law positively. Rather than worrying about all we should *not* do, we should concentrate on all we *can* do to show our love for God and others.

22.41–45 The Pharisees, Herodians, and Sadducees had asked their questions. Now Jesus turned the tables and asked them a question: 42 "What do you think of the Messiah?[r] Whose son is he?" They said to him, "The son of David." 43 He said to them, "How is it then that David by the Spirit[s] calls him Lord, saying,

44 'The Lord said to my Lord,
"Sit at my right hand,
until I put your enemies under your feet" '?

45 If David thus calls him Lord, how can he be his son?" 46 No one was able to give him an answer, nor from that day did anyone dare to ask him any more questions.

22.43 2 Sam 23.2; 2 Pet 1.20,21
22.44 Ps 110.1; Mt 26.64; Acts 2.34; Heb 1.13; 10.12
22.46 Lk 14.6; 20.40

Jesus warns against the religious leaders
(197/Mark 12.38–40; Luke 20.45–47)

23 Then Jesus said to the crowds and to his disciples, 2 "The scribes and the Pharisees sit on Moses' seat; 3 therefore, do whatever they teach you and follow it; but do not do as they do, for they do not practice what they teach. 4 They tie up heavy burdens, hard to bear,[t] and lay them on the shoulders of others; but they themselves are unwilling to lift a finger to move them. 5 They do all their deeds to be seen by others; for they make their phylacteries broad and their fringes long. 6 They love to have the place of honor at banquets and the best seats in the synagogues, 7 and to be greeted with respect in the marketplaces, and to have people call them rabbi. 8 But you are not to be called rabbi, for you have one teacher, and you are all students.[u] 9 And call no one your father on earth, for you have one Father—the one in heaven. 10 Nor are you to be called instructors, for you have one instructor, the Messiah.[v] 11 The greatest among you will be your servant. 12 All who exalt themselves will be humbled, and all who humble themselves will be exalted.

23.2 Ezra 7.6,25; Neh 8.1-4; Lk 11.46; Acts 15.10; Rom 2.17-23; Gal 6.13
23.5 Num 15.37-40; Mt 6.1,2
23.9 Mal 1.6
23.11 Mt 20.26; Mk 9.35; 10.43-45; Lk 9.48
23.12 1 Pet 5.5,6

Jesus condemns the religious leaders
(198)

13 "But woe to you, scribes and Pharisees, hypocrites! For you lock people out of the kingdom of heaven. For you do not go in yourselves, and when others are

23.13 Lk 11.39-52

[r] Or *Christ* [s] Gk *in spirit* [t] Other ancient authorities lack *hard to bear* [u] Gk *brothers* [v] Or *the Christ*

---

penetrating question—who they thought the Messiah was. The Pharisees knew the Messiah would be a descendant of David, but they did not understand he would be God himself. Jesus quoted from Psalm 110.1 to show that the Messiah would be greater than David. (Hebrews 1.13 uses the same text as proof of Christ's deity.) The most important question we will ever answer is what we believe about Christ. Other spiritual questions are irrelevant until we believe that Jesus is who he said he is.

23.2, 3 The Pharisees' traditions and their interpretations and applications of the laws had become as important to them as God's law itself. Their laws were not all bad—some were beneficial. The problem arose when the religious leaders (1) took man-made rules as seriously as God's laws, (2) told the people to obey these rules but did not do so themselves, or (3) obeyed the rules not to honor God but to make themselves look good. Usually Jesus did not condemn what they taught, but what they *were*—hypocrites.

23.5 Phylacteries were little leather boxes containing Scripture verses that very religious people wore on their forehead and arms in order to obey Deuteronomy 6.8 and Exodus 13.9, 16. But the phylacteries had become more important for the status they gave than for the truth they contained.

23.5–7 Jesus again exposed the hypocritical attitudes of the religious leaders. They knew the Scriptures but did not live by them. They didn't care about *being* holy—just *looking* holy in order to receive the people's admiration and praise. Today, like the Pharisees, many people who know the Bible do not let it change their lives. They say they follow Jesus but don't live by his standards of love. People who live this way are hypocrites. We must make sure our actions match our beliefs.

23.5–7 People desire positions of leadership not only in business but also in the church. This becomes dangerous if love for the position grows stronger than loyalty to God. This is what happened to the scribes and Pharisees. Jesus is not against all leadership—we need Christian leaders—but against leadership that serves itself rather than others.

23.11, 12 Jesus challenged society's norms. To him, greatness comes from serving—giving of yourself to help God and others. Service keeps us aware of others' needs, and it stops us from focusing only on ourselves. Jesus came as a servant. What kind of greatness do you seek?

23.13, 14 Being a religious leader in Jerusalem was very different from being a pastor in a secular society today. The nation's history, culture, and daily life centered around its relationship with God. The religious leaders were the best known, most powerful, and most respected of all leaders. Jesus made these stinging accusations because the leaders' hunger for more power, money, and status had made them lose sight of God, and their blindness was spreading to the whole nation.

going in, you stop them.[w] 15 Woe to you, scribes and Pharisees, hypocrites! For
you cross sea and land to make a single convert, and you make the new convert
twice as much a child of hell[x] as yourselves.
16 "Woe to you, blind guides, who say, 'Whoever swears by the sanctuary is
bound by nothing, but whoever swears by the gold of the sanctuary is bound by the
oath.' 17 You blind fools! For which is greater, the gold or the sanctuary that has
made the gold sacred? 18 And you say, 'Whoever swears by the altar is bound by
nothing, but whoever swears by the gift that is on the altar is bound by the oath.'
19 How blind you are! For which is greater, the gift or the altar that makes the gift
sacred? 20 So whoever swears by the altar, swears by it and by everything on it;
21 and whoever swears by the sanctuary, swears by it and by the one who dwells in
it; 22 and whoever swears by heaven, swears by the throne of God and by the one
who is seated upon it.
23 "Woe to you, scribes and Pharisees, hypocrites! For you tithe mint, dill, and
cummin, and have neglected the weightier matters of the law: justice and mercy
and faith. It is these you ought to have practiced without neglecting the others.
24 You blind guides! You strain out a gnat but swallow a camel!
25 "Woe to you, scribes and Pharisees, hypocrites! For you clean the outside of
the cup and of the plate, but inside they are full of greed and self-indulgence. 26 You
blind Pharisee! First clean the inside of the cup,[y] so that the outside also may become clean.
27 "Woe to you, scribes and Pharisees, hypocrites! For you are like whitewashed tombs, which on the outside look beautiful, but inside they are full of the
bones of the dead and of all kinds of filth. 28 So you also on the outside look righteous to others, but inside you are full of hypocrisy and lawlessness.
29 "Woe to you, scribes and Pharisees, hypocrites! For you build the tombs of
the prophets and decorate the graves of the righteous, 30 and you say, 'If we had
lived in the days of our ancestors, we would not have taken part with them in shedding the blood of the prophets.' 31 Thus you testify against yourselves that you are
descendants of those who murdered the prophets. 32 Fill up, then, the measure of
your ancestors. 33 You snakes, you brood of vipers! How can you escape being
sentenced to hell?[x] 34 Therefore I send you prophets, sages, and scribes, some of
whom you will kill and crucify, and some you will flog in your synagogues and
pursue from town to town, 35 so that upon you may come all the righteous blood
shed on earth, from the blood of righteous Abel to the blood of Zechariah son of
Barachiah, whom you murdered between the sanctuary and the altar. 36 Truly I tell
you, all this will come upon this generation.

23.16 Isa 56.10 Mt 5.33-35 15.14
23.19 Ex 29.37; 30.29
23.21 1 Kgs 8.12,13 2 Chron 6.1 Ps 26.8; 132.14
23.22 Ps 11.4 Acts 7.48,49
23.23 1 Sam 15.22 Hos 6.6 Mic 6.8 Mt 9.13; 12.7
23.25 Mk 7.4 Tit 1.15
23.27 Lk 11.44 Acts 23.3
23.31 Acts 7.51
23.32 Gen 15.16 1 Thess 2.16
23.33 Mt 3.7; 12.34 Lk 3.7
23.34 Acts 5.40; 7.58 22.19 2 Cor 11.23-25
23.35 Gen 4.8 1 Jn 3.12 Rev 18.24

[w] Other authorities add here (or after verse 12) verse 14, *Woe to you, scribes and Pharisees, hypocrites! For you devour widows' houses and for the sake of appearance you make long prayers; therefore you will receive the greater condemnation* [x] Gk *Gehenna* [y] Other ancient authorities add *and of the plate*

23.15 The Pharisees' converts were attracted to pharisaism, not to God. By getting caught up in the details of their additional laws and regulations, they missed God, to whom the laws pointed. A religion of works puts pressure on people to surpass others in what they know and do. Thus, a hypocritical teacher was likely to have students who were even more hypocritical. We must make sure we are not creating Pharisees by emphasizing outward obedience at the expense of inner renewal.

23.23, 24 It's possible to obey the details of the laws but still be disobedient in our general behavior. For example, we could be very precise and faithful about giving 10 percent of our money to God, but refuse to give one minute of our time in helping others. Tithing is important, but paying tithe does not exempt us from fulfilling God's other directives.

23.24 The Pharisees strained their water so they wouldn't accidentally swallow a gnat—an unclean insect according to the law. Meticulous about the details of ceremonial cleanliness, they nevertheless had lost their perspective on inner purity. Ceremonially clean on the outside, they had corrupt hearts.

23.25–28 Jesus condemned the Pharisees and religious leaders for appearing saintly and holy outwardly but inwardly remaining full of corruption and greed. Living our Christianity merely as a show for others is like washing a cup on the outside only. When we are clean on the inside, our cleanliness on the outside won't be a sham.

23.34–36 These prophets, wise men (sages), and scribes are probably leaders in the early church who were persecuted, scourged, and killed, as Jesus predicted. The people of Jesus' generation said they would not act as their fathers did in killing the prophets whom God had sent to them (23.30), but they were about to kill the Messiah himself and his faithful followers. Thus they would become guilty of all the righteous blood shed through the centuries.

23.35 Jesus was giving a brief history of Old Testament martyrdom. Abel was the first martyr (Genesis 4); Zacharias was the last mentioned in the Hebrew Bible, which ended with 2 Chronicles. Zacharias was a classic example of a man of God killed by those who claimed to be God's people (see 2 Chronicles 24.20, 21).

Jesus grieves over Jerusalem again
(199)

23.37 Deut 32.11 37 "Jerusalem, Jerusalem, the city that kills the prophets and stones those who
are sent to it! How often have I desired to gather your children together as a hen
23.38 Ezek 10.4,18,19 gathers her brood under her wings, and you were not willing! 38 See, your house is
23.39 Ps 118.26 left to you, desolate.[z] 39 For I tell you, you will not see me again until you say,
'Blessed is the one who comes in the name of the Lord.'"

7. Jesus teaches on the Mount of Olives

Jesus tells about the future
(201/Mark 13.1–28; Luke 21.5–24)

24.2 Jer 7.14; 26.18 Mic 3.12 Lk 19.44 **24** As Jesus came out of the temple and was going away, his disciples came to
point out to him the buildings of the temple. 2 Then he asked them, "You see
all these, do you not? Truly I tell you, not one stone will be left here upon another;
all will be thrown down."

24.3 1 Thess 5.1 3 When he was sitting on the Mount of Olives, the disciples came to him pri-
24.4 1 Jn 4.1 vately, saying, "Tell us, when will this be, and what will be the sign of your coming and of the end of the age?" 4 Jesus answered them, "Beware that no one leads
24.5 Jer 14.14; 23.21 Jn 5.43 you astray. 5 For many will come in my name, saying, 'I am the Messiah!'[a] and
they will lead many astray. 6 And you will hear of wars and rumors of wars; see that

[z] Other ancient authorities lack *desolate* [a] Or *the Christ*

THE SEVEN WOES

23.14	Not letting others enter the kingdom of heaven and not entering yourselves
23.15	Converting people away from God to be like yourselves
23.16–22	Blindly leading God's people to follow man-made traditions instead of God's Word
23.23, 24	Involving yourself in insignificant details and ignoring what is really important: justice, mercy, and faith
23.25, 26	Keeping up appearances while your private world is corrupt
23.27, 28	Acting spiritual to cover sin
23.29–36	Pretending to have learned from past history, but your present behavior shows you have learned nothing

Jesus mentioned seven ways to guarantee God's anger, often called the "seven woes." These seven statements about the religious leaders must have been spoken with a mixed tone of judgment and sorrow. They were strong and unforgettable. They are still applicable any time we become so involved in perfecting the practice of religion that we forget that God is also concerned with mercy, real love, and forgiveness.

23.37 Jesus wanted to gather his people together as a hen protects her chicks under her wings, but they wouldn't let him. Jesus also wants to protect us if we will come to him. Many times we hurt and don't know where to turn. We reject Christ's help because we don't think he can give us what we need. But who knows our needs better than our Creator? Those who turn to Jesus will find that he helps and comforts as no one else can.

23.37 Jerusalem was the capital city of God's chosen people; the ancestral home of David, Israel's greatest king; and the location of the temple, the earthly dwelling place of God. It was intended to be the center of worship of the true God and a model of justice to all people, but Jerusalem had become blind to God and insensitive to human need. Here we see the depth of Jesus' feelings for lost people and for his beloved city, which would soon be destroyed.

24.1, 2 Although no one knows exactly how this temple looked, it must have been beautiful. Herod had helped the Jews remodel and beautify it, no doubt to stay on friendly terms with his subjects. Next to the inner temple, where the sacred objects were kept and the sacrifices offered, there was a large area called the court of the Gentiles (this was where the money changers and merchants had their booths). Outside these courts were long porches. Solomon's porch was 1,562 feet long; the royal portico was decorated with 160 columns stretching along its 921-foot length. Gazing at this glorious and massive structure, the disciples found Jesus' words about its destruction difficult to believe. But the temple was indeed destroyed only 40 years later when the Romans sacked Jerusalem in A.D. 70.

24.3ff Jesus was sitting on the Mount of Olives, the very place where the prophet Zechariah predicted the Messiah would stand when he came to establish his kingdom (Zechariah 14.4). It was a fitting place for the disciples to ask Jesus when he would come into power and what they could expect then. Jesus' reply emphasized the events that would take place before the end of the age. He pointed out that his disciples should be less concerned with knowing the exact date and more concerned with being prepared—living God's way consistently so that no matter when Jesus came in glory, he would claim them as his own.

24.4 The disciples asked Jesus for the sign of his coming and of the end of the world. Jesus' first response was, "Beware that no one leads you astray." The fact is that whenever we look for signs, we become very susceptible to being deceived. There are many "false prophets" (24.11, 24) around with counterfeit signs of spiritual power and authority. The only sure way to keep from being deceived is to focus on Christ and his words. Don't look for special signs or at other people, look at Christ.

you are not alarmed; for this must take place, but the end is not yet. 7 For nation will
rise against nation, and kingdom against kingdom, and there will be famines[b] and
earthquakes in various places: 8 all this is but the beginning of the birthpangs.
9 "Then they will hand you over to be tortured and will put you to death, and
you will be hated by all nations because of my name. 10 Then many will fall away,[c]
and they will betray one another and hate one another. 11 And many false prophets
will arise and lead many astray. 12 And because of the increase of lawlessness, the
love of many will grow cold. 13 But the one who endures to the end will be saved.
14 And this good news[d] of the kingdom will be proclaimed throughout the world,
as a testimony to all the nations; and then the end will come.
15 "So when you see the desolating sacrilege standing in the holy place, as was
spoken of by the prophet Daniel (let the reader understand), 16 then those in Judea
must flee to the mountains; 17 the one on the housetop must not go down to take
what is in the house; 18 the one in the field must not turn back to get a coat. 19 Woe
to those who are pregnant and to those who are nursing infants in those days! 20 Pray
that your flight may not be in winter or on a sabbath. 21 For at that time there will
be great suffering, such as has not been from the beginning of the world until now,
no, and never will be. 22 And if those days had not been cut short, no one would be
saved; but for the sake of the elect those days will be cut short. 23 Then if anyone
says to you, 'Look! Here is the Messiah!'[e] or 'There he is!'—do not believe it.
24 For false messiahs[f] and false prophets will appear and produce great signs and
omens, to lead astray, if possible, even the elect. 25 Take note, I have told you
beforehand. 26 So, if they say to you, 'Look! He is in the wilderness,' do not go out.
If they say, 'Look! He is in the inner rooms,' do not believe it. 27 For as the lightning comes from the east and flashes as far as the west, so will be the coming of the
Son of Man. 28 Wherever the corpse is, there the vultures will gather.

24.9 Acts 7.59; 12.1
24.10 2 Tim 4.10,16
24.11 Acts 20.29; 1 Tim 4.1; 2 Pet 2.1
24.12 2 Tim 3.1-5
24.13 Mt 10.22; Rev 2.7
24.14 Mk 13.14-23; Lk 21.20-24
24.15 Dan 9.27; 11.31; 12.11
24.21 Dan 12.1; Joel 2.2; Rev 3.10; 7.14
24.22 Isa 65.8,9
24.24 2 Thess 2.9; 1 Jn 4.1-3; Rev 13.13,14
24.28 Job 39.30; Lk 17.37; Rev 19.17,18

[b] Other ancient authorities add *and pestilences* [c] Or *stumble* [d] Or *gospel* [e] Or *the Christ* [f] Or *christs*

24.9–13 You may not be facing intense persecution now, but Christians in other parts of the world are. As you hear about Christians suffering for their faith, remember that they are your brothers and sisters in Christ. Pray for them. Ask God what you can do to help them in their troubles. When one part suffers, the *whole* body suffers. But when all the parts join together to ease the suffering, the whole body benefits.

24.11 The Old Testament frequently mentions false prophets (see 2 Kings 3.13; Isaiah 44.25; Jeremiah 23.16; Ezekiel 13.2, 3; Micah 3.5; Zechariah 13.2). They were people who claimed to receive messages from God, but who preached a "health and wealth" message. They told the people only what they wanted to hear, even when the nation was not following God as it should. There were false prophets in Jesus' day, and we have them today. They are the popular leaders who tell people what they want to hear—such as "God wants you to be rich," "Do whatever your desires tell you," or "There is no such thing as sin or hell." Jesus said false teachers would come, and he warned his disciples, as he warns us, not to listen to their dangerous words.

24.12 With false teaching and loose morals comes a particularly destructive disease—the loss of true love for God and others. Sin cools your love for God and others by turning your focus on yourself. You cannot truly love if you think only of yourself.

24.13 Jesus predicted that his followers would be severely persecuted by those who hated what he stood for. In the midst of terrible persecutions, however, they could have hope, knowing that salvation was theirs. Times of trial serve to sift true Christians from false or fair-weather Christians. When you are pressured to give up and turn your back on Christ, don't do it. Remember the benefits of endurance, and continue to live for Christ.

24.14 Jesus said that before he returns, the good news of the kingdom (the message of salvation) would be preached throughout the world. This was the disciples' mission—and it is ours today. Jesus talked about the end times and final Judgment to show his followers the urgency of spreading the good news of salvation to everyone.

24.15, 16 What was this "desolating sacrilege" mentioned by both Daniel and Jesus? Rather than one specific object, event, or person, it could be seen as any deliberate attempt to mock and destroy God's presence. Daniel's prediction came true in 168 B.C. when Antiochus Epiphanes sacrificed a pig to Zeus on the sacred temple altar (Daniel 9.27; 11.30, 31). Jesus' words were remembered in A.D. 70, when Titus placed an idol on the site of the burned temple after destroying Jerusalem. In the end times the antichrist will set up a statue to himself and order everyone to worship it (2 Thessalonians 2.4; Revelation 13.14, 15). These are all "sacrileges" that mock God.

24.21, 22 Jesus, talking about the end times, telescoped near future and far future events, as did the Old Testament prophets. Many of these persecutions have already occurred; more are yet to come. But God is in control of even the length of persecutions. He will not forget his people. This is all we need to know about the future to motivate us to live rightly now.

24.23, 24 Jesus' warnings about false teachers still hold true. Upon close examination it becomes clear that many nice-sounding messages don't agree with God's message in the Bible. Only a solid foundation in God's Word can equip us to perceive the errors and distortions in false teaching.

24.24–28 In times of persecution even strong believers will find it difficult to be loyal. To keep from being deceived by false messiahs, we must understand that Jesus' return will be unmistakable (Mark 13.26): no one will doubt that it is he. If you have to be told that the Messiah has come, then he hasn't (24.27). Christ's coming will be obvious to everyone.

Jesus tells about his return
(202/Mark 13.21–31; Luke 21.25–33)

29 “Immediately after the suffering of those days
the sun will be darkened,
and the moon will not give its light;
the stars will fall from heaven,
and the powers of heaven will be shaken.
30 Then the sign of the Son of Man will appear in heaven, and then all the tribes of
the earth will mourn, and they will see ‘the Son of Man coming on the clouds of
heaven’ with power and great glory. 31 And he will send out his angels with a loud
trumpet call, and they will gather his elect from the four winds, from one end of
heaven to the other.
32 “From the fig tree learn its lesson: as soon as its branch becomes tender and
puts forth its leaves, you know that summer is near. 33 So also, when you see all
these things, you know that he[g] is near, at the very gates. 34 Truly I tell you, this
generation will not pass away until all these things have taken place. 35 Heaven and
earth will pass away, but my words will not pass away.

24.29 Isa 13.10 Ezek 32.7,8 Joel 2.31; 3.15 Mk 13.24-37 Lk 21.25-36 Acts 2.20 Rev 6.12
24.30 Dan 7.13 Zech 12.10-14 Rev 1.7
24.31 1 Cor 15.52 1 Thess 4.16 Rev 11.15
24.33 Mt 16.28 Jas 5.9

Jesus tells about remaining watchful
(203/Mark 13.32–37; Luke 21.34–38)

36 “But about that day and hour no one knows, neither the angels of heaven,
nor the Son,[h] but only the Father. 37 For as the days of Noah were, so will be the
coming of the Son of Man. 38 For as in those days before the flood they were eating
and drinking, marrying and giving in marriage, until the day Noah entered the ark,
39 and they knew nothing until the flood came and swept them all away, so too will
be the coming of the Son of Man. 40 Then two will be in the field; one will be taken
and one will be left. 41 Two women will be grinding meal together; one will be
taken and one will be left. 42 Keep awake therefore, for you do not know on what
day[i] your Lord is coming. 43 But understand this: if the owner of the house had
known in what part of the night the thief was coming, he would have stayed awake
and would not have let his house be broken into. 44 Therefore you also must be
ready, for the Son of Man is coming at an unexpected hour.
45 “Who then is the faithful and wise slave, whom his master has put in charge
of his household, to give the other slaves[j] their allowance of food at the proper
time? 46 Blessed is that slave whom his master will find at work when he arrives.
47 Truly I tell you, he will put that one in charge of all his possessions. 48 But if that
wicked slave says to himself, ‘My master is delayed,’ 49 and he begins to beat his
fellow slaves, and eats and drinks with drunkards, 50 the master of that slave will
come on a day when he does not expect him and at an hour that he does not know.
51 He will cut him in pieces[k] and put him with the hypocrites, where there will be
weeping and gnashing of teeth.

24.36 Acts 1.7 1 Thess 5.2 2 Pet 3.10
24.37 Gen 6.3; 7.1 Lk 17.26 1 Pet 3.20
24.40 Lk 17.34-36
24.42 Lk 12.29; 21.36 1 Thess 5.6 Rev 3.3,16.15
24.45 Lk 12.40-47 1 Cor 4.2 Heb 3.5
24.51 Mt 25.30

[g] Or *it* [h] Other ancient authorities lack *nor the Son* [i] Other ancient authorities read *at what hour* [j] Gk *to give them* [k] Or *cut him off*

24.30 The tribes of the earth will mourn because unbelievers will suddenly realize they have chosen the wrong side. Everything they have scoffed about will be happening, and it will be too late for them.

24.36 It is good that we don't know exactly when Christ will return. If we knew the precise date, we might be tempted to be lazy in our work for Christ. Worse yet, we might plan to keep sinning and then turn to God right at the end. Heaven is not our only goal; we have work to do here. And we must keep on doing it until death or until we see the unmistakable return of our Savior.

24.40–42 Christ's second coming will be swift and sudden. There will be no opportunity for afterthought, last-minute repentance, or bargaining. The choice we have already made will determine our eternal destiny.

24.44 Jesus' purpose in telling about his return is not to stimulate predictions and calculations about the date, but to warn us to be prepared. Will you be ready? The only safety is to obey him *today* (24.46).

24.45–47 Jesus asks us to spend the waiting time taking care of his people and doing his work here on earth, both within the church and outside it. This is the best way to prepare for Christ's return.

24.50 Knowing that Christ's return will be sudden should motivate us always to be prepared. We are not to live irresponsibly – sitting and waiting, doing nothing; seeking self-serving pleasure; using his tarrying as an excuse not to do God's work of building his kingdom; developing a false security based on precise calculations of events; or letting our curiosity about the end times divert us from doing God's work.

24.51 "Weeping and gnashing of teeth" is a phrase used to describe despair. God's coming judgment is as certain as Jesus' return to earth.

Jesus tells the parable of the ten bridesmaids
(204)

25 "Then the kingdom of heaven will be like this. Ten bridesmaids[l] took their 25.1
lamps and went to meet the bridegroom.[m] 2 Five of them were foolish, and Isa 61.10 Mt 9.15
five were wise. 3 When the foolish took their lamps, they took no oil with them; Jn 3.29 Rev 19.7
4 but the wise took flasks of oil with their lamps. 5 As the bridegroom was delayed, 21.2,9
all of them became drowsy and slept. 6 But at midnight there was a shout, 'Look! 25.5 1 Thess 4.16
Here is the bridegroom! Come out to meet him.' 7 Then all those bridesmaids[l] got 5.6
up and trimmed their lamps. 8 The foolish said to the wise, 'Give us some of your 2 Pet 3.4-9
oil, for our lamps are going out.' 9 But the wise replied, 'No! there will not be 25.7 Lk 12.35-40
enough for you and for us; you had better go to the dealers and buy some for yourselves.' 10 And while they went to buy it, the bridegroom came, and those who 25.10
were ready went with him into the wedding banquet; and the door was shut. 11 Later Lk 13.24,25
the other bridesmaids[l] came also, saying, 'Lord, lord, open to us.' 12 But he replied, 'Truly I tell you, I do not know you.' 13 Keep awake therefore, for you know 25.13 Mt 24.42 Mk 13.33
neither the day nor the hour.[n] Rev 16.15

Jesus tells the parable of the loaned money
(205)

14 "For it is as if a man, going on a journey, summoned his slaves and entrusted
his property to them; 15 to one he gave five talents,[o] to another two, to another one, 25.15
to each according to his ability. Then he went away. 16 The one who had received Rom 12.6 Eph 4.11
the five talents went off at once and traded with them, and made five more talents. 1 Pet 4.10
17 In the same way, the one who had the two talents made two more talents. 18 But
the one who had received the one talent went off and dug a hole in the ground and
hid his master's money. 19 After a long time the master of those slaves came and
settled accounts with them. 20 Then the one who had received the five talents came
forward, bringing five more talents, saying, 'Master, you handed over to me five
talents; see, I have made five more talents.' 21 His master said to him, 'Well done, 25.21
good and trustworthy slave; you have been trustworthy in a few things, I will put Mt 24.46,47 Lk 12.42-44
you in charge of many things; enter into the joy of your master.' 22 And the one with 22.28-30 2 Tim 2.12
the two talents also came forward, saying, 'Master, you handed over to me two
talents; see, I have made two more talents.' 23 His master said to him, 'Well done,
good and trustworthy slave; you have been trustworthy in a few things, I will put
you in charge of many things; enter into the joy of your master.' 24 Then the one

[l] Gk *virgins* [m] Other ancient authorities add *and the bride* [n] Other ancient authorities add *in which the Son of Man is coming* [o] A talent was worth more than fifteen years' wages of a laborer

---

25.1ff Jesus gave the following parables to clarify further what it means to be ready for his return and how to live until he comes. In the story of the bridesmaids (25.1–13), we are taught that every person is responsible for his or her own spiritual condition. The story of the talents (25.14–30) shows the necessity of using well what God has entrusted to us. The parable of the sheep and goats (25.31–46) stresses the importance of serving others in need. No parable by itself *completely* describes our preparation. Instead, each paints one part of the whole picture.

25.1ff This parable is about a wedding. On the wedding day the bridegroom went to the bride's house for the ceremony; then the bride and groom, along with a great parade, returned to the groom's house where a feast took place, often lasting a full week.

These bridesmaids were waiting for the parade, and they hoped to take part in the wedding banquet. But when the groom didn't come at the expected time, five of them were out of lamp oil. By the time they had purchased extra oil, it was too late to join the feast.

When Jesus returns to take his people to heaven, we must be ready. Spiritual preparation cannot be bought or borrowed at the last minute. Our relationship with God must be our own.

25.15 The master divided the money (talents) among his servants according to their abilities. No one received more or less than he could handle. If he failed in his assignment, his excuse could not be that he was overwhelmed. Failure could come only from laziness or hatred for the master. The talents represent any kind of resource we are given. God gives us time, gifts, and other resources according to our abilities, and he expects us to invest them wisely until he returns. We are responsible to use well what God has given us. The issue is not how much we have, but how well we use what we have.

25.21 Jesus is coming back—we know this is true. Does this mean we must drop our jobs in order to serve God? No, it means we are to use our time, talents, and treasures diligently in order to serve God completely in whatever we do. For a few people, this means changing professions. For most of us, it means doing our daily work out of love for God.

25.24–30 This last man was thinking only of himself. He hoped to play it safe and protect himself from his hard master, but he was judged for his self-centeredness. We must not make excuses to avoid doing what God calls us to do. If God truly is our Master, we must obey willingly. Our time, abilities, and money aren't ours in the first place—we are caretakers, not owners. When we ignore, squander, or abuse what we are given, we are rebellious and deserve to be punished.

who had received the one talent also came forward, saying, 'Master, I knew that
you were a harsh man, reaping where you did not sow, and gathering where you did
not scatter seed; 25 so I was afraid, and I went and hid your talent in the ground.
Here you have what is yours.' 26 But his master replied, 'You wicked and lazy
slave! You knew, did you, that I reap where I did not sow, and gather where I did
not scatter? 27 Then you ought to have invested my money with the bankers, and on
my return I would have received what was my own with interest. 28 So take the
talent from him, and give it to the one with the ten talents. 29 For to all those who
have, more will be given, and they will have an abundance; but from those who
have nothing, even what they have will be taken away. 30 As for this worthless
slave, throw him into the outer darkness, where there will be weeping and gnashing
of teeth.'

Jesus tells about the final judgment
(206)

31 "When the Son of Man comes in his glory, and all the angels with him, then
he will sit on the throne of his glory. 32 All the nations will be gathered before him,
and he will separate people one from another as a shepherd separates the sheep
from the goats, 33 and he will put the sheep at his right hand and the goats at the left.
34 Then the king will say to those at his right hand, 'Come, you that are blessed by
my Father, inherit the kingdom prepared for you from the foundation of the world;
35 for I was hungry and you gave me food, I was thirsty and you gave me something
to drink, I was a stranger and you welcomed me, 36 I was naked and you gave me
clothing, I was sick and you took care of me, I was in prison and you visited me.'
37 Then the righteous will answer him, 'Lord, when was it that we saw you hungry
and gave you food, or thirsty and gave you something to drink? 38 And when was
it that we saw you a stranger and welcomed you, or naked and gave you clothing?
39 And when was it that we saw you sick or in prison and visited you?' 40 And the
king will answer them, 'Truly I tell you, just as you did it to one of the least of these
who are members of my family,[p] you did it to me.' 41 Then he will say to those at
his left hand, 'You that are accursed, depart from me into the eternal fire prepared
for the devil and his angels; 42 for I was hungry and you gave me no food, I was
thirsty and you gave me nothing to drink, 43 I was a stranger and you did not welcome me, naked and you did not give me clothing, sick and in prison and you did
not visit me.' 44 Then they also will answer, 'Lord, when was it that we saw you
hungry or thirsty or a stranger or naked or sick or in prison, and did not take care
of you?' 45 Then he will answer them, 'Truly I tell you, just as you did not do it to

p Gk *these my brothers*

25.29 Lk 8.18; Jn 15.2; 1 Cor 15.10
25.30 Mt 8.12; Lk 13.28
25.31 Zech 14.5; Acts 1.11; 3.20; 1 Thess 4.16; 2 Thess 1.7
25.32 Ezek 20.34-38; 34.17; Rev 20.12
25.34 Lk 12.32; 1 Cor 2.9; 6.9; Heb 11.16; Rev 21.7
25.35 Isa 58.7; 2 Tim 1.16; Heb 13.2,3; Jas 2.15
25.40 Prov 14.31; 19.17; Heb 6.10
25.41 Mt 13.41; 2 Pet 2.4; Jude 6
25.45 Prov 17.5; Zech 2.8; Acts 9.5

25.29, 30 This parable describes the consequences of two attitudes to Christ's return. The person who diligently prepares for it by investing his time and talent to serve God will be rewarded. The person who has no heart for the work of the kingdom will be punished. God rewards faithfulness. Those who bear no fruit for God's kingdom cannot expect to be treated the same as the faithful.

25.31–46 God will separate his obedient followers from pretenders and unbelievers. The real evidence of our belief is the way we act. To treat all persons we encounter as if they are Jesus is no easy task. What we do for others demonstrates what we really think about Jesus' words to us – feed the hungry, give the homeless a place to stay, visit the sick. How well do your actions separate you from pretenders and unbelievers?

25.32 Jesus used sheep and goats to show the division between believers and unbelievers. Sheep and goats often grazed together but were separated when it came time to shear the sheep. Ezekiel 34.17–24 also refers to the separation of sheep and goats.

25.34–40 This parable describes acts of mercy we all can do every day. These acts do not depend on wealth, ability, or intelligence; they are simple acts freely given and freely received. We have no excuse to neglect those who have deep needs, and we cannot hand over this responsibility to the church or government. Jesus demands our personal involvement in caring for others' needs (Isaiah 58.7).

25.40 There has been much discussion about the identity of the "members of my family." Some have said they are the Jews; others say they are all Christians; still others say they are suffering people everywhere. Such a debate is much like the lawyer's earlier question to Jesus, "Who is my neighbor?" (Luke 10.29). The point of this parable is not the *who*, but the *what* – the importance of serving where service is needed. The focus of this parable is that we should love every person and serve anyone we can. Such love for others glorifies God by reflecting our love for him.

one of the least of these, you did not do it to me.' 46 And these will go away into 25.46 Dan 12.2
eternal punishment, but the righteous into eternal life." Rom 2.7,8; 6.23

C. DEATH AND RESURRECTION OF JESUS, THE KING (26.1–28.20)

After facing much opposition for his teaching, Jesus is betrayed by Judas, denied by the disciples, crucified, and dies. Three days later he rises from the dead and appears to the disciples, confirming that he is indeed King over life and death. The long-awaited King has brought in his kingdom, but it is different than expected, for he reigns in our hearts until the day he comes again to establish a new and perfect world.

Religious leaders plot to kill Jesus

(207/Mark 14.1, 2; Luke 22.1, 2)

26 When Jesus had finished saying all these things, he said to his disciples, 26.1 Mk 14.1,2
2 "You know that after two days the Passover is coming, and the Son of Man Lk 22.1,2
will be handed over to be crucified."
3 Then the chief priests and the elders of the people gathered in the palace of the 26.3 Ps 2.2
high priest, who was called Caiaphas, 4 and they conspired to arrest Jesus by stealth Jn 11.47,48
and kill him. 5 But they said, "Not during the festival, or there may be a riot among Acts 4.25,26
the people."

A woman anoints Jesus with expensive perfume

(182/Mark 14.3–9; John 12.1–11)

6 Now while Jesus was at Bethany in the house of Simon the leper,[q] 7 a woman 26.7 Mt 21.17
came to him with an alabaster jar of very costly ointment, and she poured it on his Jn 11.1
head as he sat at the table. 8 But when the disciples saw it, they were angry and said,
"Why this waste? 9 For this ointment could have been sold for a large sum, and the
money given to the poor." 10 But Jesus, aware of this, said to them, "Why do you 26.11 Deut 15.11
trouble the woman? She has performed a good service for me. 11 For you always Jn 17.11

[q] The terms *leper* and *leprosy* can refer to several diseases

25.46 Eternal punishment takes place in hell, the place of punishment after death for all those who refuse to repent (5.29). In the Bible, three words have been translated "hell."

(1) *Sheol* is used in the Old Testament to mean the grave, the place of the dead, generally thought to be under the earth. (See Job 24.19; Psalm 16.10; Isaiah 38.10.)

(2) *Hades* is the Greek word for the underworld, the realm of the dead. It is the word used in the New Testament for Sheol.

(3) *Gehenna* was named after the valley of Hinnom near Jerusalem where children were sacrificed by fire to the pagan gods (see 2 Kings 23.10; 2 Chronicles 28.3). This is the place of eternal fire (Mark 9.43) prepared for the devil, his angels, and all those who do not believe in God (25.46; Revelation 20.9, 10). This is the final and eternal state of the wicked after the resurrection and the last judgment.

When Jesus warns against unbelief, he is trying to save us from agonizing punishment.

26.3 Caiaphas was the ruling high priest during Jesus' ministry. He was the son-in-law of Annas, the previous high priest. The Roman government had taken over the process of appointing all political and religious leaders. Caiaphas served for 18 years, longer than most high priests, suggesting that he was good at cooperating with the Romans. He was the first to recommend Jesus' death in order to "save" the nation (John 11.49, 50).

26.3–5 This was a deliberate plot to kill Jesus. Without this plot, there would have been no groundswell of popular opinion against him. In fact, because of Jesus' popularity, the religious leaders were afraid to arrest him during the Passover. They did not want their actions to incite a riot.

26.6–13 Matthew and Mark place this event just before the last supper, while John places it just before the triumphal entry. Of the three, John places this event in the most likely chronological order. We must remember that the main purpose of the Gospel writers was to give an accurate record of Jesus' message, not to present an exact chronological account of his life. Matthew and Mark may have chosen to place this event here to contrast the complete devotion of Mary with the betrayal of Judas, the next event they record in their Gospels.

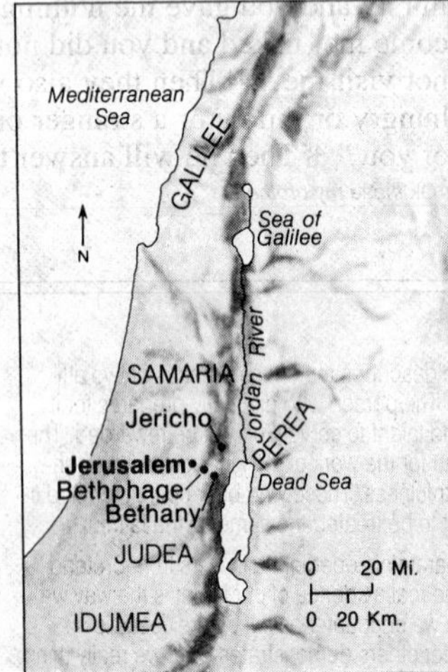

VISIT IN BETHANY
Chronologically, the events of Matthew 26.6–13 precede the events of 21.1ff. In 20.29, Jesus left Jericho, heading toward Jerusalem. Then he arrived in Bethany, where a woman anointed him. From there he went toward Bethphage where two of his disciples got the donkey that he would ride into Jerusalem.

26.7 This woman was Mary, the sister of Martha and Lazarus, who lived in Bethany (John 12.1–3). Alabaster jars were carved from a translucent gypsum. They were used to hold perfumed oil.

26.8 The disciples were all indignant, but John's Gospel singles out Judas Iscariot as especially so (John 12.4).

26.11 Jesus referred to Deuteronomy 15.11, which says, "There will never cease to be poor people in the land." This does not justify ignoring the needs of the poor. Scripture continually calls us to

have the poor with you, but you will not always have me. 12 By pouring this ointment on my body she has prepared me for burial. 13 Truly I tell you, wherever this
good news[r] is proclaimed in the whole world, what she has done will be told in
remembrance of her."

Judas agrees to betray Jesus
(208/Mark 14.10, 11; Luke 22.3–6)

14 Then one of the twelve, who was called Judas Iscariot, went to the chief
priests 15 and said, "What will you give me if I betray him to you?" They paid him
thirty pieces of silver. 16 And from that moment he began to look for an opportunity
to betray him.

[r] Or *gospel*

MARY
LAZARUS'S SISTER

Hospitality is an art. Making sure a guest is welcomed, warmed, and well fed requires creativity, organization, and teamwork. Their ability to accomplish these makes Mary and her sister Martha one of the best hospitality teams in the Bible. Their frequent guest was Jesus Christ.

For Mary, hospitality meant giving more attention to the guest himself than to the needs he might have. She would rather talk than cook. She was more interested in her guest's words than in the cleanliness of her home or the timeliness of her meals. She let her older sister Martha take care of those details. Mary's approach to events shows her to be mainly a "responder." She did little preparation—her role was participation. Unlike her sister, who had to learn to stop and listen, Mary needed to learn that action is often appropriate and necessary.

We first meet Mary during a visit Jesus paid to her home. She simply sat at his feet and listened. When Martha became irritated at her sister's lack of help, Jesus stated that Mary's choice to enjoy his company was the most appropriate response at the time. Our last glimpse of Mary shows her to have become a woman of thoughtful and worshipful action. Again she was at Jesus' feet, washing them with perfume and wiping them with her hair. She seemed to understand, better even than the disciples, why Jesus was going to die. Jesus said her act of worship would be told everywhere, along with the gospel, as an example of costly service.

What kind of hospitality does Jesus receive in your life? Are you so busy planning and running your life that you neglect precious time with him? Or do you respond to him by listening to his Word, then finding ways to worship him with your life? It is that kind of hospitality he longs for from each of us.

Strengths and accomplishments:
- Perhaps the only person who understood and accepted Jesus' coming death, taking time to anoint his body while he was still living
- Learned when to listen and when to act

Lessons from her life:
- The busy-ness of serving God can become a barrier to knowing him personally
- Small acts of obedience and service have widespread effects

Vital statistics:
- Where: Bethany
- Relatives: Sister: Martha. Brother: Lazarus

Key verses:
"By pouring this ointment on my body she has prepared me for burial. Truly I tell you, wherever this good news is proclaimed in the whole world, what she has done will be told in remembrance of her" (Matthew 26.12, 13).

Mary's story is told in Matthew 26.6–13; Mark 14.3–9; Luke 10.38–42; John 11.17–45; 12.1–11.

care for the needy. The passage in Deuteronomy continues: "I therefore command you, 'Open your hand to the poor and needy neighbor in your land.'" Rather, Jesus said this to highlight the special sacrifice Mary made for him.

26.14, 15 Why would Judas want to betray Jesus? Judas, like the other disciples, expected Jesus to start a political rebellion and overthrow Rome. As treasurer, Judas certainly assumed (as did the other disciples – see Mark 10.35–37) that he would be given an important position in Jesus' new government. But when Jesus praised Mary for pouring out perfume worth a year's salary, Judas may have realized that Jesus' kingdom was not physical or political, but spiritual. Judas's greedy desire for money and status could not be realized if he followed Jesus, so he betrayed him in exchange for money and favor from the religious leaders.

26.15 Matthew alone records the exact amount of money Judas accepted to betray Jesus – 30 pieces of silver, the price of a slave (Exodus 21.32). The religious leaders had planned to wait until after the Passover to take Jesus, but with Judas's unexpected offer, they accelerated their plans.

Disciples prepare for the Passover
(209/Mark 14.12–16; Luke 22.7–13)

17 On the first day of Unleavened Bread the disciples came to Jesus, saying, **26.17**
“Where do you want us to make the preparations for you to eat the Passover?” 18 He Ex 12.6
said, “Go into the city to a certain man, and say to him, ‘The Teacher says, My time Lev 23.5,6
is near; I will keep the Passover at your house with my disciples.’ ” 19 So the disciples did as Jesus had directed them, and they prepared the Passover meal.

Jesus and the disciples have the last supper
(211/Mark 14.17–25; Luke 22.14–30; John 13.21–30)

20 When it was evening, he took his place with the twelve;[s] 21 and while they **26.23**
were eating, he said, “Truly I tell you, one of you will betray me.” 22 And they Ps 41.9 **26.24**
became greatly distressed and began to say to him one after another, “Surely not I, Gen 3.15
Lord?” 23 He answered, “The one who has dipped his hand into the bowl with me Isa 53.8 Dan 9.26
will betray me. 24 The Son of Man goes as it is written of him, but woe to that one Lk 24.25-27,46
by whom the Son of Man is betrayed! It would have been better for that one not to 1 Pet 1.10,11
have been born.” 25 Judas, who betrayed him, said, “Surely not I, Rabbi?” He re- **26.26** Mk 14.22-26
plied, “You have said so.” Lk 22.19,20,39 1 Cor 10.16
26 While they were eating, Jesus took a loaf of bread, and after blessing it he 11.23
broke it, gave it to the disciples, and said, “Take, eat; this is my body.” 27 Then he **26.28** Ex 24.8
took a cup, and after giving thanks he gave it to them, saying, “Drink from it, all Lev 17.11 Jer 31.31
of you; 28 for this is my blood of the[t] covenant, which is poured out for many for Rom 5.15
the forgiveness of sins. 29 I tell you, I will never again drink of this fruit of the vine Heb 9.22 **26.29**
until that day when I drink it new with you in my Father’s kingdom.” Acts 10.41

[s] Other ancient authorities add *disciples* [t] Other ancient authorities add *new*

26.17 The Passover was one night and one meal, but the festival of unleavened bread, which was celebrated with it, continued for a week. The people removed all yeast from their homes in commemoration of their ancestors’ exodus from Egypt, when they did not have time to let the bread dough rise. Thousands of people poured into Jerusalem from all over the Roman Empire for this feast. For more information on how the Passover was celebrated, see the notes on Mark 14.1 and in Exodus 12.

26.23 In Jesus’ time, food was eaten from a common dish into which everyone dipped their hand.

26.26 Each name we use for this sacrament brings out a different dimension to it. It is the *Lord’s supper* because it commemorates the Passover meal Jesus ate with his disciples; it is the *eucharist* (thanksgiving) because in it we thank God for Christ’s work for us; it is *communion* because through it we commune with God and with other believers. As we eat the bread and drink the wine, we should be sober as we recall Jesus’ death and his promise to come again, grateful for God’s wonderful gift to us, and joyful as we meet with Christ and the body of believers.

26.28 How does Jesus’ blood seal the new covenant? People under the old covenant (those who lived before Jesus) could approach God only through a priest and an animal sacrifice. Now all people can come directly to God through faith because Jesus’ death has made us acceptable in God’s eyes (Romans 3.21–24).

The old covenant was a picture of the new (Jeremiah 31.31), pointing forward to the day when Jesus himself would be the final and ultimate sacrifice for sin. Rather than a lamb without blemish slain on the altar, the perfect Lamb of God was slain on the cross, a sinless sacrifice so that our sins could be forgiven once and for all. All those who believe in him receive that forgiveness.

26.29 Again Jesus assured his disciples of victory over death and of their future with him. The next few hours would bring apparent defeat, but soon they would experience the power of the Holy Spirit and witness the great spread of the gospel message. And one day, they would all be together again in God’s new kingdom.

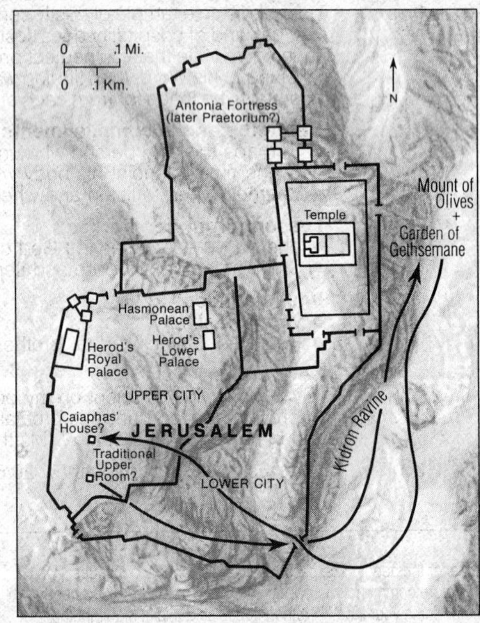

THE PASSOVER MEAL AND GETHSEMANE Jesus, who would soon be the final Passover Lamb, ate the traditional Passover meal with his disciples in the upper room of a house in Jerusalem. During the meal they partook of the wine and bread, which would be the element of future communion celebrations and then went out to the Garden of Gethsemane on the Mount of Olives.

Jesus again predicts Peter's denial
(222/Mark 14.26–31)

30 When they had sung the hymn, they went out to the Mount of Olives.
26.31 Zech 13.7
31 Then Jesus said to them, "You will all become deserters because of me this
night; for it is written,
'I will strike the shepherd,
and the sheep of the flock will be scattered.'
32 But after I am raised up, I will go ahead of you to Galilee." 33 Peter said to him,
26.34 Mt 26.75 Mk 14.30 Lk 22.34 Jn 13.38
"Though all become deserters because of you, I will never desert you." 34 Jesus said
to him, "Truly I tell you, this very night, before the cock crows, you will deny me
three times." 35 Peter said to him, "Even though I must die with you, I will not deny
you." And so said all the disciples.

Jesus agonizes in the garden
(223/Mark 14.32–42; Luke 22.39–46)

26.36 Mk 14.32-42 Lk 22.39-46 Jn 18.1
36 Then Jesus went with them to a place called Gethsemane; and he said to his
disciples, "Sit here while I go over there and pray." 37 He took with him Peter and
the two sons of Zebedee, and began to be grieved and agitated. 38 Then he said to
26.38 Jn 12.27
them, "I am deeply grieved, even to death; remain here, and stay awake with me."
26.39 Mt 20.22 Jn 5.30; 6.38 Heb 5.7
39 And going a little farther, he threw himself on the ground and prayed, "My Father, if it is possible, let this cup pass from me; yet not what I want but what you
want." 40 Then he came to the disciples and found them sleeping; and he said to
26.41 Eph 6.18 1 Pet 5.8
Peter, "So, could you not stay awake with me one hour? 41 Stay awake and pray that
you may not come into the time of trial;[u] the spirit indeed is willing, but the flesh
is weak." 42 Again he went away for the second time and prayed, "My Father, if this
cannot pass unless I drink it, your will be done." 43 Again he came and found them
sleeping, for their eyes were heavy. 44 So leaving them again, he went away and
26.45 Jn 12.23-27 13.1,31
prayed for the third time, saying the same words. 45 Then he came to the disciples
and said to them, "Are you still sleeping and taking your rest? See, the hour is at
hand, and the Son of Man is betrayed into the hands of sinners. 46 Get up, let us be
going. See, my betrayer is at hand."

Jesus is betrayed and arrested
(224/Mark 14.43–52; Luke 22.47–53; John 18.1–11)

26.47 Lk 22.47-53 Jn 18.1-12
47 While he was still speaking, Judas, one of the twelve, arrived; with him was
a large crowd with swords and clubs, from the chief priests and the elders of the

[u] Or *into temptation*

26.30 It is possible that the hymn the disciples sang was from Psalms 115–118, the traditional psalms sung as part of the Passover meal.

26.35 All the disciples declared that they would die before deserting Jesus. A few hours later, however, they all scattered. Talk is cheap. It is easy to say we are devoted to Christ, but our claims are meaningful only when they are tested in the crucible of persecution. How strong is your faith? Is it strong enough to stand under intense trial? For the second time that evening, Jesus predicted that his disciples would desert him (see Luke 22.31–38; John 13.31–38 for the first prediction).

26.37, 38 Jesus was in great anguish over his coming physical pain, separation from the Father, and death for the sins of the world. The divine course was set; but he, in his human nature, still struggled (Hebrews 5.7–9). Because of the anguish he experienced, he can relate to our suffering. His strength to obey came from his relationship with God the Father, who is also the source of our strength (John 17.11, 15, 16, 21, 26).

26.39 Jesus was not rebelling against his Father's will when he asked that the cup of suffering and separation be taken away. In fact, he reaffirmed his desire to do God's will by saying, "Yet not what I want but what you want." His prayer reveals to us his terrible suffering. His agony was worse than death as he paid for *all* sin by being separated from God. The sinless Son of God took our sins upon himself to save us from suffering and separation.

26.39 In times of suffering people sometimes wish they knew the future, or they wish they could understand the reason for their anguish. Jesus knew what lay ahead of him, and he knew the reason. Even so, his struggle was intense—more wrenching than any struggle we will ever have to face. What does it take to be able to say "Your will be done"? It takes trust in God's plans, prayer, and obedience each step of the way.

26.40, 41 Jesus used Peter's drowsiness to warn him about the kinds of temptation he would soon face. The way to overcome temptation is to be alert to it and pray. Being alert means being aware of the possibilities of temptation, sensitive to the subtleties, and spiritually equipped to fight it. Because temptation strikes where we are most vulnerable, we can't resist it alone. Prayer is essential, because God's strength can shore up our defenses and defeat Satan's power.

people. 48 Now the betrayer had given them a sign, saying, "The one I will kiss is
the man; arrest him." 49 At once he came up to Jesus and said, "Greetings, Rabbi!"
and kissed him. 50 Jesus said to him, "Friend, do what you are here to do." Then
they came and laid hands on Jesus and arrested him. 51 Suddenly, one of those with
Jesus put his hand on his sword, drew it, and struck the slave of the high priest,
cutting off his ear. 52 Then Jesus said to him, "Put your sword back into its place;
for all who take the sword will perish by the sword. 53 Do you think that I cannot
appeal to my Father, and he will at once send me more than twelve legions of
angels? 54 But how then would the scriptures be fulfilled, which say it must happen
in this way?" 55 At that hour Jesus said to the crowds, "Have you come out with
swords and clubs to arrest me as though I were a bandit? Day after day I sat in the
temple teaching, and you did not arrest me. 56 But all this has taken place, so that
the scriptures of the prophets may be fulfilled." Then all the disciples deserted him
and fled.

26.50 Ps 41.9; 55.12,13
26.52 Gen 9.6; Rev 13.10
26.53 2 Kgs 6.16,17; Ps 91.11
26.55 Mk 12.35; 14.49; Lk 4.20; 19.47; 20.1; 21.37; Jn 7.14,28; 8.20
26.56 Isa 53.7; Dan 9.26; Jn 18.15

Caiaphas questions Jesus
(226/Mark 14.53–65)

57 Those who had arrested Jesus took him to Caiaphas the high priest, in whose
house the scribes and the elders had gathered. 58 But Peter was following him at a
distance, as far as the courtyard of the high priest; and going inside, he sat with the
guards in order to see how this would end. 59 Now the chief priests and the whole
council were looking for false testimony against Jesus so that they might put him to
death, 60 but they found none, though many false witnesses came forward. At last
two came forward 61 and said, "This fellow said, 'I am able to destroy the temple of
God and to build it in three days.' " 62 The high priest stood up and said, "Have you
no answer? What is it that they testify against you?" 63 But Jesus was silent. Then
the high priest said to him, "I put you under oath before the living God, tell us if you
are the Messiah,[v] the Son of God." 64 Jesus said to him, "You have said so. But I
tell you,

From now on you will see the Son of Man
seated at the right hand of Power
and coming on the clouds of heaven."

65 Then the high priest tore his clothes and said, "He has blasphemed! Why do we
still need witnesses? You have now heard his blasphemy. 66 What is your verdict?"
They answered, "He deserves death." 67 Then they spat in his face and struck him;

[v] Or *Christ*

26.57 Mk 14.53-65
26.58 Lk 22.54,55
26.60 Deut 19.15; 1 Kgs 21.10; Ps 27.12
26.61 Mt 27.40; Jn 2.19; Acts 6.14
26.62 Mt 27.12
26.63 Lev 5.1
26.64 Ps 110.1; Dan 7.13; Acts 7.55; 1 Thess 4.16; Rev 1.7
26.65 Lev 24.16; 2 Kgs 18.37; Jn 19.7; Acts 3.15; 7.52

26.48 Judas had told the temple guards to arrest the man he greeted. This was not an arrest by Roman soldiers under Roman law, but an arrest by the religious leaders. Judas pointed Jesus out not because he was hard to recognize, but because Judas had agreed to be the formal accuser in case a trial was called. Judas was able to lead them to one of Jesus' retreats where no crowds would interfere with the arrest.

26.51–53 The man who cut off the slave's ear was Peter (John 18.10). Peter was trying to prevent what he saw as *defeat.* He didn't realize that Jesus had to die in order to have *victory.* But Jesus demonstrated perfect commitment to his Father's will. His kingdom would not be advanced with swords, but with faith and obedience.

26.55 Although the religious leaders could have arrested Jesus at any time, they came at night because they were afraid of the crowds who followed him each day (see 26.5).

26.56 A few hours earlier, this band of men had said they would rather die than desert their Lord (see the note on 26.35).

26.57 Earlier in the evening, Jesus had been questioned by Annas (the former high priest and father-in-law of Caiaphas). Annas then sent Jesus to Caiaphas's home to be questioned (John 18.12–24). Because of their haste to complete the trial and see Jesus die before the sabbath, less than 24 hours away, the religious leaders met in Caiaphas's home at night instead of waiting for daylight and meeting in the temple.

26.59 The council, also called the Sanhedrin, was the most powerful religious and political body of the Jewish people. Although the Romans controlled Israel's government, they gave the people power to handle religious disputes and some civil disputes, so the Sanhedrin made many of the local decisions affecting daily life. But a death sentence had to be approved by the Romans.

26.60, 61 The council tried to find witnesses who would distort some of Jesus' teachings. Finally they found two witnesses who distorted Jesus' words about the temple (see John 2.19). They claimed that Jesus had said he could destroy the temple – a blasphemous boast. Actually Jesus had said, "Destroy this temple, and in three days I will raise it up." Jesus, of course, was talking about his body, not the building. Ironically, the religious leaders were about to destroy Jesus' body just as he had said, and three days later he would rise from the dead.

26.64 Jesus declared his royalty in no uncertain terms. In saying he was the Son of Man, he was claiming to be the Messiah, as his listeners well knew. He knew this declaration would be his undoing, but he did not panic. He was calm, courageous, and determined.

26.67 Isa 50.6; 53.3 Mic 5.1 and some slapped him, 68 saying, "Prophesy to us, you Messiah![w] Who is it that
struck you?"

Peter denies knowing Jesus
(227/Mark 14.66–72; Luke 22.54–65; John 18.25–27)

26.69 Mk 14.66-72 Lk 22.55-62 Jn 18.25-27 69 Now Peter was sitting outside in the courtyard. A servant-girl came to him
and said, "You also were with Jesus the Galilean." 70 But he denied it before all of
them, saying, "I do not know what you are talking about." 71 When he went out to
the porch, another servant-girl saw him, and she said to the bystanders, "This man
was with Jesus of Nazareth."[x] 72 Again he denied it with an oath, "I do not know
the man." 73 After a little while the bystanders came up and said to Peter, "Certainly
you are also one of them, for your accent betrays you." 74 Then he began to curse,
and he swore an oath, "I do not know the man!" At that moment the cock crowed.
26.75 Mt 26.34 75 Then Peter remembered what Jesus had said: "Before the cock crows, you will
deny me three times." And he went out and wept bitterly.

[w] Or *Christ* [x] Gk *the Nazorean*

BETRAYED!

Delilah betrayed Samson to the Philistines.	Judges 16.16–21
Absalom betrayed David, his father.	2 Samuel 15.10–17
Jehu betrayed Joram and killed him.	2 Kings 9.14–27
Servants betrayed Joash and killed him.	2 Kings 12.20, 21
Judas betrayed Jesus.	Matthew 26.46–56

Scripture records a number of occasions in which a person or group was betrayed. The tragedies caused by these violations of trust are a strong lesson about the importance of keeping our commitments.

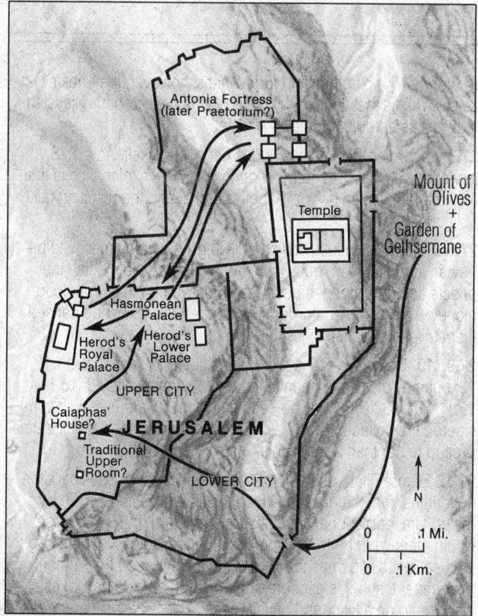

JESUS' TRIAL After Judas singled Jesus out for arrest, the mob took Jesus first to Caiaphas, the high priest. This trial, a mockery of justice, ended at daybreak with their decision to kill him—but the Jews needed Rome's permission for the death sentence. Jesus was taken to Pilate (who was probably in the Antonia Fortress), then to Herod (Luke 23.5–12), and back to Pilate who sentenced him to die.

26.65, 66 The high priest accused Jesus of blasphemy—calling himself God. To the Jews, this was a great crime, punishable by death. The religious leaders refused even to consider that Jesus' words might be true. They had decided against Jesus, and in so doing they sealed their own fate as well as his. Like the council members, you must decide whether Jesus' words are blasphemy or truth. Your decision has eternal implications.

26.69ff There were three stages to Peter's denial. First he acted confused and tried to divert attention from himself by changing the subject. Second, he denied Jesus with an oath. Third, he began to curse and swear. Believers who deny Christ often begin doing so subtly by pretending not to know him. When opportunities to discuss religious issues come up, they walk away or pretend they don't know the answers. With only a little more pressure, they can be induced to deny flatly their relationship with Christ. If you find yourself subtly diverting conversation so you don't have to talk about Christ, watch out. You may be on the road to denying him.

26.72–74 That Peter denied Christ with an oath and with cursing and swearing does not mean he used foul language. This was the kind of swearing one does in a court of law. Peter was swearing that he did not know Jesus and was invoking a curse on himself if his words were untrue. In effect he was saying, "May God strike me dead if I am lying."

The council of religious leaders condemns Jesus
(228/Mark 15.1; Luke 22.66–71)

27 When morning came, all the chief priests and the elders of the people con- 27.1 Ps 2.2
ferred together against Jesus in order to bring about his death. 2 They bound 27.2 Mt 20.19
him, led him away, and handed him over to Pilate the governor.

Judas kills himself
(229)

3 When Judas, his betrayer, saw that Jesus[y] was condemned, he repented and 27.3
brought back the thirty pieces of silver to the chief priests and the elders. 4 He said, Job 20.5 Mt 26.14
"I have sinned by betraying innocent[z] blood." But they said, "What is that to us? 2 Cor 7.10
See to it yourself." 5 Throwing down the pieces of silver in the temple, he departed; 27.5
and he went and hanged himself. 6 But the chief priests, taking the pieces of silver, Acts 1.18
said, "It is not lawful to put them into the treasury, since they are blood money."
7 After conferring together, they used them to buy the potter's field as a place to
bury foreigners. 8 For this reason that field has been called the Field of Blood to this
day. 9 Then was fulfilled what had been spoken through the prophet Jeremiah,[a] 27.9,10
"And they took[b] the thirty pieces of silver, the price of the one on whom a price had Jer 18.1-4; 19.2, 11; 32.6-9
been set,[c] on whom some of the people of Israel had set a price, 10 and they gave[d] Zech 11.12,13
them for the potter's field, as the Lord commanded me."

Jesus stands trial before Pilate
(230/Mark 15.2–5; Luke 23.1–5; John 18.28–38)

11 Now Jesus stood before the governor; and the governor asked him, "Are you 27.11
the King of the Jews?" Jesus said, "You say so." 12 But when he was accused by the 1 Tim 6.13
chief priests and elders, he did not answer. 13 Then Pilate said to him, "Do you not 27.12 Isa 53.7
hear how many accusations they make against you?" 14 But he gave him no answer, Mt 26.63 Jn 19.9
not even to a single charge, so that the governor was greatly amazed. 1 Pet 2.22

[y] Gk *he* [z] Other ancient authorities read *righteous* [a] Other ancient authorities read *Zechariah* or *Isaiah* [b] Or *I took* [c] Or *the price of the precious One* [d] Other ancient authorities read *I gave*

27.1, 2 The religious leaders had to induce the Roman government to sentence Jesus to death because they did not have the authority to do it themselves. The Romans had taken away the religious leaders' authority to inflict capital punishment. Politically, it looked better for the religious leaders anyway if someone else was responsible for killing Jesus. They wanted the death to appear Roman so the crowds couldn't blame them. They had arrested Jesus on theological grounds—blasphemy; but since this charge would be thrown out of a Roman court, they had to come up with a political reason for Jesus' death. Their strategy was to show Jesus as a rebel who claimed to be God and thus higher than Caesar.

27.2 Pilate was the Roman governor for the regions of Samaria and Judea from A.D. 26–36. Jerusalem was located in Judea. Pilate took special pleasure in demonstrating his authority over the Jews; for example, he impounded money from the temple treasuries to build an aqueduct. He was not popular, but the religious leaders had no other way to get rid of Jesus than to go to Pilate. Ironically, when Jesus, a Jew, came before him for trial, Pilate found him innocent. He could not find a single fault in Jesus, nor could he contrive one.

27.3, 4 Jesus' formal accuser (see 26.48 note) wanted to drop his charges, but the religious leaders refused to halt the trial. When he betrayed Jesus, perhaps Judas was trying to force his hand to get him to lead a revolt against Rome. This did not work, of course. Whatever his reason, Judas changed his mind, but it was too late. Many of the plans we set into motion cannot be reversed. It is best to think of the potential consequences before we launch into an action we may later regret.

27.4 The priests' job was to teach people about God and act as intercessors for them, helping with the sacrifices to cover their sins. Judas returned to the priests, exclaiming that he had sinned. Rather than helping him find forgiveness, however, the priests said, "What is that to us?" Not only had they rejected the Messiah, they had rejected their role as priests.

27.5 According to Matthew, Judas hanged himself. Acts 1.18, however, says he fell and burst open. The best explanation is that the limb from which he was hanging broke, and the resulting fall split open his body.

27.6 These chief priests felt no guilt in giving Judas money to betray an innocent man, but when Judas returned the money, the priests couldn't accept it because it was wrong to accept blood money—payment for murder! Their hatred for Jesus had caused them to lose all sense of justice.

27.9, 10 This prophecy is found specifically in Zechariah 11.12, 13, but may also have been taken from Jeremiah 17.2, 3; 18.1–4; 19.1–11; or 32.6–15. In Old Testament times, Jeremiah was considered the collector of some of the prophets' writings, so his name is cited rather than Zechariah's.

27.12 Before Pilate, the religious leaders accused Jesus of different crimes from the ones for which they had arrested him. They arrested him for blasphemy (claiming to be God), but that charge would mean nothing to the Romans. So the religious leaders had to accuse Jesus of crimes that would have concerned the Roman government, such as encouraging the people not to pay taxes, claiming to be a king, and causing riots. These accusations were not true, but the religious leaders were determined to kill Jesus, and they broke several commandments in order to do so.

27.14 Jesus' silence fulfilled the words of the prophet (Isaiah 53.7). Pilate was amazed that Jesus didn't try to defend himself. He recognized the obvious plot against Jesus and wanted to let him go, but Pilate was already under pressure from Rome to keep peace in his territory. The last thing he needed was a rebellion over

Pilate hands Jesus over to be crucified
(232/Mark 15.6–15; Luke 23.13–25; John 18.39–19.16)

15 Now at the festival the governor was accustomed to release a prisoner for the
crowd, anyone whom they wanted. 16 At that time they had a notorious prisoner,
called Jesus[e] Barabbas. 17 So after they had gathered, Pilate said to them, "Whom
do you want me to release for you, Jesus[e] Barabbas or Jesus who is called the
27.18 Messiah?"[f] 18 For he realized that it was out of jealousy that they had handed him
Acts 7.9 27.19 over. 19 While he was sitting on the judgment seat, his wife sent word to him,
Job 33.14,15 "Have nothing to do with that innocent man, for today I have suffered a great deal
27.20 because of a dream about him." 20 Now the chief priests and the elders persuaded
Acts 3.14 the crowds to ask for Barabbas and to have Jesus killed. 21 The governor again said

[e] Other ancient authorities lack *Jesus* [f] Or *the Christ*

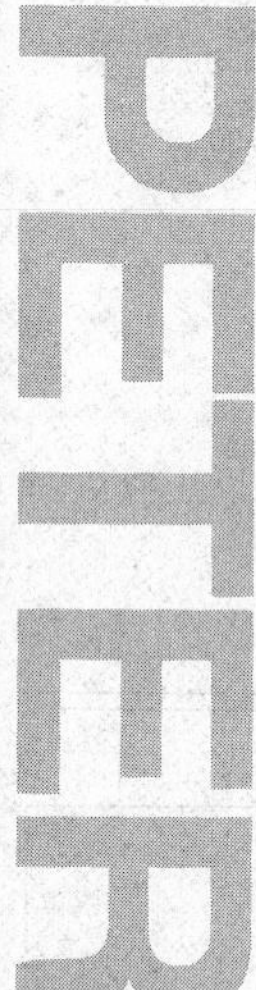

Jesus' first words to Simon Peter were "Follow me" (Mark 1.17). His last words to him were "Follow me" (John 21.22). Every step of the way between those two challenges, Peter never failed to follow—even though he often stumbled.

When Jesus entered Peter's life, this plain fisherman became a new person with new goals and new priorities. He did not become a perfect person, however, and he never stopped being Simon Peter. We may wonder what Jesus saw in Simon that made him greet this potential disciple with a new name, Peter—"the rock." Impulsive Peter certainly didn't act like a rock much of the time. But when Jesus chose his followers, he wasn't looking for models, he was looking for men. He chose people who could be changed by his love, and then he sent them out to communicate that his acceptance was available to anyone—even to those who often fail.

We may wonder what Jesus sees in us when he calls us to follow him. But we know Jesus accepted Peter, and, in spite of his failures, Peter went on to do great things for God. Are you willing to keep following Jesus, even when you fail?

Strengths and accomplishments:
- Became the recognized leader among Jesus' disciples—one of the inner group of three
- Was the first great voice of the gospel during and after Pentecost
- Probably knew Mark and gave him information for the Gospel of Mark
- Wrote 1 and 2 Peter

Weaknesses and mistakes:
- Often spoke without thinking; was brash and impulsive
- During Jesus' trial, denied three times that he even knew Jesus
- Later, found it hard to treat Gentile Christians as equals

Lessons from his life:
- Enthusiasm has to be backed up by faith and understanding or it fails
- God's faithfulness can compensate for our greatest unfaithfulness
- It is better to be a follower who fails than one who fails to follow

Vital statistics:
- Occupation: Fisherman, disciple
- Relatives: Father: Jona. Brother: Andrew
- Contemporaries: Jesus, Pilate, Herod

Key verse:
"You are Peter, and on this rock I will build my church, and the gates of Hades will not prevail against it" (Matthew 16.18).

Peter's story is told in the Gospels and the book of Acts. He is mentioned in Galatians 1.18 and 2.7–14; and he wrote the books of 1 and 2 Peter.

this quiet and seemingly insignificant man.

27.15, 16 Barabbas had taken part in a rebellion against the Roman government (Mark 15.7). Although an enemy to Rome, he may have been a hero to the Jews. Ironically, Barabbas was guilty of the crime for which Jesus was accused. *Barabbas* means "son of the father," which was actually Jesus' position with God.

27.19 For a leader who was supposed to administer justice, Pilate proved to be concerned more about political expediency than about doing what was right. He had several opportunities to make the right decision. His conscience told him Jesus was innocent; Roman law said an innocent man should not be put to death; and his wife had a troubled dream. Pilate had no good excuse to condemn Jesus, but he was afraid of the mob.

27.21 Crowds are fickle. If they loved Jesus on Sunday because they thought he was going to inaugurate his kingdom, they could easily hate him on Friday when his power appeared broken. In the face of the mass uprising against Jesus, his friends were afraid to speak up.

27.21 Faced with a clear choice, the people chose Barabbas, a revolutionary and murderer, over the Son of God. Faced with the same choice today, people are still choosing "Barabbas." They would rather have the tangible force of human power than the salvation offered by the Son of God.

to them, “Which of the two do you want me to release for you?” And they said,
“Barabbas.” 22 Pilate said to them, “Then what should I do with Jesus who is called 27.22
the Messiah?”[g] All of them said, “Let him be crucified!” 23 Then he asked, “Why, Mt 1.16
what evil has he done?” But they shouted all the more, “Let him be crucified!” 27.24
24 So when Pilate saw that he could do nothing, but rather that a riot was begin- Deut 21.5-9 Ps 26.6
ning, he took some water and washed his hands before the crowd, saying, “I am 27.25
innocent of this man’s blood;[h] see to it yourselves.” 25 Then the people as a whole Deut 19.10 Acts 5.28
answered, “His blood be on us and on our children!” 26 So he released Barabbas for 27.26
them; and after flogging Jesus, he handed him over to be crucified. Isa 53.5

Roman soldiers mock Jesus
(233/Mark 15.16–20)

27 Then the soldiers of the governor took Jesus into the governor’s headquar- 27.28
ters,[i] and they gathered the whole cohort around him. 28 They stripped him and put Lk 23.11
a scarlet robe on him, 29 and after twisting some thorns into a crown, they put it on 27.29 Ps 69.19
his head. They put a reed in his right hand and knelt before him and mocked him, 27.30
saying, “Hail, King of the Jews!” 30 They spat on him, and took the reed and struck Job 30.10 Isa 50.6
him on the head. 31 After mocking him, they stripped him of the robe and put his 27.31
own clothes on him. Then they led him away to crucify him. Isa 53.8

Jesus is led away to be crucified
(234/Mark 15.21–24; Luke 23.26–31; John 19.17)

32 As they went out, they came upon a man from Cyrene named Simon; they 27.32 Mk 15.21-32
compelled this man to carry his cross. 33 And when they came to a place called Jn 19.17-24

[g] Or *the Christ* [h] Other ancient authorities read *this righteous blood*, or *this righteous man’s blood* [i] Gk *the praetorium*

27.24 At first Pilate hesitated to give the religious leaders permission to crucify Jesus. He thought they were simply jealous of a teacher who was more popular with the people than they were. But when the Jews threatened to report Pilate to Caesar (John 19.12), he became afraid. Historical records indicate that the Jews had already threatened to lodge a formal complaint against Pilate for his stubborn flouting of their traditions – and such a complaint would most likely have led to his recall by Rome. His job was in jeopardy. The Roman government could not afford to put large numbers of troops in all the regions under their control, so one of Pilate’s main duties was to do whatever was necessary to maintain peace.

27.24 In making no decision, Pilate made the decision to let the crowds crucify Jesus. Although he washed his hands, the guilt remained. Washing your hands of a tough situation doesn’t cancel your guilt. It merely gives you a false sense of peace. Don’t make excuses – take responsibility for the decisions you make.

27.27 A cohort was a division of the Roman legion, containing about 200 men.

27.29 People often make fun of Christians for their faith, but believers can take courage from the fact that Jesus himself was mocked as greatly as anyone. Taunting may hurt our feelings, but we should never let it change our faith (see 5.11, 12).

27.32 Condemned prisoners were forced to carry their own crosses to the execution site. Jesus, weakened from the beatings he had received, was physically unable to carry his cross any farther. Thus a bystander, Simon, was forced to do so. Simon was from Cyrene, in northern Africa, and was probably one of the thousands of Jews visiting Jerusalem for the Passover.

27.33 Golgotha was a regular place of execution in a prominent public place outside the city. Executions were held there as a deterrent to criminals.

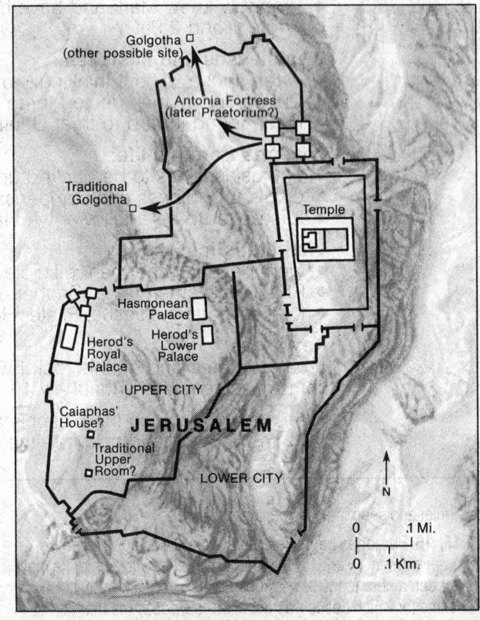

THE WAY OF THE CROSS The Roman soldiers took Jesus to the common hall (a part of the Praetorium) and mocked him, dressing him with a scarlet robe and a crown of thorns. They then led him to the crucifixion site outside the city. He was so weakened by his beatings that he could not carry his cross, and a man from Cyrene was forced to carry it to Golgotha.

27.34 Ps 69.21
27.35 Ps 22.18

Golgotha (which means Place of a Skull), 34 they offered him wine to drink, mixed with gall; but when he tasted it, he would not drink it. 35 And when they had crucified him, they divided his clothes among themselves by casting lots;[j] 36 then they sat down there and kept watch over him. 37 Over his head they put the charge against him, which read, "This is Jesus, the King of the Jews."

Jesus is placed on the cross
(235/Mark 15.25–32; Luke 23.32–43; John 19.18–27)

27.38 Isa 53.12
27.39 Ps 22.7,8
27.40 Mt 26.61 Jn 2.19

38 Then two bandits were crucified with him, one on his right and one on his left. 39 Those who passed by derided[k] him, shaking their heads 40 and saying, "You who would destroy the temple and build it in three days, save yourself! If you are the Son of God, come down from the cross." 41 In the same way the chief priests also, along with the scribes and elders, were mocking him, saying, 42 "He saved others; he cannot save himself.[l] He is the King of Israel; let him come down from the cross now, and we will believe in him. 43 He trusts in God; let God deliver him now, if he wants to; for he said, 'I am God's Son.' " 44 The bandits who were crucified with him also taunted him in the same way.

Jesus dies on the cross
(236/Mark 15.33–41; Luke 23.44–49; John 19.28–37)

27.45 Isa 50.3 Amos 8.9
27.46 Ps 22.1
27.48 Ps 69.21 Jn 19.29,30

45 From noon on, darkness came over the whole land[m] until three in the afternoon. 46 And about three o'clock Jesus cried with a loud voice, "Eli, Eli, lema sabachthani?" that is, "My God, my God, why have you forsaken me?" 47 When some of the bystanders heard it, they said, "This man is calling for Elijah." 48 At once one of them ran and got a sponge, filled it with sour wine, put it on a stick, and gave it to him to drink. 49 But the others said, "Wait, let us see whether Elijah will

[j] Other ancient authorities add *in order that what had been spoken through the prophet might be fulfilled, "They divided my clothes among themselves, and for my clothing they cast lots."* [k] Or *blasphemed* [l] Or *is he unable to save himself?* [m] Or *earth*

THE SEVEN LAST WORDS OF JESUS ON THE CROSS

"Father, forgive them; for they do not know what they are doing."	Luke 23.34
"Truly I tell you, today you will be with me in Paradise."	Luke 23.43
Speaking to John and Mary, "Woman, here is your son! . . . Here is your mother."	John 19.26, 27
"My God, my God, why have you forsaken me?"	Matthew 27.46; Mark 15.34
"I am thirsty."	John 19.28
"It is finished."	John 19.30
"Father, into your hands I commend my spirit."	Luke 23.46

The statements that Jesus made from the cross have been treasured by all who have followed him as Lord. They demonstrate both his manhood and his divinity. They also capture the last moments of all that Jesus went through to gain our forgiveness.

27.34 Wine mixed with gall was offered to Jesus to help deaden his pain, but Jesus refused. Gall is generally understood to be a narcotic that was used to reduce the pain of the crucifixion. Jesus would suffer fully conscious and with a clear mind.

27.35 The soldiers customarily took the clothing of those they crucified. These soldiers threw dice and divided Jesus' clothing among themselves, fulfilling the prophecy made by David. Much of Psalm 22 parallels Jesus' crucifixion.

27.40 This accusation was used against Jesus in his trial by the Sanhedrin (26.61). How ironic that Jesus was in the very process of fulfilling his own prophecy. Because Jesus is the Son of God who always obeys the will of the Father, he did not come down from the cross.

27.44 Later one of these thieves repented. Jesus promised that the repentant thief would join him in Paradise (Luke 23.39–43).

27.45 We do not know how this darkness occurred, but it is clear that God caused it. Nature testified to the gravity of Jesus' death, while Jesus' friends and enemies alike fell silent in the encircling gloom. The darkness on that Friday afternoon was both physical and spiritual.

27.46 Jesus was not questioning God; he was quoting the first line of Psalm 22 – a deep expression of the anguish he felt when he took on the sins of the world, causing him to be separated from his Father. *This* was what Jesus dreaded as he prayed to God in the garden to take the cup from him (26.39). The physical agony was horrible, but even worse was the period of spiritual separation from God. Jesus suffered this double death so that we would never have to experience eternal separation from God.

27.47 The bystanders misinterpreted Jesus' words and thought he was calling for Elijah. Because Elijah ascended into heaven without dying (2 Kings 2.11), they thought he would return again to rescue them from great trouble (Malachi 4.5). At their annual Passover feast, each family set an extra place for Elijah in expectation of his return.

come to save him."[n] 50 Then Jesus cried again with a loud voice and breathed his
last.[o] 51 At that moment the curtain of the temple was torn in two, from top to 27.51 Ex 26.31-33
bottom. The earth shook, and the rocks were split. 52 The tombs also were opened, Heb 10.19,20
and many bodies of the saints who had fallen asleep were raised. 53 After his resur- 27.52
rection they came out of the tombs and entered the holy city and appeared to many. Ps 69.20
54 Now when the centurion and those with him, who were keeping watch over 27.54
Jesus, saw the earthquake and what took place, they were terrified and said, "Truly Ex 20.18-20
this man was God's Son!"[p]

55 Many women were also there, looking on from a distance; they had followed
Jesus from Galilee and had provided for him. 56 Among them were Mary Magda- 27.56
lene, and Mary the mother of James and Joseph, and the mother of the sons of Lk 8.2
Zebedee.

Jesus is laid in the tomb
(237/Mark 15.42–47; Luke 23.50–56; John 19.38–42)

57 When it was evening, there came a rich man from Arimathea, named Jo- 27.57
seph, who was also a disciple of Jesus. 58 He went to Pilate and asked for the body Mk 15.42-47 Lk 23.50-56
of Jesus; then Pilate ordered it to be given to him. 59 So Joseph took the body and Jn 19.38-42
wrapped it in a clean linen cloth 60 and laid it in his own new tomb, which he had 27.60
hewn in the rock. He then rolled a great stone to the door of the tomb and went Isa 53.9
away. 61 Mary Magdalene and the other Mary were there, sitting opposite the tomb.

Guards are posted at the tomb
(238)

62 The next day, that is, after the day of Preparation, the chief priests and the 27.62
Pharisees gathered before Pilate 63 and said, "Sir, we remember what that impostor Ps 2.1-6 27.63
said while he was still alive, 'After three days I will rise again.' 64 Therefore com- 2 Cor 6.8

[n] Other ancient authorities add *And another took a spear and pierced his side, and out came water and blood*
[o] Or *gave up his spirit* [p] Or *a son of God*

HOW JESUS' TRIAL WAS ILLEGAL

1. Even before the trial began, it had been determined that Jesus must die (John 11.50; Mark 14.1). There was no "innocent before being proven guilty" approach.
2. False witnesses were sought to testify against Jesus (Matthew 26.59). Usually the religious leaders went through an elaborate system of screening witnesses to insure justice.
3. No defense for Jesus was sought or allowed (Luke 22.67–71).
4. The trial was conducted by night (Luke 22.53–55), which was illegal according to the religious leaders' own laws.
5. The high priest put Jesus under oath, but then incriminated him for what he said (Matthew 26.63–66).
6. Cases involving such serious charges were to be tried only in the Sanhedrin's regular meeting place, not in the high priest's palace (Luke 22.54).

The religious leaders were not interested in giving Jesus a fair trial. In their minds, Jesus had to die. This blind obsession led them to pervert the justice they were appointed to protect. Here are many examples of the actions taken by the religious leaders that were illegal according to their own laws.

27.51 The temple had three main parts—the courts, the holy place (where only the priests could enter), and the most holy place (where only the high priest could enter, and then only once a year, to atone for the sins of the nation—Leviticus 16.1–35). The curtain separating the holy place from the most holy place was split in two at Christ's death, symbolizing that the barrier between God and people was removed. Now all people are free to approach God because of Christ's sacrifice for our sins (see Hebrews 9.1–14; 10.19–22).

27.52, 53 Christ's death was accompanied by at least four miraculous events: darkness, the splitting of the curtain in the temple, an earthquake, and dead people rising from their tombs. Jesus' death, therefore, could not have gone unnoticed. Everyone knew something significant had happened.

27.57, 58 Joseph of Arimathea was a secret follower of Jesus. He was a religious leader, an honored member of the Sanhedrin. In the past, Joseph had been afraid to speak against the religious leaders who opposed Jesus; now he was bold, courageously asking to take Jesus' body from the cross and bury it. The disciples who publicly followed Jesus had fled, but this Jewish leader, who followed Jesus in secret, came forward and did what was right.

27.60 The tomb where Jesus was laid was probably a man-made cave cut out of one of the many limestone hills in the area. These caves were often large enough to walk into.

27.64 The religious leaders took Jesus' resurrection claims more seriously than the disciples did. The disciples didn't remember Jesus' teaching about his resurrection (20.17–19); but the religious leaders did. Because of his claims, they were almost as afraid of Jesus after his death as when he was alive. They tried to take every precaution that his body would remain in the tomb.

mand the tomb to be made secure until the third day; otherwise his disciples may go
and steal him away, and tell the people, 'He has been raised from the dead,' and the
last deception would be worse than the first." 65 Pilate said to them, "You have a
27.66 Dan 6.17 guard[q] of soldiers; go, make it as secure as you can."[r] 66 So they went with the
guard and made the tomb secure by sealing the stone.

Jesus rises from the dead
(239/Mark 16.1–8; Luke 24.1–12; John 20.1–10)

28.1 Mk 16.1-11 **28** After the sabbath, as the first day of the week was dawning, Mary Magda-
Lk 24.1-11 lene and the other Mary went to see the tomb. 2 And suddenly there was a
Jn 20.1,2,11-18 great earthquake; for an angel of the Lord, descending from heaven, came and
28.3 Dan 7.9; 10.5,6 rolled back the stone and sat on it. 3 His appearance was like lightning, and his
Rev 1.16 clothing white as snow. 4 For fear of him the guards shook and became like dead
28.5 Rev 1.17,18 men. 5 But the angel said to the women, "Do not be afraid; I know that you are
28.6 looking for Jesus who was crucified. 6 He is not here; for he has been raised, as he
Mt 12.40; 16.21 17.23; 20.19 said. Come, see the place where he[s] lay. 7 Then go quickly and tell his disciples,
28.7 'He has been raised from the dead,[t] and indeed he is going ahead of you to Galilee;
Mk 16.7 there you will see him.' This is my message for you."

Jesus appears to the women
(241) 8 So they left the tomb quickly with fear and great joy, and ran to tell his
disciples.
28.10 9 Suddenly Jesus met them and said, "Greetings!" And they came to him, took hold
Jn 20.17 Rom 8.29 of his feet, and worshiped him. 10 Then Jesus said to them, "Do not be afraid; go
Heb 2.11 and tell my brothers to go to Galilee; there they will see me."

Religious leaders bribe the guards
(242)
11 While they were going, some of the guard went into the city and told the
chief priests everything that had happened. 12 After the priests[u] had assembled with
the elders, they devised a plan to give a large sum of money to the soldiers, 13 telling

[q] Or *Take a guard* [r] Gk *you know how* [s] Other ancient authorities read *the Lord* [t] Other ancient authorities lack *from the dead* [u] Gk *they*

27.66 The Pharisees were so afraid of Jesus' predictions about his resurrection that they made sure the tomb was thoroughly sealed and guarded. Because the tomb was hewn out of rock in the side of a hill, there was only one entrance. The tomb was sealed by stringing a cord across the stone that was rolled over the entrance. The cord was sealed at each end with clay. But the religious leaders took a further precaution, asking that guards be placed at the tomb's entrance. With such precautions, the only way the tomb could be empty would be for Jesus to rise from the dead. The Pharisees failed to understand that no rock, seal, guard, or army could prevent the Son of God from rising again.

28.1 The other Mary was not Jesus' mother. She could have been the wife of Cleopas (John 19.25). Or, if she was the mother of James and John, she may have been Jesus' aunt.

28.2 The stone was not rolled away so Jesus could get out, but so others could get in and see that Jesus had indeed risen from the dead, just as he had promised.

28.5–7 The angel who announced the good news of the resurrection to the women gave them four messages: (1) *Do not be afraid.* The reality of the resurrection brings joy, not fear. When you are afraid, remember the empty tomb. (2) *He is not here.* Jesus is not dead and is not to be looked for among the dead. He is alive, with his people. (3) *Come, see.* The women could check the evidence themselves. The tomb was empty then, and is empty today. The resurrection is a historical fact. (4) *Go quickly and tell.* They were to spread the joy of the resurrection. We too are to spread the good news about Jesus' resurrection.

28.6 Jesus' resurrection is the key to the Christian faith. Why? (1) Just as he promised, Jesus rose from the dead. We can be confident, therefore, that he will accomplish all he has promised. (2) Jesus' bodily resurrection shows us that the living Christ is ruler of God's eternal kingdom, not a false prophet or imposter. (3) We can be certain of our resurrection because he was resurrected. Death is not the end – there is future life. (4) The power that brought Jesus back to life is available to us to bring our spiritually dead selves back to life. (5) The resurrection is the basis for the church's witness to the world. Jesus is more than just a human leader; he is the Son of God.

28.10 By "brothers," Jesus meant his disciples. This showed that he had forgiven them, even after they had denied and deserted him. Their relationship would now be even stronger than before.

28.10 Jesus told the women to pass a message on to the disciples – that he would meet them in Galilee, as he had previously told them (Mark 14.28). But the disciples, afraid of the religious leaders, stayed hidden behind locked doors in Jerusalem (John 20.19). So Jesus met them first there (Luke 24.36) and then later in Galilee (John 21).

28.11–15 Jesus' resurrection was already causing a great stir in Jerusalem. A group of women was moving quickly through the streets, looking for the disciples to tell them the amazing news that Jesus was alive. At the same time, a group of religious leaders was plotting how to cover up the resurrection.

Today there is still a great stir over the resurrection, and there are still only two choices – to believe that Jesus rose from the dead, or to be closed to the truth – denying it, ignoring it, or rationalizing it away.

them, "You must say, 'His disciples came by night and stole him away while we
were asleep.' 14 If this comes to the governor's ears, we will satisfy him and keep
you out of trouble." 15 So they took the money and did as they were directed. And
this story is still told among the Jews to this day.

Jesus gives the great commission
(248/Mark 16.15–18)

16 Now the eleven disciples went to Galilee, to the mountain to which Jesus
had directed them. 17 When they saw him, they worshiped him; but some doubted.
18 And Jesus came and said to them, "All authority in heaven and on earth has been
given to me. 19 Go therefore and make disciples of all nations, baptizing them in the
name of the Father and of the Son and of the Holy Spirit, 20 and teaching them to
obey everything that I have commanded you. And remember, I am with you always, to the end of the age."[v]

28.18 Mt 26.64; Eph 1.19-22; 1 Pet 3.22
28.19 Lk 24.47; Acts 2.38,41,42
28.20 Mt 1.23; 18.20; Jn 14.17-20; Heb 13.5

[v] Other ancient authorities add *Amen*

28.18 God gave Jesus authority over heaven and earth. On the basis of that authority, Jesus told his disciples to make more disciples as they preached, baptized, and taught. With this same authority, Jesus still commands us to tell others the gospel and make them disciples for the kingdom.

28.18–20 When someone is dying or leaving us, his or her last words are very important. Jesus left the disciples with these last words of instruction: they were under his authority; they were to make more disciples; they were to baptize and teach them to obey him; he would be with them always. Whereas in previous missions Jesus had sent his disciples only to the Jews (10.5, 6), their mission from now on would be worldwide. Jesus is Lord of the earth, and he died for the sins of people from all nations.

We are to go—whether it is next door or to another country—and make disciples. It is not an option, but a command to all who call Jesus "Lord." We are not all evangelists, but we have all received gifts that we can use in helping to fulfill the great commission. As we obey we have comfort in the knowledge that Jesus is always with us.

28.19 Jesus' words affirm the reality of the trinity. Some people accuse theologians of making up the concept of the trinity and reading it into Scripture. As we see here, the concept comes directly from Jesus himself. He did not say baptize them into the *names,* but into the *name* of the Father, Son, and Holy Spirit. The word *trinity* does not occur in Scripture, but it well describes the three-in-one nature of the Father, Son, and Holy Spirit.

28.19 The disciples were to baptize people because baptism unites a believer with Jesus Christ in his death to sin and resurrection to new life. Baptism shows submission to Christ, willingness to live God's way, and identification with God's covenant people.

28.20 How is Jesus present with us? Jesus was with the disciples physically until he ascended into heaven, and then spiritually through the Holy Spirit (Acts 1.4). The Holy Spirit would be Jesus' presence that would never leave them (John 14.26). Jesus continues to be with us today through his Spirit.

28.20 The Old Testament prophecies and genealogies in the book of Matthew present Jesus' credentials for being King of the world—not a military or political leader as the disciples had originally hoped, but a spiritual King who can overcome all evil and reign in the heart of every person. If we refuse to serve the King faithfully, we are disloyal subjects, fit only to be banished from the kingdom. We must make Jesus King of our lives and worship him as our Savior, King, and Lord.

OLD TESTAMENT PASSAGES QUOTED BY CHRIST

New Testament	Old Testament	Occasion
Matthew 4.4	Deuteronomy 8.3	Temptation
Matthew 4.7	Deuteronomy 6.16	
Matthew 4.10	Deuteronomy 6.13	
Matthew 5.21	Exodus 20.13	Sermon on the Mount
Matthew 5.27	Exodus 20.14	
Luke 4.18, 19	Isaiah 61.1, 2	Hometown Sermon
Matthew 9.13	Hosea 6.6	Confrontations with the Jewish Rulers
Mark 10.7, 8	Genesis 2.24	
Mark 12.29, 30	Deuteronomy 6.4, 5	
Matthew 15.7-9	Isaiah 29.13	
John 8.17	Deuteronomy 17.6	
Luke 7.27	Malachi 3.1	Tribute to John
Matthew 21.16	Psalm 8.2	Triumphal Entry
Luke 19.46	Isaiah 56.7	Temple Cleansing
Matthew 21.42, 44	Psalm 118.22, 23	Parable about Israel
Mark 12.36	Psalm 110.1	Temple Question Session
John 15.25	Psalm 35.19; 69.4	Last Passover
Matthew 27.46	Psalm 22.1	On the Cross
Luke 23.46	Psalm 31.5	

The Gospel according to MARK

Herod the Great begins to rule 37 B.C. | *Jesus is born 6/5 B.C.* | *Escape to Egypt 5/4 B.C.* | *Herod the Great dies 4 B.C.* | *Return to Nazareth 4/3 B.C.* | *Jesus visits temple as a boy A.D. 6/7*

VITAL STATISTICS

PURPOSE:
To present the person, work, and teachings of Jesus

AUTHOR:
John Mark. He was not one of the 12 disciples but he accompanied Paul on his first missionary journey (Acts 13.13).

TO WHOM WRITTEN:
The Christians in Rome, where he wrote the Gospel

DATE WRITTEN:
Between A.D. 55 and 65

SETTING:
The Roman Empire under Tiberius Caesar. The Empire, with its common language and excellent transportation and communication systems, was ripe to hear Jesus' message, which spread quickly from nation to nation.

KEY VERSE:
"For the Son of man came not to be served but to serve, and to give his life a ransom for many" (10.45).

KEY PEOPLE:
Jesus, the 12 disciples, Pilate, the Jewish religious leaders

KEY PLACES:
Capernaum, Nazareth, Caesarea Philippi, Jericho, Bethany, Mount of Olives, Jerusalem, Golgotha

SPECIAL FEATURES:
Mark was the first Gospel written. The other Gospels quote all but 31 verses of Mark. Mark records more miracles than does any other Gospel.

EVERYONE wants to be a winner. Losers are those who finish any less than first. In direct contrast are the words of Jesus, "And whoever wishes to be first among you must be slave of all. For the Son of Man came not to be served but to serve, and to give his life a ransom for many" (10.44, 45). Jesus *is* the greatest—God incarnate, our Messiah—but he entered history as a servant.

This is the message of Mark. Written to encourage Roman Christians and to prove beyond a doubt that Jesus is the Messiah, Mark presents a rapid succession of vivid pictures of Jesus in action—his true identity revealed by what he does, not by what he says (18 miracles are described, and only four parables). It is Jesus on the move.

Omitting the birth of Jesus, Mark begins with John the Baptist's preaching. Then, moving quickly past Jesus' baptism, temptation in the desert, and call of the disciples, Mark takes us directly into his public ministry. We see Jesus confronting a demon, healing a leper, and forgiving and healing the paralyzed man lowered into his presence by friends.

Next, Jesus called Matthew and had dinner with him and his questionable associates. This incident initiated the conflict with the Pharisees and other religious leaders who condemned him for eating with sinners and breaking the sabbath.

In chapter 4, Mark pauses to give a sample of Jesus' teaching—the parable of the sower and the illustration of the mustard seed—and then plunges back into the action. Jesus calmed the waves, cast out demons, and healed Jairus's daughter.

After returning to Nazareth for a few days and experiencing rejection in his hometown, Jesus commissioned the disciples to spread the good news everywhere. Opposition from Herod and the Pharisees increased and John the Baptist was beheaded, but Jesus continued to move, feeding 5,000, reaching out to the Syrophoenician woman, healing the deaf man, and feeding 4,000.

Finally it was time to confront the disciples with his true identity. Did they really know who he was? Peter proclaimed him Messiah, but then promptly showed he did not understand Jesus' mission. After the transfiguration, Jesus continued to teach and heal, confronting the Pharisees about divorce and the rich young ruler about eternal life. Blind Bartimaeus was healed.

Events rapidly move toward a climax. The last supper, the betrayal, the crucifixion, and the resurrection are dramatically portrayed, along with more examples of Jesus' teachings. Mark shows us Jesus—moving, serving, sacrificing, and saving! As you read Mark, be ready for action, be open for God's move into your life, and be challenged to move into your world to serve.

Tiberius Caesar becomes emperor 14	*John's ministry begins 26*	*Jesus begins his ministry 26/27*	*Jesus chooses twelve disciples 28*	*Jesus feeds 5,000 29*	*Jesus is crucified, rises again, and ascends 30*

THE BLUEPRINT

A. BIRTH AND PREPARATION OF JESUS, THE SERVANT (1.1–13)

Jesus did not arrive unannounced or unexpected. The Old Testament prophets had clearly predicted the coming of a great One, sent by God himself, who would offer salvation and eternal peace to Israel and the entire world. Then came John the Baptist, who announced that the long-awaited Messiah had finally come and would soon be among the people. In God's work in the world today, Jesus does not come unannounced or unexpected. Yet many still reject him. We have the witness of the Bible, but some choose to ignore it as they ignored John the Baptist in his day.

B. MESSAGE AND MINISTRY OF JESUS, THE SERVANT (1.14—3.37)
1. Jesus' ministry in Galilee
2. Jesus' ministry beyond Galilee
3. Jesus' ministry in Jerusalem

Jesus had all the power of almighty God—he raised the dead, gave sight to the blind, restored deformed bodies, and quieted stormy seas. But with all this power, Jesus came to mankind as a servant. We can use his life as a pattern for how to live today. As Jesus served God and others, so should we.

C. DEATH AND RESURRECTION OF JESUS, THE SERVANT (14.1—16.20)

Jesus came as a servant, so many did not recognize or acknowledge him as the Messiah. We, too, must be careful we don't reject God or his will because it doesn't quite fit our image of how God should be.

MEGATHEMES

THEME	EXPLANATION	IMPORTANCE
Jesus Christ	Jesus Christ alone is the Son of God. In Mark, Jesus demonstrates his divinity by overcoming disease, demons, and death. Although he had the power to be king of the earth, Jesus chose to obey the Father and die for us.	When Jesus rose from the dead, he proved that he was God, that he could forgive sin, and that he has the power to change our lives. By trusting in him for forgiveness, we can begin a new life with him as our guide.
Servant	As the Messiah, Jesus fulfilled the prophecies of the Old Testament by coming to earth. He did not come as a conquering king; he came as a servant. He helped mankind by telling them about God and healing them. Even more, by giving his life as a sacrifice for sin, he did the ultimate act of service.	Because of Jesus' example, we should be willing to serve God and others. Real greatness in Christ's kingdom is shown by service and sacrifice. Ambition, love of power or position, should not be our motive; instead, we should do God's work because we love him.
Miracles	Mark records more of Jesus' miracles than sermons. Jesus is clearly a man of power and action, not just words. Jesus did miracles to convince the people who he was and to teach the disciples his true identity as God.	The more convinced we become that Jesus is God, the more we will see his power and his love. His mighty works show us he is able to save anyone regardless of his or her past. His miracles of forgiveness bring healing, wholeness, and changed lives to those who trust him.
Spreading the gospel	Jesus directed his public ministry to the Jews first. When the Jewish leaders opposed him, Jesus also went to the non-Jewish world, healing and preaching. Roman soldiers, Syrians, and other Gentiles heard the good news. Many believed and followed him. Jesus' final message to his disciples challenged them to go into all the world and preach the gospel of salvation.	Jesus crossed national, racial, and economic barriers to spread his good news. Jesus' message of faith and forgiveness is for the whole world—not just our church, neighborhood, or nation. We must reach out beyond our own people and needs to fulfill the worldwide vision of Jesus Christ that people everywhere might hear this great message and be saved from sin and death.

KEY PLACES IN MARK

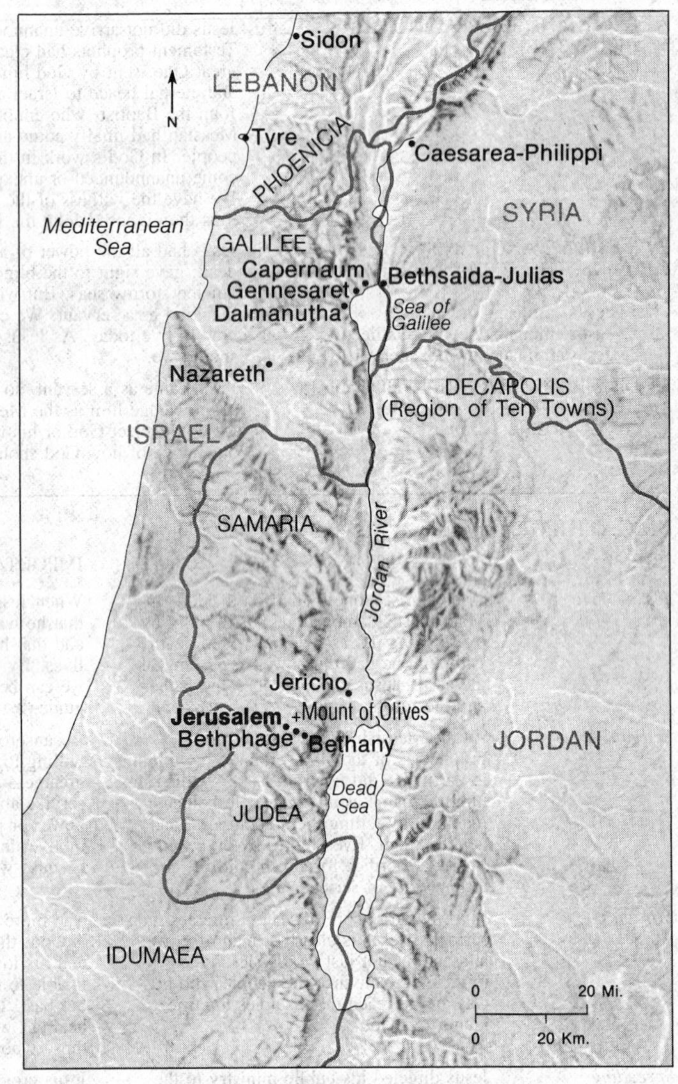

Of the four Gospels, Mark's narrative is the most chronological—that is, most of the stories are positioned in the order they actually occurred. Though the shortest of the four, the Gospel of Mark contains the most events; it is action-packed. Most of this action centers in Galilee, where Jesus began his ministry. Capernaum served as his base of operation (1.21; 2.1; 9.33), from which he would go out to cities like Bethsaida-Julias—where he healed a blind man (8.22ff); Gennesaret—where he performed many healings (6.53ff); Tyre and Sidon (to the far north)—where he cured many, cast out demons, and met the Syrophoenician woman (3.8; 7.24ff); and Caesarea-Philippi—where Peter declared him to be the Messiah (8.27ff). After his ministry in Galilee and the surrounding regions, Jesus headed for Jerusalem (10.1). Before going there, Jesus told his disciples three times that he would be crucified there and then come back to life (8.31; 9.31; 10.33, 34).

A. BIRTH AND PREPARATION OF JESUS, THE SERVANT (1.1–13)

Mark, the shortest of the four Gospels, opens with Jesus' baptism and temptation. Moving right into action, Mark quickly prepares us for Christ's ministry. The Gospel of Mark is concise, straightforward, and chronological.

John the Baptist prepares the way for Jesus
(16/Matthew 3.1–12; Luke 3.1–17)

1 The beginning of the good news[a] of Jesus Christ, the Son of God.[b]
2 As it is written in the prophet Isaiah,[c]
"See, I am sending my messenger ahead of you,[d]
who will prepare your way;
3 the voice of one crying out in the wilderness:
'Prepare the way of the Lord,
make his paths straight,' "
4 John the baptizer appeared[e] in the wilderness, proclaiming a baptism of repentance for the forgiveness of sins. 5 And people from the whole Judean countryside
and all the people of Jerusalem were going out to him, and were baptized by him in
the river Jordan, confessing their sins. 6 Now John was clothed with camel's hair,
with a leather belt around his waist, and he ate locusts and wild honey. 7 He

1.1 Ps 2.7 Mt 3.1-6,11 Lk 1.35 3.1-6,16 Jn 1.34 Rom 8.3 1 Jn 4.15
1.2,3 Isa 40.3 Mal 3.1 Jn 1.23
1.4 Acts 19.4
1.6 Lev 11.22
1.7 Jn 1.15

[a] Or *gospel* [b] Other ancient authorities lack *the Son of God* [c] Other ancient authorities read *in the prophets*
[d] Gk *before your face* [e] Other ancient authorities read *John was baptizing*

1.1 When you experience the excitement of a big event, you naturally want to tell someone. Telling the story can bring back that original thrill as you relive the experience. Reading Mark's first words, you can sense his excitement. Picture yourself in the crowd as Jesus heals and teaches. Imagine yourself as one of the disciples. Respond to his words of love and encouragement. And remember that Jesus came for us who live today as well as those who lived 2,000 years ago.

1.1 Mark was not one of the 12 disciples of Jesus, but he probably knew Jesus personally. He wrote his Gospel in the form of a fast-paced story, like a popular novel. The book portrays Jesus as a man who backed up his words with action that constantly proved who he is—the Son of God. Because he wrote the Gospel for Christians in Rome where many gods were worshiped, Mark wanted his readers to know that Jesus is *the one true* Son of God.

1.2 Why did Jesus come at this time in history? The entire civilized world was relatively peaceful under Roman rule, travel was easy, and there was a common language. The news about Jesus' life, death, and resurrection could spread quickly throughout the vast Roman Empire.

In Israel, common men and women were ready for Jesus too. There had been no God-sent prophets for 400 years, since the days of Malachi (who wrote the last book of the Old Testament). There was growing anticipation that a great prophet, or the Messiah mentioned in the Old Testament, would soon come (see Luke 3.15).

1.2, 3 Isaiah was one of the greatest prophets of the Old Testament. The second half of the book of Isaiah is devoted to the promise of salvation. Isaiah wrote about the coming of the Messiah, Jesus Christ, and the man who would announce his coming, John the Baptist ("the baptizer"). John's call to "make his paths straight" meant that people should give up their selfish way of living, renounce their sins, seek God's forgiveness, and establish a relationship with the almighty God by believing and obeying his words as found in the Bible (Isaiah 1.18–20; 57.15).

1.2, 3 Hundreds of years earlier, the prophet Isaiah had predicted that John the Baptist and Jesus would come. How did he know? God promised Isaiah that a Deliverer would come to Israel, and that a voice crying in the wilderness would prepare the way for him. Isaiah's words comforted many people as they looked forward to the Messiah, and knowing that God keeps his promises can comfort you too.

1.4 Why does the Gospel of Mark begin with the story of John the Baptist, not mentioning the story of Jesus' birth? Important Roman officials of this day were always preceded by an announcer or herald. When the herald arrived in town, the people knew that someone of prominence would soon arrive. Because Mark's audience was primarily Roman Christians, he began his book with John the Baptist, the one whose mission it was to announce the coming of Jesus, the most important man who ever lived. Roman Christians would have been less interested in Jesus' birth than in this herald.

1.4 John chose to live in the wilderness (1) to get away from distractions so he could hear God's instructions; (2) to capture the undivided attention of the people; (3) to symbolize a sharp break with the hypocrisy of the religious leaders who preferred their luxurious homes and positions of authority over doing God's work; (4) to fulfill Old Testament prophecies that said John would be a voice crying out in the wilderness (Isaiah 40.3).

1.4 In John's ministry, baptism was a visible sign that a person had decided to change his or her life, giving up a sinful and selfish way of living and turning to God. John took a known custom and gave it new meaning. The Jews often baptized non-Jews who had converted to Judaism. But to baptize a Jew as a sign of repentance was a radical departure from Jewish custom. The early church took baptism a step further, associating it with Jesus' death and resurrection (see, for example, Romans 6.3, 4; 1 Peter 3.21).

1.5 The purpose of John's preaching was to prepare people to accept Jesus as God's Son. When John challenged the people to confess sin individually, he signaled the start of a new approach to relating to God.

Is change needed in your life before you can hear and understand Jesus' message? You have to admit that you need forgiveness before you can accept it. To prepare to receive Christ, repent. Denounce the world's dead-end attractions, sinful temptations, and harmful attitudes.

1.6 John's clothes were not the latest style of his day. He dressed much like the prophet Elijah (2 Kings 1.8) in order to distinguish himself from the religious leaders whose long-flowing robes reflected their great pride in their position. John's striking appearance reinforced his striking message.

1.7, 8 Although John was the first genuine prophet in 400 years, Jesus the Messiah would be infinitely greater than he. John was pointing out how insignificant he was compared to the one who was coming. He was not even worthy of doing the most menial tasks for him, like untying his sandals. What John began, Jesus finished. What John prepared, Jesus fulfilled.

proclaimed, "The one who is more powerful than I is coming after me; I am not
worthy to stoop down and untie the thong of his sandals. 8 I have baptized you with[f] 1.8 Acts 2.4; 10.45
water; but he will baptize you with[f] the Holy Spirit."

John baptizes Jesus
(17/Matthew 3.13–17; Luke 3.21, 22)

9 In those days Jesus came from Nazareth of Galilee and was baptized by John 1.9 Mt 3.13-17
in the Jordan. 10 And just as he was coming up out of the water, he saw the heavens Lk 3.21,22
torn apart and the Spirit descending like a dove on him. 11 And a voice came from Jn 1.32-34
heaven, "You are my Son, the Beloved;[g] with you I am well pleased."

Satan tempts Jesus in the wilderness
(18/Matthew 4.1–11; Luke 4.1–13)

12 And the Spirit immediately drove him out into the wilderness. 13 He was in 1.12 Mt 4.1-11
the wilderness forty days, tempted by Satan; and he was with the wild beasts; and Lk 4.1-13
the angels waited on him. 1 Tim 3.16

[f] Or *in* [g] Or *my beloved Son*

1.8 John said Jesus would baptize with the Holy Spirit, sending the Holy Spirit to live within each believer. John's baptism with water prepared a person to receive Christ's message. It demonstrated humility and willingness to turn from sin. This was the *beginning* of the spiritual process.

When Jesus baptizes with the Holy Spirit, however, the entire person is transformed by the Spirit's power. Jesus offers to us both forgiveness of sin and the power to live for him.

1.9 If John's baptism was only for the forgiveness of sin, why was Jesus baptized? While even the greatest prophets (Isaiah, Jeremiah, Ezekiel) had to confess their sinfulness and need for repentance, Jesus didn't need to admit sin – he was sinless. Although Jesus didn't need forgiveness, he was baptized for the following reasons: (1) to begin his mission to bring the message of salvation to all people; (2) to show support for John's ministry; (3) to identify with our humanness and sin; (4) to give us an example to follow. John's baptism was different from Christian baptism in the church, because Paul had John's followers baptized again (see Acts 19.2–5).

1.9 Jesus grew up in Nazareth, where he had lived since he was a young boy (Matthew 2.22, 23). Nazareth was a small town in Galilee, located about halfway between the Sea of Galilee and the Mediterranean Sea. The city was despised and avoided by many Jews because it was an outpost for Roman troops in the region. Devout Jews hated the Romans for making them pay taxes and for showing no respect for God.

1.10, 11 The Spirit descended like a dove on Jesus, and the voice from heaven proclaimed the Father's approval of Jesus as his divine Son. That Jesus is God's divine Son is the foundation for all we read about Jesus in the Gospels. Here we see all three members of the trinity together – God the Father, God the Son, and God the Holy Spirit.

1.12, 13 Jesus left the crowds and went into the desert where he was tempted by Satan. Temptation is bad for us only when we give in. We should not hate or resent times of inner testing because through them God can strengthen our character and teach us valuable lessons. When you face Satan and must deal with his temptations and the turmoil he brings, remember Jesus. He used God's Word against Satan and won. You can do the same.

1.12, 13 Satan is an angel who rebelled against God. He is real, not symbolic, and is constantly working against God and those who obey him. He tempted Eve in the garden and persuaded her to sin; he tempted Jesus in the wilderness and did not persuade him to fall. To be tempted is not a sin. Tempting others or giving in to temptation *is* sin. For a more detailed account of Jesus' temptation, read Matthew 4.1–11.

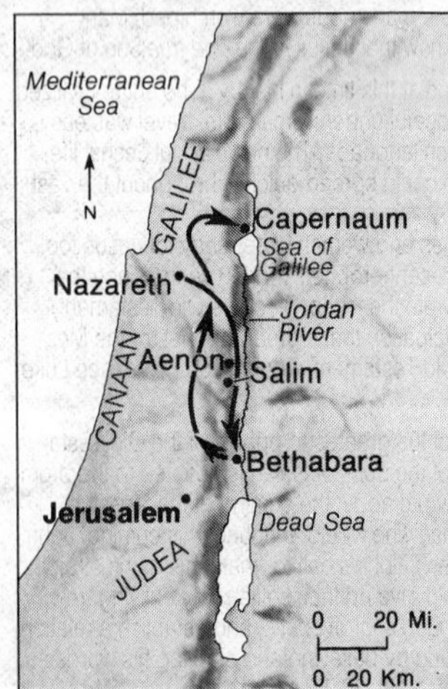

JESUS BEGINS HIS MINISTRY
When Jesus came from his home in Nazareth to begin his ministry, he first took two steps in preparation—baptism by John in the Jordan River, and temptation by Satan in the rough wilderness of Judea. After the temptations, Jesus returned to Galilee and later set up his home base in Capernaum.

1.12, 13 To identify fully with human beings, Jesus had to endure Satan's temptations. Although Jesus is God, he is also man. And as fully human, he was not exempt from Satan's attacks. Because Jesus faced temptations and overcame them, he can assist us in two important ways: (1) as an example of how to face temptation without sinning, and (2) as a helper who knows just what we need, because he went through the same experience. (See Hebrews 4.15 for more on Jesus and temptation.)

B. MESSAGE AND MINISTRY OF JESUS, THE SERVANT (1.14–13.37)

Mark tells us dramatic, action-packed stories. He gives us the most vivid account of Christ's activities. He features facts and actions, rather than teachings. Seeing Jesus live his life is the perfect example of how we should live our lives today.

1. Jesus' ministry in Galilee

Jesus preaches in Galilee

(30/Matthew 4.12–17; Luke 4.14, 15; John 4.43–45)

14 Now after John was arrested, Jesus came to Galilee, proclaiming the good
1.15 Dan 2.44; 9.24,25 news[h] of God,[i] 15 and saying, "The time is fulfilled, and the kingdom of God has
Gal 4.4 come near;[j] repent, and believe in the good news."[h]

Four fishermen follow Jesus

(33/Matthew 4.18–22)

1.16 Mt 4.18-22 16 As Jesus passed along the Sea of Galilee, he saw Simon and his brother
Lk 5.1-11 Andrew casting a net into the sea—for they were fishermen. 17 And Jesus said to
Jn 1.35-42 them, "Follow me and I will make you fish for people." 18 And immediately they
1.18 Mt 19.27 left their nets and followed him. 19 As he went a little farther, he saw James son of
Zebedee and his brother John, who were in their boat mending the nets. 20 Immediately he called them; and they left their father Zebedee in the boat with the hired
men, and followed him.

Jesus teaches with great authority

(34/Luke 4.31–37)

1.21 Lk 4.31-41 21 They went to Capernaum; and when the sabbath came, he entered the synagogue and taught. 22 They were astounded at his teaching, for he taught them as one
1.24 Jn 6.69 having authority, and not as the scribes. 23 Just then there was in their synagogue a
Acts 3.14 man with an unclean spirit, 24 and he cried out, "What have you to do with us, Jesus
Jas 2.19 of Nazareth? Have you come to destroy us? I know who you are, the Holy One of

[h] Or *gospel* [i] Other ancient authorities read *of the kingdom* [j] Or *is at hand*

1.14, 15 What is the good news of the kingdom of God? These first words spoken by Jesus in Mark give the core of his teaching: that the long-awaited Messiah has come to break the power of sin and begin God's personal reign on earth. Most of the people who heard this message were oppressed, poor, and without hope. Jesus' words were good news because they offered freedom, justice, and hope.

1.16 Fishing was a major industry around the Sea of Galilee. Fishing with nets was the most common method. Capernaum, the largest of the more than 30 fishing towns around the sea at that time, became Jesus' new home (Matthew 4.12, 13).

1.16–20 We often assume that Jesus' disciples were great men of faith from the first time they met Jesus. But they had to grow in their faith just as all believers do (14.48–50, 66–72; John 14.1–9; 20.26–29). This is apparently not the only time Jesus called Peter (Simon), James, and John to follow him (see Luke 5.1–11 and John 1.35–42 for two other times). Although it took time for Jesus' call and his message to get through, the disciples *followed.* In the same way, we may question and falter, but we must never stop following Jesus.

1.21 Because the temple in Jerusalem was too far for many Jews to travel to regularly for worship, many towns had synagogues serving both as places of worship and as schools. Beginning in the days of Ezra, about 450 B.C., a group of ten Jewish families could start a synagogue. There, during the week, Jewish boys were taught the Old Testament law and Jewish religion. Girls could not attend. Each Saturday, the sabbath, the Jewish men would gather to listen to a rabbi teach from God's Word. Because there was no permanent rabbi or teacher, it was customary for the synagogue leader to ask visiting teachers to speak. This is why Jesus often spoke in the synagogues in the towns he visited.

1.21 Jesus had recently moved to Capernaum from Nazareth (Matthew 4.12, 13). Capernaum was a thriving town with great wealth as well as great sin and decadence. Because it was the headquarters for many Roman troops, pagan influences from all over the Roman Empire were pervasive. This was an ideal place for Jesus to challenge both Jews and non-Jews with the gospel of God's kingdom.

1.22 The Jewish teachers often quoted from well-known rabbis to give their words more authority. But Jesus didn't have that need. Because he was God, he knew exactly what the Scriptures said and meant. He was the ultimate authority.

1.23 Unclean spirits, or demons, are evil spirits ruled by Satan. They work to tempt people to sin. They were not created by Satan, because God is the Creator of all; rather they are fallen angels who joined Satan in his rebellion. They can cause a person to become mute, deaf, blind, or insane. But in every case where they confronted Jesus, they lost their power. Thus God limits what they can do; they can do nothing without his permission. During Jesus' life on earth, demons were allowed to be very active to show once and for all Christ's power and authority over them.

1.23ff Many psychologists dismiss all accounts of demon possession as a primitive way to describe mental illness. Although throughout history, mental illness has often been wrongly diagnosed as demon possession, clearly a hostile outside force controlled the man described here. Mark emphasizes Jesus' conflict with evil powers to show his superiority over them, and so he records many stories about Jesus casting out demons. Jesus didn't have to conduct an elaborate exorcism ritual. His word was enough to send out the demons.

1.23, 24 The unclean spirit knew at once that Jesus was the Son (Holy One) of God. By including this event in his Gospel, Mark was establishing Jesus' credentials, showing that even the spiritual underworld recognized Jesus as the Messiah.

God." 25 But Jesus rebuked him, saying, "Be silent, and come out of him!" 26 And **1.26**
the unclean spirit, convulsing him and crying with a loud voice, came out of him. Mk 9.20
27 They were all amazed, and they kept on asking one another, "What is this? A new
teaching—with authority! He[k] commands even the unclean spirits, and they obey
him." 28 At once his fame began to spread throughout the surrounding region of
Galilee.

Jesus heals Peter's mother-in-law and many others
(35/Matthew 8.14–17; Luke 4.38–41)

29 As soon as they[l] left the synagogue, they entered the house of Simon and **1.29**
Andrew, with James and John. 30 Now Simon's mother-in-law was in bed with a Mt 8.14-17 Lk 4.18-31
fever, and they told him about her at once. 31 He came and took her by the hand and
lifted her up. Then the fever left her, and she began to serve them.

32 That evening, at sundown, they brought to him all who were sick or pos- **1.32** Mt 8.16,17
sessed with demons. 33 And the whole city was gathered around the door. 34 And he Lk 4.40,41
cured many who were sick with various diseases, and cast out many demons; and **1.34** Mk 3.12
he would not permit the demons to speak, because they knew him. Acts 16.16,17

Jesus preaches throughout Galilee
(36/Matthew 4.23–25; Luke 4.42–44)

35 In the morning, while it was still very dark, he got up and went out to a **1.35**
deserted place, and there he prayed. 36 And Simon and his companions hunted for Lk 4.42-44 Heb 5.7
him. 37 When they found him, they said to him, "Everyone is searching for you."
38 He answered, "Let us go on to the neighboring towns, so that I may proclaim the **1.38** Isa 61.1
message there also; for that is what I came out to do." 39 And he went throughout **1.39**
Galilee, proclaiming the message in their synagogues and casting out demons. Mt 4.23

Jesus heals a man with leprosy
(38/Matthew 8.1–4; Luke 5.12–16)

40 A leper[m] came to him begging him, and kneeling[n] he said to him, "If you **1.40** Jer 32.17
choose, you can make me clean." 41 Moved with pity,[o] Jesus[p] stretched out his Mt 8.2-4
hand and touched him, and said to him, "I do choose. Be made clean!" 42 Immedi- Lk 5.12-16 **1.41**
ately the leprosy[m] left him, and he was made clean. 43 After sternly warning him he Heb 2.17; 4.15

[k] Or *A new teaching! With authority he* [l] Other ancient authorities read *he* [m] The terms *leper* and *leprosy* can refer to several diseases [n] Other ancient authorities lack *kneeling* [o] Other ancient authorities read *anger* [p] Gk *he*

1.29–31 Each Gospel writer had a slightly different perspective as he wrote; thus the comparable stories in the Gospels often highlight different details. In Matthew, Jesus touched the woman's hand. In Mark, he helped her sit up. In Luke, he spoke to the fever and it left her. The accounts do not conflict. Each writer chose to emphasize different details of the story in order to highlight a certain characteristic of Jesus.

1.32, 33 The people came to Jesus in the evening as the sun was setting. This was the sabbath (1.21), their day of rest, lasting from sunset Friday to sunset Saturday. The Jewish leaders had proclaimed that it was against the law to be healed on the sabbath (Matthew 12.10; Luke 13.14). The people didn't want to break this law or the Jewish law that prohibited traveling on the sabbath, so they waited until sunset. After the sun went down, the crowds were free to find Jesus so he could heal them.

1.34 Why didn't Jesus want the demons to reveal who he was? (1) By commanding the demons to remain silent, he proved his authority and power over them. (2) Jesus wanted the people to believe he was the Messiah because of what he said and did, not because of the demons' words. (3) He wanted to reveal his identity as the Messiah according to his timetable, not according to Satan's timetable. Satan wanted the people to follow Jesus for what they could get out of him, not because he was the Son of God.

1.35 Jesus took time to pray. Finding time to pray is not easy, but prayer is the vital link between us and God. Like Jesus, we must find time away from others to talk with God, even if we have to get up before daybreak to do it!

1.39 The Romans divided the land of Israel into three separate regions: Galilee, Samaria, and Judea. Galilee was the northernmost region, an area about 60 miles long and 30 miles wide. Jesus did much of his ministry in this area, an ideal place for him to teach because there were over 250 towns concentrated there, with many synagogues.

1.40, 41 Following the law in Leviticus 13 and 14, Jewish leaders declared lepers unclean. This meant they were unfit to participate in any religious or social activity. Because the law said that contact with any unclean person made them unclean too, some people even threw rocks at lepers to keep them at a safe distance. Even the name of this disabling disease terrified people. But Jesus touched this leper.

The real value of a person is inside, not outside. Although a person's body may be diseased or deformed, the person inside is no less valuable to God. No person is too disgusting for his touch. In a sense, we are all lepers, because we have all been deformed by the ugliness of sin. But God, by sending his Son Jesus, has touched us, giving us the opportunity to be healed. When you feel repulsed by someone, stop and remember how God feels about that person—and about you.

1.43, 44 Although leprosy was incurable, many different types of skin diseases were classified together as "leprosy." According to the Old Testament laws about leprosy (Leviticus 13, 14), when a leper was cured, he or she had to go to a priest to be examined.

1.44 Lev 14.1-32 sent him away at once, 44 saying to him, "See that you say nothing to anyone; but
go, show yourself to the priest, and offer for your cleansing what Moses com-
1.45 Mk 3.7; 6.31-34 manded, as a testimony to them." 45 But he went out and began to proclaim it
freely, and to spread the word, so that Jesus[q] could no longer go into a town
openly, but stayed out in the country; and people came to him from every quarter.

Jesus heals a paralyzed man
(39/Matthew 9.2–8; Luke 5.17–26)

2.1 Mt 9.1-8 Lk 5.17-26 **2** When he returned to Capernaum after some days, it was reported that he was
at home. 2 So many gathered around that there was no longer room for them,
2.2 Eph 2.17 Heb 2.3 not even in front of the door; and he was speaking the word to them. 3 Then some
people[r] came, bringing to him a paralyzed man, carried by four of them. 4 And
when they could not bring him to Jesus because of the crowd, they removed the
roof above him; and after having dug through it, they let down the mat on which the
2.5 Ps 103.3 paralytic lay. 5 When Jesus saw their faith, he said to the paralytic, "Son, your sins
are forgiven." 6 Now some of the scribes were sitting there, questioning in their
2.7 Ps 130.4 Isa 43.25 Rom 8.33 hearts, 7 "Why does this fellow speak in this way? It is blasphemy! Who can forgive
sins but God alone?" 8 At once Jesus perceived in his spirit that they were discuss-
ing these questions among themselves; and he said to them, "Why do you raise
2.8 Heb 4.13 such questions in your hearts? 9 Which is easier, to say to the paralytic, 'Your sins
are forgiven,' or to say, 'Stand up and take your mat and walk'? 10 But so that you
may know that the Son of Man has authority on earth to forgive sins"—he said to
the paralytic— 11 "I say to you, stand up, take your mat and go to your home."
2.12 Mt 9.33 12 And he stood up, and immediately took the mat and went out before all of them;
so that they were all amazed and glorified God, saying, "We have never seen anything like this!"

Jesus eats with sinners at Matthew's house
(40/Matthew 9.9–13; Luke 5.27–32)

2.13 Mt 9.9-13 Lk 5.27-32 13 Jesus[s] went out again beside the sea; the whole crowd gathered around him,
and he taught them. 14 As he was walking along, he saw Levi son of Alphaeus

[q] Gk *he* [r] Gk *they* [s] Gk *He*

Then the leper was to give a thank offering at the temple. Jesus adhered to these laws by sending the man to the priest, demonstrating his complete regard for God's law. Sending a healed leper to a priest was also a way to verify Jesus' great miracle to the community.

2.3 The paralyzed man's need moved his friends to action, and they brought him to Jesus. When you recognize someone's need, do you act? Many people have physical and spiritual needs you can meet, either by yourself or with others who are also concerned. Human need moved these four men; let it also move you to compassionate action.

2.4 Houses in Bible times were built of stone. They had flat roofs made of mud mixed with straw. Outside stairways led to the roofs. These friends may have carried the lame man up the outside stairs to the roof. They then could easily have taken apart the mud and straw mixture to make a hole through which to lower their friend to Jesus.

2.5–7 Before saying to the paralyzed man, "Stand up," Jesus said, "Your sins are forgiven." To the Jewish leaders this was blasphemy, claiming to do something only God could do. According to the law, the punishment for this sin was death (Leviticus 24.15, 16).

The religious leaders understood correctly that Jesus was claiming divine prerogatives, but their judgment of him was wrong. Jesus was not blaspheming, because his claim was true. Jesus is God, and he proved his claim by healing the paralyzed man (2.9–12).

2.10 This is the first time in Mark that Jesus calls himself the "Son of Man." The title *Son of Man* emphasizes that Jesus is fully human, while *Son of God* (see, for example, John 20.31) emphasizes that he is fully God. As God's Son, Jesus has the authority to forgive sin. As a man, he can identify with our deepest needs and sufferings and help us overcome sin.

2.14 Levi is another name for Matthew, the disciple who wrote the Gospel of Matthew. See Matthew's Profile in Matthew 9 for more information.

2.14 Capernaum was a key military center for Roman troops as well as a thriving business community. Several major highways intersected in Capernaum, with merchants passing through from as far away as Egypt to the south and Mesopotamia to the north.

Matthew, a Jew, was appointed by the Romans to be the area's tax collector. He collected taxes from citizens as well as from merchants passing through town. Tax collectors were expected to take a commission on the taxes they collected. Most of them overcharged and vastly enriched themselves. Tax collectors were hated by the Jews because of their reputation for cheating and their support of Rome. The Jews also hated to think that some of the money collected went to support pagan religions and temples.

2.14, 15 The day that Levi met Jesus, he held a meeting at his house to introduce others to him. He didn't waste any time starting to witness! Some people feel that new believers should wait for maturity or training before they start telling others about Jesus. But like Levi, new believers can share their faith right away with whatever knowledge, skill, or experience they already have.

sitting at the tax booth, and he said to him, "Follow me." And he got up and followed him.

15 And as he sat at dinner[t] in Levi's[u] house, many tax collectors and sinners
were also sitting[v] with Jesus and his disciples — for there were many who followed
him. 16 When the scribes of[w] the Pharisees saw that he was eating with sinners and 2.16 Isa 65.5
tax collectors, they said to his disciples, "Why does he eat[x] with tax collectors and
sinners?" 17 When Jesus heard this, he said to them, "Those who are well have no 2.17 Mt 18.11 Lk 19.9,10 1 Tim 1.15
need of a physician, but those who are sick; I have come to call not the righteous but
sinners."

Religious leaders ask Jesus about fasting
(41/Matthew 9.14–17; Luke 5.33–39)

18 Now John's disciples and the Pharisees were fasting; and people[y] came and 2.18 Mt 9.14-17 Lk 5.33-39
said to him, "Why do John's disciples and the disciples of the Pharisees fast, but
your disciples do not fast?" 19 Jesus said to them, "The wedding guests cannot fast 2.19 Isa 54.5 Jn 3.29 Rev 19.7
while the bridegroom is with them, can they? As long as they have the bridegroom
with them, they cannot fast. 20 The days will come when the bridegroom is taken
away from them, and then they will fast on that day.
21 "No one sews a piece of unshrunk cloth on an old cloak; otherwise, the patch
pulls away from it, the new from the old, and a worse tear is made. 22 And no one 2.22 Gal 3.1-3
puts new wine into old wineskins; otherwise, the wine will burst the skins, and the
wine is lost, and so are the skins; but one puts new wine into fresh wineskins."[z]

The disciples pick wheat on the sabbath
(45/Matthew 12.1–8; Luke 6.1–5)

23 One sabbath he was going through the grainfields; and as they made their 2.23 Deut 23.25 Mt 12.1-8 Lk 6.1-5
way his disciples began to pluck heads of grain. 24 The Pharisees said to him,
"Look, why are they doing what is not lawful on the sabbath?" 25 And he said to

[t] Gk *reclined* [u] Gk *his* [v] Gk *reclining* [w] Other ancient authorities read *and* [x] Other ancient authorities add *and drink* [y] Gk *they* [z] Other ancient authorities lack *but one puts new wine into fresh wineskins*

2.16, 17 "Tax collectors and sinners – such scum!" the self-righteous Pharisees must have said, describing the people with whom Jesus ate. But Jesus associated with sinners because he loved them and because he knew they needed to hear what he had to say. He spent time with whoever needed or wanted to hear his message – poor, rich, bad, good. We, too, must befriend those who need Christ, even if they do not seem to be ideal companions. Are there people you have been neglecting because of their reputation? They may be the ones who most need to see and hear the message of Christ's love from you.

2.18ff John had two goals: to cause people to repent of their sin, and to prepare them for Christ's coming. His was a sobering message, and so he and his followers fasted. Fasting is both an outward sign of humility and regret for sin, and an inner discipline that clears the mind and keeps the spirit alert. Fasting empties the body of food; repentance empties the life of sin. Jesus' disciples did not need to fast to prepare for his coming, because he was with them. Jesus did not condemn fasting, however. He himself fasted for 40 days (Matthew 4.2). Nevertheless, he emphasized fasting with the right motives. The Pharisees fasted twice a week to show how holy they were. Jesus explained that if people fast only to impress others, they have twisted the purpose of fasting.

2.19 Jesus compared himself to a bridegroom. In the Bible, the image of a bride is often used for God's people, and the image of a bridegroom for the God who loves them (Isaiah 62.5; Matthew 25.1–14; Revelation 21.2).

2.22 A wine bottle was a goatskin sewed together at the edges to form a watertight bag. New wine, expanding as it aged, stretched the wineskin. New wine, therefore, could not be put into a wineskin that had already been stretched, or the taut skin would burst.

The Pharisees had become rigid like old wineskins. They could not accept faith in Jesus which cannot be contained or limited by man-made ideas or rules. Your heart, like a wineskin, can become rigid and prevent you from accepting the new life that Christ offers. Keep your heart pliable and open to accepting the life-changing truths of Jesus' message.

2.23 Jesus and his disciples were not stealing when they picked the grain. Leviticus 19.9, 10 and Deuteronomy 23.25 say that farmers were to leave the corners and edges of their fields unharvested so that some of their crop could be picked by travelers and by the poor. Just as walking on a sidewalk is not trespassing on private property, eating grain at the edge of a field was not stealing.

2.24 God's law said that crops should not be harvested on the sabbath (Exodus 34.21). This law prevented farmers from becoming greedy and ignoring God on the sabbath. It also protected laborers from being overworked.

The Pharisees interpreted the action of Jesus and his disciples – picking the grain and eating it as they walked through the fields – as harvesting; and so they judged Jesus a lawbreaker. But Jesus and the disciples clearly were not picking the grain for personal gain; they were simply looking for something to eat. The Pharisees focused so intently on the words of the rule that they missed its intent.

2.24 Many of the Pharisees were so caught up in their man-made laws that they lost sight of what was good and right. Jesus implies in Mark 3.4 that the sabbath is a day to do good. God provided the sabbath as a day of rest and worship, but he didn't mean that concern for rest should keep us from lifting a finger to help others. Don't allow your sabbath to become a time of selfish indulgence.

2.25–28 Jesus used the example of David to point out how ridiculous the Pharisees' accusations were (this incident occurred in 1 Samuel 21.1–6). God created the sabbath for our benefit, not his

2.25 Ex 25.30 29.32,33 Lev 24.9 1 Sam 21.1-6
2.27 Ex 23.12 Deut 5.14 Jn 7.21-24

them, "Have you never read what David did when he and his companions were
hungry and in need of food? 26 He entered the house of God, when Abiathar was
high priest, and ate the bread of the Presence, which it is not lawful for any but the
priests to eat, and he gave some to his companions." 27 Then he said to them, "The
sabbath was made for humankind, and not humankind for the sabbath; 28 so the Son
of Man is lord even of the sabbath."

Jesus heals a man's hand on the sabbath
(46/Matthew 12.9–14; Luke 6.6–11)

3.1 Mt 12.9-16 Lk 6.6-11,17-19

3 Again he entered the synagogue, and a man was there who had a withered
hand. 2 They watched him to see whether he would cure him on the sabbath, so
that they might accuse him. 3 And he said to the man who had the withered hand,

PROMINENT JEWISH RELIGIOUS AND POLITICAL GROUPS

Name and Selected References	Description	Agreement with Jesus	Disagreement with Jesus
PHARISEES Matthew 5.20 Matthew 23.1–36 Luke 6.2 Luke 7.36–47	Strict religious group of Jews, who advocated minute obedience to the Jewish law and traditions. Very influential in the synagogues.	Respect for the law, belief in the resurrection of the dead, committed to obeying God's will.	Rejected Jesus' claim to be Messiah because he did not follow all their traditions and associated with notoriously wicked people.
SADDUCEES Matthew 3.7 Matthew 16.11, 12 Mark 12.18	Wealthy, upper class, Jewish priestly party. Rejected the authority of the Bible beyond the five books of Moses. Profited from business in the temple. They, along with the Pharisees, were the two major parties of the Jewish council.	Showed great respect for the five books of Moses, as well as the sanctity of the temple.	Denied the resurrection of the dead. Thought the temple could also be used as a place to transact business.
SCRIBES Matthew 7.29 Mark 2.6 Mark 2.16	Professional interpreters of the law—who especially emphasized the traditions. Many scribes were Pharisees.	Respect for the law. Committed to obeying God.	Denied Jesus' authority to reinterpret the law. Rejected Jesus as Messiah because he did not obey all of their traditions.
HERODIANS Matthew 22.16 Mark 3.6 Mark 12.13	A Jewish political party of King Herod's supporters.	Unknown. In the Gospels they tried to trap Jesus with questions and plotted to kill him.	Afraid of Jesus causing political instability. They saw Jesus as a threat to their political future, at a time when they were trying to regain from Rome some of their lost political power.
ZEALOTS Luke 6.15 Acts 1.14	A fiercely dedicated group of Jewish patriots determined to end Roman rule in Israel.	Concerned about the future of Israel. Believed in the Messiah but did not recognize Jesus as the One sent by God.	Believed that the Messiah must be a political leader who would deliver Israel from Roman occupation.
ESSENES none	Jewish monastic group practicing ritual purity and personal holiness.	Emphasized justice, honesty, commitment.	Believed ceremonial rituals made them righteous.

own. We are restored both physically and spiritually when we take time to rest and focus on God. For the Pharisees, sabbath laws had become more important than sabbath rest. Both David and Jesus understood that the intent of God's law is to promote love for God and others. When we apply a law to other people, we should make sure we understand its purpose and intent so we don't make harmful or inappropriate judgments.

2.26 The bread of the Presence was the bread set before God in the tabernacle. Every sabbath, 12 baked loaves of bread were placed on the table in the holy place. Then the priests ate the old ones. (See Exodus 25.30 and Leviticus 24.5–9.)

3.2 Already the Pharisees had turned against Jesus. They were jealous of his popularity, his miracles, and his speaking authority. They valued their status in the community and their opportunity for personal gain so much that they lost sight of their goal as religious leaders – to point people toward God. They refused to acknowledge him because they were not willing to give up their treasured position and power. When Jesus exposed their attitudes, he became their enemy instead of their Messiah, and they began looking for ways to turn the people against him.

"Come forward." [4]Then he said to them, "Is it lawful to do good or to do harm on
the sabbath, to save life or to kill?" But they were silent. [5]He looked around at them
with anger; he was grieved at their hardness of heart and said to the man, "Stretch
out your hand." He stretched it out, and his hand was restored. [6]The Pharisees went 3.6
out and immediately conspired with the Herodians against him, how to destroy Mt 22.16
him.

Large crowds follow Jesus
(47/Matthew 12.15–21)

7 Jesus departed with his disciples to the sea, and a great multitude from Galilee 3.7
followed him; [8]hearing all that he was doing, they came to him in great numbers Mt 12.15-21 Lk 6.17-19
from Judea, Jerusalem, Idumea, beyond the Jordan, and the region around Tyre
and Sidon. [9]He told his disciples to have a boat ready for him because of the crowd,
so that they would not crush him; [10]for he had cured many, so that all who had
diseases pressed upon him to touch him. [11]Whenever the unclean spirits saw him, 3.11
they fell down before him and shouted, "You are the Son of God!" [12]But he sternly Mk 1.24,25,34 Lk 4.41
ordered them not to make him known. Acts 16.16,17

Jesus selects the twelve disciples
(48/Luke 6.12–16)

13 He went up the mountain and called to him those whom he wanted, and they 3.13
came to him. [14]And he appointed twelve, whom he also named apostles,[a] to be Mt 10.2-4 Lk 6.12-16
with him, and to be sent out to proclaim the message, [15]and to have authority to cast 3.14
out demons. [16]So he appointed the twelve:[b] Simon (to whom he gave the name Lk 9.1
Peter); [17]James son of Zebedee and John the brother of James (to whom he gave the 3.16 Jn 1.42
name Boanerges, that is, Sons of Thunder); [18]and Andrew, and Philip, and Bartholomew, and Matthew, and Thomas, and James son of Alphaeus, and Thaddaeus, and Simon the Cananaean, [19]and Judas Iscariot, who betrayed him.

[a] Other ancient authorities lack *whom he also named apostles* [b] Other ancient authorities lack *So he appointed the twelve*

3.5 Jesus was angry about the Pharisees' uncaring attitudes. Anger itself is not wrong. It depends on what makes us angry and what we do with our anger. Too often we express our anger in selfish and harmful ways. By contrast, Jesus expressed his anger by correcting a problem—healing the man's hand. Use your anger to find constructive solutions rather than tear people down.

3.6 The Pharisees were a Jewish religious group who zealously followed the Old Testament laws as well as their own religious traditions. They were highly respected in the community, but they hated Jesus because he challenged their proud attitudes and dishonorable motives.

The Herodians were a Jewish political party that hoped to restore Herod the Great's line to the throne. Jesus was a threat to them as well because he challenged their political ambitions. The Pharisees and Herodians, normally enemies, joined forces against Jesus because he exposed them for what they were.

3.6 The Pharisees accused Jesus of breaking their law that said medical attention could be given to no one on the sabbath except in matters of life and death. Ironically, the Pharisees themselves were breaking God's law by plotting murder.

3.7, 8 While Jesus was drawing fire from the religious leaders, he was gaining great popularity among the people. Some were curious, some sought healing, some wanted evidence to use against him, and others wanted to know if he truly was the Messiah. Most of them only dimly guessed the real meaning of what was happening among them. Today crowds still follow Jesus, and they come for the same variety of reasons. What is your primary reason for following Jesus?

3.11 The unclean spirits knew that Jesus was God's Son, but they refused to turn from their evil purpose. Knowing about Jesus, or even believing that he is God's Son, does not guarantee salvation. You must also want to follow and obey him (see also James 2.17).

3.12 Jesus warned the unclean spirits not to reveal his identity, because he did not want them to reinforce a popular misconception. The huge crowds were looking for a political and military leader who would free them from Rome's control, and they thought the Messiah predicted by the Old Testament prophets would be this kind of man. Jesus wanted to teach the people about the kind of Messiah he really was—far different from their expectations. His kingdom is spiritual. It begins not with the overthrow of governments, but with the overthrow of sin in people's hearts.

3.14 From the hundreds of people who followed him from place to place, Jesus chose 12 to be his regular companions. He did not choose these 12 because of their faith; their faith often faltered. He didn't choose them because of their talent and ability; no one stood out with unusual ability. The disciples represented a wide range of backgrounds and life experiences, but apparently they had no more leadership potential than those who were not chosen. The one characteristic they all shared was their willingness to obey Jesus. After Jesus' ascension, they were filled with the Holy Spirit and carried out special roles in the growth of the early church. We should not disqualify ourselves from service to Christ because we do not have the expected credentials. Being a good disciple is simply a matter of following Jesus with a willing heart.

3.14, 15 Why did Jesus choose 12 men? The number 12 corresponds to the 12 tribes of Israel (Matthew 19.28), showing the continuity between the old religious system and the new one based on Jesus' message. Many people followed Jesus, but these 12 received the most intense training. We see the impact of these men throughout the rest of the New Testament.

3.18 *Cananaean* is the same as *zealot*. Zealots were Jewish nationalists who opposed the Roman occupation of Palestine.

Religious leaders accuse Jesus of being Satan
(74/Matthew 12.22–37)

3.20 Mk 6.31 Then he went home; 20 and the crowd came together again, so that they could not
even eat. 21 When his family heard it, they went out to restrain him, for people were
3.22 Mt 9.34; 10.25 12.22-32 Lk 11.14-23 Jn 8.48,52 10.20 saying, "He has gone out of his mind." 22 And the scribes who came down from
Jerusalem said, "He has Beelzebul, and by the ruler of the demons he casts out
demons." 23 And he called them to him, and spoke to them in parables, "How can
Satan cast out Satan? 24 If a kingdom is divided against itself, that kingdom cannot
stand. 25 And if a house is divided against itself, that house will not be able to stand.
3.26 Mt 4.10 26 And if Satan has risen up against himself and is divided, he cannot stand, but his
3.27 Isa 49.24,25 end has come. 27 But no one can enter a strong man's house and plunder his property without first tying up the strong man; then indeed the house can be plundered.
28 "Truly I tell you, people will be forgiven for their sins and whatever blasphe-
3.29 Lk 12.10 1 Jn 5.16 mies they utter; 29 but whoever blasphemes against the Holy Spirit can never have
forgiveness, but is guilty of an eternal sin"— 30 for they had said, "He has an unclean spirit."

Jesus describes his true family
(76/Matthew 12.46–50; Luke 8.19–21)

3.31 Mt 12.46-50; 13.55 Mk 6.3 Lk 8.19-21 Jn 7.3-5 31 Then his mother and his brothers came; and standing outside, they sent to
him and called him. 32 A crowd was sitting around him; and they said to him, "Your
mother and your brothers and sisters[c] are outside, asking for you." 33 And he re-
3.34 Rom 8.29 Heb 2.11 plied, "Who are my mother and my brothers?" 34 And looking at those who sat
around him, he said, "Here are my mother and my brothers! 35 Whoever does the
will of God is my brother and sister and mother."

Jesus tells the parable of the four soils
(77/Matthew 13.1–9; Luke 8.4–8)

4.1 Mt 13.1-23 Lk 8.4-15 **4** Again he began to teach beside the sea. Such a very large crowd gathered
around him that he got into a boat on the sea and sat there, while the whole
crowd was beside the sea on the land. 2 He began to teach them many things in

[c] Other ancient authorities lack *and sisters*

3.21 With the crowds pressing in on him, Jesus didn't even take time to eat. Because of this, his friends and family came to take him home (3.31, 32), thinking he had gone "over the edge" as a religious fanatic. They were concerned for him, but they missed the point of his ministry. Even those who were closest to Jesus were slow to understand who he was and what he came to do.

3.22–27 The Pharisees could not deny Jesus' miracles and supernatural power. They refused to believe that his power was from God, however, because then they would have had to accept him as the Messiah. Their pride would not let them do that. So in an attempt to destroy his popularity among the people, they accused him of having power from Satan. Jesus' reply showed that their argument didn't make sense. (*Beelzebul* refers to Satan.)

3.27 Although God permits Satan to work in our world, God is still in control. Jesus, because he is God, has power over Satan; he is able to cast out demons and end their terrible work in people's lives. One day Satan will be bound forever (Revelation 20.10).

3.28, 29 Christians sometimes wonder if they have committed this sin of blasphemy against the Holy Spirit. Christians need not worry about this sin; it is a heart-attitude of unbelief and unrepentance. Deliberate, ongoing rejection of the work of the Holy Spirit is blasphemy, because it is rejecting God himself. The religious leaders accused Jesus of blasphemy, but ironically they were the guilty ones when they looked him in the face and called him Satan.

3.31–35 Jesus' mother was Mary (Luke 1.30, 31), and his brothers were probably the other children Mary and Joseph had after Jesus (see also 6.3). Many Christians, however, believe the ancient tradition that Jesus was Mary's only child. If this is true, the "brothers" were possibly cousins (cousins were often called brothers in those days). Some have offered yet another suggestion: when Joseph married Mary, he was a widower, and these were his children by his first marriage.

Jesus' family did not yet fully understand his ministry, as can be seen in verse 21. Jesus explained that our spiritual family forms relationships that are ultimately more important and longer lasting than those formed in our physical families.

3.33–35 God's family is open and doesn't exclude anyone. Although Jesus cared for his mother and brothers, he also cared for all those who loved him. Jesus did not show partiality; he allowed everyone the privilege of obeying God and becoming part of his family. He shows us how to relate to other believers in this new way. In our increasingly computerized, impersonal world, warm relationships among members of God's family take on major importance. The church can give loving, personalized care that many people find nowhere else.

4.2 Jesus taught the people by telling parables, short stories using familiar scenes to explain spiritual truth. This method of teaching compels the listener to think. It conceals the truth from those who are too stubborn or prejudiced to hear what is being taught. Most parables have one main point, so we must be careful not to go beyond what Jesus intended to teach.

THE TWELVE

Name	*Occupation*	*Outstanding Characteristics*	*Major Events in His Life*
SIMON PETER (son of John)	Fisherman	Impulsive; later—bold in preaching Jesus	One of three in core group of disciples; recognized Jesus as the Messiah; denied Christ and repented; preached pentecost sermon; a leader of the Jerusalem church; baptized Gentiles; wrote 1 and 2 Peter.
JAMES, son of Zebedee. He and his brother John were called the "Sons of Thunder"	Fisherman	Ambitious, short-tempered, judgmental, deeply committed to Jesus	Also in core group; he and his brother John asked Jesus for places of honor in his kingdom; wanted to command fire to fall on a Samaritan village; first disciple to be martyred.
JOHN (son of Zebedee), James's brother, and "the disciple Jesus loved"	Fisherman	Ambitious, judgmental, later—very loving	Third disciple in core group; asked Jesus for a place of honor in his kingdom; wanted to call down fire on a Samaritan village; a leader of the Jerusalem church; wrote the Gospel of John and 1, 2, 3 John and Revelation.
ANDREW (Peter's brother)	Fisherman	Eager to bring others to Jesus	Accepted John the Baptist's testimony about Jesus; told Peter about Jesus; he and Philip told Jesus that Greeks wanted to see him.
PHILIP	Fisherman	Questioning attitude	Told Nathanael about Jesus; wondered how Jesus could feed the 5,000; asked Jesus to show his followers God the Father; he and Andrew told Jesus that Greeks wanted to see him.
BARTHOLOMEW (Nathanael)	Unknown	Honesty and straight-forwardness	Initially rejected Jesus because he was from Nazareth but acknowledged Jesus as the "Son of God" and "King of Israel" when they met.
MATTHEW (Levi)	Tax collector	Despised outcast because of his dishonest career	Abandoned his corrupt (and financially profitable) way of life to follow Jesus; invited Jesus to a party with his notorious friends; wrote the Gospel of Matthew.
THOMAS (the Twin)	Unknown	Courage and doubt	Suggested the disciples go with Jesus to Bethany—even if it meant death; asked Jesus about where he was going; refused to believe Jesus was risen until he would see Jesus alive and touch his wounds.
JAMES (son of Alphaeus)	Unknown	Unknown	Became one of Jesus' disciples.
THADDAEUS (Judas, son of James)	Unknown	Unknown	Asked Jesus why he would reveal himself to his followers and not to the world.
SIMON THE ZEALOT	Unknown	Fierce patriotism	Became a disciple of Jesus.
JUDAS ISCARIOT	Unknown	Treacherous and greedy	Became one of Jesus' disciples; betrayed Jesus; killed himself.

Jesus' faithful disciples were ordinary men who became extraordinary because of Jesus Christ. Despite their confusion and misunderstanding during his lifetime, they became powerful witnesses to his resurrection. Their lives were transformed by God's power. The story of Jesus' disciples does not end with the Gospels. It continues in the book of Acts and many of the epistles.

DISCIPLES

What Jesus Said about Him	A Key Lesson from His Life	Selected References
Named him Peter, "a rock"; called him "Satan" when he urged Jesus to reject the cross; said he would become a fisherman of men's souls; he received revelation from God; he would deny Jesus; he would later be crucified for his faith.	Christians falter at times; but when they return to Jesus, he forgives them and strengthens their faith.	Matthew 4.18–20 Mark 8.29–33 Luke 22.31–34 John 21.15–19 Acts 2.14–41 Acts 10.1—11.18
Called James and John "Sons of Thunder"; said they would fish for the souls of men; they would drink the cup Jesus drank; they did not understand their own hearts.	Christians must be willing to die for Jesus.	Mark 3.17 Mark 10.35–40 Luke 9.52–56 Acts 12.1, 2
Called James and John "Sons of Thunder"; said he would fish for the souls of men; would drink the cup Jesus drank; did not understand his own heart; would take care of Jesus' mother after his death.	The transforming power of the love of Christ is available to all.	Mark 1.19 Mark 10.35–40 Luke 9.52–56 John 19.26, 27 John 21.20–24
Said he would become a fisherman of men's souls.	Christians are to tell other people about Jesus.	Matthew 4.18–20 John 1.35–42; 6.8, 9 John 12.20–22
Asked if Philip realized that to know and see him was to know and see the Father.	God uses our questions to teach us.	Matthew 10.3 John 1.43–46; 6.2–7 John 12.20–22 John 14.8–11
Called him "truly an Israelite" and a man "in whom there is no deceit."	Jesus respects honesty in people—even if they challenge him because of it.	Mark 3.18 John 1.45–51 John 21.1–13
Called him to be a disciple.	Christianity is not for people who think they're already good; it is for people who know they've failed and want help.	Matthew 9.9–13 Mark 2.15–17 Luke 5.27–32
Said Thomas believed because he actually saw Jesus after the resurrection.	Even when Christians experience serious doubts, Jesus reaches out to them to restore their faith.	Matthew 10.3 John 14.5; 20.24–29 John 21.1–13
Unknown	Unknown	Matthew 10.3 Mark 3.18 Luke 6.15
Unknown	Christians follow Jesus because they believe in him; they do not always understand the details of God's plan.	Matthew 10.3 Mark 3.18 John 14.22
Unknown	If we are willing to give up our plans for the future, we can participate in Jesus' plans.	Matthew 10.4 Mark 3.18 Luke 6.15
Called him "a devil"; said he would betray Jesus.	It is not enough to be familiar with Jesus' teachings. Jesus' true followers love and obey him.	Matthew 26.20–25 Luke 22.47, 48 John 12.4–8

parables, and in his teaching he said to them: 3 "Listen! A sower went out to sow.
4 And as he sowed, some seed fell on the path, and the birds came and ate it up.
5 Other seed fell on rocky ground, where it did not have much soil, and it sprang up
quickly, since it had no depth of soil. 6 And when the sun rose, it was scorched; and
since it had no root, it withered away. 7 Other seed fell among thorns, and the
thorns grew up and choked it, and it yielded no grain. 8 Other seed fell into good
soil and brought forth grain, growing up and increasing and yielding thirty and
sixty and a hundredfold." 9 And he said, "Let anyone with ears to hear listen!"

4.9 Mk 4.23

Jesus explains the parable of the four soils
(78/Matthew 13.10–23; Luke 8.9–18)

10 When he was alone, those who were around him along with the twelve asked
him about the parables. 11 And he said to them, "To you has been given the secret[d]
of the kingdom of God, but for those outside, everything comes in parables; 12 in
order that

'they may indeed look, but not perceive,
and may indeed listen, but not understand;
so that they may not turn again and be forgiven.' "

13 And he said to them, "Do you not understand this parable? Then how will
you understand all the parables? 14 The sower sows the word. 15 These are the ones
on the path where the word is sown: when they hear, Satan immediately comes and
takes away the word that is sown in them. 16 And these are the ones sown on rocky
ground: when they hear the word, they immediately receive it with joy. 17 But they
have no root, and endure only for a while; then, when trouble or persecution arises
on account of the word, immediately they fall away.[e] 18 And others are those sown
among the thorns: these are the ones who hear the word, 19 but the cares of the
world, and the lure of wealth, and the desire for other things come in and choke the
word, and it yields nothing. 20 And these are the ones sown on the good soil: they
hear the word and accept it and bear fruit, thirty and sixty and a hundredfold."
21 He said to them, "Is a lamp brought in to be put under the bushel basket, or
under the bed, and not on the lampstand? 22 For there is nothing hidden, except to
be disclosed; nor is anything secret, except to come to light. 23 Let anyone with ears
to hear listen!" 24 And he said to them, "Pay attention to what you hear; the measure
you give will be the measure you get, and still more will be given you. 25 For to

4.11,12 Isa 6.9; 44.18 Jer 5.21 Jn 12.39,40 Acts 28.26,27 Rom 11.8 1 Cor 2.10
4.14 Eph 3.8 Jas 1.18 1 Pet 1.23-25
4.15 2 Cor 4.4 1 Pet 5.8
4.19 Prov 23.4,5 Lk 18.24 1 Tim 6.9,10,17 1 Jn 2.15,16
4.20 Jn 15.5
4.21 Mt 5.15 Lk 8.16-18 11.33
4.22 Mt 10.26 Lk 12.2
4.23 Mt 11.15; 13.43
4.25 Mt 13.12; 25.29 Lk 6.38; 19.26 2 Cor 9.6

[d] Or *mystery* [e] Or *stumble*

4.3 Seed was sowed by hand. As the farmer walked across the field, he threw handfuls of seed onto the ground from a large bag slung across his shoulders. The plants did not grow in neat rows as with today's machine planting. No matter how skillful, no farmer could keep some of his seed from falling by the wayside, from being scattered among rocks and thorns, or from being carried off by the wind. He threw the seed liberally, however, and enough fell on good ground to ensure the harvest.

4.9 We hear with our ears, but there is a deeper kind of listening with the mind and heart that is necessary in order to gain spiritual understanding from Jesus' words. Some people in the crowd were looking for evidence to use against Jesus; others truly wanted to learn and grow. Jesus' words were for the honest seekers.

4.11, 12 Some people do not understand God's truth because they are not ready for it. God reveals truth to people who will act on it, who will make it evident in their lives. When you talk with people about God, be aware that they will not understand if they are not yet ready. Be patient, taking every chance to tell them more of the truth about God and praying that the Holy Spirit will open their minds and hearts, making them ready to receive the truth and act on it.

4.14–20 The four soils represent four different ways people respond to God's Word. Usually we think that Jesus was talking about four different kinds of people. But he may also have been talking about (1) different times or phases in a person's life, or (2) how we willingly receive God's message in some areas of our lives and resist it in others. For example, you may be open to God about your future, but closed concerning how you spend your money. You may respond like good soil to God's demand for worship, but like rocky soil to his demand to give to those in need. We must strive to be like good soil in every area of our lives at all times.

4.19 Worldly cares, illusory riches, and the desire for things plagued Roman disciples as they do us today. How easy it is for our daily routines to become overcrowded. A life packed with materialistic pursuits deafens us to God's Word. Stay free so you can hear God when he speaks.

4.21 If a lamp doesn't help people see, it is useless. Does your life show other people how to find God and how to live for him? If not, ask what "bushels" have shut out your light. Complacency, resentment, stubbornness of heart, or disobedience could keep God's light from shining through you to others.

4.24, 25 The light of Jesus' truth is revealed to us, not hidden. But we may not be able to see or to use all of that truth right now. Only as we put God's teachings into practice will we understand and see more of the truth. The truth is clear, but our ability to understand is imperfect. As we obey, we will sharpen our vision and increase our understanding (see James 1.22–25).

4.25 This verse simply means we are responsible to use well what

those who have, more will be given; and from those who have nothing, even what
they have will be taken away."

Jesus tells the parable of the growing seed
(79)

4.26,27 1 Cor 3.6,7 — 26 He also said, "The kingdom of God is as if someone would scatter seed on
the ground, 27 and would sleep and rise night and day, and the seed would sprout
4.28,29 Mt 9.37,38; Jn 4.35; 1 Cor 15.36-38; Rev 14.15 — and grow, he does not know how. 28 The earth produces of itself, first the stalk,
then the head, then the full grain in the head. 29 But when the grain is ripe, at once
he goes in with his sickle, because the harvest has come."

Jesus tells the parable of the mustard seed
(81/Matthew 13.31, 32)

4.30 Mt 13.31,32; Lk 13.18,19 — 30 He also said, "With what can we compare the kingdom of God, or what
parable will we use for it? 31 It is like a mustard seed, which, when sown upon the
4.31,32 Ezek 17.22,23 — ground, is the smallest of all the seeds on earth; 32 yet when it is sown it grows up
and becomes the greatest of all shrubs, and puts forth large branches, so that the
birds of the air can make nests in its shade."
4.33 Mt 13.34,35 — 33 With many such parables he spoke the word to them, as they were able to
4.34 Jn 10.6; 16.25 — hear it; 34 he did not speak to them except in parables, but he explained everything
in private to his disciples.

Jesus calms the storm
(87/Matthew 8.23–27; Luke 8.22–25)

4.35 Mt 8.23-27; Lk 8.22-25 — 35 On that day, when evening had come, he said to them, "Let us go across to
the other side." 36 And leaving the crowd behind, they took him with them in the
boat, just as he was. Other boats were with him. 37 A great windstorm arose, and
the waves beat into the boat, so that the boat was already being swamped. 38 But he
was in the stern, asleep on the cushion; and they woke him up and said to him,
4.39 Job 38.11; Ps 65.7; 89.9; 93.4 — "Teacher, do you not care that we are perishing?" 39 He woke up and rebuked the
wind, and said to the sea, "Peace! Be still!" Then the wind ceased, and there was
a dead calm. 40 He said to them, "Why are you afraid? Have you still no faith?"
4.41 Ps 33.8,9 — 41 And they were filled with great awe and said to one another, "Who then is this,
that even the wind and the sea obey him?"

---

we have. How much we have is not nearly as important as what we do with it.

4.26–29 This parable about the kingdom of God, recorded only by Mark, reveals that spiritual growth is a continual, gradual process that is finally consummated in a harvest of spiritual maturity. We can understand the process of spiritual growth by comparing it to the slow but certain growth of a plant.

4.30–32 Jesus used this parable to explain that although Christianity had very small beginnings, it would grow into a worldwide community of believers. When you feel alone in your stand for Christ, realize that God is building a worldwide kingdom. He has faithful followers in every part of the world, and your faith, no matter how small, can join with that of others to accomplish great things.

4.33, 34 Jesus adapted his methods to his audience's ability and desire to understand. He didn't speak in parables to confuse people, but to challenge sincere seekers to discover the meaning of his words. Much of Jesus' teaching was against hypocrisy and impure motives, characteristics of the religious leaders. Had Jesus spoken against the leaders directly, his public ministry would have been hampered. Those who listened carefully to Jesus knew what he was talking about.

4.37, 38 The Sea of Galilee is 680 feet below sea level, and it is surrounded by hills. Winds blowing across the land intensify close to the sea, causing violent and unexpected storms. The disciples were seasoned fishermen who had spent their lives fishing on this huge lake, but in this storm they panicked.

4.38–40 The disciples panicked because the storm threatened to destroy them all, and Jesus seemed unaware and unconcerned. Theirs was a physical storm, but storms come in other forms. Think about the storms in your life – the situations that cause you great anxiety. Whatever your difficulty, you have two options: You can worry and assume that Jesus no longer cares, or you can resist fear, putting your trust in him. When you feel like panicking, confess your need for God and then trust him to care for you.

4.41 The disciples lived with Jesus, but they underestimated him. They did not see that his power applied to their own situation. Jesus has been with his people for 20 centuries, and yet we, like the disciples, underestimate his power to handle crises in our lives. The disciples did not yet know enough about Jesus. We cannot make the same excuse.

Jesus sends the demons into a herd of pigs
(88/Matthew 8.28–9.1; Luke 8.26–39)

5 They came to the other side of the sea, to the country of the Gerasenes.[f] 2 And 5.1
when he had stepped out of the boat, immediately a man out of the tombs with Mt 8.28-34 Lk 8.26-39
an unclean spirit met him. 3 He lived among the tombs; and no one could restrain
him any more, even with a chain; 4 for he had often been restrained with shackles
and chains, but the chains he wrenched apart, and the shackles he broke in pieces;
and no one had the strength to subdue him. 5 Night and day among the tombs and
on the mountains he was always howling and bruising himself with stones. 6 When
he saw Jesus from a distance, he ran and bowed down before him; 7 and he shouted 5.7,8
at the top of his voice, "What have you to do with me, Jesus, Son of the Most High Lk 8.28 Acts 16.17
God? I adjure you by God, do not torment me." 8 For he had said to him, "Come out Heb 7.1
of the man, you unclean spirit!" 9 Then Jesus[g] asked him, "What is your name?"
He replied, "My name is Legion; for we are many." 10 He begged him earnestly not
to send them out of the country. 11 Now there on the hillside a great herd of swine 5.11
was feeding; 12 and the unclean spirits[h] begged him, "Send us into the swine; let us Deut 14.8 Isa 65.4
enter them." 13 So he gave them permission. And the unclean spirits came out and 5.13
entered the swine; and the herd, numbering about two thousand, rushed down the Job 1.12; 2.6; 12.16 Mt 28.18
steep bank into the sea, and were drowned in the sea. Lk 4.36 Col 2.10

14 The swineherds ran off and told it in the city and in the country. Then people Heb 2.8
came to see what it was that had happened. 15 They came to Jesus and saw the 5.15
demoniac sitting there, clothed and in his right mind, the very man who had had 1 Jn 3.8
the legion; and they were afraid. 16 Those who had seen what had happened to the 5.17
demoniac and to the swine reported it. 17 Then they began to beg Jesus[i] to leave Job 21.14; 22.17
their neighborhood. 18 As he was getting into the boat, the man who had been pos- Lk 5.8 5.18
sessed by demons begged him that he might be with him. 19 But Jesus[g] refused, and Ps 116.12

[f] Other ancient authorities read *Gergesenes*; others, *Gadarenes* [g] Gk *he* [h] Gk *they* [i] Gk *him*

5.1, 2 Although we cannot be sure why demon possession occurs, we know that unclean spirits use the body to distort and destroy man's relationship with God and likeness to him. Even today, demons are dangerous, powerful, and destructive. While it is important to recognize their evil activity so we can stay away from them, we must avoid any curiosity about or involvement with demonic forces or the occult (Deuteronomy 18.10–12). If we resist the devil and his influences, he will flee from us (James 4.7).

5.9 The unclean spirit said its name was Legion. A legion was the largest unit of the Roman army, consisting of 3,000 to 6,000 soldiers. Obviously this man was possessed by many demons.

5.10 Mark often highlights the supernatural struggle between Jesus and Satan. The demons' goal was to control the humans they inhabited; Jesus' goal was to give people freedom from sin and Satan's control. The demons knew they had no power over Jesus, so when they saw him, they begged not to be sent out of the country ("into the abyss" in Luke 8.31). Jesus granted their request to enter into the herd of swine (5.13) but ended their destructive work in people. Perhaps he let the demons destroy the pigs to demonstrate his own superiority over a very powerful yet destructive force. He could have sent them to hell, but he did not because the time for judgment had not yet come. In the end, the devil and all his evil spirits will be sent into eternal fire (Matthew 25.41).

5.11 According to Old Testament law (Leviticus 11.7), swine were "unclean" animals. This meant they could not be eaten or even touched by a Jew. This incident took place southeast of the Sea of Galilee in the Gerasene country, a Gentile region.

5.14, 15 Swineherds were those who watched over the pigs. A demoniac is someone possessed by a demon.

5.17 After such a wonderful miracle of saving a man's life, why did the people want Jesus to leave? They were afraid of his supernatural power. They may have also feared that Jesus would continue destroying their pigs. They would rather give up Jesus than lose their source of income and security.

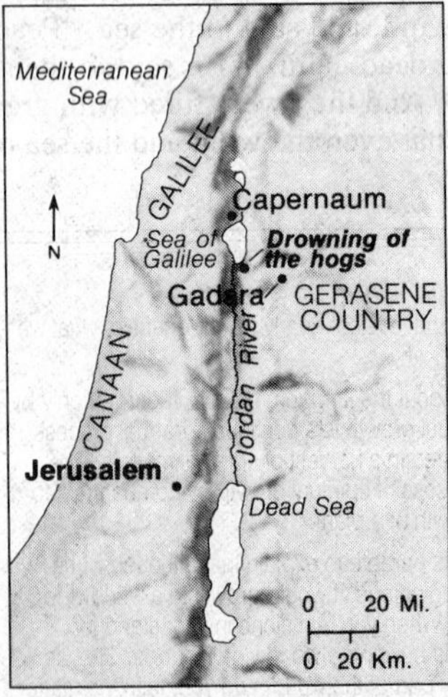

HEALING A DEMON-POSSESSED MAN
From Capernaum, Jesus and his disciples crossed the Sea of Galilee. A storm blew up unexpectedly, but Jesus calmed it. Landing in the country of the Gerasenes, Jesus sent demons out of a man and into a herd of swine that plunged over the steep bank into the sea.

5.19 Jesus told this man to tell his friends about the miraculous healing. Most of the time, Jesus urged those he healed to keep quiet. Why the difference? Here are possible answers: (1) The demon-possessed man had been alone and unable to speak. Telling others what Jesus did for him would prove that he was healed. (2) This was mainly a Gentile and pagan area, so Jesus was not expecting great crowds to follow him or religious leaders to hinder him. (3) By sending the man away with this good news, Jesus was expanding his ministry to people who were not Jews.

5.19, 20 This man had been demon possessed but now was a liv-

said to him, "Go home to your friends, and tell them how much the Lord has done
for you, and what mercy he has shown you." 20 And he went away and began to
proclaim in the Decapolis how much Jesus had done for him; and everyone was
amazed.

5.20 Isa 63.7; 1 Tim 1.13,14

Jesus heals a bleeding woman and restores a girl to life
(89/Matthew 9.18–26; Luke 8.40–56)

21 When Jesus had crossed again in the boat[j] to the other side, a great crowd
gathered around him; and he was by the sea. 22 Then one of the leaders of the synagogue named Jairus came and, when he saw him, fell at his feet 23 and begged him
repeatedly, "My little daughter is at the point of death. Come and lay your hands on
her, so that she may be made well, and live." 24 So he went with him.
And a large crowd followed him and pressed in on him. 25 Now there was a

5.21 Mt 9.1,18-26; Lk 8.40-56
5.23 Mk 6.5; 7.32; 8.23; 16.18; Lk 4.40; 13.13; Acts 6.6; 9.17; 28.8

[j] Other ancient authorities lack *in the boat*

THE TOUCH OF JESUS

What kind of people did Jesus associate with? Whom did he consider important enough to touch? Here we see many of the people Jesus came to know. Some reached out to him; he reached out to them all. Regardless of how great or unknown, rich or poor, young or old, sinner or saint—Jesus cares equally for all. No person is beyond the loving touch of Jesus.

Jesus Talked with . . .	*Reference*
A despised tax collector	Matthew 9.9
An insane hermit	Mark 5.1–15
The Roman governor	Mark 15.1–15
A young boy	Mark 9.17–27
A prominent religious leader	John 3.1–21
A homemaker	Luke 10.38–42
A lawyer	Matthew 22.35
A criminal	Luke 23.40–43
A synagogue leader	Mark 5.22
Fishermen	Matthew 4.18–20
A king	Luke 23.7–11
A poor widow	Luke 7.11–17; 21.1–4
A Roman army captain	Luke 7.1–10
A group of children	Mark 10.13–16
A prophet	Matthew 3
An adulterous woman	John 8.1–11
The Jewish council	Luke 22.66–71
A sick old woman	Mark 5.25–34
A rich man	Mark 10.17–23
A blind beggar	Mark 10.46
Jewish political leaders	Mark 12.13
A group of women	Luke 8.2, 3
The high priest	Matthew 26.62–68
An outcast with leprosy	Luke 17.11–19
A city official	John 4.46–53
A young girl	Mark 5.41, 42
A traitor	John 13.1–3, 27
A helpless and paralyzed man	Mark 2.1–12
An angry mob of soldiers and police	John 18.3–9
A woman from a foreign land	Mark 7.25–30
A doubting follower	John 20.24–29
An enemy who hated him	Acts 9.1–9

ing example of Jesus' power. He wanted to go with Jesus, but Jesus told him to go home and share his story with his friends. If you have experienced Jesus' power, you too are a living example. Are you, like this man, enthusiastic about sharing the good news with those around you? Just as we would tell others about a doctor who cured a physical disease, we should tell about Christ who cures our sin.

5.20 Decapolis, or the Ten Towns, was located southeast of the Sea of Galilee. Ten cities, each with its own independent government, formed an alliance for protection and to increase trade. These cities had been settled several centuries earlier by Greek traders and immigrants. Although Jews also lived in the area, they were not in the majority. Many people from Decapolis followed Jesus (Matthew 4.25).

5.22 Jesus recrossed the Sea of Galilee, probably landing at Capernaum. Jairus was the elected ruler of the local synagogue. He was responsible for supervising worship, running the weekly school, and caring for the building. Many synagogue rulers had close ties to the Pharisees. It is likely, therefore, that some synagogue rulers had been pressured not to support Jesus. For Jairus to bow before Jesus was a significant and perhaps daring act of respect and worship.

5.25–34 This woman had an incurable condition causing her to bleed constantly. This may have been a menstrual or uterine disorder which would have made her ritually unclean (Leviticus 15.25–27) and excluded her from most social contact. She desperately wanted Jesus to heal her, but she knew her bleeding would cause Jesus to be unclean under Jewish law if she touched him. Still, she reached out by faith and was healed. Sometimes we feel that our problems will keep us from God. But he is always ready to help. We should never allow our fear to keep us from approaching him.

woman who had been suffering from hemorrhages for twelve years. 26 She had endured much under many physicians, and had spent all that she had; and she was no
better, but rather grew worse. 27 She had heard about Jesus, and came up behind **5.27** Mk 3.10
him in the crowd and touched his cloak, 28 for she said, "If I but touch his clothes, Acts 19.11,12
I will be made well." 29 Immediately her hemorrhage stopped; and she felt in her
body that she was healed of her disease. 30 Immediately aware that power had gone **5.30** Lk 6.19
forth from him, Jesus turned about in the crowd and said, "Who touched my
clothes?" 31 And his disciples said to him, "You see the crowd pressing in on you;
how can you say, 'Who touched me?' " 32 He looked all around to see who had done
it. 33 But the woman, knowing what had happened to her, came in fear and trembling, fell down before him, and told him the whole truth. 34 He said to her, **5.34** Mk 10.52
"Daughter, your faith has made you well; go in peace, and be healed of your dis- Lk 7.50; 17.19 18.42
ease." Acts 14.9

35 While he was still speaking, some people came from the leader's house to
say, "Your daughter is dead. Why trouble the teacher any further?" 36 But overhear- **5.36** Jn 11.25,40
ing[k] what they said, Jesus said to the leader of the synagogue, "Do not fear, only
believe." 37 He allowed no one to follow him except Peter, James, and John, the
brother of James. 38 When they came to the house of the leader of the synagogue,
he saw a commotion, people weeping and wailing loudly. 39 When he had entered, **5.39** Jn 11.11
he said to them, "Why do you make a commotion and weep? The child is not dead
but sleeping." 40 And they laughed at him. Then he put them all outside, and took **5.40** Acts 9.40
the child's father and mother and those who were with him, and went in where the
child was. 41 He took her by the hand and said to her, "Talitha cum," which means, **5.41,42** Ps 33.9
"Little girl, get up!" 42 And immediately the girl got up and began to walk about Lk 7.14
(she was twelve years of age). At this they were overcome with amazement. 43 He **5.43** Mt 12.16; 17.9
strictly ordered them that no one should know this, and told them to give her some- Mk 3.12; 5.19
thing to eat. Lk 5.14

The people of Nazareth refuse to believe
(91/Matthew 13.54–58)

6 He left that place and came to his hometown, and his disciples followed him. **6.1** Mt 13.53-58
2 On the sabbath he began to teach in the synagogue, and many who heard him **6.2,3** Ps 69.8
were astounded. They said, "Where did this man get all this? What is this wisdom Mt 11.6
that has been given to him? What deeds of power are being done by his hands! 3 Is
not this the carpenter, the son of Mary[l] and brother of James and Joses and Judas
and Simon, and are not his sisters here with us?" And they took offense[m] at him.

[k] Or *ignoring*; other ancient authorities read *hearing* [l] Other ancient authorities read *son of the carpenter and of Mary* [m] Or *stumbled*

5.32–34 Jesus was not angry with this woman for touching him. He knew she had touched him, but he stopped and asked who did it in order to teach her something about faith. Although she was healed when she touched him, Jesus said her faith caused the cure. Genuine faith involves action. Faith that isn't put into action is no faith at all.

5.35, 36 Jairus's crisis made him feel confused, afraid, and without hope. Jesus' words to Jairus in the midst of crisis speak to us as well: "Do not fear, only believe." In Jesus' mind, there was both hope and promise. The next time you feel hopeless and afraid, look at your problem from Jesus' point of view. He is the source of all hope and promise.

5.38 Loud weeping and wailing was customary at a person's death. Lack of it was the ultimate disgrace and disrespect. Some people, usually women, made mourning a profession, and were paid by the dead person's family to weep over the body. On the day of death, the body was carried through the streets, followed by mourners, family members, and friends.

5.39, 40 The mourners began to laugh at Jesus when he said, "The child is not dead but sleeping." The girl was dead, but Jesus used the image of sleep to indicate that her condition was temporary, and she would be restored.

Jesus tolerated the crowd's abuse in order to teach an important lesson about maintaining hope and trust in him. Today, most of the world laughs at God's claims, which seem ridiculous to them. When you are belittled for expressing faith in Jesus and hope for eternal life, remember that unbelievers don't see from God's perspective. For a clear statement about life after death, see 1 Thessalonians 4.13, 14.

5.41, 42 Jesus not only demonstrated great power; he also showed tremendous compassion. Jesus' power over nature, evil spirits, and death was motivated by compassion – for a demon-possessed man who lived among tombs, for a diseased woman, and for the family of a dead girl. The rabbis of the day considered such people unclean. Polite society avoided them. But Jesus reached out and helped anyone in need.

5.43 Jesus told the girl's parents not to spread the news of the miracle. He wanted the facts to speak for themselves, and the time was not yet right for a major confrontation with the religious leaders. Jesus still had much to accomplish, and he didn't want people following him just to see his miracles.

6.4 Jn 4.44 4 Then Jesus said to them, "Prophets are not without honor, except in their hometown, and among their own kin, and in their own house." 5 And he could do no deed
of power there, except that he laid his hands on a few sick people and cured them.
6 And he was amazed at their unbelief.

Jesus sends out the twelve disciples
(93/Matthew 10.1–15; Luke 9.1–6)

6.7 Mt 10.1,9-14; 11.1 Then he went about among the villages teaching. 7 He called the twelve and be-
Lk 9.1-6 gan to send them out two by two, and gave them authority over the unclean spirits.
10.1-11 8 He ordered them to take nothing for their journey except a staff; no bread, no bag,
no money in their belts; 9 but to wear sandals and not to put on two tunics. 10 He said
6.11 to them, "Wherever you enter a house, stay there until you leave the place. 11 If any
Acts 13.51; 18.6 place will not welcome you and they refuse to hear you, as you leave, shake off the
Heb 10.31 dust that is on your feet as a testimony against them." 12 So they went out and pro-
6.13 Jas 5.14 claimed that all should repent. 13 They cast out many demons, and anointed with oil
many who were sick and cured them.

Herod kills John the Baptist
(95/Matthew 14.1–12; Luke 9.7–9)

6.14 Mt 14.1-12 14 King Herod heard of it, for Jesus'[n] name had become known. Some were[o]
Lk 9.7-9 saying, "John the baptizer has been raised from the dead; and for this reason these

[n] Gk *his* [o] Other ancient authorities read *He was*

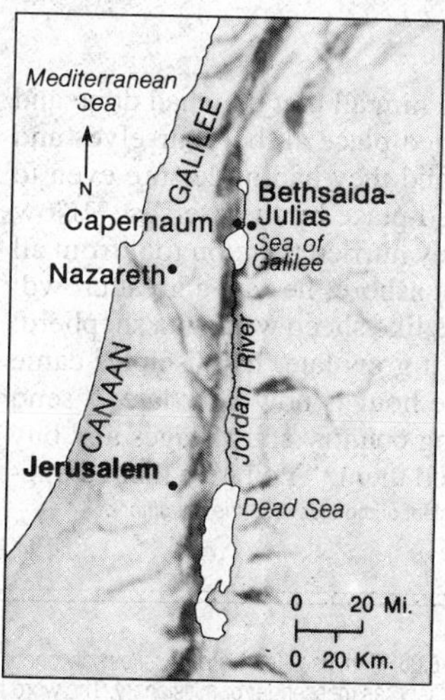

PREACHING IN GALILEE After returning to his hometown, Nazareth, from Capernaum Jesus preached in the villages of Galilee and sent his disciples out to preach as well. After meeting back in Capernaum, they left by boat to rest, only to be met by the crowds who followed the boat along the shore.

6.2, 3 Jesus was teaching effectively and wisely, but the people of his hometown saw him as only a carpenter. "He's no better than we are – he's just a common laborer," they said. They were offended that others could be impressed by him and follow him. They rejected his authority because he was one of their peers. They thought they knew him, but their preconceived notions about who he was made it impossible for them to accept his message. Don't let prejudice blind you to truth. As you learn more about Jesus, try to see him for who he really is.

6.4 Jesus said that a prophet (in other words, a worker for God) is never honored in his hometown. But that doesn't make his work any less important. A person doesn't need to be respected or honored to be useful to God. If friends, neighbors, or family don't respect your Christian work, don't let their rejection keep you from serving God.

6.5 Jesus could have done greater miracles in Nazareth, but he chose not to because of the people's pride and unbelief. The miracles he did had little effect on the people because they did not accept his message or believe he was from God. Therefore, Jesus looked elsewhere, seeking those who would respond to his miracles and message.

6.7 The disciples were sent out in pairs. Individually they could have reached more areas of the country, but this was not Christ's plan. One advantage in going out by twos was that they could strengthen and encourage each other, especially when they faced rejection. Our strength comes from God, but he meets many of our needs through our teamwork with others. As you serve him, don't try to go it alone.

6.8, 9 Mark records that the disciples were instructed to take nothing with them *except* staffs, while in the Matthew and Luke accounts Jesus told them *not* to take staffs. One explanation is that Matthew and Luke were referring to a club used for protection, whereas Mark was talking about a shepherd's crook. In any case, the point in all three accounts is the same – the disciples were to leave at once, without extensive preparation, trusting in God's care rather than in their own resources.

6.11 Pious Jews shook the dust from their feet after passing through Gentile cities or territory to show their separation from Gentile influences and practices. When the disciples shook the dust from their feet after leaving a *Jewish* town, it was a vivid sign that they wished to remain separate from people who had rejected Jesus and his message. Jesus made it clear that the listeners were responsible for what they did with the gospel. The disciples were not to blame if the message was rejected, as long as they had faithfully and carefully presented it. We are not responsible when others reject Christ's message of salvation, but we do have the responsibility to share it clearly and faithfully.

6.14, 15 Herod, along with many others, wondered who Jesus really was. Unable to accept Jesus' claim to be God's Son, many people made up their own explanations for his power and authority. Herod thought Jesus was John the Baptist come back to life, while those who were familiar with the Old Testament thought he was Elijah (Malachi 4.5). Still others believed he was a teaching prophet in the tradition of Moses, Isaiah, or Jeremiah. Today people still have to make up their minds about Jesus. Some think that if they can name what he is – prophet, teacher, good man – they can weaken the power of his claim on their lives. But what they *think* does not change who Jesus *is*.

powers are at work in him." 15 But others said, "It is Elijah." And others said, "It 6.15
is a prophet, like one of the prophets of old." 16 But when Herod heard of it, he said, Mt 16.14
"John, whom I beheaded, has been raised."
17 For Herod himself had sent men who arrested John, bound him, and put him 6.17
in prison on account of Herodias, his brother Philip's wife, because Herod[p] had Lev 18.15,16 20.21
married her. 18 For John had been telling Herod, "It is not lawful for you to have Lk 3.19 2 Tim 4.2
your brother's wife." 19 And Herodias had a grudge against him, and wanted to kill Heb 13.4
him. But she could not, 20 for Herod feared John, knowing that he was a righteous
and holy man, and he protected him. When he heard him, he was greatly perplexed;[q] and yet he liked to listen to him. 21 But an opportunity came when Herod 6.21
on his birthday gave a banquet for his courtiers and officers and for the leaders of Gen 40.20
Galilee. 22 When his daughter Herodias[r] came in and danced, she pleased Herod 6.22
and his guests; and the king said to the girl, "Ask me for whatever you wish, and Esth 5.3,6; 7.2
I will give it." 23 And he solemnly swore to her, "Whatever you ask me, I will give
you, even half of my kingdom." 24 She went out and said to her mother, "What
should I ask for?" She replied, "The head of John the baptizer." 25 Immediately she
rushed back to the king and requested, "I want you to give me at once the head of
John the Baptist on a platter." 26 The king was deeply grieved; yet out of regard for
his oaths and for the guests, he did not want to refuse her. 27 Immediately the king 6.27
sent a soldier of the guard with orders to bring John's[s] head. He went and be- Rev 6.9
headed him in the prison, 28 brought his head on a platter, and gave it to the girl.
Then the girl gave it to her mother. 29 When his disciples heard about it, they came 6.29
and took his body, and laid it in a tomb. Acts 8.2

Jesus feeds five thousand
(96/Matthew 14.13–21; Luke 9.10–17; John 6.1–15)

30 The apostles gathered around Jesus, and told him all that they had done and 6.30
taught. 31 He said to them, "Come away to a deserted place all by yourselves and Mt 14.13-22 Lk 9.10-17
rest a while." For many were coming and going, and they had no leisure even to Jn 6.1-15
eat. 32 And they went away in the boat to a deserted place by themselves. 33 Now 6.31 Mk 3.20
many saw them going and recognized them, and they hurried there on foot from all 6.34
the towns and arrived ahead of them. 34 As he went ashore, he saw a great crowd; Ps 145.8,9 Isa 61.1
and he had compassion for them, because they were like sheep without a shepherd; Mt 9.36
and he began to teach them many things. 35 When it grew late, his disciples came Heb 5.1-3
to him and said, "This is a deserted place, and the hour is now very late; 36 send 6.37 Num 11.13,22
them away so that they may go into the surrounding country and villages and buy 2 Kgs 4.43 Mt 15.33
something for themselves to eat." 37 But he answered them, "You give them some- Mk 8.4

[p] Gk *he* [q] Other ancient authorities read *he did many things* [r] Other ancient authorities read *the daughter of Herodias herself* [s] Gk *his*

6.17–19 Palestine was divided into four territories, each with a different ruler. Herod Antipas, called Herod in the Gospels, was ruler over Galilee; his brother Philip ruled over Trachonitis and Idumea. Philip's wife was Herodias, but she left him to marry Herod Antipas. When John confronted the two for committing adultery, Herodias formulated a plot to kill him. Instead of trying to get rid of her sin, she tried to get rid of the one who brought it to public attention. This is exactly what the religious leaders were trying to do to Jesus.

6.20 Herod arrested John the Baptist under pressure from his wife and advisers. Though he respected John's integrity, in the end he had him killed because of pressure from his peers and family. What you do under pressure often shows what you are really like.

6.22, 23 As a ruler under Roman authority, Herod had no kingdom to give. His offer of half his kingdom was his way to say he would give Herodias's daughter almost anything she wanted. When Herodias asked for John's head, Herod would have been greatly embarrassed in front of his guests if he had denied her request. Words are powerful. Because they can lead to great sin, we should use them with great care.

6.30 Mark uses the word *apostles* only once. *Apostle* means "one sent" as messenger or missionary. The word became an official title for Jesus' 12 disciples after his death and resurrection (Acts 1.25, 26; Ephesians 2.20).

6.31 When the disciples had returned from their mission, Jesus took them away to rest. Doing God's work is very important, but Jesus recognized that to do it effectively we need periodic rest and renewal. Jesus and his disciples, however, did not always find it easy to get the rest they needed!

6.34 This crowd was as pitiful as a flock of sheep without a shepherd. Sheep are easily scattered; without a shepherd they are in grave danger. Jesus was the Shepherd who could teach them what they needed to know and keep them from straying from God. See Psalm 23; Isaiah 40.11; and Ezekiel 34.5ff for descriptions of the Good Shepherd.

6.37 In this chapter different people have examined Jesus' life and ministry: his neighbors and family, Herod the king, and the disciples. Yet none of these appreciate him for who he is. The disciples are still pondering, still unclear, still unbelieving. They do not realize that Jesus can provide for them. They are so preoccupied with

thing to eat." They said to him, "Are we to go and buy two hundred denarii[t] worth
of bread, and give it to them to eat?" 38 And he said to them, "How many loaves
6.41 have you? Go and see." When they had found out, they said, "Five, and two fish."
1 Sam 9.13 39 Then he ordered them to get all the people to sit down in groups on the green
Mt 26.26 grass. 40 So they sat down in groups of hundreds and of fifties. 41 Taking the five
1 Tim 4.4,5

[t] The denarius was the usual day's wage for a laborer

HEROD ANTIPAS

Most people dislike having their sins pointed out, especially in public. The shame of being exposed is often stronger than the guilt brought on by the wrongdoing. Herod Antipas was a man experiencing both guilt and shame.

Herod's ruthless ambition was public knowledge, as was his illegal marriage to his brother's wife, Herodias. One man made Herod's sin a public issue. That man was John the Baptist. John had been preaching in the wilderness, and thousands flocked to hear him. Apparently it was no secret that John had rebuked Herod for his adulterous marriage. Herodias was particularly anxious to have John silenced. As a solution, Herod imprisoned John.

Herod liked John. John was probably one of the few people he met who spoke only the truth to him. But the truth about his sin was a bitter pill to swallow, and Herod wavered at the point of conflict: he couldn't afford to have John constantly reminding the people of their leader's sinfulness, but he was afraid to have John killed. He put off the choice. Eventually Herodias forced his hand, and John was executed. Of course, this only served to increase Herod's guilt.

Upon hearing about Jesus, Herod immediately identified him with John. He couldn't decide what to do about Jesus. He didn't want to repeat the mistake he had made with John, so he tried to threaten Jesus just before his final journey to Jerusalem. When the two met briefly during Jesus' trial, Jesus would not speak to Herod. Herod had proved himself a poor listener to John, and Jesus had nothing to add to John's words. Herod responded with spite and mocking. Having rejected the messenger, he found it easy to reject the Messiah.

For each person, God chooses the best possible ways to reveal himself. He uses his Word, circumstances, our minds, or other people to get our attention. He is persuasive and persistent, but never forces himself on us. To miss or resist God's message, as did Herod, is tragedy. How aware are you of God's attempts to enter your life? Have you welcomed him?

Strengths and accomplishments:
- Built the city of Tiberias and other architectural projects
- Ruled the region of Galilee for the Romans

Weaknesses and mistakes:
- Consumed with his quest for power
- Put off decisions or made wrong ones under pressure
- Divorced his wife to marry the wife of his half brother, Philip
- Imprisoned John the Baptist and later ordered his execution
- Had a minor part in the execution of Jesus

Lessons from his life:
- A life motivated by ambition is usually characterized by self-destruction
- Opportunities to do good usually come to us in the form of choices to be made

Vital statistics:
- Where: Jerusalem
- Occupation: Roman ruler of the region of Galilee and Perea
- Relatives: Father: Herod the Great. Mother: Malthace. First wife: daughter of Aretas IV. Second wife: Herodias
- Contemporaries: John the Baptist, Jesus, Pilate

Key verse:
"For Herod feared John, knowing that he was a righteous and holy man, and he protected him. When he heard him, he was greatly perplexed; and yet he liked to listen to him" (Mark 6.20).

Herod Antipas's story is told in the Gospels. He is also mentioned in Acts 4.27; 13.1.

the immensity of the task that they cannot see what is possible with God. Do you let what seems impossible about Christianity keep you from believing?

6.37–42 When Jesus asked the disciples to provide food for over 5,000 people, they sarcastically asked if they should go spend "two hundred denarii" (about eight months' wages) on bread. How do you react when you are given an impossible task? A situation that seems impossible with human means is simply an opportunity for God. The disciples did everything they could by gathering the available food and organizing the people into groups. Then, in answer to prayer, God did the impossible. When facing a seemingly impossible task, do what you can and ask God to do the rest. He may see fit to make the impossible happen.

loaves and the two fish, he looked up to heaven, and blessed and broke the loaves,
and gave them to his disciples to set before the people; and he divided the two fish
among them all. 42 And all ate and were filled; 43 and they took up twelve baskets
full of broken pieces and of the fish. 44 Those who had eaten the loaves numbered
five thousand men.

Jesus walks on water
(97/Matthew 14.22–33; John 6.16–21)

45 Immediately he made his disciples get into the boat and go on ahead to the
other side, to Bethsaida, while he dismissed the crowd. 46 After saying farewell to
them, he went up on the mountain to pray.
47 When evening came, the boat was out on the sea, and he was alone on the **6.47**
land. 48 When he saw that they were straining at the oars against an adverse wind, Mt 14.23-36 Jn 6.16-21
he came towards them early in the morning, walking on the sea. He intended to
pass them by. 49 But when they saw him walking on the sea, they thought it was a
ghost and cried out; 50 for they all saw him and were terrified. But immediately he
spoke to them and said, "Take heart, it is I; do not be afraid." 51 Then he got into the
boat with them and the wind ceased. And they were utterly astounded, 52 for they **6.52** Mk 16.14
did not understand about the loaves, but their hearts were hardened.

Jesus heals all who touch him
(98/Matthew 14.34–36)

53 When they had crossed over, they came to land at Gennesaret and moored **6.53**
the boat. 54 When they got out of the boat, people at once recognized him, 55 and Mt 14.34-36 Jn 6.24,25
rushed about that whole region and began to bring the sick on mats to wherever they
heard he was. 56 And wherever he went, into villages or cities or farms, they laid the **6.56**
sick in the marketplaces, and begged him that they might touch even the fringe of Mk 5.28 Acts 5.15
his cloak; and all who touched it were healed.

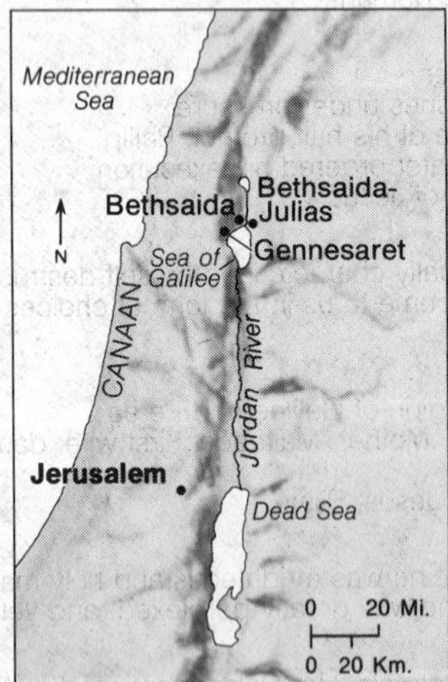

JESUS WALKS ON THE WATER
After feeding the people who had followed to hear him at Bethsaida-Julias, Jesus sent the people home, sent his disciples by boat toward Bethsaida, and went to pray. The disciples encountered a storm and Jesus walked to them on the water. They landed at Gennesaret.

6.49 The disciples were surprised to see Jesus walking beside them on the water. But they should have realized he would help them when they were in trouble. Though they had lost sight of him, he had not lost sight of them. His concern for them overcame their lack of faith. The next time you are in "deep water," remember that Christ knows your struggle and cares for you.

6.49, 50 The disciples were afraid, but Jesus' presence calmed their fears. We all experience fear. Do we try to deal with it ourselves, or do we let Jesus deal with it? In times of fear and uncertainty, it is calming to know that Christ is always with us (Matthew 28.20). To recognize his presence is the antidote for fear.

6.52 The disciples didn't want to believe, perhaps because (1) they couldn't accept the fact that this human named Jesus was really the Son of God; (2) they dared not believe that the Messiah would choose them as his followers—it was too good to be true; (3) they still did not understand the real purpose for Jesus' coming to earth. Their disbelief took the form of misunderstanding.

Even after watching Jesus miraculously feed 5,000 people, they still could not take the final step of faith and believe he was God's Son. If they had, they would not have been amazed that he could walk on water. They did not transfer the truth they already knew about him to their own lives. We read that Jesus walked on the water, and yet we often marvel that he is able to work in our lives. We must not only believe these miracles really occurred; we must also transfer the truth to our own life situations.

6.53 Gennesaret was a small fertile plain located on the west side of the Sea of Galilee. Capernaum, Jesus' home, sat at the northern edge of this plain.

6.56 A Jewish man wore an ankle-length robe called a tunic. Over the tunic he wore a waist-length vest called a tallith. Four tassels were sewn to the four lower corners of the border of the tallith. The people probably expected Jesus' healing power to be released when they touched these tassels (Matthew 9.20, 21). They may not have realized that it was faith in Jesus, not magical power, that healed them.

Jesus teaches about inner purity
(102/Matthew 15.1–20)

7.1 Mt 15.1-20
7 Now when the Pharisees and some of the scribes who had come from Jerusa-
7.2 Lk 11.38
lem gathered around him, 2 they noticed that some of his disciples were eating
with defiled hands, that is, without washing them. 3 (For the Pharisees, and all the
7.3 Gal 1.14 Col 2.8
Jews, do not eat unless they thoroughly wash their hands,[u] thus observing the tradition of the elders; 4 and they do not eat anything from the market unless they wash
it;[v] and there are also many other traditions that they observe, the washing of cups,
pots, and bronze kettles.[w]) 5 So the Pharisees and the scribes asked him, "Why do
your disciples not live[x] according to the tradition of the elders, but eat with defiled
7.6,7 Isa 29.13 Tit 1.16
hands?" 6 He said to them, "Isaiah prophesied rightly about you hypocrites, as it is
written,

'This people honors me with their lips,
but their hearts are far from me;
7 in vain do they worship me,
teaching human precepts as doctrines.'

7.9 Isa 24.4,5
8 You abandon the commandment of God and hold to human tradition."
9 Then he said to them, "You have a fine way of rejecting the commandment of
7.10 Ex 20.12; 21.17 Lev 20.19 Deut 5.16 Prov 20.20 1 Tim 5.8
God in order to keep your tradition! 10 For Moses said, 'Honor your father and your
mother'; and, 'Whoever speaks evil of father or mother must surely die.' 11 But you
say that if anyone tells father or mother, 'Whatever support you might have had
7.11 Lev 1.2
from me is Corban' (that is, an offering to God[y]) — 12 then you no longer permit
doing anything for a father or mother, 13 thus making void the word of God through
7.15 Acts 10.14,15 1 Cor 8.8 1 Tim 4.4
your tradition that you have handed on. And you do many things like this."
14 Then he called the crowd again and said to them, "Listen to me, all of you,
and understand: 15 there is nothing outside a person that by going in can defile, but
7.17 Mk 2.1,2; 3.20 9.28
the things that come out are what defile."[z]
17 When he had left the crowd and entered the house, his disciples asked him

[u] Meaning of Gk uncertain [v] Other ancient authorities read *and when they come from the marketplace, they do not eat unless they purify themselves* [w] Other ancient authorities add *and beds* [x] Gk *walk* [y] Gk lacks *to God* [z] Other ancient authorities add verse 16, *"Let anyone with ears to hear listen"*

REAL LEADERSHIP
Mark gives us some of the best insights into Jesus' character.

Herod as a leader	*Jesus as a leader*
Selfish	Compassionate
Murderer	Healer
Immoral	Just and good
Political opportunist	Servant
King over small territory	King over all creation

7.1ff The religious leaders sent some investigators from their headquarters in Jerusalem to check up on Jesus. They didn't like what they found, however, because Jesus scolded them for keeping the law in order to look holy instead of to honor God. The prophet Isaiah accused the religious leaders of his day for doing the same (Isaiah 29.13). Jesus used Isaiah's words to accuse these men.

7.3, 4 Mark explained these Jewish rituals because he was writing to a non-Jewish audience. Before each meal, devout Jews performed a short ceremony, washing their hands and arms in a specific way. The disciples did not have dirty hands, but they avoided this traditional cleansing. The Pharisees thought this ceremony cleansed them from any contact they might have had with anything considered unclean. Jesus said they were wrong in thinking they were acceptable to God because they were clean on the outside.

7.6, 7 Hypocrisy is pretending to be something you are not and have no intention of being. Jesus called the Pharisees hypocrites because they worshiped God for the wrong reasons. Their worship was not motivated by love, but by a desire for profit, for the appearance of holiness, and for increased status. We become hypocrites when we (1) pay more attention to reputation than to character, (2) carefully follow certain religious practices while allowing our hearts to remain distant from God, and (3) emphasize our virtues but others' sins.

7.8, 9 The Pharisees added hundreds of their own petty rules and regulations to God's holy laws, and then they tried to force people to follow them. These men claimed to know God's will in every detail of life. There are still religious leaders today who add rules and regulations to God's Word, causing much confusion among believers. It is idolatry to claim that your interpretation of God's Word is as important as God's Word itself. It is especially dangerous to set up nonbiblical standards for *others* to follow. Instead, look to Christ for guidance about your own behavior, and let him lead others in the details of their lives.

7.10, 11 The Pharisees used God as an excuse to avoid helping their families. They thought it was more important to put money in the temple treasury than to help their needy parents, although God's law specifically says to honor fathers and mothers (Exodus 20.12) and to care for those in need (Leviticus 25.35–43). (For an explanation of *Corban,* see the note on Matthew 15.5, 6.) We should give money and time to God, but we must never use God as an excuse to neglect our responsibilities. Helping those in need is one of the most important ways to honor God.

about the parable. 18 He said to them, "Then do you also fail to understand? Do you
not see that whatever goes into a person from outside cannot defile, 19 since it en- 7.19 Lk 11.41
ters, not the heart but the stomach, and goes out into the sewer?" (Thus he declared Acts 10.15; 11.9
all foods clean.) 20 And he said, "It is what comes out of a person that defiles. 21 For 7.20
it is from within, from the human heart, that evil intentions come: fornication, Rom 14.1-12 Col 2.16
theft, murder, 22 adultery, avarice, wickedness, deceit, licentiousness, envy, slan- 7.21
der, pride, folly. 23 All these evil things come from within, and they defile a per- Gal 5.19 Tit 1.15
son."

2. Jesus' ministry beyond Galilee

Jesus sends a demon out of a girl
(103/Matthew 15.21–28)

24 From there he set out and went away to the region of Tyre.[a] He entered a 7.24 Mt 15.21-28
house and did not want anyone to know he was there. Yet he could not escape
notice, 25 but a woman whose little daughter had an unclean spirit immediately
heard about him, and she came and bowed down at his feet. 26 Now the woman was
a Gentile, of Syrophoenician origin. She begged him to cast the demon out of her 7.27 Mt 10.5,6
daughter. 27 He said to her, "Let the children be fed first, for it is not fair to take the Acts 13.46 Rom 9.4
children's food and throw it to the dogs." 28 But she answered him, "Sir,[b] even the Eph 2.11,12
dogs under the table eat the children's crumbs." 29 Then he said to her, "For saying 7.29 Mt 9.29
that, you may go — the demon has left your daughter." 30 So she went home, found 7.30
the child lying on the bed, and the demon gone. Josh 21.45

The crowd marvels at Jesus' healings
(104/Matthew 15.29–31)

31 Then he returned from the region of Tyre, and went by way of Sidon towards

[a] Other ancient authorities add *and Sidon* [b] Or *Lord*; other ancient authorities prefix *Yes*

7.18, 19 Do we worry more about what is in our diets than what is in our hearts and minds? As they interpreted the dietary laws (Leviticus 11), the Jews believed they could be clean before God because of what they would not eat. But Jesus pointed out that sin actually begins in the attitudes and intentions of the inner person. He did not downgrade the law, but he paved the way for the change made clear in Acts 10.9–29 when God removed the cultural restrictions regarding food. We are not pure because of outward acts—we become pure on the inside as Christ renews our minds and makes us over in his image.

7.20–23 An evil action begins with a single thought. Allowing our minds to dwell on lust, envy, hate, or revenge will lead to sin. Don't defile yourself by focusing on evil. Instead, follow Paul's advice in Philippians 4.8 and think about what is true, honorable, just, pure, pleasing, and commendable.

7.24 Jesus traveled about 50 miles to Tyre and then went to Sidon. These were port cities on the Mediterranean Sea north of Israel. Both cities had flourishing trade and were very wealthy.

In David's day, Tyre was on friendly terms with Israel (2 Samuel 5.11), but soon afterward the city became known for its wickedness. Its king, Ethbaal, even claimed to be God (Ezekiel 28.1ff). Tyre rejoiced when Jerusalem was destroyed in 586 B.C., because without Israel's competition, Tyre's trade and profits would increase. It was into this evil and materialistic culture that Jesus brought his message. It is interesting that he stressed the importance of inner purity just before visiting Tyre.

7.26 This woman is called a Syrophoenician in Mark and a Canaanite in Matthew. Mark's designation refers to her political background. His Roman audience would easily identify her by the part of the empire that was her home. Matthew's description was designed for his Jewish audience, who remembered the Canaanites as bitter enemies when Israel was settling the promised land.

7.27, 28 *Dog* was a term the Jews commonly applied to any Gentiles, because the Jews considered these people no more likely than dogs to receive God's approval. Jesus, however, was not degrading the woman by using this term, but simply explaining to her God's plan to present his message first to Jews.

The woman did not try to argue. Using Jesus' choice of words, she pointed out that she was willing to be considered a dog as long as she could receive God's healing for her daughter. Ironically, many Jews would lose God's spiritual healing because they rejected Jesus, while many Gentiles, whom the Jews considered "dogs," would find salvation because they recognized Jesus.

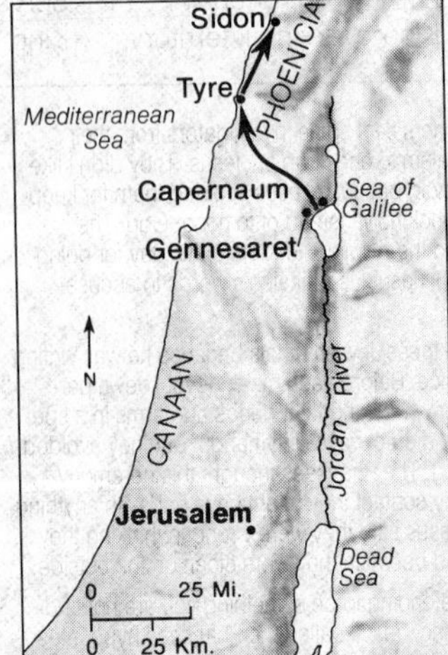

MINISTRY IN PHOENICIA
Jesus' ministry was to all people—first to Jews but also to Gentiles. Jesus took his disciples from Galilee to Tyre and Sidon, large cities in Phoenicia, where he healed a Gentile woman's daughter.

7.29 This miracle shows that Jesus' power over demons is so great that he doesn't need to be present physically in order to free someone. His power spans any distance.

7.31 Mt 15.29-31 the Sea of Galilee, in the region of the Decapolis. 32 They brought to him a deaf man
who had an impediment in his speech; and they begged him to lay his hand on him.
7.33 Mk 8.23 Jn 9.6 33 He took him aside in private, away from the crowd, and put his fingers into his
ears, and he spat and touched his tongue. 34 Then looking up to heaven, he sighed
7.34 Isa 35.5,6 Mt 11.5 Mk 6.41 Jn 11.41; 17.1 and said to him, "Ephphatha," that is, "Be opened." 35 And immediately his ears
were opened, his tongue was released, and he spoke plainly. 36 Then Jesus[c] ordered them to tell no one; but the more he ordered them, the more zealously they
7.36 Mk 5.43 proclaimed it. 37 They were astounded beyond measure, saying, "He has done everything well; he even makes the deaf to hear and the mute to speak."

Jesus feeds four thousand
(105/Matthew 15.32–39)

8 In those days when there was again a great crowd without anything to eat, he
8.2 Ps 111.4,5 145.9 Mk 1.41 Heb 2.17; 4.15 5.1-3 called his disciples and said to them, 2 "I have compassion for the crowd, because they have been with me now for three days and have nothing to eat. 3 If I send
them away hungry to their homes, they will faint on the way—and some of them
have come from a great distance." 4 His disciples replied, "How can one feed these
8.4 Num 11.21,22 2 Kgs 4.42,43 people with bread here in the desert?" 5 He asked them, "How many loaves do you
have?" They said, "Seven." 6 Then he ordered the crowd to sit down on the ground;
8.5 Mk 6.38 and he took the seven loaves, and after giving thanks he broke them and gave them
8.6 1 Tim 4.4,5 to his disciples to distribute; and they distributed them to the crowd. 7 They had also
8.7 Mt 14.19 a few small fish; and after blessing them, he ordered that these too should be distributed. 8 They ate and were filled; and they took up the broken pieces left over,
seven baskets full. 9 Now there were about four thousand people. And he sent them
8.10 Mt 15.39—16.12 away. 10 And immediately he got into the boat with his disciples and went to the
district of Dalmanutha.[d]

[c] Gk *he* [d] Other ancient authorities read *Mageda* or *Magdala*

GOSPEL ACCOUNTS FOUND ONLY IN MARK

Section	*Topic*	*Significance*
4.26–29	Story of the growing seeds	We must share the good news of Jesus with other people, but only God makes it grow in their lives.
7.31–37	Jesus heals a deaf man with a speech impediment	Jesus cares about our physical as well as spiritual needs.
8.22–26	Jesus heals the blind man of Bethsaida	Jesus is considerate because he makes sure this man's sight is fully restored.

CONTINUED MINISTRY
After taking a roundabout way back to Galilee through Decapolis (the Ten Towns), Jesus returned to Dalmanutha where Jewish leaders questioned his authority. From there he went to Bethsaida-Julias and on to Caesarea-Philippi. Here he talked with his disciples about his authority and coming events.

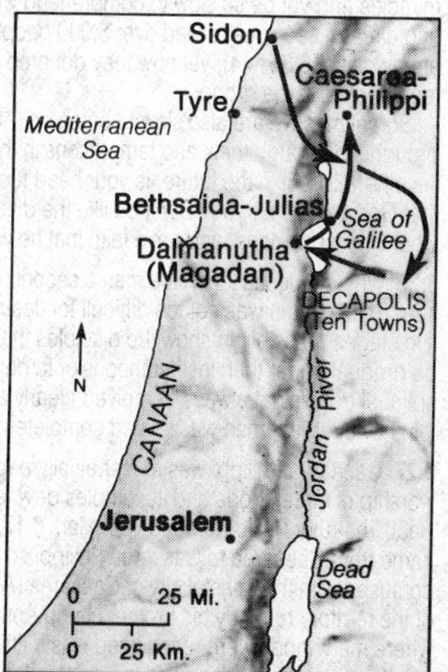

7.36 Jesus asked the people not to talk about this healing, because he didn't want to be seen simply as a miracle worker. He didn't want the people to miss his real message. We must not be so concerned about what Jesus can do for us that we forget to listen to his message.

8.1ff This is a different miracle from the feeding of the 5,000 described in chapter 6. At that time, those fed were mostly Jews. This time Jesus was ministering to a non-Jewish crowd in the Gentile region of Decapolis. Jesus' work and message were beginning to have an impact on large numbers of Gentiles. That Jesus would minister to non-Jews was very reassuring to Mark's primarily Roman audience.

8.1–3 Do you ever feel that God is so busy with important concerns that he can't possibly be aware of your needs? Just as Jesus was concerned about those people's need for food, he is concerned about our daily needs. At another time Jesus said, "Therefore do not worry, saying, 'What will we eat?' or 'What will we drink?' or 'What will we wear?' . . . your heavenly Father knows that you need all these things" (Matthew 6.31, 32). Do you have concerns that you think would not interest God? There is nothing too large for him to handle and no need too small to escape his interest.

Religious leaders ask for a sign in the sky
(106/Matthew 16.1–4)

11 The Pharisees came and began to argue with him, asking him for a sign from 8.11 Mt 12.38
heaven, to test him. 12 And he sighed deeply in his spirit and said, "Why does this 16.1-10
generation ask for a sign? Truly I tell you, no sign will be given to this generation." Lk 11.16 Jn 6.30
13 And he left them, and getting into the boat again, he went across to the other side. 1 Cor 1.22

Jesus warns against wrong teaching
(107/Matthew 16.5–12)

14 Now the disciples[e] had forgotten to bring any bread; and they had only one
loaf with them in the boat. 15 And he cautioned them, saying, "Watch out—beware 8.15 Lk 12.1
of the yeast of the Pharisees and the yeast of Herod."[f] 16 They said to one another,
"It is because we have no bread." 17 And becoming aware of it, Jesus said to them, 8.17 Mk 6.52
"Why are you talking about having no bread? Do you still not perceive or under- 8.18 Ezek 12.2
stand? Are your hearts hardened? 18 Do you have eyes, and fail to see? Do you have
ears, and fail to hear? And do you not remember? 19 When I broke the five loaves 8.19 Mt 14.20
for the five thousand, how many baskets full of broken pieces did you collect?" Mk 6.43,44 Lk 9.17
They said to him, "Twelve." 20 "And the seven for the four thousand, how many Jn 6.13
baskets full of broken pieces did you collect?" And they said to him, "Seven." 8.20 Mt 15.37
21 Then he said to them, "Do you not yet understand?" Mk 8.8,9

Jesus restores sight to a blind man
(108)

22 They came to Bethsaida. Some people[g] brought a blind man to him and
begged him to touch him. 23 He took the blind man by the hand and led him out of 8.23 Mk 7.33
the village; and when he had put saliva on his eyes and laid his hands on him, he Jn 9.6
asked him, "Can you see anything?" 24 And the man[h] looked up and said, "I can see
people, but they look like trees, walking." 25 Then Jesus[h] laid his hands on his eyes
again; and he looked intently and his sight was restored, and he saw everything
clearly. 26 Then he sent him away to his home, saying, "Do not even go into the 8.26 Mt 8.4
village."[i]

Peter says Jesus is the Messiah
(109/Matthew 16.13–20; Luke 9.18–20)

27 Jesus went on with his disciples to the villages of Caesarea Philippi; and on

[e] Gk *they* [f] Other ancient authorities read *the Herodians* [g] Gk *They* [h] Gk *he* [i] Other ancient authorities add *or tell anyone in the village*

8.11 The Pharisees had tried to explain away Jesus' previous miracles by claiming they were done by luck, coincidence, or evil power. Now they demanded a sign from heaven—something only God could do. Jesus refused their demand because he knew that even this kind of miracle would not convince them. They had already decided not to believe. Hearts can become so hard that even the most convincing facts and demonstrations will not change them.

8.15 Mark mentions the yeast of the Pharisees and Herod, while Matthew talks about the yeast of the Sadducees and Pharisees. Mark's audience, mostly non-Jews, would have known about Herod, but not necessarily about the Jewish religious sect of the Sadducees. Thus Mark quoted the part of Jesus' statement that his readers would understand. This reference to Herod means the Herodians, a group of Jews who supported the king. Many Herodians were also Sadducees.

8.15ff Yeast in this passage symbolizes evil. Just as only a small amount of yeast is needed to make a batch of bread rise, so the hardheartedness of the religious and political leaders could permeate and contaminate the entire society and make it rise up against Jesus.

8.17, 18 How could the disciples experience so many of Jesus' miracles and yet be so slow to comprehend who he was? They had already seen Jesus feed over 5,000 people with five loaves and two fish (6.35–44), yet now they doubted whether he could feed another large group.

Sometimes we are also slow to catch on. Although Christ has brought us through trials and temptations in the past, we don't believe he will do it in the future. Is your heart too closed to take in all that God can do for you? Don't be like the disciples. Remember what Christ has done, and have faith that he will do it again.

8.25 Why did Jesus touch the man a second time before he could see? This miracle was not too difficult for Jesus, but he chose to do it in stages, possibly to show the disciples that some healing would be gradual rather than instantaneous or to demonstrate that spiritual truth is not always perceived clearly at first. Before Jesus left, however, the man was healed completely.

8.27 Caesarea Philippi was an especially pagan city, known for its worship of Greek gods and its temples devoted to the ancient god Baal. The ruler Philip, referred to in Mark 6.17, changed the city's name from Caesarea to Caesarea Philippi so that it would not be confused with the coastal city of Caesarea (Acts 8.40), the capital of the territory ruled by his brother Herod Antipas. This pagan city where many gods were recognized was a fitting place for Jesus to ask the disciples to recognize him as the Son of God.

8.27 Mt 16.13-20
8.28 Mt 14.2
8.29 Jn 6.69; 11.27

the way he asked his disciples, "Who do people say that I am?" 28 And they answered him, "John the Baptist; and others, Elijah; and still others, one of the prophets." 29 He asked them, "But who do you say that I am?" Peter answered him, "You
are the Messiah."[j] 30 And he sternly ordered them not to tell anyone about him.

Jesus predicts his death the first time
(110/Matthew 16.21–28; Luke 9.21–27)

8.31 Mt 16.21-28; 17.22, 23 Lk 9.22-27
8.33 Rom 8.7
8.34 Mt 10.38 Lk 14.27
8.35 Lk 17.33 Jn 12.25 Rev 12.11
8.38 Mt 10.33 Lk 12.9 Rom 1.16 2 Thess 1.7 2 Tim 1.8; 2.12 Heb 11.16

31 Then he began to teach them that the Son of Man must undergo great suffering, and be rejected by the elders, the chief priests, and the scribes, and be killed,
and after three days rise again. 32 He said all this quite openly. And Peter took him
aside and began to rebuke him. 33 But turning and looking at his disciples, he rebuked Peter and said, "Get behind me, Satan! For you are setting your mind not on
divine things but on human things."
34 He called the crowd with his disciples, and said to them, "If any want to
become my followers, let them deny themselves and take up their cross and follow
me. 35 For those who want to save their life will lose it, and those who lose their life
for my sake, and for the sake of the gospel,[k] will save it. 36 For what will it profit
them to gain the whole world and forfeit their life? 37 Indeed, what can they give in
return for their life? 38 Those who are ashamed of me and of my words[l] in this
adulterous and sinful generation, of them the Son of Man will also be ashamed

[j] Or *the Christ* [k] Other ancient authorities read *lose their life for the sake of the gospel* [l] Other ancient authorities read *and of mine*

8.28 For the story of John the Baptist, see Mark 1.1–11 and 6.14–29. For the story of Elijah, see 1 Kings 17–20 and 2 Kings 1; 2.

8.29 Jesus asked the disciples who others thought he was; then he asked them the same question. It is not enough to know what others say about Jesus: you must know, understand, and accept for yourself that he is the Messiah. You must move from curiosity to commitment, from admiration to adoration.

8.30 Why did Jesus warn his own disciples not to tell anyone the truth about him? Jesus knew they needed more instruction about the work he would accomplish through his death and resurrection. Without more teaching, the disciples would have only half the picture. When they confessed Jesus as the Christ, they still didn't know all that it meant.

8.31 From this point on, Jesus spoke plainly and directly to his disciples about his death and resurrection. He began to prepare them for what was going to happen to him by telling them three times that he would soon die (8.31; 9.31; 10.33, 34).

8.32, 33 In this moment, Peter was not considering God's purposes, but only his natural human desires and feelings. He wanted Christ to be King, but not the suffering Servant prophesied in Isaiah 53. He was ready to receive the glory of following the Messiah, but not the persecution.

The Christian life is not a paved road to wealth and ease. It often involves hard work, persecution, privation, and deep suffering. Peter saw only part of the picture. Don't repeat his mistake—instead, focus on the good that God can bring out of apparent evil, and the resurrection that follows crucifixion.

8.33 Peter was often the spokesman for all the disciples. In singling him out, Jesus may have been addressing all of them indirectly. Unknowingly, the disciples were trying to prevent Jesus from going to the cross and thus fulfilling his mission on earth. Satan also tempted Jesus to avoid the way of the cross (Matthew 4). Whereas Satan's motives were evil, the disciples were motivated by love and admiration for Jesus. Nevertheless, the disciples' job was not to guide and protect Jesus, but to follow him. Only after Jesus' death and resurrection would they fully understand why he had to die.

8.34 The Romans, Mark's original audience, knew what taking up the cross meant. Death on a cross was a form of execution used by Rome for dangerous criminals. A prisoner carried his own cross to the place of execution, signifying submission to Rome's power.

Jesus used carrying a cross to illustrate the ultimate submission required of his followers. He is not against pleasure, nor is he saying that we should seek pain needlessly. He is talking about the heroic effort needed to follow him moment by moment, to do his will even when the work is difficult and the future looks bleak.

8.35 We should be willing to lose our lives for the sake of the gospel, not because our lives are useless but because nothing—not even life itself—can compare to what we gain with Christ. Jesus wants us to *choose* to follow him rather than to lead a life of sin and self-satisfaction. He wants us to stop trying to control our own destiny and to let him direct us. This makes good sense because, as the Creator, he knows better than we do what real life is about. He asks for submission, not self-hatred; he asks us only to lose our self-centered determination to be in charge.

8.36, 37 Many people spend all their energy seeking pleasure. Jesus said, however, that the world of pleasure centered on possessions, position, or power is ultimately worthless. Whatever you have on earth is only temporary; it cannot be exchanged for your soul. If you work hard at getting what you want, you might eventually have a "pleasurable" life, but in the end you will find it hollow and empty. Are you willing to make the pursuit of God more important than the selfish pursuit of pleasure? Follow Jesus, and you will know what it means to live abundantly now and to have eternal life as well.

8.38 Jesus constantly turns the world's perspective upside down with talk of first and last, saving and losing. Here he gives us a choice. We can reject Jesus now and be rejected by him at his second coming, or we can accept him now and be accepted by him then. Rejecting him may help us escape shame for the time being, but it will guarantee an eternity of shame later.

9 when he comes in the glory of his Father with the holy angels." 1 And he said 9.1
to them, "Truly I tell you, there are some standing here who will not taste death Mt 16.28; 24.30 Lk 9.27; 22.18
until they see that the kingdom of God has come with[m] power."

Jesus is transfigured on the mountain
(111/Matthew 17.1–13; Luke 9.28–36)

2 Six days later, Jesus took with him Peter and James and John, and led them up 9.2
a high mountain apart, by themselves. And he was transfigured before them, 3 and Mt 17.1-13 Lk 9.28-36
his clothes became dazzling white, such as no one[n] on earth could bleach them. 9.3
4 And there appeared to them Elijah with Moses, who were talking with Jesus. Dan 7.9 Mt 28.3
5 Then Peter said to Jesus, "Rabbi, it is good for us to be here; let us make three
dwellings,[o] one for you, one for Moses, and one for Elijah." 6 He did not know
what to say, for they were terrified. 7 Then a cloud overshadowed them, and from 9.7
the cloud there came a voice, "This is my Son, the Beloved;[p] listen to him!" 8 Sud- Ex 40.34 2 Pet 1.17,18
denly when they looked around, they saw no one with them any more, but only Heb 1.2; 2.3; 12.25
Jesus.
9 As they were coming down the mountain, he ordered them to tell no one about
what they had seen, until after the Son of Man had risen from the dead. 10 So they 9.11
kept the matter to themselves, questioning what this rising from the dead could Mal 4.5 Mt 11.14
mean. 11 Then they asked him, "Why do the scribes say that Elijah must come 9.12,13
first?" 12 He said to them, "Elijah is indeed coming first to restore all things. How Gen 3.15 Ps 22.6,7
then is it written about the Son of Man, that he is to go through many sufferings and Isa 50.6; 53.2,3 Dan 9.26
be treated with contempt? 13 But I tell you that Elijah has come, and they did to him Mt 11.13,14 Lk 1.17; 23.11
whatever they pleased, as it is written about him." Jn 3.14

Jesus heals a demon-possessed boy
(112/Matthew 17.14–21; Luke 9.37–43)

14 When they came to the disciples, they saw a great crowd around them, and 9.14
some scribes arguing with them. 15 When the whole crowd saw him, they were Mt 17.14-21 Lk 9.37-43
immediately overcome with awe, and they ran forward to greet him. 16 He asked
them, "What are you arguing about with them?" 17 Someone from the crowd answered him, "Teacher, I brought you my son; he has a spirit that makes him unable

[m] *Or in* [n] *Gk no fuller* [o] *Or tents* [p] *Or my beloved Son*

9.1 What did Jesus mean when he said that some of the disciples would see the kingdom come with power? There are several possibilities. He could have been foretelling his transfiguration, his resurrection and ascension, the coming of the Holy Spirit at pentecost, or his second coming. The transfiguration is a strong possibility because Mark immediately tells the story. In the transfiguration (9.2–8), Peter, James, and John saw Jesus' identity and power as the Son of God (2 Peter 1.16).

9.2 We don't know why Jesus singled out Peter, James, and John for this special revelation of Jesus' glory and purity. Perhaps they were the ones most ready to understand and accept this great truth about Jesus. These three disciples were the inner circle of the group of 12. They were among the first to hear Jesus' call (1.16–19). They headed the Gospel lists of disciples (3.16). And they were present at certain healings where others were excluded (Luke 8.51).

9.2 Jesus took the disciples to either Mount Hermon or Mount Tabor. A mountain was often associated with closeness to God and readiness to receive his words. God had appeared to both Moses (Exodus 24.12–18) and Elijah (1 Kings 19.8–18) on mountains.

9.3ff The transfiguration revealed Christ's divine nature. God's voice elevated Jesus above Moses and Elijah as the long-awaited Messiah with full divine authority. Moses represented the law, and Elijah, the prophets. Their appearance showed Jesus as the fulfillment of both the Old Testament Law and the prophetic promises.

Jesus was not a reincarnation of Elijah or Moses. He was not merely one of the prophets. As God's only Son, he far surpasses them in authority and power. Many voices try to tell us how to live and how to know God personally. Some of these are helpful; many are not. We must first listen to the Bible, and then evaluate all other authorities in light of God's revelation.

9.9, 10 Jesus told Peter, James, and John not to speak about what they had seen, because they would not fully understand it until Jesus had risen from the dead. Then they would realize that only through dying could he show his power over death and his authority to be King of all. The disciples could not be powerful witnesses for God until they had grasped this truth.

It was natural for the disciples to be confused about Jesus' death and resurrection because they could not see into the future. We, on the other hand, have God's revealed Word, the Bible, to give us the full meaning of Jesus' death and resurrection. We have no excuse for our unbelief.

9.11–13 When Jesus said Elijah had indeed come, he was speaking of John the Baptist (Matthew 17.11–13).

9.12, 13 It was difficult for the disciples to grasp the idea that their Messiah would have to suffer. The Jews who studied the Old Testament prophecies expected the Messiah to be a great king like David, who would overthrow the enemy, Rome. Their vision was limited to their own time and experience.

They could not understand that the values of God's eternal kingdom were different from the values of the world. They wanted relief from their present problems, but deliverance from sin is far more important than deliverance from physical suffering or political oppression. Our understanding of and appreciation for Jesus must go beyond what he can do for us here and now.

to speak; 18 and whenever it seizes him, it dashes him down; and he foams and
grinds his teeth and becomes rigid; and I asked your disciples to cast it out, but they
9.19 could not do so." 19 He answered them, "You faithless generation, how much
Jn 4.48 longer must I be among you? How much longer must I put up with you? Bring him
9.20 to me." 20 And they brought the boy[q] to him. When the spirit saw him, immedi-
Mk 1.26 ately it convulsed the boy,[q] and he fell on the ground and rolled about, foaming at
the mouth. 21 Jesus[r] asked the father, "How long has this been happening to him?"
And he said, "From childhood. 22 It has often cast him into the fire and into the
water, to destroy him; but if you are able to do anything, have pity on us and help
9.23 Mk 11.22-24 us." 23 Jesus said to him, "If you are able! — All things can be done for the one who
Lk 17.6 believes." 24 Immediately the father of the child cried out,[s] "I believe; help my
Jn 11.40 Acts 14.9 unbelief!" 25 When Jesus saw that a crowd came running together, he rebuked the
9.24 unclean spirit, saying to it, "You spirit that keeps this boy from speaking and hear-
Eph 2.8 ing, I command you, come out of him, and never enter him again!" 26 After crying
9.25 Acts 10.38 out and convulsing him terribly, it came out, and the boy was like a corpse, so that
most of them said, "He is dead." 27 But Jesus took him by the hand and lifted him
up, and he was able to stand. 28 When he had entered the house, his disciples asked
him privately, "Why could we not cast it out?" 29 He said to them, "This kind can
come out only through prayer."[t]

Jesus predicts his death the second time
(113/Matthew 17.22, 23; Luke 9.44, 45)

9.30 Mt 17.22,23 30 They went on from there and passed through Galilee. He did not want any-
Lk 9.43-45 one to know it; 31 for he was teaching his disciples, saying to them, "The Son of
9.31 Mt 16.21 Man is to be betrayed into human hands, and they will kill him, and three days after
Mk 8.31 Lk 9.22 being killed, he will rise again." 32 But they did not understand what he was saying
and were afraid to ask him.

The disciples argue about who would be the greatest
(115/Matthew 18.1–6; Luke 9.46–48)

33 Then they came to Capernaum; and when he was in the house he asked them,
9.34 Prov 13.10 "What were you arguing about on the way?" 34 But they were silent, for on the way
Lk 22.24,26 they had argued with one another who was the greatest. 35 He sat down, called the

[q] Gk *him* [r] Gk *He* [s] Other ancient authorities add *with tears* [t] Other ancient authorities add *and fasting*

9.18 Why couldn't the disciples cast out the evil spirit? In 6.13 we read that they cast out demons while on their mission to the villages. Perhaps they had special authority only for that trip; or perhaps their faith was faltering. Mark tells this story to show that the battle with Satan is a difficult, ongoing struggle. Victory over sin and temptation comes through faith in Jesus Christ, not through our own efforts.

9.23 Jesus' words do not mean we can automatically obtain anything we want if we just think positively. Jesus meant that anything is *possible* if we believe, because nothing is too difficult for God. We cannot have everything we pray for as if by magic; but with faith, we can have everything we need to serve him.

9.24 The attitude of trust and confidence that the Bible calls *belief* or *faith* (Hebrews 11.1, 6) is not something we can obtain without help. Faith is a gift from God (Ephesians 2.8, 9). No matter how much faith we have, we never reach the point of being self-sufficient. Faith is not stored away like money in the bank. Growing in faith is a constant process of daily renewing our trust in Jesus.

9.29 The disciples would often face difficult situations that could be resolved only through prayer. Prayer is the key that unlocks faith in our lives. Effective prayer needs both an attitude — complete dependence — and an action — asking. Prayer demonstrates our reliance on God as we humbly invite him to fill us with faith and power. There is no substitute for prayer, especially in circumstances that seem impossible.

9.30, 31 At times Jesus limited his public ministry in order to train his disciples in depth. He knew the importance of equipping them to carry on when he returned to heaven. It takes time to learn. Deep spiritual growth isn't instant, regardless of the quality of experience or teaching. If even the disciples needed to lay aside their work periodically in order to learn from the Master, how much more do we need to alternate working and learning.

9.30, 31 Leaving Caesarea Philippi, Jesus began his last tour through the region of Galilee.

9.32 Why were the disciples afraid to ask Jesus about his prediction of his death? Perhaps it was because the last time they reacted to Jesus' words they were scolded (8.32, 33). In their minds, Jesus seemed morbidly preoccupied with death. Actually it was the disciples who were wrongly preoccupied — constantly thinking about the kingdom they hoped Jesus would bring and their positions in it. If Jesus died, the kingdom as they imagined it could not come. Consequently they preferred not to talk about his predictions.

9.34 The disciples, caught up in their constant struggle for personal success, were embarrassed to answer Jesus' question. It is always painful to compare our motives with Christ's. It is not wrong for believers to be industrious or ambitious, but when ambition pushes obedience and service to one side, it becomes sin. Pride or insecurity can cause us to overvalue position and prestige. In God's kingdom, such motives are destructive. The only safe ambition is for Christ's kingdom, not our own advancement.

twelve, and said to them, "Whoever wants to be first must be last of all and servant
of all." 36 Then he took a little child and put it among them; and taking it in his arms, 9.37
he said to them, 37 "Whoever welcomes one such child in my name welcomes me, Mt 10.40 Mk 10.16
and whoever welcomes me welcomes not me but the one who sent me." Jn 13.20

The disciples forbid another to use Jesus' name
(116/Luke 9.49, 50)

38 John said to him, "Teacher, we saw someone[u] casting out demons in your 9.38 Num 11.26-29
name, and we tried to stop him, because he was not following us." 39 But Jesus 9.39
said, "Do not stop him; for no one who does a deed of power in my name will be 1 Cor 12.3
able soon afterward to speak evil of me. 40 Whoever is not against us is for us. 41 For 9.40 Mt 12.30
truly I tell you, whoever gives you a cup of water to drink because you bear the 9.41
name of Christ will by no means lose the reward. Mt 10.42

Jesus warns against temptation
(117/Matthew 18.7–9)

42 "If any of you put a stumbling block before one of these little ones who 9.42 Lk 17.1-3
believe in me,[v] it would be better for you if a great millstone were hung around
your neck and you were thrown into the sea. 43 If your hand causes you to stumble, 9.43 Deut 13.6-10
cut it off; it is better for you to enter life maimed than to have two hands and to go Mt 5.29,30
to hell,[w] to the unquenchable fire.[x] 45 And if your foot causes you to stumble, cut
it off; it is better for you to enter life lame than to have two feet and to be thrown 9.48 Isa 66.24
into hell.[w,x] 47 And if your eye causes you to stumble, tear it out; it is better for you 2 Thess 1.9
to enter the kingdom of God with one eye than to have two eyes and to be thrown 9.49 Lev 2.13
into hell,[w] 48 where their worm never dies, and the fire is never quenched. Ezek 43.24

49 "For everyone will be salted with fire.[y] 50 Salt is good; but if salt has lost its 9.50 Mt 5.13
saltiness, how can you season it?[z] Have salt in yourselves, and be at peace with Lk 14.34
one another."

[u] Other ancient authorities add *who does not follow us* [v] Other ancient authorities lack *in me* [w] Gk *Gehenna* [x] Verses 44 and 46 (which are identical with verse 48) are lacking in the best ancient authorities [y] Other ancient authorities either add or substitute *and every sacrifice will be salted with salt* [z] Or *how can you restore its saltiness?*

9.36, 37 Jesus taught the disciples to welcome children. This was a new approach in a society where children were usually treated as second-class citizens. It is important not only to treat children well, but also to teach them about Jesus. Children's ministries should never be regarded as less important than those for adults.

9.38 The disciples were jealous of a man who healed in Jesus' name, because they were more concerned about their own group's position than in helping to free those troubled by demons. We do the same today when we refuse to participate in worthy causes because (1) they are not affiliated with our denomination, (2) they do not involve the kind of people with whom we feel most comfortable, (3) they don't do things the way we are used to, (4) our efforts won't receive enough recognition. Correct theology is important, but it should never be an excuse to avoid helping those in need.

9.40 Jesus was not saying that being indifferent or neutral toward him is as good as being committed. As he explained in Matthew 12.30, "Whoever is not with me is against me." In both cases, Jesus was pointing out that neutrality toward him is not possible. Nevertheless, his followers will not all resemble each other or belong to the same groups. People who are on Jesus' side have the same goal of building up the kingdom of God, and they should not let their differences interfere with this. Those who share a common faith in Christ should cooperate. People don't have to be just like us to be following Jesus with us.

9.41, 42 Luke 9.48 states, "The least among all of you is the greatest." In Jesus' eyes, whoever welcomes a child welcomes Jesus; giving a cup of cold water to a person in need is the same as giving an offering to God. By contrast, harming others or failing to care for them is a sin, even if they are unimportant people in the world's eyes. It is possible for thoughtless, selfish people to gain a measure of worldly greatness, but lasting greatness is measured by God's standards. What do you use as your measure – personal achievement or unselfish service?

9.42 This caution against harming little ones in the faith applies both to what we do individually as teachers and examples and to what we allow in our Christian fellowship. Our thoughts and actions must be motivated by love (1 Corinthians 13) and we must be careful about judging others (Matthew 7.1–5; Romans 14.1–15.4). However, we also have a responsibility to confront flagrant sin within the church (1 Corinthians 5.12, 13).

9.43ff Jesus used startling language to stress the importance of cutting sin out of our lives. Painful discipline is required of his true followers. Giving up a relationship, job, or habit that is against God's will may seem just as painful as cutting off a hand. Our high goal, however, is worth any sacrifice; Christ is worth any possible loss. Nothing should stand in the way of faith. We must be ruthless in removing sins from our lives now in order to avoid being stuck with them for eternity. Make your choices from an eternal perspective.

9.48, 49 With these strange words, Jesus pictured the serious and eternal consequences of sin. To the Jews, worms and fire represented both internal and external pain. What could be worse?

9.50 Jesus used salt to illustrate three qualities that should be found in his people: (1) *We should remember God's faithfulness,* just as salt when used with a sacrifice recalled God's covenant with his people (Leviticus 2.13). (2) *We should make a difference in the "flavor" of the world we live in,* just as salt changes meat's flavor (see Matthew 5.13). (3) *We should counteract the moral decay in society,* just as salt preserves food from decay. When we lose this desire to "salt" the earth with the love and message of God, we become useless to him.

Jesus teaches about marriage and divorce
(173/Matthew 19.1–12)

10 He left that place and went to the region of Judea and[a] beyond the Jordan.
And crowds again gathered around him; and, as was his custom, he again
taught them.
10.2 Mt 19.3-12 2 Some Pharisees came, and to test him they asked, "Is it lawful for a man to
divorce his wife?" 3 He answered them, "What did Moses command you?" 4 They
10.4 Deut 24.1-3 said, "Moses allowed a man to write a certificate of dismissal and to divorce her."
Mt 5.31 5 But Jesus said to them, "Because of your hardness of heart he wrote this com-
10.6 mandment for you. 6 But from the beginning of creation, 'God made them male and
Gen 1.27; 2.24 female.' 7 'For this reason a man shall leave his father and mother and be joined to
10.8 1 Cor 6.16 his wife,[b] 8 and the two shall become one flesh.' So they are no longer two, but one
Eph 5.31 flesh. 9 Therefore what God has joined together, let no one separate."
10.11 Mt 5.32 10 Then in the house the disciples asked him again about this matter. 11 He said
Lk 16.18 to them, "Whoever divorces his wife and marries another commits adultery against
Rom 7.2,3 her; 12 and if she divorces her husband and marries another, she commits adultery."

Jesus blesses little children
(174/Matthew 19.13–15; Luke 18.15–17)

10.13 Mt 19.13-15 13 People were bringing little children to him in order that he might touch them;
Lk 18.15-17 and the disciples spoke sternly to them. 14 But when Jesus saw this, he was indig-
10.15 Mt 18.3 nant and said to them, "Let the little children come to me; do not stop them; for it
1 Cor 14.20 is to such as these that the kingdom of God belongs. 15 Truly I tell you, whoever
1 Pet 2.2 does not receive the kingdom of God as a little child will never enter it." 16 And he
10.16 Isa 40.11 took them up in his arms, laid his hands on them, and blessed them.

[a] Other ancient authorities lack *and* [b] Other ancient authorities lack *and be joined to his wife*

FINAL TRIP TO JUDEA
Jesus quietly left Capernaum, heading toward the borders of Judea before crossing the Jordan River. He preached there before going to Jericho. This trip from Galilee was his last; he would not return before his death.

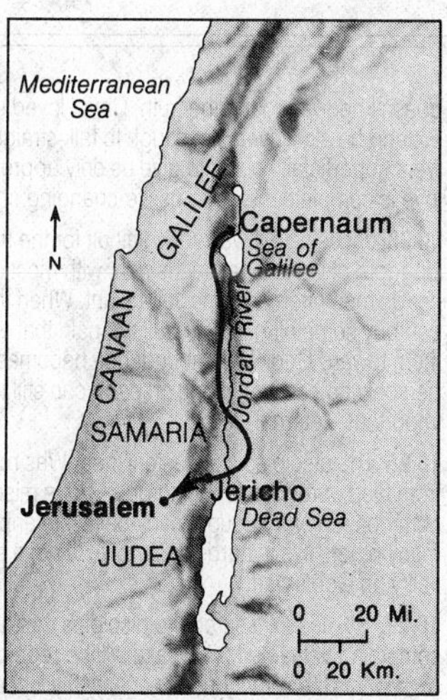

10.2 The Pharisees were trying to trap Jesus with their question. If he supported divorce, he would be upholding the Pharisees' procedures, and they doubted that he would do that. If he spoke against divorce, however, the crowds would dislike his position. More important, he might incur the wrath of Herod, who had already killed John the Baptist for speaking out against divorce and adultery (6.17–28). This is what the Pharisees wanted.

The Pharisees saw divorce as a legal issue rather than a spiritual one. Jesus used this test as an opportunity to review God's intended purpose for marriage and to expose the Pharisees' selfish motives. They were not thinking about what God intended for marriage, but had settled for marriages of convenience. In addition, they were quoting Moses unfairly and out of context. Jesus showed these legal experts how superficial their knowledge really was.

10.5–9 God allowed divorce as a concession to people's sinfulness. Divorce was not approved, but it was instituted to protect the injured party in the midst of a bad situation. Unfortunately, the Pharisees used Deuteronomy 24.1 as an excuse for divorce. Jesus explained that this was not God's intent; instead, God wants married people to consider their marriage permanent. Don't enter marriage with the option of getting out. Your marriage is more likely to be happy if from the outset you are committed to permanence. Don't be hardhearted like these Pharisees, but be hardheaded in your determination, with God's help, to stay together.

10.6–9 Women were often treated as property. Marriage and divorce were regarded as transactions similar to buying and selling land. But Jesus condemned this attitude, clarifying God's original intention—that marriage bring oneness (Genesis 2.24). Jesus held up God's ideal for marriage and told his followers to live by it.

10.13–16 Jesus was often criticized for spending too much time with the wrong people—children, tax collectors, and sinners (Matthew 9.11; Luke 15.1, 2; 19.7). Some, including the disciples, thought Jesus should be spending more time with important leaders and the devout, because this was the way to improve his position and avoid criticism. But Jesus didn't need to improve his position. He was God, and he wanted to speak to those who needed him most.

10.14 Adults are not as trusting as little children. All children need in order to feel secure is a loving look and gentle touch from someone who cares. Complete intellectual understanding is not one of their requirements. They believe us if they trust us. Jesus said that all must believe in him with this kind of childlike faith. We should not have to understand all the mysteries of the universe; it should be enough to know that God loves us and provides forgiveness for our sin. This doesn't mean we should be childish or immature, but we should trust God with a child's simplicity and purity.

Jesus speaks to the rich young man
(175/Matthew 19.16–30; Luke 18.18–30)

17 As he was setting out on a journey, a man ran up and knelt before him, and 10.17
asked him, "Good Teacher, what must I do to inherit eternal life?" 18 Jesus said to Mt 19.16-30 Lk 18.18-30
him, "Why do you call me good? No one is good but God alone. 19 You know the 10.19
commandments: 'You shall not murder; You shall not commit adultery; You shall Ex 20.12-17 Deut 5.16-20
not steal; You shall not bear false witness; You shall not defraud; Honor your father Rom 13.9
and mother.' " 20 He said to him, "Teacher, I have kept all these since my youth." 10.20
21 Jesus, looking at him, loved him and said, "You lack one thing; go, sell what you Jas 2.10 10.21
own, and give the money[c] to the poor, and you will have treasure in heaven; then Mt 6.19,20
come, follow me." 22 When he heard this, he was shocked and went away grieving, Lk 12.33 Acts 2.44,45
for he had many possessions. 1 Tim 6.17-19
23 Then Jesus looked around and said to his disciples, "How hard it will be for
those who have wealth to enter the kingdom of God!" 24 And the disciples were 10.24
perplexed at these words. But Jesus said to them again, "Children, how hard it is[d] Ps 52.7
to enter the kingdom of God! 25 It is easier for a camel to go through the eye of a
needle than for someone who is rich to enter the kingdom of God." 26 They were
greatly astounded and said to one another,[e] "Then who can be saved?" 27 Jesus 10.27
looked at them and said, "For mortals it is impossible, but not for God; for God all Jer 32.17 Heb 7.25
things are possible."
28 Peter began to say to him, "Look, we have left everything and followed 10.28
you." 29 Jesus said, "Truly I tell you, there is no one who has left house or brothers Mk 1.18
or sisters or mother or father or children or fields, for my sake and for the sake of 10.30
the good news,[f] 30 who will not receive a hundredfold now in this age—houses, Acts 14.22 1 Thess 3.3
brothers and sisters, mothers and children, and fields with persecutions—and in 2 Tim 3.12
the age to come eternal life. 31 But many who are first will be last, and the last will 10.31 Mt 20.16
be first." Lk 13.30

[c] Gk lacks *the money* [d] Other ancient authorities add *for those who trust in riches* [e] Other ancient authorities read *to him* [f] Or *gospel*

10.17–23 This young man wanted to be sure he would get eternal life, so he asked what he could *do.* He said he'd never once broken any of the laws Jesus mentioned (10.19), and perhaps he had kept the Pharisees' loophole-filled version of them. But Jesus lovingly broke through his pride with a challenge that brought out his true motives: "Sell what you own, and give the money to the poor." Here was the barrier that could keep this young man out of the kingdom: his love of money. Money represented his pride of accomplishment and self-effort. Ironically, his attitude made him unable to keep the first commandment, to let nothing be more important than God (Exodus 20.3). He could not meet the one requirement Jesus gave—to turn his whole heart and life over to God. The man came to Jesus wondering what he could do; he left seeing what he was unable to do. What barriers are keeping you from turning your life over to Christ?

10.18 When Jesus asked this question, he was saying, "Do you really know to whom you are talking?" Because only God is truly good, the man was calling Jesus God, whether or not he realized it.

10.21 What does your money mean to you? Although Jesus wanted this man to sell everything and give his money to the poor, this does not mean that all believers should sell all their possessions. Most of his followers did not sell everything, although they used their possessions to serve others. Instead, this story shows us that we must not let anything we have or desire keep us from following Jesus. We must remove all barriers to serving him fully. If Jesus asked, could you give up your house? your car? your level of income? your position on the ladder of promotion? Your reaction may show your attitude toward money—whether it is your servant or your master.

10.21 Jesus showed genuine love for this man, even though he knew he might not follow him. Love is able to give tough advice; it doesn't hedge around the truth. Christ loved us enough to die for us, and he also loves us enough to talk straight to us. If his love were superficial, he would give us only approval; but because his love is complete, he gives us life-changing challenges.

10.23 Jesus said it was very difficult for the rich to get into the kingdom of God because the rich, with most of their basic physical needs met, often become self-reliant. When they feel empty, they can buy something new to dull the pain that was meant to drive them toward God. Their abundance becomes their deficiency. The person who has everything on earth can still lack what is most important—eternal life.

10.26 The disciples were astonished. Was not wealth a blessing from God, a reward for being good? This misconception is still common today. Although many believers enjoy material prosperity, many others live in hardship. Wealth is not a sign of faith or of partiality on God's part.

10.29, 30 Jesus assured the disciples that anyone who gives up something valuable for his sake will be repaid a hundred times over in this life, although not necessarily in the same form. For example, someone may be rejected by his family for accepting Christ, but he will gain the larger family of believers. Along with these rewards, however, we receive persecution because the world hates God. Jesus emphasized persecution to make sure we do not selfishly follow him only for the rewards.

10.31 Jesus explained that in the world to come, the values of this world will be reversed. Those who seek status and importance here will have none in heaven. Those who are humble here will be great in heaven. The corrupt condition of our society encourages confusion in values. We are bombarded by messages that tell us how to be important and feel good, and Jesus' teaching on service to others seems alien. But those who have humbly served others are most qualified to be great in heaven.

Jesus predicts his death the third time
(177/Matthew 20.17–19; Luke 18.31–34)

10.32 Mt 20.17-19 Lk 18.31-34
10.33 Mt 16.21; 26.67 27.30 Mk 8.31; 9.31 14.65 Lk 9.22 1 Cor 15.3,4

32 They were on the road, going up to Jerusalem, and Jesus was walking ahead
of them; they were amazed, and those who followed were afraid. He took the
twelve aside again and began to tell them what was to happen to him, 33 saying,
"See, we are going up to Jerusalem, and the Son of Man will be handed over to the
chief priests and the scribes, and they will condemn him to death; then they will
hand him over to the Gentiles; 34 they will mock him, and spit upon him, and flog
him, and kill him; and after three days he will rise again."

Jesus teaches about serving others
(178/Matthew 20.20–28)

10.35 Mt 20.20-28
10.38 Lk 12.50
10.39 Acts 12.2 Rev 1.9
10.40 Jas 4.3

35 James and John, the sons of Zebedee, came forward to him and said to him,
"Teacher, we want you to do for us whatever we ask of you." 36 And he said to
them, "What is it you want me to do for you?" 37 And they said to him, "Grant us
to sit, one at your right hand and one at your left, in your glory." 38 But Jesus said
to them, "You do not know what you are asking. Are you able to drink the cup that
I drink, or be baptized with the baptism that I am baptized with?" 39 They replied,
"We are able." Then Jesus said to them, "The cup that I drink you will drink; and
with the baptism with which I am baptized, you will be baptized; 40 but to sit at my
right hand or at my left is not mine to grant, but it is for those for whom it has been
prepared."

10.42 Lk 22.25,26
10.43 Mk 9.35 Lk 9.48
10.45 Jn 13.14 Phil 2.7 1 Tim 2.5,6 Tit 2.14

41 When the ten heard this, they began to be angry with James and John. 42 So
Jesus called them and said to them, "You know that among the Gentiles those
whom they recognize as their rulers lord it over them, and their great ones are
tyrants over them. 43 But it is not so among you; but whoever wishes to become
great among you must be your servant, 44 and whoever wishes to be first among you
must be slave of all. 45 For the Son of Man came not to be served but to serve, and
to give his life a ransom for many."

10.32 Because Jesus had just spoken to them about facing persecution, the disciples were afraid of what they thought awaited them in Jerusalem.

10.33, 34 Jesus' death and resurrection should have come as no surprise to the disciples. Here he clearly explained to them what would happen to him. Unfortunately, they didn't really hear what he was saying. Jesus said he was the Messiah, but they thought the Messiah would be a conquering king. He spoke to them of resurrection, but they heard only his words about death. Because Jesus often spoke in parables, the disciples may have thought his words on death and resurrection were another parable they didn't understand. The Gospels include Jesus' predictions of his death and resurrection to show that they were God's plan from the beginning, not an accident.

10.35 Mark records that John and James went to Jesus with their request; in Matthew, their mother also made the request. There is no contradiction in the accounts – mother and sons were in agreement in requesting honored places in Christ's kingdom.

10.37 The disciples, like most Jews of that day, had the wrong idea of the Messiah's kingdom as predicted by the Old Testament prophets. They thought Jesus would establish an earthly kingdom that would free Israel from Rome's oppression, and James and John wanted honored places in it. But Jesus' kingdom is not of this world; it is not centered in palaces and thrones, but in the hearts and lives of his followers. The disciples did not understand this until after Jesus' resurrection.

10.38, 39 James and John said they were willing to face any trial for Christ. Both did suffer: James died as a martyr (Acts 12.2), and John was forced to live in exile (Revelation 1.9). It is easy to say we'll suffer anything for Christ, and yet most of us complain over the most minor irritations. If we say we are willing to suffer on a large scale for Christ, we must also be willing to suffer the irritations that come with serving others.

10.38–40 Jesus didn't ridicule James and John for asking, but he denied their request. We can feel free to ask God for anything, but our request may be denied. God wants to give us what is best for us, not merely what we want. He denies some requests for our own good.

10.42–45 James and John wanted the highest positions in Jesus' kingdom. But Jesus told them that true greatness comes in serving others. Peter, one of the disciples who heard this message, expands the thought in 1 Peter 5.1–4.

Most businesses, organizations, and institutions measure greatness by high personal achievement. In Christ's kingdom, however, service is the way to get ahead. The desire to be on top will hinder, not help. Rather than seeking to have your needs met, look for ways you can minister to the needs of others.

10.45 A ransom was the price paid to release a slave. Jesus paid a ransom for us, because we could not pay it ourselves. His death released all of us from our slavery to sin. The disciples thought Jesus' life and power would save them from Rome; Jesus said his *death* would save them from sin, an even greater slavery than Rome's. More about the ransom Jesus paid for us is found in 1 Peter 1.18, 19.

Jesus heals a blind beggar
(179/Matthew 20.29–34; Luke 18.35–43)

46 They came to Jericho. As he and his disciples and a large crowd were leav- **10.46** Mt 20.29-34
ing Jericho, Bartimaeus son of Timaeus, a blind beggar, was sitting by the road- Lk 18.35-43
side. 47 When he heard that it was Jesus of Nazareth, he began to shout out and say, **10.47**
"Jesus, Son of David, have mercy on me!" 48 Many sternly ordered him to be quiet, Isa 11.1 Jer 23.5,6
but he cried out even more loudly, "Son of David, have mercy on me!" 49 Jesus Rom 1.3
stood still and said, "Call him here." And they called the blind man, saying to him, Rev 22.16
"Take heart; get up, he is calling you." 50 So throwing off his cloak, he sprang up
and came to Jesus. 51 Then Jesus said to him, "What do you want me to do for you?"
The blind man said to him, "My teacher,[g] let me see again." 52 Jesus said to him, **10.52** Isa 35.5
"Go; your faith has made you well." Immediately he regained his sight and fol- Mt 9.22
lowed him on the way.

3. Jesus' ministry in Jerusalem

Jesus rides into Jerusalem on a donkey
(183/Matthew 21.1–11; Luke 19.28–44; John 12.12–19)

11 When they were approaching Jerusalem, at Bethphage and Bethany, near **11.1** Mt 21.1-9
the Mount of Olives, he sent two of his disciples 2 and said to them, "Go into Lk 19.29-40
the village ahead of you, and immediately as you enter it, you will find tied there Jn 12.12-19 Acts 1.12
a colt that has never been ridden; untie it and bring it. 3 If anyone says to you, 'Why
are you doing this?' just say this, 'The Lord needs it and will send it back here
immediately.'" 4 They went away and found a colt tied near a door, outside in the
street. As they were untying it, 5 some of the bystanders said to them, "What are
you doing, untying the colt?" 6 They told them what Jesus had said; and they allowed them to take it. 7 Then they brought the colt to Jesus and threw their cloaks **11.7**
on it; and he sat on it. 8 Many people spread their cloaks on the road, and others Zech 9.9
spread leafy branches that they had cut in the fields. 9 Then those who went ahead **11.9**
and those who followed were shouting, Ps 118.25,26

"Hosanna!
Blessed is the one who comes in the name of the Lord!
10 Blessed is the coming kingdom of our ancestor David!

[g] Aramaic *Rabbouni*

10.46 Jericho was a popular resort city rebuilt by Herod the Great in the Judean desert, not far from the Jordan River crossing. Jesus was on his way to Jerusalem (10.32) and, after crossing over from Perea, would naturally enter Jericho.

10.46 Beggars were a common sight in most towns. Because most occupations of that day required physical labor, anyone with a crippling disease or handicap was at a severe disadvantage and was usually forced to beg, even though God's laws commanded care for such needy people (Leviticus 25.35–38). Blindness was considered a curse from God for sin, but Jesus refuted this idea when he reached out to heal the blind.

11.1, 2 This was Sunday of the week Jesus would be crucified, and the great Passover festival was about to begin. Jews came to Jerusalem from all over the Roman world during this week-long celebration to remember the great exodus from Egypt (see Exodus 12.37–51). Many in the crowds had heard of or seen Jesus and were hoping he would come to the temple (John 11.55–57).

Jesus did come, not as a warring king on a horse or in a chariot, but as a peaceable king on a donkey's colt, just as Zechariah 9.9 had predicted. Jesus knew that those who heard him teach at the temple would return to their homes throughout the world and announce the coming of the Messiah.

11.9, 10 The people exclaimed "Hosanna" (meaning, "Save, I pray") because they recognized that Jesus was fulfilling the prophecy in Zechariah 9.9. (See also Psalm 24.7–10; 118.26.) They spoke of David's kingdom because of God's words to David in 2 Samuel 7.12–14. The crowd correctly saw Jesus as the fulfillment of these prophecies, but they did not understand where Jesus' kingship would lead him. This same crowd cried out "Crucify him!" when Jesus stood on trial only a few days later.

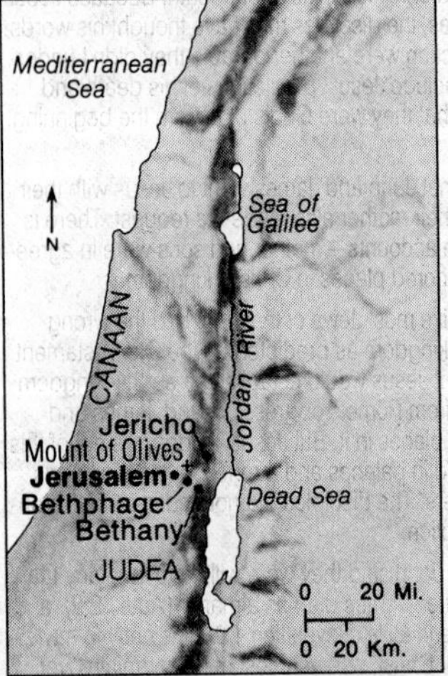

JESUS NEARS JERUSALEM
Leaving Jericho, Jesus headed toward acclaim, then crucifixion, in Jerusalem. During his last week, he stayed outside the city in Bethany, a village on the Mount of Olives, entering Jerusalem to teach, eat the Passover, and finally be crucified.

Hosanna in the highest heaven!"

11.11 Mt 21.10,17 11 Then he entered Jerusalem and went into the temple; and when he had
looked around at everything, as it was already late, he went out to Bethany with the
twelve.

Jesus clears the temple again
(184/Matthew 21.12–17; Luke 19.45–48)

11.12-14 Mt 21.18,19 12 On the following day, when they came from Bethany, he was hungry.
13 Seeing in the distance a fig tree in leaf, he went to see whether perhaps he would
find anything on it. When he came to it, he found nothing but leaves, for it was not
the season for figs. 14 He said to it, "May no one ever eat fruit from you again." And
his disciples heard it.
11.15 Mt 21.12-17 Lk 19.45-48 Jn 2.13-17 15 Then they came to Jerusalem. And he entered the temple and began to drive
out those who were selling and those who were buying in the temple, and he over-
turned the tables of the money changers and the seats of those who sold doves;

KEY CHARACTERISTICS OF CHRIST IN THE GOSPELS

Characteristic	*References*
Jesus is the Son of God	Matthew 16.15, 16; Mark 1.1 Luke 22.70, 71; John 8.24
Jesus is God who became human	John 1.1, 2, 14; 20.28
Jesus is the Christ, the Messiah	Matthew 26.63, 64; Mark 14.61, 62 Luke 9.20; John 4.25, 26
Jesus came to help sinners	Luke 5.32; Matthew 9.13
Jesus has power to forgive sins	Mark 2.9–12; Luke 24.47
Jesus has authority over death	Mark 5.22–24, 35–42 John 11.1–44; Luke 24.5, 6 Matthew 28.5, 6
Jesus has power to give eternal life	John 10.28; 17.2
Jesus healed the sick	Matthew 8.5–13; Mark 1.32–34 Luke 5.12–15; John 9.1–7
Jesus taught with authority	Mark 1.21, 22; Matthew 7.29
Jesus was compassionate	Mark 1.41; Mark 8.2; Matthew 9.36
Jesus experienced sorrow	Matthew 26.38; John 11.35
Jesus never disobeyed God	Matthew 3.15; John 8.46

11.11–21 In this passage, two unusual incidents are related: the cursing of the fig tree and the cleansing of the temple. The cursing of the fig tree was an acted-out parable related to the cleansing of the temple. The temple was supposed to be a place of worship, but true worship had disappeared. The fig tree showed promise of fruit, but it produced none. Jesus was showing his anger at religious life without substance. If you claim to have faith without putting it to work in your life, you are like the barren fig tree. Genuine faith has great potential; ask God to help you bear fruit for his kingdom.

11.13–26 Fig trees, a popular source of inexpensive food in Israel, require three years from the time they are planted until they can bear fruit. Each tree yields a great amount of fruit twice a year, in late spring and in early autumn. This incident occurred early in the spring fig season when the leaves were beginning to bud. The figs normally grow as the leaves fill out, but this tree, though full of leaves, had none. The tree looked promising but offered no fruit. Jesus' harsh words compared the nation of Israel to the fig tree. Fruitful in appearance only, Israel was spiritually barren.

11.15–17 Jesus became angry, but he did not sin. There is a place for righteous indignation. Christians are right to be upset about sin and injustice and should take a stand against them. Unfortunately, believers are often passive about these important issues and instead get angry over personal insults and petty irritations. Make sure your anger is directed toward the right issues.

11.15–17 Money changers and merchants did big business during Passover. Those who came from foreign countries had to have their money changed into temple currency, because this was the only money accepted for the temple tax and for the purchase of sacrificial animals. Often the inflated exchange rate enriched the money changers, and the exorbitant prices of animals made the merchants wealthy. Their stalls were set up in the temple's court of the Gentiles, frustrating the intentions of non-Jews who had come to worship God (Isaiah 56.6, 7). Jesus became angry because God's house of worship had become a place of extortion and a barrier to Gentiles who wanted to worship.

16 and he would not allow anyone to carry anything through the temple. 17 He was
teaching and saying, "Is it not written,
'My house shall be called a house of prayer for all the nations'?
But you have made it a den of robbers."
18 And when the chief priests and the scribes heard it, they kept looking for a way
to kill him; for they were afraid of him, because the whole crowd was spellbound
by his teaching. 19 And when evening came, Jesus and his disciples[h] went out of
the city.

11.17 Isa 56.7 Jer 7.11
11.18 Mt 21.46 Mk 12.12 Lk 4.32; 20.19 Jn 7.1

Jesus says the disciples can pray for anything
(188/Matthew 21.18–22)

20 In the morning as they passed by, they saw the fig tree withered away to its
roots. 21 Then Peter remembered and said to him, "Rabbi, look! The fig tree that
you cursed has withered." 22 Jesus answered them, "Have[i] faith in God. 23 Truly I
tell you, if you say to this mountain, 'Be taken up and thrown into the sea,' and if
you do not doubt in your heart, but believe that what you say will come to pass, it
will be done for you. 24 So I tell you, whatever you ask for in prayer, believe that
you have received[j] it, and it will be yours.
25 Whenever you stand praying, forgive, if you have anything against anyone;
so that your Father in heaven may also forgive you your trespasses."[k]

11.20 Mt 21.20-22
11.22 Mt 17.20 Lk 17.6
11.24 Mt 7.7 Lk 11.9 Jn 14.12-14; 15.7, 16.24 Jas 1.5-8
11.25 Mt 6.14,15 Eph 4.32

Religious leaders challenge Jesus' authority
(189/Matthew 21.23–27; Luke 20.1–8)

27 Again they came to Jerusalem. As he was walking in the temple, the chief
priests, the scribes, and the elders came to him 28 and said, "By what authority are
you doing these things? Who gave you this authority to do them?" 29 Jesus said to
them, "I will ask you one question; answer me, and I will tell you by what authority

11.26 Mt 21.23-27 Lk 20.1-8

[h] Gk *they*: other ancient authorities read *he* [i] Other ancient authorities read *"If you have* [j] Other ancient authorities read *are receiving* [k] Other ancient authorities add verse 26, *"But if you do not forgive, neither will your Father in heaven forgive your trespasses."*

11.22, 23 The kind of prayer that moves mountains is prayer for the fruitfulness of God's kingdom. It would seem impossible to move a mountain into the sea, so Jesus used that picture to say that God can do anything. God will answer your prayers, but not as a result of your positive mental attitude. Other conditions must be met: (1) you must be a believer; (2) you must not hold a grudge against another person; (3) you must not pray with selfish motives; (4) your request must be for the good of his kingdom. To pray effectively, you need faith in God, not faith in the object of your request. If you focus only on your request, you will have nothing if your request is refused.

11.24 Jesus, our example for prayer, prayed, "For you all things are possible; . . . . yet, not what I want, but what you want" (14.36). Our prayers are often motivated by our own interests and desires. We like to hear that we can have anything. But Jesus prayed with God's interests in mind. When we pray, we should express our desires, but want his will above ours. Check yourself to see if your prayers focus on your interests or God's.

11.27ff The religious leaders asked Jesus who gave him the authority to chase away the merchants and money changers. Their question was a trap. If Jesus said his authority was from God, they would accuse him of blasphemy; if he said his authority was his own, they would dismiss him as a fanatic. To expose their real motives, Jesus countered their question with a question about John the Baptist. The leaders' silence proved they were not interested in the truth. They simply wanted to get rid of Jesus because he was undermining their own authority.

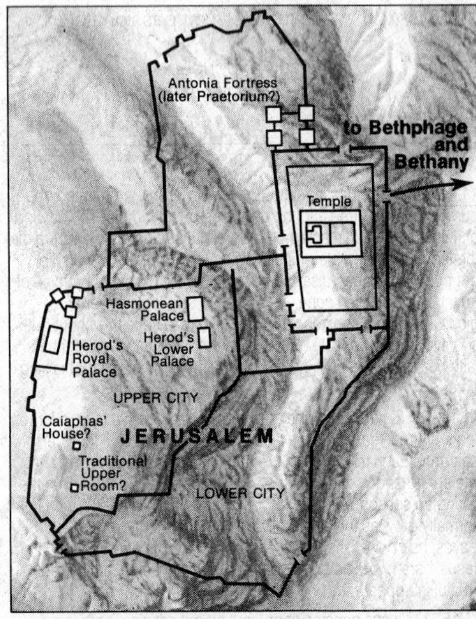

CLEANSING THE TEMPLE On Monday morning of his last week, Jesus left Bethany, entered Jerusalem, and cleansed the temple of moneychangers and merchants.

I do these things. 30 Did the baptism of John come from heaven, or was it of human
origin? Answer me." 31 They argued with one another, "If we say, 'From heaven,'
he will say, 'Why then did you not believe him?' 32 But shall we say, 'Of human
origin'?"—they were afraid of the crowd, for all regarded John as truly a prophet.
33 So they answered Jesus, "We do not know." And Jesus said to them, "Neither
will I tell you by what authority I am doing these things."

Jesus tells the parable of the wicked farmers
(191/Matthew 21.33–46; Luke 20.9–19)

12 Then he began to speak to them in parables. "A man planted a vineyard, put
a fence around it, dug a pit for the wine press, and built a watchtower; then
he leased it to tenants and went to another country. 2 When the season came, he sent
a slave to the tenants to collect from them his share of the produce of the vineyard.
3 But they seized him, and beat him, and sent him away empty-handed. 4 And again
he sent another slave to them; this one they beat over the head and insulted. 5 Then
he sent another, and that one they killed. And so it was with many others; some
they beat, and others they killed. 6 He had still one other, a beloved son. Finally he
sent him to them, saying, 'They will respect my son.' 7 But those tenants said to one
another, 'This is the heir; come, let us kill him, and the inheritance will be ours.'
8 So they seized him, killed him, and threw him out of the vineyard. 9 What then
will the owner of the vineyard do? He will come and destroy the tenants and give
the vineyard to others. 10 Have you not read this scripture:
'The stone that the builders rejected
has become the cornerstone;[l]
11 this was the Lord's doing,
and it is amazing in our eyes'?"
12 When they realized that he had told this parable against them, they wanted
to arrest him, but they feared the crowd. So they left him and went away.

Religious leaders question Jesus about paying taxes
(193/Matthew 22.15–22; Luke 20.20–26)

13 Then they sent to him some Pharisees and some Herodians to trap him in
what he said. 14 And they came and said to him, "Teacher, we know that you are
sincere, and show deference to no one; for you do not regard people with partiality,
but teach the way of God in accordance with truth. Is it lawful to pay taxes to the

[l] Or *keystone*

11.32 Mt 14.5 Mk 6.20
11.33 Job 5.12,13
12.1 Isa 5.1,2
12.5 2 Chron 24.21 36.15,16 Neh 9.26 Mt 23.34-37 Acts 7.52 1 Thess 2.15
12.6 Rom 8.3 Gal 4.4
12.7 Acts 4.27
12.8 Acts 2.23
12.9 Acts 28.23-29
12.10,11 Ps 118.22,23 Rom 9.33 Eph 2.20 1 Pet 2.5-7
12.12 Mt 11.18 Jn 7.26,30,44
12.13 Mt 22.15-40,46 Lk 20.20-40

11.30 For more information, see John the Baptist's Profile in John 1.

12.1 Parables are story illustrations that use something familiar to help us understand something new. This method of teaching compels listeners to discover truth for themselves. The message gets through only to those who are willing to listen and learn.

12.1 Israel, pictured as a vineyard, was the nation God had cultivated to bring salvation to the world. The religious leaders not only frustrated their nation's purpose; they also killed those trying to fulfill it. They were so jealous that they forgot the welfare of the very people they were supposed to be bringing to God.

12.1ff In this parable, the man who planted the vineyard is God; the vineyard is the nation Israel; the tenants are Israel's religious leaders; the slaves are the prophets and priests who remained faithful to God; the son is Jesus; and the others are the Gentiles. By telling this story, Jesus exposed the religious leaders' plot to kill him and warned that their sins would be punished.

12.10, 11 Jesus referred to himself as the stone rejected by the builders. Although he would be rejected by most of the Jewish leaders, he would become the cornerstone of a new "building," the church (Acts 4.11, 12). The cornerstone was used as a base to make sure the other stones of the building were straight and level. Likewise, Jesus' life and teaching would be the church's standard of truth.

12.13 The Pharisees were primarily a religious group concerned for ritual purity; the Herodians, a Jewish political group that approved of Herod's compromises with Rome. Normally the two groups had nothing to do with each other.

The Pharisees did not like Jesus because he exposed their hypocrisy. The Herodians also saw Jesus as a threat. Supporters of the dynasty of Herod the Great, they had lost political control when, as a result of reported unrest, Rome deposed Archelaus (Herod's son with authority over Judea), and replaced him with a Roman governor. The Herodians feared that Jesus would cause still more instability in Judea, and that Rome might react by never allowing the Roman leaders to step down and be replaced by a descendant of Herod.

12.14 Anyone who avoided paying taxes faced harsh penalties. The Jews hated to pay taxes to Rome because the money supported their oppressors and symbolized their subjection. Much of it also went to maintain the pagan temples and luxurious life-styles of Rome's upper class. The Pharisees and Herodians hoped to trap Jesus with this tax question. Either a yes or a no could lead him into trouble. A yes would mean he supported Rome, which would turn the people against him. A no would bring accusations of treason and rebellion against Rome and could lead to civil penalties.

emperor, or not? 15 Should we pay them, or should we not?" But knowing their
hypocrisy, he said to them, "Why are you putting me to the test? Bring me a
denarius and let me see it." 16 And they brought one. Then he said to them, "Whose
head is this, and whose title?" They answered, "The emperor's." 17 Jesus said to
them, "Give to the emperor the things that are the emperor's, and to God the things
that are God's." And they were utterly amazed at him.

Religious leaders question Jesus about the resurrection
(194/Matthew 22.23–33; Luke 20.27–40)

18 Some Sadducees, who say there is no resurrection, came to him and asked **12.18**
him a question, saying, 19 "Teacher, Moses wrote for us that 'if a man's brother Mt 22.23-33 Lk 20.27-38
dies, leaving a wife but no child, the man[m] shall marry the widow and raise up Acts 23.8 1 Cor 15.12
children for his brother.' 20 There were seven brothers; the first married and, when **12.19**
he died, left no children; 21 and the second married her and died, leaving no chil- Gen 38.8 Deut 25.5
dren; and the third likewise; 22 none of the seven left children. Last of all the woman **12.24**
herself died. 23 In the resurrection[n] whose wife will she be? For the seven had mar- Dan 12.2 Rom 4.17
ried her." 1 Tim 1.7 2 Pet 1.19

24 Jesus said to them, "Is not this the reason you are wrong, that you know **12.25**
neither the scriptures nor the power of God? 25 For when they rise from the dead, 1 Cor 15.42, 49,52
they neither marry nor are given in marriage, but are like angels in heaven. 26 And 1 Jn 3.2
as for the dead being raised, have you not read in the book of Moses, in the story **12.26** Ex 3.6
about the bush, how God said to him, 'I am the God of Abraham, the God of Isaac, Lk 20.37
and the God of Jacob'? 27 He is God not of the dead, but of the living; you are quite **12.27** Mt 22.32
wrong." Lk 20.38

Religious leaders question Jesus about the greatest commandment
(195/Matthew 22.34–40)

28 One of the scribes came near and heard them disputing with one another, and
seeing that he answered them well, he asked him, "Which commandment is the
first of all?" 29 Jesus answered, "The first is, 'Hear, O Israel: the Lord our God, the **12.29** Deut 6.4,5

m Gk *his brother* n Other ancient authorities add *when they rise*

12.15 A denarius was the usual day's wage for a laborer.

12.17 The Pharisees and Herodians thought they had the perfect question to trap Jesus. But Jesus answered wisely, once again exposing their self-interest and wrong motives. Jesus said that the coin bearing the emperor's image should be given to the emperor. But our lives, which bear God's image, belong to God. Are you giving God all that is rightfully his? Give your life to God – you bear his image.

12.18–23 After the Pharisees and Herodians failed to trap Jesus with their tax question, the Sadducees stepped in with a question they were sure would stump him. This was a question they had successfully used against the Pharisees, who could not come up with an answer. The Sadducees did not believe in life after death because the Pentateuch (Genesis – Deuteronomy) had no direct teaching about it, and the writings of Moses were the only Scriptures they followed. But Jesus was about to point out that Moses' books support the idea of eternal life (12.26).

12.19 According to Old Testament law, when a man died without a son, his brother had to marry the widow and produce children to care for her and allow the family line to continue. The first son of this marriage was considered the heir of the dead man (Deuteronomy 25.5, 6).

12.24 What life will be like after the resurrection is far beyond our ability to understand or imagine (Isaiah 64.4; 1 Corinthians 2.9). We need not be afraid of eternal life because of the unknowns, however. Instead of wondering what God's coming kingdom will be like, we should concentrate on our relationship with Jesus right now, because in the new kingdom we will be with him. If we learn to love and trust him *now,* we will not be afraid of what he has in store for us then.

12.25–27 Jesus' statement does not mean that people won't recognize their partners in the coming kingdom. It simply means that God's new order will not be an extension of this life, and the same physical and natural rules won't apply. Jesus' comment in verse 25 was not intended to be the final word on marriage in heaven. Instead, it was Jesus' refusal to answer the Sadducees' riddle and fall into their trap. Sidestepping their question about the much-married woman, he gave a definitive answer to their question about the resurrection.

12.26 The Sadducees' real question was not about marriage but about the doctrine of resurrection. Because the Sadducees believed only in the Pentateuch, Jesus quoted from Exodus 3.6 to prove that there is life after death. The Pharisees had overlooked this verse in their debates with the Sadducees. God spoke of Abraham, Isaac, and Jacob years after their death as if they *still lived.* God's covenant with all people exists beyond death.

12.28 By Jesus' time, the Jews had accumulated hundreds of laws – 613 by one count. Some religious leaders tried to distinguish between major and minor laws, and some taught that all laws were equally binding and that it was dangerous to make any distinctions. This teacher's question could have provoked controversy among these groups, but Jesus' answer summarized all of God's laws.

12.29–31 God's laws are not burdensome. They can be reduced to two simple principles: love God, and love others. These commands are from the Old Testament (Deuteronomy 6.5; Leviticus 19.18). When you love God completely and care for others as you care for yourself, then you have fulfilled the intent of the ten commandments and the other Old Testament laws. According to Jesus, these two commandments summarize all God's laws. Let

12.30 Lk 10.27 Lord is one; 30 you shall love the Lord your God with all your heart, and with all
your soul, and with all your mind, and with all your strength.' 31 The second is this,
12.31 Lev 19.18 Rom 13.9 'You shall love your neighbor as yourself.' There is no other commandment greater
than these." 32 Then the scribe said to him, "You are right, Teacher; you have truly
12.32 Deut 4.35,39 Isa 45.5,6,14 1 Cor 8.4-6 said that 'he is one, and besides him there is no other'; 33 and 'to love him with all
the heart, and with all the understanding, and with all the strength,' and 'to love
one's neighbor as oneself,'—this is much more important than all whole burnt
12.33 1 Sam 15.22 Hos 6.6 Mic 6.6-8 offerings and sacrifices." 34 When Jesus saw that he answered wisely, he said to
him, "You are not far from the kingdom of God." After that no one dared to ask him
any question.

Religious leaders cannot answer Jesus' question
(196/Matthew 22.41–46; Luke 20.41–44)

12.35 Mt 22.41-46 Lk 20.41-44 35 While Jesus was teaching in the temple, he said, "How can the scribes say
that the Messiah[o] is the son of David? 36 David himself, by the Holy Spirit, de-
12.36 2 Sam 23.2 Ps 110.1 clared,

'The Lord said to my Lord,
"Sit at my right hand,
until I put your enemies under your feet." '

12.37 Rom 1.3; 9.5 37 David himself calls him Lord; so how can he be his son?" And the large crowd
was listening to him with delight.

o Or *the Christ*

WHAT JESUS SAID ABOUT LOVE

In Mark 12.28 a teacher of religion asked Jesus which of all the commandments was the most important to follow. Jesus mentioned two commandments, one from Deuteronomy 6.5, the other from Leviticus 19.18. Both had to do with love. Why is love so important? Jesus said that all of the commandments were given for two simple reasons—to help us love God and love others as we should.

What else did Jesus say about love?	*Reference*
God loves us.	John 3.16
We are to love God.	Matthew 22.37
Because God loves us, he cares for us.	Matthew 6.25–34
God wants everyone to know how much he loves them.	John 17.23
God loves even those who hate him; we are to do the same.	Matthew 5.43–47; Luke 6.35
God seeks out even those most alienated from him.	Luke 15
God must be your first love.	Matthew 6.24; 10.37
You love God when you obey him.	John 14.21; 15.10
God loves Jesus his Son.	John 5.20; 10.17
Jesus loves God.	John 14.31
Those who refuse Jesus don't have God's love.	John 5.41–44
Jesus loves us just as God loves Jesus.	John 15.9
Jesus proved his love for us by dying on the cross so that we could live eternally with him.	John 3.14, 15; 15.13, 14
The love between God and Jesus is the perfect example of how we are to love others.	John 17.21–26
We are to love one another (John 13.34, 35) and demonstrate that love.	Matthew 5.40–42; 10.42
We are *not* to love the praise of men (John 12.43), selfish recognition (Matthew 23.6), earthly belongings (Luke 16.19–31), or anything more than God.	Luke 16.13
Jesus' love extends to each individual.	John 10.11–15; Mark 10.21
Jesus wants us to love him through the good and difficult times.	Matthew 26.31–35
Jesus wants our love to be genuine.	John 21.15–17

them rule your thoughts, decisions, and actions. When you are uncertain about what to do, ask yourself which course of action best demonstrates love for God and love for others.

12.32–34 This man had caught the intent of God's law as it is so often stressed in the Old Testament—that true obedience comes from the heart. Since all the Old Testament commands lead to Christ, his next step was faith in Jesus himself. This, however, was the most difficult step to take.

12.35–37 Jesus quoted Psalm 110.1 to show that the Messiah would be different from an ordinary man. The religious leaders did not understand that the Messiah would be far more than a human descendant of David; he would be God himself in human form.

Jesus warns against the religious leaders
(197/Matthew 23.1–12; Luke 20.45–47)

38 As he taught, he said, "Beware of the scribes, who like to walk around in **12.38** Mt 23.1-10,14
long robes, and to be greeted with respect in the marketplaces, 39 and to have the Lk 20.45-47
best seats in the synagogues and places of honor at banquets! 40 They devour wid- **12.39**
ows' houses and for the sake of appearance say long prayers. They will receive the Lk 11.43
greater condemnation."

A poor widow gives all she has
(200/Luke 21.1–4)

41 He sat down opposite the treasury, and watched the crowd putting money **12.41**
into the treasury. Many rich people put in large sums. 42 A poor widow came and 2 Kgs 12.9 Lk 21.1-4
put in two small copper coins, which are worth a penny. 43 Then he called his disci- Jn 8.20
ples and said to them, "Truly I tell you, this poor widow has put in more than all **12.43** Lk 8.43,44
those who are contributing to the treasury. 44 For all of them have contributed out 2 Cor 8.12
of their abundance; but she out of her poverty has put in everything she had, all she
had to live on."

Jesus tells about the future
(201/Matthew 24.1–28; Luke 21.5–24)

13 As he came out of the temple, one of his disciples said to him, "Look, **13.1**
Teacher, what large stones and what large buildings!" 2 Then Jesus asked Mt 24.1-51 Lk 21.5-36
him, "Do you see these great buildings? Not one stone will be left here upon **13.2**
another; all will be thrown down." Lk 19.43,44

3 When he was sitting on the Mount of Olives opposite the temple, Peter,
James, John, and Andrew asked him privately, 4 "Tell us, when will this be, and
what will be the sign that all these things are about to be accomplished?" 5 Then

12.38–40 Jesus again exposed the religious leaders' impure motives. The scribes, or teachers of the law, received no pay, so they depended upon the hospitality extended by devout Jews. Some of them used this custom to exploit people, cheating the poor out of everything they had and taking advantage of the rich. They acted pious to gain status, recognition, and respect.

12.38–40 Jesus warned against phonies—people who try to appear better than they are. True followers of Christ are not distinguished by showy spirituality. Reading the Bible, praying in public, or following church rituals can be phony if the motive for doing them is to be noticed or honored. Let your actions be consistent with your beliefs. Live for Christ, even when no one is looking.

12.40 The scribes' punishment would be especially great because as teachers they were responsible for shaping the faith of the people. But they saddled people with petty rules while they lived greedily and deceitfully. Their behavior oppressed and misled the people they were supposed to lead.

12.41 There were several boxes in the temple where money could be placed. Some were for collecting the temple tax from Jewish males; the others were for freewill offerings. These particular collection boxes were probably in the Court of Women.

12.41–44 In the Lord's eyes, this poor widow gave more than all the others put together, although her gift was by far the smallest. The value of a gift is not determined by its amount, but by the spirit in which it is given. A gift given grudgingly or for recognition loses its value. When you give, take heart—gifts of any size are pleasing to God when they are given out of gratitude and generosity.

13.1, 2 About 15 years before Jesus was born (20 B.C.), Herod the Great began to remodel and rebuild the temple, which had stood for nearly 500 years since the days of Ezra (Ezra 6.14, 15). Herod made the temple one of the most beautiful buildings in Jerusalem, not to honor God, but to appease the Jews whom he ruled. The magnificent building project was not completely finished until A.D. 64. Jesus' prophecy that not one stone would be left upon another was fulfilled in A.D. 70, when the Romans completely destroyed the temple and the entire city of Jerusalem.

13.3ff The disciples wanted to know when the temple would be destroyed. Jesus gave them a prophetic picture of that time, including events leading up to it. He also talked about future events connected with his return to earth to judge all people. Jesus predicted both near and distant events without putting them in chronological order. Some of the disciples lived to see the destruction of Jerusalem in A.D. 70. This event would assure them that everything else Jesus predicted would also happen.

Jesus warned his followers about the future so that they could learn how to live in the present. Many predictions Jesus made in this passage have not yet been fulfilled. He did not make them so that we would guess when they might be fulfilled, but to help us remain spiritually alert and prepared at all times, waiting for his return.

13.3, 4 The Mount of Olives rises above Jerusalem to the east. From its slopes a person can look down into the city and see the temple. Zechariah 14.1–4 predicts that the Messiah will stand on this very mountain when he returns to set up his eternal kingdom.

13.5–7 What are the signs of the end times? There have been people in every generation since Christ's resurrection claiming to know exactly when Jesus would return. No one has been right yet, however, because Christ will return on God's timetable, not man's. Jesus predicted that before his return, many believers would be misled by false teachers claiming to have revelations from God.

In Scripture, the one clear sign of Christ's return is his unmistakable appearance in the clouds, which will be seen by all people (13.26; Revelation 1.7). In other words, you do not have to wonder whether a certain person is the Messiah or whether these are the "end times." When Jesus returns, *you will know* beyond a doubt. Beware of groups who claim special knowledge of the last days, because no one knows when this time will be (13.32). Be cautious about saying, "This is it!" but be bold in your total commitment to

Jesus began to say to them, "Beware that no one leads you astray. 6 Many will come
in my name and say, 'I am he!'[p] and they will lead many astray. 7 When you hear
of wars and rumors of wars, do not be alarmed; this must take place, but the end is
still to come. 8 For nation will rise against nation, and kingdom against kingdom;
there will be earthquakes in various places; there will be famines. This is but the
beginning of the birthpangs.
9 "As for yourselves, beware; for they will hand you over to councils; and you
will be beaten in synagogues; and you will stand before governors and kings because of me, as a testimony to them. 10 And the good news[q] must first be proclaimed to all nations. 11 When they bring you to trial and hand you over, do not
worry beforehand about what you are to say; but say whatever is given you at that
time, for it is not you who speak, but the Holy Spirit. 12 Brother will betray brother
to death, and a father his child, and children will rise against parents and have them
put to death; 13 and you will be hated by all because of my name. But the one who
endures to the end will be saved.
14 "But when you see the desolating sacrilege set up where it ought not to be
(let the reader understand), then those in Judea must flee to the mountains; 15 the
one on the housetop must not go down or enter the house to take anything away;
16 the one in the field must not turn back to get a coat. 17 Woe to those who are
pregnant and to those who are nursing infants in those days! 18 Pray that it may not
be in winter. 19 For in those days there will be suffering, such as has not been from
the beginning of the creation that God created until now, no, and never will be.
20 And if the Lord had not cut short those days, no one would be saved; but for the
sake of the elect, whom he chose, he has cut short those days. 21 And if anyone says
to you at that time, 'Look! Here is the Messiah!'[r] or 'Look! There he is!'—do not

13.9 Mt 10.17-22
13.10 Rom 10.18
13.11 Lk 12.11,12; 21.14, 15 Acts 2.4; 4.8,31
13.12 Mic 7.6
13.13 Jn 15.18-21 2 Tim 4.7,8 Heb 3.6,14 Rev 2.10
13.14 Dan 9.27 11.31; 12.11 Mt 24.15
13.17 Lk 23.29
13.19 Jer 30.7 Dan 12.1 Joel 2.2 Rev 3.10
13.21 Lk 17.23

p Gk *I am* q Gk *gospel* r Or *the Christ*

JESUS' PROPHECIES IN THE OLIVET DISCOURSE

Type of Prophecy	*Old Testament References*	*Other New Testament References*
The Last Days Mark 13.1–23 Matthew 24.1–28 Luke 21.5–24	Daniel 9.26 27 Daniel 11.31 Joel 2.2	John 15.21 Revelation 11.2 1 Timothy 4.1, 2
The Second Coming of Christ Mark 13.24–27 Luke 21.25–28 Matthew 24.29–31	Isaiah 13.6–10 Ezekiel 32.7 Daniel 7.13, 14	Revelation 6.12 Mark 14.62 1 Thessalonians 4.16

In Mark 13, often called the Olivet Discourse, Jesus talked a lot about two things: the end times and his second coming. Jesus was not trying to encourage his disciples to speculate about exactly when he would return by sharing these prophecies with them. Instead, he urges all his followers to be watchful and prepared for his coming. If we serve Jesus faithfully now, we will be ready when he returns.

have your heart and life ready for his return.

13.9, 10 As the early church began to grow, most of the disciples experienced the kind of persecution Jesus was talking about. Since the time of Christ, Christians have been persecuted in their own lands and on foreign mission fields. Though you may be safe from persecution now, your vision of God's kingdom must not be limited by what happens only to you. A glance at a newspaper will show you that many Christians in other parts of the world daily face hardships and persecution. Persecutions are an opportunity for Christians to witness for Christ to those opposed to him. They serve God's desire that the gospel be proclaimed to everyone.

13.11 Jesus is not saying that studying the Bible and gaining knowledge is useless or wrong. Before and after his resurrection Jesus himself taught his disciples what to say and how to say it. But Jesus is telling us what attitude we can have when we must take a stand for the gospel. We don't have to be fearful or defensive about our faith, because the Holy Spirit will be present to give us the right words to say.

13.13 To believe in Jesus "to the end" will take perseverance, because our faith will be challenged and opposed. Severe trials will sift true Christians from fair-weather believers. Enduring to the end does not earn salvation for us, but marks us as already saved. The assurance of our salvation will keep us going through the persecution.

13.14 The "desolating sacrilege" (or abomination of desolation) Jesus mentioned is the desecration of the temple by God's enemies. This happened repeatedly in Israel's history: in 597 B.C. when Nebuchadnezzar looted the temple and took Judean captives to Babylon (2 Chronicles 36); in 168 B.C. when Antiochus Epiphanes sacrificed a pig to Zeus on the sacred temple altar (Daniel 9.27; 11.30, 31); in A.D. 70 when the Emperor Titus placed an idol on the site of the burned-out temple after the destruction of Jerusalem. In A.D. 38, just a few years after Jesus gave this warning, the Emperor Caligula made plans to put his own statue in the temple, but he died before this could be carried out.

13.20 The *elect* are God's chosen people, those who are saved. See Romans 8.29, 30 and Ephesians 1.4, 5 for more on God's choice.

believe it. 22 False messiahs[s] and false prophets will appear and produce signs and
omens, to lead astray, if possible, the elect. 23 But be alert; I have already told you
everything.

13.22 Mt 7.15; 24.24
13.23 2 Pet 3.17

Jesus tells about his return
(202/Matthew 24.29–35; Luke 21.25–33)

24 "But in those days, after that suffering,
the sun will be darkened,
and the moon will not give its light,
25 and the stars will be falling from heaven,
and the powers in the heavens will be shaken.
26 Then they will see 'the Son of Man coming in clouds' with great power and glory.
27 Then he will send out the angels, and gather his elect from the four winds, from
the ends of the earth to the ends of heaven.
28 "From the fig tree learn its lesson: as soon as its branch becomes tender and
puts forth its leaves, you know that summer is near. 29 So also, when you see these
things taking place, you know that he[t] is near, at the very gates. 30 Truly I tell you,
this generation will not pass away until all these things have taken place. 31 Heaven
and earth will pass away, but my words will not pass away.

13.24 Isa 13.10 Ezek 32.7,8 Joel 2.31; 3.15 Rev 6.12
13.26 Dan 7.13 Mt 16.27 Acts 1.11 Rev 1.7
13.27 Deut 30.3,4
13.31 Ps 102.25-27

Jesus tells about remaining watchful
(203/Matthew 24.36–51; Luke 21.34–38)

32 "But about that day or hour no one knows, neither the angels in heaven, nor
the Son, but only the Father. 33 Beware, keep alert;[u] for you do not know when the
time will come. 34 It is like a man going on a journey, when he leaves home and puts
his slaves in charge, each with his work, and commands the doorkeeper to be on the
watch. 35 Therefore, keep awake—for you do not know when the master of the
house will come, in the evening, or at midnight, or at cockcrow, or at dawn, 36 or
else he may find you asleep when he comes suddenly. 37 And what I say to you I say
to all: Keep awake."

13.32 Acts 1.7
13.33 Rom 13.11 Eph 6.17,18 Col 4.2 1 Thess 5.6
13.34 Mt 25.14
13.35-37 Lk 12.39,40

[s] Or *christs* [t] Or *it* [u] Other ancient authorities add *and pray*

13.22, 23 Is it possible for Christians to be deceived? Yes. So convincing will be the arguments and proofs from deceivers in the end times that it will be difficult *not* to fall away from Christ. If we are prepared, Jesus says, we can remain faithful. But if we are not prepared, we will not endure. To penetrate the disguises of false teachers we can ask: (1) Have their predictions come true, or do they have to revise them to fit what's already happened? (2) Does any teaching utilize a small section of the Bible to the neglect of the whole? (3) Does the teaching contradict what the Bible says about God? (4) Are the practices meant to glorify the teacher or Christ? (5) Do the teachings promote hostility toward other Christians?

13.31 In Jesus' day the world seemed concrete, dependable, and permanent. These days many people fear its destruction by nuclear war. Jesus tells us, however, that even if the earth passes away, the truth of his words will never be changed or abolished. God and his Word provide the only stability in our unstable world. How shortsighted people are who spend their time learning about this temporary world and accumulating its possessions, while neglecting the Bible and its eternal truths!

13.32 When Jesus said that even he did not know the time of the end, he was affirming his humanity. Of course God the Father knows the time, and Jesus and the Father are one. But when Jesus became a man, he voluntarily gave up the unlimited use of his divine attributes.

The emphasis of this verse is not on Jesus' lack of knowledge, but rather on the fact that no one knows. It is God the Father's secret to be revealed when he wills. No one can predict by Scripture or science the exact day of Jesus' return. Jesus is teaching that preparation, not calculation, is needed.

13.33, 34 Months of planning go into a wedding, the birth of a baby, a career change, a speaking engagement, the purchase of a home. Do you place the same importance on preparing for Christ's return, the most important event in your life? Its results will last for eternity. You dare not postpone these preparations, because you do not know when it will occur. The way to prepare is to study God's Word and live by its instructions each day.

13.35–37 The entire thirteenth chapter of Mark tells us how to live while we wait for Christ's return: (1) We are not to be misled by confusing claims or speculative interpretations of what will happen (13.5, 6). (2) We should not be afraid to tell people about Christ, despite what they might say or do to us (13.9–11). (3) We must endure by faith and not be surprised by persecutions (13.13). (4) We must be morally alert, obedient to the commands for living found in God's Word. This chapter was not given to promote discussions on prophetic timetables, but to stimulate right living for God in a world where he is largely ignored.

C. DEATH AND RESURRECTION OF JESUS, THE SERVANT (14.1 – 16.20)

Mark tells us about Jesus' ultimate deed of servanthood – dying for us on the cross. Jesus died for our sin so we wouldn't have to. Now we can have eternal fellowship with God instead of eternal suffering and death. When first written in Rome, this Gospel was encouraging to Roman Christians during times of persecution. Christ's victory through suffering can encourage us during difficult times too.

Religious leaders plot to kill Jesus

(207/Matthew 26.1–5; Luke 22.1, 2)

14.1 Mt 26.1-5 Lk 22.1,2 Jn 11.55-57 **14** It was two days before the Passover and the festival of Unleavened Bread.
The chief priests and the scribes were looking for a way to arrest Jesus[v] by
stealth and kill him; 2 for they said, "Not during the festival, or there may be a riot
among the people."

A woman anoints Jesus with expensive perfume

(182/Matthew 26.6–13; John 12.1–11)

14.3 Mt 26.6-13 Lk 7.37-39 Jn 12.1-8 3 While he was at Bethany in the house of Simon the leper,[w] as he sat at the
table, a woman came with an alabaster jar of very costly ointment of nard, and she
broke open the jar and poured the ointment on his head. 4 But some were there who
said to one another in anger, "Why was the ointment wasted in this way? 5 For this
ointment could have been sold for more than three hundred denarii,[x] and the
money given to the poor." And they scolded her. 6 But Jesus said, "Let her alone;
14.7 Deut 15.11 why do you trouble her? She has performed a good service for me. 7 For you always
have the poor with you, and you can show kindness to them whenever you wish;
14.8 Mk 16.1 Lk 24.1 Jn 19.40 but you will not always have me. 8 She has done what she could; she has anointed
my body beforehand for its burial. 9 Truly I tell you, wherever the good news[y] is
proclaimed in the whole world, what she has done will be told in remembrance of
her."

Judas agrees to betray Jesus

(208/Matthew 26.14–16; Luke 22.3–6)

14.11 Zech 11.12 1 Tim 6.10 Jude 11 10 Then Judas Iscariot, who was one of the twelve, went to the chief priests in
order to betray him to them. 11 When they heard it, they were greatly pleased, and
promised to give him money. So he began to look for an opportunity to betray him.

[v] Gk *him* [w] The terms *leper* and *leprosy* can refer to several diseases [x] The denarius was the usual day's wage for a laborer [y] Or *gospel*

14.1 The Passover commemorated the night the Israelites were freed from Egypt (Exodus 12) when God "passed over" homes marked by the blood of a lamb while killing firstborn sons in unmarked homes. The day of Passover was followed by a seven-day festival called the festival of unleavened bread. This, too, recalled the Israelites' quick escape from Egypt when they didn't have time to let their bread rise, so they baked it without yeast. This holiday found people gathering for a special meal that included lamb, wine, bitter herbs, and unleavened bread. Eventually the whole week came to be called Passover.

14.1 The Jewish leaders plotted secretly to kill Jesus – his murder was carefully planned. It was not because popular opinion had turned against him. In fact, the leaders were afraid of Jesus' popularity.

14.3 Bethany is located on the eastern slope of the Mount of Olives (Jerusalem is on the western side). This town was the home of Jesus' friends Lazarus, Mary, and Martha, who were also present at this dinner (John 11.2). The woman who anointed Jesus' feet was Mary, Lazarus's and Martha's sister (John 12.1–3). An alabaster jar was a beautiful and expensive carved vase. Nard was expensive perfume.

14.3–9 Matthew and Mark placed this event just before the last supper, while John placed it a week earlier, just before the triumphal entry. It must be remembered that the main purpose of the Gospel writers was not to present an exact chronological account of Christ's life, but to give an accurate record of his message. Matthew and Mark may have chosen to place this event here to contrast the complete devotion of Mary with the betrayal of Judas, the next event in both Gospels.

14.4, 5 Where Mark says "some," John specifically mentions Judas (John 12.4, 5). Judas's indignation over Mary's act of worship was based not on concern for the poor but on greed. Because he was the treasurer of Jesus' ministry and had embezzled funds (John 12.6), he no doubt wanted the perfume sold so that the proceeds could be put into his care.

14.6, 7 Jesus was not saying that we should neglect the poor, nor was he justifying indifference to them. He was praising Mary for her unselfish act of worship. The essence of worshiping Christ is to regard him with utmost love, respect, and devotion and to be willing to sacrifice to him what is most precious.

14.10 Why would Judas want to betray Jesus? Like the other disciples, Judas expected Jesus to start a political rebellion and overthrow Rome. As treasurer, Judas certainly assumed (as did the other disciples – see 10.35–37) that he would be given an important position in Jesus' new government. But when Jesus praised Mary for pouring out the perfume, thought to be worth a year's salary, Judas finally realized that Jesus' kingdom was not physical or political, but spiritual. Judas's greedy desire for money and status could not be realized if he followed Jesus, so he betrayed him in exchange for money and favor from the religious leaders.

Disciples prepare for the Passover
(209/Matthew 26.17–19; Luke 22.7–13)

12 On the first day of Unleavened Bread, when the Passover lamb is sacrificed, **14.12**
his disciples said to him, "Where do you want us to go and make the preparations Deut 16.5 Mt 26.17-19
for you to eat the Passover?" 13 So he sent two of his disciples, saying to them, "Go Lk 22.7-13 1 Cor 5.7,8
into the city, and a man carrying a jar of water will meet you; follow him, 14 and **14.14**
wherever he enters, say to the owner of the house, 'The Teacher asks, Where is my Ex 12.8
guest room where I may eat the Passover with my disciples?' 15 He will show you Lev 23.5
a large room upstairs, furnished and ready. Make preparations for us there." 16 So
the disciples set out and went to the city, and found everything as he had told them;
and they prepared the Passover meal.

Jesus and the disciples have the last supper
(211/Matthew 26.20–30; Luke 22.14–30; John 13.21–30)

17 When it was evening, he came with the twelve. 18 And when they had taken **14.17**
their places and were eating, Jesus said, "Truly I tell you, one of you will betray Mt 26.20-30 Lk 22.14-23
me, one who is eating with me." 19 They began to be distressed and to say to him Jn 13.21-30
one after another, "Surely, not I?" 20 He said to them, "It is one of the twelve, one
who is dipping bread[z] into the bowl[a] with me. 21 For the Son of Man goes as it is **14.21**
written of him, but woe to that one by whom the Son of Man is betrayed! It would Ps 22.1-21 Isa 53.3-8
have been better for that one not to have been born." **14.22**
22 While they were eating, he took a loaf of bread, and after blessing it he broke 1 Cor 10.16 11.23-26
it, gave it to them, and said, "Take; this is my body." 23 Then he took a cup, and **14.24**
after giving thanks he gave it to them, and all of them drank from it. 24 He said to Heb 9.13-15

[z] Gk lacks *bread* [a] Other ancient authorities read *same bowl*

14.13 The two men Jesus sent were Peter and John (Luke 22.8).

14.14, 15 Many homes had large upstairs rooms, sometimes with stairways both inside and outside the house. The preparations for the Passover would have included setting the table and buying and preparing the Passover lamb, unleavened bread, sauces, and other ceremonial food and drink.

14.19 Judas, the very man who would betray Jesus, was at the table with the others. He had already determined to betray Jesus, but in cold-blooded hypocrisy he shared the fellowship of this meal. It is easy to become enraged or shocked by what Judas did, yet professing commitment to Christ and then denying him with one's life is also betraying him. It is denying Christ's love to disobey him; it is denying his truth to distrust him; it is denying his deity to reject his authority. Do your words and actions match? If not, consider a change of mind and heart that will protect you from making a terrible mistake.

14.20 It was often the practice to eat from a common bowl.

14.22–25 Mark records the origin of the Lord's supper, also called communion or eucharist (thanksgiving), which is still celebrated in worship services today. Jesus and his disciples ate a meal, sang psalms, read Scripture, and prayed. Then Jesus took two traditional parts of the Passover meal, the passing of bread and the drinking of wine, and gave them new meaning as his body and blood. He used the bread and wine to explain the significance of what he was about to do on the cross. For more on the significance of the last supper, see 1 Corinthians 11.23–29.

14.24 Jesus' death for us on the cross seals a new covenant between God and people. The old covenant involved forgiveness of sins through the blood of an animal sacrifice (Exodus 24.6–8). But instead of a spotless lamb on the altar, Jesus offered himself, the spotless Lamb of God, as a sacrifice that would forgive sin once and for all. Jesus was the final sacrifice for sins, and his blood sealed the new agreement between God and us. Now all of us can come to God through Jesus, in full confidence that he will hear us and save us from our sins.

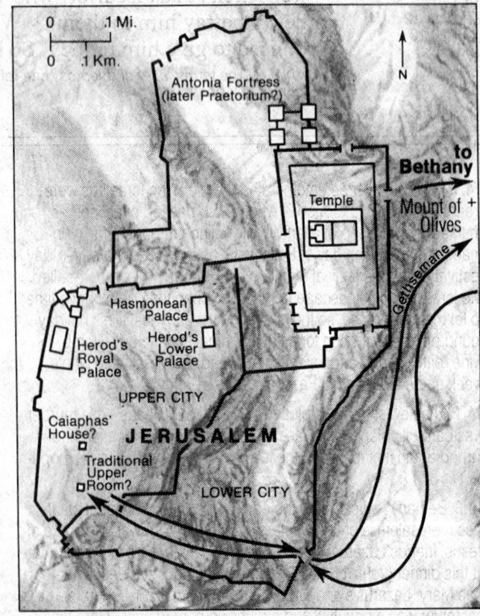

UPPER ROOM AND GETHSEMANE Jesus and the disciples ate the traditional Passover meal in an upper room in the city and then went to the Mount of Olives into a garden called Gethsemane. In the cool of the evening, Jesus prayed for strength to face the trial and suffering ahead.

them, "This is my blood of the[b] covenant, which is poured out for many. 25 Truly
I tell you, I will never again drink of the fruit of the vine until that day when I drink
it new in the kingdom of God."

[b] Other ancient authorities add *new*

JUDAS ISCARIOT

It is easy to overlook the fact that Jesus chose Judas to be his disciple. We may also forget that while Judas betrayed Jesus, *all* the disciples abandoned him. With the other disciples, Judas shared a persistent misunderstanding of Jesus' mission. They all expected Jesus to make the right political moves. When he kept talking about dying, they all felt varying degrees of anger, fear, and disappointment. They didn't understand why they had been chosen if Jesus' mission was doomed to fail.

We do not know the exact motivation behind Judas's betrayal. What is clear is that Judas allowed his desires to place him in a position where Satan could manipulate him. He accepted payment to set Jesus up for the religious leaders. He identified Jesus for the guards in the dimly lit garden of Gethsemane. It is possible that he was trying to force Jesus' hand—would he rebel against Rome and set up a new government or not?

Whatever his plan, though, at some point Judas realized he didn't like the way things were turning out. He tried to undo the evil he had done by returning the money to the priests, but it was too late. The wheels of God's sovereign plan had been set into motion. How sad that Judas ended his life in despair without ever experiencing the gift of reconciliation God could give even to him through Jesus Christ.

Human feelings toward Judas have always been mixed. Some have fervently hated him for his betrayal. Others have pitied him for not realizing what he was doing. A few have tried to make him a hero for his part in ending Jesus' earthly mission. Some have questioned God's fairness in allowing one man to bear such guilt. While there are many feelings about Judas, there are some facts to consider as well. He, by his own choice, betrayed God's Son into the hands of soldiers (Luke 22.48). He was a thief (John 12.6). Jesus knew that Judas's life of evil would not change (John 6.70). Judas's betrayal of Jesus was part of God's sovereign plan (Psalm 41.9; Zechariah 11.12, 13; Matthew 20.18; 26.20–25; Acts 1.16, 20).

In betraying Jesus, Judas made the greatest mistake in history. But the fact that Jesus knew Judas would betray him doesn't mean that Judas was a puppet of God's will. Judas made the choice. God knew what that choice would be and confirmed it. Judas didn't lose his relationship with Jesus; rather, he never found Jesus in the first place. He is called "the one destined to be lost" (John 17.12) because he was never saved.

Judas does us a favor if he makes us think a second time about our commitment to God and the presence of his Spirit within us. Are we true disciples and followers, or uncommitted pretenders? We can choose despair and death, or we can choose repentance, forgiveness, hope, and eternal life. Judas's betrayal sent Jesus to the cross to guarantee that second choice, our only chance. Will we accept his free gift, or, like Judas, betray him?

Strengths and accomplishments:
- He was chosen as one of the 12 disciples; the only non-Galilean
- He kept the money bag for the expenses of the group
- He was able to recognize the evil in his betrayal of Jesus

Weaknesses and mistakes:
- He was greedy (John 12.6)
- He betrayed Jesus
- He committed suicide instead of seeking forgiveness

Lessons from his life:
- Evil plans and motives leave us open to being used by Satan for even greater evil
- The consequences of evil are so devastating that even small lies and little wrong-doings have serious results
- God's plan and his purposes are worked out even in the worst possible events

Vital statistics:
- Where: Probably from the town of Kerioth
- Occupation: disciple of Jesus
- Relatives: Father: Simon
- Contemporaries: Jesus, Pilate, Herod, the other 11 disciples

Key verses:
"Then Satan entered into Judas called Iscariot, who was one of the twelve; he went away and conferred with the chief priests and officers of the temple police about how he might betray him to them" (Luke 22.3, 4).

Judas's story is told in the Gospels. He is also mentioned in Acts 1.18, 19.

Jesus again predicts Peter's denial
(222/Matthew 26.30–35)

26 When they had sung the hymn, they went out to the Mount of Olives. 27 And 14.27
Jesus said to them, "You will all become deserters; for it is written, Zech 13.7 Mt 26.31-35
'I will strike the shepherd, Lk 22.31-34 Jn 13.36-38
and the sheep will be scattered.'
28 But after I am raised up, I will go before you to Galilee." 29 Peter said to him, 14.28
"Even though all become deserters, I will not." 30 Jesus said to him, "Truly I tell Mk 16.7
you, this day, this very night, before the cock crows twice, you will deny me three
times." 31 But he said vehemently, "Even though I must die with you, I will not
deny you." And all of them said the same.

Jesus agonizes in the garden
(223/Matthew 26.36–46; Luke 22.39–46)

32 They went to a place called Gethsemane; and he said to his disciples, "Sit 14.32
here while I pray." 33 He took with him Peter and James and John, and began to be Mt 26.36-46 Lk 22.39-46
distressed and agitated. 34 And said to them, "I am deeply grieved, even to death; Jn 18.1
remain here, and keep awake." 35 And going a little farther, he threw himself on the 14.33 Mt 17.1
ground and prayed that, if it were possible, the hour might pass from him. 36 He Mk 9.2
said, "Abba,[c] Father, for you all things are possible; remove this cup from me; yet, Lk 9.28
not what I want, but what you want." 37 He came and found them sleeping; and he 14.35 Jn 12.27
said to Peter, "Simon, are you asleep? Could you not keep awake one hour? 38 Keep Heb 5.7
awake and pray that you may not come into the time of trial;[d] the spirit indeed is 14.36 Mt 20.22
willing, but the flesh is weak." 39 And again he went away and prayed, saying the Jn 5.30; 6.38; 18.11 Rom 8.15
same words. 40 And once more he came and found them sleeping, for their eyes Gal 4.6
were very heavy; and they did not know what to say to him. 41 He came a third time 14.38 Rom 7.23
and said to them, "Are you still sleeping and taking your rest? Enough! The hour Gal 5.17
has come; the Son of Man is betrayed into the hands of sinners. 42 Get up, let us be
going. See, my betrayer is at hand."

Jesus is betrayed and arrested
(224/Matthew 26.47–56; Luke 22.47–53; John 18.1–11)

43 Immediately, while he was still speaking, Judas, one of the twelve, arrived; 14.43
and with him there was a crowd with swords and clubs, from the chief priests, the Mt 26.47-56 Lk 22.47-53
scribes, and the elders. 44 Now the betrayer had given them a sign, saying, "The Jn 18.2-11
one I will kiss is the man; arrest him and lead him away under guard." 45 So when 14.45
he came, he went up to him at once and said, "Rabbi!" and kissed him. 46 Then they Jn 20.16
laid hands on him and arrested him. 47 But one of those who stood near drew his 14.47 Jn 18.10

[c] Aramaic for *Father* [d] Or *into temptation*

14.26 The hymn they sang was most likely taken from Psalms 115–118, traditionally sung at the Passover meal.

14.27 It's easy to think that Satan temporarily gained the upper hand in this drama about Jesus' death. But we see later that God was in control, even in the death of his Son. Satan gained no victory—everything occurred exactly as God had planned.

14.27-31 This is the second time in the same evening that Jesus predicted the disciples' denial and desertion, which probably explains their strong reaction (14.31). For Jesus' earlier prediction, see Luke 22.31–34 and John 13.36–38.

14.35, 36 Was Jesus trying to get out of his task? Jesus expressed his true feelings, but he did not deny or rebel against God's will. He reaffirmed his desire to do what God wanted. His prayer highlights the terrible suffering he had to endure—an agony worse than dying, because he had to take on the sins of the whole world. This "cup" was the agony of alienation from God, his Father, at the cross (Hebrews 5.7–9). The sinless Son of God took on our sins and was separated for a while from God in order that we could be eternally saved.

14.36 While praying, Jesus was aware of what doing the Father's will would cost him. He understood the suffering he was about to encounter, and he did not want to have to endure the horrible experience. But Christ prayed, "Not what I want, but what you want." Anything worth having costs something. What does your commitment to God cost you? Be willing to pay the price to have something worthwhile in the end.

14.38 In times of great stress, we are vulnerable to temptation, even if we have a willing spirit. Jesus gave us an example of what to do to resist: (1) pray to God (14.35); (2) seek support of friends and loved ones (14.33, 37, 40, 41); (3) focus on the purpose God has given us (14.36).

14.43-45 Judas was given a contingent of policemen and soldiers (John 18.3) in order to seize Jesus and bring him before the religious court for trial. The religious leaders had issued the warrant for Jesus' arrest, and Judas was acting as Jesus' official accuser.

14.47 According to John 18.10, the person who pulled the sword was Peter. Luke 22.51 records that Jesus immediately healed the man's ear and prevented any further bloodshed.

14.49 Ps 22.6-18 Isa 53.7-9 Dan 9.26 Lk 24.44
14.50 Ps 88.8 Jn 16.32

sword and struck the slave of the high priest, cutting off his ear. [48]Then Jesus said
to them, "Have you come out with swords and clubs to arrest me as though I were
a bandit? [49]Day after day I was with you in the temple teaching, and you did not
arrest me. But let the scriptures be fulfilled." [50]All of them deserted him and fled.
51 A certain young man was following him, wearing nothing but a linen cloth.
They caught hold of him, [52]but he left the linen cloth and ran off naked.

MAJOR EVENTS OF PASSION WEEK

Sunday through Wednesday Jesus spent each night in Bethany, just two miles east of Jerusalem on the opposite slope of the Mount of Olives. He probably stayed at the home of Mary, Martha, and Lazarus. Jesus spent Thursday night praying in the Garden of Gethsemane. Friday and Saturday nights Jesus' body lay in the garden tomb.

Day	*Event*	*References*
Sunday	Triumphal entry into Jerusalem	Matthew 21.1–11 Mark 11.1–10 Luke 19.29–40 John 12.12–19
Monday	Jesus cleanses the temple	Matthew 21.12, 13 Mark 11.15–17 Luke 19.45, 46
Tuesday	Jesus' authority challenged in the temple	Matthew 21.23–27 Mark 11.27–33 Luke 20.1–8
	Jesus teaches in stories and confronts the Jewish leaders	Matthew 21.28—23.36 Mark 12.1–40 Luke 20.9–47
	Greeks ask to see Jesus	John 12.20–26
	The Olivet Discourse	Matthew 24 Mark 13 Luke 21.5–38
	Judas agrees to betray Jesus	Matthew 26.14–16 Mark 14.10, 11 Luke 22.3–6
Wednesday	The Bible does not say what Jesus did on this day. He probably remained in Bethany with his disciples	
Thursday	The last supper	Matthew 26.26–29 Mark 14.22–25 Luke 22.14–20
	Jesus speaks to the disciples in the upper room	John 13—17
	Jesus struggles in Gethsemane	Matthew 26.36–46 Mark 14.32–42 Luke 22.39–46 John 18.1
	Jesus is betrayed and arrested	Matthew 26.47–56 Mark 14.43–52 Luke 22.47–53 John 18.2–12
Friday	Jesus is tried by Jewish and Roman authorities and denied by Peter	Matthew 26.57—27.2, 11–31 Mark 14.53—15.20 Luke 22.54—23.25 John 18.13—19.16
	Jesus is crucified	Matthew 27.31–56 Mark 15.20–41 Luke 23.26–49 John 19.17–30
Sunday	The resurrection	Matthew 28.1–10 Mark 16.1–11 Luke 24.1–12 John 20.1–18

14.50 Just hours earlier, these disciples had vowed never to desert Jesus (14.31).

14.51, 52 Tradition says that this young man might have been John Mark, the writer of this Gospel. The incident is not mentioned in any of the other accounts.

Caiaphas questions Jesus
(226/Matthew 26.57–68)

53 They took Jesus to the high priest; and all the chief priests, the elders, and
the scribes were assembled. 54 Peter had followed him at a distance, right into the
courtyard of the high priest; and he was sitting with the guards, warming himself at
the fire. 55 Now the chief priests and the whole council were looking for testimony
against Jesus to put him to death; but they found none. 56 For many gave false testimony against him, and their testimony did not agree. 57 Some stood up and gave
false testimony against him, saying, 58 "We heard him say, 'I will destroy this temple that is made with hands, and in three days I will build another, not made with
hands.' " 59 But even on this point their testimony did not agree. 60 Then the high
priest stood up before them and asked Jesus, "Have you no answer? What is it that
they testify against you?" 61 But he was silent and did not answer. Again the high
priest asked him, "Are you the Messiah,[e] the Son of the Blessed One?" 62 Jesus
said, "I am; and
'you will see the Son of Man
seated at the right hand of the Power,'
and 'coming with the clouds of heaven.' "
63 Then the high priest tore his clothes and said, "Why do we still need witnesses?
64 You have heard his blasphemy! What is your decision?" All of them condemned
him as deserving death. 65 Some began to spit on him, to blindfold him, and to
strike him, saying to him, "Prophesy!" The guards also took him over and beat
him.

14.53 Mt 26.57-68 Lk 22.54,63-71 Jn 18.12-14,19-24
14.54 Mt 26.3 Jn 18.18
14.55 Dan 6.4 1 Pet 3.16
14.56 Ps 35.11 Prov 6.16-19 19.5
14.58 Jn 2.19
14.61 Isa 53.7 1 Pet 2.23
14.62 Ps 110.1 Dan 7.13 Acts 1.11 1 Thess 4.16 Rev 1.7; 22.20
14.63 Lev 24.15,16 Acts 6.11
14.65 Isa 50.6; 53.5

[e] Or *the Christ*

14.53ff This trial by the Jewish council had two phases. A small group met at night (John 18.12–24), and then the full council met at daybreak (Luke 22.66–71). They tried Jesus for religious offenses such as calling himself the Son of God, which, according to law, was blasphemy. The trial was fixed: these religious leaders had already decided to kill Jesus (Luke 22.2).

14.55 The Romans controlled Israel, but the Jews were given some authority over religious and minor civil disputes. The Jewish ruling body called the council (or Sanhedrin) was made up of 71 of Israel's religious leaders. It was assumed that these men would be just. Instead they showed great injustice in the trial of Jesus, even to the point of making up lies to use against him (14.57).

14.58 The claim about which the false witnesses finally agreed twisted Jesus' actual words. He did not say, "I will destroy this temple;" he said, "Destroy this temple, and in three days I will raise it up" (John 2.19). Jesus was not talking about Herod's temple, but about his own body.

14.60–64 To the first question, Jesus made no reply because it was based on confusing and erroneous evidence. Not answering was wiser than trying to clarify the fabricated accusations. But if Jesus had refused to answer the second question, it could have been taken as a denial of his mission. Instead, his answer predicted a powerful role-reversal. Sitting on the right hand of power, he would come to judge his accusers, and they would have to answer *his* questions (Psalm 110.1; Revelation 20.11–13).

14.63, 64 Of all people, the high priest and members of the council should have recognized the Messiah because they knew the Scriptures thoroughly. Their job was to point people to God, but they were more concerned about preserving their reputations and holding on to their authority. They valued human security more than eternal security.

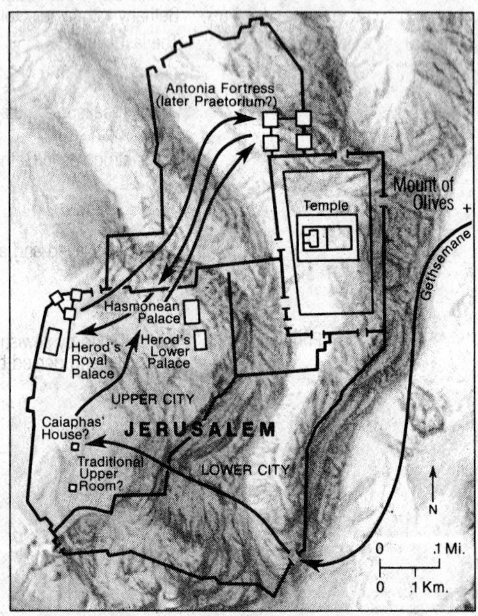

JESUS' TRIAL From Gethsemane, Jesus' trial began at the home of Caiaphas, the high priest. He was then taken to Pilate, the Roman governor. Luke records that Pilate sent him to Herod, who was in Jerusalem—presumably in one of his two palaces (Luke 23.5–12). Herod sent him back to Pilate, who sentenced him to be crucified.

Peter denies knowing Jesus
(227/Matthew 26.69–75; Luke 22.54–65; John 18.25–27)

14.66 Mt 26.69-75 — 66 While Peter was below in the courtyard, one of the servant-girls of the high
Lk 22.55-62 — priest came by. 67 When she saw Peter warming himself, she stared at him and said,
Jn 18.15-18; 25-27 — "You also were with Jesus, the man from Nazareth." 68 But he denied it, saying, "I
do not know or understand what you are talking about." And he went out into the
forecourt.[f] Then the cock crowed.[g] 69 And the servant-girl, on seeing him, began
14.70 Acts 2.7 — again to say to the bystanders, "This man is one of them." 70 But again he denied it.
Then after a little while the bystanders again said to Peter, "Certainly you are one
14.71 Prov 29.25 — of them; for you are a Galilean." 71 But he began to curse, and he swore an oath, "I
1 Cor 10.12 — do not know this man you are talking about." 72 At that moment the cock crowed for
14.72 2 Cor 7.10 — the second time. Then Peter remembered that Jesus had said to him, "Before the
cock crows twice, you will deny me three times." And he broke down and wept.

The council of religious leaders condemns Jesus
(228/Matthew 27.1, 2; Luke 22.66–71)

15.1 Jn 18.28-40 — **15** As soon as it was morning, the chief priests held a consultation with the
Acts 4.27 — elders and scribes and the whole council. They bound Jesus, led him away,
15.2 1 Tim 6.13 — and handed him over to Pilate. 2 Pilate asked him, "Are you the King of the Jews?"
15.5 Isa 53.7 — He answered him, "You say so." 3 Then the chief priests accused him of many
Jn 19.9 — things. 4 Pilate asked him again, "Have you no answer? See how many charges they
1 Pet 2.23 — bring against you." 5 But Jesus made no further reply, so that Pilate was amazed.

[f] Or *gateway* [g] Other ancient authorities lack *Then the cock crowed*

WHY DID JESUS HAVE TO DIE?

The Problem	We have all done things that are wrong, and we have failed to obey God's laws. Because of this, we have been separated from God our Creator. Separation from God is death; but, by ourselves, we can do nothing to become united with God.
Why Jesus Could Help	Jesus was not only a man; he was God's unique Son. Because Jesus never disobeyed God and never sinned, only he can bridge the gap between the sinless God and sinful mankind.
The Solution	Jesus freely offered his life for us, dying on the cross in our place, taking all our wrongdoing upon himself, and saving us from the consequences of sin—including God's judgment and death.
The Results	Jesus took our past, present, and future sins upon himself so that we could have new life. Because all our wrongdoing is forgiven, we are reconciled to God. Furthermore, Jesus' resurrection from the dead is the proof that his substitutionary sacrifice on the cross was acceptable to God, and his resurrection has become the source of new life for whoever believes that Jesus is the Son of God. All who believe in him may have this new life and live it in union with him.

14.66, 67 Caiaphas's house, where Jesus was tried (14.53), was part of a huge palace with several courtyards. John was apparently acquainted with the high priest, and he was let into the courtyard along with Peter (John 18.15, 16).

14.71 Peter's curse was more than just a common swear word. He was making the strongest denial he could think of by denying with an oath that he knew Jesus. He said, in effect, "May God strike me dead if I'm lying."

14.71 It is easy to get angry at the Jewish council and the Roman governor for their injustice in condemning Jesus, but Peter and the rest of the disciples also contributed to Jesus' pain by deserting him (14.50). While most of us are not like the Jewish and Roman leaders, we are all like the disciples, because all of us have been guilty of denying Christ as Lord in vital areas of our lives. We may pride ourselves that we have not committed certain sins, but we are all guilty of sin. Don't try to excuse yourself by pointing at others whose sins seem worse than yours.

15.1 Why did the Jewish leaders send Jesus to Pilate, the Roman governor? The Romans had taken away the Jews' right to inflict capital punishment, so in order for Jesus to be condemned to death, he had to be sentenced by a Roman leader. The Jewish leaders wanted Jesus executed on a cross, a method of death they believed brought a curse from God (see Deuteronomy 21.23). They hoped to persuade the people that Jesus was cursed, not blessed by God.

15.3, 4 The Jewish leaders had to fabricate new accusations against Jesus when they brought him before Pilate. The charge of blasphemy would mean nothing to the Roman governor, so they accused Jesus of three other crimes: (1) encouraging the people not to pay their taxes to Rome, (2) claiming he was a king – "the King of the Jews," and (3) causing riots all over the countryside. Tax evasion, treason, and terrorism – all these would be cause for Pilate's concern.

15.5 Why didn't Jesus answer Pilate's questions? It would have been futile to answer, and the time had come to give his life to save the world. He had no reason to try to prolong the trial or save himself. His was the ultimate example of self-assurance and peace, which no ordinary criminal could imitate. Nothing would stop him from completing the work he had come to earth to do (Isaiah 53.7).

Pilate hands Jesus over to be crucified
(232/Matthew 27.15–26; Luke 23.13–25; John 18.39 – 19.16)

6 Now at the festival he used to release a prisoner for them, anyone for whom
they asked. 7 Now a man called Barabbas was in prison with the rebels who had
committed murder during the insurrection. 8 So the crowd came and began to ask
Pilate to do for them according to his custom. 9 Then he answered them, "Do you **15.9**
want me to release for you the King of the Jews?" 10 For he realized that it was out Ps 2.6 Jer 23.5,6
of jealousy that the chief priests had handed him over. 11 But the chief priests stirred Mic 5.2 Lk 1.31-33
up the crowd to have him release Barabbas for them instead. 12 Pilate spoke to them Acts 3.13,14
again, "Then what do you wish me to do[h] with the man you call[i] the King of the
Jews?" 13 They shouted back, "Crucify him!" 14 Pilate asked them, "Why, what evil
has he done?" But they shouted all the more, "Crucify him!" 15 So Pilate, wishing **15.15**
to satisfy the crowd, released Barabbas for them; and after flogging Jesus, he Prov 29.25
handed him over to be crucified.

Roman soldiers mock Jesus
(233/Matthew 27.27–31)

16 Then the soldiers led him into the courtyard of the palace (that is, the gover- **15.16**
nor's headquarters[j]); and they called together the whole cohort. 17 And they Mt 27.27-31 Jn 19.1-3,16
clothed him in a purple cloak; and after twisting some thorns into a crown, they put
it on him. 18 And they began saluting him, "Hail, King of the Jews!" 19 They struck
his head with a reed, spat upon him, and knelt down in homage to him. 20 After
mocking him, they stripped him of the purple cloak and put his own clothes on him.
Then they led him out to crucify him.

[h] Other ancient authorities read *what should I do* [i] Other ancient authorities lack *the man you call* [j] Gk *the praetorium*

15.7 Barabbas was arrested for his part in a rebellion against the Roman government, and although he had committed a murder, he may have been a hero among the Jews. The fiercely independent Jews hated to be ruled by pagan Romans. They hated paying taxes to support the despised government and its gods. Most of the Roman authorities who had to settle Jewish disputes hated the Jews in return. The time was ripe for rebellion.

15.8 This crowd was most likely a group of people loyal to the Jewish leaders. But where were the disciples and the crowds who days earlier had shouted, "Hosanna in the highest heaven" (11.10)? Jesus' sympathizers were afraid of the Jewish leaders, so they went into hiding. Another possibility is that the multitude included many people who were in the Palm Sunday parade, but who turned against Jesus when they saw he was not going to be an earthly conqueror and their deliverer from Rome.

15.10 The Jews hated Pilate, but they went to him for the favor of condemning Jesus to crucifixion. Pilate could see that this was a frame-up. Why else would these people, who hated him and the Roman Empire he represented, ask him to convict of treason and give the death penalty to one of their fellow Jews?

15.13 Crucifixion was the Roman penalty for rebellion. Only slaves or those who were not Roman citizens could be crucified. If Jesus died by crucifixion, he would die the death of a rebel and slave, not of the king he claimed to be. This is just what the Jewish religious leaders wanted; this is why they whipped the mob into a frenzy. In addition, crucifixion would put the responsibility for killing Jesus on the Romans, and thus the crowds could not blame the religious leaders.

15.14, 15 Who was guilty of Jesus' death? In reality, everyone was at fault. The disciples deserted him in terror. Peter denied that he ever knew Jesus. Judas betrayed him. The crowds who had followed him stood by and did nothing. Pilate tried to blame the crowds. The religious leaders actively promoted Jesus' death. The Roman soldiers tortured him. If you had been there, watching these trials, what would your response have been?

15.15 The region of Judea where Pilate ruled as governor was little more than a hot and dusty outpost of the Roman Empire. Because it was so far from Rome, Pilate was given just a small army. His primary job was to keep peace. We know from historical records that Pilate had already been warned about other uprisings in his region. Although he may have seen no guilt in Jesus and no reason to condemn him to death, he wavered when the Jews in the crowd threatened to report him to Caesar (John 19.12). Such a report, accompanied by a riot, could cost him his position and hopes for advancement.

15.15 Although Jesus was innocent according to Roman law, Pilate caved in under political pressure. He abandoned what he knew was right. He tried to second-guess the Jewish leaders and gave a decision that would please everyone while keeping himself safe. When we lay aside God's clear statements of right and wrong and make decisions based on our audience, we fall into compromise and lawlessness. God promises to honor those who do right, not those who make everyone happy.

15.19 The soldiers "knelt down in homage to him"; in other words, they mocked Jesus by pretending to worship him.

Jesus is led away to be crucified
(234/Matthew 27.32–37; Luke 23.26–31; John 19.17)

15.21 Rom 16.13
21 They compelled a passer-by, who was coming in from the country, to carry
his cross; it was Simon of Cyrene, the father of Alexander and Rufus. 22 Then they
brought Jesus[k] to the place called Golgotha (which means the place of a skull).

[k] Gk *him*

PILATE

In Jesus' day, any death sentence had to be approved by the Roman official in charge of the administrative district. Pontius Pilate was governor of the province of Judea, where Jerusalem was located. When the Jewish leaders had Jesus in their power and wanted to kill him, they had to obtain Pilate's permission. So it was that early one morning Pilate found a crowd at his door demanding a man's death.

Pilate's relationship with the Jews had always been stormy. His Roman toughness and fairness had been weakened by cynicism, compromises, and mistakes. On several occasions his actions had deeply offended the religious leaders. The resulting riots and chaos must have made Pilate wonder what he had gotten himself into. He was trying to control people who treated their Roman conquerors without respect. Jesus' trial was another episode in Pilate's ongoing problems.

For Pilate, there was never a doubt about Jesus' innocence. Three separate times he declared Jesus not guilty. He couldn't understand what made these people want to kill Jesus, but his fear of the pressure the Jews would place on him made him decide to allow Jesus' crucifixion. Because of the people's threat to inform the emperor that Pilate hadn't eliminated a rebel against Rome, Pilate went against what he knew was right. In desperation, he chose to do wrong.

We share a common humanity with Pilate. At times we know the right and choose the wrong. He had his moment in history and now we have ours. What have we done with our opportunities and responsibilities? What judgment have we passed on Jesus?

Strength and accomplishment:
- Roman governor of Judea

Weaknesses and mistakes:
- He failed in his attempt to rule a people who were defeated militarily but never dominated by Rome
- His constant political struggles made him a cynical and uncaring compromiser, susceptible to pressure
- Although he realized Jesus was innocent, he bowed to the public demand for his execution

Lessons from his life:
- Great evil can happen when truth is at the mercy of political pressures
- Resisting the truth leaves a person without purpose or direction

Vital statistics:
- Where: Judea
- Occupation: Roman governor of Judea
- Relatives: Wife: unnamed
- Contemporaries: Jesus, Caiaphas, Herod

Key verses:
"Pilate asked him, 'What is truth?' After he had said this, he went out to the Jews again and told them, "I find no case against him. But you have a custom that I release someone for you at the Passover. Do you want me to release for you the King of the Jews?' " (John 18.38, 39).

Pilate's story is told in the Gospels. He is also mentioned in Acts 3.13; 4.27; 13.28; 1 Timothy 6.13.

15.21 Colonies of Jews existed outside Judea. Simon made a Passover pilgrimage to Jerusalem all the way from Cyrene in North Africa. His sons, Alexander and Rufus, are evidently mentioned here because they became well known in the early church (Romans 16.13).

23 And they offered him wine mixed with myrrh; but he did not take it. 24 And they 15.23 Ps 69.21
crucified him, and divided his clothes among them, casting lots to decide what each 15.24
should take. Ps 22.18

Jesus is placed on the cross
(235/Matthew 27.38–44; Luke 23.32–43; John 19.18–27)

25 It was nine o'clock in the morning when they crucified him. 26 The inscrip- 15.25 Jn 19.14
tion of the charge against him read, "The King of the Jews." 27 And with him they 15.26
crucified two bandits, one on his right and one on his left.[l] 29 Those who passed by Ps 2.6 Jer 23.5
derided[m] him, shaking their heads and saying, "Aha! You who would destroy the 15.28
temple and build it in three days, 30 save yourself, and come down from the cross!" Lk 22.37
31 In the same way the chief priests, along with the scribes, were also mocking him 15.29,30 Ps 22.7
among themselves and saying, "He saved others; he cannot save himself. 32 Let the Jn 2.19 Acts 6.14
Messiah,[n] the King of Israel, come down from the cross now, so that we may see 15.32
and believe." Those who were crucified with him also taunted him. Heb 12.2,3

Jesus dies on the cross
(236/Matthew 27.45–56; Luke 23.44–49; John 19.28–37)

33 When it was noon, darkness came over the whole land[o] until three in the 15.33 Mt 27.45-56
afternoon. 34 At three o'clock Jesus cried out with a loud voice, "Eloi, Eloi, lema Jn 19.28-30

[l] Other ancient authorities add verse 28, *And the scripture was fulfilled that says, "And he was counted among the lawless."* [m] Or *blasphemed* [n] Or *the Christ* [o] Or *earth*

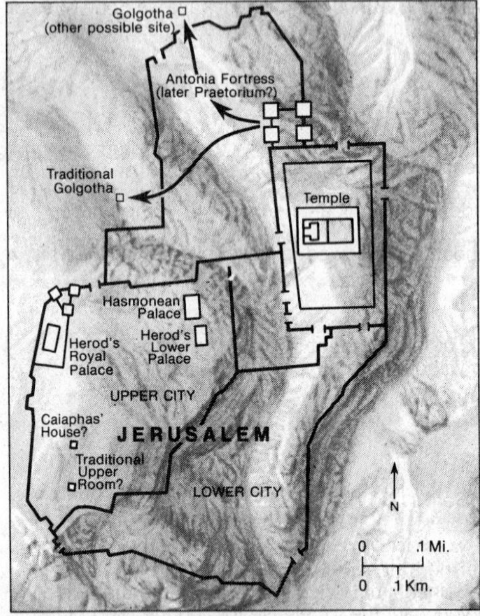

JESUS' ROUTE TO GOLGOTHA After being sentenced by Pilate, Jesus was taken from the Praetorium to a place outside the city, Golgotha, for crucifixion.

15.24 Casting lots was a way of making a decision by chance, like throwing dice or drawing straws. The soldiers cast lots to decide who would receive Jesus' clothing. Roman soldiers had the right to take for themselves the clothing of those crucified. This act fulfilled the prophecy of Psalm 22.18.

15.25 Crucifixion was a feared and shameful form of execution. The victim was forced to carry his cross along the longest possible route to the crucifixion site as a warning to bystanders. There were several shapes for crosses, and several different methods of crucifixion. Jesus was nailed to the cross; condemned men were sometimes tied to their crosses with ropes. In either case, death came by suffocation as the person lost strength and the weight of the body made breathing more and more difficult.

15.26 A sign stating the condemned man's crime was often placed on a cross as a warning. Because Jesus was never found guilty, the only accusation placed on his sign was the "crime" of being King of the Jews.

15.27 Luke records that one of these thieves repented before his death, and Jesus promised that he would be with him in Paradise (Luke 23.39–43).

15.31 Jesus could have saved himself, but he endured this suffering because of his love for us. He could have chosen not to take the pain and humiliation; he could have killed those who mocked him – but he suffered through it all because he loved even his enemies. We had a significant part in the drama that afternoon because our sin was on the cross too. Jesus died on that cross for us, and the penalty for our sin was paid by his death. The only adequate response we can make is to confess our sin and freely accept the fact that Jesus paid for it so we wouldn't have to. Don't insult God with indifference toward the greatest act of genuine love in history.

15.32 When James and John asked Jesus for the places of honor next to him in his kingdom, he told them they didn't know what they were asking (10.35–39). Now that Jesus was preparing to inaugurate his kingdom through his death, the places on his right and on his left were taken by dying men – criminals. This illustrates that Jesus' death is for *all* people. As Jesus explained to his two power-hungry disciples, a person who wants to be close to Jesus must be prepared to suffer and die as he himself was doing. The way to the kingdom is the way of the cross. If we want the glory of the kingdom, we must be willing to be united with the crucified Christ.

15.34 Jesus did not ask this question in surprise or despair. He was quoting the first line of Psalm 22. The whole psalm is a prophecy expressing the deep agony of the Messiah's death for the world's sin. Jesus knew he would be temporarily separated from God the moment he took upon himself the sins of the world.

15.34 sabachthani?" which means, "My God, my God, why have you forsaken me?"[p]
Ps 22.1 35 When some of the bystanders heard it, they said, "Listen, he is calling for Eli-
15.36 jah." 36 And someone ran, filled a sponge with sour wine, put it on a stick, and gave
Ps 69.21 it to him to drink, saying, "Wait, let us see whether Elijah will come to take him
15.38 down." 37 Then Jesus gave a loud cry and breathed his last. 38 And the curtain of the
Ex 26.31-33 Eph 2.14 temple was torn in two, from top to bottom. 39 Now when the centurion, who stood
Heb 6.19 10.19,20 facing him, saw that in this way he[q] breathed his last, he said, "Truly this man was
God's Son!"[r]

15.40 40 There were also women looking on from a distance; among them were Mary
Ps 38.11 Lk 8.2 Magdalene, and Mary the mother of James the younger and of Joses, and Salome.
41 These used to follow him and provided for him when he was in Galilee; and there
were many other women who had come up with him to Jerusalem.

Jesus is laid in the tomb

(237/Matthew 27.57–61; Luke 23.50–56; John 19.38–42)

15.42,43 42 When evening had come, and since it was the day of Preparation, that is, the
Deut 21.22,23 Mt 27.57-61 day before the sabbath, 43 Joseph of Arimathea, a respected member of the council,
Lk 23.50-56 who was also himself waiting expectantly for the kingdom of God, went boldly to
Pilate and asked for the body of Jesus. 44 Then Pilate wondered if he were already
dead; and summoning the centurion, he asked him whether he had been dead for
some time. 45 When he learned from the centurion that he was dead, he granted the
15.46 body to Joseph. 46 Then Joseph[s] bought a linen cloth, and taking down the body,[t]
Isa 53.9 Acts 13.29 wrapped it in the linen cloth, and laid it in a tomb that had been hewn out of the
rock. He then rolled a stone against the door of the tomb. 47 Mary Magdalene and
Mary the mother of Joses saw where the body[t] was laid.

Jesus rises from the dead

(239/Matthew 28.1–7; Luke 24.1–12; John 20.1–10)

16 When the sabbath was over, Mary Magdalene, and Mary the mother of
James, and Salome bought spices, so that they might go and anoint him.
2 And very early on the first day of the week, when the sun had risen, they went to

[p] Other ancient authorities read *made me a reproach* [q] Other ancient authorities add *cried out and* [r] Or *a son of God* [s] Gk *he* [t] Gk *it*

This separation was what he dreaded as he prayed in Gethsemane. The physical agony was horrible, but the spiritual alienation from God was the ultimate torture.

15.37 Jesus' loud cry was probably his last words, "It is finished" (John 19.30).

15.38 A heavy curtain hung in front of the temple room called the most holy place, a place reserved by God for himself. Symbolically, the curtain separated the holy God from sinful people. The room was entered only once a year, on the day of atonement, by the high priest as he made a sacrifice to gain forgiveness for the sins of all the people. When Jesus died, the curtain was split in two, showing that his death for our sins had opened up the way for us to approach our holy God. (Read Hebrews 9 for more on this.)

15.42ff The sabbath began at sundown on Friday and ended at sundown on Saturday. Jesus died just a few hours before sundown on Friday. It was against Jewish law to do physical work or to travel on the sabbath, but Jesus died in time for Joseph of Arimathea to remove his body, prepare it for burial, and put it in his tomb.

15.42, 43 After Jesus died on the cross, Joseph of Arimathea asked for his body and then sealed it in a new tomb. Although an honored member of the Jewish council, Joseph was a secret disciple of Jesus. Not all the Jewish leaders hated Jesus. Joseph risked his reputation to give a proper burial to his Lord. It is frightening to risk one's reputation even for what is right. If your Christian witness endangers your reputation, remember Joseph. Today he is well known in the Christian church.

15.44 Pilate was surprised that Jesus had died so quickly, so he asked an officer to verify the report. Today, in an effort to deny the resurrection, there are those who say that Jesus didn't really die. His death, however, was confirmed by the centurion, Pilate, Joseph of Arimathaea, the religious leaders, and the women who witnessed his burial.

15.46 This tomb was probably a man-made cave hewn from a hill. It was large enough to walk into. Joseph wrapped Jesus' body, placed it in the tomb, and rolled a heavy stone across the entrance. The religious leaders also watched where Jesus was buried. They stationed guards by the tomb and sealed the stone to make sure no one would steal Jesus' body and claim he had risen from the dead (Matthew 27.62–66).

15.47 These women could do very little. They couldn't speak before the Sanhedrin in Jesus' defense; they couldn't appeal to Pilate; they couldn't stand against the crowds; they couldn't overpower the Roman guards. But they did what they could. They stayed at the cross when the disciples had fled; they followed Jesus' body to its tomb; and they prepared spices for his body. Because they used the opportunities they had, they were the first to witness the resurrection. God blessed their devotion and diligence. As believers, we should take advantage of the opportunities we have and do what we *can* for Christ, instead of worrying about what we *cannot* do.

16.1, 2 The women purchased the spices on Saturday evening after the sabbath had ended so they could go to the tomb early the next morning and embalm Jesus' body as a sign of love, devotion, and respect. Bringing spices to the tomb was like bringing flowers to a grave today.

the tomb. 3 They had been saying to one another, "Who will roll away the stone for
us from the entrance to the tomb?" 4 When they looked up, they saw that the stone,
which was very large, had already been rolled back. 5 As they entered the tomb,
they saw a young man, dressed in a white robe, sitting on the right side; and they
were alarmed. 6 But he said to them, "Do not be alarmed; you are looking for Jesus
of Nazareth, who was crucified. He has been raised; he is not here. Look, there is
the place they laid him. 7 But go, tell his disciples and Peter that he is going ahead
of you to Galilee; there you will see him, just as he told you." 8 So they went out and
fled from the tomb, for terror and amazement had seized them; and they said nothing to anyone, for they were afraid.[u]

16.3 Mt 27.60 Mk 15.46
16.5 John 20.11,12 Acts 1.10; 10.30
16.6 Acts 2.23-32 Rom 1.3,4 1 Cor 15.4,12-20 Rev 1.18
16.7 Mt 26.32 Mk 14.28 Jn 21.1

The Shorter Ending of Mark

⟦And all that had been commanded them they told briefly to those around Peter. And afterward Jesus himself sent out through them, from east to west, the sacred and imperishable proclamation of eternal salvation.[v]⟧

The Longer Ending of Mark

Jesus appears to Mary Magdalene
(240/John 20.11–18)

9 ⟦Now after he rose early on the first day of the week, he appeared first to Mary
Magdalene, from whom he had cast out seven demons. 10 She went out and told
those who had been with him, while they were mourning and weeping. 11 But when
they heard that he was alive and had been seen by her, they would not believe it.

16.9 Mt 28.9,10 Lk 24.11 Jn 20.11-18

Jesus appears to two believers traveling on the road
(243/Luke 24.13–35)

12 After this he appeared in another form to two of them, as they were walking
into the country. 13 And they went back and told the rest, but they did not believe
them.

16.12 Lk 24.13-35 1 Cor 15.35-45

Jesus appears to the disciples including Thomas
(245/John 20.24–31)

14 Later he appeared to the eleven themselves as they were sitting at the table;

[u] Some of the most ancient authorities bring the book to a close at the end of verse 8. One authority concludes the book with the shorter ending; others include the shorter ending and then continue with verses 9-20. In most authorities verses 9-20 follow immediately after verse 8, though in some of these authorities the passage is marked as being doubtful. [v] Other ancient authorities add *Amen*

16.4 The angels did not roll away the stone so Jesus could get out, but so others could get in and see for themselves that Jesus had indeed risen from the dead, just as he said.

16.5 Mark says that one angel met the women at the sepulchre, while Luke mentions two angels. These accounts are not contradictory. Each Gospel writer chose to highlight different details as he explained the same story, just as eyewitnesses to a news story each may highlight a different aspect of that event. Mark probably emphasized only the angel who spoke. The unique emphasis of each Gospel shows that the four accounts were written independently. This should give us confidence that all four are true and reliable.

16.6 The resurrection is vitally important for many reasons: (1) Jesus kept his promise to rise from the dead, so we can believe he will keep all his other promises. (2) The resurrection ensures that the ruler of God's eternal kingdom will be the living Christ, not just an idea, hope, or dream. (3) Christ's resurrection gives us the assurance that we also will be resurrected. (4) The power of God that brought Christ's body back from the dead is available to us to bring our morally and spiritually dead selves back to life so we can change and grow (1 Corinthians 15.12–19). (5) The resurrection provides the substance of the church's witness to the world. We do not merely tell lessons from the life of a good teacher; we proclaim the reality of the resurrection of Jesus Christ.

16.7 The angel made special mention of Peter to show that, in spite of Peter's denials, Jesus had not denied him. Jesus had great responsibilities for Peter to fulfill in the church that was not yet born.

16.7 The angel told the disciples to meet Jesus in Galilee "as he told you" (see 14.28). This is where he called most of them to "fish for people" (Matthew 4.19), and it would be where this mission would be restated (John 21). But the disciples, filled with fear, remained behind locked doors in Jerusalem (John 20.19). Jesus met them first in Jerusalem (Luke 24.36) and later in Galilee (John 21). Then he returned to Jerusalem where he ascended into heaven from the Mount of Olives (Acts 1.12).

16.13 When the two finally realized who Jesus was, they rushed back to Jerusalem. It's not enough to read about Christ as a personality or to study his teachings. You must also believe he is God, trust him to save you, and accept him as Lord of your life. This is the difference between knowing Jesus and knowing about him. Only when you know him will you be motivated to share with others what he has done for you.

16.14 1 Cor 15.5
16.15 Col 1.23
16.16 Rom 10.9; 1 Pet 3.21
16.17 Acts 2.4; 19.6
16.18 Acts 28.5

and he upbraided them for their lack of faith and stubbornness, because they had
not believed those who saw him after he had risen.[w] 15 And he said to them, "Go
into all the world and proclaim the good news[x] to the whole creation. 16 The one
who believes and is baptized will be saved; but the one who does not believe will
be condemned. 17 And these signs will accompany those who believe: by using my
name they will cast out demons; they will speak in new tongues; 18 they will pick up
snakes in their hands,[y] and if they drink any deadly thing, it will not hurt them;
they will lay their hands on the sick, and they will recover."

[w] Other ancient authorities add, in whole or in part, *And they excused themselves, saying, "This age of lawlessness and unbelief is under Satan, who does not allow the truth and power of God to prevail over the unclean things of the spirits. Therefore reveal your righteousness now"—thus they spoke to Christ. And Christ replied to them, "The term of years of Satan's power has been fulfilled, but other terrible things draw near. And for those who have sinned I was handed over to death, that they may return to the truth and sin no more, that they may inherit the spiritual and imperishable glory of righteousness that is in heaven."* [x] Or *gospel* [y] Other ancient authorities lack *in their hands*

EVIDENCE THAT JESUS ACTUALLY DIED AND AROSE

This evidence demonstrates Jesus' uniqueness in history and proves that he is God's Son. No one else was able to predict his own resurrection and then accomplish it.

Proposed Explanations for Empty Tomb	*Evidence Against These Explanations*	*References*
Jesus was only unconscious and later revived.	A Roman soldier told Pilate Jesus was dead.	Mark 15.44, 45
	The Roman soldiers did not break Jesus' legs, because he had already died, and one of them pierced Jesus' side with a spear.	John 19.32–34
	Joseph of Arimathea and Nicodemus wrapped Jesus' body and placed it in the tomb.	John 19.38–40
The women made a mistake and went to the wrong tomb.	Mary Magdalene and Mary the mother of Joses saw Jesus placed in the tomb.	Matthew 27.59–61 Mark 15.47 Luke 23.55
	On Sunday morning Peter and John also went to the same tomb.	John 20.3–9
Unknown thieves stole Jesus' body.	The tomb was sealed and guarded by the temple police and probably Roman soldiers, too.	Matthew 27.65, 66
The disciples stole Jesus' body.	The disciples were ready to die for their faith. Stealing Jesus' body would have been admitting their faith was meaningless.	Acts 12.2
	The tomb was guarded and sealed.	Matthew 27.66
The religious leaders stole Jesus' body to secure it.	If the religious leaders had taken Jesus' body, they would have produced it to stop the rumors of his resurrection.	None

16.14 As the disciples sat together, they found it difficult to believe the stories circulating that Jesus had risen from the dead. When Jesus appeared to them, he "upbraided" (harshly rebuked) them for their lack of faith. Lack of faith had been a continual struggle for the disciples (Mark 9.19). In a short time they would preach about Jesus to those who also suffered from a lack of faith and hard hearts. This experience helped them to better understand their listeners who would also find it difficult to believe the stories of Jesus rising from the dead.

16.15 Jesus told his disciples to go into all the world telling everyone that he paid the penalty for sin and that those who believe in him can be forgiven and live eternally with God. Christian disciples today in all parts of the world are preaching this gospel to people who haven't heard it. The driving power that carries missionaries around the world and sets Christ's church in motion is the faith that comes from the resurrection. Do you ever feel as though you don't have the skill or determination to be a witness for Christ? You must personally realize that Jesus rose from the dead and lives for you today. As you grow in your relationship with him, he will give you both the opportunities and the inner strength to tell his message.

16.16 It is not the water of baptism that saves, but God's grace accepted through faith in Christ. Because of Jesus' response to the thief on the cross who died with him, we know it is possible to be saved without being baptized (Luke 23.43). Baptism alone without faith does not automatically bring a person to heaven. Those who refuse to believe will be condemned, regardless of whether or not they have been baptized.

16.18 There are times when God intervenes miraculously to protect his followers. Occasionally he gives them special powers. Paul handled a snake safely (Acts 28.5), and the disciples healed the sick (Matthew 10.1; Acts 3.7, 8). This does not mean, however, that we should test God by putting ourselves in dangerous situations.

Jesus ascends into heaven
(250/Luke 24.50–53)

19 So then the Lord Jesus, after he had spoken to them, was taken up into
heaven and sat down at the right hand of God. 20 And they went out and proclaimed
the good news everywhere, while the Lord worked with them and confirmed the
message by the signs that accompanied it.[z]]

16.19 Lk 24.50,51 Rom 8.34 Heb 1.3 Rev 3.21

z Other ancient authorities add *Amen*

16.19 When Jesus ascended into heaven, his physical presence left the disciples (Acts 1.9). Jesus' sitting at God's right hand signifies the completion of his work, his authority as God, and his coronation as King.

16.20 Mark's Gospel emphasizes Christ's power as well as his servanthood. Jesus' life and teaching turn the world upside down. The world sees power as a way to gain control over others. But Jesus, with all authority and power in heaven and earth, chose to serve others. He held children in his arms, healed the sick, washed the disciples' feet, and died for the sins of the world. Following Jesus means receiving this same power to serve. As believers, we are called to be servants of Christ. As Christ served, we are to serve.

OLD TESTAMENT EVENTS AND PEOPLE MENTIONED BY CHRIST

Old Testament Reference	*Event*	*New Testament Reference*
Genesis 1.27; 2.24	Creation of Adam and Eve	Mark 10.6-8
Genesis 4.10	Murder of Abel	Luke 11.51
Genesis 6.5-13	Corruption of Noah's day and flood	Luke 17.26, 27
Genesis 18.20; 19.24	Corruption of Lot's day and the fire	Luke 17.28, 29
Genesis 19.26	Worldliness of Lot's wife	Luke 17.32
Exodus 3.1-6	Moses and the burning bush	Luke 20.37
Exodus 16.15	Moses and the heavenly manna	John 6.31
Numbers 21.8	Moses and the brazen serpent	John 3.14
1 Samuel 21.6	David and the holy bread	Matthew 12.3, 4
1 Kings 10.1	Solomon and the Queen of Sheba	Matthew 12.42
1 Kings 17.1, 9	Elijah, the widow, and the famine	Luke 4.25, 26
2 Kings 5	Naaman and his leprosy	Luke 4.27
2 Chronicles 24.20, 21	The murder of Zechariah	Luke 11.51
Daniel 9.27; 11.31; 12.11	Daniel and the abomination of desolation	Matthew 24.15
Jonah 1.17	Jonah and the fish	Matthew 12.40; 16.4
Jonah 3.4-10	The repentance of Nineveh	Luke 11.30; Matthew 12.41

The Gospel according to LUKE

Herod the Great begins to rule 37 B.C.	Jesus is born 6/5 B.C.	Escape to Egypt 5/4 B.C.	Herod the Great dies 4 B.C.	Return to Nazareth 4/3 B.C.	Jesus visits temple as a boy A.D. 6/7

VITAL STATISTICS

PURPOSE:
To present an accurate account of the life of Christ and to present Christ as the perfect man and Savior

AUTHOR:
Luke—a doctor (Colossians 4.14), a Greek and Gentile Christian. He is the only known Gentile author in the New Testament. He was a close friend and companion of Paul. He also wrote Acts, and the two books go together.

TO WHOM WRITTEN:
Theophilus ("lover of God"), Gentiles, and people everywhere

DATE WRITTEN:
About A.D. 60

SETTING:
Luke wrote from Caesarea or from Rome.

KEY VERSES:
"Then Jesus said to him, 'Today salvation has come to this house, because he too is a son of Abraham. For the Son of Man came to seek out and to save the lost" (19.9, 10).

KEY PEOPLE:
Jesus, Elizabeth, Zechariah, John the Baptist, Mary, the disciples, Herod the Great, Pilate, Mary Magdalene

KEY PLACES:
Bethlehem, Galilee, Judea, Jerusalem

SPECIAL FEATURES:
This is the most comprehensive Gospel. The general vocabulary and diction show that the author was educated. He makes frequent references to illnesses and diagnoses. Luke stresses Jesus' relationships with people; emphasizes prayer, miracles, angels; records inspired hymns of praise; and gives a prominent place to women. Most of 9.51—18.35 is not found in any other Gospel.

EVERY birth is a miracle, and every child is a gift from God. But nearly 20 centuries ago, there was a truly miraculous birth; the Son of God was born a man. With divine Father and human mother, Jesus entered history—God in the flesh.

Luke affirms Christ's divinity, but the real emphasis of his book is to show his humanity—Jesus, the Son of God, is also the Son of Man. As a doctor, Luke was a man of science, and as a Greek, he was a man of detail. It is not surprising, then, that he begins by outlining his extensive research and explaining that he is reporting the facts (1.1–4). In addition, Luke was a close friend and traveling companion of Paul, so he could interview the other disciples, had access to other historical accounts, and was an eyewitness to the birth and growth of the early church. His Gospel and book of Acts are reliable, historical documents.

Luke's story begins with angels appearing to Zechariah and then Mary, telling them of the births of their sons. From Zechariah and Elizabeth would come John the Baptist who would prepare the way for Christ. And Mary would conceive by the Holy Spirit and bear Jesus, the Son of God. Soon after John's birth, Caesar Augustus declared a census, and so Mary and Joseph traveled to Bethlehem, the city of David, their ancient ancestor. There the child was born. Angels announced the joyous event to shepherds who rushed to the manger. When they left, they were praising God and spreading the news. Eight days later, Jesus was circumcised and then dedicated to God in the temple where Simeon and Anna confirmed his identity as the Savior, their Messiah.

Luke gives us a glimpse of Jesus at age 12—discussing theology with the teachers of the law at the temple (2.41–52). The next event occurs 18 years later, when we read of John the Baptist preaching in the wilderness. Jesus came to John to be baptized before beginning his public ministry (3.1–38). At this point, Luke traces Jesus' geneology on his stepfather Joseph's side, through David and Abraham back to Adam, underscoring his identity as the Son of Man.

After the temptation in the Judean wastelands (4.1–13), Jesus returned to Galilee and began to preach, teach, and heal (4.14—21.38). During this time, he solidified his group of 12 disciples, calling Peter, James, John (5.1–10), and Matthew (5.27–29). Later Jesus commissioned the disciples and sent them out to proclaim the kingdom of God. When they returned, he revealed to them his mission, his true identity, and what it means to be his disciple (9.18–62). His mission—to be the Savior of the world—would take him to Jerusalem (9.51–53), where he would be rejected, tried, and crucified.

While carrying his cross to Golgotha, some women in Jerusalem wept for him; but Jesus told them to weep for themselves and their children (23.28). But Luke's Gospel does not end in sadness. It concludes with the thrilling account of Jesus' resurrection from the dead, his appearances to the disciples, and his promise to send the Holy Spirit (24.1–53). Read Luke's beautifully written and accurate account of the life of Jesus, Son of Man and Son of God. Then praise God for sending the Savior for all men—our risen and triumphant Lord.

Tiberius Caesar becomes emperor 14	John's ministry begins 26	Jesus begins his ministry 26/27	Jesus chooses twelve disciples 28	Jesus feeds 5,000 29	Jesus is crucified, rises again, and ascends 30

THE BLUEPRINT

A. BIRTH AND PREPARATION OF JESUS, THE SAVIOR (1.1—4.13)	From an infant who could do nothing on his own, Jesus grew to become completely able to fulfill his mission on earth. He became fully human, developing in all ways like us. Yet he remained fully God. He took no short-cuts and was not isolated from the pressures and temptations of life. There are no short-cuts for us either as we prepare for a life of service to God.
B. MESSAGE AND MINISTRY OF JESUS, THE SAVIOR (4.14—21.38) 1. Jesus' ministry in Galilee 2. Jesus' ministry on the way to Jerusalem 3. Jesus' ministry in Jerusalem	Jesus taught great crowds of people, especially through parables, which are stories with great truths. But only those with ears to hear will understand. We should pray that God's Spirit would help us understand the implications of these truths for our lives so we can become more and more like Jesus.
C. DEATH AND RESURRECTION OF JESUS, THE SAVIOR (22.1—24.53)	The Savior of the world was arrested and executed. But death could not destroy him, and Jesus came to life again and ascended to heaven. In Luke's careful, historical account, we receive the facts about Jesus' resurrection. We must not only believe that these facts are true, but must also trust Christ as our Savior. It is shortsighted to neglect the facts, but how sad to accept the facts and neglect the forgiveness that Jesus offers to each of us.

MEGATHEMES

THEME	EXPLANATION	IMPORTANCE
Jesus Christ, the Savior	Luke describes how God's Son entered human history. Jesus lived as the perfect example of a man. After a perfect ministry, he provided a perfect sacrifice for our sin so we could be saved.	Jesus is our perfect leader and Savior. He offers forgiveness to all who will accept him as Lord of their lives and believe that what he says is true.
History	Luke was a medical doctor and historian. He put great emphasis on dates and details, connecting Jesus to events and people in history.	Luke gives details so we can believe in the reliability of the history of Jesus' life. Even more important, we can believe with certainty that Jesus is God.
People	Jesus was deeply interested in people and relationships. He showed warm concern for his followers and friends—men, women, and children.	Jesus' love for people is good news for everyone. His message is for all people in every nation. Each one of us has an opportunity to respond to him in faith.
Compassion	As a perfect human, Jesus showed tender sympathy to the poor, the despised, the hurt, and the sinful. No one was rejected or ignored by him.	Jesus is more than an idea or teacher—he cares for you. Only this kind of deep love can satisfy your need.
Holy Spirit	The Holy Spirit was present at Jesus' birth, baptism, ministry, and resurrection. As a perfect example for us, Jesus lived in dependence on the Holy Spirit.	The Holy Spirit was sent by God as confirmation of Jesus' authority. The Holy Spirit is given to enable people to live for Christ. By faith we can have the Holy Spirit's presence and power to witness and to serve.

KEY PLACES IN LUKE

Luke begins his account in the temple in Jerusalem, giving us the background for the birth of John the Baptist, then moves on to the city of Nazareth and the story of Mary, chosen to be Jesus' mother (1.26ff). As a result of Caesar's call for a census, Mary and Joseph had to travel to Bethlehem, where Jesus was born in fulfillment of prophecy (2.1ff). Jesus grew up in Nazareth and began his earthly ministry by being baptized by John (3.21, 22) and tempted by Satan (4.1ff). Much of his ministry focused in Galilee—he set up his "home" in Capernaum (4.31ff) and from there he taught throughout the region (8.1ff). Later he visited the Gerasene country where he healed a demon-possessed man (8.36ff). He fed more than 5,000 people with one lunch on the shores of the Sea of Galilee near Bethsaida-Julias (9.10ff). Jesus always traveled to Jerusalem for the major festivals, and enjoyed visiting friends in nearby Bethany (10.38ff). He healed ten lepers on the border between Galilee and Samaria (17.11), and helped a dishonest tax collector in Jericho turn his life around (19.1ff). The little villages of Bethphage and Bethany on the Mount of Olives were Jesus' resting places during his last days on earth. He was crucified outside Jerusalem's walls, but he would rise again. Two men on the road leading to Emmaus were among the first to see the resurrected Christ (24.13ff).

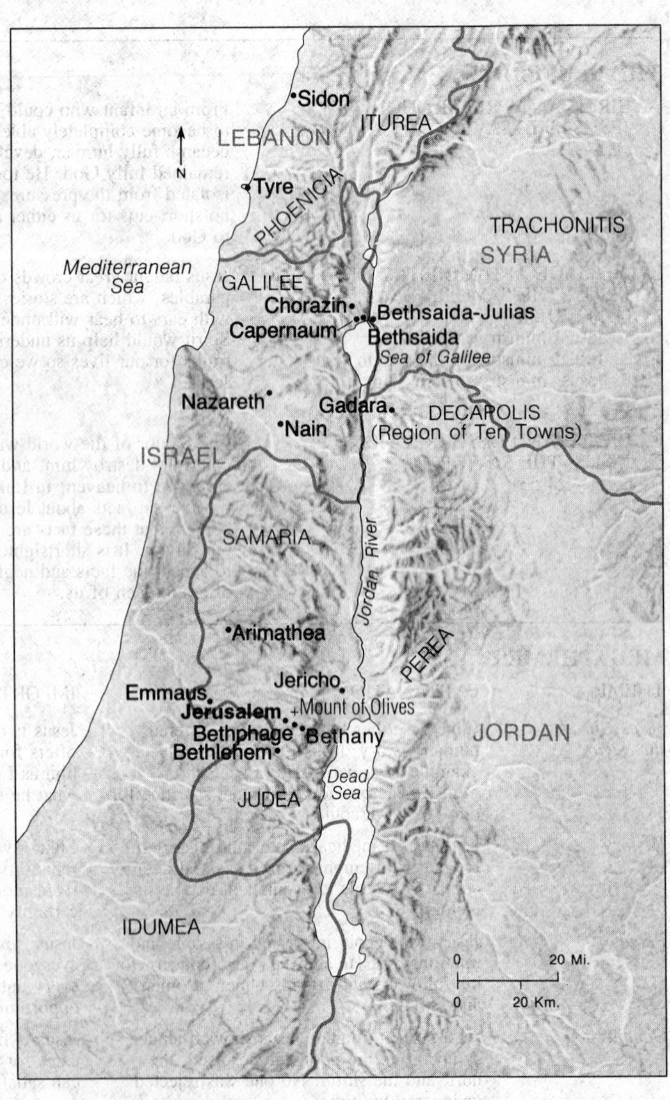

A. BIRTH AND PREPARATION OF JESUS, THE SAVIOR (1.1–4.13)

Luke gives us the most detailed account of Jesus' birth. In describing Jesus' birth, childhood, and human development, Luke lifts up the humanity of Jesus. Our Savior was the ideal man. Fully prepared, the ideal man was now ready to live the perfect life.

Luke's purpose in writing
(1)

1.1,2 Jn 15.27 Acts 1.21,22 1 Tim 3.16 Heb 2.3 2 Pet 1.16 1 Jn 1.1-4
1.3 Acts 1.1; 11.4

1 Since many have undertaken to set down an orderly account of the events that
have been fulfilled among us, [2]just as they were handed on to us by those who
from the beginning were eyewitnesses and servants of the word, [3]I too decided,
after investigating everything carefully from the very first,[a] to write an orderly
account for you, most excellent Theophilus, [4]so that you may know the truth concerning the things about which you have been instructed.

An angel promises the birth of John to Zechariah
(4)

1.5 1 Chron 24.10,19 Neh 12.4 Mt 2.1
1.6 2 Kgs 20.3 Phil 3.6
1.7 1 Sam 1.5
1.8 2 Chron 8.14
1.9 Ex 30.7,8

5 In the days of King Herod of Judea, there was a priest named Zechariah, who
belonged to the priestly order of Abijah. His wife was a descendant of Aaron, and
her name was Elizabeth. [6]Both of them were righteous before God, living blamelessly according to all the commandments and regulations of the Lord. [7]But they
had no children, because Elizabeth was barren, and both were getting on in years.
8 Once when he was serving as priest before God and his section was on duty,
[9]he was chosen by lot, according to the custom of the priesthood, to enter the sanctuary of the Lord and offer incense. [10]Now at the time of the incense offering, the
whole assembly of the people was praying outside. [11]Then there appeared to him

[a] Or *for a long time*

1.1, 2 Luke tells Jesus' story from the unique perspective of a Gentile, a physician, and the first historian of the early church. Not an eyewitness of Jesus' ministry, he nevertheless is concerned that eyewitness accounts be preserved accurately and that the foundations of Christian belief be transmitted intact to the next generation. Luke's Gospel is the source of many of Jesus' parables. In addition, more than any other Gospel, it gives specific instances of Jesus' concern for women.

1.1–4 There was a lot of interest in Jesus, and many people had written firsthand accounts of experiences with him. Luke used these accounts and all other available resources as material for an accurate and complete account of Jesus' life, teachings, and ministry. Because truth was important to him, he relied heavily on eyewitness accounts. Christianity doesn't say, "Close your eyes and believe," but rather "Check it out for yourself." The Bible encourages you to investigate its claims thoroughly (John 1.46; 21.24; Acts 17.11, 12), because your conclusion about Jesus is a life-and-death matter.

1.3 *Theophilus* means "one who loves God." The book of Acts, also written by Luke, is likewise addressed to Theophilus. This may be a general dedication to all Christian readers. More likely, Theophilus was a Roman acquaintance of Luke's with a strong interest in the new Christian religion.

1.3, 4 As a medical doctor, Luke knew the importance of thoroughness. He used his skills in observation and analysis to thoroughly investigate the stories about Jesus. His diagnosis? The gospel of Jesus Christ is true! You can read Luke's account of Jesus' life with confidence that it was written by a clear thinker and a thoughtful researcher. Because the gospel is founded on historical truth, our spiritual growth must involve careful, disciplined, and thorough investigation of God's Word so that we can understand how God has acted in history. If this kind of study is not part of your life, find a pastor, teacher, or book to help you get started and to guide you in this important part of Christian growth.

1.5 This was Herod the Great, confirmed by the Roman Senate as king of the Jews. Only half Jewish himself and eager to please his Roman superiors, he expanded and beautified the Jerusalem temple—but placed a Roman eagle over the entrance. When he helped the Jews, it was for political purposes and not because he cared about their God. Herod the Great later ordered a massacre of infants in a futile attempt to kill the infant Jesus, whom some were calling the new "King of the Jews" (Matthew 2.16–18).

1.5 A Jewish priest was a minister who worked at the temple managing its upkeep, teaching the people God's Word, and directing the worship services. At this time there were about 20,000 priests throughout the country—far too many to minister in the temple at one time. Therefore the priests were divided into 24 separate groups of about 1,000 each, according to David's directions (1 Chronicles 24.3–19).

Zechariah was a member of the Abijah division, on duty this particular week. Each morning a priest was to enter the holy place of the temple and burn incense. Lots were cast (a procedure like throwing dice) to decide who would enter the sacred room, and one day the lot fell to Zechariah. But it was not by chance that Zechariah was on duty and that he was chosen that day to enter the holy place—a once-in-a-lifetime opportunity. God was guiding the events of history to prepare the way for Jesus to come to earth.

1.6 Zechariah and Elizabeth not only went through the motions of following God's laws; they backed up their outward compliance with inward obedience. Unlike the religious leaders whom Jesus called hypocrites, they did not stop with the letter of the law. Their obedience was from the heart, and that is why they are called "righteous."

1.9 Incense was burned in the temple twice daily. When the people saw the smoke from the burning incense, they prayed. The smoke drifting heavenward symbolized their prayers ascending to God's throne.

1.11, 12 Angels are spirit beings who live in God's presence and do his will. Only two are mentioned by name in Scripture—Michael and Gabriel—but there are many who act as God's messengers. Here Gabriel (1.19) delivered a special message to Zechariah. This was not a dream or a vision. The angel appeared in visible form and spoke audible words to the priest.

an angel of the Lord, standing at the right side of the altar of incense. 12 When
Zechariah saw him, he was terrified; and fear overwhelmed him. 13 But the angel 1.13
said to him, "Do not be afraid, Zechariah, for your prayer has been heard. Your Gen 25.21 1 Sam 1.19
wife Elizabeth will bear you a son, and you will name him John. 14 You will have Lk 1.60-63
joy and gladness, and many will rejoice at his birth, 15 for he will be great in the 1.15
sight of the Lord. He must never drink wine or strong drink; even before his birth Num 6.3 Judg 13.4
he will be filled with the Holy Spirit. 16 He will turn many of the people of Israel to Jer 1.5 Mt 11.11
the Lord their God. 17 With the spirit and power of Elijah he will go before him, to 1.16
turn the hearts of parents to their children, and the disobedient to the wisdom of the Mal 4.5,6
righteous, to make ready a people prepared for the Lord." 18 Zechariah said to the 1.17 Isa 40.3
angel, "How will I know that this is so? For I am an old man, and my wife is getting Mal 4.5
on in years." 19 The angel replied, "I am Gabriel. I stand in the presence of God, Mt 11.14 Mk 9.12
and I have been sent to speak to you and to bring you this good news. 20 But now, Rom 9.5
because you did not believe my words, which will be fulfilled in their time, you 1.18 Gen 17.17
will become mute, unable to speak, until the day these things occur." 1.19
21 Meanwhile the people were waiting for Zechariah, and wondered at his Dan 8.16 9.21-23
delay in the sanctuary. 22 When he did come out, he could not speak to them, and Heb 1.14
they realized that he had seen a vision in the sanctuary. He kept motioning to them 1.20
and remained unable to speak. 23 When his time of service was ended, he went to Ezek 3.26; 24.27
his home.
24 After those days his wife Elizabeth conceived, and for five months she remained in seclusion. She said, 25 "This is what the Lord has done for me when he 1.25 Gen 30.23
looked favorably on me and took away the disgrace I have endured among my
people."

1.13 Zechariah, while offering incense on the altar, was also praying, perhaps for a son or for the coming of the Messiah. In either case, his prayer was answered. He would soon have a son who would prepare the way for the Messiah. God answers prayer in his own way and in his own time. He worked in an "impossible" situation – Zechariah's wife was barren – to bring about the fulfillment of all the prophecies concerning the Messiah. If we want to have our prayers answered, we must be open to what God can do in impossible situations. And we must wait for him to work in his way, in his time.

1.13 *John* means "the Lord is gracious," and *Jesus* means "Savior." Both names were prescribed by God, not chosen by human parents. Throughout the Gospels, God acts graciously and gives salvation to his people. He will not withhold it from anyone who sincerely comes to him.

1.15 John was set apart for special service to God. He may have been forbidden to drink as part of the nazirite vow, an ancient vow of consecration to God (see Numbers 6.1–8). Samson (Judges 13) was under the nazirite vow, and Samuel may have been also (1 Samuel 1.11).

1.15 This is Luke's first mention of the Holy Spirit, the third person of the trinity, and he refers to the Holy Spirit more than any other Gospel writer. Because Luke also wrote the book of Acts, he was thoroughly informed about the work of the Holy Spirit. He recognized and emphasized the Holy Spirit's work in directing the founding of Christianity and guiding the early church. The presence of the Spirit is God's gift given to the entire church at pentecost. Prior to that, God's Spirit was given to the faithful for special tasks. We need the Holy Spirit's help to do God's work effectively.

1.17 John's role was to be almost identical to that of an Old Testament prophet – to encourage people to turn away from sin and back to God. He is often compared to the great prophet Elijah, known for standing up to evil rulers (Malachi 4.5; Matthew 11.14; 17.10–13). See Elijah's Profile in 1 Kings 18.

1.17 In preparing people for the Messiah's arrival, John would do "heart transplants." He would take stony hearts and exchange them for hearts that were soft, pliable, trusting, and open to change. (See Ezekiel 11.19, 20 and 36.25–29 for more on "heart transplants.") Are you as open to God as you should be? Or do you need a change of heart?

1.18 When told he would have a son, Zechariah doubted the angel's word. From his human perspective, his doubts were understandable – but with God, anything is possible. Although Zechariah and Elizabeth were past the age of childbearing, God gave them a child. It is easy to doubt or misunderstand what God wants to do in our lives. Even God's people sometimes make the mistake of trusting their reason or experience rather than God. When tempted to think that one of God's promises is impossible, remember his work throughout history. God's power is not confined by narrow perspective, nor bound by human limitations.

1.20 Zechariah thought it incredible that he and his wife, at their old age, could conceive a child. But what God promises, he delivers. And he delivers *on time!* You can have complete confidence that God will keep his promises. It may not be the next day, but it will be "in their time." If you are waiting for God to answer some request or fill some need, remain patient. No matter how impossible God's promises may seem, what he has said in his Word will come true at the right time.

1.21 The people were waiting outside for Zechariah to come out and pronounce the customary blessing upon them as found in Numbers 6.22–27.

1.25 Zechariah and Elizabeth were both faithful people, and yet they were suffering. Some Jews at that time did not believe in a bodily resurrection, so their hope of immortality was in their children. In addition, children cared for their parents in their old age, and they added to the family's financial security and social status. Children were considered a blessing, and childlessness was seen as a curse. Zechariah and Elizabeth had been childless for many years, and now they were too old to expect any change in their situation. They felt humiliated and hopeless. But God was waiting for the right time to encourage them and take away their disgrace.

An angel promises the birth of Jesus to Mary
(5)

1.26 Mt 2.23 26 In the sixth month the angel Gabriel was sent by God to a town in Galilee
1.27 called Nazareth, 27 to a virgin engaged to a man whose name was Joseph, of the
Isa 7.14 house of David. The virgin's name was Mary. 28 And he came to her and said,
"Greetings, favored one! The Lord is with you."[b] 29 But she was much perplexed
1.31 by his words and pondered what sort of greeting this might be. 30 The angel said to
Mt 1.21,25 her, "Do not be afraid, Mary, for you have found favor with God. 31 And now, you

[b] Other ancient authorities add *Blessed are you among women*

ZECHARIAH

Zechariah was told before anyone else that God was setting in motion his own visit to earth. Zechariah and his wife, Elizabeth, were known for their personal holiness. They were well suited to doing a special work for God. But they shared the pain of not having children, and in Jewish culture this was considered not having God's blessing. Zechariah and Elizabeth were old, and they had stopped even asking for children.

This trip to the temple in Jerusalem for Zechariah's turn at duty had included an unexpected blessing. Zechariah was chosen to be the priest who would enter the holy place to offer incense to God for the people. Suddenly, much to his surprise and terror, he found himself face to face with an angel. The angel's message was too good to be true! But Zechariah did not respond to the news of the coming Savior as much as he expressed doubts about his own ability to father the child the angel promised him. His age spoke more loudly than God's promise. As a result, God prevented Zechariah from speaking until the promise became reality.

The record of the prayer in Luke 1 is our last glimpse of Zechariah. Like so many of God's most faithful servants, he passed quietly from the scene once his part was done. He becomes our hero for times when we doubt God yet are willing to obey. We gain hope from Zechariah that God can do great things through anyone who is available to him.

Strengths and accomplishments:
- Known as a righteous man
- Was a priest for God
- One of the few people to be directly addressed by an angel
- Fathered John the Baptist

Weakness and mistake:
- Momentarily doubted the angel's promise of a son because of his old age

Lessons from his life:
- Physical limitations do not limit God
- God accomplishes his will, sometimes in unexpected ways

Vital statistics:
- Occupation: Priest
- Relatives: Wife: Elizabeth. Son: John the Baptist

Key verses:
"Both of them were righteous before God, living blamelessly according to all the commandments and regulations of the Lord. But they had no children, because Elizabeth was barren, and both were getting on in years" (Luke 1.6, 7).

Zechariah's story is told in Luke 1.

1.26 Gabriel appeared not only to Zechariah and to Mary but also to the prophet Daniel more than 500 years earlier (Daniel 8.15–17; 9.21). Each time he appeared, he brought important messages from God.

1.26 Nazareth, Joseph's and Mary's hometown, was remote from Jerusalem, the center of Jewish life and worship. Located on a major trade route, it was frequently visited by Gentile merchants and Roman soldiers. For these reasons its reputation was tarnished among the Jews (John 1.46). Jesus was born in Bethlehem but grew up in Nazareth. Nevertheless, the people of Nazareth would reject him as the Messiah (4.22–30).

1.27, 28 Mary was young, poor, female—all characteristics that, to the people of her day, would make her seem unusable by God for any major task. But God chose Mary for a very important act of obedience. You may feel that your ability, experience, or education make you an unlikely candidate for God's service. Don't limit God's choices. He can use you if you trust him.

1.30, 31 God's favor does not automatically bring instant success or fame. His blessing on Mary, the honor of being the mother of the Messiah, would lead to much pain: her peers would ridicule her; her fiancé would come close to leaving her; her son would be rejected and murdered. But through her son would come the world's only hope, and this is why Mary has been praised by countless generations as "favored one." Her submission led to our salvation. If sorrow weighs you down and dims your hope, think of Mary and wait patiently for God to finish working out his plan.

1.31–33 *Jesus*, a Greek form of the Hebrew name *Joshua*, was a common name meaning "Savior." Just as Joshua led Israel into the promised land (see Joshua 1.1, 2), so Jesus would lead his people into eternal life. The symbolism of his name was not lost on the people of his day, who took names seriously and saw them as a source of power. In Jesus' name people were healed, demons were banished, and sins were forgiven.

will conceive in your womb and bear a son, and you will name him Jesus. 32 He will
be great, and will be called the Son of the Most High, and the Lord God will give
to him the throne of his ancestor David. 33 He will reign over the house of Jacob
forever, and of his kingdom there will be no end." 34 Mary said to the angel, "How
can this be, since I am a virgin?"[c] 35 The angel said to her, "The Holy Spirit will
come upon you, and the power of the Most High will overshadow you; therefore
the child to be born[d] will be holy; he will be called Son of God. 36 And now, your
relative Elizabeth in her old age has also conceived a son; and this is the sixth
month for her who was said to be barren. 37 For nothing will be impossible with
God." 38 Then Mary said, "Here am I, the servant of the Lord; let it be with me
according to your word." Then the angel departed from her.

1.32 2 Sam 7.11 Ps 132.11 Isa 9.6,7; 16.5 Jer 23.5
1.33 Dan 2.44 7.14,18,27 Heb 1.8
1.35 Mt 14.33; 26.63 Mk 1.1 Jn 1.34; 20.31
1.37 Gen 18.14 Rom 4.21

Mary visits Elizabeth
(6)

39 In those days Mary set out and went with haste to a Judean town in the hill
country, 40 where she entered the house of Zechariah and greeted Elizabeth.
41 When Elizabeth heard Mary's greeting, the child leaped in her womb. And Elizabeth was filled with the Holy Spirit 42 and exclaimed with a loud cry, "Blessed
are you among women, and blessed is the fruit of your womb. 43 And why has this
happened to me, that the mother of my Lord comes to me? 44 For as soon as I heard
the sound of your greeting, the child in my womb leaped for joy. 45 And blessed is
she who believed that there would be[e] a fulfillment of what was spoken to her by
the Lord."
46 And Mary[f] said,
47 "My soul magnifies the Lord,
and my spirit rejoices in God my Savior,
48 for he has looked with favor on the lowliness of his servant.

1.39 Josh 20.7; 21.9, 11
1.42 Judg 5.24
1.43 Lk 2.11
1.46 1 Sam 2.1-10 Ps 34.2,3
1.47 1 Tim 1.1; 2.3 Tit 1.3; 2.10; 3.4
1.48 1 Sam 1.11

[c] Gk *I do not know a man* [d] Other ancient authorities add *of you* [e] Or *believed, for there will be* [f] Other ancient authorities read *Elizabeth*

1.32, 33 Centuries earlier, God had promised David that his kingdom would last forever (2 Samuel 7.16). This promise was fulfilled in the coming of Jesus, a direct descendant of David, whose reign will continue throughout eternity.

1.34 The birth of Jesus to a virgin is a miracle that many people find hard to believe. These three facts can aid our faith: (1) Luke was a medical doctor, and he knew perfectly well how babies are made. It would have been just as hard for him to believe in a virgin birth as it is for us, and yet he reports it as fact. (2) Luke was a painstaking researcher who based his Gospel on eyewitness accounts. Tradition holds that he talked with Mary about the events he recorded in the first two chapters. This is her story, not a fictional invention. (3) Christians and Jews, who worship God as the Creator of the universe, should believe he has the power to create a child in a virgin's womb.

1.35 Jesus was born without the sin that entered the world through Adam. He was born holy, just as Adam was created sinless. In contrast to Adam, who disobeyed God, Jesus obeyed God and is thus able to accept sin's consequences in our place and make us acceptable to God (Romans 5.14–19).

1.38 A young unmarried girl who became pregnant risked disaster. Unless the father of the child agreed to marry her, she would probably remain unmarried for life. If her own father rejected her, she could be forced into begging or prostitution in order to earn her living. And Mary, with her story about being made pregnant by the Holy Spirit, risked being considered crazy as well. Still she said, despite the possible risks, "Let it be with me according to your word." When Mary said that, she didn't know about the tremendous opportunity she would have. She only knew God was asking her to serve him, and she willingly obeyed. Don't wait to see the bottom line before offering your life to God. Offer yourself willingly, even when the outcome seems disastrous.

1.38 The announcement of a child was met with various responses throughout Scripture. Sarah, Abraham's wife, laughed (Genesis 18.9–15). Manoah, Samson's father, panicked (Judges 13.22). Zechariah doubted (Luke 1.18). By contrast, Mary submitted. She believed the angel's words and agreed to bear the child, even under humanly impossible circumstances. God is able to do the impossible. Our response to his demands should not be laughter, fear, or doubt, but willing acceptance.

1.41–43 Apparently the Holy Spirit told Elizabeth that Mary's child was the Messiah, because Elizabeth called her young cousin "the mother of my Lord" as she greeted her. As Mary rushed off to visit her cousin, she must have been wondering if the events of the last few days were real. Elizabeth's greeting would have strengthened her faith. Mary's pregnancy may have seemed impossible, but her wise old cousin believed and rejoiced in it.

1.42, 43 Even though she herself was pregnant with a long-awaited son, Elizabeth could have envied Mary, whose son would be even greater than her own. Instead she was filled with joy that the mother of her Lord would visit her. Have you ever envied people whom God has apparently singled out for special blessing? A cure for jealousy is to rejoice with them, realizing that God uses his people in ways best suited to his purpose.

1.46–55 This song is often called the *Magnificat*, the first word in the Latin translation of this passage. It has often been used as the basis for choral music and hymns. Like Hannah, the mother of Samuel (1 Samuel 2.1–10), Mary glorified God in song for what he was going to do for the world through her. Notice that in both songs, God is pictured as a champion of the poor, the oppressed, and the despised.

1.48 When Mary said, "From now on all generations will call me blessed," was she being proud? No, she was recognizing and accepting the gift God had given her. If Mary had denied her incredible position, she would have been throwing God's blessing back at him. Pride is refusing to accept God's gifts or taking credit for what

Surely, from now on all generations will call me blessed;
49 for the Mighty One has done great things for me,
and holy is his name.
1.50 Gen 17.7 Ex 20.6 Ps 103.17 — 50 His mercy is for those who fear him
from generation to generation.
1.51 Ps 33.10; 98.1 118.15 — 51 He has shown strength with his arm;
he has scattered the proud in the thoughts of their hearts.
1.52 1 Sam 2.6 — 52 He has brought down the powerful from their thrones,
and lifted up the lowly;
1.53 Ps 34.10; 107.9 — 53 he has filled the hungry with good things,
and sent the rich away empty.
1.54 Ps 98.3 — 54 He has helped his servant Israel,
in remembrance of his mercy,
1.55 Gen 17.9 — 55 according to the promise he made to our ancestors,
to Abraham and to his descendants forever."

56 And Mary remained with her about three months and then returned to her home.

John the Baptist is born
(7)

57 Now the time came for Elizabeth to give birth, and she bore a son. 58 Her
neighbors and relatives heard that the Lord had shown his great mercy to her, and
they rejoiced with her.
1.59 Gen 17.12 Lev 12.3 Lk 2.21 Phil 13.5 — 59 On the eighth day they came to circumcise the child, and they were going to
name him Zechariah after his father. 60 But his mother said, "No; he is to be called
John." 61 They said to her, "None of your relatives has this name." 62 Then they

GOD'S UNUSUAL METHODS

One of the best ways to understand God's willingness to communicate to people is to note the various methods, some of them quite unexpected, that he has used to give his message. Following is a sample of his methods and the people he contacted.

Person/Group	*Method*	*Reference*
Jacob, Zechariah, Mary, Shepherds	Angels	Genesis 32.22–32; Luke 1.13, 30; 2.10
Jacob, Joseph, a baker, a butler, Pharaoh, Isaiah, Joseph, the wise men	Dreams	Genesis 28.10–22; 37.5–10; 40.5; 41.7, 8; Isaiah 1.1; Matthew 1.20; 2.12, 13
Belshazzar	Handwriting on the wall	Daniel 5.5–9
Balaam	Talking donkey	Numbers 22.21–35
People of Israel	Pillar of cloud and fire	Exodus 13.21, 22
Jonah	Being swallowed by a fish	Jonah 2
Abraham, Moses, Jesus at his baptism, Paul	Verbally	Genesis 12.1–4; Exodus 7.8; Matthew 3.13–17; Acts 18.9
Moses	Fire	Exodus 3.2
Us	God's Son	Hebrews 1.1, 2

God has done; humility is accepting them and using them to praise and serve him. Don't deny, belittle, or ignore your gifts. Thank God for them and use them to his glory.

1.54, 55 God kept his promise to Abraham to be merciful to his people forever (Genesis 22.16–18). Christ's birth fulfilled the promise, and Mary understood this. She was not surprised when her special son eventually announced that he was the Messiah. She had known his mission from before his birth. Some of God's promises to Israel are found in 2 Samuel 22.50, 51; Psalms 89.2–4; 103.17, 18; Micah 7.18–20.

1.56 Because travel was not easy, long visits were customary. Mary must have been a great help to Elizabeth, who was experiencing the discomforts of a first pregnancy in old age.

1.59 The circumcision ceremony was an important event in the family of a Jewish baby boy. God commanded it when he was beginning to form his holy nation (Genesis 17.4–14) and reaffirmed it through Moses (Leviticus 12.1–3). It was a time of joy when friends and family members celebrated the baby's becoming part of God's covenant with Israel.

1.59 Family lines and family names were important to the Jews. The people naturally assumed the child would receive Zechariah's name or at least a family name. Thus they were surprised that both Elizabeth and Zechariah wanted to name him John, as the angel had told them to do (see 1.13).

1.62 Zechariah's relatives talked to him by gestures, because he was apparently deaf as well as speechless and had not heard what his wife had said.

began motioning to his father to find out what name he wanted to give him. 63 He
asked for a writing tablet and wrote, "His name is John." And all of them were
amazed. 64 Immediately his mouth was opened and his tongue freed, and he began
to speak, praising God. 65 Fear came over all their neighbors, and all these things
were talked about throughout the entire hill country of Judea. 66 All who heard them
pondered them and said, "What then will this child become?" For, indeed, the hand
of the Lord was with him.

67 Then his father Zechariah was filled with the Holy Spirit and spoke this
prophecy:

68 "Blessed be the Lord God of Israel,
for he has looked favorably on his people and redeemed them.
69 He has raised up a mighty savior[g] for us
in the house of his servant David,
70 as he spoke through the mouth of his holy prophets from of old,
71 that we would be saved from our enemies and from the hand of all who
hate us.
72 Thus he has shown the mercy promised to our ancestors,
and has remembered his holy covenant,
73 the oath that he swore to our ancestor Abraham,
to grant us 74 that we, being rescued from the hands of our enemies,
might serve him without fear, 75 in holiness and righteousness
before him all our days.
76 And you, child, will be called the prophet of the Most High;
for you will go before the Lord to prepare his ways,
77 to give knowledge of salvation to his people
by the forgiveness of their sins.
78 By the tender mercy of our God,
the dawn from on high will break upon[h] us,
79 to give light to those who sit in darkness and in the shadow of death,
to guide our feet into the way of peace."

80 The child grew and became strong in spirit, and he was in the wilderness
until the day he appeared publicly to Israel.

1.66 Lk 2.19 Acts 11.21
1.67 Joel 2.28
1.68 Lk 2.38 Acts 1.6 Heb 9.12
1.69 1 Sam 2.1,10 Ps 18.2; 132.17 Ezek 29.21
1.70 Jer 23.5; 30.10 Dan 9.24 Acts 3.21 Rom 1.2-4
1.71 Ps 106.10
1.72,73 Lev 26.42 Ps 105.8; 106.45 Mic 7.20 Heb 6.13
1.75 Jer 32.39 Eph 4.24
1.76 Isa 40.3 Mal 3.1
1.77 Jer 31.34 Mk 1.4
1.78 Eph 5.14 2 Pet 1.19
1.79 Isa 9.2
1.80 Lk 2.40

Jesus is born in Bethlehem
(9)

2 In those days a decree went out from Emperor Augustus that all the world
should be registered. 2 This was the first registration and was taken while
Quirinius was governor of Syria. 3 All went to their own towns to be registered.

2.1 Mt 1.18-25

g Gk *a horn of salvation* h Other ancient authorities read *has broken upon*

1.67–79 Zechariah praised God with his first words after months of silence. In a song that is often called the *Benedictus* after the first words in the Latin translation of this passage, he prophesied the coming of a Savior who would redeem his people, and he predicted that his son John would prepare the Messiah's way. All the Old Testament prophecies were coming true—no wonder Zechariah praised God! The Messiah would come in his lifetime, and his son had been chosen to pave the way.

1.71 The Jews were eagerly awaiting the Messiah, but they thought he would come to save them from the powerful Roman Empire. They were ready for a military Savior, but not for a peaceful Messiah who would conquer sin.

1.72, 73 This was God's promise to Abraham to bless all nations through him (see Genesis 12.3). It would be fulfilled through the Messiah, Abraham's descendant.

1.76 Zechariah had just recalled hundreds of years of God's sovereign work in history, beginning with Abraham and ending in eternity. Then, in tender contrast, he personalized the story. His son had been chosen for a key role in the drama of the ages. Although God has unlimited power, he chooses to work through frail humans who begin as helpless babies. Don't minimize what God can do through those who are faithful to him.

1.80 Why did John live out in the "wilderness"? Prophets used the isolation of the uninhabited wilderness to enhance their spiritual growth and to focus their message on God. By being in the wilderness, John remained separate from the economic and political powers so that he could aim his message against them. He also remained separate from the hypocritical religious leaders of his day. His message was different from theirs, and his life proved it.

2.1 Luke was the only Gospel writer who related the events he recorded to world history. His account was addressed to a predominantly Greek audience who would have been interested in and familiar with the political situation. Palestine was under the rule of the Roman Empire; Emperor Caesar Augustus, the first Roman emperor, was in charge. The Roman rulers, considered gods, stood in contrast to the tiny baby in a manger who was truly God in the flesh.

2.1 A Roman census (registration) was taken to aid military conscription or tax collection. The Jews didn't have to serve in the Roman army, but they could not avoid paying taxes. Augustus's

2.4 1 Sam 16.1 Mic 5.2 Mt 1.16 Lk 1.27 Jn 7.42
2.7 Mt 1.25 Gal 4.4

4 Joseph also went from the town of Nazareth in Galilee to Judea, to the city of David called Bethlehem, because he was descended from the house and family of David. 5 He went to be registered with Mary, to whom he was engaged and who was expecting a child. 6 While they were there, the time came for her to deliver her child. 7 And she gave birth to her firstborn son and wrapped him in bands of cloth, and laid him in a manger, because there was no place for them in the inn.

Shepherds visit Jesus
(10)

8 In that region there were shepherds living in the fields, keeping watch over

DOUBTERS IN THE BIBLE

Doubter	*Doubtful Moment*	*Reference*
Abraham	When God told him he would be a father in old age	Genesis 17.17
Sarah	When she heard she would be a mother in old age	Genesis 18.12
Moses	When God told him to return to Egypt to lead the people	Exodus 3.10–15
Israelites	Whenever they faced difficulties in the wilderness	Exodus 16.1–3
Gideon	When told he would be a judge and lead the people	Judges 6.14–23
Zechariah	When told he would be a father in old age	Luke 1.18
Thomas	When told Jesus had risen from the dead	John 20.24–25

Many of the people God used to accomplish great things started out as real doubters. With all of them, God showed great patience. Honest doubt was not a bad starting point as long as they didn't stay there. How great a part does doubt have in your willingness to trust God?

decree went out in God's perfect timing and according to his perfect plan to bring his Son into the world.

THE JOURNEY TO BETHLEHEM
Caesar's decree for a census of the entire Roman Empire made it necessary for Joseph and Mary to leave their hometown, Nazareth, and journey the 70 miles to the Judean village of Bethlehem.

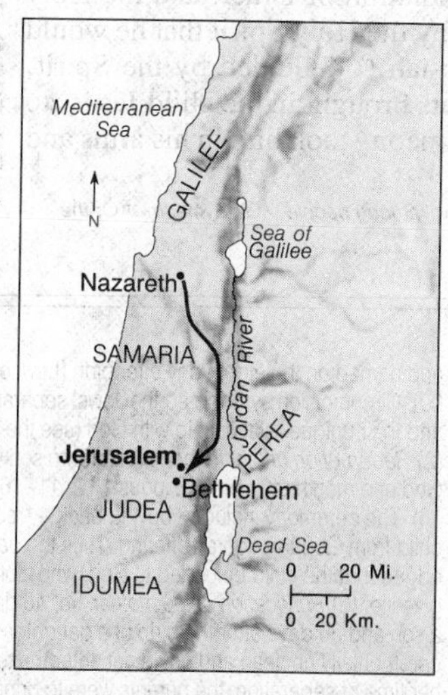

2.3–6 The government forced Joseph to make a long trip just to pay his taxes. His fiancée, who had to go with him, was going to have a baby any moment. But when they arrived in Bethlehem, they couldn't even find a place to stay. When we do God's will, we are not guaranteed a comfortable life; we are promised that everything, even our discomfort, has meaning in God's plan.

2.4 God controls all history. By the decree of Emperor Augustus, Jesus was born in the very town prophesied for his birth (Micah 5.2), even though his parents did not live there.

2.4 Joseph and Mary were both descendants of David. The Old Testament is filled with prophecies that the Messiah would be born in David's royal line (see Isaiah 11.1; Jeremiah 33.15; Ezekiel 37.24).

2.7 Bands of cloth were used to keep a baby warm and give it a sense of security. They were believed to protect its internal organs. The custom of wrapping infants this way is still practiced in many Eastern countries.

2.7 This mention of the manger is the basis for the traditional belief that Jesus was born in a stable. Stables were often caves with feeding troughs (mangers) carved into the rock walls. Despite popular Christmas card pictures, the surroundings were dark and dirty. This was not the atmosphere the Jews expected as the birthplace of the Messiah King. They thought their promised Messiah would be born in royal surroundings. We should not limit God by our expectations. He is at work wherever he is needed in our sin-darkened and dirty world.

2.7 Although our first picture of Jesus is as a baby in a manger, it must not be our last. The Christ child in the manger makes a beautiful Christmas scene, but we cannot leave him there. This tiny, helpless baby lived an amazing life, died for us, ascended to heaven, and will come back to this earth as King of kings. He will rule the world and judge all people according to their decisions about him. Do you still picture Jesus as a baby in a manger—or is he your Lord? Make sure you don't underestimate Jesus. Let him grow up in your life.

2.8 God continued to reveal his Son, but not to those we might expect. Luke records that Jesus' birth was announced to shepherds in the fields. These may have been the shepherds who supplied the lambs for the temple sacrifices, performed for the forgiveness of sin. Angels now invited these shepherds to greet the Lamb of God (John 1.36), who would take away the sins of the whole world forever.

2.8–15 What a birth announcement! The shepherds were terrified, but their fear turned to joy as the angels announced the Messiah's birth. First the shepherds ran to see the baby; then they spread the word. Jesus is *your* Messiah, *your* Savior. Do you look forward to meeting him in prayer and in his Word each day? Have you discovered a Lord so wonderful that you can't help sharing your joy with your friends?

their flock by night. 9 Then an angel of the Lord stood before them, and the glory
of the Lord shone around them, and they were terrified. 10 But the angel said to
them, "Do not be afraid; for see—I am bringing you good news of great joy for all
the people: 11 to you is born this day in the city of David a Savior, who is the Messiah,[i] the Lord. 12 This will be a sign for you: you will find a child wrapped in
bands of cloth and lying in a manger." 13 And suddenly there was with the angel a
multitude of the heavenly host,[j] praising God and saying,
14 "Glory to God in the highest heaven,
and on earth peace among those whom he favors!"[k]
15 When the angels had left them and gone into heaven, the shepherds said to
one another, "Let us go now to Bethlehem and see this thing that has taken place,
which the Lord has made known to us." 16 So they went with haste and found Mary
and Joseph, and the child lying in the manger. 17 When they saw this, they made
known what had been told them about this child; 18 and all who heard it were
amazed at what the shepherds told them. 19 But Mary treasured all these words and
pondered them in her heart. 20 The shepherds returned, glorifying and praising God
for all they had heard and seen, as it had been told them.

Mary and Joseph bring Jesus to the temple
(11)

21 After eight days had passed, it was time to circumcise the child; and he was
called Jesus, the name given by the angel before he was conceived in the womb.
22 When the time came for their purification according to the law of Moses,
they brought him up to Jerusalem to present him to the Lord 23 (as it is written in the
law of the Lord, "Every firstborn male shall be designated as holy to the Lord"),
24 and they offered a sacrifice according to what is stated in the law of the Lord, "a
pair of turtledoves or two young pigeons."
25 Now there was a man in Jerusalem whose name was Simeon;[l] this man was
righteous and devout, looking forward to the consolation of Israel, and the Holy
Spirit rested on him. 26 It had been revealed to him by the Holy Spirit that he would
not see death before he had seen the Lord's Messiah.[m] 27 Guided by the Spirit,
Simeon[n] came into the temple; and when the parents brought in the child Jesus, to
do for him what was customary under the law, 28 Simeon[o] took him in his arms and
praised God, saying,

2.9 Lk 1.11; 24.4
2.10 Mt 28.19 Acts 13.47
2.11 Mt 1.16,21 16.16,20 Acts 2.36; 10.36 Phil 2.11
2.13 Gen 28.12 Ps 103.20 Rev 5.11
2.14 Isa 57.19 Eph 2.14,18 Col 1.20 2 Thess 2.16
2.21 Gen 17.12 Lev 12.3 Mt 1.21
2.22 Lev 12.2-6
2.23 Ex 13.2,12
2.24 Lev 12.8
2.25 Isa 40.1 Mk 15.43
2.26 Ps 89.48 Jn 8.51 Heb 11.5
2.27 Rev 1.10

[i] Or *the Christ* [j] Gk *army* [k] Other ancient authorities read *peace, good will among people* [l] Gk *Symeon* [m] Or *the Lord's Christ* [n] Gk *In the Spirit, he* [o] Gk *he*

2.9, 10 The greatest event in history had just happened! The Messiah was born! For ages the Jews had waited for this, and when it finally occurred, the announcement came to humble shepherds. The good news about Jesus is that he comes to all, including the plain and the ordinary. He comes to anyone with a heart humble enough to accept him. Whoever you are, whatever you do, you can have Jesus in your life. Don't think you need extraordinary qualifications—he accepts you as you are.

2.11–14 Some of the Jews were waiting for a savior to deliver them from Roman rule; others hoped the Christ (Messiah) would deliver them from physical ailments. But Jesus, while healing their illnesses and establishing a spiritual kingdom, delivered them from sin. His work is farther reaching than anyone could imagine. He paid the price for sin and opened the way to God. He offers us more than temporary political or physical changes—he offers us new hearts that will last for eternity.

2.14 The story of Jesus' birth resounds with music that has inspired composers for 2,000 years. The angels' song is an all-time favorite. Often called the *Gloria* after its first word in the Latin translation, it is the basis of modern choral works, traditional Christmas carols, and ancient liturgical chants.

2.21–24 Jewish families went through several ceremonies soon after a baby's birth: (1) *Circumcision.* Every boy was circumcised and named on the eighth day after birth (Leviticus 12.3; Luke 1.59, 60). Circumcision symbolized the Jews' separation from Gentiles and their unique relationship with God (see the note on 1.59). (2) *Redemption of the firstborn.* A firstborn son was presented to God one month after birth (Exodus 13.2, 11–16; Numbers 18.15, 16). The ceremony included buying back—"redeeming"—the child from God through an offering. Thus the parents acknowledged that the child belonged to God, who alone has the power to give life. (3) *Purification of the mother.* For 40 days after the birth of a son and 80 days after the birth of a daughter, the mother was ceremonially unclean and could not enter the temple. At the end of her time of separation, the parents were to bring a lamb for a burnt offering and a dove for a sin offering. The priest would sacrifice these animals and declare her clean. If a lamb was too expensive, the parents could bring a second dove instead. This is what Mary and Joseph did.

Jesus was God's Son, and his family carried out these ceremonies according to God's law. He was not born above the law; instead, he fulfilled it perfectly.

2.28–32 When Mary and Joseph brought Jesus to the temple to be dedicated to God, they met an old man who told them what their child would become. Simeon's song is often called the *Nunc Dimittis,* because these are the first words of its Latin translation. Simeon could die in peace, because he had seen the Messiah.

29 "Master, now you are dismissing your servant[p] in peace,
according to your word;
30 for my eyes have seen your salvation,
31 which you have prepared in the presence of all peoples,
32 a light for revelation to the Gentiles
and for glory to your people Israel."
33 And the child's father and mother were amazed at what was being said about
him. 34 Then Simeon[q] blessed them and said to his mother Mary, "This child is
destined for the falling and the rising of many in Israel, and to be a sign that will be
opposed 35 so that the inner thoughts of many will be revealed—and a sword will
pierce your own soul too."
36 There was also a prophet, Anna[r] the daughter of Phanuel, of the tribe of
Asher. She was of a great age, having lived with her husband seven years after her
marriage, 37 then as a widow to the age of eighty-four. She never left the temple but
worshiped there with fasting and prayer night and day. 38 At that moment she came,
and began to praise God and to speak about the child[s] to all who were looking for
the redemption of Jerusalem.
39 When they had finished everything required by the law of the Lord, they
returned to Galilee, to their own town of Nazareth. 40 The child grew and became
strong, filled with wisdom; and the favor of God was upon him.

2.30 Isa 52.10; Acts 4.12
2.32 Isa 9.2; 42.6,7; 49.6; Acts 13.47; 26.23
2.34,35 Isa 8.14; Hos 14.9; Acts 24.5,14; 28.22; 1 Cor 1.23; 1 Pet 2.7,8,12
2.35 Ps 42.10; 1 Cor 11.19
2.37 Acts 21.9; 26.7; 1 Tim 5.5,9
2.38 Lam 3.25,26; Mk 15.43; Lk 24.21
2.39 Mt 2.23

[p] Gk *slave* [q] Gk *Symeon* [r] Gk *Hanna* [s] Gk *him*

TO FEAR OR NOT TO FEAR

Person	*Reference*
Abraham	Genesis 15.1
Moses	Numbers 21.34 Deuteronomy 3.2
Joshua	Joshua 8.1
Jeremiah	Lamentations 3.57
Daniel	Daniel 10.12, 19
Zechariah	Luke 1.13
Mary	Luke 1.30
Shepherds	Luke 2.10
Peter	Luke 5.10
Paul	Acts 27.23, 24
John	Revelation 1.17, 18

People in the Bible who were confronted by God or his angels all had one consistent response—fear. To each of them, God's response was always the same—don't be afraid. As soon as they sensed that God accepted them and wanted to communicate with them, then fear subsided. He had given them freedom to be his friends. Has he given you the same freedom?

2.32 The Jews were well acquainted with the Old Testament prophecies that spoke of the Messiah's blessings to their nation. They did not always give equal attention to the prophecies saying he would bring salvation to the entire world, not just the Jews (see, for example, Isaiah 49.6). Many thought he had come to save only his own people. Luke made sure his Greek audience understood that Jesus came to save *all* who believe, Gentiles as well as Jews.

2.33 Joseph and Mary were amazed for three reasons: Simeon said Jesus was a gift from God; he recognized Jesus as the Messiah; and he said Jesus would be a light to the entire world. This was at least the second time that Mary was greeted with a prophecy about her son; the first time was when Elizabeth had welcomed her as the mother of her Lord (1.42–45).

2.34, 35 Simeon prophesied that Jesus would have a paradoxical effect on Israel. Some would fall because of him (see Isaiah 8.14, 15), while others would rise again (see Malachi 4.2). With Jesus, there would be no neutral ground: people would either joyfully accept him or totally reject him. As Jesus' mother, Mary would be grieved by the widespread rejection he would face.

2.36 Although Simeon and Anna were very old, they still hoped to see the Messiah. Led by the Holy Spirit, they were among the first to bear witness to Jesus. In the Jewish culture, elders were respected, and Simeon's and Anna's prophecies carried extra weight because they were not young. Our society, however, values youthfulness over wisdom, and potential contributions by the elderly are often ignored. As Christians, we should reverse those values wherever we can. Encourage older people to share their wisdom and experience. Listen carefully when they speak. Offer them your friendship and help them find ways to continue to serve God.

2.39 Did Mary and Joseph return immediately to Nazareth, or did they remain in Bethlehem for a time (as implied in Matthew 2)? Apparently there is a gap of several years between verses 38 and 39—ample time for them to find a place to live in Bethlehem, flee to Egypt to escape Herod's wrath, and return to Nazareth when it was safe to do so.

2.40 Jesus was filled with wisdom, which is not surprising because he stayed in close contact with his heavenly Father. James 1.5 says God gives wisdom liberally to all who ask. Like Jesus, we can grow in wisdom by walking with God.

Jesus speaks with the religious teachers
(15)

41 Now every year his parents went to Jerusalem for the festival of the Passover. 42 And when he was twelve years old, they went up as usual for the festival.
43 When the festival was ended and they started to return, the boy Jesus stayed
behind in Jerusalem, but his parents did not know it. 44 Assuming that he was in the
group of travelers, they went a day's journey. Then they started to look for him
among their relatives and friends. 45 When they did not find him, they returned to 2.46 Isa 11.1-4
Jerusalem to search for him. 46 After three days they found him in the temple, sit- 2.47 Mt 7.28
ting among the teachers, listening to them and asking them questions. 47 And all Mk 1.22
who heard him were amazed at his understanding and his answers. 48 When his Jn 7.15
parents[t] saw him they were astonished; and his mother said to him, "Child, why 2.48 Mt 12.26
have you treated us like this? Look, your father and I have been searching for you Lk 4.22
in great anxiety." 49 He said to them, "Why were you searching for me? Did you not 2.49 Jn 2.16; 4.34
know that I must be in my Father's house?"[u] 50 But they did not understand what 6.38; 8.29
he said to them. 51 Then he went down with them and came to Nazareth, and was 2.50 Lk 9.45; 18.34
obedient to them. His mother treasured all these things in her heart. 2.52
52 And Jesus increased in wisdom and in years,[v] and in divine and human 1 Sam 2.26
favor.

John the Baptist prepares the way for Jesus
(16/Matthew 3.1–12; Mark 1.1–8)

3 In the fifteenth year of the reign of Emperor Tiberius, when Pontius Pilate was 3.1
governor of Judea, and Herod was ruler[w] of Galilee, and his brother Philip Mt 3.1-12 Mk 1.1-8
ruler[w] of the region of Ituraea and Trachonitis, and Lysanias ruler[w] of Abilene,

[t] Gk *they* [u] Or *be about my Father's interests?* [v] Or *in stature* [w] Gk *tetrarch*

2.41, 42 According to God's law, every male was required to go to Jerusalem three times a year for the great festivals (Deuteronomy 16.16). In the spring, the Passover was celebrated, followed immediately by the week-long festival of unleavened bread. Passover commemorated the night of the Jews' escape from Egypt when God killed the Egyptian firstborn but passed over Israelite homes (see Exodus 12.21–36). Passover was the most important of the three annual festivals.

2.43–45 At age 12, Jesus was considered almost an adult, and so he didn't spend a lot of time with his parents during the festival. Those who attended these festivals often traveled in caravans for protection from robbers along the Palestine roads. It was customary for the women and children to travel at the front of the caravan, with the men bringing up the rear. A 12-year-old boy could have been in either group, and both Mary and Joseph assumed Jesus was with the other one. But when the caravan left Jerusalem, Jesus stayed behind, absorbed in his discussion with the religious leaders.

2.46, 47 The temple school, a kind of seminary, was famous throughout Judea. The apostle Paul studied there under Gamaliel, one of its foremost teachers (Acts 22.3). At the time of the Passover, the greatest rabbis of the land would assemble to teach and to discuss great truths among themselves. The coming Messiah would no doubt have been a popular discussion topic, for everyone was expecting him soon. Jesus would have been eager to listen and to ask probing questions. It was not his youth, but the depth of his thought, that astounded these teachers.

2.48 Mary had to let go of her child and let him become a man, God's Son, the Messiah. Fearful that she hadn't been careful enough with this God-given child, she searched frantically for him. But she was looking for a boy, not the young man who was in the temple astounding the religious leaders with his questions. It is hard to let go of people or projects we have nurtured. It is both sweet and painful to see our children as adults, our students as teachers, our subordinates as managers, our inspirations as institutions. But when the time comes to step back and let go, we must do so in spite of the hurt. Then our protégés can exercise their wings, take flight, and soar to the heights God intended for them.

2.49, 50 This is the first mention of Jesus' realization that he was God's Son. But even though he knew his real Father, he did not reject his earthly parents. He went back to Nazareth with them and lived under their authority for another 18 years. God's people do not despise human relationships or family responsibilities. If the Son of God obeyed his human parents, how much more should we honor our family members! Don't use God's work to justify neglect of family.

2.50 Jesus' parents didn't understand what he meant about his Father's house. They didn't realize he was making a distinction between his earthly father and his heavenly Father. Jesus knew that he had a unique relationship with God. Although they knew he was God's Son, they didn't understand what his mission would involve. Besides, they had to raise him, along with his brothers and sisters (Matthew 13.55, 56), as a normal child. They knew he was unique, but they did not know what was going on in his mind.

2.52 The Bible does not record any events of the next 18 years of Jesus' life, but he was learning and maturing. As the oldest in a large family, he assisted Joseph in his carpentry work. Joseph probably died during this time, leaving Jesus to provide for the family. The normal routines of his daily life gave him a solid understanding of the Judean people.

2.52 The second chapter of Luke shows us that although Jesus was unique, he had a normal childhood and youth. In terms of development, he was like us. He grew physically and mentally; he related to other people; and he was loved by God. A full human life is not unbalanced. It was important to Jesus – and it should be important to all believers – to develop fully and harmoniously in each of these key areas: physical, mental, social, and spiritual.

3.1 Tiberius, the Roman emperor, ruled from A.D. 14 to 37. Pilate was the Roman governor responsible for the province of Judea; Herod (Antipas) and Philip were half brothers and sons of the cruel Herod the Great, who had been dead more than 20 years. Antipas, Philip, Pilate, and Lysanias apparently had equal powers in gov-

3.3 Mal 4.6; Acts 13.24; 19.4
3.4 Isa 40.3

[2]during the high priesthood of Annas and Caiaphas, the word of God came to John
son of Zechariah in the wilderness. [3]He went into all the region around the Jordan,
proclaiming a baptism of repentance for the forgiveness of sins, [4]as it is written in
the book of the words of the prophet Isaiah,

In societies like Israel in which a woman's value was largely measured by her ability to bear children, aging without children often led to personal hardship and public shame. For Elizabeth, a childless old age was a painful and lonely time during which she remained faithful to God.

Both Elizabeth and Zechariah came from priestly families. For two weeks each year, Zechariah had to go to the temple in Jerusalem to attend to his priestly duties. After one of those trips, Zechariah returned home excited, but speechless. He had to write down his good news, because he couldn't give it any other way. And what a wonderful surprise he had for his wife—their faded dream would become an exciting reality! Soon Elizabeth became pregnant, and she knew her child was a long-hoped-for gift from God.

News traveled fast among the family. Seventy miles to the north, in Nazareth, Elizabeth's cousin, Mary, also unexpectedly became pregnant. Within days after the angel's message that she would bear the Messiah, Mary went to visit Elizabeth. They were instantly bound together by the unique gifts God had given them. Elizabeth knew that Mary's son would be even greater than her own, for John would be the messenger for Mary's son.

When the baby was born, Elizabeth insisted on his God-given name: John. Zechariah's written agreement freed his tongue, and everyone in town wondered what would become of this obviously special child.

Elizabeth whispered her praise as she cared for God's gift. Knowing about Mary must have made her marvel at God's timing. Things had worked out even better than she could have planned. We too need to remember that God is in control of every situation. When did you last pause to recognize God's timing in the events of your life?

Strengths and accomplishments:
- Known as a deeply spiritual woman
- Showed no doubts about God's ability to fulfill his promise
- Mother of John the Baptist
- The first woman besides Mary to hear of the coming Savior

Key lessons from her life:
- God does not forget those who have been faithful to him
- God's timetable and methods do not have to conform to what we expect

Vital statistics:
- Occupation: Homemaker
- Relatives: Husband: Zechariah. Son: John the Baptist. Cousin: Mary
- Contemporaries: Joseph, Herod the Great

Key verses:
"And why has this happened to me, that the mother of my Lord comes to me? For as soon as I heard the sound of your greeting, the child in my womb leaped for joy. And blessed is she who believed that there would be a fulfillment of what was spoken to her by the Lord" (Luke 1.43–45).

Elizabeth's story is told in Luke 1.5–80.

erning their separate territories. All were subject to Rome and responsible for keeping peace in their respective lands.

3.2 Under Jewish law there was only one high priest. God appointed him from Aaron's line, and he held his position for life. By this time, however, the religious system had been corrupted, and the Roman government was appointing its own religious leaders to maintain greater control over the Jews. The Roman authorities had apparently deposed the Jewish-appointed Annas and replaced him with his son-in-law, Caiaphas. Nevertheless, Annas retained his title (see Acts 4.6) and probably also much of the power it carried. Because the Jews believed the high priest's position to be for life, they would have continued to call Annas their high priest.

3.2 This is John the Baptist, whose birth story is told in chapter 1. See his Profile in John 1.

3.2 Pilate, Herod, and Caiaphas were the most powerful leaders in Palestine, but they were upstaged by a desert prophet from rural Judea. God chose to speak through the loner John the Baptist, who has gone down in history as greater than any of the rulers of his day. How often we judge people by our culture's standards—power, wealth, beauty—and miss the truly great people through whom God works! Greatness is not measured by what you have, but by your faith in God. Like John, give yourself entirely to him so his power can work through you.

3.3 Repentance has two sides—turning away from sins and turning toward God. To be forgiven, we must do both. We can't just say we believe and then live any way we choose (see 3.7, 8), and neither can we simply live a morally correct life without reference to God, because that alone cannot bring forgiveness from sin. Determine to rid your life of any sins God points out, and put your trust in him alone to guide you.

3.4, 5 In John's day, before a king took a trip, messengers would tell the ones he was planning to visit to prepare the roads for him. Similarly John told his listeners to make their lives ready so the Lord could come to them. To prepare for Jesus' coming to us, we must focus on him, listen to his words, and respond obediently to his directions.

"The voice of one crying out in the wilderness:
'Prepare the way of the Lord,
make his paths straight.
5 Every valley shall be filled,
and every mountain and hill shall be made low,
and the crooked shall be made straight,
and the rough ways made smooth;
6 and all flesh shall see the salvation of God.' "
7 John said to the crowds that came out to be baptized by him, "You brood of
vipers! Who warned you to flee from the wrath to come? 8 Bear fruits worthy of
repentance. Do not begin to say to yourselves, 'We have Abraham as our ancestor';
for I tell you, God is able from these stones to raise up children to Abraham. 9 Even
now the ax is lying at the root of the trees; every tree therefore that does not bear
good fruit is cut down and thrown into the fire."
10 And the crowds asked him, "What then should we do?" 11 In reply he said to
them, "Whoever has two coats must share with anyone who has none; and whoever
has food must do likewise." 12 Even tax collectors came to be baptized, and they
asked him, "Teacher, what should we do?" 13 He said to them, "Collect no more
than the amount prescribed for you." 14 Soldiers also asked him, "And we, what
should we do?" He said to them, "Do not extort money from anyone by threats or
false accusation, and be satisfied with your wages."
15 As the people were filled with expectation, and all were questioning in their
hearts concerning John, whether he might be the Messiah,[x] 16 John answered all of

[x] Or *the Christ*

3.5 Isa 40.4
3.6 Isa 40.5; 52.10
3.7 Mt 3.7; Jn 8.44
3.8 Acts 26.20
3.9 Mt 3.10; 7.19; Jn 15.2,6
3.11 Jas 2.15; 1 Jn 3.17
3.12 Mt 21.32
3.13 Mic 6.8; Lk 19.8
3.14 Ex 23.1; Lev 19.11
3.15 Jn 1.19,20
3.16 Mt 3.11; Mk 1.7,8; Jn 1.26,33; 1 Cor 12.13

3.6 This book was written to a non-Jewish audience. Luke quoted from Isaiah to show that salvation is for all people, not just the Jews (Isaiah 40.3–5; 52.10). John the Baptist called all mankind to prepare to meet Jesus. That includes you, no matter what your standing is with religious organizations and authorities. Don't let feelings of being an outsider cause you to hold back. No one who wants to follow Jesus is an outsider in God's kingdom.

3.7 What motivates your faith—fear of the future, or a desire to be a better person in a better world? Some people wanted to be baptized by John so they could escape eternal punishment, but they didn't turn to God for salvation. John had harsh words for such people. He knew that God values reformation above ritual. Is your faith motivated by a desire for a new, changed life, or is it only a vaccination or an insurance policy against possible disaster?

3.8 Many of John's hearers were shocked when he said that being Abraham's descendants was not enough for God. The religious leaders relied more on their family line than on their faith for their standing with God. For them, religion was inherited. But a personal relationship with God is not handed down from parents to children. Everyone has to commit to it on his or her own. Don't rely on someone else's faith for your salvation. Put your own faith in Jesus, and then exercise it every day.

3.8, 9 Confession and a changed life are inseparable. Faith without works is lifeless (James 2.14–26). Jesus' harshest words were to the respectable religious leaders who lacked the desire for real change. They wanted to be known as religious authorities, but they didn't want to change their hearts and minds. Thus their lives were unproductive. Repentance must be tied to action, or it isn't real. Following Jesus means more than saying the words; it means acting on what he says.

3.11–14 John's message demanded at least three specific responses: (1) share what you have with those who need it, (2) whatever your job is, do it well and with fairness, and (3) be content with what you're earning. John had no time to address comforting messages to those who lived careless or selfish lives—he was calling the people to right living. What changes can you make in sharing what you have, doing your work honestly and well, and being content?

3.12 Tax collectors were notorious for their dishonesty. Romans gathered funds for their government by farming out the collection privilege to whoever promised to get the most money from a given area. This tax collector earned his own living by adding a sizable sum—whatever he could get away with—to the total and keeping this money for himself. Unless the people revolted and risked Roman fury, they had to pay whatever was demanded. Obviously they hated the tax collectors, who were dishonest, greedy, and ready to betray their own countrymen for cold cash. Yet, said John, God would accept even these men if they repented and gave up their unfair practices.

3.12–14 John's message took root in unexpected places—among the poor, the dishonest, and even the hated occupation army. These people were painfully aware of their needs. Too often we confuse respectability with right living. They are not the same. Respectability can even hinder right living if it keeps us from seeing our need for God. If you had to choose between them, would you protect your character or your reputation?

3.14 These soldiers were the Roman troops sent to keep peace in this distant province. They oppressed the poor and used their power to take advantage of all the people. John called them to repent and change their ways.

3.15 There had not been a prophet in Israel for more than 400 years. It was widely believed that when the Messiah came, prophecy would reappear (Joel 2.28, 29; Malachi 3.1; 4.5). When John burst upon the scene, the people were excited. He was obviously a great prophet, and they were sure that the eagerly awaited age of the Messiah had come. Some, in fact, thought John himself was the Messiah. John spoke like the prophets of old: turn from your sin to avoid punishment, turn to God to experience his mercy and approval. It is a message for all times and places, but John spoke it with particular urgency—he was preparing the people for the coming Messiah.

3.16 John's baptism with water symbolized the washing away of sins. It coordinated with his message of repentance and reformation. Jesus' baptism by fire includes the power needed to do God's will. It began on the day of pentecost (Acts 2) when the Holy Spirit in the form of tongues of fire came upon the believers, empowering

them by saying, "I baptize you with water; but one who is more powerful than I is
coming; I am not worthy to untie the thong of his sandals. He will baptize you
3.17 Mic 4.12 Mt 13.20 with[y] the Holy Spirit and fire. 17 His winnowing fork is in his hand, to clear his
threshing floor and to gather the wheat into his granary; but the chaff he will burn
with unquenchable fire."

Herod puts John in prison
(26)

18 So, with many other exhortations, he proclaimed the good news to the

[y] Or *in*

MARY

Motherhood is a painful privilege. Young Mary of Nazareth had the unique privilege of being mother to the very Son of God. Yet the pains and pleasures of her motherhood are understood by mothers everywhere. Mary was the only human present at Jesus' birth who also witnessed his death. She saw him arrive as her baby son, and she watched him die as her Savior.

Until Gabriel's unexpected visit, Mary's life was quite satisfactory. She had recently become engaged to a carpenter, Joseph, and was anticipating married life. But her life was about to change forever.

Angels don't usually make appointments before visiting. As if she were being congratulated for winning grand prize in a contest she had never entered, Mary found the angel's greeting puzzling and his presence frightening. What she heard next was the news almost every woman in Israel hoped to hear—that her child would be the Messiah, God's promised Savior. Mary did not doubt the message, but rather asked how pregnancy would be possible. Gabriel told her the baby would be God's Son. Her answer was the one God waits in vain to hear from so many other people: "Here am I, the servant of the Lord; let it be with me according to your word" (Luke 1.38). Later, her song of joy to Elizabeth shows us how well she knew God, for her thoughts were filled with his words from the Old Testament.

Within a few weeks of his birth, Jesus was taken to the temple to be dedicated to God. There Joseph and Mary were met by two prophets, Simeon and Anna, who recognized the child as the Messiah and praised God. Simeon added some words to Mary that must have come to her mind many times in the years that followed: "A sword will pierce your own soul too" (Luke 2.35). A big part of her painful privilege of motherhood would be to see her son rejected and crucified by the people he came to save.

We can imagine that even if she had known all she would suffer as Jesus' mother, Mary would have given the same response. Are you, like Mary, available to be used by God?

Strengths and accomplishments:
- The mother of Jesus, the Messiah
- The one human who was with Jesus from birth to death
- Willing to be available to God
- Knew and applied God's Word

Lessons from her life:
- God's best servants are often plain people available to him
- God's plans involve extraordinary events in ordinary people
- A person's character is revealed by his or her response to the unexpected

Vital statistics:
- Where: Nazareth, Bethlehem
- Occupation: Homemaker
- Relatives: Husband: Joseph. Cousins: Zechariah and Elizabeth. Children: Jesus, James, Joses, Juda, Simon, and daughters

Key verse:
"Then Mary said, 'Here am I, the servant of the Lord; let it be with me according to your word' " (Luke 1.38).

Mary's story is told throughout the Gospels. She is also mentioned in Acts 1.14.

---

them to proclaim Jesus' resurrection in many languages. The baptism by fire also symbolizes the work of the Holy Spirit in bringing God's judgment on those who refuse to repent.

3.17 John warns of impending judgment by comparing those who refuse to live for God to chaff, the useless outer husk of the grain. By contrast, he compares those who repent and reform their lives to the nourishing grain itself. The winnowing fork was a pitchfork used to toss wheat so that the kernels would separate from the blades. Those who refuse to be used by God will be discarded because they have no value in furthering God's work. Those who repent and believe, however, hold great value in God's eyes because they are beginning a new life of productive service for him.

people. 19 But Herod the ruler,[z] who had been rebuked by him because of Herodias, 3.19,20 Mt 14.3
his brother's wife, and because of all the evil things that Herod had done, 20 added Mk 6.17
to them all by shutting up John in prison. Jn 3.24

John baptizes Jesus
(17/Matthew 3.13–17; Mark 1.9–11)

21 Now when all the people were baptized, and when Jesus also had been bap- 3.21 Mt 3.13-17
tized and was praying, the heaven was opened, 22 and the Holy Spirit descended Mk 1.9-11
upon him in bodily form like a dove. And a voice came from heaven, "You are my Jn 1.32
Son, the Beloved;[a] with you I am well pleased."[b]

The ancestors of Jesus
(3/Matthew 1.1–17)

23 Jesus was about thirty years old when he began his work. He was the son (as 3.23 Num 4.3,35,
was thought) of Joseph son of Heli, 24 son of Matthat, son of Levi, son of Melchi, 39,47
son of Jannai, son of Joseph, 25 son of Mattathias, son of Amos, son of Nahum, son Mt 1.1-17; 13.55
of Esli, son of Naggai, 26 son of Maath, son of Mattathias, son of Semein, son of Jn 6.42
Josech, son of Joda, 27 son of Joanan, son of Rhesa, son of Zerubbabel, son of
Shealtiel,[c] son of Neri, 28 son of Melchi, son of Addi, son of Cosam, son of El-
madam, son of Er, 29 son of Joshua, son of Eliezer, son of Jorim, son of Matthat, 3.31
son of Levi, 30 son of Simeon, son of Judah, son of Joseph, son of Jonam, son of 2 Sam 5.14 1 Chron 3.5
Eliakim, 31 son of Melea, son of Menna, son of Mattatha, son of Nathan, son of Zech 12.12
David, 32 son of Jesse, son of Obed, son of Boaz, son of Sala,[d] son of Nahshon, 3.32 Ruth 4.18
33 son of Amminadab, son of Admin, son of Arni,[e] son of Hezron, son of Perez, 1 Chron 2.10
son of Judah, 34 son of Jacob, son of Isaac, son of Abraham, son of Terah, son of 3.34 Gen 11.24,26
Nahor, 35 son of Serug, son of Reu, son of Peleg, son of Eber, son of Shelah, 36 son 3.36
of Cainan, son of Arphaxad, son of Shem, son of Noah, son of Lamech, 37 son of Gen 11.10,12

[z] Gk *tetrarch* [a] Or *my beloved Son* [b] Other ancient authorities read *You are my Son, today I have begotten you*
[c] Gk *Salathiel* [d] Other ancient authorities read *Salmon* [e] Other ancient authorities read *Amminadab, son of Aram*; others vary widely

---

3.19, 20 In these two verses Luke flashes forward to continue his explanation about John the Baptist. See the Harmony of the Gospels for the chronological order of events.

3.19, 20 This was Herod Antipas (see Mark 6 for his Profile). Herodias was Herod's niece and also his brother's wife. She treacherously plotted John the Baptist's death (Matthew 14.1–12). The Herods were an incestuous, murderous, deceitful family. Rebuking a tyrannical Roman official who could imprison and execute him was extremely dangerous, yet that is what John did. Herod seemingly had the last word, but the story is not finished. At the last judgment, Herod, not John, will be the one in danger.

3.21 Luke emphasizes Jesus' human side. He was born to humble parents, unannounced except to shepherds and foreigners. This baptism was the first public declaration of his ministry. Instead of going to Jerusalem and identifying with the established religious leaders, Jesus went to a river and identified himself with those who were repenting of sin. When Jesus, at age 12, visited the temple, he understood his mission (2.49). Eighteen years later, at his baptism, he began carrying it out. And as he prayed, God spoke to him and confirmed his decision to act. God was breaking into human history through Jesus Christ.

3.21, 22 If baptism was a sign of repentance from sin, why did Jesus ask to be baptized? Several explanations are often given: (1) Jesus' baptism was one step in fulfilling his earthly mission of identifying with our humanity and sin; (2) by endorsing the rite of baptism, he was giving us an example to follow; (3) he was announcing the beginning of his public ministry; (4) he was being baptized for the sins of the nation. The Holy Spirit's appearance in the form of a dove showed that God's plan for salvation was centered in Jesus. Jesus was the perfect man who didn't need baptism for sin, but he was baptized anyway on our behalf.

3.21, 22 This is one of several places in Scripture where all members of the trinity are mentioned – Father, Son, and Holy Spirit. In the traditional words of the church, the one God exists in three persons but one substance, co-eternal and co-equal. No amount of explanation can adequately portray the power and intricacy of this unique relationship. There are no perfect analogies in nature because there is no other relationship like the trinity.

3.23 Imagine the Savior of the world driving nails in a small-town carpenter's shop until he was 30 years old! It seems incredible that Jesus would have been content to remain in Nazareth all that time, but he patiently trusted the Father's timing for his life and ministry. Thirty was the prescribed age for priests to begin their ministry (Numbers 4.3). Joseph was 30 years old when he began serving the king of Egypt (Genesis 41.46), and David was 30 years old when he began to reign over Judah (2 Samuel 5.4). Age 30, then, was a good time to begin an important task in the Jewish culture. Like Jesus, we need to resist the temptation to jump ahead before receiving the Spirit's direction. Are you waiting and wondering what your next step should be? Don't jump ahead – trust God's timing.

3.23 Heli was most likely Joseph's father-in-law. Thus this would be Mary's genealogy, which Luke may have received personally from her. It is fitting that Luke would show Mary's genealogy because of the prominence he gives women in his Gospel.

3.23–38 Matthew's genealogy goes back to Abraham and shows that Jesus was related to all Jews (Matthew 1). Luke's goes back to Adam, showing he is related to all human beings. This is consistent with Luke's picture of Jesus as the Savior of the whole world.

3.38 Gen 1.26,27 Isa 64.8
Methuselah, son of Enoch, son of Jared, son of Mahalaleel, son of Cainan, 38 son
of Enos, son of Seth, son of Adam, son of God.

Satan tempts Jesus in the wilderness
(18/Matthew 4.1–11; Mark 1.12, 13)

4.1 Isa 11.2; 61.1 Mt 4.1-11
4.2 Heb 2.18; 4.15
4.4 Deut 8.3 Eph 6.17
4.6 Jn 12.31; 14.30 1 Jn 5.19 Rev 13.2,7

4 Jesus, full of the Holy Spirit, returned from the Jordan and was led by the
Spirit in the wilderness, 2 where for forty days he was tempted by the devil. He
ate nothing at all during those days, and when they were over, he was famished.
3 The devil said to him, "If you are the Son of God, command this stone to become
a loaf of bread." 4 Jesus answered him, "It is written, 'One does not live by bread
alone.' "
5 Then the devil[f] led him up and showed him in an instant all the kingdoms of
the world. 6 And the devil[f] said to him, "To you I will give their glory and all this
authority; for it has been given over to me, and I give it to anyone I please. 7 If you,

[f] Gk *he*

4.1 Sometimes we feel that if the Holy Spirit leads us, it will always be "beside still waters." But that is not necessarily true. He led Jesus into the wilderness for a long and difficult time of testing, and he may also lead us into difficult situations. When facing trials, first make sure you haven't brought them on yourself through sin or unwise choices. If you find no sin to confess or unwise behavior to change, then ask God to strengthen you for your test. Finally, be careful to follow faithfully wherever the Holy Spirit leads.

4.1 Temptation often comes after a high point in our spiritual lives or ministries (see 1 Kings 18, 19 for Elijah's story of great victory followed by despair). Remember that Satan chooses the times for his attacks. We need to be on our guard in times of victory just as much as in times of discouragement. See the second note on Matthew 4.1ff for how Satan tempts us when we're vulnerable.

4.1, 2 The devil, who tempted Adam and Eve in the garden, also tempted Jesus in the wilderness. Satan is a real being, a created but rebellious fallen angel, not a symbol or an idea. He constantly fights against God and those who follow and obey God. Jesus was a prime target for his temptations. Satan succeeded with Adam and Eve, and he hoped to succeed with Jesus too.

4.1–13 Knowing and obeying God's Word is an effective weapon against temptation, the only *offensive* weapon provided in the Christian's "armor" (Ephesians 6.17). Jesus used Scripture to counter Satan's attacks, and you can too. But to use it effectively you must have faith in God's promises, because Satan also knows Scripture and is adept at twisting it to suit his purpose. Obeying the Scriptures is more important than simply having a verse to quote, so read them daily and apply them to your life. Then your "sword" will always be sharp.

4.2 Why was it necessary for Jesus to be tempted? First, temptation is part of the human experience. For Jesus to be fully human, for him to understand us completely, he had to face temptation (see Hebrews 4.15). Second, Jesus had to undo Adam's work. Adam, though created perfect, gave in to temptation and passed sin on to the whole human race. Jesus, by contrast, resisted Satan. His victory offers salvation to all of Adam's descendants (see Romans 5.12–19).

4.3 Satan frequently raises questions about what God has said. He knows that once we begin to question God, it's far easier to get us to do what he wants. Times of questioning can help us sort out our beliefs and strengthen our faith, but they can also be dangerous. If you are dealing with doubt, realize that you are especially vulnerable to temptation. Even as you search for answers, protect yourself by meditating on the unshakable truths of God's Word.

4.3 Sometimes what we are tempted to do isn't wrong in itself. Turning stones into bread wasn't necessarily bad. The sin was not in the act but in the reason for it. Satan was trying to get Jesus to take a shortcut, to solve his immediate problem at the expense of his long-range goals, to seek comfort at the sacrifice of his discipline. Satan often works that way – persuading us to take action, even right action, for the wrong reason or at the wrong time. The fact that something is not wrong in itself does not mean it is good for you at a given time. Many people sin by attempting to fulfill legitimate desires outside of God's will or ahead of his timetable. First ask, "Is the Holy Spirit leading me to do this? Or is Satan trying to get me off the track?"

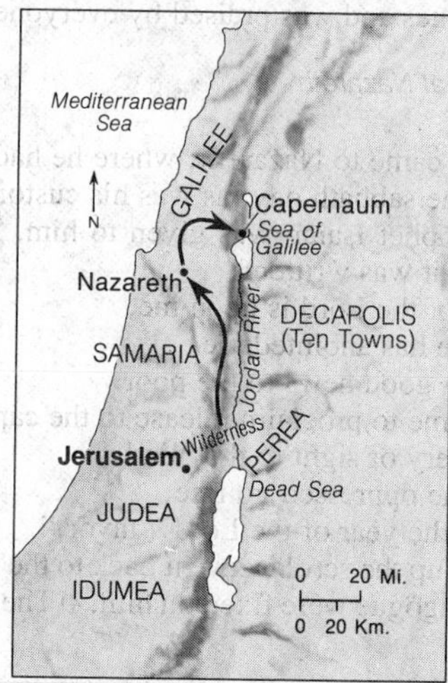

JESUS' TEMPTATION AND RETURN TO GALILEE
Jesus was tempted by Satan in the rough wilderness of Judea before returning to his boyhood home, Nazareth. John's Gospel tells of his journeys in Galilee, Samaria, and Judea (see John 1–4) before he moved to Capernaum to set up his base of operations (see Matthew 4.12, 13).

4.3ff Often we are tempted not through our weaknesses, but through our strengths. Satan tempted Jesus where he was strong. Jesus had power over stones, the kingdoms of the world, and even angels, and Satan wanted him to use that power without regard to his mission. When we give in to Satan and wrongly use our strengths, we become proud and self-reliant. Trusting in our own powers, we feel little need of God. To avoid this trap, we must realize that all our strengths are God's gifts to us, and we must dedicate them to his service.

4.6, 7 Satan arrogantly hoped to succeed in his rebellion against God by diverting Jesus from his mission and winning his worship. "This world is mine, not God's," he was saying, "and if you hope to do anything worthwhile here, you'd better recognize that fact." Jesus didn't argue with Satan about who owns the world, but he refused to validate Satan's claim by bowing to him. Jesus knew he would redeem the world through giving up his life on the cross, not through making an alliance with a corrupt angel.

then, will worship me, it will all be yours." 8 Jesus answered him, "It is written, 4.8 Deut 6.13; 10.20
'Worship the Lord your God,
and serve only him.' "
9 Then the devil[g] took him to Jerusalem, and placed him on the pinnacle of the 4.9 Mt 4.5
temple, saying to him, "If you are the Son of God, throw yourself down from here, 1 Pet 5.8
10 for it is written,
'He will command his angels concerning you,
to protect you,'
11 and 4.11 Ps 91.11
'On their hands they will bear you up,
so that you will not dash your foot against a stone.' "
12 Jesus answered him, "It is said, 'Do not put the Lord your God to the test.' " 4.12 Deut 6.16
13 When the devil had finished every test, he departed from him until an opportune 4.13 Jn 14.30
time.

B. MESSAGE AND MINISTRY OF JESUS, THE SAVIOR (4.14—21.38)

Luke accurately records the actions and teachings of Christ, helping us understand the way of salvation. There is much unique material in Luke, especially the parables of Jesus. Jesus came to teach us how to live and how to find salvation. How carefully, then, we should study the words and life of our Savior.

1. Jesus' ministry in Galilee

Jesus preaches in Galilee
(30/Matthew 4.12–17; Mark 1.14, 15; John 4.43–45)

14 Then Jesus, filled with the power of the Spirit, returned to Galilee, and a 4.14 Mt 4.12-17
report about him spread through all the surrounding country. 15 He began to teach Mk 1.14,15
in their synagogues and was praised by everyone. Jn 4.43-45

Jesus is rejected at Nazareth
(32)

16 When he came to Nazareth, where he had been brought up, he went to the 4.16 Mt 2.23
synagogue on the sabbath day, as was his custom. He stood up to read, 17 and the 13.54-58
scroll of the prophet Isaiah was given to him. He unrolled the scroll and found Mk 6.1-6
the place where it was written: Acts 13.14
18 "The Spirit of the Lord is upon me, 4.18 Isa 61.1-2 Dan 9.24
because he has anointed me
to bring good news to the poor.
He has sent me to proclaim release to the captives
and recovery of sight to the blind,
to let the oppressed go free,
19 to proclaim the year of the Lord's favor." 4.19 Lev 25.8-10
20 And he rolled up the scroll, gave it back to the attendant, and sat down. The eyes 2 Cor 6.2
of all in the synagogue were fixed on him. 21 Then he began to say to them, "Today

g Gk *he*

4.9–11 Here Satan misinterpreted Scripture. The intention of Psalm 91 is to show God's protection of his people, not to incite them to use God's power for sensational or foolish displays.

4.13 Christ's defeat of Satan in the wilderness was decisive but not final. Throughout his ministry, Jesus would confront Satan in many forms. Too often we see temptation as once and for all. In reality, we need to be constantly on guard against the devil's ongoing attacks. Where are you most susceptible to temptation right now? How are you preparing to withstand it?

4.16 Synagogues were very important in Jewish religious life. During the exile when the Jews no longer had their temple, synagogues were established as places of worship on the sabbath and as schools for young boys during the week. They continued after the temple was rebuilt. A synagogue could be set up in any town where there were at least ten Jewish families. It was run by one leader and an assistant. At the synagogue, the leader often invited a visiting rabbi to read from the Scriptures and to teach.

4.16 Jesus went to the synagogue "as was his custom." Even though he was the perfect Son of God and his local synagogue left much to be desired, he attended services every week. His example makes most excuses for not attending church sound weak and self-serving. Make regular worship a part of your life.

4.17–19 Jesus was quoting from Isaiah 61.1, 2. Isaiah pictures the deliverance of Israel from exile in Babylon as a year of jubilee when all debts are cancelled, all slaves are freed, and all property is returned to original owners (Leviticus 25). But the release from Babylonian exile had not brought the fulfillment the people had expected; they were still conquered and oppressed. So Isaiah must have been referring to a future messianic age. Jesus boldly announced, "Today this scripture has been fulfilled in your hearing." Jesus was proclaiming himself as the One who would bring this to pass, but in a way that the people would not yet be able to grasp.

4.22 Ps 45.2
4.23 Mt 4.13; 11.23 Mk 1.21-28 2.1-12 Jn 4.46-54
4.24 Mt 13.57
4.25,26 1 Kgs 17.9; 18.1 Jas 5.17
4.27 2 Kgs 5.14
4.29 Num 15.35 Acts 7.58 Heb 13.12
4.30 Jn 8.59; 10.39

this scripture has been fulfilled in your hearing." 22 All spoke well of him and were
amazed at the gracious words that came from his mouth. They said, "Is not this
Joseph's son?" 23 He said to them, "Doubtless you will quote to me this proverb,
'Doctor, cure yourself!' And you will say, 'Do here also in your hometown the
things that we have heard you did at Capernaum.' " 24 And he said, "Truly I tell
you, no prophet is accepted in the prophet's hometown. 25 But the truth is, there
were many widows in Israel in the time of Elijah, when the heaven was shut up
three years and six months, and there was a severe famine over all the land; 26 yet
Elijah was sent to none of them except to a widow at Zarephath in Sidon. 27 There
were also many lepers[h] in Israel in the time of the prophet Elisha, and none of them
was cleansed except Naaman the Syrian." 28 When they heard this, all in the synagogue were filled with rage. 29 They got up, drove him out of the town, and led him
to the brow of the hill on which their town was built, so that they might hurl him off
the cliff. 30 But he passed through the midst of them and went on his way.

Jesus teaches with great authority
(34/Mark 1.21–28)

4.31 Mt 4.13-16 Mk 1.21-34
4.32 Mt 7.28,29 Tit 2.15
4.34 Isa 49.7 Dan 9.24 Lk 1.35
4.35 Lk 4.39,41
4.37 Mic 5.4

31 He went down to Capernaum, a city in Galilee, and was teaching them on
the sabbath. 32 They were astounded at his teaching, because he spoke with authority. 33 In the synagogue there was a man who had the spirit of an unclean demon, and he cried out with a loud voice, 34 "Let us alone! What have you to do with
us, Jesus of Nazareth? Have you come to destroy us? I know who you are, the Holy
One of God." 35 But Jesus rebuked him, saying, "Be silent, and come out of him!"
When the demon had thrown him down before them, he came out of him without
having done him any harm. 36 They were all amazed and kept saying to one
another, "What kind of utterance is this? For with authority and power he commands the unclean spirits, and out they come!" 37 And a report about him began to
reach every place in the region.

Jesus heals Peter's mother-in-law and many others
(35/Matthew 8.14–17; Mark 1.29–34)

4.38 Mt 8.14-17 Mk 1.29-34
4.39 Ps 103.3

38 After leaving the synagogue he entered Simon's house. Now Simon's
mother-in-law was suffering from a high fever, and they asked him about her.
39 Then he stood over her and rebuked the fever, and it left her. Immediately she got
up and began to serve them.

[h] The terms *leper* and *leprosy* can refer to several diseases

---

4.24 Even Jesus himself was not accepted as a prophet in his hometown. Many people have a similar attitude—an expert is anyone who carries a briefcase and comes from more than 200 miles away. Don't be surprised when your Christian life and faith are not easily understood or accepted by those who know you well.

4.28 These remarks filled the people of Nazareth with rage because Jesus was saying that God sometimes chose to reach Gentiles rather than Jews. Jesus implied that his hearers were as unbelieving as the citizens of the northern kingdom of Israel in the days of Elijah and Elisha, a time notorious for its great wickedness.

4.31 Jesus had recently moved to Capernaum from Nazareth (Matthew 4.13). Capernaum was a thriving city with great wealth as well as great decadence. Because it was the headquarters for many Roman troops, word about Jesus could spread all over the Roman Empire.

4.31 Why was Jesus allowed to teach in the synagogues? Jesus was taking advantage of the policy of allowing visitors to teach. Itinerant rabbis were always welcome to speak to those gathered each sabbath in the synagogues. The apostle Paul also profited from this practice (see Acts 13.5, 14.1).

4.33 A man possessed by a demon was in the synagogue where Jesus was teaching. He made his way into the place of worship and verbally abused Jesus. It is naive to think we are sheltered from evil in the church. Satan is happy to invade our presence wherever and whenever he can. But Jesus' authority is much greater than Satan's, and where Jesus is present, demons cannot stay for long.

4.34–36 The people were amazed at Jesus' authority to cast out demons—evil spirits ruled by Satan and sent to harass people and tempt them to sin. They are fallen angels who have joined Satan in rebellion against God. Demons can cause a person to become mute, deaf, blind, or insane. Jesus faced many demons during his time on earth, and he always exerted authority over them. Not only did the devil leave this man; Luke records that the man was not even hurt.

4.36 Evil permeates our world, and it is no wonder that people are often fearful. But Jesus' power is far greater than that of Satan. The first step toward conquering fear of evil is to recognize Jesus' authority. He has overcome all evil, including Satan himself.

4.39 Jesus healed Simon's (Peter's) mother-in-law so completely that not only did the fever leave, but her strength was restored and immediately she got up and took care of others' needs. What a beautiful attitude of service she showed! God gives us health so that we may serve others.

40 As the sun was setting, all those who had any who were sick with various 4.40 Mt 8.16,17
kinds of diseases brought them to him; and he laid his hands on each of them and Mk 1.32-34
cured them. 41 Demons also came out of many, shouting, "You are the Son of 4.41
God!" But he rebuked them and would not allow them to speak, because they knew Mk 3.11
that he was the Messiah.[i]

Jesus preaches throughout Galilee
(36/Matthew 4.23–25; Mark 1.35–39)

42 At daybreak he departed and went into a deserted place. And the crowds 4.42 Mt 4.23
were looking for him; and when they reached him, they wanted to prevent him from Mk 1.35-39
leaving them. 43 But he said to them, "I must proclaim the good news of the king- 4.43
dom of God to the other cities also; for I was sent for this purpose." 44 So he con- Mk 1.14,15 Acts 10.38
tinued proclaiming the message in the synagogues of Judea.[j] Rom 15.8

Jesus provides a miraculous catch of fish
(37)

5 Once while Jesus[k] was standing beside the lake of Gennesaret, and the crowd 5.1 Mt 4.18-22
was pressing in on him to hear the word of God, 2 he saw two boats there at the Mk 1.16-20
shore of the lake; the fishermen had gone out of them and were washing their nets.
3 He got into one of the boats, the one belonging to Simon, and asked him to put out
a little way from the shore. Then he sat down and taught the crowds from the boat.
4 When he had finished speaking, he said to Simon, "Put out into the deep water and 5.4
let down your nets for a catch." 5 Simon answered, "Master, we have worked all Jn 21.6 5.5
night long but have caught nothing. Yet if you say so, I will let down the nets." Jn 21.3
6 When they had done this, they caught so many fish that their nets were beginning
to break. 7 So they signaled their partners in the other boat to come and help them.
And they came and filled both boats, so that they began to sink. 8 But when Simon 5.8
Peter saw it, he fell down at Jesus' knees, saying, "Go away from me, Lord, for I 2 Sam 6.9 Job 42.5,6
am a sinful man!" 9 For he and all who were with him were amazed at the catch of Dan 8.17
fish that they had taken; 10 and so also were James and John, sons of Zebedee, who 5.10 Ezek 47.9,10
were partners with Simon. Then Jesus said to Simon, "Do not be afraid; from now 5.11
on you will be catching people." 11 When they had brought their boats to shore, Mt 19.27 Lk 18.28
they left everything and followed him. Phil 3.7,8

[i] Or *the Christ* [j] Other ancient authorities read *Galilee* [k] Gk *he*

4.40 The villagers came to Jesus when the sun was setting because this was the sabbath (4.31), their day of rest. Sabbath lasted from sunset on Friday to sunset on Saturday. The people didn't want to break the law that prohibited travel on the sabbath, so they waited until the sabbath hours were over before coming to Jesus. Then, as Luke the physician notes, they came with all kinds of diseases, and Jesus healed every one.

4.41 Why didn't Jesus want the demons to reveal who he was? (1) He commanded them to remain silent to show his authority over them. (2) He wanted his listeners to believe he was the Messiah because of his words, not because of the demons' words. (3) He was going to reveal his identity according to God's timetable, and he would not be pushed by Satan's evil plans. The demons called Jesus "Son of God" or "Christ." But Jesus was going to show himself to be the suffering Servant before he became the great King. To reveal his identity as King too soon would stir up the crowds with the wrong expectations of what he had come to do.

4.42 Jesus had to get up very early just to get some time alone. If Jesus needed solitude for prayer and refreshment, how much more is this true for us? Don't become so busy that life turns into a flurry of activity leaving no room for quiet fellowship alone with God. No matter how much you have to do, you always have time for prayer.

4.43 The kingdom of God was good news! It was good news to the Jews, because they had been awaiting the coming of the promised Messiah ever since the Babylonian captivity. It is good news for us also, because it means freedom from slavery to sin and selfishness. The kingdom of God is here and now, because the Holy Spirit lives in the hearts of believers. Yet it is also in the future, because Jesus will return to reign over a perfect kingdom where sin and evil no longer exist.

5.1 The lake of Gennesaret was also known as the Sea of Galilee or the Sea of Tiberias.

5.2 Fishermen on the Sea of Galilee used nets, often bell-shaped with lead weights around the edges. A net was thrown flat on the water, and the lead weights caused it to sink and cover the fish. The fishermen then pulled on a cord, drawing the net around the fish. Nets had to be kept in good condition, so they were washed to remove weeds and then mended.

5.8 Simon (Peter) was awestruck at this miracle, and his first response was to feel his own insignificance in comparison to this man's greatness. Peter knew Jesus had healed the sick and cast out demons, but he was amazed that Jesus cared about his day-to-day routine and understood his needs. God is interested not only in saving us, but also in helping us in our daily activities.

5.11 There are two preconditions in coming to God. Like Peter, we must recognize our own sinfulness. And then, like these fishermen, we must realize that we can't save ourselves. If we know that we need help, and if we know that Jesus is the only one who can help us, we will be ready to leave everything and follow him.

5.11 This is the disciples' second call. After the first call (Matthew 4.18–22; Mark 1.16–20), Peter, Andrew, James, and John went

Jesus heals a man with leprosy
(38/Matthew 8.1–4; Mark 1.40–45)

12 Once, when he was in one of the cities, there was a man covered with leprosy.[l] When he saw Jesus, he bowed with his face to the ground and begged him,
"Lord, if you choose, you can make me clean." 13 Then Jesus[m] stretched out his
hand, touched him, and said, "I do choose. Be made clean." Immediately the leprosy[l] left him. 14 And he ordered him to tell no one. "Go," he said, "and show
yourself to the priest, and, as Moses commanded, make an offering for your
cleansing, for a testimony to them." 15 But now more than ever the word about
Jesus[n] spread abroad; many crowds would gather to hear him and to be cured of
their diseases. 16 But he would withdraw to deserted places and pray.

Jesus heals a paralyzed man
(39/Matthew 9.2–8; Mark 2.1–12)

17 One day, while he was teaching, Pharisees and teachers of the law were
sitting near by (they had come from every village of Galilee and Judea and from
Jerusalem); and the power of the Lord was with him to heal.[o] 18 Just then some men
came, carrying a paralyzed man on a bed. They were trying to bring him in and lay
him before Jesus;[n] 19 but finding no way to bring him in because of the crowd, they
went up on the roof and let him down with his bed through the tiles into the middle
of the crowd[p] in front of Jesus. 20 When he saw their faith, he said, "Friend,[q] your
sins are forgiven you." 21 Then the scribes and the Pharisees began to question,
"Who is this who is speaking blasphemies? Who can forgive sins but God alone?"
22 When Jesus perceived their questionings, he answered them, "Why do you raise
such questions in your hearts? 23 Which is easier, to say, 'Your sins are forgiven
you,' or to say, 'Stand up and walk'? 24 But so that you may know that the Son of
Man has authority on earth to forgive sins"—he said to the one who was
paralyzed—"I say to you, stand up and take your bed and go to your home." 25 Immediately he stood up before them, took what he had been lying on, and went to his

5.14 Lev 13.1 14.4,10,21,22
5.15 Mt 4.25 Mk 3.7 Jn 6.2
5.16 Mt 14.23 Mk 6.46
5.17 Mt 9.1-8 Mk 2.1-12
5.20 Acts 5.31
5.21 Ex 34.7 Ps 32.5; 103.3 Isa 1.18; 43.25 Dan 9.9
5.24 Acts 5.31 Col 3.13
5.25 Ps 103.1

[l] The terms *leper* and *leprosy* can refer to several diseases [m] Gk *he* [n] Gk *him* [o] Other ancient authorities read *was present to heal them* [p] Gk *into the midst* [q] Gk *Man*

---

back to fishing. They continued to watch Jesus, however, as he established his authority in the synagogue, healed the sick, and cast out demons. Now he also established his authority in their lives—he met them on their level and helped them in their work. From this point on, they left their nets and remained with Jesus. For us, to follow Jesus is more than just acknowledging him as Savior. It means leaving our past behind and devoting our future to him.

5.12 Leprosy was a feared disease because there was no known cure for it, and some forms of it were highly contagious. It had a similar emotional impact and terror associated with it as AIDS does today. (Sometimes called Hansen's disease, leprosy still exists today in a less contagious form that can be treated.) The priests monitored the disease, banishing lepers with active cases to prevent the spread of infection and readmitting lepers whose disease was in remission. Since leprosy destroyed the nerve endings, lepers often unknowingly damaged their fingers, toes, and noses. This leper had an advanced case, so he undoubtedly had lost much bodily tissue. Still, he believed Jesus could heal every trace of the disease.

5.13 Lepers were considered untouchable because people feared contracting their disease. Yet Jesus reached out and touched the leper to heal him. We may consider certain people who are diseased or handicapped to be untouchable or repulsive. We must not be afraid to reach out and touch them with God's love. Whom do you know who needs God's touch of love?

5.16 People were clamoring to hear Jesus preach and to have their diseases healed, but Jesus made sure he often withdrew to quiet, solitary places to pray. Many things clamor for our attention, and we often run ourselves ragged attending to them. Like Jesus, however, we should take time to withdraw to a quiet and deserted place to pray. Strength comes from God, and we can get it only by spending time with him.

5.17 The religious leaders spent much time defining and discussing the huge body of religious tradition that had been accumulating for more than 400 years since the Jews' return from exile. They were so concerned with these man-made traditions, in fact, that they often lost sight of Scripture. Now these leaders felt threatened because Jesus challenged their sincerity, and the people were flocking to him.

5.18, 19 In Bible times, houses were built of stone and had flat roofs made of mud mixed with straw. Outside stairways led to the roof. These men carried their friend up the stairs to the roof where they took apart as much of the mud and straw mixture as was necessary to lower him through to Jesus.

5.18–20 It wasn't the sick man's faith that impressed Jesus, but the faith of his friends. Jesus responded to their faith and healed the man. For better or worse, our faith affects others. We cannot make another person a Christian, but we can do much through our words, actions, and love to give him or her a chance to respond. Look for opportunities to bring your friends to the living Christ.

5.21 When Jesus told the paralyzed man his sins were forgiven, the Jewish leaders accused him of blasphemy—claiming to be God or to do what only God can do. In Jewish law, blasphemy was punishable by death (Leviticus 24.16). In labeling Jesus' claim to forgive sins blasphemous, the religious leaders showed they did not understand that he *is* God, and he has God's power to heal both the body and the soul. Forgiveness of sins was a sign that the messianic age had come (Isaiah 40.2; Joel 2.32; Micah 7.18, 19; Zechariah 13.1).

home, glorifying God. 26 Amazement seized all of them, and they glorified God
and were filled with awe, saying, "We have seen strange things today."

Jesus eats with sinners at Matthew's house
(40/Matthew 9.9–13; Mark 2.13–17)

27 After this he went out and saw a tax collector named Levi, sitting at the tax
booth; and he said to him, "Follow me." 28 And he got up, left everything, and
followed him.
29 Then Levi gave a great banquet for him in his house; and there was a large **5.29**
crowd of tax collectors and others sitting at the table[r] with them. 30 The Pharisees Lk 15.1
and their scribes were complaining to his disciples, saying, "Why do you eat and
drink with tax collectors and sinners?" 31 Jesus answered, "Those who are well
have no need of a physician, but those who are sick; 32 I have come to call not the **5.32**
righteous but sinners to repentance." 1 Tim 1.15

Religious leaders ask Jesus about fasting
(41/Matthew 9.14–17; Mark 2.18–22)

33 Then they said to him, "John's disciples, like the disciples of the Pharisees, **5.33**
frequently fast and pray, but your disciples eat and drink. 34 Jesus said to them, Mt 9.14-17 Mk 2.18-22
"You cannot make wedding guests fast while the bridegroom is with them, can **5.34**
you? 35 The days will come when the bridegroom will be taken away from them, Mt 22.2 Lk 14.16-23
and then they will fast in those days." 36 He also told them a parable: "No one tears 2 Cor 11.2
a piece from a new garment and sews it on an old garment; otherwise the new will Rev 19.7; 21.2
be torn, and the piece from the new will not match the old. 37 And no one puts new **5.35** Zech 13.7
wine into old wineskins; otherwise the new wine will burst the skins and will be Mt 6.16,17 Jn 7.33; 16.6,
spilled, and the skins will be destroyed. 38 But new wine must be put into fresh 20,22
wineskins. 39 And no one after drinking old wine desires new wine, but says, 'The Acts 13.2,3 1 Cor 7.5
old is good.' "[s]

The disciples pick wheat on the sabbath
(45/Matthew 12.1–8; Mark 2.23–28)

6 One sabbath[t] while Jesus[u] was going through the grainfields, his disciples **6.2** Ex 20.10
plucked some heads of grain, rubbed them in their hands, and ate them. 2 But Mk 7.2
some of the Pharisees said, "Why are you doing what is not lawful[v] on the sab-

[r] Gk *reclining* [s] Other ancient authorities read *better*; others lack verse 39 [t] Other ancient authorities read *On the second first sabbath* [u] Gk *he* [v] Other ancient authorities add *to do*

5.27 For more about Levi, who became Matthew the disciple and author of the Gospel of Matthew, see his Profile in Matthew 9.

5.28, 29 Levi responded as Jesus would want all his followers to do—he followed his Lord immediately, and he called his friends together to meet him too. Levi left a lucrative, though probably dishonest, tax-collecting business to follow Jesus. Then he held a reception for his fellow tax collectors and other notorious sinners so they could meet Jesus too. Levi, who left behind a material fortune in order to gain a spiritual fortune, was proud to be associated with Jesus.

5.30–32 The Pharisees wrapped their sin in respectability. They made themselves appear good by publicly doing good deeds and pointing at the sins of others. Jesus chose to spend time not with these proud, self-righteous religious leaders, but with people who sensed their own sin and knew they were not good enough for God. In order to come to God, we must repent; and in order to renounce our sin, we must recognize it for what it is.

5.35 Jesus knew his death was coming. After that time, fasting would be in order. Although he was fully human, Jesus knew he was God and knew why he had come—to die for the sins of the world.

5.36–39 "Wineskins" were goatskins sewed together at the edges to form watertight bags. New wine expands as it ages, so it had to be put in new, pliable wineskins. A used skin, more rigid, would burst and spill the wine. Like old wineskins, the Pharisees were too rigid to accept Jesus, who could not be contained in their traditions or rules. Christianity required new approaches, new traditions, new structures. Our church programs and ministries should not be so structured that they have no room for a fresh touch of the Spirit, a new method, or a new idea. We, too, must be careful that our hearts do not become so rigid that they prevent us from accepting the new way of thinking that Christ brings. We need to keep our hearts pliable so we can accept Jesus' life-changing message.

6.1, 2 In Jewish legal tradition, there were 39 categories of activities forbidden on the sabbath—and harvesting was one of them. The teachers of the law even went so far as to describe different methods of harvesting. One was rubbing the heads of grain between the hands, as the disciples were doing here. Since God's law said farmers were to leave the edges of their fields unplowed so travelers and the poor could eat from this bounty (Deuteronomy 23.25), the disciples were not stealing grain. Neither were they breaking the sabbath by doing their daily work on it. In fact, though they were violating the Pharisees' rules, they were not breaking any divine law.

6.2 The Pharisees thought their religious system had all the answers. They could not accept Jesus because he did not fit into their system. We could miss Christ for the same reason. Beware of

6.3 1 Sam 21.6
6.4 Ex 29.23,33 Lev 24.9

bath?" 3 Jesus answered, "Have you not read what David did when he and his companions were hungry? 4 He entered the house of God and took and ate the bread of
the Presence, which it is not lawful for any but the priests to eat, and gave some to
his companions?" 5 Then he said to them, "The Son of Man is lord of the sabbath."

Jesus heals a man's hand on the sabbath
(46/Matthew 12.9–14; Mark 3.1–6)

6.6 Mt 12.9-14 Mk 3.1-6 Lk 13.14; 14.3 Jn 9.16
6.8 1 Sam 16.7 Mt 9.4 Jn 2.24,25 6.64; 21.17 Acts 1.24 Rev 2.23
6.9 Jn 7.23

6 On another sabbath he entered the synagogue and taught, and there was a man
there whose right hand was withered. 7 The scribes and the Pharisees watched him
to see whether he would cure on the sabbath, so that they might find an accusation
against him. 8 Even though he knew what they were thinking, he said to the man
who had the withered hand, "Come and stand here." He got up and stood there.
9 Then Jesus said to them, "I ask you, is it lawful to do good or to do harm on the
sabbath, to save life or to destroy it?" 10 After looking around at all of them, he said
to him, "Stretch out your hand." He did so, and his hand was restored. 11 But they
were filled with fury and discussed with one another what they might do to Jesus.

Jesus selects the twelve disciples
(48/Mark 3.13–19)

6.12 Mk 3.13-19
6.13 Mt 10.1
6.14 Jn 1.42
6.16 Acts 1.13

12 Now during those days he went out to the mountain to pray; and he spent the
night in prayer to God. 13 And when day came, he called his disciples and chose
twelve of them, whom he also named apostles: 14 Simon, whom he named Peter,
and his brother Andrew, and James, and John, and Philip, and Bartholomew, 15 and
Matthew, and Thomas, and James son of Alphaeus, and Simon, who was called the
Zealot, 16 and Judas son of James, and Judas Iscariot, who became a traitor.

Jesus gives the beatitudes
(49/Matthew 5.1–12)

6.17 Mt 4.25
6.19 Mt 14.36 Mk 5.30

17 He came down with them and stood on a level place, with a great crowd of
his disciples and a great multitude of people from all Judea, Jerusalem, and the
coast of Tyre and Sidon. 18 They had come to hear him and to be healed of their
diseases; and those who were troubled with unclean spirits were cured. 19 And all in

---

thinking you or your church has all the answers. No religious system is big enough to contain Christ completely or to fulfill perfectly all his desires for the world.

6.3–5 Each week 12 consecrated loaves of bread, representing the 12 tribes of Israel, were placed on a table in the temple. This bread was called the bread of the Presence. After its use in the temple, it was to be eaten only by priests. Jesus, accused of sabbath-breaking, referred to a well-known story about David (1 Samuel 21.1–6). Once when fleeing from Saul, he and his men ate this consecrated bread. Their need was more important than ceremonial regulations. Jesus was appealing to the same principle: human need is more important than petty laws. By comparing himself and his disciples with David and his men, he was saying, "If you condemn me, you must also condemn David."

6.5 When Jesus said he was 'lord of the sabbath,' he meant he had the authority to overrule the Pharisees' traditions and regulations because he was the Creator of the sabbath.

6.6, 7 According to the tradition of the religious leaders, no healing could be done on the sabbath. Healing, they argued, was practicing medicine, and a person could not practice his or her profession on the sabbath. It was more important for the religious leaders to protect their laws than to free a person from suffering.

6.11 Jesus' enemies were wild with rage. Not only had he read their minds; he also flouted their laws and exposed the hatred in their hearts. It is ironic that their hatred combined with their zeal for the law drove them to plot murder – clearly against the law.

6.12 The Gospel writers note that before every important event in Jesus' life, he took time to go off by himself and pray. This time he was preparing to choose his inner circle, the 12 disciples. Make sure that all your important decisions are grounded in prayer.

6.13 Jesus had many *disciples* (learners), but he chose only 12 *apostles* (messengers). The apostles were his inner circle to whom he gave special training, and he sent them out with his own authority. In the Gospels these 12 men are usually called the disciples, but in the book of Acts they are called apostles.

6.13–16 To be his disciples, Jesus selected "ordinary" men with a mixture of backgrounds and personalities. Today, God calls "ordinary" people together to build his church. Alone we may feel unqualified to serve Christ effectively, but together we make up a group strong enough to serve God in any way. Ask for patience to accept the differences in people in your church, and build on the variety of strengths represented in your group.

6.14–16 The disciples are not always listed by the same names. For example, Peter is sometimes called Simon or Cephas. Matthew is also known as Levi. Bartholomew is thought to be the same person as Nathanael (John 1.45). Judas the brother of James is also called Thaddaeus, and Simon is called both the Zealot and the Canaanite (Mark 3.18).

6.19 Once Jesus' healing power became known, crowds gathered just to touch him. For many, he had become a symbol of good fortune, a lucky charm, or a magician. Instead of desiring God's pardon and love, they only wanted physical healing or a chance to see spectacular events. Some people still see God as a cosmic magician and prayer as a way to get him to do his tricks. But God is not a magician – he is the Master. Prayer is not a way for us to control him; it is a way for us to put ourselves under his control.

the crowd were trying to touch him, for power came out from him and healed all of
them.

20 Then he looked up at his disciples and said:
"Blessed are you who are poor,
for yours is the kingdom of God.
21 "Blessed are you who are hungry now,
for you will be filled.
"Blessed are you who weep now,
for you will laugh.

22 "Blessed are you when people hate you, and when they exclude you, revile
you, and defame you[w] on account of the Son of Man. 23 Rejoice in that day and leap
for joy, for surely your reward is great in heaven; for that is what their ancestors did
to the prophets.
24 "But woe to you who are rich,
for you have received your consolation.
25 "Woe to you who are full now,
for you will be hungry.
"Woe to you who are laughing now,
for you will mourn and weep.

26 "Woe to you when all speak well of you, for that is what their ancestors did
to the false prophets.

Jesus teaches about loving enemies
(57/Matthew 5.43–48)

27 "But I say to you that listen, Love your enemies, do good to those who hate
you, 28 bless those who curse you, pray for those who abuse you. 29 If anyone
strikes you on the cheek, offer the other also; and from anyone who takes away
your coat do not withhold even your shirt. 30 Give to everyone who begs from you;
and if anyone takes away your goods, do not ask for them again. 31 Do to others as
you would have them do to you.
32 "If you love those who love you, what credit is that to you? For even sinners
love those who love them. 33 If you do good to those who do good to you, what
credit is that to you? For even sinners do the same. 34 If you lend to those from
whom you hope to receive, what credit is that to you? Even sinners lend to sinners,
to receive as much again. 35 But love your enemies, do good, and lend, expecting

6.20 Mt 5,6,7; 8.1 11.5 Jas 2.5
6.21 Isa 55.1; 61.3 1 Cor 4.11 Rev 7.14-17
6.22 Jn 9.22; 16.2 1 Pet 2.19 3.14; 4.14
6.23 Acts 5.41; 7.51 Col 1.24
6.24 Amos 6.1 Jas 5.1
6.25 Isa 65.13 Prov 14.13
6.27 Prov 25.21 Rom 12.20
6.28 Acts 7.60
6.29 1 Cor 6.7
6.30 Deut 15.7
6.31 Phil 4.8
6.35 Lev 25.35 Ps 37.26 1 Jn 3.1

w Gk *cast out your name as evil*

6.20ff This may be Luke's account of the sermon Matthew records in Matthew 5–7, or it may be that Jesus gave a similar sermon on several different occasions. Some believe that this was not one sermon, but a composite based on Jesus' customary teachings.

6.20–26 These verses are called the *beatitudes,* from the Latin word meaning "blessing." They describe what it means to be Christ's follower. They are a standard of conduct. They contrast kingdom values with worldly values, showing what Christ's followers can expect from the world and what God will give them. They contrast fake piety with true humility. And finally, they show how Old Testament expectations are fulfilled in God's kingdom.

6.21 Some believe that the hunger of which Jesus spoke is a hunger for righteousness (Matthew 5.6). Others say this is physical hunger. In any case, in a nation where riches were seen as a sign of God's favor, Jesus startled his hearers by pronouncing blessings on the hungry. In doing so, however, he was in line with an ancient tradition. The Old Testament is full of texts proclaiming God's concern for the poor. See, for example, 1 Samuel 2.5; Psalm 146.7; Isaiah 58.6, 7; and Jesus' own mother's prayer in Luke 1.53.

6.24 If you are trying to find fulfillment only through riches, wealth may be the only reward you will ever get—and it does not last. We must not seek comfort now at the expense of eternal life.

6.26 There were many false prophets in Old Testament times. They were praised by kings and crowds because their predictions—prosperity and victory in war—were exactly what the people wanted to hear. But popularity is no guarantee of truth, and human flattery does not bring God's approval. Sadness lies ahead for those who chase after the crowd's praise rather than God's truth.

6.27 The Jews despised the Romans because they oppressed God's people, but Jesus told them to love these enemies. Such words turned many away from Christ. But Jesus wasn't talking about having affection for enemies; he was talking about an act of the will. You can't "fall into" this kind of love—it takes conscious effort. Loving our enemies means acting in their best interests. We can pray for them, and we can think of ways to help them. Jesus loved the whole world, even though the world was in rebellion against God. He asks us to follow his example by loving our enemies. Grant them the same respect and rights as you desire for yourself.

6.35 Love means action. One way to put love to work is to take the initiative in meeting specific needs. This is easy to do with people who love us, people whom we trust; but love means doing this even to those who dislike us or plan to hurt us. The money we give others should be considered a gift, not a high-interest loan that will help us more than them. Give it as though you are giving to God.

nothing in return.[x] Your reward will be great, and you will be children of the Most
6.36 High; for he is kind to the ungrateful and the wicked. 36 Be merciful, just as your
Eph 5.1,2 Father is merciful.

Jesus teaches about criticizing others
(63/Matthew 7.1–6)

6.37 37 "Do not judge, and you will not be judged; do not condemn, and you will not
Jas 4.11 be condemned. Forgive, and you will be forgiven; 38 give, and it will be given to
6.38 Ps 79.12 you. A good measure, pressed down, shaken together, running over, will be put
Prov 19.17 Mk 4.24 into your lap; for the measure you give will be the measure you get back."
Jas 2.13 39 He also told them a parable: "Can a blind person guide a blind person? Will
6.39 Mt 15.14 not both fall into a pit? 40 A disciple is not above the teacher, but everyone who is
6.40 fully qualified will be like the teacher. 41 Why do you see the speck in your neigh-
Mt 10.24 Jn 13.16; 15.20 bor's[y] eye, but do not notice the log in your own eye? 42 Or how can you say to your
6.42 neighbor,[z] 'Friend,[z] let me take out the speck in your eye,' when you yourself do
Prov 18.17 not see the log in your own eye? You hypocrite, first take the log out of your own
eye, and then you will see clearly to take the speck out of your neighbor's[y] eye.

Jesus teaches about fruit in people's lives
(66/Matthew 7.15–20)

6.43 43 "No good tree bears bad fruit, nor again does a bad tree bear good fruit; 44 for
1 Tim 3.1-9 6.44 each tree is known by its own fruit. Figs are not gathered from thorns, nor are
Mt 12.33 grapes picked from a bramble bush. 45 The good person out of the good treasure of
6.45 Rom 8.5-8 the heart produces good, and the evil person out of evil treasure produces evil; for
it is out of the abundance of the heart that the mouth speaks.

Jesus teaches about those who build houses on rock and sand
(67/Matthew 7.21–29)

6.46 Mal 1.6 46 "Why do you call me 'Lord, Lord,' and do not do what I tell you? 47 I will
Mt 25.11 show you what someone is like who comes to me, hears my words, and acts on
Rom 2.13 them. 48 That one is like a man building a house, who dug deeply and laid the foun-
6.48 1 Cor 3.11 dation on rock; when a flood arose, the river burst against that house but could not
6.49 shake it, because it had been well built.[a] 49 But the one who hears and does not act
Job 8.13 is like a man who built a house on the ground without a foundation. When the river
Prov 1.29-31 2 Pet 2.20,21 burst against it, immediately it fell, and great was the ruin of that house."

[x] Other ancient authorities read *despairing of no one* [y] Gk *brother's* [z] Gk *brother* [a] Other ancient authorities read *founded upon the rock*

6.37, 38 A forgiving spirit demonstrates that a person has received God's forgiveness. Jesus' words reflect measuring grain in a basket to insure the full amount. If we are critical rather than compassionate, we will also receive criticism. If we treat others generously, graciously, and compassionately, however, these qualities will come back to us in full measure. We are to love others, not judge them.

6.39, 40 Make sure you're following the right teachers and leaders, because you will go no farther than they do. Look for leaders who will show you more about faith and whose guidance you can trust.

6.41 Jesus doesn't mean we should ignore wrongdoing, but we are not to be so worried about others' sins that we overlook our own. We often rationalize our sins by pointing out the same mistakes in others. What kinds of specks in others' eyes are the easiest for you to criticize? Remember your own "logs" when you feel like criticizing, and you may find you have less to say.

6.42 We should not be so afraid of the label *hypocrite* that we stand still in our Christian life, hiding our faith and making no attempts to grow. A person who tries to do right but often fails is not a hypocrite. Neither is a person whose actions are different from his feelings—it is often necessary and good to set aside our feelings and do what needs doing. It is not hypocrisy to be weak in faith. A hypocrite is a person who puts on religious behavior in order to gain attention, approval, acceptance, or admiration from others.

6.45 Jesus reminds us that our speech and actions reveal our real, underlying beliefs, attitudes, and motivations. The good impressions we try to make cannot last if our hearts are deceptive. What is in your heart will come out in your speech and behavior.

6.46–49 Obeying God is like building a house on a strong, solid foundation that stands firm when storms come. When life is calm, our foundations don't seem to matter. But when crises come, our foundations are tested. Be sure your life is built on the solid foundation of knowing and trusting Jesus Christ.

6.49 Why would people build a house directly on the ground? Perhaps to save time and avoid the hard work of preparing a stone foundation. Possibly the waterfront scenery is more attractive or beach houses have higher social status than cliff houses. Perhaps they are joining their friends who have already settled in sandy areas. Maybe they haven't heard about the violent storms coming, or they have discounted the reports, or for some reason they think disaster can't happen to them. Whatever their reason, sand-builders are shortsighted, and they will be sorry. When you find yourself listening but not obeying, what are your reasons?

A Roman soldier demonstrates faith
(68/Matthew 8.5–13)

7 After Jesus[b] had finished all his sayings in the hearing of the people, he en- 7.1
tered Capernaum. 2 A centurion there had a slave whom he valued highly, and Mt 8.5-13
who was ill and close to death. 3 When he heard about Jesus, he sent some Jewish
elders to him, asking him to come and heal his slave. 4 When they came to Jesus,
they appealed to him earnestly, saying, "He is worthy of having you do this for
him, 5 for he loves our people, and it is he who built our synagogue for us." 6 And 7.6-8
Jesus went with them, but when he was not far from the house, the centurion sent Ps 33.9 Lk 4.36
friends to say to him, "Lord, do not trouble yourself, for I am not worthy to have Jn 11.43
you come under my roof; 7 therefore I did not presume to come to you. But only
speak the word, and let my servant be healed. 8 For I also am a man set under
authority, with soldiers under me; and I say to one, 'Go,' and he goes, and to
another, 'Come,' and he comes, and to my slave, 'Do this,' and the slave does it."
9 When Jesus heard this he was amazed at him, and turning to the crowd that fol- 7.9
lowed him, he said, "I tell you, not even in Israel have I found such faith." 10 When Rom 3.1,2; 9.4
those who had been sent returned to the house, they found the slave in good health.

Jesus raises a widow's son from the dead
(69)

11 Soon afterwards[c] he went to a town called Nain, and his disciples and a 7.13
large crowd went with him. 12 As he approached the gate of the town, a man who Lam 3.32 Jn 11.33,35
had died was being carried out. He was his mother's only son, and she was a Heb 4.15
widow; and with her was a large crowd from the town. 13 When the Lord saw her, 7.14
he had compassion for her and said to her, "Do not weep." 14 Then he came forward Acts 9.40 Rom 4.17

[b] Gk *he* [c] Other ancient authorities read *Next day*

7.2 A *centurion* was a Roman army officer in charge of 100 men. This man came to Jesus not as a last resort or magic charm, but because he believed Jesus was sent from God. Apparently he recognized that the Jews had God's message for mankind—he had paid to build a synagogue. Thus it was natural for him to turn to Jesus in his need.

7.3 Why did the centurion send Jewish elders to Jesus instead of going himself? Well aware of the Jewish hatred for Roman soldiers, he may not have wanted to interrupt a Jewish gathering. As an army captain, he daily delegated jobs and sent groups on missions, so this was how he chose to get his message to Jesus.

7.3 Matthew 8.5 says the Roman centurion visited Jesus himself, while Luke 7.3 says he sent Jewish elders to present his request to Jesus. In dealing with the messengers, Jesus was dealing with the centurion. For his Jewish audience, Matthew emphasized the man's faith. For his Gentile audience, Luke highlighted the good relationship between the Jewish elders and the Roman army captain.

7.9 The Roman centurion didn't come to Jesus, and he didn't expect Jesus to come to him. Just as he did not need to be present to have his orders carried out, so Jesus didn't need to be present to heal. The centurion's faith was especially amazing because he was a Gentile who had not been brought up to know a loving God.

7.11–15 The widow's situation was serious. She had lost her husband, and now her only son was dead—her last means of support. The crowd of mourners would go home, and she would be left penniless and friendless. She was probably past the age of childbearing and would not marry again. Unless a relative came to her aid, her future was bleak. She would be an easy prey for swindlers, and she would likely be reduced to begging for food. In fact, as Luke repeatedly emphasizes, she was just the kind of person Jesus came to help—and help her he did. Jesus has the power to bring hope out of any tragedy.

7.11–17 This story illustrates salvation. The whole world was dead in sin (Ephesians 2.1), just as the widow's son was dead. Being dead, we could do nothing to help ourselves—we couldn't even ask for help. But God had compassion on us, and he sent Jesus to raise us to life with him (Ephesians 2.4–7). The dead boy did not earn his second chance at life, and we cannot earn our new life in Christ. But we can accept it, praise God for it, and use it to do his will.

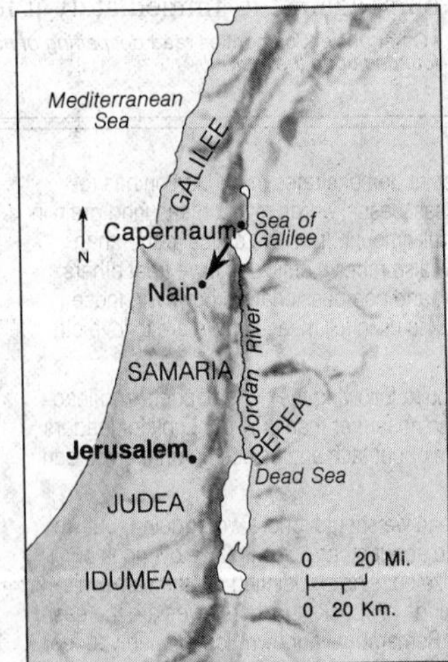

JESUS RAISES A DEAD BOY Jesus traveled to Nain, and met a funeral procession leaving the village. A widow's only son had died, leaving her virtually helpless, but Jesus brought the boy back to life. This miracle, recorded only in Luke, reveals Jesus' compassion for people's needs.

7.12 Honoring the dead was important in Jewish tradition. A funeral procession—the relatives of the dead person following the body, which was wrapped and carried on a kind of stretcher—made its way through town, and bystanders were expected to join it. In addition, hired mourners cried aloud and drew attention to the procession. The family's mourning continued for 30 days.

7.16 Lk 1.65,68 24.19 Jn 4.19; 6.14 9.17
7.17 Mt 9.26

and touched the bier, and the bearers stood still. And he said, "Young man, I say
to you, rise!" 15 The dead man sat up and began to speak, and Jesus[d] gave him to
his mother. 16 Fear seized all of them; and they glorified God, saying, "A great
prophet has risen among us!" and "God has looked favorably on his people!" 17 This
word about him spread throughout Judea and all the surrounding country.

Jesus eases John's doubt
(70/Matthew 11.1–19)

7.18 Mt 11.2-30
7.19 Ezek 21.27 Dan 9.24-26 Mic 5.2 Zech 9.9 Mal 3.1-3
7.22 Isa 29.18; 35.5 42.6; 61.1 Lk 4.18 Jas 2.5

18 The disciples of John reported all these things to him. So John summoned
two of his disciples 19 and sent them to the Lord to ask, "Are you the one who is to
come, or are we to wait for another?" 20 When the men had come to him, they said,
"John the Baptist has sent us to you to ask, 'Are you the one who is to come, or are
we to wait for another?' " 21 Jesus[e] had just then cured many people of diseases,
plagues, and evil spirits, and had given sight to many who were blind. 22 And he
answered them, "Go and tell John what you have seen and heard: the blind receive
their sight, the lame walk, the lepers[f] are cleansed, the deaf hear, the dead are
raised, the poor have good news brought to them. 23 And blessed is anyone who
takes no offense at me."

7.25 Mt 3.4 Mk 1.6
7.27 Isa 40.3 Mal 3.1; 4.5
7.29 Mt 3.5 Lk 3.12 Acts 18.25; 19.3
7.30 Acts 20.27

24 When John's messengers had gone, Jesus[d] began to speak to the crowds
about John:[g] "What did you go out into the wilderness to look at? A reed shaken
by the wind? 25 What then did you go out to see? Someone[h] dressed in soft robes?
Look, those who put on fine clothing and live in luxury are in royal palaces. 26 What
then did you go out to see? A prophet? Yes, I tell you, and more than a prophet.
27 This is the one about whom it is written,

'See, I am sending my messenger ahead of you,
who will prepare your way before you.'

28 I tell you, among those born of women no one is greater than John; yet the least
in the kingdom of God is greater than he." 29 (And all the people who heard this,
including the tax collectors, acknowledged the justice of God,[i] because they had
been baptized with John's baptism. 30 But by refusing to be baptized by him, the
Pharisees and the lawyers rejected God's purpose for themselves.)

31 "To what then will I compare the people of this generation, and what are
they like? 32 They are like children sitting in the marketplace and calling to one
another,

'We played the flute for you, and you did not dance;

[d] Gk *he* [e] Gk *He* [f] The terms *leper* and *leprosy* can refer to several diseases [g] Gk *him* [h] Or *Why then did you go out? To see someone* [i] Or *praised God*

7.16 The people thought of Jesus as a prophet because, like the Old Testament prophets, he boldly proclaimed God's message and sometimes raised the dead. Both Elijah and Elisha raised children from the dead (1 Kings 17.17–24; 2 Kings 4.18–37). The people were correct in thinking that Jesus was a prophet, but he is much more – he is God himself.

7.18–23 John was confused because the reports he received about Jesus were unexpected and incomplete. His doubts were natural, and Jesus didn't rebuke him for them. Instead, he responded in a way John would understand: he explained that he had accomplished what the Messiah was supposed to accomplish. God can handle our doubts, and he welcomes our questions. Do you have questions about Jesus – about who he is or what he expects of you? Admit them to yourself and to God, and begin looking for answers. Only as you face your doubts honestly can you begin to resolve them.

7.20–22 The proofs listed here for Jesus' being the Messiah are significant. They consist of observable deeds, not theories – actions that Jesus' contemporaries saw and reported for us to read today. The prophets had said that the Messiah would do these very acts (see Isaiah 35.5, 6; 61.1). These physical proofs helped John – and will help all of us – to recognize who Jesus is.

7.28 Of all people, no one fulfilled his God-given purpose better than John. Yet in God's kingdom, all who come after John have a greater spiritual heritage than his, because they have clearer knowledge of the purpose of Jesus' death and resurrection. John was the last of the Old Testament prophets, the last to prepare the people for the coming messianic age. Jesus was not contrasting the man John with individual Christians; he was contrasting life before Christ with life in the fullness of his kingdom.

7.29, 30 The tax collectors (who embodied evil in most people's minds) and common people heard John's message and repented. In contrast, the Pharisees and lawyers – religious leaders – rejected his words. Wanting to live their own way, they justified their own point of view and refused to listen to other ideas. Rather than trying to force your plans on God, try to discover his plan for you.

7.31–35 The religious leaders hated anyone who spoke the truth and showed up their own hypocrisy, and they did not bother to be consistent in their faultfinding. They criticized John the Baptist because he fasted and drank no wine; they criticized Jesus because he ate heartily and drank wine with publicans and sinners. Their real objection to both men, of course, had nothing to do with their dietary habits. What the Pharisees and lawyers couldn't stand was being exposed for their hypocrisy.

we wailed, and you did not weep.’
33 For John the Baptist has come eating no bread and drinking no wine, and you say, **7.33** Mt 3.4
‘He has a demon’; 34 the Son of Man has come eating and drinking, and you say, Mk 1.6 Lk 1.15
‘Look, a glutton and a drunkard, a friend of tax collectors and sinners!’ 35 Neverthe- **7.35**
less, wisdom is vindicated by all her children.” 1 Cor 1.23,24

A sinful woman anoints Jesus' feet
(72)

36 One of the Pharisees asked Jesus[j] to eat with him, and he went into the **7.36** Mt 26.6
Pharisee's house and took his place at the table. 37 And a woman in the city, who Mk 14.3
was a sinner, having learned that he was eating in the Pharisee's house, brought an Jn 11.2
alabaster jar of ointment. 38 She stood behind him at his feet, weeping, and began **7.37** Lk 8.2
to bathe his feet with her tears and to dry them with her hair. Then she continued **7.38**
kissing his feet and anointing them with the ointment. 39 Now when the Pharisee Zech 12.10
who had invited him saw it, he said to himself, “If this man were a prophet, he **7.39** Lk 15.2
would have known who and what kind of woman this is who is touching him — that Jn 7.52
she is a sinner.” 40 Jesus spoke up and said to him, “Simon, I have something to say
to you.” “Teacher,” he replied, “Speak.” 41 “A certain creditor had two debtors; **7.41** Mt 18.28
one owed five hundred denarii,[k] and the other fifty. 42 When they could not pay, he **7.42**
canceled the debts for both of them. Now which of them will love him more?” Isa 1.18; 43.25
43 Simon answered, “I suppose the one for whom he canceled the greater debt.” 44.22
And Jesus[l] said to him, “You have judged rightly.” 44 Then turning toward the **7.44** Gen 18.4
woman, he said to Simon, “Do you see this woman? I entered your house; you gave 1 Tim 5.10
me no water for my feet, but she has bathed my feet with her tears and dried them
with her hair. 45 You gave me no kiss, but from the time I came in she has not **7.45** 1 Cor 16.20
stopped kissing my feet. 46 You did not anoint my head with oil, but she has 2 Cor 13.12
anointed my feet with ointment. 47 Therefore, I tell you, her sins, which were **7.46**
many, have been forgiven; hence she has shown great love. But the one to whom 2 Sam 12.20 Ps 23.5
little is forgiven, loves little.” 48 Then he said to her, “Your sins are forgiven.” **7.49**
49 But those who were at the table with him began to say among themselves, “Who Isa 53.3
is this who even forgives sins?” 50 And he said to the woman, “Your faith has saved Mt 9.3 Mk 2.7
you; go in peace.” Jn 1.10

Women accompany Jesus and the disciples
(73)

8 Soon afterwards he went on through cities and villages, proclaiming and **8.1** Mt 4.23
bringing the good news of the kingdom of God. The twelve were with him, 2 as **8.2**
well as some women who had been cured of evil spirits and infirmities: Mary, Mk 16.9

[j] Gk *him* [k] The denarius was the usual day's wage for a laborer [l] Gk *he*

7.35 The Pharisees weren't troubled by their inconsistency toward John the Baptist and Jesus. They were good at justifying their "wisdom." Most of us can find compelling reasons to do or believe whatever suits our purposes. If we do not examine our ideas in the light of God's truth, however, we may be just as obviously self-serving as the Pharisees.

7.36 A similar incident occurred later in Jesus' ministry (see Matthew 26.6–13; Mark 14.3–9; John 12.1–11).

7.37 Alabaster jars were expensive, beautiful, carved jars containing perfume.

7.38 Although the woman was not an invited guest, she entered the house anyway and knelt behind Jesus at his feet. In Jesus' day, it was customary to recline while eating. Dinner guests lay on couches with their heads near the table, propping themselves up on one elbow and stretching their feet out behind them. The woman could easily anoint Jesus' feet without going up to the table.

7.44ff Again Luke contrasts the Pharisees with sinners — and again the sinners come out ahead. Simon had committed several social errors in neglecting to wash Jesus' feet (a courtesy extended to guests because sandaled feet got very dirty), anoint his head with oil, and offer him the kiss of greeting. Did he perhaps feel he was too good to treat Jesus as an equal? The sinful woman, by contrast, lavished tears, expensive perfume, and kisses on her Savior. In this story it is the grateful prostitute, not the stingy religious leader, whose sins are forgiven. Although it is God's grace through faith that saves us, not acts of love or generosity, this woman's act demonstrated her true faith, and Jesus honored it.

7.47 Overflowing love is the natural response to forgiveness and the consequence of faith. But only those who realize the depth of their sin can appreciate the complete forgiveness God offers them. Jesus has rescued all of his followers, whether they were once extremely wicked or conventionally good, from eternal death. Do you appreciate the wideness of his mercy? Are you grateful for his forgiveness?

7.49, 50 The Pharisees believed that only God could forgive sins, so they wondered why this man Jesus was saying the woman's sins were forgiven. They did not grasp the fact that Jesus is indeed God.

8.2, 3 Jesus raised women from degradation and servitude to fel-

8.3 Mt 14.1 called Magdalene, from whom seven demons had gone out, 3 and Joanna, the wife
of Herod's steward Chuza, and Susanna, and many others, who provided for
them[m] out of their resources.

Jesus tells the parable of the four soils
(77/Matthew 13.1–9; Mark 4.1–9)

8.4 Mt 13.1-53 Mk 4.1-34 4 When a great crowd gathered and people from town after town came to him,
he said in a parable: 5 "A sower went out to sow his seed; and as he sowed, some fell
on the path and was trampled on, and the birds of the air ate it up. 6 Some fell on the
rock; and as it grew up, it withered for lack of moisture. 7 Some fell among thorns,
and the thorns grew with it and choked it. 8 Some fell into good soil, and when it
grew, it produced a hundredfold." As he said this, he called out, "Let anyone with
ears to hear listen!"

Jesus explains the parable of the four soils
(78/Matthew 13.10–23; Mark 4.10–25)

8.10 Isa 6.9 9 Then his disciples asked him what this parable meant. 10 He said, "To you it
has been given to know the secrets[n] of the kingdom of God; but to others I speak[o]
in parables, so that

'looking they may not perceive,

[m] Other ancient authorities read *him* [n] Or *mysteries* [o] Gk lacks *I speak*

JESUS AND WOMEN

Jesus raises a widow's son from the dead	Luke 7.11–17
A sinful woman anoints Jesus' feet	Luke 7.36–50
The adulterous woman	John 8.1–11
The group of women travel with Jesus	Luke 8.1–3
Jesus visits Mary and Martha	Luke 10.38–42
Jesus heals a handicapped woman	Luke 13.10–17
Jesus heals the daughter of a Gentile woman	Mark 7.24–30
Weeping women follow Jesus on his way to the cross	Luke 23.27–31
Jesus' mother and other women gather at the cross	John 19.25–27
Jesus appears to Mary Magdalene	Mark 16.9–11
Jesus appears to other women after his resurrection	Matthew 28.8–10

As a non-Jew recording the words and works of Jesus' life, Luke demonstrates a special sensitivity to other "outsiders" with whom Jesus came into contact. For instance, Luke records five events involving women that are not mentioned in the other Gospels. In first-century Jewish culture, women were usually treated as second-class citizens and had few of the rights men had. But Jesus crossed those barriers, and Luke showed the special care Jesus had for women. Jesus treated all people with equal respect. Above are his encounters with women.

lowship and service. In Jewish culture, women were not supposed to learn from rabbis. By allowing these women to travel with him, Jesus was showing that all people are equal under God. These women supported Jesus' ministry with their own money. They owed a great debt to him, because he had cast demons out of some and had healed others.

8.2, 3 Here we catch a glimpse of a few of the people behind the scenes in Jesus' ministry. The ministry of those in the foreground is often supported by those whose work is less visible but just as essential. Offer your resources to God, whether or not you will be center stage.

8.4 Jesus often communicated spiritual truth through *parables*—short stories that take a familiar object or situation and give it a startling new twist. By linking the known with the hidden and forcing listeners to think, parables can point to spiritual truths. A parable compels listeners to discover the truth for themselves, and it conceals the truth from those too lazy or prejudiced to look for it. In reading Jesus' parables, we must be careful not to read too much into them. Most have only one point and one meaning.

8.5 Why would a farmer allow precious seed to land on the path, on rocks, or among thorns? This is not an irresponsible farmer scattering seeds at random. He is using the acceptable method of hand-seeding a large field—casting it by handfuls as he walks through the field. His goal is to get as much seed as possible to take root in good soil, but there is inevitable waste as some falls or is blown into less productive places. That some of the seed produced no crop was not the fault of the faithful farmer or of the seed. The yield depended on the condition of the soil where the seed fell. It is our responsibility to spread the seed (God's message), but we should not give up when some of our efforts fail. Remember, not every seed falls on good soil.

8.10 Why didn't the crowds understand Jesus' words? Perhaps they were looking for a military leader or political messiah and could not fit his gentle teaching style into their preconceived ideas. Perhaps they were afraid of pressure from religious leaders and did not want to look too deeply into Jesus' words. God told Isaiah that people would hear without understanding and see without perceiving (Isaiah 6.9), and this is what happened to Jesus. The parable of the soil was an accurate picture of the people's reaction to the rest of his parables.

and listening they may not understand.'
11 “Now the parable is this: The seed is the word of God. 12 The ones on the 8.11 Acts 20.27,32
path are those who have heard; then the devil comes and takes away the word from 1 Pet 1.23
their hearts, so that they may not believe and be saved. 13 The ones on the rock are 8.12 2 Cor 2.11; 4.3
those who, when they hear the word, receive it with joy. But these have no root; 2 Thess 2.10
they believe only for a while and in a time of testing fall away. 14 As for what fell Jas 1.23,24 1 Pet 5.8
among the thorns, these are the ones who hear; but as they go on their way, they are 8.14
choked by the cares and riches and pleasures of life, and their fruit does not mature. 1 Tim 6.9,10 2 Tim 4.10
15 But as for that in the good soil, these are the ones who, when they hear the word, 8.15
hold it fast in an honest and good heart, and bear fruit with patient endurance. Ps 32.2,5 Eph 2.4
16 “No one after lighting a lamp hides it under a jar, or puts it under a bed, but 2 Pet 1.5-10
puts it on a lampstand, so that those who enter may see the light. 17 For nothing is 8.16 Phil 2.15,16
hidden that will not be disclosed, nor is anything secret that will not become known
and come to light. 18 Then pay attention to how you listen; for to those who have, 8.17 Mt 10.26
more will be given; and from those who do not have, even what they seem to have 8.18 Mt 25.29
will be taken away.” Jn 15.2

Jesus describes his true family
(76/Matthew 12.46–50; Mark 3.31–35)

19 Then his mother and his brothers came to him, but they could not reach him 8.19 Mt 12.46-50
because of the crowd. 20 And he was told, “Your mother and your brothers are 13.55
standing outside, wanting to see you.” 21 But he said to them, “My mother and my Mk 3.31-35 Jn 7.5
brothers are those who hear the word of God and do it.” Acts 1.14

Jesus calms the storm
(87/Matthew 8.23–27; Mark 4.35–41)

22 One day he got into a boat with his disciples, and he said to them, “Let us go 8.22 Job 28.11; 38.11
across to the other side of the lake.” So they put out, 23 and while they were sailing Ps 29.10; 65.7
he fell asleep. A windstorm swept down on the lake, and the boat was filling with 89.9
water, and they were in danger. 24 They went to him and woke him up, shouting, Mt 8.18,23-27 Mk 4.35-41
“Master, Master, we are perishing!” And he woke up and rebuked the wind and the 8.25 Ps 33.8,9
raging waves; they ceased, and there was a calm. 25 He said to them, “Where is Mk 6.51

8.11–15 "Path" people, like many of the religious leaders, refused to believe God's message. "Rock" people, like many in the crowds who followed Jesus, believed his message but never got around to doing anything about it. "Thorn-patch" people, overcome by materialism, left no room in their lives for God. Good-soil people, in contrast to all the other groups, followed no matter what the cost. Which type of soil are you?

8.16, 17 When the light of the truth about Jesus illuminates us, it is our duty to shine that light to help others. Our witness for Christ should be public, not hidden. We should not use it for ourselves alone but for others. In order to be helpful, we need to be well placed. Seek opportunities to be there when unbelievers need help.

8.18 Applying God's Word helps us grow. This is a principle of growth in physical, mental, and spiritual life. For example, a muscle, when exercised, grows stronger, but an unused muscle grows weak and flabby. If you are not growing stronger, you are growing weaker; it is impossible for you to stand still. How are you using what God has taught you?

8.21 Jesus' true family are those who hear *and* obey his words. Hearing without obeying is not enough. As Jesus loved his mother (see John 19.25–27), so he loves us. He offers us an intimate family relationship with him.

8.23 The Sea of Galilee, actually a large lake, is still the scene of fierce storms, sometimes with waves as high as 20 feet. Jesus' disciples were not frightened without cause. Even though several of them were expert fishermen and knew how to handle a boat, their peril was real.

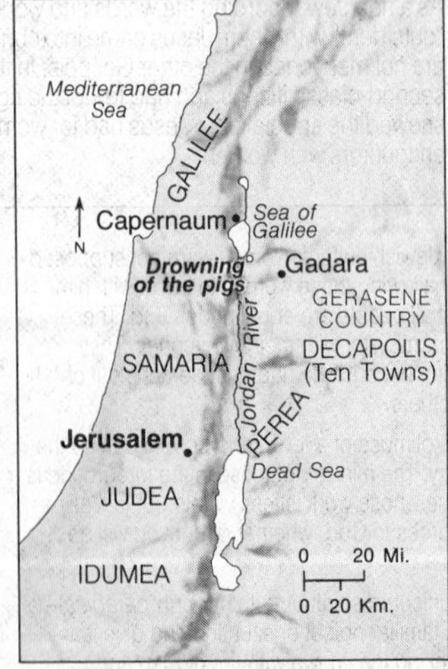

HEALING A DEMON-POSSESSED MAN
As he traveled through Galilee, Jesus gave many parables and met many people as recorded in Matthew and Mark. Later, from Capernaum, Jesus and the disciples set out in a boat, only to encounter a fierce storm. Jesus calmed the storm and, when they landed, exorcised a "legion" of demons.

8.25 When caught in the storms of life, it is easy to think God has lost control and we're at the mercy of the winds of fate. In reality, God is sovereign. Just as Jesus calmed the waves, he can calm whatever storms you may face.

your faith?" They were afraid and amazed, and said to one another, "Who then is
this, that he commands even the winds and the water, and they obey him?"

Jesus sends demons into a herd of pigs
(88/Matthew 8.28–9.1; Mark 5.1–20)

26 Then they arrived at the country of the Gerasenes,[p] which is opposite Galilee. 27 As he stepped out on land, a man of the city who had demons met him. For
a long time he had worn[q] no clothes, and he did not live in a house but in the tombs.
28 When he saw Jesus, he fell down before him and shouted at the top of his voice,
"What have you to do with me, Jesus, Son of the Most High God? I beg you, do not
torment me"— 29 for Jesus[r] had commanded the unclean spirit to come out of the
man. (For many times it had seized him; he was kept under guard and bound with
chains and shackles, but he would break the bonds and be driven by the demon into
the wilds.) 30 Jesus then asked him, "What is your name?" He said, "Legion"; for
many demons had entered him. 31 They begged him not to order them to go back
into the abyss.
32 Now there on the hillside a large herd of swine was feeding; and the demons[s] begged Jesus[t] to let them enter these. So he gave them permission. 33 Then
the demons came out of the man and entered the swine, and the herd rushed down
the steep bank into the lake and was drowned.
34 When the swineherds saw what had happened, they ran off and told it in the
city and in the country. 35 Then people came out to see what had happened, and
when they came to Jesus, they found the man from whom the demons had gone
sitting at the feet of Jesus, clothed and in his right mind. And they were afraid.
36 Those who had seen it told them how the one who had been possessed by demons
had been healed. 37 Then all the people of the surrounding country of the Gerasenes[p] asked Jesus[t] to leave them; for they were seized with great fear. So he got
into the boat and returned. 38 The man from whom the demons had gone begged
that he might be with him; but Jesus[r] sent him away, saying, 39 "Return to your
home, and declare how much God has done for you." So he went away, proclaiming throughout the city how much Jesus had done for him.

8.26 Mt 8.28-34; Mk 5.1-20
8.28 Acts 16.16,17; Phil 2.10,11
8.31 Rev 9.1; 20.3
8.32 Lev 11.7; Deut 14.8; Job 1.12; 12.16; Rev 20.7
8.35 1 Jn 3.8; Rom 16.20
8.37 1 Sam 16.4; Job 21.14; Mk 1.24; Lk 4.34; 5.8; Acts 16.39
8.38 Lk 18.43

[p] Other ancient authorities read *Gadarenes*; others, *Gergesenes* [q] Other ancient authorities read *a man of the city who had had demons for a long time met him. He wore* [r] Gk *he* [s] Gk *they* [t] Gk *him*

8.26 The Gerasene country was a Gentile region southeast of the Sea of Galilee, home of Decapolis, or the Ten Towns. These were Greek cities that belonged to no country and were self-governing. Although Jews would not have raised pigs because the Jewish religion labeled them unclean, the Gentiles had no objections to them.

8.27, 28 These demons recognized Jesus and his authority immediately. They knew who he was and what his great power could do to them. Demons, Satan's messengers, are powerful and destructive. Still active today, they attempt to distort and destroy man's relationship with God. Demons and demon possession are real. It is vital that believers recognize the power of Satan and his demons, but we shouldn't let curiosity lead us to get involved with demonic forces (Deuteronomy 18.10–12). They are defeated and powerless against those who trust in Jesus. If we resist the devil, he will leave us alone (James 4.7).

8.29–31 The demons begged Jesus to spare them from the abyss, which is also mentioned in Revelation 9.1 and 20.1–3 as the place of confinement for Satan and his messengers. They, of course, knew all about this place of confinement, and they didn't want to go there.

8.30 The demon's name was Legion. A legion was the largest unit in the Roman army, having between 3,000 and 6,000 soldiers. The man was possessed by not one, but many demons.

8.33 Why didn't Jesus just destroy these demons—or send them to the deep? Because the time for such work had not yet come. He healed many people of the destructive work of demon possession, but he did not yet destroy demons. The same question could be asked today—why doesn't Jesus stop all the evil in the world? His time for that has not yet come. But it will come. The book of Revelation portrays the future victory of Jesus over Satan, his demons, and all evil.

8.33–37 The demons destroyed the pigs and hurt the swineherds' finances, but can pigs and money compare with a human life? A man had been freed from the devils' power, but the villagers thought only about their livestock. People have always tended to value financial gain above needy people. Throughout history, most wars have been fought to protect economic interests. Much injustice and oppression, both at home and abroad, is the direct result of some individual's or company's urge to get rich. People are continually being sacrificed to money. Don't think more highly of "pigs" than of people. Think carefully about how your decisions will affect other human beings, and be willing to choose a simpler life-style if it would keep other people from being harmed.

8.38, 39 Often Jesus asked those he healed to be quiet about the healing, but he urged this man to return to his family and tell them what God had done for him. Why? (1) He knew the man would be an effective witness to those who knew his previous condition and could attest to the miraculous healing. (2) He wanted to expand his ministry by introducing his message into this Gentile area. (3) He knew that the Gentiles, since they were not expecting a Messiah, would not divert his ministry by trying to crown him king. When God touches your life, don't be afraid to share the wonderful events with your family and friends.

Jesus heals a bleeding woman and restores a girl to life
(89/Matthew 9.18–26; Mark 5.21–43)

40 Now when Jesus returned, the crowd welcomed him, for they were all waiting for him. 41 Just then there came a man named Jairus, a leader of the synagogue.
He fell at Jesus' feet and begged him to come to his house, 42 for he had an only
daughter, about twelve years old, who was dying.
As he went, the crowds pressed in on him. 43 Now there was a woman who had
been suffering from hemorrhages for twelve years; and though she had spent all she
had on physicians,[u] no one could cure her. 44 She came up behind him and touched
the fringe of his clothes, and immediately her hemorrhage stopped. 45 Then Jesus
asked, "Who touched me?" When all denied it, Peter[v] said, "Master, the crowds
surround you and press in on you." 46 But Jesus said, "Someone touched me; for I
noticed that power had gone out from me." 47 When the woman saw that she could
not remain hidden, she came trembling; and falling down before him, she declared
in the presence of all the people why she had touched him, and how she had been
immediately healed. 48 He said to her, "Daughter, your faith has made you well; go
in peace."
49 While he was still speaking, someone came from the leader's house to say,
"Your daughter is dead; do not trouble the teacher any longer." 50 When Jesus heard
this, he replied, "Do not fear. Only believe, and she will be saved." 51 When he
came to the house, he did not allow anyone to enter with him, except Peter, John,
and James, and the child's father and mother. 52 They were all weeping and wailing
for her; but he said, "Do not weep; for she is not dead but sleeping." 53 And they
laughed at him, knowing that she was dead. 54 But he took her by the hand and
called out, "Child, get up!" 55 Her spirit returned, and she got up at once. Then he
directed them to give her something to eat. 56 Her parents were astounded; but he
ordered them to tell no one what had happened.

8.40 Mt 9.1,18-26 Mk 5.21-43
8.43 Lev 15.25
8.44 Acts 5.15; 19.12
8.46 Lk 5.17; 6.19
8.50 2 Chron 20.20 Mk 9.23
8.52 Jn 11.11,13
8.54 Lk 7.14 Jn 11.43
8.55 Deut 32.39 Ps 33.9
8.56 Mt 8.4; 9.30

Jesus sends out the twelve disciples
(93/Matthew 10.1–15; Mark 6.7–13)

9 Then Jesus[w] called the twelve together and gave them power and authority
over all demons and to cure diseases, 2 and he sent them out to proclaim the
kingdom of God and to heal. 3 He said to them, "Take nothing for your journey, no

9.1 Mt 9.36–11.1
9.2 Lk 10.1,9

[u] Other ancient authorities lack *and had spent all she had on physicians* [v] Other ancient authorities add *and those who were with him* [w] Gk *he*

8.41 The synagogue was the local center of worship. The synagogue leader was responsible for administration, building maintenance, and worship supervision. It would have been quite unusual for a respected synagogue ruler to fall at the feet of an itinerant preacher and beg him to heal his daughter. Jesus honored this man's humble trust (8.50, 54–56).

8.43–48 Many people surrounded Jesus as he made his way toward Jairus's house. It was virtually impossible to get through the multitude, but one woman fought her way desperately through the crowd in order to touch Jesus. As soon as she did so, she was healed. What a difference between the crowds that are curious about Jesus and the few that reach out and touch him! Today, many people are vaguely familiar with Jesus, but nothing in their lives is changed or bettered by this slight acquaintance. It is only faith that releases God's healing power. Are you just curious about God, or do you reach out to him in faith, knowing that his mercy will bring healing to your body, soul, and spirit?

8.45 It wasn't that Jesus didn't know who had touched him, but he wanted the woman to step forward and identify herself. He wanted to teach her that his robe did not contain magical properties, but that her faith in him had healed her. He may also have wanted to teach the crowds a lesson. According to Jewish law, a man who touched a menstruating woman became ceremonially defiled (Leviticus 15.19–28). This was true whether her bleeding was normal or, as in this woman's case, the result of illness. To protect themselves from such defilement, Jewish men carefully avoided touching, speaking to, or even looking at women. By contrast, Jesus proclaimed to hundreds of people that this "unclean" woman had touched him – and then he healed her. In Jesus' mind, this suffering woman was not to be overlooked. As God's creation, she deserved attention and respect.

8.56 Jesus told the parents not to talk about their daughter's healing, because he knew the facts would speak for themselves. Besides, he was concerned for his ministry. He did not want to be known as just a miracle-worker; he wanted people to listen to his words that would heal their broken spiritual lives.

9.1–10 Note Jesus' methods of leadership. He empowered his disciples (9.1), gave them specific instructions so they knew what to do (9.3, 4), told them how to deal with tough times (9.5), and held them accountable (9.10). As you lead others, study the Master Leader's pattern. Which of these elements do you need to incorporate into your leadership?

9.2 Jesus announced his kingdom by both preaching and healing. If he had limited himself to preaching, people might have seen his kingdom as spiritual only. On the other hand, if he had healed without preaching, people might not have realized the spiritual importance of his mission. Most of his listeners expected a Messiah who would bring wealth and power to their nation; they preferred material benefits to spiritual discernment. The truth about Jesus is that he is both God and man, both spiritual and physical; and the salvation he offers is both for the soul and the body. Any group or teaching that emphasizes soul at the expense of body, or the body

9.3 Lk 10.4; 22.35
9.5 Acts 13.51
9.6 Lk 8.1

staff, nor bag, nor bread, nor money—not even an extra tunic. 4 Whatever house
you enter, stay there, and leave from there. 5 Wherever they do not welcome you,
as you are leaving that town shake the dust off your feet as a testimony against
them." 6 They departed and went through the villages, bringing the good news and
curing diseases everywhere.

Herod kills John the Baptist
(95/Matthew 14.1–12; Mark 6.14–29)

9.7 Mt 14.1-12 Mk 6.14-29
9.8 Mt 16.14
9.9 Lk 23.8

7 Now Herod the ruler[x] heard about all that had taken place, and he was perplexed, because it was said by some that John had been raised from the dead, 8 by
some that Elijah had appeared, and by others that one of the ancient prophets had
arisen. 9 Herod said, "John I beheaded; but who is this about whom I hear such
things?" And he tried to see him.

Jesus feeds five thousand
(96/Matthew 14.13–21; Mark 6.30–44; John 6.1–15)

9.10 Mt 14.13-23 Mk 6.30-46 Jn 6.1-15
9.13 Num 11.22 2 Kgs 4.42,43 Ps 78.19,20

10 On their return the apostles told Jesus[y] all they had done. He took them with
him and withdrew privately to a city called Bethsaida. 11 When the crowds found
out about it, they followed him; and he welcomed them, and spoke to them about
the kingdom of God, and healed those who needed to be cured.
12 The day was drawing to a close, and the twelve came to him and said, "Send
the crowd away, so that they may go into the surrounding villages and countryside,
to lodge and get provisions; for we are here in a deserted place." 13 But he said to
them, "You give them something to eat." They said, "We have no more than five
loaves and two fish—unless we are to go and buy food for all these people." 14 For
there were about five thousand men. And he said to his disciples, "Make them sit
down in groups of about fifty each." 15 They did so and made them all sit down.

[x] Gk *tetrarch* [y] Gk *him*

---

at the expense of soul is in danger of distorting Jesus' good news.

9.3, 4 Why were the disciples instructed to depend on others while they went from town to town preaching the gospel? Their purpose was to blanket Judea with Jesus' message, and by traveling light they could move quickly. Their dependence on others had other good effects as well: (1) it clearly showed that the Messiah had not come to offer wealth to his followers; (2) it forced the disciples to rely on God's power and not on their own provision; (3) it involved the villagers and made them more eager to hear the message. This was an excellent approach for their short-term mission; it was not intended, however, to be a permanent way of life for them.

9.4 The disciples were told to stay in only one home in each village because they were not to offend their hosts by moving to a home that was more comfortable or socially prominent. This was not a burden, because the disciples' stay in each community was short.

9.5 Shaking the dust of unaccepting towns from their feet had deep cultural implications. Pious Jews would do this after passing through Gentile cities to show their separation from Gentile practices. If the disciples shook the dust of a *Jewish* town from their feet, it would show their separation from Jews who rejected their Messiah. This action also showed that the disciples were not responsible for how the people responded to their message. Neither are we responsible if we have carefully and truthfully presented Christ and our message is rejected. Like the disciples, we must move on to others God desires to reach.

9.7 For more information on Herod, also known as Herod Antipas, see his Profile in Mark 6.

9.7, 8 It was so difficult for the people to accept Jesus as the Son of God that they tried to come up with other solutions—most of which sound quite unbelievable to us. Many thought he must be someone come back to life, perhaps John the Baptist or another prophet. Some suggested he was Elijah, the great prophet who did not die but was taken to heaven in a chariot of fire (2 Kings 2.1–11). Very few found the correct answer, as Peter did (9.20). For many people today, it is still not easy to accept Jesus as the fully human yet fully divine Son of God. People are still trying to find alternate explanations—a great prophet, a radical political leader, a self-deceived rabble-rouser. None of these explanations can account for Jesus' miracles or, especially, his glorious resurrection—so these too have to be explained away. In the end, the attempts to explain away Jesus are far more difficult to believe than the truth.

9.9 For the story of how Herod had John beheaded, see Mark 6.14–29.

9.10, 11 Jesus had tried to slip quietly away from the crowds, but they found out where he was going and followed him. Instead of showing impatience at this interruption, Jesus welcomed the people and ministered to their needs. How do you see people who interrupt your schedule—as nuisances, or as the reason for your life and ministry?

9.11 The kingdom of God was a focal point of Jesus' teaching. He explained that it was not just a future kingdom; it was among them, embodied in him, the Messiah. Even though the kingdom will not be complete until Jesus comes again in glory, we do not have to wait to taste it. The kingdom of God begins in the hearts of those who believe in Jesus. It is as present with us today as it was with the Judeans 2,000 years ago.

9.13, 14 When the disciples expressed concern about where the crowd of thousands would eat, Jesus offered a surprising solution—"You give them something to eat." They protested, focusing their attention on what they didn't have (food and money). Do you think God would ask you to do something that you and he together couldn't handle? Don't let your lack of resources blind you to seeing God's power.

16 And taking the five loaves and the two fish, he looked up to heaven, and blessed
and broke them, and gave them to the disciples to set before the crowd. 17 And all 9.17
ate and were filled. What was left over was gathered up, twelve baskets of broken Ps 145.15,16 Prov 10.22
pieces.

Peter says Jesus is the Messiah
(109/Matthew 16.13–20; Mark 8.27–30)

18 Once when Jesus[z] was praying alone, with only the disciples near him, he 9.18
asked them, "Who do the crowds say that I am?" 19 They answered, "John the Bap- Mt 16.13-20 Mk 8.27-30
tist; but others, Elijah; and still others, that one of the ancient prophets has arisen."
20 He said to them, "But who do you say that I am?" Peter answered, "The Mes- 9.20 Jn 6.69
siah[a] of God." 1 Jn 4.14,15

Jesus predicts his death the first time
(110/Matthew 16.21–28; Mark 8.31—9.1)

21 He sternly ordered and commanded them not to tell anyone, 22 saying, "The 9.22
Son of Man must undergo great suffering, and be rejected by the elders, chief Mt 16.21-28 17.22; 20.17
priests, and scribes, and be killed, and on the third day be raised." Mk 8.31—9.1,31 Lk 18.31
23 Then he said to them all, "If any want to become my followers, let them 24.6,7
deny themselves and take up their cross daily and follow me. 24 For those who want 9.23
to save their life will lose it, and those who lose their life for my sake will save it. Mt 10.38 Lk 14.27
25 What does it profit them if they gain the whole world, but lose or forfeit them- 9.24
selves? 26 Those who are ashamed of me and of my words, of them the Son of Man Mt 10.39
will be ashamed when he comes in his glory and the glory of the Father and of the 9.26 Mt 10.33
holy angels. 27 But truly I tell you, there are some standing here who will not taste 2 Tim 2.12
death before they see the kingdom of God."

[z] Gk *he* [a] Or *The Christ*

9.16, 17 Why did Jesus bother to feed these people? He could just as easily have sent them on their way. But Jesus does not ignore needs. He is concerned with every aspect of our lives—the physical as well as the spiritual. As we work to bring wholeness to people's lives, we must never ignore the fact that all of us have both physical and spiritual needs. It is impossible to minister effectively to one type of need without considering the other.

9.18–20 The Christian faith goes beyond knowing what others believe. It requires us to hold beliefs for ourselves. When Jesus asks, "Who do you say that I am?" he wants us to take a stand. Who do *you* say Jesus is?

9.21 Jesus told his disciples not to tell anyone he was the Christ, because at this point, they didn't fully understand the significance of that statement—nor would anyone else. Everyone still expected the Messiah to come as a conquering king. But Jesus, though the Messiah, still had to suffer, be rejected by the leaders, be killed, and rise from the dead. When the disciples saw all this happen to Jesus, they would understand what the Messiah came to do. Only then would they be equipped to share the gospel around the world.

9.22 This was the turning point in Jesus' instruction of his disciples. He now began teaching clearly and specifically what they could expect, so they would not need to be surprised when it happened. He explained that he would not *now* be the conquering Messiah, because he first had to suffer, die, and rise again. But one day he would return in great glory to set up his eternal kingdom.

9.23 Christians follow their Lord by imitating his life and obeying his commands. To take up the cross means to deny selfish desires to use our resources of time and money our own way, and to choose our own direction in life. Following Christ is costly now, but in the long run it is well worth the pain and effort.

9.23–26 People are willing to pay a high price for something they value. Is it any surprise that Jesus should demand this much commitment from his followers? There are at least three conditions that must be met by people who want to follow Jesus. We must be willing to deny self, to take up our crosses, and to follow him. Anything less is superficial lip service.

9.24, 25 If this present life is most important to you, you will do everything you can to protect it. You will not want to do anything that might endanger your safety, health, or comfort. By contrast, if following Jesus is most important, you may find yourself in unsafe, unhealthy, and uncomfortable places. You will risk death, but you will not fear it because of your knowledge that Jesus will raise you to eternal life. Nothing material can compensate for the loss of eternal life. Jesus' disciples are not to use their lives on earth for their own pleasure, but they should spend them serving God and people.

9.26 Luke's Greek audience would have found it difficult to understand a God who could die, just as Jesus' Jewish audience would have been perplexed by a Messiah who would let himself be captured. Both would be ashamed of Jesus if they did not look past his death to his glorious resurrection and second coming. Then they would see him not as a loser but as the Lord of the universe, who through his death brought salvation to all people.

9.27 When Jesus said some would not die without seeing the kingdom, he was referring to (1) Peter, James, and John, who would witness the transfiguration eight days later, or in a broader sense to (2) all who would witness the resurrection and ascension, or (3) all who would take part in the spread of the church after pentecost. Jesus' listeners were not going to have to wait for another, future Messiah—the kingdom was among them, and it would soon come in power.

Jesus is transfigured on the mountain
(111/Matthew 17.1–13; Mark 9.2–13)

9.29 Ex 34.29,35
9.30 2 Kgs 2.11 Rom 3.21
9.31 Rom 3.21 Col 3.4 2 Pet 1.15 1 Jn 3.2
9.32 Dan 8.18; 10.9
9.35 Ex 23.21 Deut 18.15,18 Mt 3.17 Acts 3.22 Heb 2.3 2 Pet 1.16,17

28 Now about eight days after these sayings Jesus[b] took with him Peter and
John and James, and went up on the mountain to pray. 29 And while he was praying,
the appearance of his face changed, and his clothes became dazzling white. 30 Suddenly they saw two men, Moses and Elijah, talking to him. 31 They appeared in
glory and were speaking of his departure, which he was about to accomplish at
Jerusalem. 32 Now Peter and his companions were weighed down with sleep; but
since they had stayed awake,[c] they saw his glory and the two men who stood with
him. 33 Just as they were leaving him, Peter said to Jesus, "Master, it is good for us
to be here; let us make three dwellings,[d] one for you, one for Moses, and one for
Elijah" — not knowing what he said. 34 While he was saying this, a cloud came and
overshadowed them; and they were terrified as they entered the cloud. 35 Then from
the cloud came a voice that said, "This is my Son, my Chosen;[e] listen to him!"
36 When the voice had spoken, Jesus was found alone. And they kept silent and in
those days told no one any of the things they had seen.

Jesus heals a demon-possessed boy
(112/Matthew 17.14–21; Mark 9.14–29)

9.37 Mt 17.14-21 Mk 9.14-29
9.38 Lk 7.12
9.43 Mt 17.22,23 Mk 9.30-32 2 Pet 1.16

37 On the next day, when they had come down from the mountain, a great
crowd met him. 38 Just then a man from the crowd shouted, "Teacher, I beg you to
look at my son; he is my only child. 39 Suddenly a spirit seizes him, and all at once
he[f] shrieks. It convulses him until he foams at the mouth; it mauls him and will
scarcely leave him. 40 I begged your disciples to cast it out, but they could not."
41 Jesus answered, "You faithless and perverse generation, how much longer must
I be with you and bear with you? Bring your son here." 42 While he was coming, the
demon dashed him to the ground in convulsions. But Jesus rebuked the unclean
spirit, healed the boy, and gave him back to his father. 43 And all were astounded
at the greatness of God.

Jesus predicts his death the second time
(113/Matthew 17.22, 23; Mark 9.30–32)

9.44 Mt 17.22,23
9.45 Lk 2.50; 18.34

While everyone was amazed at all that he was doing, he said to his disciples,
44 "Let these words sink into your ears: The Son of Man is going to be betrayed into
human hands." 45 But they did not understand this saying; its meaning was

[b] Gk *he* [c] Or *but when they were fully awake* [d] Or *tents* [e] Other ancient authorities read *my Beloved* [f] Or *it*

9.29, 30 Jesus took Peter, James, and John to the top of a mountain to show them who he really was – not just a great prophet, but God's own Son. Moses, representing the law, and Elijah, representing the prophets, appeared with Jesus. Then God's voice singled out Jesus as the long-awaited Messiah with divine authority. Jesus would fulfill both the law and the prophets.

9.33 When Peter suggested making three dwellings, he may have been thinking of the festival of booths, where booths were set up to commemorate the exodus, God's deliverance from slavery in Egypt. Peter wanted to keep Moses and Elijah with them. But this was not what God wanted. Peter's wish to build shelters for Jesus, Moses, and Elijah may also show he wished to build a church on three cornerstones: the law, the prophets, and Jesus. But Peter grew in his understanding, and eventually he would write of Jesus as the church's "cornerstone chosen and precious" (1 Peter 2.6).

9.33 Peter, James, and John experienced a wonderful moment on the mountain, and they didn't want to leave. Sometimes we too have such an inspiring experience that we want to stay where we are – away from the reality and problems of our daily lives. Knowing that struggles await us in the valley encourages us to linger on the mountaintop. Yet staying on top of a mountain prohibits us from ministering to others. We need times of retreat and renewal, but only so we can return to minister to the world. Our faith must make sense off the mountain as well as on it.

9.35 As God's Son, Jesus has God's power and authority; thus his words should be our final authority. Test everything you hear against Jesus' words, and you will not be led astray. Don't be hasty to seek advice and guidance from merely human sources and thereby neglect Christ's message.

9.35 God clearly identified Jesus as his Son before saying that Peter and the others were to listen to him, not to their own ideas and desires. The ability to follow Jesus comes from confidence about who he is. If we believe he is God's Son then we surely want to do what he says.

9.37–39 As the disciples came down the mountain with Jesus, they passed from a reassuring experience of God's presence to a frightening experience of evil. The beauty they had just seen made the ugliness seem even uglier. As our spiritual vision improves and allows us to see and understand God better, we will also be able to see and understand evil better. We would be overcome by its horror if we did not have Jesus with us to take us through it safely.

9.40 Why couldn't the disciples cast out the evil spirit? For a possible answer, see the note on Mark 9.18.

9.45, 46 The disciples didn't understand Jesus' words about his death. They still thought of Jesus as only an earthly king, and they were concerned about their places in the kingdom he would set up. So they ignored his words about his death and began arguing about who would be greatest.

concealed from them, so that they could not perceive it. And they were afraid to ask
him about this saying.

The disciples argue about who would be the greatest
(115/Matthew 18.1–6; Mark 9.33–37)

46 An argument arose among them as to which one of them was the greatest.
47 But Jesus, aware of their inner thoughts, took a little child and put it by his side,
48 and said to them, "Whoever welcomes this child in my name welcomes me, and
whoever welcomes me welcomes the one who sent me; for the least among all of
you is the greatest."

9.47 Mt 9.4 Jn 2.24,25
9.48 Mt 10.40 23.11,12 Lk 18.17; 22.26

The disciples forbid another from using Jesus' name
(116/Mark 9.38–41)

49 John answered, "Master, we saw someone casting out demons in your
name, and we tried to stop him, because he does not follow with us." 50 But Jesus
said to him, "Do not stop him; for whoever is not against you is for you."

9.49 Num 11.28 Mk 9.38-42

2. Jesus' ministry on the way to Jerusalem

Jesus teaches about the cost of following him
(122/Matthew 8.18–22)

51 When the days drew near for him to be taken up, he set his face to go to
Jerusalem. 52 And he sent messengers ahead of him. On their way they entered a
village of the Samaritans to make ready for him; 53 but they did not receive him,
because his face was set toward Jerusalem. 54 When his disciples James and John
saw it, they said, "Lord, do you want us to command fire to come down from
heaven and consume them?"[g] 55 But he turned and rebuked them. 56 Then[h] they
went on to another village.
57 As they were going along the road, someone said to him, "I will follow you
wherever you go." 58 And Jesus said to him, "Foxes have holes, and birds of the air
have nests; but the Son of Man has nowhere to lay his head." 59 To another he said,
"Follow me." But he said, "Lord, first let me go and bury my father." 60 But Jesus[i]
said to him, "Let the dead bury their own dead; but as for you, go and proclaim the
kingdom of God." 61 Another said, "I will follow you, Lord; but let me first say
farewell to those at my home." 62 Jesus said to him, "No one who puts a hand to the
plow and looks back is fit for the kingdom of God."

9.51 Mt 19.1,2 8.18-22 Mk 10.1; 16.19 Lk 13.22; 17.11 18.31 19.28; 24.51 Acts 1.2
9.54 2 Kgs 1.10,12
9.55 Rom 10.2
9.60 Mt 4.23
9.61 1 Kgs 19.20
9.62 Phil 3.13 Heb 6.4

[g] Other ancient authorities add *as Elijah did* [h] Other ancient authorities read *rebuked them, and said, "You do not know what spirit you are of, 56 for the Son of Man has not come to destroy the lives of human beings but to save them." Then* [i] Gk *he*

9.48 Our care for others is a measure of our greatness. How much concern do you show to others? This is a vital question that can accurately measure your greatness in God's eyes. How have you expressed your care for others lately, especially the helpless, the needy, the poor—those who can't return your love and concern? Your honest answer to that question will give you a good idea of your real greatness.

9.49, 50 The disciples were jealous. Nine of them together were unable to cast out a single evil spirit (9.40), but when they saw a man who was not one of their group casting out demons, they told him to stop. Our pride is hurt when someone else succeeds where we have failed, but Jesus says there is no room for such jealousy in the spiritual warfare of his kingdom. Share Jesus' open-arms attitude to Christian workers outside your group.

9.51 Although Jesus knew he would face persecution and death in Jerusalem, he was determined to go there. That kind of resolve should characterize our lives too. When God gives us a course of action, we must move steadily toward our destination, no matter what potential hazards await us there.

9.53 After Assyria invaded Israel, the northern kingdom, and resettled it with its own people (2 Kings 17.24–41), the mixed race that developed became known as the Samaritans. "Purebred" Jews hated these "half-breeds," and the Samaritans in turn hated the Jews. So many tensions arose between the two peoples that Jewish travelers between Galilee and southern Judea often walked around rather than through Samaritan territory, even though this lengthened their trip considerably. Jesus held no such prejudices, and he sent messengers ahead to get rooms in a Samaritan village. But the village refused to welcome these Jewish travelers.

9.54 When James and John were rejected by the Samaritan village, they didn't want to stop at shaking the dust from their feet (9.5). They wanted to retaliate by calling down fire from heaven on them, as Elijah did upon the servants of a wicked king of Israel (2 Kings 1). When others reject or scorn us, we too may feel like retaliating. We must remember that judgment belongs to God, and we must not expect him to use his power to carry out our personal vendettas.

9.62 What does Jesus want from us? Total dedication, not half-hearted commitment. We can't pick and choose among Jesus' ideas and follow him selectively; we have to accept the cross along with the crown, judgment as well as mercy. We must count the cost and be willing to abandon everything else that has given us security. With our focus on Jesus, we should allow nothing to distract us from the manner of living that he calls good and true.

Jesus sends out seventy messengers
(130)

10.2 Jer 3.15 Jn 4.35 1 Cor 12.28 2 Thess 3.1
10.3 Mt 10.16

10 After this the Lord appointed seventy[j] others and sent them on ahead of him
in pairs to every town and place where he himself intended to go. [2]He said
to them, "The harvest is plentiful, but the laborers are few; therefore ask the Lord
of the harvest to send out laborers into his harvest. [3]Go on your way. See, I am
sending you out like lambs into the midst of wolves. [4]Carry no purse, no bag, no

j Other ancient authorities read *seventy-two*

JAMES

Jesus singled out three of his 12 disciples for special training. James, his brother John, and Peter made up this inner circle. Each eventually played a key role in the early church. Peter became a great speaker, John became a major writer, and James was the first of the 12 disciples to die for the faith.

The fact that his name is always mentioned before John's indicates that James was the older brother. Zebedee, their father, owned a fishing business where they worked along with Peter and Andrew. When Peter, Andrew, and John left Galilee to see John the Baptist, James stayed back with the boats and fishing nets. Later, when Jesus called them, he was as eager as his partners to follow.

James enjoyed being in the inner circle of Jesus' disciples, but he misunderstood Jesus' purpose. He and his brother even tried to secure their role in Jesus' kingdom by asking Jesus to promise them each a special position. Like the other disciples, James had a limited view of what Jesus was doing on earth, picturing only an earthly kingdom that would overthrow Rome and restore Israel's former glory. But above all, James wanted to be with Jesus. He had found the right leader, even though he was still on the wrong timetable. It took Jesus' death and resurrection to correct his view.

James was the first of the 12 disciples to die for the gospel. He was willing to die because he knew Jesus had conquered death, the doorway to eternal life. Our expectations about life will be limited if this life is all we can see. Jesus promised eternal life to those willing to trust him. If we believe this promise, he will give us the courage to stand for him even during dangerous times.

Strengths and accomplishments:
- One of the 12 disciples
- One of a special inner circle of three with Peter and John
- First of the 12 disciples to be killed for his faith

Weaknesses and mistakes:
- Two outbursts from James indicate struggles with temper (Luke 9.54) and selfishness (Mark 10.37). Both times, he and his brother, John, spoke as one

Lesson from his life:
- Loss of life is not too heavy a price to pay for following Jesus

Vital statistics:
- Where: Galilee
- Occupation: Fisherman, disciple
- Relatives: Father: Zebedee. Mother: Salome. Brother: John
- Contemporaries: Jesus, Pilate, Herod Agrippa

Key verses:
"James and John, the sons of Zebedee, came forward to him and said to him, 'Teacher, we want you to do for us whatever we ask of you.' And he said to them, 'What is it you want me to do for you?' And they said to him, 'Grant us to sit, one at your right hand and one at your left, in your glory.' " (Mark 10.35–37).

James' story is told in the Gospels. He is also mentioned in Acts 1.13 and 12.2.

10.1, 2 Far more than 12 people had been following Jesus. Now he designated a group of 70 to prepare a number of towns that he would visit later. These disciples were not unique in their qualifications. They were not better educated, more capable, or of higher status than other followers of Jesus. What equipped them for this mission was their awareness of Jesus' power and their vision to reach all the people. It is important to dedicate our skills to God's kingdom, but we must also be equipped with his power and have a clear vision of what he wants us to do.

10.2 Jesus was sending out 35 teams of two to reach the multitudes. They were not to try to do the job without help; rather, they were to ask God for more workers. Some people, as soon as they understand the gospel, want to go to work immediately contacting unsaved people. This story suggests a different approach: begin by mobilizing people to pray. And before praying for the unsaved people, pray that other concerned disciples will join you in reaching out to them.

10.2 In Christian service, there is no unemployment. God has work enough for everyone. Don't just sit back and watch the others work—look for ways to help with the harvest.

10.3 Jesus said he was sending his disciples out "like lambs into the midst of wolves." They would have to be careful, because they would surely meet with opposition. We too are sent into the world as lambs among wolves. Be alert, and remember to face your enemies not with aggression but with love and gentleness. A dangerous mission requires sincere commitment.

sandals; and greet no one on the road. 5 Whatever house you enter, first say, 'Peace
to this house!' 6 And if anyone is there who shares in peace, your peace will rest on
that person; but if not, it will return to you. 7 Remain in the same house, eating and
drinking whatever they provide, for the laborer deserves to be paid. Do not move
about from house to house. 8 Whenever you enter a town and its people welcome
you, eat what is set before you; 9 cure the sick who are there, and say to them, 'The
kingdom of God has come near to you.'[k] 10 But whenever you enter a town and
they do not welcome you, go out into its streets and say, 11 'Even the dust of your
town that clings to our feet, we wipe off in protest against you. Yet know this: the
kingdom of God has come near.'[l] 12 I tell you, on that day it will be more tolerable
for Sodom than for that town.

13 "Woe to you, Chorazin! Woe to you, Bethsaida! For if the deeds of power
done in you had been done in Tyre and Sidon, they would have repented long ago,
sitting in sackcloth and ashes. 14 But at the judgment it will be more tolerable for
Tyre and Sidon than for you. 15 And you, Capernaum,
will you be exalted to heaven?
No, you will be brought down to Hades.

16 "Whoever listens to you listens to me, and whoever rejects you rejects me,
and whoever rejects me rejects the one who sent me."

The seventy messengers return
(131)

17 The seventy[m] returned with joy, saying, "Lord, in your name even the demons submit to us!" 18 He said to them, "I watched Satan fall from heaven like a
flash of lightning. 19 See, I have given you authority to tread on snakes and scorpions, and over all the power of the enemy; and nothing will hurt you. 20 Nevertheless, do not rejoice at this, that the spirits submit to you, but rejoice that your names
are written in heaven."

21 At that same hour Jesus[n] rejoiced in the Holy Spirit[o] and said, "I thank[p]

10.5 Mt 10.12
10.7 Mt 10.10,11; 1 Cor 9.4; 10.27; Eph 5.15; 1 Tim 5.18
10.9 Isa 2.2; Mt 3.2; 10.7; Lk 9.2
10.12 Mt 10.15
10.13 Ezek 3.6; Mt 11.21; Jn 3.5
10.15 Gen 11.4; Deut 1.28; Isa 14.13; Jer 51.53; Ezek 26.20
10.16 Mt 10.40; Jn 5.23; 13.20; 1 Thess 4.8
10.18 Jn 12.31; 1 Jn 3.8; Rev 9.1; 12.8,9
10.19 Acts 28.5
10.21 Mt 11.25; 1 Cor 1.19; 2 Cor 2.6

[k] Or *is at hand for you* [l] Or *is at hand* [m] Other ancient authorities read *seventy-two* [n] Gk *he* [o] Other authorities read *in the spirit* [p] Or *praise*

10.7 Jesus' direction to stay in one house avoided certain problems. Shifting from house to house could offend the families who first took them in. Some families might begin to compete for the disciples' presence, and some might think they weren't good enough to hear their message. If the disciples appeared not to appreciate the hospitality offered them, the village might not accept Jesus when he followed them there. In addition, by staying in one place the disciples did not have to worry continually about getting good accommodations. They could settle down and do their appointed task.

10.7 Jesus told his disciples to accept hospitality graciously, because their work entitled them to it. Ministers of the gospel deserve to be supported, and it is our responsibility to make sure they have what they need. There are several ways to support the efforts of those who serve God in his church. First, see that they have an adequate salary. Second, see that they are supported emotionally; plan a time to express appreciation for something they have done. Third, lift their spirits with encouraging surprises from time to time. Our ministers deserve to know we are giving to them cheerfully and generously.

10.8, 9 Jesus gave two rules for the disciples to follow as they traveled. They were to eat what was put before them—that is, they were to accept hospitality without being picky—and they were to heal the sick. Because of the healings, people would be willing to listen to the gospel.

10.12 Sodom was an evil city that God destroyed because of its great sinfulness (Genesis 19). The city's name is often used to symbolize wickedness and immorality. Sodom will suffer at judgment day, but cities who saw the Messiah and rejected him will suffer even more.

10.13 Tyre and Sidon were cities destroyed by God as punishment for their wickedness (see Ezekiel 26–28).

10.15 Capernaum was Jesus' base for his Galilean ministry. The city was located at an important crossroads used by traders and the Roman army, and a message proclaimed in Capernaum was likely to go far. But many people of Capernaum did not understand Jesus' miracles or believe his teaching, and the city was included among those who would be judged for rejecting him.

10.17–20 The disciples had seen tremendous results as they ministered in Jesus' name and with his authority. They were elated by the victories they had witnessed, and Jesus shared their enthusiasm. He brought them down to earth, however, by reminding them of their most important victory—that their names were registered in heaven. This honor was more important than any of their accomplishments. As we see God's wonders at work in and through us, we should not lose sight of the greatest wonder of all—our heavenly citizenship.

10.18 Jesus may have been looking ahead to his victory over Satan at the cross. John 12.31, 32 indicates that Satan would be judged and cast out at the time of Jesus' death. On the other hand, Jesus may have been warning his disciples against pride. Perhaps he was referring to Isaiah 14.12–17, which begins, "How you are fallen from heaven, O Day Star, son of Dawn!" Many interpreters identify this with Satan and explain that his pride led to all the evil we see on earth today. To his disciples, who were thrilled with their power over evil spirits, Jesus gave this stern warning: "Yours is the kind of pride that led to Satan's downfall. Be careful!"

10.21 Jesus thanked God that spiritual truth was for everyone, not just the elite. Many of life's rewards seem to go to the intelligent, the rich, the good-looking, or the powerful, but the kingdom of God

you, Father, Lord of heaven and earth, because you have hidden these things from
the wise and the intelligent and have revealed them to infants; yes, Father, for such
10.22 was your gracious will.[q] 22 All things have been handed over to me by my Father;
Mt 28.18 Jn 1.18; 3.35 and no one knows who the Son is except the Father, or who the Father is except the
5.27; 17.2 Son and anyone to whom the Son chooses to reveal him."
10.23 Mt 13.16 23 Then turning to the disciples, Jesus[r] said to them privately, "Blessed are the
10.24 eyes that see what you see! 24 For I tell you that many prophets and kings desired to
1 Pet 1.10 see what you see, but did not see it, and to hear what you hear, but did not hear it."

Jesus tells the parable of the good Samaritan (132)

10.25 Mt 22.34-40 25 Just then a lawyer stood up to test Jesus.[s] "Teacher," he said, "what must I
Mk 12.28-31 do to inherit eternal life?" 26 He said to him, "What is written in the law? What do
10.27 Deut 6.5 you read there?" 27 He answered, "You shall love the Lord your God with all your
Lev 19.18 heart, and with all your soul, and with all your strength, and with all your mind; and
10.28 Lev 18.5 your neighbor as yourself." 28 And he said to him, "You have given the right an-
Neh 9.29 swer; do this, and you will live."
Ezek 20.11 29 But wanting to justify himself, he asked Jesus, "And who is my neighbor?"
Rom 10.5 10.29 30 Jesus replied, "A man was going down from Jerusalem to Jericho, and fell into
Lk 16.15 the hands of robbers, who stripped him, beat him, and went away, leaving him half
10.31 dead. 31 Now by chance a priest was going down that road; and when he saw him,
Ps 38.11 he passed by on the other side. 32 So likewise a Levite, when he came to the place

[q] Or *for so it was well-pleasing in your sight* [r] Gk *he* [s] Gk *him*

A COLLECTION OF ATTITUDES

To the lawyer, the wounded man was a subject to discuss.

To the thieves, the wounded man was someone to use and exploit.

To the religious men, the wounded man was a problem to be avoided.

To the innkeeper, the wounded man was a customer to serve for a fee.

To the Samaritan, the wounded man was a human being worth being cared for and loved.

To Jesus, all of them and all of us were worth dying for.

The needs of others bring out various attitudes in us. Jesus used the story of the good but despised Samaritan to make clear what attitude was acceptable to him. If we are honest, we often will find ourselves in the place of the lawyer, needing to learn again who our neighbor is. Note these different attitudes toward the wounded man.

---

is equally available to all, regardless of position or abilities. We come to Jesus not through strength or brains, but through childlike trust. Jesus is not opposed to engaging in scholarly pursuits; he is opposed to spiritual pride (being wise in one's own eyes). Join Jesus in thanking God that we all have equal access to him. Trust in God's grace, not in your personal qualifications, for your citizenship in the kingdom.

10.22 Christ's mission was to reveal God the Father to people. His Word brought difficult ideas down to earth. He explained God's love through parables, teachings, and most of all his life. By examining Jesus' actions, principles, and attitudes we can understand God more clearly.

10.23, 24 The disciples had a fantastic opportunity – they were eyewitnesses to Christ, the Son of God. But for many months they took Jesus for granted, not really listening to him or obeying him. We also have a privileged position, with knowledge of 2,000 years of church history, availability of the Bible in hundreds of languages and translations, and access to many excellent pastors and speakers. Yet how often we take these for granted. Remember, with privilege comes responsibility. Because we are privileged to know so much about Christ, we must be careful to follow him.

10.24 Old Testament men of God such as David and the prophet Isaiah made many God-inspired predictions that Jesus fulfilled. As Peter later wrote, they wondered what their words meant and when they would be fulfilled (1 Peter 1.10–13). In Jesus' words, they "desired to see what you see" – the coming of God's kingdom.

10.27 This lawyer, or expert in Moses' law, was quoting Deuteronomy 6.5 and Leviticus 19.18. Jesus talked more about these laws elsewhere (see Matthew 19.16–22 and Mark 10.17–22).

10.27–37 The lawyer treated the wounded man as a topic for discussion; the thieves, as an object to exploit; the priest, as a problem to avoid; and the Levite, as an object of curiosity. Only the Samaritan treated him as a person to love.

10.27–37 From the parable we learn three principles about loving our neighbor: (1) lack of love is often easy to justify, even though it is never right; (2) our neighbor is anyone of any race or creed or social background who is in need; and (3) love means acting to meet the need. Wherever you live, there are needy people close by. There is no good rationale for refusing to help.

and saw him, passed by on the other side. 33 But a Samaritan while traveling came 10.33 Jn 4.9
near him; and when he saw him, he was moved with pity. 34 He went to him and
bandaged his wounds, having poured oil and wine on them. Then he put him on his
own animal, brought him to an inn, and took care of him. 35 The next day he took 10.35 Philem 18
out two denarii,[t] gave them to the innkeeper, and said, 'Take care of him; and
when I come back, I will repay you whatever more you spend.' 36 Which of these
three, do you think, was a neighbor to the man who fell into the hands of the robbers?" 37 He said, "The one who showed him mercy." Jesus said to him, "Go and
do likewise."

Jesus visits Mary and Martha
(133)

38 Now as they went on their way, he entered a certain village, where a woman 10.38 Jn 11.1,5,19,30, 39; 12.2
named Martha welcomed him into her home. 39 She had a sister named Mary, who
sat at the Lord's feet and listened to what he was saying. 40 But Martha was distracted by her many tasks; so she came to him and asked, "Lord, do you not care
that my sister has left me to do all the work by myself? Tell her then to help me."
41 But the Lord answered her, "Martha, Martha, you are worried and distracted by 10.41 Mt 6.25
many things; 42 there is need of only one thing.[u] Mary has chosen the better part, 10.42 Ps 27.4 Phil 3.13,14
which will not be taken away from her."

Jesus teaches his disciples about prayer
(134)

11 He was praying in a certain place, and after he had finished, one of his disci- 11.1 2 Cor 3.5
ples said to him, "Lord, teach us to pray, as John taught his disciples." 2 He 11.2 Isa 11.9; 63.16 Dan 7.14
said to them, "When you pray, say:
"Father,[v] hallowed be your name.
Your kingdom come.[w] 11.4 Eph 4.32 1 Cor 10.13 Jas 1.13 Rev 3.10
3 Give us each day our daily bread.[x]
4 And forgive us our sins,

[t] The denarius was the usual day's wage for a laborer [u] Other ancient authorities read *few things are necessary, or only one* [v] Other ancient authorities read *Our Father in heaven* [w] A few ancient authorities read *Your Holy Spirit come upon us and cleanse us.* Other ancient authorities add *Your will be done, on earth as in heaven* [x] Or *our bread for tomorrow*

10.33 There was deep hatred between Jews and Samaritans. The Jews saw themselves as pure descendants of Abraham, while the Samaritans were a mixed race produced when Jews from the northern kingdom intermarried with other peoples after Israel's exile. To this lawyer, the person least likely to act correctly would be the Samaritan. In fact, he could not bear to say "Samaritan" in answer to Jesus' question. The lawyer's attitude betrayed his lack of love, which he had earlier said the law commanded.

10.38–42 Mary and Martha both loved Jesus. On this occasion they were both serving him. But Martha thought Mary's style of serving was inferior to hers. She didn't realize that in her desire to serve, she was actually neglecting her guest. Are you so busy doing things *for* Jesus that you're not spending any time *with* him? Don't let your service become self-serving.

10.41, 42 Jesus did not blame Martha for being concerned about household chores. He was only asking her to set priorities. It is possible for service to Christ to degenerate into mere busywork that is no longer full of devotion to God.

11.1–4 Notice the order in this prayer. First Jesus praised God; then he made his requests. Praising God first puts us in the right frame of mind to tell him about our needs. Too often our prayers are more like shopping lists than conversations.

11.2–13 These verses focus on three aspects of prayer: its content (11.2–4), our persistence (11.5–10), and God's faithfulness (11.11–13).

11.3 God's provision is daily, not all at once. We cannot store it up and then cut off communication with God. And we dare not be self-satisfied. If you are running low on strength, ask yourself—how long have I been away from the Source?

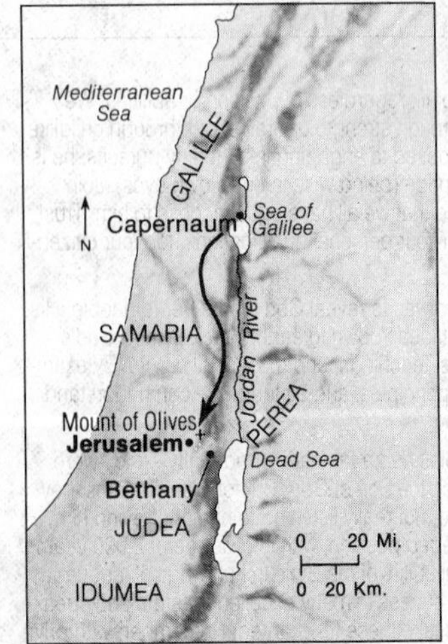

JESUS VISITS MARY AND MARTHA
Jesus, after teaching throughout Galilee, returned to Jerusalem for the Feast of Tabernacles (John 7.2). He spoke in Jerusalem and then visited his friends Mary and Martha in the tiny village of Bethany on the slope of the Mount of Olives.

11.4 When Jesus taught his disciples to pray, he made forgive-

for we ourselves forgive everyone indebted to us.
And do not bring us to the time of trial."[y]
5 And he said to them, "Suppose one of you has a friend, and you go to him at
midnight and say to him, 'Friend, lend me three loaves of bread; [6]for a friend of
mine has arrived, and I have nothing to set before him.' [7]And he answers from
11.8 within, 'Do not bother me; the door has already been locked, and my children are
Lk 18.1 with me in bed; I cannot get up and give you anything.' [8]I tell you, even though he

[y] Or *us into temptation.* Other ancient authorities add *but rescue us from the evil one* (or *from evil*)

MARTHA

Many older brothers and sisters have an irritating tendency to take charge, a habit developed while growing up. We can easily see this pattern in Martha, the older sister of Mary and Lazarus. She was used to being in control.

The fact that Martha, Mary, and Lazarus are remembered for their hospitality takes on added significance when we note that hospitality was a social requirement in their culture. It was considered shameful to turn anyone away from your door. Apparently Martha's family met this requirement very well.

Martha worried about details. She wished to please, to serve, to do the right thing—but she often succeeded in making everyone around her uncomfortable. Perhaps as the oldest she feared shame if her home did not measure up to expectations. She tried to do everything she could to make sure that wouldn't happen. As a result, she found it hard to relax and enjoy her guests, and even harder to accept Mary's lack of cooperation in all the preparations. Martha's frustration was so intense that she finally asked Jesus to settle the matter. He gently corrected her attitude and showed her that her priorities, though good, were not the best. The personal attention she gave her guests should be more important than the comforts she tried to provide for them.

Later, following her brother Lazarus's death, Martha could hardly help being herself. When she heard Jesus was finally coming, she rushed out to meet him and expressed her inward conflict of disappointment and hope. Jesus pointed out that her hope was too limited. He was not only Lord beyond death, he was Lord over death—the resurrection and the life! Moments later, Martha again spoke without thinking, pointing out that four-day-old corpses are well on their way to decomposition. Her awareness of details sometimes kept her from seeing the whole picture, but Jesus was consistently patient with her.

In our last picture of Martha, she is once again serving a meal to Jesus and his disciples. She has not stopped serving. But the Bible records her silence this time. She has begun to learn what her younger sister already knew, that worship begins with silence and listening.

Strengths and accomplishments:
- Known as a hospitable homeowner
- Believed in Jesus with growing faith
- Had a strong desire to do everything exactly right

Weaknesses and mistakes:
- Expected others to agree with her priorities
- Was overly concerned with details
- Tended to feel sorry for herself when her efforts were not recognized
- Limited Jesus' power to this life

Lessons from her life:
- Getting caught up in details can make us forget the main reasons for our actions
- There is a proper time to listen to Jesus and a proper time to work for him

Vital statistics:
- Where: Bethany
- Relatives: Sister: Mary. Brother: Lazarus

Key verse:
"But Martha was distracted by her many tasks; so she came to him and asked, 'Lord, do you not care that my sister has left me to do all the work by myself? Tell her then to help me'" (Luke 10.40).

Martha's story is told in Luke 10.38–42 and John 11.17–45.

ness the cornerstone of their relationship with God. God has forgiven our sins; we must now forgive those who have wronged us. To remain unforgiving shows we have not understood that we ourselves deeply need to be forgiven. Think of some people who have wronged you. Have you forgiven them? How will God deal with you if he treats you as you treat others?

11.8 Persistence in prayer overcomes our insensitivity, not God's. It does more to change our hearts and minds than his, helping us understand and express the intensity of our need. Persistence in prayer helps us recognize God's work.

will not get up and give him anything because he is his friend, at least because of
his persistence he will get up and give him whatever he needs.
9 "So I say to you, Ask, and it will be given you; search, and you will find;
knock, and the door will be opened for you. 10 For everyone who asks receives, and
everyone who searches finds, and for everyone who knocks, the door will be
opened. 11 Is there anyone among you who, if your child asks for[z] a fish, will give
a snake instead of a fish? 12 Or if the child asks for an egg, will give a scorpion? 13 If
you then, who are evil, know how to give good gifts to your children, how much
more will the heavenly Father give the Holy Spirit[a] to those who ask him!"

11.9 Mt 7.7; 21.22 Mk 11.24 Jn 15.7 Jas 1.6 1 Jn 3.22; 5.14
11.11 Mt 7.9
11.13 Isa 44.3 Jas 1.15

Jesus answers hostile accusations
(135)

14 Now he was casting out a demon that was mute; when the demon had gone
out, the one who had been mute spoke, and the crowds were amazed. 15 But some
of them said, "He casts out demons by Beelzebul, the ruler of the demons." 16 Others, to test him, kept demanding from him a sign from heaven. 17 But he knew what
they were thinking and said to them, "Every kingdom divided against itself becomes a desert, and house falls on house. 18 If Satan also is divided against himself,
how will his kingdom stand? — for you say that I cast out the demons by Beelzebul.
19 Now if I cast out the demons by Beelzebul, by whom do your exorcists[b] cast
them out? Therefore they will be your judges. 20 But if it is by the finger of God that
I cast out the demons, then the kingdom of God has come to you. 21 When a strong
man, fully armed, guards his castle, his property is safe. 22 But when one stronger
than he attacks him and overpowers him, he takes away his armor in which he
trusted and divides his plunder. 23 Whoever is not with me is against me, and whoever does not gather with me scatters.
24 "When the unclean spirit has gone out of a person, it wanders through waterless regions looking for a resting place, but not finding any, it says, 'I will return
to my house from which I came.' 25 When it comes, it finds it swept and put in
order. 26 Then it goes and brings seven other spirits more evil than itself, and they
enter and live there; and the last state of that person is worse than the first."
27 While he was saying this, a woman in the crowd raised her voice and said to

11.14 Mt 9.32 12.22-32,38-45 Mk 3.22-30
11.15 Mt 9.34
11.16 Mt 16.1
11.17 Jn 2.25 Rev 2.23
11.19 Mk 9.38
11.20 Ex 8.19 Jn 3.2 Acts 2.22; 10.38
11.21 Eph 2.2; 6.12 1 Pet 5.8
11.22 Isa 53.12 Col 2.15 Heb 7.25
11.26 Jn 5.14 Heb 6.4; 10.26 2 Pet 2.20
11.27 Lk 1.28,48

[z] Other ancient authorities add *bread, will give a stone; or if your child asks for* [a] Other ancient authorities read *the Father give the Holy Spirit from heaven* [b] Gk *sons*

11.13 Even though good fathers make mistakes, they treat their children well. How much better our perfect heavenly Father treats his children! The most important gift he ever gives us is the Holy Spirit (Acts 2.1–4), whom he promised to give all believers after his death, resurrection, and return to heaven (John 15.26).

11.14–23 A similar but separate event is reported in Matthew 12.22–45 and Mark 3.20–30. The event described by Luke happened in Judea while the other two took place in Galilee. According to Luke, Jesus spoke to the crowds; in Matthew and Mark he accused the Pharisees.

11.15–20 There are two common interpretations of these verses: (1) Some of the Pharisees' followers cast out demons. If this was so, the Pharisees' accusations were becoming more desperate. To accuse Jesus of being empowered by Beelzebul, the prince of demons (or Satan himself), because he was casting out demons was also to say their own people were doing Satan's work. Jesus turned the leaders' accusation against them. (2) Another possibility is that the Pharisees' followers were *not* casting out demons; and if they tried, they did not succeed. Jesus first dismisses their claim as absurd (Why would the devil cast out his own demons?). Then he engages in a little irony ("By whom do your exorcists cast them out?"). Finally he concludes that his work of casting out demons proves that the kingdom of God has arrived.

Satan, who had controlled the kingdom of this world for thousands of years, was now being controlled and defeated by Jesus and the kingdom of heaven. Jesus' kingdom began to come into power at his birth, grew as he resisted the wilderness temptations, established itself through his teachings and healings, blossomed in victory at his resurrection and at Pentecost, and will become permanent and universal at his second coming. Though these two interpretations differ, they arrive at the same conclusion – the kingdom of God has arrived with the coming of Jesus Christ.

11.21, 22 Jesus may have been referring to Isaiah 49.24–26. Regardless of how great Satan's power is, Jesus is stronger still. He will bind Satan and dispose of him for eternity (see Revelation 20.2, 10).

11.23 How does this verse relate to 9.50: "Whoever is not against you is for you"? In the earlier verse, Jesus was talking about a person who was casting out devils in Jesus' name. Those who fight evil, he was saying, are on the same side. Here, by contrast, he was talking about the conflict between God and the devil. In this battle, if a person is not on God's side, he or she is on Satan's. There is no neutral ground. Because God has already won the battle, why be on the losing side? If you aren't actively for Christ, you are against him.

11.24–26 Jesus was illustrating an unfortunate human tendency – our desire to reform often does not last long. In Judea's history, almost as soon as a good king pulled down idols, a bad king set them up again. It is not enough to be emptied of evil; we must then be filled with the power of the Holy Spirit to accomplish God's new purpose in our lives (see also Matthew 12.43–45; Galatians 5.22).

11.27, 28 Jesus was speaking to people who put extremely high

11.28 Mt 7.21 Jas 1.25

him, "Blessed is the womb that bore you and the breasts that nursed you!" 28 But he
said, "Blessed rather are those who hear the word of God and obey it!"

Jesus warns against unbelief
(136)

11.29 Mt 12.38-40
11.30 Jonah 1.17; 2.10
11.31 1 Kgs 10.1 Isa 9.6 Rom 9.5 Phil 2.10 Tit 2.13
11.32 Jn 3.5

29 When the crowds were increasing, he began to say, "This generation is an
evil generation; it asks for a sign, but no sign will be given to it except the sign of
Jonah. 30 For just as Jonah became a sign to the people of Nineveh, so the Son of
Man will be to this generation. 31 The queen of the South will rise at the judgment
with the people of this generation and condemn them, because she came from the
ends of the earth to listen to the wisdom of Solomon, and see, something greater
than Solomon is here! 32 The people of Nineveh will rise up at the judgment with
this generation and condemn it, because they repented at the proclamation of
Jonah, and see, something greater than Jonah is here!

Jesus teaches about the light within
(137)

11.33 Mt 5.15 Mk 4.21 Lk 8.16
11.34 Mt 6.22

33 "No one after lighting a lamp puts it in a cellar,[c] but on the lampstand so that
those who enter may see the light. 34 Your eye is the lamp of your body. If your eye
is healthy, your whole body is full of light; but if it is not healthy, your body is full
of darkness. 35 Therefore consider whether the light in you is not darkness. 36 If then
your whole body is full of light, with no part of it in darkness, it will be as full of
light as when a lamp gives you light with its rays."

Jesus criticizes the religious leaders
(138)

11.38 Mk 7.3
11.39 Mt 23.25 2 Tim 3.5 Tit 1.15
11.41 Isa 58.7

37 While he was speaking, a Pharisee invited him to dine with him; so he went
in and took his place at the table. 38 The Pharisee was amazed to see that he did not
first wash before dinner. 39 Then the Lord said to him, "Now you Pharisees clean
the outside of the cup and of the dish, but inside you are full of greed and wickedness. 40 You fools! Did not the one who made the outside make the inside also? 41 So
give for alms those things that are within; and see, everything will be clean for you.

[c] Other ancient authorities add *or under the bushel basket*

---

value on family ties. Their genealogies were important guarantees that they were part of God's chosen people. A man's value came from his ancestors, and a woman's value came from the sons she bore. Jesus' response to the woman meant that a person's obedience to God is more important than his or her place on the family tree. The patient work of consistent obedience is even more important than the honor of bearing a respected son.

11.29, 30 What was the sign of Jonah? God asked Jonah to preach repentance to the Gentiles (non-Jews). Jesus was affirming his message. Salvation is not only for Jews, but all people. Matthew 12.40 adds another explanation: Jesus would die and rise after three days, just as the prophet Jonah was rescued after three days in the whale's belly.

11.29–32 The cruel, warlike men of Nineveh, capital of Assyria, repented when Jonah preached to them – and Jonah did not even care about them. The heathen queen of the South (Sheba) praised the God of Israel when she heard Solomon's wisdom, and Solomon was full of faults. By contrast, Jesus, the perfect Son of God, came to people that he loved dearly – and they rejected him. Thus God's chosen people made themselves more liable to judgment than either a notoriously wicked nation or a powerful pagan queen. Compare 10.12–15 where Jesus says the evil cities of Sodom, Tyre, and Sidon will be judged less harshly than the cities in Judea and Galilee who rejected Jesus' message.

11.31, 32 The people of Nineveh and the queen of Sheba had turned to God with far less evidence than Jesus was giving his listeners – and far less than we have today. We have eyewitness reports of the risen Jesus, the continuing power of the Holy Spirit unleashed at pentecost, easy access to the Bible, and knowledge of 2,000 years of Christ's acts through his church. With the knowledge and insight available to us, our response to Christ ought to be even more complete.

11.33–36 The light is Christ; the eye represents spiritual understanding and insight. Evil desires make the eye less sensitive and blot out the light of Christ's presence. If you have a hard time seeing God at work, check your vision. Are any sinful desires blinding you to Christ?

11.37–39 This washing was done not for health reasons, but as a symbol of washing away any contamination from touching anything unclean. Not only did the Pharisees make a public show of their washing, they also commanded everyone else to follow a practice originally intended only for the priests.

11.41 The Pharisees loved to think of themselves as "clean," but their stinginess toward God and the poor proved they were not as pure as they thought. How do you use the resources God has entrusted to you? Are you generous in meeting the needs around you? Your generosity reveals much about the purity of your heart.

42 "But woe to you Pharisees! For you tithe the mint and rue and herbs of all kinds,
and neglect justice and the love of God; it is these you ought to have practiced,
without neglecting the others. 43 Woe to you Pharisees! For you love to have the
seat of honor in the synagogues and to be greeted with respect in the marketplaces.
44 Woe to you! For you are like unmarked graves, and people walk over them without realizing it."
45 One of the lawyers answered him, "Teacher, when you say these things, you
insult us too." 46 And he said, "Woe also to you lawyers! For you load people with
burdens hard to bear, and you yourselves do not lift a finger to ease them. 47 Woe
to you! For you build the tombs of the prophets whom your ancestors killed. 48 So
you are witnesses and approve of the deeds of your ancestors; for they killed them,
and you build their tombs. 49 Therefore also the Wisdom of God said, 'I will send
them prophets and apostles, some of whom they will kill and persecute,' 50 so that
this generation may be charged with the blood of all the prophets shed since the
foundation of the world, 51 from the blood of Abel to the blood of Zechariah, who
perished between the altar and the sanctuary. Yes, I tell you, it will be charged
against this generation. 52 Woe to you lawyers! For you have taken away the key of
knowledge; you did not enter yourselves, and you hindered those who were entering."
53 When he went outside, the scribes and the Pharisees began to be very hostile
toward him and to cross-examine him about many things, 54 lying in wait for him,
to catch him in something he might say.

Jesus speaks against hypocrisy
(139)

12 Meanwhile, when the crowd gathered by the thousands, so that they trampled on one another, he began to speak first to his disciples, "Beware of the
yeast of the Pharisees, that is, their hypocrisy. 2 Nothing is covered up that will not
be uncovered, and nothing secret that will not become known. 3 Therefore what-

11.42 Mt 23.23 1 Sam 15.22 Hos 6.6
11.43 Mt 23.6,7 Mk 12.38,39
11.46 Mt 23.4
11.47 Mt 23.29-36 Acts 7.51,52
11.48 Acts 8.1; 22.20
11.49 Prov 8.12,22-31 Mt 11.19; 23.34 Lk 7.35 1 Cor 1.24,30 Col 2.3
11.50 1 Thess 2.15
11.51 Gen 4.8 2 Chron 24.20,21
11.52 Mt 23.13
11.53 Mk 12.13
12.1 Mt 16.6,11,12
12.2 Mt 10.26-33 Mk 4.22 Lk 8.17

11.42 It is easy to rationalize not helping others because we have already given to the church, but a person who follows Jesus should share with needy neighbors. While tithing is important to the life of the church, our compassion must not stop there. Where we can help, we should help.

11.42–52 Jesus criticized the Pharisees and lawyers harshly because they (1) washed their hands but not their hearts, (2) remembered to tithe but forgot justice, (3) loved people's praise, (4) made impossible religious demands, (5) would not accept the truth about Jesus, and (6) prevented others from believing it as well. They went wrong by focusing on outward appearances and ignoring the inner condition of their hearts. We do the same when our service comes from a desire to be seen rather than a pure heart and love for others. People may sometimes be fooled, but God isn't. Don't be a Christian on the outside only. Bring your inner life under God's control, and your outer life will naturally reflect him.

11.44 The Old Testament laws said a person who touched a grave was unclean (Numbers 19.16). Jesus accused the Pharisees of making others unclean by their spiritual rottenness. Like graves hidden in a field, they corrupted everyone that came in contact with them.

11.45 The title of lawyer, as used here, meant an expert in religious law.

11.46 These "burdens hard to bear" were the details the Pharisees had added to God's law. To the commandment, "Remember the sabbath day, and keep it holy" (Exodus 20.8), for example, they had added instructions regarding how far a person could walk on the sabbath, which kinds of knots could be tied, and how much weight could be carried. Healing a person was considered unlawful work on the sabbath, although rescuing a trapped animal was permitted (14.5). No wonder Jesus condemned their additions to the law.

11.49 God's prophets have been persecuted and murdered throughout history. But this generation was rejecting more than a human prophet—they were rejecting God himself. This quotation is not from the Old Testament. Jesus, the greatest Prophet of all, was directly giving them God's message.

11.51 Abel's death is recorded in Genesis 4.8. For more about him, see his Profile in Genesis 5. The prophet Zechariah's death is recorded in 2 Chronicles 24.20–22 (the last book in the Hebrew canon). Why were all these sins charged against this particular generation? Because they were rejecting the Messiah himself, the one to whom all their history and prophecy was pointing.

11.52 How did the lawyers take away the "key of knowledge"? Through their erroneous interpretations of Scripture and their added man-made rules, they made God's truth hard to understand and practice. On top of that, they were bad examples, arguing their way out of the demanding rules they placed on others. Caught up in a religion of their own making, they could no longer lead the people to God. They had closed the door of God's love to the people and thrown away the key.

11.53, 54 The scribes and Pharisees hoped to arrest Jesus for blasphemy, heresy, and law breaking. They were enraged by Jesus' words about them, but they couldn't arrest him for words. They had to find a legal way to get rid of Jesus.

12.1, 2 As Jesus watched the huge crowds waiting to hear him, he warned his disciples against hypocrisy—trying to appear good when one's heart is far from God. The Pharisees could not keep their attitudes hidden forever. Their selfishness would act like yeast, and soon they would expose themselves for what they really were—power-hungry impostors, not devoted religious leaders. It is easy to be angry at the blatant hypocrisy of the Pharisees, but each of us must resist the temptation to settle for the appearance of respectability when our hearts are far from God.

ever you have said in the dark will be heard in the light, and what you have whispered behind closed doors will be proclaimed from the housetops.
4 "I tell you, my friends, do not fear those who kill the body, and after that can
do nothing more. 5 But I will warn you whom to fear: fear him who, after he has
killed, has authority[d] to cast into hell.[e] Yes, I tell you, fear him! 6 Are not five
sparrows sold for two pennies? Yet not one of them is forgotten in God's sight.
7 But even the hairs of your head are all counted. Do not be afraid; you are of more
value than many sparrows.
8 "And I tell you, everyone who acknowledges me before others, the Son of
Man also will acknowledge before the angels of God; 9 but whoever denies me
before others will be denied before the angels of God. 10 And everyone who speaks
a word against the Son of Man will be forgiven; but whoever blasphemes against
the Holy Spirit will not be forgiven. 11 When they bring you before the synagogues,
the rulers, and the authorities, do not worry about how[f] you are to defend yourselves or what you are to say; 12 for the Holy Spirit will teach you at that very hour
what you ought to say."

12.5 Heb 10.31 Rev 1.17,18
12.8 Rom 10.9-11 Rev 3.5
12.9 Mk 8.38 Lk 9.26 2 Tim 2.12
12.10 Mt 12.31,32 Mk 3.28,29 1 Jn 5.16
12.11 Ex 4.12 Mt 10.19,20 Mk 13.11 Lk 21.14,15 1 Pet 5.7

Jesus tells the parable of the rich fool
(140)

13 Someone in the crowd said to him, "Teacher, tell my brother to divide the
family inheritance with me." 14 But he said to him, "Friend, who set me to be a
judge or arbitrator over you?" 15 And he said to them, "Take care! Be on your guard
against all kinds of greed; for one's life does not consist in the abundance of possessions." 16 Then he told them a parable: "The land of a rich man produced abundantly. 17 And he thought to himself, 'What should I do, for I have no place to store
my crops?' 18 Then he said, 'I will do this: I will pull down my barns and build

12.14 Acts 7.27
12.15 1 Tim 6.6-10 Heb 13.5

[d] Or *power* [e] Gk *Gehenna* [f] Other ancient authorities add *or what*

12.4, 5 Fear of opposition or ridicule can weaken our witness for Christ. Often we cling to peace and comfort, even at the cost of our walk with God. Jesus reminds us here that we should fear God who controls eternal, not merely temporal, consequences. Don't allow fear of a person or group to keep you from standing up for Christ.

12.7 Our true value is God's estimate of our worth, not our peers'. Other people evaluate and categorize us according to how we perform, what we achieve, and how we look. But God cares for us, as for all of his creatures, because we belong to him. So we can face life without fear.

12.8, 9 We deny Jesus when we (1) hope no one will think we are Christians, (2) decide *not* to speak up for what is right, (3) are silent about our relationship with God, (4) blend into society, (5) accept our culture's non-Christian values. By contrast, we confess him when we (1) live moral, upright, Christ-honoring lives, (2) look for opportunities to share our faith with others, (3) help others in need, (4) take a stand for justice, (5) love others, (6) acknowledge our loyalty to Christ, (7) use our lives and resources to carry out his desires rather than our own.

12.10 Jesus said that the sin against the Holy Spirit is unforgivable. This has worried many sincere Christians, but it does not need to. The unforgivable sin involves deliberate and ongoing rejection of the Holy Spirit's work and thus of God himself. A person who has committed this sin has shut himself off from God so thoroughly that he is unaware of any sin at all. A person who fears having committed it shows by his concern that he has not sinned in this way.

12.11, 12 The disciples knew they could never dominate a religious dispute with the well-educated Jewish leaders. Nevertheless, they would not be left unprepared. Jesus promised that the Holy Spirit would supply the needed words. The disciples' testimony might not make them look impressive, but it would still point out God's work in the world through Jesus' life. We need to pray for opportunities to speak for God, and then trust him to help us with our words. This promise of courage, however, does not compensate for lack of preparation. Remember that these disciples had three years of teaching and practical application. We too must study God's Word. Then God will bring his truths to mind when we most need them.

12.13ff Problems like this were often brought to rabbis for them to settle. Jesus' response, though not directly to the topic, is not a change of subject. Rather, Jesus is pointing to a higher issue – a correct attitude toward the accumulation of wealth. Life is more than material goods; far more important is our relationship with God. Jesus put his finger on this questioner's heart. When we bring problems to God in prayer he often does the same – showing us how we need to change and grow in our attitude toward the problem. This answer is often not the one we were looking for, but it is more effective.

12.15 Jesus says that the good life has nothing to do with being wealthy, so beware of covetousness (greedy desire for what we don't have). This is the exact opposite of what society usually says. Advertisers spend millions of dollars to entice us to think that if we buy more and more of their products, we will be happier, more fulfilled, more comfortable. How do you respond to the constant pressure to buy? Learn to tune out expensive enticements and concentrate instead on the truly good life – living in a relationship with God and doing his work.

12.16–21 The man in Jesus' story died before he could begin to use what was stored in his big barns. Planning for retirement – preparing for life *before* death – is wise, but neglecting life *after* death is disastrous. If you accumulate wealth only to enrich yourself, with no concern for helping others, you will enter eternity empty-handed.

12.18–20 Why do you save money? To retire? To buy more expensive cars or toys? To be secure? Jesus challenges us to think beyond earthbound goals and to use what we have been given for God's kingdom. Faith, service, and obedience are the way to get rich with God.

larger ones, and there I will store all my grain and my goods. 19 And I will say to my 12.19
soul, 'Soul, you have ample goods laid up for many years; relax, eat, drink, be Prov 27.1 1 Cor 15.32
merry.' 20 But God said to him, 'You fool! This very night your life is being de- Jas 5.1-5
manded of you. And the things you have prepared, whose will they be?' 21 So it is 12.21 Hab 2.9
with those who store up treasures for themselves but are not rich toward God." 1 Tim 6.18,19

Jesus warns about worry
(141)

22 He said to his disciples, "Therefore I tell you, do not worry about your life, 12.22
what you will eat, or about your body, what you will wear. 23 For life is more than Mt 6.25-33 Phil 4.6
food, and the body more than clothing. 24 Consider the ravens: they neither sow nor 12.24
reap, they have neither storehouse nor barn, and yet God feeds them. Of how much Job 38.41 Ps 147.9
more value are you than the birds! 25 And can any of you by worrying add a single 12.25
hour to your span of life?[g] 26 If then you are not able to do so small a thing as that, Ps 39.5
why do you worry about the rest? 27 Consider the lilies, how they grow: they neither 12.27
toil nor spin;[h] yet I tell you, even Solomon in all his glory was not clothed like one 1 Kgs 10.1-10
of these. 28 But if God so clothes the grass of the field, which is alive today and
tomorrow is thrown into the oven, how much more will he clothe you—you of little
faith! 29 And do not keep striving for what you are to eat and what you are to drink,
and do not keep worrying. 30 For it is the nations of the world that strive after all 12.30
these things, and your Father knows that you need them. 31 Instead, strive for his[i] Mt 6.8 Phil 4.19
kingdom, and these things will be given to you as well.

32 "Do not be afraid, little flock, for it is your Father's good pleasure to give 12.32
you the kingdom. 33 Sell your possessions, and give alms. Make purses for your- Dan 7.27 Eph 1.5
selves that do not wear out, an unfailing treasure in heaven, where no thief comes 12.33
near and no moth destroys. 34 For where your treasure is, there your heart will be Mt 6.19-21 19.21
also. Acts 2.45; 4.34

Jesus warns about preparing for his coming
(142)

35 "Be dressed for action and have your lamps lit; 36 be like those who are waiting for their master to return from the wedding banquet, so that they may open the
door for him as soon as he comes and knocks. 37 Blessed are those slaves whom the 12.37
master finds alert when he comes; truly I tell you, he will fasten his belt and have Jn 13.4
them sit down to eat, and he will come and serve them. 38 If he comes during the
middle of the night, or near dawn, and finds them so, blessed are those slaves.

39 But know this: if the owner of the house had known at what hour the thief 12.39 1 Thess 5.2
was coming, he[j] would not have let his house be broken into. 40 You also must be Rev 16.15 12.40
ready, for the Son of Man is coming at an unexpected hour." Mk 13.32,33

[g] Or *add a cubit to your stature* [h] Other ancient authorities read *Consider the lilies; they neither spin nor weave*
[i] Other ancient authorities read *God's* [j] Other ancient authorities add *would have watched and*

12.22–34 Jesus commands us not to worry. But how can we avoid it? Only faith can free us from the anxiety caused by greed and covetousness. It is good to work and plan responsibly; it is bad to dwell on all the ways our planning could go wrong. Worry is pointless, because it can't fill any of our needs; worry is foolish, because the Creator of the universe loves us and knows what we need. He promises to meet all our real needs, not our desires.

12.31 Striving for the kingdom of God means making Jesus the Lord and King of your life. He must control every area—your work, play, plans, relationships. Is the kingdom only one of your many concerns, or is it central to all you do? Are you holding back any areas of your life from God's control? As Lord and Creator, he wants to help provide what you need as well as guide how you use what he provides.

12.33 Money seen as an end in itself quickly traps us and cuts us off from both God and the needy. The key to using money wisely is to see how much we can use for God's purposes, not how much we can accumulate for ourselves. Does God's love touch your wallet? Does your money free you to help others? If so, you are storing up lasting treasures in heaven. If your financial goals and possessions hinder you from giving, loving others, or serving, sell what you must to bring your life into perspective.

12.34 If you put your money in your business, your thoughts will center on making the business profitable. If you put it in other people, you will become concerned with their welfare. Where do you put your time, money, and energy? What do you think about most? How should you change the way you use your resources in order to reflect kingdom values more accurately?

12.35–40 Jesus repeatedly said he would leave this world but would return at some future time (see Matthew 24, 25; John 14.1–3). He also said a kingdom is being prepared for his followers. Many Greeks envisioned this as a heavenly, idealized, spiritual kingdom. Jews—like Isaiah and John, the writer of Revelation—saw it as a restored earthly kingdom.

12.40 Christ's return at an unexpected time is not a trap, a trick by which God hopes to catch us off guard. In fact, God is delaying his

12.42 Mt 24.45-51 1 Cor 4.2 1 Pet 5.4 41 Peter said, "Lord, are you telling this parable for us or for everyone?" 42 And
the Lord said, "Who then is the faithful and prudent manager whom his master will
put in charge of his slaves, to give them their allowance of food at the proper time?
43 Blessed is that slave whom his master will find at work when he arrives. 44 Truly
I tell you, he will put that one in charge of all his possessions. 45 But if that slave
says to himself, 'My master is delayed in coming,' and if he begins to beat the other
12.46 1 Thess 5.3 slaves, men and women, and to eat and drink and get drunk, 46 the master of that
slave will come on a day when he does not expect him and at an hour that he does
12.47 Num 15.31 Deut 25.1-3 not know, and will cut him in pieces,[k] and put him with the unfaithful. 47 That
slave who knew what his master wanted, but did not prepare himself or do what
12.48 Lev 5.17 Jn 9.41; 15.22 1 Tim 1.13 Jas 4.17 was wanted, will receive a severe beating. 48 But the one who did not know and did
what deserved a beating will receive a light beating. From everyone to whom much
has been given, much will be required; and from the one to whom much has been
entrusted, even more will be demanded.

Jesus warns about coming division
(143)

12.50 Mk 10.38 49 "I came to bring fire to the earth, and how I wish it were already kindled! 50 I
have a baptism with which to be baptized, and what stress I am under until it is
12.51 Mt 10.34-36 Mic 7.6 Jn 7.43; 9.16 10.19 completed! 51 Do you think that I have come to bring peace to the earth? No, I tell
you, but rather division! 52 From now on five in one household will be divided,
three against two and two against three; 53 they will be divided:

father against son
  and son against father,
mother against daughter
  and daughter against mother,
mother-in-law against her daughter-in-law
  and daughter-in-law against mother-in-law."

Jesus warns about the future crisis
(144)

12.54 Mt 16.2,3 54 He also said to the crowds, "When you see a cloud rising in the west, you
12.55 Job 37.17 immediately say, 'It is going to rain'; and so it happens. 55 And when you see the
south wind blowing, you say, 'There will be scorching heat'; and it happens. 56 You

[k] Or *cut him off*

---

return so more people will have a better chance to follow him (see 2 Peter 3.9). During this time before Christ's return, we have the *opportunity* to live out our beliefs and to reflect Jesus' love as we relate to others.

People who are ready for their Lord's return are (1) not hypocritical, but sincere (12.1), (2) not fearful, but ready to witness (12.4–9), (3) not anxious, but trusting (12.25, 26), (4) not greedy, but generous (12.34), (5) not lazy, but diligent (12.37). May your life be more like Christ's so that when he comes, you will be ready to greet him joyfully.

12.42–44 Jesus promises a reward for those who have been faithful to the Master. While we sometimes experience immediate and material rewards for our obedience to God, this is not always the case. If so, we would be tempted to boast about our achievements and do good only for what we get. Jesus said that if we look for rewards now, we will lose them later (see Mark 8.36). Our heavenly rewards will be the most accurate reflection of what we have done on earth and far greater than we can imagine.

12.48 Jesus has told us how to live until he comes: we must watch for him, work diligently, and obey his commands. Such attitudes are especially necessary for leaders. Watchful and faithful leaders will be given increased opportunities and responsibilities. The more resources, talent, and understanding we have, the more responsible we are to use them effectively. God will not hold us responsible for gifts he has not given us, but all of us have enough gifts and duties to keep us busy until Jesus comes.

12.50 The "baptism" to which Jesus referred was his coming crucifixion. He was dreading the physical pain, of course, but even worse would be the spiritual pain of complete separation from God that would accompany his death for the sins of the world.

12.51–53 In these strange and unsettling words, Jesus revealed that his coming often results in conflict. He demands a response, and close groups can be torn apart when some choose to follow him and others refuse to do so. There is no middle ground with Jesus. Loyalties must be declared and commitments made, sometimes to the severing of other relationships. Are you willing to risk your family's approval in order to gain eternal life?

12.54–57 For most of recorded history, the world's principal occupation was farming. The farmer depended directly on the weather for his livelihood. He needed just the right amounts of sun and rain – not too much, not too little – to make his living, and he grew skilled in interpreting natural signs. Jesus was announcing an earthshaking event that would be much more important than the year's crops – the coming of God's kingdom. The kingdom, like a rainstorm or a sunny day, was giving signs that it would soon arrive. But Jesus' hearers, though skilled at interpreting weather signs, were intentionally ignoring the signs of the times.

hypocrites! You know how to interpret the appearance of earth and sky, but why do **12.56**
you not know how to interpret the present time? Lk 21.30,31
57 "And why do you not judge for yourselves what is right? 58 Thus, when you **12.58**
go with your accuser before a magistrate, on the way make an effort to settle the Prov 25.8-10
case,[l] or you may be dragged before the judge, and the judge hand you over to the Mt 5.25,26
officer, and the officer throw you in prison. 59 I tell you, you will never get out until
you have paid the very last penny."

Jesus calls the people to repent
(145)

13 At that very time there were some present who told him about the Galileans
whose blood Pilate had mingled with their sacrifices. 2 He asked them, "Do **13.2**
you think that because these Galileans suffered in this way they were worse sinners Jn 9.2
than all other Galileans? 3 No, I tell you; but unless you repent, you will all perish **13.3**
as they did. 4 Or those eighteen who were killed when the tower of Siloam fell on Ezek 18.30
them— do you think that they were worse offenders than all the others living in **13.4** Isa 8.6
Jerusalem? 5 No, I tell you; but unless you repent, you will all perish just as they Jn 9.7,11
did." **13.6** Isa 5.2
6 Then he told this parable: "A man had a fig tree planted in his vineyard; and Mt 21.18,19
he came looking for fruit on it and found none. 7 So he said to the gardener, 'See Mk 11.12-14,20, 21
here! For three years I have come looking for fruit on this fig tree, and still I find Rom 2.4,5
none. Cut it down! Why should it be wasting the soil?' 8 He replied, 'Sir, let it alone **13.7** Mt 3.10
for one more year, until I dig around it and put manure on it. 9 If it bears fruit next Lk 3.9
year, well and good; but if not, you can cut it down.' " **13.8** 2 Pet 3.9

Jesus heals the handicapped woman
(146)

10 Now he was teaching in one of the synagogues on the sabbath. 11 And just **13.10**
then there appeared a woman with a spirit that had crippled her for eighteen years. Mt 4.23
She was bent over and was quite unable to stand up straight. 12 When Jesus saw her, **13.13** Mk 5.23
he called her over and said, "Woman, you are set free from your ailment." 13 When **13.14**
he laid his hands on her, immediately she stood up straight and began praising God. Ex 20.8,9
14 But the leader of the synagogue, indignant because Jesus had cured on the sab- Mt 12.9-12 Mk 3.2
bath, kept saying to the crowd, "There are six days on which work ought to be Lk 6.7; 14.3 Rom 10.1-4
done; come on those days and be cured, and not on the sabbath day." 15 But the **13.15**
Lord answered him and said, "You hypocrites! Does not each of you on the sabbath Lk 14.5
untie his ox or his donkey from the manger, and lead it away to give it water? 16 And **13.16** Lk 19.9

l Gk *settle with him*

13.1–5 Pilate may have killed the Galileans because he thought they were rebelling against Rome; those killed by the tower of Siloam may have been working for the Romans on an aqueduct there. The Pharisees, who were opposed to using force to deal with Rome, would have said the Galileans deserved to die for rebelling. The Zealots, a group of anti-Roman terrorists, would have said the aqueduct workers deserved to die for cooperating. Jesus said that neither the Galileans nor the workers should be blamed for their calamity. Instead, everyone should look to his or her own day of Judgment.

13.5 Whether a person is killed in a tragic accident or miraculously survives, it is not a measure of righteousness. Everyone will die; that's part of being human. But not everyone needs to stay dead. Jesus promises that those who believe in him will not perish but have eternal life (John 3.16).

13.6–9 In the Old Testament, a fruitful tree was often used as a symbol of godly living (see, for example, Psalm 1.3 and Jeremiah 17.7, 8). Jesus pointed out what would happen to the other kind of tree—the kind that took time and space and still produced nothing for the patient gardener. This was one way he warned his listeners that God would not tolerate forever their lack of productivity. (Luke 3.9 records John the Baptist's version of the same message.) Have you been enjoying God's special treatment without giving anything in return? If so, respond to the Gardener's patient care, and begin to bear the fruit God has created you to produce.

13.10–17 Why was healing considered work? The religious leaders saw healing as part of a doctor's profession, and practicing one's profession on the sabbath was prohibited. The synagogue leader could not see beyond the law to Jesus' compassion in healing this handicapped woman. Jesus shamed him and the other leaders by pointing out their hypocrisy. They would untie their cattle and care for them, but they refused to rejoice when a human being was freed from Satan's bondage.

13.15, 16 The Pharisees hid behind their own set of laws to avoid love's obligations. We too can use the letter of the law to rationalize away our obligation to care for others (for example, by tithing regularly, and then refusing to help a needy neighbor). But people's needs are more important than laws. Take time to help others, even if doing so might compromise your public image.

13.16 In our fallen world, disease is common. Its causes are many and often multiple—inadequate nutrition, contact with a source of infection, lowered defenses, and even direct attack by Satan.

ought not this woman, a daughter of Abraham whom Satan bound for eighteen long
13.17 years, be set free from this bondage on the sabbath day?" 17 When he said this, all
Lk 18.43 his opponents were put to shame; and the entire crowd was rejoicing at all the wonderful things that he was doing.

Jesus teaches about the kingdom of God
(147)

13.18 Gen 1.11,12 18 He said therefore, "What is the kingdom of God like? And to what should I
Ps 104.12 compare it? 19 It is like a mustard seed that someone took and sowed in the garden;
Ezek 17.22,23 Dan 4.12,21 it grew and became a tree, and the birds of the air made nests in its branches."
Mt 13.31,32 Mk 4.30-32 20 And again he said, "To what should I compare the kingdom of God? 21 It is
13.20 like yeast that a woman took and mixed in with[m] three measures of flour until all
Mt 13.33 of it was leavened."

Jesus teaches about entering the kingdom
(153)

13.22 Mt 9.35 22 Jesus[n] went through one town and village after another, teaching as he made
Mk 6.6 his way to Jerusalem. 23 Someone asked him, "Lord, will only a few be saved?" He
13.24 said to them, 24 "Strive to enter through the narrow door; for many, I tell you, will
Mt 7.13,14 try to enter and will not be able. 25 When once the owner of the house has got up and
13.26 shut the door, and you begin to stand outside and to knock at the door, saying,
Tit 1.16 'Lord, open to us,' then in reply he will say to you, 'I do not know where you come
13.27 Ps 6.18 from.' 26 Then you will begin to say, 'We ate and drank with you, and you taught
Mt 25.41 in our streets.' 27 But he will say, 'I do not know where you come from; go away
13.28 from me, all you evildoers!' 28 There will be weeping and gnashing of teeth when
Mt 8.10-12 13.41,42 you see Abraham and Isaac and Jacob and all the prophets in the kingdom of God,

[m] Gk *hid in* [n] Gk *He*

SEVEN SABBATH MIRACLES		
	Jesus sends a demon out of a man	Mark 1.21–28
	Jesus heals Peter's mother-in-law	Mark 1.29–31
	Jesus heals a lame man by Bethesda Pool	John 5.1–18
	Jesus heals a man with a withered hand	Mark 3.1–6
	Jesus restores a handicapped woman	Luke 13.10–17
	Jesus heals a man with dropsy	Luke 14.1–6
	Jesus heals a man born blind	John 9.1–16

Over the centuries, the Jewish religious leaders had added rule after rule to God's law. For example, God's law said the sabbath is a day of rest (Exodus 20.10, 11). But the religious leaders added to that law, creating one that said, "you cannot heal on the sabbath" because that is "work." Seven times Jesus healed people on the sabbath. In doing this, he was challenging these religious leaders to look beneath their rules to their true purpose—to honor God by helping those in need. Would God have been pleased if Jesus had ignored these people?

Whatever the immediate cause of our illness, we can trace its original source to Satan, the author of all the evil in our world. The Good News – the gospel – is that Jesus is more powerful than any devil or any disease. He often offers physical healing in this life; and when he returns, he will put an end to all disease and handicaps.

13.18–21 The general expectation among Jesus' hearers was that the Messiah would come as a great king and leader, freeing the nation from Rome and restoring Israel's former glory. But Jesus said his kingdom was beginning small and quietly. Like the tiny mustard seed that grows into an enormous bush or the spoonful of leaven that makes the bread dough double in size, the kingdom of God would eventually push outward until the whole world was changed.

13.22 This is the second time Luke reminds us that Jesus was intentionally going to Jerusalem (the other time is in 9.51). He knew that he was on his way to die, but he continued preaching to large crowds. The prospect of death did not deter Jesus from his mission.

13.24, 25 Finding salvation requires more concentrated effort than most people are willing to put forth. Obviously we cannot save ourselves – there is no way we can work ourselves into God's favor. The work we must do "to enter through the narrow door" is earnestly desiring to know Jesus and diligently striving to follow him whatever the cost. We dare not put off making this decision, because the door will not stay open forever.

13.26, 27 The kingdom of God will not necessarily be populated with the people we expect to find there. Some perfectly respectable religious leaders claiming allegiance to Jesus will not be there, because secretly they were morally corrupt.

13.27 The people were eager to know who would be in God's kingdom. Jesus explained that although many people know something about God, only a few have acknowledged their sins and accepted his forgiveness. Just listening to Jesus' words or admiring his miracles is not enough – we must turn from sin and trust in God to save us.

and you yourselves thrown out. [29]Then people will come from east and west, from
north and south, and will eat in the kingdom of God. [30]Indeed, some are last who
will be first, and some are first who will be last."

13.29 Rev 5.9; 7.9
13.30 Mt 19.30; 20.16

Jesus grieves over Jerusalem
(154)

31 At that very hour some Pharisees came and said to him, "Get away from
here, for Herod wants to kill you." [32]He said to them, "Go and tell that fox for
me,[o] 'Listen, I am casting out demons and performing cures today and tomorrow,
and on the third day I finish my work. [33]Yet today, tomorrow, and the next day I
must be on my way, because it is impossible for a prophet to be killed outside of
Jerusalem.' [34]Jerusalem, Jerusalem, the city that kills the prophets and stones
those who are sent to it! How often have I desired to gather your children together
as a hen gathers her brood under her wings, and you were not willing! [35]See, your
house is left to you. And I tell you, you will not see me until the time comes when[p]
you say, 'Blessed is the one who comes in the name of the Lord.' "

13.32 Lk 24.26 Heb 2.10; 5.5,9 7.28
13.33 Mt 16.21 Jn 11.7-10
13.34 Mt 23.37-39 Lk 19.41-44
13.35 Ps 69.25 118.26 Ezek 10.4,18,19 Lk 19.38; 21.24

Jesus heals a man with dropsy
(155)

14 On one occasion when Jesus[q] was going to the house of a leader of the
Pharisees to eat a meal on the sabbath, they were watching him closely.
[2]Just then, in front of him, there was a man who had dropsy. [3]And Jesus asked the
lawyers and Pharisees, "Is it lawful to cure people on the sabbath, or not?" [4]But
they were silent. So Jesus[q] took him and healed him, and sent him away. [5]Then he
said to them, "If one of you has a child[r] or an ox that has fallen into a well, will you
not immediately pull it out on a sabbath day?" [6]And they could not reply to this.

14.1 Mt 12.9-13 Mk 3.1-5 Lk 6.6-11 13.10-16

Jesus teaches about seeking honor
(156)

7 When he noticed how the guests chose the places of honor, he told them a
parable. [8]"When you are invited by someone to a wedding banquet, do not sit down
at the place of honor, in case someone more distinguished than you has been invited
by your host; [9]and the host who invited both of you may come and say to you,

[o] Gk lacks *for me* [p] Other ancient authorities lack *the time comes when* [q] Gk *he* [r] Other ancient authorities read *a donkey*

13.29 God's kingdom will include people from every part of the world. Israel's rejection of Jesus as Messiah would not stop God's plan. True Israel includes all people who believe in God. This is an important fact for Luke to stress as he directs his Gospel to a Gentile audience (see also Romans 4.16–25; Galatians 3.6–9).

13.30 There will be many surprises in God's kingdom. Some who are despised now will be greatly honored then; some influential people here will be left outside the gates. Many "great" people on this earth (in God's eyes) are virtually ignored by the rest of the world. What matters to God is not one's earthly popularity, status, wealth, heritage, or power, but one's commitment to Christ. How do your values match what the Bible tells us to value? Put God in first place, and you will join the people from all over the world who will take their places in the kingdom of heaven.

13.31–33 The Pharisees weren't interested in protecting Jesus from danger. They were trying to trap him themselves. They urged him to leave because they wanted to stop him from going to Jerusalem, not because they feared Herod. But Jesus' life, work, and death were not to be determined by Herod or the Pharisees. His life was planned and directed by God himself, and his mission would unfold in God's time according to God's plan.

13.33, 34 Why was Jesus aiming for Jerusalem? Jerusalem, the city of God, symbolized the entire nation. It was Israel's largest city and the nation's spiritual and political capital, and Jews from around the world visited it frequently. But Jerusalem had a history of rejecting God's prophets (1 Kings 19.10; 2 Chronicles 24.19; Jeremiah 2.30), and it would reject the Messiah just as it had rejected his forerunners.

14.1–6 Earlier Jesus had been invited to a Pharisee's home for discussion (7.36). This time a high-ranking Pharisee invited Jesus to his home specifically to trap him into saying or doing something for which he could be arrested. It may be surprising to see Jesus on the Pharisees' turf after he had denounced them so many times. But he was not afraid to face them, even though he knew that their purpose was to trick him into breaking their laws.

14.2 Luke, the physician, identifies this man's disease – he was suffering from *dropsy,* an abnormal accumulation of fluid in bodily tissues and cavities.

14.7–11 Jesus advised people not to rush for the best places at a feast. People today are just as eager to raise their social status, whether by being with the right people, dressing for success, or driving the right car. Whom do you try to impress? Rather than aiming for prestige, look for a place where you can serve. If God wants you to serve on a wider scale, he will invite you to take a higher place.

14.7–14 Jesus taught two lessons here. First he spoke to the guests, telling them not to seek places of honor. Service is more important in God's kingdom than status. Second he told the host not to be exclusive about whom he invites. God opens his kingdom to everyone.

'Give this person your place,' and then in disgrace you would start to take the
14.10 Prov 15.33 lowest place. 10 But when you are invited, go and sit down at the lowest place, so
18.12; 25.6,7 that when your host comes, he may say to you, 'Friend, move up higher'; then you
14.11 Ps 18.27 will be honored in the presence of all who sit at the table with you. 11 For all who
Prov 29.23 exalt themselves will be humbled, and those who humble themselves will be ex-
Mt 23.12 Lk 18.14 alted."
Jas 4.6 1 Pet 5.5 12 He said also to the one who had invited him, "When you give a luncheon or
a dinner, do not invite your friends or your brothers or your relatives or rich neigh-
14.13 Job 31.17 bors, in case they may invite you in return, and you would be repaid. 13 But when
14.14 you give a banquet, invite the poor, the crippled, the lame, and the blind. 14 And
Jn 5.28,29 you will be blessed, because they cannot repay you, for you will be repaid at the
Acts 24.15 resurrection of the righteous."

Jesus tells the parable of the great feast (157)

14.15 Mt 22.1-10 15 One of the dinner guests, on hearing this, said to him, "Blessed is anyone
14.16 who will eat bread in the kingdom of God!" 16 Then Jesus[s] said to him, "Someone
Rev 19.9 gave a great dinner and invited many. 17 At the time for the dinner he sent his slave
to say to those who had been invited, 'Come; for everything is ready now.' 18 But
they all alike began to make excuses. The first said to him, 'I have bought a piece
of land, and I must go out and see it; please accept my regrets.' 19 Another said, 'I
have bought five yoke of oxen, and I am going to try them out; please accept my
14.20 Deut 24.15 regrets.' 20 Another said, 'I have just been married, and therefore I cannot come.'
1 Cor 7.33 21 So the slave returned and reported this to his master. Then the owner of the house
14.21 became angry and said to his slave, 'Go out at once into the streets and lanes of the
Acts 13.46 town and bring in the poor, the crippled, the blind, and the lame.' 22 And the slave
said, 'Sir, what you ordered has been done, and there is still room.' 23 Then the
master said to the slave, 'Go out into the roads and lanes, and compel people to
14.24 Mt 8.12; 21.43 come in, so that my house may be filled. 24 For I tell you,[t] none of those who were
Heb 3.18,19 invited will taste my dinner.' "

Jesus teaches about the cost of being a disciple (158)

14.26 Mt 10.37,38 25 Now large crowds were traveling with him; and he turned and said to them,
Rev 12.11 26 "Whoever comes to me and does not hate father and mother, wife and children,
14.27 Mt 16.24 brothers and sisters, yes, and even life itself, cannot be my disciple. 27 Whoever
Mk 8.34 does not carry the cross and follow me cannot be my disciple. 28 For which of you,

[s] Gk *he* [t] The Greek word for *you* here is plural

14.11 How can we humble ourselves? Some people try to give the appearance of humility in order to manipulate others. Others think that humility means putting themselves down. Truly humble people compare themselves only with Christ, realize their own sinfulness, and understand their limitations. On the other hand, they also recognize their gifts and strengths and are willing to use them as Christ directs. Humility is not self-degradation; it is realistic assessment and commitment to serve.

14.15–24 The man with Jesus saw the glory of God's kingdom, but he did not yet understand how to get in. In Jesus' story, many turned down the invitation to the banquet because the timing was inconvenient. We too can resist or delay responding to God's invitation, and our excuses may sound reasonable—work duties, family responsibilities, financial need, or whatever they may be. Nevertheless, God's invitation is the most important event in our lives, no matter how inconveniently it may be timed. Are you making excuses to avoid responding to God's call? Jesus reminds us that the time will come when God will stop inviting us—then it will be too late to get into the banquet.

14.16ff It was customary to send two invitations to a party—the first to announce it, the second to tell the guests that all was ready. The guests in Jesus' story insulted the host by making excuses when he issued the second invitation. In Israel's history, God's first invitation came from Moses and the prophets; the second came from his Son. The religious leaders accepted the first invitation. They believed God had called them to be his people, but they insulted God by refusing to accept his Son. Thus, as the master in the story sent his servant into the streets to invite the needy to his banquet, so God sent his Son to the whole world of needy people to tell them that God's kingdom had arrived.

14.16ff In this chapter we read Jesus' words against seeking status, and in favor of hard work and even suffering. Let's not lose sight of the purpose of all our humility and self-sacrifice—a joyous banquet with our Lord! He is not calling us to join him in a labor camp but in a feast—the marriage supper of the Lamb (Revelation 19.6–9), when God and his beloved church will be joined forever.

14.27 Jesus' audience was well aware of what it meant to carry one's own cross. When the Romans led a criminal to his execution site, he was forced to carry the cross on which he would die. This showed his submission to Rome and warned observers that they'd better submit too. Jesus gave this teaching to get the crowds to think through their enthusiasm for him. He encouraged those who were superficial either to go deeper or to turn back. Following Christ means total submission to him—perhaps even death.

intending to build a tower, does not first sit down and estimate the cost, to see
whether he has enough to complete it? 29 Otherwise, when he has laid a foundation
and is not able to finish, all who see it will begin to ridicule him, 30 saying, 'This
fellow began to build and was not able to finish.' 31 Or what king, going out to wage
war against another king, will not sit down first and consider whether he is able
with ten thousand to oppose the one who comes against him with twenty thousand?
32 If he cannot, then, while the other is still far away, he sends a delegation and asks
for the terms of peace. 33 So therefore, none of you can become my disciple if you
do not give up all your possessions.
34 "Salt is good; but if salt has lost its taste, how can its saltiness be restored?[u]
35 It is fit neither for the soil nor for the manure pile; they throw it away. Let anyone
with ears to hear listen!"

14.33 Mt 19.27,28 Lk 18.29,30 Phil 3.7 Heb 11.26
14.34 Mt 5.13 Mk 9.50

Jesus tells the parable of the lost sheep
(159)

15 Now all the tax collectors and sinners were coming near to listen to him.
2 And the Pharisees and the scribes were grumbling and saying, "This fellow
welcomes sinners and eats with them."
3 So he told them this parable: 4 "Which one of you, having a hundred sheep and
losing one of them, does not leave the ninety-nine in the wilderness and go after the
one that is lost until he finds it? 5 When he has found it, he lays it on his shoulders
and rejoices. 6 And when he comes home, he calls together his friends and neighbors, saying to them, 'Rejoice with me, for I have found my sheep that was lost.'
7 Just so, I tell you, there will be more joy in heaven over one sinner who repents
than over ninety-nine righteous persons who need no repentance.

15.1 Mt 9.10,11 Lk 5.29,30 19.7 Acts 11.3 Gal 2.12 1 Tim 1.15,16
15.4 Ezek 34.11,12 Jn 10.11
15.6 1 Pet 2.25
15.7 Lk 5.32

Jesus tells the parable of the lost coin
(160)

8 "Or what woman having ten silver coins,[v] if she loses one of them, does not
light a lamp, sweep the house, and search carefully until she finds it? 9 When she

[u] Or *how can it be used for seasoning?* [v] Gk *drachmas,* each worth about a day's wage for a laborer

---

14.33 When a builder doesn't count the cost or figures it inaccurately, his building may be left half completed. Will your Christian life be only half built and then abandoned because you did not count the cost of commitment to Jesus? What are those costs? A Christian may face loss of social status or wealth. He may have to give up control over his money, his time, or his career. He may be hated, separated from his family, and even put to death. Following Christ does not mean a trouble-free life. We must carefully count the cost of becoming Christ's disciples so that we know what we are getting into and are not later tempted to turn back.

14.34 Salt can lose its flavor. When it gets wet and then dries, nothing is left but a tasteless residue. Many Christians blend into the world and avoid the cost of standing up for Christ. But Jesus says if Christians lose their distinctive saltiness, they become worthless. Just as salt flavors and preserves food, we are to preserve the good in the world, help keep it from spoiling, and bring new flavor to life. This requires planning, willing sacrifice, and unswerving commitment to Christ's kingdom. Being "salty" is not easy, but if a Christian fails in this function, he fails to represent Christ in the world. How salty are you?

15.2 Why were the Pharisees and scribes bothered that Jesus associated with these people? The religious leaders were always careful to stay "clean" according to Old Testament law. In fact, they went well beyond the law in their avoidance of certain people and situations and in their ritual washings. By contrast, Jesus took their concept of "cleanness" lightly. He risked defilement by touching lepers and by neglecting to wash in the Pharisees' prescribed manner, and he showed complete disregard for their sanctions against associating with certain classes of people. He came to offer salvation to sinners, to show that God loves them. Jesus didn't worry about the accusations. Instead he continued going to those who needed him, regardless of the effect they might have on his reputation.

15.3–6 It may seem foolish for the shepherd to leave 99 sheep to go search for just one. But the shepherd knew that the 99 would be safe in the sheepfold, whereas the lost sheep was in danger. Because each sheep was of high value, the shepherd knew it was worthwhile to search diligently for the lost one. God's love for each individual is so great that he seeks each one out and rejoices when he or she is "found." Jesus associated with sinners because he wanted to bring the lost sheep—people considered beyond hope—the gospel of God's kingdom. Before you were a believer, he sought you; and his love is still seeking those who are yet lost.

15.4, 5 We may be able to understand a God who would forgive sinners who come to him for mercy. But a God who tenderly searches for sinners and then joyfully forgives them must have extraordinary love! This is the kind of love that prompted Jesus to come to earth to search for lost people and save them. This is the kind of extraordinary love God has for you. If you feel far from God, don't despair. He is seaching for you.

15.8–10 Palestinian women received ten silver coins as a wedding gift. Besides their monetary value, these coins held sentimental value like that of a wedding ring, and to lose one was extremely distressing. Just as a woman would rejoice at finding her lost coin or ring, so the angels would rejoice over a repentant sinner. Each individual is precious to God. He grieves over every loss and rejoices whenever one of his children is found and brought into his kingdom. Perhaps we would have more joy in our churches if we shared Jesus' love and concern for the lost.

has found it, she calls together her friends and neighbors, saying, 'Rejoice with
15.10 Ezek 18.23 me, for I have found the coin that I had lost.' 10 Just so, I tell you, there is joy in the
presence of the angels of God over one sinner who repents."

Jesus tells the parable of the lost son
(161)

15.12 Deut 21.17 11 Then Jesus[w] said, "There was a man who had two sons. 12 The younger of
them said to his father, 'Father, give me the share of the property that will belong
to me.' So he divided his property between them. 13 A few days later the younger
son gathered all he had and traveled to a distant country, and there he squandered
his property in dissolute living. 14 When he had spent everything, a severe famine
took place throughout that country, and he began to be in need. 15 So he went and
hired himself out to one of the citizens of that country, who sent him to his fields
to feed the pigs. 16 He would gladly have filled himself with[x] the pods that the pigs
were eating; and no one gave him anything. 17 But when he came to himself he said,
'How many of my father's hired hands have bread enough and to spare, but here I
15.18 Lam 3.40 Lk 18.13,14 am dying of hunger! 18 I will get up and go to my father, and I will say to him,
"Father, I have sinned against heaven and before you; 19 I am no longer worthy to
15.20 Gen 45.14; 46.29 be called your son; treat me like one of your hired hands." ' 20 So he set off and went
to his father. But while he was still far off, his father saw him and was filled with
compassion; he ran and put his arms around him and kissed him. 21 Then the son
said to him, 'Father, I have sinned against heaven and before you; I am no longer
15.22 Isa 61.10 Zech 3.4 Rev 6.11 worthy to be called your son.'[y] 22 But the father said to his slaves, 'Quickly, bring
out a robe — the best one — and put it on him; put a ring on his finger and sandals on
15.24 Rom 11.15 Eph 2.1-5 Col 2.13 his feet. 23 And get the fatted calf and kill it, and let us eat and celebrate; 24 for this
son of mine was dead and is alive again; he was lost and is found!' And they began
to celebrate.

25 "Now his elder son was in the field; and when he came and approached the
house, he heard music and dancing. 26 He called one of the slaves and asked what
was going on. 27 He replied, 'Your brother has come, and your father has killed the
fatted calf, because he has got him back safe and sound.' 28 Then he became angry
15.29 Mt 20.11-15 and refused to go in. His father came out and began to plead with him. 29 But he
answered his father, 'Listen! For all these years I have been working like a slave for
you, and I have never disobeyed your command; yet you have never given me even

[w] Gk *he* [x] Other ancient authorities read *filled his stomach with* [y] Other ancient authorities add *treat me as one of your hired servants*

15.12 The younger son's share of the estate was one third (Deuteronomy 21.17). In most cases he would have received this at his father's death, although fathers sometimes chose to divide up their inheritance early and retire from managing their estates. What is unusual here is that the younger one initiated the division of the estate. This showed disregard for his father's authority as head of the family.

15.15, 16 According to Moses' law, pigs were unclean animals (Leviticus 11.2–8; Deuteronomy 14.8). This meant that they could not be eaten or used for sacrifices. To protect themselves from defilement, Jews would not even touch them. For a Jew to stoop to feeding pigs was a great humiliation, and for this young man to eat food the pigs had touched was to be degraded beyond belief. The younger son had truly sunk to the depths.

15.17 The younger son, like many who are rebellious and immature, wanted to be free to live as he pleased, and he had to hit bottom before he "came to himself." It often takes great sorrow and tragedy to cause people to look to the only One who can help them. Are you trying to live life your way, selfishly pushing aside any responsibility or commitment that gets in your way? Stop and look before you hit bottom, and save yourself and your family much grief.

15.20 In the two preceding stories, the seeker actively looked for the coin and the sheep, which could not return by themselves. In this story, the father watched and waited. He was dealing with a human being with a will of his own, but he was ready to greet his son if he returned. In the same way, God's love is constant and waiting. He will search for us and give us opportunities to respond, but he does not force us to come to him. Like the father, he waits patiently for us to come to our senses.

15.24 The sheep was lost because it foolishly wandered away (15.4); the coin was lost through no fault of its own (15.8); and the son left out of selfishness (15.12). God's great love reaches out and finds sinners no matter why they got lost.

15.25–31 It was hard for the elder brother to accept his younger brother when he returned, and it is just as difficult to accept "younger brothers" today. People who repent after leading notoriously sinful lives are often held in suspicion; churches are sometimes unwilling to admit them to membership. Instead, we should rejoice like the angels in heaven when an unbeliever repents and turns to God. Like the father, accept repentant sinners wholeheartedly and give them the support and encouragement they need to grow in Christ.

a young goat so that I might celebrate with my friends. 30 But when this son of yours 15.30
came back, who has devoured your property with prostitutes, you killed the fatted Prov 29.3
calf for him!' 31 Then the father[z] said to him, 'Son, you are always with me, and
all that is mine is yours. 32 But we had to celebrate and rejoice, because this brother 15.32
of yours was dead and has come to life; he was lost and has been found.' " Lk 15.7

Jesus tells the parable of the shrewd manager
(162)

16 Then Jesus[z] said to the disciples, "There was a rich man who had a
manager, and charges were brought to him that this man was squandering his
property. 2 So he summoned him and said to him, 'What is this that I hear about 16.2
you? Give me an accounting of your management, because you cannot be my Rom 14.12
manager any longer.' 3 Then the manager said to himself, 'What will I do, now that
my master is taking the position away from me? I am not strong enough to dig, and
I am ashamed to beg. 4 I have decided what to do so that, when I am dismissed as
manager, people may welcome me into their homes.' 5 So, summoning his master's
debtors one by one, he asked the first, 'How much do you owe my master?' 6 He
answered, 'A hundred jugs of olive oil.' He said to him, 'Take your bill, sit down
quickly, and make it fifty.' 7 Then he asked another, 'And how much do you owe?'
He replied, 'A hundred containers of wheat.' He said to him, 'Take your bill and
make it eighty.' 8 And his master commended the dishonest manager because he 16.8
had acted shrewdly; for the children of this age are more shrewd in dealing with Jn 12.36 Eph 5.8,9
their own generation than are the children of light. 9 And I tell you, make friends for 1 Thess 5.5
yourselves by means of dishonest wealth[a] so that when it is gone, they may welcome you into the eternal homes.[b]
10 "Whoever is faithful in a very little is faithful also in much; and whoever is 16.10
dishonest in a very little is dishonest also in much. 11 If then you have not been Mt 25.21 Lk 19.17
faithful with the dishonest wealth,[a] who will entrust to you the true riches? 12 And
if you have not been faithful with what belongs to another, who will give you what
is your own? 13 No slave can serve two masters; for a slave will either hate the one 16.13
and love the other, or be devoted to the one and despise the other. You cannot serve Mt 6.24
God and wealth."[a] 16.14 Mt 23.13,14
14 The Pharisees, who were lovers of money, heard all this, and they ridiculed 1 Tim 3.2

[z] Gk *he* [a] Gk *mammon* [b] Gk *tents*

15.30 In the story of the prodigal son, the father's response is contrasted with the older brother's. The father forgave because he was joyful. The son refused to forgive because he was bitter toward the injustice of it all. His resentment rendered him just as lost to the father's love as his younger brother had been. Don't let anything keep you from forgiving others. If you are refusing to forgive people, you are missing a wonderful opportunity of experiencing joy and sharing it with them. Make your joy grow: forgive somebody who has hurt you.

15.32 When Jesus told this story, the older brother represented the Pharisees, who were angry and resentful that sinners were being welcomed into God's kingdom. After all, they thought, we have sacrificed and done *so much* for God. How easy it is to resent God's gracious forgiveness of others whom we consider far worse sinners than ourselves. But when our self-righteousness gets in the way of rejoicing at others coming to Jesus, we are no better than the Pharisees.

16.1–8 Our use of money is a good test of the Lordship of Christ. (1) Let us use our resources wisely, because they belong to God, not us. (2) Money can be used for good or evil; let us use ours for good. (3) Money has a lot of power, so we must use it carefully and thoughtfully. (4) We must use our material goods in a way that will foster faith and obedience, essential for the next life (see 12.33, 34).

16.9 "Dishonest wealth" is money that is acquired unjustly. We are to make wise use of opportunities, not to earn heaven, but so that heaven ("eternal homes") will be a welcome experience. When we obey God's will, the unselfish use of possessions will follow.

16.10, 11 Our integrity often meets its match in money matters. God calls us to be honest even in small details we could rationalize away. Heaven's riches are far more valuable than earthly wealth. But if we are untrustworthy with our money here (no matter how much or little we have), we are unfit to handle the vast riches of God's kingdom. Don't let your integrity slip in small matters, and it will not fail you in crucial decisions either.

16.13 Money has the power to take God's place in your life. It can become your master. How can you tell if you are a slave to wealth? (1) Do you think and worry about it frequently? (2) Do you give up doing what you should do or would like to do in order to make more money? (3) Do you spend a great deal of your time caring for your possessions? (4) Is it hard for you to give money away? (5) Are you in debt?

Money is a hard master and a deceptive one. Wealth promises power and control, but it often cannot deliver. Great fortunes can be made—and lost—overnight, and no amount of money can provide health, happiness, or eternal life. How much better it is to let God be your Master. His servants have peace of mind and security both now and forever.

16.14 The Pharisees loved money and took exception to Jesus' teaching. We live in an age that measures people's worth by how much money they make. Do we laugh at Jesus' warnings against serving money? Do we try to explain them away? Do we apply

16.15 1 Sam 16.7 Jer 17.10 Mt 23.28 Heb 4.13
16.16 Mt 11.12,13
16.17 Isa 40.8 Mt 5.17,18
16.18 Mk 10.11,12 1 Cor 7.10,11
16.20 Acts 3.2
16.22 Ps 103.20,21 Mt 8.11 Jn 1.18 Heb 1.14 Jas 2.5
16.24 Mk 9.44 Lk 3.8
16.25 Job 21.7-14 Lk 6.24,25
16.26 2 Thess 1.9
16.28 Acts 2.40; 10.42 18.5
16.29 Jn 5.39,45-47 Acts 15.21 2 Tim 3.15
16.31 Jn 12.9,10

him. 15 So he said to them, "You are those who justify yourselves in the sight of
others; but God knows your hearts; for what is prized by human beings is an abomination in the sight of God.
16 "The law and the prophets were in effect until John came; since then the
good news of the kingdom of God is proclaimed, and everyone tries to enter it by
force.[c] 17 But it is easier for heaven and earth to pass away, than for one stroke of
a letter in the law to be dropped.
18 "Anyone who divorces his wife and marries another commits adultery, and
whoever marries a woman divorced from her husband commits adultery.

Jesus tells about the rich man and the beggar
(163)

19 "There was a rich man who was dressed in purple and fine linen and who
feasted sumptuously every day. 20 And at his gate lay a poor man named Lazarus,
covered with sores, 21 who longed to satisfy his hunger with what fell from the rich
man's table; even the dogs would come and lick his sores. 22 The poor man died and
was carried away by the angels to be with Abraham.[d] The rich man also died and
was buried. 23 In Hades, where he was being tormented, he looked up and saw
Abraham far away with Lazarus by his side.[e] 24 He called out, 'Father Abraham,
have mercy on me, and send Lazarus to dip the tip of his finger in water and cool
my tongue; for I am in agony in these flames.' 25 But Abraham said, 'Child,
remember that during your lifetime you received your good things, and Lazarus in
like manner evil things; but now he is comforted here, and you are in agony. 26 Besides all this, between you and us a great chasm has been fixed, so that those who
might want to pass from here to you cannot do so, and no one can cross from there
to us.' 27 He said, 'Then, father, I beg you to send him to my father's house— 28 for
I have five brothers—that he may warn them, so that they will not also come into
this place of torment.' 29 Abraham replied, 'They have Moses and the prophets;
they should listen to them.' 30 He said, 'No, father Abraham; but if someone goes
to them from the dead, they will repent.' 31 He said to him, 'If they do not listen to
Moses and the prophets, neither will they be convinced even if someone rises from
the dead.' "

[c] Or *everyone is strongly urged to enter it* [d] Gk *to Abraham's bosom* [e] Gk *in his bosom*

---

them to someone else—the Pharisees, for example? Unless we take Jesus' statements seriously, we may be acting like Pharisees ourselves.

16.15 The Pharisees acted pious to get praise from others, but God knew what was in their hearts. They considered their wealth as a sign of God's approval. God detested their wealth because it caused them to abandon true spirituality. Though prosperity may earn people's praise, it must never substitute for devotion and service to God.

16.16, 17 John the Baptist was the dividing line between the Old and New Testaments (John 1.15–18). With Jesus came the realization of all the prophets' hopes. Jesus emphasized that his kingdom fulfilled the law (the Old Testament); it did not cancel it. His was not a new system but the culmination of the old. The same God who worked through Moses was working through Jesus.

16.18 Most religious leaders of Jesus' day permitted a man to divorce his wife for nearly any reason. Jesus' teaching about divorce went beyond Moses' (Deuteronomy 24.1–4). Stricter than any of the then-current schools of thought, they shocked his hearers (see Matthew 19.10) just as they shake today's readers. Jesus says in unmistakable terms that marriage is a lifetime commitment. To leave your spouse for another person may be legal, but it is adultery in God's eyes. As you think about marriage, remember that God intends it to be a permanent commitment.

16.19–31 The Pharisees considered wealth to be a proof of righteousness. Jesus startled them with this story in which a diseased beggar is rewarded and a rich man is punished. The rich man did not go to hell because of his wealth but because he was selfish with it. He refused to feed Lazarus, take him in, or care for him. He was hardhearted in spite of his great blessings. The amount of money we have is not so important as the way we use it. What is your attitude toward your money and possessions? Do you hoard them selfishly for yourself, or do you use them to help others?

16.20 This Lazarus should not be confused with the Lazarus whom Jesus raised from the dead in John 11.

16.29–31 The rich man thought his five brothers would surely believe a messenger who was raised from the dead. But Jesus said that if they did not believe Moses and the prophets, who spoke constantly of the duty to care for the poor, not even a resurrection would convince them. Notice the irony in Jesus' statement; on his way to Jerusalem to die, he was fully aware that even when he had returned from the dead, most of the religious leaders would not accept him. They were set in their ways, and neither Scripture nor God's Son himself could shake them loose.

Jesus teaches about forgiveness and faith
(164)

17 Jesus[f] said to his disciples, "Occasions for stumbling are bound to come, 17.1
but woe to anyone by whom they come! 2 It would be better for you if a Mt 18.6,7 Mk 9.42
millstone were hung around your neck and you were thrown into the sea than for 1 Cor 8.12
you to cause one of these little ones to stumble. 3 Be on your guard! If another 17.3
disciple[g] sins, you must rebuke the offender, and if there is repentance, you must Lev 19.17 Mt 18.15,21,22
forgive. 4 And if the same person sins against you seven times a day, and turns back Jas 5.19
to you seven times and says, 'I repent,' you must forgive."
5 The apostles said to the Lord, "Increase our faith!" 6 The Lord replied, "If you 17.6
had faith the size of a[h] mustard seed, you could say to this mulberry tree, 'Be Mt 17.20; 21.21 Mk 9.23
uprooted and planted in the sea,' and it would obey you. 11.22,23
7 "Who among you would say to your slave who has just come in from plowing
or tending sheep in the field, 'Come here at once and take your place at the table'?
8 Would you not rather say to him, 'Prepare supper for me, put on your apron and
serve me while I eat and drink; later you may eat and drink'? 9 Do you thank the
slave for doing what was commanded? 10 So you also, when you have done all that 17.10
you were ordered to do, say, 'We are worthless slaves; we have done only what we 1 Cor 9.16-18
ought to have done!'"

Jesus heals ten lepers
(169)

11 On the way to Jerusalem Jesus[i] was going through the region between Sa- 17.12
maria and Galilee. 12 As he entered a village, ten lepers[j] approached him. Keeping Lev 13.45,46
their distance, 13 they called out, saying, "Jesus, Master, have mercy on us!" 17.14 Lev 14.3
14 When he saw them, he said to them, "Go and show yourselves to the priests." Mk 1.43,44

f Gk *He* g Gk *your brother* h Gk *faith as a grain of* i Gk *he* j The terms *leper* and *leprosy* can refer to several diseases

17.1–3 Jesus may have been directing this warning at the religious leaders who taught their converts their own hypocritical ways (see Matthew 23.15). They were perpetuating an evil system. A person who teaches others has a solemn responsibility (James 3.1). Like physicians, a teacher should keep this ancient oath in mind: "First, do no harm."

17.3, 4 To rebuke does not mean to point out every sin we see; it means to bring sin to a person's attention with the purpose of restoring him or her to God and to fellow humans. When you feel you must rebuke another Christian for a sin, check your attitudes before you speak. Do you love the person? Are you willing to forgive? Unless rebuke is tied to forgiveness, it will not help the sinning person.

17.5, 6 The disciples' request was genuine; they wanted the faith necessary for such radical forgiveness. But Jesus didn't directly answer their question, because the amount of faith is not as important as its genuineness. What is faith? It is total dependence on God and a willingness to do his will. It is not something we use to put on a show for others. It is complete and humble obedience to God's will, readiness to do whatever he calls us to do. The amount of faith isn't as important as the right kind of faith—faith in our all-powerful God.

17.6 A mustard seed is small, but it is alive and growing. Like a tiny seed, a small amount of genuine faith in God will take root and grow. Almost invisible at first, it will begin to spread, first underground and then visibly. Although each change will be gradual and imperceptible, soon this faith will have produced major results that will uproot and destroy competing loyalties. We don't need more faith; a tiny seed of faith is enough, if it is alive and growing.

17.7–10 If we have obeyed God, we have only done our duty and we should regard it as a privilege. Do you sometimes feel you deserve extra credit for serving God? Remember, obedience is not something extra we do; it is our duty. Jesus is not rendering our service as meaningless or useless, nor is he doing away with rewards. He is attacking unwarranted self-esteem and spiritual pride.

17.11–14 Lepers were required to try to stay away from other people and to announce their presence if they had to come near. Sometimes leprosy went into remission. If a leper thought his leprosy had gone away, he was supposed to present himself to a priest who could declare him clean (Leviticus 14). Jesus sent the ten lepers to the priest *before* they were healed—and they went! They responded in faith, and Jesus healed them on the way. Is your trust in God so strong that you act on what he says even before you see evidence that it will work?

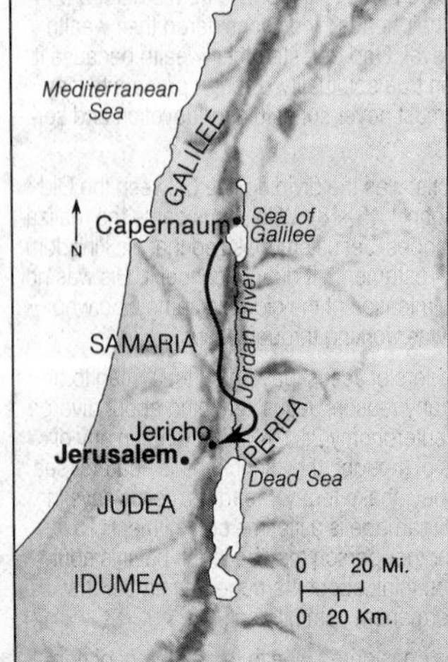

LAST TRIP FROM GALILEE
Jesus left Galilee for the last time—he would not return before his death. He passed through Samaria, met and healed ten lepers, and continued to Jerusalem. He spent some time east of the Jordan (Mark 10.1) before going to Jericho (19.1).

And as they went, they were made clean. 15Then one of them, when he saw that he
was healed, turned back, praising God with a loud voice. 16He prostrated himself
at Jesus'[k] feet and thanked him. And he was a Samaritan. 17Then Jesus asked,
"Were not ten made clean? But the other nine, where are they? 18Was none of them
found to return and give praise to God except this foreigner?" 19Then he said to
him, "Get up and go on your way; your faith has made you well."

Jesus teaches about the coming of the kingdom of God
(170)

20 Once Jesus[l] was asked by the Pharisees when the kingdom of God was
coming, and he answered, "The kingdom of God is not coming with things that can
be observed; 21 nor will they say, 'Look, here it is!' or 'There it is!' For, in fact, the
kingdom of God is among[m] you."

22 Then he said to the disciples, "The days are coming when you will long to
see one of the days of the Son of Man, and you will not see it. 23They will say to
you, 'Look there!' or 'Look here!' Do not go, do not set off in pursuit. 24For as the
lightning flashes and lights up the sky from one side to the other, so will the Son of
Man be in his day.[n] 25But first he must endure much suffering and be rejected by
this generation. 26Just as it was in the days of Noah, so too it will be in the days of
the Son of Man. 27They were eating and drinking, and marrying and being given in
marriage, until the day Noah entered the ark, and the flood came and destroyed all
of them. 28Likewise, just as it was in the days of Lot: they were eating and drinking, buying and selling, planting and building, 29but on the day that Lot left
Sodom, it rained fire and sulfur from heaven and destroyed all of them 30 — it will
be like that on the day that the Son of Man is revealed. 31On that day, anyone on
the housetop who has belongings in the house must not come down to take them
away; and likewise anyone in the field must not turn back. 32Remember Lot's wife.
33Those who try to make their life secure will lose it, but those who lose their life
will keep it. 34I tell you, on that night there will be two in one bed; one will be taken
and the other left. 35There will be two women grinding meal together; one will be
taken and the other left."[o] 37Then they asked him, "Where, Lord?" He said to
them, "Where the corpse is, there the vultures will gather."

- **17.16** 2 Kgs 17.24 Jn 8.48
- **17.19** Mt 9.22 Lk 18.42
- **17.20** Mt 12.28 Lk 11.20; 19.11 Jn 3.3; 18.36 Acts 1.6
- **17.22** Mt 9.15
- **17.23** Mt 24.23,26,27 Mk 13.21 Lk 21.8
- **17.24** 1 Tim 6.15
- **17.25** Mt 16.21 Mk 8.31 Lk 9.22
- **17.26** Gen 6.12,13 Mt 24.37-39
- **17.29** Gen 19.24-26
- **17.30** 2 Thess 1.7
- **17.33** Mt 10.39; 16.25 Jn 12.25
- **17.35** Mt 24.40,41 1 Thess 4.17
- **17.37** Job 39.30

[k] Gk *his* [l] Gk *he* [m] Or *within* [n] Other ancient authorities lack *in his day* [o] Other ancient authorities add verse 36, *"Two will be in the field; one will be taken and the other left."*

17.16 Jesus healed all ten lepers, but only one returned to thank him. It is possible to receive God's great gifts with an ungrateful spirit — nine of the lepers did so. Only the thankful leper, however, learned that his faith had played a role in his healing; and only grateful Christians grow in understanding of God's grace. God does not demand that we thank him, but he is pleased when we do so. And he uses our responsiveness to teach us more about himself.

17.16 Not only was this man a leper, he was also a Samaritan — a race despised by the Jews as idolatrous half-breeds (see the note on 10.33). Once again Luke is pointing out that God's grace is for everybody.

17.20, 21 The Pharisees asked when God's kingdom would come, not knowing that it had already arrived. The kingdom of God is not like an earthly kingdom with geographical boundaries. Instead, it begins with the work of God's Spirit in people's lives and relationships. Still today we must resist looking to institutions or programs for evidence of the progress of God's kingdom. Instead, we should look for what God is doing in people's hearts.

17.23, 24 Many will claim to be God or will claim that Jesus has returned — and many will believe them. Jesus warns us never to take such reports seriously, no matter how convincing they may sound. When Jesus returns, his power and presence will be evident to everyone. No one will need to spread the message, because all will see for themselves.

17.23–36 Life will be going on as usual on the day Christ returns. There will be no warning. Most people will be going about their everyday tasks, indifferent to the demands of God. They will be as surprised by Christ's return as the people in Noah's day were by the flood (Genesis 6 – 8) or the people in Lot's day by the destruction of Sodom (Genesis 19). We don't know the time of Christ's return, but we do know he is coming. He may come today, tomorrow, or centuries in the future. Whenever it is, we must be morally and spiritually ready. Live as if Jesus were returning today.

17.26–36 Jesus warned against false security. We are to abandon the values and attachments of this world in order to be ready for Christ's return. His return will happen suddenly, and when he comes, there will be no second chances. Some will be taken to be with him; the rest will be left behind.

17.37 To answer the disciples' question, Jesus quoted a familiar proverb. One vulture circling overhead does not mean much; but a gathering of vultures means a dead body is nearby. Likewise, one "sign of the end" may not be significant; but when many signs occur, the Second Coming is near.

Jesus tells the parable of the persistent widow
(171)

18 Then Jesus[p] told them a parable about their need to pray always and not to 18.1
lose heart. 2 He said, "In a certain city there was a judge who neither feared Rom 12.12 Eph 6.18
God nor had respect for people. 3 In that city there was a widow who kept coming Col 4.2 1 Thess 5.17
to him and saying, 'Grant me justice against my opponent.' 4 For a while he re- 18.4,5
fused; but later he said to himself, 'Though I have no fear of God and no respect for Lk 11.8
anyone, 5 yet because this widow keeps bothering me, I will grant her justice, so
that she may not wear me out by continually coming.' "[q] 6 And the Lord said,
"Listen to what the unjust judge says. 7 And will not God grant justice to his chosen 18.7 Mt 24.22
ones who cry to him day and night? Will he delay long in helping them? 8 I tell you, Rom 8.33 Rev 6.10
he will quickly grant justice to them. And yet, when the Son of Man comes, will he 18.8
find faith on earth?" 1 Tim 4.1

Jesus tells the parable of two men who prayed
(172)

9 He also told this parable to some who trusted in themselves that they were 18.9
righteous and regarded others with contempt: 10 "Two men went up to the temple to Rom 14.10
pray, one a Pharisee and the other a tax collector. 11 The Pharisee, standing by 18.11 Isa 58.2
himself, was praying thus, 'God, I thank you that I am not like other people: Mt 6.5
thieves, rogues, adulterers, or even like this tax collector. 12 I fast twice a week; I Rev 3.17
give a tenth of all my income.' 13 But the tax collector, standing far off, would not 18.13 Ps 40.12
even look up to heaven, but was beating his breast and saying, 'God, be merciful 18.14 Job 22.29
to me, a sinner!' 14 I tell you, this man went down to his home justified rather than Mt 23.12
the other; for all who exalt themselves will be humbled, but all who humble them- Lk 14.11 Jas 4.6
selves will be exalted." 1 Pet 5.5,6

Jesus blesses little children
(174/Matthew 19.13–15; Mark 10.13–16)

15 People were bringing even infants to him that he might touch them; and 18.15 Mt 19.13-15
when the disciples saw it, they sternly ordered them not to do it. 16 But Jesus called Mk 10.13-16
for them and said, "Let the little children come to me, and do not stop them; for it 18.17
is to such as these that the kingdom of God belongs. 17 Truly I tell you, whoever Mt 18.3 1 Cor 14.20
does not receive the kingdom of God as a little child will never enter it." 1 Pet 2.2

Jesus speaks to the rich young man
(175/Matthew 19.16–30; Mark 10.17–31)

18 A certain ruler asked him, "Good Teacher, what must I do to inherit eternal

[p] Gk *he* [q] *Or so that she may not finally come and slap me in the face*

18.1 To persist in prayer until the answer comes does not mean endless repetition or painfully long prayer sessions. Always praying means keeping our requests constantly before God as we live for him day by day, believing he will answer. When we thus live by faith, we are not to give up. God may delay answering, but his delays always have good reasons. As we persist in prayer we grow in character, faith, and hope.

18.3 Widows and orphans were among the most vulnerable of all God's people, and both Old Testament prophets and New Testament apostles insisted that they be properly cared for. See, for example, Exodus 22.22–24; Isaiah 1.17; 1 Timothy 5.3; James 1.27.

18.6, 7 If unjust judges respond to constant pressure, how much more will a great and loving God respond to us. If we know he loves us, we can believe he will hear our cries for help.

18.10 The people who lived near Jerusalem often went to the temple to pray. The temple was the center of their worship.

18.11–14 The Pharisee did not go to the temple to pray to God but to announce to all within earshot how good he was. The tax collector went recognizing his sin and begging for mercy. Self-righteousness is dangerous. It leads to pride, causes a person to despise others, and prevents him or her from learning anything from God. The tax collector's prayer should be our prayer, because we all need God's mercy every day. Don't let pride in your achievements cut you off from God.

18.15–17 It was customary for a mother to bring her children to a rabbi for a blessing, and that is why these mothers gathered around Jesus. The disciples, however, thought the children were unworthy of the Master's time—less important than whatever else he was doing. But Jesus welcomed them, because little children have the kind of faith and trust needed to enter God's kingdom. It is important that we introduce our children to Jesus and that we ourselves approach him with childlike attitudes of acceptance, faith, and trust.

18.18ff This ruler sought reassurance, some way of knowing for sure he had eternal life. He wanted Jesus to measure and grade his qualifications, or to give him some task he could do to assure his own immortality. So Jesus gave him a task—the one thing the rich ruler felt he could not do. "Who then can be saved?" the bystanders asked. "No one can, by his own achievements," Jesus' answer implied. "But God can do what men can't." Salvation can-

18.18 Mt 19.16-22; Mk 10.17-22
18.20 Ex 20.12-16; Deut 5.16-20
18.22 Mt 6.19-21; 1 Tim 6.18,19
18.23 Ezek 33.31
18.24 Mt 19.23-30; Mk 10.23-31; 1 Tim 6.9; Jas 2.5
18.27 Jer 32.17
18.28 Lk 5.11
18.30 Job 42.10

life?" 19 Jesus said to him, "Why do you call me good? No one is good but God
alone. 20 You know the commandments: 'You shall not commit adultery; You shall
not murder; You shall not steal; You shall not bear false witness; Honor your father
and mother.' " 21 He replied, "I have kept all these since my youth." 22 When Jesus
heard this, he said to him, "There is still one thing lacking. Sell all that you own and
distribute the money[r] to the poor, and you will have treasure in heaven; then come,
follow me." 23 But when he heard this, he became sad; for he was very rich. 24 Jesus
looked at him and said, "How hard it is for those who have wealth to enter the
kingdom of God! 25 Indeed, it is easier for a camel to go through the eye of a needle
than for someone who is rich to enter the kingdom of God."

26 Those who heard it said, "Then who can be saved?" 27 He replied, "What is
impossible for mortals is possible for God."

28 Then Peter said, "Look, we have left our homes and followed you." 29 And
he said to them, "Truly I tell you, there is no one who has left house or wife or
brothers or parents or children, for the sake of the kingdom of God, 30 who will not
get back very much more in this age, and in the age to come eternal life."

Jesus predicts his death the third time
(177/Matthew 20.17–19; Mark 10.32–34)

18.31 Ps 22; Isa 53; Lk 9.22,44-45; 17.25
18.32 Mt 16.21; 17.22; 27.2

31 Then he took the twelve aside and said to them, "See, we are going up to
Jerusalem, and everything that is written about the Son of Man by the prophets will
be accomplished. 32 For he will be handed over to the Gentiles; and he will be
mocked and insulted and spat upon. 33 After they have flogged him, they will kill
him, and on the third day he will rise again." 34 But they understood nothing about
all these things; in fact, what he said was hidden from them, and they did not grasp
what was said.

Jesus heals a blind beggar
(179/Matthew 20.29–34; Mark 10.46–52)

18.35 Mt 20.29-34; Mk 10.46-52

35 As he approached Jericho, a blind man was sitting by the roadside begging.
36 When he heard a crowd going by, he asked what was happening. 37 They told

[r] Gk lacks *the money*

---

not be earned – it is God's gift (see Ephesians 2.8–10).

18.18, 19 Jesus' question to the ruler who came and called him "Good Teacher" was, in essence, "Do you know who I am?" Undoubtedly the man did not catch the implications of Jesus' reply – that the man was right in calling him good, because Jesus truly is God.

18.22, 23 This man's wealth smoothed his life and gave him power and prestige. When Jesus told him to sell everything he owned, he was touching the man's very basis for security and identity. The man did not understand that he would be even more secure if he followed Jesus than he was with all his wealth. Jesus does not ask all believers to sell everything they have, although this may be his will for some. He does ask us all, however, to get rid of anything that has become more important to us than God. If your basis for security has shifted from God to what you own, it would be better for you to get rid of those possessions.

18.24–27 Because money represents power, authority, and success, often it is difficult for wealthy people to realize their need and their powerlessness to save themselves. The rich in talent or intelligence suffer the same difficulty. Unless God reaches down into their lives, they will not come to him. Jesus surprised some of his hearers by offering salvation to the poor; he may surprise some people today by offering it to the rich. It is difficult for a self-sufficient person to realize his need and come to Jesus, but "What is impossible for mortals is possible for God."

18.26–30 Peter and the other disciples had paid a high price – leaving their homes and jobs – to follow Jesus. But Jesus reminded Peter that following him has its benefits as well as its sacrifices. Any believer who has had to give up something to follow Christ will be paid back in this life as well as in the next. For example, if you must give up a secure job, you will find that God offers a secure relationship with himself now and forever. If you must give up your family's approval, you will gain the love of the family of God. The disciples had begun to pay the price of following Jesus, and Jesus said they would be rewarded. Don't dwell on what you have given up; think about what you have gained and give thanks for it. You can never outgive God.

18.31–34 Some predictions about what would happen to Jesus are found in Psalm 41.9 (betrayal); Psalm 22.16–18 and Isaiah 53.4–7 (crucifixion); Psalm 16.10 (resurrection). The disciples didn't understand what Jesus said, apparently because they focused on what he said about his death and ignored what he said about his resurrection. Even though Jesus spoke plainly, they would not grasp the significance of his words until they saw the risen Christ face to face.

18.35 Beggars often waited along the roads near cities, because that was where they were able to contact the most people. Usually handicapped in some way, they were unable to earn a living. Medical help was not available for their problems, and the people tended to ignore their obligation to care for the needy (Leviticus 25.35–38). Thus beggars had little hope of escaping their degrading way of life. But this blind beggar took hope in the Messiah. He shamelessly cried out for Jesus' attention, and Jesus said his faith made him see. No matter how desperate your situation may seem, if you call out to Jesus in faith, he will help you.

him, "Jesus of Nazareth[s] is passing by." 38 Then he shouted, "Jesus, Son of David, **18.38** Heb 2.17
have mercy on me!" 39 Those who were in front sternly ordered him to be quiet; but
he shouted even more loudly, "Son of David, have mercy on me!" 40 Jesus stood **18.42**
still and ordered the man to be brought to him; and when he came near, he asked Mt 9.22
him, 41 "What do you want me to do for you?" He said, "Lord, let me see again." Lk 7.50; 17.19
42 Jesus said to him, "Receive your sight; your faith has saved you." 43 Immediately **18.43** Isa 35.5
he regained his sight and followed him, glorifying God; and all the people, when Mt 9.8 Lk 19.37
they saw it, praised God. Acts 4.21

Jesus brings salvation to Zacchaeus' home
(180)

19 He entered Jericho and was passing through it. 2 A man was there named **19.1** Josh 6.26
Zacchaeus; he was a chief tax collector and was rich. 3 He was trying to see 1 Kgs 16.34
who Jesus was, but on account of the crowd he could not, because he was short in **19.4**
stature. 4 So he ran ahead and climbed a sycamore tree to see him, because he was 1 Kings 10.27 2 Chron 1.15
going to pass that way. 5 When Jesus came to the place, he looked up and said to **19.7**
him, "Zacchaeus, hurry and come down; for I must stay at your house today." 6 So Mt 9.11; 11.19 Lk 5.30; 15.2
he hurried down and was happy to welcome him. 7 All who saw it began to grumble **19.8**
and said, "He has gone to be the guest of one who is a sinner." 8 Zacchaeus stood Ex 22.1
there and said to the Lord, "Look, half of my possessions, Lord, I will give to the Num 5.7 2 Sam 12.6
poor; and if I have defrauded anyone of anything, I will pay back four times as **19.9**
much." 9 Then Jesus said to him, "Today salvation has come to this house, because Mt 15.24; 18.11 Rom 4.11,12,
he too is a son of Abraham. 10 For the Son of Man came to seek out and to save the 16,17 Gal 3.7
lost." 1 Tim 1.15

Jesus tells the parable of the king's ten servants
(181)

11 As they were listening to this, he went on to tell a parable, because he was **19.11** Acts 1.6
near Jerusalem, and because they supposed that the kingdom of God was to appear **19.12**
immediately. 12 So he said, "A nobleman went to a distant country to get royal Mt 25.14-30 Mk 13.34
power for himself and then return. 13 He summoned ten of his slaves, and gave **19.13**
them ten pounds,[t] and said to them, 'Do business with these until I come back.' 1 Pet 4.10,11

[s] Gk *the Nazorean* [t] The mina, rendered here by *pound,* was about three months' wages for a laborer

18.38 The blind man called Jesus "Son of David." This means that he understood Jesus to be the long-awaited Messiah. A poor and blind beggar could *see* that Jesus was the Messiah, while the religious leaders who saw his miracles were blinded to his identity and refused to recognize him as the Messiah.

19.1–10 To finance their great world empire, the Romans levied heavy taxes upon all nations under their control. The Jews opposed these taxes because they supported a secular government and its pagan gods, but they were still forced to pay. Tax collectors were among the most unpopular people in Israel. Jews by birth, who chose to work for Rome, were considered traitors. Besides, it was common knowledge that tax collectors made themselves rich by gouging their fellow Jews. No wonder the crowds were displeased when Jesus went home with the tax collector Zacchaeus. But despite the fact that Zacchaeus was both dishonest and a turncoat, Jesus loved him; and in response, the little tax collector was converted. In every society, certain groups of people are considered "untouchable" because of their politics, their immoral behavior, or their life-style. We should not give in to social pressure to avoid these people. Jesus loves them, and they need to hear his good news.

19.8 Judging from the crowd's reaction to him, Zacchaeus must have been a very crooked tax collector. But after he met Jesus, he realized that his life needed straightening out. By giving to the poor and making restitution—with generous interest—to those he had cheated, Zacchaeus demonstrated inward change by outward action. It is not enough to follow Jesus in your head or heart alone. You must show your changed heart by changed behavior. Has your faith resulted in action? What changes do you need to make?

19.9, 10 When Jesus said Zacchaeus was a son of Abraham and yet was lost, he must have shocked his hearers two ways. They would not have liked to acknowledge this unpopular tax-gatherer as a fellow son of Abraham, and they would not have wished to admit that sons of Abraham could be lost. But a person is not saved by a good heritage or condemned by a bad one; faith is more important than genealogy. Jesus still loves to bring the lost into his kingdom, no matter what their background or previous way of life. Through faith, they are forgiven and made new.

19.11ff The people still hoped for a political leader who would set up an earthly kingdom and get rid of Roman domination. Jesus' parable showed that his kingdom would not take this form right away. First he would go away for a while, and his followers would need to be faithful and productive during his absence. Upon his return, he would inaugurate the powerful kingdom they were expecting.

19.14 14 But the citizens of his country hated him and sent a delegation after him, saying,
Jn 1.11 'We do not want this man to rule over us.' 15 When he returned, having received
royal power, he ordered these slaves, to whom he had given the money, to be summoned so that he might find out what they had gained by trading. 16 The first came
19.17 forward and said, 'Lord, your pound has made ten more pounds.' 17 He said to him,
Lk 16.10 'Well done, good slave! Because you have been trustworthy in a very small thing,
take charge of ten cities.' 18 Then the second came, saying, 'Lord, your pound has
made five pounds.' 19 He said to him, 'And you, rule over five cities.' 20 Then the
other came, saying, 'Lord, here is your pound. I wrapped it up in a piece of cloth,
21 for I was afraid of you, because you are a harsh man; you take what you did not
19.22 deposit, and reap what you did not sow.' 22 He said to him, 'I will judge you by
Job 15.6 Mt 12.37 your own words, you wicked slave! You knew, did you, that I was a harsh man,
Tit 3.11 taking what I did not deposit and reaping what I did not sow? 23 Why then did you
not put my money into the bank? Then when I returned, I could have collected it
with interest.' 24 He said to the bystanders, 'Take the pound from him and give it to
the one who has ten pounds.' 25 (And they said to him, 'Lord, he has ten pounds!')
19.26 Mt 13.12 26 'I tell you, to all those who have, more will be given; but from those who have
Mk 4.25 nothing, even what they have will be taken away. 27 But as for these enemies of
Lk 8.18 mine who did not want me to be king over them — bring them here and slaughter
them in my presence.' "

3. Jesus' ministry in Jerusalem

Jesus rides into Jerusalem on a donkey

(183/Matthew 21.1–11; Mark 11.1–11; John 12.12–19)

28 After he had said this, he went on ahead, going up to Jerusalem.

29 When he had come near Bethphage and Bethany, at the place called the

GOSPEL ACCOUNTS FOUND ONLY IN LUKE

1.5–80	Special events leading up to birth of John the Baptist and Jesus
2.1–52	Events from Jesus' childhood
3.19, 20	Herod puts John in prison
4.16–30	Jesus is rejected at Nazareth
5.1–11	Jesus provides a miraculous catch of fish
7.11–17	Jesus raises a widow's son from the dead
7.36–50	A sinful woman anoints Jesus' feet
8.1–3	Women travel with Jesus
10.1—18.14	Events, miracles, and teaching during the months prior to Christ's death
19.1–27	Jesus meets Zacchaeus and later tells the parable of the king's ten servants
23.6–12	Jesus' trial before Herod
24.44–49	Some of Jesus' last words before his ascension

19.11ff This story showed Jesus' followers what they were to do during the time between Jesus' departure and his second coming. Because we live in that time, it applies directly to us. We have been given excellent resources to build and expand God's kingdom. Jesus expects us to use these talents so that they multiply and the kingdom grows. He asks each of us to account for what we do with his gifts. While awaiting the coming of the kingdom of God in glory, we must do Christ's work.

19.20–27 Why was the king so hard on this man who had not increased the money? He punished the man because (1) he didn't share his master's interest in the kingdom; (2) he didn't trust his master's intentions; (3) his only concern was for himself, and (4) he did nothing to use the money. Like the king in this story, God has given you gifts to use for the benefit of his kingdom. Do you want the kingdom to grow? Do you trust God to govern it fairly? Are you as concerned for others' welfare as for your own? Are you willing to use faithfully what he has entrusted to you?

19.26–27 The background of this story is civil war. Some of the king's subjects refuse to acknowledge him. As he tries to consolidate his kingdom in absentia, he discovers among his own servants one who seems more influenced by the rebels than by the loyal subjects. Like the kingdom in the story, our world is in a state of civil war. Some people are loyal to God, their King in heaven, while others refuse to acknowledge his Lordship. Even among God's servants, people can be found who act more like enemies than loyal subjects. One day the Lord will return to put an end to the civil war by destroying his enemies and recreating the earth. On which side will you be?

Mount of Olives, he sent two of the disciples, 30 saying, "Go into the village ahead
of you, and as you enter it you will find tied there a colt that has never been ridden.
Untie it and bring it here. 31 If anyone asks you, 'Why are you untying it?' just say
this, 'The Lord needs it.' " 32 So those who were sent departed and found it as he
had told them. 33 As they were untying the colt, its owners asked them, "Why are
you untying the colt?" 34 They said, "The Lord needs it." 35 Then they brought it to
Jesus; and after throwing their cloaks on the colt, they set Jesus on it. 36 As he rode
along, people kept spreading their cloaks on the road. 37 As he was now approaching the path down from the Mount of Olives, the whole multitude of the disciples
began to praise God joyfully with a loud voice for all the deeds of power that they
had seen, 38 saying,

"Blessed is the king
who comes in the name of the Lord!
Peace in heaven,
and glory in the highest heaven!"

39 Some of the Pharisees in the crowd said to him, "Teacher, order your disciples to
stop." 40 He answered, "I tell you, if these were silent, the stones would shout out."
41 As he came near and saw the city, he wept over it, 42 saying, "If you, even
you, had only recognized on this day the things that make for peace! But now they
are hidden from your eyes. 43 Indeed, the days will come upon you, when your
enemies will set up ramparts around you and surround you, and hem you in on
every side. 44 They will crush you to the ground, you and your children within you,

19.36 2 Kgs 9.13
19.38 Ps 118.26 Mt 2.2; 25.34 Lk 2.14; 13.35 1 Tim 1.17
19.40 Hab 2.11
19.41 Lk 13.34 Jn 11.35
19.43 Isa 29.3 Ezek 4.1-3 Lk 21.6,20
19.44 1 Kgs 9.6-9 Dan 9.26 Mt 24.2 Mk 13.2 Lk 21.6

LAST WEEK IN JERUSALEM
As they neared Jerusalem from Jericho (19.1), Jesus and the disciples came to the villages of Bethany and Bethphage, nestled on the eastern slope of the Mount of Olives, only a few miles outside Jerusalem. Jesus stayed in Bethany during the nights of that last week, entering Jerusalem during the day.

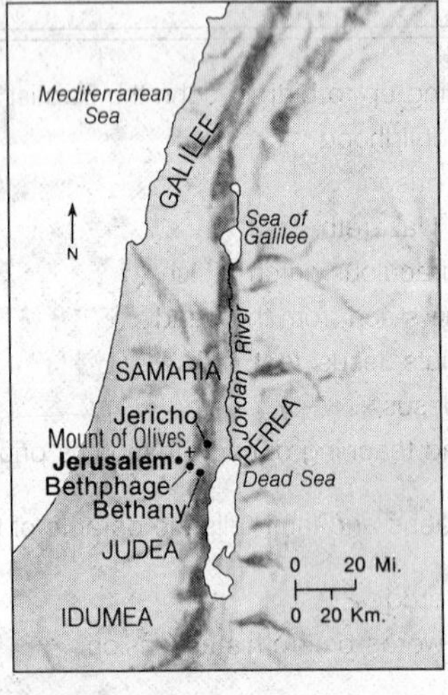

19.30–35 By this time Jesus was extremely well known. Everyone coming to Jerusalem for the Passover feast had heard of him, and, for a time, the popular mood was in his favor. "The Lord needs it" was all the disciples had to say, and the colt's owners gladly turned their animal over to them.

19.35–38 Christians celebrate this event on Palm Sunday. The people lined the highway, praising God, waving palm branches, and throwing their cloaks in front of the colt as it passed before them. "Long live the King" was the meaning of their joyful shouts, because they knew Jesus was intentionally fulfilling the prophecy in Zechariah 9.9: "Lo, your king comes to you; triumphant and victorious is he, humble and riding on a donkey, on a colt, the foal of a donkey." To announce that he was indeed the Messiah, Jesus chose a *time* when all Israel would be gathered at Jerusalem, a *place* where huge crowds could see him, and a *way* of proclaiming his mission that was unmistakable. The people went wild. They were sure their liberation was at hand.

19.38 The people who were praising God for giving them a king had the wrong idea about Jesus. They expected him to be a national leader who would restore their nation to its former glory, and thus they were deaf to the words of their prophets and blind to Jesus' real mission. When it became apparent that Jesus was not going to fulfill their hopes, many people turned against him.

19.39, 40 The Pharisees thought the crowd's words were sacrilegious and blasphemous. They didn't want someone challenging their power and authority, and they didn't want a revolt that would bring the Roman army down on them. So they asked Jesus to keep his people quiet. But Jesus said that if the people were quiet, the stones would immediately cry out. Why? Not because Jesus was setting up a powerful political kingdom, but because he was establishing God's eternal kingdom, a reason for the greatest celebration of all.

19.41–44 The Jewish leaders had rejected their king (19.47). They had gone too far. They had refused God's offer of salvation in Jesus Christ, when they were visited by God himself ("the time of your visitation"), and soon their nation would suffer. God did not turn away from the Jewish people who obeyed him, however. He continues to offer salvation to the people he loves, both Jews and Gentiles. Eternal life is within your reach – accept it while the opportunity is still offered.

19.43, 44 About 40 years after Jesus said these words, they came true. In A.D. 66, the Jews revolted against Roman control. Three years later Titus, son of the Emperor Vespasian, was sent to crush the rebellion. Roman soldiers attacked Jerusalem and broke through the northern wall but still couldn't take the city. Finally they laid siege to it, and in A.D. 70 they were able to enter the severely weakened city and burn it. Six hundred thousand Jews were killed during Titus's onslaught.

and they will not leave within you one stone upon another; because you did not
recognize the time of your visitation from God."[u]

Jesus clears the temple again
(184/Matthew 21.12–17; Mark 11.12–19)

45 Then he entered the temple and began to drive out those who were selling
19.46 Isa 56.7 Jer 7.11 things there; 46 and he said, "It is written,

'My house shall be a house of prayer';
but you have made it a den of robbers."

19.47 Mt 26.55 Lk 21.37; 22.53 Jn 18.20 47 Every day he was teaching in the temple. The chief priests, the scribes,
and the leaders of the people kept looking for a way to kill him; 48 but they did not
find anything they could do, for all the people were spellbound by what they
heard.

Religious leaders challenge Jesus' authority
(189/Matthew 21.23–27; Mark 11.27–33)

20.1 Mt 21.23-27 Mk 11.26-33 Acts 4.1; 6.12 **20** One day, as he was teaching the people in the temple and telling the good
news, the chief priests and the scribes came with the elders 2 and said to him,
20.2 Jn 2.18 Acts 4.7,10 "Tell us, by what authority are you doing these things? Who is it who gave you this
authority?" 3 He answered them, "I will also ask you a question, and you tell me:
4 Did the baptism of John come from heaven, or was it of human origin?" 5 They
20.6 Mt 14.5 Lk 7.29 discussed it with one another, saying, "If we say, 'From heaven,' he will say,
'Why did you not believe him?' 6 But if we say, 'Of human origin,' all the people
20.7 Rom 1.18,21 will stone us; for they are convinced that John was a prophet." 7 So they answered
20.8 Job 5.12,13 that they did not know where it came from. 8 Then Jesus said to them, "Neither will
I tell you by what authority I am doing these things."

Jesus tells the parable of the wicked farmers
(191/Matthew 21.33–46; Mark 12.1–12)

20.9 Isa 5.1-7 Mt 21.33-46 Mk 12.1-12 9 He began to tell the people this parable: "A man planted a vineyard, and
leased it to tenants, and went to another country for a long time. 10 When the season
20.10 2 Kgs 17.13,14 2 Chron 36.15, 16 Acts 7.52 came, he sent a slave to the tenants in order that they might give him his share of
the produce of the vineyard; but the tenants beat him and sent him away empty-
handed. 11 Next he sent another slave; that one also they beat and insulted and sent
away empty-handed. 12 And he sent still a third; this one also they wounded and
20.13 Jn 3.16 Rom 8.3 Gal 4.4 threw out. 13 Then the owner of the vineyard said, 'What shall I do? I will send my
beloved son; perhaps they will respect him.' 14 But when the tenants saw him, they
20.14 Heb 1.2 discussed it among themselves and said, 'This is the heir; let us kill him so that the
20.15 Acts 3.15 1 Thess 2.15 inheritance may be ours.' 15 So they threw him out of the vineyard and killed him.
What then will the owner of the vineyard do to them? 16 He will come and destroy
those tenants and give the vineyard to others." When they heard this, they said,

[u] Gk lacks *from God*

19.47 Who were the "leaders of the people"? This group probably included wealthy leaders in politics, commerce, and law. They had several reasons for wanting to get rid of Jesus. He had damaged business in the temple by driving the merchants out. In addition, he preached against injustice, and his teachings often favored the poor over the rich. Further, his great popularity was in danger of attracting Rome's attention, and the leaders of Israel wanted as little as possible to do with Rome.

20.1–8 This group of leaders wanted to get rid of Jesus, so they tried to trap him with their question. If Jesus answered that his authority came from God—if he stated openly that he was the Messiah and the Son of God—they would accuse him of blasphemy and bring him to trial. Jesus did not let himself be caught. Instead, he turned the question on them. Thus he exposed their motives and avoided their trap.

20.9–16 The characters in this story are easily identified. Even the religious leaders understood it. The owner of the vineyard is God; the vineyard is Israel; the tenants are the religious leaders; the slaves are the prophets and priests God sent to Israel; the son is the Messiah, Jesus; and the others are the Gentiles. Jesus' parable indirectly answered the religious leaders' question about his authority; it also showed them that he knew their plan to kill him.

"Heaven forbid!" 17 But he looked at them and said, "What then does this text 20.17 Ps 118.22
mean: Acts 4.11
'The stone that the builders rejected Eph 2.20 1 Pet 2.7,8
has become the cornerstone'?[v]
18 Everyone who falls on that stone will be broken to pieces; and it will crush any- 20.18 Isa 8.14,15
one on whom it falls." 19 When the scribes and chief priests realized that he had told Dan 2.34,35
this parable against them, they wanted to lay hands on him at that very hour, but
they feared the people.

Religious leaders question Jesus about paying taxes
(193/Matthew 22.15–22; Mark 12.13–17)

20 So they watched him and sent spies who pretended to be honest, in order to 20.20 Mt 22.15-22
trap him by what he said, so as to hand him over to the jurisdiction and authority of Mk 12.13-17
the governor. 21 So they asked him, "Teacher, we know that you are right in what
you say and teach, and you show deference to no one, but teach the way of God in
accordance with truth. 22 Is it lawful for us to pay taxes to the emperor, or not?"
23 But he perceived their craftiness and said to them, 24 "Show me a denarius.
Whose head and whose title does it bear?" They said, "The emperor's." 25 He 20.25 Lk 23.2
said to them, "Then give to the emperor the things that are the emperor's, and to Rom 13.7
God the things that are God's." 26 And they were not able in the presence of the
people to trap him by what he said; and being amazed by his answer, they became
silent.

Religious leaders question Jesus about the resurrection
(194/Matthew 22.23–33; Mark 12.18–27)

27 Some Sadducees, those who say there is no resurrection, came to him 20.27 Mt 22.15-33
28 and asked him a question, "Teacher, Moses wrote for us that if a man's brother Mk 12.18-27
dies, leaving a wife but no children, the man[w] shall marry the widow and raise Acts 23.8
up children for his brother. 29 Now there were seven brothers; the first married, 20.28 Gen 38.8
and died childless; 30 then the second 31 and the third married her, and so in the Deut 25.5
same way all seven died childless. 32 Finally the woman also died. 33 In the resur-

[v] Or *keystone* [w] Gk *his brother*

20.17–19 Quoting Psalm 118.22, Jesus showed the unbelieving leaders that even their rejection of the Messiah was prophesied in Scripture. Ignoring the cornerstone was dangerous. A person could be tripped or crushed (judged and punished). Jesus' comments were veiled, but the religious leaders had no trouble interpreting them. They immediately wanted to "lay hands on him."

20.20–26 Jesus turned his enemies' attempt to trap him into a powerful lesson: As God's followers, we have legitimate obligations to both God and the government. What is important is to keep our priorities straight. When the two authorities conflict, our duty to God always comes before our duty to the government.

20.21 These spies, pretending to be honest men, flattered Jesus before asking him their trick question, hoping to catch him off guard. But Jesus knew what they were trying to do and stayed out of their trap. Beware of flattery. With God's help, you can detect it and avoid the trap that often follows.

20.22 This was a loaded question. The Jews were enraged at having to pay taxes to Rome, thus supporting the pagan government and its gods. They hated the system that allowed tax collectors to charge exorbitant rates and keep the extra for themselves. If Jesus said they should pay taxes, they would call him a traitor to their nation and their religion. But if he said they should not, they could report him to Rome as a rebel. Jesus' questioners thought they had him this time, but he outwitted them again.

20.24 The denarius was the usual pay for one day's work.

20.27–38 The Sadducees, a group of conservative religious leaders, honored only the Pentateuch – Genesis through Deuteronomy – as Scripture. They also did not believe in a resurrection of the dead because they could find no mention of it in these books. They decided to try their hand at tricking Jesus, so they brought him a question that had always stumped the Pharisees. After addressing their question about marriage, Jesus answered their *real* question about resurrection. Basing his answer on the writings of Moses – an authority they respected – he upheld belief in resurrection.

20.34, 35 Jesus' statement does not mean people will not recognize their partners in heaven. It simply means we must not think of heaven as an extension of life as we now know it. Our relationships in this life are limited by time, death, and sin. We don't know everything about our resurrection life, but Jesus affirms that relationships will be different from what we are used to here and now.

rection, therefore, whose wife will the woman be? For the seven had married
her."

20.36 Rom 8.23; 1 Cor 15.42,49,52; 1 Jn 3.1,2
20.37 Ex 3.6; Jn 11.25; Acts 7.32; Rom 4.17; 2 Cor 5.15; Heb 11.10,35
20.40 Mt 22.41-46; Mk 12.34-37

34 Jesus said to them, "Those who belong to this age marry and are given in
marriage; 35 but those who are considered worthy of a place in that age and in the
resurrection from the dead neither marry nor are given in marriage. 36 Indeed they
cannot die anymore, because they are like angels and are children of God, being
children of the resurrection. 37 And the fact that the dead are raised Moses himself
showed, in the story about the bush, where he speaks of the Lord as the God of
Abraham, the God of Isaac, and the God of Jacob. 38 Now he is God not of the
dead, but of the living; for to him all of them are alive." 39 Then some of the scribes
answered, "Teacher, you have spoken well." 40 For they no longer dared to ask him
another question.

Religious leaders cannot answer Jesus' question
(196/Matthew 22.41–46; Mark 12.35–37)

20.42 Ps 110.1; Acts 2.34; 1 Cor 15.25

41 Then he said to them, "How can they say that the Messiah[x] is David's son?
42 For David himself says in the book of Psalms,
'The Lord said to my Lord,
"Sit at my right hand,
43 until I make your enemies your footstool."'
44 David thus calls him Lord; so how can he be his son?"

Jesus warns against the religious leaders
(197/Matthew 23.1–12; Mark 12.38–40)

20.45 Mt 23.1-7,13-14; Mk 12.38-40; Lk 11.43
20.47 Lk 12.47; Jas 4.17

45 In the hearing of all the people he said to the[y] disciples, 46 "Beware of the
scribes, who like to walk around in long robes, and love to be greeted with respect
in the marketplaces, and to have the best seats in the synagogues and places of
honor at banquets. 47 They devour widows' houses and for the sake of appearance
say long prayers. They will receive the greater condemnation."

[x] Or *the Christ* [y] Other ancient authorities read *his*

20.37, 38 The Sadducees came to Jesus with a trick question. Not believing in the resurrection, they wanted Jesus to say something they could refute. Even so, Jesus did not ignore or belittle their question. He answered it, and then went beyond it to the real issue. When people ask you tough religious questions—"How can a loving God allow people to starve?" "If God knows what I'm going to do, do I have any free choice?"—follow Jesus' example. First answer the question to the best of your ability; then look for the real issue—hurt over a personal tragedy, for example, or difficulty in making a decision. Often the spoken question is only a test, not of your ability to answer hard questions, but of your willingness to listen and care.

20.41–44 The Pharisees and Sadducees had asked their questions. Now Jesus turned the tables and asked them a question that went right to the heart of the matter—what they thought about the Messiah's identity. The Pharisees knew that the Messiah would be a descendant of David, but they did not understand that he would be more than a human descendant—he was God in the flesh. Jesus quoted from Psalm 110.1 to show that David knew the Messiah would be both man and God. The Pharisees expected only a human ruler to restore Israel's greatness as in the days of David and Solomon.

The central issue of life is what we believe about Jesus. Other spiritual questions are irrelevant unless we first decide to believe that Jesus is who he said he is. The Pharisees and Sadducees could not do this. They remained divided and confused over his identity.

20.45–47 The religious experts loved the benefits associated with their position, and they sometimes cheated the poor in order to get even more benefits. Every job has its rewards, but they should never become more important than doing the job faithfully. God will punish people who use their position of responsibility to cheat others. Whatever trust you have been given, use it to help others and not just yourself.

20.47 How strange to think that the religious leaders would receive the worst punishment. But behind their appearance of holiness and respectability, they were arrogant, crafty, selfish, and uncaring. Jesus exposed their evil hearts. He showed that despite their pious words, they neglected God's laws and did as they pleased. Religious works do not cancel sin. Jesus said God's heaviest sentence awaited these leaders because they should have been living examples of mercy and justice.

A poor widow gives all she has
(200/Mark 12.41–44)

21 He looked up and saw rich people putting their gifts into the treasury; [2]he 21.1
also saw a poor widow put in two small copper coins. [3]He said, "Truly I tell Prov 3.9,10 11.24,25
you, this poor widow has put in more than all of them; [4]for all of them have contrib- Mk 12.41-44
uted out of their abundance, but she out of her poverty has put in all she had to live
on."

Jesus tells about the future
(201/Matthew 24.1–28; Mark 13.1–23)

5 When some were speaking about the temple, how it was adorned with beauti- 21.5 Mt 24.1-22
ful stones and gifts dedicated to God, he said, [6]"As for these things that you see, Mk 13.1-23
the days will come when not one stone will be left upon another; all will be thrown 21.6 1 Kgs 9.8
down." Mic 3.12
7 They asked him, "Teacher, when will this be, and what will be the sign that Lk 19.44
this is about to take place?" [8]And he said, "Beware that you are not led astray; for 21.8
many will come in my name and say, 'I am he!'[z] and, 'The time is near!'[a] Do not Lk 17.23
go after them.
9 "When you hear of wars and insurrections, do not be terrified; for these things
must take place first, but the end will not follow immediately." [10]Then he said to
them, "Nation will rise against nation, and kingdom against kingdom; [11]there will 21.12 Mt 10.17,18
be great earthquakes, and in various places famines and plagues; and there will be Acts 4.3; 5.18 12.4; 16.24
dreadful portents and great signs from heaven. 25.23
12 "But before all this occurs, they will arrest you and persecute you; they will Rev 2.10

[z] Gk *I am* [a] Or *at hand*

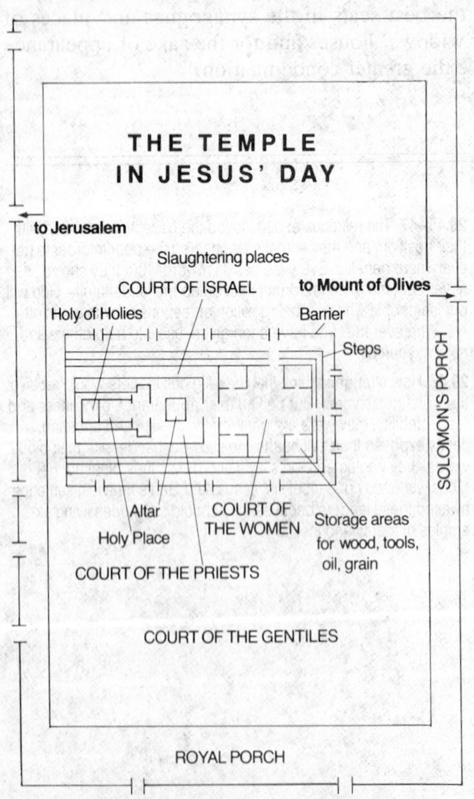

21.1, 2 Jesus was in the area of the temple called the court of the women. The treasury was located there or in an adjoining walkway. In this area were seven boxes in which worshipers could deposit their temple tax and six boxes for freewill offerings like the one this woman gave. Not only was she poor; as a widow she had few resources for making money. Her small gift was a sacrifice, but she gave it willingly.

21.1–4 This widow gave all she had, in contrast to the way most of us handle our money. When we consider giving a certain percentage of our income a great accomplishment, we resemble those who gave "out of their abundance." Here, Jesus is admiring generous and sacrifical giving. As believers, we should consider increasing our giving—whether of money, time, or talents—to a point beyond convenience or safety.

21.5, 6 The temple the disciples were admiring was not Solomon's temple—that was destroyed by the Babylonians in the seventh century B.C. This temple was built by Ezra after the return from exile in the sixth century B.C., desecrated by the Seleucids in the second century B.C., reconsecrated by the Maccabees soon afterward, and enormously expanded by Herod the Great over a 46-year period. It was a beautiful, imposing structure with a significant history, but Jesus said it would be completely destroyed. This happened in A.D. 70 when the Roman army burned Jerusalem.

21.7ff Jesus did not leave his disciples unprepared for the difficult years ahead. He warned them about false messiahs, natural disasters, and persecutions; but he assured them he would be with them to protect them and make his kingdom known through them. In the end, he promised, he would return in power and glory to save them. Jesus' warnings and promises to his disciples also apply to us as we look forward to his return.

21.12, 13 These persecutions soon began. Luke recorded many of them in the book of Acts. Paul wrote from prison that he anticipated suffering because it helped him know Christ better (Philippians 3.10; Colossians 1.24). The early church thrived despite intense persecution. In fact, late in the second century the church father Tertullian wrote, "The blood of Christians is seed," because opposition helped spread the news of Christianity.

21.13 Phil 1.12,13
21.14 Mt 10.19,20 Acts 6.10
21.16 Mic 7.6 Mt 10.21,22 Acts 7.60; 12.2
21.17 2 Tim 3.12
21.19 Rom 2.7 1 Pet 1.6-9
21.22 Isa 61.2 Dan 9.26,27 Hos 9.7 Rom 11.25 Rev 11.2
21.24 Dan 8.13 Rom 11.25 Rev 11.2

hand you over to synagogues and prisons, and you will be brought before kings and
governors because of my name. 13 This will give you an opportunity to testify. 14 So
make up your minds not to prepare your defense in advance; 15 for I will give you
words[b] and a wisdom that none of your opponents will be able to withstand or
contradict. 16 You will be betrayed even by parents and brothers, by relatives and
friends; and they will put some of you to death. 17 You will be hated by all because
of my name. 18 But not a hair of your head will perish. 19 By your endurance you
will gain your souls.
20 "When you see Jerusalem surrounded by armies, then know that its desolation has come near.[c] 21 Then those in Judea must flee to the mountains, and those
inside the city must leave it, and those out in the country must not enter it; 22 for
these are days of vengeance, as a fulfillment of all that is written. 23 Woe to those
who are pregnant and to those who are nursing infants in those days! For there will
be great distress on the earth and wrath against this people; 24 they will fall by the
edge of the sword and be taken away as captives among all nations; and Jerusalem
will be trampled on by the Gentiles, until the times of the Gentiles are fulfilled.

Jesus tells about his return
(202/Matthew 24.23–35; Mark 13.21–31)

21.25 Mt 24.29-31 Mk 13.24-27 2 Pet 3.10,12
21.27 Dan 7.13 Acts 1.11 Rev 1.7; 14.14
21.29 Mt 24.32-35 Mk 13.28-31
21.31 Mk 1.15
21.33 Isa 40.6-8 Mt 5.18 Lk 6.17 1 Pet 1.23-25

25 "There will be signs in the sun, the moon, and the stars, and on the earth
distress among nations confused by the roaring of the sea and the waves. 26 People
will faint from fear and foreboding of what is coming upon the world, for the powers of the heavens will be shaken. 27 Then they will see 'the Son of Man coming in
a cloud' with power and great glory. 28 Now when these things begin to take place,
stand up and raise your heads, because your redemption is drawing near."
29 Then he told them a parable: "Look at the fig tree and all the trees; 30 as soon
as they sprout leaves you can see for yourselves and know that summer is already
near. 31 So also, when you see these things taking place, you know that the kingdom of God is near. 32 Truly I tell you, this generation will not pass away until all
things have taken place. 33 Heaven and earth will pass away, but my words will not
pass away.

Jesus tells about remaining watchful
(203/Matthew 24.36–51; Mark 13.32–37)

21.34 Rom 13.12,13 1 Thess 5.2

34 "Be on guard so that your hearts are not weighed down with dissipation and
drunkenness and the worries of this life, and that day catch you unexpectedly,

[b] Gk *a mouth* [c] Or *is at hand*

21.14–19 Jesus warned that in the coming persecutions his followers would be betrayed by their family members and friends. Christians of every age have had to face this possibility. It is reassuring to know that even when we feel completely abandoned, the Holy Spirit stays with us. He will comfort us, protect us, and give us the words we need. This assurance can give us the courage and hope to stand firm for Christ no matter how difficult the situation.

21.18 Jesus was *not* saying believers would be exempt from harm or death during the persecutions. Remember that most of the disciples were martyred. Rather he was saying that none of his followers would suffer spiritual or eternal loss. On earth, everyone will die, but believers in Jesus will be saved for eternal life.

21.24 The "times of the Gentiles" began with Babylon's destruction of Jerusalem in 586 B.C. and the exile of the Jewish people. Israel was no longer an independent nation but was under the control of Gentile rulers. In Jesus' day, Israel was governed by the Roman Empire, and a Roman general would destroy the city in A.D. 70. Jesus was saying that the domination of God's people by his enemies would continue until God decided to end it. The "times of the Gentiles" refers not just to the repeated destructions of Jerusalem, but also to the continued and mounting persecution of God's people until the end.

21.28 The picture of the coming persecutions and natural disasters is gloomy, but ultimately it is a cause not for worry but for great joy. When believers see these events happening, they will know that the return of their Messiah is near, and they can look forward to his reign of justice and peace. Rather than being terrified by what is happening in our world, we should confidently await Christ's return to bring justice and restoration to his people.

21.34–36 Jesus told the disciples to keep a constant watch for his return. Although nearly 2,000 years have passed since he spoke these words, their truth remains: he is coming again, and we need to watch and be spiritually fit. This means working faithfully at the tasks God has given us. Don't let your mind and spirit be dulled by careless living, drinking, or the foolish pursuit of pleasure (dissipation). Be detached from the problems of life so you will be ready to move at his command.

[35]like a trap. For it will come upon all who live on the face of the whole earth. [36]Be
alert at all times, praying that you may have the strength to escape all these things
that will take place, and to stand before the Son of Man."
37 Every day he was teaching in the temple, and at night he would go out and
spend the night on the Mount of Olives, as it was called. [38]And all the people would
get up early in the morning to listen to him in the temple.

21.36 Mt 25.13 Mk 13.33 Eph 6.13,18 1 Thess 5.17 1 Jn 2.28
21.37,38 Lk 22.39 Jn 8.1,2

C. DEATH AND RESURRECTION OF JESUS, THE SAVIOR (22.1 – 24.53)

The perfect man was a high ideal in Greek culture. Written with Greeks in mind, Luke shows how Jesus was the perfect man given as the perfect sacrifice for the sin of all mankind. Christ is the ideal man — the perfect model for us to follow. We must stand in awe of his character, living up to man's highest ideals as well as God's demand for an atonement for sin. He is, at once, our model and our Savior.

Religious leaders plot to kill Jesus
(207/Matthew 26.1–5; Mark 14.1, 2)

22 Now the festival of Unleavened Bread, which is called the Passover, was
near. [2]The chief priests and the scribes were looking for a way to put Jesus[d]
to death, for they were afraid of the people.

22.1 Mt 26.1-5,14-16 Mk 14.1,2,10

Judas agrees to betray Jesus
(208/Matthew 26.14–16; Mark 14.10, 11)

3 Then Satan entered into Judas called Iscariot, who was one of the twelve; [4]he
went away and conferred with the chief priests and officers of the temple police
about how he might betray him to them. [5]They were greatly pleased and agreed to
give him money. [6]So he consented and began to look for an opportunity to betray
him to them when no crowd was present.

22.3 Jn 13.2,27
22.5 Zech 11.12 1 Tim 6.10

Disciples prepare for the Passover
(209/Matthew 26.17–19; Mark 14.12–16)

7 Then came the day of Unleavened Bread, on which the Passover lamb had to
be sacrificed. [8]So Jesus[e] sent Peter and John, saying, "Go and prepare the Passover meal for us that we may eat it." [9]They asked him, "Where do you want us to
make preparations for it?" [10]"Listen," he said to them, "when you have entered the
city, a man carrying a jar of water will meet you; follow him into the house he
enters [11]and say to the owner of the house, 'The teacher asks you, "Where is the
guest room, where I may eat the Passover with my disciples?" ' [12]He will show you
a large room upstairs, already furnished. Make preparations for us there." [13]So
they went and found everything as he had told them; and they prepared the Passover
meal.

22.7 Ex 12.3,4,17 Deut 16.1 Mt 26.17-19 Mk 14.12-16
22.8 Acts 3.1; 4.13 Gal 2.9
22.10 1 Sam 10.3

[d] Gk *him* [e] Gk *he*

21.36 Only days after telling the disciples to pray that they might escape persecution, Jesus himself asked God, if possible, to spare him the agonies of the cross (22.41, 42). It is abnormal to *want* to suffer, but as Jesus' followers we are willing to suffer if by doing so we can help build God's kingdom. We have two wonderful promises to help us as we suffer: God will always be with us (Matthew 28.20), and he will one day rescue us and give us eternal life (Revelation 21.1–4).

22.1 All Jewish males over the age of 12 were required to go to Jerusalem for the Passover festival, followed by a seven-day festival called the festival of unleavened bread. For these feasts, Jews from all over the Roman Empire converged on Jerusalem to celebrate one of the most important events in their history. To learn more about the Passover and the festival of unleavened bread, see the note on Mark 14.1.

22.3 Satan's part in the betrayal of Jesus does not remove any of the responsibility from Judas. Disillusioned because Jesus was talking about dying rather than about setting up his kingdom, Judas may have been trying to force Jesus' hand and make him use his power to prove he was the Messiah. Or perhaps Judas, not understanding Jesus' mission, no longer believed that Jesus was God's chosen one. (For more information on Judas, see his Profile in Mark 14.) Whatever Judas thought, Satan assumed that Jesus' death would end his mission and thwart God's plan. Like Judas, he did not know that Jesus' death and resurrection were the most important parts of God's plan all along.

22.7, 8 The Passover meal included lamb because of its associations with the Jews' exodus from Egypt. When the Jews were getting ready to leave, God told them to kill a lamb and paint its blood on the doorposts of their houses. They then were to prepare the meat for food. Peter and John had to buy and prepare the lamb as well as the unleavened bread, herbs, wine, and other ceremonial food.

22.10 Ordinarily women, not men, went to the well and brought home the water. So this man would have stood out in the crowd.

Jesus and the disciples have the last supper
(211/Matthew 26.20–30; Mark 14.17–26; John 13.21–30)

14 When the hour came, he took his place at the table, and the apostles with
him. 15 He said to them, "I have eagerly desired to eat this Passover with you before
I suffer; 16 for I tell you, I will not eat it[f] until it is fulfilled in the kingdom of God."
17 Then he took a cup, and after giving thanks he said, "Take this and divide it
among yourselves; 18 for I tell you that from now on I will not drink of the fruit of
the vine until the kingdom of God comes." 19 Then he took a loaf of bread, and
when he had given thanks, he broke it and gave it to them, saying, "This is my
body, which is given for you. Do this in remembrance of me." 20 And he did the
same with the cup after supper, saying, "This cup that is poured out for you is the
new covenant in my blood.[g] 21 But see, the one who betrays me is with me, and his
hand is on the table. 22 For the Son of Man is going as it has been determined, but
woe to that one by whom he is betrayed!" 23 Then they began to ask one another,
which one of them it could be who would do this.

24 A dispute also arose among them as to which one of them was to be regarded
as the greatest. 25 But he said to them, "The kings of the Gentiles lord it over them;
and those in authority over them are called benefactors. 26 But not so with you;
rather the greatest among you must become like the youngest, and the leader like
one who serves. 27 For who is greater, the one who is at the table or the one who
serves? Is it not the one at the table? But I am among you as one who serves.

28 "You are those who have stood by me in my trials; 29 and I confer on you,
just as my Father has conferred on me, a kingdom, 30 so that you may eat and drink
at my table in my kingdom, and you will sit on thrones judging the twelve tribes of
Israel.

22.14 Mt 26.20,26-29 Mk 14.17,22-25
22.16 Lk 14.15 Rev 19.9
22.19 1 Cor 10.16 11.23-26
22.20 Jer 31.31 Heb 9.15-18
22.21 Ps 41.9 Mt 26.20-25 Mk 14.17-21 Jn 13.21-30
22.22 Acts 2.23; 4.28
22.24 Mk 9.34 Lk 9.46
22.25 Mt 20.25-28 Mk 10.42-45
22.26 Mt 23.11 Mk 9.35 Lk 9.48 1 Pet 5.5
22.27 Jn 13.14 Phil 2.7
22.30 Mt 8.11; 19.28

[f] Other ancient authorities read *never eat it again* [g] Other ancient authorities lack, in whole or in part, verses 19b-20 (*which is given . . . in my blood*)

22.14–18 The Passover commemorated Israel's escape from Egypt when the blood of a lamb painted on their doorposts saved their firstborn sons from death. This event foreshadowed Jesus' work on the cross. As the spotless Lamb of God, his blood would be spilled in order to save his people from the penalty of death brought by sin.

22.17, 20 Luke mentions two glasses of wine, while Matthew and Mark mention only one. In the traditional Passover meal, the wine is served four times. Christ spoke the words about his body and his blood when he offered the fourth and last cup.

22.17–20 Christians differ in their interpretation of the meaning of the commemoration of the Lord's supper. There are three main views: (1) the bread and wine actually become Christ's body and blood; (2) the bread and wine remain unchanged, yet Christ is spiritually present by faith in and through them; (3) the bread and wine, which remain unchanged, are lasting memorials of Christ's sacrifice. No matter which view they favor, all Christians agree that the Lord's supper commemorates Christ's death on the cross for our sins and points to the coming of his kingdom in glory. When we partake of it, we show our deep gratitude for his work on our behalf and our faith is strengthened.

22.19 Jesus asked the disciples to eat the broken bread "in remembrance of me." He wanted them to remember his sacrifice, the basis for forgiveness of sins, and also his friendship, which they could continue to enjoy through the work of the Holy Spirit. Although the exact meaning of communion has been strongly debated throughout church history, Christians still take bread and wine in remembrance of their Lord, Savior, and Friend, Jesus Christ. Do not neglect participating in the Lord's supper. Let it remind you of what Christ did for you.

22.20 In Old Testament times, God agreed to forgive people's sins if they brought animals for the priests to sacrifice. When this sacrificial system was inaugurated, the agreement between God and man was sealed with the blood of animals (Exodus 24.8). But animal blood did not in itself remove sin (only God can forgive sin), and animal sacrifices had to be repeated day by day and year after year. Jesus instituted a "new covenant" or agreement between man and God. Under this new covenant, Jesus would die in the place of sinners. Unlike the blood of animals, his blood (because he is God) would truly remove the sins of all who put their faith in him. And his sacrifice would never have to be repeated; it would be good for all eternity. The prophets looked forward to this new covenant that would fulfill the old sacrificial agreement (Jeremiah 31.31–34), and John the Baptist called Jesus the "Lamb of God who takes away the sin of the world" (John 1.29).

22.21 From the accounts of Mark and John we know that the betrayer is Judas Iscariot. Although the other disciples were confused by Jesus' words, Judas knew what he meant.

22.24 The most important event in human history was about to take place, and the disciples were still arguing about their prestige in the kingdom! Looking back, we say, "This was no time to worry about status." But the disciples, wrapped up in their own concerns, did not perceive what Jesus had been trying to tell them about his approaching death and resurrection. What are your major concerns today? Twenty years from now, as you look back, will these worries look petty and inappropriate? Get your eyes off yourself and get ready for Christ's coming into human history for the second time.

22.24–27 The world's system of leadership is very different from the kingdom's. Worldly leaders are often selfish and arrogant as they claw their way to the top. (Some kings in the ancient world gave themselves the title "benefactor.") But among Christians, the leader is to be the one who *serves* best. There are different styles of leadership – some lead through public speaking, some through administering, some through relationships – but every Christian leader needs a servant's heart. Ask the people you lead how you can serve them better.

Jesus predicts Peter's denial
(212/John 13.31–38)

31 "Simon, Simon, listen! Satan has demanded[h] to sift all of you like wheat,
32 but I have prayed for you that your own faith may not fail; and you, when once
you have turned back, strengthen your brothers." 33 And he said to him, "Lord, I
am ready to go with you to prison and to death!" 34 Jesus[i] said, "I tell you, Peter,
the cock will not crow this day, until you have denied three times that you know
me."
35 He said to them, "When I sent you out without a purse, bag, or sandals, did
you lack anything?" They said, "No, not a thing." 36 He said to them, "But now, the
one who has a purse must take it, and likewise a bag. And the one who has no sword
must sell his cloak and buy one. 37 For I tell you, this scripture must be fulfilled in
me, 'And he was counted among the lawless'; and indeed what is written about me
is being fulfilled." 38 They said, "Lord, look, here are two swords." He replied, "It
is enough."

22.31 Amos 9.9 Mt 26.31-35 Mk 14.27-31 1 Pet 5.8
22.32 Ps 51.13 Jn 17.9,11,15 21.15 2 Cor 1.3,4
22.33 Jn 13.37,38
22.35 Mt 10.9,10 Lk 9.3
22.37 Isa 53.12 Mk 15.28

Jesus agonizes in the garden
(223/Matthew 26.36–46; Mark 14.32–42)

39 He came out and went, as was his custom, to the Mount of Olives; and the
disciples followed him. 40 When he reached the place, he said to them, "Pray that
you may not come into the time of trial."[j] 41 Then he withdrew from them about a
stone's throw, knelt down, and prayed, 42 "Father, if you are willing, remove this
cup from me; yet, not my will but yours be done." ⟦43 Then an angel from heaven
appeared to him and gave him strength. 44 In his anguish he prayed more earnestly,
and his sweat became like great drops of blood falling down on the ground.⟧[k]
45 When he got up from prayer, he came to the disciples and found them sleeping
because of grief, 46 and he said to them, "Why are you sleeping? Get up and pray
that you may not come into the time of trial."[j]

22.39 Mt 26.30,36-46 Mk 14.26,32-42 Jn 18.1
22.40 Mt 6.13
22.41 Mk 10.38 Jn 5.30; 6.38 18.11

[h] Or *has obtained permission* [i] Gk *He* [j] Or *into temptation* [k] Other ancient authorities lack verses 43 and 44

22.31, 32 Satan wanted to crush Simon Peter like a grain of wheat. He hoped to find only chaff and blow it away. But Jesus assured Peter that his faith, although it would falter, would not be destroyed. It would be renewed, and he would become a powerful leader.

22.33, 34 Jesus predicted that Judas would betray him and said that calamity awaited the traitor (22.22). He then predicted that Peter would deny him but then repent and lead his brethren. Betraying and denying—one is just about as bad as the other. But the two men have entirely different fates because one repented.

22.35–38 Now Jesus reversed his earlier advice regarding how to travel (9.3). The disciples were to bring a bag, money, and a sword. They would be facing hatred and persecution and would need to be prepared. When Jesus said "It is enough," he may have meant it was not time to think of using swords. In either case, mention of a sword vividly communicated the trials they were soon to face.

22.39 The Mount of Olives was located just to the east of Jerusalem. Jesus went up the southwestern slope to an olive grove called Gethsemane, which means "oil press."

22.40 Jesus asked the disciples to pray that they would not enter into temptation, because he knew he would soon be leaving them. He also knew they would need extra strength to face the temptations ahead—temptations to run away or to deny their relationship with him. They were about to see him die. Would they still think he was the Messiah? Their strongest temptation would be to think they had been deceived.

22.41, 42 Was Jesus trying to get out of his mission? It is never wrong to express our true feelings to God. Jesus exposed his dread of the coming trials, but he also reaffirmed his commitment to do what God wanted. The cup he spoke of meant the terrible agony he knew he would endure—not only the horror of the crucifixion but, even worse, the total separation from God he would have to experience in order to die for the world's sins.

22.44 Only Luke tells us of Jesus' sweat resembling great drops of blood. Jesus was in extreme agony, but he did not give up or give in. He went ahead with the mission for which he had come. The writer to the Hebrews used Jesus' experience to encourage fainthearted Christians (see Hebrews 12.3, 4).

22.46 These disciples were asleep. How tragic it is that many Christians act as if they are sound asleep when it comes to devotion to Christ and service for him. Don't be found insensitive or unprepared for Christ's work.

Jesus is betrayed and arrested
(224/Matthew 26.47–56; Mark 14.43–52; John 18.1–11)

22.47 Mt 26.47-56 47 While he was still speaking, suddenly a crowd came, and the one called
Mk 14.43-50 Judas, one of the twelve, was leading them. He approached Jesus to kiss him; 48 but
Jn 18.1-11 Jesus said to him, "Judas, is it with a kiss that you are betraying the Son of Man?"
49 When those who were around him saw what was coming, they asked, "Lord,
should we strike with the sword?" 50 Then one of them struck the slave of the high
priest and cut off his right ear. 51 But Jesus said, "No more of this!" And he touched
his ear and healed him. 52 Then Jesus said to the chief priests, the officers of the
temple police, and the elders who had come for him, "Have you come out with
22.53 swords and clubs as if I were a bandit? 53 When I was with you day after day in the
Gen 3.15 Lk 19.47 temple, you did not lay hands on me. But this is your hour, and the power of dark-
Jn 7.30 ness!"

Peter denies knowing Jesus
(227/Matthew 26.69–75; Mark 14.66–72; John 18.25–27)

54 Then they seized him and led him away, bringing him into the high priest's

JESUS' TRIAL Jesus' trial was actually a series of hearings, carefully controlled to accomplish the death of Jesus. The verdict was predecided, but certain "legal" procedures were necessary. A lot of effort went into condemning and crucifying an innocent man. Jesus went through an unfair trial in our place so that we would not have to face a fair trial and receive just punishment for our sins.

Event	*Probable reasons*	*References*
Trial before Annas (powerful ex-high priest)	Although no longer the high priest, may have still wielded much power	John 18.13–23
Trial before Caiaphas (the ruling high priest)	To gather evidence for the full council hearing to follow	Matthew 26.57–68 Mark 14.53–65 Luke 22.54, 63–65 John 18.24
Trial before the council	Formal religious trial and condemnation to death	Matthew 27.1 Mark 15.1 Luke 22.66–71
Trial before Pilate (highest Roman authority)	All death sentences needed Roman approval	Matthew 27.2, 11–14 Mark 15.1–5 Luke 23.1–6 John 18.28–38
Trial before Herod (ruler of Galilee)	A courtesy and guilt-sharing act by Pilate because Jesus was from Galilee, Herod's district	Luke 23.7–12
Trial before Pilate	Pilate's last effort to avoid condemning an obviously innocent man	Matthew 27.15–26 Mark 15.6–15 Luke 23.13–25 John 18.39—19.16

22.47 A kiss was and still is the traditional greeting among men in certain parts of the world. In this case, it was also the agreed upon signal to point out Jesus (Matthew 26.48). It is ironic that a gesture of greeting would be the means of betrayal. It was a hollow gesture because of Judas's treachery. Have any of your religious practices become empty gestures? We still betray Christ when our acts of service or giving are insincere or done merely for show.

22.50 We learn from the Gospel of John that the man who cut off the servant's ear was Peter (John 18.10).

22.53 The religious leaders had not arrested Jesus in the temple for fear of a riot. Instead, they came secretly at night, under the influence of the prince of darkness, Satan himself. Although it looked as if Satan was getting the upper hand, everything was proceeding according to God's plan. It was now time for Jesus to die.

22.54 Jesus was immediately taken to the high priest's house, even though this was the middle of the night. The Jewish leaders were in a hurry—they wanted to complete the execution before the sabbath and get on with the Passover celebration. This residence was a palace with outer walls enclosing a courtyard where servants and soldiers warmed themselves around a fire.

house. But Peter was following at a distance. 55 When they had kindled a fire in the **22.54**
middle of the courtyard and sat down together, Peter sat among them. 56 Then a Mt 26.57,58 Mk 14.53,54
servant-girl, seeing him in the firelight, stared at him and said, "This man also was Jn 18.25-27
with him." 57 But he denied it, saying, "Woman, I do not know him." 58 A little later
someone else, on seeing him, said, "You also are one of them." But Peter said,
"Man, I am not!" 59 Then about an hour later still another kept insisting, "Surely
this man also was with him; for he is a Galilean." 60 But Peter said, "Man, I do not
know what you are talking about!" At that moment, while he was still speaking, the
cock crowed. 61 The Lord turned and looked at Peter. Then Peter remembered the **22.61** Jn 13.38
word of the Lord, how he had said to him, "Before the cock crows today, you will **22.62**
deny me three times." 62 And he went out and wept bitterly. 2 Cor 7.10
63 Now the men who were holding Jesus began to mock him and beat him; **22.63** Isa 52.14
64 they also blindfolded him and kept asking him, "Prophesy! Who is it that struck Mt 26.67,68 Mk 14.65
you?" 65 They kept heaping many other insults on him. Jn 18.22

The council of religious leaders condemns Jesus
(228/Matthew 27.1, 2; Mark 15.1)

66 When day came, the assembly of the elders of the people, both chief priests **22.66** Mt 26.63-66
and scribes, gathered together, and they brought him to their council. 67 They said, 27.1
"If you are the Messiah,[l] tell us." He replied, "If I tell you, you will not believe; Mk 14.61-64 15.1
68 and if I question you, you will not answer. 69 But from now on the Son of Man **22.69**
will be seated at the right hand of the power of God." 70 All of them asked, "Are Dan 7.13,14 Acts 3.21
you, then, the Son of God?" He said to them, "You say that I am." 71 Then they Heb 1.3; 8.1
said, "What further testimony do we need? We have heard it ourselves from his
own lips!"

[l] Or *the Christ*

22.55 Peter's experiences in the next few hours would change his life. He would change from a half-hearted follower, to a repentant disciple, and finally to the kind of person Christ could use to build his church. For more information on Peter, see his Profile in Matthew 27.

22.62 Peter wept bitterly, not only because he realized he had denied his Lord, the Messiah, but also because he had turned away from a very dear friend, a person who had loved and taught him for three years. Peter had said he would *never* deny Christ, despite Jesus' prediction (22.33, 34). But when frightened, he went against all he had boldly promised. Unable to stand up for his Lord for even 12 hours, he had failed as a disciple and as a friend. We need to be aware of our own breaking points and not become overconfident or self-sufficient. If we fail, we must remember that Christ can use those who recognize their failure. From this humiliating experience Peter learned much that would help him later when he assumed leadership of the young church.

22.70 Jesus in effect agreed he was the Son of God when he simply turned around the high priest's question by saying, "You say that I am." And Jesus identified himself with God by using a familiar title for God found in the Old Testament: "I am" (Exodus 3.14). The high priest recognized Jesus' claim and accused him of blasphemy. For any other man this claim would have been blasphemy, but in this case it was true. Blasphemy, the sin of claiming to be God or of attacking him, was punishable by death. The Jewish leaders had the evidence they wanted.

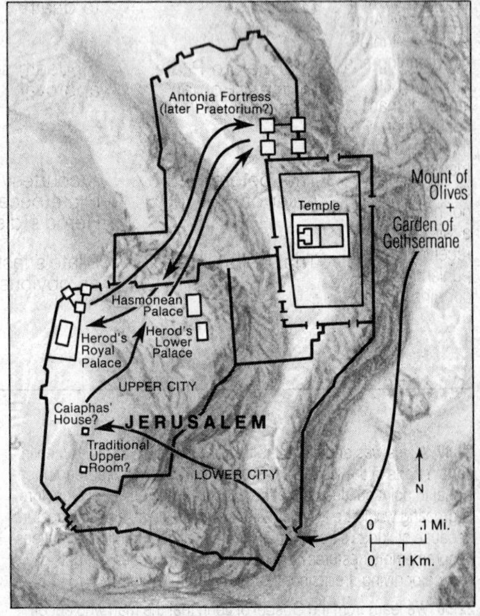

JESUS' TRIAL Taken from Gethsemane, Jesus first appeared before the Jewish council which had convened at daybreak at Caiaphas's house. From there he went first to Pilate, the Roman governor, then to Herod, tetrarch of Galilee, who was visiting in Jerusalem, and back to Pilate who, in desperation, sentenced Jesus to die.

Jesus stands trial before Pilate
(230/Matthew 27.11–14; Mark 15.2–5; John 18.28–38)

23 Then the assembly rose as a body and brought Jesus[m] before Pilate. 2 They
began to accuse him, saying, "We found this man perverting our nation,
forbidding us to pay taxes to the emperor, and saying that he himself is the Messiah, a king."[n] 3 Then Pilate asked him, "Are you the king of the Jews?" He answered, "You say so." 4 Then Pilate said to the chief priests and the crowds, "I find
no basis for an accusation against this man." 5 But they were insistent and said, "He
stirs up the people by teaching throughout all Judea, from Galilee where he began
even to this place."

23.1 Mt 27.2,11-14 Mk 15.1-5 Jn 18.28,33-38
23.2 Mt 17.24-27 Acts 17.7; 24.5
23.3 1 Tim 6.13
23.4 Jn 19.4

Jesus stands trial before Herod
(231)

6 When Pilate heard this, he asked whether the man was a Galilean. 7 And when
he learned that he was under Herod's jurisdiction, he sent him off to Herod, who
was himself in Jerusalem at that time. 8 When Herod saw Jesus, he was very glad,
for he had been wanting to see him for a long time, because he had heard about him
and was hoping to see him perform some sign. 9 He questioned him at some length,
but Jesus[o] gave him no answer. 10 The chief priests and the scribes stood by, vehemently accusing him. 11 Even Herod with his soldiers treated him with contempt
and mocked him; then he put an elegant robe on him, and sent him back to Pilate.
12 That same day Herod and Pilate became friends with each other; before this they
had been enemies.

23.7 Lk 3.1
23.8 Mt 14.1 Mk 6.14 Lk 9.9
23.9 Jn 19.9
23.12 Acts 4.27

Pilate hands Jesus over to be crucified
(232/Matthew 27.15–26; Mark 15.6–15; John 18.39—19.16)

13 Pilate then called together the chief priests, the leaders, and the people,
14 and said to them, "You brought me this man as one who was perverting the people; and here I have examined him in your presence and have not found this man

[m] Gk *him* [n] Or *is an anointed king* [o] Gk *he*

23.1 Pilate was the Roman governor of Judea, where Jerusalem was located. He seemed to take special pleasure in harassing the Jews. For example, he took money from the temple treasury and used it to build an aqueduct, and he insulted the Jewish religion by bringing imperial images into the city. As Pilate well knew, such acts could backfire. If the people lodged a formal complaint against his administration, Rome might remove him from his post. Pilate was already beginning to feel insecure in his position when the Jewish leaders brought Jesus to trial. Would he continue to badger the Jews and risk his political future, or would he give in to their demands and condemn a man who, he was quite sure, was innocent? That was the question facing Pilate that springtime Friday morning nearly 2,000 years ago. For more about Pilate, see his Profile in Mark 15.

23.7 Herod, also called Herod Antipas, was in Jerusalem that weekend for the Passover celebration. (This was the Herod who killed John the Baptist.) Pilate hoped to pass Jesus off on Herod, because he knew Jesus had lived and worked in Galilee. But Herod was not much help. He was curious about Jesus and enjoyed making fun of him. But when he sent Jesus back to Pilate, it was with the verdict of innocent. For more about Herod Antipas, see his Profile in Mark 6.

23.12 Herod was the part-Jewish ruler of Galilee and Perea. Pilate was the Roman governor of Judea and Samaria. These four provinces, together with several others, had been united under Herod the Great. But when he died in 4 B.C., the kingdom was divided among his sons, who were called not "king" but "tetrarch" (meaning "ruler of a fourth part of a region"). Archelaus, the son who had received Judea and Samaria, was removed from office within ten years, and his provinces were then ruled by a succession of Roman governors of whom Pilate was the fifth.

Herod Antipas had two advantages over Pilate: he came from a hereditary, part-Jewish monarchy, and he had held his position much longer. But Pilate had two advantages over Herod: he was a Roman citizen and an envoy of the emperor, and his position was created to replace that of Herod's ineffective half brother. It is not surprising that the two men were uneasy around each other. Jesus' trial, however, brought them together. Because Pilate recognized Herod's authority over Galilee, Herod stopped feeling threatened by the Roman politician. And because neither man knew what to do in this predicament, their common problem united them.

23.13–25 Pilate wanted to release Jesus, but the crowd loudly demanded his death, so Pilate sentenced Jesus to die. No doubt Pilate did not want to risk losing his position, which may already have been shaky, by allowing a riot to occur in his province. As a career politician, he knew the importance of compromise, and he saw Jesus more as a political threat than as a human being with rights and dignity.

When the stakes are high, it is difficult to stand up for what is right, and it is easy to see our opponents as problems to be solved rather than as people to be respected. Had Pilate been a man of real courage, he would have released Jesus no matter what the consequences. But the crowd roared, and Pilate buckled. We are like Pilate when we know what is right, but decide not to do it. When you have a difficult decision to make, don't discount the effects of peer pressure. Realize beforehand that the right decision could have unpleasant consequences: social rejection, career derailment, public ridicule. Then think of Pilate and resolve to stand up for what is right no matter what other people pressure you to do.

guilty of any of your charges against him. [15]Neither has Herod, for he sent him
back to us. Indeed, he has done nothing to deserve death. [16]I will therefore have
him flogged and release him."[p]
18 Then they all shouted out together, "Away with this fellow! Release Barabbas for us!" [19](This was a man who had been put in prison for an insurrection that
had taken place in the city, and for murder.) [20]Pilate, wanting to release Jesus,
addressed them again; [21]but they kept shouting, "Crucify, crucify him!" [22]A third
time he said to them, "Why, what evil has he done? I have found in him no ground
for the sentence of death; I will therefore have him flogged and then release him."
[23]But they kept urgently demanding with loud shouts that he should be crucified;
and their voices prevailed. [24]So Pilate gave his verdict that their demand should be
granted. [25]He released the man they asked for, the one who had been put in prison
for insurrection and murder, and he handed Jesus over as they wished.

23.15 Lk 9.9
23.16 Jn 19.1 Acts 16.37
23.17 Mt 27.15-26 Mk 15.6-15 Jn 18.39,40
23.18 Acts 3.14
23.23 Ex 23.2,3
23.24 Jn 19.16
23.25 Prov 17.15

Jesus is led away to be crucified
(234/Matthew 27.32–37; Mark 15.21–24; John 19.17)

26 As they led him away, they seized a man, Simon of Cyrene, who was coming from the country, and they laid the cross on him, and made him carry it behind
Jesus. [27]A great number of the people followed him, and among them were women
who were beating their breasts and wailing for him. [28]But Jesus turned to them and
said, "Daughters of Jerusalem, do not weep for me, but weep for yourselves and for

23.26 Mt 27.32 Mk 15.21 Jn 19.17

[p] Here, or after verse 19, other ancient authorities add verse 17, *Now he was obliged to release someone for them at the festival*

23.15 Jesus was tried six times, by both Jewish and Roman authorities, but he was never convicted of a crime deserving death. Even when condemned to execution, he had been convicted of no felony. Today, no one can find fault in Jesus. But just like Pilate, Herod, and the religious leaders, many still refuse to acknowledge him as Lord.

23.18, 19 Barabbas had been part of a rebellion against the Roman government (Mark 15.7). As a political insurgent, he was no doubt a hero among some of the Jews. How ironic it is that Barabbas, who was released, was guilty of the very crime Jesus was accused of (23.14).

23.18, 19 Who was Barabbas? Jewish men had names that identified them with their fathers. Simon Peter, for example, is called Simon son of Jonah (Matthew 16.17). Barabbas is never identified by his given name, and this name is not much help either – *bar-abbas* means "son of papa." He could have been anybody's son – and that's just the point. Barabbas, son of an unnamed father, committed a crime. Because Jesus died in his place, this man was set free. We too are sinners and criminals against God's holy law. Like Barabbas, we deserve to die. But Jesus has died in our place, for our sins, and we have been set free. We don't have to be important to accept our freedom in Christ. In fact, thanks to Jesus, God adopts us all as his own sons and daughters and gives us the right to call him Abba – "papa" (see Galatians 4.4–6).

23.22 When Pilate said he would have Jesus "flogged," he was referring to a punishment that could have killed Jesus. The usual procedure was to bare the upper half of the victim's body and tie his hands to a pillar before whipping him with a three-pronged whip. The number of lashes was determined by the severity of the crime; up to 40 were permitted under Jewish law. After being scourged, Jesus also endured other agonies as recorded in Matthew and Mark. He was slapped, struck with fists, and mocked. A crown of thorns was placed on his head, and he was beaten with a stick and stripped before being hung on the cross.

23.23, 24 Pilate did not want to give Jesus the death sentence. He thought the Jewish leaders were simply jealous and wanted to get rid of a rival. When they threatened to report Pilate to Caesar (John 19.12), however, Pilate became frightened. Historical records indicate that Pilate had already been warned by Roman authorities about tensions in this region. The last thing he needed was a riot in Jerusalem at Passover time, when the city was crowded with Jews from all over the Empire. So he turned Jesus over to the mob to do with as they pleased.

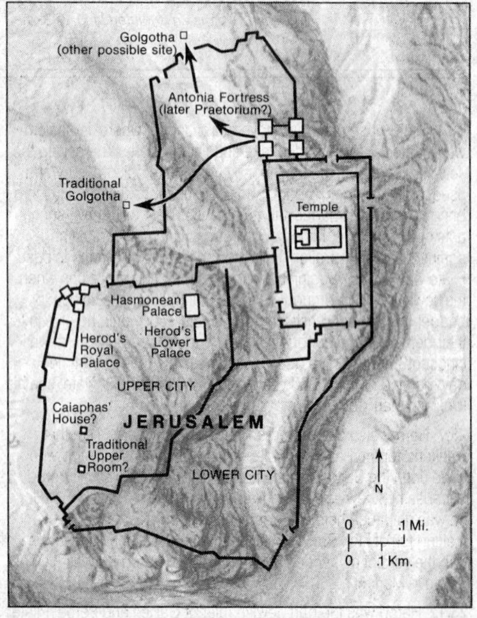

JESUS LED AWAY TO DIE As Jesus was led away through the streets of Jerusalem, he could no longer carry his cross, and Simon of Cyrene was given the burden. Jesus was crucified, along with common criminals, on a hill outside Jerusalem.

23.27–29 Luke alone mentions the tears of the Jewish women

23.29 Lk 21.23
23.30 Isa 2.19; Hos 10.8; Rev 6.16

your children. 29 For the days are surely coming when they will say, 'Blessed are
the barren, and the wombs that never bore, and the breasts that never nursed.'
30 Then they will begin to say to the mountains, 'Fall on us'; and to the hills, 'Cover
us.' 31 For if they do this when the wood is green, what will happen when it is dry?"

Jesus is placed on the cross

(235/Matthew 27.38–44; Mark 15.25–32; John 19.18–27)

23.32 Isa 53.12; Mt 27.33-44; Mk 15.22-32; Jn 19.18-24
23.34 Mt 5.44; Acts 3.17; 7.60; 1 Cor 2.8
23.35 Ps 22.16-18
23.36 Mt 27.48
23.42 Heb 8.1
23.43 2 Cor 12.3,4; Rev 2.7

32 Two others also, who were criminals, were led away to be put to death with
him. 33 When they came to the place that is called The Skull, they crucified Jesus[q]
there with the criminals, one on his right and one on his left. ⟦34 Then Jesus said,
"Father, forgive them; for they do not know what they are doing."⟧[r] And they cast
lots to divide his clothing. 35 And the people stood by, watching; but the leaders
scoffed at him, saying, "He saved others; let him save himself if he is the Messiah[s]
of God, his chosen one!" 36 The soldiers also mocked him, coming up and offering
him sour wine, 37 and saying, "If you are the King of the Jews, save yourself!"
38 There was also an inscription over him,[t] "This is the King of the Jews."
39 One of the criminals who were hanged there kept deriding[u] him and saying,
"Are you not the Messiah?[s] Save yourself and us!" 40 But the other rebuked him,
saying, "Do you not fear God, since you are under the same sentence of condemnation? 41 And we indeed have been condemned justly, for we are getting what we
deserve for our deeds, but this man has done nothing wrong." 42 Then he said,
"Jesus, remember me when you come into[v] your kingdom." 43 He replied, "Truly
I tell you, today you will be with me in Paradise."

Jesus dies on the cross

(236/Matthew 27.45–56; Mark 15.33–41; John 19.28–37)

44 It was now about noon, and darkness came over the whole land[w] until three

[q] Gk *him* [r] Other ancient authorities lack the sentence *Then Jesus . . . what they are doing* [s] Or *the Christ* [t] Other ancient authorities add *written in Greek and Latin and Hebrew* (that is, *Aramaic*) [u] Or *blaspheming* [v] Other ancient authorities read *in* [w] Or *earth*

---

while Jesus was being led through the streets to his execution. He told them not to weep for him but for themselves. He knew that in only about 40 years, Jerusalem and the temple would be destroyed by the Romans.

23.31 This proverb is difficult to interpret. Some feel it means: if the innocent Jesus (green wood) suffered at the hands of the Romans, what would happen to the guilty Jews (dry wood)?

23.32, 33 The place called The Skull, or Golgotha, was probably a hill outside Jerusalem along a main road. The Romans executed people publicly as examples to the people.

23.32, 33 When James and John asked Jesus for the places of honor next to him in his kingdom, he told them they didn't know what they were asking (Mark 10.35–39). Now that Jesus was preparing to inaugurate his kingdom through his death, the places on his right and on his left were taken by dying men—criminals. This shows that Jesus' death is for *all* people. As Jesus explained to his two position-conscious disciples, a person who wants to be close to Jesus must be prepared to suffer and die. The way to the kingdom is the way of the cross.

23.34 Jesus asked God to forgive the people who were putting him to death—Jewish leaders, Roman politicians and soldiers, bystanders—and God answered that prayer by opening up the way of salvation even to Jesus' murderers. The Roman officer and soldiers who witnessed the crucifixion said, "Truly this man was God's Son" (Matthew 27.54). Soon many priests were converted to the Christian faith (Acts 6.7). Since we are all sinners, we all played a part in putting Jesus to death. The gospel—the Good News—is that God is gracious. He will forgive us and give us new life through his Son.

23.34 Roman soldiers customarily divided up the clothing of executed criminals among themselves. When they cast lots for Jesus' clothes, they fulfilled the prophecy in Psalm 22.18.

23.38 This sign was meant to be ironic. A king, stripped and executed in public view, had obviously lost his kingdom forever. But Jesus, who turns the world's wisdom upside down, was just coming into his kingdom. His death and resurrection would strike the deathblow to Satan's rule and would establish Christ's eternal authority over the earth. Few people reading the sign that bleak afternoon understood its real meaning, but the sign was absolutely true. All was not lost. Jesus is King of the Jews—and the Gentiles, and the whole universe.

23.39-43 As this man was about to die, he turned to Christ for forgiveness, and Christ accepted him. This shows that our works don't save us—our faith in Christ does. It is never too late to turn to God. Even in his misery, Jesus had mercy on this criminal who decided to believe in him. Our lives are much more useful and fulfilling if we turn to God early, but even those who repent at the very last moment will be with God in Paradise.

23.42, 43 The dying criminal had more faith than the rest of Jesus' followers put together. Although the disciples continued to love Jesus, their hopes for the kingdom were shattered. Most of them had gone into hiding. As one of his followers sadly said two days later, "We had hoped that he was the one to redeem Israel" (24.21). By contrast, the criminal looked at the man who was dying next to him and said, "Jesus, remember me when you come into your kingdom." By all appearances, the kingdom was finished. How awe-inspiring is the faith of this man who alone saw beyond the present shame to the coming glory!

23.44 Darkness covered the entire land for about three hours in the middle of the day. All nature seemed to mourn over the stark tragedy of the death of God's Son.

in the afternoon, 45 while the sun's light failed;[x] and the curtain of the temple was 23.45 Ex 26.33
torn in two. 46 Then Jesus, crying with a loud voice, said, "Father, into your hands Heb 9.8; 10.19
I commend my spirit." Having said this, he breathed his last. 47 When the centurion 23.46
saw what had taken place, he praised God and said, "Certainly this man was inno- Ps 31.5
cent."[y] 48 And when all the crowds who had gathered there for this spectacle saw 23.47 Mt 27.54-56
what had taken place, they returned home, beating their breasts. 49 But all his ac- Mk 15.39-41 Jn 19.25
quaintances, including the women who had followed him from Galilee, stood at a
distance, watching these things.

Jesus is laid in the tomb
(237/Matthew 27.57–61; Mark 15.42–47; John 19.38–42)

50 Now there was a good and righteous man named Joseph, who, though a 23.50 Mt 27.57-61
member of the council, 51 had not agreed to their plan and action. He came from the Mk 15.42-47
Jewish town of Arimathea, and he was waiting expectantly for the kingdom of Lk 2.25,38 Jn 19.38-42
God. 52 This man went to Pilate and asked for the body of Jesus. 53 Then he took it 23.53
down, wrapped it in a linen cloth, and laid it in a rock-hewn tomb where no one had Isa 53.9
ever been laid. 54 It was the day of Preparation, and the sabbath was beginning.[z]
55 The women who had come with him from Galilee followed, and they saw the 23.55 Lk 8.2
tomb and how his body was laid. 56 Then they returned, and prepared spices and 23.56
ointments. Ex 20.10; 35.2 Lev 23.3
On the sabbath they rested according to the commandment. Deut 5.14

Jesus rises from the dead
(239/Matthew 28.1–7; Mark 16.1–8; John 20.1–10)

24 But on the first day of the week, at early dawn, they came to the tomb, 24.1
taking the spices that they had prepared. 2 They found the stone rolled away Mt 28.1-8 Mk 16.1-11
from the tomb, 3 but when they went in, they did not find the body.[a] 4 While they Jn 20.1,2,10-13
were perplexed about this, suddenly two men in dazzling clothes stood beside 24.4
them. 5 The women[b] were terrified and bowed their faces to the ground, but the Acts 1.10
men[c] said to them, "Why do you look for the living among the dead? He is not 24.5 Rev 1.17,18
here, but has risen.[d] 6 Remember how he told you, while he was still in Galilee,

[x] Or *the sun was eclipsed.* Other ancient authorities read *the sun was darkened* [y] Or *righteous* [z] Gk *was dawning*
[a] Other ancient authorities add *of the Lord Jesus* [b] Gk *They* [c] Gk *but they* [d] Other ancient authorities lack *He is not here, but has risen*

23.45 This significant event symbolized Christ's work on the cross. The temple had three parts: the courts for all the people; the holy place, where only priests could enter; and the most holy place, where the high priest alone could enter once a year to atone for the sins of the people. It was in the most holy place that the ark of the covenant, and God's presence with it, rested. The curtain that was torn was the one that closed off the most holy place from view. At Christ's death, the barrier between God and man was split in two. Now all people can approach God directly through Christ (Hebrews 9.1–14; 10.19–22).

23.50–52 Joseph of Arimathaea was a wealthy and honored member of the Jewish council. He was also a secret disciple of Jesus (John 19.38). The disciples who had publicly followed Jesus fled, but Joseph boldly took a stand that could cost him dearly. He cared enough about Jesus to ask for his body so he could give it a proper burial.

23.53 The tomb was likely a man-made cave cut out of one of the many limestone hills in the area around Jerusalem. Such a tomb was large enough to walk into. After burial, a large stone would have been rolled across the entrance (John 20.1).

23.55 The Galilean women followed Joseph to the tomb, and so they knew exactly where to find Jesus' body when they returned after the sabbath with their spices and ointments. These women could not do great things for Jesus – they were not permitted to stand up before the Jewish council or the Roman governor and testify on his behalf – but they did what they could. They stayed at the cross when most of the disciples had fled, and they got ready to embalm their Lord's body. Because of their devotion, they were the first to know about the resurrection. As believers, we may feel we can't do much for Jesus. But we are called to take advantage of the opportunities given us, doing what we *can* do and not worrying about what we cannot do.

24.1 The women brought spices to the tomb as we would bring flowers – as a sign of love and respect. Ordinarily a body was embalmed at burial and not a day and a half later, but Jesus died only a few hours before sundown Friday, when the sabbath began. By the time Joseph had received Pilate's permission to take the body and had put it in his tomb, there was no longer time for embalming. The women went home and kept sabbath as the law required, from sundown Friday to sundown Saturday, before gathering up their spices and returning to the tomb.

24.1–9 The two angels ("men in dazzling clothes") asked the women why they were looking in a tomb for someone who was alive. Often we run into people who are looking for God among the dead. They study the Bible as a mere historical document and go to church as if to a memorial service. But Jesus is not among the dead – he lives! He reigns in the hearts of Christians, and he is the head of his church. Do you look for Jesus among the living? Do you expect him to be active in the world and in the church? Look for signs of his power – they are all around you.

24.4 We learn from Matthew and John that these two men in dazzling clothes were angels. When angels appeared to people, they looked like humans.

24.6, 7 The angels reminded the women that Jesus had accu-

7 that the Son of Man must be handed over to sinners, and be crucified, and on the
24.8 Jn 2.22 third day rise again." 8 Then they remembered his words, 9 and returning from the
24.10 Mt 27.56 Lk 8.3 tomb, they told all this to the eleven and to all the rest. 10 Now it was Mary Magdalene, Joanna, Mary the mother of James, and the other women with them who told
this to the apostles. 11 But these words seemed to them an idle tale, and they did not
24.11 Mk 16.11 believe them. 12 But Peter got up and ran to the tomb; stooping and looking in, he
24.12 Lk 24.34 Jn 20.2-10 saw the linen cloths by themselves; then he went home, amazed at what had happened.[e]

Jesus appears to two believers traveling on the road
(243/Mark 16.12, 13)

13 Now on that same day two of them were going to a village called Emmaus,
about seven miles[f] from Jerusalem, 14 and talking with each other about all these
24.15 Mt 18.20 things that had happened. 15 While they were talking and discussing, Jesus himself
24.16 Jn 20.14; 21.4 came near and went with them, 16 but their eyes were kept from recognizing him.
17 And he said to them, "What are you discussing with each other while you walk
24.18 Jn 19.25 along?" They stood still, looking sad.[g] 18 Then one of them, whose name was
24.19 Acts 2.22 Cleopas, answered him, "Are you the only stranger in Jerusalem who does not
know the things that have taken place there in these days?" 19 He asked them,

[e] Other ancient authorities lack verse 12 [f] Gk *sixty stadia;* other ancient authorities read *a hundred sixty stadia*
[g] Other ancient authorities read *walk along, looking sad?"*

---

rately predicted all that had happened to him (9.22, 44; 18.31–33).

24.6, 7 The resurrection of Jesus from the dead is the central fact of Christian history. On it, the church is built; without it, there would be no Christian church today. Jesus' resurrection is unique. Other religions have strong ethical systems, concepts about paradise, and various holy Scriptures. Only Christianity has a God who became man, literally died for his people, and was raised again in power and glory to rule his church forever.

Why is the resurrection so important? (1) Because Christ was raised from the dead, we know that the kingdom of heaven has broken into earth's history. Our world is now headed for redemption, not disaster. God's mighty power is at work destroying sin, creating new lives, and preparing us for Jesus' second coming. (2) Because of the resurrection, we know that death has been conquered, and we too will be raised from the dead to live forever with Christ. (3) The resurrection gives authority to the church's witness in the world. Look at the early evangelistic sermons in the book of Acts: the apostles' most important message was the proclamation that Jesus Christ had been raised from the dead! (4) The resurrection gives meaning to the church's regular feast, the Lord's supper. Like the disciples on the Emmaus Road, we break bread with our risen Lord, who comes in power to save us. (5) The resurrection helps us find meaning even in great tragedy. No matter what happens to us as we walk with the Lord, the resurrection gives us hope for the future. (6) The resurrection assures us that Christ is alive and ruling his kingdom. He is not legend; he is alive and real. (7) God's power that brought Jesus back from the dead is available to us so that we can live for him in an evil world.

Christians can look very different from one another, and they can hold widely varying beliefs about politics, life-style, and even theology. But one central belief unites and inspires all true Christians—Jesus Christ rose from the dead! (For more on the importance of the resurrection, see 1 Corinthians 15.12–58.)

24.11, 12 People who hear about the resurrection for the first time may need time before they can comprehend this amazing story. Like the disciples, they may pass through four stages of belief. (1) At first, they may think it is a fairy tale, impossible to believe. (2) Like Peter, they may check out the facts but still be puzzled about what happened. (3) Only when they encounter Jesus personally are they able to accept the fact of the resurrection. (4) Then, as they commit themselves to Jesus and devote their lives to serving him, they begin fully to understand the reality of his presence with them.

24.12 From John 20.3, 4, we learn that another disciple ran to the tomb with Peter. That other disciple was almost certainly John, the author of the fourth Gospel.

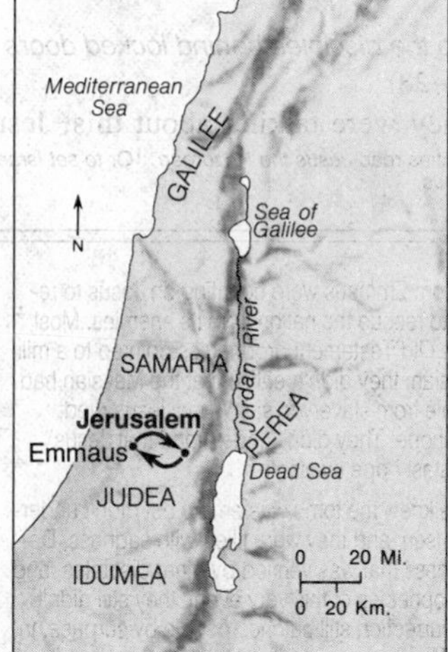

ON THE ROAD TO EMMAUS
After Jesus' death, two of his followers were walking from Jerusalem back towards Emmaus when a stranger joined them. After dinner in Emmaus, Jesus revealed himself to these men, then disappeared. They immediately returned to Jerusalem to tell the disciples the good news that Jesus was alive!

24.13ff The two disciples returning to Emmaus at first missed the significance of history's greatest event because they were too focused on their disappointments and problems. In fact, they didn't recognize Jesus when he was walking beside them. To compound the problem, they were walking in the wrong direction—away from the fellowship of believers in Jerusalem. We are likely to miss Jesus and withdraw from the strength found in other believers when we become preoccupied with our dashed hopes and frustrated plans. Only when we are looking for Jesus in our midst will we experience the power and help he can bring.

24.18 The news about Jesus' crucifixion had spread throughout Jerusalem. Because this was Passover week, Jewish pilgrims visiting the city from all over the Roman Empire now knew about his death. This was not a small, insignificant event, affecting only the disciples—the whole nation was interested.

"What things?" They replied, "The things about Jesus of Nazareth,[h] who was a
prophet mighty in deed and word before God and all the people, 20 and how our
chief priests and leaders handed him over to be condemned to death and crucified
him. 21 But we had hoped that he was the one to redeem Israel.[i] Yes, and besides
all this, it is now the third day since these things took place. 22 Moreover, some
women of our group astounded us. They were at the tomb early this morning, 23 and
when they did not find his body there, they came back and told us that they had
indeed seen a vision of angels who said that he was alive. 24 Some of those who
were with us went to the tomb and found it just as the women had said; but they did
not see him." 25 Then he said to them, "Oh, how foolish you are, and how slow of
heart to believe all that the prophets have declared! 26 Was it not necessary that the
Messiah[j] should suffer these things and then enter into his glory?" 27 Then beginning with Moses and all the prophets, he interpreted to them the things about himself in all the scriptures.

28 As they came near the village to which they were going, he walked ahead as
if he were going on. 29 But they urged him strongly, saying, "Stay with us, because
it is almost evening and the day is now nearly over." So he went in to stay with
them. 30 When he was at the table with them, he took bread, blessed and broke it,
and gave it to them. 31 Then their eyes were opened, and they recognized him; and
he vanished from their sight. 32 They said to each other, "Were not our hearts burning within us[k] while he was talking to us on the road, while he was opening the
scriptures to us?" 33 That same hour they got up and returned to Jerusalem; and they
found the eleven and their companions gathered together. 34 They were saying,
"The Lord has risen indeed, and he has appeared to Simon!" 35 Then they told what
had happened on the road, and how he had been made known to them in the breaking of the bread.

24.20 Lk 23.13 Acts 13.27
24.21 Lk 1.68 Acts 1.6
24.25 2 Cor 4.14,15
24.26 Mt 26.24 Lk 24.7,44 Jn 12.23,24 13.31,32 Acts 17.3 Heb 2.10; 5.5
24.27 Gen 3.15 Num 21.8,9 Deut 18.15,18 Ps 8.4-6; 16.8-11 22.1-22; 31.5 97.7; 110.1,2,4 118.22,26 Isa 7.14; 9.1,2,6,7 11.1-10 40.3-11 42.1-9; 49.1-10 52.10,13 53.1-12 Jer 23.5,6; 30.9 Ezek 34.23,24 Dan 9.25,26 Mic 5.2 Zech 6.12,13; 9.9 13.1,7 Mal 3.1; 4.2,5
24.34 1 Cor 15.5

Jesus appears to the disciples behind locked doors
(244/John 20.19–23)

36 While they were talking about this, Jesus himself stood among them and

[h] Other ancient authorities read *Jesus the Nazorean* [i] Or *to set Israel free* [j] Or *the Christ* [k] Other ancient authorities lack *within us*

24.21 The disciples from Emmaus were counting on Jesus to redeem Israel – that is, to rescue the nation from its enemies. Most Jews believed that the Old Testament prophecies pointed to a military and political Messiah; they didn't realize that the Messiah had come to redeem people from slavery to sin. When Jesus died, therefore, they lost all hope. They didn't understand that Jesus' death offered the greatest hope available.

24.24 These disciples knew the tomb was empty but didn't understand that Jesus had risen, and they were filled with sadness. Despite the women's witness that was verified by other disciples, and despite the biblical prophecies of this very event, they still didn't believe. Today the resurrection still catches people by surprise. In spite of 2,000 years of evidence and witness, many people refuse to believe. What more will it take? For these disciples it took the living, breathing Jesus in their midst. For many people today, it takes the presence of living, breathing Christians.

24.25 Why did Jesus call these disciples fools? Even though they well knew the biblical prophecies, they failed to understand that Christ's suffering was his path to glory. They could not understand why God did not intervene to save Jesus from the cross. They were so caught up in the world's admiration of political power and military might that they were unprepared for the reversal of values in God's kingdom – that the last will be first, and that life grows out of death. The world has not changed its values: a suffering servant is no more popular today than 2,000 years ago. But we have not only the witness of the Old Testament prophets; we have also the witness of the New Testament apostles and the history of the Christian church all pointing to Jesus' victory over death. Will we step outside the values of our culture and put our faith in Jesus? Or will we foolishly continue to be baffled by his good news?

24.25–27 After the two disciples explained their sadness and confusion, Jesus responded by going to Scripture and applying it to his ministry. When we are puzzled by questions or problems, we too can go to Scripture and find authoritative help. If we, like these two disciples, do not understand what the Bible means, we can turn to other believers who know the Bible and have the wisdom to apply it to our situation.

24.27 Beginning with the promised seed in Genesis and going through the suffering Servant in Isaiah, the pierced one in Zechariah, and the messenger of the covenant in Malachi, Jesus reintroduced these disciples to the Old Testament. Christ is the thread woven through all the Scriptures, the central theme that binds them together. Following are several key passages Jesus probably mentioned on this walk to Emmaus: Genesis 3, 12; Psalms 22, 69, 110; Isaiah 53; Jeremiah 31; Zechariah 9, 13; Malachi 3.

24.33, 34 Paul also mentions that Jesus appeared to Peter alone (1 Corinthians 15.5; note that Luke uses Peter's Hebrew name, Simon, while Paul uses his Greek surname, Cephas). This event is not described in the Gospels. Jesus showed individual concern for Peter because Peter felt completely unworthy after denying his Lord. But Peter repented, and Jesus met and forgave him. Soon God would use Peter in building Christ's church (see the first half of the book of Acts).

24.36–43 Jesus' body wasn't just a vision or a ghost – the disciples touched him, and he ate food. On the other hand, his body wasn't just a restored human body like Lazarus's (John 11) – he was able to appear and disappear. Jesus' resurrected body was even more real than before: it was now immortal. This is the kind of

24.36 Mk 16.14 said to them, "Peace be with you."[l] [37]They were startled and terrified, and thought
Jn 20.19,20 that they were seeing a ghost. [38]He said to them, "Why are you frightened, and
why do doubts arise in your hearts? [39]Look at my hands and my feet; see that it is
I myself. Touch me and see; for a ghost does not have flesh and bones as you see
that I have." [40]And when he had said this, he showed them his hands and his feet.[m]
[41]While in their joy they were disbelieving and still wondering, he said to them,
"Have you anything here to eat?" [42]They gave him a piece of broiled fish, [43]and he
took it and ate in their presence.

Jesus appears to the disciples in Jerusalem
(249)

24.44 44 Then he said to them, "These are my words that I spoke to you while I was
Lk 24.27 still with you—that everything written about me in the law of Moses, the prophets,
24.47 and the psalms must be fulfilled." [45]Then he opened their minds to understand the
Acts 2.38; 5.31; 10.43; 13.38 scriptures, [46]and he said to them, "Thus it is written, that the Messiah[n] is to suffer
26.18 and to rise from the dead on the third day, [47]and that repentance and forgiveness of
24.48 Jn 15.27 sins is to be proclaimed in his name to all nations,[o] beginning from Jerusalem.
24.49 [48]You are witnesses of these things. [49]And see, I am sending upon you what my
Isa 44.3 Joel 2.28 Father promised; so stay here in the city until you have been clothed with power
Acts 2.1-4 from on high."

Jesus ascends into heaven
(250/Mark 16.19, 20)

24.51 Mk 16.19,20 50 Then he led them out as far as Bethany, and, lifting up his hands, he blessed
Eph 1.20; 4.8 them. [51]While he was blessing them, he withdrew from them and was carried up
24.53 into heaven.[p] [52]And they worshiped him, and[q] returned to Jerusalem with great
Acts 2.46; 5.42 joy; [53]and they were continually in the temple blessing God.[r]

[l] Other ancient authorities lack *and said to them, "Peace be with you."* [m] Other ancient authorities lack verse 40 [n] Or *the Christ* [o] Or *nations. Beginning from Jerusalem you are witnesses* [p] Other ancient authorities lack *and was carried up into heaven* [q] Other ancient authorities lack *worshiped him, and* [r] Other ancient authorities add *Amen*

---

body we will be given at the resurrection of the dead (see 1 Corinthians 15.42–50).

24.44 We can assume that many days elapsed between verses 43 and 44, because Jesus and his followers traveled to Galilee and back before he returned to heaven (Matthew 28.16; John 21). In his second book, Acts, Luke makes it clear that Jesus spent 40 days with his disciples between his resurrection and ascension.

24.44–46 The law of Moses, the prophets, and the psalms is a way to describe the entire Old Testament. In other words, the entire Old Testament points to the Messiah. For example, his sufferings were prophesied in Psalm 22 and Isaiah 53; his resurrection was predicted in Psalm 16.9–11 and Isaiah 53.10, 11.

24.45 Jesus opened these people's minds to understand the Scriptures. The Holy Spirit does this in our lives today when we study the Bible. Have you ever wondered how to understand a difficult Bible passage? Besides reading surrounding passages, asking other people, and consulting reference works, pray that the Holy Spirit will open your mind to understand, giving you the needed insight to put God's Word into action in your life.

24.47 Luke wrote to the Greek-speaking world. He wanted them to know that Christ's message of God's love and forgiveness should go to all the world. We must never ignore the worldwide scope of Christ's gospel. God wants all the world to hear the good news of salvation.

24.50–53 As the disciples stood and watched, Jesus began rising into the air, and soon he disappeared into heaven. Seeing Jesus leave must have been frightening, but they knew he would keep his promise to be with them in the Spirit. This same Jesus who lived with the disciples, who died and was buried, and who rose from the dead, loves us and promises to be with us always. We can get to know him better through studying the Scriptures, praying, and allowing the Holy Spirit to make us more like him.

24.51 Jesus' physical presence left the disciples when he returned to heaven (Acts 1.9), but the Holy Spirit soon came to comfort them and empower them to spread the gospel of salvation (Acts 2.1–4). Today Jesus' work of salvation is completed, and he is sitting at God's right hand, where he has authority over heaven and earth.

24.53 Luke's Gospel portrays Jesus as the perfect example of a life lived according to God's plan—as a child living in obedience to his parents and yet amazing the religious leaders in the temple, as an adult serving God and others through preaching and healing, and finally as a condemned man suffering without complaint. This emphasis was well suited to Luke's Greek audience, who placed high value on examples and self-improvement, and who often discussed the meaning of perfection. The Greeks, however, had a hard time understanding the spiritual importance of the physical world. To them, the spiritual was always more important than the physical. To help them understand the God-man who united the spiritual and the physical, Luke emphasized that Jesus was not a phantom but a real human being who healed and fed people because he was concerned with their physical health as well as the state of their souls.

As believers living according to God's plan, we too should obey our Lord in every detail as we seek to restore people's bodies and souls to the health and salvation God has in store for them. If we want to know how to live a perfect life, we can look to Jesus as our example.

The Gospel according to JOHN

Herod the Great begins to rule 37 B.C.	Jesus is born 6/5 B.C.	Escape to Egypt 5/4 B.C.	Herod the Great dies 4 B.C.	Return to Nazareth 4/3 B.C.	Judea becomes a Roman province A.D. 6

VITAL STATISTICS

PURPOSE:
To prove conclusively that Jesus is the Son of God and that all who believe in him will have eternal life.

AUTHOR:
John, the apostle, son of Zebedee, brother of James, called a "Son of Thunder"

TO WHOM WRITTEN:
New Christians and searching non-Christians

DATE WRITTEN:
Probably A.D. 85–90

SETTING:
Written after the destruction of Jerusalem in A.D. 70 and before John's exile to the island of Patmos

KEY VERSES:
"Now Jesus did many other signs in the presence of his disciples, which are not written in this book. But these are written so that you may come to believe that Jesus is the Messiah, the Son of God, and that through believing you may have life in his name" (20.30, 31).

KEY PEOPLE:
Jesus, John the Baptist, the disciples, Mary, Martha, Lazarus, Jesus' mother, Pilate, Mary Magdalene

KEY PLACES:
Judean countryside, Samaria, Galilee, Bethany, Jerusalem

SPECIAL FEATURES:
Of the eight miracles recorded, six are unique (among the Gospels) to John, as is the "Upper Room Discourse" (chapters 14—17). Over 90% of John is unique to his Gospel—John does not contain a genealogy or any record of Jesus' birth, childhood, temptation, transfiguration, appointment of the disciples, and no parables, ascension, or great commission.

HE SPOKE, and galaxies whirled into place, stars burned the heavens, and planets began orbiting their suns—words of awesome, unlimited, unleashed power. He spoke again, and the waters and lands were filled with plants and creatures, running, swimming, growing, and multiplying—words of animating, breathing, pulsing life. Again he spoke, and man and woman were formed, thinking, speaking, and loving—words of personal and creative glory. Eternal, infinite, unlimited—he was, is, and always will be the Maker and Lord of all that exists.

And then he came in the flesh to a speck in the universe called planet Earth. The mighty Creator became a part of the creation, limited by time and space and susceptible to age, sickness, and death. But love propelled him, and so he came to rescue and save those who were lost and to give them the gift of eternity. He is *the Word;* he is Jesus, the Christ.

It is this truth that the apostle John brings to us in this book. John's Gospel is not a life of Christ; it is a powerful argument for the incarnation, a conclusive demonstration that Jesus was, and is, the very heaven-sent Son of God and the only source of eternal life.

John discloses Christ's identity with his very first words, "In the beginning was the Word, and the Word was with God, and the Word was God. He was in the beginning with God" (1.1, 2); and the rest of the book continues the theme. John, the eyewitness, chooses eight of Christ's miracles (or signs, as he calls them), to reveal Christ's divine/human nature and his life-giving mission. These signs are (1) turning water to wine (2.1–11), (2) healing the nobleman's son (4.46–54), (3) healing the cripple (5.1–9), (4) feeding the 5,000 with just a few loaves and fish (6.1–14), (5) walking on the water (6.15–21), (6) restoring sight to the blind man (9.1–41), (7) raising Lazarus from the dead (11.1–44), and, after the resurrection, (8) giving the disciples an overwhelming catch of fish (21.1–14).

In every chapter Jesus' deity is revealed. And John underscores Jesus' true identity through the titles he is given—Word, only begotten, lamb of God, Son of God, true bread, life, resurrection, vine. And the formula is "I am." When Jesus uses this phrase, he affirms his preexistence and eternal deity. Jesus says, *I am* the bread of life (6.35); *I am* the light of the world (8.12; 9.5); *I am* the gate (10.7); *I am* the good shepherd (10.11, 14); *I am* the resurrection and the life (11.25); *I am* the way, the truth, and the life (14.6); and *I am* the true vine (15.1).

The greatest sign, of course, is the resurrection, and John provides a stirring eyewitness account of finding the empty tomb. Then he records various post-resurrection appearances by Jesus.

John, the devoted follower of Christ, has given us a personal and powerful look at Jesus Christ, the eternal Son of God. As you read his story commit yourself to believe and follow him.

Tiberius Caesar becomes emperor 14	Pontius Pilate appointed governor 26	Jesus begins his ministry 26/27	Jesus and Nicodemus 27	Jesus chooses twelve disciples 28	Jesus feeds 5,000 29	Jesus is crucified, rises again, and ascends 30

THE BLUEPRINT

A. BIRTH AND PREPARATION OF JESUS, THE SON OF GOD (1.1—2.12)

John makes it clear that Jesus is not just a man; he is the eternal Son of God. He is the light of the world because he offers this gift of eternal life to all mankind. How blind and foolish to call Jesus nothing more than an unusually good man or moral teacher. Yet we sometimes act as if this were true when we casually toss around his words and go about living our own way. If Jesus is the eternal Son of God, we should pay attention to his divine identity and life-giving message.

B. MESSAGE AND MINISTRY OF JESUS, THE SON OF GOD (2.13—12.50)

1. Jesus encounters belief and unbelief from the people
2. Jesus encounters conflict with the religious leaders
3. Jesus encounters crucial events in Jerusalem

Jesus meets with individuals, preaches to great crowds, trains his disciples, and debates with the religious leaders. The message that he is the Son of God receives a mixed reaction. Some worship him, some are puzzled, some shrink back, and some move to silence him. We see the same varied reactions today. Times have changed, but people's hearts remain hard. May we see ourselves in these encounters Jesus had with people, and may our response be to worship and follow him.

C. DEATH AND RESURRECTION OF JESUS, THE SON OF GOD (13.1—21.25)

1. Jesus teaches his disciples
2. Jesus completes his mission

Jesus carefully instructed the disciples how to continue to believe even after his death, yet they could not take it in. After he died and the first reports came back that Jesus was alive, the disciples could not believe it. Thomas is especially remembered as one who refused to believe even when he heard the eyewitness accounts from other disciples. May we not be like Thomas, demanding a physical face-to-face encounter, but may we accept the eyewitness of the disciples that John has recorded in this Gospel.

MEGATHEMES

THEME	EXPLANATION	IMPORTANCE
Jesus Christ, Son of God	John shows us that Jesus is unique as God's special Son, yet he is fully God. Because he is fully God, Jesus is able to reveal God to us clearly and accurately.	Because Jesus is God's Son, we can perfectly trust what he says. By trusting him, we can gain an open mind to understand God's message and fulfill his purpose in our lives.
Eternal life	Because Jesus is God, he lives forever. Before the world began, he lived with God, and he will reign forever with him. In John we see Jesus revealed in power and magnificence even before his resurrection.	Jesus offers eternal life to us. We are invited to begin living in a personal, eternal relationship with him that begins now. Although we must grow old and die, by trusting him we can have a new life that lasts forever.
Belief	John records eight specific signs, or miracles, that show the nature of Jesus' power and love. We see his power over everything created, and we see his love of all people. These signs encourage us to believe in him.	Believing is active, living, and continuous trust in Jesus as God. When we believe in his life, his words, his death, and his resurrection, we are cleansed from sin and receive power to follow him. But we must respond to him by believing.
Holy Spirit	Jesus taught his disciples that the Holy Spirit would come after he ascended from earth. The Holy Spirit would then indwell, guide, counsel, and comfort those who follow Jesus. Through the Holy Spirit, Christ's presence and power are multiplied in all who believe.	Through God's Holy Spirit we are drawn to him in faith. We must know the Holy Spirit to understand all Jesus taught. We can experience Jesus' love and guidance as we allow the Holy Spirit to do his work in us.

Resurrection	On the third day after he died, Jesus rose from the dead. This was verified by his disciples and many eyewitnesses. This reality changed the disciples from frightened deserters to dynamic leaders in the new church. This fact is the foundation of the Christian faith.	We can be changed as the disciples were and have confidence that our bodies will one day be raised to live with Christ forever. The same power that raised Christ to life can give us the ability to follow Christ each day.

KEY PLACES IN JOHN

John's story begins as John the Baptist ministers near Bethany beyond the Jordan (1.28ff). Jesus also begins his ministry, talking to some of the men who would later become his 12 disciples. Jesus' ministry in Galilee began with a visit to a wedding in Cana (2.1ff). Then he went to Capernaum, which became his new home (2.12). He journeyed to Jerusalem for the special festivals (2.13) and there met with Nicodemus, a religious leader (3.1ff). When he left Judea, he traveled through Samaria and ministered to the Samaritans (4.1ff). Jesus did miracles in Galilee (4.46ff) and in Judea and Jerusalem (5.1ff). We follow him as he fed 5,000 near Bethsaida-Julias beside the Sea of Galilee (Sea of Tiberias) (6.1ff), walked on the water to his frightened disciples (6.16ff), preached through Galilee (7.1), returned to Jerusalem (7.2ff), preached beyond the Jordan in Perea (10.40), raised Lazarus from the dead in Bethany (11.1ff), and finally entered Jerusalem for the last time to celebrate the Passover with his disciples and give them key teachings about what was to come and how they should act. His last hours before his crucifixion were spent in the city (13.1ff), in the garden of Gethsemane (18.1ff), and finally in various buildings in Jerusalem during his trial (18.12ff). He would be crucified, but he would rise again as he had promised.

Modern names and boundaries are shown in gray.

A. BIRTH AND PREPARATION OF JESUS, THE SON OF GOD (1.1 – 2.12)

In this Gospel, John provides clear evidence that Jesus is the Son of God and that by believing in him we may have eternal life. John also provides unique material about Jesus' birth. He did not come into being when he was born, because he is eternal.

God became a human being

(2)

1 In the beginning was the Word, and the Word was with God, and the Word
was God. 2 He was in the beginning with God. 3 All things came into being
through him, and without him not one thing came into being. What has come into
being 4 in him was life,[a] and the life was the light of all people. 5 The light shines
in the darkness, and the darkness did not overcome it.
6 There was a man sent from God, whose name was John. 7 He came as a witness to testify to the light, so that all might believe through him. 8 He himself was
not the light, but he came to testify to the light. 9 The true light, which enlightens
everyone, was coming into the world.[b]
10 He was in the world, and the world came into being through him; yet the
world did not know him. 11 He came to what was his own,[c] and his own people did
not accept him. 12 But to all who received him, who believed in his name, he gave
power to become children of God, 13 who were born, not of blood or of the will of
the flesh or of the will of man, but of God.

[a] Or *3 through him. And without him not one thing came into being that has come into being. 4 In him was life* [b] Or *He was the true light that enlightens everyone coming into the world* [c] Or *to his own home*

1.1 Gen 1.1 Phil 2.6 1 Jn 5.21
1.3 1 Cor 8.6 Col 1.16,17 Heb 1.2
1.4 Jn 3.15,16,36 6.35,48; 8.12 11.25; 14.6 1 Jn 5.12,20
1.5 Jn 3.19; 9.5
1.9 1 Jn 2.8
1.12 Rom 8.15,16,29 1 Jn 3.1,23

1.1 What Jesus taught and what he did are tied inseparably to who he is. John shows Jesus as fully human and fully God. Although Jesus took upon himself full humanity and lived as a man, he never ceased to be the eternal God who has always existed, the Creator and Sustainer of all things, and the source of eternal life. This is the truth about Jesus and the foundation of all truth. If we cannot or do not believe this basic truth, we will not have enough faith to trust our eternal destiny to him. That is why John wrote this Gospel – to build faith and confidence in Jesus Christ so that we may believe he truly was and is the Son of God (20.30, 31).

1.1 John wrote to believers everywhere, both Jews and non-Jews (Gentiles). As one of Jesus' 12 disciples, John was an eyewitness, so his story is accurate. His book is not a biography (like the book of Luke) but a thematic presentation of Jesus' life. Many in John's original audience had Greek backgrounds. Greek culture encouraged worship of many mythological gods, whose supernatural characteristics were as important to Greeks as genealogies were to Jews. John shows that Jesus is not only different from but superior to these gods of mythology.

1.1ff What does John mean by *the Word? The Word* was a term used by theologians and philosophers, both Hebrew and Greek, in many different ways. In Hebrew Scripture, the Word was an agent of creation (Psalm 33.6), the source of God's message to his people through the prophets (Hosea 1.2), and God's law, his standard of holiness (Psalm 119.11). In Greek philosophy *the Word* was the divine essence that held all things together, God's ideal pattern for creation. John's description shows clearly that he is speaking of Jesus (see especially 1.14) – a human being he knew and loved, but at the same time the Creator of the universe, the ultimate revelation of God, the living picture of God's holiness, the one by whom "all things hold together" (Colossians 1.17). To Jewish readers, "the Word was God" was blasphemous. To Greek readers, "the Word was made flesh" was unthinkable. To John, this new understanding of the Word was gospel, the good news of Jesus Christ.

1.3 When God created, he made something from nothing. Since we are created beings, we have no basis for pride. Remember that you exist only because God made you, and you have special gifts only because God gave them to you. With God you are something valuable and unique; apart from God you are nothing.

1.3–5 Do you ever feel as though your life is too complex for God to understand? Remember, God created the entire universe, and nothing is too difficult for him. He created you, he is alive today, and his love is bigger than any problem you may face.

1.5 "The darkness did not overcome it" means the darkness of evil never has and never will overcome or extinguish God's light. Jesus Christ was the Creator of life, and his life brings light. In his light, we see ourselves as we really are (sinners in need of a Savior). When we follow Jesus, the Light, we can avoid walking blindly and falling into sin. He lights the path ahead of us so we can see how to live. He removes the darkness of sin from our lives. Have you allowed the light of Christ to shine into your life? Let Christ guide you, and you will never need to stumble in darkness.

1.6–8 In this book, the name *John* refers to John the Baptist. For more information on John the Baptist, see his Profile in this chapter.

1.8 We, like John the Baptist, are not the source of God's light; we merely reflect that light. Jesus Christ is the true light; he helps us see our way to God and shows us how to walk along that way. But Christ has chosen to reflect his light from his followers to an unbelieving world, perhaps because unbelievers are not able to bear the full blazing glory of his light firsthand. The word *testify* indicates our role as reflectors of Christ's light. We are never to present ourselves as the light to others, but are always to point them to Christ, the light.

1.10, 11 Although Christ created the world, the people he created didn't recognize him (1.10). Even the people chosen by God to prepare the rest of the world for the Messiah rejected him (1.11), although the entire Old Testament pointed to his coming.

1.12, 13 All who welcome Jesus Christ as Lord of their lives are reborn spiritually, receiving new life from God. Through faith in Christ, this new birth changes us from the inside out – rearranging our attitudes, desires, and motives. Being born makes you physically alive and places you in your parents' family (1.13). Being reborn makes you spiritually alive and puts you in God's family (1.12). Have you asked Christ to make you a new person? This fresh start in life is available to all who believe in Christ.

14 And the Word became flesh and lived among us, and we have seen his glory,
the glory as of a father's only son,[d] full of grace and truth. 15 (John testified to him
and cried out, "This was he of whom I said, 'He who comes after me ranks ahead
of me because he was before me.' ") 16 From his fullness we have all received,
grace upon grace. 17 The law indeed was given through Moses; grace and truth
came through Jesus Christ. 18 No one has ever seen God. It is God the only Son,[e]
who is close to the Father's heart,[f] who has made him known.

1.14 Col 2.9 1 Tim 3.16 Heb 2.14 1 Jn 1.1; 4.2,3
1.17 Ex 20.1
1.18 Ex 33.20 2 Cor 4.4,6 Col 1.15

John the Baptist declares his mission
(19)

19 This is the testimony given by John when the Jews sent priests and Levites
from Jerusalem to ask him, "Who are you?" 20 He confessed and did not deny it, but
confessed, "I am not the Messiah."[g] 21 And they asked him, "What then? Are you
Elijah?" He said, "I am not." "Are you the prophet?" He answered, "No." 22 Then
they said to him, "Who are you? Let us have an answer for those who sent us. What
do you say about yourself?" 23 He said,

"I am the voice of one crying out in the wilderness,
'Make straight the way of the Lord,' "

as the prophet Isaiah said.

24 Now they had been sent from the Pharisees. 25 They asked him, "Why then
are you baptizing if you are neither the Messiah,[g] nor Elijah, nor the prophet?"
26 John answered them, "I baptize with water. Among you stands one whom you do
not know, 27 the one who is coming after me; I am not worthy to untie the thong of

1.20 Lk 3.15 Jn 3.28
1.21 Deut 18.15 Mal 4.5 Mt 11.14
1.23 Isa 40.3
1.26 Mt 3.11 Mk 1.8 Lk 3.16
1.27 Mk 1.7

[d] Or *the Father's only Son* [e] Other ancient authorities read *It is an only Son, God,* or *It is the only Son* [f] Gk *bosom*
[g] Or *the Christ*

1.14 "And the Word became flesh" means becoming human. By doing so, Christ became (1) *the perfect teacher*—in Jesus' life we see how God thinks and therefore how we should think (Philippians 2.5–11); (2) *the perfect example*—as a model of what we are to become, he shows us how to live and gives us the power to live that way (1 Peter 2.21); (3) *the perfect sacrifice*—Jesus came as a sacrifice for all sins, and his death satisfied God's requirements for the removal of sin (Colossians 1.15–23).

1.14 Jesus is God's only and unique Son. The emphasis is on *unique.* Jesus is one of a kind and enjoys a relationship with God unlike all believers who are called "sons."

1.14 When Christ was born, God became a man. He was not part man and part God; he was completely human and completely divine (Colossians 2.9). Before Christ came, people could know God partially. After Christ came, people could know God fully, because he became visible and tangible in Christ. Christ is the perfect expression of God in human form. The two most common errors people make about Jesus are to minimize his humanity or to minimize his divinity. Jesus is both God and man.

1.17 Law and grace are both aspects of God's nature that he uses in dealing with us. Moses emphasized God's law and justice, while Jesus Christ came to highlight God's mercy, love, and forgiveness. Moses could only be the giver of the law, while Christ came to fulfill it. The nature and will of God were revealed in the law; now the nature and will of God are revealed in Jesus Christ. Rather than coming through cold stone tablets, God's revelation ("truth") now comes through a person's life. As we get to know Christ better, our understanding of God will increase.

1.18 God communicated through various people in the Old Testament, usually prophets who were told to give specific messages. But no one ever *saw* God. In Christ, God revealed his nature and essence in a way that could be seen and touched. In Christ, God became a man who lived on earth.

1.18 "Close to the Father's heart" means at his Father's side, his constant companion, and implies close intimacy.

1.19 The priests and Levites were respected religious leaders in Jerusalem. Priests served in the temple, and Levites assisted them. The leaders who came to see John were Pharisees (1.24), a group that both John the Baptist and Jesus often denounced. Many of them outwardly obeyed God's laws to look pious, while inwardly their hearts were filled with pride and greed. The Pharisees believed that their own oral traditions were just as important as God's inspired Word. For more information on the Pharisees, see the charts in Matthew 4 and Mark 3.

These leaders came to see John the Baptist for several reasons: (1) Their duty as guardians of the faith caused them to want to investigate any new preaching (Deuteronomy 13.1–5; 18.20–22). (2) They wanted to find out if he had the credentials of a prophet. (3) John had quite a following, and it was growing. They were probably jealous and wanted to see why this man was so popular.

1.21–23 In the Pharisees' minds, there were four options regarding John the Baptist's identity: he was (1) the prophet foretold by Moses (Deuteronomy 18.15), (2) Elijah (Malachi 4.5), (3) the Messiah, or (4) a false prophet. John called himself, in the words of the Old Testament prophet Isaiah, "the voice of one crying out in the wilderness" (Isaiah 40.3). The leaders kept pressing him to say who he was, because people were expecting the Messiah to come (Luke 3.15). But John emphasized only *why* he had come—to prepare the way for the Messiah. The Pharisees missed the point. They wanted to know who John was, but John wanted them to know who Jesus was.

1.25, 26 John was baptizing Jews. The Essenes (a strict, monastic sect of Judaism) practiced baptism for purification, but normally only non-Jews (Gentiles) were baptized when they converted to Judaism. When the Pharisees asked by what authority he was baptizing, they were asking who gave John the right to treat God's chosen people like Gentiles. John said, "I baptize with water"—he was merely helping the people perform a symbolic act of repentance. But soon one would come who would truly *forgive* sins, something only the Son of God—the Messiah—could do.

1.27 John the Baptist said he was not even fit to be Christ's slave, to perform the humble task of unfastening his sandals. But in Luke 7.28, Jesus said that John was the greatest of all prophets. If such a great person felt inadequate even to be Christ's slave, how much

1.28 Jn 3.26; 10.40 his sandal." [28]This took place in Bethany across the Jordan where John was baptizing.

John the Baptist proclaims Jesus as the Messiah
(20)

1.29 Isa 53.7 29 The next day he saw Jesus coming toward him and declared, "Here is the
Lamb of God who takes away the sin of the world! [30]This is he of whom I said,

JOHN THE BAPTIST

There's no getting around it—John the Baptist was unique. He wore odd clothes and ate strange food and preached an unusual message to the Judeans who went in to the wastelands to see him.

But John did not aim at uniqueness for its own sake. Instead, he aimed at obedience. He knew he had a specific role to play in the world—announcing the coming of the Savior—and he put all his energies into this task. Luke tells us that John was in the desert when God's word of direction came to him. John was ready and waiting. The angel who had announced John's birth to Zechariah had made it clear this child was to be a nazirite—one set apart for God's service. John remained faithful to that calling. This wild-looking man had no power or position in the Jewish political system, but he spoke with almost irresistible authority. People were moved by his words because he spoke the truth, challenging them to turn from their sins and baptizing them as a symbol of their repentance. They responded by the hundreds. But even as people crowded to him, he pointed beyond himself, never forgetting that his main role was to announce the coming of the Savior.

The words of truth that moved many to repentance goaded others to resistance and resentment. John even challenged Herod to admit his sin. Herodias, the woman Herod had married illegally, decided to get rid of this desert preacher. Although she was able to have him killed, she was not able to stop his message. The One John had announced was already on the move. John had accomplished his mission.

God has given each of us a purpose for living, and we can trust him to guide us. John did not have the complete Bible as we know it today, but he focused his life on the truth he knew from the available Old Testament Scriptures. Likewise, we can discover in God's Word the truths he wants us to know. And as these truths work in us, others will be drawn to him. God can use you in a way he can use no one else. Let him know your willingness to follow him today.

Strengths and accomplishments:
- The God-appointed messenger to announce the arrival of Jesus
- A preacher whose theme was repentance
- A fearless confronter
- Known for his remarkable life-style
- Uncompromising

Lessons from his life:
- God does not guarantee an easy or safe life to those who serve him
- Doing what God desires is the greatest possible life investment
- Standing for the truth is more important than life itself

Vital statistics:
- Where: Judea
- Occupation: Prophet
- Relatives: Father: Zechariah. Mother: Elizabeth. Distant cousin: Jesus
- Contemporaries: Herod, Herodias

Key verse:
"Truly I tell you, among those born of women no one has arisen greater than John the Baptist; yet the least in the kingdom of heaven is greater than he" (Matthew 11.11).

John's story is told in all four Gospels. His coming was predicted in Isaiah 40.3 and Malachi 4.5; and he is mentioned in Acts 1.5, 22; 10.37; 11.16; 13.24, 25; 18.25; 19.3, 4.

more should we lay aside our pride to serve Christ! When we truly understand who Christ is, our pride and self-importance melt away.

1.29 Every morning and evening, a lamb was sacrificed in the temple for the sins of the people (Exodus 29.38–42). Isaiah 53.7 prophesied that the Messiah, God's servant, would be led to slaughter like a lamb. To pay the penalty for sin, a life had to be given – and God chose to provide the sacrifice himself. Jesus died as the perfect sacrifice for sin. This is the way our sins are forgiven (1 Corinthians 5.7). The "sin of the world" means the sin of each individual. Jesus paid the price of *your* sin by his death. You can receive forgiveness by confessing your sin to him and asking him to forgive you.

1.30 Although John the Baptist attracted large crowds, he was content for Jesus to take the higher place. This is true humility. When you are content to do what God wants you to do and let Jesus Christ be honored for it, God will do great things through you.

'After me comes a man who ranks ahead of me because he was before me.' 31 I
myself did not know him; but I came baptizing with water for this reason, that he
might be revealed to Israel." 32 And John testified, "I saw the Spirit descending
from heaven like a dove, and it remained on him. 33 I myself did not know him, but
the one who sent me to baptize with water said to me, 'He on whom you see the
Spirit descend and remain is the one who baptizes with the Holy Spirit.' 34 And I
myself have seen and have testified that this is the Son of God."[h]

1.32 Mt 3.16 Mk 1.10 Lk 3.22
1.33 Lk 3.16 Acts 1.5
1.34 Jn 1.49; 10.36 11.27; 20.30,31

The first disciples follow Jesus
(21)

35 The next day John again was standing with two of his disciples, 36 and as he
watched Jesus walk by, he exclaimed, "Look, here is the Lamb of God!" 37 The two
disciples heard him say this, and they followed Jesus. 38 When Jesus turned and saw
them following, he said to them, "What are you looking for?" They said to him,
"Rabbi" (which translated means Teacher), "where are you staying?" 39 He said to
them, "Come and see." They came and saw where he was staying, and they remained with him that day. It was about four o'clock in the afternoon. 40 One of the
two who heard John speak and followed him was Andrew, Simon Peter's brother.
41 He first found his brother Simon and said to him, "We have found the Messiah"
(which is translated Anointed[i]). 42 He brought Simon[j] to Jesus, who looked at
him and said, "You are Simon son of John. You are to be called Cephas" (which is
translated Peter[k]).
43 The next day Jesus decided to go to Galilee. He found Philip and said to him,
"Follow me." 44 Now Philip was from Bethsaida, the city of Andrew and Peter.
45 Philip found Nathanael and said to him, "We have found him about whom Moses
in the law and also the prophets wrote, Jesus son of Joseph from Nazareth." 46 Nathanael said to him, "Can anything good come out of Nazareth?" Philip said to him,
"Come and see." 47 When Jesus saw Nathanael coming toward him, he said of
him "Here is truly an Israelite in whom there is no deceit!" 48 Nathanael asked him,
"Where did you get to know me?" Jesus answered, "I saw you under the fig tree
before Philip called you." 49 Nathanael replied, "Rabbi, you are the Son of God!

1.40 Mt 4.18-22 Mk 1.16 Lk 5.2-11
1.41 Job 23.3 Dan 9.25 Jn 4.25
1.42 Mt 16.18 1 Cor 15.5 1 Pet 2.5 Rev 21.14
1.43 Jn 6.5,6 12.20-22
1.45 Gen 3.15; 26.4 49.10 Num 21.8,9 Deut 18.15,18 Ps 2; 16.8-11,22 110; 132.11 Isa 6.5; 7.14; 9.6 11.1-10; 32.1-5 42.1-9; 49.1-13 50.6,53 Jer 23.5,6 Ezek 34.23 Dan 7.13; 9.25 Mic 5.2 Zech 3.8,9 6.12; 9.9; 13.1,7

[h] Other ancient authorities read *is God's chosen one* [i] Or *Christ* [j] Gk *him* [k] From the word for *rock* in Aramaic (*kepha*) and Greek (*petra*), respectively

---

1.31–34 At Jesus' baptism, John the Baptist declared him to be the Messiah. At this time God gave John a sign to show him that Jesus was truly sent from God (1.33). John and Jesus were related, so John probably knew who he was. But it wasn't until his baptism that he understood Jesus to be the Messiah. Jesus' baptism is described in Matthew 3.13–17; Mark 1.9–11; and Luke 3.21, 22.

1.33 John the Baptist's baptism by water was preparatory, because it was for repentance and symbolized the washing away of sins. Jesus, by contrast, would baptize with the Holy Spirit. He would send the Holy Spirit upon all believers, empowering them to live and teach the message of salvation. This began after Jesus had risen from the dead and ascended into heaven (see 20.22; Acts 2).

1.34 John the Baptist's job was to point people to Jesus, the Messiah for whom they were looking. Today people are looking for someone to give them security in an insecure world. Our job is to point them to Christ and to show that he is the one they seek.

1.35ff These new disciples used several names for Jesus: Lamb of God (1.36), Rabbi (1.38), Messiah (1.41), Son of God (1.49), King of Israel (1.49). As they got to know Jesus, their appreciation for him grew. The more time we spend getting to know Christ, the more we understand and appreciate who he is. We may be drawn to him for his teaching, but we will come to know him as the Son of God. Although these disciples made this verbal shift in a few days, they would not fully understand until three years later (Acts 2). What they so easily professed had to be worked out in experience. We may find that words of faith come easily, but deep appreciation for Christ comes with living by faith.

1.37 One of the two disciples was Andrew (1.40). The other was probably John, the writer of this book. Why did these disciples leave John the Baptist? Because that's what John wanted them to do—he pointed the way to Jesus, whom he had prepared them to follow. These were Jesus' first disciples, along with Simon Peter (1.42) and Nathanael (1.45).

1.38 When the two disciples began to follow Jesus, he asked them, "What are you looking for?" Following Christ is not enough; we must follow him for the right reasons. To follow Christ for our own purposes is asking Christ to follow us—to align with us to build our cause, not his. We must examine our motives for following him. Are we seeking his glory or ours?

1.40 Andrew accepted John the Baptist's testimony about Jesus and immediately went to tell his brother, Simon Peter, about him. There was no question in his mind that Jesus was the Messiah. Not only did he tell his brother, often Andrew was eager to introduce people to Jesus (see 6.8, 9; 12.22).

1.42 Jesus saw not only who Simon was, but who he would become. That is why he gave him a new name—Cephas in Greek, Peter in Latin (the name means "a rock"). Peter is not presented as rock-solid throughout the Gospels, but he became a solid rock in the days of the early church, as we learn in the book of Acts. By giving Simon a new name, Jesus introduced a change in character. For more on Simon Peter, see his Profile in Matthew 27.

1.49 Jn 1.34 You are the King of Israel!" 50 Jesus answered, "Do you believe because I told you
1.51 Gen 28.12 that I saw you under the fig tree? You will see greater things than these." 51 And he
said to him, "Very truly, I tell you,[l] you will see heaven opened and the angels of
God ascending and descending upon the Son of Man."

Jesus turns water into wine
(22)

2.1 Jn 1.29,35,43 **2** On the third day there was a wedding in Cana of Galilee, and the mother of
Jesus was there. 2 Jesus and his disciples had also been invited to the wedding.
3 When the wine gave out, the mother of Jesus said to him, "They have no wine."
2.4 Eccles 3.1 Mt 12.46-49 Jn 7.6; 8.20 19.26 4 And Jesus said to her, "Woman, what concern is that to you and to me? My hour
has not yet come." 5 His mother said to the servants, "Do whatever he tells you."
6 Now standing there were six stone water jars for the Jewish rites of purification,
2.6 Mk 7.3,4 Jn 3.25 each holding twenty or thirty gallons. 7 Jesus said to them, "Fill the jars with water." And they filled them up to the brim. 8 He said to them, "Now draw some out,
2.9 Jn 4.46 and take it to the chief steward." So they took it. 9 When the steward tasted the
water that had become wine, and did not know where it came from (though the
servants who had drawn the water knew), the steward called the bridegroom 10 and
said to him, "Everyone serves the good wine first, and then the inferior wine after

[l] Both instances of the Greek word for *you* in this verse are plural

JESUS' FIRST TRAVELS
After his baptism by John in the Jordan River and temptation by Satan in the wilderness (see the map in Mark 1), Jesus returned to Galilee. He visited Nazareth, Cana, and Capernaum, and then returned to Jerusalem for the Passover.

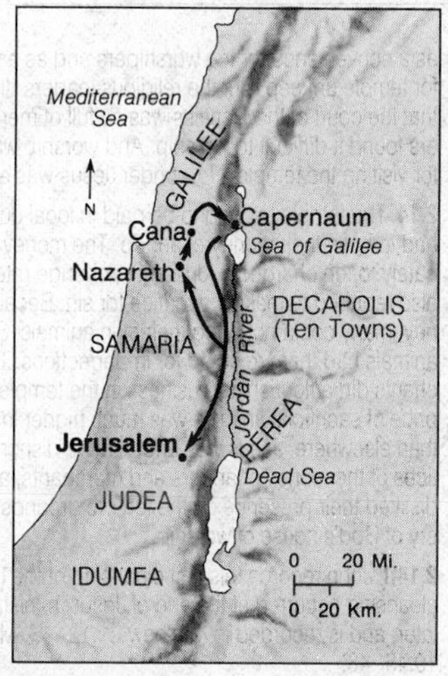

1.46 Nazareth was despised by the Jews because a Roman army garrison was located there. Nathanael's harsh comment reflected the common view. Nathanael's hometown was Cana, about four miles from Nazareth.

1.46 When Nathanael heard that the Messiah was from Nazareth, he was surprised. Philip responded, "Come and see." Fortunately, Nathanael went to meet Jesus and became a disciple. If he had acted on his prejudice without investigating further, he would have missed the Messiah! Don't let people's stereotypes about Christ cause them to miss his power and love. Invite them to come and see who he really is.

1.47–49 Jesus knew about Nathanael before the two ever met. Christ also knows what we are really like. You can't pretend to be something you're not. God knows the real you and wants *you* to follow him.

1.51 Jesus may have been referring to Jacob's dream recorded in Genesis 28.12. As the unique God-man, Jesus would be the ladder between heaven and earth. This would not be a physical experience such as the transfiguration, but spiritual insight into Jesus' true nature and purpose for coming.

2.1, 2 Jesus was on a mission to save the world, the greatest mission in history. Yet he took time to attend a wedding and take part in its festivities. We may be tempted to think we should not take time out from our "important" work for social occasions. But maybe these social occasions are part of our mission. Jesus valued these wedding festivities because they involved people, and Jesus came to be with people. Our mission can often be accomplished in joyous times of celebration with others. Jesus brings balance to your life. He is with you in times of pleasure as well as times of work.

2.1–3 Weddings in Jesus' day were week-long festivals. Banquets were prepared for many guests, and the week was spent celebrating the new life of the married couple. Often the whole town was invited. To accommodate many people, careful planning was needed. To run out of wine was more than embarrassing; it broke the strong unwritten laws of hospitality. Jesus was about to respond to a heartfelt need.

2.4 Mary was probably not asking Jesus to do a miracle; she simply hoped her son would help solve this major problem and find some wine. Tradition says that Joseph, Mary's husband, was dead, so she probably was used to asking for her son's help in difficult situations. Jesus' answer to Mary is difficult to understand, but maybe that is the point. Although Mary did not understand what Jesus was going to do, she trusted him to do the right thing. Although we believe in Jesus, we may run into situations that we cannot understand. We must always trust that he will work in the best way.

2.5 Mary submitted to Jesus' way of doing things. She recognized that Jesus was more than her human son – he was the Son of God. When we bring our problems to Christ, we may think we know how he should take care of them. But like Mary, we should submit and allow him to deal with the problem as he sees best.

2.6 The six stone water jars were normally used for ceremonial washing. When full, the jars would hold 20 to 30 gallons. According to the Jews' ceremonial law, people became symbolically unclean by touching objects of everyday life. Before eating, they poured water over their hands to cleanse themselves of any bad influences associated with what they had touched.

2.10 People look everywhere but to God for excitement and meaning. They somehow expect God to be dull and lifeless. Just as the wine Jesus made was the best, so life in him is better than life on our own. Why wait until everything else runs out before trying God? Why save the best until last?

the guests have become drunk. But you have kept the good wine until now."
11 Jesus did this, the first of his signs, in Cana of Galilee, and revealed his glory;
and his disciples believed in him.
12 After this he went down to Capernaum with his mother, his brothers, and his
disciples; and they remained there a few days.

2.11 Jn 2.23; 3.2 4.54; 6.14; 11.47 12.37

2.12 Mt 12.46-50

B. MESSAGE AND MINISTRY OF JESUS, THE SON OF GOD (2.13–12.50)

John stresses the deity of Christ. He gives us seven miracles that serve as signs that Jesus is the Messiah. In this section he records Jesus describing himself as the bread of life, the water of life, the light of the world, the door, and the good shepherd. John provides teachings of Jesus found nowhere else. This is the most theological of the four Gospels.

1. Jesus encounters belief and unbelief from the people

Jesus clears the temple

(23)

13 The Passover of the Jews was near, and Jesus went up to Jerusalem. 14 In the
temple he found people selling cattle, sheep, and doves, and the money changers
seated at their tables. 15 Making a whip of cords, he drove all of them out of the
temple, both the sheep and the cattle. He also poured out the coins of the money
changers and overturned their tables. 16 He told those who were selling the doves,

2.13 Ex 12.14 Num 28.16 Deut 16.1

2.16 Lk 2.49 Jn 14.2

2.11 When the disciples saw Jesus' miracle, they believed. The miracle showed his power over nature and revealed the way he would go about his ministry – helping others, speaking with authority, and being in personal touch with people.

2.11 Miracles are not merely superhuman happenings, but happenings that demonstrate God's power. Almost every miracle Jesus did was a renewal of fallen creation – restoring sight, making the lame walk, even restoring life to the dead. Believe in him, not because he is a superhuman, but because he is God continuing his creation, even in those of us who are poor, weak, crippled, orphaned, blind, lame, or with some other desperate need for re-creation.

2.12 Capernaum became Jesus' home base during his ministry in Galilee. Located on a major trade route, it was an important city in the region, with a Roman garrison and a customs station. At Capernaum, Matthew was called to be a disciple (Matthew 9.9). The city was also the home of several other disciples (Matthew 4.13–19) and a high-ranking government official (4.46). It had at least one major synagogue. Although Jesus made this city his base of operations in Galilee, he condemned it for the people's unbelief (Matthew 11.23; Luke 10.15).

2.13 The Passover celebration took place yearly at the temple in Jerusalem. Every Jewish male was expected to make a pilgrimage to Jerusalem during this time (Deuteronomy 16.16). This was a week-long festival – the Passover was one day, and the festival of unleavened bread lasted the rest of the week. The entire week commemorated the freeing of the Jews from slavery in Egypt (Exodus 12.1–13).

2.13 Jerusalem was both the religious and the political seat of Palestine, and the place where the Messiah was expected to arrive. The temple was located there, and many Jewish families from all over the world traveled to Jerusalem during the key feasts. The temple was built on an imposing site, a hill overlooking the city. Solomon had built the first temple on this same site almost 1,000 years earlier (949 B.C.), but his temple was destroyed by the Babylonians (2 Kings 25). The temple was rebuilt in 515 B.C., and Herod the Great enlarged and remodeled it.

2.14 The temple area was always crowded during Passover with thousands of out-of-town visitors. The religious leaders crowded it even further by allowing money changers and merchants to set up booths in the court of the Gentiles. They rationalized this practice as a convenience for the worshipers and as a way to make money for temple upkeep. But the religious leaders did not seem to care that the court of the Gentiles was so full of merchants that foreigners found it difficult to worship. And worship was the main purpose for visiting the temple. No wonder Jesus was angry!

2.14 The temple tax had to be paid in local currency, so foreigners had to have their money changed. The money changers, unfortunately, often charged exorbitant exchange rates. The people were also required to make a sacrifice for sin. Because of the long journey, many could not bring their own animals. Some who brought animals had them rejected for imperfections. Thus animal merchants did a flourishing business in the temple courtyard. The price of sacrificial animals was much higher in the temple area than elsewhere. Jesus was angry at the dishonest, greedy practices of the money changers and merchants, and he particularly disliked their presence on the temple grounds. They made a mockery of God's house of worship.

2.14ff John records this first cleansing of the temple. A second cleansing occurred at the end of Jesus' ministry, about three years later, and is recorded in Matthew 21.12–17; Mark 11.12–19; Luke 19.45–48.

2.14–16 God's temple was being misused by people who turned it into a marketplace. They forgot, or didn't care, that God's house is a place of worship, not a place for making a profit. Our attitude toward the church is wrong if we see it as a place for personal contacts or business advantage. Make sure you attend church to worship God.

2.15, 16 Jesus was obviously angry at the merchants who exploited those who had come to God's house to worship. There is a difference between uncontrolled rage and righteous indignation – yet both are called anger. We must be very careful how we use the powerful emotion of anger. It is right to be angry about injustice and sin; it is wrong to be angry over trivial personal offenses.

2.15, 16 Jesus made a whip and chased out the money changers. Does his example permit us to use violence against wrongdoers? Certain authority is granted to some, but not to all. For example, the authority to use weapons and restrain people is granted to police officers, but not to the general public. The authority to imprison people is granted to judges, but not to individual citizens. Jesus had God's authority, something we cannot have. While we want to live like Christ, we should never try to claim his authority where it has not been given to us.

2.17 Ps 69.9
2.19 Acts 6.14
2.20 Ezra 5.16
2.21 Jn 14.2,10; 17.21; 1 Cor 3.16; 6.19; 2 Cor 6.16; Eph 2.21,22; Col 2.9; 1 Pet 2.4-7
2.22 Ps 2.7; 16.10; Lk 24.8,25,26; Jn 12.16; 14.26

"Take these things out of here! Stop making my Father's house a marketplace!"
17 His disciples remembered that it was written, "Zeal for your house will consume
me." 18 The Jews then said to him, "What sign can you show us for doing this?"
19 Jesus answered them, "Destroy this temple, and in three days I will raise it up."
20 The Jews then said, "This temple has been under construction for forty-six years,
and will you raise it up in three days?" 21 But he was speaking of the temple of his
body. 22 After he was raised from the dead, his disciples remembered that he had
said this; and they believed the scripture and the word that Jesus had spoken.
23 When he was in Jerusalem during the Passover festival, many believed in his
name because they saw the signs that he was doing. 24 But Jesus on his part would
not entrust himself to them, because he knew all people 25 and needed no one to
testify about anyone; for he himself knew what was in everyone.

Nicodemus visits Jesus at night
(24)

3.1 Jn 7.50; 19.39
3.2 Acts 2.22; 10.38
3.3 Jn 1.13; 1 Pet 1.23

3 Now there was a Pharisee named Nicodemus, a leader of the Jews. 2 He came
to Jesus[m] by night and said to him, "Rabbi, we know that you are a teacher
who has come from God; for no one can do these signs that you do apart from the
presence of God." 3 Jesus answered him, "Very truly, I tell you, no one can see the
kingdom of God without being born from above."[n] 4 Nicodemus said to him,

[m] Gk *him* [n] Or *born anew*

2.17 Jesus took the evil acts in the temple as an insult against God, and thus he did not deal with them halfheartedly. He was "consumed" with righteous anger against such flagrant disrespect for God.

2.19, 20 The Jews understood Jesus to mean the temple out of which he had just driven the merchants and money changers. This was the temple Zerubbabel had built over 500 years earlier, but Herod the Great had begun remodeling it, making it much larger and far more beautiful. It had been 46 years since this remodeling had started (20 B.C.), and it still wasn't completely finished. They understood Jesus' words to mean that this imposing building could be torn down and rebuilt in three days, and they were startled.

2.21, 22 Jesus was not talking about the literal temple, but about himself. His listeners didn't realize it, but he was greater than the temple (Matthew 12.6). His words would take on meaning for his disciples after his resurrection. That Christ so perfectly fulfilled this prediction became the strongest proof for his claims to be God.

2.23–25 Jesus, the Son of God, knows all about human nature. He was well aware of the truth of Jeremiah 17.9, which states, "The heart is devious above all else; it is perverse—who can understand it?" Jesus was discerning, and he knew that the faith of some would-be followers was superficial. Some of the same people claiming to believe in Jesus at this time would later yell "Crucify him!" It's easy to believe when it is exciting and everyone else believes the same way. It is difficult to believe when you feel no other support. Be strong in your faith even when it isn't popular to believe.

3.1 Nicodemus was a ruler and a member of the Pharisees, a group of religious leaders whom Jesus and John the Baptist often criticized for being hypocrites (see the note on Matthew 3.7 for more on the Pharisees). Most Pharisees were intensely jealous of Jesus because he undermined their authority and challenged their views. But Nicodemus was searching, and he believed Jesus had some answers. A learned teacher himself, he came to Jesus to be taught. No matter how intelligent and well educated you are, you must come to Jesus with an open mind and heart so he can teach you the truth about God.

3.1ff Nicodemus came to Jesus personally, although he could have sent one of his assistants. He wanted to examine Jesus for himself to separate fact from rumor. Perhaps he was afraid of what his peers, the Pharisees, would say about his visit, so he came after dark. Later, when he understood that Jesus was truly the Messiah, he spoke up boldly in his defense (7.50, 51). Like Nicodemus, we must examine Jesus for ourselves—others cannot do it for us. Then, if we believe he is who he says, we will want to follow him and to speak up for him.

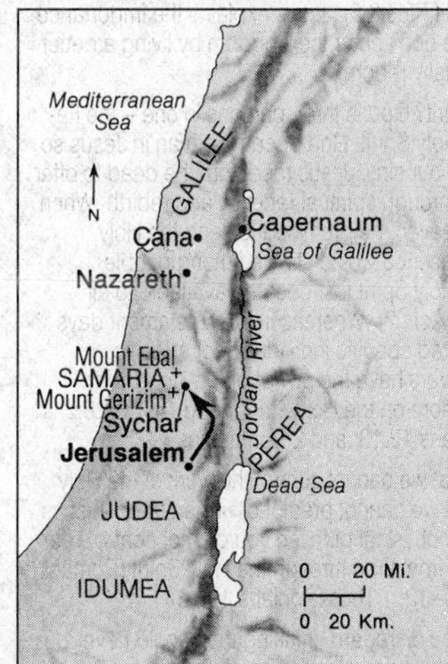

THE VISIT IN SAMARIA
Jesus went to Jerusalem for the Passover, cleansed the temple, and talked with Nicodemus, a religious leader, about eternal life. He then left Jerusalem and traveled in Judea. On his way to Galilee, he visited Sychar and other villages in Samaria. Unlike most Jews of the day, he did not try to avoid the region of Samaria.

3.3 What did Nicodemus know about the kingdom? From the Bible he knew it would be ruled by God, it would be restored on earth, and it would incorporate God's people. Jesus revealed to this devout Pharisee that the kingdom would come to the whole world (3.16), not just the Jews, and that Nicodemus wouldn't be a part of it unless he was personally born again (3.5). This was a revolutionary concept: the kingdom is personal, not national or ethnic, and its entrance requirements are repentance and spiritual rebirth. Jesus later taught that God's kingdom has *already begun* in the hearts of believers. It will be fully realized when Jesus returns to judge the world and abolish evil forever (Revelation 21, 22).

"How can anyone be born after having grown old? Can one enter a second time into
the mother's womb and be born?" 5 Jesus answered, "Very truly, I tell you, no one
can enter the kingdom of God without being born of water and Spirit. 6 What is born
of the flesh is flesh, and what is born of the Spirit is spirit.[o] 7 Do not be astonished
that I said to you, 'You[p] must be born from above.'[q] 8 The wind[o] blows where it
chooses, and you hear the sound of it, but you do not know where it comes from or
where it goes. So it is with everyone who is born of the Spirit." 9 Nicodemus said
to him, "How can these things be?" 10 Jesus answered him, "Are you a teacher of
Israel, and yet you do not understand these things?

11 "Very truly, I tell you, we speak of what we know and testify to what we
have seen; yet you[r] do not receive our testimony. 12 If I have told you about earthly
things and you do not believe, how can you believe if I tell you about heavenly
things? 13 No one has ascended into heaven except the one who descended from
heaven, the Son of Man.[s] 14 And just as Moses lifted up the serpent in the wilderness, so must the Son of Man be lifted up, 15 that whoever believes in him may have
eternal life.[t]

16 "For God so loved the world that he gave his only Son, so that everyone who
believes in him may not perish but may have eternal life.

17 "Indeed, God did not send the Son into the world to condemn the world, but
in order that the world might be saved through him. 18 Those who believe in him are

3.5 Acts 2.38 Tit 3.4,5 1 Pet 3.21
3.6 Ezek 36.26,27 Jn 1.13 Rom 8.15,16 1 Cor 15.50 Gal 4.6
3.8 Eccles 11.5 Ezek 37.5,9,10,14
3.13 Jn 6.38,42 16.28 Rom 10.6 Eph 4.9,10
3.14 Num 21.8,9
3.15 1 Jn 5.11,12
3.16 Rom 5.8; 8.32
3.17 Jn 12.47
3.18 Jn 5.24 Rom 8.1

[o] The same Greek word means both *wind* and *spirit* [p] The Greek word for *you* here is plural [q] Or *anew*
[r] The Greek word for *you* here and in verse 12 is plural [s] Other ancient authorities add *who is in heaven* [t] Some interpreters hold that the quotation concludes with verse 15

3.5, 6 "Of water and Spirit" could be referring to (1) the contrast between physical birth (water) and spiritual birth (Spirit), or (2) being regenerated by the Spirit and demonstrating that rebirth by Christian baptism. The water may also represent the cleansing action of God's Holy Spirit (Titus 3.5). Jesus explains the importance of a spiritual rebirth. We don't enter the kingdom by living a better life, but by being spiritually reborn.

3.6 Who is the Holy Spirit? God is three persons in one – the Father, the Son, and the Holy Spirit. God became a man in Jesus so that Jesus could die for our sins. Jesus rose from the dead to offer salvation to all people through spiritual renewal and rebirth. When Jesus ascended into heaven, he promised to send the Holy Spirit so his spiritual presence would still be among people (see Luke 24.49). The Holy Spirit first became available to all believers at Pentecost (Acts 2). Whereas in Old Testament days the Holy Spirit empowered specific individuals for specific purposes, now all believers have the power of the Holy Spirit available to them. For more on the Holy Spirit, read 14.16–28; Romans 8.9; 1 Corinthians 12.13; and 2 Corinthians 1.22.

3.8 Jesus explained that we cannot control the work of the Holy Spirit. He works in ways we cannot predict or understand. Just as you did not control your physical birth, so you cannot control your spiritual birth. It is a gift from God through the Holy Spirit (Romans 8.16; 1 Corinthians 2.10–12; 1 Thessalonians 1.5, 6).

3.8 Are there people you disregard, thinking they could never be brought to God – such as a world leader for whom you have never prayed or a successful person to whom you have never witnessed? Don't assume that anyone is beyond the reach of the gospel. God, through his Holy Spirit, can reach anyone, and you should pray diligently for whomever he brings to your mind. Be a witness and example to everyone with whom you have contact. God may touch those you think most unlikely – and he may use you to do it.

3.10, 11 This Jewish teacher of the Bible knew the Old Testament thoroughly, but he didn't understand what it said about the Messiah. Knowledge is not salvation. You should know the Bible; but even more important, you should understand the God it reveals and the salvation he offers.

3.14, 15 When the Israelites were wandering in the wilderness, God sent a plague of serpents to punish the people for their rebellious attitudes. Those doomed to die from snakebite could be healed by obeying God's command to look up at the elevated bronze serpent and by believing that God would heal them if they did (see Numbers 21.8, 9). Similarly, our salvation happens when we look up to Jesus, believing he will save us. God has provided this way for us to be healed of sin's deadly bite.

3.16 The entire gospel comes to a focus in this verse. God's love is not static or self-centered; it reaches out and draws others in. Here God sets the pattern of true love, the basis for all love relationships – if you love someone dearly, you are willing to pay dearly for that person's responsive love. God paid dearly with the life of his Son, the highest price he could pay. Jesus accepted our punishment, paid the price for our sins, and then offered us the new life he bought for us. When we share the gospel with others, our love must be like his. Do we willingly give up our own comfort and security so that others might join us in receiving God's love?

3.16 Some people are repulsed by the idea of eternal life because their lives are miserable. But eternal life is not an extension of man's miserable, mortal life; eternal life is God's life embodied in Christ, given to all believers now as a guarantee that they will live forever. In eternal life there is no death, sickness, evil, or sin. When we don't know Christ, we make choices as though this life is all we have. In reality, this life is just the introduction to eternity. Receive this new life by faith and begin to evaluate all that happens from God's eternal perspective.

3.16 To believe is more than intellectual agreement that Jesus is God. It means to put our trust and confidence in him that he alone can save us. It is to put him in charge of our present plans and eternal destiny. Believing is both trusting his words as reliable and relying on him for the power to change. If you have never trusted him, let this promise of everlasting life be yours.

3.18 People often try to protect themselves from their fears by putting their trust in something they do or have: their good works, their skill or intelligence, their money or possessions. But only God can save us from the one thing we really need to fear – eternal condemnation. We trust in God by recognizing the insufficiency of our own efforts to find salvation and by asking him to do his work in us. When Jesus talks about unbelievers, he means those who reject or ignore him completely, not those who have momentary doubts.

not condemned; but those who do not believe are condemned already, because they
3.19 Jn 1.4,5; 7.7 8.12; 12.46 have not believed in the name of the only Son of God. 19 And this is the judgment,
that the light has come into the world, and people loved darkness rather than light
3.20 Eph 5.11-13 because their deeds were evil. 20 For all who do evil hate the light and do not come
to the light, so that their deeds may not be exposed. 21 But those who do what is true
3.21 1 Jn 1.7 come to the light, so that it may be clearly seen that their deeds have been done in
God."[u]

John the Baptist tells more about Jesus

(25)

3.22 Jn 4.2 22 After this Jesus and his disciples went into the Judean countryside, and he
spent some time there with them and baptized. 23 John also was baptizing at Aenon
near Salim because water was abundant there; and people kept coming and were
3.24 Mt 4.12 being baptized 24 —John, of course, had not yet been thrown into prison.
3.26 Jn 1.6,7,34 25 Now a discussion about purification arose between John's disciples and a
Jew.[v] 26 They came to John and said to him, "Rabbi, the one who was with you

[u] Some interpreters hold that the quotation concludes with verse 15 [v] Other ancient authorities read *the Jews*

NICODEMUS

God specializes in finding and changing people we consider out of reach. It took awhile for Nicodemus to come out of the dark, but God was patient with this "undercover" believer.

Afraid of being discovered, Nicodemus made an appointment to see Jesus at night. Daylight conversations between Pharisees and Jesus tended to be antagonistic, but Nicodemus really wanted to learn. He probably got a lot more than he expected—a challenge to a new life! We know very little about Nicodemus, but we know that he left that evening's encounter a changed man. He came away with a whole new understanding of both God and himself.

Nicodemus next appears as part of the Jewish council. As it discussed ways to eliminate Jesus, Nicodemus raised the question of justice. Although his objection was overruled, he had spoken up. He had begun to change.

Our last picture of Nicodemus shows him joining Joseph of Arimathea in asking for Jesus' body to bury. Realizing what he was risking, Nicodemus was making a bold move. He was continuing to grow.

God looks for steady growth, not instant perfection. How well does your present level of spiritual growth match up with how long you have known Jesus?

Strengths and accomplishments:
- One of the few religious leaders who believed in Jesus
- A member of the powerful council
- A Pharisee who was attracted by Jesus' character and miracles
- Joined with Joseph of Arimathea in burying Jesus

Weakness and mistake:
- Limited by his fear of being publicly exposed as Jesus' follower

Lessons from his life:
- Unless we are born again, we can never be part of the kingdom of God
- God is able to change those we might consider unreachable
- God is patient, but persistent
- If we are available, God can use us

Vital statistics:
- Where: Jerusalem
- Occupation: Religious leader
- Contemporaries: Jesus, Annas, Caiaphas, Pilate, Joseph of Arimathea

Key verse:
"Nicodemus said to him, 'How can anyone be born after having grown old? Can one enter a second time into the mother's womb and be born?'" (John 3.4).

Nicodemus's story is told in John 3.1–21; 7.50–52; and 19.39, 40.

3.19–21 Many people don't want their lives exposed to God's light because they are afraid of what it will reveal. They don't want to be changed. Don't be surprised when these same people are threatened by your desire to obey God and do what is right, because they are afraid that the light in you may expose some of the darkness in their lives. Rather than giving in to discouragement, keep praying that people you know will come to see how much better it is to live in light than in darkness.

3.26 John the Baptist's disciples were disturbed because people were following Jesus instead of John. It is easy to grow jealous of the popularity of another person's ministry. But we must remember that our true mission is to influence people to follow Christ, not us.

across the Jordan, to whom you testified, here he is baptizing, and all are going to
him." 27 John answered, "No one can receive anything except what has been given
from heaven. 28 You yourselves are my witnesses that I said, 'I am not the Messiah,[w] but I have been sent ahead of him.' 29 He who has the bride is the bridegroom. The friend of the bridegroom, who stands and hears him, rejoices greatly at
the bridegroom's voice. For this reason my joy has been fulfilled. 30 He must increase, but I must decrease."[x]

31 The one who comes from above is above all; the one who is of the earth
belongs to the earth and speaks about earthly things. The one who comes from
heaven is above all. 32 He testifies to what he has seen and heard, yet no one accepts
his testimony. 33 Whoever has accepted his testimony has certified[y] this, that God
is true. 34 He whom God has sent speaks the words of God, for he gives the Spirit
without measure. 35 The Father loves the Son and has placed all things in his hands.
36 Whoever believes in the Son has eternal life; whoever disobeys the Son will not
see life, but must endure God's wrath.

3.27 1 Cor 4.7 Heb 5.4 **3.28** Mal 3.1 Jn 1.20,23 **3.29** Isa 62.5 2 Cor 11.2 Rev 21.9 **3.33** 1 Jn 5.10 **3.34** Lk 4.18,19 Jn 6.63 **3.35** Jn 5.20; 17.2,24 **3.36** Hab 2.4 Jn 3.16 Rom 1.17

Jesus talks to a woman at the well
(27)

4 Now when Jesus[z] learned that the Pharisees had heard, "Jesus is making and
baptizing more disciples than John" 2 — although it was not Jesus himself but
his disciples who baptized— 3 he left Judea and started back to Galilee. 4 But he had
to go through Samaria. 5 So he came to a Samaritan city called Sychar, near the plot
of ground that Jacob had given to his son Joseph. 6 Jacob's well was there, and
Jesus, tired out by his journey, was sitting by the well. It was about noon.
7 A Samaritan woman came to draw water, and Jesus said to her, "Give me a

4.4 Lk 9.52 **4.5,6** Gen 33.19 48.22 Josh 24.32 **4.7** Gen 24.11

[w] Or *the Christ* [x] Some interpreters hold that the quotation continues through verse 36 [y] Gk *set a seal to* [z] Other ancient authorities read *the Lord*

3.27 Why did John the Baptist continue to baptize after Jesus came onto the scene? Why didn't he become a disciple too? John explained that God gave him his work, and he had to continue it until God called him to do something else. John's main purpose was to point people to Christ. Even with Jesus beginning his own ministry, John could still point people to him.

3.27 John believed God had appointed him. If God appoints us to a task, it becomes a high and holy privilege. We should accept it with great enthusiasm.

3.30 John's willingness to decrease in importance shows unusual humility. Pastors and other Christian leaders can be tempted to focus more on the success of their ministries than on Christ. Beware of those who put more emphasis on their own achievements than on God's kingdom.

3.31–35 Jesus' testimony was trustworthy because he came from heaven and spoke of what he saw there. His words were the very words of God. Your whole spiritual life depends on your answer to one question, "Who is Jesus Christ?" If you accept Jesus as only a prophet or teacher, you have to reject his teaching, because he claimed to be God's Son, even God himself. The heartbeat of John's Gospel is the dynamic truth that Jesus Christ is God's Son, the Messiah, the Savior, who was from the beginning and will continue to live forever. This same Jesus has invited us to accept him and live with him eternally. When we understand Jesus' true identity, we are compelled to believe what he said.

3.34 "Gives the Spirit without measure" means that God's Spirit was upon Jesus completely and without any limit. Thus Jesus was the highest revelation of God to man (Hebrews 1.2).

3.36 Jesus says that those who believe in him *have* (not *will* have) everlasting life. To receive eternal life is to join in God's life, which by nature is eternal. Thus, eternal life begins at the moment of spiritual rebirth.

3.36 The apostle John has been demonstrating that Jesus is the true Son of God. He sets before us the greatest choice of our life. We are responsible to decide today whom we will obey (Joshua 24.15), and God wants us to choose him and live (Deuteronomy 30.15–20). The wrath of God is God's final judgment and rejection of the sinner. Putting off the choice is choosing not to follow Christ. Such indecision is spiritually fatal.

4.1–3 Already opposition was rising against Jesus, especially from the Pharisees. They resented Jesus' popularity as well as his message, which challenged much of their teachings. Because Jesus was just beginning his ministry, it wasn't yet time to confront these leaders openly; so he left Jerusalem and traveled north toward Galilee.

4.4 When the northern kingdom with its capital at Samaria fell to the Assyrians, many Jews were deported to Assyria, and foreigners were brought in to settle the land and help keep the peace (2 Kings 17.24). The intermarriage between those foreigners and the remaining Jews resulted in a mixed race, impure in the opinion of Jews who lived in the southern kingdom. Thus the pure Jews hated this mixed race called Samaritans, feeling that they had betrayed their people and nation. The Samaritans set up an alternate center for worship on Mount Gerazim (4.20) to parallel the temple at Jerusalem; but it had been destroyed 150 years earlier. The Jews did everything they could to avoid traveling through Samaria. But Jesus had no reason to live by such cultural restrictions. The route through Samaria was shorter, and that was the route he took.

4.5, 6 Jacob's well was on the property originally owned by Jacob. It was not a spring-fed well, but a well into which water seeped from rain and dew, collecting at the bottom. Wells were almost always located outside the city along the main road. Twice each day, morning and evening, women came to draw water. This woman came at noon, however, probably to avoid meeting people because of her reputation. Jesus gave this woman an extraordinary message about fresh and pure water that would quench her spiritual thirst forever.

4.7–9 This woman (1) was a Samaritan, a member of the hated

4.9 2 Kgs 17.24 Ezra 4 Mt 10.5 Jn 8.48 Acts 10.48
4.10 Isa 12.3; 44.3 Jer 2.13 1 Cor 12.13 Rev 21.6; 22.17
4.14 Jn 6.35 7.37,38
4.15 Jn 6.34
4.19 Lk 7.16
4.20 Gen 12.6,7 33.18 Judg 9.7 Deut 12.5 2 Chron 7.12
4.21 Mal 1.11 1 Tim 2.8
4.22 2 Kings 17.28-41 Isa 2.3 Acts 17.24-29 Rom 3.1,2 9.4,5
4.23,24 2 Cor 3.17,18 Phil 3.3
4.25 Deut 18.15
4.26 Mk 14.61,62 Jn 8.24; 9.35-37

drink." 8 (His disciples had gone to the city to buy food.) 9 The Samaritan woman
said to him, "How is it that you, a Jew, ask a drink of me, a woman of Samaria?"
(Jews do not share things in common with Samaritans.)[a] 10 Jesus answered her, "If
you knew the gift of God, and who it is that is saying to you, 'Give me a drink,' you
would have asked him, and he would have given you living water." 11 The woman
said to him, "Sir, you have no bucket, and the well is deep. Where do you get that
living water? 12 Are you greater than our ancestor Jacob, who gave us the well, and
with his sons and his flocks drank from it?" 13 Jesus said to her, "Everyone who
drinks of this water will be thirsty again, 14 but those who drink of the water that I
will give them will never be thirsty. The water that I will give will become in them
a spring of water gushing up to eternal life." 15 The woman said to him, "Sir, give
me this water, so that I may never be thirsty or have to keep coming here to draw
water."

16 Jesus said to her, "Go, call your husband, and come back." 17 The woman
answered him, "I have no husband." Jesus said to her, "You are right in saying, 'I
have no husband'; 18 for you have had five husbands, and the one you have now is
not your husband. What you have said is true!" 19 The woman said to him, "Sir, I
see that you are a prophet. 20 Our ancestors worshiped on this mountain, but you[b]
say that the place where people must worship is in Jerusalem." 21 Jesus said to her,
"Woman, believe me, the hour is coming when you will worship the Father neither
on this mountain nor in Jerusalem. 22 You worship what you do not know; we worship what we know, for salvation is from the Jews. 23 But the hour is coming, and
is now here, when the true worshipers will worship the Father in spirit and truth, for
the Father seeks such as these to worship him. 24 God is spirit, and those who worship him must worship in spirit and truth." 25 The woman said to him, "I know that
Messiah is coming" (who is called Christ). "When he comes, he will proclaim all
things to us." 26 Jesus said to her, "I am he,[c] the one who is speaking to you."

[a] Other ancient authorities lack this sentence [b] The Greek word for *you* here and in verses 21 and 22 is plural
[c] Gk *I am*

---

mixed race, (2) was known to be living in sin, and (3) was in a public place. No respectable Jewish man would talk to a woman under such circumstances. But Jesus did. The gospel is for every person, no matter what his or her race, social position, or past sins. We must be prepared to share this gospel at any time in any place. Jesus crossed all barriers to share the gospel, and we who follow him must do the same.

4.10 What did Jesus mean by "living water?" In the Old Testament, many verses speak of thirsting after God as one thirsts for water (Psalm 42.1; Isaiah 55.1; Jeremiah 2.13; Zechariah 13.1). God is called the fountain of life (Psalm 36.9) and the fountain of living water (Jeremiah 17.13). In saying he would bring living water that could forever quench one's thirst for God, Jesus was claiming to be the Messiah. Only the Messiah could give this gift that satisfies the soul's desire.

4.13–15 Many spiritual functions parallel physical functions. As our bodies hunger and thirst, so do our souls. But our souls need *spiritual* food and water. The woman confused the two kinds of water, perhaps because no one had ever talked with her about her spiritual hunger and thirst before. We would not think of depriving our bodies of food and water when they hunger or thirst. Why then should we deprive our souls? The living Word, Jesus Christ, and the written Word, the Bible, can satisfy our hungry and thirsty souls.

4.15 The woman mistakenly believed that if she received the water Jesus offered, she would not have to return to the well each day. She was interested in Jesus' message because she thought it could make her life easier. But if that were always the case, people would accept Christ's message for the wrong reasons. Christ did not come to take away challenges, but to change us on the inside and to empower us to deal with problems from God's perspective.

4.15 The woman did not immediately understand what Jesus was talking about. It takes time to accept something that changes the very foundations of your life. Jesus allowed the woman time to ask questions and put pieces together for herself. Sharing the gospel does not always have immediate results. When you ask people to let Jesus change their lives, give them time to weigh the matter.

4.16–20 When this woman discovered that Jesus knew all about her private life, she quickly changed the subject. Often people become uncomfortable when the conversation is too close to home, and they try to change the subject. As we witness we should gently guide the conversation back to Christ. His presence reveals sin and makes people squirm, but only he can forgive the sins and give new life.

4.20–24 The woman brought up a popular theological issue—the correct place to worship. But her question was a smokescreen to keep Jesus away from her deepest need. Jesus directed the conversation to a much more important point: the *location* of worship is not nearly so important as the *attitude* of the worshipers.

4.21–24 "God is spirit" means he is not a physical being limited to one place. He is present everywhere, and he can be worshiped anywhere, anytime. It is not where we worship that counts, but how we worship. Is your worship genuine and real? Do you have the Holy Spirit's help? How does the Holy Spirit help us worship? The Holy Spirit prays for us (Romans 8.26), teaches us the words of Christ (14.26), and assures us that we are loved (Romans 5.5).

4.22 When Jesus said, "salvation is from the Jews," he meant that only through the Jewish Messiah would the whole world find salvation. God had promised that through the Jewish race the whole earth would be blessed (Genesis 12.3). The Old Testament prophets called the Jews to be a light to the other nations of the world, telling them about God; and they predicted the Messiah's coming. The woman at the well knew of these passages and was expecting the Messiah, but she didn't realize that she was talking to him!

Jesus tells about the spiritual harvest
(28)

27 Just then his disciples came. They were astonished that he was speaking
with a woman, but no one said, "What do you want?" or, "Why are you speaking
with her?" 28 Then the woman left her water jar and went back to the city. She said
to the people, 29 "Come and see a man who told me everything I have ever done! He
cannot be the Messiah,[d] can he?" 30 They left the city and were on their way to him.
31 Meanwhile the disciples were urging him, "Rabbi, eat something." 32 But he
said to them, "I have food to eat that you do not know about." 33 So the disciples
said to one another, "Surely no one has brought him something to eat?" 34 Jesus said
to them, "My food is to do the will of him who sent me and to complete his work.
35 Do you not say, 'Four months more, then comes the harvest'? But I tell you, look
around you, and see how the fields are ripe for harvesting. 36 The reaper is already
receiving[e] wages and is gathering fruit for eternal life, so that sower and reaper
may rejoice together. 37 For here the saying holds true, 'One sows and another
reaps.' 38 I sent you to reap that for which you did not labor. Others have labored,
and you have entered into their labor."

4.29 Jn 7.26,31
4.34 Job 23.12 Jn 5.30,36 6.38; 17.4 19.28,30
4.35 Mt 9.37,38 Lk 10.2
4.36 Dan 12.3 1 Cor 3.8,9 9.17-19
4.37 Job 31.8 Mic 6.15

Many Samaritans believe in Jesus
(29)

39 Many Samaritans from that city believed in him because of the woman's
testimony, "He told me everything I have ever done." 40 So when the Samaritans
came to him, they asked him to stay with them; and he stayed there two days.
41 And many more believed because of his word. 42 They said to the woman, "It is
no longer because of what you said that we believe, for we have heard for ourselves, and we know that this is truly the Savior of the world."

4.42 Isa 49.6 Mt 1.21 Lk 2.29-31 Jn 1.29; 17.8 Acts 5.31; 13.23 Eph 2.13 Phil 3.20 1 Tim 1.15 1 Jn 4.14

Jesus preaches in Galilee
(30/Matthew 4.12–17; Mark 1.14, 15; Luke 4.14, 15)

43 When the two days were over, he went from that place to Galilee 44 (for Jesus
himself had testified that a prophet has no honor in the prophet's own country).
45 When he came to Galilee, the Galileans welcomed him, since they had seen all
that he had done in Jerusalem at the festival; for they too had gone to the festival.

4.43,44 Mt 13.57 Mk 6.4 Lk 4.24
4.45 Deut 16.16

[d] *Or the Christ* [e] *Or 35. . . the fields are already ripe for harvesting. 36 The reaper is receiving*

JESUS RETURNS TO GALILEE
Jesus stayed in Sychar for two days, then went on to Galilee. He visited Nazareth and various towns in Galilee before arriving in Cana. From there he spoke the word of healing and a government official's son in Capernaum was healed. The Gospel of Matthew tells us Jesus then settled in Capernaum (Matthew 4.12, 13).

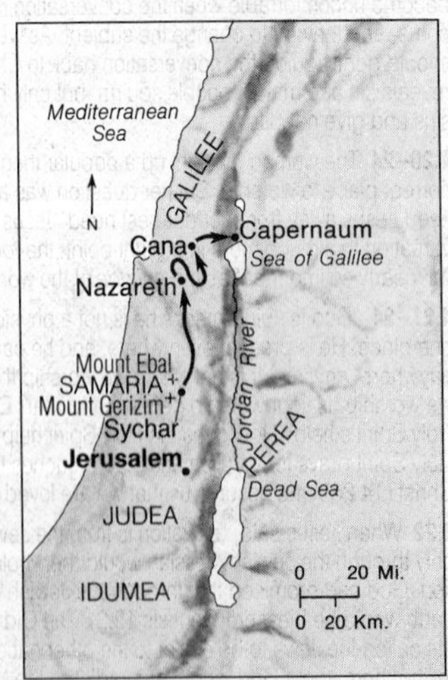

4.29, 39 The Samaritan woman immediately shared her experience with others. Despite her reputation, many took her invitation and came out to meet Jesus. Perhaps we're ashamed of sins in our past. But Christ's love changes us. He gives us new purpose, new attitudes, and new behavior. As people see these changes, they become curious. Use these opportunities to introduce them to Christ.

4.34 The "food" about which Jesus was speaking was his spiritual nourishment. Spiritual food includes more than Bible study, prayer, and attending church. It also comes from doing God's will and reaching out to others. We are nourished not only by what we take in, but also by what we give out for God. In 17.4, Jesus refers to completing his work on earth.

4.35 Sometimes Christians excuse themselves from witnessing by saying that their family or friends aren't ready to believe. Jesus, however, makes it clear that around us a continual harvest waits to be reaped. Don't let Jesus find you making excuses. Look around. You will find people ready to hear God's Word.

4.36–38 The wages Jesus offers are the joy of working for him and seeing the harvest of believers. These wages come to sower and reaper alike, because both find joy in seeing new believers come into Christ's kingdom. The phrase "others have labored" (4.38) may refer to the Old Testament prophets and John the Baptist, who paved the way for the gospel.

Jesus heals a government official's son
(31)

4.46 46 Then he came again to Cana in Galilee where he had changed the water into
Jn 2.1,11,23 wine. Now there was a royal official whose son lay ill in Capernaum. 47 When he
heard that Jesus had come from Judea to Galilee, he went and begged him to come
4.48 down and heal his son, for he was at the point of death. 48 Then Jesus said to him,
1 Cor 1.22 "Unless you[f] see signs and wonders you will not believe." 49 The official said to
Heb 2.4 him, "Sir, come down before my little boy dies." 50 Jesus said to him, "Go; your
son will live." The man believed the word that Jesus spoke to him and started on his
way. 51 As he was going down, his slaves met him and told him that his child was
alive. 52 So he asked them the hour when he began to recover, and they said to him,
4.53 "Yesterday at one in the afternoon the fever left him." 53 The father realized that
Acts 11.14 16.34 this was the hour when Jesus had said to him, "Your son will live." So he himself
4.54 believed, along with his whole household. 54 Now this was the second sign that
Jn 2.11 Jesus did after coming from Judea to Galilee.

Jesus heals a lame man by the pool
(42)

5.1 **5** After this there was a festival of the Jews, and Jesus went up to Jerusalem.
Lev 23.1,2 Deut 16.1 2 Now in Jerusalem by the Sheep Gate there is a pool, called in Hebrew[g]
Jn 2.13 Beth-zatha,[h] which has five porticoes. 3 In these lay many invalids—blind, lame,
5.2 Neh 3.1; 12.39 and paralyzed.[i] 5 One man was there who had been ill for thirty-eight years.
5.6 6 When Jesus saw him lying there and knew that he had been there a long time, he
Ps 72.13 said to him, "Do you want to be made well?" 7 The sick man answered him, "Sir,
113.5,6 Heb 4.13 I have no one to put me into the pool when the water is stirred up; and while I am

[f] Both instances of the Greek word for *you* in this verse are plural [g] That is, *Aramaic* [h] Other ancient authorities read *Bethesda*, others *Bethsaida* [i] Other ancient authorities add, wholly or in part, *waiting for the stirring of the water; 4for an angel of the Lord went down at certain seasons into the pool, and stirred up the water; whoever stepped in first after the stirring of the water was made well from whatever disease that person had.*

4.46–49 This royal official was probably an officer in Herod's service. He walked 20 miles to see Jesus and addressed him as "Sir," putting himself under Jesus even though he had legal authority over Jesus.

4.48 This miracle was more than a favor to one official; it was a sign to all the people. John's Gospel was written to all people to urge faith in Christ. Here a government official had faith that Jesus could do what he claimed. He believed; *then* he saw.

4.50 This government official not only believed Jesus could heal; he also obeyed Jesus by returning home, thus demonstrating his faith. It isn't enough for us to say we believe Jesus can take care of our problems. We need to act as if he can. When you pray about a need or problem, live as though you believe Jesus will do what he says.

4.51 Jesus' miracles were not mere illusions, the product of wishful thinking. Although the official's son was 20 miles away, he was healed when Jesus spoke the word. Distance was no problem because Christ has mastery over space. We can never put so much space between ourselves and Christ that he can no longer help us.

4.53 Notice how the official's faith grew. First, he believed enough to ask Jesus to help his son. Second, he believed Jesus' assurance that his son would live, and he acted on it. Third, he and his whole house believed in Jesus. Faith is a gift that grows as we use it.

5.1 Three festivals required all Jewish males to come to Jerusalem: (1) the Passover and festival of unleavened bread, (2) the festival of weeks (also called pentecost), and (3) the festival of booths.

5.2 A portico is a covered porch or entrance with columns.

5.3 It is unclear whether an angel actually disturbed the water, or if this was just what the people believed (see textual note). In either case, Jesus healed a man who had been waiting for 38 years to be healed.

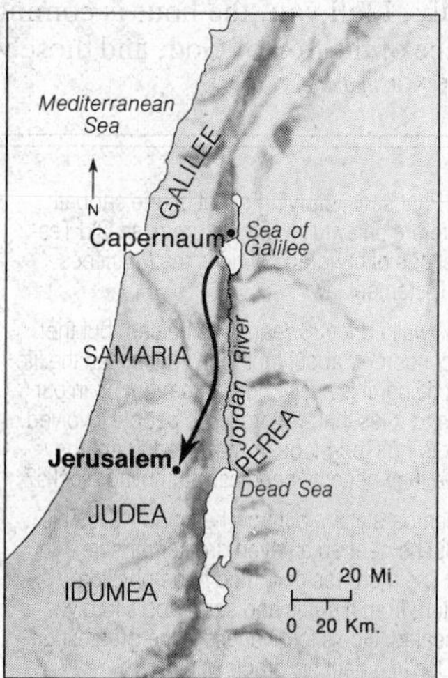

JESUS TEACHES IN JERUSALEM
Between chapters four and five of John, Jesus ministered throughout Galilee, especially in Capernaum. He had been calling certain men to follow him, but it wasn't until after this trip to Jerusalem (5.1) that he chose his 12 disciples from among them.

5.6 After 38 years, this man's problem had become a way of life. No one had ever helped him. He had no hope of ever being healed and no desire to help himself. His situation looked hopeless. But no matter how trapped you feel in your infirmities, God can minister to your deepest needs. Don't let a problem or hardship cause you to lose hope. God may have special work for you to do in spite of your condition, or even because of it. Many have ministered effectively to hurting people because they have triumphed over their own hurts.

making my way, someone else steps down ahead of me." 8 Jesus said to him,
"Stand up, take your mat and walk." 9 At once the man was made well, and he took
up his mat and began to walk.
Now that day was a sabbath. 10 So the Jews said to the man who had been cured,
"It is the sabbath; it is not lawful for you to carry your mat." 11 But he answered
them, "The man who made me well said to me, 'Take up your mat and walk.' "
12 They asked him, "Who is the man who said to you, 'Take it up and walk'?"
13 Now the man who had been healed did not know who it was, for Jesus had disappeared in[j] the crowd that was there. 14 Later Jesus found him in the temple and said
to him, "See, you have been made well! Do not sin any more, so that nothing worse
happens to you." 15 The man went away and told the Jews that it was Jesus who had
made him well. 16 Therefore the Jews started persecuting Jesus, because he was
doing such things on the sabbath. 17 But Jesus answered them, "My Father is still
working, and I also am working." 18 For this reason the Jews were seeking all the
more to kill him, because he was not only breaking the sabbath, but was also calling
God his own Father, thereby making himself equal to God.

5.8 Mt 9.6 Mk 2.11 Lk 5.24
5.10 Ex 20.10 Neh 13.19 Jer 17.21 Mt 12.2 Mk 2.24; 3.4 Lk 6.2; 13.14
5.14 Jn 8.11
5.17 Jn 9.4; 14.10
5.18 Isa 9.6 Jn 1.1,18 10.30,33; 20.28 Phil 2.6 Tit 2.13 2 Pet 1.1 1 Jn 5.21

Jesus claims to be God's Son
(43)

19 Jesus said to them, "Very truly, I tell you, the Son can do nothing on his
own, but only what he sees the Father doing; for whatever the Father[k] does, the
Son does likewise. 20 The Father loves the Son and shows him all that he himself is
doing; and he will show him greater works than these, so that you will be astonished. 21 Indeed, just as the Father raises the dead and gives them life, so also the
Son gives life to whomever he wishes. 22 The Father judges no one but has given all
judgment to the Son, 23 so that all may honor the Son just as they honor the Father.
Anyone who does not honor the Son does not honor the Father who sent him.
24 Very truly, I tell you, anyone who hears my word and believes him who sent me
has eternal life, and does not come under judgment, but has passed from death to
life.
25 "Very truly, I tell you, the hour is coming, and is now here, when the dead
will hear the voice of the Son of God, and those who hear will live. 26 For just as the

5.19 Jn 8.28; 12.49 14.10
5.21 Jn 11.25
5.22 Jn 5.27
5.23 1 Jn 2.23
5.24 Jn 20.30,31 1 Jn 3.14; 5.13
5.25 Jn 4.21; 6.63,68
5.26 Jn 1.4; 6.57 1 Jn 5.11,12

[j] Or *had left because of* [k] Gk *that one*

5.10 According to the Pharisees, carrying a mat on the sabbath was work and was therefore unlawful. It did not break an Old Testament law but was just one of hundreds of rules the Pharisees had added to the Old Testament law.

5.10 A man who hadn't walked for 38 years was healed, but the Pharisees were more concerned about their petty rules than the life and health of a human being. It is easy to get so caught up in our man-made structures and rules that we forget the people involved. Are your guidelines for living God-made or man-made? Are they helping people, or have they become needless stumbling blocks?

5.14 This man had been paralyzed, but now he could walk. This was a great miracle. But he needed an even greater miracle—to have his sins forgiven. The man was delighted to be physically healed, but he had to turn from his sins and seek God's forgiveness to be spiritually healed. God's forgiveness is the greatest gift you will ever receive. Don't neglect his gracious offer.

5.16 The Jewish leaders saw a mighty miracle of healing and a broken rule. They threw the miracle aside as they focused their attention on the broken rule, because the rule was more important to them than the miracle. God is prepared to work in our lives, but we can shut out his miracles by limiting our views about how he works.

5.17 If God stopped every kind of work on the sabbath, nature would fall into chaos and sin would overrun the world. Genesis 2.2 says that God rested on the seventh day, but this can't mean he stopped doing good. Jesus wanted to teach that when the opportunity to do good presents itself, it should not be ignored, even on the sabbath.

5.17ff Jesus was identifying himself with God, his Father. There could be no doubt as to his claim to be God. We do not have the option of believing in God while ignoring Jesus (5.23). In response to Jesus' claim, the Pharisees had two choices: to believe him or to accuse him of blasphemy. They chose the latter.

5.19–23 Because of his unity with God, Jesus lived as God wanted. Because of our identification with Jesus, we must honor him and live as he wants us to live. The questions "What would Jesus do?" and "What would Jesus have me do?" may help us make the right choices.

5.24 Eternal life—living forever with God—begins when you accept Jesus Christ as Savior. At that moment, new life begins in you (2 Corinthians 5.17). It is a completed transaction. You will still have to die physically, but when Christ returns, your body will be resurrected to live forever.

5.25 In saying that the dead would hear his voice, Jesus was talking about the spiritually dead who hear, understand, and accept him. Those who accept God's Word will have eternal life. He was also talking about the physically dead. Jesus raised several dead people while he was on earth, and at his second coming all the "dead in Christ" will rise to meet him (1 Thessalonians 4.16).

5.26 God is the source and creator of life, for there is no life apart from God, here or hereafter. The life in us is a gift from him (see Deuteronomy 30.20; Psalm 36.9). Because Jesus is eternally existent with God, the Creator, he too is "the life" (14.6). Through him we may live eternally (see 1 John 5.11).

5.27 Dan 7.13,14 Jn 9.39 Acts 10.42; 17.31
5.29 Dan 12.2 Mt 25.31-46 Acts 24.15 1 Cor 15.52
5.30 Jn 5.19; 6.38

Father has life in himself, so he has granted the Son also to have life in himself;
27 and he has given him authority to execute judgment, because he is the Son of
Man. 28 Do not be astonished at this; for the hour is coming when all who are in
their graves will hear his voice 29 and will come out—those who have done good,
to the resurrection of life, and those who have done evil, to the resurrection of
condemnation.
30 "I can do nothing on my own. As I hear, I judge; and my judgment is just,
because I seek to do not my own will but the will of him who sent me.

Jesus supports his claim
(44)

5.31 Jn 8.14
5.36 Jn 14.11; 15.24 1 Jn 5.9
5.37 Deut 4.12
5.38 1 Jn 2.14
5.39 Isa 34.16 Lk 16.29; 24.25 Acts 13.27 17.11 Rom 2.17

31 "If I testify about myself, my testimony is not true. 32 There is another who
testifies on my behalf, and I know that his testimony to me is true. 33 You sent
messengers to John, and he testified to the truth. 34 Not that I accept such human
testimony, but I say these things so that you may be saved. 35 He was a burning and
shining lamp, and you were willing to rejoice for a while in his light. 36 But I have
a testimony greater than John's. The works that the Father has given me to complete, the very works that I am doing, testify on my behalf that the Father has sent
me. 37 And the Father who sent me has himself testified on my behalf. You have
never heard his voice or seen his form, 38 and you do not have his word abiding in
you, because you do not believe him whom he has sent.
39 "You search the scriptures because you think that in them you have eternal

THE CLAIMS OF CHRIST
Those who read the life of Christ are faced with one unavoidable question—was Jesus God? Part of any reasonable conclusion has to include the fact that he did claim to be God. We have no other choice but to agree or disagree with his claim. Eternal life is at stake in the choice.

Jesus claimed to be:	*Matthew*	*Mark*	*Luke*	*John*
the fulfillment of Old Testament prophecies	5.17; 14.33; 16.16, 17; 26.31, 53–56; 27.43	14.21, 61, 62	4.16–21; 7.18–23; 18.31; 22.37; 24.44	2.22; 5.45–47; 6.45; 7.40; 10.34–36; 13.18; 15.25; 20.9
the Son of Man	8.20; 12.8; 16.27; 19.28; 20.18, 19; 24.27, 44; 25.31; 26.2, 45, 64	8.31, 38; 9.9; 10.45; 14.41	6.22; 7.33, 34; 12.8; 17.22; 18.8, 31; 19.10; 21.36	1.51; 3.13, 14; 6.27, 53; 12.23, 34
the Son of God	11.27; 14.33; 16.16, 17; 27.43	3.11, 12; 14.61, 62	8.28; 10.22	1.18; 3.35, 36; 5.18–26; 6.40; 10.36; 11.4; 17.1; 19.7
the Messiah/ the Christ	23.9, 10; 26.63, 64	8.29, 30	4.41; 23.1, 2; 24.25–27	4.25, 26; 10.24, 25; 11.27
Teacher/Master	26.18			13.13, 14
One with authority to forgive		2.1–12	7.48, 49	
Lord		5.19		13.13, 14; 20.28
Savior			19.10	3.17; 10.9

5.27 The Old Testament mentioned three signs of the coming Messiah. In this chapter, John shows that Jesus has fulfilled all three signs. All power and dominion are given to him as the Son of Man (cf. 5.27 with Daniel 7.13, 14). The lame and sick are healed (cf. 5.20, 26 with Isaiah 35.6; Jeremiah 31.8, 9). The dead are raised to life (cf. 5.21, 28 with Deuteronomy 32.39; 1 Samuel 2.6; 2 Kings 5.7).

5.29 Those who have done evil will also be resurrected, but to hear God's judgment against them.There are those who wish to live well on earth, ignore God, and see death as final rest. Jesus does not allow that option. There is a judgment to face.

5.31ff Jesus claimed to be equal with God (5.18), to give eternal life (5.24), to be the source of life (5.26), and to judge sin (5.27). These statements make it clear that Jesus claimed to be divine—an almost unbelievable claim, but one that was supported by another witness, John the Baptist.

5.39, 40 The religious leaders knew what the Bible said but failed to apply its words to their lives. They knew the teachings of the Scriptures but failed to see the Messiah to whom the Scriptures pointed. They knew the rules but missed the Savior. Entrenched in their own religious system, they refused to let the Son of God change their lives.

life; and it is they that testify on my behalf. 40 Yet you refuse to come to me to have
life. 41 I do not accept glory from human beings. 42 But I know that you do not have 5.41 Jn 7.18
the love of God in[l] you. 43 I have come in my Father's name, and you do not accept
me; if another comes in his own name, you will accept him. 44 How can you believe 5.45 Jn 9.28 Rom 2.17
when you accept glory from one another and do not seek the glory that comes from
the one who alone is God? 45 Do not think that I will accept you before the Father; 5.46 Gen 3.15; 12.3 18.18; 22.18 49.10
your accuser is Moses, on whom you have set your hope. 46 If you believed Moses,
you would believe me, for he wrote about me. 47 But if you do not believe what he Deut 18.15,18 Lk 24.27,44
wrote, how will you believe what I say?" Acts 26.22,23

Jesus feeds five thousand

(96/Matthew 14.13–21; Mark 6.30–44; Luke 9.10–17)

6 After this Jesus went to the other side of the Sea of Galilee, also called the Sea 5.47 Lk 16.31
of Tiberias.[m] 2 A large crowd kept following him, because they saw the signs
that he was doing for the sick. 3 Jesus went up the mountain and sat down there with 6.2 Mt 14.14
his disciples. 4 Now the Passover, the festival of the Jews, was near. 5 When he Mk 6.35 Lk 9.12
looked up and saw a large crowd coming toward him, Jesus said to Philip, "Where
are we to buy bread for these people to eat?" 6 He said this to test him, for he himself
knew what he was going to do. 7 Philip answered him, "Six months' wages[n] would 6.6 Num 11.21,22
not buy enough bread for each of them to get a little." 8 One of his disciples, An- 6.7 Mk 6.37
drew, Simon Peter's brother, said to him, 9 "There is a boy here who has five barley
loaves and two fish. But what are they among so many people?" 10 Jesus said, 6.9 2 Kgs 4.43,44
"Make the people sit down." Now there was a great deal of grass in the place; so 6.10 Mt 14.21
they[o] sat down, about five thousand in all. 11 Then Jesus took the loaves, and when Mk 6.43,44
he had given thanks, he distributed them to those who were seated; so also the fish, Lk 9.14
as much as they wanted. 12 When they were satisfied, he told his disciples, "Gather 6.11 1 Tim 4.4,5

[l] *Or among* [m] Gk *of Galilee of Tiberius* [n] Gk *Two hundred denarii*; the denarius was the usual day's wage for a laborer [o] Gk *the men*

5.41 Whose approval do you seek? The religious leaders enjoyed great prestige in Israel, but their stamp of approval meant nothing to Jesus. He was concerned about God's approval. This is a good principle for us. If the highest officials in the world approve of our actions, but God does not, we should be concerned. But if God approves, even though others don't, we should be content.

5.45 The Pharisees prided themselves on being the true followers of their ancestor Moses. They followed every one of his laws to the letter and even added some of their own. Jesus' warning that Moses would accuse them made them furious. Moses wrote about Jesus (Genesis 3.15; Numbers 21.9; 24.17; Deuteronomy 18.15), yet the religious leaders refused to believe Jesus when he came.

5.46 It is not known what statement of Moses Jesus had in mind. It could have been Genesis 49.10 or more likely Deuteronomy 18.18: "I will raise up for them a prophet like you from among their own people; I will put my words in the mouth of the prophet, who shall speak to them everything that I command." Most likely Jesus was chastising them for not wanting to understand the purpose of Moses' writings. Moses wrote so that people would know and obey God, and these leaders had strayed far from those intentions.

6.5 If anyone knew where to get food, it would have been Philip. He was from Bethsaida, a town about nine miles away (1.44). Jesus was testing Philip to strengthen his faith. By asking for a human solution (knowing that there was none), Jesus highlighted the powerful and miraculous act he was about to perform.

6.5–7 Jesus asked Philip where they could buy a large amount of bread. Philip started assessing the probable cost. Jesus wanted to teach him that financial resources are not the most important ones. We can limit what God does in us by assuming what is and is not possible. Is there some impossible task you feel God wants you to do? Don't let your estimate of what can't be done keep you from taking on the task. God can do the miraculous; trust him to provide the resources.

6.8, 9 Here the disciples are contrasted with the youngster who brought what he had. They certainly had more resources than the boy. But they knew they didn't have enough, so they didn't give anything at all. The boy gave what little he had, and it made all the difference. If we offer nothing to God, he will have nothing to use. But he can take what little we have and turn it into something great.

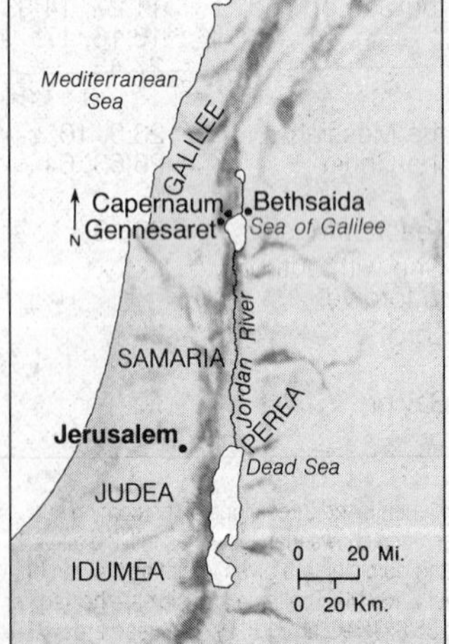

JESUS WALKS ON THE WATER Jesus fed the 5,000 on a hill near the Sea of Galilee (Tiberias) at Bethsaida-Julias. The disciples set out across the sea toward Bethsaida or Capernaum and encountered a storm—and Jesus came walking to them on the water! The boat landed at Gennesaret (Mark 6.53); then they went, by sea or by land, back to Capernaum.

6.8, 9 Jesus often performed his miracles through people. Here he took what a young child offered and used it to accomplish one of the most spectacular miracles recorded in the Gospels. Age is no barrier to Christ. You are never too young or too old to be used by him.

up the fragments left over, so that nothing may be lost." 13 So they gathered them
up, and from the fragments of the five barley loaves, left by those who had eaten,

6.14 Gen 49.10; Deut 18.15,18; Isa 7.14; 9.6; Mt 11.3; Jn 1.21; 7.40-42

they filled twelve baskets. 14 When the people saw the sign that he had done, they
began to say, "This is indeed the prophet who is to come into the world."
15 When Jesus realized that they were about to come and take him by force to
make him king, he withdrew again to the mountain by himself.

Jesus walks on water
(97/Matthew 14.22–33; Mark 6.45–52)

6.16 Mt 14.23-27; Mk 6.47-51

16 When evening came, his disciples went down to the sea, 17 got into a boat,
and started across the sea to Capernaum. It was now dark, and Jesus had not yet
come to them. 18 The sea became rough because a strong wind was blowing.
19 When they had rowed about three or four miles,[p] they saw Jesus walking on the
sea and coming near the boat, and they were terrified. 20 But he said to them, "It is
I;[q] do not be afraid." 21 Then they wanted to take him into the boat, and immediately the boat reached the land toward which they were going.

Jesus is the true bread from heaven
(99)

22 The next day the crowd that had stayed on the other side of the sea saw that
there had been only one boat there. They also saw that Jesus had not got into the
boat with his disciples, but that his disciples had gone away alone. 23 Then some
boats from Tiberias came near the place where they had eaten the bread after the
Lord had given thanks.[r] 24 So when the crowd saw that neither Jesus nor his disci-

6.27 Isa 55.2; Mt 3.17; 17.5; Mk 1.11; 9.7; Lk 3.22; Jn 1.33; 5.37; 8.18; Acts 2.22; Rom 6.23; 2 Pet 1.17,18

ples were there, they themselves got into the boats and went to Capernaum looking
for Jesus.
25 When they found him on the other side of the sea, they said to him, "Rabbi,
when did you come here?" 26 Jesus answered them, "Very truly, I tell you, you are
looking for me, not because you saw signs, but because you ate your fill of the
loaves. 27 Do not work for the food that perishes, but for the food that endures for
eternal life, which the Son of Man will give you. For it is on him that God the

6.29 1 Thess 1.3; 1 Jn 3.23

Father has set his seal." 28 Then they said to him, "What must we do to perform the
works of God?" 29 Jesus answered them, "This is the work of God, that you believe

6.31 Ex 16.4,15; Num 11.7; Neh 9.15; Ps 78.24; 105.40; Mt 12.38; Mk 8.11; 1 Cor 10.3

in him whom he has sent." 30 So they said to him, "What sign are you going to give
us then, so that we may see it and believe you? What work are you performing?
31 Our ancestors ate the manna in the wilderness; as it is written, 'He gave them
bread from heaven to eat.' " 32 Then Jesus said to them, "Very truly, I tell you, it
was not Moses who gave you the bread from heaven, but it is my Father who gives

[p] Gk *about twenty-five or thirty stadia* [q] Gk *I am* [r] Other ancient authorities lack *after the Lord had given thanks*

6.13 There is a lesson in the leftovers. God gives in abundance. He takes whatever we can offer him in time, ability, or resources and multiplies its effectiveness beyond our wildest expectations. If you take the first step in making yourself available to him, he will show you how greatly you can be used to advance the work of his kingdom.

6.14 "The prophet" is the one prophesied by Moses (Deuteronomy 18.15).

6.18 The Sea of Galilee is 650 feet below sea level, 150 feet deep, and surrounded by hills. These physical features make it susceptible to sudden windstorms, causing extremely high waves. Such storms were expected on this sea, but they were nevertheless frightening. When Jesus came to the disciples during a storm, walking on the water (three and a half miles from shore), he told them not to be afraid. We often face spiritual and emotional storms and feel tossed about like a small boat on a big lake. In spite of terrifying circumstances, we should trust our lives to Christ for his safekeeping. He can give us peace in any storm.

6.18, 19 The terrified disciples thought they were seeing a ghost (Mark 6.49). But if they had thought about all they had already seen Jesus do, they could have accepted this miracle. They were frightened—they didn't expect Jesus to come, and they weren't prepared for his help. Faith is a mind-set that *expects* God to act. When we act upon this expectation, we can overcome our fears.

6.26 Jesus criticized the people who followed him only for the physical and temporal benefits, not because they were spiritually hungry. Many people use religion to gain prestige, comfort, or even votes. But those are self-centered motives. True believers follow Jesus because they know his way is true and right.

6.28, 29 Many sincere seekers for God are puzzled about what he wants them to do. The religions of the world are people's attempts to answer this question. But Jesus' reply is brief and simple: we must believe in him whom God has sent. Satisfying God does not come from the work we *do,* but from whom we *believe.* The first step is accepting that Jesus is who he claims to be. All spiritual development is built on this affirmation. Declare to Jesus, "You are the Christ, the Son of the living God," and embark on a life of belief that is satisfying to your Creator.

you the true bread from heaven. 33 For the bread of God is that which[s] comes down
from heaven and gives life to the world." 34 They said to him, "Sir, give us this
bread always."
35 Jesus said to them, "I am the bread of life. Whoever comes to me will never
be hungry, and whoever believes in me will never be thirsty. 36 But I said to you that
you have seen me and yet do not believe. 37 Everything that the Father gives me will
come to me, and anyone who comes to me I will never drive away; 38 for I have
come down from heaven, not to do my own will, but the will of him who sent me.
39 And this is the will of him who sent me, that I should lose nothing of all that he
has given me, but raise it up on the last day. 40 This is indeed the will of my Father,
that all who see the Son and believe in him may have eternal life; and I will raise
them up on the last day."

The Jews disagree that Jesus is from heaven
(100)

41 Then the Jews began to complain about him because he said, "I am the bread
that came down from heaven." 42 They were saying, "Is not this Jesus, the son of
Joseph, whose father and mother we know? How can he now say, 'I have come
down from heaven'?" 43 Jesus answered them, "Do not complain among yourselves. 44 No one can come to me unless drawn by the Father who sent me; and I
will raise that person up on the last day. 45 It is written in the prophets, 'And they
shall all be taught by God.' Everyone who has heard and learned from the Father
comes to me. 46 Not that anyone has seen the Father except the one who is from
God; he has seen the Father. 47 Very truly, I tell you, whoever believes has eternal
life. 48 I am the bread of life. 49 Your ancestors ate the manna in the wilderness, and
they died. 50 This is the bread that comes down from heaven, so that one may eat of
it and not die. 51 I am the living bread that came down from heaven. Whoever eats
of this bread will live forever; and the bread that I will give for the life of the world
is my flesh."
52 The Jews then disputed among themselves, saying, "How can this man give

6.33 Jn 6.41,50
6.35 Jn 4.14; 6.48 7.37,38
6.37 Jn 10.28,29 17.2,24
6.38 Jn 4.34; 5.30
6.39 Jn 5.24; 10.28 17.12; 18.9 Col 3.3
6.40 Jn 1.14,18; 3.16
6.41 Jn 6.33,51,58
6.42 Jn 7.27
6.44 Jer 31.3 Hos 11.4 Jn 6.65; 12.32
6.45 Isa 54.13 Jer 31.34 Mic 4.2 1 Thess 4.9 Heb 8.10,11
6.46 Mt 11.27 Lk 10.22 2 Cor 4.6
6.48 Heb 10.5,10

s *Or he who*

6.35 People eat bread to satisfy physical hunger and to sustain physical life. We can satisfy spiritual hunger and sustain spiritual life only by a right relationship with Jesus Christ. No wonder he called himself the bread of life. But bread must be eaten to give life, and Christ must be invited into our daily walk to give spiritual life.

6.37, 38 Jesus did not work independently of God the Father, but in union with him. This gives us even more assurance of being welcomed into God's presence and being protected by him. Jesus' purpose was to do the will of God, not to satisfy his human desires. When we follow Jesus, we should have the same purpose.

6.39 Jesus said he would not lose even one person that the Father had given him. Thus anyone who makes a sincere commitment to believe in Jesus Christ as Savior is secure in God's promise of eternal life. Christ will not let his people be overcome by Satan and lose their salvation (see also 17.12; Philippians 1.6).

6.40 Those who put their faith in Christ will be resurrected from physical death to eternal life with God when Christ comes again (see 1 Corinthians 15.52; 1 Thessalonians 4.16).

6.41 When John says *Jews,* he is referring to the Jewish leaders who were hostile to Jesus, not to all the Jewish people. Both John and Jesus were Jews.

6.41 The religious leaders murmured because they could not accept Jesus' claim of divinity. They refused to believe he was God's divine Son, and they could not tolerate his message. Many people reject Christ because they cannot believe he is the Son of God. In reality, the claims he makes for their loyalty and obedience are what they can't accept. So to protect themselves from the message, they deny the messenger.

6.44 God, not man, plays the most active role in salvation. When someone chooses to believe in Jesus Christ as Savior, he does so only in response to the urging of God's Holy Spirit. God does the urging; then we decide whether or not to believe. Thus no one can believe in Jesus without God's help.

6.45 Jesus is alluding to an Old Testament view of the messianic kingdom in which all people are taught directly by God (Isaiah 54.13; Jeremiah 31.31–34). He is stressing the importance of not merely hearing, but learning. We are taught by God through the Bible, our experiences, the thoughts the Holy Spirit brings, and other Christians.

6.47 *Believes* as used here means "continues to believe." We do not believe merely once; we keep on believing or trusting Jesus.

6.47ff The religious leaders frequently asked Jesus to prove to them why he was better than the prophets they already had. Jesus here refers to the manna that Moses gave their ancestors in the wilderness (see Exodus 16). This bread was physical and temporal. The people ate it and were sustained for a day; but they had to get more bread every day, and this bread could not keep them from dying. Jesus, who is much greater than Moses, offers himself as the spiritual bread from heaven that satisfies completely and leads to eternal life.

6.51 How can Jesus give us his flesh as bread to eat? To eat living bread means to unite ourselves to Christ. We are united with Christ in two ways: (1) by believing in his death (the sacrifice of his flesh) and resurrection and (2) by devoting ourselves to living as he requires, depending on his teaching for guidance and trusting in the Holy Spirit for power.

6.54 Jn 6.39
6.56 Jn 15.4; 14.20 17.21-23
6.57 Jn 5.26; 14.19 15.5
6.58 Jn 6.31
6.59 Mt 4.23

us his flesh to eat?" 53 So Jesus said to them, "Very truly, I tell you, unless you eat
the flesh of the Son of Man and drink his blood, you have no life in you. 54 Those
who eat my flesh and drink my blood have eternal life, and I will raise them up on
the last day; 55 for my flesh is true food and my blood is true drink. 56 Those who eat
my flesh and drink my blood abide in me, and I in them. 57 Just as the living Father
sent me, and I live because of the Father, so whoever eats me will live because of
me. 58 This is the bread that came down from heaven, not like that which your
ancestors ate, and they died. But the one who eats this bread will live forever."
59 He said these things while he was teaching in the synagogue at Capernaum.

Many disciples desert Jesus
(101)

6.62 Mk 16.19 Acts 1.9 Eph 4.8
6.63 1 Cor 15.45 2 Cor 3.6 Heb 4.12
6.64 Mt 10.4 Jn 13.11
6.66 Lk 9.62 1 Jn 2.19
6.68 Jn 3.34; 5.25,26
6.69 Lk 4.34 Acts 3.14 1 Jn 2.20
6.70 Mt 10.2-4 Jn 13.2,27

60 When many of his disciples heard it, they said, "This teaching is difficult;
who can accept it?" 61 But Jesus, being aware that his disciples were complaining
about it, said to them, "Does this offend you? 62 Then what if you were to see the
Son of Man ascending to where he was before? 63 It is the spirit that gives life; the
flesh is useless. The words that I have spoken to you are spirit and life. 64 But
among you there are some who do not believe." For Jesus knew from the first who
were the ones that did not believe, and who was the one that would betray him.
65 And he said, "For this reason I have told you that no one can come to me unless
it is granted by the Father."

66 Because of this many of his disciples turned back and no longer went about
with him. 67 So Jesus asked the twelve, "Do you also wish to go away?" 68 Simon
Peter answered him, "Lord, to whom can we go? You have the words of eternal
life. 69 We have come to believe and know that you are the Holy One of God."[t]
70 Jesus answered them, "Did I not choose you, the twelve? Yet one of you is a
devil." 71 He was speaking of Judas son of Simon Iscariot,[u] for he, though one of
the twelve, was going to betray him.

[t] Other ancient authorities read *the Christ, the Son of the living God* [u] Other ancient authorities read *Judas Iscariot son of Simon;* others, *Judas son of Simon from Karyot* (Kerioth)

6.56 This was a shocking message—to eat flesh and drink blood sounded cannibalistic. The idea of drinking any blood, let alone human blood, was repugnant to the religious leaders because the law forbade it (Leviticus 17.10, 11). Jesus was not talking about literal blood, of course. He was saying that his life had to become their own, but they could not accept this concept. Later, the apostle Paul used the body and blood imagery in talking about communion (see 1 Corinthians 11.23–26).

6.63, 65 The Holy Spirit gives spiritual life; without the work of the Holy Spirit we cannot even see our need for it (14.17). All spiritual renewal begins and ends with God. He reveals truth to us, lives within us, and then enables us to respond to that truth.

6.66 Why did Jesus' words cause many of his followers to desert him? (1) They may have realized that he wasn't going to be the conquering Messiah-king they expected. (2) He refused to give in to their self-centered requests. (3) He emphasized faith, not works. (4) His teachings were difficult to understand, and some of his words were offensive. As we grow in our faith, we may be tempted to turn away because Jesus' lessons are hard. Will your response be to give up, ignore certain teachings, or reject Christ? Instead, ask God to show you what the teachings mean and how they apply to your situation. Then have the courage to act upon God's truth.

6.67 There is no middle ground with Jesus. When he asked the disciples if they would also leave, he was showing that they could either accept or reject him. Jesus was not trying to repel people with his teachings. He was simply telling the truth. The more the people heard Jesus' real message, the more they divided into two camps—the honest seekers who wanted to understand more, and those who rejected Jesus because they didn't like what they heard.

6.67, 68 After many of Jesus' followers had deserted him, he asked the 12 disciples if they were also going to leave. Peter responded, "To whom can we go? You have the words of eternal life." In his straightforward way, Peter answered for all of us—there is no other way. Though there are many philosophies and self-styled authorities, Jesus alone has the words that give eternal life. People look everywhere for eternal life and miss Christ, the only source. Stay with him, especially when you are confused or feel alone.

6.70 In response to Jesus' message, some people left; others stayed and truly believed; and some, like Judas, stayed but tried to use Jesus for personal gain. Many today turn away from Christ. Others pretend to follow, going to church for status, approval of family and friends, or business contacts. But there are only two real responses to Jesus—you either accept or reject him. How have you responded to Christ?

6.71 For more information on Judas, see his Profile in Mark 14.

2. Jesus encounters conflict with the religious leaders

Jesus' brothers ridicule him

(121)

7 After this Jesus went about in Galilee. He did not wish[v] to go about in Judea 7.1 Jn 5.18; 8.37
because the Jews were looking for an opportunity to kill him. 2 Now the Jewish 7.2
festival of Booths[w] was near. 3 So his brothers said to him, "Leave here and go to Lev 23.23,24 Deut 16.16
Judea so that your disciples also may see the works you are doing; 4 for no one who Zech 14.16
wants[x] to be widely known acts in secret. If you do these things, show yourself to 7.3 Mt 12.46
the world." 5 (For not even his brothers believed in him.) 6 Jesus said to them, "My Mk 3.31,32
time has not yet come, but your time is always here. 7 The world cannot hate you, Acts 1.14
but it hates me because I testify against it that its works are evil. 8 Go to the festival 7.6 Jn 2.4
yourselves. I am not[y] going to this festival, for my time has not yet fully come." 7.7 Jn 3.19
9 After saying this, he remained in Galilee. 15.18,19

Jesus teaches openly at the temple

(123)

10 But after his brothers had gone to the festival, then he also went, not publicly 7.11
but as it were[z] in secret. 11 The Jews were looking for him at the festival and say- Jn 11.56
ing, "Where is he?" 12 And there was considerable complaining about him among 7.12 Mt 21.45,46
the crowds. While some were saying, "He is a good man," others were saying, Lk 7.16 Jn 9.16; 10.19
"No, he is deceiving the crowd." 13 Yet no one would speak openly about him for 7.13
fear of the Jews. Jn 9.22,23
14 About the middle of the festival Jesus went up into the temple and began to 7.15 Acts 4.13; 22.3
teach. 15 The Jews were astonished at it, saying, "How does this man have such 2 Tim 3.15
learning,[a] when he has never been taught?" 16 Then Jesus answered them, "My 7.16 Jn 8.28; 12.49
teaching is not mine but his who sent me. 17 Anyone who resolves to do the will of 14.10
God will know whether the teaching is from God or whether I am speaking on my 7.17 Hos 6.1-3
own. 18 Those who speak on their own seek their own glory; but the one who seeks 7.18
the glory of him who sent him is true, and there is nothing false in him. Jn 5.41; 8.50,54 7.19
19 "Did not Moses give you the law? Yet none of you keeps the law. Why are Jn 1.17; 7.1

[v] Other ancient authorities read *was not at liberty* [w] Or *Tabernacles* [x] Other ancient authorities read *wants it* [y] Other ancient authorities add *yet* [z] Other ancient authorities lack *as it were* [a] Or *this man know his letters*

7.2 The festival of booths is described in Leviticus 23.33ff. This event occurred in October, about six months after the Passover celebration mentioned in John 6.2–5. The festival commemorated the days when the Israelites wandered in the wilderness and lived in tents (Leviticus 23.43).

7.3–5 Jesus' brothers had a difficult time believing in him. Some of these brothers would eventually become leaders in the church, but for several years they were embarrassed by him. After Jesus died and rose again, they finally believed. We today have every reason to believe because we have the full record of Jesus' miracles, death, and resurrection. We also have the evidence of what the gospel has done in people's lives through the centuries. Don't miss this opportunity to believe in God's Son.

7.7 Because the world hated Jesus, we who follow him can expect that many people will hate us as well. If circumstances are going too well, ask if you are following him as you should. We can be grateful if life goes well, but not at the cost of following Jesus half-heartedly or not at all.

7.10 Jesus came with the greatest gift ever offered, so why did he often act secretly? The religious leaders hated him and would refuse his gift of salvation no matter what he said or did. The more he taught and worked publicly, the more these leaders would cause trouble for Jesus and his followers. So it was necessary for Jesus to teach and work as quietly as possible. Many people today have the privilege of teaching, preaching, and worshiping publicly with little persecution. These believers should thankfully take advantage of their freedom.

7.13 The religious leaders had a great deal of power over the common people. It is apparent that they couldn't do much to Jesus at this time, but they threatened anyone who might publicly support him. Excommunication from the synagogue was one of the reprisals for believing in Jesus (9.22). To a Jew, this was a severe punishment.

7.13 Everyone was talking about Jesus! But when it came time to speak up for him in public, no one said a word. All were afraid. Fear can stifle our witness. Although many people talk about Christ in church, when it comes to making a public statement about their faith, they are often embarrassed. Jesus says that he will acknowledge us before God if we acknowledge him before others (Matthew 10.32). Be courageous! Speak up for Christ!

7.15 The religious leaders knew that Jesus had never attended the rabbinic schools and had no professional training. Jesus pointed to the divine source of his wisdom and insight.

7.16–18 Those who attempt to know God's will and do it will know intuitively that Jesus was telling the truth about himself. Have you ever listened to religious speakers and wondered if they were telling the truth? Test them: (1) ask if their words agree with or contradict the Bible, and (2) ask if their words point to God and doing his will or to themselves.

7.19 The Pharisees spent their days trying to achieve holiness by keeping the meticulous rules they had added to God's laws. Jesus' accusation that they didn't keep Moses' laws stung them deeply. In spite of their pompous pride in themselves and their rules, they did not even fulfill a legalistic religion, because they were living far below what the law of Moses required. Jesus' followers should do *more* than the moral law requires, not by adding to its requirements, but by going beyond the do's and don'ts to the spirit of the law.

you looking for an opportunity to kill me?" 20 The crowd answered, "You have a
demon! Who is trying to kill you?" 21 Jesus answered them, "I performed one work,
and all of you are astonished. 22 Moses gave you circumcision (it is, of course, not
from Moses, but from the patriarchs), and you circumcise a man on the sabbath.
23 If a man receives circumcision on the sabbath in order that the law of Moses may
not be broken, are you angry with me because I healed a man's whole body on the
sabbath? 24 Do not judge by appearances, but judge with right judgment."

25 Now some of the people of Jerusalem were saying, "Is not this the man
whom they are trying to kill? 26 And here he is, speaking openly, but they say nothing to him! Can it be that the authorities really know that this is the Messiah?[b]
27 Yet we know where this man is from; but when the Messiah[b] comes, no one will
know where he is from." 28 Then Jesus cried out as he was teaching in the temple,
"You know me, and you know where I am from. I have not come on my own. But
the one who sent me is true, and you do not know him. 29 I know him, because I am
from him, and he sent me." 30 Then they tried to arrest him, but no one laid hands
on him, because his hour had not yet come. 31 Yet many in the crowd believed in
him and were saying, "When the Messiah[b] comes, will he do more signs than this
man has done?"[c]

Religious leaders attempt to arrest Jesus
(124)

32 The Pharisees heard the crowd muttering such things about him, and the
chief priests and Pharisees sent temple police to arrest him. 33 Jesus then said, "I
will be with you a little while longer, and then I am going to him who sent me.
34 You will search for me, but you will not find me; and where I am, you cannot
come." 35 The Jews said to one another, "Where does this man intend to go that we
will not find him? Does he intend to go to the Dispersion among the Greeks and
teach the Greeks? 36 What does he mean by saying, 'You will search for me and you
will not find me' and 'Where I am, you cannot come'?"

37 On the last day of the festival, the great day, while Jesus was standing there,
he cried out, "Let anyone who is thirsty come to me, 38 and let the one who believes
in me drink. As[d] the scripture has said, 'Out of the believer's heart[e] shall flow
rivers of living water.' " 39 Now he said this about the Spirit, which believers in him
were to receive; for as yet there was no Spirit,[f] because Jesus was not yet glorified.

40 When they heard these words, some in the crowd said, "This is really the

7.20 Jn 8.48-52; 10.20
7.21,22 Gen 17.9,10; Lev 12.3; Jn 5.8; Acts 7.8
7.23 Jn 5.10
7.24 Isa 11.3; Jn 8.15
7.27 Jn 7.41,42; 9.29
7.28 Jn 1.18; 5.43; 8.14,26,55
7.29 Mt 11.27; Jn 3.17; 8.55; 10.15; 17.25
7.33 Jn 14.19; 16.5,10,16-18
7.34 Jn 8.21; 13.33
7.37 Isa 55.1; Rev 22.17
7.38 Isa 12.3; 44.3; 58.11; Ezek 47.1-10; Joel 3.18
7.39 Jn 14.17,18; 16.7; 20.22; Rom 8.9; 1 Cor 15.45; 2 Cor 3.17
7.40 Deut 18.15

[b] Or *the Christ* [c] Other ancient authorities read *is doing* [d] *Or come to me and drink.* [38] *The one who believes in me, as* [e] Gk *out of his belly* [f] Other ancient authorities read *for as yet the Spirit* (others, *Holy Spirit*) *had not been given*

7.20 Most of the people were probably not aware of the plot to kill Jesus (5.18). There was a small group looking for the right opportunity to kill him, but most were still trying to decide what they believed about him.

7.21–23 According to Moses' law, circumcision was to be performed eight days after a baby's birth (Genesis 17.9–14; Leviticus 12.3). This was done to all Jewish males to identify them as part of God's covenant people. If the eighth day after birth was a sabbath, the circumcision was still performed (even though it was considered work). While the religious leaders allowed certain exceptions to sabbath laws, they allowed none to Jesus, who was simply showing mercy to those who needed healing.

7.26 This chapter shows the many reactions people had toward Jesus. They called him a good man (7.12), a deceiver (7.12), a demon-possessed man (7.20), the Messiah (7.26), and the prophet (7.40). We must make up our own minds about who Jesus is, knowing that whatever we decide will have eternal consequences.

7.27 There was a popular tradition that the Messiah would simply appear. But those who believed this tradition were ignoring the scriptures that clearly predicted the Messiah's birthplace (Micah 5.2).

7.35 *Dispersion* means "scattered," and refers to all Jews living in foreign lands. Thriving communities existed in Rome, Egypt, Alexandria, Cyprus, and the cities of Greece and Asia Minor.

7.37 Jesus' words, "Let anyone who is thirsty come to me, and let the one who believes in me drink" alluded to the theme of many Bible passages that talk about the Messiah's life-giving blessings (Isaiah 12.2, 3; 44.3, 4; 58.11). In promising to give the Holy Spirit to all who believed, Jesus was claiming to be the Messiah, because that was something only the Messiah could do.

7.38 Jesus used the term *living water* in 4.10 to indicate eternal life. Here he uses the term to refer to the Holy Spirit. The two go together: wherever the Holy Spirit is accepted, he brings eternal life. Jesus teaches more about the Holy Spirit in chapters 14–16. The Holy Spirit empowered Jesus' followers at pentecost (Acts 2) and has since been available to all who believe in Jesus as Savior.

7.40–43 The crowd was asking questions about Jesus. Some believed, others were hostile, and others disqualified Jesus as the Messiah because he was from Nazareth, not Bethlehem (Micah 5.2). But Jesus *was* born in Bethlehem (Luke 2.1–7), although he grew up in Nazareth. If they had looked more carefully, they would not have jumped to the wrong conclusions. When you search for God's truth, make sure you look carefully and thoughtfully at the Bible with an open heart and mind. Don't jump to conclusions before knowing more of what the Bible says.

prophet." 41 Others said, "This is the Messiah."[g] But some asked, "Surely the Messiah[g] does not come from Galilee, does he? 42 Has not the scripture said that the
Messiah[g] is descended from David and comes from Bethlehem, the village where
David lived?" 43 So there was a division in the crowd because of him. 44 Some of
them wanted to arrest him, but no one laid hands on him.
45 Then the temple police went back to the chief priests and Pharisees, who
asked them, "Why did you not arrest him?" 46 The police answered, "Never has
anyone spoken like this!" 47 Then the Pharisees replied, "Surely you have not been
deceived too, have you? 48 Has any one of the authorities or of the Pharisees believed in him? 49 But this crowd, which does not know the law—they are accursed." 50 Nicodemus, who had gone to Jesus[h] before, and who was one of them,
asked, 51 "Our law does not judge people without first giving them a hearing to find
out what they are doing, does it?" 52 They replied, "Surely you are not also from
Galilee, are you? Search and you will see that no prophet is to arise from Galilee."

7.41,42 1 Sam 16.1; 2 Sam 7.12; Ps 132.11; Mic 5.2; Mt 1.1; 2.5-10
7.43 Jn 9.16; 10.19
7.46 Lk 4.22
7.48 1 Cor 1.20
7.50 Jn 3.1,2; 19.39
7.51 Deut 17.2-8; 19.15-19
7.52 Isa 9.1,2; Mt 4.14-16; Jn 1.46

Jesus forgives an adulterous woman
(125)

8 [[53 Then each of them went home, 1 while Jesus went to the Mount of Olives.
2 Early in the morning he came again to the temple. All the people came to him
and he sat down and began to teach them. 3 The scribes and the Pharisees brought
a woman who had been caught in adultery; and making her stand before all of them,
4 they said to him, "Teacher, this woman was caught in the very act of committing
adultery. 5 Now in the law Moses commanded us to stone such women. Now what
do you say?" 6 They said this to test him, so that they might have some charge to
bring against him. Jesus bent down and wrote with his finger on the ground. 7 When
they kept on questioning him, he straightened up and said to them, "Let anyone
among you who is without sin be the first to throw a stone at her." 8 And once again
he bent down and wrote on the ground.[i] 9 When they heard it, they went away, one

8.5 Ex 20.14; Lev 18.20; 20.10; Deut 5.18; 22.22; Job 31.9-11; Mt 5.27,28
8.7 Deut 17.7

g Or *the Christ* h Gk *him* i Other ancient authorities add *the sins of each of them*

7.44–46 Although the Romans ruled Palestine, they gave the Jewish religious leaders authority over minor civil and religious affairs. The religious leaders controlled their own temple police and gave the officers power to arrest anyone causing a disturbance or breaking any of their ceremonial laws. Because these leaders had developed hundreds of trivial laws, it was almost impossible for anyone, even the leaders themselves, not to break, neglect, or ignore at least a few of them some of the time. But these police officers couldn't find one reason to arrest Jesus. And as they listened to him to try to find evidence, they couldn't help hearing the wonderful words he said.

7.46–49 The Jewish leaders saw themselves as an elite group who alone had the truth. They resisted the truth about Christ because it wasn't *theirs* to begin with. It is easy to think that we have the truth and that those who disagree with us do not have any truth at all. But God's truth is available to everyone. Make sure your attitude is not self-centered and narrow like the Pharisees.

7.50–52 This passage offers additional insight into Nicodemus, the Pharisee who visited Jesus at night (chapter 3). Apparently Nicodemus had become a secret believer. Most of the Pharisees hated Jesus and wanted to kill him, so Nicodemus risked his reputation and high position when he spoke up for Jesus. His statement was bold, and the Pharisees immediately became suspicious. After Jesus' death, Nicodemus brought spices for his body (19.39). That is the last time he is mentioned in Scripture, but tradition says he was baptized by Peter and John and was later forced to step down from his position as a member of the council.

7.51 Nicodemus confronted the Pharisees with their failure to keep their own laws. The Pharisees saw themselves losing ground—the police came back impressed by Jesus (7.46), and one of their own, Nicodemus, was defending him. With their hypocritical motives being exposed and their prestige slowly eroding, they began to move to protect themselves. Pride would interfere with their ability to reason, and soon they would become obsessed with getting rid of Jesus just to save face. What was good and right no longer mattered; they continued to break their own laws by plotting to murder Jesus.

8.3–6 The Jewish leaders had already disregarded the law by arresting the woman without the man. The law required that both parties to adultery be stoned (Leviticus 20.10; Deuteronomy 22.22). The leaders were using the woman as a trap so they could trick Jesus. If Jesus said the woman should not be stoned, they would accuse him of violating Moses' law. If he urged them to execute her, they would report him to the Romans, who did not permit the Jews to carry out their own executions.

8.7 This is a significant statement about judging others. Because he upheld the legal penalty for adultery (stoning) Jesus could not be accused of being against the law. But by saying that only a sinless person could throw the first stone, he highlighted the importance of compassion and forgiveness. When others are caught in sin, are you quick to pass judgment? To do so is to act as though you have never sinned. It is God's role to judge, not ours. We are to show forgiveness and compassion.

8.8 Jesus may have been ignoring them by writing on the ground, writing out the ten commandments, or listing the sins of the participants.

8.9 When Jesus said that only someone who had not sinned should throw the first stone, the leaders slipped quietly away, from eldest to youngest. Evidently the older men were more aware of their sins than the younger. Age and experience often temper youthful self-righteousness. But whatever your age, take an honest look at your motives and desires. Recognize your sinful nature, ask God to forgive you, and look for ways to help others rather than hurt them.

8.11 Jn 5.14

by one, beginning with the elders; and Jesus was left alone with the woman standing before him. 10 Jesus straightened up and said to her, "Woman, where are they?
Has no one condemned you?" 11 She said, "No one, sir."[j] And Jesus said, "Neither
do I condemn you. Go your way, and from now on do not sin again."]][k]

Jesus is the light of the world
(126)

8.12 Isa 9.1,2; Jn 1.4,5,9; 3.19; 9.5; 12.35,36,46; 2 Cor 4.6
8.14 Jn 7.28; 18.37; Rev 1.5
8.16 Jn 5.30; 14.10,11; 16.32
8.17 Deut 17.6; 19.15; 2 Cor 13.1; Heb 10.28
8.18 Jn 5.37
8.19 Jn 14.7,9
8.20 Jn 7.30

12 Again Jesus spoke to them, saying, "I am the light of the world. Whoever
follows me will never walk in darkness but will have the light of life." 13 Then the
Pharisees said to him, "You are testifying on your own behalf; your testimony is
not valid." 14 Jesus answered, "Even if I testify on my own behalf, my testimony is
valid because I know where I have come from and where I am going, but you do not
know where I come from or where I am going. 15 You judge by human standards;[l]
I judge no one. 16 Yet even if I do judge, my judgment is valid; for it is not I alone
who judge, but I and the Father[m] who sent me. 17 In your law it is written that the
testimony of two witnesses is valid. 18 I testify on my own behalf, and the Father
who sent me testifies on my behalf." 19 Then they said to him, "Where is your
Father?" Jesus answered, "You know neither me nor my Father. If you knew me,
you would know my Father also." 20 He spoke these words while he was teaching
in the treasury of the temple, but no one arrested him, because his hour had not yet
come.

Jesus warns of coming judgment
(127)

8.21 Jn 7.34; 13.33
8.22 Jn 7.35,36
8.23 Jn 3.31; 15.19; 17.16; 1 Jn 4.5
8.24 Ex 3.14,15; Jn 4.26; 13.19
8.28 Jn 3.11,14,15; 5.19; 8.24; 12.32; Rom 1.4

21 Again he said to them, "I am going away, and you will search for me, but
you will die in your sin. Where I am going, you cannot come." 22 Then the Jews
said, "Is he going to kill himself? Is that what he means by saying, 'Where I am
going, you cannot come'?" 23 He said to them, "You are from below, I am from
above; you are of this world, I am not of this world. 24 I told you that you would die
in your sins, for you will die in your sins unless you believe that I am he."[n] 25 They
said to him, "Who are you?" Jesus said to them, "Why do I speak to you at all?[o]
26 I have much to say about you and much to condemn; but the one who sent me is
true, and I declare to the world what I have heard from him." 27 They did not understand that he was speaking to them about the Father. 28 So Jesus said, "When you
have lifted up the Son of Man, then you will realize that I am he,[n] and that I do

[j] Or *Lord* [k] The most ancient authorities lack 7.53—8.11; other authorities add the passage here or after 7.36 or after 21.25 or after Luke 21.38, with variations of text; some mark the passage as doubtful. [l] Gk *according to the flesh* [m] Other ancient authorities read *he* [n] Gk *I am* [o] Or *What I have told you from the beginning*

8.11 Jesus didn't condemn the woman accused of adultery, but neither did he ignore or condone her sin. He told her to go and sin no more. Jesus stands ready to forgive any sin in your life, but confession and repentance mean a change of heart. With God's help we can accept Christ's forgiveness and stop our wrongdoing.

8.12 To understand what Jesus meant by *the light of the world,* see the notes on 1.4 and 1.4, 5.

8.12 Jesus was speaking in the part of the temple known as the treasury (8.20), where candles burned to symbolize the pillar of fire that led the people of Israel through the wilderness (Exodus 13.21, 22). In this context, Jesus called himself the light of the world. The pillar of fire represented God's presence, protection, and guidance. Jesus brings God's presence, protection, and guidance. Is he the light of *your* world?

8.12 What does it mean to follow Christ? As a soldier follows his captain, so we should follow Christ, our commander. As a slave follows his master, so we should follow Christ, our Lord. As we follow the advice of a trusted counselor, so we should follow Jesus' commands to us in Scripture. As we follow the laws of our nation, so we should follow the laws of the kingdom of heaven.

8.13, 14 The Pharisees thought Jesus was either insane or a liar. Jesus provided them with a third alternative: he was telling the truth. Because most of the Pharisees refused to consider the third alternative, they never recognized him as Messiah and Lord. If you are seeking to know who Jesus is, do not close any door before looking through it honestly. Only with an open mind will you recognize the truth that he is Messiah and Lord.

8.13–18 The Pharisees argued that Jesus' claim was legally invalid because he had no other witnesses. Jesus responded that his confirming witness was God himself. He and God made two witnesses, the number required by the law (Deuteronomy 19.15).

8.20 The temple treasury was located in the court of the women. In this area, 13 collection boxes were set up to receive money offerings. Seven of the boxes were for the temple tax; the other six were for freewill offerings. On another occasion, a widow placed her money in one of these boxes, and Jesus taught a profound lesson from her action (Luke 21.1–4).

8.24 People will die in their sins if they reject Christ, because they are rejecting the only way to be rescued. Sadly, many are so taken up with the values of this world that they are blind to the priceless gift Christ offers. Where are you looking? Don't focus on this world's values and miss what is most valuable – eternal life with God.

nothing on my own, but I speak these things as the Father instructed me. 29 And the 8.29
one who sent me is with me; he has not left me alone, for I always do what is Jn 4.34; 6.38 14.10; 16.32
pleasing to him." 30 As he was saying these things, many believed in him.

Jesus speaks about God's true children
(128)

31 Then Jesus said to the Jews who had believed in him, "If you continue in my 8.31
word, you are truly my disciples; 32 and you will know the truth, and the truth will Jn 15.7
make you free." 33 They answered him, "We are descendants of Abraham and have 8.32 Rom 8.2
never been slaves to anyone. What do you mean by saying, 'You will be made 2 Cor 3.17 Gal 5.1,13
free'?" 1 Pet 2.16
34 Jesus answered them, "Very truly, I tell you, everyone who commits sin is 8.33 Lev 25.42
a slave to sin. 35 The slave does not have a permanent place in the household; the Mt 3.9
son has a place there forever. 36 So if the Son makes you free, you will be free 8.34 Rom 6.16
indeed. 37 I know that you are descendants of Abraham; yet you look for an oppor- 2 Pet 2.19
tunity to kill me, because there is no place in you for my word. 38 I declare what I 8.35 Gen 21.10
have seen in the Father's presence; as for you, you should do what you have heard Gal 4.30
from the Father."[p]
39 They answered him, "Abraham is our father." Jesus said to them, "If you 8.39 Mt 3.9
were Abraham's children, you would be doing[q] what Abraham did, 40 but now you Rom 3.28; 9.7
are trying to kill me, a man who has told you the truth that I heard from God. This Gal 3.7,29
is not what Abraham did. 41 You are indeed doing what your father does." They 8.41 Deut 32.6
said to him, "We are not illegitimate children; we have one father, God himself." Isa 63.16; 64.8
42 Jesus said to them, "If God were your Father, you would love me, for I came Mal 1.6
from God and now I am here. I did not come on my own, but he sent me. 43 Why 8.42 Jn 1.14; 3.16
do you not understand what I say? It is because you cannot accept my word. 44 You 5.43; 16.27
are from your father the devil, and you choose to do your father's desires. He was Gal 4.4
a murderer from the beginning and does not stand in the truth, because there is no 8.44 Gen 3.1,4
truth in him. When he lies, he speaks according to his own nature, for he is a liar 1 Jn 2.4; 3.8
and the father of lies. 45 But because I tell the truth, you do not believe me. 46 Which 8.45 Jn 18.37
of you convicts me of sin? If I tell the truth, why do you not believe me? 47 Whoever
is from God hears the words of God. The reason you do not hear them is that you 8.47 1 Jn 4.6
are not from God."

Jesus states he is eternal
(129)

48 The Jews answered him, "Are we not right in saying that you are a Samaritan

p Other ancient authorities read *you do what you have heard from your father* q Other ancient authorities read *If you are Abraham's children, then do*

8.32 Jesus himself is the truth that makes us free (8.36). He is the source of truth, the perfect standard of what is right. He frees us from the consequences of sin, from self-deception, and from deception by Satan. He shows us clearly the way to eternal life with God. Thus Jesus does not give us freedom to do what we want, but freedom to follow God. As we seek to serve God, Jesus' perfect truth frees us to be all that God meant us to be.

8.34, 35 Sin has a way of enslaving us, controlling us, dominating us, and dictating our actions. Jesus can free you from this slavery that keeps you from becoming the person God created you to be. If sin is restraining, mastering, or enslaving you, Christ can break its power over your life.

8.41 Jesus made a distinction between hereditary sons and *true* sons. The religious leaders were hereditary sons of Abraham (founder of the Jewish nation) and therefore claimed to be sons of God. But their actions showed them to be true sons of Satan, because they lived under Satan's guidance. True sons of Abraham (faithful followers of God) would not act as they did. Your church membership and family connections will not make you true sons of God. Your true father is the one you obey.

8.43 The religious leaders were prevented from understanding because they refused to listen. Satan used their stubbornness, pride, and prejudices to keep them from believing in Jesus.

8.44, 45 The attitudes and actions of these leaders clearly identified them as followers of Satan. They may not have been conscious of this, but their hatred of truth, their lies, and their murderous intentions indicated how much control Satan had over them. They were his tools in carrying out his plans; they spoke the same language of lies. Satan still uses people to obstruct God's work (Genesis 4.8; Romans 5.12; 1 John 3.12).

8.46 No one could accuse Jesus of a single sin. Those who hated him and wanted him dead scrutinized his behavior but could find nothing wrong. Jesus proved he was God in the flesh by his sinless life. He is the only perfect example for us to follow.

8.46, 47 In a number of places Jesus intentionally challenged his listeners to test him. He welcomed those who wanted to question his claims and character as long as they were willing to follow through on what they discovered. His challenge clarifies the two most frequent reasons that people miss encountering him: (1) they never accept his challenge to test him, or (2) they test him but are not willing to believe what they discover. Have you made either of those mistakes?

8.49 Jn 7.20
8.50 Jn 5.41,42
8.51 Jn 5.24; 11.25,26
8.53 Jn 4.12
8.54 Acts 3.13
8.55 Jn 7.29; 15.10
8.56 Gen 22.17,18; Lk 10.24; Gal 3.8,9,16; Heb 11.10,13
8.58 Ex 3.14; Isa 9.6; 43.13; Mic 5.2

and have a demon?" 49 Jesus answered, "I do not have a demon; but I honor my
Father, and you dishonor me. 50 Yet I do not seek my own glory; there is one who
seeks it and he is the judge. 51 Very truly, I tell you, whoever keeps my word will
never see death." 52 The Jews said to him, "Now we know that you have a demon.
Abraham died, and so did the prophets; yet you say, 'Whoever keeps my word will
never taste death.' 53 Are you greater than our father Abraham, who died? The
prophets also died. Who do you claim to be?" 54 Jesus answered, "If I glorify myself, my glory is nothing. It is my Father who glorifies me, he of whom you say,
'He is our God,' 55 though you do not know him. But I know him; if I would say that
I do not know him, I would be a liar like you. But I do know him and I keep his
word. 56 Your ancestor Abraham rejoiced that he would see my day; he saw it and
was glad." 57 Then the Jews said to him, "You are not yet fifty years old, and have
you seen Abraham?"[r] 58 Jesus said to them, "Very truly, I tell you, before
Abraham was, I am." 59 So they picked up stones to throw at him, but Jesus hid
himself and went out of the temple.

Jesus heals the man who was born blind
(148)

9.1 Ex 20.5; Lk 13.2; Jn 9.34
9.3 Jn 11.4
9.4 Jn 4.34; 5.19,36; 11.9; 12.35; 17.4
9.5 Isa 9.2; 42.6; 49.6; Lk 2.32; Jn 1.5,9; 3.19; 8.12; 12.46
9.6 Mk 7.33; 8.23
9.7 2 Kgs 5.14; Neh 3.15; Isa 35.5
9.8 Acts 3.2,10

9 As he walked along, he saw a man blind from birth. 2 His disciples asked him,
"Rabbi, who sinned, this man or his parents, that he was born blind?" 3 Jesus
answered, "Neither this man nor his parents sinned; he was born blind so that God's
works might be revealed in him. 4 We[s] must work the works of him who sent me[t]
while it is day; night is coming when no one can work. 5 As long as I am in the
world, I am the light of the world." 6 When he had said this, he spat on the ground
and made mud with the saliva and spread the mud on the man's eyes, 7 saying to
him, "Go, wash in the pool of Siloam" (which means Sent). Then he went and
washed and came back able to see. 8 The neighbors and those who had seen him
before as a beggar began to ask, "Is this not the man who used to sit and beg?"
9 Some were saying, "It is he." Others were saying, "No, but it is someone like
him." He kept saying, "I am the man." 10 But they kept asking him, "Then how
were your eyes opened?" 11 He answered, "The man called Jesus made mud, spread
it on my eyes, and said to me, 'Go to Siloam and wash.' Then I went and washed
and received my sight." 12 They said to him, "Where is he?" He said, "I do not
know."

[r] Other ancient authorities read *has Abraham seen you?* [s] Other ancient authorities read *I* [t] Other ancient authorities read *us*

8.51 To keep Jesus' word means to hear his words and obey them. When Jesus says those who obey won't see death, he is talking about spiritual death, not physical death. Even physical death, however, will eventually be overcome. Those who follow Jesus will be raised to live eternally with him.

8.56 God told Abraham, father of the Jewish nation, that through him all nations would be blessed (Genesis 12.1–7; 15.1–21). Abraham had been able to see this through the eyes of faith. Jesus, a descendant of Abraham, blessed all people through his death, resurrection, and offer of salvation.

8.58 This is one of the most powerful statements uttered by Jesus. When he said he existed before Abraham was born, he undeniably proclaimed his divinity. Not only did Jesus say he existed before Abraham; he also applied God's holy name (*I Am*—Exodus 3.14) to himself. This claim demands a response. It cannot be ignored. The Jewish leaders tried to stone him for blasphemy because he claimed equality with God. But Jesus is God. How have you responded to Jesus, the Son of God?

8.59 In accordance with the law in Leviticus 24.16, the religious leaders were ready to stone Jesus for claiming to be God. But somehow he escaped. They well understood what Jesus was claiming, and because they didn't believe him, they charged him with blasphemy. How ironic that they were really the blasphemers, cursing and attacking the very God they claimed to serve!

9.1ff In chapter 9, we see four different reactions to Jesus. The neighbors revealed surprise and skepticism; the Pharisees showed disbelief and prejudice; the parents believed but kept quiet for fear of excommunication; and the healed man showed consistent, growing belief.

9.2, 3 A common belief in Jewish culture was that calamity or suffering was the result of some great sin. But Christ used this man's suffering to teach about faith and to glorify God. We live in a fallen world where good behavior is not always rewarded and bad behavior not always punished. Therefore, innocent people sometimes suffer. If God took suffering away whenever we asked, we would follow him for comfort and convenience, not out of love and devotion. Regardless of the reasons for our suffering, Jesus has the power to help us deal with it. When you suffer from a disease, tragedy, or handicap, try not to ask, "Why did this happen to me?" or "What did I do wrong?" Instead, ask God to give you strength for the trial and offer you a clearer perspective on what is happening.

9.7 The pool of Siloam was made by Hezekiah. His workers built an underground tunnel from a spring outside the city walls to carry water into the city. Thus the people could always get water without fear of being attacked. This was especially important in times of siege (see 2 Kings 20.20; 2 Chronicles 32.30).

Religious leaders question the blind man
(149)

13 They brought to the Pharisees the man who had formerly been blind. 14 Now
it was a sabbath day when Jesus made the mud and opened his eyes. 15 Then the
Pharisees also began to ask him how he had received his sight. He said to them,
"He put mud on my eyes. Then I washed, and now I see." 16 Some of the Pharisees
said, "This man is not from God, for he does not observe the sabbath." But others
said, "How can a man who is a sinner perform such signs?" And they were divided.
17 So they said again to the blind man, "What do you say about him? It was your
eyes he opened." He said, "He is a prophet."
18 The Jews did not believe that he had been blind and had received his sight
until they called the parents of the man who had received his sight 19 and asked
them, "Is this your son, who you say was born blind? How then does he now see?"
20 His parents answered, "We know that this is our son, and that he was born blind;
21 but we do not know how it is that now he sees, nor do we know who opened his
eyes. Ask him; he is of age. He will speak for himself." 22 His parents said this
because they were afraid of the Jews; for the Jews had already agreed that anyone
who confessed Jesus[u] to be the Messiah[v] would be put out of the synagogue.
23 Therefore his parents said, "He is of age; ask him."
24 So for the second time they called the man who had been blind, and they said
to him, "Give glory to God! We know that this man is a sinner." 25 He answered,
"I do not know whether he is a sinner. One thing I do know, that though I was blind,
now I see." 26 They said to him, "What did he do to you? How did he open your
eyes?" 27 He answered them, "I have told you already, and you would not listen.
Why do you want to hear it again? Do you also want to become his disciples?"
28 Then they reviled him, saying, "You are his disciple, but we are disciples of
Moses. 29 We know that God has spoken to Moses, but as for this man, we do not
know where he comes from." 30 The man answered, "Here is an astonishing thing!
You do not know where he comes from, and yet he opened my eyes. 31 We know
that God does not listen to sinners, but he does listen to one who worships him and
obeys his will. 32 Never since the world began has it been heard that anyone opened
the eyes of a person born blind. 33 If this man were not from God, he could do
nothing." 34 They answered him, "You were born entirely in sins, and are you trying to teach us?" And they drove him out.

9.14 Jn 5.9
9.16 Jn 3.2; 7.12,43
9.17 Deut 18.15 Mt 21.11 Jn 4.19; 6.14
9.22 Jn 7.13; 12.42 16.2; 19.38 Acts 5.13
9.24 Josh 7.19
9.28 Jn 5.45 Rom 2.17
9.29 Jn 1.10; 8.14
9.31 Job 27.8,9 Ps 34.15; 66.18 145.19 Prov 15.29 Isa 1.15 Jer 11.11; 14.12 Mic 3.4 Zech 7.13
9.33 Jn 3.2
9.34 Jn 12.42

Jesus teaches about spiritual blindness
(150)

35 Jesus heard that they had driven him out, and when he found him, he said,
"Do you believe in the Son of Man?"[w] 36 He answered, "And who is he, sir?[x] Tell
me, so that I may believe in him." 37 Jesus said to him, "You have seen him, and the
one speaking with you is he." 38 He said, "Lord,[x] I believe." And he worshiped
him. 39 Jesus said, "I came into this world for judgment so that those who do not see

9.35 Mt 16.16 Mk 1.1
9.37 Jn 4.26
9.39 Lk 4.18,19

[u] Gk *him* [v] Or *the Christ* [w] Other ancient authorities read *the Son of God* [x] *Sir* and *Lord* translate the same Greek word

---

9.13–17 While the Pharisees questioned and debated about Jesus, people were being healed and lives were being changed. Their skepticism was based on jealousy of Jesus' popularity, not on insufficient evidence.

9.14–16 The Jewish sabbath, Saturday, was the weekly holy day of rest. The Pharisees had made a long list of specific do's and don'ts regarding the sabbath. Kneading the clay and healing the man were considered work and therefore were forbidden. Jesus may have made the clay in order to emphasize his teaching about the sabbath—that it is right to care for others' needs even if it involves working on a day of rest.

9.25 By now the man who had been blind had heard the same questions over and over. He did not know how he was healed, but he knew that his life had been miraculously changed, and he was not afraid to tell the truth. You don't need to know all the answers in order to share Christ with others. It is important to tell them how he has changed your life. Then trust that God will use your words.

9.28, 34 The man's new faith was severely tested. He was cursed and evicted from the temple. Persecution may come when you follow Jesus. You may lose friends; you may even lose your life. But no one can ever take away the eternal life Jesus gives you.

9.38 The longer this man experienced his new life through Christ, the more confident he became in the one who had healed him. He gained not only physical sight but also spiritual sight as he recognized Jesus first as a prophet (9.17), then as his Lord. When you turn to Christ, you begin to see him differently. Peter tells us to "grow in the grace and knowledge of our Lord and Savior Jesus Christ" (2 Peter 3.18). If you want to know more about Jesus, read about him in God's Word and accept his leadership in all you do.

9.40 Rom 2.19
9.41 Prov 26.12; Jn 15.22

may see, and those who do see may become blind.” 40 Some of the Pharisees near
him heard this and said to him, “Surely we are not blind, are we?” 41 Jesus said to
them, “If you were blind, you would not have sin. But now that you say, ‘We see,’
your sin remains.

Jesus is the good shepherd
(151)

10.1 Isa 56.10
10.2 Acts 20.28
10.5 Prov 19.27; Gal 1.8; Eph 4.14
10.6 2 Pet 2.22
10.8 Jer 23.1; 50.6
10.10 2 Pet 2.1
10.11 Isa 40.11; Ezek 34.11-16, 23; 37.24; Heb 13.20,21; 1 Pet 2.25; 5.4; 1 Jn 3.16; Rev 7.17

10 “Very truly, I tell you, anyone who does not enter the sheepfold by the gate
but climbs in by another way is a thief and a bandit. 2 The one who enters by
the gate is the shepherd of the sheep. 3 The gatekeeper opens the gate for him, and
the sheep hear his voice. He calls his own sheep by name and leads them out.
4 When he has brought out all his own, he goes ahead of them, and the sheep follow
him because they know his voice. 5 They will not follow a stranger, but they will
run from him because they do not know the voice of strangers.” 6 Jesus used this
figure of speech with them, but they did not understand what he was saying to
them.

7 So again Jesus said to them, “Very truly, I tell you, I am the gate for the
sheep. 8 All who came before me are thieves and bandits; but the sheep did not
listen to them. 9 I am the gate. Whoever enters by me will be saved, and will come
in and go out and find pasture. 10 The thief comes only to steal and kill and destroy.
I came that they may have life, and have it abundantly.
11 “I am the good shepherd. The good shepherd lays down his life for the

THE NAMES OF JESUS In different settings, Jesus gave himself names that pointed to special roles he was ready to fulfill for people. Some of these refer back to the Old Testament promises of the Messiah. Others were ways to help people understand him.

Reference	*Name*	*Significance*
6.27	Son of Man	Jesus' favorite reference to himself. It emphasized his humanity—but the way he used it, it was a claim to divinity.
6.35	Bread of life	Refers to his life-giving role—that he is the only source of eternal life.
8.12	Light of the world	Light is a symbol of spiritual truth. Jesus is the universal answer for man's need of spiritual truth.
10.7	Gate for the sheep	Jesus is the only way into God's kingdom.
10.11	Good shepherd	Jesus appropriated the prophetic images of the Messiah pictured in the Old Testament. This is a claim to divinity, focusing on his love and guidance.
11.25	The Resurrection and the life	Not only is Jesus the source of life, he is the power over death.
14.6	The way, the truth, and the life	Jesus is the method, the message, and the meaning for all people. With this title he summarized his purpose in coming to earth.
15.1	The vine	This title has an important second part, "you are the branches." As in so many of his other names, Jesus reminds us that just as branches gain life from the vine and cannot live apart from it, so we are completely dependent on Christ for spiritual life.

9.40, 41 The Pharisees were shocked that Jesus thought they were spiritually blind. Jesus countered that only blindness (stubbornness and stupidity) could excuse their behavior. To those who remained open (recognized how sin had truly blinded them from knowing the truth), he gave spiritual understanding and insight. But he rejected those who had become complacent, self-satisfied, and "blind."

10.1 At night, sheep were often gathered into a sheepfold to protect them from thieves, weather, or wild animals. The sheepfolds were caves, sheds, or open areas surrounded by walls made of stones or branches. The shepherd often slept in the fold to protect the sheep. Just as a shepherd cares for his sheep, Jesus, the good shepherd, cares for his flock (those who follow him). The prophet Ezekiel, in predicting the coming of the Messiah, called him a shepherd (Ezekiel 34.23).

10.10 In contrast to the thief who takes, Jesus gives. The life he gives now is abundantly richer and fuller. It is eternal, yet it begins immediately. Life in him is lived on a higher plain because of his overflowing forgiveness, love, and guidance.

10.11, 12 A hired man tends the sheep for money, while the shepherd does it for love. The shepherd owns the sheep and is committed to them. Jesus is not merely doing a job; he is committed to love us and even lay down his life for us. False teachers and false prophets do not have this commitment.

sheep. 12The hired hand, who is not the shepherd and does not own the sheep, sees
the wolf coming and leaves the sheep and runs away — and the wolf snatches them
and scatters them. 13The hired hand runs away because a hired hand does not care
for the sheep. 14I am the good shepherd. I know my own and my own know me,
15just as the Father knows me and I know the Father. And I lay down my life for the
sheep. 16I have other sheep that do not belong to this fold. I must bring them also,
and they will listen to my voice. So there will be one flock, one shepherd. 17For this
reason the Father loves me, because I lay down my life in order to take it up again.
18No one takes[y] it from me, but I lay it down of my own accord. I have power to
lay it down, and I have power to take it up again. I have received this command
from my Father."

19 Again the Jews were divided because of these words. 20Many of them were
saying, "He has a demon and is out of his mind. Why listen to him?" 21Others were
saying, "These are not the words of one who has a demon. Can a demon open the
eyes of the blind?"

10.14 Phil 3.10; 2 Tim 2.19
10.16 Isa 56.6,7; Ezek 37.21,22; Jn 11.52; 17.20-24; Eph 2.14; 3.6
10.17 Isa 53.6,7; 2 Cor 5.15; Heb 2.9; 1 Jn 3.16
10.18 Jn 11.25; 19.11; Heb 5.8; 7.16

Religious leaders surround Jesus at the temple
(152)

22 At that time the festival of the Dedication took place in Jerusalem. It was
winter, 23and Jesus was walking in the temple, in the portico of Solomon. 24So the
Jews gathered around him and said to him, "How long will you keep us in suspense? If you are the Messiah,[z] tell us plainly." 25Jesus answered, "I have told
you, and you do not believe. The works that I do in my Father's name testify to me;
26but you do not believe, because you do not belong to my sheep. 27My sheep hear
my voice. I know them, and they follow me. 28I give them eternal life, and they
will never perish. No one will snatch them out of my hand. 29What my Father has
given me is greater than all else, and no one can snatch it out of the Father's hand.[a]
30The Father and I are one."

10.23 Acts 3.11; 5.12
10.24 Lk 22.67
10.25 Jn 5.36; 10.38; 14.10,11
10.26 1 Jn 4.6
10.28 1 Jn 5.11,12
10.30 Isa 9.6; Jn 1.1; 10.38

[y] Other ancient authorities read *has taken* [z] Or *the Christ* [a] Other ancient authorities read *My Father who has given them to me is greater than all, and no one can snatch them out of the Father's hand*

10.16 The "other sheep" were non-Jews. Jesus came to save Gentiles as well as Jews. This is an insight into his worldwide mission – to die for the sins of the whole world. People tend to want to restrict God's blessings to their own group, but Jesus refuses to be limited by the fences we build.

10.17, 18 Jesus' death and resurrection, as part of God's plan for the salvation of the world, were under God's full control. No one could kill Jesus without his consent.

10.19, 20 If Jesus had been merely a man, his claims to be God would have proven him insane. But his miracles proved his words true – he really was God. The Jewish leaders could not see beyond their own prejudices, and they tried to put Jesus in a human "box." But Jesus was not limited by their restricted vision.

10.22, 23 The festival of the Dedication commemorated the cleansing of the temple under Judas Maccabeus in 164 B.C. after Antiochus Epiphanes had defiled it by sacrificing a pig on the altar of burnt offering. It was celebrated toward the end of December. This is also the present-day Feast of Lights, Hanukkah.

10.23 The portico of Solomon was a roofed walkway supported by large stone columns, just inside the walls of the temple courtyard.

10.24 Many people asking for proof do so for the wrong reasons. Most of these questioners didn't want to follow Jesus in the way he wanted to lead them. They hoped he would declare himself Messiah for one of two other reasons. First, they, along with the disciples and everyone else in the Jewish nation, would have been delighted to have him drive out the Romans. Many of them didn't think he was going to do that, however. These doubters hoped he would identify himself so they could accuse him of telling lies (as the Pharisees did in 8.13).

10.28, 29 Just as a shepherd protects his sheep, Jesus protects his people from eternal harm. While believers can expect to suffer on earth, Satan cannot harm their souls or take away their eternal life with God. There are many reasons to be afraid here on earth, because this is Satan's domain. But if you choose to follow Jesus, he will give you everlasting safety.

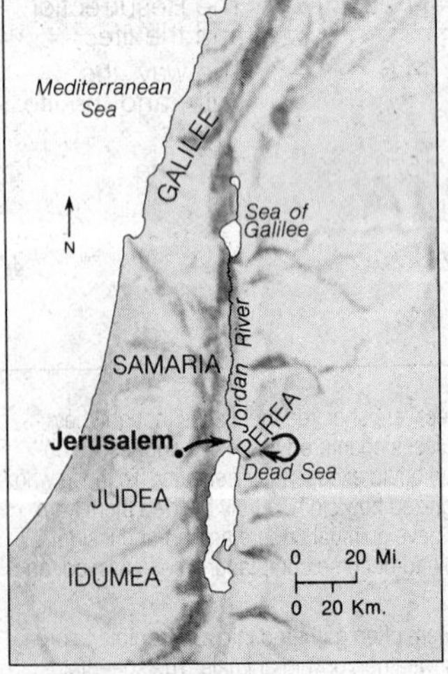

MINISTRY BEYOND THE JORDAN
Jesus had been in Jerusalem for the festival of Booths (7.2); then he preached in various towns, probably in Judea, before returning to to Jerusalem for the festival of the Dedication. He again angered the religious leaders who tried to arrest him, but he left the city and went beyond the Jordan to preach.

10.30–33 This is the clearest statement of Jesus' divinity he ever made. Jesus and his Father are not the same person, but they are one in essence and nature. Thus Jesus is not merely a good

10.33 Lev 24.15,16 Jn 1.1,18 5.18; 20.28 Rom 9.5 Phil 2.6 Tit 2.13 Heb 1.8,9 2 Pet 1.1 1 Jn 5.20
10.34 Ps 82.1,6
10.37 Jn 15.24

31 The Jews took up stones again to stone him. 32 Jesus replied, "I have shown
you many good works from the Father. For which of these are you going to stone
me?" 33 The Jews answered, "It is not for a good work that we are going to stone
you, but for blasphemy, because you, though only a human being, are making
yourself God." 34 Jesus answered, "Is it not written in your law,[b] 'I said, you are
gods'? 35 If those to whom the word of God came were called 'gods'—and the
scripture cannot be annulled— 36 can you say that the one whom the Father has
sanctified and sent into the world is blaspheming because I said, 'I am God's Son'?
37 If I am not doing the works of my Father, then do not believe me. 38 But if I do
them, even though you do not believe me, believe the works, so that you may know
and understand[c] that the Father is in me and I am in the Father." 39 Then they tried
to arrest him again, but he escaped from their hands.

10.42 Jn 7.31 8.30,31; 11.45

40 He went away again across the Jordan to the place where John had been
baptizing earlier, and he remained there. 41 Many came to him, and they were saying, "John performed no sign, but everything that John said about this man was
true." 42 And many believed in him there.

3. Jesus encounters crucial events in Jerusalem

Lazarus becomes ill and dies
(165)

11.1 Mt 21.17 Lk 10.38
11.2 Mt 26.7 Mk 14.3 Lk 7.37,38
11.4 Jn 9.3

11 Now a certain man was ill, Lazarus of Bethany, the village of Mary and her
sister Martha. 2 Mary was the one who anointed the Lord with perfume and
wiped his feet with her hair; her brother Lazarus was ill. 3 So the sisters sent a
message to Jesus,[d] "Lord, he whom you love is ill." 4 But when Jesus heard it, he
said, "This illness does not lead to death; rather it is for God's glory, so that the Son
of God may be glorified through it." 5 Accordingly, though Jesus loved Martha and

[b] Other ancient authorities read *in the law* [c] Other ancient authorities lack *and understand*; others read *and believe*
[d] Gk *him*

teacher—he is God. His claim to be God was unmistakable. The religious leaders wanted to kill him for it, because their laws said that anyone claiming to be God should die. Nothing could persuade them that Jesus' claim was true.

10.31 The Jewish leaders attempted to carry out the direction found in Leviticus 24.16 regarding those who blaspheme (claim to be God). They intended to stone Jesus.

10.34–36 Jesus referred to Psalm 82.6 where the Israelite judges are called "gods" (see also Exodus 4.16; 7.1). If God called the Israelite judges "gods" because they were agents of God's revelation and will, how could it be blasphemy for Jesus to call himself the Son of God? Jesus was rebuking them because he is the Son of God in a unique, unparalleled relationship of oneness with the Father.

10.35 "The scripture cannot be annulled" is a clear statement of the truth of the Bible. *Annull* means "to neutralize or set aside as invalid." There are many ways people attempt to nullify God's Word today. They (1) ignore it completely, (2) claim that it is for another time, (3) claim that there is no such thing as absolute truth, or (4) protest that it applies to others, but not to them. If we accept Christ as Lord, we also accept his confirmation of the Bible as God's Word.

11.1 The village of Bethany was located about two miles east of Jerusalem on the road to Jericho. It was near enough to Jerusalem for them to be in danger, but far enough away so as not to attract attention prematurely.

11.3 As their brother grew very sick, Mary and Martha turned to Jesus for help. They believed in his ability to help because they had seen his miracles. We too know of his miracles, both from Scripture and through changed lives we have seen. When we need extraordinary help, Jesus offers extraordinary resources. We should not hesitate to ask him for help.

11.4 Any trial a believer faces can ultimately bring glory to God because God can bring good out of any bad situation. When trouble comes, do you grumble, complain, and blame God, or do you see your problems as opportunities to honor him?

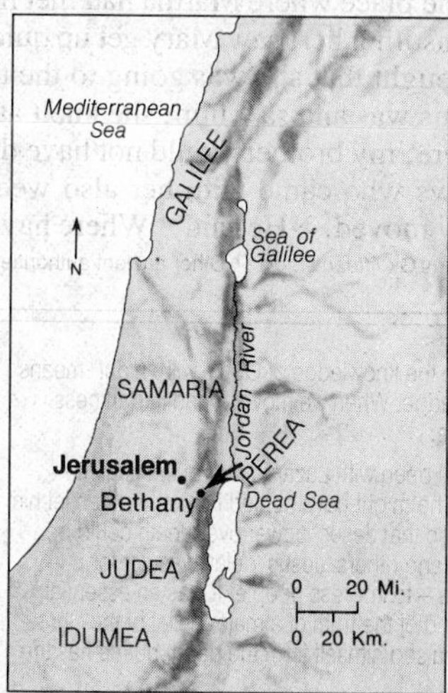

JESUS RAISES LAZARUS
Jesus had been preaching in the villages beyond the Jordan, probably in Perea, when he received the news of Lazarus's sickness. Jesus did not leave immediately, but waited two days before returning to Judea. He knew Lazarus would be dead when he arrived in Bethany, but he was going to do a great miracle.

11.5–7 Jesus loved this family and often stayed with them. He knew their pain but did not respond immediately. His delay had a specific purpose. God's timing, especially his delays, may make us think he is not answering or is not answering the way we want. But he will meet all our needs according to his perfect schedule and purpose. Patiently await his timing.

her sister and Lazarus, 6 after having heard that Lazarus[e] was ill, he stayed two
days longer in the place where he was.
7 Then after this he said to the disciples, "Let us go to Judea again." 8 The disciples said to him, "Rabbi, the Jews were just now trying to stone you, and are you
going there again?" 9 Jesus answered, "Are there not twelve hours of daylight?
Those who walk during the day do not stumble, because they see the light of this
world. 10 But those who walk at night stumble, because the light is not in them."
11 After saying this, he told them, "Our friend Lazarus has fallen asleep, but I am
going there to awaken him." 12 The disciples said to him, "Lord, if he has fallen
asleep, he will be all right." 13 Jesus, however, had been speaking about his death,
but they thought that he was referring merely to sleep. 14 Then Jesus told them
plainly, "Lazarus is dead. 15 For your sake I am glad I was not there, so that you
may believe. But let us go to him." 16 Thomas, who was called the Twin,[f] said to
his fellow disciples, "Let us also go, that we may die with him."

Jesus comforts Mary and Martha
(166)

17 When Jesus arrived, he found that Lazarus[e] had already been in the tomb
four days. 18 Now Bethany was near Jerusalem, some two miles[g] away, 19 and
many of the Jews had come to Martha and Mary to console them about their
brother. 20 When Martha heard that Jesus was coming, she went and met him, while
Mary stayed at home. 21 Martha said to Jesus, "Lord, if you had been here, my
brother would not have died. 22 But even now I know that God will give you whatever you ask of him." 23 Jesus said to her, "Your brother will rise again." 24 Martha
said to him, "I know that he will rise again in the resurrection on the last day."
25 Jesus said to her, "I am the resurrection and the life.[h] Those who believe in me,
even though they die, will live, 26 and everyone who lives and believes in me will
never die. Do you believe this?" 27 She said to him, "Yes, Lord, I believe that you
are the Messiah,[i] the Son of God, the one coming into the world."
28 When she had said this, she went back and called her sister Mary, and told
her privately, "The Teacher is here and is calling for you." 29 And when she heard
it, she got up quickly and went to him. 30 Now Jesus had not yet come to the village,
but was still at the place where Martha had met him. 31 The Jews who were with her
in the house, consoling her, saw Mary get up quickly and go out. They followed her
because they thought that she was going to the tomb to weep there. 32 When Mary
came where Jesus was and saw him, she knelt at his feet and said to him, "Lord, if
you had been here, my brother would not have died." 33 When Jesus saw her weeping, and the Jews who came with her also weeping, he was greatly disturbed in
spirit and deeply moved. 34 He said, "Where have you laid him?" They said to him,

11.8 Jn 8.59; 10.31
11.9 Ps 97.11; 119.105,130; Prov 4.18; 13.9; Lk 13.33; Jn 9.4
11.10 Job 12.24,25; Jn 12.35; 1 Jn 2.11
11.11 Dan 12.2; Acts 7.60; 1 Cor 15.51
11.16 Mt 10.3; Jn 14.5; 20.24-28; 21.2
11.17 Jn 11.39
11.20 Lk 10.38-42
11.22 Jn 9.31
11.23 Dan 12.2; Phil 3.21; 1 Thess 4.14
11.24 Jn 5.28,29; Acts 24.15
11.25 Jn 1.4; 3.36; 5.21; 6.39,40; 14.6; Col 1.18; 3.4; 1 Jn 1.1,2; 5.10,11; Rev 1.17,18
11.26 Jn 6.47-51; 8.51
11.27 Mt 16.16; Jn 4.42; 6.14,68,69

e Gk *he* f Gk *Didymus* g Gk *fifteen stadia* h Other ancient authorities lack *and the life* i Or *the Christ*

11.9, 10 "Day" means the knowledge of God's will; "night" means absence of this knowledge. When we move ahead in darkness, we are likely to stumble.

11.14, 15 If Jesus had been with Lazarus during the final moments of his sickness, he might have healed him rather than let him die. But Lazarus died so that Jesus' power over death could be shown to his disciples and others. Jesus' delay was not for purposes of showmanship – to impress people. It was an essential display of his power and of the truth of a major belief of the Christian faith. He not only raised himself from the dead, but he has the power to raise others.

11.16 The disciples knew the dangers of going with Jesus to Jerusalem, and they tried to talk him out of it. Thomas merely expressed what all of them felt. When their objections failed, they were willing to go and even die with Jesus. They may not have understood why Jesus would die, but they were loyal. There are unknown dangers in doing God's work. It is wise to consider the high cost of being Christ's disciple.

11.25, 26 Jesus has power over life and death as well as power to forgive sins. This is because he is the Creator of life (see John 14.6). He who *is* life can surely restore life. Whoever believes in him has a spiritual life that death cannot touch or diminish in any way. When we realize his power and how wonderful his offer to us really is, how can we help but commit our lives to him! Those of us who believe have wonderful assurance and certainty: "Because I live, you also will live" (14.19).

11.27 Martha is best known for being too busy to sit down and talk with Jesus (Luke 10.38–42). But here we see her as a woman of deep faith. Her statement of faith is exactly the response Jesus desires from us.

11.33–38 John stresses that we have a God who cares. This contrasts with the Greek concept of God that was popular in his day – a God with no emotions and no messy involvement with humans. Here we see many of Jesus' emotions – compassion, indignation, sorrow, even frustration. He often expressed deep emotion, and we must never be afraid to reveal our true feelings to him. He understands them because he experienced them. Be honest, and don't try to hide anything from your Savior. He truly cares.

11.35 Isa 53.3; Rom 12.15; Heb 4.15 "Lord, come and see." 35 Jesus began to weep. 36 So the Jews said, "See how he
loved him!" 37 But some of them said, "Could not he who opened the eyes of the
blind man have kept this man from dying?"

Jesus raises Lazarus from the dead
(167)

38 Then Jesus, again greatly disturbed, came to the tomb. It was a cave, and a
11.39 Jn 11.17 stone was lying against it. 39 Jesus said, "Take away the stone." Martha, the sister
of the dead man, said to him, "Lord, already there is a stench because he has been
dead four days." 40 Jesus said to her, "Did I not tell you that if you believed, you
11.41 Mt 11.25; 27.60; Lk 24.2 would see the glory of God?" 41 So they took away the stone. And Jesus looked
upward and said, "Father, I thank you for having heard me. 42 I knew that you
11.42 Jn 12.30 always hear me, but I have said this for the sake of the crowd standing here, so that
they may believe that you sent me." 43 When he had said this, he cried with a loud
11.43 Deut 32.39; 1 Sam 2.6; Lk 7.14; 8.54; Acts 3.15; 9.40 voice, "Lazarus, come out!" 44 The dead man came out, his hands and feet bound
with strips of cloth, and his face wrapped in a cloth. Jesus said to them, "Unbind
him, and let him go."

Religious leaders plot to kill Jesus
(168)

11.47 Ps 2.2; Acts 4.16 45 Many of the Jews therefore, who had come with Mary and had seen what
Jesus did, believed in him. 46 But some of them went to the Pharisees and told them
11.48 Dan 9.26,27 what he had done. 47 So the chief priests and the Pharisees called a meeting of the
council, and said, "What are we to do? This man is performing many signs. 48 If we
11.49 Mt 26.3; Lk 3.1,2 let him go on like this, everyone will believe in him, and the Romans will come and
destroy both our holy place[j] and our nation." 49 But one of them, Caiaphas, who
11.51 Ex 28.30; Num 27.21; Ezra 2.62,63 was high priest that year, said to them, "You know nothing at all! 50 You do not
understand that it is better for you to have one man die for the people than to have
the whole nation destroyed." 51 He did not say this on his own, but being high priest
11.52 Isa 49.6; Acts 13.47; Gal 3.28; Eph 2.14-19; 3.6; 1 Pet 5.9; 1 Jn 2.2 that year he prophesied that Jesus was about to die for the nation, 52 and not for the
nation only, but to gather into one the dispersed children of God. 53 So from that
day on they planned to put him to death.
54 Jesus therefore no longer walked about openly among the Jews, but went

[j] *Or our temple*; Greek *our place*

11.35 When Jesus saw the weeping and wailing, he too wept openly. Perhaps he empathized with their grief, or perhaps he was troubled at their unbelief. In either case, Jesus showed that he cares enough for us to weep with us.

11.38 Tombs at this time were usually caves carved in the limestone rock of a hillside. A tomb was often large enough for people to walk inside. Several bodies were usually placed in one tomb. After burial, a large stone was rolled across the entrance to the tomb.

11.44 Jesus raised others from the dead, including Jairus's daughter (Matthew 9.18–26; Mark 5.41, 42; Luke 8.40–56) and a widow's son (Luke 7.11–15).

11.45–53 Even when confronted point-blank with the power of Jesus' deity, some refused to believe. These eyewitnesses not only rejected him; they plotted his murder. They were so hardened that they preferred to reject God's Son rather than admit they were wrong. Beware of pride. If we allow it to grow, it can lead us into enormous sin.

11.48 The Jewish leaders thought that if they didn't stop Jesus, the Romans would punish them. Rome gave partial freedom to the Jews as long as they were quiet and obedient. Jesus' miracles often caused a disturbance. The leaders feared that Rome's displeasure would bring additional hardship to their nation.

11.51 John regarded Caiaphas's statement as a prophecy. As high priest, Caiaphas was used by God to explain Jesus' death even though Caiaphas didn't realize what he was doing.

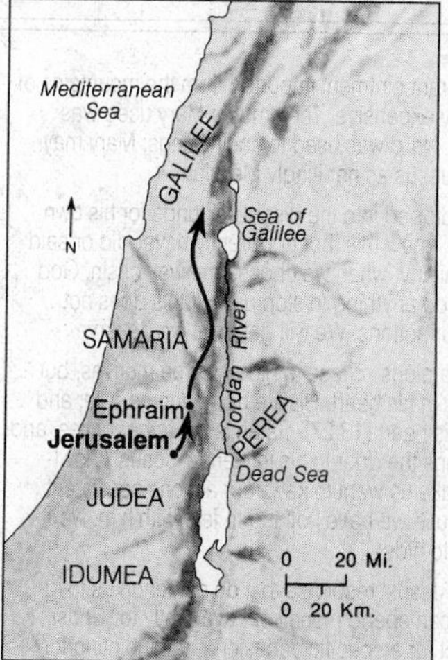

TIME WITH THE DISCIPLES
Lazarus's return to life became the last straw for the religious leaders who were bent on killing Jesus. So Jesus stopped his public ministry and took his disciples away from Jerusalem to Ephraim. From there they returned to Galilee for a while (see the map in Luke 17.)

from there to a town called Ephraim in the region near the wilderness; and he remained there with the disciples.
55 Now the Passover of the Jews was near, and many went up from the country
to Jerusalem before the Passover to purify themselves. 56 They were looking for
Jesus and were asking one another as they stood in the temple, "What do you think?
Surely he will not come to the festival, will he?" 57 Now the chief priests and the
Pharisees had given orders that anyone who knew where Jesus[k] was should let
them know, so that they might arrest him.

11.55 Ex 19.10; 2 Chron 30.17-19; Mt 26.1,2; Mk 14.1; Lk 22.1; Jn 18.28

A woman anoints Jesus with expensive perfume
(182/Matthew 26.6–13; Mark 14.3–9)

12 Six days before the Passover Jesus came to Bethany, the home of Lazarus,
whom he had raised from the dead. 2 There they gave a dinner for him. Martha served, and Lazarus was one of those at the table with him. 3 Mary took a pound
of costly perfume made of pure nard, anointed Jesus' feet, and wiped them[l] with
her hair. The house was filled with the fragrance of the perfume. 4 But Judas Iscariot, one of his disciples (the one who was about to betray him), said, 5 "Why was
this perfume not sold for three hundred denarii[m] and the money given to the poor?"
6 (He said this not because he cared about the poor, but because he was a thief; he
kept the common purse and used to steal what was put into it.) 7 Jesus said, "Leave
her alone. She bought it[n] so that she might keep it for the day of my burial. 8 You
always have the poor with you, but you do not always have me."
9 When the great crowd of the Jews learned that he was there, they came not
only because of Jesus but also to see Lazarus, whom he had raised from the dead.
10 So the chief priests planned to put Lazarus to death as well, 11 since it was on
account of him that many of the Jews were deserting and were believing in Jesus.

12.1 Jn 11.43
12.3 Lk 10.38-41; Jn 11.1,2
12.4 Jn 6.70,71
12.6 Prov 28.20,22; Jn 13.29; 1 Cor 5.10,11; 6.10; Eph 5.5; 1 Tim 6.9,10
12.7 Mt 26.10-13; Mk 14.8,9; Jn 19.40
12.8 Deut 15.11; Mk 14.7
12.10 Lk 16.31

Jesus rides into Jerusalem on a donkey
(183/Matthew 21.1–11; Mark 11.1–11; Luke 19.28–44)

12 The next day the great crowd that had come to the festival heard that Jesus
was coming to Jerusalem. 13 So they took branches of palm trees and went out to
meet him, shouting,
"Hosanna!
Blessed is the one who comes in the name of the Lord—
the King of Israel!"

12.12 Mt 21.4-9; Mk 11.7-10
12.13 Ps 118.26

[k] Gk *he* [l] Gk *his feet* [m] Three hundred denarii would be nearly a year's wages for a laborer [n] Gk lacks *She bought it*

12.3 Nard was a fragrant ointment imported from the mountains of India. Thus it was very expensive. The amount Mary used was worth a year's wages. Nard was used to anoint kings; Mary may have been anointing Jesus as her kingly Messiah.

12.4–6 Judas often dipped into the disciples' funds for his own use. Jesus, of course, knew this, but apparently never did or said anything about it. Similarly, when we choose the way of sin, God may not immediately do anything to stop us, but this does not mean he approves our actions. We will get what we deserve.

12.5, 6 Judas used a pious phrase to hide his true motives, but Jesus knew what was in his heart. His life had become a lie, and Satan was entering his heart (13.27). Satan is the father of lies, and a lying character opens the door to his influence. Jesus' knowledge of us should make us want to keep our actions consistent with our words. Because we have nothing to fear with him, we should have nothing to hide.

12.7, 8 This act and Jesus' response to it do not teach us to ignore the poor so we can spend money extravagantly for Christ. This was a unique act for a specific occasion—an anointing for Jesus' burial and a public declaration of faith in him as Messiah. Jesus' words should have taught Judas a valuable lesson about the worth of money. Unfortunately, Judas did not take heed; soon he would sell his Master's life for 30 pieces of silver.

12.10, 11 The chief priests' blindness and hardness of heart caused them to sink ever deeper into sin. They rejected the Messiah, planned to kill him, and now also plotted to murder Lazarus. One sin leads to another. From the Jewish leaders' point of view, they could accuse Jesus of blasphemy because he claimed equality with God. But Lazarus had done nothing of the kind. They wanted him dead simply because he was a living witness to Jesus' power. This is a warning to us to avoid sin. Sin leads to more sin, a downward spiral that can be stopped only by repentance and the power of the Holy Spirit.

12.13 Jesus began his last week on earth by riding into Jerusalem on a donkey under a canopy of palm branches, with crowds hailing him as their king. To announce that he was indeed the Messiah, Jesus chose a *time* when all Israel would be gathered at Jerusalem, a *place* where huge crowds could see him, and a *way* of proclaiming his mission that was unmistakable. On Palm Sunday we celebrate Jesus' triumphal entry into Jerusalem.

12.13 The people who were praising God for giving them a king had the wrong idea about Jesus. They were sure that he would be a national leader who would restore their nation to its former glory. Thus they were deaf to the words of their prophets and blind to Jesus' real mission. When it became apparent that Jesus was not going to fulfill their hopes, many people turned against him.

14 Jesus found a young donkey and sat on it; as it is written:
12.15 Zech 9.9 15 "Do not be afraid, daughter of Zion.
Look, your king is coming,
sitting on a donkey's colt!"
12.16 Jn 2.22; 7.39 16 His disciples did not understand these things at first; but when Jesus was glori-
12.17 Jn 11.42 fied, then they remembered that these things had been written of him and had been
done to him. 17 So the crowd that had been with him when he called Lazarus out of

CAIAPHAS

Caiaphas was the leader of the religious group called the Sadducees. Educated and wealthy, they were the political rulers of the nation. As the elite group, they were on fairly good terms with Rome. They hated Jesus because he endangered their secure lifestyles and taught a message they could not accept. A kingdom in which leaders *served* had no appeal to them.

Caiaphas's usual policy was to remove any threats to his power by whatever means necessary. For Caiaphas, whether Jesus should die was not in question; the only point to be settled was *when* his death should take place. Not only did Jesus have to be captured and tried; the Jewish council also needed Roman approval before they could carry out the death sentence. Caiaphas's plans were unexpectedly helped by Judas's offer to betray Christ.

Caiaphas did not realize that his schemes were actually part of a wonderful plan God was carrying out. Caiaphas's willingness to sacrifice another man to preserve his own security was clearly selfish. By contrast, Jesus' willingness to die for us was a clear example of loving self-sacrifice. Caiaphas thought he had won the battle as Jesus hung on the cross, but he did not count on the resurrection!

Caiaphas's mind was closed. He couldn't accept the resurrection even when the evidence was overwhelming, and he attempted to silence those whose lives had been forever changed by the risen Christ (Matthew 28.12, 13). Caiaphas represents those people who will not believe because they think it will cost them too much to accept Jesus as Lord. They choose the fleeting power, prestige, and pleasures of this life instead of the eternal life God offers those who receive his Son. What is your choice?

Strength and accomplishment:
- High priest for 18 years

Weaknesses and mistakes:
- One of those most directly responsible for Jesus' death
- Used his office as a means to power and personal security
- Planned Jesus' capture, carried out his illegal trial, pressured Pilate to approve the crucifixion, attempted to prevent the resurrection, and later tried to cover up the fact of the resurrection
- Kept up religious appearances while compromising with Rome
- Involved in the later persecution of Christians

Lessons from his life:
- God uses even the twisted motives and actions of his enemies to bring about his will
- When we cover selfish motives with spiritual objectives and words, God still sees our intentions

Vital statistics:
- Where: Jerusalem
- Occupation: High priest
- Relatives: Father-in-law: Annas
- Contemporaries: Jesus, Pilate, Herod Antipas

Key verses:
"But one of them, Caiaphas, who was high priest that year, said to them, 'You know nothing at all! You do not understand that it is better for you to have one man die for the people than to have the whole nation destroyed' " (John 11.49, 50).

Caiaphas is also mentioned in Matthew 26.3, 4, 57–67; Luke 3.2; John 11.49–53; John 18.13–28; and Acts 4.6.

12.16 After Jesus' resurrection, the disciples understood for the first time many of the prophecies that they had missed along the way. Jesus' words and actions took on new meaning and made more sense. In retrospect, they saw how Jesus had led them into a deeper and better understanding of his truth. Stop and think about the events in your life leading up to where you are now. How has God led you to this point? As you grow older, you will look back and see God's involvement more clearly than you do now. Let this truth encourage you to live faithfully today.

the tomb and raised him from the dead continued to testify.[o] 18 It was also because
they heard that he had performed this sign that the crowd went to meet him. 19 The
Pharisees then said to one another, "You see, you can do nothing. Look, the world
has gone after him!"

Jesus explains why he must die
(185)

20 Now among those who went up to worship at the festival were some Greeks.
21 They came to Philip, who was from Bethsaida in Galilee, and said to him, "Sir,
we wish to see Jesus." 22 Philip went and told Andrew; then Andrew and Philip
went and told Jesus. 23 Jesus answered them, "The hour has come for the Son of
Man to be glorified. 24 Very truly, I tell you, unless a grain of wheat falls into the
earth and dies, it remains just a single grain; but if it dies, it bears much fruit.
25 Those who love their life lose it, and those who hate their life in this world will
keep it for eternal life. 26 Whoever serves me must follow me, and where I am,
there will my servant be also. Whoever serves me, the Father will honor.
27 "Now my soul is troubled. And what should I say—'Father, save me from
this hour'? No, it is for this reason that I have come to this hour. 28 Father, glorify
your name." Then a voice came from heaven, "I have glorified it, and I will glorify
it again." 29 The crowd standing there heard it and said that it was thunder. Others
said, "An angel has spoken to him." 30 Jesus answered, "This voice has come for
your sake, not for mine. 31 Now is the judgment of this world; now the ruler of this
world will be driven out. 32 And I, when I am lifted up from the earth, will draw all
people[p] to myself." 33 He said this to indicate the kind of death he was to die. 34 The
crowd answered him, "We have heard from the law that the Messiah[q] remains
forever. How can you say that the Son of Man must be lifted up? Who is this Son
of Man?" 35 Jesus said to them, "The light is with you for a little longer. Walk while
you have the light, so that the darkness may not overtake you. If you walk in the

12.18 Jn 12.11
12.21 Jn 1.43,44
12.23,24 Jn 13.32; 17.1 Rom 6.4,5 1 Cor 15.36-45
12.25 Mt 20.39 Lk 9.24; 17.33
12.27 Lk 12.50; 22.53
12.28 Mt 3.17; 17.5 Mk 1.11; 9.7 Lk 3.22; 9.35 2 Pet 1.17,18
12.31 Jn 14.30; 16.11 Eph 6.12 Heb 2.14
12.32 Jn 3.14; 6.44
12.34 2 Sam 7.13 Ps 89.35,36 110.4 Isa 9.7 Ezek 37.24,25 Dan 7.14 Mic 4.7
12.35 Jn 8.12; 9.5

[o] Other ancient authorities read *with him began to testify that he had called. . .from the dead* [p] Other ancient authorities read *all things* [q] Or *the Christ*

12.18 The people flocked to Jesus because they had heard of his great miracle in raising Lazarus from the dead. Their adoration was short-lived and their commitment shallow, for in a few days they would do nothing to stop his crucifixion. Devotion based only on curiosity or popularity fades quickly.

12.20, 21 These Greeks were converts to the Jewish faith. They probably went to Philip, because though he was a Jew, he had a Greek name.

12.23–25 This is a beautiful picture of the necessary sacrifice of Jesus. Unless a grain of wheat is buried, it will not become a blade of wheat producing many more grains. Jesus had to die to pay the penalty for our sin, and to demonstrate his power over death. Jesus' resurrection proves he has eternal life. Because he is God, he can give this same eternal life to all who believe in him.

12.25 We must be so committed to living for Christ that we "hate" our lives by comparison. This does not mean that we long to die or are careless or destructive with the life God has given, but that we are willing to die if doing so will glorify Christ. We must disown the tyrannical rule of our own self-centeredness. By laying aside our striving for advantage, security, and pleasure, we can serve God lovingly and freely. Releasing control of our life and transferring control to Christ ushers in both eternal life and genuine joy in the present.

12.26 Many believed that Jesus came for the Jews only. But when Jesus said, "Whoever serves me must follow me," he was talking to these Greeks. Jesus welcomes sincere seekers, no matter who they are. His message is for everyone. Don't allow social or racial differences to become barriers to the gospel. Take the word to all people.

12.27 Jesus knew his crucifixion lay ahead, and because he was human he dreaded it. He knew he would have to take the sins of the world on himself, and he knew this would separate him from his Father. He wanted to be delivered from this horrible death, but he knew that God sent him into the world to die for our sins, in our place. Jesus said no to his human desires in order to obey his Father and bring glory to him. Although we will never have to face such a difficult task, we are still called to obedience. Whatever the Father asks, we should do his will and bring glory to his name.

12.31 The ruler of this world is Satan, an angel who rebelled against God. He is real, not symbolic, and is constantly working against God and those who obey him. He tempted Eve in the garden and persuaded her to sin; he tempted Jesus in the wilderness and did not persuade him to fall (Matthew 4.1–11). Satan has great power, but people can be delivered from his reign of spiritual darkness because of Christ's victory on the cross. And Jesus is much more powerful. His resurrection shattered Satan's deathly power (Colossians 1.13, 14).

12.32–34 The crowd could not believe the Messiah would die. They were waving palm branches for a victorious Messiah who they thought would set up a political, earthly kingdom that would never end. Jesus' words did not fit their concept of the Messiah. First he had to suffer and die—then he would one day set up his eternal kingdom. For what kind of Messiah, or Savior, are you looking? Don't try to force Jesus into your own mold—he won't fit.

12.35, 36 Jesus said he would be with them in person for only a short time, and they should take advantage of his presence while they had it. Like a light in a dark place, he would show them where to go. If they walked in his light, they would become "children of light," revealing the truth and pointing people to God. As Christians, we are to be Christ's light bearers, letting his light shine through us. How brightly is your light shining?

12.36 Eph 5.8 1 Thess 5.5 darkness, you do not know where you are going. 36 While you have the light, believe in the light, so that you may become children of light."

Most of the people do not believe in Jesus
(186)

After Jesus had said this, he departed and hid from them. 37 Although he had
12.38 Isa 53.1 Rom 10.16 performed so many signs in their presence, they did not believe in him. 38 This was
to fulfill the word spoken by the prophet Isaiah:
"Lord, who has believed our message,
and to whom has the arm of the Lord been revealed?"
39 And so they could not believe, because Isaiah also said,
12.40 Isa 6.9,10 Mt 13.14 40 "He has blinded their eyes
and hardened their heart,
so that they might not look with their eyes,
and understand with their heart and turn—
12.41 Isa 6.1 and I would heal them."
12.42 Jn 7.13,48 9.22,23; 12.11 41 Isaiah said this because[r] he saw his glory and spoke about him. 42 Nevertheless
many, even of the authorities, believed in him. But because of the Pharisees they
12.43 Jn 5.44 did not confess it, for fear that they would be put out of the synagogue; 43 for they
loved human glory more than the glory that comes from God.

[r] Other ancient witnesses read *when*

GREAT EXPECTATIONS
Wherever he went, Jesus exceeded people's expectations.

What was expected	*What Jesus did*	*Reference*
A man looked for healing	Jesus also forgave his sins	Mark 2.1–12
The disciples were expecting an ordinary day of fishing	They found the Savior	Luke 5.1–11
A widow was resigned to bury her dead son	Jesus restored her son to life	Luke 7.11–17
The religious leaders wanted a miracle	Jesus offered them the Creator of miracles	Matthew 12.38–45
A woman who wanted to be healed touched Jesus	Jesus helped her see it was her faith that made her well	Mark 5.25–34
The disciples thought the crowd should be sent home because there was no food	Jesus used a small meal to feed thousands, and there were leftovers!	John 6.1–15
The crowds looked for a political leader to set up a new kingdom to overthrow Rome's control	Jesus offered them an eternal, spiritual kingdom to overthrow sin's control	A theme throughout the Gospels
The disciples wanted to eat the Passover meal with Jesus, their Master	Jesus washed their feet, showing he was also their servant	John 13.1–20
The religious leaders wanted Jesus killed and got their wish	But Jesus rose from the dead!	John 11.53; 19.30; 20.1–29

12.37, 38 Jesus had performed many miracles, but most people still didn't believe in him. Likewise, many today won't believe despite all God does. Don't be discouraged if your witness for Christ doesn't turn as many to him as you'd like. Your job is to continue to be a faithful witness. You are responsible to reach out to others, but they are responsible for their own decisions.

12.39–41 People in Jesus' time, like those in the time of Isaiah, would not believe despite the evidence (12.37). As a result, God hardened their hearts. Does that mean God intentionally prevented these people from believing in him? No, he simply confirmed their own choices. After a lifetime of resisting God, they had become so set in their ways that they wouldn't even try to understand Jesus' message. For such people, it is virtually impossible to come to God—their hearts have been permanently hardened. Other instances of hardened hearts are recorded in Exodus 9.12, Romans 1.24–28, and 2 Thessalonians 2.8–12.

12.42, 43 Along with those who refused to believe, many believed but refused to admit it. This is just as bad, and Jesus had strong words for such people (see Matthew 10.32, 33). People who do this are afraid of rejection or ridicule. Many Jewish leaders wouldn't admit their faith in Jesus because they feared excommunication from the synagogue (which was their livelihood) and loss of their prestigious place in the community. But the praise of others is fickle and short-lived. We should be concerned much more about God's eternal acceptance than the temporary approval of other people.

Jesus summarizes his message
(187)

44 Then Jesus cried aloud: "Whoever believes in me believes not in me but in
him who sent me. 45 And whoever sees me sees him who sent me. 46 I have come as
light into the world, so that everyone who believes in me should not remain in the
darkness. 47 I do not judge anyone who hears my words and does not keep them, for
I came not to judge the world, but to save the world. 48 The one who rejects me and
does not receive my word has a judge; on the last day the word that I have spoken
will serve as judge, 49 for I have not spoken on my own, but the Father who sent me
has himself given me a commandment about what to say and what to speak. 50 And
I know that his commandment is eternal life. What I speak, therefore, I speak just
as the Father has told me."

12.45 Jn 14.9
12.46 Jn 1.4,5,9 3.19; 8.12 9.5,39
12.47 Jn 3.17; 5.45 8.15,16
12.48 Deut 18.18,19

C. DEATH AND RESURRECTION OF JESUS, THE SON OF GOD (13.1 – 21.25)

John begins his Gospel with eternity and ends with Jesus coming to earth again. He features Jesus teaching his disciples privately just before his arrest and death. We see, clearly, the deep love Jesus has for the believer, and the peace that comes from faith. Knowing the love Jesus has for believers, we too should believe and allow Jesus to forgive our sins. Only then will we experience peace in a world filled with turmoil.

1. Jesus teaches his disciples

Jesus washes the disciples' feet
(210)

13 Now before the festival of the Passover, Jesus knew that his hour had come
to depart from this world and go to the Father. Having loved his own who
were in the world, he loved them to the end. 2 The devil had already put it into the
heart of Judas son of Simon Iscariot to betray him. And during supper 3 Jesus,
knowing that the Father had given all things into his hands, and that he had come
from God and was going to God, 4 got up from the table,[s] took off his outer robe,
and tied a towel around himself. 5 Then he poured water into a basin and began to
wash the disciples' feet and to wipe them with the towel that was tied around him.
6 He came to Simon Peter, who said to him, "Lord, are you going to wash my feet?"
7 Jesus answered, "You do not know now what I am doing, but later you will understand." 8 Peter said to him, "You will never wash my feet." Jesus answered, "Unless I wash you, you have no share with me." 9 Simon Peter said to him, "Lord, not
my feet only but also my hands and my head!" 10 Jesus said to him, "One who has
bathed does not need to wash, except for the feet,[t] but is entirely clean. And you[u]

13.1 1 Cor 15.27
13.2 Lk 22.3
13.4 Lk 12.37; 22.27
13.5 Lk 7.44
13.8 Ps 51.2,7 Isa 52.14,15 Ezek 36.25 Acts 2.38 1 Cor 6.11 Eph 5.26 Tit 3.5 Heb 9.13,14 10.22
13.10 Ex 29.4 30.18-21; 40.12

[s] Gk *from supper* [t] Other ancient authorities lack *except for the feet* [u] The Greek word for *you* here is plural

12.45 We often wonder what God is like. How can we know the Creator when he doesn't make himself visible? Jesus said plainly that those who see him see God, because he *is* God. If you want to know what God is like, study the life and words of Jesus Christ.

12.48 The purpose of Jesus' first mission on earth was not to judge people, but to show them the way to find salvation and eternal life. When Christ returns, one of his main purposes will be to judge people for how they lived on earth. On the day of Judgment, those who accepted Jesus and lived his way will be raised to eternal life (1 Corinthians 15.51–57; 1 Thessalonians 4.15–18; Revelation 21.1–8); and those who rejected Jesus and lived any way they pleased will face eternal punishment (Revelation 20.11–15). Decide now which side you'll be on, because the consequences of your decision last forever.

13.1 Jesus knew he would be betrayed by one of his disciples, denied by another, and deserted by all of them for a time. Still "he loved them to the end." God knows us completely, as Jesus knew his disciples. He knows the sins we have committed and the ones we will yet commit. Still, he loves us. How do you respond to that kind of love?

13.1ff Chapters 13 – 17 tell us what Jesus said to his disciples the night before his death. All of these words were spoken in one evening when he gave final instructions to the disciples to prepare them for his death and resurrection, events that would change their lives forever.

13.1–3 For more information on Judas Iscariot, see his Profile in Mark 14.

13.1–17 Jesus was the model servant, and he showed this attitude to his disciples. Washing guests' feet when they arrived was a job for a household servant. But Jesus wrapped a towel around him, as the lowliest slave would do, and washed his disciples' feet. If Jesus, God in the flesh, is willing to serve, we his followers must also be servants, willing to serve in any way that glorifies God. Are you willing to follow Christ's example? Whom can you serve today? There is a special blessing for those who serve Christ's way (13.17).

13.6, 7 Seeing his Master behave like a slave must have confused Peter. He still did not understand Jesus' teaching that to be a leader, one must be a servant. This is not a comfortable passage for leaders who find it hard to serve those under them. How do you treat those who work for you?

13.11 Jn 6.64; 13.2
13.12 Jn 13.4
13.13 1 Cor 8.6; 12.3
13.14 Lk 22.27 Rom 12.10
13.15 Phil 2.5-7 1 Pet 5.3-5 1 Jn 2.6
13.17 Jas 1.25
13.18 Ps 41.9 2 Tim 2.19
13.20 Mt 10.40 Lk 10.16

are clean, though not all of you." 11 For he knew who was to betray him; for this
reason he said, "Not all of you are clean."
12 After he had washed their feet, had put on his robe, and had returned to the
table, he said to them, "Do you know what I have done to you? 13 You call me
Teacher and Lord—and you are right, for that is what I am. 14 So if I, your Lord and
Teacher, have washed your feet, you also ought to wash one another's feet. 15 For
I have set you an example, that you also should do as I have done to you. 16 Very
truly, I tell you, servants[v] are not greater than their master, nor are messengers
greater than the one who sent them. 17 If you know these things, you are blessed if
you do them. 18 I am not speaking of all of you; I know whom I have chosen. But
it is to fulfill the scripture, 'The one who ate my bread[w] has lifted his heel against
me.' 19 I tell you this now, before it occurs, so that when it does occur, you may
believe that I am he.[x] 20 Very truly, I tell you, whoever receives one whom I send
receives me; and whoever receives me receives him who sent me."

Jesus and the disciples have the last supper
(211/Matthew 26.20–30; Mark 14.17–26; Luke 22.14–30)

13.21 Mt 26.20-25 Mk 14.18-21 Lk 22.21-23
13.23 Jn 19.26
13.25 Jn 21.20
13.26 Jn 6.71
13.27 Lk 22.3
13.29 Jn 12.6
13.30 Lk 22.53

21 After saying this Jesus was troubled in spirit, and declared, "Very truly, I
tell you, one of you will betray me." 22 The disciples looked at one another, uncertain of whom he was speaking. 23 One of his disciples—the one whom Jesus
loved—was reclining next to him; 24 Simon Peter therefore motioned to him to ask
Jesus of whom he was speaking. 25 So while reclining next to Jesus, he asked him,
"Lord, who is it?" 26 Jesus answered, "It is the one to whom I give this piece
of bread when I have dipped it in the dish."[y] So when he had dipped the piece of
bread, he gave it to Judas son of Simon Iscariot.[z] 27 After he received the piece of
bread,[a] Satan entered into him. Jesus said to him, "Do quickly what you are going
to do." 28 Now no one at the table knew why he said this to him. 29 Some thought
that, because Judas had the common purse, Jesus was telling him, "Buy what we
need for the festival"; or, that he should give something to the poor. 30 So, after
receiving the piece of bread, he immediately went out. And it was night.

Jesus predicts Peter's denial
(212/Luke 22.31–38)

13.31,32 Lk 24.26 Jn 12.23; 17.1,5 1 Cor 15.42 Heb 5.5
13.33 Jn 7.33,34

31 When he had gone out, Jesus said, "Now the Son of Man has been glorified,
and God has been glorified in him. 32 If God has been glorified in him,[b] God will
also glorify him in himself and will glorify him at once. 33 Little children, I am with
you only a little longer. You will look for me; and as I said to the Jews so now I say
to you, 'Where I am going, you cannot come.' 34 I give you a new commandment,

[v] Gk *slaves* [w] Other ancient authorities read *ate bread with me* [x] Gk *I am* [y] Gk *dipped it* [z] Other ancient authorities read *Judas Iscariot son of Simon*; others, *Judas son of Simon from Karyot* (Kerioth) [a] Gk *After the piece of bread* [b] Other ancient authorities lack *If God has been glorified in him*

13.12ff Jesus did not wash his disciples' feet just to get them to be nice to each other. Instead, he wanted to extend his mission on earth after he was gone. The disciples were to move into the world serving God, serving each other, and serving all people to whom they took the message of salvation.

13.26 The honored guest at a meal was singled out in this way.

13.27 Satan's part in the betrayal of Jesus does not remove any of the responsibility from Judas. Disillusioned because Jesus was talking about dying rather than setting up his kingdom, Judas may have been trying to force Jesus' hand and make him use his power to prove he was the Messiah. Or perhaps Judas, not understanding Jesus' mission, no longer believed he was God's chosen one. Whatever Judas thought, Satan assumed that Jesus' death would end his mission and thwart God's plan. He did not know that Jesus' death was the most important part of God's plan.

13.27–38 John describes these few moments in clear detail. We can see that Jesus knew exactly what was going to happen. He knew about Judas and about Peter, but he did not change the situation, nor did he stop loving them. In the same way, Jesus knows exactly what you will do to hurt him. Yet he still loves you unconditionally and will forgive you. Judas couldn't understand this, and his life ended tragically. Peter understood, and despite his shortcomings, his life ended triumphantly because he never let go of his faith.

13.34 To love others was not a new commandment (see Leviticus 19.18), but to love others as much as Christ loved them was revolutionary. Now we are to love others based on Jesus' sacrificial love for us. Such love will not only bring unbelievers to Christ, it will also keep believers strong and united in a world hostile to God. Jesus was a living example of God's love. And we are to be living examples of Christ's love.

13.34, 35 Jesus says that our Christlike love will show we are his disciples. Do people see petty bickering, jealousy, and division in your church? Or do they know you are Jesus' followers by your love for one another?

that you love one another. Just as I have loved you, you also should love one
another. 35 By this everyone will know that you are my disciples, if you have love
for one another."
36 Simon Peter said to him, "Lord, where are you going?" Jesus answered,
"Where I am going, you cannot follow me now; but you will follow afterward."
37 Peter said to him, "Lord, why can I not follow you now? I will lay down my life
for you." 38 Jesus answered, "Will you lay down your life for me? Very truly, I tell
you, before the cock crows, you will have denied me three times.

13.34 Lev 19.18 Eph 5.2 1 Thess 4.9 Heb 13.1 Jas 2.8 1 Jn 2.8; 3.11 4.20,21
13.35 Acts 2.44-46
13.36 2 Pet 1.13,14

Jesus is the way to the Father
(213)

14 "Do not let your hearts be troubled. Believe[c] in God, believe also in me. 2 In
my Father's house there are many dwelling places. If it were not so, would
I have told you that I go to prepare a place for you?[d] 3 And if I go and prepare a
place for you, I will come again and will take you to myself, so that where I am,
there you may be also. 4 And you know the way to the place where I am going."[e]
5 Thomas said to him, "Lord, we do not know where you are going. How can we
know the way?" 6 Jesus said to him, "I am the way, and the truth, and the life. No
one comes to the Father except through me. 7 If you know me, you will know[f] my
Father also. From now on you do know him and have seen him."
8 Philip said to him, "Lord, show us the Father, and we will be satisfied."
9 Jesus said to him, "Have I been with you all this time, Philip, and you still do not
know me? Whoever has seen me has seen the Father. How can you say, 'Show us
the Father'? 10 Do you not believe that I am in the Father and the Father is in me?
The words that I say to you I do not speak on my own; but the Father who dwells
in me does his works. 11 Believe me that I am in the Father and the Father is in me;
but if you do not, then believe me because of the works themselves. 12 "Very truly,
I tell you, the one who believes in me will also do the works that I do and, in fact,
will do greater works than these, because I am going to the Father. 13 I will do
whatever you ask in my name, so that the Father may be glorified in the Son. 14 If
in my name you ask me[g] for anything, I will do it.

14.2 Ps 90.1 Jn 2.16,19-21 14.6
14.3 Jn 10.38 14.10,11,18,20 16.16,19-22 17.21-24
14.6 Jn 1.4,14,16 8.32; 10.9,10 11.25 Eph 2.18 1 Jn 5.20
14.7 Jn 6.46; 8.19 1 Jn 2.13
14.9 Jn 1.14,18 12.45 2 Cor 4.4 Col 1.15 Heb 1.3
14.10 Jn 5.19; 10.38 17.11,21-24
14.12 Acts 5.15 19.11,12

[c] Or *You believe* [d] Or *If it were not so, I would have told you; for I go to prepare a place for you* [e] Other ancient authorities read *Where I am going you know, and the way you know* [f] Other ancient authorities read *If you had known me, you would have known* [g] Other ancient authorities lack *me*

13.35 Love is not simply warm feelings; instead, it is an attitude that reveals itself in action. How can we love others as Jesus loves us? By helping when it's not convenient, by giving when it hurts, by devoting energy to others' welfare rather than our own, by absorbing hurts from others without complaining or fighting back. This kind of loving is hard to do. That is why people notice when you do it and know you are empowered by a supernatural source. The Bible has another beautiful description of love in 1 Corinthians 13.

13.37, 38 Peter proudly announced that he was ready to die for Jesus. But Jesus corrected him. He knew that Peter would deny him that very night to protect himself (18.25–27). In our enthusiasm, it is easy to make promises. But God knows the extent of our commitment. Paul tells us not to think of ourselves more highly than we ought (Romans 12.3). Instead of bragging, show your commitment one step at a time as you grow in your knowledge of God's Word and in your faith.

14.1–3 Jesus' words show that the way to eternal life, though unseen, is certain—as assured as your trust in Jesus. He has already prepared the way to eternal life. The only issue that may still be unsettled is your willingness to believe.

14.2, 3 There are few verses in Scripture that describe eternal life, but they are rich with promises. Here Jesus says, "I go to prepare a place," and "I will come again." We can look forward to eternal life because Jesus has promised it to all who believe in him. Although the details of life in eternity are unknown, we need not fear, because Jesus is preparing it for us and he will be with us.

14.5, 6 This is one of the most basic and important passages in Scripture. How can we know the way to God? Only through Jesus. Jesus is the way because he is both God and man. By uniting our lives with his, we are united with God. Trust Jesus to take you to the Father, and all the benefits of being God's child will be yours.

14.6 Jesus says he is the *only* way to God the Father. Some people may argue that this is too narrow. In reality, it is wide enough for the whole world, if the world chooses to accept it. Instead of worrying about how limited it sounds to have only one way, we should be saying, "Thank you, God, for providing a sure way to get to you!"

14.6 As the *way,* Jesus is our path to the Father. As the *truth,* he is the reality of all God's promises. As the *life,* he joins his divine life to ours, both now and eternally.

14.9 Jesus is the visible, tangible image of the invisible God. He is the complete revelation of what God is like. Jesus explained to Philip, who wanted to see the Father, that to know Jesus is to know God. The search for God, for truth and reality, ends in Christ. (See also Colossians 1.15; Hebrews 1.1–4.)

14.12, 13 Jesus is not saying that his disciples would do more amazing miracles—after all, raising the dead is about as amazing as you can get. Rather, the disciples, working in the power of the Holy Spirit, would carry the gospel of God's kingdom out of Palestine and into the whole world.

14.14 When Jesus says we can ask for anything, we must remember that our asking must be in his name—that is, according to

Jesus promises the Holy Spirit
(214)

14.17 Rom 8.15,16 1 Jn 3.24

15 "If you love me, you will keep[h] my commandments. 16 And I will ask the
Father, and he will give you another Advocate,[i] to be with you forever. 17 This is

[h] Other ancient authorities read *me, keep* [i] Or *Helper*

JOHN

Being loved is the most powerful motivation in the world! Our ability to love is often shaped by our experience of love. We usually love others as we have been loved.

Some of the greatest statements about God's loving nature were written by a man who experienced God's love in a unique way. John, Jesus' disciple, expressed his relationship to the Son of God by calling himself "the disciple whom Jesus loved" (John 21.20). Although Jesus' love is clearly communicated in all the Gospels, in John's Gospel it is a central theme. Because his own experience of Jesus' love was so strong and personal, John was sensitive to those words and actions of Jesus that illustrated how the one who *is* love loved others.

Jesus knew John fully and loved him fully. He gave John and his brother James the nickname "Sons of Thunder," perhaps from an occasion when the brothers asked Jesus for permission to "command fire to come down from heaven" (Luke 9.54) on a village that had refused to welcome Jesus and the disciples. In John's Gospel and letters, we see the great God of love, while the thunder of God's justice bursts from the pages of Revelation.

Jesus confronts each of us as he confronted John. We cannot know the depth of his love unless we are willing to face the fact that he knows us completely. Otherwise we are fooled into believing he must love who we pretend to be, not the sinner we actually are. John and all the disciples convince us that God is able and willing to accept us as we are. Being aware of God's love is a great motivator for change. His love is not given in exchange for our efforts; his love frees us to really live. Have you accepted that love?

Strengths and accomplishments:
- Before following Jesus, one of John the Baptist's disciples
- One of the 12 disciples and, with Peter and James, one of the inner three, closest to Jesus
- Wrote five New Testament books: the Gospel of John; 1, 2, and 3 John; and Revelation

Weaknesses and mistakes:
- Along with James, shared a tendency to outbursts of selfishness and anger
- Asked for a special position in Jesus' kingdom

Lessons from his life:
- Those who realize how much they are loved are able to love much
- When God changes a life, he does not take away personality characteristics, but puts them to effective use in his service

Vital statistics:
- Occupation: Fisherman, disciple
- Relatives: Father: Zebedee. Mother: Salome. Brother: James
- Contemporaries: Jesus, Pilate, Herod

Key verses:
"Beloved, I am writing you no new commandment, but an old commandment that you have had from the beginning; the old commandment is the word that you have heard. Yet I am writing you a new commandment that is true in him and in you, because the darkness is passing away and the true light is already shining" (1 John 2.7, 8).

John's story is told throughout the Gospels, Acts, and Revelation.

God's character and will. God will not grant requests contrary to his nature or his will, and we cannot use his name as a magic formula to fulfill our selfish desires. If we are sincerely following God and seeking to do his will, then our requests will be in line with what he wants, and he will grant them. (See also 15.16; 16.23.)

14.15, 16 Jesus was soon going to leave the disciples, but he would remain with them. How could this be? The Advocate – the Spirit of God himself – would come after Jesus was gone to care for and guide the disciples. This happened to the disciples just before Jesus' ascension (21.22), and to all the believers at pentecost (Acts 2), shortly afterwards. The Holy Spirit is the very presence of God within all believers, helping us live as God wants and building Christ's church on earth.

14.16 The word translated *Advocate* means "one who pleads in favor of another." It combines the ideas of helper, comforter, and counselor. The Holy Spirit is a powerful person on our side, working for and with us.

14.17ff The following chapters teach these truths about the Holy Spirit: he will never leave us (14.16); the world at large cannot recognize him (14.17); he lives with us and in us (14.17); he teaches us (14.26); he reminds us of Jesus' words (14.26; 15.26); he reproves us of sin, shows us God's righteousness, and announces God's judgment on evil (16.8); he guides into truth and gives insight into future events (16.13); he glorifies Christ (16.14). Many people are unaware of the Holy Spirit's activities, but to those who receive Christ's word and understand the Spirit's power, he gives a whole new way to look at life.

the Spirit of truth, whom the world cannot receive, because it neither sees him nor
knows him. You know him, because he abides with you, and he will be in[j] you.
18 "I will not leave you orphaned; I am coming to you. 19 In a little while the
world will no longer see me, but you will see me; because I live, you also will live.
20 On that day you will know that I am in my Father, and you in me, and I in you.
21 They who have my commandments and keep them are those who love me; and
those who love me will be loved by my Father, and I will love them and reveal
myself to them." 22 Judas (not Iscariot) said to him, "Lord, how is it that you will
reveal yourself to us, and not to the world?" 23 Jesus answered him, "Those who
love me will keep my word, and my Father will love them, and we will come to
them and make our home with them. 24 Whoever does not love me does not keep
my words; and the word that you hear is not mine, but is from the Father who sent
me.
25 "I have said these things to you while I am still with you. 26 But the Advocate,[k] the Holy Spirit, whom the Father will send in my name, will teach you
everything, and remind you of all that I have said to you. 27 Peace I leave with you;
my peace I give to you. I do not give to you as the world gives. Do not let your
hearts be troubled, and do not let them be afraid. 28 You heard me say to you, 'I am
going away, and I am coming to you.' If you loved me, you would rejoice that I am
going to the Father, because the Father is greater than I. 29 And now I have told you
this before it occurs, so that when it does occur, you may believe. 30 I will no longer
talk much with you, for the ruler of this world is coming. He has no power over me;
31 but I do as the Father has commanded me, so that the world may know that I love
the Father. Rise, let us be on our way.

14.18 Rom 8.9-11; 2 Cor 3.17,18
14.20 Jn 10.38; 15.4,5; 16.16,23; 17.21-24
14.21 Prov 8.17; 1 Jn 2.5; 2 Jn 6
14.22 Lk 6.14-16; Acts 10.40
14.23 Ps 91.1; Eph 3.17; 1 Jn 4.16; 5.3; Rev 3.20; 21.3
14.26 Lk 24.49; Jn 1.33; 15.26; 16.7; 20.22; 1 Jn 2.20,27
14.27 Phil 4.7; Col 3.15
14.28 1 Cor 11.3
14.29 Jn 13.19
14.30 Jn 12.31; Heb 4.15
14.31 Jn 10.18; 12.49

Jesus teaches about the vine and the branches
(215)

15 "I am the true vine, and my Father is the vinegrower. 2 He removes every
branch in me that bears no fruit. Every branch that bears fruit he prunes[l] to
make it bear more fruit. 3 You have already been cleansed[l] by the word that I have

15.1 Isa 5.1-7
15.3 Jn 17.17

[j] Or *among* [k] Or *Helper* [l] The same Greek root refers to pruning and cleansing

14.18 When Jesus said, "I am coming to you," he meant it. Although Jesus ascended to heaven, he sent the Holy Spirit to live in believers. To have the Holy Spirit is to have Jesus himself.

14.19–21 Sometimes people wish they knew the future so they could prepare for it. God has chosen not to give us this knowledge. He alone knows what will happen, but he tells us all we need to know to *prepare* for the future. When we live by his standards, he will not leave us; he will come to us, he will be within us, and he will reveal himself to us. God knows what will happen, and because he will be with us through it, we need not fear. We don't have to know the future to have faith in God; we have to have faith in God to be secure about the future.

14.21 Jesus said that his followers show their love by obeying him. Love is more than lovely words; it is commitment and conduct. If you love Christ, then prove it by obeying what he says in his Word.

14.22, 23 Because the disciples were still expecting Jesus to establish an earthly kingdom and overthrow Rome, they found it hard to understand why he did not tell the world at large that he was the Messiah. Not everyone, however, could understand his message. Since pentecost, the gospel of the kingdom has been proclaimed throughout the whole world, but not everyone is receptive to it. Jesus saves the deepest revelations of himself for those who love and obey him.

14.26 Jesus promised the disciples that the Holy Spirit would help them remember what he had been teaching them. This promise ensures the validity of the New Testament. The disciples were eyewitnesses of Jesus' life and teachings. The Holy Spirit helped them remember without taking away their individual perspective. We can be confident that the Gospels are accurate records of what Jesus taught and did (see 1 Corinthians 2.10–14). The Holy Spirit can help us as well. As we study the Bible, we can trust him to plant truth in our mind, convince us of God's will, and remind us when we stray from it.

14.27 The result of the Holy Spirit's work in our lives is deep and lasting peace. Unlike worldly peace, which is usually defined as the absence of conflict, this peace is confident assurance in any circumstance. With Christ's peace, we have no need to fear the present or the future. If your life is full of stress, allow the Holy Spirit to fill you with Christ's peace (see Philippians 4.6, 7 for more on experiencing God's peace).

14.27–29 Sin, fear, uncertainty, doubt, and numerous other forces are at war within us. The peace of God moves into our hearts and lives to restrain these hostile forces and to offer comfort in place of conflict. Jesus says he will give us that peace if we are willing to accept it from him.

14.28 As God the Son, Jesus willingly submits to God the Father. On earth, Jesus also submitted to many of the physical limitations of being human (Philippians 2.6).

14.30, 31 Although Satan, the prince of this world, was unable to overpower Jesus (Matthew 4), he still had the arrogance to try. Satan's power exists only because God allows him to act. But because Jesus is sinless, Satan has no power over him. If we obey Jesus and align ourselves closely with God's purposes, Satan can have no power over us.

14.31 "Rise, let us be on our way" suggests that chapters 15 – 17 may have been spoken en route to the garden of Gethsemane. Another view is that Jesus was asking the disciples to get ready to leave the upper room, but they did not actually do so until 18.1.

15.4 Jn 6.56; 14.20 1 Jn 4.12,13
15.5 Hos 14.8
15.6 Mt 3.10; 7.19 Heb 6.4-6
15.8 Mt 5.15,16
15.9 Jn 3.35 17.23-26
15.10 Jn 8.29 14.15,16,31
15.11 Jn 16.24; 17.13 1 Jn 1.4
15.12 1 Thess 4.9 1 Pet 4.8 1 Jn 3.11
15.13 Jn 10.11 Rom 5.6-8 Eph 5.2

spoken to you. 4 Abide in me as I abide in you. Just as the branch cannot bear fruit
by itself unless it abides in the vine, neither can you unless you abide in me. 5 I am
the vine, you are the branches. Those who abide in me and I in them bear much
fruit, because apart from me you can do nothing. 6 Whoever does not abide in me
is thrown away like a branch and withers; such branches are gathered, thrown into
the fire, and burned. 7 If you abide in me, and my words abide in you, ask for
whatever you wish, and it will be done for you. 8 My Father is glorified by this, that
you bear much fruit and become[m] my disciples. 9 As the Father has loved me, so I
have loved you; abide in my love. 10 If you keep my commandments, you will abide
in my love, just as I have kept my Father's commandments and abide in his love.
11 I have said these things to you so that my joy may be in you, and that your joy
may be complete.

12 "This is my commandment, that you love one another as I have loved you.
13 No one has greater love than this, to lay down one's life for one's friends. 14 You
are my friends if you do what I command you. 15 I do not call you servants[n] any
longer, because the servant[o] does not know what the master is doing; but I have
called you friends, because I have made known to you everything that I have heard
from my Father. 16 You did not choose me but I chose you. And I appointed you to
go and bear fruit, fruit that will last, so that the Father will give you whatever you
ask him in my name. 17 I am giving you these commands so that you may love one
another.

Jesus warns about the world's hatred
(216)

18 "If the world hates you, be aware that it hated me before it hated you. 19 If

[m] Or *be* [n] Gk *slaves* [o] Gk *slave*

15.1 The grapevine is a prolific plant; a single vine bears many grapes. In the Old Testament, grapes symbolized Israel's fruitfulness in doing God's work on the earth (Psalm 80.8; Isaiah 5.1–7; Ezekiel 19.10–14). In the Passover meal, the fruit of the vine symbolized God's goodness to his people.

15.1ff Christ is the vine, and God is the vinegrower who cares for the branches to make them fruitful. The branches are all who claim to be followers of Christ. The fruitful branches are true believers who by their living union with Christ produce much fruit. But those who become unproductive – those who turn back from following Christ after making a superficial commitment – will be separated from the vine. Unproductive followers are as good as dead and will be cut off and cast aside.

15.2, 3 Jesus makes a distinction between two kinds of pruning: (1) separating and (2) cutting back branches. Fruitful branches are cut back to promote growth. In other words, God must sometimes discipline us to strengthen our character and faith. But branches that don't bear fruit are cut off at the trunk. Not only are they worthless, but they often infect the rest of the tree. Those who won't bear fruit for God or who try to block the efforts of God's followers will be cut off from the divine flow of life.

15.5 Fruit is not limited to soul-winning. In this chapter, answered prayer, joy, and love are mentioned as fruit (15.7, 11, 12). Galatians 5.22–24 and 2 Peter 1.5–8 describe additional fruit: qualities of the Christian character.

15.5, 6 Abiding in Christ means (1) believing he is God's Son (1 John 4.15), (2) receiving him as Savior and Lord (John 1.12), (3) doing what God says (1 John 3.24), (4) continuing in faith (1 John 2.24), and (5) relating to the community of believers, Christ's body (John 15.12).

15.5–8 Many people try to do good, be honest, and do what is right. But Jesus says the only way to live a truly good life is to stay close to him, like a branch attached to the vine. Apart from him our efforts are unfruitful. Are you receiving the nourishment and life offered by Christ, the vine?

15.8 When a vine bears "much fruit," God is glorified, because daily he sent the sunshine and rain to make the crops grow, and constantly he nurtured each tiny plant and prepared it to blossom. What a moment of glory for the Lord of the harvest when the harvest is brought into the barns, safe and ready for use! He made it all happen! This farming analogy shows how God is glorified when people come into a right relationship with him and begin to "bear much fruit" in their lives.

15.11 When things are going well, we feel elated. When hardships come, we may sink into depression. But true joy transcends these waves of circumstance. Joy comes from a consistent relationship with Jesus Christ. When our lives are intertwined with his, he will help us walk through adversity without sinking into debilitating lows, and manage prosperity without moving into deceptive highs. The joy of living with Jesus Christ daily keeps us levelheaded, no matter how high or low our circumstances.

15.12, 13 We are to love one another as Jesus loved us, and he loved us enough to give his life for us. We may not have to die for someone, but there are other ways to practice sacrificial love: listening, helping, encouraging, giving. Think of someone who needs this kind of love today. Give all the love you can, and then try to give a little more.

15.15 Because Jesus Christ is Lord and Master, he should call us slaves, but instead he calls us friends. How comforting and reassuring to be chosen as his friends. Because he is Lord and Master, our obedience should be unqualified and blind. But Jesus asks us to obey him because we love him.

15.16 Jesus made the first choice – to love and to die for us, to offer us eternal life. We make the next choice – to accept or reject his offer. Without *his* choice, we would have no choice.

15.17 Christians will get plenty of hatred from the world; we need love and support from one another. Do you allow small problems to get in the way of loving other believers? Jesus commands that you love them, and he will give you the strength to do it.

you belonged to the world,[p] the world would love you as its own. Because you do
not belong to the world, but I have chosen you out of the world—therefore the
world hates you. 20 Remember the word that I said to you, 'Servants[q] are not
greater than their master.' If they persecuted me, they will persecute you; if they
kept my word, they will keep yours also. 21 But they will do all these things to you
on account of my name, because they do not know him who sent me. 22 If I had not
come and spoken to them, they would not have sin; but now they have no excuse
for their sin. 23 Whoever hates me hates my Father also. 24 If I had not done among
them the works that no one else did, they would not have sin. But now they have
seen and hated both me and my Father. 25 It was to fulfill the word that is written in
their law, 'They hated me without a cause.'
26 "When the Advocate[r] comes, whom I will send to you from the Father, the
Spirit of truth who comes from the Father, he will testify on my behalf. 27 You also
are to testify because you have been with me from the beginning.
16 "I have said these things to you to keep you from stumbling. 2 They will put
you out of the synagogues. Indeed, an hour is coming when those who kill
you will think that by doing so they are offering worship to God. 3 And they will do
this because they have not known the Father or me. 4 But I have said these things to
you so that when their hour comes you may remember that I told you about them.

Jesus teaches about the Holy Spirit
(217)

"I did not say these things to you from the beginning, because I was with you.
5 But now I am going to him who sent me; yet none of you asks me, 'Where are you
going?' 6 But because I have said these things to you, sorrow has filled your hearts.
7 Nevertheless I tell you the truth: it is to your advantage that I go away, for if I do
not go away, the Advocate[r] will not come to you; but if I go, I will send him to
you. 8 And when he comes, he will prove the world wrong about[s] sin and righteousness and judgment: 9 about sin, because they do not believe in me; 10 about
righteousness, because I am going to the Father and you will see me no longer;
11 about judgment, because the ruler of this world has been condemned.
12 "I still have many things to say to you, but you cannot bear them now.
13 When the Spirit of truth comes, he will guide you into all the truth; for he will not

15.19 Mt 10.22; 24.9 Jn 17.14 1 Jn 4.5,6
15.21 Jn 17.25 1 Pet 4.14
15.22 Jn 9.41
15.24 Jn 5.36-38 10.37,38
15.25 Ps 35.19; 69.4
15.26 Acts 2.33
15.27 Jn 19.35; 21.24 1 Jn 1.1,2
16.2 Acts 8.1; 9.1 26.9 Rev 6.9
16.3 Acts 3.17
16.4 Jn 13.19; 14.29
16.5 Jn 7.33; 13.36
16.7 Jn 14.26
16.8 1 Pet 1.2
16.9 Rom 1.18-23 3.9,10; 14.23
16.10 Acts 3.14; 7.52
16.11 Lk 10.18 Jn 12.31 Heb 2.14

p Gk *were of the world* q Gk *Slaves* r Or *Helper* s Or *convict the world of*

15.26 Once again Jesus offers hope. The Holy Spirit gives strength to endure the unreasonable hatred and evil in our world and the hostility many have toward Christ.

15.26 Jesus uses two names for the Holy Spirit—*Advocate* and *Spirit of truth.* The word *Advocate* conveys the helping, encouraging, and strengthening work of the Spirit. *Spirit of truth* points to the teaching, illuminating, and reminding work of the Spirit. The Holy Spirit ministers to both the head and the heart. "Comes from the Father" means the Spirit goes out from the Father. This is no angelic being but the divine person himself.

16.1–16 In his last moments with his disciples, Jesus (1) warned them about further persecution, (2) told them where, when, and why he was going, and (3) assured them they would not be left alone, but that the Spirit would come. He knew what lay ahead, and he did not want their faith shaken or destroyed. God wants you to know you are not alone. You have the Holy Spirit to comfort you, teach you truth, and help you.

16.2 A vivid fulfillment of this prediction happened when Stephen was expelled from the synagogue and stoned to death (Acts 7.57–60). Saul (who later became Paul), under the authority of the high priest, went through the land persecuting Christians (Acts 9.1, 2).

16.5 Although the disciples had asked Jesus about his death (13.36; 14.5), they had never wondered about its meaning. They were mostly concerned about themselves. If Jesus went, what would become of them?

16.7 Unless Jesus did what he came to do, there would be no gospel. If he did not die, he could not remove our sins; he could not rise again and defeat death. If he did not go back to the Father, the Holy Spirit would not come. Christ's presence on earth was limited to one place at a time. His leaving meant he could be present to the whole world through the Holy Spirit.

16.8–11 Three important tasks of the Holy Spirit are (1) convincing the world of its sin and calling it to repentance, (2) showing the standard of God's righteousness to anyone who believes because Christ would no longer be physically present on earth, and (3) demonstrating Christ's judgment over Satan.

16.9 According to Jesus, unbelief in him is *sin.*

16.10, 11 Christ's death on the cross made a personal relationship with God available to us. When we confess our sin, God declares us righteous and delivers us from judgment for our sins.

16.13 The truth into which the Holy Spirit guides us is the truth about Christ. He also helps us through patient practice to discern right from wrong.

16.13 Jesus said the Holy Spirit would show them "things that are to come"—the nature of their mission, the opposition they would face, and the final outcome of their efforts. They didn't fully understand these promises until the Holy Spirit came after Jesus' death and resurrection. Then the Holy Spirit revealed truths to the disci-

16.14 Phil 1.19
16.15 Mt 11.27; Jn 17.10; Col 2.9,10
16.16 Jn 14.3,19-25
16.20 Mk 16.10; Lk 23.27; Jn 20.19,20
16.21 Isa 26.16-19; Acts 13.33; Col 1.18
16.22 Jn 20.19,20
16.23 Jn 14.20; 15.16; 16.26
16.24 Jn 15.11
16.25 Jn 10.6; 16.29
16.27 Jn 8.42; 14.21; 17.8
16.28 Jn 1.14; 6.32,46; 8.42; 13.1,3; 17.11,13
16.32 Zech 13.7; Mt 26.31; Jn 8.29
16.33 Jn 14.27; Acts 14.22; Rom 5.1; 8.37; 1 Cor 15.27; 2 Cor 2.14; Eph 2.14; Col 1.20; Rev 3.19

speak on his own, but will speak whatever he hears, and he will declare to you the
things that are to come. 14 He will glorify me, because he will take what is mine and
declare it to you. 15 All that the Father has is mine. For this reason I said that he will
take what is mine and declare it to you.

Jesus teaches about using his name in prayer
(218)

16 "A little while, and you will no longer see me, and again a little while, and
you will see me." 17 Then some of his disciples said to one another, "What does he
mean by saying to us, 'A little while, and you will no longer see me, and again a
little while, and you will see me'; and 'Because I am going to the Father'?" 18 They
said, "What does he mean by this 'a little while'? We do not know what he is
talking about." 19 Jesus knew that they wanted to ask him, so he said to them, "Are
you discussing among yourselves what I meant when I said, 'A little while, and you
will no longer see me, and again a little while, and you will see me'? 20 Very truly,
I tell you, you will weep and mourn, but the world will rejoice; you will have pain,
but your pain will turn into joy. 21 When a woman is in labor, she has pain, because
her hour has come. But when her child is born, she no longer remembers the anguish because of the joy of having brought a human being into the world. 22 So you
have pain now; but I will see you again, and your hearts will rejoice, and no one
will take your joy from you. 23 On that day you will ask nothing of me.[t] Very truly,
I tell you, if you ask anything of the Father in my name, he will give it to you.[u]
24 Until now you have not asked for anything in my name. Ask and you will receive, so that your joy may be complete.

25 "I have said these things to you in figures of speech. The hour is coming
when I will no longer speak to you in figures, but will tell you plainly of the Father.
26 On that day you will ask in my name. I do not say to you that I will ask the Father
on your behalf; 27 for the Father himself loves you, because you have loved me and
have believed that I came from God.[v] 28 I came from the Father and have come into
the world; again, I am leaving the world and am going to the Father."

29 His disciples said, "Yes, now you are speaking plainly, not in any figure of
speech! 30 Now we know that you know all things, and do not need to have anyone
question you; by this we believe that you came from God." 31 Jesus answered them,
"Do you now believe? 32 The hour is coming, indeed it has come, when you will be
scattered, each one to his home, and you will leave me alone. Yet I am not alone
because the Father is with me. 33 I have said this to you, so that in me you may have
peace. In the world you face persecution. But take courage; I have conquered the
world!"

[t] Or *will ask me no question* [u] Other ancient authorities read *Father, he will give it to you in my name* [v] Other ancient authorities read *the Father*

---

ples that they wrote down in the books that now form the New Testament.

16.16 Jesus was referring to his death, now only a few hours away, and his resurrection three days later.

16.20 What a contrast between the disciples and the world! The world rejoiced as the disciples wept, but they would see him again (in three days) and rejoice. The world's values are often the opposite of God's values. This can cause Christians to feel like misfits. But even if life is difficult now, one day we will rejoice. Keep your eye on the future and on God's promises!

16.23–27 Jesus is talking about a new relationship between the believer and God. Previously, people approached God through priests. After Jesus' resurrection, any believer could approach God directly. A new day has dawned, and now all believers are priests, talking with God personally and directly (see Hebrews 10.19–23). We approach God, not because of our own merit, but because Jesus, our great High Priest, has made us acceptable to God.

16.30 The disciples believed Jesus' words because they were convinced he knew everything. But their belief was only a first step toward the great faith they would receive when the Holy Spirit came to indwell them.

16.31–33 As Christians, we should expect continuing tension with an unbelieving world that is "out of sync" with Christ, his gospel, and his people. At the same time, we can expect our relationship with Christ to produce peace and comfort, because we are "in sync" with him.

16.32 The disciples scattered after Jesus was arrested (see Mark 14.50).

16.33 Jesus sums up all he has told them this night, tying together themes from 14.27–29; 16.1–4; and 16.9–11. With these words he tells his disciples to take courage. In spite of the inevitable struggles they will face, they are not alone. Jesus does not abandon us to our struggles either. If we remember that the ultimate victory has already been won, we can claim the peace of Christ in the most troublesome times.

Jesus prays for himself
(219)

17 After Jesus had spoken these words, he looked up to heaven and said, "Father, the hour has come; glorify your Son so that the Son may glorify you,
2 since you have given him authority over all people,[w] to give eternal life to all
whom you have given him. 3 And this is eternal life, that they may know you, the
only true God, and Jesus Christ whom you have sent. 4 I glorified you on earth by
finishing the work that you gave me to do. 5 So now, Father, glorify me in your own
presence with the glory that I had in your presence before the world existed.

Jesus prays for his disciples
(220)

6 "I have made your name known to those whom you gave me from the world.
They were yours, and you gave them to me, and they have kept your word. 7 Now
they know that everything you have given me is from you; 8 for the words that you
gave to me I have given to them, and they have received them and know in truth
that I came from you; and they have believed that you sent me. 9 I am asking on
their behalf; I am not asking on behalf of the world, but on behalf of those whom
you gave me, because they are yours. 10 All mine are yours, and yours are mine;
and I have been glorified in them. 11 And now I am no longer in the world, but they
are in the world, and I am coming to you. Holy Father, protect them in your name
that[x] you have given me, so that they may be one, as we are one. 12 While I was
with them, I protected them in your name that[x] you have given me. I guarded
them, and not one of them was lost except the one destined to be lost,[y] so that the
scripture might be fulfilled. 13 But now I am coming to you, and I speak these things
in the world so that they may have my joy made complete in themselves.[z] 14 I have
given them your word, and the world has hated them because they do not belong to
the world, just as I do not belong to the world. 15 I am not asking you to take them
out of the world, but I ask you to protect them from the evil one.[a] 16 They do not
belong to the world, just as I do not belong to the world. 17 Sanctify them in the
truth; your word is truth. 18 As you have sent me into the world, so I have sent them

17.2 Jn 3.35; 6.37 10.28
17.3 Phil 3.8,10 1 Jn 5.20
17.5 Jn 1.1,2; 17.24 Phil 2.6
17.6 Jn 17.26
17.9 1 Jn 5.19
17.10 Rom 8.29,30 Eph 3.21
17.11 Jn 10.30; 17.21 Rom 12.4,5 Gal 3.28
17.12 Jn 6.39; 10.28 Acts 1.20 Heb 2.13 1 Jn 2.19
17.13 Jn 7.33; 15.11
17.14 Jn 15.19 1 Jn 3.13
17.15 1 Jn 5.18
17.17 Jn 15.3
17.18 Jn 20.21

[w] Gk *flesh* [x] Other ancient authorities read *protected in your name those whom* [y] Gk *except the son of destruction*
[z] Or *among themselves* [a] Or *from evil*

17.1ff This entire chapter is Jesus' prayer. From it, we learn that the world is a tremendous battleground where the forces under Satan's power and those under God's authority are at war. Satan and his forces are motivated by bitter hatred for Christ and his forces. Jesus prayed for his disciples, including those of us who follow him today. He prayed that God would keep his chosen believers safe from Satan's power, making them pure and holy, uniting them through his truth.

17.3 How do we receive eternal life? Jesus tells us clearly here—by knowing God the Father himself through his Son, Jesus Christ. Eternal life requires a faith commitment to Christ. When we admit our sin, turn away from it, and turn to Christ, his love lives in us by the Holy Spirit.

17.5 Before Jesus came to earth, he was one with God. Now that his mission on earth was almost finished, he was asking his Father to restore him to his original place of honor and authority. Jesus' resurrection and ascension—and Stephen's dying exclamation (Acts 7.56)—attest that Jesus did return to his exalted position at the right hand of God.

17.10 What did Jesus mean when he said he is glorified in his followers? God's glory is the revelation of his character and presence. The lives of Jesus' disciples reveal his character, and he is present to the world through them. Does your life reveal Jesus' character and presence?

17.11 Jesus is asking that the disciples be united in harmony and love as the Father, Son, and Holy Spirit are united—the strongest of all unions. (See the note on 17.21–23.)

17.12 Judas was the "one destined to be lost" who perished because he betrayed Jesus (see Psalm 41.9).

17.13 Joy is a common theme in Christ's teachings—he wants us to be joyful (see 15.11; 16.24, 33). The key to immeasurable joy is living in close contact with him, the source of all joy. When we do, we will experience God's special care and protection and see the victory God brings even when defeat seems certain.

17.14 The world hates Christians because Christians' values are different. Because Christ's followers don't cooperate with the world by joining in their sin, they are living accusations against the world's immorality. The world follows Satan's agenda, and Satan is the avowed enemy of Jesus and his people.

17.17 A follower of Christ becomes sanctified (set apart for sacred use, cleansed and made holy) through believing and obeying God's Word (Hebrews 4.12). He or she has already accepted forgiveness through Christ's sacrificial death (Hebrews 7.26, 27). But daily application of God's Word has a purifying effect on our minds and hearts. It points out sin, motivates us to confess, renews our relationship with Christ, and guides us back to the right path.

17.18 Jesus didn't ask God to take believers *out* of the world but instead to use them *in* the world. Because Jesus sends us into the world, we should not try to escape or avoid all relationships with non-Christians. We are called to be salt and light (Matthew 5.13–16), and we are to do the work God sent us to do.

17.19 1 Cor 1.30 into the world. 19 And for their sakes I sanctify myself, so that they also may be
Heb 2.11 sanctified in truth.

Jesus prays for future believers
(221)

17.20 Acts 2.40,41 20 "I ask not only on behalf of these, but also on behalf of those who will be-
17.21 lieve in me through their word, 21 that they may all be one. As you, Father, are in
Jn 10.30,38 me and I am in you, may they also be in us,[b] so that the world may believe that you
14.11; 17.11 have sent me. 22 The glory that you have given me I have given them, so that they
17.22 2 Cor 4.6 may be one, as we are one, 23 I in them and you in me, that they may become
Eph 3.16,21 completely one, so that the world may know that you have sent me and have loved
17.23 Jn 10.38 them even as you have loved me. 24 Father, I desire that those also, whom you have
16.27; 17.11 given me, may be with me where I am, to see my glory, which you have given me
17.24 Jn 1.14; 12.26 because you loved me before the foundation of the world.
25 "Righteous Father, the world does not know you, but I know you; and these
17.26 know that you have sent me. 26 I made your name known to them, and I will make
Jn 15.9 it known, so that the love with which you have loved me may be in them, and I in
them."

2. Jesus completes his mission

Jesus is betrayed and arrested
(224/Matthew 26.47–56; Mark 14.43–52; Luke 22.47–53)

18.1 2 Sam 15.23 **18** After Jesus had spoken these words, he went out with his disciples across the
2 Kgs 23.4,6,12 Kidron valley to a place where there was a garden, which he and his disci-
2 Chron 15.16 29.16; 30.14 ples entered. 2 Now Judas, who betrayed him, also knew the place, because Jesus
often met there with his disciples. 3 So Judas brought a detachment of soldiers
together with police from the chief priests and the Pharisees, and they came there

[b] Other ancient authorities read *be one in us*

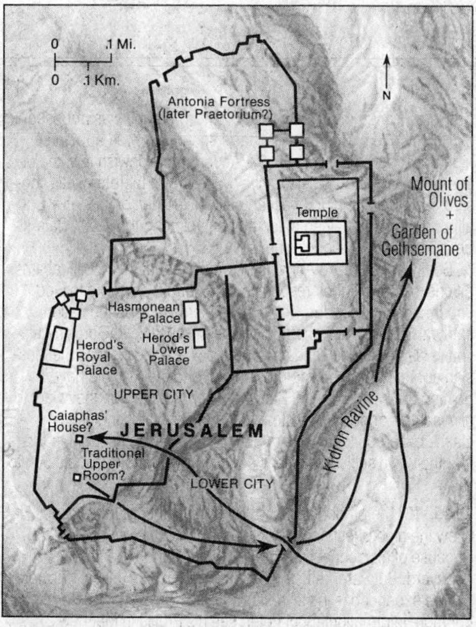

BETRAYAL IN THE GARDEN After eating the Passover meal in the upper room, Jesus and his disciples went to Gethsemane, where Judas led the temple police to arrest Jesus. Jesus was then taken to Caiaphas's house for his first of many trials.

17.20 Jesus prayed for all who would follow him, including you and others you know. He prayed for oneness (17.11), protection from evil (17.15), and sanctity (holiness) (17.17). Knowing that Jesus prayed for us should give us confidence as we work for his kingdom.

17.21–23 Jesus' great desire for his disciples was that they become one. He wanted them unified as a powerful witness to the reality of God's love. How are you helping to unify the body of Christ, the church? You can pray for other Christians, avoid gossip, build others up, work together in humility, give your time and money, lift up Christ, and refuse to get sidetracked, arguing over divisive matters.

17.21–23 Jesus prayed for unity among the believers based on the believers' oneness with him and the Father. Christians can know unity among themselves if they are living in union with God. For example, each branch living in union with the vine is united with all other branches doing the same.

18.1 This garden was the garden of Gethsemane, a place the disciples often used as a retreat from the crowds.

18.3 The police were temple police; they were Jews given authority by the religious leaders to make arrests for minor infractions. The soldiers may have been a small contingent of Roman soldiers who did not participate in the arrest but accompanied the police to make sure matters didn't get out of control.

with lanterns and torches and weapons. 4Then Jesus, knowing all that was to happen to him, came forward and asked them, "Whom are you looking for?" 5They
answered, "Jesus of Nazareth."[c] Jesus replied, "I am he."[d] Judas, who betrayed
him, was standing with them. 6When Jesus[e] said to them, "I am he,"[d] they stepped back and fell to the ground. 7Again he asked them, "Whom are you looking
for?" And they said, "Jesus of Nazareth."[c] 8Jesus answered, "I told you that I am
he.[d] So if you are looking for me, let these men go." 9This was to fulfill the word 18.9 Jn 17.12
that he had spoken, "I did not lose a single one of those whom you gave me." 18.10
10Then Simon Peter, who had a sword, drew it, struck the high priest's slave, and Mt 26.51 Mk 14.47
cut off his right ear. The slave's name was Malchus. 11Jesus said to Peter, "Put Lk 22.49,50
your sword back into its sheath. Am I not to drink the cup that the Father has given 18.11 Mt 20.22
me?" 26.39,42

Annas questions Jesus
(225)

12 So the soldiers, their officer, and the Jewish police arrested Jesus and bound 18.12
him. 13First they took him to Annas, who was the father-in-law of Caiaphas, the Mt 26.57 18.13
high priest that year. 14Caiaphas was the one who had advised the Jews that it was Lk 3.1,2
better to have one person die for the people. Acts 4.6 18.14
15 Simon Peter and another disciple followed Jesus. Since that disciple was Jn 11.50
known to the high priest, he went with Jesus into the courtyard of the high priest, 18.15 Mt 26.58
16but Peter was standing outside at the gate. So the other disciple, who was known Lk 22.54
to the high priest, went out, spoke to the woman who guarded the gate, and brought 18.16 Mt 26.69
Peter in. 17The woman said to Peter, "You are not also one of this man's disciples, 18.18
are you?" He said, "I am not." 18Now the slaves and the police had made a charcoal Mk 14.54
fire because it was cold, and they were standing around it and warming themselves. 18.19 Mt 26.59-68
Peter also was standing with them and warming himself. Mk 14.55-65 Lk 22.63-71
19 Then the high priest questioned Jesus about his disciples and about his teach- 18.20
ing. 20Jesus answered, "I have spoken openly to the world; I have always taught in Mt 26.55 Lk 4.15
synagogues and in the temple, where all the Jews come together. I have said noth- Jn 7.14,26,28

[c] Gk *the Nazorean* [d] Gk *I am* [e] Gk *he*

18.4, 5 John does not record Judas's kiss of greeting (Matthew 26.49; Mark 14.45; Luke 22.47, 48); but his kiss marked a turning point for the disciples because with Jesus' arrest, each one's life would be radically different. For the first time, Judas openly betrayed Jesus in front of the other disciples. For the first time, Jesus' loyal disciples ran away from him (Matthew 26.56). The band of disciples would undergo severe testing before they were transformed from uncertain followers to dynamic leaders.

18.6 The men may have been startled by Jesus' statement or by the words "I am," a declaration of his divinity (Exodus 3.14). Or perhaps they were overcome by his obvious power and authority.

18.10, 11 Trying to protect Jesus, Peter pulled a sword and wounded the high priest's servant. But Jesus told him to put away his sword and allow God's plan to unfold. At times it is tempting to take matters into our own hands, to force the issue. Most often such moves lead to sin. Instead we must trust God to work out his plan. Think of it – if Peter had had his way, Jesus would not have gone to the cross, and God's plan of redemption would have been halted.

18.11 The cup means the suffering, isolation, and death that Jesus would have to endure in order to atone for the sins of the world.

18.12, 13 Jesus was immediately taken to the high priest's residence, even though this was the middle of the night. The religious leaders were in a hurry – they wanted to complete the execution before the sabbath and get on with the Passover celebration. This residence was a palace whose outer walls enclosed a courtyard where servants and soldiers warmed themselves around a fire.

18.13 Both Annas and Caiaphas are called high priests. Annas was Israel's high priest from A.D. 6 to 15, when he was deposed by Roman rulers. Caiaphas, Annas's son-in-law, was appointed high priest from A.D. 18 to 36/37. According to Jewish law, the office of high priest was held for life. Many Jews, therefore, still considered Annas the high priest and still called him by that title. But although Annas retained much authority among the Jews, Caiaphas made the final decisions.

Both Caiaphas and Annas cared more about their political ambitions than about their responsibility to lead the people to God. Though religious leaders, they had become evil. As the nation's spiritual leaders, they should have been sensitive to God's revelation in his Word. They should have known that Jesus was the Messiah about whom the scriptures spoke, and they should have pointed the people to him. But when men pursue evil, they want to eliminate all opposition. Instead of honestly evaluating Jesus' claims based on their knowledge of Scripture, they sought to further their own selfish ambitions and were willing to kill God's Son to do it.

18.15, 16 The other disciple is John, the author of this Gospel. He knew the high priest and identified himself to the girl at the gate. Because of his connections, he got himself and Peter into the courtyard. But Peter refused to identify himself as Jesus' follower. Peter's experiences in the next few hours would change his life. For more information about Peter, see his Profile in Matthew 27.

18.19ff During the night, Jesus had two pre-trial hearings before he was taken before the entire Jewish council (18.24 mentions the second pre-trial hearing). The religious leaders knew they had no grounds for charging him, so they tried to build evidence against him by using false witnesses.

18.22 Isa 50.6 Mic 5.1 Jn 19.3 — ing in secret. 21 Why do you ask me? Ask those who heard what I said to them; they
know what I said." 22 When he had said this, one of the police standing nearby
struck Jesus on the face, saying, "Is that how you answer the high priest?" 23 Jesus
18.23 Mt 5.39 Acts 23.2 Heb 12.3 1 Pet 2.21-23 — answered, "If I have spoken wrongly, testify to the wrong. But if I have spoken
rightly, why do you strike me?" 24 Then Annas sent him bound to Caiaphas the high
priest.

Peter denies knowing Jesus
(227/Matthew 26.69–75; Mark 14.66–72; Luke 22.54–65)

18.25 Mt 26.73-75 — 25 Now Simon Peter was standing and warming himself. They asked him,
"You are not also one of his disciples, are you?" He denied it and said, "I am not."

THE SIX STAGES OF JESUS' TRIAL
Although Jesus' trial lasted less than 18 hours, he was taken to six different hearings.

BEFORE JEWISH AUTHORITIES	Preliminary Hearing before Annas (John 18.12–24)	Because the office of high priest was for life, Annas was still the "official" high priest in the eyes of the Jews, even though the Romans had appointed another. Thus Annas still carried much weight among the Jewish council.
	Hearing before Caiaphas (Matthew 26.57–68)	Like the hearing before Annas, this hearing was conducted at night in secrecy. It was full of illegalities that made a mockery of justice (see the chart in Matthew 28).
	Trial before the Council (Matthew 27.1, 2)	Just after daybreak, 70 members of the Jewish council met to rubber-stamp their approval of the previous hearings to make them appear legal. The purpose of this trial was not to determine justice, but to justify their own preconceptions of Jesus' guilt.
BEFORE ROMAN AUTHORITIES	First Hearing before Pilate (Luke 23.1–5)	The religious leaders had condemned Jesus to death on religious grounds, but only the Roman government could grant the death penalty. Thus, they took Jesus to Pilate, the Roman governor, and accused him of treason and rebellion, crimes for which the Roman government gave the death penalty. Pilate saw at once that Jesus was innocent, but he was afraid about the uproar being caused by the religious leaders.
	Hearing before Herod (Luke 23.6–12)	Since Jesus' home was in the region of Galilee, Pilate sent Jesus to Herod Agrippa, the ruler of Galilee, who was in Jerusalem for the Passover celebration. Herod was eager to see Jesus do a miracle, but when Jesus remained silent, Herod wanted nothing to do with him and sent him back to Pilate.
	Last Hearing before Pilate (Luke 23.13–25)	Pilate didn't like the religious leaders. He wasn't interested in condemning Jesus because he knew Jesus was innocent. However, he knew that another uprising in his district might cost him his job. First he tried to compromise with the religious leaders by having Jesus beaten, an illegal action in itself. But finally he gave in and handed Jesus over to be executed. His self-interest was stronger than his sense of justice.

18.22–27 We can easily get angry at the Jewish council for their injustice in condemning Jesus, but we must remember that Peter and the rest of the disciples also contributed to Jesus' pain by deserting and denying him (Matthew 26.56). We are all like the disciples, because all of us have been guilty of denying Christ as Lord in vital areas of our lives or of keeping secret our identity as believers in times of pressure. Don't excuse yourself by pointing at others whose sins seem worse than yours. Instead, come to Jesus for forgiveness and healing.

18.25 The other three Gospels say that Peter's three denials happened outside Caiaphas's palace. John places the first denial outside Annas's home, the other two outside Caiaphas's home. This was, no doubt, the same courtyard. The high priest's residence was large, and Annas and Caiaphas lived near each other.

18.25–27 Imagine standing outside while Jesus, your Lord and Master, is questioned. Imagine watching this man, whom you have come to believe is the long-awaited Messiah, being abused and beaten. Naturally Peter was confused and afraid. It is a serious sin to deny Christ, but Jesus forgave Peter (21.15–17). No sin is too great for Jesus to forgive if you turn from it and ask his pardon.

26 One of the slaves of the high priest, a relative of the man whose ear Peter had cut
off, asked, "Did I not see you in the garden with him?" 27 Again Peter denied it, and 18.27
at that moment the cock crowed. Jn 13.38

Jesus stands trial before Pilate

(230/Matthew 27.11–14; Mark 15.2–5; Luke 23.1–5)

28 Then they took Jesus from Caiaphas to Pilate's headquarters.[f] It was early 18.28
in the morning. They themselves did not enter the headquarters,[f] so as to avoid Mt 27.2 Mk 15.1
ritual defilement and to be able to eat the Passover. 29 So Pilate went out to them and Lk 23.1 Jn 11.55
said, "What accusation do you bring against this man?" 30 They answered, "If this Acts 11.3
man were not a criminal, we would not have handed him over to you." 31 Pilate said
to them, "Take him yourselves and judge him according to your law." The Jews
replied, "We are not permitted to put anyone to death." 32 (This was to fulfill what 18.32 Mt 20.19
Jesus had said when he indicated the kind of death he was to die.) Jn 12.32,33

33 Then Pilate entered the headquarters[f] again, summoned Jesus, and asked 18.33
him, "Are you the King of the Jews?" 34 Jesus answered, "Do you ask this on your Lk 23.3 Jn 19.12
own, or did others tell you about me?" 35 Pilate replied, "I am not a Jew, am I? Your 18.36
own nation and the chief priests have handed you over to me. What have you Isa 9.6 Dan 2.44; 7.14
done?" 36 Jesus answered, "My kingdom is not from this world. If my kingdom Mt 26.53 Lk 17.20,21
were from this world, my followers would be fighting to keep me from being Jn 6.15

[f] Gk *the praetorium*

18.27 This fulfilled Jesus' words to Peter after he promised he would never deny him (13.38).

18.28 By Jewish law, entering the house of a Gentile would cause a Jewish person to be ceremonially defiled. As a result, he could not take part in worship at the temple or celebrate the feasts until he was restored to a state of "cleanness." Afraid of being defiled, these men stayed outside the house where they had taken Jesus for trial. They kept up the ceremonial requirements of their religion while harboring murder and treachery in their hearts.

18.29 This Roman governor, Pilate, was in charge of Judea (the region where Jerusalem was located) from A.D. 26 to 36. Pilate was unpopular with the Jews because he had raided the temple treasuries for money to build an aqueduct. He did not like the Jews, but when Jesus, the King of the Jews, stood before him, Pilate found him innocent.

18.30 Pilate knew what was going on; he knew that the religious leaders hated Jesus, and he did not want to act as their executioner. They could not sentence him to death themselves—permission had to come from a Roman leader. But Pilate initially refused to sentence Jesus without sufficient evidence. Jesus' life became a pawn in a political power struggle.

18.31ff Pilate made four attempts to deal with Jesus: (1) he tried to put the responsibility on someone else (18.31); (2) he tried to find a way of escape so he could release Jesus (18.39); (3) he tried to compromise with the people—beating Jesus rather than handing him over to die (19.1–3); and (4) he tried a direct appeal to the sympathy of the accusers (19.14, 15). Everyone has to decide what to do with Jesus. Pilate tried to let everyone else decide for him—and in the end, he lost.

18.32 This prediction is recorded in Matthew 20.19. Crucifixion was a common method of execution for criminals who were not Roman citizens.

18.33 If Pilate was asking as the Roman governor, he would be inquiring whether Jesus was setting up a rebel government. But the Jews were using the word *king* to mean their religious ruler, the Messiah. Israel was a captive nation, under the authority of the Roman Empire. A rival king might have threatened Rome; a Messiah could have been a purely religious leader.

18.36, 37 Pilate asked Jesus a straightforward question and Jesus answered clearly. He is a king, but one whose kingdom is not of this world. There seems to have been no question in Pilate's mind that Jesus spoke the truth and was innocent of any crime. It also seems apparent that while recognizing the truth, Pilate chose to reject it. It is a tragedy when we fail to recognize the truth. It is a greater tragedy when we recognize the truth but fail to heed it.

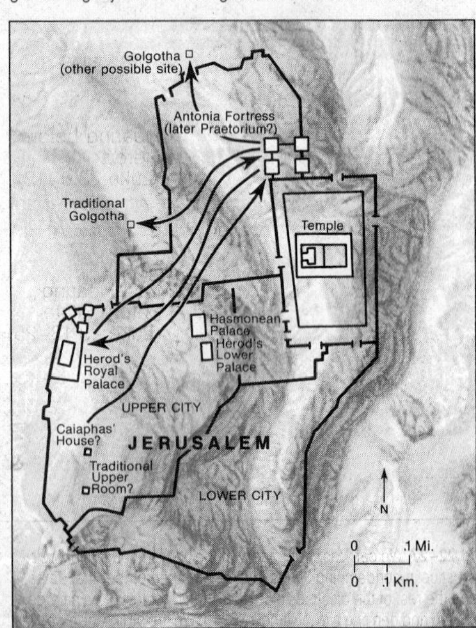

JESUS' TRIAL AND CRUCIFIXION Jesus was taken from trial before the Jewish council to trial before the Roman procurator, Pilate, in the Antonia Fortress. Pilate sent him to Herod (Luke 23.5–12), but Herod just returned Jesus to Pilate. Responding to threats from the mob, Pilate finally turned Jesus over to be crucified.

handed over to the Jews. But as it is, my kingdom is not from here." 37 Pilate asked
him, "So you are a king?" Jesus answered, "You say that I am a king. For this I was
born, and for this I came into the world, to testify to the truth. Everyone who belongs to the truth listens to my voice." 38 Pilate asked him, "What is truth?"

Pilate hands Jesus over to be crucified
(232/Matthew 27.15–26; Mark 15.6–15; Luke 23.13–25)

After he had said this, he went out to the Jews again and told them, "I find no
case against him. 39 But you have a custom that I release someone for you at the
Passover. Do you want me to release for you the King of the Jews?" 40 They
shouted in reply, "Not this man, but Barabbas!" Now Barabbas was a bandit.

19 Then Pilate took Jesus and had him flogged. 2 And the soldiers wove a crown
of thorns and put it on his head, and they dressed him in a purple robe. 3 They
kept coming up to him, saying, "Hail, King of the Jews!" and striking him on the
face. 4 Pilate went out again and said to them, "Look, I am bringing him out to you
to let you know that I find no case against him." 5 So Jesus came out, wearing the
crown of thorns and the purple robe. Pilate said to them, "Here is the man!" 6 When
the chief priests and the police saw him, they shouted, "Crucify him! Crucify him!"
Pilate said to them, "Take him yourselves and crucify him; I find no case against
him." 7 The Jews answered him, "We have a law, and according to that law he
ought to die because he has claimed to be the Son of God."

8 Now when Pilate heard this, he was more afraid than ever. 9 He entered his
headquarters[g] again and asked Jesus, "Where are you from?" But Jesus gave him
no answer. 10 Pilate therefore said to him, "Do you refuse to speak to me? Do you
not know that I have power to release you, and power to crucify you?" 11 Jesus
answered him, "You would have no power over me unless it had been given you
from above; therefore the one who handed me over to you is guilty of a greater sin."
12 From then on Pilate tried to release him, but the Jews cried out, "If you release

18.37 Jn 8.47; 1 Pet 1.23; 1 Jn 3.19; 4.6; Rev 1.5
18.39 Mt 27.15-18, 20-23; Mk 15.6-15
18.40 Lk 23.17-19
19.1 Isa 50.6; Mt 27.26-30; Mk 15.15-19; Lk 18.32,33
19.3 Jn 18.22
19.4 Jn 18.38; 2 Cor 5.21
19.6 Acts 3.13
19.7 Lev 24.15,16; Mt 26.63-66
19.9 Isa 53.7; Mt 27.12,14; Acts 8.32
19.11 Acts 2.23; 3.13; Rom 13.1

g Gk *the praetorium*

18.38 Pilate was cynical; he thought all truth was relative. To many government officials, truth was whatever the majority of people agreed with or whatever helped their own personal power and political advancement. When there is no basis for truth, there is no basis for moral right and wrong. Justice becomes whatever works or helps those in power. In Jesus and his Word we have a standard for truth and for our moral behavior.

18.40 Barabbas was a rebel against Rome and, although he had committed murder, was probably a hero among the Jews. The Jews hated being governed by Rome and paying taxes to the despised government. Barabbas, who had led a rebellion and failed, was released instead of Jesus, the only one who could truly help Israel. For more on Barabbas, see the note on Luke 23.17–19.

19.1ff To grasp the full picture of Jesus' crucifixion, read John's perspective along with the other three accounts in Matthew 27, Mark 15, and Luke 23. Each writer adds meaningful details, but each has the same message – Jesus died on the cross, in fulfillment of Old Testament prophecy, so that we could be saved from our sins and given eternal life.

19.1–3 This flogging could have killed Jesus. The usual procedure was to bare the upper half of the victim's body and tie his hands to a pillar before whipping him with a three-pronged whip. The number of lashes was determined by the severity of the crime; up to 40 were permitted under Jewish law (Deuteronomy 25.3). After being flogged, Jesus also endured other agonies recorded here and in the other Gospels.

19.2–5 The soldiers went beyond their orders to whip Jesus – they also mocked his claim to royalty by placing a crown on his head and a royal robe on his shoulders.

19.7 The truth finally came out – the religious leaders had not brought Jesus to Pilate because he was causing rebellion against Rome, but because they thought he had broken their religious laws. Blasphemy (claiming to be the Son of God), one of the most serious crimes in Jewish law, deserved the death penalty. Accusing Jesus of blasphemy would give credibility to their case in the eyes of Jews; accusing Jesus of treason would give credibility to their case in the eyes of the Romans. They didn't care which accusation Pilate listened to, as long as he would cooperate with them in killing Jesus.

19.10 Throughout the trial we see that Jesus was in control, not Pilate or the religious leaders. Pilate vacillated, the Jewish leaders reacted out of hatred and anger, but Jesus remained composed. He knew the truth, he knew God's plan, and he knew the reason for his trial. Despite the pressure and persecution, Jesus remained unmoved. It was really Pilate and the religious leaders who were on trial, not Jesus. When you are questioned or ridiculed because of your faith, remember that while you may be on trial before your accusers, they are on trial before God.

19.11 When Jesus said the man who delivered him to Pilate was guiltier than Pilate, he was not excusing Pilate for reacting to the political pressure placed on him. Pilate was responsible for his decision about Jesus. The religious leaders were guiltier because they premeditated Jesus' murder.

19.12, 13 These words pressured Pilate into allowing Jesus to be crucified. As Roman governor of the area, Pilate was expected to keep the peace. Because Rome could not afford to keep large numbers of troops in the outlying regions, they maintained control by crushing rebellions immediately with brute force. Pilate was afraid that reports to Caesar of insurrection in his region would cost him his job and perhaps even his life. When we face a tough decision, we can take the easy way out, or we can stand for what is right regardless of the cost. If we know to do right and don't do it, we sin (James 4.17).

this man, you are no friend of the emperor. Everyone who claims to be a king sets 19.12
himself against the emperor." Lk 23.2 Acts 17.7
13 When Pilate heard these words, he brought Jesus outside and sat[h] on the 19.13
judge's bench at a place called The Stone Pavement, or in Hebrew[i] Gabbatha. Mt 27.19
14 Now it was the day of Preparation for the Passover; and it was about noon. He
said to the Jews, "Here is your King!" 15 They cried out, "Away with him! Away
with him! Crucify him!" Pilate asked them, "Shall I crucify your King?" The chief 19.16
priests answered, "We have no king but the emperor." 16 Then he handed him over Mt 27.26,31 Mk 15.15
to them to be crucified. Lk 23.24

Jesus is led away to be crucified
(234/Matthew 27.32–37; Mark 15.21–24; Luke 23.26–31)

So they took Jesus; 17 and carrying the cross by himself, he went out to what is 19.17
called The Place of the Skull, which in Hebrew[i] is called Golgotha. 18 There they Num 15.36 Heb 13.12
crucified him, and with him two others, one on either side, with Jesus between 19.18
them. 19 Pilate also had an inscription written and put on the cross. It read, "Jesus Gal 3.13
of Nazareth,[j] the King of the Jews." 20 Many of the Jews read this inscription, 19.19 Isa 53.12
because the place where Jesus was crucified was near the city; and it was written in Mt 27.37 Mk 15.26
Hebrew,[i] in Latin, and in Greek. 21 Then the chief priests of the Jews said to Pilate, Lk 23.38
"Do not write, 'The King of the Jews,' but, 'This man said, I am King of the
Jews.' " 22 Pilate answered, "What I have written I have written." 23 When the sol- 19.23,24
diers had crucified Jesus, they took his clothes and divided them into four parts, Ps 22.18
one for each soldier. They also took his tunic; now the tunic was seamless, woven
in one piece from the top. 24 So they said to one another, "Let us not tear it, but cast
lots for it to see who will get it." This was to fulfill what the scripture says,

"They divided my clothes among themselves,
and for my clothing they cast lots."

25 And that is what the soldiers did. 19.25
Meanwhile, standing near the cross of Jesus were his mother, and his mother's Mt 27.55,56 Lk 8.2,3; 24.18
sister, Mary the wife of Clopas, and Mary Magdalene. 26 When Jesus saw his 19.26
mother and the disciple whom he loved standing beside her, he said to his mother, Jn 2.4; 13.23 21.24
"Woman, here is your son." 27 Then he said to the disciple, "Here is your mother."
And from that hour the disciple took her into his own home.

[h] Or *seated him* [i] That is, *Aramaic* [j] Gk *the Nazorean*

19.13 The Stone Pavement was part of the Tower of Antonia bordering the northwest corner of the temple complex.

19.15 The Jewish leaders were so desperate to get rid of Jesus that despite their intense hatred for Rome, they shouted, "We have no king but the emperor." How ironic that they feigned allegiance to Rome while rejecting their own Messiah! Their own words condemned them, because God was to be their only true King and they had abandoned every trace of loyalty to him. The priests had truly lost their reason for being – instead of turning people to God, they claimed allegiance to Rome in order to kill their Messiah.

19.17 This place called *Golgotha,* "The Place of the Skull," was probably a hill outside Jerusalem along a main road. Many executions took place here, so the Romans could use them as an example to the people.

19.18 Crucifixion was a Roman form of execution. The condemned man was forced to carry his cross along a main road to the execution site, as a warning to the people. Crosses and methods of crucifixion varied. Jesus was nailed to his cross; some people were tied with ropes. Death came by suffocation, because the weight of the body made breathing difficult as the victim lost strength. Crucifixion was a hideously slow and painful death.

19.19 This sign was meant to be ironic. A king, stripped naked and executed in public view, had obviously lost his kingdom forever. But Jesus, who turns the world's wisdom upside down, was just coming into his kingdom. His death and resurrection would strike the deathblow to Satan's rule and would establish his eternal authority over the earth. Few people reading the sign that bleak afternoon understood its real meaning, but the sign was absolutely true. All was not lost. Jesus was King of the Jews – and the Gentiles, and the whole universe.

19.20 The signboard was written in three languages: Hebrew for the native Jews; Latin for the Roman occupation forces; and Greek for foreigners and Jews visiting from other lands.

19.23, 24 Roman soldiers in charge of crucifixions customarily took the clothes of the condemned men. They cast lots to determine who would get Jesus' robe, the most valuable piece of clothing. This fulfilled the prophecy in Psalm 22.18.

19.25–27 Even while dying on the cross, Jesus was concerned about his family. He instructed John to care for Mary, his mother. Our families are precious gifts from God, and we should value and care for them under all circumstances. Neither Christian work nor responsibilities in any job excuse us from caring for our families. What can you do today to show your love to your family?

19.27 Jesus asked his close friend John, the writer of this Gospel, to care for his mother, Mary, whose husband, Joseph, was probably dead by this time. Why didn't Jesus assign this task to his brothers? As the eldest son, Jesus entrusted his mother to a person who stayed with him at the cross – and that was John.

Jesus dies on the cross
(236/Matthew 27.45–56; Mark 15.33–41; Luke 23.44–49)

28 After this, when Jesus knew that all was now finished, he said (in order to
fulfill the scripture), "I am thirsty." 29 A jar full of sour wine was standing there. So
they put a sponge full of the wine on a branch of hyssop and held it to his mouth.
30 When Jesus had received the wine, he said, "It is finished." Then he bowed his
head and gave up his spirit.
31 Since it was the day of Preparation, the Jews did not want the bodies left on
the cross during the sabbath, especially because that sabbath was a day of great
solemnity. So they asked Pilate to have the legs of the crucified men broken and the
bodies removed. 32 Then the soldiers came and broke the legs of the first and of the
other who had been crucified with him. 33 But when they came to Jesus and saw that
he was already dead, they did not break his legs. 34 Instead, one of the soldiers
pierced his side with a spear, and at once blood and water came out. 35 (He who saw
this has testified so that you also may believe. His testimony is true, and he knows[k]
that he tells the truth.) 36 These things occurred so that the scripture might be fulfilled, "None of his bones shall be broken." 37 And again another passage of scripture says, "They will look on the one whom they have pierced."

19.28 Ps 2.1-3; 22.1-21; 69.21; Isa 53; Mt 27.48-50; Mk 15.36,37; Lk 23.36
19.30 Lk 23.46; Heb 10.1-14
19.31 Num 28.17; Deut 21.22,23
19.35 Jn 20.30,31; 21.24; 1 Jn 1.1
19.36,37 Ex 12.46; Num 9.12; Ps 34.20; Zech 12.10; Rev 1.7

Jesus is laid in the tomb
(237/Matthew 27.57–61; Mark 15.42–47; Luke 23.50–56)

38 After these things, Joseph of Arimathea, who was a disciple of Jesus,
though a secret one because of his fear of the Jews, asked Pilate to let him take
away the body of Jesus. Pilate gave him permission; so he came and removed his
body. 39 Nicodemus, who had at first come to Jesus by night, also came, bringing
a mixture of myrrh and aloes, weighing about a hundred pounds. 40 They took the
body of Jesus and wrapped it with the spices in linen cloths, according to the burial
custom of the Jews. 41 Now there was a garden in the place where he was crucified,
and in the garden there was a new tomb in which no one had ever been laid. 42 And

19.39 2 Chron 16.13,14; Mt 26.12; Mk 14.8; Jn 3.1,2; 7.50; 12.7
19.40 Lk 23.56; Jn 11.44
19.41 Mt 27.60

[k] *Or there is one who knows*

19.30 Until this time, a complicated system of sacrifices atoned for sins. Sin separates people from God, and only through the sacrifice of an animal, a substitute, could people be forgiven of sin and become clean before God. But people sin continually, so frequent sacrifices were required. Jesus, however, became the final and ultimate sacrifice for sin. The word *finished* is the same as "paid in full." Jesus came to *finish* God's work of salvation (4.34; 17.4), to pay the full penalty for our sins. With his death, the complex sacrificial system ended because Jesus took all sin upon himself. Now we can freely approach God because of what Jesus did for us. Those who believe in Jesus' death and resurrection can live eternally with God and escape the penalty that comes from sin.

19.31 It was against God's law to leave the body of a dead person exposed overnight (Deuteronomy 21.23), and it was also against the law to work after sundown on Friday, when the sabbath began. This is why the religious leaders urgently wanted to get Jesus' body off the cross and buried by sundown.

19.31–35 These Romans were experienced soldiers. They knew from many previous crucifixions whether a man was dead or alive. There was no question that Jesus was dead when they checked him, so they decided not to break his legs as they had done to the other victims. Piercing his side and seeing the separation of blood and water was further proof of his death. Some people say Jesus didn't really die, that he only passed out – and that's how he "came back to life." But we have the witness of an impartial party, the Roman soldiers, that Jesus died on the cross (Mark 15.44, 45).

19.32 The Roman soldiers broke victims' legs to hurry the death process. When a person hung on a cross, death came by suffocation, but the victim could push against the cross with his legs to hold up his body and keep breathing. With broken legs, he would suffocate immediately.

19.34, 35 The graphic details of Jesus' death are especially important in John's record because he was an eyewitness.

19.36, 37 Jesus died when the lambs for the Passover meal were being slain. Not a bone was to be broken in these sacrificial lambs (Exodus 12.46; Numbers 9.12). Jesus, the Lamb of God, was the perfect sacrifice for the sins of the world (1 Corinthians 5.7).

19.38, 39 Four people were changed in the process of Jesus' death. The criminal, dying on the cross beside Jesus, asked Jesus to include him in his kingdom (Luke 23.39–43). The Roman captain proclaimed that surely Jesus was the Son of God (Mark 15.39). Joseph and Nicodemus, members of the Jewish council and secret followers of Jesus (7.50–52), came out of hiding. These men were changed more by Christ's death than by his life. They realized who he was, and that realization brought out their belief, proclamation, and action. When confronted with Jesus and his death, we should be changed – to believe, proclaim, and act.

19.38–42 Joseph of Arimathea and Nicodemus were secret followers of Jesus. They were afraid to make this known because of their positions in the Jewish community. Joseph was a leader and honored member of the Jewish council. Nicodemus, also a member of the council, had come to Jesus by night (3.1) and later tried to defend him before the other religious leaders (7.50–52). Yet they risked their reputations to bury Jesus. Are you a secret believer? Do you hide your faith from your friends and fellow workers? This is an appropriate time to step out of hiding and let others know whom you follow.

19.42 This tomb was probably a cave carved out of the stone hillside. It was large enough for a man to walk into, so Joseph and Nicodemus carried Jesus' body into it. A large stone was rolled in front of the entrance.

so, because it was the Jewish day of Preparation, and the tomb was nearby, they
laid Jesus there.

Jesus rises from the dead
(239/Matthew 28.1–7; Mark 16.1–8; Luke 24.1–12)

20 Early on the first day of the week, while it was still dark, Mary Magdalene
came to the tomb and saw that the stone had been removed from the tomb.
2 So she ran and went to Simon Peter and the other disciple, the one whom Jesus 20.2
loved, and said to them, "They have taken the Lord out of the tomb, and we do not Jn 13.23
know where they have laid him." 3 Then Peter and the other disciple set out and 20.3
went toward the tomb. 4 The two were running together, but the other disciple out- Lk 24.12
ran Peter and reached the tomb first. 5 He bent down to look in and saw the linen 20.5
wrappings lying there, but he did not go in. 6 Then Simon Peter came, following Jn 19.40
him, and went into the tomb. He saw the linen wrappings lying there, 7 and the 20.6 Lk 24.12
cloth that had been on Jesus' head, not lying with the linen wrappings but rolled up 20.7
in a place by itself. 8 Then the other disciple, who reached the tomb first, also went Jn 11.44; 19.40
in, and he saw and believed; 9 for as yet they did not understand the scripture, that 20.9
he must rise from the dead. 10 Then the disciples returned to their homes. Ps 2.7; 16.8-11

Jesus appears to Mary Magdalene
(240/Mark 16.9–11)

11 But Mary stood weeping outside the tomb. As she wept, she bent over to 20.12 Mt 28.2
look[l] into the tomb; 12 and she saw two angels in white, sitting where the body of Mk 16.5
Jesus had been lying, one at the head and the other at the feet. 13 They said to her, Lk 24.4
"Woman, why are you weeping?" She said to them, "They have taken away my 20.14 Mt 28.9
Lord, and I do not know where they have laid him." 14 When she had said this, she Mk 16.9
turned around and saw Jesus standing there, but she did not know that it was Jesus. Jn 21.4
15 Jesus said to her, "Woman, why are you weeping? Whom are you looking for?"
Supposing him to be the gardener, she said to him, "Sir, if you have carried him 20.17 Mt 28.10
away, tell me where you have laid him, and I will take him away." 16 Jesus said to Jn 16.28 Rom 8.29
her, "Mary!" She turned and said to him in Hebrew,[m] "Rabbouni!" (which means Col 1.18
Teacher). 17 Jesus said to her, "Do not hold on to me, because I have not yet as- Heb 2.11 1 Pet 1.3

[l] Gk lacks *to look* [m] That is, *Aramaic*

20.1 Other women came to the tomb along with Mary Magdalene. The other Gospel accounts give their names. For more information on Mary Magdalene, see her Profile in this chapter.

20.1 The stone was not removed from the entrance to the tomb so Jesus could get out. He could have left easily without moving the stone. It was rolled away so others could get *in* and see that Jesus was gone.

20.1ff People who hear about the resurrection for the first time may need time before they can comprehend this amazing story. Like Mary and the disciples, they may pass through four stages of belief. (1) At first, they may think it is a fabrication, impossible to believe (20.2). (2) Like Peter, they may check out the facts and still be puzzled about what happened (20.6). (3) Only when they encounter Jesus personally are they able to accept the fact of the resurrection (20.16). (4) Then, as they commit themselves to the risen Lord and devote their lives to serving him, they begin to understand fully the reality of his presence with them (20.28).

20.7 The grave clothes were left as if Jesus had passed right through them. The head piece was still rolled up in the shape of a head, and it was at about the right distance from the wrappings that had enveloped Jesus' body. A grave robber couldn't possibly have made off with Jesus' body and left the linens as if they were still shaped around it.

20.8, 9 As further proof that the disciples did not fabricate this story, we find that Peter and John were surprised that Jesus was not in the tomb. When John saw the grave clothes looking like an empty cocoon from which Jesus had emerged, he believed Jesus had risen. It wasn't until after they had seen the empty tomb that they remembered what the scriptures and Jesus had said—he would die, but he would also rise again!

20.9 Jesus' resurrection is the key to the Christian faith. Why? (1) Just as he said, Jesus rose from the dead. We can be confident, therefore, that he will accomplish all he has promised. (2) Jesus' bodily resurrection shows us that the living Christ, not a false prophet or imposter, is ruler of God's eternal kingdom. (3) We can be certain of our own resurrection because Jesus was resurrected. Death is not the end—there is future life. (4) The divine power that brought Jesus back to life is now available to us to bring our spiritually dead selves back to life. (5) The resurrection is the basis for the church's witness to the world.

20.16 Mary didn't recognize Jesus at first. Her grief had blinded her; she couldn't see him because she didn't expect to see him. Then he spoke her name, and immediately she recognized him. Imagine the love that flooded her heart when she heard her Savior saying her name. Jesus is near you, and he is calling your name. Can you, like Mary, respond to him with your devotion and allegiance?

20.17 Jesus told Mary, "Do not hold on to me" or "Do not cling to me." Mary did not want to lose Jesus again. She had not yet understood the resurrection. Perhaps she thought this was his promised second coming (14.3). But Jesus did not want to be detained by the tomb. If he did not ascend to heaven, the Holy Spirit could not come. Both he and Mary had important work to do.

cended to the Father. But go to my brothers and say to them, 'I am ascending to my
Father and your Father, to my God and your God.' " 18 Mary Magdalene went and
announced to the disciples, "I have seen the Lord"; and she told them that he had
said these things to her.

Jesus appears to the disciples behind locked doors
(244/Luke 24.36–43)

20.19 Mk 16.14 Lk 24.36-43 1 Cor 15.5,42-45
20.21 Mt 28.18-20 Jn 17.18

19 When it was evening on that day, the first day of the week, and the doors of
the house where the disciples had met were locked for fear of the Jews, Jesus came
and stood among them and said, "Peace be with you." 20 After he said this, he
showed them his hands and his side. Then the disciples rejoiced when they saw the
Lord. 21 Jesus said to them again, "Peace be with you. As the Father has sent me,

---

MARY MAGDALENE

The absence of women among the 12 disciples has bothered a few people. But it is clear that there were many women among Jesus' followers. It is also clear that Jesus did not treat women as others in his culture did; he treated them with dignity, as people with worth.

Mary of Magdala was an early follower of Jesus and certainly deserves to be called a disciple. An energetic, impulsive, caring woman, she not only traveled with Jesus, but also contributed to the needs of the group. She was present at the crucifixion and was on her way to embalm Jesus' body on Sunday morning when she discovered the empty tomb. Mary was the first to see Jesus after his resurrection.

Mary Magdalene is a heartwarming example of thankful living. Her life was miraculously freed by Jesus when he cast seven demons out of her. In every glimpse we have of her, she was acting out her appreciation for the freedom Christ had given her. That freedom allowed her to stand under Christ's cross when all the disciples except John were hiding in fear. After Jesus' death, she intended to give his body every respect. Like the rest of Jesus' followers, she never expected his bodily resurrection—but she was overjoyed to discover it.

Mary's faith was not complicated, but it was direct and genuine. She was more eager to believe and obey than to understand everything. Jesus honored her childlike faith by appearing to her first and by entrusting her with the first message of his resurrection.

Strengths and accomplishments:
- Contributed to the needs of Jesus and his disciples
- One of the few faithful followers present at Jesus' death on the cross
- First to see the risen Christ

Weakness and mistake:
- Jesus had to cast seven demons out of her

Lessons from her life:
- Those who are obedient grow in understanding
- Women are vital to Jesus' ministry
- Jesus relates to women as he created them—as equal reflectors of God's image

Vital statistics:
- Where: Magdala
- Occupation: We are not told, but she seems to have been wealthy
- Contemporaries: Jesus, the 12 disciples, Mary, Martha, Lazarus, Jesus' mother Mary

Key verse:
"Now after he rose early on the first day of the week, he appeared first to Mary Magdalene, from whom he had cast out seven demons" (Mark 16.9).

Mary Magdalene's story is told in Matthew 27; 28; Mark 15; 16; Luke 23; 24; and John 19; 20. She is also mentioned in Luke 8.2.

20.18 Mary did not meet the risen Christ until she had discovered the empty tomb. She responded with joy and obedience in telling the disciples. We cannot meet Christ until we discover that he is indeed alive, that his tomb is empty. Are you filled with joy by this good news, and do you share it with others?

20.21 Jesus again identified himself with his Father. He told the disciples by whose authority he did his work. Now he passed the job to his disciples of spreading the gospel of salvation around the world. Whatever God has asked you to do, remember: (1) your authority comes from God, and (2) Jesus has demonstrated by words and actions how to accomplish the job he has given you. As the Father sent Jesus, Jesus sends his followers.

so I send you." 22 When he had said this, he breathed on them and said to them, 20.22
"Receive the Holy Spirit. 23 If you forgive the sins of any, they are forgiven them; Jn 7.37-39 14.16-18,26
if you retain the sins of any, they are retained."

Jesus appears to the disciples including Thomas
(245/Mark 16.14)

24 But Thomas (who was called the Twin[n]), one of the twelve, was not with 20.24
them when Jesus came. 25 So the other disciples told him, "We have seen the Jn 11.16
Lord." But he said to them, "Unless I see the mark of the nails in his hands, and put
my finger in the mark of the nails and my hand in his side, I will not believe."
26 A week later his disciples were again in the house, and Thomas was with 20.28
them. Although the doors were shut, Jesus came and stood among them and said, Jn 1.1,18 10.30; 14.9
"Peace be with you." 27 Then he said to Thomas, "Put your finger here and see my Phil 2.6 Col 2.9
hands. Reach out your hand and put it in my side. Do not doubt but believe." Tit 2.13
28 Thomas answered him, "My Lord and my God!" 29 Jesus said to him, "Have you 2 Pet 1.1 1 Jn 5.20
believed because you have seen me? Blessed are those who have not seen and yet 20.29
have come to believe." 2 Cor 5.7 1 Pet 1.8
30 Now Jesus did many other signs in the presence of his disciples, which are
not written in this book. 31 But these are written so that you may come to believe[o] 20.30,31
that Jesus is the Messiah,[p] the Son of God, and that through believing you may Jn 3.15,16 5.24; 19.35
have life in his name. 21.25

Jesus appears to the disciples while they are fishing
(246)

21

After these things Jesus showed himself again to the disciples by the Sea of 21.1
Tiberias; and he showed himself in this way. 2 Gathered there together were Jn 21.14 21.2
Simon Peter, Thomas called the Twin,[n] Nathanael of Cana in Galilee, the sons of Mt 4.21,22
Zebedee, and two others of his disciples. 3 Simon Peter said to them, "I am going Jn 1.45-51
fishing." They said to him, "We will go with you." They went out and got into the
boat, but that night they caught nothing.

[n] Gk *Didymus* [o] Other ancient authorities read *may continue to believe* [p] Or *the Christ*

20.22 This is a special filling of the Holy Spirit for the disciples, a foretaste of what all believers would experience from the time of pentecost (Acts 2) and forever after. To do God's work, we need the guidance and power of the Holy Spirit. We must avoid trying to do his work in our own strength for we will not succeed.

20.22 There is life in the breath of God. Man was created but did not come alive until God breathed into him the breath of life (Genesis 2.7). His first breath made man different from all other forms of creation. Here, through the breath of Jesus, God imparted eternal, spiritual life. With this inbreathing came the power to do God's will on earth.

20.23 Jesus is telling the disciples their Spirit-powered and Spirit-guided mission—to preach the good news about Jesus so people's sins might be forgiven. The disciples did not have the power to forgive sins (only God can forgive sins), but Jesus gave them the privilege of telling new believers that their sins *have been* forgiven because they have accepted Jesus' message. All believers have this same privilege. We can announce the forgiveness of sin with certainty when we ourselves find repentance and faith.

20.24–29 Have you ever wished you could actually see Jesus, touch him, hear his words? Wouldn't you like to sit down with him and get his advice? Thomas wanted Jesus' physical presence. But God's plan is wiser. By not limiting himself to one physical body, he can be present with us at all times. Even now he is with you in the form of the Holy Spirit. You can talk to him, and you can find his words to you in the pages of the Bible. He can be as real to you as he was to Thomas.

20.25–29 Jesus wasn't hard on Thomas for his doubts. Despite his skepticism, Thomas was still loyal to the believers and to Jesus himself. Some need to doubt before they believe. If doubt leads to questions, the questions lead to answers, and the answers are accepted, then doubt has done good work. It is when doubt becomes stubbornness and stubbornness becomes a life-style that doubt harms faith. Don't stop at your doubts. Let them deepen your faith as you continue to search for the answers.

20.27 Jesus' resurrected body was unique. It was not the same kind of flesh and blood Lazarus had when he came back to life. Jesus' body was no longer subject to the same laws of nature as before his death. He could appear in a locked room, yet he was not a ghost or apparition; he could be touched and could eat. Jesus' resurrection was *literal* and *physical*—he was not a disembodied spirit.

20.29 Some people think they would believe in Jesus if they could see a definite sign or miracle. But Jesus says we are blessed if we can believe without seeing. We have all the proof we need in the words of the Bible and the testimony of believers. A physical appearance would not make Jesus any more real to us than he is now.

20.30, 31 To understand the life and mission of Jesus more fully, all we need to do is study the Gospels. John tells us that his Gospel records only a few of the many events in Jesus' life on earth. But the gospel includes everything we need to know to believe that Jesus is the Christ, the Son of God, through whom we receive eternal life.

21.1ff This chapter tells how Jesus commissioned Peter. Perhaps Peter needed special encouragement after his denial—he may have felt completely worthless. Verses 1–14 set the scene for Jesus' conversation with Peter.

4 Just after daybreak, Jesus stood on the beach; but the disciples did not know
that it was Jesus. 5 Jesus said to them, "Children, you have no fish, have you?"
21.6 Lk 5.4-7 They answered him, "No." 6 He said to them, "Cast the net to the right side of the
boat, and you will find some." So they cast it, and now they were not able to haul
21.7 Jn 13.21; 21.20 it in because there were so many fish. 7 That disciple whom Jesus loved said to
Peter, "It is the Lord!" When Simon Peter heard that it was the Lord, he put on
some clothes, for he was naked, and jumped into the sea. 8 But the other disciples
came in the boat, dragging the net full of fish, for they were not far from the land,
only about a hundred yards[q] off.
21.9 Jn 6.9,11 9 When they had gone ashore, they saw a charcoal fire there, with fish on it, and
bread. 10 Jesus said to them, "Bring some of the fish that you have just caught."
11 So Simon Peter went aboard and hauled the net ashore, full of large fish, a hundred fifty-three of them; and though there were so many, the net was not torn.

q Gk *two hundred cubits*

THOMAS

Thomas, so often remembered as "Doubting Thomas," deserves to be respected for his faith. He was a doubter, but his doubts had a purpose—he wanted to know the truth. Thomas did not idolize his doubts; he gladly believed when given reasons to do so. He expressed his doubts fully and had them answered completely. Doubting was only his way of responding, not his way of life.

Although our glimpses of Thomas are brief, his character comes through with consistency. He struggled to be faithful to what he knew, despite what he felt. At one point, when it was plain to everyone that Jesus' life was in danger, only Thomas put into words what most were feeling, "Let us also go, that we may die with him" (John 11.16). He didn't hesitate to follow Jesus.

We don't know why Thomas was absent the first time Jesus appeared to the disciples after the resurrection, but he was reluctant to believe their witness to Christ's resurrection. Not even ten friends could change his mind!

We can doubt without having to live a doubting way of life. Doubt encourages rethinking. Its purpose is more to sharpen the mind than to change it. Doubt can be used to pose the question, get an answer, and push for a decision. But doubt was never meant to be a permanent condition. Doubt is one foot lifted, poised to step forward or back. There is no motion until the foot comes down.

When you experience doubt, take encouragement from Thomas. He didn't stay in his doubt, but allowed Jesus to bring him to belief. Take encouragement also from the fact that countless other followers of Christ have struggled with doubts. The answers God gave them may help you too. Don't settle into doubts, but move on from them to decision and belief. Find another believer with whom you can share your doubts. Silent doubts rarely find answers.

Strengths and accomplishments:
- One of Jesus' 12 disciples
- Intense both in doubt and belief
- Was a loyal and honest man

Weaknesses and mistakes:
- Along with the others, abandoned Jesus at his arrest
- Refused to believe the others' claims to have seen Christ and demanded proof
- Struggled with a pessimistic outlook

Lessons from his life:
- Jesus does not reject doubts that are honest and directed toward belief
- Better to doubt out loud than to disbelieve in silence

Vital statistics:
- Where: Galilee, Judea, Samaria
- Occupation: Disciple of Jesus
- Contemporaries: Jesus, other disciples, Herod, Pilate

Key verses:
"Then he said to Thomas, 'Put your finger here and see my hands. Reach out your hand and put it in my side. Do not doubt but believe.' Thomas answered him, 'My Lord and my God!' " (John 20.27, 28).

Thomas's story is told in the Gospels. He is also mentioned in Acts 1.13.

21.5 "Children" was an affectionate greeting, not a term of condescension.

21.7 Only John recognized Jesus in the dim morning light, perhaps because he had seen Jesus perform a similar miracle earlier (Luke 5.1–11).

12 Jesus said to them, “Come and have breakfast.” Now none of the disciples dared 21.12
to ask him, “Who are you?” because they knew it was the Lord. 13 Jesus came and Acts 10.41
took the bread and gave it to them, and did the same with the fish. 14 This was now 21.14
the third time that Jesus appeared to the disciples after he was raised from the dead. Jn 20.19,26

Jesus talks with Peter
(247)

15 When they had finished breakfast, Jesus said to Simon Peter, “Simon son of 21.15
John, do you love me more than these?” He said to him, “Yes, Lord; you know that Mt 26.33 Acts 20.28
I love you.” Jesus said to him, “Feed my lambs.” 16 A second time he said to him, Eph 4.11
“Simon son of John, do you love me?” He said to him, “Yes, Lord; you know that 21.16 Heb 13.20,21
I love you.” Jesus said to him, “Tend my sheep.” 17 He said to him the third time, 1 Pet 2.25,5.2
“Simon son of John, do you love me?” Peter felt hurt because he said to him the 21.17
third time, “Do you love me?” And he said to him, “Lord, you know everything; 1 Chron 28.9 29.17
you know that I love you.” Jesus said to him, “Feed my sheep. 18 Very truly, I tell 2 Chron 6.30 Jer 17.10
you, when you were younger, you used to fasten your own belt and to go wher- Jn 2.24,25
ever you wished. But when you grow old, you will stretch out your hands, and some- 13.38 Rom 8.27
one else will fasten a belt around you and take you where you do not wish to go.” 1 Thess 2.4
19 (He said this to indicate the kind of death by which he would glorify God.) After 21.19 2 Pet 1.13,14
this he said to him, “Follow me.”

20 Peter turned and saw the disciple whom Jesus loved following them; he was 21.20
the one who had reclined next to Jesus at the supper and had said, “Lord, who is it Jn 13.23-25
that is going to betray you?” 21 When Peter saw him, he said to Jesus, “Lord, what

JESUS' APPEARANCES AFTER HIS RESURRECTION

Mary Magdalene	Mark 16.9–11; John 20.10–18
The other women at the tomb	Matthew 28.8–10
Peter in Jerusalem	Luke 24.34; 1 Corinthians 15.5
The two travelers on the road	Mark 16.12, 13
Ten disciples behind closed doors	Mark 16.14; Luke 24.36–43; John 20.19–25
All the disciples, with Thomas (excluding Judas Iscariot)	John 20.26–31; 1 Corinthians 15.5
Seven disciples while fishing	John 21.1–14
Eleven disciples on the mountain	Matthew 28.16–20
A crowd of 500	1 Corinthians 15.6
His brother James	1 Corinthians 15.7
Those who watched him ascend into heaven	Luke 24.44–49; Acts 1.3–8

The truth of Christianity rests heavily on the resurrection. If Jesus rose from the grave, who saw him? How trustworthy were the witnesses? Those who claimed to have seen the risen Jesus went on to turn the world upside down. Most of them also died for being followers of Christ. People rarely die for half-hearted belief. These are the people who saw Jesus risen from the grave.

21.15–17 In this beach scene, Jesus led Peter through an experience that would remove the cloud of his denial. Peter had denied Jesus three times. Three times Jesus asked Peter if he loved him. When Peter answered yes, Jesus told him to feed his sheep. It is one thing to say you love Jesus, but the real test is willingness to serve him. Peter had repented, and now Jesus asked him to commit his life. Peter's life changed when he finally realized who Jesus was. His occupation changed from fisherman to evangelist; his identity changed from impetuous to "rock;" and his relationship to Jesus changed – now he was forgiven and fully understood the significance of Jesus' words about his death and resurrection.

21.15–17 Jesus asked Peter three times if he loved him. The first time Jesus said, "Do you love (Greek *agape:* volitional, self-sacrificial love) me more than these?" ("these" referring to the other disciples). The second time, Jesus focused on Peter alone and still used the word translated into Greek, *agape.* The third time, Jesus used the word translated into Greek, *phileo* (signifying affection, affinity, or brotherly love) and asked, in effect, "Are you even my friend?" Each time Peter responded with the word translated into Greek as *phileo.* Jesus doesn't settle for quick, superficial answers. He has a way of getting to the heart of the matter. Peter had to face his true feelings and motives when Jesus confronted him. How would you respond if Jesus asked you, "Do you love me?" Do you really love Jesus? Are you his friend?

21.18, 19 This was a prediction of Peter's death by crucifixion. Tradition indicates that Peter was crucified for his faith – upside down, because he did not feel worthy of dying as his Lord did. Despite what his future held, Jesus told Peter to follow him. We may be uncertain and fearful about the future. But if we know God is in control, we can confidently follow Christ, no matter what.

21.21, 22 Peter asked Jesus how John would die. Jesus replied that Peter should not concern himself with that. We tend to compare our lives to those of others, whether to rationalize our own level of devotion to Christ or to question God's justice. Jesus re-

21.22 Deut 29.29; 1 Cor 4.5; 11.26; Rev 2.25; 3.11; 22.7,20
21.24 Jn 1.14; 15.27; 19.35; 1 Jn 1.1-3; 3 Jn 12
21.25 Jn 20.30,31

about him?" 22 Jesus said to him, "If it is my will that he remain until I come, what
is that to you? Follow me!" 23 So the rumor spread in the community[r] that this
disciple would not die. Yet Jesus did not say to him that he would not die, but, "If
it is my will that he remain until I come, what is that to you?"[s]

24 This is the disciple who is testifying to these things and has written them,
and we know that his testimony is true. 25 But there are also many other things that
Jesus did; if every one of them were written down, I suppose that the world itself
could not contain the books that would be written.

[r] Gk *among the brothers* [s] Other ancient authorities lack *what is that to you*

---

sponds to us the same way: "What is that to you? Follow me!"

21.23 Early church history reports that John spent several years as an exile on the island of Patmos, and then returned to Ephesus, where he died as an old man near the end of the first century.

21.25 John's stated purpose for writing his Gospel was to show that Jesus is the Son of God. He clearly and systematically presented the evidence for Jesus' claims. When evidence is presented in the courtroom, those who hear it must make a choice. Those who read the Gospel of John must also make a choice – is Jesus the Son of God, or isn't he? You are the jury. The evidence has been clearly presented. You must decide. Read John's Gospel and believe!

250 EVENTS IN THE LIFE OF CHRIST/ A HARMONY OF THE GOSPELS

All four books in the Bible that tell the story of Jesus Christ—Matthew, Mark, Luke, and John—stand alone, emphasizing a unique aspect of Jesus' life. But when these are blended into one complete account, or harmonized, we gain new insights about the life of Christ.

This harmony combines the four Gospels into a single chronological account of Christ's life on earth. It includes every chapter and verse of each Gospel, leaving nothing out.

The harmony is divided into 250 events. The title of each event is identical to the title found in the corresponding Gospel. Parallel passages found in more than one Gospel have identical titles, helping you to identify them quickly.

Each of the 250 events in the harmony is numbered. The number of the event corresponds to the number next to the title in the Bible text. When reading one of the Gospel accounts you will notice, at times, that some numbers are missing or out of sequence. The easiest way to locate these events is to refer to the harmony.

In addition, if you are looking for a particular event in the life of Christ, the harmony can help you locate it more rapidly than paging through all four Gospels. Each of the 250 events has a distinctive title keyed to the main emphasis of the passage to help you locate and remember the events.

This harmony will help you better visualize the travels of Jesus, study the four Gospels comparatively, and appreciate the unity of their message.

I. BIRTH AND PREPARATION OF JESUS CHRIST

	Event	*Matthew*	*Mark*	*Luke*	*John*
1	Luke's purpose in writing			1.1–4	
2	God became a human being				1.1–18
3	The ancestors of Jesus	1.1–17		3.23–38	
4	An angel promises the birth of John to Zachariah			1.5–25	
5	An angel promises the birth of Jesus to Mary			1.26–38	
6	Mary visits Elizabeth			1.39–56	
7	John the Baptist is born			1.57–80	
8	An angel appears to Joseph	1.18–25			
9	Jesus is born in Bethlehem			2.1–7	
10	Shepherds visit Jesus			2.8–20	
11	Mary and Joseph bring Jesus to the temple			2.21–40	
12	Visitors arrive from eastern lands	2.1–12			
13	The escape to Egypt	2.13–18			
14	The return to Nazareth	2.19–23			
15	Jesus speaks with the religious teachers			2.41–52	
16	John the Baptist prepares the way for Jesus	3.1–12	1.1–8	3.1–17	
17	John baptizes Jesus	3.13–17	1.9–11	3.21, 22	
18	Satan tempts Jesus in the wilderness	4.1–11	1.12, 13	4.1–13	
19	John the Baptist declares his mission				1.19–28

	Matthew	Mark	Luke	John
20 John the Baptist proclaims Jesus as the Messiah				1.29–34
21 The first disciples follow Jesus				1.35–51
22 Jesus turns water into wine				2.1–12

II. MESSAGE AND MINISTRY OF JESUS CHRIST

	Matthew	Mark	Luke	John
23 Jesus clears the temple				2.13–25
24 Nicodemus visits Jesus at night				3.1–21
25 John the Baptist tells more about Jesus				3.22–36
26 Herod puts John in prison			3.18–20	
27 Jesus talks to a woman at the well				4.1–26
28 Jesus tells about the spiritual harvest				4.27–38
29 Many Samaritans believe in Jesus				4.39–42
30 Jesus preaches in Galilee	4.12–17	1.14, 15	4.14, 15	4.43–45
31 Jesus heals a government official's son				4.46–54
32 Jesus is rejected at Nazareth			4.16–30	
33 Four fishermen follow Jesus	4.18–22	1.16–20		
34 Jesus teaches with great authority		1.21–28	4.31–37	
35 Jesus heals Peter's mother-in-law and many others	8.14–17	1.29–34	4.38–41	
36 Jesus preaches throughout Galilee	4.23–25	1.35–39	4.42–44	
37 Jesus provides a miraculous catch of fish			5.1–11	
38 Jesus heals a man with leprosy	8.1–4	1.40–45	5.12–16	
39 Jesus heals a paralyzed man	9.2–8	2.1–12	5.17–26	
40 Jesus eats with sinners at Matthew's house	9.9–13	2.13–17	5.27–32	
41 Religious leaders ask Jesus about fasting	9.14–17	2.18–22	5.33–39	
42 Jesus heals a lame man by the pool				5.1–18
43 Jesus claims to be God's Son				5.19–30
44 Jesus supports his claim				5.31–47
45 The disciples pick wheat on the sabbath	12.1–8	2.23–28	6.1–5	
46 Jesus heals a man's hand on the sabbath	12.9–14	3.1–6	6.6–11	
47 Large crowds follow Jesus	12.15–21	3.7–12		
48 Jesus selects the twelve disciples		3.13–19	6.12–16	
49 Jesus gives the beatitudes	5.1–12		6.17–26	
50 Jesus teaches about salt and light	5.13–16			
51 Jesus teaches about the law	5.17–20			
52 Jesus teaches about anger	5.21–26			
53 Jesus teaches about lust	5.27–30			
54 Jesus teaches about divorce	5.31, 32			
55 Jesus teaches about vows	5.33–37			
56 Jesus teaches about retaliation	5.38–42			
57 Jesus teaches about loving enemies	5.43–48		6.27–36	
58 Jesus teaches about giving to the needy	6.1–4			
59 Jesus teaches about prayer	6.5–15			
60 Jesus teaches about fasting	6.16–18			
61 Jesus teaches about money	6.19–24			
62 Jesus teaches about worry	6.25–34			
63 Jesus teaches about criticizing others	7.1–6		6.37–42	
64 Jesus teaches about asking, seeking, knocking	7.7–12			
65 Jesus teaches about the way to heaven	7.13, 14			
66 Jesus teaches about fruit in people's lives	7.15–20		6.43–45	
67 Jesus teaches about those who build houses on rock and sand	7.21–29		6.46–49	
68 A Roman soldier demonstrates faith	8.5–13		7.1–10	
69 Jesus raises a widow's son from the dead			7.11–17	
70 Jesus eases John's doubt	11.1–19		7.18–35	
71 Jesus promises rest for the soul	11.20–30			
72 A sinful woman anoints Jesus' feet			7.36–50	
73 Women accompany Jesus and the disciples			8.1–3	
74 Religious leaders accuse Jesus of being Satan	12.22–37	3.20–30		

		Matthew	Mark	Luke	John
75	Religious leaders ask Jesus for a miracle	12.38–45			
76	Jesus describes his true family	12.46–50	3.31–35	8.19–21	
77	Jesus tells the parable of the four soils	13.1–9	4.1–9	8.4–8	
78	Jesus explains the parable of the four soils	13.10–23	4.10–25	8.9–18	
79	Jesus tells the parable of the growing seed		4.26–29		
80	Jesus tells the parable of the weeds	13.24–30			
81	Jesus tells the parable of the mustard seed	13.31, 32	4.30–34		
82	Jesus tells the parable of the yeast	13.33–35			
83	Jesus explains the parable of the weeds	13.36–43			
84	Jesus tells the parable of hidden treasure	13.44			
85	Jesus tells the parable of the pearl merchant	13.45, 46			
86	Jesus tells the parable of the fishing net	13.47–53			
87	Jesus calms the storm	8.23–27	4.35–41	8.22–25	
88	Jesus sends the demons into a herd of pigs	8.28–9.1	5.1–20	8.26–39	
89	Jesus heals a bleeding woman and restores a girl to life	9.18–26	5.21–43	8.40–56	
90	Jesus heals the blind and mute	9.27–34			
91	The people of Nazareth refuse to believe	13.54–58	6.1–6		
92	Jesus urges the disciples to pray for workers	9.35–38			
93	Jesus sends out the twelve disciples	10.1–15	6.7–13	9.1–6	
94	Jesus prepares the disciples for persecution	10.16–42			
95	Herod kills John the Baptist	14.1–12	6.14–29	9.7–9	
96	Jesus feeds five thousand	14.13–21	6.30–44	9.10–17	6.1–15
97	Jesus walks on water	14.22–33	6.45–52		6.16–21
98	Jesus heals all who touch him	14.34–36	6.53–56		
99	Jesus is the true bread from heaven				6.22–40
100	The Jews disagree that Jesus is from heaven				6.41–59
101	Many disciples desert Jesus				6.60–71
102	Jesus teaches about inner purity	15.1–20	7.1–23		
103	Jesus sends a demon out of a girl	15.21–28	7.24–30		
104	The crowd marvels at Jesus' healings	15.29–31	7.31–37		
105	Jesus feeds four thousand	15.32–39	8.1–10		
106	Religious leaders ask for a sign in the sky	16.1–4	8.11–13		
107	Jesus warns against wrong teaching	16.5–12	8.14–21		
108	Jesus restores sight to a blind man		8.22–26		
109	Peter says Jesus is the Messiah	16.13–20	8.27–30	9.18–20	
110	Jesus predicts his death the first time	16.21–28	8.31—9.1	9.21–27	
111	Jesus is transfigured on the mountain	17.1–13	9.2–13	9.28–36	
112	Jesus heals a demon-possessed boy	17.14–21	9.14–29	9.37–43	
113	Jesus predicts his death the second time	17.22, 23	9.30–32	9.44, 45	
114	Peter finds the coin in the fish's mouth	17.24–27			
115	The disciples argue about who would be the greatest	18.1–6	9.33–37	9.46–48	
116	The disciples forbid another to use Jesus' name		9.38–41	9.49, 50	
117	Jesus warns against temptation	18.7–9	9.42–50		
118	Jesus warns against looking down on others	18.10–14			
119	Jesus teaches how to treat a believer who sins	18.15–20			
120	Jesus tells the parable of the unforgiving debtor	18.21–35			
121	Jesus' brothers ridicule him				7.1–9
122	Jesus teaches about the cost of following him	8.18–22		9.51–62	
123	Jesus teaches openly at the temple				7.10–31
124	Religious leaders attempt to arrest Jesus				7.32–52
125	Jesus forgives an adulterous woman				7.53–8.11
126	Jesus is the light of the world				8.12–20
127	Jesus warns of coming judgment				8.21–30
128	Jesus speaks about God's true children				8.31–47
129	Jesus states he is eternal				8.48–59
130	Jesus sends out seventy messengers			10.1–16	
131	The seventy messengers return			10.17–24	
132	Jesus tells the parable of the good Samaritan			10.25–37	
133	Jesus visits Mary and Martha			10.38–42	
134	Jesus teaches his disciples about prayer			11.1–13	
135	Jesus answers hostile accusations			11.14–28	
136	Jesus warns against unbelief			11.29–32	

	Matthew	Mark	Luke	John
137 Jesus teaches about the light within			11.33–36	
138 Jesus criticizes the religious leaders			11.37–54	
139 Jesus speaks against hypocrisy			12.1–12	
140 Jesus tells the parable of the rich fool			12.13–21	
141 Jesus warns about worry			12.22–34	
142 Jesus warns about preparing for his coming			12.35–48	
143 Jesus warns about coming division			12.49–53	
144 Jesus warns about the future crisis			12.54–59	
145 Jesus calls the people to repent			13.1–9	
146 Jesus heals the handicapped woman			13.10–17	
147 Jesus teaches about the kingdom of God			13.18–21	
148 Jesus heals the man who was born blind				9.1–12
149 Religious leaders question the blind man				9.13–34
150 Jesus teaches about spiritual blindness				9.35–41
151 Jesus is the good shepherd				10.1–21
152 Religious leaders surround Jesus at the temple				10.22–42
153 Jesus teaches about entering the kingdom			13.22–30	
154 Jesus grieves over Jerusalem			13.31–35	
155 Jesus heals a man with dropsy			14.1–6	
156 Jesus teaches about seeking honor			14.7–14	
157 Jesus tells the parable of the great feast			14.15–24	
158 Jesus teaches about the cost of being a disciple			14.25–35	
159 Jesus tells the parable of the lost sheep			15.1–7	
160 Jesus tells the parable of the lost coin			15.8–10	
161 Jesus tells the parable of the lost son			15.11–32	
162 Jesus tells the parable of the shrewd accountant			16.1–18	
163 Jesus tells about the rich man and the beggar			16.19–31	
164 Jesus tells about forgiveness and faith			17.1–10	
165 Lazarus becomes ill and dies				11.1–16
166 Jesus comforts Mary and Martha				11.17–37
167 Jesus raises Lazarus from the dead				11.38–44
168 Religious leaders plot to kill Jesus				11.45–57
169 Jesus heals ten lepers			17.11–19	
170 Jesus teaches about the coming of the kingdom of God			17.20–37	
171 Jesus tells the parable of the persistent widow			18.1–8	
172 Jesus tells the parable of two men who prayed			18.9–14	
173 Jesus teaches about marriage and divorce	19.1–12	10.1–12		
174 Jesus blesses little children	19.13–15	10.13–16	18.15–17	
175 Jesus speaks to the rich young man	19.16–30	10.17–31	18.18–30	
176 Jesus tells the parable of the workers paid equally	20.1–16			
177 Jesus predicts his death the third time	20.17–19	10.32–34	18.31–34	
178 Jesus teaches about serving others	20.20–28	10.35–45		
179 Jesus heals a blind beggar	20.29–34	10.46–52	18.35–43	
180 Jesus brings salvation to Zacchaeus's home			19.1–10	
181 Jesus tells the parable of the king's ten servants			19.11–27	
182 A woman anoints Jesus with perfume	26.6–13	14.3–9		12.1–11
183 Jesus rides into Jerusalem on a donkey	21.1–11	11.1–11	19.28–44	12.12–19
184 Jesus clears the temple again	21.12–17	11.12–19	19.45–48	
185 Jesus explains why he must die				12.20–36
186 Most of the people do not believe in Jesus				12.37–43
187 Jesus summarizes his message				12.44–50
188 Jesus says the disciples can pray for anything	21.18–22	11.20–26		
189 Religious leaders challenge Jesus' authority	21.23–27	11.27–33	20.1–8	
190 Jesus tells the parable of the two sons	21.28–32			
191 Jesus tells the parable of the wicked farmers	21.33–46	12.1–12	20.9–19	
192 Jesus tells the parable of the wedding feast	22.1–14			
193 Religious leaders question Jesus about paying taxes	22.15–22	12.13–17	20.20–26	
194 Religious leaders question Jesus about the resurrection	22.23–33	12.18–27	20.27–40	
195 Religious leaders question Jesus about the greatest commandment	22.34–40	12.28–34		
196 Religious leaders cannot answer Jesus' question	22.41–46	12.35–37	20.41–44	

	Matthew	*Mark*	*Luke*	*John*
197 Jesus warns against the religious leaders	23.1–12	12.38–40	20.45–47	
198 Jesus condemns the religious leaders	23.13–36			
199 Jesus grieves over Jerusalem again	23.37–39			
200 A poor widow gives all she has		12.41–44	21.1–4	
201 Jesus tells about the future	24.1–28	13.1–23	21.5–24	
202 Jesus tells about his return	24.29–35	13.24–31	21.25–33	
203 Jesus tells about remaining watchful	24.36–51	13.32–37	21.34–38	
204 Jesus tells the parable of the ten bridesmaids	25.1–13			
205 Jesus tells the parable of the loaned money	25.14–30			
206 Jesus tells about the final judgment	25.31–46			

III. DEATH AND RESURRECTION OF JESUS CHRIST

	Matthew	*Mark*	*Luke*	*John*
207 Religious leaders plot to kill Jesus	26.1–5	14.1, 2	22.1, 2	
208 Judas agrees to betray Jesus	26.14–16	14.10, 11	22.3–6	
209 Disciples prepare for the Passover	26.17–19	14.12–16	22.7–13	
210 Jesus washes the disciples' feet				13.1–20
211 Jesus and the disciples have the last supper	26.20–30	14.17–26	22.14–30	13.21–30
212 Jesus predicts Peter's denial			22.31–38	13.31–38
213 Jesus is the way to the Father				14.1–14
214 Jesus promises the Holy Spirit				14.15–31
215 Jesus teaches about the vine and the branches				15.1–17
216 Jesus warns about the world's hatred				15.18—16.4
217 Jesus teaches about the Holy Spirit				16.5–15
218 Jesus teaches about using his name in prayer				16.16–33
219 Jesus prays for himself				17.1–5
220 Jesus prays for his disciples				17.6–19
221 Jesus prays for future believers				17.20–26
222 Jesus again predicts Peter's denial	26.31–35	14.27–31		
223 Jesus agonizes in the garden	26.36–46	14.32–42	22.39–46	
224 Jesus is betrayed and arrested	26.47–56	14.43–52	22.47–53	18.1–11
225 Annas questions Jesus				18.12–24
226 Caiaphas questions Jesus	26.57–68	14.53–65		
227 Peter denies knowing Jesus	26.69–75	14.66–72	22.54–65	18.25–27
228 The council of religious leaders condemns Jesus	27.1, 2	15.1	22.66–71	
229 Judas kills himself	27.3–10			
230 Jesus stands trial before Pilate	27.11–14	15.2–5	23.1–5	18.28–38
231 Jesus stands trial before Herod			23.6–12	
232 Pilate hands Jesus over to be crucified	27.15–26	15.6–15	23.13–25	18.39—19.16
233 Roman soldiers mock Jesus	27.27–31	15.16–20		
234 Jesus is led away to be crucified	27.32–37	15.21–24	23.26–31	19.17
235 Jesus is placed on the cross	27.38–44	15.25–32	23.32–43	19.18–27
236 Jesus dies on the cross	27.45–56	15.33–41	23.44–49	19.28–37
237 Jesus is laid in the tomb	27.57–61	15.42–47	23.50–56	19.38–42
238 Guards are posted at the tomb	27.62–66			
239 Jesus rises from the dead	28.1–7	16.1–8	24.1–12	20.1–10
240 Jesus appears to Mary Magdalene		16.9–11		20.11–18
241 Jesus appears to the women	28.8–10			
242 Religious leaders bribe the guards	28.11–15			
243 Jesus appears to two believers traveling on the road		16.12, 13	24.13–35	
244 Jesus appears to the disciples behind locked doors			24.36–43	20.19–23
245 Jesus appears to the disciples including Thomas		16.14		20.24–31
246 Jesus appears to the disciples while fishing				21.1–14
247 Jesus talks with Peter				21.15–25

	Matthew	Mark	Luke	John
248 Jesus gives the great commission	28.16–20	16.15–18		
249 Jesus appears to the disciples in Jerusalem			24.44–49	
250 Jesus ascends into heaven		16.19, 20	24.50–53	

THE PARABLES OF JESUS

I. Teaching Parables

A. About the Kingdom of God
1. The Soils (Matthew 13.3–8; Mark 4.4–8; Luke 8.5–8)
2. The Thistles (Matthew 13.24–30)
3. The Mustard Seed (Matthew 13.31, 32; Mark 4.30–32; Luke 13.18, 19)
4. The Yeast (Matthew 13.33; Luke 13.20, 21)
5. The Treasure (Matthew 13.44)
6. The Pearl (Matthew 13.45, 46)
7. The Fishing Net (Matthew 13.47–50)
8. The Growing Wheat (Mark 4.26–29)

B. About Service and Obedience
1. The Workers in the Harvest (Matthew 20.1–16)
2. The Loaned Money (Matthew 25.14–30)
3. The Nobleman's Servants (Luke 19.11–27)
4. The Servant's Role (Luke 17.7–10)

C. About Prayer
1. The Friend at Midnight (Luke 11.5–8)
2. The Unjust Judge (Luke 18.1–8)

D. About Neighbors
1. The Good Samaritan (Luke 10.30–37)

E. About Humility
1. The Wedding Feast (Luke 14.7–11)
2. The Proud Pharisee and the Corrupt Taxpayer (Luke 18.9–14)

F. About Wealth
1. The Wealthy Fool (Luke 12.16–21)
2. The Great Feast (Luke 14.16–24)
3. The Dishonest Accountant (Luke 16.1–9)

II. Gospel Parables

A. About God's Love
1. The Lost Sheep (Matthew 18.12–14; Luke 15.3–7)
2. The Lost Coin (Luke 15.8–10)
3. The Lost Son (Luke 15.11–32)

B. About Thankfulness
1. The Forgiven Loans (Luke 7.41–43)

III. Parables of Judgment and the Future

A. About Christ's Return
1. The Ten Virgins (Matthew 25.1–13)
2. The Wise and Faithful Servants (Matthew 24.45–51; Luke 12.42–48)
3. The Traveling Boss (Mark 13.34–37)

B. About God's Values
1. The Two Sons (Matthew 21.28–32)
2. The Wicked Farmers (Matthew 21.33, 34; Mark 12.1–9; Luke 20.9–16)
3. The Unproductive Fig Tree (Luke 13.6–9)
4. The Marriage Feast (Matthew 22.1–14)
5. The Unforgiving Servant (Matthew 18.23–35)

JESUS' MIRACLES

John and the other Gospel writers were able to record only a fraction of the people who were touched and healed by Jesus. But enough of Jesus' words and works have been saved so that we also might be able to know him and be his disciples in this day. There follows a listing of the miracles that are included in the Gospels. They were supernatural events that pointed people to God, and they were acts of love by one who is love.

	Matthew	*Mark*	*Luke*	*John*
Five thousand people are fed	14.15–21	6.35–44	9.12–17	6.5–14
Stilling the storm	8.23–27	4.35–41	8.22–25	
Demons sent into the pigs	8.28–34	5.1–20	8.26–39	
Jairus's daughter raised	9.18–26	5.22–24, 35–43	8.41, 42, 49–56	
Diseased woman healed	9.20–22	5.25–34	8.43–48	
Jesus heals a paralyzed man	9.1–8	2.1–12	5.17–26	
A leper is healed at Gennesaret	8.1–4	1.40–45	5.12–15	
Peter's mother-in-law healed	8.14–17	1.29–31	4.38, 39	
A withered hand is restored	12.9–13	3.1–5	6.6–11	
A demon-possessed boy is cured	17.14–21	9.14–29	9.37–42	
Jesus walks on the sea	14.22–33	6.45–52		6.17–21
Blind Bartimaeus receives sight	20.29–34	10.46–52	18.35–43	
A girl is freed from a demon	15.21–28	7.24–30		
Four thousand are fed	15.32–38	8.1–9		
Cursing the fig tree	21.18–22	11.12–14, 20–24		
A centurion's servant is healed	8.5–13		7.1–10	
A demon is sent out of a man		1.23–27	4.33–36	
A dumb demoniac is healed	12.22		11.14	
Two blind men find sight	9.27–31			
Jesus heals the mute man	9.32, 33			
A coin in a fish's mouth	17.24–27			
A deaf and dumb man is healed		7.31–37		
A blind man sees at Bethsaida		8.22–26		
The first miraculous catch of fish			5.1–11	
A widow's son is raised			7.11–16	
A handicapped woman is healed			13.10–17	
Jesus cures a sick man			14.1–6	
Ten lepers are cured			17.11–19	
Jesus restores a man's ear			22.49–51	
Jesus turns water into wine				2.1–11
A nobleman's son is healed at Cana				4.46–54
A lame man is cured				5.1–16
Jesus heals a man born blind				9.1–7
Lazarus is raised from the dead				11.1–45
The second miraculous catch of fish				21.1–14

COMPARISON OF THE FOUR GOSPELS

All four Gospels present the life and teachings of Jesus. Each book, however, focuses on a unique facet of Jesus and his character. To understand more about the specific characteristics of Jesus, read any one of the four Gospels.

	Matthew	*Mark*	*Luke*	*John*
Jesus is . . .	The promised King	The Servant of God	The Son of Man	The Son of God
The original readers were . . .	Jews	Gentiles, Romans	Greeks	Christians throughout the world
Significant themes . . .	Jesus is the Messiah because he fulfilled Old Testament prophecy	Jesus backed up his words with action	Jesus was God but also fully human	Belief in Jesus is required for salvation
Character of the writer . . .	Teacher	Storyteller	Historian	Theologian
Greatest emphasis is on . . .	Jesus' sermons and words	Jesus' miracles and actions	Jesus' humanity	The principles of Jesus' teaching

MESSIANIC PROPHECIES AND FULFILLMENTS

For the Gospel writers, one of the main reasons for believing in Jesus was the way his life fulfilled the Old Testament prophecies about the Messiah. Following is a list of some of the main prophecies.

	Old Testament Prophecies	New Testament Fulfillment
1. Messiah was to be born in Bethlehem	Micah 5.2	Matthew 2.1–6 Luke 2.1–20
2. Messiah was to be born of a virgin	Isaiah 7.14	Matthew 1.18–25 Luke 1.26–38
3. Messiah was to be a prophet like Moses	Deuteronomy 18.15, 18, 19	John 7.40
4. Messiah was to enter Jerusalem in triumph	Zechariah 9.9	Matthew 21.1–9 John 12.12–16
5. Messiah was to be rejected by his own people	Isaiah 53.1, 3 Psalm 118.22	Matthew 26.3, 4 John 12.37–43 Acts 4.1–12
6. Messiah was to be betrayed by one of his followers	Psalm 41.9	Matthew 26.14–16, 47–50 Luke 22.19–23
7. Messiah was to be tried and condemned	Isaiah 53.8	Luke 23.1–25 Matthew 27.1, 2
8. Messiah was to be silent before his accusers	Isaiah 53.7	Matthew 27.12–14 Mark 15.3–4, Luke 23.8–10
9. Messiah was to be struck and spat upon by his enemies	Isaiah 50.6	Matthew 26.67 Matthew 27.30 Mark 14.65
10. Messiah was to be mocked and taunted	Psalm 22.7, 8	Matthew 27.39–44 Luke 23.11, 35
11. Messiah was to die by crucifixion	Psalm 22.14, 16, 17	Matthew 27.31 Mark 15.20, 25
12. Messiah was to suffer with criminals and pray for his enemies	Isaiah 53.12	Matthew 27.38 Mark 15.27, 28 Luke 23.32–34
13. Messiah was to be given vinegar and gall	Psalm 69.21	Matthew 27.34 John 19.28–30
14. Others were to cast lots for Messiah's garments	Psalm 22.18	Matthew 27.35 John 19.23, 24
15. Messiah's bones were not to be broken	Exodus 12.46	John 19.31–36
16. Messiah was to die as a sacrifice for sin	Isaiah 53.5, 6, 8, 10, 11, 12	John 1.29; 11.49–52 Acts 10.43; 13.38, 39
17. Messiah was to be raised from the dead	Psalm 16.10	Acts 2.22–32 Matthew 28.1–10
18. Messiah is now at God's right hand	Psalm 110.1	Mark 16.19 Luke 24.50, 51

The ACTS of the Apostles

Jesus crucified; Pentecost; church begun A.D. 30	*Stephen martyred; Paul's conversion 35*	*Paul returns to Tarsus 38*	*Barnabas goes to find Paul 43*	*James martyred; Peter in prison 44*	*Paul's first missionary journey 46-48*	*Jerusalem council 50*	*Paul's second missionary journey 50-52*

VITAL STATISTICS

PURPOSE:
To give an accurate account of the birth and growth of the Christian church

AUTHOR:
Luke (a Gentile physician)

TO WHOM WRITTEN:
Theophilus

DATE WRITTEN:
Between A.D. 63 and 70

SETTING:
Acts is the connecting link between Christ's life and the life of the church, between the Gospels and the Epistles

KEY VERSE:
"But you will receive power when the Holy Spirit has come upon you; and you will be my witnesses in Jerusalem, in all Judea and Samaria, and to the ends of the earth" (1.8).

KEY PEOPLE:
Peter, John, James, Stephen, Philip, Paul, Barnabas, Cornelius, James (Jesus' brother), Timothy, Lydia, Silas, Titus, Apollos, Agabus, Ananias, Felix, Festus, Agrippa, Luke

KEY PLACES:
Jerusalem, Samaria, Lydda, Joppa, Antioch, Cyprus, Antioch in Pisidia, Iconium, Lystra, Derbe, Philippi, Thessalonica, Beroea, Athens, Corinth, Ephesus, Caesarea, Malta, Rome

SPECIAL FEATURES:
Acts is a sequel to the Gospel of Luke. Because it ends so abruptly, Luke may have planned to write a third book, continuing the story.

WITH a flick of the fingers, friction occurs and a spark leaps from match to tinder. A small flame burns the edges and grows, fueled by wood and air. Heat builds, and soon the kindling is licked by orange-red tongues. Higher and wider it spreads, consuming the wood. The flame has become a fire.

Nearly 2,000 years ago, a match was struck in Palestine. At first, just a few in that corner of the world were touched and warmed; but the fire spread beyond Jerusalem and Judea out to the world and to all people. Acts provides an eyewitness account of the flame and fire—the birth and spread of the church. Beginning in Jerusalem with a small group of disciples, the message traveled across the Roman Empire. Empowered by the Holy Spirit, this courageous band preached, taught, healed, and demonstrated love in synagogues, schools, homes, markets, and courtrooms; on streets, hills, ships, and desert roads—wherever God sent them, lives and history were changed.

Written by Luke as a sequel to his Gospel, Acts is an accurate historical record of the early church. But Acts is also a theological book, with lessons and living examples of the work of the Holy Spirit, church relationships and organization, the implications of grace, and the law of love. And Acts is an apologetic work, building a strong case for the validity of Christ's claims and promises.

The book of Acts begins with the outpouring of the promised Holy Spirit and the commencement of the proclamation of the gospel of Jesus Christ. This Spirit-inspired evangelism began in Jerusalem and eventually spread to Rome, covering most of the Roman Empire. The gospel first went to the Jews; but they, as a nation, rejected it. A remnant of Jews, of course, gladly received the good news. But the continual rejection of the gospel by the vast majority of the Jews led to the ever-increasing proclamation of the gospel to the Gentiles. This was according to Jesus' plan: the gospel was to go from Jerusalem, to Judea, to Samaria, and to the ends of the earth (1.8). This, in fact, is the pattern that the Acts narrative follows. The glorious proclamation begins in Jerusalem (chapters 1—7), goes to Judea and Samaria (chapter 8 and following), and to the countries beyond Judea (11.19; 13.4 and on to the end of Acts). The second half of Acts is focused primarily on Paul's missionary journeys to many countries north of the Mediterranean Sea. He, with his companions, takes the gospel first to the Jews and then to the Gentiles. Some of the Jews believe, and many of the Gentiles receive the good news with joy. New churches are started, and new believers begin to grow in the Christian life.

As you read Acts, put yourself in the place of the disciples—feel with them as they are filled with the Holy Spirit, and thrill with them as they see thousands respond to the gospel message. Sense their commitment as they give every ounce of talent and treasure to Christ. And as you read, watch the Spirit-led boldness of these first-century believers, who through suffering and in the face of death take every opportunity to tell of their crucified and risen Lord. Then decide to be a 20th-century version of those men and women of God.

Paul's third missionary journey 53-57	Nero becomes emperor 54	Paul imprisoned in Caesarea 57-59	Paul's voyage to Rome 59	Paul released from prison 62	Paul martyred 67?	Rome destroys Jerusalem 70

THE BLUEPRINT

A. PETER'S MINISTRY (1.1—12.25)
1. Establishment of the church
2. Expansion of the church

After the resurrection of Jesus Christ, Peter preached boldly and performed many miracles. This demonstrates vividly the source and effects of Christian power. Because of the Holy Spirit, God's people were empowered so they could accomplish their tasks. The Holy Spirit is still available to empower believers today. We should turn to the Holy Spirit to give us the strength, courage, and insight to accomplish our work for God.

B. PAUL'S MINISTRY (13.1—28.31)
1. First missionary journey
2. Meeting of the church council
3. Second missionary journey
4. Third missionary journey
5. Paul on trial

Paul's missionary adventures show us the progress of Christianity. The gospel could not be confined to one corner of the world. This was a faith that offered hope to all mankind. We too should venture forth and share in this heroic task to witness for Christ in all the world.

MEGATHEMES

THEME	EXPLANATION	IMPORTANCE
Church beginnings	Acts is the history of how Christianity was founded and organized and solved its problems. The community of believers began by faith in the risen Christ and in the power of the Holy Spirit, who enabled them to witness, to love, and to serve.	New churches are continually being founded. By faith in Jesus Christ and in the power of the Holy Spirit, the church can be a vibrant agent for change. As we face new problems, Acts gives important remedies for solving them.
Holy Spirit	The church did not start or grow by its own power or enthusiasm. The disciples were empowered by God's Holy Spirit. He was the promised Comforter and Guide sent when Jesus went to heaven.	The Holy Spirit's work demonstrated that Christianity was supernatural. Thus the church became more Holy Spirit-conscious than problem-conscious. By faith, any believer can claim the Holy Spirit's power to do Christ's work.
Church growth	Acts presents the history of a dynamic, growing community of believers from Jerusalem to Syria, Africa, Asia, and Europe. In the first century it spread from believing Jews to non-Jews in 39 cities and 30 countries, islands, or provinces.	When the Holy Spirit works, there is movement, excitement, and growth. He gives us the motivation, energy, and ability to get the gospel to the whole world. How are you fitting into God's plan for expanding Christianity? What is your place in this movement?
Witnessing	Peter, John, Philip, Paul, Barnabas, and thousands more witnessed to their new faith in Christ. By personal testimony, preaching, or defense before authorities, they told the story with boldness and courage to groups of all sizes.	We are God's people, chosen to be part of his plan to reach the world. In love and by faith, we can have the Holy Spirit's help as we witness or preach. Witnessing is also beneficial to us because it strengthens our faith as we confront those who challenge it.
Opposition	Through imprisonment, beatings, plots, and riots, Christians were persecuted by both Jews and Gentiles. But the opposition became a catalyst for the spread of Christianity. This showed that Christianity was not the work of man, but of God.	God can work through any opposition. When severe treatment from hostile unbelievers comes, realize that it has come because you have been a faithful witness and you have looked for the opportunity to present the good news about Christ. Seize the opportunities that opposition brings.

KEY PLACES IN ACTS

Modern names and boundaries are shown in gray.

The apostle Paul, whose missionary journeys fill much of this book, traveled tremendous distances as he tirelessly spread the gospel across much of the Roman Empire. His combined trips, by land and ship, equal more than 13,000 airline miles, to say nothing of the circuitous land routes he walked and climbed.

1 **Judea** Jesus ascended to heaven from the Mount of Olives outside Jerusalem, and his followers returned to the city to await the infilling of the Holy Spirit, which occurred at Pentecost. Peter gave a powerful sermon that was heard by Jews from across the empire. The Jerusalem church grew, but Stephen was martyred for his faith by Jewish leaders who did not believe in Jesus (1.1—7.59).

2 **Samaria** After Stephen's death, persecution of Christians intensified, but it caused the believers to leave Jerusalem and spread the gospel to other cities in the empire. Philip took the gospel into Samaria, and even to a man from Ethiopia (8.1–40).

3 **Syria** Paul began his story as a persecutor of Christians, only to be met by Jesus himself on the road to Damascus. He became a believer, but his new faith caused opposition, so he returned to Tarsus, his home, for safety. Barnabas sought out Paul in Tarsus and brought him to the church in Antioch in Syria, where they worked together. Meanwhile, Peter had received a vision that led him to Caesarea, where he presented the gospel to a Gentile family, who became believers (9.1–12.25).

4 **Cyprus and Galatia** Paul and Barnabas were dedicated by the church in Antioch in Syria for God's work of spreading the gospel to other cities. They set off on their first missionary journey through Cyprus and Galatia (13.1—14.28).

5 **Jerusalem** Controversy between Jewish Christians and Gentile Christians over the matter of keeping the law led to a special council, with delegates from the churches in Antioch and Jerusalem meeting in Jerusalem. Together, they resolved the conflict and the news was taken back to Antioch (15.1–35).

6 **Macedonia** Barnabas traveled to Cyprus while Paul took a second missionary journey. He revisited the churches in Galatia and headed toward Ephesus, but the Holy Spirit said no. He then turned north toward Bithynia and Pontus, but again was told not to go. He then received the "Macedonian call," and followed the Spirit's direction into the cities of Macedonia (15.36—17.14).

7 **Achaia** Paul traveled from Macedonia to Athens and Corinth in Achaia, then traveled by ship to Ephesus before returning to Caesarea, Jerusalem, and finally back to Antioch (17.15—18.22).

8 **Ephesus** Paul's third missionary journey took him back through Cilicia and Galatia, this time straight to Ephesus in Asia. He visited other cities in Asia before going back to Macedonia and Achaia. He returned to Jerusalem by ship, despite his knowledge that arrest awaited him there (18.23—23.30).

9 **Caesarea** Paul was arrested in Jerusalem and taken to Antipatris, then on to Caesarea under Roman guard. Paul always took advantage of any opportunity to share the gospel, and he did so before many Gentile leaders. But because Paul appealed to Caesar, he began the long journey to Rome (23.31—26.32).

10 **Rome** After storms, layovers in Crete, and shipwreck on the island of Malta, Paul arrived in Sicily, and finally in Italy, where he traveled by land, under guard, to his long-awaited destination, Rome, the capital of the empire (27.1—28.31).

A. PETER'S MINISTRY (1.1 – 12.25)

The book of Acts begins where the Gospels leave off, reporting on the actions of the apostles and the work of the Holy Spirit. Beginning in Jerusalem, the church is established and grows rapidly, then faces intense persecution, which drives the believers out into the surrounding areas. Through this dispersion, Samaritans and Gentiles hear the good news and believe.

1. Establishment of the church

Jesus ascends to heaven

1.1 Lk 1.3
1.3 Mk 16.12,14 Lk 24.33-36 Jn 20.19,26 21.1,14
1.4 Jn 14.16,17,26 Lk 24.49
1.6 Dan 7.27 Amos 9.11 1 Cor 15.7

1 In the first book, Theophilus, I wrote about all that Jesus did and taught from
the beginning 2 until the day when he was taken up to heaven, after giving
instructions through the Holy Spirit to the apostles whom he had chosen. 3 After his
suffering he presented himself alive to them by many convincing proofs, appearing
to them during forty days and speaking about the kingdom of God. 4 While staying[a] with them, he ordered them not to leave Jerusalem, but to wait there for the
promise of the Father. "This," he said, "is what you have heard from me; 5 for John
baptized with water, but you will be baptized with[b] the Holy Spirit not many days
from now."

6 So when they had come together, they asked him, "Lord, is this the time when
you will restore the kingdom to Israel?" 7 He replied, "It is not for you to know the

[a] Or *eating* [b] Or *by*

1.1 The book of Acts continues the story Luke began in his Gospel, covering the 30 years after Jesus' ascension. In that short time the church was established, and the gospel of salvation was taken throughout the world, even to the capital of the Roman Empire. Those preaching the gospel, though ordinary people with human frailties and limitations, were empowered by the Holy Spirit to turn the world "upside down" (17.6). Throughout the book of Acts we learn about the nature of the church and how we today are also to go about turning our world upside down.

1.1 Luke's first writing was the Gospel of Luke; it was also addressed to Theophilus, whose name means "dear friend who loves God." (See note on Luke 1.3.)

1.1ff Verses 1–11 are the bridge between the events recorded in the Gospels and the beginning of the church. Jesus spent 40 days teaching his disciples, and they were changed drastically. Before, they had argued with each other, deserted their Lord, even lied about knowing Jesus. Here, in a series of meetings with the living, resurrected Christ, the disciples had many questions answered. They became convinced about the resurrection, learned about the kingdom of God, and learned about their power source – the Holy Spirit. By reading the Bible, we can sit with the resurrected Christ in his school of discipleship. By believing in him, we can receive his power by the Holy Spirit to be new people. By joining with other Christians in his church, we can take part in doing his work on earth.

1.1–3 Luke says that the disciples were eyewitnesses to all that had happened to Jesus Christ – his life before his crucifixion ("suffering"), and the 40 days after his resurrection as he taught them more about the kingdom of God. Today there are still people who doubt Jesus' resurrection. But look at the change the resurrection made in the disciples' lives. At Jesus' death, they scattered. They were disillusioned and feared for their lives. After seeing the resurrected Christ, they were fearless and risked everything to spread the good news about him around the world. They faced imprisonment, beatings, rejection, and martyrdom yet never compromised their mission. These men would not have risked their lives for something they knew was a fraud. They knew Jesus was raised from the dead, and the early church was fired with their enthusiasm to tell others. It is important to know this so we can have confidence in their testimony. Twenty centuries later we can still be confident that our faith is based on fact.

1.3 Jesus explained that with his coming, the kingdom of God was inaugurated. But the kingdom of God will not be fully realized until Jesus Christ comes again to judge all people and remove all evil from the world. Before that time, believers are to work to spread God's kingdom across the world. The book of Acts records how this was begun. What the early church started, we must continue.

1.4, 5 The *trinity* is a description of the unique relationship of God the Father, the Son, and the Holy Spirit. If Jesus had stayed on earth, his physical presence would have limited the spread of the gospel, because physically he could be in only one place at a time. After his ascension, he would be spiritually present everywhere through the Holy Spirit. The Holy Spirit was sent so that God would be with and within his followers after Jesus returned to heaven. His Spirit would comfort them, guide them to know his truth, remind them of Jesus' words, give them the right words to say, and fill them with power (see John 14 – 16).

1.5 At Pentecost (2.1–4) the Holy Spirit was made available to all who believe in Jesus. We receive the Holy Spirit (are baptized by him) when we receive Jesus Christ. The baptism of the Holy Spirit must be understood in the light of his total work in Christians.

(1) The Spirit marks the beginning of the Christian experience. We cannot belong to Christ without his Spirit (Romans 8.9); we cannot be united to Christ without his Spirit (1 Corinthians 6.17); we cannot be adopted as his children without his Spirit (Romans 8.14–17; Galatians 4.6, 7); we cannot be in the body of Christ except by baptism in the Spirit (1 Corinthians 12.13).

(2) The Spirit is the power of our new lives. He begins a lifelong process of change as we become more like Christ (Galatians 3.3; Philippians 1.6). When we receive Christ by faith, we begin an immediate personal relationship with God. The Holy Spirit works in us to help us become like Christ.

(3) The Spirit unites the Christian community in Christ (Ephesians 2.19–22). The Holy Spirit can be experienced by all, and he works through all (1 Corinthians 12.11; Ephesians 4.4).

1.6 During the years of Jesus' ministry on earth, the disciples continually wondered about his kingdom. When would it come? What would be their role? In the traditional view, the Messiah would be an earthly conqueror who would free Israel from Rome. But the kingdom Jesus spoke about was first a *spiritual* kingdom established in the hearts and lives of believers. God's presence and power dwell in believers in the person of the Holy Spirit.

1.6, 7 Like other Jews, the disciples chafed under their Roman rulers. They wanted Jesus to free Israel from Roman power and then become their king. Jesus replied that God the Father sets the timetable for all events – worldwide, national, and personal. If you want changes that God isn't making immediately, don't become impatient. Instead, trust God's timetable.

times or periods that the Father has set by his own authority. 8 But you will receive
power when the Holy Spirit has come upon you; and you will be my witnesses in
Jerusalem, in all Judea and Samaria, and to the ends of the earth." 9 When he had
said this, as they were watching, he was lifted up, and a cloud took him out of their
sight. 10 While he was going and they were gazing up toward heaven, suddenly two
men in white robes stood by them. 11 They said, "Men of Galilee, why do you stand
looking up toward heaven? This Jesus, who has been taken up from you into
heaven, will come in the same way as you saw him go into heaven."

Matthias is chosen to replace Judas

12 Then they returned to Jerusalem from the mount called Olivet, which is near
Jerusalem, a sabbath day's journey away. 13 When they had entered the city, they
went to the room upstairs where they were staying, Peter, and John, and James, and
Andrew, Philip and Thomas, Bartholomew and Matthew, James son of Alphaeus,
and Simon the Zealot, and Judas son of[c] James. 14 All these were constantly devoting themselves to prayer, together with certain women, including Mary the mother
of Jesus, as well as his brothers.

15 In those days Peter stood up among the believers[d] (together the crowd numbered about one hundred twenty persons) and said, 16 "Friends,[e] the scripture had
to be fulfilled, which the Holy Spirit through David foretold concerning Judas, who
became a guide for those who arrested Jesus— 17 for he was numbered among us
and was allotted his share in this ministry." 18 (Now this man acquired a field with
the reward of his wickedness; and falling headlong,[f] he burst open in the middle

1.7 Mt 24.36 1 Thess 5.1,2
1.8 Mt 28.19 Lk 24.48,49 Jn 15.27 Acts 2.4; 8.1 Rom 10.18
1.11 Zech 14.4 Rev 1.7
1.12 Lk 24.50
1.13 Lk 22.12 Acts 12.12; 20.8
1.14 Mt 10.2-4 Mk 3.16-19 Lk 6.14-16
1.16 Ps 41.9 Jn 18.3
1.17 Jn 6.70,71 Acts 1.24,25 20.24; 21.19
1.18 Mt 26.14,15 27.3-10

[c] *Or the brother of* [d] Gk *brothers* [e] Gk *Men, brothers* [f] *Or swelling up*

1.8 Power from the Holy Spirit is not limited to strength beyond the ordinary—it involves courage, boldness, confidence, insight, ability, and authority. The disciples would need all these to fulfill their mission. If you believe in Jesus Christ, you can experience the power of the Holy Spirit in your life.

1.8 Jesus promised the disciples that they would receive power to witness after they received the Holy Spirit. Notice the progression: (1) they received the Holy Spirit, (2) he gave them power, and (3) they witnessed with extraordinary results. Often we try to reverse the order and witness by our own power and authority. Witnessing is not showing what we can do for God. It is showing and telling what God has done for us.

1.8 Jesus instructed his disciples to witness to people of all nations about him (Matthew 28.19, 20). But they were told to wait first for the Holy Spirit. God has important work for you to do for him, but you must do it by the power of the Holy Spirit. We often like to get on with the job, even if it means running ahead of God. But waiting is sometimes part of God's plan. Are you waiting and listening for God's complete instructions, or are you running ahead of his plans? We need God's timing and power to be truly effective.

1.8 This verse describes a series of ever-widening circles. The gospel was to spread, geographically, from Jerusalem, into Judea and Samaria, and finally to the whole world. It would begin with the devout Jews in Jerusalem and Samaria, spread to the mixed race in Samaria, and finally be offered to the Gentiles in the uttermost parts of the earth. God's gospel has not reached its final destination if someone in your family, your workplace, your school, or your community hasn't heard about Jesus Christ. Make sure that you are contributing in some way to the ever-widening circle of God's loving message.

1.9 It was important for the disciples to see Jesus ascend. Then they knew without a doubt that he was God and that his home was in heaven.

1.9–11 After 40 days with his disciples (1.3), Jesus ascended into heaven. Two angels proclaimed to the disciples that one day Jesus would return in the same way he went—bodily and visibly. History is not haphazard; it is moving toward a specific point—the return of Jesus to judge and rule over the earth. We should be ready for his sudden return (1 Thessalonians 5.2), not by standing around "looking up toward heaven," but by working hard to share the gospel so others will be able to share in God's great blessings.

1.12, 13 After Christ ascended into heaven, the disciples immediately returned to Jerusalem and had a prayer meeting. Jesus had said they would be baptized with the Holy Spirit in a few days, so they waited and prayed. When you face a difficult task, an important decision, or a baffling dilemma, don't rush into the work and just hope it happens the way it should. Instead, your first step should be to pray for the Holy Spirit's power and guidance.

1.13 The Zealots were a radical political party working for the violent overthrow of Roman rule in Israel.

1.14 At this time, Jesus' brothers are with the disciples. During Jesus' lifetime, they did not believe he was the Messiah, but his resurrection must have convinced them. Jesus' special appearance to James, one of his brothers, may have been an especially significant event in their conversion (see 1 Corinthians 15.7).

1.15–26 This was the first church business meeting. The small group of 11 had already grown to more than 120. The main order of business was to appoint a new disciple, or apostle, as the twelve were now called. While the apostles waited, they were doing what they could—praying, seeking God's guidance, and getting organized. Waiting for God to work does not mean sitting around doing nothing. We must do what we can, while we can, as long as we don't run ahead of God.

1.16, 17 How could someone who had been with Jesus daily betray him? Judas received the same calling and teaching as everyone else. But he chose to reject Christ's warning as well as his offers of mercy. He hardened his heart and joined in the plot with Jesus' enemies to betray him. Judas remained unrepentant to the end, and he finally committed suicide. Although Jesus predicted this would happen, it was Judas's choice. Those privileged to be *close* to the truth are not necessarily *committed* to the truth. See Judas's Profile in Mark 14 for more information on his life.

1.18 Matthew says Judas hanged himself (Matthew 27.5); Acts says he fell. The traditional explanation is that when Judas hanged himself, the rope or branch broke, Judas fell, and his body burst open.

and all his bowels gushed out. 19 This became known to all the residents of Jerusalem, so that the field was called in their language Hakeldama, that is, Field of
Blood.) 20 "For it is written in the book of Psalms,

'Let his homestead become desolate,
and let there be no one to live in it';

and

'Let another take his position of overseer.'

21 So one of the men who have accompanied us during all the time that the Lord
Jesus went in and out among us, 22 beginning from the baptism of John until the day
when he was taken up from us—one of these must become a witness with us to his
resurrection." 23 So they proposed two, Joseph called Barsabbas, who was also
known as Justus; and Matthias. 24 Then they prayed and said, "Lord, you know
everyone's heart. Show us which one of these two you have chosen 25 to take the
place[g] in this ministry and apostleship from which Judas turned aside to go to his
own place." 26 And they cast lots for them, and the lot fell on Matthias; and he was
added to the eleven apostles.

1.20 Ps 69.25; 109.8
1.21,22 Mk 1.1-4; Acts 1.2; 2.32
1.24 1 Sam 16.7; Acts 6.6; 15.8
1.25 Acts 1.17; Rom 1.5
1.26 Lev 16.8; Josh 14.1,2; 1 Sam 14.41; Prov 16.33

The Holy Spirit comes at Pentecost

2 When the day of Pentecost had come, they were all together in one place.
2 And suddenly from heaven there came a sound like the rush of a violent wind,
and it filled the entire house where they were sitting. 3 Divided tongues, as of fire,
appeared among them, and a tongue rested on each of them. 4 All of them were
filled with the Holy Spirit and began to speak in other languages, as the Spirit gave
them ability.

5 Now there were devout Jews from every nation under heaven living in Jerusalem. 6 And at this sound the crowd gathered and was bewildered, because each one
heard them speaking in the native language of each. 7 Amazed and astonished, they
asked, "Are not all these who are speaking Galileans? 8 And how is it that we hear,

2.1 Lev 23.15,16; Deut 16.9,10; Acts 1.14,15; 20.16
2.4 Mk 16.7; Acts 4.8,31; 10.46; 13.9; 19.6; 1 Cor 12.10; 13.1; Eph 5.18
2.7 Mt 26.73; Acts 1.11

[g] Other ancient authorities read *the share*

1.21, 22 There were many who consistently followed Jesus throughout his ministry on earth. The 12 disciples were his inner circle, but others shared their deep love for and commitment to Jesus.

1.21–25 The apostles had to choose a replacement for Judas Iscariot. They outlined specific criteria for making the choice. When the "finalists" had been chosen, the apostles prayed, asking God to guide the selection process. This gives us a good example of how to proceed when we are making important decisions. Set up criteria consistent with the Bible, examine the alternatives, and pray for wisdom and guidance to reach a wise decision.

1.26 The disciples became *apostles. Disciple* means follower or learner, and *apostle* means messenger or missionary. These men now had the special assignment of spreading the good news of Jesus' death and resurrection.

2.1 Held 50 days after Passover, Pentecost was also called the festival of weeks. It was one of three major annual feasts (Deuteronomy 16.16), a festival of thanksgiving for the harvested crops. Jesus was crucified at Passover, and he ascended 40 days later. The Holy Spirit came 50 days after the crucifixion, 10 days after the ascension. Jews of many nations gathered in Jerusalem for this festival. Thus Peter's speech (2.14ff) was given to an international audience, and it resulted in a worldwide harvest of new believers—the first converts to Christianity.

2.3, 4 This was a fulfillment of John the Baptist's words about the Holy Spirit's baptizing with fire (Luke 3.16), and of the prophet Joel's words about the outpouring of the Holy Spirit (Joel 2.28, 29).

Why tongues of fire? Tongues symbolize speech and the communication of the gospel. "Divided tongues" means the fire separated and rested on each of them. Fire symbolizes God's purifying presence, burning away the undesirable elements of our lives and setting our hearts aflame to ignite the lives of others. On Mount Sinai, God confirmed the validity of the Old Testament law with fire from heaven (Exodus 19.16–18). At Pentecost, God confirmed the validity of the Holy Spirit's ministry by sending fire. At Mount Sinai, fire came down on one place; at Pentecost, fire came down on many believers, symbolizing that God's presence is now available to all who believe in him.

2.3, 4 God made his presence known to this group of believers in a spectacular way—violent wind, fire, and his Holy Spirit. Would you like God to reveal himself to you in such recognizable ways? He may, but be wary of forcing your expectations on God. In 1 Kings 19.10–13, Elijah also needed a message from God. There was a great wind, then an earthquake, and finally a fire. But God's message came in a "sound of sheer silence." God may use dramatic methods to work in your life—or he may speak in gentle whispers. Wait patiently and always listen.

2.4–11 These people literally spoke in other languages—a miraculous attention-getter for the international crowd gathered in town for the feast. All the nationalities represented recognized their own languages being spoken. But more than miraculous speaking drew people's attention; they saw the presence and power of the Holy Spirit. The apostles continued to minister in the power of the Holy Spirit wherever they went.

2.7, 8 Christianity is not limited to any race or group of people. Christ offers salvation to all people without regard to nationality. Visitors in Jerusalem were surprised to hear the apostles speaking in their native languages, but they need not have been. God works all kinds of miracles to spread the gospel, using many languages as he calls all people to become his followers. No matter what your race, color, nationality, or language, God speaks to you. Are you listening?

each of us, in our own native language? 9 Parthians, Medes, Elamites, and residents
of Mesopotamia, Judea and Cappadocia, Pontus and Asia, 10 Phrygia and Pamphylia, Egypt and the parts of Libya belonging to Cyrene, and visitors from Rome,
both Jews and proselytes, 11 Cretans and Arabs—in our own languages we hear
them speaking about God's deeds of power." 12 All were amazed and perplexed,
saying to one another, "What does this mean?" 13 But others sneered and said,
"They are filled with new wine."

Peter preaches to the crowd

14 But Peter, standing with the eleven, raised his voice and addressed them,
"Men of Judea and all who live in Jerusalem, let this be known to you, and listen
to what I say. 15 Indeed, these are not drunk, as you suppose, for it is only nine
o'clock in the morning. 16 No, this is what was spoken through the prophet Joel:

17 'In the last days it will be, God declares,
that I will pour out my Spirit upon all flesh,
and your sons and your daughters shall prophesy,
and your young men shall see visions,
and your old men shall dream dreams.
18 Even upon my slaves, both men and women,
in those days I will pour out my Spirit;
and they shall prophesy.
19 And I will show portents in the heaven above
and signs on the earth below,
blood, and fire, and smoky mist.
20 The sun shall be turned to darkness
and the moon to blood,
before the coming of the Lord's great and glorious day.
21 Then everyone who calls on the name of the Lord shall be saved.'

22 "You that are Israelites,[h] listen to what I have to say: Jesus of Nazareth,[i] a
man attested to you by God with deeds of power, wonders, and signs that God did
through him among you, as you yourselves know— 23 this man, handed over to you
according to the definite plan and foreknowledge of God, you crucified and killed
by the hands of those outside the law. 24 But God raised him up, having freed him
from death,[j] because it was impossible for him to be held in its power. 25 For David
says concerning him,

h Gk *Men, Israelites* i Gk *the Nazorean* j Gk *the pains of death*

2.9 Acts 6.9; 19.10 1 Pet 1.1
2.10 Ex 12.48 Mt 23.15; 27.32 Acts 13.13; 16.6
2.13 1 Cor 2.14; 14.23 Eph 5.18
2.16 Joel 2.28-32
2.17 Isa 44.3 Ezek 11.10 36.27 Zech 12.10 Acts 10.45
2.18 1 Cor 12.10
2.20 Mt 24.29
2.21 Ps 55.16 88.9; 116.2,4,13, 17; 145.18 Acts 9.14,21; 22.16 Rom 10.13
2.22 Jn 17.4 Acts 10.38 Heb 2.4
2.23 Acts 3.17,18 1 Pet 1.11,20 Rev 13.8
2.24 Acts 3.15 10.40; 17.31
2.25-27 Ps 16.8-11 Acts 13.30-35

2.9–11 Why are all these places mentioned? This is a list of many lands from which Jews came to the festivals in Jerusalem. These Jews were not living in Palestine because they had been dispersed throughout the world through captivities and persecutions. The Jews who responded to Peter's message returned to their homelands with God's good news of salvation. Thus God prepared the way for the spread of the gospel. As you read Acts, you will see how the way was often prepared for Paul and others by people who became believers at Pentecost. The church at Rome, for example, was begun by such Jewish believers.

2.14 Peter had been an unstable leader during Jesus' ministry, letting his bravado be his downfall, even denying that he knew Jesus (John 18.15–18, 25–27). But Christ forgave and restored him (John 21). This is a new Peter, humble but bold. His confidence came from the Holy Spirit, who made him a powerful and dynamic speaker. Have you ever felt as if you've made such bad mistakes that God could never forgive and use you? No matter what sins you have committed, God promises to forgive you and make you useful for his kingdom. Allow him to forgive you and use you effectively to serve him.

2.14ff Peter tells the people why they should listen to the believers: because the Old Testament prophecies had been entirely fulfilled in Jesus (2.14–21), because Jesus is the Messiah (2.25–36), and because the risen Christ could change their lives (2.37–40).

2.15 Peter answers accusations that they are all drunk (2.13) by saying it was much too early in the day for that.

2.16–21 Not everything mentioned in Joel 2.28, 29 was happening that particular morning. The "last days" include all the days between Christ's first and second comings, another way of saying "from now on." "The Lord's great and glorious day" (2.20) denotes the whole Christian age. Even Moses yearned for the Lord to pour his Spirit on everyone (Numbers 11.29). At Pentecost the Holy Spirit was released throughout the entire world—to men, women, slaves, Jews, Gentiles. Now *everyone* can receive the Spirit. This was a revolutionary thought for first-century Jews.

2.23 Everything that happened was under God's control. His plans were never disrupted by the Roman government or the Jewish officials. This was especially comforting to those facing oppression during the time of the early Christian church.

2.24 Peter began with a public proclamation of the resurrection at a time when it could be verified by many witnesses. This was a

A JOURNEY THROUGH THE BOOK OF ACTS

Beginning with a brief summary of Jesus' last days on earth with his disciples, his ascension, and the replacement for Judas Iscariot, Luke moves quickly to his subject—the spread of the gospel and the growth of the church. Pentecost, celebrated by the filling of the Holy Spirit (2.1–13) and Peter's powerful sermon (2.14–42), was the beginning. Then the Jerusalem church grew daily through the bold witness of Peter and John and the love of the believers (2.43—4.37). The infant church was not without problems, however, with external opposition (resulting in imprisonment, beatings, and death) and internal deceit and complaining. Greek-speaking Jewish believers were appointed to help with the administration of the church to free the apostles to preach. Stephen and Philip were among the first deacons, and Stephen became the church's first martyr (5.1—8.3).

Instead of stopping Christianity, opposition and persecution served as catalysts for its spread because the believers took the message with them wherever they fled (8.4). Soon there were converts throughout Samaria and even in Ethiopia (8.5–40).

At this point, Luke introduces us to a bright young Jew, zealous for the law and intent on ridding Judaism of the Jesus heresy. But on the way to Damascus to capture believers, Saul was converted, confronted in person by the risen Christ (9.1–9). Through the ministry of Ananias and the sponsorship of Barnabas, Saul (Paul) was welcomed into the fellowship and then sent to Tarsus for safety (9.10–30).

Meanwhile, the church continued to thrive throughout Judea, Galilee, and Samaria. Luke recounts Peter's preaching and how he healed Aeneas in Lydda and Dorcas in Joppa (9.31–43). While in Joppa, Peter learned through a vision that he could take the gospel to the "unclean" Gentiles. Peter understood and he faithfully shared the truth with Cornelius, whose entire household became believers (chapter 10). This was startling news to the Jerusalem church; but when Peter told his story, they praised God for his plan for *all* people to hear the good news (11.1–18). This pushed the church into even wider circles as the message was preached to Greeks in Antioch, where Barnabas went to encourage the believers and find Paul (11.20–26).

To please the Jewish leaders, Herod joined in the persecution of the Jerusalem church, killing James (John's brother) and imprisoning Peter. But God freed Peter, and he walked from prison to a prayer meeting on his behalf at John Mark's house (chapter 12).

Here Luke shifts the focus to Paul's ministry. Commissioned by the Antioch church for a missionary tour (13.1–3), Paul and Barnabas took the gospel to Cyprus and south Galatia with great success (13.4—14.28). But the Jewish-Gentile controversy still smoldered, and with so many Gentiles responding to Christ, it threatened to divide the church. So a council met in Jerusalem to rule on the relationship of Gentile Christians to the Old Testament laws. After hearing both sides, James (Jesus' brother and the leader of the Jerusalem church) resolved the issue and sent messengers to the churches with the decision (15.1–31).

After the council, Paul and Silas preached in Antioch. Then they left for Syria and Cilicia as Barnabas and Mark sailed for Cyprus (15.36–41). On this second missionary journey, Paul and Silas traveled throughout Macedonia and Achaia, establishing churches in Philippi, Thessalonica, Beroea, Corinth, and Ephesus before returning to Antioch (16.1—18.21). Luke also tells of the ministry of Apollos (18.24–28).

On Paul's third missionary trip he traveled through Galatia, Phrygia, Macedonia, and Achaia, encouraging and teaching the believers (19.1—21.9). During this time, he felt compelled to go to Jerusalem; and although he was warned by Agabus and others of impending imprisonment (21.10–12), he continued his journey in that direction.

While in Jerusalem, Paul was accosted in the temple by an angry mob and taken into protective custody by the Roman commander (21.17—22.30). Now we see Paul as a prisoner and on trial before the Jewish council (23.1–9), Governor Felix (23.22—24.27), and Festus and Agrippa (25.1—26.32). In each case, Paul gave a strong and clear witness for his Lord.

Because he appealed to Caesar, however, they sent him to Rome for the final hearing of his case. But on the way the ship was destroyed in a storm, and the sailors and prisoners had to swim ashore. Even in this circumstance Paul shared his faith (27.1—28.11). Eventually the journey continued and Paul arrived in Rome, where he was held under house arrest while awaiting trial (28.12–31).

Luke ends Acts abruptly with the encouraging word that Paul had freedom in his captivity to talk to visitors and guards with boldness, "proclaiming the kingdom of God and teaching about the Lord Jesus Christ with all boldness and without hindrance" (28.31).

---

powerful statement because many of the people listening to Peter's words had been in Jerusalem 50 days earlier at Passover and may have seen or heard about the crucifixion of this "great teacher." Jesus' resurrection was the ultimate sign that what he said about himself was true. Without the resurrection, we would have no reason to believe in Jesus.

'I saw the Lord always before me,
for he is at my right hand so that I will not be shaken;
26 therefore my heart was glad, and my tongue rejoiced;
moreover my flesh will live in hope.
27 For you will not abandon my soul to Hades,
or let your Holy One experience corruption.
28 You have made known to me the ways of life;
you will make me full of gladness with your presence.'

29 "Fellow Israelites,[k] I may say to you confidently of our ancestor David that
he both died and was buried, and his tomb is with us to this day. 30 Since he was a
prophet, he knew that God had sworn with an oath to him that he would put one of
his descendants on his throne. 31 Foreseeing this, David[l] spoke of the resurrection
of the Messiah,[m] saying,

'He was not abandoned to Hades,
nor did his flesh experience corruption.'

32 This Jesus God raised up, and of that all of us are witnesses. 33 Being therefore
exalted at[n] the right hand of God, and having received from the Father the promise
of the Holy Spirit, he has poured out this that you both see and hear. 34 For David
did not ascend into the heavens, but he himself says,

'The Lord said to my Lord,
"Sit at my right hand,
35 until I make your enemies your footstool." '

36 Therefore let the entire house of Israel know with certainty that God has made
him both Lord and Messiah,[o] this Jesus whom you crucified."

37 Now when they heard this, they were cut to the heart and said to Peter and
to the other apostles, "Brothers,[k] what should we do?" 38 Peter said to them, "Repent, and be baptized every one of you in the name of Jesus Christ so that your sins
may be forgiven; and you will receive the gift of the Holy Spirit. 39 For the promise
is for you, for your children, and for all who are far away, everyone whom the Lord
our God calls to him." 40 And he testified with many other arguments and exhorted
them, saying, "Save yourselves from this corrupt generation." 41 So those who welcomed his message were baptized, and that day about three thousand persons were
added. 42 They devoted themselves to the apostles' teaching and fellowship, to the
breaking of bread and the prayers.

The believers become the first church

43 Awe came upon everyone, because many wonders and signs were being
done by the apostles. 44 All who believed were together and had all things in com-

2.29 1 Kings 2.10; Neh 3.16; Acts 13.35,36
2.30 2 Sam 7.12-14; Ps 89.3,4; Lk 1.32; 2 Tim 2.8
2.31 Acts 13.35,36
2.33 Lk 24.49; Jn 14.26; Acts 1.4,8; Eph 4.8; Phil 2.9; Heb 10.12
2.34 Ps 110.1
2.35 1 Cor 15.25
2.36 Lk 2.11; Acts 5.31
2.37 Zech 12.10; Acts 16.30
2.38 Mk 16.16; Lk 24.47; Acts 3.19; 5.31; 8.12; 22.16
2.39 Isa 44.3; Joel 2.32; Rom 9.8; Eph 2.13,17
2.40 Phil 2.15
2.42 Acts 20.7
2.44 Acts 4.32-37

[k] Gk *Men, brothers* [l] Gk *he* [m] Or *the Christ* [n] Or *by* [o] Or *Christ*

2.25–32 Peter quotes from Psalm 16.8–11, a psalm written by David. He explains that David was not writing about himself, because he died and was buried (2.29). Instead, he wrote as a prophet (2.30), speaking of the Messiah who would be resurrected. The audience understood *Hades* (2.27) as the grave, not the place of final punishment. The emphasis here is that Jesus' body was *not* left to decay, but was resurrected and glorified.

2.33 "He has poured out this that you both see and hear" could be translated, "gave him the authority to send the Holy Spirit with the results you are seeing and hearing today."

2.37 After Peter's powerful, Spirit-filled message, the people were deeply moved and asked, "What should we do?" This is the basic question we must ask. It is not enough to be sorry for our sins – we must let God forgive them, and then we must live like forgiven people. Has God spoken to you through his Word or through the words of another believer? Like Peter's audience, ask God what you should do, and then obey.

2.38, 39 If you want to follow Christ, you must "repent, and be baptized." To repent means to *turn from* sin, changing the direction of your life from selfishness and rebellion against God's laws. At the same time, you must *turn to* Christ, depending on him for forgiveness, mercy, guidance, and purpose. We cannot save ourselves – only God can save us. Baptism identifies us with Christ and with the community of believers. It is a condition of discipleship and a sign of faith.

2.40–43 About 3,000 people became new believers when Peter preached the good news about Christ. These new Christians were joined with the other believers, taught by the apostles, and included in the prayer meetings and fellowship. New believers in Christ need to be in groups where they can learn God's Word, pray, and mature in the faith. If you have just begun a relationship with Christ, seek out other believers for fellowship, prayer, and teaching. This is the way to grow.

2.42 "Breaking of bread" means communion services that were celebrated in remembrance of Jesus and were patterned after the last supper that Jesus had with his disciples before his death (Matthew 26.26–29).

2.44 Recognizing the other believers as brothers and sisters in the family of God, the Christians in Jerusalem shared all they had so that all could benefit from God's gifts. It is tempting – especially if

2.45 Isa 58.7 mon; 45 they would sell their possessions and goods and distribute the proceeds[p] to
all, as any had need. 46 Day by day, as they spent much time together in the temple,
they broke bread at home[q] and ate their food with glad and generous[r] hearts,
2.47 Acts 4.4; 6.7 Rom 14.18,19 47 praising God and having the goodwill of all the people. And day by day the Lord
added to their number those who were being saved.

Peter heals a crippled beggar

3 One day Peter and John were going up to the temple at the hour of prayer, at
three o'clock in the afternoon. 2 And a man lame from birth was being carried
in. People would lay him daily at the gate of the temple called the Beautiful Gate
so that he could ask for alms from those entering the temple. 3 When he saw Peter
and John about to go into the temple, he asked them for alms. 4 Peter looked intently at him, as did John, and said, "Look at us." 5 And he fixed his attention on
3.6 Acts 4.10 1 Pet 4.10 them, expecting to receive something from them. 6 But Peter said, "I have no silver
or gold, but what I have I give you; in the name of Jesus Christ of Nazareth,[s] stand
up and walk." 7 And he took him by the right hand and raised him up; and immedi-
3.8 Isa 35.6 ately his feet and ankles were made strong. 8 Jumping up, he stood and began to
walk, and he entered the temple with them, walking and leaping and praising God.
3.9 Acts 4.16,21 9 All the people saw him walking and praising God, 10 and they recognized him as
3.10 Jn 9.8 the one who used to sit and ask for alms at the Beautiful Gate of the temple; and
they were filled with wonder and amazement at what had happened to him.

Peter preaches in the temple

3.12 2 Cor 3.5 11 While he clung to Peter and John, all the people ran together to them in the
portico called Solomon's Portico, utterly astonished. 12 When Peter saw it, he ad-
3.13 Lk 23.4 Phil 2.9-11 dressed the people, "You Israelites,[t] why do you wonder at this, or why do you
stare at us, as though by our own power or piety we had made him walk? 13 The God

[p] Gk *them* [q] Or *from house to house* [r] Or *sincere* [s] Gk *the Nazorean* [t] Gk *Men, Israelites*

we have material wealth – to cut ourselves off from one another, each taking care of his own, each providing for and enjoying his own little piece of the world. But as part of God's spiritual family, it is our responsibility to help one another in every way possible. God's family works best when its members work together.

2.46 A common misconception about the first Christians (who were Jews) was that they rejected the Jewish religion. But these believers saw Jesus' message and resurrection as the fulfillment of everything they knew and believed from the Old Testament. The Jewish believers at first did not separate from the rest of the Jewish community. They still went to the temple and synagogues for worship and instruction in God's Word. But their belief in Jesus created great friction with Jews who didn't believe that Jesus was the Messiah. Thus, believing Jews were forced to meet in private homes for communion, prayer, and teaching about Christ. By the end of the first century, many of these Jewish believers were excommunicated from their synagogues.

2.47 A healthy Christian community attracts people to Christ. The Jerusalem church's zeal for worship and brotherly love was contagious. A healthy, loving church will grow. What are you doing to make your church the kind of place that will attract others to Christ?

3.1 The Jews observed three times of prayer – morning (9.00 a.m.), afternoon (3.00 p.m.), and evening (sunset). At these times devout Jews and Gentiles who believed in God often went to the temple to pray. Peter and John were going to the temple at 3.00 p.m.

3.2 The Beautiful Gate was an entrance to the temple, not to the city. It was one of the favored entrances, and many people passed through it on their way to worship. The lame man was begging where he would be seen by the most people.

3.2 Giving money to beggars was considered praiseworthy in Jewish religion. So the beggar wisely placed himself where pious people might see him on their way to worship at the temple.

3.5, 6 The lame beggar asked for money, but Peter gave him something much better – the use of his legs. We often ask God to solve a small problem, but he wants to give us a new life and help for *all* our problems. When we ask God for help, he may say, "I've got something even better for you." Ask God for what you want, but don't be surprised when he gives you what you really *need.*

3.6 "In the name of Jesus Christ" means "by the authority of Jesus Christ." The apostles were doing this healing through the Holy Spirit's power, not their own.

3.7–10 In his excitement the formerly lame man began to jump and walk around. He also praised God! And then others were also awed by God's power. Don't forget to thank people who help you, but also remember to praise God for his care and protection.

3.11 A portico was a covered porch or entrance with columns.

3.11ff Peter had an audience, and he capitalized on the opportunity to share Jesus Christ. He clearly presented his message by telling (1) who Jesus is, (2) how they had rejected him, (3) why their rejection was fatal, and (4) what they needed to do to change the situation. He told them that they still had a choice: God still offered them the opportunity to believe and receive Jesus as their Messiah and as their Lord. Displays of God's mercy and grace, such as the healing of this lame man, often create teachable moments. Pray to have courage like Peter to see these opportunities and speak up for Christ.

3.13, 14 Pilate had decided to release Jesus, but the people had clamored to have Barabbas, a murderer, released instead (see John 19.1–16). When Peter said "whom you handed over and rejected," he meant it literally. Jesus' trial and death had occurred right there in Jerusalem only weeks earlier. It wasn't an event of the distant past – most of these people had heard about it, and some had probably taken part in condemning him.

of Abraham, the God of Isaac, and the God of Jacob, the God of our ancestors has
glorified his servant[u] Jesus, whom you handed over and rejected in the presence of
Pilate, though he had decided to release him. 14 But you rejected the Holy and
Righteous One and asked to have a murderer given to you, 15 and you killed the
Author of life, whom God raised from the dead. To this we are witnesses. 16 And
by faith in his name, his name itself has made this man strong, whom you see and
know; and the faith that is through Jesus[v] has given him this perfect health in the
presence of all of you.
17 "And now, friends,[w] I know that you acted in ignorance, as did also your
rulers. 18 In this way God fulfilled what he had foretold through all the prophets,
that his Messiah[x] would suffer. 19 Repent therefore, and turn to God so that your
sins may be wiped out, 20 so that times of refreshing may come from the presence
of the Lord, and that he may send the Messiah[y] appointed for you, that is, Jesus,
21 who must remain in heaven until the time of universal restoration that God announced long ago through his holy prophets. 22 Moses said, 'The Lord your God
will raise up for you from your own people[w] a prophet like me. You must listen to
whatever he tells you. 23 And it will be that everyone who does not listen to that
prophet will be utterly rooted out of the people.' 24 And all the prophets, as many
as have spoken, from Samuel and those after him, also predicted these days. 25 You
are the descendants of the prophets and of the covenant that God gave to your ancestors, saying to Abraham, 'And in your descendants all the families of the earth
shall be blessed.' 26 When God raised up his servant,[u] he sent him first to you, to
bless you by turning each of you from your wicked ways."

3.15 Acts 2.24; 5.31,32 Heb 2.10; 5.9
3.17 Lk 23.34 Acts 13.27 1 Cor 2.8 1 Tim 1.13
3.18 Ps 22; 41.9 69.4,21 Isa 50.6; 53.4-11 Zech 12.10; 13.7 1 Pet 1.10
3.19 Acts 2.38; 26.20
3.21 Rom 8.21
3.22 Deut 18.15,18 Jn 1.20,21 7.40,41,52
3.23 Deut 18.19
3.25 Gen 12.3; 22.18 Rom 9.4-8
3.26 Acts 13.46

Peter and John face the Sanhedrin

4 While Peter and John[z] were speaking to the people, the priests, the captain of
the temple, and the Sadducees came to them, 2 much annoyed because they
were teaching the people and proclaiming that in Jesus there is the resurrection of

4.1 Lk 22.4

[u] Or *child* [v] Gk *him* [w] Gk *brothers* [x] Or *his Christ* [y] Or *the Christ* [z] Gk *While they*

3.15 The religious leaders thought they had put an end to Jesus when they crucified him. But their confidence was shaken when Peter told them that Jesus was alive again and that this time they could not harm him. Peter's message emphasized that (1) they and their religious leaders killed Jesus (3.17), (2) God brought him back to life, and (3) the apostles were witnesses to this fact. After pointing out the sin and injustice of these leaders, Peter showed the significance of the resurrection, God's triumph and power over death.

3.16 Jesus, not the apostles, received the glory for the healing of the lame man. In those days a man's name represented his character; it stood for his authority and power. By using Jesus' name, Peter showed who gave him the authority and power to heal. The apostles did not emphasize what they could do, but what God could do through them. Jesus' name is not to be used as magic—it must be used by faith. When we pray in Jesus' name, we must remember that it is Christ himself, not merely the sound of his name, who gives our prayers their power.

3.18 These prophecies are found in Psalm 22, Isaiah 50.6, and Isaiah 53. Peter was explaining the kind of Messiah God sent to earth. The Jews expected a great ruler, not a suffering servant.

3.19 John the Baptist prepared the way for Jesus by preaching repentance. The apostles' call to salvation also included repentance—acknowledging personal sin and turning away from it. Many people want the benefits of being identified with Christ without turning from sin and admitting their own disobedience. The key to forgiveness is confessing your sin and turning from it (see 2.38).

3.19, 20 When we repent, God promises not only to wipe away our sin, but to bring spiritual refreshment. Repentance may at first seem painful because it is hard to give up certain sins. But God will give you a better way. As Hosea promised, "Let us press on to know the Lord; his appearing is as sure as the dawn; he will come to us like showers, like the spring rains that water the earth" (Hosea 6.3). Do you feel a need to be refreshed?

3.21 The "time of universal restoration" points to the Second Coming, the last Judgment, and the removal of sin from the world.

3.21, 22 Most Jews thought that Joshua was this prophet predicted by Moses (Deuteronomy 18.15). Peter was saying that the prophet was Jesus Christ. Peter wanted to show them that their long-awaited Messiah had come! He and all the apostles were calling the Jewish nation to realize what they had done to their Messiah, to repent, and to believe. From this point on in Acts, we see many Jews rejecting the gospel. So the message went also to the Gentiles, many of whom were open to receive Jesus.

3.24 The prophet Samuel lived during the transition between the judges and the kings of Israel, and he was seen as the first in a succession of prophets. He anointed David king, founding David's royal line, from which the Messiah eventually came. All the prophets pointed forward to a future Messiah. For more on Samuel, see his Profile in 1 Samuel 8.

3.25 God promised Abraham that he would bless the world through his descendants, the Jewish race (Genesis 12.3), from which the Messiah would come. God intended the Jewish nation to be a separate and holy nation that would teach the world about God, introduce the Messiah, and then carry on his work in the world. After the days of Solomon, the nation gave up its mission to tell the world about God. Here too, in apostolic times, Israel rejected its Messiah.

4.1 The priests were the chief priests who had special influence and were often close relatives of the high priests. The captain of the temple was the leader of the temple police, who were guards set around the temple to insure order. The Sadducees were members of a small but powerful Jewish religious sect who did not be-

4.3 Acts 5.18
4.4 Acts 4.21
4.6 Mt 26.3; Lk 3.1,2; Jn 11.49; 18.13
4.7 Mt 21.23
4.8 Lk 12.1
4.10 Acts 2.22,24; 3.6
4.11 Ps 118.22; Isa 28.16; Mt 21.42; Rom 9.33
4.12 Mt 1.21; Acts 10.43; Rom 3.24; 1 Tim 2.5
4.13 Mt 11.25; 1 Cor 1.27
4.16 Jn 11.47; Acts 3.7-10
4.17 Jn 15.20,21

the dead. 3 So they arrested them and put them in custody until the next day, for it
was already evening. 4 But many of those who heard the word believed; and they
numbered about five thousand.
5 The next day their rulers, elders, and scribes assembled in Jerusalem, 6 with
Annas the high priest, Caiaphas, John,[a] and Alexander, and all who were of the
high-priestly family. 7 When they had made the prisoners[b] stand in their midst,
they inquired, "By what power or by what name did you do this?" 8 Then Peter,
filled with the Holy Spirit, said to them, "Rulers of the people and elders, 9 if we are
questioned today because of a good deed done to someone who was sick and are
asked how this man has been healed, 10 let it be known to all of you, and to all the
people of Israel, that this man is standing before you in good health by the name of
Jesus Christ of Nazareth,[c] whom you crucified, whom God raised from the dead.
11 This Jesus[d] is

'the stone that was rejected by you, the builders;
it has become the cornerstone.'[e]

12 There is salvation in no one else, for there is no other name under heaven given
among mortals by which we must be saved."
13 Now when they saw the boldness of Peter and John and realized that they
were uneducated and ordinary men, they were amazed and recognized them as
companions of Jesus. 14 When they saw the man who had been cured standing beside them, they had nothing to say in opposition. 15 So they ordered them to leave
the council while they discussed the matter with one another. 16 They said,
"What will we do with them? For it is obvious to all who live in Jerusalem that a
notable sign has been done through them; we cannot deny it. 17 But to keep it from

[a] Other ancient authorities read *Jonathan* [b] Gk *them* [c] Gk *the Nazorean* [d] Gk *This* [e] Or *keystone*

---

lieve in the resurrection of the dead. They were the religious leaders who gained financially by cooperating with the Romans. Most of those who engineered and carried out Jesus' arrest and crucifixion were from these three groups.

4.2, 3 Peter and John spoke to the people during the afternoon prayer time. The Sadducees moved in quickly to investigate. Because they did not believe in the resurrection, they were disturbed by what the apostles were saying. Peter and John were refuting one of their fundamental beliefs and thus threatening their authority as religious teachers. Even under Roman rule, the Sadducees had almost unlimited power over the temple grounds. Thus they were able to arrest Peter and John for no reason other than teaching something that contradicted their beliefs.

4.3 Not often will sharing the gospel send us to prison as it did Peter and John. Still, we run risks in trying to win others to Christ. We might be willing to face a night in prison if it would bring 5,000 people to Christ, but shouldn't we also be willing to suffer for even one? What do you risk in witnessing – rejection, persecution? Whatever the risks, realize that nothing done for God is ever wasted.

4.5, 6 The rulers, elders, scribes, and priests made up the Sanhedrin, or Jewish supreme court – the same council that had condemned Jesus to death (Luke 22.66). It had 70 members plus the current high priest, who presided. The Sadducees held a majority in this ruling group. These were the wealthy, intellectual, and powerful men of Jerusalem. Jesus' followers stood before this council just as he had.

4.6 Annas had been deposed as high priest by the Romans, who then appointed Caiaphas, Annas's son-in-law, in his place. But because the Jews considered the office of high priest a lifetime position, they still called Annas by that title and gave him respect and authority within the council. Annas and Caiaphas had played significant roles in Jesus' trial (John 18.24, 28). It did not please them that the man they thought they had sacrificed for the good of the nation (John 11.49–51) had followers who were just as persistent and promised to be just as troublesome as he was.

4.7 The council asked Peter and John by whose power they had healed the man (3.6, 7) and by what authority they preached (3.12–26). The actions and words of Peter and John threatened these religious leaders who, for the most part, were more interested in their reputations and positions than in God. Through the help of the Holy Spirit (Mark 13.11), Peter spoke boldly before the council, actually putting the council on trial by showing them that the One they had crucified had risen again. Instead of being defensive, the apostles were going on the offensive, boldly speaking out for God and presenting the gospel to these leaders.

4.11 The cornerstone unites two walls at the corner of a building and holds the building together. Peter said the Jews rejected Jesus, but now he has become the cornerstone of the church (Psalm 118.22; Mark 12.10; 1 Peter 2.7). Without him there would be no church, because it could not stand.

4.12 Many people react negatively to the fact that there is no other name than that of Jesus to call upon for salvation. Yet this is not something the church decided; it is the specific teaching of Jesus himself (John 14.6). If God designated Jesus to be the Savior of the world, no one else can be his equal. Christians are to be open-minded on many issues, but not on how we are saved from sin. No other religious teacher could die for our sins; no other religious teacher came to earth as God's only Son; no other religious teacher rose from the dead. Our focus should be on Jesus, whom God offered as the way to have an eternal relationship with himself. There is no other name or way!

4.13 Knowing that Peter and John were uneducated, the council was amazed at what being with Jesus had done for them. A changed life convinces people of Jesus' power. One of your greatest testimonies is the difference others see in your life and attitudes since you have believed in Jesus.

4.13–18 Although the evidence was overwhelming and irrefutable (changed lives and a healed man), the religious leaders refused to believe in Christ and continued to try to suppress the truth. Don't be surprised if some people reject you and your positive witness for Christ. When minds are closed, even the clearest presentation of the facts can't open them. But don't give up. Pray for those people and continue to spread the gospel.

spreading further among the people, let us warn them to speak no more to anyone
in this name." 18 So they called them and ordered them not to speak or teach at all
in the name of Jesus. 19 But Peter and John answered them, "Whether it is right in
God's sight to listen to you rather than to God, you must judge; 20 for we cannot
keep from speaking about what we have seen and heard." 21 After threatening
them again, they let them go, finding no way to punish them because of the people,
for all of them praised God for what had happened. 22 For the man on whom this
sign of healing had been performed was more than forty years old.

4.18 Acts 5.28
4.19 Acts 5.29
4.20 Acts 1.8; 1 Cor 9.16; 1 Jn 1.1
4.21 Mt 21.26; Lk 20.6; 22.2; Acts 3.7,8

The believers pray for boldness

23 After they were released, they went to their friends[f] and reported what the
chief priests and the elders had said to them. 24 When they heard it, they raised their
voices together to God and said, "Sovereign Lord, who made the heaven and the
earth, the sea, and everything in them, 25 it is you who said by the Holy Spirit
through our ancestor David, your servant:[g]

'Why did the Gentiles rage,
and the peoples imagine vain things?
26 The kings of the earth took their stand,
and the rulers have gathered together
against the Lord and against his Messiah.'[h]

27 For in this city, in fact, both Herod and Pontius Pilate, with the Gentiles and the
peoples of Israel, gathered together against your holy servant[g] Jesus, whom you
anointed, 28 to do whatever your hand and your plan had predestined to take place.
29 And now, Lord, look at their threats, and grant to your servants[i] to speak your
word with all boldness, 30 while you stretch out your hand to heal, and signs and
wonders are performed through the name of your holy servant[g] Jesus." 31 When
they had prayed, the place in which they were gathered together was shaken; and
they were all filled with the Holy Spirit and spoke the word of God with boldness.

4.24 Ex 20.11; Ps 103.1; 107.1; 146.6
4.25,26 Ps 2.1,2
4.27 Isa 61.1; Lk 23.12; Acts 3.13
4.28 Acts 2.23
4.29 Eph 6.19; 2 Thess 3.1
4.30 Acts 3.6,16; 5.12
4.31 Acts 2.2,4; 16.26; Phil 1.14

The believers share their possessions

32 Now the whole group of those who believed were of one heart and soul, and
no one claimed private ownership of any possessions, but everything they owned

4.32 Acts 2.44; Phil 2.2

[f] *Gk their own* [g] *Or child* [h] *Or his Christ* [i] *Gk slaves*

4.20 We may sometimes be afraid to share our faith in Christ because people might feel uncomfortable and disapprove. But Peter and John's zeal for the Lord was so strong that they could not keep quiet, even when threatened. If your courage to witness for God has weakened, pray that your boldness may increase. Remember Jesus' promise, "Everyone therefore who acknowledges me before others, I also will acknowledge before my Father in heaven" (Matthew 10.32).

4.24–30 Notice how the believers prayed. First they praised God; then they told God their specific problem and asked for his help. They did not ask God to remove the problem, but to help them deal with it. This is a model for us to follow when we pray. We may ask God to remove our problems, and he may choose to do so. But we must recognize that often he will leave the problem in place and give us the strength and courage to deal with it.

4.27 This was Herod Antipas, appointed by the Romans to rule over the territory of Galilee. For more information on Herod, see his Profile in Mark 6. Pontius Pilate was the Roman governor over Judea. He bent to pressure from the crowd and sentenced Jesus to death. For more information on Pilate, see his Profile in Mark 15.

4.28 *Predestined* means that God is the sovereign Lord of all events and rules history to fulfill his purpose. What his will determines, his power carries out. No army, government, or council could stand in his way.

4.29–31 Boldness is not reckless impulsiveness. Boldness requires courage to press through our fears and do what we know is right. How can we be more bold? Like the disciples, we need to pray with others for that courage. To gain boldness, you can (1) pray for the power of the Holy Spirit to give you courage, (2) look for opportunities in your family and neighborhood to talk about Christ, (3) realize that rejection, social discomfort, and embarrassment are not persecution, and (4) start where you are by being bolder in small ways.

4.32 Differences of opinion are inevitable among human personalities and can actually be helpful, if handled well. But spiritual unity is essential – loyalty, commitment, and love for God and his Word. Without spiritual unity, the church could not survive. Paul wrote the letter of 1 Corinthians to urge the church in Corinth toward greater unity.

4.32 None of these Christians felt that what they had was their own, and so they were able to give and share, eliminating poverty among them. They would not let a brother or sister suffer when others had plenty. How do you feel about your possessions? We should adopt the attitude, "Everything we have comes from God, and we are only sharing what is already his."

4.32–35 The early church was able to share possessions and property as a result of the unity brought by the Holy Spirit working in and through the believers' lives. This is different from communism because (1) it was voluntary sharing; (2) it didn't involve *all* private property, but only as much as was needed; (3) it was not a membership requirement in order to be a part of the church. The spiritual unity and generosity of these early believers attracted others to them. This organizational structure is not a biblical command, but it offers vital principles for us to follow.

4.33 Lk 24.48
4.36 Acts 9.27; 11.19-30; 12.25; 13.1-4; 15.39
4.37 Prov 11.24,25

was held in common. 33 With great power the apostles gave their testimony to the
resurrection of the Lord Jesus, and great grace was upon them all. 34 There was not
a needy person among them, for as many as owned lands or houses sold them and
brought the proceeds of what was sold. 35 They laid it at the apostles' feet, and it
was distributed to each as any had need. 36 There was a Levite, a native of Cyprus,
Joseph, to whom the apostles gave the name Barnabas (which means "son of encouragement"). 37 He sold a field that belonged to him, then brought the money,
and laid it at the apostles' feet.

The judgment of Ananias and Sapphira

5.2 Acts 4.37; 1 Tim 6.10
5.3 Num 30.1,2; Deut 23.21; Eccles 5.4; Isa 29.15
5.5 Ezek 11.13

5 But a man named Ananias, with the consent of his wife Sapphira, sold a piece
of property; 2 with his wife's knowledge, he kept back some of the proceeds,
and brought only a part and laid it at the apostles' feet. 3 "Ananias," Peter asked,
"why has Satan filled your heart to lie to the Holy Spirit and to keep back part of the
proceeds of the land? 4 While it remained unsold, did it not remain your own? And
after it was sold, were not the proceeds at your disposal? How is it that you have
contrived this deed in your heart? You did not lie to us[j] but to God!" 5 Now when
Ananias heard these words, he fell down and died. And great fear seized all who
heard of it. 6 The young men came and wrapped up his body,[k] then carried him out
and buried him.
7 After an interval of about three hours his wife came in, not knowing what had
happened. 8 Peter said to her, "Tell me whether you and your husband sold the land
for such and such a price." And she said, "Yes, that was the price." 9 Then Peter
said to her, "How is it that you have agreed together to put the Spirit of the Lord to
the test? Look, the feet of those who have buried your husband are at the door, and
they will carry you out." 10 Immediately she fell down at his feet and died. When
the young men came in they found her dead, so they carried her out and buried her
beside her husband. 11 And great fear seized the whole church and all who heard of
these things.

5.9 Deut 6.16; Mt 4.7; Lk 4.12; 1 Cor 10.9

The apostles heal many people

5.12 Mk 16.15-20; Jn 10.23; Heb 2.4

12 Now many signs and wonders were done among the people through the
apostles. And they were all together in Solomon's Portico. 13 None of the rest
dared to join them, but the people held them in high esteem. 14 Yet more than ever

[j] Gk *to men* [k] Meaning of Gk uncertain

4.36 Barnabas was a respected leader of the church. He was a Levite by birth, a member of the Jewish tribe that carried out temple duties. But his family moved to Cyprus. He traveled with Paul on his first missionary journey (13.1ff). For more information on Barnabas, see his Profile in chapter 13.

5.1ff In Acts 5.1 – 8.3 we see both internal and external problems facing the early church. Inside, there was dishonesty (5.1–11) and adminstrative headaches (6.1–7). Outside, the church was being pressured by persecution. While church leaders were careful and sensitive in dealing with the internal problems, there was not much they could do to prevent the external pressures. Through it all, the leaders kept their focus on what was most important – spreading the gospel of Jesus Christ.

5.3 Even after the Holy Spirit had come, the believers were not immune to Satan's temptations. Although Satan was defeated by Christ at the cross, he was still actively trying to make the believers stumble – as he does today (Ephesians 6.12; 1 Peter 5.8). Satan's overthrow is inevitable, but it will not occur until the last days, when Christ returns to judge the world (Revelation 20.10).

5.3ff The sin Ananias and Sapphira committed was not stinginess or holding back part of the money – it was their choice whether or not to sell the land and how much to give. Their sin was lying to God and God's people – saying they gave the whole amount but holding back some for themselves and trying to make themselves appear more generous than they really were. This act was judged harshly because dishonesty and covetousness are destructive in a church, preventing the Holy Spirit from working effectively. All lying is bad, but when we lie to try to deceive God and his people about our relationship with him, we destroy our testimony for Christ.

5.11 God's judgment on Ananias and Sapphira produced shock and fear among the believers, making them realize how seriously God regards sin in the church.

5.12 Solomon's Portico was part of the temple complex built by King Herod the Great in an attempt to strengthen his relationship with the Jews. A portico is an entrance or porch supported by columns. Jesus taught and performed miracles in the temple many times. When the apostles went to the temple, they were near the same religious leaders who had conspired to put Jesus to death.

5.13 Although the believers greatly respected the apostles, they did not dare join them in the temple or work beside them. They were afraid to face the same kind of persecution the apostles had just faced (4.17).

5.14 What makes Christianity attractive? It is easy to be drawn to churches because of programs, good speakers, size, beautiful facilities, or fellowship. People were attracted to the early church by God's power and miracles, the generosity, sincerity, honesty, and unity of the members, and the character of the leaders. Have our standards slipped? God wants to add to his *church,* not just to programs or congregations.

believers were added to the Lord, great numbers of both men and women, 15 so that
they even carried out the sick into the streets, and laid them on cots and mats, in
order that Peter's shadow might fall on some of them as he came by. 16 A great
number of people would also gather from the towns around Jerusalem, bringing
the sick and those tormented by unclean spirits, and they were all cured.

The apostles meet furious opposition

17 Then the high priest took action; he and all who were with him (that is, the
sect of the Sadducees), being filled with jealousy, 18 arrested the apostles and put
them in the public prison. 19 But during the night an angel of the Lord opened the
prison doors, brought them out, and said, 20 "Go, stand in the temple and tell the
people the whole message about this life." 21 When they heard this, they entered
the temple at daybreak and went on with their teaching.

When the high priest and those with him arrived, they called together the council
and the whole body of the elders of Israel, and sent to the prison to have them
brought. 22 But when the temple police went there, they did not find them in the
prison; so they returned and reported, 23 "We found the prison securely locked and
the guards standing at the doors, but when we opened them, we found no one inside." 24 Now when the captain of the temple and the chief priests heard these
words, they were perplexed about them, wondering what might be going on.
25 Then someone arrived and announced, "Look, the men whom you put in prison
are standing in the temple and teaching the people!" 26 Then the captain went with
the temple police and brought them, but without violence, for they were afraid of
being stoned by the people.

27 When they had brought them, they had them stand before the council. The
high priest questioned them, 28 saying, "We gave you strict orders not to teach in
this name,[l] yet here you have filled Jerusalem with your teaching and you are
determined to bring this man's blood on us." 29 But Peter and the apostles answered, "We must obey God rather than any human authority.[m] 30 The God of our
ancestors raised up Jesus, whom you had killed by hanging him on a tree. 31 God
exalted him at his right hand as Leader and Savior that he might give repentance to
Israel and forgiveness of sins. 32 And we are witnesses to these things, and so is the
Holy Spirit whom God has given to those who obey him."

5.17 Acts 4.1,2
5.18 Lk 21.12
5.19 Ps 34.7; Acts 12.7; 16.26; Heb 1.14
5.20 Jn 6.63,68; 17.3; 1 Jn 5.11
5.21 Acts 4.5,6
5.26 Mt 14.5; 21.26
5.28 Mt 23.35; 27.25; Acts 2.23; 3.15; 4.18; 7.52
5.29 Acts 4.19
5.30 Acts 10.39-41; 1 Pet 2.24
5.31 Isa 9.6; Mt 1.21; Acts 2.33; Phil 2.9; Heb 2.10; 12.2; Rev 1.5
5.32 Lk 24.28; Jn 15.26; Rom 8.16; Heb 2.4

[l] Other ancient authorities read *Did we not give you strict orders not to teach in this name?* [m] Gk *than men*

5.15 If people in Peter's shadow were healed, they were not healed by Peter's shadow, but by God's power working through Peter.

5.16 What did these miraculous healings do for the early church? (1) They attracted believers. (2) They confirmed the truth of the apostles' teaching. (3) They demonstrated that the power of the Messiah who had been crucified and risen was now with his followers.

5.17 The religious leaders were jealous – Peter and the apostles were already commanding more respect than they had ever received. The difference, however, was that the religious leaders demanded respect and reverence for themselves; the apostles' goal was to bring respect and reverence to God. The apostles were respected not because they demanded it, but because they deserved it.

5.17, 18 The apostles had power to do miracles, great boldness in preaching, and God's presence in their lives; yet they were not free from hatred and persecution. They were arrested, put in jail, beaten, and slandered by community leaders. Faith in God does not make troubles disappear; it makes troubles appear less fearsome because it puts them in the right perspective. You cannot expect everyone to react favorably when you share something as dynamic as your faith in Christ. Some will be jealous, frightened, or threatened. Expect some negative reactions, but remember that you must be more concerned about serving God than about the reactions of people (see 5.29).

5.21 The "council and the whole body of the elders" were not two different groups – this phrase simply means they convened the entire group, the 70 men of the council (also called the Sanhedrin). This was going to be no small trial. The religious leaders would do anything to stop these apostles from challenging their authority, threatening their secure position, and exposing their hypocritical motives to the people.

5.21 The temple at daybreak was a busy place. Many people stopped at the temple to pray and worship at sunrise. The apostles were already there, ready to tell them the good news.

5.21 Suppose someone threatened to kill you if you didn't stop talking about God. You might be tempted to keep quiet. But after being threatened by powerful leaders, arrested, jailed, and miraculously released, the apostles went back to preaching. This was nothing less than God's power working through them (4.13)! When we are convinced of the truth of Christ's resurrection and have experienced the presence and power of his Holy Spirit, we can have the confidence to speak out for Christ.

5.29 The apostles knew their priorities. While we should try to keep peace with everyone (Romans 12.18), conflict with the world and its authorities is sometimes inevitable for a Christian (John 15.18). There will be situations where you cannot obey both God and man. Then you must obey God and trust his Word. Let Jesus' words in Luke 6.22, 23 encourage you: "Blessed are you when people hate you, and when they exclude you, revile you, and defame you on account of the Son of Man."

5.33 Acts 2.37; 7.54
5.36 Acts 8.9
5.37 Lk 2.1
5.38 Ps 127.1
5.39 Prov 21.30 Isa 46.9,10 Mt 16.18 Acts 9.5 1 Cor 1.25
5.40 Mt 10.17 Mk 13.9
5.41 Mt 5.11,12 Jn 15.20,21 Rom 5.3 Phil 1.29 Heb 10.34 1 Pet 4.13,14,16

33 When they heard this, they were enraged and wanted to kill them. 34 But a
Pharisee in the council named Gamaliel, a teacher of the law, respected by all the
people, stood up and ordered the men to be put outside for a short time. 35 Then he
said to them, "Fellow Israelites,[n] consider carefully what you propose to do to
these men. 36 For some time ago Theudas rose up, claiming to be somebody, and a
number of men, about four hundred, joined him; but he was killed, and all who
followed him were dispersed and disappeared. 37 After him Judas the Galilean rose
up at the time of the census and got people to follow him; he also perished, and all
who followed him were scattered. 38 So in the present case, I tell you, keep away
from these men and let them alone; because if this plan or this undertaking is of
human origin, it will fail; 39 but if it is of God, you will not be able to overthrow
them — in that case you may even be found fighting against God!"
They were convinced by him, 40 and when they had called in the apostles, they
had them flogged. Then they ordered them not to speak in the name of Jesus, and
let them go. 41 As they left the council, they rejoiced that they were considered
worthy to suffer dishonor for the sake of the name. 42 And every day in the temple
and at home[o] they did not cease to teach and proclaim Jesus as the Messiah.[p]

The church appoints seven to help

6.1 Ex 18.17 Acts 2.47; 4.35 1 Tim 5.3

6 Now during those days, when the disciples were increasing in number, the
Hellenists complained against the Hebrews because their widows were being
neglected in the daily distribution of food. 2 And the twelve called together the
whole community of the disciples and said, "It is not right that we should neglect

[n] Gk *Men, Israelites* [o] Or *from house to house* [p] Or *the Christ*

5.34 The Pharisees were the other major party in the Jewish council with the Sadducees (5.17). They were the strict keepers of the law — not only God's law, but hundreds of other rules they had added to God's law. They were careful about outward purity, but many had hearts full of impure motives. Jesus confronted the Pharisees often during his ministry on earth.

5.34 Gamaliel was an unexpected ally for the apostles, although he probably did not support their teachings. He was a distinguished member of the council and a teacher. While he may have saved their lives, his real intentions were to keep the council from being divided over them and to avoid arousing the Romans. The apostles were popular with the people, and killing them might start a riot. Gamaliel's advice to the council gave the apostles some breathing room to continue their work. The council waited and hoped that this would all fade away harmlessly. They couldn't have been more wrong. Ironically, Paul, later one of the greatest apostles, was tutored by Gamaliel (22.3).

5.39 Gamaliel presented some sound advice about reacting to religious movements. Unless they endorse obviously dangerous doctrines or practices, it is often wiser to be tolerant rather than repressive. Sometimes only time will tell if they are merely the work of men or if God is trying to say something through them. Next time a group promotes differing religious ideas, consider Gamaliel's advice, "You may even be found fighting against God."

5.40–42 Peter and John were warned repeatedly not to preach, but they continued in spite of the threats. We, too, should live as Christ has asked, sharing our faith no matter what the cost. We may not be beaten or thrown in jail, but we may be ridiculed, ostracized, or slandered. To what extent are you willing to suffer for the sake of sharing the gospel with others?

5.41 Have you ever thought of persecution as a blessing? This beating suffered by Peter and John was the first time any of the apostles had been physically abused for their faith. These men knew how Jesus had suffered, and they praised God that he allowed them to be persecuted like their Lord. If you are mocked or persecuted for your faith, it isn't because you're doing something wrong, but that God has counted you "worthy to suffer dishonor for the sake of the name."

5.42 Home Bible studies are not new. As the believers needed to grow in their new faith, home Bible studies met their needs, as well as introducing new people to the Christian faith. During later times of persecution, this became the primary method of passing on Bible knowledge. Christians throughout the world still use this as a strategy under persecution and as a way to build up believers.

6.1 When we read the descriptions of the early church — the miracles, the sharing and generosity — we may wish we could have been a part of this "perfect" church. In reality, they had problems just as we do today. No church has ever been or will ever be perfect until Christ and his followers are united at his second coming. All churches have problems. If your church's shortcomings distress you, ask yourself: "Would a perfect church allow me to be a member?" Then do what you can to make your church better. A church does not have to be perfect to be faithful.

6.1ff Another internal problem developed in the early church. The Hebrews, native Jewish Christians, spoke Aramaic, a semitic language. The Hellenists, Greek-speaking Christians, were probably Jews from other lands who were converted at Pentecost. The Greek-speaking Christians complained that their widows were being unfairly treated. This favoritism was probably not intentional, but caused by the language barrier. To correct the situation, the apostles put seven respected Greek-speaking men in charge of the food distribution program. This ended the problem and allowed the apostles to keep their focus on teaching and preaching the good news about Jesus.

6.2 "The twelve" are the 11 original disciples and Matthias, who was chosen to replace Judas Iscariot (1.26).

6.2–4 As the early church increased in size, so did their needs. One was to organize the distribution of food to the poor. The apostles needed to focus on preaching, so they chose others to administer the food program. Each person has a necessary part to play in the life of the church (see 1 Corinthians 12). If you are in a position of leadership and find yourself overwhelmed by responsibilities, determine *your* God-given abilities and priorities and then find others to help. If you are not in leadership, you have gifts that can be used by God in various areas of the church's ministry. Offer these gifts in service to him.

the word of God in order to wait on tables.[q] 3 Therefore, friends,[r] select from 6.3 Acts 2.4
among yourselves seven men of good standing, full of the Spirit and of wisdom, Eph 5.18 1 Tim 3.7,8
whom we may appoint to this task, 4 while we, for our part, will devote ourselves 6.4
to prayer and to serving the word." 5 What they said pleased the whole community, Acts 1.14; 2.42
and they chose Stephen, a man full of faith and the Holy Spirit, together with Phi- 6.5 Acts 8.5; 21.8
lip, Prochorus, Nicanor, Timon, Parmenas, and Nicolaus, a proselyte of Antioch. 6.6
6 They had these men stand before the apostles, who prayed and laid their hands on Num 8.10
them. Acts 1.24; 13.3 1 Tim 4.14
7 The word of God continued to spread; the number of the disciples increased 2 Tim 1.6 6.7
greatly in Jerusalem, and a great many of the priests became obedient to the faith. Acts 12.24; 19.20

Stephen is arrested

8 Stephen, full of grace and power, did great wonders and signs among the 6.8 Jn 14.12
people. 9 Then some of those who belonged to the synagogue of the Freedmen (as 6.9
it was called), Cyrenians, Alexandrians, and others of those from Cilicia and Asia, Mt 27.32
stood up and argued with Stephen. 10 But they could not withstand the wisdom and 6.10 Ex 4.12
the Spirit[s] with which he spoke. 11 Then they secretly instigated some men to say, Lk 21.15
"We have heard him speak blasphemous words against Moses and God." 12 They 6.11 Mt 26.59
stirred up the people as well as the elders and the scribes; then they suddenly con- 6.12
fronted him, seized him, and brought him before the council. 13 They set up false Lk 20.1
witnesses who said, "This man never stops saying things against this holy place and 6.13 Mt 26.59
the law; 14 for we have heard him say that this Jesus of Nazareth[t] will destroy this Acts 7.58;21.28
place and will change the customs that Moses handed on to us." 15 And all who sat 6.14 Jn 2.19-21
in the council looked intently at him, and they saw that his face was like the face of Heb 9; 10 6.15
an angel. Mt 28.3

Stephen addresses the Sanhedrin

7 Then the high priest asked him, "Are these things so?" 2 And Stephen replied: 7.2 Gen 15.7
"Brothers[u] and fathers, listen to me. The God of glory appeared to our ances- 7.3
tor Abraham when he was in Mesopotamia, before he lived in Haran, 3 and said to Gen 12.1

[q] Or *keep accounts* [r] Gk *brothers* [s] Or *spirit* [t] Gk *the Nazorean* [u] Gk *Men, brothers*

6.3 This administrative task was not taken lightly. Notice the requirements for the men who were to handle the feeding program: (1) of good standing, with reputations for being honest, (2) full of the Holy Spirit, and (3) wise. People who carry heavy responsibilities and work closely with others should have these qualities. We must look for honest, spiritually mature, and wise men and women to lead our churches.

6.4 The apostles' priorities were correct. The ministry of the Word should never be neglected because of administrative burdens. Pastors should never try, or be expected, to do everything. Instead, the work of the church should be spread out among its members.

6.6 Spiritual leadership is serious business and must not be taken lightly by the church or the leaders. In the early church, the chosen men were commissioned (set apart by prayer and laying on of hands) by the apostles. Laying hands on someone, an ancient Jewish practice, was a way to set a person apart for special service (see Numbers 27.23; Deuteronomy 34.9).

6.7 Jesus had told the apostles that they were to witness first in Jerusalem (1.8). In a short time, their message had infiltrated the entire city and all levels of society. Even some priests were being converted, going against the directives of the council and endangering their position.

6.7 The word of God spread like ripples on a pond where, from a single center, each wave touches the next, spreading wider and farther. The gospel still spreads in the same way today. You don't have to change the world single-handedly – it is enough just to be part of the wave, touching those around you, who in turn will touch others until all have felt the movement. You should never feel that your part is insignificant or unimportant.

6.8–10 The most important prerequisite for any kind of Christian service is to be filled with faith and the power of the Holy Spirit. By the Spirit's power, Stephen was a good administrator (6.3), miracle worker (6.8), and evangelist (6.10). By the Spirit's power, you can exercise the gifts God has given you.

6.9 "The Freedmen" was a group of Jewish slaves who had been freed by Rome and had formed their own synagogue in Jerusalem.

6.11 These men lied about Stephen, causing him to be arrested and brought before the Jewish council. The Sadducees, the dominant party in the council, accepted and studied only the writings of Moses (Genesis through Deuteronomy). In their view, to curse Moses was a crime. But from Stephen's speech (chapter 7), we learn that this accusation was false. Stephen based his review of Israel's history on Moses' writings.

6.14 When Stephen was brought before the council of religious leaders, the accusation against him was the same that the religious leaders had used against Jesus (Matthew 26.59–61). They falsely accused Stephen of wanting to do away with Moses' laws because they knew that the Sadducees, who controlled the council, believed *only* in Moses' laws.

7.1 This high priest was Caiphas, the same man who had earlier questioned and condemned Jesus (John 18.24).

7.2ff Stephen launched into a long speech about Israel's relationship with God. From Old Testament history he showed that the Jews had constantly rejected God's message and his prophets, and that this council had rejected the Messiah, God's Son. He made three main points: (1) Israel's history is the history of God's acts in the world; (2) people worshiped God long before there was

7.4 Gen 11.31; 12.4 Heb 11.8
7.5 Gen 12.7 13.15,16 17.7,8; 26.3
7.6 Ex 12.40 Gal 3.17 1 Pet 2.11
7.7 Ex 3.12

him, 'Leave your country and your relatives and go to the land that I will show
you.' 4Then he left the country of the Chaldeans and settled in Haran. After his
father died, God had him move from there to this country in which you are now
living. 5He did not give him any of it as a heritage, not even a foot's length, but
promised to give it to him as his possession and to his descendants after him, even
though he had no child. 6And God spoke in these terms, that his descendants would
be resident aliens in a country belonging to others, who would enslave them and
mistreat them during four hundred years. 7'But I will judge the nation that they
serve,' said God, 'and after that they shall come out and worship me in this place.'

STEPHEN

Around the world, the gospel has most often taken root in places prepared by the blood of martyrs. Before a person can *give* his life for the gospel, however, he must first *live* his life for the gospel. One way God trains his servants is to place them in insignificant positions. Their desire to serve Christ is translated into the reality of serving others. Stephen was an effective administrator and messenger before becoming a martyr.

Stephen was named among the managers of food distribution in the early church. Long before violent persecution broke out against Christians, there was already social ostracism. Jews who accepted Jesus as Messiah were usually cut off from their families. As a result, the believers depended on each other for support. The sharing of homes, food, and resources was both a practical and necessary mark of the early church. Eventually, the number of believers made it necessary to organize the sharing. People were being overlooked. There were complaints. Those chosen to help manage were chosen for their integrity and sensitivity to God.

Stephen, besides being a good administrator, was also a powerful speaker. When confronted in the temple by various antagonistic groups, Stephen's logic in responding was convincing. This is clear from the defense he made before the court. He presented a summary of the Jews' own history and made powerful applications that stung his listeners. During his defense Stephen must have known he was speaking his own death sentence. Members of the court could not stand to have their evil motives exposed. They stoned him to death while he prayed for their forgiveness. His final words show how much like Jesus he had become in a short time. His death had a lasting impact on young Saul (Paul) of Tarsus, who would move from being a violent persecutor of Christians to being one of the greatest champions of the gospel the church has known.

Stephen's life is a continual challenge to all Christians. Because he was the first to die for the faith, his sacrifice raises questions: How many risks do we take in being Jesus' followers? Would we be willing to die for him? Are we really willing to live for him?

Strengths and accomplishments:
- One of seven leaders chosen to supervise food distribution to the needy in the early church
- Known for his spiritual qualities of faith, wisdom, grace, and power, and for the Spirit's presence in his life
- Outstanding leader, teacher, and debater
- First to give his life for the gospel

Lessons from his life:
- Striving for excellence in small assignments prepares one for greater responsibilities
- Real understanding of God always leads to practical and compassionate actions toward people

Vital statistics:
- Church responsibilities: Deacon—distributing food to the needy
- Contemporaries: Paul, Caiaphas, Gamaliel, the apostles

Key verses:
"While they were stoning Stephen, he prayed, 'Lord Jesus, receive my spirit.' Then he knelt down and cried out in a loud voice, 'Lord, do not hold this sin against them.' When he had said this, he died" (Acts 7.59, 60).

Stephen's story is told in Acts 6.3—8.2. He is also mentioned in Acts 11.19; 22.20.

a temple, because God does not live in a temple; (3) Jesus' death was just one more example of Israel's rebellion and rejection of God.

7.2ff Stephen wasn't really defending himself. Instead, he took the offensive, seizing the opportunity to summarize his teaching about Jesus. Stephen was accusing these religious leaders of failing to obey God's laws—the laws they prided themselves in following so meticulously. This was the same accusation Jesus had leveled against them. When we witness for Christ, we don't need to be on the defensive. Instead we can simply share our faith.

8 Then he gave him the covenant of circumcision. And so Abraham[v] became the
father of Isaac and circumcised him on the eighth day; and Isaac became the father
of Jacob, and Jacob of the twelve patriarchs.
9 "The patriarchs, jealous of Joseph, sold him into Egypt; but God was with
him, 10 and rescued him from all his afflictions, and enabled him to win favor and
to show wisdom when he stood before Pharaoh, king of Egypt, who appointed him
ruler over Egypt and over all his household. 11 Now there came a famine throughout
Egypt and Canaan, and great suffering, and our ancestors could find no food. 12 But
when Jacob heard that there was grain in Egypt, he sent our ancestors there on their
first visit. 13 On the second visit Joseph made himself known to his brothers, and
Joseph's family became known to Pharaoh. 14 Then Joseph sent and invited his
father Jacob and all his relatives to come to him, seventy-five in all; 15 so Jacob
went down to Egypt. He himself died there as well as our ancestors, 16 and their
bodies[w] were brought back to Shechem and laid in the tomb that Abraham had
bought for a sum of silver from the sons of Hamor in Shechem.

17 "But as the time drew near for the fulfillment of the promise that God had
made to Abraham, our people in Egypt increased and multiplied 18 until another
king who had not known Joseph ruled over Egypt. 19 He dealt craftily with our race
and forced our ancestors to abandon their infants so that they would die. 20 At this
time Moses was born, and he was beautiful before God. For three months he was
brought up in his father's house; 21 and when he was abandoned, Pharaoh's daughter adopted him and brought him up as her own son. 22 So Moses was instructed in
all the wisdom of the Egyptians and was powerful in his words and deeds.

23 "When he was forty years old, it came into his heart to visit his relatives, the
Israelites.[x] 24 When he saw one of them being wronged, he defended the oppressed
man and avenged him by striking down the Egyptian. 25 He supposed that his kinsfolk would understand that God through him was rescuing them, but they did not
understand. 26 The next day he came to some of them as they were quarreling and
tried to reconcile them, saying, 'Men, you are brothers; why do you wrong each
other?' 27 But the man who was wronging his neighbor pushed Moses[y] aside, saying, 'Who made you a ruler and a judge over us? 28 Do you want to kill me as you
killed the Egyptian yesterday?' 29 When he heard this, Moses fled and became a
resident alien in the land of Midian. There he became the father of two sons.

30 "Now when forty years had passed, an angel appeared to him in the wilderness of Mount Sinai, in the flame of a burning bush. 31 When Moses saw it, he was
amazed at the sight; and as he approached to look, there came the voice of the Lord:
32 'I am the God of your ancestors, the God of Abraham, Isaac, and Jacob.' Moses
began to tremble and did not dare to look. 33 Then the Lord said to him, 'Take off
the sandals from your feet, for the place where you are standing is holy ground. 34 I
have surely seen the mistreatment of my people who are in Egypt and have heard
their groaning, and I have come down to rescue them. Come now, I will send you
to Egypt.'

35 "It was this Moses whom they rejected when they said, 'Who made you a
ruler and a judge?' and whom God now sent as both ruler and liberator through the
angel who appeared to him in the bush. 36 He led them out, having performed wonders and signs in Egypt, at the Red Sea, and in the wilderness for forty years. 37 This

[v] Gk *he* [w] Gk *they* [x] Gk *his brothers, the sons of Israel* [y] Gk *him*

7.8 Gen 17.9,10 21.1,2; 25.26 35.23-26 1 Chron 1.34 Mt 1.2
7.9 Gen 37.4,11,28 39.2 Ps 105.17
7.10 Gen 42.6 Ps 37.23; 105.21
7.11 Gen 41.54
7.12 Gen 42.2
7.13 Gen 45.1-4
7.14 Gen 45.9; 46.27 Deut 10.22
7.15 Gen 49.33 Ex 1.6
7.16 Gen 23.16
7.17,18 Gen 15.13 Ex 1.7,8
7.19 Ex 1.10,15,16
7.20 Ex 2.1,2 Heb 11.23
7.22 1 Kgs 4.30
7.23 Ex 2.11
7.24 Ex 2.12
7.27,28 Ex 2.14
7.29 Ex 2.15
7.30 Ex 3.2 Deut 33.16
7.32 Ex 3.6
7.33 Josh 5.15
7.34 Ex 3.7,10
7.35 Ex 14.19 Num 20.16
7.36 Ex 7.3; 12.40,41
7.37 Deut 18.15 Mt 17.5 Acts 3.22

7.8 Circumcision was a sign of the promise or covenant made between God, Abraham, and the entire nation of Israel (Genesis 17.9–13). Stephen's speech summarized Israel's history, and so it summarized how this covenant fared during that time. Stephen pointed out that God always kept his side of the promise, but Israel failed again and again to uphold its end. Although the Jews in Stephen's day still circumcised their baby boys, they failed to obey God. The people's hearts were far from God. Their lack of faith and lack of obedience meant that they had failed to keep their side of the covenant.

7.17, 18 Stephen's review of Jewish history gives a clear testimony of God's faithfulness and sovereignty. Despite the continued failures of his chosen people and swirling world events, God was working out his plan. When faced by a confusing array of circumstances, remember that: (1) God is in control – nothing surprises him; (2) this world is not all there is – it will pass away, but God is eternal; (3) God is just, and he will make things right – punishing the wicked and rewarding the faithful; (4) God wants to use you (like Joseph, Moses, and Stephen) to make a difference in the world.

7.37 The Jews originally thought this "prophet" was Joshua. But Moses was prophesying of the coming Messiah (Deuteronomy

is the Moses who said to the Israelites, 'God will raise up a prophet for you from
your own people[z] as he raised me up.' 38 He is the one who was in the congregation
in the wilderness with the angel who spoke to him at Mount Sinai, and with our
ancestors; and he received living oracles to give to us. 39 Our ancestors were unwilling to obey him; instead, they pushed him aside, and in their hearts they turned
back to Egypt, 40 saying to Aaron, 'Make gods for us who will lead the way for us;
as for this Moses who led us out from the land of Egypt, we do not know what has
happened to him.' 41 At that time they made a calf, offered a sacrifice to the idol,
and reveled in the works of their hands. 42 But God turned away from them and
handed them over to worship the host of heaven, as it is written in the book of the
prophets:

'Did you offer to me slain victims and sacrifices
forty years in the wilderness, O house of Israel?
43 No; you took along the tent of Moloch,
and the star of your god Rephan,
the images that you made to worship;
so I will remove you beyond Babylon.'

44 "Our ancestors had the tent of testimony in the wilderness, as God[a] directed
when he spoke to Moses, ordering him to make it according to the pattern he had
seen. 45 Our ancestors in turn brought it in with Joshua when they dispossessed the
nations that God drove out before our ancestors. And it was there until the time of
David, 46 who found favor with God and asked that he might find a dwelling place
for the house of Jacob.[b] 47 But it was Solomon who built a house for him. 48 Yet the
Most High does not dwell in houses made with human hands;[c] as the prophet says,

49 'Heaven is my throne,
and the earth is my footstool.
What kind of house will you build for me, says the Lord,
or what is the place of my rest?
50 Did not my hand make all these things?'

51 "You stiff-necked people, uncircumcised in heart and ears, you are forever
opposing the Holy Spirit, just as your ancestors used to do. 52 Which of the prophets

7.38 Ex 19.2,3,17; Deut 32.47; Rom 3.2
7.39 Num 14.3
7.40 Ex 32.1,23
7.42 Deut 17.2,3; Josh 24.20; 2 Kgs 17.16; Amos 5.25-27
7.44 Ex 25.8,40; Heb 8.5
7.45 Josh 3.13,14; 18.1; 22.19; 2 Sam 7.6; 1 Chron 17.5; 21.29; 2 Chron 1.3
7.46 2 Sam 7.1-14; 1 Kgs 8.17; Ps 132.1-5
7.47 2 Sam 7.12,13; 1 Kgs 8.20
7.48 2 Chron 2.6; Isa 57.15; Eph 2.22; 1 Pet 2.5
7.49,50 Isa 66.1-2
7.51 Ex 32.9; Isa 48.4; Ezek 44.9
7.52 2 Chron 36.16; Mt 23.30-34

[z] Gk *your brothers* [a] Gk *he* [b] Other ancient authorities read *for the God of Jacob* [c] Gk *with hands*

THE EFFECTS OF STEPHEN'S DEATH

Stephen's death was not in vain. Below are some of the events that were by-products (either directly or indirectly) of the persecution that began with Stephen's martyrdom.

1. Philip's evangelistic tour (Acts 8.4–40)
2. Paul's conversion (Acts 9.1–30)
3. Peter's missionary tour (Acts 9.32—11.18)
4. The church in Antioch in Syria founded (Acts 11.19ff)

18.15). Peter also quotes this verse in referring to the Messiah (3.22).

7.38 Stephen used the word *ekklesia* (translated "church") to describe the congregation or people of God in the wilderness. This word means "called out ones" and was used by the first-century Christians to describe their own community or "church." Stephen's point was that the giving of the law through Moses to the Jews was the sign of the covenant. By *obedience*, then, would they continue to be God's covenant people. Because they disobeyed (7.39), they broke the covenant and forfeited their right to be the chosen people.

7.38 From Galatians 3.19 and Hebrews 2.2, it appears that God gave the law to Moses through angels. Exodus 31.18 says God wrote the ten commandments himself ("written with the finger of God"). Apparently God used angelic messengers to deliver his law to Moses.

7.42 The *host of heaven* refers to their practice of worshiping deities associated with stars and planets.

7.43 Here Stephen gives more details of the idolatry referred to in verse 40. These were idols worshiped by Israel during their wilderness wanderings (Exodus 32.4). Molech (Moloch) is the god associated with child sacrifice, and Rephan is an Egyptian god. Amos also names Assyrian deities worshiped by Israel (Amos 5.25–27).

7.44–50 Stephen had been accused of speaking against the temple (6.13). Although he recognized the importance of the temple, he knew that it was not more important than God. God is not limited; he doesn't live only in a house of worship, but wherever hearts of faith are open to receive him (Isaiah 66.1, 2). Solomon knew this when he prayed at the dedication of the temple (2 Chronicles 6.18). God wants to live in us . . . in you.

7.52 Indeed many prophets were persecuted: Jeremiah (Jeremiah 38.1–6); Isaiah (tradition says he was killed by King Manasseh; see 2 Kings 21.16); Amos (Amos 7.10–13); Zechariah (2 Chronicles 24.20–22); Elijah (1 Kings 19.1, 2). Jesus also told a parable about how the Jews had constantly rejected God's messages and persecuted his messengers (Luke 20.9–19). The Righteous One refers to the Messiah.

did your ancestors not persecute? They killed those who foretold the coming of the
Righteous One, and now you have become his betrayers and murderers. 53 You are
the ones that received the law as ordained by angels, and yet you have not kept it."

Stephen is martyred by stoning

54 When they heard these things, they became enraged and ground their teeth
at Stephen.[d] 55 But filled with the Holy Spirit, he gazed into heaven and saw the
glory of God and Jesus standing at the right hand of God. 56 "Look," he said, "I see
the heavens opened and the Son of Man standing at the right hand of God!" 57 But
they covered their ears, and with a loud shout all rushed together against him.
58 Then they dragged him out of the city and began to stone him; and the witnesses
laid their coats at the feet of a young man named Saul. 59 While they were stoning
Stephen, he prayed, "Lord Jesus, receive my spirit." 60 Then he knelt down and
8 cried out in a loud voice, "Lord, do not hold this sin against them." When he
had said this, he died.[e] 1 And Saul approved of their killing him.

2. Expansion of the church

Widespread persecution scatters the believers

That day a severe persecution began against the church in Jerusalem, and all
except the apostles were scattered throughout the countryside of Judea and Samaria. 2 Devout men buried Stephen and made loud lamentation over him. 3 But
Saul was ravaging the church by entering house after house; dragging off both men
and women, he committed them to prison.

4 Now those who were scattered went from place to place, proclaiming the
word. 5 Philip went down to the city[f] of Samaria and proclaimed the Messiah[g] to
them. 6 The crowds with one accord listened eagerly to what was said by Philip,
hearing and seeing the signs that he did, 7 for unclean spirits, crying with loud

[d] Gk *him* [e] Gk *fell asleep* [f] Other ancient authorities read *a city* [g] Or *the Christ*

7.53 Ex 20.1; Gal 3.19
7.55 Mt 26.64; Heb 1.3,13
7.56 Mt 3.16; Heb 9.24
7.58 Lev 24.14-16; Deut 17.7
7.59 Ps 31.5; Lk 23.46
7.60 Mt 5.44; Lk 6.28; 23.34
8.3 Acts 9.1; 22.4; 26.10; 1 Cor 15.9; Gal 1.13
8.4 Acts 11.19
8.5 Acts 6.5
8.7 Mt 10.1

7.55, 56 Stephen saw the glory of God and Jesus the Messiah standing at God's right hand. Stephen's words are similar to Jesus' words spoken before the council (Matthew 26.64; Mark 14.62; Luke 22.69). Stephen's vision supported Jesus' claim and angered the Jewish leaders who had condemned Jesus to death for blasphemy. They would not tolerate Stephen's words, so they mobbed him and killed him. People may not kill us for witnessing about Christ, but they will let us know they don't want to hear the truth and will often try to silence us. Keep honoring God in your conduct and words; though many may turn against you and your message, some will follow Christ. Remember, Stephen's death made a profound impact on Paul, who later became the world's greatest missionary. Even those who oppose you may later turn to Christ.

7.58 Saul is also called Paul (see 13.9), the great missionary who wrote many of the letters in the New Testament. Saul was his Hebrew name; Paul, his Greek name, was used after his conversion. When Luke introduces him, Paul is hating and persecuting Jesus' followers. This is a great contrast to the Paul about whom Luke will write for most of the rest of the book of Acts—a devoted follower of Christ and a gifted gospel preacher. Paul was uniquely qualified to talk to the Jews about Jesus because he had once persecuted those who believed in Jesus, and he understood how the opposition felt. Paul is a powerful example of how no one is impossible for God to reach and change.

7.59 The penalty for blasphemy, speaking irreverently about God, was death by stoning (Leviticus 24.14). The religious leaders, in a rage and without trial, had Stephen stoned. They did not understand that Stephen's words were true because they were not seeking the truth. They only wanted support for their own views.

7.60 As Stephen died, he repeated Jesus' words on the cross (Luke 23.34). The early believers were glad to suffer as Jesus had suffered, because that meant they were counted worthy (5.41). Stephen was ready to suffer like Jesus, even to the point of asking forgiveness for his murderers. Such a forgiving response comes only from the Holy Spirit. The Spirit can also help us respond as Stephen did and love our enemies (Luke 6.27). How would you react if someone hurt you because of what you believed?

8.1–4 Persecution forced the Christians out of Jerusalem and into Judea and Samaria—thus fulfilling the next part of Jesus' command (see 1.8). The persecution helped spread the gospel. God would bring great results from the believers' suffering.

8.4 Persecution forced the believers out of their homes in Jerusalem, and with them went the gospel. Sometimes we have to become uncomfortable before we'll move. We may not want it, but discomfort may be the best thing for us because God may be working through our hurts. When you are tempted to complain about uncomfortable or painful circumstances, stop and ask if God might be preparing you for a special task.

8.5 This is not the apostle Philip (see John 1.43, 44), but a Greek-speaking Jew, "of good standing, full of the Spirit and of wisdom" (6.3), who was one of the seven deacons chosen to help with the food distribution program in the church (6.5).

8.5 Israel was divided into three main regions—Galilee in the north, Samaria in the middle, and Judea in the south. The city of Samaria (in the region of Samaria) had been the capital of the northern kingdom of Israel in the days of the divided kingdom, before it was conquered by Assyria in 722 B.C. The Assyrian king took many captives, leaving only the poorest people in the land and resettling it with foreigners. These foreigners intermarried with the Jews who were left, and the mixed race became known as Samaritans. The Samaritans were considered half-breeds by the "pure" Jews in the southern kingdom of Judah, and there was intense hatred between the two groups. But Jesus himself went into Samaria (John 4), and he commanded his followers to spread the gospel even there (1.8).

shrieks, came out of many who were possessed; and many others who were paralyzed or lame were cured. [8]So there was great joy in that city.

Philip and Simon the sorcerer

8.9 Acts 5.36; 13.6 — 9 Now a certain man named Simon had previously practiced magic in the city
and amazed the people of Samaria, saying that he was someone great. [10]All of
them, from the least to the greatest, listened to him eagerly, saying, "This man is
the power of God that is called Great." [11]And they listened eagerly to him because
8.12 Acts 1.3; 2.38 — for a long time he had amazed them with his magic. [12]But when they believed
8.13 Acts 19.11 — Philip, who was proclaiming the good news about the kingdom of God and the
name of Jesus Christ, they were baptized, both men and women. [13]Even Simon

MISSIONARIES OF THE NEW TESTAMENT AND THEIR JOURNEYS

Name	*Journey Purpose*	*Scripture Reference in Acts*
Philip	One of the first to preach the gospel outside Jerusalem	8.4–40
Peter and John	Visited new Samaritan believers to encourage them	8.14–25
Paul (journey to Damascus)	Set out to capture Christians but was captured by Christ	9.1–25
Peter	Led by God to one of the first Gentile families to become Christian—Cornelius's family	9.32—10.48
Barnabas	Went to Antioch as an encourager; traveled on to Troas to bring Paul back to Jerusalem from Antioch	11.25–30
Barnabas, Paul, John Mark	Left Antioch for Cyprus, Pamphylia, and Galatia on the first missionary journey	13.1—14.28
Barnabas and John Mark	After a break with Paul, they left Antioch for Cyprus	15.36–41
Paul, Silas, Timothy, Luke	Left Antioch to revisit churches in Galatia, then traveled on to Asia, Macedonia, and Achaia on a second missionary journey	15.36—18.22
Apollos	Left Alexandria for Ephesus; learned the complete gospel story from Priscilla and Aquila; preached in Athens and Corinth	18.24–28
Paul, Timothy, Erastus	Third major missionary journey revisiting churches in Galatia, Asia, Macedonia, and Achaia	18.23; 19.1—21.14

PHILIP'S MINISTRY
To escape persecution in Jerusalem, Philip fled to Samaria, where he continued preaching the gospel. While he was there, an angel commanded him to meet an Ethiopian official on the road between Jerusalem and Gaza. The man became a believer before continuing to Ethiopia. Philip then went from Azotus to Caesarea.

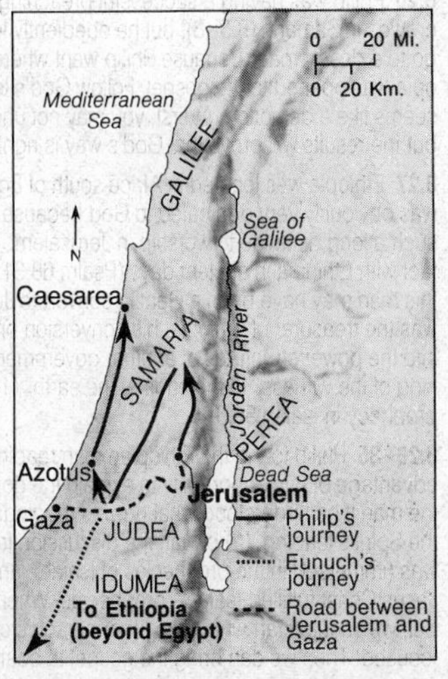

8.7 Jesus encountered and cast out many demons during his ministry on earth. Demons, or evil spirits, are ruled by Satan. They are fallen angels who joined Satan in his rebellion against God, and they can cause a person to be mute, deaf, blind, or insane. They also tempt people to sin. Although they can be powerful, they are not able to read our minds and cannot be everywhere at once. Demons are real and active, but Jesus has authority over them, and he gave this authority to his followers. Although he allows Satan to work in our world, God is in complete control. He can cast demons out and end their destructive work in people's lives. Eventually Satan and his demons will be put into the lake of fire forever, ending their evil work in the world (Revelation 20.10).

8.9–11 In the days of the early church, sorcerers and magicians were numerous and influential. They worked wonders, performed healings and exorcisms, and practiced astrology. Their wonders may simply have been tricks or possibly empowered by Satan. Simon had done so many wonders that some even thought he was the Messiah; but his powers did not come from God (see 8.18–24).

himself believed. After being baptized, he stayed constantly with Philip and was
amazed when he saw the signs and great miracles that took place.
14 Now when the apostles at Jerusalem heard that Samaria had accepted the
word of God, they sent Peter and John to them. 15 The two went down and prayed
for them that they might receive the Holy Spirit 16 (for as yet the Spirit had not
come[h] upon any of them; they had only been baptized in the name of the Lord
Jesus). 17 Then Peter and John[i] laid their hands on them, and they received the
Holy Spirit. 18 Now when Simon saw that the Spirit was given through the laying on
of the apostles' hands, he offered them money, 19 saying, "Give me also this power
so that anyone on whom I lay my hands may receive the Holy Spirit." 20 But Peter
said to him, "May your silver perish with you, because you thought you could
obtain God's gift with money! 21 You have no part or share in this, for your heart is
not right before God. 22 Repent therefore of this wickedness of yours, and pray to
the Lord that, if possible, the intent of your heart may be forgiven you. 23 For I see
that you are in the gall of bitterness and the chains of wickedness." 24 Simon answered, "Pray for me to the Lord, that nothing of what you[j] have said may happen
to me."
25 Now after Peter and John[k] had testified and spoken the word of the Lord,
they returned to Jerusalem, proclaiming the good news to many villages of the
Samaritans.

Philip and the Ethiopian official

26 Then an angel of the Lord said to Philip, "Get up and go toward the south[l]
to the road that goes down from Jerusalem to Gaza." (This is a wilderness road.)
27 So he got up and went. Now there was an Ethiopian eunuch, a court official of the
Candace, queen of the Ethiopians, in charge of her entire treasury. He had come to
Jerusalem to worship 28 and was returning home; seated in his chariot, he was reading the prophet Isaiah. 29 Then the Spirit said to Philip, "Go over to this chariot and

8.14 Acts 8.1
8.15 Acts 2.38; 19.2
8.16 Acts 10.48
8.17 Acts 2.4
8.20 Mic 3.11,12; Mt 10.8; Acts 2.38
8.21 Jer 17.9; Eph 5.5
8.22 Isa 55.7; Dan 4.27
8.23 Heb 12.15
8.24 Gen 20.7; Ex 8.8; Num 21.7; Job 42.8
8.26 Ps 91.11; Heb 1.14
8.27 1 Kgs 8.41,42; Ps 68.29; Isa 43.6; 53.7; 56.3; Zeph 3.10

[h] Gk *fallen* [i] Gk *they* [j] The Greek word for *you* and the verb *pray* are plural [k] Gk *after they* [l] Or *go at noon*

8.14 Peter and John were sent to Samaria to find out whether or not the Samaritans were truly becoming believers. The Jewish Christians, even the apostles, were still unsure whether Gentiles (non-Jews) and half-Jews could receive the Holy Spirit. It wasn't until Peter's experience with Cornelius (chapter 10) that the apostles became fully convinced that the Holy Spirit was for all people. It was John who had asked Jesus if they should call fire down from heaven to burn up a Samaritan village that refused to welcome them (Luke 9.51–55). Now he and Peter went to the Samaritans to pray with them.

8.15–17 This was a crucial moment in the spread of the gospel and the growth of the church. Peter and John had to go to Samaria to help keep this new group of believers from becoming separated from other believers. When Peter and John saw the Holy Spirit working in these people, they were assured that the Holy Spirit worked through *all* believers—Gentiles and mixed races as well as the "pure" Jews.

8.15–17 Many scholars believe that God chose to have a dramatic filling of his Spirit as a sign at this special moment in history—the spread of the gospel into Samaria through the powerful, effective preaching of believers. Normally, the Holy Spirit enters a person's life at conversion. This was a special event. This would be repeated with Cornelius and his family (10.44–47), a sign that the uncircumcised Gentiles could receive the gospel.

8.17–22 "Everything has a price" seems to be true in our world of bribes, wealth, and materialism. Simon thought he could buy the Holy Spirit's power, but Peter harshly rebuked him. The only way to receive God's power is to do as Peter told Simon—turn from sin, ask God for forgiveness, and be filled with his Spirit. No amount of money can buy salvation, forgiveness of sin, or God's power. These are only gained by repentance and belief in Christ as Savior.

8.23 *Gall of bitterness* means jealousy and sin in your heart.

8.24 The last time a parent or friend rebuked you, were you hurt, angry, or defensive? Learn a lesson from Simon and his reaction to what Peter told him. He exclaimed, "Pray for me to the Lord." If you are rebuked for a serious mistake, it is for your good. Admit your error, repent quickly, and ask for prayer.

8.26 Philip was having a successful preaching ministry to great crowds in Samaria (8.5–8), but he obediently left that ministry to go to a desert road. Because Philip went where God sent him, Ethiopia was opened to the gospel. Follow God's leading, even if it seems like a demotion. At first, you may not understand his plans, but the results will prove that God's way is right.

8.27 Ethiopia was located in Africa south of Egypt. The eunuch was obviously very dedicated to God because he had traveled such a long distance to worship in Jerusalem. The Jews had contact with Ethiopia in ancient days (Psalm 68.31; Jeremiah 38.7), so this man may have been a Gentile convert to Judaism. Because he was the treasurer of Ethiopia, his conversion brought Christianity into the power structures of another government. This is the beginning of the witness "to the ends of the earth" (1.8). See the prophecy in Isaiah 56.3–5.

8.29–35 Philip found the Ethiopian man reading Scripture. Taking advantage of this opportunity to explain the gospel, Philip asked the man if he understood what he was reading. Philip (1) followed the Spirit's leading, (2) began the discussion from where the man was (immersed in the prophecies of Isaiah), and (3) explained how Jesus Christ fulfilled Isaiah's prophecies. When we share the gospel, we should start where the other person's concerns are focused. Then we can bring the gospel to bear on those concerns.

join it.” 30 So Philip ran up to it and heard him reading the prophet Isaiah. He asked,
8.31 2 Cor 3.14 “Do you understand what you are reading?” 31 He replied, “How can I, unless
someone guides me?” And he invited Philip to get in and sit beside him. 32 Now the
8.32,33 Isa 53.7,8 Phil 2.7,8 passage of the scripture that he was reading was this:

“Like a sheep he was led to the slaughter,
and like a lamb silent before its shearer,
so he does not open his mouth.
33 In his humiliation justice was denied him.
Who can describe his generation?
For his life is taken away from the earth.”

34 The eunuch asked Philip, “About whom, may I ask you, does the prophet say
8.35 Lk 24.27 Acts 18.28 this, about himself or about someone else?” 35 Then Philip began to speak, and
starting with this scripture, he proclaimed to him the good news about Jesus. 36 As
they were going along the road, they came to some water; and the eunuch said,
8.37 Mt 16.16; 28.19 Mk 16.16 Jn 6.69; 11.27 Rom 10.10 “Look, here is water! What is to prevent me from being baptized?”[m] 38 He commanded the chariot to stop, and both of them, Philip and the eunuch, went down
into the water, and Philip[n] baptized him. 39 When they came up out of the water,
8.39 1 Kgs 18.12 2 Kgs 2.16 Ezek 3.12 the Spirit of the Lord snatched Philip away; the eunuch saw him no more, and went
on his way rejoicing. 40 But Philip found himself at Azotus, and as he was passing
through the region, he proclaimed the good news to all the towns until he came to
Caesarea.

Paul is converted on the way to Damascus

9.1 Gal 1.13 1 Tim 1.13 **9** Meanwhile Saul, still breathing threats and murder against the disciples of the
Lord, went to the high priest 2 and asked him for letters to the synagogues at
9.3 1 Cor 15.8 Damascus, so that if he found any who belonged to the Way, men or women, he
might bring them bound to Jerusalem. 3 Now as he was going along and approaching Damascus, suddenly a light from heaven flashed around him. 4 He fell to the

[m] Other ancient authorities add all or most of verse 37, *And Philip said, “If you believe with all your heart, you may.” And he replied, “I believe that Jesus Christ is the Son of God.”* [n] Gk *he*

8.30, 31 The eunuch begged Philip to explain a passage of Scripture that he did not understand. When we have trouble understanding the Bible, we should ask others to help us. We must never let our insecurity or pride get in the way of understanding God's Word.

8.35 Some think the Old Testament is not relevant today, but Philip led this man to faith in Jesus Christ by using the Old Testament. Jesus Christ is found in the pages of both the Old and New Testaments. God's entire Word is applicable to all people in all ages. Don't avoid or neglect to use the Old Testament. It too is God's Word.

8.38 Baptism was a sign of identification with Christ and with the Christian community. Although there were no witnesses besides Philip, it was still important for the eunuch to take this step.

8.39, 40 Why was Philip suddenly transported to a different city? This miraculous sign showed the urgency of bringing the Gentiles to belief in Christ. Azotus is Ashdod, the ancient Philistine capital. Philip settled there for the next 20 years (21.8).

9.2 Paul was so zealous for his Jewish beliefs that he began a persecution campaign against anyone who believed in Christ (“any who belonged to the Way”). Why would the Jews in Jerusalem want to persecute Christians as far away as Damascus? There are several possibilities: (1) to seize the Christians who had fled, (2) to contain and prevent the spread of Christianity to other major cities, (3) to keep the Christians from causing any trouble with Rome, (4) to advance Paul's career and build his reputation as a true Pharisee, zealous for the law, (5) to unify the factions of Judaism by giving them a common enemy.

9.2–5 As Paul traveled to Damascus, pursuing Christians, he was confronted by the risen Christ and brought face to face with the truth of the gospel. Sometimes God breaks into a life in a spectacular manner, and sometimes conversion is a quiet experience. Beware of people who insist that you must have a particular type of conversion experience. The right way to come to faith in Jesus is whatever way God brings *you.*

9.3 Damascus, a key commercial city, was located about 175 miles northeast of Jerusalem in the Roman province of Syria. Several trade routes linked Damascus to other cities throughout the Roman world. Paul may have thought that by stamping out Christianity in Damascus, he could prevent its spread to other areas.

9.3–5 Paul refers to this experience as the start of his new life in Christ (1 Corinthians 9.1; 15.8; Galatians 1.15, 16). At the center of this wonderful experience was Jesus Christ. Paul did not see a vision; he saw the risen Christ himself (9.17). Paul acknowledged Jesus as Lord, confessed his own sin, surrendered his life to Christ, and resolved to obey. True conversion comes from a personal encounter with Jesus Christ and leads to a new life in relationship with him.

ground and heard a voice saying to him, "Saul, Saul, why do you persecute me?"
5 He asked, "Who are you, Lord?" The reply came, "I am Jesus, whom you are
persecuting. 6 But get up and enter the city, and you will be told what you are to
do." 7 The men who were traveling with him stood speechless because they heard
the voice but saw no one. 8 Saul got up from the ground, and though his eyes were
open, he could see nothing; so they led him by the hand and brought him into
Damascus. 9 For three days he was without sight, and neither ate nor drank.

10 Now there was a disciple in Damascus named Ananias. The Lord said to him
in a vision, "Ananias." He answered, "Here I am, Lord." 11 The Lord said to him,
"Get up and go to the street called Straight, and at the house of Judas look for a man
of Tarsus named Saul. At this moment he is praying, 12 and he has seen in a vision[o]
a man named Ananias come in and lay his hands on him so that he might regain his
sight." 13 But Ananias answered, "Lord, I have heard from many about this man,
how much evil he has done to your saints in Jerusalem; 14 and here he has authority
from the chief priests to bind all who invoke your name." 15 But the Lord said to
him, "Go, for he is an instrument whom I have chosen to bring my name before
Gentiles and kings and before the people of Israel; 16 I myself will show him how
much he must suffer for the sake of my name." 17 So Ananias went and entered the
house. He laid his hands on Saul[p] and said, "Brother Saul, the Lord Jesus, who
appeared to you on your way here, has sent me so that you may regain your sight
and be filled with the Holy Spirit." 18 And immediately something like scales fell
from his eyes, and his sight was restored. Then he got up and was baptized, 19 and
after taking some food, he regained his strength.

Paul preaches boldly

For several days he was with the disciples in Damascus, 20 and immediately he
began to proclaim Jesus in the synagogues, saying, "He is the Son of God." 21 All

9.5 Acts 5.39
9.7 Dan 10.7 Acts 22.9; 26.14
9.10 Acts 10.3 11.5; 12.9; 22.12
9.11 Acts 21.39
9.13 Acts 26.10
9.14 1 Cor 1.2
9.15 Acts 13.2 22.21; 26.1-18 Rom 1.1,5 11.13 Gal 1.15,16 Eph 3.7 1 Tim 2.7 2 Tim 1.11
9.16 Acts 20.23 21.11 2 Cor 11.23-27
9.17 Acts 2.4; 13.52 22.12,13
9.19 Acts 26.20

[o] Other ancient authorities lack *in a vision* [p] Gk *him*

PAUL TRAVELS TO DAMASCUS
Many Christians fled Jerusalem when persecution began after Stephen's death, seeking refuge in other cities and countries. Paul tracked them down, even traveling 150 miles to Damascus in Syria to bring Christians back in chains to Jerusalem. But as he neared the ancient city, he discovered that God had other plans for him (9.15).

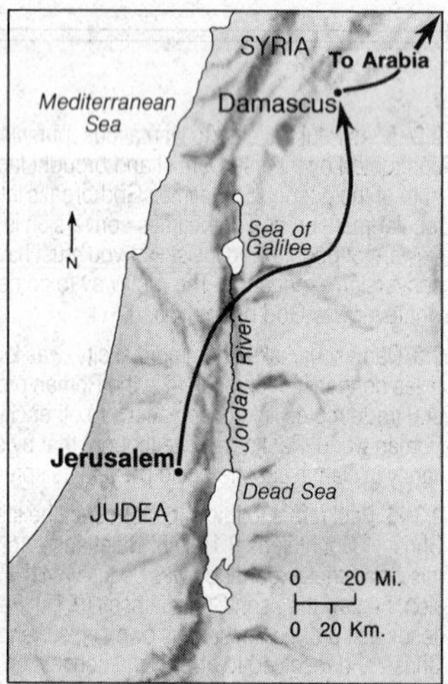

9.5 Paul thought he was pursuing heretics, but he was persecuting Jesus himself. Anyone who persecutes believers today is also guilty of persecuting Jesus (see Matthew 25.40, 45), because believers are the body of Christ on earth.

9.8 Paul opened his eyes but could not see—he was temporarily blinded (see 9.17, 18).

9.13, 14 "Not him, Lord, that's impossible. He could never become a Christian!" In essence, that's what Ananias said when God told him of Paul's conversion. After all, Paul had pursued believers to their death. Despite these understandable feelings, Ananias obeyed God and ministered to Paul. We must not limit God, because he can do anything. We must obey, following God's leading even to difficult people and places.

9.15, 16 Faith in Christ brings great blessings but often great suffering too. Paul would suffer for his faith (see 2 Corinthians 11.23–27). God calls us to commitment, not to comfort. He promises to be with us through suffering and hardship, not to spare us from them.

9.17 Ananias found Paul, as he had been instructed, and greeted him as "Brother Saul." Ananias feared this meeting because Paul had come to Damascus to capture the believers and take them in chains to Jerusalem (9.2). But in obedience to the Holy Spirit, he greeted Paul lovingly. It is not always easy to show love to others, especially when we are afraid of them or doubt their motives. Nevertheless, we must follow Jesus' command (John 13.34) and Ananias's example, showing loving acceptance to other believers.

9.17, 18 Although there is no mention of a special filling of the Holy Spirit for Paul, his changed life and subsequent accomplishments bear strong witness of the Holy Spirit's presence and power in his life. Evidently, the Holy Spirit filled Paul when he received his sight and was baptized. See the note on 8.15–17 for more on the filling of the Holy Spirit.

9.20 Immediately after receiving his sight and being with the believers in Damascus, Paul went to the synagogue to tell the Jews about Jesus Christ. Some Christians counsel new believers to wait until they are thoroughly grounded in their faith before attempting to share the gospel. Paul took time alone to learn about Jesus before beginning his worldwide ministry, but he did not wait to witness. Although we should not rush into a ministry unprepared, we do not need to wait before telling others what has happened to us.

9.21 Gal 1.13
9.22 Acts 18.28
9.23 Gal 1.17,18
9.24 2 Cor 11.32

who heard him were amazed and said, "Is not this the man who made havoc in
Jerusalem among those who invoked this name? And has he not come here for the
purpose of bringing them bound before the chief priests?" 22 Saul became increasingly more powerful and confounded the Jews who lived in Damascus by proving
that Jesus[q] was the Messiah.[r]
23 After some time had passed, the Jews plotted to kill him, 24 but their plot

[q] Gk *that this* [r] Or *the Christ*

PHILIP

Jesus' last words to his followers were a command to take the gospel everywhere, but his followers seemed reluctant to leave Jerusalem. It took intense persecution to scatter them from Jerusalem and into Judea and Samaria, where Jesus had instructed them to go. Philip, one of the deacons in charge of food distribution, left Jerusalem and, like most Jewish Christians, spread the gospel wherever he went; but unlike most of them, he did not limit his audience to other Jews. He went directly to Samaria, the last place many Jews would go, due to age-old prejudice.

The Samaritans responded in large numbers. When word got back to Jerusalem, Peter and John were sent to evaluate Philip's ministry. They quickly became involved themselves, seeing firsthand God's acceptance of those who previously were considered unacceptable.

In the middle of all this success and excitement, God directed Philip out to the desert for an appointment with an Ethiopian eunuch, another foreigner who had been in Jerusalem. Philip went immediately. His effectiveness in sharing the gospel with this man placed a Christian in a significant position in a distant country and may well have had an effect on an entire nation.

Philip ended up in Caesarea, where events allowed him to be Paul's host many years later. Paul, who as the leading persecutor of the Christians had been instrumental in pushing Philip and others out of Jerusalem, had himself become an effective believer. The conversion of the Gentiles begun by Philip was continued across the entire Roman Empire by Paul.

Whether or not you are a follower of Christ, Philip's life presents a challenge. To those still outside the gospel, he is a reminder that the good news is for you also. To those who have accepted Christ, he is a reminder that we are not free to disqualify anyone from hearing about Jesus. How much like Philip would your neighbors say you are?

Strengths and accomplishments:
- One of the seven organizers of food distribution in the early church
- An evangelist, one of the first traveling missionaries
- One of the first to obey Jesus' command to take the gospel to all people
- A careful student of the Bible who could explain its meaning clearly

Lessons from his life:
- God finds great and various uses for those willing to obey wholeheartedly
- The gospel is universal good news
- The whole Bible, not just the New Testament, helps us understand more about Jesus
- Both mass response (the Samaritans) and individual response (the man from Ethiopia) to the gospel are valuable

Vital statistics:
- Occupation: Deacon, evangelist
- Relatives: Four daughters
- Contemporaries: Paul, Stephen, the apostles

Key verse:
"Then Philip began to speak, and starting with this scripture, he proclaimed to him the good news about Jesus" (Acts 8.35).

Philip's story is told in Acts 6.1–7; 8.5–40; 21.8–10.

9.21, 22 Paul's arguments were powerful because he was a brilliant scholar. But what was more convincing was his changed life. People knew what he taught was real because they could see the evidence in the way he lived. It is important to know what the Bible teaches and how to defend the faith, but your words should be backed up with a changed life.

9.23 According to Galatians 1.17, 18, Paul left Damascus and traveled to Arabia, the desert region just southeast of Damascus, where he lived for three years. It is unclear whether his three-year stay occurred between verses 22 and 23, or between verses 25 and 26. Some commentators say that "some time" could mean a long period of time. They suggest that when Paul returned to Damascus, the governor under Aretas ordered his arrest (2 Corinthians 11.32), in an effort to keep peace with influential Jews.

The other possibility is that Paul's night escape occurred during his first stay in Damascus, just after his conversion, when the Pharisees were especially upset over his defection from their ranks. He would have fled to Arabia to spend time alone with God and to let the Jewish religious leaders cool down. Regardless of which theory is correct, there was a period of at least three years between Paul's conversion (9.3–6) and his trip to Jerusalem (9.26).

became known to Saul. They were watching the gates day and night so that they
might kill him; 25 but his disciples took him by night and let him down through an
opening in the wall,[s] lowering him in a basket.
26 When he had come to Jerusalem, he attempted to join the disciples; and they
were all afraid of him, for they did not believe that he was a disciple. 27 But Barnabas took him, brought him to the apostles, and described for them how on the
road he had seen the Lord, who had spoken to him, and how in Damascus he had
spoken boldly in the name of Jesus. 28 So he went in and out among them in Jerusalem, speaking boldly in the name of the Lord. 29 He spoke and argued with the
Hellenists; but they were attempting to kill him. 30 When the believers[t] learned of
it, they brought him down to Caesarea and sent him off to Tarsus.
31 Meanwhile the church throughout Judea, Galilee, and Samaria had peace
and was built up. Living in the fear of the Lord and in the comfort of the Holy
Spirit, it increased in numbers.

9.25 Josh 2.15 1 Sam 19.12
9.26 Acts 22.17,18
9.27 Acts 4.36 11.24; 13.2
9.31 Acts 5.11; 8.1

Peter heals Aeneas and Dorcas

32 Now as Peter went here and there among all the believers,[u] he came down
also to the saints living in Lydda. 33 There he found a man named Aeneas, who had
been bedridden for eight years, for he was paralyzed. 34 Peter said to him, "Aeneas,
Jesus Christ heals you; get up and make your bed!" And immediately he got up.
35 And all the residents of Lydda and Sharon saw him and turned to the Lord.
36 Now in Joppa there was a disciple whose name was Tabitha, which in Greek
is Dorcas.[v] She was devoted to good works and acts of charity. 37 At that time she
became ill and died. When they had washed her, they laid her in a room upstairs.
38 Since Lydda was near Joppa, the disciples, who heard that Peter was there, sent
two men to him with the request, "Please come to us without delay." 39 So Peter got
up and went with them; and when he arrived, they took him to the room upstairs.
All the widows stood beside him, weeping and showing tunics and other clothing
that Dorcas had made while she was with them. 40 Peter put all of them outside, and
then he knelt down and prayed. He turned to the body and said, "Tabitha, get up."

9.32 Acts 8.14
9.34 Mt 9.6 Jn 5.8 Acts 3.6; 4.10
9.35 Acts 11.21
9.36 Prov 31.31 1 Tim 2.9,10 5.10 Tit 3.8 Jas 1.27
9.40 1 Kgs 17.19-23 2 Kgs 4.32-36 Mt 9.25 Mk 5.41,42 Jn 11.43

[s] Gk *through the wall* [t] Gk *brothers* [u] Gk *all of them* [v] The name Tabitha in Aramaic and the name Dorcas in Greek mean *a gazelle*

9.26, 27 It is difficult to change your reputation, and Paul had a terrible reputation with the Christians. But Barnabas, a Jewish convert (mentioned in 4.36), became the bridge between Paul and the apostles. New Christians (especially those with tarnished reputations) need sponsors, people who will come alongside, encourage, teach, and introduce them to other believers. Find ways that you can become a Barnabas to new believers.

9.27 Galatians 1.18, 19 says that Paul was in Jerusalem only 15 days and that he met only with Peter and James.

9.29, 30 In these short sentences we can see two characteristics of Paul, even as a new believer in Christ. He was bold, and he stirred up controversy. These would characterize Paul's ministry the rest of his life. The Hellenists were Greek-speaking Jews.

9.31 Paul's visit to Tarsus helped quiet conflicts with the Jews and allowed Paul time to prove his commitment. After Paul, the most zealous persecutor, was converted, the church enjoyed a brief time of relative peace.

9.36 The important harbor city of Joppa sits 125 feet above sea level overlooking the Mediterranean Sea. Joppa was the town into which the cedars of Lebanon were floated to be shipped to Jerusalem and used in the temple construction (2 Chronicles 2.16; Ezra 3.7). The prophet Jonah left the port of Joppa on his ill-fated trip (Jonah 1.3).

9.36–42 Dorcas made an enormous impact on her community by being "devoted to good works," such as making coats and other garments for the poor (9.39). When she died, the room was filled with mourners, people she had helped. And when she was brought back to life, the news raced through the town. God uses great preachers like Peter and Paul, but he also uses those who have gifts of kindness, like Dorcas. Rather than wishing you had other gifts, make good use of the gifts God has given you.

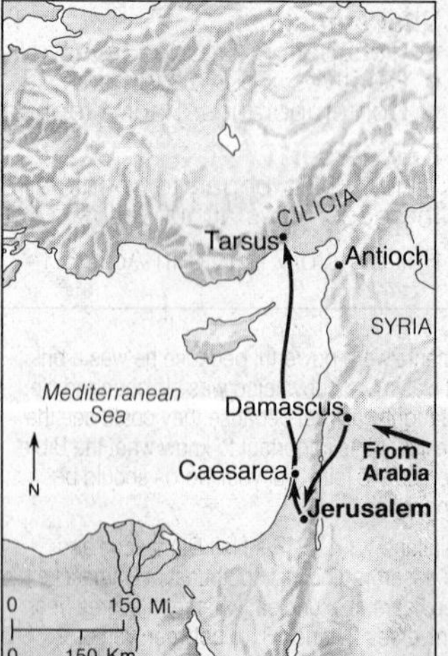

PAUL'S RETURN TO TARSUS
At least three years elapsed between Acts 9.22 and 9.26. After time alone in Arabia (see Galatians 1.16–18), Paul returned to Damascus and then to Jerusalem. The apostles were reluctant to believe this former persecutor could be one of them. He escaped to Caesarea where he caught a ship and returned to Tarsus.

Then she opened her eyes, and seeing Peter, she sat up. 41 He gave her his hand and
helped her up. Then calling the saints and widows, he showed her to be alive.
9.42 Jn 11.45; 12.11 42 This became known throughout Joppa, and many believed in the Lord. 43 Meanwhile he stayed in Joppa for some time with a certain Simon, a tanner.

GREAT ESCAPES IN THE BIBLE

Who escaped	*Reference*	*What happened*	*What the escape accomplished*	*Application*
Jacob	Genesis 31.1–55	Left his father-in-law, Laban, after almost 20 years of service	Allowed Jacob to return home for Isaac's death and for reconciliation with Esau, his brother	A time away from home often puts the really important things into perspective
Moses	Exodus 2.11–15	Fled Egypt after killing an Egyptian in defense of a fellow Israelite	Saved his own life and began another part of God's training	God fits even our mistakes into his plan
Israelites	Exodus 12.28–42	Escaped Egypt after 430 years, most of that time in slavery	God confirmed his choice of Abraham's descendants	God will not forget his promises
Spies	Joshua 2.1–24	Escaped searchers in Jericho by hiding in Rahab's house	Prepared the destruction of Jericho and preserved Rahab, who would become one of David's ancestors—as well as an ancestor of Jesus	God's plan weaves lives together in a pattern beyond our understanding
Ehud	Judges 3.15–30	Assassinated the Moabite King Eglon, but escaped undetected	Broke the control of Moab over Israel and began 80 years of peace	Punishments by God are often swift and deadly
Samson	Judges 16.1–3	Escaped a locked city by ripping the gates from their hinges	Merely postponed Samson's self-destruction because of his lack of self-control	Without dependence on God and his guidance, even great ability is wasted
Elijah	1 Kings 19.1–18	Fled into the desert out of fear of Queen Jezebel	Preserved Elijah's life, but also displayed his human weakness	Even at moments of real success, our personal weaknesses are our greatest challenges
Paul	Acts 9.23–25	Lowered over the wall in a basket to get out of Damascus	Saved this new Christian for great service to God	God has a purpose for every life, which becomes a real adventure for those willing to cooperate
Peter	Acts 12.1–11	Freed from prison by an angel	Saved Peter for God's further plans for his life	God can use extraordinary means to carry out his plan—often when we least expect it
Paul and Silas	Acts 16.22–40	Chains loosened and doors opened by an earthquake, but they chose not to leave the prison	Pointed out the powerlessness of men before God	When our dependence and attention are focused on God rather than our problems, he is able to offer help in unexpected ways

9.43 In Joppa, Peter stayed at the home of Simon, a tanner. Tanners made animal hides into leather. It is significant that Peter was at Simon's house, because tanning involved contact with dead animals, and Jewish law considered it an unclean job. Peter was already beginning to break down his prejudice against people and customs that did not adhere to Jewish religious traditions.

Peter and Cornelius

10 In Caesarea there was a man named Cornelius, a centurion of the Italian
Cohort, as it was called. 2He was a devout man who feared God with all his
household; he gave alms generously to the people and prayed constantly to God.
3One afternoon at about three o'clock he had a vision in which he clearly saw an
angel of God coming in and saying to him, "Cornelius." 4He stared at him in terror
and said, "What is it, Lord?" He answered, "Your prayers and your alms have
ascended as a memorial before God. 5Now send men to Joppa for a certain Simon
who is called Peter; 6he is lodging with Simon, a tanner, whose house is by the
seaside." 7When the angel who spoke to him had left, he called two of his slaves
and a devout soldier from the ranks of those who served him, 8and after telling
them everything, he sent them to Joppa.
9 About noon the next day, as they were on their journey and approaching the
city, Peter went up on the roof to pray. 10He became hungry and wanted something
to eat; and while it was being prepared, he fell into a trance. 11He saw the heaven
opened and something like a large sheet coming down, being lowered to the ground
by its four corners. 12In it were all kinds of four-footed creatures and reptiles and
birds of the air. 13Then he heard a voice saying, "Get up, Peter; kill and eat." 14But
Peter said, "By no means, Lord; for I have never eaten anything that is profane or
unclean." 15The voice said to him again, a second time, "What God has made
clean, you must not call profane." 16This happened three times, and the thing was
suddenly taken up to heaven.
17 Now while Peter was greatly puzzled about what to make of the vision that
he had seen, suddenly the men sent by Cornelius appeared. They were asking for
Simon's house and were standing by the gate. 18They called out to ask whether
Simon, who was called Peter, was staying there. 19While Peter was still thinking
about the vision, the Spirit said to him, "Look, three[w] men are searching for you.
20Now get up, go down, and go with them without hesitation; for I have sent
them." 21So Peter went down to the men and said, "I am the one you are looking
for; what is the reason for your coming?" 22They answered, "Cornelius, a centurion, an upright and God-fearing man, who is well spoken of by the whole Jewish

10.1 Acts 8.40; 27.1
10.2 Gen 18.19 Josh 24.15
10.3 Ps 34.7 Heb 1.14
10.4 2 Chron 7.15 Ps 65.1,2 141.2 Prov 15.29 Heb 6.10; 13.16 Jas 5.16 1 Pet 3.2 Rev 5.8; 8.4
10.9 Ps 55.17 Acts 11.5
10.11 Ezek 1.1-3 Mt 3.16 Acts 7.56 Rev 19.11
10.14 Lev 11.4-7 20.25 Deut 14.3-5 Ezek 4.14
10.15 Mt 15.11 Rom 14.14,17, 20 1 Cor 10.25 1 Tim 4.4 Tit 1.15
10.19 Acts 8.29; 11.12
10.20 Mt 28.19 Mk 16.15 Acts 15.7

[w] One ancient authority reads *two*; others lack the word

10.1 This Caesarea, sometimes called Palestinian Caesarea, was located on the coast of the Mediterranean Sea, 32 miles north of Joppa. The largest and most important port city on the Mediterranean in Palestine, it served as the capital of the Roman province of Judea. This was the first city to have Gentile Christians and a non-Jewish church.

10.1 This Roman officer was a *centurion,* a commander of 100 soldiers. *Cohort* could be translated "regiment." Although stationed in Caesarea, Cornelius would probably return soon to Rome. Thus his conversion was a major stepping-stone for spreading the gospel to the capital city.

10.2 "What will happen to the heathen who have never heard about Christ?" This question is often asked about God's justice. Cornelius wasn't a Christian, but he was seeking God, and he was reverent and generous. Giving alms is making donations to the poor. Therefore God sent Peter to tell Cornelius about Christ. Cornelius is an example that God "rewards those who seek him" (Hebrews 11.6). Those who sincerely seek God will find him! God made Cornelius's knowledge complete.

10.4 God saw Cornelius's sincere faith. His prayers and charitable giving (alms) were a "memorial before God" or like a sacrificial offering. God answers the sincere prayers of those who seek him by sending the right person or the right information at the right time.

10.12 According to Jewish law, certain foods were forbidden (see Leviticus 11). The food laws made it difficult for Jews to eat with Gentiles without risking defilement. In fact, the Gentiles themselves were often seen as "unclean." Peter's vision meant that he should not look upon the Gentiles as inferior people whom God would not redeem. Before having the vision, Peter would have thought that a Gentile Roman officer could not accept Christ. Afterward, he understood that he should go with the messengers into a Gentile home and tell Cornelius the good news of salvation in Jesus Christ.

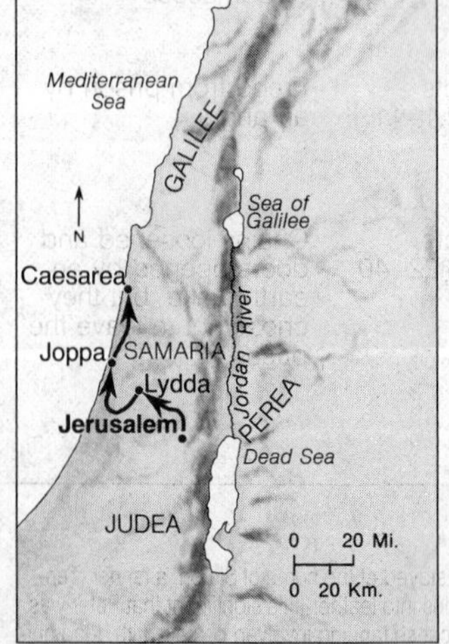

PETER'S MINISTRY
Peter traveled to the ancient crossroads town of Lydda, where he healed crippled Aeneas. The believers in Joppa, an old port city, sent for him after a wonderful woman died. Peter went and brought her back to life. While in Joppa, Peter had a vision that led him to take the gospel to Cornelius, a Gentile, in Caesarea.

10.22 Acts 10.2
10.23 Acts 10.45; 11.12
10.24 Acts 8.40; 10.1

nation, was directed by a holy angel to send for you to come to his house and to hear
what you have to say." 23 So Peter[x] invited them in and gave them lodging.
The next day he got up and went with them, and some of the believers[y] from
Joppa accompanied him. 24 The following day they came to Caesarea. Cornelius
was expecting them and had called together his relatives and close friends. 25 On

[x] Gk *he* [y] Gk *brothers*

PAUL

No person, apart from Jesus himself, shaped the history of Christianity like the apostle Paul. Even before he was a believer, his actions were significant. His frenzied persecution of Christians following Stephen's death got the church started in obeying Christ's final command to take the gospel worldwide. Paul's personal encounter with Jesus changed his life. He never lost his fierce intensity, but from then on it was channeled for spreading the good news.

Paul was very religious. His training under Gamaliel was the finest available. His intentions and efforts were sincere. He was a good Pharisee, knew the Bible, and sincerely believed that this Christian movement was dangerous to Judaism. Thus Paul hated the Christian faith and persecuted Christians without mercy.

Paul got permission to travel to Damascus to capture Christians and bring them back to Jersualem. But God had other plans for Paul and stopped him in his hurried tracks on the Damascus road. Paul personally met Jesus Christ, and his life was never the same.

Until Paul's conversion, little had been done about carrying the gospel to non-Jews. Philip had preached in Samaria and to an Ethiopian man; Cornelius, a Gentile, was converted under Peter; and in Antioch in Syria, some Greeks had joined the believers. When Barnabas was sent from Jerusalem to check on this situation, he went to Tarsus to find Paul and bring him to Antioch, and together they worked among the believers there. They were then sent on a missionary journey, the first of three Paul would take that would carry the gospel across the Roman Empire.

The thorny issue of whether Gentile believers had to obey Jewish laws before they could become Christians caused many problems in the early church. Paul worked hard to convince the Jews that Gentiles were acceptable to God, but he spent even more time convincing the Gentiles that they were acceptable to God. The lives Paul touched were changed and challenged by meeting Christ through him.

When Paul met Jesus, he found the One with the reason for living and dying, and he became totally sold out for Christ. God did not waste any part of Paul—his background, his training, his citizenship, his mind, or even his weaknesses. Are you willing to let God do the same for you? You will never know all he can do with you until you allow him to have all that you are!

Strengths and accomplishments:
- Transformed by God from a persecutor of Christians to a preacher for Christ
- Preached for Christ throughout the Roman Empire on three missionary journeys
- Wrote letters to various churches that became part of the New Testament
- Was never afraid to face an issue head-on and deal with it
- Was sensitive to God's leading and, despite his strong personality, always did as God directed
- Is often called the apostle to the Gentiles

Weaknesses and mistakes:
- Witnessed and approved of Stephen's stoning
- Set out to destroy Christianity by persecuting Christians

Lessons from his life:
- The good news is that forgiveness and eternal life are a gift of God's grace received by faith in Christ and available to all people
- Obedience flows from a relationship with God, but obedience will never create or earn that relationship
- Real freedom doesn't come until we no longer have to prove our freedom
- God does not waste our time—he will use our past and present so we may serve him with our future

Vital statistics:
- Where: Born in Tarsus, but became a world traveler for Christ
- Occupation: Trained as a Pharisee, learned the tentmaking trade, served as a missionary
- Contemporaries: Gamaliel, Stephen, the apostles, Luke, Barnabas, Mark, Timothy, James

Key verse:
"For to me, living is Christ and dying is gain" (Philippians 1.21).

Paul's story is told in Acts 7.58—28.31 and throughout his New Testament letters.

Peter's arrival Cornelius met him, and falling at his feet, worshiped him. 26 But
Peter made him get up, saying, "Stand up; I am only a mortal." 27 And as he talked
with him, he went in and found that many had assembled; 28 and he said to them,
"You yourselves know that it is unlawful for a Jew to associate with or to visit a
Gentile; but God has shown me that I should not call anyone profane or unclean.
29 So when I was sent for, I came without objection. Now may I ask why you sent
for me?"

30 Cornelius replied, "Four days ago at this very hour, at three o'clock, I was
praying in my house when suddenly a man in dazzling clothes stood before me.
31 He said, 'Cornelius, your prayer has been heard and your alms have been remembered before God. 32 Send therefore to Joppa and ask for Simon, who is called
Peter; he is staying in the home of Simon, a tanner, by the sea.' 33 Therefore I sent
for you immediately, and you have been kind enough to come. So now all of us are
here in the presence of God to listen to all that the Lord has commanded you to
say."

Peter preaches in Cornelius's house

34 Then Peter began to speak to them: "I truly understand that God shows no
partiality, 35 but in every nation anyone who fears him and does what is right is
acceptable to him. 36 You know the message he sent to the people of Israel, preaching peace by Jesus Christ—he is Lord of all. 37 That message spread throughout
Judea, beginning in Galilee after the baptism that John announced: 38 how God
anointed Jesus of Nazareth with the Holy Spirit and with power; how he went about
doing good and healing all who were oppressed by the devil, for God was with him.
39 We are witnesses to all that he did both in Judea and in Jerusalem. They put him
to death by hanging him on a tree; 40 but God raised him on the third day and allowed him to appear, 41 not to all the people but to us who were chosen by God as
witnesses, and who ate and drank with him after he rose from the dead. 42 He commanded us to preach to the people and to testify that he is the one ordained by God
as judge of the living and the dead. 43 All the prophets testify about him that everyone who believes in him receives forgiveness of sins through his name."

44 While Peter was still speaking, the Holy Spirit fell upon all who heard the
word. 45 The circumcised believers who had come with Peter were astounded that

10.26 Lk 4.8 Acts 14.14 Col 2.18 Rev 19.10; 22.9
10.28 Jn 4.9 Acts 11.3; 15.9 Gal 2.12
10.30 Acts 10.3-6
10.31 Prov 14.31 Dan 10.12 Mt 6.4; 10.42 Heb 6.10
10.34 Rom 2.11 Col 3.11,25
10.35 Rom 3.9-24 Eph 2.13; 3.6
10.36 Rom 5.1 Eph 2.17
10.38 Lk 4.18,19
10.39 Lk 24.40
10.40,41 Jn 21.13
10.42 Mt 28.19 2 Cor 5.10
10.43 Isa 53.11 Jer 31.34
10.44 Acts 11.15; 15.8

10.26 This act of worship could have caused Peter to become prideful. After all, a Roman centurion was bowing before him. Instead, Peter pointed Cornelius to Christ. We too should remember our mortality whenever we are flattered or honored, and use the opportunity to give glory to God.

10.34, 35 Perhaps the greatest barrier to the spread of the gospel in the first century was the Jewish-Gentile conflict. Most of the early believers were Jewish, and to them it was scandalous even to think of associating with Gentiles. But God told Peter to take the gospel to a Roman, and Peter obeyed despite his background and personal feelings. (Later he struggled with this again—see Galatians 2.11–14.) God was making it clear that the good news of Christ is for everyone! We should not allow any barrier—language, culture, prejudice, geography, economic class, or education—to keep us from telling others about Christ.

10.35 In every nation there are hearts bent toward God, ready to receive the gospel—but someone must take it to them. Seeking God is not enough—people must find him. How then shall seekers find God without someone to point the way? Is God asking you to show someone the way to him? (See Romans 10.14, 15.)

10.37–43 Peter's brief and powerful sermon contains a concise statement of the gospel: Jesus' perfect life; his death on the cross; his resurrection, personally witnessed and experienced by Peter; Jesus' fulfillment of the Scriptures; and the necessity of personal faith in him. A sermon or witness for Christ does not need to be long to be effective. It should be Spirit-led and should center on Christ.

10.43 Two examples of prophets writing about Jesus and his forgiveness of sin are Isaiah 52.13–53.12 and Ezekiel 36.25, 26.

10.45 Cornelius and Peter were very different people. Cornelius was wealthy, a Gentile, and a military man. Peter was a Jewish fisherman turned preacher. But God's plan included both of them. In Cornelius's house that day, a new chapter in Christian history was written as a Jewish Christian leader and a Gentile Christian convert each discovered something significant about God at work in the other person. Cornelius needed Peter and his gospel to know he could be saved. Peter needed Cornelius and his salvation experience to know Gentiles were included in God's plan. You and another believer may also need each other to understand how God works!

10.45 "The circumcised believers" could be translated "the Jewish believers" (see also 11.2).

10.47, 48 In this case, the people were baptized *after* they received the Holy Spirit, publicly declaring their allegiance to Christ and identification with the Christian community.

10.46 Acts 2.4,19.6
10.47 Acts 8.36; 11.17
10.48 Acts 2.38 8.16; 19.5

the gift of the Holy Spirit had been poured out even on the Gentiles, 46 for they
heard them speaking in tongues and extolling God. Then Peter said, 47 "Can anyone
withhold the water for baptizing these people who have received the Holy Spirit
just as we have?" 48 So he ordered them to be baptized in the name of Jesus Christ.
Then they invited him to stay for several days.

CORNELIUS

The early days of Christianity were exciting as God's Spirit moved and people's lives were changed. Converts were pouring in from surprising backgrounds. Even the dreaded Saul (Paul) became a Christian, and non-Jews were responding to the good news about Jesus. Among the first of these was the Roman centurion, Cornelius.

Because of frequent outbreaks of violence, Roman soldiers had to be stationed throughout Israel to keep peace. But most Romans, hated as conquerors, did not get along well in the nation. As an army officer, Cornelius was in a difficult position. He represented Rome, but his home was in Caesarea. During his years in Israel, he had himself been conquered by the God of Israel. He had a reputation as a godly man who put his faith into action, and he was respected by the Jews.

Four significant aspects of Cornelius's character are noted in Acts. He actively sought after God, he revered God, he was generous in meeting other people's needs, and he prayed. God told him to send for Peter, because Peter would give him more knowledge about the God he was already seeking to please. And Cornelius obeyed.

When Peter entered Cornelius's home, he broke a whole list of Jewish rules. Peter confessed he wasn't all that comfortable, but here was an eager audience, and he couldn't hold back his message. No sooner had he started sharing the gospel and God demonstrated his overwhelming approval by filling that Roman family with the Holy Spirit. Peter saw he had no choice but to baptize them and welcome them as equals in the growing Christian church. Another step had been taken in carrying the gospel to the whole world.

Cornelius is a welcome example of God's willingness to use extraordinary means to reach those who truly desire to know him. He does not play favorites, and he does not hide from those who want to find him. God sent his Son because he loves the whole world—and that includes Peter, Cornelius, and you.

Strengths and accomplishments:
- Was a godly and generous Roman
- Although an officer in the occupying army, he seems to have been well respected by the Jews
- He responded to God and encouraged his family to do the same
- His conversion helped the young church realize that the good news was for all people, both Jews and Gentiles

Lessons from his life:
- God reaches those who want to know him
- The gospel is open to all people
- There are those eager to believe all over the world
- When we are willing to seek the truth and be obedient to the light God gives us, God will reward us richly

Vital statistics:
- Where: Caesarea
- Occupation: Roman centurion
- Contemporaries: Philip, Peter, the other apostles

Key verse:
"He was a devout man who feared God with all his household; he gave alms generously to the people and prayed constantly to God" (Acts 10.2).

Cornelius's story is told in Acts 10.1—11.18.

10.48 Cornelius wanted Peter to stay with him for several days. He was a new believer and realized his need for teaching and fellowship. Are you as eager to learn more about Christ? Recognize your need to be with more mature Christians, and strive to learn from them.

Peter defends his preaching to Gentiles

11 Now the apostles and the believers[z] who were in Judea heard that the Gentiles had also accepted the word of God. 2 So when Peter went up to Jerusalem, the circumcised believers[a] criticized him, 3 saying, "Why did you go to **11.3**
uncircumcised men and eat with them?" 4 Then Peter began to explain it to them, Mt 9.11 Acts 10.28
step by step, saying, 5 "I was in the city of Joppa praying, and in a trance I saw a Gal 2.12
vision. There was something like a large sheet coming down from heaven, being **11.5**
lowered by its four corners; and it came close to me. 6 As I looked at it closely I saw Acts 10.9,10
four-footed animals, beasts of prey, reptiles, and birds of the air. 7 I also heard a
voice saying to me, 'Get up, Peter; kill and eat.' 8 But I replied, 'By no means, **11.8**
Lord; for nothing profane or unclean has ever entered my mouth.' 9 But a second Ezek 4.14
time the voice answered from heaven, 'What God has made clean, you must not **11.12**
call profane.' 10 This happened three times; then everything was pulled up again to Jn 16.13
heaven. 11 At that very moment three men, sent to me from Caesarea, arrived at the Acts 10.23; 15.7 **11.13**
house where we were. 12 The Spirit told me to go with them and not to make a Acts 10.30
distinction between them and us.[b] These six brothers also accompanied me, and **11.14**
we entered the man's house. 13 He told us how he had seen the angel standing in his Acts 10.2; 16.15 18.8
house and saying, 'Send to Joppa and bring Simon, who is called Peter; 14 he will 1 Cor 1.16
give you a message by which you and your entire household will be saved.' 15 And **11.15**
as I began to speak, the Holy Spirit fell upon them just as it had upon us at the Acts 2.4 **11.16**
beginning. 16 And I remembered the word of the Lord, how he had said, 'John Isa 44.3 Joel 2.28
baptized with water, but you will be baptized with the Holy Spirit.' 17 If then God Mt 3.11
gave them the same gift that he gave us when we believed in the Lord Jesus Christ, Jn 1.26,33
who was I that I could hinder God?" 18 When they heard this, they were silenced. **11.17** Acts 10.47
And they praised God, saying, "Then God has given even to the Gentiles the re- 15.8,9
pentance that leads to life." **11.18** Rom 10.12; 15.9

The Gentile church in Antioch

19 Now those who were scattered because of the persecution that took place **11.19**
over Stephen traveled as far as Phoenicia, Cyprus, and Antioch, and they spoke the Acts 8.1; 13.1 14.25-27; 15.3
word to no one except Jews. 20 But among them were some men of Cyprus and **11.20**
Cyrene who, on coming to Antioch, spoke to the Hellenists[c] also, proclaiming the Acts 6.1

[z] Gk *brothers* [a] Gk lacks *believers* [b] Or *not to hesitate* [c] Other ancient authorities read *Greeks*

11.1 A Gentile was anyone who was not a Jew; the Jewish believers are sometimes referred to as "the circumcised believers" (11.2). Most Jewish believers thought God offered salvation only to the Jews because God had given his law to them (Exodus 19, 20). A group in Jerusalem believed that Gentiles could be saved, but only if they followed all the Jewish laws and traditions – in essence, if they became Jews. Both were mistaken. God chose the Jews and taught them his laws so they could bring the message of salvation to *all* people (see Genesis 12.3; Psalm 22.27; Isaiah 42.4; 49.6; 56.3–7; 60.1–3; Jeremiah 16.19–21; Zechariah 2.11; Malachi 1.11; Romans 15.9–12).

11.2–18 When Peter brought the news of Cornelius's conversion back to Jerusalem, the believers were shocked that he had eaten with Gentiles. After they heard the whole story, however, they began praising God (11.18). Their reactions teach us how to handle disagreements with other Christians. Before judging the behavior of fellow believers, it is important to hear them out. The Holy Spirit may have something important to teach us through them.

11.8 God had promised throughout Scripture that he would reach the Gentiles. This began with his general promise to Abraham (Genesis 12.3; 18.18) and became very specific in Malachi's statement: "For from the rising of the sun to its setting my name is great among the nations" (Malachi 1.11). But this was an extremely difficult truth for Jews, even Jewish believers, to accept. The Jewish believers understood how certain prophecies were fulfilled in Christ, but they overlooked other Old Testament teachings. Too often we are inclined to accept only the parts of God's Word that appeal to us, ignoring the teachings we don't like. We must accept all of God's Word as absolute truth.

11.12ff Peter's defense for eating with Gentiles was a simple restatement of what happened. He brought six witnesses with him to back him up, and then he quoted Jesus' promise about the coming of the Holy Spirit (11.16). These Gentiles' lives had been changed, and that was all the evidence Peter and the other believers needed. Changed lives are an equally powerful evidence today.

11.16 Jesus had also demonstrated clearly that he and his message were for all people. He preached in Samaria (John 4.1–42); in the country of the Gerasenes, populated by Greeks (Mark 5.1–20); and he even reached out to Romans (Luke 7.1–10). The apostles shouldn't have been surprised that they were to do the same.

11.18 The intellectual questions ended and the theological discussion stopped with the report that God had given the Holy Spirit to the Gentiles. This was a turning point for the early church. They had to accept those whom God had chosen, even if they were Gentiles. But joy over the conversion of Gentiles was not unanimous. This continued to be a struggle for some Jewish Christians throughout the first century.

11.19–21 When the church accepted Peter's testimony that the gospel was also for Gentiles, Christianity exploded into Gentile areas and large numbers became believers. The seeds of this missionary work had been sown after Stephen's death when many believing Jews were persecuted and scattered, settling in faraway cities and spreading the gospel.

11.21 Lk 1.66 — Lord Jesus. 21 The hand of the Lord was with them, and a great number became
believers and turned to the Lord. 22 News of this came to the ears of the church in
11.23 Deut 10.20 — Jerusalem, and they sent Barnabas to Antioch. 23 When he came and saw the grace
1 Cor 15.58 Col 2.6 — of God, he rejoiced, and he exhorted them all to remain faithful to the Lord with
11.24 Acts 2.4,47 5.14 — steadfast devotion; 24 for he was a good man, full of the Holy Spirit and of faith.
And a great many people were brought to the Lord. 25 Then Barnabas went to Tar-
sus to look for Saul, 26 and when he had found him, he brought him to Antioch. So
it was that for an entire year they met with[d] the church and taught a great many
11.27 Acts 2.17; 13.1 — people, and it was in Antioch that the disciples were first called "Christians."
1 Cor 16.1 — 27 At that time prophets came down from Jerusalem to Antioch. 28 One of them
2 Cor 9.1 11.28 Acts 21.10 — named Agabus stood up and predicted by the Spirit that there would be a severe
famine over all the world; and this took place during the reign of Claudius. 29 The
11.29 Rom 15.25,26 — disciples determined that according to their ability, each would send relief to the
11.30 1 Pet 5.1 — believers[e] living in Judea; 30 this they did, sending it to the elders by Barnabas and
Saul.

[d] Or *were guests of* [e] Gk *brothers*

BARNABAS AND PAUL IN ANTIOCH
Persecution spread the believers into Phoenicia, Cyprus, and Antioch, and the gospel went with them. Most spoke only to Jews, but in Antioch, some Gentiles were converted. The church sent Barnabas to investigate, and he was pleased with what he found. Barnabas went to Tarsus to bring Paul back to Antioch.

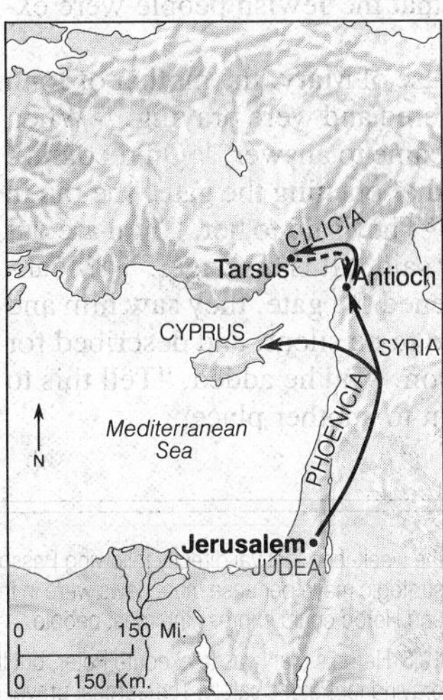

11.20, 21 It was in Antioch that Christianity was launched on its worldwide mission and where the believers aggressively preached to the Gentiles (non-Jews who did not worship God). Philip had preached in Samaria, but the Samaritans were part Jewish (8.5); Peter preached to Cornelius, but he already worshiped God (10.2). Believers who scattered after the outbreak of persecution in Jerusalem spread the gospel to other Jews in the lands they fled to (11.19). At this time, the believers began actively sharing the good news with Gentiles.

11.22 With the exception of Jerusalem, Antioch of Syria played a more important role in the early church than any other city. After Rome and Alexandria, Antioch was the largest city in the Roman world. In Antioch, the first Gentile church was founded, and the believers were first called Christians (11.26). Paul used the city as his home base during his missionary journeys. Antioch was the center of worship for several pagan cults, promoting much sexual immorality and other forms of evil common to pagan religions. It was also a vital commercial center – the gateway to the eastern world. Antioch was a key city both to Rome and to the early church.

11.22–26 Barnabas gives us a wonderful example of how to help new Christians. He demonstrated strong faith; he ministered joyfully with kindness and encouragement; he taught them further lessons about God (see 9.26–30). Remember Barnabas when you see new believers, and think of ways to help them grow in their faith.

11.25 Paul had been sent to his home in Tarsus to protect him from danger after his conversion caused an uproar among the Jewish leaders in Jerusalem (9.26–30). He stayed there for several years before Barnabas brought him to help the church at Antioch.

11.26 The young church at Antioch was a curious mixture of Jews (who spoke Greek or Aramaic) and Gentiles. It is significant that this is the first place where the believers were called Christians (or "Christ-ones"), because all they had in common was Christ – not race, culture, or even language. Christ can cross all boundaries and unify all people.

11.26 Barnabas and Paul stayed at Antioch for a full year, teaching the new believers. They could have left for new cities, but they saw the importance of follow-through and training. Have you helped someone believe in God? Spend time teaching and encouraging that person. Are you a new believer? Remember, you are just beginning your Christian life. Your faith needs to grow and mature through consistent Bible study and teaching.

11.27, 28 Prophets were found not only in the Old Testament, but also in the early church. Their role was to present God's will to the people and to instruct them in God's Word. Sometimes, like Agabus, they also had the gift of predicting the future.

11.28, 29 There were serious food shortages during the reign of the Roman emperor Claudius (A.D. 41–54) because of a drought that extended across much of the Roman Empire for many years. It is significant that the church in Antioch assisted the church in Jerusalem. The daughter church had grown enough to be able to help the established church.

11.29 The people of Antioch were motivated to give generously because they cared about the needs of others. This is "cheerful giving," which the Bible commends (2 Corinthians 9.7). Reluctant giving reflects a lack of concern for people. Focus your concern on the needy, and you will be motivated to give.

11.30 Elders were appointed to manage the affairs of the congregation. At this point, not much is known about their responsibilities, but it appears that their main role was to respond to the believers' needs.

An angel rescues Peter from prison

12 About that time King Herod laid violent hands upon some who belonged to 12.1
the church. 2 He had James, the brother of John, killed with the sword. Mt 10.17
3 After he saw that it pleased the Jews, he proceeded to arrest Peter also. (This was 12.2 Mt 4.21
during the festival of Unleavened Bread.) 4 When he had seized him, he put him in 12.3
prison and handed him over to four squads of soldiers to guard him, intending to Ex 12.14,15
bring him out to the people after the Passover. 5 While Peter was kept in prison, the 12.4 Jn 21.18
church prayed fervently to God for him. 12.5
6 The very night before Herod was going to bring him out, Peter, bound with 2 Cor 1.11 Eph 6.18
two chains, was sleeping between two soldiers, while guards in front of the door
were keeping watch over the prison. 7 Suddenly an angel of the Lord appeared and 12.7
a light shone in the cell. He tapped Peter on the side and woke him, saying, "Get Acts 5.19; 21.33 Heb 1.14
up quickly." And the chains fell off his wrists. 8 The angel said to him, "Fasten your
belt and put on your sandals." He did so. Then he said to him, "Wrap your cloak
around you and follow me." 9 Peter[f] went out and followed him; he did not realize 12.9
that what was happening with the angel's help was real; he thought he was seeing Ps 126.1 Acts 10.3
a vision. 10 After they had passed the first and the second guard, they came before 12.10
the iron gate leading into the city. It opened for them of its own accord, and they Acts 5.19; 16.26
went outside and walked along a lane, when suddenly the angel left him. 11 Then 12.11
Peter came to himself and said, "Now I am sure that the Lord has sent his angel and Job 5.19
rescued me from the hands of Herod and from all that the Jewish people were ex- Ps 33.18,19 34.7; 97.10
pecting." Dan 3.28; 6.22 2 Pet 2.9
12 As soon as he realized this, he went to the house of Mary, the mother of John 12.12
whose other name was Mark, where many had gathered and were praying. 13 When Acts 12.25 13.5; 15.37
he knocked at the outer gate, a maid named Rhoda came to answer. 14 On recogniz- Col 4.10 1 Pet 5.13
ing Peter's voice, she was so overjoyed that, instead of opening the gate, she ran in
and announced that Peter was standing at the gate. 15 They said to her, "You are out 12.15
of your mind!" But she insisted that it was so. They said, "It is his angel." 16 Mean- Mt 18.10
while Peter continued knocking; and when they opened the gate, they saw him and
were amazed. 17 He motioned to them with his hand to be silent, and described for 12.17
them how the Lord had brought him out of the prison. And he added, "Tell this to Acts 15.35; 21.18
James and to the believers.[g]" Then he left and went to another place.

[f] Gk *He* [g] Gk *brothers*

12.1 This King Herod was Herod Agrippa I, the son of Aristobulus and grandson of Herod the Great. His sister was Herodias, who was responsible for the death of John the Baptist (see Mark 6.17–28). He was partly Jewish. The Romans had appointed him to rule over most of Palestine, including the territories of Galilee, Perea, Judea, and Samaria. He moved against the Christians in order to please the Jewish leaders who opposed them, hoping that would solidify his position. Agrippa I died suddenly in A.D. 44 (see 12.20–23). His death is also recorded by the historian Josephus.

12.2 James and John were two of the original 12 disciples who followed Jesus. They had asked Jesus for special recognition in his kingdom (Mark 10.35–40). Jesus said that being part of his kingdom often means suffering for him (drink from the same cup—Mark 10.38, 39). James and John did indeed suffer—Herod executed James, and later John was exiled (see Revelation 1.9).

12.2–11 Why did God allow James to die and yet miraculously save Peter? Life is full of difficult questions like this. Why is one child physically handicapped and another child athletically gifted? Why do people die seemingly before realizing their potential? These are questions we cannot possibly answer in this life because we do not see all that God sees. He has chosen to allow evil in this world for a time. But we can trust his leading because he has promised to destroy all evil eventually. In the meantime, we know he will help us use our suffering to strengthen us and glorify him. For more on this question, see the notes on Job 1.1ff; 2.10; 3.23–26.

12.3 Peter was arrested during the festival of Unleavened Bread, the week-long festival directly following Passover. This was a strategic move because more Jews were in the city than usual, and Herod could impress the most people.

12.5 Herod's plan was to execute Peter, but the believers were praying for Peter's safety. The earnest prayer of the church significantly affected the outcome of these events. Prayer changes things, so pray often and with confidence.

12.7 God sent an angel to rescue Peter. Angels are God's messengers. They are divinely created beings with supernatural powers, and they sometimes take on human appearance in order to talk to people. Angels should not be worshiped because they are not divine. They also serve God.

12.12 John Mark wrote the Gospel of Mark. His mother's house was large enough to accommodate a meeting of many believers. An upstairs room in this house may have been the location of Jesus' last supper with his disciples (Luke 22.8ff).

12.13–15 The prayers of the little group of believers were answered, even as they prayed. But when the answer arrived at the door, they didn't believe it. We should be people of faith who believe that God answers the prayers of those who seek his will. When you pray, believe you'll get an answer. And when the answer comes, don't be surprised—be thankful!

12.17 This James was Jesus' brother, who became a leader in the Jerusalem church (15.13; Galatians 1.19). The James who was killed (12.2) was John's brother and one of the original 12 disciples.

18 When morning came, there was no small commotion among the soldiers
12.19 Acts 8.40; 16.27 over what had become of Peter. 19 When Herod had searched for him and could not
find him, he examined the guards and ordered them to be put to death. Then Peter[h]
went down from Judea to Caesarea and stayed there.

The judgment of Herod

20 Now Herod was angry with the people of Tyre and Sidon. So they came to
him in a body; and after winning over Blastus, the king's chamberlain, they asked

[h] Gk *he*

HEROD AGRIPPA I

For good or evil, families have lasting and powerful influence on their children. Traits and qualities are passed on to the next generation, and often the mistakes and sins of the parents are repeated by the children. Four generations of the Herod family are mentioned in the Bible. Each leader left his evil mark: Herod the Great murdered Bethlehem's children; Herod Antipas was involved in Jesus' trial and had John the Baptist executed; Herod Agrippa I murdered the apostle James; and Herod Agrippa II was one of Paul's judges.

Herod Agrippa I related fairly well to his Jewish subjects. Because he had a Jewish grandmother of royal blood (Mariamne), he was grudgingly accepted by the people. Although as a youth he had been temporarily imprisoned by the Emperor Tiberias, he was now trusted by Rome and got along well with the Emperors Caligula and Claudius.

An unexpected opportunity for Herod to gain new favor with the Jews was created by the Christian movement. Gentiles began to be accepted into the church in large numbers. Many Jews had been tolerating this new movement as a sect within Judaism, but its rapid growth alarmed them. Persecution of Christians was revived, and even the apostles were not spared. James was killed, and Peter was thrown into prison.

But soon, Herod made a fatal error. During a visit to Caesarea, the people called him a god, and he accepted their praise. Immediately Herod was struck with a painful disease, and he died within a week.

Like his grandfather, uncle, and son after him, Herod Agrippa I came close to the truth but missed it. Because religion was important only as an aspect of politics, he had no reverence and no qualms about taking praise that only God should receive. His mistake is a common one. Whenever we are proud of our own abilities and accomplishments, not recognizing them as gifts from God, we repeat Herod's sin.

Strengths and accomplishments:
- Was a capable administrator and negotiator
- Managed to maintain good relations with the Jews in his region and with Rome

Weaknesses and mistakes:
- Arranged the murder of the apostle James
- Imprisoned Peter with plans to execute him
- Allowed the people to praise him as a god

Lessons from his life:
- Those who set themselves against God are doomed to ultimate failure
- There is great danger in accepting praise that only God deserves
- Family traits can influence children toward great good or great evil

Vital statistics:
- Where: Jerusalem
- Occupation: Roman-appointed king of the Jews
- Relatives: Grandfather: Herod the Great. Father: Aristobulus. Uncle: Herod Antipas. Sister: Herodias. Wife: Cypros. Son: Herod Agrippa II. Daughters: Bernice, Mariamne, Drusilla
- Contemporaries: Emperors Tiberias, Caligula, and Claudius. James, Peter, the other apostles

Key verse:
"And immediately, because he had not given the glory to God, an angel of the Lord struck him down, and he was eaten by worms and died" (Acts 12.23).

Herod Agrippa I's story is told in Acts 12.1–23.

12.19 Under Roman law, guards who allowed a prisoner to escape were subject to the same punishment the prisoner was to receive. Thus these 16 guards were sentenced to death.

12.19 The Jews considered Jerusalem their capital, but the Romans made Caesarea their headquarters in Palestine. This is where Herod Agrippa lived.

12.20 These coastal cities, Tyre and Sidon, were free and self-governing but economically dependent on Judea (see the map in the introduction of Acts for their location). We don't know why Herod was displeased with them, but representatives from those cities were trying to appease him through his chamberlain (royal secretary).

for a reconciliation, because their country depended on the king's country for food.
21 On an appointed day Herod put on his royal robes, took his seat on the platform,
and delivered a public address to them. 22 The people kept shouting, "The voice of
a god, and not of a mortal!" 23 And immediately, because he had not given the glory
to God, an angel of the Lord struck him down, and he was eaten by worms and
died.
24 But the word of God continued to advance and gain adherents. 25 Then after
completing their mission Barnabas and Saul returned to[i] Jerusalem and brought
with them John, whose other name was Mark.

12.23 Deut 28.58,59; 1 Sam 25.37,38; 2 Sam 24.16; 2 Kgs 19.35; Isa 42.8; 48.11; Dan 4.30-37; Rev 15.3,4
12.24 Isa 55.11; Acts 6.7; 19.20
12.25 Acts 11.29,30; 15.37

B. PAUL'S MINISTRY (13.1—28.31)

The book focuses now on the ministry to the Gentiles and the spread of the church around the world, and Paul replaces Peter as the central figure in the book. Paul completes three missionary journeys and ends up being imprisoned in Jerusalem and transported to Rome. The book of Acts ends abruptly, showing that the history of the church is not yet complete. We are to be a part of the sequel.

1. First missionary journey

Barnabas and Paul are sent out to preach

13 Now in the church at Antioch there were prophets and teachers: Barnabas,
Simeon who was called Niger, Lucius of Cyrene, Manaen a member of the
court of Herod the ruler,[j] and Saul. 2 While they were worshiping the Lord and
fasting, the Holy Spirit said, "Set apart for me Barnabas and Saul for the work to
which I have called them." 3 Then after fasting and praying they laid their hands on
them and sent them off.

13.1 Acts 11.22; Rom 16.21
13.2 Eph 3.7-9
13.3 Acts 6.6

Paul curses a sorcerer in Cyprus

4 So, being sent out by the Holy Spirit, they went down to Seleucia; and from
there they sailed to Cyprus. 5 When they arrived at Salamis, they proclaimed the
word of God in the synagogues of the Jews. And they had John also to assist them.
6 When they had gone through the whole island as far as Paphos, they met a certain

13.5 1 Pet 5.13
13.6 Ex 7.11; Mt 7.15; 2 Tim 3.8

[i] Other ancient authorities read *from* [j] Gk *tetrarch*

12.23 Herod died a horrible death with intense pain; he was literally eaten alive, from the inside out, by maggots or worms. To be eaten by worms was considered to be the most disgraceful way to die. Pride is a serious sin, and in this case, God chose to punish it immediately. God does not immediately punish all sin, but he *will* (Hebrews 9.27). Accept Christ's offer of forgiveness today. No one can afford to wait.

12.25 John Mark was Barnabas's nephew. His mother, Mary, often opened her home to the apostles (12.12), so John Mark would have been exposed to most of the great men and teachings of the early church. Later, John Mark joined Paul and Barnabas on their first missionary journey, but for unknown reasons, he left them in the middle of the trip. John Mark was criticized for abandoning the mission, but he wrote the Gospel of Mark and was later acclaimed by Paul as a vital help in the growth of the early church.

13.1 What variety there is in the church! The common thread among these five men was their deep faith in Christ. We must never exclude anyone whom Christ has called to follow him.

13.2, 3 The church set apart Barnabas and Paul to the work God had for them. To *set apart* means to dedicate for a special purpose. We too should dedicate our pastors, missionaries, and Christian workers for their tasks. We can also dedicate ourselves with our time, money, and talents for God's work. Ask God what he wants you to set apart to him.

13.2, 3 This was the beginning of Paul's first missionary journey. The church was involved in sending Paul and Barnabas, but it was God's plan. Why did Paul and Barnabas go where they did? (1) The Holy Spirit led them. (2) They followed the communication routes of the Roman Empire—this made travel easier. (3) They visited key population and cultural centers to reach as many people as possible. (4) They went to cities with synagogues, speaking first to the Jews in hopes that they would see Jesus as the Messiah and help spread the good news to everyone.

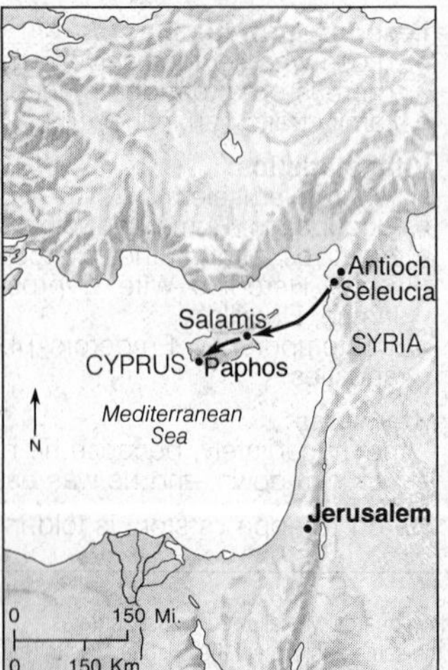

MINISTRY IN CYPRUS
The leaders of the church in Antioch chose Paul and Barnabas to take the gospel westward. Along with John Mark, they boarded ship at Seleucia and set out across the Mediterranean for Cyprus. They preached in Salamis, the largest city, and went across the island to Paphos.

13.4 Located in the Mediterranean Sea, the island of Cyprus, with a large Jewish population, was Barnabas's home. Their first stop was in familiar territory.

magician, a Jewish false prophet, named Bar-Jesus. 7 He was with the proconsul,
Sergius Paulus, an intelligent man, who summoned Barnabas and Saul and wanted
to hear the word of God. 8 But the magician Elymas (for that is the translation of his
name) opposed them and tried to turn the proconsul away from the faith. 9 But Saul,
also known as Paul, filled with the Holy Spirit, looked intently at him 10 and said,
"You son of the devil, you enemy of all righteousness, full of all deceit and villainy, will you not stop making crooked the straight paths of the Lord? 11 And now
listen—the hand of the Lord is against you, and you will be blind for a while,
unable to see the sun." Immediately mist and darkness came over him, and he went
about groping for someone to lead him by the hand. 12 When the proconsul saw

13.9 Acts 2.4; 4.8
13.10 Mt 13.38; Jn 8.44; 2 Pet 2.15; 1 Jn 3.8
13.11 2 Kgs 6.18

JOHN MARK

Mistakes are effective teachers. Their consequences have a way of making lessons painfully clear. But those who learn from their mistakes are likely to develop wisdom. John Mark was a good learner who just needed some time and encouragement.

Mark was eager to do the right thing, but he had trouble staying with a task. In his Gospel, Mark mentions a young man (probably referring to himself) who fled in such fear during Jesus' arrest that he left his clothes behind. This tendency to run was to reappear later when Paul and Barnabas took him as their assistant on their first missionary journey. At the second stop, Mark left them and returned to Jerusalem. It was a decision Paul did not easily accept. In preparing for their second journey two years later, Barnabas again suggested Mark as a traveling companion, but Paul flatly refused. As a result, the team was divided. Barnabas took Mark with him, and Paul chose Silas. Barnabas was patient with Mark, and the young man repaid his investment. Paul and Mark were later reunited, and the older apostle became a close friend of the young disciple.

Mark was a valuable companion to three early Christian leaders—Barnabas, Paul, and Peter. The material in Mark's Gospel seems to have come mostly from Peter. Mark's role as a serving assistant allowed him to be an observer. He heard Peter's accounts of the years with Jesus over and over, and he was one of the first to put Jesus' life in writing.

Barnabas played a key role in Mark's life. He stood beside the young man despite his failure, giving him patient encouragement. Mark challenges us to learn from our mistakes and appreciate the patience of others. Is there a Barnabas in your life you need to thank for his or her encouragment to you?

Strengths and accomplishments:
- Wrote the Gospel of Mark
- He and his mother provided their home as one of the main meeting places for the Christians in Jerusalem
- Persisted beyond his youthful mistakes
- Was an assistant and traveling companion to three of the greatest early missionaries

Weaknesses and mistakes:
- Was probably the nameless young man described in the Gospel of Mark who fled in panic when Jesus was arrested
- Left Paul and Barnabas for unknown reasons during the first missionary journey

Lessons from his life:
- Personal maturity usually comes from a combination of time and mistakes
- Mistakes are not usually as important as what can be learned from them
- Effective living is not measured as much by what we accomplish as by what we overcome in order to accomplish it
- Encouragement can change a person's life

Vital statistics:
- Where: Jerusalem
- Occupation: Missionary-in-training, Gospel writer, traveling companion
- Relatives: Mother: Mary. Uncle: Barnabas
- Contemporaries: Paul, Peter, Timothy, Luke, Silas

Key verse:
"Only Luke is with me. Get Mark and bring him with you, for he is useful in my ministry" (Paul writing in 2 Timothy 4.11).

John Mark's story is told in Acts 12.12—13.13 and 15.36–39. He is also mentioned in Colossians 4.10, 11; 2 Timothy 4.11; Philemon 1.24; 1 Peter 5.13.

13.6, 7 A proconsul is a high Roman official. Here he is governor of the island. Such leaders often kept private wizards. Bar-Jesus realized that if Sergius Paulus believed in Jesus, he'd soon be out of a job.

13.10 The Holy Spirit led Paul to confront Bar-Jesus with his sin. There is a time for being nice and a time for direct confrontation. Ask God to show you the difference and for the courage to do what is right.

what had happened, he believed, for he was astonished at the teaching about the
Lord.

Paul preaches to the Jews in Antioch in Pisidia

13 Then Paul and his companions set sail from Paphos and came to Perga in
Pamphylia. John, however, left them and returned to Jerusalem; 14 but they went on
from Perga and came to Antioch in Pisidia. And on the sabbath day they went into
the synagogue and sat down. 15 After the reading of the law and the prophets, the
officials of the synagogue sent them a message, saying, "Brothers, if you have any
word of exhortation for the people, give it." 16 So Paul stood up and with a gesture
began to speak:

"You Israelites,[k] and others who fear God, listen. 17 The God of this people
Israel chose our ancestors and made the people great during their stay in the land of
Egypt, and with uplifted arm he led them out of it. 18 For about forty years he put
up with[l] them in the wilderness. 19 After he had destroyed seven nations in the land
of Canaan, he gave them their land as an inheritance 20 for about four hundred fifty
years. After that he gave them judges until the time of the prophet Samuel. 21 Then
they asked for a king; and God gave them Saul son of Kish, a man of the tribe of
Benjamin, who reigned for forty years. 22 When he had removed him, he made
David their king. In his testimony about him he said, 'I have found David, son of
Jesse, to be a man after my heart, who will carry out all my wishes.' 23 Of this

13.13 Acts 14.24,25 15.38
13.14 Acts 14.19,21, 24
13.15 Lk 14.16 Acts 15.21 2 Cor 3.14
13.16 Acts 10.2; 13.26
13.17 Deut 7.6-8 Acts 7.36
13.19,20 Deut 7.1 Judg 2.16
13.21 1 Sam 8.5; 10.1
13.22 1 Sam 16.1,13

[k] Gk *Men, Israelites* [l] Other ancient authorities read *cared for*

13.13 No reason is given why John Mark left Paul and Barnabas. Some suggestions are: (1) he was homesick, (2) he resented the change in leadership from Barnabas (his uncle) to Paul, (3) he became ill (this may have affected all of them – see Galatians 4.13), (4) he was unable to withstand the rigors and dangers of the missionary journey, (5) he may have planned to go only that far but had not communicated this to Paul and Barnabas. Paul accused John Mark of lacking courage and commitment, calling him a deserter (see 15.37, 38). It is clear from Paul's later letters, however, that he grew to respect Mark (Colossians 4.10) and needed him in his work (2 Timothy 4.11).

13.14 This is Antioch of Pisidia, different from Antioch of Syria where there was already a flourishing church (11.26). Antioch of Pisidia was a hub of good roads and trade and had a large Jewish population.

13.14 When they went to a new town to witness for Christ, Paul and Barnabas went first to the synagogue. The Jews who were there believed in God and diligently studied the Scriptures. Tragically, however, many could not accept Jesus as the promised Messiah because they had the wrong idea of what kind of Messiah he would be. He was not a military king who would overthrow Rome's control, but a servant king who would defeat sin in people's hearts. (Only later, when he returns, will he rule the nations of the world.) Paul and Barnabas did not separate themselves from the synagogues but tried to show clearly that the Scriptures the Jews studied pointed to Jesus.

13.14, 15 What happened in a synagogue service? First the *Shema* was recited (this is Deuteronomy 6.4, which Jews repeated several times daily). Certain prayers were given; then there was a reading from the law (the books of Genesis through Deuteronomy), a reading from the prophets intending to illustrate the law, and a sermon. The synagogue leader decided who was to lead the service and give the sermon. A different person was chosen to lead each week. Because it was customary for the synagogue leader to invite visiting rabbis to speak, Paul and Barnabas usually had an open door when they first went to a synagogue. But as soon as they spoke about Jesus as Messiah, the door slammed. They were usually not invited back by the religious leaders, and sometimes they were thrown out of town!

13.16 Paul's opening remarks indicate that the audience contained Jews and Gentile proselytes, who were called "others who fear God."

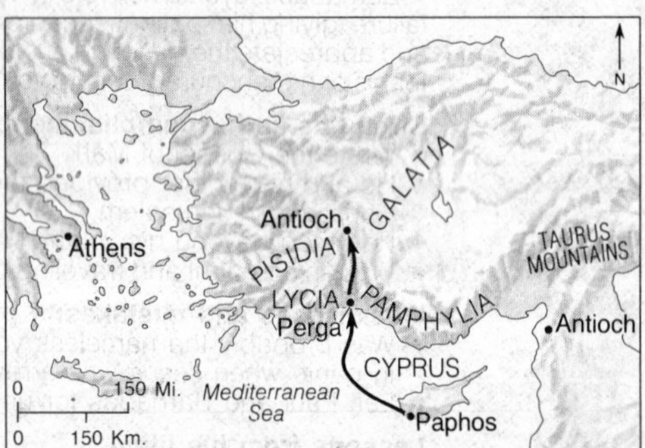

MINISTRY IN PAMPHYLIA AND GALATIA Paul, Barnabas, and John Mark left Paphos and landed at Perga in the humid region of Pamphylia, a narrow strip of land between the sea and the Taurus Mountains. John Mark deserted them in Perga, but Paul and Barnabas traveled up the steep road into the higher elevation of Pisidia in Galatia. When the Jews rejected his message, Paul preached to Gentiles, and the Jews drove Paul and Barnabas out of the Pisidian city of Antioch.

13.16ff Paul's message to the Jews in the synagogue in Antioch began with an emphasis on God's covenant with Israel. This was a point of agreement, because all Jews were proud to be God's chosen people. Then Paul went on to explain how the gospel fulfilled the covenant. Some Jews found this message hard to take.

13.23–30 Paul began where his listeners were and then introduced them to Christ. Because he was speaking to devout Jews, he began with the covenant, Abraham, David, and other familiar themes. Later, when speaking to the Greek philosophers in Athens (17.22–32), he began by talking about what he had observed in their city. In both cases, however, he centered the sermon around Christ and emphasized the resurrection. When you share the good news, begin where your audience is – then tell them about Christ.

13.23 Isa 11.1 Lk 1.32; 2.11
13.24 Mk 1.1-14
13.25 Mt 3.11 Mk 1.7 Lk 3.16 Jn 1.26,27
13.27 Acts 3.17 1 Cor 2.8

man's posterity God has brought to Israel a Savior, Jesus, as he promised; 24 before
his coming John had already proclaimed a baptism of repentance to all the people
of Israel. 25 And as John was finishing his work, he said, 'What do you suppose that
I am? I am not he. No, but one is coming after me; I am not worthy to untie the
thong of the sandals[m] on his feet.'
26 "My brothers, you descendants of Abraham's family, and others who fear
God, to us[n] the message of this salvation has been sent. 27 Because the residents of
Jerusalem and their leaders did not recognize him or understand the words of the
prophets that are read every sabbath, they fulfilled those words by condemning

[m] Gk *untie the sandals* [n] Other ancient authorities read *you*

BARNABAS

Every group needs an "encourager" because everyone needs encouragement at one time or another. However, the value of encouragement is often missed because it tends to be private rather than public. In fact, people most need encouragement when they feel most alone. A man named Joseph was such an encourager that he earned the nickname "son of encouragement," or Barnabas, from the Jerusalem Christians.

Barnabas was drawn to people he could encourage, and he was a great help to those around him. It is delightful that wherever Barnabas encouraged Christians, non-Christians flocked to become believers!

Barnabas's actions were crucial to the early church. In a way, we can thank him for most of the New Testament. God used his relationship with Paul at one point and with Mark at another to keep these two men going when either might have failed. Barnabas did wonders with encouragement!

When Paul arrived in Jerusalem for the first time following his conversion, the local Christians were understandably reluctant to welcome him. They thought his story was a trick to capture more Christians. Only Barnabas was willing to risk his life to meet with Paul and then convince the others that their former enemy was now a vibrant believer in Jesus. We can only wonder what might have happened to Paul without Barnabas.

It was Barnabas who encouraged Mark to go with him and Paul to Antioch. Mark joined them on their first missionary journey, but decided during the trip to return home. Later, Barnabas wanted to invite Mark to join them for another journey, but Paul would not agree. As a result, the partners went separate ways, Barnabas with Mark and Paul with Silas. This actually doubled the missionary effort. Barnabas's patient encouragement was confirmed by Mark's eventual effective ministry. Paul and Mark were later reunited in missionary efforts.

As Barnabas's life shows, we are rarely in situations where there isn't someone we can encourage. Our tendency, however, is to criticize instead of help. It may be important at times to point out someone's shortcomings, but before we have the right to do this, we must build that person's trust through encouragement. Are you prepared to encourage those you come in contact with today?

Strengths and accomplishments:
- Was one of the first to sell possessions to help the Christians in Jerusalem
- Was the first to travel with Paul as a missionary team
- Was an encourager, as his nickname shows, and thus one of the most quietly influential people in the early days of Christianity
- Called an apostle, although not one of the original twelve

Weakness and mistake:
- With Peter, temporarily stayed aloof from Gentile believers until Paul corrected him

Lessons from his life:
- Encouragement is one of the most effective ways to help
- Sooner or later, true obedience to God will involve risk
- There is always someone who needs encouragement

Vital statistics:
- Where: Cyprus, Jerusalem, Antioch
- Occupation: Missionary, teacher
- Relatives: Sister: Mary. Nephew: John Mark
- Contemporaries: Peter, Silas, Paul, Herod Agrippa I

Key verses:
"When he came and saw the grace of God, he rejoiced, and he exhorted them all to remain faithful to the Lord with steadfast devotion; for he was a good man, full of the Holy Spirit and of faith. And a great many people were brought to the Lord" (Acts 11.23, 24).

Barnabas's story is told in Acts 9.27—15.39. He is also mentioned in 1 Corinthians 9.6; Galatians 2.1, 9, 13; Colossians 4.10.

him. 28 Even though they found no cause for a sentence of death, they asked Pilate
to have him killed. 29 When they had carried out everything that was written about
him, they took him down from the tree and laid him in a tomb. 30 But God raised
him from the dead; 31 and for many days he appeared to those who came up
with him from Galilee to Jerusalem, and they are now his witnesses to the people.
32 And we bring you the good news that what God promised to our ancestors
33 he has fulfilled for us, their children, by raising Jesus; as also it is written in
the second psalm,

'You are my Son;
today I have begotten you.'

34 As to his raising him from the dead, no more to return to corruption, he has
spoken in this way,

'I will give you the holy promises made to David.'

35 Therefore he has also said in another psalm,

'You will not let your Holy One experience corruption.'

36 For David, after he had served the purpose of God in his own generation, died,[o]
was laid beside his ancestors, and experienced corruption; 37 but he whom God
raised up experienced no corruption. 38 Let it be known to you therefore, my brothers, that through this man forgiveness of sins is proclaimed to you; 39 by this Jesus[p]
everyone who believes is set free from all those sins[q] from which you could not be
freed by the law of Moses. 40 Beware, therefore, that what the prophets said does
not happen to you:

41 'Look, you scoffers!
Be amazed and perish,
for in your days I am doing a work,
a work that you will never believe, even if someone tells you.' "

42 As Paul and Barnabas[r] were going out, the people urged them to speak
about these things again the next sabbath. 43 When the meeting of the synagogue
broke up, many Jews and devout converts to Judaism followed Paul and Barnabas,
who spoke to them and urged them to continue in the grace of God.

Paul turns to the Gentiles

44 The next sabbath almost the whole city gathered to hear the word of the
Lord.[s] 45 But when the Jews saw the crowds, they were filled with jealousy; and
blaspheming, they contradicted what was spoken by Paul. 46 Then both Paul and
Barnabas spoke out boldly, saying, "It was necessary that the word of God should
be spoken first to you. Since you reject it and judge yourselves to be unworthy of
eternal life, we are now turning to the Gentiles. 47 For so the Lord has commanded
us, saying,

'I have set you to be a light for the Gentiles,
so that you may bring salvation to the ends of the earth.' "

48 When the Gentiles heard this, they were glad and praised the word of the
Lord; and as many as had been destined for eternal life became believers. 49 Thus

[o] Gk *fell asleep* [p] Gk *this* [q] Gk *all* [r] Gk *they* [s] Other ancient authorities read *God*

13.28 Acts 3.14
13.29 Lk 23.52,53
13.30 Mt 28.6 Acts 2.24
13.31 Lk 24.48 Acts 1.11 1 Cor 15.5
13.32 Rom 1.2-4 Gal 3.16
13.33 Ps 2.7 Heb 1.5; 5.5
13.34 Isa 55.3
13.35 Ps 16.10
13.36 1 Kgs 2.10
13.37 Acts 2.24 1 Cor 15.42
13.38 Jer 31.34 Col 1.13,14
13.39 Isa 53.11 Rom 3.28; 10.4 Gal 2.16
13.41 Hab 1.5
13.45 Acts 14.2; 18.6 1 Thess 2.15,16 Jude 10
13.46 Deut 32.21 Rom 1.16; 10.19
13.47 Isa 42.6; 49.6 Lk 2.32
13.48 Rom 8.29,30 Eph 1.4,5,11 1 Pet 1.2

13.38, 39 This is the good news of the gospel—that forgiveness of sins and freedom from guilt are available to all people through faith in Christ—including *you.* Have you received this forgiveness? Are you refreshed by it each day?

13.42 These Gentiles were the "others who fear God"; they worshiped with the Jews (see 13.16).

13.42–45 The Jewish leaders brought theological arguments against Paul and Barnabas, but the Bible tells us that the real reason for their denunciation was that "they were filled with jealousy." When we see others succeeding where we haven't or receiving the affirmation we crave, it is hard to rejoice with them. Jealousy is our natural reaction. But how tragic it is when our own jealous feelings make us try to stop God's work. If a work is God's work, rejoice in it—no matter who is doing it.

13.46 Why was it necessary for the gospel to go first to the Jews? God planned that through the Jewish nation *all* the world would come to know God (Genesis 12.3). Paul, a Jew himself, loved his people (Romans 9.1–5) and wanted to give them every opportunity to join him in proclaiming God's salvation. Unfortunately, many Jews did not recognize Jesus as Messiah, and they did not understand that God was offering salvation to anyone, Jew or Gentile, who comes to him through faith in Christ.

13.47 God had planned for Israel to be this light (Isaiah 49.6). Through Israel came Jesus, the light of the nations (Luke 2.32). This light would spread out and enlighten the Gentiles.

13.50 Instead of hearing the truth, the Jewish leaders stirred up opposition and ran Paul and Barnabas out of town. When confronted by a disturbing truth, people often turn away and refuse to

13.51 Mt 10.14 Lk 9.5 Acts 18.6 2 Tim 3.11 the word of the Lord spread throughout the region. 50 But the Jews incited the devout women of high standing and the leading men of the city, and stirred up persecu-
tion against Paul and Barnabas, and drove them out of their region. 51 So they shook
13.52 1 Pet 1.8 the dust off their feet in protest against them, and went to Iconium. 52 And the disciples were filled with joy and with the Holy Spirit.

Paul and Barnabas preach boldly at Iconium

14 The same thing occurred in Iconium, where Paul and Barnabas[t] went into
the Jewish synagogue and spoke in such a way that a great number of both
14.2 2 Tim 3.11 Jews and Greeks became believers. 2 But the unbelieving Jews stirred up the Gentiles and poisoned their minds against the brothers. 3 So they remained for a long
14.3 Mk 16.20 Rom 15.19 Heb 2.4 time, speaking boldly for the Lord, who testified to the word of his grace by granting signs and wonders to be done through them. 4 But the residents of the city were
14.4 Acts 27.4,5 19.9; 28.24 divided; some sided with the Jews, and some with the apostles. 5 And when an
attempt was made by both Gentiles and Jews, with their rulers, to mistreat them and
14.5 Acts 14.19; 16.1 1 Thess 2.14-16 to stone them, 6 the apostles[t] learned of it and fled to Lystra and Derbe, cities of
Lycaonia, and to the surrounding country; 7 and there they continued proclaiming
the good news.

Paul heals a cripple in Lystra

14.8 Acts 3.2 8 In Lystra there was a man sitting who could not use his feet and had never
walked, for he had been crippled from birth. 9 He listened to Paul as he was speak-
14.10 Isa 35.6 Acts 3.8 ing. And Paul, looking at him intently and seeing that he had faith to be healed,
10 said in a loud voice, "Stand upright on your feet." And the man[u] sprang up
14.11 Acts 28.6 and began to walk. 11 When the crowds saw what Paul had done, they shouted
in the Lycaonian language, "The gods have come down to us in human form!"

[t] Gk *they* [u] Gk *he*

listen. When God's Spirit points out needed changes in our lives, we must listen to him. Otherwise we may be pushing the truth so far away that it no longer affects us.

13.51 Often Jews would shake the dust off their feet when leaving a Gentile town, on the way back to their own land. This symbolized cleansing themselves from the contamination of those who did not worship God. For Paul and Barnabas to do this to Jews demonstrated that Jews who reject the gospel are not truly part of Israel and are no better than pagans.

13.51 Jesus had told his disciples to shake from their feet the dust of any village that would not accept or listen to them (Mark 6.11). The disciples were not to blame if the message was rejected as long as they had faithfully presented it. When we share Christ carefully and sensitively, God does not hold us responsible for the other person's decision.

14.3, 4 We may wish we could perform a miraculous act that would convince everyone once and for all that Jesus is the Lord. But we see here that even if we could perform a miracle, it wouldn't convince everyone. God gave these men power to do great wonders as proof, but people were still divided. Don't spend your time and energy wishing for miracles. Sow your seeds of good news on the best ground you can find in the best way you can, and leave the convincing to the Holy Spirit.

14.6 Iconium (14.1), Lystra, and Derbe were three cities Paul visited in the region of Galatia. Paul wrote a letter to these churches – the letter to the Galatians – because many Jewish Christians were claiming that non-Jewish Christians couldn't be saved unless they followed Jewish laws and customs. Paul's letter refuted this and brought the believers back to a right understanding of faith in Jesus (see Galatians 3.3, 5). Paul wrote his letter soon after leaving the region (see the note on 14.28).

14.11 "The Lycaonian language" means their local dialect.

14.11, 12 Zeus and Hermes (also known as Jupiter and Mercury) were two popular gods in the Roman world. People from Lystra claimed that these gods had once visited their city. According to legend, no one offered them hospitality except an old couple, so Zeus and Hermes killed the rest of the people and rewarded the old couple. When the citizens of Lystra saw the miracles of Paul and Barnabas, they assumed that the gods were revisiting them. Remembering what had happened to their citizens before, they immediately honored Paul and Barnabas and showered them with gifts.

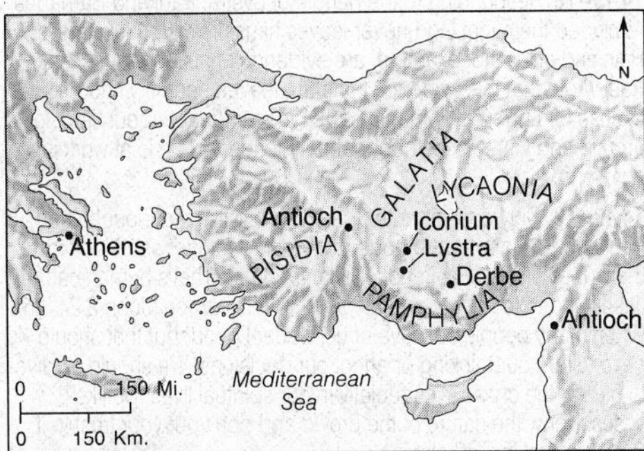

CONTINUED MINISTRY IN GALATIA Paul and Barnabas, thrown out of Antioch in Pisidia, descended the mountains, going east into Lycaonia. They went first to Iconium, a commercial center on the road between Asia and Syria. After preaching there, they had to flee to Lystra, 25 miles south. Paul was stoned in Lystra, but he and Barnabas traveled the 50 miles to Derbe, a frontier town. The pair then boldly retraced their steps.

12 Barnabas they called Zeus, and Paul they called Hermes, because he was the
chief speaker. 13 The priest of Zeus, whose temple was just outside the city,[v]
brought oxen and garlands to the gates; he and the crowds wanted to offer sacrifice.
14 When the apostles Barnabas and Paul heard of it, they tore their clothes and
rushed out into the crowd, shouting, 15 "Friends,[w] why are you doing this? We are
mortals just like you, and we bring you good news, that you should turn from
these worthless things to the living God, who made the heaven and the earth and the
sea and all that is in them. 16 In past generations he allowed all the nations to
follow their own ways; 17 yet he has not left himself without a witness in doing
good—giving you rains from heaven and fruitful seasons, and filling you with
food and your hearts with joy." 18 Even with these words, they scarcely restrained
the crowds from offering sacrifice to them.

19 But Jews came there from Antioch and Iconium and won over the crowds.
Then they stoned Paul and dragged him out of the city, supposing that he was dead.
20 But when the disciples surrounded him, he got up and went into the city. The next
day he went on with Barnabas to Derbe.

Paul and Barnabas appoint elders on the return trip home

21 After they had proclaimed the good news to that city and had made many
disciples, they returned to Lystra, then on to Iconium and Antioch. 22 There they
strengthened the souls of the disciples and encouraged them to continue in the faith,
saying, "It is through many persecutions that we must enter the kingdom of God."
23 And after they had appointed elders for them in each church, with prayer and
fasting they entrusted them to the Lord in whom they had come to believe.

24 Then they passed through Pisidia and came to Pamphylia. 25 When they had
spoken the word in Perga, they went down to Attalia. 26 From there they sailed back
to Antioch, where they had been commended to the grace of God for the work[x] that
they had completed. 27 When they arrived, they called the church together and
related all that God had done with them, and how he had opened a door of faith for
the Gentiles. 28 And they stayed there with the disciples for some time.

14.13 Dan 2.46
14.15 Ex 20.11; Deut 32.21; Jer 14.22; Mt 16.16; 1 Thess 1.9; Rev 14.7; 19.10
14.16 Ps 81.12
14.17 Deut 11.14; Ps 65.10-12; 147.8; Acts 17.27; Rom 1.19,20
14.19 Acts 13.45; 2 Cor 1.8; 11.25; 2 Tim 3.11
14.20 Acts 14.6
14.22 Mt 10.38; 16.24; Jn 15.18; Rom 8.17; 2 Tim 2.11; 3.12
14.23 Tit 1.5
14.24 Acts 13.13,14
14.26 Acts 11.26; 13.1-3
14.27 1 Cor 16.9; Col 4.3; Rev 3.8

[v] Or *The priest of Zeus-Outside-the-City* [w] Gk *Men* [x] Or *committed in the grace of God to the work*

14.15–18 Responding to the people of Lystra, Paul and Barnabas reminded them that God never leaves himself "without a witness." Rain and crops, for example, are evidence of his goodness. Later Paul wrote that this evidence in nature leaves people without an excuse for unbelief (Romans 1.20). When in doubt about God, look around and you will see abundant evidence that he is at work in our world.

14.18, 19 Only days after the people in Lystra had thought that Paul and Barnabas were gods and wanted to offer sacrifices to them, they stoned Paul and left him for dead. That's human nature. Jesus understood how changeable crowds can be (John 2.24, 25). When many people approve of us, we feel good, but that should never cloud our thinking or affect our decisions. We should not live to please the crowd—especially in our spiritual lives. Be like Jesus. Know the nature of the crowd and don't put your trust in it. Put your trust in God alone.

14.18–20 Paul and Barnabas were persistent in their preaching of the good news, considering the cost to themselves to be nothing in comparison with obedience to Christ. They had just narrowly escaped being stoned in Iconium (14.1–7), but Jews from Antioch and Iconium tracked Paul down, stoned him, and left him for dead. But Paul got up and went back into the city to preach the good news. That's true commitment! Being a disciple of Christ calls for costly commitment. As Christians, we no longer belong to ourselves, but to our Lord, for whom we are called to suffer.

14.21, 22 Paul and Barnabas returned to visit the believers in all the cities where they had recently been threatened and physically attacked. They knew the dangers they faced, yet they believed they had a responsibility to encourage the new believers. No matter how inconvenient or uncomfortable the task may seem, we must always support new believers who need our help and encouragement. It was not convenient or comfortable for Jesus to go to the cross for us!

14.23 Part of the reason Paul and Barnabas risked their lives to return to these cities was to organize the churches' leadership. They were not just following up on a loosely knit group; they were helping the believers get organized with spiritual leaders who could help them grow. Churches grow under Spirit-led leaders, both laypersons and pastors. Pray for your church leaders and support them; and if God urges you, humbly accept the responsibility of a leadership role in your church.

14.28 Paul probably wrote his letter to the Galatians while he was staying in Antioch (A.D. 48 or 49) after completing his first missionary journey. There are several theories as to what part of Galatia Paul was addressing, but most agree that Iconium, Lystra, and Derbe were part of that region. Galatians was probably written before the Jerusalem council (Acts 15), because in the letter, the question of whether Gentile believers should be required to follow Jewish law was not yet resolved. The council met to solve that problem.

2. Meeting of the church council

The leaders meet in Jerusalem

15.1 Lev 12.3 Gal 5.2 Phil 3.2,3
15.2 Gal 2.1-10
15.3 Acts 14.27
15.5 1 Cor 7.18 Gal 5.2-11
15.7 Acts 10.19-29

15 Then certain individuals came down from Judea and were teaching the
brothers, "Unless you are circumcised according to the custom of Moses,
you cannot be saved." 2 And after Paul and Barnabas had no small dissension and
debate with them, Paul and Barnabas and some of the others were appointed to go
up to Jerusalem to discuss this question with the apostles and the elders. 3 So they
were sent on their way by the church, and as they passed through both Phoenicia
and Samaria, they reported the conversion of the Gentiles, and brought great joy to
all the believers.[y] 4 When they came to Jerusalem, they were welcomed by the
church and the apostles and the elders, and they reported all that God had done with
them. 5 But some believers who belonged to the sect of the Pharisees stood up and
said, "It is necessary for them to be circumcised and ordered to keep the law of
Moses."

6 The apostles and the elders met together to consider this matter. 7 After there

[y] Gk *brothers*

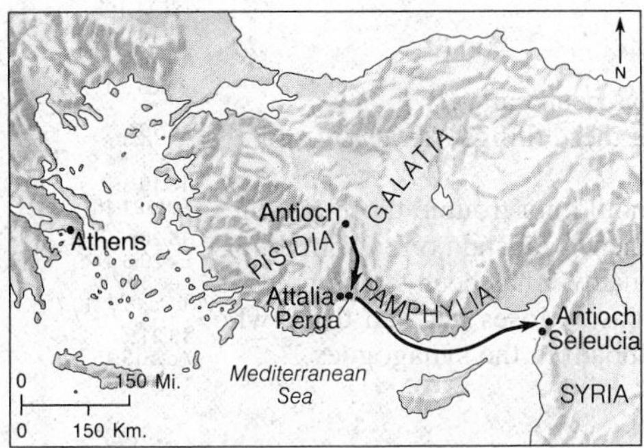

THE END OF THE FIRST JOURNEY From Antioch in Pisidia, Paul and Barnabas went down the mountains back to Pamphylia on the coast. Stopping first in Perga, where they had landed, they went west to Attalia, the main port that sent goods from Asia to Syria and Egypt. There they found a ship bound for Seleucia, the port of Antioch in Syria. This ended their first missionary journey.

15.1 The real problem for the Jewish Christians was not over whether Gentiles could be saved, but whether Gentiles had to adhere to the laws of Moses. The test of following these laws was circumcision. The Jewish Christians were worried because soon there would be more Gentile than Jewish Christians. And they were afraid of weakening moral standards among believers if they did not follow Jewish laws. Paul, Barnabas, and the other church leaders believed that the Old Testament law was very important, but it was not a prerequisite to salvation. The law cannot save; only faith in Jesus Christ is what a person needs to be saved.

15.1ff The delegates to the council at Jerusalem came from the churches in Jerusalem and Antioch. The conversion of Gentiles was raising an urgent question for the early church—do the Gentiles have to adhere to the laws of Moses and other Jewish traditions to be saved? One group of Jewish Christians insisted that following the law, including circumcision, was necessary for salvation. The Gentiles, however, did not think they needed to become Jewish first in order to become Christians. So Paul and Barnabas discussed this problem with the leaders of the church. The council upheld the convictions expressed by Paul and Barnabas that following the Jewish laws, including circumcision, was not essential for salvation and that Jewish and Gentile Christians could eat together without the Jews' becoming defiled.

15.2 The question of whether the Gentile believers should obey the law of Moses to be saved was an important one. The controversy intensified largely due to the success of the new Gentile churches. The conservatives in the Jerusalem church were led by converted Pharisees (15.5) who preferred a legalistic religion to one based on faith alone. If the conservatives had won, the Gentiles would have been required to be circumcised and converted to Judaism. This would have seriously limited Christianity to a sect within Judaism. There is some Pharisee in each one of us. We may unwittingly mistake upholding tradition, structure, and legal requirements for obeying God. Make sure the gospel brings freedom and life to those you are trying to reach.

15.2ff It is helpful to see how the churches in Antioch and Jerusalem resolved their conflict: (1) the church in Antioch sent a delegation to help seek a solution; (2) the delegates met with the church leaders to give their reports and set another date to continue the discussion; (3) Paul and Barnabas gave their report; (4) James summarized the reports and made the decision; (5) everyone abided by the decision; (6) the council sent a letter with delegates back to Antioch to report the decision.

This is a wise way to handle conflicts within the church. Problems must be confronted, and all sides of the argument must be given a fair hearing. The discussion should be held before leaders who are spiritually mature and trusted to make wise decisions. Everyone should then abide by the decisions.

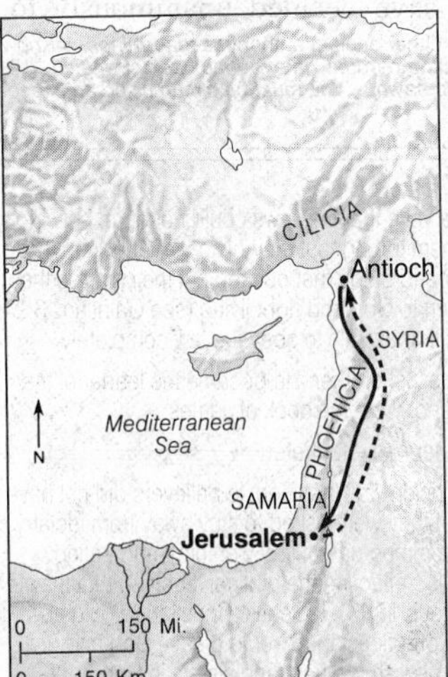

THE JERUSALEM COUNCIL A dispute arose when some Judeans taught that Gentile believers had to be circumcised to be saved. Paul and Barnabas went to Jerusalem to discuss this situation with the leaders there. After the Jerusalem council made its decision, Paul and Barnabas returned to Antioch with the news.

had been much debate, Peter stood up and said to them, "My brothers,[z] you know
that in the early days God made a choice among you, that I should be the one
through whom the Gentiles would hear the message of the good news and become
believers. 8 And God, who knows the human heart, testified to them by giving them
the Holy Spirit, just as he did to us; 9 and in cleansing their hearts by faith he has
made no distinction between them and us. 10 Now therefore why are you putting
God to the test by placing on the neck of the disciples a yoke that neither our ancestors nor we have been able to bear? 11 On the contrary, we believe that we will be
saved through the grace of the Lord Jesus, just as they will."

12 The whole assembly kept silence, and listened to Barnabas and Paul as they
told of all the signs and wonders that God had done through them among the Gentiles. 13 After they finished speaking, James replied, "My brothers,[z] listen to me.
14 Simeon has related how God first looked favorably on the Gentiles, to take from
among them a people for his name. 15 This agrees with the words of the prophets,
as it is written,

16 'After this I will return,
and I will rebuild the dwelling of David, which has fallen;
from its ruins I will rebuild it,
and I will set it up,
17 so that all other peoples may seek the Lord—
even all the Gentiles over whom my name has been called.
Thus says the Lord, who has been making these things 18 known from
long ago.'[a]

19 Therefore I have reached the decision that we should not trouble those Gentiles
who are turning to God, 20 but we should write to them to abstain only from things
polluted by idols and from fornication and from whatever has been strangled[b] and
from blood. 21 For in every city, for generations past, Moses has had those who
proclaim him, for he has been read aloud every sabbath in the synagogues."

The council sends a letter to Gentile believers

22 Then the apostles and the elders, with the consent of the whole church, decided to choose men from among their members[c] and to send them to Antioch with
Paul and Barnabas. They sent Judas called Barsabbas, and Silas, leaders among the
brothers, 23 with the following letter: "The brothers, both the apostles and the elders, to the believers[d] of Gentile origin in Antioch and Syria and Cilicia, greetings.
24 Since we have heard that certain persons who have gone out from us, though with
no instructions from us, have said things to disturb you and have unsettled your
minds,[e] 25 we have decided unanimously to choose representatives[f] and send

15.8 1 Chron 28.9 Jer 17.10 Acts 10.44,47 Heb 4.13
15.9 Acts 10.43 Rom 10.11,12
15.10 Mt 23.4 Gal 5.1
15.11 Rom 3.23,24 5.15 2 Cor 13.14 Eph 1.7,8; 2.8
15.12 Acts 14.27; 15.4
15.13 Acts 12.17
15.15 Isa 11.10 54.1-5
15.16 Amos 9.11,12
15.18 Isa 45.21
15.19 Acts 21.15
15.20 Ex 20.3,4 Lev 3.17 1 Cor 8.7; 10.7
15.21 Acts 13.15
15.22 Acts 1.23 15.27; 16.19 17.4 1 Pet 5.12
15.24 Gal 1.7; 2.4; 5.12 Tit 1.10

[z] Gk *Men, brothers* [a] Other ancient authorities read *things. 18Known to God from of old are all his works.'* [b] Other ancient authorities lack *and from whatever has been strangled* [c] Gk *from among them* [d] Gk *brothers* [e] Other ancient authorities add *saying, 'You must be circumcised and keep the law,'* [f] Gk *men*

15.10 If the law was a yoke that the Jews could not bear, how did having the law help them throughout their history? Paul wrote that the law was a teacher and guide that pointed out their sins so they could repent and return to God and right living (see Galatians 3.24, 25). It was, and still is, impossible to obey the law completely.

15.13 This James is Jesus' brother. He became the leader of the church in Jerusalem and wrote the book of James.

15.14 Simeon is another name for Peter.

15.20, 21 James' decision was that Gentile believers did not have to be circumcised. But they were asked to stay away from idolatry, sexual immorality (a common part of idol worship), and eating meat of unbled animals (reflecting the biblical teaching that the life is in the blood—Leviticus 17.14). If Gentile Christians would abstain from these three practices, they would please God and get along better with their Jewish brothers and sisters in Christ. Of course, there were other actions inappropriate for believers, but the Jews were especially concerned about these three. This compromise helped the church grow unhindered by the cultural differences of Jews and Gentiles. When we share our message across cultural and economic boundaries, we must be sure that the requirements for faith we set up are those of God, not of people.

15.22 Apostleship was not a church office, but a position and function based on specific gifts. Elders were appointed to lead and manage the church. In this meeting, apostles submitted to the decision of an elder—James, Jesus' brother.

15.22 Silas would later accompany Paul on his second missionary journey in place of Barnabas, who visited different cities with John Mark.

15.23–29 This letter answered their questions and brought great joy to the Gentile Christians in Antioch (15.31). Beautifully written, it appeals to the Holy Spirit's guidance and explains what is to be done as though the readers already know it. It is helpful when believers learn to be careful not only in what they say, but also in how they say it. We may be correct in our content, but we can lose our audience by our tone of voice or attitude.

15.26 Acts 13.50 14.19 1 Cor 15.30 2 Cor 11.23,26

15.29 Lev 17.14 Acts 21.25 Rev 2.14

15.32 Acts 13.1

15.33 Mt 4.24 Acts 6.9; 11.20 15.41 Gal 1.21

them to you, along with our beloved Barnabas and Paul, 26 who have risked their
lives for the sake of our Lord Jesus Christ. 27 We have therefore sent Judas and
Silas, who themselves will tell you the same things by word of mouth. 28 For it has
seemed good to the Holy Spirit and to us to impose on you no further burden than
these essentials: 29 that you abstain from what has been sacrificed to idols and from
blood and from what is strangled[g] and from fornication. If you keep yourselves
from these, you will do well. Farewell."

30 So they were sent off and went down to Antioch. When they gathered the
congregation together, they delivered the letter. 31 When its members[h] read it, they
rejoiced at the exhortation. 32 Judas and Silas, who were themselves prophets, said
much to encourage and strengthen the believers.[i] 33 After they had been there for
some time, they were sent off in peace by the believers[i] to those who had sent
them.[j] 35 But Paul and Barnabas remained in Antioch, and there, with many others, they taught and proclaimed the word of the Lord.

[g] Other ancient authorities lack *and from what is strangled* [h] Gk *When they* [i] Gk *brothers* [j] Other ancient authorities add verse 34, *But it seemed good to Silas to remain there*

THE FIRST CHURCH CONFERENCE

Group	Position	Reasons
Judaizers (some Jewish Christians)	Gentiles must become Jewish first to be eligible for salvation	1. They were devout, practicing Jews who found it difficult to set aside a tradition of gaining merit with God by keeping the law 2. They thought grace was too easy for the Gentiles 3. They were afraid of seeming too non-Jewish in their new faith—which could lead to death 4. The demands on the Gentiles were a way of maintaining control and authority in the movement
Gentile Christians	Faith in Christ as Savior is the only requirement for salvation	1. To submit to Jewish demands would be to doubt what God had already done for them by faith alone 2. They resisted exchanging a system of Jewish rituals for their pagan rituals—neither of which had power to save 3. They sought to obey Christ by baptism (rather than by circumcision) as a sign of their new faith
Peter and James	Faith is the only requirement, but there must be evidence of change by rejecting parts of the old life-style	1. They tried to distinguish between what was still true from God's Word and what was just human tradition 2. They had Christ's command to preach to all the world 3. They wanted to preserve unity 4. They saw that Christianity could never survive as just a sect within Judaism

As long as most of the first Christians were Jewish, there was little difficulty in welcoming new believers; however, Gentiles (non-Jews) began to accept Jesus' offer of salvation. The evidence from their lives and the presence of God's Spirit in them showed that God was accepting them. Some of the early Christians believed that non-Jewish Christians needed to meet certain conditions before they could be worthy to accept Christ. The issue could have destroyed the church, so a conference was called in Jerusalem and the issue was formally settled there, although it continued to be a problem for many years following. Above is an outline of the three points of view at the conference.

15.31 The debate over circumcision could have split the church, but Paul, Barnabas, and the Jews in Antioch made the right decision – they sought counsel from the church leaders and God's Word. Our differences should be settled the same way, by seeking wise counsel and abiding by the decisions. Don't let disagreements divide you from other believers. Third-party assistance is a sound method for resolving problems and preserving unity.

3. Second missionary journey

Paul and Barnabas separate

36 After some days Paul said to Barnabas, "Come, let us return and visit the
believers[k] in every city where we proclaimed the word of the Lord and see how
they are doing." 37 Barnabas wanted to take with them John called Mark. 38 But
Paul decided not to take with them one who had deserted them in Pamphylia and
had not accompanied them in the work. 39 The disagreement became so sharp that
they parted company; Barnabas took Mark with him and sailed away to Cyprus.
40 But Paul chose Silas and set out, the believers[k] commending him to the grace of
the Lord. 41 He went through Syria and Cilicia, strengthening the churches.

15.36 Acts 13.4,13, 14,51 14.5,6,24-28
15.37 Col 4.10 2 Tim 4.11
15.38 Acts 13.13

Timothy joins Paul and Silas at Lystra

16 Paul[l] went on also to Derbe and to Lystra, where there was a disciple named
Timothy, the son of a Jewish woman who was a believer; but his father was
a Greek. 2 He was well spoken of by the believers[k] in Lystra and Iconium. 3 Paul
wanted Timothy to accompany him; and he took him and had him circumcised
because of the Jews who were in those places, for they all knew that his father was
a Greek. 4 As they went from town to town, they delivered to them for observance
the decisions that had been reached by the apostles and elders who were in Jerusalem. 5 So the churches were strengthened in the faith and increased in numbers
daily.

16.1 Acts 14.5,6 Phil 2.19-22 2 Tim 1.2,5; 3.15
16.3 1 Cor 9.20 Gal 2.3; 5.2
16.5 Acts 9.31

Paul has a vision directing them to Macedonia

6 They went through the region of Phrygia and Galatia, having been forbidden
by the Holy Spirit to speak the word in Asia. 7 When they had come opposite
Mysia, they attempted to go into Bithynia, but the Spirit of Jesus did not allow
them; 8 so, passing by Mysia, they went down to Troas. 9 During the night Paul had
a vision: there stood a man of Macedonia pleading with him and saying, "Come
over to Macedonia and help us." 10 When he had seen the vision, we immediately

16.7 Rom 8.9
16.8 2 Cor 2.12 2 Tim 4.13
16.9 Num 12.6 Acts 10.3,30

[k] Gk *brothers* [l] Gk *He*

15.36–39 Paul and Barnabas disagreed sharply over Mark. Paul didn't want to take Mark along because he had left them earlier (13.13). This disagreement caused the two great preachers to form two teams, opening up two missionary endeavors instead of one. God works even through conflict and disagreements. Later, Mark became vital to Paul's ministry (Colossians 4.10). Christians do not always agree, but problems can be solved by agreeing to disagree and letting God work his will.

15.40 Paul's second missionary journey, this time with Silas as his partner, began approximately three years after his first one ended. The two visited many of the cities covered on Paul's first journey, plus others. This journey laid the groundwork for the church in Greece.

15.40 Silas had been involved in the Jerusalem council and was one of the two men chosen to represent the Jerusalem church by taking the letter and decision back to Antioch (15.22). Paul, from the Antioch church, chose Silas, from the Jerusalem church, and they traveled together to many cities to spread the good news. This teamwork revealed the church's unity after the decision at the Jerusalem council.

16.1 Timothy is the first second-generation Christian mentioned in the New Testament. His mother, Eunice, and grandmother, Lois (2 Timothy 1.5), had become believers and had faithfully influenced him for the Lord. Although Timothy's father apparently was not a Christian, the faithfulness of his mother and grandmother prevailed. Never underestimate the far-reaching consequences of raising one small child to love the Lord.

16.2, 3 Timothy and his mother, Eunice, were from Lystra. Eunice had probably heard Paul's preaching when he was there during his first missionary journey (14.6–18). Timothy was the son of a Jewish mother and Greek father – to the Jews, a half-breed like a Samaritan. So Paul asked Timothy to be circumcised to remove some of the stigma he may have had with Jewish believers. Timothy was not required to be circumcised (the Jerusalem council had decided that – chapter 15), but he voluntarily did this to overcome any barriers to his witness for Christ. Sometimes we need to go beyond the minimum requirements in order to help our audience receive our testimony.

16.6 We don't know how the Holy Spirit told Paul that he and his men should not go into Asia. It may have been through a prophet, a vision, an inner conviction, or some other circumstance. To know God's will does not mean we must hear his voice. He leads in different ways. When seeking God's will (1) make sure your plan is in harmony with God's Word; (2) ask mature Christians for their advice; (3) check your own motives – are you seeking to do what you want or what you think God wants? – and (4) pray for God to open and close the doors of circumstances.

16.7–9 The "Spirit of Jesus" is another name for the Holy Spirit. The Holy Spirit closed the door twice for Paul, so he must have wondered which geographical direction to take in spreading the gospel. Then, in a vision (16.9), Paul was given definite direction, and he and his companions obediently traveled into Greece. The Holy Spirit guides us to the right places, but he also guides us away from the wrong places. As we seek God's will, it is important to know what God wants us to do and where he wants us to go, but it is equally important to know what God does not want us to do and where he does not want us to go.

16.10 The use of the pronoun *we* indicates that Luke, the author of the Gospel of Luke and of this book, joined Paul, Silas, and Timothy on their journey. He was an eyewitness to most of the remaining incidents in this book.

tried to cross over to Macedonia, being convinced that God had called us to proclaim the good news to them.

Lydia is converted in Philippi

16.11 11 We set sail from Troas and took a straight course to Samothrace, the follow-
2 Cor 2.12 ing day to Neapolis, 12 and from there to Philippi, which is a leading city of the
16.12 Acts 20.6 district[m] of Macedonia and a Roman colony. We remained in this city for some
1 Thess 2.2 days. 13 On the sabbath day we went outside the gate by the river, where we supposed there was a place of prayer; and we sat down and spoke to the women who
16.14 had gathered there. 14 A certain woman named Lydia, a worshiper of God, was
a) Rev 1.11 2.18-29 listening to us; she was from the city of Thyatira and a dealer in purple cloth. The
b) Acts 13.43 18.7 Lord opened her heart to listen eagerly to what was said by Paul. 15 When she and
16.15 her household were baptized, she urged us, saying, "If you have judged me to be
Acts 16.14 faithful to the Lord, come and stay at my home." And she prevailed upon us.

The Philippian jailer is converted

16.16 16 One day, as we were going to the place of prayer, we met a slave girl who
Lev 19.31; 20.6 had a spirit of divination and brought her owners a great deal of money by fortune-
Deut 18.10,11 1 Sam 28.3,7,8 telling. 17 While she followed Paul and us, she would cry out, "These men are
16.18 slaves of the Most High God, who proclaim to you[n] a way of salvation." 18 She
Mk 1.25,34 kept doing this for many days. But Paul, very much annoyed, turned and said to the
16.17 spirit, "I order you in the name of Jesus Christ to come out of her." And it came out
that very hour.

[m] Other authorities read *a city of the first district* [n] Other ancient authorities read *to us*

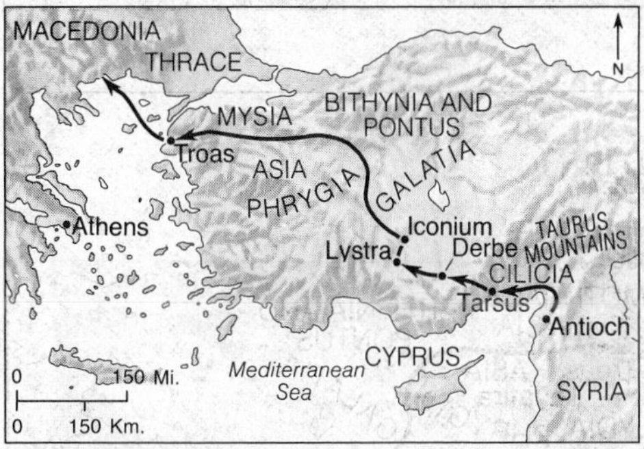

THE SECOND JOURNEY BEGINS Paul and Silas set out on a second missionary journey to visit the cities Paul had preached in earlier. This time they set out by land rather than sea, traveling the Roman road through Cilicia and the Cilician Gates—a gorge through the Taurus Mountains—then northwest toward Derbe, Lystra, and Iconium. The Spirit told them not to go into Asia, so they turned northward toward Bithynia. Again the Spirit said no, so they turned west through Mysia to the harbor city of Troas.

16.12 Philippi was the key city in the region of Macedonia (northern Greece today). Paul founded a church during this visit (A.D. 50–51). Later Paul wrote a letter to the church, the book of Philippians, probably from a prison in Rome (A.D. 61). The letter was personal and tender, showing Paul's deep love and friendship for the believers there. In it he thanked them for a gift they had sent, alerted them to a coming visit by Timothy and Epaphroditus, urged the church to clear up any disunity, and encouraged the believers not to give in to persecution.

16.13 Inscribed on the arches outside the city of Philippi was a prohibition against bringing an unrecognized religion into the city; therefore, this prayer meeting was held outside the city, beside the river.

16.13, 14 After following the Holy Spirit's leading into Macedonia, Paul made his first evangelistic contact with a small group of women. Paul never allowed sexual or cultural boundaries to keep him from preaching the gospel. He preached to these women; and Lydia, an influential merchant, believed. This opened the way for ministry in that region. God often worked in and through women in the early church.

16.14 Lydia was a merchant of purple cloth, so she was probably wealthy. Purple cloth was valuable and expensive. It was often worn as a sign of nobility or royalty.

16.14ff Luke highlights the stories of three individuals who became believers through Paul's ministry in Philippi: Lydia, the influential businesswoman (16.14), the demon-possessed slave girl (16.16–18), and the jailer (16.27–30). The gospel was affecting all strata of society, just as it does today.

16.15 Why was Lydia's household baptized when Lydia believed? Baptism was a public sign of identification with Christ and the Christian community. Although not all members of her household may have chosen to follow Christ (we don't know), it was now a Christian home.

16.16 This girl had a spirit of divination, meaning she had fortune-telling ability from evil spirits. Fortune-telling was a common practice in Greek and Roman culture. There were many superstitious methods by which people thought they could foretell future events, from interpreting omens in nature to communicating with the spirits of the dead. This young slave girl had an evil spirit, and she made her master rich by interpreting signs and telling people their fortunes. The master was exploiting her unfortunate condition for personal gain.

16.17, 18 What the slave girl said was true, although the source of her knowledge was a demon. Why did a demon announce the truth about Paul, and why did this annoy Paul? If Paul accepted the demon's words, he would appear to be linking the gospel and demon-related activities. This would damage his message about Christ. Truth and evil do not mix.

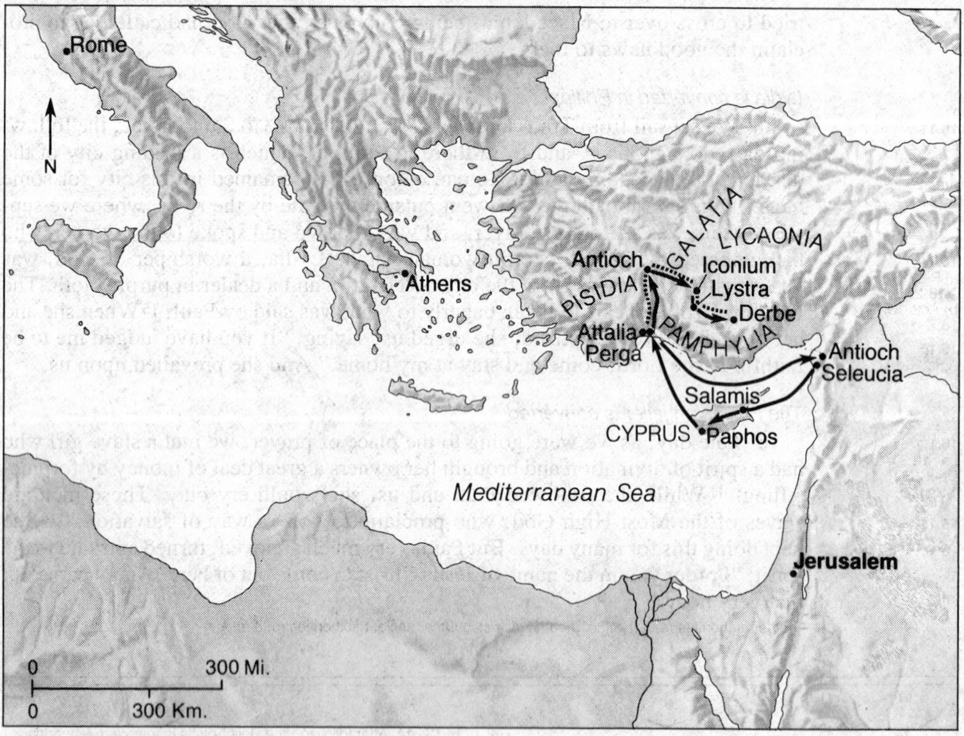

PAUL'S FIRST MISSIONARY JOURNEY (ACTS 13.1—14.28)

PAUL'S SECOND MISSIONARY JOURNEY (ACTS 15.36—18.22)

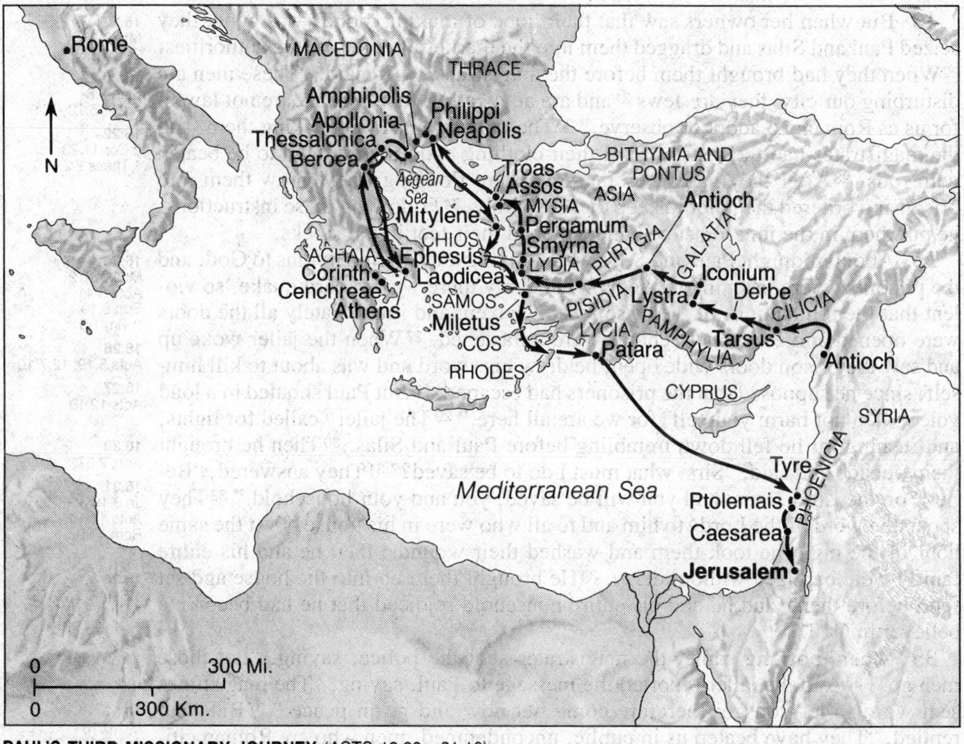

Rome
MACEDONIA
THRACE
Amphipolis
Apollonia
Philippi
Neapolis
Thessalonica
Beroea
N
Aegean Sea
Troas
Assos
BITHYNIA AND PONTUS
ASIA
MYSIA
Antioch
Mitylene
Pergamum
CHIOS
Smyrna
PHRYGIA
GALATIA
ACHAIA
Ephesus
LYDIA
Iconium
Corinth
Laodicea
Cenchreae
PISIDIA
Lystra
Derbe
SAMOS
Athens
Miletus
PAMPHYLIA
CILICIA
COS
LYCIA
Tarsus
Patara
Antioch
RHODES
CYPRUS
SYRIA
PHOENICIA
Tyre
Mediterranean Sea
Ptolemais
Caesarea
Jerusalem
0 300 Mi.
0 300 Km.

PAUL'S THIRD MISSIONARY JOURNEY (ACTS 18.23—21.16)

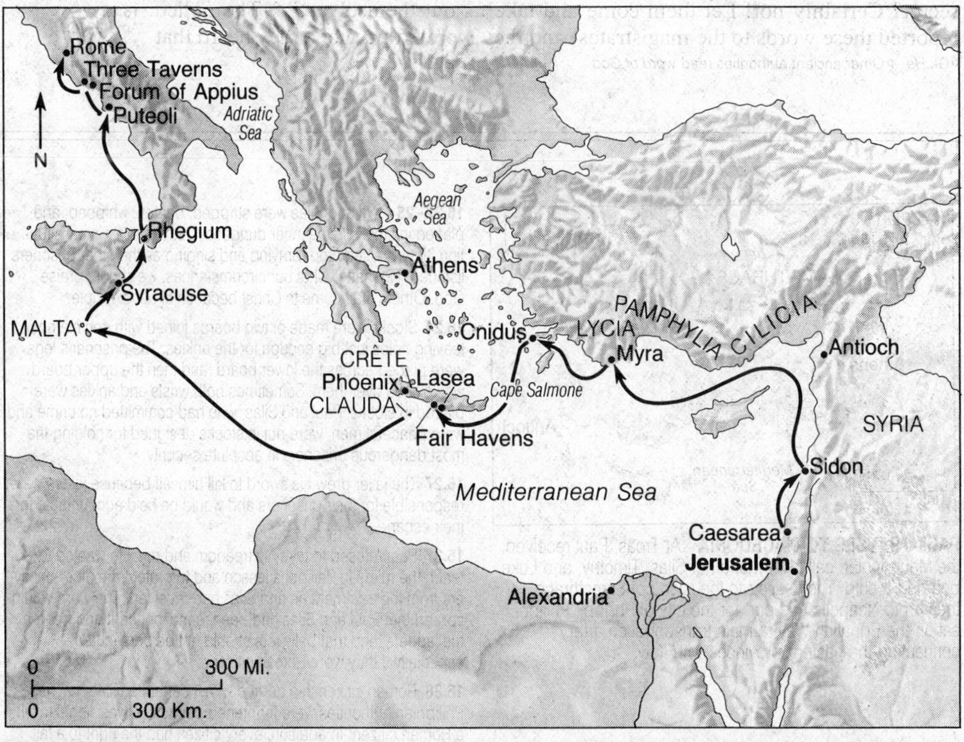

Rome
Three Taverns
Forum of Appius
Puteoli
Adriatic Sea
N
Aegean Sea
Rhegium
Athens
Syracuse
MALTA
PAMPHYLIA
CILICIA
LYCIA
Cnidus
Myra
Antioch
CRETE
Phoenix
Lasea
Cape Salmone
CLAUDA
Fair Havens
SYRIA
Sidon
Mediterranean Sea
Caesarea
Jerusalem
Alexandria
0 300 Mi.
0 300 Km.

PAUL'S JOURNEY TO ROME (ACTS 21.17—28.31)

19 But when her owners saw that their hope of making money was gone, they **16.19**
seized Paul and Silas and dragged them into the marketplace before the authorities. Mt 10.18; 2 Cor 6.5
20 When they had brought them before the magistrates, they said, "These men are **16.20,21**
disturbing our city; they are Jews 21 and are advocating customs that are not lawful Esth 3.8; Acts 16.12; 17.6
for us as Romans to adopt or observe." 22 The crowd joined in attacking them, and **16.22**
the magistrates had them stripped of their clothing and ordered them to be beaten 2 Cor 11.23; 1 Thess 2.2
with rods. 23 After they had given them a severe flogging, they threw them into
prison and ordered the jailer to keep them securely. 24 Following these instructions,
he put them in the innermost cell and fastened their feet in the stocks.
25 About midnight Paul and Silas were praying and singing hymns to God, and **16.25**
the prisoners were listening to them. 26 Suddenly there was an earthquake, so vio- Mt 5.10-12; Acts 5.41
lent that the foundations of the prison were shaken; and immediately all the doors Eph 5.19; 2 Tim 1.8
were opened and everyone's chains were unfastened. 27 When the jailer woke up **16.26**
and saw the prison doors wide open, he drew his sword and was about to kill him- Acts 5.19; 12.7,10
self, since he supposed that the prisoners had escaped. 28 But Paul shouted in a loud **16.27** Acts 12.19
voice, "Do not harm yourself, for we are all here." 29 The jailer[o] called for lights,
and rushing in, he fell down trembling before Paul and Silas. 30 Then he brought **16.30**
them outside and said, "Sirs, what must I do to be saved?" 31 They answered, "Be- Acts 2.37
lieve on the Lord Jesus, and you will be saved, you and your household." 32 They **16.31** Jn 3.16,36
spoke the word of the Lord[p] to him and to all who were in his house. 33 At the same Acts 11.14; Rom 10.9
hour of the night he took them and washed their wounds; then he and his entire
family were baptized without delay. 34 He brought them up into the house and set **16.34**
food before them; and he and his entire household rejoiced that he had become a 1 Sam 2.1,2; 1 Chron 16.10
believer in God. Ps 119.111; Rom 5.2
35 When morning came, the magistrates sent the police, saying, "Let those 1 Pet 1.8
men go." 36 And the jailer reported the message to Paul, saying, "The magistrates
sent word to let you go; therefore come out now and go in peace." 37 But Paul **16.37**
replied, "They have beaten us in public, uncondemned, men who are Roman citi- Mt 10.16; Acts 22.25-29
zens, and have thrown us into prison; and now are they going to discharge us in
secret? Certainly not! Let them come and take us out themselves." 38 The police **16.38**
reported these words to the magistrates, and they were afraid when they heard that Acts 22.29

[o] Gk *He* [p] Other ancient authorities read *word of God*

PAUL TRAVELS TO MACEDONIA At Troas, Paul received the Macedonian call (16.9), and he, Silas, Timothy, and Luke boarded a ship. They sailed to the island of Samothrace, then on to Neapolis, the port for the city of Philippi. Philippi sat on the Egnatian Way, a main transportation artery connecting the eastern provinces with Italy.

16.22–25 Paul and Silas were stripped, beaten, whipped, and placed in stocks in the inner dungeon. Despite this dismal situation, they praised God, praying and singing as the other prisoners listened. No matter what our circumstances, we should praise God. Others may come to Christ because of our example.

16.24 Stocks were made of two boards joined with iron clamps, leaving holes just big enough for the ankles. The prisoner's legs were placed across the lower board, and then the upper board was closed over them. Sometimes both wrists and ankles were placed in stocks. Paul and Silas, who had committed no crime and were peaceful men, were put in stocks designed for holding the most dangerous prisoners in absolute security.

16.27 The jailer drew his sword to kill himself because jailers were responsible for their prisoners and would be held accountable for their escape.

16.37 Paul refused to take his freedom and run. He wanted to teach the rulers in Philippi a lesson and to protect the other believers from the treatment he and Silas had received. The word would spread that Paul and Silas had been found innocent and freed by the leaders, and that believers should not be persecuted—especially if they were Roman citizens.

16.38 Roman citizenship carried with it certain privileges. These Philippian authorities were frightened because it was illegal to whip a Roman citizen. In addition, every citizen had the right to a fair trial—which Paul and Silas had not been given.

16.40 Acts 16.14,15

they were Roman citizens; 39 so they came and apologized to them. And they took them out and asked them to leave the city. 40 After leaving the prison they went to Lydia's home; and when they had seen and encouraged the brothers and sisters[q] there, they departed.

[q] Gk *brothers*

SILAS

The lives of the first Christian missionaries can be described with many words, but "boring" is not one of them. There were days of great excitement as men and women who had never heard of Jesus responded to the gospel. There were dangerous journeys over land and sea. Health risks and hunger were part of the daily routine. And there was open and hostile resistance to Christianity in many cities. Silas was one of the first missionaries, and he found out that serving Jesus Christ was certainly not boring!

Silas's name appears in Acts at the end of the first church conference on the Jewish/Gentile problem. The majority of early Christians were Jews who realized Jesus was the fulfillment of God's Old Testament promises to his people; however, the universal application of those promises had been overlooked. Thus, many felt that becoming Jewish was a prerequisite to becoming a Christian. The idea that God could accept a Gentile pagan was too incredible. But Gentiles began to accept Christ as Savior, and the transformation of their lives and the presence of God's Spirit confirmed their conversions. Some Jews were still reluctant, though, and insisted that these new Christians take on various Jewish customs. The issue came to a boiling point at the Jerusalem meeting but was peacefully resolved. Silas was one of the representatives from Jerusalem sent with Paul and Barnabas back to Antioch with an official letter of welcome and acceptance to the Gentile Christians. Having fulfilled this mission, Silas returned to Jerusalem. Within a short time, however, he was back in Antioch at Paul's request to join him on his second missionary journey.

Paul, Silas, and Timothy began a far-ranging ministry that included some exciting adventures. Paul and Silas spent a night singing in a Philippian prison after being severely beaten. An earthquake, the loosing of their chains, and the resulting panic led to the conversion of their jailer. Later, they narrowly missed another beating in Thessalonica, prevented by an evening escape. In Beroea there was more trouble, but Silas and Timothy stayed to teach the young believers while Paul traveled on to Athens. The team was finally reunited in Corinth. In each place they visited, they left behind a small group of Christians.

Silas leaves the story as suddenly as he entered it. Peter mentions him as the co-author of 1 Peter, but we do not know when he joined Peter. He was an effective believer before leaving Jerusalem, and he doubtless continued to minister after his work with Paul was completed. He took advantage of opportunities to serve God and was not discouraged by the setbacks and opposition he met along the way. Silas, though not the most famous of the early missionaries, was certainly a hero worth imitating.

Strengths and accomplishments:
- Was a leader in the Jerusalem church
- Represented the church in carrying the "acceptance letter" prepared by the Jerusalem council to the Gentile believers in Antioch
- Was closely associated with Paul from the second missionary journey on
- When imprisoned with Paul in Philippi, sang songs of praise to God
- Worked as a writing secretary for both Paul and Peter, using "Silvanus" as his pen name

Lessons from his life:
- Partnership is a significant part of effective ministry
- God never guarantees that his servants will not suffer
- Obedience to God will often mean giving up what makes us feel secure

Vital statistics:
- Where: Roman citizen living in Jerusalem
- Occupation: One of the first career missionaries
- Contemporaries: Paul, Timothy, Peter, Mark, Barnabas

Key verses:
"We have decided unanimously to choose representatives and send them to you, along with our beloved Barnabas and Paul, who have risked their lives for the sake of our Lord Jesus Christ. We have therefore sent Judas and Silas, who themselves will tell you the same things by word of mouth" (Acts 15.25–27).

Silas's story is told in Acts 15.22—19.10. He is also mentioned in 2 Corinthians 1.19; 1 Thessalonians 1.1; 2 Thessalonians 1.1; 1 Peter 5.12.

Paul preaches in Thessalonica

17 After Paul and Silas[r] had passed through Amphipolis and Apollonia, they
came to Thessalonica, where there was a synagogue of the Jews. 2 And Paul
went in, as was his custom, and on three sabbath days argued with them from the
scriptures, 3 explaining and proving that it was necessary for the Messiah[s] to suffer
and to rise from the dead, and saying, "This is the Messiah,[s] Jesus whom I am
proclaiming to you." 4 Some of them were persuaded and joined Paul and Silas, as
did a great many of the devout Greeks and not a few of the leading women. 5 But
the Jews became jealous, and with the help of some ruffians in the marketplaces
they formed a mob and set the city in an uproar. While they were searching for Paul
and Silas to bring them out to the assembly, they attacked Jason's house. 6 When
they could not find them, they dragged Jason and some believers[t] before the city
authorities,[u] shouting, "These people who have been turning the world upside
down have come here also, 7 and Jason has entertained them as guests. They are all
acting contrary to the decrees of the emperor, saying that there is another king
named Jesus." 8 The people and the city officials were disturbed when they heard
this, 9 and after they had taken bail from Jason and the others, they let them go.

Those at Beroea search the Scriptures

10 That very night the believers[t] sent Paul and Silas off to Beroea; and when
they arrived, they went to the Jewish synagogue. 11 These Jews were more recep-

17.1 Phil 4.16; 1 Thess 1.1
17.2 Acts 9.20; 13.5,14; 14.1; 17.10,17; 19.8
17.3 Lk 24.26; Acts 3.18; 9.22; 18.5
17.5 Rom 16.21
17.6 Acts 16.20,21
17.7 Lk 23.2

[r] Gk *they* [s] Or *the Christ* [t] Gk *brothers* [u] Gk *politarchs*

17.1 Thessalonica was one of the wealthiest and most influential cities in Macedonia. This is the first city Paul visited where his teachings attracted a large group of socially prominent citizens. The church he planted grew quickly, but in A.D. 50–51, Paul was forced out of the city by a mob (17.5, 6, 10). Paul later sent Timothy back to Thessalonica to see how the Christians were doing. Soon afterward, Paul wrote two letters to the Thessalonian believers (1 and 2 Thessalonians), encouraging them to remain faithful and to refuse to listen to false teachers who tried to refute their beliefs.

17.1, 2 A synagogue, a group of Jews who gathered for teaching and prayer, could be established wherever there were ten Jewish males. Paul's regular practice was to preach in synagogues as long as the Jews allowed it. Often those who weren't Jews came to these services and heard Paul's preaching. For a description of a synagogue service, see the note on 13.14, 15.

17.2, 3 When Paul spoke in the synagogues, he wisely began by talking about Old Testament writings and explaining how the Messiah fulfilled them, moving from the known to the unknown. This is a good strategy for us. When we witness for Christ, we should begin where people are, affirming the truth they do know, and then present Christ, the One who is Truth.

17.5 The Jewish leaders didn't refute the theology of Paul and Silas, but they were jealous of the popularity of these itinerant preachers. Their motives for causing the uproar were rooted in personal jealousy, not doctrinal purity.

17.6 We don't know much about Jason except that he evidently was the local host and sponsor of Paul and Silas; thus he took the heat for all the problems. Jason is just one of many "unsung heroes" who faithfully played their part to help spread the gospel. Because of his courage, Paul and Silas were able to minister more effectually. You may not receive much attention (and maybe only grief) for your service for Christ. But God wants to use you. Lives will be changed because of your courage and faithfulness.

17.6 What a reputation these early Christians had; they were truly "turning the world upside down!" The power of the gospel revolutionized lives, crossed all social barriers, threw open prison doors, caused people to care deeply for one another, and stirred them to worship God. Our world needs to be turned upside down, to be transformed. The gospel is not in the business of merely improving programs and conduct, but of dynamically transforming lives. Take courage and ask God how you can help turn your world upside down.

MINISTRY IN MACEDONIA
Luke stayed in Philippi while Paul, Silas, and Timothy continued on the Egnatian Way to Amphipolis, Apollonia, and Thessalonica. But trouble arose in Thessalonica, and they fled to Beroea. When their enemies from Thessalonica pursued them, Paul set out by sea to Athens, leaving Silas and Timothy to encourage the believers.

17.7 The Jewish leaders had difficulty manufacturing an accusation that would be heard by the city government. The Romans did not care about theological disagreements between the Jews and these preachers. Treason, however, was a serious offense in the Roman Empire. Although Paul and Silas were not advocating rebellion against Roman law, their loyalty to another king sounded suspicious.

17.8, 9 Jason posted bail—putting up cash for freedom. By doing so, he promised that the trouble would cease or his own property and possibly his life would be taken.

17.11 How do you evaluate sermons and teachings? The people in Beroea opened the Scriptures for themselves and searched for truths to verify or disprove the message they heard. Always compare what you hear with what the Bible says. A preacher or teacher who gives God's true message will never contradict or explain away anything in God's Word.

17.11 Isa 34.16 Lk 16.29 Jn 5.39 Acts 26.22,23
17.13 1 Thess 2.15
17.14 Mt 10.23
17.15 Acts 18.5 1 Thess 3.1

tive than those in Thessalonica, for they welcomed the message very eagerly and
examined the scriptures every day to see whether these things were so. 12 Many of
them therefore believed, including not a few Greek women and men of high standing. 13 But when the Jews of Thessalonica learned that the word of God had been
proclaimed by Paul in Beroea as well, they came there too, to stir up and incite the
crowds. 14 Then the believers[v] immediately sent Paul away to the coast, but Silas
and Timothy remained behind. 15 Those who conducted Paul brought him as far as
Athens; and after receiving instructions to have Silas and Timothy join him as soon
as possible, they left him.

In Athens Paul tells about the unknown God

17.16 Acts 18.1
17.18 1 Cor 1.20-24 4.10

16 While Paul was waiting for them in Athens, he was deeply distressed to see
that the city was full of idols. 17 So he argued in the synagogue with the Jews and
the devout persons, and also in the marketplace[w] every day with those who happened to be there. 18 Also some Epicurean and Stoic philosophers debated with
him. Some said, "What does this babbler want to say?" Others said, "He seems to
be a proclaimer of foreign divinities." (This was because he was telling the good
news about Jesus and the resurrection.) 19 So they took him and brought him to the
Areopagus and asked him, "May we know what this new teaching is that you are
presenting? 20 It sounds rather strange to us, so we would like to know what it
means." 21 Now all the Athenians and the foreigners living there would spend their
time in nothing but telling or hearing something new.
22 Then Paul stood in front of the Areopagus and said, "Athenians, I see how

[v] Gk *brothers* [w] Or *civic center*, Gk *agora*

THE BOOKS OF THE NEW TESTAMENT: WHEN WERE THEY WRITTEN?

Book	*Approximate Date*	*Book*	*Approximate Date*
Galatians	49	Jude	65
James	49	1 Timothy	64
1, 2 Thessalonians	51/52	1 Peter	64/65
1, 2 Corinthians	55	Titus	64
Romans	57	Acts	66/68
Mark	58/60	2 Peter	66/68
Ephesians	60	2 Timothy	66/67
Colossians	60	Hebrews	68/70
Philemon	60	John	85
Philippians	61	1, 2, 3 John	85/90
Matthew	61/64	Revelation	95
Luke	61/64		

17.15 Athens, with its magnificent buildings and many gods, was a center for Greek culture, philosophy, and education. Philosophers and educated men were always ready to hear something new, so they invited Paul to speak to them at Mars Hill (the Areopagus – 17.18, 19).

17.18 The Epicureans and Stoics were the dominant philosophers in Greek culture. The Epicureans believed that seeking happiness or pleasure was the primary goal of life. By contrast, the Stoics placed thinking above feeling and tried to live in harmony with nature and reason, suppressing their desire for pleasure. Thus, they were very disciplined.

17.19 For a time the council or high court met on the Areopagus, a low hill in Athens near the Acropolis. As Paul stood there and spoke about the one true God, his audience could look down on the city and see the many idols representing gods that Paul claimed were worthless.

17.22 Paul was well prepared to speak to this group. He came from Tarsus, an educational center, and had the training and knowledge to present his beliefs clearly and persuasively. Paul was a rabbi, taught by the finest scholar of his day, Gamaliel, and he had spent much of his life thinking and reasoning through the Scriptures.

It is not enough to teach or preach with conviction. Like Paul, we must be prepared. The more we know about the Bible, what it means, and how to apply it to our lives, the more convincing our words will be. This does not mean we should avoid presenting the gospel until we feel adequately prepared. We should work with what we know, but always want to know more in order to reach more people and answer their questions and arguments more effectively.

17.22ff Paul's address is a good example of how to communicate the gospel. Paul did not begin by reciting Jewish history, as he usually did, for this would have been meaningless to his Greek audience. He began by building a case for the one true God, using examples they understood (17.22, 23). Then he established common ground by emphasizing what they agreed about God (17.24–29). Finally he moved his message to the person of Christ, centering on the resurrection (17.30, 31). When you witness to others, you can use Paul's approach: use examples, establish common ground, and then move people toward a decision about Jesus Christ.

extremely religious you are in every way. 23 For as I went through the city and
looked carefully at the objects of your worship, I found among them an altar with
the inscription, 'To an unknown god.' What therefore you worship as unknown,
this I proclaim to you. 24 The God who made the world and everything in it, he who
is Lord of heaven and earth, does not live in shrines made by human hands, 25 nor
is he served by human hands, as though he needed anything, since he himself gives
to all mortals life and breath and all things. 26 From one ancestor[x] he made all
nations to inhabit the whole earth, and he allotted the times of their existence and
the boundaries of the places where they would live, 27 so that they would search for
God[y] and perhaps grope for him and find him—though indeed he is not far from
each one of us. 28 For 'In him we live and move and have our being'; as even some
of your own poets have said,

'For we too are his offspring.'

29 Since we are God's offspring, we ought not to think that the deity is like gold, or
silver, or stone, an image formed by the art and imagination of mortals. 30 While
God has overlooked the times of human ignorance, now he commands all people
everywhere to repent, 31 because he has fixed a day on which he will have the world
judged in righteousness by a man whom he has appointed, and of this he has given
assurance to all by raising him from the dead."

32 When they heard of the resurrection of the dead, some scoffed; but others
said, "We will hear you again about this." 33 At that point Paul left them. 34 But
some of them joined him and became believers, including Dionysius the Areopa-
gite and a woman named Damaris, and others with them.

The governor releases Paul at Corinth

18 After this Paul[z] left Athens and went to Corinth. 2 There he found a Jew
named Aquila, a native of Pontus, who had recently come from Italy with his
wife Priscilla, because Claudius had ordered all Jews to leave Rome. Paul[a] went
to see them, 3 and, because he was of the same trade, he stayed with them, and they
worked together—by trade they were tentmakers. 4 Every sabbath he would argue
in the synagogue and would try to convince Jews and Greeks.

5 When Silas and Timothy arrived from Macedonia, Paul was occupied with
proclaiming the word,[b] testifying to the Jews that the Messiah[c] was Jesus. 6 When

17.23 Jn 4.22; 2 Thess 2.4
17.24 1 Kgs 8.27; Isa 42.5; Acts 7.48,49
17.25 Ps 50.10-12; Dan 4.35; Rom 11.36
17.26 Job 12.23; 14.5
17.27 Jer 23.23,24; Acts 14.17; Rom 1.20
17.28 Col 1.17-19; Heb 1.3
17.29 Isa 40.18-25; Rom 1.23
17.30 Acts 14.16,17; Rom 3.25
17.31 Acts 2.24; 10.42; Rom 2.16; 4.25
18.2 Rom 16.3; 1 Cor 16.19
18.3 Acts 20.34; 1 Cor 4.12; 9.15; 2 Cor 11.7
18.5 Acts 17.3; 18.28

[x] Gk *From one*; other ancient authorities read *From one blood* [y] Other ancient authorities read *the Lord* [z] Gk *he*
[a] Gk *He* [b] Gk *with the word* [c] Or *the Christ*

17.23 The Athenians built an idol to the unknown god for fear of missing blessings or receiving punishment. Paul's opening statement to the men of Athens was about their unknown god. Paul was not endorsing this god, but using the inscription as a point of entry for his witness to the one true God.

17.23 Paul explained the one true God to these educated men of Athens; although they were, in general, very religious, they did not know him. Today we have a "Christian" society, but to most people, God is still unknown. We need to proclaim who he is and make it clear what he did for all mankind through his Son Jesus Christ. We cannot assume that even religious people around us truly know Jesus or understand the importance of faith in him.

17.27, 28 God is in his creation and close to every one of us. But he is not trapped in his creation—he is transcendent. God is the Creator, not the creation. This means that God is sovereign and in control, while at the same time he is close and personal. Let the Creator of the universe rule your life.

17.30, 31 Paul did not leave his message unfinished. He confronted his listeners with Jesus' resurrection and its meaning to all people—either blessing or punishment. The Greeks had no concept of judgment. Most of them preferred worshiping many gods instead of just one, and the concept of resurrection was unbelievable and offensive to them. But Paul did not hold back the truth, no matter what they might think of it. He changed his approach to fit his audience, but he never changed his basic message.

17.32–34 Paul's speech received a mixed reaction: some laughed, some kept searching for more information, and a few believed. Dionysius was a member of the council that met at the Areopagus. Don't hesitate to tell others about Christ because you fear that some will not believe you. Don't expect a unanimously positive response to your witnessing. Even if only a few believe, it's worth the effort.

18.1 Corinth was the political and commercial center of Greece, surpassing Athens in importance. It had a reputation for great wickedness and immorality. A temple to Aphrodite—goddess of love and war—had been built on the large hill behind the city. In this popular religion, people worshiped the goddess by giving money to the temple and taking part in sexual acts with male and female temple prostitutes. Paul found Corinth a challenge and a great ministry opportunity. Later, he wrote a series of letters to the Corinthians dealing in part with the problems of immorality. First and Second Corinthians are two of those letters.

18.2, 3 Each Jewish boy learned a trade and tried to earn his living with it. Paul and Aquila had been trained in tentmaking, cutting and sewing the woven cloth of goat's hair into tents. Many tents were used to house soldiers, and so these tents may have been sold to the Roman army. As a tentmaker, Paul was able to go wherever God led him, carrying his livelihood with him. The word "tentmaker" in Greek was also used to describe a leather worker.

18.6 Ezek 3.18,19 Mt 10.14 27.24,25 Acts 13.46 20.26; 28.26-28

18.8 1 Cor 1.2,14

18.10 Isa 41.10 Jer 1.18 2 Tim 2.19

they opposed and reviled him, in protest he shook the dust from his clothes[d] and
said to them, "Your blood be on your own heads! I am innocent. From now on I
will go to the Gentiles." 7 Then he left the synagogue[e] and went to the house of a
man named Titius[f] Justus, a worshiper of God; his house was next door to the
synagogue. 8 Crispus, the official of the synagogue, became a believer in the Lord,
together with all his household; and many of the Corinthians who heard Paul
became believers and were baptized. 9 One night the Lord said to Paul in a vision,
"Do not be afraid, but speak and do not be silent; 10 for I am with you, and no one
will lay a hand on you to harm you, for there are many in this city who are my

[d] Gk *reviled him, he shook out his clothes* [e] Gk *left there* [f] Other ancient authorities read *Titus*

LUKE

One of the essential qualities of a good doctor is compassion. People need to know that their doctor cares. Even if he or she doesn't know what is wrong or isn't sure what to do, real concern is always a doctor's good medicine. Doctor Luke was a person of compassion.

Although we know few facts of his life, Luke has left us a strong impression of himself by what he wrote. In his Gospel, he emphasizes Jesus Christ's compassion. He vividly recorded both the power demonstrated by Christ's life and the care with which he treated people. Luke highlighted the relationships Jesus had with women. His writing in Acts is full of sharp verbal pictures of real people caught up in the greatest events of history. As a writer, Luke made a contribution whose value cannot be measured.

Luke was also a doctor. He had a traveling medical practice as Paul's companion. Since the gospel was often welcomed with whips and stones, the doctor was seldom without patients. It is even possible that Paul's "thorn in the flesh" was some kind of physical ailment that needed Luke's regular attention. Paul deeply appreciated Luke's skills and faithfulness.

God also made special use of Luke as the historian of the early church. Repeatedly, the details of Luke's descriptions have been proven accurate. The first words in his Gospel indicate his interest in the truth.

Luke's compassion reflected his Lord's. His skill as a doctor helped Paul. His passion for the facts as he recorded the life of Christ, the spread of the early church, and the lives of Christianity's missionaries gives us dependable sources for the basis of our faith. He accomplished all this while staying out of the spotlight. Perhaps his greatest example is the challenge to greatness even when we are not the center of attention.

Strengths and accomplishments:
- A humble, faithful, and useful companion of Paul
- A well-educated and trained physician
- A careful and exact historian
- Writer of both the Gospel of Luke and the Acts of the Apostles

Lessons from his life:
- The words we leave behind will be a lasting picture of who we are
- Even the most successful person needs the personal care of others
- Excellence is shown by how we work when no one is noticing

Vital statistics:
- Where: Probably met Paul in Troas
- Occupation: Doctor, historian, traveling companion
- Contemporaries: Paul; Timothy, Silas, Peter

Key verses:
"Since many have undertaken to set down an orderly account of the events that have been fulfilled among us, just as they were handed on to us by those who from the beginning were eyewitnesses and servants of the word, I too decided, after investigating everything carefully from the very first, to write an orderly account for you, most excellent Theophilus, so that you may know the truth concerning the things about which you have been instructed" (Luke 1.1–4).

Luke includes himself in the *we* sections of Acts 16—28. He is also mentioned in Luke 1.3; Acts 1.1; Colossians 4.14; 2 Timothy 4.11; Philemon 1.24.

18.6 Paul told the Jews he had done all he could for them. Because they rejected Jesus as their Messiah, he would go to the Gentiles, who would be more receptive.

18.10 In a vision, Christ told Paul that he had many people in Corinth. Sometimes we can feel alone or isolated, especially when we see wickedness all around us and we are persecuted for our faith. Usually, however, there are others in the neighborhood or community who also follow Christ. Ask God to lead you to them.

18.10, 11 Others who became Christians in Corinth were Phoebe (Romans 16.1 – Cenchreae was the port city of Corinth), Tertius (Romans 16.22), Erastus (Romans 16.23), Quartus (Romans 16.23), Chloe (1 Corinthians 1.11), Gaius (1 Corinthians 1.14), Stephanas and his household (1 Corinthians 16.15), Fortunatus (1 Corinthians 16.17), and Achaicus (1 Corinthians 16.17).

people." 11 He stayed there a year and six months, teaching the word of God among
them.
12 But when Gallio was proconsul of Achaia, the Jews made a united attack on 18.12 Rom 15.26
Paul and brought him before the tribunal. 13 They said, "This man is persuading 1 Thess 1.7; 2.16
people to worship God in ways that are contrary to the law." 14 Just as Paul was
about to speak, Gallio said to the Jews, "If it were a matter of crime or serious
villainy, I would be justified in accepting the complaint of you Jews; 15 but since it 18.15
is a matter of questions about words and names and your own law, see to it your- Acts 23.29 25.19
selves; I do not wish to be a judge of these matters." 16 And he dismissed them from
the tribunal. 17 Then all of them[g] seized Sosthenes, the official of the synagogue, 18.17
and beat him in front of the tribunal. But Gallio paid no attention to any of these Acts 18.8 1 Cor 1.1
things.

The return to Jerusalem and Antioch

18 After staying there for a considerable time, Paul said farewell to the believ- 18.18 Num 6.2,18
ers[h] and sailed for Syria, accompanied by Priscilla and Aquila. At Cenchreae he Rom 16.1
had his hair cut, for he was under a vow. 19 When they reached Ephesus, he left 1 Cor 9.20
them there, but first he himself went into the synagogue and had a discussion with 18.19 Eph 1.1
the Jews. 20 When they asked him to stay longer, he declined; 21 but on taking leave Rev 1.11; 2.1
of them, he said, "I[i] will return to you, if God wills." Then he set sail from 18.21 Acts 19.1
Ephesus. Jas 4.15

4. Third missionary journey

Apollos is instructed at Ephesus

22 When he had landed at Caesarea, he went up to Jerusalem[j] and greeted the 18.23
church, and then went down to Antioch. 23 After spending some time there he de- Isa 35.3 Gal 1.2; 4.14
parted and went from place to place through the region of Galatia[k] and Phrygia,
strengthening all the disciples. 18.24 Tit 3.13
24 Now there came to Ephesus a Jew named Apollos, a native of Alexandria.

[g] Other ancient authorities read *all the Greeks* [h] Gk *brothers* [i] Other ancient authorities read *I must at all costs keep the approaching festival in Jerusalem, but I* [j] Gk *went up* [k] Gk *the Galatian region*

18.11 During the year and a half that Paul stayed in wicked Corinth, he established a church and wrote two letters to the believers in Thessalonica (the books of 1 and 2 Thessalonians). Although he had been in Thessalonica for only a short time (17.1–15), he commended the believers there for their loving deeds, strong faith, and steadfast hope. While encouraging them to stay away from immorality, he dealt with the themes of salvation, suffering, and the second coming of Jesus Christ. He told them to continue to work hard while they awaited Christ's return.

18.12 Gallio was governor of Achaia (modern Greece) and the brother of Seneca the philosopher. He came to power in A.D. 51–52. The tribunal was the outdoor place where the civil court was held.

18.13 Paul was unjustly charged with treason. He was not encouraging obedience to a human king other than Caesar (see 17.7), nor was he speaking against the Roman Empire. Instead he was speaking about Christ's eternal kingdom.

18.14–16 This was an important judicial decision for the spread of the gospel in the Roman Empire. Judaism was a recognized religion under Roman law. As long as Christians were seen as part of Judaism, the court refused to hear cases brought against them. If they had claimed to be a new religion, they could easily have been outlawed by the government. In effect Gallio was saying, "I don't understand all your terminology and finer points of theology. Handle the matter yourself and don't bother me."

18.17 Crispus had been the leader of the synagogue, but he and his family were converted and joined the Christians (18.8). Sosthenes was chosen to take his place. The mob could have been Greeks venting their feelings against the Jews for causing turmoil. Or they may have been mixed with Jews who beat Sosthenes for losing the case and leaving the synagogue worse off than before. A Sosthenes is mentioned in 1 Corinthians 1.1, and many believe this was the same man who, in time, became a convert and companion of Paul.

18.18 This vow Paul took was probably a temporary nazirite vow that ended with shaving his head and offering the hair as a sacrifice (Numbers 6.18).

18.19 Ephesus was situated on an important trade route and was the main city of the Roman province of Asia. This was the location of the temple to the goddess Artemis (Acts 19.21–41). The city was a meeting place of many cultural influences. There was a sizable Jewish population living there who enjoyed special privileges.

18.22 This verse marks the end of Paul's second missionary journey and the beginning of the third, which lasted from A.D. 53–57. Leaving the church at Antioch (his home base), Paul headed toward Ephesus, but along the way he revisited the churches in Galatia and Phrygia (18.23). The heart of this trip was a lengthy stay (two to three years) in Ephesus. Before returning to Jerusalem, he also visited believers in Macedonia and Greece.

18.23 The region of Galatia and Phrygia is the area in south Galatia where Paul had previously preached the gospel (Acts 13.1–14.28).

18.25 Acts 18.2,18 19.3
18.27 1 Cor 3.6
18.28 Ps 22 Isa 7.14 9.6; 53 Jer 23.5,6 Dan 9.25,26 Mic 5.2 Lk 24.27

He was an eloquent man, well-versed in the scriptures. 25 He had been instructed in
the Way of the Lord; and he spoke with burning enthusiasm and taught accurately
the things concerning Jesus, though he knew only the baptism of John. 26 He began
to speak boldly in the synagogue; but when Priscilla and Aquila heard him, they
took him aside and explained the Way of God to him more accurately. 27 And when
he wished to cross over to Achaia, the believers[l] encouraged him and wrote to the
disciples to welcome him. On his arrival he greatly helped those who through grace
had become believers, 28 for he powerfully refuted the Jews in public, showing by
the scriptures that the Messiah[m] is Jesus.

[l] *Gk brothers* [m] *Or the Christ*

MINISTRY IN CORINTH AND EPHESUS
Paul left Athens and traveled on to Corinth, one of the greatest commercial centers of the empire, located on a narrow neck of land offering direct passage between the Aegean and Adriatic seas. When Paul left from the port of Corinth at Cenchreae, he visited Ephesus. He then traveled to Caesarea, from which he went on to Jerusalem to report on his trip before returning to Antioch.

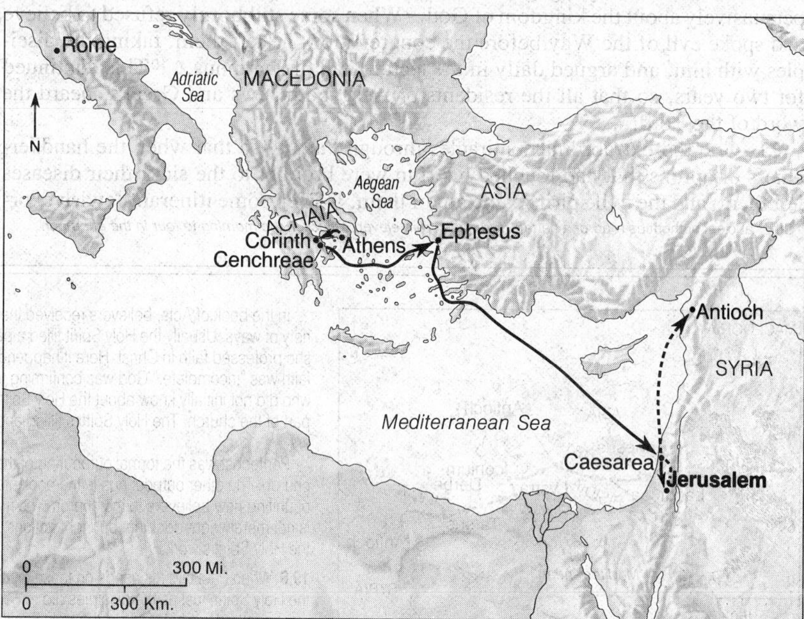

18.25, 26 Apollos had heard only what John the Baptist had said about Jesus (see Luke 3.1–18), so his message was not the complete story. John focused on repentance from sin, the first step. But the whole message is to repent from sin and then believe in Christ. Apollos did not know about Jesus' life, crucifixion, and resurrection. Nor did he know about the coming of the Holy Spirit. Priscilla and Aquila explained everything to him.

18.27, 28 Apollos was from Alexandria in Egypt, the second largest city in the Roman Empire, home of a great university. There was a thriving Jewish population in Alexandria. Apollos was a scholar, orator, and debater, and after his knowledge about Christ was made more complete, God greatly used these gifts to strengthen and encourage the church. Reason is a powerful tool in the right hands and the right situation. Apollos used it to convince many in Greece of the truth of the gospel. You don't have to turn off your mind when you turn to Christ. If you have an ability in logic or debate, use it to bring others to God.

18.27, 28 Not all the work of a minister or missionary is drudgery, setback, or suffering. Chapter 18 is triumphant, showing victories in key cities and the addition of exciting new leaders such as Priscilla, Aquila, and Apollos, to the church. Rejoice in the victories Christ brings, and don't let the hazards create a negative mindset.

18.27, 28 When Apollos crossed over to the province of Achaia, he probably went to the city of Corinth. Using the scriptures, he taught that Jesus is the Messiah. This was the same approach used by the apostle Paul (18.5). His teaching was so powerful that it became one of the factions in the church in Corinth (1 Corinthians 1.12). But Apollos did not promote division in the church, and Paul nowhere blamed Apollos for encouraging those who claimed to be part of the faction that was loyal to him.

18.28 *Messiah* means "Christ" or "Anointed One." The Jews were waiting for the Messiah to come, but there was confusion about what he would do. The main idea current at the time was that the Messiah would deliver his people from the Roman occupation. This was far from the purpose of Jesus, who came to save all people from their sins. Jesus avoided the use of the title of Messiah since it would have been misunderstood. But the early Christians triumphantly proclaimed that he was indeed the Messiah and waiting at God's right hand until all enemies would be placed at this feet.

Christians in Ephesus receive the Holy Spirit

19 While Apollos was in Corinth, Paul passed through the interior regions and
came to Ephesus, where he found some disciples. 2 He said to them, "Did
you receive the Holy Spirit when you became believers?" They replied, "No, we
have not even heard that there is a Holy Spirit." 3 Then he said, "Into what then
were you baptized?" They answered, "Into John's baptism." 4 Paul said, "John baptized with the baptism of repentance, telling the people to believe in the one who
was to come after him, that is, in Jesus." 5 On hearing this, they were baptized in
the name of the Lord Jesus. 6 When Paul had laid his hands on them, the Holy Spirit
came upon them, and they spoke in tongues and prophesied— 7 altogether there
were about twelve of them.

19.1 Acts 28.21
19.2 Acts 8.15,16
19.3 Lk 7.29
19.4 Acts 1.5; 11.16
19.5 Acts 8.12,16 10.48 Gal 3.27
19.6 Acts 2.4; 10.46

Paul ministers powerfully in Ephesus

8 He entered the synagogue and for three months spoke out boldly, and argued
persuasively about the kingdom of God. 9 When some stubbornly refused to believe
and spoke evil of the Way before the congregation, he left them, taking the disciples with him, and argued daily in the lecture hall of Tyrannus.[n] 10 This continued
for two years, so that all the residents of Asia, both Jews and Greeks, heard the
word of the Lord.

11 God did extraordinary miracles through Paul, 12 so that when the handker-
chiefs or aprons that had touched his skin were brought to the sick, their diseases
left them, and the evil spirits came out of them. 13 Then some itinerant Jewish exor-

19.8 Acts 1.3; 28.23,31
19.11 Mk 16.20
19.12 2 Kgs 4.29 Jn 14.12 Acts 5.15
19.13 Mt 12.26-28 Mk 9.38,39 Lk 9.49,50 11.19

[n] Other ancient authorities read *of a certain Tyrannus, from eleven o'clock in the morning to four in the afternoon*

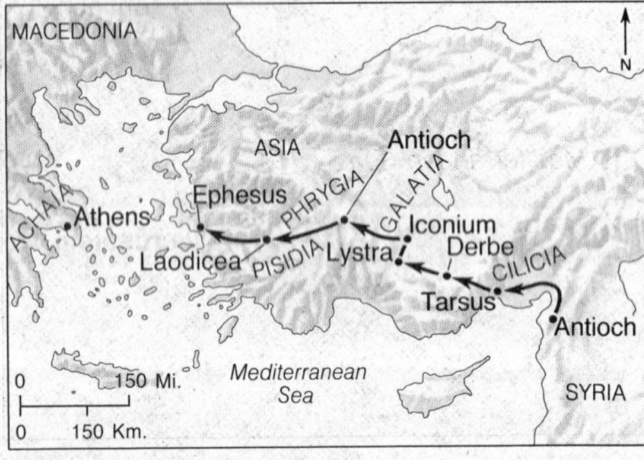

PAUL TAKES A THIRD JOURNEY What prompted Paul's third journey may have been the spread of his opponents' message in the churches Paul had planted. So he hurried north, then west, returning to many of the cities he had previously visited. This time, however, he stayed on a more direct westward route toward Ephesus.

19.1 Ephesus was the capital and leading business center of the Roman province of Asia (part of present-day Turkey). A hub of sea and land transportation, it ranked with Antioch in Syria and Alexandria in Egypt as one of the great cities on the Mediterranean Sea. Paul stayed in Ephesus for a little over two years. There he wrote his first letter to the Corinthians to counter several problems they were facing. Later, while imprisoned in Rome, Paul wrote a letter to the Ephesian church (the book of Ephesians).

19.2–4 John's baptism was a sign of repentance from sin only, not a sign of new life in Christ. Like Apollos (18.24–26), these Ephesian believers needed further instruction on the message and ministry of Jesus Christ. They believed in Jesus as the Messiah, but they did not understand the significance of his death and resurrection or the work of the Holy Spirit. Becoming a Christian involves turning from sin (repentance) and turning to Christ (faith). These "believers" were incomplete.

In the book of Acts, believers received the Holy Spirit in a variety of ways. Usually the Holy Spirit filled a person as soon as he or she professed faith in Christ. Here it happened later because their faith was "incomplete." God was confirming to these believers, who did not initially know about the Holy Spirit, that they were a part of the church. The Holy Spirit's filling endorsed them as believers.

Pentecost was the formal outpouring of the Holy Spirit to the church. The other outpourings in the book of Acts were God's way of uniting new believers to the church. The mark of the true church is not merely right doctrine, but right actions, the true evidence of the Holy Spirit's work.

19.6 When Paul laid his hands on these disciples, they received the Holy Spirit, just as the disciples did at Pentecost, and there were outward, visible signs of the Holy Spirit's presence. This also happened when the Holy Spirit came upon Gentiles (non-Jews, see 10.45–47).

19.9 Paul probably spoke in a lecture hall at this school. Such halls were used in the morning for teaching philosophy, but were empty during the hot part of the day (about 11 a.m. to 4 p.m.). Because many people did not work during those hours, they came to hear Paul's preaching.

19.10 Luke refers to Asia Minor or modern-day Turkey. During this time, Paul and his co-workers spread the gospel throughout the land.

19.13 "Itinerant Jewish exorcists" were people who traveled from town to town making a living by claiming to heal and cast out demons. Often they would recite a whole list of names in their incantation to be sure of including the right deity. Here they were trying to use Jesus' name in an effort to match Paul's power.

19.13–16 Many Ephesians engaged in exorcism and occult practices for profit (see 19.18, 19). The sons of Sceva were impressed by the work of Paul, whose power to cast out demons came from God's Holy Spirit, not from witchcraft, and was obviously more powerful than theirs. They discovered, however, that no one can control or duplicate God's power. These men were calling upon the name without knowing the person. The power to change people comes from Christ. It cannot be tapped by reciting his name like a magic charm. He works his power only through those he chooses.

cists tried to use the name of the Lord Jesus over those who had evil spirits, saying,
"I adjure you by the Jesus whom Paul proclaims." 14 Seven sons of a Jewish high
priest named Sceva were doing this. 15 But the evil spirit said to them in reply,
"Jesus I know, and Paul I know; but who are you?" 16 Then the man with the evil
spirit leaped on them, mastered them all, and so overpowered them that they fled
out of the house naked and wounded. 17 When this became known to all residents
of Ephesus, both Jews and Greeks, everyone was awestruck; and the name of the
Lord Jesus was praised. 18 Also many of those who became believers confessed and
disclosed their practices. 19 A number of those who practiced magic collected their

19.15 Mt 8.29 Mk 1.24 Lk 4.34 Acts 16.16-18 Jas 2.19
19.17 Lk 7.16
19.18 Isa 30.22 Jer 3.13

AQUILA, PRISCILLA

Some couples know how to make the most of life. They complement each other, utilize each other's strengths, and form an effective team. Their united efforts affect those around them. Aquila and Priscilla were such a couple. They are never mentioned separately in the Bible. In marriage and ministry, they were always together.

Priscilla and Aquila met Paul in Corinth while Paul was on his second missionary journey. They had just been expelled from Rome by Emperor Claudius's decree against the Jews. Their home was as movable as the tents they made to support themselves. They opened their home to Paul, and he joined them in tentmaking. He shared with them his wealth of spiritual wisdom.

Priscilla and Aquila made the most of their spiritual education. They listened carefully to sermons and evaluated what they heard. When they heard Apollos speak, they were impressed by his ability, but realized that the content of his message was not complete. Instead of open confrontation, the couple quietly took Apollos home and shared with him what he needed to know. Until then, Apollos had only known John the Baptist's message about Christ. Priscilla and Aquila told him about Jesus' life, death, and resurrection, and the reality of God's indwelling Spirit. He continued to preach powerfully—but now with the full story.

As for Priscilla and Aquila, they went on using their home as a warm place for training and worship. Back in Rome years later, they hosted one of the house churches that developed. The early Christians did not meet in church buildings but in the homes of members. This informal atmosphere provided opportunity for intimate fellowship.

In an age when the focus is mostly on what happens *between* husband and wife, Aquila and Priscilla are an example of what can happen *through* husband and wife. Their effectiveness together speaks about their relationship with each other. Their hospitality opened the doorway of salvation to many. The Christian home is still one of the best tools for spreading the gospel. Do guests find Christ in your home?

Strengths and accomplishments:
- Was an outstanding husband/wife team who ministered in the early church
- Supported themselves by tentmaking while serving Christ
- Were close friends of Paul
- Explained to Apollos the full message of Christ

Lessons from their lives:
- Couples can have an effective ministry together
- The home is a valuable tool for evangelism
- Every believer needs to be well educated in the faith, whatever his or her role in the church

Vital statistics:
- Where: Originally from Rome, moved to Corinth, then Ephesus
- Occupation: Tentmakers
- Contemporaries: Emperor Claudius, Paul, Timothy, Apollos

Key verses:
"Greet Prisca and Aquila, who work with me in Christ Jesus, and who risked their necks for my life, to whom not only I give thanks, but also all the churches of the Gentiles" (Romans 16.3, 4).

Their story is told in Acts 18. They are also mentioned in Romans 16.3–5; 1 Corinthians 16.19; 2 Timothy 4.19 (Priscilla is sometimes called Prisca).

19.18, 19 Ephesus was a center for black magic and other occult practices. The people sought spells to give them wealth, happiness, and success in marriage. Superstition and sorcery were commonplace. God clearly forbids such practices (Deuteronomy 18.9–13). You cannot be a believer and hold on to the occult, black magic, or sorcery. Once you begin to dabble in these areas, it is extremely easy to become obsessed by them because Satan is very powerful. But God's power is even greater (1 John 4.4; Revelation 20.10). If you are mixed up in the occult, learn a lesson from the Ephesians and get rid of anything that could lure you into such practices.

books and burned them publicly; when the value of these books[o] was calculated,
it was found to come to fifty thousand silver coins. 20 So the word of the Lord grew 19.20 Acts 6.7; 12.24
mightily and prevailed. 19.10

The craftsmen cause a riot

21 Now after these things had been accomplished, Paul resolved in the Spirit to
go through Macedonia and Achaia, and then to go on to Jerusalem. He said, "After
I have gone there, I must also see Rome." 22 So he sent two of his helpers, Timothy 19.22
and Erastus, to Macedonia, while he himself stayed for some time longer in Asia. Acts 16.9 Rom 16.23
23 About that time no little disturbance broke out concerning the Way. 24 A man 2 Tim 4.20
named Demetrius, a silversmith who made silver shrines of Artemis, brought no 19.23 2 Cor 1.8
little business to the artisans. 25 These he gathered together, with the workers of the 19.24
same trade, and said, "Men, you know that we get our wealth from this business. Acts 16.16,19
26 You also see and hear that not only in Ephesus but in almost the whole of Asia 19.25 1 Tim 6.10
this Paul has persuaded and drawn away a considerable number of people by saying 19.26
that gods made with hands are not gods. 27 And there is danger not only that this 1 Chron 16.26 Ps 115.4
trade of ours may come into disrepute but also that the temple of the great goddess Isa 44.10-20
Artemis will be scorned, and she will be deprived of her majesty that brought all 46.7 Jer 16.20
Asia and the world to worship her." Acts 17.29 1 Cor 8.4
28 When they heard this, they were enraged and shouted, "Great is Artemis of 19.28
the Ephesians!" 29 The city was filled with the confusion; and people[p] rushed Jer 50.38
together to the theater, dragging with them Gaius and Aristarchus, Macedonians Hab 2.18-20 19.29
who were Paul's travel companions. 30 Paul wished to go into the crowd, but the Acts 20.4; 27.2
disciples would not let him; 31 even some officials of the province of Asia,[q] who Rom 16.23 1 Cor 1.14
were friendly to him, sent him a message urging him not to venture into the theater. Col 4.10
32 Meanwhile, some were shouting one thing, some another; for the assembly was Philem 24 19.32
in confusion, and most of them did not know why they had come together. 33 Some Acts 21.34
of the crowd gave instructions to Alexander, whom the Jews had pushed forward. 19.33 1 Tim 1.20
And Alexander motioned for silence and tried to make a defense before the people. 2 Tim 4.14
34 But when they recognized that he was a Jew, for about two hours all of them
shouted in unison, "Great is Artemis of the Ephesians!" 35 But when the town clerk
had quieted the crowd, he said, "Citizens of Ephesus, who is there that does not
know that the city of the Ephesians is the temple keeper of the great Artemis and of
the statue that fell from heaven?[r] 36 Since these things cannot be denied, you ought

[o] Gk *them* [p] Gk *they* [q] Gk *some of the Asiarchs* [r] Meaning of Gk uncertain

---

19.21 Why did Paul say he had to go to Rome? Wherever he went, he could see Rome's influence. Paul wanted to take the message of Christ to the world's center of influence and power.

19.22 Paul mentions Timothy in more detail in the books of 1 and 2 Timothy. Erastus was a committed follower of Christ who was not only Paul's helpful assistant, but also the city treasurer of Corinth (see Romans 16.23).

19.23 "The Way" refers to those who followed the way of Christ—the Christians.

19.24 Artemis was a goddess of fertility. She was represented by a carved female figure with many breasts. A large statue of her (which was said to have come from heaven, from Jupiter, the king of the gods, 19.35) was in the great temple at Ephesus, one of the wonders of the ancient world. The festival of Artemis involved wild orgies and carousing. Obviously the religious and commercial life of Ephesus reflected this pagan deity.

19.25–27 When Paul preached in Ephesus, Demetrius and his fellow shrinemakers did not quarrel with his doctrine. Their anger boiled because his preaching threatened their profits. They made statues of the Greek goddess Artemis (her Roman counterpart was Diana) and her temple. If people started believing in God and discarding the idols, their livelihood would suffer.

Jesus does not promise that we will escape persecution, but that he will give us a way through it. He also promises not to send us through persecution alone. He said, "I am with you always, to the end of the age" (Matthew 28.20).

19.27 Demetrius's strategy for stirring up a riot was to appeal to the people's love of money and then hide their greed behind the mask of patriotism and religious loyalty. The rioters couldn't see the selfish motives for their rioting—instead they saw themselves as heroes for the sake of their land and beliefs.

19.29 Paul often sought others to help him in his work. On this occasion, his traveling companions were Aristarchus (who would accompany him on other journeys; see 20.3, 4 and 27.1, 2), and Gaius (probably not the same Gaius mentioned in Romans 16.23 or 1 Corinthians 1.14).

19.30 Paul wanted to go to the theater to speak up and defend his companions, but the other believers wouldn't let him go, fearing for his safety.

19.30, 31 These men were government officials responsible for the religious and political order of the region. Paul's message had reached all levels of society, crossing all social barriers and giving Paul friends in high places.

19.33, 34 The mob had become anti-Jewish as well as anti-Christian. This Alexander may have been pulled forward by the Jews as a spokesman to explain that the Jews had no part in the Christian community, and thus had no part in the economic problem of the silversmiths.

to be quiet and do nothing rash. 37 You have brought these men here who are neither
temple robbers nor blasphemers of our[s] goddess. 38 If therefore Demetrius and the
artisans with him have a complaint against anyone, the courts are open, and there
are proconsuls; let them bring charges there against one another. 39 If there is anything further[t] you want to know, it must be settled in the regular assembly. 40 For
we are in danger of being charged with rioting today, since there is no cause that we
can give to justify this commotion." 41 When he had said this, he dismissed the
assembly.

[s] Other ancient authorities read *your* [t] Other ancient authorities read *about other matters*

APOLLOS

Some people have an amazing natural talent for public speaking. A few even have a great message to go along with it. When Apollos arrived in Ephesus shortly after Paul's departure, he made an immediate impact. He spoke boldly in public, interpreting and applying the Old Testament effectively. He debated opponents forcefully and effectively. It didn't take long for him to be noticed by Priscilla and Aquila.

The couple quickly realized that Apollos did not have the whole story. His preaching was based on the Old Testament and John the Baptist's message. He was probably urging people to repent and prepare for the coming Messiah. Priscilla and Aquila took Apollos home with them and brought him up to date on all that had happened. As they told him of the life of Jesus, his death and resurrection, and the coming of the Holy Spirit, Apollos must have seen scripture after scripture become clear. He was filled with new energy and boldness, now that he had the complete gospel.

Apollos next decided to travel to Achaia. His friends in Ephesus were able to send along a glowing letter of introduction. He quickly became the verbal champion of the Christians in Corinth, debating the opponents of the gospel in public. As often happens, Apollos's abilities eventually created a problem. Some of the Corinthians began to follow Apollos rather than his message. Paul had to confront the Corinthians about their divisiveness. They had been forming little groups named after their favorite preacher. Apollos left Corinth and hesitated to return. Paul wrote warmly of Apollos as a fellow minister who had "watered" the seeds of the gospel that Paul had planted in Corinth. Paul last mentions Apollos briefly to Titus. He was still a traveling representative of the gospel who deserved Titus's help.

Although his natural abilities could have made him proud, Apollos proved himself willing to learn. Because Apollos did not hesitate to be a student, he became an even better teacher. How much does your willingness to learn affect God's efforts to help you become all he wants you to be?

Strengths and accomplishments:
- A gifted and persuasive preacher and apologist in the early church
- Willing to be taught
- Mentioned as the possible author of Hebrews

Lessons from his life:
- Effective communication of the gospel includes an accurate message delivered with God's power
- A clear verbal defense of the gospel can be a real encouragement to believers, while convincing non-believers of its truth

Vital statistics:
- Where: From Alexandria in Egypt
- Occupation: Traveling preacher, apologist
- Contemporaries: Priscilla, Aquila, Paul

Key verses:
"He had been instructed in the Way of the Lord; and he spoke with burning enthusiasm and taught accurately the things concerning Jesus, though he knew only the baptism of John. He began to speak boldly in the synagogue; but when Priscilla and Aquila heard him, they took him aside and explained the Way of God to him more accurately" (Acts 18.25, 26).

Apollos's story is told in Acts 18.24—19.1. He is also mentioned in 1 Corinthians 1.12; 3.4–6, 22; 4.1, 6; 16.12; Titus 3.13.

19.38 A proconsul served as a civil magistrate of a Roman province.

19.40 The city of Ephesus was under the domination of the Roman Empire. The main responsibility of the local city leaders was simply to maintain peace and order. If they failed to control the people, Rome would remove them from office.

19.41 The riot in Ephesus showed Paul that it was time to move on. But it also showed that the law still provided some protection for Christians as they confronted the worship of the goddess Diana in the most idolatrous religion in Asia.

Paul raises Eutychus from the dead at Troas

20 After the uproar had ceased, Paul sent for the disciples; and after encouraging them and saying farewell, he left for Macedonia. 2 When he had gone
through those regions and had given the believers[u] much encouragement, he came
to Greece, 3 where he stayed for three months. He was about to set sail for Syria **20.3**
when a plot was made against him by the Jews, and so he decided to return through Acts 9.24; 20.19 23.12,13
Macedonia. 4 He was accompanied by Sopater son of Pyrrhus from Beroea, by Ar- 2 Cor 11.26
istarchus and Secundus from Thessalonica, by Gaius from Derbe, and by Timo- **20.4** Acts 16.1
thy, as well as by Tychicus and Trophimus from Asia. 5 They went ahead and were 19.22,29; 21.29 Eph 6.21
waiting for us in Troas; 6 but we sailed from Philippi after the days of Unleavened 2 Tim 4.12,20
Bread, and in five days we joined them in Troas, where we stayed for seven days. Tit 3.12
7 On the first day of the week, when we met to break bread, Paul was holding **20.6** Ex 23.15
a discussion with them; since he intended to leave the next day, he continued speak- 2 Cor 2.12
ing until midnight. 8 There were many lamps in the room upstairs where we were **20.7** Acts 2.42
meeting. 9 A young man named Eutychus, who was sitting in the window, began to 1 Cor 10.16,17 11.20-34; 16.2
sink off into a deep sleep while Paul talked still longer. Overcome by sleep, he fell Rev 1.10
to the ground three floors below and was picked up dead. 10 But Paul went down, **20.10**
and bending over him took him in his arms, and said, "Do not be alarmed, for his 1 Kgs 17.21 2 Kgs 4.34
life is in him." 11 Then Paul went upstairs, and after he had broken bread and eaten, Mt 9.23-25
he continued to converse with them until dawn; then he left. 12 Meanwhile they had Mk 5.39-42
taken the boy away alive and were not a little comforted.

Paul's farewell to the elders of Ephesus

13 We went ahead to the ship and set sail for Assos, intending to take Paul on
board there; for he had made this arrangement, intending to go by land himself.
14 When he met us in Assos, we took him on board and went to Mitylene. 15 We **20.15**
sailed from there, and on the following day we arrived opposite Chios. The next Acts 21.4,12 24.17
day we touched at Samos, and[v] the day after that we came to Miletus. 16 For Paul 2 Tim 4.20
had decided to sail past Ephesus, so that he might not have to spend time in Asia, **20.18** Acts 18.19
he was eager to be in Jerusalem, if possible, on the day of Pentecost. 19.1,10
17 From Miletus he sent a message to Ephesus, asking the elders of the church
to meet him. 18 When they came to him, he said to them:

[u] Gk *given them* [v] Other ancient authorities add *after remaining at Trogyllium*

20.1–3 While in Greece, Paul spent much of his time in Corinth. From there he wrote the letter to the Romans. Although he had not yet been to Rome, believers had already started a church there (2.10; 18.2). Paul wrote that he planned to visit the Roman believers. The letter to the Romans is a theological essay on the meaning of salvation and faith, an explanation of the relation between Jews and Gentiles in Christ, and a list of practical guidelines for the church.

20.4 These men traveling with Paul represented churches he had started in Asia. Each man was carrying an offering from his home church to the believers in Jerusalem. By having each man deliver the gift, the gifts had a personal touch and the unity of the believers was strengthened. This was also an effective way to teach the church about giving because the men were able to report to their churches what they had seen. Paul discussed this gift in one of his letters to the Corinthian church (see 2 Corinthians 8.1–21).

20.5, 6 The use of *us* and *we* shows that this is where Luke again joins the group. The last *we* was in chapter 16.

20.6 Jewish believers celebrated the Passover (which was immediately followed by the festival of Unleavened Bread) according to Moses' instructions (see Exodus 12.43–51) even if they couldn't go to Jerusalem.

20.7 A fellowship meal—much like a potluck supper—was eaten just before the Lord's supper was celebrated with the breaking of bread and drinking of the cup.

20.8, 9 The many lamps were candles in lanterns. These and the gathered assembly in an upstairs room probably made it very warm. This no doubt helped Eutychus fall asleep, as well as the fact that Paul spoke for a long time. Eutychus was 8–14 years old (the age of a "young man").

THROUGH MACEDONIA AND ACHAIA
A riot in Ephesus sent Paul to Troas, then through Macedonia to the region of Achaia. In Achaia he went to Corinth to deal with problems there. Paul had planned to sail from there straight to Antioch in Syria, but a plot against his life was discovered. So he retraced his steps through Macedonia.

20.21 Lk 24.47 Acts 2.38 11.18; 26.20
20.22 Acts 19.21
20.23 Acts 9.16 21.4,11,33
20.24 Acts 21.13 2 Tim 4.7
20.26 Acts 18.6
20.28 Jn 21.15-17 1 Pet 1.19; 5.2 Rev 5.9
20.29 Ezek 22.27 Mt 7.15 Jn 10.10,12
20.31 Acts 19.10
20.32 Jn 17.17 Acts 9.31; 26.18 Eph 1.18 Col 3.24 1 Pet 1.4; 2.2
20.33 1 Sam 12.3 1 Cor 9.12 2 Cor 7.2 11.8,9; 12.17

"You yourselves know how I lived among you the entire time from the first day
that I set foot in Asia, 19 serving the Lord with all humility and with tears, enduring
the trials that came to me through the plots of the Jews. 20 I did not shrink from
doing anything helpful, proclaiming the message to you and teaching you publicly
and from house to house, 21 as I testified to both Jews and Greeks about repentance
toward God and faith toward our Lord Jesus. 22 And now, as a captive to the
Spirit,[w] I am on my way to Jerusalem, not knowing what will happen to me there,
23 except that the Holy Spirit testifies to me in every city that imprisonment and
persecutions are waiting for me. 24 But I do not count my life of any value to myself, if only I may finish my course and the ministry that I received from the Lord
Jesus, to testify to the good news of God's grace.
25 "And now I know that none of you, among whom I have gone about proclaiming the kingdom, will ever see my face again. 26 Therefore I declare to you
this day that I am not responsible for the blood of any of you, 27 for I did not shrink
from declaring to you the whole purpose of God. 28 Keep watch over yourselves
and over all the flock, of which the Holy Spirit has made you overseers, to shepherd
the church of God[x] that he obtained with the blood of his own Son.[y] 29 I know that
after I have gone, savage wolves will come in among you, not sparing the flock.
30 Some even from your own group will come distorting the truth in order to entice
the disciples to follow them. 31 Therefore be alert, remembering that for three years
I did not cease night or day to warn everyone with tears. 32 And now I commend you
to God and to the message of his grace, a message that is able to build you up and
to give you the inheritance among all who are sanctified. 33 I coveted no one's silver

[w] Or *And now, bound in the spirit* [x] Other ancient authorities read *of the Lord* [y] Or *with his own blood*; Gk *with the blood of his Own*

PAUL TRAVELS FROM TROAS TO MILETUS
From Troas, Paul traveled overland to Assos, then boarded a ship to Mitylene and Samos on its way to Miletus. He summoned the elders of the Ephesian church to say farewell to them because he knew he would probably not see them again.

20.16 Paul had missed attending the Passover feast in Jerusalem, so he was especially interested in arriving on time for Pentecost, which was 50 days after Passover. He was carrying with him gifts for the Jerusalem believers from churches in Asia and Greece (see Romans 15.25, 26; 1 Corinthians 16.1ff; 2 Corinthians 8, 9). The Jerusalem church was experiencing difficult times. Paul may have been anxious to deliver this gift to the believers at Pentecost because it was a day of celebration and thanksgiving to God for his provision.

20.18–21 The way of the believer is not an easy road; being a Christian does not solve all problems. Paul sowed humbly and "with tears," but he never quit, never gave up. The message of salvation was so important that he never missed an opportunity to share it. And although he preached his message in different ways to fit different audiences, the message remained the same—turning away from sin and turning to Christ by faith. The Christian life will have its rough times, its tears, and its joys, but we should always be ready to tell others what good things God has done for us. His blessings far outweigh life's difficulties.

20.22 "Captive to the Spirit" could be translated, "drawn irresistibly by the Holy Spirit."

20.23 The Holy Spirit showed Paul that he would be imprisoned and would suffer. Even knowing this, Paul did not shrink from fulfilling his mission. His strong character was a good example to the Ephesian elders, some of whom would also suffer for Christ.

20.24 We often feel that life is a failure unless we're getting a lot out of it: recognition, fun, money, success. But Paul thought life was worth *nothing* unless he used it for God's work. What he put *into* life was far more important than what he got out. Which is more important to you—what you get out of life, or what you put into it?

20.24 Singlemindedness is a quality needed by anyone who wishes to do God's work. Paul was a singleminded person, and the most important goal of his life was to tell others about Christ (Philippians 3.7–13). It is no wonder that Paul was the greatest missionary who ever lived. God is looking for more men and women who focus on that one great task God has given them to do.

20.31, 36–38 Paul's relationship with these believers is a beautiful example of Christian fellowship. He had cared for them and loved them, even cried over their needs. They responded with love and care for him and sorrow over his leaving. They had prayed together and comforted one another. Like Paul, you can build strong relationships with other Christians by sharing, caring, sorrowing, rejoicing, and praying with them. You will gather others around you only by giving yourself away to them.

20.33 Paul was satisfied with whatever he had, wherever he was, as long as he could do God's work. Examine your attitudes toward wealth and comfort. If you focus more on what you don't have than on what you do have, it's time to reexamine your priorities and put God's work back in first place.

or gold or clothing. 34 You know for yourselves that I worked with my own hands
to support myself and my companions. 35 In all this I have given you an example
that by such work we must support the weak, remembering the words of the Lord
Jesus, for he himself said, 'It is more blessed to give than to receive.' "
36 When he had finished speaking, he knelt down with them all and prayed.
37 There was much weeping among them all; they embraced Paul and kissed him,
38 grieving especially because of what he had said, that they would not see him
again. Then they brought him to the ship.

Paul continues to Jerusalem

21 When we had parted from them and set sail, we came by a straight course to
Cos, and the next day to Rhodes, and from there to Patara.[z] 2 When we
found a ship bound for Phoenicia, we went on board and set sail. 3 We came in sight
of Cyprus; and leaving it on our left, we sailed to Syria and landed at Tyre, because
the ship was to unload its cargo there. 4 We looked up the disciples and stayed there
for seven days. Through the Spirit they told Paul not to go on to Jerusalem. 5 When
our days there were ended, we left and proceeded on our journey; and all of them,
with wives and children, escorted us outside the city. There we knelt down on the
beach and prayed 6 and said farewell to one another. Then we went on board the
ship, and they returned home.
7 When we had finished[a] the voyage from Tyre, we arrived at Ptolemais; and
we greeted the believers[b] and stayed with them for one day. 8 The next day we left
and came to Caesarea; and we went into the house of Philip the evangelist, one of
the seven, and stayed with him. 9 He had four unmarried daughters[c] who had the
gift of prophecy. 10 While we were staying there for several days, a prophet named
Agabus came down from Judea. 11 He came to us and took Paul's belt, bound his
own feet and hands with it, and said, "Thus says the Holy Spirit, 'This is the way
the Jews in Jerusalem will bind the man who owns this belt and will hand him over
to the Gentiles.' " 12 When we heard this, we and the people there urged him not to
go up to Jerusalem. 13 Then Paul answered, "What are you doing, weeping and
breaking my heart? For I am ready not only to be bound but even to die in Jerusalem
for the name of the Lord Jesus." 14 Since he would not be persuaded, we remained
silent except to say, "The Lord's will be done."
15 After these days we got ready and started to go up to Jerusalem. 16 Some of
the disciples from Caesarea also came along and brought us to the house of Mnason
of Cyprus, an early disciple, with whom we were to stay.

5. Paul on trial

Paul arrives at Jerusalem

17 When we arrived in Jerusalem, the brothers welcomed us warmly. 18 The

20.34 1 Cor 4.12 1 Thess 2.9 2 Thess 3.8
20.35 2 Cor 8.9 1 Thess 4.11 5.14 Heb 13.1,3
21.4 Acts 20.23; 21.11
21.5 Acts 20.36
21.8 Acts 6.3,5 8.26,40 Eph 4.11
21.9 Joel 2.28 Acts 2.17
21.10 Acts 11.28
21.11 Acts 20.23; 21.3 Eph 6.20
21.13 Acts 20.24 2 Cor 4.10 Col 1.24
21.14 Mt 26.42

[z] Other ancient authorities add *and Myra* [a] Or *continued* [b] Gk *brothers* [c] Gk *four daughters, virgins,*

20.34 Paul was a tentmaker, and he supported himself with this trade. Paul worked to show he was free of covetousness, not to grow rich. He supported himself and others working with him (he also mentions this in some of his letters; see Philippians 4.11–13; 1 Thessalonians 2.9).

20.35 These words of Jesus are not recorded in the Gospels. Obviously, not all of Jesus' words were written down (John 21.25); this saying may have been passed on orally through the apostles.

21.4 Did Paul disobey the Holy Spirit by going to Jerusalem? No. More likely, the Holy Spirit warned these believers about the suffering Paul would face in Jerusalem. They drew the conclusion that he should not go because of that danger. This is supported by 21.10–12 where the local believers, after hearing that Paul would be turned over to the Romans, begged him to turn back.

21.8 This is the Philip mentioned in 6.5 and 8.26–40.

21.9 Obviously the gift of prophecy was given to both men and women. Women actively participated in God's work (2.17; Philippians 4.3). Other women who prophesied include Miriam (Exodus 15.20), Deborah (Judges 4.4), Huldah (2 Kings 22.14), Noadiah (Nehemiah 6.14), Isaiah's wife (Isaiah 8.3), and Anna (Luke 2.36–38).

21.10 Fifteen years earlier, Agabus had predicted the famine in Jerusalem (11.27–29).

21.13, 14 Paul knew he would be imprisoned in Jerusalem. Although his friends pleaded with him to not go there, he knew he had to because God wanted him to. No one enjoys pain, but a faithful disciple wants above all else to please God. Our desire to please God should overshadow our desire to avoid hardship and suffering. When we really want to do God's will, we must accept all that comes with it—even the pain. Then we can say with Paul, "The Lord's will be done."

21.18 James, Jesus' brother, was the leader of the Jerusalem church (15.13–21; Galatians 1.19; 2.9). He was called an apostle even though he wasn't one of the original twelve who followed Jesus.

21.19 Rom 15.18
21.20 Acts 15.1,5 Gal 3.10,11
21.21 Acts 16.3 Gal 2.3
21.23 Acts 18.18
21.24 Num 6.2,13-21 1 Cor 9.20
21.25 Acts 15.19-29

next day Paul went with us to visit James; and all the elders were present. 19 After
greeting them, he related one by one the things that God had done among the Gentiles through his ministry. 20 When they heard it, they praised God. Then they said
to him, "You see, brother, how many thousands of believers there are among the
Jews, and they are all zealous for the law. 21 They have been told about you that you
teach all the Jews living among the Gentiles to forsake Moses, and that you tell
them not to circumcise their children or observe the customs. 22 What then is to be
done? They will certainly hear that you have come. 23 So do what we tell you. We
have four men who are under a vow. 24 Join these men, go through the rite of purification with them, and pay for the shaving of their heads. Thus all will know that
there is nothing in what they have been told about you, but that you yourself observe and guard the law. 25 But as for the Gentiles who have become believers,
we have sent a letter with our judgment that they should abstain from what has
been sacrificed to idols and from blood and from what is strangled[k] and from

[k] Other ancient authorities lack *and from what is strangled*

PAUL RETURNS TO JERUSALEM
The ship sailed from Miletus to Cos, Rhodes, and Patara. Paul and his companions then boarded a cargo ship bound for Phoenicia. They passed Cyprus and landed at Tyre, then Ptolemais, and finally Caesarea, where Paul disembarked and returned by land to Jerusalem.

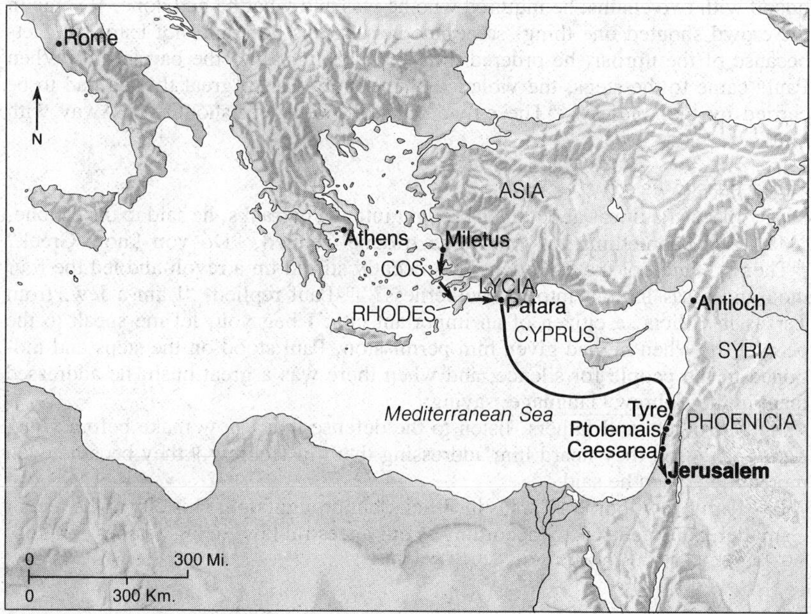

21.21 The Jerusalem council (Acts 15) had settled the issue of circumcision of Gentile believers. Evidently there was a rumor that Paul had gone far beyond their decision, even forbidding Jews to circumcise their children. This, of course, was not true, and so Paul willingly submitted to Jewish custom to show that he was not working against the council's decision and that he was still Jewish in his life-style. Sometimes we must go the second mile to avoid offending others, especially when offending them would hinder God's work.

21.23, 24 Evidently these four men had made a religious vow. Because Paul was to participate with them in the vow (apparently he was asked to pay for some part of it), he would need to be sprinkled with water as part of the purification ceremony in order to enter the temple. Paul submitted himself to this Jewish custom to keep peace in the Jerusalem church. Although Paul was a man of strong conviction, he was willing to compromise on nonessential points, becoming all things to all men that he might win some (1 Corinthians 9.19–23). Often a church is split over disagreements about minor issues or traditions. Like Paul, we should remain firm on Christian essentials but flexible on nonessentials. Of course, no one should violate his true convictions, but sometimes we need to exercise the gift of mutual submission for the sake of the gospel.

21.23, 24 There are two ways to think of the Jewish laws. Paul rejects one and accepts the other. (1) Paul rejects the idea that the Old Testament laws bring salvation to those who keep them. Our salvation is freely given by God's gracious act. We receive it by faith. The laws are of no value for salvation except to show us our sin. (2) Paul accepts the view that the Old Testament laws prepared us for and taught us about the coming of Jesus Christ. Christ fulfilled the law and released us from its burden of guilt. But the law still teaches us many valuable principles and gives us guidelines for living. Paul was not observing the laws to be saved. He was simply keeping the laws as custom to avoid offending those he wished to reach with the gospel (see Romans 3.21–31; 7.4–6; 13.9, 10). For more on the law, see Galatians 3.23–29; 4.21–31, and the chart in Galatians 3.

fornication." 26 Then Paul took the men, and the next day, having purified
himself, he entered the temple with them, making public the completion of the days
of purification when the sacrifice would be made for each of them.

Paul is arrested at the temple

27 When the seven days were almost completed, the Jews from Asia, who had
seen him in the temple, stirred up the whole crowd. They seized him, 28 shouting,
"Fellow Israelites, help! This is the man who is teaching everyone everywhere
against our people, our law, and this place; more than that, he has actually brought
Greeks into the temple and has defiled this holy place." 29 For they had previously
seen Trophimus the Ephesian with him in the city, and they supposed that Paul had
brought him into the temple. 30 Then all the city was aroused, and the people rushed
together. They seized Paul and dragged him out of the temple, and immediately the
doors were shut. 31 While they were trying to kill him, word came to the tribune of
the cohort that all Jerusalem was in an uproar. 32 Immediately he took soldiers and
centurions and ran down to them. When they saw the tribune and the soldiers, they
stopped beating Paul. 33 Then the tribune came, arrested him, and ordered him to be
bound with two chains; he inquired who he was and what he had done. 34 Some in
the crowd shouted one thing, some another; and as he could not learn the facts
because of the uproar, he ordered him to be brought into the barracks. 35 When
Paul[e] came to the steps, the violence of the mob was so great that he had to be
carried by the soldiers. 36 The crowd that followed kept shouting, "Away with
him!"

Paul speaks to the crowd

37 Just as Paul was about to be brought into the barracks, he said to the tribune,
"May I say something to you?" The tribune[f] replied, "Do you know Greek?
38 Then you are not the Egyptian who recently stirred up a revolt and led the four
thousand assassins out into the wilderness?" 39 Paul replied, "I am a Jew, from
Tarsus in Cilicia, a citizen of an important city; I beg you, let me speak to the
people." 40 When he had given him permission, Paul stood on the steps and motioned to the people for silence; and when there was a great hush, he addressed
them in the Hebrew[g] language, saying:

22 "Brothers and fathers, listen to the defense that I now make before you."
2 When they heard him addressing them in Hebrew,[g] they became even
more quiet. Then he said:
3 "I am a Jew, born in Tarsus in Cilicia, but brought up in this city at the feet of
Gamaliel, educated strictly according to our ancestral law, being zealous for God,

21.27 Acts 24.18
21.28 Mt 5.11 Lk 6.22; 11.49 21.12; 23.2 Jn 15.10 Acts 6.13 16.20,21; 17.6 24.5,6 1 Cor 4.12
21.29 Acts 20.4 2 Tim 4.20
21.32 Acts 23.27
21.33 Acts 20.23; 28.20 Eph 6.20
21.36 Lk 23.18 Jn 19.15 Acts 22.22
21.39 Acts 9.11 2 Cor 11.22 Gal 3.5 1 Pet 3.15; 4.16
21.40 Acts 26.14
22.3 Acts 5.34-40 26.5 Rom 10.2 2 Cor 11.22 Gal 1.14 Phil 3.5

[e] Gk *he* [f] Gk *He* [g] That is, *Aramaic*

21.28, 29 These men knew how effective Paul's work had been in Asia. Their strategy was to discredit Paul so his work would be weakened. Be alert when you hear accusations against God's workers. Someone may be trying to discredit them or to hinder their work. Keep an open mind and pray for the workers. They will be strengthened by your support.

21.31 Because Jerusalem was under Roman control, an uproar in the city would be investigated by Roman authorities. The ruler at this time was Claudius Lysias (23.26). This tribune was the commander of the cohort (a special group, part of a legion) of Roman soldiers. He was the senior Roman official in Jerusalem.

21.37, 38 By speaking in Greek, Paul showed that he was a cultured man and not just a common rebel starting riots in the streets. The language grabbed the commander's attention and gave Paul protection and the opportunity to give his defense.

21.37, 38 The historian Josephus tells of an Egyptian who led a revolt of 4,000 people in Jerusalem in A.D. 54 and then disappeared. The commander assumed that Paul was this rebel.

21.40—22.2 Paul was speaking in Hebrew, the language of the Old Testament and of Judaism. He used Hebrew not only to communicate in the language of his listeners, but also to show that he was a devout Jew and had respect for the Jewish laws and customs. Paul spoke Greek to the Roman officials and Hebrew to the Jews. To minister to people most effectively, use their language.

22.3 Gamaliel was the most honored rabbi of the first century. He was well known and respected as an expert on religious law and as a voice for moderation (5.34). Paul was showing his credentials as a well-educated man trained under the most respected Jewish rabbi.

22.3 By saying "as all of you are today," Paul acknowledged their sincere motives in trying to kill him and recognized that he would have done the same to Christian leaders a few years earlier. Paul always tried to establish a common point of contact with his audience before launching into a full-scale defense of Christianity. When you witness for Christ, first identify yourself with your audience. They are much more likely to listen if they feel a common bond with you.

22.4 Acts 8.3; 1 Tim 1.13
22.5 Acts 9.2,3
22.6 Acts 9.3-8; 26.12,13
22.8 Acts 26.15
22.9 Dan 10.7; Acts 9.7; 26.13
22.11 Acts 9.8
22.12,13 Acts 9.10,17,18
22.14 Acts 3.13; 26.16; 1 Cor 9.1; 15.8; Gal 1.12
22.15 Acts 26.16
22.16 Ps 116.13; Acts 2.38; Rom 10.13; 1 Cor 6.11; Heb 10.22
22.19 Acts 8.3; 22.4; 26.11
22.20 Acts 7.58-8.1
22.21 Acts 13.2; 18.6; 26.17; Rom 15.15,16; 1 Tim 2.7

just as all of you are today. 4 I persecuted this Way up to the point of death by
binding both men and women and putting them in prison, 5 as the high priest and the
whole council of elders can testify about me. From them I also received letters to
the brothers in Damascus, and I went there in order to bind those who were there
and to bring them back to Jerusalem for punishment.
6 "While I was on my way and approaching Damascus, about noon a great light
from heaven suddenly shone about me. 7 I fell to the ground and heard a voice
saying to me, 'Saul, Saul, why are you persecuting me?' 8 I answered, 'Who are
you, Lord?' Then he said to me, 'I am Jesus of Nazareth[h] whom you are persecuting.' 9 Now those who were with me saw the light but did not hear the voice of the
one who was speaking to me. 10 I asked, 'What am I to do, Lord?' The Lord said to
me, 'Get up and go to Damascus; there you will be told everything that has been
assigned to you to do.' 11 Since I could not see because of the brightness of that
light, those who were with me took my hand and led me to Damascus.
12 "A certain Ananias, who was a devout man according to the law and well
spoken of by all the Jews living there, 13 came to me; and standing beside me, he
said, 'Brother Saul, regain your sight!' In that very hour I regained my sight and
saw him. 14 Then he said, 'The God of our ancestors has chosen you to know his
will, to see the Righteous One and to hear his own voice; 15 for you will be his
witness to all the world of what you have seen and heard. 16 And now why do you
delay? Get up, be baptized, and have your sins washed away, calling on his name.'
17 "After I had returned to Jerusalem and while I was praying in the temple, I
fell into a trance 18 and saw Jesus[i] saying to me, 'Hurry and get out of Jerusalem
quickly, because they will not accept your testimony about me.' 19 And I said,
'Lord, they themselves know that in every synagogue I imprisoned and beat those
who believed in you. 20 And while the blood of your witness Stephen was shed, I
myself was standing by, approving and keeping the coats of those who killed him.'
21 Then he said to me, 'Go, for I will send you far away to the Gentiles.' "

Paul reveals his Roman citizenship

22.22 Acts 21.36; 25.24
22.25 Acts 16.37
22.29 Acts 16.38

22 Up to this point they listened to him, but then they shouted, "Away with
such a fellow from the earth! For he should not be allowed to live." 23 And while
they were shouting, throwing off their cloaks, and tossing dust into the air, 24 the
tribune directed that he was to be brought into the barracks, and ordered him to be
examined by flogging, to find out the reason for this outcry against him. 25 But
when they had tied him up with thongs,[j] Paul said to the centurion who was standing by, "Is it legal for you to flog a Roman citizen who is uncondemned?" 26 When
the centurion heard that, he went to the tribune and said to him, "What are you
about to do? This man is a Roman citizen." 27 The tribune came and asked Paul,[i]
"Tell me, are you a Roman citizen?" And he said, "Yes." 28 The tribune answered,
"It cost me a large sum of money to get my citizenship." Paul said, "But I was born
a citizen." 29 Immediately those who were about to examine him drew back from
him; and the tribune also was afraid, for he realized that Paul was a Roman citizen
and that he had bound him.

[h] Gk *the Nazorean* [i] Gk *him* [j] Or *up for the lashes*

22.6ff After gaining a hearing and establishing common ground with his audience, Paul gave his testimony. That is, he shared how he had come to faith in Christ. Sound reasoning is good, but it is also important to simply share what Christ has done in our lives. But no matter how we present the message, not everyone will accept it, as Paul knew. We must faithfully and responsibly give the gospel, and leave the results to God.

22.21, 22 These people listened intently to Paul, but the word *Gentile* brought out all their anger and pride. They were supposed to be a light to the Gentiles, telling them about the one true God. But they had renounced that mission by becoming separatist and exclusive. God's plan, however, was not thwarted; the Gentiles would hear the good news through Jewish Christians such as Paul and Peter.

22.25–28 Paul's question stopped the officers because, by law, a Roman citizen could not be punished until he had been proven guilty of a crime. Paul was born a Roman citizen, whereas the commander had purchased his citizenship. Buying citizenship was a common practice and a good source of money for the Roman government. Bought citizenship was considered inferior to citizenship by birth.

Paul appears before the Sanhedrin

30 Since he wanted to find out what Paul[k] was being accused of by the Jews,
the next day he released him and ordered the chief priests and the entire council to
meet. He brought Paul down and had him stand before them.

23 While Paul was looking intently at the council he said, "Brothers,[l] up to
this day I have lived my life with a clear conscience before God." 2 Then the
high priest Ananias ordered those standing near him to strike him on the mouth. 3 At
this Paul said to him, "God will strike you, you whitewashed wall! Are you sitting
there to judge me according to the law, and yet in violation of the law you order me
to be struck?" 4 Those standing nearby said, "Do you dare to insult God's high
priest?" 5 And Paul said, "I did not realize, brothers, that he was high priest; for it
is written, 'You shall not speak evil of a leader of your people.' "
6 When Paul noticed that some were Sadducees and others were Pharisees, he
called out in the council, "Brothers, I am a Pharisee, a son of Pharisees. I am on
trial concerning the hope of the resurrection[m] of the dead." 7 When he said this, a
dissension began between the Pharisees and the Sadducees, and the assembly was
divided. 8 (The Sadducees say that there is no resurrection, or angel, or spirit; but
the Pharisees acknowledge all three.) 9 Then a great clamor arose, and certain
scribes of the Pharisees' group stood up and contended, "We find nothing wrong
with this man. What if a spirit or an angel has spoken to him?" 10 When the dissension became violent, the tribune, fearing that they would tear Paul to pieces, ordered the soldiers to go down, take him by force, and bring him into the barracks.
11 That night the Lord stood near him and said, "Keep up your courage! For
just as you have testified for me in Jerusalem, so you must bear witness also in
Rome."

The plan to kill Paul

12 In the morning the Jews joined in a conspiracy and bound themselves by an
oath neither to eat nor drink until they had killed Paul. 13 There were more than
forty who joined in this conspiracy. 14 They went to the chief priests and elders and
said, "We have strictly bound ourselves by an oath to taste no food until we have
killed Paul. 15 Now then, you and the council must notify the tribune to bring him
down to you, on the pretext that you want to make a more thorough examination of
his case. And we are ready to do away with him before he arrives."
16 Now the son of Paul's sister heard about the ambush; so he went and gained

23.1 1 Cor 4.4; 2 Cor 1.12; 4.2; Heb 13.18
23.2 Jn 18.22; Acts 24.1
23.3 Lev 19.15; Ezek 13.10-15; Jn 7.51
23.5 Ex 22.28
23.8 Mt 22.23; Mk 12.18; Lk 20.27; Acts 24.5
23.9 Prov 16.7; Jn 12.29; Acts 5.39; 22.7
23.11 Ps 46.1; Isa 41.10; 43.2; Acts 18.9; 22.1-21; 27.23
23.12 Acts 9.23
23.15 Ps 37.32
23.16 Job 5.12,13

k Gk *he* l Gk *Men, brothers* m Gk *concerning hope and resurrection*

22.30 Paul used his persecution as an opportunity for him to witness. Even his enemies were creating a platform for him to address the entire Jewish council. If we are sensitive to the Holy Spirit's leading, we will see increased opportunities to share our faith, even in the face of opposition.

23.2–5 Josephus, a respected first-century historian, described Ananias as profane, greedy, and hot-tempered. Paul's outburst came as a result of the illegal command Ananias had given. He had violated Jewish law by assuming that Paul was guilty without a trial and ordering his punishment (see Deuteronomy 19.15). Paul didn't recognize Ananias as the high priest, probably because Ananias's command broke the law he was pledged to represent. As Christians, we are to represent Christ. When those around us say, "I didn't know you were a Christian," we have failed to represent him as we should. We are not merely Christ's followers; we are his representatives to others.

23.6–8 The Sadducees and Pharisees were two groups of religious leaders, but with strikingly different beliefs. The Pharisees believed in a bodily resurrection, but the Sadducees did not. They adhered only to Genesis through Deuteronomy, which contain no explicit teaching on resurrection. Paul's words moved the debate away from himself and toward their raging controversy about the resurrection. The Jewish council was split.

23.6–8 Paul's sudden insight that the council was a mixture of Sadducees and Pharisees is an example of the power Jesus promised to believers (Mark 13.9–11). God will help us when we are under fire for our faith. Like Paul, we should always be ready to present our testimony. The Holy Spirit will give us power to speak boldly.

23.14, 15 When the Pharisee-Sadducee controversy died down, the religious leaders refocused their attention on Paul. To these leaders, politics and position had become more important than God. They were ready to plan another murder, as they had done with Jesus. But, as always, God was in control.

23.16 This is the only biblical reference to Paul's family, leading some scholars to believe that they had disowned Paul when he became a Christian. Paul wrote of having suffered the loss of everything for Christ (Philippians 3.8). Paul's nephew was able to see Paul even though Paul was in protective custody, because Roman prisoners were accessible to their relatives and friends who could bring them food and other amenities.

23.16–22 It is easy to overlook children, assuming that they aren't old enough to do much for the Lord. But a young boy played an important part in protecting Paul's life. God can use anyone, of any age, who is willing to yield to him. Jesus made it clear that children are important (Matthew 18.2–6). Give children the importance God gives them.

entrance to the barracks and told Paul. 17 Paul called one of the centurions and said,
"Take this young man to the tribune, for he has something to report to him." 18 So
he took him, brought him to the tribune, and said, "The prisoner Paul called me and
asked me to bring this young man to you; he has something to tell you." 19 The
tribune took him by the hand, drew him aside privately, and asked, "What is it that
you have to report to me?" 20 He answered, "The Jews have agreed to ask you to
bring Paul down to the council tomorrow, as though they were going to inquire
23.21 Ps 10.9 more thoroughly into his case. 21 But do not be persuaded by them, for more than
37.12,13,32 forty of their men are lying in ambush for him. They have bound themselves by an
oath neither to eat nor drink until they kill him. They are ready now and are waiting
for your consent." 22 So the tribune dismissed the young man, ordering him, "Tell
no one that you have informed me of this."

Paul is sent to Caesarea

23 Then he summoned two of the centurions and said, "Get ready to leave by
nine o'clock tonight for Caesarea with two hundred soldiers, seventy horsemen,
and two hundred spearmen. 24 Also provide mounts for Paul to ride, and take him
safely to Felix the governor." 25 He wrote a letter to this effect:
23.27 26 "Claudius Lysias to his Excellency the governor Felix, greetings. 27 This
Acts 21.33 man was seized by the Jews and was about to be killed by them, but when I had
22.25-29 learned that he was a Roman citizen, I came with the guard and rescued him.
23.28 Acts 22.30 28 Since I wanted to know the charge for which they accused him, I had him brought

UNSUNG HEROES IN ACTS

When we think of the success of the early church, we often think of the work of the apostles. But the church could have died if it hadn't been for the "unsung" heroes, the men and women who through some small but committed act moved the church forward.

Hero	*Reference*	*Heroic action*
Lame beggar	3.9–12	After his healing, he praised God. With the crowds gathering to see what happened, Peter used the opportunity to tell many about Jesus.
Five deacons	6.2–5	Everyone has heard of Stephen and many know of Philip, but there were five other men chosen to be deacons. They not only laid the foundation for service in the church, but their hard work also gave the apostles the time they needed to preach the gospel.
Ananias	9.10–19	He had the responsibility of being the first to demonstrate Christ's love to Paul after his conversion.
Cornelius	10.30–35	His example showed Peter that the gospel was for *all* people, Jews and Gentiles.
Rhoda	12.13–15	Her persistence brought Peter inside Mary's home where he would be safe.
James	15.13–21	He took command of the Jerusalem council and had the courage and discernment to make a decision that would affect literally millions of Christians over many generations.
Lydia	16.13–15	She opened her home to Paul, from which he led many to Christ and founded a church in Philippi.
Jason	17.5–9	He risked his life for the gospel by allowing Paul to stay in his home. He stood up for what was true and right, even though he faced persecution for it.
Paul's nephew	23.16–24	He saved Paul's life by telling officials of a murder plot.
Julius	27.1, 43	He spared Paul when the other soldiers wanted to kill him.

23.23, 24 The Roman commander ordered Paul sent to Caesarea. Jerusalem was the seat of Jewish government, but Caesarea was the Roman headquarters for the area. God works in amazing and amusing ways. There were infinite possibilities of ways God could use to get Paul to Caesarea, but he chose to use the Roman army to deliver Paul from his enemies. God's ways are not our ways. Ours are limited; his are not. Don't limit God by asking him to respond your way. When God intervenes, anything can happen, much more and much better than you could ever anticipate.

23.26 Felix was the Roman governor or procurator of Judea from A.D. 52 to 59. This was the same position Pontius Pilate had held. While the Jews were given much freedom to govern themselves, the governor ran the army, kept the peace, and gathered the taxes.

23.26 How did Luke know what was written in the letter from Claudius Felix? In his concern for historical accuracy, Luke used many documents to make sure his writings were correct (see Luke 1.1–4). This letter was probably read aloud in court when Paul came before Felix to answer the Jews' accusations. Also, because Paul was a Roman citizen, a copy may have been given to him as a courtesy.

to their council. 29 I found that he was accused concerning questions of their law,
but was charged with nothing deserving death or imprisonment. 30 When I was informed that there would be a plot against the man, I sent him to you at once, ordering his accusers also to state before you what they have against him.[n]"
31 So the soldiers, according to their instructions, took Paul and brought him
during the night to Antipatris. 32 The next day they let the horsemen go on with him,
while they returned to the barracks. 33 When they came to Caesarea and delivered
the letter to the governor, they presented Paul also before him. 34 On reading the
letter, he asked what province he belonged to, and when he learned that he was
from Cilicia, 35 he said, "I will give you a hearing when your accusers arrive." Then
he ordered that he be kept under guard in Herod's headquarters.[o]

Paul appears before Felix

24 Five days later the high priest Ananias came down with some elders and an
attorney, a certain Tertullus, and they reported their case against Paul to the
governor. 2 When Paul[p] had been summoned, Tertullus began to accuse him, saying:
"Your Excellency,[q] because of you we have long enjoyed peace, and reforms
have been made for this people because of your foresight. 3 We welcome this in
every way and everywhere with utmost gratitude. 4 But, to detain you no further, I
beg you to hear us briefly with your customary graciousness. 5 We have, in fact,
found this man a pestilent fellow, an agitator among all the Jews throughout the
world, and a ringleader of the sect of the Nazarenes.[r] 6 He even tried to profane the
temple, and so we seized him.[s] 8 By examining him yourself you will be able to
learn from him concerning everything of which we accuse him."
9 The Jews also joined in the charge by asserting that all this was true.
10 When the governor motioned to him to speak, Paul replied:
"I cheerfully make my defense, knowing that for many years you have been a
judge over this nation. 11 As you can find out, it is not more than twelve days since
I went up to worship in Jerusalem. 12 They did not find me disputing with anyone
in the temple or stirring up a crowd either in the synagogues or throughout the city.
13 Neither can they prove to you the charge that they now bring against me. 14 But

23.29 Acts 18.15; 25.19; 26.31; 28.18
23.30 Acts 24.8,19; 25.16
23.33 Acts 8.40
23.34 Acts 21.39
23.35 Acts 24.1,19; 25.16
24.1 Acts 21.26,27; 23.2,24-30
24.5 Mt 5.11; Lk 23.2; Jn 15.20; Acts 16.20,21; 17.6; 24.14; 1 Thess 2.14-16; 2 Tim 3.2; 1 Pet 2.12,19
24.6 Jn 18.31; Acts 21.28
24.7 Acts 21.33
24.8 Acts 23.30
24.12 Acts 15.8
24.13 Acts 15.7
24.14 Lk 24.27; Acts 9.2; 26.22; 2 Tim 1.3

[n] Other ancient authorities add *Farewell* [o] Gk *praetorium* [p] Gk *he* [q] Gk lacks *Your Excellency* [r] Gk *Nazoreans*
[s] Other ancient authorities add *and we would have judged him according to our law. 7 But the chief captain Lysias came and with great violence took him out of our hands, 8 commanding his accusers to come before you.*

IMPRISONMENT IN CAESAREA
Paul brought news of his third journey to the elders of the Jerusalem church, who rejoiced at his ministry. But Paul's presence soon stirred up the Jews, who persuaded the Romans to arrest him. A plot to kill Paul was uncovered, so Paul was taken by night to Antipatris, then transferred to the provincial prison in Caesarea.

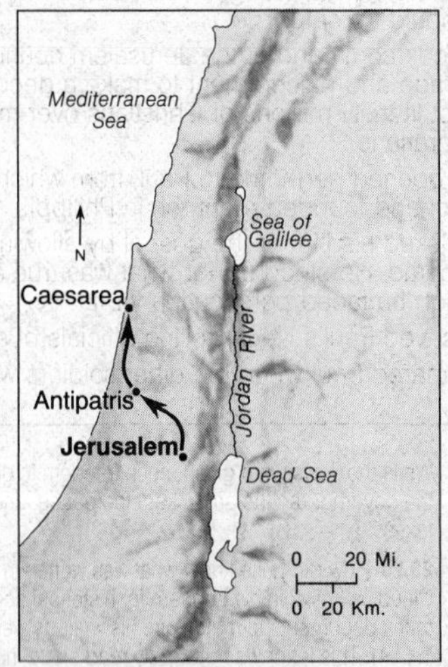

24.1 The accusers arrived—Ananias, the high priest; Tertullus, the attorney; and several Jewish leaders. They traveled 60 miles to Caesarea, the Roman center of government, to give their false accusations against Paul. Their murder plot had failed (23.12–15), but they persisted in trying to kill him. This attempted murder was both premeditated and persistent.

24.2ff Tertullus was a special orator called to present the religious leaders' case before the Roman governor. He made three accusations against Paul: (1) he was a renegade, inciting the Jews around the world; (2) he was the ringleader of an unrecognized religious sect, which was against Roman law; and (3) he had profaned the temple. The religious leaders hoped that these accusations would persuade Felix to execute Paul in order to keep the peace in Palestine.

24.5 "A pestilent fellow" could be translated "a troublemaker." While this charge was insulting, it was too vague to be a substantial legal charge. *Nazarenes* referred to the Christians—named here after Jesus' hometown.

24.10ff Tertullus and the religious leaders seemed to have a strong argument against Paul, but Paul refuted their accusations point by point. Paul was also able to present the gospel message through his defense. Paul's accusers were unable to present specific evidence to support their general accusations. For example, Paul was accused of starting trouble among the Jews in Turkey (Asia, 24.18, 19), but the Jews in Turkey were not present to confirm this. This is another example of Paul using every opportunity to witness for Christ (see 24.14, 24).

this I admit to you, that according to the Way, which they call a sect, I worship the
God of our ancestors, believing everything laid down according to the law or written in the prophets. [15] I have a hope in God—a hope that they themselves also
accept—that there will be a resurrection of both[t] the righteous and the unrighteous. [16] Therefore I do my best always to have a clear conscience toward God and
all people. [17] Now after some years I came to bring alms to my nation and to offer
sacrifices. [18] While I was doing this, they found me in the temple, completing the
rite of purification, without any crowd or disturbance. [19] But there were some Jews
from Asia—they ought to be here before you to make an accusation, if they have
anything against me. [20] Or let these men here tell what crime they had found when
I stood before the council, [21] unless it was this one sentence that I called out while
standing before them, 'It is about the resurrection of the dead that I am on trial
before you today.'"

22 But Felix, who was rather well informed about the Way, adjourned the hearing with the comment, "When Lysias the tribune comes down, I will decide your
case." [23] Then he ordered the centurion to keep him in custody, but to let him have
some liberty and not to prevent any of his friends from taking care of his needs.

24 Some days later when Felix came with his wife Drusilla, who was Jewish,
he sent for Paul and heard him speak concerning faith in Christ Jesus. [25] And as he
discussed justice, self-control, and the coming judgment, Felix became frightened
and said, "Go away for the present; when I have an opportunity, I will send for
you." [26] At the same time he hoped that money would be given him by Paul, and for
that reason he used to send for him very often and converse with him.

27 After two years had passed, Felix was succeeded by Porcius Festus; and
since he wanted to grant the Jews a favor, Felix left Paul in prison.

Paul appears before Festus

25 Three days after Festus had arrived in the province, he went up from Caesarea to Jerusalem [2] where the chief priests and the leaders of the Jews gave
him a report against Paul. They appealed to him [3] and requested, as a favor to them
against Paul,[u] to have him transferred to Jerusalem. They were, in fact, planning
an ambush to kill him along the way. [4] Festus replied that Paul was being kept at
Caesarea, and that he himself intended to go there shortly. [5] "So," he said, "let
those of you who have the authority come down with me, and if there is anything
wrong about the man, let them accuse him."

6 After he had stayed among them not more than eight or ten days, he went
down to Caesarea; the next day he took his seat on the tribunal and ordered Paul to
be brought. [7] When he arrived, the Jews who had gone down from Jerusalem surrounded him, bringing many serious charges against him, which they could not
prove. [8] Paul said in his defense, "I have in no way committed an offense against

[t] Other ancient authorities read *of the dead, both of* [u] Gk *him*

24.15 Dan 12.2; Mt 22.31,32; Jn 5.28,29; Acts 23.6; 26.6-8; 1 Thess 4.14; Rev 20.12
24.16 Acts 23.1
24.17 Acts 11.29; Rom 15.25-28; 1 Cor 16.3; 2 Cor 8.4
24.18 Acts 21.26,27
24.21 Acts 23.6
24.23 Acts 27.3; 28.16
24.25 Acts 10.42; Gal 5.23; Tit 2.12; 2 Pet 1.6
24.26 Acts 24.17
24.27 Acts 25.9, 24-27; 26.24
25.2 Acts 23.12-21; 24.1
25.7 Esth 3.8; Acts 24.13,27
25.8 Acts 6.13; 24.12; 28.17; Rom 13.1-7

24.22 Felix had been governor for six years and would have known about the Christians, a topic of conversation among the Roman leaders. The Christians' peaceful life-styles had shown the Romans that Christians didn't go around starting riots.

24.22 "Who was rather well informed about the Way" could be translated, "who knew much about Christians and that they didn't go around starting riots."

24.25 Paul's talk with Felix became so personal that Felix felt convicted. Felix, like Herod Antipas (Mark 6.17, 18), had taken another man's wife. Paul's words were interesting until they focused on "justice, self-control, and the coming judgment." Many people will be glad to discuss the gospel with you as long as it doesn't touch their lives too personally. When it does, some will resist or leave. But this is what the gospel is all about—God's power to change lives. The gospel is not effective until it moves from principles and doctrine into a life-changing dynamic. When someone resists or runs from your witness, you have made the gospel personal.

24.27 Felix lost his job as governor and was called back to Rome. Porcius Festus took over as governor in late 59 or early 60. He was more just than Felix, who had kept Paul in prison for two years, hoping that perhaps Paul would bribe him and to keep the Jews happy. When Festus came into office, he immediately ordered Paul's trial to resume.

24.27 The Jews were in the majority, and the political leaders wanted to defer to them to help keep the peace. Paul seemed to incite problems among the Jews everywhere he went. By keeping him in prison, Felix left office on good terms with the Jews.

25.1–9 Although two years had passed, the Jewish leaders still were looking for a way to kill Paul. They told Festus about Paul and tried to convince him to hold the trial in Jerusalem (so they could set an ambush). But God and Paul thwarted their schemes again.

25.6 The tribunal was the outdoor place where the civil court was held. It was a powerful symbol of Roman authority.

the law of the Jews, or against the temple, or against the emperor." 9 But Festus,
wishing to do the Jews a favor, asked Paul, "Do you wish to go up to Jerusalem and
be tried there before me on these charges?" 10 Paul said, "I am appealing to the **25.10**
emperor's tribunal; this is where I should be tried. I have done no wrong to the Acts 25.21 26.32
Jews, as you very well know. 11 Now if I am in the wrong and have committed **25.11**
something for which I deserve to die, I am not trying to escape death; but if there Acts 23.11 27.24; 28.19
is nothing to their charges against me, no one can turn me over to them. I appeal to
the emperor." 12 Then Festus, after he had conferred with his council, replied,
"You have appealed to the emperor; to the emperor you will go."

13 After several days had passed, King Agrippa and Bernice arrived at Caesarea to welcome Festus. 14 Since they were staying there several days, Festus laid **25.14**
Paul's case before the king, saying, "There is a man here who was left in prison by Acts 24.27
Felix. 15 When I was in Jerusalem, the chief priests and the elders of the Jews in- **25.15**
formed me about him and asked for a sentence against him. 16 I told them that it was Acts 25.2 **25.16**
not the custom of the Romans to hand over anyone before the accused had met the Acts 23.30
accusers face to face and had been given an opportunity to make a defense against
the charge. 17 So when they met here, I lost no time, but on the next day took my
seat on the tribunal and ordered the man to be brought. 18 When the accusers stood
up, they did not charge him with any of the crimes[v] that I was expecting. 19 Instead **25.19**
they had certain points of disagreement with him about their own religion and about Acts 18.15 23.29
a certain Jesus, who had died, but whom Paul asserted to be alive. 20 Since I was at 1 Cor 15.2-8
a loss how to investigate these questions, I asked whether he wished to go to Jerusalem and be tried there on these charges.[w] 21 But when Paul had appealed to be kept
in custody for the decision of his Imperial Majesty, I ordered him to be held until
I could send him to the emperor." 22 Agrippa said to Festus, "I would like to hear **25.22**
the man myself." "Tomorrow," he said, "you will hear him." Acts 9.15

Paul witnesses to Agrippa

23 So on the next day Agrippa and Bernice came with great pomp, and they
entered the audience hall with the military tribunes and the prominent men of the
city. Then Festus gave the order and Paul was brought in. 24 And Festus said, "King **25.24**
Agrippa and all here present with us, you see this man about whom the whole Acts 22.22
Jewish community petitioned me, both in Jerusalem and here, shouting that he
ought not to live any longer. 25 But I found that he had done nothing deserving **25.25**
death; and when he appealed to his Imperial Majesty, I decided to send him. 26 But Acts 23.22
I have nothing definite to write to our sovereign about him. Therefore I have
brought him before all of you, and especially before you, King Agrippa, so that,
after we have examined him, I may have something to write — 27 for it seems to me
unreasonable to send a prisoner without indicating the charges against him."

[v] Other ancient authorities read *with anything* [w] Gk *on them*

25.10, 11 Every Roman citizen had the right to appeal to Caesar. This didn't mean that Caesar himself would hear the case, but that his case would be tried by the highest courts in the Empire. Festus saw Paul's appeal as a way to send him out of the country and thus calm the Jews. Paul wanted to go to Rome to preach the gospel (Romans 1.10), and he knew his appeal would give him the opportunity. To go there as a prisoner was better than not to go at all.

25.11 Paul knew he was blameless of the charges against him and could appeal to Caesar's judgment. He knew his rights as a Roman citizen and as an innocent person. Paul had met his responsibilities as a Roman, and so he had the opportunity to claim Rome's protection. The good reputation and clear conscience that result from our walk with God can help us remain guiltless before God and blameless before the world.

25.13 This was Herod Agrippa II, son of Herod Agrippa I, and a descendant of Herod the Great. He had power over the temple, controlled the temple treasury, and could appoint and remove the high priest. Bernice was the sister of Herod Agrippa II. She married her uncle Herod Chalcis, became a mistress to her brother Agrippa II, and then became mistress to the emperor Titus. Here Agrippa and Bernice were making an official visit to Festus. Agrippa, of Jewish descent, could help clarify this "Jewish situation" to the Roman governor. Agrippa and Festus were anxious to cooperate in governing their neighboring territories.

25.19 Even though Festus knew little about Christianity, he understood that the resurrection was central to Christian belief.

25.23ff Paul was in prison, but that didn't stop him from making the most of his situation. Military officers and prominent city leaders met in the palace room with Agrippa to hear this case. Paul saw this new audience as yet another opportunity to present the gospel. Rather than complain about your present situation, look for ways to use every opportunity to serve God and share him with others. Your problems may be opportunities in disguise.

26.4 Phil 3.5
26.6 Gen 3.15
22.18; 26.4
Deut 18.15
Isa 7.14; 9.6,7
Jer 23.5,6
33.14
Ezek 34.23
37.24
Dan 9.24
Mal 3.1; 4.2
Acts 13.32,33
26.7 Phil 3.11
26.8 Dan 12.2
26.9 Jn 15.21; 16.2
1 Tim 1.13
26.10 Acts 8.3; 22.5
26.11 Acts 9.1; 22.19
26.15 Acts 9.5; 22.8
26.16 Acts 22.15
Gal 1.12
Col 1.25
1 Tim 1.12
26.17 Acts 13.46-48
22.21
Rom 11.13
15.16
Gal 1.15,16
2.7-9
1 Tim 2.7
2 Tim 1.11
26.18 Isa 35.5; 42.6,7
Lk 1.77,79
Eph 1.11; 5.8
Col 1.13
1 Pet 2.9
26.20 Mt 3.8
Acts 9.20,26
13.46
26.21 Acts 21.30
26.22 Jn 5.46
Rom 3.21,22
26.23 Ps 2.7
6.8-11,22
Isa 53.1-12
Lk 24.26,27,46,
47
Rom 1.3,4
1 Cor 15.20
Col 1.18
Rev 1.5
26.24 1 Cor 1.23

26 Agrippa said to Paul, "You have permission to speak for yourself." Then
Paul stretched out his hand and began to defend himself:
2 "I consider myself fortunate that it is before you, King Agrippa, I am to make
my defense today against all the accusations of the Jews, 3 because you are especially familiar with all the customs and controversies of the Jews; therefore I beg of
you to listen to me patiently.
4 "All the Jews know my way of life from my youth, a life spent from the beginning among my own people and in Jerusalem. 5 They have known for a long time,
if they are willing to testify, that I have belonged to the strictest sect of our religion
and lived as a Pharisee. 6 And now I stand here on trial on account of my hope in the
promise made by God to our ancestors, 7 a promise that our twelve tribes hope to
attain, as they earnestly worship day and night. It is for this hope, your Excellency,[x] that I am accused by Jews! 8 Why is it thought incredible by any of you that
God raises the dead?
9 "Indeed, I myself was convinced that I ought to do many things against the
name of Jesus of Nazareth.[y] 10 And that is what I did in Jerusalem; with authority
received from the chief priests, I not only locked up many of the saints in prison,
but I also cast my vote against them when they were being condemned to death.
11 By punishing them often in all the synagogues I tried to force them to blaspheme;
and since I was so furiously enraged at them, I pursued them even to foreign cities.
12 "With this in mind, I was traveling to Damascus with the authority and commission of the chief priests, 13 when at midday along the road, your Excellency,[x]
I saw a light from heaven, brighter than the sun, shining around me and my companions. 14 When we had all fallen to the ground, I heard a voice saying to me in the
Hebrew[z] language, 'Saul, Saul, why are you persecuting me? It hurts you to kick
against the goads.' 15 I asked, 'Who are you, Lord?' The Lord answered, 'I am
Jesus whom you are persecuting. 16 But get up and stand on your feet; for I have
appeared to you for this purpose, to appoint you to serve and testify to the things in
which you have seen me[a] and to those in which I will appear to you. 17 I will rescue
you from your people and from the Gentiles—to whom I am sending you 18 to open
their eyes so that they may turn from darkness to light and from the power of Satan
to God, so that they may receive forgiveness of sins and a place among those who
are sanctified by faith in me.'
19 "After that, King Agrippa, I was not disobedient to the heavenly vision,
20 but declared first to those in Damascus, then in Jerusalem and throughout the
countryside of Judea, and also to the Gentiles, that they should repent and turn to
God and do deeds consistent with repentance. 21 For this reason the Jews seized me
in the temple and tried to kill me. 22 To this day I have had help from God, and so
I stand here, testifying to both small and great, saying nothing but what the prophets and Moses said would take place: 23 that the Messiah[b] must suffer, and that, by
being the first to rise from the dead, he would proclaim light both to our people and
to the Gentiles."
24 While he was making this defense, Festus exclaimed, "You are out of your
mind, Paul! Too much learning is driving you insane!" 25 But Paul said, "I am not

[x] Gk *O king* [y] Gk *the Nazorean* [z] That is, *Aramaic* [a] Other ancient authorities read *the things that you have seen* [b] Or *the Christ*

26.3ff This speech is a good example of Paul's powerful oratory. Beginning with a compliment to Agrippa, he tells his story, including the resurrection of Christ, and the royal audience was spellbound.

26.14 An ox goad was a sharp stick used to prod cattle. "It hurts you to kick against the goads" (ox goads) could be translated, "You are only hurting yourself."

26.17, 18 Paul took every opportunity to remind his audience that the Gentiles have an equal share in God's inheritance. This inheritance is the promise and blessing of the covenant God made with Abraham (see Ephesians 2.19; 1 Peter 1.3, 4). Paul's mission was to preach the good news to the Gentiles.

26.24 Paul was risking his life for an argument that was offensive to the Jews and unbelievable to the Gentiles. Jesus received the same response to his message (Mark 3.21; John 10.20). To a worldly, materialistic mind, it seems insane to risk so much to gain what seems to be so little. But as you follow Christ, you discover that temporary possessions look small next to even the smallest eternal reward.

out of my mind, most excellent Festus, but I am speaking the sober truth. 26 Indeed **26.26**
the king knows about these things, and to him I speak freely; for I am certain that Acts 26.3
none of these things has escaped his notice, for this was not done in a corner.
27 King Agrippa, do you believe the prophets? I know that you believe." 28 Agrippa
said to Paul, "Are you so quickly persuading me to become a Christian?"[c] 29 Paul
replied, "Whether quickly or not, I pray to God that not only you but also all who
are listening to me today might become such as I am—except for these chains."
30 Then the king got up, and with him the governor and Bernice and those who
had been seated with them; 31 and as they were leaving, they said to one another, **26.31**
"This man is doing nothing to deserve death or imprisonment." 32 Agrippa said to Acts 23.9; 25.25 **26.32**
Festus, "This man could have been set free if he had not appealed to the emperor." Acts 25.11

Paul sails for Rome

27 When it was decided that we were to sail for Italy, they transferred Paul and **27.1**
some other prisoners to a centurion of the Augustan Cohort, named Julius. Acts 25.12,25
2 Embarking on a ship of Adramyttium that was about to set sail to the ports along **27.2**
the coast of Asia, we put to sea, accompanied by Aristarchus, a Macedonian from Acts 19.29; 20.4
Thessalonica. 3 The next day we put in at Sidon; and Julius treated Paul kindly, and Col 4.10 **27.3**
allowed him to go to his friends to be cared for. 4 Putting out to sea from there, we Mt 11.21 Acts 24.23
sailed under the lee of Cyprus, because the winds were against us. 5 After we had 27.43; 28.16
sailed across the sea that is off Cilicia and Pamphylia, we came to Myra in Lycia.
6 There the centurion found an Alexandrian ship bound for Italy and put us on **27.6**
board. 7 We sailed slowly for a number of days and arrived with difficulty off Acts 28.11
Cnidus, and as the wind was against us, we sailed under the lee of Crete off Salmone. 8 Sailing past it with difficulty, we came to a place called Fair Havens, near
the city of Lasea.
9 Since much time had been lost and sailing was now dangerous, because even
the Fast had already gone by, Paul advised them, 10 saying, "Sirs, I can see that the **27.10**
voyage will be with danger and much heavy loss, not only of the cargo and the ship, Amos 3.7
but also of our lives." 11 But the centurion paid more attention to the pilot and to the
owner of the ship than to what Paul said. 12 Since the harbor was not suitable for
spending the winter, the majority was in favor of putting to sea from there, on the
chance that somehow they could reach Phoenix, where they could spend the winter. It was a harbor of Crete, facing southwest and northwest.

The storm at sea

13 When a moderate south wind began to blow, they thought they could
achieve their purpose; so they weighed anchor and began to sail past Crete, close to

[c] Or *Quickly you will persuade me to play the Christian*

26.26 Paul was appealing to the *facts*—people were still alive who had heard Jesus and seen his miracles; the empty tomb could still be seen; and the Christian message was turning the world upside down (17.6). The history of Jesus' life and the early church are facts that are still open for us to examine. We still have eyewitness accounts of Jesus' life in the Bible as well as historical and archaeological records of the early church to study. Examine the events and facts as verified by many witnesses. Reconfirm your faith with the truth of these accounts.

26.28, 29 Agrippa answered Paul's presentation with a sarcastic remark. Paul didn't react to the brush-off, but made a personal appeal to which he hoped all his listeners would respond. Paul's response is a good example for us as we tell others about God's plan of salvation. A sincere personal appeal or personal testimony can show the depth of our concern and break through hardened hearts.

26.28, 29 Paul's heart is revealed here: he was more concerned for the salvation of these strangers than for the removal of his own bonds. Ask God to give you a burning desire to see others come to Christ—a desire so strong that it overshadows your problems.

27.1 Use of the pronoun *we* indicates that Luke accompanied Paul on this journey. Aristarchus is the man who was dragged into the amphitheater at the beginning of the riot in Ephesus (19.29; 20.4; Philemon 1.24).

27.1–3 Julius, a hardened Roman centurion, was assigned to guard Paul. Obviously he had to remain close to Paul at all times. Through this contact, Julius developed a respect for Paul. He gave Paul a certain amount of freedom (27.3) and later spared his life (27.43). How would your character look up close and personal?

27.9 The Fast was the day of atonement. Ships in ancient times had no compasses and navigated by the stars. Overcast weather made sailing almost impossible and very dangerous. Sailing was doubtful in September and impossible by November. This event occurred in October (A.D. 59).

27.12 Although this was not the best time to sail, the master of the ship didn't want to spend the winter in Lasea, and so he took a chance. At first the winds and weather were favorable, but then the deadly storm arose.

the shore. 14But soon a violent wind, called the northeaster, rushed down from
Crete.[d] 15Since the ship was caught and could not be turned head-on into the wind,
we gave way to it and were driven. 16By running under the lee of a small island
called Cauda[e] we were scarcely able to get the ship's boat under control. 17After
hoisting it up they took measures[f] to undergird the ship; then, fearing that they
27.18 would run on the Syrtis, they lowered the sea anchor and so were driven. 18We
Jonah 1.5 were being pounded by the storm so violently that on the next day they began to
throw the cargo overboard, 19and on the third day with their own hands they threw
27.21 the ship's tackle overboard. 20When neither sun nor stars appeared for many days,
Acts 27.10 and no small tempest raged, all hope of our being saved was at last abandoned.
27.23 Acts 18.9; 23.11 21 Since they had been without food for a long time, Paul then stood up among
27.44 them and said, "Men, you should have listened to me and not have set sail from
2 Tim 4.17 Crete and thereby avoided this damage and loss. 22I urge you now to keep up your
27.24 Isa 41.10,14 courage, for there will be no loss of life among you, but only of the ship. 23For last
43.1,2 Acts 19.21 night there stood by me an angel of the God to whom I belong and whom I worship,
23.11; 25.11 24and he said, 'Do not be afraid, Paul; you must stand before the emperor; and

[d] Gk *it* [e] Other ancient authorities read *Clauda* [f] Gk *helps*

HEROD AGRIPPA II

Like great-grandfather, like grandfather, like father, like son—this tells the story of Herod Agrippa II. He inherited the effects of generations of powerful men with flawed personalities. Each son followed his father in weaknesses, mistakes, and missed opportunities. Each generation had a confrontation with God, but each failed to realize the importance of the decision. Herod Agrippa's great-uncle, Herod Antipas, actually met Jesus during his trial, but failed to see Jesus for who he was. Agrippa II heard the gospel from Paul, but considered the message mild entertainment. He found it humorous that Paul actually tried to convince him to become a Christian.

Like so many before and after, Agrippa II stopped within hearing distance of the kingdom of God. He left himself without excuse. He heard the gospel but decided it wasn't worth responding to personally. Unfortunately, his mistake isn't uncommon. Many who read his story also will not believe. Their problem, like his, is not really that the gospel isn't convincing or that they don't need to know God personally; it is that they choose not to respond.

What has been your response to the gospel? Has it turned your life around and given you the hope of eternal life, or has it been a message to resist or reject? Perhaps it has just been entertainment. It may seem like too great a price to give God control of your life, but it is an even greater price by far to live eternally apart from him because you chose not to be his child.

Strengths and accomplishments:
- Was the last of the Herod dynasty that ruled parts of Palestine from 40 B.C. to A.D. 100
- Continued his father's success in mediating between Rome and Palestine
- Continued the family tradition of building and improving cities

Weaknesses and mistakes:
- Was not convinced by the gospel and consciously rejected it
- Carried on an incestuous relationship with his sister Bernice

Lessons from his life:
- Families pass on both positive and negative influences to children
- There are no guarantees of multiple opportunities to respond to God

Vital statistics:
- Occupation: Ruler of northern and eastern Palestine
- Relatives: Great-grandfather: Herod the Great. Father: Herod Agrippa I. Great-uncle: Herod Antipas. Sisters: Bernice, Drusilla
- Contemporaries: Paul, Felix, Festus, Peter, Luke

Key verse:
"Agrippa said to Paul, 'Are you so quickly persuading me to become a Christian?' " (Acts 26.28).

Herod Agrippa II's story is told in Acts 25.13—26.32.

27.17 The measures they took included passing ropes under the ship to hold it together. "Run on the Syrtis" meant running onto the sandbars of Syrtis, two bays on the northern coast of Africa.

27.21 Why would Paul talk to the crew this way? Paul was not taunting them with an "I told you so," but was reminding them that, with God's guidance, he had predicted this very problem (27.10). In the future, they listened to him (27.30–32) and their lives were spared because of it.

indeed, God has granted safety to all those who are sailing with you.' 25 So keep up
your courage, men, for I have faith in God that it will be exactly as I have been told.
26 But we will have to run aground on some island."

The shipwreck

27 When the fourteenth night had come, as we were drifting across the sea of
Adria, about midnight the sailors suspected that they were nearing land. 28 So they
took soundings and found twenty fathoms; a little farther on they took soundings
again and found fifteen fathoms. 29 Fearing that we might run on the rocks, they let
down four anchors from the stern and prayed for day to come. 30 But when the
sailors tried to escape from the ship and had lowered the boat into the sea, on the
pretext of putting out anchors from the bow, 31 Paul said to the centurion and
the soldiers, "Unless these men stay in the ship, you cannot be saved." 32 Then
the soldiers cut away the ropes of the boat and set it adrift.

33 Just before daybreak, Paul urged all of them to take some food, saying, "Today is the fourteenth day that you have been in suspense and remaining without
food, having eaten nothing. 34 Therefore I urge you to take some food, for it will
help you survive; for none of you will lose a hair from your heads." 35 After he had
said this, he took bread; and giving thanks to God in the presence of all, he broke
it and began to eat. 36 Then all of them were encouraged and took food for themselves. 37 (We were in all two hundred seventy-six[g] persons in the ship.) 38 After
they had satisfied their hunger, they lightened the ship by throwing the wheat into
the sea.

39 In the morning they did not recognize the land, but they noticed a bay with

27.25 2 Chron 20.20 Lk 1.45 Heb 6.17

27.34 Mt 10.30 Lk 12.7; 21.18

27.35 Mt 14.19 Jn 6.11 1 Tim 4.4,5

27.38 Jonah 1.5 Acts 27.18

g Other ancient authorities read *seventy-six*; others, *about seventy-six*

PAUL'S JOURNEY TO ROME

One of Paul's most important journeys was to Rome, but he didn't get there the way he expected. It turned out to be more of a legal journey than a missionary journey because through a series of legal trials and transactions, Paul was delivered to Rome where his presentation of the gospel would penetrate even into the walls of the emperor's palace. Sometimes when our plans don't work out as we want them to, they work out even better than we expected.

Reference	*What happened*
21.30–34	When Paul arrived in Jerusalem, a riot broke out. Seeing the riot, Roman soldiers put Paul into protective custody. Paul asked for a chance to defend himself to the people. His speech was interrupted by the crowd when he spoke about the Gentiles.
22.24, 25	A Roman commander ordered a beating to get a confession from Paul. Paul claimed Roman citizenship and escaped the whip.
22.30	Paul was brought before the Jewish council. Because of his Roman citizenship, he was rescued from the religious leaders who wanted to kill him.
23.10	The Roman commander put Paul back under protective custody.
23.21–24	Due to a plot to kill Paul, the commander transferred him to Caesarea, which was under Governor Felix's control.
23.35	Paul was in prison until the Jews arrived to accuse him. Paul defended himself before Felix.
24.25, 26	Paul was in prison for two years, speaking occasionally to Felix and Drusilla.
24.27	Felix was replaced by Festus.
25.1, 10	New accusations were brought against Paul—Jews wanted him back in Jerusalem for a trial. Paul claimed his right to a hearing before Caesar.
25.12	Festus promised to send him to Rome.
25.13, 14	Festus discussed Paul's case with Agrippa II.
26.1	Agrippa and Festus heard Paul speak. Paul again told his story.
26.24–28	Agrippa interrupted with sarcastic rejection of the gospel.
26.30–32	Group consensus was that Paul was guilty of nothing and could be released if he had not appealed to Rome.
27.1, 2	Paul left for Rome, by courtesy of the Roman Empire.

27.27 The sea of Adria referred to the central part of the Mediterranean Sea between Italy, Crete, and the northern coast of Africa.

27.28 Soundings were made by throwing a weighted, marked line into the water. When the lead hit the bottom, sailors could tell the depth of the water from the marks on the rope.

a beach, on which they planned to run the ship ashore, if they could. 40 So they cast
off the anchors and left them in the sea. At the same time they loosened the ropes
that tied the steering-oars; then hoisting the foresail to the wind, they made for the
27.41 2 Cor 11.25 beach. 41 But striking a reef,[h] they ran the ship aground; the bow stuck and remained immovable, but the stern was being broken up by the force of the waves.
42 The soldiers' plan was to kill the prisoners, so that none might swim away and
escape; 43 but the centurion, wishing to save Paul, kept them from carrying out their
plan. He ordered those who could swim to jump overboard first and make for the
27.44 Ps 107.30 land, 44 and the rest to follow, some on planks and others on pieces of the ship. And
so it was that all were brought safely to land.

Paul is bitten by a snake on Malta

28.1 Acts 27.26 **28** After we had reached safety, we then learned that the island was called
Malta. 2 The natives showed us unusual kindness. Since it had begun to rain
and was cold, they kindled a fire and welcomed all of us around it. 3 Paul had gathered a bundle of brushwood and was putting it on the fire, when a viper, driven out
28.4 Lk 13.2,4 by the heat, fastened itself on his hand. 4 When the natives saw the creature hanging
28.5 Mk 16.18 Lk 10.19 from his hand, they said to one another, "This man must be a murderer; though he
has escaped from the sea, justice has not allowed him to live." 5 He, however,
28.6 Acts 14.11 shook off the creature into the fire and suffered no harm. 6 They were expecting him
to swell up or drop dead, but after they had waited a long time and saw that nothing

[h] Gk *place of two seas*

THE TRIP TOWARD ROME
Paul began his 2,000-mile trip to Rome at Caesarea. To avoid the open seas, the ship followed the coastline. At Myra, Paul was put on a vessel bound for Italy. It arrived with difficulty at Cnidus, then went to Crete, landing at the port of Fair Havens. The next stop was Phoenix, but the ship was blown south around the island of Clauda, then drifted for two weeks until it was shipwrecked on the island of Malta.

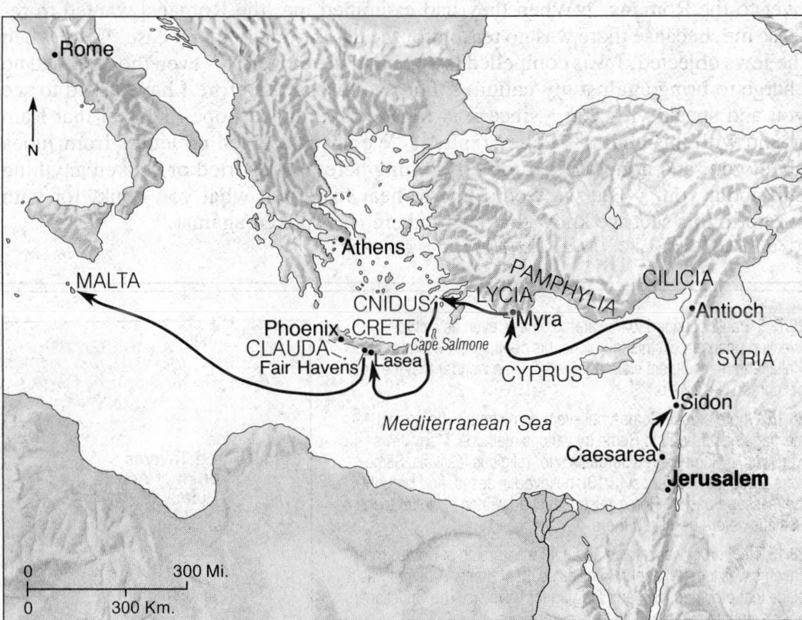

27.42, 43 The soldiers would pay with their own lives if any of their prisoners escaped. Their instinctive reaction was to kill the prisoners so they wouldn't get away. Julius, the centurion, was impressed with Paul and wanted to save his life. Julius was the highest ranking official and could make this decision. This act preserved Paul for his later ministry in Rome and fulfilled Paul's prediction that all people on the ship would be saved (27.22).

28.1 The island of Malta is 60 miles south of Sicily. It had excellent harbors and was ideally located for trade.

28.2 The natives of Malta were of Phoenician ancestry.

28.3 God had promised safe passage to Paul, and he would let nothing stop his servant. The poisonous snake that bit Paul was unable to harm him. Our lives are in God's hands, to continue or end in his good timing. God still had work for Paul to do.

28.6 These people were very superstitious and believed in many gods. When they saw that Paul was unhurt by the poisonous snake, they thought he was a god. A similar situation is reported in 14.11–18.

unusual had happened to him, they changed their minds and began to say that he
was a god.
7 Now in the neighborhood of that place were lands belonging to the leading
man of the island, named Publius, who received us and entertained us hospitably
for three days. 8 It so happened that the father of Publius lay sick in bed with fever 28.8
and dysentery. Paul visited him and cured him by praying and putting his hands on Mk 5.23 Acts 19.11
him. 9 After this happened, the rest of the people on the island who had diseases 1 Cor 12.9,28
also came and were cured. 10 They bestowed many honors on us, and when we were Jas 5.14
about to sail, they put on board all the provisions we needed.

Paul lives under guard in Rome

11 Three months later we set sail on a ship that had wintered at the island, an 28.11
Alexandrian ship with the Twin Brothers as its figurehead. 12 We put in at Syracuse Acts 27.6
and stayed there for three days; 13 then we weighed anchor and came to Rhegium.
After one day there a south wind sprang up, and on the second day we came to
Puteoli. 14 There we found believers[i] and were invited to stay with them for seven
days. And so we came to Rome. 15 The believers[i] from there, when they heard of
us, came as far as the Forum of Appius and Three Taverns to meet us. On seeing
them, Paul thanked God and took courage.
16 When we came into Rome, Paul was allowed to live by himself, with the 28.16
soldier who was guarding him. Acts 24.33; 27.3
17 Three days later he called together the local leaders of the Jews. When they 28.17
had assembled, he said to them, "Brothers, though I had done nothing against our Acts 24.12; 25.8
people or the customs of our ancestors, yet I was arrested in Jerusalem and handed
over to the Romans. 18 When they had examined me, the Romans[j] wanted to re- 28.18
lease me, because there was no reason for the death penalty in my case. 19 But when Acts 23.29
the Jews objected, I was compelled to appeal to the emperor — even though I had no 28.19
charge to bring against my nation. 20 For this reason therefore I have asked to see Acts 25.11; 26.32 28.20
you and speak with you,[k] since it is for the sake of the hope of Israel that I am Acts 26.6
bound with this chain." 21 They replied, "We have received no letters from Judea
about you, and none of the brothers coming here has reported or spoken anything 28.22
evil about you. 22 But we would like to hear from you what you think, for with Acts 24.14 1 Pet 2.12; 3.16
regard to this sect we know that everywhere it is spoken against." 4.16

[i] Gk *brothers* [j] Gk *they* [k] Or *I have asked you to see me and speak with me*

28.7, 8 Paul continued to minister to others, even as a shipwrecked prisoner. On this trip alone, his centurion, the leader of Malta, and many others were affected. It is no wonder that the gospel spread like wildfire.

28.15 Where did the Roman believers come from? The gospel message had spread to Rome by various methods. Many Jews who lived in Rome visited Jerusalem for religious festivals. Some were present at Pentecost (2.10), believed in Jesus, and brought the message back to Rome. Also, Paul had written his letter to the Romans before he visited there.

28.15 The Forum was a town about 43 miles south of Rome; Three Taverns was located about 35 miles south of Rome. A *tavern* was a place that provided food and lodging for travelers. The Christians openly went to meet Paul and encourage him.

28.17 The Edict of Claudius expelling Jews from Rome (18.2) must have been temporary, because Jewish leaders were back in Rome.

28.17–20 Paul wanted to preach the gospel in Rome, and he eventually got there – in chains, through shipwreck, and after many trials. Although he may have wished for an easier passage, he knew that God had blessed him greatly in allowing him to meet the believers in Rome and preach the message to both Jews and Gentiles in that great city. God worked all things for good (Romans 8.28) for Paul. You can trust him to do the same for you. God may not make you comfortable or secure, but he will provide the opportunity to do his work.

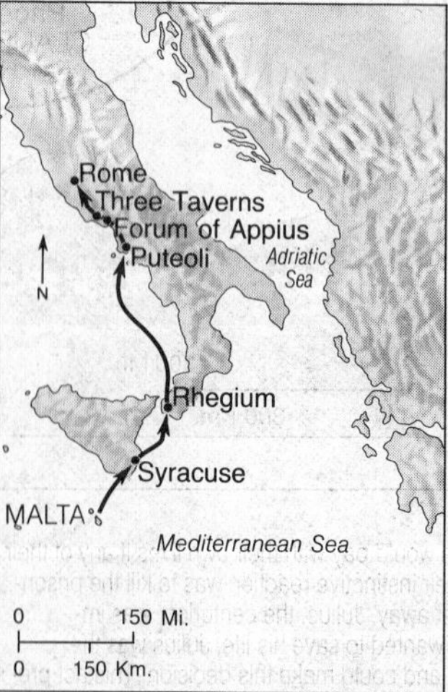

PAUL ARRIVES IN ROME
The shipwreck occurred on Malta, where the ship's company spent three months. Finally another ship gave them passage for the 100 miles to Syracuse, capital of Sicily, then on to Rhegium, finally dropping anchor at Puteoli. Paul was taken along the Appian Way to the Forum, and to the Three Taverns before arriving in Rome.

28.22 Christians were denounced everywhere by the Romans because they were seen as a threat to the Roman establishment. They believed in one God, whereas the Romans had many gods,

28.23 Lk 24.27 Acts 1.3; 23.11 28.31
28.24 Acts 14.4
28.25-27 Isa 6.9-10 Jn 12.39,40

23 After they had set a day to meet with him, they came to him at his lodgings
in great numbers. From morning until evening he explained the matter to them,
testifying to the kingdom of God and trying to convince them about Jesus both from
the law of Moses and from the prophets. 24 Some were convinced by what he had
said, while others refused to believe. 25 So they disagreed with each other; and as
they were leaving, Paul made one further statement: "The Holy Spirit was right in
saying to your ancestors through the prophet Isaiah,
26 'Go to this people and say,
You will indeed listen, but never understand,
and you will indeed look, but never perceive.
27 For this people's heart has grown dull,
and their ears are hard of hearing,
and they have shut their eyes;
so that they might not look with their eyes,
and listen with their ears,
and understand with their heart and turn—
and I would heal them.'

28.28 Ps 98.3 Lk 2.30-32 Acts 9.15 13.26,46
28.31 Acts 20.25 28.23

28 Let it be known to you then that this salvation of God has been sent to the Gentiles; they will listen."[l]
30 He lived there two whole years at his own expense[m] and welcomed all who
came to him, 31 proclaiming the kingdom of God and teaching about the Lord Jesus
Christ with all boldness and without hindrance.

[l] Other ancient authorities add verse 29, *And when he had said these words, the Jews departed, arguing vigorously among themselves* [m] Or *in his own hired dwelling*

---

including Caesar. The Christians were committed to an authority higher than Caesar.

28.23 Paul used the Old Testament to teach the Jews that Jesus was the Messiah, the fulfillment of God's promises. The book of Romans, written ten years earlier, reveals the ongoing dialogue Paul had with the Jews in Rome.

28.27 Paul was quoting from Isaiah 6.9, 10.

28.30 While Paul was under house arrest, he did more than speak to the Jews. He wrote letters, commonly called his Prison Epistles, to the Ephesians, Colossians, and Philippians. He also wrote personal letters, such as the one to Philemon. Luke was with Paul in Rome (2 Timothy 4.11). Timothy often visited him (Philippians 1.1; Colossians 1.1; Philemon 1), as did Tychicus (Ephesians 6.21), Epaphroditus (Philippians 4.18), and Mark (Colossians 4.10). Paul witnessed to the Roman guard (Philippians 1.13) and was involved with the Roman believers.

28.30 Tradition says that Paul was released after two years of house arrest in Rome and then set off on a fourth missionary journey. Some reasons for this tradition are as follows: (1) Luke does not give us an account of his trial before Caesar, and Luke was a detailed chronicler; (2) the prosecution had two years to bring the case to trial, and time may have run out; (3) in his letter to the Philippians, written during his imprisonment in Rome, Paul implied that he would soon be released and would do further traveling; (4) Paul mentions several places where he intended to take the gospel, but he never visited those places in his first three journeys; and (5) early Christian literature talks plainly about other travels by Paul.

It may be that during Paul's time of freedom, he continued to travel extensively, even going to Spain (see Romans 15.24, 28) and back to the churches in Greece. The books of 1 Timothy and Titus were written during this time. Later, Paul was imprisoned again, probably in Rome, where he wrote his last epistle (2 Timothy).

28.31 Why does the book of Acts end here and so abruptly? The book is not about the life of Paul, but about the spread of the gospel, and that has been clearly presented. God apparently thought it was not necessary for someone to write an additional book describing the continuing history of the early church. Now that the gospel had been preached and established at the center of trade and government, it would spread across the world.

28.31 The book of Acts deals with the history of the Christian church and its expansion in ever-widening circles touching Jerusalem, Antioch, Ephesus, and Rome—the most influential cities in the Western world. Acts also shows the mighty miracles and testimonies of the heroes and martyrs of the early church—Peter, Stephen, James, Paul. All the ministry was prompted and held together by the Holy Spirit working in the lives of ordinary people—merchants, travelers, slaves, jailers, church leaders, males, females, Gentiles, Jews, rich, poor. Many unsung heroes of the faith continued the work, through the Holy Spirit, in succeeding generations, changing the world with a changeless message—that Jesus Christ is Savior and Lord for all who call upon him. Today we can be the unsung heroes in the continuing story of the spread of the gospel. It is that same message that we Christians are to take to our world so that many more may hear and believe.

The Letter of Paul to the ROMANS

VITAL STATISTICS

PURPOSE:
To introduce Paul to the Romans and to give a sample of his message before he arrives in Rome

AUTHOR:
Paul

TO WHOM WRITTEN:
The Christians in Rome and believers everywhere

DATE WRITTEN:
About A.D. 57, from Corinth, as Paul was preparing for his visit to Jerusalem.

SETTING:
Apparently Paul had finished his work in the east, and he planned to visit Rome on his way to Spain after first bringing a collection to Jerusalem for the poor Christians there (15.22–28). The Roman church was mostly Jewish but also contained a great number of Gentiles.

KEY VERSE:
"Therefore, since we are justified by faith, we have peace with God through our Lord Jesus Christ" (5.1).

KEY PEOPLE:
Paul, Phoebe

KEY PLACE:
Rome

SPECIAL FEATURES:
Paul writes Romans as an organized and carefully presented statement of his faith—it does not have the form of a typical letter. He does, however, spend considerable time greeting people in Rome at the end of the letter.

KNOWLEDGEABLE and experienced, the District Attorney makes his case. Calling key witnesses to the stand, he presents the evidence. After discrediting the testimonies of witnesses for the defense by skillfully cross-examining them, he concludes with an airtight summary and stirring challenge for the jury. The announced verdict is no surprise. "Guilty" states the foreman; and justice is served.

The apostle Paul was intelligent, articulate, and committed to his calling. Like a skilled lawyer, he presents the case for the gospel clearly and forthrightly in his letter to the believers in Rome.

Paul had heard of the church at Rome, but he had never been there, nor had any of the other apostles. Evidently the church was begun by Jews who had come to faith during Pentecost (Acts 2). They spread the faith on their return to Rome and the church grew.

Although many barriers separated them, Paul felt a bond with these Romans. They were his brothers and sisters in Christ, and he longed to see them face to face. He had never met most of the believers there, yet he loved them. He sent this letter to introduce himself and to make a clear declaration of the faith.

After a brief introduction, Paul presents the facts of the gospel (1.3) and declares his allegiance to it (1.16, 17). He continues by building an airtight case for the lostness of mankind and the necessity for God's intervention (1.18—3.20).

Then Paul presents the good news—salvation is available to all, regardless of a person's identity, sin, or heritage. We are saved by *grace* (unearned, undeserved favor from God) through *faith* (complete trust) in Christ and his finished work. Through him we can stand before God justified, "not guilty" (3.21—5.21). With this foundation Paul moves directly into a discussion of the freedom that comes from being saved—freedom from the power of sin (6.1–23), freedom from the domination of the law (7.1–25), freedom to become like Christ and discover God's limitless love (8.1–39).

Speaking directly to his Jewish brothers and sisters, Paul shares his concern for them and explains how they fit into God's plan (9.1—11.12). God has made the way for Jews and Gentiles to be united in the body of Christ—both groups can praise God for his wisdom and love (11.13–36).

Paul explains what it means to live in complete submission to Christ—using spiritual gifts to serve others (12.3–8), genuinely loving others (12.9–21), and being good citizens (13.1–14). Freedom must be guided by love as we build each other up in the faith, being sensitive and helpful to those who are weak (14.1—15.4). Paul stresses unity, especially between Gentiles and Jews (15.5–13). He concludes by reviewing his reasons for writing, outlining his personal plans (15.22–33), greeting his friends, and giving a few final thoughts and greetings from his traveling companions (16.1–27).

As you read Romans, reexamine your commitment to Christ and reconfirm your relationships with other believers in Christ's body.

THE BLUEPRINT

A. WHAT TO BELIEVE (1.1—11.36) 1. Sinfulness of mankind 2. Forgiveness of sin through Christ 3. Freedom from sin's grasp 4. Israel's past, present, and future	Paul clearly sets forth the foundations of the Christian faith. All men are sinful; Christ died to forgive sin; we are made right with God through faith; this begins a new life with a new relationship with God. Like a sports team that constantly reviews the basics, we will be greatly helped in our faith by keeping close to these foundations. If we study Romans carefully, we will never be at a loss to know what to believe.
B. HOW TO BEHAVE (12.1—16.27) 1. Personal responsibility 2. Personal notes	Paul gives clear, practical guidelines for the believers in Rome. The Christian life is not abstract theology unconnected with life, but has practical implications which will affect how we choose to behave each day. It is not enough merely to know the gospel; we must let it transform our lives and let God impact every aspect of our lives.

MEGATHEMES

THEME	EXPLANATION	IMPORTANCE
Sin	Sin means refusing to do God's will and failing to do all that God wants. Since Adam's rebellion against God, our nature is to disobey him. Our sin cuts us off from God. Sin causes us to want to live our own way rather than God's way. Because God is morally perfect, just, and fair, he is right to condemn sin.	Each person has sinned, either by rebelling against God or by ignoring his will. No matter what our background or how hard we try to live good and moral lives, we cannot earn salvation or remove our sin. Only Christ can save us.
Salvation	Our sin points out our need to be forgiven and cleansed. Although we don't deserve it, God, in his kindness, reached out to love and forgive us. He provides the way for us to be saved. Christ's death paid the penalty for our sin.	It is good news that God saves us from our sin. But we must believe in Jesus Christ and that he forgave our sin in order to enter into a wonderful new relationship with God.
Growth	By God's power, believers are sanctified—made holy. This means we are set apart from sin, enabled to obey and to become more like Christ. When we are growing in our relationship with Christ, the Holy Spirit frees us from the demands of the law and from fear of judgment.	Because we are free from sin's control, the law's demands, and fear of God's punishment, we can grow in our relationship with Christ. By trusting in the Holy Spirit and allowing him to help us, we can overcome sin and temptation.
Sovereignty	God oversees and cares about his people—past, present, and future. God's ways of dealing with people are always fair. Because God is in charge of all creation, he can save whomever he wills.	Because of God's mercy, both Jews and Gentiles can be saved. We all must respond to his mercy and accept his gracious offer of forgiveness. Because he is sovereign, let him reign in your heart.
Service	When our purpose is to give credit to God for his love, power, and perfection in all we do, we can serve him properly. Serving him unifies all believers and enables them to show love and sensitivity to others.	Each one of us can't be fully Christlike by ourselves—it takes the entire body of Christ to fully express Christ. By actively and vigorously building up other believers, Christians can be a symphony of service to God.

A. WHAT TO BELIEVE (1.1—11.36)

Paul begins his message to the Romans by vividly portraying the sinfulness of all mankind, explaining how forgiveness is available through faith in Christ, and showing what believers experience in life through their new faith. In this section, we learn of the centrality of faith to becoming a Christian and to living the Christian life. Apart from faith, we have no hope in life.

1. Sinfulness of mankind

1 Paul, a servant[a] of Jesus Christ, called to be an apostle, set apart for the gospel **1.2**
of God, 2 which he promised beforehand through his prophets in the holy scrip- Rom 3.21 Tit 1.2
tures, 3 the gospel concerning his Son, who was descended from David according **1.3**
to the flesh 4 and was declared to be Son of God with power according to the spirit[b] Mt 1.1-17 **1.5**
of holiness by resurrection from the dead, Jesus Christ our Lord, 5 through whom Acts 9.15
we have received grace and apostleship to bring about the obedience of faith among Rom 16.26 Gal 1.16
all the Gentiles for the sake of his name, 6 including yourselves who are called to Eph 3.8,9
belong to Jesus Christ, **1.6** 1 Cor 1.3
7 To all God's beloved in Rome, who are called to be saints: 2 Cor 1.2 Eph 1.1,2
Grace to you and peace from God our Father and the Lord Jesus Christ.

Paul declares the power of the gospel

8 First, I thank my God through Jesus Christ for all of you, because your faith

[a] Gk *slave* [b] Or *Spirit*

1.1 Paul wrote this letter to the church in Rome. Neither he nor the other church leaders, James and Peter, had yet been to Rome. The Roman church was established by believers who had been at Jerusalem for Pentecost (Acts 2.10) and travelers who had heard the good news in other places and brought it back to Rome (for example, Priscilla and Aquila, Acts 18.2; Romans 16.3–5). Paul wrote the letter to the Romans during his ministry in Corinth (at the end of his third missionary journey just before returning to Jerusalem; Acts 20.3; Romans 15.25) to encourage the believers and to express his desire to visit them someday (within three years he would). The Roman church had no New Testament, because the Gospels were not yet being circulated in their final written form. Thus, this letter may well have been the first piece of Christian literature the Roman believers had seen. Written to both Jewish and Gentile Christians, the letter to the Romans is a systematic presentation of the Christian faith.

1.1 When Paul, a devout Jew who had at first persecuted the Christians, became a believer, God used him to spread the gospel throughout the world. Although it was as a prisoner, Paul did eventually preach in Rome (Acts 28), perhaps even to Caesar himself. Paul's Profile is found in Acts 10.

1.1 Paul humbly calls himself a servant of Jesus Christ and an apostle ("one who is sent"). For a Roman citizen—which Paul was—to choose to be a servant was unthinkable. But Paul chose to be completely dependent on and obedient to his beloved Master. What is your attitude toward Christ, your Master? Our willingness to serve and obey Jesus Christ enables us to be useful and usable servants to do work for him—work that really matters.

1.2 Some of the prophecies predicting the good news of Jesus Christ are Genesis 12.3; Psalms 16.10; 40.6–10; 118.22; Isaiah 11.1ff; Zechariah 9.9–11; 12.10; Malachi 4.1–6.

1.3, 4 Paul states that Jesus is the Son of God, the promised Messiah, and the resurrected Lord. Paul called Jesus a descendant of King David to emphasize that Jesus truly fulfilled the Old Testament Scriptures predicting that the Messiah would come from David's line. With this statement of faith, Paul declared his agreement with the teaching of all Scripture and of the apostles.

1.3–5 Here Paul summarizes the good news about Jesus Christ who (1) came as a human ("according to the flesh" means by natural descent), (2) was part of the Jewish royal line through David, (3) died and was raised from the dead, and (4) opened the door for God's kindness to be poured out on us. The book of Romans is an expansion of these themes.

1.5, 6 Christians have both privilege and a great responsibility. Paul and the apostles received forgiveness ("grace") as an undeserved privilege. But they also received the responsibility ("apostleship") to share the message of God's forgiveness with others ("obedience of faith among all the Gentiles"). God also graciously forgives our sins when we believe in him as Lord. In doing this, we are committing ourselves to begin a new life. Paul's new life also involved a God-given responsibility—to witness of God's good news to the world as a missionary. God may or may not call you to be an overseas missionary, but he does call you (and all believers) to witness and be an example of the changed life Jesus Christ has begun in you.

1.6, 7 Paul says that those who become Christians are *called* (summoned or invited) by Jesus Christ (1) to become part of God's family, and (2) to be holy people ("to be saints," set apart, dedicated for his service). What a wonderful expression of what it means to be a Christian! In being reborn into God's family we have the greatest love and the greatest inheritance. Because of all that God has done for us, we should strive to be his holy people.

1.6–12 Paul showed his love for the Roman Christians by expressing God's love for them and his own thanks and prayers for them. To have an effect on people's lives, you first need to love them and believe in them. Paul's passion to teach these people began with his love for them. Thank God for your Christian brothers and sisters, and let them know how deeply you care for them.

1.7 Rome was the capital of the Roman Empire, which had spread over most of Europe, North Africa, and the Near East. In New Testament times, Rome was experiencing a "golden age." This was a time of world peace. The city was wealthy, literary, and artistic. It was a cultural center, but it was also morally decadent. The Romans worshiped many pagan gods, and even some of the emperors were worshiped. In contrast to this, the followers of Christ believed in only one God and lived by his high moral standards.

1.7 Christianity was at odds with the Romans' dependence on their military strength. Many Romans were naively pragmatic, believing that any means to accomplish the intended task was good. And for them, nothing worked better than physical might. The Romans trusted in their strong military power to protect them against all enemies. Christians in every age need to be reminded that God is the only permanent source of our security and salvation, and at the same time he is "our Father"!

1.9 Eph 1.16 Phil 1.3 1 Thess 1.2 2 Tim 1.3 Philem 4-7
1.10 Jas 4.15
1.11 Rom 15.29
1.13 Rom 15.22,23
1.14 Ps 40.9 1 Cor 9.16

is proclaimed throughout the world. 9 For God, whom I serve with my spirit by
announcing the gospel[c] of his Son, is my witness that without ceasing I remember
you always in my prayers, 10 asking that by God's will I may somehow at last succeed in coming to you. 11 For I am longing to see you so that I may share with you
some spiritual gift to strengthen you— 12 or rather so that we may be mutually
encouraged by each other's faith, both yours and mine. 13 I want you to know,
brothers and sisters,[d] that I have often intended to come to you (but thus far have
been prevented), in order that I may reap some harvest among you as I have among
the rest of the Gentiles. 14 I am a debtor both to Greeks and to barbarians, both to
the wise and to the foolish 15 — hence my eagerness to proclaim the gospel to you
also who are in Rome.

c Gk *my spirit in the gospel* d Gk *brothers*

THE GOSPEL GOES TO ROME
When Paul wrote his letter to the church in Rome, he had not yet been there, but he had taken the gospel "from Jerusalem and as far around as Illyricum" (15.19). He planned to visit and preach in Rome one day, and hoped to continue to take the gospel farther west—even to Spain.

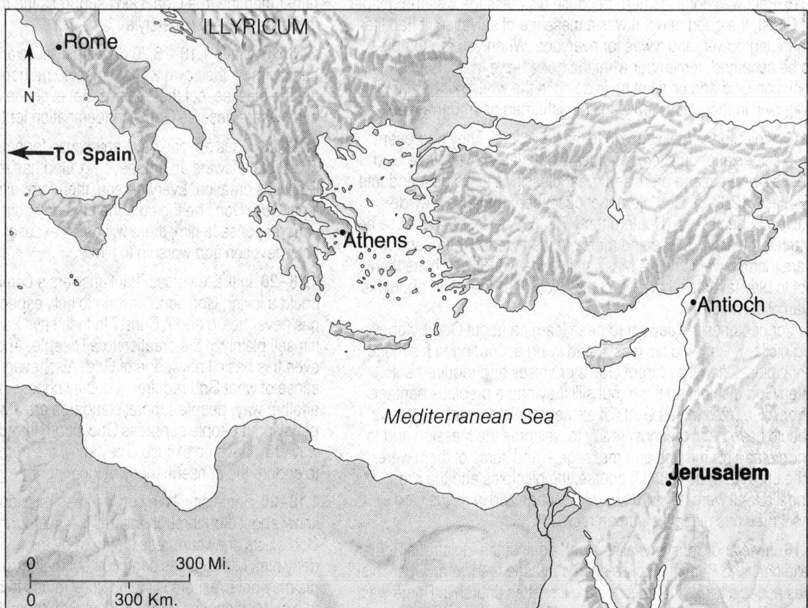

1.8 Paul used the phrase "I thank my God through Jesus Christ" to emphasize that Christ is the one and only mediator between God and man. Through Christ, God sends his love and forgiveness to us; through Christ, we send our thanks to God (see 1 Timothy 2.5).

1.8 The Roman Christians, at the Western world's political power center, were highly visible. Fortunately, their reputation was excellent; their strong faith was making itself known around the world. When people talk about your congregation or your denomination, what do they say? Are their comments accurate? Would you rather they noticed other features? What is the best way to get the public to recognize your faith?

1.9, 10 When you pray continually about a concern, don't be surprised at how God answers. Paul prayed to visit Rome so he could teach the Christians there. When he finally arrived, it was as a prisoner (see Acts 28.16). Paul prayed for a safe trip, and he did arrive safely—after getting arrested, slapped in the face, shipwrecked, and bitten by a poisonous snake. God's ways of answering our prayers are often far from what we expect. When you sincerely pray, God will answer—although sometimes with timing and in ways you do not expect.

1.11, 12 Paul prayed for the chance to visit these Christians so that he could encourage them with his gift of faith and be encouraged by theirs. As God's missionary, he could help them understand the meaning of the good news about Jesus. As God's devoted people, they could offer him fellowship and comfort. When Christians gather, everyone should give *and* receive. Our mutual faith gives us a common language and a common purpose for encouraging one another.

1.13 By the end of his third missionary journey, Paul had traveled through Syria, Galatia, Asia, Macedonia, and Achaia. The churches in these areas consisted mostly of Gentile believers.

1.14 By *Greeks* and *barbarians,* Paul was referring to civilized and uncivilized people; *wise* and *foolish* refers to educated and uneducated people. What was Paul's debt? After his experience with Christ on the Damascus Road (Acts 9), his whole life was consumed with spreading the good news of salvation. His debt was to Christ for being his Savior, and it was payable to the entire world. He paid his debt of love by proclaiming Christ's salvation to *all* people—both Jews and Gentiles, across all cultural, social, racial, and economic lines. We owe Christ this same debt of love because he took on the punishment we deserve for our sin. Although we cannot repay him for all he has done, we can demonstrate our gratitude by showing his love to others.

16 For I am not ashamed of the gospel; it is the power of God for salvation to **1.16** 2 Tim 1.8-12
everyone who has faith, to the Jew first and also to the Greek. 17 For in it the righ- **1.17** Hab 2.4
teousness of God is revealed through faith for faith; as it is written, "The one who
is righteous will live by faith."[e]

God's anger at sin

18 For the wrath of God is revealed from heaven against all ungodliness and
wickedness of those who by their wickedness suppress the truth. 19 For what can be **1.19** Jn 1.9
known about God is plain to them, because God has shown it to them. 20 Ever since Acts 14.17
the creation of the world his eternal power and divine nature, invisible though they **1.20** Ps 19.1
are, have been understood and seen through the things he has made. So they are Acts 17.24

[e] Or *The one who is righteous through faith will live*

1.16 Paul was not ashamed, because his message was the gospel of Christ, the good news. It was a message of salvation, it had life-changing power, and it was for everyone. When you are tempted to be ashamed, remember what the good news is all about. If you focus on God and on what he is doing in the world rather than on your own inadequacy, you won't be ashamed or embarrassed.

1.16 Why did the message go to the Jews first? They had been God's special people for more than 2,000 years, ever since God chose Abraham and promised great blessings to his descendants (Genesis 12.1–3). God did not choose them because they deserved to be chosen (Deuteronomy 7.7, 8; 9.4–6), but because he wanted to show his love and mercy to them, teach them, and prepare them to welcome his Messiah into the world. He chose them not to play favorites, but so that they would tell the world about his plan of salvation.

For centuries the Jews had been learning about God by obeying his laws, keeping his feasts, and living according to his moral principles. Often they forgot God's promises and requirements; often God disciplined them; but still they had a precious heritage of belief in the one true God. Of all the people on earth, the Jews should have been the most ready to welcome the Messiah and to understand his mission and message—and some of them were (see Luke 2.25, 36–38). Of course, the disciples and the great apostle Paul were faithful Jews who recognized in Jesus God's most precious gift to the human race.

1.16 Jews and Christians alike stood against the idolatrous Roman religions, and Roman officials often confused the two groups. This was especially easy to do since the Christian church in Rome was originally composed of Jewish converts who attended the feast of Pentecost (see Acts 2.1ff). By the time Paul wrote this letter to the Romans, however, many Gentiles had joined the church. The Jews and the Gentiles needed to know the relationship between Judaism and Christianity.

1.17 The gospel shows us both how righteous God is in his plan for us to be saved, and also how we may be made fit for eternal life. By trusting Christ, our relationship with God is made right. "Through faith for faith" means that from start to finish God declares us to be righteous because of faith and faith alone.

1.17 Paul was quoting Habakkuk 2.4. Habakkuk may have understood *life* to mean this present life only, but Paul extends this statement to include eternal life. As we trust God, we are saved: we find life both now and forever.

1.18 *Wrath* implies judgment against sin, not just being angry. Why is God angry at sinful people? Because they have substituted the truth about him with a fantasy of their own imagination (1.25). They have stifled the truth God naturally reveals to all people in order to believe anything that supports their own self-centered lifestyles. God cannot tolerate sin because his nature is morally perfect. He cannot ignore or condone such willful rebellion. He wants to remove the sin and restore the sinner—if the sinner does not distort or reject the truth. But his anger erupts against those who persist in sinning. Make sure you are not pursuing a fantasy rather than the true God. Don't suppress the truth about him merely to protect your own life-style.

1.18ff Romans 1.18–3.20 develops Paul's argument that no one can claim by their own work or merit to be good in God's sight—not the masses, not the Romans, not even the Jews. All people everywhere deserve God's condemnation for their sin.

1.18–20 Does anyone have an excuse for not believing in God? The Bible answers an emphatic *no.* God has revealed what he is like in his creation. Every person, therefore, either accepts or rejects God. Don't be fooled. When the day comes for God to judge your response to him, there will be no excuses. Begin today to give your devotion and worship to him.

1.18–20 In these verses, Paul answers a common objection: How could a loving God send anyone to hell, especially someone who has never heard about Christ? In fact, says Paul, God has revealed himself plainly in the creation to *all* people. And yet people reject even this basic knowledge of God. Also, everyone has an inner sense of what God requires, but they choose not to live up to it. Put another way, people's moral standards are always better than their behavior. If people suppress God's truth in order to live their own way, they have no excuse. They know the truth, and they will have to endure the consequences of ignoring it.

1.18–20 Some say, "Why do we need missionaries if people can know about God through nature?" (1) Although people know that God exists, they suppress that truth by their wickedness and thus deny him. Missionaries can point out their error. (2) Although people may believe there is a God, they refuse to commit themselves to him. Missionaries can help persuade them. (3) Missionaries can convince people who reject God of the dangerous consequences of their actions. (4) Most importantly, though nature reveals God, people need to be told about Jesus and how through him they can have a personal relationship with God. (5) Missionaries are needed to help the church obey the great commission of our Lord (Matthew 28.19, 20).

Knowing that God exists is not enough. People must learn that God is loving. They must understand what he did to show that love to us. They must be shown how to accept his forgiveness of their sins. (See also 10.14, 15.)

1.20 What kind of God does nature reveal? Nature shows us a God of might, intelligence, and intricate detail; a God of order and beauty; a God who controls powerful forces. That is *general* revelation. Through *special* revelation (the Bible and the coming of Jesus), we learn about God's love, forgiveness, and promise of eternal life. God has graciously given us both sources that we might more completely believe in him.

1.20 God reveals his nature and personal qualities through creation, even though nature's testimony has been distorted by the Fall. Adam's sin resulted in a divine curse upon the whole natural order (Genesis 3.17–19); thorns and thistles were an immediate result, and natural disasters have been common from Adam's day to ours. In Romans 8.19–21, Paul says that nature itself is eagerly awaiting its own redemption from the effects of sin (see Revelation 22.3).

1.21 2 Kgs 17.15; Ps 106.13; Eph 4.17,18
1.22 Jer 10.14; 1 Cor 1.20
1.23 Ps 106.20; Isa 40.18; Jer 2.11
1.24 Lev 18.22

without excuse; 21 for though they knew God, they did not honor him as God or give
thanks to him, but they became futile in their thinking, and their senseless minds
were darkened. 22 Claiming to be wise, they became fools; 23 and they exchanged
the glory of the immortal God for images resembling a mortal human being or birds
or four-footed animals or reptiles.
24 Therefore God gave them up in the lusts of their hearts to impurity, to the
degrading of their bodies among themselves, 25 because they exchanged the truth
about God for a lie and worshiped and served the creature rather than the Creator,
who is blessed forever! Amen.

FAITH

Faith is a word with many meanings. It can mean faithfulness (Matthew 24.45). It can mean absolute trust, as shown by some of the people who came to Jesus for healing (Luke 7.2–10). It can mean confident hope (Hebrews 11.1). Or, as James points out, it can even mean a barren belief that does not result in good works (James 2.14–26). What does Paul mean when, in Romans, he speaks of saving faith?

We must be very careful to understand faith as Paul uses the word, because he ties faith so closely to salvation. It is *not* something we must do in order to earn salvation—if that were true, then faith would be just one more work, and Paul clearly states that human works can never save us (Galatians 2.16). Instead, faith is a gift God gives us *because* he is saving us (Ephesians 2.8). It is God's grace, not our faith, that saves us. In his mercy, however, when he saves us he gives us faith—a relationship with his Son that helps us become like him. Through the faith he gives us, he carries us from death into life (John 5.24).

Even in Old Testament times grace, not works, was the basis of salvation. As Hebrews points out, "it is impossible for the blood of bulls and goats to take away sins" (10.4). God intended for his people to look beyond the animal sacrifices to him, but all too often they, instead, put their confidence in fulfilling the requirements of the law—that is, performing the required sacrifices. When Jesus triumphed over death, he cancelled the charges against us and opened the way to the Father (Colossians 2.12–15). Because he is merciful, he offers us faith. How tragic if we turn faith into a work and try to develop it on our own! We can never come to God through our own faith, any more than his Old Testament people could come through their own sacrifices. Instead, we must accept his gracious offer with thanksgiving and allow him to plant the seed of faith within us.

1.21–24 How could intelligent people turn to idolatry? Idolatry begins when people reject what they know about God. Instead of looking to him as the Creator and sustainer of life, they see themselves as the center of the universe. They soon invent "gods" that are convenient projections of their own selfish plans and decrees. These gods may be wooden figures, but they may also be goals such as money, power, or comfort. They may even be misrepresentations of God himself – making God in our image, instead of the reverse. The common denominator is this – idolators worship the things God made rather than God himself. Is there anything you feel you can't live without? Is there any priority greater than God? Do you have a dream you would sacrifice everything to realize? Does God take first place? Do you worship God or idols of your own making?

1.21–32 Paul clearly portrays the inevitable downward spiral into sin. First people reject God; next they make up their own ideas of what a god should be and do; then they fall into sin – sexual sin, greed, hatred, envy, murder, fighting, lying, bitterness, gossip. Finally they grow to hate God and encourage others to do so. God does not cause this steady progression toward evil. Rather, when people reject him, he allows them to live as they choose. God gives them up or commits them to experience the natural consequences of their sin. Once caught in the downward spiral, no one can pull himself out. Sinners must trust Christ alone to put them on the path of escape.

1.23 When Paul says that men exchanged God's glory for images of birds, animals, and reptiles, he seems to deliberately state man's wickedness in the terms used in the Genesis narrative of Adam's fall (see Genesis 1.20–26). When we worship the creature instead of the Creator, we lose sight of our own identity as higher than the animals – made in the image of God.

1.24–32 These people chose to reject God, and God allowed them to do it. God does not usually stop us from making choices against his will. He lets us declare our supposed independence from him, even though he knows that in time we will become slaves to our own rebellious choices – we will lose our freedom not to sin. Does life without God look like freedom to you? Look more closely. There is no worse slavery than slavery to sin.

1.25 People tend to believe lies that reinforce their own selfish, personal beliefs. Today more than ever we need to be careful about what we allow to form our beliefs. With TV, music, movies, and the rest of the media often presenting sinful life-styles and unwholesome values, we find ourselves constantly bombarded by attitudes and beliefs that are totally opposed to the Bible. Be careful about what you allow to form your opinions. The Bible is the only standard of truth. Evaluate all other opinions in light of its teachings.

26 For this reason God gave them up to degrading passions. Their women ex- **1.26**
changed natural intercourse for unnatural, 27 and in the same way also the men, 1 Thess 4.5 Jude 1
giving up natural intercourse with women, were consumed with passion for one **1.27**
another. Men committed shameless acts with men and received in their own per- Lev 18.22; 20.13 1 Cor 6.9,10
sons the due penalty for their error.
28 And since they did not see fit to acknowledge God, God gave them up to a **1.28**
debased mind and to things that should not be done. 29 They were filled with every Eph 5.4
kind of wickedness, evil, covetousness, malice. Full of envy, murder, strife, deceit, craftiness, they are gossips, 30 slanderers, God-haters,[f] insolent, haughty, **1.30** 2 Tim 3.2
boastful, inventors of evil, rebellious toward parents, 31 foolish, faithless, heart- **1.31**
less, ruthless. 32 They know God's decree, that those who practice such things de- 2 Tim 3.3 **1.32**
serve to die — yet they not only do them but even applaud others who practice them. Rom 6.21,23

God's judgment of sin

2 Therefore you have no excuse, whoever you are, when you judge others; for in **2.1**
passing judgment on another you condemn yourself, because you, the judge, 2 Sam 12.5-9 Mt 7.1
are doing the very same things. 2 You say,[g] "We know that God's judgment on **2.3**
those who do such things is in accordance with truth." 3 Do you imagine, whoever Prov 11.21
you are, that when you judge those who do such things and yet do them yourself, **2.4** Ex 34.5,6
you will escape the judgment of God? 4 Or do you despise the riches of his kindness 2 Pet 3.9
and forbearance and patience? Do you not realize that God's kindness is meant to **2.5** Ps 110.5
lead you to repentance? 5 But by your hard and impenitent heart you are storing up Jas 5.3

[f] Or *God-hated* [g] Gk lacks *You say*

1.26, 27 God's plan for natural sexual relationships is his ideal for his creation. Unfortunately, sin distorts the natural use of God's gifts. Sin often means not only denying God, but also denying the way we are made. When people say that any sex act is acceptable so long as nobody gets hurt, they are fooling themselves. In the long run (and often in the short run), sin hurts people – individuals, families, whole societies. How sad that people who worship the things God made instead of the Creator so often distort and destroy the very things they claim to value!

1.26, 27 Homosexuality was as widespread in Paul's day as it is in ours. Many pagan practices encouraged it. God is willing to receive anyone who comes to him in faith and Christians should love and accept others no matter what their background. Yet, homosexuality is strictly forbidden in Scripture (Leviticus 18.22). Homosexuality is considered an acceptable practice by many in our world today – even by some churches. But society does not set the standard for God's law. Many homosexuals believe that their desires are normal and that they have a right to express them. But God does not obligate nor encourage us to fulfill all of our desires (even normal ones). All desires that violate his laws must be controlled.

If you have these desires, you can and must resist acting upon them. Consciously avoid places or activities you know will kindle temptations of this kind. Don't underestimate the power of Satan to tempt you nor the potential for serious harm if you yield to these temptations. Remember, God can and will forgive sexual sins just as he forgives other sins. Surrender yourself to the grace and mercy of God, asking him to show you the way out of sin and into the light of his freedom and love. Prayer, Bible study, and strong support in a Christian church can help you to gain strength to resist these powerful temptations. If you are already deeply involved in homosexual behavior, seek help from a trustworthy, professional, pastoral counselor.

1.32 How were these people aware of God's death penalty? Human beings, created in God's image, have a basic moral nature and a conscience. This truth is understood beyond religious circles. Psychologists, for example, say that the rare person who has no conscience has a serious personality disorder, one that is extremely difficult to treat. Most people instinctively know when they do wrong – but they may not care. Some people will even risk an early death for the freedom to indulge their desires now. "I know it's wrong, but I really want it," they say; or, "I know it's dangerous, but it's worth the risk." For such people, part of the "fun" is going against God's law, the community's moral standards, common sense, or their own sense of right and wrong. But deep down inside they know that sin deserves the punishment of death (6.23).

2.1 Whenever we find ourselves feeling justifiably angry about someone's sin, we should be careful. We need to speak out against sin, but we must do so in a spirit of humility. Often the sins we notice most clearly in others are the ones that have taken root in us. If we look closely at ourselves, we may find that we are committing the same sin in more socially acceptable forms. For example, a person who gossips may be very critical of others who gossip.

2.1ff When Paul's letter was read in the Roman church, no doubt many heads nodded as he condemned idol worshipers, homosexual practices, and violent people. But what surprise his listeners must have felt when he turned on them and said, "You are just as bad!" Paul was emphatically stressing that *nobody* is good enough to save himself or herself. If we want to avoid punishment and live eternally with Christ, all of us, whether we have been murderers and molesters or honest, hardworking, solid citizens, must depend totally on God's grace. Paul is not discussing whether some sins are worse than others. Any sin is enough to cause us to depend on Jesus Christ for salvation and eternal life. We have all sinned repeatedly, and there is no way apart from Christ to be saved from sin's consequences.

2.4 In his kindness, God holds back his judgment, giving people time to repent. It is easy to mistake God's patience for approval of the wrong way we are living. Self-evaluation is difficult, and it is even more difficult to expose our conduct to God and let him tell us where we need to change. But as Christians we must pray constantly that God will point out our sins, so that he can heal them. Unfortunately, we are more likely to be amazed at God's patience with others than humbled at his patience with us.

2.5–11 Although God does not usually punish us immediately for sin, his eventual judgment is certain. We don't know exactly when it will happen, but we know that no one will escape that final encounter with the Creator. For more on judgment, see John 12.48 and Revelation 20.11–15.

wrath for yourself on the day of wrath, when God's righteous judgment will be
revealed. 6 For he will repay according to each one's deeds: 7 to those who by patiently doing good seek for glory and honor and immortality, he will give eternal
life; 8 while for those who are self-seeking and who obey not the truth but wickedness, there will be wrath and fury. 9 There will be anguish and distress for everyone
who does evil, the Jew first and also the Greek, 10 but glory and honor and peace for
everyone who does good, the Jew first and also the Greek. 11 For God shows no
partiality.
12 All who have sinned apart from the law will also perish apart from the law,
and all who have sinned under the law will be judged by the law. 13 For it is not the
hearers of the law who are righteous in God's sight, but the doers of the law who
will be justified. 14 When Gentiles, who do not possess the law, do instinctively
what the law requires, these, though not having the law, are a law to themselves.
15 They show that what the law requires is written on their hearts, to which their
own conscience also bears witness; and their conflicting thoughts will accuse or
perhaps excuse them 16 on the day when, according to my gospel, God, through
Jesus Christ, will judge the secret thoughts of all.

2.6 Mt 16.27
2.7 Mt 25.46; Lk 8.15; 2 Cor 4.17; Heb 10.36; Jude 21; Rev 2.7
2.8 Isa 3.11; 2 Thess 2.12
2.11 Job 34.19
2.12-15 Mt 7.21-26; Jn 13.17; Acts 10.35; Jas 1.22
2.16 Jn 5.22; Acts 10.42; Rom 16.25,26; Rev 20.12

God's law is broken

17 But if you call yourself a Jew and rely on the law and boast of your relation
to God 18 and know his will and determine what is best because you are instructed
in the law, 19 and if you are sure that you are a guide to the blind, a light to those
who are in darkness, 20 a corrector of the foolish, a teacher of children, having in
the law the embodiment of knowledge and truth, 21 you, then, that teach others, will
you not teach yourself? While you preach against stealing, do you steal? 22 You that
forbid adultery, do you commit adultery? You that abhor idols, do you rob temples? 23 You that boast in the law, do you dishonor God by breaking the law? 24 For,

2.21 Mt 23.3
2.22 Mal 3.8
2.23 Jn 5.45
2.24 2 Sam 12.14; Isa 52.5; Ezek 36.20

SALVATION'S FREEWAY

Romans 3.23	Everyone has sinned.
Romans 6.23	The penalty for our sin is death.
Romans 5.8	Jesus Christ died for sin.
Romans 10.8–10	To be forgiven for our sin, we must believe and confess that Jesus is Lord. Salvation comes through Jesus Christ.

2.7 Paul says that those who patiently *do* God's will will find eternal life. He is not contradicting his previous statement that salvation comes by faith alone (1.16, 17). We are not saved by good works. But when we commit our lives fully to God, we want to please him and do his will. As such, our good works are a grateful *response* to what God has done, not a prerequisite to earning his grace.

2.12–15 People are not condemned for what they don't know, but for what they do with what they know. Those who know God's written Word and his law will be judged by them. Those who have never seen a Bible still know right from wrong. They will be judged because they did not keep even those standards their own consciences dictated. Our modern-day sense of fair play and the rights of the individual often balks at God's judgment. But keep in mind, people violate the standards they create for themselves.

2.12–15 If you traveled around the world, you would find evidence in every society and culture of God's moral law. For example, all cultures prohibit murder, and yet in all societies that law has been broken. We belong to a stubborn race. We know what's right, but we insist on doing what is wrong. It is not enough to know what's right; we must also do it. Admit to yourself and to God that you fit the human pattern and frequently fail to live up to your own standards (much less to God's standards). That's the first step to forgiveness and healing.

2.17ff Paul continues to argue that all stand guilty before God. After describing the fate of the unbelieving, pagan Gentiles, he moves to that of the religiously privileged. Despite their knowledge of God's will, they are guilty because they too have refused to live by their beliefs. Those of us who have grown up in Christian families are the religiously privileged of today. Paul's condemnation applies to us if we do not live up to what we know.

2.21, 22 Paul explained to the Jews that they needed to teach *themselves,* not others, by their law. They knew the law so well that they had learned how to excuse their own actions while criticizing others. But the law is more than legalistic minimum requirements—it is a guideline for living according to God's will. It is also a reminder that we cannot please God without a proper relationship to him. As Jesus pointed out, even withholding what rightfully belongs to someone else is stealing (Mark 7.9–13), and looking on another person with lustful, adulterous intent is adultery (Matthew 5.27, 28). Before we accuse others, we must look at ourselves and see if that sin, in any form, exists within us.

2.21–27 These verses are a scathing criticism of hypocrisy. It is much easier to tell others how to behave than to behave properly ourselves. It is easier to say the right words than to allow them to take root in our lives. Do you ever advise others to do something you are unwilling to do yourself? Make sure your actions match your words.

2.24 If you claim to be one of God's people, your life should reflect what God is like. When you disobey God, you dishonor his name. People may even speak evil of God because of you. What do people think about God from watching your life?

as it is written, "The name of God is blasphemed among the Gentiles because of
you."
25 Circumcision indeed is of value if you obey the law; but if you break the law,
your circumcision has become uncircumcision. 26 So, if those who are uncircumcised keep the requirements of the law, will not their uncircumcision be regarded as
circumcision? 27 Then those who are physically uncircumcised but keep the law
will condemn you that have the written code and circumcision but break the law.
28 For a person is not a Jew who is one outwardly, nor is true circumcision something external and physical. 29 Rather, a person is a Jew who is one inwardly, and
real circumcision is a matter of the heart—it is spiritual and not literal. Such a
person receives praise not from others but from God.

God remains faithful

3 Then what advantage has the Jew? Or what is the value of circumcision?
2 Much, in every way. For in the first place the Jews[h] were entrusted with the
oracles of God. 3 What if some were unfaithful? Will their faithlessness nullify the
faithfulness of God? 4 By no means! Although everyone is a liar, let God be proved
true, as it is written,

"So that you may be justified in your words,
and prevail in your judging."[i]

5 But if our injustice serves to confirm the justice of God, what should we say? That
God is unjust to inflict wrath on us? (I speak in a human way.) 6 By no means! For
then how could God judge the world? 7 But if through my falsehood God's truthfulness abounds to his glory, why am I still being condemned as a sinner? 8 And why
not say (as some people slander us by saying that we say), "Let us do evil so that
good may come"? Their condemnation is deserved!

All people are sinners

9 What then? Are we any better off?[j] No, not at all; for we have already

[h] Gk *they* [i] Gk *when you are being judged* [j] Or *at any disadvantage?*

2.25 Gal 5.3
2.26 Acts 10.34
2.28 Mt 3.9; Jn 8.39; Gal 6.15; Rev 2.9
2.29 Jn 1.47; Rom 7.6; 2 Cor 3.6; Phil 3.3; Col 2.11; 1 Pet 3.4
3.2 Deut 4.8; Ps 147.19; Acts 7.38
3.3 Num 23.18,19
3.4 Ps 51.4; 62.9
3.5 Rom 5.8; 7.7; Gal 3.15
3.6 Job 34.17
3.7 Rom 9.19,20
3.8 Rom 5.20

2.25–29 *Circumcision* refers to God's special covenant with his people. It was required of all Jewish males (Genesis 17.9–14). According to Paul, being a Jew (being circumcised) meant nothing if the person didn't obey God's laws. On the other hand, the Gentiles (the uncircumcised) would receive God's love and approval if they obeyed God's laws. Paul goes on to explain that a "real Jew" (one who pleases God) is not someone who has been circumcised (a Jew "outwardly") but someone whose heart is right with God and obeys him (a Jew "inwardly").

2.28, 29 To be a Jew meant you were in God's family, an heir to all his promises. Yet Paul made it clear that membership in God's family is based on internal, not external, qualities. All whose hearts are right with God are real Jews—that is, part of God's family (see also Galatians 3.7). Attending church or being baptized, confirmed, or accepted for membership are not enough, just as circumcision was not enough for the Jews. God desires our devotion and obedience. (See also Deuteronomy 10.16; Jeremiah 4.4 for more on "circumcising the heart.")

3.1ff In this chapter Paul contends that everyone stands guilty before God. Paul has dismantled the common excuses of people who refuse to admit they are sinners: (1) "There is no God" or "I follow my conscience"—1.18–32; (2) "I'm not as bad as other people"—2.1–16; (3) "I'm a church member" or "I'm a religious person"—2.17–29. No one will be exempted from God's judgment on sin. Every person must accept that he or she is sinful and condemned by God. Only then can we understand and receive God's wonderful gift of salvation.

3.1ff What a depressing picture Paul is painting! All of us—pagan Gentiles, humanitarians, or religious people—are condemned by our own actions. The law, which God gave to show the way to live, holds up our evil deeds to public view. Is there any hope for us? Yes, says Paul. The law condemns us, it is true, but the law is not the basis of our hope. God himself is. He, in his righteousness and wonderful love, offers us eternal life. We receive our salvation not through law but through faith in Jesus Christ. We do not—cannot—earn it; we accept it as a gift from our loving heavenly Father. In fact, as Paul notes at the very end of the chapter and develops in chapter 4, this was originally the point of the law.

3.2 The Jewish nation had many advantages. (1) They were entrusted with God's law (the "oracles" or utterances of God, Exodus 19, 20; Deuteronomy 4.8). (2) They were the race through whom the Messiah came to earth (Isaiah 11.1–10; Matthew 1.1–17). (3) They were the beneficiaries of covenants with God himself (Genesis 17.1–16; Exodus 19.3–6). But these privileges did not make them better than anyone else (see 3.9). In fact, because of them, the Jews were even more responsible to live up to God's requirements.

3.4 This promise that God's words will always prove true ("be justified in your words"), no matter what anyone says or does, is both a comfort and a challenge. It is a comfort to have a solid and unchanging foundation on which to build our lives. It is a challenge to make the changes that God's words require. If you have been struggling with habits, attitudes, or ideas that do not agree with God's words, a fresh recognition that God has spoken to you in the Bible will help you change.

3.5–8 Some may think that they don't have to worry about sin because (1) it's God's job to forgive; (2) God is so loving, he won't judge us; (3) sin isn't so bad—it teaches us valuable lessons, or (4) we need to stay in touch with the culture around us. It is far too easy to take God's grace for granted. But God cannot overlook sin. Sinners, no matter how many excuses they make, will have to answer to God for their sin.

3.9 Rom 1.18-32 2.1-29 Gal 3.21,22 | charged that all, both Jews and Greeks, are under the power of sin, [10] as it is written:
"There is no one who is righteous, not even one;
3.10 Ps 14.1-3 53.1-4
11 there is no one who has understanding,
there is no one who seeks God.
12 All have turned aside, together they have become worthless;
there is no one who shows kindness,
there is not even one."
3.13 Ps 5.9; 140.3
13 "Their throats are opened graves;
they use their tongues to deceive."
3.14 Ps 10.7
"The venom of vipers is under their lips."
3.15 Prov 1.16 Isa 59.7
14 "Their mouths are full of cursing and bitterness."
15 "Their feet are swift to shed blood;
16 ruin and misery are in their paths,
3.18 Ps 36.1
17 and the way of peace they have not known."
3.19 Rom 2.2,12
18 "There is no fear of God before their eyes."
3.20 Ps 143.2 Acts 13.39 Rom 4.15; 7.7 Gal 2.16; 3.11
19 Now we know that whatever the law says, it speaks to those who are under
the law, so that every mouth may be silenced, and the whole world may be held
accountable to God. [20] For "no human being will be justified in his sight" by deeds
prescribed by the law, for through the law comes the knowledge of sin.

2. Forgiveness of sin through Christ

Christ took our punishment

3.21 Rom 1.2,17
21 But now, apart from law, the righteousness of God has been disclosed, and
is attested by the law and the prophets, [22] the righteousness of God through faith in

CRUCIAL CONCEPTS IN ROMANS

ELECTION Romans 9.10–13	God's choice of an individual or group for a specific purpose or destiny.
JUSTIFICATION Romans 4.25; 5.18	God's act of declaring us "not guilty" for our sins.
PROPITIATION/EXPIATION Romans 3.25	The removal of God's punishment for sin through the perfect sacrifice of Jesus Christ.
REDEMPTION Romans 3.24; 8.23	Jesus Christ has paid the price so we can go free. The price of sin is death; Jesus paid the price.
SANCTIFICATION Romans 5.2; 15.16	Becoming more and more like Jesus Christ through the work of the Holy Spirit.
GLORIFICATION Romans 8.18, 19	The ultimate state of the believer after death when he or she becomes like Christ (1 John 4.4).

3.10–12 Paul is referring to Psalm 14.1–3. "There is no one who is righteous" means "no one is innocent." Every person is valuable in God's eyes because God created us in his image and he loves us. But no one is righteous (that is, no one can earn right standing with God). Though valuable, we have fallen into sin. But God, through Jesus his Son, has redeemed us and will forgive us if we return to him in faith.

3.10–18 Paul uses these Old Testament references to show that humanity in general, in its present sinful condition, is unacceptable before God. Have you ever thought to yourself, "Well, I'm not too bad. I'm a pretty good person"? Look at these verses and see if any of them apply to you. Have you ever lied? Have you ever hurt someone's feelings by your words or tone of voice? Are you bitter toward anyone? Do you become angry with those who strongly disagree with you? In thought, word, and deed you, like everyone else in the world, stand guilty before God. We must remember who we are in his sight – alienated sinners. Don't deny that you are a sinner. Instead, allow your desperate need to point you toward Christ.

3.19 The last time someone accused you of wrongdoing, what was your reaction? Denial, argument, and defensiveness? The Bible tells us the world stands hushed and guilty before Almighty God. No excuses or arguments are left. Have you reached the point with God where you are ready to hang up your defenses and await his decision? If not, stop now and admit your sin to him. If you have, the next five verses are truly good news for you!

3.20, 31 In these verses we see two functions of God's law. First, it shows us where we go wrong. Because of the law, we know we are helpless sinners who must come to Jesus Christ for mercy. Second, the moral code revealed in the law can serve to guide our actions by holding up God's moral standards. We do not earn salvation by keeping the law (no one except Christ ever kept or could keep God's law perfectly), but we do please God when our lives conform to his revealed will for us.

3.21–29 After all this bad news about our sinfulness and God's condemnation, Paul now gives the wonderful news. There is a way to be declared not guilty – by trusting Jesus Christ to take away our sins. Trusting means putting our confidence in him to forgive our sins, to make us right with God, and to empower us to live the way he taught us. God's solution is available to all of us regardless of our background or past behavior.

Jesus Christ[k] for all who believe. For there is no distinction, 23 since all have 3.24
sinned and fall short of the glory of God; 24 they are now justified by his grace as a Eph 1.7; 2.8 1 Pet 1.18,19
gift, through the redemption that is in Christ Jesus, 25 whom God put forward as a 3.25
sacrifice of atonement[l] by his blood, effective through faith. He did this to show Lev 16.15 Acts 17.30
his righteousness, because in his divine forbearance he had passed over the sins Heb 9.13,14 1 Pet 1.19
previously committed; 26 it was to prove at the present time that he himself is righ- 1 Jn 2.2; 4.10
teous and that he justifies the one who has faith in Jesus.[m] 3.27 1 Cor 1.29
27 Then what becomes of boasting? It is excluded. By what law? By that of Eph 2.9
works? No, but by the law of faith. 28 For we hold that a person is justified by faith 3.28 Acts 13.39
apart from works prescribed by the law. 29 Or is God the God of Jews only? Is he 3.29
not the God of Gentiles also? Yes, of Gentiles also, 30 since God is one; and he will Rom 9.24 10.12; 15.9
justify the circumcised on the ground of faith and the uncircumcised through that Gal 3.28
same faith. 31 Do we then overthrow the law by this faith? By no means! On the 3.31 Mt 5.17
contrary, we uphold the law. Lk 20.16

Abraham was justified by faith

4 What then are we to say was gained by[n] Abraham, our ancestor according to 4.2
the flesh? 2 For if Abraham was justified by works, he has something to boast 1 Cor 1.31
about, but not before God. 3 For what does the scripture say? "Abraham believed 4.3 Gen 15.6
God, and it was reckoned to him as righteousness." 4 Now to one who works, Gal 3.6 Jas 2.23
wages are not reckoned as a gift but as something due. 5 But to one who without

[k] Or *through the faith of Jesus Christ* [l] Or *a place of atonement* [m] Or *who has the faith of Jesus* [n] Other ancient authorities read *say about*

3.23 Some sins seem bigger than others because their obvious consequences are much more serious. Murder, for example, seems to us to be worse than hatred, and adultery seems worse than lust. But this does not mean that because we do lesser sins, we deserve eternal life. All sin makes us sinners, and all sin cuts us off from our holy God. All sin, therefore, leads to death (because it disqualifies us from living with God), regardless of how great or small it seems. Don't minimize "little" sins or overrate "big" ones. They all separate us from God. But they all can be forgiven!

3.24 *Justified* means to be declared not guilty. When a judge in a court of law declares the defendant not guilty, all the charges are removed from his record. Legally, it is as if the person had never been accused. When God forgives our sins, our record is wiped clean. It is as though we had never sinned.

3.24 Redemption refers to Christ setting sinners free from slavery to sin. In Old Testament times, a person's debts could result in his being sold as a slave. The next of kin could redeem him – buy his freedom. Christ purchased our freedom with his life.

3.25 Christ is our sacrifice of atonement. In other words, he died in our place, for our sins. God is justifiably angry at sinners. They have rebelled against him and cut themselves off from his life-giving power. But God declares Christ's death as the appropriate, designated sacrifice for our sin. Christ then stands in our place, having paid the penalty of death for our sin and completely satisfying God's demands. His sacrifice brings pardon, deliverance, and freedom.

3.25 What happened to people who lived before Christ came and died for sin? If God condemned them, is he being unfair? If he saved them, was Christ's sacrifice unnecessary? Paul shows that God forgave all human sin at the cross of Jesus. Old Testament believers looked forward by faith to Christ's coming and were saved, even though they did not know Jesus' name or the details of his earthly life. Unlike the Old Testament believers, you know about the God who loved the world so much that he gave his own Son (John 3.16). Have you put your trust in him?

3.27, 28 Most religions prescribe specific duties that must be performed to make a person acceptable to God. Christianity is unique in teaching that the good works we do will not make us right with God. No amount of human achievement or progress in personal development will close the gap between God's moral perfection and our imperfect daily performance. Good deeds are important, but they will not earn us eternal life. We are saved only by trusting in what God has done for us (see Ephesians 2.8–10).

3.28 Why does God save us by faith alone? (1) Faith eliminates the pride of human effort because faith is not a work that we do. (2) Faith exalts what God has done, not what people do. (3) Faith admits that we can't keep the law or measure up to God's standards – we need help. (4) Faith is based on our relationship with God, not our performance for God.

3.31 If we are saved by faith, does this mean that we no longer need to obey God's laws? Just the opposite! In fact, only when we trust Jesus can we truly obey him. There were some misunderstandings between the Jewish and Gentile Christians in Rome. Worried Jewish Christians were asking Paul, "Does faith wipe out everything Judaism stands for? Does it cancel our Scriptures, put an end to our customs, declare that God is no longer working through us?" (This is essentially the question used to open chapter 3.) "Absolutely not!" says Paul. When we understand the way of salvation through faith, we understand the Jewish religion better. We know why Abraham was chosen, why the law was given, why God worked patiently with Israel for centuries. Faith does not wipe out the Old Testament. Rather, it makes God's dealings with the Jewish people understandable. In chapter 4, Paul will expand on this theme (see also 5.20, 21; 8.3, 4; 13.9, 10; Galatians 3.24–29; and 1 Timothy 1.8 for more on this concept).

4.1–3 The Jews were proud to be called children of Abraham. Paul used Abraham as a good example of someone who was saved by faith. By emphasizing faith, Paul was not saying God's laws are unimportant (4.13) but that it is impossible to be saved simply by obeying them. For more about Abraham, see his Profile in Genesis 18.

4.4 This verse means that if a person could earn right standing with God by being good, salvation wouldn't be free. It would be an obligation. Relying on our goodness is futile; all we can do is cast ourselves on God's mercy and grace.

4.5 When some people learn that they are saved by God through faith, they start to worry. "Do I have enough faith?" they wonder. "Is my faith strong enough to save me?" These people miss the point. It is Jesus Christ who saves us, not *our* feelings or actions, and he is strong enough to save us no matter how weak our faith is. Jesus

works trusts him who justifies the ungodly, such faith is reckoned as righteousness.
6 So also David speaks of the blessedness of those to whom God reckons righteousness apart from works:

7 "Blessed are those whose iniquities are forgiven,
and whose sins are covered;
8 blessed is the one against whom the Lord will not reckon sin."

9 Is this blessedness, then, pronounced only on the circumcised, or also on the
uncircumcised? We say, "Faith was reckoned to Abraham as righteousness."
10 How then was it reckoned to him? Was it before or after he had been circumcised? It was not after, but before he was circumcised. 11 He received the sign of
circumcision as a seal of the righteousness that he had by faith while he was still
uncircumcised. The purpose was to make him the ancestor of all who believe without being circumcised and who thus have righteousness reckoned to them, 12 and
likewise the ancestor of the circumcised who are not only circumcised but who also
follow the example of the faith that our ancestor Abraham had before he was circumcised.

13 For the promise that he would inherit the world did not come to Abraham or
to his descendants through the law but through the righteousness of faith. 14 If it is
the adherents of the law who are to be the heirs, faith is null and the promise is void.
15 For the law brings wrath; but where there is no law, neither is there violation.

16 For this reason it depends on faith, in order that the promise may rest on
grace and be guaranteed to all his descendants, not only to the adherents of the law
but also to those who share the faith of Abraham (for he is the father of all of us,
17 as it is written, "I have made you the father of many nations")—in the presence
of the God in whom he believed, who gives life to the dead and calls into existence
the things that do not exist. 18 Hoping against hope, he believed that he would
become "the father of many nations," according to what was said, "So numerous
shall your descendants be." 19 He did not weaken in faith when he considered his
own body, which was already[o] as good as dead (for he was about a hundred years
old), or when he considered the barrenness of Sarah's womb. 20 No distrust made
him waver concerning the promise of God, but he grew strong in his faith as he
gave glory to God, 21 being fully convinced that God was able to do what he had

4.4,5 Josh 24.2 Acts 13.38,39 Rom 11.6 Gal 2.16
4.6 1 Cor 1.30 2 Cor 5.19
4.7 Ps 32.1,2
4.8 Ps 32.1,2 2 Cor 5.19
4.9 Gen 15.6 Rom 3.30
4.10 Gen 15.6 17.10,11
4.11 Gen 17.1-11 Lk 19.9 Jn 8.39 Rom 4.16
4.13 Gen 12.3; 17.4-6 22.17,18 Rom 9.8 Gal 3.16,29
4.14 Gal 3.18
4.15 Rom 3.20; 7.7 1 Cor 15.55,56 Gal 3.10
4.16 Rom 9.8 Col 3.11
4.17 Gen 17.5 Isa 51.2 Jn 5.21 1 Cor 1.28-30
4.18 Gen 15.5
4.19 Gen 17.17; 18.11 Heb 11.11,12

o Other ancient authorities lack *already*

---

offers us salvation as a gift, because he loves us, not because we have earned it through our powerful faith. What, then, is the role of faith? Faith is believing and trusting in Jesus Christ, reaching out to accept his wonderful gift of salvation.

4.6–8 What can we do to get rid of guilt? King David was guilty of terrible sins—adultery, murder, lies—and yet he experienced the joy of forgiveness. We too can have this joy when we (1) quit denying our guilt and recognize we have sinned, (2) admit our guilt to God and ask his forgiveness, and (3) let go of our guilt and believe God has forgiven us. This can be difficult when a sin has taken root and grown over many years, when it is very serious, or when it involves others. We must remember that Jesus is willing and able to forgive every sin. In view of the tremendous price he paid on the cross, it is arrogant to think that any of our sins are too great for him to cover. Even though our faith is weak, our conscience is sensitive, and our memory haunts us, God's Word declares that sins confessed are sins forgiven (1 John 1.9).

4.10 Circumcision was a sign to others and a personal seal or certification for the Jews that they were God's special people. Circumcision of all Jewish boys set the Jewish people apart from the nations who worshiped other gods; thus it was a very important ceremony. God gave the blessing and the command for this ceremony to Abraham (Genesis 17.9–14).

4.10–12 Rituals did not earn any reward for Abraham; he was blessed long before the circumcision ceremony was introduced. Abraham found favor with God by faith alone, before he was circumcised. Genesis 12.1–4 tells of God's call to Abraham when he was 75 years old; the circumcision ceremony was introduced when he was 99 (Genesis 17.1–14). Ceremonies and rituals serve as reminders of our faith, and they instruct new and younger believers. But we should not think that they give us any special merit before God. They are outward signs that demonstrate inward belief and trust. The focus of our faith should be on Christ and his saving actions, not on our own actions.

4.16 Paul explains that Abraham pleased God through his faith alone, before he ever heard about the rituals that would become so important to the Jewish people. We too are saved by faith plus nothing. It is not by loving God and doing good that we are saved; neither is it by faith plus love or faith plus good works. We are saved only through faith in Christ, trusting him to forgive all our sins. For more on Abraham, see his Profile in Genesis 18.

4.17 The promise (or covenant) God gave Abraham stated that Abraham would be the father of many nations (Genesis 17.2–4) and that the entire world would be blessed through him (Genesis 12.3). This promise was fulfilled in Jesus Christ. Jesus was from Abraham's line, and the whole world was blessed through him.

4.21 Abraham never doubted that God would fulfill his promise. His life was marked by mistakes, sins, and failures as well as by wisdom and goodness, but he consistently trusted God. His faith was strengthened by the obstacles he faced, and his life is an example of faith in action. If he had looked only at his own resources for subduing Canaan and founding a nation, he would have given up in despair. But he looked to God, obeyed him, and waited for God to fulfill his promise to him.

promised. 22 Therefore his faith[p] "was reckoned to him as righteousness." 23 Now
the words, "it was reckoned to him," were written not for his sake alone, 24 but for
ours also. It will be reckoned to us who believe in him who raised Jesus our Lord
from the dead, 25 who was handed over to death for our trespasses and was raised
for our justification.

Faith brings joy

5 Therefore, since we are justified by faith, we[q] have peace with God through
our Lord Jesus Christ, 2 through whom we have obtained access[r] to this grace
in which we stand; and we[s] boast in our hope of sharing the glory of God. 3 And not
only that, but we[s] also boast in our sufferings, knowing that suffering produces
endurance, 4 and endurance produces character, and character produces hope, 5 and
hope does not disappoint us, because God's love has been poured into our hearts
through the Holy Spirit that has been given to us.
6 For while we were still weak, at the right time Christ died for the ungodly.
7 Indeed, rarely will anyone die for a righteous person—though perhaps for a good
person someone might actually dare to die. 8 But God proves his love for us in that
while we still were sinners Christ died for us. 9 Much more surely then, now that we
have been justified by his blood, will we be saved through him from the wrath of
God.[t] 10 For if while we were enemies, we were reconciled to God through the
death of his Son, much more surely, having been reconciled, will we be saved by

4.22 Rom 4.3
4.23 Acts 13.30; Rom 15.4; 1 Cor 10.11; 2 Tim 3.16
5.1 Eph 2.14; Col 1.20
5.2 Heb 3.6; 10.19
5.3 Mt 5.11; Phil 2.17
5.5 2 Cor 1.22
5.6 Gal 2.20; 4.4
5.8 Jn 3.16; 15.13; 1 Pet 3.18
5.9 1 Thess 1.10; 1 Jn 1.7
5.10 2 Cor 5.18

[p] Gk *Therefore it* [q] Other ancient authorities read *let us* [r] Other ancient authorities add *by faith* [s] Or *let us* [t] Gk *the wrath*

4.25 When we believe, an exchange takes place. We give Christ our sins, and he gives us his goodness and forgiveness (see 2 Corinthians 5.21). There is nothing we can do to earn this. Only through Christ can we receive God's goodness. What an incredible bargain for us! But, sadly, many still choose to pass it up to continue "enjoying" their sin.

5.1 We now have peace *with God,* which may differ from peaceful feelings such as calmness and tranquility. Peace with God means that we have been reconciled with him. There is no more hostility between us, no sin blocking our relationship with him. Peace with God is possible only because Jesus paid the price for our sins with his death on the cross.

5.1–5 These verses introduce a section that contains some difficult concepts. To understand the next four chapters, it helps to keep in mind the two-sided reality of the Christian life. On the one hand, we are complete in Christ (our acceptance with him is secure). On the other hand, we are growing in Christ (we are becoming more and more like him). At the same time we have the status of kings and the duties of slaves. We feel both the presence of Christ and the pressure of sin. We enjoy the peace that comes from being made right with God, but we still face daily problems that help us grow. If we remember these two sides of the Christian life, we will not become discouraged as we face temptations and problems. Instead, we will learn to depend on the power available to us from Christ, who lives in us by the Holy Spirit.

5.2 Paul states that, as believers, we now stand in a place of highest privilege ("this grace in which we stand"). Not only has God declared us not guilty, but he has also drawn us close to him. Instead of enemies, we have become his friends—in fact, his own children (John 15.15; Galatians 4.5).

5.2–5 As Paul states clearly in 1 Corinthians 13.13, faith, hope, and love are at the heart of the Christian life. Our relationship with God begins with *faith,* which helps us realize that we are delivered from our past by Christ's death. *Hope* grows as we learn all that God has in mind for us; it gives us the promise of the future. And God's *love* fills our lives and gives us the ability to reach out to others.

5.3, 4 For first-century Christians, suffering was the rule rather than the exception. Paul tells us that in the future we will *become,* but until then we must *overcome.* This means we will experience difficulties that help us grow. "Boast in our sufferings" means rejoicing in suffering, not because we like pain or deny its tragedy, but because we know God is using life's difficulties and Satan's attacks to build our character. The problems we run into will develop our patience—which in turn will strengthen our character, deepen our trust in God, and give us greater confidence about the future. You probably find your patience tested in some way every day. Thank God for these opportunities to grow, and deal with them in his strength (see also James 1.2–4; 1 Peter 1.6, 7).

5.5, 6 All three members of the trinity are involved in salvation. The Father loved us so much that he sent his Son to bridge the gap between us (John 3.16). The Father and the Son send the Holy Spirit to fill our lives with love and to enable us to live by his power (Acts 1.8). With all this loving care, how can we do less than serve him completely!

5.6 We were weak and helpless because we could do nothing on our own to save ourselves. Someone had to come and rescue us. Not only did Christ come at a good time in history; he came at exactly the right time—according to God's own schedule. God controls all history, and he controlled the timing, methods, and results of Jesus' death.

5.8 *While we still were sinners*—these are amazing words. God sent Jesus Christ to die for us, not because we were good enough, but because he loved us. Whenever you feel uncertain about God's love for you, remember that he loved you even before you turned to him. If God loved you when you were a rebel, he can surely strengthen you now that you love him in return.

5.9, 10 The love that caused Christ to die is the same love that sends the Holy Spirit to live in us and guide us every day. The power that raised Christ from the dead is the same power that saved you and is available to you in your daily life. Be assured that having begun a life with Christ, you have a reserve of power and love to call on each day to help you meet every challenge or trial. You can pray for God's power and love as you need it.

his life. 11 But more than that, we even boast in God through our Lord Jesus Christ,
through whom we have now received reconciliation.

Adam and Christ contrasted

12 Therefore, just as sin came into the world through one man, and death came
through sin, and so death spread to all because all have sinned— 13 sin was indeed
in the world before the law, but sin is not reckoned when there is no law. 14 Yet
death exercised dominion from Adam to Moses, even over those whose sins were
not like the transgression of Adam, who is a type of the one who was to come.
15 But the free gift is not like the trespass. For if the many died through the one
man's trespass, much more surely have the grace of God and the free gift in the
grace of the one man, Jesus Christ, abounded for the many. 16 And the free gift is
not like the effect of the one man's sin. For the judgment following one trespass
brought condemnation, but the free gift following many trespasses brings justification. 17 If, because of the one man's trespass, death exercised dominion through
that one, much more surely will those who receive the abundance of grace and the
free gift of righteousness exercise dominion in life through the one man, Jesus
Christ.
18 Therefore just as one man's trespass led to condemnation for all, so one
man's act of righteousness leads to justification and life for all. 19 For just as by the
one man's disobedience the many were made sinners, so by the one man's obedience the many will be made righteous. 20 But law came in, with the result that the

5.12 Gen 2.17 Ezek 18.4 Rom 6.23 1 Cor 15.21,22,56
5.13 1 Jn 3.4
5.14 Hos 6.7 1 Cor 15.45
5.15 Isa 53.11
5.17 Gen 2.17 3.6,19 1 Cor 15.21
5.18 Rom 4.25 Heb 2.9
5.19 Rom 11.32 Phil 2.8
5.20 Lk 7.47 Jn 15.22 Gal 3.19 1 Tim 1.14

WHAT WE HAVE AS CHILDREN

What we have as Adam's children	*What we have as God's children*
Ruin 5.9	Rescue 5.8
Sin 5.12, 15, 21	Righteousness 5.18
Death 5.12, 16, 21	Eternal life 5.17, 21
Separation from God 5.18	Relationship with God 5.11, 19
Disobedience 5.12, 19	Obedience 5.19
Judgment 5.18	Deliverance 5.10, 11
Law 5.20	Grace 5.20

5.11 God is holy and will not be associated with sin. All people are sinful, and so they are separated from God. In addition, all sin deserves punishment. Instead of punishing us with the death we deserve, however, Christ took our sins upon himself and took our punishment by dying on the cross. Now we can "boast in God." Through faith in *his* work, we become close to God rather than enemies and outcasts.

5.12 How can we be declared guilty for something Adam did thousands of years ago? Many feel it isn't right for God to judge us because of Adam's sin. Yet each of us confirms our solidarity with Adam by our own sins each day. We are made of the same stuff, prone to rebel, and we are judged for the sins *we* commit. Because we are sinners, it isn't fairness we need—it's mercy.

5.13, 14 Paul has shown that keeping the law does not bring salvation. Now he adds that breaking the law is not what brings death. Death is the result of Adam's sin and of the sins we all commit, even if they don't resemble Adam's. Paul reminds his readers that for thousands of years the law had not yet been explicitly given, and yet people died. The law was added, he explains in 5.20, to help people see their sinfulness, to show them the seriousness of their offenses, and to drive them to God for mercy and pardon. This was true in Moses' day, and it is still true today. Sin is a deep rupture between who we are and who we were created to be. The law points out our sin and places the responsibility for it squarely on our shoulders. But it offers no remedy. When we're convicted of sin, we must turn to Jesus Christ for healing.

5.14 Adam is a *type*, figure, or example. He is the counterpart of Christ. Just as Adam was a representative of first humanity, so is Christ the first representative of a new, spiritual humanity.

5.15–19 We are all born into Adam's physical family—the family line that leads to certain death. All of us reap the results of Adam's sin. We have inherited his guilt, a sinful nature (the tendency to sin), and God's punishment. Because of Jesus, however, we can trade judgment for forgiveness. We can trade our sin for Jesus' goodness. Christ offers us the opportunity to be born into his spiritual family—the family line that begins with forgiveness and leads to eternal life. If we do nothing, we have death through Adam; but if we come to God by faith, we have life through Christ. Which family line do you now belong to?

5.17 What a promise to those who love Christ! We can reign ("exercise dominion") over sin's power, over death's threats, and over Satan's attacks. Eternal life is ours now and forever. In the power and protection of Jesus Christ, we can overcome temptation. See 8.17 for more on our privileged position in Christ.

5.20 As a sinner, separated from God, you see his law from below, as a ladder to be climbed to get to God. Perhaps you have repeatedly tried to climb it, only to fall to the ground every time you have advanced one or two rungs. Or perhaps the sheer height of the ladder is so overwhelming that you have never even started up. In either case, what relief you should feel to see Jesus with open arms offering to lift you above the ladder of the law, to take you directly to God! Once Jesus lifts you into God's presence, you are free to obey—out of love, not necessity; through God's power, not your own. You know that if you stumble, you will not fall back to the ground. Instead, you will be caught and held in Christ's loving arms.

trespass multiplied; but where sin increased, grace abounded all the more, 21 so 5.21
that, just as sin exercised dominion in death, so grace might also exercise dominion Jn 1.17 Rom 6.23
through justification[u] leading to eternal life through Jesus Christ our Lord.

3. Freedom from sin's grasp

Sin's power is broken

6 What then are we to say? Should we continue in sin in order that grace may 6.1
abound? 2 By no means! How can we who died to sin go on living in it? 3 Do Rom 3.5,8; 6.15
you not know that all of us who have been baptized into Christ Jesus were baptized 6.2 Col 2.20; 3.3
into his death? 4 Therefore we have been buried with him by baptism into death, so 6.3
that, just as Christ was raised from the dead by the glory of the Father, so we too Gal 3.27
might walk in newness of life. 6.4 Eph 4.22
5 For if we have been united with him in a death like his, we will certainly be 6.5
united with him in a resurrection like his. 6 We know that our old self was crucified Jn 14.19,20
with him so that the body of sin might be destroyed, and we might no longer be 6.6 Gal 2.20
enslaved to sin. 7 For whoever has died is freed from sin. 8 But if we have died with Col 2.11,12
Christ, we believe that we will also live with him. 9 We know that Christ, being 6.7 1 Pet 4.1
raised from the dead, will never die again; death no longer has dominion over him. 6.8
10 The death he died, he died to sin, once for all; but the life he lives, he lives to Jn 14.19
God. 11 So you also must consider yourselves dead to sin and alive to God in Christ 6.9 Acts 2.24
Jesus. 6.11
12 Therefore, do not let sin exercise dominion in your mortal bodies, to make Col 2.20; 3.3
you obey their passions. 13 No longer present your members to sin as instruments[v] 6.12 Eph 4.22
of wickedness, but present yourselves to God as those who have been brought from 6.13
death to life, and present your members to God as instruments[v] of righteousness. 2 Cor 5.14 Col 3.5
14 For sin will have no dominion over you, since you are not under law but under 6.14
grace. Rom 7.4,6

[u] Or *righteousness* [v] Or *weapons*

6.1–8.39 This section deals with *sanctification*—the change God makes in our lives as we grow in the faith. Chapter 6 explains that believers are free from sin's control. Chapter 7 discusses the continuing struggle believers have with sin. Chapter 8 describes how we can have victory over sin.

6.1, 2 If God loves to forgive, why not give him more to forgive? If forgiveness is guaranteed, do we have the freedom to sin as much as we want? Paul's forceful answer is *No!* Such an attitude—deciding ahead of time to take advantage of God—shows that a person does not understand the seriousness of sin. God's forgiveness does not make sin less serious; his Son's death shows us the dreadful seriousness of sin. Jesus paid with his life so we could be forgiven. The availability of God's mercy must not become an excuse for careless living and moral laxness.

6.1–4 In the church in Paul's day, immersion was the usual form of baptism—that is, new Christians were completely "buried" in water. They understood this form of baptism to symbolize the death and burial of the old way of life. Coming up out of the water symbolized resurrection to new life with Christ. If we think of our old, sinful life as dead and buried, we have a powerful motive to resist sin. We can consciously choose to treat the desires and temptations of the old nature as if they were dead. Then we can continue to enjoy our wonderful new life with Jesus (see Galatians 3.27 and Colossians 3.1–4 for more on this concept).

6.5ff We can enjoy our new life in Christ because we are united with him in his death and resurrection. Our evil desires, our bondage to sin, and our love of sin died with him. Now, united by faith with him in his resurrection life, we have unbroken fellowship with God and freedom from sin's hold on us. For more on the difference between our new life in Christ and our old sinful nature, read Ephesians 4.21–24 and Colossians 3.3–15.

6.6 The power and penalty of sin died with Christ on the cross. Our "old self," our sinful nature, died once and for all, so we are freed from its power. The "body of sin" is not the human body, but our rebellious sin-loving nature inherited from Adam. Though our body willingly cooperates with our sinful nature, we must not regard the body as evil. It is the sin in us. And it is this power of sin at work in our body that is defeated. Paul has already stated that through faith in Christ we stand acquitted, "not guilty" before God. Here Paul emphasizes that we need no longer live under sin's power. God does not take us out of the world or make us robots—we will still feel like sinning, and sometimes we will sin. The difference is that before we were saved, we were slaves to our sinful nature, but now we can choose to live for Christ (see Galatians 2.20).

6.8 Because of Christ's death and resurrection, his followers need never fear death. This frees us to fellowship with him and do his will. This will affect all our activities—work, worship, play, Bible study, quiet times, and times caring for others. When you know that you need not fear death, you will experience new vigor in life.

6.11 "Consider yourselves dead to sin" means that we should regard our old sin nature as dead. We are fully fenced off (because of our union and identification with Christ) from all the old ways of believing and behaving. We are no longer answerable to those motives, desires, and goals. Let us consider ourselves to be what God has in fact made us. We have a new start, and the Holy Spirit will help us become in our daily experience what Christ has declared us to be.

6.14, 15 If we're no longer under the law but under grace, are we now free to sin and disregard the ten commandments? Paul says, "Of course not." When we were under the law, sin was our master—the law does not justify us or help us overcome sin. But now we are bound to Christ. He is our Master, and he gives us power to do good rather than evil.

6.16 Jn 8.34; 1 Cor 6.9,15; 2 Pet 2.19
6.17 2 Tim 1.13
6.18 1 Cor 7.22; Gal 5.1; 1 Pet 2.16
6.19 Mt 6.24
6.21 Jer 12.13; Gal 6.8
6.22 Jn 8.32; Rom 8.2; 1 Cor 7.22; 1 Pet 1.9; 2.16
6.23 Mt 25.46; Jn 3.16; 4.10; Gal 6.8

Slaves to righteousness

15 What then? Should we sin because we are not under law but under grace? By
no means! 16 Do you not know that if you present yourselves to anyone as obedient
slaves, you are slaves of the one whom you obey, either of sin, which leads to
death, or of obedience, which leads to righteousness? 17 But thanks be to God that
you, having once been slaves of sin, have become obedient from the heart to the
form of teaching to which you were entrusted, 18 and that you, having been set free
from sin, have become slaves of righteousness. 19 I am speaking in human terms
because of your natural limitations.[w] For just as you once presented your members
as slaves to impurity and to greater and greater iniquity, so now present your members as slaves to righteousness for sanctification.

20 When you were slaves of sin, you were free in regard to righteousness. 21 So
what advantage did you then get from the things of which you now are ashamed?
The end of those things is death. 22 But now that you have been freed from sin and
enslaved to God, the advantage you get is sanctification. The end is eternal life.
23 For the wages of sin is death, but the free gift of God is eternal life in Christ Jesus
our Lord.

[w] Gk *the weakness of your flesh*

WHAT HAS GOD DONE ABOUT SIN?	*He has given us . . .*		*Principle*	*Importance*
	New life	6.2, 3	Sin's power is broken.	We can be certain that sin's power is broken.
		6.4	Sin-loving nature is buried.	
		6.6	You are no longer under sin's control.	
	New nature	6.5	Now you share his new life.	We can see ourselves as unresponsive to the old power and alive to the new.
		6.11	Look upon your old sin nature as dead and unresponsive, and instead be alive to God.	
	New freedom	6.12	Do not let sin control you.	We can commit ourselves to obey Christ in perfect freedom.
		6.13	Give yourselves completely to God.	
		6.14	You are free.	
		6.16	You can choose your own master.	

6.16–18 In certain skilled crafts, an apprentice works under a master, who trains, shapes, and molds the apprentice in the finer points of his craft. All people choose a master and pattern themselves after him. Without Jesus, we would have no choice—we would have to apprentice ourselves to sin, and the results would be guilt, suffering, and separation from God. Thanks to Jesus, however, we can now choose God as our Master. Following him, we can enjoy new life and learn how to work for him. Are you still serving your first master, sin? Or have you apprenticed yourself to God?

6.17 To obey from the heart means to give yourself fully to God, to love him "with all your heart, and with all your soul, and with all your mind" (Matthew 22.37). And yet so often our efforts to know and obey God's commands can best be described as "halfhearted." How do you rate your heart's obedience? God wants to give you the power to obey him with all your heart.

6.17 The "form of teaching" delivered to them is the good news that Jesus died for their sins and was raised to give them new life. Many believe this refers to the early church's statement of faith found in 1 Corinthians 15.1–11.

6.19 Paul used a human analogy in case they did not grasp his meaning. He wanted to speak clearly to those who were confused and becoming entangled in sin.

6.19–22 It is impossible to be neutral. Every person has a master—either God or sin. A Christian is not someone who cannot sin, but someone who is no longer a slave to sin. He belongs to God.

6.22 *Sanctification* means the process of being made holy. We are made holy by faith in Jesus Christ, but we also go through a lifelong process of growing in our faith and practice.

6.23 You are free to choose between two masters, but you are not free to change the consequences of your choice. Each of the two masters pays with his own kind of currency. The currency of sin is death. That is all you can expect or hope for in life without God. Christ's currency is eternal life—new life with God that begins on earth and continues forever with God. What choice have you made?

6.23 Eternal life is a free gift from God. If it is a gift, then it is not something that we earn, nor something that must be paid back. Consider the foolishness of someone who receives a gift given out of love and then offers to pay for it. A gift cannot be purchased. A more appropriate response to a loved one who offers a gift is graceful acceptance with gratitude. Our salvation is a gift of God, not something of our own doing (Ephesians 2.8, 9). He saved us because of his mercy, not because of any works of righteousness that we have done (Titus 3.5). How much more we should accept with thanksgiving the gift that God has freely given to us.

No longer bound to the law

7 Do you not know, brothers and sisters[x]—for I am speaking to those who
know the law—that the law is binding on a person only during that person's
lifetime? 2 Thus a married woman is bound by the law to her husband as long as he
lives; but if her husband dies, she is discharged from the law concerning the husband. 3 Accordingly, she will be called an adulteress if she lives with another man
while her husband is alive. But if her husband dies, she is free from that law, and
if she marries another man, she is not an adulteress.
4 In the same way, my friends,[x] you have died to the law through the body of
Christ, so that you may belong to another, to him who has been raised from the
dead in order that we may bear fruit for God. 5 While we were living in the flesh,
our sinful passions, aroused by the law, were at work in our members to bear fruit
for death. 6 But now we are discharged from the law, dead to that which held us
captive, so that we are slaves not under the old written code but in the new life of
the Spirit.

7.2 Mt 19.5,6 1 Cor 7.39
7.3 Mt 5.32 Mk 10.12 Lk 16.18 1 Cor 6.9 Heb 13.4
7.4 Rom 6.2 Gal 5.18 1 Pet 2.24
7.5 Rom 6.21; 8.8 Gal 5.19-21
7.6 2 Cor 3.6 Gal 5.22 Phil 3.3

God's law reveals sin

7 What then should we say? That the law is sin? By no means! Yet, if it had not
been for the law, I would not have known sin. I would not have known what it is
to covet if the law had not said, "You shall not covet." 8 But sin, seizing an opportunity in the commandment, produced in me all kinds of covetousness. Apart from
the law sin lies dead. 9 I was once alive apart from the law, but when the commandment came, sin revived 10 and I died, and the very commandment that promised life
proved to be death to me. 11 For sin, seizing an opportunity in the commandment,
deceived me and through it killed me. 12 So the law is holy, and the commandment
is holy and just and good.
13 Did what is good, then, bring death to me? By no means! It was sin, working

7.7 Ex 20.17 Rom 3.20 4.15; 5.20
7.8 1 Cor 15.56
7.10 Ezek 20.13 2 Cor 3.7
7.11 Gen 3.13
7.12 Ps 19.8 1 Tim 1.8

[x] Gk *brothers*

7.1ff Paul shows that the law is powerless to save the sinner (7.7–14), the lawkeeper (7.15–22), and even the man with a new nature (7.23–25). The sinner is condemned by the law; the lawkeeper can't live up to it; and the man with the new nature finds his obedience to the law sabotaged by the effects of his old nature. Once again, Paul declares that salvation cannot be found by obeying the law. No matter who we are, only Jesus Christ can set us free.

7.2–6 Paul uses marriage to illustrate our relationship to the law. When a spouse dies, the law of marriage no longer applies. Because we have died with Christ, the law can no longer condemn us. We "rose again" when Christ was resurrected and, as new people, we belong to Christ. His Spirit enables us to produce good fruit for God. We now serve not by obeying a set of rules, but out of renewed hearts and minds that overflow with love for God.

7.4 When a person "dies" to the old life and "belongs" to Christ, a new life begins. An unbeliever's mindset is centered on his own personal gratification. His source of power is his own self-determination. By contrast, the center of a Christian's life is God. God supplies the power for the Christian's daily living. Believers find that their whole way of looking at the world changes when they come to Christ.

7.5 "In the flesh" does not mean in our skin and bones, but in the mindset of the "old self" (see 6.6). When the law says, "You shall not," our old nature rebelled and desired to do that very thing.

7.6 Some people try to earn their way to God by keeping a set of rules (obeying the ten commandments, attending church faithfully, or doing good works), but all they earn for their efforts is frustration and discouragement. However, because of Christ's sacrifice, the way to God is already open, and we can become his children simply by putting our faith in him. No longer trying to reach God by keeping rules, we can become more and more like Jesus as we live with him day by day. Let the Holy Spirit turn your eyes away from your own performance and toward Jesus. He will free you to serve him out of love and gratitude. This is living "in the new life of the Spirit."

7.6 Keeping the rules, laws, and customs of Christianity doesn't save us. Even if we could keep our actions pure, we would still be doomed because our hearts and minds are perverse and rebellious. Like Paul, we can find no relief in the synagogue or church until we look to Jesus Christ himself for our salvation, which he freely gives us. When we do come to Jesus, we are flooded with relief and gratitude. Will we keep the rules any better? Most likely, but we will be motivated by love and gratitude, not by the desire to get God's approval. We will not be merely submitting to an external code, but willingly and lovingly seeking to do God's will.

7.9–11 Where there is no law, there is no sin, because people cannot know their actions are sinful unless a law forbids those actions. God's law makes people realize that they are sinners, doomed to die, and yet it offers no help. Sin is real, and it is dangerous. Imagine a sunny day at the beach. You plunge into the surf. Then you notice a sign on the pier: "No swimming. Sharks in water." Your day is ruined. Is it the sign's fault? Are you angry with the people who put it up? The law is like the sign. It is essential, and we are grateful for it—but it doesn't get rid of the sharks.

7.11 Sin deceives people by misusing the law. In the garden of Eden (Genesis 3), the serpent deceived Eve by taking her focus off the freedom she had and putting it on the one restriction God had made. Ever since then, we have all been rebels. Sin looks good to us precisely because God has said it is wrong. Instead of paying attention to his warnings, we use them as a "to do" list. When we are tempted to rebel, we need to look at the law from a wider perspective—in the light of God's grace and mercy. If we focus on his great love for us, we will understand that he only restricts us from actions and attitudes that ultimately will harm us.

death in me through what is good, in order that sin might be shown to be sin, and
through the commandment might become sinful beyond measure.

The struggle within

14 For we know that the law is spiritual; but I am of the flesh, sold into slavery
under sin.[y] 15 I do not understand my own actions. For I do not do what I want, but
I do the very thing I hate. 16 Now if I do what I do not want, I agree that the law is
good. 17 But in fact it is no longer I that do it, but sin that dwells within me. 18 For
I know that nothing good dwells within me, that is, in my flesh. I can will what is
right, but I cannot do it. 19 For I do not do the good I want, but the evil I do not want
is what I do. 20 Now if I do what I do not want, it is no longer I that do it, but sin
that dwells within me.

21 So I find it to be a law that when I want to do what is good, evil lies close at
hand. 22 For I delight in the law of God in my inmost self, 23 but I see in my members another law at war with the law of my mind, making me captive to the law of
sin that dwells in my members. 24 Wretched man that I am! Who will rescue me
from this body of death? 25 Thanks be to God through Jesus Christ our Lord!

So then, with my mind I am a slave to the law of God, but with my flesh I am a
slave to the law of sin.

The Holy Spirit frees us from sin

8 There is therefore now no condemnation for those who are in Christ Jesus.
2 For the law of the Spirit[z] of life in Christ Jesus has set you[a] free from the law
of sin and of death. 3 For God has done what the law, weakened by the flesh, could

7.14 Rom 3.9; 6.6
7.15 1 Kgs 21.20-25; Gal 5.17
7.16 1 Tim 1.8
7.18 Gen 8.21; Jn 3.6; Rom 8.3
7.21 Rom 8.2
7.22 Ps 1.2
7.23-25 Rom 8.2; 1 Cor 15.57; Gal 5.17; Col 2.11; Jas 4.1; 1 Pet 2.11
8.2 Rom 8.11; 2 Cor 3.6; Gal 2.19; 5.1

[y] Gk *sold under sin* [z] Or *spirit* [a] Here the Greek word *you* is singular number; other ancient authorities read *me* or *us*

7.14 "I am of the flesh, sold into slavery under sin" speaks of the old nature. It seeks to rebel and be independent of him. If I, being a Christian, try to struggle with sin in my own strength, I am slipping into the grasp of sin's power.

7.15 Paul gives three lessons he learned in trying to deal with his old sinful desires. (1) Knowledge is not the answer (7.9). Paul felt fine as long as he did not understand what the law demanded. When he learned the truth, he knew he was doomed. (2) Self-determination (struggling in my own strength) doesn't succeed (7.15). Paul found himself sinning in ways that weren't even attractive to him. (3) Becoming a Christian does not stamp out all sin and temptation from one's life (7.22–25).

Being born again takes a moment of faith, but becoming like Christ is a lifelong process. Paul compares Christian growth to a strenuous race or fight (1 Corinthians 9.24–27; 2 Timothy 4.7). Thus, as Paul has been emphasizing since the beginning of this letter, *no one* in the world is innocent; no one deserves to be saved—not the pagan who doesn't know God's laws, not the Christian or Jew who knows them and tries to keep them. All of us must depend totally on the work of Christ for our salvation. We cannot earn it by our good behavior.

7.15 This is more than the cry of one desperate man—it describes the experience of any Christian struggling against sin or trying to please God by keeping rules and laws without the Spirit's help. We must never underestimate the power of sin. We must never attempt to fight it in our own strength. Satan is a crafty tempter, and we have a great ability to make excuses. Instead of trying to overcome sin with human willpower, we must take hold of the tremendous power of Christ that is available to us. This is God's provision for victory over sin—he sends the Holy Spirit to live in us and give us power. And when we fall, he lovingly reaches out to help us up.

7.17–20 "The devil made me do it." "I didn't do it; the sin in me did it." These sound like good excuses, but we are responsible for our actions. We must never use the power of sin or Satan as an excuse, because they are defeated enemies. Without Christ's help, sin is stronger than we are, and sometimes we are unable to defend ourselves against its attacks. That is why we should never stand up to sin all alone. Jesus Christ, who has conquered sin once and for all, promises to fight by our side. If we look to him for help, we will not have to give in to sin.

7.23–25 The sin deep within us is sometimes called the flesh or the "law in our members." This is our vulnerability to sin, referring to everything within us that is more loyal to our old way of selfish living than to God.

7.23–25 This inward struggle with sin was as real for Paul as it is for us. From Paul we learn what to do about it. Whenever he felt lost, he would return to the beginning of his spiritual life, remembering that he had already been freed by Jesus Christ. When you feel confused and overwhelmed by sin's appeal, follow his example: thank God that he has given you freedom through Jesus Christ. Let Christ's power lift you up to real victory over sin.

8.1 "Not guilty; let him go free"—what would those words mean to you if you were on death row? The fact is that the whole human race *is* on death row, justly condemned for repeatedly breaking God's holy law. Without Jesus we would have no hope at all. But thank God! He has declared us not guilty and has offered us freedom from sin and power to do his will.

8.1ff The *flesh* as used throughout this chapter refers not to our human bodies, but to the power of sin. Sin is present and tries to utilize our body, but shouldn't be equated with the body (see 6.6).

8.2 This "Spirit of life" is the Holy Spirit. He was present at the creation of the world (Genesis 1.2), and he is the power behind the rebirth of every Christian. He gives us the power we need to live the Christian life.

8.3 Jesus gave himself as a *sacrifice* for our sins. In Old Testament times, animal sacrifices were continually offered at the temple. The sacrifices showed the Israelites the seriousness of sin: blood had to be shed before sins could be pardoned (see Leviticus 17.11). But animal blood could not really remove sins (Hebrews 10.4). The sacrifices could only point to Jesus' sacrifice, which paid the final penalty for sin.

not do: by sending his own Son in the likeness of sinful flesh, and to deal with sin,[b]
he condemned sin in the flesh, 4so that the just requirement of the law might be
fulfilled in us, who walk not according to the flesh but according to the Spirit.[c]
5For those who live according to the flesh set their minds on the things of the flesh,
but those who live according to the Spirit[c] set their minds on the things of the
Spirit.[c] 6To set the mind on the flesh is death, but to set the mind on the Spirit[c] is
life and peace. 7For this reason the mind that is set on the flesh is hostile to God;
it does not submit to God's law—indeed it cannot, 8and those who are in the flesh
cannot please God.

9 But you are not in the flesh; you are in the Spirit,[c] since the Spirit of God
dwells in you. Anyone who does not have the Spirit of Christ does not belong to
him. 10But if Christ is in you, though the body is dead because of sin, the Spirit[c]
is life because of righteousness. 11If the Spirit of him who raised Jesus from the
dead dwells in you, he who raised Christ[d] from the dead will give life to your
mortal bodies also through[e] his Spirit that dwells in you.

12 So then, brothers and sisters,[f] we are debtors, not to the flesh, to live according to the flesh— 13for if you live according to the flesh, you will die; but if by
the Spirit you put to death the deeds of the body, you will live. 14For all who are led
by the Spirit of God are children of God. 15For you did not receive a spirit of slavery to fall back into fear, but you have received a spirit of adoption. When we cry,
"Abba![g] Father!" 16it is that very Spirit bearing witness[h] with our spirit that we are
children of God, 17and if children, then heirs, heirs of God and joint heirs with
Christ— if, in fact, we suffer with him so that we may also be glorified with him.

The future glory

18 I consider that the sufferings of this present time are not worth comparing
with the glory about to be revealed to us. 19For the creation waits with eager long-

8.3 Acts 13.39; 2 Cor 5.21; Phil 2.7; Heb 2.14; 4.15
8.4 Gal 5.16,25
8.5 Gal 5.19-22
8.6 Gal 6.8
8.9 Jn 14.17,18,23; Phil 1.19
8.10 2 Cor 13.5; Col 1.26,27
8.11 1 Cor 6.14; 15.45
8.13 Gal 6.8; Col 3.5
8.14 Gal 3.26
8.15 Gal 4.5,6
8.16 2 Cor 1.22; Eph 1.13
8.17 Tit 3.7
8.18 2 Cor 4.17; 1 Pet 1.6,7

[b] Or *and as a sin offering* [c] Or *spirit* [d] Other ancient authorities read *the Christ* or *Christ Jesus* or *Jesus Christ* [e] Other ancient authorities read *on account of* [f] Gk *brothers* [g] Aramaic for *Father* [h] Or *15a spirit of adoption, by which we cry, "Abba! Father!" 16The Spirit itself bears witness*

8.5, 6 Paul divides people into two categories—those who let themselves be controlled by their sinful natures, and those who follow after the Holy Spirit. All of us would be in the first category if Jesus hadn't offered us a way out. Once we have said yes to Jesus, we will want to continue following him because his way brings life and peace. Daily we must consciously choose to center our lives on God. Use the Bible to discover God's guidelines, and then follow them. In every perplexing situation ask yourself, "What would Jesus want me to do?" When the Holy Spirit points out what is right, do it eagerly. For more on our lower natures versus our new life in Christ, see 6.6–8, Ephesians 4.22–24; Colossians 3.3–15.

8.9 Have you ever worried about whether or not you really are a Christian? A Christian is anyone who has the Spirit of God living in him. If you have sincerely trusted Christ for your salvation and acknowledged him as Lord, then the Holy Spirit has come into your life, and you are a Christian. You won't know the Holy Spirit has come if you are waiting for a certain feeling; you will know he has come because Jesus promised he would. When the Holy Spirit is working within you, you will believe that Jesus Christ is God's Son and that eternal life comes through him (1 John 5.5); you will begin to act as Christ directs (Romans 8.5; Galatians 5.22, 23); you will find help in your daily problems and in your praying (Romans 8.26, 27); you will be empowered to serve God and do his will (Acts 1.8; Romans 12.6ff); and you will become part of God's plan to build up his church (Ephesians 4.12, 13).

8.11 The Holy Spirit is God's promise or guarantee of eternal life for those who believe in him. He is in us now by faith, and by faith we are certain to live with Christ forever. See Romans 8.23; 1 Corinthians 6.14; 2 Corinthians 4.14; 1 Thessalonians 4.14.

8.13 "Put to death the deeds of the body" means to regard as dead the power of sin in your body (see 6.11 and Galatians 5.24). When we regard sin's appeal as dead and lifeless, we can ignore temptation when it comes.

8.14–17 Paul uses adoption to illustrate the believer's new relationship with God. In Roman culture, the adopted person lost all rights in his old family and gained all the rights of a legitimate child in his new family. He became a full heir to his new father's estate. Likewise, when a person becomes a Christian, he gains all the privileges and responsibilities of a child in God's family. One of these outstanding privileges is being led by the Spirit (see Galatians 4.5, 6). We may not always feel like we belong to God, but the Holy Spirit is our witness. His inward presence reminds us of who we are and encourages us with his love (5.5).

8.14–17 We are no longer cringing and fearful slaves; instead, we are the Master's children. What a privilege! Because we are God's children, we share in great treasures as joint-heirs. God has already given us his best gifts: his Son, forgiveness, and eternal life; and he encourages us to ask him for whatever we need.

8.17 There is a price for being identified with Jesus. Along with the great treasures, Paul mentions the suffering that Christians must face. What kinds of suffering are we to endure? For first-century believers, there was economic and social persecution, and some faced death. We too must pay a price for following Jesus. In many parts of today's world, Christians face pressures just as severe as those faced by Christ's first followers. Even in countries where Christianity is tolerated or encouraged, Christians must not become complacent. To live as Jesus did—serving others, giving up one's own rights, resisting pressures to conform to the world—always exacts a price. Nothing we suffer, however, can compare to the great price Jesus paid to save us.

8.19–22 Sin has caused all creation to fall from the perfect state in which God created it. It is subject to futility and bondage by God so that it cannot fulfill its intended purpose. One day it will be trans-

8.20
Gen 3.17-19
8.21
Acts 3.21
Rev 21.1
8.22
Jer 12.4,11
8.23
Lk 20.36
2 Cor 1.22; 5.3-6
Phil 3.21
8.24
2 Cor 5.7
1 Thess 5.8
Heb 11.1
8.26
Mt 20.22
Jn 14.16
8.27
1 Thess 2.4
1 Jn 5.14
8.28
2 Cor 4.17
2 Tim 1.9
8.29
a)Eph 1.5
1 Pet 1.2
b)Heb 1.6

ing for the revealing of the children of God; 20 for the creation was subjected to
futility, not of its own will but by the will of the one who subjected it, in hope 21 that
the creation itself will be set free from its bondage to decay and will obtain the
freedom of the glory of the children of God. 22 We know that the whole creation has
been groaning in labor pains until now; 23 and not only the creation, but we ourselves, who have the first fruits of the Spirit, groan inwardly while we wait for
adoption, the redemption of our bodies. 24 For in[i] hope we were saved. Now hope
that is seen is not hope. For who hopes[j] for what is seen? 25 But if we hope for what
we do not see, we wait for it with patience.
26 Likewise the Spirit helps us in our weakness; for we do not know how to
pray as we ought, but that very Spirit intercedes[k] with sighs too deep for words.
27 And God,[l] who searches the heart, knows what is the mind of the Spirit, because
the Spirit[m] intercedes for the saints according to the will of God.[n]
28 We know that all things work together for good[o] for those who love God,
who are called according to his purpose. 29 For those whom he foreknew he also
predestined to be conformed to the image of his Son, in order that he might be the
firstborn within a large family.[p] 30 And those whom he predestined he also called;
and those whom he called he also justified; and those whom he justified he also
glorified.

[i] Or *by* [j] Other ancient authorities read *awaits* [k] Other ancient authorities add *for us* [l] Gk *the one* [m] Gk *he* or *it* [n] Gk *according to God* [o] Other ancient authorities read *God makes all things work together for good*, or *in all things God works for good* [p] Gk *among many brothers*

---

formed. Until that time it looks forward to the resurrection of God's children ("the freedom of the glory of the children of God").

8.19–22 Christians see the world as it is – physically decaying and spiritually infected with sin. But Christians do not need to be pessimistic, because they have hope. They look forward to the new heaven and new earth God has promised, and they wait for God's new order that will free the world of sin, sickness, and evil. In the meantime, they go with Christ into the world where they heal people's bodies and souls and fight the evil effects of sin in the world.

8.23 We will be resurrected with bodies, but they will be glorified bodies like the body Christ now has in heaven (see 1 Corinthians 15.25–58). We have the *first fruits,* the first installment or down payment of the Holy Spirit as a guarantee of our resurrection life (see 2 Corinthians 1.22; 5.5; Ephesians 1.14).

8.24, 25 It is natural for children to trust their parents, even though parents sometimes fail to keep their promises. Our heavenly Father, however, never makes promises he won't keep. Nevertheless, his plan may take more time than we expect. Rather than acting like impatient children as we wait for God's will to unfold, we should place our confidence in his goodness and wisdom, and wait patiently.

8.24, 25 In Romans, Paul presents the idea that salvation is past, present, and future. It is past because we *were* saved the moment we believed in Jesus Christ as Savior (3.21–26; 5.1–11; 6.1–11, 22, 23); our new life (eternal life) begins. And it is present because we *are being* saved; that is sanctification (see the note on 6.1 – 8.39). But at the same time, we have not fully received all the benefits and blessings of salvation that will be ours when Christ's new kingdom is completely established. That's our future salvation. While we can be confident of our salvation, we still look ahead with hope and trust toward the complete change of body and personality that lies beyond this life, when we will be like Christ (1 John 3.2).

8.26, 27 As a believer in Christ, you are not left to your own resources to cope with problems. Even when you don't know the right words to pray, the Holy Spirit prays with and for you, and God answers. With God helping you pray, you don't need to be afraid to come before him. Ask the Holy Spirit to plead for you "according to the will of God." Then, when you bring your requests to God, trust that he will always do what is best.

8.28 God works out all things – not just isolated incidents – for our good. This does not mean that all that happens to us is good. Evil is prevalent in our fallen world, but God is able to turn it around for our long-range good. Note that God is not working to make us happy, but to fulfill his purpose. Note also that this promise is not for everybody. It can be claimed only by those who love God and are *called.* Those who are "called" are those the Holy Spirit convinces and enables to receive Christ. Such people have a new perspective, a new mindset on life. They trust in God, not life's treasures; they look to their security in heaven, not on earth; they learn to accept, not resent, pain and persecution because God is with them.

8.29 God's ultimate goal for us is to make us like Christ (1 John 3.2). As we become more and more like him, we discover our true selves, the persons we were created to be. How can we be conformed to his image? By reading and heeding his Word, by studying his life on earth through the Gospels, by being filled with his Spirit, and by doing his work in the world.

8.29, 30 Some believe these verses mean that before the beginning of the world, God chose or *predestined* certain people to receive his gift of salvation. They point to verses like Ephesians 1.11 which says we are "destined according to the purpose of him who accomplishes all things according to his counsel and will." Others believe that God *foreknew* those who would respond to him and upon those he set his mark. What is clear is that God's purpose for people was not an afterthought; it was settled before the foundation of the world. And God does not lose track of a single one. People are to serve and honor God. If you have believed in him, you can rejoice in the fact that God has always known you. His love is eternal. His wisdom and power are supreme. He will guide and protect you until you one day stand in his presence.

8.30 *Called* means summoned or invited. For more on justification and glorification, see the chart in chapter 3.

Nothing can separate us from God's love

31 What then are we to say about these things? If God is for us, who is against
us? 32 He who did not withhold his own Son, but gave him up for all of us, will he
not with him also give us everything else? 33 Who will bring any charge against
God's elect? It is God who justifies. 34 Who is to condemn? It is Christ Jesus, who
died, yes, who was raised, who is at the right hand of God, who indeed intercedes
for us.[q] 35 Who will separate us from the love of Christ? Will hardship, or distress,
or persecution, or famine, or nakedness, or peril, or sword? 36 As it is written,

"For your sake we are being killed all day long;
we are accounted as sheep to be slaughtered."

37 No, in all these things we are more than conquerors through him who loved us.
38 For I am convinced that neither death, nor life, nor angels, nor rulers, nor things
present, nor things to come, nor powers, 39 nor height, nor depth, nor anything else
in all creation, will be able to separate us from the love of God in Christ Jesus our
Lord.

8.31 Ps 118.6
8.32 Jn 3.16
8.33 Isa 50.8,9
8.34 Heb 7.25; 1 Jn 2.1
8.35 2 Cor 4.7-12
8.36 Ps 44.22
8.37 Jn 16.33
8.38 1 Cor 15.57; 1 Jn 5.4
8.38 Jn 10.28; Col 3.3

4. Israel's past, present, and future

God's sovereignty

9 I am speaking the truth in Christ—I am not lying; my conscience confirms it
by the Holy Spirit— 2 I have great sorrow and unceasing anguish in my heart.
3 For I could wish that I myself were accursed and cut off from Christ for the sake
of my own people,[r] my kindred according to the flesh. 4 They are Israelites, and to
them belong the adoption, the glory, the covenants, the giving of the law, the worship, and the promises; 5 to them belong the patriarchs, and from them, according
to the flesh, comes the Messiah,[s] who is over all, God blessed forever.[t] Amen.
6 It is not as though the word of God had failed. For not all Israelites truly
belong to Israel, 7 and not all of Abraham's children are his true descendants; but "It
is through Isaac that descendants shall be named for you." 8 This means that it is not
the children of the flesh who are the children of God, but the children of the promise are counted as descendants. 9 For this is what the promise said, "About this
time I will return and Sarah shall have a son." 10 Nor is that all; something similar

9.1-3 Ex 32.32
9.4 Gen 17.2; Deut 4.13; 7.6; Eph 2.12
9.5 bN)Jn 1.1,14; Tit 2.13; 2 Pet 1.1; 1 Jn 5.20
9.6 Num 23.19; Gal 6.16
9.7 Heb 11.17,18
9.8 Gal 3.29
9.9 Gen 18.10

[q] Or *Is it Christ Jesus . . . for us?* [r] Gk *my brothers* [s] Or *the Christ* [t] Or *Messiah, who is God over all, blessed forever*; or *Messiah. May he who is God over all be blessed forever*

8.31–34 Do you ever think that because you aren't good enough for God, he will not save you? Do you ever feel as if salvation is for everyone else but you? Then these verses are especially for you. If God gave his Son for you, he isn't going to hold back the gift of salvation! If Christ gave his life for you, he isn't going to turn around and condemn you! He will not withhold anything you need to live for him. The book of Romans is more than a theological explanation of God's redeeming grace—it is a letter of comfort and confidence addressed to you.

8.33 The *elect* refers to those chosen by God. They are not chosen because of any merit or work they have done, but because God in his mercy freely chooses them to be saved.

8.34 Paul says that Jesus is interceding for us in heaven. God has acquitted us and removed our sin and guilt, so it is Satan, not God, who accuses us. And when Satan accuses, Jesus, the advocate for our defense, stands at God's right hand to present our case. For more on the concept of Christ as our advocate, see the notes in Hebrews 4.14 and 7.25.

8.35, 36 These words were written to a church that would soon undergo terrible persecution. In just a few years, Paul's hypothetical situations would turn into painful realities. This passage reaffirms God's profound love for his people. No matter what happens to us or where we are, we can never be lost to his love. When suffering comes, it should not drive us away from God, but help us to identify with him further and allow his love to reach us and heal us.

8.35–39 These verses contain one of the most comforting promises in all Scripture. Believers have always had to face hardships in many forms: persecution, illness, imprisonment, even death. These could cause them to fear that they have been abandoned by Christ. But Paul exclaims that it is *impossible* to be separated from Christ. His death for us is proof of his unconquerable love. Nothing can stop his constant presence with us. God tells us how great his love is so that we will feel totally secure in him. If we believe these overwhelming assurances, we will not be afraid.

8.38 *Rulers* and *powers* are unseen forces of evil in the universe. These are Satan and his fallen angels (see Ephesians 6.12). In Christ we are super-conquerors, and his love will protect us from any such forces.

9.1–3 Paul expressed concern for his Jewish "kindred" by saying he would willingly take their punishment if that could save them. While the only one who can save us is Christ, Paul showed a rare depth of love. Like Jesus, he was willing to sacrifice himself for others. How concerned are you for those who don't know Christ? Are you willing to give your time, money, energy, comfort, and safety to see them come to faith in Jesus?

9.4 The Jews viewed God's choosing of Israel in the Old Testament as being like adoption. They were undeserving and without rights as natural children. Yet God adopted them and granted them the status of his sons and daughters.

9.6 God's promises were made to Abraham. This is the *covenant.* Covenant people, the true children of Abraham, are not just his biological descendants. They are all those who trust in God and in what Jesus Christ has done for them. (See also 2.29; Galatians 3.7.)

9.10-13 Gen 25.21-23 Deut 21.15 Mal 1.2,3
9.14 Deut 32.4 2 Chron 19.7
9.15 Ex 33.19
9.16 Ps 115.3 Eph 2.8
9.17 Ex 9.16 Prov 16.4
9.18 Ex 4.21; 14.4 Josh 11.20 Jn 12.40
9.19 Job 9.12
9.20 Isa 29.16; 45.9 64.8
9.21 Jer 18.6 2 Tim 2.20
9.22 Prov 16.4 Rom 2.4 1 Thess 5.9
9.23 Acts 9.15 Rom 8.29
9.24 Rom 3.29
9.25 Hos 2.23
9.26 Hos 1.10 1 Pet 2.10
9.27 Isa 10.22 Rom 11.5
9.28 Isa 28.22
9.29 Isa 1.9; 13.19 Lam 3.22

happened to Rebecca when she had conceived children by one husband, our ancestor Isaac. 11 Even before they had been born or had done anything good or bad (so
that God's purpose of election might continue, 12 not by works but by his call) she
was told, "The elder shall serve the younger." 13 As it is written,

"I have loved Jacob,
but I have hated Esau."

14 What then are we to say? Is there injustice on God's part? By no means!
15 For he says to Moses,

"I will have mercy on whom I have mercy,
and I will have compassion on whom I have compassion."

16 So it depends not on human will or exertion, but on God who shows mercy. 17 For
the scripture says to Pharaoh, "I have raised you up for the very purpose of showing
my power in you, so that my name may be proclaimed in all the earth." 18 So then
he has mercy on whomever he chooses, and he hardens the heart of whomever he
chooses.

19 You will say to me then, "Why then does he still find fault? For who can
resist his will?" 20 But who indeed are you, a human being, to argue with God? Will
what is molded say to the one who molds it, "Why have you made me like this?"
21 Has the potter no right over the clay, to make out of the same lump one object for
special use and another for ordinary use? 22 What if God, desiring to show his wrath
and to make known his power, has endured with much patience the objects of wrath
that are made for destruction; 23 and what if he has done so in order to make known
the riches of his glory for the objects of mercy, which he has prepared beforehand
for glory— 24 including us whom he has called, not from the Jews only but also
from the Gentiles? 25 As indeed he says in Hosea,

"Those who were not my people I will call 'my people,'
and her who was not beloved I will call 'beloved.' "
26 "And in the very place where it was said to them, 'You are not my
people,'
there they shall be called children of the living God."

27 And Isaiah cries out concerning Israel, "Though the number of the children
of Israel were like the sand of the sea, only a remnant of them will be saved; 28 for
the Lord will execute his sentence on the earth quickly and decisively."[u] 29 And as
Isaiah predicted,

"If the Lord of hosts had not left survivors[v] to us,
we would have fared like Sodom
and been made like Gomorrah."

[u] Other ancient authorities read *for he will finish his work and cut it short in righteousness, because the Lord will make the sentence shortened on the earth* [v] Or *descendants*; Gk *seed*

9.11 Jews were proud of the fact that their lineage came from Isaac whose mother was Sarah (Abraham's legitimate wife), rather than Ishmael whose mother was Hagar (Sarah's handmaiden). Paul asserts that no one can claim to be chosen by God because of his or her heritage or good works. God freely chooses to save whomever he wills. The doctrine of election teaches that it is God's goodness and mercy that save us, and not our own merit.

9.12–14 Was it right for God to choose Jacob, the younger, to be over Esau? "I have loved Jacob, but I have hated Esau" refers to the nations of Israel and Edom rather than to the individual brothers. He chose Jacob to continue the family line of the faithful. But he did not exclude Esau from knowing and loving him. Keep in mind the kind of God we worship: he is sovereign; he works for our good in everything; he is trustworthy; he will save all who believe in him. When we understand these qualities of God, we know his choices are good even if we don't understand all his reasons.

9.16 God's mercy does not depend on our desire or effort, but on his compassion and decision to give it to us.

9.17, 18 Paul quotes from Exodus 9.16 where God foretells how Pharaoh would be used to demonstrate God's power. Paul used this argument to show that salvation was God's proper work, not man's. God's judgment on Pharaoh's sin was to harden his heart, to confirm his disobedience so that the consequences of his rebellion would be his punishment.

9.21 With this illustration, Paul is not saying that some of us are worth more than others, but simply that the Creator has control over what he has created. The created object, therefore, has no right to demand anything from its Creator—its very existence depends on him. Keeping this perspective removes any temptation to have great pride in personal achievement.

9.25, 26 Seven hundred years before Jesus' birth, Hosea told of God's intention to bring Gentiles into his family after the Jews rejected his plan. Verse 25 is a quotation from Hosea 2.23 and verse 26 is from Hosea 1.10.

9.27–29 Isaiah prophesied that only a small number—a remnant—of God's original people, the Jews, would be saved. Paul saw this happening in every city where he preached. Even though he went to the Jews first, relatively few ever accepted the message. Verses 27 and 28 are based on Isaiah 10.22, 23; and 9.29 is from Isaiah 1.9.

Israel's unbelief of the gospel

30 What then are we to say? Gentiles, who did not strive for righteousness, **9.30** Gal 2.16
have attained it, that is, righteousness through faith; 31 but Israel, who did strive for Heb 11.7
the righteousness that is based on the law, did not succeed in fulfilling that law. **9.31**
32 Why not? Because they did not strive for it on the basis of faith, but as if it were Isa 51.1 Gal 5.4
based on works. They have stumbled over the stumbling stone, 33 as it is written, **9.32**
"See, I am laying in Zion a stone that will make people stumble, a rock Isa 8.14,15
that will make them fall, **9.33** Ps 118.22
and whoever believes in him[w] will not be put to shame." Isa 28.16

10 Brothers and sisters,[x] my heart's desire and prayer to God for them is that
they may be saved. 2 I can testify that they have a zeal for God, but it is not
enlightened. 3 For, being ignorant of the righteousness that comes from God, and **10.3** Rom 1.17
seeking to establish their own, they have not submitted to God's righteousness. Phil 3.9
4 For Christ is the end of the law so that there may be righteousness for everyone **10.4** Gal 3.24
who believes. **10.5**
5 Moses writes concerning the righteousness that comes from the law, that "the Lev 18.4,5 Ezek 20.11,
person who does these things will live by them." 6 But the righteousness that comes 13,21
from faith says, "Do not say in your heart, 'Who will ascend into heaven?' " (that Rom 7.10 **10.6**
is, to bring Christ down) 7 "or 'Who will descend into the abyss?' " (that is, to bring Deut 30.11-14
Christ up from the dead). 8 But what does it say? **10.7** 1 Cor 15.3,4
"The word is near you, **10.8**
on your lips and in your heart" Deut 30.14
(that is, the word of faith that we proclaim); 9 because[y] if you confess with your lips **10.9** Mt 10.32
that Jesus is Lord and believe in your heart that God raised him from the dead, you Lk 12.8 Acts 2.24; 16.31
will be saved. 10 For one believes with the heart and so is justified, and one con- Rom 4.24

[w] *Or trusts in it* [x] Gk *Brothers* [y] *Or namely, that*

9.31–33 Sometimes we are like these people, trying to get right with God by keeping his laws. We may think church attendance, church work, giving offerings, and being nice will be enough. After all, we've played by the rules, haven't we? But Paul's words sting—this approach never succeeds. Paul explains that God's plan is not for those who try to earn his favor by being good; it is for those who realize that they can never be good enough and so must depend on Christ. Only by putting our faith in what Jesus Christ has done will we be saved. If we do that, we will never be disappointed ("put to shame").

9.32 The Jews had a worthy goal—to honor God. But they tried to achieve it the wrong way—by rigid and painstaking obedience to the law. Some of them became more dedicated to the law than to God. They thought if they kept the law, God would have to accept them as his people. But God cannot be controlled. The Jews did not see that their Scriptures, the Old Testament, taught salvation by faith and not by human effort (see Genesis 15.6).

9.32 The "stumbling stone" was Jesus. The Jews did not believe in him because he didn't meet their expectations for the Messiah. Some people still stumble over Christ because salvation by faith doesn't make sense to them. They would rather try to work their way to God, or else they expect him simply to overlook their sins. Others stumble over Christ because his values are the opposite of the world's. He asks for humility, and many are unwilling to humble themselves before him. He requires obedience, and many refuse to put their wills at his disposal.

10.1 What will happen to the Jewish people who believe in God but not in Christ? Since they believe in the same God, won't they be saved? If that were true, Paul would not have worked so hard and sacrificed so much to teach them about Christ. Because Jesus is the most complete revelation of God, we cannot fully know God apart from Christ; and because God appointed Jesus to bring God and man together, we cannot come to God by another path. The Jews, like everyone else, can find salvation only through Jesus Christ (John 14.6; Acts 4.12). Like Paul, we should wish that all Jews might be saved. We should pray for them and lovingly share the good news with them.

10.3–5 Rather than living by faith in God, the Jews established customs and traditions (in addition to God's law) to try to make themselves acceptable in God's sight. But human effort, no matter how sincere, can never substitute for the goodness God offers us by faith. The only way to *earn* salvation is to be perfect—and that is impossible. We can only hold out our empty hands and receive salvation as a gift.

10.4 Christ is the "end of the law" in two ways. He fulfills the purpose and goal of the law (Matthew 5.17) in that he perfectly exemplified God's desires on earth. But he is also the termination of the law because in comparison to Christ, the law is powerless to save.

10.5 In order to be saved by the law, a person would have to live a perfect life, not sinning once. Why did God give the law when he knew people couldn't keep it? According to Paul, one reason the law was given was to show people how guilty they are (Galatians 3.19). The law was a shadow of Christ—that is, the sacrificial system educated the people so that when the true sacrifice came, they would be able to understand his work. The system of ceremonial laws was to last until the coming of Christ. The law points to Christ, the reason for all those animal sacrifices.

10.6–8 Paul adapts Moses' farewell challenge from Deuteronomy 30.11–14 to apply to Christ. Christ has provided our salvation through his incarnation (coming to earth) and resurrection (coming back from the dead). God's salvation is right in front of us. He will come to us wherever we are. All we need to do is to respond and accept his gift of salvation. The *abyss* as used here refers to the grave or Hades, the place of the dead.

10.8–13 Have you ever been asked, "How do I become a Christian?" These verses give you the beautiful answer—salvation is as close as your own mouth and heart. People think it must be a complicated process, but it is not. If we believe in our hearts and say with our mouths that Christ is the risen Lord, we will be saved.

10.11 Isa 28.16
10.12 Acts 15.9; Eph 2.4-7
10.13 Joel 2.32; Acts 2.21
10.14 Acts 8.28-31; Tit 1.3
10.15 Isa 52.7; Rom 1.15; 15.20
10.16 Isa 53.1; Jn 12.38; Heb 4.2
10.17 Gal 3.2,5; Col 3.16
10.18 Ps 19.4
10.19 Deut 32.21
10.20 Isa 65.1,2
10.21 1 Sam 12.22; Jer 31.37

fesses with the mouth and so is saved. 11 The scripture says, "No one who believes
in him will be put to shame." 12 For there is no distinction between Jew and Greek;
the same Lord is Lord of all and is generous to all who call on him. 13 For, "Everyone who calls on the name of the Lord shall be saved."
14 But how are they to call on one in whom they have not believed? And how
are they to believe in one of whom they have never heard? And how are they to hear
without someone to proclaim him? 15 And how are they to proclaim him unless they
are sent? As it is written, "How beautiful are the feet of those who bring good
news!" 16 But not all have obeyed the good news;[z] for Isaiah says, "Lord, who has
believed our message?" 17 So faith comes from what is heard, and what is heard
comes through the word of Christ.[a]
18 But I ask, have they not heard? Indeed they have; for
"Their voice has gone out to all the earth,
and their words to the ends of the world."
19 Again I ask, did Israel not understand? First Moses says,
"I will make you jealous of those who are not a nation;
with a foolish nation I will make you angry."
20 Then Isaiah is so bold as to say,
"I have been found by those who did not seek me;
I have shown myself to those who did not ask for me."
21 But of Israel he says, "All day long I have held out my hands to a disobedient and
contrary people."

11.1 1 Sam 12.22; Jer 31.36,37; 2 Cor 11.22; Phil 3.5
11.2 1 Kgs 19.10
11.4 1 Kgs 19.18
11.5 2 Kgs 19.4
11.6 Rom 4.4,5

God's mercy on Israel

11 I ask, then, has God rejected his people? By no means! I myself am an Israelite, a descendant of Abraham, a member of the tribe of Benjamin. 2 God has
not rejected his people whom he foreknew. Do you not know what the scripture
says of Elijah, how he pleads with God against Israel? 3 "Lord, they have killed
your prophets, they have demolished your altars; I alone am left, and they are seeking my life." 4 But what is the divine reply to him? "I have kept for myself seven
thousand who have not bowed the knee to Baal." 5 So too at the present time there
is a remnant, chosen by grace. 6 But if it is by grace, it is no longer on the basis of
works, otherwise grace would no longer be grace.[b]

[z] Or *gospel* [a] Or *about Christ;* other ancient authorities read *of God* [b] Other ancient authorities add *But if it is by works, it is no longer on the basis of grace, otherwise work would no longer be work*

10.11 This verse must be read in context. Paul is not saying Christians will never be disappointed (put to shame). There will be times when people will let us down and when circumstances will take a turn for the worse. Paul is saying that God will keep his side of the bargain—those who call on him will be saved.

10.14, 15 We must take God's great message of salvation to others so they can respond to the good news. How will your loved ones and neighbors hear it unless someone tells them? Is God calling you to take a part in making his message known in your community? Think of one person who needs to hear the good news, and think of something you can do to help him or her hear it. Then take that step as soon as possible.

10.18–20 Many Jews who looked for the Messiah refused to believe in him when he came. God offered his salvation to the Gentiles ("those who are not a nation" and "foolish nation"); thus many Gentiles who didn't even know about a Messiah found and believed in him. Some "religious" people are spiritually blind, while those who have never been in a church are sometimes the most responsive to God's message. Because appearances are deceiving and we can't see into people's hearts, beware of judging beforehand who will respond to the gospel and who will not.

11.1ff In this chapter Paul points out that not *all* Jews have rejected God's message of salvation. Paul himself, after all, was a Jew, and so were Jesus' disciples and nearly all of the early Christian missionaries.

11.2 Elijah was a great reforming prophet who challenged the northern kingdom of Israel to repent. See his Profile in 1 Kings 18 for more information.

11.2 God chose the Jews ("his people whom he foreknew") to be the people through whom the rest of the world could find salvation. But this did not mean the entire Jewish nation would be saved; only those who were faithful to God were considered true Jews (11.5). We are saved through faith in Christ, not because we are part of a certain nation, religion, or family. On what are you depending for salvation?

11.6 Do you think it's easier for God to love you when you're good? Do you secretly suspect that God chose you because you deserved it? Do you think some people's behavior is so bad that God couldn't possibly save them? If you ever think this way, you don't entirely understand that salvation is by grace, a free gift. It cannot be earned, in whole or in part; it can only be accepted with thankfulness and praise.

7 What then? Israel failed to obtain what it was seeking. The elect obtained it,
but the rest were hardened, 8 as it is written,

"God gave them a sluggish spirit,
eyes that would not see
and ears that would not hear,
down to this very day."

9 And David says,

"Let their table become a snare and a trap,
a stumbling block and a retribution for them;
10 let their eyes be darkened so that they cannot see,
and keep their backs forever bent."

11 So I ask, have they stumbled so as to fall? By no means! But through their
stumbling[c] salvation has come to the Gentiles, so as to make Israel[d] jealous.
12 Now if their stumbling[c] means riches for the world, and if their defeat means
riches for Gentiles, how much more will their full inclusion mean!

13 Now I am speaking to you Gentiles. Inasmuch then as I am an apostle to the
Gentiles, I glorify my ministry 14 in order to make my own people[e] jealous, and
thus save some of them. 15 For if their rejection is the reconciliation of the world,
what will their acceptance be but life from the dead! 16 If the part of the dough
offered as first fruits is holy, then the whole batch is holy; and if the root is holy,
then the branches also are holy.

17 But if some of the branches were broken off, and you, a wild olive shoot,
were grafted in their place to share the rich root[f] of the olive tree, 18 do not boast
over the branches. If you do boast, remember that it is not you that support the root,
but the root that supports you. 19 You will say, "Branches were broken off so that
I might be grafted in." 20 That is true. They were broken off because of their unbelief, but you stand only through faith. So do not become proud, but stand in awe.
21 For if God did not spare the natural branches, perhaps he will not spare you.[g]
22 Note then the kindness and the severity of God: severity toward those who have
fallen, but God's kindness toward you, provided you continue in his kindness; oth-

11.7 Mk 6.52 2 Cor 3.14,15
11.8 Deut 29.4 Isa 6.9-13 29.10 Mt 13.14 Jn 12.40 Acts 28.26,27
11.9 Ps 69.22
11.10 Ps 69.23
11.11 Ezek 18.23 33.11 Acts 18.6
11.12 Jer 30.3-9,11 Zech 2.11
11.13 Acts 9.15
11.14 Rom 9.3 1 Cor 9.20 2 Tim 1.9
11.15 Lk 15.24,32 Rom 5.11
11.17 Jer 11.16 Eph 2.11-16
11.18 Jn 4.22 1 Cor 10.12
11.20 Rom 12.16 Phil 2.12
11.22 Jn 15.2 Heb 3.6

c Gk *transgression* d Gk *them* e Gk *my flesh* f Other ancient authorities read *the richness* g Other ancient authorities read *neither will he spare you*

11.7, 8 "The rest were hardened" was God's punishment for their sin. It was a confirmation of their stubbornness. As judgment, he removed their ability to see and repent, and let them have their own way. Thus they would experience the consequences of their rebellion. A sluggish spirit refers to being unresponsive, slow to move.

11.8–10 These verses describe the punishment for hardened hearts predicted by the prophet Isaiah (Isaiah 6.9–13). If people refuse to hear God's good news, they eventually will be unable to understand it. Paul saw this happening in the Jewish congregations he visited on his missionary journeys. (Verse 8 is based on Deuteronomy 29.4 and Isaiah 29.10. Verses 9 and 10 are from Psalm 69.22, 23.)

11.11ff Paul had a vision for a church where Jews and Gentiles would be united in their love of God and in obedience to Christ. While respecting God's law, this ideal church would look to Christ alone for salvation. One's ethnic background and social status would be irrelevant (see Galatians 3.28)—what mattered would be one's faith in Christ.

But Paul's vision has not yet been realized. Many Jewish people rejected the good news. They depended on their heritage for salvation, and they did not have the obedient heart that was so important to the Old Testament prophets and to Paul.

Once Gentiles became dominant in many of the churches, they began rejecting Jews and even persecuting them. Unfortunately, this practice has recurred through the centuries.

True Christians should not persecute anyone. Both Christians and Jews have done so much to damage the cause of the God they claim to serve that Paul's vision often seems impossible to fulfill.

Yet God chose the Jews, just as he chose the Christians, and he is still working to unite Jew and Gentile in a new Israel, a new Jerusalem, ruled by his Son.

11.13–15 Paul was appointed a missionary to the Gentiles. He reminded his Jewish brothers of this, hoping they too would want to be saved. The Jews were rejected, and thus Gentiles were offered salvation. But when a Jew comes to Christ, there is great rejoicing, as if a dead person had come back to life.

11.16–25 Speaking to Gentile Christians, Paul warns them not to feel superior because God rejected some Jews. The Jewish religion, he says, is like the root of an unproductive tree, and the Jewish people are the tree's natural branches. Gentile believers have been grafted into the tree like a wild olive branch to inject new vitality into the old tree. Both Jews and Gentiles share its nourishment and depend on Christ for life; neither can rest on heritage, culture, or theological beliefs for salvation.

11.23 2 Cor 3.14-16 erwise you also will be cut off. 23 And even those of Israel,[h] if they do not persist
in unbelief, will be grafted in, for God has the power to graft them in again. 24 For
if you have been cut from what is by nature a wild olive tree and grafted, contrary
to nature, into a cultivated olive tree, how much more will these natural branches
be grafted back into their own olive tree.

God's mercy on all

11.25 Lk 21.24 Rom 11.12; 16.25 Eph 3.3-6 25 So that you may not claim to be wiser than you are, brothers and sisters,[i] I
want you to understand this mystery: a hardening has come upon part of Israel,
11.26 Ps 14.7 Isa 59.20 Jer 3.18 until the full number of the Gentiles has come in. 26 And so all Israel will be saved;
as it is written,
"Out of Zion will come the Deliverer;
he will banish ungodliness from Jacob."
11.27 Jer 31.31 Heb 8.8; 10.16 27 "And this is my covenant with them,
when I take away their sins."
28 As regards the gospel they are enemies of God[j] for your sake; but as regards
11.29 Num 23.18-24 Heb 7.21 election they are beloved, for the sake of their ancestors; 29 for the gifts and the
calling of God are irrevocable. 30 Just as you were once disobedient to God but have
now received mercy because of their disobedience, 31 so they have now been
disobedient in order that, by the mercy shown to you, they too may now[k] receive
11.32 Rom 3.9 Gal 3.22 mercy. 32 For God has imprisoned all in disobedience so that he may be merciful to
all.
11.33 Job 11.7; 15.8 Eph 3.8,10 33 O the depth of the riches and wisdom and knowledge of God! How unsearchable are his judgments and how inscrutable his ways!
11.34 Isa 40.13 1 Cor 2.16 34 "For who has known the mind of the Lord?
Or who has been his counselor?"
11.35 Job 35.7; 41.11 Col 1.16 35 "Or who has given a gift to him,
to receive a gift in return?"
11.36 1 Cor 8.6 36 For from him and through him and to him are all things. To him be the glory
forever. Amen.

[h] Gk lacks *of Israel* [i] Gk *brothers* [j] Gk lacks *of God* [k] Other ancient authorities lack *now*

11.22 "Continue in his kindness" refers to steadfast perseverance in faith. This perseverence is a proof of the reality of faith and a by-product of salvation, not a means to it.

11.26 Some say the phrase "and so all Israel will be saved" means that the majority of Jews in the final generation before Christ's return will turn to Christ for salvation. Others say that Paul is using the term *Israel* for the "spiritual" nation of Israel made up of everyone – Jew and Gentile – who has received salvation through faith in Christ. Thus *all Israel* (or all believers) will receive God's promised gift of salvation. Still others say that *all Israel* means Israel as a whole will have a role in Christ's kingdom. Their identity as a people won't be discarded. God chose the nation of Israel, and he has never rejected it. He also chose the church, through Jesus Christ, and he will never reject it either. This does not mean, of course, that all Jews or all church members will be saved. It is possible to belong to a nation or to an organization without ever responding in faith. But just because some people have rejected Christ does not mean that God stops working with either Israel or the church. He continues to offer salvation freely to all. Still others say that the phrase "and so" means "in this way" or "this is how," referring to the necessity of faith in Christ.

11.28–32 In this passage Paul shows how the Jews and the Gentiles benefit each other. Whenever God shows mercy to one group, the other shares the blessing. In God's original plan, the Jews would be the source of God's blessing to the Gentiles (see Genesis 12.3). When the Jews neglected this mission, God blessed the Gentiles anyway through the Jewish Messiah. He still maintained his love for the Jews because of his promises to Abraham, Isaac, and Jacob ("for the sake of their ancestors"). But someday the faithful Jews will share in God's mercy. God's plans will not be thwarted: he will "be merciful to all." For a beautiful picture of Jews and Gentiles being blessed together, see Isaiah 60.

11.29 The privileges and invitation of God [given to Israel] can never be withdrawn.

11.34, 35 The implication of these questions is that no one has fully understood the mind of the Lord. No one has been his counselor. And God owes nothing to any one of us. Isaiah and Jeremiah asked similar questions to show that we are unable to give advice to God or criticize his ways (Isaiah 40.13; Jeremiah 23.18). God alone is the possessor of absolute power and absolute wisdom.

11.36 In the final analysis, we are all absolutely dependent on God. He is the source of all things, including ourselves. He is the power that sustains and rules the world that we live in. And God works out all things to bring glory to himself. The all-powerful God deserves our praise.

B. HOW TO BEHAVE (12.1—16.27)

Moving from theological to practical, Paul gives guidelines for living as a redeemed people in a fallen world. We are to give ourselves to Christ as living sacrifices, obey the government, love our neighbors, and take special care of those who are weak in the faith. He closes with personal remarks. Throughout this section, we learn how to live our faith each day.

1. Personal responsibility

A living sacrifice to God

12 I appeal to you therefore, brothers and sisters,[l] by the mercies of God, to **12.1**
present your bodies as a living sacrifice, holy and acceptable to God, which Rom 6.12,13
is your spiritual[m] worship. 2 Do not be conformed to this world,[n] but be trans- **12.2** Gal 1.4
formed by the renewing of your minds, so that you may discern what is the will of Eph 4.23
God—what is good and acceptable and perfect.[o] Col 3.10
3 For by the grace given to me I say to everyone among you not to think of **12.3** 1 Cor 12.7
yourself more highly than you ought to think, but to think with sober judgment, Phil 2.3-5
each according to the measure of faith that God has assigned. 4 For as in one body **12.4,5** 1 Cor 10.17
we have many members, and not all the members have the same function, 5 so we, 12.12-14
who are many, are one body in Christ, and individually we are members one of **12.6** 1 Pet 4.10,11
another. 6 We have gifts that differ according to the grace given to us: prophecy, in **12.8**
proportion to faith; 7 ministry, in ministering; the teacher, in teaching; 8 the ex- 1 Pet 5.2

l Gk *brothers* m Or *reasonable* n Gk *age* o Or *what is the good and acceptable and perfect will of God*

12.1 When sacrificing an animal according to God's law, a priest killed the animal, cut it in pieces, and placed it on the altar. Sacrifice was important, but even in the Old Testament, God made it clear that obedience from the heart was much more important (see 1 Samuel 15.22; Psalm 40.6; Amos 5.21–24). God wants us to offer ourselves, not animals, as *living* sacrifices—daily laying aside our own desires to follow him, putting all our energy and resources at his disposal and trusting him to guide us. We do this out of gratitude that our sins have been forgiven.

12.1, 2 God has good, acceptable, and perfect plans for his children. He wants us to be new people with renewed minds, living to honor and obey him. Because he wants only what is best for us, and because he gave his Son to make our new lives possible, we should joyfully volunteer as living sacrifices for his service.

12.2 Christians are called to "not be conformed to this world" with its behavior and customs that are usually selfish and often corrupting. Many Christians wisely decide that much worldly behavior is off-limits for them. Our refusal to conform to this world's values, however, must go even deeper than the level of behavior and customs—it must be firmly founded in our minds—"be transformed by the renewing of your minds." It is possible to avoid most worldly customs and still be proud, covetous, selfish, stubborn, and arrogant. Only when the Holy Spirit renews, reeducates, and redirects our minds will we be truly transformed (see 8.5).

12.3 Healthy self-esteem is important because some of us think too little of ourselves. On the other hand, some of us overestimate ourselves. The key to an honest and accurate evaluation is knowing the basis of our self-worth—our identity in Christ. Apart from him, we aren't capable of very much by eternal standards; in him, we are valuable and capable of worthy service. Evaluating yourself by the worldly standards of success and achievement can cause you to think too much about your worth in the eyes of others and miss your true value in God's eyes.

12.4, 5 Paul uses the concept of the human body to teach how Christians should live and work together. Just as the parts of the body function under the direction of the brain, so Christians are to work together under the command and authority of Jesus Christ (see 1 Corinthians 12.12–31; Ephesians 4.1–16).

12.4–8 God gives us gifts so we can build up his church. To use them effectively, we must (1) realize that all gifts and abilities come from God; (2) understand that not everyone has the same gifts; (3) know who we are and what we do best; (4) dedicate our gifts to God's service and not to our personal success; (5) be willing to utilize our gifts wholeheartedly, not holding back anything from God's service.

12.6 God's gifts differ in nature, power, and effectiveness according to his wisdom and graciousness, not according to our faith. The "measure of faith" (12.3) or the proportion of faith means that God will give the spiritual power necessary and appropriate to carry out each responsibility. We cannot, by our own effort or willpower, drum up more faith and thus be more effective teachers or servants. These are God's gifts to his church, and he gives faith and power as he wills. Our role is to be faithful and to seek ways to serve others with what Christ has given us.

12.6 *Prophecy* in Scripture is not always predicting the future. Often it means preaching God's messages (1 Corinthians 14.1–3).

12.6–8 Look at this list of gifts and imagine the kinds of people who would have each gift. Prophets are often bold and articulate. Servers (those in ministry) are faithful and loyal. Teachers are clear thinkers. Preachers (exhorter) know how to motivate others. Givers are generous and trusting. Leaders are good organizers and managers. Comforters are caring people who are happy to give their time to others. It would be difficult for one person to embody all these gifts. An assertive prophet would not usually make a good counselor, and a generous giver might fail as an administrator. When you identify your own gifts (and this list is far from complete),

12.9 1 Tim 1.5
12.10 Phil 2.3,4; 1 Thess 4.9
12.11 Acts 18.25
12.12 Heb 3.6; 10.32
12.13 Heb 6.10; 13.1-3
12.14 1 Pet 3.9
12.15 Job 30.25
12.16 Phil 2.2; 4.2
12.17 Prov 20.22
12.20 Mt 5.44
12.21 1 Pet 2.21

horter, in exhortation; the giver, in generosity; the leader, in diligence; the compassionate, in cheerfulness.
9 Let love be genuine; hate what is evil, hold fast to what is good; 10 love one
another with mutual affection; outdo one another in showing honor. 11 Do not lag in
zeal, be ardent in spirit, serve the Lord.[p] 12 Rejoice in hope, be patient in suffering,
persevere in prayer. 13 Contribute to the needs of the saints; extend hospitality to
strangers.
14 Bless those who persecute you; bless and do not curse them. 15 Rejoice with
those who rejoice, weep with those who weep. 16 Live in harmony with one
another; do not be haughty, but associate with the lowly;[q] do not claim to be wiser
than you are. 17 Do not repay anyone evil for evil, but take thought for what is noble
in the sight of all. 18 If it is possible, so far as it depends on you, live peaceably with
all. 19 Beloved, never avenge yourselves, but leave room for the wrath of God;[r] for
it is written, "Vengeance is mine, I will repay, says the Lord." 20 No, "if your enemies are hungry, feed them; if they are thirsty, give them something to drink; for by
doing this you will heap burning coals on their heads." 21 Do not be overcome by
evil, but overcome evil with good.

[p] Other ancient authorities read *serve the opportune time* [q] Or *give yourselves to humble tasks* [r] Gk *the wrath*

---

ask how you can use them to build up God's family. At the same time, realize that your gifts can't do the work of the church all alone. Be thankful for people whose gifts are completely different from yours. Let your strengths balance their weaknesses, and be grateful that their abilities make up for your deficiencies. Together you can build his church.

12.9 Most of us have learned how to pretend to love others—how to speak kindly, avoid hurting their feelings, and appear to take an interest in them. We may even be skilled in pretending to feel moved with compassion when we hear of others' needs or to be indignant when we learn of injustice. But God calls us to genuine and sincere love that goes far beyond pretense and politeness. Genuine love requires concentration and effort. It means helping others become better people. It demands our time, money, and personal involvement. No individual has the capacity to express love to a whole community, but the body of Christ in your town has. Look for people who need your love, and look for ways you and your fellow believers can love your community for Christ.

12.10 We can honor others in one of two ways. One involves ulterior motives. We honor our bosses so they will reward us, our employees so they will work harder, the wealthy so they will contribute to our cause, the powerful so they will use their power for us and not against us. God's other way involves love. As Christians, we should honor people because they have been created in God's image, because they are our brothers and sisters in Christ, because they have a unique contribution to Christ's church. Does God's way of honoring others sound too difficult for your competitive nature? Why not try to outdo one another in showing honor? Put others first!

12.12 To "rejoice in hope" means that we should look forward with happy anticipation to all that God has in store for us. We don't have to fear the future when it is in his hands.

12.13 Christian hospitality differs from social entertaining. Entertaining focuses on the host—the home must be spotless; the food must be well prepared and abundant; the host must appear relaxed and good natured. Hospitality, by contrast, focuses on the guests. Their needs—whether for a place to stay, nourishing food, a listening ear, or acceptance—are the primary concern. Hospitality can happen in a messy home. It can happen around a dinner table where the main dish is canned soup. It can even happen while the host and the guest are doing chores together. Don't be afraid to offer hospitality just because you are too tired, too busy, or not wealthy enough to entertain.

12.17–21 These verses summarize the real core of Christian living. If we love someone the way Christ loves us, we will be willing to forgive. If we have experienced God's grace, we will want to pass it on to others. And remember, grace is *undeserved* favor. By giving an enemy a drink, we're not excusing his misdeeds. We're recognizing him, forgiving him, and loving him in spite of his sins—just as Christ did in our case.

12.19–21 In this day of constant lawsuits and incessant demands for legal rights, Paul's command sounds almost impossible. When someone hurts you deeply, instead of giving him what he deserves, Paul says to befriend him. Why does Paul tell us to forgive our enemies? (1) Forgiveness may break a cycle of retaliation and lead to mutual reconciliation. (2) It may make the enemy feel ashamed and change his ways. (3) By contrast, returning evil for evil hurts you just as much as it hurts your enemy. Even if your enemy never repents, forgiving him will free you of a heavy load of bitterness.

12.19–21 Forgiveness involves both attitudes and actions. If you find it hard to *feel* forgiving of someone who has hurt you, try to *act* forgiving. If appropriate, tell this person you would like to heal your relationship. Give him a helping hand. Send her a gift. Smile at him. Many times you will discover that right actions lead to right feelings.

12.20 What does it mean to "heap burning coals" on someone's head? This may refer to an Egyptian tradition of carying a pan of burning charcoal on one's head as a public act of repentance. By referring to this proverb, Paul was saying that we should treat our enemies with kindness so that they will become ashamed and turn from their sins. The best way to get rid of enemies is to turn them into friends.

Obedience to the government

13 Let every person be subject to the governing authorities; for there is no au- **13.1** Dan 2.21; 4.32
thority except from God, and those authorities that exist have been instituted Jn 19.11
by God. 2 Therefore whoever resists authority resists what God has appointed, and Tit 3.1
those who resist will incur judgment. 3 For rulers are not a terror to good conduct, **13.3** 1 Pet 2.14
but to bad. Do you wish to have no fear of the authority? Then do what is good, and
you will receive its approval; 4 for it is God's servant for your good. But if you do
what is wrong, you should be afraid, for the authority[s] does not bear the sword in
vain! It is the servant of God to execute wrath on the wrongdoer. 5 Therefore one **13.5** Eccles 8.2
must be subject, not only because of wrath but also because of conscience. 6 For the 1 Pet 2.13
same reason you also pay taxes, for the authorities are God's servants, busy with
this very thing. 7 Pay to all what is due them—taxes to whom taxes are due, revenue **13.7** Mt 17.24,25
to whom revenue is due, respect to whom respect is due, honor to whom honor is 22.21
due. Lk 20.25

Love fulfills God's requirements

8 Owe no one anything, except to love one another; for the one who loves **13.8** Mt 7.12; 22.39
another has fulfilled the law. 9 The commandments, "You shall not commit adul- Jn 13.34
tery; You shall not murder; You shall not steal; You shall not covet"; and any other **13.9** Ex 20.13-17
commandment, are summed up in this word, "Love your neighbor as yourself."
10 Love does no wrong to a neighbor; therefore, love is the fulfilling of the law. **13.10** Gal 5.13,14
11 Besides this, you know what time it is, how it is now the moment for you to **13.11** 1 Cor 7.29
wake from sleep. For salvation is nearer to us now than when we became believers; 1 Thess 5.6
12 the night is far gone, the day is near. Let us then lay aside the works of darkness Jas 5.8 1 Pet 4.7
and put on the armor of light; 13 let us live honorably as in the day, not in reveling Rev 1.3

[s] Gk *it*

13.1 Are there times when we should not obey the government? We can never allow government to force us to disobey God. Jesus and his apostles never disobeyed the government for personal reasons; when they disobeyed, it was in order to follow their higher loyalty to God. Their disobedience was not cheap: they were threatened, beaten, thrown into jail, tortured, and executed for their convictions. Like them, if we are compelled to disobey, we must be ready to accept the consequences.

13.1ff Christians understand Romans 13 in different ways. All Christians agree that we are to live at peace with the state as long as the state allows us to live by our religious convictions. For hundreds of years, however, there have been at least three interpretations of how we are to do this.

(1) Some Christians believe that the state is so corrupt that Christians should have as little to do with it as possible. Although they should be good citizens as long as they can do so without compromising their beliefs, they should not work for the government, vote, or serve in the military.

(2) Others believe God has given the state authority in certain areas and the church authority in others. Christians can be loyal to both and can work for either. They should not, however, confuse the two. In this view, church and state are concerned with two totally different spheres—the spiritual and the physical—and thus complement each other but do not work together.

(3) Still others believe that Christians have a responsibility to make the state better. They can do this politically, by electing Christian or other high-principled leaders. They can also do this morally, by serving as an influence for good in society. In this view, church and state ideally work together for the good of all.

None of these views advocate rebelling against or refusing to obey the government's laws or regulations unless they clearly require you to violate the moral standards revealed by God. Wherever we find ourselves, we must be responsible citizens, as well as responsible Christians.

13.3, 4 When the police are unjust, good people are afraid. In these verses, Paul is talking about police who are doing their duty. When the police are just, people who are doing right have nothing to fear.

13.8 How can we *owe* love to others? We are permanently in debt to Christ for the lavish love he has poured out on us. The only way we can even begin to repay this debt is by loving others in turn. Christ's love will always be infinitely greater than ours, so we will always have the obligation to love our neighbors.

13.9 Somehow many of us have gotten the idea that self-love is wrong. But if this were the case, it would be pointless to love our neighbors as ourselves. But Paul explains what he means by self-love. Even if you have low self-esteem, you probably don't willingly let yourself go hungry. You clothe yourself reasonably well. You make sure there's a roof over your head if you can. You try not to let yourself be cheated or injured. And you get angry if someone tries to ruin your marriage. This is the kind of love we need to have for our neighbors. Do we see that others are fed, clothed, and housed as well as they can be? Are we concerned about issues of social justice? Loving others as ourselves means to be actively working to see that their needs are met. Interestingly, people who focus on others rather than on themselves rarely suffer from low self-esteem.

13.10 Christians must obey the law of love, which supersedes both religious and civil laws. How easy it is to excuse our indifference to others merely because we have no legal obligation to help them, even to justify harming them if our actions are technically legal! But Jesus does not leave loopholes in the law of love. Whenever love demands it, we are to go beyond human legal requirements and imitate the God of love. See James 2.8, 9; 4.11; and 1 Peter 2.16, 17 for more about this law of love.

13.12–14 Some people are surprised that Paul lists quarreling and jealousy with the gross and obvious sins of drunkenness and debauchery. Like Jesus in his Sermon on the Mount (Matthew 5–7), Paul considers attitudes as important as actions. Just as hatred can lead to murder, so quarreling can lead to fighting and jealousy can lead to stealing or violence. When Christ returns, he wants to find his people clean on the inside as well as on the outside.

13.12,13 Eph 5.11; 6.13 Col 3.5-10 Jas 3.14

and drunkenness, not in debauchery and licentiousness, not in quarreling and jealousy. 14 Instead, put on the Lord Jesus Christ, and make no provision for the flesh,
to gratify its desires.

Weak and strong believers

14.1 1 Cor 9.22
14.2 1 Cor 10.25
14.3 Col 2.16
14.5 Gal 4.10
14.6 1 Cor 10.31 1 Tim 4.3
14.7 1 Cor 6.19 2 Cor 5.15 Gal 2.20
14.8 Phil 1.20 1 Thess 5.10
14.9 Phil 2.11 Rev 1.18
14.10 Mt 25.31,32 Rom 2.16 2 Cor 5.10

14 Welcome those who are weak in faith,[t] but not for the purpose of quarreling
over opinions. 2 Some believe in eating anything, while the weak eat only
vegetables. 3 Those who eat must not despise those who abstain, and those who
abstain must not pass judgment on those who eat; for God has welcomed them.
4 Who are you to pass judgment on servants of another? It is before their own lord
that they stand or fall. And they will be upheld, for the Lord[u] is able to make them
stand.
5 Some judge one day to be better than another, while others judge all days to
be alike. Let all be fully convinced in their own minds. 6 Those who observe the
day, observe it in honor of the Lord. Also those who eat, eat in honor of the Lord,
since they give thanks to God; while those who abstain, abstain in honor of the Lord
and give thanks to God.
7 We do not live to ourselves, and we do not die to ourselves. 8 If we live, we
live to the Lord, and if we die, we die to the Lord; so then, whether we live or
whether we die, we are the Lord's. 9 For to this end Christ died and lived again, so
that he might be Lord of both the dead and the living.
10 Why do you pass judgment on your brother or sister?[v] Or you, why do you

[t] Or *conviction* [u] Other ancient authorities read *for God* [v] Gk *brother*

13.14 How do we "put on the Lord Jesus Christ"? First we identify with Christ by being baptized (Galatians 3.27). This shows our solidarity with other Christians. Second, we exemplify the qualities Jesus showed while he was here on earth (love, humility, truth, service). In a sense, we role play what Jesus would do in our situation (see Ephesians 4.24–32; Colossians 3.10–17). We also must not give our desires any opportunity to lead us into sin. Avoid those situations that open the door to gratifying sinful desires.

14.1 Who is weak in faith and who is strong? We are all weak in some areas and strong in others. Our faith is strong in an area if we can survive contact with sinners without falling into their patterns. It is weak in an area if we must avoid certain activities, people, or places in order to protect our spiritual life. It is important to take a self-inventory in order to find out our strengths and weaknesses. Whenever in doubt, we should ask, "Can I do that without sinning? Can I influence others for good, rather than being influenced by them?"

In areas of strength, we should not fear being defiled by the world; rather we should go and serve God. In areas of weakness, we need to be cautious. If we have a strong faith but shelter it, we are not doing Christ's work in the world. If we have a weak faith but expose it, we are being extremely foolish.

14.1 This verse assumes there will be differences of opinion in the church. Paul says we are not to quarrel about issues that are matters of opinion. Differences of opinion should not be feared or avoided, but accepted and handled with love. Don't expect everyone, even in the best church, to agree on every subject. Through sharing ideas we can come to a fuller understanding of what the Bible teaches. Accept, listen to, and respect others. Differences of opinion need not cause division. They can be a source of learning and richness in our relationships.

14.1ff What is weak faith? Paul is speaking about immature faith, faith that has not yet developed the muscle it needs to stand against external pressures. For example, if a person who once worshiped idols became a Christian, he might understand perfectly well that Christ saved him through faith and that idols have no real power. Still, because of his past associations, he might be badly shaken if he knowingly ate meat that had been used in idol worship as part of a heathen ritual. If a person who once worshiped God on the required Jewish holy days became a Christian, he might well know that Christ saved him through faith, not through his keeping of the law. Still, when the feast days came, he might feel empty and unfaithful if he didn't dedicate them to God.

Paul responds to both weak brothers in love. Both are acting according to their consciences, but their honest scruples do not need to be made into rules for the church. Certainly some issues are central to the faith and worth fighting for – but many are based on individual differences and should not be legislated. Our principle should be: "In essentials, unity; in nonessentials, liberty; in everything, love."

14.2 "Eating anything" refers to eating meat offered to idols; eating only vegetables refers to one weaker in the faith who eats only vegetables and refuses to eat meat that has been offered to idols. But how would Christians end up eating meat that had been offered to idols? The ancient system of sacrifice was at the center of the religious, social, and domestic life of the Roman world. After a sacrifice was presented to a god in a heathen temple, only part of it was burned. The remainder was often sent to the market to be sold. Thus a Christian might easily – even unknowingly – buy such meat in the marketplace or eat it at the home of a friend. Should a Christian question the source of his meat? Some thought there was nothing wrong with eating meat that had been offered to idols, since idols were not real gods. Others carefully checked the source of their meat, or else gave up meat altogether, in order to avoid a guilty conscience. The problem was especially acute for Christians who had once been idol worshipers. For them, such a strong reminder of their pagan days might weaken their newfound faith. Paul also deals with this problem in 1 Corinthians 8.

14.10–12 Each person is accountable to Christ, not to others. While the church must be uncompromising in its stand against activities expressly forbidden by Scripture (adultery, homosexuality, murder, theft), it should not create additional rules and regulations and give them equal standing with God's law. Many times Christians base their moral judgments on opinion, personal dislikes, or cultural bias rather than on the Word of God. When they do this, they show that their own faith is weak. They do not think God is powerful enough to guide his children. When we stand before God's court of justice ("judgment seat"), we won't be worried about what our Christian neighbor has done (see 2 Corinthians 5.10).

despise your brother or sister?[w] For we will all stand before the judgment seat of
God.[x] 11 For it is written,

"As I live, says the Lord, every knee shall bow to me,
and every tongue shall give praise to[y] God."

12 So then, each of us will be accountable to God.[z]
13 Let us therefore no longer pass judgment on one another, but resolve instead
never to put a stumbling block or hindrance in the way of another.[a] 14 I know and
am persuaded in the Lord Jesus that nothing is unclean in itself; but it is unclean for
anyone who thinks it unclean. 15 If your brother or sister[w] is being injured by what
you eat, you are no longer walking in love. Do not let what you eat cause the ruin
of one for whom Christ died. 16 So do not let your good be spoken of as evil. 17 For
the kingdom of God is not food and drink but righteousness and peace and joy in the
Holy Spirit. 18 The one who thus serves Christ is acceptable to God and has human
approval. 19 Let us then pursue what makes for peace and for mutual upbuilding.
20 Do not, for the sake of food, destroy the work of God. Everything is indeed
clean, but it is wrong for you to make others fall by what you eat; 21 it is good not
to eat meat or drink wine or do anything that makes your brother or sister[w] stumble.[b] 22 The faith that you have, have as your own conviction before God. Blessed
are those who have no reason to condemn themselves because of what they approve. 23 But those who have doubts are condemned if they eat, because they do not
act from faith;[c] for whatever does not proceed from faith[c] is sin.[d]

Live to please others

15 We who are strong ought to put up with the failings of the weak, and not to
please ourselves. 2 Each of us must please our neighbor for the good purpose
of building up the neighbor. 3 For Christ did not please himself; but, as it is written,
"The insults of those who insult you have fallen on me." 4 For whatever was written
in former days was written for our instruction, so that by steadfastness and by the
encouragement of the scriptures we might have hope. 5 May the God of steadfastness and encouragement grant you to live in harmony with one another, in accord-

14.11 Isa 45.23
14.12 Mt 12.36
14.13 Mt 7.1; 1 Cor 8.9
14.14 1 Cor 8.7
14.15 1 Cor 8.11
14.16 1 Cor 10.29,30; Tit 2.5
14.17 Rom 15.13; Gal 5.22
14.19 Ps 34.14
14.20 Acts 10.15; 1 Cor 8.9
14.21 1 Cor 8.13
14.22 1 Jn 3.21
15.1,2 1 Cor 9.19,22; 10.23,24; Phil 2.4,5
15.3 Ps 69.9
15.4 2 Tim 3.16
15.5 2 Cor 1.3,4

[w] Gk *brother* [x] Other ancient authorities read *of Christ* [y] Or *confess* [z] Other ancient authorities lack *to God*
[a] Gk *of a brother* [b] Other ancient authorities add *or be upset or be weakened* [c] Or *conviction* [d] Other authorities, some ancient, add here 16.25-27

14.13 Both strong and weak Christians can cause their brothers to stumble. The strong but insensitive Christian may flaunt his freedom and intentionally offend others' consciences. The scrupulous but weak Christian tries to fence others in with petty rules and regulations, thus causing dissension. Paul wants his readers to be both strong in the faith and sensitive to others' needs. Because we are all strong in some areas and weak in others, we need constantly to monitor the effect of our behavior on others.

14.13ff Some Christians use an invisible weaker brother to support their own opinions, prejudices, or standards. "You must live by these standards," they say, "or you will be offending the weaker brother." In truth, you will often be offending no one but the speaker. While Paul urges us to be sensitive to those whose faith may be harmed by our actions, we should not sacrifice our liberty in Christ just to satisfy the selfish motives of those who are trying to force their opinions on us. Neither fear nor criticize them, but follow Christ as closely as you can.

14.14 At the Jerusalem council (Acts 15), the Jewish church in Jerusalem asked the Gentile church in Antioch not to eat meat offered to idols. Paul was at the Jerusalem council, and he accepted this request, not because he felt this practice was wrong in itself, but because this practice would deeply offend many Jewish believers. Paul did not think the issue was worth dividing the church; his desire was to promote unity.

14.20, 21 Sin is not just a private matter. Everything we do affects others, and we have to think of them constantly. God created us to be interdependent, not independent. We who are strong in our faith must, without pride or condescension, treat others with love, patience, and self-restraint.

14.23 We try to steer clear of actions forbidden by Scripture, of course; but sometimes Scripture is silent. Then we should follow our conscience. "Whatever does not proceed from faith is sin" means to go against a conviction and leaves a person with a guilty or uneasy conscience. When God shows us something is wrong for us, we should avoid it. But we should not look down on other Christians who exercise their freedom in those areas.

15.2 If we merely set out to please our neighbors, we would be people-pleasers. Paul was against that (see Galatians 1.10). But we are to set aside willfulness and self-pleasing for the sake of building them up for good. Our Christian convictions must not be a disguise for cold-hearted treatment of our brothers and sisters.

15.4 The knowledge of the Scriptures affects our attitude toward the present and the future. The more we know about what God has done in years past, the greater the confidence we have about what he will do in the days ahead. We should read our Bibles diligently to increase our trust that God's will is best for us.

15.5–7 To accept Jesus' lordship in all areas of life means to share his values and his perspective. Just as we take Jesus' view on the authority of Scripture, the nature of heaven, and the resurrection, we are to have his attitude of love toward other Christians as well. As we grow in faith and come to know Jesus better, we become more capable of maintaining this attitude throughout each day. Christ's attitude is explained in more detail in Philippians 2.

ance with Christ Jesus, 6 so that together you may with one voice glorify the God
and Father of our Lord Jesus Christ.

Fellowship among believers

7 Welcome one another, therefore, just as Christ has welcomed you, for the
glory of God. 8 For I tell you that Christ has become a servant of the circumcised on
behalf of the truth of God in order that he might confirm the promises given to the
patriarchs, 9 and in order that the Gentiles might glorify God for his mercy. As it is
written,

"Therefore I will confess[e] you among the Gentiles,
and sing praises to your name";

10 and again he says,

"Rejoice, O Gentiles, with his people";

11 and again,

"Praise the Lord, all you Gentiles,
and let all the peoples praise him";

12 and again Isaiah says,

"The root of Jesse shall come,
the one who rises to rule the Gentiles;
in him the Gentiles shall hope."

13 May the God of hope fill you with all joy and peace in believing, so that you may
abound in hope by the power of the Holy Spirit.

2. Personal notes

Paul explains his reason for writing

14 I myself feel confident about you, my brothers and sisters,[f] that you yourselves are full of goodness, filled with all knowledge, and able to instruct one
another. 15 Nevertheless on some points I have written to you rather boldly by way
of reminder, because of the grace given me by God 16 to be a minister of Christ
Jesus to the Gentiles in the priestly service of the gospel of God, so that the offering
of the Gentiles may be acceptable, sanctified by the Holy Spirit. 17 In Christ Jesus,
then, I have reason to boast of my work for God. 18 For I will not venture to speak
of anything except what Christ has accomplished[g] through me to win obedience
from the Gentiles, by word and deed, 19 by the power of signs and wonders, by the
power of the Spirit of God,[h] so that from Jerusalem and as far around as Illyricum
I have fully proclaimed the good news[i] of Christ. 20 Thus I make it my ambition to
proclaim the good news,[i] not where Christ has already been named, so that I do
not build on someone else's foundation, 21 but as it is written,

"Those who have never been told of him shall see,
and those who have never heard of him shall understand."

Paul explains his travel plans

22 This is the reason that I have so often been hindered from coming to you.

15.6 Rev 1.6
15.7 Rom 5.2
15.8 Mt 15.24; Acts 3.25,26; Rom 3.3,4; 2 Cor 1.20
15.9 Ps 18.49; Rom 9.23
15.10 Deut 32.43
15.11 Ps 117.1
15.12 Isa 11.10; Rev 5.5; 22.16
15.14 2 Pet 1.12; 1 Jn 2.21
15.15,16 Acts 9.15; Gal 1.15; 2.7-9; 1 Tim 2.7
15.17 Phil 3.3
15.18 Rom 1.5
15.19 Acts 19.11; 1 Cor 2.4
15.20 Rom 1.15; 1 Cor 3.10; 2 Cor 10.13,15
15.21 Isa 52.14,15

e Or *thank* f Gk *brothers* g Gk *speak of those things that Christ has not accomplished* h Other ancient authorities read *of the Spirit* or *of the Holy Spirit* i Or *gospel*

15.8 This verse means that Jesus came to bring the truth to the Jews (the circumcised) and to show that God is true to his promises.

15.12 The *root of Jesse* refers to Christ being the heir from the family line of Jesse, David's father (1 Samuel 16.1).

15.17 Paul was not proud of what he had done, but of what God had done through him. Being proud of God's work is not a sin—it is worship. If you are not sure whether your pride is selfish or holy, ask yourself this question: Are you just as proud of what God is doing through other people as of what he is doing through you?

15.19 Illyricum was a Roman territory on the Adriatic Sea between present-day Italy and Greece. It covered much the same territory as present-day Yugoslavia. See the map in chapter 1.

15.20–23 Paul wanted to visit the church at Rome, but he had delayed his visit because he had heard many good reports about the believers there and he knew they were doing well on their own. It was more important for him to preach in areas that had not yet heard the good news.

23 But now, with no further place for me in these regions, I desire, as I have for
many years, to come to you 24 when I go to Spain. For I do hope to see you on my
journey and to be sent on by you, once I have enjoyed your company for a little
while. 25 At present, however, I am going to Jerusalem in a ministry to the saints;
26 for Macedonia and Achaia have been pleased to share their resources with the
poor among the saints at Jerusalem. 27 They were pleased to do this, and indeed
they owe it to them; for if the Gentiles have come to share in their spiritual blessings, they ought also to be of service to them in material things. 28 So, when I have
completed this, and have delivered to them what has been collected,[j] I will set out
by way of you to Spain; 29 and I know that when I come to you, I will come in the
fullness of the blessing[k] of Christ.

30 I appeal to you, brothers and sisters,[l] by our Lord Jesus Christ and by the
love of the Spirit, to join me in earnest prayer to God on my behalf, 31 that I may be
rescued from the unbelievers in Judea, and that my ministry[m] to Jerusalem may
be acceptable to the saints, 32 so that by God's will I may come to you with joy and
be refreshed in your company. 33 The God of peace be with all of you.[n] Amen.

Paul greets his friends

16 I commend to you our sister Phoebe, a deacon[o] of the church at Cenchreae,
2 so that you may welcome her in the Lord as is fitting for the saints, and help
her in whatever she may require from you, for she has been a benefactor of many
and of myself as well.

3 Greet Prisca and Aquila, who work with me in Christ Jesus, 4 and who risked
their necks for my life, to whom not only I give thanks, but also all the churches of
the Gentiles. 5 Greet also the church in their house. Greet my beloved Epaenetus,
who was the first convert[p] in Asia for Christ. 6 Greet Mary, who has worked very
hard among you. 7 Greet Andronicus and Junia,[q] my relatives[r] who were in prison
with me; they are prominent among the apostles, and they were in Christ before I
was. 8 Greet Ampliatus, my beloved in the Lord. 9 Greet Urbanus, our co-worker in
Christ, and my beloved Stachys. 10 Greet Apelles, who is approved in Christ. Greet
those who belong to the family of Aristobulus. 11 Greet my relative[s] Herodion.

15.23 Acts 19.21
15.24 Acts 15.3
15.26 1 Cor 16.1,5; 2 Cor 8.1; 9.2
15.27 1 Cor 9.11
15.29 Acts 19.21
15.30 2 Cor 1.11; Col 1.8; 4.12
15.31 2 Cor 8.4; 2 Thess 3.2
15.32 2 Cor 7.13; 2 Tim 1.16; Philem 7
15.33 Heb 13.20
16.1 Acts 18.18
16.2 Phil 2.29
16.5 1 Cor 16.15,19; Col 4.15; Philem 1,2
16.7 Rom 16.11,21; 2 Cor 11.23; Col 4.10; Philem 23
16.10 1 Cor 1.11
16.11 Rom 16.7,21

[j] Gk *have sealed to them this fruit* [k] Other ancient authorities add *of the gospel* [l] Gk *brothers* [m] Other ancient authorities read *my bringing of a gift* [n] One ancient authority adds 16.25-27 here [o] Or *minister* [p] Gk *first fruits* [q] Or *Junias*; other ancient authorities read *Julia* [r] Or *compatriots* [s] Or *compatriot*

15.23, 24 Paul was referring to the completion of his work in Corinth ("in these regions"), the city from which he most likely wrote this letter. Most of Paul's three-month stay in Achaia (see Acts 20.3) was probably spent in Corinth. He believed he had done what God wanted him to do there – he was now looking forward to taking the gospel to new lands west of Rome. When Paul eventually went to Rome, however, it was as a prisoner (see Acts 28). Tradition says that Paul was released for a time, and that he used this opportunity to go to Spain to preach the good news. This journey is not mentioned in the book of Acts.

15.27 If the Gentiles had received the gospel ("spiritual blessings") originally from Jerusalem, surely they would want to offer financial help ("material things").

15.28 Paul's future plan was to go to Spain because Spain was at the very western end of the civilized world. He wanted to extend Christianity there. Also, Spain had many great minds and influential leaders in the Roman world (Lucan, Martial, Seneca, Nero) and perhaps Paul thought Christianity would advance greatly in such an atmosphere.

15.30 Too often we view prayer as a time for comfort, reflection, or making our requests known to God. But here Paul urges believers to join in the struggle by means of prayer. Prayer is also a weapon in all believers' armor as we intercede for others who join in the fight against Satan. Do your prayers reflect that urgency?

15.33 This phrase sounds like the end of the book, and it does signal the end of Paul's teaching. He concludes his letter, then, with personal greetings and remarks.

16.1, 2 Phoebe was a *deacon* or *servant.* She apparently was wealthy and helped support Paul's ministry. She was highly regarded in the church and may have delivered this letter from Corinth to Rome. This provides evidence that women had important roles in the early church. Cenchreae, the town where Phoebe lived, was the eastern port of Corinth, six miles from the city center.

16.3 Priscilla (Prisca) and Aquila were a married couple who became Paul's close friends. They, along with all other Jews, had been expelled from Rome by the emperor (Acts 18.2, 3), and they had moved to Corinth. There they met Paul and invited him to live with them. They were Christians before they met Paul, and probably told him much about the Roman church. Like Paul, Priscilla and Aquila were missionaries. They helped believers in Ephesus (Acts 18.18–28), in Rome when they were allowed to return, and again at Ephesus (2 Timothy 4.19).

16.5ff Paul's personal greetings went to Romans and Greeks, Jews and Gentiles, men and women, prisoners and prominent citizens. The church's base was broad: it crossed cultural, social, and economic lines. From this list we learn that the Christian community was mobile. Though Paul had not yet been to Rome, he had met these people in other places on his journeys.

16.7 Andronicus and Junia were "prominent among the apostles" – very likely they had distinguished themselves as missionaries. Scholars are not sure whether the second name should be Junias (masculine) or Junia (feminine). If Junia is correct, some suggest she was Andronicus's wife. *Relatives* means brothers in Christ or compatriots.

Greet those in the Lord who belong to the family of Narcissus. 12 Greet those workers in the Lord, Tryphaena and Tryphosa. Greet the beloved Persis, who has
worked hard in the Lord. 13 Greet Rufus, chosen in the Lord; and greet his
mother—a mother to me also. 14 Greet Asyncritus, Phlegon, Hermes, Patrobas,
Hermas, and the brothers and sisters[t] who are with them. 15 Greet Philologus,
Julia, Nereus and his sister, and Olympas, and all the saints who are with them.
16 Greet one another with a holy kiss. All the churches of Christ greet you.

16.13 Mk 15.21 Eph 1.4 2 Jn 1
16.16 1 Thess 5.26 1 Pet 5.14

Paul gives final instructions

17 I urge you, brothers and sisters,[t] to keep an eye on those who cause dissensions and offenses, in opposition to the teaching that you have learned; avoid them.
18 For such people do not serve our Lord Christ, but their own appetites,[u] and by
smooth talk and flattery they deceive the hearts of the simple-minded. 19 For while
your obedience is known to all, so that I rejoice over you, I want you to be wise in
what is good and guileless in what is evil. 20 The God of peace will shortly crush
Satan under your feet. The grace of our Lord Jesus Christ be with you.[v]
21 Timothy, my co-worker, greets you; so do Lucius and Jason and Sosipater,
my relatives.[w]
22 I Tertius, the writer of this letter, greet you in the Lord.[x]
23 Gaius, who is host to me and to the whole church, greets you. Erastus, the
city treasurer, and our brother Quartus, greet you.[y]

25 Now to God[z] who is able to strengthen you according to my gospel and the
proclamation of Jesus Christ, according to the revelation of the mystery that was
kept secret for long ages 26 but is now disclosed, and through the prophetic writings
is made known to all the Gentiles, according to the command of the eternal God, to
bring about the obedience of faith— 27 to the only wise God, through Jesus Christ,
to whom[a] be the glory forever! Amen.[b]

16.17 Acts 15.1-29 1 Cor 5.9 2 Thess 3.6 1 Tim 6.3 2 Tim 3.5,6 Tit 3.10 2 Jn 10
16.18 Phil 3.19 Col 2.4 2 Pet 2.3
16.19 Mt 10.16
16.20 Gen 3.15
16.21 Acts 13.1; 16.1 17.5 1 Tim 1.2
16.25 1 Cor 2.1,7; 4.1 Eph 3.3-5 1 Col 1.27; 2.2 2 Tim 1.10 1 Pet 1.20
16.26 Rom 1.2,5

[t] Gk *brothers* [u] Gk *their own belly* [v] Other ancient authorities lack this sentence [w] Or *compatriots* [x] Or *I Tertius, writing this letter in the Lord, greet you* [y] Other ancient authorities add verse 24, *The grace of our Lord Jesus Christ be with all of you. Amen.* [z] Gk *the one* [a] Other ancient authorities lack *to whom*. The verse then reads, *to the only wise God be the glory through Jesus Christ forever. Amen.* [b] Other ancient authorities lack 16.25-27 or include it after 14.23 or 15.33; others put verse 24 after verse 27

16.17–20 When we read books or listen to sermons, we should check the content of what is written or said and not be fooled by smooth style. Christians who study God's Word do not need to be fooled, even if superficial listeners are easily taken in. For an example of believers who carefully checked God's Word, see Acts 17.10–12.

16.21 Timothy was a key person in the growth of the early church, traveling with Paul on his second missionary journey (Acts 16.1–3). Later Paul wrote two letters to him as he worked to strengthen the churches in Ephesus—1 and 2 Timothy. See his Profile in the book of 1 Timothy.

16.25–27 Paul exclaims that it is wonderful to be alive when God's secret—his way of saving the Gentiles—is becoming known throughout the world! All the Old Testament prophecies were coming true, and God was using Paul to tell this good news.

16.25–27 As Jerusalem was the center of Jewish life, Rome was the world's political, religious, social, and economic center. There the major governmental decisions were made, and from there the gospel spread to the ends of the earth. The church in Rome was a cosmopolitan mixture of Jews, Gentiles, slaves, free people, men, women, Roman citizens, and world travelers; therefore, it had potential for both great influence and great conflict.

Paul had not yet been to Rome to meet all the Christians there, and, of course, he has not yet met us. We too live in a cosmopolitan setting with the entire world open to us. We also have the potential for both widespread influence and wrenching conflict. We should listen carefully to Paul and apply his teaching about unity, service, and love.

The First Letter of Paul to the CORINTHIANS

VITAL STATISTICS

PURPOSE:
To identify problems in the Corinthian church, to offer solutions, and to teach the believers how to live for Christ in a corrupt society

AUTHOR:
Paul

TO WHOM WRITTEN:
The church in Corinth

DATE WRITTEN:
About A.D. 55, near the end of Paul's three-year ministry in Ephesus during his third missionary journey

SETTING:
Corinth was a major cosmopolitan city, a seaport and major trade center—the most important city in Achaia. It was also filled with idolatry and immorality. The church was largely made up of Gentiles. Paul had established this church on his second missionary journey.

KEY VERSE:
"Now I appeal to you, brothers and sisters, by the name of our Lord Jesus Christ, that all of you be in agreement and that there be no divisions among you, but that you be united in the same mind and the same purpose" (1.10).

KEY PEOPLE:
Paul, Timothy, members of Chloe's household

KEY PLACES:
Worship meetings in Corinth

SPECIAL FEATURES:
This is a strong, straightforward letter.

ON A BED of grass, a chameleon's skin turns green. On the earth, it becomes brown. The animal changes to match the environment. Many creatures blend into nature with God-given camouflage suits to aid their survival. It's natural to fit in and adapt to the environment. But followers of Christ are *new creations,* born from above and changed from within, with values and life-styles that confront the world and clash with accepted morals. True believers don't blend in very well.

The Christians in Corinth were struggling with their environment. Surrounded by corruption and every conceivable sin, they felt the pressure to adapt. They knew they were free in Christ, but what did this freedom mean? How should they view idols or sexuality? What should they do about marriage, women in the church, and the gifts of the Spirit? These were more than theoretical questions—the church was being undermined by immorality and spiritual immaturity. Their faith was being tried in the crucible of immoral Corinth, and some of them were failing the test.

Paul heard of their struggles and wrote this letter to address their problems, heal their divisions, and answer their questions. Paul confronted them with their sin and their need for corrective action and clear commitment to Christ.

After a brief introduction (1.1–9), Paul immediately turns to the question of unity (1.10—4.21). He emphasizes the clear and simple gospel message around which all believers should rally; he explains the role of church leaders; and he urges them to grow up in their faith.

Paul then deals with the immorality of certain church members and lawsuits among Christians (5.1—6.8). He tells them to exercise church discipline and to settle their internal matters themselves. Because so many of the problems in the Corinthian church involved sex, Paul denounces sexual sin in the strongest possible terms (6.9–20).

Next Paul answers some questions that the Corinthians had. Because prostitution and immorality were pervasive, marriages in Corinth were in shambles, and Christians weren't sure how to react. Paul gives pointed and practical answers (7.1–40). Concerning the question of meat sacrificed to idols, Paul suggests that we show complete commitment to Christ and sensitivity to other believers, especially weaker brothers and sisters (8.1—11.2).

Paul goes on to talk about worship, and he carefully explains the role of women, the Lord's supper, and spiritual gifts (11.3—14.39). Sandwiched in the middle of this section is his magnificent description of the greatest gift—love (chapter 13). Then Paul concludes with a discussion of the resurrection (15.1–58), some final thoughts, greetings, and a benediction (16.1–24).

In this letter Paul confronts the Corinthians about their sins and shortcomings. And 1 Corinthians calls all Christians to be careful not to blend in with the world, accepting its values and life-styles. We must live Christ-centered, blameless, loving lives that make a difference for God. As you read 1 Corinthians, examine your values in light of complete commitment to Christ.

THE BLUEPRINT

A. PAUL ADDRESSES CHURCH PROBLEMS (1.1—6.20) 1. Divisions in the church 2. Disorders in the church	Without Paul's presence, the Corinthian church had fallen into divisiveness and disorder. This resulted in many problems which Paul addressed squarely. We must be concerned for unity and order in our local churches, but we should not mistake inactivity for order and cordiality for unity. We too must squarely address problems in our churches.
B. PAUL ANSWERS CHURCH QUESTIONS (7.1—16.24) 1. Instruction on Christian marriage 2. Instruction on Christian freedom 3. Instruction on public worship 4. Instruction on the resurrection	The Corinthians had sent Paul a list of questions, and he answered them in a way to correct abuses in the church and to show how important it is that they live what they believe. Paul gives us a Christian approach to problem-solving. He analyzed the problem thoroughly to uncover the underlying issue, and then highlighted the biblical values that should guide our actions.

MEGATHEMES

THEME	EXPLANATION	IMPORTANCE
Loyalties	The Corinthians were rallying around various church leaders and teachers—Peter, Paul, and Apollos. These loyalties led to intellectual pride and created a spirit of division in the church.	Our loyalty to human leaders or human wisdom must never divide Christians into camps. We must care for our fellow believers, not strive with them. Your allegiance must be to Christ. Let him lead you.
Immorality	Paul received a report of uncorrected sexual sin in the church at Corinth. The people had grown indifferent to immorality. Others had misconceptions about marriage. We are to live morally, keeping our bodies ready to serve God at all times.	Christians must never compromise with sinful ideas and practices. We should not blend in with people around us. You must live up to God's standard of morality and not condone immoral behavior even if society accepts it.
Freedom	Paul taught freedom of choice on practices not expressly forbidden in Scripture. Some believers felt certain actions—like buying meat from animals used in pagan rituals—were corrupt by association. Others felt free from the law to do such actions without sin.	We are free in Christ, yet we must not abuse our Christian freedom by being inconsiderate and insensitive to others. We must never encourage others to do wrong by anything we do. Let love guide your behavior.
Worship	Paul addressed disorder in worship. People were taking the Lord's supper without first confessing sin. There was misuse of spiritual gifts and confusion over women's roles in the church.	Worship must be carried out properly and in an orderly manner. Everything we do to worship God should be done in a manner worthy of his high honor. Make sure that worship is harmonious, useful, and builds up all believers.
Resurrection	Some people denied that Christ rose from the dead. Others felt that people would not physically be resurrected. Christ's resurrection assures us that we will have new, living bodies after we die. The hope of the resurrection forms the secret of Christian confidence.	Since we will be raised again to life after we die, our lives are not in vain. We must stay faithful to God in our morality and our service. We are to live today knowing we will spend eternity with Christ.

A. PAUL ADDRESSES CHURCH PROBLEMS (1.1–6.20)

Through various sources, Paul had received reports of problems in the Corinthian church, including jealousy, divisiveness, sexual immorality, and failure to discipline members. Churches today must also address the problems they face. We can learn a great deal by observing how Paul handled these delicate situations.

1 Paul, called to be an apostle of Christ Jesus by the will of God, and our brother 1.1 Acts 18.17
Sosthenes, Rom 1.1
2 To the church of God that is in Corinth, to those who are sanctified in Christ
Jesus, called to be saints, together with all those who in every place call on the
name of our Lord Jesus Christ, both their Lord[a] and ours: 1.3
3 Grace to you and peace from God our Father and the Lord Jesus Christ. Rom 1.7

1. Divisions in the church

Paul thanks God

4 I give thanks to my[b] God always for you because of the grace of God that has 1.4,5
been given you in Christ Jesus, 5 for in every way you have been enriched in him, 2 Cor 8.7; 9.11 1.7
in speech and knowledge of every kind— 6 just as the testimony of[c] Christ has Phil 3.20
been strengthened among you— 7 so that you are not lacking in any spiritual gift as 2 Pet 3.12 1.8
you wait for the revealing of our Lord Jesus Christ. 8 He will also strengthen you to Phil 1.6
the end, so that you may be blameless on the day of our Lord Jesus Christ. 9 God is 1 Thess 5.23 2 Thess 3.3
faithful; by him you were called into the fellowship of his Son, Jesus Christ our 1.9
Lord. 1 Jn 1.3

[a] Gk *theirs* [b] Other ancient authorities lack *my* [c] Or *to*

1.1 Paul wrote this letter to the church in Corinth while he was visiting Ephesus during his third missionary journey (Acts 19.1–20.1). Corinth and Ephesus faced each other across the Aegean Sea. Paul knew the Corinthian church well because he had spent 18 months in Corinth during his second missionary journey (Acts 18.1–18). While in Ephesus, he heard about problems in Corinth (1.11). About the same time, a delegation from the Corinthian church visited Paul to ask his advice about their conflicts (16.17). Paul's purpose in writing was to correct those problems and to answer questions church members had asked in a previous letter (7.1).

1.1 Paul was specially called by God to preach about Jesus Christ. Each Christian has a job to do, a role to take, or a contribution to make. One assignment may seem more spectacular than another, but all are necessary to carry out God's greater plans for the world (12.12–27). Be available to God by placing your gifts at his service. As you discover what he calls you to do, be ready to do it.

1.1 Sosthenes may have been Paul's secretary who wrote this letter as Paul dictated it. He was the Jewish synagogue leader in Corinth (Acts 18.17) who was beaten during an attack on Paul, and then later became a believer. Sosthenes was well known to the members of the Corinthian church, and so Paul included his familiar name in the opening of the letter.

1.2 Corinth was a giant cultural melting pot with great diversion of wealth, religions, intellect, and moral standards. It had a reputation for being fiercely independent and as decadent as any city in the world. The Romans destroyed Corinth in 146 B.C. after a rebellion. But in 46 B.C., the Roman Emperor Julius Caesar rebuilt it because of its strategic seaport. By Paul's day (A.D. 50), the Romans had made Corinth the capital of Achaia (present-day Greece). It was a large city, offering Rome great profits through trade as well as the military protection of its ports. But the city's prosperity made it ripe for all sorts of corruption. Idolatry flourished, and there were more than a dozen pagan temples employing at least a thousand prostitutes.

1.2 A personal invitation makes a person feel wanted and welcome. We are "called to be saints;" God personally invites us to be citizens of his eternal kingdom. But Jesus Christ, God's Son, is the only one who can bring us into this glorious kingdom, because he is the only one who removes our sins. *Sanctified* means we are chosen or set apart by Christ for his service. We accept God's invitation by accepting his Son, Jesus Christ, and trusting in the work he did on the cross to forgive our sins.

1.2 By including a salutation to "all those who in every place call on the name of our Lord Jesus Christ," Paul made it clear that this was not a private letter. Although it dealt with specific issues facing the church at Corinth, all believers could learn from it. The Corinthian church included a great cross-section of believers—wealthy merchants, common laborers, former temple prostitutes, and middle-class families. Because of the wide diversity of people and backgrounds, Paul took great pains to stress both spiritual unity and Christian morality.

1.3 Grace is God's free gift of salvation given to us in Christ. Receiving it brings us peace (see Romans 5.1). In a world of noise, confusion, and relentless pressures, people long for peace. Many give up the search, thinking it impossible to find, but true peace of heart and mind is available to us through faith in Jesus Christ.

1.4–7 In this letter, Paul wrote some strong words to the Corinthians, but he began on a positive note. He affirmed their privilege of being in God's family, the power God gave them to speak out for him and understand his truth, and the reality of their spiritual gifts. When we must correct others, it helps to begin by affirming what God has already accomplished in them.

1.7 The Corinthian church members had all the spiritual gifts they needed to live the Christian life, to witness for Christ, and to stand against the paganism and immorality of Corinth. But instead of using what God had given them, they were arguing over which gifts were more important. Paul addresses this issue in depth in chapters 12–14.

1.7–9 Paul guaranteed the Corinthian believers that God would consider them free from sin (blameless) when Christ returns (see Ephesians 1.7–10). This guarantee was not because of their great gifts or performance, but because of what Jesus Christ accomplished for them through his death and resurrection. *All* who obey God's Word will be considered free from sin when Jesus Christ returns (see also 1 Thessalonians 3.13; Hebrews 9.28). If you have faith in Christ, even if it is weak, you *are* and *will be* saved.

1.10 1 Cor 11.18 Phil 1.27
1.12 Jn 1.42 Acts 18.24 1 Cor 3.4
1.13 Acts 2.38 Eph 4.5
1.14 Acts 18.8
1.16 1 Cor 16.15

Paul appeals for harmony

10 Now I appeal to you, brothers and sisters,[d] by the name of our Lord Jesus
Christ, that all of you be in agreement and that there be no divisions among you, but
that you be united in the same mind and the same purpose. 11 For it has been reported to me by Chloe's people that there are quarrels among you, my brothers and
sisters.[e] 12 What I mean is that each of you says, "I belong to Paul," or "I belong
to Apollos," or "I belong to Cephas," or "I belong to Christ." 13 Has Christ been
divided? Was Paul crucified for you? Or were you baptized in the name of Paul? 14 I
thank God[f] that I baptized none of you except Crispus and Gaius, 15 so that no one
can say that you were baptized in my name. 16 (I did baptize also the household of

[d] Gk *brothers* [e] Gk *my brothers* [f] Other ancient authorities read *I am thankful*

CORINTH AND EPHESUS
Paul wrote this letter to Corinth during his three-year visit in Ephesus during his third missionary journey. The two cities sat across from each other on the Aegean Sea—both were busy and important ports. Titus may have carried this letter from Ephesus to Corinth (2 Corinthians 12.18).

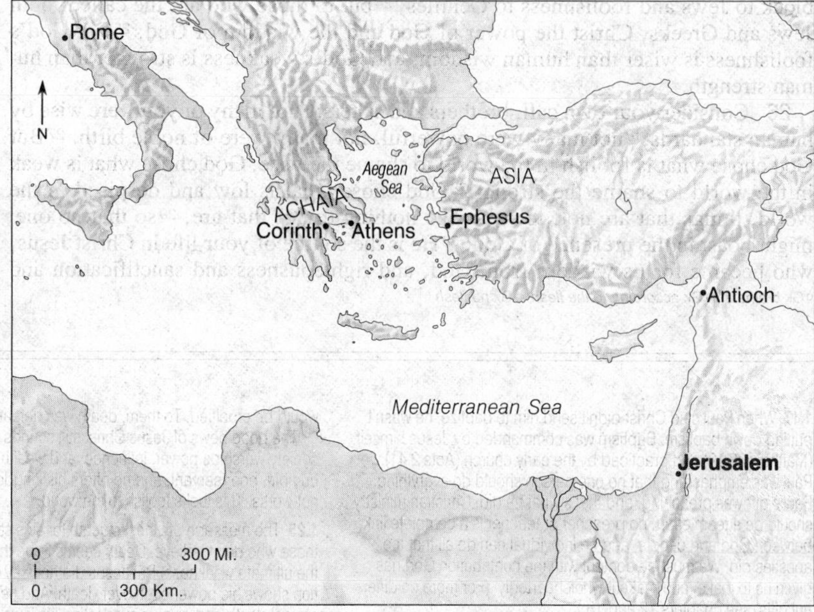

1.10 Paul founded the church in Corinth on his second missionary journey. Eighteen months after he left, the people began arguing, divisions arose, and some slipped back into an immoral life-style. Paul wrote this letter to correct the situation, to clear up confusion about right and wrong, and to remove the immorality among them. Corinthians had a reputation for jumping from fad to fad; Paul wanted to keep Christianity from degenerating into another fad.

1.10 By saying "brothers and sisters," Paul was emphasizing that all Christians are part of God's family. Believers share a unity that runs even deeper than that of blood brothers and sisters.

1.10, 11 To "be in agreement," allow for "no divisions among you," and "be united in the same mind and the same purpose" does not require everyone to believe exactly the same. There is a difference between having opposing viewpoints and being divisive. A group of people will not completely agree on every issue, but they can work together harmoniously if they agree on what truly matters—Jesus Christ as Lord of all. In your church, talk and behave in a way that will reduce arguments and increase harmony. Petty differences should never divide Christians.

1.12ff In this large and diverse Corinthian church, the believers favored different preachers. Because there was as yet no written New Testament, the believers depended heavily on preaching and teaching for spiritual insight into the meaning of the Old Testament. Some followed Paul, who had founded their church; some who had heard Peter (Cephas) in Jerusalem followed him; while others listened only to Apollos, an eloquent and popular preacher who had had a dynamic ministry in Corinth (Acts 18.24; 19.1). Although these three preachers were united in their message, their personalities attracted different people. At this time the church was in danger of dividing. By mentioning Jesus Christ ten times in the first ten verses, Paul makes it clear whom all preachers and teachers should emphasize. God's message is much more important than any human messenger.

1.12, 13 Paul says that the Corinthians' arguing had "divided Christ." This is a graphic picture of what happens when the church (the body of Christ) is divided. With the many churches and styles of worship available today, we could get caught up in the same game of "my preacher is better than yours!" To do so would divide Christ again. But Christ is not divided, and his true followers should not allow anything to divide them. Don't let your appreciation for any teacher, preacher, or author lead you into intellectual pride. Our allegiance must be to Christ and to the unity he desires.

Stephanas; beyond that, I do not know whether I baptized anyone else.) 17 For
Christ did not send me to baptize but to proclaim the gospel, and not with eloquent
wisdom, so that the cross of Christ might not be emptied of its power.

Christ brings us life from God

18 For the message about the cross is foolishness to those who are perishing,
but to us who are being saved it is the power of God. 19 For it is written,
"I will destroy the wisdom of the wise,
and the discernment of the discerning I will thwart."
20 Where is the one who is wise? Where is the scribe? Where is the debater of this
age? Has not God made foolish the wisdom of the world? 21 For since, in the wisdom of God, the world did not know God through wisdom, God decided, through
the foolishness of our proclamation, to save those who believe. 22 For Jews demand
signs and Greeks desire wisdom, 23 but we proclaim Christ crucified, a stumbling
block to Jews and foolishness to Gentiles, 24 but to those who are the called, both
Jews and Greeks, Christ the power of God and the wisdom of God. 25 For God's
foolishness is wiser than human wisdom, and God's weakness is stronger than human strength.
26 Consider your own call, brothers and sisters:[g] not many of you were wise by
human standards,[h] not many were powerful, not many were of noble birth. 27 But
God chose what is foolish in the world to shame the wise; God chose what is weak
in the world to shame the strong; 28 God chose what is low and despised in the
world, things that are not, to reduce to nothing things that are, 29 so that no one[i]
might boast in the presence of God. 30 He is the source of your life in Christ Jesus,
who became for us wisdom from God, and righteousness and sanctification and

g Gk *brothers* h Gk *according to the flesh* i Gk *no flesh*

1.17 Acts 26.17; 2 Cor 10.10; 11.16
1.18 Acts 17.18; 1 Cor 2.14; 2 Cor 2.15,16
1.19 Isa 29.14
1.20 Job 12.17; Isa 44.25
1.21 Lk 10.21
1.22 Mt 12.38
1.23 Isa 8.14,15; Mt 11.6
1.25 2 Cor 4.7; 13.4
1.26 Mt 11.25; Jn 7.48; 1 Cor 2.8
1.28 Job 34.19
1.29 Eph 2.8-10
1.30 2 Cor 5.21

1.17 When Paul said Christ didn't send him to baptize, he wasn't putting down baptism. Baptism was commanded by Jesus himself (Matthew 28.19) and practiced by the early church (Acts 2.41). Paul was emphasizing that no one person should do everything. Paul's gift was preaching, and that's what he did. Christian ministry should be a team effort; no preacher or teacher is a complete link between God and people, and no individual can do all that the apostles did. We must be content with the contribution God has given us to make, and make it wholeheartedly. (For more on different gifts, see chapters 12 and 13.)

1.17 Some speakers use impressive words, but they are weak on content. Paul stressed solid content and practical help for his listeners. He wanted them to be impressed with his *message,* not just his style (see 2.1–5). You don't need to be a great speaker with a large vocabulary to share the gospel effectively. The persuasive power is in the story, not the storyteller. Paul was not against those who carefully prepare what they say (see 2.6), but against those who try to impress others only with their knowledge or speaking ability.

1.19 Paul summarizes Isaiah 29.14 to emphasize a point Jesus often made: God's way of thinking is not like the world's way (normal human wisdom). And God offers eternal life that the world can never give. We can spend a lifetime accumulating human wisdom and never learn how to have a personal relationship with God. We must come to Christ to learn this important truth.

1.22, 23 Many Jews considered the good news of Jesus Christ to be foolish, because they thought the Messiah would be a conquering king accompanied by signs and miracles. Jesus had not restored David's throne as they expected. Besides, he was executed as a criminal, and how could a criminal be a savior? Greeks, too, considered the gospel foolish: they did not believe in a bodily resurrection; they did not see in Jesus the powerful characteristics of their mythological gods; and they thought no reputable person would be crucified. To them, death was defeat, not victory.

The good news of Jesus Christ still sounds foolish to many. Our society worships power, influence, and wealth. Jesus came as a humble, poor servant, and he offers his kingdom to those with faith, not works. This looks foolish to the world.

1.25 The message of Christ's death for sins sounds foolish to those who don't believe. Death seems to be the end of the road, the ultimate weakness. But Jesus did not stay dead. His resurrection shows his power even over death. And he will save us from eternal death and give us everlasting life if we trust him as Savior and Lord. This sounds so simple that many people won't accept it. They try other ways to obtain eternal life (being good, being wise, etc.). But their attempts will not work. The "foolish" people who simply accept Christ's offer are actually the wisest of all, because they alone will live eternally with God.

1.27 Is Christianity against rational thinking? Christians do believe in using the mind to weigh the evidence and make wise choices. Paul was declaring that no amount of human knowledge can replace or bypass Christ's work on the cross. If it could, Christ would be available only to the intellectually gifted and well educated, not to the ordinary person or child.

1.28–31 Paul continued to emphasize that the way to receive salvation is so simple that *any* person who wants to can understand it. Skill does not get a person into God's kingdom – simple faith does – so no one can boast that his or her achievements helped him or her secure eternal life. Salvation is totally from God through Jesus' death. There is *nothing* we can do to earn our salvation; we need only accept what Jesus has already done for us.

1.30 God is the source of our personal and living relationship with Christ. Our union and identification with him results in our having God's wisdom (Colossians 2.3), possessing right standing with God (*righteousness,* 2 Corinthians 5.21), being holy (*sanctification,* 1 Thessalonians 4.3–7), and having the penalty for our sins paid by Jesus (*redemption,* Mark 10.45).

1.31 Jer 9.23,24 2 Cor 10.17
2.1 1 Cor 1.17
2.2 Gal 6.14 Phil 3.8
2.3 2 Cor 10.1 Gal 4.13
2.4 1 Cor 4.20
2.6 Eph 4.13 Heb 5.14
2.7 Rom 8.29; 16.25 Eph 3.3-5
2.8 Acts 13.27
2.9 Isa 64.4; 65.17
2.10 Jn 14.26 15.26; 16.13-15

redemption, 31 in order that, as it is written, "Let the one who boasts, boast in[j] the
Lord."

The Spirit gives wisdom

2 When I came to you, brothers and sisters,[k] I did not come proclaiming the
mystery[l] of God to you in lofty words or wisdom. 2 For I decided to know
nothing among you except Jesus Christ, and him crucified. 3 And I came to you in
weakness and in fear and in much trembling. 4 My speech and my proclamation
were not with plausible words of wisdom,[m] but with a demonstration of the Spirit
and of power, 5 so that your faith might rest not on human wisdom but on the power
of God.

6 Yet among the mature we do speak wisdom, though it is not a wisdom of this
age or of the rulers of this age, who are doomed to perish. 7 But we speak God's
wisdom, secret and hidden, which God decreed before the ages for our glory.
8 None of the rulers of this age understood this; for if they had, they would not have
crucified the Lord of glory. 9 But, as it is written,

"What no eye has seen, nor ear heard,
nor the human heart conceived,
what God has prepared for those who love him"—

10 these things God has revealed to us through the Spirit; for the Spirit searches
everything, even the depths of God. 11 For what human being knows what is truly

[j] Or *of* [k] Gk *brothers* [l] Other ancient authorities read *testimony* [m] Other ancient authorities read *the persuasiveness of wisdom*

HIGHLIGHTS OF 1 CORINTHIANS		
	The Meaning of the Cross 1.18—2.16	Be considerate of one another because of what Christ has done for us. There is no place for pride or a know-it-all attitude. We are to have the mind of Christ.
	The Story of the Last Supper 11.23–29	The Last supper is a time of reflection on Christ's final words to his disciples before he died on the cross; we must celebrate this in an orderly and correct manner.
	The Poem of Love 13.1–13	Love is to guide all we do. We have different gifts, abilities, likes, dislikes—but we are called, without exception, to love.
	The Christian's Destiny 15.42–58	We are promised by Christ who died for us that, as he came back to life after death, so our perishable bodies will be exchanged for heavenly bodies. Then we will live and reign with Christ.

2.1 Paul was referring to his first visit to Corinth during his second missionary journey (A.D. 51), when he founded the church (Acts 18.1ff).

2.1–5 A brilliant scholar, Paul could have overwhelmed his listeners with intellectual arguments and persuasive oratory. Instead he shared the simple message of Jesus Christ by allowing the Holy Spirit to guide his words. In sharing the gospel with others, we should follow Paul's example and keep our message simple and basic. The Holy Spirit will give power to our words and use them to bring glory to Jesus.

2.4 Paul's confidence was not in his keen intellect or speaking ability but in his knowledge that the Holy Spirit was helping and guiding him. Paul was not denying the importance of study and preparation for preaching—he had a thorough education in the Scriptures. Effective preaching must combine studious preparation with the work of the Holy Spirit. Don't use Paul as an excuse for not studying or preparing.

2.7 God's "wisdom, secret and hidden" was his offer of salvation to all people. Originally unknown to mankind, this plan became crystal clear when Jesus rose from the dead. His resurrection proved that he had power over sin and death and could now offer us this power as well (see also 1 Peter 1.10–12). God's plan, however, is still hidden to unbelievers because they either refuse to accept it, choose to ignore it, or simply haven't heard about it.

2.8 Jesus was misunderstood and rejected by those whom the world considered wise and great. He was put to death by the rulers in Palestine—the high priest, King Herod, Pilate, and the Pharisees and Sadducees. Jesus' rejection by these rulers was predicted in Isaiah 53.3 and Zechariah 12.10, 11.

2.9 We cannot imagine all that God has in store for us, both in this life and for eternity. He will create a new heaven and a new earth (Isaiah 65.17; Revelation 21.1), and we will live with him forever. Until then, his Holy Spirit comforts and guides us. Knowing our wonderful and eternal future gives us hope and courage to press on in this life, to endure hardship, and to avoid giving in to temptation. This world is not all there is. The best is yet to come.

2.10 The "depths of God" are God's plans—Jesus' resurrection and the promise of salvation, revealed only to those who believe that what God says is true. Those who believe in the resurrection and put their faith in Christ will know all they need to know to be saved. This knowledge, however, can't be grasped by even the wisest people unless they accept God's message. All who reject God's message are foolish, no matter how wise the world thinks they are.

human except the human spirit that is within? So also no one comprehends what is
truly God's except the Spirit of God. 12 Now we have received not the spirit of the
world, but the Spirit that is from God, so that we may understand the gifts bestowed
on us by God. 13 And we speak of these things in words not taught by human wisdom but taught by the Spirit, interpreting spiritual things to those who are
spiritual.[n]
14 Those who are unspiritual[o] do not receive the gifts of God's Spirit, for they
are foolishness to them, and they are unable to understand them because they are
spiritually discerned. 15 Those who are spiritual discern all things, and they are
themselves subject to no one else's scrutiny.
16 "For who has known the mind of the Lord
so as to instruct him?"
But we have the mind of Christ.

Paul condemns division in the church

3 And so, brothers and sisters,[p] I could not speak to you as spiritual people, but
rather as people of the flesh, as infants in Christ. 2 I fed you with milk, not solid
food, for you were not ready for solid food. Even now you are still not ready, 3 for
you are still of the flesh. For as long as there is jealousy and quarreling among you,
are you not of the flesh, and behaving according to human inclinations? 4 For when
one says, "I belong to Paul," and another, "I belong to Apollos," are you not
merely human?
5 What then is Apollos? What is Paul? Servants through whom you came to
believe, as the Lord assigned to each. 6 I planted, Apollos watered, but God gave
the growth. 7 So neither the one who plants nor the one who waters is anything, but
only God who gives the growth. 8 The one who plants and the one who waters have
a common purpose, and each will receive wages according to the labor of each.
9 For we are God's servants, working together; you are God's field, God's building.
10 According to the grace of God given to me, like a skilled master builder I

2.11 Prov 20.27 Rom 11.33
2.12 Rom 8.15 1 Cor 1.27
2.13 Mt 16.23 Rom 8.5 2 Pet 1.20,21
2.15 Prov 28.5
2.16 Ps 25.14 Jn 15.15 Rom 11.34
3.1 Gal 6.1 Eph 4.14
3.2 Heb 5.12-13 1 Pet 2.2,3
3.3 Rom 13.12-13
3.5 Rom 12.3,6 2 Cor 6.4
3.6 Acts 18.4; 19.1
3.8 Rev 2.23; 22.12
3.9 Eph 2.20 Col 2.7 1 Pet 2.5
3.10 Rom 15.20 1 Pet 4.11

[n] Or *interpreting spiritual things in spiritual language,* or *comparing spiritual things with spiritual* [o] Or *natural*
[p] Gk *brothers*

2.13 Paul's words are authoritative because their source is the Holy Spirit. Paul was not merely giving his views or his impression of what God had said. Under the inspiration of the Holy Spirit, he wrote the very thoughts and words of God.

2.14, 15 Non-Christians cannot understand God, and they cannot grasp the concept that God's Spirit lives in believers. Don't expect most people to approve of or understand your decision to follow Christ. It all seems silly to them. Just as a tone-deaf person cannot appreciate fine music, the person who rejects God cannot understand God's beautiful message. The lines of communication are broken, and he cannot hear what God is saying to him.

2.15, 16 No one can comprehend God (Romans 11.34), but by his Spirit believers have insight into some of God's plans, thoughts, and actions. By his Holy Spirit we can begin to know his thoughts, discuss them with him, and expect his answers to our prayers. Are you spending enough time with Christ to have his very mind in you? An intimate relationship with Christ comes only from consistent time spent in his presence and in his Word. Read Philippians 2.5ff for more on the mind of Christ.

3.1–3 Paul called the Corinthians infants in the Christian life because they were not yet spiritually healthy and mature. The proof was that they quarreled like children. Immature Christians are controlled by their own desires ("of the flesh"); mature believers, by God's desires. How much influence do your desires have on your life? Your goal should be to let God's desires be yours. Being controlled by your own desires will stunt your growth.

3.6 Paul planted the seed of God's Word in people's hearts. He was a missionary pioneer; he brought the message of salvation. Apollos's role was to water—to help the believers grow stronger in the faith. Paul founded the church in Corinth, and Apollos built on that foundation. Tragically, the believers in Corinth had split into factions, pledging loyalty to different teachers (see 1.11–13). After the preachers' work is completed, God keeps on making Christians grow. Our leaders should be respected, but we should never place them on pedestals that create barriers between people or as a substitute for Christ.

3.7–9 God's work involves many different individuals with a variety of gifts and abilities. There are no superstars in this task, only team members performing their own special roles. We become useful members of God's team by setting aside our desires to receive glory for what we do. Don't seek the praise that comes from people because it is comparatively worthless. Instead, seek approval from God.

3.10, 11 The foundation of the church—of all believers—is Jesus Christ. Paul laid this foundation when he began the church at Corinth. Whoever builds the church—officers, teachers, preachers, parents, and others—must build with high-quality materials (right doctrine and right living, 3.12ff) that meet God's standards. Paul was not criticizing Apollos, but challenging future church leaders to have sound preaching and teaching.

3.10–17 In the church built on Jesus Christ, each church member would be mature, spiritually sensitive, and doctrinally sound. However, the Corinthian church was filled with "wood, hay, straw," members who were immature, insensitive to one another, and eagerly accepting wrong doctrine (3.1–4). No wonder they had so many problems. Local church members should be deeply committed to Christ. Can your Christian character stand the test?

laid a foundation, and someone else is building on it. Each builder must choose
with care how to build on it. 11 For no one can lay any foundation other than the one
that has been laid; that foundation is Jesus Christ. 12 Now if anyone builds on the
foundation with gold, silver, precious stones, wood, hay, straw— 13 the work of
each builder will become visible, for the Day will disclose it, because it will be
revealed with fire, and the fire will test what sort of work each has done. 14 If what
has been built on the foundation survives, the builder will receive a reward. 15 If the
work is burned up, the builder will suffer loss; the builder will be saved, but only
as through fire.
16 Do you not know that you are God's temple and that God's Spirit dwells in
you?[q] 17 If anyone destroys God's temple, God will destroy that person. For God's
temple is holy, and you are that temple.
18 Do not deceive yourselves. If you think that you are wise in this age, you
should become fools so that you may become wise. 19 For the wisdom of this world
is foolishness with God. For it is written,
"He catches the wise in their craftiness,"
20 and again,
"The Lord knows the thoughts of the wise,
that they are futile."
21 So let no one boast about human leaders. For all things are yours, 22 whether Paul
or Apollos or Cephas or the world or life or death or the present or the future—all
belong to you, 23 and you belong to Christ, and Christ belongs to God.

Paul counsels his beloved children

4 Think of us in this way, as servants of Christ and stewards of God's mysteries.
2 Moreover, it is required of stewards that they be found trustworthy. 3 But with
me it is a very small thing that I should be judged by you or by any human court.
I do not even judge myself. 4 I am not aware of anything against myself, but I am
not thereby acquitted. It is the Lord who judges me. 5 Therefore do not pronounce
judgment before the time, before the Lord comes, who will bring to light the things
now hidden in darkness and will disclose the purposes of the heart. Then each one
will receive commendation from God.

[q] In verses 16 and 17 the Greek word for *you* is plural

3.11 Isa 28.16 Mt 16.18 1 Pet 2.4
3.13 2 Tim 1.12,18 4.8
3.14 1 Cor 9.25 Gal 6.4
3.15 Jude 23
3.16 2 Cor 6.16 Eph 2.21
3.17 Heb 3.1
3.18 Isa 5.21 1 Cor 8.2 Gal 6.3
3.19 Job 5.13 1 Cor 1.20
3.20 Ps 94.11
3.21 Rom 8.28,32
3.22 Rom 8.38
3.23 1 Cor 11.3
4.1 Rom 16.25-27 Eph 3.3-5
4.5 Mt 7.1 Rom 2.16,29 2 Cor 5.10 Rev 20.12

3.11 A building is only as solid as its foundation. The foundation of our lives is Jesus Christ; he is our base, our reason for being. Everything we are and do must fit into the pattern provided by him. Are you building your life on the only real and lasting foundation, or are you building on a faulty foundation such as wealth, security, or success?

3.13–15 Two ways to destroy a building are to tamper with the foundation or to build with inferior materials. The church must be built on Christ, not on any other person or principle. Christ will evaluate each minister's contribution to the life of the church, and the day of judgment (the Day) will reveal the sincerity of each person's work. God will determine whether or not they have been faithful to Jesus' instructions. Good work will be rewarded; unfaithful or inferior work will be discounted. "The builder will be saved, but only as through fire" means that unfaithful workers will be saved, but like people escaping from a burning building. All their possessions (accomplishments) will be lost.

3.16, 17 Just as our bodies are the "temple of the Holy Spirit" (6.19), so also the local church or Christian community is God's temple. Just as the Jews' temple in Jerusalem was not to be defiled, the church is not to be spoiled and ruined by divisions, controversy, or other sins as members come together to worship God.

3.18–21 Paul is not telling the Corinthian believers to neglect the pursuit of knowledge. He is warning them that if worldly wisdom holds them back from God, it is not wisdom at all. God's way of thinking and evaluating is far more valuable, even though it may seem foolish to the world (1.27). The Corinthians were using so-called worldly wisdom to evaluate their leaders and teachers. Their pride made them value the presentation of the message more than its content.

3.22 Paul said that both life and death are our servants. While nonbelievers are victims of life, swept along by its current and wondering if there is meaning to it, believers use life well because they understand its true purpose. Nonbelievers can only fear death. For believers, however, death holds no terrors, because Christ has conquered them all. Death is only the beginning of eternal life with God. (Note: Cephas is Peter.)

4.1, 2 Paul urged the Corinthians to think of him, Peter (Cephas), and Apollos not as leaders of parties, but as servants of Christ and stewards (trusted administrators) of God's mysteries (see the note on 2.7). A servant does what his master tells him to do. We must do what God tells us to do in the Bible and through his Holy Spirit. Each day God presents us with needs and opportunities that challenge us to do what we know is right.

4.5 It is tempting to judge a fellow Christian, evaluating whether or not he or she is a good follower of Christ. But only God knows a person's heart, and he is the only one with the right to judge. Paul's warning to the Corinthians should also warn us. We are to confront those who are sinning (see 5.12, 13), but we must not judge who is a better servant for Christ. When you judge someone, you automatically consider yourself better, and that is pride.

6 I have applied all this to Apollos and myself for your benefit, brothers and
sisters,[r] so that you may learn through us the meaning of the saying, "Nothing
beyond what is written," so that none of you will be puffed up in favor of one
against another. 7 For who sees anything different in you?[s] What do you have that
you did not receive? And if you received it, why do you boast as if it were not a
gift?
8 Already you have all you want! Already you have become rich! Quite apart
from us you have become kings! Indeed, I wish that you had become kings, so that
we might be kings with you! 9 For I think that God has exhibited us apostles as last
of all, as though sentenced to death, because we have become a spectacle to the
world, to angels and to mortals. 10 We are fools for the sake of Christ, but you are
wise in Christ. We are weak, but you are strong. You are held in honor, but we in
disrepute. 11 To the present hour we are hungry and thirsty, we are poorly clothed
and beaten and homeless, 12 and we grow weary from the work of our own hands.
When reviled, we bless; when persecuted, we endure; 13 when slandered, we speak
kindly. We have become like the rubbish of the world, the dregs of all things, to
this very day.
14 I am not writing this to make you ashamed, but to admonish you as my
beloved children. 15 For though you might have ten thousand guardians in Christ,
you do not have many fathers. Indeed, in Christ Jesus I became your father through
the gospel. 16 I appeal to you, then, be imitators of me. 17 For this reason I sent[t] you
Timothy, who is my beloved and faithful child in the Lord, to remind you of my
ways in Christ Jesus, as I teach them everywhere in every church. 18 But some of
you, thinking that I am not coming to you, have become arrogant. 19 But I will
come to you soon, if the Lord wills, and I will find out not the talk of these arrogant
people but their power. 20 For the kingdom of God depends not on talk but on
power. 21 What would you prefer? Am I to come to you with a stick, or with love
in a spirit of gentleness?

4.6 1 Cor 1.12,31 4.18
4.7 Jn 3.27 Rom 12.3,6 1 Pet 4.10
4.8 Rev 3.17
4.9 Ps 44.22 Rom 8.36 2 Cor 4.11
4.10 2 Cor 11.19,20 13.9
4.11 Acts 23.2 Rom 8.35
4.12 Mt 5.44 Acts 18.2,3 1 Tim 4.9,10 1 Pet 3.9
4.14 2 Cor 6.13 12.14
4.15 Rom 15.20 Gal 4.19
4.16 Phil 3.17
4.17 Acts 16.1; 19.22 1 Tim 1.2
4.19 Acts 19.21 2 Cor 1.15
4.20 1 Thess 1.5
4.21 2 Cor 1.23; 2.1

[r] Gk *brothers* [s] Or *Who makes you different from another?* [t] Or *am sending*

4.6, 7 How easy it is for us to become attached to a spiritual leader. When someone has helped us, it's natural to feel loyalty. But Paul warns against having such pride in our favorite leaders that we cause divisions in the church. Any true spiritual leader is a representative of Christ and has nothing to offer that God hasn't given him. Don't let your loyalty cause fighting, slander, or broken relationships. Make sure your deepest loyalties are to Christ and not to his human agents. Those who spend more time debating church leadership than declaring Christ's message don't have Christ as their top priority.

4.6–13 The Corinthians had split into various cliques, each following its favorite preacher (Paul, Apollos, Peter, etc.). Each clique really believed it was the only one who had the whole truth, and thus felt spiritually proud ("puffed up"). But Paul told the groups not to boast about being tied to a particular preacher, because each preacher was simply a humble servant who had suffered for the same message of salvation in Jesus Christ. No preacher of God has more status than another.

4.15 In Paul's day, a guardian was a slave who was assigned as a special tutor and caretaker of a child. Paul was portraying his special affection for them (greater than a slave) and his special role (more than a tutor). In an attempt to unify the church, Paul appealed to his relationship with them. By *father,* he meant he was the church's founder. Because he started the church, he could be trusted to have its best interests at heart. Paul's tough words were motivated by love—like the love a good father has for his children (see also 1 Thessalonians 2.11).

4.16 Paul told the Corinthians to follow his example. He was able to make this statement because he walked close to God, spent time in God's Word and in prayer, and was aware of God's presence in his life at all times. God was his example; therefore, his life could be an example to other Christians. Paul wasn't expecting others to copy everything he did, because people are all different. But they should copy those aspects of his beliefs and Christian conduct that modeled Christ's way of living.

4.17 Timothy had traveled with Paul on his second missionary journey (see Acts 16.1–3) and was a key person in the growth of the early church. Timothy may have delivered this letter to Corinth, but more likely he arrived there shortly after the letter (see 16.10). His role was to see that Paul's advice was received, read, and implemented. He was then to return to Paul and report on the church's progress.

4.18–20 Some people talk a lot about faith, but that's all it is—talk. They may know all the right words to say, but their lives don't reflect God's power. Paul says the kingdom of God is to be *lived,* not just discussed. There is a big difference between knowing the right words and living them out. Don't be content to have the right answers about Christ. Let your life show that God's power is really working in you.

4.19 It is not known whether Paul ever returned to Corinth, but it is likely. In 2 Corinthians 2.1, he says he decided not to make "another painful visit," implying that he had had a previous painful confrontation with the Corinthian believers.

2. Disorders in the church

Paul condemns immorality in the church

5.1 Lev 18.7,8 2 Cor 7.12 Eph 5.3
5.3,4 Mt 18.15-18 Jn 20.23 2 Cor 2.5-10 13.3,4
5.5 Acts 26.18 1 Tim 1.20
5.6 Mt 13.33; 16.6,11 Gal 5.9
5.7 Ex 12.21 Isa 53.7 1 Pet 1.19 Rev 5.6
5.9 2 Cor 6.14
5.10 Jn 17.15

5 It is actually reported that there is sexual immorality among you, and of a kind
that is not found even among pagans; for a man is living with his father's wife.
[2]And you are arrogant! Should you not rather have mourned, so that he who has
done this would have been removed from among you?
3 For though absent in body, I am present in spirit; and as if present I have
already pronounced judgment [4]in the name of the Lord Jesus on the man who has
done such a thing.[u] When you are assembled, and my spirit is present with the
power of our Lord Jesus, [5]you are to hand this man over to Satan for the destruction
of the flesh, so that his spirit may be saved in the day of the Lord.[v]
6 Your boasting is not a good thing. Do you not know that a little yeast leavens
the whole batch of dough? [7]Clean out the old yeast so that you may be a new batch,
as you really are unleavened. For our paschal lamb, Christ, has been sacrificed.
[8]Therefore, let us celebrate the festival, not with the old yeast, the yeast of malice
and evil, but with the unleavened bread of sincerity and truth.
9 I wrote to you in my letter not to associate with sexually immoral persons—
[10]not at all meaning the immoral of this world, or the greedy and robbers, or

[u] *Or on the man who has done such a thing in the name of the Lord Jesus* [v] Other ancient authorities add *Jesus*

CHURCH DISCIPLINE
The church, at times, must exercise discipline toward members who have sinned. But church discipline must be handled carefully, straightforwardly, and in love.

Situations	*Steps* (Matthew 18.15–17)
Unintentional error and/or private sin	1. Go to the brother or sister, reprove him or her in private.
Public sin and/or those done with prior knowledge and flagrantly	2. If he/she does not listen, go with one or two witnesses.
	3. If he/she refuses to listen, take the matter before the church.

After these steps have been carried out, the next steps are:

1. Remove the one in error from the fellowship (1 Corinthians 5.2–13).
2. The church gives united disapproval, but forgiveness and comfort are in order if he/she chooses to repent (2 Corinthians 2.5–8).
3. Do not associate with the disobedient person; and if you must, speak to him/her as one who needs a warning (2 Thessalonians 3.14, 15.)
4. After two warnings, reject the person from the fellowship (Titus 3.10).

5.1ff The church must discipline flagrant sin among its members—such actions, left unchecked, can polarize and paralyze a church. The correction, however, is never to be vengeful. Instead, it is intended to bring about a cure. The Corinthian believers had a specific sin in their midst, but they had refused to deal with it. In this case, a man was having an affair with his mother (or stepmother), and the church members were trying to ignore the situation. Paul was telling the church that it had a responsibility to maintain the standards of morality found in God's Word. God tells us not to judge others, but he also tells us not to tolerate flagrant sin. It will be a dangerous influence on other believers (5.6).

5.5 To "hand this man over to Satan" means to exclude him from the fellowship of believers. Without the spiritual support of Christians, this man would be left alone with his sin and Satan, and perhaps this emptiness would drive him to repentance. "For the destruction of the flesh" means either that he would experience bodily illness, the natural result of his sinful state, or that the experience would bring him to God to destroy his sinful nature. Putting someone out of the church should be a last resort in disciplinary action. It should not be done out of vengeance, but out of love, just as parents punish children to correct them. The church's role is to help the offender, not to hurt him, motivating him to repent of his sins and to return to the fellowship of the church.

5.6 Paul was talking to those who wanted to ignore this church problem. They didn't realize that allowing public sin to exist in the church affects all its members. Paul was not expecting anyone to be sinless—all believers struggle with sin daily. Instead, he was speaking against those who deliberately sinned, felt no guilt, and would not repent. This kind of sin cannot be tolerated in the church because it affects others. We have a responsibility to other believers. Yeast makes bread dough rise. A little bit affects the whole batch. Blatant sins, left uncorrected, confuse and divide the congregation. While believers should encourage, pray for, and build up one another, they must also be intolerant of sin when it jeopardizes the spiritual health of the church.

5.7, 8 As the Hebrews prepared for their exodus from slavery in Egypt, they were commanded to prepare bread without yeast ("unleavened bread") because they didn't have time to wait for it to rise. Yeast also was a symbol of sin, so they were commanded to clean all of it out of the house (Exodus 12.15; 13.7). Christ is our Passover (paschal lamb), the perfect sacrifice for our sin. Because he has delivered us from the slavery of sin, we should have nothing to do with the sins of the past ("old leaven").

5.9 Paul was referring to an earlier letter to the Corinthian church, often called the lost letter because it has not been preserved.

5.10, 11 Paul made it clear that we should not dissociate ourselves from unbelievers—otherwise, we could not carry out Christ's command to tell them about salvation (Matthew 28.18–20). But we are to distance ourselves from the person who claims to be a Christian, yet indulges in sins explicitly forbidden in Scripture and then rationalizes his actions. By rationalizing sin, a person harms others for whom Christ died and dims the image of God in

idolaters, since you would then need to go out of the world. 11 But now I am writing to you not to associate with anyone who bears the name of brother or sister[w]
who is sexually immoral or greedy, or is an idolater, reviler, drunkard, or robber.
Do not even eat with such a one. 12 For what have I to do with judging those outside? Is it not those who are inside that you are to judge? 13 God will judge those
outside. "Drive out the wicked person from among you."

5.11 Mt 18.17; Rom 16.17; 2 Jn 1.10
5.12 1 Tim 3.7
5.13 Heb 13.4

Believers should not sue each other

6 When any of you has a grievance against another, do you dare to take it to court
before the unrighteous, instead of taking it before the saints? 2 Do you not
know that the saints will judge the world? And if the world is to be judged by you,
are you incompetent to try trivial cases? 3 Do you not know that we are to judge
angels—to say nothing of ordinary matters? 4 If you have ordinary cases, then, do
you appoint as judges those who have no standing in the church? 5 I say this to your
shame. Can it be that there is no one among you wise enough to decide between one
believer[w] and another, 6 but a believer[w] goes to court against a believer[w]—and
before unbelievers at that?
7 In fact, to have lawsuits at all with one another is already a defeat for you.
Why not rather be wronged? Why not rather be defrauded? 8 But you yourselves
wrong and defraud—and believers[x] at that.

6.1 Mt 18.15-17
6.2 Dan 7.18,22; Lk 22.30; Rev 2.26; 20.4
6.3 2 Pet 2.4; Jude 6
6.5 1 Cor 4.14; 15.34
6.7 Prov 20.22; Mt 5.39; Rom 12.17; 1 Thess 5.15
6.8 1 Thess 4.6

Use your body to give God glory

9 Do you not know that wrongdoers will not inherit the kingdom of God? Do
not be deceived! Fornicators, idolaters, adulterers, male prostitutes, sodomites,
10 thieves, the greedy, drunkards, revilers, robbers—none of these will inherit the
kingdom of God. 11 And this is what some of you used to be. But you were washed,
you were sanctified, you were justified in the name of the Lord Jesus Christ and in
the Spirit of our God.
12 "All things are lawful for me," but not all things are beneficial. "All things

6.9,10 Isa 3.11; Acts 20.32; Gal 5.21; Eph 5.5
6.11 Acts 22.16; Rom 8.30; 1 Cor 1.2,30; Heb 10.22

[w] Gk *brother* [x] Gk *brothers*

himself. A church that includes such people is hardly fit to be the light of the world. This distorts the picture of Christ it presents to the world. Church leaders must be ready to correct, in love, for the sake of spiritual unity.

5.12 The Bible consistently tells us not to criticize people by gossiping or making rash judgments. At the same time, however, we are to judge and deal with sin that can hurt others. Paul's instructions are not to be used to handle trivial matters or to take revenge; nor are they to be applied to individual problems between believers. These verses are instructions for dealing with open sin in the church, with a person who claims to be a Christian and yet who sins without remorse. The church is to confront and discipline such a person in love. Also see the notes on 4.5 and 5.1ff.

6.1–6 In chapter 5, Paul explained what to do with open immorality in the congregation. In chapter 6, he teaches them how the congregation should handle smaller problems between believers. Society has set up a legal system where disagreements can be solved in courts. But Paul declares that disagreeing Christians should not have to go to a secular court to resolve their differences. As Christians we have the Holy Spirit and the mind of Christ, so why should we turn to those who lack God's wisdom? Because of all that we have been given as believers, and because of the authority that we will have in the future to judge the world and the angels, we should be able to deal with the disputes among ourselves. The saints are the same as believers. See John 5.22 and Revelation 3.21 for more on judging the world. Judging angels is mentioned in 2 Peter 2.4 and Jude 1.6.

6.6 Why did Paul say Christians should not take their disagreements to unbelievers in secular courts? (1) If the judge and jury are not Christians, they are unlikely to be sensitive to Christian values. (2) The basis for going to court is often revenge; this should never be a Christian's motive. (3) Lawsuits make the church look bad, causing unbelievers to focus on its problems rather than its purpose.

6.9–11 Paul is describing characteristics of unbelievers. He doesn't mean that adulterers, male prostitutes, homosexuals ("sodomites"), thieves, or greedy people are automatically and irrevocably excluded from heaven. Christians come from all backgrounds, including these. They may still struggle with evil desires, but they should not continue in these practices. In 6.11, Paul clearly stated that even those who sin in these ways can have their lives changed by Christ. However, those who say they are Christians but persist in these practices with no remorse will not inherit the kingdom of God. Such people need to reevaluate their lives to see if they truly believe in Christ.

6.9–11 In a permissive society it is easy for Christians to overlook or tolerate some immoral behaviors (greed, drunkenness, etc.) while remaining outraged at others (homosexuality, thievery). We cannot take part in sin or condone it in any way, nor should we be selective about what we condemn or excuse. Staying away from generally accepted sin is difficult, but it is no harder for us than it

6.13 Mt 5.17 Col 2.22 1 Thess 4.3
6.14 Acts 2.24 Eph 1.19,20
6.16 Gen 2.24 Mt 19.5,6
6.17 2 Cor 3.17 Eph 5.30
6.18 1 Thess 4.3,4
6.19 Rom 14.7,8 2 Cor 6.16

are lawful for me," but I will not be dominated by anything. 13 "Food is meant for
the stomach and the stomach for food,"[y] and God will destroy both one and the
other. The body is meant not for fornication but for the Lord, and the Lord for the
body. 14 And God raised the Lord and will also raise us by his power. 15 Do you not
know that your bodies are members of Christ? Should I therefore take the members
of Christ and make them members of a prostitute? Never! 16 Do you not know that
whoever is united to a prostitute becomes one body with her? For it is said, "The
two shall be one flesh." 17 But anyone united to the Lord becomes one spirit with
him. 18 Shun fornication! Every sin that a person commits is outside the body; but
the fornicator sins against the body itself. 19 Or do you not know that your body is
a temple[z] of the Holy Spirit within you, which you have from God, and that you
are not your own? 20 For you were bought with a price; therefore glorify God in
your body.

[y] The quotation may extend to the word *other* [z] Or *sanctuary*

was for the Corinthians. God expects his followers in any age to have high standards.

6.11 Paul emphasizes God's action in making them new people. The three aspects of God's work are all part of our salvation: our sins were washed away, we were set apart for special use ("sanctified"), and we were pronounced not guilty ("justified") for our sins.

6.12 Apparently the church was quoting and misapplying the words "all things are lawful for me." Some Christians in Corinth were excusing their sins by saying that (1) Christ had taken away all sin, and so they had complete freedom to live as they pleased, or (2) what they were doing was not strictly forbidden by Scripture. Paul answered both these excuses. (1) While Christ has taken away our sin, this does not give us freedom to go on doing what we know is wrong. The New Testament specifically forbids many sins (see 6.9, 10) that were originally prohibited in the Old Testament (see Romans 12.9–21; 13.8–10). (2) Some actions are not sinful in themselves, but they are not appropriate because they can control our lives and lead us away from God. (3) Some actions may hurt others. Anything we do that hurts rather than helps others is not right.

6.12, 13 Many of the world's religions teach that the soul or spirit is important and the body is not; and Christianity has sometimes been influenced by these ideas. In truth, however, Christianity is a very physical religion. We worship a God who created a physical world and pronounced it good. He promises us a new earth where real people have transformed physical lives – not a pink cloud where disembodied souls listen to harp music. At the heart of Christianity is the story of God himself taking on flesh and blood and coming to live with us, offering both physical healing and spiritual restoration.

We humans, like Adam, are a combination of dust and spirit. Just as our spirits affect our bodies, so our physical bodies affect our spirits. We cannot commit sin with our bodies without damaging our souls, because our bodies and souls are inseparably joined. In the new earth we will have resurrection bodies that are not corrupted by sin. Then we will enjoy the fullness of our salvation.

6.12, 13 Freedom is a mark of the Christian faith – freedom from sin and guilt, and freedom to use and enjoy anything that comes from God. But Christians should not abuse this freedom and hurt themselves or others. Drinking too much leads to alcoholism, gluttony leads to obesity. Be careful that what God has allowed you to enjoy doesn't grow into a bad habit that controls you. For more about Christian freedom and everyday behavior, read chapter 8.

6.13 Sexual sin (fornication) is a temptation we cannot escape. In movies and on television, sex outside marriage is treated as a normal, even desirable, part of life, while marriage is often shown as confining and joyless. We can even be looked down upon by others if we are suspected of being pure. But God does not forbid sexual sin just to be difficult. He knows its power to destroy us physically and spiritually. No one should underestimate the power of sexual sin. It has devastated countless lives and destroyed families, churches, communities, and even nations. God wants to protect us from damaging ourselves and others, and so he offers to fill us – our loneliness, our desires – with himself.

6.15–17 This teaching about sexual sin and prostitutes was especially important for the Corinthian church because the temple of the goddess Aphrodite was in Corinth. It employed more than a thousand prostitutes, and sex was part of the worship ritual. Paul clearly stated that Christians are to have no part in sexual sin, even if it is acceptable and popular in our culture.

6.18 As Christians we are free to be all we can be for God; we are not free *from* God. God created sex to be a beautiful and essential ingredient of marriage, but sexual sin – sex outside the marriage relationship – *always* hurts someone. It hurts God because it shows we prefer following our own desires instead of the leading of the Holy Spirit. It hurts others because it violates the commitment so necessary to a relationship. It often brings disease to our bodies, and it deeply affects our personalities, which respond in anguish when we harm ourselves physically and spiritually.

6.19, 20 What did Paul mean when he said that our bodies belong to God? Many people say they have the right to do whatever they want with their own bodies. Although they think this is freedom, they are really enslaved to their own desires. When we become Christians, the Holy Spirit fills and lives in us. Therefore, we no longer own our bodies. We have been "bought with a price" refers to slaves purchased at auction. Christ's death freed us from sin, but also obligates us to his service. If you live in a building owned by someone else, you don't violate the building rules. Because your body belongs to God, you must not violate his standards for living.

B. PAUL ANSWERS CHURCH QUESTIONS (7.1—16.24)

After discussing disorders in the church, Paul moves to the list of questions which the Corinthians had sent him, including subjects of marriage, singleness, eating meat offered to idols, clothing in worship, orderliness in the Lord's supper, spiritual gifts, and the resurrection. Questions which plague churches today are remarkably similar to these, so we can receive specific guidance in these areas.

1. Instruction on Christian marriage

Questions about marriage

7 Now concerning the matters about which you wrote: "It is well for a man not 7.1
to touch a woman." 2 But because of cases of sexual immorality, each man 1 Cor 7.8,26
should have his own wife and each woman her own husband. 3 The husband should 7.2 Prov 5.19
give to his wife her conjugal rights, and likewise the wife to her husband. 4 For the 7.3
wife does not have authority over her own body, but the husband does; likewise the Ex 21.10 1 Pet 3.7
husband does not have authority over his own body, but the wife does. 5 Do not 7.5
deprive one another except perhaps by agreement for a set time, to devote your- 1 Thess 3.5
selves to prayer, and then come together again, so that Satan may not tempt you
because of your lack of self-control. 6 This I say by way of concession, not of com- 7.6 2 Cor 8.8; 11.17
mand. 7 I wish that all were as I myself am. But each has a particular gift from God, 7.7
one having one kind and another a different kind. Mt 19.12 1 Cor 9.5; 12.11
8 To the unmarried and the widows I say that it is well for them to remain unmarried as I am. 9 But if they are not practicing self-control, they should marry. For 7.9 1 Tim 5.14
it is better to marry than to be aflame with passion.
10 To the married I give this command—not I but the Lord—that the wife 7.10 Mal 2.14,16
should not separate from her husband 11 (but if she does separate, let her remain Mt 5.32; 19.5,6 Mk 10.10-12
unmarried or else be reconciled to her husband), and that the husband should not Lk 16.18
divorce his wife.
12 To the rest I say—I and not the Lord—that if any believer[a] has a wife who 7.12 2 Cor 11.17

[a] Gk *brother*

7.1 The Corinthians had written to Paul asking him several questions relating to the Christian life and problems in the church. The first was whether or not it was good to be married ("to touch a woman"). Paul answers these questions in the remainder of this letter.

7.1ff Christians in Corinth were surrounded by sexual temptation. The city had a reputation even among pagans for sexual immorality and religious prostitution. It was to this kind of society that Paul delivered these instructions on sex and marriage. The Corinthians needed special, specific instructions because of their culture's immoral standards. For more on Paul's teaching on marriage, see Ephesians 5.

7.3–5 Sexual temptations are difficult to withstand because they appeal to the normal and natural desires God has given us. Marriage provides God's way to satisfy these natural sexual desires and to strengthen the partners against temptation. Married couples have the responsibility to care for each other; therefore, husbands and wives should not withhold themselves sexually from one another, but should fulfill each other's needs and desires. (See also the note on 10.13.)

7.3–11 The Corinthian church was in turmoil because of the immorality of the culture around them. Some Greeks, in rejecting immorality, rejected sex and marriage altogether. The Corinthian Christians wondered if this was what they should do also, so they asked Paul several questions: "Because sex is perverted, shouldn't we also abstain in marriage?" "If my spouse is unsaved, should I seek a divorce?" "Should unmarried people and widows not marry?" Paul answered many of these questions by saying, "For now, stay put. Be content in the situation where God has placed you. Don't seek to be married or single. Live God's way, one day at a time, and he will show you what to do."

7.4 Spiritually, our bodies belong to God when we become Christians, because Jesus Christ bought us by paying the price to release us from sin (see 6.19, 20). Physically, our bodies belong to our spouses, because God designed marriage so that through the union of husband and wife, the two become one (Genesis 2.24). Paul stressed complete equality in sexual relationships. Neither male nor female should seek dominance or autonomy.

7.7 Both marriage and singleness are gifts from God. One is not morally better than the other, and both are valuable to accomplishing God's purposes. It is important for us, therefore, to accept our present situation. When Paul said he wished that more people could get along without marrying, he was expressing his desire that more people would devote themselves *completely* to the ministry without the added concerns of spouse and family, as he had done. He was not criticizing marriage—after all, it is God's created way of providing companionship and populating the earth.

7.9 Sexual pressure is not the best motive for getting married, but it is better to marry the right person than to be aflame with passion. Many new believers in Corinth thought that all sex was wrong, and so engaged couples were deciding not to get married. In this passage, Paul was telling couples who wanted to marry that they should not frustrate their normal sexual drives by avoiding marriage. This does not mean, however, that people who have trouble controlling themselves should marry the first person who comes along. It is better to deal with the pressure of desire than to deal with an unhappy marriage.

7.10, 11 Because of their desire to serve Christ, some people in the Corinthian church thought they ought to divorce their pagan spouses and marry Christians. But Paul affirmed the marriage commitment. God's ideal is for marriages to stay together—even when one spouse is not a believer. The Christian spouse should try to win the other to Christ. It would be easy to rationalize leaving; however, Paul made a strong case for staying with the unbelieving spouse and being a positive influence on the marriage. Paul, like Jesus, believed that marriage is permanent (see Mark 10.1–9).

7.12 Paul's *command* about the permanence of marriage (7.10) comes from the Old Testament and from Jesus. His *suggestion* in

is an unbeliever, and she consents to live with him, he should not divorce her.
13 And if any woman has a husband who is an unbeliever, and he consents to live
7.14 Ezra 9.2 Mal 2.15 with her, she should not divorce him. 14 For the unbelieving husband is made holy
through his wife, and the unbelieving wife is made holy through her husband. Otherwise, your children would be unclean, but as it is, they are holy. 15 But if the
unbelieving partner separates, let it be so; in such a case the brother or sister is not
7.16 1 Pet 3.1 bound. It is to peace that God has called you.[b] 16 Wife, for all you know, you might
save your husband. Husband, for all you know, you might save your wife.

Believers should be content where they are

7.17 1 Cor 4.17 11.16; 14.33 17 However that may be, let each of you lead the life that the Lord has assigned,
to which God called you. This is my rule in all the churches. 18 Was anyone at the
7.18 Acts 15.4-19 Gal 5.2 time of his call already circumcised? Let him not seek to remove the marks of
circumcision. Was anyone at the time of his call uncircumcised? Let him not seek
7.19 Rom 2.25 Gal 5.6; 6.15 Col 3.11 circumcision. 19 Circumcision is nothing, and uncircumcision is nothing; but obeying the commandments of God is everything. 20 Let each of you remain in the con-
dition in which you were called.
7.21 Gal 3.28 21 Were you a slave when called? Do not be concerned about it. Even if you
can gain your freedom, make use of your present condition now more than ever.[c]
7.22 Gal 5.13 Eph 6.6 1 Pet 2.16 22 For whoever was called in the Lord as a slave is a freed person belonging to the
Lord, just as whoever was free when called is a slave of Christ. 23 You were bought
7.23 1 Cor 6.20 with a price; do not become slaves of human masters. 24 In whatever condition you
were called, brothers and sisters,[d] there remain with God.

Questions about singleness

7.25 2 Cor 4.1 25 Now concerning virgins, I have no command of the Lord, but I give my
7.26 Lk 21.23 opinion as one who by the Lord's mercy is trustworthy. 26 I think that, in view of the
impending[e] crisis, it is well for you to remain as you are. 27 Are you bound to a

[b] Other ancient authorities read *us* [c] Or *avail yourself of the opportunity* [d] Gk *brothers* [e] Or *present*

---

this verse is based on God's command, and he applies it to the situation the Corinthians were facing. Paul ranked the command above the suggestion because one is an eternal principle while the other is a specific application. Nevertheless, for people in similar situations, Paul's suggestion is the best advice they will get. Paul was a man of God, an apostle; and he had the mind of Christ.

7.14 The blessings that flow to believers don't stop there, but extend to others. God regards the marriage as "sanctified" (set apart for his use) by the presence of one Christian spouse. The other does not receive salvation automatically, but is helped by this relationship. The children of such a marriage are to be regarded as Christians (because of God's blessing on the family unit) until they are old enough to decide for themselves.

7.15, 16 This verse is misused by some as a loophole to get out of marriage. But Paul's statements were given to encourage the Christian spouse to try to get along with the unbeliever and make the marriage work. If, however, the unbelieving spouse insisted on leaving, Paul said to let him or her go. The only alternative would be for the Christian to deny his or her faith to preserve the marriage, and that would be worse than dissolving the marriage. Paul's purpose in writing this was to urge the married couples to seek unity, not separation (see 7.17; 1 Peter 3.1, 2).

7.17 Apparently the Corinthians were ready to make wholesale changes without thinking through the ramifications. Paul was writing to say that people should be Christians where they are. You can do God's work and demonstrate your faith *anywhere.* If you became a Christian after marriage, and your spouse is not a believer, remember that you don't have to be married to a Christian to live for Christ. Don't assume that you are in the wrong place, stuck with the wrong person. You may be just where God wants you (see 7.20).

7.18, 19 The ceremony of circumcision was an important part of the Jews' relationship with God. In fact, before Christ came, circumcision was commanded by God for those who claimed to follow him (Genesis 17.9–14). But after Christ's death, circumcision was no longer necessary (Acts 15; Romans 4.9–11; Galatians 5.2–4; Colossians 2.11). Pleasing God and obeying him is more important than observing traditional ceremonies.

7.20 Often we are so concerned about what we *could* be doing for God somewhere else that we miss great opportunities right where we are. Paul said that when someone becomes a Christian, he should usually continue with the work he has previously been doing – provided it isn't immoral or unethical. Every job can become Christian work when you realize that the purpose of your life is to honor, serve, and speak out for Christ. Because God has placed you where you are, look carefully for opportunities to serve him there.

7.23 Slavery was common throughout the Roman Empire. Some Christians in the Corinthian church were slaves. Paul said that although they were slaves to men, they were free from the power of sin in their lives. People today are slaves to sin until they commit their lives to Christ, who alone can conquer sin's power. Sin, pride, and fear no longer have claim over us, just as a slaveowner no longer has power over the slaves he has sold. The Bible says we become Christ's slaves when we become Christians (Romans 6.18), but this actually means we gain our freedom, because sin no longer controls us.

7.26 Paul saw the impending persecution that the Roman government would soon bring upon Christians. He gave this practical advice because being unmarried would mean less suffering and more freedom to throw one's life into the cause of Christ (7.29), even to the point of fearlessly dying for him. Paul's advice reveals his single-minded devotion to spreading the good news.

wife? Do not seek to be free. Are you free from a wife? Do not seek a wife. 28 But
if you marry, you do not sin, and if a virgin marries, she does not sin. Yet those
who marry will experience distress in this life,[f] and I would spare you that. 29 I **7.29**
mean, brothers and sisters,[g] the appointed time has grown short; from now on, let Rom 13.11 1 Cor 7.31
even those who have wives be as though they had none, 30 and those who mourn as 1 Pet 4.7
though they were not mourning, and those who rejoice as though they were not
rejoicing, and those who buy as though they had no possessions, 31 and those who **7.31**
deal with the world as though they had no dealings with it. For the present form of Ps 39.6 Jas 4.14
this world is passing away. 1 Jn 2.17

32 I want you to be free from anxieties. The unmarried man is anxious about the
affairs of the Lord, how to please the Lord; 33 but the married man is anxious about
the affairs of the world, how to please his wife, 34 and his interests are divided. And **7.34**
the unmarried woman and the virgin are anxious about the affairs of the Lord, so Lk 10.40
that they may be holy in body and spirit; but the married woman is anxious about 1 Tim 5.5
the affairs of the world, how to please her husband. 35 I say this for your own benefit, not to put any restraint upon you, but to promote good order and unhindered
devotion to the Lord.

36 If anyone thinks that he is not behaving properly toward his fiancée,[h] if his
passions are strong, and so it has to be, let him marry as he wishes; it is no sin. Let
them marry. 37 But if someone stands firm in his resolve, being under no necessity
but having his own desire under control, and has determined in his own mind to
keep her as his fiancée,[h] he will do well. 38 So then, he who marries his fiancée[h] **7.38**
does well; and he who refrains from marriage will do better. Heb 13.4

39 A wife is bound as long as her husband lives. But if the husband dies,[i] she **7.39** Rom 7.2
is free to marry anyone she wishes, only in the Lord. 40 But in my judgment she is 2 Cor 6.14
more blessed if she remains as she is. And I think that I too have the Spirit of God. **7.40** 1 Cor 7.6,25

2. Instruction on Christian freedom

Questions about food offered to idols

8 Now concerning food sacrificed to idols: we know that "all of us possess **8.1**
knowledge." Knowledge puffs up, but love builds up. 2 Anyone who claims to Acts 15.20 Rom 14.19
know something does not yet have the necessary knowledge; 3 but anyone who **8.3**
loves God is known by him. Gal 4.9 2 Tim 2.19
4 Hence, as to the eating of food offered to idols, we know that "no idol in the

[f] Gk *in the flesh* [g] Gk *brothers* [h] Gk *virgin* [i] Gk *falls asleep*

7.28 Many people naively think that marriage will solve all their problems. Here are some problems marriage won't solve: (1) loneliness, (2) sexual temptation, (3) satisfaction of one's deepest emotional needs, (4) elimination of life's difficulties. Marriage alone does not hold two people together, but commitment does—commitment to Christ and to each other despite conflicts and problems. As wonderful as it is, marriage does not automatically solve every problem. Whether married or single, we must be content with our situation and focus on Christ, not loved ones, to solve our problems.

7.29 Paul urges all believers to make the most of their time before Christ's return. Every person in every generation should have this sense of urgency about telling the good news to others. Life is short no matter how long we live.

7.29–31 Paul urged the believers to not regard marriage, home, or financial security as the ultimate goals of life. As far as possible, we should live unhindered by the cares of this world, not getting involved with burdensome mortgages, budgets, investments, or bills that will keep us from doing God's work. A married man, as Paul pointed out (7.33), must take care of his earthly responsibilities—but he should keep them modest and manageable.

7.32–34 Some single people feel tremendous pressure to be married. They think their lives can be complete only with a spouse. But Paul underlined one advantage of being single—the potential of a greater focus on Christ and his work. If you are unmarried, use your special opportunity to serve Christ wholeheartedly.

7.38 When Paul says the unmarried person does better, he was talking about the potential time available for service to God. The single person does not have the responsibility of caring for a spouse and raising a family. Singleness, however, does not insure service to God—that is up to the commitment of the individual.

7.40 Paul's advice comes from the Holy Spirit, who guides and equips both single and married people to fulfill their roles.

8.1 Meat bought in the marketplace was likely to have been symbolically offered to an idol in one of the many pagan temples. Animals were brought to a temple, killed before an idol as part of a pagan religious ceremony, and then taken to butchers who sold the meat in a temple restaurant or in the marketplace. The believers wondered if by eating such meat, they were somehow participating in the worship of pagan idols.

8.1–3 Love is more important than knowledge. Knowledge makes us look good and feel important, but one can easily develop an arrogant, know-it-all attitude. Many people with strong opinions are unwilling to listen and learn from God and others. We can obtain God's knowledge only by loving him (see James 3.17, 18).

8.4–9 Paul addresses these words to believers who weren't bothered by eating meat that had been sacrificed to idols. Although idols were not real, and the pagan ritual of sacrificing to them was

8.6 Jn 1.3 Acts 17.28 Eph 4.6 Col 1.16
8.7 1 Cor 8.4
8.8 Rom 14.17
8.9 Rom 14.1,13,21 1 Cor 8.10 10.28 Gal 5.13
8.10 Acts 15.20
8.11 Rom 14.15,20 1 Cor 8.4
8.12 Rom 14.20
8.13 Rom 14.21 1 Cor 10.32 2 Cor 6.3; 11.29

world really exists," and that "there is no God but one." 5 Indeed, even though there
may be so-called gods in heaven or on earth—as in fact there are many gods and
many lords— 6 yet for us there is one God, the Father, from whom are all things
and for whom we exist, and one Lord, Jesus Christ, through whom are all things
and through whom we exist.
7 It is not everyone, however, who has this knowledge. Since some have
become so accustomed to idols until now, they still think of the food they eat as
food offered to an idol; and their conscience, being weak, is defiled. 8 "Food will
not bring us close to God."[j] We are no worse off if we do not eat, and no better off
if we do. 9 But take care that this liberty of yours does not somehow become a
stumbling block to the weak. 10 For if others see you, who possess knowledge,
eating in the temple of an idol, might they not, since their conscience is weak, be
encouraged to the point of eating food sacrificed to idols? 11 So by your knowledge
those weak believers for whom Christ died are destroyed.[k] 12 But when you thus
sin against members of your family,[l] and wound their conscience when it is weak,
you sin against Christ. 13 Therefore, if food is a cause of their falling,[m] I will never
eat meat, so that I may not cause one of them[n] to fall.

The rights of apostles

9.1 Acts 9.3; 18.9 1 Tim 2.7 2 Tim 1.11
9.2 2 Cor 3.2

9 Am I not free? Am I not an apostle? Have I not seen Jesus our Lord? Are you
not my work in the Lord? 2 If I am not an apostle to others, at least I am to you;
for you are the seal of my apostleship in the Lord.
3 This is my defense to those who would examine me. 4 Do we not have the

[j] The quotation may extend to the end of the verse [k] Gk *the weak brother . . . is destroyed* [l] Gk *against the brothers* [m] Gk *my brother's falling* [n] Gk *cause my brother*

STRONGER, WEAKER BROTHERS

Advice to:

Stronger believer	Don't be proud of your maturity; don't flaunt your freedom. Act in love so you do not cause a weaker brother to stumble.
Weaker believer	Although you may not feel the same freedom in some areas as in others, take your time, pray to God, but do not force others to adhere to your stipulations. You would hinder other believers by making up rules and standards for how everyone ought to behave. Make sure your convictions are based on God's Word, not your opinions.
Pastors and leaders	Teach correctly from God's Word, helping Christians understand what is right and wrong in God's eyes, and helping them see that they can have varied opinions on other issues and still be unified. Don't allow potential problems to get out of hand, causing splits and divisions.

Paul advises those who are more mature in the faith about how they must care about their brothers and sisters in Christ who have more tender consciences; those "weaker" brothers and sisters are advised concerning their growth; and pastors and leaders are instructed on how to deal with the conflicts that easily could arise between these groups.

meaningless, eating such meat offended Christians with more sensitive consciences. Paul says, therefore, that if a weaker or less mature believer misunderstood their actions, they should, out of consideration, avoid eating meat offered to idols.

8.10–13 Christian freedom does not mean "anything goes." It means that our salvation is not determined by legalism, good works, or rules, but by the free gift of God (Ephesians 2.8, 9). Christian freedom, then, is inseparably tied to Christian responsibility. New believers are often very sensitive to what is right or wrong, what they should or shouldn't do. Some actions may be perfectly all right for us to do, but may harm a Christian brother or sister who is still young in the faith and learning what the Christian life is all about. We must be careful not to offend a sensitive or younger Christian or, by our example, to cause him or her to sin. When we love others, our freedom should be less important to us than strengthening the faith of a brother or sister in Christ.

9.1 Some Corinthians were questioning Paul's authority, so Paul gives his credentials—he actually saw and talked with the resurrected Christ, who called him to be an apostle (Acts 93–18). Such credentials make the advice he gives in this letter more persuasive.

9.1 Changed lives were the evidence that God was using Paul. Does your faith have an impact on others? You can help others grow spiritually if you let God use you and make you effective.

9.4ff Paul uses himself as an illustration of giving up personal rights. Paul had the right to hospitality, to be married, to bring guests, and to be paid for his work. But he willingly gave up these rights to win people to Christ. When your focus is on living for Christ, your rights become comparatively unimportant.

9.4–10 Jesus said that workers are worthy of their pay (Luke 10.7). Paul echoed this thought and urged the church to be sure to pay their Christian workers. We have the responsibility to care for our pastors, teachers, and other spiritual leaders and to see that they are fairly and adequately compensated.

right to our food and drink? 5 Do we not have the right to be accompanied by a
believing wife,[o] as do the other apostles and the brothers of the Lord and Cephas?
6 Or is it only Barnabas and I who have no right to refrain from working for a living?
7 Who at any time pays the expenses for doing military service? Who plants a vineyard and does not eat any of its fruit? Or who tends a flock and does not get any of
its milk?
8 Do I say this on human authority? Does not the law also say the same? 9 For
it is written in the law of Moses, "You shall not muzzle an ox while it is treading
out the grain." Is it for oxen that God is concerned? 10 Or does he not speak entirely
for our sake? It was indeed written for our sake, for whoever plows should plow in
hope and whoever threshes should thresh in hope of a share in the crop. 11 If we
have sown spiritual good among you, is it too much if we reap your material benefits? 12 If others share this rightful claim on you, do not we still more?
Nevertheless, we have not made use of this right, but we endure anything rather
than put an obstacle in the way of the gospel of Christ. 13 Do you not know that
those who are employed in the temple service get their food from the temple, and
those who serve at the altar share in what is sacrificed on the altar? 14 In the same
way, the Lord commanded that those who proclaim the gospel should get their
living by the gospel.
15 But I have made no use of any of these rights, nor am I writing this so that
they may be applied in my case. Indeed, I would rather die than that — no one will
deprive me of my ground for boasting! 16 If I proclaim the gospel, this gives me no
ground for boasting, for an obligation is laid on me, and woe to me if I do not
proclaim the gospel! 17 For if I do this of my own will, I have a reward; but if not
of my own will, I am entrusted with a commission. 18 What then is my reward? Just
this: that in my proclamation I may make the gospel free of charge, so as not to
make full use of my rights in the gospel.
19 For though I am free with respect to all, I have made myself a slave to all,
so that I might win more of them. 20 To the Jews I became as a Jew, in order to win
Jews. To those under the law I became as one under the law (though I myself am
not under the law) so that I might win those under the law. 21 To those outside the
law I became as one outside the law (though I am not free from God's law but am
under Christ's law) so that I might win those outside the law. 22 To the weak I
became weak, so that I might win the weak. I have become all things to all people,
that I might by all means save some. 23 I do it all for the sake of the gospel, so that
I may share in its blessings.
24 Do you not know that in a race the runners all compete, but only one receives
the prize? Run in such a way that you may win it. 25 Athletes exercise self-control
in all things; they do it to receive a perishable wreath, but we an imperishable one.

o Gk *a sister as wife*

9.5 Mt 8.14; 12.46 Mk 6.2,3 Lk 6.15
9.6 2 Thess 3.8
9.7 Deut 20.6 Prov 27.18 2 Cor 10.4 2 Tim 4.7 1 Pet 5.2
9.9 Deut 25.4 1 Tim 5.18
9.10 Rom 4.23 2 Tim 2.6
9.12 2 Cor 6.3; 11.7,12
9.13 Lev 6.16 Num 5.9,10
9.14 Mt 10.10 Lk 10.7 1 Tim 5.17
9.15 Acts 18.3; 20.33 2 Cor 11.8-10
9.16 Acts 9.15 Rom 1.14
9.17 Eph 3.1-8 Phil 1.16,17 Col 1.25
9.19 Gal 5.13
9.20 Acts 16.3 21.20-27 Rom 11.14
9.21 Rom 2.8-11 Gal 3.2
9.22 Rom 14.1; 15.1
9.24 Heb 12.1
9.25 1 Tim 6.12 2 Tim 2.5 1 Pet 5.4 Rev 2.10; 3.11

9.5 Cephas is Peter. The brothers of Jesus attained leadership status in the church at Jerusalem. James, for example, led the way to an agreement in the meeting in Acts 15, and wrote the book of James.

9.13 As part of their pay, priests in the temple received a portion of the offerings as their food (see Numbers 18.8–24).

9.16 Preaching the gospel was Paul's gift and calling, and he said he couldn't stop preaching even if he wanted to. He was driven by the desire to do what God wanted, using his gifts for God's glory. What special gifts has God given you? Are you motivated, like Paul, to honor God with your gifts?

9.19–27 In 9.19–22 Paul asserted that he had freedom to do anything; in 9.24–27 he emphasizes a life of strict discipline. The Christian life involves both freedom and discipline. The goal of Paul's life was to glorify God and bring people to Christ. Thus he stayed free of any philosophical position or material entanglement that could sidetrack him, while he strictly disciplined himself to carry out his goal. For Paul, both freedom and discipline were important tools to be used in God's service.

9.22, 23 Paul gives several important principles for ministry: (1) find common ground with those you contact; (2) avoid a know-it-all attitude; (3) make others feel accepted; (4) be sensitive to their needs and concerns; and (5) look for opportunities to tell them about Christ. These principles are just as valid for us as they were for Paul.

9.24–27 Winning a race requires purpose and discipline. Paul uses this illustration to explain that the Christian life takes hard work, self-denial, and grueling preparation. As Christians, we are running toward our heavenly reward. The essential disciplines of prayer, Bible study, and worship equip us to run with vigor and stamina. Don't merely observe from the grandstand; don't just turn out to jog a couple of laps each morning. Train diligently, because your spiritual progress depends upon it.

9.25 At times we must even give up something good in order to do what God wants. Each individual's special duties determine the discipline and denial he must accept. With the goal of pleasing God, our denial seems like nothing compared to the eternal, imperishable reward that will be ours.

9.26 2 Tim 4.7,8 — 26 So I do not run aimlessly, nor do I box as though beating the air; 27 but I punish
9.27 2 Cor 13.5 — my body and enslave it, so that after proclaiming to others I myself should not be
disqualified.

Avoiding idol worship

10.1 Ex 13.21,22; 14.15-22 — **10** I do not want you to be unaware, brothers and sisters,[p] that our ancestors
were all under the cloud, and all passed through the sea, 2 and all were bap-
10.3,4 Ex 16.4,13-15; 17.5,6; Num 20.11; Ps 78.15 — tized into Moses in the cloud and in the sea, 3 and all ate the same spiritual food,
4 and all drank the same spiritual drink. For they drank from the spiritual rock that
followed them, and the rock was Christ. 5 Nevertheless, God was not pleased with
10.5 Num 14.29,37; 26.65 — most of them, and they were struck down in the wilderness.
6 Now these things occurred as examples for us, so that we might not desire evil
10.8 Num 25.1-9 — as they did. 7 Do not become idolaters as some of them did; as it is written, "The
people sat down to eat and drink, and they rose up to play." 8 We must not indulge
10.9 Ex 17.2,7 — in sexual immorality as some of them did, and twenty-three thousand fell in a single
10.10 Heb 10.25 — day. 9 We must not put Christ[q] to the test, as some of them did, and were destroyed
by serpents. 10 And do not complain as some of them did, and were destroyed by the

[p] Gk *brothers* [q] Other ancient authorities read *the Lord*

WHY WE DON'T GIVE UP

Perseverance, persistence, the prize!! The Christian life was never promised as an easy way to live; instead, Paul constantly reminds us that we must have a purpose and a plan because times will be difficult and Satan will attack. But we never persevere without the promise of a prize—a promise God will keep.

Reference	*The Purpose*	*The Plan*	*The Prize*
1 Corinthians 9.24–27	• Run your race to win • Run straight to the goal	• Deny yourself whatever is potentially harmful • Discipline your body, training it	• A heavenly reward that never disappears
Galatians 6.7–10	• Don't get tired of doing right • Don't get discouraged and give up • Be kind to everyone	• Plant the good things of the Spirit	• Reap everlasting life
Ephesians 6.10–20	• Put on all of God's armor • Pray all the time	• Use all the pieces of God's armor provided for you	• Standing safe against all the strategies and tricks of Satan
Philippians 3.12–14	• Keep working for the day when you will be all God wants you to be	• Forget the past, look forward to what lies ahead	• The heavenly prize to which God calls us
2 Timothy 2.3–13	• Teach these great truths to people who will pass them on • Hold on to your faith, even when you feel too weak to have any left	• Take your suffering as a soldier, and don't get tied up in worldly affairs • Follow the Lord's rules, as an athlete must do in order to win • Work hard, like a farmer who tends his fields for the harvest	• We will live with Christ; we will sit and rule with him • He always remains faithful to us and always carries out his promises

9.27 When Paul says he might be declared unfit and ordered to stand aside (disqualified), he does not mean he could lose his salvation, but rather that he could lose his privilege of telling others about Christ. It is easy to tell others how to live and then not to take our own advice. We must be careful to practice what we preach.

10.1ff In chapter 9 Paul used himself as an example of a mature Christian who disciplines himself to better serve God. In chapter 10, he uses Israel as an example of spiritual immaturity shown by their overconfidence and lack of self-discipline.

10.1–5 The cloud and sea mentioned here refer to Israel's escape from slavery in Egypt when God led them by a cloud and brought them safely through the Red Sea (Exodus 14). The spiritual food and drink are the miraculous provisions God gave as they traveled through the wilderness (Exodus 15; 16).

10.2 "Baptized into Moses" means that just as we are united in Christ by baptism, so were the Israelites united under Moses' leadership in the events of the exodus.

10.7–10 The incident referred to in 10.7 is when the Israelites made a golden calf and worshiped it in the wilderness (Exodus 32). The incident in 10.8 is recorded in Numbers 25.1–9 when the Israelites engaged in sexually immoral behavior with Moabite women and worshiped Baal-peor. The reference in 10.9 is to the Israelites complaining about their food (Numbers 21.5, 6). They put God to the test by seeing how far they could go. In 10.10, Paul refers to when the people complained against God (Numbers 14.2, 36). The destroyer is the destroying angel (Exodus 12.23).

destroyer. 11 These things happened to them to serve as an example, and they were
written down to instruct us, on whom the ends of the ages have come. 12 So if you
think you are standing, watch out that you do not fall. 13 No testing has overtaken
you that is not common to everyone. God is faithful, and he will not let you be
tested beyond your strength, but with the testing he will also provide the way out so
that you may be able to endure it.
14 Therefore, my dear friends,[r] flee from the worship of idols. 15 I speak as to
sensible people; judge for yourselves what I say. 16 The cup of blessing that we
bless, is it not a sharing in the blood of Christ? The bread that we break, is it not a
sharing in the body of Christ? 17 Because there is one bread, we who are many are
one body, for we all partake of the one bread. 18 Consider the people of Israel;[s] are
not those who eat the sacrifices partners in the altar? 19 What do I imply then? That
food sacrificed to idols is anything, or that an idol is anything? 20 No, I imply that
what pagans sacrifice, they sacrifice to demons and not to God. I do not want you
to be partners with demons. 21 You cannot drink the cup of the Lord and the cup of
demons. You cannot partake of the table of the Lord and the table of demons. 22 Or
are we provoking the Lord to jealousy? Are we stronger than he?
23 "All things are lawful," but not all things are beneficial. "All things are lawful," but not all things build up. 24 Do not seek your own advantage, but that of the
other. 25 Eat whatever is sold in the meat market without raising any question on the
ground of conscience, 26 for "the earth and its fullness are the Lord's." 27 If an unbeliever invites you to a meal and you are disposed to go, eat whatever is set before
you without raising any question on the ground of conscience. 28 But if someone

10.11 Rom 4.23
10.12 Rom 11.20
10.14 1 Jn 5.21
10.16 Mt 26.26-29 Acts 2.42 1 Cor 11.25-27
10.17 Rom 12.4,5 1 Cor 12.12,13
10.18 Deut 12.17 Lev 7.15
10.20 Deut 32.16,17 Ps 106.36,37
10.21 Isa 65.11 2 Cor 6.15
10.22 Ezek 22.14
10.23 Rom 14.19
10.24 Rom 15.1,2
10.25 1 Tim 4.4
10.26 Ps 24.1; 105.12
10.27 Lk 10.8,9

[r] Gk *my beloved* [s] Gk *Israel according to the flesh*

10.11 Today's pressures make it easy to ignore or forget the lessons of the past. But Paul cautions us to remember the lessons the Israelites learned about God so we can avoid repeating their errors. The key to remembering is to study the Bible regularly so that these lessons remind us how God wants us to live. We need not repeat their mistakes!

10.11 Did Paul think the world was going to end soon? Neither Paul nor even Jesus himself knew when the end of the world would come – God alone knows (Mark 13.32). We have been living in the "ends of the ages" since Christ's ascension. We are to be ready for Christ's return at any moment. Anyone close to Christ feels, with Paul, the urgency of spreading the gospel.

10.13 In a culture filled with moral depravity and pressures, Paul gives strong encouragement to the Corinthians about temptation. He says: (1) wrong desires and temptations happen to everyone, so don't feel you've been singled out; (2) others have resisted temptation, and so can you; (3) any temptation can be resisted, because God will help you resist it. God helps you resist temptation by helping you (1) recognize those people and situations that give you trouble, (2) run from anything you know is wrong, (3) choose to do only what is right, (4) pray for God's help, and (5) seek friends who love God and can offer help when you are tempted. Running from a tempting situation is your first step to victory (see 2 Timothy 2.22).

10.14 Idol worship was the major form of religion in Corinth. There were several pagan temples in the city, and they were very popular. The statues of wood or stone were not bad in themselves, but people gave them credit for what only God could do, such as provide good weather, crops, and children. Idolatry is still a serious problem today, but it takes a different form. We don't put our trust in statues of wood and stone, but in paper money and plastic cards. Trusting anything for what God alone provides is idolatry. Our modern idols are those symbols of power, pleasure, or prestige that we so highly regard. When we understand contemporary parallels to idolatry, Paul's words to "flee from the worship of idols" become much more meaningful.

10.16–21 The idea of unity with God through eating a sacrifice was strong in Judaism and Christianity as well as paganism. In Old Testament days, when a Jew offered a sacrifice, he ate a part of that sacrifice as a way of restoring his unity with God, against whom he had sinned (Deuteronomy 12.17, 18). Similarly, Christians participate in Christ's once-for-all sacrifice when they eat the bread and drink the wine symbolizing his body and blood. Recent converts from paganism could not help being affected if they knowingly ate meat offered to idols.

10.21 As followers of Christ we must give him our total allegiance. We cannot, as Paul explains, eat both at the Lord's table and at the table of demons. Eating at the Lord's table means communing with Christ and identifying with his death. Eating at the demons' table means identifying with Satan by worshiping or promoting heathen (or evil) activities. Are you trying to lead two lives, following the desires of both Christ and the crowd? The Bible says you can't do both at the same time.

10.22–24 Sometimes it's hard to know when to defer to the weaker believer. Paul gives a simple rule of thumb to help in making the decision – we should be sensitive and gracious. While some actions may not be wrong, they may not be in the best interest of others. While we have freedom in Christ, we shouldn't exercise our freedom at the cost of hurting a Christian brother or sister. We are not to consider only ourselves, but we must be sensitive to others. For more on the proper attitude toward a weaker believer, see the notes in 8.10–13 and Romans 14.

10.25–27 Paul gives one answer to the dilemma – to buy whatever meat is sold at the market without asking whether it was offered to idols. It doesn't matter anyway, and no one's conscience will be troubled. When we become too worried about our every action, we become legalistic and cannot enjoy life. Everything belongs to God, and he has given us all things to enjoy. If we know something is a problem, then we can deal with it, but we need not go looking for problems.

10.28–33 Why should we be limited by another person's conscience? Simply because we are to do all things to God's glory, even our eating and drinking. Nothing we do should cause another believer to stumble. We do what is best for others so that they might be saved. On the other hand, Christians should not make a career out of being the weaker person with over-legalistic con-

10.31 Mt 5.15,16 Jn 15.8 Rom 14.6 Phil 1.11
10.32 Acts 24.16 1 Cor 8.13
10.33 Rom 11.14 15.1-2 1 Cor 9.22 13.1-8
11.1 1 Cor 4.16

says to you, "This has been offered in sacrifice," then do not eat it, out of consideration for the one who informed you, and for the sake of conscience — 29 I mean the
other's conscience, not your own. For why should my liberty be subject to the
judgment of someone else's conscience? 30 If I partake with thankfulness, why
should I be denounced because of that for which I give thanks?
31 So, whether you eat or drink, or whatever you do, do everything for the
glory of God. 32 Give no offense to Jews or to Greeks or to the church of God, 33 just
as I try to please everyone in everything I do, not seeking my own advantage, but
11 that of many, so that they may be saved. 1 Be imitators of me, as I am of
Christ.

3. Instruction on public worship

Questions about covering the head in worship

2 I commend you because you remember me in everything and maintain the
traditions just as I handed them on to you. 3 But I want you to understand that Christ

---

MAKING CHOICES IN SENSITIVE ISSUES

If I choose one course of action:
... does it help my witness for Christ? (9.19–22)
... am I motivated by a desire to help others to know Christ? (9.23; 10.33)
... does it help me do my best? (9.25)
... is it against a specific command in Scripture and would thus cause me to sin? (10.12)
... is it best and helpful? (10.23, 33)
... am I thinking only of myself, or do I truly care about the other person? (10.24)
... am I acting lovingly or selfishly? (10.28–31)
... does it glorify God? (10.31)
... will it encourage someone else to sin? (10.32)

All of us make hundreds of choices every day. Most choices have no right or wrong attached to them—like what you wear or what you eat. But we always face decisions that carry a little more weight. We don't want to do wrong, and we don't want to cause others to do wrong, so how can we make such decisions?

---

sciences. Christian leaders and teachers should carefully teach about the freedom we have in matters not expressly forbidden by Scripture.

10.31 God's love must so permeate our motives that all we do is for his glory. Keep this as a guiding principle by asking, "Is this action glorifying God?" or "How can I honor God through this action?"

10.33 Paul's criterion for all his actions was not what he liked best, but what was best for those around him. The opposite attitude would be: (1) being insensitive and doing what we want, no matter who is hurt by it; (2) being oversensitive and doing nothing, for fear someone may be displeased; (3) being a "yes person" by going along with everything, trying to gain approval from people rather than from God. In this age of "me first" and "looking out for number one," Paul's startling statement is a good standard. If we make the good of others one of our primary goals, we will develop a serving attitude that pleases God.

11.1 Why did Paul say, "Be imitators of me"? Paul wasn't being proud – he did not think of himself as sinless. At this time, however, the Corinthian believers did not know much about the life and ministry of Christ. Paul could not tell them to imitate Jesus, because the Gospels had not yet been written, so they did not know what Jesus was like. The best way to point these new Christians to Christ was to point them to a Christian whom they trusted (see also Galatians 4.12; Philippians 3.17; 1 Thessalonians 1.6; 2.14; 2 Thessalonians 3.7, 9). Paul had been in Corinth almost two years and had built a relationship of trust with many of these new believers.

11.1ff In this section Paul's main concern is irreverence in worship. We need to read it in the context of the situation in Corinth. The matter of wearing hats or head coverings, although seemingly insignificant, had become a big problem because two cultural backgrounds were colliding. Jewish women always covered their heads in worship. For a woman to uncover her head in public was a sign of loose morals. On the other hand, Greek women were used to worshiping without head coverings.

In this letter Paul had already spoken about divisions in the church and scruples. Both are involved in this issue. Paul's solution comes from his desire for unity among church members and appropriateness in the worship service. He accepted God's sovereignty in creating the rules for relationships.

11.2–16 This section focuses primarily on attitudes toward worship, not on marriage or the role of women in the church. While Paul's specific instructions may be cultural (women covering their heads in worship), the principles behind his specific instructions are timeless, including respect for spouse, reverence and appropriateness in worship, and focusing all of life on God. If anything you do can easily offend members and divide the church, then change your ways to promote church unity. Thus Paul told the women who were not wearing head coverings to wear them; not because it was a scriptural command, but because it kept the congregation from dividing over a petty issue that served only to take people's minds off Christ.

is the head of every man, and the husband[t] is the head of his wife,[u] and God is the
head of Christ. 4 Any man who prays or prophesies with something on his head
disgraces his head, 5 but any woman who prays or prophesies with her head unveiled disgraces her head—it is one and the same thing as having her head shaved.
6 For if a woman will not veil herself, then she should cut off her hair; but if it is
disgraceful for a woman to have her hair cut off or to be shaved, she should wear
a veil. 7 For a man ought not to have his head veiled, since he is the image and
reflection[v] of God; but woman is the reflection[v] of man. 8 Indeed, man was not
made from woman, but woman from man. 9 Neither was man created for the sake
of woman, but woman for the sake of man. 10 For this reason a woman ought to
have a symbol of[w] authority on her head,[x] because of the angels. 11 Nevertheless,
in the Lord woman is not independent of man or man independent of woman. 12 For
just as woman came from man, so man comes through woman; but all things come
from God. 13 Judge for yourselves: is it proper for a woman to pray to God with her
head unveiled? 14 Does not nature itself teach you that if a man wears long hair, it
is degrading to him, 15 but if a woman has long hair, it is her glory? For her hair is
given to her for a covering. 16 But if anyone is disposed to be contentious—we have
no such custom, nor do the churches of God.

11.3 Gen 3.16; 1 Cor 3.23; 7.17; Gal 4.4; Eph 5.23; Phil 2.7
11.5 Lk 2.36; Acts 21.9
11.6 Num 5.18
11.7 Gen 1.26; Jas 3.9
11.8 Gen 2.21; 1 Tim 2.13
11.9 Gen 2.18
11.12 Rom 11.36
11.13 Lk 12.57
11.16 1 Tim 6.4

Order at the Lord's supper

17 Now in the following instructions I do not commend you, because when you
come together it is not for the better but for the worse. 18 For, to begin with, when
you come together as a church, I hear that there are divisions among you; and to
some extent I believe it. 19 Indeed, there have to be factions among you, for only so
will it become clear who among you are genuine. 20 When you come together, it is
not really to eat the Lord's supper. 21 For when the time comes to eat, each of you

11.18,19 1 Cor 1.10; 2 Pet 2.1; 1 Tim 4.1; 1 Jn 2.19
11.21 Jude 12

[t] The same Greek word means *man* or *husband* [u] Or *head of the woman* [v] Or *glory* [w] Gk lacks *a symbol of*
[x] Or *have freedom of choice regarding her head*

11.3 In the phrase, "the husband is the head of his wife," *head* is not used to indicate control or supremacy, but rather, "the source of." Because man was created first, the woman derives her existence from man, as man does from Christ, and Christ from God. Paul was evidently correcting some excesses in worship that the emancipated Corinthian women had engaged in.

11.3 Submission is a key element in the smooth functioning of any business, government, or family. God ordained submission in certain relationships to prevent chaos. It is essential to understand that submission is not surrender, withdrawal, or apathy. It does not mean inferiority, because God created all people in his image, and all have equal value. Submission is mutual commitment and cooperation.

Thus God calls for submission among *equals.* He did not make the man superior; he made a way for the man and woman to work together. Jesus Christ, although equal with God the Father, submitted to him to carry out the plan for salvation. Likewise, although equal to man under God, the wife should submit to her husband for the sake of their marriage and family. Submission between equals is submission by choice, not by force. We serve God in these relationships by willingly submitting to others in our church, to our spouses, and to our government leaders.

11.9–11 God created lines of authority in order for his created world to function smoothly. Although there must be lines of authority, even in marriage, there should *not* be lines of superiority. God created men and women with unique and complementary characteristics. One sex is not better than the other. We must not let the issue of authority and submission become a wedge to destroy oneness in marriage. Instead, we should use our unique gifts to strengthen our marriages and to glorify God.

11.10 "A woman ought to have a symbol of authority on her head, because of the angels" means that the woman should wear a covering on her head as a sign that she is under the man's authority. This is a fact even the angels understand as they observe Christians in worship. See the note on 11.1ff for an explanation of head coverings.

11.14, 15 In talking about head coverings and length of hair, Paul is saying that believers should look and behave in ways that are honorable within their own culture. In many cultures long hair on men is considered appropriate and masculine. In Corinth, it was thought to be a sign of male prostitution in the pagan temples. And women with short hair were labeled prostitutes. Paul was saying that in the Corinthian culture, Christian women should keep their long hair. If short hair on women was a sign of prostitution, then a Christian woman with short hair would find it even more difficult to be a believable witness for Jesus Christ. Paul wasn't saying we should adopt all the practices of our culture, but that we should avoid appearances and behavior that detract from our ultimate goal of being believable witnesses for Jesus Christ and demonstrating our Christian faith.

11.17–34 The Lord's supper (11.20) is a visible representation of the gospel, the death of Christ for our sins. It reminds us of Christ's death and the glorious hope of his return. It strengthens our faith through fellowship with Christ and with other believers.

11.19 Paul allows that there might be differences ("factions") among church members. When they develop into self-willed divisions, they are destructive to the congregation. Those who cause division only highlight those who are genuine believers.

11.21, 22 When the Lord's supper was celebrated in the early church, it included a feast or fellowship meal followed by communion. In the church in Corinth, the fellowship meal had become a time when some ate and drank excessively while others went hungry. There was little sharing and caring. This certainly did not demonstrate the unity and love that should characterize the church, nor was it a preparation for communion. Paul condemned these

11.22 Lev 19.30; 1 Cor 10.32; Jas 2.6
11.23 Mt 26.26-28; Mk 14.22-24; Lk 22.17-20; 1 Cor 10.16; Gal 1.12
11.25 Lk 22.20; 2 Cor 3.6
11.26 Acts 1.11; Rev 1.7
11.27 Heb 10.29
11.28 Mt 26.20-22; 2 Cor 13.5; Gal 6.4
11.31 1 Jn 1.9; Rev 3.19
11.32 2 Sam 7.14; Job 5.17; Ps 94.12; Amos 3.2; Heb 12.5-7
11.34 1 Cor 4.19

goes ahead with your own supper, and one goes hungry and another becomes
drunk. 22 What! Do you not have homes to eat and drink in? Or do you show contempt for the church of God and humiliate those who have nothing? What should I
say to you? Should I commend you? In this matter I do not commend you!
23 For I received from the Lord what I also handed on to you, that the Lord
Jesus on the night when he was betrayed took a loaf of bread, 24 and when he had
given thanks, he broke it and said, "This is my body that is for[y] you. Do this in
remembrance of me." 25 In the same way he took the cup also, after supper, saying,
"This cup is the new covenant in my blood. Do this, as often as you drink it, in
remembrance of me." 26 For as often as you eat this bread and drink the cup, you
proclaim the Lord's death until he comes.
27 Whoever, therefore, eats the bread or drinks the cup of the Lord in an unworthy manner will be answerable for the body and blood of the Lord. 28 Examine
yourselves, and only then eat of the bread and drink of the cup. 29 For all who eat
and drink[z] without discerning the body,[a] eat and drink judgment against themselves. 30 For this reason many of you are weak and ill, and some have died.[b] 31 But
if we judged ourselves, we would not be judged. 32 But when we are judged by the
Lord, we are disciplined[c] so that we may not be condemned along with the world.
33 So then, my brothers and sisters,[d] when you come together to eat, wait for
one another. 34 If you are hungry, eat at home, so that when you come together, it
will not be for your condemnation. About the other things I will give instructions
when I come.

[y] Other ancient authorities read *is broken for* [z] Other ancient authorities add *in an unworthy manner,* [a] Other ancient authorities read *the Lord's body* [b] Gk *fallen asleep* [c] Or *When we are judged, we are being disciplined by the Lord* [d] Gk *brothers*

---

actions and reminded the church of the real purpose of the Lord's supper.

11.24, 25 What does the Lord's supper mean? The early church remembered that Jesus taught about the Lord's supper on the night of the Passover (Luke 22.13–20). Just as Passover celebrated deliverance from slavery in Egypt, so the Lord's Supper celebrates deliverance from sin by Christ's death.

Christians have several opinions about what Christ meant when he said, "This is my body." (1) Some believe that the wine and bread actually become Christ's physical blood and body. (2) Others believe that the bread and wine remain unchanged, but Christ is spiritually present with the bread and wine. (3) Still others believe that the bread and wine symbolize Christ's body and blood. Christians agree, however, that participating in the Lord's supper is essential to Christian faith and that Christ's presence, however we understand it, strengthens us spiritually.

11.25 What is this new covenant? With the old covenant, people could approach God only through the priests and the sacrificial system. Jesus' death on the cross brought in the new covenant or agreement between God and us. Now all people can personally approach God and communicate with him. The people of Israel first entered into this agreement after their exodus from Egypt (Exodus 24), and it was designed to point to the day when Jesus Christ would come. The new covenant completes, rather than replaces, the old covenant, fulfilling everything the old covenant looked forward to (see Jeremiah 31.31–34). Eating the bread and drinking the cup shows we are remembering Christ's death for us and renewing our commitment to serve him.

11.25 Jesus said, "Do this, as often as you drink it, in remembrance of me." How do we remember Christ in the Lord's supper? By thinking about what he did and why he did it. If the Lord's supper becomes just a ritual or pious habit, it no longer remembers Christ, and it loses its significance.

11.27ff Paul gave specific instructions on how the Lord's supper should be observed. (1) We should take the Lord's supper thoughtfully because we are proclaiming that Christ died for our sins (11.26). (2) We should take it worthily with due reverence and respect (11.29). (3) We should examine ourselves for any unconfessed sin or resentful attitudes (11.28). We are to be prepared and ready, based on our belief in and love for Christ. (4) We should be considerate of others (11.33), waiting until everyone is present and eating in an orderly and unified manner.

11.27–34 When Paul said no one should take the Lord's supper in an unworthy manner, he was speaking to the church members who were rushing into it without thinking of its meaning. Those who did so were "answerable for the body and blood of the Lord." This means instead of honoring his sacrifice, they were sharing in the guilt of those who crucified Christ. In reality, *no one* is worthy to take the Lord's supper. We are all sinners saved by grace. This is why we should prepare ourselves for communion through healthy introspection, confession of sin, and resolution of differences with others. These actions remove the barriers to our relationship with Christ and with other believers. Awareness of your sin should not keep you away from communion but should drive you to it.

11.29 "Without discerning the body" means not understanding what the Lord's supper means and not distinguishing it from a normal meal. He who does so condemns himself (see 11.27).

11.30 That some of the people had died may have been a special supernatural judgment on the Corinthian church. It highlights the seriousness of the communion service. The Lord's supper is not to be taken lightly; this new agreement cost Jesus his life. It is not a meaningless ritual, but a sacrament given by Christ to help strengthen our faith.

11.34 People should come to this meal desiring to fellowship with other believers and prepare for the Lord's supper to follow, not coming to fill up on a big dinner. "If you are hungry, eat at home" means that they should eat dinner beforehand, so as to come to the fellowship meal in the right frame of mind.

Paul teaches about spiritual gifts

12 Now concerning spiritual gifts,[e] brothers and sisters,[f] I do not want you to **12.1**
be uninformed. 2 You know that when you were pagans, you were enticed 1 Cor 14.1 **12.2**
and led astray to idols that could not speak. 3 Therefore I want you to understand Isa 46.7
that no one speaking by the Spirit of God ever says "Let Jesus be cursed!" and no **12.3**
one can say "Jesus is Lord" except by the Holy Spirit. Rom 10.9 1 Jn 4.2
4 Now there are varieties of gifts, but the same Spirit; 5 and there are varieties of **12.4**
services, but the same Lord; 6 and there are varieties of activities, but it is the same Eph 4.4
God who activates all of them in everyone. 7 To each is given the manifestation of **12.6** Eph 1.23
the Spirit for the common good. 8 To one is given through the Spirit the utterance
of wisdom, and to another the utterance of knowledge according to the same Spirit, **12.9**
9 to another faith by the same Spirit, to another gifts of healing by the one Spirit, Mt 17.19,20
10 to another the working of miracles, to another prophecy, to another the discern- **12.10** Acts 2.4
ment of spirits, to another various kinds of tongues, to another the interpretation of 1 Jn 4.1
tongues. 11 All these are activated by one and the same Spirit, who allots to each **12.11** Rom 12.6-8
one individually just as the Spirit chooses. Eph 4.7

Believers are the body of Christ

12 For just as the body is one and has many members, and all the members of **12.12**
the body, though many, are one body, so it is with Christ. 13 For in the one Spirit Rom 12.4 1 Cor 10.17
we were all baptized into one body—Jews or Greeks, slaves or free—and we were 12.27
all made to drink of one Spirit. **12.13** Jn 6.63; 7.37-39
14 Indeed, the body does not consist of one member but of many. 15 If the foot Rom 6.5
would say, "Because I am not a hand, I do not belong to the body," that would not Gal 3.27,28 Eph 2.13-16,18
make it any less a part of the body. 16 And if the ear would say, "Because I am not Col 3.11
an eye, I do not belong to the body," that would not make it any less a part of the
body. 17 If the whole body were an eye, where would the hearing be? If the whole

[e] Or *spiritual persons* [f] Gk *brothers*

12.1ff The spiritual gifts given to each person by the Holy Spirit are special abilities that are to be used to minister to the needs of the body of believers. This chapter is not an exhaustive list of spiritual gifts (see Romans 12; Ephesians 4; 1 Peter 4.10, 11 for more examples). There are many gifts. People have different gifts; some people have more than one gift, and one gift is not superior to another. They all come from the Holy Spirit, and their purpose is to build up Christ's body, the church.

12.1ff Instead of building and unifying the Corinthian church, spiritual gifts were splitting it. They had become symbols of spiritual power, causing rivalries because some thought they were more "spiritual" than others according to their gifts. This was a terrible misuse of spiritual gifts, because their purpose is always to help the church function more effectively, not to divide it. We can be divisive if we insist on using our gift our own way without being sensitive to others. We must never use gifts as a means of manipulating others or serving our own self-esteem.

12.3 Anyone can claim to speak for God, and the world is full of false teachers. Paul gives us a test to help us discern whether or not a messenger is really from God: does he or she confess Christ as Lord? Don't naively accept the words of all who claim to speak for God; test their credentials by finding what they teach about Christ.

12.9 All Christians have faith. Some, however, have the spiritual gift of faith which is an unusual measure of trust in the Holy Spirit's power.

12.10, 11 "Prophecy" is not just predicting the future; it can also mean preaching God's Word with power. "Discernment of spirits" means the ability to discern whether a person who claims to speak for God is doing so, or is speaking by an evil spirit. (Paul discusses tongues and their interpretation in more detail in chapter 14.) No matter what gift(s) a person has, each gift is given by the Holy Spirit. "Allots to each one individually" means that the Holy Spirit decides which gifts each one of us should have. We are responsible to sharpen and use our gifts, but we can take no credit for what God has freely given us.

12.12 Paul compares the body of Christ to a human body. Each part has a specific function that is necessary to the body as a whole. The parts are different for a purpose, and in their differences they must work together. Christians must avoid two common errors: (1) being too proud of their abilities, or (2) thinking they have nothing to give to the body of believers. Instead of comparing ourselves to one another, we must use our different gifts, together, to spread the good news of salvation.

12.13 The church is composed of many types of people from a variety of backgrounds with a multitude of gifts and abilities. It is easy for these differences to divide people, as was the case in Corinth. But despite the differences, all believers have one thing in common—faith in Christ. On this essential truth the church finds unity. All believers are baptized by one Holy Spirit into one body of believers, the church. We don't lose our individual identities, but we have an overriding oneness in Christ. When a person becomes a Christian, the Holy Spirit takes up residence, and he or she is born into God's family. "To drink of one Spirit" means that the same Holy Spirit completely fills our innermost beings. As members of God's family, we may have different interests and gifts, but we have a common goal.

12.14–24 Using the analogy of the body, Paul emphasizes the importance of each church member (see the note on 12.12). If a seemingly insignificant part is taken away, the whole body becomes less effective. Thinking that your gift is more important than someone else's is spiritual pride. We should not look down on those who seem unimportant, and we should not be jealous of others who have impressive gifts. Instead, we must use the gifts we have been given and encourage others to use theirs. If we don't, the body of believers will be less effective.

body were hearing, where would the sense of smell be? 18 But as it is, God arranged
the members in the body, each one of them, as he chose. 19 If all were a single
member, where would the body be? 20 As it is, there are many members, yet one
body. 21 The eye cannot say to the hand, "I have no need of you," nor again the head
to the feet, "I have no need of you." 22 On the contrary, the members of the body
that seem to be weaker are indispensable, 23 and those members of the body that we
think less honorable we clothe with greater honor, and our less respectable members are treated with greater respect; 24 whereas our more respectable members do
not need this. But God has so arranged the body, giving the greater honor to the
inferior member, 25 that there may be no dissension within the body, but the members may have the same care for one another. 26 If one member suffers, all suffer
together with it; if one member is honored, all rejoice together with it.

27 Now you are the body of Christ and individually members of it. 28 And God
has appointed in the church first apostles, second prophets, third teachers; then
deeds of power, then gifts of healing, forms of assistance, forms of leadership,
various kinds of tongues. 29 Are all apostles? Are all prophets? Are all teachers? Do
all work miracles? 30 Do all possess gifts of healing? Do all speak in tongues? Do
all interpret? 31 But strive for the greater gifts. And I will show you a still more
excellent way.

The characteristics of love

13 If I speak in the tongues of mortals and of angels, but do not have love, I am
a noisy gong or a clanging cymbal. 2 And if I have prophetic powers, and
understand all mysteries and all knowledge, and if I have all faith, so as to remove
mountains, but do not have love, I am nothing. 3 If I give away all my possessions,
and if I hand over my body so that I may boast,[g] but do not have love, I gain
nothing.

4 Love is patient; love is kind; love is not envious or boastful or arrogant 5 or
rude. It does not insist on its own way; it is not irritable or resentful; 6 it does not
rejoice in wrongdoing, but rejoices in the truth. 7 It bears all things, believes all
things, hopes all things, endures all things.

8 Love never ends. But as for prophecies, they will come to an end; as for
tongues, they will cease; as for knowledge, it will come to an end. 9 For we know
only in part, and we prophesy only in part; 10 but when the complete comes, the
partial will come to an end. 11 When I was a child, I spoke like a child, I thought like
a child, I reasoned like a child; when I became an adult, I put an end to childish
ways. 12 For now we see in a mirror, dimly,[h] but then we will see face to face. Now

12.18 Rom 12.6; 1 Cor 12.28
12.27 Rom 12.4,5; 1 Cor 12.12; Eph 1.22,23; 4.12; 5.23,30; Col 1.24
12.28 Num 11.16,17; Acts 13.1; Rom 12.6-8; Eph 2.20; 3.5; 4.11; 1 Tim 5.17; Heb 13.17
12.31 1 Cor 14.1-39
13.1 1 Tim 1.5
13.2 Mk 17.20; Lk 17.6
13.3 Mt 6.1,2
13.4 1 Pet 4.8
13.5 Phil 2.4; 4.8
13.6 Ps 10.3; Prov 10.12; 2 Thess 2.12
13.7 Gal 6.2
13.10 Isa 60.19; Jer 31.34
13.12 2 Cor 3.18; 5.7; 1 Jn 3.2

[g] Other ancient authorities read *body to be burned* [h] Gk *in a riddle*

12.25, 26 What is your response when a fellow Christian is honored? How do you respond when someone is suffering? We are called to rejoice with those who rejoice and weep with those who weep (Romans 12.15). Too often, unfortunately, we are jealous of those who rejoice and separate ourselves from those who weep. Believers are in the world together – there is no such thing as private or individualistic Christianity. We shouldn't stop with enjoying only our own relationship with God; we need to get involved in the lives of others.

12.30 Paul discusses the subject of speaking in and interpreting tongues in more detail in chapter 14.

12.31 The greater gifts are those that are more beneficial to the body of Christ. Paul has already made it clear that one gift is not superior to another, but he urges the believers to discover how they can serve Christ's body with the gifts God has given them. Your spiritual gifts are not for your own self-advancement. They were given to you for serving God and enhancing the spiritual growth of the body of believers.

13.1ff In chapter 12 Paul gave evidence of the Corinthians' lack of love; chapter 13 defines real love; and chapter 14 shows how love works. Love is more important than all the spiritual gifts exercised in the church body. Great faith, acts of dedication or sacrifice, and miracle-working power produce very little without love. Love makes our actions and gifts useful. Although people have different gifts, love is available to everyone.

13.4–7 Our society confuses love and lust. Unlike lust, God's kind of love is directed outward toward others, not inward toward ourselves. It is utterly unselfish. This love is not natural. It is possible only if God helps us set aside our own desires and instincts, so we can give love while expecting nothing in return. Thus the closer we come to Christ, the more love we will show to others.

13.10 God gives us spiritual gifts for life on earth in order to build up, serve, and strengthen fellow Christians. The spiritual gifts are for the church. In eternity, we will be made perfect and complete and will be in the very presence of God. We will no longer need the spiritual gifts, so they will come to an end.

13.12 Paul offers a glimpse into the future to give us hope that one day we will be complete when we see God face to face. This truth should strengthen our faith – we don't have all the answers now, but then we will. Someday we will see Christ in person and be able to see with God's perspective.

I know only in part; then I will know fully, even as I have been fully known. 13 And
now faith, hope, and love abide, these three; and the greatest of these is love.

Paul teaches about the gifts of prophecy and tongues

14 Pursue love and strive for the spiritual gifts, and especially that you may
prophesy. 2 For those who speak in a tongue do not speak to other people but
to God; for nobody understands them, since they are speaking mysteries in the
Spirit. 3 On the other hand, those who prophesy speak to other people for their
upbuilding and encouragement and consolation. 4 Those who speak in a tongue
build up themselves, but those who prophesy build up the church. 5 Now I would
like all of you to speak in tongues, but even more to prophesy. One who prophesies
is greater than one who speaks in tongues, unless someone interprets, so that the
church may be built up.
6 Now, brothers and sisters,[i] if I come to you speaking in tongues, how will I
benefit you unless I speak to you in some revelation or knowledge or prophecy or
teaching? 7 It is the same way with lifeless instruments that produce sound, such as
the flute or the harp. If they do not give distinct notes, how will anyone know what
is being played? 8 And if the bugle gives an indistinct sound, who will get ready for
battle? 9 So with yourselves; if in a tongue you utter speech that is not intelligible,
how will anyone know what is being said? For you will be speaking into the air.
10 There are doubtless many different kinds of sounds in the world, and nothing is
without sound. 11 If then I do not know the meaning of a sound, I will be a foreigner
to the speaker and the speaker a foreigner to me. 12 So with yourselves; since you
are eager for spiritual gifts, strive to excel in them for building up the church.
13 Therefore, one who speaks in a tongue should pray for the power to interpret. 14 For if I pray in a tongue, my spirit prays but my mind is unproductive.
15 What should I do then? I will pray with the spirit, but I will pray with the mind
also; I will sing praise with the spirit, but I will sing praise with the mind also.
16 Otherwise, if you say a blessing with the spirit, how can anyone in the position
of an outsider say the "Amen" to your thanksgiving, since the outsider does not
know what you are saying? 17 For you may give thanks well enough, but the other
person is not built up. 18 I thank God that I speak in tongues more than all of you;
19 nevertheless, in church I would rather speak five words with my mind, in order
to instruct others also, than ten thousand words in a tongue.

[i] Gk *brothers*

13.13 Mt 22.37-39
14.1 Lev 19.18; Num 11.25; Mt 22.37-40; Mk 12.29-31; Rom 12.6; 13.8-10; 1 Cor 12.1; Gal 5.14; Eph 5.2; Col 3.14; 1 Tim 1.5; Jas 2.8
14.2 Mk 16.17; Acts 2.4; 10.46,47; 19.6
14.3 Rom 14.19
14.4 1 Cor 12.10,30; 14.18,19,26-28
14.6 Rom 6.17; 1 Cor 12.8; 13.2; Eph 1.16,17
14.8 Num 10.9; Jer 4.19; Ezek 33.2-6; Joel 2.1
14.12 Rom 14.19
14.13 1 Cor 12.10
14.15 Ps 47.6,7; Eph 5.19; Col 3.16
14.16 1 Chron 16.36; Neh 5.13; 8.6; Ps 106.48
14.17 Rom 14.19

13.13 In morally corrupt Corinth, love had become a mixed-up term with little meaning. Today people are still confused about love. Love is the greatest of all human qualities, and it is an attribute of God himself (1 John 4.8). It involves unselfish service to others; it gives evidence that you care. *Faith* is the foundation and content of God's message; *hope* is the attitude and focus; *love* is the action. When faith and hope are in line, you are free to love completely because you understand how God loved.

14.1 Prophecy may involve predicting future events, but its main purpose is to communicate God's Word to people, providing insight, warning, correction, and encouragement.

14.2 The gift of speaking in unknown tongues was a concern of the Corinthian church because it had caused disorder in worship. Speaking in tongues is a legitimate gift of the Holy Spirit, but the Corinthian believers were using it as a sign of spiritual superiority rather than as a means to spiritual unity. Spiritual gifts are beneficial only when they are properly used to help everyone in the church. We should not exercise them only to make *ourselves* feel good.

14.2ff Paul makes several points about speaking in tongues: (1) it is a spiritual gift from God (14.2); (2) it is a desirable gift even though it isn't a requirement of faith (12.28–31); (3) it is less important than prophecy and teaching (14.4). Although Paul himself spoke in tongues, he stresses prophecy (preaching) because it benefits the whole church, while speaking in tongues primarily benefits the speaker. Public worship must be understandable and beneficial to the whole church.

14.5–12 As musical instruments must play each note for the music to be clear, so Paul said words preached in the hearers' language are more clear and helpful. There are many languages in the world (14.10), and people who speak different languages can rarely understand each other. So it is with speaking in tongues. Although this gift is helpful to many for private worship, and helpful for public worship with interpretation, Paul says he would rather speak five words that his hearers can understand than 10,000 that they cannot (14.19).

14.13–20 If a person has the gift of speaking in tongues, he should also pray for the gift of knowing what he has said (interpretation) so he can tell people afterwards. This way, the entire church is helped by this gift.

14.15 There is a proper place for the intellect in Christianity. In praying and singing, both the mind and the spirit are to be fully engaged. When we sing, we should also think about the meaning of the words. When we pour out our feelings to God in prayer, we should also think. True Christianity is neither barren intellectualism nor thoughtless emotionalism. See also Ephesians 1.17, 18; Philippians 1.9–11; Colossians 1.9.

14.20 Mt 11.25 Rom 16.19 Eph 4.14 Heb 5.12
14.21 Isa 28.11 Jn 10.34
14.22 1 Cor 14.1
14.23 Acts 2.12,13
14.24 1 Cor 14.1
14.25 Isa 45.14 Zech 8.23 Heb 4.12,13

20 Brothers and sisters,[j] do not be children in your thinking; rather, be infants
in evil, but in thinking be adults. 21 In the law it is written,

"By people of strange tongues
and by the lips of foreigners
I will speak to this people;
yet even then they will not listen to me,"

says the Lord. 22 Tongues, then, are a sign not for believers but for unbelievers,
while prophecy is not for unbelievers but for believers. 23 If, therefore, the whole
church comes together and all speak in tongues, and outsiders or unbelievers enter,
will they not say that you are out of your mind? 24 But if all prophesy, an unbeliever
or outsider who enters is reproved by all and called to account by all. 25 After the
secrets of the unbeliever's heart are disclosed, that person will bow down before
God and worship him, declaring, "God is really among you."

Worship in an orderly way

14.26 Rom 14.19 1 Cor 12.8-10 14.2-6 Eph 4.12-13 5.19
14.27 1 Cor 12.10 14.2,5,13 1 Thess 5.20,21
14.31 Rom 12.6
14.32 1 Jn 4.1
14.33 1 Cor 4.17; 7.17
14.34 1 Cor 11.3,16 1 Tim 2.11 Tit 2.5 1 Pet 3.1
14.36 Isa 2.3
14.37 1 Cor 2.15 2 Cor 10.7 1 Jn 4.6
14.39 1 Cor 12.31 1 Thess 5.20

26 What should be done then, my friends?[j] When you come together, each one
has a hymn, a lesson, a revelation, a tongue, or an interpretation. Let all things be
done for building up. 27 If anyone speaks in a tongue, let there be only two or at
most three, and each in turn; and let one interpret. 28 But if there is no one to interpret, let them be silent in church and speak to themselves and to God. 29 Let two or
three prophets speak, and let the others weigh what is said. 30 If a revelation is made
to someone else sitting nearby, let the first person be silent. 31 For you can all
prophesy one by one, so that all may learn and all be encouraged. 32 And the spirits
of prophets are subject to the prophets, 33 for God is a God not of disorder but of
peace.

(As in all the churches of the saints, 34 women should be silent in the churches.
For they are not permitted to speak, but should be subordinate, as the law also says.
35 If there is anything they desire to know, let them ask their husbands at home. For
it is shameful for a woman to speak in church.[k] 36 Or did the word of God originate
with you? Or are you the only ones it has reached?)

37 Anyone who claims to be a prophet, or to have spiritual powers, must acknowledge that what I am writing to you is a command of the Lord. 38 Anyone who
does not recognize this is not to be recognized. 39 So, my friends,[l] be eager to
prophesy, and do not forbid speaking in tongues; 40 but all things should be done
decently and in order.

[j] Gk *brothers* [k] Other ancient authorities put verses 34-35 after verse 40 [l] Gk *my brothers*

14.22–25 The way the Corinthians were speaking in tongues was helping no one because believers did not understand what was being said, and unbelievers thought the people speaking in tongues were crazy. Speaking in tongues was supposed to be a *sign* to unbelievers (as it was in Acts 2). After speaking in tongues, believers were supposed to explain what was said and give the credit to God. The unsaved people would then be convinced of a spiritual reality and motivated to search the Christian faith further. While this is one way to reach unbelievers, Paul says that clear preaching is usually better (14.5).

14.26ff Everything done in worship services must be beneficial to the worshipers. This principle touches every aspect – singing, preaching, and the exercise of spiritual gifts. Those contributing to the service (singers, speakers, readers) must have love as their chief motivation, giving useful words or help that will strengthen the faith of other believers.

14.33 In worship, everything must be done in harmony and with order. Even when the gifts of the Holy Spirit are being exercised, there is no excuse for disorder. When there is chaos, the church is not allowing God to work among the believers as he would like.

14.34, 35 Does this mean that women should not speak in church services today? It is clear from 11.5 that women prayed and prophesied in public worship. It is also clear in chapters 12 – 14 that women have spiritual gifts, and they are encouraged to exercise them in the body of Christ. Women have much to contribute and can participate in worship services.

In the Corinthian culture, women were not allowed to confront men in public. Apparently some of the women who had become Christians thought their Christian freedom gave them the right to question the men in public worship. This was causing division in the church. In addition, women of that day did not receive formal religious education as did the men. Women may have been raising questions in the worship service which could have been answered at home without disrupting the church service. Paul was asking the women not to flaunt their Christian freedom during the worship service. The purpose of Paul's words was to promote unity, not to teach about women's role in the church.

14.40 Worship is vital to the life of an individual and to the whole church. Our church services should be conducted in an orderly way so that we can worship, be taught, and be prepared to serve God. Those who are responsible for planning worship should make sure it has order and direction rather than chaos and confusion.

4. Instruction on the resurrection

The resurrection of Christ

15 Now I would remind you, brothers and sisters,[m] of the good news[n] that I
proclaimed to you, which you in turn received, in which also you stand,
2 through which also you are being saved, if you hold firmly to the message that I
proclaimed to you—unless you have come to believe in vain.
3 For I handed on to you as of first importance what I in turn had received: that
Christ died for our sins in accordance with the scriptures, 4 and that he was buried,
and that he was raised on the third day in accordance with the scriptures, 5 and that
he appeared to Cephas, then to the twelve. 6 Then he appeared to more than five
hundred brothers and sisters[m] at one time, most of whom are still alive, though
some have died.[o] 7 Then he appeared to James, then to all the apostles. 8 Last of all,
as to one untimely born, he appeared also to me. 9 For I am the least of the apostles,
unfit to be called an apostle, because I persecuted the church of God. 10 But by the
grace of God I am what I am, and his grace toward me has not been in vain. On the
contrary, I worked harder than any of them—though it was not I, but the grace of
God that is with me. 11 Whether then it was I or they, so we proclaim and so you
have come to believe.

15.3 Isa 53.5 Lk 24.25-27 1 Pet 2.24
15.4 Lk 24.25-27
15.5 Mk 16.14 Lk 24.34,35 Jn 20.19
15.6 Lk 24.13-31,36 Jn 20.19,26,30
15.8 Acts 9.3-12
15.9 Acts 8.3 2 Cor 12.11 Eph 3.8
15.10 2 Cor 11.23 Eph 2.7 1 Tim 4.10

The resurrection of the dead

12 Now if Christ is proclaimed as raised from the dead, how can some of you
say there is no resurrection of the dead? 13 If there is no resurrection of the dead,
then Christ has not been raised; 14 and if Christ has not been raised, then our proclamation has been in vain and your faith has been in vain. 15 We are even found to be
misrepresenting God, because we testified of God that he raised Christ—whom he
did not raise if it is true that the dead are not raised. 16 For if the dead are not raised,
then Christ has not been raised. 17 If Christ has not been raised, your faith is futile
and you are still in your sins. 18 Then those also who have died[o] in Christ have
perished. 19 If for this life only we have hoped in Christ, we are of all people most
to be pitied.

15.12 2 Tim 2.18
15.13 1 Thess 4.14
15.17 Rom 4.25
15.18 1 Thess 4.16
15.19 2 Tim 3.12

[m] Gk *brothers* [n] Or *gospel* [o] Gk *fallen asleep*

15.2 Most churches have people who do not yet believe. Some are moving in the direction of belief, and others are simply pretending. Imposters, however, are not to be removed (see Matthew 13.28, 29), for that is the Lord's work alone. The good news about Jesus Christ saves us *if* we firmly believe it and faithfully follow it.

15.5–8 There will always be people who say that Jesus didn't rise from the dead. Paul assures us that many people saw Jesus after his resurrection: Peter (Cephas); the disciples; more than 500 Christian believers (most of whom were still alive, although some had died); James (Jesus' brother); all the apostles; and finally Paul himself. The resurrection is an historical fact. Don't be discouraged by doubters who deny the resurrection. Be filled with hope because of the knowledge that one day you, and they, will see the living proof when Christ returns. (For more evidence on the resurrection, see the chart in Mark 16.)

15.7 This James is Jesus' brother, who at first did not believe Jesus was the Messiah (John 7.5). After seeing the resurrected Christ, he became a believer and ultimately a leader of the church in Jerusalem (Acts 15.13). He wrote the New Testament book of James.

15.8, 9 Paul's most important credential to be an apostle was that he was an eyewitness of the risen Christ (see Acts 9.3–6). "Untimely born" means he was a special case. The other apostles saw Christ in the flesh. But Paul was in the next generation of believers—yet Christ appeared to him.

15.9, 10 As a zealous Pharisee, Paul had been an enemy of the Christian church—even to the point of capturing and persecuting believers (see Acts 9.1–3). Thus he felt unworthy to be called an apostle (a chosen messenger) of Christ. Though the most influential of the apostles, Paul was deeply humble. He knew he had worked hard and accomplished much, but only because God had poured kindness and grace (unmerited favor) upon him. True humility is not convincing yourself that you are worthless, but recognizing God's work in you. It is having God's perspective on who you are and acknowledging his grace in developing your abilities.

15.10 Paul speaks of working harder than the other apostles. This was not an arrogant boast because he knew that his power came from God and that it didn't matter who worked hardest. Because of his prominent position as a Pharisee, Paul's conversion made him the object of even greater persecution than the other apostles, thus he had to work harder to preach the same message.

15.12ff Most Greeks did not believe that people's bodies would be resurrected after death. They saw the afterlife as something that happened only to the soul. According to Greek philosophers, the soul was the real person, imprisoned in a physical body, and at death the soul was released. There was no immortality for the body, but the soul entered an eternal state. Christianity, by contrast, affirms that the body and soul will be united after resurrection. The church at Corinth was in the heart of Greek culture. Thus many believers had a difficult time believing in a bodily resurrection. Paul wrote this part of his letter to clear up this confusion about the resurrection.

15.13–18 The resurrection of Christ is the center of the Christian faith. Because Christ rose from the dead as he promised, we know that what he said is true—he is God. Because he rose, we have certainty that our sins are forgiven. Because he rose, he lives and represents us to God. Because he rose and defeated death, we know we will also rise.

15.19 Why does Paul say believers should be pitied if there were

15.20 Col 1.18
15.21 Rom 5.12
15.22 Rom 5.14-18
15.23 1 Thess 4.15-17
15.24 Dan 7.14; 2 Cor 4.14
15.25 Ps 110.1; Heb 1.13
15.26 Heb 2.14; Rev 1.18; 20.14; 21.4
15.27 Ps 8.6; Eph 1.22; Heb 2.8
15.28 1 Cor 3.23; 11.3; Phil 3.21
15.30 2 Cor 11.26
15.31 2 Cor 4.10
15.32 1 Cor 16.8; 2 Cor 1.8
15.34 Eph 5.14; 1 Cor 6.5

20 But in fact Christ has been raised from the dead, the first fruits of those who
have died.[p] 21 For since death came through a human being, the resurrection of the
dead has also come through a human being; 22 for as all die in Adam, so all will be
made alive in Christ. 23 But each in his own order: Christ the first fruits, then at his
coming those who belong to Christ. 24 Then comes the end,[q] when he hands over
the kingdom to God the Father, after he has destroyed every ruler and every authority and power. 25 For he must reign until he has put all his enemies under his
feet. 26 The last enemy to be destroyed is death. 27 For "God[r] has put all things in
subjection under his feet." But when it says, "All things are put in subjection," it is
plain that this does not include the one who put all things in subjection under him.
28 When all things are subjected to him, then the Son himself will also be subjected
to the one who put all things in subjection under him, so that God may be all in all.
29 Otherwise, what will those people do who receive baptism on behalf of the
dead? If the dead are not raised at all, why are people baptized on their behalf?
30 And why are we putting ourselves in danger every hour? 31 I die every day!
That is as certain, brothers and sisters,[s] as my boasting of you—a boast that I
make in Christ Jesus our Lord. 32 If with merely human hopes I fought with wild
animals at Ephesus, what would I have gained by it? If the dead are not raised,

"Let us eat and drink,
for tomorrow we die."

33 Do not be deceived:

"Bad company ruins good morals."

34 Come to a sober and right mind, and sin no more; for some people have no knowledge of God. I say this to your shame.

The resurrection body

35 But someone will ask, "How are the dead raised? With what kind of body do

[p] Gk *fallen asleep* [q] Or *Then come the rest* [r] Gk *he* [s] Gk *brothers*

---

only earthly value to Christianity? In Paul's day, Christianity often brought a person persecution, ostracism from family, and, in many cases, poverty. There were few tangible benefits for being a Christian in that society. It was certainly not a step up the social or career ladder. Even more important, however, is the fact that if Christ had not been resurrected from death, Christians could not be forgiven for their sins and would have no hope of eternal life.

15.20 First fruits were the first part of the harvest that faithful Jews brought to the temple as an offering (Leviticus 23.10ff). Although Christ was not the first to rise from the dead (he raised Lazarus and others), he was the first to never die again. He is the forerunner for us, the proof of our eventual resurrection to eternal life.

15.21 Death came into the world as a result of Adam and Eve's sin. In Romans 5.12–21, Paul explained why Adam's sin brought sin to all people, how death and sin spread to all humans because of this first sin, and the parallel between Adam's death and Christ's death.

15.24–28 This is not a chronological sequence of events, and no specific time for these events is given. Paul's point is that the resurrected Christ will conquer all evil, including death. See Revelation 20.14 for the final destruction of death.

15.25–28 Although God the Father and God the Son are equal, each has a special work to do and area of sovereign control (15.28). Christ is not inferior to the Father, but his work is to defeat all evil on earth. First he defeated sin and death on the cross; and in the final days, he will defeat Satan and all evil. World events may seem out of control and justice may seem scarce. But God is in control, allowing evil to remain for a time until he sends Jesus to earth again. Then Christ will present to God a perfect new world.

15.29 Some believers were baptized on behalf of others who had died unbaptized. Nothing more is known about this practice, but it affirms a belief in resurrection. Paul is not approving it, but is illustrating his argument that the resurrection is a reality.

15.30–34 If death ended it all, enjoying the moment would be all that matters. But Christians know that there is life beyond the grave and that our life on earth is only a preparation for our life that will never end. What you do today matters for eternity. In light of eternity, sin is a foolish gamble.

15.31, 32 "I die every day" refers to Paul's daily exposure to danger. There is no evidence that Paul actually "fought with wild animals at Ephesus," but rather he was referring to the savage opposition he had faced.

15.33 Keeping company with those who deny the resurrection could corrupt good Christian character. Don't let your relationships with unbelievers lead you away from Christ or cause your faith to waver.

15.35ff Paul launches into a discussion about what our resurrected bodies will be like. If you could select your own body, what kind would you choose—strong, athletic, beautiful? Paul explains that we will be recognized in our resurrected bodies, yet they will be better than we can imagine, for they will be made to live forever. We will still have our own personalities and individualities, but these will be perfected through Christ's work. The Bible does not reveal everything that our resurrected bodies will be able to do, but we know they will be perfect, without sickness or disease (see Philippians 3.21).

15.35ff Paul compares the resurrection of our bodies with the growth in a garden. Seeds placed in the ground don't grow unless they "die" first. The plant that grows is very different looking from the seed, because God gives it a new "body." There are different kinds of bodies—people, animals, fish, birds. Even the angels in heaven have bodies that are different in beauty and glory. Our resurrected bodies will be very different in some ways, but not all, from our earthly bodies.

they come?" 36 Fool! What you sow does not come to life unless it dies. 37 And as
for what you sow, you do not sow the body that is to be, but a bare seed, perhaps
of wheat or of some other grain. 38 But God gives it a body as he has chosen, and
to each kind of seed its own body. 39 Not all flesh is alike, but there is one flesh for
human beings, another for animals, another for birds, and another for fish. 40 There
are both heavenly bodies and earthly bodies, but the glory of the heavenly is one
thing, and that of the earthly is another. 41 There is one glory of the sun, and another
glory of the moon, and another glory of the stars; indeed, star differs from star in
glory.

42 So it is with the resurrection of the dead. What is sown is perishable, what
is raised is imperishable. 43 It is sown in dishonor, it is raised in glory. It is sown in
weakness, it is raised in power. 44 It is sown a physical body, it is raised a spiritual
body. If there is a physical body, there is also a spiritual body. 45 Thus it is written,
"The first man, Adam, became a living being"; the last Adam became a life-giving
spirit. 46 But it is not the spiritual that is first, but the physical, and then the
spiritual. 47 The first man was from the earth, a man of dust; the second man is[t]
from heaven. 48 As was the man of dust, so are those who are of the dust; and as is
the man of heaven, so are those who are of heaven. 49 Just as we have borne the
image of the man of dust, we will[u] also bear the image of the man of heaven.

50 What I am saying, brothers and sisters,[v] is this: flesh and blood cannot inherit the kingdom of God, nor does the perishable inherit the imperishable. 51 Listen, I will tell you a mystery! We will not all die,[w] but we will all be changed, 52 in
a moment, in the twinkling of an eye, at the last trumpet. For the trumpet will
sound, and the dead will be raised imperishable, and we will be changed. 53 For this
perishable body must put on imperishability, and this mortal body must put on
immortality. 54 When this perishable body puts on imperishability, and this mortal
body puts on immortality, then the saying that is written will be fulfilled:

"Death has been swallowed up in victory."
55 "Where, O death, is your victory?
Where, O death, is your sting?"

56 The sting of death is sin, and the power of sin is the law. 57 But thanks be to God,
who gives us the victory through our Lord Jesus Christ.

58 Therefore, my beloved,[x] be steadfast, immovable, always excelling in the
work of the Lord, because you know that in the Lord your labor is not in vain.

15.36 Jn 12.23,24
15.38 Gen 1.11 Ps 104.14
15.42 Dan 12.3 Mt 13.43 1 Cor 15.50
15.43 Phil 3.21 Col 3.4
15.45 Gen 2.7 Jn 5.21 Rom 8.2 2 Cor 3.17 Col 3.4 1 Pet 3.18
15.47 Gen 3.19 Jn 3.13,31
15.48 Phil 3.20,21
15.49 Gen 5.3 Rom 8.29 Phil 3.21 1 Jn 3.2
15.50 Mt 16.17 Jn 3.3,5
15.51 2 Cor 5.2-4 Phil 3.21 1 Thess 4.15,16
15.52 Mt 24.31
15.53 2 Cor 5.4
15.54 Isa 25.8
15.55 Hos 13.14 Rom 4.15
15.57 Rom 7.23-25 1 Jn 5.4

[t] Other ancient authorities add *the Lord* [u] Other ancient authorities read *let us* [v] Gk *brothers* [w] Gk *fall asleep*
[x] Gk *beloved brothers*

15.42–44 Our present bodies are perishable and liable to decay. Our resurrection bodies will be transformed. These spiritual bodies will not be limited by the laws of nature. This does not necessarily mean we'll be superpeople, but our bodies will be different and more capable than our present earthly bodies. Our spiritual bodies will not be weak, will never get sick, and will never die.

15.45 The "last Adam" refers to Christ. Because Christ rose from the dead, he is a life-giving spirit. This means that he entered into a new form of existence. He is the source of the spiritual life that will result in our resurrection. Christ's new glorified human body now suits his new glorified life – just as Adam's human body was suitable to his natural life. When we will be resurrected, God will give us a transformed, eternal body suited to our new eternal life.

15.50–53 We all face limitations. Those who have physical, mental, or emotional handicaps are especially aware of this. Some may be blind, but they can see a new way to live. Some may be deaf, but they can hear God's good news. Some may be lame, but they can walk in God's love. In addition, they have the encouragement that those handicaps are only temporary. Paul tells us we shall all be given new bodies when Christ returns, and these bodies will be without handicaps, never to die or become sick. This can give us hope in our suffering.

15.51, 52 "We will not all die" means that Christians alive at that day will not have to die but will be transformed immediately. A trumpet blast will usher in the new heaven and earth. The Jews would understand the significance of this, because trumpets were always blown to signal the start of great festivals and other extraordinary events (Numbers 10.10).

15.54–56 Satan seemed to be victorious in the garden of Eden (Genesis 3) and when Jesus died on the cross. But God turned Satan's apparent victory into defeat when Jesus Christ rose from the dead (Colossians 2.15; Hebrews 2.14, 15). Thus death is no longer a source of dread or fear. Christ overcame it, and one day we will also. The law will no longer make sinners out of us because we cannot keep it. Death has been defeated, and we have hope beyond the grave.

15.58 Paul says that because of the resurrection, nothing we do is wasted. Sometimes we hesitate to do good because we don't see any results. But if we can maintain a heavenly perspective, we understand that we don't often see the good that results from our efforts. If we truly believe that Christ has won the ultimate victory, it must affect the way we live right now. Don't let discouragement over an apparent lack of results keep you from working. Do the good that you have opportunity to do, knowing your work will have eternal results.

Directions for the offering

16 Now concerning the collection for the saints: you should follow the directions I gave to the churches of Galatia. 2 On the first day of every week, each
of you is to put aside and save whatever extra you earn, so that collections need not
be taken when I come. 3 And when I arrive, I will send any whom you approve with
letters to take your gift to Jerusalem. 4 If it seems advisable that I should go also,
they will accompany me.

Paul's final instructions

5 I will visit you after passing through Macedonia—for I intend to pass through
Macedonia— 6 and perhaps I will stay with you or even spend the winter, so that
you may send me on my way, wherever I go. 7 I do not want to see you now just in
passing, for I hope to spend some time with you, if the Lord permits. 8 But I will
stay in Ephesus until Pentecost, 9 for a wide door for effective work has opened to
me, and there are many adversaries.

10 If Timothy comes, see that he has nothing to fear among you, for he is doing
the work of the Lord just as I am; 11 therefore let no one despise him. Send him on
his way in peace, so that he may come to me; for I am expecting him with the
brothers.

12 Now concerning our brother Apollos, I strongly urged him to visit you with
the other brothers, but he was not at all willing[y] to come now. He will come when
he has the opportunity.

13 Keep alert, stand firm in your faith, be courageous, be strong. 14 Let all that
you do be done in love.

15 Now, brothers and sisters,[z] you know that members of the household of
Stephanas were the first converts in Achaia, and they have devoted themselves to
the service of the saints; 16 I urge you to put yourselves at the service of such people,
and of everyone who works and toils with them. 17 I rejoice at the coming of Stephanas and Fortunatus and Achaicus, because they have made up for your absence;
18 for they refreshed my spirit as well as yours. So give recognition to such persons.

[y] Or *it was not at all God's will for him* [z] Gk *brothers*

16.1 2 Cor 8.4; 9.1
16.2 Lk 24.1; Acts 20.7; Rev 1.10
16.3 2 Cor 8.19-21
16.5 Acts 19.21; 1 Cor 4.19; 2 Cor 1.15,16
16.6 Acts 15.3; 17.5
16.7 Acts 18.21
16.8 Acts 2.1
16.9 Acts 14.27; 19.8-10; 2 Cor 2.12
16.10 Acts 16.1; Rom 16.21
16.11 1 Tim 4.12,13
16.12 Acts 18.24; 1 Cor 1.12; Tit 3.13
16.13 Mt 24.42; Phil 1.27; 4.1; 1 Thess 3.7,8; 2 Thess 2.15
16.16 1 Thess 5.12,13

PHYSICAL AND RESURRECTION BODIES

Physical Bodies	*Resurrection Bodies*
Die and decay	Never die
Embarrassing	Full of glory
Weak and sick	Full of strength
Human	Superhuman
Natural	Spiritual
From the dust	From heaven

We all have bodies—each looks different, each has different abilities and weaknesses. But as physical, earthly bodies, they are all alike. All believers are promised life after death and bodies like Christ's (15.49), resurrection bodies.

16.1ff Paul had just said that no good work is ever wasted (15.58). In this chapter he mentions some practical works that have value for all Christians.

16.1–4 The Christians in Jerusalem were suffering from poverty and famine, so Paul was collecting money for them (Romans 15.25–31; 2 Corinthians 8.4; 9.1ff). He suggests that believers set aside a certain amount each week and give it to the church until he arrives to take it on to Jerusalem. Paul had planned to go straight to Corinth from Ephesus, but he changed his mind (2 Corinthians 1; 2). When he finally arrived, he took the gift and delivered it to the Jerusalem church (Acts 21.18; 24.17).

16.10, 11 Paul was sending Timothy ahead to Corinth. Paul respected Timothy and had worked closely with him (Philippians 2.22; 1 Timothy 1.2). Although Timothy was young, Paul encouraged the Corinthian church to welcome him because he was doing the Lord's work. God's work is not limited by age. Paul wrote two personal letters to Timothy that have been preserved in the Bible (1 and 2 Timothy).

16.12 Apollos, who had preached in Corinth, was doing evangelistic work in Greece (see Acts 18.24–28; 1 Corinthians 3.3ff). Apollos didn't go to Corinth right away, partly because he knew of the factions there and didn't want to cause any more divisions.

16.13, 14 As the Corinthians awaited Paul's next visit, they were directed to (1) be alert to spiritual dangers, (2) stand true to the Lord, (3) behave maturely, (4) be strong, and (5) do all things with kindness and love. Today, as we await the return of Christ, we should follow the same instructions.

19 The churches of Asia send greetings. Aquila and Prisca, together with the
church in their house, greet you warmly in the Lord. 20 All the brothers and sisters[a]
send greetings. Greet one another with a holy kiss.

16.19 Rom 16.5 Philem 2 Rev 1.4,11

21 I, Paul, write this greeting with my own hand. 22 Let anyone be accursed
who has no love for the Lord. Our Lord, come![b] 23 The grace of the Lord Jesus be
with you. 24 My love be with all of you in Christ Jesus.[c]

16.21 Gal 6.11 Col 4.18 2 Thess 3.17

[a] Gk *brothers* [b] Gk *Marana tha.* These Aramaic words can also be read *Maran atha,* meaning *Our Lord has come*
[c] Other ancient authorities add *Amen*

16.19 Aquila and Prisca (Priscilla) were tentmakers (or leather workers) whom Paul met in Corinth (Acts 18.1–3). They followed Paul to Ephesus and lived there with him, helping to teach others about Jesus (Romans 16.3–5). Many in the Corinthian church would have known this Christian couple. They are also mentioned in Acts 18.18, 26; Romans 16.3; 2 Timothy 4.19.

16.20 Kissing and embracing were normal ways of greeting one another in Paul's day. Paul encouraged its use as a way to greet Christians, and it would help break down the divisions in this church.

16.21 Paul had a helper, or secretary, who wrote this letter while he dictated. Paul wrote the final words, however, in his own handwriting. This is similar to adding a handwritten postscript (P.S.) to a typewritten letter. It also served to verify that this was a genuine letter from the apostle, not a forgery.

16.22 The Lord Jesus Christ is coming back to earth again. To Paul, this was a glad hope, the best he could look forward to. He was not afraid of seeing Christ – he could hardly wait! Do you share Paul's eager anticipation? Those who love Christ are looking forward to that wonderful time of his return (Titus 2.13). To those who did not love the Lord, however, Paul says let them be cursed.

16.24 The church at Corinth was a church in trouble. Paul lovingly and forcefully confronts their problems and points them back to Christ. He deals with divisions and conflicts, selfishness, inconsiderate use of freedom, disorder in worship, misuse of spiritual gifts, and wrong attitudes about the resurrection.

In every church, there are enough problems to split it. We should not ignore or gloss over problems in our church or in our lives. Instead, like Paul, we should deal with problems head on as they arise. The lesson for us in 1 Corinthians is that unity and love in a church are far more important than leaders and labels.

The Second Letter of Paul to the CORINTHIANS

SLITHERING through the centuries, the serpent whispers his silver-lined promises, beguiling, deceiving, and tempting—urging men and women to reject God and to follow him. Satan's emissaries have been many—false prophets contradicting God's ancient spokesmen, "pious" leaders hurling blasphemous accusations, and heretical teachers infiltrating churches. And the deception continues. Our world is filled with cults, "isms," and ideologies, all claiming to be the way to God.

Paul constantly struggled with those who would mislead God's people, and he poured his life into spreading the good news to the uttermost parts of the world. During three missionary trips and other travels, he proclaimed Christ, made converts, and established churches. But often young believers were easy prey for false teachers. False teachers were a constant threat to the gospel and the early church. So Paul had to spend much time warning and correcting these new Christians.

The church at Corinth was weak. Surrounded by idolatry and immorality, they struggled with their Christian faith and life-style. Through personal visits and letters, Paul tried to instruct them in the faith, resolve their conflicts, and solve some of their problems. First Corinthians was sent to deal with specific moral issues in the church and to answer questions about sex, marriage, and tender consciences. That letter confronted the issues directly and was well received by most. But there were false teachers who denied Paul's authority and slandered him. Paul then wrote 2 Corinthians to defend his position and to denounce those who were twisting the truth.

Second Corinthians was a difficult letter for Paul to write because he had to list his credentials as an apostle. Paul was reluctant to do so as a humble servant of Christ, but he knew it was necessary. Paul also knew that most of the believers in Corinth had taken his previous words to heart and were beginning to mature in their faith. He affirmed their commitment to Christ.

Second Corinthians begins with Paul reminding his readers of (1) their relationship to him—Paul had always been honest and straightforward with them (1.12–14), (2) his itinerary—he was planning to visit them again (1.15—2.3), and (3) his previous letter (2.4–11). Paul then moves directly to the subject of false teachers (2.17), and he reviews his ministry among them to demonstrate the validity of his message and to urge them not to turn away from the truth (3.1—7.16).

Paul next turns to the issue of collecting money for the poor Christians in Jerusalem. He tells them how others have given, and he urges them to show their love in a tangible way as well (8.1—9.15). Paul then gives a strong defense for his authority as a genuine apostle while pointing out the deception of the false apostles (10.1—13.13).

As you read this intensely personal letter, listen to Paul's words of love and exhortation, and be committed to the truth of God's Word, prepared to reject all false teaching.

VITAL STATISTICS

PURPOSE:
To affirm his own ministry, defend his authority as an apostle, and refute the false teachers in Corinth

AUTHOR:
Paul

TO WHOM WRITTEN:
The church in Corinth, and Christians everywhere

DATE WRITTEN:
About A.D. 55–57, from Macedonia

SETTING:
Paul had already written three letters to the Corinthians (two are now lost). In 1 Corinthians (the second of these letters), he used strong words to correct and teach. Most of the church had responded in the right spirit; there were, however, those who were denying Paul's authority and questioning his motives.

KEY VERSE:
"So we are ambassadors for Christ, since God is making his appeal through us; we entreat you on behalf of Christ, be reconciled to God" (5.20).

KEY PEOPLE:
Paul, Timothy, Titus, false teachers

KEY PLACES:
Corinth, Jerusalem

SPECIAL FEATURES:
This is an intensely personal and autobiographical letter.

THE BLUEPRINT

1. Paul explains his actions (1.1—2.13)
2. Paul defends his ministry (2.14—7.16)
3. Paul defends the collection (8.1—9.15)
4. Paul defends his authority (10.1—13.13)

In responding to the attacks on his character and authority, Paul explains the nature of Christian ministry and, as an example, openly shares about his ministry. This is an important letter for all who wish to be involved in any kind of Christian ministry because it has much to teach us about how we should handle our ministries today. Like Paul, those involved in ministry should be blameless, sincere, confident, caring, open, and willing to suffer for the sake of Christ.

MEGATHEMES

THEME	EXPLANATION	IMPORTANCE
Trials	Paul experienced great suffering, persecution, and opposition in his ministry. He even struggled with a personal weakness—a "thorn in the flesh." Through it all, Paul affirmed God's faithfulness.	God is faithful. His strength is sufficient for any trial. When trials come, they keep us from pride and teach us dependence on God. He comforts us so we can comfort others.
Church discipline	Paul defends his role in church discipline. Neither immorality nor false teaching could be ignored. The church was to be neither lax nor too severe in administering discipline. The church was to restore the corrected person when he or she repented.	The goal of all discipline in the church should be correction, not vengeance. For churches to be effective, they must confront and solve problems, not ignore them. In everything, we must act in love.
Hope	To encourage the Corinthians as they faced trials, Paul reminded them that they would receive new bodies in heaven. This would be a great victory in contrast to their present suffering.	To know we will receive new bodies offers us hope. No matter what adversity we face, we can keep going. Our faithful service will result in triumph.
Giving	Paul organized a collection of funds for the poor in the Jerusalem church. Many of the Asian churches gave money. Paul explains and defends his beliefs about giving, and he urges the Corinthians to follow through on their previous commitment.	Like the Corinthians, we should follow through on our financial commitments. Our giving must be generous, sacrificial, according to a plan, and based on need. Our generosity not only helps those in need, but enables them to thank God.
Sound doctrine	False teachers were challenging Paul's ministry and authority as an apostle. Paul asserts his authority in order to preserve correct Christian doctrine. His sincerity, his love for Christ, and his concern for the people were his defense.	We should share Paul's concern for correct teaching in our churches. But in so doing, we must share his motivation—love for Christ and people—and be sincere.

1. Paul explains his actions

1 Paul, an apostle of Christ Jesus by the will of God, and Timothy our brother, 1.1
To the church of God that is in Corinth, including all the saints throughout 1 Cor 1.1 2 Cor 1.19
Achaia: Eph 1.1

1.1 Paul visited Corinth on his second missionary journey and founded a church (Acts 18.1ff). He later wrote several letters to the believers in Corinth, two of which are included in the Bible. Paul's first letter to the Corinthians is lost (1 Corinthians 5.9–11), his second letter to them is our book of 1 Corinthians, his third letter is lost (2.6–9; 7.12), and his fourth letter is our book of 2 Corinthians. Second Corinthians was written less than a year after 1 Corinthians.

Paul wrote 1 Corinthians to deal with divisions in the church. When his advice was not taken and their problems weren't solved, Paul visited Corinth a second time, which was painful both for him and for the church (2.1). He then planned a third visit, but delayed it and wrote 2 Corinthians instead. After writing 2 Corinthians, he visited Corinth once more (Acts 20.2, 3).

1.1 Paul had great respect for Timothy (see also Philippians 2.19, 20; 1 Timothy 1.2), one of his traveling companions (Acts 16.1–3). Timothy had accompanied Paul to Corinth on his second missionary journey, and Paul had recently sent him there to minister (1 Corinthians 4.17; 16.10). Timothy's report to Paul about the crisis in the Corinthian church prompted Paul to make an unplanned visit to the church to deal with the problem in person (see 2.1). For more information on Timothy, see his Profile in 1 Timothy.

1.1 The Romans had made Corinth the capital of Achaia (the southern half of present-day Greece). The city was a flourishing trade center because of its seaport. With the thousands of merchants and sailors who disembarked there each year, it had deve-

2 Grace to you and peace from God our Father and the Lord Jesus Christ.

We pass on God's comfort to others

3 Blessed be the God and Father of our Lord Jesus Christ, the Father of mercies
and the God of all consolation, 4 who consoles us in all our affliction, so that we
may be able to console those who are in any affliction with the consolation with
which we ourselves are consoled by God. 5 For just as the sufferings of Christ are
abundant for us, so also our consolation is abundant through Christ. 6 If we are
being afflicted, it is for your consolation and salvation; if we are being consoled, it
is for your consolation, which you experience when you patiently endure the same
sufferings that we are also suffering. 7 Our hope for you is unshaken; for we know
that as you share in our sufferings, so also you share in our consolation.
8 We do not want you to be unaware, brothers and sisters,[a] of the affliction we
experienced in Asia; for we were so utterly, unbearably crushed that we despaired
of life itself. 9 Indeed, we felt that we had received the sentence of death so that we
would rely not on ourselves but on God who raises the dead. 10 He who rescued us
from so deadly a peril will continue to rescue us; on him we have set our hope that
he will rescue us again, 11 as you also join in helping us by your prayers, so that
many will give thanks on our[b] behalf for the blessing granted us through the
prayers of many.

[a] Gk *brothers* [b] Other ancient authorities read *your*

1.3 Eph 1.3; 1 Pet 1.3
1.4 Isa 51.12; 66.13; 2 Cor 7.6
1.5 2 Cor 4.10; Phil 3.10; Col 1.24
1.6 2 Cor 4.15; 2 Tim 2.10; 4.10
1.7 Rom 8.17; 2 Tim 2.12
1.9 Jer 17.5,7
1.10 2 Pet 2.9
1.11 Rom 15.30; 2 Cor 4.15; Phil 1.19; Philem 22

DIFFERENCES BETWEEN 1 AND 2 CORINTHIANS
The two letters to the Corinthian church found in the Bible are very different, with different tones and focuses.

1 Corinthians	*2 Corinthians*
Practical	Personal
Focuses on the character of the Corinthian church	Focuses on Paul as he bares his soul and tells of his love for the Corinthian church
Deals with questions on marriage, freedom, spiritual gifts, and order in the church	Deals with the problem of false teachers, whereby Paul defends his authority and the truth of his message
Paul instructs in matters concerning the church's well-being	Paul gives his testimony because he knows they trust him and that acceptance of his advice is vital to the church's well-being
Contains advice to help the church against the pagan influences in the wicked city of Corinth	Contains testimony to help the church against the havoc caused by false teachers

loped a reputation as one of the most immoral cities in the ancient world; its many heathen temples included sexual immorality along with idol worship. In fact, the Greek word for practicing sexual immorality was "to Corinthianize." A Christian church in the city would face many pressures and conflicts. For more information on Corinth, see the first note in 1 Corinthians 1.2.

1.3–5 Many think that when God consoles us, our hardships should go away. But if that were always so, people would turn to God only to be relieved of pain and not out of love for him. We must understand that being *consoled* can also mean receiving strength, encouragement, and hope to deal with our hardships. The more we suffer, the more comfort God gives us. If you are feeling overwhelmed, allow God to comfort you. Remember that every trial you endure will help you comfort other people suffering similar hardships.

1.5 The "sufferings of Christ" are those afflictions we experience for doing Christ's ministry. At the same time, Christ suffers in his people as they are united with him. In Acts 9.4, 5 Christ questioned Paul for persecuting him. This implies that Christ suffered with the early Christians when they were persecuted.

1.6, 7 Paul explains that he and his companions suffered greatly for bringing "consolation and salvation" to the Corinthians. But as God consoled Paul, he would console the Corinthian believers when they suffered for their faith. God would give them the strength to endure.

1.8–10 Paul does not give details about their "affliction" in Asia, although his accounts of all three missionary journeys record many difficult trials he faced (Acts 13.2 – 14.28; Acts 15.40 – 21.17). He does write that they felt doomed to die, and realized they could do nothing to help themselves – they simply had to trust in God.

1.8–10 We often depend on our own skills and abilities when life seems easy, but we turn to God when we feel unable to help ourselves. Depending on God is not defeat or weakness, but a realization of our own powerlessness without him and our need for his constant contact. God is our source of power, and we receive his help by keeping in touch with him. With this attitude, problems will drive us to God rather than away from him. Learn how to rely on God daily.

1.11 Paul requests prayer for himself and his companions as they travel to spread God's message. Pray for pastors, teachers, missionaries, and others who are spreading the gospel. Satan will challenge anyone making a real difference for God.

Paul's change of plans

12 Indeed, this is our boast, the testimony of our conscience: we have behaved
in the world with frankness[c] and godly sincerity, not by earthly wisdom but by the
grace of God—and all the more toward you. 13 For we write you nothing other than
what you can read and also understand; I hope you will understand until the end—
14 as you have already understood us in part—that on the day of the Lord Jesus we
are your boast even as you are our boast.

15 Since I was sure of this, I wanted to come to you first, so that you might have
a double favor;[d] 16 I wanted to visit you on my way to Macedonia, and to come
back to you from Macedonia and have you send me on to Judea. 17 Was I vacillating
when I wanted to do this? Do I make my plans according to ordinary human standards,[e] ready to say "Yes, yes" and "No, no" at the same time? 18 As surely as God
is faithful, our word to you has not been "Yes and No." 19 For the Son of God, Jesus
Christ, whom we proclaimed among you, Silvanus and Timothy and I, was not
"Yes and No"; but in him it is always "Yes." 20 For in him every one of God's
promises is a "Yes." For this reason it is through him that we say the "Amen," to
the glory of God. 21 But it is God who establishes us with you in Christ and has
anointed us, 22 by putting his seal on us and giving us his Spirit in our hearts as a
first installment.

23 But I call on God as witness against me: it was to spare you that I did not
come again to Corinth. 24 I do not mean to imply that we lord it over your faith;
rather, we are workers with you for your joy, because you stand firm in the faith.

2 1 So I made up my mind not to make you another painful visit. 2 For if I cause
you pain, who is there to make me glad but the one whom I have pained? 3 And
I wrote as I did, so that when I came, I might not suffer pain from those who should
have made me rejoice; for I am confident about all of you, that my joy would be the

1.12 Acts 23.1; 1 Cor 2.4; 2 Cor 2.17; 4.15
1.14 2 Cor 5.12; Phil 4.1; 1 Thess 2.19
1.15 Rom 1.11,12; 1 Cor 4.19
1.16 1 Cor 16.5
1.17 2 Cor 10.2
1.19 Ex 3.14; Mt 16.16; 26.63; Lk 1.35; Acts 9.20; 18.5; Heb 13.8
1.20 Rom 15.8,9; Rev 3.14
1.21 1 Jn 2.20,27
1.22 2 Cor 5.5; Eph 1.13,14; 4.30; 2 Tim 2.19; Rev 2.17
1.23 1 Cor 4.21
1.24 Rom 11.20; 1 Cor 15.1,2

[c] Other ancient authorities read *holiness* [d] Other ancient authorities read *pleasure* [e] Gk *according to the flesh*

1.12–14 Paul knew the importance of honesty (frankness) and sincerity in word and action, especially in a situation as in Corinth, where constructive criticism was necessary. So Paul did not come with impressive human knowledge (earthly wisdom). God wants us to be real and transparent in all our relationships. If we aren't, we may end up lowering ourselves to spreading rumors, gossiping, and second-guessing.

1.15–17 Paul had recently made a brief, unscheduled visit to Corinth which was very painful for him and the church (see 2.1). After that visit, he told the church when he would return. But Paul changed his original travel plans. Instead of sailing from Ephesus to Corinth before going to Macedonia, he traveled from Ephesus directly to Macedonia, where he wrote a letter to the Corinthians that caused him much anguish. He had made his original plans thinking the church would have solved its problems. When the time came for Paul's scheduled trip to Corinth, however, the crisis had not been fully resolved (although progress was being made in some areas; 7.11–16). So he wrote a letter instead (2.3, 4; 7.8), because another visit would only have made matters worse. Thus Paul stayed away from Corinth because he was concerned over the church's unity, not because he was fickle.

1.17–20 Paul's change of plans caused some of his accusers to say he couldn't be trusted, hoping to undermine his authority. Paul says that he is not the type of person to say "yes" when he means "no." Paul explains that it was not indecision but concern for their feelings that forced him to change his plans. The reason for his trip—to bring joy (1.24)—could not be accomplished with the present crisis. He didn't want to visit them only to rebuke them severely (1.23). Just as the Corinthians could trust God to keep his promises, they could trust Paul as God's representative to keep his. He would still visit them, but at a better time.

1.19, 20 All of God's promises of what the Messiah would be like are fulfilled in Christ ("in him every one of God's promises is a 'Yes' "). Jesus was completely faithful in his ministry; he never sinned (1 Peter 3.18); he faithfully died for us (Hebrews 2.9); and now he faithfully intercedes for us (Romans 8.34; Hebrews 4.14, 15). Because Jesus Christ is faithful, Paul wanted to be faithful in his ministry.

1.21, 22 Paul mentions two gifts God gives when we become believers: (1) a *seal* that is his "mark of ownership" to show who our Master is, and (2) the Holy Spirit who guarantees that we belong to him (Ephesians 1.13, 14). The Holy Spirit guarantees that salvation is ours now, and that we will receive so much more when Christ returns. The great comfort and power the Holy Spirit gives in this life is a foretaste or down payment ("first installment") of the benefits of our eternal life in God's presence. With the privilege of belonging to God comes the responsibility of identifying ourselves as his faithful servants. Don't be ashamed to let others know you are his.

1.23 The Corinthian church had written to Paul with questions about their faith (see 1 Corinthians 7.1). In response, Paul wrote 1 Corinthians. But they did not follow Paul's instructions.

Paul had planned to visit them again, but instead wrote a sorrowful letter (7.8, 9) to give them another chance to change their ways. He didn't want to visit and repeat the same advice for the same problems. He wrote that emotional letter to encourage them to follow the advice he had already given in previous letters and visits.

2.1 Paul's phrase, "another painful visit," indicates that he had already made one difficult trip to Corinth (see the notes on 1.1; 1.15–17) since founding the church. He went there to deal with those in the church who were attacking and undermining his authority as an apostle of Jesus Christ, thus confusing other believers.

2.3 Paul's last letter, referred to here, was not the book of 1 Corinthians, but a letter written between 1 and 2 Corinthians, just after his unplanned, painful visit (2.1). Paul refers to this letter again in 7.8.

2.4 2 Cor 2.9; 7.8,9
joy of all of you. 4 For I wrote you out of much distress and anguish of heart and
with many tears, not to cause you pain, but to let you know the abundant love that
I have for you.

Reinstate the repentant sinner

2.5,6 1 Cor 5.1-5 2 Cor 7.11
2.7 Gal 6.1 Eph 4.32
2.10 1 Cor 5.4
2.11 2 Cor 4.4; 11.3 1 Pet 5.8
2.12 Acts 14.27 2 Cor 4.3; 10.14

5 But if anyone has caused pain, he has caused it not to me, but to some
extent—not to exaggerate it—to all of you. 6 This punishment by the majority is
enough for such a person; 7 so now instead you should forgive and console him, so
that he may not be overwhelmed by excessive sorrow. 8 So I urge you to reaffirm
your love for him. 9 I wrote for this reason: to test you and to know whether you are
obedient in everything. 10 Anyone whom you forgive, I also forgive. What I have
forgiven, if I have forgiven anything, has been for your sake in the presence of
Christ. 11 And we do this so that we may not be outwitted by Satan; for we are not
ignorant of his designs.
12 When I came to Troas to proclaim the good news of Christ, a door was

PAUL SEARCHES FOR TITUS
Paul had searched for Titus, hoping to meet him in Troas and receive news about the Corinthian church. When he did not find Titus in Troas, he went on to Macedonia (2.13), most likely to Philippi, where he found Titus.

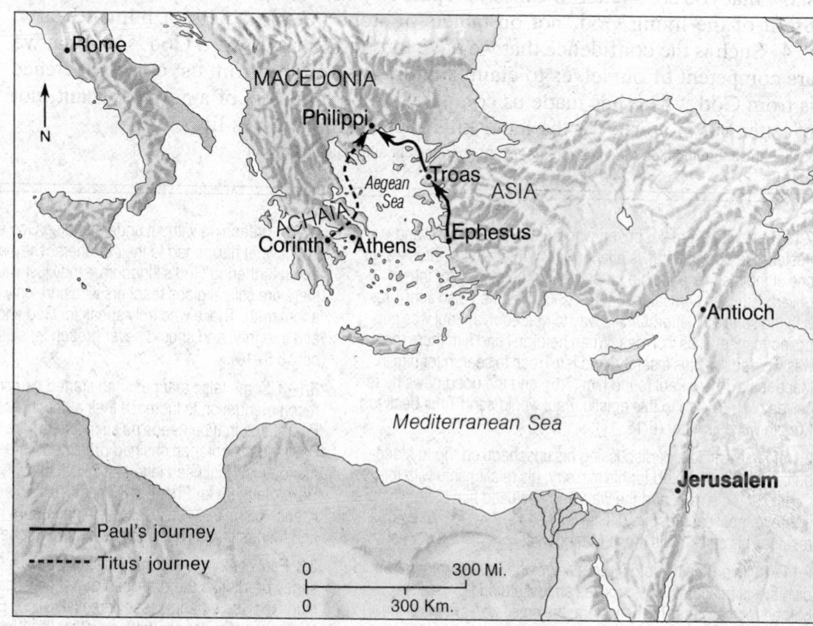

2.4 Paul did not enjoy reprimanding his friends and fellow believers, but he cared enough for the Corinthians to confront them about their wrongdoing. Proverbs 27.6 says: "Well meant are the wounds a friend inflicts, but profuse are the kisses of an enemy." Sometimes our friends make choices that we know are wrong. If we ignore their behavior and let them continue, we aren't showing love to them. We show love by honestly sharing our concerns in order to help them do and be their very best for God. When we don't move to help, we show that we are more concerned about being well liked than about what will happen to them.

2.5–11 Paul explains that it is time to forgive the man who had been punished by the church and had subsequently repented. He now needs friendship and comfort. Satan would gain an advantage if they permanently separate this man from the congregation rather than forgiving and restoring him. This may be the man who required the disciplinary action described in 1 Corinthians 5 or the chief opponent of Paul who had caused Paul the anguish described in 2.1–11. The sorrowful letter taken by Titus had finally brought about the repentance of the Corinthians (7.8–14), and their discipline of the man had led to his repentance. Church discipline should seek restoration. Two mistakes in church discipline should be avoided—being too lenient and not correcting mistakes, or being too harsh and not forgiving. There is a time to confront and a time to comfort.

2.11 We use church discipline in order to keep the church pure and to help wayward people repent. But Satan tries to harm the church by tempting it to use discipline in an unforgiving way. This causes those exercising discipline to become proud of their purity, and it causes the one being disciplined to become bitter and perhaps leave the church entirely. We must remember that our purpose in discipline is to *restore* a person to the fellowship, not to destroy him or her. We must be cautious that personal anger is not vented under the guise of church discipline.

opened for me in the Lord; 13 but my mind could not rest because I did not find my
brother Titus there. So I said farewell to them and went on to Macedonia.

2. Paul defends his ministry

The fragrance of Christ

14 But thanks be to God, who in Christ always leads us in triumphal procession, and through us spreads in every place the fragrance that comes from knowing
him. 15 For we are the aroma of Christ to God among those who are being saved and
among those who are perishing; 16 to the one a fragrance from death to death, to the
other a fragrance from life to life. Who is sufficient for these things? 17 For we are
not peddlers of God's word like so many;[f] but in Christ we speak as persons of
sincerity, as persons sent from God and standing in his presence.

God's great new covenant

3 Are we beginning to commend ourselves again? Surely we do not need, as
some do, letters of recommendation to you or from you, do we? 2 You yourselves are our letter, written on our[g] hearts, to be known and read by all; 3 and you
show that you are a letter of Christ, prepared by us, written not with ink but with the
Spirit of the living God, not on tablets of stone but on tablets of human hearts.
4 Such is the confidence that we have through Christ toward God. 5 Not that we
are competent of ourselves to claim anything as coming from us; our competence
is from God, 6 who has made us competent to be ministers of a new covenant, not
of letter but of spirit; for the letter kills, but the Spirit gives life.

2.13 2 Cor 7.5,6
2.14 Col 2.15
2.15 Eph 5.2
2.16 Lk 2.34; Jn 9.39; 2 Cor 3.5
2.17 2 Cor 4.2
3.2 1 Cor 9.2
3.3 Ex 24.12; Jer 31.33; Ezek 36.26
3.5 1 Cor 15.10
3.6 Jer 31.31; Jn 6.63; Rom 8.2

f Other ancient authorities read *like the others* g Other ancient authorities read *your*

2.13 Titus was a Greek convert whom Paul greatly loved and trusted (the book of Titus is a letter Paul wrote to him). Titus was one of the men responsible for collecting the money for the poverty-stricken Jerusalem church (8.6). Paul had also sent Titus with the sorrowful letter. On his way to Macedonia, Paul was supposed to meet Titus in Troas. When he didn't find him there, he was worried for Titus's safety, and left Troas to search for him in Macedonia. There Paul found him (7.6), and the good news he received (7.8–16) led to this epistle. Paul would send Titus back to Corinth with this letter (8.16, 17).

2.14ff In the middle of discussing his unscheduled trip to Macedonia, Paul thanks God for his ministry, his relationship with the Corinthian believers, and the way God has used him to help others wherever he went, despite difficulties (2.14–7.4). In 7.5, Paul resumes his story of his trip to Macedonia.

2.14–16 In a Roman victory procession, the Roman general would display his treasures and captives amidst a cloud of incense burned for the gods. To the victors, the smell was sweet; to the captives in the parade, it was the stench of slavery and death. When Christians preach the gospel, it is good news to some and repulsive to others. Believers recognize the life-giving fragrance of this news. To nonbelievers, however, it smells foul, like death—their own.

2.14–16 Believers are to be like a sweet aroma whose fragrance others can't help noticing. Just as we cannot control a person's opinion about a perfume's fragrance, we cannot control a person's reaction to our Christian message and actions. But if we remain true to Christ, his Spirit working in us will attract others.

2.16, 17 Paul asks "who is sufficient" for the task of representing Christ? Our adequacy is always from God (1 Corinthians 15.10; 2 Corinthians 3.5). He has already commissioned and sent us (see Matthew 28.18–20). He has given us the Holy Spirit to speak with Christ's power. He keeps his eye upon us, protecting us as we work for him. Thus, if we realize that God makes us competent and useful, we can overcome our feelings of inadequacy. Serving him, therefore, requires that we focus on what he can do through us, not on what we can't do by ourselves.

2.17 Some preachers in Paul's day were "peddlers of God's word," preaching without understanding God's message or caring about what happened to their listeners. They weren't concerned about furthering God's kingdom—they just wanted money. Today there are still religious teachers who care only about money, not about truth. Those who truly speak for God should have sincerity and integrity, and should never preach for selfish reasons (1 Timothy 6.5–10).

3.1–3 Some false teachers had started carrying forged letters of recommendation to increase their authority. In no uncertain terms, Paul states that he needs no such letters. The believers to whom Paul and his companions had preached were enough of a recommendation. Paul used letters of introduction, however, many times. He wrote them for Phoebe (Romans 16.1, 2) and Timothy (1 Corinthians 16.10, 11). These letters helped Paul's trusted companions and friends find a welcome in various churches.

3.3 Paul uses powerful imagery from famous Old Testament passages predicting the promised day of new hearts and new beginnings for God's people (see Jeremiah 31.33; Ezekiel 11.19; 36.26). No human minister can take credit for this process of conversion. It is the work of God's Spirit. We do not become believers by following some manual or using some technique. Our conversion is a result of God's implanting his Spirit in our hearts, giving us new power to live for him.

3.4, 5 Paul is not boasting; he gives God the credit for all his accomplishments. While the false teachers boasted of their own power and prestige, Paul expressed his humility before God. No one can claim to be adequate without God's help. No one is competent to carry out the responsibilities of God's calling in his or her own strength. Without the Holy Spirit's enabling, natural talent can carry us only so far. As Christ's witnesses, we need the character and special strength that only God gives.

3.6 "The letter kills, but the Spirit gives life" means that trying to be saved by keeping the Old Testament laws ends in death. Only by trusting in God can a person receive eternal life through the Holy Spirit. No one but Jesus has ever fulfilled the law perfectly, and thus the whole world is condemned to death. The law makes people realize their sin, but it cannot give life. Under the New Testament (or covenant, which means promise or agreement), eternal

7 Now if the ministry of death, chiseled in letters on stone tablets,[h] came in
glory so that the people of Israel could not gaze at Moses' face because of the glory
of his face, a glory now set aside, 8 how much more will the ministry of the Spirit
come in glory? 9 For if there was glory in the ministry of condemnation, much more
does the ministry of justification abound in glory! 10 Indeed, what once had glory
has lost its glory because of the greater glory; 11 for if what was set aside came
through glory, much more has the permanent come in glory!
12 Since, then, we have such a hope, we act with great boldness, 13 not like
Moses, who put a veil over his face to keep the people of Israel from gazing at the
end of the glory that[i] was being set aside. 14 But their minds were hardened. Indeed, to this very day, when they hear the reading of the old covenant, that same
veil is still there, since only in Christ is it set aside. 15 Indeed, to this very day
whenever Moses is read, a veil lies over their minds; 16 but when one turns to the
Lord, the veil is removed. 17 Now the Lord is the Spirit, and where the Spirit of the
Lord is, there is freedom. 18 And all of us, with unveiled faces, seeing the glory of
the Lord as though reflected in a mirror, are being transformed into the same image
from one degree of glory to another; for this comes from the Lord, the Spirit.

Satan blinds, but God gives light

4 Therefore, since it is by God's mercy that we are engaged in this ministry, we
do not lose heart. 2 We have renounced the shameful things that one hides; we
refuse to practice cunning or to falsify God's word; but by the open statement of the
truth we commend ourselves to the conscience of everyone in the sight of God.
3 And even if our gospel is veiled, it is veiled to those who are perishing. 4 In their
case the god of this world has blinded the minds of the unbelievers, to keep them
from seeing the light of the gospel of the glory of Christ, who is the image of God.

[h] Gk *on stones* [i] Gk *of what*

3.7 Ex 34.29-35 Deut 9.10
3.8 Gal 3.5
3.9 Rom 1.17; 3.21
3.12 1 Thess 2.2
3.13 Ex 34.33 Rom 10.4 Gal 3.23
3.14 Isa 6.10 Jn 12.40 Rom 11.7 2 Cor 4.4
3.16 Isa 25.7 1 Cor 2.10
3.17 Rom 8.9 1 Cor 15.45 Phil 1.19
4.2 2 Cor 2.17 1 Thess 2.3,5
4.4 Jn 1.18 12.31,40,45 Eph 6.12 Col 1.15 Heb 1.3

life comes from the Holy Spirit. He gives new life to all who believe in Christ. The moral law (ten commandments) still points out sin and shows us how to obey God, but forgiveness comes only through the grace and mercy of Christ (see Romans 7.10–8.2).

3.7–11 Paul contrasts the glory of the ten commandments with the glory of the life-giving Spirit. If the law which leads to death, was glorious, how much more glorious is God's plan to give us life through his Spirit! The sacrifice of Jesus Christ is far superior to the Old Testament system of sacrifice (see Hebrews 8, 10 for a more complete discussion). If Christianity was superior to the Judaism of the Old Testament, which was the highest form of religion on earth, it will surely be superior to any other religion we may come across. Because God's plan is wonderful by comparison to any other, we dare not reject it or treat it casually.

3.9 Paul is saying that if the old covenant had its glory (and certainly it did), just imagine how glorious the new covenant is. The law was wonderful because, although it condemned us, it pointed us to Christ. But in the new covenant, the law and the promise are fulfilled. Christ has come—by faith we can be justified (made right with God)!

3.13–18 When Moses came down Mount Sinai with the ten commandments, his face glowed from being in God's presence (Exodus 34.29–35). He put on a veil to keep the people from being terrified by the brightness of his face. Paul adds that his veil kept them from seeing the glory fade away. Moses and his veil illustrate the fading of the old system and the veiling of the people's minds and understanding with their pride, hardness of heart, and refusal to repent. The veil kept them from understanding the references to Christ in the Scriptures. When anyone becomes a Christian, Christ removes the veil (3.16), giving eternal life and freedom from trying to be saved by keeping laws. And without the veil, we can be like mirrors reflecting God's glory.

3.17 Those who were trying to be saved by keeping the Old Testament law were soon tied up in rules and ceremonies. But now, through the Holy Spirit, God provides freedom from sin and condemnation (Romans 8.1). When we trust Christ to save us, he removes our heavy burden of trying to please him and our guilt for failing to do so. By trusting him we are loved, accepted, forgiven, and freed to live for him. "Where the Spirit of the Lord is, there is freedom."

3.18 The glory that the Spirit imparts to the believer is more excellent and lasts longer than that which Moses experienced. By beholding the nature of God with unveiled minds, we can be more like him. In the gospel, we see the truth about Christ, and it transforms us morally as we understand and apply it. Through Christ's life, we understand how wonderful God is and what he is really like. As our knowledge deepens, the Holy Spirit helps us to change. Becoming Christlike is a progressive experience (see Romans 8.29; Galatians 4.19; Philippians 3.21; 1 John 3.2). The more closely we follow him, the more we will be like him.

4.2 Preachers, teachers, and anyone else who talks about Jesus Christ must remember that they stand in God's presence—he hears every word. When you tell people about Christ, be careful not to distort the message to please your audience. Proclaim the truth of God's Word.

4.3, 4 The good news is open and revealed to everyone, except to those who refuse to believe. Satan is "the god of this world." His work is to deceive, and he has blinded those who don't believe in Christ (see 11.14, 15). The allure of money, power, and pleasure blinds people to the light of Christ's gospel. Those who refuse Christ, preferring their own pursuits, have unknowingly made Satan their god.

5 For we do not proclaim ourselves; we proclaim Jesus Christ as Lord and ourselves
as your slaves for Jesus' sake. 6 For it is the God who said, "Let light shine out of
darkness," who has shone in our hearts to give the light of the knowledge of the
glory of God in the face of Jesus Christ.
7 But we have this treasure in clay jars, so that it may be made clear that this
extraordinary power belongs to God and does not come from us. 8 We are afflicted
in every way, but not crushed; perplexed, but not driven to despair; 9 persecuted,
but not forsaken; struck down, but not destroyed; 10 always carrying in the body the
death of Jesus, so that the life of Jesus may also be made visible in our bodies.
11 For while we live, we are always being given up to death for Jesus' sake, so that
the life of Jesus may be made visible in our mortal flesh. 12 So death is at work in
us, but life in you.
13 But just as we have the same spirit of faith that is in accordance with
scripture—"I believed, and so I spoke"—we also believe, and so we speak, 14 because we know that the one who raised the Lord Jesus will raise us also with Jesus,
and will bring us with you into his presence. 15 Yes, everything is for your sake, so
that grace, as it extends to more and more people, may increase thanksgiving, to
the glory of God.
16 So we do not lose heart. Even though our outer nature is wasting away, our
inner nature is being renewed day by day. 17 For this slight momentary affliction is
preparing us for an eternal weight of glory beyond all measure, 18 because we look
not at what can be seen but at what cannot be seen; for what can be seen is temporary, but what cannot be seen is eternal.

Earthly bodies are weak

5 For we know that if the earthly tent we live in is destroyed, we have a building
from God, a house not made with hands, eternal in the heavens. 2 For in this
tent we groan, longing to be clothed with our heavenly dwelling— 3 if indeed,

4.5 1 Cor 9.19
4.6 Gen 1.3; Ps 36.9; Jn 8.12; 12.46; Eph 5.8,14; 1 Pet 2.9
4.7 2 Tim 2.20
4.9 Rom 8.35,36
4.10 1 Cor 15.31; Gal 6.17; Phil 3.10; Col 1.24; 2 Tim 2.11
4.13 Ps 116.10
4.14 Acts 2.24; 1 Thess 2.19
4.16 Eph 3.16; Col 3.10
4.17 Rom 8.18; 1 Pet 1.6,7
4.18 Rom 8.24; 2 Cor 5.7
5.1 Heb 11.10; 2 Pet 1.13

4.5 The focus of Paul's preaching was Christ, not himself. When you witness, tell people about what Christ has done, and not about your abilities and accomplishments. People must be introduced to Christ, not to you. And if you hear someone preaching himself or his own ideas rather than Christ, beware—he is a false teacher.

4.5 Paul willingly served the Corinthian church even though the people disappointed him. Serving people requires a sacrifice of time and personal desires. Being Christ's follower means serving others, even when they do not measure up to our expectations.

4.7 The supremely valuable message of salvation in Jesus Christ has been entrusted by God to frail and fallible human beings (clay jars). Paul's focus, however, was not on the perishable container but on its priceless contents—God's power dwelling in us. Though we are weak, God uses us to spread his good news, and he gives us power to do his work. Knowing that the power is his, not ours, keeps us from pride and motivates us to keep daily contact with God, our power source. Our responsibility is to let people see God through us.

4.8–12 Paul reminds us that though we may be at the end of the rope, we are never at the end of hope. Our perishable bodies are subject to sin and suffering, but God never abandons us. Because Christ has won victory over death, we have eternal life. All our risks, humiliations, and trials are opportunities for Christ to demonstrate his power and presence through us.

4.15–18 Paul faced sufferings, trials, and distress as he preached the good news. But he knew that they would one day be over, and he would obtain God's rest and rewards. As we face great troubles, it's easy to focus on the pain rather than on our ultimate goal. Just as athletes concentrate on the finish line and ignore their discomfort, we too must focus on the reward for our faith and the joy that lasts forever. No matter what happens to us in this life, we have the assurance of eternal life when all suffering will end.

4.16 It is easy to quit. We all have faced problems in our relationships or work that caused us to want to lay down the tools and walk away. Rather than giving up when persecution wore him down, Paul concentrated on experiencing the inner strength from the Holy Spirit (Ephesians 3.16). Don't let fatigue, pain, or criticism force you off the job. Renew your commitment to serving Christ. Don't forsake your eternal reward because of the intensity of today's pain. Your very weakness allows the resurrection power of Christ to strengthen you moment by moment.

4.17 Our troubles ("slight momentary affliction") should not diminish our faith or disillusion us. We should realize that there is a purpose in our suffering. Problems and human limitations have several benefits: (1) they remind us of Christ's suffering for us; (2) they keep us from pride; (3) they cause us to look beyond this brief life; (4) they prove our faith to others; and (5) they give God the opportunity to demonstrate his power. See your troubles as opportunities!

4.18 Our ultimate hope in terrible illness, persecution, or pain is realizing that this life is not all there is—there is life after death! Knowing that we will live forever with God in a place without sin and suffering helps us live above the pain we must face in this life.

5.1–10 Paul contrasts our earthly bodies ("earthly tent") and our future resurrection bodies ("building from God, a house not made with hands, eternal in the heavens"). Paul clearly states that our present bodies make us groan, but when we die we will not be spirits without bodies ("be found naked"). We will have new bodies that will be perfect for our everlasting life.

Paul wrote as he did because the church at Corinth was in the heart of Greek culture, and many believers had difficulty with the concept of bodily resurrection. Greeks did not believe in a bodily resurrection. Most saw the afterlife as something that happened only to the soul, with the real person imprisoned in a physical body. At death the soul is released. There is no immortality for the

5.4 1 Cor 15.53,54
5.5 Rom 8.23; 2 Cor 1.22; Eph 1.14
5.7 1 Cor 13.12
5.8 Phil 1.23
5.10 Mt 16.27; 1 Cor 3.13-15; Rev 22.12
5.12 2 Cor 1.14; 3.1
5.14 Rom 5.15; Gal 2.20
5.15 Rom 14.7-9; 1 Pet 4.2
5.16 Mt 12.50
5.17 Isa 65.17; Gal 6.15; Eph 4.24; Rev 21.5
5.18 Rom 5.10; Col 1.20-22
5.19 Isa 43.25; Rom 3.24; 4.28
5.20 Rom 5.10

when we have taken it off[j] we will not be found naked. 4 For while we are still in
this tent, we groan under our burden, because we wish not to be unclothed but to be
further clothed, so that what is mortal may be swallowed up by life. 5 He who has
prepared us for this very thing is God, who has given us the Spirit as a guarantee.
6 So we are always confident; even though we know that while we are at home
in the body we are away from the Lord— 7 for we walk by faith, not by sight. 8 Yes,
we do have confidence, and we would rather be away from the body and at home
with the Lord. 9 So whether we are at home or away, we make it our aim to please
him. 10 For all of us must appear before the judgment seat of Christ, so that each
may receive recompense for what has been done in the body, whether good or evil.

Be reconciled to God

11 Therefore, knowing the fear of the Lord, we try to persuade others; but we
ourselves are well known to God, and I hope that we are also well known to your
consciences. 12 We are not commending ourselves to you again, but giving you an
opportunity to boast about us, so that you may be able to answer those who boast
in outward appearance and not in the heart. 13 For if we are beside ourselves, it is
for God; if we are in our right mind, it is for you. 14 For the love of Christ urges us
on, because we are convinced that one has died for all; therefore all have died.
15 And he died for all, so that those who live might live no longer for themselves,
but for him who died and was raised for them.
16 From now on, therefore, we regard no one from a human point of view;[k]
even though we once knew Christ from a human point of view,[k] we know him no
longer in that way. 17 So if anyone is in Christ, there is a new creation: everything
old has passed away; see, everything has become new! 18 All this is from God, who
reconciled us to himself through Christ, and has given us the ministry of reconciliation; 19 that is, in Christ God was reconciling the world to himself,[l] not counting
their trespasses against them, and entrusting the message of reconciliation to us.
20 So we are ambassadors for Christ, since God is making his appeal through us; we

[j] Other ancient authorities read *put it on* [k] Gk *according to the flesh* [l] Or *God was in Christ reconciling the world to himself*

body, and the soul enters an eternal state. But the Bible teaches that the body and soul are inseparable.

Paul describes our resurrected bodies in more detail in 1 Corinthians 15.46–58. We will still have personalities and recognizable differences in our resurrected bodies, but through Christ's work, our bodies will be better than we can imagine. The Bible does not tell us everything about our resurrected bodies, but we know they will be perfect, without sickness or disease (see Philippians 3.21).

5.5 The Holy Spirit within us is our guarantee that God will give us everlasting bodies at the resurrection (1.22). We have eternity in us now! Such hope should give us great courage and patience to endure anything we might experience.

5.6–8 Paul was not afraid to die because he was confident of spending eternity with Christ. Of course, facing the unknown may cause us anxiety and leaving loved ones hurts deeply, but if we believe in Jesus Christ, we can share Paul's hope and confidence of eternal life with Christ.

5.8 For those who believe in Christ, death is only a prelude to eternal life with God. We will continue to live in body and in spirit. Let this hope give you confidence and inspire you to faithful service.

5.9, 10 While eternal life is a free gift given on the basis of God's grace (Ephesians 2.8, 9), each of us will still be judged by Christ. This judgment will reward us for how we have lived. God's gracious gift of salvation does not free us from the requirement for faithful obedience. All Christians must give account for how they have lived (see Matthew 16.27; Romans 14.10–12; 1 Corinthians 3.10–15).

5.12 Those who "boast in outward appearance and not in the heart" are the false preachers (see 2.17) who were concerned only about getting ahead in this world. They were preaching the gospel for money, while Paul and his companions were preaching out of concern for eternity. You can identify false preachers by finding out what really motivates them. If they are more concerned about themselves than Christ, avoid them and their message.

5.13–15 Everything Paul and his companions did was to honor God. Christ's love controlled their lives. Because Christ died for us, we also are dead to our old lives. Like Paul, we should no longer live to please ourselves; we should spend our lives pleasing Christ who died for us and rose from the grave.

5.17 Christians are brand new people on the *inside.* The Holy Spirit gives them new life, and they are not the same anymore. We are not reformed, rehabilitated, or reeducated – we are recreated (new creations), living in vital union with Christ (Colossians 2.6, 7). We are not merely turning over a new leaf; we are beginning a new life under a new Master.

5.18, 19 God brings us back to himself (reconciles us) by blotting out our sins (see also Ephesians 2.13–18) and making us righteous. We are no longer strangers, foreigners, or enemies to God when we trust in Christ. Because we have been reconciled to God, we have the privilege to encourage others to do the same.

5.20 An ambassador is an official representative from one country to another. As believers, we are Christ's ambassadors, sent with his message of reconciliation to the world. An ambassador of reconciliation has an important responsibility. We dare not take this responsibility lightly. How well are you fulfilling your commission as Christ's ambassador?

entreat you on behalf of Christ, be reconciled to God. 21 For our sake he made him 5.21 Isa 53.6,9
to be sin who knew no sin, so that in him we might become the righteousness of Gal 3.13
God. Heb 4.15; 7.26

Paul patiently endures hardship

6 As we work together with him,[m] we urge you also not to accept the grace of 6.1 1 Cor 3.9
God in vain. 2 For he says, 6.2
"At an acceptable time I have listened to you, Isa 49.8
and on a day of salvation I have helped you." 6.3 1 Cor 8.9; 9.12
See, now is the acceptable time; see, now is the day of salvation! 3 We are putting 6.4
no obstacle in anyone's way, so that no fault may be found with our ministry, 4 but 2 Cor 4.8 11.23-28
as servants of God we have commended ourselves in every way: through great 6.5
endurance, in afflictions, hardships, calamities, 5 beatings, imprisonments, riots, 1 Cor 4.11
labors, sleepless nights, hunger; 6 by purity, knowledge, patience, kindness, holi- 6.6 2 Cor 11.6
ness of spirit, genuine love, 7 truthful speech, and the power of God; with the weap- 6.7 1 Cor 2.4
ons of righteousness for the right hand and for the left; 8 in honor and dishonor, in 2 Cor 2.17; 4.2
ill repute and good repute. We are treated as impostors, and yet are true; 9 as un- 6.8 Mt 27.63
known, and yet are well known; as dying, and see—we are alive; as punished, and 1 Cor 4.10,13
yet not killed; 10 as sorrowful, yet always rejoicing; as poor, yet making many rich; 2 Cor 4.2 6.10
as having nothing, and yet possessing everything. 2 Cor 8.9
11 We have spoken frankly to you Corinthians; our heart is wide open to you. 6.11 2 Cor 7.3
12 There is no restriction in our affections, but only in yours. 13 In return—I speak 6.12
as to children—open wide your hearts also. 2 Cor 12.15

Be separate from unbelievers

14 Do not be mismatched with unbelievers. For what partnership is there be- 6.14 Deut 7.3; 22.10
tween righteousness and lawlessness? Or what fellowship is there between light Eph 5.6,7
and darkness? 15 What agreement does Christ have with Beliar? Or what does a 1 Jn 1.6,7

m Gk *As we work together*

5.21 When we trust in Christ, we make a trade—our sin for his goodness. Our sin was poured into Christ at his crucifixion. His righteousness is poured into us at our conversion. This is what Christians mean by Christ's atonement for sin. In the world, bartering works only when two people exchange goods of relatively equal value. But God offers to trade his righteousness for our sin—something of immeasurable worth for something worthless. How grateful we should be for his goodness to us.

6.1 How could the Corinthian believers toss aside God's message ("accept the grace of God in vain")? Perhaps they were doubting Paul and his words, confused by the false teachers who taught a different message. The people heard God's message, but did not let it affect what they said and did. How often does God's message reach you in vain?

6.2 God offers salvation to all people. Many people put off a decision for Christ, thinking there will be a better time—but they could easily miss their opportunity altogether. There is no time like the present to receive God's forgiveness. Don't let anything hold you back from coming to God.

6.3 In everything he did, Paul always considered what his actions communicated about Jesus Christ. If you are a believer, you are a minister for God. In the course of each day, non-Christians observe you. Don't let your careless or undisciplined actions be another person's excuse for rejecting God.

6.7 See Romans 13.2; 2 Corinthians 10.3–5; and Ephesians 6.10–18 for more about the armor of righteousness. Weapons for the right had are offensive weapons; those for the left hand are defensive. No soldier is fully prepared for battle without both.

6.8–10 What a difference knowing Jesus can make! He cares for us in spite of what the world thinks. Christians don't have to give in to public opinion and pressure. Paul stood true to God whether people praised him or condemned him. He remained active, joyous, and content in the most difficult conditions. Don't let circumstances or people's expectations control you. Be firm as you stand true to God, and refuse to compromise his standards for living.

6.11–13 "Our heart is wide open" and "there is no restriction in our affections" means that Paul had told the Corinthian believers his true feelings for them, how much he loved them. The Corinthians were reacting coldly to Paul's words, but Paul explained that his harsh words come from his love for them. It is easy to react against those whom God has placed over us in leadership rather than to accept their exhortations as a sign of their love for us. We need an open rather than a hardened heart toward God's messengers.

6.12 This verse could be translated, "we are not withholding our affection from you, but you are withholding yours from us."

6.14–17 Paul urged believers not to form binding relationships with nonbelievers because this might weaken their Christian commitment, integrity, or standards. It would be a mismatch (also translated "unequally yoked"). Earlier, Paul had explained that this did not mean isolating oneself from nonbelievers (see 1 Corinthians 5.9, 10). Paul even told Christians to stay with their nonbelieving spouses (1 Corinthians 7.12, 13). Paul wanted believers to be active in their witness for Christ to nonbelievers, but they should not lock themselves into personal or business relationships that could cause them to compromise the faith. Believers should avoid situations that would force them to divide their loyalties.

6.15 *Beliar* is a name Paul uses for Satan. For those who have discovered God's kingdom of light, there can be no contact or compromise with the kingdom of darkness (1 Corinthians 10.20, 21).

6.16 Ex 25.8; 29.45 Jer 31.33 Ezek 36.28
6.17 Isa 52.11
6.18 Jer 31.1,9 Hos 1.10
7.1 1 Pet 1.22 1 Jn 3.3
7.2 2 Cor 6.12
7.3 2 Cor 6.11
7.4 1 Cor 1.4 2 Cor 7.14; 8.24 10.8 Phil 2.17
7.5 2 Cor 2.13; 4.8
7.6 2 Cor 2.13; 7.13 2 Thess 2.16
7.8 2 Cor 2.2-4
7.10 2 Sam 12.13 Jer 31.18-20 Mt 26.75 27.4,5

believer share with an unbeliever? 16 What agreement has the temple of God with
idols? For we[n] are the temple of the living God; as God said,

"I will live in them and walk among them,
and I will be their God,
and they shall be my people.
17 Therefore come out from them,
and be separate from them, says the Lord,
and touch nothing unclean;
then I will welcome you,
18 and I will be your father,
and you shall be my sons and daughters,
says the Lord Almighty."

7 Since we have these promises, beloved, let us cleanse ourselves from every
defilement of body and of spirit, making holiness perfect in the fear of God.

The church's repentance gives Paul joy

2 Make room in your hearts[o] for us; we have wronged no one, we have corrupted no one, we have taken advantage of no one. 3 I do not say this to condemn
you, for I said before that you are in our hearts, to die together and to live together.
4 I often boast about you; I have great pride in you; I am filled with consolation; I
am overjoyed in all our affliction.

5 For even when we came into Macedonia, our bodies had no rest, but we were
afflicted in every way—disputes without and fears within. 6 But God, who consoles the downcast, consoled us by the arrival of Titus, 7 and not only by his coming, but also by the consolation with which he was consoled about you, as he told
us of your longing, your mourning, your zeal for me, so that I rejoiced still more.
8 For even if I made you sorry with my letter, I do not regret it (though I did regret
it, for I see that I grieved you with that letter, though only briefly). 9 Now I rejoice,
not because you were grieved, but because your grief led to repentance; for you felt
a godly grief, so that you were not harmed in any way by us. 10 For godly grief
produces a repentance that leads to salvation and brings no regret, but worldly grief

[n] Other ancient authorities read *you* [o] Gk lacks *in your hearts*

PRINCIPLES OF CONFRONTATION IN 2 CORINTHIANS

Method	*Reference*
Be firm	7.9; 10.2
Affirm all you see that is good	7.4
Be accurate and honest	7.14; 8.21
Know the facts	11.22–27
Follow up after the confrontation	7.13; 12.14
Be gentle after being firm	7.15; 13.11–13
Speak words that reflect Christ's message, not your own ideas	10.3; 10.12, 13; 12.19
Use discipline only when all else fails	13.2

Sometimes rebuke is necessary, but it must be used with caution. The purpose of any rebuke, confrontation, or discipline is to help people, not hurt them.

6.17 Separation from the world involves more than keeping our distance from sinners; it means staying close to God (see 7.1, 2). It involves more than avoiding entertainment that leads to sin; it extends into how we spend our time and money. There is no way to separate ourselves totally from all sinful influences. Nevertheless, we are to resist the sin around us, not give up and give in.

7.1 Cleansing ourselves is a twofold action: turning *away* from sin, and turning *toward* God. "Making holiness perfect" means the Corinthians were to have nothing to do with paganism. They were to make a clean break with their past and give themselves to God alone.

7.5 Here Paul resumes the story that he left in 2.13, where he says he went to Macedonia to look for Titus.

7.8ff "My letter" refers to the third letter (now lost) that Paul wrote the Corinthians. Apparently it had caused the people to begin to change. For an explanation of the chronology of Paul's letters to Corinth, see the note on 1.1.

7.10 "Godly grief produces a repentance that leads to salvation" means the sorrow for our sins that results in changed behavior. Many people are sorry only for the effects of their sins or for being caught ("worldly grief"). Compare Peter's remorse and repentance with Judas's bitterness and suicide. Both denied Christ. One repented and was restored to faith and service; the other took his own life.

produces death. 11 For see what earnestness this godly grief has produced in you,
what eagerness to clear yourselves, what indignation, what alarm, what longing,
what zeal, what punishment! At every point you have proved yourselves guiltless
in the matter. 12 So although I wrote to you, it was not on account of the one who
did the wrong, nor on account of the one who was wronged, but in order that your
zeal for us might be made known to you before God. 13 In this we find comfort.
In addition to our own consolation, we rejoiced still more at the joy of Titus,
because his mind has been set at rest by all of you. 14 For if I have been somewhat
boastful about you to him, I was not disgraced; but just as everything we said to you
was true, so our boasting to Titus has proved true as well. 15 And his heart goes out
all the more to you, as he remembers the obedience of all of you, and how you
welcomed him with fear and trembling. 16 I rejoice, because I have complete confidence in you.

7.11 Jer 50.4,5 Zech 12.10 2 Cor 2.6
7.12 1 Cor 5.1-5
7.13 Rom 15.32 2 Cor 2.13; 7.6
7.15 2 Cor 2.9 Phil 2.12
7.16 2 Cor 2.3 2 Thess 3.4 Philem 21

3. Paul defends the collection

Generous giving glorifies the Lord

8 We want you to know, brothers and sisters,[p] about the grace of God that has
been granted to the churches of Macedonia; 2 for during a severe ordeal of affliction, their abundant joy and their extreme poverty have overflowed in a wealth
of generosity on their part. 3 For, as I can testify, they voluntarily gave according
to their means, and even beyond their means, 4 begging us earnestly for the privilege[q] of sharing in this ministry to the saints— 5 and this, not merely as we expected; they gave themselves first to the Lord and, by the will of God, to us, 6 so
that we might urge Titus that, as he had already made a beginning, so he should
also complete this generous undertaking[r] among you. 7 Now as you excel in
everything—in faith, in speech, in knowledge, in utmost eagerness, and in our
love for you[s]—so we want you to excel also in this generous undertaking.[r]
8 I do not say this as a command, but I am testing the genuineness of your love
against the earnestness of others. 9 For you know the generous act[t] of our Lord
Jesus Christ, that though he was rich, yet for your sakes he became poor, so that by
his poverty you might become rich. 10 And in this matter I am giving my advice: it

8.1 Acts 16.9
8.4 Acts 24.17 Rom 15.25 1 Cor 16.1,3
8.5 Mt 25.40 Heb 13.16
8.6 2 Cor 12.18
8.7 Prov 22.9; 28.27 Mt 19.21 Mk 10.21 Lk 18.22 1 Cor 1.5; 12.13 2 Cor 9.8
8.9 Mt 8.20 Lk 9.58 Phil 2.6,7

[p] Gk *brothers* [q] Gk *grace* [r] Gk *this grace* [s] Other ancient authorities read *your love for us* [t] Gk *the grace*

7.11 It is difficult to be confronted with our sin, and even more difficult to get rid of sin. Paul praises the Corinthians for clearing up an especially troublesome situation (see the note on 2.5–11). Do you tend to be defensive when confronted? Don't let pride keep you from admitting your sins. Accept correction as a tool for your growth, and do all you can to correct problems that are pointed out to you.

8.1ff Paul, writing from Macedonia, hoped that news of the generosity of these churches would encourage the Corinthian believers and motivate them to solve their problems and unite in fellowship.

8.2–5 During his third missionary journey, Paul collected money for the impoverished believers in Jerusalem. The churches in Macedonia—Philippi, Thessalonica, and Beroea—gave money even though they were poor, and they gave more than Paul expected. This was sacrificial giving—they were poor themselves, but they wanted to help. The point of giving is not so much the amount we give, but why and how we give. God does not want gifts given grudgingly. Instead, he wants us to give as these churches did—out of dedication to him, love for fellow believers, and the joy of helping those in need, and because it was right to do so. How well does your giving measure up to the standards set by the Macedonian churches?

8.3–6 The kingdom of God spreads through believers' concern and eagerness to help others. Here we see several churches joining to help others beyond their own circle of friends and their own city. Explore ways you might link up with a ministry outside your city, either through your church or through a Christian organization. By joining with other believers to do God's work, you increase Christian unity and help the kingdom to grow.

8.7, 8 The Corinthian believers excelled in everything—they had strong faith, good preaching, much knowledge, much enthusiasm, much love. Paul wanted them to also be leaders in generosity. Giving is a natural response of love. Paul did not order the Corinthians to give, but he encouraged them to prove that their love was sincere. When you love someone, you want to give him your time and attention and to provide for his needs. If you refuse to help, your love may not be as genuine as you say.

8.9 There is no evidence that Jesus was any poorer than most first-century Palestinians; rather, Jesus became poor by giving up his rights as God and becoming human. In his incarnation God voluntarily became man—the wholly human person, Jesus of Nazareth. As a man, Jesus was subject to place, time, and other human limitations. He did not give up his eternal power when he became human, but he did set aside his glory and his rights. In response to the Father's will, he limited his power and knowledge. He became "poor" when he became human, because he set aside so much. Yet by doing so, he made us "rich," because we received salvation and eternal life.

What made Jesus' humanity unique was his freedom from sin. In his full humanity, we can see everything about God's character that can be conveyed in human terms. The incarnation is explained further in these Bible passages: John 1.1–14; Romans 1.2–5; Philippians 2.6–11; 1 Timothy 3.16; Hebrews 2.14; 1 John 1.1–3.

8.10–15 The Corinthian church had money, and apparently they planned to collect money for the Jerusalem churches a year previously (see also 9.2). Paul challenges them to act on their plans. Four principles of giving emerge here: (1) your willingness to give

8.10 Prov 19.17 Mt 10.42 1 Tim 6.18 Heb 13.16
is appropriate for you who began last year not only to do something but even to
desire to do something— 11 now finish doing it, so that your eagerness may be
matched by completing it according to your means. 12 For if the eagerness is there,
8.12 Mk 12.43 2 Cor 9.7
the gift is acceptable according to what one has—not according to what one does
not have. 13 I do not mean that there should be relief for others and pressure on you,
8.14 Acts 4.34,35
but it is a question of a fair balance between 14 your present abundance and their
need, so that their abundance may be for your need, in order that there may be a fair
8.15 Ex 16.18
balance. 15 As it is written,

> "The one who had much did not have too much,
> and the one who had little did not have too little."

8.16 2 Cor 2.13,14
16 But thanks be to God who put in the heart of Titus the same eagerness for
8.17 2 Cor 12.18
you that I myself have. 17 For he not only accepted our appeal, but since he is more
eager than ever, he is going to you of his own accord. 18 With him we are sending
8.18 2 Cor 12.18
the brother who is famous among all the churches for his proclaiming the good
news;[u] 19 and not only that, but he has also been appointed by the churches to travel
8.19 Acts 14.23 1 Cor 16.3
with us while we are administering this generous undertaking[v] for the glory of the
Lord himself[w] and to show our goodwill. 20 We intend that no one should blame us
8.21 Prov 3.4 Rom 12.17 Phil 4.8 1 Pet 2.12
about this generous gift that we are administering, 21 for we intend to do what is
right not only in the Lord's sight but also in the sight of others. 22 And with them we
are sending our brother whom we have often tested and found eager in many matters, but who is now more eager than ever because of his great confidence in you.
8.23 Phil 2.25
23 As for Titus, he is my partner and co-worker in your service; as for our brothers,
8.24 2 Cor 7.4
they are messengers[x] of the churches, the glory of Christ. 24 Therefore openly
before the churches, show them the proof of your love and of our reason for boasting about you.

God prizes cheerful givers

9.1 Rom 15.26 Gal 2.10 1 Thess 4.9
9 Now it is not necessary for me to write you about the ministry to the saints,
2 for I know your eagerness, which is the subject of my boasting about you to
the people of Macedonia, saying that Achaia has been ready since last year; and

[u] Or *the gospel* [v] Gk *this grace* [w] Other ancient authorities lack *himself* [x] Gk *apostles*

NEEDS FOR A FUNDRAISING PROJECT

Information	8.4
Definite purpose	8.4
Readiness and willingness	9.7
Dedication	8.5
Leadership	8.7
Enthusiasm	8.7, 8, 11
Persistence	8.2ff
Honesty and integrity	8.21
Accountability	9.3
Someone to keep it moving	8.18–22

The topic of fundraising is not one to be avoided or one that should embarrass us, but all fundraising efforts should be planned and conducted responsibly.

cheerfully is more important than the amount you give; (2) you should strive to fulfill your financial commitments; (3) if you give to others in need, they will in turn help you when you are in need; (4) you should give as a response to Christ, not for anything you can get out of it. How you give reflects your devotion to Christ.

8.12 How do you decide how much to give? What about differences in the financial resources Christians have? Paul gives the Corinthian church several principles to follow: (1) each person should follow through on previous promises (8.10; 9.3); (2) each person should give as much as he is able (8.12; 9.6); (3) each person must make up his own mind how much to give (9.7); and (4) each person should give in proportion to what God has given (9.10). God gives to us so we can give to others.

8.12 Paul says that we should give of what we have, not what we don't have. Sacrificial giving must be responsible. Paul wants believers to give generously, but not to the extent that those who depend on the givers must go without having their basic needs met. Give until it hurts, but don't give so that it hurts your family and/or relatives needing your financial support.

8.18–21 Another "brother" traveled with Paul and Titus, a man who was elected by the churches to also take the large financial gift to Jerusalem. Paul explains that by traveling together there could be no suspicion and people would know that the gift was being handled honestly. The church did not need to worry that they would misuse the money.

your zeal has stirred up most of them. 3 But I am sending the brothers in order that
our boasting about you may not prove to have been empty in this case, so that you
may be ready, as I said you would be; 4 otherwise, if some Macedonians come with
me and find that you are not ready, we would be humiliated—to say nothing of
you—in this undertaking.[y] 5 So I thought it necessary to urge the brothers to go on
ahead to you, and arrange in advance for this bountiful gift that you have promised,
so that it may be ready as a voluntary gift and not as an extortion.
6 The point is this: the one who sows sparingly will also reap sparingly, and the
one who sows bountifully will also reap bountifully. 7 Each of you must give as you
have made up your mind, not reluctantly or under compulsion, for God loves a
cheerful giver. 8 And God is able to provide you with every blessing in abundance,
so that by always having enough of everything, you may share abundantly in every
good work. 9 As it is written,
"He scatters abroad, he gives to the poor;
his righteousness[z] endures forever."
10 He who supplies seed to the sower and bread for food will supply and multiply
your seed for sowing and increase the harvest of your righteousness.[z] 11 You will
be enriched in every way for your great generosity, which will produce thanksgiving to God through us; 12 for the rendering of this ministry not only supplies the
needs of the saints but also overflows with many thanksgivings to God. 13 Through
the testing of this ministry you glorify God by your obedience to the confession of
the gospel of Christ and by the generosity of your sharing with them and with all
others, 14 while they long for you and pray for you because of the surpassing grace
of God that he has given you. 15 Thanks be to God for his indescribable gift!

9.3 1 Cor 16.2
9.5 Gen 33.11
9.6 Prov 11.24; 19.17; Lk 6.38; Gal 6.7,9
9.7 Ex 35.5; Deut 15.7-10; Rom 12.8; 2 Cor 8.12
9.8 Prov 28.27; Phil 4.19
9.9 Ps 112.9
9.10 Hos 10.12; Mt 6.1
9.11 2 Cor 1.11; 4.16
9.12 2 Cor 8.14
9.13 Mt 5.16; Heb 13.16
9.15 Jas 1.17

4. Paul defends his authority

Paul's authority is discredited

10 I myself, Paul, appeal to you by the meekness and gentleness of Christ—I
who am humble when face to face with you, but bold toward you when I am
away!— 2 I ask that when I am present I need not show boldness by daring to oppose those who think we are acting according to human standards.[a] 3 Indeed, we
live as human beings,[b] but we do not wage war according to human standards;[a]
4 for the weapons of our warfare are not merely human,[c] but they have divine
power to destroy strongholds. We destroy arguments 5 and every proud obstacle

10.1 1 Cor 2.3
10.2 1 Cor 4.18,21
10.4 Jer 1.10; Eph 6.13-17; 1 Thess 5.8
10.5 Isa 2.11

y Other ancient authorities add *of boasting* z Or *benevolence* a Gk *according to the flesh* b Gk *in the flesh* c Gk *fleshly*

9.3–5 Paul reminds the Corinthians to fulfill the commitment they had already made (see also 8.10–12). They said they would collect a financial gift to send to the church in Jerusalem. Paul was sending a few men ahead of him to make sure their gift was ready, so it would be a real gift and not look like people had to give under pressure at the last minute ("as a voluntary gift and not as an extortion"). He is holding them accountable to keep their promise, so that neither Paul nor the Corinthians would be embarrassed.

9.6–8 People may hesitate to give generously to God if they worry about having enough money left over to meet their own needs. Paul assures the Corinthians that God is able to meet their needs. The person who gives only a little will receive only a little in return. Don't let a lack of faith keep you from giving freely and generously.

9.7 Our attitude when we give is more important than the amount we give. We don't have to be embarrassed if we can give only a small gift. God is concerned about *how* we give from the resources we have (see Mark 12.41–44). According to that standard, the giving of the Macedonian churches was difficult to match.

9.10 God gives us resources to use and invest for him. Paul uses the illustration of seeds to explain that the resources God gives us are not to be hidden, foolishly devoured, or thrown away. Instead, they should be cultivated in order to produce more crops. When we invest what God has given us in his work, he will provide us with even more to give.

9.12–14 Paul emphasizes the spiritual rewards for those who give generously to God's work. We should not expect to become wealthy through giving. Those who receive your gifts will be helped, will praise God, and will pray for you. As you bless others, you will be blessed.

10.1, 2 Paul's opponents questioned his authority. From 7.8–16 we know that the majority of Corinthian believers sided with Paul. However, a minority continued to slander him, saying that he was bold in his letters but had no authority in person. Chapters 10–13 are Paul's response to this charge.

10.3–6 We, like Paul, are merely weak humans, but we don't need to use human plans and methods to win our battles. God's mighty weapons are available to us as we fight against Satan's "strongholds." The Christian must choose whose methods to use, God's or man's. Paul assures us that God's mighty weapons—prayer, faith, hope, love, God's Word, the Holy Spirit—are powerful and effective (see Ephesians 6.13–18)! These weapons can break down the proud human arguments against God, and the walls Satan builds to keep people from finding God. When dealing with the pride that keeps people from a relationship with Christ, we may be tempted to use our own methods. But nothing can break down these barriers like God's weapons.

10.5 Paul uses military terminology to describe this warfare against sin and Satan. God must be the commander-in-chief—

10.6 2 Cor 2.9; 7.15 13.2
10.7 Jn 7.24 1 Cor 9.1; 14.37 2 Cor 11.23 1 Jn 4.6
10.10 1 Cor 1.17; 2.3 2 Cor 11.6 Gal 4.13

raised up against the knowledge of God, and we take every thought captive to obey
Christ. 6 We are ready to punish every disobedience when your obedience is complete.
7 Look at what is before your eyes. If you are confident that you belong to
Christ, remind yourself of this, that just as you belong to Christ, so also do we.
8 Now, even if I boast a little too much of our authority, which the Lord gave for
building you up and not for tearing you down, I will not be ashamed of it. 9 I do not
want to seem as though I am trying to frighten you with my letters. 10 For they say,

PAUL'S CREDENTIALS

One of Paul's biggest problems with the church in Corinth was his concern that they viewed him as no more than a blustering preacher; thus, they were not taking seriously his advice in his letters and on his visits. Paul addressed this attitude in the letter of 2 Corinthians, pointing out his credentials as an apostle of Christ and why they should take his advice.

1.1; 1.21; 4.1	Commissioned by God
1.18; 4.2	Spoke truthfully
1.12	Acted with purity, sincerity, and dependence on God alone in his dealings with them
1.13, 14	Was straightforward and sincere in his letters
1.22	Had God's Holy Spirit
2.4; 6.11; 11.11	Loved the Corinthian believers
2.17	Spoke with integrity and Christ's power
3.2, 3	Worked among them and changed their lives
3.4; 12.6	Lived as an example to the believers
4.1, 16	Never gave up
4.2	Taught the Bible with integrity
4.5	Had Christ as the center of his message
4.8–12; 6.4, 5, 9, 10	Endured persecution as he taught the good news
5.11	Worked to win others and to please God
5.12	Was well-intentioned and honest
5.18–20	Was Christ's ambassador, called to tell the good news
6.3, 4	Tried to live a blameless life so others would not be kept from God because of his actions
6.6	Led a wholesome life, understood the gospel, and displayed patience with the Corinthians
6.7	Was truthful and filled with God's power
6.8	Stood true to God first and always
7.2; 11.7–9	Never cheated, wronged, or took advantage of anyone
8.20, 21	Handled their money offering to be sent to Jerusalem in a responsible, blameless manner
10.1–6	Used God's weapons, not his own, for God's work
10.7, 8	Had the power and authority of Christ
10.12, 13	Wanted to measure up to God's plan, not glorify himself
10.14, 15	Had authority because he taught them the good news
11.23–33	Endured pain and danger as he fulfilled his calling
12.2–4	Was blessed with an astounding vision
12.7–10	Was constantly humbled by a "thorn in the flesh" that God refused to take away
12.12	Did miracles among them
12.19	Was always motivated to build up others spiritually
13.4	Was filled with God's power
13.5, 6	Stood the test
13.9	Was always concerned that his spiritual children become mature believers

even our thoughts must submit to his control as we live for him.

10.7–9 Those who opposed Paul portrayed him as weak and powerless, but Paul reminds the Corinthians that he claimed the power and authority of Christ. False teachers were encouraging the believers to ignore Paul, but Paul explains that the words in his letters were to be taken seriously. Paul had authority because he and his companions were the first to bring the good news to Corinth (10.14). On the basis of this authority, Paul wrote to help them grow.

10.10 Some said that Paul's speaking was "contemptible." Evidently, some were judging Paul by comparing him to other speakers they had heard, and Paul was not the most powerful preacher (although he was an excellent debater). But he responded obediently to God's call, and he introduced Christianity to the Roman Empire. Preaching ability is not the first prerequisite of a great leader!

"His letters are weighty and strong, but his bodily presence is weak, and his speech
contemptible." 11 Let such people understand that what we say by letter when absent, we will also do when present.
12 We do not dare to classify or compare ourselves with some of those who 10.12
commend themselves. But when they measure themselves by one another, and 2 Cor 3.1; 5.12
compare themselves with one another, they do not show good sense. 13 We, 10.13 Rom 12.3
however, will not boast beyond limits, but will keep within the field that God has 10.14
assigned to us, to reach out even as far as you. 14 For we were not overstepping our 1 Cor 9.1
limits when we reached you; we were the first to come all the way to you with the 10.15 Rom 15.20
good news[d] of Christ. 15 We do not boast beyond limits, that is, in the labors of 2 Thess 1.3
others; but our hope is that, as your faith increases, our sphere of action among you 10.16 Acts 19.21
may be greatly enlarged, 16 so that we may proclaim the good news[d] in lands 10.17
beyond you, without boasting of work already done in someone else's sphere of Jer 9.24 1 Cor 1.31
action. 17 "Let the one who boasts, boast in the Lord." 18 For it is not those who 10.18
commend themselves that are approved, but those whom the Lord commends. Prov 27.2

Paul and the false apostles

11 I wish you would bear with me in a little foolishness. Do bear with me! 2 I 11.2
feel a divine jealousy for you, for I promised you in marriage to one hus- Hos 2.19 1 Cor 4.15
band, to present you as a chaste virgin to Christ. 3 But I am afraid that as the serpent 11.3 Gen 3.4
deceived Eve by its cunning, your thoughts will be led astray from a sincere and 1 Tim 1.3; 4.1
pure[e] devotion to Christ. 4 For if someone comes and proclaims another Jesus than 2 Pet 3.17 Jude 4
the one we proclaimed, or if you receive a different spirit from the one you re- Rev 12.9
ceived, or a different gospel from the one you accepted, you submit to it readily 11.4 Rom 8.15
enough. 5 I think that I am not in the least inferior to these super-apostles. 6 I may Gal 1.6-8
be untrained in speech, but not in knowledge; certainly in every way and in all 11.6
things we have made this evident to you. Eph 3.4 11.7
7 Did I commit a sin by humbling myself so that you might be exalted, because Acts 18.3

[d] Or *the gospel* [e] Other ancient authorities lack *and pure*

10.12, 13 Paul criticizes the false teachers who were trying to prove their goodness by comparing themselves with others rather than with God's standards. When we compare ourselves with others, we may feel pride because we think we're better. But when we measure ourselves against God's standards, it becomes obvious that we have no basis for pride. Don't worry about other people's accomplishments. Instead, continually ask: How does my life measure up to what God wants? How does my life compare to Jesus Christ?

10.17, 18 When we do something well, we want to tell others and be recognized. But recognition is dangerous—it can lead to inflated pride. How much better to seek the praise of God rather than men. Then, when we receive praise, we will be free to give God the credit. How should you live differently in order to receive God's commendation?

11.1 Paul asks the Corinthian believers to bear with him as he talks "a little foolishness." In other words, Paul feels foolish rehearsing his credentials as a preacher of the gospel (11.16–21). But he feels he must do this to silence the false teachers (11.13).

11.2 This verse could also be translated, "I am anxious that your love should be for Christ alone, just as a pure maiden saves her love for one man only."

11.3 The Corinthians' pure and simple devotion to Christ was being threatened by false teaching. Paul did not want the believers to lose their single-minded love for Christ. Keeping Christ first in our lives can be very difficult when we have so many distractions threatening to sidetrack our faith. Just as Eve lost her focus by listening to the serpent, we too can lose our focus by letting our lives become overcrowded and confused. Is there anything that weakens your commitment to keep Christ first in your life? How can you minimize the distractions that threaten your devotion to him?

11.3, 4 The Corinthian believers fell for smooth talk and messages that sounded good and seemed to make sense. Today there are many false teachings that seem to make sense. Don't believe anyone simply because he sounds like an authority or says words you like to hear. Search the Bible and check the teaching with God's Word. The Bible should be your authoritative guide to all teaching. Don't listen to any "authoritative preacher" who contradicts God's Word.

11.4 The false teachers distorted the truth about Christ and ended up preaching a different Christ, a different spirit than the Holy Spirit, and a different way of salvation. Because the Bible is God's infallible Word, those who teach anything different from what it says are both mistaken and misleading.

11.5 Paul is saying that these marvelous teachers ("super-apostles") are no better than he is. They may be better speakers, but they speak lies and are servants of Satan.

11.6 Paul, a brilliant thinker, was not a trained, spellbinding speaker. Although his ministry was effective (see Acts 17), he was not trained in the Greek schools of oratory and speech making, as many of the false teachers probably were. Paul believed in a simple presentation of the gospel (see 1 Corinthians 1.17), and some people thought this showed simplemindedness. Thus his speaking performance was often used against him by false teachers. In all our teaching and preaching, content is far more important than the presentation. A simple, clear presentation that helps listeners understand will be of great value.

11.7 The Corinthians may have thought that preachers can be judged by how much money they demand. A good speaker would charge a large sum, a fair speaker would be a little cheaper, and a poor speaker would speak for free. The false teachers may have argued that because Paul asked no fee for his preaching, he must be an amateur, with little authority. Believers today must be careful not to assume that every speaker who is well known and demands

I proclaimed God's good news[f] to you free of charge? 8 I robbed other churches by
11.9 2 Cor 12.14 accepting support from them in order to serve you. 9 And when I was with you and
was in need, I did not burden anyone, for my needs were supplied by the friends[g]
who came from Macedonia. So I refrained and will continue to refrain from bur-
11.11 dening you in any way. 10 As the truth of Christ is in me, this boast of mine will not
2 Cor 7.3; 12.15 be silenced in the regions of Achaia. 11 And why? Because I do not love you? God
11.12 1 Cor 9.12 knows I do!
11.13 Gal 1.7 12 And what I do I will also continue to do, in order to deny an opportunity to
Rev 2.2 those who want an opportunity to be recognized as our equals in what they boast
11.14 Rev 12.9 about. 13 For such boasters are false apostles, deceitful workers, disguising themselves as apostles of Christ. 14 And no wonder! Even Satan disguises himself as an
11.15 Rom 2.6; 3.8 angel of light. 15 So it is not strange if his ministers also disguise themselves as
Phil 3.19 ministers of righteousness. Their end will match their deeds.

Paul's many trials

11.17 2 Cor 7.4 16 I repeat, let no one think that I am a fool; but if you do, then accept me as a
fool, so that I too may boast a little. 17 What I am saying in regard to this boastful
11.18 Phil 3.3 confidence, I am saying not with the Lord's authority, but as a fool; 18 since many
11.20 boast according to human standards,[g] I will also boast. 19 For you gladly put up
Gal 2.4; 4.9 with fools, being wise yourselves! 20 For you put up with it when someone makes
11.22 Acts 22.3 slaves of you, or preys upon you, or takes advantage of you, or puts on airs, or
Rom 11.1 Phil 3.5 gives you a slap in the face. 21 To my shame, I must say, we were too weak for that!
11.23 Rom 8.36 But whatever anyone dares to boast of — I am speaking as a fool — I also dare to
1 Cor 15.10 16.23 boast of that. 22 Are they Hebrews? So am I. Are they Israelites? So am I. Are they
descendants of Abraham? So am I. 23 Are they ministers of Christ? I am talking like
11.25 Acts 14.19 a madman — I am a better one: with far greater labors, far more imprisonments,
16.22; 27.41 with countless floggings, and often near death. 24 Five times I have received from
11.26 Acts 9.23 the Jews the forty lashes minus one. 25 Three times I was beaten with rods. Once I
13.50; 14.5 received a stoning. Three times I was shipwrecked; for a night and a day I was
17.5; 19.23 21.31; 23.10 adrift at sea; 26 on frequent journeys, in danger from rivers, danger from bandits,
Gal 2.4 danger from my own people, danger from Gentiles, danger in the city, danger in
11.27 1 Cor 4.11 the wilderness, danger at sea, danger from false brothers and sisters;[h] 27 in toil and
1 Thess 2.9 hardship, through many a sleepless night, hungry and thirsty, often without food,

[f] Gk *the gospel of God* [g] Gk according to the flesh [h] Gk *brothers*

---

a large honorarium is superior at explaining and applying God's Word.

11.7–12 Paul could have asked the Corinthian church for financial support. Jesus himself taught that those who minister for God should be supported by the people to whom they minister (Matthew 10.10). But Paul thought that asking for support in Corinth could be misunderstood. There were many false teachers who hoped to make a good profit from preaching (2.17), and Paul might look like one of them. Paul separated himself completely from these false teachers in order to silence those who only claimed to do God's work.

11.14, 15 In one popular version of the story of Eve's temptation, Satan disguised himself as an angel. Paul may have been thinking of this story, or he could have been referring to Satan's typical devices. In either case, nothing could be more deceitful than Satan, the prince of darkness (Ephesians 6.12; Colossians 1.13), disguising himself as an angel of light. In the same way, when the false teachers claimed to represent Christ, they were lying shamelessly.

11.14, 15 Satan and his servants can deceive us by appearing to be attractive, good, and moral. Many unsuspecting people follow smooth-talking, Bible-quoting leaders into cults that alienate them from their families and practice immorality and deceit. Don't be fooled by external appearances. Our impressions alone are not an accurate indicator of who is or isn't a true follower of Christ; so it helps to ask these questions: (1) Do their teachings confirm Scripture (Acts 17.11)? (2) Do the teachers affirm and proclaim that Jesus Christ is God who came into the world as a man to save people from their sins (1 John 4.1–3)? (3) Is their life-style consistent with biblical morality (Matthew 12.33–37)?

11.22, 23 Paul presents his credentials to counteract the charges that the false teachers were making against him. He felt foolish speaking like this, but his list of credentials would silence any doubts about his authority. He wants to keep the Corinthians from slipping under the spell of the false teachers and turning away from the gospel. Paul also gave a list of his credentials in his letter to the Philippians (see Philippians 3.4–8).

11.23–29 Paul was angry that the false teachers had impressed and deceived the Corinthians (11.13–15). Therefore, he had to reestablish his credibility and authority by listing the trials he had endured in his service for Christ. Some of these trials are recorded in the book of Acts (Acts 14.19; 16.22–24). Because Paul wrote this letter during his third missionary journey (Acts 18.23 – 21.17), his trials weren't over. He would experience yet further difficulties and humiliations for the cause of Christ (see Acts 21.30–33; 22.24–30). He was sacrificing his life for the gospel, something the false teachers would never do. The trials and hurts we experience for Christ's sake build our character, demonstrate our faith, and prepare us to work for the Lord.

11.25 Sea travel was not as safe as it is today. Paul had been shipwrecked three times, and he would face another accident on his voyage to Rome (see Acts 27). By this time, Paul had probably made at least eight or nine voyages.

cold and naked. 28 And, besides other things, I am under daily pressure because of
my anxiety for all the churches. 29 Who is weak, and I am not weak? Who is made
to stumble, and I am not indignant?
30 If I must boast, I will boast of the things that show my weakness. 31 The God
and Father of the Lord Jesus (blessed be he forever!) knows that I do not lie. 32 In
Damascus, the governor[i] under King Aretas guarded the city of Damascus in order
to[j] seize me, 33 but I was let down in a basket through a window in the wall,[k] and
escaped from his hands.

11.28 Acts 20.18 Rom 1.14
11.29 1 Cor 9.22
11.31 Rom 9.5
11.32 Acts 9.24
11.33 Acts 9.25

Paul's vision and his thorn

12 It is necessary to boast; nothing is to be gained by it, but I will go on to
visions and revelations of the Lord. 2 I know a person in Christ who fourteen
years ago was caught up to the third heaven—whether in the body or out of the
body I do not know; God knows. 3 And I know that such a person — whether in the
body or out of the body I do not know; God knows — 4 was caught up into Paradise
and heard things that are not to be told, that no mortal is permitted to repeat. 5 On
behalf of such a one I will boast, but on my own behalf I will not boast, except of
my weaknesses. 6 But if I wish to boast, I will not be a fool, for I will be speaking
the truth. But I refrain from it, so that no one may think better of me than what is
seen in me or heard from me, 7 even considering the exceptional character of the
revelations. Therefore, to keep[l] me from being too elated, a thorn was given me
in the flesh, a messenger of Satan to torment me, to keep me from being too
elated.[m] 8 Three times I appealed to the Lord about this, that it would leave me,
9 but he said to me, "My grace is sufficient for you, for power[n] is made perfect in
weakness." So, I will boast all the more gladly of my weaknesses, so that the power
of Christ may dwell in me. 10 Therefore I am content with weaknesses, insults,
hardships, persecutions, and calamities for the sake of Christ; for whenever I am
weak, then I am strong.

12.1 Gal 1.12
12.2 Deut 10.14 Acts 22.17 Rom 16.7 Gal 1.22
12.4 Lk 23.43 Rev 2.7
12.5 1 Cor 2.3
12.7 Job 2.7 Lk 13.16 Gal 4.13
12.8 Mt 26.44
12.9 Isa 40.29; 42.10 1 Cor 10.13 Eph 3.16 Phil 4.13 Heb 2.18 1 Pet 4.14 2 Pet 2.9

Paul's concern for the Corinthians

11 I have been a fool! You forced me to it. Indeed you should have been the

[i] Gk *ethnarch* [j] Other ancient authorities read *and wanted to* [k] Gk *through the wall* [l] Other ancient authorities read *To keep* [m] Other ancient authorities lack *to keep me from being too elated* [n] Other ancient authorities read *my power*

11.28, 29 Not only did Paul face beatings and perils, he also carried the daily concern for the young churches, worrying that they were staying true to the gospel and free from false teachings and inner strife. Paul was concerned for individuals in the churches he served. If God has placed you in a position of leadership and authority, treat people with Paul's kind of empathy and concern.

11.32 King Aretas, king of the Nabateans (Edomites) from A.D. 9 to 40, appointed a governor to oversee the Nabatean segment of the population in Damascus. Somehow the Jews in Damascus were able to enlist this governor to help them try to capture Paul (see Acts 9.22–25). Paul gives a "for instance" here, describing his escape from Damascus in a basket let down from a hole in the city wall. Paul recounts this incident to show what he had endured for Christ. The false teachers couldn't make such claims.

12.2, 3 Paul continues his "foolish boasting," as he called it, by telling about visions and revelations he had from the Lord. "I know a person" means he was speaking about himself. He explained that he didn't know if he was taken in his body or in his spirit, but he was in paradise ("the third heaven"). This incident cannot be positively matched with a recorded event in Paul's career, although some think this may have been when he was stoned and left for dead (Acts 14.19, 20). Paul told about this incident to show that he had been uniquely touched by God.

12.7, 8 We don't know what Paul's thorn in the flesh was, because he doesn't tell us. Some have suggested that it was malaria, epilepsy, or a disease of the eyes (see Galatians 4.13–15). Whatever the case, it was a chronic and debilitating physical problem, which at times kept him from working. This thorn was a hindrance to his ministry, and he prayed for its removal; but God refused. Paul was a very self-sufficient person, so this thorn was difficult for him. It kept Paul humble, reminded him of his need for constant contact with God, and benefited those around him as they saw God at work in his life.

12.9 Although God did not remove Paul's physical affliction, he promised to demonstrate his power in Paul. The fact that God's power shows up in weak people should give us courage. If we recognize our limitations, we will not congratulate ourselves. Instead, we will turn to God to seek pathways for effectiveness. We must rely on God for our effectiveness rather than on simple energy, effort, or talent. Our weakness not only helps develop Christian character; it also deepens our worship, because in admitting our weakness, we affirm God's strength.

12.10 When we are strong in abilities or resources, we are tempted to do God's work on our own, and that leads to pride. When we are weak, allowing God to fill us with *his* power, then we are stronger than we could ever be on our own. God does not intend for us to seek to be weak, passive, or ineffective – life provides enough hindrances and setbacks without us creating them. When they come, we must depend on God. Only his power makes us effective for him and helps us do work that has lasting value.

12.11–15 Paul is not merely revealing his feelings; he is defending his authority as an apostle of Jesus Christ. He was hurt that the church in Corinth doubted and questioned him, so he defends himself for the cause of the gospel, not to satisfy his ego. When

12.12
Rom 15.18,19
1 Cor 9.1,2
12.13
1 Cor 1.7; 9.12
2 Cor 11.7
12.14
1 Cor 4.14
9.19; 10.33
2 Cor 13.1
12.15
2 Cor 1.6; 6.12
1 Thess 2.8
Phil 2.17
12.16
2 Cor 11.9
12.17
2 Cor 7.2; 9.5
12.18
2 Cor 8.6,18
12.19
Rom 9.1
1 Cor 10.33
2 Cor 5.12
12.20
1 Cor 4.21
12.21
1 Cor 5.1
2 Cor 2.1,4
Gal 5.19
Phil 3.18

ones commending me, for I am not at all inferior to these super-apostles, even
though I am nothing. 12 The signs of a true apostle were performed among you with
utmost patience, signs and wonders and mighty works. 13 How have you been
worse off than the other churches, except that I myself did not burden you? Forgive
me this wrong!

14 Here I am, ready to come to you this third time. And I will not be a burden,
because I do not want what is yours but you; for children ought not to lay up for
their parents, but parents for their children. 15 I will most gladly spend and be spent
for you. If I love you more, am I to be loved less? 16 Let it be assumed that I did not
burden you. Nevertheless (you say) since I was crafty, I took you in by deceit.
17 Did I take advantage of you through any of those whom I sent to you? 18 I urged
Titus to go, and sent the brother with him. Titus did not take advantage of you, did
he? Did we not conduct ourselves with the same spirit? Did we not take the same
steps?

19 Have you been thinking all along that we have been defending ourselves
before you? We are speaking in Christ before God. Everything we do, beloved, is
for the sake of building you up. 20 For I fear that when I come, I may find you not
as I wish, and that you may find me not as you wish; I fear that there may perhaps
be quarreling, jealousy, anger, selfishness, slander, gossip, conceit, and disorder.
21 I fear that when I come again, my God may humble me before you, and that I
may have to mourn over many who previously sinned and have not repented of the
impurity, sexual immorality, and licentiousness that they have practiced.

Paul's final advice

13.1
Num 35.30
Deut 19.15
Acts 18.1
13.3
Mt 10.20
1 Cor 7.40; 9.2
13.4
Rom 1.4; 6.4
Phil 2.7,8
1 Pet 3.18
13.5
Jn 14.20; 17.23
Rom 8.10
1 Cor 9.27; 11.28
Gal 4.19
Col 1.27

13 This is the third time I am coming to you. "Any charge must be sustained by
the evidence of two or three witnesses." 2 I warned those who sinned previously and all the others, and I warn them now while absent, as I did when present
on my second visit, that if I come again, I will not be lenient— 3 since you desire
proof that Christ is speaking in me. He is not weak in dealing with you, but is
powerful in you. 4 For he was crucified in weakness, but lives by the power of God.
For we are weak in him,[o] but in dealing with you we will live with him by the
power of God.

5 Examine yourselves to see whether you are living in the faith. Test yourselves. Do you not realize that Jesus Christ is in you?—unless, indeed, you fail to
meet the test! 6 I hope you will find out that we have not failed. 7 But we pray to God
that you may not do anything wrong—not that we may appear to have met the test,

[o] Other ancient authorities read *with him*

---

you are "put on trial," do you think only about saving your reputation or are you more concerned about what people will think about Christ?

12.13 Paul explains that the only thing he did for the other churches that he didn't do in Corinth was to become a burden—to ask the believers to feed and house him. When he said, "Forgive me this wrong," he was being sarcastic. He actually did more for the Corinthians than for any other church, but still they misunderstood him.

12.14 Paul had founded the church in Corinth on his first visit there (Acts 18.1). He subsequently made a second visit (2.1). This would be his third visit (see also 13.1). He explains that, as before, he doesn't want to be paid, fed, or housed; he only wants the believers to grow with the spiritual food he will feed them.

12.16–19 Although Paul asked nothing of the Corinthian believers, some doubters were still saying that Paul must have been crafty and made money from them somehow. But Paul again explains that everything he did for the believers was for their edification, not to enrich himself.

12.20, 21 After reading this catalog of sins, it is hard to believe that these are the people Paul said had great gifts and were leaders (8.7). Paul feared that the practices of wicked Corinth had invaded the congregation. He writes sternly, hoping they will straighten up their lives before he arrives. We must live differently than unbelievers, not letting secular society dictate how we are to treat others. Don't let culture invade your practices at church.

13.2 When Paul arrived the third time in Corinth, he would not be lenient toward the unrepentant sinners. His actions could include (1) confronting and publicly denouncing their behavior; (2) exercising church discipline by calling them before the church leaders; or (3) excommunicating them from the church.

13.5 The Corinthians were to examine and test themselves to see if they really were Christians. Just as we get physical check-ups, Paul urges us to give ourselves spiritual check-ups. We should look for a growing awareness of Christ's presence and power in our lives. Only then will we know if we are true Christians or imposters. If we're not taking active steps to grow closer to God, we are withdrawing farther away from him.

but that you may do what is right, though we may seem to have failed. [8]For we
cannot do anything against the truth, but only for the truth. [9]For we rejoice when
we are weak and you are strong. This is what we pray for, that you may become
perfect. [10]So I write these things while I am away from you, so that when I come,
I may not have to be severe in using the authority that the Lord has given me for
building up and not for tearing down.

11 Finally, brothers and sisters,[p] farewell.[q] Put things in order, listen to my
appeal,[r] agree with one another, live in peace; and the God of love and peace will
be with you. [12]Greet one another with a holy kiss. All the saints greet you.

13 The grace of the Lord Jesus Christ, the love of God, and the communion of[s]
the Holy Spirit be with all of you.

[p] Gk *brothers* [q] Or *rejoice* [r] Or *encourage one another* [s] Or *and the sharing in*

13.9 1 Cor 4.10; Eph 4.12-16; 1 Thess 3.10

13.10 Tit 1.13

13.11 Rom 12.16; 15.33; 1 Cor 1.10; 1 Pet 3.8

13.13 Rom 5.5; 16.20; Phil 2.1

13.8, 9 Just as parents want their children to grow into mature adults, so Paul wanted the Corinthians to grow into mature believers. As we share the good news, our goal should be not merely to see others profess faith or begin attending church, but to see them become mature in their faith. Don't set your sights too low.

13.11 Paul's closing words—what he wants the Corinthians to remember about the needs for their church—are still fitting for the church today. When these qualities are not present, there are problems that must be dealt with. These traits do not come to a church by glossing over problems, conflicts, and difficulties. They are not produced by neglect, denial, withdrawal, or bitterness. They are the by-products of the extremely hard work of solving problems. Just as Paul and the Corinthians had to hammer out difficulties to bring peace, so we must apply the principles of God's Word and not just hear them.

13.13 Paul's farewell blessing invokes all three members of the trinity—Father, Son, and Holy Spirit. Although the doctrine of the trinity is not explicitly taught in Scripture, verses such as this one show that it was believed.

13.13 Paul was dealing with an ongoing problem in the Corinthian church. He could have refused to communicate until they cleared up their situation, but he loved them and reached out to them again with the love of Christ. Love, however, means that sometimes we must confront those we care about. Both authority and personal concern are needed in dealing with people who are ruining their lives with sin. But there are several wrong approaches in confronting others, and these can further break relationships rather than heal them. We can be legalistic and blast people with the laws they should be obeying. We can turn away from them because we don't want to face the situation. We can isolate them by gossiping about their problem and turning others against them as well. Or, like Paul, we can seek to build relationships by taking a better approach—sharing, communicating, and caring. This is a difficult approach that can drain us emotionally; but it is best for the other person, and it is the only Christlike way to deal with others' sin.

The Letter of Paul to the GALATIANS

A FAMILY, executing their carefully planned escape at midnight, dashing for the border . . . a man standing outside prison walls, gulping fresh air, awash in the new sun . . . a young woman with every trace of the ravaging drug gone from her system . . . they are FREE! With fresh anticipation, they can begin life anew.

Whether fleeing oppression, stepping out of prison, or breaking a strangling habit, freedom means life. There is nothing so exhilarating as knowing that the past is forgotten and that new options await. People yearn to be free.

The book of Galatians is the charter of Christian freedom. In this profound letter, Paul proclaims the reality of our liberty in Christ—freedom from the law and the power of sin to serve our living Lord.

Most of the first converts and early leaders in the church were Jewish Christians who proclaimed Jesus as their Messiah. As Jewish Christians, they struggled with a dual identity: their Jewishness constrained them to be strict followers of the law; their newfound faith in Christ invited them to celebrate a holy liberty. They wondered how Gentiles (non-Jews) could be part of the kingdom of heaven.

This controversy tore the early church. Judaizers—an extremist Jewish faction within the church—taught that Gentile Christians had to submit to Jewish laws and traditions *in addition to* believing in Christ. As a missionary to the Gentiles, Paul had to confront this issue many times.

Galatians was written, therefore, to refute the Judaizers and to call believers back to the pure gospel. The Good News is for all people—Jews and Gentiles alike. Salvation is by God's grace through faith in Christ Jesus *and nothing else*. Faith in Christ means true freedom.

After a brief introduction (1.1–5), Paul addresses those who were accepting the Judaizer's twisted gospel (1.6–9). He summarizes the controversy including his personal confrontation with Peter and other church leaders (1.10—2.16). He then demonstrates that salvation is by faith alone by alluding to his conversion (2.17–21), appealing to his readers' own experience of the Good News (3.1–5), and showing how the Old Testament teaches grace (3.6–20). Next, he explains the purpose of God's laws and the relationship between law, God's promises, and Christ (3.21—4.31).

Having laid the foundation, Paul builds his case for Christian liberty. We are saved by faith, not by works (5.1–12); our freedom means we are free to love and serve one another, not to do wrong (5.13–26); and Christians should bear one another's burdens and be kind to one another (6.1–10). In 6.11–18, Paul takes the pen into his own hand and shares his final thoughts.

As you read Galatians, try to understand this first-century conflict between law and grace, faith and works, but also be aware of modern parallels. Like Paul, defend the truth of the gospel and reject all those who would add to or twist this truth. You are *free* in Christ—step into the light and celebrate!

VITAL STATISTICS

PURPOSE:
To refute the Judaizers (who taught that Gentile believers must obey the Jewish law in order to be saved), and to call Christians to faith and freedom in Christ

AUTHOR:
Paul

TO WHOM WRITTEN:
The churches in southern Galatia founded on Paul's first missionary journey (including Iconium, Lystra, Derbe)

DATE WRITTEN:
About A.D. 49, from Antioch, prior to the Jerusalem council (A.D. 50)

SETTING:
The most pressing controversy of the early church was the relationship of new believers, particularly Gentiles, to the Jewish laws. This was especially a problem for the converts and young churches that Paul founded on his first missionary journey. Paul writes to correct this problem. Later, at the council in Jerusalem, the conflict was officially resolved by the church leaders.

KEY VERSE:
"For freedom Christ has set us free. Stand firm, therefore, and do not submit again to a yoke of slavery" (5.1).

KEY PEOPLE:
Paul, Peter, Barnabas, Titus, Abraham, false teachers

KEY PLACES:
Galatia, Jerusalem

SPECIAL FEATURES:
This letter is not addressed to any specific body of believers and was probably circulated to several churches in Galatia.

THE BLUEPRINT

1. Authenticity of the gospel (1.1—2.21)
2. Superiority of the gospel (3.1—5.1)
3. Freedom of the gospel (5.2—6.18)

In response to attacks from false teachers, Paul wrote to defend his apostleship and to defend the authority of the gospel. The Galatians were beginning to turn from faith to legalism. The struggle between the gospel and legalism is still a crisis. Many today would have us return to trying to earn God's favor through following rituals or obeying a set of rules. As Christians, we are not boxed in, but set free. To preserve our freedom, we must stay close to Christ and resist any who promote subtle ways of trying to earn our salvation.

MEGATHEMES

THEME	EXPLANATION	IMPORTANCE
Law	A group of Jewish teachers insisted that non-Jewish believers must obey Jewish law and traditional rules. They believed a person was saved by following the law of Moses (with emphasis on circumcision, the sign of the covenant), in addition to faith in Christ. Paul opposed them by showing that the law can't save anyone.	We can't be saved by keeping the Old Testament law, even the ten commandments. The law served as a guide to point out our need to be forgiven. Christ fulfilled the obligations of the law for us. We must turn to him to be saved. He alone can make us right with God.
Faith	We are saved from God's judgment and penalty for sin by God's gracious gift to us. We receive salvation by faith—trusting in him—not in anything else. Becoming a Christian is in no way based on our initiative, wise choice, or good character. We can be right with God only by believing in him.	Your acceptance with God comes by believing in Christ alone. You must never add to or twist this truth. We are saved by faith, not by the good that we do. Have you placed your whole trust and confidence in Christ? He alone can forgive you and bring you into a relationship with God.
Freedom	Galatians is our charter of Christian freedom. We are not under the jurisdiction of Jewish laws and traditions, nor under the authority of Jerusalem. Faith in Christ brings true freedom from sin and from the futile attempt to be right with God by keeping the law.	We are free in Christ, and yet freedom is a privilege. We are not free to disobey Christ or be immoral, but we are free to serve the risen Christ. Let us use our freedom to love and to serve, not to do wrong.
Holy Spirit	We become Christians through the work of the Holy Spirit. He brings new life; even our faith to believe is a gift from him. The Holy Spirit instructs, guides, leads, and gives us power. He ends our bondage to evil desires, and he creates in us love, joy, peace, and many other wonderful changes.	When the Holy Spirit leads us, he produces his fruit in us. Just as we are saved by faith, not works, we also grow by faith. By believing, we can have the Holy Spirit within us, helping us live for Christ. Obey Christ by following the Holy Spirit's leading.

1. Authenticity of the gospel

1 Paul an apostle—sent neither by human commission nor from human authorities, but through Jesus Christ and God the Father, who raised him from the
dead— 2 and all the members of God's family[a] who are with me,

a Gk *all the brothers*

1.1 Paul and Barnabas had just completed their first missionary journey (Acts 13.2—14.28). They had visited Iconium, Lystra, and Derbe, cities in the Roman province of Galatia (present-day Turkey). Upon returning to Antioch, Paul was accused by some Jew-

1.4 Jn 15.19; 17.14 Rom 4.25
1.5 Rom 11.36

To the churches of Galatia:
3 Grace to you and peace from God our Father and the Lord Jesus Christ, 4 who
gave himself for our sins to set us free from the present evil age, according to the
will of our God and Father, 5 to whom be the glory forever and ever. Amen.

There is no other gospel

6 I am astonished that you are so quickly deserting the one who called you in the

CITIES IN GALATIA
Paul visited several cities in Galatia on each of his three missionary journeys. On his first journey he went through Antioch in Pisidia, Iconium, Lystra, and Derbe, then retraced his steps; on his second journey he went by land from Antioch in Syria through the four cities in Galatia; on his third journey he also went through those cities on the main route to Ephesus.

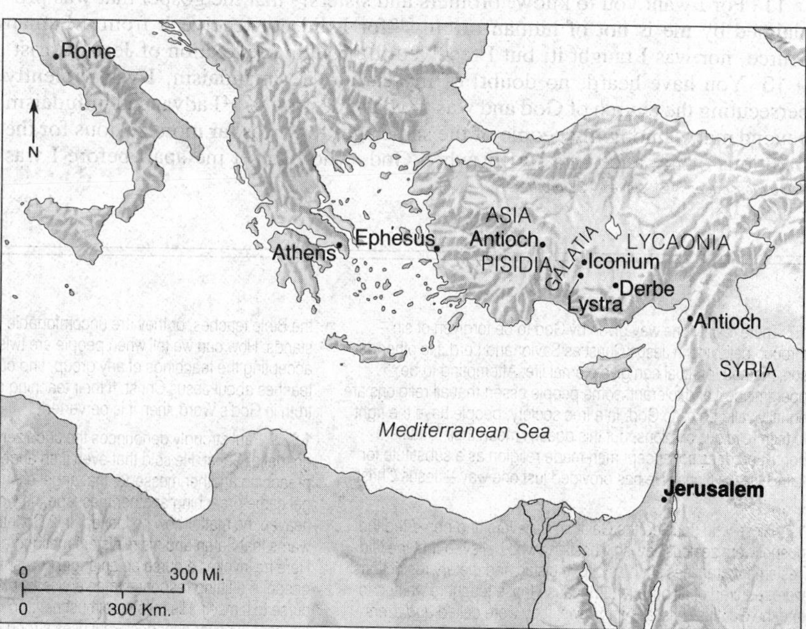

ish Christians of diluting Christianity to make it more appealing to Gentiles. These Jewish Christians disagreed with Paul's statements that Gentiles did not have to follow many of the religious laws that the Jews had obeyed for centuries. Some of Paul's accusers had even followed him to those Galatian cities and told the Gentile converts they had to be circumcised and follow all the Jewish laws and customs in order to be saved. According to these men, Gentiles had to first become Jews in order to become Christians.

In response to this threat, Paul wrote this letter to the Galatian churches. In it, he explains that following the Old Testament laws or the Jewish laws will not bring salvation. A person is saved by grace through faith. Paul wrote this letter about A.D. 49, shortly before the meeting of the Jerusalem council, which settled the law versus grace controversy (Acts 15).

1.1 Paul was called to be an apostle by Jesus Christ himself. He presented his credentials at the very outset of this letter, because some people in Galatia were questioning his authority.

1.1 For more information about Paul's life, see his Profile in Acts 10. Paul had been a Christian for about fifteen years at this time.

1.2 In Paul's time, *Galatia* was the Roman province located in the center section of present-day Turkey. Much of the region rests on a large and fertile plateau, and large numbers of people had moved to the region because of its favorable agriculture. One of Paul's goals during his missionary journeys was to visit regions with large population centers in order to reach as many people as possible.

1.3–5 God's plan all along was to save us by Jesus' death. We have been delivered from the power of this evil world – a world ruled by Satan, full of cruelty, tragedy, temptation, and deception. Being rescued from this evil world doesn't mean we are taken out of it, but that we are no longer enslaved to it. We have been saved to live for God, and we have been promised eternal life with him.

1.6 Some people were preaching a "different gospel." They taught that to be saved, Gentile believers had to follow Jewish laws and customs, especially the rite of circumcision. Faith in Christ was not enough. This message undermined the truth of the good news that salvation is a gift, not a reward for certain works. Jesus Christ has made this gift available to all people, not just to Jews. Beware of people who say that we need to do more than believe in Christ to be saved. When people set up additional requirements for salvation, they deny the power of Christ's death on the cross (see 3.1–5).

grace of Christ and are turning to a different gospel— 7 not that there is another
gospel, but there are some who are confusing you and want to pervert the gospel of
Christ. 8 But even if we or an angel[b] from heaven should proclaim to you a gospel
contrary to what we proclaimed to you, let that one be accursed! 9 As we have said
before, so now I repeat, if anyone proclaims to you a gospel contrary to what you
received, let that one be accursed!
10 Am I now seeking human approval, or God's approval? Or am I trying to
please people? If I were still pleasing people, I would not be a servant[c] of Christ.

1.7 Acts 15.1; Gal 5.10
1.8 2 Cor 11.14
1.9 Deut 4.2; 12.32; Prov 30.6; Rev 22.18
1.10 1 Thess 2.4

Paul received the gospel from God

11 For I want you to know, brothers and sisters,[d] that the gospel that was proclaimed by me is not of human origin; 12 for I did not receive it from a human
source, nor was I taught it, but I received it through a revelation of Jesus Christ.
13 You have heard, no doubt, of my earlier life in Judaism. I was violently
persecuting the church of God and was trying to destroy it. 14 I advanced in Judaism
beyond many among my people of the same age, for I was far more zealous for the
traditions of my ancestors. 15 But when God, who had set me apart before I was

1.12 1 Cor 2.10; Eph 3.3
1.13 Acts 8.3; 9.21; 22.3-5; 26.4-11
1.15 Acts 9.15; 15.10; Eph 2.3

[b] Or *a messenger* [c] Gk *slave* [d] Gk *brothers*

1.7 There is only one way given by God to be forgiven of sin—through believing in Jesus Christ as Savior and Lord. No other person, method, or ritual can give eternal life. Attempting to be open-minded and tolerant, some people assert that all religions are equally valid paths to God. In a free society, people have the right to their religious opinions, but this doesn't mean their ideas are right. God does not accept man-made religion as a substitute for faith in Jesus Christ. He has provided just one way—Jesus Christ (John 14.6).

1.7 Those who troubled the Galatian believers and perverted the gospel were zealous Jewish Christians who believed that the Old Testament practices such as circumcision and dietary restrictions were required of all believers. Because these teachers wanted to turn the Gentile Christians into Jews, they were called *Judaizers.* Some time after the letter to the Galatians was sent, Paul met with the apostles in Jerusalem to discuss this matter further (see Acts 15).

1.7 The Galatian Christians were mainly Greek, unfamiliar with Jewish laws and customs. The Judaizers were an extreme faction of Jewish Christians. Both groups believed in Christ, but their lifestyles differed considerably. We do not know why the Judaizers traveled to teach their mistaken notions to the new Gentile converts. They may have been motivated by (1) a sincere wish to integrate Judaism with the new Christian faith, (2) a sincere love for their Jewish heritage, or (3) a jealous desire to destroy Paul's authority. Whether or not these Judaizers were sincere, their teaching threatened these new churches and had to be countered. When Paul called their teaching a perversion of the gospel, he was not rejecting everything Jewish. He himself was a Jew who worshiped in the temple and attended the religious festivals. But he was concerned that *nothing* get in the way of the simple truth of his message—that salvation, to Jews and Gentiles alike, is by faith in Jesus Christ alone.

1.7 A perversion or twisting of the truth is more difficult to spot than an outright lie. The Judaizers were twisting the truth about Christ. They claimed to follow him, but they denied that Jesus' work on the cross was sufficient for salvation. There will always be people who twist the good news. Either they do not understand what the Bible teaches, or they are uncomfortable with the truth as it stands. How can we tell when people are twisting the truth? Before accepting the teachings of any group, find out what the group teaches about Jesus Christ. If their teaching does not match the truth in God's Word, then it is perverted.

1.8, 9 Paul strongly denounces the Judaizers' perversion of the gospel of Christ. He said that even if an angel from heaven comes preaching another message, that angel should be cursed. If an angel came preaching another message, he would not be from heaven, no matter how he looked. In 2 Corinthians 11.14, 15, Paul warns that Satan and his ministers masquerade as angels of light. Here he invokes a curse on an angel who spreads a false gospel—a fitting response to an emissary of hell. Paul extends that curse to himself. His message must never change, for the truth of the gospel never changes. Paul uses strong language because he is dealing with a life-and-death issue.

1.10 Paul had to speak harshly to the Christians in Galatia because they were in serious danger. He did not apologize for his straightforward words, knowing that he could not serve Christ faithfully if he allowed the Galatian Christians to remain on the wrong track. Whom are you trying to please—other people or God? Pray for the courage to put God's approval first.

1.11ff Why should the Galatians listen to Paul instead of the Judaizers? Paul answers this implicit question by furnishing his credentials: his message was directly from Christ (1.12); he had been an exemplary Jew (1.13, 14); he had a special conversion experience (1.15, 16; see also Acts 9.1–9); he was confirmed in his ministry by the other apostles (1.18, 19; 2.1–9). Paul also presented his credentials to the Corinthian and Philippian churches (2 Corinthians 11, 12; Philippians 3.4–9).

1.12 We do not know the details of this other revelation. Paul is referring to something other than his experience on the road to Damascus. The point is that these words are more than his own speculations or ideas.

1.13, 14 Paul had been one of the most religious Jews of his day, scrupulously keeping the law and relentlessly persecuting Christians (see Acts 9.1, 2). Before his conversion he had been even more zealous for the law than the Judaizers were. He had surpassed his contemporaries in religious knowledge and practice. Paul was sincere in his zeal—but wrong. When he met Jesus Christ, his life changed. Now he directs all his energies toward building up the Christian church.

1.16 Rom 1.17; 8.3, 10; Col 1.27
1.17 1 Jn 3.8
1.18 Acts 9.26
1.19 Mt 13.55; Acts 12.17; 15.13; 21.18; 1 Cor 15.7
1.23 Acts 9.20

born and called me through his grace, was pleased 16 to reveal his Son to me,[e] so
that I might proclaim him among the Gentiles, I did not confer with any human
being, 17 nor did I go up to Jerusalem to those who were already apostles before me,
but I went away at once into Arabia, and afterwards I returned to Damascus.
18 Then after three years I did go up to Jerusalem to visit Cephas and stayed
with him fifteen days; 19 but I did not see any other apostle except James the Lord's
brother. 20 In what I am writing to you, before God, I do not lie! 21 Then I went into
the regions of Syria and Cilicia, 22 and I was still unknown by sight to the churches
of Judea that are in Christ; 23 they only heard it said, "The one who formerly was
persecuting us is now proclaiming the faith he once tried to destroy." 24 And they
glorified God because of me.

[e] Gk *in me*

THE MARKS OF THE TRUE GOSPEL AND OF FALSE GOSPELS

Marks of a false gospel

2.21	Treats Christ's death as meaningless
3.12	Says people must obey the law in order to be saved
4.10	Tries to find favor with God by observing certain rituals
5.4	Counts on keeping laws to erase sin

Marks of the true gospel

1.11, 12	Teaches that the source of the gospel is God
2.20	Knows that life is obtained through death; we trust in the God who loved us and died for us so that we might die to sin and live for him
3.14	Explains that all believers have the Holy Spirit through faith
3.21, 22	Declares that we cannot be saved by keeping laws; the only way of salvation is by faith in Christ, which is available to all
3.26–28	Says that all believers are one in Christ, so there is no basis for discrimination of any kind
5.24, 25	Proclaims that we are free from the grip of sin and the Holy Spirit's power fills and guides us

1.15, 16 Because God was guiding his ministry, Paul wasn't doing anything God hadn't already planned and given him power to do. The great prophets Isaiah and Jeremiah knew that God had called them, even before they were born, to do special work for him (see Isaiah 49.1; Jeremiah 1.5). God knows you intimately as well, and he chose you to be his even before you were born (see Psalm 139). He wants you to draw close to him and to fulfill the job he has given you to do.

1.15–24 Paul tells of his conversion to show that his message came directly from God. God commissioned him to preach the good news to the Gentiles. After his call, Paul did not consult with anyone; instead he spent three years in the deserts of Arabia. Then he spoke with Peter and James, but he had no other contact with Jewish Christians for several more years. During those years, he was preaching to the Gentiles the message God had given him. His good news did not come from any person; it came from God.

1.16 The word *Jew* refers not only to nationality but also to religion. To be fully Jewish, a person must have descended from Abraham. In addition, a faithful Jew adheres to the Jewish laws. *Gentiles* are non-Jews, whether in nationality or in religion. In Paul's day, Jews thought of all Gentiles as pagans. Jews avoided Gentiles, believing that contact with Gentiles brought spiritual corruption. Although Gentiles could become Jews in religion by undergoing circumcision and by following Jewish laws and customs, they were never fully accepted.

Many Jews had difficulty understanding that God's message is for Jews and Gentiles alike. Some Jews thought Gentiles had to become Jews before they could become Christians. But God planned to save both Jews and Gentiles. He had revealed this plan through Old Testament prophets (see, for example, Genesis 12.3; Isaiah 42.6; 66.19), he had fulfilled it through Jesus Christ, and he was proclaiming it to the Gentiles through Paul.

1.18 Paul is talking about his first visit to Jerusalem as a Christian, as recorded in Acts 9.26–30. Cephas is another name for Peter.

1.21 Because of opposition in Jerusalem (see Acts 9.29, 30), Paul had gone to Syria and Cilicia. In those remote areas, he had no opportunity to receive instruction from the apostles.

1.24 Paul's changed life brought many comments from those who saw him or heard about him. His new life astonished them. They glorified God, because only God could have turned this zealous persecutor of Christians into a Christian himself. We may not have had as dramatic a change as Paul had, but still our new lives should honor God in every way. When people look at you, do they recognize that God has made changes in you? If not, perhaps you are not living as you should.

The apostles accepted Paul

2 Then after fourteen years I went up again to Jerusalem with Barnabas, taking
Titus along with me. 2 I went up in response to a revelation. Then I laid before
them (though only in a private meeting with the acknowledged leaders) the gospel
that I proclaim among the Gentiles, in order to make sure that I was not running, or
had not run, in vain. 3 But even Titus, who was with me, was not compelled to be
circumcised, though he was a Greek. 4 But because of false believers[f] secretly
brought in, who slipped in to spy on the freedom we have in Christ Jesus, so that
they might enslave us— 5 we did not submit to them even for a moment, so that the
truth of the gospel might always remain with you. 6 And from those who were supposed to be acknowledged leaders (what they actually were makes no difference to
me; God shows no partiality)—those leaders contributed nothing to me. 7 On the
contrary, when they saw that I had been entrusted with the gospel for the uncircumcised, just as Peter had been entrusted with the gospel for the circumcised 8 (for he
who worked through Peter making him an apostle to the circumcised also worked
through me in sending me to the Gentiles), 9 and when James and Cephas and John,
who were acknowledged pillars, recognized the grace that had been given to me,
they gave to Barnabas and me the right hand of fellowship, agreeing that we should
go to the Gentiles and they to the circumcised. 10 They asked only one thing, that
we remember the poor, which was actually what I was[g] eager to do.

[f] Gk *false brothers* [g] Or *had been*

2.1 Acts 15.2-29
2.2 Gal 1.6
2.3 Acts 16.3
2.4 Gal 1.7; 4.3,9; 5.1
2.5 Gal 1.6; 2.14
2.6 Acts 10.34; Rom 2.11; 2 Cor 12.11; Gal 6.3
2.7 Acts 13.46; 1 Thess 2.4
2.8 Acts 9.15; 13.2; 22.21; 26.17; 1 Cor 15.10
2.9 Rom 1.5
2.10 Acts 11.30; 24.17

2.1 Paul was converted around A.D. 35. The fourteen years he mentions are probably calculated from the time of his conversion. Therefore, this trip to Jerusalem was not his first. He made his first trip to Jerusalem around A.D. 38 (see Acts 9.26–30); and other trips to Jerusalem in approximately A.D. 44 (Acts 11.29, 30; Galatians 2.1–10), A.D. 49/50 (Acts 15), A.D. 52 (Acts 18.22; "the church" refers to the church in Jerusalem), and A.D. 57 (Acts 21.15ff). Paul probably visited Jerusalem on several other occasions as well.

2.1 Barnabas and Titus were two of Paul's close friends. Barnabas and Paul visited Galatia together on their first missionary journey. Paul wrote a personal letter to Titus, a faithful believer and church leader serving on the island of Crete (see the book of Titus). For more information on Barnabas, see his Profile in Acts 13. For more information on Titus, see the letter Paul wrote to him in the New Testament.

2.1 After his conversion Paul spent many years preparing for the ministry to which God had called him. This preparation period included time alone with God (1.16, 17), as well as time conferring with other Christians. Often new Christians, in their zeal, want to begin a full-time ministry without investing the necessary time studying the Bible and learning from qualified teachers. We need not wait to share Christ with our friends, but we may need more preparation before embarking on a special ministry, whether volunteer or full-time. While we wait for God's timing, we should continue to study, learn, and grow.

2.2 God told Paul, by a revelation, to confer with the church leaders in Jerusalem about the message he was preaching to the Gentiles, so they would understand what he was doing and approve. The essence of Paul's message to both Jews and Gentiles was that God's salvation is offered to all people regardless of race, sex, nationality, wealth, social standing, education, or anything else. Forgiveness comes through trusting in Christ (see Romans 10.8–13).

2.2, 3 Even though God had specifically sent Paul to the Gentiles (Acts 9.15, 16), Paul needed to discuss his gospel message with the leaders of the Jerusalem church (Acts 15). This meeting prevented a major split in the church, and it formally acknowledged the apostles' approval of Paul's preaching. Sometimes we avoid conferring with others because we fear that problems or arguments may develop. Instead, we should openly discuss our plans and actions with others. This helps everyone understand the situation better, reduces gossip, and builds unity in the church.

2.3–5 When Paul took Titus, a Greek Christian, to Jerusalem, the Judaizers (false believers) said he should be circumcised. Paul adamantly refused to give in to their demands. The apostles agreed that circumcision was an unnecessary rite for Gentile converts. Several years later, Paul circumcised Timothy, another Greek Christian (Acts 16.3). Unlike Titus, however, Timothy was half Jewish. Paul did not deny Jews the right to be circumcised; he was simply saying that Gentiles should not be asked to become Jews before becoming Christians.

2.4 These false believers were most likely from the sect of the Pharisees (Acts 15.5). These were the most strict religious leaders of Judaism, some of whom had been converted. We don't know if these were agents of well-meaning converts or those trying to pervert Christianity. Most agree that neither Peter nor James had any part in this conspiracy.

2.6 It's easy to rate people on the basis of their official status and to be intimidated by powerful people. But Paul was not intimidated by the "acknowledged leaders," because all believers are equal in Christ. We should show respect for our spiritual leaders, but our ultimate allegiance must be to Christ. We are to serve him with our whole being. He doesn't rate us according to our status; he looks at the attitude of our hearts (1 Samuel 16.7).

2.6 "Contributed nothing to me" means that the apostles had nothing to add to Paul's preaching. He had the complete truth and was preaching it correctly.

2.7–9 The church leaders (pillars), James, Peter (Cephas), and John realized that God was using Paul to reach the Gentiles, just as Peter was being used so greatly to reach the Jews. After hearing Paul's message, they gave Paul and Barnabas their approval (the right hand of fellowship) to continue working among the Gentiles.

2.10 The apostles referred to the poor of Jerusalem. While many Gentile converts were financially comfortable, the Jerusalem church suffered a severe famine in Palestine (see Acts 11.28–30). So on his journeys, Paul gathered funds for the Jewish Christians (Acts 24.17; Romans 15.25–29; 1 Corinthians 16.1–4; 2 Corinthians 8). The need for believers to care for the poor is a constant theme of Scripture. But often we do nothing, caught up in meeting our own needs and desires. Or we just don't see enough poor peo-

Paul publicly opposed Peter

11 But when Cephas came to Antioch, I opposed him to his face, because he
2.12 Acts 10.28 11.2,3 stood self-condemned; 12 for until certain people came from James, he used to eat
with the Gentiles. But after they came, he drew back and kept himself separate for
fear of the circumcision faction. 13 And the other Jews joined him in this hypocrisy,
2.14 Acts 11.3 so that even Barnabas was led astray by their hypocrisy. 14 But when I saw that they
were not acting consistently with the truth of the gospel, I said to Cephas before
2.15 Acts 15.10 Eph 2.3 Phil 3.4 them all, "If you, though a Jew, live like a Gentile and not like a Jew, how can you
compel the Gentiles to live like Jews?"[h]
15 We ourselves are Jews by birth and not Gentile sinners; 16 yet we know that
2.16 Acts 13.39 Rom 1.17; 3.20 8.3 Heb 7.18 a person is justified[i] not by the works of the law but through faith in Jesus Christ.[j]
And we have come to believe in Christ Jesus, so that we might be justified by faith
in Christ,[k] and not by doing the works of the law, because no one will be justified

[h] Some interpreters hold that the quotation extends into the following paragraph [i] Or *reckoned as righteous;* and so elsewhere [j] Or *the faith of Jesus Christ* [k] Or *the faith of Christ*

JUDAIZERS VS. PAUL

What the Judaizers said about Paul	*Paul's defense*
They said he was perverting the truth.	He received his message from Christ himself (1.11, 12).
They said he was a traitor to the Jewish faith.	Paul was one of the most dedicated Jews of his time. Yet, in the midst of one of his most zealous acts, God transformed him through a revelation of the good news about Jesus (1.13–16; Acts 9.1–30).
They said he compromised and watered down his message for the Gentiles.	The other apostles declared that the message Paul preached was the true gospel (2.1–10).
They said he was disregarding the law of Moses.	Far from downgrading the law, Paul puts the law in its proper place. He says it shows people where they have sinned and it points them to Christ (3.19–29).

As the debate raged between the Gentile Christians and the Judaizers, Paul found it necessary to write to the churches in Galatia. The Judaizers were trying to undermine Paul's authority and taught a false gospel. In reply, Paul defended his authority as an apostle and the truth of his message. The debate over Jewish laws and Gentile Christians was officially resolved at the Jerusalem council (Acts 15), yet it continued to be a point of contention after that time.

ple to remember their needs. The world is filled with poor people, here and overseas. What can you do to help?

2.11 Antioch in Syria (distinguished from Antioch in Pisidia) was a major trade center in the ancient world. Heavily populated by Greeks, it eventually became a strong Christian center. In Antioch the believers were first called Christians (Acts 11.26). Antioch in Syria became the headquarters for the Gentile church and Paul's base of operations.

2.11 Although Peter (Cephas) was a leader of the church, he was acting like a hypocrite. Paul knew he had to confront Peter before his actions damaged the church. Therefore, Paul publicly confronted Peter. Note, however, that Paul did not go to the other leaders, nor did he write letters to the churches telling them not to follow Peter's example. Instead, he confronted Peter face to face. Sometimes sincere Christians, even Christian leaders, make mistakes. And it may take other sincere Christians to get them back on track. If you are convinced that someone is doing harm to himself or the church, try the direct approach. There is no place for backstabbing in the body of Christ.

2.11ff The Judaizers accused Paul of watering down the gospel to make it easier for Gentiles to accept, while Paul accused the Judaizers of nullifying the truth of the gospel by adding conditions to it. The basis of salvation was the issue—is salvation through Christ alone, or does it come through Christ *and* adherence to the law? The argument came to a head when Peter, Paul, the Judaizers, and some Gentile Christians all gathered together in Antioch to share a meal. Peter probably thought that by staying aloof from the Gentiles he was promoting harmony—he did not want to offend the friends of James. But Paul charged that Peter's action violated the gospel. By joining the Judaizers, Peter implicitly supported their claim that Christ was not sufficient for salvation. Compromise is an important element in getting along with others, but we should never compromise the truth of God's Word. If we feel we have to change our Christian beliefs to match those of our companions, we are on dangerous ground.

2.15, 16 If the Jewish laws cannot save (justify) us, why should we still obey the ten commandments and other Old Testament laws? Paul is not saying the law is bad, because in another letter he wrote, "the law is holy" (Romans 7.12). Instead, he is saying that the law can never make us acceptable to God. The law still has an important role to play in the life of a Christian. The law: (1) guards us from sin by giving us standards for behavior; (2) convicts us of sin, leaving us the opportunity to get in tune with God by asking his forgiveness; (3) drives us to trust in the sufficiency of Christ because we can never keep the ten commandments perfectly. The law cannot possibly save us. But after we have become Christians, it can be a valuable guide for living as God requires.

by the works of the law. 17 But if, in our effort to be justified in Christ, we ourselves
have been found to be sinners, is Christ then a servant of sin? Certainly not! 18 But
if I build up again the very things that I once tore down, then I demonstrate that I
am a transgressor. 19 For through the law I died to the law, so that I might live to
God. I have been crucified with Christ; 20 and it is no longer I who live, but it is
Christ who lives in me. And the life I now live in the flesh I live by faith in the Son
of God,[l] who loved me and gave himself for me. 21 I do not nullify the grace of
God; for if justification[m] comes through the law, then Christ died for nothing.

2.17 1 Jn 3.8
2.19 Rom 6.2,14; 7.4 8.2 Heb 9.14
2.20 Rom 6.6 2 Cor 5.15
2.21 Heb 7.11

2. Superiority of the gospel

The law and faith

3 You foolish Galatians! Who has bewitched you? It was before your eyes that
Jesus Christ was publicly exhibited as crucified! 2 The only thing I want to
learn from you is this: Did you receive the Spirit by doing the works of the law or
by believing what you heard? 3 Are you so foolish? Having started with the Spirit,
are you now ending with the flesh? 4 Did you experience so much for nothing?—if
it really was for nothing. 5 Well then, does God[n] supply you with the Spirit and
work miracles among you by your doing the works of the law, or by your believing
what you heard?
6 Just as Abraham "believed God, and it was reckoned to him as righteousness," 7 so, you see, those who believe are the descendants of Abraham. 8 And the
scripture, foreseeing that God would justify the Gentiles by faith, declared the gospel beforehand to Abraham, saying, "All the Gentiles shall be blessed in you."
9 For this reason, those who believe are blessed with Abraham who believed.

3.1 1 Cor 1.23
3.2 Acts 2.38 Rom 10.17
3.3 Heb 7.16
3.4 2 Jn 8
3.5 Phil 1.19
3.6 Gen 15.6 Rom 4.3
3.7 Jn 8.39
3.8 Gen 12.3

[l] *Or by the faith of the Son of God* [m] *Or righteousness* [n] *Gk he*

2.17–19 Through studying the Old Testament Scripture, Paul realized he could not be saved by obeying God's laws. The prophets knew that God's plan of salvation did not rest upon keeping the law (see the chart in chapter 3 for references). Because we have all been infected by sin, we cannot keep God's laws perfectly. Fortunately, God has provided a way of salvation that depends on Jesus Christ, not on our own efforts. Even though we know this truth, we must guard against the temptation of using service, good works, charitable giving, or any other efforts as a substitute for faith.

2.20 How have we been crucified with Christ? *Legally,* God looks at us as if we died with Christ. Because our sins died with him, we are no longer condemned (Colossians 2.13–15). *Relationally,* we have become one with Christ, and his experiences are ours. Our Christian life began when, in unity with him, we died to our old life (see Romans 6.5–11). *In our daily life,* we must regularly crucify sinful desires that keep us from following Christ. This too is a kind of dying with him (Luke 9.23–25).

And yet the focus of Christianity is not dying, but living. Because we have been crucified with Christ, we have also been raised with him (Romans 6.5). *Legally,* we have been reconciled with God (2 Corinthians 5.19) and are free to grow into Christ's likeness (Romans 8.29). And *in our daily life,* we have Christ's resurrection power as we continue to fight sin (Ephesians 1.19, 20). Christ lives in us—this is our reason for living and our hope for the future (Colossians 1.27).

2.21 Believers today may still be in danger of treating Christ's death as meaningless. How? By replacing Jewish legalism with their own brand of Christian legalism, they give people extra laws to obey. By believing they can earn God's favor by what they do, they are not trusting completely in Christ's work on the cross. By struggling to appropriate God's power to change them (sanctification), they are not resting in God's power to save them (justification). If we could be saved by being good, then Christ did not have to die. But the cross is the only way to salvation.

3.1 The Galatian believers had become fascinated by the false teachers' arguments, almost as though they had been bewitched. Magic was common in Paul's day (Acts 8.9–11; 13.6, 7). Magicians used both illusions and Satan's power to perform miracles. People were drawn into the magician's mysterious rites, not recognizing their dangerous source.

3.2, 3 The believers in Galatia, many of whom may have been in Jerusalem at Pentecost and received the Holy Spirit there, knew they didn't receive God's Spirit by obeying the Jewish laws. "Ending with the flesh" means trying to reach maturity by mere human effort. Paul stresses that just as we were saved by faith in Christ, so also we grow by faith in Christ. The Galatians took a step backward when they decided to insist on keeping the Jewish laws. We must realize that we grow spiritually because of God's work in us, not by following special rules.

3.5 This is a rhetorical question. The Galatians knew they received the Holy Spirit when they believed, not when they obeyed the law. People still feel insecure in their faith, because faith alone seems too easy. People still try to get closer to God by following rules. By asking these questions, Paul hoped to get the Galatians to focus again on Christ as the center of their faith.

3.5 The Holy Spirit gives Christians great power to live for God. Some Christians want more than this. They want to live in a state of perpetual excitement. The tedium of everyday living leads them to conclude that something is wrong spiritually. Often the Holy Spirit's greatest work is teaching us to persist, to keep on doing what is right even when it no longer seems interesting or exciting. The Galatians quickly turned from Paul's good news to the teachings of the newest teachers in town; they needed the Holy Spirit's gift of persistence. If the Christian life seems ordinary, you may need the Spirit to stir you up. Every day offers a challenge to live for Christ.

3.6–9 The main argument of the Judaizers was that Gentiles had to become Jews in order to become Christians. Paul exposes the flaw in this argument by showing that real children of Abraham are those who have faith, not those who keep the law. Abraham himself was saved by his faith (Genesis 15.6). All believers in every age and from every nation share Abraham's blessing. This is a comforting promise to us, a great heritage for us, and a solid foundation for living.

3.10 Deut 27.26 10 For all who rely on the works of the law are under a curse; for it is written,
"Cursed is everyone who does not observe and obey all the things written in the
3.11 Hab 2.4 book of the law." 11 Now it is evident that no one is justified before God by the law;
3.12 Lev 18.5 for "The one who is righteous will live by faith."[o] 12 But the law does not rest on
faith; on the contrary, "Whoever does the works of the law[p] will live by them."
3.13 Deut 21.23 13 Christ redeemed us from the curse of the law by becoming a curse for us — for it
3.14 Isa 44.3 is written, "Cursed is everyone who hangs on a tree" — 14 in order that in Christ
Acts 2.33 Jesus the blessing of Abraham might come to the Gentiles, so that we might receive
Eph 1.13 the promise of the Spirit through faith.

The law and the promise

3.15 Heb 9.17 15 Brothers and sisters,[q] I give an example from daily life: once a person's
will[r] has been ratified, no one adds to it or annuls it. 16 Now the promises were
3.16 Gen 22.17,18 made to Abraham and to his offspring;[s] it does not say, "And to offsprings,"[t] as
of many; but it says, "And to your offspring,"[s] that is, to one person, who is
3.17 Ex 12.40 Christ. 17 My point is this: the law, which came four hundred thirty years later, does
Rom 4.13,14 not annul a covenant previously ratified by God, so as to nullify the promise. 18 For
3.18 Rom 4.14 if the inheritance comes from the law, it no longer comes from the promise; but
Heb 6.14 God granted it to Abraham through the promise.
19 Why then the law? It was added because of transgressions, until the

[o] Or *The one who is righteous through faith will live* [p] Gk *does them* [q] Gk *Brothers* [r] Or *covenant* (as in verse 17)
[s] Gk *seed* [t] Gk *seeds*

WHAT IS THE LAW?
Part of the Jewish law included those laws found in the Old Testament. When Paul says that non-Jews (Gentiles) are no longer bound by these laws, he is not saying that the Old Testament laws do not apply to us today. He is saying certain types of laws may not apply to us. In the Old Testament there were three categories of laws:

Ceremonial law	This kind of law relates specifically to Israel's worship (see, for example, Leviticus 1.1–13). Its primary purpose was to point forward to Jesus Christ. Therefore, these laws were no longer necessary after Jesus' death and resurrection. While we are no longer bound by ceremonial laws, the principles behind them—to worship and love a holy God—still apply. The Jewish Christians often accused the Gentile Christians of violating the ceremonial law.
Civil law	This type of law dictated Israel's daily living (see Deuteronomy 24.10, 11, for example). Because modern society and culture are so radically different, some of these guidelines cannot be followed specifically. But the principles behind the commands should guide our conduct. At times, Paul asked Gentile Christians to follow some of these laws not because they had to, but to promote unity.
Moral law	This sort of law is the direct command of God—for example, the ten commandments (Exodus 20.1–17). It requires strict obedience. It reveals the nature and will of God, and it still applies to us today. We are to obey this moral law not to obtain salvation, but to live in ways pleasing to God.

3.10 Paul quotes Deuteronomy 27.26 to prove that, contrary to what the Judaizers claimed, the law cannot justify and save – it can only condemn. Breaking even one commandment brings a person under condemnation. Because everyone has broken the commandments, everyone is condemned. The law can do nothing to reverse the condemnation (Romans 3.20–24). But Christ took the curse of the law upon himself when he hung on the cross. He did this so we wouldn't have to bear our own punishment. The only condition is that we accept Christ's death on our behalf as the means to be saved (Colossians 1.20–23).

3.11 Trying to be right with God (justified) by our own effort doesn't work. Good intentions such as "I'll do better next time" or "I'll never do that again" usually end in failure. Paul points to Habakkuk's declaration (Habakkuk 2.4) that by trusting God – believing in his provision for our sins and living each day in his power – we can break this cycle of failure.

3.17 God kept his promise to Abraham (Genesis 17.7, 8) – he has not revoked it, though thousands of years have passed. He saved Abraham through his faith, and he blessed the world through Abraham by sending the Messiah as one of his descendants. Circumstances may change, but God remains constant and does not break his promises. He has promised to forgive our sins through Jesus Christ, and we can be sure he will do so.

3.18, 19 The law has two functions. On the positive side, it reveals the nature and will of God and shows people how to live. On the negative side, it points out people's sins and shows them that it is impossible to please God by trying to obey all his laws completely. God's promise to Abraham dealt with his faith; the law focuses on actions. The covenant with Abraham shows that faith is the only way to be saved; the law shows how to obey him. Faith does not annul the law; but the more we know God, the more we see how sinful we are. Then we are driven to depend on our faith in Christ alone for our salvation.

offspring[u] would come to whom the promise had been made; and it was ordained through angels by a mediator. 20 Now a mediator involves more than one
party; but God is one.
21 Is the law then opposed to the promises of God? Certainly not! For if a law
had been given that could make alive, then righteousness would indeed come
through the law. 22 But the scripture has imprisoned all things under the power of
sin, so that what was promised through faith in Jesus Christ[v] might be given to
those who believe.

3.19 Ex 20.19 Deut 5.5; 33.2 Jn 15.22 Acts 7.53 1 Tim 1.9 Heb 2.2
3.20 1 Tim 2.5
3.22 Rom 11.32

Sons of God through faith

23 Now before faith came, we were imprisoned and guarded under the law until
faith would be revealed. 24 Therefore the law was our disciplinarian until Christ
came, so that we might be justified by faith. 25 But now that faith has come, we are
no longer subject to a disciplinarian, 26 for in Christ Jesus you are all children of
God through faith. 27 As many of you as were baptized into Christ have clothed
yourselves with Christ. 28 There is no longer Jew or Greek, there is no longer slave
or free, there is no longer male and female; for all of you are one in Christ Jesus.
29 And if you belong to Christ, then you are Abraham's offspring,[u] heirs according
to the promise.
4 My point is this: heirs, as long as they are minors, are no better than slaves,
though they are the owners of all the property; 2 but they remain under guardians and trustees until the date set by the father. 3 So with us; while we were minors,
we were enslaved to the elemental spirits[w] of the world. 4 But when the fullness of
time had come, God sent his Son, born of a woman, born under the law, 5 in order

3.24 Mt 5.17
3.28 Jn 10.16; 17.21 1 Cor 12.13 Col 3.10,11
3.29 Gen 21.10 Rom 8.17; 9.7 Heb 11.18
4.3 Heb 9.10
4.4 Mk 1.15 Jn 1.14 Eph 1.10 Heb 2.14
4.5 Mt 20.28 Rom 8.14,15

[u] Gk *seed* [v] *Or through the faith of Jesus Christ* [w] *Or the rudiments*

3.20 When God gave his promise to Abraham, he did it by himself alone, without angels or Moses as mediators. Although it is not mentioned in Exodus, Jews believed the ten commandments were given to Moses by angels (Stephen referred to this in his speech, see Acts 7.53). Paul was showing the superiority of salvation and growth by faith over trying to be saved by keeping the Jewish laws. Christ is the best and only way given by God for us to come to him (1 Timothy 2.5).

3.21, 22 Before faith in Christ delivered us, we were trapped by sin, beaten down by past mistakes, and choked by desires we knew were wrong. God knew we were sin's prisoners. But he provided a way of escape—faith in Jesus Christ. Without Christ, everyone is caught in sin's grasp, and only those who place their faith in Christ ever get out of it. Look to him—he is reaching out to set you free.

3.24, 25 The law teaches us the *need* for salvation; God's grace *gives* us that salvation. The Old Testament still applies today. In it, God reveals his nature, his will for man, his moral laws, and his guidelines for living.

3.26, 27 In Roman society, a youth coming of age laid aside the robe of childhood and put on a new toga. This represented his move into adult citizenship with full rights and responsibilities. Paul combines this understanding with baptism. By becoming Christians and being baptized, they were becoming spiritually grown up and ready to take on the privileges and responsibilities of the mature. Paul is saying, "You have laid aside the old clothes of the law, and now you are putting on Christ's new robe of righteousness" (see 2 Corinthians 5.21; Ephesians 4.23, 24).

3.28 Jewish males greeted each new day by praying, "Lord, I thank you that I am not a Gentile, a slave, or a woman." The role of women was enhanced by Christianity. Faith in Christ transcends these differences and makes all believers one in Christ.

3.28 It's our natural inclination to feel uncomfortable around those who are different from us and to gravitate toward those who resemble us. But when we allow our differences to separate us from our fellow believers, we are disregarding clear biblical teaching. Make a point of seeking out and appreciating people who are not just like you and your friends. You may find that you both have a lot in common.

3.29 The original covenant with Abraham was intended for the whole world, not just for his descendants (see Genesis 12.3). All believers partake of this covenant and are blessed as children of Abraham.

4.3–7 The "elemental spirits of the world" are the basics of the legalistic religion of Judaism. Paul uses the illustration of slavery to show that before Christ came and died for sins, people were in bondage to the law. Thinking they could be saved by it, they became enslaved to trying—and failing—to keep it. But the good news is that we who were once slaves are now God's very own children with an intimate relationship with him. Because of Christ, there is no reason to be afraid of God. We can come boldly into his presence, knowing he will welcome us as his family members.

4.4 "When the fullness of time had come" God sent Jesus to earth to die for our sins. For centuries the Jews were wondering when their Messiah would come—but God's timing was perfect. We may sometimes wonder if God will ever respond to our prayers. But we must never doubt him or give up hope. At the right time he will respond. Are you waiting for his timing? Trust his judgment for your best interests.

4.4, 5 Jesus was born of a woman—he was human. He was born as a Jew—he was subject to God's law and fulfilled it perfectly. Thus Jesus was the perfect sacrifice, because although he was fully human, he never sinned. His death bought freedom for us who were enslaved to sin so we could be adopted into God's family.

4.5–7 Under Roman law, an adopted child was guaranteed all legal rights to his father's property. He was not a second-class son; he was equal to any other sons, biological or adopted, in his father's family. "Abba" is an Aramaic word for father. It was used by Christ in prayer in Mark 14.36. As adopted children of God, we share with Jesus all rights to God's resources. As God's heirs, we can claim what he has provided for us—our full identity as his children (see Romans 8.15–17).

to redeem those who were under the law, so that we might receive adoption as
children. 6 And because you are children, God has sent the Spirit of his Son into
our[x] hearts, crying, "Abba![y] Father!" 7 So you are no longer a slave but a child,
and if a child then also an heir, through God.[z]

Paul's concern for the Galatians

8 Formerly, when you did not know God, you were enslaved to beings that by
nature are not gods. 9 Now, however, that you have come to know God, or rather
to be known by God, how can you turn back again to the weak and beggarly elemental spirits?[a] How can you want to be enslaved to them again? 10 You are observing special days, and months, and seasons, and years. 11 I am afraid that my
work for you may have been wasted.

12 Friends,[b] I beg you, become as I am, for I also have become as you are. You

4.7 Rom 8.16,17
4.8 2 Chron 13.9; Rom 1.25; 1 Cor 8.4; Eph 2.12; 1 Thess 1.9
4.9 Col 2.20
4.10 Rom 14.5; Col 2.16

[x] Other ancient authorities read *your* [y] Aramaic for *Father* [z] Other ancient authorities read *an heir of God through Christ* [a] Or *beggarly rudiments* [b] Gk *Brothers*

THREE DISTORTIONS OF CHRISTIANITY: Almost from the beginning there were forces at work within Christianity that could have destroyed or sidetracked the movement. Of these, three created many problems then and have continued to reappear in other forms even today. The three aberrations are contrasted to true Christianity:

Group	*Their definition of a Christian*	*Their genuine concern*	*The danger*	*Application question*
Judaized Christianity	Christians are Jews who have recognized Jesus as the promised Savior. Therefore any Gentile desiring to become a Christian must first become a Jew.	Having a high regard for God's Word and his choice of Jews as his people, they did not want to see God's commands over-looked or broken.	Tends to add human traditions and standards to God's law. Also subtracts from the Scriptures God's clear concern for all nations.	Do you appreciate God's choice of a unique people through which he offered forgiveness and eternal life to all peoples?
Legalized Christianity	Christians are those who live by a long list of "don'ts." God's favor is earned by good behavior.	Recognized that real change brought about by God should lead to changes in behavior.	Tends to make God's love something to earn rather than to accept freely. Would reduce Christianity to a set of impossible rules and transform the good news into bad news.	As important as change in action is, can you see that God may be desiring different changes in you than in others?
Law-less Christianity	Christians live above the law. They need no guidelines. God's Word is not as important as our personal sense of God's guidance.	Recognized that forgiveness from God cannot be based on our ability to live up to his perfect standards. It must be received by faith as a gift made possible by Christ's death on the cross.	Forgets that Christians are still human and fail consistently when trying to live only by what they "feel" God wants.	Do you recognize the ongoing need for God's expressed commands as you live out your gratitude for his great salvation?
True Christianity	Christians are those who believe inwardly and outwardly that Jesus' death has allowed God to offer them forgiveness and eternal life as a gift. They have accepted that gift by faith and are seeking to live a life of obedient gratitude for what God has done for them.	Christianity is both private and public; heart-belief and mouth-confession. Our relationship to God and the power he provides result in obedience. Having received the gift of forgiveness and eternal life, we are now daily challenged to live that life with his help.	Avoids the above dangers.	How would those closest to you describe your Christianity? Do they think you live *so* that God will accept you or do they know that you live *because* God has accepted you in Christ?

have done me no wrong. 13 You know that it was because of a physical infirmity 4.12 Gal 6.14
that I first announced the gospel to you; 14 though my condition put you to the test, 4.13
you did not scorn or despise me, but welcomed me as an angel of God, as Christ 1 Cor 2.3
Jesus. 15 What has become of the good will you felt? For I testify that, had it been Gal 1.6
possible, you would have torn out your eyes and given them to me. 16 Have I now 4.14 Mt 10.40
become your enemy by telling you the truth? 17 They make much of you, but for no 1 Thess 2.13
good purpose; they want to exclude you, so that you may make much of them. 18 It 4.16 Amos 5.10
is good to be made much of for a good purpose at all times, and not only when I am 4.17
present with you. 19 My little children, for whom I am again in the pain of childbirth Rom 10.2
until Christ is formed in you, 20 I wish I were present with you now and could 4.19 1 Cor 4.15
change my tone, for I am perplexed about you. Eph 3.17; 4.13

Abraham's two children

21 Tell me, you who desire to be subject to the law, will you not listen to the
law? 22 For it is written that Abraham had two sons, one by a slave woman and the 4.22
other by a free woman. 23 One, the child of the slave, was born according to the Gen 16.15; 21.2
flesh; the other, the child of the free woman, was born through the promise. 24 Now 4.23 Gen 18.10
this is an allegory: these women are two covenants. One woman, in fact, is Hagar, Rom 9.7,8
from Mount Sinai, bearing children for slavery. 25 Now Hagar is Mount Sinai in 4.24 Deut 32.2-4
Arabia[c] and corresponds to the present Jerusalem, for she is in slavery with her
children. 26 But the other woman corresponds to the Jerusalem above; she is free, 4.26 Heb 12.22
and she is our mother. 27 For it is written, Rev 3.12; 21.2

"Rejoice, you childless one, you who bear no children, 4.27 Isa 54.1
 burst into song and shout, you who endure no birthpangs;
for the children of the desolate woman are more numerous
 than the children of the one who is married." 4.28

28 Now you,[d] my friends,[e] are children of the promise, like Isaac. 29 But just as at Rom 4.16 Gal 3.29
that time the child who was born according to the flesh persecuted the child who 4.29 Gen 21.9
was born according to the Spirit, so it is now also. 30 But what does the scripture 4.30
say? "Drive out the slave and her child; for the child of the slave will not share Gen 21.10 Jn 8.35
the inheritance with the child of the free woman." 31 So then, friends,[e] we are Gal 3.8

[c] Other ancient authorities read *For Sinai is a mountain in Arabia* [d] Other ancient authorities read *we* [e] Gk *brothers*

4.13, 14 Paul's physical infirmity was a sickness he was enduring while he visited the Galatian churches. The world is often callous to people's pain and misery. Paul commended the Galatians for not rejecting him, even though his condition was revolting (he doesn't explain what was wrong with him). Such caring was what Jesus meant when he called us to serve the homeless, hungry, sick, and imprisoned as if they were Jesus himself (Matthew 25.34–40). Do you avoid those in pain or facing difficulty—or are you willing to care for them as if they were Jesus Christ himself?

4.15 Paul sensed that the Galatians had lost the joy of their salvation because of legalism. Legalism can take away joy because (1) it makes people feel guilty rather than loved; (2) it produces self-hatred rather than humility; (3) it stresses performance over relationship; (4) it points out how far short we fall rather than how far we've come because of what Christ did for us. If you feel guilty and inadequate, check your focus. Are you putting your faith in Christ or in rule-keeping?

4.16 Paul did not gain great popularity when he rebuked the Galatians for turning away from their first faith in Christ. Human nature hasn't changed much—we still get angry when we're scolded. But don't write off someone who challenges you. There may be truth in what he or she says. Receive his or her words with humility; carefully think them over. If you discover that you need to change an attitude or action, take steps to do it.

4.17 "They" refers to false teachers who claimed to be religious authorities, experts in Judaism and Christianity. Appealing to the believers' desire to do what is right, they drew quite a following. Paul says, however, that they are wrong and that their motives are selfish. False teachers are often respectable and persuasive. That is why all teachings need to be checked with the Bible.

4.19 Paul led many people to Christ and helped them mature spiritually. Perhaps one reason for his success as a spiritual father was the deep concern he felt for his spiritual children; he compared his pain over their faithlessness to the pain of childbirth. We should have the same intense care for those to whom we are spiritual parents. When you lead people to Christ, remember to stand by them to help them grow.

4.21ff People are saved because of their faith in Christ, not because of what they do. Paul contrasts those who are enslaved to the law (represented by Hagar, the slave woman) with those who are free from the law (represented by Sarah, the free woman). Hagar's abuse of Sarah (Genesis 16.4) was like the persecution Gentile Christians were getting from the Judaizers, who insisted on keeping the law in order to be saved. Eventually Sarah triumphed, because her son was promised by God, just as those who worship Christ in faith will also triumph.

4.24 Paul explains that what happened to Sarah and Hagar is an allegory or picture of the relationship between God and humankind. Paul is using a type of argument that was common in his day and that was probably being used against him by his opponents.

5.1 Jn 8.32; Acts 15.10
5.2 Acts 15.1
5.5 Rom 8.23
5.6 Col 3.11; 1 Thess 1.3
5.7 1 Cor 9.24
5.8 Rom 8.28
5.9 1 Cor 5.6
5.11 1 Cor 1.23; 15.30

children, not of the slave but of the free woman. 5 1 For freedom Christ has set
us free. Stand firm, therefore, and do not submit again to a yoke of slavery.

3. Freedom of the gospel

Living in the freedom of Christ

2 Listen! I, Paul, am telling you that if you let yourselves be circumcised,
Christ will be of no benefit to you. 3 Once again I testify to every man who lets
himself be circumcised that he is obliged to obey the entire law. 4 You who want to
be justified by the law have cut yourselves off from Christ; you have fallen away
from grace. 5 For through the Spirit, by faith, we eagerly wait for the hope of righteousness. 6 For in Christ Jesus neither circumcision nor uncircumcision counts for
anything; the only thing that counts is faith working[f] through love.
7 You were running well; who prevented you from obeying the truth? 8 Such
persuasion does not come from the one who calls you. 9 A little yeast leavens the
whole batch of dough. 10 I am confident about you in the Lord that you will not
think otherwise. But whoever it is that is confusing you will pay the penalty. 11 But
my friends,[g] why am I still being persecuted if I am still preaching circumcision?

[f] *Or made effective* [g] *Gk brothers*

VICES AND VIRTUES

The Bible mentions many specific actions and attitudes that are either right or wrong. Look at the list included here. Are there too many characteristics from the wrong column that are influencing you?

VICES (Neglecting God and others)	*VIRTUES (The by-products of living for God)*
Impure thoughts *(Galatians 5.19)*	Love *(Galatians 5.22)*
Lust *(Galatians 5.19)*	Joy *(Galatians 5.22)*
Hatred *(Galatians 5.20)*	Peace *(Galatians 5.22)*
Fighting *(Galatians 5.20)*	Patience *(Longsuffering) (Galatians 5.22)*
Jealousy *(Galatians 5.20)*	Kindness *(Gentleness) (Galatians 5.22)*
Anger *(Galatians 5.20)*	Goodness *(Galatians 5.22)*
Trying to be first *(Galatians 5.20)*	Faithfulness *(Galatians 5.22)*
Complaining *(Galatians 5.20)*	Meekness *(Galatians 5.23)*
Criticizing *(Galatians 5.20)*	Self-control *(Galatians 5.23)*
Thinking you're always right *(Galatians 5.20)*	
Envy *(Galatians 5.21)*	
Murder *(Galatians 5.21; Revelation 22.12–16)*	
Idolatry *(Galatians 5.20; Ephesians 5.5)*	
Spiritism *(Galatians 5.20)*	
Drunkenness *(Galatians 5.21)*	
Wild parties *(Galatians 5.21)*	
Cheating *(1 Corinthians 6.8)*	
Adultery *(1 Corinthians 6.9, 10)*	
Homosexuality *(1 Corinthians 6.9, 10)*	
Greed *(1 Corinthians 6.9, 10; Ephesians 5.5)*	
Stealing *(1 Corinthians 6.9, 10)*	
Lying *(Revelation 22.12–16)*	

5.1 Christ died to set us free from sin and from a long list of laws and regulations. Christ came to set us free – not free to do whatever we want, because that would lead back into slavery to our selfish desires. Rather, thanks to Christ, we are now free and able to do what was impossible before – to live unselfishly. Those who appeal to their freedom so they can have their own way or indulge their desires are falling back into sin. Do you merely enjoy your freedom from rules and sin, or do you use your freedom to serve others?

5.2 Trying to be saved by keeping the law and being saved by grace are two entirely different approaches. "Christ will be of no benefit to you" means Christ's provision for our salvation will not help us if we are trying to save ourselves. Obeying the law does not make it any easier for God to save us. All we can do is accept his grace through faith.

5.3, 4 These verses mean that if a person counts on finding favor with God by being circumcised, he must also obey the rest of God's law completely. Trying to save ourselves by keeping all God's laws only separates us from God.

5.6 We are saved by faith, not by works. But love for others and for God is the response of those whom God has forgiven. God's forgiveness is complete, and Jesus said that those who are forgiven much love much (Luke 7.47). Because faith expresses itself through love, you can check your love for others as a way to monitor your faith.

5.9 A little yeast causes a whole lump of dough to rise. It only takes one wrong person to infect all the others.

5.11 Persecution proved that Paul was preaching the true gospel. If he taught what the false teachers taught, no one would be offended. But because he taught the truth, he was persecuted by both Jews and Judaizers. Have friends or loved ones rejected you because you have taken a stand for Christ? Paul's experience reminds us that this is to be expected. Jesus said not to be surprised if the world hates you, because it hated him (John 15.18, 19). Just as Paul continued faithfully proclaiming the message about Christ, you should continue doing the work God has given you to do – in spite of the obstacles others may put in your way.

In that case the offense of the cross has been removed. 12 I wish those who unsettle 5.12 Acts 15.1
you would castrate themselves! 1 Cor 5.13
13 For you were called to freedom, brothers and sisters;[h] only do not use your 5.13
freedom as an opportunity for self-indulgence,[i] but through love become slaves to 1 Pet 2.16
one another. 14 For the whole law is summed up in a single commandment, "You 5.14 Lev 19.18
shall love your neighbor as yourself." 15 If, however, you bite and devour one an- Rom 13.8
other, take care that you are not consumed by one another.

Living by the Holy Spirit's power

16 Live by the Spirit, I say, and do not gratify the desires of the flesh. 17 For 5.16 Rom 6.12; 8.4-6
what the flesh desires is opposed to the Spirit, and what the Spirit desires is opposed 5.17
to the flesh; for these are opposed to each other, to prevent you from doing what Rom 7.15,23
you want. 18 But if you are led by the Spirit, you are not subject to the law. 19 Now 5.18 Rom 6.14; 8.14
the works of the flesh are obvious: fornication, impurity, licentiousness, 20 idola- 5.19
try, sorcery, enmities, strife, jealousy, anger, quarrels, dissensions, factions, Rom 13.12,13
21 envy,[j] drunkenness, carousing, and things like these. I am warning you, as I 5.21 1 Cor 6.9
warned you before: those who do such things will not inherit the kingdom of God. Eph 5.5 Rev 22.15
22 By contrast, the fruit of the Spirit is love, joy, peace, patience, kindness, 5.22
generosity, faithfulness, 23 gentleness, and self-control. There is no law against Jas 3.17
such things. 24 And those who belong to Christ Jesus have crucified the flesh with

h Gk *brothers* i Gk *the flesh* j Other ancient authorities add *murder*

Our wrong desires are:	*The fruit of the Spirit is:*
Evil	Good
Destructive	Productive
Easy to ignite	Difficult to ignite
Difficult to stifle	Easy to stifle
Self-centered	Self-giving
Oppressive and possessive	Liberating and nurturing
Decadent	Uplifting
Sinful	Holy
Deadly	Abundant life

OUR WRONG DESIRES VS. THE FRUIT OF THE SPIRIT

The will of the Holy Spirit is in constant opposition to our sinful desires. The two are on opposite sides of the spiritual battle.

5.13 Paul distinguishes between freedom to sin and freedom to serve. Freedom to sin is no freedom at all, because it enslaves you to Satan, others, or your own evil desires. People who are slaves to sin are not free to live righteously. Christians, by contrast, should not be slaves to sin because they are free to do right and glorify God through their actions.

5.14, 15 When we are not motivated by love, we become critical of others. We stop looking for good in them and see only their faults. Soon the unity of believers is broken. Have you talked behind someone's back? Have you focused on others' shortcomings instead of their strengths? Remind yourself of Jesus' command to love others as you love yourself (Matthew 22.39). When you begin to feel critical of someone, make a list of that person's positive qualities. If there are problems that need to be addressed, it is better to confront in love than to gossip.

5.16–18 If your desire is to have the qualities listed in 5.22, 23, then you know the Holy Spirit is leading you. At the same time, be careful not to confuse your feelings with the Spirit's leading. Being led by the Holy Spirit involves the desire to hear, the readiness to obey God's Word, and the sensitivity to discern between your feelings and his promptings. Live each day controlled and guided by the Holy Spirit. Then the words of Christ will be in your mind, the love of Christ will be behind your actions, and the power of Christ will help you control your selfish desires.

5.17 Paul describes the two forces at work within us – the Holy Spirit and "the flesh" (our evil inclinations). Paul is not saying that these forces are equal. The Holy Spirit is infinitely stronger, but *we* are weak. Left to our own wisdom, we will make wrong choices. If we try to walk in the Spirit by our own human effort, we will fail. Our only way to freedom from our evil desires is through the empowering of the Holy Spirit (see Romans 8.9; Ephesians 4.23, 24; Colossians 3.3–8).

5.19–21 We all have evil desires, and we can't ignore them. In order for us to follow the Holy Spirit's guidance, we must deal with them decisively (crucify them – 5.24). These desires include obvious sins such as sexual immorality and witchcraft. They also include less obvious sins such as ambition, anger, and envy. Those who ignore such sins or refuse to deal with them reveal that they have not received the gift of faith leading to a transformed life.

5.22, 23 The fruit of the Spirit is the spontaneous work of the Holy Spirit in us. The Spirit produces these character traits that are found in the nature of Christ. They are the by-products of Christ's control – we can't obtain them by *trying* to get them. If we want the fruit of the Spirit to grow in us, we must join our lives to his (see John 15.4, 5). We must know him, love him, remember him, and imitate him. As a result, we will fulfill the intended purpose of the law – loving God and people. Which of these qualities do you desire the Spirit to produce in you?

5.23 Because the God who sent the law also sent the Spirit, the by-products of the Spirit-filled life are in perfect harmony with the intent of God's law. A person who exhibits the fruit of the Spirit fulfills the law far better than a person who observes the rituals but has little love in his heart.

5.24 In order to accept Christ as Savior, we need to turn from our

5.25 Gal 5.16
5.26 Phil 2.3

its passions and desires. 25If we live by the Spirit, let us also be guided by the
Spirit. 26Let us not become conceited, competing against one another, envying one
another.

We will reap what we sow

6.1 1 Jn 5.16
6.2 Rom 15.1
6.3 Rom 12.3 2 Cor 3.5; 12.11
6.6 1 Cor 9.11,14

6 My friends,[k] if anyone is detected in a transgression, you who have received
the Spirit should restore such a one in a spirit of gentleness. Take care that you
yourselves are not tempted. 2Bear one another's burdens, and in this way you will
fulfill[l] the law of Christ. 3For if those who are nothing think they are something,
they deceive themselves. 4All must test their own work; then that work, rather than
their neighbor's work, will become a cause for pride. 5For all must carry their own
loads.

6.8 Job 4.8 Rom 8.9-14 Jas 3.18
6.9 Mt 24.13 2 Thess 3.13
6.10 Jn 9.4 Eph 2.19 1 Tim 6.18 Heb 3.6

6 Those who are taught the word must share in all good things with their
teacher.
7 Do not be deceived; God is not mocked, for you reap whatever you sow. 8If
you sow to your own flesh, you will reap corruption from the flesh; but if you sow
to the Spirit, you will reap eternal life from the Spirit. 9So let us not grow weary in
doing what is right, for we will reap at harvest-time, if we do not give up. 10So
then, whenever we have an opportunity, let us work for the good of all, and especially for those of the family of faith.

Paul's final warning

6.11 1 Cor 16.21
6.13 Rom 2.25

11 See what large letters I make when I am writing in my own hand! 12It is
those who want to make a good showing in the flesh that try to compel you to
be circumcised—only that they may not be persecuted for the cross of Christ.
13Even the circumcised do not themselves obey the law, but they want you to be

[k] Gk *Brothers* [l] Other ancient authorities read *in this way fulfill*

sins and willingly nail our natural evil desires to the cross. This doesn't mean, however, that we will never see traces of those desires again. As Christians we still have the capacity to sin, but we have been set free from sin's power over us and no longer have to give in to it. We must daily commit our sinful tendencies to God's control, daily crucify them, and moment by moment draw on the Spirit's power to overcome them (see 2.20; 6.14).

5.25 God is interested in every part of our lives, not just the spiritual part. As we live by the Holy Spirit's power, we need to submit every aspect of our lives to God—emotional, physical, social, intellectual, vocational. Paul says, "You're saved, so live like it!" The Holy Spirit is the source of your new life, so walk with him. Don't let anything or anyone else determine your values and standards in any area of your life.

5.26 We all need a certain amount of approval from others. But those who go out of their way to secure honors or to win popularity with a lot of people show they are not following the Holy Spirit's leading. Those who look to God for approval won't need to seek it from others. As God's sons and daughters, we have his Holy Spirit as the loving guarantee of his approval.

6.1–3 No Christian should ever think he or she is totally independent and doesn't need help from others, and no one should feel excused from the task of helping. The body of Christ—the church—functions only when the members work together for the common good. Do you know someone who needs help? Is there a Christian brother or sister who needs correction or encouragement? Humbly and gently reach out to that person (John 13.34, 35).

6.4 When you do your very best, you feel good about the results. There is no need to compare yourself with others. People make comparisons for many reasons. Some point out others' flaws in order to feel better about themselves. Others simply want reassurance that they are doing well. When you are tempted to compare, look at Jesus Christ. His example will inspire you to do your very best, and his loving acceptance will comfort you when you fall short of your expectations.

6.6 Paul says that students should take care of the material needs of their teachers (1 Corinthians 9.7–12). It is easy to receive the benefit of good Bible teaching and then to take our spiritual leaders for granted, ignoring their financial and physical needs. We should care for them, not grudgingly or reluctantly, but with a generous spirit, showing honor and appreciation for all they have done (1 Timothy 5.17, 18).

6.7, 8 It would certainly be a surprise if you planted corn and pumpkins came up. It's a natural law to reap what we sow. It's true in other areas too. If you gossip about your friends, you will lose their friendship. Every action has results. If you plant to please your own desires ("sow to your own flesh"), you'll reap a crop of sorrow and evil. If you plant to please God, you'll reap joy and everlasting life. What kind of seeds are you sowing?

6.9, 10 It is discouraging to continue to do right and receive no word of thanks or see no tangible results. But Paul challenges the Galatians and us to keep on doing what is right and to trust God for the results. In due time, we will reap a harvest of blessing.

6.11 Up to this point, Paul had dictated the letter to a scribe. Now he takes the pen into his own hands to write his final, personal greetings. He did this in other letters as well, to add emphasis to his words and to validate that the letter was genuine.

6.13 Some of the Judaizers were emphasizing circumcision as proof of holiness—but ignoring the other Jewish laws. People often choose a certain principle or prohibition and make it the measure of faith. Some may abhor drunkenness but ignore gluttony. Others may despise promiscuity but tolerate prejudice. The Bible in its entirety is our rule of faith and practice. We cannot pick and choose the mandates we will follow.

circumcised so that they may boast about your flesh. 14 May I never boast of 6.14
anything except the cross of our Lord Jesus Christ, by which[m] the world has been Rom 6.2,3,6 1 Cor 2.2
crucified to me, and I to the world. 15 For[n] neither circumcision nor uncircumci- Col 2.20
sion is anything; but a new creation is everything! 16 As for those who will 6.16
follow this rule — peace be upon them, and mercy, and upon the Israel of God. Phil 3.3
17 From now on, let no one make trouble for me; for I carry the marks of Jesus 6.17
branded on my body. 2 Cor 1.5; 4.10 Col 1.24
18 May the grace of our Lord Jesus Christ be with your spirit, brothers and 6.18
sisters.[o] Amen. 2 Tim 4.22

[m] Or *through whom* [n] Other ancient authorities add *in Christ Jesus* [o] Gk *brothers*

6.14 The world is full of enticements. Daily we are confronted with subtle cultural pressures and overt propaganda. The only way to escape these destructive influences is to ask God to help kill our interest in them, just as Paul did. How much do the interests of this world matter to you? (See 2.20 and 5.24 for more on this concept.)

6.15 It is easy to get caught up with the externals. Beware of those who emphasize actions we should or shouldn't do, with no concern for the inward condition of the heart. Living a "good" life without an inward change leads to a shallow and empty spiritual walk. What matters to God is that we be completely changed from the inside out (2 Corinthians 5.17).

6.18 Paul's letter to the Galatians boldly declares the freedom of the Christian. Doubtless these early Christians in Galatia wanted to grow in the Christian life, but they were being misled by those who said this could be done only by keeping certain Jewish laws.

How strange it would be for a prisoner who had been set free to walk back into his or her cell and refuse to leave! How strange for an animal, released from a trap, to go back inside it! How sad for a believer to be freed from the bondage of sin, only to return to rigid conformity to a set of rules and regulations!

If you believe in Jesus Christ, you have been set free. Instead of going back into some form of slavery, whether legalism or sin, use your freedom to live for Christ and serve him as he desires.

The Letter of Paul to the EPHESIANS

OUR CHURCHES come in all styles and shapes—secret meetings in homes; wide-open gatherings in amphitheaters; worship services packing thousands into a sanctuary while an overflow crowd watches on closed circuit television; handfuls who kneel in urban storefronts. Buildings will vary, but the church is not confined to four walls. The church of Jesus Christ is *people,* his people, of every race and nation who love Christ and are committed to serving him.

The "church age" began at Pentecost (Acts 2). Born in Jerusalem, the church spread rapidly through the ministry of the apostles and the early believers. Fanned by persecution, the gospel flame then spread to other cities and nations. On three courageous journeys, Paul and his associates established local assemblies in scores of Gentile cities.

One of the most prominent of those churches was at Ephesus. It was established in A.D. 53 on Paul's homeward journey to Jerusalem. But he returned a year later, on his third missionary trip, and stayed there for three years, preaching and teaching with great effectiveness (Acts 19.1–20). At another time, he met with the Ephesian elders, and he sent Timothy to serve as their leader (1 Timothy 1.3). Just a few years later, Paul was sent as a prisoner to Rome. In Rome, he was visited by messengers from various churches, including Tychicus of Ephesus. Paul wrote this letter to the church and sent it with Tychicus. Not written to counteract heresy or to confront any specific problem, Ephesians is a letter of encouragement. In it Paul describes the nature and appearance of the church, and he challenges believers to function as the living body of Christ on earth.

After a warm greeting (1.1, 2), Paul affirms the nature of the church—the glorious fact that believers in Christ have been showered with God's kindness (1.3–8), chosen for greatness (1.9–12), marked by the Holy Spirit (1.13, 14), filled with his power (1.15–23), freed from sin's curse and bondage (2.1–10), and brought near to God (2.11–19). As part of God's "house," we stand with the prophets, apostles, Jews, Gentiles, and Christ himself (2.20—3.11). Then, as though overcome with emotion by remembering all that God has done, Paul challenges them to live close to Christ and breaks into spontaneous praise (3.12–21).

Paul then turns his attention to the implications of being in the body of Christ, the church. Believers should have unity in their commitment to Christ and their use of spiritual gifts (4.1–16). They should have the highest moral standards (4.17—6.9). For the individual, this means rejecting heathen practices (4.17—5.20), and for the family, this means mutual submission and love (5.21—6.9).

Paul then reminds them that the church is in a constant battle with the forces of darkness and that they should use every spiritual weapon at their disposal (6.10–17). He concludes by asking for their prayers, commissioning Tychicus, and giving a benediction (6.18–24).

As you read this masterful description of the church, thank God for the diversity and unity in his family, pray for your brothers and sisters across the world, and draw close to those in your local church.

VITAL STATISTICS

PURPOSE:
To strengthen the believers in Ephesus in their Christian faith by explaining the nature and purpose of the church, the body of Christ

AUTHOR:
Paul

TO WHOM WRITTEN:
The church at Ephesus, and all believers everywhere

DATE WRITTEN:
About A.D. 60, from Rome during Paul's imprisonment there

SETTING:
The letter was not written to confront any heresy or problem in the churches. It was sent with Tychicus to strengthen and encourage the churches in the area. Paul had spent over three years with the Ephesian church. As a result, Paul was very close to them. Paul met with the elders of the Ephesian church for the last time at Miletus (Acts 20.17–38)—a meeting that was filled with great sadness because Paul was leaving them for the last time. Because there are no specific references to people or problems in the Ephesian church and because the words "at Ephesus" (1.1) are not present in the earliest manuscripts, Paul may have intended this to be a circular letter to be read to all the churches in the area.

KEY VERSE:
"There is one body and one Spirit, just as you were called to the one hope of your calling" (4.4).

KEY PEOPLE:
Paul, Tychicus

SPECIAL FEATURES:
Several pictures of the church are presented: body, temple, mystery, new man, bride, and soldier. This epistle became a circular letter distributed to many of the early churches.

THE BLUEPRINT

1. Unity in Christ (1.1—3.21)
2. Unity in the church (4.1—6.24)

In this letter, Paul explains the wonderful things that we have received through Christ and refers to the church as a body, a temple, a bride, and a soldier. These all illustrate unity of purpose and show how each individual member is a part which must work together with all the other parts. In our own lives, we should work to eradicate all backbiting, gossip, criticism, jealousy, anger, and bitterness, because these are barriers to unity in the church.

MEGATHEMES

THEME	EXPLANATION	IMPORTANCE
God's purpose	According to God's eternal, loving plan, he directs, carries out, and sustains our salvation.	When we respond to Christ's love by trusting in him, his purpose becomes our mission. Have you committed yourself to fulfilling God's purpose?
Christ the center	Christ is exalted as the central meaning of the universe and the focus of history. He is the head of the body, the church. He is the Creator and Sustainer of all creation.	Because Christ is central to everything, his power must be central in us. Begin by placing all your priorities in his control.
Living church	Paul describes the nature of the church. The church, under Christ's control, is a living body, a family, a dwelling. God gives believers special abilities by his Holy Spirit to build the church.	We are part of Christ's body, and we must live in vital union with him. Our conduct must be consistent with this living relationship. Use your God-given abilities to equip believers for service. Fulfill your role in the living church.
New family	Because God through Christ paid our penalty for sin and forgave us, we have been reconciled—brought near to him. We are a new society, a new family. Being united with Christ means we are to treat one another as family members.	We are one family in Christ; so there should be no barriers, no divisions, no basis for discrimination. We all belong to him, so we should live in harmony with one another.
Christian conduct	Paul encourages all Christians to wise, dynamic Christian living, for with privileges goes family responsibility. As a new community, we are to have Christ's new standards.	God provides his Holy Spirit to enable us to live his way. To utilize his power, we must lay aside our evil desires and draw upon the power of his new life. Submit your will to Christ, and seek to love others.

1. Unity in Christ

1 Paul, an apostle of Christ Jesus by the will of God,
To the saints who are in Ephesus and are faithful[a] in Christ Jesus: **1.2** Rom 1.7
2 Grace to you and peace from God our Father and the Lord Jesus Christ. Tit 1.4

[a] Other ancient authorities lack *in Ephesus,* reading *saints who are also faithful*

1.1 Paul wrote this letter to the church at Ephesus (the *saints* or believers) to give them in-depth teaching about how to nurture and maintain the unity of the church. He wanted to put this important information in written form, because he was in prison for preaching the gospel and could not visit the churches himself. Paul mentions no particular problems or local situations, and he offers no personal greetings. This was probably a circular letter—it was first sent to Ephesus and then circulated to neighboring local churches.

1.1 Paul had been a Christian for nearly 30 years. He had taken three missionary trips and established churches all around the Mediterranean Sea. When he wrote Ephesians, he was under house arrest in Rome (see Acts 28.16ff). Though a prisoner, he was free to have visitors and write letters. For more information on Paul, see his Profile in Acts 10.

1.1 Ephesus was one of the five major cities in the Roman Empire, along with Rome, Corinth, Antioch, and Alexandria. Paul first visited Ephesus on his second missionary journey (Acts 18.19–21). During his third missionary journey, he stayed there almost three years (Acts 19). He later met again with the elders of the Ephesian church at Miletus (Acts 20.16–38). Ephesus was a commercial, political, and religious center for all of Asia Minor. The temple to the Greek goddess Artemis was located there.

God's overflowing kindness

1.3 Eph 1.20; 2.6
1.4 1 Pet 1.2,20
1.5 Rom 8.15,29
1.7 Heb 9.12 Rev 5.9

3 Blessed be the God and Father of our Lord Jesus Christ, who has blessed us
in Christ with every spiritual blessing in the heavenly places, 4 just as he chose us
in Christ[b] before the foundation of the world to be holy and blameless before him
in love. 5 He destined us for adoption as his children through Jesus Christ, according to the good pleasure of his will, 6 to the praise of his glorious grace that he freely
bestowed on us in the Beloved. 7 In him we have redemption through his blood, the
forgiveness of our trespasses, according to the riches of his grace 8 that he lavished

[b] Gk *in him*

LOCATION OF EPHESUS
Ephesus was a strategic city, ranking in importance with Alexandria in Egypt and Antioch in Syria as a port. It lay on the most western edge of Asia Minor (modern-day Turkey), the most important port on the Aegean Sea on the main route from Rome to the east.

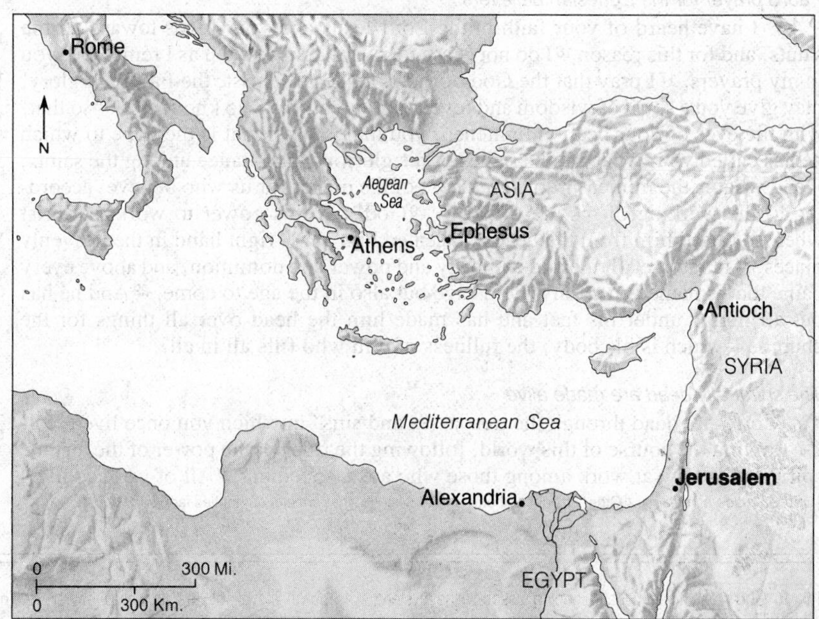

1.1 "Faithful in Christ Jesus"—what an excellent reputation! Such a label would be an honor for any believer. What would it take for others to characterize you as faithful to Christ Jesus? Hold fast to your faith, one day at a time; faithfully obey God, even in the details of life. Then, like the Ephesians, you will be known as one who is faithful to the Lord.

1.3 "Every spiritual blessing in the heavenly places" means all the benefits of knowing God—salvation, the gifts of the Spirit, power to do God's will, the hope of living forever with Christ. Because we have an intimate relationship with Christ, we can enjoy these blessings now. Other references to heaven in this letter include 1.20; 2.6; 3.10. They show Christ in his victorious, exalted role as ruler of all.

1.4 Paul says God "chose us" to emphasize that salvation depends totally on God. We are not saved because we deserve it, but because God is gracious and freely gives it. We did not influence God's decision to save us; he did it according to his plan. Thus there is no way to take credit for our salvation or to find room for pride. The mystery of salvation originated in the timeless mind of God long before we existed. It is hard to understand how God could accept us. But because of Christ, we are holy and blameless in his eyes. God chose us, and when we belong to him through Jesus Christ, he looks at us as if we had never sinned.

1.5 *Destined* means "marked out beforehand." This is another way of saying salvation is God's work and not our own doing. God has adopted us as his own children. Through Jesus' sacrifice, he has brought us into his family and made us heirs along with Jesus (Romans 8.17). In Roman law, adopted children had the same rights and privileges as natural children. Paul uses this term to show how strong our relationship to God is. For more on the meaning of adoption, see Galatians 4.5–7.

1.6 "Bestowed on us in the Beloved" means God graciously accepts us now that we belong to his dearly loved Son.

1.7 To speak of Jesus' blood was an important first-century way of speaking of Christ's death. His death points to two wonderful truths—redemption and forgiveness. *Redemption* was the price paid to gain freedom for a slave (Leviticus 25.47–54). Through his death, Jesus paid the price to release us from slavery to sin. *Forgiveness* was granted in Old Testament times on the basis of the shedding of animals' blood (Leviticus 17.11). Now we are forgiven on the basis of the shedding of Jesus' blood, because he died and was the perfect and final sacrifice. (See also Romans 5.9; Ephesians 2.13; Colossians 1.20; Hebrews 9.22; 1 Peter 1.19.)

1.7, 8 Grace is God's voluntary and loving favor given to those he saves. We can't earn it, nor do we deserve it. No religious or moral effort can gain it, because it comes only from God's mercy and love. Without his grace, no person can be saved.

on us. With all wisdom and insight 9 he has made known to us the mystery of his 1.9 Col 1.26,27; 2.2
will, according to his good pleasure that he set forth in Christ, 10 as a plan for the 1.10
fullness of time, to gather up all things in him, things in heaven and things on earth. Gal 4.4
11 In Christ we have also obtained an inheritance,[c] having been destined according 1.11 Rom 9.11
to the purpose of him who accomplishes all things according to his counsel and
will, 12 so that we, who were the first to set our hope on Christ, might live for the 1.12 Jas 1.18
praise of his glory. 13 In him you also, when you had heard the word of truth, the 1.13 2 Cor 1.22
gospel of your salvation, and had believed in him, were marked with the seal of the Col 1.5
promised Holy Spirit; 14 this[d] is the pledge of our inheritance toward redemption as 1.14 Rom 8.23
God's own people, to the praise of his glory. 2 Cor 1.22; 5.5

Paul's prayer for the Ephesian believers

15 I have heard of your faith in the Lord Jesus and your love[e] toward all the
saints, and for this reason 16 I do not cease to give thanks for you as I remember you 1.16 Col 1.9
in my prayers. 17 I pray that the God of our Lord Jesus Christ, the Father of glory, 1.17 1 Cor 2.9-12
may give you a spirit of wisdom and revelation as you come to know him, 18 so that,
with the eyes of your heart enlightened, you may know what is the hope to which 1.18 Acts 26.18
he has called you, what are the riches of his glorious inheritance among the saints, 1.19 Phil 3.21
19 and what is the immeasurable greatness of his power for us who believe, according to the working of his great power. 20 God[f] put this power to work in Christ 1.20 Acts 2.24
when he raised him from the dead and seated him at his right hand in the heavenly 1.22 Col 2.19
places, 21 far above all rule and authority and power and dominion, and above every
name that is named, not only in this age but also in the age to come. 22 And he has 1.23 Col 3.11
put all things under his feet and has made him the head over all things for the
church, 23 which is his body, the fullness of him who fills all in all.

The spiritually dead are made alive

2 You were dead through the trespasses and sins 2 in which you once lived, fol- 2.3 Gal 5.16
lowing the course of this world, following the ruler of the power of the air, the Tit 3.3
spirit that is now at work among those who are disobedient. 3 All of us once lived

[c] Or *been made a heritage* [d] Other ancient authorities read *who* [e] Other ancient authorities lack *and your love*
[f] Gk *He*

1.9, 10 God was not intentionally keeping a secret ("the mystery of his will"), but his plan for the world could not be fully understood until Christ rose from the dead. His purpose for sending Christ was to unite Jews and Gentiles in one body with Christ as the head. Many people still do not understand God's plan, but when the time is right ("the fullness of time"), he will gather us to be with him forever. Then everyone will understand. On that day, all people will bow to Jesus as Lord, either because they love him or because they fear his power (see Philippians 2.10, 11).

1.11 God's purpose is to offer salvation to the world, just as he planned to do long ago. God is sovereign; he is in charge. When your life seems chaotic, rest in this truth: Jesus is Lord, and God is in control. His purpose to save you cannot be thwarted, no matter what evil Satan may bring.

1.13, 14 The Holy Spirit is God's seal that we belong to him and his guarantee that he will do what he has promised. He is like a down payment, a pledge, a validating signature on the contract. The presence of the Holy Spirit in us demonstrates the genuineness of our faith, proves that we are his children, and secures eternal life for us. His power works in us transforming us now, and is a taste of the total change we will experience in eternity.

1.16, 17 Paul prays that the Ephesians might really understand who Christ is. Christ is our model, and the more we know of him, the more we will be like him. Study Jesus' life in the Bible to see what he was like on earth 2,000 years ago, and get to know him in prayer now. Personal knowledge of Christ is life-changing!

1.19, 20 The world fears the power of the atom, yet we belong to the God of the universe who not only created that atomic power but also raised Jesus Christ from the dead. God's incomparable power is available to help those who believe. There is nothing too difficult for him.

1.20–22 Having been raised from the dead, Christ is now the supreme head of the church, the ultimate authority over the world. Christ is the Messiah, God's Anointed One, the One Israel longed for, the One who would set their broken world right. As Christians we can be confident that God has won the final victory and is in control of everything. We need not fear any dictator, nation, death, or Satan himself. The contract has been signed and sealed; we are waiting just a short while for delivery. Paul says, in Romans 8.37–39, that nothing can separate us from God and his love.

1.22, 23 When reading Ephesians, it is important to remember that it was written primarily to the entire church, not merely to an individual. Christ is the head and we are the body of his church (Paul uses this metaphor in Romans 12.4, 5; 1 Corinthians 12.12–27; and Colossians 3.15 as well as throughout the book of Ephesians). The image of the body shows the church's unity. Each member is involved with all the others as they go about doing Christ's work on earth. We should not attempt to work, serve, or worship merely on our own. We need the entire body.

2.2 "The ruler of the power of the air" was understood by Paul's readers to mean Satan and the evil spiritual forces they believed inhabited the region between earth and sky. Satan is thus pictured as ruling the evil spiritual world—the demons and those who are against Christ. *Satan* means "the Adversary." He is also called the devil (4.27). In the resurrection, Christ was victorious over Satan and his power. Therefore, Jesus Christ is the permanent ruler of the whole world; Satan is only the temporary ruler of the part of the world that chooses to follow him.

2.4 Jn 3.16 among them in the passions of our flesh, following the desires of flesh and senses,
2.5 Rom 5.6; 6.4 and we were by nature children of wrath, like everyone else. [4]But God, who is rich
in mercy, out of the great love with which he loved us [5]even when we were dead
2.6 Eph 1.3,20 through our trespasses, made us alive together with Christ[g]—by grace you have
Col 2.12 been saved— [6]and raised us up with him and seated us with him in the heavenly
2.7 Tit 3.4 places in Christ Jesus, [7]so that in the ages to come he might show the immeasurable
riches of his grace in kindness toward us in Christ Jesus. [8]For by grace you have
2.8 Jn 4.10 been saved through faith, and this is not your own doing; it is the gift of God— [9]not
Rom 4.16 the result of works, so that no one may boast. [10]For we are what he has made us,
2.9 Rom 3.20 created in Christ Jesus for good works, which God prepared beforehand to be our
Tit 3.5 way of life.

[g] Other ancient authorities read *in Christ*

OUR TRUE IDENTITY IN CHRIST

Romans 3.24	We are declared "not guilty" of sin.
Romans 8.1	No condemnation awaits us.
Romans 8.2	We are free from the vicious circle of sin and death.
1 Corinthians 1.2	We are acceptable to God through Jesus Christ.
1 Corinthians 1.30	We are pure and holy.
1 Corinthians 15.22	We will rise again.
2 Corinthians 3.17	We are free from trying to be saved by being good enough.
2 Corinthians 5.17	We are brand new people inside.
2 Corinthians 5.21	We are full of God's goodness.
Galatians 3.28	We are one in Christ with all other believers.
Ephesians 1.3	We are blessed with every spiritual blessing in heaven.
Ephesians 1.4	We are holy, faultless, and covered with God's love.
Ephesians 1.5, 6	We belong to Christ.
Ephesians 1.7	Our sins are taken away and we are forgiven.
Ephesians 1.10, 11	We will live with Christ forever.
Ephesians 1.13	We are marked as belonging to God by the Holy Spirit.
Ephesians 2.6	We have been lifted from the grave to sit with Christ in glory.
Ephesians 2.10	We have been given new lives.
Ephesians 2.13	We have been brought near to God.
Ephesians 3.6	We will receive great blessings.
Ephesians 3.12	We can come fearlessly into God's presence.
Ephesians 5.29, 30	We are part of Christ's body, the church.
Colossians 2.10	We have everything because we have Christ; we are filled with God.
Colossians 2.11	We are set free from our evil desires.
2 Timothy 2.10	We will have eternal glory.

2.3 The fact that all people, without exception, commit sin proves that we have a sinful nature. Does this mean only Christians do good? Of course not—many people do good to others. On a relative scale, many are moral, kind, and law-abiding. Comparing these people to criminals, we would say that they are very good indeed. But on God's absolute scale, *no one* is good enough to earn salvation. Only through being united with Christ's perfect life can we become good in God's sight. "Children of wrath" refers to those who are destined, because of their rejection of Christ, to receive God's wrath.

2.4, 5 In the previous verses Paul talks about our old sinful nature (2.1–3). Here Paul emphasizes that we do not need to live any longer under sin's power. The penalty of sin and its power over us were destroyed by Christ on the cross. Through faith in Christ we stand acquitted, "not guilty," before God (Romans 3.21, 22). God does not take us out of the world or make us robots—we will still feel like sinning, and sometimes we will sin. The difference is that before we became Christians, we were dead in sin and slaves to our sinful nature. But now we are alive with Christ (see also Galatians 2.20).

2.6 Because of Christ's resurrection, we know that our bodies will also be raised from the dead (1 Corinthians 15.2–23) and that we have been given the power to live as Christians now (1.19). These ideas are combined in Paul's image of sitting with Christ in "heavenly places." Our eternal life with Christ is certain, because we are united in his powerful victory.

2.8, 9 When someone gives you a gift, do you say, "That's very nice—now how much do I owe you?" No, the appropriate response to a gift is "Thank you." Yet how often Christians, even after they have been given the gift of salvation, feel obligated to try to work their way to God. Because our salvation and even our faith are gifts, we should respond with gratitude, praise, and joy.

2.8–10 We become Christians through God's unmerited grace, not as the result of any effort, ability, intelligent choice, or act of service on our part. However, out of gratitude for this free gift, we will seek to help and serve others with kindness, charity, and goodness, and not merely to please ourselves. While no action or work we do can help us obtain salvation, God's intention is that our salvation will result in works of service. We are not saved merely for our own benefit but to serve him and build up the church (4.12).

Christ is the way to peace

11 So then, remember that at one time you Gentiles by birth,[h] called "the uncir- 2.11
cumcision" by those who are called "the circumcision"—a physical circumcision Rom 2.28 Col 2.11
made in the flesh by human hands— 12 remember that you were at that time without 2.12
Christ, being aliens from the commonwealth of Israel, and strangers to the cove- Rom 9.4,8 Gal 4.8
nants of promise, having no hope and without God in the world. 13 But now in 2.13
Christ Jesus you who once were far off have been brought near by the blood of Acts 2.39
Christ. 14 For he is our peace; in his flesh he has made both groups into one and has 2.14
broken down the dividing wall, that is, the hostility between us. 15 He has abolished 1 Cor 12.13
the law with its commandments and ordinances, that he might create in himself one 2.15 2 Cor 5.17
new humanity in place of the two, thus making peace, 16 and might reconcile both Gal 3.28
groups to God in one body[i] through the cross, thus putting to death that hostility 2.16 Col 1.20
through it.[j] 17 So he came and proclaimed peace to you who were far off and peace
to those who were near; 18 for through him both of us have access in one Spirit to the 2.18
Father. 19 So then you are no longer strangers and aliens, but you are citizens with Jn 14.6,17-20
the saints and also members of the household of God, 20 built upon the foundation 2.20
of the apostles and prophets, with Christ Jesus himself as the cornerstone.[k] 21 In Ps 118.22 Isa 28.16
him the whole structure is joined together and grows into a holy temple in the Lord; Mt 16.18; 21.42
22 in whom you also are built together spiritually[l] into a dwelling place for God. 1 Cor 3.11 Rev 21.14

Paul's special mission to Gentiles

3 This is the reason that I Paul am a prisoner for[m] Christ Jesus for the sake of you 3.2
Gentiles— 2 for surely you have already heard of the commission of God's Rom 16.25 3.3
grace that was given me for you, 3 and how the mystery was made known to me by Col 1.25-27

[h] Gk *in the flesh* [i] Or *reconcile both of us in one body for God* [j] Or *in him,* or *in himself* [k] Or *keystone* [l] Gk *in the Spirit* [m] Or *of*

2.11 Pious Jews ("the circumcision") considered all non-Jews (the "uncircumcision") ceremonially unclean. They thought of themselves as pure and clean because of their national heritage and religious ceremonies. Paul points out that Jews and Gentiles alike are unclean before God and need to be cleansed by Christ. In order to realize how great a gift salvation is, we need to remember our former natural, unclean condition.

2.11–13 Jews and Gentiles alike could be guilty of spiritual pride–Jews for thinking their ceremonies elevated them above everyone else, Gentiles for forgetting the hopelessness of their condition apart from Christ. Spiritual pride blinds us to our own faults and magnifies the faults of others. Be careful not to become proud of your salvation. Instead, humbly thank God for what he has done, and encourage others who might be struggling in their faith.

2.11–16 Before Christ's coming, Gentiles and Jews kept apart from each other. Jews considered Gentiles beyond God's saving power and therefore without hope. Gentiles resented Jewish claims. Christ revealed the total sinfulness of both Jews and Gentiles, and then he offered his salvation to both. Only Christ breaks down the walls of prejudice, reconciles all believers to God, and unifies us in one body.

2.14 There are many barriers that can divide us from other Christians: age, appearance, intelligence, political persuasion, economic status, race, theological perspective. One of the best ways to stifle Christ's love is to cater only to those for whom we have natural affinity. Fortunately, Christ has knocked down the barriers and unified all believers in one family. His cross should be the focus of our unity. The Holy Spirit helps us look beyond the barriers to the unity we are called to enjoy.

2.14ff Christ has broken down the walls people build between themselves. Because these walls have been removed, we can come to real unity with people who are not like us. This is true reconciliation. Because of Christ's death, we are all one family (2.14); our anger against each other has disappeared (2.16); we can all approach God through the Holy Spirit (2.18); we are no longer strangers to God (2.19); and we are all part of a beautiful temple with Christ as our cornerstone (2.20, 21).

2.15 By his death, Christ ended the angry resentment between Jews and Gentiles, caused by the Jewish laws which favored the Jews and excluded the Gentiles. Christ died to annul that whole system of Jewish laws. Then he took the two groups that had been opposed to each other and made them parts of himself. Thus he fused all believers together to become one new "person."

2.17, 18 The Jews were near to God because they already knew of him through the Scriptures and worshiped him in their religious ceremonies. The Gentiles were "far off" because they knew little or nothing about God. Because neither group could be saved by good works, knowledge, or sincerity, both needed to hear about the salvation available through Jesus Christ. Both Jews and Gentiles are now free to come to God through Christ.

2.19–21 A church building is sometimes called God's house. In reality, God's house is not a building, but a group of people. He lives in us and shows himself to a watching world through us. People can see that God is love and that Jesus is Lord as we live in harmony with each other and with what God says in his Word. We are citizens of God's kingdom and members of his household.

2.20 What does it mean to be built on the foundation of the apostles and the prophets? It means that the church is not built on modern ideas, but rather on the spiritual heritage given to us in the Old and New Testaments.

3.1 Paul was under house arrest in Rome for preaching about Christ. The religious leaders, who felt threatened by Christ's teachings and didn't believe he was the Messiah, pressured the Romans to arrest Paul and bring him to trial for treason and for causing rebellion among the Jews. Paul had appealed for his case to be heard by the emperor, and he was awaiting trial (see Acts 28.16–31). Even though he was under arrest, Paul maintained his firm belief that God was in control of all that happened to him. Do circumstances make you wonder if God has lost control of this world? Like Paul, remember that no matter what happens, God directs the world's affairs.

3.2, 3 God had given Paul the special work of preaching the good

3.5 Eph 1.17
3.6 Gal 3.14; Eph 2.14-16
3.7 Rom 15.18; Col 1.23
3.8 1 Cor 15.9; Col 2.2,3,9,10
3.9 1 Cor 2.7
3.10 1 Cor 2.7; Eph 1.21; 6.12; 1 Pet 3.22
3.11 Eph 1.11
3.12 Eph 2.18; Heb 4.16

revelation, as I wrote above in a few words, 4 a reading of which will enable you to
perceive my understanding of the mystery of Christ. 5 In former generations this
mystery[n] was not made known to humankind, as it has now been revealed to his
holy apostles and prophets by the Spirit: 6 that is, the Gentiles have become fellow
heirs, members of the same body, and sharers in the promise in Christ Jesus
through the gospel.
7 Of this gospel I have become a servant according to the gift of God's grace
that was given me by the working of his power. 8 Although I am the very least of all
the saints, this grace was given to me to bring to the Gentiles the news of the boundless riches of Christ, 9 and to make everyone see[o] what is the plan of the mystery
hidden for ages in[p] God who created all things; 10 so that through the church the
wisdom of God in its rich variety might now be made known to the rulers and
authorities in the heavenly places. 11 This was in accordance with the eternal purpose that he has carried out in Christ Jesus our Lord, 12 in whom we have access to
God in boldness and confidence through faith in him.[q] 13 I pray therefore that you[r]
may not lose heart over my sufferings for you; they are your glory.

[n] Gk *it* [o] Other ancient authorities read *to bring to light* [p] Or *by* [q] Or *the faith of him* [r] Or *I*

OUR LIVES BEFORE AND AFTER CHRIST

Before	*After*
Under God's curse	Loved by God
Doomed because of our sins	Shown God's mercy and given salvation
Went along with the crowd	Stand for Christ and truth
God's enemies	God's children
Enslaved to Satan	Free in Christ to love, serve, and sit with him
Followed our evil thoughts and passions	Taken from the grave to glory
Under God's anger	Given undeserved favor
Spiritually dead	Given new spiritual life

news to the Gentiles, shown to Paul in a revelation. "As I wrote above in a few words" may refer to a previous letter which was not preserved by the church, or it may refer to an earlier part of this letter (especially 1.9ff; 2.11ff).

3.5, 6 God's plan was hidden from previous generations, not because God wanted to keep something from his people, but because he would reveal it to everyone in his perfect timing. God planned to have Jews and Gentiles comprise one body, the church. It was known in the Old Testament that the Gentiles would receive salvation (Isaiah 49.6); but it was never revealed in the Old Testament that all Gentile and Jewish believers would become equal in the body of Christ. Yet this equality was accomplished when Jesus broke down the "dividing wall" and created the "one new humanity" (2.14, 15).

3.7 God gave the apostle Paul the ability to share effectively the gospel of Christ. You may not be an apostle or even an evangelist, but God will give you opportunities to tell others about Christ, and with the opportunities he will provide the ability, courage, and power. Whenever an opportunity presents itself, make yourself available to God. As you focus on the other person and his or her needs, God will communicate your caring attitude. Your words will be natural, loving, and compelling.

3.8 When Paul described himself as "the very least of all the saints," he was saying that without God's help, he would never be able to do God's work. Yet God chose him to share the gospel with the Gentiles and gave him the power to do it. If we feel useless, we may be right—except that we have forgotten what a difference God makes. How does God want to use you? Draw upon his power, do your part, and faithfully perform the special role you play in God's plan.

3.10 The "rulers and authorities in the heavenly places" are either angels (see 1 Peter 1.12), or perhaps hostile forces opposed to God (2.2; 6.12).

3.12 It is an awesome privilege to be admitted into God's presence. Most of us would be apprehensive in the presence of a powerful ruler. But thanks to Christ, we can enter directly into God's presence through prayer. We know we'll be welcomed with open arms because we are God's children through our unity with Christ. Don't be afraid of God. Talk with him about everything. He is waiting to hear from you.

3.13 Why should Paul's suffering make the Ephesians feel honored ("they are your glory")? If Paul had not preached the gospel, he would not be in jail—but then the Ephesians would not have heard the good news and been converted either. As a mother endures the pain of childbirth in order to bring new life into the world, Paul endured the pain of persecution in order to bring new believers to Christ. Obeying Christ is never easy. He calls us to take up our crosses and follow him (Matthew 16.24)—that is, to be willing to endure pain so that God's message of salvation can reach the entire world. We should feel honored that others have suffered and sacrificed for us so that we might benefit from it.

The magnitude of God's love

14 For this reason I bow my knees before the Father,[s] 15 from whom every
family[t] in heaven and on earth takes its name. 16 I pray that, according to the riches
of his glory, he may grant that you may be strengthened in your inner being with
power through his Spirit, 17 and that Christ may dwell in your hearts through faith,
as you are being rooted and grounded in love. 18 I pray that you may have the power
to comprehend, with all the saints, what is the breadth and length and height and
depth, 19 and to know the love of Christ that surpasses knowledge, so that you may
be filled with all the fullness of God.

20 Now to him who by the power at work within us is able to accomplish abundantly far more than all we can ask or imagine, 21 to him be glory in the church and
in Christ Jesus to all generations, forever and ever. Amen.

3.14 Phil 2.9,10
3.16 Phil 4.13,19; Col 1.11
3.17 Jn 14.23; Col 1.27; 2.7
3.18 Jn 1.16; Col 2.9,10
3.19 Col 2.10
3.21 1 Tim 1.17

2. Unity in the church

We are one body in Christ

4 I therefore, the prisoner in the Lord, beg you to lead a life worthy of the calling
to which you have been called, 2 with all humility and gentleness, with patience, bearing with one another in love, 3 making every effort to maintain the unity
of the Spirit in the bond of peace. 4 There is one body and one Spirit, just as you
were called to the one hope of your calling, 5 one Lord, one faith, one baptism,
6 one God and Father of all, who is above all and through all and in all.

7 But each of us was given grace according to the measure of Christ's gift.
8 Therefore it is said,

"When he ascended on high he made captivity itself a captive;
he gave gifts to his people."

9 (When it says, "He ascended," what does it mean but that he had also descended[u]

4.2 Col 3.12,13
4.4 Rom 12.5; 1 Cor 12.12,13
4.5 1 Cor 8.6
4.7 Rom 12.3
4.8 Ps 68.18
4.9 Jn 3.13; Acts 2.27; 1 Pet 3.18

[s] Other ancient authorities add *of our Lord Jesus Christ* [t] Gk *fatherhood* [u] Other ancient authorities add *first*

3.14, 15 The great family of God includes all who have believed in him in the past, all who believe in the present, and all who will believe in the future. We are all a family because we have the same Father. He is the source of all creation, the rightful owner of everything. God promises his love and power to his family, the church (3.16–21). If we want to receive his blessings, it is important that we stay in contact with other believers in the body of Christ. Those who isolate themselves from God's family and try to go it alone cut themselves off from God's power.

3.17–19 God's love is total, says Paul. It reaches every corner of our experience. It is *long*—it continues the length of our lives. It is *deep*—it reaches to the depths of discouragement, despair, and even death. It is *wide*—it covers the breadth of our own experience, and it reaches out to the whole world. It is *high*—it rises to the heights of our celebration and elation. When you feel shut out or isolated, remember that you can never be lost to God's love. For another hymn to God's immeasurable and inexhaustible love, see Paul's words in Romans 8.38, 39.

3.21 This *doxology*—hymn of praise to God—ends Part One of Ephesians, in which Paul describes the timeless role of the church. In Part Two (chapters 4–6), he will explain how church members should live in order to bring about the unity God wants. As in most of his books, Paul first lays a doctrinal foundation, and then makes practical applications of the truths he has presented.

4.1, 2 God has chosen us to be Christ's representatives on earth. In light of this truth, Paul challenges us to live worthy of the name "Christian," meaning *Christ's one*. This includes being humble, gentle, patient, understanding, and peaceful. People are watching your life. Can they see Christ in you? How well are you doing as his representative?

4.1–6 "There is one body," says Paul. Unity does not just happen; we have to work at it. Often differences among people can lead to division, but this should not be true in the church. Instead of concentrating on what divides us, we should remember what unites us: *one* body, *one* Spirit, *one* future ("calling"), *one* Lord, *one* faith, *one* baptism, *one* God! Have you learned to appreciate people who are different from you? Can you see how their differing gifts and viewpoints can help the church as it does God's work? Learn to enjoy the way we members of Christ's body complement one another. (See 1 Corinthians 12.12, 13 for more on this thought.)

4.2 No one is ever going to be perfect here on earth, so we must accept and love other Christians in spite of their faults. When we see faults in fellow believers, we should be patient and gentle. Is there someone whose actions or personality really annoys you? Rather than dwelling on that person's weaknesses or looking for faults, pray for him or her. Then do even more—spend time together and see if you can learn to like him or her.

4.3 Unity is one of the Holy Spirit's important roles. He leads, but we have to be willing to be led. We do that by focusing on God, not on ourselves. For more about who the Holy Spirit is and what he does, see the notes on John 3.6; Acts 1.5; and Ephesians 1.13, 14.

4.4–7 All believers in Christ belong to one body; all are united under one Head, Christ himself (see 1 Corinthians 12.12–26). Each believer has God-given abilities that can strengthen the whole body. Your special ability may seem small or large, but it is yours to use in God's service. Ask God to use your unique gifts to contribute to the strength and health of the body of believers.

4.6 God is *above all*—this shows his overruling care (transcendence). He is *through all and in all*—this shows his active presence in the world and in the lives of believers (immanence). Any view of God that violates either his transcendence or his immanence is not a true picture of him.

4.8 In Psalm 68.18, God is pictured as a conqueror marching to the gates and taking tribute from the fallen city. Paul uses that picture to teach that Christ, in his crucifixion and resurrection, was victorious over Satan. When he ascended to heaven, he gave gifts to the church, some of which he discusses in 4.11–13.

4.10 1 Tim 3.16 Heb 4.14; 8.1 1 Pet 3.22
4.11 1 Cor 12.28
4.12 1 Cor 14.26
4.13 Col 2.2
4.14 Mt 11.7 1 Cor 14.20 Eph 6.11
4.15,16 Col 2.19

into the lower parts of the earth? 10 He who descended is the same one who ascended far above all the heavens, so that he might fill all things.) 11 The gifts he
gave were that some would be apostles, some prophets, some evangelists, some
pastors and teachers, 12 to equip the saints for the work of ministry, for building up
the body of Christ, 13 until all of us come to the unity of the faith and of the knowledge of the Son of God, to maturity, to the measure of the full stature of Christ.
14 We must no longer be children, tossed to and fro and blown about by every wind
of doctrine, by people's trickery, by their craftiness in deceitful scheming. 15 But
speaking the truth in love, we must grow up in every way into him who is the head,
into Christ, 16 from whom the whole body, joined and knit together by every liga-
ment with which it is equipped, as each part is working properly, promotes the
body's growth in building itself up in love.

Living as a new person

4.17 Jn 1.4,5 Acts 17.30; 26.18

17 Now this I affirm and insist on in the Lord: you must no longer live
as the Gentiles live, in the futility of their minds. 18 They are darkened in their

THE ONENESS OF ALL BELIEVERS

Believers are one in:	*Our unity is experienced in:*
Body	The fellowship of believers—the church
Spirit	The Holy Spirit who activates the fellowship
Hope	That glorious future to which we are all called
Lord	Christ, to whom we all belong
Faith	Our singular commitment to Christ
Baptism	Baptism—the sign of entry into the church
God	God, who is our Father and keeps us for eternity

Too often believers are separated because of minor differences in doctrine. But Paul here shows those areas where Christians must agree to attain true unity. When believers have this unity of spirit, petty differences should never be allowed to dissolve that unity.

4.9 The "lower parts of the earth" may be (1) the earth itself (lowly by comparison to heaven), (2) the grave, or (3) Hades (many believe Hades is the resting place of souls between death and resurrection). However we understand it, Christ is Lord of the whole universe, past, present, and future. Nothing or no one is hidden from him. The Lord of all came to earth and faced death to rescue all people. No one is beyond his reach.

4.11, 12 Our oneness in Christ does not destroy our individuality. The Holy Spirit has given each Christian special gifts for building up the church. Now that we have these gifts, it is crucial to use them. Are you spiritually mature, exercising the gifts God has given you? If you know what your gifts are, look for opportunities to serve. If you don't know, ask God to show you, perhaps with the help of your minister or Christian friends. Then, as you begin to recognize your special area of service, use your gifts to strengthen and encourage the church.

4.12 God has given his church an enormous responsibility—to make disciples in every nation (Matthew 28.18–20). This involves preaching, teaching, healing, nurturing, giving, administering, building, and many other tasks. If we had to fulfill this command as individuals, we might as well give up without trying—it would be impossible. But God calls us as members of his body. Some of us can do one task; some can do another. Together we can obey him more fully than any of us could alone. It is a human tendency to overestimate what we can do by ourselves and to underestimate what we can do as a group. The truth is just the opposite. As the body of Christ, we can do more functioning together than we would dream possible working by ourselves.

4.14–16 Christ is the truth (John 14.6), and the Holy Spirit who guides the church is the Spirit of truth (John 16.13). Satan, by contrast, is the father of lies (John 8.44). As followers of Christ, we must be committed to the truth. This means both that our words will be honest and that our actions will reflect Christ's integrity. Speaking the truth in love is not always easy or pleasant; but it is necessary if the church is going to do Christ's work in the world.

4.15, 16 Some Christians fear that any mistake will destroy their witness for the Lord. They see their own weaknesses, and they know that many non-Christians seem to have stronger characters than they do. How can they be new and different persons, holy and good? The answer is that Jesus forms us into a body—a group of individuals who are united in purpose and in love for one another and for Christ. If an individual stumbles, the rest of the group is there to pick him up and help him walk with his Lord again. If an individual sins, he can find restoration through the church (Galatians 6.1). As part of Christ's body, you will reflect part of Christ's character and do part of his work. As you grow to be more like him, you will better appreciate your brothers and sisters in Christ.

4.17 Living in "the futility of their minds" refers to the natural tendency of human beings to think their way away from God. Intellectual pride, rationalizations, and excuses all keep people from God. Don't be surprised if people can't grasp the gospel. Without faith, left to their own understanding, it seems foolish.

4.17–24 People should be able to see a difference between Christians and non-Christians because of the way Christians live. Paul tells the Ephesians to leave behind the old life of sin now that they are followers of Christ. Living the Christian life is a process. Although we have a new nature, we don't automatically have all good thoughts and attitudes when we become new people in Christ. But if we keep listening to God, we will be changing all the time. As you look back over last year, do you see a process of change for the better in your thoughts, attitudes, and actions? Although change may be slow, it comes about if you trust God to change you. For more about our new nature as believers see Romans 6.6; 8.9; Galatians 5.16–26; Colossians 3.3–8.

understanding, alienated from the life of God because of their ignorance and hardness of heart. 19 They have lost all sensitivity and have abandoned themselves to
licentiousness, greedy to practice every kind of impurity. 20 That is not the way you
learned Christ! 21 For surely you have heard about him and were taught in him, as
truth is in Jesus. 22 You were taught to put away your former way of life, your old
self, corrupt and deluded by its lusts, 23 and to be renewed in the spirit of your minds,
24 and to clothe yourselves with the new self, created according to the likeness of
God in true righteousness and holiness.
25 So then, putting away falsehood, let all of us speak the truth to our neighbors, for we are members of one another. 26 Be angry but do not sin; do not let the
sun go down on your anger, 27 and do not make room for the devil. 28 Thieves must
give up stealing; rather let them labor and work honestly with their own hands, so
as to have something to share with the needy. 29 Let no evil talk come out of your
mouths, but only what is useful for building up,[v] as there is need, so that your
words may give grace to those who hear. 30 And do not grieve the Holy Spirit of
God, with which you were marked with a seal for the day of redemption. 31 Put
away from you all bitterness and wrath and anger and wrangling and slander, together with all malice, 32 and be kind to one another, tenderhearted, forgiving one
5 another, as God in Christ has forgiven you.[w] 1 Therefore be imitators of God,
as beloved children, 2 and live in love, as Christ loved us[x] and gave himself up
for us, a fragrant offering and sacrifice to God.
3 But fornication and impurity of any kind, or greed, must not even be mentioned among you, as is proper among saints. 4 Entirely out of place is obscene,
silly, and vulgar talk; but instead, let there be thanksgiving. 5 Be sure of this, that
no fornicator or impure person, or one who is greedy (that is, an idolater), has any
inheritance in the kingdom of Christ and of God.

Living as a child of the light

6 Let no one deceive you with empty words, for because of these things the
wrath of God comes on those who are disobedient. 7 Therefore do not be associated
with them. 8 For once you were darkness, but now in the Lord you are light. Live

4.19 Rom 1.24 Col 3.5
4.22 Rom 6.6 Jas 1.21
4.23 Rom 12.2
4.24 2 Cor 5.17
4.25 Zech 8.16
4.27 Jas 4.7
4.28 1 Thess 4.11
4.29 Mt 12.34 Rom 14.19 Col 4.6
4.30 Isa 63.10 1 Thess 5.19
4.31 Col 3.8 1 Pet 2.1
4.32 Col 3.12,13
5.1 Mt 5.45
5.2 2 Cor 2.15
5.4 Rom 1.28
5.5 1 Cor 6.9 Gal 5.21
5.8 Isa 9.2 Jn 8.12 1 Jn 2.9

[v] Other ancient authorities read *building up faith* [w] Other ancient authorities read *us* [x] Other ancient authorities read *you*

4.25 Lying to each other disrupts unity by creating conflicts and destroying trust. It tears down relationships and leads to open war in a church.

4.26, 27 The Bible doesn't tell us we shouldn't feel angry, but it points out that it is important to handle our anger properly. If ventilated thoughtlessly, anger can hurt others and destroy relationships. If bottled up inside, it can cause us to become bitter and destroy us from within. Paul tells us to deal with our anger immediately in a way that builds relationships rather than destroying them. If we nurse our anger, we will give Satan an opportunity to divide us. Are you angry with someone right now? What can you do to resolve your differences? Don't let the day end before you begin to work on mending your relationship.

4.28–32 We can cause the Holy Spirit sorrow by the way we live. Paul warns us against bad language, meanness, improper use of anger, quarrels, harsh words, and bad attitudes toward others. Instead of acting that way, we should be forgiving, just as God has forgiven us. Are you grieving or pleasing God with your attitudes and actions? Act in love toward your brothers and sisters in Christ, just as God acted in love by sending his Son to die for your sins.

4.30 The Holy Spirit within us is a sign that we belong to God. For more on this thought, see the note on 1.13, 14.

4.32 This is Christ's law of forgiveness as taught in the Gospels (Matthew 6.14, 15; 18.35; Mark 11.25). We also see it in the Lord's prayer—"Forgive us our debts, as we also have forgiven our debtors." God does not forgive us because we forgive others, but out of his great mercy. As we come to understand his mercy, however, we will want to be like him. Having received forgiveness, we will pass it on to others. Those who are unwilling to forgive have not become one with Christ, who was willing to forgive even those who crucified him (Luke 23.34).

5.1, 2 Just as children imitate their parents, we should imitate Christ. His great love for us led him to sacrifice himself so that we might live. Our love for others should be of the same kind—a love that goes beyond affection to self-sacrificing service.

5.4 Foul language or vulgar, obscene talk is so common that we begin to take it for granted. Paul cautions, however, that vulgar speech should have no place in the Christian's conversation because it does not reflect God's gracious presence in us. How can we praise God and remind others of his goodness when we are speaking coarsely?

5.5–7 Paul is not forbidding all contact with unbelievers. Jesus taught his followers to befriend sinners and lead them to him (Luke 5.30–32). Instead, Paul is speaking against condoning or adapting the life-style of people who excuse, love, and recommend bad behavior—whether they are in the church or outside of it. Such people can quickly pollute the church, and endanger its unity and purpose. We must befriend unbelievers if we are to lead them to Christ, but we must be wary of those who are viciously evil, immoral, or opposed to all that Christianity stands for. Such people are more likely to influence us for evil than we are likely to influence them for good.

5.8 Your actions should reflect your faith. We should live above reproach morally so that we can reflect God's goodness to others. Jesus stressed this in the Sermon on the Mount (Matthew 5.15, 16).

5.11 Lev 19.17 1 Cor 5.9
5.13 Jn 3.20 Heb 4.13
5.14 Isa 26.19; 51.17 52.1; 60.1 Jn 5.25 Rom 6.4,5; 13.11
5.17 1 Thess 4.3
5.18 Prov 20.1; 23.31 Jn 7.37-39 1 Cor 12.13
5.19 1 Cor 14.26 Col 3.16 Jas 5.13

as children of light— 9for the fruit of the light is found in all that is good and right
and true. 10Try to find out what is pleasing to the Lord. 11Take no part in the unfruitful works of darkness, but instead expose them. 12For it is shameful even to
mention what such people do secretly; 13but everything exposed by the light becomes visible, 14for everything that becomes visible is light. Therefore it says,

"Sleeper, awake!
Rise from the dead,
and Christ will shine on you."

15 Be careful then how you live, not as unwise people but as wise, 16making
the most of the time, because the days are evil. 17So do not be foolish, but understand what the will of the Lord is. 18Do not get drunk with wine, for that is debauchery; but be filled with the Spirit, 19as you sing psalms and hymns and
spiritual songs among yourselves, singing and making melody to the Lord in your
hearts, 20giving thanks to God the Father at all times and for everything in the name
of our Lord Jesus Christ.

Wives and husbands

5.21 1 Pet 5.5
5.22 Gen 3.16
5.23 1 Cor 11.3

21 Be subject to one another out of reverence for Christ.
22 Wives, be subject to your husbands as you are to the Lord. 23For the husband is the head of the wife just as Christ is the head of the church, the body of
which he is the Savior. 24Just as the church is subject to Christ, so also wives ought
to be, in everything, to their husbands.

5.10–14 It is important to avoid the unfruitful works of darkness (any pleasure or activity that results in sin), but we must go even further. Paul instructs us to rebuke and expose them, because often our silence is interpreted as approval. God needs people who will take a stand for what is right. Which evil pleasures should you reject, and when should you lovingly speak out for what is true and right?

5.14 This is not a direct quote from Scripture but was probably taken from a hymn well known to the Ephesians. The hymn seems to have been based on Isaiah 26.19; 51.17; 52.1; 60.1; and Malachi 4.2. Paul is appealing to the Ephesians to wake up and realize the dangerous condition into which some of them have been slipping.

5.15, 16 By saying, "the days are evil," Paul communicates his sense of urgency because of evil's pervasiveness. We need the same sense of urgency because our days are also difficult. We must keep our standards high, act wisely, and do good whenever we can.

5.17 It is not enough to *know* what God wants us to do; we must also *do* it. We must follow our beliefs with actions.

5.18 Paul contrasts being drunk with wine, which produces harmful effects, to being filled with the Spirit, which produces positive effects. What matters is not how much of the Holy Spirit we have, but how much of us the Holy Spirit has. We need to submit daily to his leading and draw on his power. Some effects of being filled with the Holy Spirit are mentioned in 5.19–21.

5.20 When you feel down, you may find it difficult to give thanks. Take heart—God works all things out for good if we love him and are fitting into his purpose (Romans 8.28). Thank God, not for your problems, but for the strength he is building in you through the difficult experiences of your life. You can be sure that God's perfect love will see you through.

5.21, 22 Being subject to another person (also called submission) is an often misunderstood concept. It does not mean becoming a doormat. Christ—at whose name "every knee should bend, in heaven and on earth and under the earth" (Philippians 2.10)—submitted his will to the Father, and we honor Christ by following his example. When we submit to God, we become more willing to obey his command to submit to others; that is, to subordinate our rights to theirs. In a marriage relationship, both husband and wife are called to submit. For the wife, this means willingly following her husband's leadership in Christ. For the husband, it means putting aside his own interests in order to care for his wife. Submission is rarely a problem in homes where both spouses have a strong relationship with Christ and where each is concerned for the happiness of the other.

5.22–24 In Paul's day, women, children, and slaves were to submit to the head of the family—slaves until they were freed, male children until they grew up, and women and girls their whole lives. Paul emphasized the equality of all believers in Christ (Galatians 3.28), but he did not suggest overthrowing Roman society to achieve it. Instead, he counseled all believers to submit to one another by choice—wives to husbands and also husbands to wives; slaves to masters and also masters to slaves; children to parents and also parents to children. This kind of mutual submission preserves order and harmony in the family while it increases love and respect among family members.

5.22–24 Although some people have distorted Paul's teaching on submission by giving unlimited authority to husbands, we cannot get around it—Paul told wives to submit to their husbands. The fact that a teaching is not popular is no reason to discard it. According to the Bible, the man is the spiritual head of the family and his wife should acknowledge his leadership. But real spiritual leadership involves service. Just as Christ served the disciples, even to the point of washing their feet, so the husband is to serve his wife. A wise and Christ-honoring husband will not take advantage of his role, and a wise and Christ-honoring wife will not try to undermine her husband's leadership. Either approach causes disunity and friction in marriage.

5.22–26 Why does Paul tell wives to submit and husbands to love? Perhaps Christian women, newly freed in Christ, found submission difficult; and Christian men, used to the Roman custom of giving unlimited power to the head of the family, were not used to treating their wives with respect and love. Of course both husbands and wives should submit to each other (5.21), just as both should love each other.

25 Husbands, love your wives, just as Christ loved the church and gave himself 5.26
up for her, 26 in order to make her holy by cleansing her with the washing of water Jn 15.3; 17.17 Tit 3.5
by the word, 27 so as to present the church to himself in splendor, without a spot or Heb 10.22
wrinkle or anything of the kind—yes, so that she may be holy and without blemish. 5.27 Col 1.22
28 In the same way, husbands should love their wives as they do their own bodies. Rev 21.2
He who loves his wife loves himself. 29 For no one ever hates his own body, but he 5.28 1 Pet 3.7
nourishes and tenderly cares for it, just as Christ does for the church, 30 because we 5.30
are members of his body.[y] 31 "For this reason a man will leave his father and 1 Cor 6.15
mother and be joined to his wife, and the two will become one flesh." 32 This is a 5.31 Gen 2.24
great mystery, and I am applying it to Christ and the church. 33 Each of you, how- 5.33
ever, should love his wife as himself, and a wife should respect her husband. 1 Pet 3.1,2,5

Children and parents

6 Children, obey your parents in the Lord,[z] for this is right. 2 "Honor your father 6.1 Prov 23.22
and mother"—this is the first commandment with a promise: 3 "so that it may 6.2
be well with you and you may live long on the earth." Ex 20.12 Mt 15.4
4 And, fathers, do not provoke your children to anger, but bring them up in the 6.4
discipline and instruction of the Lord. Col 3.21

Slaves and masters

5 Slaves, obey your earthly masters with fear and trembling, in singleness of 6.5
heart, as you obey Christ; 6 not only while being watched, and in order to please Col 3.22

[y] Other ancient authorities add *of his flesh and of his bones* [z] Other ancient authorities lack *in the Lord*

5.25ff Some Christians have thought Paul was negative about marriage because of the counsel he gave in 1 Corinthians 7.32–38. These verses in Ephesians, however, show a high view of marriage. Here marriage is not a practical necessity or a cure for lust, but a picture of the relationship between Christ and his church! Why the apparent difference? Paul's counsel in 1 Corinthians was designed for a state of emergency during a time of persecution and crisis. Paul's counsel to the Ephesians is more the biblical ideal for marriage. Marriage, for Paul, is a holy union, a living symbol, a precious relationship that needs tender, self-sacrificing care.

5.25–30 Paul devotes twice as many words to telling husbands to love their wives as to telling wives to submit to their husbands. How should a man love his wife? (1) He should be willing to sacrifice everything for her. (2) He should make her well-being of primary importance. (3) He should care for her as he cares for his body. No wife needs to fear submitting to a man who treats her in this way.

5.26, 27 Christ's death sanctifies and cleanses the church. He cleanses us from the old ways of sin and sets us apart for his special sacred service (Hebrews 10.29; 13.12). Christ cleansed the church by the "washing" of baptism. Through baptism we are prepared for entrance into the church just as oriental brides were prepared for marriage by a ceremonial bath. It is God's Word that cleanses us (John 17.17; Titus 3.5).

5.31–33 The union of husband and wife merges two persons in such a way that little can affect one without also affecting the other. Oneness in marriage does not mean losing your personality in the personality of the other. Instead, it means caring for your spouse as you care for yourself, learning to anticipate the other person's needs, helping the other person become all he or she can be. The creation story tells of God's plan that husband and wife should be one (Genesis 2.24), and Jesus also referred to this plan (Matthew 19.4–6).

6.1, 2 There is a difference between obeying and honoring. To obey means to do as one is told; to honor means to respect and love. Children are not commanded to disobey God in obeying their parents. Adult children are not asked to be subservient to domineering parents. Children are to obey while under their parents' care, but the responsibility to honor parents is for life.

6.1–4 If our faith in Christ is real, it will usually prove itself at home, in our relationships with those who know us best. Children and parents have a responsibility to each other. Children should honor their parents even if the parents are demanding and unfair. Parents should care gently for their children, even if the children are disobedient and unpleasant. Ideally, of course, Christian parents and Christian children will relate to each other with thoughtfulness and love. This will happen if both parents and children put the others' interests above their own—that is, if they submit to one another.

6.3 Some societies honor their elders. They respect their wisdom, they defer to their authority, and they pay attention to their comfort and happiness. This is how Christians should act. Where elders are respected, long life is a blessing, not a burden to them.

6.4 The purpose of parental discipline is to help children grow, not to hurt or discourage them (see also Colossians 3.21). Parenting is not easy—it takes lots of patience to raise children in a loving, Christ-honoring manner. But frustration and anger should not be causes for discipline. Instead, parents should act in love, treating their children as Jesus treats the people he loves. This is vital to children's development and to their understanding of what Christ is like.

6.5 Slaves played a significant part in Roman culture. There were several million of them in the Roman Empire at this time. Because many slaves and owners had become Christians, the early church had to deal straightforwardly with the question of master/slave relations. Paul's statement neither condemns nor condones slavery. Instead, it tells masters and slaves how to live together in Christian households. In Paul's day, women, children, and slaves had few rights. In the church, however, they had freedoms that society denied them. Paul tells husbands, parents, and masters to be caring.

6.6, 7 Paul's instructions encourage responsibility and integrity on the job. Christian employees should do their jobs as if Jesus Christ were their supervisor. And Christian employers should treat their employees fairly and with respect. Can you be trusted to do your best, even when the boss is not around? Do you work hard and with enthusiasm? Do you treat your employees as people, not machines? Remember that no matter whom you work for, and no matter who works for you, the One you ultimately want to please is your Father in heaven.

6.6 Col 3.22,23
6.8 Rom 2.6; 2 Cor 5.10; Col 3.24
6.9 Job 31.13,14; Col 4.1
6.11 Rom 13.12; 1 Thess 5.8
6.12 Eph 3.10
6.13 Jas 4.7
6.14 Isa 11.5; 59.17; 1 Thess 5.8

them, but as slaves of Christ, doing the will of God from the heart. 7 Render service
with enthusiasm, as to the Lord and not to men and women, 8 knowing that whatever good we do, we will receive the same again from the Lord, whether we are
slaves or free.

9 And, masters, do the same to them. Stop threatening them, for you know that
both of you have the same Master in heaven, and with him there is no partiality.

Wearing the whole armor of God

10 Finally, be strong in the Lord and in the strength of his power. 11 Put on the
whole armor of God, so that you may be able to stand against the wiles of the devil.
12 For our[a] struggle is not against enemies of blood and flesh, but against the rulers,
against the authorities, against the cosmic powers of this present darkness, against
the spiritual forces of evil in the heavenly places. 13 Therefore take up the whole
armor of God, so that you may be able to withstand on that evil day, and having
done everything, to stand firm. 14 Stand therefore, and fasten the belt of truth

[a] Other ancient authorities read *your*

GOD'S ARMOR FOR US

We are engaged in a spiritual battle—all believers find themselves subject to Satan's attacks because they are no longer on Satan's side. Thus, Paul tells us to use *every piece* of God's armor to resist Satan's attacks and to stand true to God in the midst of them.

Piece of Armor	*Use*	*Application*
Strong Belt	Truth	Satan fights with lies, and sometimes his lies *sound* like truth; but only believers have God's truth, which can defeat Satan's lies.
Breastplate	God's approval	Satan often attacks our hearts—the seat of our emotions, self-worth, and trust. God's approval is the breastplate that protects our hearts. He approves of us because he loves us and sent his Son to die for us.
Shoes	Readiness to spread the Good News	Satan wants us to think that telling others the good news is a worthless and hopeless task—the size of the task is too big and the negative responses are too much to handle. But the "shoes" God gives us are the motivation to continue to proclaim the true peace which is available in God—news everyone needs to hear.
Shield	Faith	What *we* see are Satan's attacks in the form of insults, setbacks, and temptations. But the shield of faith protects us from Satan's flaming arrows. With God's perspective, we can see beyond our circumstances and know that ultimate victory is ours.
Helmet	Salvation	Satan wants to make us doubt God, Jesus, and our salvation. The helmet protects our minds from doubting God's saving work for us.
Sword	The Spirit, the Word of God	The sword is the only weapon of *offense* in this list of armor. There are times when we need to take the offensive against Satan. When we are tempted, we need to trust in the truth of God's Word.

6.9 Although Christians may be at different levels in earthly society, we are all equal before God. He does not play favorites; no one is more important than anyone else. Paul's letter to Philemon stresses the same point: Philemon, the master, and Onesimus, his slave, were brothers in Christ.

6.10–17 In the Christian life we battle against "rulers and authorities" (the powerful evil forces of fallen angels headed by Satan, who is a vicious fighter; see 1 Peter 5.8). To withstand their attacks, we must depend on God's strength and use every piece of his armor. Paul is giving this counsel not only to the church, the body of Christ, but also to all individuals within the church. The whole body needs to be armed. As you do battle against "the cosmic powers of this present darkness," fight in the strength of the church, whose power comes from the Holy Spirit.

6.12 These who are not "blood and flesh" are demons over whom Satan has control. They are not mere fantasies – they are very real. We face a powerful army whose goal is to defeat Christ's church. When we believe in Christ, these beings become our enemies, and they try every device to turn us away from him and back to sin. Although we are assured of victory, we must engage in the struggle until Christ returns, because Satan is constantly battling against all who are on the Lord's side. We need supernatural power to defeat Satan, and God has provided that in his Holy Spirit within us and his armor surrounding us. If you feel discouraged, remember Jesus' words to Peter: "On this rock I will build my church, and the gates of Hades will not prevail against it" (Matthew 16.18).

around your waist, and put on the breastplate of righteousness. 15 As shoes for your
feet put on whatever will make you ready to proclaim the gospel of peace. 16 With
all of these,[b] take the shield of faith, with which you will be able to quench all the
flaming arrows of the evil one. 17 Take the helmet of salvation, and the sword of the
Spirit, which is the word of God.
18 Pray in the Spirit at all times in every prayer and supplication. To that end
keep alert and always persevere in supplication for all the saints. 19 Pray also for
me, so that when I speak, a message may be given to me to make known with
boldness the mystery of the gospel,[c] 20 for which I am an ambassador in chains.
Pray that I may declare it boldly, as I must speak.

Paul's final greetings

21 So that you also may know how I am and what I am doing, Tychicus will tell
you everything. He is a dear brother and a faithful minister in the Lord. 22 I am
sending him to you for this very purpose, to let you know how we are, and to
encourage your hearts.
23 Peace be to the whole community,[d] and love with faith, from God the Father and the Lord Jesus Christ. 24 Grace be with all who have an undying love for
our Lord Jesus Christ.[e]

6.15 Isa 52.7
6.16 1 Jn 5.4
6.17 Isa 59.17 Jn 6.63 1 Thess 5.8 Heb 4.12
6.18 Rom 8.26 Phil 4.6
6.19 Col 4.3,4
6.21 Acts 20.4 2 Tim 4.12 Tit 3.12
6.22 Col 4.7,8
6.23 2 Thess 3.16

b Or *In all circumstances* c Other ancient authorities lack *of the gospel* d Gk *to the brothers* e Other ancient authorities add *Amen*

6.18 How can anyone pray all the time? One way is to make quick, brief prayers your habitual response to every situation you meet throughout the day. Another way is to order your life around God's desires and teachings so that your very life becomes a prayer. You don't have to isolate yourself from other people and from daily work in order to pray constantly. You can make prayer your life and your life a prayer while living in a world that needs God's powerful influence.

6.19, 20 Undiscouraged and undefeated, Paul wrote powerful letters of encouragement from prison. Paul does not ask the Ephesians to pray that his chains would be removed, but that he will continue to speak boldly for Christ in spite of them. God can use us in any circumstance to do his will. Even as we pray for a change in our circumstances, we should also pray that God will accomplish his plan through us, right where we are. Knowing God's eternal purpose for us helps us through the difficult times.

6.21 Tychicus is also mentioned in Acts 20.4, Colossians 4.7, 2 Timothy 4.12, and Titus 3.12.

6.24 This letter was written to the church at Ephesus, but it was also meant for circulation among other churches. In this epistle, Paul presents the supremacy of Christ, gives information on both the nature of the church and on how church members should live, and stresses the unity of all believers – male, female, parent, child, master, slave – regardless of sex, nationality, or social rank. The home and the church are difficult places to live the Christian life, because our real self comes through to those who know us well. Close relationships between imperfect people can lead to trouble – or to increased faith and deepened dependence on God. We can build unity in our churches through willing submission to Christ's leadership and humble service to one another.

The Letter of Paul to the PHILIPPIANS

THE WORD *happiness* evokes visions of unwrapping gifts on Christmas morning, strolling hand in hand with the one you love, being surprised on your birthday, responding with unbridled laughter to a comedian, or vacationing in an exotic locale. Everyone wants to be happy; we make chasing this elusive ideal a lifelong pursuit: spending money, collecting things, and searching for new experiences. But if happiness depends upon our circumstances, what happens when the toys rust, loved ones die, health deteriorates, money is stolen, and the party's over? Often happiness flees and despair sets in.

In contrast to *happiness* stands *joy*. Running deeper and stronger, joy is the quiet, confident assurance of God's love and work in our lives, that he will be there no matter what! Happiness depends on happenings, but joy depends on Christ.

Philippians is Paul's joy letter. The church in that Macedonian city had been a great encouragement to Paul. The Philippian believers had enjoyed a very special relationship with Paul, so he wrote them a personal expression of his love and affection. They had brought him great joy (4.1). Philippians is also a joyful book because it emphasizes the real joy of the Christian life. The concept of *rejoicing* or *joy* appears sixteen times, and the pages radiate this positive message, culminating in the exhortation to "Rejoice in the Lord always; again I will say, Rejoice" (4.4).

In a life dedicated to serving Christ, Paul had faced excruciating poverty, abundant wealth, and everything in between. He even wrote this joyful letter from prison. Whatever the circumstances, Paul had learned to be content (4.11, 12), finding real joy as he focused all of his attention and energy on knowing Christ (3.8) and obeying him (3.12, 13).

Paul's desire to know Christ above all else is wonderfully expressed in the following words: "I regard everything as loss because of the surpassing value of knowing Christ Jesus my Lord. For his sake I have suffered the loss of all things, and I regard them as rubbish, in order that I may gain Christ and be found in him. . . . I want to know Christ and the power of his resurrection and the sharing of his sufferings by becoming like him in his death" (3.8–10). May we share Paul's aspiration and seek to know Jesus Christ more and more. Rejoice with Paul in Philippians, and rededicate yourself to finding joy in Christ.

VITAL STATISTICS

PURPOSE:
To thank the Philippians for the gift they had sent him and to strengthen these believers by showing them that true joy comes from Jesus Christ alone

AUTHOR:
Paul

TO WHOM WRITTEN:
All the Christians at Philippi and all believers everywhere

DATE WRITTEN:
About A.D. 61, from Rome during Paul's imprisonment there

SETTING:
Paul and his companions began the church at Philippi on his second missionary journey (Acts 16.11–40). This was the first church established on the European continent. The Philippian church had sent a gift with Epaphroditus (one of their members) to be delivered to Paul (4.18). Paul was in a Roman prison at the time. He writes this letter to thank them for their gift and to encourage them in their faith.

KEY VERSE:
"Rejoice in the Lord always; again I will say, Rejoice" (4.4).

KEY PEOPLE:
Paul, Timothy, Epaphroditus, Euodias, and Syntyche

KEY PLACE:
Philippi

THE BLUEPRINT

1. Joy in suffering (1.1–30)
2. Joy in serving (2.1–30)
3. Joy in believing (3.1–4.1)
4. Joy in giving (4.2–23)

Although Paul was writing from prison, joy is a dominant theme in this letter. The secret of his joy is grounded in his relationship with Christ. People today desperately want to be happy but are tossed and turned by daily successes, failures, and inconveniences. Christians are to be joyful in every circumstance, even when things are going badly, even when we feel like complaining, even when no one else is joyful. Christ still reigns and we still know him, so we can rejoice at all times.

MEGATHEMES

THEME	EXPLANATION	IMPORTANCE
Humility	Christ showed true humility when he laid aside his rights and privileges as God to become human. He poured out his life to pay the penalty we deserve. Laying aside self-interest is essential to all our relationships.	We are to take Christ's attitude in serving others. We must renounce personal recognition and merit. When we give up our self-interest, we can serve with joy, love, and kindness.
Self-sacrifice	Christ suffered and died so we might have eternal life. With courage and faithfulness, Paul sacrificed himself for the ministry. He preached the gospel even while he was in prison.	Christ gives us power to lay aside our personal needs and concerns. To utilize his power, we must imitate those leaders who show self-denying concern for others. We dare not be self-centered.
Unity	In every church, in every generation, there are divisive influences (issues, loyalties, and conflicts). In the midst of hardships, it is easy to turn on one another. Paul encouraged the Philippians to agree with one another, stop complaining, and work together.	As believers, we should contend against a common enemy, not against one another. When we are unified in love, Christ's strength is most abundant. Keep before you the ideals of teamwork, consideration of others, and unselfishness.
Christian living	Paul shows us how to live successful Christian lives. We can become mature by being so identified with Christ that his attitude of humility and sacrifice rules us. Christ is both our source of power and our guide.	Developing our character begins with God's work in us. But growth also requires discipline, obedience, and relentless concentration on our part.
Joy	Believers can have profound contentment, serenity, and peace no matter what happens. This joy comes from knowing Christ personally and from depending on his strength rather than our own.	We can have joy, even in hardship. Joy does not come from outward circumstances but from inward strength. As Christians, we must not rely on what we have or what we experience to give us joy, but on Christ within us.

1. Joy in suffering

1 Paul and Timothy, servants[a] of Christ Jesus, 1.1
To all the saints in Christ Jesus who are in Philippi, with the bishops[b] and Acts 16.1,12
deacons:[c] Col 1.1

[a] Gk *slaves* [b] Or *overseers* [c] Or *overseers and helpers*

1.1 This is a personal letter to the Philippians, not intended for general circulation to all the churches as was the letter to the Ephesians. Paul wanted to thank the believers for helping him when he had a need. He also wanted to tell them why he could be full of joy despite his imprisonment and coming trial. In this uplifting letter, Paul devotes only a small space to correcting the Philippians and warning them about potential problems. *Saints* refers to the whole body of believers.

1.1 On Paul's first missionary journey, he visited towns close to his headquarters in Antioch of Syria. On his second and third journeys, he traveled even farther. Because of the great distance between the congregations which Paul had founded, he could no longer personally oversee them all. Thus he was compelled to write letters to teach and encourage the believers. Fortunately, Paul had a staff of volunteers (including Timothy, Mark, and Epaphras) who personally delivered these letters and often remained with the congregations for a while to teach and encourage them.

1.1 For more information on Paul, see his Profile in Acts 10. Timothy's Profile is found in 1 Timothy 2.

2 Grace to you and peace from God our Father and the Lord Jesus Christ.

Paul's prayer for the Philippian believers

3 I thank my God every time I remember you, 4constantly praying with joy in
every one of my prayers for all of you, 5because of your sharing in the gospel from
the first day until now. 6I am confident of this, that the one who began a good work

1.3 Col 1.3
1.6 1 Cor 1.8

LOCATION OF PHILIPPI
Philippi sat on the Egnatian Way, the main transportation route in Macedonia, an extension of the Appian Way, which joined the Eastern Empire with Italy.

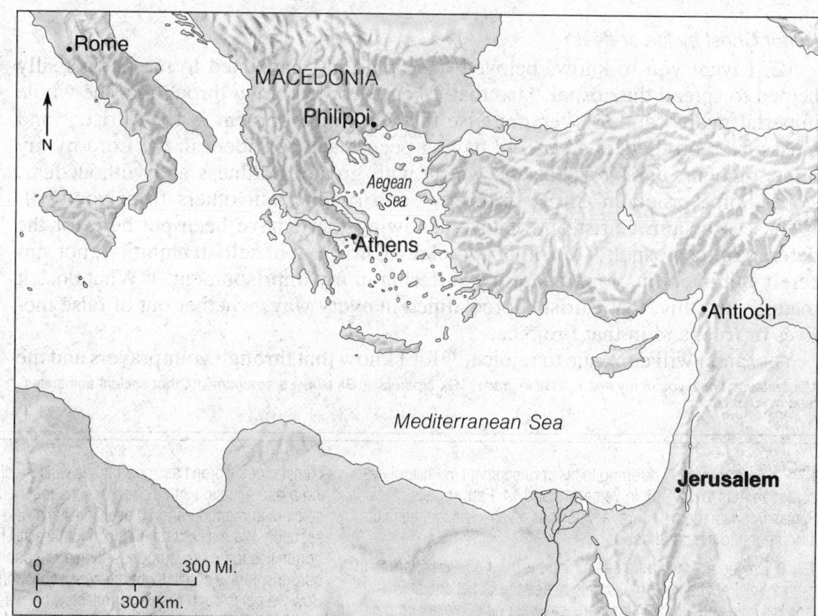

1.1 The Roman colony of Philippi was located in northern Greece (called Macedonia in Paul's day). Philip II of Macedon (the father of Alexander the Great) took the town from ancient Thrace in about 357 B.C., enlarged and strengthened it, and gave it his name. This thriving commercial center sat at the crossroads between Europe and Asia. In about A.D. 50, Paul, Silas, Timothy, and Luke crossed the Aegean Sea from Asia Minor and landed at Philippi (Acts 16.11–40). The church in Philippi consisted mostly of Gentile (non-Jewish) believers. Because they were not familiar with the Old Testament, Paul did not specifically quote any Old Testament passages in this letter.

1.1 Bishops and deacons led the early Christian churches. Bishops were the *overseers* (pastors or elders); their qualifications and duties are explained in detail in 1 Timothy 3.1–7 and Titus 1.5–9. The qualifications and duties of deacons are spelled out in 1 Timothy 3.8–13.

1.4 This is the first of many times Paul uses the word *joy* in his letter. The Philippians were a source of joy when he prayed. By helping Paul, they were helping Christ's cause. The Philippians were willing to be used by God for whatever task he had in store for them. When others think about you, are you a source of joy for them? Do your acts of kindness lift others up?

1.4, 5 The Philippians first heard the good news about ten years earlier when Paul and his companions visited Philippi (during Paul's second missionary journey) and founded the church there.

1.5 When Paul said that the Philippians were "sharing in the gospel," he was pointing out their valuable contribution in spreading God's Word. They did this through their practical help when he was in Philippi and through their financial support when he was in prison. As we help our ministers, missionaries, and evangelists through prayer, hospitality, and financial donations, we become partners with them.

1.6 The God who begins his good work in us continues it through our lives and will finish it when we meet him face to face. God's work *for* us began when Christ died on the cross to forgive our sins. His work *in* us begins when the Holy Spirit comes into our hearts, enabling us to be more like Christ every day. Paul is describing the process of Christian growth and maturity that begins when we accept Christ and continues until he returns. Have you experienced Christ beginning his work in you? Then you can be assured that your progress is in his able care.

1.6 Do you sometimes feel as if you'll never make progress in your spiritual life? When God starts a project, he finishes it! As with the Philippians, God will help you grow in grace until he has completed his work in your life. When you are discouraged, remember that God won't give up on you. He promises to finish the work he has begun. When you feel incomplete, unfinished, or distressed by your shortcomings, remember God's promise and provision. Don't let your present condition rob you of the joy of knowing Christ or keep you from growing.

among you will bring it to completion by the day of Jesus Christ. 7 It is right for me
to think this way about all of you, because you hold me in your heart,[d] for all of
you share in God's grace[e] with me, both in my imprisonment and in the defense
and confirmation of the gospel. 8 For God is my witness, how I long for all of you
with the compassion of Christ Jesus. 9 And this is my prayer, that your love may
overflow more and more with knowledge and full insight 10 to help you to determine what is best, so that in the day of Christ you may be pure and blameless,
11 having produced the harvest of righteousness that comes through Jesus Christ for
the glory and praise of God.

Honor Christ by life or death

12 I want you to know, beloved[f] that what has happened to me has actually
helped to spread the gospel, 13 so that it has become known throughout the whole
imperial guard[g] and to everyone else that my imprisonment is for Christ; 14 and
most of the brothers and sisters,[f] having been made confident in the Lord by my
imprisonment, dare to speak the word[h] with greater boldness and without fear.
15 Some proclaim Christ from envy and rivalry, but others from goodwill.
16 These proclaim Christ out of love, knowing that I have been put here for the
defense of the gospel; 17 the others proclaim Christ out of selfish ambition, not sincerely but intending to increase my suffering in my imprisonment. 18 What does it
matter? Just this, that Christ is proclaimed in every way, whether out of false motives or true; and in that I rejoice.
Yes, and I will continue to rejoice, 19 for I know that through your prayers and the

1.7 2 Cor 7.3; Eph 3.1; 6.20; 2 Tim 1.8
1.9 Col 1.9; 1 Thess 3.12; Philem 6
1.10 Rom 12.2; 1 Cor 1.8
1.11 Jn 15.4
1.12 Lk 21.12,13
1.13 Acts 28.30,31
1.14 Phil 1.20
1.15 Phil 2.3
1.17 1 Cor 9.17
1.19 Acts 16.7; Rom 8.9; 2 Cor 1.11

[d] Or *because I hold you in my heart* [e] Gk *in grace* [f] Gk *brothers* [g] Gk *whole praetorium* [h] Other ancient authorities read *word of God*

1.7 Paul was probably referring to his imprisonment in Philippi, recorded in Acts 16.22–36. In verses 13 and 14, Paul speaks of his Roman imprisonment. Wherever Paul was, even in prison, he faithfully preached the good news.

1.7, 8 Do you ever yearn to see a friend with whom you share fond memories? Paul had such a longing to see the Christians at Philippi. His love and affection for them was based not merely on past experiences, but upon the unity that comes when believers draw upon Christ's love. All Christians are part of God's family and thus share equally in the transforming power of his love. Do you feel a deep love for fellow Christians, both friends and strangers? Let Christ's love motivate you to love other Christians and to express that love in the way you treat them.

1.9 Often the best way to influence someone is to pray for him or her. Paul's prayer for the Philippians was that they would be unified. Their love was to result in greater knowledge of Christ and greater insight (moral discernment). This love wasn't based on feelings but on what Christ had done for them. As we grow in Christ's love, our hearts and minds must grow together. Are your love and insight growing?

1.10 Paul prays that the Philippian believers will "determine what is best"—in other words, that they would have the ability to differentiate between right and wrong, good and bad, vital and trivial. We ought to pray for discernment as well, so that we can maintain our Christian morals and values. Hebrews 5.14 emphasizes the need for discernment.

1.10 The "day of Christ" refers to the time when God will judge the world through Jesus Christ. We should live each day as though he could return at any moment.

1.11 The "harvest of righteousness" includes all of the character traits flowing from a right relationship with God. There is no way for us to gain this other than through Christ. See Galatians 5.22, 23 for the fruit of the Spirit.

1.12–14 Being imprisoned could cause many people to become bitter or to give up, but Paul saw it as one more opportunity to spread the good news of Christ. Paul realized that his current circumstances weren't as important as what he did with them. Turning a bad situation into a good one, he reached out to the Roman soldiers and encouraged those Christians who were afraid of persecution. We may not be in prison, but we still have plenty of opportunities to be discouraged—times of indecision, financial burdens, family conflict, church conflict, or work-related stress. How we act in such situations reflects what we believe. Like Paul, look for opportunities to demonstrate your faith even in bad situations. Whether or not the situation improves, your faith will grow stronger.

1.13 How did Paul end up in Roman prison? While he was visiting Jerusalem, some Jews had him arrested for preaching the gospel, but he appealed to Caesar to hear his case (Acts 21.15–25.12). He was then escorted by soldiers to Rome, where he was placed under house arrest while awaiting trial—a trial not for breaking the law, but for preaching about Christ. At that time, the Roman authorities did not consider this to be a serious charge. A few years later, however, Rome took a different view of Christianity and made every effort to stamp it out. Paul's house arrest allowed him some degree of freedom. He could have visitors, continue to preach, and write letters such as this one. A brief record of Paul's time in Rome is found in Acts 28.11–31. "Throughout the whole imperial guard" refers to the Praetorian guard, the elite troops housed in the emperor's palace.

1.14 When we speak boldly for Christ, or live faithfully for him during difficult situations, we encourage others to do the same. Be an encouragement by the way that you live.

1.15–18 Paul had an amazingly selfless attitude. He knew that some were preaching to build their own reputations, taking advantage of Paul's imprisonment to try to make a name for themselves. Regardless of the motives of these preachers, Paul rejoices that the gospel is being preached. Many Christians serve for the wrong reasons and God doesn't excuse their motives. But we should be glad if God uses their message, regardless of their motives.

1.19–21 This is not Paul's final imprisonment in Rome. Awaiting trial, he knows that he can be either released or executed. However, he trusts Christ to work it out for his good ("this will turn out for my deliverance"). Paul's prayer is that when he stands trial, he

1.20 Rom 5.5; 14.8 1 Cor 6.20 Eph 6.19
1.21 Gal 2.20 Col 1.27
1.22 Rom 1.13
1.23 2 Cor 5.8 2 Tim 4.6
1.27 Acts 4.32
1.28 Mt 10.28 2 Tim 2.11 Heb 13.6
1.29 Mt 5.11,12 Acts 5.41
1.30 Acts 16.19 Col 2.1 1 Thess 2.2

help of the Spirit of Jesus Christ this will turn out for my deliverance. 20 It is my
eager expectation and hope that I will not be put to shame in any way, but that by
my speaking with all boldness, Christ will be exalted now as always in my body,
whether by life or by death. 21 For to me, living is Christ and dying is gain. 22 If I am
to live in the flesh, that means fruitful labor for me; and I do not know which I
prefer. 23 I am hard pressed between the two: my desire is to depart and be with
Christ, for that is far better; 24 but to remain in the flesh is more necessary for you.
25 Since I am convinced of this, I know that I will remain and continue with all of
you for your progress and joy in faith, 26 so that I may share abundantly in your
boasting in Christ Jesus when I come to you again.

27 Only, live your life in a manner worthy of the gospel of Christ, so that,
whether I come and see you or am absent and hear about you, I will know that you
are standing firm in one spirit, striving side by side with one mind for the faith of
the gospel, 28 and are in no way intimidated by your opponents. For them this is
evidence of their destruction, but of your salvation. And this is God's doing. 29 For
he has graciously granted you the privilege not only of believing in Christ, but of
suffering for him as well— 30 since you are having the same struggle that you saw
I had and now hear that I still have.

2. Joy in serving

Be humble like Christ

2.1 2 Cor 13.14 Col 3.12
2.2 1 Pet 3.8

2 If then there is any encouragement in Christ, any consolation from love, any
sharing in the Spirit, any compassion and sympathy, 2 make my joy complete:
be of the same mind, having the same love, being in full accord and of one mind.
3 Do nothing from selfish ambition or conceit, but in humility regard others as

---

will speak boldly for Christ and not be ashamed. Whether he lives or dies, Paul wants to be an honor to Christ. As it turned out, he was released from this imprisonment but arrested again two or three years later. Only faith in Christ could sustain Paul in such adversity.

1.20, 21 To those who don't believe in God, life on earth is all there is, and so it is natural for them to strive for what this world values—money, popularity, power, pleasure, and prestige. For Paul, however, life means developing eternal values and telling others about Christ, who alone can help us see life from an eternal perspective. Paul's whole purpose in life was to speak out boldly for Christ and to become more like him. Thus Paul confidently states that dying would be even better than living, because in death he would be spared from the troubles of the world and he would see Christ face to face (1 John 3.2, 3). If you're not ready to die, then you're not ready to live. Be sure of your eternal destiny so you will then be free to serve—devoting your life to what really counts without fear of death.

1.22 Living in the flesh refers to living in the body. It does not refer to living according to the evil desires of our human nature as in Romans 8.1.

1.24 Paul had a purpose for living when he served the Philippians and others. We also need a purpose for living that goes beyond providing for our own physical needs. Whom can you serve or help? What is your purpose for living?

1.27 Paul encourages the believers to fight side by side, striving or contending for the faith. How sad that much time and effort are lost in some churches by fighting against one another instead of uniting against the real opposition! It takes a courageous church to resist in-fighting and to maintain a common purpose to serve Christ.

1.29 Paul considered it a privilege to suffer for Christ. We do not naturally consider suffering a privilege. But when we suffer for faithfully representing Christ, our message and example will have an effect (see Acts 5.41). Suffering has these additional benefits: (1) it takes our eyes off of earthly comforts; (2) it weeds out superficial believers; (3) it strengthens the faith of those who endure; (4) it serves as an example to others who may follow. Suffering for our faith doesn't mean we have done something wrong. In fact, it may mean the opposite, verifying that we have been faithful. Use suffering to build your character. Don't resent it or let it tear you down.

1.30 Throughout his life Paul suffered for spreading the good news. Like the Philippians, we are in conflict with anyone who would discredit the saving message of Christ. All true believers are in this fight together, uniting for the same cause, against the same enemy.

2.1 If there is to be unity in the church, Christians must feel and show kindness and affectionate sympathy to fellow believers.

2.1-5 Many people—even Christians—live only to make a good impression on others or to please themselves. But "selfish ambition" brings discord. Paul therefore stresses spiritual unity, asking the Philippians to love one another and to work together with one heart and purpose ("being in full accord and of one mind"). When we work together, caring for the problems of others as if they were our problems, we demonstrate Christ's example of putting others first, and we create unity. Don't be so concerned about making a good impression or meeting your own needs that you strain relationships in God's family.

2.3 Selfish ambition can ruin a church, but genuine humility can build it. Being humble means having a true perspective of ourselves (see Romans 12.3). It does not mean that we should put ourselves down. Before God, we are sinners, saved only by his grace; but we *are* saved and therefore have great worth in God's kingdom. We are to lay aside selfishness, treating others with respect and common courtesy. Considering others' interests as more important than our own links us with Christ, who is a true example of humility.

better than yourselves. 4 Let each of you look not to your own interests, but to
the interests of others. 5 Let the same mind be in you that was[i] in Christ Jesus,
6 who, though he was in the form of God,
did not regard equality with God
as something to be exploited,
7 but emptied himself,
taking the form of a slave,
being born in human likeness.
And being found in human form,
8 he humbled himself
and became obedient to the point of death—
even death on a cross.

9 Therefore God also highly exalted him
and gave him the name
that is above every name,
10 so that at the name of Jesus
every knee should bend,
in heaven and on earth and under the earth,
11 and every tongue should confess
that Jesus Christ is Lord,
to the glory of God the Father.

[i] *Or that you have*

2.3 Rom 12.10,16; 1 Pet 5.5
2.4 Rom 15.1,2; 1 Cor 10.24
2.6 Isa 9.6; Jn 1.1,2
2.7 Jn 1.14; Gal 4.4
2.8 Heb 5.8; 12.2
2.9 Eph 1.20,21; Heb 1.4
2.10 Rom 14.11

2.4 Philippi was a cosmopolitan city. The composition of the church reflected great diversity with people from a variety of backgrounds and walks of life. Acts 16 gives us some indication of the diverse makeup of this church. For example, Lydia was a Jewish convert from Asia, a wealthy merchant (Acts 16.14); the slave girl (Acts 16.16, 17) was probably a native Greek; and the jailer serving this colony of the empire was probably Roman (Acts 16.25–36). With so many different backgrounds among the members, unity must have been difficult to maintain. Although there is no evidence of division in this church, its unity had to be safeguarded (3.2; 4.2). Paul encourages them to guard against any selfishness, prejudice, or jealousy that might lead to dissension. Showing genuine interest in others is a positive step toward maintaining unity among believers.

2.5 Jesus Christ was humble, willing to give up his rights in order to obey God and serve people. Like Christ's, our attitude must be to serve out of love for God and for others, not out of guilt or fear. Remember you can choose your attitude. You can approach life expecting to be served or you can be willing to serve others. See Mark 10.45 for more on Christ's attitude of service.

2.5–7 The *incarnation* was the act of the eternally existent Son of God voluntarily assuming a human body and human nature. Without ceasing to be God, he became a human being, the man called Jesus. He did not give up his deity to become human, but he set aside the right to his glory and power. In submission to the Father's will, he limited his power and knowledge. Jesus of Nazareth was subject to place, time, and many other human limitations. What made his humanity unique was his freedom from sin. In his full humanity, Jesus showed us everything about God's character that can be conveyed in human terms. The incarnation is explained further in these passages: John 1.1–14; Romans 1.2–5; 2 Corinthians 8.9; 1 Timothy 3.16; Hebrews 2.14; and 1 John 1.1–3.

2.5–11 These verses are probably from a hymn sung by the early Christian church. The passage holds many parallels to the prophecy of the suffering servant in Isaiah 53. As a hymn, it was not meant to be a complete statement about the nature and work of Christ. Several key characteristics of Jesus Christ, however, are praised in this passage: (1) he has always existed with God; (2) he is equal to God, because he *is* God (John 1.1ff; Colossians 1.15–19); (3) though he is God, he became a man in order to fulfill God's plan of salvation for all people; (4) he did not just pretend to have a man's body—he actually became a man to identify with humanity's sins; (5) he voluntarily laid aside his divine rights and privileges out of love for his Father; (6) he died on the cross for our sins, so we wouldn't have to face eternal death; (7) God glorified him because of his obedience; (8) God raised him to his original position at the Father's right hand where he will reign forever as our Lord and Judge.

How can we do anything less than praise him as our Lord and dedicate ourselves to his service?

2.5–11 Often people excuse selfishness, pride, or evil by claiming their rights. They think, "I can cheat on this test; after all, I deserve to pass this class," or "I can spend all this money on myself—I worked for it," or "I can get an abortion; I have a right to control my own body." But as believers, we should have a different attitude; one of humility that enables us to lay aside our rights in order to serve others. If we claim to follow Christ, we must also try to live as he showed us. We should serve others, even when we are not likely to get recognition for our efforts. Are you selfishly clinging to your rights, or are you willing to serve?

2.8 Death on a cross (crucifixion) was the form of capital punishment that the Romans used for notorious criminals. It was excruciatingly painful and humiliating. Prisoners were nailed or tied to a cross and left to die. Death might not come for several days, and usually came by suffocation as the weight of the weakened body made breathing more and more difficult. Jesus died as one who was cursed (Galatians 3.13). How amazing that the perfect man should die this most shameful death so that we would not have to face eternal punishment!

2.9–11 At the last Judgment, even those who are condemned will recognize Jesus' authority and right to rule. People can choose to regard him as Lord now, as a step of willing and loving commitment, or be forced to acknowledge him as Lord when he returns. He may return at any moment. Are you prepared to meet him?

2.13 Rom 8.28 1 Cor 12.6 Heb 13.20,21
2.14 Rom 14.1
2.15 Mt 5.45 Jn 12.36 Eph 5.1
2.16 1 Thess 2.19,20
2.17 Rom 15.16 Col 1.24

Shine like lights in a dark world

12 Therefore, my beloved, just as you have always obeyed me, not only in my
presence, but much more now in my absence, work out your own salvation with
fear and trembling; 13 for it is God who is at work in you, enabling you both to will
and to work for his good pleasure.
14 Do all things without murmuring and arguing, 15 so that you may be blameless and innocent, children of God without blemish in the midst of a crooked and
perverse generation, in which you shine like stars in the world. 16 It is by your
holding fast to the word of life that I can boast on the day of Christ that I did not run
in vain or labor in vain. 17 But even if I am being poured out as a libation over the
sacrifice and the offering of your faith, I am glad and rejoice with all of you—
18 and in the same way you also must be glad and rejoice with me.

2.20 1 Cor 16.10
2.21 1 Cor 10.24 13.5
2.22 1 Cor 4.17 1 Tim 1.2
2.24 Phil 1.25
2.25 Phil 4.18

Those who will soon come to you

19 I hope in the Lord Jesus to send Timothy to you soon, so that I may be
cheered by news of you. 20 I have no one like him who will be genuinely concerned
for your welfare. 21 All of them are seeking their own interests, not those of Jesus
Christ. 22 But Timothy's[j] worth you know, how like a son with a father he has
served with me in the work of the gospel. 23 I hope therefore to send him as soon as
I see how things go with me; 24 and I trust in the Lord that I will also come soon.
25 Still, I think it necessary to send to you Epaphroditus—my brother and co-
worker and fellow soldier, your messenger[k] and minister to my need; 26 for he has
been longing for[l] all of you, and has been distressed because you heard that he was
ill. 27 He was indeed so ill that he nearly died. But God had mercy on him, and not
only on him but on me also, so that I would not have one sorrow after another. 28 I
am the more eager to send him, therefore, in order that you may rejoice at seeing

[j] Gk *his* [k] Gk *apostle* [l] Other ancient authorities read *longing to see*

2.12 *Therefore* ties this verse to the previous section. "Work out your own salvation" means "take your faith seriously" and that the entire church was to work together to rid themselves of divisions and discord. The Philippian Christians needed to be especially careful to obey Christ, now that Paul wasn't there to continually remind them about what was right. We too must be careful about how we believe and live, especially when we are on our own. In the absence of cherished Christian leaders, we must focus our attention and devotion even more on Christ so that we won't be sidetracked.

2.13 What do you do when you don't feel like obeying? God has not left us alone in our struggles to do his will. He wants to come alongside and within us to help. He helps us want to obey him. Then he gives us the power to do what he wants. The secret to a changed life is to submit to Christ's control and let him work. Next time, ask God to help you want to do his will.

2.13 To be like Christ, we must condition ourselves to think like Christ. To change our desires to be more like Christ's, we need the power of the indwelling Spirit (1.19), the influence of faithful Christians, obedience to God's Word (not just exposure to it), and sacrificial service. Often it is in *doing* God's will that we gain the *desire* for it (see 4.8, 9). Do what he wants and trust him to change your desires.

2.14–16 Why are complaining (murmuring) and arguing so harmful? If all that people know about a church is that its members constantly argue, complain, and gossip, they get a false impression of Christ and the gospel. Belief in Christ should unite those who trust him. If your church is always complaining and arguing, it lacks the unifying power of Jesus Christ. Stop arguing with other Christians or complaining about people and conditions within the church. Let the world see Christ.

2.14–16 Our lives should be characterized by moral purity, patience, and peacefulness, so that we will "shine like stars" in a crooked and perverse world. A transformed life is an effective witness to the power of God's Word. Are you shining brightly, or are you clouded by complaints and arguing? Shine out for God.

2.17 A *libation* was a drink offering, poured out to God as a sacrifice on the altar. The drink offering was an important part of the sacrificial system of the Jews (for an explanation, see Numbers 28.7). Because this church had little Jewish background, the drink offering may refer to the wine poured out to pagan deities prior to important public events. Paul regarded his life as a sacrifice.

2.17 Even if he had to die, Paul was content, knowing he had helped the Philippians live for Christ. When you're totally committed to serving Christ, sacrifice for the faith of others is a joyous reward.

2.19 Timothy was with Paul in Rome at the time Paul wrote this letter. He traveled with Paul on his second missionary journey when the church at Philippi was begun. For more information on Timothy, see his Profile in 1 Timothy 2.

2.21 Paul observed that most believers are too preoccupied with their own needs to spend time working for Christ. Don't let your schedule and concerns crowd out your Christian service and love for others.

2.22 Just as a skilled workman trains an apprentice, Paul prepared Timothy to carry on the ministry in his absence. Who are you apprenticing for God's work?

2.23 Paul was in prison (awaiting either his trial or its verdict) for preaching about Christ. He was telling the Philippians that when he learned of the court's decision, he would send Timothy to them with the news. He was ready to accept any verdict (1.21–26).

2.25 Epaphroditus delivered money from the Philippians to Paul; then he returned with this thank you letter to Philippi. Epaphroditus may have been an elder in Philippi (2.25–30; 4.18) who, while staying with Paul, became ill (2.27, 30). After his recovery, he returned home. He is mentioned only in Philippians.

him again, and that I may be less anxious. 29 Welcome him then in the Lord with all 2.29
joy, and honor such people, 30 because he came close to death for the work of Rom 16.2 1 Cor 16.18
Christ,[m] risking his life to make up for those services that you could not give me. 1 Thess 5.12 1 Tim 5.17

3 Finally, my brothers and sisters,[n] rejoice[o] in the Lord.

3. Joy in believing

All is worthless compared to knowing Christ

To write the same things to you is not troublesome to me, and for you it is a
safeguard. 3.2
2 Beware of the dogs, beware of the evil workers, beware of those who mutilate Gal 5.2
the flesh![p] 3 For it is we who are the circumcision, who worship in the Spirit of 3.3 Deut 30.6
God[q] and boast in Christ Jesus and have no confidence in the flesh— 4 even though Jn 4.21-24
I, too, have reason for confidence in the flesh. Rom 2.29; 7.6 Col 2.11
If anyone else has reason to be confident in the flesh, I have more: 5 circumcised 3.5
on the eighth day, a member of the people of Israel, of the tribe of Benjamin, a Acts 22.3; 23.6 Rom 11.1
Hebrew born of Hebrews; as to the law, a Pharisee; 6 as to zeal, a persecutor of the 2 Cor 11.22
church; as to righteousness under the law, blameless. 3.6 Acts 8.3; 22.4
7 Yet whatever gains I had, these I have come to regard as loss because of Gal 1.13
Christ. 8 More than that, I regard everything as loss because of the surpassing value 3.7 Mt 13.44
of knowing Christ Jesus my Lord. For his sake I have suffered the loss of all things, Lk 14.33

[m] Other ancient authorities read *of the Lord* [n] Gk *my brothers* [o] Or *farewell* [p] Gk *the mutilation* [q] Other ancient authorities read *worship God in spirit*

2.29, 30 The world honors those who are intelligent, beautiful, rich, and powerful. What people should the church honor? Paul indicates that we should honor those who give their lives for the sake of Christ, going where we cannot go ourselves. This is what our missionaries do for us today, providing ministry where we are not able to go.

3.1 Paul reviewed the basics with these believers as a safeguard. The Bible is our safeguard both morally and theologically. When we read it individually and publicly in church, it alerts us to corrections we need to make in our thoughts, attitudes, and actions.

3.2, 3 *Dogs, evil workers* and *those who mutilate the flesh* all refer to the same group, the Judaizers. *Judaizers* were Jewish Christians who wrongly believed that it was essential for Gentiles to follow all the Old Testament Jewish laws, especially the rite of circumcision, in order to receive salvation. Many Judaizers were motivated by spiritual pride. Because they had invested so much time and effort in keeping their laws, they couldn't accept the fact that all their efforts wouldn't bring them a step closer to salvation.

Paul criticized the Judaizers because they looked at Christianity backwards—thinking that what they *did* (*circumcision*—cutting or mutilating the flesh) made them believers rather than the free gift of grace given by Christ. What believers do is a *result* of faith, not a *prerequisite* to faith. This had been confirmed by the early church leaders at the Jerusalem council eleven years earlier (Acts 15). Who are the Judaizers of our day? They are those who say that one must add something to simple faith. No person should add anything to Christ's offer of salvation through faith.

3.2, 3 It is easy to place more emphasis on religious effort ("confidence in the flesh") than on internal faith; but God values the attitude of our hearts above all else. Don't judge people's spirituality by their fulfillment of duties or level of human activity. And don't think you will satisfy God by feverishly doing his work. God notices all you do for him and will reward you for it, but only if it comes as a loving response to his free gift of salvation.

3.4–6 At first glance, it seems that Paul is boasting about his achievements. But he is actually doing the opposite, showing that human achievements, no matter how impressive, cannot earn a person salvation and eternal life with God. Paul had impressive credentials: upbringing, nationality, family background, inheritance, orthodoxy, activity, and morality (see 2 Corinthians 11; Galatians 1.13–24, for more of his credentials). But Paul's relationship with Christ wasn't based on what he had done, but on God's grace. Paul did not depend on his works to please God, because even the most impressive credentials fall short of God's holy standards. Are you depending on Christian parents, church affiliation, or just being good to make you right with God? Accomplishments or reputation cannot earn salvation. Salvation comes only through faith in Christ.

3.5 Paul belonged to the tribe of Benjamin, a heritage greatly esteemed among the Jews. From this tribe came Israel's first king, Saul (1 Samuel 10.20–24). When the kingdom was divided after Solomon's death, only the tribes of Benjamin and Judah remained loyal to David's line (1 Kings 12.20, 21). In addition, Benjamin and Judah were the only two tribes to return to Israel after the exile (Ezra 4.1). Paul was also a Pharisee, a very devout Jewish sect that scrupulously kept its own numerous rules in addition to the laws of Moses. Jewish listeners would have been impressed by both of these credentials.

3.6 Why did Paul, a devout Jewish leader, persecute the church? Agreeing with the leaders of the religious establishment, Paul thought Christianity was heretical and blasphemous. Because Jesus did not meet his expectations of what the Messiah would be like, Paul assumed that Jesus' claims were false—and therefore wicked. In addition, he saw Christianity as a political menace because it threatened to disrupt the fragile harmony between the Jews and the Roman government.

3.7 When Paul speaks of his *gains,* he is referring to his credentials, credits, and successes. After showing he could beat the Judaizers at their own game (who they were and what they had done), he now shows that it is the wrong game. Be careful of considering past achievements so important that they get in the way of your relationship with Christ.

3.8 After considering everything he had accomplished in his life, Paul says that it was all worthless when compared with knowing Christ. This is a profound statement about values: a person's relationship with Christ is more important than anything else. To know Christ should be our ultimate goal. Consider your values. Do you place anything above your relationship with Christ? If your priorities are wrong, how will you reorder them?

3.9 Rom 1.17 9.30; 10.3
3.10 Jn 17.3 Rom 8.17,29 Eph 1.19,20 1 Pet 4.13

and I regard them as rubbish, in order that I may gain Christ 9 and be found in him,
not having a righteousness of my own that comes from the law, but one that comes
through faith in Christ,[r] the righteousness from God based on faith. 10 I want to
know Christ[s] and the power of his resurrection and the sharing of his sufferings by
becoming like him in his death, 11 if somehow I may attain the resurrection from the
dead.

Forget the past and reach to the goal

3.13 Lk 9.62 Heb 6.1
3.14 2 Tim 4.7,8 Heb 12.1

12 Not that I have already obtained this or have already reached the goal;[t] but
I press on to make it my own, because Christ Jesus has made me his own. 13 Beloved,[u] I do not consider that I have made it my own;[v] but this one thing I do:
forgetting what lies behind and straining forward to what lies ahead, 14 I press on

[r] Or *through the faith of Christ* [s] Gk *him* [t] Or *have already been made perfect* [u] Gk *Brothers* [v] Other ancient authorities read *my own yet*

THREE STAGES OF PERFECTION

1. *Perfect Relationship*	We are perfect because of our eternal union with the infinitely perfect Christ. When we become his children, we are declared "not guilty," thus righteous, because of what Christ, God's beloved Son, has done for us. This perfection is absolute and unchangeable, and it is this perfect relationship that guarantees that we will one day be "completely perfect" (below). See Colossians 2.8–10; Hebrews 10.8–14.
2. *Perfect Progress*	We can grow and mature spiritually as we continue to trust Christ, learn more about him, draw closer to him, and obey him. Our progress is changeable (in contrast to our relationship, above) because it depends on our daily walk—at times in life we mature more than at other times. But we are growing toward perfection if we work toward it. These good works do not perfect us; rather, as God perfects us, we do good works for him. See Philippians 3.1–15.
3. *Completely Perfect*	When Christ returns to take us into his eternal kingdom, we will be glorified and made completely perfect. See Philippians 3.20, 21

All phases of perfection are grounded in faith in Christ and what he has done, not what we can do for him. We cannot perfect ourselves; only God can work in and through us "by the day of Jesus Christ" (1.6).

3.9 No amount of lawkeeping, self-improvement, discipline, or religious effort can make us right with God. Righteousness comes only from God. We are made righteous (receive right standing with him) by trusting in Christ. He exchanges our sin and shortcomings for his complete righteousness. See 2 Corinthians 5.21 for more on Christ's gift of righteousness.

3.10 Paul gave up everything – family, friendship, and freedom – in order to know Christ and his resurrection power. We also have access to this knowledge and this power, but we may have to make sacrifices to enjoy it fully. What are you willing to give up in order to know Christ? A few minutes each day for prayer and Bible study? Your friend's approval? Some of your plans or pleasures? Whatever it is, knowing Christ is worth any sacrifice.

3.10 When we are united with Christ by trusting in him, we experience the power that raised him from the dead. That same mighty power helps us live morally renewed and regenerated lives. But before we can walk in newness of life, we must also die to sin (be "like him in his death"). Just as the resurrection gives us his power to live for him, his crucifixion marks the death of our old sinful nature. We can't know the victory of resurrection without applying the crucifixion.

3.11 When Paul says, "somehow I may attain the resurrection," he is not implying uncertainty or doubt. He is unsure of the way that he will meet God, whether by execution or by natural death. He does not doubt that he will be raised, but attainment of it is within God's power and not his own.

3.11 Just as Christ was exalted after his resurrection, so we will one day share Christ's glory (Revelation 22.1–7). Paul knows that he might die soon, but he has faith that he will be raised to life again.

3.12–14 Paul says his goal is to know Christ, to be like Christ, and to be all Christ has in mind for him. This goal absorbs all his energy. This is a helpful example for us. We should not let anything take our eyes off our goal – Christ. With the singlemindedness of an athlete in training, we must lay aside everything harmful and forsake anything that may distract us from being effective Christians. What is holding you back?

3.13, 14 Paul had reason to feel sorrow about the past ("what lies behind") – he had held the coats of those who stoned Stephen, the first Christian martyr (Acts 7.57, 58, he is called Saul here). We have all done things for which we are ashamed, and we all live in the tension of what we have been and what we want to be. Because our hope is in Christ, however, we can let go of past guilt and look forward to what he will help us become. Don't dwell on your past. Instead, grow in the knowledge of God by concentrating on your relationship with him *now.* Realize that you are forgiven, and then move on to a life of faith and obedience. Look forward to a fuller and more meaningful life because of your hope in Christ.

toward the goal for the prize of the heavenly[w] call of God in Christ Jesus. 15 Let
those of us then who are mature be of the same mind; and if you think differently
about anything, this too God will reveal to you. 16 Only let us hold fast to what we
have attained.
17 Brothers and sisters,[x] join in imitating me, and observe those who live according to the example you have in us. 18 For many live as enemies of the cross of
Christ; I have often told you of them, and now I tell you even with tears. 19 Their
end is destruction; their god is the belly; and their glory is in their shame; their
minds are set on earthly things. 20 But our citizenship[y] is in heaven, and it is from
there that we are expecting a Savior, the Lord Jesus Christ. 21 He will transform the
body of our humiliation[z] that it may be conformed to the body of his glory,[a] by the
4 power that also enables him to make all things subject to himself. 1 Therefore,
my brothers and sisters,[b] whom I love and long for, my joy and crown, stand
firm in the Lord in this way, my beloved.

3.15 1 Cor 2.6; 14.20 Gal 5.10 Phil 1.9,10
3.16 Gal 6.16
3.17 1 Cor 4.16 1 Pet 5.3
3.18 Gal 6.14
3.20 Eph 2.16,19 Col 3.1,3
3.21 Mt 17.2; 28.18 1 Cor 15.43-53 1 Jn 3.2

4. Joy in giving

Think about pure and lovely things

2 I urge Euodia and I urge Syntyche to be of the same mind in the Lord. 3 Yes,
and I ask you also, my loyal companion,[c] help these women, for they have struggled beside me in the work of the gospel, together with Clement and the rest of my
co-workers, whose names are in the book of life.
4 Rejoice[d] in the Lord always; again I will say, Rejoice.[d] 5 Let your gentleness
be known to everyone. The Lord is near. 6 Do not worry about anything, but in

4.3 Rev 3.5; 20.12 21.27
4.4 Phil 3.1
4.5 Heb 10.25,37 1 Pet 4.7

w Gk *upward* x Gk *Brothers* y Or *commonwealth* z Or *our humble bodies* a Or *his glorious body* b Gk *my brothers* c Or *loyal Syzygus* d Or *Farewell*

3.15, 16 Sometimes striving for Christian maturity can be so difficult that it leaves us drained and discouraged. We may feel as though we can never please God with our lives. By *mature,* Paul does not mean flawless in every detail. Mature Christians press on in the Holy Spirit's power, knowing that Christ will reveal and fill any discrepancy between what they are and what they should be. Christ's provision is no excuse for lagging devotion, but it provides relief and assurance for those who feel driven.

3.17 Paul challenges the Philippians to pursue Christ-likeness by imitating him. This does not mean, of course, that they should copy everything he did; he just stated that he was not perfect (3.12). But as he focused his life on being like Christ, so should they. None of the Gospels had yet been circulated, so Paul could not tell them to read the Bible to see what Christ was like. Therefore he urges them to imitate him. That Paul could tell people to follow his example is a testimony to his character. Can you do the same? What kind of follower would a new Christian become if he or she imitated you?

3.17–21 Paul criticizes not only the Judaizers (see the note on 3.2, 3), but also the self-indulgent Christians. These are people who claim to be Christians but don't live up to Christ's model of servanthood and sacrifice. They satisfy their own desires before even thinking about the needs of others. Freedom in Christ does not mean freedom to be selfish. It means having the opportunity to serve and to become the best person you can be.

3.20 Citizens of Philippi had the same rights and privileges as the citizens of Rome, because Philippi was a Roman colony. Likewise, we Christians will one day experience all the special privileges of our heavenly citizenship, because we belong to Christ.

3.21 The phrase, "body of our humiliation," does not imply any negative attitude toward the human body. However, the bodies we receive when we are raised from the dead will be glorious bodies, like Christ's resurrected body. Those who struggle with pain, physical limitations, or disabilities can have wonderful hope in the resurrection. For a more detailed discussion of our new bodies, see 1 Corinthians 15.35ff and 2 Corinthians 5.1–10.

4.1 How do we stand firm in the Lord? This refers to what Paul has just taught in 3.20, 21. The way to stand firm is to keep our eyes on Christ, remember that this world is not our home, and focus on the fact that Christ will bring everything under his control.

4.2, 3 Paul does not warn the Philippian church of doctrinal errors, but he does discuss some relational problems. These two women had been workers for Christ in the church. Their broken relationship was no small matter, because many had become believers through their efforts. It is possible to believe in Christ, work hard for his kingdom, and yet have broken relationships with others who are committed to the same cause. But there is no excuse for remaining unreconciled. To whom do you need to be reconciled?

4.3 The identity of this "loyal companion" remains a mystery. It could be Epaphroditus (the bearer of this letter), or a comrade of Paul in prison. It could also be someone named Syzygus, another way to interpret the word for "loyal companion."

4.3 Those "whose names are written in the book of life" are all who are marked for salvation through their faith in Christ (see also Luke 10.17–20; Revelation 20.11–15).

4.4 It seems strange that a man in prison would tell a church to rejoice. But Paul's words teach us an important lesson – our inner attitudes do not have to reflect our outward circumstances. Paul is filled with joy, because he knows that no matter what happens to him, Jesus Christ is with him. Several times in this letter, Paul urges the Philippians to be joyful, probably because they need to hear it. It's easy to get discouraged about unpleasant circumstances or to take unimportant events too seriously. If you aren't joyful, you may not be looking at life from the right perspective.

4.4, 5 Ultimate joy comes from Christ dwelling within us. Christ is

4.6 Mt 6.25 1 Pet 5.7

everything by prayer and supplication with thanksgiving let your requests be made
known to God. 7 And the peace of God, which surpasses all understanding, will
guard your hearts and your minds in Christ Jesus.

4.8 1 Thess 5.22

8 Finally, beloved,[e] whatever is true, whatever is honorable, whatever is just,
whatever is pure, whatever is pleasing, whatever is commendable, if there is any
excellence and if there is anything worthy of praise, think about[f] these things.
9 Keep on doing the things that you have learned and received and heard and seen
in me, and the God of peace will be with you.

4.9 Rom 15.33

e Gk *brothers* f Gk *take account of*

TRAINING FOR THE CHRISTIAN LIFE
As a great amount of training is needed for athletic activities, so we must train diligently for the Christian life. Such training takes time, dedication, energy, continued practice, and vision. We must all commit ourselves to the Christian life, but we must first know the rules as prescribed in God's Word (2 Timothy 2.5).

Reference	*Metaphors*	*Training*	*Our Goal as Believers*
1 Corinthians 9.24–27	Race	Deny yourself many things in order to do your best.	We train ourselves to run the race of life. So we keep our eyes on Christ—the goal—and don't get sidetracked or slowed down. When we do this, we will win a reward in Christ's kingdom.
Philippians 3.13, 14	Race	Put all your energies toward winning the race.	Living the Christian life demands all of our energy. We can forget the past and strain for the goal because we know Christ promises eternity with him at the race's end.
1 Timothy 4.7–10	Exercise	Spiritual exercise will help you grow in faith and character.	As we must repeat exercises to tone our bodies, so we must steadily repeat spiritual exercises to be spiritually fit. When we do this, we will be better Christians, living in accordance with God's will. Such a life will attract others to Christ and pay dividends in this present life and the next.
2 Timothy 4.7, 8	Fight	Fighting long and hard without giving up.	The Christian life is a fight against evil forces from without and temptation from within. If we stay true to God through it all, he promises an end, a rest, and a crown.

near, and at his second coming we will fully realize this ultimate joy. Then, he who dwells within us will fulfill his final purposes for us.

4.5 We are to be reasonable, fair minded, and charitable to those outside the church, not just to fellow believers. This means we are not to retaliate against unfairness nor be overly vocal about our personal rights.

4.6, 7 Imagine never worrying about anything! It seems like an impossibility—we all have worries on the job, in our homes, at school. But Paul's advice is to turn our worries into prayers. Do you want to worry less? Then pray more! Whenever you start to worry, stop and pray.

4.7 God's peace is different from the world's peace (see John 14.27). It is not found in positive thinking, in absence of conflict, or in good feelings. Real peace comes from knowing that because God is in control, our citizenship in Christ's kingdom is sure, our destiny is set, and our victory over sin is certain. Let God's peace defend your heart against worry.

4.8 What we put into our minds determines what comes out in our words and actions. Paul tells us to program our minds with thoughts that are true, honorable, just, pure, pleasing, commendable, excellent, and praiseworthy. Do you have problems with impure thoughts and daydreams? Examine what you are putting into your mind through television, books, conversations, movies, and magazines. Replace harmful input with wholesome material. Above all, read God's Word and pray. Ask him to help you focus your mind on what is good and pure. It takes practice, but it can be done.

4.9 It's not enough to hear or read God's Word, or even to know it well. We must also do what it says. How easy it is to listen to a sermon and forget what the preacher said. How easy it is to read the Bible and not think about how to live differently. How easy it is to debate what a passage means and not live out that meaning. Exposure to God's Word is not enough. It must lead to obedience.

Paul is grateful for their gift

10 I rejoice[g] in the Lord greatly that now at last you have revived your concern
for me; indeed, you were concerned for me, but had no opportunity to show it.[h]
11 Not that I am referring to being in need; for I have learned to be content with
whatever I have. 12 I know what it is to have little, and I know what it is to have
plenty. In any and all circumstances I have learned the secret of being well-fed and
of going hungry, of having plenty and of being in need. 13 I can do all things
through him who strengthens me. 14 In any case, it was kind of you to share my
distress.

15 You Philippians indeed know that in the early days of the gospel, when I left
Macedonia, no church shared with me in the matter of giving and receiving, except
you alone. 16 For even when I was in Thessalonica, you sent me help for my needs
more than once. 17 Not that I seek the gift, but I seek the profit that accumulates to
your account. 18 I have been paid in full and have more than enough; I am fully
satisfied, now that I have received from Epaphroditus the gifts you sent, a fragrant
offering, a sacrifice acceptable and pleasing to God. 19 And my God will fully satisfy every need of yours according to his riches in glory in Christ Jesus. 20 To our
God and Father be glory forever and ever. Amen.

Paul's final greetings

21 Greet every saint in Christ Jesus. The friends[i] who are with me greet you.
22 All the saints greet you, especially those of the emperor's household.

23 The grace of the Lord Jesus Christ be with your spirit.[j]

4.10 2 Cor 11.9
4.11 1 Tim 6.6
4.12 1 Cor 4.11; 2 Cor 11.9
4.13 Jn 15.5; 2 Cor 12.9
4.14 Heb 10.33,34
4.15 Rom 15.26; 2 Cor 11.8,9; Phil 1.5
4.17 Tit 3.14
4.18 2 Cor 9.12; Heb 13.16
4.19 Ps 23.1; Prov 8.21; 2 Cor 9.8
4.22 2 Cor 13.13
4.23 2 Tim 4.22

[g] Gk *I rejoiced* [h] Gk lacks *to show it* [i] Gk *brothers* [j] Other ancient authorities add *Amen*

4.10 In 1 Corinthians 9.11–18, Paul said he didn't accept gifts from the Corinthian church because he didn't want to be accused of preaching only to get money. But Paul maintained that it was a church's responsibility to support God's ministers (1 Corinthians 9.14). Here he accepts the Philippians' gift because they gave it willingly, and he was in need.

4.10–14 Are you content in any circumstance you face? Paul knew how to be content whether he had much or little. The secret was drawing upon Christ's power for strength. Do you have great needs? Or are you discontented because you don't have what you want? Learn to rely on God's promises and Christ's power to help you be content. If you always want more, ask God to remove that desire and teach you contentment in every situation. He will supply all your needs, but in a way that he knows is best for you (see the note on 4.19 for more on God supplying our needs).

4.12, 13 Paul was content because he could see life from God's point of view. He focused on what he was supposed to *do,* not what he felt he should *have.* He had his priorities straight and was grateful for everything God had given him. He detached himself from nonessentials so that he could concentrate on the eternal. Often the desire for more or better possessions is really a longing to fill an empty place in one's life. To what are you drawn when you feel empty inside? How can you find true contentment? The answer lies in your perspective, your priorities, and your source of power.

4.13 Can we really do everything? The power we receive in union with Christ is sufficient to do his will and to face the challenges that arise from doing it. He does not grant us superhuman ability to accomplish anything we can imagine without regard to his interests. As we contend for our faith, we will face troubles, pressures, and trials. As they come, ask Christ to strengthen you.

4.14 The Philippians shared in Paul's financial support while he was in prison.

4.17 When we give to those in need, there is not only benefit to the receiver, but we are benefited as well. It was not the Philippians' gift, but their spirit of love and devotion that Paul appreciated most. "Profit that accumulates to your account" means storing up treasure in heaven (see Matthew 19.21).

4.18 This is a reference to a thank offering, a "sacrifice acceptable . . . to God" (Leviticus 7.12–15 contains the instructions for thank offerings). Although the Greek and Roman Christians were not Jews and had not offered sacrifices according to the Old Testament laws, they were well acquainted with the pagan rituals of offering sacrifices.

4.19 We can trust that God will always meet our needs. Whatever we need on earth he will always supply, even if it is the courage to face death as Paul was. Whatever we need in heaven he will supply. We must remember, however, the difference between our wants and our needs. Most people want to feel good and avoid discomfort or pain. We may not get all that we want. By trusting in Christ our attitudes and appetites can change from wanting everything to accepting his provision and power to live for him.

4.22 There were many Christians ("saints") in Rome. Some were even in Caesar's household. Perhaps Paul, while awaiting trial, was making converts of the Roman civil service! Paul sends greetings from these Roman Christians to the believers at Philippi. The gospel had spread to all strata of society, linking people who had no other bond but Christ. The Roman Christians and the Philippian Christians were brothers and sisters because of their unity in Christ. Believers today are also linked to others across cultural, economic, and social barriers. Because all believers are brothers and sisters in Christ, let us live like God's true family.

4.23 In many ways the Philippian church was a model congregation. It was made up of many different kinds of people who were learning to work together. But recognizing that problems could arise, in his thank you letter, Paul prepares the Philippians for the difficulties that can crop up among believers. Though a prisoner in Rome, Paul had learned the true secret of joy and peace—imitating Christ and serving others. By focusing our minds on Christ we will learn unity, humility, joy, and peace. We will also be motivated to live for him. We can live confidently for him because "the grace of the Lord Jesus Christ" (4.23) is with us.

The Letter of Paul to the COLOSSIANS

REMOVE the head coach, and the team flounders; break the fuel line, and the car won't run; unplugged, the electrical appliance has no power; without the head, the body dies. Whether for leadership, power, or life, connections are vital!

Colossians is a book of connections. Writing from prison in Rome, Paul combatted false teachings which had infiltrated the Colossian church. The problem was "syncretism," combining ideas from other philosophies and religions (such as paganism, strains of Judaism, and Greek thought) with Christian truth. The resulting heresy later became known as "gnosticism," emphasizing special knowledge (*gnosis* in Greek) and denying Christ as God and Savior. To combat this devious error, Paul stressed Christ's deity—his connection with the Father—and his sacrificial death on the cross for sin. Only by being connected with Christ through faith can anyone have eternal life and only through a continuing connection with him can anyone have power for living. Christ is God incarnate and the *only* way to forgiveness and peace with God the Father. Paul also emphasized believers' connections with each other as Christ's body on earth.

Paul's introduction to the Colossians includes a greeting, a note of thanksgiving, and a prayer for spiritual wisdom and strength for these brothers and sisters in Christ (1.1–12). He then moves into a doctrinal discussion of the person and work of Christ (1.13–23), stating that Christ is the "image of the invisible God" (1.15), the Creator (1.16), the "head of the body, the church" (1.18), and the "firstborn from the dead" (1.18). His death on the cross makes it possible for us to stand in the presence of God (1.22).

Paul then explains how the world's teachings are totally empty when compared with God's plan, and he challenges the Colossians to reject shallow answers and to live in union with Christ (1.23—2.23).

Against this theological backdrop, Paul turns to practical considerations—what the divinity, death, and resurrection of Jesus should mean to all believers (3.1—4.6). Because our eternal destiny is sure, heaven should fill our thoughts (3.1–4), sexual impurity and other worldly lusts should not be named among us (3.5–8), and truth, love, and peace should mark our lives (3.9–15). Our love for Christ should also translate into love for others—friends, fellow believers, spouses, children, parents, slaves, and masters (3.16—4.1). We should constantly communicate with God through prayer (4.2–4), and we should take every opportunity to tell others the good news (4.5, 6). In Christ we have everything we need for salvation and for living the Christian life.

Paul had probably never visited Colosse, so he concludes this epistle with personal comments about their common Christian associations, providing a living lesson of the connectedness of the body of Christ.

Read Colossians as a book for an embattled church in the first century, but read it also for its timeless truths. Gain a fresh appreciation for Christ as the *fullness* of God and the *only* source for living the Christian life. Know that he is your leader, head, and power source, and make sure of your connection to him.

VITAL STATISTICS

PURPOSE:
To combat errors in the church and to show that believers have everything they need in Christ

AUTHOR:
Paul

TO WHOM WRITTEN:
The church at Colosse, a city in Asia Minor, and all believers everywhere

DATE WRITTEN:
About A.D. 60, during Paul's imprisonment in Rome

SETTING:
Paul had never visited Colosse—evidently the church had been founded by Epaphras and other converts from Paul's missionary travels. The church, however, had been infiltrated by religious relativism, with some believers attempting to combine elements of paganism and secular philosophy with Christian doctrine. Paul confronts these false teachings and affirms the sufficiency of Christ.

KEY VERSES:
"For in him the whole fullness of deity dwells bodily, and you have come to fullness in him, who is the head of every ruler and authority" (2.9, 10).

KEY PEOPLE:
Paul, Timothy, Tychicus, Onesimus, Aristarchus, Mark, Epaphras

KEY PLACES:
Colosse, Laodicea (4.15, 16)

SPECIAL FEATURES:
Christ is presented as having absolute supremacy and sole sufficiency. Colossians has similarities to Ephesians, probably because it was written at about the same time, but it has a different emphasis.

THE BLUEPRINT

1. What Christ has done (1.1—2.23)
2. What Christians should do (3.1—4.18)

In this letter Paul clearly teaches that Christ has paid for sin, that Christ has reconciled us to God, and that Christ gives us the pattern and the power to grow spiritually. Because Christ is the exact likeness of God, when we learn what he is like, we see what we need to become. Since Christ is Lord over all creation, we should crown him Lord over our lives. Since Christ is the head of the body, his church, we should nurture our vital connection to him.

MEGATHEMES

THEME	EXPLANATION	IMPORTANCE
Christ is God	Jesus Christ is God in the flesh, Lord of all creation, and Lord of the new creation. He is the expressed reflection of the invisible God. He is eternal, preexistent, omnipotent, equal with the Father. He is supreme and complete.	Because Christ is supreme, our lives must be Christ centered. To recognize him as God means to regard our relationship with him most vital and to make his interests our top priority.
Christ is head of the church	Because Christ is God, he is the head of the church, his true believers. Christ is the founder, the leader, and the highest authority on earth. He requires first place in all our thoughts and activities.	To acknowledge him as our head, we must welcome his leadership in all we do or think. No person, group, or church can regard any loyalty as more critical than that of loyalty to Christ.
Union with Christ	Because our sin has been forgiven and we have been reconciled to God, we have a union with Christ that can never be broken. In our faith connection with him, we identify with his death, burial, and resurrection.	We should live in constant contact and communication with God. When we do, we all will be unified with Christ and with one another.
Man-made religion	False teachers were promoting a heresy that stressed self-made rules (legalism). They also sought spiritual growth by discipline of the body (asceticism) and visions (mysticism). This search created pride in their self-centered efforts.	We must not cling to our own ideas and try to blend them into Christianity. Nor should we let our hunger for a more fulfilling Christian experience cause us to trust in a teacher, a group, or a system of thought more than in Christ himself. Christ is our hope and our true source of wisdom.

1. What Christ has done

1 Paul, an apostle of Christ Jesus by the will of God, and Timothy our brother, 1.1 Eph 1.1
2 To the saints and faithful brothers and sisters[a] in Christ in Colossae: 1.2 Rom 1.7
Grace to you and peace from God our Father.

a Gk *brothers*

1.1 Colossians, along with Philippians, Ephesians, and Philemon, is called a *prison epistle*, because Paul wrote it from prison in Rome. This prison was actually a house where Paul was kept under close guard at all times (probably chained to a soldier) but given certain freedoms not offered to most prisoners. He was allowed to write letters and to see any visitors he wanted to see.

1.1 Paul was an apostle "by the will of God." Paul often established his credentials as chosen and sent by God because he was not one of the original 12 disciples. *Apostle* means chosen and sent by God as a missionary or ambassador. *By the will of God* means that he was appointed – this was not just a matter of his own personal aspirations.

1.1 Paul and Timothy worked together on other New Testament letters: 2 Corinthians, Philippians, 1 and 2 Thessalonians, and Philemon. Paul also wrote two letters to Timothy (1 and 2 Timothy). For more information on these men, two of the greatest missionaries of the early church, see Paul's Profile in Acts 10 and Timothy's Profile in 1 Timothy.

1.2 *Saints* means "holy ones" and refers to the whole body of believers, made holy by Christ and set apart for service to him.

1.2 The city of Colosse was 100 miles east of Ephesus on the Lycus River. It was not as influential as the nearby city of Laodicea, but as a trading center it was a crossroads for ideas and religions. Colosse had a large Jewish population – many Jews fled there when they were forced out of Jerusalem under the persecutions of Antiochus III and IV, almost 200 years before Christ. The church in

Paul's prayer for the Colossian believers

3 In our prayers for you we always thank God, the Father of our Lord Jesus
Christ, [4] for we have heard of your faith in Christ Jesus and of the love that you have
for all the saints, [5] because of the hope laid up for you in heaven. You have heard
of this hope before in the word of the truth, the gospel [6] that has come to you. Just
as it is bearing fruit and growing in the whole world, so it has been bearing fruit
among yourselves from the day you heard it and truly comprehended the grace
of God. [7] This you learned from Epaphras, our beloved fellow servant.[b] He is a

1.4 Eph 1.15
1.5 Eph 1.13; 1 Pet 1.4
1.7 Col 4.12,13; Philem 23

[b] Gk *slave*

THE COLOSSIAN HERESY
Paul answered the various tenets of the Colossian heresy that threatened the church. This heresy was a "mixed bag," containing elements from several different heresies, some of which contradicted each other (as the chart shows).

The Heresy	*Reference*	*Paul's Answer*
Spirit is good; matter is evil.	1.15–20	God created heaven and earth for his glory.
One must follow ceremonies, rituals, and restrictions in order to be saved or perfected.	2.11, 16–23; 3.11	These were only shadows that ended when Christ came. He is all you need to be saved.
One must deny the body and live in strict asceticism.	2.20–23	This is no help in conquering evil thoughts and desires; instead, it leads to pride.
Angels must be worshiped.	2.18	Angels are not to be worshiped; Christ alone is worthy of worship.
Christ could not be both human and divine.	1.15–20; 2.2, 3	Christ is God in the flesh; he is the eternal One, head of the body, first in everything, supreme.
One must obtain "secret knowledge" in order to be saved or perfected—and this was not available to everyone.	2.2, 18	God's secret is Christ, and he has been revealed to all.
One must adhere to human wisdom, tradition, and philosophies.	2.4, 8–10; 3.15–17	By themselves, these can be misleading and shallow because they have human origin; instead, we should remember what Christ taught and follow his words as our ultimate authority.
It is even better to combine aspects of several religions.	2.10	You have everything when you have Christ; he is all-sufficient.
There is nothing wrong with immorality.	3.1–11	Get rid of sin and evil because you have been chosen by God and must live a new life as a representative of the Lord Jesus.

Colosse was founded by Epaphras (1.7), one of Paul's converts. Paul had not yet visited this church. His purpose in writing was to refute heretical teachings about Christ that had been causing confusion among the Christians there.

1.2, 3 In Paul's day, letters frequently began with the writer's name, followed by a greeting of peace. Paul usually added Christian elements to his greetings, reminding his readers of his call by God to spread the message of Christ, emphasizing that his authority came from God, and giving thanks for God's blessings.

1.4, 5 Throughout this letter Paul combats a heresy related to *gnosticism* (see the note on 2.4ff). Gnostics believed it took special knowledge to be accepted by God; for them, even if they claimed to be Christians, Christ alone was not the way of salvation (1.20). In his introductory comments, therefore, Paul commends the Colossians for their faith, hope, and love (1 Corinthians 13.13). He deliberately omits any mention of *knowledge* because of the heresy. It is not *what* we know that makes us Christians, but *whom* we know. Knowing Christ is knowing God.

1.5 *Gospel* means "good news" and refers to Christ's message of salvation by grace through faith.

1.5 When Paul says that our hope is laid up in heaven, he is emphasizing the security of the believer. Because we know that our future destination and salvation are sure, we are free to live for Christ and love others (1 Peter 1.3, 4). When you find yourself doubting or wavering in your faith or love, remember your destination – heaven.

1.6 Wherever Paul went, he preached the gospel – to Gentile audiences, to hostile Jewish leaders, and even to his Roman guards. Whenever people believed in the message he spoke, they were changed. God's Word is not just for our information, it is for our transformation! Becoming a Christian means beginning a whole new relationship with God, not just turning over a new leaf or determining to do right. New believers have a changed purpose, direction, attitude, and behavior. They no longer seek to serve themselves, but to "bear fruit" for God. What "fruit" has God's Word produced in your life? What fruit do you still lack?

1.7 Epaphras founded the church at Colosse while Paul was living in Ephesus (Acts 19.10). He may have been converted in Ephesus, then returned to Colosse, his hometown. For some reason, Epaphras visited Rome and there told Paul about the problem with the Colossian heresy. This prompted Paul to write this letter. Epaphras is also mentioned in Philemon 1.23 (the Colossian church met in Philemon's house).

faithful minister of Christ on your[c] behalf, 8 and he has made known to us your
love in the Spirit.
9 For this reason, since the day we heard it, we have not ceased praying for you
and asking that you may be filled with the knowledge of God's[d] will in all spiritual
wisdom and understanding, 10 so that you may lead lives worthy of the Lord, fully
pleasing to him, as you bear fruit in every good work and as you grow in the knowledge of God. 11 May you be made strong with all the strength that comes from his
glorious power, and may you be prepared to endure everything with patience,
while joyfully 12 giving thanks to the Father, who has enabled[e] you[f] to share in the
inheritance of the saints in the light. 13 He has rescued us from the power of darkness and transferred us into the kingdom of his beloved Son, 14 in whom we have
redemption, the forgiveness of sins.[g]

[c] Other ancient authorities read *our* [d] Gk *his* [e] Other ancient authorities read *called* [f] Other ancient authorities read *us* [g] Other ancient authorities add *through his blood*

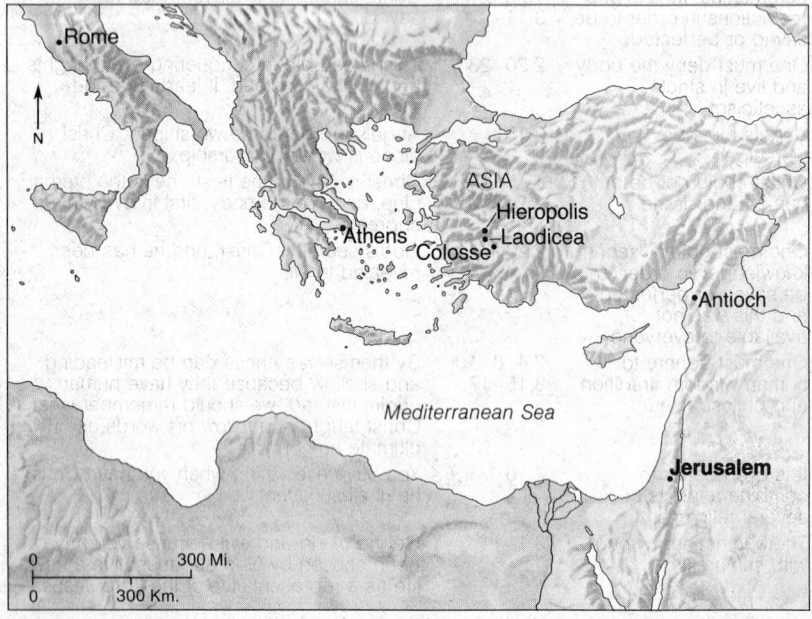

1.9 Rom 12.2 Eph 1.15-17
1.10 Jn 15.16 Eph 4.1 1 Thess 2.12
1.11 Acts 5.41 Eph 3.16,20
1.12 Acts 26.18 Eph 1.11; 5.20
1.13 Acts 26.18 Heb 2.14,15
1.14 Eph 1.7

Rome
N
ASIA
Hieropolis
Laodicea
Athens
Colosse
Antioch
Mediterranean Sea
Jerusalem
0 300 Mi.
0 300 Km.

LOCATION OF COLOSSE
Paul had no doubt been through Laodicea on his third missionary journey, as it lay on the main route to Ephesus, but he had never been to Colosse. Though a large city with a significant population, Colosse was smaller and less important than the nearby cities of Laodicea and Hieropolis.

1.8 Because of their love for one another, Christians can have an impact that goes far beyond their neighborhoods and communities. Christian love for others comes from the Holy Spirit (see Galatians 5.22). The Bible speaks of it as an action and attitude, not just an emotion. It is a by-product of our new life in Christ (see Romans 5.5; 1 Corinthians 13). Christians have no excuse for not loving others, because Christian love is a decision to *act* in the best interests of others.

1.9–14 Paul is exposing a heresy in the Colossian church that was similar to *gnosticism* (see the note on 2.4ff for more information). Gnostics valued the accumulation of knowledge, but Paul points out that knowledge in itself is empty. To be worth anything, it must lead to a changed life and right living. His prayer for the Colossians (1.9–14) has two dimensions – that they might *understand* what God wants, and that they might also have the power *to do* God's will. Knowledge is not merely to be accumulated; it should give us direction for living. Knowledge of God is not a secret that only a few can discover; it is open to everyone. God wants us to learn more about him, as well as to put that belief into practice by helping others.

1.9–14 Sometimes we wonder how to pray for missionaries and other leaders we have never met. Paul had never met the Colossians, but he faithfully prayed for them. His prayers teach us how to pray for others, whether we know them or not. We can request that they (1) understand God's will, (2) gain spiritual wisdom, (3) please and honor God, (4) do kind things for others, (5) know God better and better, (6) be filled with God's strength, (7) endure in faith, (8) stay full of Christ's joy, and (9) always be thankful. All believers have these same basic needs. When you don't know how to pray for someone, remember Paul's prayer pattern for the Colossians.

1.13 True believers have been transferred from darkness to light, from slavery to freedom, from guilt to forgiveness, and from the power of Satan to the power of God. We have been rescued from a rebel kingdom to serve the rightful King. Our conduct should reflect our new allegiance.

1.14 In verses 12–14, Paul lists five benefits God secured for us when Christ died on the cross: (1) he made us qualified to share his inheritance and be part of his kingdom (see also 2 Corinthians

Person and work of Christ

1.15 2 Cor 4.4
1.16 Jn 1.3
1.17 Jn 1.1,2; 8.58
1.18 Eph 1.22,23
1.19 Col 2.9
1.21 Rom 5.10 2 Cor 5.18,19 Eph 2.3,12

15 He is the image of the invisible God, the firstborn of all creation; 16 for in[h]
him all things in heaven and on earth were created, things visible and invisible,
whether thrones or dominions or rulers or powers—all things have been created
through him and for him. 17 He himself is before all things, and in[h] him all things
hold together. 18 He is the head of the body, the church; he is the beginning, the
firstborn from the dead, so that he might come to have first place in everything.
19 For in him all the fullness of God was pleased to dwell, 20 and through him God
was pleased to reconcile to himself all things, whether on earth or in heaven, by
making peace through the blood of his cross.
21 And you who were once estranged and hostile in mind, doing evil deeds,

[h] Or *by*

HOW TO PRAY FOR OTHER CHRISTIANS
How many people in your life could be touched if you prayed in this way?

1. Be thankful for their faith and changed lives (1.3)
2. Ask God to help them know what he wants them to do (1.9)
3. Ask God to give them deep spiritual understanding (1.9)
4. Ask God to help them live for him (1.10)
5. Ask God to give them more knowledge of himself (1.10)
6. Ask God to give them strength for endurance (1.11)
7. Ask God to fill them with joy, strength, and thankfulness (1.11)

5.21); (2) he rescued us from Satan's domination and made us his children (see also 2.15); (3) he brought us into his eternal kingdom (see also Ephesians 1.5, 6); (4) he bought our freedom ("redemption") from sin and judgment (see also Hebrews 9.12); and (5) he forgave all our sins (see also Ephesians 1.7). Thank God for what you have received in Christ.

1.15, 16 This is one of the strongest statements about the divine nature of Christ found anywhere in the Bible. Jesus is not only equal to God (Philippians 2.6), he is God (John 10.30, 38; 12.45; 14.1–11). He not only reflects God, he also reveals God to us (John 1.18; 14.9). He came from heaven, not from the dust of the ground (1 Corinthians 15.47) and is Lord of all (Romans 9.5; 10.11–13; Revelation 1.5; 17.14). He is completely holy (Hebrews 7.26–28; 1 Peter 1.19; 2.22; 1 John 3.5), and he has authority to judge the world (Romans 2.16; 2 Corinthians 5.10; 2 Timothy 4.1). Therefore, Christ is supreme over all creation, including the spirit world. We, like the Colossian believers, must believe that Jesus is God, or our Christian faith is hollow, misdirected, and meaningless. This is a central truth of Christianity. We should oppose those who say that Jesus was merely a prophet or good teacher.

1.15–23 In the Colossian church, there were several misconceptions about Christ that Paul directly refutes:

(1) They believed that matter is evil, so they said God would not have come to earth as a true human being in bodily form. Paul states that Christ is the exact likeness of God, is himself God, and yet died on the cross as a human being.

(2) They believed that God did not create the world because he would not have created evil. Paul says that Jesus Christ, who was also God in the flesh, is the Creator of both heaven and earth.

(3) They said Christ was not the unique Son of God, but rather one of many intermediaries between God and people. Paul explains that Christ existed before anything else and is the firstborn of those resurrected.

(4) They refused to see Christ as the source of salvation, insisting that people could find God through special and secret knowledge. Paul states that a person can be saved through Christ alone. When we share the gospel, we must keep the focus on Christ.

1.16 Because the false teachers believed the physical world was evil, they thought God himself could not have created it. If Christ were God, they reasoned, he would be in charge only of the spiritual world. But Paul explains that both the spiritual and physical worlds were created by and are under the authority of Christ himself. This implies earthly governments as well as the spiritual world that the heretics were so concerned about. He has no equal and no rival. He is the Lord of all. For more on the connection between the spiritual and physical dimension, see the first note on 1 Corinthians 6.12, 13.

1.17 God is not only the Creator of the world, but also the Sustainer of it. By him everything is held together, protected, and prevented from disintegrating into chaos. Because Christ is the Sustainer of all life, none of us is independent of him. We are all his servants who must daily trust him to protect and care for us.

1.18 The resurrection (Christ is "firstborn from the dead") proves Christ's lordship over the material world. All who trust in Christ will also defeat death and rise again to live eternally with him (1 Corinthians 15.20; 1 Thessalonians 4.14). Because of his death on the cross, Christ is exalted and elevated to the status that was rightfully his (see Philippians 2.5–11). Because he is spiritually supreme (preeminent) in the universe, we should surely give him first place in all our thoughts and activities. See the second note on Luke 24.6, 7 for more about Christ's resurrection.

1.19 Christ is fully divine (see the note on Philippians 2.5–7). Christ has always been God and will always be God. When we have Christ, we have all of God in human form. Don't diminish any aspect of Christ—either his humanity or his divinity.

1.20 Christ's death provided a way for all people to come to God (to be reconciled). It removed the sin that keeps us from having a right relationship with our Creator. This does not mean that everyone has been saved, but that the way has been cleared for anyone who will trust Christ to be saved. We can have peace with God and be reconciled to him by giving our lives to Christ, who died in our place. Is there a distance between you and God? Be reconciled to God. Come to him through Christ.

1.21 Because we are alienated from God, we are strangers to his way of thinking. Sin corrupts our way of thinking about God. Wrong thinking leads to sin, which further perverts and destroys our thoughts about him. When we were out of harmony with God, our natural condition was to be totally hostile to his standards. See Romans 1.21–32 for more on the perverted thinking of unbelievers.

1.21, 22 *No one* is good enough to save himself. If we want to live eternally with Christ, we must depend totally on God's grace. This is true whether we have been murderers or honest, hardworking citizens. We have all sinned repeatedly, and *any* sin is enough to require us to come to Jesus Christ for salvation and eternal life. Apart from Christ, there is no way for our sin to be forgiven.

22 he has now reconciled[i] in his fleshly body[j] through death, so as to present you
holy and blameless and irreproachable before him— 23 provided that you continue
securely established and steadfast in the faith, without shifting from the hope promised by the gospel that you heard, which has been proclaimed to every creature
under heaven. I, Paul, became a servant of this gospel.

Paul's mission and concern

24 I am now rejoicing in my sufferings for your sake, and in my flesh I am
completing what is lacking in Christ's afflictions for the sake of his body, that is,
the church. 25 I became its servant according to God's commission that was given
to me for you, to make the word of God fully known, 26 the mystery that has been
hidden throughout the ages and generations but has now been revealed to his saints.
27 To them God chose to make known how great among the Gentiles are the riches
of the glory of this mystery, which is Christ in you, the hope of glory. 28 It is he
whom we proclaim, warning everyone and teaching everyone in all wisdom, so
that we may present everyone mature in Christ. 29 For this I toil and struggle with
all the energy that he powerfully inspires within me.

2 For I want you to know how much I am struggling for you, and for those in
Laodicea, and for all who have not seen me face to face. 2 I want their hearts
to be encouraged and united in love, so that they may have all the riches of assured
understanding and have the knowledge of God's mystery, that is, Christ himself,[k]
3 in whom are hidden all the treasures of wisdom and knowledge. 4 I am saying this
so that no one may deceive you with plausible arguments. 5 For though I am absent

1.22 Rom 7.4 Eph 1.4; 5.27
1.23 Eph 3.17 Col 1.5,6
1.24 Phil 2.17; 3.10 2 Tim 1.8
1.25 Eph 3.2
1.27 Rom 8.10; 9.23,24 Eph 3.8,9,16
1.28 Eph 4.13 Col 4.12
1.29 Eph 1.19
2.2 Mt 11.25-27 Phil 3.8
2.3 Isa 11.2 Rom 11.33 Eph 3.8

[i] Other ancient authorities read *you have now been reconciled* [j] Gk *in the body of his flesh* [k] Other ancient authorities read *of the mystery of God, both of the Father and of Christ*

1.22, 23 The way to be blameless is to trust Jesus Christ to take our sin away. We must remain "established and steadfast" in the truth of the gospel, putting our confidence in Christ alone to forgive our sins, to make us right with God, and to empower us to live the way he desires. When a judge declares the defendant "not guilty," he has been acquitted of all the charges. Legally, it is as if the person had never been accused. When God forgives our sins, our record is wiped clean. From his perspective, it is as though we had never sinned. God's solution is available to you. No matter what you have done or what you have been like, God's forgiveness is for you.

1.24 When Paul says he is "completing what is lacking in Christ's afflictions," he does not mean Christ's suffering and death were inadequate to save us. Nor does he mean that there is a predetermined amount of suffering that must be paid by all believers. Paul is simply saying that suffering is unavoidable in bringing the good news of Christ to the world. It is called Christ's suffering because all Christians are related to Christ. When we suffer, Christ feels it with us. But this suffering can be endured joyfully because it changes lives and brings people into God's kingdom (see 1 Peter 4.1, 2, 12–19). For more about how Paul could be glad despite his suffering, see the note on Philippians 1.29.

1.26, 27 The false teachers in the Colossian church believed spiritual perfection was a secret and hidden plan that only a few privileged people would discover. Their secret plan was meant to be exclusive. Paul says that he proclaims God's Word in its fullness, not just as part of the plan. Paul calls God's plan a "mystery that has been hidden throughout the ages," not in the sense that only a few would understand, but because it was hidden until Christ came. God's secret plan is "Christ in you, the hope of glory"—he planned to have his Son, Jesus Christ, live in all who believe in him—even Gentiles like the Colossians. Do you know him? He is not hidden if you will come to him.

1.28, 29 Paul wanted believers to mature spiritually. Like Paul, we must work and strive wholeheartedly, like an athlete, but we must not do it in our own strength alone. We have the power of God's Spirit working in us. We can learn and grow daily motivated by love, not fear or pride, knowing that God gives the power to become mature.

1.28, 29 Christ's message is for everyone; so everywhere Paul and Timothy went they brought the good news to all who would listen. An effective presentation of the gospel includes warning and teaching. The warning is that without Christ, people are doomed to eternal separation from God. The teaching is that salvation is available through faith in Christ. As Christ works in you, tell others about him, warning and teaching them in love. Do you know someone who needs to hear this message?

2.1 Laodicea was located a few miles northwest of Colosse. Like the church at Colosse, the Laodicean church was probably founded by one of Paul's converts while Paul was staying in Ephesus (Acts 19.10). The city was wealthy, a center of trade and commerce. But later, Christ would criticize the believers for their lukewarm commitment to him (Revelation 3.14–22). The fact that Paul wanted this letter to be passed on to the Laodicean church (4.16) indicates that false teaching had spread there as well. Paul was counting on ties of love to bring the churches together to stand against this heresy and to encourage each other to remain true to God's plan of salvation in Christ.

2.4ff The problem Paul was combatting in the Colossian church was similar to *gnosticism* (from the Greek word for *knowledge*). This heresy (a teaching contrary to biblical doctrine) attacked Christianity in several basic ways: (1) It insisted that important secret knowledge was hidden from most believers; Paul, however, said that in Christ we have all we need of God's provision for us. (2) It taught that the body was evil; Paul countered that God himself dwelt in a body—that is, he was embodied in Jesus Christ. (3) It contended that Christ only seemed to be human, but was not; Paul insisted that Jesus is fully human and fully God.

Gnosticism became fashionable in the second century. Even in Paul's day, these ideas sounded attractive to many, and they could easily seduce a church that didn't know Christian doctrine well. Aspects of this early heresy still pose significant problems for many in the church today. We combat heresy by becoming thoroughly acquainted with God's Word through personal study and sound Bible teaching.

in body, yet I am with you in spirit, and I rejoice to see your morale and the firm-
ness of your faith in Christ.

New life in Christ

2.6 Col 1.10
2.7 Eph 2.20; 3.17

6 As you therefore have received Christ Jesus the Lord, continue to live your
lives[l] in him, 7 rooted and built up in him and established in the faith, just as you
were taught, abounding in thanksgiving.

2.8 Col 2.20,23
2.9 Jn 1.14
2.10 Eph 1.21; 3.19 1 Pet 3.22
2.12 Rom 6.4,5 Eph 2.6

8 See to it that no one takes you captive through philosophy and empty deceit,
according to human tradition, according to the elemental spirits of the universe,[m]
and not according to Christ. 9 For in him the whole fullness of deity dwells bodily,
10 and you have come to fullness in him, who is the head of every ruler and authority. 11 In him also you were circumcised with a spiritual circumcision,[n] by putting
off the body of the flesh in the circumcision of Christ; 12 when you were buried with
him in baptism, you were also raised with him through faith in the power of God,

[l] Gk *to walk* [m] Or *the rudiments of the world* [n] Gk *a circumcision made without hands*

SALVATION BY FAITH

	Religion by Self-effort	*Salvation by Faith*
Goal	Please God by our own good works	Trust in Christ and then live to please God
Means	Practice, diligent service, discipline, and obedience, in hope of reward	Confess, submit, and commit yourself to Christ's control
Power	Good, honest effort through self-determination	The Holy Spirit in us helps us do good work for Christ's kingdom
Control	Self-motivation; self-control	Christ in me; I in Christ
Results	Chronic guilt, apathy, depression, failure, constant desire for approval	Joy, thankfulness, love, guidance, service, forgiveness

Salvation by faith in Christ sounds too easy for many people. They would rather think that they have done something to save themselves. Their religion becomes one of self-effort that leads either to disappointment or pride, but finally to eternal death. Christ's simple way is the only way, and it alone leads to eternal life.

2.6, 7 Receiving Christ as Lord of your life is the beginning of life with Christ. But you must continue to follow his leadership by being rooted, built up, and established in the faith. Every day he desires to guide you and help you with your daily problems. You can live for Christ by (1) committing your life and submitting your will to him (Romans 12.1, 2); (2) seeking to learn from him, his life, and his teachings (3.16); and (3) recognizing the Holy Spirit's power in you (Acts 1.8; Galatians 5.22).

2.7 Paul uses the illustration of our being rooted in or connected to Christ. As plants draw nourishment from the soil through their roots, so we draw our life-giving strength from Christ. The more we draw our life from him, the less we will be fooled by those who falsely claim to have life's answers (2.8).

2.8 Paul writes against any philosophy of life based only on human ideas and experiences. Paul himself was a gifted philosopher, so he is not condemning philosophy. He was condemning teaching that credits humanity, not Christ, with being the answer to life's problems and thus becomes a false religion. There are many self-made approaches to life's problems that totally disregard God. To resist heresy, you must use your mind, keep your eyes on Christ, and study God's Word.

2.8 The phrase "elemental spirits of the universe" most likely refers to the gods or deities that ruled over individual nations and groups of people. The Colossians had been set free from them and their philosophies. See 1 Corinthians 8.4–6 for Paul's attitude toward these deities.

2.9 Again Paul asserts Christ's deity. "In him the whole fullness of deity dwells bodily" means that in Christ there is all of God in a human body. When we have Christ, we have everything we need for salvation and right living. See the note on 1.15, 16 for more on this subject.

2.10 When we know Jesus Christ, we don't need to seek God by means of other religions, cults, or unbiblical philosophies as the Colossians were doing. Christ alone holds the answers to the true meaning of life, because Christ *is* life. He is the unique source of knowledge and power for the Christian life. No Christian needs anything else than what Christ has provided to be saved. We are complete in him.

2.11, 12 Jewish males were circumcised as a sign of the Jews' covenant with God (Genesis 17.9–14). With the death of Christ, circumcision was no longer necessary as a step of faith. Now our commitment to God is written on our hearts, not our bodies. Christ sets us free from our evil desires by a spiritual operation, not a bodily one. Baptism is the new sign of the covenant.

2.12 In baptism, we are identified with Christ. Remembering that our old, sinful life is dead and buried, we have a powerful motive to resist sin. Not wanting the desires of our past to come back to power again, we can consciously choose to treat our desires as if they are dead. Then we will continue to enjoy our wonderful new life with Jesus (see Galatians 3.27 and Colossians 3.1–4).

2.12–15 Before we believed in Christ, our nature was evil. We disobeyed, rebelled, and ignored him (even at our best, we fell far short of loving him with all our heart, soul, and mind). The Christian, however, has a new nature. God has crucified the old rebellious nature (Romans 6.6) and replaced it with a new, loving nature (3.9, 10). The penalty for sin was paid when Christ died on the cross. God has declared us not guilty, and we need no longer live under sin's power. God does not take us out of the world or make us robots—we will still feel like sinning, and sometimes we will sin. The difference is that before we were saved, we were slaves to our sinful nature, but now we are free to live for Christ (see Galatians 2.20).

who raised him from the dead. 13 And when you were dead in trespasses and the
uncircumcision of your flesh, God[o] made you[p] alive together with him, when he
forgave us all our trespasses, 14 erasing the record that stood against us with its legal
demands. He set this aside, nailing it to the cross. 15 He disarmed[q] the rulers and
authorities and made a public example of them, triumphing over them in it.

2.13 Eph 2.1,5
2.14 Eph 2.15
2.15 Jn 12.31; 2 Cor 2.14

Freedom from legalism

16 Therefore do not let anyone condemn you in matters of food and drink or of
observing festivals, new moons, or sabbaths. 17 These are only a shadow of what is
to come, but the substance belongs to Christ. 18 Do not let anyone disqualify you,
insisting on self-abasement and worship of angels, dwelling[r] on visions,[s] puffed
up without cause by a human way of thinking,[t] 19 and not holding fast to the head,
from whom the whole body, nourished and held together by its ligaments and sinews, grows with a growth that is from God.

2.16 1 Chron 23.31; Rom 14.3,5; Gal 4.10
2.17 Heb 8.5; 10.1
2.19 Eph 1.22,23; 4.15,16

[o] Gk *he* [p] Other ancient authorities read *made us*; others, *made* [q] Or *divested himself of* [r] Other ancient authorities read *not dwelling* [s] Meaning of Gk uncertain [t] Gk *by the mind of his flesh*

TRUST: YESTERDAY, TODAY, AND TOMORROW!

Living under the lordship of Christ means realizing that each day brings new opportunities to trust Christ and experience his powerful work in us. Have you trusted this day to Christ?

1. Trusting Christ = living in vital union with Christ day by day (Colossians 2.2–7)
2. Accepting Christ as head or Lord = he is in control (Colossians 1.15–18; 2.19; 3.10, 17)
3. Experiencing the power of the Holy Spirit = God's mighty energy at work in us (Colossians 1.11, 28, 29)
4. Inward and outward results =
   - assurance of forgiveness (Colossians 2.15)
   - freedom from evil desires (Colossians 2.11)
   - happiness (joy) (Colossians 2.7)
   - personal growth (Colossians 1.28)
   - opportunities to tell others the gospel (Colossians 1.4, 28)
   - thankfulness to God (Colossians 2.7)
5. Direction = God becoming involved in our decisions (Colossians 3.1, 16)

2.14 The record that was erased was the legal demands of the Old Testament law. It opposed us by its demands for payment for our sin. Although no one can be saved by merely keeping that code, the moral truths and principles in the Old Testament still teach and guide today.

2.14 We can enjoy our new life in Christ because we have joined him in his death and resurrection. Our evil desires, our bondage to sin, and our love of sin died with him. And the law has been "nailed to the cross." Now, joining Christ in his resurrection life, we can have unbroken fellowship with God and freedom from sin. Our debt for sin has been paid in full; our sins are swept away and forgotten by God; and we can be clean and new. For more on the difference between our new life in Christ and our old sinful nature, read Ephesians 4.23, 24 and Colossians 3.3–15.

2.15 These rulers and authorities are not the demonic forces but, as in 2.10, are more likely the angels who were mediators of the law (Galatians 3.19). The Colossian false teachers were encouraging worship of angels. But at his death, Christ surpassed the position and authority of any angel. So rather than fear angels or worship them, we should see them as deposed rulers. Paul meant no disrespect toward angels, but he showed that they are not to be compared with Christ. Some scholars believe these powers are the powers of Rome. Christ's resurrection stripped the power away from a world empire that seemed to temporarily defeat him.

2.16, 17 Paul told the Colossian Christians not to let others criticize their diet or their religious ceremonies. Instead of outward observance, they should focus on faith in Christ alone. Our worship, traditions, and ceremonies can help bring us close to God, but we should never criticize fellow Christians whose traditions differ from ours. More important than how we worship is that we all worship Christ. Don't worry about others' judgment. You are responsible to Christ.

2.17 Old Testament laws, holidays, and feasts pointed toward Christ. Paul calls them a shadow of the reality to come – Christ himself. When Christ came, he dispelled the shadows. If we have Christ, we have what we need to know and please God.

2.18 The false teachers were proud of their humility! This false humility brought attention and praise to themselves rather than to God. True humility means seeing ourselves as we really are from God's perspective, and acting accordingly. People today practice false humility when they talk themselves down so that others will think they are spiritual. False humility is self-centered; true humility is God-centered. Don't feel disqualified or rejected by God because you don't follow others' religious standards.

2.18 The false teachers claimed that God was far away and could be approached only through various levels of angels. They taught that people had to worship angels in order to reach God. This is unscriptural. The Bible teaches that angels are God's servants, and it forbids worshiping them (Exodus 20.3, 4; Revelation 22.8, 9). As you grow in your Christian faith, let God's Word be your guide, not the opinions of other people.

2.18 The expression "human way of thinking" means that these people had a self-made religion. The false teachers were trying to deny the body by saying it was evil, but their desire for attention from others showed they were actually obsessed by it.

2.19 The fundamental problem with the false teachers was that they were not connected to Christ, the Head of the body of believers. If they had been joined to him, they could not have taught false doctrine or lived immorally. Anyone who teaches about God without being connected to him by faith should not be trusted.

2.20 Rom 6.2 Gal 2.20; 4.9
2.22 Mt 15.9 1 Cor 6.13
2.23 1 Tim 4.3

20 If with Christ you died to the elemental spirits of the universe,[u] why do you
live as if you still belonged to the world? Why do you submit to regulations, 21 "Do
not handle, Do not taste, Do not touch"? 22 All these regulations refer to things that
perish with use; they are simply human commands and teachings. 23 These have
indeed an appearance of wisdom in promoting self-imposed piety, humility, and
severe treatment of the body, but they are of no value in checking self-indulgence.[v]

2. What Christians should do

Principles of Christian living

3.1 Mt 6.33 Eph 2.6

3 So if you have been raised with Christ, seek the things that are above, where
Christ is, seated at the right hand of God. 2 Set your minds on things that are
above, not on things that are on earth, 3 for you have died, and your life is hidden

[u] *Or the rudiments of the world* [v] *Or are of no value, serving only to indulge the flesh*

FROM DEATH TO LIFE

1. Because Christ died for us, we have been crucified with him.	Romans 6.2–13; 7.4–6 2 Corinthians 5.14 Galatians 2.20; 5.24; 6.14 Colossians 2.20; 3.3–5 1 Peter 2.24
2. Our old, rebellious nature died with Christ.	Romans 6.6; 7.4–6 Colossians 3.9, 10
3. Christ's resurrection guarantees our new life now and eternal life with him later.	Romans 6.4, 11 Colossians 2.12, 13; 3.1, 3

The Bible uses many illustrations to teach what happens when we choose to let Jesus be Lord of our lives. Following are some of the most vivid pictures:

This process is acted out in baptism (Colossians 2.12), based on our faith in Christ:

(1) The old evil nature dies (crucified); (2) We are ready to receive a new life (buried); (3) Christ gives us new life (resurrected).

2.20 The "elemental spirits of the universe" or "rudiments of the world" are the beliefs in pagan deities. See 2.8 for more on Paul's view of non-Christian philosophy.

2.20; 3.1 How do we die with Christ, and how are we raised with him? When a person becomes a Christian, he or she is given new life through the power of the Holy Spirit. See the notes on 2.12–15.

2.20–23 People should be able to see a difference between the way Christians and non-Christians live. Still, we should not expect instant maturity of new Christians. Christian growth is a lifelong process. Although we have a new nature, we don't automatically have all good thoughts and attitudes when we become new people in Christ. But if we keep listening to God, we will be changing all the time. As you look over the last year, what changes have you seen in your thoughts and attitudes? Change may be slow, but your life will change significantly if you trust God to change you.

2.20–24 We cannot reach up to God by following rules of self-denial and rituals or by practicing religion. Paul isn't saying all rules are bad (see the note on Galatians 2.15, 16). But the keeping of laws or rules will not earn salvation. The good news is that God reaches down to man, and we respond. Self-made religions focus on human effort; Christianity focuses on Christ's work. Believers must put aside sinful desires, but doing so is the by-product of our new life in Christ, not the cause of it. Our salvation does not depend on our own discipline and rule-keeping, but on the power of Christ's death and resurrection.

2.22, 23 We can guard against self-made religions ("human commands and teachings") by asking these questions of any religious group: (1) Does it stress self-made rules and taboos rather than God's grace? (2) Does it foster a critical spirit about others, or does it exercise discipline discreetly and lovingly? (3) Does it stress formulas, secret knowledge, or special visions more than the word of God? (4) Does it elevate self-righteousness, honoring those who keep the rules, rather than elevating Christ? (5) Does it neglect Christ's universal church, claiming to be an elite group? (6) Does it teach humiliation of the body as a means to spiritual growth rather than focusing on the growth of the whole person?

2.23 To the Colossians, the discipline demanded by the false teachers seemed good. Legalism still attracts many people today. Following a long list of religious rules requires strong self-discipline and can make a person appear moral. But religious rules cannot change a person's heart. Only the Holy Spirit can do that.

3.1ff In chapter 2, Paul exposed the wrong reasons for self-denial. In chapter 3, he explains true Christian behavior – putting on the new nature by accepting Christ and regarding the old nature as dead. We change our moral and ethical behavior by letting Christ live within us, so that he can shape us into what we *should* be.

3.1, 2 Seeking the things that are above means trying to put heaven's priorities into daily practice. Setting our minds on things that are above means concentrating on the eternal rather than on the temporal. See Philippians 4.9 and Colossians 3.15 for more on Christ's rule in our hearts and minds.

3.2, 3 "For you have died" means we should have as little desire for this world as a dead person has. The Christian's real home is where Christ lives (John 14.2, 3). This gives us a different perspective on our lives here on earth. To "set your minds on things that are above" means to look at life from God's perspective and to seek what he desires. This is the antidote to materialism; we gain the proper perspective on material goods when we take God's view of them. The more we see the life around us as God sees it, the more we live in harmony with him. We must not become too attached to what is only temporary.

3.3 What does it mean for a believer's life to be "hidden with Christ in God"? *Hidden* means concealed and safe. This is not only a future hope, but an accomplished fact right now. Take heart that your salvation is sure, and live each day for Christ.

with Christ in God. 4 When Christ who is your[w] life is revealed, then you also will
be revealed with him in glory.
5 Put to death, therefore, whatever in you is earthly: fornication, impurity, passion, evil desire, and greed (which is idolatry). 6 On account of these the wrath of
God is coming on those who are disobedient.[x] 7 These are the ways you also once
followed, when you were living that life.[y] 8 But now you must get rid of all such
things—anger, wrath, malice, slander, and abusive[z] language from your mouth.
9 Do not lie to one another, seeing that you have stripped off the old self with its
practices 10 and have clothed yourselves with the new self, which is being renewed
in knowledge according to the image of its creator. 11 In that renewal[a] there is no
longer Greek and Jew, circumcised and uncircumcised, barbarian, Scythian, slave
and free; but Christ is all and in all!
12 As God's chosen ones, holy and beloved, clothe yourselves with compassion, kindness, humility, meekness, and patience. 13 Bear with one another and, if
anyone has a complaint against another, forgive each other; just as the Lord[b] has
forgiven you, so you also must forgive. 14 Above all, clothe yourselves with love,

3.4 1 Cor 15.43; 1 Jn 3.2
3.5 Mk 7.21-23; Gal 5.19; Eph 5.3,5
3.7 Eph 2.2
3.8 Eph 4.22,29; Jas 1.21
3.10 Rom 8.29; 12.2
3.11 Rom 10.12; 1 Cor 12.13; Gal 3.28
3.13 Eph 4.32
3.14 Rom 13.8

[w] Other authorities read *our* [x] Other ancient authorities lack *on those who are disobedient* (Gk *the children of disobedience*) [y] Or *living among such people* [z] Or *filthy* [a] Gk *its creator,* [11]*where* [b] Other ancient authorities read *just as Christ*

SINS VS. SIGNS OF LOVE

Sins of Sexual Attitude and Behavior	*Sins of Speech*	*Signs of love*
Evil desires	Anger expressed	Tender-hearted mercy
Sexual sin	Cursing	Kindness
Impurity	Dirty language	Humility
Lust	Lying	Patience
Shameful desires		Gentleness
		Forgiveness

In Colossians 3.5 Paul tells us to consider ourselves dead to list 1. In 3.8 he tells us to cast off list 2. In 3.12 we're told to practice list 3. List 1 deals with sins of sexual attitudes and behavior—they are particularly destructive because of what they do to destroy any group or church. List 2 deals with sins of speech—these are the relationship-breakers. List 3 contains the relationship-builders, which we are to express as members of Christ's body.

3.4 Christ gives us power to help us live now, and he gives us hope for the future—he will return. In the rest of this chapter, Paul explains how Christians should act *now* in order to be prepared for Christ's return.

3.5 "Put to death . . . whatever in you is earthly" means we should consider ourselves dead and unresponsive to evil desires, sexual sin, impurity, lustful desires, and materialism. Just like diseased limbs of a tree, they must be cut off before they destroy us. We must make a conscious, daily decision to remove anything that supports or feeds these desires and to rely on the Holy Spirit's power.

3.6 The "wrath of God" refers to God's judgment on those kinds of behavior, culminating in the future and final punishment of evil. When tempted to sin, remember that eventually you must stand before God.

3.9 Lying to one another disrupts unity by destroying trust. It tears down relationships and may lead to severe conflict in a church. So don't exaggerate, pass on rumors or gossip, or say things to build up your own image. Be committed to telling the truth.

3.9, 10 To strip off the old self and be clothed with the new self was not so much mystical but practical and moral. It means be done with your old way of life and commit yourself to Christ's way. Paul may be appealing to the commitment the believers had made in their baptism and urging them to remain true to their confession of faith. They were to strip off the old life and put on the new way of living given by Christ and guided by the Holy Spirit. If you have made such a commitment, are you remaining true to it?

3.10 The Christian is in a continuing education program. The more we know of Christ and his work, the more we are being changed to be like him. Because this process is lifelong, we must never stop learning and obeying. There is no justification for drifting along, but there is an incentive to find the rich treasures of growing in him. It takes practice, review, patience, and concentration to keep in line with his will. See also the note on 2.12–15.

3.11 The Christian should have no barriers of nationality, race, education, social standing, wealth, religion, or power. Christ breaks down all barriers and accepts all people who come to him. Nothing should keep us from telling others about Christ or accepting into our fellowship any and all believers (Ephesians 2.14, 15). Christians should be in the business of building bridges, not walls. *Barbarian* was another name for Greek. A *Scythian* was the lowest type of barbarian slave.

3.12–17 Paul offers a strategy to help us live for God day by day: (1) imitate Christ's merciful, forgiving attitude (3.12, 13); (2) let love guide your life (3.14); (3) let the peace of Christ reign in your heart (3.15); (4) always be thankful (3.15); (5) keep God's Word in you at all times (3.16); (6) live as Jesus Christ's representative (3.17).

3.13 The key to forgiving others is remembering how much God has forgiven you. Is it difficult for you to forgive someone who has wronged you a little when God has forgiven you so much? Realizing God's infinite love and forgiveness can help you love and forgive others.

3.14, 15 Christians should live in perfect harmony. This does not eliminate all differences in opinion, but loving Christians will work together despite their differences. Such love is not a feeling, but a decision to meet others' needs (see 1 Corinthians 13). It leads to peace between individuals and among the members of the body of believers. Do problems in your relationship with other Christians

3.15 Eph 2.14-16 which binds everything together in perfect harmony. 15 And let the peace of Christ
Phil 4.7 rule in your hearts, to which indeed you were called in the one body. And be thank-
3.16 ful. 16 Let the word of Christ[c] dwell in you richly; teach and admonish one another
Eph 5.19 in all wisdom; and with gratitude in your hearts sing psalms, hymns, and spiritual
3.17 songs to God.[d] 17 And whatever you do, in word or deed, do everything in the
Eph 5.20 name of the Lord Jesus, giving thanks to God the Father through him.

Principles for relationships

3.18 18 Wives, be subject to your husbands, as is fitting in the Lord. 19 Husbands,
Eph 5.22 3.19 love your wives and never treat them harshly.
Eph 5.25 20 Children, obey your parents in everything, for this is your acceptable duty in
3.20 the Lord. 21 Fathers, do not provoke your children, or they may lose heart.
Eph 6.1 22 Slaves, obey your earthly masters[e] in everything, not only while being watched
3.21-22 Eph 6.4-6 and in order to please them, but wholeheartedly, fearing the Lord.[e] 23 Whatever
your task, put yourselves into it, as done for the Lord and not for your masters,[f]
3.25 24 since you know that from the Lord you will receive the inheritance as your
Acts 10.34 reward; you serve[g] the Lord Christ. 25 For the wrongdoer will be paid back for

[c] Other ancient authorities read *of God*, or *of the Lord* [d] Other ancient authorities read *to the Lord* [e] In Greek the same word is used for *master* and *Lord* [f] Gk *not for men* [g] Or *you are slaves of*, or *be slaves of*

RULES OF SUBMISSION

Wives, submit to your husbands (3.18).	*Husbands,* be loving and kind toward your wives (3.19).
Children, obey your parents (3.20).	*Parents,* don't scold your children so much that they become discouraged and quit trying (3.21).
Slaves, obey your masters (3.22).	*Masters,* be just and fair toward your slaves (4.1).
(*Employees,* work hard for your employers.)	(*Employers,* be just and fair with your employees.)

The New Testament includes many instructions concerning relationships. Most people read these instructions for the other person and ignore the ones that apply to themselves. But you can't control another person's behavior, only your own. Start by following your own instructions and not insisting on the obedience of others first.

cause open conflicts or mutual silence? Consider what you can do to heal those relationships with love.

3.15 The word *rule* comes from athletics: Paul tells us to let Christ's peace be umpire or referee in our hearts. Our hearts are the center of conflict, because there our feelings and desires clash – our fears and hopes, our distrust and trust, our jealousy and love. How can we deal with these constant conflicts and live as God wants? Paul explains that we must decide between conflicting elements by using the rule of peace – which choice will promote peace in our souls and in our churches? For more on the peace of Christ, see Philippians 4.9.

3.16 Although the early Christians had access to the Old Testament and freely used it, they did not yet have the New Testament or any other Christian books to study. Their stories and teachings about Christ were memorized and passed on from person to person. Sometimes they were set to music, and so music became an important part of Christian worship and education.

3.17 Doing everything in the name of the Lord Jesus means bringing honor to Christ in every aspect and activity of daily living. As a Christian, you represent Christ at all times – wherever you go, whatever you say. What impression do people have of Christ when they see or talk with you? What changes do you need to make for your life to honor Christ?

3.18 – 4.1 Paul describes three relationships: (1) husbands and wives, (2) parents and children, and (3) masters and slaves. In each case there is mutual responsibility to submit and love, to obey and encourage, to work hard and be fair. Examine your family and work relationships. Do you relate to others as God intended? See Ephesians 5.21 – 6.9 for similar instructions.

3.19 Christian marriage involves mutual submission, subordinating our personal desires for the good of the loved one and submitting ourselves to Christ as Lord. For more on submission, see the notes on Ephesians 5.21–33.

3.20, 21 Children must be handled with care. They need firm discipline administered in love. Don't alienate them by nagging, deriding, or destroying their self-respect so that they lose heart.

3.22 – 4.1 Paul does not condemn or condone slavery, but he explains that Christ transcends all divisions between people. Slaves are told to work hard as though their master were Christ himself (3.22–25); but masters should be just and fair (4.1). Perhaps Paul was thinking specifically of Onesimus and Philemon – the slave and master whose conflict lies behind the letter to Philemon (see the book of Philemon). Philemon was a slaveowner in the Colossian church, and Onesimus had been his slave (4.9).

3.23 Since the creation, God has given us work to do. If we could regard work as an act of worship or service to God, our attitude would take some of the drudgery and boredom out of it. We could work without complaining or resentment if we would treat our job problems as the cost of discipleship.

4 whatever wrong has been done, and there is no partiality. 1 Masters, treat your
slaves justly and fairly, for you know that you also have a Master in heaven.

2 Devote yourselves to prayer, keeping alert in it with thanksgiving. 3 At the
same time pray for us as well that God will open to us a door for the word, that we
may declare the mystery of Christ, for which I am in prison, 4 so that I may reveal
it clearly, as I should.
5 Conduct yourselves wisely toward outsiders, making the most of the time.[h]
6 Let your speech always be gracious, seasoned with salt, so that you may know
how you ought to answer everyone.

Paul's final greetings

7 Tychicus will tell you all the news about me; he is a beloved brother, a faithful
minister, and a fellow servant[i] in the Lord. 8 I have sent him to you for this very
purpose, so that you may know how we are[j] and that he may encourage your
hearts; 9 he is coming with Onesimus, the faithful and beloved brother, who is one
of you. They will tell you about everything here.
10 Aristarchus my fellow prisoner greets you, as does Mark the cousin of Barnabas, concerning whom you have received instructions — if he comes to you, welcome him. 11 And Jesus who is called Justus greets you. These are the only ones of
the circumcision among my co-workers for the kingdom of God, and they have
been a comfort to me. 12 Epaphras, who is one of you, a servant[i] of Christ Jesus,
greets you. He is always wrestling in his prayers on your behalf, so that you may
stand mature and fully assured in everything that God wills. 13 For I testify for him
that he has worked hard for you and for those in Laodicea and in Hierapolis.
14 Luke, the beloved physician, and Demas greet you. 15 Give my greetings to the
brothers and sisters[k] in Laodicea, and to Nympha and the church in her house.
16 And when this letter has been read among you, have it read also in the church of

4.1 Lev 19.13 Eph 6.9
4.2 Eph 6.18
4.4 Eph 6.20
4.5 Eph 5.15,16
4.6 Eph 4.29 1 Pet 3.15
4.7 Acts 20.4 Eph 6.21,22
4.9 Philem 10
4.10 Acts 12.12; 15.37 19.29; 20.4 27.2 2 Tim 4.11
4.11 Acts 11.2
4.14 2 Tim 4.10,11 Philem 24
4.15 Rom 16.5 1 Cor 16.19 Philem 2
4.16 1 Thess 5.27

h Or *opportunity* i Gk *slave* j Other authorities read *that I may know how you are* k Gk *brothers*

4.1 "Masters," employers, and leaders should be right and fair, treating employees, followers, and volunteers justly. Remember, you are accountable to your Master in heaven.

4.2 Have you ever grown tired of praying for something or someone? Paul says we are to devote ourselves to prayer and be watchful. Persistence demonstrates our faith that God answers our prayers. Faith shouldn't die if the answers come slowly, because the delay may be God's way of working his will in your life. When you feel tired of praying, remind yourself that God is present, always listening, always acting — maybe not in ways you had hoped, but in ways he knows are best.

4.3 The "mystery of Christ" is God's good news of salvation, the gospel. Paul's life was focused on telling others about Christ, explaining and preaching the wonderful mystery of Christ.

4.5 We should be wise in our contacts with non-Christians (outsiders), making the most of our chances to tell them the good news of salvation. What opportunities do you have?

4.6 When we tell others about Christ, it is important always to be gracious in what we say. No matter how much sense the message makes, we will lose our effectiveness if we are not courteous. Just as we like to be respected, we must respect others if we want them to listen to what we have to say.

4.7 Tychicus was one of Paul's personal respresentatives and probably the bearer of the letters to the Colossians and Ephesians (see also Ephesians 6.21, 22). He accompanied Paul to Jerusalem with the collection for the church (Acts 20.4).

4.10 Mark accompanied Paul and Barnabas on their first missionary journey (Acts 12.25) but then left in the middle of the trip for unknown reasons (Acts 13.13). Barnabas and Mark were relatives. When Paul refused to take Mark on another journey, Barnabas and Mark journeyed together to preach the good news (Acts 15.37–41). Mark also worked with Peter (Acts 12.12, 13; 1 Peter 5.13). Later, Mark and Paul were reconciled (Philemon 1.24). Mark wrote the Gospel of Mark. His Profile is in Acts 13.

4.12 Epaphras founded the Colossian church (see the note on 1.7), and his report to Paul in Rome caused Paul to write this letter. Epaphras was a hero of the Colossian church, because he was one of those who had helped keep the church together in spite of growing troubles. His earnest prayers for the believers show his deep love and concern for them.

4.13 Laodicea was located a few miles northwest of Colosse; Hierapolis was about five miles north of Laodicea. See the note on 2.1 for more about Laodicea.

4.14 Luke spent much time with Paul, not only accompanying him on most of his third missionary journey, but sitting with him in the prison at Rome. Luke wrote the Gospel of Luke and the book of Acts. His Profile is in Acts 18. Demas was faithful to Paul for a while, but then deserted him (2 Timothy 4.10).

4.15 The early Christians often met in homes. Church buildings were not common until the third century.

4.16 Some suggest that the letter to Laodicea may be the book of Ephesians, and the "letter from Laodicea" is the same letter returned. It is also possible that there was a special letter to the Laodiceans, of which we have no record today. Paul wrote several letters that have been lost (see, for example, 2 Corinthians 2.3 and note).

4.17 Paul's letter to Philemon is also addressed to Archippus (Philemon 1.2). Paul called him "our fellow soldier." He may have been a Roman soldier who had become a member of the Colossian church, or he may have been Philemon's son.

4.17 2 Tim 4.5 Philem 2

the Laodiceans; and see that you read also the letter from Laodicea. 17 And say to
Archippus, "See that you complete the task that you have received in the Lord."

4.18 Heb 13.3

18 I, Paul, write this greeting with my own hand. Remember my chains. Grace
be with you.[l]

[l] Other ancient authorities add *Amen*

4.18 Paul usually dictated his letters to a scribe, but often ended with a short note in his own handwriting (see also 1 Corinthians 16.21; Galatians 6.11). This attested to the authenticity of the letter and deterred false teachers from writing letters in the name of Paul. It also gave the letters a personal touch.

4.18 To understand the letter to the Colossians, we need to know that the church was facing pressure from a cult-like heresy that promised deeper spiritual life through secret knowledge (an early form of gnosticism). The false teachers destroyed faith in Christ by undermining Christ's humanity and divinity and attempting to divide the physical and spiritual.

Paul makes it clear in Colossians that Christ alone is the source of our spiritual life, the head of the body of believers. He is Lord of both the physical and spiritual worlds. The path to deeper spiritual life is not through religious duties, special knowledge, or secrets; it is only through a clear connection with the Lord Jesus Christ. We must never let anything come between us and our Savior.

The First Letter of Paul to the THESSALONIANS

VITAL STATISTICS

PURPOSE:
To strengthen the Thessalonian Christians in their faith and give them the assurance of Christ's return

AUTHOR:
Paul

TO WHOM WRITTEN:
The church at Thessalonica and all believers everywhere

DATE WRITTEN:
About A.D. 51 from Corinth; one of Paul's earliest letters

SETTING:
The church at Thessalonica was very young, having been established only two or three years before this letter was written. The Thessalonian Christians needed to mature in their faith. In addition, there was a misunderstanding concerning Christ's second coming—some thought Christ would return immediately and were confused when their loved ones died, because they expected him to return beforehand. Also, believers were being persecuted.

KEY VERSE:
"For since we believe that Jesus died and rose again, even so, through Jesus, God will bring with him those who have died" (4.14).

KEY PEOPLE:
Paul, Timothy, Silas

KEY PLACE:
Thessalonica

SPECIAL FEATURES:
Paul received from Timothy a favorable report about the Thessalonians. However, he wrote this letter to correct their misconceptions about the resurrection and the second coming of Christ.

SLOWLY they walk, one by one, scattering the leaves and trampling the grass under measured and heavy steps. The minister's words still echoing in their minds, they hear workmen moving toward the terrible place, preparing to cover the casket of their loved one. Death, the enemy, has torn the bonded relationships of family and friends, leaving only memories and tears and loneliness.

But like a golden shaft of sun piercing the winter sky, a singular truth shatters the oppressive gloom—death is not the end! Christ is the victor over death, and there is hope of the resurrection through him.

As with every member of the human family, first-century Christians came face to face with their mortality. Many of them met early deaths at the hands of those who hated Christ and all allied with him. Whether at the hands of zealous Jews (like Paul before his conversion), angry Greeks, or ruthless Roman authorities, persecution included stonings, beatings, crucifixions, torture, and death. To be a follower of Christ meant to give up everything.

Paul established the church in Thessalonica during his second missionary journey (in about A.D. 51). He wrote this letter a short time later to encourage the young believers there. He wanted to assure them of his love, to praise them for their faithfulness during persecution, and to remind them of their hope—the sure return of their Lord and Savior.

Paul begins this letter with a note of affirmation, thanking God for the strong faith and good reputation of the Thessalonians (1.1–10). Then Paul reviews their relationship—how he and his companions brought the gospel to them (2.1–12), how they accepted the message (2.13–16), and how he longed to be with them again (2.17–20). Because of his concern, Paul sent Timothy to encourage them in their faith (3.1–13).

Paul then presents the core of his message—exhortation and comfort. He challenges them to please God in their daily living by avoiding all sexual sin (4.1–8), loving one another (4.9, 10), and living as good citizens in a sinful world (4.11, 12).

Paul comforts the Thessalonians by reminding them of the hope of the resurrection (4.13–18). Then he warns them to be prepared at all times, for Jesus Christ could return at any moment. When Christ returns, those Christians who are alive and those who have died will be raised to new life (5.1–11).

Paul then gives the Thessalonians a handful of reminders on how to prepare themselves for the Second Coming—warn the lazy (5.14), comfort the frightened (5.14), care for the weak (5.14), be patient with everyone (5.14), do good to everyone (5.15), always be joyful (5.16), pray continually (5.17), be thankful (5.18), test everything that is taught (5.20, 21), and stay away from evil (5.22). Paul concludes his letter with two benedictions and a request for prayer.

As you read this letter, listen carefully to Paul's practical advice for Christian living. And when burdened by grief and overwhelmed by sorrow, take hope in the reality of Christ's return, the resurrection, and eternal life!

THE BLUEPRINT

1. Faithfulness to the Lord (1.1—3.13) 2. Watchfulness for the Lord (4.1—5.28)	Paul and his companions were faithful to bring the gospel to the Thessalonians in the midst of persecution. The Thessalonians had only recently become Christians and yet remained faithful to the Lord, despite the fact that the apostles were not with them. Others have been faithful in bringing God's Word to us. We must remain faithful and live with the expectation that Christ will return at any time.

MEGATHEMES

THEME	EXPLANATION	IMPORTANCE
Persecution	Paul and the new Christians at Thessalonica experienced persecution because of their faith in Christ. We can expect trials and troubles as well. We need to stand firm in our faith in the midst of trials, being strengthened by the Holy Spirit.	The Holy Spirit helps us to remain strong in faith, able to show genuine love to others and maintain our moral character even when we are being persecuted, slandered, or oppressed.
Paul's ministry	Paul expressed his concern for this church even while he was being slandered. Paul's commitment to share the gospel in spite of difficult circumstances is a model we should follow.	Paul not only delivered his message, but gave of himself. In our ministries, we must become like Paul—faithful and bold, yet sensitive and self-sacrificing.
Hope	One day all believers, both those who are alive and those who have died, will be united with Christ. To those Christians who die before Christ's return, there is hope—the hope of the resurrection of the body.	If we believe in Christ, we will live with him forever. All those who belong to Jesus Christ—from throughout history—will be present with him at his second coming. We can be confident that we will be with loved ones who have trusted in Christ.
Being prepared	No one knows the time of Christ's return. We are to live moral and holy lives, ever watchful for his coming. Believers must not neglect daily responsibilities, but always work and live as unto the Lord.	The gospel is not only what we believe, but also how we must live. The Holy Spirit leads us in faithfulness, so we can avoid lust and fraud. Live as though you expect Christ's return at any time. Don't be caught unprepared.

1. Faithfulness to the Lord

1 Paul, Silvanus, and Timothy,
To the church of the Thessalonians in God the Father and the Lord Jesus
Christ:
Grace to you and peace.

Paul commends the faith of the Thessalonian believers

2 We always give thanks to God for all of you and mention you in our prayers,
constantly 3 remembering before our God and Father your work of faith and labor
of love and steadfastness of hope in our Lord Jesus Christ. 4 For we know, brothers
and sisters[a] beloved by God, that he has chosen you, 5 because our message of the
gospel came to you not in word only, but also in power and in the Holy Spirit and
with full conviction; just as you know what kind of persons we proved to be among
you for your sake. 6 And you became imitators of us and of the Lord, for in spite of
persecution you received the word with joy inspired by the Holy Spirit, 7 so that you
became an example to all the believers in Macedonia and in Achaia. 8 For the word
of the Lord has sounded forth from you not only in Macedonia and Achaia, but in
every place your faith in God has become known, so that we have no need to speak
about it. 9 For the people of those regions[b] report about us what kind of welcome
we had among you, and how you turned to God from idols, to serve a living and
true God, 10 and to wait for his Son from heaven, whom he raised from the
dead—Jesus, who rescues us from the wrath that is coming.

1.1 Rom 1.7; 2 Thess 1.1; 1 Pet 5.12
1.2 2 Thess 1.3
1.3 Heb 6.10; Jas 2.17
1.4 Col 3.12; 2 Thess 2.13; 2 Pet 1.10
1.5 1 Cor 2.4; 2 Cor 6.6; 2 Thess 3.7
1.6 Acts 17.1-6; 1 Cor 4.16
1.8 Rom 1.8; 10.18; 2 Thess 3.1
1.10 Heb 9.28

a Gk *brothers* b Gk *For they*

1.1 Paul and his companions probably arrived in Thessalonica in the early summer of A.D. 50. They planted the first Christian church in that city, but had to leave in a hurry because their lives were threatened (Acts 17.1–10). At the first opportunity, probably when he stopped at Corinth, Paul sent Timothy back to Thessalonica to see how the new believers were doing. Timothy returned to Paul with good news: the Christians in Thessalonica were remaining firm in the faith and were unified. But the Thessalonians did have some questions about their new faith. Paul had not had time to answer all their questions during his brief visit, and in the meantime, other questions had arisen. So Paul wrote this letter to answer their questions and to commend them on their faithfulness to Christ.

1.1 For more information on Paul, see his Profile in Acts 10. Timothy's Profile is in 1 Timothy. Silas (Silvanus) accompanied Paul on his second missionary journey (Acts 15.36–17.15). He helped Paul establish the church in Thessalonica (Acts 17.1–9). He is also mentioned in 2 Corinthians 1.19, 2 Thessalonians 1.1, and in 1 Peter 5.12. His Profile is found in Acts 16.

1.1 Thessalonica was the capital and largest city (about 200,000 population) of the Roman province of Macedonia. The most important Roman highway (the Egnatian Way)—extending from Rome all the way to the Orient—went through Thessalonica. This highway, along with the city's thriving seaport, made Thessalonica one of the wealthiest and most flourishing trade centers in the Roman Empire. Recognized as a free city, Thessalonica was allowed self-rule and was exempted from most of the restrictions placed by Rome on other cities in the empire. However, with its international flavor came many pagan religions and cultural influences that challenged the faith of the young Christians there.

1.3 The Thessalonians stood firm when they were persecuted (1.6; 3.1–4, 7, 8). Paul commends these young Christians for their strong faith, loving deeds, and deep commitment to Christ. These characteristics are the marks of effective Christians in any age.

1.5 The gospel came "in power"; it had a powerful effect on the Thessalonians. Whenever the Bible is heard and obeyed, lives are changed! Christianity is more than a collection of interesting facts; it is the power of God to everyone who believes. What has God's power done in your life since you first believed?

1.5 The Holy Spirit changes people when they believe the good news. When we tell others about Christ, we must depend on the Holy Spirit to open their eyes and convince them that they need salvation. His power changes them—not our cleverness or persuasion. Without the work of the Holy Spirit, our words are meaningless. The Holy Spirit not only convicts people of sin but also assures them of the truth of the gospel. (For more information on the Holy Spirit, see John 14.23–26; 15.26, 27; and the notes on John 3.6 and Acts 1.5.)

1.5 Paul says, "You know what kind of persons we proved to be." The Thessalonians could see that what Paul, Silas, and Timothy were preaching was true, because they lived it. Does your life confirm or contradict what you say you believe?

1.6 The message of salvation, though received with great joy, brought the Thessalonians sorrow because it led to persecution from both Jews and Gentiles (3.2–4; Acts 17.5). Having believed the gospel message and accepted new life in Christ, apparently many Thessalonians believed they would never die. Then, when believers began to die under persecution, they started to question their faith. Many of Paul's comments throughout this letter are addressed to these people as he explains what happens when believers die (see 4.13ff).

1.9, 10 All of us should respond to the good news as the Thessalonians did: *turn* from sin, *serve* God, and *wait* for Jesus' return. We should turn from sin, because Christ is coming to judge the earth; we should be fervent in our service, because we have little time before he returns. We should be prepared for Jesus to return because we don't know when he will come.

1.10 Paul emphasizes Christ's second coming throughout this book. Because the Thessalonian church is being persecuted, Paul encourages them to look forward to the deliverance Christ would bring. A believer's hope is in the return of Jesus, our great God and Savior (Titus 2.13). Our perspective on life remains incomplete without this hope. Just as surely as Christ was raised from the dead and ascended into heaven, he will return (Acts 1.11).

Paul reviews his relationship with the Thessalonians

2 You yourselves know, brothers and sisters,[c] that our coming to you was not in
vain, 2but though we had already suffered and been shamefully mistreated at
Philippi, as you know, we had courage in our God to declare to you the gospel of
God in spite of great opposition. 3For our appeal does not spring from deceit or
impure motives or trickery, 4but just as we have been approved by God to be entrusted with the message of the gospel, even so we speak, not to please mortals, but
to please God who tests our hearts. 5As you know and as God is our witness, we
never came with words of flattery or with a pretext for greed; 6nor did we seek
praise from mortals, whether from you or from others, 7though we might have

2.2 Acts 16.22; 17.2 Phil 1.30
2.3 2 Cor 4.2 2 Pet 1.16
2.4 Prov 17.3 1 Cor 7.25 Gal 1.10 1 Tim 1.11

[c] Gk *brothers*

LOCATION OF THESSALONICA
Paul visited Thessalonica on his second and third missionary journeys. It was a seaport and trade center located on the Egnatian Way, a busy international highway. Paul probably wrote his two letters to the Thessalonians from Corinth.

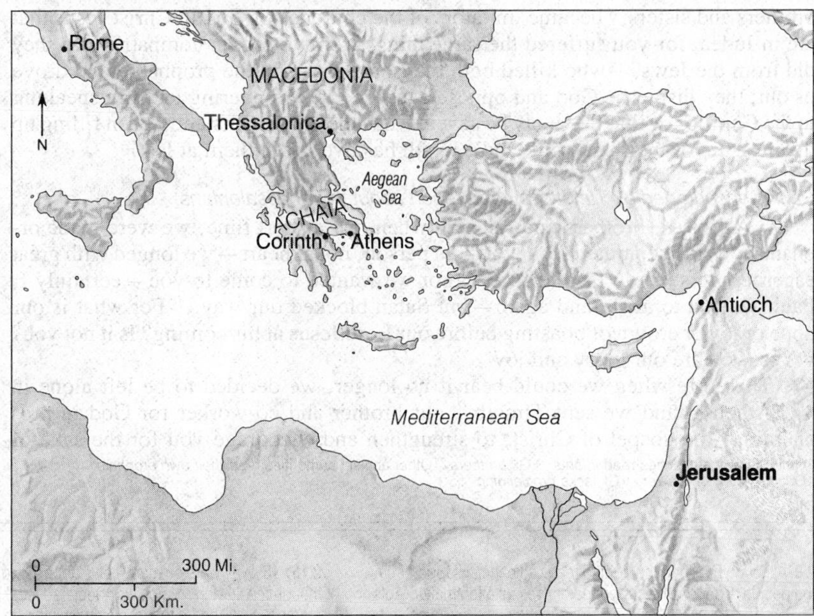

2.1 "Our coming to you" refers to Paul's first visit to Thessalonica (see Acts 17.1–9).

2.2 The Thessalonians knew that Paul had been imprisoned in Philippi just prior to coming to Thessalonica (see Acts 16.11–17.1). Fear of imprisonment did not keep Paul from preaching the good news. If God wants us to do something, he will give us the strength and courage to do it despite the obstacles that may come our way.

2.3 This pointed statement may be a response to accusations from the Jewish leaders who had stirred up the crowds (Acts 17.5). Paul did not seek money, fame, or popularity by sharing the gospel. He demonstrates the sincerity of his motives by showing that he and Silas had suffered for sharing the gospel in Philippi. People become involved in ministry for a variety of reasons, not all of them good or pure. When their bad motives are exposed, all of Christ's work suffers. When you get involved in ministry, do so out of love for Christ and others.

2.4–8 In trying to persuade people, we may be tempted to alter our position just enough to make our message more palatable, or to use flattery or praise. Paul never changed his *message* to make it more acceptable, but he did tailor his *methods* to each audience. Although our presentation must be altered to be appropriate to the situation, the truth of the gospel must never be compromised.

2.5 It's disgusting to hear someone "butter up" someone else. Flattery is phony and a false cover-up for a person's real intentions. Christians should not be flatterers. Those who proclaim God's truth have a special responsibility to be honest. Are you always honest and straightforward in your words and actions? Or do you tell people what they want to hear in order to get what you want or to get ahead?

2.6–8 When Paul was with the Thessalonians, he didn't flatter them, didn't take their money, didn't seek their praise, and wasn't a burden to them. He and Silas completely focused their efforts on presenting God's message of salvation to the Thessalonians. This was important! The Thessalonian believers had their lives changed by God, not Paul; it was Christ's message they believed, not Paul's. When we witness for Christ, our focus should not be on the impression we make. As true ministers of Christ, we should point to him, not to ourselves.

2.7 Gentleness is often overlooked as a personal trait in our society. Power and assertiveness gain more respect, even though none of us likes to be bullied. Gentleness is love in action—being considerate, meeting the needs of others, allowing time for the other person to talk, and being willing to learn. It is an essential trait for both men and women. Maintain a gentle attitude in your relationships with others.

made demands as apostles of Christ. But we were gentle[d] among you, like a nurse
tenderly caring for her own children. 8 So deeply do we care for you that we are
determined to share with you not only the gospel of God but also our own selves,
because you have become very dear to us.
9 You remember our labor and toil, brothers and sisters;[e] we worked night and
day, so that we might not burden any of you while we proclaimed to you the gospel
of God. 10 You are witnesses, and God also, how pure, upright, and blameless our
conduct was toward you believers. 11 As you know, we dealt with each one of you
like a father with his children, 12 urging and encouraging you and pleading that you
lead a life worthy of God, who calls you into his own kingdom and glory.
13 We also constantly give thanks to God for this, that when you received the
word of God that you heard from us, you accepted it not as a human word but as
what it really is, God's word, which is also at work in you believers. 14 For you,
brothers and sisters,[e] became imitators of the churches of God in Christ Jesus that
are in Judea, for you suffered the same things from your own compatriots as they
did from the Jews, 15 who killed both the Lord Jesus and the prophets,[f] and drove
us out; they displease God and oppose everyone 16 by hindering us from speaking
to the Gentiles so that they may be saved. Thus they have constantly been filling up
the measure of their sins; but God's wrath has overtaken them at last.[g]

Paul is encouraged by Timothy's good report about the Thessalonians

17 As for us, brothers and sisters,[e] when, for a short time, we were made orphans by being separated from you—in person, not in heart—we longed with great
eagerness to see you face to face. 18 For we wanted to come to you—certainly I,
Paul, wanted to again and again—but Satan blocked our way. 19 For what is our
hope or joy or crown of boasting before our Lord Jesus at his coming? Is it not you?
20 Yes, you are our glory and joy!

3 Therefore when we could bear it no longer, we decided to be left alone in
Athens; 2 and we sent Timothy, our brother and co-worker for God in proclaiming[h] the gospel of Christ, to strengthen and encourage you for the sake of

2.8 Rom 1.11; 15.29 2 Cor 12.15
2.9 Acts 18.3 2 Cor 11.9 2 Thess 3.8
2.10 1 Thess 1.5
2.11 1 Cor 4.14
2.12 Eph 4.1 Col 1.10 1 Pet 1.15
2.13 Heb 4.2,12
2.14 Acts 17.5 1 Thess 1.6
2.15 Mt 5.12 Lk 24.20 Acts 7.52
2.16 Acts 9.23; 13.50 14.19; 17.5
2.17 1 Thess 3.10
2.18 Rom 1.13; 15.22
2.19 1 Thess 3.13 Rev 1.7; 22.12
2.20 2 Cor 1.14
3.1 Acts 17.15
3.2 Rom 16.21

[d] Other ancient authorities read *infants* [e] Gk *brothers* [f] Other ancient authorities read *their own prophets*
[g] Or *completely* or *forever* [h] Gk lacks *proclaiming*

2.9 Although Paul had the right to receive financial support from the people he taught, he supported himself as a tentmaker (Acts 18.3) so that he wouldn't be a burden to the new Thessalonian believers.

2.11 No loving father would neglect the safety of his children, allowing them to walk into circumstances that might be harmful or fatal. In the same way, we must take new believers under our wing until they are mature enough to stand firm in their faith. We must help new Christians become strong enough to influence others for the gospel.

2.11, 12 By his words and example, Paul encouraged the Thessalonians to live in such a way that would be worthy of God. Is there anything about your daily life that would embarrass God? What do people think of God from watching you?

2.13 In the New Testament, *word of God* usually refers to the preaching of the gospel, the Old Testament, or Jesus Christ himself. Today we often apply it only to the Bible. Remember that Jesus Christ himself is the Word (John 1.1).

2.14 Just as the Jewish Christians in Jerusalem were persecuted by their own people, so the Gentile Christians in Thessalonica were persecuted by their fellow Gentiles. Persecution is discouraging, especially when it comes from your own people. When you take a stand for Christ, you may face opposition, disapproval, and ridicule from your neighbors, friends, and even family members.

2.14 When Paul refers to the Jews, he is talking about certain Jews who opposed his preaching of the gospel. He does not mean all Jews. Many of Paul's converts were Jewish. Paul himself was a Jew (2 Corinthians 11.22).

2.15, 16 Why were so many Jews opposed to Christianity? (1) Although the Jewish religion was declared legal by the Roman government, it still had a tenuous relationship with the government. At this time, Christianity was viewed as a sect of Judaism. The Jews were afraid that reprisals leveled against the Christians might be stretched to include them. (2) The Jewish leaders thought Jesus was a false prophet and they didn't want his teachings to spread. (3) They feared that if many Jews were drawn away, their own political position might be weakened. (4) They were proud of their special status as "God's chosen people," and they resented the fact that Gentiles were full members within the Christian church.

2.18 Satan is real. He is called "the god of this world" (2 Corinthians 4.4) and "the ruler of the power of the air" (Ephesians 2.2). We don't know exactly what hindered Paul from returning to Thessalonica—opposition, illness, travel complications, or a direct attack by Satan—but Satan worked in some way to keep him away. Many of the difficulties that prevent us from accomplishing God's work can be attributed to Satan (see Ephesians 6.12).

2.20 The ultimate reward for Paul's ministry was not money, prestige, or fame, but new believers whose lives had been changed by God through the preaching of the gospel. No matter what ministry God has given to you, your highest reward and greatest joy should be the "trophies of faith"—those who come to believe in Christ and are growing in him.

3.1–3 Some think that troubles are always caused by sin or a lack of faith. Trials may be a part of God's plan for believers. Experiencing problems and persecutions can build character (James 1.2–4), patience (Romans 5.3–5), and sensitivity toward others

your faith, 3 so that no one would be shaken by these persecutions. Indeed, you
yourselves know that this is what we are destined for. 4 In fact, when we were with
you, we told you beforehand that we were to suffer persecution; so it turned out, as
you know. 5 For this reason, when I could bear it no longer, I sent to find out about
your faith; I was afraid that somehow the tempter had tempted you and that our
labor had been in vain.
6 But Timothy has just now come to us from you, and has brought us the good
news of your faith and love. He has told us also that you always remember us
kindly and long to see us—just as we long to see you. 7 For this reason, brothers
and sisters,[i] during all our distress and persecution we have been encouraged
about you through your faith. 8 For we now live, if you continue to stand firm in the
Lord. 9 How can we thank God enough for you in return for all the joy that we feel
before our God because of you? 10 Night and day we pray most earnestly that we
may see you face to face and restore whatever is lacking in your faith.
11 Now may our God and Father himself and our Lord Jesus direct our way to
you. 12 And may the Lord make you increase and abound in love for one another
and for all, just as we abound in love for you. 13 And may he so strengthen your
hearts in holiness that you may be blameless before our God and Father at the coming of our Lord Jesus with all his saints.

3.4 1 Thess 2.14
3.5 Mt 4.3; 1 Cor 7.5; 2 Cor 11.3
3.6 Phil 1.8
3.8 Phil 4.1
3.10 2 Cor 13.9; 1 Thess 1.2,3; 2 Tim 1.3
3.11 2 Thess 3.5
3.12 Phil 1.9
3.13 Zech 14.5; 1 Cor 1.8; 1 Thess 2.19; 4.17; Jude 14; Rev 22.12

2. Watchfulness for the Lord

Live to please God

4 Finally, brothers and sisters,[i] we ask and urge you in the Lord Jesus that, as
you learned from us how you ought to live and to please God (as, in fact, you
are doing), you should do so more and more. 2 For you know what instructions we
gave you through the Lord Jesus. 3 For this is the will of God, your sanctification:

4.1 Eph 4.1
4.3,4 Heb 13.4; 1 Pet 3.7

[i] Gk *brothers*

who also face trouble (2 Corinthians 1.3–7). Problems are unavoidable for God's people. Your troubles may be a sign of effective Christian living.

3.1–4 Because Paul could not return to Thessalonica (2.18), he sent Timothy as his representative. According to Acts 17.10, Paul left Thessalonica and went to Beroea. When trouble broke out in Beroea, some Christians took Paul to Athens, while Silas and Timothy stayed behind (Acts 17.13–15). Then Paul directed Silas and Timothy to join him in Athens. Later Paul sent Timothy to encourage the Thessalonian Christians to be strong in their faith in the face of persecution and other troubles.

3.4 Some people turn to God with the hope of escaping suffering on earth. But God doesn't promise that. Instead he gives us power to grow through our sufferings. The Christian life involves obedience to Christ despite temptations and hardships.

3.5 Satan (the tempter) is the most powerful of the evil spirits. His power can affect both the spiritual world (Ephesians 2.1–3; 6.10–12) and the physical world (2 Corinthians 12.7–10). Satan even tempted Jesus (Matthew 4.1–11). But Jesus defeated Satan when he died on the cross for our sins and rose again to bring us new life. At the proper time God will overthrow Satan forever (Revelation 20.7–10).

3.7, 8 During persecution or pressure, believers should encourage one another. The lives of those who stand firm in their faith encourage both ministers and teachers (who can see the benefit of their work in those who remain faithful), and also those who are new in their faith.

3.9, 10 It is great joy for a Christian to see another person come to faith in Christ and mature in that faith. Paul experienced this joy countless times. He thanked God for those who had come to know Christ and for their strong faith. He also prayed for their continued growth. If there are new Christians who have brought you joy, thank God for them and support them as they continue to grow in the faith.

3.11 Paul wanted to return to Thessalonica. We have no record that he was able to do so; but when he was traveling through Asia on his third journey, he was joined by Aristarchus and Secundus, who were from Thessalonica (Acts 20.4, 5).

3.11–13 The "coming of our Lord Jesus with all his saints" refers to the second coming of Christ when he will establish his eternal kingdom. At that time, Christ will gather all believers, those who have died and those who are alive, into one united family under his rule. All believers from all times, including these Thessalonians, will be with Christ in his kingdom.

3.12 If we are full of God's love, it will abound and overflow to others. It's not enough merely to be courteous to others; we must actively and persistently show love to them. Our love should be growing continually. If your capacity to love has remained unchanged for some time, ask God to fill you again with his never-ending supply. Then look for opportunities to express his love.

4.1–8 Sexual standards were very low in the Roman Empire, and in many societies today they are not any higher. The temptation to engage in sexual intercourse outside the marriage relationship has always been powerful. Giving in to that temptation can have disastrous results. Sexual sins always hurt someone: families, businesses, churches. Besides the physical consequences, there are also spiritual consequences. For more on why sexual sin is so harmful, see the note on 1 Corinthians 6.18.

4.1–8 Sexual desires and activities must be placed under Christ's control. God created sex for procreation, pleasure, and as an expression of love between a husband and wife. Sexual experience must be limited to the marriage relationship to avoid hurting ourselves, our relationship to God, and our relationships with others.

4.3 *Sanctification* is the process of living the Christian life. The Holy Spirit works in us conforming us into the image of Christ (Romans 8.29).

that you abstain from fornication; 4 that each one of you know how to control your
own body[j] in holiness and honor, 5 not with lustful passion, like the Gentiles who
do not know God; 6 that no one wrong or exploit a brother or sister[k] in this matter,
because the Lord is an avenger in all these things, just as we have already told you
beforehand and solemnly warned you. 7 For God did not call us to impurity but in
holiness. 8 Therefore whoever rejects this rejects not human authority but God, who
also gives his Holy Spirit to you.
9 Now concerning love of the brothers and sisters,[l] you do not need to have
anyone write to you, for you yourselves have been taught by God to love one another; 10 and indeed you do love all the brothers and sisters[l] throughout Macedonia. But we urge you, beloved,[l] to do so more and more, 11 to aspire to live quietly,
to mind your own affairs, and to work with your hands, as we directed you, 12 so
that you may behave properly toward outsiders and be dependent on no one.

Remember the hope of the resurrection

13 But we do not want you to be uninformed, brothers and sisters,[l] about those
who have died,[m] so that you may not grieve as others do who have no hope. 14 For
since we believe that Jesus died and rose again, even so, through Jesus, God will
bring with him those who have died.[m] 15 For this we declare to you by the word of
the Lord, that we who are alive, who are left until the coming of the Lord, will by
no means precede those who have died.[m] 16 For the Lord himself, with a cry of
command, with the archangel's call and with the sound of God's trumpet, will
descend from heaven, and the dead in Christ will rise first. 17 Then we who are
alive, who are left, will be caught up in the clouds together with them to meet the
Lord in the air; and so we will be with the Lord forever. 18 Therefore encourage one
another with these words.

5 Now concerning the times and the seasons, brothers and sisters,[l] you do not
need to have anything written to you. 2 For you yourselves know very well that
the day of the Lord will come like a thief in the night. 3 When they say, "There is

4.6 1 Cor 6.8 Heb 13.4
4.7 Lev 11.44 1 Pet 1.15
4.8 Rom 5.5 1 Jn 3.24
4.9 Jer 31.34 Jn 6.45; 13.34 1 Jn 2.20,27
4.10 1 Thess 3.12
4.11 Eph 4.28 2 Thess 3.11,12
4.13 Lev 19.28 Deut 14.1,2 Eph 2.12
4.14 1 Cor 15.18,52
4.15 1 Cor 15.52
4.16 Mt 24.30 Acts 1.11 1 Cor 15.52 2 Thess 1.7
4.17 Acts 1.9
5.2 2 Pet 3.10
5.3 Isa 26.17

[j] Or *how to take a wife for himself* [k] Gk *brother* [l] Gk *brothers* [m] Gk *fallen asleep*

THE EVENTS OF CHRIST'S RETURN

1. Christ will return visibly with a mighty shout.
2. There will be an unmistakable cry from an angel.
3. There will be a trumpet fanfare such as has never been heard.
4. Believers in Christ who are dead will rise from their graves.
5. Believers who are alive will be lifted into the clouds and meet Christ.

While Christians have often disagreed about what events will lead up to the return of Christ, there has been less disagreement about what will happen once Christ does return.

4.11, 12 There is more to Christian living than simply loving other Christians. We must be responsible in all areas of life. Some of the Thessalonian Christians had adopted a life of idleness, depending on others for handouts. Some Greeks looked down on manual labor. So Paul told them to work hard and live a quiet life. You can hardly be effective when you share your faith with others if they don't respect you. Whatever you do, do it faithfully and be a positive force in society.

4.13ff The Thessalonians wondered why many of their fellow believers had died and what would happen to them when Christ returned. Paul wanted the Thessalonians to understand that death is not the end of the story. When Christ returns, all believers—dead and alive—will be reunited, never to suffer or die again.

4.15 What does Paul mean when he says, "this we declare to you by the word of the Lord"? Either this was something that God revealed directly to Paul, or it was a teaching of Jesus that had been passed along orally by the apostles and other Christians.

4.15–18 Knowing exactly *when* the dead will be raised, in relation to the other events at the Second Coming, is not as important as knowing why Paul wrote these words—to challenge believers to comfort and encourage one another when loved ones die. This passage can be a great comfort when any believer dies. The same love that should unite believers in this life (4.9) will unite believers when Christ returns and reigns for eternity.

4.15–18 Because Jesus Christ came back to life, so will all believers. All Christians, including those living when he returns, will live with Jesus forever. Therefore, we need not despair when loved ones die or world events take a tragic turn. God will turn our tragedies to triumphs, our poverty to riches, our pain to glory, and our defeat to victory. All believers throughout history will stand reunited in God's very presence, safe and secure. As Paul comforted the Thessalonians with the promise of the resurrection, so we should comfort and reassure one another with this great hope.

4.16 An *archangel* is a high or holy angel appointed to a special task. Michael is the only archangel mentioned in the New Testament (see Jude 1.9).

5.1 "The times and the seasons" refers to the knowledge of what will happen in the future, specifically the return of Christ.

5.1–3 Efforts to determine the date of Christ's return are foolish. Don't be misled by anyone who claims to know. We are told here that no one knows and that even believers will be surprised. The Lord will return suddenly and unexpectedly, warns Paul, so be

5.4 Lk 21.34; 1 Jn 2.8
5.5 Jn 12.36; Acts 26.18; Eph 5.8
5.8 Isa 59.17; Rom 8.24; 1 Pet 1.13
5.9 Rom 5.9; 2 Tim 2.19

peace and security," then sudden destruction will come upon them, as labor pains
come upon a pregnant woman, and there will be no escape! 4 But you, beloved,[n]
are not in darkness, for that day to surprise you like a thief; 5 for you are all children
of light and children of the day; we are not of the night or of darkness. 6 So then let
us not fall asleep as others do, but let us keep awake and be sober; 7 for those who
sleep sleep at night, and those who are drunk get drunk at night. 8 But since we
belong to the day, let us be sober, and put on the breastplate of faith and love, and
for a helmet the hope of salvation. 9 For God has destined us not for wrath but for
obtaining salvation through our Lord Jesus Christ, 10 who died for us, so that
whether we are awake or asleep we may live with him. 11 Therefore encourage one
another and build up each other, as indeed you are doing.

n Gk *brothers*

CHECKLIST FOR ENCOURAGERS
The command to "encourage others" is found throughout the Bible. In 5.11–23, Paul gives many specific examples of how we can encourage others.

Reference	*Example*	*Suggested application*
5.11	Build each other up.	Point out to someone a quality you appreciate in him or her.
5.12	Give honor to leaders.	Look for ways to cooperate.
5.13	Think highly of leaders.	Withhold your next critical comment about those in positions of responsibility.
5.13	Give wholehearted love.	Say "thank you" to your leaders for their efforts.
5.13	Avoid quarreling.	Search for ways to get along with others.
5.14	Warn the lazy.	Challenge someone to join you in a project.
5.14	Comfort the frightened.	Encourage those who are frightened by reminding them of God's promises.
5.14	Tenderly care for the weak.	Support those who are weak by loving them and praying for them.
5.14	Practice patience.	Think of a situation that tries your patience and plan ahead of time how you can stay calm.
5.15	Resist revenge.	Instead of planning to get even with those who mistreat you, do good to them.
5.16	Rejoice.	Remember that even in the midst of turmoil, God is in control.
5.17	Pray continuously.	God is always with you—talk to him.
5.18	Be thankful.	Make a list of all the gifts God has given you, giving thanks to God for each one.
5.19	Do not smother the Holy Spirit.	Cooperate with the Spirit the next time he prompts you to participate in a Christian meeting.
5.20	Do not scoff at those who prophesy.	Receive God's Word from those who speak for him.
5.22	Keep away from evil.	Avoid situations where you will be drawn into temptation.
5.23	Count on God's constant help.	Realize that the Christian life is to be lived not in our own strength, but through God's power.

ready! Because no one knows when Jesus will come back to earth, we should be ready at all times. Suppose he were to return today. How would he find you living? Are you ready to meet him? Live each day prepared to welcome Christ.

5.2 The day of the Lord is a future time when God will intervene directly and dramatically in world affairs. Predicted and discussed often in the Old Testament (Isaiah 13.6–12; Joel 2.28–32; Zephaniah 1.14–18), the day of the Lord will include both punishment and blessing. Christ will judge sin and set up his eternal kingdom.

5.8 For more about the Christian's armor, see Ephesians 6.13–17.

5.9–11 As you near the end of a long race, your legs ache, your throat burns, and your whole body cries out for you to stop. This is when friends and fans are most valuable. Their encouragement helps you push through the pain to the finish. In the same way, Christians are to encourage one another. A word of encouragement offered at the right moment can be the difference between finishing well and collapsing along the way. Look around you. Be sensitive to others' need for encouragement, and offer supportive words or actions.

Paul's final instructions

12 But we appeal to you, brothers and sisters,[o] to respect those who labor
among you, and have charge of you in the Lord and admonish you; 13 esteem them
very highly in love because of their work. Be at peace among yourselves. 14 And we
urge you, beloved[o] to admonish the idlers, encourage the faint hearted, help the
weak, be patient with all of them. 15 See that none of you repays evil for evil, but
always seek to do good to one another and to all. 16 Rejoice always, 17 pray without
ceasing, 18 give thanks in all circumstances; for this is the will of God in Christ
Jesus for you. 19 Do not quench the Spirit. 20 Do not despise the words of prophets,[p]
21 but test everything; hold fast to what is good; 22 abstain from every form of evil.
23 May the God of peace himself sanctify you entirely; and may your spirit and
soul and body be kept sound[q] and blameless at the coming of our Lord Jesus
Christ. 24 The one who calls you is faithful, and he will do this.
25 Beloved,[r] pray for us.
26 Greet all the brothers and sisters[o] with a holy kiss. 27 I solemnly command
you by the Lord that this letter be read to all of them.[s]
28 The grace of our Lord Jesus Christ be with you.[t]

[o] Gk *brothers* [p] Gk *despise prophecies* [q] Or *complete* [r] Gk *Brothers* [s] Gk *to all the brothers* [t] Other ancient authorities add *Amen*

5.14 2 Thess 3.6
5.15 Lev 19.18; Rom 12.17; Gal 6.10
5.16 Phil 4.4
5.17 Eph 6.18
5.19 Eph 4.30; 2 Tim 1.6
5.20 1 Cor 14.1
5.21 1 Jn 4.1
5.23 2 Pet 3.14
5.24 1 Cor 1.9
5.27 Col 4.16

5.12 "Those who labor among you, and have charge of you in the Lord" refers to elders and deacons in the church.

5.12, 13 How can you honor your pastor and other church leaders? Express your appreciation, tell them how you have been helped by their leadership and teaching, and thank them for their ministry in your life. If you say nothing, how will they know where you stand? Remember, they need and deserve your support and love.

5.14 Don't lie down with the lazy; warn them. Don't yell at the frightened or weak; encourage and help them. At times it's difficult to distinguish between laziness and fear. Two people may be doing nothing—one because he is lazy and the other out of fear of doing something wrong. The key to ministry is sensitivity: sensing the condition of each person and offering the appropriate remedy for each situation. You can't effectively help until you know the problem. You can't apply the medicine until you know where the wound is.

5.16–18 Our joy, prayers, and thankfulness to God should not fluctuate with our circumstances or feelings. Obeying these three commands—rejoice, keep praying, and give thanks—often goes against our natural inclinations. When we make a conscious decision to do what God says, however, we will begin to see people in a new perspective. When we do God's will, we will find it easier to be joyful and thankful.

5.17 We cannot spend all our time on our knees, but it is possible to have a prayerful attitude at all times. This attitude is built upon acknowledging our dependence on God, realizing his presence within us, and determining to obey him fully. We then find it natural to pray frequent, spontaneous, short prayers. A prayerful attitude is not a substitute for regular times of prayer, but should be an outgrowth of those times.

5.18 Paul was not teaching that we should thank God *for* everything that happens to us, but *in* everything. Evil does not come from God, so we should not thank him for it. But when evil strikes, we can still be thankful for God's presence and for the good he will accomplish through the distress.

5.19 By warning us not to quench the Spirit, Paul means we should not ignore or toss aside the gifts the Holy Spirit gives. Here, he mentions prophecy (5.20); in 1 Corinthians 14.39, he mentions tongues. Sometimes spiritual gifts are controversial and cause division in a church. Rather than trying to solve the problems, some Christians prefer to smother the gifts. This impoverishes the church. We should not stifle the Holy Spirit's work in anyone's life but encourage the full expression of these gifts to benefit the whole body of Christ.

5.20, 21 We shouldn't make fun of those who don't agree with what we believe, but we should always check their words against the Bible. We are on dangerous ground if we scoff at a person who speaks the truth. Instead we should carefully check out what people say, accepting what is true and rejecting what is false.

5.22–24 As Christians, we cannot avoid all evil because we live in a sinful world. We can, however, make sure that we don't give evil a foothold by avoiding tempting situations and concentrating on obeying God.

5.23 The spirit, soul, and body are not distinct parts of a person. This expression is Paul's way of saying that God must be involved in *every* aspect of our lives. It is wrong to think we can separate our spiritual lives from everything else, obeying God only in some ethereal sense or living for him only one day each week. Christ must control *all* of us, not just a "religious" part.

5.27 For every Christian to hear this letter, it had to be read in a public meeting—there were not enough copies to circulate. Paul wanted to make sure everyone had the opportunity to hear his message because he was answering important questions and offering needed encouragement.

5.28 The Thessalonian church was young, and they needed help and encouragement. Both the persecution they faced and the temptations of their pagan culture were potential problems for these new Christians. Paul wrote, therefore, to strengthen their faith and bolster their resistance to persecution and temptation. We too have a responsibility to help new believers, to make sure they continue in their faith and don't become sidetracked by wrong beliefs or practices. First Thessalonians can better equip us to help our brothers and sisters in Christ.

The Second Letter of Paul to the THESSALONIANS

"BUT I thought he said . . . ," "I'm sure he meant . . . ," "It is clear to me that we should . . . ," "I disagree. I think we must . . ."

Effective communication is difficult; often the message sent is *not* the message received in the home, marketplace, neighborhood, or church. Even when clearly stated or written, words can be misinterpreted and misunderstood, especially when filtered through the sieve of prejudices and preconceptions.

Paul faced this problem with the Thessalonians. He had written to help them grow in the faith, comforting and encouraging them by affirming the reality of Christ's return. Just a few months later, however, word came from Thessalonica that some had misunderstood his teaching about the Second Coming. His announcement that Christ could come at any moment had caused some to stop working and just wait, rationalizing their laziness by pointing to Paul's teaching. Adding fuel to this fire was the continued persecution of the church. Many felt that indeed this must be the "day of the Lord."

Responding quickly, Paul sent his second epistle to this young church. In it he gave further instruction concerning the Second Coming and the day of the Lord (2.1, 2). Second Thessalonians, therefore, continues the subject of 1 Thessalonians and is a call to continued courage and consistent conduct.

The letter begins with Paul's trademark—a personal greeting and a statement of thanksgiving for their faith (1.1–3). He mentions their patience in spite of their crushing troubles and hardships (1.4) and uses this to broach the subject of Christ's return. At that time, Christ will vindicate the righteous who endure and will punish the wicked (1.5–12).

Paul then directly answers the misunderstanding concerning the timing of the events of the end times. He tells them not to listen to rumors and reports that the day of the Lord has already begun (2.1, 2) because a number of events must occur before he returns (2.3–12). Meanwhile, they should stand firm for Christ's truth (2.13–15), receive God's comfort and hope (2.16, 17), pray for strength and that the Lord's message will spread (3.1–5), and warn those who are lazy (3.6–15). Paul ends with personal greetings and a benediction (3.16–18).

Almost 2,000 years later, we stand much closer to the time of Christ's return; but we also would be wrong to see his imminent appearance as an excuse for idle waiting and heavenward gazing. Being prepared for his coming means spreading the gospel, reaching out to those in need, and building the church, his body. As you read 2 Thessalonians, then, see clearly the reality of his return and your responsibility to live for him until that day.

VITAL STATISTICS

PURPOSE:
To clear up the confusion about the second coming of Christ

AUTHOR:
Paul

TO WHOM WRITTEN:
The church at Thessalonica and all believers everywhere

DATE WRITTEN:
About A.D. 51 or 52, a few months after 1 Thessalonians, from Corinth

SETTING:
Many in the church were confused about the timing of Christ's return. Because of mounting persecution, they thought the day of the Lord must be imminent, and they interpreted Paul's first letter to say that the Second Coming would be at any moment. In light of this misunderstanding, many persisted in being lazy and disorderly with the excuse of waiting for Christ's return.

KEY VERSE:
"May the Lord direct your hearts to the love of God and to the steadfastness of Christ" (3.5).

KEY PEOPLE:
Paul, Silas, Timothy

KEY PLACE:
Thessalonica

SPECIAL FEATURES:
This is a follow-up letter to 1 Thessalonians. In this epistle, Paul indicates various events that must precede the second coming of Christ.

THE BLUEPRINT

1. The bright hope of Christ's return (1.1—2.17)
2. Living in the light of Christ's return (3.1–18)

Paul wrote to encourage those who were facing persecution and to correct a misunderstanding about the timing of Christ's return. The teaching about the Lord's return promoted idleness in this young church. The imminent coming of Christ should never make us lazy; we should be even more busy—living purely, using our time well, and working for his kingdom. We must work not only during easy times when it is convenient, but also during difficult times. Christians must patiently wait, watch, and work for Christ's return.

MEGATHEMES

THEME	EXPLANATION	IMPORTANCE
Persecution	Paul encouraged the church to have patience in spite of troubles and hardships. God will bring victory to his faithful followers and judge those who persecute them.	God promises to reward our faith by giving us his power and helping us bear persecution. Suffering for our faith will strengthen us to serve Christ. We must be faithful to him.
Christ's return	Since Paul had said that the Lord would come at any moment, some of the Thessalonian believers had stopped work in order to wait for Christ.	Christ will return and bring total victory to all who trust in him. If we are ready, we need not be concerned about *when* he will return. We should stand firm, keep working, and wait for Christ.
Great rebellion	Before Christ's return, there will be a great rebellion against God led by the man of rebellion (the antichrist). God will remove all the restraints on evil before he brings judgment on the rebels. The antichrist will attempt to deceive many.	We should not be afraid when we see evil increase. God is in control, no matter how evil the world becomes. God guards us during Satan's attacks. We can have victory over evil by remaining faithful to God.
Persistence	Because church members had quit working and become disorderly and disobedient, Paul chastised them for their laziness. He called them to show courage and true Christian conduct.	We must never get so tired of doing right that we quit. We can be persistent by making the most of our time and talent. Our endurance will be rewarded.

1. The bright hope of Christ's return

1 Paul, Silvanus, and Timothy,
To the church of the Thessalonians in God our Father and the Lord Jesus **1.1** 1 Thess 1.1
Christ:
2 Grace to you and peace from God our[a] Father and the Lord Jesus Christ. **1.2** Rom 1.7

[a] Other ancient authorities read *the*

1.1 Paul wrote this letter from Corinth less than a year after he wrote 1 Thessalonians. He and his companions, Timothy and Silas (Silvanus), had visited Thessalonica on Paul's second missionary journey (Acts 17.1–10). They started the first church there, but Paul had to leave suddenly because of persecution. This prompted him to write his first letter (1 Thessalonians), which contains words of comfort and encouragement. Paul then heard how the Thessalonians had responded to this letter. The good news was that they continued to grow in their faith. But the bad news was that false teachings about Christ's return were spreading, leading many to quit their jobs and wait for the end of the world. So Paul wrote to them again. While the purpose of Paul's first letter was to comfort the Thessalonians with the assurance of Christ's second coming, the purpose of his second letter is to correct false teaching about the Second Coming.

1.1 Paul, Silas, and Timothy were together in Corinth (Acts 18.5). Paul writes this letter on behalf of all three of them. He often included Timothy as a co-sender of his letters (see Philippians 1.1; Colossians 1.1; 1 Thessalonians 1.1). For more information about Paul, see his Profile in Acts 10. Timothy's Profile is found in 1 Timothy, and Silas's Profile is in Acts 16.

1.1 Thessalonica was the capital and largest city of the Roman province of Macedonia. The most important Roman highway—extending from Rome to the Orient—went through Thessalonica. This highway, along with the city's thriving seaport, made Thessalonica one of the wealthiest and most flourishing trade centers in the Roman Empire. Recognized as a free city, Thessalonica was allowed self-rule and was exempted from most of the restrictions placed by Rome on other cities. Because of this open climate, however, the city had many pagan religions and cultural influences that challenged the Christians' faith.

Paul encourages those experiencing persecution

1.3 Job 17.9 Ps 84.7
1.5 2 Tim 2.12
1.6 Ex 23.22 Rev 6.10
1.7 Mk 8.38 Rev 14.13
1.8 Ps 79.6 Rom 2.8 Heb 10.27
1.9 Isa 2.19

3 We must always give thanks to God for you, brothers and sisters,[b] as is right,
because your faith is growing abundantly, and the love of everyone of you for one
another is increasing. 4 Therefore we ourselves boast of you among the churches of
God for your steadfastness and faith during all your persecutions and the afflictions
that you are enduring.
5 This is evidence of the righteous judgment of God, and is intended to make
you worthy of the kingdom of God, for which you are also suffering. 6 For it is
indeed just of God to repay with affliction those who afflict you, 7 and to give relief
to the afflicted as well as to us, when the Lord Jesus is revealed from heaven with
his mighty angels 8 in flaming fire, inflicting vengeance on those who do not know
God and on those who do not obey the gospel of our Lord Jesus. 9 These will suffer
the punishment of eternal destruction, separated from the presence of the Lord and

[b] Gk *brothers*

LOCATION OF THESSALONICA
After Paul visited Thessalonica on his second missionary journey, he went on to Beroea, Athens, and Corinth (Acts 17, 18). From Corinth, Paul wrote his two letters to the Thessalonian church.

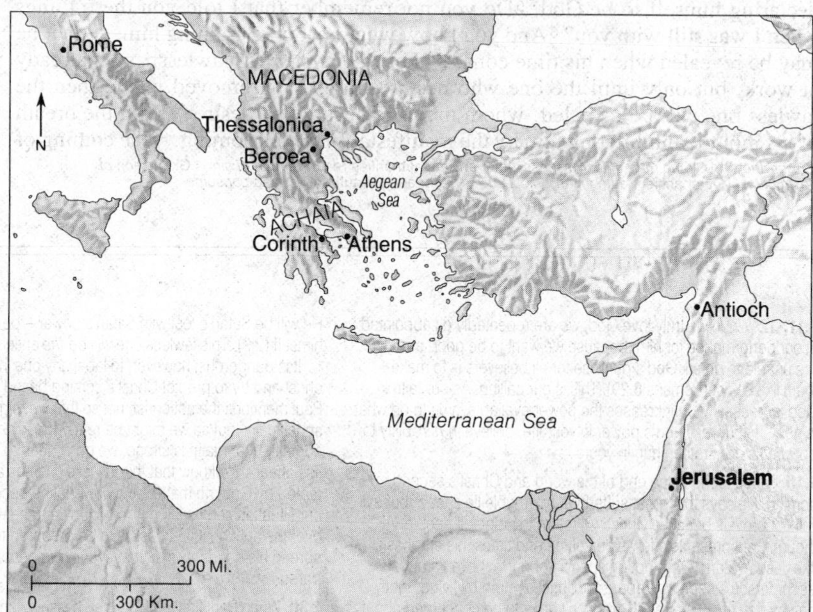

1.3 Regardless of his letters' contents, Paul's style was affirming. He began most of his letters by stating what he most appreciated about his readers and the joy he felt because of their faith in God.

1.4 The keys to surviving suffering are patience (steadfastness) and faith. When we are faced with crushing troubles and hardships we can have faith that God is using them for our good and for his glory. Knowing that God is fair and just will give us patience in our suffering, because we trust that he has not forgotten us. In his timing, he will relieve our suffering and punish those who persecute us. Can you trust God's timing?

1.4–6 Paul was persecuted during his first visit to Thessalonica (Acts 17.5–9). No doubt those who responded to his message and became Christians continued to be persecuted by both Jews and Gentiles. In Paul's first letter to the Thessalonians, he said that Christ's return would bring deliverance from persecution and judgment on the persecutors. But this caused the people to expect Christ's return right away to rescue and vindicate them. Thus Paul points out that while waiting for God's kingdom, believers can learn patience and faith from their suffering.

1.5 As we live for Christ, we will experience troubles and hardships, because we are trying to be God's people in a perverse world. Some say that troubles come from sin or lack of faith, but Paul teaches that they may be a part of God's plan for believers. Our problems help us look upward and forward, not inward (Mark 13.35, 36; Philippians 3.13, 14); they help build strong character (Romans 5.3, 4); and they help us be sensitive to others who also must struggle (2 Corinthians 1.3–5). Your troubles may be a sign of your taking a stand for Christ.

1.5, 6 There are two dimensions of the comfort mentioned by Paul. We can be comforted in knowing that our sufferings strengthen us, making us ready for Christ's kingdom. We can also take comfort in the fact that one day everyone will stand before God; then, wrongs will be righted, judgment will be pronounced, and evil will be terminated.

1.7–9 The "punishment of eternal destruction" that Paul describes is hell – the place of eternal separation from God. In hell, people no longer have any hope for salvation. Those doomed to hell didn't want to know God and refused to accept his offer of salvation. They will be allowed to stay away from him – forever.

from the glory of his might, 10 when he comes to be glorified by his saints and to be
marveled at on that day among all who have believed, because our testimony to you
was believed. 11 To this end we always pray for you, asking that our God will make
you worthy of his call and will fulfill by his power every good resolve and work of
faith, 12 so that the name of our Lord Jesus may be glorified in you, and you in him,
according to the grace of our God and the Lord Jesus Christ.

1.10 Jn 17.10; Eph 3.21
1.11 Eph 4.1; 1 Thess 1.3
1.12 Phil 2.9

Paul predicts the coming of the lawless one

2 As to the coming of our Lord Jesus Christ and our being gathered together to
him, we beg you, brothers and sisters,[c] 2 not to be quickly shaken in mind or
alarmed, either by spirit or by word or by letter, as though from us, to the effect that
the day of the Lord is already here. 3 Let no one deceive you in any way; for that day
will not come unless the rebellion comes first and the lawless one[d] is revealed, the
one destined for destruction.[e] 4 He opposes and exalts himself above every so-
called god or object of worship, so that he takes his seat in the temple of God,
declaring himself to be God. 5 Do you not remember that I told you these things
when I was still with you? 6 And you know what is now restraining him, so that he
may be revealed when his time comes. 7 For the mystery of lawlessness is already
at work, but only until the one who now restrains it is removed. 8 And then the
lawless one will be revealed, whom the Lord Jesus[f] will destroy[g] with the breath
of his mouth, annihilating him by the manifestation of his coming. 9 The coming of

2.1 Mt 24.31
2.2 2 Thess 2.15; 3.17
2.3 1 Tim 4.1
2.4 Isa 14.13; Mt 24.15; 1 Cor 8.5,6
2.7 Gen 6.3; 1 Jn 4.3
2.8 Isa 11.4; Mt 25.31; Rev 19.15

[c] Gk *brothers* [d] Gk *the man of lawlessness*; other ancient authorities read *the man of sin* [e] Gk *the son of destruction* [f] Other ancient authorities lack *Jesus* [g] Other ancient authorities read *consume*

1.11, 12 When we truly love God, we are repeatedly disappointed in our performance for him, because we want to be good and yet are unable to do so. God's purpose for all believers is to make them like Christ (Romans 8.29). This is our calling. As our faith in God increases, God increases the power available in us to do what is right. If you want God's power in your life, believe in *his* ability to do what is right rather than in yours.

2.1ff Paul describes the end of the world and Christ's second coming. He says that great suffering and trouble lie ahead, but evil will not prevail, because Christ will return to judge all people. Although Paul presents a few signs of the end times, his emphasis, like Jesus' (Mark 13), is not on specific or current events but on each person's need to prepare for Christ's return by living rightly day by day. If we are ready, we won't have to be concerned about what or when it will happen. God is in control of all events. (See 1 Thessalonians 4, 5 for Paul's earlier teaching on this subject.)

2.1, 2 In the Bible, the *day of the Lord* is used in two ways: meaning the end times (beginning with Christ's birth and continuing until today), and meaning the final Judgment Day (yet to come). Because some false teachers were saying that Judgment Day had come, many believers were waiting expectantly for their vindication and relief from suffering. But the Judgment Day had not yet come; other events must happen first.

2.1, 2 *Spirit, word,* and *letter* could refer to the fact that false teaching came from: (1) someone claiming to have had a divine revelation; (2) someone passing on a teaching as though it were from Paul; or (3) someone distributing a letter supposedly written by Paul.

2.3 Throughout history there have been antichrists—individuals who epitomized evil (being hostile to everything Christ stands for, see 1 John 2.18; 4.3; 2 John 1.7). Antichrists have lived in every generation and will continue to work their evil. Then, just before Christ's second coming, a "lawless one," completely evil, will arise. He will be Satan's tool with Satan's power—perhaps even Satan himself (2.9). This lawless one will be *the* antichrist.

It is dangerous, however, to label any one individual as the antichrist and try to predict Christ's coming based on that assumption. Paul mentions the antichrist, not so that we might identify him specifically, but so we might be ready for anything that threatens our faith. If our faith is strong, we don't need to be afraid of what lies ahead. We know that this lawless one has already been defeated by God, no matter how powerful he becomes or how terrible our situation seems. God is in control, and he will be victorious over the antichrist. Our task is to be prepared for Christ and to spread his good news so that even more people will also be prepared.

2.3ff When Paul first wrote to the Thessalonians, they were in danger of losing hope in the Second Coming. Then they shifted to the opposite extreme—some of them thought Jesus would be coming any minute. Paul tries to restore the balance by describing certain events that would happen before Christ's return.

2.7 "The mystery of lawlessness is already at work" means that the work this antichrist will do is already going on. *Mystery* means something no one can discover, but that God will reveal. The mystery of iniquity (also translated *lawlessness*) is the hidden, subtle, underlying force from which all sin springs. Civilization still has a veneer of decency through law enforcement, education, science, and reason. Although we are horrified by criminal acts, we have yet to see the real horror of complete lawlessness. This will happen when "the one who now restrains it is removed"—when the one holding back this man of sin steps out of the way, and the forces that are restraining complete lawlessness are removed. Why will God allow this to happen? To show people and nations their own sinfulness, and to show them by bitter experience the true alternative to the Lordship of Christ. People totally without God can act no better than vicious animals. Lawlessness, to a certain extent, is already going on, but the lawless one has not yet arrived.

2.7 Who restrains the lawless one? Three possibilities have been suggested: (1) government and law, which help to curb evil; (2) the ministry and activity of the church and the effects of the gospel; or

2.9 Mt 24.24 Eph 2.2 Rev 13.13 **2.11** Mt 24.5 Rom 1.24,28 **2.12** Rom 1.32; 2.8

the lawless one is apparent in the working of Satan, who uses all power, signs,
lying wonders, 10 and every kind of wicked deception for those who are perishing,
because they refused to love the truth and so be saved. 11 For this reason God sends
them a powerful delusion, leading them to believe what is false, 12 so that all who
have not believed the truth but took pleasure in unrighteousness will be condemned.

Believers should stand firm

2.13 Eph 1.4 1 Pet 1.2 **2.14** Jn 17.22 Rom 8.29,30 1 Thess 2.12 **2.15** 1 Cor 11.2; 16.13 **2.16** Jn 3.16 **2.17** 1 Thess 3.2; 5.11

13 But we must always give thanks to God for you, brothers and sisters[h] beloved by the Lord, because God chose you as the first fruits[i] for salvation through
sanctification by the Spirit and through belief in the truth. 14 For this purpose he
called you through our proclamation of the good news,[j] so that you may obtain the
glory of our Lord Jesus Christ. 15 So then, brothers and sisters,[h] stand firm and
hold fast to the traditions that you were taught by us, either by word of mouth or by
our letter.

16 Now may our Lord Jesus Christ himself and God our Father, who loved us
and through grace gave us eternal comfort and good hope, 17 comfort your hearts
and strengthen them in every good work and word.

2. Living in the light of Christ's return

Paul requests prayer

3.1 1 Thess 1.8; 5.25 **3.2** Rom 15.30,31 **3.3** Jn 17.15 1 Cor 1.9 2 Pet 2.9

3 Finally, brothers and sisters,[h] pray for us, so that the word of the Lord may
spread rapidly and be glorified everywhere, just as it is among you, 2 and that
we may be rescued from wicked and evil people; for not all have faith. 3 But the
Lord is faithful; he will strengthen you and guard you from the evil one.[k] 4 And we
have confidence in the Lord concerning you, that you are doing and will go on
doing the things that we command. 5 May the Lord direct your hearts to the love of
God and to the steadfastness of Christ.

[h] Gk *brothers* [i] Other ancient authorities read *from the beginning* [j] Or *through our gospel* [k] Or *from evil*

---

(3) the Holy Spirit. The Bible is not clear on who this "restrainer" is, only that he will not restrain forever. But we should not fear this time – God is far stronger than the man of sin, and he will save his people.

2.9 This lawless one will use "power, signs, lying wonders" to deceive and draw a following. Miracles from God can help strengthen our faith and lead people to Christ, but all miracles are not necessarily from God. Christ's miracles were significant not just because of their power, but because of their purpose – to help, to heal, and to point us to God. The lawless one will have power to do amazing things, but his power will be from Satan. He will use this power to destroy and to lead people away from God and toward himself. If any so-called religious personality draws attention only to himself, his or her work is not from God.

2.10–12 This lawless one with his power and miracles will deceive those who have refused to believe God's truth. God gives people freedom to turn their backs on him and believe Satan's lies. If they say no to the truth, they will experience the consequences of their sin.

2.13 Paul consistently taught that salvation begins and ends with God. We can do nothing to be saved on our own merit – we must accept God's gift of salvation (see the note on Ephesians 1.4). There is no other way to receive forgiveness from sin. Paul is encouraging the Thessalonian believers by reminding them that they are chosen as the *first fruits* (the first and best of the harvest offered to God). *Sanctification* is the process of Christian growth through which the Holy Spirit makes us like Christ (Romans 8.29).

2.14 God worked through Paul and his companions to tell the good news so that people could share in Christ's glory. It may seem strange that God works through us – fallible, unfaithful, untrustworthy human creatures. But he has given us the fantastic privilege of accomplishing his great mission – telling the world how to find salvation.

2.15 Paul knew that the Thessalonians would face pressure from persecutions, false teachers, worldliness, and apathy to waver from the truth and to leave the faith. So he urged them to "stand firm" and hold on to the truth they had been taught both through his letters and in person. We also may face persecution, false teachings, worldliness, and apathy. We should hold on to the truth of Christ's teachings because our lives depend on it. Never forget the reality of his life and love!

3.1–3 Beneath the surface of the routine of daily life, a fierce struggle among invisible spiritual powers is being waged. Our main defense is prayer that God will protect us from evil and that he will make us strong. (See also comments on Ephesians 6.10–19 concerning our armor for spiritual warfare.) The following guidelines can help you prepare for and survive satanic attacks: (1) take the threat of spiritual attack seriously; (2) pray for strength and help from God; (3) study the Bible to recognize Satan's style and tactics; (4) memorize Scripture so it will be a source of help no matter where you are; (5) associate with those who speak the truth; and (6) practice what you are taught by spiritual leaders.

Paul admonishes the church against laziness

6 Now we command you, beloved,[l] in the name of our Lord Jesus Christ, to
keep away from believers who are[m] living in idleness and not according to the
tradition that they[n] received from us. 7 For you yourselves know how you ought to
imitate us; we were not idle when we were with you, 8 and we did not eat anyone's
bread without paying for it; but with toil and labor we worked night and day, so that
we might not burden any of you. 9 This was not because we do not have that right,
but in order to give you an example to imitate. 10 For even when we were with you,
we gave you this command: Anyone unwilling to work should not eat. 11 For we
hear that some of you are living in idleness, mere busybodies, not doing any work.
12 Now such persons we command and exhort in the Lord Jesus Christ to do their
work quietly and to earn their own living. 13 Brothers and sisters,[o] do not be weary
in doing what is right.

14 Take note of those who do not obey what we say in this letter; have nothing
to do with them, so that they may be ashamed. 15 Do not regard them as enemies,
but warn them as believers.[p]

Paul's final greetings

16 Now may the Lord of peace himself give you peace at all times in all ways.
The Lord be with all of you.

17 I, Paul, write this greeting with my own hand. This is the mark in every
letter of mine; it is the way I write. 18 The grace of our Lord Jesus Christ be with all
of you.[q]

3.6 Rom 16.17; 1 Cor 5.4; 11.2; 1 Thess 5.14
3.8 Acts 18.3; 1 Thess 2.9
3.9 Mt 10.10; 1 Cor 9.4; 1 Tim 5.17; 1 Pet 5.3
3.10 1 Thess 4.11
3.11 1 Tim 5.13
3.12 Rom 12.11; 1 Thess 4.1,11
3.15 Gal 6.1; 1 Thess 5.14
3.16 Rom 15.33
3.17 1 Cor 16.21; Gal 6.11; Col 4.18; Philem 19

[l] Gk *brothers* [m] Gk *from every brother who is* [n] Other ancient authorities read *you* [o] Gk *Brothers* [p] Gk *a brother*
[q] Other ancient authorities add *Amen*

3.6–10 Paul is talking here about the person who is lazy. Paul explains that when he and his companions were in Thessalonica, they worked hard, purchasing what they needed rather than becoming a burden to any of the believers. The rule they followed was, "Anyone unwilling to work should not eat." There's a difference between leisure and laziness. Relaxation and recreation provide a necessary and much needed balance; but when it is time to work, Christians should be responsible. We should make the most of our talent and time, doing all we can to provide for ourselves and our dependents. Rest when you should be resting, and work when you should be working.

3.6–15 Some people in the Thessalonian church were falsely teaching that since Christ would return any day, people should set aside their responsibilities, quit work, do no future planning, and just wait for the Lord. But their lack of activity only led them into sin. They became a burden to the church, which was supporting them; they wasted time that could have been used for helping others; and they became "busybodies" (3.11). They may have thought they were being more spiritual by not working, but Paul tells them to be responsible and get back to work. Being ready for Christ means obeying him in every area of life. Because we know Christ is coming, we must live in such a way that our faith and our daily practice will please him when he arrives.

3.11, 12 A "busybody" is a gossip. A lazy person who doesn't work ends up filling his or her time with less than helpful activities, like gossip. Rumors and hearsay are tantalizing, exciting to hear, and make us feel like insiders. But they tear people down. If you often find your nose in other people's business, you may be underemployed. Look for a task to do for Christ or for your family, and get to work.

3.14, 15 Paul counsels the church to stop supporting financially and associating with those who persist in their laziness. Hunger and loneliness can be very effective means in making the idle person become productive. Paul is not advising coldness or cruelty, but the kind of tough love one would show a brother.

3.18 The book of 2 Thessalonians is especially meaningful for those who are being persecuted or are under pressure for their faith. In chapter 1 we are told what suffering can do for us. In chapter 2 we are assured of final victory. In chapter 3 we are encouraged to continue living responsibly in spite of difficult circumstances. Christ's return is more than a doctrine; it is a promise. It is not just for the future; it has a vital impact on how we live now.

The First Letter of Paul to TIMOTHY

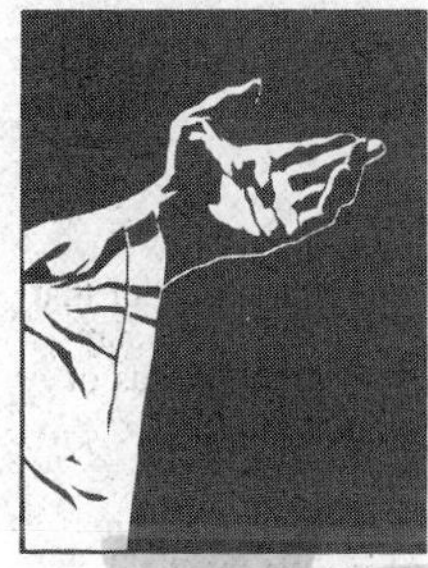

WITHOUT trying, we model our values. Parents in particular demonstrate to their children what they consider important. "Like father, like son" is not just a well-worn cliché; it is a truth often repeated in our homes. And experience proves that children often follow the life-styles of their parents, repeating their successes and mistakes.

Timothy is a prime example of one who was influenced by godly relatives. His mother, Eunice, and grandmother, Lois, were Jewish believers who helped shape his life and spiritual growth (2 Timothy 1.5; 3.15). The first "second generation" Christian mentioned in the New Testament, Timothy became Paul's protegé and pastor of the church at Ephesus. As a young minister, Timothy faced all sorts of pressures, conflicts, and challenges from the church and his surrounding culture. To counsel and encourage Timothy, Paul sent this very personal letter.

Paul wrote 1 Timothy in about A.D. 64, probably just prior to his final Roman imprisonment. Because he had appealed to Caesar, Paul was sent as a prisoner to Rome (see Acts 25—28). Most scholars believe that Paul was released in about A.D. 62 (possibly because the "statute of limitations" had expired), and that during the next few years he was able to travel. During this time, he wrote 1 Timothy and Titus. Soon, however, Emperor Nero began his campaign to eliminate Christianity. It is believed that during this time, Paul was imprisoned again and eventually executed. During this second Roman imprisonment, Paul wrote 2 Timothy. Titus and the two letters to Timothy, the "pastoral epistles," gave guidelines for aspiring church leaders.

Paul's first letter to Timothy affirms their relationship (1.2). Paul begins his fatherly advice, warning Timothy about false teachers (1.3–11) and urging him to cling tightly to his faith in Christ (1.12–20). Next Paul considers public worship, emphasizing the importance of prayer (2.1–7) and order in church meetings (2.8–15). This leads to a discussion of the qualifications of church leaders—pastors (elders) and deacons. Here Paul lists specific criteria for each office (3.1–16).

Paul speaks again about false teachers, telling Timothy how to recognize them and respond to them (4.1–16). Next, he gives practical advice on pastoral care to the young and old (5.1, 2), widows (5.3–16), elders (5.17–25), and slaves (6.1, 2). Paul concludes by exhorting Timothy to guard his motives (6.3–10), to stand firm in his faith (6.11, 12), to live above reproach (6.13–16), and to minister faithfully (6.17–21).

First Timothy holds many lessons. If you are a church leader, take note of Paul's relationship with this young disciple—his careful counsel and guidance. Measure yourself against the qualifications Paul gives for elders and deacons. If you are young in the faith, follow the example of godly Christian leaders, like Timothy, who imitated Paul's life. If you are a parent, remind yourself of the profound effect a Christian home can have on family members—a faithful mother and grandmother led Timothy to Christ, and his ministry helped change the world.

VITAL STATISTICS

PURPOSE:
To give encouragement and instruction to Timothy, a young leader

AUTHOR:
Paul

TO WHOM WRITTEN:
Timothy, young church leaders, and all believers everywhere

DATE WRITTEN:
About A.D. 64, from Rome or Macedonia (possibly Philippi), probably just prior to Paul's final imprisonment in Rome

SETTING:
Timothy was one of Paul's closest companions. Paul had sent Timothy to the church at Ephesus to counter the false teaching that had arisen there (1 Timothy 1.3, 4). Timothy probably served for a time as a leader in the church at Ephesus. Paul hoped to visit Timothy (3.14, 15; 4.13), but in the meantime, he wrote this letter to give Timothy practical advice for the ministry.

KEY VERSE:
"Let no one despise your youth, but set the believers an example in speech and conduct, in love, in faith, in purity" (4.12).

KEY PEOPLE:
Paul, Timothy

KEY PLACE:
Ephesus

SPECIAL FEATURES:
First Timothy is a personal letter and a handbook of church administration and discipline.

THE BLUEPRINT

1. Instructions on right belief (1.1–20)
2. Instructions for the church (2.1—3.16)
3. Instructions for leaders (4.1—6.21)

Paul advised Timothy on such practical topics as qualifications for church leaders, public worship, confronting false teaching, and how to treat various groups of people within the church. Right belief and right behavior are critical for anyone who desires to lead or serve effectively in the church. We should all believe rightly, participate in church actively, and minister to one another lovingly.

MEGATHEMES

THEME	EXPLANATION	IMPORTANCE
Sound doctrine	Paul instructed Timothy to preserve the Christian faith by teaching sound doctrine and modeling right living. Timothy had to oppose false teachers who were leading church members away from belief in salvation by faith in Jesus Christ alone.	We must know the truth in order to defend it. We must cling to the belief that Christ came to save us. We should stay away from those who twist the words of the Bible for their own purposes.
Public worship	Prayer in public worship must be done with a proper attitude toward God and fellow believers.	Christian character must be evident in every aspect of worship. We must rid ourselves of any anger, resentment, or offensive behavior that might disrupt worship or damage church unity.
Church leadership	Paul gives specific instructions concerning the qualifications for church leaders so that the church might honor God and run smoothly.	Church leaders must be wholly committed to Christ. If you are a new or young Christian, don't be anxious to become a leader in the church. Seek to develop your Christian character first. Be sure to seek God, not your own ambition.
Personal discipline	It takes discipline to be a leader in the church. Timothy, like all pastors, had to guard his motives, minister faithfully, and live above reproach. Any pastor must keep morally and spiritually fit.	To stay in good spiritual shape, you must discipline yourself to study God's Word and to obey it. Put your spiritual abilities to work!
Caring church	The church has a responsibility to care for the needs of all its members, especially the sick, the poor, and the widowed. Caring must go beyond good intentions.	Caring for the family of believers demonstrates our Christ-like attitude and exhibits genuine love to nonbelievers.

1. Instructions on right belief

1 Paul, an apostle of Christ Jesus by the command of God our Savior and of Christ Jesus our hope, **1.1** Tit 1.3; 3.4

2 To Timothy, my loyal child in the faith: **1.2** Acts 16.1; 2 Tim 1.2

Grace, mercy, and peace from God the Father and Christ Jesus our Lord.

1.1 This letter was written to Timothy in A.D. 64 or 65, after Paul's first imprisonment in Rome (Acts 28.16–31). Paul was apparently released from prison for several years, and during that time he revisited many churches in Asia and Macedonia. When he and Timothy returned to Ephesus, they found widespread false teaching in the church. Paul had warned the Ephesian elders to be on guard against the false teachers who inevitably would come after he had left (Acts 20.17–31). Paul sent Timothy to lead the Ephesian church while he moved on to Macedonia. From there Paul wrote this letter of encouragement and instruction to help Timothy deal with the difficult situation in the Ephesian church. Later, Paul was arrested again and brought back to a Roman prison.

1.1 Paul calls himself an *apostle*, "one who is sent." Paul was sent by Jesus Christ to give the message of salvation to the Gentiles (Acts 9.1–20). For more information on Paul, see his Profile in Acts 10.

1.1 How was Paul an apostle "by the command of God"? In Acts 13.2, the Holy Spirit, through the prophets, said, "Set apart for me Barnabas and Saul for the work to which I have called them." In Romans 16.25, 26 and Titus 1.3, Paul regards this commission as directly from God.

1.1 In adventure stories, the hero often rescues defenseless victims at the last possible moment. Within this fictional world, the bold adventurer is the only hope for the victims. Within the reality of this life, our only hope is Jesus Christ. Only he can save us. Where have you placed your hope?

Paul warns about false teachers

1.3,4 Acts 19.1,10; 20.1-3; Gal 1.6,7; 1 Tim 4.7; 6.3,4; Tit 3.9
1.5 Rom 13.8; Gal 5.14; 2 Tim 1.5; 2.22; 1 Pet 3.16
1.6 Tit 1.10
1.8 Rom 7.12,16
1.9 Gal 3.19; Rev 21.8
1.11 2 Cor 4.4

3 I urge you, as I did when I was on my way to Macedonia, to remain in Ephesus so that you may instruct certain people not to teach any different doctrine, 4 and
not to occupy themselves with myths and endless genealogies that promote speculations rather than the divine training[a] that is known by faith. 5 But the aim of such
instruction is love that comes from a pure heart, a good conscience, and sincere
faith. 6 Some people have deviated from these and turned to meaningless talk, 7 desiring to be teachers of the law, without understanding either what they are saying
or the things about which they make assertions.
8 Now we know that the law is good, if one uses it legitimately. 9 This means
understanding that the law is laid down not for the innocent but for the lawless and
disobedient, for the godless and sinful, for the unholy and profane, for those who
kill their father or mother, for murderers, 10 fornicators, sodomites, slave traders,
liars, perjurers, and whatever else is contrary to the sound teaching 11 that conforms
to the glorious gospel of the blessed God, which he entrusted to me.

God's mercy on Paul

1.13 Lk 23.34; Acts 8.3; 26.9; 1 Cor 15.9

12 I am grateful to Christ Jesus our Lord, who has strengthened me, because he
judged me faithful and appointed me to his service, 13 even though I was formerly
a blasphemer, a persecutor, and a man of violence. But I received mercy because
I had acted ignorantly in unbelief, 14 and the grace of our Lord overflowed for me

[a] Or *plan*

1.3 Paul first visited Ephesus on his second missionary journey (Acts 18.19–21). Later, on his third missionary journey, he stayed there for almost three years (Acts 19, 20). Ephesus, along with Rome, Corinth, Antioch, and Alexandria, was one of the major cities in the Roman Empire. It was a center for the commerce, politics, and religions of Asia Minor, and the place where the temple dedicated to the goddess Artemis (Diana) was located.

1.3, 4 The church at Ephesus was probably plagued by the same heresy that threatened the church at Colossae, the false doctrine that to be acceptable to God one had to gain certain hidden knowledge and worship angels (Colossians 2.8, 18). Thinking that it would aid in their salvation, some Ephesians constructed genealogies of angels. The false teachers were motivated by their own interests rather than Christ's. They embroiled the church in endless and irrelevant questions and controversies, taking precious time away from the study of the truth. We often enter into worthless and irrelevant discussions today, but such disputes crowd out the life-changing message of Christ. Stay away from religious speculation and pointless theological arguments. They may seem harmless at first, but they have a way of sidetracking us from the central message of the gospel—the person and work of Jesus Christ.

1.3–11 There are many leaders and authorities today who demand allegiance, many of whom would have us turn from Christ to follow them. When they seem knowledgable in their use of the Bible, their influence is dangerously subtle. How can you recognize false teaching? (1) It promotes controversies instead of helping people come to Jesus (1.4). (2) It is often promoted by teachers whose motivation is to make a name for themselves (1.7). (3) It is contrary to the true teaching of the Scriptures (1.6, 7; 4.1–3). To protect yourself from the deception of false teachers, you should learn what the Bible teaches and remain steadfast in your faith in Christ alone.

1.5 The false teachers were motivated by curiosity, power, and prestige. By contrast, genuine Christian teachers are motivated by love that comes from purity, a good conscience, and faith. It may be exciting to impress people with our great knowledge, but position based on falsehood is ultimately worthless. Teachers and leaders who truly follow Christ will find lasting, eternal rewards as they see God's truth spread throughout the world and his love transform people everywhere.

1.6 Arguing about details of the Bible can take us on interesting, but irrelevant, tangents and cause us to miss the intent of God's message. The false teachers at Ephesus constructed vast speculative systems and then argued about the minor details of their wholly imaginary ideas. We should allow nothing to distract us from the good news of salvation in Jesus Christ, the main point of Scripture. We should know what the Bible says, apply it to our lives daily, and teach it to others. When we do this we will be able to evaluate all teachings in light of the central truth about Jesus.

1.7 Paul is speaking against the teachers of the law who were engaging in philosophical speculation based on the Pentateuch (the first five books of the Old Testament, written by Moses).

1.7–11 The false teachers wanted to become famous as teachers of God's law, but they didn't even understand its purpose. The law was not meant to give believers a list of commands for every occasion, but to show nonbelievers their sin and bring them to God. For more of what Paul says about our relationship to the law, see Romans 5.20, 21; 13.9, 10; Galatians 3.24–29.

1.10 *Sodomites* are practicing homosexuals. There are those who attempt to legitimize homosexuality as an acceptable alternative life-style. Even some Christians say people have a right to choose their sexual preference. But the Bible specifically calls homosexual behavior sin (see Leviticus 18.22; Romans 1.18–32; 1 Corinthians 6.9–11). We must be careful, however, to condemn only the practice, not the people. Those who commit homosexual acts are not to be feared, ridiculed, or hated. God can forgive them and transform their lives. The church should be a haven of forgiveness and healing for repentant homosexuals without compromising its stance against homosexual behavior. For more on this subject see the notes on Romans 1.26, 27.

1.12–17 People can feel so guilt-ridden by their past that they think God could never forgive and accept them. But consider Paul's past. He had scoffed at the teachings of Jesus ("a blasphemer"), hunting down and murdering God's people ("a persecutor, and a man of violence") before coming to faith in Christ (Acts 9.1–9). God forgave Paul and used him mightily for his kingdom. No matter how bad your past, he can also forgive and use you.

1.14 When we become Christians, we often feel that our faith in God and our love for him and for others is inadequate. But we can be confident that Christ will help our faith and love grow as our relationship with him deepens.

with the faith and love that are in Christ Jesus. 15 The saying is sure and worthy of 1.15
full acceptance, that Christ Jesus came into the world to save sinners — of whom I Lk 19.10 Rom 5.8
am the foremost. 16 But for that very reason I received mercy, so that in me, as the 1.16
foremost, Jesus Christ might display the utmost patience, making me an example Eph 2.7
to those who would come to believe in him for eternal life. 17 To the King of the 1.17
ages, immortal, invisible, the only God, be honor and glory forever and ever.[b] 1 Tim 6.15,16
Amen.

Cling tightly to the faith

18 I am giving you these instructions, Timothy, my child, in accordance with 1.18
the prophecies made earlier about you, so that by following them you may fight the 2 Cor 10.4
good fight, 19 having faith and a good conscience. By rejecting conscience, certain 1.19
persons have suffered shipwreck in the faith; 20 among them are Hymenaeus and 1 Tim 6.12
Alexander, whom I have turned over to Satan, so that they may learn not to blas- 1.20 1 Cor 5.5
pheme. 2 Tim 2.17; 4.14

2. Instructions for the church

Instructions about worship

2 First of all, then, I urge that supplications, prayers, intercessions, and thanks- 2.1
givings be made for everyone, 2 for kings and all who are in high positions, so Eph 6.18
that we may lead a quiet and peaceable life in all godliness and dignity. 3 This is 2.2 Rom 13.1
right and is acceptable in the sight of God our Savior, 4 who desires everyone to be 2.4
saved and to come to the knowledge of the truth. 5 For 2 Tim 2.25

[b] Gk *to the ages of the ages*

1.15 In this well-known verse, Paul summarizes the good news: Jesus came into the world to save sinners, and no sinner is beyond his saving power. (See Luke 5.32 for Jesus' purpose for being on earth.) Jesus didn't come merely to show us how to live a better life, or to challenge us to be better people. He came to offer us salvation that leads to eternal life. Have you accepted his offer?

1.15 Paul calls himself the *foremost* of sinners. We think of Paul as a great hero of the faith, but he never saw himself that way because he remembered his life before Christ. The more Paul understood God's grace, the more he was aware of his own sinfulness. Humility and gratitude should mark the life of every Christian. Never forget that you too are a sinner saved by God's grace.

1.17 This verse is a typical doxology given by Paul as a natural, emotional response to these reflections of the mercies of God. Paul is so moved by God's love that he breaks into spontaneous praise.

1.18 Paul highly valued the gift of prophecy (1 Corinthians 14.1). Through it important messages of warning and encouragement came to the church. Just as pastors are ordained, set apart for ministry in churches today, Timothy was set apart for ministry when elders laid their hands on him (see 4.14). Apparently at this ceremony, several believers prophesied about Timothy's gifts and strengths. These words from the Lord must have encouraged Timothy throughout his ministry.

1.19 How can you have a good conscience? Treasure your faith in Christ more than anything else and do what you know is right. Each time you deliberately ignore your conscience, you harden your heart a bit. Over time, your capacity to tell right from wrong will diminish. As you walk with God, he will speak to you through your conscience, letting you know the difference between right and wrong. Be sure to act on those inner tugs to do what is right—then your conscience will remain clear.

1.20 We don't know who Alexander was—he may have been an associate of Hymenaeus. Hymenaeus's error is explained in 2 Timothy 2.17, 18. He weakened people's faith by teaching that the resurrection had already occurred. Paul says that he turned him over "to Satan," meaning that Paul had removed him from the fellowship of the church. He did this so that Hymenaeus would see his error and repent. The ultimate purpose of this discipline was not punishment, but correction. The church today is often too lax in disciplining Christians who deliberately sin. Deliberate disobedience should be handled quickly and sternly to prevent the entire congregation from being affected. But it must be done in a way that strives to bring the offender back to Christ and into the loving embrace of the church. The definition of discipline includes these words: strengthening, purifying, training, correcting, perfecting. Therefore, condemnation, suspicion, withholding forgiveness, or permanent exile should not be part of church discipline.

2.1–4 Although God is all-powerful and all-knowing, he has chosen to let us help him change the world through our prayers. How this works is a mystery to us because of our limited understanding, but it is a reality. Paul urges us to pray for each other and for our leaders in government. Our earnest prayers will have powerful results (James 5.16).

2.2 Paul's command to pray for kings is remarkable considering that Nero was emperor at this time (A.D. 54–68) and persecution was a growing threat to believers. Nero was a notoriously cruel ruler. Later, when he needed a scapegoat for the great fire that destroyed much of Rome in A.D. 64, he blamed the Roman Christians to take the focus off himself. Persecution erupted throughout the Roman Empire. Not only were Christians denied certain privileges in society, some were even publicly butchered, burned, or fed to animals. Social ostracism was widespread.

2.2 When our lives are going along peacefully and quietly, it is difficult to remember to pray for those in authority over us. We can easily take good government for granted. It's easier to remember to pray when we are having problems. Burt we should remember to pray for those in authority around the world so that their societies will be open to the spread of the gospel.

2.4 Both Peter and Paul said that God longs for all to be saved (see 2 Peter 3.9). This does not mean that all *will* be saved, because the Bible makes it clear that many reject him (Matthew 25.31–46; John 12.44–50; Hebrews 10.26–29). The gospel has a universal scope; it is not limited to people of one race, one sex, or one national background. God loves the whole world and sent his Son to save sinners. Never assume that anyone is outside God's mercy or beyond his reach.

TIMOTHY

Painful lessons are usually doorways to new opportunities. Even the apostle Paul had much to learn. Shortly after his disappointing experience with John Mark, Paul recruited another eager young man, Timothy, to be his assistant. Paul's intense personality may have been too much for John Mark to handle. It could easily have been the same for Timothy. But Paul seems to have learned a lesson in patience from his old friend Barnabas. As a result, Timothy became a "son" to Paul.

Timothy probably became a Christian after Paul's first missionary visit to Lystra (Acts 16.1–5). He already had solid Jewish training in the Scriptures from his mother and grandmother. By Paul's second visit, Timothy had grown into a respected disciple of Jesus in his hometown. He did not hesitate to join Paul and Silas on their journey. His willingness to be circumcised as an adult is clearly a mark of his commitment (Timothy's mixed Greek/Jewish background could have created problems on their missionary journeys, because many of their audiences would be made up of Jews who were concerned with the strict keeping of this tradition). The circumcision helped to avoid that potential problem.

Beyond the tensions of his mixed racial background, Timothy seemed to struggle with a naturally timid character and an overawareness of his youthfulness. Unfortunately, many who share Timothy's character are quickly written off as too great a risk to deserve much responsibility. By God's grace, Paul saw great potential in Timothy. Paul demonstrated his confidence in Timothy by entrusting him with important responsibilities. Paul sent Timothy as his personal representative to Corinth during a particularly tense time (1 Corinthians 4.14–17). Although Timothy was apparently ineffective in that difficult mission, Paul did not give up on him. He continued to travel with Paul.

Our last pictures of Timothy come from the most personal letters in the New Testament: 1 and 2 Timothy. In them, the aging apostle Paul was near the end of his life, but his burning desire to continue his mission had not dimmed. Paul was writing to one of his closest friends—they had traveled, suffered, cried, and laughed together. They shared the intense joy of people responding to the good news and the agonies of seeing the gospel rejected and distorted. Paul left Timothy in Ephesus to oversee the young church there (1 Timothy 1.3, 4). He wrote to encourage Timothy and give him needed direction. These letters have provided comfort and help to countless other "Timothys" through the years. When you face a challenge that is beyond your abilities, read 1 and 2 Timothy, and remember that others have shared your experience.

Strengths and accomplishments:

- Became a believer after Paul's first missionary journey and joined him for his other two journeys
- Was a respected Christian in his hometown
- Was Paul's special representative on several occasions
- Received two personal letters from Paul
- Probably knew Paul better than any other person. Timothy became like a son to the apostle.

Weaknesses and mistakes:

- Struggled with a timid and reserved nature
- He allowed others to look down upon his youthfulness
- He was apparently unable to correct some of the problems in the church at Corinth when Paul sent him there

Lessons from his life:

- Youthfulness should not be an excuse for ineffectiveness
- Our inadequacies and inabilities should not keep us from being available to God

Key verses:

"I have no one like him who will be genuinely concerned for your welfare. All of them are seeking their own interests, not those of Jesus Christ. But Timothy's worth you know, how like a son with a father he has served with me in the work of the gospel" (Philippians 2.20–22).

Vital statistics:

- Where: Lystra
- Occupation: Missionary, pastor
- Relatives: Mother: Eunice. Grandmother: Lois. Greek father
- Contemporaries: Paul, Silas, Luke, Mark, Peter, Barnabas

Timothy's story is told in Acts, starting in chapter 16. He is also mentioned in Romans 16.21; 1 Corinthians 4.17; 16.10, 11; 2 Corinthians 1.1, 19; Philippians 1.1; 2.19–23; Colossians 1.1; 1 Thessalonians 1.1–10; 2.3, 4; 3.2–6; 1 and 2 Timothy; Philemon 1.1; Hebrews 13.23.

there is one God;
there is also one mediator between God and humankind,
Christ Jesus, himself human,
6 who gave himself a ransom for all
—this was attested at the right time. 7 For this I was appointed a herald and an
apostle (I am telling the truth,[c] I am not lying), a teacher of the Gentiles in faith and
truth.
8 I desire, then, that in every place the men should pray, lifting up holy hands
without anger or argument; 9 also that the women should dress themselves modestly
and decently in suitable clothing, not with their hair braided, or with gold, pearls,
or expensive clothes, 10 but with good works, as is proper for women who profess
reverence for God. 11 Let a woman[d] learn in silence with full submission. 12 I permit no woman[d] to teach or to have authority over a man;[e] she is to keep silent.
13 For Adam was formed first, then Eve; 14 and Adam was not deceived, but the
woman was deceived and became a transgressor. 15 Yet she will be saved through

2.5 Rom 8.35
2.6 Gal 4.4
2.7 Acts 9.15; 1 Cor 9.1; 2 Tim 1.1
2.8 Ps 24.4; 63.4
2.9 1 Pet 3.3
2.11 1 Cor 14.34
2.12 Tit 2.5
2.13 Gen 2.7,22
2.14,15 Gen 3.6,13,16

[c] Other ancient authorities add *in Christ* [d] Or *wife* [e] Or *her husband*

2.5, 6 We human beings are separated from God by sin, and only one person in the universe is our mediator and can stand between us and bring us together again—Jesus, who is both God and man. Jesus' sacrifice brought new life to all people. Have you let him bring you to the Father?

2.6 Jesus gave his life as a "ransom for all" (see also Mark 10.45). A ransom was the price paid to release a slave from captivity. Jesus, our mediator, gave his life in exchange for ours. By his death, he paid our penalty for sin.

2.7 Paul says he is a herald (preacher). He was given the special privilege of announcing Christianity to the Gentiles. He gives his credentials as an apostle in 1 Corinthians 15.7–11.

2.8 Besides displeasing God, it is difficult to pray when we have sinned or when we feel angry and resentful. That is why Jesus told us to interrupt our prayers, if necessary, to make peace with others (Matthew 5.23, 24). God wants us to obey him immediately and thoroughly. Our goal should be to have a right relationship with God and also with others.

2.9, 10 Apparently, some Christian women were trying to gain respect by looking beautiful rather than becoming Christ-like in character. Some may have thought they could win unbelieving husbands through their appearance (see Peter's counsel to such women in 1 Peter 3.1–6). It is not unscriptural for a woman to want to be attractive. Beauty, however, begins inside a person. A gentle, modest, loving character gives a light to the face that cannot be duplicated by the best cosmetics and jewelry. A carefully groomed and well-decorated exterior is artificial and cold unless inner beauty is present.

2.9–15 To understand these verses, we must understand the situation in which Paul and Timothy worked. In first-century Jewish culture, women were not allowed to study. When Paul said women should *learn* quietly and humbly, he was offering them an amazing new opportunity. Paul did not want the Ephesian women to teach because they didn't yet have enough knowledge or experience. The Ephesian church had a particular problem with false teachers. Evidently the women were especially susceptible to their teaching (2 Timothy 3.1–9), because they did not yet have enough biblical knowledge to see through the false claims. In addition, some of the women were apparently flaunting their new-found Christian freedom by wearing inappropriate clothing (2.9). Paul was telling Timothy not to put anyone (in this case, women) into positions of leadership who were not yet mature in the faith (see 5.22). The same principle applies to churches today (see the note on 3.6).

2.12 Some interpret this passage to mean that women should never teach in the assembled church. However, other commentators say that Paul's words "I permit no woman to teach" can be more literally translated "I am not permitting." Paul did not forbid women from ever teaching men. Paul's commended co-worker, Priscilla, taught Apollos, the great preacher (Acts 18.24–26). In addition, Paul frequently mentioned other women who held positions of responsibility in the church. Phoebe worked in the church (Romans 16.1). Mary, Tryphena, and Tryphosa were the Lord's workers (Romans 16.6, 12), as were Euodias and Syntyche (Philippians 4.2). Paul was here prohibiting the Ephesian women, not all women, from teaching (see the note on 2.9–15).

In Paul's reference to women being silent in church meetings, the word *silent* expresses an attitude of quietness and composure. (A different Greek word is usually used to mean "complete silence.") In addition, Paul himself acknowledges that women publicly prayed and prophesied (1 Corinthians 11.5). Apparently, however, the women in the Ephesian church were abusing their newly acquired Christian freedom. Because these women were new converts and uneducated, they did not yet have the necessary experience, knowledge, or maturity to teach those who already had extensive biblical education.

2.13, 14 In previous letters Paul had talked about male/female roles in marriage (Ephesians 5.21–33; Colossians 3.18, 19). Here he talks about male/female roles within the church. Some scholars see these verses about Adam and Eve as an illustration of what was happening in the Ephesian church. Just as Eve had been deceived in the garden of Eden, so the women in the church were being deceived by false teachers. And just as Adam was the first human created by God, so the men in the church in Ephesus should be the first to speak and teach, because they had more education. This view, then, stresses that Paul's teaching here is not universal, but applies to churches with similar problems. Other scholars, however, contend that the roles Paul points out are God's design for his created order. God established these roles to maintain harmony in both the family and the church.

2.14 Paul is not excusing Adam for his part in the Fall (Genesis 3.6, 7, 17–19). On the contrary, in his letter to the Romans, Paul placed the primary blame for mankind's sinful nature on Adam (Romans 5.12–21).

2.15 There are several ways to understand "saved through childbearing": (1) Man sinned, and so men were condemned to hard labor. Woman sinned, and so women were condemned to pain in childbearing. Both men and women, however, can be saved through trusting Christ and obeying him. (2) Women who fulfill their God-given roles are demonstrating true commitment and obedience to Christ. One of the most important roles for a wife and mother is to care for her family. (3) The childbirth mentioned here refers to the birth of Jesus Christ. Women (and men) are saved childbearing, provided they continue in faith and love and holiness, with modesty.

Standards for church leaders

3 The saying is sure:[f] whoever aspires to the office of bishop[g] desires a noble
task. 2 Now a bishop[h] must be above reproach, married only once,[i] temperate, sensible, respectable, hospitable, an apt teacher, 3 not a drunkard, not violent
but gentle, not quarrelsome, and not a lover of money. 4 He must manage his own
household well, keeping his children submissive and respectful in every way—
5 for if someone does not know how to manage his own household, how can he take
care of God's church? 6 He must not be a recent convert, or he may be puffed up
with conceit and fall into the condemnation of the devil. 7 Moreover, he must be
well thought of by outsiders, so that he may not fall into disgrace and the snare of
the devil.
8 Deacons likewise must be serious, not double-tongued, not indulging in
much wine, not greedy for money; 9 they must hold fast to the mystery of the faith
with a clear conscience. 10 And let them first be tested; then, if they prove themselves blameless, let them serve as deacons. 11 Women[j] likewise must be serious,
not slanderers, but temperate, faithful in all things. 12 Let deacons be married only
once,[k] and let them manage their children and their households well; 13 for those
who serve well as deacons gain a good standing for themselves and great boldness
in the faith that is in Christ Jesus.
14 I hope to come to you soon, but I am writing these instructions to you so that,
15 if I am delayed, you may know how one ought to behave in the household of
God, which is the church of the living God, the pillar and bulwark of the truth.
16 Without any doubt, the mystery of our religion is great:

He[l] was revealed in flesh,
vindicated[m] in spirit,[n]

3.1 Acts 20.28
3.2 Tit 1.6,8
3.3 Tit 1.7
3.4 1 Tim 3.12
3.7 2 Cor 8.21 2 Tim 2.26
3.8 Phil 1.1
3.9 1 Tim 1.19
3.12 1 Tim 3.2,4
3.13 Mt 25.21
3.15 Mt 16.16-18 Eph 2.21
3.16 Isa 7.14 Mt 4.11 Jn 1.14 Rom 1.3,4 Acts 1.9 1 Jn 4.2,3; 5.6

[f] Some interpreters place these words at the end of the previous paragraph. Other ancient authorities read *The saying is commonly accepted* [g] Or *overseer* [h] Or *an overseer* [i] Gk *the husband of one wife* [j] Or *Their wives*, or *Women deacons* [k] Gk *be husbands of one wife* [l] Gk *Who*; other ancient authorities read *God*; others, *Which* [m] Or *justified* [n] Or *by the Spirit*

spiritually because of the most important birth, that of Christ himself. (4) From the lessons learned through the trials of childbearing, women can develop qualities that teach them about love, trust, submission, and service.

3.1–13 The word *bishop* can refer to a pastor, church leader, or presiding elder. It is good to want to be a spiritual leader, but the standards are high. Paul enumerates some of the qualifications here. Do you hold a position of spiritual leadership, or would you like to be a leader some day? Check yourself against Paul's standard of excellence. Those with great responsibility must meet high expectations.

3.2 When Paul says church leaders (bishops) should be married only once, he is prohibiting both polygamy and promiscuity. This does not prohibit an unmarried man from becoming an leader or a widowed leader from remarrying.

3.4, 5 Christian workers and volunteers sometimes make the mistake of thinking their work is so important that they are justified in ignoring their families. Spiritual leadership, however, must begin at home. If a man is not willing to care for, discipline, and teach his children, he is not qualified to lead the church. Don't allow your volunteer activities to detract from your family responsibilities.

3.6 New believers should become secure and strong in the faith before taking leadership roles in the church. Too often, when the church is desperate for workers, they place new believers into positions of responsibility for which they are unqualified. New faith needs to mature, and that takes time. New believers should have a place of service, but not be put into leadership positions until they are firmly grounded in their faith, with a solid Christian life-style and a knowledge of God's Word.

3.8–13 *Deacon* means "one who serves." This position was begun by the apostles in the Jerusalem church (Acts 6.1–6) to care for the physical needs of the congregation, especially the needs of the Greek-speaking widows. Deacons were leaders in the church, and their qualifications resemble those of the elders (bishops). In some churches today, the office of deacon has lost its importance. New Christians are asked to serve in this position, but that is not the New Testament pattern. Paul says that those who would be deacons should first be tested with lesser responsibilities.

3.11 Some have translated *women* as "women helpers" or "deaconesses." It is unclear whether this verse refers to wives of deacons or female leaders of the church (such as Phoebe, the deaconess mentioned in Romans 16.1). In either case, Paul expects the behavior of prominent women in the church to be just as responsible and blameless as that of prominent men.

3.15 To be a church leader is a heavy responsibility because the church belongs to the living God. Church leaders should not be elected because they are popular, nor should they be allowed to push their way to the top. Instead they should be chosen by the church because of their respect for truth, both in doctrine and in their personal lives.

3.15 The lists of qualifications for church office show that living a blameless and pure life requires effort and self-discipline. All believers, even if they never plan to be church leaders, should strive to follow these guidelines because they are consistent with what God says is true and right. The strength to do so comes from Christ.

3.16 This short hymn affirms the humanity and divinity of Christ. As a man, Jesus lived a perfect life, and so he is a perfect example for how to live. As God, Jesus gives us the power to do what is right. It is possible to live a godly life—follow Christ.

seen by angels,
proclaimed among Gentiles,
believed in throughout the world,
taken up in glory.

3. Instructions for elders

Paul gives guidelines for teaching

4 Now the Spirit expressly says that in later[o] times some will renounce the faith **4.1**
by paying attention to deceitful spirits and teachings of demons, 2 through the Jn 16.13 2 Thess 2.3
hypocrisy of liars whose consciences are seared with a hot iron. 3 They forbid mar- 2 Pet 2.1 1 Jn 4.6
riage and demand abstinence from foods, which God created to be received with **4.2**
thanksgiving by those who believe and know the truth. 4 For everything created by Eph 4.19
God is good, and nothing is to be rejected, provided it is received with thanksgiv- **4.3**
ing; 5 for it is sanctified by God's word and by prayer. Prov 18.22 Col 2.16
6 If you put these instructions before the brothers and sisters,[p] you will be a Heb 13.4
good servant[q] of Christ Jesus, nourished on the words of the faith and of the sound **4.4** 1 Cor 10.26
teaching that you have followed. 7 Have nothing to do with profane myths and old Tit 1.15
wives' tales. Train yourself in godliness, 8 for, while physical training is of some **4.6** 2 Tim 3.14
value, godliness is valuable in every way, holding promise for both the present life **4.8**
and the life to come. 9 The saying is sure and worthy of full acceptance. 10 For to this Col 2.23
end we toil and struggle,[r] because we have our hope set on the living God, who is **4.10** 1 Tim 2.4; 3.15
the Savior of all people, especially of those who believe. **4.11**
11 These are the things you must insist on and teach. 12 Let no one despise your 1 Tim 5.7
youth, but set the believers an example in speech and conduct, in love, in faith, in **4.12** 1 Cor 16.11
purity. 13 Until I arrive, give attention to the public reading of scripture,[s] to exhort- Tit 2.7
ing, to teaching. 14 Do not neglect the gift that is in you, which was given to you

[o] Or *the last* [p] Gk *brothers* [q] Or *deacon* [r] Other ancient authorities read *suffer reproach* [s] Gk *to the reading*

4.1 The "later times" began with Christ's resurrection and will continue until his return, when he will set up his kingdom and judge all mankind.

4.1, 2 False teachers were and still are a threat to the church. Jesus and the apostles repeatedly warned against them (see, for example, Mark 13.21–23; Acts 20.28–31; 2 Thessalonians 2.1–12; 2 Peter 3.3–7). The danger Timothy faced in Ephesus seems to have come from certain people in the church who followed some Greek philosophers who taught that the body is evil and that only the soul matters. They refused to believe that the God of creation was good, because his very contact with the physical world would soil him. Though these Greek-influenced church members honored Jesus, they could not believe he was truly human. Their teachings, if left unchecked, would greatly distort Christian truth.

It is not enough that a teacher appears to know what he is talking about, is disciplined and moral, and says he is speaking for God. If his words contradict the Bible, his teaching is false. Like Timothy, we must guard against any teaching that causes believers to dilute or reject parts of their faith. Such false teaching can be very direct or extremely subtle.

4.1–5 Why did Paul say the false teachers taught the "teachings of demons"? Satan deceives people by offering a clever imitation of the real thing. The false teachers gave stringent rules (such as forbidding people to marry or eat meat) and this made them appear self-disciplined and righteous. Their strict disciplines for the body, however, could not remove sin (see Colossians 2.20–23). We must look beyond a teacher's methods and disciplines to his teaching about Jesus Christ. His conclusions about Christ show the source of his message.

4.4, 5 In opposition to the false teachers, Paul affirmed that everything God made is good (see Genesis 1) and *sanctified* (set apart for his use). We should ask his blessing on his created gifts that give us pleasure and thank him for them. This doesn't mean we should abuse what God has made (for example, gluttony abuses God's gift of good food, lust abuses God's gift of love, and murder abuses God's gift of life). Instead of abusing, we should enjoy these gifts by using them to serve and honor God. Have you thanked God for the good things he has made? Are you using them in ways pleasing to you *and* to God?

4.7–10 Are you in shape both physically and spiritually? In our society, much emphasis is placed on physical fitness, but Paul declared that spiritual health (godliness) is even more important. We must develop our faith by using the abilities God has given us in the service of the church (see 4.14–16). Are you developing your spiritual muscles?

4.10 Christ is the mediator and ransom for all, but his salvation becomes effective for only those who trust him.

4.12, 13 Timothy was a young pastor. It would be easy for older Christians to look down on him because of his youth. He had to earn the respect of his elders by setting an example in his teaching, life, love, faith, and purity. Regardless of your age, God can use you. Whether you are young or old, don't think of your age as a handicap. Live so others can see Christ in you.

4.14 Timothy's commission as a church leader was confirmed by prophecy (see also 1.18) and by the laying on of hands by the elders of the church. He was not a self-appointed leader. If you aspire to church leadership, seek the counsel of mature Christians who know you well and who will hold you accountable.

4.14, 15 As a young leader in a church with a lot of problems, Timothy may have felt intimidated. The elders and prophets encouraged him and charged him to use his spiritual abilities responsibly. Highly skilled and talented athletes lose their abilities if their muscles aren't toned by constant use. Our talents are improved by exercise, but failing to use them causes them to waste away from lack of practice and nourishment. What gifts and abilities has God given you? Use them regularly in serving God and others. (See Romans 12.1–8; 2 Timothy 1.6–8 for more on using well the abilities God has given us.)

4.14 Acts 6.6 1 Tim 1.8 2 Tim 1.6 through prophecy with the laying on of hands by the council of elders.[t] 15 Put these
things into practice, devote yourself to them, so that all may see your progress.
16 Pay close attention to yourself and to your teaching; continue in these things, for
in doing this you will save both yourself and your hearers.

Caring for different groups in the church

5.1 Lev 19.32 Tit 2.2,6 **5** Do not speak harshly to an older man,[u] but speak to him as to a father, to
younger men as brothers, 2 to older women as mothers, to younger women as
sisters—with absolute purity.
5.4 Mt 15.4 Eph 6.2 1 Tim 2.3 3 Honor widows who are really widows. 4 If a widow has children or grandchildren, they should first learn their religious duty to their own family and make some
repayment to their parents; for this is pleasing in God's sight. 5 The real widow, left
5.5 Lk 2.37 1 Pet 3.5 alone, has set her hope on God and continues in supplications and prayers night and
5.6 Jas 5.5 day; 6 but the widow[v] who lives for pleasure is dead even while she lives. 7 Give
these commands as well, so that they may be above reproach. 8 And whoever does
not provide for relatives, and especially for family members, has denied the faith
and is worse than an unbeliever.
5.10 Gen 18.3,4 Acts 9.36 9 Let a widow be put on the list if she is not less than sixty years old and has
been married only once;[w] 10 she must be well attested for her good works, as one
5.12 Heb 6.4-6 who has brought up children, shown hospitality, washed the saints' feet, helped the
afflicted, and devoted herself to doing good in every way. 11 But refuse to put youn-
5.13 2 Thess 3.11 Tit 1.11 ger widows on the list; for when their sensual desires alienate them from Christ,
they want to marry, 12 and so they incur condemnation for having violated their first
5.14 1 Cor 7.9 1 Tim 3.15 Tit 2.5 pledge. 13 Besides that, they learn to be idle, gadding about from house to house;
and they are not merely idle, but also gossips and busybodies, saying what they
should not say. 14 So I would have younger widows marry, bear children, and man-
5.15 1 Tim 1.20 age their households, so as to give the adversary no occasion to revile us. 15 For

[t] Gk *by the presbytery* [u] Or *an elder,* or *a presbyter* [v] Gk *she* [w] Gk *the wife of one husband*

5.2 Men in the ministry can avoid improper attitudes toward women by treating them as family members. If men see women as fellow members in God's family, they will protect them and help them grow spiritually.

5.3ff Paul wants Christian families to be as self-supporting as possible. He insists that children and grandchildren take care of the widows in their families (5.4); he suggested that younger widows remarry and start new families (5.14); and he ordered the church not to support lazy members who refused to work (2 Thessalonians 3.10). Nevertheless, when necessary, the believers pooled their resources (Acts 2.44–47); they gave generously to help disaster-ridden churches (1 Corinthians 16.1–4); and they took care of a large number of widows (Acts 6.1–6). The church has always had limited resources, and it has always had to balance financial responsibility with generosity. It only makes sense for members to work as hard as they can and to be as independent as possible so they can adequately care for themselves and for less fortunate members. When church members are both responsible and generous, everyone's needs can be met.

5.3–5 Because there were no pensions, no social security, no life insurance, and few honorable jobs for women, widows were usually unable to support themselves. The responsibility for caring for the helpless naturally falls first on their families, the people whose lives are closely linked with theirs. Paul stressed the importance of families caring for the needs of widows, not leaving it for the church to do, so the church can care for widows who have no families to turn to ("real widows," 5.16). A widow who had no children or other family members to support her was doomed to poverty. From the beginning, the church took care of its widows, who in turn gave valuable service to the church.

The church should support those who have no families, and it should also help the others—whether elderly, young, handicapped, ill, or poverty-stricken—with their emotional and spiritual needs. Often families who are caring for their own helpless members have heavy burdens. They may need extra money, a listening ear, a helping hand, or a word of encouragement. Interestingly, those who are helped often turn around and help others so that the church turns into a circle of caring. Don't wait for them to ask. Take the initiative and look for ways to serve them.

5.8 Almost everyone has relatives, family of some kind. Family relationships are so important in God's eyes, Paul says, that a person who neglects his or her family responsibilities has "denied the faith." Are you doing your part to meet the needs of those included in your family circle?

5.9–16 Apparently some older widows were "put on the list," meaning they took a vow committing themselves to work for the church in exchange for financial support. Paul lists a few qualifications for these church workers—these widows should be at least 60 years old, should have been faithful to their husbands, and should be well thought of for their kind deeds. Younger widows should not be included in this group because they may desire to marry again and have to break their vow (5.11, 12).

Three out of four women today eventually are widowed, and many of the older women in our churches have lost their husbands. Does your church provide an avenue of service for these women? Could you help match their gifts and abilities with your church's needs? Often their maturity and wisdom can be of great service in the church.

5.10 "Washed the saints' feet" means having helped and served other believers with humility, following Jesus' example when he washed the feet of his disciples at the last supper (John 13.1–17).

5.15 "Turned away to follow Satan" refers to their immoral conduct that identified them with their pagan neighbors.

some have already turned away to follow Satan. 16 If any believing woman[x] has 5.16
relatives who are really widows, let her assist them; let the church not be burdened, Ruth 2.18
so that it can assist those who are real widows.
17 Let the elders who rule well be considered worthy of double honor,[y] espe- 5.17
cially those who labor in preaching and teaching; 18 for the scripture says, "You Rom 12.8 Gal 6.6
shall not muzzle an ox while it is treading out the grain," and, "The laborer de- 1 Thess 5.12
serves to be paid." 19 Never accept any accusation against an elder except on the 5.18 Deut 25.4
evidence of two or three witnesses. 20 As for those who persist in sin, rebuke them Lk 10.7
in the presence of all, so that the rest also may stand in fear. 21 In the presence of 5.19 Mt 18.16
God and of Christ Jesus and of the elect angels, I warn you to keep these instruc- 5.20
tions without prejudice, doing nothing on the basis of partiality. 22 Do not ordain[z] Deut 13.11 2 Cor 7.11
anyone hastily, and do not participate in the sins of others; keep yourself pure. Eph 5.11
23 No longer drink only water, but take a little wine for the sake of your stom- 5.21 1 Tim 6.13
ach and your frequent ailments.
24 The sins of some people are conspicuous and precede them to judgment, 5.22 1 Tim 4.14
while the sins of others follow them there. 25 So also good works are conspicuous; 5.23 1 Tim 3.8
and even when they are not, they cannot remain hidden.
6 Let all who are under the yoke of slavery regard their masters as worthy of all 5.24 Rev 14.13
honor, so that the name of God and the teaching may not be blasphemed. 6.1 Tit 2.9
2 Those who have believing masters must not be disrespectful to them on the ground 6.2
that they are members of the church;[a] rather they must serve them all the more, 1 Tim 4.11
since those who benefit by their service are believers and beloved.[b]

Avoid worthless arguments and the longing to be rich

Teach and urge these duties. 3 Whoever teaches otherwise and does not agree 6.3 Tit 1.1
with the sound words of our Lord Jesus Christ and the teaching that is in accordance 6.4
with godliness, 4 is conceited, understanding nothing, and has a morbid craving for 1 Cor 8.2
controversy and for disputes about words. From these come envy, dissension, slan- 6.5 Rom 16.17
der, base suspicions, 5 and wrangling among those who are depraved in mind and 2 Tim 3.8

[x] Other ancient authorities read *believing man or woman;* others, *believing man* [y] Or *compensation* [z] Gk *Do not lay hands on* [a] Gk *are brothers* [b] Or *since they are believers and beloved, who devote themselves to good deeds*

5.17, 18 Faithful and diligent church leaders should be supported and appreciated. Too often they are targets for criticism because the congregation has unrealistic expectations. How do you treat your church leaders? Do you enjoy finding fault, or do you show your appreciation? Do they receive enough financial support to allow them to live without worry and provide for the needs of their families? Both Jesus and Paul emphasized the importance of supporting those who lead and teach us (see Galatians 6.6 and the notes on Luke 10.7 and 1 Corinthians 9.4–10).

5.17, 18 Preaching and teaching are closely related. Preaching is proclaiming God's Word and confronting listeners with the truth of Scripture. Teaching is explaining the truth in Scripture, helping learners understand difficult passages, and helping them apply God's Word to daily life. Paul says these "elders who rule well" are worthy of double honor. Unfortunately, however, we often take them for granted. Think of how you can honor your preachers and teachers.

5.19–21 Church leaders are not exempt from sin, faults, and mistakes. But they are often criticized for the wrong reasons — minor imperfections, failure to meet someone's expectations, personality clashes. Thus Paul said that complaints should not even be heard unless two or three witnesses will confirm them. Sometimes church leaders should be confronted about their behavior, and sometimes they should be rebuked. But all rebuking must be done fairly, lovingly, and for the purpose of restoration.

5.21 "Elect angels" are all those angels who did not rebel against God like Satan did.

5.21 We must not treat others with partiality, giving preferential treatment to some and ignoring others. Make sure you honor people for who they are in Christ, not who they are in the world.

5.22 Paul says a church should never be in a hurry about choosing its leaders, especially the pastor, because we may overlook major problems or sins. It is a serious responsibility to choose church leaders. They must have strong faith and be morally upright, having the qualities described in 3.1–13 and Titus 1.5–9. Not everyone who wants to be a church leader is eligible. Be certain of an applicant's qualifications before asking him to be a leader in the church.

5.23 It is unclear why Paul gave this advice to Timothy. Perhaps contaminated water had led to Timothy's indigestion and so he should not drink only water. Whatever the reason, this statement is not an invitation to overindulgence or alcoholism.

6.1, 2 In Paul's culture there was a great social and legal gulf separating masters and slaves. But as Christians, masters and slaves became spiritual equals, brothers and sisters in the faith (Galatians 3.28). Paul does not speak against the institution of slavery, but he gives guidelines for Christian slaves and Christian masters. His counsel for the master/slave relationship can be applied to the employer/employee relationship today. Employees should work hard, showing respect for their employers. In turn, employers should be fair (Ephesians 6.5–9; Colossians 3.22–25). Our work should reflect our faithfulness to and love for Christ.

6.3–5 Paul tells Timothy to stay away from those who just want to make money from preaching, and who have strayed from the sound teachings of the gospel into minute doctrinal differences that caused strife in the church. A person's understanding of the finer points of theology should not become the basis for lording it over others or making money. Stay away from those who just want to argue.

6.6 Phil 4.11; 1 Tim 4.8
6.7 Job 1.21
6.8 Heb 13.5
6.9 Mt 13.22

bereft of the truth, imagining that godliness is a means of gain.[c] 6 Of course, there
is great gain in godliness combined with contentment; 7 for we brought nothing into
the world, so that[d] we can take nothing out of it; 8 but if we have food and clothing,
we will be content with these. 9 But those who want to be rich fall into temptation
and are trapped by many senseless and harmful desires that plunge people into ruin
and destruction. 10 For the love of money is a root of all kinds of evil, and in their
eagerness to be rich some have wandered away from the faith and pierced themselves with many pains.

Paul's final instructions

6.11 2 Tim 2.22
6.12 1 Tim 1.19; 2 Tim 2.2-4; 4.7
6.13 Jn 18.37
6.14 1 Thess 3.13
6.15 1 Tim 1.17; Rev 17.14; 19.16
6.16 Ex 33.20; 2 Chron 5.14; Ps 104.2; Jn 1.18; 5.26; 1 Tim 1.17
6.17 Lk 12.20
6.19 Mt 6.20; 1 Tim 6.12
6.20 2 Tim 2.16
6.21 1 Tim 1.19; 2 Tim 2.18

11 But as for you, man of God, shun all this; pursue righteousness, godliness,
faith, love, endurance, gentleness. 12 Fight the good fight of the faith; take hold of
the eternal life, to which you were called and for which you made[e] the good confession in the presence of many witnesses. 13 In the presence of God, who gives life
to all things, and of Christ Jesus, who in his testimony before Pontius Pilate made
the good confession, I charge you 14 to keep the commandment without spot or
blame until the manifestation of our Lord Jesus Christ, 15 which he will bring about
at the right time—he who is the blessed and only Sovereign, the King of kings and
Lord of lords. 16 It is he alone who has immortality and dwells in unapproachable
light, whom no one has ever seen or can see; to him be honor and eternal dominion.
Amen.

17 As for those who in the present age are rich, command them not to be
haughty, or to set their hopes on the uncertainty of riches, but rather on God who
richly provides us with everything for our enjoyment. 18 They are to do good, to be
rich in good works, generous, and ready to share, 19 thus storing up for themselves
the treasure of a good foundation for the future, so that they may take hold of the
life that really is life.

20 Timothy, guard what has been entrusted to you. Avoid the profane chatter
and contradictions of what is falsely called knowledge; 21 by professing it some
have missed the mark as regards the faith.

Grace be with you.[f]

c Other ancient authorities add *Withdraw yourself from such people* d Other ancient authorities read *world—it is certain that* e Gk *confessed* f The Greek word for *you* here is plural; in other ancient authorities it is singular. Other ancient authorities add *Amen*

6.6 This statement is the key to spiritual growth and personal fulfillment. We should honor God and center our lives on him (godliness, see Matthew 6.33), and we should be content with what God is doing in our lives (contentment, see Philippians 4.11–13).

6.6–10 Despite almost overwhelming evidence to the contrary, most people still believe that money brings happiness. Rich people craving greater riches can be caught in an endless cycle that only ends in ruin and destruction. How can you keep away from the love of money? Paul gives us some guidelines: (1) realize that one day riches will all be gone (6.7, 17); (2) be content with what you have (6.8); (3) monitor what you are willing to do to get more money (6.9, 10); (4) love people more than money (6.11); (5) love God's work more than money (6.11); (6) freely share what you have with others (6.18). (See Proverbs 30.7–9.)

6.8 There is a difference between *needs* and *wants*. We may have all we need to live, but we let ourselves become anxious and discontent over what we merely want. Like Paul, we can choose to be content without having all we want. The only alternative is to be slaves to our desires.

6.11, 12 Paul uses active and forceful words to describe the Christian life: pursue, fight, take hold. Some think that Christianity is passive, waiting for God to act. But we must have an *active* faith—obeying God with courage and doing what we know is right. Is it time for action on your part? Don't wait. Get going!

6.13 Jesus' trial before Pilate is recorded in the Gospels: Matthew 27.11–26; Mark 15.1–15; Luke 23.1–25; John 18.28–19.16.

6.13–16 Paul concludes with a charge to Timothy to keep "the commandment," referring to the commands Christ has given to his church, or to Timothy's promise to serve Christ. Timothy's own confession of faith is compared with Christ's before Pilate.

6.14 *Manifestation* refers to Christ's return.

6.17–19 Ephesus was a wealthy city, and the Ephesian church probably had many wealthy members. Paul advises Timothy to deal with that potential problem by teaching that having riches carries great responsibility. Those who have money must be generous, not arrogant because they have a lot to give. They must be careful not to put their trust in money instead of in the living God for their security. Even if we don't have material wealth, we can be rich in good works toward others. No matter how poor we are, we have something to share with someone.

6.21 The book of 1 Timothy provides guiding principles for local churches, including rules for public worship and qualifications for bishops (elders, pastors), deacons, and special church workers (widows). Paul tells the church leaders to correct unsound doctrine and to deal lovingly and fairly with all people in the church. The church is not organized for the sake of organization, but so Christ can be honored and glorified. While studying these guidelines, don't lose sight of what is most important in the life of the church—knowing God, working together in loving harmony, and taking God's good news to the world.

The Second Letter of Paul to TIMOTHY

VITAL STATISTICS

PURPOSE:
To give final instructions and encouragement to Timothy, pastor of the church at Ephesus

AUTHOR:
Paul

TO WHOM WRITTEN:
Timothy

DATE WRITTEN:
About A.D. 66 or 67 from prison in Rome. After a year or two of freedom, Paul was arrested again and executed under Emperor Nero.

SETTING:
Paul is virtually alone in prison; only Luke is with him. He writes this letter to pass the torch to the new generation of church leaders. He also asks for visits from his friends, for his books, and especially the parchments—possibly parts of the Old Testament, the Gospels, and other biblical manuscripts.

KEY VERSE:
"Do your best to present yourself to God as one approved by him, a worker who has no need to be ashamed, rightly explaining the word of truth" (2.15).

KEY PEOPLE:
Paul, Timothy, Luke, Mark, and others

KEY PLACES:
Rome, Ephesus

SPECIAL FEATURES:
Because this is Paul's last letter, it reveals his heart and his priorities—sound doctrine, steadfast faith, confident endurance, and enduring love.

"FAMOUS last words" is more than a cliché. When notable men and women of influence are about to die, the world waits to hear their final words of insight and wisdom. Then those quotes are repeated worldwide. This is also true with a dying loved one. Gathered at his or her side, the family strains to hear every whispered syllable of blessing, encouragement, and advice, knowing that this will be the final message.

One of the most knowledgeable, influential, and beloved men of history was the apostle Paul. And we have his famous last words.

Paul was facing death. He was not dying of a disease in a sterile hospital with loved ones gathered near. He was very much alive, but his condition was terminal. Convicted as a follower of Jesus of Nazareth, he lay in a cold Roman prison, cut off from the world, with just a visitor or two and his writing materials. Paul knew that soon he would be executed (4.6), and so he wrote his final thoughts to his "son" Timothy, passing to him the torch of leadership, reminding him of what was truly important, and encouraging him in the faith. Imagine how Timothy must have read and reread every word—this was the last message from his beloved mentor, Paul. Because of the situation and the recipient, this is the most intimate and moving of all Paul's letters, and his last.

Paul's introduction is tender as the love he has for Timothy seeps from every phrase (1.1–5). He then reminds Timothy of the qualities necessary for a faithful minister of Jesus Christ (1.6—2.13). Timothy should remember his call and use his gifts with boldness (1.6–12), hold tightly to the truth (1.13–18), prepare others to follow him in the ministry (2.1, 2), be disciplined and ready to suffer hardship (2.3–7), and keep his eyes and mind focused on Christ (2.8–13). Paul challenges Timothy to hold to sound doctrine, rejecting error and foolish discussions and knowing the Word (2.14–19), and to keep his life pure (2.20–26).

Next, Paul warns Timothy of the opposition that he and other believers would face in the last days from self-centered people who use the church for their own gain and who teach new and false doctrines (3.1–9). He tells Timothy to be prepared for them by remembering his example (3.10, 11), understanding the real source of the opposition (3.12, 13), and finding strength and power in the word of God (3.14–17). Then Paul gives Timothy a stirring charge—to preach the Word (4.1–4) and to fulfill his ministry until the end (4.5–8).

Paul concludes with personal requests and items of information. In these final words, he reveals his loneliness and his strong love for his brothers and sisters in Christ (4.9–22).

There has never been another person like Paul, the missionary apostle. He was a man of deep faith, undying love, constant hope, tenacious conviction, and profound insight. And he was inspired by the Holy Spirit to give us God's message. As you read 2 Timothy, know that you are reading the last words of this great man of God—last words to Timothy and to all who would claim to follow Christ. Recommit yourself to stand courageously for the truth, knowing the Word and empowered by the Holy Spirit.

THE BLUEPRINT

1. Foundations of Christian service (1.1—2.26)
2. Difficult times for Christian service (3.1—4.22)

Paul gives helpful advice to Timothy to remain solidly grounded in Christian service and endure suffering during the difficult days to come. It is easy for us to serve Christ for the wrong reasons: because it is exciting, rewarding, or personally enriching. Without a proper foundation, however, we will find it easy to quit during difficult times. All believers need a strong foundation for their service, because Christian service does not get easier as we grow older, and it will become no easier as we near the last days.

MEGATHEMES

THEME	EXPLANATION	IMPORTANCE
Boldness	In the face of opposition and persecution, Timothy was to carry out his ministry unashamed and unafraid. Paul urged him to utilize boldly the gifts of preaching and teaching that the Holy Spirit had given him.	The Holy Spirit helps us to be wise and strong. God honors our confident testimony even when we suffer. To get over our fear of what people might say or do, we must take our eyes off of people and look only to God.
Faithfulness	Christ was faithful to all of us in dying for our sin. Paul was a faithful minister even when he was in prison. Paul urged Timothy to maintain not only sound doctrine, but also loyalty, diligence, and endurance.	We can count on opposition, suffering, and hardship as we serve Christ. But this shows that our faithfulness is having an effect on others. As we trust Christ, he counts us worthy to suffer and will give us the strength we need to be steadfast.
Preaching and Teaching	Paul and Timothy were active in preaching and teaching the good news about Jesus Christ. Paul encouraged Timothy not only to carry the torch of truth but also to train others, passing on to them sound doctrine and enthusiasm for Christ's mission.	We must prepare people to transmit God's Word to others so that they might pass it on. Does your church carefully train others to teach?
Error	In the final days before Christ returns, there will be false teachers, spiritual dropouts, and heresy. The remedy for error is to have a solid program for teaching Christians.	Because of the deception and false teaching, we must be disciplined and ready to reject error by knowing God's Word. Know the word of God as your sure defense against error and confusion.

1. Foundations of Christian service

1 Paul, an apostle of Christ Jesus by the will of God, for the sake of the promise
of life that is in Christ Jesus,
2 To Timothy, my beloved child:
Grace, mercy, and peace from God the Father and Christ Jesus our Lord.

Paul encourages Timothy to be faithful

3 I am grateful to God — whom I worship with a clear conscience, as my ancestors did — when I remember you constantly in my prayers night and day. 4 Recalling
your tears, I long to see you so that I may be filled with joy. 5 I am reminded of your
sincere faith, a faith that lived first in your grandmother Lois and your mother Eunice and now, I am sure, lives in you. 6 For this reason I remind you to rekindle the
gift of God that is within you through the laying on of my hands; 7 for God did not
give us a spirit of cowardice, but rather a spirit of power and of love and of self-
discipline.
8 Do not be ashamed, then, of the testimony about our Lord or of me his prisoner, but join with me in suffering for the gospel, relying on the power of God,
9 who saved us and called us with a holy calling, not according to our works but
according to his own purpose and grace. This grace was given to us in Christ Jesus
before the ages began, 10 but it has now been revealed through the appearing of our
Savior Christ Jesus, who abolished death and brought life and immortality to light
through the gospel. 11 For this gospel I was appointed a herald and an apostle and
a teacher,[a] 12 and for this reason I suffer as I do. But I am not ashamed, for I know

1.1 Tit 1.1,2; 1 Jn 5.10,11,20
1.2 1 Tim 1.2
1.3 Acts 23.1; 24.14; Rom 1.9
1.4 Acts 20.37
1.5 Acts 16.1
1.6 Acts 8.18; 1 Tim 4.14
1.7 Rom 8.15
1.8 Eph 3.1
1.9 Rom 8.28-30; 11.29; Eph 1.4; 2.9; 1 Thess 4.7; Tit 3.5
1.12 1 Tim 6.20; 1 Pet 4.19

[a] Other ancient authorities add *of the Gentiles*

1.1 This is a somber letter. Paul was imprisoned for the last time, and he knew he would soon die. Unlike his first imprisonment in Rome, when he was in a house (Acts 28.16, 23, 30) and continued to teach, this time he was probably confined to a cold dungeon, awaiting his death (4.6–8). Emperor Nero had begun a major persecution in A.D. 64 as part of his plan to pass the blame for the great fire of Rome from himself to the Christians. This persecution spread across the empire and included social ostracism, public torture, and murder. As Paul waited to die, he wrote a letter to his dear friend Timothy, a younger man who was like a son to him (1.2). These are the last words we have from Paul, written in approximately A.D. 66–67.

1.2 Paul's second letter to Timothy was written about two to four years after his first letter. Timothy had been Paul's traveling companion on the second and third missionary journeys, and Paul had left him in Ephesus to help the church there (1 Timothy 1.3, 4). For more information on Timothy, see his Profile in 1 Timothy. For more information on the great missionary, Paul, see his Profile in Acts 10.

1.3 Paul consistently prayed for Timothy, his friend, his fellow traveler, his son in the faith, and a strong leader in the Christian church. Although the two men were separated from each other, their prayers provided a source of mutual encouragement. We too should pray consistently for others, especially for those with whom we do God's work.

1.4 We don't know when Paul and Timothy last parted, but it was probably when Paul was arrested and taken to Rome for his second imprisonment. The tears they shed at parting reveal the depth of their relationship.

1.5 Timothy's mother and grandmother, Eunice and Lois, were early Christian converts, possibly through Paul's ministry in their home city, Lystra (Acts 16.1). They communicated their strong Christian faith to Timothy, even though his father was probably not a believer. Don't hide your light at home: our families are fertile fields for planting gospel seeds. Let your parents, children, spouse, brothers, and sisters know of your faith in Jesus, and be sure they see Christ's love, helpfulness, and joy in you.

1.6 At the time of his ordination, Timothy received special gifts of the Spirit to enable him to serve the church (see 1 Timothy 4.14). In telling Timothy to "rekindle" those gifts, Paul was encouraging him to persevere. Timothy did not need new revelations or new gifts; he needed the courage and self-discipline to hang on to the truth and use the gifts he had already received (see 1.13, 14). If he would step out boldly in faith and proclaim the gospel once again, the Holy Spirit would go with him and give him power. Use the gift you have, and you will find that God will give you the power you need.

1.6, 7 Timothy was experiencing great opposition to his message and to himself as a leader. His youth, his association with Paul, and his leadership had come under fire from believers and nonbelievers alike. Paul urged him to be bold. When we allow people to intimidate us, we neutralize our effectiveness for God. The power of the Holy Spirit can help us overcome our fear of what some might say or do to us so we can continue to do God's work.

1.7 Paul mentions three characteristics of the effective Christian leader: power, love, and self-discipline. These are available to us because the Holy Spirit lives in us. See Galatians 5.22, 23 for a list of characteristics resulting from the Holy Spirit living in us.

1.8 In this time of mounting persecution, Timothy may have been afraid to continue preaching the gospel. His fears were based on fact. As Paul warned him, suffering would come: Timothy, like Paul, would be jailed for preaching the gospel (Hebrews 13.23). But Paul promised Timothy that God would give him strength and that he would be ready when it was his turn to suffer. Even when we are not persecuted, it can be difficult to share our faith in Christ. Fortunately we, like Paul and Timothy, can call on the Holy Spirit to give us courage. Don't be ashamed to tell others about Christ.

1.9, 10 This is a brief synopsis of the gospel. God loves us, chose us, and sent Christ to die for us. We can have eternal life through faith in him, because he broke the power of death with his resurrection. We do not deserve to be saved, but God offers us salvation anyway. All we have to do is believe and accept his offer.

1.11 Paul was a *herald* to preach to all, an *apostle* to speak with authority, and a *teacher* to help people understand the message.

1.12 Paul was in prison, but that did not stop his ministry. He carried it on through others like Timothy. Paul had lost all his material possessions, but he would never lose his faith. He trusted God to use him regardless of his circumstances. If your situation looks

the one in whom I have put my trust, and I am sure that he is able to guard until that
day what I have entrusted to him.[b] 13 Hold to the standard of sound teaching that
you have heard from me, in the faith and love that are in Christ Jesus. 14 Guard the
good treasure entrusted to you, with the help of the Holy Spirit living in us.
15 You are aware that all who are in Asia have turned away from me, including
Phygelus and Hermogenes. 16 May the Lord grant mercy to the household of Onesiphorus, because he often refreshed me and was not ashamed of my chain; 17 when
he arrived in Rome, he eagerly[c] searched for me and found me 18 — may the Lord
grant that he will find mercy from the Lord on that day! And you know very well
how much service he rendered in Ephesus.

Good soldiers are not afraid to suffer

2 You then, my child, be strong in the grace that is in Christ Jesus; 2 and what
you have heard from me through many witnesses entrust to faithful people who
will be able to teach others as well. 3 Share in suffering like a good soldier of Christ
Jesus. 4 No one serving in the army gets entangled in everyday affairs; the soldier's
aim is to please the enlisting officer. 5 And in the case of an athlete, no one is
crowned without competing according to the rules. 6 It is the farmer who does the
work who ought to have the first share of the crops. 7 Think over what I say, for the
Lord will give you understanding in all things.
8 Remember Jesus Christ, raised from the dead, a descendant of David — that is

1.13 Rom 6.17 1 Tim 1.14 2 Tim 3.14 Heb 10.23
1.14 Rom 8.9,11,16 Gal 4.6
1.15 2 Tim 4.10
1.16 2 Tim 4.19 Philem 7
1.18 Heb 6.10
2.1 Eph 3.16; 6.10 Col 1.11
2.2 1 Cor 15.3-7 2 Tim 2.13
2.3 1 Cor 9.7
2.4 2 Pet 2.20
2.5 1 Cor 9.25

[b] Or *what has been entrusted to me* [c] Or *promptly*

---

bleak, give your concerns to Christ. He will guard your faith and safely guard all you have entrusted to him until the day of his return. For more on our security in Christ, see Romans 8.38, 39.

1.12 The phrase "guard . . . what I have entrusted to him" could mean: (1) Paul knew God would guard the souls of those converted through his preaching; (2) he trusted God to guard his own soul until the Second Coming; or (3) he was confident that, though he was in prison and facing death, God would carry out the gospel ministry through others such as Timothy. Paul may have expressed his confidence to encourage Timothy, who was discouraged by the problems in Ephesus and fearful of persecution. Even in prison, Paul knew God was still in control. No matter what setbacks or problems we face, we can trust fully in God.

1.13, 14 Timothy was in a time of transition. He had been Paul's bright young helper; soon he would be on his own as leader of a church in a difficult environment. Although his responsibilities were changing, Timothy was not without help. He had everything he needed to face the future, if he would hold on tightly to it. When you are facing difficult transitions, it is good to follow Paul's advice to Timothy and look back at your experience. Who is the foundation of your faith? How can you build on the foundation that has already been laid? What gifts has the Holy Spirit given you? Use the gifts you have already been given.

1.15, 16 Nothing more is known about Phygelus and Hermogenes, who evidently opposed Paul's ministry. These men serve as a warning that even leaders can fall. Onesiphorus is given as a positive example in contrast to these men. *Asia* is Asia Minor, or modern Turkey.

2.1 How can someone be *strong* in grace? Grace means undeserved favor. Just as we are saved by grace (Ephesians 2.8, 9), we should live by grace (Colossians 2.6). This means trusting completely in Christ and *his* power, not trying to live the Christian life in our strength alone. Receive and utilize Christ's power. He will give you the strength to do his work.

2.2 If the church consistently followed this advice, it would expand geometrically as well-taught believers would teach others and commission them, in turn, to teach still others. Disciples need to be equipped to pass their faith on. Our work is not done until new believers are able to make disciples of others (see Ephesians 4.12, 13).

2.3–7 As Timothy preached and taught, he would face suffering, but he would be able to endure, because the results were well worth it. Paul uses a comparison with soldiers, athletes, and farmers who must discipline themselves and be willing to sacrifice to achieve the results they want. Like soldiers, we have to give up worldly security and endure rigorous discipline. Like athletes, we must train hard and follow the rules. Like farmers, we must work extremely hard and be patient. But we should keep going despite suffering because of the thought of victory, the vision of winning, and the hope of harvest. We will see that our suffering is worthwhile when we see our goal of glorifying God, winning people to Christ, and one day living eternally with him.

2.7 Paul tells Timothy to reflect on his words and God would give him understanding. God speaks through the Bible, his Word, but we need to be open and receptive to him. As you read the Bible, ask God to show you his timeless truths and the application to your life. Then consider what you have read by thinking it through and meditating on it. God will give you understanding.

2.8 False teachers were a problem in Ephesus (see Acts 20.29, 30; 1 Timothy 1.3–11). At the heart of false teaching is an incorrect view of Christ. In Timothy's day many asserted that Christ is divine, but not human — God, but not man. These days we often hear that he is human, but not divine — man, but not God. Either view destroys the good news that Jesus Christ has taken our sins on himself and has reconciled us to God. In this verse, Paul firmly states that Jesus is fully man ("a descendant of David") and fully God ("raised from the dead"). This is an important doctrine for all Christians. For more on this key concept, see the note on Philippians 2.5–7.

my gospel, 9 for which I suffer hardship, even to the point of being chained like a
criminal. But the word of God is not chained. 10 Therefore I endure everything for
the sake of the elect, so that they may also obtain the salvation that is in Christ
Jesus, with eternal glory. 11 The saying is sure:
If we have died with him, we will also live with him;
12 if we endure, we will also reign with him;
if we deny him, he will also deny us;
13 if we are faithless, he remains faithful—
for he cannot deny himself.

2.8 Acts 2.24 13.33,34 Rom 1.3,4
2.9 Phil 1.7
2.11 Rom 6.5,8
2.12 Rom 8.17
2.13 1 Cor 1.9

Good workers are not ashamed of their work

14 Remind them of this, and warn them before God[d] that they are to avoid
wrangling over words, which does no good but only ruins those who are listening.
15 Do your best to present yourself to God as one approved by him, a worker who
has no need to be ashamed, rightly explaining the word of truth. 16 Avoid profane
chatter, for it will lead people into more and more impiety, 17 and their talk will
spread like gangrene. Among them are Hymenaeus and Philetus, 18 who have
swerved from the truth by claiming that the resurrection has already taken place.
They are upsetting the faith of some. 19 But God's firm foundation stands, bearing

2.14 1 Tim 1.4; 6.4 Tit 3.9
2.17 1 Tim 1.20
2.18 1 Cor 15.12-20
2.19 Num 16.5 Nah 1.7 Jn 10.14

[d] Other ancient authorities read *the Lord*

2.9 Paul was in chains in prison because of the gospel he preached. The truth about Jesus was no more popular in Paul's day than in ours, but it still reaches receptive hearts. When Paul said Jesus was God, he angered the Jews who had condemned Jesus for blasphemy; but many Jews became followers of Christ (1 Corinthians 1.24). He angered the Romans who worshiped the emperor as god; but even some in Caesar's household turned to Jesus (Philippians 4.22). When Paul said Jesus was man, he angered the Greeks who thought divinity was soiled if it had any contact with humanity; still many Greeks accepted the faith (Acts 11.20, 21). The truth that Jesus is one person with two united natures has never been easy to understand, but it is being believed by people every day. Despite the opposition, continue to proclaim Christ. Some will listen and believe.

2.10 We are free to choose between life and death, and yet God has chosen us (we are his elect). This is a mystery our finite minds cannot easily grasp. But even if we do not completely understand it, we can still choose Jesus and be grateful that he has chosen us.

2.10 When Paul says "obtain the salvation," is he contradicting grace? Salvation is not something that can be worked for as Paul taught in Ephesians 2.8, 9. Paul is referring to being faithful to the end, not to a way to earn salvation.

2.11–13 God is faithful to his children; and although we may suffer great hardships here, he promises that someday we will live eternally with him. What will this involve? It means that believers will live in Christ's kingdom and that we will share in the administration of that kingdom. This was Paul's comfort as he went through suffering and faced death, and it can be ours, too. Are you facing hardships? Don't turn away from God—he promises you a wonderful future with him. For more information about living eternally with God, see Matthew 16.24–27; 19.28–30; Luke 22.28–30; Romans 5.17; 6.8; 8.10, 11, 17; 1 Corinthians 15.42–58; Colossians 3.3, 4; 1 Thessalonians 4.13–18; Revelation 3.21; 21.1—22.21.

2.13 Jesus is faithful. He will stay by our side even when we have endured so much that we seem to have no faith left. We may be faithless at times, but Jesus remains faithful to his promise to be with us always, "to the end of the age" (see Matthew 28.20; Romans 8.38, 39). Turning against him and refusing his help will break our communication with God. But he never turns his back on us even though we turn our backs on him.

2.14, 15 Paul urged Timothy to remind the believers not to argue over unimportant details or have foolish discussions ("profane chatter," 2.16), because such arguments are confusing, useless, and even harmful. False teachers loved to cause strife and divisions by quibbling over unimportant details (see 1 Timothy 6.3–5). To handle God's Word correctly, we must study and know what it says so we can understand what it means ("rightly explaining the word of truth").

2.15 Because God will examine what kind of workers we have been for him, we should build our lives on his Word and build his Word into our lives—it alone tells us how to live for him and serve him. Believers who ignore the Bible will certainly be ashamed at the judgment. Consistent and diligent study of God's Word is vital; otherwise we will be lulled into neglecting God and our true purpose for living.

2.16 In important areas of Christian teaching, we must carefully work through our disagreements. But when we bicker long hours over words and theories that are not central to the Christian faith and life, we only provoke anger and hurt feelings. Even if such profane chatter reaches a resolution, it gains little ground for the kingdom. Learning and discussing are not bad unless they keep believers constantly focusing on false doctrine or unhelpful trivialities. Don't let anything keep you from your work and service to God.

2.17, 18 Hymenaeus is also mentioned in 1 Timothy 1.20. Paul had turned him over to Satan because of his false teaching concerning the resurrection.

2.18 The false teachers were denying the resurrection of the body. They believed that when a person became a Christian, he was spiritually reborn, and that was the only resurrection there would ever be. To them, resurrection was symbolic and spiritual, not physical. Paul clearly teaches, however, that believers will be resurrected after they die, and their bodies as well as their souls will live eternally with Christ (1 Corinthians 15.35ff; 2 Corinthians 5.1–10; 1 Thessalonians 4.15–18). We cannot shape the doctrines of Scripture to match our opinions. If we try, we are putting ourselves above God. Instead, we must shape our opinions into beliefs that match God's Word.

2.19 False teachers are still spouting lies. Some distort the truth; some dilute it; and some simply delete it by saying it no longer applies. No matter how many people follow the liars, God's truth never changes, is never shaken, and will never fade. When we know and believe God's truth, he will never forsake us. God's solid foundation stands firm.

2.20 Rom 9.21
2.21 2 Tim 3.17
2.22 1 Tim 6.11
2.23 1 Tim 6.4; Tit 3.9
2.24 1 Tim 3.2,3; Tit 1.7-9
2.25 1 Tim 2.4; Tit 3.2; 1 Pet 3.15
2.26 Eph 4.27; 6.11; 1 Tim 3.7

this inscription: "The Lord knows those who are his," and, "Let everyone who calls
on the name of the Lord turn away from wickedness."
20 In a large house there are utensils not only of gold and silver but also of wood
and clay, some for special use, some for ordinary. 21 All who cleanse themselves of
the things I have mentioned[e] will become special utensils, dedicated and useful to
the owner of the house, ready for every good work. 22 Shun youthful passions and
pursue righteousness, faith, love, and peace, along with those who call on the Lord
from a pure heart. 23 Have nothing to do with stupid and senseless controversies;
you know that they breed quarrels. 24 And the Lord's servant[f] must not be quarrelsome but kindly to everyone, an apt teacher, patient, 25 correcting opponents with
gentleness. God may perhaps grant that they will repent and come to know the
truth, 26 and that they may escape from the snare of the devil, having been held
captive by him to do his will.[g]

2. Difficult times for Christian service

The last days characterized by sinfulness

3.1 1 Tim 4.1; Jude 18
3.2 Lk 16.14; Rom 1.30; 1 Tim 1.9
3.3 Rom 1.31
3.5 1 Tim 5.8
3.6 Jude 4
3.8 Ex 7.11
3.9 Ex 8.18; 9.11

3 You must understand this, that in the last days distressing times will come.
2 For people will be lovers of themselves, lovers of money, boasters, arrogant,
abusive, disobedient to their parents, ungrateful, unholy, 3 inhuman, implacable,
slanderers, profligates, brutes, haters of good, 4 treacherous, reckless, swollen
with conceit, lovers of pleasure rather than lovers of God, 5 holding to the outward
form of godliness but denying its power. Avoid them! 6 For among them are those
who make their way into households and captivate silly women, overwhelmed by
their sins and swayed by all kinds of desires, 7 who are always being instructed and
can never arrive at a knowledge of the truth. 8 As Jannes and Jambres opposed
Moses, so these people, of corrupt mind and counterfeit faith, also oppose the
truth. 9 But they will not make much progress, because, as in the case of those two
men,[h] their folly will become plain to everyone.

[e] Gk *of these things* [f] Gk *slave* [g] Or *by him, to do his* (that is, God's) *will* [h] Gk lacks *two men*

2.20, 21 Here Paul urges Timothy to be the kind of person Christ can use for his highest purposes. Don't settle for less. Make sure your life is fully in God's control, so that his will can be carried out through you.

2.22 Running away or shunning something is sometimes considered cowardly. But wise people realize that removing themselves physically from temptation is often the most courageous action to take. Timothy, a young man, was warned to shun anything that produced evil thoughts (1 Timothy 6.11). If you experience a recurring temptation that is difficult to resist, remove yourself physically from the situation. Knowing when to run is as important in spiritual battle as knowing when and how to fight.

2.23–26 As a teacher, Timothy helped those who were confused about the truth. Paul's advice to him, and to all who teach God's truth, is to be kind and gentle, patiently and courteously explaining the truth. Good teaching never promotes quarrels or foolish arguments. Whether you are teaching Sunday school, leading a Bible study, or preaching in church, remember to listen to people's questions and treat them respectfully, while avoiding getting embroiled in foolish debates. If you do this, they will be more willing to hear what you have to say and perhaps turn from their error.

3.1 Paul's reference to the *last days* reveals his sense of urgency. The last days began after Jesus' resurrection, when the Holy Spirit came upon the believers at Pentecost. They will continue until his second coming. In other words, *we* are living in the last days. Make the most of the time God has given you.

3.1ff In many parts of the world today it does not seem especially difficult to be a Christian – people aren't jailed for reading the Bible or executed for preaching Christ. There is a comfortableness about superficial Christianity. But Paul's descriptive list of behavior in the last days describes our society – even, unfortunately, many Christians. Don't give in to society's pressures. Stand up against evil by living as God would have his people live.

3.5 The *form* or appearance of godliness includes going to church, knowing Christian doctrine, using Christian clichés, and following a community's Christian traditions. Such practices can make a person look good. But if the inner attitudes of belief, love, and worship are lacking, the outer appearance is meaningless. Paul warns us not to be deceived by people who only appear to be Christians. It may be difficult to distinguish them from true Christians at first, but their lives will give them away. The characteristics described in 3.2–4 are unmistakable.

3.6, 7 Because of their cultural background, women in the Ephesian church had had no formal religious training. They enjoyed their new freedom to study Christian truths, but their eagerness to learn made them a target for false teachers. Paul warns Timothy to watch out for men who would take advantage of these women. New believers need to grow in their knowledge of the Word, because ignorance can make them vulnerable to deception.

3.7 It is possible to be a perpetual student and never graduate. This verse is not decrying study and learning; it is warning about learning for learning's sake. Honest seekers are looking for answers. Remember this as you study God's Word. Seek to find God's truth and will for your life.

3.8, 9 According to tradition, Jannes and Jambres were two of the magicians who counterfeited Moses' miracles before Pharaoh (Exodus 7.11, 12). Moses exposed and defeated them (Exodus 8.18, 19), just as God would overthrow the false teachers who were plaguing the Ephesian church.

3.9 Sin has consequences, and no one will get away with it forever. Live each day as if your actions will one day be known to everyone. Now is the time to change anything you wouldn't want revealed later.

Paul's charge to Timothy

10 Now you have observed my teaching, my conduct, my aim in life, my faith,
my patience, my love, my steadfastness, 11 my persecutions and suffering the
things that happened to me in Antioch, Iconium, and Lystra. What persecutions I
endured! Yet the Lord rescued me from all of them. 12 Indeed, all who want to live
a godly life in Christ Jesus will be persecuted. 13 But wicked people and impostors
will go from bad to worse, deceiving others and being deceived. 14 But as for you,
continue in what you have learned and firmly believed, knowing from whom you
learned it, 15 and how from childhood you have known the sacred writings that are
able to instruct you for salvation through faith in Christ Jesus. 16 All scripture is
inspired by God and is[i] useful for teaching, for reproof, for correction, and for
training in righteousness, 17 so that everyone who belongs to God may be profi-
cient, equipped for every good work.

4 In the presence of God and of Christ Jesus, who is to judge the living and the
dead, and in view of his appearing and his kingdom, I solemnly urge you:
2 proclaim the message; be persistent whether the time is favorable or unfavorable;
convince, rebuke, and encourage, with the utmost patience in teaching. 3 For the
time is coming when people will not put up with sound doctrine, but having itching
ears, they will accumulate for themselves teachers to suit their own desires, 4 and

3.10 1 Tim 6.11
3.11 Acts 13.14,45, 50; 14.19 2 Cor 1.5 11.23-27
3.12 1 Thess 3.3
3.15 Jn 5.47 Rom 10.17
3.16 Rom 15.4 2 Pet 1.20,21
3.17 1 Tim 6.11 2 Tim 2.21
4.1 Acts 10.42
4.2 1 Tim 5.10 Tit 1.13
4.3 2 Tim 3.1

[i] Or *Every scripture inspired by God is also*

3.11 In Lystra, Timothy's hometown, Paul was stoned and left for dead (Acts 14.19); and this was only one incident among many. In 2 Corinthians 11.23–33 he summarizes his lifetime of suffering for the sake of the gospel. Paul mentions his suffering here to contrast his experience with that of the false teachers.

3.12 Paul tells Timothy that those who obey God and live for Christ will be persecuted. Don't be surprised when people misunderstand, criticize, and even try to hurt you because of what you believe and how you live. Don't give up. Continue to live as you know you should. God is the only one you need to please.

3.13 Don't expect false teachers and evil people to reform and change on their own. Left alone, they will go from bad to worse. If you have the opportunity, correct them. Fight for the truth to protect younger Christians.

3.14 Besieged by false teachers and the inevitable pressures of a growing ministry, Timothy could easily have abandoned his faith or modified his doctrine. Once again Paul counsels him to look to his past and to hold to the basic teachings about Jesus that are eternally true. Like Timothy, we are surrounded by false teachings, and most of us are very busy. But we must not allow our society to distort or crowd out God's eternal truth. Spend time every day reflecting on the foundation of your Christian faith found in God's Word, the great truths on which you build your life. Thank God for and express appreciation to the devoted men and women who taught them to you.

3.15 Timothy was one of the first second-generation Christians: he became a Christian not because an evangelist preached a powerful sermon, but because his mother and grandmother taught him the holy Scriptures when he was a small child (1.5). The evangelist's work is important, but the parent's work is just as important. At home and in church, we should realize that teaching small children is both an opportunity and a responsibility. Jesus wanted little children to come to him (Matthew 19.13–15). Like Timothy's mother and grandmother, Eunice and Lois, do your part in leading them to Christ.

3.15 For Timothy, the sacred writings were the Old Testament—Genesis to Malachi. The Old Testament is important, because it points to Jesus Christ. And faith in Christ makes the whole Bible intelligible.

3.16 The Bible is not a collection of stories, fables, myths, or merely human ideas about God. It is not just a human book. Through the Holy Spirit God revealed his person and plan to certain believers, who wrote down God's message for his people (2 Peter 1.20, 21). This process is known as *inspiration.* The writers wrote from their own personal, historical, and cultural contexts. But even though they used their own minds, talents, language, and style, they wrote what God wanted them to write. Scripture is completely trustworthy, because God was in control of its writing, and its words are entirely authoritative for our faith and lives. The Bible is inspired. Read it and use it to guide your conduct.

3.16 The whole Bible is God's inspired Word. Because it is inspired and trustworthy, we should *read* it and *apply* it to our lives. The Bible is our standard for testing everything else that claims to be true. It is our safeguard against false teaching and our source of guidance for how we should live. It is our only source of knowledge about how we can be saved. God wants to show you what is true and equip you to live for him. How much time do you spend in God's Word? Read it regularly to discover God's truth and become confident in your life and faith. Develop a plan for reading the whole Bible, not just the same familiar passages.

3.17 In our zeal for the *truth* of Scripture, we must never forget its *purpose*—to equip us to do good to others. We should not study God's Word simply to increase our own knowledge or to prepare us to win arguments. We should study Scripture so that we will know how to do Christ's work in the world. Our knowledge of God's Word is not useful unless it leads us to good works.

4.1, 2 It was important for Timothy to preach the gospel so that the Christian faith could spread throughout the world. We believe in Christ today because people like Timothy were faithful to their mission. It is still vitally important for believers to spread the gospel. Half the people who have ever lived are alive today, and most of them do not know Jesus. He is coming soon, and he wants to find his faithful believers ready for him. It may be inconvenient to take a stand for Christ or to tell others about his love, but preaching the word of God is the most important responsibility the church and its members have been given. Be prepared, courageous, and sensitive to God-given opportunities to tell the good news.

4.2 Paul told Timothy to "convince, rebuke, and encourage." It is difficult to accept correction, to be told we have to change. But no matter how much the truth hurts, we must be willing to listen to it so we can more fully obey God.

4.3 "Having itching ears" means hearing only what they want to hear.

4.5 2 Tim 1.8
4.6 Phil 1.23
4.7 1 Cor 9.24-27 Phil 3.12-14 1 Tim 6.12
4.8 1 Cor 9.25 2 Tim 1.12

will turn away from listening to the truth and wander away to myths. 5 As for you,
always be sober, endure suffering, do the work of an evangelist, carry out your
ministry fully.
6 As for me, I am already being poured out as a libation, and the time of my
departure has come. 7 I have fought the good fight, I have finished the race, I have
kept the faith. 8 From now on there is reserved for me the crown of righteousness,
which the Lord, the righteous judge, will give me on that day, and not only to me
but also to all who have longed for his appearing.

Paul's final words

4.9 2 Tim 1.4
4.10 Col 4.14 Philem 24
4.11 Col 4.10,14
4.12 Acts 20.4 Eph 6.21
4.16 Acts 7.60 1 Cor 13.5
4.17 Ps 22.21 Acts 9.15 2 Tim 3.11 Tit 1.3

9 Do your best to come to me soon, 10 for Demas, in love with this present
world, has deserted me and gone to Thessalonica; Crescens has gone to Galatia,[j]
Titus to Dalmatia. 11 Only Luke is with me. Get Mark and bring him with you, for
he is useful in my ministry. 12 I have sent Tychicus to Ephesus. 13 When you come,
bring the cloak that I left with Carpus at Troas, also the books, and above all the
parchments. 14 Alexander the coppersmith did me great harm; the Lord will pay
him back for his deeds. 15 You also must beware of him, for he strongly opposed
our message.
16 At my first defense no one came to my support, but all deserted me. May it
not be counted against them! 17 But the Lord stood by me and gave me strength, so
that through me the message might be fully proclaimed and all the Gentiles might
hear it. So I was rescued from the lion's mouth. 18 The Lord will rescue me from

[j] Other ancient authorities read *Gaul*

4.5 "Always be sober" means to "keep your head." To keep cool when jolted by people or circumstances, don't react quickly. In any work of ministry, keeping your head makes you morally alert to temptation, calm under pressure, and vigilant when facing heavy responsibility.

4.5–8 As he neared the end of his life, Paul could confidently say he had been faithful to his call. Thus he faced death calmly; he knew he would be rewarded by Christ. Is your life preparing you for death? Do you share Paul's confident expectation of meeting Christ? The good news is that the heavenly reward is not just for giants of the faith, like Paul, but for all who are eagerly looking forward to Jesus' second coming. Paul gave these words to encourage Timothy, and us, that no matter how difficult the fight seems—keep fighting. We will discover when we are with Jesus Christ that it was all worth it.

4.6 A *libation* was a drink offering poured out to the Lord as a sacrifice on the altar.

4.8 In Roman athletic games, a laurel wreath was given to the winners. A symbol of triumph and honor, it was the most coveted prize in ancient Rome. This is probably what Paul was referring to when he spoke of a "crown." But his would be a crown of righteousness. See 2 Corinthians 5.10 and the note on Matthew 19.27 for more on the rewards awaiting us for our faith and deeds. Although Paul would not receive an earthly reward, he would be rewarded in heaven. Whatever we may face—discomfort, persecution, or death—we know our reward is with Christ in heaven.

4.9 Paul was virtually alone and probably lonely. No one had been there at his trial to speak in his defense (4.16), and Demas and others had left the faith (4.10). Only Luke had returned (4.11).

4.10 Demas had been one of Paul's co-workers (Colossians 4.14; Philemon 1.24), but he deserted Paul because he was "in love with this present world." In other words, he loved worldly values and worldly pleasures. There are two ways to love the world. God loves the world as he created it and as it could be if it were rescued from evil. Others, like Demas, love the world as it is, sin and all. Do you love the world as it could be if justice were done, the hungry were fed, and people loved one another? Or do you love what the world has to offer—wealth, power, pleasure—even if gaining it means hurting people and neglecting the work God has given you to do?

4.10 Crescens and Titus had left, but not for the same reasons as Demas. Paul does not criticize or condemn them.

4.11, 12 Mentioning Demas reminded Paul of more faithful co-workers. Only Luke was with him, and Paul was feeling lonely. Tychicus, one of his most trusted companions (Acts 20.4; Ephesians 6.21; Colossians 4.7; Titus 3.12), had already left for Ephesus. He missed his young helpers Timothy and Mark. Mark had left Paul and Barnabas on the first missionary journey, and this had greatly angered Paul (Acts 13.13; 15.36–41). But Mark later proved himself a worthy helper, and Paul recognized him as a good friend and trusted Christian leader (Colossians 4.10; Philemon 1.24). Mark wrote the Gospel of Mark.

4.13 Paul's arrest was probably so sudden that he was not allowed to return home to gather his personal belongings. As a prisoner in a damp and chilly dungeon, Paul asked Timothy to bring him a coat. Even more than the coat, he wanted his parchments. These may have included parts of the Old Testament, the Gospels, copies of his own letters, or other important documents.

4.14, 15 Alexander may have been a witness against Paul at his trial. He is also mentioned in 1 Timothy 1.20, and may be the Alexander in Acts 19.33, 34.

4.17 With his mentor in prison and his church in turmoil, Timothy was not feeling very brave. Paul may be subtly telling him that the Lord has called him to preach and will give him the courage to do so. God always gives us the strength to do what he has commanded. This strength may not be evident, however, until we step out in faith and actually begin doing the task.

4.17 Paul was probably literally "rescued from the lion's mouth," because Nero often had Christians killed by throwing them to the lions in the Coliseum.

4.18 Paul was affirming his belief in eternal life after death, not that he wouldn't die. Paul knew the end was near, and he was ready for it. Paul was confident in God's power and sovereignty, even as he faced death. Anyone facing a life-and-death struggle can be comforted and encouraged knowing that God will bring each believer safely through death to his heavenly kingdom.

every evil attack and save me for his heavenly kingdom. To him be the glory for- **4.18** Ps 121.7
ever and ever. Amen. Rom 11.36

19 Greet Prisca and Aquila, and the household of Onesiphorus. 20 Erastus re- **4.19** Acts 18.2
mained in Corinth; Trophimus I left ill in Miletus. 21 Do your best to come before 2 Tim 1.16
winter. Eubulus sends greetings to you, as do Pudens and Linus and Claudia and all **4.20** Acts 19.22; 20.4
the brothers and sisters.[k] **4.22**
22 The Lord be with your spirit. Grace be with you.[l] Gal 6.18

[k] Gk *all the brothers* [l] The Greek word for *you* here is plural. Other ancient authorities add *Amen*

4.19, 20 Priscilla (Prisca) and Aquila were fellow Christian leaders with whom Paul had lived and worked (Acts 18.2, 3). Onesiphorus visited and encouraged Paul in jail. Erastus was one of Paul's trusted companions (Acts 19.22), as was Trophimus (Acts 20.4; 21.29).

4.19–22 Paul ends the final chapter in his book and in his life by greeting those who were closest to him. Although he had spent most of his life traveling, he developed close and lasting friendships. Too often we rush through our days barely touching anyone's life. Like Paul, take time to build your life into others through lasting relationships.

4.22 As Paul reached the end of his life, he could look back and know he had been faithful to God's call. Now it was time to pass the torch to the next generation, preparing leaders to take his place so that the world would continue to hear the life-changing message of Jesus Christ. Timothy was Paul's living legacy, a product of Paul's faithful teaching, discipleship, and example. Because of Paul's work with many believers, including Timothy, the world is full of believers today who are also carrying on the work. What legacy will you leave behind? Whom are you training to carry on your work? It is our responsibility to keep God's Word alive for the next generation.

The Letter of Paul to TITUS

THE VACUUM produced when a strong leader departs can devastate a movement, organization, or institution. Dependent upon his or her skill, style, and personality, associates and subordinates flounder or vie for control. Soon efficiency and vitality are lost, and decline and demise follow. Often this pattern is repeated in churches. Great speakers and teachers gather a following, and soon a church is flourishing. It is alive, vital, and effective. Lives are being changed and souls led into the kingdom. But when this catalyst leaves or dies, with him or her goes the drive and the heart of the organization.

People flocked to hear Paul's teaching. Educated, articulate, motivated, and filled with the Holy Spirit, this man of faith faithfully proclaimed the good news throughout the Roman Empire—lives were changed and churches begun. But Paul knew that the church must be built on Christ, not on a person. And he knew that eventually he would not be there to build, encourage, discipline, and teach. So he trained young pastors to assume leadership in the church after he was gone. Paul urged them to center their lives and preaching on the word of God (2 Timothy 3.16, 17) and to train others to carry on the ministry (2 Timothy 2.2).

Titus was a Greek believer. Taught and nurtured by Paul, he stood before the leaders of the church in Jerusalem as a living example of what Christ was doing among the Gentiles (Galatians 2.1–3). Like Timothy, he was one of Paul's trusted traveling companions and closest friends. Later he became Paul's special ambassador (2 Corinthians 7.5–16) and eventually the overseer of the churches on Crete (Titus 1.5). Slowly and carefully, Paul developed Titus into a mature Christian and a responsible leader. The letter to Titus is another step in this discipleship process. As with Timothy, Paul tells Titus how to organize and lead the churches.

Paul begins with a longer than usual greeting and introduction, outlining the leadership progression—Paul's ministry (1.1–3), Titus's responsibilities (1.4, 5), and those leaders whom Titus would appoint and train (1.5). Paul then lists pastoral qualifications (1.6–9) and contrasts them with the false leaders and teachers (1.10–16).

Next, Paul emphasizes the importance of good works in the life of the Christian, telling Titus how to relate to the various age groups in the church (2.2–6). He urges Titus to be a good example of a mature believer (2.7, 8) and to teach with courage and conviction (2.9–15). He then discusses the general responsibilities of Christians in society—Titus should remind the people of these (3.1–8), and he should avoid divisive arguments (3.9–11). Paul concludes with a few matters of itinerary and personal greetings (3.12–15).

Paul's letter to Titus is brief, but it is an important link in the discipleship process—helping a young man grow into leadership in the church. As you read this pastoral epistle, you will gain insight into the organization and life of the early church and principles for structuring contemporary churches. But you should also see how to be a responsible Christian leader. Read the Epistle to Titus and determine, like Paul, to train men and women to lead and teach others.

VITAL STATISTICS

PURPOSE:
To advise Titus in his responsibility of supervising the churches on the island of Crete

AUTHOR:
Paul

TO WHOM WRITTEN:
Titus, a Greek, probably converted to Christ through Paul's ministry, who had become Paul's special representative to the island of Crete

DATE WRITTEN:
About A.D. 64, around the same time 1 Timothy was written; probably from Macedonia when Paul traveled in between his Roman imprisonments

SETTING:
Paul sent Titus to organize and oversee the churches on Crete. This letter tells him how to do this job.

KEY VERSE:
"I left you behind in Crete for this reason, so that you should put in order what remained to be done, and should appoint elders in every town, as I directed you" (1.5).

KEY PEOPLE:
Paul, Titus

KEY PLACES:
Crete, Nicopolis

SPECIAL FEATURES:
Titus is very similar to 1 Timothy with its instructions to pastors (elders).

THE BLUEPRINT

1. Leadership in the church (1.1–16)
2. Right living in the church (2.1–15)
3. Right living in society (3.1–15)

Paul calls for church order and right living on an island known for laziness, gluttony, lying, and evil. The Christians are to be disciplined as individuals and orderly as a church. We need to obey this message in our day when discipline is not respected or rewarded by our society. Although others may not regard our efforts, we must live upright lives, obey the government, and control our speech. We should live together peacefully in the church and be living examples of our faith in society.

MEGATHEMES

THEME	EXPLANATION	IMPORTANCE
A Good Life	The good news of salvation is that we can't be saved by living a good life; we are saved only by faith in Jesus Christ. But the gospel transforms people's lives, so that they eventually perform good works. Our service won't save us, but we are saved to serve.	A good life is a witness to the gospel's power. As Christians, we must have commitment and discipline to serve. Are you putting your faith in action by serving others?
Character	Titus's responsibility at Crete was to appoint pastors (elders) on Crete to maintain proper organization and discipline, so Paul listed the qualities needed for the eldership. Their conduct in their homes revealed their fitness for service in the church.	It's not enough to be educated or have a following to be Christ's kind of leader. You must have self-control, spiritual and moral fitness, and Christian character. Who you are is just as important as what you can do.
Church Relationships	Church teaching was to relate to various groups. Older Christians were to teach and to be examples to younger men and women. Every age and group has a lesson to learn and a role to play.	Right living and right relationship go along with right doctrine. Treat relationships with other believers as an outgrowth of your faith.
Citizenship	Christians must be good citizens in society, not just in church. Believers must obey the government and work honestly.	How you fulfill your civic duties is a witness to the watching world. Your community life should reflect Christ's love as much as your church life does.

1. Leadership in the church

1 Paul, a servant[a] of God and an apostle of Jesus Christ, for the sake of the faith
of God's elect and the knowledge of the truth that is in accordance with godliness, 2 in the hope of eternal life that God, who never lies, promised before the ages 1.2 1 Tim 1.9
began— 3 in due time he revealed his word through the proclamation with which I 1.3 Acts 9.15 2 Tim 4.17
have been entrusted by the command of God our Savior,

a Gk *slave*

1.1 Paul wrote this letter between his first and second imprisonments in Rome (before he wrote 2 Timothy) to guide Titus in working with the churches on the island of Crete. Paul had visited Crete with Titus and left him there to minister. There was a strong pagan influence on this small island, because Crete was a center for training Roman soldiers. Therefore, the church in Crete needed strong Christian leadership.

1.1 In one short phrase, Paul gives us insight into his reason for living. He calls himself a servant of God—that is, he was committed to obeying God. This obedience led him to spend his life telling others about Christ. How would you describe your purpose in life? To what are you devoted? For more information on Paul, see his Profile in Acts 10.

1.1 Paul calls himself "an apostle." Even though he was not one of the original 12, he was specially called by God to bring the good news to the Gentiles (Acts 9.1–16 for an account of his call). The word *apostle* means messenger or missionary. *God's elect* refers to God's choice of his people, the church.

1.2 Apparently lying was common in Crete (see 1.12). Paul makes it clear at the start that God does not lie. The foundation of our faith is trust in God's character. Because he *is* truth, he is the *source* of all truth and cannot lie. Believing in him leads to godliness, living a God-honoring life-style (1.1). The eternal life he has promised will be ours because he keeps his promises. Build your faith on the foundation of a trustworthy God who never lies.

1.3 God is called "our Savior," as is Jesus Christ (1.4). *God* here means the "Father." Jesus did the work of salvation by dying for our sins and therefore is our Savior. God planned the work of sal-

4 To Titus, my loyal child in the faith we share:
Grace[b] and peace from God the Father and Christ Jesus our Savior.

Qualifications for church leaders

1.5 Acts 14.23
1.6 1 Tim 3.2-4
1.7 1 Cor 4.1,2; 1 Tim 3.2,3
1.8 1 Tim 3.2,3
1.9 2 Thess 2.15

5 I left you behind in Crete for this reason, so that you should put in order what
remained to be done, and should appoint elders in every town, as I directed you:
6 someone who is blameless, married only once,[c] whose children are believers, not
accused of debauchery and not rebellious. 7 For a bishop,[d] as God's steward, must
be blameless; he must not be arrogant or quick-tempered or addicted to wine or
violent or greedy for gain; 8 but he must be hospitable, a lover of goodness, prudent, upright, devout, and self-controlled. 9 He must have a firm grasp of the word
that is trustworthy in accordance with the teaching, so that he may be able both to
preach with sound doctrine and to refute those who contradict it.

[b] Other ancient authorities read *Grace, mercy,* [c] Gk *husband of one wife* [d] Or *an overseer*

TITUS GOES TO CRETE
Tradition says that after Paul was released from prison in Rome (before his second and final Roman imprisonment), he and Titus traveled together for a while. They stopped in Crete; and when it was time for Paul to go, he left Titus behind to help the churches there.

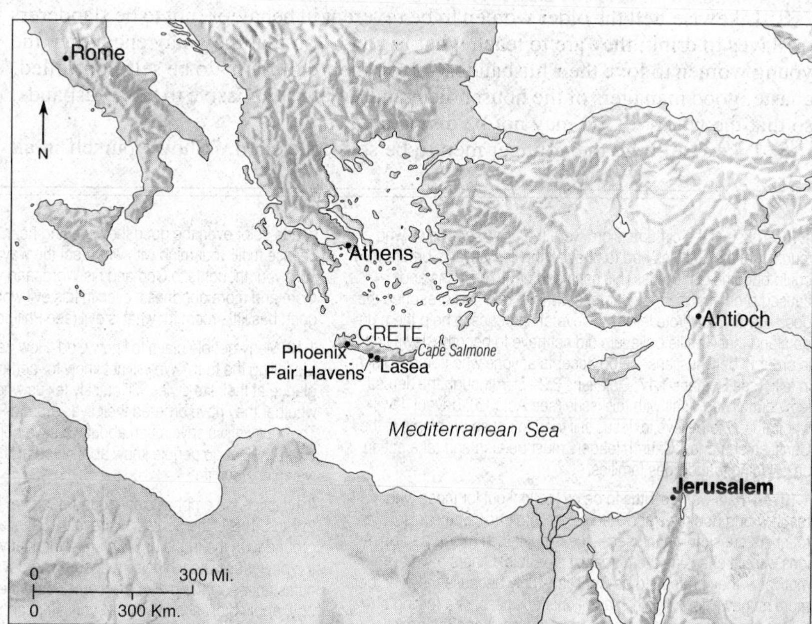

vation and forgives our sins; thus, he is also our Savior. Both the Father and the Son acted to save us from our sins.

1.4 Titus, a Greek, was one of Paul's most trusted and dependable co-workers. Paul sent Titus to Corinth on several special missions to help the church in its troubles (2 Corinthians 7, 8). Paul and Titus also traveled together to Jerusalem (Galatians 2.3) and Crete (1.5). Paul left Titus in Crete to lead the new churches springing up on the island. Titus is last mentioned by Paul in 2 Timothy 4.10, his last recorded letter. Titus had leadership ability, so Paul gave him leadership responsibility, urging him to use his abilities well.

1.5 Crete, a small island in the Mediterranean Sea, had a large population of Jews. The churches there were probably founded by Cretan Jews who had been in Jerusalem at Pentecost (Acts 2.11) more than 30 years before Paul wrote this letter.

1.5 "What remained to be done" refers to the establishment of correct teaching and the appointing of elders in every town.

1.5 Paul had appointed elders in various churches during his journeys (Acts 14.23). He could not stay in each church, but he knew that these new churches needed strong spiritual leadership. The men chosen were to lead the churches by teaching sound doctrine, helping believers mature spiritually, and equipping them to live for Jesus Christ despite the opposition.

1.5–9 Paul briefly describes some qualifications the *elders* or *bishops* should have. He gave Timothy a similar set of instructions for the church in Ephesus (see 1 Timothy 3.1–7; 5.22). Notice that most of the qualifications involve character, not knowledge or skill. A person's life-style and relationships provide a window into his character. Consider these qualifications as you evaluate a person for a position of leadership in your church. While it is important to have leaders who can effectively preach God's Word, it is even more important that they live out God's Word and be examples for others to follow.

Warning against false teachers

10 There are also many rebellious people, idle talkers and deceivers, especially
those of the circumcision; 11 they must be silenced, since they are upsetting whole
families by teaching for sordid gain what it is not right to teach. 12 It was one of
them, their very own prophet, who said,
"Cretans are always liars, vicious brutes, lazy gluttons."
13 That testimony is true. For this reason rebuke them sharply, so that they may
become sound in the faith, 14 not paying attention to Jewish myths or to commandments of those who reject the truth. 15 To the pure all things are pure, but to the
corrupt and unbelieving nothing is pure. Their very minds and consciences are corrupted. 16 They profess to know God, but they deny him by their actions. They are
detestable, disobedient, unfit for any good work.

1.10 Acts 15.1; 2 Cor 11.13; 1 Tim 1.6
1.11 1 Tim 5.13; 6.5
1.13 1 Tim 5.20
1.14 Col 2.22; 2 Tim 4.4
1.15 Rom 14.14
1.16 1 Tim 5.8; 2 Tim 3.8

2. Right living in the church

2 But as for you, teach what is consistent with sound doctrine. 2 Tell the older
men to be temperate, serious, prudent, and sound in faith, in love, and in endurance.
3 Likewise, tell the older women to be reverent in behavior, not to be slanderers
or slaves to drink; they are to teach what is good, 4 so that they may encourage the
young women to love their husbands, to love their children, 5 to be self-controlled,
chaste, good managers of the household, kind, being submissive to their husbands,
so that the word of God may not be discredited.
6 Likewise, urge the younger men to be self-controlled. 7 Show yourself in all

2.1 1 Tim 6.3; Tit 1.9
2.3 1 Pet 3.3,4
2.5 Eph 5.22; Col 3.18; 1 Tim 5.14
2.7 1 Tim 4.12; 1 Pet 5.3

1.10 "Those of the circumcision" were the *Judaizers,* Jews who taught that the Gentiles had to obey all the Jewish laws before they could become Christians. This confused new Christians and caused problems in many churches where Paul had preached the good news. Paul wrote letters to several churches to help them understand that Gentile believers did not have to become Jews first in order to be Christians – God accepts anyone who comes to him in faith (see Romans 1.17; Galatians 3.2–7). Although the Jerusalem council had dealt with this issue (see Acts 15), devout Jews who refused to believe in Jesus still tried to cause problems in the Christian churches. Church leaders must be alert and take action on anything that divides families.

1.10–14 Paul warned Titus to be on the lookout for those who teach wrong doctrines and lead others into error. Some false teachers are simply confused – they speak their misguided opinions without checking them against the Bible. Others have evil motives – they pretend to be Christians only because they can get more money ("sordid gain"), additional business, or a feeling of power from being a leader in the church. Jesus and the apostles repeatedly warned against false teachers (see Mark 13.22; Acts 20.29; 2 Thessalonians 2.3–12; 2 Peter 3.3–7), because their teachings attack the foundations of truth and integrity upon which the Christian faith is built.

You can recognize false teachers because they will (1) focus more attention on themselves than on Christ; (2) ask you to do something that will compromise or dilute your faith; (3) deemphasize the divine nature of Christ or the inspiration of the Bible; or (4) urge believers to make decisions based more on human judgment than on prayer and biblical guidelines.

1.12 Paul was quoting a line from a poem by Epimenides, a poet and philosopher who had lived in Crete 600 years earlier. Paul used this familiar phrase to make the point that Titus's ministry and leadership were very much needed.

1.15 Some people see good all around them, while others see nothing but evil. What is the difference? Our souls become filters through which we perceive goodness or evil. The pure of heart (those who have Christ in control of their lives) learn to see goodness and purity even in this evil world. But "corrupt and unbelieving" people find evil in everything, because their evil minds and hearts color even the good they see and hear. Whatever you choose to fill your mind with will affect the way you think and act. Turn your thoughts to God and his Word, and you will discover more and more goodness, even in this evil world. A mind filled with good has little room for what is evil (see Philippians 4.8).

1.16 Many people claim to know God. How can we know if they are telling the truth? We will not know for certain in this life, but a glance at their life-styles will quickly tell us what they value and whether they have ordered their lives around kingdom priorities. The way we live says much about what we believe (see 1 John 2.4–6). What do people know about God and about your faith by watching your life?

2.1 Notice the emphasis on "sound doctrine" in these instructions to Titus. This is the *content* of the faith. Believers must be grounded in the truths of Scripture – then they won't be swayed by the powerful oratory of false teachers, the devastation of tragic circumstances, or the pull of emotions. Learn the Word, study theology, apply biblical principles to your life, and *do* what you learn.

2.1–8 Having people of all ages makes the church strong, but it also brings potential for problems. Paul counsels Titus on how to help various groups of people. The older people should teach the younger, by words *and* by example. This is how values are passed on from generation to generation.

2.2, 5 *Temperance* or self-control was an important aspect in early Christianity. The Christian community was made up of people from differing backgrounds and viewpoints, making conflict inevitable. Christians existed in a pagan and often hostile world. To keep above reproach, men and women needed wisdom and discernment to be discreet and to master their wills, tongues, and passions so that Christ would not be dishonored. Do you strive to exhibit self-control?

2.3–5 Women who were new Christians were to learn how to have harmony in the home by watching older women who had been Christians for some time. We have the same need today. Younger wives and mothers should learn to live in a Christian manner – loving their husbands and caring for their children – by observing exemplary women of God. If you are of an age or position where people look up to you, make sure that your example motivates younger believers to live in a way that honors God.

2.8 1 Pet 2.12
2.9 Eph 6.5
2.11 Jn 1.9; 1 Tim 2.4; 2 Tim 1.10
2.13 Isa 9.6; Jn 1.1; 20.28; Rom 9.5; 2 Pet 1.1; 1 Jn 5.20
2.14 Deut 7.6; 14.2; Eph 2.10; 1 Pet 2.9; 1 Jn 1.7
2.15 1 Tim 4.12

respects a model of good works, and in your teaching show integrity, gravity, 8 and
sound speech that cannot be censured; then any opponent will be put to shame,
having nothing evil to say of us.
9 Tell slaves to be submissive to their masters and to give satisfaction in every
respect; they are not to talk back, 10 not to pilfer, but to show complete and perfect
fidelity, so that in everything they may be an ornament to the doctrine of God our
Savior.
11 For the grace of God has appeared, bringing salvation to all,[e] 12 training us
to renounce impiety and worldly passions, and in the present age to live lives that
are self-controlled, upright, and godly, 13 while we wait for the blessed hope and
the manifestation of the glory of our great God and Savior,[f] Jesus Christ. 14 He it
is who gave himself for us that he might redeem us from all iniquity and purify for
himself a people of his own who are zealous for good deeds.
15 Declare these things; exhort and reprove with all authority.[g] Let no one look
down on you.

3. Right living in society

Obey the government

3.2 Eph 4.31; 2 Tim 2.25
3.3 1 Cor 6.9-11
3.5 Rom 3.20; 8.16; Gal 2.16; 4.6; Eph 2.9

3 Remind them to be subject to rulers and authorities, to be obedient, to be ready
for every good work, 2 to speak evil of no one, to avoid quarreling, to be gentle, and to show every courtesy to everyone. 3 For we ourselves were once foolish,
disobedient, led astray, slaves to various passions and pleasures, passing our days
in malice and envy, despicable, hating one another. 4 But when the goodness and
loving kindness of God our Savior appeared, 5 he saved us, not because of any
works of righteousness that we had done, but according to his mercy, through the

[e] Or *has appeared to all, bringing salvation* [f] Or *of the great God and our Savior* [g] Gk *commandment*

2.6 This advice given to young men was very important. In ancient Greek society, the role of the husband/father was not viewed as a nurturing role, but merely a functional one. Many young men today have been raised in families where fathers have neglected their responsibilities to their wives and children. Husbands and fathers who are good examples of Christian living are extremely important role models for young men who need to *see* how it is done.

2.7 When Paul encourages young men to have *gravity* in their teaching, he wants them to be reverent and purposeful, not boring. Christianity should never be intentionally gloomy. Don't let the seriousness of the gospel cause you to repel others by your grim disposition.

2.7, 8 Paul urged Titus to be a good example to those around him so that others might see his good deeds and imitate him. His life would give his words greater impact. If you want someone to act a certain way, be sure that you live that way yourself. Then you will earn the right to be heard, and your life will reinforce what you teach.

2.8 Paul counsels Titus to be "sound" (sensible and reasonable) in his conversation so that he would avoid criticism. Such conversation comes from careful Bible study and by listening before speaking. This is especially important when teaching or confronting others about spiritual or moral issues. If we are impulsive, unreasonable, and confusing, we are likely to start arguments rather than to convince people of the truth.

2.9, 10 Slavery was common in Paul's day. Paul does not condemn slavery in any of his letters, but he advises slaves and masters to be loving and responsible in their conduct (see also Ephesians 6.5–9). The standards set by Paul apply to any employee/employer relationship. Employees should always do their best work and be trustworthy, not just when the employer is watching. Businesses in the United States lose millions of dollars a year to employee theft and time-wasting. If all Christian employees followed Paul's advice at work, what a transformation it would make!

2.11–14 The power to live as a Christian comes from the Holy Spirit. Because Christ died and rescued us from sin, we are free from sin's control. God gives us the power and understanding to live according to his will and to do good. Then we will look forward to Christ's wonderful (manifestation) return with eager expectation and hope.

2.12 It is not enough to renounce sin and evil desires; we must also live actively for God. To fight against lust we must say no to temptation, but we must also say yes to active service for Christ.

2.14 Christ's redeeming us opens the way for him to purify us. *Redeem* means to purchase our release from the captivity of sin with a ransom (see Mark 10.45 for more on Christ as our ransom). We are not only free from the sentence of death for our sin, but we are also purified from sin's influence as we grow in Christ.

2.15 Paul told Titus to teach the Scriptures as well as to live them. We must also teach, exhort, and rebuke others when necessary. It is easy to feel afraid when others are older, more influential in the community, or wealthier. Like Titus, we should not let ourselves be threatened when we are trying to minister to others or provide leadership in the church.

3.1, 2 As Christians, our first allegiance is to Jesus as Lord, but we also must obey our government and its leaders. Christians are not above the law. Obeying the civil law is only the beginning of our Christian responsibility; we must do what we can to be good citizens. In a democracy, this means participation and willingness to serve. (See Acts 5.29 and Romans 13.1ff for more on the Christian's attitude toward government.)

3.3–8 Paul summarizes what Christ does for us when he saves us. We move from a life full of sin to one led by God's Holy Spirit. *All* our sins, not merely some, are washed away. Water may refer to the water of baptism. In receiving baptism, the individual identifies with the Christian community.

3.4–6 All persons of the trinity participate in the work of salvation. Based upon the redemptive work of his Son, the Father forgives and sends the Holy Spirit to wash away our sins and continually renew us.

water[h] of rebirth and renewal by the Holy Spirit. 6 This Spirit he poured out on us
richly through Jesus Christ our Savior, 7 so that, having been justified by his grace,
we might become heirs according to the hope of eternal life. 8 The saying is sure.

Avoid useless arguments

I desire that you insist on these things, so that those who have come to believe in
God may be careful to devote themselves to good works; these things are excellent
and profitable to everyone. 9 But avoid stupid controversies, genealogies, dissensions, and quarrels about the law, for they are unprofitable and worthless. 10 After
a first and second admonition, have nothing more to do with anyone who causes
divisions, 11 since you know that such a person is perverted and sinful, being self-
condemned.

Paul's final instructions

12 When I send Artemas to you, or Tychicus, do your best to come to me at
Nicopolis, for I have decided to spend the winter there. 13 Make every effort to send
Zenas the lawyer and Apollos on their way, and see that they lack nothing. 14 And
let people learn to devote themselves to good works in order to meet urgent needs,
so that they may not be unproductive.

15 All who are with me send greetings to you. Greet those who love us in the
faith.

Grace be with all of you.[i]

3.6 Joel 2.28
3.7 Rom 8.17
3.9 1 Tim 1.4; 2 Tim 2.14,16, 23
3.10 Mt 18.15-17; Rom 16.2
3.12 Acts 20.4; 2 Tim 4.12,21; Col 4.9
3.13 Acts 18.24
3.14 Rom 12.13; Phil 1.11; Tit 3.8; 2 Pet 1.8

[h] Gk *washing* [i] Other ancient authorities add *Amen*

3.9 Paul warns Titus, as he warned Timothy, not to get involved in foolish and unprofitable arguments (2 Timothy 2.14). This does not mean we should refuse to study, discuss, and examine different interpretations of difficult Bible passages. Paul is warning against petty quarrels, not honest discussion that leads to wisdom. As foolish arguments develop, it is best to turn the discussion back to a helpful direction or politely excuse yourself.

3.9 The false teachers were basing their heresies on genealogies and speculations about the law (see 1 Timothy 1.3, 4). Similar to the false teachers in Ephesus and Colosse, they were building their case on genealogies of angels. We should avoid false teachers, not even bothering to react to their pretentious positions. Our overreaction can sometimes give more attention to their points of view.

3.9–11 A person must be warned when he or she is causing division that threatens the unity of the church. This warning should not be a heavy-handed action, but should correct the individual's divisive nature and restore him or her to fellowship. A person who refuses to be corrected should be put outside the fellowship. As Paul says, he is "self-condemned"—he is sinning and he knows it. (See also Matthew 18.15–18 and 2 Thessalonians 3.14, 15 for help in handling such problems in the church.)

3.12 The city of Nicopolis was on the western coast of Greece. Artemas or Tychicus would take over Titus's work on the island of Crete, so Titus could meet Paul in Nicopolis. Tychicus was one of Paul's trusted companions (Acts 20.4; Ephesians 6.21; Colossians 4.7). Titus would have to leave quickly because sea travel was dangerous in the winter months.

3.13 Apollos was a famous Christian preacher. A native of Alexandria in North Africa, he became a Christian in Ephesus and was trained by Aquila and Priscilla (Acts 18.24–28; 1 Corinthians 1.12).

3.15 The letters of Paul to Titus and Timothy are his last writings and mark the end of his life and ministry. These letters are rich treasures for us today because they give vital information for church leadership. They provide a strong model for elders, pastors, and other Christian leaders as they develop younger leaders to continue the work, following Paul's example of preparing Timothy and Titus to carry on his ministry. For practical guidelines on church leadership and problem solving, carefully study the principles found in these letters.

The Letter of Paul to PHILEMON

AT THE FOREMAN'S signal, the giant ball is released, and with dynamite force and a reverberating crash, it meets the wall, snapping bricks like twigs and scattering pieces of mortar. Repeatedly, the powerful pendulum works, and soon the barrier has been reduced to rubble. Then it is carted away so that construction can begin.

Life has many walls and fences that divide, separate, and compartmentalize. Not made of wood or stone, they are personal obstructions, blocking people from each other and from God. But Christ came as the great wall remover, tearing down the sin partition that separates us from God and blasting the barriers that keep us from each other. His death and resurrection opened the way to eternal life to bring all who believe into the family of God (see Ephesians 2:14–18).

Roman, Greek, and Jewish cultures were littered with barriers as society assigned people to classes and expected them to stay in their place—men and women, enslaved and free, rich and poor, Jews and Gentiles, Greeks and barbarians, pious and heathen. But with the message of Christ, the walls came down, and Paul could declare, "There is no longer Greek and Jew, circumcised and uncircumcised, barbarian, Scythian, slave and free; but Christ is all and in all!" (Colossians 3.11).

This life-changing truth forms the backdrop for the letter to Philemon. One of three personal letters in the Bible, the epistle to Philemon is Paul's personal plea for a slave. Onesimus "belonged" to Philemon, a member of the Colossian church and Paul's friend. But Onesimus, the slave, had stolen from his master and run away. He ran to Rome where he met Paul, and there he responded to the good news and came to faith in Christ (1.10). So Paul writes to Philemon and reintroduces Onesimus to him, explaining that he is sending him back, not just as a slave but as a brother (1.11, 12, 16). Tactfully he asks Philemon to accept and forgive his servant (1.10, 14, 15, 20). The barriers of the past and the new ones erected by Onesimus's desertion and theft should divide them no longer—they are one in Christ.

This small book is a masterpiece of grace and tact and is a profound demonstration of the power of Christ and of true Christian fellowship in action. What barriers are in your home, neighborhood, and church? What separates you from fellow believers—race? status? wealth? education? personality? As with Philemon, God calls you to unity, breaking down those walls and embracing your brothers and sisters in Christ.

VITAL STATISTICS

PURPOSE:
To convince Philemon to forgive his runaway slave, Onesimus, and to accept him as a brother in the faith

AUTHOR:
Paul

TO WHOM WRITTEN:
Philemon, who was probably a wealthy member of the Colossian church

DATE WRITTEN:
About A.D. 60, during Paul's first imprisonment in Rome, at about the same time Ephesians and Colossians were written

SETTING:
Slavery was very common in the Roman Empire, and evidently some Christians had slaves. Paul does not condemn the institution in his writings, but he makes a radical statement by calling this slave Philemon's brother in Christ.

KEY VERSES:
"Perhaps this is the reason he was separated from you for a while, so that you might have him back forever, no longer as a slave but more than a slave, a beloved brother—especially to me but how much more to you, both in the flesh and in the Lord" (1.15, 16).

KEY PEOPLE:
Paul, Philemon, Onesimus

KEY PLACES:
Colosse, Rome

SPECIAL FEATURES:
This is a private, personal letter to a friend.

THE BLUEPRINT

1. Paul's appreciation of Philemon (1.1–7)
2. Paul's appeal for Onesimus (1.8–25)

Paul pleads for Onesimus, a runaway slave. Paul's intercession for him illustrates what Christ has done for us. As Paul interceded for a slave, so Christ intercedes for us, slaves to sin. As Onesimus was reconciled to Philemon, so we are reconciled to God through Christ. As Paul offered to pay the debts of a slave, so Christ paid our debt of sin. Like Onesimus, we must return to God our Master and serve him.

MEGATHEMES

THEME	EXPLANATION	IMPORTANCE
Forgiveness	Philemon was Paul's friend and legal owner of the slave, Onesimus. Paul asked him not to punish Onesimus, but to forgive and restore him as a new Christian brother.	Christian relationships must be full of forgiveness and acceptance. Can you forgive those who have wronged you?
Barriers	Slavery was widespread in the Roman Empire, but no one is lost to God or beyond his love. Slavery was a barrier between people, but Christian love and fellowship are to overcome such barriers.	In Christ we are one family. No walls of race, economic or political differences should separate us. Let Christ work through you to remove barriers between Christian brothers and sisters.
Respect	Paul was a friend of both Philemon and Onesimus. He had the authority as an apostle to tell Philemon what to do. Yet Paul chose to appeal to his friend in Christian love rather than to order him.	Tactful persuasion accomplishes a great deal more than commands, when dealing with people. Remember to exhibit courtesy and respect in dealing with people.

1. Paul's appreciation of Philemon

1 Paul, a prisoner of Christ Jesus, and Timothy our brother,[a] **1.1**
To Philemon our dear friend and co-worker, 2 to Apphia our sister,[b] to Archip- Eph 4.1 2 Tim 1.8
pus our fellow soldier, and to the church in your house: Philem 9,23,24
3 Grace to you and peace from God our Father and the Lord Jesus Christ. **1.2** Rom 16.5
4 When I remember you[c] in my prayers, I always thank my God 5 because I 1 Cor 16.29
hear of your love for all the saints and your faith toward the Lord Jesus. 6 I pray that Col 4.17 **1.6**
the sharing of your faith may become effective when you perceive all the good that Phil 1.9
we[d] may do for Christ. 7 I have indeed received much joy and encouragement from **1.7**
your love, because the hearts of the saints have been refreshed through you, my 2 Cor 7.13 2 Tim 1.16
brother.

2. Paul's appeal for Onesimus

8 For this reason, though I am bold enough in Christ to command you to do your **2.8**
duty, 9 yet I would rather appeal to you on the basis of love — and I, Paul, do this as 1 Thess 2.6

[a] Gk *the brother* [b] Gk *the sister* [c] From verse 4 through verse 21, *you* is singular [d] Other ancient authorities read *you* (plural)

1.1 Paul wrote this letter from Rome in about A.D. 60, when he was under house arrest (see Acts 28.30, 31). Onesimus was a domestic slave who belonged to Philemon, a wealthy man and a member of the church in Colosse. Onesimus had run away from Philemon and made his way to Rome where he met Paul, who apparently led him to Christ (1.10). Paul convinced Onesimus that running from his problems wouldn't solve them, and he persuaded Onesimus to return to his master. Paul wrote this letter to Philemon to ask him to be reconciled to his runaway slave.

1.1 For more information on Paul's life, see his Profile in Acts 10. Timothy's name is included with Paul's in 2 Corinthians, 1 Thessalonians, 2 Thessalonians, Philippians, Colossians, and Philemon – the last three of these letters are from a group known as the "prison epistles." Timothy was one of Paul's trusted companions; Paul wrote two letters to him – 1 and 2 Timothy.

1.1 Philemon was a Greek landowner living in Colosse. He was converted under Paul's ministry, and the Colossian church met in his home. Onesimus was one of Philemon's slaves.

1.2 Apphia may have been Philemon's wife. Archippus may have been Philemon's son or possibly an elder of the Colossian church. In either case, Paul included him as a recipient of the letter, possibly so Archippus could read the letter with Philemon and encourage him to follow Paul's advice.

1.2 The early churches often met in people's homes. Because of sporadic persecutions and the great expense involved, church buildings were not constructed at this time.

1.7 Paul reflects on Philemon's kindness, love, and comfort. He had opened his heart and his home to the church. We should do likewise, opening ourselves and our homes to others, offering Christian fellowship to refresh people's spirits.

an old man, and now also as a prisoner of Christ Jesus.[e] 10 I am appealing to you
for my child, Onesimus, whose father I have become during my imprisonment.
11 Formerly he was useless to you, but now he is indeed useful[f] both to you and to
me. 12 I am sending him, that is, my own heart, back to you. 13 I wanted to keep him
with me, so that he might be of service to me in your place during my imprisonment
for the gospel; 14 but I preferred to do nothing without your consent, in order that
your good deed might be voluntary and not something forced. 15 Perhaps this is the
reason he was separated from you for a while, so that you might have him back
forever, 16 no longer as a slave but more than a slave, a beloved brother—especially
to me but how much more to you, both in the flesh and in the Lord.

17 So if you consider me your partner, welcome him as you would welcome
me. 18 If he has wronged you in any way, or owes you anything, charge that to my
account. 19 I, Paul, am writing this with my own hand: I will repay it. I say nothing
about your owing me even your own self. 20 Yes, brother, let me have this benefit
from you in the Lord! Refresh my heart in Christ. 21 Confident of your obedience,
I am writing to you, knowing that you will do even more than I say.

22 One thing more—prepare a guest room for me, for I am hoping through your
prayers to be restored to you.

23 Epaphras, my fellow prisoner in Christ Jesus, sends greetings to you,[g]
24 and so do Mark, Aristarchus, Demas, and Luke, my fellow workers.

25 The grace of the Lord Jesus Christ be with your spirit.[h]

1.13 Phil 1.7; 2.30
1.14 2 Cor 9.7
1.15 Gen 45.5,8 Rom 8.28
1.16 Mt 23.8 1 Cor 7.22 Col 3.22
1.17 2 Cor 8.23
1.19 2 Thess 3.17
1.22 Phil 1.24-26
1.23 Col 1.7; 4.12
1.24 Acts 12.12 19.29; 27.2 Col 4.10,14 Philem 1
1.25 Gal 6.18 2 Tim 4.22

[e] Or *as an ambassador of Christ Jesus, and now also his prisoner* [f] The name Onesimus means *useful* or (compare verse 20) *beneficial* [g] Here *you* is singular [h] Other ancient authorities add *Amen*

1.8, 9 Because Paul was an elder and an apostle, he could have used his authority with Philemon, commanding him to deal kindly with his runaway slave. But Paul bases his request not on his own authority, but on Philemon's Christian commitment. Paul wants Philemon's heartfelt, not grudging, obedience. When you know something is right and you have the power to demand it, do you appeal to your authority or the other person's commitment? Here Paul provides a good example of how to deal with a possible conflict between Christian friends.

1.10 A master had the legal right to kill a runaway slave. Onesimus feared for his life. So Paul wrote this letter to Philemon to help him understand his new relationship with Onesimus. Onesimus was now a Christian brother, not a mere possession.

1.10ff In prison, Paul led Onesimus to the Lord. Paul asks Philemon to forgive his runaway slave who had become a Christian, and even beyond forgiveness, to accept Onesimus as a brother. As Christians, we should forgive as we have been forgiven (Matthew 6.12; Ephesians 4.31, 32).

1.11–15 *Onesimus* means "useful." Paul uses a play on words, saying that Onesimus had not been much use to Philemon in the past, but is now very useful to both Philemon and Paul. Although Paul wants to keep Onesimus with him, he is sending Onesimus back, requesting that Philemon accept him not only as a forgiven runaway servant, but also as a brother in Christ.

1.15, 16 Slavery was widespread throughout the Roman Empire. In these early days, Christians did not have the political power to change the slavery system. Paul didn't condemn or condone slavery but worked to transform relationships. The gospel begins to change social structures by changing the *people* within those structures. (See also 1 Corinthians 7.20–24; Ephesians 6.5–9; Colossians 3.22–4.1 for more on master/slave relationships.)

1.16 What a difference Onesimus's status as a Christian made in his relationship to Philemon. He was no longer merely a servant, he was also a brother. Now both Onesimus and Philemon were members of God's family—equals in Christ. A Christian's status as a member of God's family transcends all other distinctions among believers. Do you look down on any fellow Christians? Remember, they are your brothers and sisters, your equals before Christ (Galatians 3.28).

1.17–19 Paul genuinely loved Onesimus. Paul shows his love by personally guaranteeing payment for any stolen goods or injuries for which Onesimus might be responsible. Paul's investment in the life of this new believer certainly encouraged and strengthened Onesimus's faith. Are there young believers who need you to demonstrate such self-sacrifice toward them? Be grateful when you can invest in the lives of others, helping them with Bible study, prayer, encouragement, support, and friendship.

1.19 Philemon owed himself to Paul, meaning that Paul had led Philemon to Christ. Because Paul is Philemon's spiritual father, he hopes Philemon will feel a debt of gratitude that he will repay by accepting Onesimus with a spirit of forgiveness.

1.22 Paul was released from prison soon after writing this letter, but the Bible doesn't say whether or not he returned to Colosse.

1.23 Epaphras was well known to the Colossians, because he had founded the church there (Colossians 1.7). He was a hero to this church, helping to hold it together in spite of growing persecution and struggles with false doctrine. His report to Paul about the problems in Colosse had prompted Paul to write his letter to the Colossians. Epaphras's greeting and prayers for the Colossian Christians reveal his deep love for them (Colossians 4.12, 13). He is in prison with Paul for preaching the gospel.

1.24 Mark, Aristarchus, Demas, and Luke are also mentioned in Colossians 4.10, 14. Mark had accompanied Paul and Barnabas on their first missionary journey (Acts 12.25ff). Mark also wrote the Gospel of Mark. Luke had accompanied Paul on his third missionary journey and was the writer of the Gospel of Luke and the book of Acts. Demas was faithful to Paul for a while but then deserted him (see 2 Timothy 4.10).

1.25 Paul urges Philemon to be reconciled to his slave, receiving him as a brother and fellow member of God's family. *Reconciliation* means reestablishing relationship. Christ has reconciled us to God and to others. Many barriers come between people—race, social status, sex, personality differences—but Christ can break down these barriers. Jesus Christ changed Onesimus's relationship to Philemon from slave to brother. Christ can transform our most hopeless relationships into deep and loving friendships.

The Letter to the HEBREWS

VITAL STATISTICS

PURPOSE:
To present the sufficiency and superiority of Christ

AUTHOR:
Paul, Luke, Barnabas, Apollos, Silas, Philip, Priscilla, and others have been suggested because the name of the author is not given in the biblical text itself. Whoever it was speaks of Timothy as "brother" (13.23).

TO WHOM WRITTEN:
Hebrew Christians who may have been considering a return to Judaism, perhaps because of immaturity, due to their lack of understanding of biblical truths. They seem to be "second-generation" Christians (2.3).

DATE WRITTEN:
Probably before the destruction of the temple in Jerusalem in A.D. 70, since the religious sacrifices and ceremonies are referred to in the book, but no mention is made of the temple's destruction

SETTING:
These Jewish Christians were probably undergoing fierce persecution, socially and physically, both from Jews and from Romans. Christ had not returned to establish his kingdom, and the people needed to be reassured that Christianity was true and that Jesus was indeed the Messiah.

KEY VERSE:
"He is the reflection of God's glory and the exact imprint of God's very being, and he sustains all things by his powerful word. When he had made purification for sins, he sat down at the right hand of the Majesty on high" (1.3).

KEY PEOPLE:
Old Testament men and women of faith (chapter 11)

SPECIAL FEATURES:
Although Hebrews is called a "letter" (13.22), it has the form and the content of a sermon.

CONSCIENTIOUS consumers shop for value, the best products for the money. Wise parents desire only the best for their children, nourishing their growing bodies, minds, and spirits. Individuals with integrity seek the best investment of time, talents, and treasures. In every area, to settle for less would be wasteful, foolish, and irresponsible. Yet that is a natural pull, to move toward what is convenient and comfortable.

Judaism was not second-rate or easy. Divinely designed, it was the best religion, expressing true worship and devotion to God. The commandments, the rituals, and the prophets described God's promises and revealed the way to forgiveness and salvation. But Christ came, fulfilling the Law and the Prophets, conquering sin, shattering all barriers to God, and freely providing eternal life.

This message was difficult for Jews to accept. Although they had sought the Messiah for centuries, they were entrenched in thinking and worshiping in traditional forms. Following Jesus seemed to repudiate their marvelous heritage and profound Scriptures. With caution and questions they listened to the gospel, but many rejected it and sought to eliminate this "heresy." Those who did accept Jesus as the Messiah often found themselves slipping back into the old, familiar routines, trying to live a hybrid faith.

Hebrews is a masterful document written to Jews who were considering Jesus or struggling with this new faith. The message of Hebrews is that Christianity is superior, because Christ is supreme and is completely sufficient for salvation.

Hebrews begins by emphasizing that the old (Judaism) and the new (Christianity) are both religions "revealed" by God (1.1–3). In the doctrinal section which follows (1.4—10.23), the writer shows how Jesus is greater than angels (1.4—2.18), better than their leaders (3.1–4.13), and superior to their priests (4.14—7.28). Christianity surpasses Judaism because it has a better covenant (8.1–13), a better sanctuary (9.1–10), and a more sufficient sacrifice for sins (9.1—10.18).

Having established the superiority of Christianity, the writer moves on to the practical implications of following Christ. The readers are exhorted to hold on to their new faith, encourage each other, and look forward to Christ's return (10.19–25). They are warned about the consequences of rejecting Christ's sacrifice for them (10.26–31) and reminded of the rewards for faithfulness (10.32–39). Then the author explains how to live by faith, giving illustrations of the faithful men and women in the history of Israel (11.1–40) and of daily living (12.1–17). This section ends by comparing the old covenant with the new (12.18–29). The writer concludes with moral exhortations (13.1–17), a request for prayer (13.18, 19), and a benediction followed by greetings (13.20–25).

Whatever you are considering as the focus of life, Christ is better. He is the perfect revelation of God, the final and complete sacrifice for sin, the compassionate and understanding mediator, and the *only* way to eternal life. Read Hebrews and begin to see history and life from God's perspective. Then give yourself unreservedly and completely to Christ. Don't settle for anything less.

THE BLUEPRINT

A. THE SUPERIORITY OF CHRIST (1.1—10.18) 1. Christ is greater than the angels 2. Christ is greater than Moses 3. Christ is greater than the Old Testament priesthood 4. The new covenant is greater than the old	The superiority of Christ over everyone and everything is clearly demonstrated by the author. Christianity supersedes all other religions and can never be surpassed. Where can one find anything better than Christ? Living in Christ is having the best there is in life. All competing religions are deceptions or cheap imitations.
B. THE SUPERIORITY OF FAITH (10.19—13.25)	Jews who had become Christians in the first century were tempted to fall back into Judaism because of uncertainty, the security of customs, and persecution. Today believers are also tempted to fall back into legalism, fulfilling minimum religious requirements, rather than pressing on in genuine faith. We must strive to live by faith each day.

MEGATHEMES

THEME	EXPLANATION	IMPORTANCE
Christ Is Superior	Hebrews reveals Jesus' true identity as God. He is the ultimate authority. He is greater than any religion or any angel. He is superior to any Jewish leader (such as Abraham, Moses, or Joshua) and superior to any priest. He is the complete revelation of God.	Jesus alone can forgive your sin. He has secured your forgiveness and salvation by his death on the cross. You can find peace with God and real meaning for life by believing in Christ. Don't accept any alternative or substitute for him.
High Priest	In the Old Testament, the high priest represented the Jews before God. Jesus Christ links us with God. There is no other way to reach God. Because Jesus Christ lived a sinless life, he is the perfect substitute to die for our sin. He is our perfect representative with God.	Jesus guarantees our access to God the Father. He intercedes for us so we can boldly come to the Father with our needs. When we are weak we can come confidently to God for forgiveness and ask his help.
Sacrifice	Christ's sacrifice was the ultimate fulfillment of all that the Old Testament sacrifices represented—God's forgiveness for sin. Because Christ is the perfect sacrifice for our sin, our sins are completely forgiven—past, present, and future.	Christ removed sin, which barred us from God's presence and fellowship. But we must accept his sacrifice for us. By believing in him we are no longer guilty, but cleansed and made whole. His sacrifice makes the way for us to have eternal life.
Maturity	Though we are saved from sin when we believe in Christ, we are given the task of going on and growing in our faith. Through our relationship with Christ we can live blameless lives, be set aside for his special use, and develop maturity.	The process of maturing in our faith takes time. Daily commitment and service produce maturity. When we are mature in our faith, we are not easily swayed or shaken by temptations or worldly concerns.
Faith	Faith is confident trust in God's promises. God's greatest promise is that we can be saved through Jesus.	If you trust in Jesus Christ for your complete salvation, he will transform you completely. A life of obedience and complete trust is pleasing to God.
Endurance	Faith enables Christians to face trials. Genuine faith includes the commitment to stay true to God when we are under fire. Endurance builds character and leads to victory.	You can have victory in your trials if you don't give up or turn your back on Christ. Stay true to Christ and pray for endurance.

A. THE SUPERIORITY OF CHRIST (1.1—10.18)

The relationship of Christianity to Judaism was a critical issue in the early church. The author clears up confusion by carefully explaining how Christ is superior to angels, Moses, and high priests. The new covenant is shown to be far superior to the old. This can be of great encouragement to us and help us avoid drifting away from our faith in Christ.

1. Christ is greater than the angels

God's Son compared to the angels

1 Long ago God spoke to our ancestors in many and various ways by the prophets, 2 but in these last days he has spoken to us by a Son,[a] whom he appointed
heir of all things, through whom he also created the worlds. 3 He is the reflection of
God's glory and the exact imprint of God's very being, and he sustains[b] all things
by his powerful word. When he had made purification for sins, he sat down at the
right hand of the Majesty on high, 4 having become as much superior to angels as
the name he has inherited is more excellent than theirs.

5 For to which of the angels did God ever say,
"You are my Son;
today I have begotten you"?
Or again,
"I will be his Father,
and he will be my Son"?
6 And again, when he brings the firstborn into the world, he says,
"Let all God's angels worship him."
7 Of the angels he says,
"He makes his angels winds,
and his servants flames of fire."
8 But of the Son he says,
"Your throne, O God,[c] is forever and ever,
and the righteous scepter is the scepter of your[d] kingdom.
9 You have loved righteousness and hated wickedness;
therefore God, your God, has anointed you

1.1 Num12.6-8
1.2 Ps 2.8 Jn 1.1,3,18; 8.25
1.3 Ps 110.1 Jn 14.9 2 Cor 4.4 Col 1.15
1.4 Eph 1.21 Phil 2.9
1.5 a)Ps 2.7 Rev 1.5 b)2 Sam 7.14
1.6 Ps 89.27; 97.7
1.7 Ps 104.4
1.8,9 Ps 45.6,7

[a] Or *the Son* [b] Or *bears along* [c] Or *God is your throne* [d] Other ancient authorities read *his*

1.1 The book of Hebrews describes in detail how Jesus Christ fulfills the promises and prophecies of the Old Testament. The Jews believed in the Old Testament, but most rejected Jesus as the long-awaited Messiah. The recipients of this letter seem to have been Jewish Christians. They were well-versed in Scripture, and they had professed faith in Christ. Whether through doubt, persecution, or false teaching, however, they may have been in danger of giving up their Christian faith and returning to Judaism.

The authorship of this book is uncertain. Several names have been suggested, including Luke, Barnabas, Apollos, Priscilla, and Paul. Most scholars do not believe Paul was the author, because the writing style of Hebrews is quite different from that of his epistles. In addition, Paul identified himself in his other letters and appealed to his authority as an apostle, whereas this writer of Hebrews never gives his or her name and appeals to eyewitnesses of Jesus' ministry for authority. Nevertheless, the author of Hebrews evidently knew Paul well. Hebrews was probably written by one of Paul's close associates who often heard him preach.

1.1, 2 God used many approaches to send his messages to people in Old Testament times. He spoke to Isaiah in visions (Isaiah 6), to Jacob in a dream (Genesis 28.10–22), and to Abraham and Moses personally (Genesis 18; Exodus 31.18). Jewish people familiar with these stories would not have found it hard to believe that God was still revealing his will, but it was astonishing for them to think that God had revealed *himself* by speaking through his Son, Jesus Christ. Jesus is the fulfillment and culmination of God's revelation through the centuries. When we know him, we have all we need to be saved from our sin and to have a perfect relationship with God.

1.2, 3 Not only is Jesus God's spokesman, he is God himself—the very God who spoke in Old Testament times. He is eternal; he worked with the Father in creating the world (John 1.3; Colossians 1.16). He is the full revelation of God, the "exact imprint." You can have no clearer view of God than by looking at him. Jesus Christ is the complete expression of God in a human body.

1.3 The book of Hebrews links God's saving power with his creative power. In other words, the power that brought the universe into being and that keeps it operating is the very power that removes (purifies) our sins. How mistaken we would be ever to think that God couldn't forgive us. No sin is too big for the Ruler of the universe to handle. He can and will forgive us when we come to him through his Son. That Jesus *sat down* means the work is complete. Christ's sacrifice was final.

1.4 The name Jesus inherited that is more excellent is "Son of God." This name given to him by his Father is greater than the names and titles of the angels.

1.4ff False teachers in many of the early churches taught that God could be approached only through angels. Instead of worshiping God directly, followers of these heretics bowed to angels. Hebrews clearly denounces such teaching as false. Some thought of Jesus as the highest angel of God. But Jesus is not a superior angel; and, in any case, angels are not to be worshiped (see Colossians 2.18; Revelation 19.1–10). We should not regard any intermediaries or authorities as greater than Christ. Jesus is God. He alone deserves our worship.

1.5, 6 Jesus is God's firstborn Son. In Jewish families the firstborn son held the place of highest privilege and responsibility. The Jewish Christians reading this message would understand that as God's firstborn, Jesus was superior to any created being.

with the oil of gladness beyond your companions."
10 And,
"In the beginning, Lord, you founded the earth,
and the heavens are the work of your hands;
11 they will perish, but you remain;
they will all wear out like clothing;
12 like a cloak you will roll them up,
and like clothing[e] they will be changed.
But you are the same,
and your years will never end."
13 But to which of the angels has he ever said,
"Sit at my right hand
until I make your enemies a footstool for your feet"?
14 Are not all angels[f] spirits in the divine service, sent to serve for the sake of those
who are to inherit salvation?

1.10-12 Ps 102.25-27
1.13 Ps 110.1 Mt 22.44
1.14 Ps 34.7; 91.11 Rom 8.17 Heb 2.3

Warning against drifting away

2 Therefore we must pay greater attention to what we have heard, so that we do
not drift away from it. 2 For if the message declared through angels was valid,
and every transgression or disobedience received a just penalty, 3 how can we escape if we neglect so great a salvation? It was declared at first through the Lord, and

2.2 Deut 5.5; 33.2 Acts 7.38,53 Gal 3.19
2.3 Heb 1.1,2; 10.29

[e] Other ancient authorities lack *like clothing* [f] Gk *all of them*

CHRIST AND THE ANGELS

Hebrews passage	*Old Testament passage*	*How Christ is higher than the angels*
1.5, 6	Psalm 2.7	Christ is called Son of God, a title never given to an angel.
1.7, 14	Psalm 104.4	Angels are important, but are servants under God.
1.8, 9	Psalm 45.6	Christ's kingdom is forever.
1.10	Psalm 102.25	Christ is the Creator of the world.
1.13	Psalm 110.1	Christ is given unique honor by God.

The writer of Hebrews quotes from the Old Testament repeatedly in demonstrating Christ's greatness in comparison to the angels. His audience of first-century Jewish Christians had developed an imbalanced belief in angels and their role. Christ's lordship is affirmed without disrespect to God's valued angelic messengers.

1.10–12 The author of Hebrews quotes Psalm 102.25–27. In the quotation, he regards God as the speaker and applies the words to the Son Jesus. That the earth and the heavens rolled up like a cloak reveals that the earth is not permanent or indestructible (a position held by many Greek and Roman philosophies). Jesus' authority is established over all of creation, so we dare not treat any created object or earthly resource as more important than he is.

1.11, 12 Because the readers of Hebrews experienced the rejection of their fellow Jews, they often felt isolated. Many were tempted to exchange the changeless Christ for their familiar old faith. The writer of Hebrews warns them not to do this: Christ is our *only* security in a changing world. Whatever may happen in this world, Christ remains forever changeless. If we trust him, we are absolutely secure because we stand on the firmest foundation in the universe—Jesus Christ. A famous hymn captures this truth: "On Christ the solid rock I stand, all other ground is sinking sand."

1.12 What does it mean that Christ is changeless ("you are the same")? It means that his character will never change. He persistently shows his love to us. He is always fair, just, and merciful to us who are so undeserving. Be thankful that Christ is changeless—he will always help you when you need it and offer forgiveness when you fall.

1.14 Angels are God's messengers, spiritual beings created by God and under his authority (Colossians 1.16). They have several functions: serving believers (1.14), protecting the helpless (Matthew 18.10, 11), proclaiming God's messages (Revelation 14.6–12), and executing God's judgment (Acts 12.1–23; Revelation 20.1–3).

2.1–3 The author calls his readers to pay attention to the truth they have heard so that they won't drift away into false teachings. This is hard work. It involves focusing our minds, bodies, and senses. Listening to Christ means not merely hearing, but also obeying (see James 1.22–25). We must listen carefully and be ready to carry out his instructions.

2.2, 3 "The message declared through angels" refers to the teaching that angels, as messengers for God, brought the law to Moses (see Galatians 3.19). A central theme of Hebrews is that Christ is infinitely greater than all other proposed means to God. "Your previous faith was good," the author says to his Jewish readers, "but that faith pointed to Christ." Just as Christ is greater than angels, so his message is more important than theirs. No one will escape God's punishment if he or she is indifferent to the salv[illegible] offered by Christ.

2.3 Eyewitnesses to Jesus' ministry had handed down t[illegible] ings to the readers of this book. These readers were [illegible] generation believers who had not seen Christ in th[illegible] like us; we have not seen Jesus personally. We [illegible] Jesus on the eyewitness accounts recorded [illegible] 20.29 for Jesus' encouragement to those [illegible] having seen him.

it was attested to us by those who heard him, 4 while God added his testimony by
signs and wonders and various miracles, and by gifts of the Holy Spirit, distributed
according to his will.

Christ came as a human being

5 Now God[g] did not subject the coming world, about which we are speaking,
to angels. 6 But someone has testified somewhere,

"What are human beings that you are mindful of them,[h]
or mortals, that you care for them?[i]
7 You have made them for a little while lower[j] than the angels;
you have crowned them with glory and honor,[k]
8 subjecting all things under their feet."

Now in subjecting all things to them, God[g] left nothing outside their control. As it
is, we do not yet see everything in subjection to them, 9 but we do see Jesus, who
for a little while was made lower[l] than the angels, now crowned with glory and
honor because of the suffering of death, so that by the grace of God[m] he might taste
death for everyone.
10 It was fitting that God,[g] for whom and through whom all things exist, in
bringing many children to glory, should make the pioneer of their salvation perfect
through sufferings. 11 For the one who sanctifies and those who are sanctified all
have one Father.[n] For this reason Jesus[g] is not ashamed to call them brothers and
sisters,[o] 12 saying,

"I will proclaim your name to my brothers and sisters,[o]
in the midst of the congregation I will praise you."

13 And again,

"I will put my trust in him."

And again,

"Here am I and the children whom God has given me."

14 Since, therefore, the children share flesh and blood, he himself likewise
shared the same things, so that through death he might destroy the one who has the

2.4 Mk 6.14
2.5 Heb 6.5
2.6 Ps 8.4-6
2.8 1 Cor 15.27
2.9 Acts 2.33; Phil 2.6-9
2.10 Lk 13.32; 24.46; Acts 3.15; Rom 11.36; Heb 5.9
2.11 Mt 28.10; Jn 20.17; Rom 8.29; Heb 10.10; 13.12
2.12 Ps 22.22
2.13 Isa 8.17,18; Jn 17.6,9, 11,12
2.14 Jn 1.14; Rom 8.3; 1 Cor 15.54,55; 2 Tim 1.10; 1 Jn 3.8

[g] Gk *he* [h] Gk *What is man that you are mindful of him?* [i] Gk *or the son of man that you care for him?* In the Hebrew of Psalm 8.4-6 both *man* and *son of man* refer to all humankind [j] Or *them only a little lower* [k] Other ancient authorities add *and set them over the works of your hands* [l] Or *who was made a little lower* [m] Other ancient authorities read *apart from God* [n] Gk *are all of one* [o] Gk *brothers*

2.4 "While God added his testimony" continues the thought from 2.3. Those who heard Jesus speak and passed on his words also had God's affirmation that their words were true by the "signs and wonders and various miracles, and by gifts of the Holy Spirit." In the book of Acts, miracles and gifts of the Spirit authenticated the gospel wherever it was preached (see Acts 9.31–42; 14.1–20). Paul, who discussed spiritual gifts in Romans 12, 1 Corinthians 12–14, and Ephesians 4, taught that their purpose is to build up the church, making it strong and mature. When we see the gifts of the Spirit in an individual or congregation, we know God is truly present. As we receive God's gifts, we should recognize him and thank him for them.

2.8, 9 God put Jesus in charge of everything, and Jesus revealed himself to us. We do not yet see Jesus reigning on earth, but we can picture him in his heavenly glory. When you are confused by events of the day and anxious about the future, strive to keep Jesus' true position and authority in mind. He is Lord of all, and one ... he will rule on earth as he does now in heaven. Remember, ...th will give stability to your decisions day by day.

2. ...d's kindness to us led Christ to his death. What a startling ... Jesus did not come into the world to gain status or politic... to suffer and die so that we could have eternal life ("bri... ...ldren to glory"). If it is difficult for us to identify with Ch... ...titude, perhaps we need to evaluate our own motives. ...rested in power or participation, domination or ... ...giving?

2.10 How was Je... ...ugh suffering? Jesus' suffering made him a perfect leader, or pioneer, of our salvation (see the notes on 5.8 and 5.9). He did not need to suffer for his own salvation because he was God in human form. His perfect obedience (which led to his suffering) demonstrates that he was the complete sacrifice for us. Through suffering, he completed the work necessary for our own salvation. Our suffering can make us more sensitive servants of God. People who have known pain are able to reach out with compassion to others who hurt. If you have suffered, ask God how your experience can be used to help others.

2.11–13 We who have been set apart for God's service, cleansed, and made holy (sanctified) by Jesus now have the same Father he has, so he is not ashamed to call us his brothers and sisters. Various psalms look forward to Christ and his work in the world. Here the writer quotes a portion of Psalm 22, a messianic psalm. Because God has adopted all believers as his children, Jesus calls them his brothers and sisters.

2.14, 15 Jesus had to become human ("flesh and blood") so he could die and rise again, in order to destroy the devil's power over death (Romans 6.5–11). Only then could he deliver those who had lived in constant fear of death, and free them to live for him. When we belong to God, we need not fear death because we know that death is only the beginning of eternal life (1 Corinthians 15).

2.14, 15 Christ's death and resurrection free us from the fear of death because death has been defeated. Every person must die, but death is not the end; instead, it is the doorway to a new life. All who dread death should have the opportunity to know the hope that Christ's victory brings. How can you share this truth with those close to you?

power of death, that is, the devil, 15 and free those who all their lives were held in
slavery by the fear of death. 16 For it is clear that he did not come to help angels, but
the descendants of Abraham. 17 Therefore he had to become like his brothers and
sisters[p] in every respect, so that he might be a merciful and faithful high priest in
the service of God, to make a sacrifice of atonement for the sins of the people.
18 Because he himself was tested by what he suffered, he is able to help those who
are being tested.

2.17 Phil 2.7 Heb 3.1; 4.15 5.1 1 Jn 2.2
2.18 Heb 4.15; 5.2

2. Christ is greater than Moses

Jesus compared to Moses

3 Therefore, brothers and sisters,[p] holy partners in a heavenly calling, consider
that Jesus, the apostle and high priest of our confession, 2 was faithful to the
one who appointed him, just as Moses also "was faithful in all[q] God's[r] house."
3 Yet Jesus[s] is worthy of more glory than Moses, just as the builder of a house has
more honor than the house itself. 4 (For every house is built by someone, but the
builder of all things is God.) 5 Now Moses was faithful in all God's[r] house as a
servant, to testify to the things that would be spoken later. 6 Christ, however, was
faithful over God's[r] house as a son, and we are his house if we hold firm[t] the
confidence and the pride that belong to hope.

3.1 Jn 17.3
3.3 2 Cor 3.7-11
3.5 Deut 18.15,18
3.6 a)Eph 2.19-22 1 Tim 3.15 1 Pet 2.5 b)Mt 10.22 Rom 11.22

[p] Gk *brothers* [q] Other ancient authorities lack *all* [r] Gk *his* [s] Gk *this one* [t] Other ancient authorities add *to the end*

LESSONS FROM CHRIST'S HUMANITY

Christ is the perfect human		
	leader	and he wants to lead you
	model	and he is worth imitating
	sacrifice	and he died for you
	conqueror	and he conquered death to give you eternal life
	High Priest	and he is merciful, loving, and understanding

God, in Christ, became a living, breathing human being. Hebrews points out many reasons why this is so important.

2.16, 17 In the Old Testament, the high priest was the mediator between God and his people. His job was to regularly offer animal sacrifices according to the law and to intercede with God for the people's sins. Jesus Christ is now our high priest. He came to earth as a human being; therefore, he understands our weaknesses and is merciful to us. He has *once and for all* paid the penalty for our sins by his own sacrificial death (atonement), and he can be depended upon to restore our broken relationship with God. We are released from sin's domination over us when we commit ourselves fully to Christ, trusting completely in what he has done for us (see the note on 4.14 for more about Jesus as the high priest).

2.18 Knowing that Christ suffered pain and faced temptation helps us face our trials. He understands our struggles because he himself faced them as a human being (2.16). We can trust him to help us survive suffering and overcome temptation. When you face trials, go to Jesus for strength and patience. He understands your needs and is able to help (see 4.14–16).

3.1 This verse would have been especially meaningful to Jewish Christians. For Jews, the highest human authority was the high priest. For Christians, the highest human authorities were God's apostles. Jesus, God's apostle (meaning "sent one") and high priest is the ultimate authority in the church.

3.1–6 The author uses different pictures to explain Jesus' relationship to believers: he is (1) the apostle ("sent one") of God, to whom we should listen; (2) our high priest, by whom we come to God the Father; and (3) the ruler of God's house ("faithful over God's house as a son"), whom we should obey. The Bible is filled with different names and pictures of Jesus Christ, and each one reveals something more about his nature and ministry. What do these images teach you about your relationship to Jesus?

3.2, 3 To the Jewish people, Moses was a great hero; he brought their ancestors, the Israelites, from Egyptian bondage to the promised land. He also wrote the first five books of the Old Testament and was the prophet through whom God gave the law; therefore, he was the greatest prophet in the Scriptures. But Jesus is to be more highly regarded as the central figure of faith than Moses, who was merely a human servant. Jesus is more than human – he is God himself (1.3). As Moses led the people of Israel out of Egyptian bondage, so Christ leads us out of slavery to sin. Why settle for Moses, the author of Hebrews asks its readers, when you can have Jesus Christ who appointed Moses?

3.5 Moses was faithful to God's calling not only to deliver Israel, but also to prepare the way for the Messiah ("to testify to the things that would be spoken later"). All the Old Testament believers served the same way. Thus, knowing the Old Testament is the best foundation for understanding the New Testament. In reading the Old Testament, we see (1) how God used people to accomplish his purposes, (2) how God used events and personalities to illustrate important truths, (3) how, through prophets, God announced the Messiah, and (4) how, through the system of sacrifices, God prepared people to understand the Messiah's work. If you include the Old Testament in your regular Bible reading, the New Testament will grow clearer and more meaningful to you.

3.6 Because Christ lives in us as believers, we can remain faithful and confident to the end. We are not saved by being steadfast and firm in our faith, but our perseverance reveals that our faith is real. Without this enduring faithfulness, we could easily be blown away by the winds of temptation, false teaching, or persecution. (See also 3.14.)

Now is the time to listen to God

7 Therefore, as the Holy Spirit says, [3.7 2 Sam 23.2]
“Today, if you hear his voice, [Ps 95.7,8]
8 do not harden your hearts as in the rebellion, [Acts 1.16]
as on the day of testing in the wilderness,
9 where your ancestors put me to the test, [3.9 Ps 95.9]
though they had seen my works 10 for forty years. [Acts 7.36]
Therefore I was angry with that generation, [3.10 Ps 95.10]
and I said, ‘They always go astray in their hearts,
and they have not known my ways.’
11 As in my anger I swore, [3.11 Ps 95.11]
‘They will not enter my rest.’ ”
12 Take care, brothers and sisters,[u] that none of you may have an evil, unbelieving
heart that turns away from the living God. 13 But exhort one another every day, as [3.13 Eph 4.22]
long as it is called “today,” so that none of you may be hardened by the deceitfulness of sin. 14 For we have become partners of Christ, if only we hold our first [3.14 Heb 3.6]
confidence firm to the end. 15 As it is said, [3.15 Ps 95.7]
“Today, if you hear his voice,
do not harden your hearts as in the rebellion.”
16 Now who were they who heard and yet were rebellious? Was it not all those who [3.16 Deut 1.34,35]
left Egypt under the leadership of Moses? 17 But with whom was he angry forty
years? Was it not those who sinned, whose bodies fell in the wilderness? 18 And to [3.17 1 Cor 10.5]
whom did he swear that they would not enter his rest, if not to those who were
disobedient? 19 So we see that they were unable to enter because of unbelief.

A rest for God's people

4 Therefore, while the promise of entering his rest is still open, let us take care
that none of you should seem to have failed to reach it. 2 For indeed the good [4.2 1 Thess 2.13]
news came to us just as to them; but the message they heard did not benefit them,
because they were not united by faith with those who listened.[v] 3 For we who have [4.3 Ps 95.11]
believed enter that rest, just as God[w] has said,
“As in my anger I swore,
‘They shall not enter my rest,’ ”
though his works were finished at the foundation of the world. 4 For in one place it [4.4 Gen 2.2 Ex 31.17]

[u] Gk *brothers* [v] Other ancient authorities read *it did not meet with faith in those who listened* [w] Gk *he*

3.7–15 In many places, the Bible warns us not to “harden” our hearts. This means setting ourselves against God so that we are no longer able to turn to him for forgiveness. The Israelites became hardhearted when they disobeyed God's command to conquer the promised land (here called “the rebellion,” see Numbers 13, 14; see also Numbers 20 and Psalm 95). Be careful to obey God's Word and not allow your heart to become hardened.

3.11 God's *rest* has several meanings in Scripture: (1) the seventh day of creation and the weekly sabbath commemorating it (Genesis 2.2; Hebrews 4.4–9); (2) the promised land of Canaan (Deuteronomy 12.8–12; Psalm 95); (3) peace with God now because of our relationship with Christ through faith (Matthew 12.28; Hebrews 4.1, 3, 8–11); and (4) our future eternal life with Christ (Hebrews 4.8–11). All of these meanings were probably familiar to the Jewish Christian readers of Hebrews.

3.12–14 Our hearts lead us away from the living God when we stubbornly refuse to believe him. If we persist in our unbelief, God will eventually leave us alone in our sin. But God can give us new hearts, new desires, and new spirits (Ezekiel 36.22–27). To prevent having an unbelieving heart, stay in fellowship with other believers, talk daily about your mutual faith, be aware of the deceitfulness of sin (it attracts but also destroys), and encourage each other with love and concern.

3.15–19 The Israelites failed to enter the promised land because they did not believe in God's protection, and they did not believe that God would help them conquer the giants in the land (see Numbers 14, 15). So God sent them into the wilderness to wander for 40 years. This was an unhappy alternative to the wonderful gift he had planned for them. Lack of trust in God always prevents us from receiving his best.

4.1–3 Some of the Jewish Christians who received this letter of Hebrews may have been on the verge of turning back from their promised rest in Christ, just as the people in Moses' day turned back from the promised land. In both cases, the difficulties of the present moment overshadowed the reality of God's promise, and the people doubted that God would fulfill his promises. When we trust our own efforts instead of Christ's power, we too are in danger of turning back. Our own efforts are never adequate; only Christ can see us through.

4.2 The Israelites of Moses' day illustrate a problem facing many who fill our churches today. They know a great deal about Christ, but they do not know him personally – they don't mix their knowledge with faith. Let the good news about Christ benefit your life. Believe in him and then act on what you know. Trust in Christ and do what he says.

4.4 God rested on the seventh day not because he was tired, but to indicate the completion of creation. The world was perfect, and he was well satisfied with it. This rest is a foretaste of our eternal joy when creation is renewed and restored, when every mark of sin has been removed, and the world is perfect again. Our rest in

speaks about the seventh day as follows, "And God rested on the seventh day from
all his works." 5 And again in this place it says, "They shall not enter my rest."
6 Since therefore it remains open for some to enter it, and those who formerly received the good news failed to enter because of disobedience, 7 again he sets a certain day—"today"—saying through David much later, in the words already
quoted,

"Today, if you hear his voice,
do not harden your hearts."

8 For if Joshua had given them rest, God[x] would not speak later about another day.
9 So then, a sabbath rest still remains for the people of God; 10 for those who enter
God's rest also cease from their labors as God did from his. 11 Let us therefore make
every effort to enter that rest, so that no one may fall through such disobedience as
theirs.

12 Indeed, the word of God is living and active, sharper than any two-edged
sword, piercing until it divides soul from spirit, joints from marrow; it is able to
judge the thoughts and intentions of the heart. 13 And before him no creature is
hidden, but all are naked and laid bare to the eyes of the one to whom we must
render an account.

4.6 Num 14.26-30 Heb 3.18
4.7 Ps 95.7
4.8 Josh 22.4
4.10 Rev 14.13
4.11 2 Pet 2.6
4.12 Isa 49.2 Jer 23.29 1 Cor 14.24,25 Eph 6.17 1 Pet 1.23
4.13 2 Chron 16.9 Jn 2.25

3. Christ is greater than the Old Testament priesthood

Jesus Christ is our high priest

14 Since, then, we have a great high priest who has passed through the heavens,
Jesus, the Son of God, let us hold fast to our confession. 15 For we do not have a
high priest who is unable to sympathize with our weaknesses, but we have one who
in every respect has been tested[y] as we are, yet without sin. 16 Let us therefore
approach the throne of grace with boldness, so that we may receive mercy and find
grace to help in time of need.

4.14 Heb 2.17; 3.1
4.15 2 Cor 5.21 Heb 2.17,18
4.16 Heb 7.19; 10.19,22

[x] Gk *he* [y] Or *tempted*

Christ begins when we trust him to complete his good and perfect work in us (see the note on 3.11).

4.6, 7 God gave Israel the opportunity to enter Canaan, but they failed because they didn't trust him (Numbers 13, 14). Now God offers another opportunity to enter his ultimate place of rest—he invites us to come to Christ. To enter his rest, you must believe that God has this relationship in mind for you; you must cease from your own efforts to create it; you must trust in Jesus to bring you God's rest; and you must determine to follow him in obedience. *Now* is the best time to find peace with God. Tomorrow may be too late.

4.8–11 God wants us to enter his rest. For the Israelites of Moses' time, this rest was the promised land. For Christians, it is peace with God now and eternal life in a new earth later. We do not need to wait for the next life to enjoy God's rest and peace; we may have it daily now! Our daily rest in the Lord will not end with death, but will become an eternal rest in the home Christ is preparing for us (John 14.1–4).

4.11 If Jesus has provided for our rest through faith, why must we "make every effort" for it? This is not the struggle of good works to obtain salvation, nor is it a mystical struggle to overcome selfishness. It refers to making every effort to obtain what God has provided. Salvation is not to be taken for granted. It requires decision and commitment to appropriate the gift God offers.

4.12 The word of God is not merely a collection of words from God, a vehicle for communicating ideas; it is living, life-changing, and dynamic as it works in us. With the incisiveness of a surgeon's knife, God's Word reveals who we are and what we are not. It penetrates the core of our moral and spiritual life. It discerns what is within us, both good and evil. The demands of God's Word require decisions. We must not only listen to the Word; we must also let it shape our lives.

4.13 Nothing can be hidden from God. He knows about everyone everywhere, and everything about us is wide open to his all-seeing eyes. He sees all we do and knows all we think. When we are unaware of his presence, he is there. When we try to hide from him, he sees us. We can have no secrets from God. It is comforting that although God knows us intimately, he still loves us.

4.14 To the Jews, the high priest was the highest religious authority in the land. He alone entered the Holy of Holies in the temple once a year to make atonement for the sins of the whole nation (Leviticus 16). Like the high priest, Jesus mediates between God and us. As humanity's representative, he intercedes for us before God. As God's representative, he assures us of God's forgiveness. Jesus has more authority than the Jewish high priests because he is truly God and truly man. Unlike the high priest who could go before God only once a year, Christ is always at God's right hand, interceding for us. He is always available when we pray.

4.15 Jesus is like us because he experienced a full range of temptations as a human being throughout his life. We can be comforted knowing that Jesus faced temptation—he can sympathize with us. We can be inspired knowing that Jesus faced temptation without giving in to sin. He shows us that we do not have to sin when facing the seductive lure of temptation. Jesus is the only perfect human being who has ever lived.

4.16 Prayer is our approach to God, and we are to come "with boldness." Some Christians approach God meekly with heads hung, afraid to ask him to meet their needs. Others pray flippantly with little thought. Come with reverence, because he is your King. But also come with bold assurance, because he is your Friend and Counselor.

5 Every high priest chosen from among mortals is put in charge of things pertaining to God on their behalf, to offer gifts and sacrifices for sins. 2 He is able to
deal gently with the ignorant and wayward, since he himself is subject to weakness;
3 and because of this he must offer sacrifice for his own sins as well as for those of
the people. 4 And one does not presume to take this honor, but takes it only when
called by God, just as Aaron was.
5 So also Christ did not glorify himself in becoming a high priest, but was appointed by the one who said to him,
"You are my Son,
today I have begotten you";
6 as he says also in another place,
"You are a priest forever,
according to the order of Melchizedek."
7 In the days of his flesh, Jesus[z] offered up prayers and supplications, with
loud cries and tears, to the one who was able to save him from death, and he was
heard because of his reverent submission. 8 Although he was a Son, he learned
obedience through what he suffered; 9 and having been made perfect, he became
the source of eternal salvation for all who obey him, 10 having been designated by
God a high priest according to the order of Melchizedek.

Go beyond elementary principles

11 About this[a] we have much to say that is hard to explain, since you have
become dull in understanding. 12 For though by this time you ought to be teachers,
you need someone to teach you again the basic elements of the oracles of God. You
need milk, not solid food; 13 for everyone who lives on milk, being still an infant,
is unskilled in the word of righteousness. 14 But solid food is for the mature, for
those whose faculties have been trained by practice to distinguish good from evil.
6 Therefore let us go on toward perfection,[b] leaving behind the basic teaching
about Christ, and not laying again the foundation: repentance from dead works
and faith toward God, 2 instruction about baptisms, laying on of hands, resurrection

5.1 Lev 4.3; 9.7 Heb 2.17; 7.27; 8.3,4
5.2 Heb 2.18; 7.28
5.3 Heb 7.27; 9.7
5.4 Ex 28.1 Num 16.40
5.5 Ps 2.7 Acts 13.33 Heb 1.5
5.6 Ps 110.4
5.7 Ps 22.1-4 Mt 26.39,53
5.8 Phil 2.8 Heb 1.2
5.10 Heb 2.17; 6.20
5.12 1 Cor 3.1,2
5.13 1 Cor 14.20 Eph 4.13,14
5.14 1 Cor 2.6,14
6.1 Phil 3.13-16 Heb 5.12,16
6.2 Acts 6.6; 8.17 17.31; 19.4

[z] Gk *he* [a] Or *him* [b] Or *toward maturity*

5.4–6 This chapter stresses both Christ's divine appointment and his humanity. The writer uses two Old Testament verses to show Christ's divine appointment—Psalms 2.7 and 110.4. In the days when this book was written, the Romans chose the high priest in Jerusalem. In the Old Testament, however, God chose Aaron, and only his descendants could be high priests. Christ, like Aaron, was chosen by God.

5.6 Melchizedek was a priest of Salem (now called Jerusalem). His Profile is found in Genesis 16. Melchizedek's position is explained in Hebrews 7.

5.7 Jesus was in great agony as he prepared to face death (Luke 22.41–44). Although he cried out to God asking to be delivered, he was prepared to suffer humiliation, separation from his Father, and death in order to do God's will. At times we will undergo trials, not because we want to suffer, but because we want to obey God. Let Jesus' obedience sustain and encourage you in times of trial. You can face anything when you know Jesus Christ is with you.

5.7 Have you ever felt that God didn't hear your prayers? Be sure you are praying with reverent submission, willing to do what God wants. God responds to his obedient children.

5.8 Jesus' human life was not a script that he passively followed. It was a life he chose freely (John 10.17, 18). It was a continuous process of making the will of God the Father his own. He chose to obey, even though obedience led to suffering and death. Because he obeyed perfectly even under trial, he can help us obey, no matter how difficult obedience seems to be.

5.9 Christ was always morally perfect. By obeying, he demonstrated his perfection to us, not to God or to himself. In the Bible, *perfection* means completeness or maturity. By sharing our experience of suffering, Christ shared our human experience completely. He is now able to offer eternal salvation to those who obey him. See Philippians 2.5–11 for Christ's attitude in taking human form.

5.12, 13 "Oracles of God" means the words of God or the revelation from God. These Jewish Christians were immature. Some of them should have been teaching others, but they had not applied the basics to their own lives. They were reluctant to move beyond age-old traditions, established doctrines, and discussion of the basics. They wouldn't be able to understand the high-priestly role of Christ unless they moved out of their comfortable position, cut some of their Jewish ties, and stopped trying to blend in with their culture. Commitment to Christ moves people out of the "comfort zone."

5.12–14 In order to grow from an infant Christian to a mature Christian, we must learn discernment. We must train our consciences, our senses, our minds, and our bodies to distinguish right from wrong. Can you recognize temptation before it traps you? Can you tell correct use of Scripture from mistaken uses?

5.14 Our capacity to feast on deeper knowledge of God ("solid food") is determined by our spiritual growth. Too often we want God's banquet before we are spiritually capable of digesting it. As you grow in the Lord and put into practice what you have learned, your capacity to understand will grow even greater.

6.1, 2 Certain basics are essential for all believers. Those principles that all Christians must know include the importance of faith, the foolishness of trying to be saved by works, the meaning of baptism, spiritual gifts, and the facts of resurrection and eternal life. To become mature in our understanding, we need to move beyond (but not away from) the basics to a more complete understanding

6.4 Mt 7.22; Jn 4.10; 6.32; Eph 2.8; Heb 10.26,32; 2 Pet 2.20; 1 Jn 5.16
6.5 Heb 2.5; 1 Pet 2.3
6.6 Heb 10.26,29
6.10 Mt 10.42; 25.40; Jn 13.20; 1 Thess 1.3
6.11 Col 2.2; Heb 3.6; 10.22
6.12 Heb 1.14; 10.36; 13.7
6.13 Gen 22.16; Gal 3.16

of the dead, and eternal judgment. 3 And we will do[c] this, if God permits. 4 For it
is impossible to restore again to repentance those who have once been enlightened,
and have tasted the heavenly gift, and have shared in the Holy Spirit, 5 and have
tasted the goodness of the word of God and the powers of the age to come, 6 and
then have fallen away, since on their own they are crucifying again the Son of God
and are holding him up to contempt. 7 Ground that drinks up the rain falling on it
repeatedly, and that produces a crop useful to those for whom it is cultivated, receives a blessing from God. 8 But if it produces thorns and thistles, it is worthless
and on the verge of being cursed; its end is to be burned over.

9 Even though we speak in this way, beloved, we are confident of better things
in your case, things that belong to salvation. 10 For God is not unjust; he will not
overlook your work and the love that you showed for his sake[d] in serving the
saints, as you still do. 11 And we want each one of you to show the same diligence
so as to realize the full assurance of hope to the very end, 12 so that you may not
become sluggish, but imitators of those who through faith and patience inherit the
promises.

God's certain promise gives hope

13 When God made a promise to Abraham, because he had no one greater by
whom to swear, he swore by himself, 14 saying, "I will surely bless you and multiply you." 15 And thus Abraham,[e] having patiently endured, obtained the promise.

[c] Other ancient authorities read *let us do* [d] Gk *for his name* [e] Gk *he*

THE CHOICES OF MATURITY
One way to evaluate spiritual maturity is by looking at the choices we make. The writer of Hebrews notes many of the ways those choices change with personal growth.

Mature choices	*Versus*	*Immature choices*
Teaching others	rather than . . .	just being taught.
Developing depth of understanding	rather than . . .	struggling with the basics.
Self-evaluation	rather than . . .	self-criticism.
Seeking unity	rather than . . .	disunity.
Desiring spiritual challenges	rather than . . .	desiring entertainment.
Careful study and observation	rather than . . .	opinions and half-hearted efforts.
Active faith	rather than . . .	cautious apathy and doubt.
Confidence	rather than . . .	fear.
Feelings and experiences evaluated in the light of God's Word	rather than . . .	experiences evaluated according to feelings.

of the faith. And this is what the author intends to do (6.3). Mature Christians should be teaching new Christians the basics. Then, acting on what they know, the mature will learn even more from God's Word.

6.3 These Christians needed to move beyond the basics of their faith to understanding Christ as the perfect high priest and fulfillment of all the Old Testament prophecies. Rather than arguing about the respective merits of Judaism and Christianity, they needed to depend on Christ and live effectively for him.

6.4–6 In the first century, a pagan who investigated Christianity and then went back to paganism made a clean break with the church. But for Jewish Christians who decided to return to Judaism, the break was less obvious. Their life-style remained relatively unchanged. But by deliberately turning away from Christ, they were cutting themselves off from God's forgiveness. Those who persevere in believing are true saints; those who continue to reject Christ are unbelievers, no matter how well they behave.

6.6 Some think this verse refers to believers who renounce their Christianity or else to unbelievers who come close to salvation, then turn away. Either way, those who reject Christ will not be saved. Christ died once for all. He will not be crucified again. Apart from his cross, there is no other possible way of salvation. However, the author does not indicate that his readers are in danger of renouncing Christ (see 6.9). He is warning against hardness of heart that would make repentance inconceivable for the sinner.

6.7, 8 Land that produces a good crop receives loving care, but land that produces thorns and thistles has to be burned off so the farmer can start over. An unproductive Christian life falls under God's condemnation. We are not saved by works or conduct, but what we do is the *evidence* of our faith.

6.10 It's easy to get discouraged thinking God has forgotten us. But God is never unfair. He never forgets or overlooks our hard work for him. Presently you may not be receiving the rewards and acclaim that this life has to offer, but God knows your every effort of love and ministry. Let God's love for you and his intimate knowledge of your service for him bolster you as you face disappointment and rejection here on earth.

6.11, 12 Hope keeps the Christian from feeling dull or becoming bored. Like an athlete, train hard and run well, remembering the reward that lies ahead (Philippians 3.14).

6.15 Abraham waited patiently—it was 25 years from the time God promised him a son (Genesis 17.16) to Isaac's birth (Genesis 21.1–3). Because our trials and temptations are so intense, they seem to last an eternity. Both the Bible and the testimony of mature Christians encourage us to wait for God's timing, even when our needs seem too great to wait any longer.

16 Human beings, of course, swear by someone greater than themselves, and an 6.16
oath given as confirmation puts an end to all dispute. 17 In the same way, when God Gal 3.15
desired to show even more clearly to the heirs of the promise the unchangeable 6.17 Ps 110.4
character of his purpose, he guaranteed it by an oath, 18 so that through two un- Heb 11.9
changeable things, in which it is impossible that God would prove false, we who 6.18 Tit 1.2
have taken refuge might be strongly encouraged to seize the hope set before us. Heb 3.6
19 We have this hope, a sure and steadfast anchor of the soul, a hope that enters the 6.19 Lev 16.15,16
inner shrine behind the curtain, 20 where Jesus, a forerunner on our behalf, has Heb 9.7
entered, having become a high priest forever according to the order of Melchize- 6.20 Heb 4.14; 5.6
dek. 9.24

Melchizedek compared to Abraham

7 This "King Melchizedek of Salem, priest of the Most High God, met Abraham 7.1
as he was returning from defeating the kings and blessed him"; 2 and to him Gen 14.17-20 Ps 110.4
Abraham apportioned "one-tenth of everything." His name, in the first place, Heb 5.6,10
means "king of righteousness"; next he is also king of Salem, that is, "king of
peace." 3 Without father, without mother, without genealogy, having neither beginning of days nor end of life, but resembling the Son of God, he remains a priest
forever.

4 See how great he is! Even[f] Abraham the patriarch gave him a tenth of the 7.4
spoils. 5 And those descendants of Levi who receive the priestly office have a com- Gen 14.20
mandment in the law to collect tithes[g] from the people, that is, from their kin- 7.5 Num 18.21,26
dred,[h] though these also are descended from Abraham. 6 But this man, who does 7.6
not belong to their ancestry, collected tithes[g] from Abraham and blessed him who Rom 4.13 Gal 3.16
had received the promises. 7 It is beyond dispute that the inferior is blessed by the
superior. 8 In the one case, tithes are received by those who are mortal; in the other, 7.8
by one of whom it is testified that he lives. 9 One might even say that Levi himself, Heb 5.6
who receives tithes, paid tithes through Abraham, 10 for he was still in the loins of
his ancestor when Melchizedek met him.

Christ is like Melchizedek

11 Now if perfection had been attainable through the levitical priesthood—for 7.11
the people received the law under this priesthood—what further need would there Gal 2.21 Heb 7.17,18
have been to speak of another priest arising according to the order of Melchizedek,

[f] Other ancient authorities lack *Even* [g] Or *a tenth* [h] Gk *brothers*

6.17 God's promises are unchangeable and trustworthy, because God is unchangeable and trustworthy. When God promised Abraham a son, he took an oath in his own name. The oath was as good as his name, and his name was as good as his divine nature.

6.18, 19 God's two unchangeable realities are his own nature and his own promise. God embodies all truth, and therefore he cannot lie. Because God is truth, you can be secure in his promises; you don't need to wonder if he will change his plans. For the true seeker who comes to God in belief, God gives an unconditional promise of acceptance. When you ask God with openness, honesty, and sincerity to save you from your sins, *he will do it.* This assurance should give you courage and hope.

6.19, 20 The curtain referred to in the text hung across the entrance from the Holy Place to the Holy of Holies, the two innermost chambers of the temple. This curtain prevented anyone from entering, gazing into, or even getting a fleeting glimpse of the interior of the Holy of Holies (see also 9.1–8). The high priest could enter there only once a year to stand before God's presence and atone for the sins of the entire nation. But Christ is in God's presence at all times, not just once a year, as the high priest who can continually intercede for us.

7.1, 2 *Melchizedek* means "king of righteousness," and *Salem* (Jerusalem) means "peace."

7.2ff The writer of Hebrews uses this story from Genesis 14.17–20 to show that Christ is even greater than Abraham, father of the Jewish nation, and Levi (Abraham's descendant). Therefore, the Jewish priesthood (made up of Levi's descendants) was inferior to Melchizedek's priesthood (a type of Christ's priesthood).

7.3–10 Melchizedek was a priest of the Most High God (see the note on Genesis 14.18 and his Profile in Genesis 16). He is said to be a priest forever (Psalm 110.4), because his priesthood has no record of beginning or end—he was a priest of God in Salem (Jerusalem) long before the nation of Israel and the regular priesthood began.

7.7 The "inferior is blessed by the superior" means a person who has the power to bless is always greater than the person he blesses.

7.11–16 Jesus' high-priestly role was superior to that of any priest of Levi, because the Messiah was a priest of a higher rank (Psalm 110.4). If the Jewish priests and their laws had been able to save people, why would God need to send Christ as a priest, who came not from the tribe of Levi (the priestly tribe), but from the tribe of Judah? The animal sacrifices had to be repeated, and they offered only temporary forgiveness; but Christ's sacrifice was offered once, and it offers total and permanent forgiveness. Under the new covenant, the levitical priesthood was canceled in favor of Christ's role as high priest. Because Christ is our high priest, we need to pay attention to him. No minister, leader, or Christian friend can substitute for his work and his role in our salvation.

rather than one according to the order of Aaron? 12 For when there is a change in the
priesthood, there is necessarily a change in the law as well. 13 Now the one of whom
these things are spoken belonged to another tribe, from which no one has ever
served at the altar. 14 For it is evident that our Lord was descended from Judah, and
in connection with that tribe Moses said nothing about priests.

15 It is even more obvious when another priest arises, resembling Melchizedek, 16 one who has become a priest, not through a legal requirement concerning
physical descent, but through the power of an indestructible life. 17 For it is attested
of him,

"You are a priest forever,
according to the order of Melchizedek."

7.14 Gen 49.10 Isa 11.1 Mt 1.3 Lk 3.33 Rom 1.3 Rev 5.5
7.17 Ps 110.4

ABRAHAM IN THE NEW TESTAMENT

Abraham was an ancestor of Jesus Christ	Matthew 1.1, 2, 17; Luke 3.23, 34	Jesus Christ was human; he was born into the line of Abraham, whom God had chosen to be the father of a great nation through which the whole world would be blessed. We are blessed because of what Jesus Christ, Abraham's descendant, did for us.
Abraham was the father of the Jewish nation	Matthew 3.9; Luke 3.8; Acts 13.26; Romans 4.1; 11.1; 2 Corinthians 11.22; Hebrews 6.13, 14	God wanted to set apart a nation for himself, a nation that would tell the world about him. He began with a man of faith who, though old and childless, believed God's promise of innumerable descendants. We can trust God to do the impossible when we have faith.
Abraham was honored by God	Hebrews 7.4	God honors those who trust him. Although the world may disdain us if we trust in God, God promises to honor us.
Abraham, because of his faith, now sits in the kingdom with Christ.	Matthew 8.11; Luke 13.28; 16.23–31	Abraham followed God, and now he is enjoying his reward—eternity with God. We will one day meet Abraham, because we have been promised eternity as well.
God *is* Abraham's God; thus Abraham is alive with God	Matthew 22.32; Mark 12.26; Luke 20.37; Acts 7.32	As Abraham lives forever, we will live forever because we, like Abraham, have chosen the life of faith.
Abraham received great promises from God	Luke 1.55, 72, 73; Acts 3.25; 7.17, 18; Galatians 3.6, 14–16; Hebrews 6.13–15	Many of the promises God made to Abraham seemed impossible to be realized, but Abraham trusted God. The promises to believers in God's Word also seem too incredible to believe, but we can trust God to keep all his promises.
Abraham followed God	Acts 7.2–8; Hebrews 11.8, 17–19	Abraham followed God's leading from his homeland to an unknown territory, which became the Jews' promised land. When we follow God, even before he makes all his plans clear to us, we will never be disappointed.
God blessed Abraham because of his faith	Romans 4; Galatians 3.6–9, 14–29; Hebrews 11.8, 17–19; James 2.21–24	Abraham showed faith in times of disappointment, trial, and testing. Because of his faith, God counted him righteous, his "friend." God accepts us because of our faith.
Abraham is the father of all those who come to God by faith	Romans 9.6–8; Galatians 3.6–9, 14–29	The Jews are Abraham's children, and Christ was his descendant. We are Christ's brothers and sisters; thus all believers are Abraham's children and God's children. Abraham was righteous because of his faith; we are made righteous by faith in Christ. The promises made to Abraham apply to us because of Christ.

18 There is, on the one hand, the abrogation of an earlier commandment because it
was weak and ineffectual 19 (for the law made nothing perfect); there is, on the
other hand, the introduction of a better hope, through which we approach God.
20 This was confirmed with an oath; for others who became priests took their
office without an oath, 21 but this one became a priest with an oath, because of the
one who said to him,

"The Lord has sworn
and will not change his mind,
'You are a priest forever' "—

22 accordingly Jesus has also become the guarantee of a better covenant.
23 Furthermore, the former priests were many in number, because they were
prevented by death from continuing in office; 24 but he holds his priesthood permanently, because he continues forever. 25 Consequently he is able for all time to
save[i] those who approach God through him, since he always lives to make intercession for them.
26 For it was fitting that we should have such a high priest, holy, blameless,
undefiled, separated from sinners, and exalted above the heavens. 27 Unlike the
other[j] high priests, he has no need to offer sacrifices day after day, first for his own
sins, and then for those of the people; this he did once for all when he offered
himself. 28 For the law appoints as high priests those who are subject to weakness,
but the word of the oath, which came later than the law, appoints a Son who has
been made perfect forever.

7.18 Rom 8.3 Gal 4.9
7.19 Acts 13.39 Rom 3.20; 5.2 Gal 2.16 Heb 6.18; 9.9 10.19-22
7.21 Num 23.19 Ps 110.4
7.24 Isa 9.6,7 Jn 12.34 Rev 1.18
7.25 Rom 8.34 1 Tim 2.5 1 Jn 2.1
7.26 2 Cor 5.21 1 Pet 2.22
7.27 Lev 9.7 16.6,11,15 Rom 6.10 Eph 5.2 Heb 5.3; 9.7,12
7.28 Heb 2.10; 5.1,2

4. The new covenant is greater than the old

Christ is the high priest of the new covenant

8 Now the main point in what we are saying is this: we have such a high priest,
one who is seated at the right hand of the throne of the Majesty in the heavens,
2 a minister in the sanctuary and the true tent[k] that the Lord, and not any mortal, has
set up. 3 For every high priest is appointed to offer gifts and sacrifices; hence it is
necessary for this priest also to have something to offer. 4 Now if he were on earth,

8.1 Col 3.1
8.2 Ex 33.7
8.3 Eph 5.2

[i] Or *able to save completely* [j] Gk lacks *other* [k] Or *tabernacle*

7.18, 19 The law (commandment) was not intended to save people, but to point out sin (see Romans 3.20; 5.20) and to point toward Christ (see Galatians 3.24, 25). Salvation comes through Christ whose sacrifice brings forgiveness for our sins. Being ethical, working diligently to help others, and giving to charity are all commendable, but they cannot save us or make us right with God.

7.22–24 This "better covenant" is also called the new covenant or new testament. It is new and better because it allows us to go directly to God through Christ. We no longer need to rely on sacrificed animals and priests to obtain God's forgiveness. This new covenant is better because, while all the priests died, Christ lives forever. Priests and sacrifices could not save people, but Christ truly saves. You have access to Christ. He is available to you, but do you go to him with your needs?

7.25 No one can add to what Jesus did to save us; our past, present, and future sins are all forgiven, and Jesus is with the Father as a sign that our sins are forgiven. If you are a Christian, remember that Christ has paid the price for your sins once and for all. (See also 9.24–28.)

7.25 As our high priest, Christ is our advocate, the mediator between us and God. He looks after our interests and intercedes for us with God. The Old Testament high priest went before God once a year to plead for the forgiveness of the nation's sins; Christ makes perpetual intercession before God for us. Christ's continuous presence in heaven with the Father assures us that our sins have been paid for and forgiven (see Romans 8.33, 34; Hebrews 2.17, 18; 4.15, 16; 9.24). This wonderful assurance frees us from guilt and fear of failure.

7.27 In Old Testament times when animals were sacrificed, they were cut into pieces, the parts were washed, the fat was burned, the blood was sprinkled, and the meat was boiled. Blood was demanded as atonement for sins, and God accepted animal blood to cover the people's sins (Leviticus 17.11). Because of the sacrificial system, the Israelites were generally aware that sin costs and that they themselves were sinful. Many people take Christ's work on the cross for granted. They don't realize how costly it was for Jesus to secure our forgiveness—it cost him his life (1 Peter 1.18, 19).

7.27 Because Christ died *once* and *for all*, he finished all sacrifices. He forgave sins—past, present, and future. The Jews did not need to go back to the old system because Christ, the perfect sacrifice, completed the work of redemption. You don't have to look for another way to have your sins forgiven—Christ was the final sacrifice for you.

7.28 These verses help explain why Jesus had to die. As we better understand the Jewish sacrificial system, we see that Jesus' death served as the perfect atonement for our sins. His death brings us eternal life. How callous, how cold, how stubborn it would be to refuse God's greatest gift.

8.4 Under the old Jewish system, priests were chosen only from the tribe of Levi, and sacrifices were offered daily on the altar for forgiveness of sins (see 7.12–14). This system would not have allowed Jesus to be a priest because he was from the tribe of Judah. But his perfect sacrifice ended all need for further priests and sacrifices.

The use of the present tense, "there are priests who offer gifts" indicates that this book was written before A.D. 70, when the temple in Jerusalem was destroyed, ending the sacrifices.

8.5 Ex 25.40 Col 2.17 Heb 9.23
8.6 2 Cor 3.6 Heb 7.22
8.7 Heb 7.11
8.8-11 Jer 31.31-34

he would not be a priest at all, since there are priests who offer gifts according to
the law. 5 They offer worship in a sanctuary that is a sketch and shadow of the
heavenly one; for Moses, when he was about to erect the tent,[l] was warned, "See
that you make everything according to the pattern that was shown you on the mountain." 6 But Jesus[m] has now obtained a more excellent ministry, and to that degree
he is the mediator of a better covenant, which has been enacted through better
promises. 7 For if that first covenant had been faultless, there would have been no
need to look for a second one.

8 God[n] finds fault with them when he says:
"The days are surely coming, says the Lord,
when I will establish a new covenant with the house of Israel
and with the house of Judah;
9 not like the covenant that I made with their ancestors,
on the day when I took them by the hand to lead them out of the land of
Egypt;
for they did not continue in my covenant,
and so I had no concern for them, says the Lord.
10 This is the covenant that I will make with the house of Israel
after those days, says the Lord:

[l] Or *tabernacle* [m] Gk *he* [n] Gk *He*

THE OLD AND NEW COVENANTS

Like pointing out the similarities and differences between the photograph of a person and the actual person, the writer of Hebrews shows the connection between the old mosaic covenant and the new messianic covenant. He proves that the old covenant was a shadow of the real Christ.

The Old Covenant under Moses	*The New Covenant in Christ*	*Application*
Gifts and sacrifices by those guilty of sin	Self-sacrifice by the guiltless Christ	Christ died for you
Focused on a physical building where one goes to worship	Focuses on the reign of Christ in the hearts of believers	God is directly involved in your life
A model	A reality	Not temporal, but eternal
Limited promises	Limitless promises	We can trust God's promises to us
Failed agreement by people	Faithful agreement by Christ	Christ has kept the agreement where people couldn't
External standards and rules	Internal standards—a new heart	God sees both actions and motives—we are accountable to God, not rules
Limited access to God	Unlimited access to God	God is personally available
Based on fear	Based on love and forgiveness	Forgiveness keeps our failures from destroying the agreement
Legal cleansing	Personal cleansing	God's cleansing is complete
Continual sacrifice	Conclusive sacrifice	Christ's sacrifice was perfect and final
Obey the rules	Serve the living God	We have a relationship, not regulations
Forgiveness earned	Forgiveness freely given	We have true and complete forgiveness
Repeated yearly	Completed by Christ's death	Christ's death can be applied to your sin
Man's effort	God's grace	Initiated by God's love for you
Available to some	Available to all	Available to you

8.5 The pattern for the tabernacle built by Moses was given by God. It was a pattern of the spiritual reality of Christ's sacrifice. There is no tabernacle in heaven of which the earthly is a copy, but rather the earthly tabernacle was an expression of eternal, theological principles.

8.8–12 This passage quotes Jeremiah 31.31–34 and compares the new covenant (or agreement) with the old. The old covenant was the covenant of law between God and Israel. The new and better way is the covenant of grace – Christ's offer to forgive our sins and bring us to God through his sacrificial death. This covenant is new in extent – it goes beyond Israel and Judah to all the Gentile nations. It is new in application, because it is written in our hearts and minds. It offers a new way to forgiveness, not through animal sacrifice but through faith.

8.10 If our hearts are not changed, following God's rules will be unpleasant and difficult. We will rebel against being told how to live. The Holy Spirit, however, gives us new desires. He helps us want to obey God (see Philippians 2.12, 13). With new hearts, we find that serving God is our greatest joy.

8.10, 11 Under God's new covenant, God's law is inside us. It is no longer an external set of rules and principles. The Holy Spirit reminds us of Christ's words, quickens our consciences, influences our motives and desires, and makes us want to obey. Now doing God's will is something we desire with all our heart and mind.

I will put my laws in their minds,
and write them on their hearts,
and I will be their God,
and they shall be my people.
11 And they shall not teach one another 8.11
or say to each other, 'Know the Lord,' Jn 6.45 1 Jn 2.27
for they shall all know me,
from the least of them to the greatest.
12 For I will be merciful toward their iniquities,
and I will remember their sins no more."
13In speaking of "a new covenant," he has made the first one obsolete. And what 8.13
is obsolete and growing old will soon disappear. Heb 12.24

Rules for worship under the old covenant

9 Now even the first covenant had regulations for worship and an earthly sanctu- 9.1
ary. 2For a tent[o] was constructed, the first one, in which were the lampstand, Ex 25.8
the table, and the bread of the Presence;[p] this is called the Holy Place. 3Behind the 9.2 Ex 25.23,31
second curtain was a tent[o] called the Holy of Holies. 4In it stood the golden altar 9.3
of incense and the ark of the covenant overlaid on all sides with gold, in which there Ex 26.31,33
were a golden urn holding the manna, and Aaron's rod that budded, and the tablets 9.4 Ex 16.33
of the covenant; 5above it were the cherubim of glory overshadowing the mercy 25.10,16 30.1; 31.18
seat.[q] Of these things we cannot speak now in detail. 9.5
6 Such preparations having been made, the priests go continually into the first Lev 16.2
tent[o] to carry out their ritual duties; 7but only the high priest goes into the second, 9.7 Ex 30.10
and he but once a year, and not without taking the blood that he offers for himself Lev 16.11
and for the sins committed unintentionally by the people. 8By this the Holy Spirit Num 15.25
indicates that the way into the sanctuary has not yet been disclosed as long as the 9.8 Jn 14.6
first tent[o] is still standing. 9This is a symbol[r] of the present time, during which 9.9
gifts and sacrifices are offered that cannot perfect the conscience of the worshiper, Gal 3.21,22
10but deal only with food and drink and various baptisms, regulations for the body 9.10
imposed until the time comes to set things right. Rom 14.17 Eph 2.15

Christ is the perfect offering for sin

11 But when Christ came as a high priest of the good things that have come,[s] 9.11 Mk 14.58
then through the greater and perfect[t] tent[o] (not made with hands, that is, not of 9.12
this creation), 12he entered once for all into the Holy Place, not with the blood of Lev 4.3
goats and calves, but with his own blood, thus obtaining eternal redemption. 13For 9.13 Num 19.2,9

[o] Or *tabernacle* [p] Gk *the presentation of the loaves* [q] Or *the place of atonement* [r] Gk *parable* [s] Other ancient authorities read *good things to come* [t] Gk *more perfect*

9.1 The earthly sanctuary refers to the tabernacle that God instructed Moses to set up (see Exodus 36–40).

9.5 Cherubim are mighty angels.

9.6–8 The high priest could enter the Holy of Holies (9.3; or the "second" tent, 9.7), the innermost room of the tabernacle, one day each year to atone for the nation's sins. The Holy of Holies was a small room that contained the ark of the covenant (a gold-covered chest containing the original stone tablets on which the ten commandments were written, a jar of manna, and Aaron's rod). The top of the chest served as the "mercy seat" (the altar) on which the blood was sprinkled by the high priest on the day of atonement. The Holy of Holies was the most sacred spot on earth for the Jews. Only the high priest could enter – the other priests and the common people were forbidden to come into the room. Their only access to God was through the high priest, who offered a sacrifice and used its blood to atone first for his own sins and then for the people's sins (see also 10.19).

9.10 The people had to keep the Old Testament dietary laws and ceremonial cleansing laws until Christ came with God's new and better way.

9.12 This imagery comes from the day of atonement rituals described in Leviticus 16. Redemption refers to the process of paying the price (ransom) to free a slave. By his death, Christ freed us from the slavery of sin forever.

9.12–14 Though you know Christ, you may believe that you have to work hard to make yourself good enough for God. But rules and rituals have never cleansed people's hearts. By Jesus' blood alone (1) our consciences are cleared, (2) we are freed from death and can live to serve God, and (3) we are freed from sin's power. If you are carrying a load of guilt because you can't be good enough for God, take another look at Jesus' death and what it means for you. Christ can heal your conscience and deliver you from the frustration of trying to earn God's favor.

9.13, 14 When the people sacrificed animals, God regarded their faith and obedience, cleansed the people from sin, and made them *ceremonially* acceptable according to Old Testament law.

and I will write them on their minds,"
17 he also adds,
"I will remember[e] their sins and their lawless deeds no more."
18 Where there is forgiveness of these, there is no longer any offering for sin.

B. THE SUPERIORITY OF FAITH (10.19–13.25)

Moving from argument to instruction, the author cites many examples of those who have demonstrated faith throughout history. Living by faith is far better than merely fulfilling rituals and rules. This can challenge us to grow in faith and to live in obedience to God each day.

Living by faith

19 Therefore, my friends,[f] since we have confidence to enter the sanctuary by
the blood of Jesus, 20 by the new and living way that he opened for us through the
curtain (that is, through his flesh), 21 and since we have a great priest over the house
of God, 22 let us approach with a true heart in full assurance of faith, with our hearts
sprinkled clean from an evil conscience and our bodies washed with pure water.
23 Let us hold fast to the confession of our hope without wavering, for he who has
promised is faithful. 24 And let us consider how to provoke one another to love and
good deeds, 25 not neglecting to meet together, as is the habit of some, but encouraging one another, and all the more as you see the Day approaching.
26 For if we willfully persist in sin after having received the knowledge of the
truth, there no longer remains a sacrifice for sins, 27 but a fearful prospect of judgment, and a fury of fire that will consume the adversaries. 28 Anyone who has violated the law of Moses dies without mercy "on the testimony of two or three
witnesses." 29 How much worse punishment do you think will be deserved by those
who have spurned the Son of God, profaned the blood of the covenant by which
they were sanctified, and outraged the Spirit of grace? 30 For we know the one who
said, "Vengeance is mine, I will repay." And again, "The Lord will judge his people." 31 It is a fearful thing to fall into the hands of the living God.
32 But recall those earlier days when, after you had been enlightened, you
endured a hard struggle with sufferings, 33 sometimes being publicly exposed to
abuse and persecution, and sometimes being partners with those so treated. 34 For
you had compassion for those who were in prison, and you cheerfully accepted the

10.20 Jn 10.9; 14.6
10.21 1 Tim 3.15
10.22 Ezek 36.25; 2 Cor 7.1; Eph 3.12; 1 Jn 3.21
10.23 1 Cor 1.9; 10.13
10.25 Acts 2.42; 2 Pet 3.9
10.26 Num 15.30; 1 Tim 2.4; 2 Pet 2.20; 1 Jn 5.16
10.27 Ezek 36.5
10.29 Mt 12.31
10.30 Deut 32.35,36; Ps 50.4; 135.14
10.32 Gal 3.4
10.33 Phil 1.7; 1 Thess 2.14

[e] Gk *on their minds and I will remember* [f] Gk *Therefore, brothers*

10.17 The writer concludes his argument with this powerful statement that God will never remember our sins. Christ forgives completely, so there is no need to confess our past sins repeatedly. As believers, we can be confident that the sins we confess and renounce are forgiven and forgotten.

10.19 The Holy of Holies (sanctuary) in the temple was sealed from view by a curtain (10.20). Only the high priest could enter this holy room, and he did so only once a year on the day of atonement when he made the sacrifice for the nation's sins. But now, Jesus' death has removed the curtain, and all believers may walk into God's presence at any time (see also 6.19, 20).

10.22–25 We have significant privileges with our new life in Christ: (1) we have personal access to God through Christ and can approach him without an elaborate system (10.22); (2) we may grow in faith, overcome doubts and questions, and deepen our relationship with God (10.23); (3) we may enjoy encouragement from one another (10.24); (4) we may worship together (10.25).

10.25 To neglect Christian meetings is to give up the encouragement and help of other Christians. We gather together to share our faith and to strengthen one another in the Lord. As we get closer to the "Day" when Christ will return, we will face many spiritual struggles and even persecution. Anti-Christian forces will grow in strength. Difficulties should never be excuses for missing church services. Rather, as difficulties arise, we should make an even greater effort to be faithful in attendance.

10.26 When people deliberately reject Christ's offer of salvation, they reject God's most precious gift. They ignore the leading of the Holy Spirit, the one who communicates to us God's saving love. This warning was given to Jewish Christians who were tempted to reject Christ for Judaism, but it applies to anyone who rejects Christ for another religion or, having understood Christ's atoning work, deliberately turns away from it (see also Numbers 15.30, 31 and Mark 3.28–30). The point is that there is no acceptable sacrifice for sin other than the death of Christ on the cross. If someone deliberately rejects the sacrifice of Christ after clearly understanding the gospel teaching about it, then there is no way for that person to be saved, because God has not provided any other name under heaven by whom we can be saved (see Acts 4.12).

10.31 This judgment is for those who have rejected God's mercy. For those who accept Christ's love and accept his salvation, the coming judgment is no cause for worry. Being saved through his grace, they have nothing to fear (see 1 John 4.18).

10.34–37 Hebrews encourages believers, when facing persecution and pressure, to persevere in their Christian faith and conduct. We don't usually think of suffering as good for us, but it can build our character and our patience. During times of great stress, we may feel God's presence more clearly and find help from Christians we never thought would care. Knowing that Jesus is with us in our suffering and that he will return one day to put an end to all pain, we grow in our faith and our relationship with him (see Romans 5.3–5).

plundering of your possessions, knowing that you yourselves possessed something better and more lasting. 35 Do not, therefore, abandon that confidence of
yours; it brings a great reward. 36 For you need endurance, so that when you have
done the will of God, you may receive what was promised.
37 For yet "in a very little while,
the one who is coming will come and will not delay;
38 but my righteous one will live by faith.
My soul takes no pleasure in anyone who shrinks back."
39 But we are not among those who shrink back and so are lost, but among those
who have faith and so are saved.

10.34 Mt 5.12 Heb 13.3
10.36 Col 3.24 Heb 9.15
10.37,38 Lk 18.8 Hab 2.3,4

Great heroes of faith

11 Now faith is the assurance of things hoped for, the conviction of things not
seen. 2 Indeed, by faith[g] our ancestors received approval. 3 By faith we understand that the worlds were prepared by the word of God, so that what is seen was
made from things that are not visible.[h]
4 By faith Abel offered to God a more acceptable[i] sacrifice than Cain's.
Through this he received approval as righteous, God himself giving approval to his
gifts; he died, but through his faith[j] he still speaks. 5 By faith Enoch was taken so
that he did not experience death; and "he was not found, because God had taken
him." For it was attested before he was taken away that "he had pleased God."
6 And without faith it is impossible to please God, for whoever would approach him
must believe that he exists and that he rewards those who seek him. 7 By faith
Noah, warned by God about events as yet unseen, respected the warning and built
an ark to save his household; by this he condemned the world and became an heir
to the righteousness that is in accordance with faith.
8 By faith Abraham obeyed when he was called to set out for a place that he was
to receive as an inheritance; and he set out, not knowing where he was going. 9 By

11.1 Rom 8.24 Heb 3.6,14
11.2 Heb 11.3
11.3 Gen 1.1-31 John 1.3 Rom 1.19,20 4.20 Heb 1.2
11.4 Gen 4.3-5
11.5 Gen 5.22-24
11.6 Jn 3.18,36
11.7 Gen 6.13-22 Rom 3.22 Phil 3.9
11.8 Gen 12.1-4

[g] Gk *by this* [h] Or *was not made out of visible things* [i] Gk *greater* [j] Gk *through it*

10.35–38 The writer encourages his readers not to abandon their faith in times of persecution, but to show by their endurance that their faith was real. Faith means resting in what Christ has done for us in the past, but it also means hoping for what he will do for us in the future (see Romans 8.12–25; Galatians 3.10–13).

11.1 Do you remember how you felt when you were younger and your birthday approached? You were excited and anxious. You knew you would certainly receive gifts and other special treats. But some things would be a surprise. Birthdays combine assurance and anticipation, and so does faith! Faith is the conviction based on past experience that God's new and fresh surprises will surely be ours.

11.1 Two words describe our faith: assurance and conviction. These two qualities need a secure beginning and ending point. The beginning point of faith is believing in God's character—he *is* who he says. The end point is believing in God's promises—he will *do* what he says. When we believe that God will fulfill his promises even though we don't see those promises materializing yet, we demonstrate true faith (see John 20.24–31).

11.3 God called the universe into existence out of nothing; he declared that it was to be, and it was. Our faith is in the God who created the entire universe by his word. God's Word has awesome power. When he speaks, do you listen and respond? How can you better prepare yourself to respond to his Word?

11.4 Cain and Abel were Adam and Eve's first two sons. Abel offered a sacrifice that pleased God, while Cain's sacrifice was unacceptable. Abel's Profile is found in Genesis 5. Cain's Profile is in Genesis 6. Abel's sacrifice (an animal substitute) was more acceptable to God, both because it was a blood sacrifice, and because of Abel's attitude when he offered it.

11.6 Believing that God exists is only the beginning; even the demons believe that much (James 2.19, 20). God will not settle for your mere acknowledgment of his existence. He wants a personal, dynamic relationship with you that will transform your life. Those who seek him will find that they are rewarded with God's intimate presence.

11.6 Sometimes we wonder about the fate of those who haven't heard of Christ and have not even had a Bible to read. God assures us that all who honestly seek him—who act in faith on the knowledge of God that they possess—will be rewarded. When you tell others the gospel, encourage them to be honest and diligent in their search for truth. Those who hear the gospel are responsible for what they have heard (see 2 Corinthians 6.1, 2).

11.7 Noah experienced rejection because he was different from his neighbors. God commanded him to build a huge boat in the middle of dry land, and although God's command seemed foolish, Noah obeyed. Noah's obedience made him appear strange to his neighbors, just as the new beliefs of Jewish Christians made them stand out. As you obey God, don't be surprised if others regard you as "different." Your obedience makes their disobedience stand out. Remember, if God asks you to do something, he will give you the necessary strength to carry out that task. For more information on Noah, see his Profile in Genesis 7.

11.8–10 Abraham's life was filled with faith. At God's command, he left home and went to another land—obeying without question (Genesis 12.1ff). He believed the covenant that God made with him (Genesis 12.2, 3; 13.14–16; 15.1–6). In obedience to God, Abraham was even willing to sacrifice his son Isaac (Genesis 22.1–19). Do not be surprised if God asks you to give up secure, familiar surroundings to carry out his will. For further information on Abraham, see his Profile in Genesis 18.

faith he stayed for a time in the land he had been promised, as in a foreign land,
living in tents, as did Isaac and Jacob, who were heirs with him of the same promise. 10 For he looked forward to the city that has foundations, whose architect and
builder is God. 11 By faith he received power of procreation, even though he was
too old—and Sarah herself was barren—because he considered him faithful who
had promised.[k] 12 Therefore from one person, and this one as good as dead, descendants were born, "as many as the stars of heaven and as the innumerable grains
of sand by the seashore."

13 All of these died in faith without having received the promises, but from a
distance they saw and greeted them. They confessed that they were strangers and
foreigners on the earth, 14 for people who speak in this way make it clear that they
are seeking a homeland. 15 If they had been thinking of the land that they had left
behind, they would have had opportunity to return. 16 But as it is, they desire a
better country, that is, a heavenly one. Therefore God is not ashamed to be called
their God; indeed, he has prepared a city for them.

17 By faith Abraham, when put to the test, offered up Isaac. He who had received the promises was ready to offer up his only son, 18 of whom he had been
told, "It is through Isaac that descendants shall be named for you." 19 He considered
the fact that God is able even to raise someone from the dead—and figuratively
speaking, he did receive him back. 20 By faith Isaac invoked blessings for the future
on Jacob and Esau. 21 By faith Jacob, when dying, blessed each of the sons of Joseph, "bowing in worship over the top of his staff." 22 By faith Joseph, at the end
of his life, made mention of the exodus of the Israelites and gave instructions about
his burial.[l]

23 By faith Moses was hidden by his parents for three months after his birth,
because they saw that the child was beautiful; and they were not afraid of the king's

11.10 Heb 11.16; 12.22 Rev 21.2
11.11 Gen 17.19 21.1-3
11.12 Gen 15.5 Rom 4.19
11.13 Gen 23.4 Mt 13.17 Jn 8.56 Heb 11.39
11.14 Heb 13.14
11.15 Gen 24.6
11.16 Gen 26.24 Ex 3.6,15 Phil 3.20
11.17 Gen 22.1,2 Jas 2.21
11.18 Gen 21.12
11.19 Rom 4.21
11.20 Gen 27.27-29
11.21 Gen 47.31; 48.5
11.22 Gen 50.24,25 Ex 13.19
11.23 Ex 1.16; 2.2

[k] Other ancient authorities read *By faith Sarah herself, though barren, received power to conceive, even when she was too old, because she considered him faithful who had promised.* [l] Gk *his bones*

11.11, 12 Sarah was Abraham's wife. They were unable to have children through many years of their marriage. God promised Abraham a son, but Sarah doubted that she could become pregnant in her old age. At first she laughed, but afterwards, she believed (Genesis 18). For more information on Sarah, see her Profile in Genesis 19.

11.13 That we are "strangers and foreigners" may be an awareness forced upon us by circumstances. It may come late in life or as the result of difficult times. But this world is not our home. We cannot live here forever (see also 1 Peter 1.1). It is best for us not to be so attached to this world's desires and possessions that we can't move out at God's command.

11.13–16 These people of faith died without receiving all that God had promised, but they never lost their vision of heaven ("a homeland"). Many Christians become frustrated and defeated because their needs, wants, expectations, and demands are not immediately met when they believe in Christ. They become impatient and want to quit. Are you discouraged because your goal seems far away? Take courage from these heroes of faith who lived and died without seeing the fruit of their faith on earth, and yet continued to believe (see 11.36–39).

11.17–19 Abraham was willing to give up his son when God commanded him to do so (Genesis 22.1–19). God did not let Abraham take Isaac's life, because God had given the command to test Abraham's faith. Instead of taking Abraham's son, God gave him a whole nation of descendants through Isaac. If you are afraid to trust God with your most prized possession, dream, or person, pay attention to Abraham's example. Because Abraham was willing to give up everything for God, he received back more than he could have imagined. What we receive, however, is not always immediate, or in the form of material possessions. After all, material possessions should be among the least satisfying of rewards. Our best and greatest rewards await us in eternity.

11.20 Isaac was the son promised to Abraham and Sarah in their old age. It was through Isaac that God fulfilled his promise to give Abraham countless descendants. Isaac had twin sons, Jacob and Esau. God chose the younger son, Jacob, through whom to continue his promise to Abraham. For more information on Isaac, see his Profile in Genesis 23.

11.21 Jacob was Isaac's son and Abraham's grandson. Jacob's sons became the fathers of Israel's 12 tribes. Even when Jacob (also called "Israel") was dying in a strange land, he believed the promise that Abraham's descendants would be like the sand on the seashore and that Israel would become a great nation (Genesis 48.1–22). True faith helps us see beyond the grave. For more information on Jacob and Esau, see their Profiles in Genesis 26 and 27.

11.22 Joseph, one of Jacob's sons, was sold into slavery by his jealous brothers (Genesis 37). Eventually, Joseph was sold again, this time to an officer of the pharaoh of Egypt. Because of his faithfulness to God, however, Joseph was given a top-ranking position in Egypt. Although Joseph could have used that position to build a personal empire, he remembered God's promise to Abraham. After he had been reconciled to his brothers, he brought his family to be near him and requested that his bones be taken to the promised land when the Jews eventually left Egypt (Genesis 50.24, 25). Faith means trusting in God and doing what he wants, regardless of the circumstances. For more information on Joseph, see his Profile in Genesis 37.

11.23 Moses' parents trusted God for their son's life. They were not merely proud parents, they were believers who had faith that God would care for him. As a parent, have you trusted God enough to take care of your children? God has a plan for every person, and your important task is to pray for and prepare your children to do the work God has planned for them to do. Faith allows us to entrust even our children to God.

edict.[m] 24 By faith Moses, when he was grown up, refused to be called a son of
Pharaoh's daughter, 25 choosing rather to share ill-treatment with the people of God
than to enjoy the fleeting pleasures of sin. 26 He considered abuse suffered for the
Christ[n] to be greater wealth than the treasures of Egypt, for he was looking ahead
to the reward. 27 By faith he left Egypt, unafraid of the king's anger; for he persevered as though[o] he saw him who is invisible. 28 By faith he kept the Passover and
the sprinkling of blood, so that the destroyer of the firstborn would not touch the
firstborn of Israel.[p]

29 By faith the people passed through the Red Sea as if it were dry land, but
when the Egyptians attempted to do so they were drowned. 30 By faith the walls of
Jericho fell after they had been encircled for seven days. 31 By faith Rahab the prostitute did not perish with those who were disobedient,[q] because she had received
the spies in peace.

32 And what more should I say? For time would fail me to tell of Gideon,
Barak, Samson, Jephthah, of David and Samuel and the prophets— 33 who through
faith conquered kingdoms, administered justice, obtained promises, shut the
mouths of lions, 34 quenched raging fire, escaped the edge of the sword, won
strength out of weakness, became mighty in war, put foreign armies to flight.
35 Women received their dead by resurrection. Others were tortured, refusing to
accept release, in order to obtain a better resurrection. 36 Others suffered mocking
and flogging, and even chains and imprisonment. 37 They were stoned to death,
they were sawn in two,[r] they were killed by the sword; they went about in skins of
sheep and goats, destitute, persecuted, tormented— 38 of whom the world was not
worthy. They wandered in deserts and mountains, and in caves and holes in the
ground.

39 Yet all these, though they were commended for their faith, did not receive

11.25 Ex 2.10-12 Ps 84.10
11.27 Ex 10.28; 12.37 Heb 11.1
11.28 Ex 12.1-13,21-30
11.29 Ex 14.13-31
11.30 Josh 6.20
11.31 Josh 2.9; 6.23 Jas 2.25
11.32 Judg 4.6; 6.11 11.1; 13.24 1 Sam 1.20 16.1
11.33 Dan 6.22
11.34 1 Sam 14.13 1 Kgs 19.3 2 Kgs 20.7
11.35 Acts 22.25
11.36 Gen 39.20 Jer 20.2; 37.15
11.37 2 Chron 24.21 Acts 7.58; 14.19

m Other ancient authorities add *By faith Moses, when he was grown up, killed the Egyptian, because he observed the humiliation of his people* (Gk *brothers*) n Or *the Messiah* o Or *because* p Gk *would not touch them*
q Or *unbelieving* r Other ancient authorities add *they were tempted*

11.24–28 Moses became one of Israel's greatest leaders, a prophet and a lawgiver. But when he was born, his people were slaves in Egypt, and the Egyptian officials had ordered that all Hebrew baby boys were to be killed. Moses was spared, however, and Pharaoh's daughter raised Moses in Pharaoh's own household (Exodus 1, 2)! It took faith for Moses to give up his place in the palace, but he could do it because he saw the fleeting nature of great wealth and prestige. It is easy to be deceived by the temporary benefits of wealth, popularity, status, and achievement, and to be blind to the long-range benefits of God's kingdom. Faith helps us look beyond the world's value system to see the eternal values of God's kingdom. For more information on Moses, see his Profile in Exodus 15.

11.31 When Joshua planned the conquest of Jericho, he sent spies to investigate the fortifications of the city. The spies met Rahab, who had two strikes against her—she was a Gentile and a prostitute. But she showed that she had faith in God by welcoming the spies and by trusting God to spare her and her family when the city was destroyed. Faith helps us change and do what is right regardless of our past or the disapproval of others. For more information on Rahab, see her Profile in Joshua 2.

11.32–40 These verses summarize the lives of other great men and women of faith. Some experienced outstanding victories, even over death. But others were severely mistreated, tortured, and even killed. Having a steadfast faith in God does not guarantee a happy, carefree life. On the contrary, our faith almost guarantees us some form of abuse from the world. While we are on earth, we may never see the purpose of our suffering. But we know that God will keep his promises to us. Do you believe that God will keep his promises to you?

11.33–35 The Old Testament records the lives of various people who experienced these great victories. Deborah won battles (Judges 4; 5). Joshua overthrew kingdoms (the book of Joshua). Nehemiah ruled God's people well (the book of Nehemiah). Daniel was kept from harm in the den of lions (Daniel 6). Shadrach, Meshach, and Abednego were kept from harm in the fiery furnace (Daniel 3). Elijah escaped the swords of evil Queen Jezebel's henchmen (1 Kings 19.2ff). Hezekiah became strong after sickness (2 Kings 20). Gideon had great power in battle (Judges 7). A widow's son was brought back to life by the prophet Elisha (2 Kings 4.8–37).

We, too, can experience victory through faith in Christ. Our victories from oppressors may be like those of the Old Testament saints, but more likely, our victories will be directly related to the role God wants us to play. Even though our bodies may die, we will live forever because of Christ. In the promised resurrection, even death will be defeated and Christ's victory will be made complete.

11.36–39 Many think that pain is the exception in the Christian life. When suffering occurs they say, "Why me?" They feel that God has deserted them or perhaps was not as dependable as they thought. In reality, however, we live in an evil world with much suffering, even for believers. But God is still in control. He allows some Christians to become martyrs for the faith, and he allows others to survive persecution. Rather than asking, "Why me?" it is much more helpful to ask, "Why not me?" Our faith and the values of this world are on a collision course. If we expect pain and suffering to come, we will not be shocked when it hits. But we can also take comfort in knowing that Jesus suffered too. He understands our fears, our weaknesses, our disappointments (see 2.16–18; 4.14–16). He promised never to leave us (Matthew 28.18–20), and he intercedes on our behalf (7.24, 25). In times of pain, persecution, or suffering we should trust confidently in Christ alone.

11.39, 40 Hebrews 11 has been called faith's hall of fame. No doubt the author surprised his readers by this conclusion: these mighty Jewish heroes did not receive God's total reward, because they died before Christ came. In God's plan, they and the Christian

11.40 Rom 11.26; Rev 6.11
12.1 1 Cor 9.24; Phil 3.12-14
12.2 Ps 110.1; 2 Cor 3.18; Heb 2.9,10; 1 Pet 1.11
12.3 Jn 15.20
12.4 Heb 10.32
12.5 Job 5.17; Prov 3.11
12.6 Prov 3.12; Ps 94.12; Jas 1.12; Rev 3.19
12.7 Deut 8.5
12.8 1 Pet 5.9
12.9 Isa 38.16
12.10 2 Pet 1.4
12.11 1 Pet 1.6
12.12 Isa 35.3
12.13 Prov 4.26; Gal 6.1

what was promised, 40 since God had provided something better so that they would
not, apart from us, be made perfect.

God's discipline proves his love

12 Therefore, since we are surrounded by so great a cloud of witnesses, let us
also lay aside every weight and the sin that clings so closely,[s] and let us run
with perseverance the race that is set before us, 2 looking to Jesus the pioneer and
perfecter of our faith, who for the sake of[t] the joy that was set before him endured
the cross, disregarding its shame, and has taken his seat at the right hand of the
throne of God.
3 Consider him who endured such hostility against himself from sinners,[u] so
that you may not grow weary or lose heart. 4 In your struggle against sin you have
not yet resisted to the point of shedding your blood. 5 And you have forgotten the
exhortation that addresses you as children—
"My child, do not regard lightly the discipline of the Lord,
or lose heart when you are punished by him;
6 for the Lord disciplines those whom he loves,
and chastises every child whom he accepts."
7 Endure trials for the sake of discipline. God is treating you as children; for what
child is there whom a parent does not discipline? 8 If you do not have that discipline
in which all children share, then you are illegitimate and not his children. 9 Moreover, we had human parents to discipline us, and we respected them. Should we not
be even more willing to be subject to the Father of spirits and live? 10 For they
disciplined us for a short time as seemed best to them, but he disciplines us for our
good, in order that we may share his holiness. 11 Now, discipline always seems
painful rather than pleasant at the time, but later it yields the peaceful fruit of righteousness to those who have been trained by it.
12 Therefore lift your drooping hands and strengthen your weak knees, 13 and
make straight paths for your feet, so that what is lame may not be put out of joint,
but rather be healed.

[s] Other ancient authorities read *sin that easily distracts* [t] Or *who instead of* [u] Other ancient authorities read *such hostility from sinners against themselves*

---

believers (who were also enduring much testing) would be rewarded together. Once again Hebrews shows that Christianity offers a better way than Judaism.

11.40 There is a solidarity among believers (see 12.23). Old and New Testament believers will be glorified together. We are one in the body of Christ not only with all those alive, but also with all those who ever lived. It takes all of us to be complete (perfect) in him.

12.1 This great "cloud of witnesses" is composed of the people described in chapter 11. Their faithfulness is a constant encouragement to us. We do not struggle alone, and we are not the first to struggle with the problems we face. Others have run the race and won, and their witness stirs us to run and win also. What an inspiring heritage we have!

12.1–4 The Christian life involves hard work. It requires us to give up whatever endangers our relationship with God, to run patiently, and to struggle against sin with the power of the Holy Spirit. To live effectively, we must keep our eyes on Jesus. We stumble when we look away from him, at ourselves, or the circumstances surrounding us. We are running for Christ, not ourselves, and we must always keep him in sight.

12.3 When we face hardship and discouragement, it is easy to lose sight of the big picture. But we're not alone; there is help. Many have already made it through life enduring far more difficult circumstances than we have experienced. Suffering is the training ground for Christian maturity. It develops our patience and makes our final victory sweet.

12.4 These readers were facing difficult times of persecution, but none of them had yet died for their faith. Because they were still alive, the writer urged them to continue to run their race. Just as Christ did not give up, neither should they.

12.5–11 Who loves his child more—the father who allows the child to do what will harm him, or the one who corrects, trains, and even punishes the child to help him learn what is right? It's never pleasant to be corrected and disciplined by God, but his discipline is a sign of his deep love for us. When God corrects you, see it as proof of his love and ask him what he is trying to teach you.

12.11 We may respond to discipline in several ways: (1) we can accept it with resignation; (2) we can accept it with self-pity, thinking we really don't deserve it; (3) we can be angry and resent God for it; or (4) we can accept it gratefully as the appropriate response from a loving Father.

12.12, 13 God is not only a disciplining parent, but also a demanding coach who pushes us to our limits and requires our lives to be disciplined. Although we may not feel strong enough to push on to victory, we will be able to obtain it as we follow Christ and draw upon his strength. Then we can use our growing strength to help those around us who are weak and struggling.

12.12, 13 The word *therefore* is a clue that what follows is important! We must not live with only our own survival in mind. Others will follow our example, and we have a responsibility to them if we claim to live for Christ. Does your example make it easier for others to believe, follow, and mature in Christ? Or would those who follow you end up confused and misled?

Warning against refusing to listen

14 Pursue peace with everyone, and the holiness without which no one will see **12.14**
the Lord. 15 See to it that no one fails to obtain the grace of God; that no root of Rom 6.22; 14.19
bitterness springs up and causes trouble, and through it many become defiled. **12.15** Deut 29.18
16 See to it that no one becomes like Esau, an immoral and godless person, who sold Heb 4.1
his birthright for a single meal. 17 You know that later, when he wanted to inherit **12.16** Gen 25.33
the blessing, he was rejected, for he found no chance to repent,[v] even though he **12.17**
sought the blessing[w] with tears. Gen 27.34

18 You have not come to something[x] that can be touched, a blazing fire, and **12.18**
darkness, and gloom, and a tempest, 19 and the sound of a trumpet, and a voice Ex 19.12,16
whose words made the hearers beg that not another word be spoken to them. 20 (For **12.19** Ex 20.19
they could not endure the order that was given, "If even an animal touches the **12.20**
mountain, it shall be stoned to death." 21 Indeed, so terrifying was the sight that Ex 19.12
Moses said, "I tremble with fear.") 22 But you have come to Mount Zion and to the **12.22**
city of the living God, the heavenly Jerusalem, and to innumerable angels in festal Ps 68.17 Gal 4.26
gathering, 23 and to the assembly[y] of the firstborn who are enrolled in heaven, and Rev 3.12; 14.1
to God the judge of all, and to the spirits of the righteous made perfect, 24 and to 21.2 **12.23**
Jesus, the mediator of a new covenant, and to the sprinkled blood that speaks a Heb 2.12
better word than the blood of Abel. **12.24** Gen 4.10

25 See that you do not refuse the one who is speaking; for if they did not escape Ex 24.8
when they refused the one who warned them on earth, how much less will we **12.25**
escape if we reject the one who warns from heaven! 26 At that time his voice shook Num 16
the earth; but now he has promised, "Yet once more I will shake not only the earth **12.26** Ex 19.18
but also the heaven." 27 This phrase, "Yet once more," indicates the removal of **12.27**
what is shaken—that is, created things—so that what cannot be shaken may re- Mt 24.35 2 Pet 3.10
main. 28 Therefore, since we are receiving a kingdom that cannot be shaken, let us **12.28**
give thanks, by which we offer to God an acceptable worship with reverence and Dan 2.44
awe; 29 for indeed our God is a consuming fire.

Holy and obedient lives

13 Let mutual love continue. 2 Do not neglect to show hospitality to strangers,
for by doing that some have entertained angels without knowing it. 3 Re- **13.3**
member those who are in prison, as though you were in prison with them; those Mt 25.36 Col 4.18

[v] Or *no chance to change his father's mind* [w] Gk *it* [x] Other ancient authorities read *a mountain* [y] Or *angels, and to the festal gathering* [23]*and assembly*

12.14 The readers were familiar with the ceremonial cleansing ritual that prepared them for worship, and they knew they had to be holy or clean in order to enter the temple. Sin always blocks our vision of God, so if we want to see God, we must renounce sin and obey him (see Psalm 24.3, 4). Holiness is coupled with peace—staying out of quarrels. A right relationship with God leads to right relationships with fellow believers. Although we will not always feel love toward all other believers, we must pursue peace as we become more Christlike.

12.15 Like a small root that grows into a great tree, bitterness springs up in our hearts and overshadows even our deepest Christian relationships. Bitterness comes when we allow disappointment to grow into resentment, or when we nurse grudges over past hurts. Bitterness brings with it jealousy, dissension, and immorality. When the Holy Spirit fills us, however, he can heal the hurt that causes bitterness.

12.16, 17 Esau's story shows us that mistakes and sin sometimes have lasting consequences (Genesis 25.29–34; 27.36). Even repentance and forgiveness do not always eliminate sin's consequences. How often do you make decisions based on what you want now, rather than on what you need long-term? Evaluate the long-range effects of your decisions and actions.

12.18–24 What a contrast between the people's terrified approach to God at Mount Sinai and their joyful approach at Mount Zion! What a difference Jesus has made! Before he came, God seemed distant and threatening. After he came, God welcomes us through Christ into his presence. Accept his invitation!

12.22 As Christians, we are partakers in the heavenly Jerusalem right now, because Christ rules our lives, the Holy Spirit is always with us, and we experience close fellowship with other believers. The full and ultimate rewards and reality of the heavenly Jerusalem are depicted in Revelation 21.

12.27–29 Eventually the world will crumble, and only God's kingdom will last. Those who follow Christ are part of this kingdom, and they will withstand the shaking, sifting, and burning. When we feel unsure about the future, we can take confidence from these verses. Whatever happens here, our future is built on a solid foundation that cannot be destroyed. Don't put your confidence in what will be destroyed; instead, build your life on Christ and his unshakable kingdom. (See Matthew 7.24–29 for the importance of building on a solid foundation.)

12.29 There is a big difference between the flame of a candle and the roaring blast of a forest fire. We cannot even stand near a raging fire. Even with sophisticated fire-fighting equipment, it is often beyond human control. God is not within our control, either. We cannot force him to do anything for us through our prayers. He cannot be contained. Yet, he is a God of compassion. He has saved us from sin, and he will save us from death. But all that is worthless and sinful will be consumed by the fire of his wrath. Only what is good, dedicated to God, and righteous will remain. He is a raging fire that cannot be contained.

who are being tortured, as though you yourselves were being tortured.[z] 4 Let marriage be held in honor by all, and let the marriage bed be kept undefiled; for God
will judge fornicators and adulterers. 5 Keep your lives free from the love of
money, and be content with what you have; for he has said, "I will never leave you
or forsake you." 6 So we can say with confidence,

"The Lord is my helper;
  I will not be afraid.
What can anyone do to me?"

7 Remember your leaders, those who spoke the word of God to you; consider
the outcome of their way of life, and imitate their faith. 8 Jesus Christ is the same
yesterday and today and forever. 9 Do not be carried away by all kinds of strange
teachings; for it is well for the heart to be strengthened by grace, not by regulations
about food,[a] which have not benefited those who observe them. 10 We have an
altar from which those who officiate in the tent[b] have no right to eat. 11 For the
bodies of those animals whose blood is brought into the sanctuary by the high priest
as a sacrifice for sin are burned outside the camp. 12 Therefore Jesus also suffered
outside the city gate in order to sanctify the people by his own blood. 13 Let us then
go to him outside the camp and bear the abuse he endured. 14 For here we have no
lasting city, but we are looking for the city that is to come. 15 Through him, then,
let us continually offer a sacrifice of praise to God, that is, the fruit of lips that
confess his name. 16 Do not neglect to do good and to share what you have, for such
sacrifices are pleasing to God.

13.4 1 Cor 7.38
13.5 Gen 28.15; Ps 37.25
13.6 Ps 118.6
13.7 Heb 6.12
13.8 Jn 8.58
13.9 Eph 4.14; Col 2.16
13.10 1 Cor 10.18
13.11 Lev 4.12,21
13.12 Jn 19.17; Heb 9.12
13.13 1 Pet 4.14
13.14 Heb 10.34; 11.10
13.15 Lev 7.12; Ps 50.14; 1 Pet 2.5

[z] Gk *were in the body* [a] Gk *not by foods* [b] Or *tabernacle*

13.1–5 Real love toward others produces tangible actions: (1) kindness to strangers (13.2); (2) sympathy for those who are in prison and those who have been mistreated (13.3); (3) respect for your marriage vows (13.4); and (4) satisfaction with what you have (13.5). Make sure that your love runs deep enough to affect your hospitality, sympathy, fidelity, and contentment.

13.2 Three Old Testament people entertained angels without knowing it: (1) Abraham (Genesis 18.1ff), (2) Gideon (Judges 6.11ff), and (3) Manoah (Judges 13.2ff). Some people say they cannot be hospitable because their homes are not large enough or nice enough. But even if you have no more than a table and two chairs in a rented room, there are people who would be grateful to spend time in your home. Are there visitors to your church with whom you could share a meal? Do you know single people who would enjoy an evening of conversation? Is there any way your home could meet the needs of traveling missionaries? Hospitality simply means making other people feel comfortable and at home.

13.3 We are to have sympathy for those in prison, especially for (but not limited to) Christians imprisoned for their faith. Jesus said that his true followers would represent him as they visit those in prison (Matthew 25.36).

13.5 How can we learn to be content? Strive to live with less rather than desiring more; give away from your abundance rather than accumulating more; relish what you have rather than resenting what you're missing. See God's love in what he has provided, and remember that money and possessions will all pass away. (See Philippians 4.11 for more on contentment, and 1 John 2.17 for the futility of earthly desires.)

13.5, 6 We become contented when we realize God's sufficiency for our needs. Christians who become materialistic are saying by their actions that God can't take care of them – or at least won't take care of them the way they want. Insecurity can lead to the love of money, whether we are rich or poor. The only antidote is to trust God to meet all our needs.

13.7 If you are a Christian, you owe much to others who have taught you and modeled for you what you needed to know about the gospel and Christian living. Continue following the good examples of those who have invested themselves in you by investing your life through evangelism, service, and Christian education.

13.8 Though human leaders have much to offer, we must keep our eyes on Christ, our ultimate leader. Unlike any human leaders, he will never change. Christ has been and will be the same forever. In a changing world we can trust our unchanging Lord.

13.9 Apparently some were teaching that keeping the Old Testament ceremonial laws and rituals (such as not eating certain foods) was important to salvation. But these laws were useless for conquering a person's evil thoughts and desires (Colossians 2.23). The laws could influence conduct, but they could not change the heart. Lasting changes in conduct begin when the Holy Spirit lives in each person.

13.13 The Jewish Christians were being ridiculed and persecuted by Jews who didn't believe in Jesus the Messiah. Most of the book of Hebrews tells them how Christ is greater than the sacrificial system. Here the writer drives home the point of his lengthy argument: It may be necessary to leave the "camp" and suffer with Christ. To be outside the camp meant to be unclean. But Jesus suffered humiliation and uncleanness outside the Jerusalem gates on their behalf. The time had come for Jewish Christians to declare their loyalty to Christ above any other loyalty, to choose to follow the Messiah whatever suffering that might entail. They needed to move outside the safe confinement of their past, traditions, and ceremonies to live for Christ. Is there anything holding you back from complete loyalty to Jesus Christ?

13.14 We should not be attached to this world, because all that we are and have here is temporary. Only our relationship with God and our service to him will last. Don't store up your treasures here, store them in heaven (Matthew 6.19–21).

13.15, 16 If these Jewish Christians, because of their witness to the Messiah, could no longer worship with other Jews, they could consider praise and acts of service their sacrifices – ones they could offer anywhere, anytime. This must have reminded them of the prophet Hosea's words, "Take away all guilt; accept that which is good, and we will offer the fruit of our lips" (Hosea 14.2). A "sacrifice of praise" today would include thanking Christ for his sacrifice on the cross and telling others about it. Acts of kindness and sharing with others are particularly pleasing to God even when they go unnoticed by others.

17 Obey your leaders and submit to them, for they are keeping watch over your
souls and will give an account. Let them do this with joy and not with sighing—for
that would be harmful to you.

13.17 Ezek 3.17 33.2,7 Acts 20.28

Final words

18 Pray for us; we are sure that we have a clear conscience, desiring to act
honorably in all things. 19 I urge you all the more to do this, so that I may be restored
to you very soon.
20 Now may the God of peace, who brought back from the dead our Lord Jesus,
the great shepherd of the sheep, by the blood of the eternal covenant, 21 make you
complete in everything good so that you may do his will, working among us[c] that
which is pleasing in his sight, through Jesus Christ, to whom be the glory forever
and ever. Amen.

13.18 Acts 24.16
13.19 Philem 22
13.20 Isa 40.11 Ezek 31.23 37.24 Zech 9.11 Jn 10.11
13.21 Rom 11.36 Phil 2.13 1 Pet 5.10

22 I appeal to you, brothers and sisters,[d] bear with my word of exhortation, for
I have written to you briefly. 23 I want you to know that our brother Timothy has
been set free; and if he comes in time, he will be with me when I see you. 24 Greet
all your leaders and all the saints. Those from Italy send you greetings. 25 Grace be
with all of you.[e]

13.23 Acts 16.1 1 Thess 3.2

[c] Other ancient authorities read *you* [d] Gk *brothers* [e] Other ancient authorities add *Amen*

13.17 The task of church leaders is to help people mature in Christ. Cooperative followers greatly ease the burden of leadership. Does your conduct give your leaders reason to report joyfully about you?

13.18, 19 The writer recognizes the need for prayer. Christian leaders are especially vulnerable to criticism from others, pride (if they succeed), depression (if they fail), and Satan's constant efforts to destroy their work for God. They desperately need our prayers! For whom should you regularly pray?

13.21 This verse includes two significant results of Christ's death and resurrection. God works in us to make us the kind of people that would please him, and he equips us to do the kind of *work* that would please him. Let God change you from within, then use you to help others.

13.23 We have no record of Timothy's imprisonment, but obviously he had been in prison because we learn here that he had been released. For more about Timothy, see his Profile in 1 Timothy 2.

13.24, 25 Hebrews is a call to Christian maturity. It was addressed to first-century Jewish Christians, but it applies to Christians of any age or background. Christian maturity means making Christ the beginning and end of our faith. To mature, we must center our lives on him, not depending on religious ritual, not falling back into sin, not trusting in ourselves, and not letting anything come between us and Christ. Christ is sufficient and superior.

The Letter of JAMES

"MIRACULOUS!" . . . "Revolutionary!" . . . "Greatest ever!" We are inundated by a flood of extravagant claims as we flip the television dial or magazine pages. The messages leap out at us. The products assure that they are new, improved, fantastic, and will change our lives. For only a few dollars, we can have "cleaner clothes," "whiter teeth," "glamorous hair," and "tastier food." Automobiles, perfume, diet drinks, and mouthwash are guaranteed to bring happiness, friends, and the good life. And just before an election, no one can match the politicians' promises. But talk is cheap, and too often we soon realize that the boasts were hollow, quite far from the truth.

"Jesus is the answer!" . . . "Believe in God!" . . . "Follow me to church!" Christians also make great claims, but are often guilty of belying them with their actions. Professing to trust God and to be his people, they cling tightly to the world and its values. Possessing all the right answers, they contradict the gospel with their lives.

With energetic style and crisp, well-chosen words, James confronts this conflict head-on. It is not enough to talk the Christian faith, he says, we must live it. "What good is it, my brothers and sisters, if you say you have faith but do not have works? Can faith save you?" (2.14). The proof of the reality of our faith is a changed life.

Genuine faith will inevitably produce good works. This is the central theme of James's epistle, around which he supplies practical advice on living the Christian life.

James begins his epistle by outlining some general characteristics of the Christian life (1.1–27). Next, he exhorts Christians to act justly in society (2.1–13). He follows this practical advice with a theological discourse on the relationship between faith and action (2.14–26). Then James shows the importance of controlling one's speech (3.1–12). In 3.13–18, James distinguishes two kinds of wisdom, earthly and heavenly. Then he encourages his readers to turn from evil desires and obey God (4.1–12). James reproves those who trust in their own plans and possessions (4.13—5.6). Finally, he exhorts his readers to be patient with each other (5.7–11), to be straightforward in their promises (5.12), to pray for each other (5.13–18), and to help one another remain faithful to God (5.19, 20).

This epistle could be considered a how-to book on Christian living. Confrontation, challenge, and commitment await you in its pages. Read James and become a *doer* of the Word (1.22–25).

VITAL STATISTICS

PURPOSE:
To expose hypocritical practices and to teach right Christian behavior

AUTHOR:
James, Jesus' brother, a leader in the Jerusalem church

TO WHOM WRITTEN:
First-century Jewish Christians residing in Gentile communities outside Palestine, and to all Christians everywhere

DATE WRITTEN:
Probably A.D. 49, prior to the Jerusalem council held in A.D. 50

SETTING:
This letter expresses James's concern for persecuted Christians who were once part of the Jerusalem church

KEY VERSE:
"But someone will say, 'You have faith and I have works.' Show me your faith apart from your works, and I by my works will show you my faith" (2.18).

THE BLUEPRINT

1. Genuine religion (1.1–27)
2. Genuine faith (2.1—3.12)
3. Genuine wisdom (3.13—5.20)

James wrote to Jewish Christians who had been scattered throughout the Mediterranean world because of persecution. In their hostile surroundings they were tempted to let intellectual agreement pass for true faith. This letter can have rich meaning for us as we are reminded that genuine faith transforms lives. We are encouraged to put our faith into action. It is easy to say we have faith, but true faith will produce loving actions toward others.

MEGATHEMES

THEME	EXPLANATION	IMPORTANCE
Living Faith	James wants believers not only to hear the truth, but also to do it. He contrasts empty faith (claims without conduct) with faith that works. Commitment to love and to serve is evidence of true faith.	Living faith makes a difference. Make sure your faith is more than just a statement—it should also result in action. Seek ways of putting your faith to work.
Trials	In the Christian life there are trials and temptations. Successfully overcoming these adversities produces maturity and strong character.	Don't resent troubles when they come. Pray for wisdom; God will supply all that you will need to face persecution or adversity. He will give you patience and keep you strong in times of trial.
Law of Love	We are saved by God's gracious mercy, not by keeping the law. But Christ gave us a special command, "You shall love your neighbor as yourself" (Matthew 19.19). We are to love and serve those around us.	Keeping the law of love shows that our faith is vital and real. When we show love to others, we are overcoming our own selfishness.
Wise Speech	Wisdom shows itself in speech. We are responsible for the destructive results of our talk. The wisdom of God that helps control the tongue can help control all our actions.	Accepting God's wisdom will affect your speech. Your words will convey true humility and lead to peace. Think before you speak and allow God to give you self-control.
Wealth	James taught Christians not to compromise with worldly attitudes about wealth. Because the glory of wealth fades, Christians should store up God's treasures through sincere service. Christians must not show partiality to the wealthy, nor be prejudiced against the poor.	All of us are accountable for how we use what we have. We should not hoard wealth, but be generous toward others. In addition, we should not be impressed by the wealthy nor look down on those who are poor.

1. Genuine religion

1 James, a servant[a] of God and of the Lord Jesus Christ,
To the twelve tribes in the Dispersion:
Greetings.

Enduring trials and temptations

2 My brothers and sisters,[b] whenever you face trials of any kind, consider it

a Gk *slave* b Gk *brothers*

1.1 The writer of this letter, a leader of the church in Jerusalem (see Acts 12.17; 15.13), was James, Jesus' brother, not James the apostle. The book of James was one of the earliest epistles, probably written before A.D. 50. After Stephen was martyred (Acts 7.55–8.3), persecution increased, and Christians in Jerusalem were scattered throughout the Roman world. *Dispersion* means "those scattered" and refers to all Jews living in foreign lands. There were thriving Jewish communities in Rome, Alexandria, Cyprus, and cities in Greece and Asia Minor. Because these early believers did not have the support of established Christian churches, James wrote to them as a concerned leader, to encourage them in their faith during that difficult time.

1.2, 3 James doesn't say *if* we face trials, but *when* we face them. He assumes we will have trials and that it is possible to profit from them. We are not required to pretend to be happy when we face pain, but to have a positive outlook because of the results trials will bring. James tells us to turn our hardships into times of learning. Rough times can teach us patience. For other passages dealing with patience (also called perseverance and steadfastness), see Romans 2.7; 5.3–5; 8.24, 25; 2 Corinthians 6.3–7; 2 Peter 1.2–9.

1.3
Rom 2.7; 5.3-5
1.5
Prov 2.3-13
Mt 7.7-11
Jas 3.17
1.6
Mt 21.22
Mk 11.22-24
1.9
Deut 15.7-11
Prov 17.5
Lk 14.11
1.10,11
Isa 40.7
1 Pet 1.24
1.12
Job 5.17-19
Prov 3.11,12
2 Tim 4.8
Heb 10.32-34
Jas 5.11
Rev 2.10; 3.11

nothing but joy, 3 because you know that the testing of your faith produces endurance; 4 and let endurance have its full effect, so that you may be mature and complete, lacking in nothing.
5 If any of you is lacking in wisdom, ask God, who gives to all generously and
ungrudgingly, and it will be given you. 6 But ask in faith, never doubting, for the
one who doubts is like a wave of the sea, driven and tossed by the wind; 7, 8 for the
doubter, being double-minded and unstable in every way, must not expect to receive anything from the Lord.
9 Let the believer[c] who is lowly boast in being raised up, 10 and the rich in
being brought low, because the rich will disappear like a flower in the field. 11 For
the sun rises with its scorching heat and withers the field; its flower falls, and its
beauty perishes. It is the same way with the rich; in the midst of a busy life, they
will wither away.
12 Blessed is anyone who endures temptation. Such a one has stood the test and
will receive the crown of life that the Lord[d] has promised to those who love him.

[c] Gk *brother* [d] Gk *he;* other ancient authorities read *God*

CHAPTER SUMMARY

Chapter 1	Confident Stand	What a Christian has
Chapter 2	Compassionate Service	What a Christian does
Chapter 3	Careful Speech	What a Christian says
Chapter 4	Contrite Submission	What a Christian feels
Chapter 5	Concerned Sharing	What a Christian gives

1.2–4 We can't really know the depth of our character until we see how we react under pressure. It is easy to be kind to others when everything is going well, but can we still be kind when others are treating us unfairly? God wants to make us mature and complete, not to keep us from all pain. Instead of complaining about our struggles, we should see them as opportunities for growth. Thank God for promising to be with you in rough times. Ask him to help you solve your problems or give you the strength to endure them. Then be patient. God will not leave you alone with your problems; he will stay close and help you grow.

1.5 By *wisdom,* James is talking not only about knowledge, but the ability to make wise decisions in difficult circumstances. If we need wisdom, we can pray to God, and he will supply what we need. Christians don't have to grope about in the dark, hoping to stumble upon answers. We can ask for God's wisdom to guide our choices.

1.5 *Wisdom* means practical discernment. It begins with respect for God, leads to right living, and results in increased ability to tell right from wrong. God is willing to give us this wisdom; but we will be unable to receive it if our goals are self-centered instead of God-centered. To learn God's will, we need to read his Word and ask him to show us how to obey it. Then we must do what he tells us.

1.6 God does not grant every thoughtless or selfish request. To "ask in faith" means asking with confidence that God will align our desires with his purposes. For more on this concept, read the note on Matthew 21.22.

1.6 A mind that wavers is not completely convinced that God's way is best. It treats God's Word like any human advice, retaining the option of disobedience. It vacillates between feelings, the world's ideas, and God's commands. If your faith is new, weak, or struggling, remember God is trustworthy; be loyal to him. To stabilize your wavering or doubtful mind, commit yourself wholeheartedly to God.

1.6–8 If you have ever seen the constant rolling of huge waves at sea, you know how restless they are—subject to the forces of wind, gravity, and tide. Doubt leaves a person as unsettled as the restless waves. If you want to stop being tossed about, rely on God to show you what is best for you. Ask him for wisdom, and trust that he will give it to you. Then your decisions will be sure and solid.

1.9 Christians who aren't exalted in this world should be glad, because they are great in the Lord's eyes. This "believer who is lowly" is a person of humble circumstances, without status or wealth. Such people are often overlooked, even in our churches today, but they are not overlooked by God. Strive to treat each person as Christ would treat him or her.

1.9–11 The poor should be glad that riches mean nothing to God; otherwise they would be considered unworthy. The rich should be glad that money means nothing to God, because money is easily lost. We find true wealth by developing our spiritual life, not our financial assets. God is interested in what is lasting (our souls), not in what is temporary (our money and possessions). See Mark 4.18, 19 for Jesus' words on this subject.

1.10, 11 If wealth, power, and status mean nothing to God, why do we attribute so much importance to them and so much honor to those who possess them? Do your material possessions give you goals and your only reason for living? If they were gone, what would be left? What you have in your heart, not your bank account, matters to God and endures for eternity.

1.12 The crown of life is like the victory wreath given to winning athletes (see 1 Corinthians 9.25). God's crown of life is not glory and honor here on earth, but the reward of eternal life—living with him forever.

1.12–15 Temptation comes from evil desires within, not from God. It begins with an evil thought. It becomes sin when we dwell on the thought and allow it to become an action. Like a snowball rolling downhill, sin grows more destructive the more we let it have its way. The best time to stop a temptation is before it is too great or moving too fast to control. See Matthew 4.1–11; 1 Corinthians 10.13; and 2 Timothy 2.22 for more about escaping temptation.

13 No one, when tempted, should say, “I am being tempted by God”; for God can- **1.13**
not be tempted by evil and he himself tempts no one. 14 But one is tempted by one’s Gen 22.1 Rom 9.19,20
own desire, being lured and enticed by it; 15 then, when that desire has conceived,
it gives birth to sin, and that sin, when it is fully grown, gives birth to death. 16 Do **1.16**
not be deceived, my beloved.[e] 1 Cor 6.9
17 Every generous act of giving, with every perfect gift, is from above, coming **1.17**
down from the Father of lights, with whom there is no variation or shadow due to Gen 1.1-5, 14-16
change.[f] 18 In fulfillment of his own purpose he gave us birth by the word of truth, Ps 19.1-8; 136.7
so that we would become a kind of first fruits of his creatures. Heb 13.8

Listening and doing

19 You must understand this, my beloved:[e] let everyone be quick to listen, **1.19**
slow to speak, slow to anger; 20 for your anger does not produce God’s righteous- Prov 10.19
ness. 21 Therefore rid yourselves of all sordidness and rank growth of wickedness, 15.18; 17.27,28
and welcome with meekness the implanted word that has the power to save your Eph 4.26,31
souls. **1.21** Rom 13.12,13 1 Pet 1.23
22 But be doers of the word, and not merely hearers who deceive themselves. **1.22**
23 For if any are hearers of the word and not doers, they are like those who look at Mt 7.24 12.50; 28.20
themselves[g] in a mirror; 24 for they look at themselves and, on going away, imme- Lk 6.46-49 Jn 13.17
diately forget what they were like. 25 But those who look into the perfect law, the **1.25**
law of liberty, and persevere, being not hearers who forget but doers who 2 Cor 3.17,18
act—they will be blessed in their doing. Gal 5.1 1 Pet 2.16
26 If any think they are religious, and do not bridle their tongues but deceive **1.26**
their hearts, their religion is worthless. 27 Religion that is pure and undefiled before Prov 13.3; 21.23
God, the Father, is this: to care for orphans and widows in their distress, and to **1.27** Deut 14.29
keep oneself unstained by the world. 24.17-20

[e] Gk *my beloved brothers* [f] Other ancient authorities read *variation due to a shadow of turning* [g] Gk *at the face of his birth*

1.13, 14 People who live for God often wonder why they still have temptations. Does God tempt them? God *tests* people, but he does not *tempt* them by trying to seduce them into sin. He allows Satan to tempt them, however, in order to refine their faith and to help them grow in their dependence upon Christ. We can resist the tempta tion to sin by turning to God for strength and choosing to obey his Word.

1.13–15 It is easy to blame others and make excuses for evil thoughts and wrong actions. Excuses include (1) it's the other person's fault; (2) I couldn't help it; (3) everybody's doing it; (4) it was just a mistake; (5) nobody's perfect; (6) the devil made me do it; (7) I was pressured into it; (8) I didn't know it was wrong. A person who makes excuses is trying to shift the blame from himself or herself to something or someone else. A Christian, on the other hand, accepts responsibility for his or her wrongs, confesses them, and asks God for forgiveness.

1.17 The Bible often compares goodness with light and evil with darkness. For other passages where God is pictured as light, see Psalm 27.1, Isaiah 60.19–22, John 1.1–14.

1.18 First-century Christians were the first generation to believe in Jesus Christ as Messiah. James calls them "a kind of first fruits of his creatures." The Jewish leaders would be well aware of the practice of offering the first crops to ripen just prior to harvest as an act of worship, and also as a blessing on the rest of the harvest. In 1 Corinthians 15.20, Paul refers to Christ as the first fruit of those who have died.

1.19 When we talk too much and listen too little, we communicate to others that we think our ideas are much more important than theirs. James wisely advises us to reverse this process. Put a mental stopwatch on your conversations and keep track of how much you talk and how much you listen. When people talk with you, do they feel that their viewpoints and ideas have value?

1.19, 20 This verse speaks of anger that erupts when our egos are bruised—"*I* am hurt;" "*My* opinions are not being heard." When injustice and sin occur, we *should* become angry because others are being hurt. But we should not become angry when we fail to win an argument, or when we feel neglected. Selfish anger never helps anybody.

1.21 James advises us to get rid of all that is wrong in our lives and "welcome with meekness" (humility) the salvation message we have received ("the implanted word"), because it alone can save us.

1.22–25 It is important to know what God's Word says, but it is much more important to obey it. We can measure the effectiveness of our Bible study time by the effect it has on our behavior and attitudes.

1.25 "The law of liberty" could also be called "the perfect law that gives freedom." It seems paradoxical that a law could give us freedom, but God's law points out sin in us and gives us the opportunity to ask God's forgiveness (see Romans 7.7, 8). As Christians, we are saved by God's grace, and salvation frees us from sin's control. As believers, we are free to live as God created us to live. Of course, this does not mean that we are free to do as we please (see 1 Peter 2.16). We are now free to obey God.

1.27 In the first century, orphans and widows had very little means of economic support. Unless a family member was willing to care for them, they were reduced to begging, selling themselves as slaves, or starving. By caring for these powerless people, the church put God's Word into practice. When we give with no hope of receiving in return, we show what it means to serve others.

1.27 To keep ourselves unstained by the world, we need to commit ourselves to Christ's ethical and moral system, not the world's. We are not to adapt to the world's value system based on money, power, and pleasure. True faith means nothing if we are contaminated with such values.

2. Genuine faith

Do not favor the rich

2.1 Lev 19.15 Deut 16.19 Prov 24.23 1 Cor 2.8
2.4 Jn 7.24
2.5 Prov 8.17-21 Mt 5.3; 11.6 Lk 6.20; 12.21 1 Cor 1.27 2 Cor 6.10
2.8 Lev 19.18 Mt 7.12 Rom 13.8
2.10 Deut 27.26 Mt 5.18,19 Gal 5.3

2 My brothers and sisters,[h] do you with your acts of favoritism really believe in
our glorious Lord Jesus Christ?[i] 2 For if a person with gold rings and in fine
clothes comes into your assembly, and if a poor person in dirty clothes also comes
in, 3 and if you take notice of the one wearing the fine clothes and say, "Have a seat
here, please," while to the one who is poor you say, "Stand there," or, "Sit at my
feet,"[j] 4 have you not made distinctions among yourselves, and become judges
with evil thoughts? 5 Listen, my beloved brothers and sisters.[k] Has not God chosen
the poor in the world to be rich in faith and to be heirs of the kingdom that he has
promised to those who love him? 6 But you have dishonored the poor. Is it not the
rich who oppress you? Is it not they who drag you into court? 7 Is it not they who
blaspheme the excellent name that was invoked over you?

8 You do well if you really fulfill the royal law according to the scripture, "You
shall love your neighbor as yourself." 9 But if you show partiality, you commit sin
and are convicted by the law as transgressors. 10 For whoever keeps the whole law

[h] Gk *My brothers* [i] Or *hold the faith of our glorious Lord Jesus Christ without acts of favoritism* [j] Gk *Sit under my footstool* [k] Gk *brothers*

SHOWING FAVORITISM
Why it is wrong to show favoritism to the wealthy:

1. It is inconsistent with Christ's teachings.
2. It results from evil thoughts.
3. It belittles people made in God's image.
4. It is a by-product of selfish motives.
5. It goes against the biblical definition of love.
6. It shows a lack of mercy to those less fortunate.
7. It is hypocritical.
8. It is sin.

2.1ff In this chapter James argues for the necessity of good works. He presents three principles of faith: (1) Commitment is an essential part of faith. You cannot be a Christian simply by affirming the right doctrines or agreeing with biblical facts (2.19). You must commit your mind and heart to Christ. (2) Good works are the natural by-products of true faith. A genuine Christian will have a changed life (2.18). (3) Faith without good works doesn't do anybody any good – it is useless (2.14–17). These statements are consistent with Paul's teaching that we receive salvation by faith alone. Paul emphasizes the purpose of faith – to bring salvation. James emphasizes the results of faith – a changed life.

2.1–7 James condemns acts of favoritism. Often we treat a well-dressed, impressive-looking person better than someone who looks poor. We do this because we would rather identify with successful people than with apparent failures. The irony, as James reminds us, is that the supposed winners may have gained their impressive life-style at our expense. In addition, the rich find it hard to identify with the Lord Jesus, who came as a humble servant. Are you easily impressed by status, wealth, or fame? Are you partial to the "haves" while ignoring the "have-nots"? This attitude is sin. God views all people as equals; and if he favors anyone, it is the poor and the powerless. We should follow his example.

2.2–4 Why is it wrong to judge a person by his or her economic status? Wealth may indicate intelligence, wise decisions, and hard work. On the other hand, it may mean only that a person had the good fortune of being born into a wealthy family. Or it can even be the sign of greed, dishonesty, and selfishness. By honoring someone just because he or she dresses well, we are making appearance more important than character. We sometimes do this because (1) poverty makes us uncomfortable; we don't want to face our responsibilities to those who have less than we do; (2) we too want to be wealthy, and we hope to use the rich person as a means to that end; (3) we want the rich person to join our church and help support it financially. All these motives are selfish; they view neither the rich nor the poor person as a human being in need of fellowship. If we say that Christ is Lord of our lives, then we must live as he requires, showing no favoritism and loving all people regardless of whether they are rich or poor.

2.2–4 We are often partial to the rich because we mistakenly assume that riches are a sign of God's blessing and approval. But God does not promise us earthly rewards or riches; in fact, Christ calls us to be ready to suffer for him and give up everything in order to hold on to eternal life (Matthew 6.19–21; 19.28–30; Luke 12.14–34; Romans 8.15–21; 1 Timothy 6.17–19). We will have untold riches in eternity if we are faithful in our present life (Luke 6.35; John 12.23–25; Galatians 6.7–10; Titus 3.4–8).

2.5 When James speaks about the poor, he is talking about those who have no money, and also those whose simple values are despised by much of our affluent society. Perhaps they prefer serving to managing, human relationships to financial security, peace to power. This does not mean that the poor will automatically go to heaven and the rich to hell. Poor people, however, are usually more aware of their powerlessness. Thus it is often easier for them to acknowledge their need for salvation. One of the greatest barriers to salvation for the rich is pride. For the poor, it is bitterness.

2.8 The royal law is the law of our great King Jesus Christ who said, "love one another as I have loved you" (John 15.12). This law, originally summarized in Leviticus 19.18, is reinforced by Christ in Matthew 22.37–40 and taught by Paul in Romans 13.8 and Galatians 5.14.

2.8, 9 We must treat all people as we would want to be treated. We should not ignore the rich, because then we would be withholding our love. But we must not favor them for what they can do for us, while ignoring the poor who can offer us little in return.

2.10 Christians must not use this verse to justify sinning. We dare not say: "Because I can't keep every demand of God, why even try?" James reminds us that if we've broken just one law, we are sinners. We can't decide to keep part of God's law and ignore the rest. You can't break the law a little bit; if you have broken it at all, you need Christ to pay for your sin. Measure yourself, not someone else, against God's standards. Ask for forgiveness where you need it, and then renew your effort to put your faith into practice.

but fails in one point has become accountable for all of it. 11 For the one who said,
"You shall not commit adultery," also said, "You shall not murder." Now if you do
not commit adultery but if you murder, you have become a transgressor of the law.
12 So speak and so act as those who are to be judged by the law of liberty. 13 For
judgment will be without mercy to anyone who has shown no mercy; mercy triumphs over judgment.

2.11 Ex 20.13,14 Deut 5.17,18 Mt 19.18
2.12 Jas 1.25
2.13 Mt 18.32-35

Faith results in good works

14 What good is it, my brothers and sisters,[l] if you say you have faith but do
not have works? Can faith save you? 15 If a brother or sister is naked and lacks daily
food, 16 and one of you says to them, "Go in peace; keep warm and eat your fill,"
and yet you do not supply their bodily needs, what is the good of that? 17 So faith
by itself, if it has no works, is dead.
18 But someone will say, "You have faith and I have works." Show me your
faith apart from your works, and I by my works will show you my faith. 19 You
believe that God is one; you do well. Even the demons believe — and shudder. 20 Do
you want to be shown, you senseless person, that faith apart from works is barren?
21 Was not our ancestor Abraham justified by works when he offered his son Isaac
on the altar? 22 You see that faith was active along with his works, and faith was
brought to completion by the works. 23 Thus the scripture was fulfilled that says,
"Abraham believed God, and it was reckoned to him as righteousness," and he was
called the friend of God. 24 You see that a person is justified by works and not by
faith alone. 25 Likewise, was not Rahab the prostitute also justified by works when
she welcomed the messengers and sent them out by another road? 26 For just as the
body without the spirit is dead, so faith without works is also dead.

2.16 1 Jn 3.17
2.17 Gal 5.6 1 Pet 1.5-9
2.18 Mt 7.16 Rom 3.28
2.19 Deut 6.4 Isa 43.10 44.6,8 Mt 8.28,29
2.21 Gen 22.16-18
2.22 Heb 11.17
2.23 Gen 15.6 Isa 41.8 Rom 4.3-5
2.25 Josh 2.4,6,15 Heb 11.31

Controlling the tongue

3 Not many of you should become teachers, my brothers and sisters,[l] for you
know that we who teach will be judged with greater strictness. 2 For all of us
make many mistakes. Anyone who makes no mistakes in speaking is perfect, able

3.1 Mt 23.8-10 Rom 2.17-24

[l] Gk *brothers*

2.12 As Christians we are saved by God's free gift (grace) through faith, not by keeping the law. But as Christians, we are also required to obey Christ. The apostle Paul taught "for all of us must appear before the judgment seat of Christ" (2 Corinthians 5.10) to be judged for our conduct. God's grace does not cancel our duty to obey him; it gives it a new basis. It is no longer an external set of rules, but it is a "law of liberty" – one we joyfully and willingly carry out, because we love God and because we have the power of his Holy Spirit to carry it out (see 1.25).

2.13 Only God in his mercy can forgive our sins. We can't earn forgiveness by forgiving others. But when we withhold forgiveness from others after having received it ourselves, it shows that we don't understand or appreciate God's mercy toward us (see Matthew 6.14, 15; Ephesians 4.31, 32).

2.14 Intellectual assent – agreement with a set of Christian teachings – is incomplete faith. True faith transforms our conduct as well as our thoughts. If our lives remain unchanged, we don't truly believe the truths we claim to believe.

2.17 We cannot earn our way into heaven by serving and obeying God. But such "works" show that our commitment to God is real. Works of loving service are not a substitute for, but a verification of, our faith in Christ.

2.18 At first glance, this verse seems to contradict Romans 3.28, "a person is justified by faith apart from works prescribed by the law." Deeper investigation, however, shows that the teachings of James and Paul are not at odds. While it is true that our good works can never earn salvation, true faith always results in a changed life and good works. Paul speaks against those who try to be saved by works instead of true faith; James speaks against those who confuse mere intellectual assent with true faith. After all, even demons know who Jesus is, but they don't obey him (2.19). True faith involves a commitment of your whole self to God.

2.21–24 James says Abraham was *justified* (declared righteous) because of what he *did*. Paul says he was justified because of what he *believed* (Romans 4.1–5). James and Paul are not contradicting, but complementing each other. Let's not infer that the truth is a compromise between these two statements. We are not justified by works in any way. True faith always results in works, but the works do not justify us. Belief brings us salvation; active obedience demonstrates that our belief is genuine.

2.25 Rahab lived in Jericho, a city the Israelites conquered as they entered the promised land (Joshua 2). When Israel's spies came to the city, she hid them and helped them escape. In this way she demonstrated faith in God's purpose for Israel. As a result, she and her family were saved when the city was destroyed. Hebrews 11.31 lists Rahab among the heroes of faith.

3.1 Teaching was a highly valued and respected profession in Jewish culture, and many Jews who embraced Christianity wanted to become teachers. James warned that although it is good to aspire to teach, the teachers' responsibility is great because their words affect others' spiritual lives. If you are in a teaching or leadership role, how is your example affecting those you lead?

3.2, 3 What you say and what you *don't* say are both important. Proper speech is not only saying the right words at the right time, but controlling your desire to say what you shouldn't. Examples of wrongly using the tongue include gossiping, putting others down, bragging, manipulating, false teaching, exaggerating, complaining, flattering, and lying. Before you speak, ask, "Is what I want to say true? Is it necessary? Is it kind?"

3.3 Ps 32.9 to keep the whole body in check with a bridle. 3 If we put bits into the mouths of
horses to make them obey us, we guide their whole bodies. 4 Or look at ships:
though they are so large that it takes strong winds to drive them, yet they are guided
3.5 Prov 26.20 by a very small rudder wherever the will of the pilot directs. 5 So also the tongue is
a small member, yet it boasts of great exploits.
3.6 Ps 120.3 How great a forest is set ablaze by a small fire! 6 And the tongue is a fire. The
Prov 6.12-19 tongue is placed among our members as a world of iniquity; it stains the whole
10.11; 16.27 Mt 15.11 body, sets on fire the cycle of nature,[m] and is itself set on fire by hell.[n] 7 For every
Mk 7.15,16 species of beast and bird, of reptile and sea creature, can be tamed and has been
3.8 Ps 140.3 tamed by the human species, 8 but no one can tame the tongue—a restless evil, full
Rom 3.13 of deadly poison. 9 With it we bless the Lord and Father, and with it we curse those
3.9 Gen 1.26,27; 5.1 who are made in the likeness of God. 10 From the same mouth come blessing and
1 Cor 11.7 cursing. My brothers and sisters,[o] this ought not to be so. 11 Does a spring pour
3.12 Mt 7.16 forth from the same opening both fresh and brackish water? 12 Can a fig tree, my
brothers and sisters,[p] yield olives, or a grapevine figs? No more can salt water
yield fresh.

3. Genuine wisdom

Wisdom from heaven

13 Who is wise and understanding among you? Show by your good life that
3.14 Rom 13.13 your works are done with gentleness born of wisdom. 14 But if you have bitter envy
3.15 Jas 1.17 and selfish ambition in your hearts, do not be boastful and false to the truth. 15 Such
wisdom does not come down from above, but is earthly, unspiritual, devilish.

[m] Or *wheel of birth* [n] Gk *Gehenna* [o] Gk *My brothers* [p] Gk *my brothers*

SPEECH	*When our speech is motivated by:*	*It is full of:*
	Satan	Jealousy Selfishness Earthly concerns and desires Unspiritual thoughts and ideas Disorder Evil
	God and his wisdom	Mercy Love for others Peace Courtesy Yielding to others Sincerity, straightforwardness Quiet gentleness Goodness

3.6 James compares the damage the tongue can do to that of a raging fire—the tongue's wickedness has its source in hell itself. The uncontrolled tongue can do terrible damage. Satan uses the tongue to divide people and pit them against one another. Idle words are damaging because they spread destruction quickly, and no one can stop the results once they are spoken. We dare not be careless with our words thinking we can apologize later, because even if we do, the scars remain. A few words spoken in anger can destroy a relationship that took years to build. Before you speak, remember that words are like fire—you can neither control nor reverse the damage they can do.

3.8 If no human being can control the tongue, why bother trying? Even if we may not achieve perfect control of it in this life, we can still learn enough control to reduce the damage it can do. It is better to fight a fire than to go around setting new ones! Remember that we are not fighting the tongue's fire in our own strength. The Holy Spirit will give us increasing power to monitor and control what we say. As Christians we are not sinless, but we should never stop growing.

3.9–12 Our contradictory speech often puzzles us. At times it is right and pleasing to God, but at other times it is violent and destructive. Which of these reflects our true identity? The tongue gives us a picture of our basic human nature. We are good—made in God's image; but we are also bad—fallen and sinful. God works to change us from the inside out. As the Holy Spirit purifies our hearts, he also gives us self-control so that we will speak words that please God.

3.13–18 Have you ever known anyone who claimed to be wise, but acted foolishly? True wisdom can be measured by the depth of one's character. Just as you can identify a tree by the type of fruit it produces, you can evaluate your wisdom by the way you act. Foolishness leads to disorder, but wisdom leads to peace and goodness.

3.14, 15 Bitter envy and selfish ambition are inspired by the devil. It is so easy for us to be drawn into wrong desires by the pressures of society and sometimes even by well-meaning Christians. By listening to the advice "Assert yourself," "Go for it," "Set high goals," we can be drawn into greed and destructive competitiveness. Seeking God's wisdom delivers us from the need to compare ourselves to others and from desiring what they have.

16 For where there is envy and selfish ambition, there will also be disorder and
wickedness of every kind. 17 But the wisdom from above is first pure, then peaceable, gentle, willing to yield, full of mercy and good fruits, without a trace of partiality or hypocrisy. 18 And a harvest of righteousness is sown in peace for[q] those
who make peace.

Drawing near to God

4 Those conflicts and disputes among you, where do they come from? Do they
not come from your cravings that are at war within you? 2 You want something
and do not have it; so you commit murder. And you covet[r] something and cannot
obtain it; so you engage in disputes and conflicts. You do not have, because you do
not ask. 3 You ask and do not receive, because you ask wrongly, in order to spend
what you get on your pleasures. 4 Adulterers! Do you not know that friendship with
the world is enmity with God? Therefore whoever wishes to be a friend of the world
becomes an enemy of God. 5 Or do you suppose that it is for nothing that the scripture says, "God[s] yearns jealously for the spirit that he has made to dwell in us"?
6 But he gives all the more grace; therefore it says,

"God opposes the proud,
but gives grace to the humble."

7 Submit yourselves therefore to God. Resist the devil, and he will flee from you.
8 Draw near to God, and he will draw near to you. Cleanse your hands, you sinners,
and purify your hearts, you double-minded. 9 Lament and mourn and weep. Let
your laughter be turned into mourning and your joy into dejection. 10 Humble yourselves before the Lord, and he will exalt you.
11 Do not speak evil against one another, brothers and sisters.[t] Whoever
speaks evil against another or judges another, speaks evil against the law and
judges the law; but if you judge the law, you are not a doer of the law but a judge.
12 There is one lawgiver and judge who is able to save and to destroy. So who, then,
are you to judge your neighbor?

[q] *Or by* [r] *Or you murder and you covet* [s] *Gk He* [t] *Gk brothers*

3.16 1 Cor 3.3
3.17 Rom 12.9-11,18; 2 Cor 6.6; Phil 1.11; Heb 12.10,11
4.2 1 Jn 3.15
4.4 Jn 15.19; 1 Jn 2.15
4.5 1 Cor 6.19; 2 Cor 6.16
4.6 Ps 138.6; Prov 3.34; 29.23; Mt 23.12; 1 Pet 5.5
4.7 Rom 14.11; Eph 5.21; 6.11,12; 1 Pet 5.6,8,9
4.8 Ps 73.28; Isa 1.16; 55.6,7
4.9 Lk 6.25
4.11 Mt 7.1; 2 Cor 12.20; 2 Tim 3.3; 1 Pet 2.1
4.12 Mt 10.28; Rom 2.1; 14.4,13; Jas 5.9

4.1–3 Conflicts and disputes among believers are always harmful. James tells us that these quarrels result from evil desires within us—we want more possessions, more money, higher status, more recognition. When we want badly enough to fulfill these desires, we fight in order to do so. Instead of aggressively grabbing what we want, we should ask God to help us get rid of our selfish desires and trust him to give us what we really need.

4.2, 3 James mentions the most common problems in prayer: not asking, asking for the wrong things, asking for the wrong reasons. Do you talk to God at all? When you do, what do you talk about? Do you ask only to satisfy your desires? Do you seek God's approval for what you already plan to do? Your prayers will become powerful when you allow God to change your desires so that they perfectly correspond to his will for you (1 John 3.21, 22).

4.3, 4 There is nothing wrong with wanting a pleasurable life. God gives us good gifts that he wants us to enjoy (1.17; Ephesians 4.7; 1 Timothy 4.4, 5). But having friendship with the world involves seeking pleasure at others' expense or at the expense of obeying God. Pleasure that keeps us from pleasing God is sinful; pleasure from God's rich bounty is good.

4.4–6 The cure for evil desires is humility (see Proverbs 16.18, 19; 1 Peter 5.5, 6). Pride makes us self-centered and leads us to conclude that we deserve all we can see, touch, or imagine. It creates greedy appetites for far more than we need. We can be released from our self-centered desires by humbling ourselves before God, realizing that all we need is his approval. When the Holy Spirit fills us, we realize that this world's seductive attractions are only cheap substitutes for what God has to offer.

4.7 Although God and Satan are at war, we don't have to wait until the end to see who will win. God has *already* defeated Satan (Colossians 2.13–15; Revelation 12.10–12), and when Christ returns, Satan and all he stands for will be eliminated forever (Revelation 20.10–15). Satan is here now, however, and he is trying to win us over to his evil cause. With the Holy Spirit's power, we can resist the devil, and he will flee from us.

4.7–10 How can you draw near to God? James gives five ways: (1) *Submit to God* (4.7). Realize that you need his forgiveness, and be willing to follow him. (2) *Resist the devil* (4.7). Don't allow him to entice and tempt you. (3) *Cleanse your hands . . . and purify your hearts* (that is, lead a pure life) (4.8). Be cleansed from sin, replacing it with God's purity. (4) *Lament and mourn and weep* in sincere grief for your sins (4.9). Don't be afraid to express deep heartfelt sorrow for them. (5) *Humble yourself before the Lord,* and he will lift you up (4.10; 1 Peter 5.6).

4.10 Humbling ourselves means recognizing that our worth comes from God alone. It is working with his power according to his guidance, not with our own independent effort. Although we do not deserve God's favor, he reaches out to us in love and gives us worth and dignity, despite our human shortcomings.

4.11, 12 Jesus summarized the law as love to God and neighbor (Matthew 22.37–40), and Paul said love demonstrated toward a neighbor fully satisfies the law (Romans 13.6–10). When we fail to love, we are actually breaking God's law. Examine your attitude and actions toward others. Do you build people up or tear them down? When you're ready to criticize someone, remember God's law of love and say something good instead. Saying something beneficial to others will cure you of finding fault and increase your ability to obey God's law of love.

Trust God in making future plans

13 Come now, you who say, "Today or tomorrow we will go to such and such
4.14 Ps 102.3 a town and spend a year there, doing business and making money." [14]Yet you do
not even know what tomorrow will bring. What is your life? For you are a mist that
4.16 1 Cor 4.7,8; 5.6 appears for a little while and then vanishes. [15]Instead you ought to say, "If the Lord
wishes, we will live and do this or that." [16]As it is, you boast in your arrogance; all
4.17 Lk 12.47,48 Rom 2.17-23 such boasting is evil. [17]Anyone, then, who knows the right thing to do and fails to
do it, commits sin.

Warning to the rich

5.1 Prov 11.4,28 Isa 13.6 Mt 19.23,24 **5** Come now, you rich people, weep and wail for the miseries that are coming to
you. [2]Your riches have rotted, and your clothes are moth-eaten. [3]Your gold
and silver have rusted, and their rust will be evidence against you, and it will eat

FAITH THAT WORKS
James offers a larger number of similarities to the Sermon on the Mount than any other book in the New Testament. James relied heavily on Jesus' teachings.

Lesson	*Reference*
When your life is full of difficulties and persecutions, be happy. A reward awaits you.	James 1.2 Matthew 5.10–12
You are to be perfect, strong in character, full and complete.	James 1.4 Matthew 5.48
Ask God and he will answer.	James 1.5; 5.15 Matthew 7.7–12
Those who are humble, who don't amount to much by the world's standards, should be very glad.	James 1.9 Matthew 5.3
Watch out for your anger . . . it can be dangerous.	James 1.20 Matthew 5.22
Be merciful to others, as God is merciful to you.	James 2.13 Matthew 5.7; 6.14
Your faith must prove itself by helping others.	James 2.14–16 Matthew 7.21–23
Happy are those who strive for peace; peacemakers plant seeds of peace and reap a harvest of goodness.	James 3.17, 18 Matthew 5.9
You cannot serve God *and* money, pleasures, or evil. Friendship with evil makes you an enemy of God.	James 4.4 Matthew 6.24
When we humble ourselves and realize our need for God, he will come to us and encourage us.	James 4.10 Matthew 5.3, 4
Don't criticize or speak evil of others; it works against God's command to love one another.	James 4.11 Matthew 7.1, 2
Treasures on earth will only erode and disappear—we must store eternal treasures in heaven.	James 5.2 Matthew 6.19
Be patient in suffering, as God's prophets were patient.	James 5.10 Matthew 5.12
Be honest in your speech so you can say a simple "yes" or "no" and always be trusted.	James 5.12 Matthew 5.33–37

4.13–16 It is good to have goals, but goals can disappoint us if we leave God out of them. There is no point in making plans as though God does not exist, because the future is in his hands. What would you like to be doing ten years from now? One year from now? Tomorrow? How will you react if God steps in and rearranges your plans? Plan ahead, but hold on to your plans loosely. If you put God's desires at the center of your planning, he will never disappoint you.

4.14 Life is short no matter how long we live. Don't be deceived into thinking you have lots of remaining time to live for Christ, to enjoy your loved ones, or to do what you know you should. Live for God today! Then, no matter when your life ends, you will have fulfilled God's plan for you.

4.17 We tend to think that *doing* wrong is sin. But James tells us that sin is also *not* doing right. (These two kinds of sin are sometimes called sins of commission and sins of omission.) It is a sin to lie; it can also be a sin to know the truth and not tell it. It is a sin to speak evil of someone; it is also a sin to avoid him when you know he needs your friendship. We should be willing to help as the Holy Spirit guides us. If God has directed you to some kind act to do, some service to render, or some relationship to restore, do it. You will experience a renewed and refreshed vitality to your Christian faith.

5.1–6 James proclaims the worthlessness of riches, not the worthlessness of the rich. Today's money will be worthless when Christ returns, so we should spend our time accumulating treasures that will be worthwhile in God's eternal kingdom. Money is not the problem; Christian leaders need money to live and support their families; missionaries need money to help them spread the gospel; churches need money to do their work effectively. It is the *love* of money that leads to evil (1 Timothy 6.10). This is a warning to all Christians who are tempted to adopt worldly standards rather than God's standards (Romans 12.1, 2) and an encouragement to all those who are oppressed by the rich. Also read Matthew 6.19–21 to see what Jesus says about riches.

your flesh like fire. You have laid up treasure[u] for the last days. 4 Listen! The 5.4 Ex 2.23,24
wages of the laborers who mowed your fields, which you kept back by fraud, cry Lev 19.13
out, and the cries of the harvesters have reached the ears of the Lord of hosts. 5 You Deut 24.14,15 Ps 9.12
have lived on the earth in luxury and in pleasure; you have fattened your hearts in Jer 22.13
a day of slaughter. 6 You have condemned and murdered the righteous one, who 5.5 Lk 16.19
does not resist you.

Patience in suffering

7 Be patient, therefore, beloved,[v] until the coming of the Lord. The farmer 5.7 2 Pet 3.4-13
waits for the precious crop from the earth, being patient with it until it receives the
early and the late rains. 8 You also must be patient. Strengthen your hearts, for the 5.8 Rom 8.25; 13.11
coming of the Lord is near.[w] 9 Beloved,[x] do not grumble against one another, so Heb 10.25-37
that you may not be judged. See, the Judge is standing at the doors! 10 As an exam- 5.9 1 Cor 4.5
ple of suffering and patience, beloved,[v] take the prophets who spoke in the name
of the Lord. 11 Indeed we call blessed those who showed endurance. You have 5.10 Jer 2.30
heard of the endurance of Job, and you have seen the purpose of the Lord, how the Mt 5.11,12
Lord is compassionate and merciful. 5.11 Job 1.20-22
12 Above all, my beloved,[v] do not swear, either by heaven or by earth or by 2.7-10
any other oath, but let your "Yes" be yes and your "No" be no, so that you may not 5.12 Mt 5.33-37
fall under condemnation. 23.16-22

Faithful prayer

13 Are any among you suffering? They should pray. Are any cheerful? They 5.14 Mk 6.13
should sing songs of praise. 14 Are any among you sick? They should call for the Tit 1.5
elders of the church and have them pray over them, anointing them with oil in the 5.15 Mt 21.22
name of the Lord. 15 The prayer of faith will save the sick, and the Lord will raise
them up; and anyone who has committed sins will be forgiven. 16 Therefore confess 5.16 Mt 18.15-18

[u] *Or will eat your flesh, since you have stored up fire* [v] *Gk brothers* [w] *Or is at hand* [x] *Gk Brothers*

5.6 The "righteous one" is a defenseless person, probably a poor laborer. Poor people who could not pay their debts were thrown into prison or forced to sell all their possessions. At times, they were even forced to sell their family members into slavery. With no opportunity to work off their debts, poor people often died of starvation. God called this murder. Hoarding money, exploiting employees, and living self-indulgently will not escape God's notice.

5.7, 8 The farmer must wait patiently for his crops to grow; he cannot hurry the process. But he does not take the summer off and hope that all goes well in the fields. There is much work to do to ensure a good harvest. In the same way, we must wait patiently for Christ's return. We cannot make him come back any sooner. But while we wait, there is much work we can do to advance God's kingdom. Both the farmer and the Christian must live by faith, looking toward the future reward for their labors. Don't live as if Christ will never come. Work faithfully to build his kingdom—the King *will* come when the time is ripe.

5.9 When things go wrong, we tend to blame others for our miseries (see the second note on Genesis 3.11–13). Blaming others is easier than owning our share of the responsibility, but it is both destructive and sinful. Before you judge others for their shortcomings, remember that Christ the Judge will come to evaluate each of us (Matthew 7.1–5). He will not let us get away with shifting the blame to others.

5.10, 11 For more on the topic of suffering, see the notes on Job 1.1ff; 2.10; 3.23–26; 4.7, 8; 23.14; 42.17; and Job's Profile in Job 3.

5.12 A person with a reputation for exaggeration or lying often can't get anyone to believe him on his word alone. Christians should never become like that. Always be honest so that others will believe your simple yes or no. By avoiding lies, half-truths, and omissions of the truth, you will become known as a trustworthy person.

5.14, 15 James refers to someone who is incapacitated physically. In Scripture, oil was both a medicine (see the parable of the Good Samaritan in Luke 10.30–37) and a symbol of the Spirit of God (as used in anointing kings, see 1 Samuel 16.1–13). Thus oil can represent both the medical and the spiritual spheres of life. Christians should not separate the physical and the spiritual—Jesus Christ is Lord over both the body and the spirit.

5.14, 15 People in the church are not alone. Members of Christ's body should be able to count on others for support and prayer, especially when they are sick or suffering. The elders should be on call to respond to the illness of any member, and the church should stay alert to pray for the needs of all its members.

5.15 "The prayer of faith," does not refer to the faith of the sick person, but to the faith of the people praying. God heals, not faith, and all prayers are subject to God's will. But our prayers are part of God's healing process. That is why God often waits for our prayers of faith before intervening to heal a person.

5.16 Christ has made it possible for us to go directly to God for forgiveness. But confessing our sins to one another still has an important place in the life of the church. (1) If we have sinned against an individual, we must ask him or her to forgive us. (2) If our sin has affected the church, we must confess it publicly. (3) If we need loving support as we struggle with a sin, we should confess it to those who are able to provide that support. (4) If, after confessing a private sin to God, we still don't feel his forgiveness, we may wish to confess that sin to a fellow believer and hear him or her assure us of God's pardon. In Christ's kingdom, every believer is a priest to other believers (1 Peter 2.9). We must help others come to Christ and tell them of Christ's forgiveness.

5.16–18 The Christian's most powerful resource is communion with God through prayer. The results are often greater than we thought were possible. Some people see prayer as a last resort to be tried when all else fails. This is backwards. Prayer should come

your sins to one another, and pray for one another, so that you may be healed. The
5.17 1 Kgs 17.1-7 18.36-39 prayer of the righteous is powerful and effective. 17 Elijah was a human being like
us, and he prayed fervently that it might not rain, and for three years and six months
it did not rain on the earth. 18 Then he prayed again, and the heaven gave rain and
the earth yielded its harvest.

Restore wandering believers

5.19 Prov 19.27 Mt 18.15 1 Tim 6.10 2 Pet 3.17 19 My brothers and sisters,[y] if anyone among you wanders from the truth and
is brought back by another, 20 you should know that whoever brings back a sinner
from wandering will save the sinner's[z] soul from death and will cover a multitude
of sins.

[y] Gk *My brothers* [z] Gk *his*

---

first. Because God's power is infinitely greater than ours, it only makes sense to rely on it—especially because God encourages us to do so.

5.17 For more about the great prophet Elijah, read his Profile in 1 Kings 18.

5.19, 20 Clearly the person who has wandered away is a believer who has fallen into sin—one who is no longer living a life consistent with his beliefs. Christians disagree over whether or not it is possible for people to lose their salvation, but all agree that those who move away from their faith are in serious trouble and need to repent. James urges Christians to help backsliders return to God. By taking the initiative, praying for the person, and acting in love, we can meet the person where he or she is and bring him back to God.

5.20 The book of James emphasizes faith in action. Right living is the evidence and result of faith. The church must serve with compassion, speak lovingly and truthfully, live in obedience to God's commands, and love one another. The body of believers ought to be an example of heaven on earth, drawing people to Christ through love for God and one another. If we truly believe God's Word, we will *live* it day by day. God's Word is not merely something we read or think about, but something we do. Belief, faith, and trust must have hands and feet—ours!

The First Letter of PETER

VITAL STATISTICS

PURPOSE:
To offer encouragement to suffering Christians

AUTHOR:
Peter

TO WHOM WRITTEN:
Jewish Christians driven out of Jerusalem and scattered throughout Asia Minor, and to all believers everywhere

DATE WRITTEN:
About A.D. 62–64 from Rome

SETTING:
Peter was probably in Rome when the great persecution under Emperor Nero began. (Peter was eventually executed during this persecution.) Throughout the Roman Empire, Christians were being tortured and killed for their faith, and the church in Jerusalem was being scattered throughout the Mediterranean world.

KEY VERSE:
"That the genuineness of your faith . . . may be found to result in praise and glory and honor when Jesus Christ is revealed" (1.7).

KEY PEOPLE:
Peter, Silvanus, Mark

KEY PLACES:
Jerusalem, Rome, and the regions of Pontus, Galatia, Cappadocia, Asia Minor, and Bithynia

SPECIAL FEATURES:
Peter used several images that were very special to him because Jesus had used them when he revealed certain truths to Peter. Peter's name (which means "stone") had been given to him by Jesus. Peter's conception of the church—a spiritual house composed of living stones built upon Christ as the foundation—came from Christ. Jesus encouraged Peter to care for the church as a shepherd tending the flock. Thus, it is not surprising to see Peter using living stones (2.5–9) and shepherds and sheep (2.25; 5.2, 4) to describe the church.

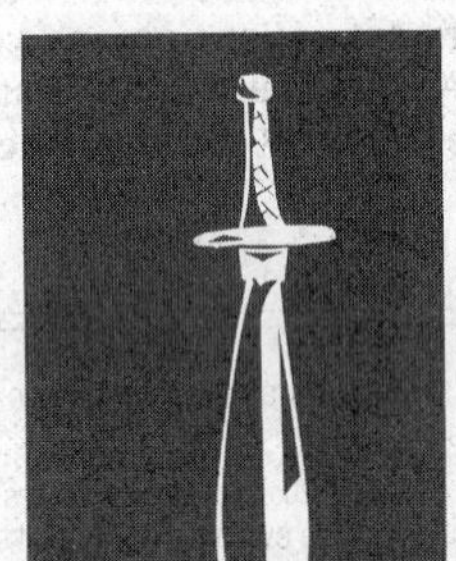

CRUSHED, overwhelmed, devastated, torn—these waves of feeling wash over those who suffer, blinding all vision of hope and threatening to destroy them. Suffering has many forms—physical abuse, debilitating disease, social ostracism, persecution. The pain and anguish tempt one to turn back, to surrender, to give in.

Many first-century followers of Christ were suffering, abused and persecuted for believing and obeying Jesus. Beginning in Jerusalem at the hands of their Jewish brothers, the pattern spread to the rest of the world—wherever Christians gathered—and climaxed when Rome determined to rid the empire of those who would not bow to Caesar . . . the "Christ-ones."

Peter knew persecution firsthand. Beaten and jailed, his life had been threatened often. He had seen fellow Christians die and the church scattered. But he knew Christ, and nothing could shake his confidence in his risen Lord. In this personal context, Peter wrote to the church scattered and suffering for the faith, giving comfort and hope, and urging continued loyalty to Christ.

Peter begins by thanking God for salvation (1.2–6). He explains to his readers that trials will refine their faith (1.7–9). They should believe in spite of their circumstances; for many in past ages believed in God's plan of salvation—even the prophets of old who wrote about it, but didn't understand it. But now salvation has been revealed in Christ (1.10–13).

In response to such a great salvation, Peter commands them to live holy lives (1.14–16), to reverently fear and trust God (1.17–21), to be honest and loving (2.1–3a), and to become like Christ (2.3b–4).

Jesus Christ, as the "cornerstone chosen and precious" upon whom the church is to be built (2.5, 6), is also the Stone that was rejected, causing those who are disobedient to fall (2.7, 8). But the church, built upon this Stone, is to be God's holy priesthood (2.9, 10).

Next, Peter explains how believers should live during difficult times (2.11—4.11). Christians should be above reproach (2.12–17), imitating Christ in all their social roles—masters and servants, husbands and wives, church members and neighbors (2.18—3.17). Christ should be our model for obedience to God in the midst of great suffering (3.18—4.11).

Peter then outlines the right attitude to have about persecution: expect it (4.12), be thankful for the privilege of suffering for Christ (4.13–18), and trust God for deliverance (4.19).

Next, Peter gives some special instructions—elders should feed God's flock (5.1–4), younger men should follow the leadership of the elders (5.5, 6), and everyone should trust God and resist Satan (5.7–11).

Peter concludes by introducing Silvanus and by giving personal greetings from himself, the church in Rome, and Mark (5.12–14).

When you suffer for doing what is right, remember that following Christ is a costly commitment. When persecuted for your faith, rejoice that you have been counted worthy to suffer for Christ. He suffered for us; as his followers, we should expect nothing less. As you read 1 Peter, remember that trials will come to refine your faith. When they come, remain faithful to God.

THE BLUEPRINT

1. God's great blessings to his people (1.1—2.10)
2. The conduct of God's people in the midst of suffering (2.11—4.19)
3. The shepherding of God's people in the midst of suffering (5.1–14)

Peter wrote to Jewish Christians who were experiencing persecution for their faith. He wrote to comfort them with the hope of eternal life and to challenge them to continue living holy lives. Those who suffer for being Christians become partners with Christ in his suffering. As we suffer, we must remember that Christ is both our hope in the midst of suffering and our example of how to endure suffering faithfully.

MEGATHEMES

THEME	EXPLANATION	IMPORTANCE
Salvation	Our salvation is a gracious gift from God. God chose us out of his love for us, Jesus died to pay the penalty for our sin, and the Holy Spirit cleansed us from sin when we believed. Eternal life is a wonderful privilege for those who trust in Christ.	Our safety and security are in God. If we experience joy in relationship with Christ now, how much greater will our joy be when he returns and we see him face to face. Such a hope should motivate us to serve Christ with greater commitment.
Persecution	Peter offers faithful believers comfort and hope. We should expect ridicule, rejection, and suffering because we are Christians. Persecution makes us stronger because it refines our faith. We can face persecution victoriously as Christ did, if we rely on him.	Christians still suffer for what they believe. We should expect persecution, but we don't have to be terrified by it. The fact that we will live eternally with Christ should give us the confidence, patience, and hope to stand firm even when we are persecuted.
God's Family	We are privileged to belong to God's family, a community with Christ as the Founder and Foundation. Everyone in this community is related—we are all brothers and sisters, loved equally by God.	Because Christ is the foundation of our family, we must be devoted, loyal, and faithful to him. By obeying him, we show that we are his children. We must accept the challenge to live differently from the society around us.
Family Life	Peter encouraged the wives of unbelievers to submit to their husbands' authority as a means to winning them to Christ. He urged all family members to treat others with sympathy, love, tenderness, and humility.	We must treat our families lovingly. Though it's never easy, willing service is the best way to influence loved ones. To gain the strength we need for self-discipline and submission, we need to pray for God's help.
Judgment	God will judge everyone with perfect justice. We all will face God. He will punish evildoers and those who persecute God's people. Those who love him will be rewarded with life forever in his presence.	Because all are accountable to God, we can leave judgment of others to him. We must not hate or resent those who persecute us. We should realize that we will be held responsible for how we live each day.

1. God's great blessings to his people

1 Peter, an apostle of Jesus Christ, 1.1 Acts 2.9,10 Gal 1.2
To the exiles of the Dispersion in Pontus, Galatia, Cappadocia, Asia, and Bithynia, 2 who have been chosen and destined by God the Father and sanctified by
the Spirit to be obedient to Jesus Christ and to be sprinkled with his blood:
May grace and peace be yours in abundance.

The hope of eternal life

3 Blessed be the God and Father of our Lord Jesus Christ! By his great mercy 1.3 1 Jn 3.3
he has given us a new birth into a living hope through the resurrection of Jesus 1.4
Christ from the dead, 4 and into an inheritance that is imperishable, undefiled, and 2 Tim 4.8
unfading, kept in heaven for you, 5 who are being protected by the power of God 1.5 2 Thess 2.13
through faith for a salvation ready to be revealed in the last time. 6 In this you re- 1.6
joice,[a] even if now for a little while you have had to suffer various trials, 7 so that Rom 5.2

[a] Or *Rejoice in this*

1.1 The apostle Peter wrote this letter to encourage believers who were facing trials and persecution under Emperor Nero. During most of the first century, Christians were not hunted down and killed throughout the Roman Empire. They could, however, expect social and economic persecution from three main sources: the Romans, the Jews, and their own families. All would be misunderstood; some would be harassed; a few would be tortured and even put to death.

The legal status of Christians in the Roman Empire was unclear. Many Romans still thought of Christians as a Jewish sect; and because the Jewish religion was legal, they considered Christianity legal also—as long as Christians went along with the empire's laws. However, if Christians refused to worship the emperor or join the army, or if they were involved in civil disturbances (such as the one in Ephesus recorded in Acts 19.23ff), they might be punished by the civil authorities.

Many Jews did not appreciate being legally associated with Christians. As the book of Acts frequently records, they harmed Christians physically, drove them out of town, or attempted to turn Roman officials against them. Saul, later the great apostle Paul, was an early Jewish persecutor of Christians.

Another source of persecution was the Christian's own family. Under Roman law, the head of the household had absolute authority over all its members. Unless the ruling male became a Christian, the wife, children and servants who were believers might well face extreme hardship. If they were sent away, they would have no place to turn but the church; if they were beaten, no court of law would uphold their interests.

Peter may have been writing especially for new Christians and those planning to be baptized. Peter wanted to warn them about what lay ahead, and they needed his encouraging words to help them face it. This letter is still helpful for any Christians facing trials. Many Christians around the world are living under governments more repressive than the Roman Empire of the first century. Christians everywhere are subject to misunderstanding, ridicule, and even harassment by unbelieving friends, employers, and family members. None of us is exempt from catastrophe, pain, illness, and death—trials that, like persecution, make us draw heavily on God's grace. For today's readers, as well as for Peter's original audience, the theme of this letter is *hope*.

1.1 Peter (also called Simon and Cephas) was one of the 12 disciples chosen by Jesus (Mark 1.16–18; John 1.42) and, with James and John, was part of the inner group Jesus singled out for special training and fellowship. Peter was one of the first to recognize Jesus as the Messiah, God's Son; and Jesus gave him a special leadership role in the church (Matthew 16.16–19; Luke 22.31, 32; John 21.15–19). Although during Jesus' trial Peter denied knowing Jesus, he repented and became a great apostle. For more information on Peter, see his Profile in Matthew 27.

1.1 This letter is addressed to "the exiles of the Dispersion," or to the Jewish Christians scattered throughout the world as a result of persecution against believers in and around Jerusalem. The first believers and leaders of the early church were Jews. When they became Christians, they didn't give up their Jewish heritage, just as we didn't give up our nationalities when we became Christians. Because of persecution, these believers had been scattered throughout the Roman world (this is described in Acts 8.1–4). Persecution didn't quench the gospel; instead, it introduced it to the whole empire. Thus the churches to whom Peter wrote also included Gentile Christians.

1.2 Peter encouraged his readers by this strong declaration that they were *chosen and destined* by God the Father. At one time, only the nation of Israel could claim to be God's chosen people; but through Christ, all believers—Jews, former Jews, and Gentiles—belong to God. Our salvation and security rest in the free and merciful choice of the almighty God; no trials or persecutions can rob us of the eternal life he gives to us who believe in him.

1.2 This verse mentions all three members of the trinity—God the Father, God the Son, and God the Holy Spirit. All members of the trinity work to bring about our salvation. The Father chose us before we chose him (Ephesians 1.4). The Son died for us while we were still sinners (Romans 5.6–10). The Holy Spirit brings us salvation and sets us apart (sanctifies us) for God's service (2 Thessalonians 2.13).

1.3 The term *new birth* refers to spiritual birth—the Holy Spirit's act of bringing believers into God's family. Jesus used this term when he explained salvation to Nicodemus (see John 3).

1.3-6 Do you need encouragement? Peter's words offer joy and hope in times of trouble, and he bases his confidence on what God has done for us in Christ Jesus. We're called to *live* in the hope of eternal life (1.3). Our hope is not only for the future: eternal life begins when we believe in God and join his family. No matter what pain or trial we face in this life, we know it is not our final experience. One day we will live with Christ forever.

1.4 The Jews looked forward to an inheritance in the promised land of Canaan (Numbers 32.19; Deuteronomy 2.12; 19.9). Christians now look forward to a family inheritance in the eternal city of God. God has reserved the inheritance; it will never grow dim or decay; it will be unstained by sin. The best part is that you have an inheritance if you have trusted him.

1.5 God will help us remain true to our faith, whatever difficult times we must face. The "last time" is the Judgment Day of Christ described in Romans 14.10 and Revelation 20.11–15. We may have to endure trials, persecution, or violent death, but our souls cannot be harmed if we have accepted Christ's gift of salvation. We know we will receive the promised rewards.

1.7 Job 23.10 Isa 48.10 Jas 1.3
1.8 Jn 20.29 Eph 3.19 1 Jn 4.2
1.10 Gen 49.10 Mt 13.17; 26.24 Col 3.4
1.11 Ps 22.6 Mt 26.24 Rom 8.9 2 Pet 1.21
1.12 Acts 2.2-4

the genuineness of your faith — being more precious than gold that, though perishable, is tested by fire — may be found to result in praise and glory and honor when
Jesus Christ is revealed. 8 Although you have not seen[b] him, you love him; and
even though you do not see him now, you believe in him and rejoice with an indescribable and glorious joy, 9 for you are receiving the outcome of your faith, the
salvation of your souls.
10 Concerning this salvation, the prophets who prophesied of the grace that was
to be yours made careful search and inquiry, 11 inquiring about the person or time
that the Spirit of Christ within them indicated when it testified in advance to the
sufferings destined for Christ and the subsequent glory. 12 It was revealed to them
that they were serving not themselves but you, in regard to the things that have now
been announced to you through those who brought you good news by the Holy
Spirit sent from heaven — things into which angels long to look!

[b] Other ancient authorities read *known*

THE CHURCHES OF PETER'S LETTER
Peter addressed his letter to the churches located through Bithynia, Pontus, Asia, Galatia, and Cappadocia. Paul had evangelized many of these areas; others had churches that were begun by the Jews who were in Jerusalem on the day of Pentecost and heard Peter's powerful sermon (see Acts 2.9–11)

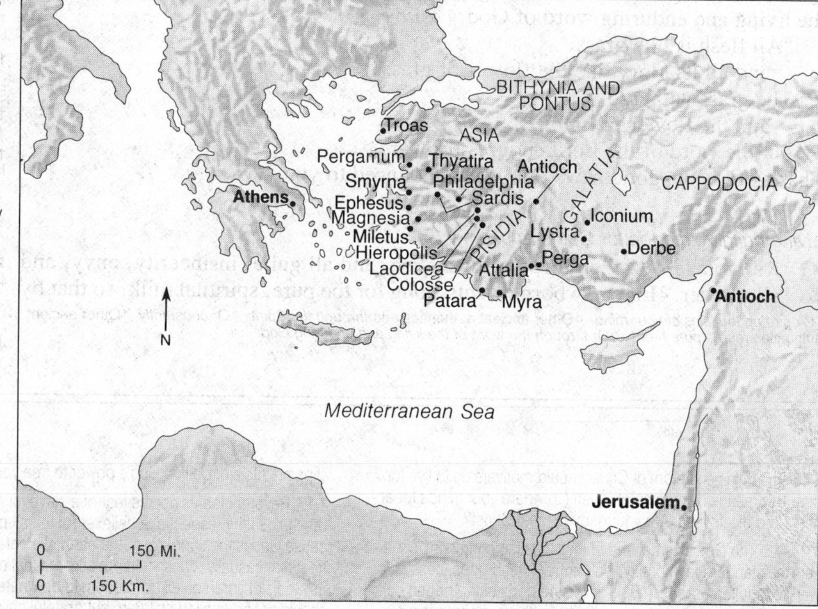

1.7 Why were Christians the target of persecution? (1) They refused to worship the emperor as a god and thus were viewed as atheists and traitors. (2) They refused to worship at pagan temples, so business for these money-making enterprises dropped wherever Christianity took hold. (3) They didn't support the Roman ideals of self, power, and conquest; and the Romans scorned the Christian ideal of self-sacrificing service. (4) They exposed and rejected the horrible immorality of pagan culture.

1.7 Peter mentions suffering several times in this letter: 1.6, 7; 3.13–17; 4.12–19; 5.9. When he speaks of trials, he is not talking about natural disasters or God's punishments, but the response of an unbelieving world to people of faith. All believers face such trials when they let their light shine into the darkness. We must accept trials as part of the refining process that burns away impurities, preparing us to meet Christ. Trials teach us patience (Romans 5.3, 4; James 1.2, 3) and help us grow to be the kind of people God wants.

1.7 As gold is heated, impurities float to the top and can be skimmed off. Steel is tempered or strengthened by heating it in fire. Likewise, our trials, struggles, and persecutions strengthen our faith and make us useful to God.

1.10–13 Although the plan of salvation was a mystery to the Old Testament prophets, they still suffered persecution and some died for God. Some Jewish Christians reading Peter's letter, by contrast, had seen Jesus for themselves and knew why he came. They based their assurance on Jesus' death and resurrection. With their firsthand knowledge and personal experience of Jesus, their faith could be even stronger than that of the Old Testament prophets.

1.11 The Spirit of Christ is another name for the Holy Spirit. Before Jesus left his ministry on earth to return to heaven, he promised to send his Holy Spirit, the Advocate, to teach, help, and guide his followers (John 14.15–17, 26; 16.7). The Holy Spirit would tell them all about Jesus and reveal his glory (John 15.26; 16.14). The Old Testament prophets, writing under the Holy Spirit's inspiration (2 Peter 1.20, 21), described the coming Messiah. The New Testament apostles, through the inspiration of the same Spirit, preached the crucified and risen Lord.

A call to holy living

13 Therefore prepare your minds for action;[c] discipline yourselves; set all your
hope on the grace that Jesus Christ will bring you when he is revealed. 14 Like
obedient children, do not be conformed to the desires that you formerly had in
ignorance. 15 Instead, as he who called you is holy, be holy yourselves in all your
conduct; 16 for it is written, "You shall be holy, for I am holy."
17 If you invoke as Father the one who judges all people impartially according
to their deeds, live in reverent fear during the time of your exile. 18 You know that
you were ransomed from the futile ways inherited from your ancestors, not with
perishable things like silver or gold, 19 but with the precious blood of Christ, like
that of a lamb without defect or blemish. 20 He was destined before the foundation
of the world, but was revealed at the end of the ages for your sake. 21 Through him
you have come to trust in God, who raised him from the dead and gave him glory,
so that your faith and hope are set on God.
22 Now that you have purified your souls by your obedience to the truth[d] so
that you have genuine mutual love, love one another deeply[e] from the heart.[f]
23 You have been born anew, not of perishable but of imperishable seed, through
the living and enduring word of God.[g] 24 For

"All flesh is like grass
    and all its glory like the flower of grass.
The grass withers,
    and the flower falls,
25 but the word of the Lord endures forever."

That word is the good news that was announced to you.

Living building stones for God's house

2 Rid yourselves, therefore, of all malice, and all guile, insincerity, envy, and
all slander. 2 Like newborn infants, long for the pure, spiritual milk, so that by

1.13 1 Thess 5.6
1.14 Rom 12.2 Eph 4.18
1.15 2 Cor 7.1 1 Thess 4.7 1 Jn 3.3
1.16 Lev 11.44,45
1.17 Deut 10.17 Ps 89.26
1.18 Isa 52.3
1.19 Ex 12.5 Jn 1.29 Heb 9.14
1.20 Gal 4.4 2 Tim 1.9,10
1.21 Rom 4.24
1.22 Jn 13.34 Rom 12.10
1.23 Jn 1.13; 3.3
1.24 Isa 40.6-8
2.1 Eph 4.22,25,31

[c] Gk *gird up the loins of your mind* [d] Other ancient authorities add *through the Spirit* [e] Or *constantly* [f] Other ancient authorities read *a pure heart* [g] Or *through the word of the living and enduring God*

1.13 The imminent return of Christ should motivate us to live for him. This means being mentally alert ("prepare your minds for action") and disciplined. Are you ready to meet Christ?

1.14–16 The God of Israel and of the Christian church is holy—he sets the standard for morality. Unlike the Roman gods, he is not warlike, adulterous, or spiteful. Unlike the gods of the pagan cults popular in the first century, he is not bloodthirsty or promiscuous. He is a God of mercy and justice who cares personally for each of his followers. Our holy God expects us to imitate him by following his high moral standards. Like him, we should be both merciful and just; like him, we should sacrifice ourselves for others.

1.15, 16 After people commit their lives to Christ, they still feel a pull back to their old ways. Peter tells us to be like our heavenly Father—holy in everything we do. Holiness means being totally devoted or dedicated to God, set aside for his special use, and set apart from sin and its influence. We're to be set apart and different, not blending in with the crowd, yet not being different just for the sake of being different. What make us different are God's qualities in our lives. Our focus and priorities must be his. All this is in direct contrast to our old ways (1.14). We cannot become holy on our own, but God gives us his Holy Spirit to help us obey and to give us power to overcome sin. Don't use the excuse that you can't help slipping into sin. Call on God's power to free you from sin's grip.

1.17 Reverent fear is not the fear of a slave for a ruthless master, but the healthy respect of a believer for the all-powerful God. Because God is the Judge of all the earth, we dare not ignore him or treat him casually. We should not assume that our privileged status as God's children gives us freedom to do whatever we want. We should not be spoiled children, but grateful children who love to show respect for our heavenly Father.

1.18, 19 A slave was "ransomed" when someone paid money to buy his or her freedom. God ransomed us from the tyranny of sin, not with money, but with the precious blood of his own Son (Romans 6.6, 7; 1 Corinthians 6.20; Colossians 2.13, 14; Hebrews 9.12). We could not escape from sin on our own; only the life of God's Son could free us.

1.20 Christ's sacrifice for our sins was not an afterthought, not something God decided to do when the world got out of control. This plan was set in motion by the all-knowing, eternal God long before the world was created. What a comfort it must have been to Jewish believers to know that Christ's coming and his work of salvation were planned by God long before the world began. This assured them that the law was not being scrapped because it didn't work, but that both the law *and* the coming of Christ were part of God's eternal plan.

1.22 Genuine love involves selfless giving, so a self-centered person can't truly love. God's love and forgiveness free you to take your eyes off yourself and to meet others' needs. By sacrificing his life, Christ showed that he truly loves you. Now you can love others by following his example and giving of yourself sacrificially.

2.2 Mt 18.3; 19.14 Eph 4.15 Heb 6.5
2.5 Isa 61.6; 66.21 Eph 2.21 1 Tim 3.15 Rev 1.6
2.6 Isa 28.16 Rom 9.32,33 Eph 2.20
2.7 Ps 118.22 Mt 21.42
2.8 Isa 8.14 Lk 2.34,35
2.9 Ex 19.6 Deut 7.6; 10.15 Isa 43.20 Acts 26.18
2.10 Hos 1.10; 2.23 Rom 9.25; 10.19

it you may grow into salvation— 3 if indeed you have tasted that the Lord is good.
4 Come to him, a living stone, though rejected by mortals yet chosen and precious in God's sight, and 5 like living stones, let yourselves be built[h] into a spiritual
house, to be a holy priesthood, to offer spiritual sacrifices acceptable to God
through Jesus Christ. 6 For it stands in scripture:
"See, I am laying in Zion a stone,
a cornerstone chosen and precious;
and whoever believes in him[i] will not be put to shame."
7 To you then who believe, he is precious; but for those who do not believe,
"The stone that the builders rejected
has become the very head of the corner,"
8 and
"A stone that makes them stumble,
and a rock that makes them fall."
They stumble because they disobey the word, as they were destined to do.
9 But you are a chosen race, a royal priesthood, a holy nation, God's own people,[j] in order that you may proclaim the mighty acts of him who called you out of
darkness into his marvelous light.
10 Once you were not a people,
but now you are God's people;
once you had not received mercy,
but now you have received mercy.

[h] Or *you yourselves are being built* [i] Or *it* [j] Gk *a people for his possession*

1.24, 25 Quoting Isaiah 40.6–8, Peter reminds the believers that everything in this life—possessions, accomplishments, people—will eventually fade away and disappear. Only God's will, Word, and work are permanent. We must stop grasping the temporary and focus our time, money, and energy on the permanent—the word of God and our eternal life in Christ.

2.2, 3 One characteristic all children share is that they want to grow up, to be like the big kids or their parents. When we are born again, we become spiritual infants. If we are healthy, we will yearn to grow. How sad it is that some people never grow up. The need for milk is a natural instinct for a baby and a sign of growth. Once we see our need for God's Word and begin to find nourishment in Christ, our spiritual appetite will increase, and we will start to mature. How strong is your desire for God's Word?

2.4–8 In describing the church as God's building, Peter draws on several Old Testament texts familiar to his Jewish Christian readers: Psalm 118.22; Isaiah 8.14; 28.16. Peter's readers would have understood the cornerstone to be Israel; now Peter applies the image to Christ. Once again Peter shows that the church does not cancel the Jewish heritage, but fulfills it.

2.4–8 Peter portrays the church as a living, spiritual house, with Christ as the foundation and each believer as a stone. Paul portrays it as a body, with Christ as the head and each believer as a member (see, for example, Ephesians 4.15, 16). Both pictures emphasize *community.* One stone is not a temple or even a wall; one body part is useless without the others. In our individualistic society, it is easy to forget our interdependence with other Christians. When God calls you to a task, remember that he is also calling others to work with you. Together your individual efforts will be multiplied. Look for those people and join with them to build a beautiful house for God.

2.6 Christians will sometimes face disappointment ("be put to shame") in this life, but their trust in God is never misplaced. God will not let them down. We can safely put our confidence in him, because the eternal life he promises is certain.

2.6–8 No doubt Peter often thought of Jesus' words to him right after he confessed that Jesus was "the Messiah, the Son of the living God": "You are Peter, and on this rock I will build my church, and the gates of Hades will not prevail against it" (Matthew 16.16–18). What is the stone that really counts in the building of the church? Peter answers: Christ himself. What are the characteristics of Christ, the cornerstone? (1) He is completely trustworthy; (2) he is precious to believers; (3) and, though rejected by some, he is the most important part of the church.

2.8 Jesus Christ is called "a stone that makes them stumble, and a rock that makes them fall." Some will stumble over him because they reject him or refuse to believe he is who he says he is. But Psalm 118.22 says that "the stone that the builders rejected has become the chief cornerstone," the most important part of God's building, the church. In the same way today, people who refuse to believe in Christ have made the greatest mistake of their lives. They have stumbled over the one person who could save them and give meaning to their lives, and they have fallen into God's hands for judgment.

2.9 Christians sometimes speak of "the priesthood of all believers." In Old Testament times, people did not approach God directly. A priest acted as intermediary between God and sinful man. With Christ's victory on the cross, that changed. Now we can come directly into God's presence without fear (Hebrews 4.16), and we are given the responsibility of bringing others to him also (2 Corinthians 5.18–21). When we are united with Christ as members of his body, we join in his priestly work of reconciling God and man.

2.9, 10 People often base their self-concept on their accomplishments, but our relationship with Christ is far more important than our jobs, our successes, our wealth, or our knowledge. We have been chosen by God as his very own, and we have been called to represent him to others. Remember that your value comes from being one of God's children, not from what you can achieve. You have worth because of what *God does,* not because of what you do.

2. The conduct of God's people in the midst of suffering

Obey those in authority

11 Beloved, I urge you as aliens and exiles to abstain from the desires of the
flesh that wage war against the soul. 12 Conduct yourselves honorably among the
Gentiles, so that, though they malign you as evildoers, they may see your honorable deeds and glorify God when he comes to judge.[k]

13 For the Lord's sake accept the authority of every human institution,[l]
whether of the emperor as supreme, 14 or of governors, as sent by him to punish
those who do wrong and to praise those who do right. 15 For it is God's will that by
doing right you should silence the ignorance of the foolish. 16 As servants[m] of God,
live as free people, yet do not use your freedom as a pretext for evil. 17 Honor
everyone. Love the family of believers.[n] Fear God. Honor the emperor.

18 Slaves, accept the authority of your masters with all deference, not only
those who are kind and gentle but also those who are harsh. 19 For it is a credit to
you if, being aware of God, you endure pain while suffering unjustly. 20 If you
endure when you are beaten for doing wrong, what credit is that? But if you endure
when you do right and suffer for it, you have God's approval. 21 For to this you have
been called, because Christ also suffered for you, leaving you an example, so that
you should follow in his steps.

22 "He committed no sin,
    and no deceit was found in his mouth."

23 When he was abused, he did not return abuse; when he suffered, he did not
threaten; but he entrusted himself to the one who judges justly. 24 He himself bore
our sins in his body on the cross,[o] so that, free from sins, we might live for righ-

2.11 Rom 12.1; 13.14
2.12 Phil 2.15 Tit 2.8
2.13 Rom 13.1
2.14 Rom 13.3,4
2.15 1 Pet 2.12; 3.17
2.16 Jn 8.32 1 Cor 7.22 Jas 1.25
2.17 Rom 12.10; 13.7
2.18 Eph 6.5 Jas 3.17
2.20 1 Pet 3.14,17
2.21 Mt 11.29; 16.24 Acts 14.22
2.22 Isa 53.9 2 Cor 5.21
2.24 Isa 53.4,5,11

[k] Gk *God on the day of visitation* [l] Or *every institution ordained for human beings* [m] Gk *slaves* [n] Gk *Love the brotherhood* [o] Or *carried up our sins in his body to the tree*

2.11 As believers, we are "aliens and exiles" in this world because our real home is with God. Heaven is not the pink-cloud-and-harp existence popular in cartoons. Heaven is where God lives. It operates according to God's principles and values, and it is eternal and unshakable. Heaven came to earth in the Jewish sanctuary (the tabernacle and temple) where God's presence dwelt. It came in a fuller way in the person of Jesus Christ, "God with us." It permeated the entire world as the Holy Spirit came to indwell every believer.

Someday, after God judges and destroys all sin, the kingdom of heaven will rule every corner of this earth. John saw this day in a vision, and he cried out, "See, the home of God is among mortals. He will dwell with them as their God; they will be his peoples, and God himself will be with them" (Revelation 21.3). Our true loyalty should be to our real home in heaven, not to this earth, because it will be destroyed. Our loyalty should be to God's truth, his way of life, his dedicated people. Because we are loyal to God, we often will feel like strangers in a world that would prefer to ignore God.

2.12 Peter's advice sounds like Jesus' in Matthew 5.16: If your actions are above reproach, even hostile people will end up praising God. Peter's readers were scattered among unbelieving Gentiles who were inclined to believe vicious lies about Christians. Attractive, gracious, upright behavior on the part of Christians could show these rumors to be false and could even win some of the unsaved critics to the Lord's side. Don't write off people because they misunderstand Christianity; instead, show them Christ by your life. The day may come when those who criticize you will praise God with you.

2.12–17 When Peter told his readers to respect the civil government, he was speaking of the Roman Empire under Nero, a notoriously cruel tyrant. Obviously he was not telling believers to compromise their consciences; as Peter had told the high priest years before, "We must obey God rather than any human authority" (Acts 5.29). But in most aspects of daily life, it was possible and desirable for Christians to live according to the law of their land. Today, some Christians live in freedom while others live under repressive governments. All are commanded to cooperate with the rulers as far as conscience will allow. We are to do this "for the Lord's sake"—so that his good news and his people will be respected. If we are to be persecuted, it should be for obeying God, and not for breaking moral or civil laws. For more about the Christian government, see the note on Romans 13.1ff.

2.16 We are free from keeping the law as a means to earning salvation. However, we are still to obey, out of gratitude for our free salvation, the teachings of the ten commandments, for they are an expression of God's will for us.

2.18–23 Many Christians were household slaves. It would be easy for them to submit to masters who were gentle and kind. But Peter encouraged loyalty and persistence even in the face of unjust treatment. In the same way, we should submit to our employers whether they are kind or harsh. By so doing, we may win them to Christ by our good example. Paul gave similar advice in his letters (see Ephesians 6.5–9; Colossians 3.22–25), as did Jesus (Matthew 5.46; Luke 6.32–36).

2.21 There are many reasons why we suffer. Some suffering is the direct result of our own sin; some happens because of our foolishness; and some is the result of living in a fallen world. Peter is writing about suffering that comes as a result of doing good. Christ never sinned, and yet he suffered so that we could be set free. When we follow Christ's example and live for others, we too may suffer. Our goal should be to face suffering as he did—with patience, calmness, and confidence that God is in control of the future.

2.21–25 Peter had learned about suffering from Jesus. He knew that Jesus' suffering was part of God's plan (Matthew 16.21–23; Luke 24.25–27, 44–47) and was intended to save us (Matthew 20.28; 26.28). He also knew that all who follow Jesus must be prepared to suffer (Mark 8.34, 35). Peter learned these truths with Jesus and passed them on to us.

2.24 Christ died for *our* sins, in *our* place, so we would not have to suffer the punishment we deserve. This is called *substitutionary atonement*.

2.25 Heb 13.20; 1 Pet 5.4
3.1 1 Cor 7.16; 9.19; Eph 5.22
3.3 Isa 3.16-24; 1 Tim 2.9
3.4 Ps 45.13; Rom 2.29; 7.22
3.5 1 Tim 5.5
3.6 Gen 18.12
3.7 Mt 5.23,24; 18.19; Eph 5.25; Col 3.19

teousness; by his wounds[p] you have been healed. 25 For you were going astray like
sheep, but now you have returned to the shepherd and guardian of your souls.

Wives and husbands

3 Wives, in the same way, accept the authority of your husbands, so that, even
if some of them do not obey the word, they may be won over without a word
by their wives' conduct, 2 when they see the purity and reverence of your lives. 3 Do
not adorn yourselves outwardly by braiding your hair, and by wearing gold ornaments or fine clothing; 4 rather, let your adornment be the inner self with the lasting
beauty of a gentle and quiet spirit, which is very precious in God's sight. 5 It was in
this way long ago that the holy women who hoped in God used to adorn themselves
by accepting the authority of their husbands. 6 Thus Sarah obeyed Abraham and
called him lord. You have become her daughters as long as you do what is good and
never let fears alarm you.
7 Husbands, in the same way, show consideration for your wives in your life
together, paying honor to the woman as the weaker sex,[q] since they too are also
heirs of the gracious gift of life—so that nothing may hinder your prayers.

[p] Gk *bruise* [q] Gk *vessel*

SUBMISSION
Submission is:

Functional	a distinguishing of our roles and the work we do
Relational	a loving acknowledgement of another's value as a person
Reciprocal	a mutual, humble cooperation with one another
Universal	an acknowledgement by the church of the all-encompassing lordship of Jesus Christ

Submission is voluntarily cooperating with anyone out of love and respect for God first, then secondly, love and respect for that person. Submitting to nonbelievers is difficult, but it is a vital part of leading them to Jesus Christ. We are not called to submit to nonbelievers to the point that we compromise our relationship with God, but we must look for every opportunity to humbly serve in the power of God's Spirit.

3.1ff When a man became a Christian, he usually would bring his whole family into the church with him (see, for example, the story of the conversion of the Philippian jailer, Acts 16.29–33). By contrast, a woman who became a Christian usually came into the church alone. Under Roman law, the husband and father had absolute authority over all members of his household, including his wife. Demanding her rights as a free woman in Christ could endanger her marriage if her husband disapproved. Peter reassures Christian women married to unbelievers that they did not need to preach to their husbands. Under the circumstances, their best approach would be loving service: they should show their husbands the kind of self-giving love that Christ showed the church. By being exemplary wives, they would please their husbands. At the very least, the men would then allow them to continue practicing their "strange" religion. At best, their husbands would join them and become Christians too.

3.1–7 A changed life speaks loudly and clearly, and it is often the most effective way to influence a family member. Peter instructs Christian wives to develop inner beauty rather than being overly concerned about their appearance. Their husbands would be won by their love rather than by their looks. Live your Christian faith quietly and consistently in your home, and your family will see Christ in you.

3.3 We should not be obsessed by fashion, but neither should we be so unconcerned that we do not bother to care for ourselves. Hygiene, neatness, and grooming are important, but even more important are a person's attitude and spirit. True beauty begins inside.

3.5 Accepting authority means cooperating voluntarily with someone else out of love and respect for God and for that person. Ideally, this *submission* is mutual ("Be subject to one another out of reverence for Christ"—Ephesians 5.21). Even when it is one-sided, however, it can be an effective Christian strategy. Jesus Christ submitted to death so that we could be saved; we may sometimes have to submit to unpleasant circumstances so that others will see Christ in us. (Christian submission never requires us to disobey God or to participate in what our conscience forbids.) One-sided submission requires tremendous strength. We could not do it without the power of the Holy Spirit working in us.

3.7 When Peter calls women the "weaker sex" he does not imply moral or intellectual inferiority, but he is recognizing women's physical limitations. Women in his day, if unprotected by men, were vulnerable to attack, abuse, and financial disaster. Women's lives may be easier today, but they are still vulnerable to criminal attack and family abuse. And in spite of increased opportunities in the workplace, most women still earn considerably less than most men, and the vast majority of the nations' poor are single mothers and their children. A man who honors his wife as a member of the weaker sex will protect, respect, help, and stay with her. He will not expect her to work full-time outside and full-time at home; he will lighten her load wherever he can. He will be sensitive to her needs, and he will relate to her with courtesy, consideration, insight, and tact.

3.7 If a man does not treat his wife kindly, his prayers will become ineffective, because a living relationship with God depends on right relationships with others. Jesus said that if you have a problem with a fellow believer, you must make it right with that person before coming to worship (Matthew 5.23, 24). This principle carries over into family relationships. If men use their position to mistreat their wives, their relationship with God will suffer.

Suffering for doing good

8 Finally, all of you, have unity of spirit, sympathy, love for one another, a
tender heart, and a humble mind. 9 Do not repay evil for evil or abuse for abuse;
but, on the contrary, repay with a blessing. It is for this that you were called—that
you might inherit a blessing. 10 For

"Those who desire life
and desire to see good days,
let them keep their tongues from evil
and their lips from speaking deceit;
11 let them turn away from evil and do good;
let them seek peace and pursue it.
12 For the eyes of the Lord are on the righteous,
and his ears are open to their prayer.
But the face of the Lord is against those who do evil."

13 Now who will harm you if you are eager to do what is good? 14 But even if
you do suffer for doing what is right, you are blessed. Do not fear what they fear,[r]
and do not be intimidated, 15 but in your hearts sanctify Christ as Lord. Always be
ready to make your defense to anyone who demands from you an accounting for the
hope that is in you; 16 yet do it with gentleness and reverence.[s] Keep your conscience clear, so that, when you are maligned, those who abuse you for your good
conduct in Christ may be put to shame. 17 For it is better to suffer for doing good,
if suffering should be God's will, than to suffer for doing evil. 18 For Christ also
suffered[t] for sins once for all, the righteous for the unrighteous, in order to bring
you[u] to God. He was put to death in the flesh, but made alive in the spirit, 19 in
which also he went and made a proclamation to the spirits in prison, 20 who in former times did not obey, when God waited patiently in the days of Noah, during the

[r] Gk *their fear* [s] Or *respect* [t] Other ancient authorities read *died* [u] Other ancient authorities read *us*

3.8 Rom 12.16; Eph 4.32
3.9 Lk 6.28; Rom 12.14,17; Heb 6.14; 12.17
3.10-12 Ps 34.12-16
3.13 Prov 16.7
3.14 Isa 8.12,13
3.15 Col 4.6; 2 Tim 2.25; 1 Pet 1.3,17
3.16 1 Pet 2.12; 3.21
3.17 1 Pet 2.20,21; 4.15,19
3.19 1 Pet 4.6
3.20 Gen 6.3; 7.1; Heb 11.7; 1 Pet 1.9,22; 2.25; 4.19

3.8 Peter lists five key elements that should characterize any group of believers: (1) harmony ("have unity of spirit")—pursuing the same goals; (2) sympathy—being responsive to others' needs; (3) love—seeing one another as brothers and sisters; (4) tender hearts—being affectionately sensitive; and (5) humble minds—being willing to encourage one another and rejoice in each other's successes. These five qualities go a long way toward helping believers serve God effectively.

3.8, 9 Peter developed the qualities of tenderness and humility the hard way. In his early days with Christ, these attitudes did not come naturally to his impulsive, strong personality (see Mark 8.31–33; John 13.6–9 for examples of Peter's blustering). But the Holy Spirit changed Peter, molding his strong personality to God's use and teaching him tenderness and humility.

3.9 In our fallen world, it is often acceptable to tear people down verbally or get back at them if we feel hurt. Peter, remembering Jesus' teaching to turn the other cheek (Matthew 5.39), encourages his readers to pay back wrongs by praying for the offenders. In God's kingdom, revenge is unacceptable behavior. So is insulting a person, no matter how indirectly it is done. Rise above getting back at those who hurt you. Instead of reacting angrily to these people, pray for them.

3.10 For more about controlling your tongue, see the notes in James 3.2, 3; 3.6; 3.8; 3.13–18.

3.11 Too often we see peace as merely the absence of conflict, and we think peacemaking is a passive role. But an effective peacemaker actively pursues peace. He or she builds good relationships, knowing that peace is a by-product of commitment. The peacemaker anticipates problems and deals with them before they occur. When conflicts arise, he or she brings them into the open and deals with them before they grow unmanageable. Making peace can be harder work than waging war, but it results not in death but in life and happiness.

3.14, 15 Rather than fear our enemies, we are to quietly trust in ("sanctify") God as the Lord. We must believe that Christ, not our enemies, is truly in control of all events. When he rules our thoughts and emotions, we cannot be shaken by anything our enemies may do.

3.15 Some Christians believe faith is a personal matter that should be kept to oneself. It is true that we shouldn't be boisterous or obnoxious in sharing our faith, but we should always be ready to answer, gently and respectfully, when asked about our faith, our life-style, or our Christian perspective. Can others see your hope in Christ? Are you prepared to tell them what Christ has done in your life?

3.16 You may not be able to keep people from attacking you, but you can at least stop supplying them with ammunition. As long as you do what is right, their accusations will be empty and will only embarrass them. Keep your conduct above criticism!

3.18–20 The meaning of making a proclamation "to the spirits in prison" is not completely clear, and commentators have explained it different ways. The traditional interpretation is that Christ, between his death and resurrection, announced salvation to God's faithful followers who had been waiting for their salvation during the whole Old Testament era. Matthew records that when Jesus died, "many bodies of the saints who had fallen asleep were raised. After his resurrection they came out of the tombs" (Matthew 27.52, 53). Other commentators think this passage says that Christ's Spirit was in Noah as he preached to those imprisoned by sin (but now in hell). Still others hold that Christ went to Hades to proclaim his victory and final condemnation to the fallen angels imprisoned there since Noah's day (see 2 Peter 2.4).

In any case, the passage shows that Christ's good news is not limited. It has been preached in the past as well as in the present; it has gone to the dead as well as to the living. God has given everyone the opportunity to come to him, but this does not imply a second chance for those who reject Christ in this life.

building of the ark, in which a few, that is, eight persons, were saved through
water. 21 And baptism, which this prefigured, now saves you — not as a removal of
dirt from the body, but as an appeal to God for[v] a good conscience, through the
resurrection of Jesus Christ, 22 who has gone into heaven and is at the right hand of
God, with angels, authorities, and powers made subject to him.

Continue to love each other in the midst of suffering

4 Since therefore Christ suffered in the flesh,[w] arm yourselves also with the
same intention (for whoever has suffered in the flesh has finished with sin),
2 so as to live for the rest of your earthly life[x] no longer by human desires but by the
will of God. 3 You have already spent enough time in doing what the Gentiles like
to do, living in licentiousness, passions, drunkenness, revels, carousing, and lawless idolatry. 4 They are surprised that you no longer join them in the same excesses
of dissipation, and so they blaspheme.[y] 5 But they will have to give an accounting
to him who stands ready to judge the living and the dead. 6 For this is the reason the
gospel was proclaimed even to the dead, so that, though they had been judged in the
flesh as everyone is judged, they might live in the spirit as God does.
7 The end of all things is near;[z] therefore be serious and discipline yourselves
for the sake of your prayers. 8 Above all, maintain constant love for one another, for
love covers a multitude of sins. 9 Be hospitable to one another without complaining. 10 Like good stewards of the manifold grace of God, serve one another with
whatever gift each of you has received. 11 Whoever speaks must do so as one speaking the very words of God; whoever serves must do so with the strength that God
supplies, so that God may be glorified in all things through Jesus Christ. To him
belong the glory and the power forever and ever. Amen.

[v] Or *a pledge to God from* [w] Other ancient authorities add *for us*; others, *for you* [x] Gk *rest of the time in the flesh*
[y] Or *they malign you* [z] Or *is at hand*

3.21 Heb 9.14 10.22; 13.18
3.22 Mk 16.19 Rom 8.38
4.1 Rom 6.7 Gal 2.20 Col 3.5 1 Pet 2.21
4.2 Rom 6.2,11
4.3 Rom 13.13 Eph 2.2; 4.17
4.4 Eph 5.18 1 Pet 3.16
4.5 Acts 10.42 17.31 Rom 14.10
4.7 Rom 13.11-13
4.8 1 Pet 1.22
4.10 Rom 12.6-8

3.21 Peter says that Noah's salvation *through water* was a *prefigure* or symbol of baptism, a ceremony of water. In baptism we identify with Jesus Christ, who separates us from the lost and gives us new life. It is not the ceremony by itself that saves us, but faith in Christ's death and resurrection. Baptism is the symbol of the transformation that happens in the hearts of those who believe (Romans 6.3–5; Galatians 3.27; Colossians 2.12). By identifying themselves with Christ through baptism, Peter's readers could never turn back, even under the pressure of persecution. Public baptism would keep them from the temptation to renounce their faith.

4.1, 2 Some people will do anything to avoid pain. As followers of Christ, however, we should be willing and prepared to do God's will and to suffer for it if necessary. Sin loses its power when we suffer if we focus on Christ and what he wants us to do. When our bodies are in pain or our lives in jeopardy, our real values show up clearly, and sinful pleasures seem less important. If anyone suffers for doing right and still faithfully obeys in spite of suffering, that person has made a clean break with sin.

4.3, 4 A person whose life changes radically at conversion may experience contempt from his or her old friends. He or she may be scorned not only because he refuses to participate in certain activities, but also because his priorities have changed and he is now heading in the opposite direction. His very life incriminates their sinful activities. Mature Christians should help new believers resist such pressures by encouraging them to be faithful to Christ. *Dissipation* is wasteful expenditure and intemperate pursuit of pleasure, especially drinking to excess.

4.5 The basis of salvation is whether we have believed in Jesus (Acts 16.31), but the basis for judgment is how we have lived. Those who inflict persecution are marked for punishment when they stand before God. Believers have nothing to fear, however, because Jesus will be the final Judge over all (John 5.22; 2 Timothy 4.1).

4.5, 6 Many people in the early church had concerns about life after death. In Thessalonica, Christians worried that loved ones who died before Christ's return might never see him (1 Thessalonians 4.13–18). Peter's readers needed to be reminded that the dead (both the faithful and their oppressors) will be judged. The judgment will be perfectly fair, he points out, because even the dead have heard the gospel (see also 3.18, 19). The good news was first announced when Jesus Christ preached on the earth, but it has been operating since before the creation of the world (Ephesians 1.4), and it affects all people, the dead as well as the living.

4.7–9 We should live expectantly, because Christ is coming. Getting ready to meet Christ involves continually growing in love for God and for others (see Jesus' summary of the law in Matthew 22.37–40). It is important to pray regularly, and it is also important to reach out to needy people. Your possessions, status, and power will mean nothing in God's kingdom, but you will spend eternity with other people. Invest your time and talents where they will make an eternal difference.

4.9 For more about hospitality, see the note on Romans 12.13.

4.10, 11 Some people, well aware of their abilities, believe they have the right to use them as they please. Others feel that they have no special talents at all. Peter addresses both groups in these verses. Everyone has some gifts; find yours and use them. All our abilities should be used in serving others; none are for our own exclusive enjoyment. Peter mentions speaking and serving. Paul lists these and other abilities in Romans 12.6–8; 1 Corinthians 12.8–11; Ephesians 4.11.

4.11 How is God glorified when we use our abilities? When we use them as he directs, to help others, they will see Jesus in us and praise him for the help they have received. Peter may have been thinking of Jesus' words, "Let your light shine before others, so that they may see your good works and give glory to your Father in heaven" (Matthew 5.16).

Suffering for being a Christian

12 Beloved, do not be surprised at the fiery ordeal that is taking place among
you to test you, as though something strange were happening to you. 13 But rejoice
insofar as you are sharing Christ's sufferings, so that you may also be glad and
shout for joy when his glory is revealed. 14 If you are reviled for the name of Christ,
you are blessed, because the spirit of glory,[a] which is the Spirit of God, is resting
on you.[b] 15 But let none of you suffer as a murderer, a thief, a criminal, or even as
a mischief maker. 16 Yet if any of you suffers as a Christian, do not consider it a
disgrace, but glorify God because you bear this name. 17 For the time has come for
judgment to begin with the household of God; if it begins with us, what will be the
end for those who do not obey the gospel of God? 18 And

"If it is hard for the righteous to be saved,
what will become of the ungodly and the sinners?"

19 Therefore, let those suffering in accordance with God's will entrust themselves to
a faithful Creator, while continuing to do good.

4.13 Rom 8.17 Phil 3.10 2 Tim 2.12
4.14 Mt 5.11 Jn 15.21 2 Cor 4.10 Heb 11.26
4.15 1 Thess 4.11 1 Tim 5.13
4.16 Acts 5.41; 28.22
4.17 Jer 25.29 Rom 2.9 2 Thess 1.8
4.18 Lk 23.31

3. The shepherding of God's people in the midst of suffering

5 Now as an elder myself and a witness of the sufferings of Christ, as well as one
who shares in the glory to be revealed, I exhort the elders among you 2 to tend
the flock of God that is in your charge, exercising the oversight,[c] not under compulsion but willingly, as God would have you do it[d]—not for sordid gain but eagerly. 3 Do not lord it over those in your charge, but be examples to the flock. 4 And
when the chief shepherd appears, you will win the crown of glory that never fades
away. 5 In the same way, you who are younger must accept the authority of the

5.1 Lk 24.48
5.2 Jn 21.16 Acts 20.28
5.4 1 Cor 9.25 Heb 13.20,21
5.5 Jas 4.6

[a] Other ancient authorities add *and of power* [b] Other ancient authorities add *On their part he is blasphemed, but on your part he is glorified* [c] Other ancient authorities lack *exercising the oversight* [d] Other ancient authorities lack *as God would have you do it*

4.14–16 Again Peter brings to mind Jesus' words: "Blessed are you when people revile you and persecute you and utter all kinds of evil against you falsely on my account" (Matthew 5.11). Christ will send his Spirit to strengthen those who are persecuted for their faith. This does not mean that all suffering is the result of good Christian conduct. Sometimes a person will grumble, "He's just picking on me because I'm a Christian," when it's obvious to everyone else that the person's own unpleasant behavior is the cause of his problems. It may take careful thought or wise counsel to determine the real cause of our suffering. We can be assured, however, that whenever we suffer because of our loyalty to Christ, he will be with us all the way.

4.16 It is not shameful to suffer for being a Christian. When Peter and John were persecuted for preaching the good news, they rejoiced because such persecution was a mark of God's approval of their work (Acts 5.41). Don't seek out suffering, and don't try to avoid it. Instead, keep on doing what is right regardless of the suffering it might bring.

4.17, 18 This is not final judgment but God's refining discipline (Hebrews 12.7). God often allows believers to sin and then experience the consequences. He does this for several reasons: (1) to show us our potential for sinning, (2) to encourage us to turn from sin and more constantly depend on him, (3) to prepare us to face other, even stronger temptations in the future, and (4) to help us stay faithful and keep on trusting him. If believers need earthly discipline (judgment) from God, how much more will unbelievers receive it? If it is hard for the righteous to be saved (only because of God's mercy, or as some say, barely saved through persecution), what chance do those have who reject Christ?

4.19 God created the world, and he has faithfully ordered it and kept it since the creation. Because we know he is faithful, we can count on him to fulfill his promises to us. If he can oversee the forces of nature, surely he can see us through the trials we face.

5.1 Elders were church officers providing supervision, protection, discipline, instruction, and direction for the other believers. *Elder* simply means "older." Both Greeks and Jews gave positions of great honor to wise older men, and the Christian church continued this pattern of leadership. Elders carried great responsibility, and they were expected to be good examples.

5.1, 2 Peter, one of Jesus' 12 disciples, was one of the three who saw Christ's glory at the transfiguration (Mark 9.1–13; 2 Peter 1.16–18). Often the spokesman for the apostles, he witnessed Jesus' death and resurrection, preached at Pentecost, and became a pillar of the Jerusalem church. But writing to the elders, he identifies himself as a fellow elder, not a superior. He asks them to "tend the flock of God," exactly what Jesus had told him to do (John 21.15–17). Peter was taking his own advice as he worked along with the other elders in caring for God's faithful people. His identification with the elders is a powerful example of Christian leadership, where authority is based on service, not power (Mark 10.42–45).

5.2–5 Peter describes several characteristics of good leaders in the church: (1) they realize they are caring for God's flock, not their own; (2) they lead out of eagerness to serve, not out of obligation; (3) they are concerned for what they can give, not for what they can get; (4) they lead by example, not force. All of us lead others in some way. Whatever our role, our leadership should be in line with these characteristics.

5.4 The chief shepherd is Jesus Christ. This refers to his second coming, when he will judge all people.

5.5 Both young and old can benefit from Peter's instructions. Pride often keeps elders from trying to understand young people and young people from listening to their elders. Peter told both young and old to be humble and serve each other. Young men should follow the leadership of older men, who should lead by example. Respect your elders, listen to those younger than you, and be humble enough to admit that you can learn from each other.

elders.[e] And all of you must clothe yourselves with humility in your dealings with
one another, for

"God opposes the proud,
but gives grace to the humble."

6 Humble yourselves therefore under the mighty hand of God, so that he may
exalt you in due time. 7 Cast all your anxiety on him, because he cares for you.
8 Discipline yourselves, keep alert.[f] Like a roaring lion your adversary the devil
prowls around, looking for someone to devour. 9 Resist him, steadfast in your faith,
for you know that your brothers and sisters[g] in all the world are undergoing the
same kinds of suffering. 10 And after you have suffered for a little while, the God
of all grace, who has called you to his eternal glory in Christ, will himself restore,
support, strengthen, and establish you. 11 To him be the power forever and ever.
Amen.

Peter's final greetings

12 Through Silvanus, whom I consider a faithful brother, I have written this
short letter to encourage you and to testify that this is the true grace of God. Stand
fast in it. 13 Your sister church[h] in Babylon, chosen together with you, sends you
greetings; and so does my son Mark. 14 Greet one another with a kiss of love.
Peace to all of you who are in Christ.[i]

5.6 Jas 4.10
5.7 Mt 6.25; Heb 13.5
5.8 Job 1.7; Jas 4.7; 1 Pet 1.13
5.9 Acts 14.22; Heb 12.8
5.10 Rom 16.25; 2 Thess 2.17; 2 Tim 2.10; 1 Pet 1.6; 4.10
5.12 Acts 11.23; 2 Cor 1.19; Heb 13.22
5.14 Rom 16.16; Eph 6.23

[e] Or *of those who are older* [f] Or *be vigilant* [g] Gk *your brotherhood* [h] Gk *She who is* [i] Other ancient authorities add *Amen*

5.6 We often worry about our position and status, hoping to get proper recognition for what we do. But Peter advises us to remember that God's recognition counts more than human praise. God is able and willing to bless us according to his own timing. Humbly obey God regardless of present circumstances, and in his good time—either in this life or in the next—he will lift you up.

5.7 Carrying your worries, stress, and daily struggles by yourself shows that you have not trusted God fully with your life. It takes humility, however, to recognize that God cares, to admit your need, and to let others in his family help you. Sometimes we think that struggles caused by our own sin and foolishness are not God's concern. But when we turn to him in repentance, he will bear the weight even of those struggles. Letting God have your worries is active, not passive. Don't submit to circumstances, but to the Lord who controls circumstances.

5.8, 9 Lions attack sick, young, or straggling animals; they choose victims who are alone or not alert. Peter warns us to watch out for Satan when we are suffering or persecuted. Feeling alone, weak, helpless, and cut off from other believers, so focused on our troubles that we forget to watch for danger, we are especially vulnerable to Satan's attacks. During times of suffering, seek other Christians for support. Keep your eyes on Christ, and resist the devil. Then, says James, "he will flee from you" (James 4.7).

5.10 When we are suffering, we feel as though our pain will never end. Peter shows these faithful Christians the wider perspective. In comparison with eternity, their suffering would last only "a little while." Some of Peter's readers would be delivered in their own lifetimes. Others would be released from their suffering through death. All of God's faithful followers are assured of an eternal life with Christ where there will be no suffering (Revelation 21.4).

5.12 Silvanus, also called Silas, was one of the men chosen to deliver the letter from the Jerusalem council to the church in Antioch (Acts 15.22). He accompanied Paul on his second missionary journey (Acts 15.40—18.11), helped Paul write his letters to the Thessalonians (1 Thessalonians 1.1; 2 Thessalonians 1.1), and ministered with Timothy in Corinth (2 Corinthians 1.19).

5.13 *Babylon* was broadly understood by believers to be a reference to Rome. Just as the nation of Israel was under captivity to Babylon, so the Christians were the new Israel and were exiles in a foreign land.

5.13 Mark, also called John Mark, was known to many of this letter's readers because he had traveled widely (Acts 12.25—13.13; 15.36–41) and was recognized as a leader in the church (Colossians 4.10; Philemon 1.24). Mark was probably with the disciples at the time of Jesus' arrest (Mark 14.51, 52). Tradition holds that Peter was Mark's main source of information when he wrote the Gospel of Mark.

5.14 Peter wrote this letter just before the cruel Emperor Nero began persecuting Christians in Rome and throughout the empire. Afraid for his life, Peter had three times denied even knowing Jesus (John 18.15–27). But here, having learned how to stand firm in an evil world, he encourages other Christians who are facing persecution for their faith. Peter himself lived by the words he wrote, because he was martyred for his faith. Those who stand for Christ will be persecuted, because the world is ruled by Christ's greatest enemy. But just as the small group of early believers stood against persecution, so we must be willing to stand for our faith with the patience, endurance, and courage that Peter exhibited.

The Second Letter of PETER

VITAL STATISTICS

PURPOSE:
To warn Christians about false teachers and to exhort them to grow in their faith and knowledge of Christ

AUTHOR:
Peter

TO WHOM WRITTEN:
The church at large

DATE WRITTEN:
About A.D. 67, three years after 1 Peter was written, possibly from Rome

SETTING:
Peter knows that his time on earth is limited (1.13, 14), so he is writing about what is on his heart, warning believers of what will happen when he is gone—especially about false teachers. He reminds them of the unchanging truth of the gospel.

KEY VERSE:
"His divine power has given us everything needed for life and godliness, through the knowledge of him who called us by his own glory and goodness" (1.3).

KEY PEOPLE:
Peter, Paul

SPECIAL FEATURES:
The date and destination are uncertain, and the authorship has been disputed. Because of this, 2 Peter was the last book admitted to the canon of the New Testament Scripture. Also, there are similarities between 2 Peter and Jude.

WARNINGS have many forms—lights, signs, sights, sounds, smells, feelings, and written words. With varied focus, their purpose is the same—to advise wariness and caution because of imminent danger. Responses to these warnings will also vary, from disregard and neglect to evasive or corrective action. How a person reacts to a warning is usually determined by the situation and the source. An impending storm is treated differently than an onrushing automobile, and the counsel of a trusted friend is heeded much more than the flippant remark by a stranger or the fearful guess of a child.

Second Peter is a letter of warning—from an authority none other than the courageous, experienced, and faithful apostle. And it is the last communication from this great warrior of Christ. Soon thereafter he would die, martyred for the faith.

Previously Peter had written to comfort and encourage believers in the midst of suffering and persecution—an external onslaught. But three years later, in this epistle with his last words, he writes to warn them of an internal attack—complacency and heresy. He speaks of holding fast to the nonnegotiable facts of the faith, of growing and maturing in the faith, and of rejecting all who would twist the truth. This would ensure Christ-honoring individuals and Christ-centered churches.

After a brief greeting (1.1), Peter gives the antidote for stagnancy and shortsightedness in the Christian life (1.2–11). Then he explains that his days are numbered (1.12–15) and that the believers should listen to his messages and the words of Scripture (1.16–21).

Next, Peter gives a blunt warning about false teachers (2.1–22). They will become prevalent in the last days (2.1, 2), they will do or say anything for money (2.3), they will laugh at the things of God (2.2, 10, 11), they will do whatever they feel like doing (2.12–17), they will be proud and boastful (2.18, 19), and they will be judged and punished by God (2.3–10, 20–22).

Peter concludes his brief letter by explaining why he has written it (3.1–18)—to remind them of God's Word, that predicted the coming of false teachers and gives the reasons for the delay in Christ's return (3.1–13), and to encourage them to beware of heresies and to grow in their faith (3.14–18).

Addressed to "those who have received a faith as precious as ours," 2 Peter could have been written to us. Our world is filled with false prophets and teachers who claim to have the truth and who clamor for attention and allegiance. Listen carefully to Peter's message and heed his warning. Determine to grow in your knowledge of Christ and to reject all those who preach anything but that which is consistent with God's Word.

THE BLUEPRINT

1. Guidance for growing Christians (1.1–21)
2. Danger to growing Christians (2.1–22)
3. Hope for growing Christians (3.1–18)

While Peter wrote his first letter to teach about handling persecution (trials from without), he wrote this letter to teach about handling heresy (trials from within). False teachers are often subtly deceitful. Believers today must still be vigilant against falling into false doctrine, heresy, and cults. This letter gives us clues to help detect false teaching.

MEGATHEMES

THEME	EXPLANATION	IMPORTANCE
Diligence	If our faith is real, it will be evident in our faithful behavior. If people are diligent in Christian growth, they won't backslide or be deceived by false teachers.	Growth is essential. It begins with faith and culminates in love for others. To keep growing we need to know God, keep on following him, and remember what he taught us. We must remain diligent in faithful obedience and Christian growth.
False Teachers	Peter warns the church to beware of false teachers. These teachers were proud of their position, promoted sexual sin, and advised against keeping the ten commandments. Peter countered them by pointing to the Spirit-inspired Scriptures as our authority.	Christians need discernment to be able to resist false teachers. God can rescue us from their lies if we stay true to his Word, the Bible, and reject those who twist the truth.
Christ's Return	One day Christ will create a new heaven and earth where we will live forever. As Christians, our hope is in this promise. But with Christ's return comes his judgment on all who refuse to believe.	The cure for complacency, lawlessness, and heresy is found in the confident assurance that Christ will return. God is still giving unbelievers time to repent. To be ready, Christians must keep on trusting and resist the pressure to give up waiting for Christ's return.

1. Guidance for growing Christians

1.1 2 Cor 4.13 Eph 4.5 1 Pet 1.1,7; 2.7
1 Simeon[a] Peter, a servant[b] and apostle of Jesus Christ,
To those who have received a faith as precious as ours through the righteousness of our God and Savior Jesus Christ:[c]

1.2 2 Pet 3.18
2 May grace and peace be yours in abundance in the knowledge of God and of
Jesus our Lord.

Character qualities to develop in life

3 His divine power has given us everything needed for life and godliness,

[a] Other ancient authorities read *Simon* [b] Gk *slave* [c] Or *of our God and the Savior Jesus Christ*

1.1 First Peter was written around the time that the Roman Emperor Nero began his persecution of Christians. Second Peter was written two or three years later (between A.D. 66 and 68), after persecution had intensified. First Peter was a letter of encouragement to the Christians who suffered, but 2 Peter focuses on the church's internal problems, especially the false teachers who were causing people to doubt and turn away from Christianity. Second Peter combats their heresies by denouncing the evil motives of the false teachers and reaffirming Christianity's truths – the authority of Scripture, the primacy of faith, and the certainty of Christ's return.

1.2 Many believers want more of God's grace and peace, but they are unwilling to put forth the effort to get to know him better through Bible study and prayer. To enjoy the privileges God offers us freely, we have to combine getting to know him better ("knowledge of God") with complete trust.

1.3, 4 The power to grow doesn't come from within us, but from God. Because we don't have the resources to live full of "glory and goodness," God makes us "participants of the divine nature" to keep us from sin and help us live for him. When we are born again, God by his Spirit empowers us with his own moral goodness. See John 3.6; 14.17–23; 2 Corinthians 5.21; and 1 Peter 1.22, 23.

through the knowledge of him who called us by[d] his own glory and goodness.
4 Thus he has given us, through these things, his precious and very great promises,
so that through them you may escape from the corruption that is in the world because of lust, and may become participants of the divine nature. 5 For this very
reason, you must make every effort to support your faith with goodness, and goodness with knowledge, 6 and knowledge with self-control, and self-control with endurance, and endurance with godliness, 7 and godliness with mutual[e] affection,
and mutual[e] affection with love. 8 For if these things are yours and are increasing
among you, they keep you from being ineffective and unfruitful in the knowledge
of our Lord Jesus Christ. 9 For anyone who lacks these things is nearsighted and
blind, and is forgetful of the cleansing of past sins. 10 Therefore, brothers and sisters,[f] be all the more eager to confirm your call and election, for if you do this, you
will never stumble. 11 For in this way, entry into the eternal kingdom of our Lord
and Savior Jesus Christ will be richly provided for you.
12 Therefore I intend to keep on reminding you of these things, though you
know them already and are established in the truth that has come to you. 13 I think
it right, as long as I am in this body,[g] to refresh your memory, 14 since I know that
my death[h] will come soon, as indeed our Lord Jesus Christ has made clear to me.
15 And I will make every effort so that after my departure you may be able at any
time to recall these things.

Paying attention to Scripture

16 For we did not follow cleverly devised myths when we made known to you
the power and coming of our Lord Jesus Christ, but we had been eyewitnesses of
his majesty. 17 For he received honor and glory from God the Father when that
voice was conveyed to him by the Majestic Glory, saying, "This is my Son, my
Beloved,[i] with whom I am well pleased." 18 We ourselves heard this voice come
from heaven, while we were with him on the holy mountain.

1.3 2 Thess 2.14
1.4 1 Jn 2.15,16
1.6 Gal 5.22
1.7 Jn 13.34,35; Rom 12.10; 1 Pet 1.22
1.8 Jn 15.1-6; Col 1.10; 2 Pet 1.3
1.9 2 Cor 4.3,4
1.10 Mt 22.14; Rom 8.28-31; 1 Thess 1.4; Jude 24
1.11 2 Tim 4.18; 2 Pet 2.20
1.13,14 Jn 13.36; 21.18; 2 Tim 4.6; 2 Pet 1.12; 3.1
1.16 Mt 17.1-5; 28.18; Mk 13.26; Lk 9.28-32; Eph 4.14; 1 Thess 2.19; 1 Tim 1.4
1.17 Heb 1.3

d Other ancient authorities read *through* e Gk *brotherly* f Gk *brothers* g Gk *tent* h Gk *the putting off of my tent*
i Other ancient authorities read *my beloved Son*

1.5–9 Faith is more than belief in certain facts; it must result in action, growth in Christian character, and moral discipline, or it dies away because it does not demonstrate a truly transformed life (James 2.14–17). Peter lists several of faith's actions: learning to know God better, developing patience, doing God's will, loving others. These actions do not come automatically; they require hard work. They are not optional; all of them must be a continual part of the Christian life. We don't finish one and start on the next, but we work on them all together. God empowers and enables us, but he also assigns us the responsibility of learning and growing. We should not be surprised or resentful of the process.

1.6 False teachers were saying that self-control is not needed because works do not help the believer anyway (2.19). It is true that works cannot save us, but it is absolutely false to think they are unimportant. We are saved so that we can grow to resemble Christ and so that we can serve others. God wants to produce his character in us. But to do this, he demands our discipline and effort. As we obey Christ who guides us by his Spirit, we will develop self-control, not only of food and drink, but also of our emotions.

1.9 Our faith must go beyond what we believe; it must become a dynamic part of all we do, resulting in good works and spiritual maturity. Salvation does not depend on good works, but it results in good works. A person who claims to be saved while remaining unchanged does not understand faith or what God has done for him.

1.10 Peter wants to rouse the complacent believers who have listened to the false teachers and believe that because salvation is not based on good works they can live as they want. If you truly belong to the Lord, he says, your hard work will prove it. If you're not working for God, maybe you don't belong to him. If you are the Lord's – and your hard work backs up your claim to be chosen by God ("call and election") – you will never be led astray by false teaching or glamorous sin.

1.12–15 Outstanding coaches constantly review the basics of the sport with their teams, and good athletes can execute the fundamentals consistently well. We must not neglect the basics of our faith when we go on to study deeper truths. Just as an athlete needs constant practice, we need constant reminders of the fundamentals of our faith and of how we came to believe in the first place. Don't allow yourself to remain bored or impatient with messages on the basics of the Christian life. Instead, take the attitude of an athlete who continues to practice and refine the basics even as he learns more advanced skills.

1.13, 14 Peter knows that he will soon die. Many years before, Christ had prepared Peter for the kind of death he would face (see John 21.18, 19). Now Peter knows his death is at hand. Peter was martyred for the faith in about A.D. 68. One tradition says he was crucified upside down, at his own request, because he did not feel worthy to die in the same manner as his Master.

1.16–18 Peter is referring to the transfiguration when Jesus' divine identity was revealed to him and two other disciples, James and John (see Matthew 17.1–8; Mark 9.2–8; Luke 9.28–36).

1.16–21 This section is a strong statement on the inspiration of Scripture. Peter affirms that the Old Testament prophets wrote God's messages, and he puts himself and the other apostles in the same category, because they also proclaim God's truth. The Bible is not a collection of fables or of human ideas about God. It is God's very words given *through* people *to* people. Peter emphasizes his authority as an eyewitness as well as the God-inspired authority of Scripture to prepare for his attack on the false teachers. If these wicked men contradict the apostles and the Bible, their message cannot come from God.

1.19 Lk 1.78,79; 2 Cor 4.6; 1 Pet 1.10-12
1.20 Rom 12.6
1.21 Jn 14.26; 1 Cor 2.13

19 So we have the prophetic message more fully confirmed. You will do well
to be attentive to this as to a lamp shining in a dark place, until the day dawns and
the morning star rises in your hearts. 20 First of all you must understand this, that no
prophecy of scripture is a matter of one's own interpretation, 21 because no prophecy ever came by human will, but men and women moved by the Holy Spirit spoke
from God.[j]

2. Danger to growing Christians

2.1 Deut 13.1-3; Mt 7.15; 2 Cor 11.13; 1 Tim 4.1; Jude 4
2.3 1 Tim 6.5; Jude 16
2.4 Jude 6; Rev 20.1-3
2.5 Gen 6.13-22; 1 Pet 3.20
2.6 Gen 19.24,25; Mt 10.15; 11.23; Rom 9.29; Jude 7
2.7 Gen 19.5,16,29; 2 Pet 3.17
2.9 Jude 6
2.10 2 Pet 3.3; Jude 8,16,18

2 But false prophets also arose among the people, just as there will be false
teachers among you, who will secretly bring in destructive opinions. They will
even deny the Master who bought them—bringing swift destruction on themselves. 2 Even so, many will follow their licentious ways, and because of these
teachers[k] the way of truth will be maligned. 3 And in their greed they will exploit
you with deceptive words. Their condemnation, pronounced against them long
ago, has not been idle, and their destruction is not asleep.
4 For if God did not spare the angels when they sinned, but cast them into hell[l]
and committed them to chains[m] of deepest darkness to be kept until the judgment;
5 and if he did not spare the ancient world, even though he saved Noah, a herald of
righteousness, with seven others, when he brought a flood on a world of the ungodly; 6 and if by turning the cities of Sodom and Gomorrah to ashes he condemned
them to extinction[n] and made them an example of what is coming to the ungodly;[o]
7 and if he rescued Lot, a righteous man greatly distressed by the licentiousness of
the lawless 8 (for that righteous man, living among them day after day, was tormented in his righteous soul by their lawless deeds that he saw and heard), 9 then
the Lord knows how to rescue the godly from trial, and to keep the unrighteous
under punishment until the day of judgment 10—especially those who indulge their
flesh in depraved lust, and who despise authority.

[j] Other ancient authorities read *but moved by the Holy Spirit saints of God spoke* [k] Gk *because of them* [l] Gk *Tartaros* [m] Other ancient authorities read *pits* [n] Other ancient authorities lack *to extinction* [o] Other ancient authorities read *an example to those who were to be ungodly*

1.19 Christ is the "morning star," and when he returns, he will shine in his full glory. Until that day we have the Scripture as a lamp, and the Holy Spirit to illuminate Scripture for us and guide us as we seek the truth. For more on Christ as the morning star, see Luke 1.78; Ephesians 5.14; Revelation 2.28; 22.16.

1.21 "Men and women moved by the Holy Spirit spoke from God" means that the Scripture did not come from the creative work of the prophets' own invention or ecstasy. God inspired the writers, so their message is authentic and reliable. God used the talents, education, and cultural background of each writer (they were not mindless robots); but God cooperated with the writers in such a way to insure that the message he intended was faithfully communicated in the very words they wrote.

2.1 Jesus had told the disciples that false teachers would come (Matthew 24.11; Mark 13.22, 23). Peter had heard these words, and now he is seeing them come true. Just as false prophets had contradicted the true prophets in Old Testament times (see, for example, Jeremiah 23.16–40; 28.1–17) telling people only what they wanted to hear, so false teachers twisted Christ's teachings and the words of his apostles. These teachers belittled the significance of Jesus' life, death, and resurrection. Some claimed he couldn't be God; others claimed he couldn't have been a real man. They allowed and even encouraged all kinds of wrong and immoral acts, especially sexual sin. We must be careful to avoid false teachers today. Any book, tape series, or TV message must be evaluated by God's Word. Beware of special meanings or interpretations that belittle Christ or his work.

2.3 Teachers should be paid by the people they teach, but these false teachers were attempting to make more money by distorting the truth and saying what people wanted to hear. They were more interested in making money than in teaching truth. Peter and Paul both condemned greedy, lying teachers (see 1 Timothy 6.5). Before you send money to any appeal, evaluate it carefully. Is the teacher or preacher clearly serving God or promoting his/her own interests? Will the money be used to promote valid ministry, or will it merely finance further promotions?

2.4–6 If God did not spare angels, or people who lived before the flood, or the citizens of Sodom and Gomorrah, he would not spare these false teachers. Some would have us believe that God will save all people because he is so loving. But we are foolish if we think he will cancel the last Judgment. These three examples should warn us clearly that God judges sin and that unrepentant sinners cannot escape.

2.7–9 Just as God rescued Lot from Sodom, so he is able to rescue us from the temptations and trials we face in a wicked world. Lot was not sinless, but he put his trust in God and was spared when Sodom was destroyed. For more information on Lot, see his Profile in Genesis 14. Also God will judge those who cause the temptations and trials, so we need never worry if justice will be done.

2.10–12 The glorious ones may be angels, all the glories of the unseen world, or more probably, fallen angels. A similar passage is found in Jude 1.8–10. Whichever they are, the false teachers scoffed at the spiritual realities they did not understand, taking Satan's power lightly and thinking they had the ability to judge evil. Many in our world today mock the supernatural. They deny the reality of the spiritual world and claim that only what can be seen and felt is real. Like the false teachers of Peter's day, they are fools who will be proven wrong in the end. Don't take Satan and his supernatural powers of evil lightly or feel arrogant about how defeated he will be. Although Satan will be destroyed completely, he is at work now trying to lure complacent or arrogant Christians over to his side.

Bold and willful, they are not afraid to slander the glorious ones,[p] 11 whereas
angels, though greater in might and power, do not bring against them a slanderous
judgment from the Lord.[q] 12 These people, however, are like irrational animals,
mere creatures of instinct, born to be caught and killed. They slander what they do
not understand, and when those creatures are destroyed,[r] they also will be destroyed, 13 suffering[s] the penalty for doing wrong. They count it a pleasure to revel
in the daytime. They are blots and blemishes, reveling in their dissipation[t] while
they feast with you. 14 They have eyes full of adultery, insatiable for sin. They
entice unsteady souls. They have hearts trained in greed. Accursed children!
15 They have left the straight road and have gone astray, following the road of Balaam son of Bosor,[u] who loved the wages of doing wrong, 16 but was rebuked for
his own transgression; a speechless donkey spoke with a human voice and restrained the prophet's madness.
17 These are waterless springs and mists driven by a storm; for them the deepest
darkness has been reserved. 18 For they speak bombastic nonsense, and with licentious desires of the flesh they entice people who have just[v] escaped from those who
live in error. 19 They promise them freedom, but they themselves are slaves of corruption; for people are slaves to whatever masters them. 20 For if, after they have
escaped the defilements of the world through the knowledge of our Lord and Savior
Jesus Christ, they are again entangled in them and overpowered, the last state has
become worse for them than the first. 21 For it would have been better for them
never to have known the way of righteousness than, after knowing it, to turn back
from the holy commandment that was passed on to them. 22 It has happened to them
according to the true proverb,

"The dog turns back to its own vomit,"

and,

"The sow is washed only to wallow in the mud."

2.11 Jude 9
2.13 Rom 13.13 Phil 3.19
2.14 Eph 2.3 2 Pet 2.18; 3.16
2.15 Num 22.5-7,17 Deut 23.4 Acts 13.10 2 Pet 2.13 Jude 11 Rev 2.14
2.16 Num 22.21-28
2.17 Jude 12,13
2.18 Eph 4.17-19 2 Pet 2.2,14,20 Jude 16
2.19 Jn 8.34 Rom 6.16 Gal 5.13
2.20 Mt 12.43-45 Lk 11.26 2 Tim 2.4 2 Pet 1.2; 2.18
2.21 Ezek 18.24 1 Tim 6.14 Heb 6.4; 10.26 Jas 4.17
2.22 Prov 26.11

3. Hope for growing Christians

3 This is now, beloved, the second letter I am writing to you; in them I am trying
to arouse your sincere intention by reminding you 2 that you should remember
the words spoken in the past by the holy prophets, and the commandment of the
Lord and Savior spoken through your apostles. 3 First of all you must understand
this, that in the last days scoffers will come, scoffing and indulging their own lusts
4 and saying, "Where is the promise of his coming? For ever since our ancestors
died,[w] all things continue as they were from the beginning of creation!" 5 They
deliberately ignore this fact, that by the word of God heavens existed long ago and

3.1 Acts 3.21
3.3 1 Tim 4.1 Jude 18
3.4 Jer 17.15
3.5,6 Gen 1.6,9,10 7.10-12 Ps 24.2; 136.6 Heb 11.3

p Or *angels*; Gk *glories* q Other ancient authorities read *before the Lord*; others lack the phrase r Gk *in their destruction* s Other ancient authorities read *receiving* t Other ancient authorities read *love feasts* u Other ancient authorities read *Beor* v Other ancient authorities read *actually* w Gk *our fathers fell asleep*

2.13, 14 The feast was part of the celebration of the Lord's supper. It was a full meal, ending with communion. The false teachers, although they were sinning openly, took part in these meals with everyone else in the church. In one of the greatest of hypocritical acts, they attended a sacred feast designed to promote love and unity among believers, while at the same time they gossiped and slandered those who disagreed with their opinions. As Paul told the Corinthians, "Whoever, therefore, eats the bread or drinks the cup of the Lord in an unworthy manner will be answerable for the body and blood of the Lord" (1 Corinthians 11.27). These men were guilty of more than false teaching and evil pleasures; they were guilty of leading others away from God's Son, Jesus. *Dissipation* is wasteful expenditure and intemperate pursuit of pleasure, especially drinking to excess.

2.15 Balaam was hired by a pagan king to curse Israel. He did what God told him for a while (Numbers 22–24), but eventually his evil motives and desire for money won out (Numbers 25.1–3; 31.16). Like the false teachers of Peter's day, Balaam used religion for personal advancement, a sin God does not take lightly.

2.19 A person is a slave to whatever controls him or her. Many believe freedom means doing anything we want. But no one is ever completely free in that sense. If we refuse to follow God, we will follow our own sinful desires and become enslaved to what our bodies want. If we submit our lives to Christ, he will free us from slavery to sin. Christ frees us to serve him, resulting in our ultimate good.

2.20–22 Peter is speaking of a person who has learned about Christ and how to be saved, and has even been positively influenced by Christians, but then rejects the truth and returns to his sin. This person is worse off than before, because he or she has rejected the only way out of sin, the only way of salvation. Like a man sinking in quicksand who refuses to grab the rope thrown to him, the person who turns away from Christ casts aside his only means of escape (see the note on Luke 11.24–26).

3.3, 4 Scoffers in the last days would say Jesus was never coming back, but Peter refutes their argument by explaining God's mastery over time. The "last days" are the time between Christ's first and second comings; thus we, like Peter, live in the last days. We must do the work to which God has called us and believe he will return as he promised.

3.7
Isa 66.15
Mt 10.15
1 Cor 3.13
2 Thess 1.8
Heb 12.29
3.9
Isa 30.18
Rom 2.4; 13.11
1 Tim 2.4
Rev 2.21
3.10
Mt 24.43
1 Cor 1.8
1 Thess 5.2
Rev 3.3
3.12
Ps 50.3
Isa 24.19; 34.4
1 Cor 1.7
3.13
Isa 60.21
65.17,25
Rev 21.1,27
3.14
1 Pet 1.7
3.15
Rom 2.4
Col 1.25-27
3.16
Isa 28.13
Heb 5.11
2 Pet 3.2
3.17
1 Cor 10.12
Eph 4.14
2 Pet 2.18
Rev 2.5
3.18
2 Pet 1.2,8

an earth was formed out of water and by means of water, 6 through which the world
of that time was deluged with water and perished. 7 But by the same word the
present heavens and earth have been reserved for fire, being kept until the day of
judgment and destruction of the godless.

8 But do not ignore this one fact, beloved, that with the Lord one day is like a
thousand years, and a thousand years are like one day. 9 The Lord is not slow about
his promise, as some think of slowness, but is patient with you,[x] not wanting any
to perish, but all to come to repentance. 10 But the day of the Lord will come like a
thief, and then the heavens will pass away with a loud noise, and the elements will
be dissolved with fire, and the earth and everything that is done on it will be disclosed.[y]

11 Since all these things are to be dissolved in this way, what sort of persons
ought you to be in leading lives of holiness and godliness, 12 waiting for and hastening[z] the coming of the day of God, because of which the heavens will be set ablaze
and dissolved, and the elements will melt with fire? 13 But, in accordance with his
promise, we wait for new heavens and a new earth, where righteousness is at home.

14 Therefore, beloved, while you are waiting for these things, strive to be
found by him at peace, without spot or blemish; 15 and regard the patience of our
Lord as salvation. So also our beloved brother Paul wrote to you according to the
wisdom given him, 16 speaking of this as he does in all his letters. There are some
things in them hard to understand, which the ignorant and unstable twist to their
own destruction, as they do the other scriptures. 17 You therefore, beloved, since
you are forewarned, beware that you are not carried away with the error of the
lawless and lose your own stability. 18 But grow in the grace and knowledge of our
Lord and Savior Jesus Christ. To him be the glory both now and to the day of
eternity. Amen.[a]

[x] Other ancient authorities read *on your account* [y] Other ancient authorities read *will be burned up* [z] Or *earnestly desiring* [a] Other ancient authorities lack *Amen*

3.7 In Noah's day the earth was judged by water; at the Second Coming it will be judged by fire. This fire is described in Revelation 19.20; 20.10–15.

3.8, 9 God may have seemed slow to these believers as they faced persecution every day and longed to be delivered. But God is not slow; he just is not on our timetable (Psalm 90.4). Jesus is waiting so that more sinners will repent and turn to him. We must not sit and wait for him, but live in the realization that time is short and we have important work to do. Be ready to meet him any time, even today; yet plan your course of service as if he may not return for many years.

3.10, 11 Christ's second coming will be sudden and terrible for those who do not believe in him. But if we are morally clean and spiritually alert, it won't come as a surprise. For other prophetic pictures of the day of the Lord, see Isaiah 34.4; Joel 3.15, 16; Matthew 24; Mark 13; Luke 21; Revelation 6.12–17. Realizing that the earth is going to be burned up, we should put our confidence in what is lasting and eternal and not be bound to earth and its treasures or pursuits. Do you spend more of your time piling up possessions, or striving to develop Christlike character?

3.13 God's purpose for people is not destruction but re-creation (see Isaiah 66.22; Revelation 21, 22). He will purify the heavens and earth with fire, and he will then create them anew. We can joyously look forward to the restoration of God's good world.

3.14 We should not become lazy and complacent because Christ has not yet returned. Instead, we should live in eager expectation of his coming. What would you like to be doing when Christ returns? Is that the way you are living each day?

3.15, 16 By the time of Peter's writing, Paul's letters already had a widespread reputation. Notice that Peter speaks of Paul's letters as if they are on a level with "other scriptures." Already the early church was thinking of them as inspired by God.

3.15–18 Peter and Paul had very different backgrounds and personalities, and they preached from different viewpoints. Paul emphasized salvation by grace, not law, while Peter preferred to talk about Christian life and service. The two men did not contradict each other, however, and they always held each other in high esteem. The false teachers intentionally misused Paul's writings by twisting them to condone lawlessness. No doubt this made them popular, because people always like to have their favorite sins justified, but it totally destroyed Paul's message. Paul may have been thinking of teachers like these when he wrote Romans 6.15: "What then? Should we sin because we are not under law but under grace? By no means!" Peter warns his readers to avoid the mistakes of these wicked teachers by growing in the knowledge of Jesus. The better we know Jesus, the less attractive false teaching will be.

3.18 Peter concludes this brief letter as he began, by urging his readers to get to know God better and better. This is the most important step in refuting false teachers. No matter where we are in our spiritual journey, no matter how mature we are in our faith, the sinful world always challenges our faith. We still have much room for growth. If every day we find some way to draw closer to Christ, we will be prepared to stand for truth in all circumstances.

The First Letter of JOHN

VITAL STATISTICS

PURPOSE:
To reassure Christians in their faith and to counter false teachings

AUTHOR:
The apostle John

TO WHOM WRITTEN:
The letter is untitled and was written to no particular church. It was sent as a pastoral letter to several Gentile congregations. It was also written to all believers everywhere.

DATE WRITTEN:
Probably between A.D. 85 and 90 from Ephesus

SETTING:
John was an older man and perhaps the only surviving apostle at this time. He had not yet been banished to the island of Patmos where he would live in exile. As an eyewitness of Christ, he wrote authoritatively to give this new generation of believers assurance and confidence in God and in their faith.

KEY VERSE:
"I write these things to you who believe in the name of the Son of God, so that you may know that you have eternal life" (5.13).

KEY PEOPLE:
John, Jesus

SPECIAL FEATURES:
John is the apostle of love, and love is mentioned throughout this letter. There are a number of similarities between this letter and John's Gospel—in vocabulary, style, and main ideas. John uses brief statements and simple words, and he features sharp contrasts—light and darkness, truth and error, God and Satan, life and death, love and hate.

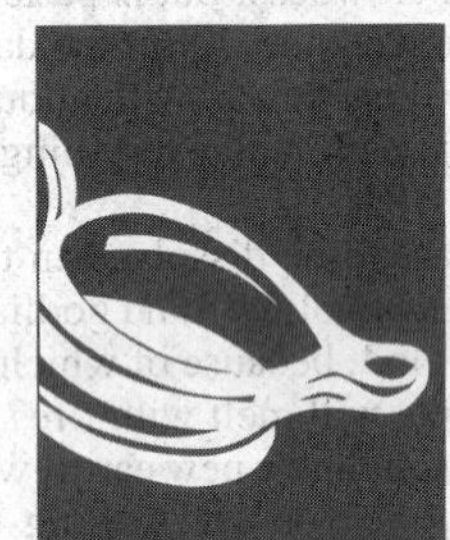

"A GOOD MAN . . . yes . . . perhaps one of the best who ever lived . . . but just a man," say many. Others disagree, claiming that he suffered from delusions of grandeur—a "messiah complex." And the argument rages over Jesus' true identity. Suggestions have ranged from "simple teacher" to "egomaniac" and "misguided fool." Whoever he was, all agree, Jesus left his mark on history.

Hearing these discussions, even Christians can begin to wonder and doubt. Is Jesus really God? Did he come to save sinners like us? Does God care about me?

First John was written to dispel doubts and to build assurance by presenting a clear picture of Christ. Entering history, Jesus was and is God in the flesh and God in focus—seen, heard, and touched by the author of this epistle, John the apostle. John walked and talked with Jesus, saw him heal, heard him teach, watched him die, met him arisen, and saw him ascend. John knew God—he had lived with him and had seen him work. And John enjoyed fellowship with the Father and his Son all the days of his life.

As the elder statesman in the church, he writes this letter to his "little children." In it he presents God as light, as love, and as life. He explains in simple and practical terms what it means to have fellowship with God.

At the same time, false teachers had entered the church, denying the incarnation of Christ. John wrote to correct their serious errors. So, John's letter is a model for us to follow as we combat modern heresies.

John opens this letter by giving his credentials as an eyewitness of the incarnation and by stating his reason for writing (1.1–4). He then presents God as "light," symbolizing absolute purity and holiness (1.5–7), and he explains how believers can walk in God's light and have fellowship with him (1.8–10) with Christ as their advocate (2.1, 2). John urges them to obey Christ fully and to love all the members of God's family (2.3–17). He warns his readers of "antichrists" and the antichrist who will try to lead them away from the truth (2.18–29).

In the next section, John presents God as "love"—giving, dying, forgiving, and blessing (3.1—4.21). Because God loves us, he calls us his children and makes us like Christ (3.1, 2). This truth should motivate us to live close to him (3.3–6). We can be sure of our family relationship with God when our lives are filled with good works and love for others (3.7–24). Again, John warns of false teachers who twist the truth. We should reject these false teachers (4.1–6) as we continue to live in God's love (4.7–21).

In the last section, John presents God as "life" (5.1–21). God's life is in his Son. To have his Son is to have eternal life.

Do you know God? Do you know Christ? Do you know that you have eternal life? First John was written to help you know the reality of God in your life through faith in Christ, to assure you that you have eternal life, and to encourage you to remain in fellowship with the God who is light and love. Read this letter written by one overwhelmed by God's love, and with renewed confidence, pass on his love to others.

THE BLUEPRINT

1. God is light (1.1—2.29)
2. God is love (2.29—4.21)
3. God is life (5.1–21)

John wrote about the most vital aspects of faith so readers would know Christian truth from error. He emphasizes the basics of faith so we can be confident in our faith. In our dark world, God is light. In our cold world, God brings the warmth of love. In our dying world, God brings life. When we feel a lack of confidence, these truths bring us certainty.

MEGATHEMES

THEME	EXPLANATION	IMPORTANCE
Sin	Even Christians sin. Sin requires God's forgiveness and Christ's death provides it for us. Determining to live according to God's standards in the Bible shows our lives are being transformed.	We cannot deny our sin nature, maintain that we are "above" sinning, or minimize the consequences of sin in our relationship with God. We must resist the attraction of sin, yet we must confess when we do sin.
Love	Christ commands us to love others as he did. This love is evidence that we are truly saved. God is the Creator of love; he cares that his children love each other.	Love means putting others first, being unselfish. Love is action—showing others we care—not just saying it. To show love we must give sacrificially of our time and money to meet the needs of others.
Family of God	We become God's children by believing in Christ. God's life in us enables us to love our fellow family members.	How we treat others shows who our Father is. Live as a faithful, loving family member.
Truth and Error	Teaching that the body does not matter, false teachers encouraged believers to throw off moral restraints. They also taught that Christ wasn't really a man and that we must be saved by having some special mystical knowledge. The result was that people became indifferent to sin.	God is truth and light, so the more we get to know him the better we can keep focused on the truth. Don't be led astray by any teaching that denies Christ's deity or humanity. Check the message; test the claims.
Assurance	God is in control of heaven and earth. Because his Word is true, we can have assurance of eternal life and victory over sin. By faith we can be certain of our eternal destiny with him.	Assurance of our relationship with God is a promise, but it is also a way of life. We build our confidence by trusting in God's Word and in Christ's provision for our sin.

1. God is light

Jesus Christ is God's Son

1 We declare to you what was from the beginning, what we have heard, what we 1.1
have seen with our eyes, what we have looked at and touched with our hands, Jn 1.1,4,14 1 Jn 4.14
concerning the word of life— 2 this life was revealed, and we have seen it and 1.2
testify to it, and declare to you the eternal life that was with the Father and was Jn 1.1-4 19.35; 20.30,31
revealed to us— 3 we declare to you what we have seen and heard so that you also 1 Jn 5.11,13,20
may have fellowship with us; and truly our fellowship is with the Father and with
his Son Jesus Christ. 4 We are writing these things so that our[a] joy may be com- 1.4
plete. Jn 15.11

Living in the light of God

5 This is the message we have heard from him and proclaim to you, that God is 1.5
light and in him there is no darkness at all. 6 If we say that we have fellowship with Jn 1.9; 8.12
him while we are walking in darkness, we lie and do not do what is true; 7 but if we 1.7 Heb 9.14
walk in the light as he himself is in the light, we have fellowship with one another, 1.8
and the blood of Jesus his Son cleanses us from all sin. 8 If we say that we have no Prov 20.9

a Other ancient authorities read *your*

1.1 First John was written by John, one of Jesus' original 12 disciples. He was the "disciple whom Jesus loved" (John 21.20) and, along with Peter and James, had a special relationship with Jesus. This letter was written between A.D. 85–90 from Ephesus, before John's exile to the island of Patmos (see Revelation 1.9). Jerusalem had been destroyed in A.D. 70, and Christians were scattered throughout the empire. By the time John wrote this epistle, Christianity had been around for more than a generation. It had faced and survived severe persecution. The main problem confronting the church at this time was declining commitment: many believers were conforming to the world's standards, failing to stand up for Christ, and compromising their faith. False teachers were plentiful, and they accelerated the church's downward slide away from the Christian faith.

John wrote this letter to put believers back on track, to show the difference between light and darkness (truth and error), and to encourage the church to grow in genuine love for God and for one another. He also wrote to assure true believers that they possessed eternal life and to help them know their faith was genuine—so they could enjoy all the benefits of being God's children. For more about John, see his Profile in John 14.

1.1–5 John opens his first letter to the churches much as he opened his Gospel, emphasizing that Christ (the Word of life) is eternal, that God came into the world as a man, that he, John, was an eyewitness to Jesus' life, and that Jesus brings light and life.

1.3 As an eyewitness to Jesus' ministry, John was qualified to teach the truth about him. The readers of this letter had not seen and heard Jesus themselves, but they could trust that what John wrote was accurate. We are like those second-and third-generation Christians. Though we have not personally seen, heard, or touched Jesus, we have the New Testament record of his eyewitnesses, and we can trust that they spoke the truth about him. See John 20.29.

1.3, 4 There are three principles to true Christian fellowship. First, it is grounded in the testimony of the God's Word. Without this underlying strength, togetherness is impossible. Second, it is mutual, depending on the unity of believers. Third, it is daily renewed through the Holy Spirit. True fellowship combines social and spiritual interaction, and it is made possible only by a living relationship with Christ.

1.5, 6 Light represents what is good, pure, true, holy, and reliable. Darkness represents sin and evil. To say "God is light" means that God is perfectly holy and true, and that he alone can guide us out of the darkness of sin. Light is also related to truth, in that it exposes whatever exists, whether it is good or bad. In the dark, good and evil look alike; in the light, they can be clearly distinguished. Just as darkness cannot exist in the presence of light, sin cannot exist in the presence of a holy God. If we want to have a relationship with God, we must put aside our sinful ways of living. To claim that we belong to him but live for ourselves is hypocrisy. Christ will expose and judge such deceit.

1.6 John confronts the first of three claims of the false teachers: that we can have fellowship with God and still walk in darkness. False teachers who thought the body was evil or worthless taught one of two approaches to behavior: either they insisted on denying bodily desires through rigid discipline, or they approved of gratifying every physical lust because the body was going to be destroyed anyway. Obviously the second approach was more popular! Here John exposes the error in both these approaches. Faith is not real unless it results in changed lives and good works, and people cannot be true believers if they continue to sin. The body itself is not evil, because Jesus himself has a human body.

1.7 How does Jesus' blood cleanse us from every sin? In Old Testament times, believers symbolically transferred their sins to an animal, which they then sacrificed (see a description of this ceremony in Leviticus 4). The animal died in their place to pay for their sin and to allow them to continue living in God's favor. God graciously forgave them because of their faith in him, and because they obeyed his commandments concerning the sacrifice. Those sacrifices anticipated the day when Christ would completely remove sin. Real cleansing from sin came with Jesus, the "Lamb of God who takes away the sin of the world" (John 1.29). Sin, by its very nature, brings death—that is a fact as certain as the law of gravity. Jesus did not die for his own sins; he had none. Instead, by a transaction we may never fully understand, he died for the sins of the world. When we commit our lives to Christ and thus identify ourselves with him, his death becomes ours. He has paid the penalty for our sins, and his blood has cleansed us. Just as he rose from the grave, we rise to a new life of fellowship with him (Romans 6.4).

1.8 John attacks the second claim of the false teachers: that people had no natural tendency toward sin, that their sinful nature had been eliminated, and that they were now incapable of sinning. This is at best self-deception, and at worst a lie. They refused to take sin seriously. They wanted to be considered Christians, but they saw no need to confess and repent. The death of Christ did not mean much to them, because they didn't think they needed it. Instead of repenting and being cleansed by Christ's blood, they were encouraging sin among believers. In this life we are always capable of sinning, so we should never let down our guard.

1.8–10 The false teachers denied not only that sin breaks our fellowship with God (1.6) and that they had a sin nature in them (1.8),

1.9 Heb 9.14
1.10 Prov 20.9
2.1 Rom 8.34; 1 Tim 2.5; Heb 7.25; 9.24
2.2 Jn 1.29; 4.42; Rom 3.25; Heb 2.17; 1 Jn 4.10
2.3 1 Jn 3.22,24
2.5 Jn 14.23
2.6 Jn 6.56,57; 15.4

sin, we deceive ourselves, and the truth is not in us. 9 If we confess our sins, he who
is faithful and just will forgive us our sins and cleanse us from all unrighteousness.
10 If we say that we have not sinned, we make him a liar, and his word is not in us.

2 My little children, I am writing these things to you so that you may not sin. But
if anyone does sin, we have an advocate with the Father, Jesus Christ the righteous; 2 and he is the atoning sacrifice for our sins, and not for ours only but also for
the sins of the whole world.

3 Now by this we may be sure that we know him, if we obey his commandments. 4 Whoever says, "I have come to know him," but does not obey his commandments, is a liar, and in such a person the truth does not exist; 5 but whoever
obeys his word, truly in this person the love of God has reached perfection. By this
we may be sure that we are in him: 6 whoever says, "I abide in him," ought to walk
just as he walked.

JOHN COUNTERS FALSE TEACHINGS

John counters two major strands in the false teachings of the heretics in this epistle:

1.6, 8, 10	They denied the reality of sin. John says that if we continue in sin, we can't claim to belong to God. If we say we have no sin, we are only fooling ourselves and refusing to accept the truth.
2.22; 4.1–3	They denied that Jesus was the Messiah—God in the flesh. John said that if we believe that Jesus was God incarnate and trust him for our salvation, we are children of God.

but also that their conduct involved any sin (1.10). This is a lie that ignores one basic truth: all people are sinners by nature and by practice. At conversion all our sins are forgiven – past, present, and future. Yet even after we become Christians, we still sin and must confess. This kind of confession is not to gain God's acceptance, but to remove the barrier to fellowship that our sin has put between us and him. It is difficult, however, for many people to admit their faults and shortcomings, even to God. It takes humility and honesty to recognize our weaknesses, and most of us would rather pretend we are strong. But we need not fear revealing our sins to God – he knows them already. He will not push us away, no matter what we've done. Instead he will draw us to himself.

1.9 Confession is supposed to free us to enjoy fellowship with Christ. It should ease our consciences and lighten our cares. But some Christians do not understand how it works. They feel so guilty that they confess the same sins over and over, and then they wonder if they might have forgotten something. Other Christians believe that God forgives them when they confess, but if they died with unconfessed sins, they would be forever lost. These Christians do not understand that God *wants* to forgive us. He allowed his beloved Son to die just so he could pardon us. When we come to Christ, he forgives all the sins we have committed or will ever commit. We don't need to confess the sins of the past all over again, and we don't need to fear that he will reject us if we don't keep our slate perfectly clear. Of course we should continue to confess our sins, but not because failure to do so will make us lose our salvation. Our relationship with Christ is secure. Instead, we should confess so that we can enjoy maximum fellowship and joy with him.

True confession also involves a commitment not to continue in sin. We wouldn't be genuinely confessing our sins to God if we planned to commit them again and just wanted temporary forgiveness. We should also pray for strength to defeat temptation the next time we face it.

1.9 If God has forgiven us for our sins because of Christ's death, why must we confess our sins? In admitting our sins and receiving Christ's cleansing, we are: (1) agreeing with God that our sin truly was sin and that we are willing to turn from it, (2) ensuring that we don't conceal our sins from him and consequently, from ourselves, and (3) recognizing our tendency to sin and relying on his power to overcome it.

2.1 John uses the address "little children" in a warm, fatherly way. He is not talking down to his readers but is showing affection for them. At this writing, John was a very old man. He had spent almost all his life in ministry, and many of his readers were indeed his spiritual children.

2.1, 2 To people who are feeling guilty and condemned, John offers reassurance. They know they have sinned, and Satan (called "the accuser" in Revelation 12.10) is demanding the death penalty. When you feel this way, don't give up hope – the best defense attorney in the universe is pleading your case. Jesus Christ, your advocate, is the Judge's Son. He has already suffered your penalty in your place. You can't be tried again for a case that is no longer on the docket. United with Christ, you are as safe as he is. Don't be afraid to ask him to plead your case – he has already won it (see Romans 8.33, 34; Hebrews 7.24, 25).

2.2 Jesus Christ is the atoning sacrifice (propitiation) for our sins (see also 4.10). He can stand before God as our mediator, because his death satisfied the wrath of God against sin and paid the death penalty for our sin. Thus he both satisfies God's requirement and removes our sin. In him we are forgiven and cleansed.

2.2 Sometimes it's difficult to forgive those who wrong us. Imagine how hard it would be to forgive everyone no matter what they had done! This is what God has done in Jesus. No one, no matter what he or she has done, is beyond forgiveness. All a person has to do is turn from his or her sin, receive Christ's forgiveness, and commit his or her life to him.

2.3–6 How can you be sure you belong to Christ? This passage gives two ways to know: a Christian should do what Christ says and live as Christ wants. What does Christ tell us to do? John answers in 3.23: "Believe in the name of his Son Jesus Christ and love one another." True Christian faith results in loving behavior; that is why John says our behavior can assure us that we belong to Christ.

2.6 Walking "as he walked" or living as Christ did doesn't mean choosing 12 disciples, performing great miracles, and being crucified. We cannot merely copy Christ's life – much of what Jesus did had to do with his identity as God's Son, his special role in dying for sin, and the cultural context of the first-century Roman world. To live today as Christ did, we must obey his teachings and follow his example of complete obedience to God and loving service to people.

7 Beloved, I am writing you no new commandment, but an old commandment
that you have had from the beginning; the old commandment is the word that you
have heard. 8 Yet I am writing you a new commandment that is true in him and in
you, because[b] the darkness is passing away and the true light is already shining.
9 Whoever says, "I am in the light," while hating a brother or sister,[c] is still in the
darkness. 10 Whoever loves a brother or sister[d] lives in the light, and in such a
person[e] there is no cause for stumbling. 11 But whoever hates another believer[f] is
in the darkness, walks in the darkness, and does not know the way to go, because
the darkness has brought on blindness.

12 I am writing to you, little children,
because your sins are forgiven on account of his name.
13 I am writing to you, fathers,
because you know him who is from the beginning.
I am writing to you, young people,
because you have conquered the evil one.
14 I write to you, children,
because you know the Father.
I write to you, fathers,
because you know him who is from the beginning.
I write to you, young people,
because you are strong
and the word of God abides in you,
and you have overcome the evil one.

2.7 1 Jn 3.2,11,23 2 Jn 5,6
2.8 Jn 1.9; 13.34 Eph 5.8 1 Thess 5.4
2.11 Jn 12.35 2 Cor 4.4 2 Pet 1.9 1 Jn 2.9; 3.15
2.12 Lk 24.27 Acts 4.12 1 Cor 6.11 1 Jn 2.1
2.13 1 Jn 1.1; 4.4
2.14 Eph 6.10 1 Jn 1.1; 1.10 2.13

Do not love this evil world

15 Do not love the world or the things in the world. The love of the Father is not
in those who love the world; 16 for all that is in the world—the desire of the flesh,
the desire of the eyes, the pride in riches—comes not from the Father but from the
world. 17 And the world and its desire[g] are passing away, but those who do the will
of God live forever.

2.15 Mt 6.24 Rom 12.2 Jas 1.27; 4.4
2.16 Prov 27.20 Rom 13.14

[b] Or *that* [c] Gk *hating a brother* [d] Gk *loves a brother* [e] Or *in it* [f] Gk *hates a brother* [g] Or *the desire for it*

2.7, 8 The commandment to love others is both old and new. It is old, because it comes from the Old Testament (Leviticus 19.18). It is new, because Jesus interpreted it in a radically new way (John 13.34, 35). In the Christian church, love is not only showing respect; it is also self-sacrifice and servanthood (John 15.13). In fact, it can be defined as "selfless giving," reaching beyond friends to enemies and persecutors (Matthew 5.43–48). Love should be the unifying force and the identifying mark of the Christian community. It is the key to walking in the light, because we cannot grow spiritually while we hate others. Our growing relationship with God will result in growing relationships with others.

2.9–11 Does this mean that if you dislike anyone you aren't a Christian? These verses are not talking about disliking a disagreeable Christian brother or sister. There will always be people we will not like as well as others. John's words focus on the attitude that causes us to ignore or despise others, to treat them as irritants, competitors, or enemies. Christian love is not a feeling but a choice. We can choose to be concerned with people's well-being and treat them with respect, whether or not we feel affection toward them. If we choose to love others, God will help us express our love.

2.12–14 John is writing to believers of all ages, his "little children," who had experienced forgiveness through Jesus. The older men ("fathers") were mature in the faith and had a long-standing relationship with Christ. The younger men had struggled with Satan's temptations and had won. The boys and girls had learned about Christ and were just beginning their spiritual journey. Each stage of life builds upon the other. As children learn about Christ, they grow in their ability to win battles with temptation. As young adults move from victory to victory, they grow in their relationship with Christ. Older adults, having known Christ for years, have developed the wisdom needed to teach young people and start the cycle all over again. Has your Christian growth reached the maturity appropriate for your stage in life?

2.15, 16 Some people think that worldliness is limited to external behavior—the people we associate with, the places we go, the activities we enjoy. Worldliness is also internal, because it begins in the heart and is characterized by three attitudes: (1) *the desire of the flesh*—preoccupation with gratifying physical desires; (2) *the desire of the eyes*—craving and accumulating things, materialism; and (3) *pride in riches*—obsession with one's status or importance. When the serpent tempted Eve (Genesis 3.6), he tempted her in these areas. Also, when the devil tempted Jesus in the wilderness, these were his three areas of attack (see Matthew 4.1–11).

By contrast, God values self-control, a spirit of generosity, and humble service. It is possible to avoid worldly pleasures while still harboring worldly attitudes in one's heart. It is also possible, like Jesus, to love sinners and spend time with them while maintaining the values of God's kingdom. What values are most important to you? Do your actions reflect the world's values or God's values?

2.17 When our attachment to possessions is strong, it's hard to believe that what we want will one day pass away. It may be even harder to believe that the person who does the will of God will live forever. But this was John's conviction based on the facts of Jesus' life, death, resurrection, and promises. Knowing that this evil world and our desires for its pleasures will end gives us courage to control our behavior and continue doing God's will.

Warning against antichrists

18 Children, it is the last hour! As you have heard that antichrist is coming, so
2.19 now many antichrists have come. From this we know that it is the last hour. 19 They
Mt 24.24 2 Tim 2.19 went out from us, but they did not belong to us; for if they had belonged to us, they
would have remained with us. But by going out they made it plain that none of them
2.20 belongs to us. 20 But you have been anointed by the Holy One, and all of you have
Jn 14.26 1 Jn 2.27 knowledge.[h] 21 I write to you, not because you do not know the truth, but because
2.23 you know it, and you know that no lie comes from the truth. 22 Who is the liar but
Jn 8.19; 16.3 17.3 the one who denies that Jesus is the Christ?[i] This is the antichrist, the one who
1 Jn 4.15; 5.1 denies the Father and the Son. 23 No one who denies the Son has the Father; every-
2.24 1 Jn 1.3; 2.7 one who confesses the Son has the Father also. 24 Let what you heard from the
2 Jn 9 beginning abide in you. If what you heard from the beginning abides in you, then
2.25 Jn 3.15; 6.40 you will abide in the Son and in the Father. 25 And this is what he has promised us,[j]
17.3 eternal life.

[h] Other ancient authorities read *you know all things* [i] Or *the Messiah* [j] Other ancient authorities read *you*

A BOOK OF CONTRASTS

One of the distinct features of John's writing style was his habit of noting both sides of a conflict. He wrote to show the difference between real Christianity and anything else. Here are some of his favorite contrasts.

Contrast between:	*Passage*
Light and darkness	1.5
The new rule and the old commandment	2.7, 8
Loving God and loving the world	2.15, 16
Christ and antichrist	2.18
Truth and falsehood	2.20, 21
Child of God and child of Satan	3.1–10
Eternal life and eternal death	3.14
Love and hatred	3.15, 16
True teaching and false teaching	4.1–3
Love and fear	4.18, 19
Having life and not having life	5.11, 12

2.18–21 John is talking about the last days, the time between Christ's first and second comings. The first-century readers of 1 John lived in the last days, and so do we. During this time, antichrists (false teachers who pretend to be Christians and lure weak members away from Christ) will appear. Finally, just before the world ends, one great antichrist will arise (Revelation 13; 19.20; 20.10). We do not need to fear these evil people, however. The Holy Spirit shows us their errors, so we are not deceived. However, we must teach God's Word clearly and carefully to the peripheral, weak members among us so they won't fall prey to these teachers "who come to you in sheep's clothing but inwardly are ravenous wolves" (Matthew 7.15).

2.19 The antichrists were not total strangers to the church; they once belonged to it, but they did not continue. John does not say why they left; it is clear that their reasons for joining in the first place were wrong. Some people may call themselves Christians for less than the best reasons. Perhaps going to church is a family tradition. Maybe they like the social and business contacts they make there. Or possibly going to church is a long-standing habit, and they have never stopped to ask themselves why they do it. What is your main reason for being a Christian? Unless it is a Christ-centered reason, you may not really belong. You don't have to settle for less than the best. You can become personally acquainted with Jesus Christ and become a loyal, trustworthy follower.

2.20 *Anointing* usually means pouring on special olive oil. This oil was used to appoint kings and special servants for service (1 Samuel 16.1, 13), and also was used by the church when someone was ill (James 5.14). "You have been anointed by the Holy One" means "the Holy Spirit has come upon you." When a person becomes a Christian, he or she receives the Holy Spirit. One way the Holy Spirit helps the believer and the church is by communicating truth. Jesus is the truth (John 14.6), and the Holy Spirit guides believers to him (John 16.13). People who are against Christ are also against his truth, and the Holy Spirit is not working in their lives. When we are led by the Spirit, we can stand against false teachers and the antichrist. Ask him to guide you each day (see 2.27).

2.22, 23 Apparently the antichrists in John's day were attempting to be loyal to God while denying and opposing Christ. This, John firmly states, is impossible. Because Jesus is God's Son and the Messiah, to deny Christ is to reject God's way of revealing himself to the world. A person who accepts Christ as God's Son, however, accepts God the Father at the same time. The two are one and cannot be separated. Many cultists today call themselves Christians but deny that Jesus is divine. We must expose these heresies and oppose such teachings so that the weak believers among us do not succumb to their teachings.

2.24 These Christians had heard the gospel, very likely from John himself. They knew that Christ was God's Son, that he died for their sins and was raised to give them new life, and that he would return and establish his kingdom in its fulness. But they were being infiltrated by teachers who denied these basic doctrines of the Christian faith, and some of the believers were in danger of succumbing to false arguments. John encourages them to hold on to the Christian truth they heard at the beginning of their walk with Christ. It is important to grow in our knowledge of the Lord, to deepen our understanding through careful study, and to teach these truths to others. But no matter how much we learn, we must never abandon the basic truths about Christ. Jesus will always be God's Son, and his sacrifice for our sins is permanent. No truth will ever contradict these teachings in the Bible.

26 I write these things to you concerning those who would deceive you. 27 As
for you, the anointing that you received from him abides in you, and so you do not
need anyone to teach you. But as his anointing teaches you about all things, and is
true and is not a lie, and just as it has taught you, abide in him.[k]
28 And now, little children, abide in him, so that when he is revealed we may
have confidence and not be put to shame before him at his coming.

2.27 Jer 31.33 Jn 14.16,26 16.13 1 Cor 2.10-12
2.28 Mk 8.38 Lk 17.30 1 Thess 2.19

2. God is love

We are God's children

29 If you know that he is righteous, you may be sure that everyone who does
3 right has been born of him. 1 See what love the Father has given us, that we
should be called children of God; and that is what we are. The reason the world
does not know us is that it did not know him. 2 Beloved, we are God's children now;
what we will be has not yet been revealed. What we do know is this: when he[k] is
revealed, we will be like him, for we will see him as he is. 3 And all who have this
hope in him purify themselves, just as he is pure.
4 Everyone who commits sin is guilty of lawlessness; sin is lawlessness. 5 You
know that he was revealed to take away sins, and in him there is no sin. 6 No one
who abides in him sins; no one who sins has either seen him or known him. 7 Little
children, let no one deceive you. Everyone who does what is right is righteous, just
as he is righteous. 8 Everyone who commits sin is a child of the devil; for the devil
has been sinning from the beginning. The Son of God was revealed for this purpose, to destroy the works of the devil. 9 Those who have been born of God do not

3.1 Jn 1.11,12 17.26 Rom 8.16 Eph 1.4,5
3.2 Jn 17.24 Rom 8.19,29 1 Cor 15.49
3.3 1 Thess 5.25 1 Pet 1.7-9
3.5 Jn 1.29 2 Cor 5.21
3.8 Mt 13.38 Jn 8.44; 16.11
3.9 1 Pet 1.3

[k] Or *it*

2.26, 27 Christ promised to send the Holy Spirit to teach his followers and remind them of all that he had taught (John 14.26). As a result, Christians have the Holy Spirit within them ("anointing") to keep them from going astray. In addition, they have the God-inspired Scriptures, against which they can test questionable teachings. To stay true to Christ, we must follow his Word and his Spirit. Let the Holy Spirit help you discern truth from error. For more about who the Holy Spirit is and what he does, see the notes on John 3.6; Acts 1.5; and Ephesians 3.5.

2.27 Christ lives (abides) in us, and we also live in Christ. This means that we place our total trust in him, rely on him for guidance and strength, and live as he wants us to live. It implies a personal, life-giving relationship. John uses the same idea in John 15.5, where he speaks of Christ as the vine and his followers as the branches (see also 3.24; 4.15).

2.28, 29 The visible proof of being a Christian is right behavior. Many people do good works but don't have faith in Jesus Christ. Others claim to have faith but rarely produce good works. A deficit in either faith or right behavior will be a cause for shame when Christ returns. Because true faith always results in good works, those who claim to have faith *and* who consistently live rightly are true believers. Good works cannot produce salvation (see Ephesians 2.8, 9), but they are necessary proof that true faith has actually occurred (James 2.14–17).

3.1 As believers, our self-worth is based on the fact that God loves us and calls us his children. We are his children *now,* not just sometime in the distant future. Knowing that we are his children encourages us to live as Jesus did. For other references about being part of God's family, see Romans 8.14–17; Galatians 3.26, 27; 4.6, 7.

3.1ff Verse 1 tells us who we are—members of God's family ("children of God"). Verse 2 tells us who we are becoming—reflections of God. The rest of the chapter tells us what we have as we grow to resemble God: (1) victory over sin (3.4–9); (2) love for others (3.10–18); and (3) confidence before God (3.19–24).

3.2, 3 The Christian life is a process of becoming more and more like Christ (see Romans 8.29). This process will not be complete until we see Christ face to face (1 Corinthians 13.12; Philippians 3.21), but knowing that it is our ultimate goal should motivate us to purify ourselves. To purify means to keep morally straight, free from the corruption of sin. God also purifies us, but there is action we must take to remain morally fit (see 1 Timothy 5.22; James 4.8; 1 Peter 1.22).

3.4ff There is a difference between committing a sin and remaining in sin. Even the most faithful believers sometimes commit sins, but they do not cherish a particular sin and choose to commit it. A believer who commits a sin repents, confesses, and is forgiven. A person who remains in sin, by contrast, is not sorry for what he or she is doing. Thus this person never confesses and never receives forgiveness. Such a person is against God, no matter what religious claims he or she makes.

3.5 Under the Old Testament sacrifice system, a lamb without blemish was offered as a sacrifice for sin. Jesus is "the Lamb of God who takes away the sin of the world" (John 1.29). Because he lived a perfect life and sacrificed himself for our sins, we can be completely forgiven (2.2). We can look back to his death for us and know we need never suffer eternal death (1 Peter 1.18–20).

3.8, 9 We all have areas where temptation is strong and habits are hard to conquer. These weaknesses give Satan a foothold, so we must deal with them. If we are struggling with a particular sin, however, these verses are not directed at us, even if for the time we seem to keep on sinning. John is not talking about people whose victories are still incomplete; he is talking about people who make a practice of sinning and look for ways to justify it.

Three steps are necessary to find victory over prevailing sin: (1) seek the power of the Holy Spirit and God's Word; (2) stay away from tempting situations; and (3) seek the help of the body of Christ—their accountability and prayers.

3.9 "God's seed abides in them" means that true believers do not make a practice of sinning, because God's new life has been born into them.

3.9 "Those who have been born of God cannot sin" means that true believers do not make a practice of sinning, nor do they become indifferent to God's moral law. All believers still sin, but they are working for victory over sin.

sin, because God's seed abides in them;[l] they cannot sin, because they have been
born of God. 10 The children of God and the children of the devil are revealed in this
way: all who do not do what is right are not from God, nor are those who do not
love their brothers and sisters.[m]

We must love other Christians

11 For this is the message you have heard from the beginning, that we should
love one another. 12 We must not be like Cain who was from the evil one and murdered his brother. And why did he murder him? Because his own deeds were evil
and his brother's righteous. 13 Do not be astonished, brothers and sisters,[n] that the
world hates you. 14 We know that we have passed from death to life because we
love one another. Whoever does not love abides in death. 15 All who hate a brother
or sister[m] are murderers, and you know that murderers do not have eternal life
abiding in them. 16 We know love by this, that he laid down his life for us—and we
ought to lay down our lives for one another. 17 How does God's love abide in anyone who has the world's goods and sees a brother or sister[o] in need and yet refuses
help?

18 Little children, let us love, not in word or speech, but in truth and action.
19 And by this we will know that we are from the truth and will reassure our hearts
before him 20 whenever our hearts condemn us; for God is greater than our hearts,
and he knows everything. 21 Beloved, if our hearts do not condemn us, we have
boldness before God; 22 and we receive from him whatever we ask, because we
obey his commandments and do what pleases him.

23 And this is his commandment, that we should believe in the name of his Son
Jesus Christ and love one another, just as he has commanded us. 24 All who obey
his commandments abide in him, and he abides in them. And by this we know that
he abides in us, by the Spirit that he has given us.

3.10 Rom 13.8-14; 1 Jn 2.9; 4.8
3.11 Jn 13.34; 15.12; 2 John 5,6
3.12 Gen 4.3-8
3.13 Jn 15.18; 17.14
3.14 Jn 5.24; 13.35
3.15 Mt 5.21,22; Gal 5.21
3.16 Jn 3.16; 15.13; Rom 5.8; Eph 5.2,25
3.17 Lk 3.11; Jas 2.15
3.18 Rom 12.9
3.19 Jn 18.37
3.22 Mt 21.22; Jn 8.29; 9.31; Jas 5.16
3.24 Rom 8.9

[l] Or *because the children of God abide in him* [m] Gk *his brother* [n] Gk *brothers* [o] Gk *brother*

3.9 We are "born of God" when the Holy Spirit lives in us and gives us Jesus' new life. Being born again is more than a fresh start; it is a rebirth, receiving a new family name based on Christ's death for us. God forgives us and totally accepts us. The Holy Spirit gives us new minds and hearts, lives in us, and begins helping us be like Christ. Our perspective changes too. We have a mind that is renewed day by day by the Holy Spirit (see Romans 12.2; Ephesians 4.22–24). So we must begin to think and act differently. See John 3.1–21 for more on being born again.

3.12, 13 Cain killed his brother, Abel, when God accepted Abel's offering and not his (Genesis 4.1–16). Abel's offering showed that Cain was not giving his best to God, and Cain's jealous anger drove him to murder. People who are morally upright expose and shame those who aren't. If we live for God, the world will often hate us, because we make them painfully aware of their immoral way of living.

3.15 John echoes Jesus' words that whoever hates another person is a murderer at heart (Matthew 5.21, 22). Christianity is a religion of the heart; outward compliance alone is not enough. Bitterness against someone who has wronged you is an evil cancer within you and will eventually destroy you. Don't let a "root of bitterness" (Hebrews 12.15) grow in you or your church.

3.16 Real love is an action, not a feeling. It produces selfless, sacrificial giving. The greatest act of love is giving oneself for others. How can we lay down our lives? By serving others with no thought of receiving anything in return. Sometimes it is easier to say we'll die for others than to truly live for them—this involves putting others' desires first. Jesus taught this same principle of love in John 15.13.

3.17, 18 These verses give an example of how to lay down our lives for others—to help those in need. This is strikingly similar to James's teaching (James 2.14–17). How clearly do your actions say you really love others? Are you as generous as you should be with your money, possessions, and time?

3.19, 20 Many are afraid they don't love others as they should. They feel guilty because they think they are not doing enough to show proper love to Christ. Their consciences bother them. John has these people in mind in this letter. How do we escape the gnawing accusations of our conscience? Not by ignoring them or rationalizing our behavior, but by setting our hearts on God's love. If we feel guilty, we should remind ourselves that God knows our motives as well as our actions. His voice of assurance is stronger than our conscience. If we are in Christ, he will not condemn us (Romans 8.1; Hebrews 9.14, 15). So if you are living for the Lord but feel you are not good enough, remind yourself that God is greater than your conscience.

3.21, 22 If your conscience is clear, you can come to God without fear, confident that your requests will be heard. John reaffirms Jesus' promise, "Ask, and it will be given you" (Matthew 7.7; see also Matthew 21.22; John 9.31; 15.7). You will receive if you obey, because when you obey, you ask in line with God's will. Of course this does not mean you can have anything you want, like instant riches. If you are truly seeking God's will, there are some requests you will not make.

3.23 In the Bible, a person's name stands for his character. It represents who he really is. We are to believe not only in Jesus' words, but also in his very person as the Son of God. Moreover, to believe "in the name" means to pattern your life after Christ's, to become more like him by uniting yourself with him.

3.24 The mutual relationship, abiding in him as he abides in us, shows itself in Christians who keep these three essential commands: (1) believe in Christ, (2) love the brothers and sisters, and (3) live morally upright. The Spirit's presence is not only spiritual and mystical, but it is also practical. Our conduct verifies his presence.

Distinguish truth from false teaching

4 Beloved, do not believe every spirit, but test the spirits to see whether they are
from God; for many false prophets have gone out into the world. 2 By this you
know the Spirit of God: every spirit that confesses that Jesus Christ has come in the
flesh is from God, 3 and every spirit that does not confess Jesus[p] is not from God.
And this is the spirit of the antichrist, of which you have heard that it is coming; and
now it is already in the world. 4 Little children, you are from God, and have conquered them; for the one who is in you is greater than the one who is in the world.
5 They are from the world; therefore what they say is from the world, and the world
listens to them. 6 We are from God. Whoever knows God listens to us, and whoever
is not from God does not listen to us. From this we know the spirit of truth and the
spirit of error.

Love comes from God

7 Beloved, let us love one another, because love is from God; everyone who
loves is born of God and knows God. 8 Whoever does not love does not know God,
for God is love. 9 God's love was revealed among us in this way: God sent his only
Son into the world so that we might live through him. 10 In this is love, not that we
loved God but that he loved us and sent his Son to be the atoning sacrifice for our
sins. 11 Beloved, since God loved us so much, we also ought to love one another.
12 No one has ever seen God; if we love one another, God lives in us, and his love
is perfected in us.

p Other ancient authorities read *does away with Jesus* (Gk *dissolves Jesus*)

4.1 1 Thess 5.20
4.2 1 Cor 12.3; 1 Jn 1.2; 2.23
4.4 Jn 12.31; 14.30; Rom 8.31
4.5 Jn 15.19; 17.14,16
4.6 Jn 8.47; 10.27; 14.17; 1 Cor 14.37; 1 Tim 4.1
4.8 Ex 34.4,5; Mic 7.18; 1 Jn 4.7,16
4.10 Jn 15.16; Rom 5.8,10; Tit 3.4,5
4.12 Jn 1.18; 14.23; 1 Tim 6.16

4.1, 2 "Do not believe every spirit, but test the spirits" means we shouldn't believe everything we hear just because someone says it is a message inspired by God. There are many ways to test teachers to see if their message is truly from God. One is to check their words with what God says in the Bible. Other tests include their commitment to the body of believers (2.19), their life-style (3.23, 24), and the fruit of their ministry (4.6). But the most important test of all, says John, is what they believe about Christ. Do they teach that Jesus is fully God and fully man? Our world is filled with voices claiming to speak for God. Give them these tests to see if they are indeed speaking God's truth.

4.1–3 Some people believe everything they read or hear. Unfortunately, many ideas printed and taught are not true. Christians should have faith, but they should not be gullible. Verify every message you hear, even if the person who brings it says it's from God. If the message is truly from God, it will be consistent with Christ's teachings.

4.3 The antichrist will be a person who epitomizes all that is evil, and he will be readily received by an evil world. He is more fully described in 2 Thessalonians 2.3–12 and Revelation 13.

4.4 It is easy to be frightened by the wickedness we see all around us and overwhelmed by the problems we face. Evil is obviously much stronger than we are. John assures us, however, that God is even stronger. He will conquer all evil—and his Spirit and his Word live in our hearts!

4.6 False teachers are popular with the world because, like the false prophets of the Old Testament, they tell people what they want to hear. John warns that Christians who faithfully teach God's Word will not win any popularity contests in the world. People don't want to hear their sins denounced; they don't want to listen to demands that they change their behavior. A false teacher will be well received by non-Christians who never are won to Christ.

4.7ff Everyone believes that love is important, but love is usually thought of as a feeling. In reality, love is a choice and an action, as 1 Corinthians 13.4–7 shows. God is the source of our love: he loved us enough to sacrifice his Son for us. Jesus is our example of what it means to love; everything he did in life and death was supremely loving. The Holy Spirit gives us the power to love; he lives in our hearts and makes us more and more like Jesus. God's love always involves a choice and an action, and our love should be like his. How well do you display your love for God in the choices you make and the actions you take?

4.8 John says, "God is love," not "Love is God." Our world, with its shallow and selfish view of love, has turned these words around and contaminated our understanding of love. The world thinks that love is what makes a person feel good, and that it is all right to sacrifice moral principles and others' rights in order to obtain such "love." But that isn't real love; it is the exact opposite—selfishness. And God is not that kind of "love." Real love is like God who is holy, just, and perfect. If we truly know God, we will love as he does.

4.9 Jesus is God's *only* Son. While all believers are sons and daughters of God, only Jesus lives in this special, unique relationship (see John 1.18; 3.16).

4.9, 10 Love explains (1) why God creates—because he loves, he creates people to love; (2) why God cares—because he loves them, he cares for sinful people; (3) why we are free to choose—he wants a loving response from us; (4) why Christ died—his love for us caused him to seek a solution to the problem of sin; and (5) why we receive eternal life—his love expresses itself to us forever.

4.10 Nothing sinful or evil can exist in God's presence. He is absolute goodness. He cannot overlook, condone, or excuse sin as though it never happened. He loves us, but his love does not make him morally lax. If we trust in Christ, however, we will not have to bear the penalty for our sins (1 Peter 2.24). We will be acquitted (Romans 5.18) by his atoning sacrifice.

4.12 If no one has ever seen God, how can we ever know him? John in his Gospel said, "the only Son, who is close to the Father's heart, who has made him known" (John 1.18). Jesus is the complete expression of God in human form, and he has revealed God to us. When we love one another, the invisible God reveals himself to others through us, and his love is made complete ("perfected").

4.13 Jn 14.20 Rom 8.9
4.14 Jn 1.14; 3.17 4.42
4.15 Mt 16.16 Jn 6.69 Rom 10.9
4.17 Mt 10.15 Jas 2.13
4.18 Rom 8.15
4.21 Lev 19.18 Mt 5.43; 22.37 Jn 13.34

13 By this we know that we abide in him and he in us, because he has given us
of his Spirit. 14 And we have seen and do testify that the Father has sent his Son as
the Savior of the world. 15 God abides in those who confess that Jesus is the Son of
God, and they abide in God. 16 So we have known and believe the love that God has
for us.

God is love, and those who abide in love abide in God, and God abides in them.
17 Love has been perfected among us in this: that we may have boldness on the day
of judgment, because as he is, so are we in this world. 18 There is no fear in love,
but perfect love casts out fear; for fear has to do with punishment, and whoever
fears has not reached perfection in love. 19 We love[q] because he first loved us.
20 Those who say, "I love God," and hate their brothers or sisters,[r] are liars; for
those who do not love a brother or sister[s] whom they have seen, cannot love God
whom they have not seen. 21 The commandment we have from him is this: those
who love God must love their brothers and sisters[r] also.

[q] Other ancient authorities add *him*; others add *God* [r] Gk *brothers* [s] Gk *brother*

HERESIES Most of the eyewitnesses to Jesus' ministry had died by the time John composed this epistle. Some of the second- or third-generation Christians began to have doubts about what they had been taught about Jesus. Some Christians with a Greek background had a hard time believing that Jesus was human as well as divine because in Platonic thought the spirit was all-important. The body was only a prison from which one desired to escape. Heresies developed from a uniting of this kind of Platonic thought and Christianity.

A particularly widespread false teaching, later called *Docetism* (from a Greek word meaning "to seem"), held that Jesus was actually a spirit who only appeared to have a body. In reality he cast no shadow and left no footprints; he was God, but not man. Another heretical teaching, related to *Gnosticism* (from a Greek word meaning "knowledge"), held that all physical matter was evil, the spirit was good, and only the intellectually enlightened could enjoy the benefits of religion. Both groups found it hard to believe in a Savior who was fully human.

John answers these false teachers as an eyewitness to Jesus' life on earth. He saw Jesus, talked with him, touched him—he knew that Jesus was more than a mere spirit. In the very first sentence of his letter, John establishes that Jesus had been alive before the world began and also that he lived as a man among men. In other words, he was both divine and human.

Through the centuries, many heretics have denied that Jesus was both God and man. In John's day people had trouble believing he was man; today more people have problems seeing him as God. But Jesus' divine-human nature is the pivotal issue of Christianity. Before you accept what religious teachers say about any topic, listen carefully to what they believe about Jesus. To deny either his divinity or his humanity is to consider him less than Christ, the Savior.

4.12 Some people love to be with others. They befriend strangers easily and always are surrounded by many friends. Other people are shy or reserved. They have a few friends, but they are uncomfortable talking with people they don't know or mingling in crowds. Shy people don't need to become extroverts in order to love others. John isn't telling us *how many* people to love, but *how much* to love the people we already know. Our job is to love faithfully the people God has given us to love, whether there are two or two hundred of them. If God sees that we are ready to love others, he will bring them to us. No matter how shy we are, we don't need to be afraid of the love commandment. God provides us the strength to do what he asks.

4.13 When we become Christians, we receive the Holy Spirit. God's presence in our lives is proof that we really belong to him. He also gives us the power to love (Romans 5.5; 8.9; 2 Corinthians 1.22). Rely on that power as you reach out to others. As you do so, you will gain confidence. See also Romans 8.16.

4.17 The day of Judgment is that time when all people will appear before Christ and be held accountable for their actions. With God living in us through Christ, we have no reason to fear this day because we have been saved from punishment. Instead, we can look forward to the day of Judgment, because it will mean the end of sin and the beginning of a face-to-face relationship with Jesus Christ.

4.18 If we ever are afraid of the future, eternity, heaven, or God's judgment, we can remind ourselves of God's love. We know he loves us perfectly (Romans 8.38, 39). We can resolve our fears first by focusing on his immeasurable love for us, then by allowing him to love others through us. His love will quiet your fears and give you confidence.

4.19 God's love is the source of all human love, and it spreads like fire. In loving his children, he kindles a flame in their hearts. In turn, they love others, who are warmed by God's love through them.

4.20, 21 It is easy to say we love God when that love doesn't cost us anything more than weekly attendance at religious services. But the real test of our love for God is how we treat the people right in front of us – our family members and fellow believers. We cannot truly love God while neglecting to love those who are created in his image.

3. God is life

5 Everyone who believes that Jesus is the Christ[t] has been born of God, and
everyone who loves the parent loves the child. 2 By this we know that we love
the children of God, when we love God and obey his commandments. 3 For the love
of God is this, that we obey his commandments. And his commandments are not
burdensome, 4 for whatever is born of God conquers the world. And this is the
victory that conquers the world, our faith. 5 Who is it that conquers the world but
the one who believes that Jesus is the Son of God?
6 This is the one who came by water and blood, Jesus Christ, not with the water
only but with the water and the blood. And the Spirit is the one that testifies, for the
Spirit is the truth. 7 There are three that testify:[u] 8 the Spirit and the water and the
blood, and these three agree. 9 If we receive human testimony, the testimony of
God is greater; for this is the testimony of God that he has testified to his Son.
10 Those who believe in the Son of God have the testimony in their hearts. Those
who do not believe in God[v] have made him a liar by not believing in the testimony
that God has given concerning his Son. 11 And this is the testimony: God gave us
eternal life, and this life is in his Son. 12 Whoever has the Son has life; whoever
does not have the Son of God does not have life.
13 I write these things to you who believe in the name of the Son of God, so that
you may know that you have eternal life.
14 And this is the boldness we have in him, that if we ask anything according
to his will, he hears us. 15 And if we know that he hears us in whatever we ask, we
know that we have obtained the requests made of him. 16 If you see your brother or
sister[w] committing what is not a mortal sin, you will ask, and God[x] will give life
to such a one—to those whose sin is not mortal. There is sin that is mortal; I do not
say that you should pray about that. 17 All wrongdoing is sin, but there is sin that is
not mortal.
18 We know that those who are born of God do not sin, but the one who was

5.1 Jn 1.11 8.41,42
5.3 Mic 6.8 Mt 11.30 1 Jn 2.3
5.5 1 Cor 15.57
5.6 Hag 2.5 Mt 18.16 Jn 15.26; 19.34 Rev 19.11,13
5.9 Mt 3.16,17 Jn 5.31-38; 8.18
5.10 Jn 3.18,33 Rom 8.16 Gal 4.6
5.11 Jn 1.4
5.12 Jn 14.6; 17.2,3
5.13 Jn 20.31
5.14 Mt 7.7 Jn 14.13 15.7
5.16 Num 15.30 Jer 7.16; 14.11 Mk 3.29 Heb 6.4; 10.26 Jas 5.15
5.18 Jn 10.28,29

[t] Or *the Messiah* [u] A few other authorities read (with variations) *7 There are three that testify in heaven, the Father, the Word, and the Holy Spirit, and these three are one. 8 And there are three that testify on earth:* [v] Other ancient authorities read *in the Son* [w] Gk *your brother* [x] Gk *he*

5.1, 2 When we become Christians, we become part of God's family, with fellow believers as our brothers and sisters. It is God who determines who the other family members are, not us. We are simply called to accept and love them. How well do you treat your fellow family members?

5.3, 4 Jesus never promised that obeying him would be easy. But the hard work and self-discipline of serving Christ are no burden to those who love him. And if our load starts to feel heavy, we can always trust Christ to help us bear it (see Matthew 11.28–30).

5.6–8 The phrase "came by water and blood" may refer to Jesus' baptism and his crucifixion. At this time, there was a false teaching in circulation that said Jesus was God only between his baptism and his death—that is, he was merely human until he was baptized, at which time "the Christ" then descended upon him, but then later left him before his death on the cross. But if Jesus died only as a man, he could not have taken upon himself the sins of the world, and Christianity would be an empty religion. Only an act of God could take away the punishment that we deserve for our sin.

5.7–9 In the Gospels, God twice clearly declared that Jesus is his Son—once at Jesus' baptism (Matthew 3.16, 17), and once at his transfiguration (Matthew 17.5).

5.12 Whoever believes in God's Son has eternal life. He is all you need. You don't need to *wait* for it, because eternal life begins today. You don't need to *work* for it, because it is already yours. You don't need to *worry* about it, because you have been given eternal life by God himself, and it is guaranteed.

5.13 Some people *hope* they will be given eternal life. John says we can *know* we have it. Our certainty is based on God's promise that he has given us eternal life through his Son. This is true whether you feel close to God or distant from him. Eternal life is based not on feelings, but on facts. You can know that you have eternal life if you believe God's truth. If you aren't sure that you are a Christian, ask yourself: "Have I honestly committed my life to him as my Savior and Lord?" If so, you know by faith that you are indeed a child of God.

5.14, 15 The emphasis here is on God's will, not our will. When we communicate with God, we don't demand what we want; rather, we discuss with him what *he* wants for us. If we align our prayers to his will, he will listen; and we can be certain that if he listens, he will give us a definite answer. Start praying with confidence!

5.16, 17 A *mortal sin* is one that leads to death. Commentators differ widely in their thoughts about what this mortal sin is, and whether the death it causes is physical or spiritual. Paul wrote that some Christians had died because they took communion "in an unworthy manner" (1 Corinthians 11.27–30), and Ananias and Sapphira were struck dead when they lied to God (Acts 5.1–11). Blasphemy against the Holy Spirit results in spiritual death (Mark 3.29), and the book of Hebrews describes the spiritual death of the person who turns against Christ (Hebrews 6.4–6). John was probably thinking of the people who had left the Christian fellowship and joined the antichrists. By rejecting the only way of salvation, these people were putting themselves out of reach of prayer. In most cases, however, even if we know what the mortal sin is, we have no sure way of knowing if a certain person has committed it. Therefore we should continue praying for our loved ones and Christian brothers and sisters, leaving the judging up to God. Note that John says, "I do not say that you should pray about that," rather than "You cannot pray about that." He recognized the lack of certainty.

5.18, 19 Christians commit sins, of course, but they ask God to

5.20 Lk 24.45 Jn 1.1,18; 14.20 15.5; 17.3,21,23 1 Jn 5.5,10 Rev 3.7

5.21 1 Cor 10.7 1 Thess 1.9

born of God protects them, and the evil one does not touch them. 19 We know that
we are God's children, and that the whole world lies under the power of the evil
one. 20 And we know that the Son of God has come and has given us understanding
so that we may know him who is true;[y] and we are in him who is true, in his Son
Jesus Christ. He is the true God and eternal life.
21 Little children, keep yourselves from idols.[z]

[y] Other ancient authorities read *know the true God* [z] Other ancient authorities add *Amen*

forgive them, and then they continue serving him. God has freed them from their slavery to Satan, and he keeps them safe from Satan's continued attacks. The rest of the world does not have the Christian's freedom to obey God. Unless they come to Christ in faith, they have no choice but to obey Satan. There is no middle ground; people either belong to God and obey him, or they live under Satan's control.

5.21 An idol is anything that substitutes for the true faith, anything that robs Christ of his full deity and humanity, any human idea that claims to be more authoritative than the Bible, any loyalty that replaces God as the center of our lives.

5.21 What we think about Jesus Christ is central to our teaching, preaching, and living. Jesus is the God-man, fully God and fully human at the same time. He came to earth to die in our place for our sins. Through faith in him, we can have eternal life and the power to do his will. What is your answer to the most important question you could ever ask—who is Jesus Christ?

The Second Letter of JOHN

VITAL STATISTICS

PURPOSE:
To emphasize the basics of following Christ—truth and love—and to warn against false teachers

AUTHOR:
The apostle John

TO WHOM WRITTEN:
To "the elect lady" and her household—or possibly to a local church

DATE WRITTEN:
About the same time as 1 John, around A.D. 90, from Ephesus

SETTING:
Evidently this woman and her family were involved in one of the churches that John was overseeing—they had developed a strong friendship. John was warning her of the false teachers who were becoming prevalent in some of the churches.

KEY VERSE:
"And this is love, that we walk according to his commandments; this is the commandment just as you have heard it from the beginning—you must walk in it" (1.6).

KEY PEOPLE:
John, the elect lady, and her children

TRUTH and *love* are frequently discussed in our world, but seldom practiced.

From politicians to salesmen, people conveniently ignore or conceal facts and use words to enhance positions or sell products. Perjury is common, and integrity and credibility are endangered species. Words, twisted in meaning and torn from context, have become mere tools for ego building. It is not surprising that we have to "swear" to tell the truth.

And what about love? Our world is filled with its words—popular songs, greeting cards, media counselors, and romantic novels shower us with notions and dreams of ethereal, idyllic relationships and feelings. Real love, however, is scarce—selfless giving, caring, sharing, and even dying. We yearn to love and be loved but see few living examples of real love. Plentiful are those who grasp, hoard, and watch out for "number one."

Christ is the antithesis of society's prevailing values—falsehood and self-centeredness—for *he is truth and love*, in person. Therefore, all who claim loyalty to him must be committed to these ideals—following the truth and living the truth; reflecting love and acting with love toward one another.

The apostle John had seen Truth and Love firsthand—he had been with Jesus. So affected was this disciple that all of his writings (the Gospel of John, the letters of 1, 2, and 3 John, and the book of Revelation) are filled with this theme—truth and love are vital to the Christian and are inseparable in the Christian life. Second John, his brief letter to a dear friend, is no different. John says to follow the truth and obey God (1.4), watch out for false leaders (1.7), and love God and each other (1.6).

Second John will take just a few minutes to read, but its message should last a lifetime. As you reflect on these few paragraphs penned by the wise and aged follower of Christ, recommit yourself to being a person of truth, of love, and of obedience to the Lord.

THE BLUEPRINT

1. Watch out for false teachers (1.1–11)
2. John's final words (1.12, 13)

False teachers were a dangerous problem for the church to which John was writing. His warning against giving hospitality to false teachers may sound harsh and unloving to many today. Yet these men were teaching heresy that could seriously harm many believers—for eternity.

MEGATHEMES

THEME	EXPLANATION	IMPORTANCE
Truth	Following God's Word, the Bible, is essential to Christian living because God is truth. Christ's true followers consistently obey his truth.	To be loyal to Christ's teaching we must seek to know the Bible, but never twist its message to our own needs or purposes, nor encourage others who misuse it.
Love	Christ's command is for Christians to love one another. This is the basic ingredient of true Christianity.	To obey Christ fully, we must believe his command to love others. Helping, giving, and meeting needs put love into practice.
False Leaders	We must be wary of religious leaders who are not true to Christ's teaching. We should not give them a platform to spread false teaching.	Don't encourage those who are contrary to Christ. Politely remove yourself from association with false leaders. Be aware of what's being taught in your church.

1.2 Jn 8.32 14.16,17 2 Cor 4.7,10 1 Jn 1.8; 3.18
1.5 Jn 13.34; 15.12 Eph 5.2 1 Pet 1.22
1.6 Jn 14.15 15.10,14 Rom 13.8 1 Jn 2.7; 4.7-12
1.7 1 Tim 4.1-5 2 Pet 2.1-3 1 Jn 2.18,26 4.1-3
1.8 Phil 3.14; 4.1
1.9 Jn 8.31; 15.7 1 Jn 2.23,24

1. Watch out for false teachers

1 The elder to the elect lady and her children, whom I love in the truth, and not
only I but also all who know the truth, 2 because of the truth that abides in us and
will be with us forever:
3 Grace, mercy, and peace will be with us from God the Father and from[a] Jesus
Christ, the Father's Son, in truth and love.
4 I was overjoyed to find some of your children walking in the truth, just as we
have been commanded by the Father. 5 But now, dear lady, I ask you, not as though
I were writing you a new commandment, but one we have had from the beginning,
let us love one another. 6 And this is love, that we walk according to his commandments; this is the commandment just as you have heard it from the beginning—you
must walk in it.
7 Many deceivers have gone out into the world, those who do not confess that
Jesus Christ has come in the flesh; any such person is the deceiver and the antichrist! 8 Be on your guard, so that you do not lose what we[b] have worked for, but
may receive a full reward. 9 Everyone who does not abide in the teaching of Christ,
but goes beyond it, does not have God; whoever abides in the teaching has both the

[a] Other ancient authorities add *the Lord* [b] Other ancient authorities read *you*

1.1 The "elder" is John, one of Jesus' 12 disciples and the writer of the Gospel of John, three epistles, and the book of Revelation. For more information about him, see his Profile in John 14. This letter was written shortly after 1 John to warn about false teachers. The salutation, "to the elect lady and her children," could refer to a specific woman, or to a church whose identity is no longer known. Perhaps the church from where John wrote was Ephesus.

1.1–4 The "truth" is the truth about Jesus Christ, as opposed to the lies of the false teachers (see 1 John 2.21–23).

1.5, 6 The love Christians should have for one another is a recurrent New Testament theme. Yet love for one's neighbor is an old command first appearing in the third book of Moses (Leviticus 19.18). We can show love in many ways: by avoiding prejudice and discrimination, by accepting people, by listening, helping, giving, serving, and refusing to judge. But just knowing God's command is not enough. We must put it into practice. (See also Matthew 22.37–39 and 1 John 2.7, 8.)

1.7 In John's day, many false teachers taught that spirit was good and matter was evil; therefore, they reasoned that Jesus could not have been both God and man. In strong terms, John warns against this kind of teaching. There are still many false teachers who promote an understanding of Jesus that is not biblical. They are dangerous because they twist the truth and undermine the foundations of Christian faith. They may use the right words but change the meanings. The way your teachers live shows a lot about what they believe about Christ. For more on testing teachers, see 1 John 4.1.

1.8 The full reward to which John refers is not salvation but the rewards of loyal service. All who value the truth and persistently hold to it will win their full reward. Those who live for themselves and justify it by teaching false doctrines will lose that reward (see Matthew 7.21–23).

Father and the Son. 10 Do not receive into the house or welcome anyone who comes
to you and does not bring this teaching; 11 for to welcome is to participate in the evil
deeds of such a person.

1.10
Rom 16.17
1 Cor 5.11
Tit 3.10

2. John's final words

12 Although I have much to write to you, I would rather not use paper and ink;
instead I hope to come to you and talk with you face to face, so that our joy may be
complete.
13 The children of your elect sister send you their greetings.[c]

[c] Other ancient authorities add *Amen*

1.10 John instructs the believers not to give hospitality to false teachers. They were to do nothing that would encourage the heretics in their propagation of falsehoods. In addition, if believers invited them in, it would show that they were approving of what the false teachers said and did. It may seem rude to turn people away, even if they are teaching heresy, but how much better to be faithful to God than merely courteous to people! John is not condemning hospitality to unbelievers, but rather the supporting of those who are dedicated to opposing the true teachings of God. Note that John adds that a person who supports a false teacher in any way shares that teacher's wicked work.

1.13 False teaching is serious business, and we dare not overlook it. It is so serious that John wrote this letter especially to warn against it. There are so many false teachings in our world today that we might be tempted to take them lightly. Instead, we should realize the dangers they pose and actively refuse to give heresies any foothold.

The Third Letter of JOHN

WHEN company arrives at the door, with them comes the promise of soiled floors, dirty dishes, altered schedules, personal expense, and inconvenience. From sharing a meal to providing a bed, *hospitality* costs . . . in time, energy, and money. But how we treat others reflects our true values, what is really important to us. Do we see people as objects or inconveniences, or as unique creations of a loving God? And which is more important to God, a person or a carpet? Perhaps the most effective way to demonstrate God's values and Christ's love to others is to invite and welcome guests into our homes.

For Gaius, hospitality was a habit, and his reputation for friendship and generosity, especially to traveling teachers and missionaries (1.5) had spread. To affirm and thank him for his Christian life–style, and to encourage him in his faith, John wrote this personal note.

John's format for this epistle centers around three men—Gaius, the example of one who follows Christ and loves others (1.1–8); Diotrephes, the self-proclaimed church leader who does not reflect God's values (1.9–11); and Demetrius, who also follows the Truth (1.12). John encourages Gaius to practice hospitality, cling to the truth, and do what is right.

Although this is a personal letter, we can "look over the shoulder" of Gaius and apply its lessons to our lives. As you read 3 John, with which man do you identify? Are you a Gaius, generously giving to others? A Demetrius, loving the truth? Or a Diotrephes, looking out for yourself and your "things"? Determine to reflect Christ's values in your relationships, opening your home and touching others with his love.

VITAL STATISTICS

PURPOSE:
To commend Gaius for his hospitality and to encourage him in his Christian life

AUTHOR:
The apostle John

TO WHOM WRITTEN:
Gaius, a prominent Christian in one of the churches known to John

DATE WRITTEN:
About A.D. 90, from Ephesus

SETTING:
Church leaders traveled from town to town helping to establish new congregations. They depended on the hospitality of fellow believers. Gaius was one who welcomed them into his home.

KEY VERSE:
"Beloved, you do faithfully whatever you do for the friends, even though they are strangers to you" (1.5).

KEY PEOPLE:
John, Gaius, Diotrephes, Demetrius

THE BLUEPRINT

1. God's children live by the standards of the gospel (1.1–12)
2. John's final words (1.13–15)

John wrote to commend Gaius, who was taking care of traveling teachers and missionaries, and to warn against people like Diotrephes, who are proud and refuse to listen to spiritual leaders in authority. If we are to live in the truth of the gospel, we must look for ways to support pastors, Christian workers, and missionaries today. All Christians should work together to support God's work, both at home and around the world.

MEGATHEMES

THEME	EXPLANATION	IMPORTANCE
Hospitality	John wrote to encourage those who were kind to others. Genuine hospitality for traveling Christian workers was needed then and is still important.	Faithful Christian teachers and missionaries need our support. Whenever you can extend hospitality to others, it will make you a partner in their ministry.
Pride	Diotrephes not only refused to offer hospitality, but he set himself up as a church boss. Pride disqualified him as a real leader.	Christian leaders must shun pride and its effects on them. Be careful not to misuse your position of leadership.
Faithfulness	Gaius and Demetrius were commended for their faithful work in the church. They were held up as examples of faithful, selfless servants.	Don't take for granted Christian workers who serve faithfully. Be sure to encourage them so they won't grow weary of serving.

1. God's children live by the standards of the gospel

1 The elder to the beloved Gaius, whom I love in truth.
2 Beloved, I pray that all may go well with you and that you may be in good
health, just as it is well with your soul. 3 I was overjoyed when some of the friends[a]
arrived and testified to your faithfulness to the truth, namely how you walk in the
truth. 4 I have no greater joy than this, to hear that my children are walking in the
truth.
5 Beloved, you do faithfully whatever you do for the friends,[a] even though
they are strangers to you; 6 they have testified to your love before the church. You
will do well to send them on in a manner worthy of God; 7 for they began their
journey for the sake of Christ,[b] accepting no support from non-believers.[c] 8 Therefore we ought to support such people, so that we may become co-workers with the
truth.
9 I have written something to the church; but Diotrephes, who likes to put him-

1.4 1 Cor 4.15 Gal 4.19
1.5 Rom 12.13 Heb 13.2 1 Pet 4.10,11
1.6 Col 1.10
1.7 Mt 10.9-14 Mk 6.8-13 Lk 9.3-5 10.4-11 Acts 20.33
1.9 Phil 2.3

a Gk *brothers* b Gk *for the sake of the name* c Gk *the Gentiles*

1.1 This letter gives us an important glimpse into the life of the early church. Third John, addressed to Gaius, is about the need for hospitality to traveling preachers and other believers. It also warns against a would-be church dictator.

1.1 The "elder," John, was one of Jesus' 12 disciples and the writer of the Gospel of John, three epistles, and the book of Revelation. For more information about him, see his Profile in John 14. We have no further information about Gaius, but he is someone John loved dearly. Perhaps he had shared his home and hospitality with John at some time during John's travels. If so, John would have appreciated his actions, because traveling preachers depended on hospitality to survive (see Matthew 10.11–16).

1.2 John was concerned for Gaius's physical *and* spiritual well-being. This was in direct contrast to the popular heresy of the day that taught the separation of spirit and matter and despised the physical side of life. Still today, many people fall into this way of thinking. This non-Christian attitude logically leads to one of two responses: neglect of the body and physical health, or indulgence of the body's sinful desires. God is concerned for both your body and your soul. As responsible Christians, we should neither neglect nor indulge ourselves, but care for our physical needs and discipline our bodies so we are at our best for God's service.

1.4 John says "my children" because, as a result of his preaching, he was the spiritual father of many, including Gaius.

1.5 In the church's early days, traveling prophets, evangelists, and teachers were helped on their way by people like Gaius who housed and fed them. Hospitality is a lost art in many churches today. We would do well to invite more people for meals—fellow church members, young people, traveling missionaries, those in need, visitors. This is an active and much-appreciated way to show your love. In fact it is probably more important today. Because of our individualistic, self-centered society, there are many lonely people who wonder if anyone cares whether they live or die. If you find such a lonely person, show him or her that *you* care!

1.7 The traveling missionaries neither asked for nor accepted anything from non-believers, because they didn't want anyone questioning their motives for preaching. God's true preachers do not preach to make money, but out of love for God. It is the church's responsibility to care for Christian workers; this should never be left to nonbelievers.

1.7, 8 When you help someone who is spreading the gospel, you are in a very real way a partner in the ministry. This is the other side of the principle in 2 John 1.10 (see the note there). Not everyone should go to the mission field; those who work for Christ at home are vital to the ministry of those who go and need support. We can support missionaries by praying for them and by giving them our money, hospitality, and time.

1.9 This letter to which John refers was neither 1 or 2 John, but another letter that no longer exists.

1.9, 10 All we know about Diotrephes is that he wanted to control the church. John denounces (1) his refusal to listen to other spiritual leaders, (2) his slander of the leaders, (3) his bad example in refusing to welcome any gospel teachers, and (4) his attempt to excommunicate those who opposed his leadership. Sins such as pride, jealousy, and slander are still present in the church, and when a leader makes a habit of encouraging sin and discouraging

1.10 3 Jn 5

self first, does not acknowledge our authority. 10 So if I come, I will call attention
to what he is doing in spreading false charges against us. And not content with
those charges, he refuses to welcome the friends,[d] and even prevents those who
want to do so and expels them from the church.

1.11 Ps 34.14; 1 Cor 4.16; 11.1; 1 Jn 2.29; 3.6,9

11 Beloved, do not imitate what is evil but imitate what is good. Whoever does
good is from God; whoever does evil has not seen God. 12 Everyone has testified
favorably about Demetrius, and so has the truth itself. We also testify for him,[e]
and you know that our testimony is true.

2. John's final words

1.13 2 Jn 12

1.14 2 Jn 12

13 I have much to write to you, but I would rather not write with pen and ink;
14 instead I hope to see you soon, and we will talk together face to face.
15 Peace to you. The friends send you their greetings. Greet the friends there,
each by name.

[d] Gk *brothers* [e] Gk lacks *for him*

right actions, he must be stopped. If no one speaks up, great harm can come to the church. We must confront sin in the church; if we try to avoid it, it will continue to grow. A true Christian leader is a servant, not an autocrat!

1.12 We know nothing about Demetrius except that he probably carried this letter from John to Gaius. The book of Acts mentions an Ephesian silversmith named Demetrius who opposed Paul (Acts 19.24ff), but this is probably another man. In contrast to the corrupt Diotrephes, Demetrius had a high regard for truth. John personifies truth as a witness to Demetrius's character and teaching. In other words, if truth itself could speak, it would speak on Demetrius's behalf. When Demetrius arrived, Gaius would have certainly opened his home to him.

1.14 Whereas 2 John emphasizes the need to refuse hospitality to false teachers, 3 John urges continued hospitality to those who teach the truth. Hospitality is a strong sign of support for people and their work. It means giving them of your means so their stay will be comfortable and their work and travel easier. Actively look for creative ways to show hospitality to God's workers. It may be in the form of a letter of encouragement, a "care" package, financial support, an open home, or prayer.

The Letter of JUDE

VITAL STATISTICS

PURPOSE:
To remind the church of the need for constant vigilance—to keep strong in the faith and to defend it against heresy

AUTHOR:
Jude, James's brother and Jesus' half-brother

TO WHOM WRITTEN:
Jewish Christians and all believers everywhere

DATE WRITTEN:
About A.D. 65

SETTING:
From the first century on, the church has been threatened by heresy and false teaching—we must always be on our guard.

KEY VERSE:
"Beloved, while eagerly preparing to write to you about the salvation we share, I find it necessary to write and appeal to you to contend for the faith that was once for all entrusted to the saints" (1.3).

KEY PEOPLE:
Jude, James, Jesus

TO PROTECT from harm, to guard from attack, to repulse enemies—for centuries rugged defenders have built walls, launched missiles, and waged wars, expending material and human resources in battle to save nations and cities. And with total commitment and courageous abandon, individuals have fought for their families. It is a rule of life that we fight for survival, defending with all our strength what is most precious to us, from every real or imagined attack.

God's Word and the gift of eternal life have infinite value and have been entrusted to Christ's faithful followers. There are many people who live in opposition to God and his followers. They twist God's truth, seeking to deceive and destroy the unwary. But God's truth must go forth, carried and defended by those who have committed their lives to God's Son. It is an important task, an awesome responsibility, and a profound privilege to have this commission.

This was Jude's message to Christians everywhere. Opposition would come and godless teachers would arise, but Christians should "contend for the faith" (1.3) by rejecting all falsehood and immorality (1.4–19), remembering God's mighty acts of rescue and punishment (1.5–11, 14–16) and the warnings of the apostles (1.17–19). His readers are to build up their own faith through prayer (1.20), keeping close to Christ (1.21), helping others (1.22, 23), and hating sin (1.23). Then Jude concludes with a glorious benediction of praise to God (1.24, 25).

How much do you value God's Word, the fellowship of the church, and obedience to Jesus Christ? There are many false teachers waiting to destroy your Christ-centered life, the credibility of God's Word, and the unity of the body of Christ. Read Jude and determine to stand firm in your faith and defend God's truth at all costs. *Nothing* is more valuable.

THE BLUEPRINT

1. The danger of false teachers (1.1–16)
2. The duty to fight for God's truth (1.17–25)

Jude wrote to motivate Christians everywhere to action. He wanted them to recognize the dangers of false teaching, to protect themselves and other believers, and to win back those who had already been deceived. Jude was writing against godless teachers who were saying that Christians could do as they pleased without fear of God's punishment. While few teach this heresy openly in the church today, many in the church act as though this were true. This letter contains a warning against living a nominal Christian life.

MEGATHEMES

THEME	EXPLANATION	IMPORTANCE
False teachers	Jude warns against false teachers and leaders who reject the lordship of Christ, undermine the faith of others, and lead them astray. These leaders and any who follow them will be punished.	We must stoutly defend Christian truth. Make sure that you avoid leaders and teachers who change the Bible to suit their own purposes. Genuine servants of God will faithfully portray Christ in their words and conduct.
Apostasy	Jude also warns against apostasy—turning away from Christ. We are to remember that God punishes rebellion against him. We must be careful not to drift away from a faithful commitment to Christ.	Those who do not seek to know the truth in God's Word are susceptible to apostasy. Christians must guard against any false teachings that would distract them from the truth preached by the apostles and written in God's Word.

1. The danger of false teachers

1.1 Mt 13.55

1.3 Acts 20.27 1 Cor 15.3-9 Tit 1.4 2 Pet 3.1,2 Jude 20

1.4 2 Tim 3.6 1 Pet 2.16 2 Pet 2.1-4,10, 18-22 2 Jn 7

1 Jude,[a] a servant[b] of Jesus Christ and brother of James,
To those who are called, who are beloved[c] in[d] God the Father and kept safe for[d]
Jesus Christ:
2 May mercy, peace, and love be yours in abundance.
3 Beloved, while eagerly preparing to write to you about the salvation we share,
I find it necessary to write and appeal to you to contend for the faith that was once
for all entrusted to the saints. 4 For certain intruders have stolen in among you,
people who long ago were designated for this condemnation as ungodly, who pervert the grace of our God into licentiousness and deny our only Master and Lord,
Jesus Christ.[e]

a Gk *Judas* b Gk *slave* c Other ancient authorities read *sanctified* d Or *by* e Or *the only Master and our Lord Jesus Christ*

1.1 The letter of Jude focuses on *apostasy*—when people turn away from God's truth and embrace false teachings. Jude reminds his readers of God's judgment on those who left the faith in the past. This letter is a warning against false teachers—in this case, probably gnostic teachers (see the note on Colossians 2.4ff for a description of the gnostic heresy). Gnostics opposed two of the basic foundations of Christianity—the incarnation of Christ and Christian ethics. Jude wrote to combat these false teachings and to encourage true doctrine and right conduct.

1.1 Jude was a brother of James, who was one of the leaders in the early church. Both of these men were Jesus' half-brothers. Mary was their mother. Joseph was the father of James and Jude, and although Mary was Jesus' true mother, God was Jesus' true Father.

1.3 Jude emphasizes the important relationship between correct doctrine and true faith. The truth of the Bible must not be compromised, because it gives us the real facts about Jesus and salvation. The Bible is inspired by God and should never be twisted or manipulated; when it is, we become confused over right and wrong and lose sight of the only path that leads to eternal life. Before writing about salvation, then, Jude felt he had to set his readers back on the right track, calling them back to the basics of their faith. Then the way to salvation would be clearer. *Saints* refers to all believers.

1.4 Even some of our churches today have false ("ungodly") teachers who "intrude" and twist the Bible's teachings to justify their own opinions, life-style, or wrong behavior. This may give them temporary freedom to do as they wish, but they will discover that in twisting Scripture they are playing with fire. God will judge them for excusing, tolerating, and promoting sin.

1.4 Because people think theology is dry, they avoid studying the Bible. Those who refuse to learn correct doctrine, however, are susceptible to false teaching because they are not fully grounded in God's truth. We must understand the basic doctrines of our faith so that we can recognize false doctrines and prevent them from hurting us and others.

1.4 Many first-century false teachers taught that Christians could do whatever they liked without fear of God's punishment. They took a light view of God's holiness and his justice. Paul refutes this same kind of false teaching in Romans 6.1–23. Even today, some Christians minimize the sinfulness of sin, believing that how they live has little to do with their faith. They may do well to ask, "Does the way I live show that I am sincere about my faith?" Those who truly have faith will show it by their deep respect for God and their sincere desire to live according to the principles in his Word.

5 Now I desire to remind you, though you are fully informed, that the Lord,
who once for all saved[f] a people out of the land of Egypt, afterward destroyed
those who did not believe. 6 And the angels who did not keep their own position,
but left their proper dwelling, he has kept in eternal chains in deepest darkness for
the judgment of the great Day. 7 Likewise, Sodom and Gomorrah and the surrounding cities, which, in the same manner as they, indulged in sexual immorality and
pursued unnatural lust,[g] serve as an example by undergoing a punishment of eternal fire.
8 Yet in the same way these dreamers also defile the flesh, reject authority, and
slander the glorious ones.[h] 9 But when the archangel Michael contended with the
devil and disputed about the body of Moses, he did not dare to bring a condemnation of slander[i] against him, but said, "The Lord rebuke you!" 10 But these people
slander whatever they do not understand, and they are destroyed by those things
that, like irrational animals, they know by instinct. 11 Woe to them! For they go the
way of Cain, and abandon themselves to Balaam's error for the sake of gain, and
perish in Korah's rebellion. 12 These are blemishes[j] on your love-feasts, while
they feast with you without fear, feeding themselves.[k] They are waterless clouds
carried along by the winds; autumn trees without fruit, twice dead, uprooted;
13 wild waves of the sea, casting up the foam of their own shame; wandering stars,
for whom the deepest darkness has been reserved forever.
14 It was also about these that Enoch, in the seventh generation from Adam,
prophesied, saying, "See, the Lord is coming[l] with ten thousands of his holy ones,
15 to execute judgment on all, and to convict everyone of all the deeds of ungodliness that they have committed in such an ungodly way, and of all the harsh things

1.5 Ex 14.21-31 Num 14.20-24 Deut 2.14,15 1 Cor 10.5-10
1.6 2 Pet 2.4,9 Rev 12.9
1.8 2 Pet 2.10
1.9 Deut 34.6 Dan 10.13,20, 21; 12.1 Zech 3.2 Rev 12.7
1.11 Gen 4.3-16 Num 16.1-35 22.20-33 26.5-11; 31.16 Hab 2.6-19 2 Pet 2.15-16 Rev 2.14
1.12 Mt 15.13 1 Cor 11.20-22 Phil 3.19
1.13 Isa 57.20 2 Pet 2.17 Jude 6 Rev 20.10; 21.8
1.14 Gen 5.18-24 1 Chron 1.1-4

[f] Other ancient authorities read *though you were once for all fully informed, that Jesus* (or *Joshua*) *who saved* [g] Gk *went after other flesh* [h] Or *angels;* Gk *glories* [i] Or *condemnation for blasphemy* [j] Or *reefs* [k] Or *without fear. They are shepherds who care only for themselves* [l] Gk *came*

1.5–7 Jude gives three examples of rebellion: (1) the children of Israel—who, although they were delivered from Egypt, refused to trust God and enter the promised land (Numbers 14.26–39); (2) the angels—although they were once pure, holy, and living in God's presence, some gave in to pride and joined Satan to rebel against God (2 Peter 2.4); and (3) the cities of Sodom and Gomorrah—which were so full of sin that God wiped them off the face of the earth (Genesis 19.1–29). If the chosen people, angels, and sinful cities were punished, how much more would these false teachers be severely judged?

1.7 Many people don't want to believe that God sentences people to hell ("eternal fire") for rejecting him. But this is clearly taught in Scripture. Sinners who don't seek forgiveness from God will face eternal separation from him. Jude gives this warning to all who rebel against, ignore, or reject God.

1.8 The "glorious ones" here probably refer to angels. Just as the men of Sodom insulted angels (Genesis 19), these false teachers, to whom Jude refers, scoff at any authority. For information on the danger of insulting even the fallen angels, see the note on 2 Peter 2.10–12.

1.9 This incident is not recorded any other place in Scripture. Moses' death is recorded in Deuteronomy 34. Here Jude is making use of an ancient book called *Enoch.* The book of Enoch demonstrated that Moses was taken immediately into God's presence after his death. Two other saints in the Old Testament were also taken into God's presence (only they were taken before they died)—Enoch (Genesis 5.21–24) and Elijah (2 Kings 2.1–15). Moses and Elijah appeared with Jesus at the transfiguration (Matthew 17.1–9).

1.10 False teachers claimed that they possessed secret knowledge that gave them authority. Their "knowledge" of God was esoteric—mystical and beyond human understanding. In reality, the nature of God *is* beyond our understanding. But God, in his grace, has chosen to reveal himself to us—in his Word, and supremely in Jesus Christ. Therefore, we must seek to know all we can about what he has revealed, even though we cannot fully comprehend God with our finite human minds. Beware of those who claim to have all the answers and who belittle what they do not understand.

1.11 Jude offers three examples of men who did whatever they wanted (1.10)—Cain, who murdered his brother out of vengeful jealousy (Genesis 4.1–16); Balaam, who prophesied to get money, not out of obedience to God's command (Numbers 22–24); and Korah, who rebelled against God's divinely appointed leaders, wanting the power for himself (Numbers 16.1–35). These stories illustrate attitudes that are typical of false teachers—pride, selfishness, jealousy, greed, lust for power, and disregard of God's will.

1.12 When the Lord's supper was celebrated in the early church, believers ate a full meal before taking part in the communion with the bread and wine. The meal was called a love-feast and was designed to be a sacred time of fellowship to prepare one's heart for communion. However, the false teachers were joining these love-feasts, causing "blemishes" in what should be a time of rejoicing in the Lord. In several of the churches, however, this meal had turned into a time of gluttony and drunken revelry. In Corinth, for example, some people hastily gobbled food while others went hungry (1 Corinthians 11.20–22). No church function should be an occasion for selfishness, gluttony, greed, disorder, or other sins that destroy unity or take one's mind away from the real purpose for assembling together.

1.12 The false teachers were "twice dead." They were useless because they weren't producing fruit; and they weren't even believers, so they were rooted up and burned.

1.14 Enoch is mentioned briefly in Genesis 5.21–24. This quotation is from a book of the Apocrypha called I Enoch.

1.14 Other places where Jesus is mentioned as coming with angels ("holy ones") are Matthew 16.27 and 24.31. Daniel 7.10 speaks of God judging mankind in the presence of millions of angels.

1.16 1 Thess 4.3-8 Jas 1.14,15 1 Pet 2.3,10,18

that ungodly sinners have spoken against him." 16 These are grumblers and malcontents; they indulge their own lusts; they are bombastic in speech, flattering people
to their own advantage.

2. The duty to fight for God's truth

1.17 Heb 2.3 2 Pet 3.2
1.19 1 Cor 2.14
1.20 Acts 9.31 Rom 8.15,26,27
1.21 Heb 9.28
1.23 Rom 11.14 1 Cor 5.5
1.24,25 Rom 14.4; 16.25 2 Cor 4.14 Eph 3.20

17 But you, beloved, must remember the predictions of the apostles of our Lord
Jesus Christ; 18 for they said to you, "In the last time there will be scoffers, indulging their own ungodly lusts." 19 It is these worldly people, devoid of the Spirit, who
are causing divisions. 20 But you, beloved, build yourselves up on your most holy
faith; pray in the Holy Spirit; 21 keep yourselves in the love of God; look forward to
the mercy of our Lord Jesus Christ that leads to[m] eternal life. 22 And have mercy on
some who are wavering; 23 save others by snatching them out of the fire; and have
mercy on still others with fear, hating even the tunic defiled by their bodies.[n]
24 Now to him who is able to keep you from falling, and to make you stand
without blemish in the presence of his glory with rejoicing, 25 to the only God our
Savior, through Jesus Christ our Lord, be glory, majesty, power, and authority,
before all time and now and forever. Amen.

[m] Gk *Christ to* [n] Gk *by the flesh.* The Greek text of verses 22-23 is uncertain at several points

1.17 Other apostles also warned about false teachers—see Acts 20.29; 1 Timothy 4.1; 2 Timothy 3.1–5; 2 Peter 2.1–3; 2 John 1.7.

1.18 The *last time* is a common phrase referring to the time between Jesus' first and second comings. We live in the last times.

1.20 To "pray in the Holy Spirit" means to pray in the power and strength of the Holy Spirit. He prays for us (Romans 8.26, 27), opens our minds to Jesus (John 14.26), and teaches us about him (John 15.26).

1.21 To "keep yourselves in the love of God" means to live close to him and his people, not listening to false teachers who would pull you away from him (John 15.9, 10).

1.22, 23 Effective witnessing saves people from God's judgment. We witness to some through our compassion and kindness; to others we witness as if we are snatching them from the fire of hell itself. "Hating even the tunic defiled by their bodies" means we are to hate the sin, but we must witness to and love the sinner. Unbelievers, no matter how successful they seem by worldly standards, are lost and in need of salvation. We should not take witnessing lightly—it is a matter of life and death.

1.23 In trying to find common ground with those to whom we witness, we must be careful not to fall into the quicksand of compromise. When reaching out to others, we must be sure our own footing is safe and secure. Be careful not to become so much like non-Christians that no one can tell who you are or what you believe. Influence them for Christ—don't allow them to influence you to sin!

1.24, 25 As the epistle begins, so it ends—with assurance. God keeps believers from falling prey to false teachers. Although false teachers are widespread and dangerous, we don't have to be afraid if we trust God and are rooted and grounded in him.

1.24, 25 To be sinless and perfect ("without blemish") will be the ultimate condition of the believer when he or she finally sees Christ face to face. When we are forgiven of our sins and given our new bodies, we will be like Christ (1 John 3.2). Coming into Christ's presence will be more wonderful than we could ever imagine!

1.24, 25 The audience to whom Jude wrote was susceptible to heresies and to temptations toward immoral living. Jude encourages the believers to remain firm in their faith and trust in God's promises for their future. This was all the more important because they were living in a time of increased apostasy. We too are living in the last days, much closer to the end than were the original readers of this letter. We too are susceptible to doctrinal error. We too are tempted to give in to sin. Although there is much false teaching around us, we need not fear or give up in despair—God can keep us from falling, and if we remain faithful, he guarantees that he will bring us into his presence and give us everlasting joy.

THE REVELATION to John

VITAL STATISTICS

PURPOSE:
To reveal the full identity of Christ and to give warning and hope to believers

AUTHOR:
The apostle John

TO WHOM WRITTEN:
The seven churches in Asia and all believers everywhere

DATE WRITTEN:
About A.D. 95, from Patmos

SETTING:
Most scholars believe that the seven churches of Asia to whom John writes were experiencing the persecution which took place under Emperor Domitian (A.D. 90–95). It seems that the Roman authorities had exiled John to the island of Patmos (off the coast of Asia). John, who had been an eyewitness of the incarnate Christ, has a vision of the glorified Christ. God also reveals to him what is to take place in the future—judgment and the ultimate triumph of God over evil.

KEY VERSE:
"Blessed is the one who reads aloud the words of the prophecy, and blessed are those who hear and who keep what is written in it; for the time is near" (1.3).

KEY PEOPLE:
John, Jesus

KEY PLACES:
Patmos, the seven churches, the new Jerusalem

SPECIAL FEATURES:
Revelation is written in "apocalyptic" form—a type of Jewish literature which uses symbolic imagery to communicate hope (the ultimate triumph of God) to those in the midst of persecution. The events are ordered according to literary, rather than strictly chronological, patterns.

WITH TINY wrinkles and cries, he entered through a stable door and, wrapped in strips of cloth, took his first nap on a bed of straw. He grew to manhood in obscure and dusty Nazareth in Roman-occupied Palestine, his gentle hands becoming strong and calloused in Joseph's woodworking shop. As a man, he walked through the countryside and city, touching individuals, preaching to crowds, and training 12 men to carry on his work. At every step he was hounded by those seeking to rid the world of his influence. Finally, falsely accused and tried, he was condemned to a disgraceful execution. And he died—spat upon, cursed, pierced, and hung heavenward for all to deride. Jesus, the God-man, Isaiah's suffering servant, humbly living, loving, giving, and dying . . . to bring life.

Jesus will return. But this time, the risen and ascended one will burst into history, announced and flanked by angels, with an ear-splitting shout and trumpet blast. And all the world will see and know—he is Christ, he is King, he is Lord! Those who love him will rejoice, greeting their Savior with songs and hearts overflowing with joy. But his enemies will be filled with fear. Allied with Satan in a final attempt to finish him, they will marshal and march their legions against the armies of God. But who can withstand God's wrath? Christ will win the battle and reign victorious forever! Jesus, the humble suffering Servant, is also the powerful, conquering King and Judge.

This is the message of John's final book, revealing Jesus' true and full identity. Written to first-century believers who had been torn and nearly crushed by persecution, Revelation is a book of hope. John, the beloved apostle and eyewitness of Jesus, proclaims that their victorious Lord will surely return to vindicate the righteous and judge the wicked. But Revelation is also a book of warning. Things are not as they should be in the churches, so Christ calls them to live in righteousness.

Although Jesus gave this revelation of himself to John nearly 2,000 years ago, it still stands as a warning to God's people today. We can take heart as we understand John's vision of hope—Christ will return to rescue his people and settle accounts with all who defy him.

John begins this book by explaining how he received this revelation from God (1.1-20). He then records specific messages from Jesus to the seven churches in Asia (2.1—3.22). Suddenly the scene shifts as a mosaic of dramatic and majestic images bursts into view before John's eyes. This series of visions portray the future rise of evil, culminating in the antichrist (4.1—18.24). Then follows the triumph of the King of kings, the marriage of the Lamb, the final Judgment, and the coming of the new Jerusalem (19.1—22.5). Revelation concludes with the promise of Christ's soon return (22.6–21), and John breathes a prayer which has been echoed by Christians through the centuries, "Amen. Come, Lord Jesus!" (22.20).

As you read the book of Revelation, marvel with John at the wondrous panorama of God's revealed plan. Listen as Christ warns the churches, and root out any sin that blocks your relationship with him. Have hope, knowing that God is in control, Christ's victory is assured, and all who trust him will be saved.

THE BLUEPRINT

A. LETTERS TO THE CHURCHES (1.1—3.22)	The vision John received opens with instructions for him to write to seven churches. He both commends them for their strengths and warns them about their flaws. Each letter was directed to a church then in existence, but also represents conditions in the church throughout history. Both in the church and in our individual lives, we must constantly fight against the temptation to become loveless, immoral, lenient, compromising, lifeless, or casual about our faith. The letters make it clear how our Lord feels about these qualities.
B. MESSAGE FOR THE CHURCH (4.1—22.21) 1. Worshiping God in heaven 2. Opening the seven seals 3. Sounding the seven trumpets 4. Observing the great conflict 5. Pouring out the seven plagues 6. Seizing the final victory 7. Making all things new	This revelation is both a warning to Christians who have grown apathetic and an encouragement to those who are faithfully enduring the struggles in this world. It reassures us that good will triumph over evil and gives us hope in difficult times and direction when we are wavering in our faith. Christ's message to the church is a message of hope for all believers in every generation.

MEGATHEMES

THEME	EXPLANATION	IMPORTANCE
God's sovereignty	God is sovereign. He is greater than any power in the universe. God is not to be compared with any leader, government, or religion. He controls history for the purpose of uniting true believers in loving fellowship with him.	Though Satan's power may temporarily increase, we are not to be led astray. God is all-powerful. He is in control. He will safely bring his true family into eternal life. Because he cares for us, we can trust him with our very lives.
Christ's return	Christ came to earth as a "Lamb," the symbol of his perfect sacrifice for our sin. He will return as the triumphant "Lion," the rightful ruler and conqueror. He will defeat Satan, settle accounts with all those who reject him, and bring his faithful people into eternity.	Assurance of Christ's return gives suffering Christians the strength to endure. We can look forward to his return as King and Judge. Since no one knows the time when he will appear, we must be ready at all times by keeping our faith strong.
God's faithful people	John wrote to encourage the church to resist the demands to worship the Roman emperor. He warns all God's faithful people to be devoted only to Christ. Revelation identifies who the faithful people are and what they should be doing until Christ returns.	You can take your place in the ranks of God's faithful people by believing in Christ. Victory is sure for those who resist temptation and make loyalty to Christ their top priority.
Judgment	One day God's anger toward sin will be fully and completely unleashed. Satan will be defeated with all of his agents. False religion will be destroyed. God will reward the faithful with eternal life, but all who refuse to believe in him will face eternal punishment.	Evil and injustice will not prevail forever. God's final judgment will put an end to these. We need to be certain of our commitment to Jesus if we want to escape this great final judgment. No one who rejects Christ will escape God's punishment.
Hope	One day God will create a new heaven and a new earth. All believers will live with him forever in perfect peace and security. Those who have already died will be raised to life. These promises for the future bring us hope.	Our great hope is that what Christ promises will be true. When we have confidence in our final destination, we can follow Christ with unwavering dedication no matter what we must face. We can be encouraged by hoping in Christ's return.

A. LETTERS TO THE CHURCHES (1.1–3.22)

Near the end of his life, John received a vision from Christ, which he recorded for the benefit of the seven churches in Asia and for Christians throughout history. This is the only book in the Bible that promises a blessing to those who listen to its words and do what it says.

1 The revelation of Jesus Christ, which God gave him to show his servants[a] what must soon take place; he made[b] it known by sending his angel to his servant[c] John, 2 who testified to the word of God and to the testimony of Jesus Christ, even to all that he saw.

3 Blessed is the one who reads aloud the words of the prophecy, and blessed are those who hear and who keep what is written in it; for the time is near.

1.1 Dan 2.28-45 Rev 1.9; 5.7 17.1 22.6,8,16
1.3 Rev 3.11 22.7,10

John's greetings and praise to God

4 John to the seven churches that are in Asia:

Grace to you and peace from him who is and who was and who is to come, and from the seven spirits who are before his throne, 5 and from Jesus Christ, the faithful witness, the firstborn of the dead, and the ruler of the kings of the earth.

1.4 Ex 3.14 Zech 3.9; 4.2-6
1.5 Rev 3.14; 17.14

[a] Gk *slaves* [b] Gk *and he made* [c] Gk *slave*

1.1 Revelation is a book about the future *and* about the present. It offers future hope to all believers, especially those who have suffered for their faith, by proclaiming Christ's final victory over evil and the reality of eternal life with him. It also gives present guidance as it teaches us about Jesus Christ and how we should live for him now. With graphic pictures we learn that (1) Jesus Christ is coming again, (2) evil will be judged, and (3) the dead will be raised for judgment, resulting in eternal life or eternal destruction.

1.1 According to tradition, John, the author, was the only one of Jesus' original 12 disciples who was not killed for the faith. He also wrote the Gospel of John and the letters of 1, 2, and 3 John. When John wrote Revelation, he was in exile on the island of Patmos in the Aegean Sea, sent there by the Romans for his witness about Jesus Christ. For more information on John, see his Profile in John 14.

1.1 This book is the revelation *of, concerning,* or *from* Jesus Christ. The book of Revelation unveils Christ's full identity and God's plan for the end of the world, and it focuses on Jesus Christ, his second coming, his victory over evil, and the establishment of his kingdom. As you read and study Revelation, don't focus so much on the timetable of these events or the details of John's imagery that you miss the main message – the infinite love, power, and justice of the Lord Jesus Christ.

1.1 The book of Revelation is *apocalyptic* (meaning uncovered, unveiled, or revealed) in style. This style of ancient literature usually featured spectacular and mysterious imagery and was written in the name of an ancient hero. John was acquainted with Jewish apocalyptic works, but his book is different in several ways: (1) he uses his own name rather than the name of an ancient hero; (2) he denounces evil and exhorts people to high, Christian standards; (3) he offers hope rather than gloom. John was not a psychic attempting to predict the future; he was a prophet of God describing what God showed him.

1.1 For more about angels, see the note on 5.11.

1.1 Jesus gave his message to John in a vision, allowing him to see and record certain future events so they could be an encouragement to all believers. The vision includes many signs and symbols because they convey the essence of what is to happen. What John saw, in most cases, was indescribable, so he uses illustrations to explain what it was *like.* When reading this symbolic language, we don't have to understand every detail – John didn't. Instead, realize that John's imagery is used to show us that Christ is indeed the glorious and victorious Lord of all.

1.1–3 The book of Revelation reveals future events, but there is not the gloomy pessimism we might expect. The drama of these unfolding events is spectacular, but there is nothing to fear if you are on the winning side. When you think about the future, walk with confidence because Christ, the Victor, walks with you.

1.3 Revelation is a book of prophecy that is both *prediction* (foretelling future events) and *proclamation* (preaching about who God is and what he will do). Prophecy is more than telling the future. Behind the predictions are important principles about God's character and promises. As we read we can know God better and trust him completely.

1.3 The usual news reports – filled with violence, scandal, and political haggling – are depressing, and many wonder where the world is heading. God's plan for the future, however, provides inspiration and encouragement because we know he will intervene in history to conquer evil. John encourages churches to read this book aloud so everyone can hear it, apply it ("keep what is written in it"), and be assured of the fact that God will triumph.

1.3 When John says, "the time is near," he is urging his readers to be ready at all times for the last Judgment and the establishment of God's kingdom. We do not know when these events will occur, but we must always be prepared. They will happen quickly, and there will be no second chance to change sides.

1.4 Jesus told John to write to seven churches who knew and trusted him and who had read his earlier letters (see 1.11). The letters are addressed so that they could be read and passed on in a systematic fashion, following the main Roman road clockwise around the province of Asia (present-day Turkey).

1.4 The "seven spirits" is another name for the Holy Spirit. The number seven is used throughout the Revelation to symbolize completeness and perfection. John may have adopted this concept from the seven ways the Spirit ministers found in Isaiah 11.2. For more about the Holy Spirit, see the notes on John 3.6 and Acts 1.5.

1.4–6 The trinity – the Father ("who is and who was and who is to come"), the Son (Jesus Christ), and the Holy Spirit ("the seven spirits") – is the source of all truth (John 14.6, 17; 1 John 2.27; Revelation 19.11). Thus we can be assured that John's message is reliable and is God's Word to us.

1.5 Others had risen from the dead – people whom the prophets, Jesus, and the apostles had brought back to life during their ministries. But later these people died again. Jesus was the "firstborn of the dead" – the first who rose from death *to die no more.*

1.5, 6 Many hesitate to witness about their faith in Christ because they don't feel that the change in their lives has been spectacular enough. But you qualify as a witness for Jesus because of what he has done for you, not because of what you have done for him.

1.6 Dan 4.34 Rom 11.36 1 Pet 2.5,9 Jude 24,25
1.7 Jn 19.36,37

To him who loves us and freed[d] us from our sins by his blood, [6]and made[e] us
to be a kingdom, priests serving[f] his God and Father, to him be glory and dominion forever and ever. Amen.
[7] Look! He is coming with the clouds;
every eye will see him,

[d] Other ancient authorities read *washed* [e] Gk *and he made* [f] Gk *priests to*

A JOURNEY THROUGH THE BOOK OF REVELATION

Revelation is a complex book that has baffled interpreters for centuries. We can avoid a great deal of confusion by understanding the literary structure of this book. This will allow us to understand the individual scenes within the overall structure of Revelation and keep us from getting unnecessarily bogged down in the details of each vision. John gives hints throughout the book which indicate a change of scene, a change of subject, or a flashback to an earlier scene.

In chapter one, John relates the circumstances which led to the writing of this book (1.1–20). In chapters two and three, Jesus gives special messages to the seven churches of Asia Minor (2.1—3.22).

Suddenly John is caught up into heaven where he sees a vision of God Almighty on his throne. All of Christ's followers and the heavenly angels are worshiping him (4.1–11). John watches as God gives a scroll with seven seals to the Worthy Lamb, Jesus Christ, (5.1–14). The Lamb begins to open the seals one by one. As each seal is opened, a new vision appears.

As the first four seals are opened, riders appear on different color horses—war, famine, disease, and death are in their path (6.1–8). As the fifth seal is opened, John sees those in heaven who have been martyred for their faith in Christ (6.9–11).

A set of contrasting images appears at the opening of the sixth seal. On one side, there is a huge earthquake, stars falling from the sky, and the sky rolling up like a scroll (6.12–17). On the other side, multitudes are before the great throne, worshiping and praising God and the Lamb (7.1–17).

Finally, the seventh seal is opened (8.1–5), unveiling a series of God's judgments announced by seven angels with seven trumpets. The first four angels bring hail, fire, a volcano, and a poisonous star—the sun and moon are darkened (8.6–13). The fifth trumpet announces the coming of locusts with the power to sting (9.1–12). The sixth trumpet heralds the coming of an army of warriors on horses (9.13–21). In chapter 10.1–11, John is given a small scroll to eat. Following this, John is commanded to measure the temple of God (11.1–3). He sees two prophets ("witnesses") who proclaim God's judgment on the earth for three and a half years (11.4–13).

Finally the seventh trumpet blasts, calling the rival forces of good and evil to the final battle. On one side is Satan and his forces; on the other side stands Jesus Christ with his forces (11.14—13.18). In the midst of this call to battle, John sees three angels announcing the final Judgment (14.1–13). Two angels begin to reap this harvest of judgment upon the earth (14.14–20). Following upon the heels of these two angels are seven more angels who pour out God's judgment upon the earth from seven bowls (15.1—16.21). One of these angels from the group of seven reveals to John a vision of a "great whore" called Babylon (symbolizing the Roman Empire) riding a scarlet beast (17.1–18). After the defeat of Babylon (18.1–24), a great multitude in heaven shouts praise to God for his mighty victory (19.1–21).

The final three chapters of the book of Revelation catalogue the events which finalize Christ's victory over the enemy: Satan's 1,000 year imprisonment (20.1–10), the final Judgment (20.11–15), and the creation of a new earth and a new Jerusalem (21.1—22.5). An angel then gives John final instructions concerning the visions he has seen and what to do once he has written them all down (22.6–11).

Revelation concludes with the promise of Christ's soon return, an offer to drink of the water of life which runs through the main street of the new Jerusalem, and a warning to those who read the book (22.12–21). May we pray with John, "Amen. Come, Lord Jesus!" (22.20).

The Bible ends with a message of warning and hope for men and women of every generation. Christ is victorious and all evil has been done away with. As you read the book of Revelation, marvel at God's grace in the salvation of the saints and his power over the evil forces of Satan, and remember the hope of this victory to come.

Christ demonstrated his great love by setting us free from our sins through his death on the cross ("freed us from our sins by his blood"), guaranteeing us a place in his kingdom, and making us priests to administer God's love to others. The fact that the all-powerful God has offered eternal life to you is nothing short of spectacular.

1.5–9 Jesus is portrayed as an all-powerful King, victorious in battle, glorious in peace. He is not just a humble earthly teacher, he is the glorious God. When you read John's description of his vision, keep in mind his words are not just good advice; they are truth from the King of kings. Don't just read it for its interesting and amazing portrayal of the future. Let the truth about Christ penetrate your life, deepen your faith in him, and strengthen your commitment to follow him no matter what the cost.

1.7 John is announcing the return of Jesus to earth (see also Matthew 24; Mark 13; 1 Thessalonians 4.15–18). Jesus' second coming will be *visible* and *victorious.* All people will see him arrive (Mark 13.26), and they will *know* it is Jesus. When he comes, he will conquer evil and judge all people according to their deeds (20.11–15).

1.7 "Those who pierced him" could refer to the Roman soldiers who pierced Jesus' side as he hung on the cross or the Jews who were responsible for his death. John saw this event with his own eyes, and he never forgot the horror of it (see John 19.34, 35; see also Zechariah 12.10).

even those who pierced him;
and on his account all the tribes of the earth will wail.
So it is to be. Amen.
8 "I am the Alpha and the Omega," says the Lord God, who is and who was and **1.8** Isa 41.4; 48.12
who is to come, the Almighty. Rev 21.6; 22.13

The vision of Christ

9 I, John, your brother who share with you in Jesus the persecution and the **1.9** Rom 8.17
kingdom and the patient endurance, was on the island called Patmos because of the 2 Thess 3.5
word of God and the testimony of Jesus.[g] 10 I was in the spirit[h] on the Lord's day, Rev 1.6; 3.10
and I heard behind me a loud voice like a trumpet 11 saying, "Write in a book what **1.11** Rev 1.2,19
you see and send it to the seven churches, to Ephesus, to Smyrna, to Pergamum, to 2.1,18,24
Thyatira, to Sardis, to Philadelphia, and to Laodicea." 3.1,4,7,14
12 Then I turned to see whose voice it was that spoke to me, and on turning I **1.12** Zech 4.2-6
saw seven golden lampstands, 13 and in the midst of the lampstands I saw one like **1.13** Dan 10.5,6
the Son of Man, clothed with a long robe and with a golden sash across his chest.
14 His head and his hair were white as white wool, white as snow; his eyes were like **1.14** Dan 7.9,10
a flame of fire, 15 his feet were like burnished bronze, refined as in a furnace, and **1.15** Dan 10.6
his voice was like the sound of many waters. 16 In his right hand he held seven stars,
and from his mouth came a sharp, two-edged sword, and his face was like the sun **1.16** Rev 1.20; 2.12
shining with full force. 10.1; 19.15
17 When I saw him, I fell at his feet as though dead. But he placed his right **1.17,18** Isa 41.4
hand on me, saying, "Do not be afraid; I am the first and the last, 18 and the living Ezek 1.27,28 Dan 8.17,18
one. I was dead, and see, I am alive forever and ever; and I have the keys of Death 10.8,9,17-19
and of Hades. 19 Now write what you have seen, what is, and what is to take place Lk 24.5
after this. 20 As for the mystery of the seven stars that you saw in my right hand, and **1.20** Zech 4.2

[g] Or *testimony to Jesus* [h] Or *in the Spirit*

1.8 Alpha and Omega are the first and last letters of the Greek alphabet. Christ is the beginning and the end, the eternal Lord and Ruler of the past, present, and future (see also 4.8; Isaiah 44.6; 48.12–15). Without him you have nothing that is eternal, nothing that can change your life, nothing that can save you from sin. Is Christ your reason for living, the "Alpha and Omega" of your life? Honor the One who is the beginning and the end of all existence, wisdom, and power.

1.9 Patmos is a small rocky island in the Aegean Sea, about 50 miles offshore from the city of Ephesus on the Asia Minor seacoast (see map).

1.9 John describes himself as a *brother* and one who shares with them "the persecution," indicating that the church was undergoing intense persecution as he was writing this letter. In exile for preaching the gospel, John encourages the faith of his Christian brothers and sisters. The whole church, as the body of Christ, should experience joy and suffering together. Follow John's example in your relationships with other Christians: encourage them to be steadfast and faithful, and remind them of their future reward with God (see also Romans 5.2–5).

1.9 The Christian church was facing severe persecution. Almost all believers were socially, politically, or economically suffering because of this empire-wide persecution, and some were even being killed for their faith. John was exiled to Patmos because he refused to stop preaching the gospel. We may not be harassed or harmed for our faith as the early Christians were, but even with our freedom, few of us have the courage to share God's Word with others. If we hesitate to share our faith during easy times, how will we do during times of persecution?

1.12, 13 The seven golden lampstands are the seven churches in Asia (1.11, 20), and Jesus stands among them. No matter what the churches would face, Jesus would protect them with his all-encompassing love and reassuring power. Through his Spirit, Jesus Christ is still among the churches today. When a church faces persecution, it should remember his presence and deep love and care. When wracked by internal strife and conflict, the church should remember Christ's concern for purity and his intolerance of sin.

1.13, 14 This man "like the Son of Man" is Christ himself. The title *Son of Man* occurs many times in the New Testament in reference to Jesus as the Messiah. John recognized Jesus because he lived with him for three years and had seen him both as the Galilean preacher and as the glorified Son of God at the transfiguration (Matthew 17.1–8). Here Jesus appears as the mighty Son of Man. His white hair indicates his wisdom and divine nature (see also Daniel 7.9); his flaming eyes symbolize judgment of all evil; the golden sash across his chest reveals him as the high priest who goes into God's presence to obtain forgiveness of sin for those who believe in him.

1.16 The sword in Jesus' mouth symbolizes the power and force of his message. His words of judgment are sharp as swords (Isaiah 49.2; Hebrews 4.12).

1.17, 18 As the Roman government stepped up its persecution of Christians, John must have wondered if the church could survive and stand against the opposition. But Jesus appeared in glory and splendor, reassuring John that he and his fellow believers would have God's strength to face these trials. If you are facing difficult problems, remember that the power available to John and the early church is also available to you (see 1 John 4.4).

1.17, 18 Our sins have convicted and sentenced us, but Jesus holds the keys of Death and of Hades. He alone can free us from eternal bondage to Satan. He alone has the power and authority to set us free from sin's control. Believers don't have to fear death or hell because Christ holds the keys to both. All we must do is turn from sin and turn to him in faith. When we attempt to control our lives and disregard God, we set a course that leads directly to hell. But when we place our lives in Christ's hands, he restores us now and resurrects us later to an eternal, peaceful relationship with him.

the seven golden lampstands: the seven stars are the angels of the seven churches, and the seven lampstands are the seven churches.

The loveless church

2.1 Rev 1.11-16
2.2 2 Cor 11.13 1 Jn 4.1 Rev 2.19

2 "To the angel of the church in Ephesus write: These are the words of him who holds the seven stars in his right hand, who walks among the seven golden lampstands:
2 "I know your works, your toil and your patient endurance. I know that you

INTERPRETING THE BOOK OF REVELATION
Over the centuries, four main approaches to interpreting the book of Revelation have developed. Each approach has had capable supporters, but none has proved itself the only way to read this book. However, the most basic application question for each approach can be summarized by asking yourself, "Will this help me become a better follower of Jesus Christ today?"

Approach	*Description*	*Challenge*	*Caution*
PRETERIST VIEW	John is writing to encourage Christians in his own day who are experiencing persecution from the Roman Empire.	To gain the same kind of encouragement John's first readers gained from the vivid images of God's sovereignty.	Do not forget that most biblical prophecy has both an immediate and a future application.
FUTURIST VIEW	Except for the first three chapters, John is describing events which will occur at the end of history.	To see in contemporary events many of the characteristics John describes and realize the end could come at any time.	Do not assume that we have "figured out" the future, since Jesus said no man will know the day of his return before it happens.
HISTORICIST VIEW	The book of Revelation is a presentation of history from John's day until the second coming of Christ and beyond.	To note the consistency of man's evil throughout history and recognize that names may change but the rebellion against God has not.	Be careful before identifying current events or leaders as fulfilling aspects of the book of Revelation.
IDEALIST VIEW	The book of Revelation is a symbolic representation of the continual struggle of good and evil. It does not refer to any particular historical events. It is applicable at any point in history.	Read the book to gain insight into the past, to prepare for the future, and to live obediently and confidently in the present.	Do not avoid the book because it is difficult. Try to understand Revelation within its broader literary context.

1.20 Who are the "angels of the seven churches"? Some say these are angels designated to guard the churches; others say they are elders or pastors of the local churches. Because each of the seven letters in chapters 2 and 3 was written to a leader and because the letters contain reprimands, it is doubtful that these leaders are actual angels. However, these leaders (pastors) or messengers are accountable to God for the churches they represent.

2.1 Ephesus was the capital of Asia Minor, a center of land and sea trade, and, along with Alexandria and Antioch in Syria, one of the three most influential cities in the eastern part of the Roman Empire. The temple to Diana, one of the ancient wonders of the world, was located in this city, and a major industry was the manufacture of idols of this goddess (see Acts 19.21–41). Paul ministered in Ephesus for three years and warned the Ephesians that false teachers would come and try to draw people away from the faith (see Acts 20.29–31). False teachers did indeed cause problems in the Ephesian church, but the church resisted them, as we can see from Paul's letter to them (see the book of Ephesians). John spent much of his ministry in this city and knew that they had resisted false teaching (2.2).

2.1 The one who "walks among the seven golden lampstands" (the seven churches) is Jesus (1.11–13). He holds the "seven stars" (leaders of the churches) "in his right hand," indicating his power and authority over the churches and their leaders. Ephesus had become a large, proud church, and Jesus' message reminds them that he alone is the head of the body of believers.

2.1ff Does God care about your church? If you are tempted to doubt it, look more closely at these seven letters. The Lord of the universe knew each of these churches and its precise situation. In each letter, Jesus tells John to write about specific people, places, and events. He praises believers for their successes and tells them how to correct their failures. Just as Jesus cared for each of these churches, he cares for yours. He wants it to reach its greatest potential. The group of believers with whom you worship and serve is God's vehicle for changing the world.

2.2 Over a long period of time, the church in Ephesus had steadfastly refused to tolerate sin among its members. This was not easy in a city noted for the immoral sexual practices associated with the worship of the goddess Artemis (her Roman name is Diana, see Acts 19.21ff). We also live in times of widespread sin and sexual immorality. It is popular to be open-minded toward many types of sin, calling them personal choices or alternative life-styles. But when Christians begin to tolerate sin in the church, they lower the standards and compromise the church's witness. Remember, God's approval is infinitely more important than the world's.

2.2, 3 Christ commends the church at Ephesus for (1) working hard, (2) being patient, (3) resisting sin, (4) critically examining the claims of false apostles, and (5) suffering patiently without quitting. Every church should have these characteristics. But these good efforts should spring from our love for Jesus Christ. Brotherly love is an authentic proof of the gospel (John 13.34; 1 John 3.18, 19). In the battle for maintaining sound teaching and moral and doctrinal purity, it is possible to lose a charitable spirit. Prolonged conflict can weaken or destroy our patience and affection.

cannot tolerate evildoers; you have tested those who claim to be apostles but are **2.3** Jn 15.21
not, and have found them to be false. 3 I also know that you are enduring patiently Heb 12.1-13
and bearing up for the sake of my name, and that you have not grown weary. 4 But **2.4** Jer 2.2
I have this against you, that you have abandoned the love you had at first. 5 Remem- **2.5**
ber then from what you have fallen; repent, and do the works you did at first. If not, Hos 14.1 Rev 1.20; 3.3,19
I will come to you and remove your lampstand from its place, unless you repent. **2.6**
6 Yet this is to your credit: you hate the works of the Nicolaitans, which I also hate. Num 31.15,16 Rev 2.15
7 Let anyone who has an ear listen to what the Spirit is saying to the churches. To **2.7**
everyone who conquers, I will give permission to eat from the tree of life that is in Prov 3.18 11.30; 13.12
the paradise of God. Rev 22.2,14

The persecuted church

8 "And to the angel of the church in Smyrna write: These are the words of the **2.8** Rev 1.8,11,
first and the last, who was dead and came to life: 17,18
9 "I know your affliction and your poverty, even though you are rich. I know **2.9**
the slander on the part of those who say that they are Jews and are not, but are a Rev 1.9 2.13,24
synagogue of Satan. 10 Do not fear what you are about to suffer. Beware, the devil **2.10**
is about to throw some of you into prison so that you may be tested, and for ten days Dan 1.12,14 3.16-18
you will have affliction. Be faithful until death, and I will give you the crown of Rev 3.10; 12.11

2.4 Paul had once commended the church at Ephesus for its love for God and others (Ephesians 1.15), but many of the church founders had died, and the second-generation believers had lost their zeal for God. They were a busy church—the members did much to benefit themselves and the community—but they were busy for the wrong reasons. Work for God must be motivated by love for God, or it will not last.

2.4, 5 Just as when a man and woman fall in love, so also new believers rejoice at their new-found forgiveness. But when they lose sight of the seriousness of sin, they begin to lose the thrill of our forgiveness (see 2 Peter 1.9). In the first steps of your Christian life, you may have had enthusiasm without knowledge. Do you now have knowledge without enthusiasm? Both are necessary if you are to keep your love for God intense and untarnished (see Hebrews 10.32, 35). Do you love God with the same fervor as when you were a new Christian?

2.5 For Jesus to "remove your lampstand from its place" would mean that the church would cease to be an effective church. Just as the seven-branched candlestick in the temple gave light for the priests to see, the churches were to give light to their surrounding communities. But Jesus warned that their lights could go out. In fact, Jesus himself would extinguish any light that did not fulfill its purpose. The church had to repent of its sins.

2.6 The Nicolaitans were believers who compromised their faith in order to enjoy some of the sinful practices of Ephesian society. The name *Nicolaitans* may have come from the Hebrew word for "Balaamites." Balaam was a prophet who induced the Israelites to carry out their lustful desires (see 2.14 and Numbers 31.16). When we want to take part in an activity that we know is wrong, we often make excuses to justify our behavior, saying that it isn't as bad as it seems or it won't hurt our faith. Christ has strong words for those who look for excuses to sin.

2.6 Through John, Jesus commends the church at Ephesus for hating the wicked deeds of the Nicolaitans. Note that they didn't hate the people, just their sinful actions. Accept and love all people, and refuse to tolerate all evil. God cannot tolerate sin, and he expects us to stand against it. The world needs Christians who will stand for God's truth and point people toward right living.

2.7 To *conquer* is to be victorious by believing, persevering, remaining faithful, and living as one who follows Christ. Such a life brings great rewards (21.7).

2.7 In the garden of Eden were two trees—the tree of life and the tree of the knowledge of good and evil (see Genesis 2.9). Eating from the tree of life brought eternal life with God; eating from the tree of knowledge brought realization of good and evil. When Adam and Eve ate from the tree of knowledge, they disobeyed God's command. So they were excluded from Eden and barred from eating from the tree of life. Eventually, evil will be destroyed, and believers will be brought into a restored paradise. In the new earth, no tree of knowledge will tempt people to sin. Instead, everyone will eat from the tree of life and will live forever.

2.8 The city of Smyrna was about 25 miles north of Ephesus. It was nicknamed "Port of Asia" because it had an excellent harbor on the Aegean Sea. The church in this city struggled against two hostile forces: a Jewish population strongly opposed to Christianity, and a non-Jewish population that was loyal to Rome and supported emperor worship. Persecution and suffering were inevitable in an environment like this.

2.9, 10 Persecution comes from the devil, not from God. Satan, the devil, will cause Christians to be thrown into prison and even killed. But we need not fear death, because it will only result in our receiving the crown of life. Satan may harm our earthly bodies, but he can do us no spiritual harm. The "synagogue of Satan" means that these Jews were serving Satan's purposes, not God's, when they gathered to worship. "Ten days" means that although persecution will be intense, it will be relatively short. It has a definite beginning and end, and God remains in complete control.

2.9–11 Pain is part of life, but it is never easy to suffer, no matter what the cause. Jesus commends the church at Smyrna for its faith in suffering. He then encourages the believers by saying that they need not fear the future if they remain faithful. Don't let difficult times turn you away from God. Instead let them draw you toward greater faithfulness. Trust God and remember your heavenly reward (see also 22.12–14).

2.10 Smyrna was famous for its athletic games. A crown was the victory wreath, the trophy for the champion at the games. If we have been faithful, we will receive the prize of victory—eternal life (James 1.12). The message to the Smyrna church is to remain faithful during suffering because God is in control and his promises are reliable. Jesus never says that by being faithful to him we will avoid troubles, suffering, and persecution. Rather, we must be faithful to him *in* our sufferings. Only then will our faith prove to be genuine. We can remain faithful by keeping our eyes on Christ and on what he promises us now and in the future (see Philippians 3.13, 14; 2 Timothy 4.8).

2.11 Rev 2.7,29 20.6,14

life. [11]Let anyone who has an ear listen to what the Spirit is saying to the churches.
Whoever conquers will not be harmed by the second death.

The lenient church

2.13 Rev 14.12 2.14 Num 31.16 1 Cor 6.13-20 2 Pet 2.15 Rev 2.20

12 "And to the angel of the church in Pergamum write: These are the words of
him who has the sharp two-edged sword:
13 "I know where you are living, where Satan's throne is. Yet you are holding
fast to my name, and you did not deny your faith in me[i] even in the days of Antipas
my witness, my faithful one, who was killed among you, where Satan lives. [14]But

[i] Or *deny my faith*

THE SEVEN CHURCHES
The seven churches were located on a major Roman road. A letter carrier would leave the island of Patmos (where John was exiled), arriving first at Ephesus. He would travel north to Smyrna and Pergamum, turn southeast to Thyatira, and continue on to Sardis, Philadelphia, and Laodicea—in the exact order in which the letters were dictated.

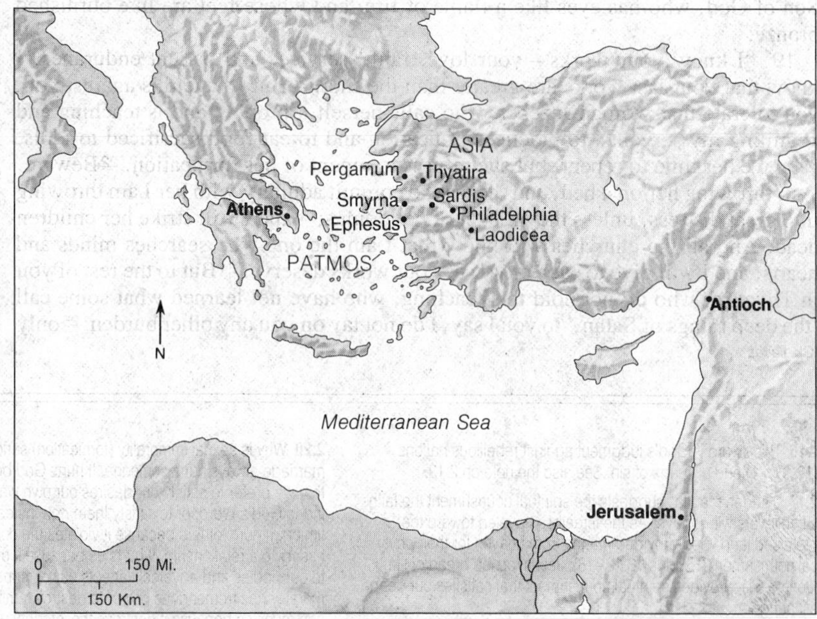

2.11 Believers and unbelievers alike experience physical death. All people will be resurrected, but believers will be raised to eternal life with God while unbelievers will be raised to be punished with a second death and eternal separation from God (see also 20.14; 21.8, 27; 22.15).

2.12 The city of Pergamum was built on a hill 1,000 feet above the surrounding countryside, creating a natural fortress. It was a sophisticated city, a center of Greek culture and education, with a 200,000-volume library. But it was also the center of four cults, rivaling Ephesus in idol worship. The city's chief god was Asclepius, whose symbol was a serpent, and who was considered the god of healing. People came to Pergamum from all over the world to seek healing from this god.

2.12 Just as the Romans used their swords for authority and judgment, Jesus' sharp, double-edged sword represents God's ultimate authority and judgment. It may also represent God's future separation of believers from unbelievers. Unbelievers cannot experience the eternal rewards of living in God's kingdom.

2.13 As the center for four idolatrous cults (Zeus, Dionysius, Asclepius, and Athene), Pergamum is called the city "where Satan's throne is." Surrounded by worship of Satan and the Roman emperor, the church at Pergamum refused to deny Christ even when Satan's worshipers martyred one of their members. Standing firm against the strong pressures and temptations of society is never easy, but the alternative is much worse (2.11).

2.13–15 It was not easy to be a Christian in Pergamum. Believers experienced great pressure to compromise or leave the faith. (For information on the Nicolaitans, see the note on 2.6.) Nothing is known about Antipas except that he did *not* compromise. Antipas was faithful, and he died for his faith. Apparently, however, some in the church were tolerating those who taught or practiced what Christ opposed. *Compromise* can be defined as blending qualities of two opposing elements or a concession of principles. Cooperate with people as much as you can, but avoid any alliance, partnership, or participation that leads to immoral practices.

2.14 There is room for differences of opinion among Christians in some areas, but there is no room for heresy and moral impurity. Your town may not participate in idol feasts, but it probably has pornography, sexual sin, cheating, gossiping, and lying. Don't tolerate sin under the pressure to be open-minded.

2.14–16 Balak was a king who feared the large number of Israelites traveling through his country, so he hired Balaam to pronounce a curse on them. At first Balaam refused, but an offer of money changed his mind (Numbers 22 – 24). Later he influenced the Israelites to turn to idol worship (Numbers 31.16; also see 2 Peter 2.15; Jude 1.11). Here Christ rebukes the church for tolerating those who, like Balaam, lead people away from God.

I have a few things against you: you have some there who hold to the teaching of
Balaam, who taught Balak to put a stumbling block before the people of Israel, so
that they would eat food sacrificed to idols and practice fornication. 15 So you also **2.15**
have some who hold to the teaching of the Nicolaitans. 16 Repent then. If not, I will Rev 2.6
come to you soon and make war against them with the sword of my mouth. 17 Let **2.16** 2 Thess 2.8
anyone who has an ear listen to what the Spirit is saying to the churches. To every- Rev 1.16; 2.5 22.7
one who conquers I will give some of the hidden manna, and I will give a white **2.17**
stone, and on the white stone is written a new name that no one knows except the Jn 6.49-58 Rev 2.7; 14.3
one who receives it. 19.12

The compromising church

18 "And to the angel of the church in Thyatira write: These are the words of the **2.18**
Son of God, who has eyes like a flame of fire, and whose feet are like burnished Rev 1.11,14 2.24
bronze: **2.19**
19 "I know your works—your love, faith, service, and patient endurance. I Rev 2.2
know that your last works are greater than the first. 20 But I have this against you: **2.20** 1 Kgs 16.31
you tolerate that woman Jezebel, who calls herself a prophet and is teaching and 2 Kgs 9.7
beguiling my servants[j] to practice fornication and to eat food sacrificed to idols. **2.21** Rev 9.20
21 I gave her time to repent, but she refuses to repent of her fornication. 22 Beware, **2.22**
I am throwing her on a bed, and those who commit adultery with her I am throwing Rev 17.2
into great distress, unless they repent of her doings; 23 and I will strike her children **2.23** Mt 16.27
dead. And all the churches will know that I am the one who searches minds and Lk 16.15
hearts, and I will give to each of you as your works deserve. 24 But to the rest of you **2.24**
in Thyatira, who do not hold this teaching, who have not learned what some call Rev 2.18; 3.11 **2.25**
'the deep things of Satan,' to you I say, I do not lay on you any other burden; 25 only Rev 3.11

[j] Gk *slaves*

2.16 This sword is God's judgment against rebellious nations (19.15, 21) and all forms of sin. See also the note on 2.12.

2.17 "Hidden manna" suggests the spiritual nourishment the faithful believers will receive. As the Israelites traveled toward the promised land, God provided manna from heaven for their physical nourishment (Exodus 16.13–18). Jesus, as the bread of life (John 6.51), provides spiritual nourishment that satisfies our deepest hunger.

2.17 It is unclear what the white stones are or exactly what the names on them will be. Because they relate to the hidden manna, they may be symbols of the believer's eternal "nourishment," or eternal life. The stones are significant because each will bear the new name of a person who truly believes in Christ. Each stone is the evidence that a person has been accepted by God and declared worthy to receive eternal life. A person's name represented his or her character. God will give us new names and new hearts.

2.18 Thyatira was a working man's town, with many trade guilds for cloth making, dyeing, and pottery. Lydia, Paul's first convert in Philippi, was a merchant from Thyatira (Acts 16.14). The city was basically secular, with no focus on any particular religion.

2.19 The believers in Thyatira were commended for growing in good deeds. We should not feel satisfied when our church only rejoices in the salvation of its members or the comfort of gathering for worship. We should grow in love, faith, and acts of service. Because the times are critical, we must spend our days wisely and faithfully.

2.20 A woman in the church in Thyatira was teaching that immorality was not a serious matter for believers. Her name may have been Jezebel, or John may have used the name Jezebel to symbolize the kind of wrong she was doing. Jezebel, a heathen queen of Israel, was considered the most evil woman who ever lived (see 1 Kings 19.1, 2; 21.1–15; 2 Kings 9.7–10, 30–37; and Jezebel's Profile in 1 Kings 21).

2.20 Why is sexual immorality (fornication) serious? Sex outside marriage always hurts someone. It hurts God because it shows that we prefer to satisfy our desires our own way instead of according to God's Word, or to satisfy them *now* instead of waiting for his timing. It hurts others because it violates the commitment so necessary to a relationship. It hurts us because it often brings disease to our bodies and adversely affects our personalities. Sexual immorality has tremendous power to destroy families, churches, and communities because it destroys the integrity upon which these relationships are built. God wants to protect us from hurting ourselves and others; thus we must have no part in sexual immorality, even if our culture accepts it.

2.20 In heathen temples, meat was often offered to idols. Then the meat that wasn't burned was sold to shoppers in the temple marketplace. Eating meat offered to idols wasn't wrong in itself because the idols were only wood and stone objects, but it could violate the principle of sensitivity toward weaker Christian brothers and sisters who would be bothered by it (see 1 Corinthians 8 and the note on Romans 14.2). Jezebel was obviously more concerned about her own selfish pleasure and freedom than about the needs and concerns of believers.

2.21 Jezebel refused God's invitation to repent. To repent means to change our mind and direction from our way to God's way. It means turning from sin and its disastrous consequences to God and eternal life. In his mercy, God has given us time to decide to follow him. Only our stubborn willfulness stands in the way.

2.23 We cannot hide from Christ, because he knows what is in our minds and hearts. The sins we try to hide from God need to be confessed to him.

2.24, 25 The "deep things of Satan" were either false teachings advocated by heretics, or secret insights by so-called believers guaranteed to promote deeper spiritual life. We should hold tightly to the basics of our Christian faith and receive with caution and counsel any new teaching that takes us away from the Bible, the fellowship of our church, or our basic confession of faith.

hold fast to what you have until I come. 26 To everyone who conquers and continues
to do my works to the end,
I will give authority over the nations;
27 to rule[k] them with an iron rod,
as when clay pots are shattered—
28 even as I also received authority from my Father. To the one who conquers I will
also give the morning star. 29 Let anyone who has an ear listen to what the Spirit is
saying to the churches.

The lifeless church

3 "And to the angel of the church in Sardis write: These are the words of him
who has the seven spirits of God and the seven stars:
"I know your works; you have a name of being alive, but you are dead. 2 Wake
up, and strengthen what remains and is on the point of death, for I have not found
your works perfect in the sight of my God. 3 Remember then what you received and
heard; obey it, and repent. If you do not wake up, I will come like a thief, and you
will not know at what hour I will come to you. 4 Yet you have still a few persons in
Sardis who have not soiled their clothes; they will walk with me, dressed in white,
for they are worthy. 5 If you conquer, you will be clothed like them in white robes,
and I will not blot your name out of the book of life; I will confess your name before
my Father and before his angels. 6 Let anyone who has an ear listen to what the
Spirit is saying to the churches.

[k] Or *to shepherd*

2.26 Dan 7.22; Mt 10.22; 19.28
2.27 Ps 2.8,9
2.28 2 Pet 1.19; Rev 22.16
3.1 Rev 1.4,11,16; 3.8,15
3.3 Mt 24.42,43; 1 Thess 5.2-6; 1 Pet 3.10
3.4 Rev 3.5; 4.4; 6.11; 19.14
3.5 Ps 49.28; Mt 10.32; Lk 10.20; 12.8; Rev 13.8; 17.8; 20.12
3.6 Rev 2.7

THE NAMES OF JESUS

Reference	*Jesus' name*	*Reference*	*Jesus' name*
1.8	Alpha and Omega, Beginning to End	5.5	Root of David
1.8	Lord	5.6	Lamb
1.8	Almighty	7.17	Shepherd
1.13	Son of Man	12.10	Messiah
1.18	He that lives, and was dead, and is alive forevermore	19.11	Faithful and True
2.18	Son of God	19.13	Word of God
3.14	Witness	19.16	King of kings
4.11	Creator	19.16	Lord of lords
5.5	Lion of the tribe of Judah	22.16	The morning star

Scattered among the vivid images of the book of Revelation is a large collection of names for Jesus. Each one tells something of his character and highlights a particular aspect of his role within God's plan of redemption.

2.26, 27 Christ says that everyone who conquers (those who remain faithful until the end and continue to please him) will rule over his enemies and reign with him as he judges evil. We will participate with God as he judges evil when his enemies are shattered (see also Psalm 2.8, 9; Isaiah 30.14; Jeremiah 19.11; 1 Corinthians 6.2, 3; Revelation 12.5; 19.15; 20.3, 4 for more about God's judgment).

2.28 Christ is called the morning star in 2.28 and 22.16, as well as in 2 Peter 1.19. A morning star appears just before dawn, when the night is coldest and darkest. When the world is at its bleakest point, Christ will burst onto the scene, exposing evil with his light of truth and bringing his promised reward.

3.1 The wealthy city of Sardis was actually in two locations. The older section of the city was on the mountain. When its population outgrew it, a newer section was built in the valley below.

3.1 The "seven spirits of God" is another name for the Holy Spirit (see the note on 1.4), and "the seven stars" are the church leaders or angels of the seven churches. See the note on 1.20 for this interpretation.

3.1 The problem in the Sardis church was not heresy, but spiritual death. In spite of its reputation for being active, Sardis was infested with sin. Its deeds were evil and its clothes soiled. The Spirit has no words of commendation for this church that looked good on the outside but was corrupt on the inside.

3.3 The church at Sardis was urged to hold on to the Christian truth they had heard when they first believed in Christ, to get back to the basics of the faith. It is important to grow in our knowledge of the Lord, to deepen our understanding through careful study. But no matter how much we learn, we must never abandon the basic truths about Christ. Jesus will always be God's Son, and his sacrifice for our sins is permanent. No new truth from God will ever contradict these biblical teachings.

3.5 To be clothed in white robes means to be set apart for God and made pure. Christ promises future honor and eternal life to those who stand firm in their faith. The names of all believers are registered in the book of life. This book symbolizes God's knowledge of who belongs to him. They are guaranteed a listing in the book of life and introduced to the hosts of heaven as belonging to Christ (see Luke 12.8, 9).

The obedient church

7 "And to the angel of the church in Philadelphia write:
These are the words of the holy one, the true one,
who has the key of David,
who opens and no one will shut,
who shuts and no one opens:
8 "I know your works. Look, I have set before you an open door, which no one
is able to shut. I know that you have but little power, and yet you have kept my
word and have not denied my name. 9 I will make those of the synagogue of Satan
who say that they are Jews and are not, but are lying—I will make them come and
bow down before your feet, and they will learn that I have loved you. 10 Because
you have kept my word of patient endurance, I will keep you from the hour of trial
that is coming on the whole world to test the inhabitants of the earth. 11 I am coming
soon; hold fast to what you have, so that no one may seize your crown. 12 If you
conquer, I will make you a pillar in the temple of my God; you will never go out of
it. I will write on you the name of my God, and the name of the city of my God, the
new Jerusalem that comes down from my God out of heaven, and my own new
name. 13 Let anyone who has an ear listen to what the Spirit is saying to the
churches.

The lukewarm church

14 "And to the angel of the church in Laodicea write: The words of the Amen,
the faithful and true witness, the origin[l] of God's creation:
15 "I know your works; you are neither cold nor hot. I wish that you were either
cold or hot. 16 So, because you are lukewarm, and neither cold nor hot, I am about
to spit you out of my mouth. 17 For you say, 'I am rich, I have prospered, and I need
nothing.' You do not realize that you are wretched, pitiable, poor, blind, and naked. 18 Therefore I counsel you to buy from me gold refined by fire so that you may

3.7 Isa 6.3; 22.22 Mt 16.19
3.8 Acts 14.27 Rev 2.13
3.9 Rev 2.9
3.10 2 Tim 2.12 2 Pet 2.9 Rev 2.10; 3.8
3.11 Rev 2.10,25 22.7,12,20
3.12 1 Kgs 7.21 Jer 1.18 Ezek 48.35 Gal 4.26,27 Heb 12.22 Rev 14.1,21 21.2; 22.4
3.14 Col 1.15-18
3.15 Rom 12.11
3.17 Mt 5.3 1 Cor 4.8
3.18 1 Cor 3.12,13 1 Pet 1.7

[l] Or *beginning*

3.7 Philadelphia was founded by the citizens of Pergamum. Built in a frontier area as a gateway to the central plateau of Asia Minor, Philadelphia kept barbarians out of the region and brought in Greek culture and language. The city was destroyed by an earthquake in A.D. 17. Aftershocks kept the people so worried that most of them lived outside the city limits.

3.7 The "key of David" represents Christ's authority to open the door of invitation into his future kingdom. After it is open, no one can close it—salvation is assured. Once it is closed, no one can open it—judgment is certain.

3.10 "I will keep you from the hour of trial" can also be translated, "I will keep you from failing in the hour of testing." Some believe that there will be a future time of great tribulation from which true believers will be spared. Others interpret this to mean that the church will go through the time of tribulation and that God will keep them strong in spite of it. Still others believe this refers to times of great trial in general, the church's suffering through the ages. Whatever the case, our emphasis should be on patiently obeying God no matter what we may face.

3.11 Christians have differing gifts, abilities, experience, and levels of maturity. God doesn't expect us all to be the same, but he does expect us to use our assets for him. The Philadelphians are commended for their efforts to obey (3.8) and encouraged to hold tightly to their faith. Use what you have to live for Christ. God will commend you for it.

3.12 The new Jerusalem is the future dwelling of the people of God (21.2). Our citizenship will be in God's future kingdom. Everything will be new, pure, and secure.

3.14 Laodicea was the wealthiest of the seven cities, known for its banking industry, manufacture of wool, a medical school, and eye salve. But the city always had a problem with its water supply. At one time an aqueduct was built to bring water to the city from hot springs. But by the time the water reached the city, it was neither hot nor refreshingly cool—only lukewarm. The church had become as bland as the tepid water that came into the city.

3.14 Christ is the final word ("Amen"), the faithful and true witness, and the Creator.

3.15 Lukewarm water makes a disgusting drink. The church in Laodicea had become lukewarm and thus distasteful and repugnant. The believers didn't stand for anything; indifference had led them to idleness. By neglecting to do anything for Christ, the church had become hardened and self-satisfied, and was destroying itself. God does not want us to be cold, but there is more hope for a rebel to repent than for a halfhearted, in-name-only Christian who thinks he or she is self-sufficient. Don't settle for following God half way. Let Christ fire up your faith and get you into the action.

3.17 Some believers falsely assume that having lots of material possessions is a sign of God's spiritual blessing. Laodicea was a wealthy city, and the church was also rich. But what the Laodiceans could see and buy had become more valuable to them than what is unseen and eternal. Wealth, luxury, and ease can make people feel confident, satisfied, and complacent. But no matter how much you possess or how much money you make, you will have nothing if you don't have a vital relationship with Christ. How does your current level of wealth affect your spiritual desire? Instead of centering your life on comfort and luxury, find your true riches in Christ.

3.18 Laodicea was known for its great wealth—but Christ told the Laodiceans to buy their gold from him. The city was proud of its cloth and dyeing industries—but Christ told them to purchase white garments from him (his righteousness). Laodicea prided itself on its precious eye salve that healed many eye problems—but Christ told them to get medicine from him to heal their eyes so they could see the truth (John 9.39). Christ is showing the Laodiceans

3.19 Job 5.17 Heb 12.6 Rev 2.5
3.21 Mt 19.28 Rev 5.5; 6.2 17.14; 20.4
3.22 Rev 2.7

be rich; and white robes to clothe you and to keep the shame of your nakedness
from being seen; and salve to anoint your eyes so that you may see. 19 I reprove and
discipline those whom I love. Be earnest, therefore, and repent. 20 Listen! I am
standing at the door, knocking; if you hear my voice and open the door, I will come
in to you and eat with you, and you with me. 21 To the one who conquers I will give
a place with me on my throne, just as I myself conquered and sat down with my
Father on his throne. 22 Let anyone who has an ear listen to what the Spirit is saying
to the churches."

B. MESSAGE FOR THE CHURCH (4.1–22.21)

Moving from the conditions within the churches in Asia to the future of the universal church, John sees the course of coming events in a way similar to Daniel and Ezekiel. Many of these passages contain clear spiritual teachings, but others seem beyond our ability to understand. The clear teaching of this book is that God will defeat all evil in the end. We must live in obedience to Jesus Christ, the coming Conqueror and Judge.

1. Worshiping God in heaven

The glorious throne

4.1 Ezek 1.1 Rev 1.10,19 11.12; 19.11
4.2 Isa 6.1 Rev 4.9
4.3 Ezek 1.28; 28.13
4.4 Mt 19.28 2 Tim 2.12

4 After this I looked, and there in heaven a door stood open! And the first voice,
which I had heard speaking to me like a trumpet, said, "Come up here, and I
will show you what must take place after this." 2 At once I was in the spirit,[m] and
there in heaven stood a throne, with one seated on the throne! 3 And the one seated
there looks like jasper and carnelian, and around the throne is a rainbow that looks
like an emerald. 4 Around the throne are twenty-four thrones, and seated on the
thrones are twenty-four elders, dressed in white robes, with golden crowns on their
heads. 5 Coming from the throne are flashes of lightning, and rumblings and peals
of thunder, and in front of the throne burn seven flaming torches, which are the

[m] Or *in the Spirit*

that true value is not in material possessions, but in a right relationship with God. Their possessions and achievements were valueless compared with the everlasting future of Christ's kingdom.

3.19 God would discipline this lukewarm church unless they turned from their indifference toward him. His purpose in discipline is not to punish, but to bring people back to him. Are you lukewarm in your devotion to God? God may use loving discipline to move you out of your uncaring attitude. You can avoid God's discipline by drawing close to him again through confession, service, worship, and Bible study. Just as the spark of love can be rekindled in marriage, so the Holy Spirit can reignite our zeal for God when we allow him to work in our hearts.

3.20 The Laodicean church was complacent and rich. They felt fulfilled, but they didn't have Christ's presence. He knocked at the door of their hearts, but they were so busy enjoying worldly pleasures that they didn't hear him. The pleasures of this world—money, security, material possessions—can be dangerous, because their temporary satisfaction makes us indifferent to God's offer of lasting satisfaction. If you find yourself feeling indifferent to church, to God, or to the Bible, you have begun to shut God out of your life. Leave the door of your heart constantly open to God, and you won't need to worry about missing his knock. Letting him in is your only hope of lasting fulfillment.

3.20 Jesus is knocking on the door of our hearts every time we sense that we should turn to him. He wants to have fellowship with us, and he wants us to open up to him. He is patient and persistent in trying to get through to us—not breaking and entering, but knocking. He allows us to decide whether or not to open our lives to him. Don't keep his life-changing presence and power on the other side of the door. Invite Christ in.

3.22 At the end of each letter to these churches, the believers are urged to listen to and take to heart what is written to them. Although a different message is addressed to each church, all the messages contain warnings and principles for everyone. Which letter speaks most directly to your church? Which has the greatest bearing upon your own spiritual condition at this time? How will you respond?

4.1 Chapters 4 and 5 give a glimpse into Christ's glory. Here we see into the throne room of heaven. God is on the throne and orchestrating all the events that John will record. The world is not spinning out of control; the God of the universe will carry out his plans as Christ initiates the final battle with the forces of evil. John shows us heaven before showing us earth so that we will not be frightened by future events.

4.1 The "first voice" that sounded like a trumpet blast was the voice of Christ (see 1.10, 11).

4.2 John says he was "in the spirit" four times in the book of Revelation (1.10; 4.2; 17.3; 21.10). This expression means that the Holy Spirit was giving him a vision—showing him situations and events he could not see with mere human eyesight. All true prophecy comes from God through the Holy Spirit (2 Peter 1.20, 21).

4.4 Who are these 24 elders? Because there were 12 tribes of Israel in the Old Testament and 12 apostles in the New Testament, the 24 elders in this vision probably represent all the redeemed of God for all time (both before and after Christ's death and resurrection). They symbolize all those—both Jews and Gentiles—who are now part of God's family. The 24 elders show us that *all* the redeemed of the Lord are worshiping him.

4.5 In Revelation, lightning and thunder are associated with significant events in heaven, reminding us of the lightning and thunder at Mount Sinai when God gave the people his laws (Exodus 19.16). The Old Testament often uses such imagery for God's power and majesty (Psalm 77.18).

4.5 The "seven spirits of God" is another name for the Holy Spirit (see the note on 1.4). See also Zechariah 4.2–6, where the seven flaming torches are equated with the one Spirit.

seven spirits of God; 6 and in front of the throne there is something like a sea of
glass, like crystal.
Around the throne, and on each side of the throne, are four living creatures, full
of eyes in front and behind: 7 the first living creature like a lion, the second living
creature like an ox, the third living creature with a face like a human face, and the
fourth living creature like a flying eagle. 8 And the four living creatures, each of
them with six wings, are full of eyes all around and inside. Day and night without
ceasing they sing,

"Holy, holy, holy,
the Lord God the Almighty,
who was and is and is to come."

9 And whenever the living creatures give glory and honor and thanks to the one who
is seated on the throne, who lives forever and ever, 10 the twenty-four elders fall
before the one who is seated on the throne and worship the one who lives forever
and ever; they cast their crowns before the throne, singing,

11 "You are worthy, our Lord and God,
to receive glory and honor and power,
for you created all things,
and by your will they existed and were created."

The scroll and the Lamb

5 Then I saw in the right hand of the one seated on the throne a scroll written on
the inside and on the back, sealed[n] with seven seals; 2 and I saw a mighty angel
proclaiming with a loud voice, "Who is worthy to open the scroll and break its
seals?" 3 And no one in heaven or on earth or under the earth was able to open the
scroll or to look into it. 4 And I began to weep bitterly because no one was found
worthy to open the scroll or to look into it. 5 Then one of the elders said to me, "Do
not weep. See, the Lion of the tribe of Judah, the Root of David, has conquered, so
that he can open the scroll and its seven seals."
6 Then I saw between the throne and the four living creatures and among the

4.5 Ex 25.31-39 Zech 4.2-6 Rev 1.4; 5.6
4.6 Ezek 1.5-14 10.12,14 Rev 15.7; 19.4
4.7 Ezek 1.10; 10.21
4.9 Dan 4.34; 12.7 Rev 4.2; 10.6
4.10 Rev 4.4 5.8,14; 10.6
4.11 Rev 10.6
5.1 Isa 29.11 Ezek 2.9 Dan 12.4
5.3 Phil 2.10
5.5 Gen 49.9 Isa 11.1,10 Heb 2.10 7.14,25 Rev 22.16

[n] *Or written on the inside, and sealed on the back*

4.6 Glass was very rare in New Testament times, and crystal-clear glass was impossible to find. The "sea of glass, like crystal" highlights both the magnificence and holiness of God.

4.6, 7 Just as the seven flaming torches symbolize the Holy Spirit, so the four creatures represent the qualities and character of God. These creatures are not real animals, but like the cherubim (the highest of the angels) they guard God's throne, lead others in worship, and proclaim God's holiness. God's attributes symbolized in the animal-like appearance of these four beings are majesty and power (the lion), faithfulness (the ox), intelligence (the human), and sovereignty (the eagle). The Old Testament prophet Ezekiel saw four similar beings in one of his visions (Ezekiel 1.5–10).

4.10 The elders "cast their crowns before the throne" acknowledging that all authority and honor belong to the Lord.

4.11 The point of this chapter is summed up in this verse: all beings in heaven and earth will praise and honor God because he is the Creator and Sustainer of everything.

5.1 In John's day, books were written on scrolls—pieces of papyrus or vellum up to 30 feet long, rolled up and sealed with clay or wax. The scroll that John sees contains the full account of what God has in store for the world. The seven seals indicate the importance of its contents. The seals are throughout the scroll so that as each one is broken, more of the scroll can be read to reveal another phase of God's plan for the end of the world. Only Christ is worthy to break the seals and open the scroll (5.3–5).

5.1ff Chapter 5 continues the glimpse into heaven begun in chapter 4.

5.5 The Lion, Jesus, proved himself worthy to break the seals and open the scroll by living a perfect life of obedience to God, dying on the cross for the sins of the world, and rising from the dead to show his power and authority over evil and death. Only Christ conquered sin, death, hell, and Satan himself; only he can be trusted with the world's future. The Root of David refers to Jesus being from David's family line, fulfilling the Old Testament prophecy (Isaiah 9.6, 7; 11.1).

5.5, 6 Jesus Christ is pictured as both a Lion (symbolizing his authority and power) and a Lamb (symbolizing his submission to God's will). One of the elders calls John to look at the Lion, but when John looks he sees a Lamb. Christ the Lamb was the perfect sacrifice for the sins of all mankind; therefore, only he can save us from the terrible events revealed by the scroll. Christ the Lamb won the greatest battle of all. He defeated all the forces of evil by dying on the cross. The role of Christ the Lion will be to lead the battle where Satan is finally defeated (19.19–21). Christ the Lion is victorious because of what Christ the Lamb has already done. We will participate in his victory not because of our effort or goodness, but because our wills are pledged completely to his service.

5.6 John sees the Lamb "as if it had been slaughtered." The wounds inflicted on Jesus' body during his trial and crucifixion could still be seen (see John 20.24–31). Jesus was called the Lamb of God by John the Baptist (John 1.29). In the Old Testament, lambs were sacrificed to cover sins: Jesus, the Lamb of God, died as the final sacrifice for all sins (see Isaiah 53.7; Hebrews 10.1–12, 18).

5.6 The horns symbolize strength and power (see 1 Kings 22.11; Zechariah 1.18). Although Christ is a sacrificial lamb, he is in no way weak. In Zechariah 4.2–10, the eyes are equated with the seven torches and the one Spirit.

5.6 Isa 53.7 Zech 3.9; 4.10 Dan 8.3 1 Pet 1.19 Rev 1.4; 4.5
5.8 Rev 4.4,10; 5.6,11 8.3,4; 14.2; 15.2
5.9 1 Pet 2.6 Rev 4.11; 7.9 14.3; 15.3,4
5.10 Ex 19.6 1 Pet 2.5-9 Rev 1.6; 3.21 20.4

elders a Lamb standing as if it had been slaughtered, having seven horns and seven
eyes, which are the seven spirits of God sent out into all the earth. 7 He went and
took the scroll from the right hand of the one who was seated on the throne. 8 When
he had taken the scroll, the four living creatures and the twenty-four elders fell
before the Lamb, each holding a harp and golden bowls full of incense, which are
the prayers of the saints. 9 They sing a new song:

"You are worthy to take the scroll
    and to open its seals,
for you were slaughtered and by your blood you ransomed for God
    saints from[o] every tribe and language and people and nation;
10 you have made them to be a kingdom and priests serving[p] our God,
    and they will reign on earth."

[o] Gk *ransomed for God from* [p] Gk *priests to*

EVENTS IN REVELATION DESCRIBED ELSEWHERE IN THE BIBLE

Other Reference	*Revelation Reference*	*Event*
Ezekiel 1.22–28	4.2, 3; 10.1–3	Glowing rainbow around God's throne
Isaiah 53.7	5.6–8	Christ is pictured as a Lamb
Psalm 96	5.9–14	New song
Zechariah 1.7–11; 6.1–8	6.1–8	Horses and horsemen
Isaiah 2.19–22	6.12; 8.5; 11.13	Earthquake
Joel 2.28–32; Acts 2.14–21	6.12	Moon turns blood-red
Mark 13.21–25	6.13	Stars falling from the heavens
Isaiah 34.1–4	6.14	Heavens rolled up like a scroll
Zephaniah 1.14–18; 1 Thessalonians 5.1–3	6.15–17	God's inescapable anger
Jeremiah 49.35–39	7.1	Four winds of judgment
Luke 8.26–34	9.1, 2; 17.3–8	Bottomless pit (or "the deep")
Joel 1.2—2.11	9.3–11	Plague of locusts
Luke 21.20–24	11.1–3	Trampling of the holy city of Jerusalem
Zechariah 4	11.4–6	Two olive trees as prophets
Daniel 7	13.1–10	A beast rising out of the sea
2 Thessalonians 2.7–14	13.11–15	Wondrous signs and miracles done by evil beings
Jeremiah 25.15–29	14.9–12	Drinking the cup of God's wrath
Isaiah 21.1–10	18.2, 3	"Babylon" falls
Matthew 22.1–14	19.5–8	Wedding banquet of the Lamb
Ezekiel 38, 39	20.7–10	Conflict with Gog and Magog
John 5.19–30	20.11–15	Judging of all people
Ezekiel 37.21–28	21.3	God lives among mankind
Isaiah 25.1–8	21.4	Our tears will be wiped away forever
Genesis 2.8–14	22.1, 2	Trees of life
1 Corinthians 13.11, 12	22.3–5	We will see God face to face
Daniel 7.18–28	22.5	Believers shall reign with God forever

5.9, 10 People from every nation are praising God before his throne. God's message of salvation and eternal life is not limited to a specific culture, race, or country. Anyone who comes to God in repentance and faith is accepted by him and will be part of his kingdom. Don't allow prejudice or bias to stop you from sharing Christ with others. Christ welcomes all kinds of people.

5.9, 10 The song of God's people praises Christ's work. He (1) was slain, (2) ransomed them with his blood, (3) gathered them into a kingdom, (4) made them priests, and (5) appointed them to reign upon the earth. Jesus has already died and paid the penalty for sin. He is now gathering us into his kingdom and making us priests. In the future we will reign with him. Realizing the glorious future that awaits us, we can find strength to face our present difficulties.

5.10 The believers' song praises Christ for bringing them into the kingdom and making them priests. While now we may be depised and mocked for our faith, (John 15.17–27), in the future we will reign over all the earth (Luke 22.29, 30). Christ's death made all believers priests of God – the channels of blessing between God and humankind (1 Peter 2.5–9).

11 Then I looked, and I heard the voice of many angels surrounding the throne
and the living creatures and the elders; they numbered myriads of myriads and
thousands of thousands, 12 singing with full voice,
"Worthy is the Lamb that was slaughtered
to receive power and wealth and wisdom and might
and honor and glory and blessing!"
13 Then I heard every creature in heaven and on earth and under the earth and in the
sea, and all that is in them, singing,
"To the one seated on the throne and to the Lamb
be blessing and honor and glory and might
forever and ever!"
14 And the four living creatures said, "Amen!" And the elders fell down and worshiped.

5.11 Ps 68.17 Heb 12.22 Rev 4.4,6
5.12 Zech 13.7 Rev 1.6; 4.11
5.13 Phil 2.10,11
5.14 Rev 4.6,10

2. Opening the seven seals

The seals

6 Then I saw the Lamb open one of the seven seals, and I heard one of the four
living creatures call out, as with a voice of thunder, "Come!"[q] 2 I looked, and
there was a white horse! Its rider had a bow; a crown was given to him, and he came
out conquering and to conquer.
3 When he opened the second seal, I heard the second living creature call out,
"Come!"[q] 4 And out came[r] another horse, bright red; its rider was permitted to
take peace from the earth, so that people would slaughter one another; and he was
given a great sword.
5 When he opened the third seal, I heard the third living creature call out,
"Come!"[q] I looked, and there was a black horse! Its rider held a pair of scales in his
hand, 6 and I heard what seemed to be a voice in the midst of the four living creatures saying, "A quart of wheat for a day's pay,[s] and three quarts of barley for a
day's pay,[s] but do not damage the olive oil and the wine!"
7 When he opened the fourth seal, I heard the voice of the fourth living creature
call out, "Come!"[q] 8 I looked and there was a pale green horse! Its rider's name was
Death, and Hades followed with him; they were given authority over a fourth of the
earth, to kill with sword, famine, and pestilence, and by the wild animals of the
earth.

6.1 Rev 5.1,6
6.2 Zech 6.1-3 Rev 10.3,4 14.14; 19.11
6.3 Rev 4.7
6.4 Zech 1.8; 6.2 Mt 10.34 Jn 19.11
6.5 Ezek 4.16 Zech 6.2
6.8 Prov 5.5 Jer 15.2 Hos 13.14 Zech 6.3 Mt 11.23 Rev 1.18; 20.14

[q] Or *"Go!"* [r] Or *went* [s] Gk *a denarius*

5.11 Angels are spiritual beings, created by God to help carry out his work on earth. They bring messages (Luke 1.26–28), protect God's people (Daniel 6.22), offer encouragement (Genesis 16.7ff), give guidance (Exodus 14.19), bring punishment (2 Samuel 24.16), patrol the earth (Ezekiel 1.9–14), and fight the forces of evil (2 Kings 6.16–18; Revelation 20.1). There are both good and evil angels (12.7). Evil angels are allied with Satan and have considerably less power and authority. Eventually, the main role of the good angels will be to offer continuous praise to God (see also 19.1–3).

5.14 The scene in chapter 5 shows us that only the Lamb, Jesus Christ, is worthy to open the scroll (the events of history). Jesus, not Satan, holds the future. Jesus Christ is in control, and he alone is worthy to set into motion the events of the last days of history.

6.1ff This is the first of three seven-part judgments. The trumpets (chapters 8, 9) and the bowls (chapter 16) are the other two. As each seal is opened, Christ the Lamb sets in motion the events that will bring about the end of human history. This scroll is not completely opened until the seventh seal is opened (8.1). The contents of the scroll reveal humankind's depravity and portray God's authority over the events of human history.

6.2ff Four horses appear as the first four seals are opened. The horses represent God's judgment of people's sin and rebellion. God is directing human history – even using his enemies to accomplish his purposes. The four horses are a foretaste of the final judgments yet to come. Some view this chapter as a parallel to the Olivet Discourse (see Matthew 24). The imagery of four horses is also found in Zechariah 6.1–8.

6.2–8 Each of the four horses is a different color. Some assume that the white horse represents victory with Christ its rider, because Christ later rides to victory on a white horse – 19.11. But because the other three horses relate to judgment and destruction, this rider on a white horse would not be Christ. The four are part of the unfolding judgment of God, and it would be premature for Christ to ride forth as conqueror. The other colored horses represent different kinds of judgment: red for warfare and bloodshed; black for famine and death; pale green for disease and wild animal attacks. The reference to wheat and barley illustrates famine conditions, but the worst is yet to come.

6.8 It is not clear whether Hades was on a separate horse than

6.9 2 Tim 4.6
6.10 Ps 79.10; Zech 1.12; Lk 18.7
6.11 Dan 12.13; 2 Thess 1.7; Heb 4.9; 11.40
6.12 Joel 2.10; Mt 24.29
6.13 Rev 8.10; 9.1
6.14 Ps 102.26; Heb 1.10-12; 2 Pet 3.10
6.16 2 Thess 1.7-9
6.17 Isa 13.6; 63.4; Mal 3.2

9 When he opened the fifth seal, I saw under the altar the souls of those who had
been slaughtered for the word of God and for the testimony they had given; 10 they
cried out with a loud voice, "Sovereign Lord, holy and true, how long will it be
before you judge and avenge our blood on the inhabitants of the earth?" 11 They
were each given a white robe and told to rest a little longer, until the number would
be complete both of their fellow servants[t] and of their brothers and sisters,[u] who
were soon to be killed as they themselves had been killed.

12 When he opened the sixth seal, I looked, and there came a great earthquake;
the sun became black as sackcloth, the full moon became like blood, 13 and the stars
of the sky fell to the earth as the fig tree drops its winter fruit when shaken by a gale.
14 The sky vanished like a scroll rolling itself up, and every mountain and island
was removed from its place. 15 Then the kings of the earth and the magnates and the
generals and the rich and the powerful, and everyone, slave and free, hid in the
caves and among the rocks of the mountains, 16 calling to the mountains and rocks,
"Fall on us and hide us from the face of the one seated on the throne and from the
wrath of the Lamb; 17 for the great day of their wrath has come, and who is able to
stand?"

The 144,000 sealed by God

7.1 Jer 49.36; Zech 6.5; Mt 24.31
7.3 Ezek 9.4,6; Dan 6.16; Eph 4.30; 2 Tim 2.19; Rev 14.1; 22.4

7 After this I saw four angels standing at the four corners of the earth, holding
back the four winds of the earth so that no wind could blow on earth or sea or
against any tree. 2 I saw another angel ascending from the rising of the sun, having
the seal of the living God, and he called with a loud voice to the four angels who
had been given power to damage earth and sea, 3 saying, "Do not damage the earth
or the sea or the trees, until we have marked the servants[t] of our God with a seal
on their foreheads."

[t] Gk *slaves* [u] Gk *brothers*

Death or merely went along with Death, but the horsemen described in verses 2–8 are commonly referred to as the four horsemen of the apocalypse.

6.8 The four horsemen are given control of one-fourth of the earth, indicating that God is still limiting his judgment – it is not yet complete. With these judgments there is still time for believers to turn to Christ and away from their sin. In this case, the limited punishment demonstrates not only God's wrath on sin, but also his merciful love in giving people yet another opportunity to turn to him before he brings final judgment.

6.9 The altar represents the altar of sacrifice in the temple, where animals were sacrificed to atone for sins. Instead of the animals' blood at the foot of the altar, John saw the souls of martyrs who had died for preaching God's Word. These martyrs were told that still more would lose their lives for their belief in Christ (6.11). In the face of warfare, famine, persecution, and death, Christians will be called on to stand firmly for what they believe. Only those who endure to the end will be rewarded by God (Mark 13.13).

6.9–11 The martyrs are eager for God to bring justice to the earth, but they are told to wait. God is not waiting until a certain number of martyrs is reached, but he is promising that those who suffer and die for their faith will not be forgotten. They will be singled out by God for special honor. We may wish for justice immediately, as these martyrs did, but we must be patient. God works on his own timetable, and he promises justice. No suffering for the sake of God's kingdom, however, is wasted.

6.12 The sixth seal changes the scene back to the physical world. The first five judgments were directed toward specific areas, but this judgment is universal. Everyone will be afraid when the earth itself trembles.

6.15–17 At the sight of God sitting on the throne, all human beings, great and small, will be terrified, calling for the mountains to fall on them so they will not have to face the judgment of the Lamb. This picture is not intended to frighten believers. For them, the Lamb is a gentle Savior. But those generals, emperors, or kings who have shown no fear of God and have arrogantly flaunted their unbelief will find that they were wrong – in that day they will have to face God's wrath. No one who has rejected God can survive the day of his wrath, but those who belong to Christ will receive a reward instead of punishment. Do you belong to Christ? If so, you need not fear these final days.

7.1ff The sixth seal has been opened, and the people of the earth have tried to hide from God, saying, "Who is able to stand?" (6.12–17). Just when all hope seems lost, four angels hold back the four winds of judgment until God's people are marked as his own. Only then will God open the seventh seal (8.1).

7.2 A seal on a scroll or document identified and protected its contents. God places his own seal on his followers, identifying them as his own and guaranteeing his protection over their souls. This shows how valuable we are to him. Our physical bodies may be beaten, maimed, or even destroyed, but *nothing* can harm our souls when we have been marked by God. See Ephesians 1.13 for the seal of the Holy Spirit.

7.3 God's seal is placed on the foreheads of his servants. This seal is the exact opposite of the mark of the beast explained in 13.16. These two marks place the people in two distinct categories – those owned by God and those owned by Satan.

4 And I heard the number of those who were sealed, one hundred forty-four **7.4**
thousand, sealed out of every tribe of the people of Israel: Rev 9.16 14.1,3
5 From the tribe of Judah twelve thousand sealed,
from the tribe of Reuben twelve thousand,
from the tribe of Gad twelve thousand,
6 from the tribe of Asher twelve thousand,
from the tribe of Naphtali twelve thousand,
from the tribe of Manasseh twelve thousand,
7 from the tribe of Simeon twelve thousand,
from the tribe of Levi twelve thousand,
from the tribe of Issachar twelve thousand,
8 from the tribe of Zebulun twelve thousand,
from the tribe of Joseph twelve thousand,
from the tribe of Benjamin twelve thousand sealed.

The great crowd

9 After this I looked, and there was a great multitude that no one could count, **7.9**
from every nation, from all tribes and peoples and languages, standing before the Rev 3.5; 6.11; 5.9
throne and before the Lamb, robed in white, with palm branches in their hands.
10 They cried out in a loud voice, saying, **7.10**
"Salvation belongs to our God who is seated on the throne, and to the Rev 5.13 12.10; 19.1; 22.3
Lamb!"
11 And all the angels stood around the throne and around the elders and the four **7.11**
living creatures, and they fell on their faces before the throne and worshiped God, Rev 4.4,6,10
12 singing, **7.12** Rev 5.12,14
"Amen! Blessing and glory and wisdom
and thanksgiving and honor
and power and might
be to our God forever and ever! Amen." **7.13** Rev 7.9
13 Then one of the elders addressed me, saying, "Who are these, robed in **7.14**
white, and where have they come from?" 14 I said to him, "Sir, you are the one that Rev 6.11; 22.14

7.4–8 The number 144,000 is 12 x 12 x 1,000, symbolizing completeness—*all* God's followers will be brought safely to him; not one will be overlooked or forgotten. God seals these believers either by withdrawing them from the earth (this is called the Rapture) or by giving them special strength and courage to make it through this time of great persecution. If they were to endure persecution, the seal would not necessarily guarantee protection from physical harm—many would die (see 6.11)—but God would protect them from spiritual harm. No matter what happens, they will be brought to their reward of eternal life. Their destiny is secure. These believers will not fall away from God even in intense persecution.

This is not saying that 144,000 individuals must be sealed before the persecution comes, but that when it begins, the faithful will have already been marked by God, and they will remain true to him until the end.

7.4–8 This is a different list from the usual listing of the 12 tribes in the Old Testament, because it is a symbolic list of God's true followers. (1) Judah is mentioned first because Judah is the tribe both of David and of Jesus the Messiah (Genesis 49.8–12; Matthew 1.1). (2) Levi had no tribal allotment because of the Levites' work for God in the temple (Deuteronomy 18.1), but here the tribe is given a place as a reward for faithfulness. (3) Dan and Ephraim are not mentioned, because they were known for rebellion and idolatry, traits unacceptable in God's followers (Genesis 49.17). (4) The two tribes representing Joseph (usually called Ephraim and Manasseh, after Joseph's sons) are here called Joseph and Manasseh, because of Ephraim's rebellion. See Genesis 49 for the story of the beginning of these 12 tribes.

7.9 Who is this great multitude? While some interpreters identify it as the martyrs described in 6.9, it may also be the same group as the 144,000 just mentioned (7.4–8). The 144,000 were sealed by God before the great time of persecution; the great multitude was spared, as God had promised. Before, they were being prepared; here, they are victorious. This crowd in heaven is composed of all those who have remained faithful to God throughout the generations. No true believer need ever worry about being included in the right group. God includes and protects each of us, and we are guaranteed a place in God's presence.

7.10 People try many methods to remove the guilt of sin—good works, intellectual pursuits, and even casting blame on others. The multitude in heaven, however, praises God, saying that salvation comes from him and from the Lamb. Salvation from sin's penalty can come only through Jesus Christ. Have you had the guilt of sin removed by Christ?

7.11 More information about the elders is found in the note on 4.4. The four creatures are explained further in the note on 4.6.

7.14 The great tribulation ("ordeal") has been explained in several ways. Some believe it refers to the suffering of believers through the ages; others believe there will be a specific time of intense tribulation. In either case, these believers come through their times of suffering by remaining loyal to God. Because they remain faithful, God will give them eternal life with him (7.17).

7.14 It is difficult to imagine how blood could whiten any cloth. But the blood of Jesus Christ is the world's greatest purifier because it removes the stain of sin. White symbolizes sinless perfection, or holiness, that can be given to people only by the death of the the sinless Lamb of God on our behalf. This is a picture of how we are

knows." Then he said to me, "These are they who have come out of the great ordeal; they have washed their robes and made them white in the blood of the Lamb.

7.15 Rev 4.9; 11.19; 22.3

15 For this reason they are before the throne of God,
and worship him day and night within his temple,
and the one who is seated on the throne will shelter them.

7.16 Isa 49.10

16 They will hunger no more, and thirst no more;
the sun will not strike them,
nor any scorching heat;

7.17 Isa 25.8; 35.10; Rev 21.4,6; 22.1

17 for the Lamb at the center of the throne will be their shepherd,
and he will guide them to springs of the water of life,
and God will wipe away every tear from their eyes."

The seventh seal

8.2 Mt 18.10; 1 Cor 15.52

8 When the Lamb opened the seventh seal, there was silence in heaven for about
half an hour. 2 And I saw the seven angels who stand before God, and seven
trumpets were given to them.

8.3 Heb 9.4

8.4 Ps 141.2

8.5 Lev 16.12; 1 Kgs 19.11; Ezek 10.2; Rev 16.18

3 Another angel with a golden censer came and stood at the altar; he was given
a great quantity of incense to offer with the prayers of all the saints on the golden
altar that is before the throne. 4 And the smoke of the incense, with the prayers of
the saints, rose before God from the hand of the angel. 5 Then the angel took the
censer and filled it with fire from the altar and threw it on the earth; and there were
peals of thunder, rumblings, flashes of lightning, and an earthquake.

3. Sounding the seven trumpets

The trumpets

8.7 Joel 2.30; Zech 13.8,9; Mt 7.25-27

6 Now the seven angels who had the seven trumpets made ready to blow them.
7 The first angel blew his trumpet, and there came hail and fire, mixed with
blood, and they were hurled to the earth; and a third of the earth was burned up, and
a third of the trees were burned up, and all green grass was burned up.

8.8 Ex 7.17; Zech 13.8,9; Rev 16.2

8.9 Rev 8.7-12; 9.15,18

8 The second angel blew his trumpet, and something like a great mountain,
burning with fire, was thrown into the sea. 9 A third of the sea became blood, a third
of the living creatures in the sea died, and a third of the ships were destroyed.

8.10 Isa 14.12; Rev 6.13; 9.1; 12.4; 16.4

8.11 Ex 15.23; Heb 12.15

10 The third angel blew his trumpet, and a great star fell from heaven, blazing
like a torch, and it fell on a third of the rivers and on the springs of water. 11 The
name of the star is Wormwood. A third of the waters became wormwood, and
many died from the water, because it was made bitter.

8.12 Ex 10.21; Zech 13.8

12 The fourth angel blew his trumpet, and a third of the sun was struck, and a
third of the moon, and a third of the stars, so that a third of their light was darkened;
a third of the day was kept from shining, and likewise the night.

---

saved by faith (see Isaiah 1.18; Romans 3.21–26).

7.16, 17 God will provide for his children's needs in their eternal home, where there will be no hunger, thirst, or pain, and he will wipe away all tears. When you are suffering or torn apart by sorrow, take comfort in this promise of complete protection and relief.

7.17 In verses 1–8 we see the believers receiving a seal to protect them through a time of great tribulation and suffering; in verses 9–17 we see the believers finally with God in heaven. All who have been faithful through the ages are singing before God's throne. Their tribulations and sorrows are over: no more tears for sin, because all their sins are forgiven; no more tears for suffering, because all their suffering is over; no more tears for death, because all believers have been resurrected to die no more.

8.1, 2 When the seventh seal is opened, the seven trumpet judgments are revealed. In the same way, the seventh trumpet will announce the seven bowl judgments in 11.15 and 16.1–21. The trumpet judgments, like the seal judgments, are only partial. God's final and complete judgment has not yet come.

8.3 A censer filled with live coals was used in temple worship. Incense was poured on the coals, and the sweet-smelling smoke drifted upwards, symbolizing believers' prayers ascending to God (see Exodus 30.7–9).

8.6 The trumpet blasts have three purposes: (1) to warn that judgment is certain, (2) to call the forces of good and evil to battle, and (3) to announce the return of the King, the Messiah. These warnings urge us to make sure that our faith is firmly fixed on Christ.

8.7–12 Because only one-third of the earth is destroyed by these trumpet judgments, this is only a partial judgment from God. His full wrath is yet to be unleashed.

8.11 Wormwood is a very bitter substance. It stands for the bitterness of God's judgment.

13 Then I looked, and I heard an eagle crying with a loud voice as it flew in
midheaven, "Woe, woe, woe to the inhabitants of the earth, at the blasts of the
other trumpets that the three angels are about to blow!"
9 And the fifth angel blew his trumpet, and I saw a star that had fallen from
heaven to earth, and he was given the key to the shaft of the bottomless pit; 2 he
opened the shaft of the bottomless pit, and from the shaft rose smoke like the smoke
of a great furnace, and the sun and the air were darkened with the smoke from the
shaft. 3 Then from the smoke came locusts on the earth, and they were given authority like the authority of scorpions of the earth. 4 They were told not to damage the
grass of the earth or any green growth or any tree, but only those people who do not
have the seal of God on their foreheads. 5 They were allowed to torture them for
five months, but not to kill them, and their torture was like the torture of a scorpion
when it stings someone. 6 And in those days people will seek death but will not find
it; they will long to die, but death will flee from them.
7 In appearance the locusts were like horses equipped for battle. On their heads
were what looked like crowns of gold; their faces were like human faces, 8 their hair
like women's hair, and their teeth like lions' teeth; 9 they had scales like iron breastplates, and the noise of their wings was like the noise of many chariots with horses
rushing into battle. 10 They have tails like scorpions, with stingers, and in their tails
is their power to harm people for five months. 11 They have as king over them the
angel of the bottomless pit; his name in Hebrew is Abaddon,[v] and in Greek he is
called Apollyon.[w]
12 The first woe has passed. There are still two woes to come.
13 Then the sixth angel blew his trumpet, and I heard a voice from the four[x]
horns of the golden altar before God, 14 saying to the sixth angel who had the trumpet, "Release the four angels who are bound at the great river Euphrates." 15 So the
four angels were released, who had been held ready for the hour, the day, the
month, and the year, to kill a third of humankind. 16 The number of the troops of

8.13 Rev 3.10; 9.12
9.1 Isa 14.12; Lk 8.31; 10.18; Rev 3.10; 8.10; 17.8; 20.1
9.2 Joel 2.2,30
9.3 Ex 10.4,5,12-15; Rev 9.5,7,10
9.4 Ex 12.23; Rev 6.6; 7.2,3
9.6 Job 3.21; Rev 6.16
9.7 Joel 2.4
9.8 Joel 1.6
9.9 Joel 2.5
9.11 Job 26.6; Prov 15.11; Lk 8.31; Jn 12.31; 14.30; Rev 9.1
9.12 Rev 8.13; 11.14
9.13 Ex 30.2-10; Heb 9.24; 10.21; Rev 8.3
9.14 Gen 2.14; 15.18; Rev 7.1; 16.12
9.15 Rev 9.18; 20.7

[v] That is, *Destruction* [w] That is, *Destroyer* [x] Other ancient authorities lack *four*

8.13 Habakkuk used an eagle to symbolize swiftness and destruction (see Habakkuk 1.8). The picture here is of a strong, powerful bird flying over all the earth, warning of the terrors yet to come. While both believers and unbelievers experience the terrors described in verses 7–12, the "inhabitants of the earth" are the unbelievers who will meet spiritual harm with the next three trumpet judgments. God has guaranteed believers protection from spiritual harm (7.2, 3).

8.13 In 6.10, the martyrs call out to God, "How long . . . before you judge and avenge our blood?" As we see the world's wickedness, we too may cry out to God, "How long?" In the following chapters, the judgment comes at last. We may be distressed and impatient, but God has his plan and his timing, and we must learn to trust him to know what is best. Judgment is coming – be sure of that. Thank God for the time he has given you to turn from sin. Use the available time to work to help others turn to him.

9.1 It is not known whether this "star" who fell from heaven is Satan, a fallen angel, Christ, or a good angel. Most likely it is a good angel, because the key to the bottomless pit is normally held by Christ (1.17, 18), but it is temporarily given to this other being from heaven (see also 20.1). This being, whoever he may be, is still under God's control and authority. The bottomless pit represents the place of the demons and of Satan, the Prince of demons (9.11). See also Luke 8.31 for another reference to the bottomless pit.

9.3 The prophet Joel described a locust plague as a foreshadowing of the day of the Lord, meaning God's coming judgment (Joel 2.1–10). In the Old Testament, locusts were symbols of destruction because they destroyed vegetation. Here, however, they symbolize an invasion of demons called to torture people who do not believe in God. The limitations placed on the demons (they could only torment people for five months) show that they are under God's authority.

9.3ff Most likely these locusts are demons – evil spirits ruled by Satan. They were not created by Satan, because God is the Creator of all. Rather, they are fallen angels who joined Satan in his rebellion. God limits what they can do; they can do nothing without his permission. Their main purpose on earth is to destroy, prevent, or distort people's relationship with God. Because they are in a corrupt and degenerate state, their appearance reflects the distortion of their spirits. While it is important to recognize their evil activity so we can stay away from them, we should avoid any curiosity about or involvement with demonic forces or the occult.

9.11 The locust-demons have a leader whose name in Hebrew means "destruction," and in Greek "the destroyer." This may be a play on words by John to show that those who worship the great god Apollo worship only a demon.

9.13 The altar in the Jerusalem temple had four projections, one at each corner, called the horns of the altar (see Exodus 27.2).

9.14 The word "angels" here means fallen angels or demons. These four unidentified demons will be exceedingly evil and destructive. But note that they do not have the power to release themselves and do their evil work on earth. Instead, they are held back by God and will be released by him at a specific time, doing only what he allows them to do.

9.15 Here one-third of all people are killed. In 6.7, 8, one-fourth of mankind was killed. Thus, over one-half of the people in the world will have been killed by God's great judgments. Even more would have died if God had not set limits on the destruction.

9.16 In John's day this number of warriors in an army was inconceivable, but today there are countries and alliances that could easily amass this many soldiers. This huge army, led by the four demons, will be sent out to destroy one-third of the earth's population. But the judgment is still not complete.

9.16 Dan 7.10; 11.40 Rev 5.11; 7.4
9.17 Dan 8.2; 9.21

cavalry was two hundred million; I heard their number. 17 And this was how I saw
the horses in my vision: the riders wore breastplates the color of fire and of sapphire[y] and of sulfur; the heads of the horses were like lions' heads, and fire and
smoke and sulfur came out of their mouths. 18 By these three plagues a third of
humankind was killed, by the fire and smoke and sulfur coming out of their
mouths. 19 For the power of the horses is in their mouths and in their tails; their tails
are like serpents, having heads; and with them they inflict harm.

9.20 Deut 4.28 Ps 115.4-7 Dan 5.23 Mic 5.13 Acts 7.41 1 Cor 10.20 Rev 2.21
9.21 Rev 7.2

20 The rest of humankind, who were not killed by these plagues, did not repent
of the works of their hands or give up worshiping demons and idols of gold and
silver and bronze and stone and wood, which cannot see or hear or walk. 21 And
they did not repent of their murders or their sorceries or their fornication or their
thefts.

The angel with the small scroll

10.1 Mt 17.2 Rev 1.15,16 4.3; 5.2; 18.1
10.3 Ps 29.3-9 Rev 4.5
10.4 Dan 8.26; 12.4 Rev 1.10; 22.10

10 And I saw another mighty angel coming down from heaven, wrapped in a
cloud, with a rainbow over his head; his face was like the sun, and his legs
like pillars of fire. 2 He held a little scroll open in his hand. Setting his right foot on
the sea and his left foot on the land, 3 he gave a great shout, like a lion roaring. And
when he shouted, the seven thunders sounded. 4 And when the seven thunders had
sounded, I was about to write, but I heard a voice from heaven saying, "Seal up
what the seven thunders have said, and do not write it down." 5 Then the angel
whom I saw standing on the sea and the land

raised his right hand to heaven

10.6 Rev 4.9,11; 16.17 21.6
10.7 Amos 3.7 Rev 11.15

6 and swore by him who lives forever and ever,
who created heaven and what is in it, the earth and what is in it, and the sea and
what is in it: "There will be no more delay, 7 but in the days when the seventh angel
is to blow his trumpet, the mystery of God will be fulfilled, as he announced to his
servants[z] the prophets."

10.8 Rev 10.2
10.9 Jer 15.16 Ezek 2.8; 3.1-3

8 Then the voice that I had heard from heaven spoke to me again, saying, "Go,
take the scroll that is open in the hand of the angel who is standing on the sea and
on the land." 9 So I went to the angel and told him to give me the little scroll; and
he said to me, "Take it, and eat; it will be bitter to your stomach, but sweet as honey
in your mouth." 10 So I took the little scroll from the hand of the angel and ate it; it
was sweet as honey in my mouth, but when I had eaten it, my stomach was made
bitter.

10.11 Rev 5.9

11 Then they said to me, "You must prophesy again about many peoples and
nations and languages and kings."

[y] Gk *hyacinth* [z] Gk *slaves*

9.20, 21 These people are so hardhearted that even plagues do not drive them to God. People don't usually fall into immorality and evil suddenly – they slip into it a little at a time until, hardly realizing what has happened, they are irrevocably mired in their wicked ways. Any person who allows sin to take root in his life may find himself in this predicament. Temptation entertained today becomes sin tomorrow, then a habit the next day, then death and separation from God forever (see James 1.15). Thinking that you could never become this evil is the first step toward a hard heart.

10.1–6 The purpose of this mighty angel is clear – to announce the final judgments on the earth. His right foot on the sea and left foot on the land (10.2) indicate that his words deal with all creation, not just a limited part as with the seal and trumpet judgments. The seventh trumpet (11.15) will usher in the seven bowl judgments, that will bring an end to the present world. When this universal judgment comes, God's truth will prevail.

10.2 There are two scrolls in Revelation. The first contains a revelation of judgments against evil (5.1ff). The contents of the second little scroll are not indicated, but it may also contain a revelation of judgment.

10.4 Throughout history people have wanted to know what will happen in the future. God reveals some of the future events in this book. But John was stopped from describing certain parts of his vision. An angel also told the prophet Daniel that some visions he saw were not to be revealed yet to everyone (Daniel 12.9); and Jesus told his disciples that the time of the end is known by no one but God (Mark 13.32, 33). God has revealed all we need to know to live for him now. In our desire to be ready for the end, we must not place more emphasis on speculation about the last days than on living for God while we wait.

10.7 When God's plan for human history is completely revealed, all prophecy will have been fulfilled. The end of the age will have arrived (see 11.15 and Ephesians 1.9, 10).

10.9, 10 The prophet Ezekiel had a vision in which he was told to swallow a scroll filled with judgments against the nation of Israel (Ezekiel 3.1ff). It was sweet in his mouth, but its contents brought destruction – just like the the scroll John was told to eat. God's Word is sweet to us as believers because it brings encouragement. But it will be bitter to our stomach because of the coming judgment we must pronounce on unbelievers.

The two witnesses

11 Then I was given a measuring rod like a staff, and I was told, "Come and
measure the temple of God and the altar and those who worship there, 2 but
do not measure the court outside the temple; leave that out, for it is given over to the
nations, and they will trample over the holy city for forty-two months. 3 And I will
grant my two witnesses authority to prophesy for one thousand two hundred sixty
days, wearing sackcloth."
4 These are the two olive trees and the two lampstands that stand before the
Lord of the earth. 5 And if anyone wants to harm them, fire pours from their mouth
and consumes their foes; anyone who wants to harm them must be killed in this
manner. 6 They have authority to shut the sky, so that no rain may fall during the
days of their prophesying, and they have authority over the waters to turn them into
blood, and to strike the earth with every kind of plague, as often as they desire.
7 When they have finished their testimony, the beast that comes up from the
bottomless pit will make war on them and conquer them and kill them, 8 and their
dead bodies will lie in the street of the great city that is prophetically[a] called
Sodom and Egypt, where also their Lord was crucified. 9 For three and a half days
members of the peoples and tribes and languages and nations will gaze at their dead
bodies and refuse to let them be placed in a tomb; 10 and the inhabitants of the earth
will gloat over them and celebrate and exchange presents, because these two prophets had been a torment to the inhabitants of the earth.
11 But after the three and a half days, the breath[b] of life from God entered
them, and they stood on their feet, and those who saw them were terrified. 12 Then
they[c] heard a loud voice from heaven saying to them, "Come up here!" And they
went up to heaven in a cloud while their enemies watched them. 13 At that moment
there was a great earthquake, and a tenth of the city fell; seven thousand people
were killed in the earthquake, and the rest were terrified and gave glory to the God
of heaven.
14 The second woe has passed. The third woe is coming very soon.

The seventh trumpet

15 Then the seventh angel blew his trumpet, and there were loud voices in
heaven, saying,

11.1 Zech 2.1 Rev 21.15
11.2 Ezek 40.17-20 Lk 21.24 Rev 12.6; 13.5
11.3 Rev 2.13; 12.6
11.4 Zech 4.3,11,14
11.5 2 Kgs 1.10-12
11.6 Ex 7.19
11.7 Rev 13.1,7
11.8 Rev 14.8; 16.9 17.5,18; 18.24
11.9 Ps 79.2
11.10 Neh 8.10 Mt 10.22
11.11 Ezek 37.5,9-14
11.12 2 Kgs 2.11 Mt 17.1-9 Acts 1.9 Rev 4.1
11.13 Jn 9.24 Rev 6.12 16.9,11,18,19
11.14 Rev 8.13; 9.12

[a] Or *allegorically*; Gk *spiritually* [b] Or *the spirit* [c] Other ancient authorities read *I*

11.1ff This temple is most likely a symbol of the church (all true believers), because there will be no temple in the New Jerusalem (21.22). John measured the temple to show that God is building walls of protection around his people to spare them from spiritual harm, and that there is a place reserved for all believers who remain faithful to God.

11.2 Those worshiping inside the temple will be protected spiritually, but those on the outside will face great suffering. This is a way of saying that true believers will be protected through persecution, but those who refuse to believe will be destroyed.

11.3 These two witnesses bear strong resemblance to Moses and Elijah, two of God's great prophets. With God's power, Moses called plagues down upon the nation of Egypt (see Exodus 8–11). Elijah defeated the prophets of Baal (1 Kings 18). Both of these men appeared with Christ at his transfiguration (see Matthew 17.1–7).

11.3 In the book of Revelation, numbers are likely to have symbolic rather than literal meanings. The 1,260 days equal 3 1/2 years. As half of the perfect number, seven, 3 1/2 can indicate incompletion, imperfection, or even evil. Notice the events predicted for this time period: trouble (Daniel 12.7), the holy city is trampled (11.2), the woman takes refuge in the wilderness (12.6), and the devil-inspired beast controls the earth (13.5). Some commentators link the 3 1/2 years with the period of famine in the days of Elijah (Luke 4.25; James 5.17). Because Malachi predicted the return of Elijah before the last judgment (Malachi 4.5), and because the events in Daniel and Revelation pave the way for the Second Coming, perhaps John is making this connection. It is possible, of course, that the 3 1/2 years are literal. If so, we will clearly recognize them when they are over! Whether symbolic or literal, however, they indicate that evil's reign will have a definite end.

11.7 This beast could be Satan or an agent of Satan.

11.8, 9 Jerusalem, once the holy city and the capital of Israel, is now enemy territory. It is compared with Sodom and with Egypt, both well known for their evil. At the time of John's writing, Jerusalem had been destroyed by the Romans in 70 A.D., nearly a million Jews were slaughtered, and the temple treasures were carried off to Rome.

11.10 The whole world rejoices at the deaths of these two witnesses who have caused trouble by saying what the people didn't want to hear—words about their sin, their need for repentance, and the coming punishment. Sinful people hate those who call attention to their sin and who urge them to repent. They hated Christ, and they hate his followers (1 John 3.13). When you obey Christ and take a stand against sin, be prepared to draw the world's hatred. But remember that the great reward awaiting you in heaven far outweighs any suffering you face now.

11.15 The seventh trumpet is blown, announcing the arrival of the King. The coming judgments are no longer partial but complete in their destruction. God is in control, and he unleashes his full wrath upon the evil world that refuses to turn to him (9.20, 21). When his wrath begins, there will be no escape.

11.15 Dan 2.44; 7.14,27; Acts 4.26; Rev 8.2; 10.7; 12.10; 16.17
11.16 Mt 19.28; Rev 4.4,10
11.17 Rev 1.8; 19.6

"The kingdom of the world has become the kingdom of our Lord
and of his Messiah,[d]
and he will reign forever and ever."
16 Then the twenty-four elders who sit on their thrones before God fell on their
faces and worshiped God, 17 singing,
"We give you thanks, Lord God Almighty,
who are and who were,
for you have taken your great power
and begun to reign.

11.18 Ps 2.1; Dan 7.10; Acts 10.42; Rev 10.7; 13.16; 19.5; 20.12

18 The nations raged,
but your wrath has come,
and the time for judging the dead,
for rewarding your servants,[e] the prophets
and saints and all who fear your name,
both small and great,
and for destroying those who destroy the earth."

11.19 Rev 4.5; 15.5

19 Then God's temple in heaven was opened, and the ark of his covenant was
seen within his temple; and there were flashes of lightning, rumblings, peals of
thunder, an earthquake, and heavy hail.

4. Observing the great conflict

The woman and the dragon

12.2 Isa 26.17; 66.6-9; Mic 4.9,10
12.3 Isa 27.1; Rev 13.1,2; 17.3,9,12,16
12.5 Ps 2.9; Rev 2.27; 19.15
12.6 Rev 11.3; 13.5; 17.18

12 A great portent appeared in heaven: a woman clothed with the sun, with the
moon under her feet, and on her head a crown of twelve stars. 2 She was
pregnant and was crying out in birthpangs, in the agony of giving birth. 3 Then
another portent appeared in heaven: a great red dragon, with seven heads and ten
horns, and seven diadems on his heads. 4 His tail swept down a third of the stars of
heaven and threw them to the earth. Then the dragon stood before the woman who
was about to bear a child, so that he might devour her child as soon as it was born.
5 And she gave birth to a son, a male child, who is to rule[f] all the nations with a rod
of iron. But her child was snatched away and taken to God and to his throne; 6 and
the woman fled into the wilderness, where she has a place prepared by God, so that
there she can be nourished for one thousand two hundred sixty days.

[d] Gk *Christ* [e] Gk *slaves* [f] Or *to shepherd*

11.16 For more on the 24 elders, see the note on 4.4.

11.18 In the Bible, God gives rewards to his people according to what they deserve. Throughout the Old Testament, obedience often brought reward in this life (Deuteronomy 28), but obedience and immediate reward are not always linked. If they were, good people would always be rich, and suffering would always be a sign of sin. If we were quickly rewarded for every faithful deed, we would soon think we were pretty good. Before long, we would be doing many good deeds for purely selfish reasons. While it is true that God will reward us for our earthly deeds (see 20.12), our greatest reward is eternal life in his presence.

11.19 In Old Testament days, the ark of the covenant ("ark of his covenant") was the most sacred treasure of the Israelite nation. For more information about the ark, see the note on Exodus 37.1.

12.1 – 14.20 The seventh trumpet (11.15) ushers in the bowl judgments (15.1 – 16.21), but in the intervening chapters (12 – 14), John sees the conflict between God and Satan. He sees the source of all sin, evil, persecution, and suffering on the earth, and he understands why the great battle between the forces of God and Satan must soon take place. In these chapters the nature of evil is exposed, and Satan is seen in all his wickedness.

12.1-6 A *portent* is an omen or prophetic sign of something to come. The woman represents God's faithful people who have been awaiting the Messiah; the crown of 12 stars represents the 12 tribes of Israel. God set apart the Jews for himself (Romans 9.4, 5), and that nation gave birth to the Messiah. The male child (12.5) is Jesus, born to a devout Jew, Mary (Luke 1.26–33). Evil King Herod immediately tried to destroy the infant Jesus (Matthew 2.13–20). Herod's desire to kill this newborn king, whom he saw as a threat to his throne, was motivated by Satan (the great red dragon), who wanted to kill the world's Savior. The heavenly pageant of Revelation 12 shows that Christ's quiet birth in the town of Bethlehem had cosmic significance.

12.3, 4 The great red dragon, Satan, has seven heads, ten horns, and seven crowns ("diadems"), representing his power and the kingdoms of the world over which he rules. The stars that plunge to earth with him are usually considered to be the angels who fell with Satan and became his demons. According to Hebrew tradition, one-third of all the angels in heaven fell with Satan. For more on demons, see the notes on 9.3ff and in Mark 5.

12.6 The wilderness represents a place of spiritual refuge and protection from Satan. By aiding the woman's escape into the wilderness, God offers security to all true believers. Satan always attacks God's people, but God keeps them spiritually secure. Some will experience physical harm, but all will be protected from spiritual harm. God will not let Satan take the souls of his true followers.

12.6 The 1,260 days (3 1/2 years) is the same length of time that the dragon is allowed to control the earth (13.5) and that the holy city is trampled (see the note on 11.3).

7 And war broke out in heaven; Michael and his angels fought against the
dragon. The dragon and his angels fought back, 8 but they were defeated, and there
was no longer any place for them in heaven. 9 The great dragon was thrown down,
that ancient serpent, who is called the Devil and Satan, the deceiver of the whole
world—he was thrown down to the earth, and his angels were thrown down with
him.
10 Then I heard a loud voice in heaven, proclaiming,
"Now have come the salvation and the power
and the kingdom of our God
and the authority of his Messiah,[g]
for the accuser of our comrades[h] has been thrown down,
who accuses them day and night before our God.
11 But they have conquered him by the blood of the Lamb
and by the word of their testimony,
for they did not cling to life even in the face of death.
12 Rejoice then, you heavens
and those who dwell in them!
But woe to the earth and the sea,
for the devil has come down to you
with great wrath,
because he knows that his time is short!"
13 So when the dragon saw that he had been thrown down to the earth, he pursued[i] the woman who had given birth to the male child. 14 But the woman was
given the two wings of the great eagle, so that she could fly from the serpent into
the wilderness, to her place where she is nourished for a time, and times, and half
a time. 15 Then from his mouth the serpent poured water like a river after the
woman, to sweep her away with the flood. 16 But the earth came to the help of the
woman; it opened its mouth and swallowed the river that the dragon had poured
from his mouth. 17 Then the dragon was angry with the woman, and went off to

12.7 Dan 10.13; 12.1 Jude 9 Rev 12.3
12.9 Gen 3.1 Zech 3.1,2 Mt 4.10 Lk 10.18 Rev 12.3,15 20.2-10
12.10 Rev 7.10; 11.15
12.11 Rev 2.10; 6.9 7.14; 15.2
12.12 Rev 8.13 10.6; 12.9; 13.6 18.20
12.14 Ex 19.4 Dan 7.25; 12.7 Rev 17.3,18
12.15 Hos 5.10
12.17 Rev 1.2; 11.7 13.7; 14.1

g Gk *Christ* h Gk *brothers* i Or *persecuted*

12.7 This event fulfills Daniel 12.1ff. Michael is a high-ranking angel. One of his responsibilities is to guard God's community of believers.

12.7ff Much more happened at Christ's birth, death, and resurrection than most people realize. A battle between the forces of good and evil was under way. With Christ's resurrection, Satan's ultimate defeat was assured. Some believe that Satan's fall to earth took place at Jesus' resurrection or ascension and that the 1,260 days (3 1/2 years) is a symbolic way of referring to the time between Christ's first and second comings. Others say that Satan's defeat occurs in the middle of a literal seven-year tribulation period, following the Rapture of the church, and preceding the Second Coming of Christ and the beginning of his 1,000-year reign. Whatever the case, we must remember that Christ is victorious—Satan has already been defeated by Christ's death on the cross (12.10–12).

12.9 Satan is not just a symbol or legend; he is very real. Originally he was an angel of God, but through his pride, he became corrupt and evil. Satan is God's enemy, constantly trying to hinder God's work, but he is limited by God's power and can do only what he is permitted to do (Job 1.6–2.8). The name *Satan* means "Adversary" or "Accuser" (12.10). He actively looks for people to attack (1 Peter 5.8, 9). He likes to seek out believers who are vulnerable in their faith, spiritually weak, or isolated from other believers.

Even though God permits Satan to do his work in this world, God is still in control. And Jesus has complete power over Satan—he defeated Satan when he died and rose again for the sins of mankind. One day Satan will be bound forever, never again to do his evil work (see 20.10).

12.10 Many believe that until this time, Satan still had access to God (see the note on Job 1.7ff). But here his access is forever barred (see also 9.1). He can no longer accuse people before God (see how Satan made accusations about Job before God in Job 1.6ff).

12.11 The critical blow to Satan came when the Lamb, Jesus Christ, shed his blood for our sins. The victory is won by sacrifice—Christ's death in our place to pay the penalty for our sin, and the sacrifices we make because of our faith in him. As we face the battle with Satan, we should not fear it or try to escape from it, but loyally serve Christ who alone brings victory (see Romans 8.34–39).

12.12 The devil begins to step up his persecution because he knows that "his time is short." We are living in the last days, and Satan's work has become more intense. Even though Satan is very powerful, as we can see by the condition of our world, he is always under God's control. One of the reasons God allows Satan to work evil and bring temptation is so that those who pretend to be Christ's followers will be weeded out from his true believers. Satan knows that the great confrontation with Jesus is near. He is desperately trying to recruit as great an enemy force as possible for this final battle.

12.17 While the woman (12.1) represents faithful Jews and the child (12.5) represents Christ, the rest of her children could be either Jewish believers or all believers. Most likely it refers to all believers.

12.17 The apostle Paul tells us we are in a spiritual battle (Ephesians 6.10–12). John says the war is still being waged, but the outcome is already determined. Satan and his followers have been defeated and will be destroyed. Nevertheless, Satan is battling daily to bring more into his ranks and to keep his own from defecting to God's side. Those who belong to Christ have gone into battle on God's side, and he has guaranteed them victory. God will not lose the war, but we must make certain not to lose the battle for

make war on the rest of her children, those who keep the commandments of God
and hold the testimony of Jesus.

The two beasts

13 18 Then the dragon[j] took his stand on the sand of the seashore. 1 And I saw
a beast rising out of the sea; and on its horns were ten diadems, and on its
heads were blasphemous names. 2 And the beast that I saw was like a leopard, its
feet were like a bear's, and its mouth was like a lion's mouth. And the dragon gave
it his power and his throne and great authority. 3 One of its heads seemed to have
received a death-blow, but its mortal wound[k] had been healed. In amazement the
whole earth followed the beast. 4 They worshiped the dragon, for he had given his
authority to the beast, and they worshiped the beast, saying, "Who is like the beast,
and who can fight against it?"
5 The beast was given a mouth uttering haughty and blasphemous words, and it
was allowed to exercise authority for forty-two months. 6 It opened its mouth to
utter blasphemies against God, blaspheming his name and his dwelling, that is,
those who dwell in heaven. 7 Also it was allowed to make war on the saints and to
conquer them.[l] It was given authority over every tribe and people and language
and nation, 8 and all the inhabitants of the earth will worship it, everyone whose
name has not been written from the foundation of the world in the book of life of the
Lamb that was slaughtered.[m]
9 Let anyone who has an ear listen:
10 If you are to be taken captive,
into captivity you go;
if you kill with the sword,

13.1 Dan 7.2-8 Rev 13.4,12 17.12
13.2 Dan 7.4-6 Rev 2.13; 12.3
13.3 2 Thess 2.9-12 Rev 13.12,14 17.8
13.4 Rev 13.2,12
13.5 Dan 7.8,11,20, 25; 11.36 2 Thess 2.3 Rev 11.2
13.6 Rev 7.15; 12.12
13.7 Rev 5.9; 11.7
13.8 Dan 12.1 1 Pet 1.19,20
13.10 Mt 26.52 Heb 6.12

[j] Gk *Then he*; other ancient authorities read *Then I stood* [k] Gk *the plague of its death* [l] Other ancient authorities lack this sentence [m] Or *written in the book of life of the Lamb that was slaughtered from the foundation of the world*

our own souls. Don't waver in your commitment to Christ. A great spiritual battle is being fought, and there is no time for indecision.

13.1 *Diadems* are crowns. This beast was initially identified with Rome because the Roman Empire, in its early days, had an evil life-style, persecuted believers, and opposed God and his followers. But the beast also symbolizes the antichrist—not Satan, but someone under Satan's power and control. This antichrist looks like a combination of the four beasts that Daniel saw centuries earlier in a vision (Daniel 7). As the dragon (12.17) is in opposition to God, so the beast from the sea is against Christ and may be seen as Satan's false messiah. The early Roman Empire was strong and also anti-Christ (or against Christ's standards); many other individual powers throughout history have been anti-Christ. Many Christians believe that Satan's evil will culminate in a final antichrist, one who will focus all the powers of evil against Jesus Christ and his followers.

13.1ff Chapter 13 introduces Satan's two evil accomplices: (1) the beast that rises out of the sea (13.1ff) and (2) the beast that rises out of the earth (13.11ff). Together, the three evil beings form an unholy trinity in direct opposition to God the Father, the Son, and the Holy Spirit.

When Satan tempted Jesus in the wilderness, he wanted Jesus to show his power by turning stones into bread, to do miracles by jumping from a high place, and to gain political power by worshiping Satan (see Matthew 4.1–11). Satan's plan was to rule the world through Jesus, but Jesus refused to do Satan's bidding. Thus Satan turns to the fearsome beasts described in Revelation. To the beast from the sea he gives political power. To the beast from the earth he gives power to do miracles. Both beasts work together to capture the control of the whole world. This unholy trinity—the dragon, the beast, and the false prophet (see 16.13)—unite in a desperate attempt to overthrow God, but their efforts are doomed to failure. See what becomes of them in 19.19–21 and 20.10.

13.3ff Because the beast, the antichrist, is a false messiah, he will be a counterfeit of Christ and will even stage a false resurrection (13.14). People will follow and worship him because they are awed by his power and miracles (13.3, 4). He will unite the world under his leadership (13.7, 8), and he will control the world economy (13.16, 17). People are impressed by power and will follow those who display it forcefully or offer it to their followers. But in following the beast, they are only fooling themselves: he uses his power to manipulate others, to point to himself, and to promote evil plans. God, by contrast, uses his infinitely greater power to love and build up. Don't be misled by claims of great miracles or reports about a resurrection or reincarnation of someone claiming to be Christ. When Jesus returns, he will reveal himself to all believers (Matthew 24.23–28).

13.5 The power given to the beast is limited by God. He allows the beast to have power only for a short time. Even while the beast is in power, God is still in control (11.15; 12.10–12).

13.7 The beast will conquer God's people and rule over them, but he cannot harm them spiritually. He will establish worldwide dominance and demand that everyone worship him. And many *will* worship him—everyone except true believers. This will result in temporary suffering for God's people, but they will be rewarded with an eternal life in the end.

13.8 See the note on 3.5 for more information on the book of life.

13.10 In this time of persecution, being faithful to Christ could bring imprisonment and even execution. Some believers will be hurt and some killed. But all that the beast and his followers can do to believers is harm them physically; no spiritual harm can come to those whose faith in God is sincere. All believers will enter God's presence perfected and purified by the blood of the Lamb (7.9–17).

13.10 The times of great persecution that John sees will be an opportunity for believers to endure and grow. The tough times we face right now are also opportunities for spiritual growth. Don't fall into Satan's trap and turn away from God during difficult times. Instead, use them as opportunities for growth.

with the sword you must be killed.
Here is a call for the endurance and faith of the saints.
11 Then I saw another beast that rose out of the earth; it had two horns like a
lamb and it spoke like a dragon. 12 It exercises all the authority of the first beast on
its behalf, and it makes the earth and its inhabitants worship the first beast, whose
mortal wound[n] had been healed. 13 It performs great signs, even making fire come
down from heaven to earth in the sight of all; 14 and by the signs that it is allowed
to perform on behalf of the beast, it deceives the inhabitants of earth, telling them
to make an image for the beast that had been wounded by the sword[o] and yet lived;
15 and it was allowed to give breath[p] to the image of the beast so that the image of
the beast could even speak and cause those who would not worship the image of the
beast to be killed. 16 Also it causes all, both small and great, both rich and poor,
both free and slave, to be marked on the right hand or the forehead, 17 so that no one
can buy or sell who does not have the mark, that is, the name of the beast or the
number of its name. 18 This calls for wisdom: let anyone with understanding calculate the number of the beast, for it is the number of a person. Its number is six
hundred sixty-six.[q]

13.11 Rev 13.1,4
13.12 2 Thess 2.4 Rev 14.9; 19.20
13.13 Ex 7.11; 19.9-11 Mt 24.24 2 Thess 2.9 2 Tim 3.8 Rev 11.15 16.14; 19.20
13.14 2 Thess 2.9 Rev 12.9 13.3,8,12
13.15 Dan 3.3 7.20,25 Rev 20.4
13.16 Ps 49.2 Rev 14.9 19.17,18

The Lamb and the 144,000

14 Then I looked, and there was the Lamb, standing on Mount Zion! And with
him were one hundred forty-four thousand who had his name and his Father's name written on their foreheads. 2 And I heard a voice from heaven like the
sound of many waters and like the sound of loud thunder; the voice I heard was like
the sound of harpists playing on their harps, 3 and they sing a new song before the
throne and before the four living creatures and before the elders. No one could learn
that song except the one hundred forty-four thousand who have been redeemed
from the earth. 4 It is these who have not defiled themselves with women, for they

14.1 Dan 12.5 Heb 12.22 Rev 3.12; 5.6 7.4
14.3 Rev 2.17; 4.4,6
14.4 Mt 19.12 2 Cor 11.2 Rev 5.9; 7.13-17

[n] Gk *whose plague of its death* [o] Or *that had received the plague of the sword* [p] Or *spirit* [q] Other ancient authorities read *six hundred sixteen*

13.11ff The first beast rose out of the sea (13.1), but this second beast rises out of the earth. Later identified as the false prophet (16.13; 19.20), this beast is a counterfeit of the Holy Spirit. It seems to do good, but the purpose of its miracles is to deceive.

13.14 Throughout the Bible, miracles are proofs of God's power, love, and authority. But here there are counterfeit miracles performed to deceive. This is similar to Pharaoh's magicians who duplicated Moses' signs in Egypt. True signs and miracles point us to Jesus Christ, but miracles alone can be deceptive. That is why we must ask with each miracle, "Is this consistent with what God says in the Bible?" The second beast here gains influence through the signs and wonders it can perform in the presence of the first beast. The second beast orders the people to worship a statue of the first beast – a direct flouting of the second commandment (Exodus 20.4–6). Allowing the Bible to guide our faith and practice will keep us from being deceived by false signs, however convincing they may appear. Any teaching that contradicts God's Word is false.

13.16, 17 In every generation, Christians need to maintain a healthy skepticism about society's pleasures and rewards. In our educational, economic, and civic structures, there are incentives. Cooperating Christians must always approve what is good and healthy about our society, but we must stand against sin. In some cases, such as Satan's system described here, the system or structure becomes so evil that there is no way to cooperate with it.

13.16–18 This mark, also called "the mark of the beast," is designed to mock the mark God places on his followers (7.2, 3). Just as God marks his people to save them, so Satan's beast marks its people to save them from the persecution that Satan will inflict upon God's followers. Identifying this mark is not as important as identifying the purpose of the mark. Those who accept it are showing their allegiance to Satan, their willingness to operate within the economic system he promotes, and their rebellion against God. To refuse the mark means to commit oneself entirely to God, preferring death to compromising one's faith in Christ.

13.18 The meaning of this number has been discussed more than any other part of the book of Revelation. The three sixes have been said to represent many things, including the number of humans or the unholy trinity of Satan, the first beast, and the false prophet (16.13). If the number seven is looked upon as the "perfect number" in the Bible, and if three sevens represent complete perfection, then the number 666 falls completely short of perfection. The first readers of this book probably applied the number to the Emperor Nero, who symbolized all the evils of the Roman Empire. (The Greek letters of Nero's name represent numbers which total 666.) Whatever specific application the number is given, it symbolizes the worldwide dominion and complete evil of this unholy trinity designed to undo Christ's work and overthrow him.

14.1ff Chapter 13 described the onslaught of evil that will occur when Satan and his helpers control the world. Chapter 14 gives a glimpse of eternity to show believers what awaits them if they endure. The Lamb is the Messiah. Mount Zion, often another name for Jerusalem (the capital of Israel), is contrasted with the worldly empire. The 144,000 represent believers who have endured persecutions on earth and now are ready to enjoy the eternal benefits and blessings of life with God forever. The three angels contrast the destiny of believers with that of unbelievers.

14.4 These people are true believers whose robes have been washed and purified by Christ's blood through his death ("redeemed from humankind," see the first note on 7.14). In the Old Testament, idolatry was often portrayed as spiritual adultery (see the book of Hosea). Their virginity is best understood symbolically, meaning that they are free from involvement with the pagan world system; these believers are spiritually pure; they have remained faithful to Christ, they followed him exclusively, and have received God's reward for staying committed to him. "First fruits" refers to

14.5 Heb 9.14 1 Pet 2.22 Jude 24

are virgins; these follow the Lamb wherever he goes. They have been redeemed
from humankind as first fruits for God and the Lamb, 5 and in their mouth no lie was
found; they are blameless.

The three angels

14.6 Rev 5.9
14.7 Ps 124.8 Dan 8.19 Acts 14.15 Rev 4.11
14.8 Jer 51.7,8 Nah 3.19 Rev 16.19 17.2-5 18.2,3,10
14.9 Rev 13.14,16
14.10 Ps 75.8 Ezek 38.22 Mk 8.38 2 Thess 1.7 Rev 16.19 19.20; 20.15 21.8
14.11 Rev 13.17
14.12 Rev 2.13 12.17; 13.10

6 Then I saw another angel flying in midheaven, with an eternal gospel to proclaim to those who live[r] on the earth—to every nation and tribe and language and
people. 7 He said in a loud voice, "Fear God and give him glory, for the hour of his
judgment has come; and worship him who made heaven and earth, the sea and the
springs of water."
8 Then another angel, a second, followed, saying, "Fallen, fallen is Babylon
the great! She has made all nations drink of the wine of the wrath of her fornication."
9 Then another angel, a third, followed them, crying with a loud voice, "Those
who worship the beast and its image, and receive a mark on their foreheads or on
their hands, 10 they will also drink the wine of God's wrath, poured unmixed into
the cup of his anger, and they will be tormented with fire and sulfur in the presence
of the holy angels and in the presence of the Lamb. 11 And the smoke of their torment goes up forever and ever. There is no rest day or night for those who worship
the beast and its image and for anyone who receives the mark of its name."
12 Here is a call for the endurance of the saints, those who keep the commandments of God and hold fast to the faith of[s] Jesus.
13 And I heard a voice from heaven saying, "Write this: Blessed are the dead
who from now on die in the Lord." "Yes," says the Spirit, "they will rest from their
labors, for their deeds follow them."

The harvest of the earth

14.14 Ezek 1.26
14.15 Mt 13.39-41

14 Then I looked, and there was a white cloud, and seated on the cloud was one
like the Son of Man, with a golden crown on his head, and a sharp sickle in his
hand! 15 Another angel came out of the temple, calling with a loud voice to the one

[r] Gk *sit* [s] Or *to their faith in*

dedicating the first part of the harvest as holy to God (Exodus 23.19; see also James 1.18).

14.6, 7 Some believe this is a final, worldwide appeal to all people to recognize the one true God. No one will have the excuse of never hearing God's truth. Others, however, see this as an announcement of judgment rather than an appeal. The people of the world have had their chance to proclaim their allegiance to God, and now God's great judgment is about to begin. Because you are reading this, you have already heard God's truth. You know that God's final judgment will not be put off forever. Have you joyfully received the everlasting good news? Have you confessed your sins and trusted in Christ to save you? If so, you have nothing to fear from God's judgment. The Judge of all the earth is your Savior!

14.8 Babylon was both an evil city and an immoral empire, a world center for idol worship. Babylon ransacked Jerusalem and carried the people of Judah into captivity (see 2 Kings 24 and 2 Chronicles 36). Just as Babylon was the Jews' worst enemy, the Roman Empire was the worst enemy of the early Christians. John, who did not dare speak against Rome openly, applied the name *Babylon* to this enemy of God's people (Rome)—and, by extension, to all God's enemies of all times.

14.9–11 Those who worship the beast, accept his mark on their foreheads and hands, and operate according to his world economic system will ultimately face God's judgment. Our world values money, power, and pleasure over God's leadership. To get what the world values, many people deny God and violate Christian principles. Thus they must drink the cup of God's wrath (see Psalm 75; Isaiah 51.17).

14.11 The ultimate result of sin is unending separation from God. Because human beings are created in God's image with an inborn thirst for fellowship with him, separation from God will be the ultimate torment and misery. Sin always brings misery, but in this life we can choose to repent and restore our relationship with God. In eternity there will no longer be the opportunity to repent. If in this life we choose to be independent of God, in the next life we will be separated from him forever. Nobody is forced to choose eternal separation from God and nobody suffers this fate by accident. Jesus invites all of us to open the door of our hearts to him (3.20). If we do this, we will enjoy everlasting fellowship with Christ.

14.12 This news about God's ultimate triumph should encourage God's people to endure, remaining firm through every trial and persecution. They can do this, God promises, by obeying the commands in God's Word and by trusting in Jesus. The secret to enduring, therefore, is trust and obedience. Trust God to give you patience to endure even the small trials you face daily; obey him, even when obedience is unattractive or dangerous.

14.13 While it is true that money, fame, and belongings can't be taken with us after death, God's people can produce fruit that survives and follows us. God will remember our love, kindness, and faithfulness, and those who accept Christ through our witness will join us in the new earth. Be sure that your values are in line with God's values, and decide today to produce fruit that lasts forever.

14.14–17 This is an image of judgment: Christ is separating the faithful from the unfaithful like a farmer harvesting his crops. This is a time of joy for the Christians who have been persecuted and martyred—they will receive their long-awaited reward. Christians should not fear the last judgment. Jesus said, "Very truly, I tell you, anyone who hears my word and believes him who sent me has eternal life, and does not come under judgment, but has passed from death to life" (John 5.24).

who sat on the cloud, "Use your sickle and reap, for the hour to reap has come,
because the harvest of the earth is fully ripe." 16 So the one who sat on the cloud
swung his sickle over the earth, and the earth was reaped.
17 Then another angel came out of the temple in heaven, and he too had a sharp
sickle. 18 Then another angel came out from the altar, the angel who has authority
over fire, and he called with a loud voice to him who had the sharp sickle, "Use
your sharp sickle and gather the clusters of the vine of the earth, for its grapes are
ripe." 19 So the angel swung his sickle over the earth and gathered the vintage of the
earth, and he threw it into the great wine press of the wrath of God. 20 And the wine
press was trodden outside the city, and blood flowed from the wine press, as high
as a horse's bridle, for a distance of about two hundred miles.[t]

14.18 Joel 3.13 Rev 6.9; 8.3 14.15
14.19 Deut 32.32,33 Isa 62.2,3 Rev 16.8; 19.15
14.20 Gen 49.11 Lam 1.15 Ezek 39.17-21 Heb 13.11,12

5. Pouring out the seven plagues

The angels with the last plagues

15 Then I saw another portent in heaven, great and amazing: seven angels with
seven plagues, which are the last, for with them the wrath of God is ended.
2 And I saw what appeared to be a sea of glass mixed with fire, and those who
had conquered the beast and its image and the number of its name, standing beside
the sea of glass with harps of God in their hands. 3 And they sing the song of Moses,
the servant[u] of God, and the song of the Lamb:

"Great and amazing are your deeds,
  Lord God the Almighty!
Just and true are your ways,
  King of the nations![v]
4 Lord, who will not fear
  and glorify your name?
For you alone are holy.
  All nations will come
  and worship before you,
for your judgments have been revealed."

15.1 Rev 14.10; 15.6
15.2 Rev 4.6; 5.8 12.11
15.3,4 Ex 15.1 Deut 32.3 Ps 86.9 Jer 10.7 Dan 9.11 Rev 5.9; 14.7

5 After this I looked, and the temple of the tent[w] of witness in heaven was
opened, 6 and out of the temple came the seven angels with the seven plagues,
robed in pure bright linen,[x] with golden sashes across their chests. 7 Then one of
the four living creatures gave the seven angels seven golden bowls full of the wrath
of God, who lives forever and ever; 8 and the temple was filled with smoke from the
glory of God and from his power, and no one could enter the temple until the seven
plagues of the seven angels were ended.

15.5 Rev 11.19
15.6 Rev 1.13 14.5; 15.6
15.8 Ex 19.18 1 Kgs 8.10 Isa 6.4

[t] Gk *one thousand six hundred stadia* [u] Gk *slave* [v] Other ancient authorities read *the ages* [w] Or *tabernacle*
[x] Other ancient authorities read *stone*

14.19 A wine press is a large vat or trough where grapes are collected and then smashed. The juice flows out of a duct that leads into a large holding vat. The wine press is often used in the Bible as a symbol of God's wrath and punishment of sin (Isaiah 63.3–6; Lamentations 1.15; Joel 3.12, 13).

15.1 A *portent* is an omen or prophetic sign of something to come. The seven last plagues are also called the seven bowl judgments. They actually begin in chapter 16. Unlike the previous plagues, these are universal and will culminate in the abolition of all evil ("the wrath of God is ended") and the end of the world.

15.2 This is similar to the "sea of glass" described in 4.6, located before the throne of God. This time it is mixed with fire to represent wrath and judgment. Those who stand on it are victorious over Satan and his evil beast. They are pure because they have been faithful to God to the end.

15.3, 4 The song of Moses celebrated Israel's deliverance from Egypt (Exodus 15). The song of the Lamb celebrates the ultimate deliverance of God's people from the power of Satan.

15.5–8 The "temple of the tent of witness" is a Greek translation for the Hebrew "tent of meeting" (see Exodus 40.34, 35). It refers to the time of the exodus in the wilderness when the ark of the covenant (the symbol of God's presence among his people) resided in the tabernacle. The angels coming out of the temple are clothed in pure, bright linen with golden sashes across their chests. Their clothes, reminiscent of the high priest's clothing, show that they are free from corruption, immorality, and injustice. The smoke that fills the temple is the manifestation of God's glory and wrath. There is no escape from this judgment.

15.8 Our eternal reign with Christ won't begin until all evil is destroyed by his judgment. The faithful must wait for his timetable to be revealed.

The bowls of God's wrath

16 Then I heard a loud voice from the temple telling the seven angels, "Go and
pour out on the earth the seven bowls of the wrath of God."
2 So the first angel went and poured his bowl on the earth, and a foul and painful sore came on those who had the mark of the beast and who worshiped its image.
3 The second angel poured his bowl into the sea, and it became like the blood
of a corpse, and every living thing in the sea died.
4 The third angel poured his bowl into the rivers and the springs of water, and
they became blood. 5 And I heard the angel of the waters say,
"You are just, O Holy One, who are and were,
for you have judged these things;
6 because they shed the blood of saints and prophets,
you have given them blood to drink.
It is what they deserve!"
7 And I heard the altar respond,
"Yes, O Lord God, the Almighty,
your judgments are true and just!"
8 The fourth angel poured his bowl on the sun, and it was allowed to scorch
them with fire; 9 they were scorched by the fierce heat, but they cursed the name of
God, who had authority over these plagues, and they did not repent and give him
glory.
10 The fifth angel poured his bowl on the throne of the beast, and its kingdom
was plunged into darkness; people gnawed their tongues in agony, 11 and cursed the
God of heaven because of their pains and sores, and they did not repent of their
deeds.
12 The sixth angel poured his bowl on the great river Euphrates, and its water
was dried up in order to prepare the way for the kings from the east. 13 And I saw
three foul spirits like frogs coming from the mouth of the dragon, from the mouth
of the beast, and from the mouth of the false prophet. 14 These are demonic spirits,
performing signs, who go abroad to the kings of the whole world, to assemble them
for battle on the great day of God the Almighty. 15 ("See, I am coming like a thief!
Blessed is the one who stays awake and is clothed,[y] not going about naked and
exposed to shame.") 16 And they assembled them at the place that in Hebrew is
called Harmagedon.

[y] Gk *and keeps his robes*

16.1 Rev 11.19; 15.1
16.2 Ex 9.9-11 Rev 8.7 13.15-17
16.3 Ex 7.17-21 Rev 8.8,9
16.4 Ex 17.7 Rev 8.10; 11.16
16.5 Rev 1.4,8; 4.8 6.10; 11.17
16.6 Deut 32.42,43 2 Kgs 24.4 Isa 49.26
16.7 Rev 1.8; 6.9 14.18; 15.3; 19.2
16.8 Rev 6.12
16.9 Rev 11.13
16.10 Ex 10.21 Mt 8.12 Rev 8.12 9.1,2; 13.2
16.11 Rev 2.21
16.12 Dan 11.43-45 Rev 9.13,14
16.13 Rev 12.3 13.1,11,14
16.14 Rev 6.17 17.14; 19.19
16.15 1 Thess 5.2 Rev 3.3,18
16.16 Judg 5.19 Zech 12.10,11 Rev 19.19

16.1ff The bowl judgments are God's final and complete judgments upon the earth. The end has come. There are many similarities between the bowl judgments and the trumpet judgments (8.6–11.19), but there are three main differences: (1) these judgments are complete, where the trumpet judgments are partial; (2) the trumpet judgments still give unbelievers the opportunity to repent, but the bowl judgments do not; and (3) humankind is indirectly affected by several of the trumpet judgments but directly attacked by all the bowl judgments.

16.7 The significance of the altar itself crying out is that everyone and everything will be praising God, acknowledging his righteousness and perfect justice.

16.9–21 People know that these judgments come from God, because they curse him for sending them. But they still refuse to recognize God's authority and repent of their sins. Christians should not be surprised at the hostility and hardness of heart of unbelievers. Even when the power of God is fully and completely revealed, many will still refuse to repent. If you find yourself ignoring God more and more, turn back to him now before your heart becomes too hard to repent (see the note on 9.20, 21 for more on hard hearts).

16.12 The Euphrates River was a natural protective boundary against the empires to the east (Babylon, Assyria, Persia). If it dried up, nothing could hold back invading armies. The armies of the east symbolize unhindered judgment.

16.13, 14 These miracle-working demons ("foul spirits") that come from the unholy trinity unite the rulers of the world for battle against God. The demons that come from the mouths of the three evil rulers signify the verbal enticements and propaganda that will draw people to their evil cause. For more about demons, see the note on 9.3ff.

16.15 Christ will return unexpectedly (1 Thessalonians 5.1–6), so we must be ready when he returns. We can prepare ourselves by standing firm in temptation and by being committed to God's moral standards. In what ways does your life show either your readiness or your lack of preparation for Christ's return?

16.16 This battlefield called Harmagedon (also called Armageddon) is near the city of Meggido (southeast of the modern port of Haifa) that guarded a large plain in northern Israel. It is a strategic location near a prominent international highway leading north from Egypt through Israel, along the coast, and on to Babylon. Megiddo overlooked the entire plain southward toward Galilee and westward toward Mount Gilboa.

16.16 Sinful men will unite to fight against God in a final display of rebellion. Many are already united against Christ and his people—those who stand for truth, peace, justice, and morality. Your personal battle with evil foreshadows the great battle pictured here, where God will meet evil and destroy it once and for all. Be strong and courageous as you battle against sin and evil: you are fighting on the winning side.

17 The seventh angel poured his bowl into the air, and a loud voice came out of
the temple, from the throne, saying, "It is done!" 18 And there came flashes of lightning, rumblings, peals of thunder, and a violent earthquake, such as had not occurred since people were upon the earth, so violent was that earthquake. 19 The
great city was split into three parts, and the cities of the nations fell. God remembered great Babylon and gave her the wine-cup of the fury of his wrath. 20 And
every island fled away, and no mountains were to be found; 21 and huge hailstones,
each weighing about a hundred pounds,[z] dropped from heaven on people, until
they cursed God for the plague of the hail, so fearful was that plague.

16.17 Dan 12.7-13 Rev 11.15; 21.6
16.18 Mt 24.21 Rev 4.5; 6.12
16.19 Rev 14.8,10
16.20 Rev 6.14; 20.11
16.21 Ex 9.18-25 Rev 11.19; 16.9

6. Seizing the final victory

The great whore and the scarlet beasts

17 Then one of the seven angels who had the seven bowls came and said to me,
"Come, I will show you the judgment of the great whore who is seated on
many waters, 2 with whom the kings of the earth have committed fornication, and
with the wine of whose fornication the inhabitants of the earth have become
drunk." 3 So he carried me away in the spirit[a] into a wilderness, and I saw a woman
sitting on a scarlet beast that was full of blasphemous names, and it had seven heads
and ten horns. 4 The woman was clothed in purple and scarlet, and adorned with
gold and jewels and pearls, holding in her hand a golden cup full of abominations
and the impurities of her fornication; 5 and on her forehead was written a name, a
mystery: "Babylon the great, mother of whores and of earth's abominations." 6 And
I saw that the woman was drunk with the blood of the saints and the blood of the
witnesses to Jesus.

When I saw her, I was greatly amazed. 7 But the angel said to me, "Why are you
so amazed? I will tell you the mystery of the woman, and of the beast with seven
heads and ten horns that carries her. 8 The beast that you saw was, and is not, and
is about to ascend from the bottomless pit and go to destruction. And the inhabitants of the earth, whose names have not been written in the book of life from the
foundation of the world, will be amazed when they see the beast, because it was
and is not and is to come.

9 "This calls for a mind that has wisdom: the seven heads are seven mountains
on which the woman is seated; also, they are seven kings, 10 of whom five have
fallen, one is living, and the other has not yet come; and when he comes, he must
remain only a little while. 11 As for the beast that was and is not, it is an eighth but
it belongs to the seven, and it goes to destruction. 12 And the ten horns that you saw

17.1 Jer 51.13 Rev 17.5,15 19.2; 21.9
17.2 Jer 51.7-9 Rev 14.8; 17.8 18.3,9
17.3 Rev 1.10; 12.3,6 13.1
17.5 2 Thess 2.7 Rev 16.19 17.2,7
17.6 Dan 7.21,25 Rev 6.9; 16.6 12.11
17.8 Rev 11.7; 13.1-8; 12,14
17.9 Rev 17.3
17.11 Rev 18.19
17.12 Dan 7.20-22 Rev 17.16 18.10,17,19

[z] Gk *weighing about a talent* [a] Or *in the Spirit*

16.17–21 For more information on Babylon and what it represents in Revelation, see the note on 14.8. The city's division into three sections is a symbol of its complete destruction.

17.1ff The destruction of Babylon mentioned in 16.17–21 is now described in greater detail. The "great whore," called Babylon, represented the early Roman Empire with its many gods and the blood of Christian martyrs on its hands. The water stands for either sea commerce or a well-watered (well-provisioned) city. The great whore represents the seductiveness of the governmental system as it used immoral means to gain its own pleasure, prosperity, and advantage. In contrast to the whore, Christ's bride, the church is pure and obedient (19.6–9). The wicked city of Babylon stands in contrast to the heavenly city of Jerusalem (21.10–22.5). The original readers easily identified Babylon with Rome, but it also symbolizes any system that is hostile to God (see 17.5).

17.3 The scarlet beast is either the dragon of 12.3, or the beast from the sea described in 13.1.

17.6 Throughout history people have been killed for their faith. Over the last century, millions have been killed by oppressive governments, and many of these were believers. The woman's drunkenness shows her pleasure in her evil accomplishments and her false feeling of triumph over the church. But every martyr who fell before her sword only strengthened the faith of the church.

17.8 In chapter 12 we met the dragon (Satan). In chapter 13 we saw the beast from the sea and the power he received from Satan. In chapters 14–16 we see God's great judgments. In this chapter, a scarlet animal similar to the beast and the dragon appears as an ally of the "great whore." The phrase, "was and is not and is to come" means the beast was alive, dead, and then will come back to life. The beast's resurrection symbolizes the persistence of evil. This resurgence of evil power will convince many to join forces with Satan, but those who choose the side of evil condemn themselves to the devil's fate – eternal torment.

17.8 For more information on the book of life, see the note on 3.5.

17.9–11 Here John is referring to Rome, the city famous for its seven hills. Many say this city also symbolizes all evil in the world – any person, religion, group, government, or structure that is against Christ. Whatever view is taken of the seven hills and seven kings, this section indicates the climax of Satan's struggle against God. Evil's power is limited and its destruction is on the horizon.

17.12 The ten horns represent kings of nations yet to arise. Rome will be followed by other powers. Rome is a good example of how the antichrist's system will work, demanding complete allegiance,

17.14 Mt 22.14 1 Tim 6.15 1 Pet 2.9 Rev 3.21; 16.14
17.15 Isa 8.7 Jer 47.2 Rev 13.7; 17.1
17.16 Jer 50.41,42 Ezek 16.37 Dan 7.5 Rev 18.8,19
17.17 Rev 10.7; 17.13
17.18 Rev 11.8; 16.19

are ten kings who have not yet received a kingdom, but they are to receive authority
as kings for one hour, together with the beast. [13]These are united in yielding their
power and authority to the beast; [14]they will make war on the Lamb, and the Lamb
will conquer them, for he is Lord of lords and King of kings, and those with him are
called and chosen and faithful."
15 And he said to me, "The waters that you saw, where the whore is seated, are
peoples and multitudes and nations and languages. [16]And the ten horns that you
saw, they and the beast will hate the whore; they will make her desolate and naked;
they will devour her flesh and burn her up with fire. [17]For God has put it into their
hearts to carry out his purpose by agreeing to give their kingdom to the beast, until
the words of God will be fulfilled. [18]The woman you saw is the great city that rules
over the kings of the earth."

The fall of Babylon

18.1 Ezek 43.2 Rev 10.1
18.2 Isa 13.19-22 14.23; 21.8,9 Rev 14.8

18 After this I saw another angel coming down from heaven, having great authority; and the earth was made bright with his splendor. [2]He called out with
a mighty voice,
"Fallen, fallen is Babylon the great!
It has become a dwelling place of demons,
a haunt of every foul and hateful bird,
a haunt of every foul and hateful beast.[b]

18.3 Ezek 27.9-25 Rev 17.2

3 For all the nations have drunk[c]
of the wine of the wrath of her fornication,
and the kings of the earth have committed fornication with her,
and the merchants of the earth have grown rich from the power[d] of her
luxury."

18.4 Gen 19.12,13 Isa 52.11 Jer 51.6,9,45

4 Then I heard another voice from heaven saying,
"Come out of her, my people,
so that you do not take part in her sins,
and so that you do not share

[b]Some ancient authorities lack *a haunt of every foul and hateful beast* [c]Other ancient authorities read *she has made all nations drink* [d]Or *resources*

HOW CAN A PERSON KEEP AWAY FROM THE EVIL SYSTEM?
Here are some suggestions:

1. People must always be more important than products.
2. Keep away from pride in your own programs, plans, and successes.
3. Remember that God's will and Word must never be compromised.
4. People must always be considered above the making of money.
5. Do what is right, no matter what the cost.
6. Be involved in businesses that provide worthwhile products or services—not just things that feed the world's desires.

---

and ruling by raw power, oppression, and slavery. Whoever the ten kings are, they will give their power to the antichrist and will wage war against the Lamb.

17.16 In a dramatic turn of events, the whore's allies turn on her and destroy her. This is how evil operates. Destructive by its very nature, it discards its own adherents when they cease to serve its purposes. An unholy alliance is an uneasy alliance, because each partner puts its own interests first.

17.17 These satanic allies will carry out God's purposes. No matter what happens, we must trust that God is still in charge, he overrules all the plans and intrigues of the Evil One, and his plans will happen just as he says. He even uses people opposed to him as tools to execute his will. Although he allows evil to permeate this present world, the new earth will never know sin.

18.1ff This chapter shows the complete destruction of Babylon, John's metaphorical name for the evil world power and all it represents. Everyone who tries to block God's purposes will come to a violent end. For more information on how the book of Revelation uses the name *Babylon,* see the note on 14.8.

18.2, 3 Merchants in the Roman Empire grew rich by exploiting the sinful pleasures of their society. Many business people today do the same thing. Businesses and governments are often based on greed, money, and power. Many bright individuals are tempted to take advantage of an evil system to enrich themselves. Christians are warned to stay free from the enchantment of money, status, and the "good life." We are to live according to the values Christ exemplified: service, giving, self-sacrifice, obedience, and truth.

18.4–8 Babylon lived in luxury and pleasure. She thought, "I rule as a queen . . . I will never see grief." The powerful, wealthy people of this world are susceptible to this same attitude. A person who is financially comfortable often feels invulnerable, secure, and in control, without need of God or anyone else. This kind of attitude defies God, and God's judgment against it is harsh. We are told to avoid Babylon's sins. If you are financially secure, don't become complacent and deluded by the myth of self-sufficiency. Use your resources to help others and advance God's kingdom.

in her plagues;
5 for her sins are heaped high as heaven,
and God has remembered her iniquities.
6 Render to her as she herself has rendered,
and repay her double for her deeds;
mix a double draught for her in the cup she mixed.
7 As she glorified herself and lived luxuriously,
so give her a like measure of torment and grief.
Since in her heart she says,
'I rule as a queen;
I am no widow,
and I will never see grief,'
8 therefore her plagues will come in a single day—
pestilence and mourning and famine—
and she will be burned with fire;
for mighty is the Lord God who judges her."

9 And the kings of the earth, who committed fornication and lived in luxury
with her, will weep and wail over her when they see the smoke of her burning;
10 they will stand far off, in fear of her torment, and say,
"Alas, alas, the great city,
Babylon, the mighty city!
For in one hour your judgment has come."

11 And the merchants of the earth weep and mourn for her, since no one buys
their cargo anymore, 12 cargo of gold, silver, jewels and pearls, fine linen, purple,
silk and scarlet, all kinds of scented wood, all articles of ivory, all articles of costly
wood, bronze, iron, and marble, 13 cinnamon, spice, incense, myrrh, frankincense,
wine, olive oil, choice flour and wheat, cattle and sheep, horses and chariots,
slaves—and human lives.[e]
14 "The fruit for which your soul longed
has gone from you,
and all your dainties and your splendor
are lost to you,
never to be found again!"
15 The merchants of these wares, who gained wealth from her, will stand far off, in
fear of her torment, weeping and mourning aloud,
16 "Alas, alas, the great city,
clothed in fine linen,
in purple and scarlet,
adorned with gold,
with jewels, and with pearls!
17 For in one hour all this wealth has been laid waste!"

And all shipmasters and seafarers, sailors and all whose trade is on the sea, stood
far off 18 and cried out as they saw the smoke of her burning,

[e] Or *chariots, and human bodies and souls*

18.5 Jer 51.9 Jon 1.2 Rev 16.19
18.6 Ps 137.8 Jer 51.24 Rev 17.4
18.7 Isa 47.7,8
18.8 Isa 47.9 Jer 50.31,34 Rev 17.16
18.9 Ps 58.10 Jer 50.46 Ezek 26.16 Dan 4.14 Rev 17.2
18.10 Num 16.34 Amos 5.16 Rev 14.8
18.11 Ezek 27.27 Rev 18.3
18.13 1 Tim 1.10
18.16 Lk 16.19 Rev 17.4
18.17 Isa 47.9 Ezek 27.27-36 Jonah 1.6 Rev 17.16
18.18 Ezek 27.30,32 Rev 13.4

18.9, 10 Those who are tied to the world's system will lose everything when it is taken away. What they have worked over a lifetime to build up will be destroyed in one hour. Those who work only for material rewards will have nothing when they die or when their possessions are destroyed. What can we take with us to the new earth? Our faith, our Christian character, and our relationships with other believers. These are more important than any amount of money, power, or pleasure.

18.9–19 Those who are in control of various parts of the economic system will mourn at Babylon's fall. The political leaders will mourn because they were the overseers of Babylon's wealth and were in a position to enrich themselves greatly. The merchants will mourn because Babylon, the greatest customer for their goods, is gone. The sea captains will no longer have anywhere to bring their goods because the merchants have nowhere to sell them. The fall of the evil world system affects all who enjoyed and depended on it. No one will remain unaffected by Babylon's fall.

18.11–13 This list of various merchandise illustrates the extreme materialism of this society. Few of these goods are necessities—most are luxuries. The society had become so self-indulgent that people were willing to use evil means to gratify their desires. Even people had become commodities—"human lives," slaves, were sold to Babylon.

18.11–19 God's people should not live for money, because money will be worthless in eternity. Instead, they should keep on guard constantly against greed, a sin that is always ready to take over their lives.

"What city was like the great city?"

18.19 Ezek 27.30

19 And they threw dust on their heads, as they wept and mourned, crying out,
"Alas, alas, the great city,
where all who had ships at sea
grew rich by her wealth!
For in one hour she has been laid waste.

18.20 Jer 51.48 Lk 11.49,50 Rev 6.10 12.12; 19.2

20 Rejoice over her, O heaven,
you saints and apostles and prophets!
For God has given judgment for you against her."

18.21 Jer 51.63,64 Dan 11.19

21 Then a mighty angel took up a stone like a great millstone and threw it into
the sea, saying,
"With such violence Babylon the great city
will be thrown down,
and will be found no more;

18.22 Ezek 26.13

22 and the sound of harpists and minstrels and of flutists and trumpeters
will be heard in you no more;
and an artisan of any trade
will be found in you no more;
and the sound of the millstone
will be heard in you no more;

18.23 Prov 4.18,19 Jer 7.34; 16.9 Nah 3.4

23 and the light of a lamp
will shine in you no more;
and the voice of bridegroom and bride
will be heard in you no more;
for your merchants were the magnates of the earth,
and all nations were deceived by your sorcery.

18.24 Mt 23.35-36 Rev 16.6; 17.6

24 And in you[f] was found the blood of prophets and of saints,
and of all who have been slaughtered on earth."

The marriage supper of the Lamb

19.1 Jer 51.48 Jonah 2.9 Mt 6.13 Rev 4.11 7.10; 12.10

19 After this I heard what seemed to be the loud voice of a great multitude in
heaven, saying,
"Hallelujah!
Salvation and glory and power to our God,

19.2 Rev 6.10 16.7; 17.1; 18.20

2 for his judgments are true and just;
he has judged the great whore
who corrupted the earth with her fornication,
and he has avenged on her the blood of his servants."[g]

19.3 Isa 34.10 Rev 4.4; 14.11

3 Once more they said,
"Hallelujah!
The smoke goes up from her forever and ever."

19.4 Rev 4.10; 5.14

4 And the twenty-four elders and the four living creatures fell down and worshiped
God who is seated on the throne, saying,
"Amen. Hallelujah!"

19.5 Rev 11.18

5 And from the throne came a voice saying,
"Praise our God,
all you his servants,[g]
and all who fear him,
small and great."

[f] Gk *her* [g] Gk *slaves*

19.1ff Praise is the heartfelt response to God by those who love him. The more you get to know God and realize what he has done, the more you will respond with praise. Praise is at the heart of true worship. Let your praise for God flow out of your realization of who he is and how much he loves you.

19.1, 2 The identity of this "great whore" is explained in the note on 17.1.

19.1-8 A great multitude in heaven initiates the chorus of praise to God for his victory (19.1–3). Then the 24 elders (identified in the note on 4.4) join the chorus (19.4). Finally, the great choir of heaven once again praises God – the wedding banquet of the Lamb has come (19.6–8). See Matthew 25.1–13 where Christ compares the coming of his kingdom to a wedding for which we must be prepared.

6 Then I heard what seemed to be the voice of a great multitude, like the sound of 19.6
many waters and like the sound of mighty thunderpeals, crying out, Rev 11.15

"Hallelujah!
For the Lord our God
the Almighty reigns.
7 Let us rejoice and exult 19.7
and give him the glory, Ps 45.10-16 Mt 25.1-10
for the marriage of the Lamb has come, Eph 5.25-32 Rev 21.2
and his bride has made herself ready;
8 to her it has been granted to be clothed 19.8
with fine linen, bright and pure"— Ps 45.13; 132.9 Rev 15.4,6

for the fine linen is the righteous deeds of the saints. 19.14
9 And the angel said[h] to me, "Write this: Blessed are those who are invited to 19.9
the marriage supper of the Lamb." And he said to me, "These are true words of Lk 14.15; 22.16 Rev 21.5; 22.6
God." 10 Then I fell down at his feet to worship him, but he said to me, "You must 19.10
not do that! I am a fellow servant[i] with you and your comrades[j] who hold the Rev 22.8,9
testimony of Jesus.[k] Worship God! For the testimony of Jesus[k] is the spirit of
prophecy."

The rider on the white horse

11 Then I saw heaven opened, and there was a white horse! Its rider is called 19.11 Isa 11.4
Faithful and True, and in righteousness he judges and makes war. 12 His eyes are Rev 1.14; 3.14
like a flame of fire, and on his head are many diadems; and he has a name inscribed 6.2
that no one knows but himself. 13 He is clothed in a robe dipped in[l] blood, and his 19.12 Rev 2.17
name is called The Word of God. 14 And the armies of heaven, wearing fine linen, 19.13 Isa 63.1-3
white and pure, were following him on white horses. 15 From his mouth comes a Jn 1.1,14
sharp sword with which to strike down the nations, and he will rule[m] them with a 19.14 Mt 28.3
rod of iron; he will tread the winepress of the fury of the wrath of God the Al- Rev 3.4; 4.4
mighty. 16 On his robe and on his thigh he has a name inscribed, "King of kings and 19.15 Isa 11.4; 63.3
Lord of lords." 2 Thess 2.8
17 Then I saw an angel standing in the sun, and with a loud voice he called to 19.16 Rev 2.17; 17.14
all the birds that fly in midheaven, "Come, gather for the great supper of God, 18 to 19.17
eat the flesh of kings, the flesh of captains, the flesh of the mighty, the flesh of Isa 56.9 Jer 12.9
horses and their riders—flesh of all, both free and slave, both small and great." Ezek 39.17-20
19 Then I saw the beast and the kings of the earth with their armies gathered to make

h Gk *he said* i Gk *slave* j Gk *brothers* k Or *to Jesus* l Other ancient authorities read *sprinkled with* m Or *will shepherd*

19.7, 8 This is the culmination of human history—the judgment of the wicked and the marriage feast of the Lamb and his bride. The bride is the church—all faithful believers from all time. The bride's clothing contrasts with the gaudy clothing of the great whore of 17.4 and 18.16. The bride's clothing is the righteousness of the saints. These are not religious works by any merit of believers, but the work of Christ to save us (7.9, 14).

19.10 Jesus is the central focus of God's revelation and his redemptive plan (as announced by the prophets). As you read the book of Revelation, don't get bogged down in all the details of the awesome visions; remember that the overarching theme in all the visions is the ultimate victory of Jesus Christ over evil.

19.11 The name "Faithful and True" contrasts with the faithless and deceitful Babylon described in chapter 18.

19.11–21 John's vision shifts again. Heaven opens and Jesus appears, this time not as a Lamb, but as a warrior on a white horse (symbolizing victory). Jesus came first as a Lamb to be a sacrifice for sin, but he will return as a Conqueror and King to execute judgment (2 Thessalonians 1.7–10). His first coming brought forgiveness; his second coming will bring judgment. The battle lines have now been drawn between God and evil, and the world is waiting for the King to ride onto the field.

19.12 *Diadems* are crowns. Although Jesus is called the "Faithful and True" (19.11), "The Word of God" (19.13), and the "King of kings, and Lord of lords" (19.16), this verse implies that no name can do him justice. He is greater than any description or expression the human mind can devise for him.

19.13 For more about the symbolism of Jesus' garments being dipped in blood, see the note on 7.14.

19.16 This title indicates God's sovereignty. Most of the world is worshiping the beast, the antichrist, whom they believe has all power and authority. Then suddenly out of heaven rides Christ and his army of angels—the "King of kings, and Lord of lords." His entrance signals the end of the false powers.

19.17 This "great supper of God" is a grim contrast to the wedding banquet of the Lamb (19.7). One is a celebration; the other, devastation.

19.19 The beast is identified in the note on 13.1.

19.19–21 The battle lines are drawn, and the greatest confrontation in the history of the world is about to begin. The antichrist and the false prophet have gathered the governments and armies of the earth under the antichrist's rule. They believe they have come of their own volition; in reality, God has summoned them to battle in order to defeat them. That they would even presume to fight

19.19 Rev 13.1 16.14,16; 18.9
19.20 Dan 2.40-45 7.7,11-14 2 Thess 2.8-11 Rev 13.11-16

war against the rider on the horse and against his army. 20 And the beast was captured, and with it the false prophet who had performed in its presence the signs by
which he deceived those who had received the mark of the beast and those who
worshiped its image. These two were thrown alive into the lake of fire that burns
with sulfur. 21 And the rest were killed by the sword of the rider on the horse, the
sword that came from his mouth; and all the birds were gorged with their flesh.

The 1,000 years

20.1 Rev 1.18; 9.1
20.2 Rev 12.9
20.4 Dan 7.9,18, 22,27 Mt 19.28 2 Tim 2.12 Rev 3.21 6.9,13
20.5 Ezek 37.2-14 Lk 14.14 Jn 5.28,29 Rom 11.15
20.6 1 Pet 2.9 Rev 1.6; 5.10 20.14; 21.8

20 Then I saw an angel coming down from heaven, holding in his hand the key
to the bottomless pit and a great chain. 2 He seized the dragon, that ancient
serpent, who is the Devil and Satan, and bound him for a thousand years, 3 and
threw him into the pit, and locked and sealed it over him, so that he would deceive
the nations no more, until the thousand years were ended. After that he must be let
out for a little while.
4 Then I saw thrones, and those seated on them were given authority to judge.
I also saw the souls of those who had been beheaded for their testimony to Jesus[n]
and for the word of God. They had not worshiped the beast or its image and had not
received its mark on their foreheads or their hands. They came to life and reigned
with Christ a thousand years. 5 (The rest of the dead did not come to life until the
thousand years were ended.) This is the first resurrection. 6 Blessed and holy are
those who share in the first resurrection. Over these the second death has no power,
but they will be priests of God and of Christ, and they will reign with him a thousand years.

The destruction of Satan

20.7 Rev 20.2
20.8 Ezek 38.2

7 When the thousand years are ended, Satan will be released from his prison
8 and will come out to deceive the nations at the four corners of the earth, Gog and
Magog, in order to gather them for battle; they are as numerous as the sands of the

[n] Or *for the testimony of Jesus*

---

against God shows how their pride and rebellion have perverted their thinking. There really is no fight, however, because the victory was won when Jesus died on the cross for sin and rose from the dead. Thus the evil leaders are immediately captured and sent to their punishment, and the forces of evil are annihilated.

19.20 The lake of fire is the final destination of the wicked. It is different from the bottomless pit referred to in 9.1. The antichrist and the false prophet are thrown into the lake of fire. Then their leader, Satan himself, is thrown there (20.10), and finally Death and Hades (Hell) (20.14). Afterward, everyone whose name is not recorded in the book of life will be sent to the same fate (20.15).

20.1 The angel and bottomless pit are explained in the notes on 9.1 and 19.20.

20.2 The dragon, Satan, is discussed in more detail in the notes on 12.3, 4 and 12.9. The dragon is not bound in chains for punishment – that occurs in 20.10 – but so that he cannot deceive the nations.

20.2–4 The 1,000 years are often referred to as the *millennium* (Latin for "one thousand"). Just how and when this 1,000 years takes place is understood differently among Christian scholars. The three major positions on this issue are called postmillennialism, premillennialism, and amillennialism.

(1) *Postmillennialism* looks for a literal 1,000-year period of peace on earth brought in by the church. At the end of the 1,000 years, Satan will be unleashed once more, but then Christ will return to defeat him and reign forever. Christ's second coming does not occur until after the 1,000-year period.

(2) *Premillennialism* also views the 1,000 years as a literal time period, but holds that Christ's second coming initiates his 1,000-year reign and this reign occurs before the final removal of Satan.

(3) *Amillennialism* understands the 1,000-year period to be symbolic of the time between Christ's ascension and his return. This millennium is the reign of Christ in the hearts of believers and in his church; thus it is the same as the church age. This period will end with the second coming of Christ.

These different views about the millennium need not cause division and controversy in the church, because each one acknowledges what is most crucial to Christianity – Christ will return, defeat Satan, and reign forever! Whatever and whenever the millennium is, Jesus Christ will unite all believers; therefore, we should not let this issue divide us.

20.3 John doesn't say why God once again releases Satan, but it is part of his plan for judging the world. Perhaps it is to expose those who rebel against God in their hearts and confirm those who are truly faithful to God. Whatever the reason, Satan's release results in the final destruction of all evil (20.12–15).

20.4 The beast's mark is explained in the note on 13.16–18.

20.5, 6 Christians hold two basic views concerning this first resurrection. (1) Some believe the first resurrection is spiritual (in our hearts at salvation), and that the millennium is our spiritual reign with Christ between his first and second comings. During this time, we are priests of God because Christ reigns in our hearts. In this view, the second resurrection is the bodily resurrection of all people for judgment. (2) Others believe the first resurrection occurs after Satan has been set aside. It is a physical resurrection of believers who then reign with Christ on the earth for a literal 1,000 years. The second resurrection occurs at the end of this millennium in order to judge unbelievers who have died.

20.6 The second death is spiritual death – everlasting separation from God (see 21.8).

20.7–9 Gog and Magog symbolize all the forces of evil who band together to battle God. Noah's son, Japheth, had a son named Magog (Genesis 10.2). Ezekiel presents Gog as a leader of forces against Israel (Ezekiel 38, 39).

sea. 9 They marched up over the breadth of the earth and surrounded the camp of the
saints and the beloved city. And fire came down from heaven[o] and consumed
them. 10 And the devil who had deceived them was thrown into the lake of fire and
sulfur, where the beast and the false prophet were, and they will be tormented day
and night forever and ever.

20.9 Ps 87.2 Ezek 38.9,22 Lk 9.54; 17.29
20.10 Mt 25.41,46 Rev 14.10; 19.20

The final judgment

11 Then I saw a great white throne and the one who sat on it; the earth and the
heaven fled from his presence, and no place was found for them. 12 And I saw the
dead, great and small, standing before the throne, and books were opened. Also
another book was opened, the book of life. And the dead were judged according to
their works, as recorded in the books. 13 And the sea gave up the dead that were in
it, Death and Hades gave up the dead that were in them, and all were judged according to what they had done. 14 Then Death and Hades were thrown into the lake
of fire. This is the second death, the lake of fire; 15 and anyone whose name was not
found written in the book of life was thrown into the lake of fire.

20.12 Rom 14.10-12
20.13 Mt 16.27
20.14 1 Cor 15.26; 53 Rev 20.6,10,15
20.15 Rev 3.5; 20.12

7. Making all things new

The new earth

21 Then I saw a new heaven and a new earth; for the first heaven and the first
earth had passed away, and the sea was no more. 2 And I saw the holy city,
the new Jerusalem, coming down out of heaven from God, prepared as a bride
adorned for her husband. 3 And I heard a loud voice from the throne saying,

"See, the home[p] of God is among mortals.
He will dwell[p] with them as their God;[q]
they will be his peoples,[r]
and God himself will be with them;[s]
4 he will wipe every tear from their eyes.
Death will be no more;
mourning and crying and pain will be no more,
for the first things have passed away."

21.1 Isa 65.17; 66.22 2 Pet 3.10,13
21.2 Jer 31.23 Heb 11.10; 12.22
21.3 2 Cor 6.16
21.4 Isa 25.8; 35.10 61.3 Rev 7.17

[o] Other ancient authorities read *from God, out of heaven,* or *out of heaven from God* [p] Gk *tabernacle* [q] Other ancient authorities lack *as their God* [r] Other ancient authorities read *people* [s] Other ancient authorities add *and be their God*

20.9 This is not a typical battle where the outcome is in doubt during the heat of the conflict. Here there is no contest. Two mighty forces of evil – those of the beast (19.19) and of Satan (20.8) – unite to do battle against God. The Bible uses just two verses to describe each battle – the evil beast and his forces are captured and thrown into the lake of fire (19.20, 21), and fire from God consumes Satan and his attacking armies (20.9, 10). For God, it is as easy as that. There will be no doubt, no worry, no second thoughts for believers about whether they have chosen the right side. If you have chosen God, you will experience this tremendous victory with Christ.

20.10 Satan's power is not eternal – he will meet his doom. He began his evil work in humankind at the beginning (Genesis 3.1–6) and continues it today, but he will be destroyed when he is thrown into the lake of fire. Satan was released from the bottomless pit ("his prison," 20.7), but he will never be released from the lake of fire. He will never be a threat to anyone again.

20.12–15 At the Judgment, the books are opened. They represent God's judgment, and in them are recorded the deeds of everyone, good or evil. We are not saved by works, but works are seen as clear evidence of a person's actual relationship with God. The book of life contains the names of those who have put their trust in Christ to save them.

20.14 Death and Hades are thrown into the lake of fire. God's judgment is finished. The lake of fire is the ultimate destination of everything wicked – Satan, the beast, the false prophet, the demons, Death, Hades, and all those whose names are not recorded in the book of life because they did not place their faith in Jesus Christ. John's vision does not permit any gray areas in God's judgment. If by faith we have not identified with Christ, confessing him as Lord, there is no hope, no second chance, no other appeal.

21.1 The earth as we know it will not last forever. After God's great judgment, he will create a new earth (see Romans 8.18–21; 2 Peter 3.7–13). God had also promised Isaiah that he would create a new and eternal earth (Isaiah 65.17; 66.22). The sea in John's time was viewed as dangerous and changeable, and also the source of the beast (13.1). We don't know how the new earth will look or where it will be, but God and his followers – those whose names are written in the book of life – will be united to live there forever. Will you be there?

21.2, 3 The new Jerusalem is where God dwells among his people ("the home of God is among mortals"). Instead of our going up to meet him, he comes down to be with us, just as God became man in Jesus Christ and lived among us (John 1.14). Wherever God reigns, there is peace, security, and love.

21.2–4 Have you ever wondered what eternity will be like? The "holy city, the new Jerusalem" is described as the place where there will be no death, pain, sorrow, or crying. What a wonderful truth! No matter what you are going through, it's not the last word – God has written the final chapter, and it is about true fulfillment and eternal joy for those who love him. We do not know as much as we would like, but it is enough to know that eternity with God will be more wonderful than we can imagine.

21.5 Isa 43.19; 2 Cor 5.17
21.6 Rev 1.8; 22.17
21.7 Rom 8.17,32
21.8 Deut 20.8; Mal 3.5; 1 Cor 6.9,10; Gal 5.19-21

5 And the one who was seated on the throne said, "See, I am making all things
new." Also he said, "Write this, for these words are trustworthy and true." 6 Then
he said to me, "It is done! I am the Alpha and the Omega, the beginning and the
end. To the thirsty I will give water as a gift from the spring of the water of life.
7 Those who conquer will inherit these things, and I will be their God and they will
be my children. 8 But as for the cowardly, the faithless,[t] the polluted, the murderers, the fornicators, the sorcerers, the idolaters, and all liars, their place will be in
the lake that burns with fire and sulfur, which is the second death."

The new Jerusalem

21.9 Rev 21.2
21.10 Ezek 40.1,2; 2 Cor 12.2-4
21.11 Job 28.17; Isa 60.1; Ezek 48.35
21.12 Ezek 48.31-34
21.14 Eph 2.20; Heb 11.10
21.15 Ezek 40.3; Zech 2.1,3

9 Then one of the seven angels who had the seven bowls full of the seven last
plagues came and said to me, "Come, I will show you the bride, the wife of the
Lamb." 10 And in the spirit[u] he carried me away to a great, high mountain and
showed me the holy city Jerusalem coming down out of heaven from God. 11 It has
the glory of God and a radiance like a very rare jewel, like jasper, clear as crystal.
12 It has a great, high wall with twelve gates, and at the gates twelve angels, and on
the gates are inscribed the names of the twelve tribes of the Israelites; 13 on the east
three gates, on the north three gates, on the south three gates, and on the west three
gates. 14 And the wall of the city has twelve foundations, and on them are the twelve
names of the twelve apostles of the Lamb.
15 The angel[v] who talked to me had a measuring rod of gold to measure the city
and its gates and walls. 16 The city lies foursquare, its length the same as its width;

[t] Or *the unbelieving* [u] Or *in the Spirit* [v] Gk *He*

THE BEGINNING AND THE END
The Bible records for us the beginning of the world and the end of the world. The story of mankind, from beginning to end—from the fall into sin to the redemption of Christ and God's ultimate victory over evil—is found in the pages of the Bible.

Genesis	*Revelation*
The sun is created	The sun is not needed
Satan is victorious	Satan is defeated
Sin enters the human race	Sin is banished
People run and hide from God	People are invited to live with God forever
People are cursed	The curse is removed
Tears are shed, with sorrow for sin	No more sin, no more tears or sorrow
The garden and earth are cursed	God's city is glorified, the earth is made new
The fruit from the tree of life is not to be eaten	God's people may eat from the tree of life
Paradise is lost	Paradise is regained
People are doomed to death	Death is defeated, believers live forever with God

21.5 God is the Creator. The Bible begins with the majestic story of his creation of the universe, and it concludes with his creation of a new heaven and earth. This is a tremendous hope and encouragement for the believer. When we are with Christ, we will be like him. We will be made perfect.

21.7, 8 The "cowardly" are not those who are fainthearted in their faith or who sometimes doubt or question, but those who turn back from following God. They are not brave enough to stand up for Christ; they are not humble enough to accept his authority over their lives. They are put in the same list as the unrepentant, abominable, murderers, liars, idolaters, the immoral, and sorcerers.

People who overcome endure to the end (Mark 13.13). They will receive the blessings God promised: (1) eating from the tree of life (2.7), (2) escaping from the lake of fire (the "second death," 2.11), (3) receiving a special name (2.17), (4) having power over the nations (2.26), (5) being included in the book of life (3.5), (6) being a pillar in God's spiritual temple (3.12), and (7) sitting with Christ on his throne (3.21). Those who can endure the testing of evil and remain faithful will be rewarded by God.

21.8 The lake is explained in the notes on 19.20 and 20.14. The second death is spiritual death, meaning either eternal torment or destruction. In either case, it is permanent separation from God.

21.10ff The description given here is symbolic and shows us that our new home with God will defy description.

21.12–14 The new Jerusalem is a picture of God's future home for his people. The 12 tribes of Israel (21.12) probably represent all the faithful in the Old Testament; the 12 apostles (21.14) represent the church. Thus, both believing Gentiles and Jews who have been faithful to God will live together in the new earth.

21.15–17 The city's measurements are symbolic of a place that will hold all God's people. Given in cubits, these measurements are all multiples of 12, the number for God's people: there were 12 tribes in Israel and 12 apostles who started the church. The walls are 144 cubits across; there are 12 layers in the walls and 12 gates in the city; and the height, length, and breadth are all the same, 12,000 furlongs (1,500 miles). The new Jerusalem is a perfect cube, the same shape as the most holy place in the temple (1 Kings 6.20). These measurements illustrate that this new home will be perfect for us.

and he measured the city with his rod, fifteen hundred miles;[w] its length and width
17 and height are equal. He also measured its wall, one hundred forty-four cubits[x]
18 by human measurement, which the angel was using. The wall is built of jasper,
19 while the city is pure gold, clear as glass. The foundations of the wall of the city
are adorned with every jewel; the first was jasper, the second sapphire, the third
20 agate, the fourth emerald, the fifth onyx, the sixth carnelian, the seventh chrysolite, the eighth beryl, the ninth topaz, the tenth chrysoprase, the eleventh jacinth,
21 the twelfth amethyst. And the twelve gates are twelve pearls, each of the gates is
a single pearl, and the street of the city is pure gold, transparent as glass.
22 I saw no temple in the city, for its temple is the Lord God the Almighty and
23 the Lamb. And the city has no need of sun or moon to shine on it, for the glory
24 of God is its light, and its lamp is the Lamb. The nations will walk by its light,
25 and the kings of the earth will bring their glory into it. Its gates will never be shut
26 by day—and there will be no night there. People will bring into it the glory and
27 the honor of the nations. But nothing unclean will enter it, nor anyone who practices abomination or falsehood, but only those who are written in the Lamb's book
of life.

21.17 Rev 13.18
21.18-20 Isa 54.11,12; Rev 4.3,6
21.22 Ps 90.1; Jn 4.21-24; 17.23,24
21.23 Isa 60.19,20; Rev 21.25
21.24 Ps 72.10; Isa 60.3; 66.10-14
21.25 Isa 60.11,20; Rev 22.5
21.26 Ps 72.10; Isa 49.23
21.27 Isa 52.1; Rev 3.5; 22.14,15

The river of Life

22 Then the angel[y] showed me the river of the water of life, bright as crystal,
2 flowing from the throne of God and of the Lamb through the middle of the
street of the city. On either side of the river, is the tree of life[z] with its twelve kinds
of fruit, producing its fruit each month; and the leaves of the tree are for the healing
3 of the nations. Nothing accursed will be found there any more. But the throne of
4 God and of the Lamb will be in it, and his servants[a] will worship him; they will
5 see his face, and his name will be on their foreheads. And there will be no more
night; they need no light of lamp or sun, for the Lord God will be their light, and
they will reign forever and ever.
6 And he said to me, "These words are trustworthy and true, for the Lord, the
God of the spirits of the prophets, has sent his angel to show his servants[a] what
must soon take place."

22.1 Ezek 47.1,2; Jn 7.37-39; Rev 7.17
22.2 Gen 2.9; Ezek 47.12; Rev 2.7; 22.14
22.3 Rev 7.15
22.4 1 Cor 13.12; Rev 7.3; 14.1
22.5 Rev 21.23,25

The promise of Jesus' return

7 "See, I am coming soon! Blessed is the one who keeps the words of the prophecy of this book."

22.6,7 Rev 1.3; 21.5

8 I, John, am the one who heard and saw these things. And when I heard and

[w] Gk *twelve thousand stadia* [x] That is, almost seventy-five yards [y] Gk *he* [z] Or *the Lamb.* [2] *In the middle of the street of the city, and on either side of the river, is the tree of life* [a] Gk *slaves*

21.18–21 The picture of walls made of jewels reveals that the new Jerusalem will be a place of purity and durability—it will last forever.

21.22–24 The temple, center of God's presence among his people, was the primary place of worship. No temple is needed in the new city because God's presence will be everywhere. He will be worshiped throughout the city, and nothing will hinder us from being with him.

21.25–27 Not everyone will be allowed into the new Jerusalem, only "those who are written in the Lamb's book of life." (The book of life is explained in the notes on 3.5 and 20.12.) Don't think you'll get in because of your background, personality, or good behavior. Eternal life is available to you only because of what Jesus, the Lamb, has done. Trust him today to secure your citizenship in his new creation.

22.1 The water of life is a symbol of eternal life. Jesus used this same image with the Samaritan woman (John 4.7–14). It pictures the fullness of life with God and the eternal blessings that come when we believe in him and satisfy our spiritual thirst (see 22.17).

22.2 These trees of life are like the tree of life in the garden of Eden (Genesis 2.9). After Adam and Eve sinned, they were forbidden to eat from the tree of life because they could not have eternal life as long as they were under sin's control. But because of the forgiveness of sin through the blood of Jesus, there will be no evil or sin in this city. We will be able to eat freely from the tree of life when sin's control over us is destroyed and our eternity with God is secure.

22.2 Why would the nations need to be healed if all evil is gone? John is quoting from Ezekiel 47.12, where water flowing from the temple produces trees with healing leaves. He is not implying that there will be illness in the new earth; he is emphasizing that the water of life produces health and strength wherever it goes.

22.3 "Nothing accursed" will be in God's presence. This fulfills Zechariah's prophecy (see Zechariah 14.11).

22.8, 9 Hearing or reading an eyewitness account is the next best thing to seeing the event yourself. John witnessed the events reported in Revelation and wrote them down so we could "see" and believe as he did. If you have read this far, you have "seen." Have you also believed?

22.8, 9 The first of the ten commandments is "You shall have no

22.8 Rev 1.1-4
22.9 Rev 19.10
22.10 Rev 1.3
22.11 Ezek 3.27; Dan 12.10
22.12 Mt 16.27; Rev 22.7
22.13 Rev 1.8,17; 21.6
22.14 Rev 21.2,12,27
22.15 Gal 5.19-21
22.16 Isa 11.1; Mt 1.1; 2.2
22.17 Jn 7.37-39

saw them, I fell down to worship at the feet of the angel who showed them to me;
9 but he said to me, "You must not do that! I am a fellow servant[b] with you and your
comrades[c] the prophets, and with those who keep the words of this book. Worship
God!"
10 And he said to me, "Do not seal up the words of the prophecy of this book,
for the time is near. 11 Let the evildoer still do evil, and the filthy still be filthy, and
the righteous still do right, and the holy still be holy."

12 "See, I am coming soon; my reward is with me, to repay according to everyone's work. 13 I am the Alpha and the Omega, the first and the last, the beginning
and the end."
14 Blessed are those who wash their robes,[d] so that they will have the right to
the tree of life and may enter the city by the gates. 15 Outside are the dogs and
sorcerers and fornicators and murderers and idolaters, and everyone who loves and
practices falsehood.
16 "It is I, Jesus, who sent my angel to you with this testimony for the churches.
I am the root and the descendant of David, the bright morning star."
17 The Spirit and the bride say, "Come."

[b] Gk *slave* [c] Gk *brothers* [d] Other ancient authorities read *do his commandments*

WHAT WE KNOW ABOUT ETERNITY

Reference	*Description*
John 14.2, 3	A place prepared for us
John 20.19, 26	Unlimited by physical properties (1 Corinthians 15.23)
1 John 3.2	We shall be like Jesus
1 Corinthians 15	We will have new bodies
1 Corinthians 2.9	Our experience will be wonderful
Revelation 21.1	A new environment
Revelation 21.3	A new experience of God's presence (1 Corinthians 13.12)
Revelation 21.4	New emotions
Revelation 21.4	There will be no more death

The Bible devotes much less space to describing eternity than it does to convincing people that eternal life is available as a free gift from God. Most of the brief descriptions of eternity would be more accurately called hints, since they use terms and ideas from present experience to describe what we cannot fully grasp until we are there ourselves. These references hint at aspects of what our future will be like if we have accepted Christ's gift of eternal life.

other gods before me" (Exodus 20.3). Jesus said that the greatest command of Moses' laws was "You shall love the Lord your God with all your heart, and with all your soul, and with all your mind" (Matthew 22.37). Here, at the end of the Bible, this truth is reiterated. The angel instructs John to "Worship God." God alone is worthy of our worship and adoration. He is above all creation, even the angels. Are there people, ideas, goals, or possessions that occupy the central place in your life, crowding God out? Worship *only* God by allowing nothing to distract you from your devotion to him.

22.10, 11 The angel tells John what to do after his vision is over. Instead of sealing up what he has written, as Daniel was commanded to do (Daniel 12.4–12), John is to leave the book open to let others see it, so that all can read and understand. Daniel's message was sealed because it was not a message for Daniel's time. But the book of Revelation was a message for John's time, and it is equally relevant today. As Christ's return gets closer, there is a greater polarization between God's followers and Satan's followers. We must read the book of Revelation, hear its message, and be prepared for Christ's imminent return.

22.12–14 Those who "wash their robes" are people purifying themselves from a sinful way of life. They are daily striving to remain faithful and ready for Christ's return. This concept is also explained in the note on 7.14.

22.14 In Eden, Adam and Eve were barred from the tree of life because of their sin (Genesis 3.22–24). In the new earth, God's people will eat from the tree of life because their sins have been removed by Christ's death and resurrection. Those who eat the fruit of this tree will live forever. If you have trusted Christ as Savior, he has forgiven your sins, and so you will have the right to eat from this tree. For more on this concept, see the first note on 22.2.

22.15 The exact location of these sinners is not known, nor is it relevant. They are outside. They were judged and condemned in 21.7, 8. John's emphasis is that nothing evil and no sinner will be in God's presence to corrupt or harm any of the faithful.

22.16 Jesus is both David's root and his descendant. As the Creator, he existed long before David. As a human, however, he was one of David's direct descendants (see Isaiah 11.1–5; Matthew 1.1–17). As the Messiah, he is the "bright morning star," the light of salvation to all.

22.17 Both the Holy Spirit and the bride, the church, extend the invitation to all the world to come to Jesus and experience the joys of salvation in Christ.

22.17 When Jesus met the Samaritan woman at the well, he told her of the living water that he could supply (John 4.10–15). This image is used again as Christ invites anyone to come and drink of the water of life. The gospel is unlimited in scope – all people, everywhere, may come. Salvation cannot be earned, but God gives it freely. We live in a world desperately thirsty for living water, and many are dying of thirst. But it's still not too late. Let us invite everyone to come and drink.

And let everyone who hears say, "Come."
And let everyone who is thirsty come.
Let anyone who wishes take the water of life as a gift.
18 I warn everyone who hears the words of the prophecy of this book: if anyone
adds to them, God will add to that person the plagues described in this book; [19]if
anyone takes away from the words of the book of this prophecy, God will take
away that person's share in the tree of life and in the holy city, which are described
in this book.
20 The one who testifies to these things says, "Surely I am coming soon."
Amen. Come, Lord Jesus!
21 The grace of the Lord Jesus be with all the saints. Amen.[e]

[e] Other ancient authorities lack *all*; others lack *the saints*; others lack *Amen*

22.18 Deut 4.2; 12.32 Prov 30.5,6 Rev 15.6-16

22.19 Ex 32.33 Deut 4.2 Rev 3.5 21.10; 22.5

22.20 Heb 9.28 Rev 1.2; 22.7,16

22.18, 19 This warning is given to those who might purposefully distort the message in this book. Moses gave a similar warning in Deuteronomy 4.1–4. We too must handle the Bible with care and great respect so that we do not distort its message, even unintentionally. We should be quick to put its principles into practice in our lives. No human explanation or interpretation of God's Word should be elevated to the same authority as the text itself.

22.20 We don't know the day or the hour, but Jesus is coming soon and unexpectedly. This is good news to those who trust him, but a terrible message for those who have rejected him and stand to be punished. *Soon* means at any moment, and we must be ready for him, always prepared for his return. Would Jesus' sudden appearance catch you off guard?

22.21 The *saints* refers to all those who believe in Christ. Revelation closes human history as Genesis opened it – in paradise. But there is one distinct difference in Revelation – evil is gone forever. Genesis describes Adam and Eve walking and talking with God; Revelation describes people worshiping him face to face. Genesis describes a garden with an evil serpent; Revelation describes a perfect city with no evil. The garden of Eden was destroyed by sin; but paradise is re-created in the new Jerusalem.

The book of Revelation ends with an urgent request: "Come, Lord Jesus!" In a world of problems, persecution, evil, and immorality, Christ calls us to persevere in our faith. Our efforts to better our world are important, but their results cannot compare with the transformation that Christ will bring about when he returns. He alone controls human history, forgives sin, and will re-create the earth and bring lasting peace.

INDEX TO NOTES

This is an index to the notes, charts, maps, and personality profiles in the *Life Application Bible*. Every entry concerning a note has a Bible reference and a page number; every entry concerning a chart, map, or personality profile has a page number. In some instances, a Bible reference is followed by a number in parentheses to indicate that there is more than one note on that particular scripture. For example, Rv 1.1(2) means that the reader should look up the second note with the heading of 1.1 in Revelation. In most cases, the entries follow in biblical/canonical order (i.e., from Genesis to Revelation). In some cases, however, the entries follow a chronological order – this is especially true with important people in the Bible. Following the general index are special indexes: Index to Charts, Index to Maps, and Index to Personality Profiles. Because of the emphasis on application in the *Life Application Bible,* these indexes are helpful guides for personal and group Bible Study, sermon preparation, or teaching.

INDEX

FAITHFULNESS

FALSE PROPHET, THE

FALSE TEACHERS, TEACHINGS & PROPHETS

FAME

FAMILY, FAMILIES

GOD, KINGDOM OF

GODLINESS

GODS/GODDESSES

GOD'S LAW

GOD'S WILL

GOD'S WORD

GOG

GOLD

GOLDEN CALF

GOLDEN RULE

GOLGOTHA

GOLIATH

GOMER

GOOD, GOODNESS

LIFE LESSONS FROM BIBLE PEOPLE (from PROFILES)

LOVE FEAST

LOVINGKINDNESS

LOYALTY

LUCIFER

LUKE

LUKE, GOSPEL OF

LUKEWARM

LUST

LYDDA

LYDIA

LYING

OBLIGATION

OBSESSION

OBSTACLES

OBVIOUS

OCCULT

ODDS

OFFENDING OTHERS

OFFERING

OFFERINGS

OG (king of Bashan)

OIL

OINTMENTS

OLD COVENANT

OLD TESTAMENT

OLIVES, MOUNT OF

ONENESS

ONESIMUS

OPEN/OPENNESS

OPINION(S)

PROCRASTINATION

PRODUCTIVITY

PROFITS

PROGRESS

PROMISED LAND

PROMISE(S)

PROMOTION

PROOF

PROPERTY

PROPHECY

INDEX TO CHARTS

INDEX TO MAPS

Note: maps concerning Jesus' ministry are given in chronological order — see Harmony of the Gospels.

INDEX TO PERSONALITY PROFILES